SOUTHERN STARS

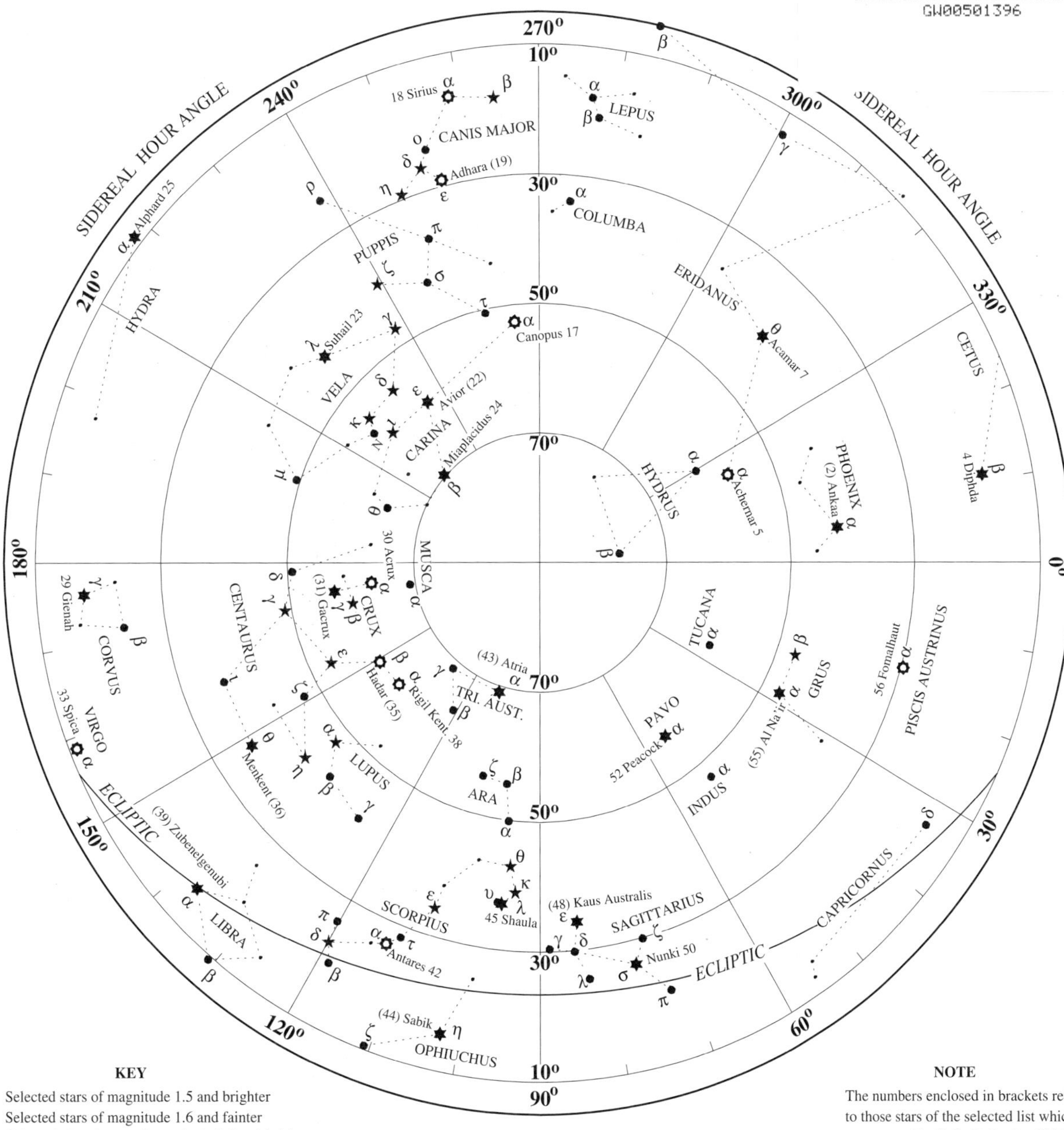

KEY

- Selected stars of magnitude 1.5 and brighter
- Selected stars of magnitude 1.6 and fainter
- Other tabulated stars of magnitude 2.5 and brighter
- Other tabulated stars of magnitude 2.6 and fainter
- Untabulated stars

NOTE

The numbers enclosed in brackets refer to those stars of the selected list which are not used in Sight Reduction Tables H.O. 249, A.P. 3270, N.P. 303.

EQUATORIAL STARS (SHA 180° to 360°)

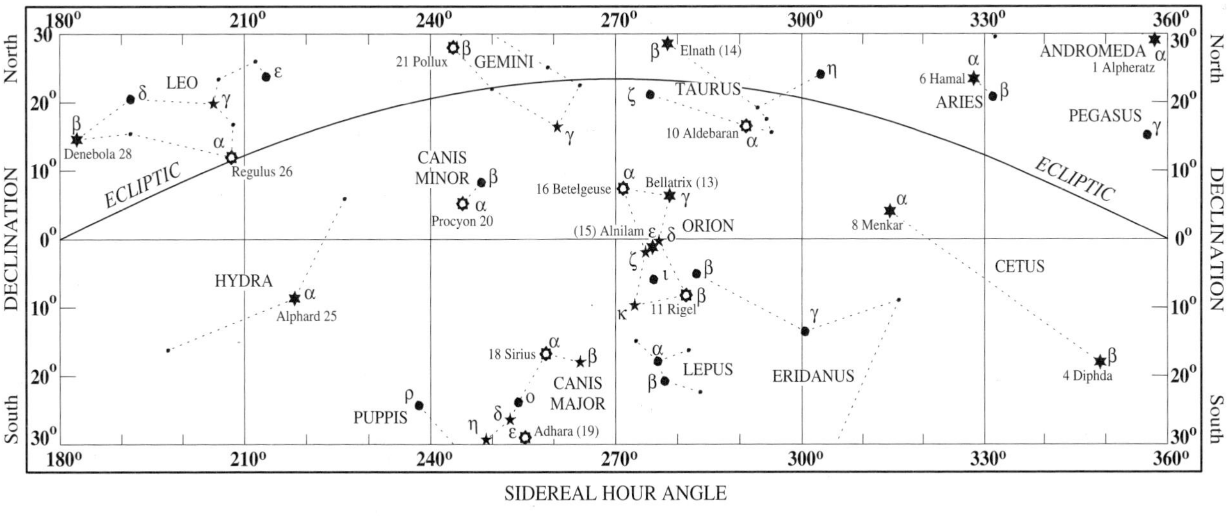

Alphabetical Order					Order of SHA				
Name	No.	Mag. Visual	SHA	Dec	Name	No.	Mag. Visual	SHA	Dec
			° ′	° ′				° ′	° ′
Acamar	7	3·2	315 18	S 40 15	*Markab	57	2·5	13 37	N 15 17
ACHERNAR	5	0·5	335 26	S 57 10	FOMALHAUT	56	1·2	15 23	S 29 33
ACRUX	30	1·3	173 08	S 63 11	*Al Na'ir	55	1·7	27 42	S 46 53
*Adhara	19	1·5	255 12	S 29 00	Enif	54	2·4	33 46	N 9 57
ALDEBARAN	10	0·9	290 48	N 16 32	DENEB	53	1·3	49 31	N 45 20
Alioth	32	1·8	166 20	N 55 53	Peacock	52	1·9	53 18	S 56 41
Alkaid	34	1·9	152 58	N 49 14	ALTAIR	51	0·8	62 07	N 8 55
*Al Na'ir	55	1·7	27 42	S 46 53	Nunki	50	2·0	75 57	S 26 17
*Alnilam	15	1·7	275 45	S 1 12	VEGA	49	0·0	80 38	N 38 48
Alphard	25	2·0	217 55	S 8 43	*Kaus Australis	48	1·9	83 42	S 34 23
Alphecca	41	2·2	126 10	N 26 40	*Eltanin	47	2·2	90 46	N 51 29
Alpheratz	1	2·1	357 43	N 29 10	Rasalhague	46	2·1	96 06	N 12 33
ALTAIR	51	0·8	62 07	N 8 55	Shaula	45	1·6	96 21	S 37 07
*Ankaa	2	2·4	353 15	S 42 13	*Sabik	44	2·4	102 11	S 15 45
ANTARES	42	1·0	112 25	S 26 28	*Atria	43	1·9	107 26	S 69 03
ARCTURUS	37	0·0	145 55	N 19 06	ANTARES	42	1·0	112 25	S 26 28
*Atria	43	1·9	107 26	S 69 03	Alphecca	41	2·2	126 10	N 26 40
*Avior	22	1·9	234 18	S 59 33	Kochab	40	2·1	137 20	N 74 06
*Bellatrix	13	1·6	278 31	N 6 22	*Zubenelgenubi	39	2·8	137 04	S 16 06
BETELGEUSE	16	0·1–1·2	271 00	N 7 25	RIGIL KENT.	38	−0·3	139 50	S 60 54
CANOPUS	17	−0·7	263 56	S 52 42	ARCTURUS	37	0·0	145 55	N 19 06
CAPELLA	12	0·1	280 33	N 46 01	*Menkent	36	2·1	148 06	S 36 27
DENEB	53	1·3	49 31	N 45 20	*HADAR	35	0·6	148 47	S 60 27
Denebola	28	2·1	182 33	N 14 29	Alkaid	34	1·9	152 58	N 49 14
Diphda	4	2·0	348 55	S 17 54	SPICA	33	1·0	158 30	S 11 14
Dubhe	27	1·8	193 50	N 61 40	Alioth	32	1·8	166 20	N 55 53
*Elnath	14	1·7	278 11	N 28 37	*Gacrux	31	1·6	172 00	S 57 12
*Eltanin	47	2·2	90 46	N 51 29	ACRUX	30	1·3	173 08	S 63 11
Enif	54	2·4	33 46	N 9 57	Gienah	29	2·6	175 51	S 17 38
FOMALHAUT	56	1·2	15 23	S 29 33	Denebola	28	2·1	182 33	N 14 29
*Gacrux	31	1·6	172 00	S 57 12	Dubhe	27	1·8	193 50	N 61 40
Gienah	29	2·6	175 51	S 17 38	REGULUS	26	1·4	207 42	N 11 54
*HADAR	35	0·6	148 47	S 60 27	Alphard	25	2·0	217 55	S 8 43
Hamal	6	2·0	328 00	N 23 32	Miaplacidus	24	1·7	221 40	S 69 47
*Kaus Australis	48	1·9	83 42	S 34 23	Suhail	23	2·2	222 52	S 43 30
Kochab	40	2·1	137 20	N 74 06	*Avior	22	1·9	234 18	S 59 33
*Markab	57	2·5	13 37	N 15 17	POLLUX	21	1·1	243 27	N 27 59
Menkar	8	2·5	314 14	N 4 09	PROCYON	20	0·4	244 59	N 5 11
*Menkent	36	2·1	148 06	S 36 27	*Adhara	19	1·5	255 12	S 29 00
Miaplacidus	24	1·7	221 40	S 69 47	SIRIUS	18	−1·5	258 33	S 16 44
Mirfak	9	1·8	308 39	N 49 55	CANOPUS	17	−0·7	263 56	S 52 42
Nunki	50	2·0	75 57	S 26 17	BETELGEUSE	16	0·1–1·2	271 00	N 7 25
Peacock	52	1·9	53 18	S 56 41	*Alnilam	15	1·7	275 45	S 1 12
POLLUX	21	1·1	243 27	N 27 59	*Elnath	14	1·7	278 11	N 28 37
PROCYON	20	0·4	244 59	N 5 11	*Bellatrix	13	1·6	278 31	N 6 22
Rasalhague	46	2·1	96 06	N 12 33	CAPELLA	12	0·1	280 33	N 46 01
REGULUS	26	1·4	207 42	N 11 54	RIGEL	11	0·1	281 11	S 8 11
RIGEL	11	0·1	281 11	S 8 11	ALDEBARAN	10	0·9	290 48	N 16 32
RIGIL KENT.	38	−0·3	139 50	S 60 54	Mirfak	9	1·8	308 39	N 49 55
*Sabik	44	2·4	102 11	S 15 45	Menkar	8	2·5	314 14	N 4 09
Schedar	3	2·2	349 39	N 56 37	Acamar	7	3·2	315 18	S 40 15
Shaula	45	1·6	96 21	S 37 07	Hamal	6	2·0	328 00	N 23 32
SIRIUS	18	−1·5	258 33	S 16 44	ACHERNAR	5	0·5	335 26	S 57 10
SPICA	33	1·0	158 30	S 11 14	Diphda	4	2·0	348 55	S 17 54
Suhail	23	2·2	222 52	S 43 30	Schedar	3	2·2	349 39	N 56 37
VEGA	49	0·0	80 38	N 38 48	*Ankaa	2	2·4	353 15	S 42 13
*Zubenelgenubi	39	2·8	137 04	S 16 06	Alpheratz	1	2·1	357 43	N 29 10

The star numbers and names are the same as in *The Nautical Almanac*.

* Not in the tabular pages of Volume **1**.

NP 303 / AP 3270

Rapid
Sight Reduction Tables for Navigation

VOLUME 1

Selected Stars

Epoch 2015·0

PUBLISHED BY THE UNITED KINGDOM HYDROGRAPHIC OFFICE

UNITED KINGDOM EDITION

To be obtained from Agents for the sale of
Admiralty Charts and Publications

ISBN 978-0-7077-41338

Printed in the United Kingdom by the United Kingdom Hydrographic Office

CONTENTS

DEDICATION

This book is dedicated to The Royal Greenwich Observatory (RGO). It is poignant to note that the RGO was originally established in 1675 in order to "... find out the so-much-desired longitude of places for the perfecting of the art of navigation".

ACKNOWLEDGEMENTS

I would like to thank S.A. Bell and my colleagues at HMNAO and J. Bangert, S. Urban and his team at the U.S. Naval Observatory.

Technical Support

HMNAO welcomes your comments, criticisms, suggestions, and reports of any problems that you encounter when using this book. We regret that we cannot respond directly to any telephone inquiries or correspondence sent by e-mail or FAX. We appreciate your understanding and cooperation in this regard.

Please send all correspondence concerning AP 3270/NP 303 to HM Nautical Almanac Office at the address given on the following page.

HM Nautical Almanac Office
http://www.ukho.gov.uk/hmnao
2012 May

FOREWORD

Rapid Sight Reduction Tables for Navigation consist of three volumes of comprehensive tables of altitude and azimuth designed for the rapid reduction of astronomical sights. These volumes were originally entitled *Sight Reduction Tables for Air Navigation*. The modified title and change in emphasis of the explanation, examples and auxiliary tables are due to their popularity for marine navigation, however, the format and star selection of main tabular material remains unchanged.

The present volume (Volume **1**) contains tables for selected stars for all latitudes, calculated for the epoch of 2015·0, and replaces the previous edition calculated for the epoch of 2010·0; it is intended for use for about 5 years, centered about 2015·0. Volume **2** for latitudes 0°–40°and Volume **3** for latitudes 39°–89°are permanent tables for integral degrees of declination. They provide sight reduction for bodies with declinations within 30° north or south of the equator, which includes the Sun, the Moon, the navigational planets and many navigational stars.

The time argument in the examples is denoted by UT (Universal Time), strictly this is UT1, which may differ by up to 0·9 seconds from the broadcast time signal UTC. In the past it was known as GMT (Greenwich Mean Time).

HM Nautical Almanac Office and the Nautical Almanac Office of the US Naval Observatory have co-operated in the preparation of these tables. All these pages have been produced and typeset in TEX by HM Nautical Almanac Office.

Ian Moncrieff CBE
Chief Executive

The United Kingdom Hydrographic Office
Admiralty Way
Taunton, TA1 2DN
England

This page is blank

Typeset by HM Nautical Almanac Office using $\TeX$

1. INTRODUCTION

These tables, designated as Volume **1** of the three-volume series of AP 3270 / NP 303 *Rapid Sight Reduction Tables for Navigation*, contain the position, altitude and true azimuth (H_c, Z_n), of seven selected stars for the complete ranges of latitudes and hour angle of Aries. The arrangement provides, for any position and time, the best selection of seven of the stars available for observation and, for these seven stars, data for presetting before observation and for accurate reduction of the sights after observation.

Volume **1** may be used without reference to an almanac. Thus it also contains the tables for calculating the Greenwich hour angle of Aries (GHA♈), dip, refraction, and conversion of arc to time. There is a sight reduction form and the tables of corrections for movement of the vessel, and movement of the body when special reduction techniques are used. In addition there are star charts to assist with identification, a list of the positions of the 57 navigational stars and tables for *Polaris*. If observations are made of stars other than those in the main tabulations, then they can be reduced by the use of Volumes **2** or **3**, provided the declinations are less than 30° north or south.

With the normal procedure of plotting a sight from an assumed position (AP), no interpolation is required for the stars tabulated.

These tables may be used to calculate an observed position to an accuracy of 0·5 nautical miles, where an observed position is the point on the earth's surface where two or more position lines intersect. *The Nautical Almanac* and the six volume series *Sight Reduction Tables for Marine Navigation* can produce an observed position to between 0·2 and 0·3 nautical miles. The concise sight reduction tables in *The Nautical Almanac* produce much less accurate observed positions at 1·0 nautical mile, and in certain cases this increases to 2·0 nautical miles. On the other hand the software *NavPac* will calculate an observed position to an accuracy of 0·15 nautical miles. These errors are quoted from *The Admiralty Manual of Navigation*, volume 2 (BR 45(2)), produced by the Fleet Publications and Graphics Organisation.

This introduction and examples are aimed at illustrating how to use this volume for marine navigation. It is not a text book on astro-navigation. AP 3270 was originally designed for air navigation. The format of the main tabulations of altitude and azimuth of the stars are unchanged. It is only the explanation, examples and some of the auxiliary tables that have been updated for use by marine navigators. Air navigators use bubble sextants, fly high above the ground and at speed causing large changes in position in a very short time. Thus, those tables dealing with speed, Coriolis forces, dome refraction, and refraction at height have been removed or modified. Those who require these tables, which do not depend on time, should check our web site (www.ukho.gov.uk/hmnao).

2. THE ALTITUDE & AZIMUTH TABLES FOR SELECTED STARS

The computed altitudes (H_c) and the true azimuths (Z_n) of the selected stars are tabulated in the main tables to the nearest minute of arc and nearest degree, respectively.

Seven stars have been selected for each latitude and each entry of LHA ♈, and the selection is unchanged for each group of 15 entries of LHA ♈ (30° for latitudes over 69°, 15° for lower latitudes); within each such group the order of arrangement is that of the azimuths corresponding to the first entry. These are the same seven stars that the software *NavPac* chooses as the 'best 7 stars'. For each selection of seven stars, three are marked with a diamond symbol (◆) as being most suitable for a three-star fix.

A total of 41 stars is used, of which 19 are of the first magnitude (brighter than magnitude 1·5) and 17 of the second magnitude. The names of first-magnitude stars are given in capital letters. A complete list of the 57 stars selected for astro-navigation is given on page ii. An asterisk is printed beside those stars not used in this volume.

Many factors were considered in selecting the stars, including azimuth, magnitude, altitude and continuity. Continuity was sought in regard to both latitude and hour angle, particularly for latitude where changes are not immediately evident by inspection.

The tabulated positions of the stars have been calculated from the positions for the fixed epoch and mean equinox of J2015·0. Since observations are made at different epochs (dates) corrections for precession and nutation may, strictly speaking, be necessary.

Tabulations are given for every whole degree of *latitude* from 89° north to 89° south. From 69° north to 69° south all data for a single latitude appear on two facing pages; from 70° to the poles, both north and south, the data for a single latitude appear on one page.

The vertical argument on each page is the local hour angle of the first point of Aries (LHA♈). It ranges from 0° to 360°; in general the interval is 1°, but between latitudes 70° and the poles it is increased to 2°. LHA♈ is calculated from the following formula

$$\text{LHA}\Upsilon = \text{GHA}\Upsilon \begin{array}{c} -\text{ west} \\ +\text{ east} \end{array} \text{longitude}$$

3. AUXILIARY TABLES, STAR CHARTS AND PLOTS

This section describes the various auxiliary tables and charts that are included in this volume.

3.1 Star Charts

There are four charts that show the constellations and the relative positions and magnitudes of the 173 navigational stars that are published in *The Nautical Almanac*. This includes the 57 stars that are printed on page ii and the 41 used in these tables. They may be identified on the chart by name and number. Those with their number enclosed in brackets are not used in this volume. A few other stars are included to make the constellation patterns recognizable.

The two polar charts, for the northern and southern stars, are centered on their respective poles with declinations from about 10° to the pole. The two equatorial charts are for the stars with declinations within 30° of the equator, and sidereal hour angle (SHA) from 0° to 180°, and from 180° to 360°. The ecliptic, the apparent path of the Sun, is shown on each chart.

3.2 The Navigational Stars

The 57 stars used in navigation are listed on page ii and are the same stars that are given in the daily pages of *The Nautical Almanac* and include the 41 stars used in the main tabulations. The stars are listed in alphabetic and SHA order. The lists contain proper name, number (same number that is used in *The Nautical Almanac*), visual magnitude, and SHA and declination. The positions are for epoch and mean equinox of 2015·0 and thus, for strict accuracy, a correction for precession and nutation may be needed (see 3.4). Those stars with asterisks (*) are not tabulated in this volume. However, if their declination is less than 30° north or south, then they may be reduced using Volumes **2** or **3**.

3.3 Greenwich Hour Angle of Aries

The local hour angle of Aries (LHA♈) is an argument of most of the tables; the main tabulations, the precession and nutation table, and the Pole Star tables. It is formed from the longitude and the Greenwich hour angle of Aries. GHA♈ is given in Table **4** and is calculated from the Greenwich date and Universal Time (UT).

The table has been split into three parts. The first, (a), gives GHA♈ for the first of each month at 00^h UT for the 10-year period for which this volume is valid. The other two tables give the increments for day of the month and hours (b), and minutes and seconds (c). The GHA♈ for the particular instant is the sum of the three quantities, removing multiples of 360° as required.

The GHA♈ is tabulated here to the nearest minute of arc. If greater accuracy is required then use *The Nautical Almanac*.

3.4 Correction for Precession and Nutation

The altitudes and azimuths of stars that are tabulated in this volume are calculated for the epoch and mean equinox of J2015·0. However, observations are made at various epochs, and the correction for precession and nutation (Table **5**) allows for the change in the positions of the stars from the epoch of the tabulations to that of the observations. Thus, for strict accuracy, it is necessary to apply this correction to a position line or fix, deduced from these tables.

Each entry in the table consists of the distance (in bold type) in nautical miles, and the direction (true bearing) in which the position line or fix is to be moved (see 5.1.2). The table is entered firstly by the year, then by choosing the column entry with nearest latitude and finally the row entry nearest the LHA♈ of the observation; no interpolation is necessary, though in extreme cases near the beginning or end of a year values midway towards those of the previous or following years may be taken.

The corrections in Table **5** are to the nearest 0′·1 in distance and 1° in true bearing for 2011–2019. Their omission will not give rise to a positional error greater than 1′·2 in the years 2013–2016. The corrections are applicable only to sights reduced with this volume of tables.

3.5 Altitude Corrections due to the Observer's Position

These corrections are applied to the sextant altitude (H_S) in order to form the observed altitude (H_O) — the altitude that may be directly compared with the calculated (tabulated) altitude (H_C).

The height of the observer's eye above the ground effects the sextant altitude as do the atmospheric conditions that are prevailing at the time of the observations. Usually both these are constant for a set of observations, but this need not necessarily be the case.

Another correction that should not be omitted is the sextant index error (IE). This type of error is not discussed here, but is included when the correction for dip is applied.

3.5.1 Dip of the Horizon The visible horizon is used as a 'base' from which the altitude of the star is measured. However, where an observer sees the horizon depends on their height above the ground and the bending of the light by the atmosphere as it travels from the horizon to the observer's eye. This effect is called dip and it is always negative. The dip (D) and the sextant index error (IE) must be applied to the sextant altitude to give the apparent altitude (H_a), viz:

$$H_a = H_S + \mathrm{IE} + D$$

Navigators using bubble sextants must set the dip to zero. The apparent altitude, the altitude of the star corrected for index error and the effect of looking towards the horizon are required in order to calculate refraction.

The dip table, Table **8**a, is a critical table, tabulated for height in metres and feet and is very similar to that given in *The Nautical Almanac*. Here the height of eye of the observer is tabulated from the ground to 50·0 m (164·7 ft) and gives dip to the nearest 0′·1. Alternatively, the following expressions may be used

$$D = -1'.76\sqrt{h} \quad \text{metres} \qquad \text{or} \qquad D = -0'.97\sqrt{h} \quad \text{feet.}$$

3.5.2 Refraction The light from objects (stars, Sun, planets, Moon) is bent as it passes through the atmosphere. This bending, refraction (R), causes the object to appear closer to the zenith. Table **8**b gives the amount of refraction, to be applied to the apparent altitude (H_a), ie. the quantity from the table is subtracted from H_a to give the observed altitude, viz.:

$$H_o = H_a + R$$

where R is tabulated with a negative sign and H_a, the apparent altitude, is the sextant altitude corrected for index error and dip.

It is recommended to observe objects away from the horizon where the effect of refraction is unpredictable and large. Refraction is a function of the atmospheric conditions along the path of the ray of light as it travels through the atmosphere. The standard temperature and pressure specified in *The Nautical Almanac* are 10°C and 1010 mb pressure, respectively. For the record, Table **8**b is now tabulated for *The Nautical Almanac* standard atmospheric conditions which are, from 2004, a temperature of 10°C, 1010 mb pressure, 80% humidity, wavelength 0·50169 μm, latitude 45°, and temperature gradient (lapse rate) of 0·0065°Km^{-1}. Of all these parameters it is the changes in temperature and pressure that produce the most significant differences in the tabulated values of refraction.

To cater for non-standard atmospheric conditions Table **8**c gives a correction to the refraction obtained from Table **8**b for a range of temperatures (−30°C to +40°C) and pressures (970 mb to 1050 mb). Locate the zone letter (A, B, . . ., N) in the top graph where the arguments of temperature and pressure at the time of the observation intersect. Then find the entry in the table below where the column with the zone letter crosses the row with the apparent altitude. Interpolation may be necessary, however, due to the uncertainty at low altitudes this will probably not lead to a more accurate correction.

These refraction tables (Table **8**b,c) are suitable for all objects when refraction on its own is being considered. However, there are altitude correction tables for the Sun and Moon that combine corrections for refraction, semi-diameter and parallax.

3.6 Altitude Corrections due to Changes in Position

These corrections allow for the movement of the vessel during the observations (MOO), and change in position of the body (MOB) when special techniques are used. They may be applied to the observed altitude, the tabulated altitude, or the intercept (position line). To minimize errors, always apply the corrections to the same quantities. All examples in this volume apply the corrections to the intercept.

3.6.1 Change in the Position of the Observer In practice this correction (MOO), for the change in position of the observer, is often made on the plotting chart by transferring the position line for the motion of the vessel. Table **1** tabulates this correction for every 2° of *relative* azimuth and for movement of the vessel (distance made good) between the time of the observations and the time of the fix. Care must be taken to ensure that the correct sign is used. This depends on whether the fix is **later** or **earlier** than the observation, and where the correction is applied; the observed altitude, the tabulated altitude, or the intercept (position line). A table at the bottom of the page gives these options.

In previous editions, this quantity was tabulated in terms of the speed and the change occurring in 4^m and 1^m (Alternative Table 1), rather than distance made good. For marine navigation this correction is often negligible, because speeds are relatively slow and observations, such as star observations, are made over a short time span (during nautical twilight). However, in adverse weather conditions, it might be necessary to combine morning and evening observations. Alternatively, when there is sufficient moonlight to illuminate the horizon, it would be possible to observe a star outside this period of twilight (see page xxii). In both these circumstances, assuming the vessel is moving, this correction could be significant.

The correction, in minutes of arc, is given by

$$\text{DMG}\cos(\text{Rel.Z}_\text{n}) = \text{DMG}\cos(\text{Z}_\text{n} - C)$$

where DMG is the distance made good in nautical miles and the relative azimuth, Rel.Z_n, is the difference between the azimuth of the star (Z_n) and the vessels true track (C). DMG may be estimated, ignoring the effects of wind, tide and variable speed, by $(\text{UT}_\text{f} - \text{UT})V$ where $(\text{UT}_\text{f} - \text{UT})$, is the time between the fix and the observation, in hours, and V is the speed in knots; Table **1** is tabulated in terms of the distance made good (DMG), and relative azimuth.

3.6.2 Change in the Position of the Body The body's position changes when special reduction techniques (see section 5.2.5) are used which first assumes that all the observations are taken at the same time (the time of the fix). Thus only one LHA♈ is calculated and used to look up the tables. A correction (MOB) is then needed for each observation to allow for the change during the interval of time between the fix and the actual observation.

Table **2** tabulates for every 5° of latitude and 3° of azimuth (Z_n), the altitude correction due to the change in position of the body during one minute of time. The arithmetic is made much simpler if one of the observations is made at the time of the fix, and the interval between the fix and the remainder of the observations are made at intervals of exact multiples of a minute. However, if required an interpolation table for seconds of time is given below the main table. Care must be taken to ensure that the correct sign is used. This, like the correction for MOO, depends on whether the fix is **later** or **earlier** than the observation, and where the correction is applied; the observed altitude, the tabulated altitude, or the intercept (position line). A table beneath the main table gives these options.

This correction, in minutes of arc, is given by

$$15{\cdot}0411\,(\text{UT}_\text{f} - \text{UT})\cos Lat\,\sin \text{Z}_\text{n}$$

where $\text{UT}_\text{f} - \text{UT}$, the difference in time between the fix and the time of the observation is expressed in minutes of time. Table **2** is tabulated for a minute interval, $\text{UT}_\text{f} - \text{UT} = 1^\text{m}$.

3.7 Polaris Tables

The tables for *Polaris* (Table **6** and Table **7**) give Q the polar distance (90°– Declination) and the true azimuth (Z_n) and are based on the position of *Polaris* for epoch 2015·0 and is therefore not as accurate as those calculated for each year. Greater accuracy is achieved by applying the precession and nutation corrections given in Table **5**. The actual position, SHA and declination, used to generate these tables is given between the tables.

The Q correction is a function of LHA♈ and is tabulated to 1′ as a critical table (Table **6**) on page 329. It is the quantity to be added to the observed altitude (H_o) of *Polaris* to give latitude. Refraction is not included.

The azimuth (Table **7**) of *Polaris* is given to 0°·1, for latitudes up to N70° and for all hour angles.

3.8 Rapid Sight Reduction Form

A blank sight reduction form is given at the back (page 333) of this volume. This closely follows the format of the examples. However, some minor modifications have been made to ensure that it fits onto an A4 page. To help the user, the example in section 5.2.4 has been repeated using this form (see page 332).

The form covers observations of four stars. The information for each star is contained within a column. These are preceded by the column (first) that contains a summary of the instructions. Each block of this column contains the step number and main function, in bold. Subsequent lines give a reminder of the actions needed, the arguments required, and the symbol for the quantity calculated or extracted from the tables. The arguments needed for entering the tables are indicated in parentheses. In the example form the arguments are only included and/or repeated for each observation if they change or are not obvious.

The form may be freely copied and/or downloaded from our web site (www.ukho.gov.uk/hmnao).

4. NOMENCLATURE AND TERMINOLOGY

The following is a list of symbols and their definition that are used in this volume.

AP — Assumed position, sometimes referred to as the chosen position. The latitude and longitude closest to the dead reckoning or estimated position (DR/EP) that have the following properties. The assumed latitude is the DR (or EP) latitude rounded to the nearest degree. Similarly, the assumed longitude is the longitude closest to the DR longitude that makes the LHA♈ a whole degree, or even degree for latitudes above 69°. This allows the tables to be entered easily without interpolation.

C — True track (or course) of the vessel. *C* is measured from true north through east, south, west and back to north. The range is from 0° to 360°.

D — Dip of the horizon see section 3.5.1.

Date — Greenwich date, or local date.

DMG — Distance made good.

DR — Dead Reckoning position. Position based on course and speed only.

DWE — Deck Watch Error. The error in the watch used to make the observations.

EP — Estimated position. The most accurate position that can be obtained by calculation and estimation alone; including leeway and tidal effects.

Epoch — An arbitrary fixed instant, identified by date and time.

GHA♈ — Greenwich hour angle of Aries is tabulated in Table **4**. The range of GHA♈ is from 0° to 360° starting at 0° on the Greenwich meridian increasing to the west, back to 360° on the Greenwich meridian. It is a function of the Greenwich date and UT time.

GMT — Greenwich mean time. In this context the name (GMT) is synonymous with Universal Time (UT see 4.1).

H_a — Apparent altitude. This is the sextant altitude (H_s) corrected for index error (IE) and dip (*D*). It is needed for calculating refraction.

H_c — Calculated altitude, sometimes called the tabulated altitude. It is the altitude tabulated in the tables for a given latitude and LHA♈. Since the tables are valid for several years a small correction may be required for precession and nutation (see 3.4).

H_o — Observed altitude, sometimes referred to as the true altitude. For stars it is the apparent altitude (H_a) corrected for refraction (*R*). The Sun, Moon and planets require additional corrections for semi-diameter and parallax.

H_s — Sextant altitude. The altitude measured by a sextant between the visible horizon and the object on an arc towards the observer's zenith.

IE — Sextant index error. *On the arc* errors are *negative*, they reduce the sextant altitude. *Off the arc* errors are *positive*, and increase the sextant altitude.

Lat — Latitude. The sign convention is north is positive, south is negative. The range is from −90° to +90°.

LHA♈ — Local hour angle of Aries is given by

$$\text{LHA}♈ = \text{GHA}♈ \begin{matrix} -\text{ west} \\ +\text{ east} \end{matrix} \text{ longitude}$$

and increases to the west from 0° on the local meridian to 360°.

Long — Longitude. The sign convention is east is positive, west is negative. The range is −180° to +180°.

p — Intercept, $p = H_o - H_c$, may be *positive* or *negative*, and thus the position line should be plotted *towards*, or *away* from the direction of the star, respectively (see 5.2.1).

R	Atmospheric refraction see section 3.5.2. The bending of the light ray as it passes through the atmosphere. The amount of refraction depends on the apparent altitude (H_a) and the atmospheric conditions, in particular the temperature and pressure. The apparent altitude is always greater than the observed altitude (H_o).
SHA	Sidereal hour angle. The range is 0° to 360°.
UT	Universal Time, the time scale required for use in sight reduction. Radio time signals are usually based on the system of Universal Coordinated Time (UTC). A correction may be required to convert from UTC to UT (see 4.1).
Rel.Z_n	Relative azimuth, Rel.$Z_n = Z_n - C$, where C is the true course of the vessel.
Z_n	Azimuth (true) or true bearing. Z_n is measured from true north through east, south, west and back to north. The range is from 0° to 360°.
ZT	Zone time correction. The time correction to be applied to the local time to give Universal Time (UT). Usually the ZT is added for west longitudes and subtracted for east longitudes, $$\text{UT} = \text{local time} \ {}^{+}_{-}\ \text{ZT for} \ {}^{\text{west}}_{\text{east}}\ \text{longitude}$$ If appropriate, allow for daylight saving (or summer) time. Remember, the ZT might cause the date to change.

4.1 Time Scales, UT, UT1 and UTC

It is necessary to record the time of each observation and convert it, as necessary, to UT1. UT1, usually denoted by UT, is the time argument of the tables for GHA♈ and thus for LHA♈. The navigator relies on radio time signals to ensure that the accuracy of the deck watch used to time observations is maintained. UTC, which is promulgated by radio time signals and many GPS receivers, is at present, kept within $0\overset{s}{.}9$ of UT1. This difference,

$$\text{DUT} = \text{UT1} - \text{UTC}$$

is at present kept small, and to the accuracy of these tables it may be ignored. Values of UT1 − UTC are published by the International Earth Rotation and Reference Systems Service (IERS, see http:/www.iers.org/).

However, if UTC and UT are allowed to diverge (there are proposals for this), then navigators will probably need to adapt their procedures. A correction must then be made to the time of each observation. Alternatively the longitude deduced from astronomical observations must be corrected by the corresponding amount. This correction, in minutes of arc, to be added to the longitude is given by

$$-15 \times \frac{\text{DUT}}{60}$$

where DUT is given in seconds of time. DUT1, UT1 − UTC rounded to the nearest $0\overset{m}{.}1$, is also promulgated by some radio time signals.

The table below gives the corrections for small values of DUT:

DUT	Correction to longitude
$2\overset{s}{.}0$	0′.5
$1\overset{s}{.}0$	0′.2
$0\overset{s}{.}5$	0′.1

Negative values of DUT move the longitude to the east, while positive values move the longitude to the west.

Please check our web site (www.ukho.gov.uk/hmnao) where more information is available.

5. USE OF THESE TABLES

The tables are intended to be used for two distinct operations—the planning of observations, and their reduction.

5.1 Planning Sextant Observations

Since only seven stars are given it is essential to refer to the tables before observations are made, in order to ensure that the data will be available for their reduction. This is done by estimating your position and thus the LHA♈ for the proposed time of observations and fix. These quantities may be found from a knowledge of the DR (or EP) position and GHA♈, which may be calculated from Table **4** or an appropriate almanac such as *The Nautical Almanac*. On reference to the tables this information gives immediately the seven stars available, together with their altitudes and azimuths. From these seven stars, the observer can select those which best suit the particular requirements and the prevailing conditions; these tabulated altitudes and azimuths make identification easy, and enable the sextant to be preset to the approximate altitude for each observation.

It should be noted that this preliminary calculation of LHA♈ may often be modified to serve as a basis for the reduction of the sights, without further reference to Table **4** or an almanac (see section 5.2.5).

If observations are made of stars other than those selected and if their declinations are less than 30° north or south (see page ii), then Volumes **2** or **3** of these tables may be used.

5.1.1 Method of Planning Observations The following procedure and example illustrates the process of selecting stars for observation.

Step 1. Estimate the approximate position (latitude and longitude) at the proposed time of the fix. The zone time correction will also be needed.

Step 2. Convert the local date and proposed time of the fix (observations) to the Greenwich date and UT time using the zone time correction (ZT).

Step 3. Calculate GHA♈ (Table **4** or an appropriate almanac such as *The Nautical Almanac*) from the Greenwich date and UT time. Add or subtract multiples of 360° so that GHA♈ is between 0° and 360° if appropriate.

Step 4. Calculate LHA♈ from the estimated longitude (east longitudes are positive, and west longitudes are negative) and GHA♈. Ensure that LHA♈ is between 0° and 360° by adding or subtracting multiples of 360°.

Step 5. From the estimate of the latitude and LHA♈, both rounded to the nearest degree, look up the appropriate page of the main tabulations and extract the calculated altitude (H_c) and azimuth (Z_n) of the seven stars.

Step 6. Note any further information that might be needed, such as how long the chosen set of stars will be valid, and the effect of changing the latitude by a degree.

5.1.2 Example of Planning Observations An example illustrating how a navigator will plan to make some observations in order to determine their position.

Example. During the morning of 2013 January 10 a navigator proposes to make a series of observations at $06^h\ 54^m$ local time. At that time the estimated (DR) position is N 44° 35′, E 160° 28′, with a zone time of -11^h.

		d	h m
1	Estimated position at the time is N 44° 35′, E 160° 28′		
2	Convert local date and time	2013 January 10	06 54
	Zone Correction	ZT =	−11 00
	Greenwich Date and UT time	2013 January 9	19 54

				°	′
3	GHA♈ from Table **4**:	for 2013 January 1	(a) =	100	49
		for 19^h UT on day 9	(b) =	293	40
		for 54^m	(c) =	13	32
	Sum (a) + (b) + (c) = GHA♈ for 2013 January 9, 19^h 54^m UT:		GHA♈ =	408	01
4	Longitude, added if east, subtracted if west			+160	28
	Sum		=	568	29
	Remove multiples of 360°			−360	
	Local hour angle of Aries		LHA♈ =	208	29

5 The seven selected stars for latitude 45° N, LHA♈ 208° (page 71) are:-

	VEGA ◆	*Rasalhague*	*ARCTURUS*	*SPICA* ◆	*REGULUS*	*POLLUX* ◆	*Dubhe*
	° ′	° ′	° ′	° ′	° ′	° ′	° ′
Hc	38 15	32 43	63 37	33 27	32 23	18 26	60 44
Zn	070	106	167	188	253	291	320

6 All the stars are at convenient altitudes between 18° and 64°.
The symbol (◆) indicates that *VEGA*, *SPICA*, and *POLLUX* are the best stars to choose for a 3-star fix, although *POLLUX* is becoming close to the horizon.
All the stars have magnitudes brighter than 1·5 except *Rasalhague* and *Dubhe* (names not in capitals).
No change in this selection will take place for about 54^m before or 6^m after the proposed time. This information is found by noting the LHA♈ when the particular set of selected stars change. Then, every degree of LHA♈ is equivalent to 4^m of time. In this case (194°·5 − 208°) × 60/15 = −13·5 × 4 = 54^m before, or (209°·5 − 208°) × 60/15 = +1·5 × 4 = 6^m after the proposed time.
The same stars are tabulated for latitude 44°N, but for 46°N, *DENEB* and *CAPELLA* replace *SPICA* and *Dubhe*.

The navigator will accordingly plan the programme of observations from among these stars, bearing in mind the phase of the Moon and the weather, which may make observing impossible. In this example, the Moon, 2 days from new, had not long risen in the south-east. The new Moon occurs 2013 January 11 at 19^h 44^m UT.

5.2 Finding Position from Sextant Observations

The methods and examples of sight reduction given here, illustrate how to use these tables efficiently to find your position from sextant observations, by calculating the intercept and azimuth and then plotting the resulting position lines on a chart.

In general terms "sight reduction" or "reduction of sights" is the process of comparing sextant observations with the equivalent calculated data, and thus determining a position — a fix.

The navigator must first make an initial estimate of position. This may either be a dead reckoning (DR) or estimated position (EP). The techniques given here concentrate on methods that rely on paper and pencil, tables and charts. Thus for best results the navigator should use the most accurate position available. Other techniques for determining a fix from sights are given in *NavPac and Compact Data* or *The Nautical Almanac*.

This method then involves adopting an assumed position (AP), close to the DR/EP, from which the sight is plotted. This position may vary for each sight and may be adjusted for various assumptions. These assumptions may be corrected at this stage or applied to the position line (intercept). It is good practice to always apply these corrections in a consistent manner. In this explanation these corrections are always made to the intercept (see below).

Having adopted a latitude, (the DR/EP latitude rounded to the nearest whole degree), and longitude, such that the LHA is a whole number of degrees, or even degrees for latitudes above 69°, the main tables may then be used to find the calculated (or tabulated) altitude (H_c) and true azimuth (bearing) (Z_n) of the star.

In order to make a valid comparison both the calculated altitude (H_c) and the sextant altitude (H_s) must be on the same system and with respect to the same origin. Thus, when reducing **star** observations, the sextant altitude (H_s) must be corrected for sextant index error (IE), dip (3.5.1), and refraction (3.5.2) to give the observed (H_o) altitude. These corrections cannot be made to the tabulated positions since they are functions of the following quantities; the particular sextant, height of eye of the observer above the horizon, and the atmospheric conditions, such as temperature and pressure, at the time of the observations.

The comparison between the observed and calculated altitudes may then be made. It is called the intercept (p) and is the difference between them ($H_o - H_c$).

However, depending on the practice and assumptions of the navigator, it may be necessary to apply corrections to the intercept, or the assumed position. These corrections are for the movement of the observer (MOO), when the observations are made over an extended interval (see 5.2.4), or for the movement of the body (MOB) when only one assumed position (at a fixed time) is adopted (see section 5.2.5).

Thus, in the first case, the position line may be advanced or retarded to another time by running it "on" or "back" along the ships course or course made good when the tidal stream and ocean currents, etc. are included. In extreme cases a correction to allow for precession and nutation (see Table **5** and the example on page xx) may be necessary.

Finally, the intercept (p), adjusted as necessary, and true azimuth (Z_n), which is given in the tables, are then used to plot the position line. The intersection of two position lines determines an observed position. When position lines of three stars are plotted, they should form a triangle, a cocked-hat, the area within which should contain the fix. The errors and uncertainties of this fix are not dealt with in this publication.

5.2.1 Sight Reduction Method The following steps give the procedure for calculating the intercept and azimuth of an observation and the resulting position line plot.

Step 1. Estimate the approximate position (DR/EP), the latitude and longitude, at the time that the fix is required. The time zone correction will also be needed.

Step 2. Convert the local date and time of the fix, and each of the observations, to their respective Greenwich date and UT time using the time zone correction (ZT), remembering to apply any errors (DWE) due to inaccuracies of the watch used to make the observation.

If the vessel has moved location significantly between observations and the time of the fix, or if special reduction techniques are used then record the difference between the time of the fix and the time of each observation. Note too whether the time of the fix is later or earlier than each of the observations. Corrections for these assumptions are made at step 8.

Step 3. Calculate the GHA♈ (Table **4** or an appropriate almanac such as *The Nautical Almanac*) for the time of the observation, i.e. from its Greenwich date and UT time. Add or subtract multiples of 360° to put GHA♈ between 0° and 360° if appropriate.

Step 4. For each observation (if appropriate) adopt an assumed position (AP) such that the sum of the assumed longitude (east longitudes are positive, and west longitudes are negative) and the respective GHA♈ gives the LHA♈ to a whole number of degrees, or an even degree for latitudes above 69°. Ensure that LHA♈ is between 0° and 360° by adding or subtracting multiples of 360°.

Step 5. Correct the sextant altitude (H_s) of the star by allowing for index error, dip (Table **8**a and the height of the observer's eye above the horizon), and refraction (Table **8**b) to give the observed altitude (H_o).

An additional correction for refraction (Table **8**c) may be needed if the temperature and pressure are different from the standard conditions (see 3.5.2) and the object is low in the sky.

Step 6. Extract the tabulated (calculated) altitude (H_C) and azimuth (Z_n) of the star from the main tabulations. These are found by going to the page for the assumed latitude (the estimated latitude rounded to the nearest degree). Then find the entry (left-hand column in bold) with the value of LHA♈ (Step 4) and name of the star observed; which gives, without interpolation, the calculated altitude (H_C) and azimuth (Z_n). Note: the azimuth is recorded after the calculation for the intercept as both are required for plotting.

Step 7. Calculate the intercept $p = H_O - H_C$. The intercept will be *positive* (towards) if the observed altitude is *greater* than the tabulated altitude. On the other hand the intercept will be *negative* (away) if the observed altitude is *less* than the tabulated altitude.

Step 8. Apply any relevant corrections to the intercept:
(a) for movement of the observer (MOO). The vessel has changed its position considerably between the time of the observations and the time of the fix (see 5.2.4);
(b) for movement of the object (MOB). Section 5.2.5 explains the details and the advantages of adopting an assumed position at the time of the fix and then making corrections for this assumption;
(c) for precession and nutation (Table **5**). This correction is normally ignored and only necessary in extreme cases, i.e., when the date is far from the epoch (2015·0) of the volume, or when maximum precision is required (see example on page xx).
It is possible to apply all these corrections at other stages of the calculation.

Step 9. Plot the position lines from the intercept (p), corrected as necessary, and azimuth (Z_n) to determine the fix.
For each observation in turn mark the assumed position and then plot its position line.
First establish whether the position line is *towards* or *away* from the direction of the star. If the intercept is *positive*, then the position line is plotted *towards* the direction (azimuth) of the star. On the other hand if the intercept is *negative*, then the position line is plotted in the opposite direction to (i.e. *away* from) the star.
Then draw the position line perpendicular to the direction of the star, where the direction of the star (Z_n) is measured at the assumed position (AP) used for that observation. The line is drawn at a distance given by the intercept, *towards* or *away from* the direction of the star.
Three position lines should define a small triangular area (cocked-hat) within which the fix is located. However, due to errors that may exist in the sextant, the observations, refraction, etc., the fix may be located outside the cocked-hat. Analysis of the accuracy of sextant observations and the resulting position lines may be found in other manuals e.g. *The Admiralty Manual of Navigation*.

Simply summarized: (1) estimate position at the time of fix, (2) convert dates and times to UT, (3) calculate GHA♈, (4) adopt an assumed position and form the LHA♈, (5) correct sextant altitudes, (6) extract the tabulated (calculated) altitude and true azimuth, (7) calculate the intercept, (8) apply any corrections if appropriate, and finally (9) plot the position line on the chart.

A sight reduction form (see 3.8) giving these steps is printed at the back of this volume. It may be freely copied or downloaded from our web site (www.ukho.gov.uk/hmnao).

5.2.2 Reduction of a Single Observation The following example follows the steps given above, but for one observation only.

Example. During the evening of 2012 December 5 in DR position N 24° 07′, W 47° 53′, zone time of $+3^h$, an observation of *Vega* is obtained at $18^h\ 07^m\ 58^s$ local time. The sextant reading is 33° 58′·1 with an index error of 2′·1 *off the arc* (+2′·1) and a height of eye of 6 metres (20 feet), under normal atmospheric conditions (10°C, 1010 mb pressure).

1	Estimated position N 24° 07′, W 47° 53′					
				d	h m s	
2	Convert local date and time 2012 December 5				18 07 58	
	Zone Correction	ZT	=		+3 00 00	
	Greenwich Date and UT on 2012 December 5				21 07 58	
3	Use Table **4** to calculate GHA ♈:				°	′
	2012 Dec. 1	*(a)*	=		70	15
	21^h UT day 5	*(b)*	=		319	48
	$07^m\ 58^s$	*(c)*	=		2	00
	Sum		=		392	03
	Remove multiples of 360°				−360	
		GHA♈	=		32	03
4	Calculate LHA♈: (360° added)				+360	
					392	03
	Assumed longitude (west, subtract)		=		−48	03
		LHA♈	=		**344**	
5	Correct the sextant altitude of *VEGA*:				°	′
	Sextant altitude	Hs	=		33	58·1
	Index error	IE	=			+2·1
	Dip, Table **8**a, 6 m	*D*	=			−4·3
	Apparent altitude	Ha	=		33	55·9
	Refraction, Table **8**b, Ha	*R*	=			−1·4
	Additional refraction, Table **8**c 10°C 1010mb					0·0
	Observed altitude	Ho	=		33	54·5
6	Extract tabulated altitude, page 113					
	Assumed latitude 24°N, LHA♈ 344°	Hc	=		34	03
7	Intercept, Ho − Hc	*p*	=			−8·5
	Ho < Hc, *p* −ve, intercept is				*away*	8·5
	Azimuth (true bearing)	Zn	=		302	
8	Precession and nutation (c), Table **5**					
	2012, 24° N, LHA♈344°				1′·5	247°

9 The centre of the plot shows the assumed position (AP) at N 24°, W 48° 03′, while the DR position is N 24° 07′, W 47° 53′. The position line for *VEGA* is then drawn perpendicular to the true direction (302°) to *VEGA* and at a distance of 8′·5 from the AP on the opposite (*away*) side to the direction to the star. The azimuth line is not normally drawn, but is often indicated by the small bars at each end of the position line pointing in the direction of the star.

The plot illustrates that the position line (the darker line) corrected for precession and nutation and its associated assumed position may be achieved by moving either the position line or the assumed position. In this particular example this correction is significant as it is greater than or equal to 1′·5.

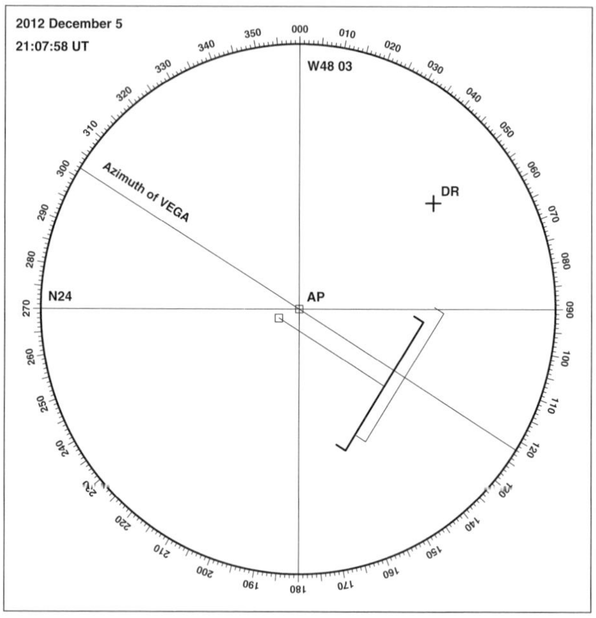

5.2.3 A 3-Star Fix The following example together with its position line plot, illustrates the use of the tables for the reduction of a typical set of observations and the determination of a fix.

The fix is usually required for some instant during, or near, the period of the observations. In the following example the observations are taken in rapid succession and any movement of the vessel during this time is negligible. No special techniques are used.

Example. On 2013 June 25 at $20^h\ 47^m$ local time the DR position will be N 45° 45′, W 26° 05′, zone correction $+2^h$. Determine a fix at this time from observations of *VEGA*, *ARCTURUS* and *Dubhe*. The observations were taken at $20^h\ 44^m\ 15^s$, $20^h\ 47^m\ 33^s$ and $20^h\ 51^m\ 55^s$ local time, and the sextant altitudes were 53° 05′·6, 60° 16′·1 and 50° 37′·4, respectively. The observer's height of eye was 6 m (20ft.) and the temperature and pressure were 10°C and 1010 mb, respectively. The index error of the sextant was 2′·1 *on the arc* (−2′·1) and there was negligible motion of the vessel between observations.

1 Estimated position N 45° 45′, W 26° 05′, 2013 June 25 at 20h 47m local time.

No.			*VEGA*		*ARCTURUS*		*Dubhe*	
2	Convert observations time to UT: 2013 June 25		h m s		h m s		h m s	
	Local time		20 44 15		20 47 33		20 51 55	
	Zone Correction		+2		+2		+2	
	UT		22 44 15		22 47 33		22 51 55	
3	GHAϒ from Table **4**:			° ′		° ′		° ′
	2013 June 1 (a)			249 39				
	Day 25 at 22h UT (b)			354 34				
	Sum (a) + (b)			604 13				
	Remove multiples of 360°			−360				
	2013 June 25 at 22h UT = (a) + (b) −360°		22	244 13	22	244 13	22	244 13
	Correction for minutes and seconds (c)		44 15	11 06	47 33	11 55	51 55	13 01
	Sum GHAϒ for given UT		22 44 15	255 19	22 47 33	256 08	22 51 55	257 14
4	Assumed longitude, subtract because west			−26 19		−26 08		−26 14
	LHAϒ= Sum			**229**		**230**		**231**
5	Correct sextant altitudes:			° ′		° ′		° ′
	Sextant altitude	H_s		53 05·6		60 16·1		50 37·4
	Index error	IE		−2·1		−2·1		−2·1
	Dip, Table **8**a, height 6 m	*D*		−4·3		−4·3		−4·3
	Apparent altitude	H_a		52 59·2		60 09·7		50 31·0
	Refraction, Table **8**b, H_a	*R*		−0·7		−0·6		−0·8
	Additional refraction, Table **8**c 10°C, 1010 mb			0·0		0·0		0·0
	Observed altitude	H_o		52 58·5		60 09·1		50 30·2
6	Extract tabulated altitude & azimuth, page 69,							
	Assumed Lat. 46° N, LHAϒ see step 4	H_c		52 46		60 05		50 39
7	Intercept, $p = H_o - H_c$			+12·5		+4·1		−8·8
		p		*towards* 12·5		*towards* 4·1		*away* 8·8
	Azimuth (true bearing)	Z_n		083°		211°		317°

8 The correction (a) MOO is negligible in this example as the time of the fix is very close to the time of the observations. No special techniques have been used so correction (b) MOB is not applicable. The correction for precession and nutation (c) is small (0′.5, 309°) and has been ignored, but may be treated as in the previous example.

9 The plot shows the three position lines indicated by arrows at each end. Each is plotted with respect to the appropriate assumed position; latitude N 46°, W 26° 19′ (AP1), N 46°, W 26° 08′ (AP2) and N 46°, W 26° 14′ (AP3), respectively (see step 4).

From the diagram it is clear that for *Dubhe* the intercept is *away*.

The fix is indicated by the area of the cocked-hat, but may lie outside it, depending on the size of the band of error on either side of each position line.

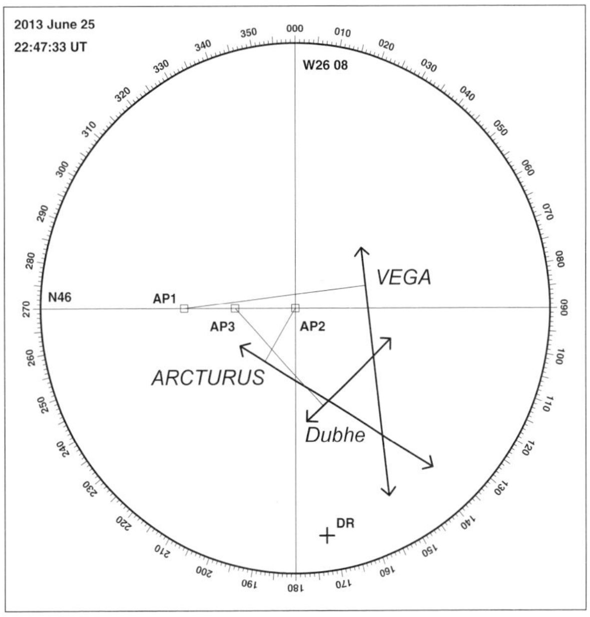

5.2.4 A 3-Star Fix with Movement of the Observer The following example illustrates the case when there have been significant changes in the position of the observer between the observations. For the Sun (see Volumes **2** or **3**) this is often the case with morning and afternoon sights. With stars, which are observed during twilight, the movement of the vessel during this period may usually be ignored. However, in cloudy conditions it may sometimes be necessary to combine observations from one evening with those taken the next morning, for example. It is also possible, when there is sufficient moonlight to illuminate the horizon, to make observations outside the nautical twilight period.

Example. On the evening of 2014 October 9 it was decided to take a fix at $18^h\ 35^m$ local time (before the end of nautical twilight). The DR position at that time was estimated to be N 24° 15′ W 051° 05′, with a zone correction of 3^h behind UT. Using the tables (see 5.1) it was established that the best three stars for a fix would be *Nunki*, *Alphecca*, and *Alpheratz*. However, observations of only two of the stars had been made before the sky clouded over. The observations were made at $18^h\ 27^m\ 01^s$ and $18^m\ 39^m$ 52 local time, and the watch was 4^s fast. The stars observed were *Nunki* and *Alphecca*, with sextant altitudes of 39° 54′.7 and 37° 53′.3, respectively. At the time of these observations the temperature was 15°C and the barometric pressure was 1000 mb. Assuming a visible horizon, it was noted that *Alphecca* would only be available for reduction for about 30^m, while both *Alpheratz* and *Nunki* were tabulated for a further $1^h.7$, with *Alpheratz* gaining in altitude. Luckily, later the same evening, after the end of nautical twilight, the sky began to clear from the east and the rising-full moon (Oct. 8) illuminated the horizon allowing an observation of the third star, *Alpheratz*, with sextant altitude of 35° 18′.0 at $19^h\ 13^m\ 16^s$ deck watch time. The temperature had decreased to 10°C but the pressure remained the same. The error of the watch was unchanged, as was the sextant index error of 2′.1 *on the arc* (−2′.1). The height of eye, for all observations was 6 m (20ft.). The navigator estimated that the distance made good (DMG) between the two sets of observations was 9 nautical miles, and the track (course) of the vessel had been 356°T. The following is the reduction and plot of the position lines.

1 Estimated position at the time of fix is N 24° 15′, W 51° 05′

2 Convert times:

	h m s
Local time of Fix 2014 October 9	18 35 00
Zone Correction	+3
UT of Fix	21 35 00

Convert time of observations of	*Nunki*	*Alphecca*	*Alpheratz*
	h m s	h m s	h m s
Local watch time of observations (DWT)	18 27 01	18 39 52	19 13 16
Watch Error (DWE)	−4	−4	−4
Local time	18 26 57	18 39 48	19 13 12
Zone Correction	+3	+3	+3
UT of Observations	21 26 57	21 39 48	22 13 12
UT of Fix			21 35 00
Time of Fix - Time of observation			− 38 12
The Fix is			earlier
than the observation by			38 12

	h m s	° ′	h m s	° ′	h m s	° ′
3 GHAϒ from Table **4**:						
2014 October 1 (a)		9 39		9 39		9 39
Day 9 at UT^h	21	323 45	21	323 45	22	338 47
2014 Oct. 9 at UT^h= (a) + (b)		333 24		333 24		348 26
Correction for minutes and seconds (c)	26 57	6 45	39 48	9 59	13 12	3 19
Sum = GHAϒ for given UT	21 26 57	340 09	21 39 48	343 23	22 13 12	351 45
4 Assumed longitude, subtract because west		−51 09		−51 23		−50 45
LHAϒ = Sum		**289**		**292**		**301**

Continued . . .

			Nunki	*Alphecca*	*Alpheratz*
	repeating last line of step 4	LHA♈	**289°**	**292°**	**301°**
5	Correct sextant altitudes:		° ′	° ′	° ′
	Sextant altitude	H_s	39 54·7	37 53·3	35 18·0
	Index error	IE	−2·1	−2·1	−2·1
	Dip, Table **8**a, height 6 m	*D*	−4·3	−4·3	−4·3
	Apparent altitude	H_a	39 48·3	37 46·9	35 11·6
	Refraction, Table **8**b, H_a	*R*	−1·2	−1·2	−1·4
	Additional refraction, Table **8**c, *T*°C, 1000 mb		0·0	0·0	0·0
	Observed altitude	H_o	39 47·1	37 45·7	35 10·2
6	Extract tabulated altitude & azimuth, page 113, Assumed Lat. 24° N, LHA♈ see step 4	H_c	39 30	37 49	35 33
7	Intercept $p = H_o - H_c$		+17·1	−3·3	−22·8
	Azimuth (true bearing)	Z_n	186°	286°	070°
8	Correction (a) for motion of vessel:				360°
	Add or subtract 360° as appropriate				430°
	True course (track) of vessel	*C*			356°
	Relative bearing = $Z_n - C$	Rel.Z_n			74°
	Table **1**, DMG = 9 nm, Z = 74°, earlier	MOO			−2·5
	Intercept, corrected				−25·3
		p	*towards* 17·1	*away* 3·3	*away* 25·3
	Azimuth (true bearing), see step **7**	Z_n	186°	286°	070°

Special care must be taken with the sign of MOO. In the above example, the value from the table, after interpolation, was +2′·5. However, the rules given below Table **1** indicate that since the time of the fix was *earlier* than the time of the observation and the sign from the table was positive (+), then the correction must be *subtracted* from the intercept. Alternatively, in this case, a negative (time of fix − time of observation) multiplied by a positive value from the table, gives a negative (−) correction. Note that although the time difference is not explicitly used it will probably be needed for calculating the distance made good. The formula for calculating this correction is given in 3.6.1, and is $(UT_f - UT)\, V \cos(\text{Rel.}Z_n)$, where the distance made good may be given by DMG = $(UT_f - UT)\, V$, (time in hours × speed (V) in knots), and ignores factors such as wind, tide and variable speed of the vessel.

9 The plot shows the three assumed positions at N 24°, W 51° 09′ (AP1), N 24° W 51° 23′ (AP2), and N 24°, W50° 45′ (AP3).

The position line of *Alpheratz* is shown plotted with respect to the assumed position (AP3) at the time of observation together with its azimuth line. The cocked-hat of position lines, the darker lines, includes the transferred position of *Alpheratz* which is indicated by the double arrows at each end of the line.

The fix is indicated by the area of the cocked-hat, but may lie outside it, depending on the size of the band of error on either side of each position line.

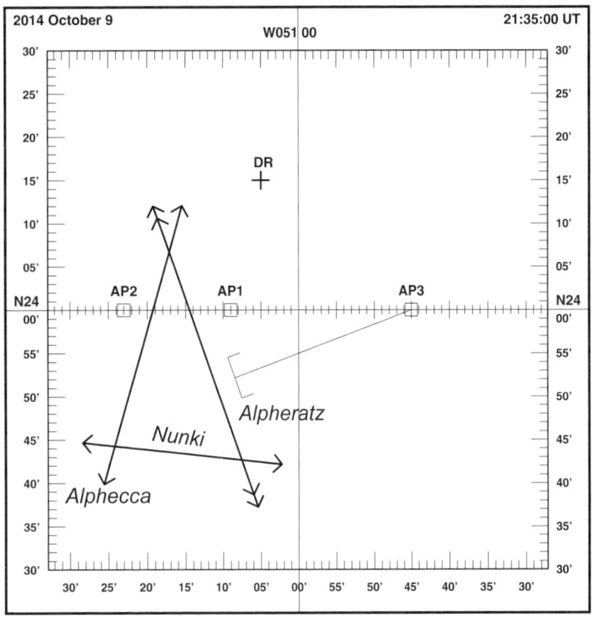

5.2.5 Special Techniques for Rapid Reduction This technique may be used when observations have been planned (see 5.1). The advantage being that the same assumed position and LHA♈, and thus H_C's and Z_n's from the planning stage are re-used in the actual reduction of the observations. This reduces the amount of calculation considerably.

Thus the following example illustrates how to perform the calculation at a fixed time (the time planned, usually the time of the fix) and the correction that has to be applied to correct to the time of observation. This correction allows for the effect of the rotation of the sky between the time of fix and the time of observation and is referred to as the movement of the body (MOB). In this example MOB is applied to the intercept.

In order to use this technique it is necessary to form the difference (see step 2) between the time of the observations and the time of the fix (the time the GHA♈ will be calculated). Note, also, whether the fix is after (later) the observation, when the interval is positive, or before (earlier) the observation, when the interval is negative. This time interval is needed later (step 8b) for calculating the total correction (MOB), since the table (Table **2**) only gives the movement during a 1^m interval.

The following example illustrates the advantages of using this special technique after planning your observations and is a continuation of the example in section 5.1.

Example. On the morning of 2013 January 10 the skies are clear and the navigator proceeds with the planned fix (see 5.1.2). The current estimate of the position (DR) at 06^h 54^m local time is N 44° 40′, E 160° 05′, with a zone time of -11^h. The most suitable stars for this morning's 3 star fix have been selected. Thus, observations of *VEGA*, *POLLUX* and *SPICA*, are taken with sextant readings of 38° 10′.2, 18° 38′.0, and 33° 19′.7, respectively. The watch used to time the observations was fast by 4 seconds (-4^s), and the timings were:-

Observations of	*VEGA*		*POLLUX*		*SPICA*	
Convert observation times to UT	Date	h m s	Date	h m s	Date	h m s
Watch time of observations	2013 Jan. 10	06 51 04	2013 Jan. 10	06 51 34	2008 Jan. 10	06 58 04
Watch error (DWE)		−04		−04		−04
Local time of observations		06 51 00		06 51 30		06 58 00
Zone Correction		−11		−11		−11
UT of observations	2013 Jan. 9	19 51 00	2013 Jan. 9	19 51 30	2013 Jan. 9	19 58 00

The navigator's height of eye was 6 m (20ft.) and the temperature and pressure was 10°C and 1010 mb, respectively. The sextant index error was 2′.1 *on the arc* (−2′.1) and vessel was on a course of 323°T at a speed of 12 knots.

Note that the current estimate of position is different from that used in the planning example, but the tabulated latitude is still 45° N. The vessel may have reduced speed. The difference in the estimate of position might matter if one needed to use a different tabulated latitude (i.e. if the assumed latitude was now 46° N). The result of this would be to change the calculated altitude (H_C) and thus reduce the size of the intercepts. The choice of stars could, however, be different.

1 Estimated position at the time of fix N 44° 40′, E 160° 05′

2 Converted times (see above)	*VEGA*	*POLLUX*	*SPICA*
	h m s	h m s	h m s
UT of Fix: 2013 January 9	19 54 00	19 54 00	19 54 00
UT of observation	19 51 00	19 51 30	19 58 00
Time of Fix − time of Observation (UT_f−UT)	+3 00	+2 30	−4 00
The Fix is	later	later	earlier
than the observation by	3 00	2 30	4 00

3 GHA♈ from Table **4**:				°	′
2013 January 1 (a)				100	49
Day 9 at 19^h UT (b)	19			293	40
Correction for minutes and seconds (c)		54	00	13	32
Sum	19	54	00	408	01
Remove multiples of 360°				−360	
GHA♈ for given UT				48	01
4 Assumed longitude, add because east				+159	59
LHA♈ = Sum				**208**	

		VEGA	*POLLUX*	*SPICA*
5 Correct sextant altitudes:		° ′	° ′	° ′
Sextant altitude	H_s	38 10·2	18 38·0	33 19·7
Index error	IE	−2·1	−2·1	−2·1
Dip, Table **8**a, height 6 m	*D*	−4·3	−4·3	−4·3
Apparent altitude	H_a	38 03·8	18 31·6	33 13·3
Refraction, Table **8**b, H_a	*R*	−1·2	−2·9	−1·5
Additional refraction, Table **8**c (10°C, 1010 mb)		0·0	0·0	0·0
Observed altitude	H_o	38 02·6	18 28·7	33 11·8
6 Extract tabulated altitude & azimuth: page 71				
Assumed Lat. 45° N, LHA♈ 208°	H_c	38 15	18 26	33 27
7 Intercept, $H_o - H_c$		−12·4	+2·7	−15·2
8 Correction (b) for fixed LHA♈208° (see below)	MOB	+30·0	−24·8	+6·0
Intercept, corrected	*p*	+17·6	−22·1	−9·2
		towards 17·6	*away* 22·1	*away* 9·2
Azimuth (true bearing)	Z_n	070°	291°	188°

9 The plot shows the DR position at N 44° 40′, E 160° 05′ and the assumed position at N 45°, E 159° 59′ (AP).

The three un-corrected position lines (lighter) are those plotted with respect to the assumed position. Applying the corrections for MOB transfers the original "cocked-hat" to the final position shown in bold.

The fix is indicated by the area of the cocked-hat, but may lie outside it, depending on the size of the band of error on either side of each position line.

The table below illustrates how the correction (MOB), given in step 8 above, for using a fixed value of LHA♈ has been calculated. The calculation is simpler if the observations are made at multiples of whole minutes from the time of the fix. Care is needed to ensure enough figures are kept when interpolating and then multiplying.

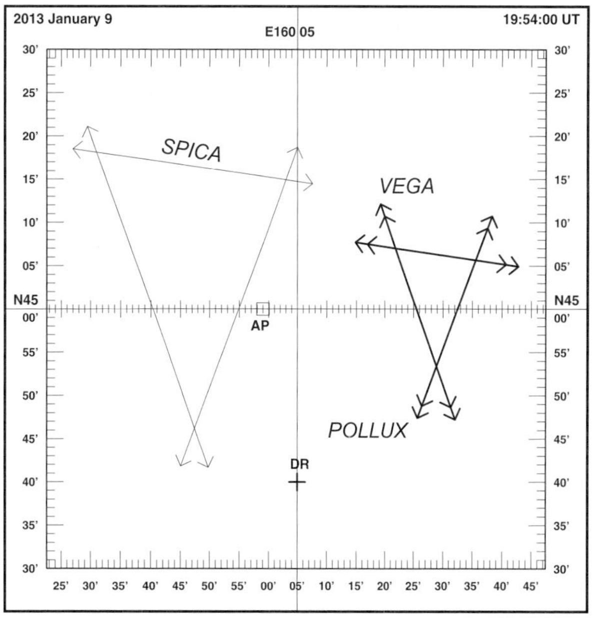

In particular, looking up Table **2**, with latitude N 45° azimuth 291° (*POLLUX*), the correction for 1^m is −9·9, no interpolation is needed as 291° is a tabular value. Interpolation is unnecessary for latitude in this example. The correction for this star for $+2^m\ 30^s$ using Table **2** is calculated from (+2·5) × (−9·9) = −24′·8. Alternatively, the correction for whole minutes may be calculated from Table **2** and the correction for the remaining fraction of a minute from the small table at the bottom of the page (which may also require interpolation) as follows (−9·9 × 2) − 5·0 = −24′·8. The values tabulated in the table at the bottom of the page are (value from Table **2** × seconds/60). The formulae for calculating this correction is given in 3.6.2, and is $15{\cdot}0411(UT_f - UT)\cos Lat \sin Z_n$, where $(UT_f - UT)$ is the time in minutes.

		VEGA		*POLLUX*		*SPICA*	
Azimuth (true bearing)	Zn		070°		291°		188°
		m s	′	m s	′	m s	′
Table **2** correction; N 45°, Zn		+1	+10·0	+1	− 9·9	+1	− 1·5
Time Interval, see step 2	minutes	+3	+30·0	+2	− 19·8	−4	+ 6·0
	seconds	00	+ 0·0	30	− 5·0	00	0·0
Correction for fixed LHA♈ = 208°	MOB	+3 00	+30·0	+2 30	−24·8	−4 00	+6·0

5.3 Method of finding Latitude from Polaris

The *Polaris* tables may be used to find latitude. They may also be used to plot a position line. The method is given below together with an example.

Step 1. Estimate the longitude at the time of the observation.

Step 2. Convert the date and time of the observation to its respective Greenwich date and UT time using the zone time correction (ZT), remembering to apply any errors (DWE) due to inaccuracies of the watch used to make the observation.

Step 3. Calculate GHA♈ (Table **4**), from the Greenwich date and UT time of the observation. Remove multiples of 360° if necessary.

Step 4. Form LHA♈ from the GHA♈ and the estimated longitude (east longitudes are positive, west longitudes are negative). Ensure that LHA♈ is between 0° and 360° by adding or subtracting multiples of 360°.

Step 5. Correct the sextant altitude (H_S) of *Polaris* by allowing for sextant index error, dip (Table **8**a), and refraction (Table **8**b,c) to give the observed altitude (H_O).

Step 6. Enter Table **6** with LHA♈ to give the *Q* correction. The latitude is the sum of *Q* and the observed altitude of *Polaris* (H_O).

Step 7. The true azimuth (Z_n) of *Polaris* is found by entering Table **7** with the latitude (nearest tabular value) and LHA♈ found in step 4. Interpolation in LHA♈ may sometimes be necessary.

Example. On the evening of 2013 January 9 at $20^h\ 23^m\ 20^s$ UT, in longitude W 48° 06′, an observation was made of the altitude of *Polaris*. The sextant reading was 54° 29′·8 with an index error of on the arc (−2′·1), while the height of eye, temperature and pressure were, 6 m (20 ft.), −8°C, and 1020 mb, respectively. The latitude is found as follows:

1	Estimated longitude W 48° 06′		
2	2013 January 9 $20^h\ 23^m\ 20^s$ UT		
3	GHA♈ from Table **4**:		° ′
	2013 Jan. 1	(a) =	100 49
	20^h UT day 9	(b) =	308 42
	$23^m\ 20^s$	(c) =	5 51
	Sum (a) + (b) + (c) = GHA ♈	=	415 22
4	Longitude (west negative)	=	−48 06
			367 16
	LHA♈ (360° removed) LHA♈	=	7 16

				°	′
5	Correct the sextant altitude:				
	Sextant altitude	H_S	=	54	29·8
	Index error	IE	=		−2·1
	Dip, Table **8**a, 6 m	*D*	=		−4·3
	Apparent altitude	H_a	=	54	23·4
	Refraction, Table **8**b,c, H_a, and	*R*	=		−0·7
	Additional refraction −8°C, 1020 mb				−0·1
	Observed altitude	H_O	=	54	22·6
6	Table **6**, LHA♈ 7° 16′	*Q*	=		−33
	Latitude = H_O + *Q*		=	53	49·6
7	Azimuth of *Polaris*, Table **7**, N 55° LHA♈ 7°	Zn	=	0°·7	

In step 5, an entry is made for non-standard refraction. In this case this correction could be ignored as the apparent altitude (H_a) is greater than 50°. However, to demonstrate the use of Table **8**c, the top graph is entered with the temperature of −8°C and pressure of 1020 mb, which give the zone letter 'C'. The bottom table is then entered with the zone letter just found and the apparent altitude. In this example H_a has been rounded to the nearest tabular value of 50°.

Using the calculated latitude it is possible to calculate the altitude of *Polaris* and thus the intercept. Thus a position line may be plotted, which is always almost a parallel of latitude, as the azimuth (see Table **7**) is always within a degree or two of north (0°). A correction is theoretically necessary for precession and nutation. However, Table **5** indicates that, in this case, the deduced position line should be shifted a distance of 0·7 mile in direction 232°.

RAPID
SIGHT REDUCTION TABLES
FOR
NAVIGATION

TABULATIONS FOR

SELECTED STARS

EPOCH J2015·0

LAT 89°N

LHA ♈	Hc	Zn	Hc	Zn	Hc	Zn	Hc	Zn	Hc	Zn	Hc	Zn	Hc	Zn
	Dubhe		POLLUX		◆ CAPELLA		Alpheratz		◆ DENEB		VEGA		◆ ARCTURUS	
0	60 42	013	27 32	063	46 11	100	30 10	178	45 59	230	38 57	261	18 17	326
2	60 42	015	27 34	065	46 13	102	30 10	180	45 57	232	38 55	263	18 15	328
4	60 43	017	27 36	067	46 15	104	30 10	182	45 55	234	38 53	265	18 14	330
6	60 44	019	27 38	069	46 17	106	30 10	184	45 54	236	38 51	267	18 13	332
8	60 44	021	27 40	071	46 19	108	30 10	186	45 52	238	38 49	269	18 12	334
10	60 45	023	27 42	073	46 21	110	30 10	188	45 50	240	38 47	271	18 11	336
12	60 46	025	27 44	075	46 23	112	30 10	190	45 48	242	38 45	273	18 11	338
14	60 47	027	27 46	077	46 25	114	30 09	192	45 46	244	38 43	275	18 10	340
16	60 48	029	27 48	079	46 27	116	30 09	194	45 44	246	38 41	277	18 09	342
18	60 49	031	27 50	081	46 29	118	30 08	196	45 43	248	38 38	279	18 09	344
20	60 50	033	27 52	083	46 31	120	30 08	198	45 41	250	38 36	281	18 08	346
22	60 51	035	27 54	085	46 33	122	30 07	200	45 39	252	38 34	283	18 08	348
24	60 52	037	27 56	087	46 34	124	30 06	202	45 37	254	38 32	285	18 07	350
26	60 54	039	27 58	089	46 36	126	30 05	204	45 35	256	38 30	287	18 07	352
28	60 55	041	28 01	091	46 38	128	30 04	206	45 33	259	38 28	289	18 07	354
	Dubhe		POLLUX		◆ CAPELLA		Alpheratz		◆ DENEB		VEGA		◆ ARCTURUS	
30	60 56	043	28 03	093	46 39	130	30 03	208	45 30	261	38 26	291	18 06	356
32	60 58	045	28 05	095	46 41	132	30 02	210	45 28	263	38 24	293	18 06	358
34	60 59	046	28 07	097	46 43	134	30 01	212	45 26	265	38 23	295	18 06	000
36	61 01	048	28 09	099	46 44	136	30 00	214	45 24	267	38 21	297	18 06	002
38	61 03	050	28 11	101	46 45	138	29 59	216	45 22	269	38 19	299	18 06	004
40	61 04	052	28 13	103	46 47	140	29 58	218	45 20	271	38 17	301	18 07	006
42	61 06	054	28 15	105	46 48	142	29 56	220	45 18	273	38 15	303	18 07	008
44	61 08	056	28 17	107	46 49	144	29 55	222	45 16	275	38 14	305	18 07	010
46	61 09	058	28 19	109	46 51	146	29 54	224	45 14	277	38 12	307	18 08	012
48	61 11	060	28 21	111	46 52	148	29 52	226	45 12	279	38 10	309	18 08	014
50	61 13	062	28 23	113	46 53	150	29 51	228	45 10	281	38 09	311	18 09	016
52	61 15	064	28 25	115	46 54	152	29 49	230	45 08	283	38 07	313	18 09	018
54	61 17	066	28 27	117	46 55	154	29 47	232	45 06	284	38 06	315	18 10	020
56	61 19	068	28 29	119	46 56	156	29 46	234	45 04	286	38 04	317	18 11	022
58	61 21	070	28 30	121	46 56	158	29 44	236	45 02	288	38 03	319	18 11	024
	◆ ARCTURUS		REGULUS		POLLUX		◆ CAPELLA		Alpheratz		◆ DENEB		VEGA	
60	18 12	026	11 51	087	28 32	123	46 57	160	29 42	238	45 00	290	38 01	321
62	18 13	028	11 53	089	28 34	125	46 58	162	29 40	240	44 58	292	38 00	323
64	18 14	030	11 55	091	28 36	127	46 58	164	29 39	242	44 56	294	37 59	325
66	18 15	032	11 57	093	28 37	129	46 59	166	29 37	244	44 54	296	37 58	327
68	18 16	034	11 59	095	28 39	131	46 59	168	29 35	246	44 52	298	37 57	329
70	18 18	036	12 02	097	28 40	133	47 00	170	29 33	248	44 50	300	37 56	331
72	18 19	038	12 04	099	28 42	135	47 00	172	29 31	250	44 48	302	37 55	333
74	18 20	040	12 06	101	28 43	137	47 00	174	29 29	252	44 47	304	37 54	335
76	18 22	042	12 08	104	28 45	139	47 01	176	29 27	254	44 45	306	37 53	337
78	18 23	044	12 10	106	28 46	141	47 01	179	29 25	256	44 43	308	37 52	339
80	18 24	046	12 12	108	28 47	143	47 01	181	29 23	258	44 42	310	37 51	341
82	18 26	048	12 14	110	28 49	145	47 01	183	29 21	260	44 40	312	37 51	343
84	18 28	050	12 16	112	28 50	147	47 01	185	29 19	262	44 38	314	37 50	345
86	18 29	052	12 18	114	28 51	149	47 00	187	29 17	264	44 37	316	37 50	347
88	18 31	054	12 20	116	28 52	151	47 00	189	29 15	266	44 36	318	37 49	349
	◆ ARCTURUS		REGULUS		POLLUX		◆ CAPELLA		Alpheratz		◆ DENEB		VEGA	
90	18 33	056	12 21	118	28 53	153	47 00	191	29 12	268	44 34	320	37 49	351
92	18 34	058	12 23	120	28 54	155	46 59	193	29 10	270	44 33	322	37 48	353
94	18 36	060	12 25	122	28 55	157	46 59	195	29 08	272	44 32	324	37 48	355
96	18 38	062	12 27	124	28 55	159	46 58	197	29 06	274	44 30	326	37 48	357
98	18 40	064	12 29	126	28 56	161	46 58	199	29 04	276	44 29	328	37 48	359
100	18 42	066	12 30	128	28 57	163	46 57	201	29 02	278	44 28	330	37 48	001
102	18 44	068	12 32	130	28 57	165	46 56	203	29 00	280	44 27	332	37 48	003
104	18 46	070	12 33	132	28 58	167	46 55	205	28 58	282	44 26	334	37 48	005
106	18 48	072	12 35	134	28 58	169	46 54	207	28 56	284	44 25	336	37 48	007
108	18 49	074	12 36	136	28 59	171	46 53	209	28 54	286	44 25	338	37 49	009
110	18 52	076	12 38	138	28 59	173	46 52	211	28 52	288	44 24	340	37 49	010
112	18 54	078	12 39	140	28 59	175	46 51	213	28 50	290	44 23	342	37 49	012
114	18 56	080	12 41	142	28 59	177	46 50	215	28 48	292	44 22	344	37 50	014
116	18 58	082	12 42	144	28 59	179	46 49	217	28 46	294	44 22	346	37 50	016
118	19 00	084	12 43	146	28 59	181	46 47	219	28 44	296	44 21	348	37 51	018
	VEGA		◆ ARCTURUS		REGULUS		POLLUX		◆ CAPELLA		Alpheratz		◆ DENEB	
120	37 52	020	19 02	086	12 44	148	28 59	183	46 46	221	28 42	298	44 21	350
122	37 52	022	19 04	088	12 45	150	28 59	185	46 45	223	28 40	300	44 21	352
124	37 53	024	19 06	090	12 46	152	28 59	188	46 43	225	28 39	302	44 20	354
126	37 54	026	19 08	092	12 47	154	28 59	190	46 42	227	28 37	304	44 20	356
128	37 55	028	19 10	094	12 48	156	28 58	192	46 40	229	28 35	306	44 20	358
130	37 56	030	19 12	096	12 49	158	28 58	194	46 38	231	28 34	308	44 20	000
132	37 57	032	19 14	098	12 50	160	28 57	196	46 37	233	28 32	310	44 20	001
134	37 58	034	19 16	100	12 51	162	28 57	198	46 35	235	28 30	312	44 20	003
136	38 00	036	19 19	102	12 51	164	28 56	200	46 33	237	28 29	314	44 20	005
138	38 01	038	19 21	104	12 52	166	28 55	202	46 32	239	28 27	316	44 21	007
140	38 02	040	19 23	106	12 52	168	28 54	204	46 30	241	28 26	318	44 21	009
142	38 04	042	19 25	108	12 53	170	28 53	206	46 28	243	28 25	320	44 21	011
144	38 05	044	19 27	110	12 53	172	28 53	208	46 26	245	28 23	322	44 22	013
146	38 06	046	19 29	112	12 53	174	28 52	210	46 24	248	28 22	324	44 22	015
148	38 08	048	19 30	114	12 53	176	28 50	212	46 22	250	28 21	326	44 23	017
	◆ DENEB		VEGA		◆ ARCTURUS		REGULUS		POLLUX		◆ CAPELLA		Alpheratz	
150	44 23	019	38 10	050	19 32	116	12 54	178	28 49	214	46 20	252	28 20	328
152	44 24	021	38 11	052	19 34	118	12 54	180	28 48	216	46 18	254	28 19	330
154	44 25	023	38 13	054	19 36	120	12 54	182	28 47	218	46 16	256	28 17	332
156	44 26	025	38 15	056	19 38	122	12 53	184	28 46	220	46 14	258	28 17	334
158	44 27	027	38 16	058	19 40	124	12 53	186	28 44	222	46 12	260	28 16	336
160	44 28	029	38 18	060	19 41	126	12 53	188	28 43	224	46 10	262	28 15	338
162	44 29	031	38 20	062	19 43	128	12 53	190	28 41	226	46 08	264	28 14	340
164	44 30	033	38 22	064	19 45	130	12 52	192	28 40	228	46 06	266	28 13	342
166	44 31	035	38 24	066	19 46	132	12 52	194	28 38	230	46 04	268	28 13	344
168	44 32	037	38 26	068	19 48	134	12 51	196	28 37	232	46 02	270	28 12	346
170	44 34	039	38 28	070	19 49	136	12 51	198	28 35	234	46 00	272	28 12	348
172	44 35	041	38 30	072	19 51	138	12 50	200	28 33	236	45 57	274	28 11	350
174	44 36	043	38 32	074	19 52	140	12 49	202	28 31	238	45 55	276	28 11	352
176	44 38	045	38 34	076	19 53	142	12 49	204	28 30	240	45 53	278	28 11	354
178	44 39	047	38 36	078	19 55	144	12 48	206	28 28	242	45 51	280	28 11	356

LHA ♈	Hc	Zn	Hc	Zn	Hc	Zn	Hc	Zn	Hc	Zn	Hc	Zn	Hc	Zn
	◆ DENEB		VEGA		◆ ARCTURUS		REGULUS		POLLUX		◆ CAPELLA		Alpheratz	
180	44 41	049	38 38	080	19 56	146	12 47	208	28 26	244	45 49	282	28 10	358
182	44 42	051	38 40	082	19 57	148	12 46	210	28 24	246	45 47	284	28 10	000
184	44 44	053	38 42	084	19 58	150	12 45	212	28 22	248	45 45	286	28 10	002
186	44 46	055	38 44	086	19 59	152	12 43	214	28 20	250	45 43	288	28 11	004
188	44 47	057	38 46	088	20 00	154	12 42	216	28 18	252	45 41	290	28 11	006
190	44 49	059	38 48	090	20 01	156	12 41	218	28 16	254	45 39	292	28 11	008
192	44 51	061	38 50	092	20 02	158	12 40	220	28 14	256	45 37	293	28 11	010
194	44 53	063	38 52	094	20 03	160	12 38	222	28 12	258	45 35	295	28 12	012
196	44 55	065	38 54	096	20 03	162	12 37	224	28 10	260	45 33	297	28 12	014
198	44 57	067	38 57	098	20 04	164	12 35	226	28 08	262	45 32	299	28 13	016
200	44 59	069	38 59	100	20 04	166	12 34	228	28 06	264	45 30	301	28 13	018
202	45 01	071	39 01	102	20 05	168	12 32	230	28 04	266	45 28	303	28 14	020
204	45 03	073	39 03	104	20 05	170	12 31	232	28 02	268	45 26	305	28 15	022
206	45 05	075	39 05	106	20 06	172	12 29	234	28 00	270	45 25	307	28 15	023
208	45 07	077	39 07	108	20 06	174	12 27	236	27 58	272	45 23	309	28 16	025
	Alpheratz		◆ DENEB		VEGA		◆ ARCTURUS		REGULUS		POLLUX		◆ CAPELLA	
210	28 17	027	45 09	079	39 09	110	20 06	176	12 26	238	27 55	274	45 21	311
212	28 18	029	45 11	081	39 11	112	20 06	178	12 24	240	27 53	276	45 20	313
214	28 19	031	45 13	083	39 13	114	20 06	180	12 22	242	27 51	278	45 18	315
216	28 20	033	45 15	085	39 14	116	20 06	182	12 20	244	27 49	280	45 17	317
218	28 22	035	45 17	087	39 16	118	20 06	184	12 18	246	27 47	282	45 15	319
220	28 23	037	45 19	089	39 18	120	20 06	186	12 16	248	27 45	284	45 14	321
222	28 24	039	45 21	091	39 20	122	20 06	188	12 14	250	27 43	286	45 13	323
224	28 25	041	45 23	093	39 22	124	20 05	190	12 12	252	27 41	288	45 12	325
226	28 27	043	45 25	095	39 23	126	20 05	192	12 10	254	27 39	290	45 10	327
228	28 28	045	45 27	097	39 25	128	20 05	194	12 08	256	27 37	292	45 09	329
230	28 30	047	45 29	099	39 27	130	20 04	196	12 06	258	27 35	294	45 08	331
232	28 31	049	45 32	101	39 28	132	20 03	198	12 04	260	27 33	296	45 07	333
234	28 33	051	45 34	103	39 30	134	20 03	200	12 02	262	27 31	298	45 06	335
236	28 35	053	45 36	105	39 31	136	20 02	202	12 00	264	27 30	300	45 06	337
238	28 36	055	45 38	107	39 33	138	20 01	204	11 58	266	27 28	302	45 05	339
	Alpheratz		◆ DENEB		VEGA		◆ ARCTURUS		REGULUS		POLLUX		◆ CAPELLA	
240	28 38	057	45 40	109	39 34	140	20 00	206	11 56	268	27 26	304	45 04	341
242	28 40	059	45 42	111	39 35	142	19 59	208	11 54	270	27 24	306	45 03	343
244	28 42	061	45 44	113	39 37	144	19 58	210	11 52	272	27 23	308	45 03	345
246	28 44	063	45 45	115	39 38	146	19 57	212	11 50	274	27 21	310	45 02	347
248	28 45	065	45 47	117	39 39	148	19 56	214	11 48	276	27 19	312	45 02	349
250	28 47	067	45 49	119	39 40	150	19 55	216	11 45	278	27 18	314	45 02	351
252	28 49	069	45 51	121	39 41	152	19 54	218	11 43	280	27 16	316	45 01	353
254	28 51	071	45 53	123	39 42	154	19 52	220	11 41	282	27 15	318	45 01	355
256	28 53	073	45 55	125	39 43	156	19 51	222	11 39	284	27 14	320	45 01	357
258	28 55	075	45 56	127	39 44	158	19 49	224	11 37	286	27 12	322	45 01	359
260	28 57	077	45 58	129	39 44	160	19 48	226	11 35	288	27 11	324	45 01	001
262	28 59	079	46 00	131	39 45	162	19 46	228	11 33	290	27 10	326	45 01	003
264	29 01	081	46 01	133	39 46	164	19 45	230	11 31	292	27 09	328	45 01	004
266	29 04	083	46 03	135	39 46	166	19 43	232	11 29	294	27 08	330	45 01	006
268	29 06	085	46 04	137	39 47	168	19 42	234	11 27	296	27 07	332	45 01	008
	◆ CAPELLA		Alpheratz		◆ DENEB		VEGA		◆ ARCTURUS		Dubhe		POLLUX	
270	45 02	010	29 08	087	46 05	139	39 47	171	19 40	236	61 25	286	27 06	334
272	45 02	012	29 10	089	46 07	141	39 47	173	19 38	238	61 23	288	27 05	336
274	45 03	014	29 12	091	46 08	143	39 48	175	19 36	240	61 21	290	27 04	338
276	45 03	016	29 14	093	46 09	145	39 48	177	19 34	242	61 19	292	27 03	340
278	45 04	018	29 16	095	46 11	147	39 48	179	19 33	244	61 17	294	27 02	342
280	45 04	020	29 18	097	46 12	149	39 48	181	19 31	246	61 15	296	27 02	344
282	45 05	022	29 20	099	46 13	151	39 48	183	19 29	248	61 13	297	27 01	346
284	45 06	024	29 22	101	46 14	153	39 48	185	19 27	250	61 11	299	27 01	348
286	45 07	026	29 24	103	46 15	155	39 47	187	19 25	252	61 10	301	27 00	350
288	45 08	028	29 26	105	46 15	157	39 47	189	19 23	254	61 08	303	27 00	352
290	45 09	030	29 28	107	46 16	159	39 47	191	19 21	256	61 06	305	27 00	354
292	45 10	032	29 30	109	46 17	161	39 46	193	19 19	258	61 04	307	27 00	355
294	45 11	034	29 32	111	46 18	163	39 46	195	19 17	260	61 03	309	26 59	357
296	45 12	036	29 34	113	46 18	165	39 45	197	19 15	262	61 01	311	26 59	359
298	45 14	038	29 36	115	46 19	167	39 45	199	19 12	264	61 00	313	26 59	001
	POLLUX		◆ CAPELLA		Alpheratz		◆ DENEB		VEGA		◆ ARCTURUS		Dubhe	
300	26 59	003	45 15	040	29 38	117	46 19	169	39 44	201	19 10	266	60 58	315
302	27 00	005	45 16	042	29 40	119	46 19	171	39 43	203	19 08	268	60 57	317
304	27 00	007	45 18	044	29 42	121	46 20	173	39 42	205	19 06	270	60 55	319
306	27 00	009	45 19	046	29 43	123	46 20	175	39 41	207	19 04	272	60 54	321
308	27 01	011	45 21	048	29 45	125	46 20	177	39 40	209	19 02	274	60 53	323
310	27 01	013	45 22	050	29 47	127	46 20	180	39 39	211	19 00	276	60 51	325
312	27 01	015	45 24	052	29 49	129	46 20	182	39 38	213	18 58	278	60 50	327
314	27 02	017	45 26	054	29 50	131	46 20	184	39 37	215	18 56	280	60 49	329
316	27 03	019	45 27	056	29 52	133	46 20	186	39 36	217	18 54	282	60 48	331
318	27 03	021	45 29	058	29 53	135	46 20	188	39 35	219	18 52	284	60 47	333
320	27 04	023	45 31	060	29 55	137	46 19	190	39 33	221	18 50	286	60 46	335
322	27 05	025	45 33	062	29 56	139	46 19	192	39 32	223	18 48	288	60 45	337
324	27 06	027	45 34	064	29 57	141	46 18	194	39 30	225	18 46	290	60 44	339
326	27 07	029	45 36	066	29 59	143	46 18	196	39 29	227	18 44	292	60 44	340
328	27 08	031	45 38	068	30 00	145	46 17	198	39 27	229	18 42	294	60 43	342
	POLLUX		◆ CAPELLA		Alpheratz		◆ DENEB		VEGA		◆ ARCTURUS		Dubhe	
330	27 09	033	45 40	070	30 01	147	46 17	200	39 26	231	18 40	296	60 42	344
332	27 10	035	45 42	072	30 02	149	46 16	202	39 24	233	18 38	298	60 42	346
334	27 12	037	45 44	074	30 03	151	46 15	204	39 22	235	18 36	300	60 41	348
336	27 13	039	45 46	076	30 04	153	46 14	206	39 21	237	18 34	302	60 41	350
338	27 14	041	45 48	078	30 05	155	46 13	208	39 19	239	18 33	304	60 41	352
340	27 16	043	45 50	080	30 06	157	46 12	210	39 17	241	18 31	306	60 41	354
342	27 17	045	45 52	082	30 07	160	46 11	212	39 15	243	18 29	308	60 40	356
344	27 19	047	45 54	084	30 07	162	46 10	214	39 13	245	18 28	310	60 40	358
346	27 20	049	45 57	086	30 08	164	46 09	216	39 11	247	18 26	312	60 40	000
348	27 22	051	45 59	088	30 09	166	46 07	218	39 09	249	18 25	314	60 40	002
350	27 23	053	46 01	090	30 09	168	46 06	220	39 07	251	18 23	316	60 40	004
352	27 25	055	46 03	092	30 09	170	46 05	222	39 05	253	18 22	318	60 40	006
354	27 27	057	46 05	094	30 10	172	46 03	224	39 03	255	18 20	320	60 41	008
356	27 29	059	46 07	096	30 10	174	46 02	226	39 01	257	18 19	322	60 41	010
358	27 30	061	46 09	098	30 10	176	46 00	228	38 59	259	18 18	324	60 41	011

LAT 88°N

LAT 88°N

LHA ♈	Hc Zn	Hc Zn	Hc Zn	Hc Zn	Hc Zn	Hc Zn	Hc Zn	LHA ♈	Hc Zn	Hc Zn	Hc Zn	Hc Zn	Hc Zn	Hc Zn	Hc Zn
	Dubhe	POLLUX	◆CAPELLA	Alpheratz	◆DENEB	VEGA	◆ARCTURUS		◆DENEB	VEGA	◆ARCTURUS	REGULUS	POLLUX	◆CAPELLA	Alpheratz
0	59 43 013	27 05 063	46 21 098	31 10 178	46 37 231	39 06 262	17 27 326	180	44 01 048	38 27 079	20 45 146	13 40 208	28 52 244	45 37 283	27 10 358
2	59 44 015	27 09 064	46 25 101	31 10 180	46 33 233	39 02 264	17 24 328	182	44 04 050	38 31 081	20 48 148	13 38 210	28 48 246	45 33 285	27 10 000
4	59 46 017	27 12 066	46 29 103	31 10 182	46 30 235	38 57 266	17 22 330	184	44 07 052	38 35 083	20 50 150	13 36 212	28 44 248	45 29 287	27 10 002
6	59 47 019	27 16 068	46 33 105	31 10 184	46 27 237	38 53 268	17 20 332	186	44 11 054	38 39 085	20 52 152	13 33 214	28 40 250	45 25 289	27 11 004
8	59 48 021	27 20 070	46 37 107	31 10 186	46 23 239	38 49 270	17 18 334	188	44 14 056	38 43 087	20 54 154	13 31 216	28 37 252	45 21 290	27 11 006
10	59 50 022	27 24 072	46 41 109	31 09 188	46 19 241	38 45 272	17 17 336	190	44 18 058	38 48 089	20 56 156	13 28 218	28 32 254	45 17 292	27 11 008
12	59 51 024	27 28 074	46 45 111	31 09 190	46 16 243	38 41 274	17 15 338	192	44 21 060	38 52 091	20 57 158	13 26 220	28 28 256	45 13 294	27 12 010
14	59 53 026	27 32 076	46 49 113	31 08 192	46 12 245	38 37 276	17 14 340	194	44 25 062	38 56 093	20 59 160	13 23 222	28 24 258	45 09 296	27 13 011
16	59 55 028	27 36 078	46 53 115	31 07 194	46 08 247	38 32 278	17 12 342	196	44 29 064	39 00 095	21 00 162	13 20 224	28 20 260	45 05 298	27 14 013
18	59 57 030	27 40 080	46 56 117	31 06 196	46 04 249	38 28 280	17 11 344	198	44 32 066	39 04 097	21 02 164	13 17 226	28 16 263	45 02 300	27 15 015
20	59 59 032	27 45 082	47 00 119	31 05 198	46 00 251	38 24 282	17 10 346	200	44 36 068	39 08 099	21 03 166	13 14 228	28 12 265	44 58 302	27 16 017
22	60 02 034	27 49 084	47 04 121	31 03 200	45 56 253	38 20 284	17 09 348	202	44 40 070	39 13 101	21 04 168	13 11 230	28 08 267	44 55 304	27 17 019
24	60 04 036	27 53 086	47 07 123	31 02 202	45 52 255	38 16 286	17 08 350	204	44 44 072	39 17 103	21 04 170	13 08 232	28 04 269	44 51 306	27 19 021
26	60 07 038	27 57 088	47 11 125	31 00 204	45 48 257	38 12 288	17 07 352	206	44 48 074	39 21 105	21 05 172	13 04 234	27 59 271	44 48 308	27 20 023
28	60 09 039	28 01 090	47 14 127	30 58 206	45 44 260	38 08 290	17 07 354	208	44 52 076	39 25 107	21 06 174	13 01 236	27 55 273	44 45 310	27 22 025
	Dubhe	POLLUX	◆CAPELLA	Alpheratz	◆DENEB	VEGA	◆ARCTURUS		Alpheratz	◆DENEB	VEGA	◆ARCTURUS	REGULUS	POLLUX	◆CAPELLA
30	60 12 041	28 05 092	47 17 129	30 56 208	45 40 262	38 04 292	17 07 356	210	27 24 027	44 56 078	39 29 109	21 06 176	12 57 238	27 51 274	44 41 312
32	60 15 043	28 10 094	47 21 131	30 54 210	45 36 264	38 00 294	17 06 358	212	27 26 029	45 00 080	39 33 111	21 06 178	12 54 240	27 47 276	44 38 314
34	60 18 045	28 14 096	47 24 133	30 52 212	45 32 266	37 57 296	17 06 000	214	27 28 031	45 04 082	39 37 113	21 06 180	12 50 242	27 43 278	44 35 316
36	60 21 047	28 18 098	47 27 135	30 50 214	45 27 268	37 53 298	17 06 002	216	27 30 033	45 09 084	39 40 115	21 06 182	12 46 244	27 39 280	44 33 318
38	60 24 049	28 22 100	47 30 137	30 47 216	45 23 270	37 49 300	17 07 004	218	27 33 035	45 13 085	39 44 117	21 06 184	12 43 246	27 34 282	44 30 320
40	60 27 051	28 26 102	47 32 139	30 45 218	45 19 272	37 46 302	17 07 006	220	27 35 037	45 17 087	39 48 119	21 06 186	12 39 248	27 30 284	44 27 322
42	60 30 053	28 30 104	47 35 141	30 42 220	45 15 274	37 42 304	17 07 008	222	27 38 039	45 21 089	39 51 121	21 05 188	12 35 250	27 26 286	44 25 324
44	60 34 055	28 34 106	47 38 143	30 39 222	45 11 276	37 39 306	17 08 010	224	27 40 041	45 25 091	39 55 123	21 04 190	12 31 252	27 22 288	44 22 326
46	60 37 057	28 38 108	47 40 145	30 37 225	45 06 278	37 35 308	17 09 012	226	27 43 043	45 29 093	39 58 125	21 04 192	12 27 254	27 18 290	44 20 328
48	60 41 059	28 42 110	47 42 147	30 34 227	45 02 280	37 32 310	17 10 014	228	27 46 045	45 34 095	40 02 127	21 03 194	12 23 256	27 15 292	44 18 330
50	60 44 061	28 46 112	47 45 149	30 30 229	44 58 281	37 29 312	17 11 016	230	27 49 047	45 38 098	40 05 129	21 02 196	12 19 258	27 11 294	44 16 332
52	60 48 063	28 50 114	47 47 152	30 27 231	44 54 283	37 26 314	17 12 018	232	27 52 049	45 42 100	40 08 131	21 00 198	12 15 260	27 07 296	44 14 333
54	60 52 065	28 54 116	47 49 154	30 24 233	44 50 285	37 23 316	17 13 020	234	27 55 051	45 46 102	40 11 133	20 59 200	12 10 262	27 03 298	44 12 335
56	60 55 066	28 57 118	47 50 156	30 21 235	44 46 287	37 20 318	17 15 022	236	27 59 053	45 50 104	40 14 135	20 58 202	12 06 264	27 00 300	44 10 337
58	60 59 068	29 01 121	47 52 158	30 17 237	44 42 289	37 17 320	17 16 024	238	28 02 055	45 54 106	40 17 138	20 56 204	12 02 266	26 56 302	44 09 339
	◆ARCTURUS	REGULUS	POLLUX	◆CAPELLA	Alpheratz	◆DENEB	VEGA		Alpheratz	◆DENEB	VEGA	◆ARCTURUS	REGULUS	POLLUX	◆CAPELLA
60	17 18 026	11 48 087	29 05 123	47 54 160	30 14 239	44 38 291	37 14 322	240	28 05 057	45 58 108	40 20 140	20 54 206	11 58 268	26 52 304	44 07 341
62	17 20 028	11 53 089	29 08 125	47 55 162	30 10 241	44 34 293	37 12 324	242	28 09 059	46 02 110	40 23 142	20 52 208	11 54 270	26 49 306	44 06 343
64	17 22 030	11 57 091	29 12 127	47 56 164	30 06 243	44 30 295	37 09 326	244	28 13 061	46 06 112	40 25 144	20 50 210	11 50 272	26 46 308	44 05 345
66	17 24 032	12 01 093	29 15 129	47 57 166	30 03 245	44 27 297	37 07 327	246	28 16 063	46 10 114	40 28 146	20 48 212	11 45 274	26 42 310	44 04 347
68	17 26 034	12 05 095	29 18 131	47 58 168	29 59 247	44 23 299	37 05 329	248	28 20 065	46 14 116	40 30 148	20 46 214	11 41 276	26 39 312	44 03 349
70	17 29 036	12 09 097	29 21 133	47 59 170	29 55 249	44 19 301	37 03 331	250	28 24 067	46 18 118	40 32 150	20 43 216	11 37 278	26 36 314	44 02 351
72	17 31 038	12 13 099	29 24 135	48 00 172	29 51 251	44 16 303	37 01 333	252	28 28 069	46 21 120	40 34 152	20 41 218	11 33 280	26 33 316	44 02 353
74	17 34 039	12 18 101	29 27 137	48 00 174	29 47 253	44 12 305	36 59 335	254	28 32 071	46 25 122	40 36 154	20 38 220	11 29 282	26 30 318	44 01 355
76	17 37 041	12 22 103	29 30 139	48 00 176	29 43 255	44 09 307	36 57 337	256	28 36 073	46 28 124	40 38 156	20 35 222	11 25 284	26 28 320	44 01 357
78	17 40 043	12 26 105	29 33 141	48 01 178	29 39 257	44 06 309	36 56 339	258	28 40 075	46 32 126	40 39 158	20 32 224	11 21 286	26 25 322	44 01 359
80	17 42 045	12 30 107	29 35 143	48 01 181	29 35 259	44 02 311	36 55 341	260	28 44 077	46 35 128	40 41 160	20 29 226	11 17 288	26 23 324	44 01 001
82	17 45 047	12 34 109	29 38 145	48 01 183	29 31 261	43 59 313	36 53 343	262	28 48 079	46 38 130	40 42 162	20 26 228	11 13 290	26 20 326	44 01 002
84	17 49 049	12 38 111	29 40 147	48 00 185	29 27 263	43 56 315	36 52 345	264	28 52 081	46 42 132	40 43 164	20 23 230	11 09 292	26 18 328	44 01 004
86	17 52 051	12 41 113	29 42 149	48 00 187	29 22 265	43 53 317	36 51 347	266	28 56 083	46 45 134	40 45 166	20 20 232	11 05 294	26 16 330	44 01 006
88	17 55 053	12 45 115	29 44 151	47 59 189	29 18 267	43 51 319	36 50 349	268	29 00 085	46 48 136	40 45 168	20 16 234	11 01 296	26 14 332	44 02 008
	◆ARCTURUS	REGULUS	POLLUX	◆CAPELLA	Alpheratz	◆DENEB	VEGA		◆CAPELLA	Alpheratz	◆DENEB	VEGA	◆ARCTURUS	Dubhe	POLLUX
90	17 59 055	12 49 117	29 46 153	47 59 191	29 14 269	43 48 321	36 49 351	270	44 03 010	29 04 087	46 50 138	40 46 170	20 13 237	61 08 287	26 12 334
92	18 02 057	12 53 119	29 48 155	47 58 193	29 10 271	43 45 323	36 49 353	272	44 03 012	29 09 089	46 53 140	40 47 172	20 10 239	61 04 289	26 10 336
94	18 06 059	12 56 121	29 50 157	47 57 195	29 06 273	43 43 325	36 48 355	274	44 04 014	29 13 091	46 56 142	40 47 174	20 06 241	61 00 291	26 08 338
96	18 09 061	13 00 123	29 52 159	47 56 197	29 01 275	43 41 327	36 48 357	276	44 06 016	29 17 093	46 58 144	40 48 177	20 02 243	60 56 293	26 07 340
98	18 13 063	13 03 125	29 53 161	47 54 199	28 57 277	43 38 329	36 48 359	278	44 07 018	29 21 095	47 01 146	40 48 179	19 58 245	60 52 295	26 05 342
100	18 17 065	13 07 127	29 54 163	47 53 201	28 53 279	43 36 330	36 48 001	280	44 08 020	29 25 097	47 03 148	40 48 181	19 55 247	60 49 297	26 04 344
102	18 21 067	13 10 129	29 55 165	47 51 203	28 49 281	43 34 332	36 48 003	282	44 10 022	29 29 099	47 05 151	40 48 183	19 51 249	60 45 299	26 03 346
104	18 24 069	13 13 131	29 56 167	47 49 205	28 45 283	43 32 334	36 48 005	284	44 11 024	29 34 101	47 07 153	40 47 185	19 47 251	60 41 301	26 02 348
106	18 28 071	13 16 133	29 57 169	47 48 208	28 41 285	43 31 336	36 49 006	286	44 13 026	29 38 103	47 09 155	40 47 187	19 43 253	60 38 303	26 01 350
108	18 32 073	13 19 135	29 58 171	47 46 210	28 37 287	43 29 338	36 49 008	288	44 15 028	29 42 105	47 11 157	40 47 189	19 39 255	60 34 305	26 01 352
110	18 36 075	13 22 137	29 59 173	47 43 212	28 33 289	43 27 340	36 50 010	290	44 17 030	29 46 107	47 12 159	40 46 191	19 35 257	60 31 307	26 00 354
112	18 40 077	13 25 139	29 59 175	47 41 214	28 29 291	43 26 342	36 51 012	292	44 19 031	29 50 109	47 14 161	40 45 193	19 31 259	60 27 309	26 00 356
114	18 45 079	13 28 141	29 59 177	47 39 216	28 25 293	43 25 344	36 52 014	294	44 21 033	29 54 111	47 15 163	40 44 195	19 27 261	60 24 311	25 59 357
116	18 49 081	13 30 143	29 59 179	47 36 218	28 21 295	43 24 346	36 53 016	296	44 24 035	29 58 113	47 16 165	40 43 197	19 22 263	60 21 313	25 59 359
118	18 53 083	13 33 145	29 59 181	47 34 220	28 17 297	43 23 348	36 54 018	298	44 26 037	30 01 115	47 17 167	40 41 199	19 18 265	60 18 314	25 59 001
	VEGA	◆ARCTURUS	REGULUS	POLLUX	◆CAPELLA	Alpheratz	◆DENEB		POLLUX	◆CAPELLA	Alpheratz	◆DENEB	VEGA	◆ARCTURUS	Dubhe
120	36 55 020	18 57 085	13 35 147	29 59 184	47 31 222	28 14 299	43 22 350	300	26 00 003	44 29 039	30 05 117	47 18 169	40 40 201	19 14 267	60 15 316
122	36 57 022	19 01 087	13 37 149	29 59 186	47 28 224	28 10 301	43 21 352	302	26 00 005	44 31 041	30 09 119	47 19 171	40 38 203	19 10 269	60 12 318
124	36 59 024	19 05 089	13 39 151	29 58 188	47 25 226	28 06 303	43 21 354	304	26 00 007	44 34 043	30 13 121	47 19 173	40 37 205	19 06 271	60 10 320
126	37 00 026	19 10 091	13 41 154	29 58 190	47 22 228	28 03 305	43 20 356	306	26 01 009	44 37 045	30 16 123	47 20 175	40 35 207	19 02 273	60 07 322
128	37 02 028	19 14 093	13 43 156	29 57 192	47 19 230	28 00 307	43 20 358	308	26 02 011	44 40 047	30 20 125	47 20 177	40 33 209	18 57 275	60 04 324
130	37 04 030	19 18 095	13 45 158	29 56 194	47 16 232	27 56 309	43 20 000	310	26 03 013	44 43 049	30 23 127	47 20 179	40 31 211	18 53 277	60 02 326
132	37 06 032	19 22 097	13 46 160	29 55 196	47 12 234	27 53 311	43 20 001	312	26 04 015	44 46 051	30 26 129	47 20 182	40 28 214	18 49 279	60 00 328
134	37 09 034	19 26 099	13 47 162	29 54 198	47 09 236	27 50 313	43 20 003	314	26 05 017	44 50 053	30 30 131	47 20 184	40 26 216	18 45 281	59 58 330
136	37 11 036	19 30 101	13 49 164	29 52 200	47 05 238	27 47 314	43 21 005	316	26 06 019	44 53 055	30 33 133	47 19 186	40 24 218	18 41 283	59 56 332
138	37 14 038	19 34 103	13 50 166	29 51 202	47 02 240	27 44 316	43 21 007	318	26 07 021	44 57 057	30 36 135	47 19 188	40 21 220	18 37 285	59 54 333
140	37 16 040	19 39 105	13 51 168	29 49 204	46 58 242	27 41 318	43 22 009	320	26 09 023	45 00 059	30 39 137	47 18 190	40 18 222	18 33 287	59 52 335
142	37 19 042	19 43 107	13 52 170	29 47 206	46 54 244	27 38 320	43 22 011	322	26 11 025	45 04 061	30 41 139	47 18 192	40 15 224	18 29 289	59 50 337
144	37 22 044	19 47 109	13 52 172	29 46 208	46 50 246	27 36 322	43 23 013	324	26 13 027	45 07 063	30 44 141	47 17 194	40 12 226	18 25 291	59 49 339
146	37 25 046	19 50 111	13 53 174	29 44 210	46 47 248	27 33 324	43 24 015	326	26 15 029	45 11 065	30 47 143	47 16 196	40 09 228	18 21 293	59 47 341
148	37 28 047	19 54 113	13 53 176	29 41 212	46 43 251	27 31 326	43 25 017	328	26 17 031	45 15 067	30 49 145	47 14 198	40 06 230	18 17 295	59 46 343
	◆DENEB	VEGA	◆ARCTURUS	REGULUS	POLLUX	◆CAPELLA	Alpheratz		POLLUX	◆CAPELLA	Alpheratz	◆DENEB	VEGA	◆ARCTURUS	Dubhe
150	43 27 019	37 31 049	19 58 115	13 54 178	29 39 214	46 39 253	27 29 328	330	26 19 033	45 19 069	30 51 147	47 13 200	40 03 232	18 13 297	59 45 345
152	43 28 021	37 34 051	20 02 117	13 54 180	29 37 216	46 35 255	27 26 330	332	26 21 035	45 23 071	30 54 149	47 11 202	40 00 234	18 10 299	59 44 347
154	43 30 023	37 37 053	20 06 119	13 54 182	29 34 218	46 31 257	27 24 332	334	26 24 037	45 27 073	30 56 151	47 10 204	39 56 236	18 06 300	59 43 349
156	43 31 025	37 41 055	20 09 121	13 53 184	29 32 220	46 27 259	27 23 334	336	26 26 039	45 31 075	30 58 153	47 08 206	39 53 238	18 02 302	59 42 350
158	43 33 027	37 44 057	20 13 123	13 53 186	29 29 222	46 22 261	27 21 336	338	26 29 041	45 35 077	31 00 155	47 06 208	39 49 240	17 59 304	59 41 352
160	43 35 029	37 48 059	20 16 125	13 53 188	29 26 224	46 18 263	27 19 338	340	26 32 043	45 39 079	31 01 157	47 04 211	39 45 242	17 55 306	59 41 354
162	43 37 031	37 51 061	20 20 127	13 52 190	29 23 226	46 14 265	27 18 340	342	26 35 045	45 43 081	31 03 159	47 02 213	39 42 244	17 52 308	59 40 356
164	43 39 032	37 55 063	20 23 129	13 51 192	29 20 228	46 10 267	27 16 342	344	26 38 047	45 47 082	31 04 161	46 59 215	39 38 246	17 49 310	59 40 358
166	43 42 034	37 59 065	20 26 131	13 50 194	29 17 230	46 06 269	27 15 344	346	26 41 049	45 51 084	31 05 163	46 57 217	39 34 248	17 46 312	59 40 000
168	43 44 036	38 03 067	20 29 133	13 49 196	29 13 232	46 02 271	27 14 346	348	26 44 051	45 56 086	31 07 165	46 54 219	39 30 250	17 43 314	59 40 002
170	43 47 038	38 07 069	20 32 135	13 48 198	29 10 234	45 57 273	27 13 348	350	26 47 053	46 00 088	31 08 167	46 52 221	39 26 252	17 40 316	59 40 004
172	43 49 040	38 11 071	20 35 137	13 47 200	29 07 236	45 53 275	27 12 350	352	26 51 055	46 04 090	31 08 169	46 49 223	39 22 254	17 37 318	59 41 005
174	43 52 042	38 15 073	20 38 139	13 45 202	29 03 238	45 49 277	27 12 352	354	26 54 057	46 08 092	31 09 172	46 46 225	39 18 256	17 34 320	59 41 007
176	43 55 044	38 19 075	20 40 141	13 43 204	28 59 240	45 45 279	27 11 354	356	26 58 059	46 12 094	31 10 174	46 43 227	39 14 258	17 32 322	59 42 009
178	43 58 046	38 23 077	20 43 143	13 42 206	28 56 242	45 41 281	27 11 356	358	27 01 061	46 16 096	31 10 176	46 40 229	39 10 260	17 29 324	59 43 011

 LAT 87°N

LHA ♈	Hc	Zn	Hc	Zn	Hc	Zn	Hc	Zn	Hc	Zn	Hc	Zn	Hc	Zn
	Dubhe		POLLUX		◆ CAPELLA		Alpheratz		◆ DENEB		VEGA		◆ ARCTURUS	
0	58 45	013	26 37	062	46 29	097	32 10	178	47 14	232	39 13	263	16 37	326
2	58 46	014	26 42	064	46 35	099	32 10	180	47 09	234	39 07	265	16 33	328
4	58 48	016	26 48	066	46 41	101	32 10	182	47 04	236	39 01	267	16 30	330
6	58 50	018	26 54	068	46 47	104	32 10	184	46 59	238	38 55	269	16 27	332
8	58 52	020	27 00	070	46 53	106	32 09	186	46 53	240	38 48	271	16 24	334
10	58 54	022	27 06	072	47 00	108	32 09	188	46 48	242	38 42	273	16 22	336
12	58 57	024	27 12	074	47 05	110	32 08	190	46 42	244	38 36	275	16 19	338
14	58 59	025	27 18	076	47 11	112	32 07	192	46 36	246	38 30	277	16 17	340
16	59 02	027	27 24	078	47 17	114	32 05	194	46 31	248	38 23	279	16 15	342
18	59 05	029	27 30	080	47 23	116	32 03	196	46 25	250	38 17	281	16 13	344
20	59 08	031	27 36	082	47 28	118	32 02	198	46 19	252	38 11	283	16 12	346
22	59 12	033	27 43	084	47 34	120	32 00	200	46 13	254	38 05	285	16 10	348
24	59 15	035	27 49	086	47 39	122	31 57	202	46 07	256	37 59	287	16 09	350
26	59 19	037	27 55	088	47 45	124	31 55	204	46 01	259	37 53	289	16 08	352
28	59 22	038	28 01	090	47 50	126	31 52	206	45 54	261	37 47	291	16 07	354
	Dubhe		POLLUX		◆ CAPELLA		Alpheratz		◆ DENEB		VEGA		◆ ARCTURUS	
30	59 26	040	28 08	092	47 55	128	31 49	209	45 48	263	37 41	293	16 07	356
32	59 31	042	28 14	094	48 00	130	31 46	211	45 42	265	37 35	295	16 06	358
34	59 35	044	28 20	096	48 04	132	31 43	213	45 36	267	37 30	297	16 06	000
36	59 39	046	28 26	098	48 09	134	31 39	215	45 29	269	37 24	299	16 06	002
38	59 44	048	28 33	100	48 13	136	31 36	217	45 23	271	37 19	301	16 07	004
40	59 49	050	28 39	102	48 18	138	31 32	219	45 17	273	37 13	303	16 07	006
42	59 53	052	28 45	104	48 22	141	31 28	221	45 11	275	37 08	305	16 08	008
44	59 58	053	28 51	106	48 26	143	31 24	223	45 04	277	37 03	307	16 09	010
46	60 04	055	28 57	108	48 29	145	31 19	225	44 58	279	36 58	308	16 10	012
48	60 09	057	29 03	110	48 33	147	31 15	227	44 52	280	36 53	310	16 11	014
50	60 14	059	29 09	112	48 36	149	31 10	229	44 46	282	36 49	312	16 13	016
52	60 20	061	29 15	114	48 39	151	31 05	231	44 40	284	36 44	314	16 15	018
54	60 25	063	29 20	116	48 42	153	31 00	233	44 34	286	36 40	316	16 17	020
56	60 31	065	29 26	118	48 45	155	30 55	235	44 28	288	36 35	318	16 19	022
58	60 36	067	29 31	120	48 48	157	30 50	237	44 22	290	36 31	320	16 21	024
	◆ ARCTURUS		REGULUS		POLLUX		◆ CAPELLA		Alpheratz		◆ DENEB		VEGA	
60	16 24	025	11 45	087	29 37	122	48 50	159	30 45	239	44 16	292	36 27	322
62	16 27	027	11 52	089	29 42	124	48 52	162	30 39	241	44 10	294	36 24	324
64	16 30	029	11 58	091	29 47	126	48 54	164	30 34	243	44 04	296	36 20	326
66	16 33	031	12 04	093	29 52	128	48 55	166	30 28	245	43 59	298	36 16	328
68	16 36	033	12 11	095	29 57	130	48 57	168	30 22	247	43 53	300	36 13	330
70	16 40	035	12 17	097	30 02	132	48 58	170	30 16	249	43 48	302	36 10	332
72	16 44	037	12 23	099	30 06	134	48 59	172	30 10	251	43 43	304	36 07	334
74	16 48	039	12 29	101	30 11	136	49 00	174	30 04	253	43 37	306	36 05	336
76	16 52	041	12 35	103	30 15	138	49 00	176	29 58	255	43 32	308	36 02	338
78	16 56	043	12 41	105	30 19	140	49 01	178	29 52	257	43 28	310	36 00	339
80	17 00	045	12 47	107	30 23	142	49 01	181	29 46	259	43 23	312	35 58	341
82	17 05	047	12 53	109	30 27	144	49 01	183	29 40	261	43 18	314	35 56	343
84	17 09	049	12 59	111	30 30	147	49 00	185	29 34	263	43 14	316	35 54	345
86	17 14	051	13 05	113	30 34	149	48 59	187	29 28	265	43 09	318	35 53	347
88	17 19	053	13 11	115	30 37	151	48 59	189	29 21	267	43 05	319	35 51	349
	◆ ARCTURUS		REGULUS		POLLUX		◆ CAPELLA		Alpheratz		◆ DENEB		VEGA	
90	17 24	055	13 16	117	30 40	153	48 57	191	29 15	269	43 01	321	35 50	351
92	17 30	057	13 22	119	30 43	155	48 56	193	29 09	271	42 57	323	35 49	353
94	17 35	059	13 27	121	30 45	157	48 55	195	29 02	273	42 54	325	35 49	355
96	17 40	061	13 33	123	30 48	159	48 53	198	28 56	275	42 50	327	35 48	357
98	17 46	063	13 38	125	30 50	161	48 51	200	28 50	277	42 47	329	35 48	359
100	17 52	065	13 43	127	30 52	163	48 49	202	28 44	279	42 44	331	35 48	001
102	17 57	067	13 48	129	30 53	165	48 46	204	28 38	281	42 41	333	35 48	003
104	18 03	069	13 53	131	30 55	167	48 44	206	28 31	283	42 38	335	35 48	004
106	18 09	071	13 57	133	30 56	169	48 41	208	28 25	285	42 35	337	35 49	006
108	18 15	073	14 02	135	30 57	171	48 38	210	28 19	287	42 33	339	35 50	008
110	18 21	075	14 06	137	30 58	173	48 34	212	28 13	289	42 31	341	35 51	010
112	18 27	077	14 10	139	30 59	175	48 31	214	28 07	291	42 29	342	35 52	012
114	18 33	079	14 14	141	30 59	177	48 27	216	28 02	293	42 27	344	35 54	014
116	18 39	081	14 18	143	30 59	179	48 23	219	27 56	295	42 26	346	35 55	016
118	18 46	083	14 22	145	30 59	181	48 19	221	27 50	297	42 24	348	35 57	018
	VEGA		◆ ARCTURUS		REGULUS		POLLUX		◆ CAPELLA		Alpheratz		◆ DENEB	
120	35 59	020	18 52	085	14 25	147	30 59	184	48 15	223	27 45	299	42 23	350
122	36 01	022	18 58	087	14 29	149	30 58	186	48 11	225	27 39	301	42 22	352
124	36 04	024	19 04	089	14 32	151	30 58	188	48 06	227	27 34	303	42 21	354
126	36 06	026	19 11	091	14 35	153	30 57	190	48 02	229	27 29	305	42 21	356
128	36 09	028	19 17	093	14 37	155	30 56	192	47 57	231	27 24	307	42 20	358
130	36 12	029	19 23	095	14 40	157	30 54	194	47 52	233	27 19	309	42 20	000
132	36 15	031	19 29	097	14 42	159	30 53	196	47 47	235	27 14	311	42 20	001
134	36 19	033	19 36	099	14 44	161	30 51	198	47 42	237	27 09	313	42 20	003
136	36 22	035	19 42	101	14 46	164	30 49	200	47 36	239	27 05	315	42 21	005
138	36 26	037	19 48	103	14 48	166	30 47	202	47 31	241	27 00	317	42 22	007
140	36 30	039	19 54	105	14 49	168	30 44	204	47 25	243	26 56	319	42 22	009
142	36 34	041	20 00	107	14 51	170	30 41	206	47 20	245	26 52	321	42 24	011
144	36 38	043	20 06	109	14 52	172	30 39	208	47 14	247	26 48	323	42 25	013
146	36 42	045	20 12	111	14 53	174	30 35	210	47 08	249	26 44	325	42 26	015
148	36 47	047	20 18	113	14 53	176	30 32	212	47 02	252	26 41	327	42 28	017
	◆ DENEB		VEGA		◆ ARCTURUS		REGULUS		POLLUX		◆ CAPELLA		Alpheratz	
150	42 30	019	36 52	049	20 24	115	14 53	178	30 29	214	46 56	254	26 38	329
152	42 32	020	36 56	051	20 29	117	14 54	180	30 25	216	46 50	256	26 34	330
154	42 34	022	37 01	053	20 35	119	14 54	182	30 21	218	46 44	258	26 31	332
156	42 37	024	37 06	055	20 40	121	14 53	184	30 17	221	46 38	260	26 29	334
158	42 39	026	37 12	057	20 46	123	14 53	186	30 13	223	46 32	262	26 26	336
160	42 42	028	37 17	059	20 51	125	14 52	188	30 09	225	46 25	264	26 23	338
162	42 45	030	37 22	061	20 56	127	14 51	190	30 04	227	46 19	266	26 21	340
164	42 49	032	37 28	063	21 01	129	14 50	192	30 00	229	46 13	268	26 19	342
166	42 52	034	37 33	064	21 06	131	14 48	194	29 55	231	46 07	270	26 17	344
168	42 56	036	37 39	066	21 10	133	14 47	196	29 50	233	46 00	272	26 16	346
170	42 59	038	37 45	068	21 15	135	14 45	198	29 45	235	45 54	274	26 14	348
172	43 03	040	37 51	070	21 19	137	14 43	200	29 40	237	45 48	276	26 13	350
174	43 07	042	37 57	072	21 23	139	14 41	202	29 34	239	45 42	278	26 12	352
176	43 12	043	38 03	074	21 27	141	14 38	204	29 29	241	45 35	280	26 11	354
178	43 16	045	38 09	076	21 31	143	14 36	206	29 23	243	45 29	282	26 11	356

LHA ♈	Hc	Zn	Hc	Zn	Hc	Zn	Hc	Zn	Hc	Zn	Hc	Zn	Hc	Zn
	◆ DENEB		VEGA		◆ ARCTURUS		REGULUS		POLLUX		◆ CAPELLA		Alpheratz	
180	43 21	047	38 15	078	21 35	145	14 33	208	29 18	245	45 23	284	26 11	358
182	43 25	049	38 21	080	21 38	147	14 30	210	29 12	247	45 17	286	26 10	000
184	43 30	051	38 27	082	21 42	149	14 26	212	29 06	249	45 11	287	26 10	002
186	43 35	053	38 34	084	21 45	151	14 23	214	29 00	251	45 05	289	26 11	004
188	43 40	055	38 40	086	21 48	153	14 19	216	28 54	253	44 59	291	26 11	006
190	43 45	057	38 46	088	21 50	155	14 16	218	28 48	255	44 53	293	26 12	008
192	43 51	059	38 52	090	21 53	157	14 12	220	28 42	257	44 48	295	26 13	009
194	43 56	061	38 59	092	21 55	160	14 08	222	28 36	259	44 42	297	26 14	011
196	44 02	063	39 05	094	21 57	162	14 03	224	28 30	261	44 36	299	26 15	013
198	44 07	065	39 11	096	21 59	164	13 59	226	28 24	263	44 31	301	26 17	015
200	44 13	067	39 17	098	22 01	166	13 54	228	28 17	265	44 26	303	26 19	017
202	44 19	069	39 24	100	22 02	168	13 49	230	28 11	267	44 21	305	26 21	019
204	44 25	071	39 30	102	22 03	170	13 44	232	28 05	269	44 15	307	26 23	021
206	44 31	073	39 36	104	22 04	172	13 39	234	27 59	271	44 10	309	26 25	023
208	44 37	075	39 42	106	22 05	174	13 34	236	27 52	273	44 06	311	26 28	025
	Alpheratz		◆ DENEB		VEGA		◆ ARCTURUS		REGULUS		POLLUX		◆ CAPELLA	
210	26 30	027	44 43	077	39 48	108	22 06	176	13 29	238	27 46	275	44 01	313
212	26 33	029	44 49	079	39 54	110	22 06	178	13 24	240	27 40	277	43 56	315
214	26 37	031	44 55	081	40 00	112	22 06	180	13 18	242	27 34	279	43 52	317
216	26 40	033	45 01	083	40 05	114	22 06	182	13 13	244	27 27	281	43 48	319
218	26 43	035	45 08	084	40 11	116	22 06	184	13 07	246	27 21	283	43 44	320
220	26 47	037	45 14	086	40 17	118	22 05	186	13 01	248	27 15	285	43 40	322
222	26 51	039	45 20	088	40 22	121	22 05	188	12 55	250	27 09	287	43 36	324
224	26 55	041	45 26	090	40 28	123	22 04	190	12 49	252	27 03	289	43 33	326
226	26 59	043	45 33	092	40 33	125	22 02	192	12 43	254	26 57	291	43 29	328
228	27 03	045	45 39	094	40 38	127	22 01	194	12 37	256	26 51	293	43 26	330
230	27 08	047	45 45	096	40 43	129	21 59	196	12 31	258	26 46	295	43 23	332
232	27 13	048	45 51	098	40 48	131	21 57	198	12 25	260	26 40	297	43 20	334
234	27 17	050	45 58	101	40 52	133	21 55	200	12 19	262	26 34	299	43 17	336
236	27 22	052	46 04	103	40 57	135	21 53	202	12 12	264	26 29	301	43 15	338
238	27 27	054	46 10	105	41 01	137	21 51	204	12 06	266	26 24	303	43 13	340
	Alpheratz		◆ DENEB		VEGA		◆ ARCTURUS		REGULUS		POLLUX		◆ CAPELLA	
240	27 32	056	46 16	107	41 05	139	21 48	206	12 00	268	26 18	305	43 10	342
242	27 38	058	46 22	109	41 10	141	21 45	208	11 54	270	26 13	307	43 09	343
244	27 43	060	46 28	111	41 13	143	21 42	210	11 47	272	26 08	309	43 07	345
246	27 49	062	46 34	113	41 17	145	21 39	213	11 41	274	26 04	311	43 05	347
248	27 54	064	46 39	115	41 21	147	21 35	215	11 35	276	25 59	313	43 04	349
250	28 00	066	46 45	117	41 24	149	21 31	217	11 28	278	25 54	315	43 03	351
252	28 06	068	46 51	119	41 27	151	21 28	219	11 22	280	25 50	317	43 02	353
254	28 12	070	46 56	121	41 30	154	21 24	221	11 16	282	25 46	318	43 01	355
256	28 18	072	47 01	123	41 33	156	21 19	223	11 10	284	25 42	320	43 01	357
258	28 24	074	47 07	125	41 35	158	21 15	225	11 04	286	25 38	322	43 01	359
260	28 30	076	47 12	127	41 37	160	21 11	227	10 58	288	25 34	324	43 01	001
262	28 36	078	47 17	129	41 39	162	21 06	229	10 52	290	25 30	326	43 01	002
264	28 42	080	47 21	131	41 41	164	21 01	231	10 46	292	25 27	328	43 01	004
266	28 48	082	47 26	133	41 43	166	20 56	233	10 40	294	25 24	330	43 02	006
268	28 54	084	47 31	135	41 44	168	20 51	235	10 35	296	25 21	332	43 03	008
	◆ CAPELLA		Alpheratz		◆ DENEB		VEGA		◆ ARCTURUS		Dubhe		POLLUX	
270	43 04	010	29 01	086	47 35	137	41 45	170	20 46	237	60 49	289	25 18	334
272	43 05	012	29 07	088	47 39	140	41 46	172	20 41	239	60 43	291	25 15	336
274	43 06	014	29 13	090	47 43	142	41 47	174	20 35	241	60 37	293	25 13	338
276	43 08	016	29 19	092	47 47	144	41 48	176	20 30	243	60 32	295	25 11	340
278	43 10	018	29 26	094	47 50	146	41 48	179	20 24	245	60 26	297	25 08	342
280	43 12	020	29 32	096	47 54	148	41 48	181	20 18	247	60 20	299	25 07	344
282	43 14	021	29 38	098	47 57	150	41 48	183	20 13	249	60 15	301	25 05	346
284	43 16	023	29 44	100	48 00	152	41 47	185	20 07	251	60 10	303	25 04	348
286	43 19	025	29 51	102	48 03	154	41 47	187	20 01	253	60 04	304	25 02	350
288	43 22	027	29 57	104	48 06	156	41 46	189	19 55	255	59 59	306	25 01	352
290	43 25	029	30 03	106	48 08	158	41 45	191	19 49	257	59 54	308	25 00	354
292	43 28	031	30 09	108	48 10	160	41 43	193	19 42	259	59 49	310	25 00	356
294	43 31	033	30 15	110	48 12	163	41 42	195	19 36	261	59 45	312	25 00	358
296	43 34	035	30 21	112	48 14	165	41 40	197	19 30	263	59 40	314	24 59	359
298	43 38	037	30 26	114	48 16	167	41 38	199	19 24	265	59 36	316	24 59	001
	POLLUX		◆ CAPELLA		Alpheratz		◆ DENEB		VEGA		◆ ARCTURUS		Dubhe	
300	25 00	003	43 42	039	30 32	116	48 17	169	41 36	202	19 17	267	59 31	318
302	25 00	005	43 46	041	30 38	118	48 18	171	41 33	204	19 11	269	59 27	319
304	25 01	007	43 50	042	30 43	120	48 19	173	41 31	206	19 05	271	59 23	321
306	25 02	009	43 54	044	30 48	122	48 19	175	41 28	208	18 59	273	59 19	323
308	25 03	011	43 59	046	30 54	124	48 20	177	41 25	210	18 52	275	59 16	325
310	25 04	013	44 04	048	30 59	126	48 20	179	41 22	212	18 46	277	59 12	327
312	25 06	015	44 08	050	31 04	128	48 20	182	41 18	214	18 40	279	59 09	329
314	25 07	017	44 13	052	31 09	130	48 20	184	41 15	216	18 34	281	59 06	331
316	25 09	019	44 18	054	31 13	132	48 19	186	41 11	218	18 28	283	59 03	332
318	25 11	021	44 23	056	31 18	134	48 18	188	41 07	220	18 21	285	59 00	334
320	25 14	023	44 29	058	31 22	137	48 17	190	41 03	222	18 15	287	58 57	336
322	25 16	025	44 34	060	31 27	139	48 16	192	40 58	224	18 09	289	58 55	338
324	25 19	027	44 39	062	31 31	141	48 15	194	40 54	226	18 04	291	58 52	340
326	25 22	029	44 45	064	31 35	143	48 13	196	40 49	228	17 58	293	58 50	342
328	25 25	031	44 51	066	31 38	145	48 11	199	40 45	231	17 52	295	58 48	343
	POLLUX		◆ CAPELLA		Alpheratz		◆ DENEB		VEGA		◆ ARCTURUS		Dubhe	
330	25 28	033	44 57	068	31 42	147	48 09	201	40 40	233	17 46	297	58 47	345
332	25 32	035	45 02	070	31 45	149	48 07	203	40 35	235	17 41	299	58 45	347
334	25 36	037	45 08	072	31 48	151	48 04	205	40 29	237	17 35	301	58 44	349
336	25 39	038	45 14	074	31 51	153	48 02	207	40 24	239	17 30	303	58 43	351
338	25 43	040	45 20	076	31 54	155	47 59	209	40 19	241	17 25	305	58 42	353
340	25 48	042	45 26	078	31 57	157	47 55	211	40 13	243	17 20	307	58 41	354
342	25 52	044	45 33	080	31 59	159	47 52	213	40 08	245	17 15	309	58 41	356
344	25 56	046	45 39	081	32 01	161	47 49	215	40 02	247	17 10	311	58 40	358
346	26 01	048	45 45	083	32 03	163	47 45	217	39 56	249	17 05	313	58 40	000
348	26 06	050	45 51	085	32 05	165	47 41	219	39 50	251	17 01	315	58 40	002
350	26 11	052	45 58	087	32 06	167	47 37	222	39 44	253	16 56	317	58 41	004
352	26 16	054	46 04	089	32 07	169	47 33	224	39 38	255	16 52	319	58 41	005
354	26 21	056	46 10	091	32 08	171	47 28	226	39 32	257	16 48	321	58 42	007
356	26 26	058	46 16	093	32 09	174	47 24	228	39 26	259	16 44	323	58 43	009
358	26 31	060	46 23	095	32 10	176	47 19	230	39 20	261	16 40	324	58 44	011

 LAT 86°N

LHA ♈	Hc Zn	Hc Zn	Hc Zn	Hc Zn	Hc Zn	Hc Zn	Hc Zn
	Dubhe	POLLUX	◆ CAPELLA	Alpheratz	◆ DENEB	VEGA	◆ ARCTURUS
0	57 46 012	26 09 062	46 36 096	33 10 178	47 51 233	39 20 264	15 47 327
2	57 48 014	26 16 064	46 44 098	33 10 180	47 44 235	39 12 266	15 42 329
4	57 50 016	26 24 066	46 53 100	33 10 182	47 37 237	39 04 268	15 38 331
6	57 53 018	26 31 068	47 01 102	33 10 184	47 30 239	38 55 270	15 34 332
8	57 56 019	26 39 069	47 09 104	33 09 186	47 23 241	38 47 272	15 30 334
10	57 58 021	26 47 071	47 17 107	33 08 188	47 15 243	38 39 274	15 27 336
12	58 02 023	26 55 073	47 25 109	33 07 190	47 08 245	38 30 276	15 24 338
14	58 05 025	27 03 075	47 33 111	33 05 192	47 00 247	38 22 278	15 21 340
16	58 09 027	27 11 077	47 41 113	33 03 194	46 52 249	38 14 280	15 18 342
18	58 12 028	27 19 079	47 48 115	33 01 196	46 44 251	38 05 282	15 15 344
20	58 17 030	27 28 081	47 56 117	32 59 198	46 36 253	37 57 284	15 13 346
22	58 21 032	27 36 083	48 03 119	32 56 201	46 28 255	37 49 286	15 11 348
24	58 25 034	27 44 085	48 11 121	32 53 203	46 20 258	37 41 288	15 10 350
26	58 30 036	27 53 087	48 18 123	32 49 205	46 12 260	37 33 290	15 09 352
28	58 35 037	28 01 089	48 25 125	32 46 207	46 04 262	37 25 292	15 08 354
	Dubhe	POLLUX	◆ CAPELLA	Alpheratz	◆ DENEB	VEGA	◆ ARCTURUS
30	58 40 039	28 09 091	48 31 127	32 42 209	45 55 264	37 18 294	15 07 356
32	58 46 041	28 18 093	48 38 129	32 38 211	45 47 266	37 10 295	15 06 358
34	58 51 043	28 26 095	48 44 131	32 33 213	45 39 268	37 02 297	15 06 000
36	58 57 045	28 34 097	48 51 133	32 28 215	45 30 270	36 55 299	15 06 002
38	59 03 047	28 43 099	48 57 136	32 24 217	45 22 272	36 48 301	15 07 004
40	59 09 048	28 51 101	49 02 138	32 18 219	45 14 274	36 41 303	15 08 006
42	59 16 050	28 59 103	49 08 140	32 13 221	45 05 276	36 34 305	15 09 008
44	59 22 052	29 07 105	49 13 142	32 07 223	44 57 278	36 27 307	15 10 010
46	59 29 054	29 15 107	49 18 144	32 02 225	44 49 279	36 21 309	15 11 012
48	59 36 056	29 23 109	49 23 146	31 55 227	44 40 281	36 14 311	15 13 014
50	59 43 058	29 31 111	49 27 148	31 49 229	44 32 283	36 08 313	15 15 016
52	59 50 059	29 39 113	49 32 150	31 43 232	44 24 285	36 02 315	15 18 018
54	59 57 061	29 46 115	49 36 153	31 36 234	44 16 287	35 56 317	15 20 019
56	60 04 063	29 54 117	49 39 155	31 29 236	44 08 289	35 50 319	15 23 021
58	60 12 065	30 01 120	49 43 157	31 22 238	44 00 291	35 45 321	15 26 023
	◆ ARCTURUS	REGULUS	POLLUX	◆ CAPELLA	Alpheratz	◆ DENEB	VEGA
60	15 30 025	11 42 087	30 08 122	49 46 159	31 15 240	43 53 293	35 40 323
62	15 34 027	11 51 089	30 15 124	49 49 161	31 08 242	43 45 295	35 35 324
64	15 38 029	11 59 091	30 22 126	49 51 163	31 00 244	43 37 297	35 30 326
66	15 42 031	12 07 093	30 29 128	49 54 165	30 53 246	43 30 299	35 26 328
68	15 46 033	12 16 095	30 36 130	49 56 168	30 45 248	43 23 301	35 21 330
70	15 51 035	12 24 097	30 42 132	49 57 170	30 37 250	43 16 303	35 17 332
72	15 56 037	12 32 099	30 48 134	49 59 172	30 29 252	43 09 305	35 13 334
74	16 01 039	12 41 101	30 54 136	50 00 174	30 21 254	43 02 307	35 10 336
76	16 06 041	12 49 103	31 00 138	50 00 176	30 13 256	42 55 309	35 07 338
78	16 12 043	12 57 105	31 05 140	50 01 178	30 05 258	42 49 311	35 04 340
80	16 18 045	13 05 107	31 10 142	50 01 181	29 57 260	42 43 312	35 01 342
82	16 24 047	13 13 109	31 15 144	50 00 183	29 49 262	42 37 314	34 58 344
84	16 30 049	13 21 111	31 20 146	50 00 185	29 40 264	42 31 316	34 56 345
86	16 37 051	13 29 113	31 25 148	49 59 187	29 32 266	42 25 318	34 54 347
88	16 43 053	13 36 115	31 29 150	49 58 189	29 24 268	42 19 320	34 52 349
	◆ ARCTURUS	REGULUS	POLLUX	◆ CAPELLA	Alpheratz	◆ DENEB	VEGA
90	16 50 055	13 44 117	31 33 152	49 56 191	29 15 270	42 14 322	34 51 351
92	16 57 057	13 51 119	31 37 154	49 55 194	29 07 272	42 09 324	34 50 353
94	17 04 059	13 58 121	31 40 157	49 52 196	28 59 274	42 04 326	34 49 355
96	17 11 061	14 05 123	31 43 159	49 50 198	28 50 276	42 00 328	34 48 357
98	17 19 063	14 12 125	31 46 161	49 47 200	28 42 278	41 55 330	34 48 359
100	17 26 065	14 19 127	31 49 163	49 44 202	28 34 280	41 51 331	34 48 001
102	17 34 067	14 26 129	31 51 165	49 41 204	28 25 282	41 47 333	34 48 003
104	17 41 069	14 32 131	31 53 167	49 37 206	28 17 284	41 44 335	34 49 004
106	17 49 071	14 38 133	31 55 169	49 33 209	28 09 286	41 40 337	34 49 006
108	17 57 073	14 44 135	31 57 171	49 29 211	28 01 288	41 37 339	34 50 008
110	18 05 075	14 50 137	31 58 173	49 25 213	27 53 290	41 34 341	34 52 010
112	18 13 077	14 56 139	31 59 175	49 20 215	27 45 292	41 32 343	34 53 012
114	18 21 079	15 01 141	31 59 177	49 15 217	27 38 294	41 29 345	34 55 014
116	18 30 081	15 06 143	31 59 179	49 10 219	27 30 296	41 27 346	34 57 016
118	18 38 083	15 11 145	31 59 182	49 05 221	27 23 298	41 25 348	35 00 018
	VEGA	◆ ARCTURUS	REGULUS	POLLUX	◆ CAPELLA	Alpheratz	◆ DENEB
120	35 03 020	18 46 085	15 16 147	31 59 184	48 59 223	27 15 300	41 24 350
122	35 05 022	18 55 087	15 20 149	31 58 186	48 53 226	27 08 302	41 23 352
124	35 09 023	19 03 089	15 24 151	31 57 188	48 47 228	27 01 304	41 22 354
126	35 12 025	19 11 091	15 28 153	31 56 190	48 41 230	26 54 305	41 21 356
128	35 16 027	19 20 093	15 32 155	31 54 192	48 34 232	26 47 307	41 20 358
130	35 20 029	19 28 095	15 35 157	31 52 194	48 28 234	26 41 309	41 20 000
132	35 24 031	19 36 097	15 38 159	31 50 196	48 21 236	26 34 311	41 20 001
134	35 28 033	19 45 099	15 41 161	31 48 198	48 14 238	26 28 313	41 20 003
136	35 33 035	19 53 101	15 44 163	31 45 200	48 07 240	26 22 315	41 21 005
138	35 38 037	20 01 103	15 46 165	31 42 202	47 59 242	26 16 317	41 22 007
140	35 43 039	20 09 105	15 48 167	31 39 204	47 52 244	26 11 319	41 23 009
142	35 48 041	20 17 107	15 50 170	31 35 206	47 44 246	26 05 321	41 25 011
144	35 54 043	20 25 109	15 51 172	31 31 209	47 36 248	26 00 323	41 26 013
146	36 00 044	20 33 111	15 52 174	31 27 211	47 29 251	25 55 325	41 28 015
148	36 06 046	20 41 113	15 53 176	31 23 213	47 21 253	25 51 327	41 30 016
	◆ DENEB	VEGA	◆ ARCTURUS	REGULUS	POLLUX	◆ CAPELLA	Alpheratz
150	41 33 018	36 12 048	20 49 115	15 53 178	31 18 215	47 13 255	25 46 329
152	41 36 020	36 18 050	20 56 117	15 54 180	31 13 217	47 05 257	25 42 331
154	41 39 022	36 25 052	21 04 119	15 53 182	31 08 219	46 56 259	25 38 333
156	41 42 024	36 31 054	21 11 121	15 53 184	31 03 221	46 48 261	25 34 335
158	41 46 026	36 38 056	21 18 123	15 52 186	30 57 223	46 40 263	25 31 337
160	41 49 028	36 45 058	21 25 125	15 51 188	30 51 225	46 32 265	25 28 338
162	41 53 030	36 52 060	21 32 127	15 50 190	30 45 227	46 23 267	25 25 340
164	41 58 031	37 00 062	21 38 129	15 49 192	30 39 229	46 15 269	25 22 342
166	42 02 033	37 07 064	21 45 131	15 47 194	30 33 231	46 06 271	25 20 344
168	42 07 035	37 15 066	21 51 133	15 44 196	30 26 233	45 58 273	25 18 346
170	42 12 037	37 23 068	21 57 135	15 42 198	30 19 235	45 50 275	25 16 348
172	42 17 039	37 30 070	22 03 137	15 39 200	30 12 237	45 41 277	25 14 350
174	42 22 041	37 38 072	22 09 139	15 36 202	30 05 239	45 33 279	25 13 352
176	42 28 043	37 46 074	22 14 141	15 33 204	29 58 241	45 25 281	25 12 354
178	42 34 045	37 54 076	22 19 143	15 29 206	29 50 243	45 17 283	25 11 356

LHA ♈	Hc Zn	Hc Zn	Hc Zn	Hc Zn	Hc Zn	Hc Zn	Hc Zn
	◆ DENEB	VEGA	◆ ARCTURUS	REGULUS	POLLUX	◆ CAPELLA	Alpheratz
180	42 40 047	38 02 078	22 24 145	15 26 208	29 43 245	45 09 285	25 11 358
182	42 46 049	38 11 079	22 29 147	15 22 210	29 35 247	45 00 286	25 10 000
184	42 52 050	38 19 081	22 33 149	15 17 212	29 27 249	44 52 288	25 10 002
186	42 59 052	38 27 083	22 37 151	15 13 214	29 20 252	44 45 290	25 11 004
188	43 05 054	38 35 085	22 41 153	15 08 216	29 12 254	44 37 292	25 12 006
190	43 12 056	38 44 087	22 45 155	15 03 218	29 04 256	44 29 294	25 12 007
192	43 19 058	38 52 089	22 48 157	14 57 220	28 55 258	44 22 296	25 14 009
194	43 27 060	39 01 091	22 51 159	14 52 222	28 47 260	44 14 298	25 15 011
196	43 34 062	39 09 093	22 54 161	14 46 224	28 39 262	44 07 300	25 17 013
198	43 41 064	39 17 095	22 57 163	14 40 226	28 31 264	44 00 302	25 19 015
200	43 49 066	39 26 097	22 59 166	14 34 228	28 22 266	43 53 304	25 21 017
202	43 57 068	39 34 099	23 01 168	14 28 230	28 14 268	43 46 306	25 24 019
204	44 04 070	39 42 101	23 02 170	14 21 232	28 06 270	43 39 308	25 27 021
206	44 12 072	39 50 103	23 04 172	14 14 234	27 57 272	43 32 310	25 30 023
208	44 20 074	39 58 105	23 05 174	14 08 236	27 49 274	43 26 312	25 33 025
	Alpheratz	◆ DENEB	VEGA	◆ ARCTURUS	REGULUS	POLLUX	◆ CAPELLA
210	25 37 027	44 28 076	40 06 108	23 06 176	14 00 238	27 41 276	43 20 313
212	25 41 029	44 36 078	40 14 110	23 06 178	13 53 241	27 32 278	43 14 315
214	25 45 031	44 45 080	40 22 112	23 06 180	13 46 243	27 24 280	43 08 317
216	25 49 033	44 53 082	40 30 114	23 06 182	13 38 245	27 16 282	43 03 319
218	25 54 035	45 01 083	40 38 116	23 06 184	13 31 247	27 08 283	42 57 321
220	25 59 036	45 10 085	40 45 118	23 05 186	13 23 249	26 59 285	42 52 323
222	26 04 038	45 18 087	40 52 120	23 04 188	13 15 251	26 51 287	42 47 325
224	26 09 040	45 26 089	41 00 122	23 03 190	13 07 253	26 43 289	42 42 327
226	26 15 042	45 35 091	41 07 124	23 01 192	12 59 255	26 36 291	42 38 329
228	26 21 044	45 43 093	41 13 126	22 59 194	12 51 257	26 28 293	42 34 331
230	26 26 046	45 51 095	41 20 128	22 57 196	12 43 259	26 20 295	42 30 332
232	26 33 048	46 00 097	41 27 130	22 54 198	12 35 261	26 13 297	42 26 334
234	26 39 050	46 08 099	41 33 132	22 52 200	12 26 263	26 05 299	42 23 336
236	26 45 052	46 16 102	41 39 134	22 49 202	12 18 265	25 58 301	42 19 338
238	26 52 054	46 24 104	41 45 136	22 45 205	12 10 267	25 51 303	42 16 340
	Alpheratz	◆ DENEB	VEGA	◆ ARCTURUS	REGULUS	POLLUX	◆ CAPELLA
240	26 59 056	46 32 106	41 51 138	22 42 207	12 01 269	25 44 305	42 14 342
242	27 06 058	46 40 108	41 56 141	22 38 209	11 53 271	25 37 307	42 11 344
244	27 13 060	46 48 110	42 01 143	22 34 211	11 45 273	25 31 309	42 09 346
246	27 20 062	46 56 112	42 06 145	22 29 213	11 36 275	25 24 311	42 07 347
248	27 28 064	47 04 114	42 11 147	22 24 215	11 28 277	25 18 313	42 05 349
250	27 35 066	47 12 116	42 15 149	22 20 217	11 20 279	25 12 315	42 04 351
252	27 43 068	47 19 118	42 20 151	22 14 219	11 11 281	25 06 317	42 03 353
254	27 51 070	47 26 120	42 23 153	22 09 221	11 03 283	25 01 319	42 02 355
256	27 59 072	47 34 122	42 27 155	22 04 223	10 55 284	24 55 321	42 01 357
258	28 07 074	47 41 124	42 30 157	21 58 225	10 47 286	24 50 323	42 01 359
260	28 15 076	47 47 126	42 34 159	21 52 227	10 39 288	24 45 325	42 01 001
262	28 23 078	47 54 128	42 36 162	21 45 229	10 31 290	24 40 327	42 01 002
264	28 31 080	48 01 130	42 39 164	21 39 231	10 23 292	24 36 328	42 01 004
266	28 40 082	48 07 132	42 41 166	21 32 233	10 16 294	24 32 330	42 02 006
268	28 48 084	48 13 135	42 43 168	21 26 235	10 08 296	24 28 332	42 03 008
	◆ CAPELLA	Alpheratz	◆ DENEB	VEGA	◆ ARCTURUS	Dubhe	POLLUX
270	42 04 010	28 56 085	48 19 137	42 45 170	21 19 237	60 29 291	24 24 334
272	42 06 012	29 04 087	48 24 139	42 46 172	21 12 239	60 21 293	24 20 336
274	42 08 014	29 13 089	48 30 141	42 47 174	21 04 241	60 13 295	24 17 338
276	42 10 015	29 21 091	48 35 143	42 47 176	20 57 243	60 06 296	24 14 340
278	42 12 017	29 30 093	48 40 145	42 48 179	20 49 245	59 58 298	24 11 342
280	42 15 019	29 38 095	48 45 147	42 48 181	20 42 247	59 51 300	24 09 344
282	42 18 021	29 46 097	48 49 149	42 48 183	20 34 249	59 44 302	24 07 346
284	42 21 023	29 55 099	48 53 152	42 47 185	20 26 251	59 37 304	24 05 348
286	42 24 025	30 03 101	48 57 154	42 46 187	20 18 253	59 30 306	24 03 350
288	42 28 027	30 11 104	49 00 156	42 45 189	20 10 255	59 23 308	24 02 352
290	42 32 029	30 19 106	49 04 158	42 44 191	20 02 257	59 17 310	24 01 354
292	42 36 031	30 27 108	49 07 160	42 42 193	19 54 259	59 10 311	24 00 356
294	42 40 032	30 35 110	49 09 162	42 40 196	19 45 261	59 04 313	24 00 358
296	42 45 034	30 43 112	49 12 164	42 37 198	19 37 263	58 58 315	23 59 359
298	42 50 036	30 51 114	49 14 167	42 35 200	19 29 265	58 52 317	23 59 001
	POLLUX	◆ CAPELLA	Alpheratz	◆ DENEB	VEGA	◆ ARCTURUS	Dubhe
300	24 00 003	42 55 038	30 58 116	49 16 169	42 32 202	19 20 267	58 47 319
302	24 00 005	43 00 040	31 06 118	49 17 171	42 28 204	19 12 269	58 41 320
304	24 01 007	43 06 042	31 13 120	49 18 173	42 25 206	19 04 271	58 36 322
306	24 02 009	43 11 044	31 20 122	49 19 175	42 21 208	18 55 273	58 31 324
308	24 04 011	43 17 046	31 27 124	49 20 177	42 17 210	18 47 275	58 26 326
310	24 06 013	43 23 048	31 34 126	49 20 179	42 13 212	18 39 277	58 22 328
312	24 08 015	43 30 049	31 41 128	49 20 182	42 08 215	18 30 279	58 17 330
314	24 10 017	43 36 051	31 47 130	49 20 184	42 03 217	18 22 281	58 13 331
316	24 13 019	43 43 053	31 54 132	49 19 186	41 58 219	18 14 283	58 09 333
318	24 15 021	43 49 055	32 00 134	49 18 188	41 53 221	18 06 285	58 06 335
320	24 18 023	43 56 057	32 06 136	49 17 190	41 47 223	17 58 287	58 02 337
322	24 22 025	44 04 059	32 11 138	49 15 192	41 41 225	17 50 289	57 59 339
324	24 25 027	44 11 061	32 17 140	49 13 195	41 35 227	17 42 291	57 56 340
326	24 29 028	44 18 063	32 22 142	49 11 197	41 29 229	17 34 293	57 53 342
328	24 33 030	44 26 065	32 27 144	49 08 199	41 22 231	17 27 295	57 51 344
	POLLUX	◆ CAPELLA	Alpheratz	◆ DENEB	VEGA	◆ ARCTURUS	Dubhe
330	24 38 032	44 33 067	32 32 146	49 05 201	41 16 233	17 19 297	57 49 346
332	24 42 034	44 41 069	32 36 148	49 02 203	41 09 235	17 12 299	57 47 347
334	24 47 036	44 49 071	32 41 151	48 59 205	41 02 237	17 05 301	57 45 349
336	24 52 038	44 57 073	32 45 153	48 55 207	40 55 239	16 57 303	57 44 351
338	24 58 040	45 05 075	32 48 155	48 51 210	40 48 242	16 50 305	57 42 353
340	25 03 042	45 13 077	32 52 157	48 47 212	40 40 244	16 44 307	57 41 355
342	25 09 044	45 21 079	32 55 159	48 42 214	40 33 246	16 37 309	57 41 356
344	25 15 046	45 29 080	32 58 161	48 37 216	40 25 248	16 31 311	57 40 358
346	25 21 048	45 38 082	33 00 163	48 32 218	40 17 250	16 24 313	57 40 000
348	25 27 050	45 46 084	33 03 165	48 27 220	40 09 252	16 18 315	57 40 002
350	25 34 052	45 54 086	33 05 167	48 22 222	40 01 254	16 13 317	57 41 003
352	25 40 054	46 03 088	33 06 169	48 16 224	39 53 256	16 07 319	57 41 005
354	25 47 056	46 11 090	33 08 171	48 10 227	39 45 258	16 02 321	57 42 007
356	25 54 058	46 19 092	33 09 173	48 04 229	39 37 260	15 56 323	57 43 009
358	26 01 060	46 28 094	33 10 176	47 57 231	39 29 262	15 51 325	57 45 011

LAT 85°N

LHA ♈	Hc	Zn	Hc	Zn	Hc	Zn	Hc	Zn	Hc	Zn	Hc	Zn	Hc	Zn
	Dubhe		POLLUX		◆CAPELLA		Alpheratz		◆DENEB		VEGA		◆ARCTURUS	
0	56 48	012	25 40	061	46 42	095	34 10	178	48 27	234	39 26	265	14 57	327
2	56 50	014	25 49	063	46 53	097	34 10	180	48 18	236	39 16	267	14 51	329
4	56 53	015	25 59	065	47 03	099	34 10	182	48 09	238	39 05	269	14 46	331
6	56 56	017	26 08	067	47 13	101	34 10	184	48 00	240	38 55	271	14 41	333
8	56 59	019	26 18	069	47 24	103	34 09	186	47 51	242	38 45	273	14 36	335
10	57 02	021	26 28	071	47 34	105	34 08	188	47 42	244	38 34	275	14 32	337
12	57 06	022	26 38	073	47 44	108	34 06	190	47 32	246	38 24	277	14 28	338
14	57 10	024	26 48	075	47 54	110	34 04	192	47 23	248	38 13	279	14 24	340
16	57 15	026	26 58	077	48 03	112	34 01	194	47 13	250	38 03	281	14 21	342
18	57 19	028	27 08	079	48 13	114	33 59	197	47 03	252	37 53	283	14 18	344
20	57 24	029	27 18	081	48 23	116	33 55	199	46 53	254	37 43	284	14 15	346
22	57 30	031	27 29	083	48 32	118	33 52	201	46 43	257	37 32	286	14 13	348
24	57 35	033	27 39	085	48 41	120	33 48	203	46 33	259	37 23	288	14 11	350
26	57 41	035	27 49	087	48 50	122	33 44	205	46 22	261	37 13	290	14 09	352
28	57 47	036	28 00	089	48 59	124	33 39	207	46 12	263	37 03	292	14 08	354
	Dubhe		POLLUX		◆CAPELLA		Alpheratz		◆DENEB		VEGA		◆ARCTURUS	
30	57 54	038	28 10	091	49 07	126	33 34	209	46 02	265	36 53	294	14 07	356
32	58 00	040	28 21	093	49 16	128	33 29	211	45 51	267	36 44	296	14 06	358
34	58 07	042	28 31	095	49 24	130	33 23	213	45 41	269	36 35	298	14 06	000
36	58 14	044	28 42	097	49 31	133	33 18	215	45 30	271	36 25	300	14 06	002
38	58 21	045	28 52	099	49 39	135	33 11	218	45 20	273	36 16	302	14 07	004
40	58 29	047	29 02	101	49 46	137	33 05	220	45 09	275	36 08	304	14 08	006
42	58 37	049	29 13	103	49 53	139	32 58	222	44 59	277	35 59	306	14 09	008
44	58 45	051	29 23	105	50 00	141	32 51	224	44 49	279	35 51	308	14 11	010
46	58 53	053	29 33	107	50 06	143	32 43	226	44 38	280	35 43	310	14 13	012
48	59 01	054	29 43	109	50 13	146	32 36	228	44 28	282	35 35	312	14 15	014
50	59 10	056	29 53	111	50 18	148	32 28	230	44 18	284	35 27	313	14 17	016
52	59 19	058	30 02	113	50 24	150	32 20	232	44 08	286	35 19	315	14 20	017
54	59 28	060	30 12	115	50 29	152	32 11	234	43 58	288	35 12	317	14 24	019
56	59 37	062	30 21	117	50 34	154	32 03	236	43 48	290	35 05	319	14 27	021
58	59 46	064	30 30	119	50 38	156	31 54	238	43 38	292	34 58	321	14 31	023
	◆ARCTURUS		Dubhe		POLLUX		◆CAPELLA		Alpheratz		◆DENEB		VEGA	
60	14 36	025	59 55	065	30 40	121	50 42	159	31 45	240	43 29	294	34 52	323
62	14 40	027	60 05	067	30 48	123	50 46	161	31 36	242	43 19	296	34 46	325
64	14 45	029	60 15	069	30 57	125	50 49	163	31 27	244	43 10	298	34 40	327
66	14 50	031	60 25	071	31 05	127	50 52	165	31 17	246	43 01	300	34 34	329
68	14 56	033	60 35	073	31 14	129	50 54	167	31 07	248	42 52	302	34 29	331
70	15 02	035	60 45	075	31 22	131	50 56	170	30 58	250	42 43	304	34 24	332
72	15 08	037	60 55	077	31 29	133	50 58	172	30 48	252	42 34	306	34 19	334
74	15 14	039	61 05	079	31 37	135	50 59	174	30 38	254	42 26	307	34 15	336
76	15 21	041	61 15	081	31 44	138	51 00	176	30 28	256	42 18	309	34 11	338
78	15 28	043	61 26	083	31 51	140	51 01	178	30 17	258	42 10	311	34 07	340
80	15 35	045	61 36	085	31 58	142	51 01	181	30 07	261	42 02	313	34 04	342
82	15 43	047	61 46	087	32 04	144	51 00	183	29 57	263	41 54	315	34 01	344
84	15 51	049	61 57	089	32 10	146	51 00	185	29 46	265	41 47	317	33 58	346
86	15 59	051	62 07	090	32 16	148	50 59	187	29 36	267	41 40	319	33 56	347
88	16 07	053	62 18	092	32 21	150	50 57	189	29 26	269	41 33	321	33 53	349
	◆ARCTURUS		REGULUS		POLLUX		◆CAPELLA		Alpheratz		◆DENEB		VEGA	
90	16 15	055	14 11	117	32 26	152	50 55	192	29 15	271	41 27	322	33 52	351
92	16 24	057	14 20	119	32 31	154	50 53	194	29 05	272	41 21	324	33 50	353
94	16 33	059	14 29	121	32 35	156	50 50	196	28 54	274	41 15	326	33 49	355
96	16 42	060	14 38	123	32 39	158	50 47	198	28 44	276	41 09	328	33 48	357
98	16 51	062	14 47	125	32 43	160	50 44	200	28 33	278	41 04	330	33 48	359
100	17 00	064	14 55	127	32 46	163	50 40	203	28 23	280	40 58	332	33 48	001
102	17 10	066	15 03	129	32 49	165	50 36	205	28 13	282	40 54	334	33 48	002
104	17 19	068	15 12	131	32 52	167	50 31	207	28 03	284	40 49	336	33 49	004
106	17 29	070	15 19	133	32 54	169	50 26	209	27 53	286	40 45	337	33 50	006
108	17 39	072	15 27	135	32 56	171	50 21	211	27 43	288	40 41	339	33 51	008
110	17 49	074	15 34	137	32 57	173	50 15	214	27 33	290	40 38	341	33 53	010
112	17 59	076	15 41	139	32 58	175	50 09	216	27 23	292	40 34	343	33 55	012
114	18 09	078	15 48	141	32 59	177	50 03	218	27 13	294	40 31	345	33 57	014
116	18 20	080	15 54	143	32 59	179	49 56	220	27 04	296	40 29	347	34 00	016
118	18 30	082	16 00	145	32 59	182	49 50	222	26 55	298	40 27	348	34 03	017
	VEGA		◆ARCTURUS		REGULUS		POLLUX		◆CAPELLA		Alpheratz		◆DENEB	
120	34 06	019	18 40	084	16 06	147	32 59	184	49 42	224	26 45	300	40 25	350
122	34 10	021	18 51	086	16 12	149	32 58	186	49 35	226	26 36	302	40 23	352
124	34 14	023	19 01	088	16 17	151	32 57	188	49 27	229	26 28	304	40 22	354
126	34 18	025	19 12	090	16 22	153	32 55	190	49 19	231	26 19	306	40 21	356
128	34 22	027	19 22	092	16 27	155	32 53	192	49 11	233	26 11	308	40 20	358
130	34 27	029	19 33	094	16 31	157	32 51	194	49 03	235	26 03	310	40 20	000
132	34 32	031	19 43	096	16 35	159	32 48	196	48 54	237	25 55	312	40 20	001
134	34 38	033	19 53	098	16 38	161	32 45	198	48 45	239	25 47	314	40 21	003
136	34 44	034	20 04	100	16 41	163	32 41	200	48 36	241	25 40	316	40 21	005
138	34 50	036	20 14	102	16 44	165	32 38	203	48 27	243	25 32	317	40 22	007
140	34 56	038	20 24	104	16 47	167	32 33	205	48 17	245	25 25	319	40 24	009
142	35 03	040	20 34	106	16 49	169	32 29	207	48 08	247	25 19	321	40 26	011
144	35 10	042	20 44	108	16 50	172	32 24	209	47 58	249	25 12	323	40 28	012
146	35 17	044	20 54	110	16 52	174	32 19	211	47 48	252	25 06	325	40 30	014
148	35 24	046	21 04	112	16 53	176	32 13	213	47 38	254	25 00	327	40 33	016
	◆DENEB		VEGA		◆ARCTURUS		REGULUS		POLLUX		◆CAPELLA		Alpheratz	
150	40 36	018	35 32	048	21 14	114	16 53	178	32 07	215	47 28	256	24 55	329
152	40 39	020	35 40	050	21 23	116	16 54	180	32 01	217	47 18	258	24 50	331
154	40 43	022	35 48	052	21 32	118	16 53	182	31 55	219	47 08	260	24 45	333
156	40 47	024	35 56	054	21 41	120	16 53	184	31 48	221	46 57	262	24 40	335
158	40 51	025	36 05	055	21 50	122	16 52	186	31 41	223	46 47	264	24 36	337
160	40 56	027	36 13	057	21 59	124	16 51	188	31 34	225	46 37	266	24 32	339
162	41 01	029	36 22	059	22 08	126	16 49	190	31 26	228	46 26	268	24 28	341
164	41 06	031	36 31	061	22 16	128	16 47	192	31 18	230	46 16	270	24 25	342
166	41 12	033	36 40	063	22 24	130	16 45	194	31 10	232	46 05	272	24 22	344
168	41 18	035	36 50	065	22 32	133	16 42	196	31 02	234	45 55	274	24 19	346
170	41 24	037	36 59	067	22 39	135	16 39	198	30 53	236	45 44	276	24 17	348
172	41 30	038	37 09	069	22 47	137	16 36	200	30 45	238	45 34	278	24 15	350
174	41 37	040	37 19	071	22 54	139	16 32	202	30 36	240	45 24	280	24 13	352
176	41 44	042	37 29	073	23 01	141	16 28	204	30 26	242	45 13	282	24 12	354
178	41 51	044	37 39	075	23 07	143	16 23	206	30 17	244	45 03	284	24 11	356

LHA ♈	Hc	Zn	Hc	Zn	Hc	Zn	Hc	Zn	Hc	Zn	Hc	Zn	Hc	Zn
	◆DENEB		VEGA		◆ARCTURUS		REGULUS		POLLUX		◆CAPELLA		Alpheratz	
180	41 58	046	37 49	077	23 13	145	16 19	208	30 08	246	44 53	286	24 11	358
182	42 06	048	37 59	079	23 19	147	16 13	210	29 58	248	44 43	287	24 10	000
184	42 14	050	38 10	081	23 25	149	16 08	212	29 48	250	44 33	289	24 11	002
186	42 22	052	38 20	083	23 30	151	16 02	214	29 38	252	44 23	291	24 11	004
188	42 30	054	38 30	085	23 35	153	15 56	216	29 28	254	44 14	293	24 12	005
190	42 39	055	38 41	087	23 39	155	15 50	218	29 18	256	44 04	295	24 13	007
192	42 47	057	38 51	089	23 44	157	15 43	220	29 08	258	43 55	297	24 14	009
194	42 56	059	39 02	091	23 47	159	15 36	223	28 58	260	43 45	299	24 16	011
196	43 05	061	39 12	093	23 51	161	15 29	225	28 47	262	43 36	301	24 19	013
198	43 15	063	39 23	095	23 54	163	15 22	227	28 37	264	43 27	303	24 21	015
200	43 24	065	39 33	097	23 57	165	15 14	229	28 27	266	43 19	305	24 24	017
202	43 33	067	39 43	099	23 59	167	15 06	231	28 16	268	43 10	307	24 27	019
204	43 43	069	39 54	101	24 01	170	14 58	233	28 06	270	43 02	309	24 31	021
206	43 53	071	40 04	103	24 03	172	14 49	235	27 55	272	42 54	310	24 35	023
208	44 03	073	40 14	105	24 05	174	14 41	237	27 45	274	42 46	312	24 39	025
	Alpheratz		◆DENEB		VEGA		◆ARCTURUS		REGULUS		POLLUX		◆CAPELLA	
210	24 43	027	44 13	075	40 24	107	24 06	176	14 32	239	27 34	276	42 38	314
212	24 48	028	44 23	077	40 34	109	24 06	178	14 23	241	27 24	278	42 31	316
214	24 53	030	44 33	079	40 44	111	24 06	180	14 13	243	27 14	280	42 24	318
216	24 58	032	44 44	081	40 54	113	24 06	182	14 04	245	27 03	282	42 17	320
218	25 04	034	44 54	083	41 03	115	24 06	184	13 55	247	26 53	284	42 10	322
220	25 11	036	45 04	084	41 13	117	24 05	186	13 45	249	26 43	286	42 04	324
222	25 17	038	45 15	086	41 22	119	24 03	188	13 35	251	26 33	288	41 58	325
224	25 23	040	45 25	088	41 31	121	24 02	190	13 25	253	26 23	290	41 52	327
226	25 30	042	45 36	090	41 40	123	24 00	192	13 15	255	26 13	292	41 47	329
228	25 37	044	45 46	092	41 48	125	23 57	194	13 05	257	26 04	294	41 41	331
230	25 45	046	45 57	094	41 57	127	23 54	196	12 55	259	25 54	296	41 36	333
232	25 52	048	46 07	096	42 05	129	23 51	199	12 44	261	25 45	298	41 32	335
234	26 00	050	46 17	098	42 13	132	23 48	201	12 34	263	25 36	300	41 28	337
236	26 08	052	46 28	100	42 21	134	23 44	203	12 24	265	25 27	302	41 24	338
238	26 17	054	46 38	103	42 28	136	23 40	205	12 13	267	25 18	304	41 20	340
	Alpheratz		◆DENEB		VEGA		◆ARCTURUS		Dubhe		POLLUX		◆CAPELLA	
240	26 25	056	46 48	105	42 35	138	23 35	207	62 40	263	25 09	306	41 16	342
242	26 34	057	46 58	107	42 42	140	23 30	209	62 30	265	25 01	307	41 13	344
244	26 43	059	47 08	109	42 49	142	23 25	211	62 19	267	24 53	309	41 11	346
246	26 52	061	47 18	111	42 55	144	23 20	213	62 09	269	24 45	311	41 08	348
248	27 01	063	47 28	113	43 01	146	23 14	215	61 59	271	24 37	313	41 06	349
250	27 11	065	47 37	115	43 07	148	23 08	217	61 48	273	24 30	315	41 04	351
252	27 20	067	47 47	117	43 12	151	23 01	219	61 38	275	24 22	317	41 03	353
254	27 30	069	47 56	119	43 17	153	22 54	221	61 27	277	24 15	319	41 02	355
256	27 40	071	48 05	121	43 21	155	22 47	223	61 17	279	24 09	321	41 01	357
258	27 50	073	48 14	123	43 26	157	22 40	225	61 07	281	24 02	323	41 01	359
260	28 00	075	48 22	125	43 30	159	22 32	227	60 56	283	23 56	325	41 01	001
262	28 10	077	48 31	127	43 33	161	22 25	229	60 46	285	23 50	327	41 01	002
264	28 20	079	48 39	129	43 36	163	22 17	231	60 36	287	23 45	329	41 02	004
266	28 30	081	48 47	132	43 39	166	22 08	233	60 26	289	23 39	331	41 03	006
268	28 41	083	48 55	134	43 42	168	22 00	235	60 16	291	23 34	333	41 04	008
	◆CAPELLA		Alpheratz		◆DENEB		VEGA		◆ARCTURUS		Dubhe		POLLUX	
270	41 05	010	28 51	085	49 02	136	43 44	170	21 51	237	60 07	292	23 30	335
272	41 07	012	29 02	087	49 09	138	43 45	172	21 42	240	59 57	294	23 25	336
274	41 10	013	29 12	089	49 16	140	43 46	174	21 33	242	59 48	296	23 21	338
276	41 12	015	29 22	091	49 23	142	43 47	176	21 24	244	59 38	298	23 18	340
278	41 15	017	29 33	093	49 29	144	43 48	179	21 14	246	59 29	300	23 14	342
280	41 18	019	29 43	095	49 35	147	43 48	181	21 05	248	59 20	302	23 11	344
282	41 22	021	29 54	097	49 40	149	43 48	183	20 55	250	59 11	304	23 09	346
284	41 26	023	30 04	099	49 46	151	43 47	185	20 45	252	59 03	305	23 06	348
286	41 30	024	30 14	101	49 51	153	43 46	187	20 35	254	58 54	307	23 04	350
288	41 34	026	30 25	103	49 55	155	43 44	189	20 25	256	58 46	309	23 03	352
290	41 39	028	30 35	105	49 59	158	43 42	191	20 15	258	58 38	311	23 01	354
292	41 44	030	30 45	107	50 03	160	43 40	194	20 05	260	58 30	313	23 00	356
294	41 50	032	30 55	109	50 07	162	43 37	196	19 54	262	58 23	314	23 00	358
296	41 55	034	31 05	111	50 10	164	43 34	198	19 44	264	58 15	316	22 59	359
298	42 01	036	31 14	113	50 12	166	43 31	200	19 34	266	58 08	318	22 59	001
	POLLUX		◆CAPELLA		Alpheratz		◆DENEB		VEGA		◆ARCTURUS		Dubhe	
300	23 00	003	42 07	038	31 24	115	50 15	168	43 27	202	19 23	268	58 01	320
302	23 01	005	42 14	039	31 33	117	50 16	171	43 23	204	19 13	270	57 55	322
304	23 02	007	42 21	041	31 42	119	50 18	173	43 19	207	19 02	272	57 48	323
306	23 03	009	42 28	043	31 52	121	50 19	175	43 14	209	18 52	274	57 42	325
308	23 05	011	42 35	045	32 00	123	50 20	177	43 09	211	18 41	276	57 36	327
310	23 07	013	42 43	047	32 09	125	50 20	179	43 03	213	18 31	278	57 31	329
312	23 10	015	42 50	049	32 17	127	50 20	182	42 57	215	18 21	280	57 25	330
314	23 13	017	42 58	051	32 26	129	50 19	184	42 51	217	18 10	282	57 20	332
316	23 16	019	43 06	053	32 34	132	50 19	186	42 45	219	18 00	284	57 15	334
318	23 19	021	43 15	054	32 41	134	50 17	188	42 38	221	17 50	286	57 11	336
320	23 23	023	43 24	056	32 49	136	50 16	190	42 31	224	17 40	288	57 07	337
322	23 27	024	43 32	058	32 56	138	50 13	193	42 23	226	17 30	289	57 03	339
324	23 32	026	43 41	060	33 03	140	50 11	195	42 16	228	17 20	291	56 59	341
326	23 37	028	43 50	062	33 09	142	50 08	197	42 08	230	17 11	293	56 56	343
328	23 42	030	44 00	064	33 16	144	50 05	199	42 00	232	17 01	295	56 53	344
	POLLUX		◆CAPELLA		Alpheratz		◆DENEB		VEGA		◆ARCTURUS		Dubhe	
330	23 47	032	44 09	066	33 22	146	50 01	201	41 51	234	16 52	297	56 50	346
332	23 53	034	44 19	068	33 27	148	49 57	204	41 43	236	16 42	299	56 48	348
334	23 59	036	44 29	070	33 33	150	49 53	206	41 34	238	16 33	301	56 46	349
336	24 05	038	44 38	072	33 38	152	49 48	208	41 25	240	16 25	303	56 44	351
338	24 12	040	44 48	074	33 42	154	49 43	210	41 16	242	16 16	305	56 43	353
340	24 18	042	44 59	076	33 47	157	49 38	212	41 07	244	16 08	307	56 42	355
342	24 26	044	45 09	078	33 51	159	49 32	214	40 57	246	15 59	309	56 41	356
344	24 33	046	45 19	079	33 54	161	49 26	217	40 47	248	15 51	311	56 40	358
346	24 41	048	45 29	081	33 58	163	49 19	219	40 38	251	15 44	313	56 40	000
348	24 48	050	45 40	083	34 01	165	49 13	221	40 28	253	15 36	315	56 40	002
350	24 56	051	45 50	085	34 03	167	49 06	223	40 18	255	15 29	317	56 41	003
352	25 05	053	46 00	087	34 05	169	48 58	225	40 08	257	15 22	319	56 42	005
354	25 13	055	46 11	089	34 07	171	48 51	227	39 57	259	15 15	321	56 43	007
356	25 22	057	46 21	091	34 08	173	48 43	229	39 47	261	15 09	323	56 44	009
358	25 31	059	46 32	093	34 10	175	48 35	232	39 37	263	15 02	325	56 46	010

 LAT 84°N

LHA ♈	Hc	Zn	Hc	Zn	Hc	Zn	Hc	Zn	Hc	Zn	Hc	Zn	Hc	Zn
	Dubhe		POLLUX		◆ CAPELLA		Alpheratz		◆ DENEB		VEGA		◆ ARCTURUS	
0	55 49	012	25 11	061	46 47	094	35 10	178	49 02	235	39 31	265	14 06	327
2	55 52	013	25 22	063	47 00	096	35 10	180	48 51	237	39 19	267	14 00	329
4	55 55	015	25 33	065	47 12	098	35 10	182	48 41	239	39 06	269	13 53	331
6	55 58	017	25 45	067	47 25	100	35 10	184	48 30	241	38 54	271	13 47	333
8	56 02	018	25 56	069	47 37	102	35 08	186	48 19	243	38 41	273	13 42	335
10	56 06	020	26 08	071	47 49	104	35 07	188	48 08	245	38 29	275	13 37	337
12	56 11	022	26 20	072	48 01	106	35 05	190	47 56	247	38 16	277	13 32	339
14	56 15	024	26 32	074	48 13	109	35 02	192	47 44	249	38 04	279	13 28	341
16	56 21	025	26 44	076	48 25	111	34 59	195	47 33	251	37 52	281	13 24	342
18	56 26	027	26 56	078	48 37	113	34 56	197	47 21	253	37 39	283	13 20	344
20	56 32	029	27 08	080	48 48	115	34 52	199	47 09	255	37 27	285	13 17	346
22	56 38	030	27 21	082	48 59	117	34 48	201	46 56	258	37 15	287	13 14	348
24	56 45	032	27 33	084	49 11	119	34 43	203	46 44	260	37 03	289	13 12	350
26	56 51	034	27 46	086	49 21	121	34 38	205	46 32	262	36 51	291	13 10	352
28	56 59	036	27 58	088	49 32	123	34 33	207	46 19	264	36 40	293	13 08	354
	Dubhe		POLLUX		◆ CAPELLA		Alpheratz		◆ DENEB		VEGA		◆ ARCTURUS	
30	57 06	037	28 11	090	49 42	125	34 27	209	46 07	266	36 28	295	13 07	356
32	57 14	039	28 23	092	49 52	127	34 20	212	45 54	268	36 17	297	13 07	358
34	57 22	041	28 36	094	50 02	130	34 13	214	45 42	270	36 06	299	13 06	000
36	57 30	042	28 48	096	50 12	132	34 06	216	45 29	272	35 55	301	13 06	002
38	57 39	044	29 01	098	50 21	134	33 59	218	45 17	274	35 44	303	13 07	004
40	57 48	046	29 13	100	50 30	136	33 51	220	45 04	276	35 34	304	13 08	006
42	57 57	048	29 26	102	50 38	138	33 43	222	44 52	278	35 24	306	13 10	008
44	58 06	049	29 38	104	50 47	140	33 34	224	44 39	279	35 14	308	13 11	010
46	58 16	051	29 50	106	50 54	143	33 25	226	44 27	281	35 04	310	13 14	012
48	58 26	053	30 02	108	51 02	145	33 16	228	44 15	283	34 55	312	13 17	014
50	58 36	055	30 14	110	51 09	147	33 06	230	44 02	285	34 45	314	13 20	015
52	58 46	057	30 25	112	51 15	149	32 57	233	43 50	287	34 37	316	13 23	017
54	58 57	058	30 37	114	51 22	151	32 46	235	43 39	289	34 28	318	13 27	019
56	59 08	060	30 48	116	51 27	154	32 36	237	43 27	291	34 20	320	13 32	021
58	59 19	062	30 59	118	51 33	156	32 26	239	43 15	293	34 12	321	13 36	023
	◆ ARCTURUS		Dubhe		POLLUX		◆ CAPELLA		Alpheratz		◆ DENEB		VEGA	
60	13 41	025	59 30	064	31 10	121	51 38	158	32 15	241	43 04	295	34 04	323
62	13 47	027	59 41	066	31 21	123	51 42	160	32 04	243	42 52	297	33 57	325
64	13 53	029	59 53	068	31 31	125	51 46	163	31 52	245	42 41	299	33 50	327
66	13 59	031	60 04	069	31 42	127	51 50	165	31 41	247	42 30	301	33 43	329
68	14 06	033	60 16	071	31 51	129	51 53	167	31 29	249	42 20	303	33 37	331
70	14 13	035	60 28	073	32 01	131	51 55	169	31 18	251	42 09	304	33 31	333
72	14 20	037	60 40	075	32 10	133	51 57	172	31 06	253	41 59	306	33 25	335
74	14 28	039	60 52	077	32 19	135	51 59	174	30 54	255	41 49	308	33 20	336
76	14 36	041	61 05	079	32 28	137	52 00	176	30 41	257	41 39	310	33 15	338
78	14 44	043	61 17	081	32 37	139	52 01	178	30 29	259	41 30	312	33 11	340
80	14 53	045	61 29	083	32 45	141	52 01	181	30 17	261	41 21	314	33 07	342
82	15 02	047	61 42	085	32 52	143	52 00	183	30 04	263	41 12	316	33 03	344
84	15 11	049	61 54	087	33 00	145	51 59	185	29 52	265	41 03	317	33 00	346
86	15 21	050	62 07	089	33 06	148	51 58	187	29 39	267	40 55	319	32 57	348
88	15 30	052	62 19	091	33 13	150	51 56	190	29 27	269	40 47	321	32 54	349
	◆ ARCTURUS		REGULUS		POLLUX		◆ CAPELLA		Alpheratz		◆ DENEB		VEGA	
90	15 40	054	14 38	116	33 19	152	51 54	192	29 14	271	40 39	323	32 52	351
92	15 51	056	14 49	118	33 25	154	51 51	194	29 02	273	40 32	325	32 51	353
94	16 01	058	15 00	120	33 30	156	51 48	196	28 49	275	40 25	327	32 49	355
96	16 12	060	15 10	122	33 35	158	51 44	199	28 37	277	40 18	329	32 48	357
98	16 23	062	15 21	125	33 39	160	51 40	201	28 24	279	40 11	330	32 48	359
100	16 34	064	15 31	127	33 43	162	51 35	203	28 12	281	40 05	332	32 48	001
102	16 46	066	15 41	129	33 47	165	51 30	205	28 00	283	40 00	334	32 48	002
104	16 57	068	15 51	131	33 50	167	51 24	208	27 48	285	39 54	336	32 49	004
106	17 09	070	16 00	133	33 53	169	51 18	210	27 35	287	39 50	338	32 50	006
108	17 21	072	16 09	135	33 55	171	51 12	212	27 23	289	39 45	340	32 52	008
110	17 33	074	16 18	137	33 57	173	51 05	214	27 12	291	39 41	341	32 54	010
112	17 45	076	16 26	139	33 58	175	50 58	216	27 00	293	39 37	343	32 56	012
114	17 57	078	16 34	141	33 59	177	50 50	219	26 49	295	39 34	345	32 59	014
116	18 09	080	16 42	143	33 59	179	50 42	221	26 37	297	39 30	347	33 02	015
118	18 22	082	16 50	145	33 59	182	50 34	223	26 26	299	39 28	349	33 05	017
	VEGA		◆ ARCTURUS		REGULUS		POLLUX		◆ CAPELLA		Alpheratz		◆ DENEB	
120	33 09	019	18 34	084	16 57	147	33 59	184	50 25	225	26 15	300	39 26	350
122	33 14	021	18 47	086	17 03	149	33 58	186	50 16	227	26 05	302	39 24	352
124	33 18	023	18 59	088	17 10	151	33 56	188	50 07	229	25 54	304	39 22	354
126	33 23	025	19 12	090	17 15	153	33 54	190	49 57	232	25 44	306	39 21	356
128	33 29	027	19 24	092	17 21	155	33 52	192	49 47	234	25 34	308	39 20	358
130	33 35	028	19 37	094	17 26	157	33 49	194	49 37	236	25 24	310	39 20	000
132	33 41	030	19 49	096	17 31	159	33 46	196	49 26	238	25 15	312	39 20	001
134	33 47	032	20 02	098	17 35	161	33 42	199	49 15	240	25 05	314	39 21	003
136	33 54	034	20 14	100	17 39	163	33 38	201	49 04	242	24 57	316	39 22	005
138	34 01	036	20 27	102	17 42	165	33 33	203	48 53	244	24 48	318	39 23	007
140	34 09	038	20 39	104	17 45	167	33 28	205	48 42	246	24 40	320	39 25	009
142	34 17	040	20 51	106	17 48	169	33 22	207	48 30	248	24 32	322	39 27	010
144	34 25	042	21 03	108	17 50	171	33 16	209	48 19	251	24 24	324	39 29	012
146	34 33	043	21 15	110	17 51	174	33 10	211	48 07	253	24 17	325	39 32	014
148	34 42	045	21 26	112	17 53	176	33 03	213	47 55	255	24 10	327	39 35	016
	◆ DENEB		VEGA		◆ ARCTURUS		REGULUS		POLLUX		◆ CAPELLA		Alpheratz	
150	39 39	018	34 51	047	21 38	114	17 53	178	32 56	215	47 42	257	24 03	329
152	39 43	020	35 01	049	21 49	116	17 54	180	32 49	218	47 30	259	23 57	331
154	39 47	021	35 10	051	22 01	118	17 53	182	32 41	220	47 18	261	23 51	333
156	39 52	023	35 20	053	22 12	120	17 53	184	32 33	222	47 05	263	23 46	335
158	39 57	025	35 30	055	22 22	122	17 52	186	32 24	224	46 53	265	23 41	337
160	40 03	027	35 41	057	22 33	124	17 50	188	32 16	226	46 40	267	23 36	339
162	40 09	029	35 51	059	22 43	126	17 48	190	32 06	228	46 28	269	23 32	341
164	40 15	031	36 02	061	22 53	128	17 46	192	31 57	230	46 15	271	23 28	343
166	40 21	032	36 13	062	23 03	130	17 43	194	31 47	232	46 03	273	23 24	345
168	40 28	034	36 24	064	23 12	132	17 40	196	31 37	234	45 50	275	23 21	346
170	40 35	036	36 36	066	23 21	134	17 36	198	31 27	236	45 38	277	23 18	348
172	40 43	038	36 47	068	23 30	136	17 32	200	31 16	238	45 25	279	23 16	350
174	40 51	040	36 59	070	23 39	138	17 27	202	31 05	240	45 13	281	23 14	352
176	40 59	042	37 11	072	23 47	140	17 22	204	30 54	242	45 01	283	23 12	354
178	41 07	043	37 23	074	23 55	142	17 17	206	30 43	244	44 49	285	23 11	356

LHA ♈	Hc	Zn	Hc	Zn	Hc	Zn	Hc	Zn	Hc	Zn	Hc	Zn	Hc	Zn
	◆ DENEB		VEGA		◆ ARCTURUS		REGULUS		POLLUX		◆ CAPELLA		Alpheratz	
180	41 16	045	37 35	076	24 02	145	17 11	208	30 32	246	44 36	286	23 11	358
182	41 25	047	37 47	078	24 09	147	17 05	210	30 20	249	44 24	288	23 10	000
184	41 35	049	37 59	080	24 16	149	16 59	213	30 08	251	44 13	290	23 11	002
186	41 44	051	38 12	082	24 22	151	16 52	215	29 57	253	44 01	292	23 11	004
188	41 54	053	38 24	084	24 28	153	16 44	217	29 45	255	43 49	294	23 12	005
190	42 04	055	38 37	086	24 34	155	16 37	219	29 32	257	43 38	296	23 13	007
192	42 15	057	38 49	088	24 39	157	16 29	221	29 20	259	43 27	298	23 15	009
194	42 25	058	39 02	090	24 44	159	16 20	223	29 08	261	43 16	300	23 17	011
196	42 36	060	39 14	092	24 48	161	16 12	225	28 55	263	43 05	302	23 20	013
198	42 47	062	39 27	094	24 52	163	16 03	227	28 43	265	42 55	304	23 23	015
200	42 58	064	39 39	096	24 55	165	15 53	229	28 30	267	42 44	305	23 27	017
202	43 10	066	39 52	098	24 58	167	15 44	231	28 18	269	42 34	307	23 30	019
204	43 21	068	40 04	100	25 00	169	15 34	233	28 05	271	42 24	309	23 35	021
206	43 33	070	40 17	102	25 03	172	15 24	235	27 53	273	42 15	311	23 39	023
208	43 45	072	40 29	104	25 04	174	15 13	237	27 40	275	42 05	313	23 44	024
	Alpheratz		◆ DENEB		VEGA		◆ ARCTURUS		REGULUS		POLLUX		◆ CAPELLA	
210	23 50	026	43 57	074	40 41	106	25 05	176	15 03	239	27 28	277	41 56	315
212	23 55	028	44 09	076	40 53	108	25 06	178	14 52	241	27 15	279	41 48	317
214	24 02	030	44 21	078	41 05	110	25 06	180	14 41	243	27 03	281	41 39	319
216	24 08	032	44 33	080	41 17	112	25 06	182	14 30	245	26 51	283	41 31	320
218	24 15	034	44 46	082	41 28	114	25 05	184	14 18	247	26 39	284	41 23	322
220	24 22	036	44 58	083	41 39	116	25 04	186	14 07	249	26 26	286	41 16	324
222	24 30	038	45 11	085	41 51	118	25 03	188	13 55	251	26 14	288	41 08	326
224	24 37	040	45 23	087	42 01	120	25 01	190	13 43	253	26 03	290	41 02	328
226	24 46	042	45 36	089	42 12	122	24 58	192	13 31	255	25 51	292	40 55	330
228	24 54	044	45 48	091	42 23	125	24 55	195	13 19	257	25 39	294	40 49	331
230	25 03	045	46 01	093	42 33	127	24 52	197	13 06	259	25 28	296	40 43	333
232	25 12	047	46 13	095	42 43	129	24 48	199	12 54	261	25 17	298	40 38	335
234	25 21	049	46 26	097	42 52	131	24 44	201	12 42	263	25 06	300	40 32	337
236	25 31	051	46 38	099	43 02	133	24 39	203	12 29	265	24 55	302	40 28	339
238	25 41	053	46 50	101	43 11	135	24 34	205	12 17	267	24 45	304	40 23	341
	Alpheratz		◆ DENEB		VEGA		◆ ARCTURUS		Dubhe		POLLUX		◆ CAPELLA	
240	25 51	055	47 03	104	43 19	137	24 29	207	62 46	265	24 34	306	40 19	342
242	26 01	057	47 15	106	43 28	139	24 23	209	62 34	267	24 24	308	40 16	344
244	26 12	059	47 27	108	43 36	141	24 17	211	62 21	269	24 15	310	40 12	346
246	26 23	061	47 39	110	43 43	144	24 10	213	62 09	271	24 05	312	40 10	348
248	26 34	063	47 50	112	43 51	146	24 03	215	61 56	273	23 56	314	40 07	350
250	26 45	065	48 02	114	43 58	148	23 55	217	61 44	275	23 47	316	40 05	351
252	26 57	067	48 13	116	44 04	150	23 48	219	61 31	277	23 38	317	40 03	353
254	27 08	069	48 25	118	44 10	152	23 39	221	61 19	279	23 30	319	40 02	355
256	27 20	071	48 35	120	44 16	154	23 31	224	61 07	281	23 22	321	40 01	357
258	27 32	073	48 46	122	44 21	157	23 22	226	60 54	283	23 14	323	40 01	359
260	27 44	075	48 57	124	44 26	159	23 13	228	60 42	285	23 07	325	40 01	000
262	27 56	077	49 07	126	44 30	161	23 04	230	60 30	287	23 00	327	40 01	002
264	28 08	078	49 17	129	44 34	163	22 54	232	60 18	288	22 53	329	40 02	004
266	28 21	080	49 27	131	44 37	165	22 44	234	60 06	290	22 47	331	40 03	006
268	28 33	082	49 36	133	44 40	168	22 34	236	59 55	292	22 41	333	40 04	008
	◆ CAPELLA		Alpheratz		◆ DENEB		VEGA		◆ ARCTURUS		Dubhe		POLLUX	
270	40 06	010	28 46	084	49 45	135	44 43	170	22 23	238	59 43	294	22 36	335
272	40 08	011	28 58	086	49 54	137	44 45	172	22 12	240	59 32	296	22 30	337
274	40 11	013	29 11	088	50 02	139	44 46	174	22 02	242	59 20	298	22 26	339
276	40 14	015	29 23	090	50 10	142	44 47	176	21 50	244	59 09	299	22 21	340
278	40 18	017	29 36	092	50 18	144	44 48	179	21 39	246	58 59	301	22 17	342
280	40 21	019	29 48	094	50 25	146	44 48	181	21 27	248	58 48	303	22 14	344
282	40 26	020	30 01	096	50 32	148	44 47	183	21 16	250	58 38	305	22 10	346
284	40 30	022	30 13	098	50 38	150	44 47	185	21 04	252	58 27	307	22 08	348
286	40 35	024	30 25	100	50 44	153	44 45	187	20 52	254	58 17	308	22 05	350
288	40 41	026	30 38	102	50 50	155	44 43	189	20 40	256	58 08	310	22 03	352
290	40 46	028	30 50	104	50 55	157	44 41	192	20 28	258	57 58	312	22 02	354
292	40 52	030	31 02	106	50 59	159	44 38	194	20 15	260	57 49	314	22 00	356
294	40 59	031	31 14	108	51 03	161	44 35	196	20 03	262	57 40	316	22 00	358
296	41 05	033	31 26	110	51 07	164	44 31	198	19 50	264	57 32	317	21 59	359
298	41 12	035	31 38	112	51 11	166	44 27	200	19 38	266	57 23	319	21 59	001
	POLLUX		◆ CAPELLA		Alpheratz		◆ DENEB		VEGA		◆ ARCTURUS		Dubhe	
300	22 00	003	41 20	037	31 49	115	51 13	168	44 23	203	19 25	268	57 15	321
302	22 01	005	41 27	039	32 00	117	51 16	170	44 18	205	19 13	270	57 07	322
304	22 02	007	41 35	041	32 11	119	51 17	173	44 12	207	19 00	272	57 00	324
306	22 04	009	41 44	043	32 22	121	51 19	175	44 06	209	18 48	274	56 53	326
308	22 06	011	41 52	044	32 33	123	51 20	177	44 00	211	18 35	276	56 46	328
310	22 09	013	42 01	046	32 43	125	51 20	179	43 53	213	18 23	278	56 39	329
312	22 12	015	42 10	048	32 54	127	51 20	182	43 46	216	18 10	280	56 33	331
314	22 15	017	42 20	050	33 04	129	51 19	184	43 39	218	17 58	282	56 27	333
316	22 19	019	42 30	052	33 13	131	51 18	186	43 31	220	17 46	284	56 21	335
318	22 23	020	42 40	054	33 22	133	51 17	188	43 23	222	17 34	286	56 16	336
320	22 28	022	42 50	056	33 31	135	51 15	191	43 14	224	17 22	288	56 11	338
322	22 33	024	43 00	057	33 40	137	51 12	193	43 05	226	17 10	290	56 07	340
324	22 38	026	43 11	059	33 48	139	51 09	195	42 56	228	16 58	292	56 03	341
326	22 44	028	43 22	061	33 56	141	51 05	197	42 46	231	16 47	294	55 59	343
328	22 50	030	43 33	063	34 04	144	51 01	200	42 36	233	16 35	296	55 55	345
	POLLUX		◆ CAPELLA		Alpheratz		◆ DENEB		VEGA		◆ ARCTURUS		Dubhe	
330	22 56	032	43 44	065	34 11	146	50 57	202	42 26	235	16 24	298	55 52	346
332	23 03	034	43 56	067	34 18	148	50 52	204	42 16	237	16 13	300	55 49	348
334	23 10	036	44 07	069	34 25	150	50 47	206	42 05	239	16 02	302	55 47	350
336	23 18	038	44 19	071	34 31	152	50 41	209	41 55	241	15 52	304	55 45	351
338	23 25	040	44 31	073	34 37	154	50 35	211	41 43	243	15 41	305	55 43	353
340	23 34	041	44 43	075	34 42	156	50 28	213	41 32	245	15 31	307	55 42	355
342	23 42	043	44 55	077	34 47	158	50 21	215	41 21	247	15 21	309	55 41	356
344	23 51	045	45 07	078	34 51	160	50 14	217	41 09	249	15 12	311	55 40	358
346	24 00	047	45 20	080	34 55	163	50 06	220	40 57	251	15 03	313	55 40	000
348	24 09	049	45 32	082	34 59	165	49 58	222	40 45	253	14 54	315	55 40	002
350	24 19	051	45 45	084	35 02	167	49 49	224	40 33	255	14 45	317	55 41	003
352	24 29	053	45 57	086	35 04	169	49 40	226	40 21	257	14 36	319	55 42	005
354	24 39	055	46 10	088	35 06	171	49 31	228	40 09	259	14 28	321	55 43	007
356	24 49	057	46 22	090	35 08	173	49 22	230	39 56	261	14 21	323	55 45	008
358	25 00	059	46 35	092	35 09	175	49 12	232	39 44	263	14 13	325	55 47	010

LHA ♈	Hc	Zn	Hc	Zn	Hc	Zn	Hc	Zn	Hc	Zn	Hc	Zn	Hc	Zn
	Dubhe		POLLUX		◆ CAPELLA		Alpheratz		◆ DENEB		VEGA		◆ ARCTURUS	
0	54 50	011	24 41	060	46 51	093	36 10	178	49 36	236	39 36	266	13 16	327
2	54 53	013	24 54	062	47 06	095	36 10	180	49 24	238	39 21	268	13 08	329
4	54 57	015	25 07	064	47 20	097	36 10	182	49 11	240	39 06	270	13 01	331
6	55 01	016	25 20	066	47 35	099	36 09	184	48 59	242	38 52	272	12 54	333
8	55 05	018	25 34	068	47 49	101	36 08	186	48 45	244	38 37	274	12 48	335
10	55 10	020	25 48	070	48 04	103	36 06	188	48 32	246	38 23	276	12 42	337
12	55 15	021	26 01	072	48 18	105	36 04	190	48 19	248	38 08	278	12 36	339
14	55 20	023	26 15	074	48 32	107	36 01	193	48 05	250	37 54	280	12 31	341
16	55 26	025	26 30	076	48 46	110	35 58	195	47 51	252	37 39	282	12 26	343
18	55 32	026	26 44	078	48 59	112	35 53	197	47 37	254	37 25	284	12 22	344
20	55 39	028	26 58	080	49 13	114	35 49	199	47 23	257	37 11	286	12 18	346
22	55 46	030	27 13	082	49 26	116	35 44	201	47 09	259	36 57	288	12 15	348
24	55 54	031	27 27	084	49 39	118	35 38	203	46 54	261	36 43	290	12 13	350
26	56 01	033	27 42	086	49 52	120	35 32	206	46 40	263	36 30	292	12 10	352
28	56 10	035	27 56	088	50 04	122	35 26	208	46 25	265	36 16	294	12 09	354
	Dubhe		POLLUX		◆ CAPELLA		Alpheratz		◆ DENEB		VEGA		◆ ARCTURUS	
30	56 18	036	28 11	090	50 17	124	35 19	210	46 11	267	36 03	296	12 07	356
32	56 27	038	28 25	092	50 29	126	35 11	212	45 56	269	35 50	297	12 07	358
34	56 36	040	28 40	094	50 40	129	35 03	214	45 42	271	35 37	299	12 06	000
36	56 46	041	28 55	096	50 51	131	34 55	216	45 27	273	35 24	301	12 07	002
38	56 55	043	29 09	098	51 02	133	34 46	218	45 12	275	35 12	303	12 07	004
40	57 06	045	29 24	100	51 13	135	34 37	220	44 58	277	35 00	305	12 08	006
42	57 16	047	29 38	102	51 23	137	34 27	223	44 43	279	34 48	307	12 10	008
44	57 27	048	29 52	104	51 33	140	34 17	225	44 29	280	34 36	309	12 12	010
46	57 38	050	30 06	106	51 42	142	34 06	227	44 15	282	34 25	311	12 15	012
48	57 49	052	30 20	108	51 51	144	33 56	229	44 00	284	34 14	313	12 18	013
50	58 01	054	30 34	110	51 59	146	33 44	231	43 46	286	34 04	314	12 22	015
52	58 13	055	30 48	112	52 07	149	33 33	233	43 32	288	33 53	316	12 26	017
54	58 25	057	31 01	114	52 14	151	33 21	235	43 18	290	33 43	318	12 31	019
56	58 37	059	31 15	116	52 21	153	33 09	237	43 05	292	33 34	320	12 36	021
58	58 50	061	31 28	118	52 27	155	32 56	239	42 51	294	33 25	322	12 41	023
	◆ ARCTURUS		Dubhe		POLLUX		◆ CAPELLA		Alpheratz		◆ DENEB		VEGA	
60	12 47	025	59 03	062	31 41	120	52 33	158	32 44	241	42 38	296	33 16	324
62	12 53	027	59 16	064	31 53	122	52 39	160	32 31	243	42 25	298	33 07	326
64	13 00	029	59 29	066	32 05	124	52 43	162	32 18	245	42 12	300	32 59	327
66	13 08	031	59 42	068	32 17	126	52 47	165	32 04	247	41 59	301	32 52	329
68	13 15	033	59 56	070	32 29	128	52 51	167	31 51	250	41 47	303	32 44	331
70	13 23	035	60 10	072	32 40	130	52 54	169	31 37	252	41 35	305	32 37	333
72	13 32	037	60 24	073	32 51	132	52 57	171	31 23	254	41 23	307	32 31	335
74	13 41	039	60 38	075	33 02	135	52 59	174	31 09	256	41 12	309	32 25	337
76	13 50	041	60 52	077	33 12	137	53 00	176	30 55	258	41 00	311	32 19	339
78	14 00	042	61 06	079	33 22	139	53 01	178	30 40	260	40 50	313	32 14	340
80	14 10	044	61 21	081	33 31	141	53 01	181	30 26	262	40 39	314	32 10	342
82	14 20	046	61 35	083	33 40	143	53 00	183	30 11	264	40 29	316	32 05	344
84	14 31	048	61 50	085	33 49	145	52 59	185	29 57	266	40 19	318	32 02	346
86	14 42	050	62 04	087	33 57	147	52 58	188	29 42	268	40 09	320	31 58	348
88	14 54	052	62 19	089	34 05	149	52 55	190	29 27	270	40 00	322	31 55	350
	◆ ARCTURUS		REGULUS		POLLUX		◆ CAPELLA		Alpheratz		◆ DENEB		VEGA	
90	15 05	054	15 04	116	34 12	151	52 53	192	29 13	272	39 51	324	31 53	351
92	15 17	056	15 17	118	34 19	154	52 49	194	28 58	274	39 42	325	31 51	353
94	15 30	058	15 30	120	34 25	156	52 45	197	28 44	276	39 34	327	31 50	355
96	15 42	060	15 42	122	34 31	158	52 41	199	28 29	278	39 27	329	31 49	357
98	15 55	062	15 55	124	34 36	160	52 36	201	28 15	280	39 19	331	31 48	359
100	16 08	064	16 07	126	34 41	162	52 30	204	28 00	281	39 12	333	31 48	001
102	16 21	066	16 18	128	34 45	164	52 24	206	27 46	283	39 06	334	31 48	002
104	16 35	068	16 30	130	34 49	166	52 17	208	27 32	285	39 00	336	31 49	004
106	16 48	070	16 41	132	34 52	169	52 10	210	27 18	287	38 54	338	31 50	006
108	17 02	072	16 51	134	34 54	171	52 03	213	27 04	289	38 49	340	31 52	008
110	17 16	074	17 01	136	34 56	173	51 54	215	26 50	291	38 44	342	31 55	010
112	17 30	076	17 11	139	34 58	175	51 46	217	26 37	293	38 39	343	31 57	012
114	17 44	078	17 21	141	34 59	177	51 37	219	26 23	295	38 36	345	32 00	013
116	17 59	080	17 30	143	34 59	179	51 27	222	26 10	297	38 32	347	32 04	015
118	18 13	082	17 39	145	34 59	182	51 17	224	25 57	299	38 29	349	32 08	017
	VEGA		◆ ARCTURUS		REGULUS		POLLUX		◆ CAPELLA		Alpheratz		◆ DENEB	
120	32 13	019	18 28	084	17 47	147	34 59	184	51 07	226	25 45	301	38 26	351
122	32 18	021	18 42	086	17 55	149	34 57	186	50 56	228	25 32	303	38 24	352
124	32 23	023	18 57	087	18 02	151	34 56	188	50 45	230	25 20	305	38 22	354
126	32 29	024	19 11	089	18 09	153	34 53	190	50 34	233	25 08	307	38 21	356
128	32 35	026	19 26	091	18 15	155	34 50	192	50 22	235	24 57	309	38 20	358
130	32 42	028	19 41	093	18 21	157	34 47	194	50 10	237	24 45	310	38 20	000
132	32 49	030	19 55	095	18 27	159	34 43	197	49 58	239	24 34	312	38 20	001
134	32 56	032	20 10	097	18 32	161	34 39	199	49 45	241	24 24	314	38 21	003
136	33 04	034	20 24	099	18 36	163	34 34	201	49 32	243	24 13	316	38 22	005
138	33 13	036	20 39	101	18 40	165	34 28	203	49 19	245	24 03	318	38 23	007
140	33 21	037	20 53	103	18 44	167	34 22	205	49 05	247	23 54	320	38 25	009
142	33 30	039	21 07	105	18 47	169	34 16	207	48 52	250	23 45	322	38 28	010
144	33 40	041	21 21	107	18 49	171	34 09	209	48 38	252	23 36	324	38 30	012
146	33 50	043	21 35	109	18 51	173	34 01	212	48 24	254	23 27	326	38 34	014
148	34 00	045	21 49	112	18 52	176	33 53	214	48 10	256	23 19	328	38 38	016
	◆ DENEB		VEGA		◆ ARCTURUS		REGULUS		POLLUX		◆ CAPELLA		Alpheratz	
150	38 42	018	34 10	047	22 02	114	18 53	178	33 45	216	47 56	258	23 12	330
152	38 46	019	34 21	049	22 15	116	18 54	180	33 36	218	47 41	260	23 04	331
154	38 51	021	34 32	050	22 29	118	18 53	182	33 27	220	47 27	262	22 58	333
156	38 57	023	34 44	052	22 41	120	18 53	184	33 18	222	47 12	264	22 51	335
158	39 03	025	34 55	054	22 54	122	18 51	186	33 08	224	46 58	266	22 45	337
160	39 09	027	35 07	056	23 06	124	18 50	188	32 57	226	46 43	268	22 40	339
162	39 16	028	35 20	058	23 18	126	18 47	190	32 46	228	46 29	270	22 35	341
164	39 23	030	35 32	060	23 30	128	18 45	192	32 35	231	46 14	272	22 30	343
166	39 30	032	35 45	062	23 41	130	18 41	194	32 24	233	45 59	274	22 26	345
168	39 38	034	35 58	064	23 52	132	18 37	196	32 12	235	45 45	276	22 23	347
170	39 47	036	36 11	066	24 03	134	18 33	198	32 00	237	45 30	278	22 19	348
172	39 55	037	36 25	068	24 13	136	18 28	200	31 48	239	45 16	280	22 17	350
174	40 05	039	36 38	069	24 23	138	18 23	202	31 35	241	45 01	282	22 15	352
176	40 14	041	36 52	071	24 33	140	18 17	204	31 22	243	44 47	284	22 13	354
178	40 24	043	37 06	073	24 42	142	18 11	207	31 09	245	44 33	285	22 11	356

LHA ♈	Hc	Zn	Hc	Zn	Hc	Zn	Hc	Zn	Hc	Zn	Hc	Zn	Hc	Zn
	◆ DENEB		VEGA		◆ ARCTURUS		REGULUS		POLLUX		◆ CAPELLA		Alpheratz	
180	40 34	045	37 20	075	24 51	144	18 04	209	30 56	247	44 19	287	22 11	358
182	40 44	047	37 34	077	24 59	146	17 57	211	30 42	249	44 05	289	22 10	000
184	40 55	048	37 49	079	25 07	148	17 49	213	30 28	251	43 51	291	22 11	002
186	41 06	050	38 03	081	25 15	151	17 41	215	30 14	253	43 38	293	22 11	003
188	41 18	052	38 17	083	25 22	153	17 32	217	30 00	255	43 24	295	22 12	005
190	41 29	054	38 32	085	25 28	155	17 23	219	29 46	257	43 11	297	22 14	007
192	41 41	056	38 47	087	25 34	157	17 14	221	29 32	259	42 58	299	22 16	009
194	41 53	058	39 01	089	25 40	159	17 04	223	29 17	261	42 46	301	22 19	011
196	42 06	060	39 16	091	25 45	161	16 54	225	29 03	263	42 33	303	22 22	013
198	42 19	061	39 30	093	25 49	163	16 44	227	28 48	265	42 21	304	22 25	015
200	42 32	063	39 45	095	25 53	165	16 33	229	28 34	267	42 09	306	22 29	017
202	42 45	065	40 00	097	25 57	167	16 22	231	28 19	269	41 57	308	22 34	019
204	42 58	067	40 14	099	25 59	169	16 10	233	28 04	271	41 46	310	22 38	020
206	43 12	069	40 28	101	26 02	171	15 58	235	27 50	273	41 35	312	22 44	022
208	43 25	071	40 43	103	26 04	174	15 46	237	27 35	275	41 24	314	22 50	024
	Alpheratz		◆ DENEB		VEGA		◆ ARCTURUS		REGULUS		POLLUX		◆ CAPELLA	
210	22 56	026	43 39	073	40 57	105	26 05	176	15 34	239	27 21	277	41 14	315
212	23 02	028	43 53	075	41 11	107	26 06	178	15 21	241	27 06	279	41 04	317
214	23 10	030	44 08	077	41 25	109	26 06	180	15 08	243	26 52	281	40 54	319
216	23 17	032	44 22	079	41 39	111	26 06	182	14 55	245	26 37	283	40 45	321
218	23 25	034	44 36	081	41 52	113	26 05	184	14 41	247	26 23	285	40 36	323
220	23 33	036	44 51	082	42 05	115	26 04	186	14 28	249	26 09	287	40 27	325
222	23 42	038	45 05	084	42 19	117	26 02	188	14 14	251	25 55	289	40 19	326
224	23 51	039	45 20	086	42 31	120	26 00	190	14 00	253	25 42	291	40 11	328
226	24 01	041	45 34	088	42 44	122	25 57	193	13 46	255	25 28	293	40 03	330
228	24 10	043	45 49	090	42 56	124	25 53	195	13 32	257	25 15	295	39 56	332
230	24 21	045	46 04	092	43 08	126	25 49	197	13 18	259	25 01	297	39 49	334
232	24 31	047	46 18	094	43 20	128	25 45	199	13 03	261	24 48	299	39 43	335
234	24 42	049	46 33	096	43 31	130	25 40	201	12 49	263	24 36	300	39 37	337
236	24 53	051	46 47	098	43 42	132	25 35	203	12 34	265	24 23	302	39 32	339
238	25 05	053	47 02	100	43 53	134	25 29	205	12 20	267	24 11	304	39 27	341
	Alpheratz		◆ DENEB		VEGA		◆ ARCTURUS		Dubhe		POLLUX		◆ CAPELLA	
240	25 17	055	47 16	102	44 03	137	25 22	207	62 51	267	23 59	306	39 22	343
242	25 29	057	47 30	105	44 13	139	25 15	209	62 36	269	23 47	308	39 18	344
244	25 41	059	47 44	107	44 23	141	25 08	211	62 21	271	23 36	310	39 14	346
246	25 54	060	47 58	109	44 32	143	25 00	213	62 07	273	23 25	312	39 11	348
248	26 06	062	48 12	111	44 40	145	24 52	216	61 52	275	23 14	314	39 08	350
250	26 19	064	48 26	113	44 48	147	24 43	218	61 38	277	23 04	316	39 06	352
252	26 33	066	48 39	115	44 56	150	24 34	220	61 23	279	22 54	318	39 04	353
254	26 46	068	48 52	117	45 03	152	24 24	222	61 09	281	22 44	320	39 02	355
256	27 00	070	49 05	119	45 10	154	24 14	224	60 54	283	22 35	322	39 01	357
258	27 14	072	49 18	121	45 16	156	24 04	226	60 40	284	22 26	323	39 01	359
260	27 28	074	49 30	123	45 22	158	23 53	228	60 26	286	22 18	325	39 01	000
262	27 42	076	49 42	126	45 27	161	23 42	230	60 12	288	22 10	327	39 01	002
264	27 56	078	49 54	128	45 31	163	23 31	232	59 58	290	22 02	329	39 02	004
266	28 10	080	50 05	130	45 35	165	23 19	234	59 45	292	21 55	331	39 03	006
268	28 25	082	50 16	132	45 39	167	23 07	236	59 31	294	21 48	333	39 05	008
	◆ CAPELLA		Alpheratz		◆ DENEB		VEGA		◆ ARCTURUS		Dubhe		POLLUX	
270	39 07	009	28 39	084	50 27	134	45 42	170	22 55	238	59 18	296	21 41	335
272	39 10	011	28 54	086	50 37	136	45 44	172	22 42	240	59 05	297	21 35	337
274	39 13	013	29 09	088	50 47	139	45 46	174	22 30	242	58 52	299	21 30	339
276	39 16	015	29 23	090	50 57	141	45 47	176	22 17	244	58 39	301	21 25	341
278	39 20	017	29 38	092	51 06	143	45 48	178	22 03	246	58 27	303	21 20	342
280	39 25	018	29 52	094	51 14	145	45 48	181	21 50	248	58 15	304	21 16	344
282	39 29	020	30 07	096	51 22	148	45 47	183	21 36	250	58 03	306	21 12	346
284	39 35	022	30 22	098	51 30	150	45 46	185	21 22	252	57 51	308	21 09	348
286	39 40	024	30 36	100	51 37	152	45 45	187	21 08	254	57 40	310	21 06	350
288	39 46	026	30 50	102	51 44	154	45 43	190	20 54	256	57 29	311	21 04	352
290	39 53	027	31 05	104	51 50	157	45 40	192	20 40	258	57 18	313	21 02	354
292	40 00	029	31 19	106	51 55	159	45 37	194	20 25	260	57 07	315	21 01	356
294	40 07	031	31 33	108	52 00	161	45 33	196	20 11	262	56 57	317	21 00	358
296	40 15	033	31 47	110	52 05	163	45 28	199	19 56	264	56 47	318	20 59	359
298	40 23	035	32 00	112	52 09	166	45 23	201	19 42	266	56 38	320	20 59	001
	POLLUX		◆ CAPELLA		Alpheratz		◆ DENEB		VEGA		◆ ARCTURUS		Dubhe	
300	21 00	003	40 32	036	32 14	114	52 12	168	45 18	203	19 27	268	56 28	322
302	21 01	005	40 40	038	32 27	116	52 15	170	45 12	205	19 13	270	56 19	323
304	21 03	007	40 50	040	32 40	118	52 17	173	45 06	207	18 58	272	56 11	325
306	21 05	009	40 59	042	32 53	120	52 19	175	44 59	210	18 43	274	56 03	327
308	21 07	011	41 09	044	33 05	122	52 20	177	44 51	212	18 29	276	55 55	328
310	21 10	013	41 20	046	33 18	124	52 20	179	44 43	214	18 14	278	55 47	330
312	21 14	015	41 30	047	33 29	126	52 20	182	44 35	216	18 00	280	55 40	332
314	21 18	017	41 41	049	33 41	128	52 19	184	44 26	218	17 46	282	55 34	333
316	21 22	018	41 52	051	33 52	131	52 18	186	44 17	221	17 31	284	55 27	335
318	21 27	020	42 04	053	34 03	133	52 16	189	44 07	223	17 17	286	55 21	337
320	21 32	022	42 16	055	34 14	135	52 13	191	43 57	225	17 03	288	55 16	338
322	21 38	024	42 28	057	34 24	137	52 10	193	43 46	227	16 49	290	55 10	340
324	21 44	026	42 40	059	34 34	139	52 07	196	43 35	229	16 36	292	55 06	342
326	21 51	028	42 53	060	34 43	141	52 03	198	43 24	231	16 22	294	55 01	343
328	21 58	030	43 05	062	34 52	143	51 58	200	43 13	233	16 09	296	54 57	345
	POLLUX		◆ CAPELLA		Alpheratz		◆ DENEB		VEGA		◆ ARCTURUS		Dubhe	
330	22 05	032	43 19	064	35 01	145	51 53	202	43 01	235	15 56	298	54 54	347
332	22 13	034	43 32	066	35 09	147	51 47	205	42 49	238	15 43	300	54 51	348
334	22 21	035	43 45	068	35 17	150	51 40	207	42 36	240	15 31	302	54 48	350
336	22 30	037	43 59	070	35 24	152	51 33	209	42 23	242	15 18	304	54 46	352
338	22 39	039	44 13	072	35 30	154	51 26	211	42 10	244	15 06	306	54 44	353
340	22 49	041	44 27	074	35 37	156	51 18	214	41 57	246	14 55	308	54 42	355
342	22 58	043	44 41	076	35 42	158	51 10	216	41 44	248	14 43	310	54 41	357
344	23 09	045	44 55	078	35 48	160	51 01	218	41 30	250	14 32	312	54 40	358
346	23 19	047	45 09	079	35 52	162	50 52	220	41 16	252	14 21	313	54 40	000
348	23 30	049	45 24	081	35 56	165	50 42	223	41 02	254	14 11	315	54 40	002
350	23 41	051	45 38	083	36 00	167	50 32	225	40 48	256	14 01	317	54 41	003
352	23 53	053	45 53	085	36 03	169	50 22	227	40 34	258	13 51	319	54 42	005
354	24 04	055	46 07	087	36 06	171	50 11	229	40 19	260	13 42	321	54 43	006
356	24 16	057	46 22	089	36 08	173	50 00	231	40 05	262	13 33	323	54 45	008
358	24 29	058	46 37	091	36 09	175	49 48	233	39 50	264	13 24	325	54 48	010

LHA ♈	Hc	Zn	Hc	Zn	Hc	Zn	Hc	Zn	Hc	Zn	Hc	Zn	Hc	Zn
	POLLUX		◆CAPELLA		Hamal		Alpheratz		◆DENEB		VEGA		◆Alioth	
0	24 11	060	46 54	092	30 14	146	37 10	177	50 10	237	39 39	267	48 04	349
2	24 26	062	47 11	094	30 23	148	37 10	180	49 55	239	39 22	269	48 01	350
4	24 41	064	47 27	096	30 32	150	37 10	182	49 41	241	39 06	271	47 58	352
6	24 56	066	47 44	098	30 40	152	37 09	184	49 26	243	38 49	273	47 56	354
8	25 11	068	48 00	100	30 48	154	37 08	186	49 11	245	38 32	275	47 55	355
10	25 27	070	48 17	102	30 55	156	37 06	188	48 56	247	38 16	277	47 54	357
12	25 43	072	48 33	104	31 01	159	37 03	191	48 40	249	37 59	279	47 53	359
14	25 59	073	48 49	106	31 07	161	36 59	193	48 25	251	37 43	281	47 53	000
16	26 15	075	49 05	108	31 12	163	36 55	195	48 09	253	37 26	283	47 53	002
18	26 31	077	49 21	111	31 17	165	36 51	197	47 53	256	37 10	285	47 54	004
20	26 47	079	49 36	113	31 21	167	36 46	199	47 36	258	36 54	287	47 55	005
22	27 04	081	49 52	115	31 24	169	36 40	202	47 20	260	36 38	289	47 57	007
24	27 20	083	50 07	117	31 27	171	36 33	204	47 04	262	36 23	291	47 59	009
26	27 37	085	50 21	119	31 29	174	36 26	206	46 47	264	36 07	292	48 02	010
28	27 54	087	50 36	121	31 31	176	36 19	208	46 30	266	35 52	294	48 05	012
	◆Alioth		POLLUX		◆CAPELLA		Hamal		Alpheratz		◆DENEB		VEGA	
30	48 09	014	28 10	089	50 50	123	31 32	178	36 11	210	46 14	268	35 37	296
32	48 13	015	28 27	091	51 04	126	31 32	180	36 02	212	45 57	270	35 22	298
34	48 18	017	28 44	093	51 17	128	31 32	182	35 53	214	45 40	272	35 07	300
36	48 23	019	29 00	095	51 30	130	31 31	184	35 43	217	45 24	274	34 53	302
38	48 28	020	29 17	097	51 43	132	31 29	186	35 33	219	45 07	276	34 39	304
40	48 35	022	29 33	099	51 55	134	31 27	189	35 22	221	44 50	278	34 25	306
42	48 41	024	29 50	101	52 07	137	31 24	191	35 11	223	44 34	279	34 12	307
44	48 48	025	30 06	103	52 18	139	31 21	193	34 59	225	44 17	281	33 59	309
46	48 55	027	30 22	105	52 29	141	31 17	195	34 47	227	44 01	283	33 46	311
48	49 03	029	30 38	107	52 39	143	31 12	197	34 35	229	43 45	285	33 33	313
50	49 11	031	30 54	109	52 49	146	31 07	199	34 22	231	43 29	287	33 21	315
52	49 20	032	31 10	111	52 58	148	31 01	201	34 09	234	43 13	289	33 10	317
54	49 29	034	31 25	113	53 06	150	30 55	204	33 55	236	42 57	291	32 59	319
56	49 39	036	31 41	115	53 14	152	30 48	206	33 41	238	42 42	293	32 48	320
58	49 49	037	31 56	117	53 22	155	30 40	208	33 27	240	42 27	295	32 37	322
	◆Alioth		POLLUX		◆CAPELLA		Hamal		Alpheratz		◆DENEB		VEGA	
60	49 59	039	32 10	119	53 29	157	30 32	210	33 12	242	42 12	297	32 27	324
62	50 10	041	32 25	122	53 35	159	30 23	212	32 57	244	41 57	298	32 18	326
64	50 21	043	32 39	124	53 40	162	30 14	214	32 42	246	41 42	300	32 09	328
66	50 32	044	32 52	126	53 45	164	30 05	216	32 27	248	41 28	302	32 00	330
68	50 44	046	33 06	128	53 49	166	29 55	218	32 11	250	41 14	304	31 52	331
70	50 57	048	33 19	130	53 53	169	29 44	221	31 55	252	41 00	306	31 44	333
72	51 09	050	33 31	132	53 56	171	29 33	223	31 39	254	40 47	308	31 37	335
74	51 22	051	33 44	134	53 58	174	29 21	225	31 23	256	40 34	310	31 30	337
76	51 35	053	33 55	136	54 00	176	29 09	227	31 07	258	40 21	311	31 24	339
78	51 49	055	34 07	138	54 01	178	28 57	229	30 51	260	40 09	313	31 18	341
80	52 02	057	34 18	140	54 01	181	28 44	231	30 34	262	39 57	315	31 13	342
82	52 17	058	34 28	143	54 00	183	28 31	233	30 18	264	39 45	317	31 08	344
84	52 31	060	34 38	145	53 59	185	28 17	235	30 01	266	39 34	319	31 03	346
86	52 46	062	34 47	147	53 57	188	28 04	237	29 44	268	39 23	320	31 00	348
88	53 00	064	34 56	149	53 54	190	27 49	239	29 28	270	39 13	322	30 56	350
	◆ARCTURUS		REGULUS		POLLUX		◆CAPELLA		Alpheratz		◆DENEB		VEGA	
90	14 30	054	15 31	116	35 05	151	53 51	192	29 11	272	39 03	324	30 54	352
92	14 44	056	15 45	118	35 12	153	53 47	195	28 54	274	38 53	326	30 51	353
94	14 58	058	16 00	120	35 20	155	53 43	197	28 38	276	38 44	328	30 50	355
96	15 12	060	16 14	122	35 26	158	53 37	199	28 21	278	38 35	329	30 49	357
98	15 27	062	16 28	124	35 32	160	53 31	202	28 04	280	38 27	331	30 48	359
100	15 41	064	16 42	126	35 38	162	53 25	204	27 48	282	38 19	333	30 48	001
102	15 57	066	16 55	128	35 43	164	53 18	206	27 32	284	38 12	335	30 48	002
104	16 12	068	17 08	130	35 47	166	53 10	209	27 16	286	38 05	337	30 49	004
106	16 27	069	17 21	132	35 50	168	53 02	211	27 00	288	37 58	338	30 51	006
108	16 43	071	17 33	134	35 54	171	52 53	213	26 44	290	37 52	340	30 53	008
110	16 59	073	17 45	136	35 56	173	52 43	216	26 28	292	37 47	342	30 55	010
112	17 15	075	17 56	138	35 58	175	52 33	218	26 13	294	37 42	344	30 58	011
114	17 31	077	18 07	140	35 59	177	52 23	220	25 58	296	37 37	345	31 02	013
116	17 48	079	18 17	142	35 59	179	52 12	222	25 43	297	37 34	347	31 06	015
118	18 04	081	18 27	144	35 59	182	52 00	225	25 28	299	37 30	349	31 11	017
	VEGA		◆ARCTURUS		REGULUS		POLLUX		◆CAPELLA		Alpheratz		◆DENEB	
120	31 16	019	18 21	083	18 37	147	35 58	184	51 48	227	25 14	301	37 27	351
122	31 21	021	18 37	085	18 46	149	35 57	186	51 36	229	24 59	303	37 25	352
124	31 28	022	18 54	087	18 54	151	35 55	188	51 23	231	24 46	305	37 23	354
126	31 34	024	19 11	089	19 02	153	35 52	190	51 10	234	24 32	307	37 21	356
128	31 41	026	19 27	091	19 10	155	35 49	192	50 56	236	24 19	309	37 20	358
130	31 49	028	19 44	093	19 16	157	35 45	195	50 42	238	24 06	311	37 20	000
132	31 57	030	20 01	095	19 23	159	35 41	197	50 28	240	23 54	313	37 20	001
134	32 05	032	20 17	097	19 28	161	35 35	199	50 13	242	23 42	315	37 21	003
136	32 14	033	20 34	099	19 34	163	35 30	201	49 58	244	23 30	317	37 22	005
138	32 24	035	20 50	101	19 38	165	35 23	203	49 43	246	23 19	318	37 24	007
140	32 34	037	21 07	103	19 42	167	35 16	205	49 28	249	23 08	320	37 26	008
142	32 44	039	21 23	105	19 46	169	35 09	208	49 12	251	22 57	322	37 29	010
144	32 55	041	21 39	107	19 48	171	35 01	210	48 56	253	22 47	324	37 32	012
146	33 06	043	21 55	109	19 51	173	34 52	212	48 40	255	22 38	326	37 36	014
148	33 17	044	22 10	111	19 52	176	34 43	214	48 24	257	22 29	328	37 40	015
	◆DENEB		VEGA		◆ARCTURUS		REGULUS		POLLUX		◆CAPELLA		Alpheratz	
150	37 44	017	33 29	046	22 26	113	19 53	178	34 34	216	48 08	259	22 20	330
152	37 50	019	33 41	048	22 41	115	19 54	180	34 24	218	47 51	261	22 12	332
154	37 55	021	33 54	050	22 56	117	19 53	182	34 13	220	47 35	263	22 04	333
156	38 02	023	34 07	052	23 11	119	19 53	184	34 02	223	47 18	265	21 57	335
158	38 08	024	34 20	054	23 25	121	19 51	186	33 50	225	47 02	267	21 50	337
160	38 15	026	34 34	056	23 39	123	19 49	188	33 38	227	46 45	269	21 44	339
162	38 23	028	34 48	057	23 53	125	19 46	190	33 26	229	46 28	271	21 38	341
164	38 31	030	35 02	059	24 07	127	19 43	192	33 13	231	46 12	273	21 33	343
166	38 39	032	35 16	061	24 20	129	19 39	194	33 00	233	45 55	275	21 28	345
168	38 48	033	35 31	063	24 32	132	19 35	196	32 46	235	45 38	277	21 24	347
170	38 58	035	35 46	065	24 45	134	19 30	198	32 33	237	45 22	279	21 21	348
172	39 08	037	36 01	067	24 57	136	19 24	200	32 18	239	45 05	281	21 18	350
174	39 18	039	36 17	069	25 08	138	19 18	203	32 04	241	44 49	283	21 15	352
176	39 29	041	36 33	071	25 19	140	19 12	205	31 49	243	44 33	285	21 13	354
178	39 40	042	36 48	073	25 30	142	19 04	207	31 34	246	44 17	286	21 12	356

LAT 82°N

LHA ♈	Hc	Zn	Hc	Zn	Hc	Zn	Hc	Zn	Hc	Zn	Hc	Zn	Hc	Zn
	◆DENEB		VEGA		◆ARCTURUS		REGULUS		POLLUX		◆CAPELLA		Alpheratz	
180	39 51	044	37 04	075	25 40	144	18 57	209	31 19	248	44 01	288	21 11	358
182	40 03	046	37 21	076	25 49	146	18 48	211	31 03	250	43 45	290	21 10	000
184	40 15	048	37 37	078	25 58	148	18 40	213	30 47	252	43 29	292	21 11	002
186	40 28	050	37 53	080	26 07	150	18 30	215	30 31	254	43 14	294	21 11	003
188	40 40	051	38 10	082	26 15	152	18 20	217	30 15	256	42 59	296	21 13	005
190	40 54	053	38 26	084	26 22	155	18 10	219	29 59	258	42 44	298	21 14	007
192	41 07	055	38 43	086	26 29	157	17 59	221	29 43	260	42 29	300	21 17	009
194	41 21	057	39 00	088	26 35	159	17 48	223	29 26	262	42 15	301	21 20	011
196	41 35	059	39 16	090	26 41	161	17 37	225	29 10	264	42 01	303	21 23	013
198	41 50	061	39 33	092	26 46	163	17 25	227	28 53	266	41 47	305	21 27	015
200	42 04	063	39 50	094	26 51	165	17 12	229	28 36	268	41 33	307	21 32	017
202	42 19	064	40 06	096	26 55	167	16 59	231	28 20	270	41 20	309	21 37	018
204	42 34	066	40 23	098	26 58	169	16 46	233	28 03	272	41 07	311	21 42	020
206	42 50	068	40 39	100	27 01	171	16 32	235	27 46	274	40 55	312	21 48	022
208	43 05	070	40 56	102	27 03	174	16 19	237	27 30	276	40 43	314	21 55	024
	Alpheratz		◆DENEB		VEGA		◆ARCTURUS		REGULUS		POLLUX		◆CAPELLA	
210	22 02	026	43 21	072	41 12	104	27 05	176	16 04	239	27 13	278	40 31	316
212	22 09	028	43 37	074	41 28	106	27 06	178	15 50	241	26 56	280	40 19	318
214	22 18	030	43 53	076	41 44	108	27 06	180	15 35	243	26 40	282	40 08	320
216	22 26	032	44 10	078	42 00	110	27 06	182	15 20	245	26 24	283	39 58	321
218	22 35	034	44 26	080	42 15	112	27 05	184	15 05	247	26 08	285	39 48	323
220	22 44	035	44 42	082	42 31	115	27 04	186	14 49	249	25 52	287	39 38	325
222	22 54	037	44 59	083	42 46	117	27 01	188	14 33	251	25 36	289	39 29	327
224	23 05	039	45 16	085	43 01	119	26 59	191	14 17	253	25 20	291	39 20	329
226	23 15	041	45 32	087	43 15	121	26 55	193	14 01	255	25 05	293	39 11	330
228	23 27	043	45 49	089	43 29	123	26 51	195	13 45	257	24 49	295	39 03	332
230	23 38	045	46 06	091	43 43	125	26 47	197	13 29	259	24 34	297	38 56	334
232	23 50	047	46 22	093	43 57	127	26 42	199	13 12	261	24 20	299	38 48	336
234	24 03	049	46 39	095	44 10	129	26 36	201	12 56	263	24 05	301	38 42	338
236	24 15	051	46 56	097	44 22	132	26 30	203	12 39	265	23 51	303	38 36	339
238	24 28	052	47 12	099	44 35	134	26 23	205	12 22	267	23 37	305	38 30	341
	Alpheratz		◆DENEB		VEGA		◆ARCTURUS		Dubhe		POLLUX		◆CAPELLA	
240	24 42	054	47 28	101	44 47	136	26 15	207	62 53	269	23 23	307	38 25	343
242	24 55	056	47 45	103	44 58	138	26 07	210	62 36	271	23 10	309	38 20	345
244	25 09	058	48 01	105	45 09	140	25 59	212	62 19	273	22 57	310	38 16	346
246	25 24	060	48 17	108	45 19	142	25 50	214	62 03	275	22 45	312	38 12	348
248	25 38	062	48 33	110	45 29	145	25 40	216	61 46	277	22 33	314	38 09	350
250	25 53	064	48 48	112	45 39	147	25 30	218	61 30	279	22 21	316	38 06	352
252	26 08	066	49 04	114	45 48	149	25 20	220	61 13	281	22 09	318	38 04	353
254	26 24	068	49 19	116	45 56	151	25 09	222	60 57	282	21 59	320	38 03	355
256	26 39	070	49 34	118	46 04	154	24 58	224	60 40	284	21 48	322	38 01	357
258	26 55	072	49 48	120	46 11	156	24 46	226	60 24	286	21 38	324	38 01	359
260	27 11	074	50 03	122	46 17	158	24 33	228	60 08	288	21 28	326	38 01	000
262	27 27	075	50 17	125	46 23	160	24 21	230	59 53	290	21 19	327	38 01	002
264	27 43	077	50 30	127	46 29	163	24 08	232	59 37	292	21 10	329	38 02	004
266	28 00	079	50 43	129	46 33	165	23 54	234	59 22	293	21 02	331	38 03	006
268	28 16	081	50 56	131	46 37	167	23 41	236	59 06	295	20 54	333	38 05	008
	◆CAPELLA		Alpheratz		◆DENEB		VEGA		◆ARCTURUS		Dubhe		POLLUX	
270	38 08	009	28 33	083	51 09	133	46 41	169	23 27	239	58 51	297	20 47	335
272	38 11	011	28 49	085	51 20	136	46 43	172	23 12	241	58 37	299	20 40	337
274	38 14	013	29 06	087	51 32	138	46 46	174	22 57	243	58 22	301	20 34	339
276	38 18	015	29 23	089	51 43	140	46 47	176	22 42	245	58 08	302	20 28	341
278	38 23	016	29 39	091	51 53	142	46 48	178	22 27	247	57 54	304	20 23	343
280	38 28	018	29 56	093	52 03	145	46 48	181	22 12	249	57 40	306	20 18	344
282	38 33	020	30 13	095	52 13	147	46 47	183	21 56	251	57 27	307	20 14	346
284	38 39	022	30 29	097	52 22	149	46 46	185	21 40	253	57 14	309	20 10	348
286	38 45	023	30 46	099	52 30	151	46 44	188	21 24	255	57 01	311	20 07	350
288	38 52	025	31 02	101	52 38	154	46 42	190	21 08	257	56 48	313	20 04	352
290	39 00	027	31 19	103	52 45	156	46 39	192	20 52	259	56 36	314	20 02	354
292	39 07	029	31 35	105	52 51	158	46 35	194	20 35	261	56 24	316	20 01	356
294	39 16	031	31 51	107	52 57	161	46 30	197	20 19	263	56 13	318	20 00	358
296	39 24	032	32 07	109	53 02	163	46 25	199	20 02	265	56 02	319	19 59	359
298	39 34	034	32 22	111	53 07	165	46 19	201	19 46	267	55 51	321	19 59	001
	POLLUX		◆CAPELLA		Alpheratz		◆DENEB		VEGA		◆ARCTURUS		Dubhe	
300	20 00	003	39 43	036	32 38	113	53 11	168	46 13	203	19 29	269	55 41	323
302	20 01	005	39 53	038	32 53	115	53 14	170	46 06	206	19 12	271	55 31	324
304	20 03	007	40 04	040	33 08	117	53 16	172	45 59	208	18 55	273	55 21	326
306	20 05	009	40 14	041	33 23	120	53 18	175	45 51	210	18 39	275	55 12	328
308	20 08	011	40 26	043	33 37	122	53 20	177	45 42	212	18 22	277	55 03	329
310	20 12	013	40 37	045	33 51	124	53 20	179	45 33	215	18 06	279	54 55	331
312	20 16	015	40 49	047	34 05	126	53 20	182	45 23	217	17 49	281	54 47	332
314	20 20	016	41 02	049	34 18	128	53 19	184	45 13	219	17 33	283	54 40	334
316	20 25	018	41 14	050	34 31	130	53 17	186	45 02	221	17 17	284	54 33	336
318	20 30	020	41 27	052	34 44	132	53 15	189	44 51	223	17 00	286	54 26	337
320	20 37	022	41 41	054	34 56	134	53 12	191	44 39	226	16 44	288	54 20	339
322	20 43	024	41 54	056	35 08	136	53 09	194	44 27	228	16 29	290	54 14	341
324	20 50	026	42 08	058	35 19	138	53 05	196	44 14	230	16 13	292	54 09	342
326	20 58	028	42 23	060	35 30	141	53 00	198	44 01	232	15 58	294	54 04	344
328	21 06	030	42 37	061	35 40	143	52 54	201	43 48	234	15 43	296	53 59	345
	POLLUX		◆CAPELLA		Hamal		Alpheratz		◆DENEB		VEGA		◆Alioth	
330	21 14	031	42 52	063	27 05	115	35 50	145	52 48	203	43 34	236	49 45	323
332	21 23	033	43 07	065	27 20	117	35 59	147	52 41	205	43 20	238	49 36	325
334	21 32	035	43 22	067	27 35	119	36 08	149	52 34	207	43 06	241	49 26	327
336	21 42	037	43 38	069	27 49	121	36 16	151	52 26	210	42 51	243	49 17	328
338	21 52	039	43 53	071	28 04	123	36 24	153	52 17	212	42 36	245	49 09	330
340	22 03	041	44 09	073	28 17	125	36 31	156	52 08	214	42 21	247	49 01	332
342	22 14	043	44 25	075	28 31	127	36 38	158	51 58	217	42 06	249	48 53	333
344	22 26	045	44 42	077	28 44	129	36 44	160	51 48	219	41 50	251	48 46	335
346	22 38	047	44 58	078	28 57	131	36 49	162	51 37	221	41 34	253	48 39	337
348	22 50	049	45 14	080	29 09	133	36 54	164	51 26	223	41 18	255	48 32	338
350	23 03	050	45 31	082	29 21	135	36 58	167	51 14	226	41 02	257	48 27	340
352	23 16	052	45 47	084	29 33	137	37 02	169	51 02	228	40 45	259	48 21	342
354	23 29	054	46 04	086	29 44	139	37 05	171	50 50	230	40 29	261	48 16	344
356	23 43	056	46 21	088	29 54	142	37 07	173	50 37	232	40 12	263	48 12	345
358	23 57	058	46 37	090	30 05	144	37 09	175	50 23	234	39 56	265	48 08	347

LAT 81°N

LHA ♈	Hc	Zn	Hc	Zn	Hc	Zn	Hc	Zn	Hc	Zn	Hc	Zn	Hc	Zn
	POLLUX		◆CAPELLA		Hamal		Alpheratz		◆DENEB		VEGA		◆Alioth	
0	23 41	060	46 56	091	31 04	145	38 10	177	50 42	238	39 42	268	47 05	349
2	23 58	062	47 15	093	31 14	148	38 10	180	50 26	240	39 23	270	47 02	350
4	24 14	063	47 33	095	31 24	150	38 10	182	50 10	242	39 04	272	46 59	352
6	24 31	065	47 52	097	31 33	152	38 09	184	49 53	244	38 45	274	46 57	354
8	24 48	067	48 11	099	31 42	154	38 07	186	49 36	246	38 27	276	46 55	355
10	25 06	069	48 29	101	31 50	156	38 05	189	49 19	248	38 08	278	46 54	357
12	25 23	071	48 47	103	31 57	158	38 02	191	49 01	250	37 50	280	46 53	359
14	25 41	073	49 06	105	32 03	160	37 58	193	48 43	252	37 31	282	46 53	000
16	25 59	075	49 24	107	32 09	163	37 53	195	48 25	255	37 13	284	46 53	002
18	26 18	077	49 41	109	32 15	165	37 48	197	48 07	257	36 55	285	46 54	004
20	26 36	079	49 59	112	32 19	167	37 42	200	47 49	259	36 37	287	46 55	005
22	26 54	081	50 16	114	32 23	169	37 36	202	47 30	261	36 19	289	46 57	007
24	27 13	083	50 33	116	32 26	171	37 28	204	47 12	263	36 01	291	47 00	008
26	27 32	085	50 50	118	32 29	173	37 20	206	46 53	265	35 44	293	47 03	010
28	27 50	087	51 06	120	32 31	176	37 12	208	46 34	267	35 27	295	47 06	012
	◆Alioth		POLLUX		◆CAPELLA		Hamal		Alpheratz		◆DENEB		VEGA	
30	47 11	013	28 09	089	51 23	122	32 32	178	37 02	211	46 16	269	35 10	297
32	47 15	015	28 28	091	51 38	124	32 32	180	36 53	213	45 57	271	34 53	299
34	47 20	017	28 47	093	51 53	127	32 32	182	36 42	215	45 38	273	34 37	301
36	47 26	018	29 05	095	52 08	129	32 31	184	36 31	217	45 19	275	34 21	302
38	47 32	020	29 24	097	52 23	131	32 29	187	36 19	219	45 01	277	34 05	304
40	47 39	022	29 43	099	52 37	133	32 26	189	36 07	221	44 42	279	33 50	306
42	47 46	023	30 01	101	52 50	136	32 23	191	35 55	224	44 24	280	33 35	308
44	47 54	025	30 20	103	53 03	138	32 19	193	35 41	226	44 05	282	33 20	310
46	48 02	027	30 38	105	53 15	140	32 15	195	35 28	228	43 47	284	33 06	312
48	48 11	028	30 56	107	53 27	143	32 09	197	35 14	230	43 29	286	32 52	314
50	48 20	030	31 14	109	53 38	145	32 03	200	34 59	232	43 11	288	32 39	315
52	48 29	032	31 31	111	53 48	147	31 57	202	34 44	234	42 53	290	32 26	317
54	48 39	033	31 49	113	53 58	150	31 50	204	34 29	236	42 35	292	32 13	319
56	48 50	035	32 06	115	54 07	152	31 42	206	34 13	238	42 18	294	32 01	321
58	49 01	037	32 23	117	54 16	154	31 33	208	33 57	240	42 01	296	31 50	323
	◆Alioth		POLLUX		◆CAPELLA		Hamal		Alpheratz		◆DENEB		VEGA	
60	49 12	038	32 40	119	54 24	157	31 24	210	33 40	242	41 44	297	31 39	325
62	49 24	040	32 56	121	54 31	159	31 14	212	33 23	245	41 28	299	31 28	326
64	49 37	042	33 12	123	54 37	161	31 04	215	33 06	247	41 12	301	31 18	328
66	49 49	043	33 27	125	54 43	164	30 53	217	32 49	249	40 56	303	31 08	330
68	50 02	045	33 42	127	54 48	166	30 41	219	32 31	251	40 40	305	30 59	332
70	50 16	047	33 57	129	54 52	169	30 29	221	32 14	253	40 25	307	30 50	334
72	50 30	049	34 11	131	54 55	171	30 17	223	31 56	255	40 10	308	30 42	335
74	50 44	050	34 25	134	54 58	173	30 04	225	31 37	257	39 55	310	30 35	337
76	50 59	052	34 39	136	55 00	176	29 50	227	31 19	259	39 41	312	30 28	339
78	51 14	054	34 51	138	55 00	178	29 36	229	31 01	261	39 27	314	30 21	341
80	51 29	056	35 04	140	55 01	181	29 22	231	30 42	263	39 14	316	30 15	343
82	51 45	057	35 16	142	55 00	183	29 07	233	30 23	265	39 01	317	30 10	344
84	52 01	059	35 27	144	54 59	186	28 52	236	30 05	267	38 49	319	30 05	346
86	52 17	061	35 37	146	54 56	188	28 36	238	29 46	269	38 37	321	30 01	348
88	52 33	063	35 48	149	54 53	190	28 20	240	29 27	271	38 25	323	29 57	350
	◆ARCTURUS		REGULUS		POLLUX		◆CAPELLA		Alpheratz		◆DENEB		VEGA	
90	13 55	054	15 57	116	35 57	151	54 50	193	29 08	273	38 14	324	29 54	352
92	14 10	056	16 14	118	36 06	153	54 45	195	28 50	275	38 03	326	29 52	353
94	14 26	058	16 30	120	36 14	155	54 40	198	28 31	277	37 53	328	29 50	355
96	14 42	060	16 46	122	36 22	157	54 34	200	28 12	279	37 43	330	29 49	357
98	14 58	061	17 02	124	36 29	160	54 27	202	27 54	281	37 34	332	29 48	359
100	15 15	063	17 17	126	36 35	162	54 20	205	27 35	283	37 25	333	29 48	001
102	15 32	065	17 32	128	36 40	164	54 11	207	27 17	284	37 17	335	29 48	002
104	15 49	067	17 47	130	36 45	166	54 03	209	26 59	286	37 10	337	29 49	004
106	16 06	069	18 01	132	36 49	168	53 53	212	26 41	288	37 02	339	29 51	006
108	16 24	071	18 15	134	36 53	171	53 43	214	26 23	290	36 56	340	29 53	008
110	16 42	073	18 28	136	36 55	173	53 32	216	26 06	292	36 50	342	29 56	010
112	17 00	075	18 41	138	36 57	175	53 20	219	25 49	294	36 44	344	30 00	011
114	17 18	077	18 53	140	36 59	177	53 08	221	25 32	296	36 39	346	30 04	013
116	17 36	079	19 05	142	36 59	179	52 56	223	25 15	298	36 35	347	30 08	015
118	17 55	081	19 16	144	36 59	182	52 43	226	24 58	300	36 31	349	30 13	017
	VEGA		◆ARCTURUS		REGULUS		POLLUX		◆CAPELLA		Alpheratz		◆DENEB	
120	30 19	019	18 13	083	19 27	146	36 58	184	52 29	228	24 42	302	36 28	351
122	30 25	020	18 32	085	19 37	148	36 57	186	52 15	230	24 26	304	36 25	353
124	30 32	022	18 51	087	19 47	150	36 54	188	52 00	232	24 11	305	36 23	354
126	30 39	024	19 10	089	19 56	153	36 51	190	51 45	235	23 56	307	36 22	356
128	30 47	026	19 28	091	20 04	155	36 48	193	51 30	237	23 41	309	36 21	358
130	30 56	028	19 47	093	20 12	157	36 43	195	51 14	239	23 27	311	36 20	000
132	31 05	029	20 06	095	20 19	159	36 38	197	50 57	241	23 13	313	36 20	001
134	31 14	031	20 25	097	20 25	161	36 32	199	50 41	243	22 59	315	36 21	003
136	31 24	033	20 43	099	20 31	163	36 26	201	50 24	245	22 46	317	36 22	005
138	31 35	035	21 02	101	20 36	165	36 18	204	50 07	248	22 34	319	36 24	007
140	31 46	037	21 20	103	20 41	167	36 11	206	49 49	250	22 22	321	36 27	008
142	31 57	038	21 38	105	20 45	169	36 02	208	49 32	252	22 10	322	36 30	010
144	32 09	040	21 56	107	20 48	171	35 53	210	49 14	254	21 59	324	36 33	012
146	32 21	042	22 14	109	20 50	173	35 43	212	48 56	256	21 48	326	36 37	014
148	32 34	044	22 32	111	20 52	176	35 33	214	48 37	258	21 38	328	36 42	015
	◆DENEB		VEGA		◆ARCTURUS		REGULUS		POLLUX		◆CAPELLA		Alpheratz	
150	36 47	017	32 47	046	22 49	113	20 53	178	35 22	217	48 19	260	21 28	330
152	36 53	019	33 01	048	23 06	115	20 54	180	35 10	219	48 00	262	21 19	332
154	36 59	021	33 15	049	23 23	117	20 53	182	34 58	221	47 42	264	21 10	334
156	37 06	022	33 30	051	23 40	119	20 52	184	34 46	223	47 23	266	21 02	336
158	37 13	024	33 44	053	23 56	121	20 51	186	34 33	225	47 04	268	20 55	337
160	37 21	026	34 00	055	24 12	123	20 49	188	34 19	227	46 45	270	20 48	339
162	37 30	028	34 15	057	24 28	125	20 46	190	34 05	229	46 27	272	20 41	341
164	37 39	029	34 31	059	24 43	127	20 42	192	33 51	232	46 08	274	20 36	343
166	37 48	031	34 47	061	24 58	129	20 38	194	33 36	234	45 49	276	20 31	345
168	37 58	033	35 04	062	25 12	131	20 33	196	33 20	236	45 31	278	20 26	347
170	38 09	035	35 20	064	25 26	133	20 27	199	33 05	238	45 12	280	20 22	349
172	38 20	036	35 38	066	25 39	135	20 21	201	32 49	240	44 54	282	20 18	350
174	38 31	038	35 55	068	25 52	137	20 14	203	32 32	242	44 35	284	20 16	352
176	38 43	040	36 12	070	26 05	140	20 06	205	32 16	244	44 17	285	20 13	354
178	38 55	042	36 30	072	26 17	142	19 58	207	31 59	246	43 59	287	20 12	356

LHA ♈	Hc	Zn	Hc	Zn	Hc	Zn	Hc	Zn	Hc	Zn	Hc	Zn	Hc	Zn
	◆DENEB		VEGA		◆ARCTURUS		REGULUS		POLLUX		◆CAPELLA		Alpheratz	
180	39 08	044	36 48	074	26 28	144	19 49	209	31 41	248	43 41	289	20 11	358
182	39 21	045	37 06	076	26 39	146	19 40	211	31 24	250	43 24	291	20 10	000
184	39 34	047	37 24	078	26 49	148	19 30	213	31 06	252	43 06	293	20 11	002
186	39 48	049	37 43	080	26 59	150	19 19	215	30 48	254	42 49	295	20 11	003
188	40 03	051	38 01	082	27 08	152	19 08	217	30 30	256	42 32	297	20 13	005
190	40 17	053	38 20	083	27 16	154	18 57	219	30 11	258	42 16	299	20 15	007
192	40 33	054	38 39	085	27 24	156	18 45	221	29 53	260	41 59	300	20 18	009
194	40 48	056	38 57	087	27 31	159	18 32	223	29 34	262	41 43	302	20 21	011
196	41 04	058	39 16	089	27 38	161	18 19	225	29 16	264	41 27	304	20 25	013
198	41 20	060	39 35	091	27 44	163	18 05	227	28 57	266	41 12	306	20 29	015
200	41 36	062	39 54	093	27 49	165	17 51	230	28 38	268	40 57	308	20 34	016
202	41 53	064	40 12	095	27 54	167	17 37	232	28 20	270	40 42	309	20 40	018
204	42 10	065	40 31	097	27 57	169	17 22	234	28 01	272	40 28	311	20 46	020
206	42 27	067	40 50	099	28 01	171	17 06	236	27 42	274	40 14	313	20 53	022
208	42 44	069	41 08	101	28 03	173	16 51	238	27 23	276	40 01	315	21 00	024
	Alpheratz		◆DENEB		VEGA		◆ARCTURUS		REGULUS		POLLUX		◆CAPELLA	
210	21 08	026	43 02	071	41 26	103	28 05	176	16 35	240	27 05	278	39 47	317
212	21 16	028	43 20	073	41 45	105	28 06	178	16 18	242	26 46	280	39 35	318
214	21 25	030	43 38	075	42 03	107	28 06	180	16 02	244	26 28	282	39 23	320
216	21 35	031	43 56	077	42 20	110	28 06	182	15 45	246	26 10	284	39 11	322
218	21 45	033	44 15	079	42 38	112	28 05	184	15 27	248	25 51	286	38 59	324
220	21 55	035	44 33	081	42 55	114	28 03	186	15 10	250	25 33	288	38 49	326
222	22 07	037	44 52	082	43 12	116	28 01	188	14 52	252	25 16	290	38 38	327
224	22 18	039	45 10	084	43 29	118	27 58	191	14 34	254	24 58	292	38 28	329
226	22 30	041	45 29	086	43 46	120	27 54	193	14 16	256	24 41	294	38 19	331
228	22 43	043	45 48	088	44 02	122	27 49	195	13 58	258	24 24	296	38 10	333
230	22 56	045	46 06	090	44 17	124	27 44	197	13 40	260	24 07	297	38 02	334
232	23 09	046	46 25	092	44 33	126	27 38	199	13 21	262	23 50	299	37 54	336
234	23 23	048	46 44	094	44 47	129	27 32	201	13 02	264	23 34	301	37 46	338
236	23 37	050	47 03	096	45 02	131	27 25	203	12 44	266	23 18	303	37 39	340
238	23 52	052	47 21	098	45 16	133	27 17	206	12 25	268	23 03	305	37 33	341
	Alpheratz		◆DENEB		VEGA		◆ARCTURUS		Dubhe		POLLUX		◆CAPELLA	
240	24 07	054	47 40	100	45 29	135	27 09	208	62 53	271	22 48	307	37 27	343
242	24 22	056	47 58	102	45 42	137	27 00	210	62 34	273	22 33	309	37 22	345
244	24 38	058	48 16	104	45 55	140	26 50	212	62 15	275	22 18	311	37 18	347
246	24 54	060	48 35	106	46 07	142	26 40	214	61 57	277	22 04	313	37 14	348
248	25 10	062	48 52	109	46 18	144	26 29	216	61 38	279	21 51	315	37 10	350
250	25 27	063	49 10	111	46 29	146	26 18	218	61 20	280	21 38	316	37 07	352
252	25 44	065	49 28	113	46 39	149	26 06	220	61 01	282	21 25	318	37 05	354
254	26 01	067	49 45	115	46 48	151	25 53	222	60 43	284	21 13	320	37 03	355
256	26 18	069	50 02	117	46 57	153	25 41	224	60 25	286	21 01	322	37 02	357
258	26 36	071	50 18	119	47 05	155	25 27	227	60 07	288	20 49	324	37 01	359
260	26 54	073	50 34	121	47 13	158	25 13	229	59 49	290	20 39	326	37 01	000
262	27 12	075	50 50	124	47 20	160	24 59	231	59 31	291	20 28	328	37 01	002
264	27 30	077	51 06	126	47 26	162	24 44	233	59 14	293	20 19	330	37 02	004
266	27 48	079	51 21	128	47 31	165	24 29	235	58 57	295	20 09	331	37 04	006
268	28 07	081	51 35	130	47 36	167	24 14	237	58 40	297	20 01	333	37 06	007
	◆CAPELLA		Alpheratz		◆DENEB		VEGA		◆ARCTURUS		Dubhe		POLLUX	
270	37 09	009	28 25	083	51 49	132	47 40	169	23 58	239	58 23	298	19 52	335
272	37 12	011	28 44	085	52 03	135	47 43	171	23 41	241	58 07	300	19 45	337
274	37 16	013	29 03	087	52 16	137	47 45	174	23 25	243	57 51	302	19 38	339
276	37 20	014	29 22	089	52 29	139	47 47	176	23 08	245	57 35	304	19 31	341
278	37 25	016	29 40	091	52 41	141	47 48	178	22 51	247	57 20	305	19 25	343
280	37 31	018	29 59	093	52 52	144	47 48	181	22 33	249	57 05	307	19 20	345
282	37 37	020	30 18	095	53 03	146	47 47	183	22 16	251	56 50	309	19 15	346
284	37 43	021	30 37	097	53 13	148	47 46	185	21 58	253	56 35	310	19 11	348
286	37 50	023	30 55	099	53 22	151	47 44	188	21 40	255	56 21	312	19 08	350
288	37 58	025	31 14	101	53 31	153	47 41	190	21 22	257	56 07	314	19 05	352
290	38 06	027	31 32	103	53 39	155	47 37	192	21 03	259	55 54	315	19 03	354
292	38 15	028	31 50	105	53 47	158	47 33	195	20 45	261	55 41	317	19 01	356
294	38 24	030	32 08	107	53 54	160	47 28	197	20 26	263	55 28	319	19 00	358
296	38 34	032	32 26	109	54 00	163	47 22	199	20 07	265	55 16	320	18 59	359
298	38 44	034	32 44	111	54 05	165	47 15	202	19 49	267	55 04	322	18 59	001
	POLLUX		◆CAPELLA		Alpheratz		◆DENEB		VEGA		◆ARCTURUS		Dubhe	
300	19 00	003	38 54	035	33 01	113	54 09	167	47 08	204	19 30	269	54 53	323
302	19 02	005	39 06	037	33 18	115	54 13	170	47 00	206	19 11	271	54 42	325
304	19 04	007	39 17	039	33 35	117	54 16	172	46 52	208	18 52	273	54 31	327
306	19 06	009	39 29	041	33 52	119	54 18	175	46 42	211	18 34	275	54 21	328
308	19 09	011	39 42	043	34 08	121	54 19	177	46 32	213	18 15	277	54 12	330
310	19 13	013	39 55	044	34 24	123	54 20	179	46 22	215	17 56	279	54 03	332
312	19 17	014	40 08	046	34 40	125	54 20	182	46 11	217	17 38	281	53 54	333
314	19 22	016	40 22	048	34 55	127	54 19	184	45 59	220	17 20	283	53 46	335
316	19 28	018	40 36	050	35 09	129	54 17	187	45 47	222	17 01	285	53 38	336
318	19 34	020	40 50	052	35 24	132	54 15	189	45 34	224	16 43	287	53 30	338
320	19 41	022	41 05	053	35 38	134	54 11	191	45 21	226	16 25	289	53 24	339
322	19 48	024	41 20	055	35 51	136	54 07	194	45 07	228	16 08	291	53 17	341
324	19 56	026	41 36	057	36 04	138	54 02	196	44 53	231	15 50	293	53 11	343
326	20 04	028	41 52	059	36 16	140	53 57	199	44 38	233	15 33	294	53 06	344
328	20 13	029	42 08	061	36 28	142	53 50	201	44 23	235	15 16	296	53 01	346
	POLLUX		◆CAPELLA		Hamal		Alpheratz		◆DENEB		VEGA		◆Alioth	
330	20 23	031	42 25	062	27 30	114	36 39	144	53 43	203	44 07	237	48 57	324
332	20 33	033	42 41	064	27 47	116	36 50	147	53 35	206	43 51	239	48 46	326
334	20 43	035	42 59	066	28 03	118	37 00	149	53 27	208	43 35	241	48 36	327
336	20 54	037	43 16	068	28 20	120	37 09	151	53 18	210	43 18	243	48 26	329
338	21 06	039	43 33	070	28 36	122	37 18	153	53 08	213	43 02	246	48 17	331
340	21 18	041	43 51	072	28 52	124	37 26	155	52 57	215	42 44	248	48 08	332
342	21 30	043	44 09	074	29 07	126	37 33	158	52 46	217	42 27	250	47 59	334
344	21 43	044	44 27	076	29 22	129	37 40	160	52 35	220	42 09	252	47 51	336
346	21 56	046	44 45	077	29 36	131	37 46	162	52 22	222	41 51	254	47 44	337
348	22 10	048	45 04	079	29 50	133	37 52	164	52 09	224	41 33	256	47 37	339
350	22 25	050	45 22	081	30 04	135	37 57	166	51 56	227	41 15	258	47 30	341
352	22 39	052	45 41	083	30 17	137	38 01	169	51 42	229	40 56	260	47 24	342
354	22 54	054	46 00	085	30 29	139	38 04	171	51 28	231	40 38	262	47 19	344
356	23 10	056	46 18	087	30 41	141	38 07	173	51 13	233	40 19	264	47 14	345
358	23 25	058	46 37	089	30 53	143	38 09	175	50 58	235	40 00	266	47 09	347

 LAT 80°N

LHA ♈	Hc Zn	Hc Zn	Hc Zn	Hc Zn	Hc Zn	Hc Zn	Hc Zn
	POLLUX	◆CAPELLA	Hamal	Alpheratz	◆DENEB	VEGA	◆Alioth
0	23 11 059	46 56 090	31 53 145	39 10 177	51 14 239	39 43 269	46 06 349
2	23 29 061	47 17 092	32 05 147	39 10 180	50 56 241	39 23 271	46 03 351
4	23 47 063	47 38 094	32 16 149	39 10 182	50 37 243	39 02 273	46 00 352
6	24 06 065	47 59 096	32 26 152	39 09 184	50 19 245	38 41 275	45 57 354
8	24 25 067	48 19 098	32 35 154	39 07 186	50 00 247	38 20 277	45 55 355
10	24 44 069	48 40 100	32 44 156	39 04 189	49 40 249	38 00 279	45 54 357
12	25 04 071	49 00 102	32 52 158	39 01 191	49 21 252	37 39 280	45 53 359
14	25 24 073	49 21 104	33 00 160	38 56 193	49 01 254	37 19 282	45 53 000
16	25 44 074	49 41 106	33 07 162	38 51 195	48 41 256	36 58 284	45 53 002
18	26 04 076	50 01 108	33 12 165	38 45 198	48 20 258	36 38 286	45 54 003
20	26 24 078	50 20 110	33 18 167	38 39 200	48 00 260	36 18 288	45 56 005
22	26 45 080	50 40 113	33 22 169	38 31 202	47 39 262	35 59 290	45 58 007
24	27 05 082	50 59 115	33 26 171	38 23 204	47 19 264	35 39 292	46 01 008
26	27 26 084	51 18 117	33 28 173	38 14 207	46 58 266	35 20 294	46 04 010
28	27 47 086	51 36 119	33 30 176	38 04 209	46 37 268	35 01 296	46 08 012
	◆Alioth	POLLUX	◆CAPELLA	Hamal	Alpheratz	◆DENEB	VEGA
30	46 12 013	28 07 088	51 54 121	33 32 178	37 54 211	46 16 270	34 42 297
32	46 17 015	28 28 090	52 12 123	33 32 180	37 43 213	45 56 272	34 24 299
34	46 23 016	28 49 092	52 29 126	33 32 182	37 31 215	45 35 274	34 06 301
36	46 29 018	29 10 094	52 46 128	33 30 184	37 19 218	45 14 276	33 48 303
38	46 36 020	29 31 096	53 02 130	33 28 187	37 06 220	44 53 278	33 31 305
40	46 43 021	29 51 098	53 17 132	33 26 189	36 52 222	44 33 279	33 14 307
42	46 51 023	30 12 100	53 33 135	33 22 191	36 38 224	44 12 281	32 58 309
44	46 59 025	30 32 102	53 47 137	33 18 193	36 23 226	43 52 283	32 42 310
46	47 08 026	30 53 104	54 01 139	33 13 195	36 08 228	43 32 285	32 26 312
48	47 18 028	31 13 106	54 14 142	33 07 198	35 52 230	43 12 287	32 11 314
50	47 28 029	31 33 108	54 27 144	33 00 200	35 36 233	42 52 289	31 56 316
52	47 38 031	31 52 110	54 39 146	32 53 202	35 19 235	42 32 291	31 42 318
54	47 49 033	32 12 112	54 50 149	32 44 204	35 02 237	42 13 293	31 28 319
56	48 01 034	32 31 114	55 00 151	32 36 206	34 44 239	41 54 294	31 15 321
58	48 13 036	32 50 116	55 10 154	32 26 208	34 26 241	41 35 296	31 02 323
	◆Alioth	REGULUS	POLLUX	◆CAPELLA	Alpheratz	◆DENEB	VEGA
60	48 25 038	11 19 086	33 08 118	55 19 156	34 08 243	41 16 298	30 50 325
62	48 38 039	11 40 088	33 26 120	55 27 158	33 49 245	40 58 300	30 38 327
64	48 52 041	12 00 090	33 44 123	55 34 161	33 30 247	40 40 302	30 27 328
66	49 05 043	12 21 092	34 02 125	55 40 163	33 11 249	40 23 304	30 16 330
68	49 20 044	12 42 094	34 19 127	55 46 166	32 51 251	40 06 305	30 06 332
70	49 35 046	13 03 096	34 35 129	55 51 168	32 31 253	39 49 307	29 56 334
72	49 50 048	13 24 097	34 51 131	55 54 171	32 11 255	39 32 309	29 48 336
74	50 05 049	13 44 099	35 06 133	55 57 173	31 51 257	39 16 311	29 39 337
76	50 21 051	14 05 101	35 21 135	55 59 176	31 30 259	39 01 313	29 32 339
78	50 38 053	14 25 103	35 36 137	56 00 178	31 10 261	38 46 314	29 24 341
80	50 55 055	14 45 105	35 50 140	56 01 181	30 49 263	38 31 316	29 18 343
82	51 12 056	15 05 107	36 03 142	56 00 183	30 28 265	38 17 318	29 12 345
84	51 29 058	15 25 109	36 15 144	55 58 186	30 08 267	38 03 320	29 07 346
86	51 47 060	15 44 111	36 27 146	55 56 188	29 47 269	37 50 321	29 02 348
88	52 05 062	16 04 113	36 39 148	55 52 191	29 26 271	37 37 323	28 58 350
	◆ARCTURUS	REGULUS	POLLUX	◆CAPELLA	Alpheratz	◆DENEB	VEGA
90	13 19 054	16 23 115	36 49 150	55 48 193	29 05 273	37 25 325	28 55 352
92	13 36 055	16 41 117	36 59 153	55 43 196	28 44 275	37 13 327	28 52 353
94	13 53 057	17 00 119	37 08 155	55 37 198	28 24 277	37 02 328	28 50 355
96	14 11 059	17 18 122	37 17 157	55 30 200	28 03 279	36 51 330	28 49 357
98	14 29 061	17 35 124	37 25 159	55 22 203	27 42 281	36 41 332	28 48 359
100	14 48 063	17 52 126	37 32 161	55 14 205	27 22 283	36 32 334	28 48 001
102	15 06 065	18 09 128	37 38 164	55 05 208	27 02 285	36 23 335	28 48 002
104	15 25 067	18 25 130	37 43 166	54 55 210	26 42 287	36 14 337	28 50 004
106	15 45 069	18 41 132	37 48 168	54 44 213	26 22 289	36 07 339	28 51 006
108	16 04 071	18 56 134	37 52 170	54 32 215	26 02 291	35 59 341	28 54 008
110	16 24 073	19 11 136	37 55 173	54 20 217	25 43 293	35 53 342	28 57 009
112	16 44 075	19 25 138	37 57 175	54 07 220	25 24 295	35 47 344	29 01 011
114	17 04 077	19 39 140	37 59 177	53 53 222	25 05 296	35 41 346	29 05 013
116	17 25 079	19 52 142	37 59 179	53 39 224	24 47 298	35 36 348	29 10 015
118	17 45 081	20 05 144	37 59 182	53 24 227	24 28 300	35 32 349	29 16 017
	VEGA	◆ARCTURUS	REGULUS	POLLUX	◆CAPELLA	Alpheratz	◆DENEB
120	29 22 018	18 06 083	20 17 146	37 58 184	53 09 229	24 11 302	35 29 351
122	29 29 020	18 27 085	20 28 148	37 56 186	52 53 231	23 53 304	35 26 353
124	29 36 022	18 47 086	20 39 150	37 54 188	52 36 233	23 36 306	35 23 354
126	29 45 024	19 08 088	20 49 152	37 50 191	52 20 236	23 19 308	35 22 356
128	29 53 026	19 29 090	20 58 154	37 46 193	52 02 238	23 03 310	35 21 358
130	30 02 027	19 50 092	21 07 157	37 41 195	51 44 240	22 47 311	35 20 000
132	30 12 029	20 11 094	21 15 159	37 35 197	51 26 242	22 32 313	35 20 001
134	30 23 031	20 31 096	21 22 161	37 29 199	51 07 244	22 17 315	35 21 003
136	30 34 033	20 52 098	21 28 163	37 21 202	50 48 246	22 02 317	35 22 005
138	30 45 034	21 13 100	21 34 165	37 13 204	50 29 249	21 49 319	35 24 006
140	30 57 036	21 33 102	21 39 167	37 04 206	50 10 251	21 35 321	35 27 008
142	31 10 038	21 53 104	21 43 169	36 55 208	49 50 253	21 22 323	35 30 010
144	31 23 040	22 13 106	21 47 171	36 45 211	49 30 255	21 10 325	35 34 012
146	31 37 042	22 33 108	21 50 173	36 34 213	49 10 257	20 58 326	35 39 013
148	31 51 044	22 53 110	21 52 175	36 22 215	48 49 259	20 47 328	35 44 015
	◆DENEB	VEGA	◆ARCTURUS	REGULUS	POLLUX	◆CAPELLA	Alpheratz
150	35 50 017	32 05 045	23 12 112	21 53 178	36 10 217	48 29 261	20 36 330
152	35 56 019	32 20 047	23 31 114	21 54 180	35 57 219	48 08 263	20 26 332
154	36 03 020	32 36 049	23 50 116	21 53 182	35 44 221	47 47 265	20 17 334
156	36 10 022	32 52 051	24 09 118	21 52 184	35 30 224	47 27 267	20 08 336
158	36 19 024	33 08 053	24 27 121	21 50 186	35 15 226	47 06 269	19 59 338
160	36 27 026	33 25 054	24 45 123	21 48 188	35 00 228	46 45 271	19 52 339
162	36 37 027	33 42 056	25 02 125	21 45 190	34 44 230	46 24 273	19 45 341
164	36 46 029	34 00 058	25 19 127	21 41 192	34 28 232	46 03 275	19 38 343
166	36 57 031	34 17 060	25 35 129	21 36 194	34 11 234	45 43 277	19 33 345
168	37 08 032	34 36 062	25 51 131	21 30 197	33 54 236	45 22 279	19 27 347
170	37 19 034	34 54 064	26 07 133	21 24 199	33 36 238	45 01 281	19 23 349
172	37 31 036	35 13 066	26 22 135	21 17 201	33 19 240	44 41 283	19 19 350
174	37 44 038	35 32 067	26 36 137	21 09 203	33 00 243	44 21 285	19 16 352
176	37 57 039	35 52 069	26 50 139	21 01 205	32 42 245	44 01 286	19 14 354
178	38 10 041	36 11 071	27 04 141	20 52 207	32 23 247	43 41 288	19 12 356

LHA ♈	Hc Zn	Hc Zn	Hc Zn	Hc Zn	Hc Zn	Hc Zn	Hc Zn
	◆DENEB	VEGA	◆ARCTURUS	REGULUS	POLLUX	◆CAPELLA	Alpheratz
180	38 24 043	36 31 073	27 16 143	20 42 209	32 03 249	43 21 290	19 11 358
182	38 39 045	36 51 075	27 28 146	20 31 211	31 44 251	43 02 292	19 10 000
184	38 53 047	37 11 077	27 40 148	20 20 213	31 24 253	42 42 294	19 11 002
186	39 09 048	37 32 079	27 51 150	20 08 215	31 04 255	42 24 296	19 12 003
188	39 25 050	37 52 081	28 01 152	19 56 217	30 44 257	42 05 297	19 13 005
190	39 41 052	38 13 083	28 10 154	19 43 219	30 23 259	41 47 299	19 15 007
192	39 57 054	38 33 085	28 19 156	19 30 222	30 03 261	41 29 301	19 18 009
194	40 14 056	38 54 087	28 27 158	19 15 224	29 42 263	41 11 303	19 22 011
196	40 32 057	39 15 089	28 34 160	19 01 226	29 21 265	40 54 305	19 26 013
198	40 49 059	39 36 090	28 41 163	18 46 228	29 01 267	40 37 307	19 31 015
200	41 07 061	39 57 092	28 47 165	18 30 230	28 40 269	40 20 308	19 37 016
202	41 26 063	40 17 094	28 52 167	18 14 232	28 19 271	40 04 310	19 43 018
204	41 45 065	40 38 096	28 56 169	17 57 234	27 58 273	39 48 312	19 50 020
206	42 03 066	40 59 098	29 00 171	17 40 236	27 37 275	39 33 314	19 57 022
208	42 23 068	41 19 100	29 03 173	17 23 238	27 17 277	39 18 315	20 05 024
	Alpheratz	◆DENEB	VEGA	◆ARCTURUS	REGULUS	POLLUX	◆CAPELLA
210	20 14 026	42 42 070	41 40 103	29 05 176	17 05 240	26 56 279	39 04 317
212	20 23 027	43 02 072	42 00 105	29 06 178	16 47 242	26 35 281	38 50 319
214	20 33 029	43 22 074	42 20 107	29 06 180	16 28 244	26 15 283	38 36 321
216	20 44 031	43 42 076	42 40 109	29 06 182	16 09 246	25 55 284	38 23 322
218	20 55 033	44 02 078	43 00 111	29 05 184	15 50 248	25 35 286	38 11 324
220	21 06 035	44 23 080	43 19 113	29 03 186	15 31 250	25 15 288	37 59 326
222	21 19 037	44 43 081	43 38 115	29 00 189	15 11 252	24 55 290	37 48 328
224	21 31 039	45 04 083	43 57 117	28 57 191	14 51 254	24 36 292	37 37 329
226	21 45 041	45 25 085	44 15 119	28 52 193	14 31 256	24 17 294	37 26 331
228	21 58 042	45 45 087	44 33 121	28 47 195	14 11 258	23 58 296	37 17 333
230	22 13 044	46 06 089	44 51 123	28 42 197	13 50 260	23 39 298	37 07 335
232	22 27 046	46 27 091	45 08 126	28 35 199	13 30 262	23 21 300	36 59 336
234	22 43 048	46 48 093	45 25 128	28 28 201	13 09 264	23 03 302	36 51 338
236	22 58 050	47 09 095	45 41 130	28 20 204	12 48 266	22 45 303	36 43 340
238	23 15 052	47 29 097	45 57 132	28 11 206	12 27 268	22 28 305	36 36 342
	Alpheratz	◆DENEB	VEGA	◆ARCTURUS	Dubhe	POLLUX	◆CAPELLA
240	23 31 054	47 50 099	46 12 134	28 02 208	62 51 273	22 11 307	36 30 343
242	23 48 055	48 10 101	46 26 137	27 52 210	62 30 275	21 55 309	36 24 345
244	24 05 057	48 31 103	46 40 139	27 41 212	62 09 277	21 39 311	36 19 347
246	24 23 059	48 51 105	46 54 141	27 29 214	61 49 279	21 24 313	36 15 348
248	24 41 061	49 11 107	47 06 143	27 17 216	61 28 280	21 09 315	36 11 350
250	25 00 063	49 31 110	47 18 146	27 05 218	61 08 282	20 54 317	36 08 352
252	25 18 065	49 50 112	47 30 148	26 51 221	60 47 284	20 40 319	36 05 354
254	25 37 067	50 09 114	47 41 150	26 38 223	60 27 286	20 26 320	36 03 355
256	25 57 069	50 28 116	47 51 153	26 23 225	60 07 288	20 13 322	36 02 357
258	26 16 071	50 47 118	48 00 155	26 08 227	59 48 289	20 01 324	36 01 359
260	26 36 073	51 05 120	48 08 157	25 53 229	59 28 291	19 49 326	36 01 000
262	26 56 074	51 23 123	48 16 160	25 37 231	59 09 293	19 38 328	36 01 002
264	27 16 076	51 40 125	48 23 162	25 20 233	58 50 295	19 27 330	36 02 004
266	27 37 078	51 57 127	48 29 164	25 03 235	58 31 296	19 17 332	36 04 006
268	27 57 080	52 14 129	48 34 167	24 46 237	58 12 298	19 07 333	36 06 007
	◆CAPELLA	Alpheratz	◆DENEB	VEGA	◆ARCTURUS	Dubhe	POLLUX
270	36 09 009	28 18 082	52 29 131	48 39 169	24 28 239	57 54 300	18 58 335
272	36 13 011	28 38 084	52 45 134	48 42 171	24 10 241	57 36 302	18 50 337
274	36 17 013	28 59 086	53 00 136	48 45 174	23 52 243	57 19 303	18 42 339
276	36 22 014	29 20 088	53 14 138	48 47 176	23 33 245	57 01 305	18 35 341
278	36 27 016	29 41 090	53 27 141	48 48 178	23 14 247	56 44 307	18 28 343
280	36 33 018	30 02 092	53 40 143	48 48 181	22 55 249	56 28 308	18 22 345
282	36 40 019	30 22 094	53 52 145	48 47 183	22 35 251	56 12 310	18 17 346
284	36 47 021	30 43 096	54 04 148	48 46 185	22 15 254	55 56 311	18 13 348
286	36 55 023	31 04 098	54 15 150	48 43 188	21 55 256	55 41 313	18 09 350
288	37 03 025	31 24 100	54 25 152	48 40 190	21 35 258	55 25 315	18 06 352
290	37 12 026	31 45 102	54 34 155	48 36 193	21 14 260	55 11 316	18 03 354
292	37 22 028	32 05 104	54 42 157	48 31 195	20 54 262	54 57 318	18 01 356
294	37 32 030	32 25 106	54 50 160	48 25 197	20 33 263	54 43 320	18 00 358
296	37 43 032	32 45 108	54 57 162	48 18 200	20 12 265	54 30 321	17 59 359
298	37 54 033	33 05 110	55 03 165	48 11 202	19 52 267	54 17 323	18 00 001
	POLLUX	◆CAPELLA	Alpheratz	◆DENEB	VEGA	◆ARCTURUS	Dubhe
300	18 00 003	38 05 035	33 24 112	55 08 167	48 03 204	19 31 269	54 04 324
302	18 02 005	38 18 037	33 43 114	55 12 170	47 54 207	19 10 271	53 53 326
304	18 04 007	38 30 039	34 02 116	55 15 172	47 44 209	18 49 273	53 41 327
306	18 07 009	38 44 040	34 21 118	55 18 174	47 34 211	18 28 275	53 30 329
308	18 10 011	38 57 042	34 39 120	55 19 177	47 23 213	18 08 277	53 20 331
310	18 15 012	39 12 044	34 57 123	55 20 179	47 11 216	17 47 279	53 10 332
312	18 19 014	39 26 046	35 14 125	55 20 182	46 58 218	17 27 281	53 00 334
314	18 25 016	39 41 047	35 31 127	55 19 184	46 45 220	17 06 283	52 51 335
316	18 31 018	39 57 049	35 47 129	55 17 187	46 31 223	16 46 285	52 43 337
318	18 38 020	40 13 051	36 03 131	55 14 189	46 17 225	16 26 287	52 35 338
320	18 45 022	40 29 053	36 19 133	55 10 192	46 02 227	16 06 289	52 27 340
322	18 53 024	40 46 054	36 34 135	55 05 194	45 47 229	15 46 291	52 21 341
324	19 02 025	41 03 056	36 48 137	55 00 197	45 31 231	15 27 293	52 14 343
326	19 11 027	41 21 058	37 02 140	54 53 199	45 14 234	15 08 295	52 08 345
328	19 21 029	41 38 060	37 15 142	54 46 202	44 57 236	14 49 297	52 03 346
	POLLUX	◆CAPELLA	Hamal	Alpheratz	◆DENEB	VEGA	◆Alioth
330	19 31 031	41 57 062	27 54 114	37 28 144	54 38 204	44 40 238	48 09 325
332	19 43 033	42 15 064	28 13 116	37 40 146	54 29 206	44 22 240	47 57 326
334	19 54 035	42 34 065	28 32 118	37 51 148	54 20 209	44 03 242	47 45 328
336	20 06 037	42 53 067	28 50 120	38 01 151	54 09 211	43 45 244	47 35 329
338	20 19 039	43 12 069	29 08 122	38 11 153	53 58 214	43 26 246	47 24 331
340	20 32 040	43 32 071	29 25 124	38 20 155	53 46 216	43 07 249	47 14 333
342	20 46 042	43 52 073	29 42 126	38 29 157	53 34 218	42 47 251	47 05 334
344	21 00 044	44 12 075	29 59 128	38 37 159	53 20 221	42 27 253	46 56 336
346	21 15 046	44 32 077	30 15 130	38 43 162	53 07 223	42 07 255	46 48 338
348	21 30 048	44 52 078	30 31 132	38 50 164	52 52 225	41 47 257	46 41 339
350	21 46 050	45 13 080	30 46 134	38 55 166	52 37 227	41 27 259	46 33 341
352	22 02 052	45 33 082	31 00 137	39 00 168	52 21 230	41 06 261	46 27 343
354	22 19 054	45 54 084	31 15 139	39 03 171	52 05 232	40 46 263	46 21 344
356	22 36 055	46 15 086	31 28 141	39 06 173	51 49 234	40 25 265	46 15 346
358	22 53 057	46 36 088	31 41 143	39 09 175	51 31 236	40 04 267	46 11 347

LAT 79°N

LHA ♈	Hc	Zn	Hc	Zn	Hc	Zn	Hc	Zn	Hc	Zn	Hc	Zn	Hc	Zn
	POLLUX		◆CAPELLA		Hamal		Alpheratz		◆DENEB		VEGA		◆Alioth	
0	22 40	059	46 56	089	32 42	145	40 10	177	51 45	240	39 44	270	45 07	349
2	23 00	061	47 19	091	32 55	147	40 10	180	51 25	242	39 21	272	45 03	351
4	23 20	063	47 42	093	33 07	149	40 10	182	51 04	244	38 58	274	45 00	352
6	23 40	065	48 04	095	33 19	151	40 09	184	50 43	246	38 36	275	44 57	354
8	24 01	066	48 27	097	33 29	153	40 07	187	50 22	248	38 13	277	44 55	356
10	24 22	068	48 50	099	33 39	156	40 04	189	50 01	251	37 50	279	44 54	357
12	24 44	070	49 12	101	33 48	158	40 00	191	49 39	253	37 28	281	44 53	359
14	25 05	072	49 35	103	33 56	160	39 55	193	49 17	255	37 05	283	44 53	000
16	25 27	074	49 57	105	34 04	162	39 49	196	48 55	257	36 43	285	44 53	002
18	25 49	076	50 19	107	34 10	164	39 42	198	48 33	259	36 21	287	44 54	003
20	26 12	078	50 41	109	34 16	167	39 35	200	48 10	261	35 59	289	44 56	005
22	26 34	080	51 02	111	34 21	169	39 27	202	47 47	263	35 38	291	44 58	007
24	26 57	082	51 23	114	34 25	171	39 18	205	47 25	265	35 16	293	45 01	008
26	27 19	084	51 44	116	34 28	173	39 08	207	47 02	267	34 55	294	45 05	010
28	27 42	086	52 05	118	34 30	176	38 57	209	46 39	269	34 35	296	45 09	011
	◆Alioth		POLLUX		◆CAPELLA		Hamal		Alpheratz		◆DENEB		VEGA	
30	45 14	013	28 05	088	52 25	120	34 32	178	38 45	211	46 16	271	34 14	298
32	45 19	015	28 28	090	52 44	122	34 32	180	38 33	214	45 53	273	33 54	300
34	45 25	016	28 51	091	53 03	125	34 32	182	38 20	216	45 30	275	33 35	302
36	45 32	018	29 14	093	53 22	127	34 30	184	38 06	218	45 07	277	33 15	304
38	45 39	019	29 37	095	53 40	129	34 28	187	37 52	220	44 45	279	32 57	305
40	45 47	021	29 59	097	53 58	131	34 25	189	37 37	222	44 22	280	32 38	307
42	45 55	022	30 22	099	54 14	134	34 21	191	37 21	225	44 00	282	32 20	309
44	46 05	024	30 45	101	54 31	136	34 16	193	37 05	227	43 37	284	32 03	311
46	46 14	026	31 07	103	54 46	138	34 10	196	36 48	229	43 15	286	31 45	313
48	46 24	027	31 29	105	55 01	141	34 04	198	36 30	231	42 54	288	31 29	314
50	46 35	029	31 51	107	55 15	143	33 56	200	36 12	233	42 32	290	31 13	316
52	46 47	031	32 13	110	55 28	146	33 48	202	35 53	235	42 10	292	30 57	318
54	46 58	032	32 34	112	55 41	148	33 39	204	35 34	237	41 49	293	30 42	320
56	47 11	034	32 55	114	55 53	150	33 29	207	35 15	240	41 28	295	30 28	322
58	47 24	035	33 16	116	56 03	153	33 19	209	34 55	242	41 08	297	30 14	323
	◆Alioth		REGULUS		POLLUX		◆CAPELLA		Alpheratz		◆DENEB		VEGA	
60	47 37	037	11 14	085	33 37	118	56 13	155	34 35	244	40 48	299	30 00	325
62	47 51	039	11 37	087	33 57	120	56 23	158	34 14	246	40 28	301	29 48	327
64	48 06	040	12 00	089	34 16	122	56 31	160	33 53	248	40 08	303	29 35	329
66	48 21	042	12 23	091	34 35	124	56 38	163	33 31	250	39 49	304	29 24	331
68	48 37	044	12 46	093	34 54	126	56 44	165	33 10	252	39 31	306	29 13	332
70	48 53	045	13 08	095	35 12	128	56 49	168	32 48	254	39 12	308	29 03	334
72	49 09	047	13 31	097	35 30	130	56 54	171	32 26	256	38 54	310	28 53	336
74	49 26	049	13 54	099	35 47	133	56 57	173	32 04	258	38 37	311	28 44	338
76	49 43	050	14 16	101	36 04	135	56 59	176	31 41	260	38 20	313	28 35	339
78	50 01	052	14 39	103	36 20	137	57 00	178	31 18	262	38 04	315	28 28	341
80	50 19	054	15 01	105	36 35	139	57 01	181	30 56	264	37 48	317	28 21	343
82	50 38	055	15 23	107	36 50	141	57 00	183	30 33	266	37 32	318	28 14	345
84	50 57	057	15 45	109	37 04	143	56 58	186	30 10	268	37 17	320	28 09	346
86	51 16	059	16 06	111	37 17	146	56 55	188	29 47	270	37 03	322	28 04	348
88	51 36	060	16 27	113	37 30	148	56 51	191	29 24	272	36 49	324	27 59	350
	◆ARCTURUS		REGULUS		POLLUX		◆CAPELLA		Alpheratz		◆DENEB		VEGA	
90	12 43	053	16 48	115	37 41	150	56 47	193	29 01	274	36 36	325	27 56	352
92	13 02	055	17 09	117	37 52	152	56 41	196	28 39	276	36 23	327	27 53	354
94	13 21	057	17 29	119	38 03	155	56 34	198	28 16	278	36 11	329	27 50	355
96	13 40	059	17 49	121	38 12	157	56 26	201	27 53	280	35 59	331	27 49	357
98	14 00	061	18 08	123	38 21	159	56 18	203	27 31	282	35 48	332	27 48	359
100	14 20	063	18 27	125	38 29	161	56 08	206	27 08	284	35 38	334	27 48	001
102	14 41	065	18 46	127	38 35	164	55 58	208	26 46	285	35 28	336	27 49	002
104	15 02	067	19 03	129	38 42	166	55 46	211	26 24	287	35 19	337	27 50	004
106	15 23	069	19 21	131	38 47	168	55 34	213	26 02	289	35 11	339	27 52	006
108	15 45	071	19 38	133	38 51	170	55 21	216	25 41	291	35 03	341	27 54	008
110	16 06	073	19 54	136	38 54	173	55 07	218	25 20	293	34 56	343	27 58	009
112	16 28	074	20 10	138	38 57	175	54 53	221	24 59	295	34 49	344	28 02	011
114	16 50	076	20 25	140	38 59	177	54 38	223	24 38	297	34 43	346	28 07	013
116	17 13	078	20 40	142	38 59	179	54 22	225	24 18	299	34 38	348	28 12	015
118	17 35	080	20 53	144	38 59	182	54 05	228	23 58	301	34 33	349	28 18	016
	◆VEGA		ARCTURUS		◆REGULUS		POLLUX		◆CAPELLA		Alpheratz		DENEB	
120	28 25	018	17 58	082	21 07	146	38 58	184	53 48	230	23 39	302	34 29	351
122	28 33	020	18 21	084	21 19	148	38 56	186	53 30	232	23 19	304	34 26	353
124	28 41	022	18 43	086	21 31	150	38 53	188	53 12	234	23 01	306	34 24	354
126	28 50	024	19 06	088	21 42	152	38 49	191	52 53	237	22 42	308	34 22	356
128	28 59	025	19 29	090	21 52	154	38 45	193	52 34	239	22 25	310	34 21	358
130	29 09	027	19 52	092	22 02	156	38 39	195	52 14	241	22 07	312	34 20	000
132	29 20	029	20 15	094	22 10	159	38 33	197	51 53	243	21 51	314	34 20	001
134	29 31	031	20 38	096	22 18	161	38 25	200	51 33	245	21 34	315	34 21	003
136	29 43	032	21 01	098	22 26	163	38 17	202	51 12	248	21 18	317	34 23	005
138	29 56	034	21 23	100	22 32	165	38 08	204	50 51	250	21 03	319	34 25	006
140	30 09	036	21 46	102	22 38	167	37 58	206	50 29	252	20 49	321	34 28	008
142	30 23	038	22 08	104	22 42	169	37 48	209	50 07	254	20 34	323	34 31	010
144	30 37	040	22 30	106	22 46	171	37 36	211	49 45	256	20 21	325	34 36	012
146	30 52	041	22 52	108	22 49	173	37 24	213	49 23	258	20 08	327	34 40	013
148	31 07	043	23 14	110	22 52	175	37 11	215	49 00	260	19 56	328	34 46	015
	DENEB		◆VEGA		ARCTURUS		◆REGULUS		POLLUX		◆CAPELLA		Alpheratz	
150	34 52	017	31 23	045	23 35	112	22 53	178	36 58	218	48 37	262	19 44	330
152	34 59	018	31 39	047	23 56	114	22 54	180	36 43	220	48 15	264	19 33	332
154	35 07	020	31 56	048	24 17	116	22 53	182	36 28	222	47 52	266	19 23	334
156	35 15	022	32 14	050	24 37	118	22 52	184	36 13	224	47 29	268	19 13	336
158	35 24	023	32 32	052	24 57	120	22 50	186	35 57	226	47 06	270	19 04	338
160	35 33	025	32 50	054	25 17	122	22 47	188	35 40	228	46 43	272	18 56	340
162	35 43	027	33 09	056	25 36	124	22 44	190	35 22	231	46 20	274	18 48	341
164	35 54	029	33 28	058	25 55	126	22 39	192	35 04	233	45 58	276	18 41	343
166	36 05	030	33 47	059	26 13	128	22 34	195	34 46	235	45 35	278	18 35	345
168	36 17	032	34 07	061	26 31	130	22 28	197	34 27	237	45 12	280	18 29	347
170	36 29	034	34 27	063	26 48	133	22 21	199	34 08	239	44 50	282	18 24	349
172	36 42	036	34 48	065	27 04	135	22 13	201	33 48	241	44 27	284	18 20	351
174	36 56	037	35 09	067	27 20	137	22 04	203	33 28	243	44 05	285	18 17	352
176	37 10	039	35 30	069	27 36	139	21 55	205	33 07	245	43 43	287	18 14	354
178	37 25	041	35 51	071	27 50	141	21 45	207	32 46	247	43 22	289	18 12	356

LHA ♈	Hc	Zn	Hc	Zn	Hc	Zn	Hc	Zn	Hc	Zn	Hc	Zn	Hc	Zn
	DENEB		◆VEGA		ARCTURUS		◆REGULUS		POLLUX		◆CAPELLA		Alpheratz	
180	37 40	042	36 13	072	28 04	143	21 34	209	32 25	249	43 00	291	18 11	358
182	37 56	044	36 35	074	28 18	145	21 23	211	32 03	251	42 39	293	18 10	000
184	38 12	046	36 57	076	28 31	147	21 10	213	31 41	253	42 18	295	18 11	002
186	38 29	048	37 20	078	28 43	150	20 57	216	31 19	255	41 57	296	18 12	003
188	38 46	050	37 42	080	28 54	152	20 44	218	30 57	257	41 37	298	18 13	005
190	39 03	051	38 05	082	29 04	154	20 29	220	30 35	259	41 17	300	18 16	007
192	39 22	053	38 27	084	29 14	156	20 14	222	30 12	261	40 57	302	18 19	009
194	39 40	055	38 50	086	29 23	158	19 59	224	29 49	263	40 38	304	18 23	011
196	39 59	057	39 13	088	29 31	160	19 43	226	29 27	265	40 19	305	18 28	013
198	40 18	058	39 36	090	29 38	162	19 26	228	29 04	267	40 01	307	18 33	014
200	40 38	060	39 59	092	29 45	165	19 09	230	28 41	269	39 43	309	18 39	016
202	40 58	062	40 22	094	29 50	167	18 51	232	28 18	271	39 25	311	18 46	018
204	41 18	064	40 45	096	29 55	169	18 33	234	27 55	273	39 08	312	18 53	020
206	41 39	066	41 07	098	29 59	171	18 14	236	27 32	275	38 51	314	19 01	022
208	42 00	067	41 30	100	30 02	173	17 55	238	27 09	277	38 35	316	19 10	024
	Alpheratz		◆DENEB		VEGA		◆ARCTURUS		REGULUS		POLLUX		◆CAPELLA	
210	19 20	025	42 21	069	41 52	102	30 04	176	17 35	240	26 47	279	38 19	318
212	19 30	027	42 43	071	42 15	104	30 06	178	17 15	242	26 24	281	38 04	319
214	19 41	029	43 05	073	42 37	106	30 06	180	16 54	244	26 02	283	37 50	321
216	19 52	031	43 27	075	42 59	108	30 06	182	16 34	246	25 40	285	37 36	323
218	20 04	033	43 49	077	43 20	110	30 05	184	16 12	248	25 18	287	37 22	325
220	20 17	035	44 11	079	43 42	112	30 02	186	15 51	250	24 56	289	37 09	326
222	20 30	037	44 34	081	44 03	114	29 59	189	15 29	252	24 34	291	36 57	328
224	20 44	038	44 56	082	44 24	116	29 56	191	15 07	254	24 13	293	36 45	330
226	20 59	040	45 19	084	44 44	118	29 51	193	14 45	256	23 52	294	36 34	332
228	21 14	042	45 42	086	45 04	120	29 45	195	14 23	258	23 31	296	36 23	333
230	21 30	044	46 05	088	45 23	123	29 39	197	14 00	260	23 11	298	36 13	335
232	21 46	046	46 28	090	45 43	125	29 32	200	13 38	262	22 51	300	36 04	337
234	22 02	048	46 51	092	46 01	127	29 24	202	13 15	264	22 31	302	35 55	338
236	22 20	050	47 14	094	46 19	129	29 15	204	12 52	266	22 12	304	35 47	340
238	22 37	051	47 36	096	46 37	131	29 05	206	12 29	268	21 53	306	35 39	342
	Alpheratz		◆DENEB		VEGA		◆ARCTURUS		Alioth		POLLUX		◆CAPELLA	
240	22 55	053	47 59	098	46 53	134	28 55	208	62 27	241	21 35	308	35 33	343
242	23 14	055	48 22	100	47 10	136	28 44	210	62 06	244	21 17	309	35 26	345
244	23 33	057	48 44	102	47 25	138	28 32	212	61 46	246	21 00	311	35 21	347
246	23 52	059	49 06	104	47 40	140	28 19	215	61 25	248	20 43	313	35 16	349
248	24 12	061	49 28	106	47 54	143	28 06	217	61 03	250	20 26	315	35 12	350
250	24 32	063	49 50	108	48 08	145	27 52	219	60 41	252	20 10	317	35 08	352
252	24 53	065	50 12	111	48 21	147	27 37	221	60 19	255	19 55	319	35 05	354
254	25 14	066	50 33	113	48 33	150	27 22	223	59 57	257	19 40	321	35 03	355
256	25 35	068	50 54	115	48 44	152	27 06	225	59 35	259	19 26	322	35 02	357
258	25 56	070	51 15	117	48 54	154	26 49	227	59 12	261	19 12	324	35 01	359
260	26 18	072	51 35	119	49 03	157	26 32	229	58 50	263	18 59	326	35 01	000
262	26 40	074	51 55	121	49 12	159	26 14	231	58 27	265	18 47	328	35 01	002
264	27 02	076	52 14	124	49 20	162	25 56	234	58 04	267	18 35	330	35 02	004
266	27 24	078	52 33	126	49 27	164	25 38	236	57 41	269	18 24	332	35 04	006
268	27 47	080	52 51	128	49 32	166	25 18	238	57 18	271	18 13	334	35 07	007
	◆CAPELLA		Alpheratz		◆DENEB		VEGA		◆ARCTURUS		Alioth		POLLUX	
270	35 10	009	28 09	082	53 09	130	49 37	169	24 59	240	56 55	273	18 03	335
272	35 14	011	28 32	084	53 26	133	49 41	171	24 39	242	56 33	275	17 54	337
274	35 19	012	28 55	086	53 42	135	49 44	174	24 19	244	56 10	277	17 46	339
276	35 24	014	29 18	088	53 58	137	49 47	176	23 58	246	55 47	279	17 38	341
278	35 30	016	29 40	089	54 13	140	49 48	178	23 37	248	55 24	281	17 31	343
280	35 36	017	30 03	091	54 28	142	49 48	181	23 15	250	55 02	282	17 24	345
282	35 43	019	30 26	093	54 41	145	49 47	183	22 54	252	54 40	284	17 19	347
284	35 51	021	30 49	095	54 54	147	49 45	186	22 32	254	54 18	286	17 14	348
286	36 00	023	31 12	097	55 06	149	49 43	188	22 10	256	53 56	288	17 10	350
288	36 09	024	31 34	099	55 18	152	49 39	190	21 48	258	53 34	290	17 06	352
290	36 19	026	31 57	101	55 28	154	49 34	193	21 25	260	53 13	291	17 03	354
292	36 29	028	32 19	103	55 38	157	49 29	195	21 02	262	52 51	293	17 01	356
294	36 40	029	32 42	105	55 46	159	49 22	198	20 40	264	52 31	295	17 00	358
296	36 51	031	33 03	107	55 54	162	49 15	200	20 17	266	52 10	297	16 59	359
298	37 03	033	33 25	110	56 00	164	49 07	202	19 54	268	51 50	298	17 00	001
	POLLUX		◆CAPELLA		Alpheratz		◆DENEB		VEGA		◆ARCTURUS		Alioth	
300	17 00	003	37 16	035	33 47	112	56 06	167	48 58	205	19 31	270	51 30	300
302	17 02	005	37 29	036	34 08	114	56 11	169	48 48	207	19 08	272	51 10	302
304	17 04	007	37 43	038	34 29	116	56 15	172	48 37	209	18 45	274	50 51	304
306	17 08	009	37 58	040	34 49	118	56 18	174	48 25	212	18 23	276	50 32	305
308	17 11	011	38 13	041	35 09	120	56 19	177	48 13	214	18 00	278	50 13	307
310	17 16	012	38 28	043	35 29	122	56 20	179	47 59	216	17 37	280	49 55	309
312	17 21	014	38 44	045	35 48	124	56 20	182	47 45	219	17 15	281	49 38	310
314	17 27	016	39 00	047	36 07	126	56 19	184	47 31	221	16 52	283	49 20	312
316	17 34	018	39 17	048	36 25	128	56 16	187	47 15	223	16 30	285	49 04	314
318	17 41	020	39 35	050	36 43	130	56 13	190	46 59	226	16 08	287	48 47	315
320	17 49	022	39 52	052	37 00	133	56 09	192	46 43	228	15 46	289	48 31	317
322	17 58	024	40 11	054	37 16	135	56 03	195	46 25	230	15 25	291	48 16	319
324	18 08	025	40 29	056	37 32	137	55 57	197	46 08	232	15 04	293	48 01	320
326	18 18	027	40 48	057	37 47	139	55 50	200	45 49	234	14 43	295	47 47	322
328	18 29	029	41 08	059	38 02	141	55 42	202	45 30	237	14 22	297	47 33	324
	POLLUX		◆CAPELLA		Hamal		Alpheratz		◆DENEB		VEGA		◆Alioth	
330	18 40	031	41 28	061	28 18	113	38 16	144	55 33	205	45 11	239	47 20	325
332	18 52	033	41 48	063	28 39	115	38 29	146	55 23	207	44 51	241	47 07	327
334	19 05	035	42 08	065	28 59	117	38 42	148	55 12	209	44 31	243	46 54	328
336	19 18	036	42 29	066	29 19	119	38 54	150	55 00	212	44 10	245	46 43	330
338	19 32	038	42 50	068	29 39	121	39 05	152	54 48	214	43 50	247	46 32	332
340	19 47	040	43 12	070	29 59	123	39 15	155	54 35	217	43 28	249	46 21	333
342	20 02	042	43 33	072	30 17	126	39 24	157	54 20	219	43 07	251	46 11	335
344	20 17	044	43 55	074	30 36	128	39 33	159	54 06	221	42 45	254	46 01	336
346	20 33	046	44 17	076	30 54	130	39 40	161	53 50	224	42 23	256	45 53	338
348	20 50	048	44 40	077	31 11	132	39 47	164	53 34	226	42 00	258	45 44	340
350	21 07	049	45 02	079	31 28	134	39 53	166	53 17	228	41 38	260	45 37	341
352	21 25	051	45 25	081	31 44	136	39 58	168	53 00	231	41 15	262	45 30	343
354	21 43	053	45 47	083	31 59	138	40 03	171	52 42	233	40 53	264	45 23	344
356	22 02	055	46 10	085	32 14	140	40 06	173	52 23	235	40 30	266	45 17	346
358	22 21	057	46 33	087	32 29	143	40 08	175	52 04	237	40 07	268	45 12	348

LHA ♈	Hc	Zn	Hc	Zn	Hc	Zn	Hc	Zn	Hc	Zn	Hc	Zn	Hc	Zn
	POLLUX		◆ CAPELLA		Hamal		Alpheratz		◆ DENEB		VEGA		◆ Alioth	
0	22 09	059	46 54	088	33 31	144	41 10	177	52 14	241	39 44	270	44 09	349
2	22 30	060	47 19	090	33 45	147	41 10	180	51 52	243	39 19	272	44 04	351
4	22 52	062	47 44	092	33 59	149	41 10	182	51 30	245	38 54	274	44 01	352
6	23 14	064	48 09	094	34 11	151	41 09	184	51 07	247	38 29	276	43 58	354
8	23 37	066	48 34	096	34 23	153	41 06	187	50 44	250	38 05	278	43 55	356
10	24 00	068	48 59	098	34 34	155	41 03	189	50 20	252	37 40	280	43 54	357
12	24 23	070	49 23	100	34 44	158	40 59	191	49 56	254	37 16	282	43 53	359
14	24 47	072	49 48	102	34 53	160	40 53	194	49 32	256	36 51	284	43 53	000
16	25 11	074	50 12	104	35 01	162	40 47	196	49 08	258	36 27	286	43 53	002
18	25 35	075	50 36	106	35 08	164	40 40	198	48 44	260	36 03	288	43 54	003
20	25 59	077	51 00	108	35 14	166	40 31	200	48 19	262	35 40	289	43 56	005
22	26 23	079	51 24	110	35 20	169	40 22	203	47 54	264	35 16	291	43 59	006
24	26 48	081	51 47	112	35 24	171	40 12	205	47 29	266	34 53	293	44 02	008
26	27 13	083	52 10	115	35 28	173	40 01	207	47 04	268	34 30	295	44 06	010
28	27 37	085	52 32	117	35 30	175	39 49	210	46 40	270	34 08	297	44 10	011
	◆ Alioth		POLLUX		◆ CAPELLA		Hamal		Alpheratz		◆ DENEB		VEGA	
30	44 15	013	28 02	087	52 54	119	35 31	178	39 36	212	46 15	272	33 46	299
32	44 21	014	28 27	089	53 16	121	35 32	180	39 23	214	45 50	274	33 24	300
34	44 28	016	28 52	091	53 37	123	35 31	182	39 08	216	45 25	276	33 03	302
36	44 35	017	29 17	093	53 57	126	35 30	184	38 53	219	45 00	278	32 42	304
38	44 42	019	29 42	095	54 17	128	35 28	187	38 37	221	44 35	280	32 22	306
40	44 51	021	30 07	097	54 37	130	35 24	189	38 21	223	44 11	281	32 02	308
42	45 00	022	30 32	099	54 55	133	35 20	191	38 03	225	43 46	283	31 42	310
44	45 10	024	30 56	101	55 13	135	35 14	193	37 45	227	43 22	285	31 23	311
46	45 20	025	31 21	103	55 31	137	35 08	196	37 27	229	42 58	287	31 05	313
48	45 31	027	31 45	105	55 47	140	35 01	198	37 08	232	42 35	289	30 47	315
50	45 43	028	32 09	107	56 03	142	34 53	200	36 48	234	42 11	291	30 29	317
52	45 55	030	32 33	109	56 18	145	34 44	202	36 27	236	41 48	292	30 12	318
54	46 07	032	32 56	111	56 32	147	34 34	205	36 06	238	41 25	294	29 56	320
56	46 21	033	33 19	113	56 45	150	34 23	207	35 45	240	41 02	296	29 41	322
58	46 35	035	33 42	115	56 57	152	34 11	209	35 23	242	40 40	298	29 25	324
	◆ Alioth		REGULUS		POLLUX		◆ CAPELLA		Alpheratz		◆ DENEB		VEGA	
60	46 49	036	11 09	085	34 04	117	57 08	155	35 01	244	40 18	300	29 11	326
62	47 04	038	11 34	087	34 26	119	57 18	157	34 38	246	39 57	301	28 57	327
64	47 20	040	11 59	089	34 48	121	57 27	160	34 15	248	39 36	303	28 44	329
66	47 36	041	12 24	091	35 09	123	57 35	162	33 52	251	39 15	305	28 32	331
68	47 53	043	12 49	093	35 29	126	57 42	165	33 28	253	38 55	307	28 20	333
70	48 10	044	13 14	095	35 49	128	57 48	168	33 04	255	38 35	309	28 09	334
72	48 28	046	13 39	097	36 09	130	57 53	170	32 40	257	38 16	310	27 58	336
74	48 46	048	14 03	099	36 28	132	57 56	173	32 16	259	37 57	312	27 48	338
76	49 05	049	14 28	101	36 46	134	57 59	175	31 51	261	37 39	314	27 39	340
78	49 24	051	14 52	103	37 03	136	58 00	178	31 26	263	37 21	315	27 31	341
80	49 43	053	15 17	105	37 20	139	58 01	181	31 02	265	37 04	317	27 23	343
82	50 03	054	15 41	107	37 36	141	58 00	183	30 37	267	36 47	319	27 16	345
84	50 24	056	16 04	109	37 52	143	57 58	186	30 12	269	36 31	321	27 10	347
86	50 45	058	16 28	111	38 06	145	57 55	189	29 47	271	36 15	322	27 05	348
88	51 06	059	16 51	113	38 20	147	57 50	191	29 22	272	36 00	324	27 00	350
	◆ ARCTURUS		REGULUS		POLLUX		◆ CAPELLA		Alpheratz		◆ DENEB		VEGA	
90	12 07	053	17 14	115	38 33	150	57 45	194	28 57	274	35 46	326	26 56	352
92	12 28	055	17 36	117	38 45	152	57 38	196	28 32	276	35 32	327	26 53	354
94	12 48	057	17 58	119	38 57	154	57 31	199	28 07	278	35 19	329	26 51	355
96	13 10	059	18 20	121	39 07	156	57 22	202	27 43	280	35 07	331	26 49	357
98	13 31	061	18 41	123	39 17	159	57 13	204	27 18	282	34 55	333	26 48	359
100	13 53	063	19 02	125	39 25	161	57 02	207	26 54	284	34 44	334	26 48	001
102	14 15	065	19 22	127	39 33	163	56 50	209	26 30	286	34 33	336	26 49	002
104	14 38	067	19 41	129	39 40	166	56 38	212	26 06	288	34 24	338	26 50	004
106	15 01	068	20 01	131	39 45	168	56 24	214	25 42	290	34 14	339	26 52	006
108	15 25	070	20 19	133	39 50	170	56 10	217	25 19	292	34 06	341	26 55	008
110	15 48	072	20 37	135	39 54	172	55 54	219	24 56	293	33 58	343	26 59	009
112	16 12	074	20 54	137	39 57	175	55 38	221	24 33	295	33 51	344	27 03	011
114	16 36	076	21 11	139	39 59	177	55 21	224	24 11	297	33 45	346	27 08	013
116	17 00	078	21 27	142	39 59	179	55 04	226	23 49	299	33 39	348	27 14	015
118	17 25	080	21 42	144	39 59	182	54 45	229	23 27	301	33 34	349	27 21	016
	◆ VEGA		ARCTURUS		◆ REGULUS		POLLUX		◆ CAPELLA		Alpheratz		DENEB	
120	27 28	018	17 50	082	21 56	146	39 58	184	54 26	231	23 06	303	33 30	351
122	27 36	020	18 14	084	22 10	148	39 56	186	54 07	233	22 45	305	33 27	353
124	27 45	022	18 39	086	22 23	150	39 52	189	53 46	236	22 25	307	33 24	355
126	27 54	023	19 04	088	22 35	152	39 48	191	53 25	238	22 05	308	33 22	356
128	28 05	025	19 29	090	22 46	154	39 43	193	53 04	240	21 46	310	33 21	358
130	28 16	027	19 54	092	22 57	156	39 37	195	52 42	242	21 27	312	33 20	000
132	28 27	029	20 19	094	23 06	158	39 30	198	52 20	244	21 09	314	33 20	001
134	28 39	030	20 44	096	23 15	160	39 22	200	51 57	247	20 51	316	33 21	003
136	28 52	032	21 09	098	23 23	163	39 13	202	51 34	249	20 34	318	33 23	005
138	29 06	034	21 33	100	23 30	165	39 03	205	51 11	251	20 19	319	33 25	006
140	29 20	036	21 58	102	23 36	167	38 52	207	50 47	253	20 02	321	33 28	008
142	29 35	037	22 22	104	23 41	169	38 40	209	50 23	255	19 47	323	33 32	010
144	29 50	039	22 46	106	23 46	171	38 28	211	49 59	257	19 32	325	33 37	011
146	30 06	041	23 10	108	23 49	173	38 14	214	49 34	259	19 18	327	33 42	013
148	30 23	043	23 34	110	23 51	175	38 00	216	49 10	261	19 05	329	33 48	015
	DENEB		◆ VEGA		ARCTURUS		◆ REGULUS		POLLUX		◆ CAPELLA		Alpheratz	
150	33 55	016	30 40	044	23 57	112	23 53	178	37 45	218	48 45	263	18 52	330
152	34 02	018	30 58	046	24 20	114	23 54	180	37 29	220	48 20	265	18 40	332
154	34 10	020	31 16	048	24 43	116	23 53	182	37 13	222	47 55	267	18 29	334
156	34 19	021	31 35	050	25 05	118	23 52	184	36 56	225	47 30	269	18 18	336
158	34 29	023	31 54	052	25 27	120	23 50	186	36 38	227	47 05	271	18 08	338
160	34 39	025	32 14	053	25 49	122	23 47	188	36 19	229	46 40	273	17 59	340
162	34 50	027	32 35	055	26 10	124	23 43	190	36 00	231	46 16	275	17 51	341
164	35 01	028	32 55	057	26 30	126	23 38	193	35 41	233	45 51	277	17 43	343
166	35 13	030	33 16	059	26 50	128	23 32	195	35 20	235	45 26	279	17 37	345
168	35 26	032	33 38	061	27 09	130	23 25	197	35 00	237	45 01	281	17 31	347
170	35 39	033	34 00	062	27 28	132	23 17	199	34 38	240	44 37	283	17 25	349
172	35 53	035	34 22	064	27 46	134	23 09	201	34 17	242	44 13	285	17 21	351
174	36 08	037	34 45	066	28 04	136	23 00	203	33 54	244	43 49	286	17 17	352
176	36 23	039	35 08	068	28 21	139	22 49	205	33 32	246	43 25	288	17 14	354
178	36 39	040	35 31	070	28 37	141	22 38	207	33 09	248	43 01	290	17 12	356

LAT 78°N

LHA ♈	Hc	Zn	Hc	Zn	Hc	Zn	Hc	Zn	Hc	Zn	Hc	Zn	Hc	Zn
	DENEB		◆ VEGA		ARCTURUS		◆ REGULUS		POLLUX		◆ CAPELLA		Alpheratz	
180	36 56	042	35 55	072	28 52	143	22 26	209	32 46	250	42 38	292	17 11	358
182	37 13	044	36 18	074	29 07	145	22 14	212	32 22	252	42 15	294	17 10	000
184	37 30	045	36 43	075	29 21	147	22 00	214	31 58	254	41 52	295	17 11	002
186	37 48	047	37 07	077	29 34	149	21 46	216	31 34	256	41 30	297	17 12	003
188	38 07	049	37 31	079	29 46	151	21 31	218	31 10	258	41 08	299	17 14	005
190	38 26	051	37 56	081	29 58	154	21 15	220	30 45	260	40 46	301	17 16	007
192	38 45	052	38 20	083	30 09	156	20 59	222	30 21	262	40 25	303	17 20	009
194	39 05	054	38 45	085	30 19	158	20 42	224	29 56	264	40 04	304	17 24	011
196	39 26	056	39 10	087	30 27	160	20 24	226	29 31	266	39 44	306	17 29	013
198	39 47	058	39 35	089	30 35	162	20 06	228	29 06	268	39 24	308	17 35	014
200	40 08	059	40 00	091	30 43	164	19 47	230	28 41	270	39 05	310	17 41	016
202	40 30	061	40 25	093	30 49	167	19 28	232	28 16	272	38 46	311	17 49	018
204	40 52	063	40 50	095	30 54	169	19 08	234	27 51	274	38 27	313	17 57	020
206	41 14	065	41 15	097	30 58	171	18 47	236	27 26	276	38 09	315	18 06	022
208	41 37	067	41 39	099	31 02	173	18 26	238	27 02	278	37 52	317	18 15	024
	Alpheratz		◆ DENEB		VEGA		◆ ARCTURUS		REGULUS		POLLUX		◆ CAPELLA	
210	18 26	025	42 00	068	42 04	101	31 04	175	18 05	240	26 37	280	37 35	318
212	18 37	027	42 23	070	42 28	103	31 06	178	17 43	242	26 12	282	37 19	320
214	18 48	029	42 47	072	42 53	105	31 06	180	17 20	245	25 48	283	37 03	322
216	19 01	031	43 11	074	43 17	107	31 06	182	16 58	247	25 24	285	36 48	323
218	19 14	033	43 35	076	43 40	109	31 04	184	16 35	249	25 00	287	36 33	325
220	19 28	035	43 59	078	44 04	111	31 02	187	16 11	251	24 36	289	36 19	327
222	19 42	036	44 23	080	44 27	113	30 59	189	15 48	253	24 13	291	36 06	328
224	19 57	038	44 48	081	44 50	115	30 55	191	15 24	255	23 50	293	35 53	330
226	20 13	040	45 13	083	45 12	117	30 49	193	14 59	256	23 27	295	35 41	332
228	20 29	042	45 38	085	45 34	120	30 43	195	14 35	258	23 04	297	35 29	334
230	20 46	044	46 02	087	45 55	122	30 36	198	14 11	260	22 42	299	35 19	335
232	21 04	046	46 27	089	46 16	124	30 28	200	13 46	262	22 21	300	35 09	337
234	21 22	047	46 52	091	46 37	126	30 19	202	13 21	264	21 59	302	34 59	339
236	21 41	049	47 17	093	46 57	128	30 10	204	12 56	266	21 38	304	34 50	340
238	22 00	051	47 42	095	47 16	131	29 59	206	12 31	268	21 18	306	34 42	342
	Alpheratz		◆ DENEB		VEGA		◆ ARCTURUS		Alioth		POLLUX		◆ CAPELLA	
240	22 19	053	48 07	097	47 35	133	29 48	208	62 55	243	20 58	308	34 35	344
242	22 39	055	48 32	099	47 52	135	29 35	211	62 32	245	20 39	310	34 28	345
244	23 00	057	48 56	101	48 10	137	29 22	213	62 09	248	20 20	312	34 22	347
246	23 21	059	49 21	103	48 26	140	29 08	215	61 46	250	20 01	313	34 17	349
248	23 43	060	49 45	105	48 42	142	28 54	217	61 22	252	19 44	315	34 13	350
250	24 05	062	50 09	107	48 57	144	28 38	219	60 59	254	19 26	317	34 09	352
252	24 27	064	50 32	109	49 11	147	28 22	221	60 34	256	19 10	319	34 06	354
254	24 49	066	50 56	112	49 24	149	28 05	223	60 10	258	18 54	321	34 03	355
256	25 12	068	51 19	114	49 37	152	27 48	226	59 46	261	18 38	323	34 02	357
258	25 36	070	51 41	116	49 48	154	27 30	228	59 21	263	18 23	325	34 01	359
260	25 59	072	52 04	118	49 58	156	27 11	230	58 56	265	18 09	326	34 01	000
262	26 23	074	52 25	120	50 08	159	26 52	232	58 31	267	17 56	328	34 01	002
264	26 47	075	52 47	123	50 17	161	26 32	234	58 06	269	17 43	330	34 03	004
266	27 11	077	53 08	125	50 24	164	26 11	236	57 41	271	17 31	332	34 05	005
268	27 36	079	53 28	127	50 31	166	25 50	238	57 16	273	17 19	334	34 07	007
	◆ CAPELLA		Alpheratz		◆ DENEB		VEGA		◆ ARCTURUS		Alioth		POLLUX	
270	34 11	009	28 00	081	53 47	129	50 36	168	25 29	240	56 52	274	17 09	336
272	34 15	011	28 25	083	54 06	132	50 41	171	25 07	242	56 27	276	16 59	337
274	34 20	012	28 50	085	54 25	134	50 44	173	24 45	244	56 02	278	16 50	339
276	34 26	014	29 15	087	54 42	136	50 46	176	24 22	246	55 37	280	16 41	341
278	34 32	016	29 40	089	54 59	139	50 48	178	23 59	248	55 13	282	16 34	343
280	34 39	017	30 05	091	55 15	141	50 48	181	23 36	250	54 48	284	16 27	345
282	34 47	019	30 29	093	55 30	144	50 47	183	23 12	252	54 24	286	16 20	347
284	34 55	021	30 54	095	55 44	146	50 45	186	22 48	254	54 00	287	16 15	348
286	35 04	022	31 19	097	55 58	149	50 42	188	22 24	256	53 37	289	16 10	350
288	35 14	024	31 44	099	56 10	151	50 38	191	22 00	258	53 13	291	16 07	352
290	35 25	026	32 09	101	56 22	154	50 33	193	21 35	260	52 50	293	16 04	354
292	35 36	027	32 33	103	56 33	156	50 27	196	21 11	262	52 27	294	16 01	356
294	35 47	029	32 57	105	56 42	159	50 19	198	20 46	264	52 05	296	16 00	358
296	36 00	031	33 21	107	56 51	161	50 11	200	20 21	266	51 42	298	15 59	359
298	36 13	032	33 45	109	56 58	164	50 02	203	19 56	268	51 21	300	16 00	001
	POLLUX		◆ CAPELLA		Alpheratz		◆ DENEB		VEGA		◆ ARCTURUS		Alioth	
300	16 01	003	36 27	034	34 08	111	57 05	166	49 52	205	19 31	270	50 59	301
302	16 02	005	36 41	036	34 32	113	57 10	169	49 41	208	19 06	272	50 38	303
304	16 05	007	36 56	038	34 54	115	57 14	172	49 29	210	18 41	274	50 17	305
306	16 08	009	37 11	039	35 17	117	57 17	174	49 16	212	18 17	276	49 57	306
308	16 12	011	37 27	041	35 39	119	57 19	177	49 02	215	17 52	278	49 37	308
310	16 17	012	37 44	043	36 00	121	57 20	179	48 47	217	17 27	280	49 17	310
312	16 23	014	38 01	044	36 21	123	57 20	182	48 32	219	17 03	282	48 58	311
314	16 30	016	38 19	046	36 42	126	57 18	185	48 16	222	16 38	284	48 40	313
316	16 37	018	38 37	048	37 02	128	57 16	187	47 59	224	16 14	286	48 22	314
318	16 45	020	38 56	050	37 21	130	57 12	190	47 41	226	15 50	288	48 04	316
320	16 54	022	39 15	051	37 40	132	57 07	192	47 23	229	15 27	289	47 47	318
322	17 03	023	39 35	053	37 58	134	57 01	195	47 04	231	15 03	291	47 31	319
324	17 13	025	39 55	055	38 16	136	56 54	198	46 44	233	14 40	293	47 15	321
326	17 24	027	40 16	057	38 33	139	56 46	200	46 24	235	14 17	295	46 59	323
328	17 36	029	40 37	058	38 49	141	56 37	203	46 03	237	13 55	297	46 44	324
	POLLUX		◆ CAPELLA		Hamal		Alpheratz		◆ DENEB		VEGA		◆ Alioth	
330	17 49	031	40 58	060	28 41	113	39 04	143	56 27	205	45 42	240	46 30	326
332	18 02	033	41 20	062	29 04	115	39 19	145	56 16	208	45 20	242	46 16	327
334	18 15	034	41 42	064	29 27	117	39 33	148	56 04	210	44 58	244	46 03	329
336	18 30	036	42 05	066	29 49	119	39 46	150	55 51	213	44 35	246	45 51	331
338	18 45	038	42 28	067	30 10	121	39 58	152	55 37	215	44 12	248	45 39	332
340	19 01	040	42 51	069	30 31	123	40 09	154	55 22	218	43 49	250	45 27	334
342	19 17	042	43 14	071	30 52	125	40 19	157	55 07	220	43 25	252	45 17	335
344	19 34	044	43 38	073	31 12	127	40 29	159	54 50	222	43 01	254	45 06	337
346	19 51	046	44 02	075	31 32	129	40 37	161	54 33	225	42 37	256	44 57	338
348	20 09	047	44 26	076	31 51	131	40 45	163	54 15	227	42 13	259	44 48	340
350	20 28	049	44 50	078	32 09	134	40 51	166	53 57	229	41 48	261	44 40	342
352	20 47	051	45 15	080	32 27	136	40 57	168	53 37	232	41 24	263	44 32	343
354	21 07	053	45 40	082	32 44	138	41 02	170	53 17	234	40 59	265	44 25	345
356	21 27	055	46 04	084	33 00	140	41 05	173	52 57	236	40 34	267	44 19	346
358	21 48	057	46 29	086	33 16	142	41 08	175	52 36	239	40 09	269	44 13	348

LHA ♈	Hc	Zn	Hc	Zn	Hc	Zn	Hc	Zn	Hc	Zn	Hc	Zn	Hc	Zn
	POLLUX		◆ CAPELLA		Hamal		Alpheratz		◆ DENEB		VEGA		◆ Alioth	
0	21 37	058	46 51	087	34 20	144	42 10	177	52 43	242	39 43	271	43 10	350
2	22 00	060	47 18	089	34 35	146	42 10	180	52 19	244	39 16	273	43 05	351
4	22 24	062	47 45	091	34 50	148	42 10	182	51 54	246	38 49	275	43 01	353
6	22 48	064	48 12	093	35 03	151	42 08	184	51 30	249	38 22	277	42 58	354
8	23 12	066	48 39	095	35 16	153	42 06	187	51 04	251	37 56	279	42 56	356
10	23 37	067	49 06	097	35 28	155	42 02	189	50 39	253	37 29	281	42 54	357
12	24 02	069	49 33	099	35 39	157	41 57	191	50 13	255	37 03	283	42 53	359
14	24 28	071	50 00	101	35 49	160	41 51	194	49 47	257	36 37	285	42 53	000
16	24 53	073	50 26	103	35 58	162	41 45	196	49 20	259	36 11	286	42 53	002
18	25 19	075	50 52	105	36 06	164	41 37	198	48 54	261	35 45	288	42 54	003
20	25 46	077	51 18	107	36 13	166	41 27	201	48 27	263	35 19	290	42 56	005
22	26 12	079	51 44	109	36 19	169	41 17	203	48 00	265	34 54	292	42 59	006
24	26 38	081	52 09	111	36 23	171	41 06	205	47 33	267	34 29	294	43 02	008
26	27 05	083	52 34	113	36 27	173	40 54	208	47 06	269	34 05	296	43 06	009
28	27 32	085	52 59	116	36 30	175	40 41	210	46 39	271	33 41	297	43 11	011
	◆ Alioth		POLLUX		◆ CAPELLA		Hamal		Alpheratz		◆ DENEB		VEGA	
30	43 17	013	27 59	087	53 23	118	36 31	178	40 27	212	46 12	273	33 17	299
32	43 23	014	28 26	088	53 46	120	36 32	180	40 12	215	45 45	275	32 53	301
34	43 30	016	28 53	090	54 10	122	36 31	182	39 57	217	45 18	277	32 31	303
36	43 37	017	29 20	092	54 32	125	36 30	185	39 40	219	44 52	279	32 08	305
38	43 46	019	29 47	094	54 54	127	36 27	187	39 23	221	44 25	281	31 46	306
40	43 55	020	30 14	096	55 15	129	36 23	189	39 05	223	43 58	282	31 25	308
42	44 04	022	30 40	098	55 36	132	36 19	191	38 46	226	43 32	284	31 04	310
44	44 15	023	31 07	100	55 56	134	36 13	194	38 26	228	43 06	286	30 43	312
46	44 26	025	31 34	102	56 15	136	36 06	196	38 06	230	42 40	288	30 23	314
48	44 37	026	32 00	104	56 33	139	35 58	198	37 45	232	42 15	290	30 04	315
50	44 50	028	32 26	106	56 50	141	35 49	200	37 23	234	41 49	292	29 45	317
52	45 03	029	32 52	108	57 06	144	35 39	203	37 01	237	41 25	293	29 27	319
54	45 16	031	33 17	110	57 22	146	35 28	205	36 38	239	41 00	295	29 10	321
56	45 30	033	33 42	112	57 36	149	35 16	207	36 15	241	40 36	297	28 53	322
58	45 45	034	34 07	114	57 50	152	35 04	209	35 51	243	40 12	299	28 37	324
	◆ Alioth		REGULUS		POLLUX		◆ CAPELLA		Alpheratz		◆ DENEB		VEGA	
60	46 01	036	11 04	085	34 31	117	58 02	154	35 27	245	39 48	300	28 21	326
62	46 17	037	11 31	087	34 55	119	58 13	157	35 02	247	39 25	302	28 07	328
64	46 34	039	11 58	089	35 19	121	58 23	159	34 37	249	39 03	304	27 53	329
66	46 51	040	12 25	091	35 42	123	58 32	162	34 11	251	38 40	306	27 39	331
68	47 09	042	12 52	093	36 04	125	58 40	165	33 46	253	38 19	307	27 26	333
70	47 27	044	13 19	095	36 26	127	58 47	167	33 20	255	37 58	309	27 14	335
72	47 46	045	13 46	097	36 47	129	58 52	170	32 54	257	37 37	311	27 03	336
74	48 05	047	14 13	099	37 08	131	58 56	173	32 27	259	37 17	313	26 53	338
76	48 25	048	14 39	101	37 28	134	58 59	175	32 01	261	36 57	314	26 43	340
78	48 46	050	15 06	103	37 47	136	59 00	178	31 34	263	36 38	316	26 34	341
80	49 07	052	15 32	105	38 05	138	59 01	181	31 07	265	36 20	318	26 26	343
82	49 28	053	15 58	107	38 23	140	59 00	183	30 40	267	36 02	319	26 18	345
84	49 50	055	16 24	109	38 40	143	58 57	186	30 13	269	35 44	321	26 12	347
86	50 12	057	16 49	111	38 56	145	58 54	189	29 46	271	35 28	323	26 06	348
88	50 35	058	17 14	113	39 11	147	58 49	192	29 19	273	35 12	324	26 01	350
	◆ ARCTURUS		REGULUS		POLLUX		◆ CAPELLA		Alpheratz		◆ DENEB		VEGA	
90	11 31	053	17 39	115	39 25	149	58 43	194	28 52	275	34 56	326	25 57	352
92	11 53	055	18 03	117	39 38	152	58 36	197	28 25	277	34 42	328	25 53	354
94	12 16	057	18 27	119	39 51	154	58 28	199	27 59	279	34 28	330	25 51	355
96	12 38	059	18 51	121	40 02	156	58 18	202	27 32	281	34 14	331	25 49	357
98	13 02	061	19 14	123	40 13	158	58 07	205	27 06	283	34 02	333	25 48	359
100	13 25	062	19 36	125	40 22	161	57 55	207	26 39	284	33 50	335	25 48	001
102	13 50	064	19 58	127	40 30	163	57 42	210	26 13	286	33 39	336	25 49	002
104	14 14	066	20 19	129	40 38	165	57 28	212	25 47	288	33 28	338	25 50	004
106	14 39	068	20 40	131	40 44	168	57 13	215	25 22	290	33 18	340	25 52	006
108	15 04	070	21 00	133	40 49	170	56 58	217	24 57	292	33 09	341	25 56	007
110	15 30	072	21 19	135	40 53	172	56 41	220	24 32	294	33 01	343	25 59	009
112	15 56	074	21 38	137	40 56	175	56 23	222	24 07	296	32 53	345	26 04	011
114	16 22	076	21 56	139	40 58	177	56 04	225	23 43	298	32 47	346	26 10	013
116	16 48	078	22 13	141	40 59	179	55 45	227	23 20	299	32 41	348	26 16	014
118	17 14	080	22 30	143	40 59	182	55 25	230	22 56	301	32 35	350	26 23	016
	◆ VEGA		ARCTURUS		◆ REGULUS		POLLUX		◆ CAPELLA		Alpheratz		DENEB	
120	26 31	018	17 41	082	22 46	145	40 58	184	55 04	232	22 34	303	32 31	351
122	26 40	020	18 08	084	23 01	148	40 55	186	54 42	234	22 11	305	32 27	353
124	26 49	021	18 35	085	23 15	150	40 52	189	54 20	237	21 49	307	32 24	355
126	26 59	023	19 02	087	23 28	152	40 47	191	53 57	239	21 28	309	32 22	356
128	27 10	025	19 29	089	23 40	154	40 41	193	53 33	241	21 07	311	32 21	358
130	27 22	027	19 56	091	23 52	156	40 35	196	53 10	243	20 47	312	32 20	000
132	27 34	028	20 23	093	24 02	158	40 27	198	52 45	246	20 27	314	32 20	001
134	27 48	030	20 49	095	24 12	160	40 18	200	52 20	248	20 08	316	32 21	003
136	28 01	032	21 16	097	24 20	162	40 08	203	51 55	250	19 50	318	32 23	005
138	28 16	034	21 43	099	24 28	165	39 57	205	51 30	252	19 32	320	32 26	006
140	28 31	035	22 10	101	24 35	167	39 45	207	51 04	254	19 15	322	32 29	008
142	28 47	037	22 36	103	24 40	169	39 33	209	50 38	256	18 58	323	32 33	010
144	29 04	039	23 02	105	24 45	171	39 19	212	50 11	258	18 43	325	32 38	011
146	29 21	041	23 28	107	24 49	173	39 04	214	49 45	260	18 28	327	32 44	013
148	29 39	042	23 54	109	24 51	175	38 49	216	49 18	262	18 13	329	32 50	015
	DENEB		◆ VEGA		ARCTURUS		◆ REGULUS		POLLUX		◆ CAPELLA		Alpheratz	
150	32 57	016	29 57	044	24 19	111	24 53	178	38 32	218	48 51	264	18 00	331
152	33 05	018	30 16	046	24 44	113	24 54	180	38 15	221	48 24	266	17 47	332
154	33 14	020	30 36	048	25 09	115	24 53	182	37 57	223	47 58	268	17 35	334
156	33 23	021	30 56	049	25 33	117	24 52	184	37 38	225	47 31	270	17 23	336
158	33 33	023	31 17	051	25 57	119	24 49	186	37 19	227	47 04	272	17 13	338
160	33 44	025	31 38	053	26 20	121	24 46	188	36 59	229	46 37	274	17 03	340
162	33 56	026	32 00	055	26 43	123	24 42	190	36 38	232	46 10	276	16 54	342
164	34 08	028	32 22	056	27 05	126	24 36	193	36 16	234	45 43	278	16 46	343
166	34 21	030	32 45	058	27 27	128	24 30	195	35 54	236	45 16	280	16 39	345
168	34 35	031	33 08	060	27 48	130	24 23	197	35 32	238	44 50	282	16 32	347
170	34 49	033	33 32	062	28 08	132	24 14	199	35 08	240	44 23	284	16 27	349
172	35 04	035	33 56	064	28 28	134	24 05	201	34 45	242	43 57	285	16 22	351
174	35 20	036	34 20	066	28 47	136	23 55	203	34 21	244	43 31	287	16 18	352
176	35 36	038	34 45	067	29 06	138	23 44	205	33 56	246	43 06	289	16 15	354
178	35 53	040	35 10	069	29 23	140	23 31	208	33 31	248	42 40	291	16 12	356

LAT 77°N

LHA ♈	Hc	Zn	Hc	Zn	Hc	Zn	Hc	Zn	Hc	Zn	Hc	Zn	Hc	Zn
	DENEB		◆ VEGA		ARCTURUS		◆ REGULUS		POLLUX		◆ CAPELLA		Alpheratz	
180	36 11	041	35 35	071	29 40	142	23 19	210	33 06	251	42 15	293	16 11	358
182	36 29	043	36 01	073	29 56	145	23 05	212	32 40	253	41 51	294	16 10	000
184	36 48	045	36 27	075	30 11	147	22 50	214	32 14	255	41 26	296	16 11	002
186	37 07	047	36 53	077	30 26	149	22 35	216	31 48	257	41 02	298	16 12	003
188	37 27	048	37 20	078	30 39	151	22 18	218	31 22	259	40 39	300	16 14	005
190	37 47	050	37 46	080	30 52	153	22 01	220	30 55	261	40 15	302	16 17	007
192	38 08	052	38 13	082	31 03	155	21 43	222	30 29	263	39 53	303	16 20	009
194	38 30	054	38 40	084	31 14	158	21 25	224	30 02	265	39 30	305	16 25	011
196	38 52	055	39 07	086	31 24	160	21 06	226	29 35	267	39 08	307	16 30	012
198	39 14	057	39 33	088	31 33	162	20 46	229	29 08	269	38 47	309	16 37	014
200	39 37	059	40 00	090	31 40	164	20 25	231	28 41	270	38 26	310	16 44	016
202	40 00	061	40 27	092	31 47	167	20 04	233	28 14	272	38 06	312	16 52	018
204	40 24	062	40 54	094	31 53	169	19 42	235	27 47	274	37 46	314	17 00	020
206	40 48	064	41 21	096	31 58	171	19 20	237	27 20	276	37 27	315	17 10	022
208	41 13	066	41 48	098	32 01	173	18 57	239	26 53	278	37 08	317	17 20	023
	Alpheratz		◆ DENEB		VEGA		◆ ARCTURUS		REGULUS		POLLUX		◆ CAPELLA	
210	17 31	025	41 37	068	42 15	100	32 04	175	18 34	241	26 27	280	36 50	319
212	17 43	027	42 02	069	42 41	102	32 06	178	18 10	243	26 00	282	36 32	320
214	17 56	029	42 28	071	43 08	104	32 06	180	17 46	245	25 34	284	36 16	322
216	18 09	031	42 54	073	43 34	106	32 06	182	17 21	247	25 08	286	35 59	324
218	18 23	032	43 19	075	43 59	108	32 04	184	16 56	249	24 42	288	35 44	326
220	18 38	034	43 46	077	44 25	110	32 02	187	16 31	251	24 16	290	35 29	327
222	18 54	036	44 12	079	44 50	112	31 58	189	16 05	253	23 51	291	35 14	329
224	19 10	038	44 39	080	45 15	114	31 53	191	15 39	255	23 26	293	35 01	331
226	19 27	040	45 05	082	45 39	117	31 48	193	15 13	257	23 02	295	34 48	332
228	19 45	042	45 32	084	46 03	119	31 41	195	14 47	259	22 37	297	34 36	334
230	20 03	043	45 59	086	46 27	121	31 33	198	14 20	261	22 14	299	34 24	336
232	20 22	045	46 26	088	46 50	123	31 25	200	13 54	263	21 50	301	34 13	337
234	20 41	047	46 53	090	47 12	125	31 15	202	13 27	265	21 27	303	34 03	339
236	21 01	049	47 20	092	47 34	128	31 04	204	13 00	267	21 05	304	33 54	341
238	21 22	051	47 47	094	47 55	130	30 53	207	12 33	269	20 43	306	33 45	342
	Alpheratz		◆ DENEB		VEGA		◆ ARCTURUS		Alioth		POLLUX		◆ CAPELLA	
240	21 43	053	48 14	096	48 15	132	30 40	209	63 21	245	20 21	308	33 37	344
242	22 05	054	48 41	098	48 35	134	30 27	211	62 56	247	20 00	310	33 30	346
244	22 27	056	49 07	100	48 54	137	30 13	213	62 31	249	19 40	312	33 24	347
246	22 50	058	49 34	102	49 12	139	29 57	215	62 06	252	19 20	314	33 18	349
248	23 13	060	50 00	104	49 29	141	29 41	217	61 40	254	19 01	316	33 13	351
250	23 36	062	50 26	106	49 45	144	29 25	220	61 14	256	18 42	317	33 09	352
252	24 00	064	50 52	108	50 01	146	29 07	222	60 48	258	18 24	319	33 06	354
254	24 25	066	51 17	110	50 16	149	28 49	224	60 21	260	18 07	321	33 04	355
256	24 50	067	51 42	113	50 29	151	28 30	226	59 55	262	17 50	323	33 02	357
258	25 15	069	52 07	115	50 42	153	28 10	228	59 28	264	17 34	325	33 01	359
260	25 40	071	52 31	117	50 53	156	27 50	230	59 01	266	17 19	327	33 01	000
262	26 06	073	52 55	119	51 04	158	27 29	232	58 34	268	17 05	328	33 01	002
264	26 32	075	53 19	121	51 13	161	27 07	234	58 07	270	16 51	330	33 03	004
266	26 58	077	53 41	124	51 22	163	26 45	236	57 40	272	16 38	332	33 05	005
268	27 24	079	54 03	126	51 29	166	26 22	238	57 13	274	16 26	334	33 08	007
	◆ CAPELLA		Alpheratz		◆ DENEB		VEGA		◆ ARCTURUS		Alioth		POLLUX	
270	33 12	009	27 51	081	54 25	128	51 35	168	25 59	241	56 46	276	16 14	336
272	33 16	010	28 17	083	54 46	131	51 40	171	25 35	243	56 19	278	16 03	338
274	33 21	012	28 44	084	55 06	133	51 44	173	25 11	245	55 53	280	15 54	339
276	33 27	014	29 11	086	55 25	135	51 46	176	24 46	247	55 26	282	15 44	341
278	33 34	015	29 38	088	55 44	138	51 48	178	24 21	249	55 00	283	15 36	343
280	33 42	017	30 05	090	56 01	140	51 48	181	23 56	251	54 34	285	15 29	345
282	33 50	019	30 32	092	56 18	143	51 47	183	23 30	253	54 08	287	15 22	347
284	33 59	020	30 59	094	56 34	145	51 45	186	23 04	255	53 42	289	15 16	349
286	34 09	022	31 26	096	56 49	148	51 41	188	22 38	257	53 16	290	15 11	350
288	34 19	024	31 53	098	57 03	150	51 37	191	22 12	259	52 51	292	15 07	352
290	34 30	025	32 19	100	57 16	153	51 31	193	21 45	261	52 26	294	15 04	354
292	34 42	027	32 46	102	57 27	156	51 24	196	21 19	263	52 02	296	15 02	356
294	34 55	029	33 12	104	57 38	158	51 16	198	20 52	265	51 38	297	15 00	358
296	35 08	030	33 38	106	57 47	161	51 07	201	20 25	267	51 14	299	14 59	359
298	35 22	032	34 04	108	57 56	163	50 57	203	19 58	269	50 51	301	15 00	001
	POLLUX		◆ CAPELLA		Alpheratz		◆ DENEB		VEGA		◆ ARCTURUS		Alioth	
300	15 01	003	35 37	034	34 29	110	58 03	166	50 46	206	19 31	270	50 27	302
302	15 03	005	35 52	035	34 55	112	58 09	169	50 34	208	19 04	272	50 05	304
304	15 05	007	36 08	037	35 19	114	58 13	171	50 21	211	18 37	274	49 43	306
306	15 09	009	36 25	039	35 44	117	58 17	174	50 06	213	18 10	276	49 21	307
308	15 13	010	36 42	040	36 08	119	58 19	177	49 51	215	17 43	278	49 00	309
310	15 19	012	37 00	042	36 31	121	58 20	179	49 35	218	17 17	280	48 39	310
312	15 25	014	37 18	044	36 54	123	58 20	182	49 18	220	16 50	282	48 19	312
314	15 32	016	37 37	046	37 17	125	58 18	185	49 00	222	16 24	284	47 59	314
316	15 40	018	37 57	047	37 38	127	58 15	187	48 42	225	15 58	286	47 40	315
318	15 48	020	38 17	049	38 00	129	58 11	190	48 22	227	15 32	288	47 21	317
320	15 58	021	38 38	051	38 20	131	58 06	193	48 02	229	15 06	290	47 03	318
322	16 08	023	38 59	052	38 40	134	57 59	195	47 41	232	14 41	292	46 45	320
324	16 19	025	39 20	054	38 59	136	57 52	198	47 20	234	14 16	294	46 28	322
326	16 31	027	39 42	056	39 18	138	57 43	201	46 58	236	13 52	295	46 12	323
328	16 44	029	40 05	058	39 35	140	57 33	203	46 35	238	13 28	297	45 56	325
	POLLUX		◆ CAPELLA		Hamal		Alpheratz		◆ DENEB		VEGA		◆ Alioth	
330	16 57	031	40 28	059	29 04	112	39 52	143	57 21	206	46 12	241	45 40	326
332	17 11	032	40 52	061	29 29	114	40 08	145	57 09	208	45 48	243	45 26	328
334	17 26	034	41 15	063	29 53	116	40 23	147	56 56	211	45 24	245	45 12	329
336	17 41	036	41 40	065	30 17	118	40 37	149	56 41	213	44 59	247	44 58	331
338	17 58	038	42 04	066	30 41	120	40 51	152	56 26	216	44 34	249	44 46	333
340	18 15	040	42 29	068	31 04	122	41 03	154	56 10	218	44 09	251	44 33	334
342	18 32	042	42 54	070	31 26	125	41 14	156	55 52	221	43 43	253	44 22	336
344	18 50	043	43 20	072	31 48	127	41 25	159	55 34	223	43 17	255	44 11	337
346	19 09	045	43 46	074	32 10	129	41 34	161	55 15	226	42 51	257	44 01	339
348	19 29	047	44 12	076	32 30	131	41 42	163	54 56	228	42 24	259	43 52	340
350	19 49	049	44 38	077	32 50	133	41 50	166	54 35	231	41 58	261	43 43	342
352	20 09	051	45 04	079	33 10	135	41 56	168	54 14	233	41 31	263	43 35	343
354	20 31	053	45 31	081	33 28	137	42 01	170	53 52	235	41 04	265	43 27	345
356	20 52	054	45 58	083	33 46	140	42 05	173	53 30	237	40 37	267	43 21	346
358	21 15	056	46 24	085	34 03	142	42 08	175	53 07	240	40 10	269	43 15	348

LHA ♈	Hc	Zn	Hc	Zn	Hc	Zn	Hc	Zn	Hc	Zn	Hc	Zn	Hc	Zn
	POLLUX		◆ CAPELLA		Hamal		Alpheratz		◆ DENEB		VEGA		◆ Alioth	
0	21 05	058	46 48	086	35 08	144	43 10	177	53 11	243	39 41	272	42 11	350
2	21 30	060	47 17	088	35 25	146	43 10	180	52 45	245	39 12	274	42 06	351
4	21 56	062	47 46	090	35 41	148	43 10	182	52 18	248	38 44	276	42 02	353
6	22 21	063	48 15	092	35 56	150	43 08	184	51 51	250	38 15	278	41 58	354
8	22 47	065	48 44	094	36 10	152	43 05	187	51 24	252	37 46	280	41 56	356
10	23 14	067	49 12	095	36 22	155	43 01	189	50 56	254	37 17	282	41 54	357
12	23 41	069	49 41	097	36 34	157	42 56	192	50 28	256	36 49	283	41 53	359
14	24 08	071	50 10	100	36 45	159	42 50	194	49 59	258	36 21	285	41 53	000
16	24 36	073	50 39	102	36 55	162	42 42	196	49 31	260	35 53	287	41 53	002
18	25 04	075	51 07	104	37 03	164	42 33	199	49 02	262	35 26	289	41 55	003
20	25 32	076	51 35	106	37 11	166	42 24	201	48 33	264	34 58	291	41 57	005
22	26 00	078	52 03	108	37 17	168	42 13	203	48 04	266	34 31	293	41 59	006
24	26 29	080	52 30	110	37 23	171	42 00	206	47 35	268	34 05	294	42 03	008
26	26 57	082	52 57	112	37 27	173	41 47	208	47 06	270	33 38	296	42 07	009
28	27 26	084	53 24	114	37 30	175	41 33	210	46 37	272	33 13	298	42 12	011
	◆ Alioth		POLLUX		◆ CAPELLA		Hamal		Alpheratz		◆ DENEB		VEGA	
30	42 18	012	27 55	086	53 50	117	37 31	178	41 18	213	46 08	274	32 47	300
32	42 25	014	28 24	088	54 16	119	37 32	180	41 02	215	45 40	276	32 22	302
34	42 32	015	28 53	090	54 41	121	37 31	182	40 45	217	45 11	278	31 58	303
36	42 40	017	29 22	092	55 06	123	37 30	185	40 27	220	44 42	280	31 34	305
38	42 49	018	29 51	094	55 30	126	37 27	187	40 08	222	44 13	281	31 10	307
40	42 58	020	30 20	096	55 53	128	37 23	189	39 48	224	43 45	283	30 47	309
42	43 09	021	30 49	098	56 15	131	37 17	192	39 27	226	43 17	285	30 25	310
44	43 19	023	31 17	100	56 37	133	37 11	194	39 06	228	42 49	287	30 03	312
46	43 31	024	31 46	102	56 58	135	37 04	196	38 44	231	42 21	289	29 42	314
48	43 43	026	32 14	104	57 18	138	36 55	198	38 21	233	41 54	291	29 21	316
50	43 57	027	32 42	106	57 37	140	36 45	201	37 58	235	41 27	292	29 01	317
52	44 10	029	33 10	108	57 55	143	36 34	203	37 34	237	41 00	294	28 42	319
54	44 25	031	33 38	110	58 12	146	36 23	205	37 09	239	40 34	296	28 23	321
56	44 40	032	34 05	112	58 27	148	36 10	208	36 44	241	40 08	298	28 06	323
58	44 56	034	34 32	114	58 42	151	35 56	210	36 18	244	39 43	299	27 48	324
	◆ Alioth		REGULUS		POLLUX		◆ CAPELLA		Alpheratz		◆ DENEB		VEGA	
60	45 12	035	10 59	085	34 58	116	58 56	153	35 52	246	39 18	301	27 32	326
62	45 29	037	11 28	087	35 24	118	59 08	156	35 25	248	38 53	303	27 16	328
64	45 47	038	11 57	089	35 49	120	59 19	159	34 58	250	38 29	305	27 01	330
66	46 05	040	12 26	091	36 14	122	59 29	161	34 31	252	38 05	306	26 47	331
68	46 24	041	12 55	093	36 38	124	59 38	164	34 03	254	37 42	308	26 33	333
70	46 43	043	13 24	095	37 02	127	59 45	167	33 35	256	37 19	310	26 20	335
72	47 03	044	13 53	097	37 25	129	59 51	170	33 07	258	36 57	311	26 08	336
74	47 24	046	14 22	098	37 47	131	59 55	172	32 38	260	36 36	313	25 57	338
76	47 45	048	14 50	100	38 09	133	59 59	175	32 09	262	36 15	315	25 47	340
78	48 07	049	15 19	102	38 30	135	60 00	178	31 41	264	35 55	316	25 37	342
80	48 29	051	15 47	104	38 50	138	60 01	181	31 12	266	35 35	318	25 28	343
82	48 52	052	16 15	106	39 09	140	60 00	184	30 43	268	35 16	320	25 21	345
84	49 15	054	16 43	108	39 27	142	59 57	186	30 14	270	34 58	322	25 13	347
86	49 39	056	17 10	110	39 44	144	59 53	189	29 45	272	34 40	323	25 07	349
88	50 03	057	17 37	112	40 01	147	59 48	192	29 16	274	34 23	325	25 02	350
	◆ ARCTURUS		REGULUS		POLLUX		◆ CAPELLA		Alpheratz		◆ DENEB		VEGA	
90	10 55	053	18 04	114	40 16	149	59 41	195	28 47	276	34 06	327	24 57	352
92	11 19	055	18 30	116	40 31	151	59 33	197	28 18	277	33 51	328	24 54	354
94	11 43	057	18 56	118	40 44	153	59 24	200	27 49	279	33 36	330	24 51	355
96	12 07	059	19 21	120	40 57	156	59 13	203	27 21	281	33 22	332	24 49	357
98	12 32	060	19 46	122	41 08	158	59 02	205	26 52	283	33 08	333	24 48	359
100	12 58	062	20 10	124	41 19	160	58 48	208	26 24	285	32 56	335	24 48	001
102	13 24	064	20 34	126	41 28	163	58 34	211	25 56	287	32 44	337	24 49	002
104	13 50	066	20 57	129	41 36	165	58 19	213	25 28	289	32 32	338	24 50	004
106	14 17	068	21 19	131	41 43	167	58 02	216	25 01	291	32 22	340	24 53	006
108	14 44	070	21 41	133	41 48	170	57 45	218	24 34	292	32 12	341	24 56	007
110	15 11	072	22 02	135	41 53	172	57 26	221	24 07	294	32 04	343	25 00	009
112	15 39	074	22 22	137	41 56	175	57 07	223	23 41	296	31 55	345	25 05	011
114	16 07	076	22 41	139	41 58	177	56 46	226	23 15	298	31 48	346	25 11	013
116	16 35	077	23 00	141	41 59	179	56 25	228	22 50	300	31 42	348	25 18	014
118	17 03	079	23 18	143	41 59	182	56 03	231	22 25	302	31 36	350	25 25	016
	◆ VEGA		ARCTURUS		◆ REGULUS		POLLUX		◆ CAPELLA		Alpheratz		DENEB	
120	25 34	018	17 32	081	23 35	145	41 58	184	55 40	233	22 01	304	31 32	351
122	25 43	019	18 01	083	23 51	147	41 55	186	55 16	236	21 37	305	31 28	353
124	25 53	021	18 30	085	24 06	149	41 51	189	54 52	238	21 13	307	31 24	355
126	26 04	023	18 59	087	24 21	152	41 46	191	54 27	240	20 50	309	31 22	356
128	26 16	025	19 28	089	24 34	154	41 40	194	54 02	242	20 28	311	31 21	358
130	26 28	026	19 57	091	24 46	156	41 32	196	53 36	245	20 06	313	31 20	000
132	26 42	028	20 26	093	24 58	158	41 24	198	53 09	247	19 45	314	31 20	001
134	26 56	030	20 55	095	25 08	160	41 14	201	52 42	249	19 25	316	31 21	003
136	27 10	032	21 24	097	25 17	162	41 03	203	52 15	251	19 05	318	31 23	005
138	27 26	033	21 52	099	25 26	164	40 52	205	51 48	253	18 46	320	31 26	006
140	27 42	035	22 21	101	25 33	167	40 39	208	51 20	255	18 28	322	31 29	008
142	27 59	037	22 49	103	25 39	169	40 25	210	50 51	258	18 10	324	31 34	009
144	28 17	038	23 18	105	25 44	171	40 10	212	50 23	260	17 53	325	31 39	011
146	28 35	040	23 46	107	25 48	173	39 54	214	49 54	262	17 37	327	31 45	013
148	28 54	042	24 13	109	25 51	175	39 37	217	49 25	264	17 22	329	31 52	014
	DENEB		◆ VEGA		ARCTURUS		◆ REGULUS		POLLUX		◆ CAPELLA		Alpheratz	
150	32 00	016	29 14	044	24 41	111	25 53	178	39 19	219	48 57	266	17 07	331
152	32 08	018	29 34	045	25 07	113	25 54	180	39 00	221	48 28	268	16 54	333
154	32 17	019	29 55	047	25 34	115	25 53	182	38 41	223	47 59	270	16 41	334
156	32 27	021	30 17	049	26 00	117	25 52	184	38 20	226	47 30	271	16 28	336
158	32 38	023	30 39	051	26 26	119	25 49	186	37 59	228	47 01	273	16 17	338
160	32 50	024	31 02	052	26 51	121	25 45	188	37 37	230	46 32	275	16 07	340
162	33 02	026	31 25	054	27 16	123	25 41	191	37 15	232	46 03	277	15 57	342
164	33 15	028	31 49	056	27 40	125	25 35	193	36 52	234	45 34	279	15 48	343
166	33 29	029	32 13	058	28 03	127	25 28	195	36 28	237	45 05	281	15 41	345
168	33 43	031	32 38	060	28 26	129	25 20	197	36 03	239	44 37	283	15 34	347
170	33 59	033	33 03	061	28 48	131	25 11	199	35 38	241	44 09	285	15 28	349
172	34 15	034	33 29	063	29 10	134	25 01	201	35 12	243	43 41	286	15 23	351
174	34 32	036	33 55	065	29 30	136	24 50	204	34 46	245	43 13	288	15 18	352
176	34 49	038	34 22	067	29 50	138	24 38	206	34 20	247	42 46	290	15 15	354
178	35 07	039	34 48	069	30 09	140	24 25	208	33 53	249	42 19	292	15 13	356

LAT 76°N

LHA ♈	Hc	Zn	Hc	Zn	Hc	Zn	Hc	Zn	Hc	Zn	Hc	Zn	Hc	Zn
	DENEB		◆ VEGA		ARCTURUS		◆ REGULUS		POLLUX		◆ CAPELLA		Alpheratz	
180	35 26	041	35 16	070	30 27	142	24 11	210	33 26	251	41 52	294	15 11	358
182	35 45	043	35 43	072	30 45	144	23 56	212	32 58	253	41 25	295	15 10	000
184	36 05	044	36 11	074	31 01	146	23 40	214	32 30	255	40 59	297	15 11	002
186	36 26	046	36 39	076	31 17	149	23 23	216	32 02	257	40 34	299	15 12	003
188	36 47	048	37 07	078	31 32	151	23 05	218	31 33	259	40 08	301	15 14	005
190	37 09	049	37 36	080	31 45	153	22 47	220	31 05	261	39 44	302	15 17	007
192	37 31	051	38 04	081	31 58	155	22 28	223	30 36	263	39 19	304	15 21	009
194	37 54	053	38 33	083	32 10	157	22 08	225	30 07	265	38 55	306	15 26	011
196	38 17	055	39 02	085	32 20	160	21 47	227	29 38	267	38 32	307	15 32	012
198	38 41	056	39 31	087	32 30	162	21 25	229	29 09	269	38 09	309	15 39	014
200	39 06	058	40 00	089	32 38	164	21 03	231	28 40	271	37 47	311	15 46	016
202	39 30	060	40 29	091	32 46	166	20 40	233	28 11	273	37 25	313	15 55	018
204	39 56	062	40 58	093	32 52	169	20 17	235	27 42	275	37 04	314	16 04	020
206	40 21	063	41 27	095	32 57	171	19 53	237	27 13	277	36 44	316	16 14	021
208	40 48	065	41 56	097	33 01	173	19 28	239	26 45	279	36 24	318	16 25	023
	Alpheratz		◆ DENEB		VEGA		◆ ARCTURUS		REGULUS		POLLUX		◆ CAPELLA	
210	16 37	025	41 14	067	42 25	099	33 04	175	19 03	241	26 16	281	36 05	319
212	16 50	027	41 41	069	42 53	101	33 06	178	18 38	243	25 47	282	35 46	321
214	17 03	029	42 08	070	43 22	103	33 06	180	18 11	245	25 19	284	35 28	323
216	17 18	030	42 36	072	43 50	105	33 06	182	17 45	247	24 51	286	35 11	324
218	17 33	032	43 03	074	44 18	107	33 04	184	17 18	249	24 24	288	34 54	326
220	17 49	034	43 31	076	44 45	109	33 01	187	16 51	251	23 56	290	34 38	328
222	18 05	036	44 00	078	45 12	111	32 57	189	16 23	253	23 29	292	34 23	329
224	18 23	038	44 28	079	45 39	113	32 52	191	15 55	255	23 02	294	34 08	331
226	18 41	040	44 57	081	46 06	116	32 46	193	15 27	257	22 36	296	33 55	333
228	19 00	041	45 26	083	46 32	118	32 39	196	14 59	259	22 10	297	33 42	334
230	19 19	043	45 54	085	46 57	120	32 30	198	14 30	261	21 44	299	33 29	336
232	19 39	045	46 23	087	47 22	122	32 21	200	14 01	263	21 19	301	33 18	337
234	20 00	047	46 52	089	47 46	124	32 10	202	13 32	265	20 55	303	33 07	339
236	20 22	049	47 21	091	48 10	127	31 59	205	13 03	267	20 31	305	32 57	341
238	20 44	050	47 50	093	48 33	129	31 46	207	12 34	269	20 07	307	32 48	342
	Alpheratz		◆ DENEB		VEGA		◆ ARCTURUS		Alioth		POLLUX		◆ CAPELLA	
240	21 06	052	48 19	095	48 55	131	31 33	209	63 46	247	19 44	308	32 40	344
242	21 30	054	48 48	097	49 16	134	31 18	211	63 19	249	19 22	310	32 32	346
244	21 54	056	49 17	099	49 37	136	31 03	213	62 52	251	19 00	312	32 25	347
246	22 18	058	49 46	101	49 57	138	30 46	216	62 24	253	18 38	314	32 19	349
248	22 43	060	50 14	103	50 16	141	30 29	218	61 56	256	18 18	316	32 14	351
250	23 08	061	50 42	105	50 34	143	30 11	220	61 28	258	17 58	318	32 10	352
252	23 34	063	51 10	107	50 51	145	29 52	222	60 59	260	17 39	319	32 06	354
254	24 00	065	51 38	109	51 07	148	29 32	224	60 31	262	17 20	321	32 04	356
256	24 26	067	52 05	111	51 21	150	29 11	226	60 02	264	17 02	323	32 02	357
258	24 53	069	52 32	114	51 35	153	28 50	228	59 33	266	16 45	325	32 01	359
260	25 20	071	52 58	116	51 48	155	28 28	231	59 04	268	16 29	327	32 01	000
262	25 48	073	53 24	118	52 00	158	28 05	233	58 35	270	16 14	329	32 01	002
264	26 16	074	53 49	120	52 10	160	27 42	235	58 06	272	15 59	330	32 03	004
266	26 44	076	54 14	123	52 19	163	27 18	237	57 37	274	15 45	332	32 05	005
268	27 12	078	54 38	125	52 27	165	26 53	239	57 08	276	15 32	334	32 08	007
	◆ CAPELLA		Alpheratz		◆ DENEB		VEGA		◆ ARCTURUS		Alioth		POLLUX	
270	32 12	009	27 41	080	55 02	127	52 34	168	26 28	241	56 39	277	15 19	336
272	32 17	010	28 09	082	55 24	130	52 39	171	26 02	243	56 10	279	15 08	338
274	32 23	012	28 38	084	55 46	132	52 43	173	25 36	245	55 42	281	14 57	339
276	32 29	014	29 07	086	56 08	134	52 46	176	25 10	247	55 13	283	14 48	341
278	32 36	015	29 36	088	56 28	137	52 48	178	24 43	249	54 45	285	14 39	343
280	32 44	017	30 05	090	56 47	139	52 48	181	24 16	251	54 17	286	14 31	345
282	32 53	018	30 34	092	57 06	142	52 47	183	23 48	253	53 50	288	14 24	347
284	33 03	020	31 03	094	57 23	144	52 44	186	23 20	255	53 22	290	14 17	349
286	33 13	022	31 32	096	57 39	147	52 41	189	22 52	257	52 55	292	14 12	350
288	33 24	023	32 01	098	57 55	150	52 36	191	22 23	259	52 28	293	14 08	352
290	33 36	025	32 30	100	58 09	152	52 30	194	21 55	261	52 02	295	14 04	354
292	33 49	027	32 58	102	58 22	155	52 22	196	21 26	263	51 36	297	14 02	356
294	34 02	028	33 27	104	58 33	158	52 13	199	20 57	265	51 10	298	14 00	358
296	34 16	030	33 55	106	58 44	160	52 03	201	20 28	267	50 44	300	13 59	359
298	34 31	032	34 22	108	58 53	163	51 52	204	19 59	269	50 19	302	14 00	001
	POLLUX		◆ CAPELLA		Alpheratz		◆ DENEB		VEGA		◆ ARCTURUS		Alioth	
300	14 01	003	34 47	033	34 50	110	59 01	166	51 40	206	19 30	271	49 55	303
302	14 03	005	35 03	035	35 17	112	59 08	168	51 27	209	19 01	273	49 31	305
304	14 06	007	35 20	037	35 44	114	59 13	171	51 12	211	18 32	275	49 07	307
306	14 10	009	35 38	038	36 10	116	59 17	174	50 56	214	18 03	277	48 44	308
308	14 14	010	35 56	040	36 36	118	59 19	177	50 40	216	17 35	279	48 22	310
310	14 20	012	36 15	042	37 02	120	59 20	179	50 22	219	17 06	280	48 00	311
312	14 27	014	36 35	043	37 26	122	59 20	182	50 04	221	16 37	282	47 38	313
314	14 34	016	36 55	045	37 51	124	59 18	185	49 44	223	16 09	284	47 17	314
316	14 43	018	37 16	047	38 14	127	59 15	188	49 24	226	15 41	286	46 57	316
318	14 52	020	37 37	048	38 37	129	59 10	190	49 03	228	15 13	288	46 37	318
320	15 02	021	37 59	050	39 00	131	59 04	193	48 41	230	14 46	290	46 17	319
322	15 13	023	38 22	052	39 21	133	58 57	196	48 18	233	14 19	292	45 59	321
324	15 25	025	38 45	054	39 42	135	58 49	198	47 55	235	13 52	294	45 41	322
326	15 37	027	39 09	055	40 02	138	58 39	201	47 31	237	13 26	296	45 23	324
328	15 51	029	39 33	057	40 21	140	58 28	204	47 06	239	13 00	298	45 06	325
	POLLUX		◆ CAPELLA		Hamal		Alpheratz		◆ DENEB		VEGA		◆ Alioth	
330	16 05	030	39 57	059	29 26	112	40 39	142	58 15	207	46 41	241	44 50	327
332	16 20	032	40 22	060	29 53	114	40 57	144	58 02	209	46 15	244	44 35	328
334	16 36	034	40 48	062	30 20	116	41 13	147	57 47	212	45 49	246	44 20	330
336	16 53	036	41 14	064	30 46	118	41 29	149	57 31	214	45 22	248	44 06	331
338	17 10	038	41 40	066	31 11	120	41 43	151	57 14	217	44 55	250	43 52	333
340	17 28	040	42 06	067	31 36	122	41 57	154	56 56	219	44 28	252	43 39	335
342	17 47	041	42 33	069	32 00	124	42 09	156	56 37	222	44 00	254	43 27	336
344	18 07	043	43 01	071	32 24	126	42 20	158	56 18	224	43 32	256	43 16	338
346	18 27	045	43 28	073	32 47	128	42 31	161	55 57	227	43 03	258	43 05	339
348	18 48	047	43 56	075	33 09	130	42 40	163	55 35	229	42 35	260	42 55	341
350	19 09	049	44 24	076	33 31	133	42 48	165	55 13	232	42 06	262	42 46	342
352	19 31	050	44 53	078	33 52	135	42 54	168	54 50	234	41 37	264	42 37	344
354	19 54	052	45 21	080	34 12	137	43 00	170	54 26	236	41 08	266	42 29	345
356	20 17	054	45 50	082	34 32	139	43 04	172	54 01	239	40 39	268	42 22	347
358	20 41	056	46 19	084	34 50	141	43 08	175	53 36	241	40 10	270	42 16	348

LHA ♈	Hc	Zn	Hc	Zn	Hc	Zn	Hc	Zn	Hc	Zn	Hc	Zn	Hc	Zn
	◆POLLUX		CAPELLA		Hamal		◆Alpheratz		DENEB		◆VEGA		Alioth	
0	20 33	058	46 43	085	35 56	143	44 10	177	53 37	244	39 39	273	41 11	350
2	21 00	059	47 13	087	36 14	145	44 10	180	53 09	247	39 08	275	41 06	351
4	21 27	061	47 45	088	36 32	148	44 10	182	52 40	249	38 37	277	41 02	353
6	21 54	063	48 16	090	36 48	150	44 08	185	52 11	251	38 06	279	40 59	354
8	22 22	065	48 47	092	37 03	152	44 05	187	51 42	253	37 35	280	40 56	356
10	22 50	067	49 18	094	37 17	154	44 01	189	51 12	255	37 05	282	40 54	357
12	23 19	069	49 49	096	37 29	157	43 55	192	50 42	257	36 35	284	40 53	359
14	23 48	070	50 19	098	37 41	159	43 48	194	50 11	259	36 05	286	40 53	000
16	24 18	072	50 50	100	37 52	161	43 40	197	49 41	261	35 35	288	40 53	002
18	24 47	074	51 20	102	38 01	164	43 30	199	49 10	263	35 06	290	40 55	003
20	25 17	076	51 51	105	38 09	166	43 19	201	48 39	265	34 37	291	40 57	005
22	25 48	078	52 21	107	38 16	168	43 07	204	48 08	267	34 08	293	41 00	006
24	26 18	080	52 50	109	38 22	171	42 54	206	47 37	269	33 40	295	41 03	008
26	26 49	082	53 19	111	38 26	173	42 40	209	47 06	271	33 12	297	41 08	009
28	27 20	084	53 48	113	38 29	175	42 25	211	46 35	273	32 44	299	41 13	011
	Alioth		◆POLLUX		CAPELLA		◆Hamal		Alpheratz		DENEB		◆VEGA	
30	41 19	012	27 51	085	54 16	115	38 31	178	42 08	213	46 04	275	32 17	300
32	41 26	014	28 21	087	54 44	118	38 32	180	41 51	216	45 33	277	31 51	302
34	41 34	015	28 53	089	55 12	120	38 31	182	41 32	218	45 02	279	31 25	304
36	41 43	017	29 24	091	55 38	122	38 29	185	41 13	220	44 31	281	30 59	306
38	41 52	018	29 55	093	56 04	125	38 26	187	40 52	222	44 01	282	30 34	307
40	42 02	020	30 26	095	56 29	127	38 22	189	40 31	225	43 31	284	30 10	309
42	42 13	021	30 56	097	56 54	129	38 16	192	40 09	227	43 01	286	29 46	311
44	42 24	023	31 27	099	57 17	132	38 09	194	39 45	229	42 31	288	29 23	313
46	42 36	024	31 58	101	57 40	134	38 01	196	39 22	231	42 02	290	29 00	314
48	42 49	026	32 28	103	58 02	137	37 52	199	38 57	233	41 33	291	28 38	316
50	43 03	027	32 58	105	58 22	139	37 41	201	38 32	236	41 04	293	28 17	318
52	43 18	029	33 28	107	58 42	142	37 30	203	38 06	238	40 36	295	27 57	320
54	43 33	030	33 58	109	59 01	145	37 17	206	37 39	240	40 08	297	27 37	321
56	43 49	032	34 27	111	59 18	147	37 03	208	37 12	242	39 40	298	27 18	323
58	44 05	033	34 56	113	59 34	150	36 48	210	36 44	244	39 13	300	26 59	325
	Alioth		◆POLLUX		CAPELLA		◆Hamal		Alpheratz		DENEB		◆VEGA	
60	44 23	035	35 24	115	59 49	153	36 32	212	36 16	246	38 46	302	26 42	326
62	44 41	036	35 52	117	60 03	155	36 14	215	35 47	248	38 20	304	26 25	328
64	44 59	038	36 19	120	60 15	158	35 56	217	35 18	250	37 54	305	26 09	330
66	45 19	039	36 46	122	60 26	161	35 37	219	34 49	252	37 29	307	25 54	332
68	45 38	041	37 12	124	60 35	164	35 17	221	34 19	254	37 05	309	25 39	333
70	45 59	042	37 37	126	60 43	167	34 56	224	33 49	257	36 41	310	25 26	335
72	46 20	044	38 02	128	60 50	169	34 34	226	33 19	259	36 17	312	25 13	337
74	46 42	045	38 26	130	60 55	172	34 12	228	32 48	261	35 55	314	25 01	338
76	47 04	047	38 50	133	60 58	175	33 48	230	32 18	262	35 33	315	24 50	340
78	47 27	048	39 12	135	61 00	178	33 24	232	31 47	264	35 11	317	24 40	342
80	47 51	050	39 34	137	61 01	181	32 59	234	31 16	266	34 50	319	24 31	344
82	48 15	052	39 54	139	60 59	184	32 34	236	30 45	268	34 30	320	24 23	345
84	48 39	053	40 14	142	60 57	187	32 08	239	30 14	270	34 10	322	24 15	347
86	49 05	055	40 33	144	60 52	189	31 41	241	29 43	272	33 52	324	24 08	349
88	49 30	056	40 51	146	60 47	192	31 13	243	29 12	274	33 34	325	24 03	350
	Alioth		◆REGULUS		POLLUX		◆CAPELLA		Alpheratz		◆DENEB		VEGA	
90	49 56	058	18 28	114	41 08	148	60 39	195	28 41	276	33 16	327	23 58	352
92	50 23	059	18 56	116	41 23	151	60 30	198	28 10	278	33 00	329	23 54	354
94	50 50	061	19 24	118	41 38	153	60 20	201	27 39	280	32 44	330	23 51	355
96	51 17	063	19 51	120	41 52	155	60 09	203	27 09	282	32 29	332	23 49	357
98	51 45	064	20 18	122	42 04	158	59 56	206	26 38	284	32 15	333	23 48	359
100	52 13	066	20 44	124	42 15	160	59 41	209	26 08	285	32 01	335	23 48	001
102	52 42	068	21 09	126	42 25	163	59 26	212	25 38	287	31 48	337	23 49	002
104	53 11	069	21 34	128	42 34	165	59 09	214	25 09	289	31 37	338	23 50	004
106	53 40	071	21 58	130	42 41	167	58 51	217	24 40	291	31 26	340	23 53	006
108	54 09	073	22 21	132	42 47	170	58 31	219	24 11	293	31 15	342	23 57	007
110	54 39	075	22 44	134	42 52	172	58 11	222	23 43	295	31 06	343	24 01	009
112	55 09	076	23 06	137	42 56	175	57 50	225	23 15	297	30 58	345	24 06	011
114	55 39	078	23 27	139	42 58	177	57 28	227	22 47	298	30 50	347	24 13	012
116	56 10	080	23 47	141	42 59	179	57 04	230	22 20	300	30 43	348	24 20	014
118	56 41	082	24 06	143	42 59	182	56 40	232	21 53	302	30 37	350	24 28	016
	◆VEGA		ARCTURUS		◆REGULUS		POLLUX		◆CAPELLA		Alpheratz		DENEB	
120	24 37	018	17 23	081	24 24	145	42 57	184	56 15	234	21 27	304	30 32	351
122	24 47	019	17 54	083	24 42	147	42 54	187	55 50	237	21 02	306	30 28	353
124	24 57	021	18 24	085	24 58	149	42 50	189	55 24	239	20 37	307	30 25	355
126	25 09	023	18 55	087	25 13	151	42 45	191	54 57	241	20 12	309	30 22	356
128	25 21	024	19 26	089	25 28	154	42 38	194	54 29	244	19 49	311	30 21	358
130	25 34	026	19 58	091	25 41	156	42 30	196	54 01	246	19 26	313	30 20	000
132	25 49	028	20 29	093	25 53	158	42 21	199	53 32	248	19 03	315	30 20	001
134	26 03	030	21 00	094	26 04	160	42 10	201	53 03	250	18 42	317	30 21	003
136	26 19	031	21 30	096	26 15	162	41 59	203	52 34	252	18 21	318	30 23	004
138	26 36	033	22 01	098	26 23	164	41 46	206	52 04	255	18 00	320	30 26	006
140	26 53	035	22 32	100	26 31	167	41 32	208	51 34	257	17 41	322	30 30	008
142	27 11	036	23 02	102	26 38	169	41 17	210	51 04	259	17 22	324	30 35	009
144	27 30	038	23 33	104	26 43	171	41 00	213	50 33	261	17 04	326	30 40	011
146	27 49	040	24 03	106	26 48	173	40 43	215	50 02	263	16 47	327	30 47	013
148	28 10	042	24 32	108	26 51	175	40 25	217	49 32	265	16 30	329	30 54	014
	DENEB		◆VEGA		ARCTURUS		◆REGULUS		POLLUX		◆CAPELLA		Alpheratz	
150	31 02	016	28 31	043	25 02	110	26 53	177	40 06	220	49 01	267	16 15	331
152	31 11	018	28 52	045	25 30	112	26 54	180	39 45	222	48 30	269	16 00	333
154	31 21	019	29 14	047	25 59	114	26 53	182	39 24	224	47 58	271	15 46	335
156	31 31	021	29 37	048	26 27	116	26 52	184	39 02	226	47 27	273	15 34	336
158	31 43	022	30 01	050	26 55	118	26 49	186	38 39	228	46 56	274	15 22	338
160	31 55	024	30 25	052	27 22	120	26 45	188	38 16	231	46 26	276	15 10	340
162	32 08	026	30 50	054	27 48	123	26 40	191	37 51	233	45 55	278	15 00	342
164	32 22	027	31 15	055	28 14	125	26 33	193	37 26	235	45 24	280	14 51	344
166	32 36	029	31 41	057	28 39	127	26 26	195	37 00	237	44 54	282	14 43	345
168	32 52	031	32 07	059	29 04	129	26 17	197	36 34	239	44 23	284	14 35	347
170	33 08	032	32 34	061	29 28	131	26 08	199	36 07	241	43 53	286	14 29	349
172	33 25	034	33 02	063	29 51	133	25 57	202	35 39	244	43 23	287	14 23	351
174	33 43	036	33 29	064	30 13	135	25 45	204	35 11	246	42 54	289	14 19	353
176	34 01	037	33 58	066	30 34	137	25 32	206	34 43	248	42 25	291	14 15	354
178	34 20	039	34 26	068	30 55	140	25 18	208	34 14	250	41 56	293	14 13	356

LAT 75°N

LHA ♈	Hc	Zn	Hc	Zn	Hc	Zn	Hc	Zn	Hc	Zn	Hc	Zn	Hc	Zn
	◆DENEB		VEGA		◆ARCTURUS		REGULUS		◆POLLUX		CAPELLA		Alpheratz	
180	34 40	041	34 55	070	31 15	142	25 03	210	33 45	252	41 27	294	14 11	358
182	35 01	042	35 24	071	31 33	144	24 46	212	33 15	254	40 59	296	14 10	000
184	35 22	044	35 54	073	31 51	146	24 29	214	32 45	256	40 32	298	14 11	002
186	35 44	046	36 24	075	32 08	148	24 11	217	32 15	258	40 04	300	14 12	003
188	36 06	047	36 54	077	32 24	151	23 52	219	31 44	260	39 38	301	14 14	005
190	36 29	049	37 24	079	32 39	153	23 33	221	31 14	262	39 11	303	14 18	007
192	36 53	051	37 55	081	32 52	155	23 12	223	30 43	264	38 45	305	14 22	009
194	37 17	052	38 26	083	33 05	157	22 50	225	30 12	266	38 20	306	14 27	011
196	37 42	054	38 57	084	33 16	159	22 28	227	29 41	268	37 55	308	14 33	012
198	38 08	056	39 28	086	33 27	162	22 05	229	29 10	270	37 31	310	14 40	014
200	38 34	057	39 59	088	33 36	164	21 41	231	28 39	272	37 08	311	14 48	016
202	39 00	059	40 30	090	33 44	166	21 17	233	28 08	273	36 45	313	14 57	018
204	39 27	061	41 01	092	33 51	169	20 51	235	27 37	275	36 22	315	15 07	020
206	39 54	063	41 32	094	33 56	171	20 25	237	27 06	277	36 01	316	15 18	021
208	40 22	064	42 03	096	34 01	173	19 59	239	26 35	279	35 39	318	15 30	023
	Alpheratz		◆DENEB		VEGA		◆ARCTURUS		REGULUS		POLLUX		◆CAPELLA	
210	15 43	025	40 50	066	42 33	098	34 04	175	19 32	241	26 05	281	35 19	320
212	15 56	027	41 19	068	43 04	100	34 06	178	19 05	243	25 34	283	34 59	321
214	16 11	029	41 48	070	43 35	102	34 06	180	18 37	245	25 04	285	34 40	323
216	16 26	030	42 17	071	44 05	104	34 06	182	18 08	247	24 34	287	34 22	325
218	16 42	032	42 46	073	44 35	106	34 04	184	17 39	249	24 05	289	34 04	326
220	16 59	034	43 16	075	45 04	108	34 01	187	17 10	251	23 35	290	33 47	328
222	17 17	036	43 46	077	45 34	110	33 57	189	16 40	253	23 06	292	33 31	330
224	17 35	038	44 17	079	46 03	113	33 51	191	16 10	255	22 38	294	33 16	331
226	17 54	039	44 47	080	46 31	115	33 44	194	15 40	257	22 10	296	33 01	333
228	18 15	041	45 18	082	46 59	117	33 37	196	15 10	259	21 42	298	32 48	334
230	18 35	043	45 49	084	47 27	119	33 28	198	14 39	261	21 15	300	32 35	336
232	18 57	045	46 20	086	47 53	121	33 17	200	14 08	263	20 48	301	32 22	338
234	19 19	047	46 51	088	48 20	123	33 06	203	13 38	265	20 22	303	32 11	339
236	19 42	048	47 22	090	48 45	126	32 53	205	13 07	267	19 56	305	32 01	341
238	20 05	050	47 53	092	49 10	128	32 40	207	12 36	269	19 31	307	31 51	343
	Alpheratz		◆DENEB		VEGA		◆ARCTURUS		Dubhe		POLLUX		◆CAPELLA	
240	20 30	052	48 24	094	49 34	130	32 25	209	62 11	282	19 07	309	31 42	344
242	20 54	054	48 55	096	49 57	133	32 09	212	61 41	284	18 43	311	31 34	346
244	21 20	056	49 26	098	50 20	135	31 53	214	61 11	286	18 19	312	31 27	347
246	21 46	057	49 56	100	50 41	137	31 35	216	60 41	287	17 57	314	31 21	349
248	22 12	059	50 27	102	51 02	140	31 16	218	60 11	289	17 35	316	31 15	351
250	22 39	061	50 57	104	51 21	142	30 57	220	59 42	291	17 14	318	31 10	352
252	23 06	063	51 27	106	51 40	145	30 36	222	59 13	292	16 53	320	31 07	354
254	23 34	065	51 57	108	51 57	147	30 15	225	58 45	294	16 33	321	31 04	356
256	24 03	067	52 26	110	52 13	150	29 53	227	58 16	296	16 14	323	31 02	357
258	24 31	068	52 55	112	52 28	152	29 30	229	57 49	297	15 56	325	31 01	359
260	25 00	070	53 24	115	52 42	155	29 06	231	57 21	299	15 39	327	31 01	000
262	25 30	072	53 52	117	52 55	157	28 41	233	56 54	300	15 22	329	31 01	002
264	26 00	074	54 19	119	53 06	160	28 16	235	56 27	302	15 07	331	31 03	004
266	26 30	076	54 46	121	53 16	162	27 50	237	56 01	303	14 52	332	31 05	005
268	27 00	078	55 12	124	53 25	165	27 24	239	55 36	305	14 38	334	31 09	007
	◆CAPELLA		Alpheratz		◆DENEB		VEGA		◆ARCTURUS		Dubhe		POLLUX	
270	31 13	009	27 30	080	55 38	126	53 32	168	26 57	241	55 10	306	14 25	336
272	31 18	010	28 01	082	56 02	128	53 38	170	26 29	243	54 45	308	14 12	338
274	31 24	012	28 32	083	56 26	131	53 43	173	26 01	245	54 21	309	14 01	340
276	31 31	013	29 03	085	56 49	133	53 46	176	25 33	248	53 57	311	13 51	341
278	31 38	015	29 34	087	57 11	136	53 48	178	25 04	250	53 34	312	13 41	343
280	31 47	017	30 05	089	57 32	138	53 48	181	24 35	252	53 11	314	13 33	345
282	31 56	018	30 36	091	57 53	141	53 47	183	24 05	254	52 49	315	13 25	347
284	32 06	020	31 07	093	58 12	143	53 44	186	23 35	256	52 27	316	13 19	349
286	32 17	022	31 38	095	58 30	146	53 40	189	23 05	258	52 06	318	13 13	350
288	32 29	023	32 09	097	58 46	149	53 35	191	22 35	260	51 46	319	13 08	352
290	32 42	025	32 39	099	59 02	151	53 28	194	22 04	261	51 26	321	13 05	354
292	32 55	026	33 10	101	59 16	154	53 20	197	21 33	263	51 06	322	13 02	356
294	33 09	028	33 40	103	59 29	157	53 10	199	21 02	265	50 48	324	13 00	358
296	33 24	030	34 10	105	59 40	160	52 59	202	20 31	267	50 30	325	12 59	359
298	33 40	031	34 40	107	59 50	162	52 47	204	20 00	269	50 12	326	13 00	001
	POLLUX		◆CAPELLA		Alpheratz		◆DENEB		VEGA		◆ARCTURUS		Dubhe	
300	13 01	003	33 57	033	35 10	109	59 59	165	52 34	207	19 29	271	49 55	328
302	13 03	005	34 14	035	35 39	111	60 06	168	52 19	209	18 58	273	49 39	329
304	13 06	007	34 32	036	36 08	113	60 12	171	52 03	212	18 27	275	49 24	331
306	13 10	009	34 51	038	36 36	115	60 16	174	51 46	214	17 56	277	49 09	332
308	13 15	010	35 10	040	37 04	117	60 19	176	51 28	217	17 25	279	48 55	334
310	13 21	012	35 30	041	37 31	119	60 20	179	51 09	219	16 55	281	48 41	335
312	13 28	014	35 51	043	37 58	122	60 20	182	50 49	222	16 24	283	48 28	336
314	13 36	016	36 12	045	38 24	124	60 18	185	50 28	224	15 54	285	48 16	338
316	13 45	018	36 35	046	38 50	126	60 14	188	50 06	226	15 24	286	48 05	339
318	13 55	019	36 57	048	39 15	128	60 09	191	49 43	229	14 55	288	47 54	340
320	14 06	021	37 21	050	39 39	130	60 03	193	49 19	231	14 25	290	47 44	342
322	14 18	023	37 45	051	40 02	132	59 55	196	48 54	233	13 56	292	47 35	343
324	14 30	025	38 09	053	40 24	135	59 45	199	48 29	236	13 28	294	47 26	345
326	14 44	027	38 34	055	40 46	137	59 35	202	48 03	238	13 00	296	47 18	346
328	14 58	028	39 00	056	41 07	139	59 22	205	47 36	240	12 32	298	47 11	347
	◆POLLUX		CAPELLA		Hamal		◆Alpheratz		DENEB		◆VEGA		Alioth	
330	15 13	030	39 26	058	29 48	111	41 27	142	59 09	207	47 09	242	44 00	327
332	15 30	032	39 52	060	30 17	113	41 45	144	58 54	210	46 41	245	43 43	329
334	15 46	034	40 19	061	30 45	115	42 03	146	58 38	213	46 13	247	43 28	330
336	16 04	036	40 47	063	31 13	117	42 20	148	58 20	215	45 44	249	43 13	332
338	16 23	038	41 15	065	31 41	119	42 36	151	58 02	218	45 15	251	42 59	333
340	16 42	039	41 43	067	32 07	121	42 50	153	57 42	220	44 46	253	42 45	335
342	17 02	041	42 12	068	32 34	124	43 04	156	57 22	223	44 16	255	42 32	336
344	17 23	043	42 41	070	32 59	126	43 16	158	57 00	225	43 46	257	42 20	338
346	17 44	045	43 10	072	33 24	128	43 27	160	56 37	228	43 15	259	42 09	339
348	18 07	047	43 40	074	33 48	130	43 37	163	56 14	230	42 45	261	41 58	341
350	18 30	048	44 10	075	34 12	132	43 46	165	55 50	233	42 14	263	41 49	342
352	18 53	050	44 40	077	34 34	134	43 53	168	55 25	235	41 43	265	41 40	344
354	19 17	052	45 10	079	34 56	136	43 59	170	54 59	238	41 12	267	41 31	345
356	19 42	054	45 41	081	35 17	139	44 04	172	54 32	240	40 41	269	41 24	347
358	20 07	056	46 12	083	35 37	141	44 07	175	54 05	242	40 10	271	41 17	348

LAT 74°N

LHA ♈	Hc Zn	Hc Zn	Hc Zn	Hc Zn	Hc Zn	Hc Zn	Hc Zn
	◆ POLLUX	CAPELLA	Hamal	◆ Alpheratz	DENEB	◆ VEGA	Alioth
0	20 01 057	46 36 084	36 44 143	45 09 177	54 03 246	39 35 274	40 12 350
2	20 29 059	47 09 086	37 04 145	45 10 180	53 32 248	39 02 276	40 07 351
4	20 58 061	47 42 087	37 22 147	45 10 182	53 01 250	38 29 278	40 03 353
6	21 27 063	48 15 089	37 39 149	45 08 185	52 30 252	37 57 279	39 59 354
8	21 56 064	48 49 091	37 56 152	45 05 187	51 58 254	37 24 281	39 56 356
10	22 27 066	49 22 093	38 11 154	45 00 190	51 26 256	36 52 283	39 54 357
12	22 57 068	49 55 095	38 25 156	44 54 192	50 54 258	36 20 285	39 53 359
14	23 28 070	50 27 097	38 37 159	44 46 194	50 22 260	35 48 287	39 53 000
16	23 59 072	51 00 099	38 49 161	44 37 197	49 49 263	35 16 289	39 53 002
18	24 31 074	51 33 101	38 59 163	44 27 199	49 16 265	34 45 290	39 55 003
20	25 03 076	52 05 103	39 07 166	44 15 202	48 43 266	34 14 292	39 57 005
22	25 35 077	52 37 105	39 15 168	44 02 204	48 10 268	33 44 294	40 00 006
24	26 07 079	53 09 107	39 21 170	43 48 207	47 37 270	33 14 296	40 04 008
26	26 40 081	53 40 110	39 26 173	43 33 209	47 04 272	32 44 297	40 09 009
28	27 13 083	54 11 112	39 29 175	43 16 211	46 31 274	32 15 299	40 14 010
	Alioth	◆ POLLUX	CAPELLA	◆ Hamal	Alpheratz	DENEB	◆ VEGA
30	40 21 012	27 45 085	54 42 114	39 31 178	42 58 214	45 58 276	31 47 301
32	40 28 013	28 18 087	55 11 116	39 32 180	42 39 216	45 25 278	31 18 303
34	40 36 015	28 51 089	55 41 119	39 31 182	42 19 218	44 52 280	30 51 304
36	40 45 016	29 25 091	56 10 121	39 29 185	41 58 221	44 20 282	30 24 306
38	40 55 018	29 58 093	56 38 123	39 26 187	41 36 223	43 48 283	29 57 308
40	41 05 019	30 31 095	57 05 126	39 21 189	41 13 225	43 16 285	29 32 310
42	41 17 021	31 04 096	57 31 128	39 15 192	40 49 227	42 44 287	29 06 311
44	41 29 022	31 36 098	57 57 131	39 07 194	40 25 230	42 12 289	28 42 313
46	41 42 024	32 09 100	58 21 133	38 59 197	39 59 232	41 41 290	28 18 315
48	41 55 025	32 41 102	58 45 136	38 49 199	39 32 234	41 10 292	27 55 316
50	42 10 027	33 14 104	59 08 138	38 37 201	39 05 236	40 40 294	27 33 318
52	42 25 028	33 45 106	59 29 141	38 25 204	38 37 238	40 10 296	27 11 320
54	42 41 030	34 17 108	59 49 144	38 11 206	38 09 241	39 40 297	26 50 322
56	42 58 031	34 48 111	60 08 146	37 56 208	37 40 243	39 11 299	26 30 323
58	43 15 033	35 19 113	60 26 149	37 40 211	37 10 245	38 43 301	26 10 325
	Alioth	◆ POLLUX	CAPELLA	◆ Hamal	Alpheratz	DENEB	◆ VEGA
60	43 33 034	35 49 115	60 42 152	37 22 213	36 40 247	38 14 302	25 52 327
62	43 52 036	36 19 117	60 57 155	37 04 215	36 09 249	37 47 304	25 34 328
64	44 12 037	36 48 119	61 11 157	36 44 217	35 38 251	37 20 306	25 17 330
66	44 32 039	37 17 121	61 23 160	36 24 220	35 07 253	36 53 308	25 01 332
68	44 53 040	37 45 123	61 33 163	36 02 222	34 35 255	36 27 309	24 46 333
70	45 14 042	38 12 125	61 42 166	35 40 224	34 03 257	36 02 311	24 31 335
72	45 37 043	38 39 128	61 49 169	35 16 226	33 30 259	35 37 313	24 18 337
74	46 00 045	39 05 130	61 54 172	34 52 228	32 58 261	35 13 314	24 05 339
76	46 23 046	39 30 132	61 58 175	34 27 231	32 25 263	34 50 316	23 54 340
78	46 47 048	39 54 134	62 00 178	34 01 233	31 52 265	34 27 317	23 43 342
80	47 12 049	40 17 136	62 01 181	33 34 235	31 19 267	34 05 319	23 33 344
82	47 37 051	40 40 139	61 59 184	33 07 237	30 46 269	33 44 321	23 24 345
84	48 03 052	41 01 141	61 56 187	32 39 239	30 13 271	33 23 322	23 17 347
86	48 29 054	41 21 143	61 52 190	32 10 241	29 40 273	33 03 324	23 10 349
88	48 56 055	41 41 146	61 45 193	31 41 243	29 07 275	32 44 326	23 04 350
	Alioth	◆ REGULUS	POLLUX	◆ CAPELLA	Alpheratz	◆ DENEB	VEGA
90	49 24 057	18 53 114	41 59 148	61 37 196	28 34 277	32 26 327	22 59 352
92	49 52 058	19 23 116	42 16 150	61 27 198	28 01 278	32 08 329	22 55 354
94	50 20 060	19 52 118	42 31 153	61 16 201	27 29 280	31 52 331	22 51 355
96	50 49 062	20 21 120	42 46 155	61 03 204	26 56 282	31 36 332	22 49 357
98	51 18 063	20 50 122	42 59 157	60 49 207	26 24 284	31 21 334	22 48 359
100	51 48 065	21 17 124	43 11 160	60 34 210	25 52 286	31 07 335	22 48 001
102	52 18 066	21 45 126	43 22 162	60 16 212	25 20 288	30 53 337	22 49 002
104	52 49 068	22 11 128	43 32 165	59 58 215	24 49 290	30 41 339	22 51 004
106	53 20 070	22 37 130	43 40 167	59 38 218	24 18 291	30 29 340	22 53 006
108	53 51 071	23 02 132	43 46 170	59 17 221	23 47 293	30 18 342	22 57 007
110	54 22 073	23 26 134	43 52 172	58 55 223	23 17 295	30 09 343	23 02 009
112	54 54 075	23 49 136	43 56 174	58 32 226	22 48 297	30 00 345	23 07 011
114	55 26 077	24 12 138	43 58 177	58 08 228	22 18 299	29 52 347	23 14 012
116	55 59 078	24 33 140	43 59 179	57 43 231	21 50 301	29 44 348	23 22 014
118	56 31 080	24 54 143	43 59 182	57 17 233	21 21 302	29 38 350	23 30 016
	◆ VEGA	ARCTURUS	◆ REGULUS	POLLUX	◆ CAPELLA	Alpheratz	DENEB
120	23 39 017	17 13 081	25 13 145	43 57 184	56 50 236	20 54 304	29 33 352
122	23 50 019	17 46 083	25 32 147	43 54 187	56 22 238	20 27 306	29 28 353
124	24 01 021	18 19 084	25 49 149	43 50 189	55 54 240	20 00 308	29 25 355
126	24 13 023	18 52 086	26 06 151	43 44 192	55 25 243	19 34 310	29 22 356
128	24 27 024	19 25 088	26 21 153	43 36 194	54 55 245	19 09 311	29 21 358
130	24 41 026	19 58 090	26 36 155	43 28 196	54 25 247	18 45 313	29 20 000
132	24 55 028	20 31 092	26 49 158	43 18 199	53 54 249	18 21 315	29 20 001
134	25 11 029	21 04 094	27 01 160	43 06 201	53 23 252	17 58 317	29 22 003
136	25 28 031	21 37 096	27 12 162	42 54 204	52 51 254	17 36 319	29 24 004
138	25 45 033	22 10 098	27 21 164	42 40 206	52 20 256	17 14 320	29 27 006
140	26 04 034	22 42 100	27 30 166	42 25 208	51 47 258	16 53 322	29 31 008
142	26 23 036	23 15 102	27 37 169	42 08 211	51 15 260	16 34 324	29 35 009
144	26 43 038	23 47 104	27 43 171	41 51 213	50 42 262	16 14 326	29 41 011
146	27 03 040	24 19 106	27 47 173	41 32 215	50 09 264	15 56 327	29 48 013
148	27 25 041	24 51 108	27 51 175	41 12 218	49 36 266	15 39 329	29 56 014
	DENEB	◆ VEGA	ARCTURUS	◆ REGULUS	POLLUX	◆ CAPELLA	Alpheratz
150	30 04 016	27 47 043	25 22 110	27 53 177	40 52 220	49 03 268	15 22 331
152	30 14 017	28 10 045	25 53 112	27 54 180	40 30 222	48 30 270	15 07 333
154	30 24 019	28 33 046	26 24 114	27 53 182	40 07 225	47 57 272	14 52 335
156	30 35 021	28 58 048	26 54 116	27 51 184	39 43 227	47 24 274	14 39 336
158	30 47 022	29 22 050	27 23 118	27 48 186	39 19 229	46 51 276	14 26 338
160	31 00 024	29 48 052	27 52 120	27 44 189	38 53 231	46 18 277	14 14 340
162	31 14 025	30 14 053	28 20 122	27 39 191	38 27 233	45 46 279	14 03 342
164	31 28 027	30 41 055	28 48 124	27 32 193	38 00 236	45 13 281	13 53 344
166	31 44 029	31 08 057	29 15 126	27 24 195	37 33 238	44 41 283	13 45 345
168	32 00 030	31 36 058	29 41 128	27 15 197	37 04 240	44 09 285	13 37 347
170	32 17 032	32 05 060	30 07 131	27 04 200	36 35 242	43 37 286	13 30 349
172	32 35 034	32 34 062	30 31 133	26 52 202	36 06 244	43 05 288	13 24 351
174	32 54 035	33 03 064	30 55 135	26 40 204	35 36 246	42 34 290	13 19 353
176	33 13 037	33 33 065	31 18 137	26 26 206	35 05 248	42 03 292	13 16 354
178	33 34 038	34 03 067	31 41 139	26 11 208	34 34 250	41 32 293	13 13 356

LHA ♈	Hc Zn	Hc Zn	Hc Zn	Hc Zn	Hc Zn	Hc Zn	Hc Zn
	◆ DENEB	VEGA	◆ ARCTURUS	REGULUS	◆ POLLUX	CAPELLA	Alpheratz
180	33 55 040	34 34 069	32 02 141	25 54 210	34 03 252	41 02 295	13 11 358
182	34 16 042	35 05 071	32 22 144	25 37 213	33 31 254	40 33 297	13 10 000
184	34 39 043	35 36 073	32 41 146	25 19 215	32 59 256	40 03 299	13 11 002
186	35 02 045	36 08 074	32 59 148	24 59 217	32 27 258	39 34 300	13 12 003
188	35 25 047	36 40 076	33 16 150	24 39 219	31 55 260	39 06 302	13 15 005
190	35 50 048	37 12 078	33 32 152	24 18 221	31 22 262	38 38 304	13 18 007
192	36 15 050	37 45 080	33 47 155	23 56 223	30 49 264	38 11 305	13 23 009
194	36 40 052	38 18 082	34 00 157	23 33 225	30 16 266	37 44 307	13 28 010
196	37 07 053	38 50 084	34 13 159	23 09 227	29 43 268	37 18 309	13 35 012
198	37 33 055	39 23 086	34 24 162	22 44 229	29 10 270	36 53 310	13 42 014
200	38 01 057	39 56 087	34 33 164	22 19 231	28 37 272	36 28 312	13 51 016
202	38 29 058	40 29 089	34 42 166	21 52 234	28 04 274	36 04 314	14 00 018
204	38 57 060	41 02 091	34 49 168	21 25 236	27 31 276	35 40 315	14 11 019
206	39 26 062	41 36 093	34 55 171	20 58 238	26 58 278	35 17 317	14 22 021
208	39 55 064	42 08 095	35 00 173	20 30 240	26 25 280	34 55 319	14 35 023
	Alpheratz	◆ DENEB	VEGA	◆ ARCTURUS	REGULUS	POLLUX	◆ CAPELLA
210	14 48 025	40 25 065	42 41 097	35 04 175	20 01 242	25 53 282	34 33 320
212	15 03 027	40 56 067	43 14 099	35 06 178	19 31 244	25 21 283	34 12 322
214	15 18 028	41 26 069	43 47 101	35 06 180	19 01 246	24 49 285	33 52 323
216	15 34 030	41 57 070	44 19 103	35 06 182	18 31 248	24 17 287	33 33 325
218	15 51 032	42 28 072	44 51 105	35 04 185	18 00 250	23 45 289	33 14 327
220	16 09 034	43 00 074	45 23 107	35 00 187	17 29 252	23 14 291	32 57 328
222	16 28 036	43 32 076	45 54 109	34 56 189	16 57 254	22 44 293	32 40 330
224	16 48 037	44 04 078	46 25 112	34 50 191	16 26 256	22 13 294	32 23 332
226	17 08 039	44 37 079	46 56 114	34 43 194	15 53 258	21 43 296	32 08 333
228	17 29 041	45 09 081	47 26 116	34 34 196	15 21 260	21 14 298	31 53 335
230	17 51 043	45 42 083	47 55 118	34 25 198	14 48 261	20 45 300	31 40 336
232	18 14 045	46 15 085	48 24 120	34 14 201	14 16 263	20 17 302	31 27 338
234	18 38 046	46 48 087	48 52 123	34 01 203	13 43 265	19 49 304	31 15 340
236	19 02 048	47 21 089	49 20 125	33 48 205	13 10 267	19 22 305	31 04 341
238	19 27 050	47 54 091	49 47 127	33 33 207	12 37 269	18 55 307	30 54 343
	Alpheratz	◆ DENEB	VEGA	◆ ARCTURUS	Dubhe	POLLUX	◆ CAPELLA
240	19 53 052	48 27 093	50 13 129	33 17 210	61 57 284	18 29 309	30 44 344
242	20 19 054	49 00 095	50 38 132	33 01 212	61 25 286	18 03 311	30 36 346
244	20 46 055	49 33 097	51 02 134	32 43 214	60 53 288	17 39 313	30 28 348
246	21 13 057	50 06 099	51 25 137	32 24 216	60 22 289	17 15 314	30 22 349
248	21 41 059	50 38 101	51 47 139	32 03 218	59 51 291	16 52 316	30 16 351
250	22 10 061	51 11 103	52 09 141	31 42 221	59 20 292	16 29 318	30 11 352
252	22 39 063	51 43 105	52 29 144	31 20 223	58 50 294	16 07 320	30 07 354
254	23 09 064	52 15 107	52 47 146	30 57 225	58 20 295	15 46 322	30 04 356
256	23 39 066	52 46 109	53 05 149	30 34 227	57 50 297	15 26 323	30 02 357
258	24 09 068	53 17 111	53 21 152	30 09 229	57 21 298	15 07 325	30 01 359
260	24 40 070	53 48 113	53 36 154	29 43 231	56 52 300	14 49 327	30 01 000
262	25 11 072	54 18 116	53 50 157	29 17 234	56 23 301	14 31 329	30 01 002
264	25 43 074	54 48 118	54 03 159	28 50 236	55 55 303	14 14 331	30 03 004
266	26 15 075	55 17 120	54 13 162	28 23 238	55 28 304	13 59 332	30 06 005
268	26 47 077	55 45 122	54 23 165	27 54 240	55 01 306	13 44 334	30 09 007
	◆ CAPELLA	Alpheratz	◆ DENEB	VEGA	◆ ARCTURUS	Dubhe	POLLUX
270	30 14 008	27 19 079	56 12 125	54 31 167	27 26 242	54 34 307	13 30 336
272	30 19 010	27 52 081	56 39 127	54 37 170	26 56 244	54 08 309	13 17 338
274	30 25 012	28 24 083	57 05 130	54 42 173	26 26 246	53 43 310	13 05 340
276	30 32 013	28 57 085	57 30 132	54 46 175	25 56 248	53 18 312	12 54 341
278	30 40 015	29 30 087	57 54 135	54 48 178	25 25 250	52 53 313	12 44 343
280	30 49 016	30 03 089	58 17 137	54 48 181	24 54 252	52 29 315	12 35 345
282	30 59 018	30 36 090	58 39 140	54 47 184	24 22 254	52 06 316	12 27 347
284	31 10 020	31 10 092	59 00 143	54 44 186	23 50 256	51 43 317	12 20 349
286	31 21 021	31 43 094	59 19 145	54 39 189	23 18 258	51 21 319	12 14 350
288	31 34 023	32 15 096	59 37 148	54 33 192	22 45 260	51 00 320	12 09 352
290	31 47 025	32 48 098	59 54 151	54 26 194	22 13 262	50 39 322	12 05 354
292	32 01 026	33 21 100	60 10 153	54 17 197	21 40 264	50 19 323	12 02 356
294	32 16 028	33 53 102	60 24 156	54 07 200	21 07 266	49 59 324	12 00 358
296	32 32 029	34 26 104	60 36 159	53 55 202	20 34 268	49 40 326	11 59 359
298	32 49 031	34 57 106	60 48 162	53 42 205	20 01 270	49 22 327	12 00 001
	POLLUX	◆ CAPELLA	Alpheratz	◆ DENEB	VEGA	◆ ARCTURUS	Dubhe
300	12 01 003	33 06 033	35 29 108	60 57 165	53 27 207	19 28 272	49 04 329
302	12 03 005	33 24 034	36 00 110	61 05 168	53 11 210	18 55 273	48 47 330
304	12 07 007	33 43 036	36 31 112	61 11 171	52 54 213	18 22 275	48 31 331
306	12 11 009	34 03 037	37 01 115	61 16 173	52 36 215	17 49 277	48 16 333
308	12 16 010	34 24 039	37 31 117	61 19 176	52 16 218	17 16 279	48 01 334
310	12 23 012	34 45 041	38 00 119	61 20 179	51 55 220	16 44 281	47 47 335
312	12 30 014	35 07 042	38 29 121	61 20 182	51 33 223	16 11 283	47 33 337
314	12 39 016	35 29 044	38 57 123	61 17 185	51 10 225	15 39 285	47 20 338
316	12 48 018	35 53 046	39 25 125	61 14 188	50 47 227	15 07 287	47 08 339
318	12 59 019	36 17 047	39 51 127	61 08 191	50 22 230	14 36 289	46 57 341
320	13 10 021	36 41 049	40 17 130	61 01 194	49 56 232	14 05 290	46 47 342
322	13 23 023	37 07 051	40 42 132	60 52 197	49 30 234	13 34 292	46 37 344
324	13 36 025	37 33 052	41 06 134	60 42 200	49 02 237	13 03 294	46 28 345
326	13 50 027	37 59 054	41 30 136	60 30 202	48 34 239	12 33 296	46 20 346
328	14 05 028	38 26 056	41 52 139	60 17 205	48 06 241	12 04 298	46 12 348
	◆ POLLUX	CAPELLA	Hamal	◆ Alpheratz	DENEB	◆ VEGA	Alioth
330	14 22 030	38 54 057	30 10 111	42 13 141	60 02 208	47 36 243	43 09 328
332	14 39 032	39 22 059	30 40 113	42 34 143	59 46 211	47 07 246	42 52 329
334	14 57 034	39 50 061	31 11 115	42 53 146	59 28 214	46 36 248	42 36 331
336	15 15 036	40 19 062	31 40 117	43 11 148	59 09 216	46 05 250	42 20 332
338	15 35 037	40 49 064	32 10 119	43 28 150	58 49 219	45 34 252	42 05 334
340	15 56 039	41 19 066	32 38 121	43 44 153	58 28 221	45 03 254	41 51 335
342	16 17 041	41 49 068	33 07 123	43 58 155	58 05 224	44 31 256	41 37 337
344	16 39 043	42 20 069	33 34 125	44 12 158	57 42 227	43 58 258	41 25 338
346	17 02 045	42 51 071	34 01 127	44 24 160	57 17 229	43 26 260	41 13 340
348	17 25 046	43 22 073	34 27 129	44 34 162	56 52 232	42 53 262	41 02 341
350	17 50 048	43 54 075	34 52 132	44 44 165	56 25 234	42 20 264	40 51 343
352	18 15 050	44 26 076	35 16 134	44 52 167	55 58 236	41 47 266	40 42 344
354	18 40 052	44 58 078	35 39 136	44 58 170	55 30 239	41 14 268	40 33 346
356	19 07 054	45 31 080	36 02 138	45 03 172	55 02 241	40 41 270	40 26 347
358	19 33 055	46 04 082	36 23 140	45 07 175	54 33 243	40 08 272	40 19 349

LAT 73°N

LAT 73°N

LHA ♈	Hc	Zn	Hc	Zn	Hc	Zn	Hc	Zn	Hc	Zn	Hc	Zn	Hc	Zn
	◆POLLUX		CAPELLA		Hamal		◆Alpheratz		DENEB		◆VEGA		Alioth	
0	19 28	057	46 29	083	37 32	142	46 09	177	54 27	247	39 31	275	39 13	350
2	19 58	059	47 04	084	37 53	144	46 10	180	53 54	249	38 56	276	39 08	352
4	20 28	061	47 39	086	38 12	147	46 10	182	53 21	251	38 21	278	39 03	353
6	20 59	062	48 14	088	38 31	149	46 08	185	52 48	253	37 47	280	38 59	354
8	21 30	064	48 49	090	38 48	151	46 04	187	52 14	256	37 12	282	38 56	356
10	22 02	066	49 24	092	39 05	154	45 59	190	51 40	258	36 38	284	38 54	357
12	22 35	068	49 59	094	39 19	156	45 52	192	51 06	260	36 04	286	38 53	359
14	23 07	070	50 34	096	39 33	158	45 44	195	50 31	262	35 30	287	38 53	000
16	23 40	071	51 09	098	39 45	161	45 34	197	49 56	264	34 57	289	38 53	002
18	24 14	073	51 44	100	39 56	163	45 23	200	49 21	266	34 24	291	38 55	003
20	24 47	075	52 18	102	40 06	166	45 11	202	48 46	268	33 51	293	38 57	005
22	25 21	077	52 52	104	40 14	168	44 57	205	48 11	270	33 19	294	39 00	006
24	25 56	079	53 26	106	40 20	170	44 42	207	47 36	271	32 48	296	39 04	007
26	26 30	081	54 00	108	40 25	173	44 25	209	47 01	273	32 16	298	39 09	009
28	27 05	083	54 33	111	40 29	175	44 07	212	46 26	275	31 46	300	39 15	010
	Alioth		◆POLLUX		CAPELLA		◆Hamal		Alpheratz		DENEB		◆VEGA	
30	39 22	012	27 40	084	55 05	113	40 31	178	43 48	214	45 51	277	31 15	301
32	39 30	013	28 15	086	55 37	115	40 32	180	43 28	217	45 16	279	30 46	303
34	39 38	015	28 50	088	56 09	117	40 31	182	43 06	219	44 42	281	30 17	305
36	39 47	016	29 25	090	56 40	120	40 29	185	42 44	221	44 07	282	29 48	307
38	39 58	018	30 00	092	57 10	122	40 25	187	42 20	224	43 33	284	29 20	308
40	40 09	019	30 35	094	57 39	124	40 20	190	41 55	226	42 59	286	28 53	310
42	40 20	020	31 10	096	58 08	127	40 14	192	41 30	228	42 26	288	28 27	312
44	40 33	022	31 45	098	58 35	129	40 06	194	41 03	230	41 53	290	28 01	313
46	40 47	023	32 20	100	59 02	132	39 56	197	40 36	233	41 20	291	27 36	315
48	41 01	025	32 54	102	59 28	135	39 45	199	40 07	235	40 47	293	27 11	317
50	41 16	026	33 28	104	59 52	137	39 33	202	39 38	237	40 15	295	26 48	319
52	41 32	028	34 02	106	60 15	140	39 20	204	39 08	239	39 44	296	26 25	320
54	41 49	029	34 36	108	60 37	143	39 05	206	38 38	241	39 12	298	26 03	322
56	42 06	031	35 09	110	60 58	145	38 49	209	38 07	243	38 42	300	25 42	324
58	42 24	032	35 42	112	61 17	148	38 31	211	37 35	246	38 12	301	25 21	325
	Alioth		◆POLLUX		CAPELLA		◆Hamal		Alpheratz		DENEB		◆VEGA	
60	42 43	034	36 14	114	61 35	151	38 12	213	37 03	248	37 42	303	25 02	327
62	43 03	035	36 46	116	61 51	154	37 53	215	36 30	250	37 13	305	24 43	329
64	43 23	036	37 17	118	62 06	157	37 32	218	35 57	252	36 44	306	24 25	330
66	43 45	038	37 48	120	62 19	160	37 10	220	35 24	254	36 16	308	24 08	332
68	44 07	039	38 18	122	62 30	163	36 47	222	34 50	256	35 49	310	23 52	334
70	44 29	041	38 47	125	62 40	166	36 23	225	34 16	258	35 22	311	23 37	335
72	44 53	042	39 15	127	62 48	169	35 57	227	33 41	260	34 56	313	23 23	337
74	45 16	044	39 43	129	62 54	172	35 31	229	33 07	262	34 31	315	23 10	339
76	45 41	045	40 10	131	62 58	175	35 05	231	32 32	264	34 06	316	22 57	340
78	46 06	047	40 36	134	63 00	178	34 37	233	31 57	266	33 43	318	22 46	342
80	46 32	048	41 01	136	63 01	181	34 08	235	31 22	268	33 19	320	22 36	344
82	46 59	050	41 24	138	62 59	184	33 39	238	30 47	270	32 57	321	22 26	345
84	47 26	051	41 47	140	62 56	187	33 09	240	30 12	271	32 35	323	22 18	347
86	47 54	053	42 09	143	62 51	190	32 39	242	29 37	273	32 15	324	22 11	349
88	48 22	054	42 30	145	62 44	193	32 07	244	29 02	275	31 55	326	22 04	350
	Alioth		◆REGULUS		POLLUX		◆CAPELLA		Alpheratz		◆DENEB		VEGA	
90	48 51	056	19 17	113	42 49	147	62 35	196	28 27	277	31 35	328	21 59	352
92	49 20	057	19 48	115	43 08	150	62 24	199	27 52	279	31 17	329	21 55	354
94	49 50	059	20 20	117	43 25	152	62 12	202	27 18	281	30 59	331	21 52	355
96	50 20	061	20 51	119	43 40	155	61 58	205	26 43	283	30 43	332	21 49	357
98	50 51	062	21 21	121	43 55	157	61 43	208	26 09	285	30 27	334	21 48	359
100	51 22	064	21 51	123	44 08	159	61 25	211	25 35	286	30 12	336	21 48	001
102	51 54	065	22 20	126	44 19	162	61 07	213	25 02	288	29 58	337	21 49	002
104	52 26	067	22 48	128	44 29	164	60 47	216	24 29	290	29 45	339	21 51	004
106	52 58	069	23 15	130	44 38	167	60 25	219	23 56	292	29 33	340	21 54	006
108	53 31	070	23 42	132	44 45	169	60 03	222	23 24	294	29 21	342	21 57	007
110	54 04	072	24 07	134	44 51	172	59 39	224	22 52	295	29 11	344	22 02	009
112	54 38	074	24 32	136	44 55	174	59 14	227	22 20	297	29 02	345	22 08	011
114	55 12	075	24 56	138	44 58	177	58 47	229	21 49	299	28 53	347	22 15	012
116	55 46	077	25 19	140	44 59	179	58 20	232	21 19	301	28 46	348	22 23	014
118	56 20	079	25 41	142	44 59	182	57 52	234	20 49	303	28 39	350	22 32	016
	◆VEGA		ARCTURUS		◆REGULUS		POLLUX		◆CAPELLA		Alpheratz		DENEB	
120	22 42	017	17 03	080	26 02	144	44 57	184	57 23	237	20 20	304	28 33	352
122	22 53	019	17 38	082	26 22	147	44 54	187	56 53	239	19 51	306	28 29	353
124	23 05	021	18 13	084	26 41	149	44 49	189	56 23	242	19 23	308	28 25	355
126	23 18	022	18 48	086	26 58	151	44 42	192	55 52	244	18 56	310	28 23	356
128	23 32	024	19 23	088	27 15	153	44 34	194	55 20	246	18 29	312	28 21	358
130	23 47	026	19 58	090	27 30	155	44 25	197	54 48	248	18 04	313	28 20	000
132	24 02	027	20 33	092	27 44	157	44 14	199	54 15	251	17 38	315	28 20	001
134	24 19	029	21 08	094	27 57	160	44 02	202	53 41	253	17 14	317	28 22	003
136	24 36	031	21 43	096	28 09	162	43 48	204	53 08	255	16 51	319	28 24	004
138	24 55	032	22 18	098	28 19	164	43 34	206	52 34	257	16 28	321	28 27	006
140	25 14	034	22 53	100	28 28	166	43 17	209	51 59	259	16 06	322	28 31	008
142	25 34	036	23 27	101	28 36	169	43 00	211	51 25	261	15 45	324	28 36	009
144	25 55	038	24 01	103	28 42	171	42 41	214	50 50	263	15 25	326	28 42	011
146	26 17	039	24 35	105	28 47	173	42 21	216	50 15	265	15 06	328	28 49	012
148	26 39	041	25 09	107	28 50	175	42 00	218	49 40	267	14 47	329	28 57	014
	DENEB		◆VEGA		ARCTURUS		◆REGULUS		POLLUX		◆CAPELLA		Alpheratz	
150	29 06	016	27 03	043	25 42	109	28 53	177	41 37	221	49 05	269	14 30	331
152	29 16	017	27 27	044	26 15	111	28 54	180	41 14	223	48 30	271	14 13	333
154	29 27	019	27 52	046	26 48	113	28 53	182	40 50	225	47 55	273	13 58	335
156	29 39	020	28 17	048	27 20	115	28 51	184	40 24	227	47 20	275	13 44	337
158	29 52	022	28 44	049	27 51	118	28 48	186	39 58	230	46 45	277	13 30	338
160	30 05	024	29 10	051	28 22	120	28 43	189	39 31	232	46 10	278	13 18	340
162	30 20	025	29 38	053	28 52	122	28 38	191	39 03	234	45 36	280	13 06	342
164	30 35	027	30 06	054	29 21	124	28 30	193	38 34	236	45 01	282	12 56	344
166	30 51	028	30 35	056	29 50	126	28 22	195	38 04	238	44 27	284	12 46	345
168	31 08	030	31 05	058	30 18	128	28 12	197	37 34	241	43 53	286	12 38	347
170	31 26	032	31 35	060	30 46	130	28 01	200	37 03	243	43 19	287	12 31	349
172	31 45	033	32 05	061	31 12	132	27 48	202	36 32	245	42 46	289	12 25	351
174	32 05	035	32 36	063	31 38	134	27 34	204	36 00	247	42 13	291	12 20	353
176	32 25	036	33 08	065	32 02	137	27 19	206	35 27	249	41 40	293	12 16	354
178	32 46	038	33 40	067	32 26	139	27 03	208	34 54	251	41 08	294	12 13	356

LHA ♈	Hc	Zn	Hc	Zn	Hc	Zn	Hc	Zn	Hc	Zn	Hc	Zn	Hc	Zn
	◆DENEB		VEGA		◆ARCTURUS		REGULUS		◆POLLUX		CAPELLA		Alpheratz	
180	33 08	040	34 12	068	32 48	141	26 46	211	34 21	253	40 36	296	12 11	358
182	33 31	041	34 45	070	33 10	143	26 28	213	33 47	255	40 05	298	12 10	000
184	33 55	043	35 18	072	33 30	145	26 08	215	33 13	257	39 34	299	12 11	002
186	34 19	045	35 52	074	33 50	148	25 47	217	32 39	259	39 04	301	12 12	003
188	34 44	046	36 26	076	34 08	150	25 26	219	32 04	261	38 34	303	12 15	005
190	35 10	048	37 00	077	34 25	152	25 03	221	31 29	263	38 05	304	12 19	007
192	35 36	049	37 34	079	34 41	154	24 39	223	30 55	265	37 36	306	12 23	009
194	36 03	051	38 09	081	34 55	157	24 15	226	30 20	267	37 08	308	12 29	010
196	36 31	053	38 43	083	35 09	159	23 49	228	29 45	269	36 41	309	12 36	012
198	36 59	054	39 18	085	35 20	161	23 23	230	29 09	271	36 14	311	12 44	014
200	37 28	056	39 53	087	35 31	164	22 56	232	28 34	273	35 47	312	12 53	016
202	37 57	058	40 28	088	35 40	166	22 28	234	27 59	275	35 22	314	13 03	018
204	38 27	059	41 03	090	35 48	168	21 59	236	27 24	276	34 57	316	13 14	019
206	38 57	061	41 38	092	35 55	171	21 30	238	26 50	278	34 33	317	13 26	021
208	39 28	063	42 13	094	36 00	173	21 00	240	26 15	280	34 10	319	13 40	023
	Alpheratz		◆DENEB		VEGA		◆ARCTURUS		REGULUS		POLLUX		◆CAPELLA	
210	13 54	025	40 00	064	42 48	096	36 03	175	20 29	242	25 41	282	33 47	321
212	14 09	027	40 32	066	43 23	098	36 06	178	19 58	244	25 06	284	33 25	322
214	14 25	028	41 04	068	43 58	100	36 06	180	19 26	246	24 32	286	33 04	324
216	14 42	030	41 37	070	44 32	102	36 06	182	18 54	248	23 59	288	32 44	325
218	15 00	032	42 10	071	45 06	104	36 04	185	18 21	250	23 26	289	32 24	327
220	15 19	034	42 43	073	45 40	106	36 00	187	17 48	252	22 53	291	32 05	329
222	15 39	035	43 17	075	46 14	108	35 55	189	17 14	254	22 20	293	31 48	330
224	16 00	037	43 51	077	46 47	111	35 49	192	16 40	256	21 48	295	31 31	332
226	16 21	039	44 25	078	47 19	113	35 41	194	16 06	258	21 17	297	31 14	333
228	16 44	041	45 00	080	47 51	115	35 32	196	15 32	260	20 45	298	30 59	335
230	17 07	043	45 34	082	48 23	117	35 21	199	14 57	262	20 15	300	30 45	337
232	17 31	044	46 09	084	48 54	119	35 10	201	14 22	264	19 45	302	30 31	338
234	17 56	046	46 44	086	49 24	122	34 57	203	13 47	266	19 15	304	30 19	340
236	18 22	048	47 19	088	49 54	124	34 42	205	13 12	268	18 47	306	30 07	341
238	18 48	050	47 54	090	50 22	126	34 26	208	12 37	269	18 18	307	29 56	343
	Alpheratz		◆DENEB		VEGA		◆ARCTURUS		Dubhe		POLLUX		◆CAPELLA	
240	19 15	051	48 29	091	50 50	128	34 10	210	61 41	286	17 51	309	29 46	345
242	19 43	053	49 04	093	51 17	131	33 51	212	61 08	288	17 24	311	29 38	346
244	20 11	055	49 39	095	51 43	133	33 32	214	60 34	289	16 58	313	29 30	348
246	20 41	057	50 14	097	52 08	136	33 12	217	60 01	291	16 33	315	29 23	349
248	21 10	059	50 49	099	52 32	138	32 50	219	59 29	292	16 08	316	29 17	351
250	21 40	060	51 23	101	52 55	141	32 28	221	58 57	294	15 44	318	29 12	352
252	22 11	062	51 58	103	53 17	143	32 04	223	58 25	295	15 21	320	29 07	354
254	22 42	064	52 32	106	53 37	146	31 40	225	57 53	297	14 59	322	29 04	356
256	23 14	066	53 05	108	53 56	148	31 14	228	57 22	298	14 38	324	29 02	357
258	23 46	068	53 38	110	54 14	151	30 48	230	56 51	300	14 18	325	29 01	359
260	24 19	069	54 11	112	54 30	154	30 21	232	56 21	301	13 58	327	29 01	000
262	24 52	071	54 43	114	54 45	156	29 53	234	55 51	303	13 40	329	29 01	002
264	25 26	073	55 15	117	54 59	159	29 24	236	55 22	304	13 22	331	29 03	004
266	25 59	075	55 46	119	55 10	162	28 55	238	54 53	306	13 05	333	29 06	005
268	26 33	077	56 16	121	55 21	164	28 24	240	54 25	307	12 50	334	29 10	007
	◆CAPELLA		Alpheratz		◆DENEB		VEGA		◆ARCTURUS		Dubhe		POLLUX	
270	29 14	008	27 08	079	56 46	124	55 29	167	27 54	242	53 57	308	12 35	336
272	29 20	010	27 42	080	57 15	126	55 36	170	27 22	244	53 30	310	12 21	338
274	29 26	012	28 17	082	57 43	129	55 42	173	26 50	246	53 04	311	12 09	340
276	29 34	013	28 52	084	58 10	131	55 46	175	26 18	248	52 37	313	11 57	342
278	29 42	015	29 27	086	58 36	134	55 48	178	25 45	250	52 12	314	11 46	343
280	29 52	016	30 02	088	59 01	136	55 48	181	25 12	252	51 47	315	11 37	345
282	30 02	018	30 37	090	59 24	139	55 46	184	24 38	254	51 23	317	11 28	347
284	30 13	020	31 12	092	59 47	141	55 43	186	24 04	256	50 59	318	11 21	349
286	30 25	021	31 47	094	60 08	144	55 39	189	23 30	258	50 36	320	11 15	351
288	30 39	023	32 22	096	60 28	147	55 32	192	22 56	260	50 14	321	11 09	352
290	30 53	024	32 57	098	60 46	150	55 24	195	22 21	262	49 52	322	11 05	354
292	31 07	026	33 31	100	61 03	153	55 14	197	21 46	264	49 31	324	11 02	356
294	31 23	027	34 06	102	61 19	155	55 03	200	21 11	266	49 10	325	11 00	358
296	31 40	029	34 40	104	61 32	158	54 50	203	20 36	268	48 50	326	10 59	359
298	31 57	031	35 14	106	61 44	161	54 36	205	20 01	270	48 31	328	11 00	001
	POLLUX		◆CAPELLA		Alpheratz		◆DENEB		VEGA		◆ARCTURUS		Dubhe	
300	11 01	003	32 16	032	35 48	108	61 55	164	54 20	208	19 26	272	48 13	329
302	11 03	005	32 35	034	36 21	110	62 03	167	54 03	211	18 51	274	47 55	330
304	11 07	007	32 55	035	36 54	112	62 10	170	53 44	213	18 16	276	47 38	332
306	11 12	008	33 15	037	37 26	114	62 15	173	53 24	216	17 41	278	47 22	333
308	11 17	010	33 37	039	37 58	116	62 19	176	53 03	218	17 06	279	47 07	334
310	11 24	012	33 59	040	38 29	118	62 20	179	52 41	221	16 32	281	46 52	336
312	11 32	014	34 22	042	39 00	120	62 20	182	52 17	223	15 58	283	46 38	337
314	11 41	016	34 46	044	39 30	122	62 17	185	51 53	226	15 24	285	46 25	339
316	11 51	017	35 11	045	39 59	125	62 13	188	51 27	228	14 50	287	46 12	340
318	12 02	019	35 36	047	40 27	127	62 07	191	51 00	231	14 16	289	46 01	341
320	12 14	021	36 02	048	40 55	129	61 59	194	50 33	233	13 43	291	45 50	343
322	12 27	023	36 28	050	41 22	131	61 50	197	50 04	235	13 11	293	45 39	344
324	12 41	025	36 56	052	41 48	133	61 38	200	49 35	238	12 39	294	45 30	345
326	12 57	026	37 23	053	42 13	136	61 25	203	49 05	240	12 07	296	45 22	347
328	13 13	028	37 52	055	42 37	138	61 11	206	48 34	242	11 36	298	45 14	348
	◆POLLUX		CAPELLA		Hamal		◆Alpheratz		DENEB		◆VEGA		Alioth	
330	13 30	030	38 21	057	30 30	110	43 00	140	60 55	209	48 03	244	42 18	328
332	13 48	032	38 50	058	31 03	112	43 22	143	60 37	212	47 31	247	42 00	330
334	14 07	034	39 21	060	31 35	114	43 42	145	60 18	214	46 59	249	41 43	331
336	14 27	035	39 51	062	32 07	116	44 02	147	59 57	217	46 26	251	41 27	333
338	14 47	037	40 22	063	32 38	118	44 20	150	59 35	220	45 52	253	41 11	334
340	15 09	039	40 54	065	33 09	120	44 37	152	59 12	223	45 19	255	40 56	336
342	15 31	041	41 26	067	33 39	122	44 53	155	58 48	225	44 45	257	40 42	337
344	15 55	043	41 58	068	34 08	125	45 07	157	58 23	228	44 10	259	40 29	339
346	16 19	044	42 31	070	34 37	127	45 20	160	57 56	230	43 36	261	40 16	340
348	16 44	046	43 04	072	35 04	129	45 31	162	57 29	233	43 01	263	40 05	341
350	17 10	048	43 38	074	35 31	131	45 41	165	57 00	235	42 26	265	39 54	343
352	17 36	050	44 12	075	35 57	133	45 50	167	56 31	238	41 51	267	39 44	344
354	18 03	052	44 46	077	36 22	135	45 57	170	56 01	240	41 16	269	39 35	346
356	18 31	053	45 20	079	36 46	138	46 03	172	55 30	242	40 41	271	39 27	347
358	18 59	055	45 55	081	37 10	140	46 07	175	54 59	245	40 06	273	39 20	349

LAT 72°N

LHA ♈	◆POLLUX Hc	Zn	CAPELLA Hc	Zn	Hamal Hc	Zn	◆Alpheratz Hc	Zn	DENEB Hc	Zn	◆VEGA Hc	Zn	Alioth Hc	Zn
0	18 55	057	46 21	082	38 19	142	47 09	177	54 50	248	39 26	275	38 14	350
2	19 27	058	46 58	083	38 41	144	47 10	180	54 15	250	38 49	277	38 08	352
4	19 59	060	47 35	085	39 02	146	47 10	182	53 40	253	38 12	279	38 03	353
6	20 31	062	48 12	087	39 22	149	47 08	185	53 04	255	37 36	281	37 59	355
8	21 04	064	48 49	089	39 41	151	47 04	187	52 28	257	36 59	283	37 56	356
10	21 38	066	49 26	091	39 58	153	46 58	190	51 52	259	36 23	285	37 54	357
12	22 12	067	50 03	093	40 14	156	46 51	192	51 16	261	35 47	286	37 53	359
14	22 46	069	50 40	095	40 29	158	46 42	195	50 39	263	35 12	288	37 53	000
16	23 21	071	51 17	097	40 42	161	46 32	198	50 02	265	34 37	290	37 53	002
18	23 56	073	51 53	099	40 53	163	46 20	200	49 25	267	34 02	292	37 55	003
20	24 32	075	52 30	101	41 04	165	46 06	203	48 48	269	33 28	293	37 57	004
22	25 08	076	53 06	103	41 12	168	45 51	205	48 11	271	32 54	295	38 01	006
24	25 44	078	53 42	105	41 19	170	45 35	207	47 34	273	32 21	297	38 05	007
26	26 20	080	54 18	107	41 25	173	45 17	210	46 57	274	31 48	299	38 10	009
28	26 57	082	54 53	109	41 29	175	44 58	212	46 20	276	31 16	300	38 16	010

LHA ♈	Alioth Hc	Zn	◆POLLUX Hc	Zn	CAPELLA Hc	Zn	◆Hamal Hc	Zn	Alpheratz Hc	Zn	DENEB Hc	Zn	◆VEGA Hc	Zn
30	38 23	012	27 34	084	55 28	111	41 31	178	44 38	215	45 43	278	30 44	302
32	38 31	013	28 11	086	56 02	114	41 32	180	44 16	217	45 07	280	30 13	304
34	38 40	014	28 48	088	56 36	116	41 31	182	43 53	220	44 30	282	29 42	305
36	38 50	016	29 25	090	57 09	118	41 29	185	43 29	222	43 54	283	29 12	307
38	39 00	017	30 02	091	57 41	121	41 25	187	43 03	224	43 18	285	28 43	309
40	39 12	019	30 39	093	58 13	123	41 19	190	42 37	227	42 42	287	28 14	310
42	39 24	020	31 16	095	58 43	126	41 12	192	42 09	229	42 07	289	27 47	312
44	39 37	022	31 53	097	59 13	128	41 04	195	41 41	231	41 32	290	27 19	314
46	39 51	023	32 29	099	59 42	131	40 54	197	41 12	233	40 58	292	26 53	315
48	40 06	024	33 06	101	60 09	133	40 42	199	40 42	236	40 23	294	26 27	317
50	40 22	026	33 42	103	60 36	136	40 29	202	40 11	238	39 50	295	26 03	319
52	40 39	027	34 18	105	61 01	139	40 14	204	39 39	240	39 17	297	25 39	321
54	40 56	029	34 54	107	61 25	141	39 58	207	39 07	242	38 44	299	25 15	322
56	41 14	030	35 29	109	61 47	144	39 41	209	38 33	244	38 12	300	24 53	324
58	41 33	032	36 04	111	62 08	147	39 22	211	38 00	246	37 40	302	24 32	326

LHA ♈	Alioth Hc	Zn	◆POLLUX Hc	Zn	CAPELLA Hc	Zn	◆Hamal Hc	Zn	Alpheratz Hc	Zn	DENEB Hc	Zn	◆VEGA Hc	Zn
60	41 53	033	36 38	113	62 27	150	39 03	214	37 26	248	37 09	304	24 11	327
62	42 14	034	37 12	115	62 45	153	38 41	216	36 51	250	36 38	305	23 52	329
64	42 35	036	37 45	118	63 01	156	38 19	218	36 16	252	36 08	307	23 33	331
66	42 57	037	38 18	120	63 15	159	37 55	221	35 40	254	35 39	309	23 15	332
68	43 20	039	38 49	122	63 28	162	37 31	223	35 04	257	35 10	310	22 58	334
70	43 44	040	39 21	124	63 38	165	37 05	225	34 28	259	34 42	312	22 42	336
72	44 08	042	39 51	126	63 47	168	36 38	227	33 52	260	34 15	314	22 28	337
74	44 33	043	40 20	128	63 53	171	36 11	229	33 15	262	33 49	315	22 14	339
76	44 59	045	40 49	131	63 58	175	35 42	232	32 38	264	33 23	317	22 01	341
78	45 25	046	41 17	133	64 00	178	35 13	234	32 01	266	32 58	318	21 49	342
80	45 52	048	41 43	135	64 01	181	34 42	236	31 24	268	32 34	320	21 38	344
82	46 20	049	42 09	137	63 59	184	34 11	238	30 47	270	32 10	322	21 28	346
84	46 48	051	42 33	140	63 55	187	33 39	240	30 10	272	31 48	323	21 20	347
86	47 17	052	42 57	142	63 50	190	33 07	242	29 33	274	31 26	325	21 12	349
88	47 46	053	43 19	145	63 42	193	32 34	244	28 56	276	31 05	326	21 05	351

LHA ♈	Alioth Hc	Zn	◆REGULUS Hc	Zn	POLLUX Hc	Zn	◆CAPELLA Hc	Zn	Alpheratz Hc	Zn	◆DENEB Hc	Zn	VEGA Hc	Zn
90	48 17	055	19 40	113	43 40	147	63 32	197	28 19	278	30 45	328	21 00	352
92	48 47	056	20 14	115	43 59	149	63 21	200	27 42	280	30 25	330	20 55	354
94	49 18	058	20 47	117	44 18	152	63 08	203	27 06	281	30 07	331	20 52	356
96	49 50	060	21 20	119	44 34	154	62 52	206	26 30	283	29 50	333	20 49	357
98	50 22	061	21 52	121	44 50	157	62 35	209	25 54	285	29 33	334	20 48	359
100	50 55	063	22 24	123	45 04	159	62 17	212	25 18	287	29 17	336	20 48	001
102	51 28	064	22 54	125	45 16	162	61 57	214	24 43	289	29 03	337	20 49	002
104	52 02	066	23 24	127	45 27	164	61 35	217	24 08	290	28 49	339	20 51	004
106	52 36	067	23 53	129	45 37	167	61 12	220	23 33	292	28 36	341	20 54	006
108	53 10	069	24 22	131	45 44	169	60 47	223	22 59	294	28 24	342	20 58	007
110	53 45	071	24 49	133	45 51	172	60 21	226	22 26	296	28 13	344	21 03	009
112	54 20	072	25 15	136	45 55	174	59 54	228	21 53	298	28 04	345	21 09	011
114	54 56	074	25 41	138	45 58	177	59 26	231	21 20	299	27 55	347	21 17	012
116	55 31	075	26 05	140	45 59	179	58 57	233	20 48	301	27 47	349	21 25	014
118	56 07	077	26 29	142	45 59	182	58 27	236	20 17	303	27 40	350	21 34	016

LHA ♈	◆VEGA Hc	Zn	ARCTURUS Hc	Zn	◆REGULUS Hc	Zn	POLLUX Hc	Zn	◆CAPELLA Hc	Zn	Alpheratz Hc	Zn	DENEB Hc	Zn
120	21 45	017	16 53	080	26 51	144	45 57	184	57 55	238	19 46	305	27 34	352
122	21 56	019	17 30	082	27 12	146	45 53	187	57 23	241	19 16	307	27 29	353
124	22 09	021	18 07	084	27 32	148	45 48	189	56 51	243	18 46	308	27 25	355
126	22 22	022	18 44	086	27 51	151	45 41	192	56 17	245	18 17	310	27 23	356
128	22 37	024	19 21	088	28 08	153	45 33	194	55 43	248	17 50	312	27 21	358
130	22 52	026	19 58	089	28 25	155	45 23	197	55 09	250	17 22	314	27 20	000
132	23 09	027	20 35	091	28 40	157	45 11	199	54 34	252	16 56	315	27 20	001
134	23 26	029	21 12	093	28 53	159	44 58	202	53 58	254	16 30	317	27 22	003
136	23 45	031	21 49	095	29 06	162	44 43	204	53 23	256	16 05	319	27 24	004
138	24 04	032	22 26	097	29 17	164	44 27	207	52 46	258	15 41	321	27 27	006
140	24 24	034	23 02	099	29 26	166	44 10	209	52 10	260	15 18	322	27 32	008
142	24 45	036	23 39	101	29 34	168	43 51	212	51 33	262	14 56	324	27 37	009
144	25 07	037	24 15	103	29 41	171	43 31	214	50 56	264	14 35	326	27 43	011
146	25 30	039	24 51	105	29 46	173	43 09	217	50 19	266	14 15	328	27 51	012
148	25 54	041	25 27	107	29 50	175	42 47	219	49 42	268	13 56	330	27 59	014

LHA ♈	DENEB Hc	Zn	◆VEGA Hc	Zn	ARCTURUS Hc	Zn	◆REGULUS Hc	Zn	POLLUX Hc	Zn	◆CAPELLA Hc	Zn	Alpheratz Hc	Zn
150	28 09	015	26 18	042	26 02	109	29 53	177	42 23	221	49 05	270	13 37	331
152	28 19	017	26 44	044	26 37	111	29 54	180	41 58	224	48 28	272	13 20	333
154	28 30	019	27 10	046	27 11	113	29 53	182	41 32	226	47 51	274	13 04	335
156	28 43	020	27 37	047	27 45	115	29 51	184	41 05	228	47 14	276	12 48	337
158	28 56	022	28 04	049	28 18	117	29 48	186	40 36	230	46 37	278	12 34	338
160	29 10	023	28 33	051	28 51	119	29 43	189	40 07	233	46 01	279	12 21	340
162	29 25	025	29 02	052	29 23	121	29 36	191	39 38	235	45 24	281	12 09	342
164	29 41	027	29 31	054	29 55	123	29 29	193	39 07	237	44 48	283	11 58	344
166	29 58	028	30 02	056	30 25	125	29 20	195	38 35	239	44 12	285	11 48	346
168	30 16	030	30 33	057	30 55	127	29 09	198	38 03	241	43 36	286	11 40	347
170	30 35	031	31 04	059	31 24	130	28 57	200	37 30	243	43 01	288	11 32	349
172	30 55	033	31 36	061	31 52	132	28 44	202	36 57	246	42 26	290	11 26	351
174	31 15	034	32 09	063	32 19	134	28 29	204	36 23	248	41 51	292	11 20	353
176	31 37	036	32 42	064	32 46	136	28 13	207	35 48	250	41 17	293	11 16	354
178	31 59	038	33 16	066	33 11	138	27 56	209	35 13	252	40 43	295	11 13	356

LHA ♈	◆DENEB Hc	Zn	VEGA Hc	Zn	◆ARCTURUS Hc	Zn	REGULUS Hc	Zn	◆POLLUX Hc	Zn	CAPELLA Hc	Zn	Alpheratz Hc	Zn
180	32 22	039	33 50	068	33 35	141	27 38	211	34 38	254	40 10	297	11 11	358
182	32 46	041	34 24	070	33 58	143	27 18	213	34 02	256	39 37	298	11 10	000
184	33 11	042	34 59	071	34 20	145	26 57	215	33 26	258	39 05	300	11 11	002
186	33 36	044	35 35	073	34 40	147	26 35	217	32 50	260	38 33	302	11 12	003
188	34 02	046	36 10	075	35 00	150	26 12	220	32 13	262	38 01	303	11 15	005
190	34 29	047	36 46	077	35 18	152	25 48	222	31 36	264	37 31	305	11 19	007
192	34 57	049	37 22	078	35 35	154	25 23	224	31 00	266	37 01	307	11 24	009
194	35 25	051	37 59	080	35 50	156	24 57	226	30 23	268	36 31	308	11 30	010
196	35 54	052	38 35	082	36 05	159	24 30	228	29 45	269	36 02	310	11 37	012
198	36 24	054	39 12	084	36 17	161	24 02	230	29 08	271	35 34	311	11 46	014
200	36 54	055	39 49	086	36 29	163	23 33	232	28 31	273	35 07	313	11 55	016
202	37 25	057	40 26	088	36 38	166	23 03	234	27 54	275	34 40	315	12 06	018
204	37 56	059	41 03	090	36 47	168	22 33	236	27 17	277	34 14	316	12 18	019
206	38 28	060	41 40	091	36 54	170	22 01	238	26 41	279	33 49	318	12 30	021
208	39 01	062	42 17	093	36 59	173	21 30	240	26 04	281	33 24	319	12 44	023

LHA ♈	Alpheratz Hc	Zn	◆DENEB Hc	Zn	VEGA Hc	Zn	◆ARCTURUS Hc	Zn	REGULUS Hc	Zn	POLLUX Hc	Zn	◆CAPELLA Hc	Zn
210	12 59	025	39 34	064	42 54	095	37 03	175	20 57	242	25 28	283	33 00	321
212	13 15	026	40 07	065	43 31	097	37 05	178	20 24	244	24 52	284	32 37	323
214	13 32	028	40 41	067	44 08	099	37 06	180	19 50	246	24 16	286	32 15	324
216	13 50	030	41 15	069	44 44	101	37 06	182	19 16	248	23 41	288	31 54	326
218	14 09	032	41 50	070	45 21	103	37 03	185	18 41	250	23 05	290	31 34	327
220	14 29	033	42 25	072	45 57	105	37 00	187	18 06	252	22 31	292	31 14	329
222	14 50	035	43 01	074	46 32	107	36 54	189	17 31	254	21 57	293	30 55	331
224	15 12	037	43 37	076	47 07	110	36 48	192	16 55	256	21 23	295	30 38	332
226	15 35	039	44 13	077	47 42	112	36 39	194	16 19	258	20 49	297	30 21	334
228	15 58	041	44 49	079	48 16	114	36 30	196	15 42	260	20 17	299	30 05	335
230	16 23	042	45 25	081	48 50	116	36 18	199	15 06	262	19 44	301	29 50	337
232	16 48	044	46 02	083	49 23	118	36 06	201	14 29	264	19 13	302	29 35	338
234	17 14	046	46 39	085	49 55	121	35 52	203	13 52	266	18 42	304	29 22	340
236	17 41	048	47 16	087	50 27	123	35 36	206	13 15	268	18 12	306	29 10	342
238	18 09	049	47 53	088	50 57	125	35 19	208	12 38	270	17 42	308	28 59	343

LHA ♈	Alpheratz Hc	Zn	◆DENEB Hc	Zn	VEGA Hc	Zn	◆ARCTURUS Hc	Zn	Dubhe Hc	Zn	POLLUX Hc	Zn	◆CAPELLA Hc	Zn
240	18 38	051	48 30	090	51 27	128	35 01	210	61 24	288	17 13	310	28 49	345
242	19 07	053	49 07	092	51 56	130	34 42	213	60 49	289	16 45	311	28 39	346
244	19 37	055	49 44	094	52 24	132	34 22	215	60 14	291	16 17	313	28 31	348
246	20 08	056	50 21	096	52 51	135	34 00	217	59 39	292	15 50	315	28 24	349
248	20 39	058	50 58	098	53 17	137	33 37	219	59 05	294	15 25	317	28 17	351
250	21 11	060	51 35	100	53 41	140	33 13	221	58 32	295	15 00	318	28 12	353
252	21 43	062	52 11	102	54 05	142	32 48	224	57 58	297	14 35	320	28 08	354
254	22 16	064	52 47	104	54 27	145	32 22	226	57 25	298	14 12	322	28 04	356
256	22 49	065	53 23	106	54 47	148	31 55	228	56 53	300	13 50	324	28 02	357
258	23 23	067	53 58	109	55 06	150	31 26	230	56 21	301	13 28	326	28 01	359
260	23 58	069	54 33	111	55 24	153	30 58	232	55 50	303	13 08	327	28 01	000
262	24 33	071	55 07	113	55 40	156	30 28	234	55 18	304	12 48	329	28 02	002
264	25 08	073	55 41	115	55 55	158	29 57	237	54 48	305	12 30	331	28 03	004
266	25 43	074	56 15	118	56 07	161	29 26	239	54 18	307	12 12	333	28 06	005
268	26 19	076	56 47	120	56 18	164	28 54	241	53 49	308	11 56	334	28 10	007

LHA ♈	◆CAPELLA Hc	Zn	Alpheratz Hc	Zn	◆DENEB Hc	Zn	VEGA Hc	Zn	◆ARCTURUS Hc	Zn	Dubhe Hc	Zn	POLLUX Hc	Zn
270	28 15	008	26 55	078	57 19	122	56 28	167	28 21	243	53 20	310	11 40	336
272	28 21	010	27 32	080	57 50	125	56 35	170	27 48	245	52 51	311	11 26	338
274	28 28	011	28 08	082	58 20	127	56 41	172	27 14	247	52 24	312	11 12	340
276	28 35	013	28 45	084	58 49	130	56 45	175	26 40	249	51 56	314	11 00	342
278	28 44	015	29 22	086	59 17	132	56 47	178	26 05	251	51 30	315	10 49	343
280	28 54	016	29 59	087	59 43	135	56 48	181	25 30	253	51 04	316	10 39	345
282	29 05	018	30 36	089	60 09	138	56 46	184	24 54	255	50 39	318	10 30	347
284	29 17	019	31 13	091	60 33	140	56 43	187	24 18	257	50 14	319	10 22	349
286	29 29	021	31 50	093	60 56	143	56 38	189	23 42	259	49 50	320	10 15	351
288	29 43	022	32 27	095	61 18	146	56 31	192	23 05	261	49 27	322	10 10	352
290	29 58	024	33 04	097	61 38	149	56 22	195	22 29	263	49 04	323	10 06	354
292	30 13	026	33 41	099	61 56	152	56 12	198	21 52	265	48 42	324	10 02	356
294	30 30	027	34 17	101	62 13	155	55 59	201	21 15	267	48 21	326	10 00	358
296	30 47	029	34 54	103	62 28	158	55 45	203	20 38	268	48 00	327	09 59	359
298	31 06	030	35 30	105	62 41	161	55 30	206	20 01	270	47 40	328	10 00	001

LHA ♈	◆CAPELLA Hc	Zn	Hamal Hc	Zn	Alpheratz Hc	Zn	◆DENEB Hc	Zn	VEGA Hc	Zn	◆ARCTURUS Hc	Zn	Dubhe Hc	Zn
300	31 25	032	21 42	080	36 05	107	62 52	164	55 13	209	19 24	272	47 21	330
302	31 45	034	22 19	082	36 41	109	63 02	167	54 54	211	18 47	274	47 03	331
304	32 06	035	22 56	084	37 15	111	63 09	170	54 34	214	18 10	276	46 45	332
306	32 27	037	23 33	086	37 50	113	63 15	173	54 13	217	17 33	278	46 29	334
308	32 50	038	24 10	088	38 24	115	63 19	176	53 50	219	16 56	280	46 12	335
310	33 13	040	24 47	090	38 57	117	63 20	179	53 26	222	16 20	282	45 57	336
312	33 38	041	25 24	092	39 30	119	63 19	182	53 00	224	15 44	284	45 43	338
314	34 02	043	26 01	094	40 01	122	63 17	185	52 34	227	15 08	285	45 29	339
316	34 28	045	26 38	096	40 33	124	63 12	189	52 06	229	14 32	287	45 16	340
318	34 55	046	27 15	098	41 03	126	63 06	192	51 38	232	13 57	289	45 04	342
320	35 22	048	27 51	100	41 33	128	62 57	195	51 08	234	13 22	291	44 52	343
322	35 50	049	28 28	101	42 01	131	62 47	198	50 38	236	12 48	293	44 42	344
324	36 18	051	29 04	103	42 29	133	62 35	201	50 07	239	12 14	295	44 32	345
326	36 47	053	29 40	105	42 56	135	62 20	204	49 35	241	11 40	296	44 23	347
328	37 17	054	30 16	107	43 21	137	62 05	207	49 02	243	11 07	298	44 15	348

LHA ♈	◆POLLUX Hc	Zn	CAPELLA Hc	Zn	Hamal Hc	Zn	◆Alpheratz Hc	Zn	DENEB Hc	Zn	◆VEGA Hc	Zn	Alioth Hc	Zn
330	12 38	030	37 48	056	30 51	109	43 46	140	61 47	210	48 28	245	41 27	329
332	12 57	032	38 19	058	31 25	111	44 09	142	61 28	213	47 54	248	41 08	330
334	13 17	033	38 50	059	32 00	114	44 31	145	61 07	215	47 20	250	40 50	332
336	13 38	035	39 22	061	32 33	116	44 52	147	60 45	218	46 45	252	40 33	333
338	13 59	037	39 55	063	33 07	118	45 12	149	60 21	221	46 09	254	40 17	335
340	14 22	039	40 28	064	33 39	120	45 30	152	59 56	224	45 34	256	40 01	336
342	14 46	041	41 02	066	34 11	122	45 47	154	59 30	226	44 58	258	39 47	337
344	15 11	042	41 36	068	34 42	124	46 02	157	59 02	229	44 21	260	39 33	339
346	15 36	044	42 10	069	35 12	126	46 16	159	58 34	232	43 45	262	39 20	340
348	16 02	046	42 45	071	35 42	128	46 28	162	58 04	234	43 08	264	39 08	342
350	16 29	048	43 20	073	36 11	131	46 39	164	57 34	237	42 31	266	38 57	343
352	16 57	049	43 56	074	36 38	133	46 49	167	57 03	239	41 54	268	38 46	345
354	17 26	051	44 32	076	37 05	135	46 56	169	56 30	241	41 17	270	38 37	346
356	17 55	053	45 08	078	37 31	137	47 02	172	55 58	244	40 40	272	38 28	347
358	18 25	055	45 44	080	37 55	139	47 07	174	55 24	246	40 03	274	38 21	349

 LAT 71°N

LHA ♈	Hc	Zn	Hc	Zn	Hc	Zn	Hc	Zn	Hc	Zn	Hc	Zn	Hc	Zn
	◆ POLLUX		CAPELLA		Hamal		◆ Alpheratz		DENEB		◆ VEGA		Alioth	
0	18 22	056	46 12	081	39 06	141	48 09	177	55 12	249	39 20	276	37 15	350
2	18 55	058	46 50	082	39 30	144	48 10	180	54 35	252	38 41	278	37 09	352
4	19 29	060	47 29	084	39 52	146	48 10	182	53 57	254	38 02	280	37 04	353
6	20 03	062	48 08	086	40 13	148	48 07	185	53 20	256	37 24	282	37 00	355
8	20 37	063	48 47	088	40 33	151	48 03	187	52 42	258	36 46	283	36 57	356
10	21 13	065	49 26	090	40 52	153	47 57	190	52 03	260	36 08	285	36 54	357
12	21 48	067	50 05	092	41 09	155	47 49	193	51 25	262	35 30	287	36 53	359
14	22 25	069	50 44	093	41 24	158	47 40	195	50 46	264	34 53	289	36 53	000
16	23 01	071	51 23	095	41 38	160	47 29	198	50 07	266	34 16	290	36 53	002
18	23 38	072	52 02	097	41 51	163	47 16	200	49 28	268	33 40	292	36 55	003
20	24 16	074	52 41	099	42 02	165	47 02	203	48 49	270	33 04	294	36 58	004
22	24 53	076	53 19	101	42 11	168	46 46	205	48 10	272	32 28	296	37 01	006
24	25 31	078	53 57	104	42 18	170	46 28	208	47 31	274	31 54	297	37 05	007
26	26 10	080	54 35	106	42 24	173	46 09	210	46 52	275	31 19	299	37 11	009
28	26 48	082	55 12	108	42 29	175	45 49	213	46 13	277	30 45	301	37 17	010
	Alioth		◆ POLLUX		CAPELLA		◆ Hamal		Alpheratz		DENEB		◆ VEGA	
30	37 24	011	27 27	083	55 49	110	42 31	178	45 27	215	45 34	279	30 12	302
32	37 33	013	28 06	085	56 26	112	42 32	180	45 03	218	44 56	281	29 39	304
34	37 42	014	28 45	087	57 01	115	42 31	182	44 39	220	44 18	283	29 07	306
36	37 52	016	29 24	089	57 37	117	42 29	185	44 13	223	43 40	284	28 36	307
38	38 03	017	30 03	091	58 11	119	42 24	187	43 46	225	43 02	286	28 05	309
40	38 15	018	30 42	093	58 45	122	42 18	190	43 18	227	42 25	288	27 35	311
42	38 28	020	31 21	095	59 18	124	42 11	192	42 49	230	41 48	290	27 06	313
44	38 41	021	32 00	097	59 49	127	42 02	195	42 18	232	41 11	291	26 38	314
46	38 56	023	32 39	099	60 20	129	41 51	197	41 47	234	40 35	293	26 10	316
48	39 12	024	33 17	101	60 50	132	41 38	200	41 15	236	39 59	295	25 43	317
50	39 28	025	33 55	102	61 18	135	41 24	202	40 42	238	39 24	296	25 17	319
52	39 45	027	34 33	104	61 45	137	41 09	205	40 09	241	38 49	298	24 52	321
54	40 03	028	35 11	106	62 11	140	40 52	207	39 34	243	38 15	300	24 28	322
56	40 22	030	35 48	109	62 35	143	40 33	209	38 59	245	37 41	301	24 05	324
58	40 42	031	36 25	111	62 58	146	40 14	212	38 24	247	37 08	303	23 42	326
	Alioth		◆ POLLUX		CAPELLA		◆ Hamal		Alpheratz		DENEB		◆ VEGA	
60	41 03	033	37 02	113	63 19	149	39 52	214	37 47	249	36 35	304	23 21	327
62	41 24	034	37 37	115	63 38	152	39 30	216	37 11	251	36 03	306	23 00	329
64	41 46	035	38 12	117	63 56	155	39 06	219	36 33	253	35 32	308	22 41	331
66	42 09	037	38 47	119	64 11	158	38 41	221	35 56	255	35 01	309	22 22	332
68	42 33	038	39 21	121	64 24	161	38 15	223	35 18	257	34 31	311	22 04	334
70	42 58	040	39 54	123	64 36	165	37 47	226	34 40	259	34 02	312	21 48	336
72	43 23	041	40 26	126	64 45	168	37 19	228	34 01	261	33 34	314	21 32	337
74	43 49	042	40 57	128	64 52	171	36 49	230	33 22	263	33 06	316	21 18	339
76	44 16	044	41 28	130	64 57	174	36 19	232	32 44	265	32 39	317	21 04	341
78	44 43	045	41 57	132	65 00	178	35 48	234	32 05	267	32 13	319	20 52	342
80	45 11	047	42 26	135	65 01	181	35 16	237	31 26	269	31 48	320	20 40	344
82	45 40	048	42 53	137	64 59	184	34 43	239	30 47	271	31 23	322	20 30	346
84	46 10	050	43 19	139	64 55	187	34 09	241	30 08	273	30 59	324	20 21	347
86	46 40	051	43 44	142	64 49	191	33 34	243	29 29	274	30 37	325	20 13	349
88	47 10	053	44 08	144	64 40	194	32 59	245	28 50	276	30 15	327	20 06	351
	Alioth		◆ REGULUS		POLLUX		◆ CAPELLA		Alpheratz		◆ DENEB		VEGA	
90	47 42	054	20 04	113	44 30	146	64 30	197	28 11	278	29 54	328	20 00	352
92	48 14	056	20 39	115	44 51	149	64 17	200	27 32	280	29 34	330	19 56	354
94	48 46	057	21 15	117	45 10	151	64 03	203	26 54	282	29 14	331	19 52	356
96	49 19	059	21 49	119	45 28	154	63 46	207	26 16	284	28 56	333	19 49	357
98	49 53	060	22 23	121	45 45	156	63 28	210	25 38	285	28 39	335	19 48	359
100	50 27	062	22 56	123	46 00	159	63 08	213	25 01	287	28 23	336	19 48	001
102	51 02	063	23 29	125	46 13	161	62 46	216	24 23	289	28 07	338	19 49	002
104	51 37	065	24 00	127	46 25	164	62 22	218	23 47	291	27 53	339	19 51	004
106	52 12	066	24 31	129	46 35	166	61 57	221	23 10	293	27 39	341	19 54	005
108	52 48	068	25 01	131	46 43	169	61 31	224	22 35	294	27 27	342	19 58	007
110	53 24	069	25 30	133	46 50	172	61 03	227	21 59	296	27 16	344	20 04	009
112	54 01	071	25 58	135	46 55	174	60 34	229	21 25	298	27 06	346	20 10	010
114	54 38	072	26 25	137	46 58	177	60 03	232	20 50	300	26 56	347	20 18	012
116	55 16	074	26 51	140	46 59	179	59 32	235	20 17	302	26 48	349	20 27	014
118	55 53	076	27 16	142	46 59	182	59 00	237	19 44	303	26 41	350	20 37	015
	◆ VEGA		ARCTURUS		◆ REGULUS		POLLUX		◆ CAPELLA		Alpheratz		DENEB	
120	20 48	017	16 43	080	27 39	144	46 57	184	58 26	240	19 11	305	26 35	352
122	21 00	019	17 21	082	28 02	146	46 53	187	57 52	242	18 40	307	26 30	353
124	21 13	020	18 00	083	28 23	148	46 47	190	57 17	244	18 09	309	26 26	355
126	21 27	022	18 39	085	28 43	150	46 40	192	56 42	247	17 39	310	26 23	356
128	21 42	024	19 18	087	29 02	153	46 31	195	56 06	249	17 09	312	26 21	358
130	21 58	025	19 57	089	29 19	155	46 20	197	55 29	251	16 41	314	26 20	000
132	22 15	027	20 36	091	29 35	157	46 07	200	54 52	253	16 13	316	26 20	001
134	22 34	029	21 15	093	29 49	159	45 53	202	54 14	255	15 46	317	26 22	003
136	22 53	030	21 54	095	30 03	162	45 38	205	53 36	258	15 20	319	26 24	004
138	23 13	032	22 33	097	30 14	164	45 21	207	52 58	260	14 55	321	26 28	006
140	23 34	034	23 12	099	30 24	166	45 02	210	52 19	262	14 31	323	26 32	007
142	23 56	035	23 50	101	30 33	168	44 42	212	51 41	264	14 08	324	26 38	009
144	24 19	037	24 28	103	30 40	171	44 20	215	51 02	266	13 45	326	26 44	011
146	24 43	039	25 06	105	30 46	173	43 57	217	50 23	268	13 24	328	26 52	012
148	25 08	040	25 44	106	30 50	175	43 33	219	49 44	269	13 04	330	27 01	014
	DENEB		◆ VEGA		ARCTURUS		◆ REGULUS		POLLUX		◆ CAPELLA		Alpheratz	
150	27 11	015	25 34	042	26 21	108	30 53	177	43 08	222	49 05	271	12 45	331
152	27 22	017	26 00	044	26 58	110	30 54	180	42 41	224	48 25	273	12 26	333
154	27 33	018	26 28	045	27 34	112	30 53	182	42 13	226	47 47	275	12 09	335
156	27 46	020	26 56	047	28 10	115	30 51	184	41 44	229	47 08	277	11 53	337
158	28 00	022	27 25	049	28 45	117	30 47	187	41 15	231	46 29	279	11 39	338
160	28 15	023	27 54	050	29 20	119	30 42	189	40 44	233	45 50	280	11 25	340
162	28 31	025	28 25	052	29 54	121	30 35	191	40 12	235	45 12	282	11 12	342
164	28 48	026	28 56	054	30 27	123	30 27	193	39 39	238	44 34	284	11 01	344
166	29 05	028	29 28	055	31 00	125	30 17	196	39 06	240	43 56	286	10 50	346
168	29 24	029	30 00	057	31 31	127	30 06	198	38 32	242	43 19	287	10 41	347
170	29 44	031	30 33	059	32 02	129	29 53	200	37 57	244	42 42	289	10 33	349
172	30 04	033	31 07	060	32 32	131	29 39	202	37 22	246	42 05	291	10 26	351
174	30 26	034	31 41	062	33 01	133	29 24	205	36 46	248	41 29	292	10 21	353
176	30 48	036	32 16	064	33 29	136	29 07	207	36 09	250	40 53	294	10 16	354
178	31 11	037	32 51	065	33 55	138	28 49	209	35 32	252	40 17	296	10 13	356

LHA ♈	Hc	Zn	Hc	Zn	Hc	Zn	Hc	Zn	Hc	Zn	Hc	Zn	Hc	Zn
	◆ DENEB		VEGA		◆ ARCTURUS		REGULUS		◆ POLLUX		CAPELLA		Schedar	
180	31 36	039	33 27	067	34 21	140	28 29	211	34 55	254	39 43	297	37 50	353
182	32 01	040	34 03	069	34 45	142	28 08	213	34 17	256	39 08	299	37 45	354
184	32 26	042	34 40	071	35 09	145	27 46	216	33 39	258	38 34	301	37 42	356
186	32 53	044	35 17	072	35 31	147	27 23	218	33 00	260	38 01	302	37 39	357
188	33 20	045	35 54	074	35 51	149	26 58	220	32 22	262	37 28	304	37 38	358
190	33 48	047	36 32	076	36 11	151	26 33	222	31 43	264	36 56	306	37 37	000
192	34 17	048	37 10	078	36 29	154	26 06	224	31 04	266	36 25	307	37 37	001
194	34 47	050	37 48	079	36 45	156	25 38	226	30 25	268	35 54	309	37 39	003
196	35 17	052	38 27	081	37 00	158	25 10	228	29 46	270	35 24	310	37 41	004
198	35 48	053	39 05	083	37 14	161	24 40	230	29 07	272	34 54	312	37 44	005
200	36 20	055	39 44	085	37 26	163	24 09	232	28 28	274	34 26	314	37 48	007
202	36 52	056	40 23	087	37 37	166	23 38	235	27 49	276	33 58	315	37 53	008
204	37 25	058	41 02	089	37 46	168	23 06	237	27 10	277	33 30	317	37 59	009
206	37 58	060	41 41	091	37 53	170	22 33	239	26 31	279	33 04	318	38 06	011
208	38 32	061	42 20	092	37 59	173	21 59	241	25 53	281	32 38	320	38 14	012
	Alpheratz		◆ DENEB		VEGA		◆ ARCTURUS		REGULUS		POLLUX		◆ CAPELLA	
210	12 05	025	39 07	063	42 59	094	38 03	175	21 25	243	25 15	283	32 14	321
212	12 21	026	39 42	065	43 38	096	38 05	177	20 50	245	24 37	285	31 50	323
214	12 39	028	40 17	066	44 17	098	38 06	180	20 14	247	23 59	287	31 27	325
216	12 58	030	40 53	068	44 56	100	38 06	182	19 38	249	23 22	288	31 04	326
218	13 18	032	41 30	070	45 34	102	38 03	185	19 01	251	22 45	290	30 43	328
220	13 39	033	42 06	071	46 12	104	37 59	187	18 24	253	22 09	292	30 23	329
222	14 01	035	42 44	073	46 50	106	37 54	189	17 47	255	21 33	294	30 03	331
224	14 24	037	43 21	075	47 27	109	37 46	192	17 09	256	20 57	296	29 44	332
226	14 48	039	43 59	077	48 04	111	37 37	194	16 31	258	20 22	297	29 27	334
228	15 13	040	44 37	078	48 40	113	37 27	197	15 52	260	19 48	299	29 10	335
230	15 38	042	45 16	080	49 16	115	37 15	199	15 14	262	19 14	301	28 54	337
232	16 05	044	45 54	082	49 51	117	37 02	201	14 35	264	18 41	303	28 40	339
234	16 33	046	46 33	084	50 25	120	36 47	204	13 56	266	18 08	304	28 26	340
236	17 01	047	47 12	085	50 59	122	36 30	206	13 17	268	17 36	306	28 13	342
238	17 30	049	47 51	087	51 32	124	36 12	208	12 38	270	17 05	308	28 01	343
	Alpheratz		◆ DENEB		VEGA		◆ ARCTURUS		Dubhe		POLLUX		◆ CAPELLA	
240	18 00	051	48 30	089	52 03	126	35 53	211	61 05	290	16 35	310	27 51	345
242	18 31	053	49 09	091	52 34	129	35 33	213	60 28	291	16 05	312	27 41	346
244	19 02	054	49 48	093	53 04	131	35 11	215	59 52	292	15 36	313	27 32	348
246	19 34	056	50 27	095	53 33	134	34 48	217	59 16	294	15 08	315	27 25	350
248	20 07	058	51 06	097	54 01	136	34 23	220	58 40	295	14 41	317	27 18	351
250	20 40	060	51 44	099	54 27	139	33 58	222	58 05	297	14 15	319	27 13	353
252	21 15	061	52 23	101	54 52	142	33 31	224	57 31	298	13 49	320	27 08	354
254	21 49	063	53 01	103	55 15	144	33 03	226	56 56	300	13 25	322	27 05	356
256	22 24	065	53 39	105	55 38	147	32 34	229	56 23	301	13 01	324	27 02	357
258	23 00	067	54 17	107	55 58	150	32 05	231	55 49	302	12 39	326	27 01	359
260	23 36	069	54 54	109	56 17	152	31 34	233	55 17	304	12 17	327	27 01	000
262	24 13	070	55 30	112	56 35	155	31 02	235	54 44	305	11 57	329	27 02	002
264	24 50	072	56 06	114	56 50	158	30 30	237	54 13	306	11 37	331	27 03	004
266	25 27	074	56 42	116	57 04	161	29 57	239	53 42	308	11 19	333	27 06	005
268	26 05	076	57 16	119	57 16	164	29 23	241	53 11	309	11 01	335	27 10	007
	◆ CAPELLA		Alpheratz		◆ DENEB		VEGA		◆ ARCTURUS		Alkaid		Dubhe	
270	27 15	008	26 43	078	57 50	121	57 26	166	28 48	243	54 22	267	52 41	311
272	27 22	010	27 21	079	58 23	123	57 34	169	28 13	245	53 43	269	52 12	312
274	27 29	011	28 00	081	58 55	126	57 41	172	27 38	247	53 04	270	51 43	313
276	27 37	013	28 38	083	59 27	128	57 45	175	27 01	249	52 25	272	51 15	315
278	27 46	014	29 17	085	59 57	131	57 47	178	26 24	251	51 46	274	50 47	316
280	27 56	016	29 56	087	60 25	134	57 48	181	25 47	253	51 07	276	50 20	317
282	28 08	018	30 35	089	60 53	136	57 46	184	25 10	255	50 28	278	49 54	318
284	28 20	019	31 14	091	61 19	139	57 43	187	24 32	257	49 50	280	49 28	320
286	28 33	021	31 53	092	61 44	142	57 37	190	23 53	259	49 11	281	49 04	321
288	28 48	022	32 32	094	62 07	145	57 29	193	23 15	261	48 33	283	48 39	322
290	29 03	024	33 11	096	62 29	148	57 20	195	22 36	263	47 55	285	48 16	324
292	29 19	025	33 50	098	62 49	151	57 09	198	21 57	265	47 18	286	47 53	325
294	29 36	027	34 28	100	63 07	154	56 55	201	21 18	267	46 40	288	47 31	326
296	29 55	028	35 07	102	63 23	157	56 40	204	20 39	269	46 03	290	47 10	328
298	30 14	030	35 45	104	63 38	160	56 24	207	20 00	271	45 27	291	46 49	329
	◆ CAPELLA		Hamal		Alpheratz		◆ DENEB		VEGA		◆ ARCTURUS		Dubhe	
300	30 34	032	21 32	080	36 23	106	63 50	163	56 05	209	19 21	273	46 29	330
302	30 55	033	22 11	082	37 00	108	64 00	166	55 45	212	18 42	274	46 10	331
304	31 17	035	22 49	084	37 37	110	64 08	170	55 24	215	18 03	276	45 52	333
306	31 39	036	23 28	086	38 13	112	64 15	173	55 01	218	17 25	278	45 35	334
308	32 03	038	24 07	088	38 49	115	64 18	176	54 36	220	16 46	280	45 18	335
310	32 27	039	24 46	089	39 24	117	64 20	179	54 10	223	16 08	282	45 02	337
312	32 52	041	25 25	091	39 59	119	64 19	182	53 43	225	15 30	284	44 47	338
314	33 18	043	26 05	093	40 33	121	64 17	186	53 15	228	14 52	286	44 33	339
316	33 45	044	26 43	095	41 06	123	64 12	189	52 45	230	14 14	287	44 19	341
318	34 13	046	27 22	097	41 38	125	64 05	192	52 15	233	13 37	289	44 07	342
320	34 41	047	28 01	099	42 09	128	63 55	195	51 43	235	13 01	291	43 55	343
322	35 10	049	28 39	101	42 40	130	63 44	198	51 11	237	12 24	293	43 44	344
324	35 40	051	29 18	103	43 09	132	63 31	202	50 37	240	11 49	295	43 34	346
326	36 11	052	29 56	105	43 38	134	63 15	205	50 03	242	11 13	297	43 25	347
328	36 42	054	30 33	107	44 05	137	62 58	208	49 28	244	10 39	298	43 16	348
	◆ POLLUX		CAPELLA		Hamal		◆ Alpheratz		DENEB		◆ VEGA		Alioth	
330	11 46	030	37 14	055	31 10	109	44 31	139	62 39	211	48 53	246	40 35	329
332	12 06	032	37 46	057	31 47	111	44 56	142	62 18	214	48 17	249	40 16	331
334	12 27	033	38 19	059	32 23	113	45 20	144	61 56	217	47 40	251	39 57	332
336	12 49	035	38 53	060	32 59	115	45 42	146	61 31	219	47 03	253	39 39	334
338	13 12	037	39 27	062	33 34	117	46 03	149	61 06	222	46 26	255	39 22	335
340	13 35	039	40 02	063	34 09	119	46 23	151	60 39	225	45 48	257	39 06	336
342	14 00	040	40 37	065	34 42	121	46 41	154	60 11	228	45 10	259	38 51	338
344	14 26	042	41 13	067	35 15	123	46 57	156	59 41	230	44 31	261	38 37	339
346	14 53	044	41 49	068	35 48	126	47 12	159	59 11	233	43 52	263	38 23	341
348	15 20	046	42 25	070	36 19	128	47 25	161	58 39	235	43 14	265	38 11	342
350	15 49	047	43 02	072	36 49	130	47 37	164	58 06	238	42 35	267	37 59	343
352	16 18	049	43 39	074	37 19	132	47 47	167	57 33	240	41 56	269	37 49	345
354	16 48	051	44 17	075	37 47	134	47 55	169	56 59	243	41 16	271	37 39	346
356	17 19	053	44 55	077	38 15	137	48 02	172	56 24	245	40 37	273	37 30	348
358	17 50	055	45 33	079	38 41	139	48 06	174	55 48	247	39 58	274	37 22	349

LAT 70°N

LHA ♈	Hc	Zn	Hc	Zn	Hc	Zn	Hc	Zn	Hc	Zn	Hc	Zn	Hc	Zn
	◆POLLUX		CAPELLA		Hamal		◆Alpheratz		DENEB		◆VEGA		Alioth	
0	17 49	056	46 01	079	39 52	141	49 09	177	55 32	251	39 13	277	36 16	351
2	18 23	058	46 42	081	40 18	143	49 10	180	54 53	253	38 32	279	36 10	352
4	18 58	060	47 22	083	40 42	145	49 10	182	54 13	255	37 51	281	36 04	353
6	19 34	061	48 03	085	41 04	148	49 07	185	53 34	257	37 11	282	36 00	355
8	20 10	063	48 44	087	41 26	150	49 03	188	52 53	259	36 31	284	35 57	356
10	20 47	065	49 25	089	41 45	153	48 56	190	52 13	261	35 52	286	35 54	357
12	21 25	067	50 06	090	42 03	155	48 48	193	51 32	263	35 12	288	35 53	359
14	22 03	068	50 47	092	42 20	157	48 38	196	50 51	265	34 33	289	35 53	000
16	22 41	070	51 28	094	42 35	160	48 26	198	50 10	267	33 55	291	35 53	002
18	23 20	072	52 09	096	42 48	162	48 12	201	49 29	269	33 17	293	35 55	003
20	23 59	074	52 50	098	43 00	165	47 57	203	48 48	271	32 39	295	35 58	004
22	24 39	076	53 30	100	43 09	167	47 40	206	48 07	273	32 02	296	36 01	006
24	25 19	077	54 10	102	43 18	170	47 21	208	47 26	275	31 26	298	36 06	007
26	25 59	079	54 50	104	43 24	172	47 01	211	46 46	277	30 50	300	36 12	009
28	26 39	081	55 30	106	43 28	175	46 39	213	46 05	278	30 14	301	36 18	010
	Alioth		◆POLLUX		CAPELLA		◆Hamal		Alpheratz		DENEB		◆VEGA	
30	36 26	011	27 20	083	56 09	109	43 31	177	46 15	216	45 24	280	29 40	303
32	36 34	013	28 01	085	56 48	111	43 32	180	45 51	218	44 44	282	29 05	305
34	36 44	014	28 42	087	57 26	113	43 31	183	45 24	221	44 04	284	28 32	306
36	36 54	015	29 23	088	58 03	115	43 28	185	44 57	223	43 24	285	27 59	308
38	37 06	017	30 04	090	58 40	118	43 24	188	44 28	226	42 45	287	27 27	310
40	37 18	018	30 45	092	59 16	120	43 18	190	43 58	228	42 06	289	26 56	311
42	37 31	020	31 26	094	59 51	123	43 09	193	43 27	230	41 27	290	26 26	313
44	37 45	021	32 07	096	60 25	125	43 00	195	42 55	232	40 49	292	25 56	315
46	38 01	022	32 47	098	60 58	128	42 48	198	42 22	235	40 11	294	25 27	316
48	38 17	024	33 28	100	61 29	131	42 35	200	41 48	237	39 34	295	24 59	318
50	38 34	025	34 08	102	62 00	133	42 20	203	41 13	239	38 57	297	24 32	319
52	38 52	027	34 48	104	62 29	136	42 03	205	40 38	241	38 20	299	24 06	321
54	39 10	028	35 28	106	62 57	139	41 45	207	40 01	243	37 45	300	23 40	323
56	39 30	029	36 07	108	63 23	142	41 26	210	39 24	246	37 10	302	23 16	324
58	39 51	031	36 46	110	63 47	145	41 04	212	38 47	248	36 35	303	22 53	326
	Alioth		◆POLLUX		CAPELLA		◆Hamal		Alpheratz		DENEB		◆VEGA	
60	40 12	032	37 24	112	64 10	148	40 42	215	38 08	250	36 01	305	22 30	328
62	40 34	033	38 02	114	64 31	151	40 18	217	37 30	252	35 28	307	22 09	329
64	40 57	035	38 39	116	64 50	154	39 53	219	36 50	254	34 55	308	21 48	331
66	41 21	036	39 16	118	65 07	157	39 26	222	36 11	256	34 23	310	21 29	333
68	41 46	038	39 51	120	65 21	161	38 58	224	35 31	258	33 52	311	21 10	334
70	42 11	039	40 26	123	65 34	164	38 29	226	34 51	260	33 22	313	20 53	336
72	42 37	040	41 01	125	65 44	167	37 59	228	34 10	262	32 52	314	20 37	337
74	43 04	042	41 34	127	65 52	171	37 28	231	33 29	264	32 23	316	20 22	339
76	43 32	043	42 06	129	65 57	174	36 56	233	32 48	266	31 55	318	20 08	341
78	44 01	045	42 37	132	66 00	178	36 22	235	32 08	268	31 28	319	19 55	342
80	44 30	046	43 08	134	66 01	181	35 48	237	31 26	269	31 01	321	19 43	344
82	45 00	047	43 36	136	65 59	184	35 13	239	30 45	271	30 36	322	19 32	346
84	45 30	049	44 04	139	65 54	188	34 38	241	30 04	273	30 11	324	19 23	347
86	46 02	050	44 31	141	65 48	191	34 01	243	29 24	275	29 47	325	19 14	349
88	46 34	052	44 56	143	65 39	194	33 24	246	28 43	277	29 24	327	19 07	351
	Alioth		◆REGULUS		POLLUX		◆CAPELLA		Alpheratz		◆DENEB		VEGA	
90	47 06	053	20 27	112	45 20	146	65 27	198	28 02	279	29 03	329	19 01	352
92	47 39	055	21 04	114	45 42	148	65 13	201	27 22	281	28 42	330	18 56	354
94	48 13	056	21 41	116	46 03	151	64 58	204	26 41	282	28 22	332	18 52	356
96	48 47	058	22 18	118	46 22	153	64 40	208	26 01	284	28 03	333	18 50	357
98	49 22	059	22 54	120	46 40	156	64 20	211	25 22	286	27 45	335	18 48	359
100	49 58	060	23 29	122	46 56	158	63 58	214	24 42	288	27 28	336	18 48	001
102	50 34	062	24 03	124	47 10	161	63 34	217	24 04	290	27 12	338	18 49	002
104	51 10	063	24 36	127	47 22	164	63 09	220	23 25	291	26 57	339	18 51	004
106	51 47	065	25 09	129	47 33	166	62 42	223	22 47	293	26 43	341	18 54	005
108	52 25	066	25 40	131	47 42	169	62 13	225	22 10	295	26 30	343	18 59	007
110	53 03	068	26 11	133	47 49	171	61 43	228	21 33	297	26 18	344	19 05	009
112	53 41	070	26 41	135	47 54	174	61 12	231	20 56	298	26 07	346	19 11	010
114	54 19	071	27 09	137	47 58	177	60 40	234	20 20	300	25 58	347	19 19	012
116	54 58	073	27 36	139	47 59	179	60 06	236	19 45	302	25 49	349	19 29	014
118	55 38	074	28 03	141	47 59	182	59 32	239	19 11	304	25 42	350	19 39	015
	◆VEGA		ARCTURUS		◆REGULUS		POLLUX		◆CAPELLA		Alpheratz		DENEB	
120	19 50	017	16 32	079	28 28	144	47 57	185	58 56	241	18 37	305	25 35	352
122	20 03	019	17 12	081	28 51	146	47 52	187	58 20	243	18 04	307	25 30	353
124	20 16	020	17 53	083	29 14	148	47 46	190	57 43	246	17 31	309	25 26	355
126	20 31	022	18 34	085	29 35	150	47 38	192	57 05	248	17 00	311	25 23	357
128	20 47	024	19 15	087	29 55	152	47 29	195	56 27	250	16 29	312	25 21	358
130	21 04	025	19 56	089	30 13	155	47 17	198	55 48	253	15 59	314	25 20	000
132	21 22	027	20 37	091	30 30	157	47 04	200	55 08	255	15 30	316	25 20	001
134	21 41	028	21 18	093	30 46	159	46 49	203	54 28	257	15 02	318	25 22	003
136	22 01	030	21 59	094	30 59	161	46 32	205	53 48	259	14 35	319	25 24	004
138	22 22	032	22 40	096	31 12	164	46 14	208	53 08	261	14 08	321	25 28	006
140	22 44	033	23 20	098	31 23	166	45 54	210	52 27	263	13 43	323	25 33	007
142	23 07	035	24 01	100	31 32	168	45 32	213	51 47	265	13 19	325	25 38	009
144	23 31	037	24 41	102	31 39	170	45 09	215	51 06	267	12 55	326	25 45	011
146	23 56	038	25 21	104	31 45	173	44 45	218	50 25	269	12 33	328	25 53	012
148	24 22	040	26 01	106	31 50	175	44 19	220	49 44	271	12 12	330	26 03	014
	DENEB		◆VEGA		ARCTURUS		◆REGULUS		POLLUX		◆CAPELLA		Schedar	
150	26 13	015	24 49	042	26 40	108	31 53	177	43 52	222	49 03	273	39 53	332
152	26 24	017	25 17	043	27 19	110	31 54	180	43 24	225	48 22	274	39 34	334
154	26 36	018	25 45	045	27 57	112	31 53	182	42 54	227	47 41	276	39 17	335
156	26 50	020	26 15	047	28 35	114	31 51	184	42 24	229	47 00	278	39 00	336
158	27 04	021	26 45	048	29 12	116	31 47	187	41 52	232	46 19	280	38 44	338
160	27 20	023	27 16	050	29 49	118	31 41	189	41 19	234	45 39	281	38 29	339
162	27 36	024	27 48	051	30 24	120	31 34	191	40 46	236	44 59	283	38 15	341
164	27 54	026	28 20	053	31 00	122	31 25	193	40 11	238	44 19	285	38 02	342
166	28 12	028	28 53	055	31 34	124	31 15	196	39 36	241	43 40	287	37 49	343
168	28 32	029	29 27	056	32 07	127	31 03	198	39 00	243	43 00	288	37 38	345
170	28 52	031	30 02	058	32 40	129	30 50	200	38 23	245	42 22	290	37 28	346
172	29 14	032	30 37	060	33 11	131	30 35	203	37 45	247	41 43	292	37 18	347
174	29 36	034	31 13	061	33 42	133	30 18	205	37 07	249	41 05	293	37 10	349
176	29 59	035	31 49	063	34 11	135	30 00	207	36 29	251	40 28	295	37 02	350
178	30 24	037	32 26	065	34 40	137	29 41	209	35 50	253	39 51	297	36 56	352

LHA ♈	Hc	Zn	Hc	Zn	Hc	Zn	Hc	Zn	Hc	Zn	Hc	Zn	Hc	Zn
	◆DENEB		VEGA		◆ARCTURUS		REGULUS		◆POLLUX		CAPELLA		Schedar	
180	30 49	039	33 03	067	35 07	140	29 20	211	35 10	255	39 15	298	36 50	353
182	31 15	040	33 41	068	35 33	142	28 58	214	34 30	257	38 39	300	36 46	354
184	31 42	042	34 19	070	35 58	144	28 35	216	33 50	259	38 03	301	36 42	356
186	32 09	043	34 58	072	36 21	146	28 10	218	33 10	261	37 29	303	36 39	357
188	32 38	045	35 37	073	36 43	149	27 44	220	32 29	263	36 54	305	36 38	358
190	33 07	046	36 17	075	37 03	151	27 17	222	31 48	265	36 21	306	36 37	000
192	33 37	048	36 57	077	37 22	153	26 49	224	31 08	267	35 48	308	36 37	001
194	34 08	049	37 37	079	37 40	156	26 20	227	30 27	269	35 16	309	36 39	003
196	34 39	051	38 17	080	37 56	158	25 49	229	29 45	271	34 45	311	36 41	004
198	35 12	053	38 58	082	38 11	161	25 18	231	29 04	272	34 14	312	36 44	005
200	35 45	054	39 39	084	38 23	163	24 46	233	28 23	274	33 44	314	36 49	007
202	36 18	056	40 19	086	38 35	165	24 13	235	27 43	276	33 15	316	36 54	008
204	36 53	057	41 00	088	38 44	168	23 39	237	27 02	278	32 47	317	37 00	009
206	37 28	059	41 41	090	38 52	170	23 04	239	26 21	280	32 19	319	37 07	011
208	38 03	061	42 23	092	38 58	173	22 28	241	25 41	282	31 52	320	37 15	012
	Alpheratz		◆DENEB		VEGA		◆ARCTURUS		REGULUS		POLLUX		◆CAPELLA	
210	11 10	024	38 39	062	43 04	093	39 03	175	21 52	243	25 01	283	31 27	322
212	11 28	026	39 16	064	43 44	095	39 05	177	21 15	245	24 21	285	31 02	323
214	11 46	028	39 53	066	44 25	097	39 06	180	20 38	247	23 42	287	30 38	325
216	12 06	030	40 30	067	45 06	099	39 05	182	20 00	249	23 03	289	30 14	326
218	12 27	031	41 08	069	45 46	101	39 03	185	19 21	251	22 24	291	29 52	328
220	12 49	033	41 47	071	46 26	103	38 59	187	18 42	253	21 46	292	29 31	330
222	13 12	035	42 26	072	47 06	105	38 53	190	18 03	255	21 08	294	29 11	331
224	13 36	037	43 05	074	47 45	107	38 45	192	17 23	257	20 31	296	28 51	333
226	14 01	038	43 45	076	48 24	110	38 36	194	16 43	259	19 54	298	28 33	334
228	14 27	040	44 25	077	49 03	112	38 24	197	16 02	261	19 18	299	28 16	336
230	14 54	042	45 05	079	49 41	114	38 12	199	15 22	263	18 43	301	27 59	337
232	15 22	044	45 45	081	50 18	116	37 57	202	14 41	264	18 08	303	27 44	339
234	15 51	045	46 26	083	50 54	118	37 42	204	14 00	266	17 34	305	27 29	340
236	16 20	047	47 06	084	51 30	121	37 24	206	13 19	268	17 01	306	27 16	342
238	16 51	049	47 47	086	52 05	123	37 05	209	12 38	270	16 28	308	27 04	343
	Alpheratz		◆DENEB		VEGA		Rasalhague		◆ARCTURUS		Dubhe		◆CAPELLA	
240	17 22	051	48 28	088	52 39	125	30 37	153	36 45	211	60 44	291	26 53	345
242	17 54	052	49 09	090	53 12	128	30 56	155	36 23	213	60 06	293	26 43	347
244	18 27	054	49 50	092	53 43	130	31 12	157	36 00	216	59 28	294	26 34	348
246	19 01	056	50 31	094	54 14	133	31 27	159	35 35	218	58 51	295	26 26	350
248	19 35	058	51 12	096	54 44	135	31 41	162	35 09	220	58 14	297	26 19	351
250	20 10	059	51 53	098	55 12	138	31 53	164	34 42	222	57 37	298	26 13	353
252	20 46	061	52 34	100	55 39	141	32 04	166	34 14	225	57 02	300	26 08	354
254	21 22	063	53 14	102	56 04	143	32 13	169	33 44	227	56 26	301	26 05	356
256	21 59	065	53 54	104	56 28	146	32 20	171	33 14	229	55 51	302	26 02	357
258	22 36	066	54 34	106	56 50	149	32 26	173	32 43	231	55 17	304	26 01	359
260	23 14	068	55 13	108	57 10	152	32 30	175	32 10	233	54 43	305	26 01	000
262	23 52	070	55 52	110	57 29	154	32 32	178	31 37	235	54 09	306	26 02	002
264	24 31	072	56 30	113	57 46	157	32 33	180	31 03	238	53 37	308	26 04	004
266	25 10	074	57 08	115	58 01	160	32 32	182	30 28	240	53 04	309	26 07	005
268	25 50	075	57 44	117	58 14	163	32 30	185	29 52	242	52 33	310	26 11	007
	◆CAPELLA		Alpheratz		◆DENEB		VEGA		◆ARCTURUS		Alkaid		Dubhe	
270	26 16	008	26 30	077	58 20	120	58 24	166	29 15	244	54 25	268	52 02	312
272	26 22	010	27 10	079	58 56	122	58 33	169	28 38	246	53 44	270	51 31	313
274	26 30	011	27 50	081	59 30	125	58 40	172	28 00	248	53 03	272	51 01	314
276	26 38	013	28 31	083	60 03	127	58 45	175	27 22	250	52 22	274	50 32	315
278	26 48	014	29 12	084	60 35	130	58 47	178	26 43	252	51 41	275	50 04	317
280	26 59	016	29 53	086	61 06	132	58 48	181	26 04	254	51 00	277	49 36	318
282	27 11	017	30 33	088	61 36	135	58 46	184	25 25	256	50 19	279	49 09	319
284	27 23	019	31 15	090	62 04	138	58 42	187	24 45	258	49 39	281	48 42	321
286	27 37	021	31 56	092	62 31	141	58 36	190	24 04	260	48 59	282	48 17	322
288	27 52	022	32 37	094	62 56	144	58 28	193	23 24	262	48 19	284	47 52	323
290	28 08	024	33 17	096	63 19	147	58 18	196	22 43	264	47 39	286	47 27	324
292	28 25	025	33 58	098	63 41	150	58 05	199	22 02	265	47 00	288	47 04	326
294	28 43	027	34 39	100	64 01	153	57 51	202	21 21	267	46 21	289	46 41	327
296	29 02	028	35 19	102	64 18	156	57 35	205	20 40	269	45 42	291	46 19	328
298	29 22	030	35 59	104	64 34	159	57 17	207	19 59	271	45 04	292	45 58	329
	◆CAPELLA		Hamal		Alpheratz		◆DENEB		VEGA		◆ARCTURUS		Dubhe	
300	29 43	031	21 22	080	36 39	106	64 47	163	56 57	210	19 18	273	45 37	331
302	30 04	033	22 02	082	37 18	108	64 59	166	56 36	213	18 37	275	45 18	332
304	30 27	034	22 43	083	37 57	110	65 07	169	56 13	216	17 56	277	44 59	333
306	30 51	036	23 24	085	38 36	112	65 14	172	55 48	218	17 16	279	44 41	335
308	31 15	038	24 05	087	39 13	114	65 18	176	55 22	221	16 35	280	44 23	336
310	31 41	039	24 46	089	39 51	116	65 20	179	54 54	224	15 55	282	44 07	337
312	32 07	041	25 27	091	40 27	118	65 19	183	54 25	226	15 15	284	43 51	338
314	32 34	042	26 08	093	41 03	120	65 16	186	53 55	229	14 35	286	43 37	340
316	33 02	044	26 49	095	41 38	122	65 11	189	53 23	231	13 56	288	43 23	341
318	33 31	045	27 29	097	42 12	125	65 03	193	52 51	234	13 17	290	43 10	342
320	34 00	047	28 10	098	42 46	127	64 53	196	52 17	236	12 39	291	42 57	343
322	34 31	048	28 51	100	43 18	129	64 41	199	51 43	238	12 01	293	42 46	345
324	35 02	050	29 31	102	43 49	131	64 26	202	51 07	241	11 23	295	42 36	346
326	35 34	052	30 11	104	44 20	134	64 09	206	50 31	243	10 46	297	42 26	347
328	36 06	053	30 50	106	44 49	136	63 51	209	49 54	245	10 10	299	42 18	348
	◆POLLUX		CAPELLA		Hamal		◆Alpheratz		DENEB		◆VEGA		Alioth	
330	10 54	030	36 39	055	31 30	108	45 17	138	63 30	212	49 16	247	39 44	330
332	11 14	031	37 13	056	32 08	110	45 43	141	63 08	215	48 38	250	39 23	331
334	11 36	033	37 48	058	32 46	112	46 08	143	62 43	218	48 00	252	39 04	333
336	11 59	035	38 23	060	33 24	114	46 32	146	62 17	221	47 20	254	38 46	334
338	12 24	037	38 58	061	34 01	116	46 54	148	61 50	223	46 41	256	38 28	335
340	12 49	039	39 35	063	34 38	119	47 15	151	61 21	226	46 01	258	38 11	337
342	13 15	040	40 11	064	35 13	121	47 34	153	60 51	229	45 20	260	37 56	338
344	13 42	042	40 49	066	35 48	123	47 52	156	60 19	232	44 40	262	37 41	339
346	14 10	044	41 26	068	36 22	125	48 08	158	59 46	234	43 59	264	37 27	341
348	14 38	046	42 04	069	36 55	127	48 22	161	59 13	237	43 18	266	37 14	342
350	15 08	047	42 43	071	37 28	129	48 35	164	58 38	239	42 37	268	37 02	344
352	15 39	049	43 22	073	37 59	132	48 45	166	58 02	242	41 56	270	36 51	345
354	16 10	051	44 01	074	38 29	134	48 54	169	57 26	244	41 15	272	36 40	346
356	16 42	053	44 41	076	38 58	136	49 01	172	56 48	246	40 34	273	36 31	348
358	17 15	054	45 21	078	39 26	138	49 06	174	56 10	249	39 53	275	36 23	349

 LAT 69°N

LHA ♈	◆ POLLUX	CAPELLA	Hamal	◆ Alpheratz	DENEB	◆ VEGA	Alioth
	Hc Zn	Hc Zn	Hc Zn	Hc Zn	Hc Zn	Hc Zn	Hc Zn
0	17 15 056	45 50 078	40 39 140	50 09 177	55 51 252	39 05 278	35 17 351
1	17 33 057	46 11 079	40 52 141	50 10 178	55 30 253	38 43 279	35 13 351
2	17 51 058	46 32 080	41 06 143	50 10 180	55 10 254	38 22 280	35 10 352
3	18 10 058	46 53 081	41 18 144	50 10 181	54 49 255	38 01 281	35 07 353
4	18 28 059	47 14 082	41 31 145	50 10 182	54 28 257	37 40 281	35 05 353
5	18 46 060	47 36 083	41 43 146	50 09 184	54 07 258	37 19 282	35 02 354
6	19 05 061	47 57 084	41 55 147	50 07 185	53 46 259	36 58 283	35 00 355
7	19 24 062	48 19 085	42 06 149	50 05 186	53 25 260	36 37 284	34 58 355
8	19 43 063	48 40 086	42 17 150	50 02 188	53 04 261	36 16 285	34 57 356
9	20 02 064	49 01 086	42 28 151	49 59 189	52 42 262	35 56 286	34 56 357
10	20 22 065	49 23 087	42 38 152	49 55 190	52 21 263	35 35 287	34 54 357
11	20 41 065	49 44 088	42 48 153	49 51 192	52 00 264	35 14 287	34 54 358
12	21 01 066	50 06 089	42 58 155	49 46 193	51 38 265	34 54 288	34 53 359
13	21 21 067	50 27 090	43 07 156	49 41 195	51 17 266	34 33 289	34 53 000
14	21 40 068	50 49 091	43 15 157	49 36 196	50 56 267	34 13 290	34 53 000

LHA ♈	Alioth	◆ POLLUX	CAPELLA	Hamal	◆ Alpheratz	DENEB	◆ VEGA
15	34 53 001	22 00 069	51 10 092	43 23 158	49 30 197	50 34 268	33 53 291
16	34 53 002	22 21 070	51 32 093	43 31 160	49 23 199	50 13 268	33 33 292
17	34 54 002	22 41 071	51 53 094	43 38 161	49 16 200	49 51 269	33 13 293
18	34 55 003	23 01 072	52 15 095	43 45 162	49 08 201	49 30 270	32 53 293
19	34 56 004	23 22 072	52 36 096	43 52 163	49 00 202	49 08 271	32 34 294
20	34 58 004	23 42 073	52 58 097	43 57 165	48 52 204	48 47 272	32 14 295
21	35 00 005	24 03 074	53 19 098	44 03 166	48 43 205	48 25 273	31 55 296
22	35 02 006	24 24 075	53 40 099	44 08 167	48 34 206	48 04 274	31 35 297
23	35 04 006	24 44 076	54 01 100	44 12 168	48 24 208	47 42 275	31 16 298
24	35 06 007	25 05 077	54 22 101	44 17 170	48 14 209	47 21 276	30 57 298
25	35 09 008	25 26 078	54 44 102	44 20 171	48 03 210	46 59 277	30 39 299
26	35 12 008	25 47 079	55 05 103	44 23 172	47 52 212	46 38 278	30 20 300
27	35 15 009	26 08 080	55 25 104	44 26 174	47 40 213	46 17 278	30 01 301
28	35 19 010	26 30 081	55 46 105	44 28 175	47 29 214	45 56 279	29 43 302
29	35 23 010	26 51 081	56 07 106	44 30 176	47 16 215	45 34 280	29 25 303

LHA ♈	Alioth	◆ POLLUX	ALDEBARAN	◆ Hamal	Alpheratz	DENEB	◆ VEGA
30	35 27 011	27 12 082	32 08 134	44 31 177	47 04 217	45 13 281	29 07 303
31	35 31 012	27 33 083	32 24 135	44 32 179	46 51 218	44 52 282	28 49 304
32	35 36 013	27 55 084	32 39 137	44 32 180	46 37 219	44 31 283	28 31 305
33	35 40 013	28 16 085	32 53 138	44 32 181	46 24 220	44 10 284	28 14 306
34	35 45 014	28 38 086	33 08 139	44 31 183	46 10 221	43 49 285	27 56 307
35	35 51 015	28 59 087	33 22 140	44 30 184	45 55 223	43 29 285	27 39 308
36	35 56 015	29 21 088	33 35 141	44 28 185	45 40 224	43 08 286	27 22 308
37	36 02 016	29 42 089	33 49 142	44 26 186	45 25 225	42 47 287	27 05 309
38	36 08 017	30 04 090	34 02 143	44 23 188	45 10 226	42 27 288	26 49 310
39	36 14 017	30 25 091	34 14 144	44 20 189	44 54 227	42 06 289	26 32 311
40	36 21 018	30 47 092	34 27 145	44 17 190	44 38 229	41 46 290	26 16 312
41	36 28 019	31 08 093	34 39 147	44 13 192	44 22 230	41 26 290	26 00 312
42	36 35 019	31 30 093	34 51 148	44 08 193	44 05 231	41 06 291	25 45 313
43	36 42 020	31 51 094	35 02 149	44 03 194	43 49 232	40 46 292	25 29 314
44	36 49 021	32 12 095	35 13 150	43 58 195	43 32 233	40 26 293	25 14 315

LHA ♈	Alioth	◆ POLLUX	ALDEBARAN	◆ Hamal	Alpheratz	DENEB	◆ VEGA
45	36 57 021	32 34 096	35 23 151	43 52 197	43 14 234	40 06 294	24 59 316
46	37 05 022	32 55 097	35 33 152	43 45 198	42 57 236	39 47 294	24 44 316
47	37 13 023	33 16 098	35 43 154	43 38 199	42 39 237	39 27 295	24 29 317
48	37 22 023	33 38 099	35 53 155	43 31 200	42 21 238	39 08 296	24 14 318
49	37 30 024	33 59 100	36 02 156	43 23 202	42 02 239	38 48 297	24 00 319
50	37 39 025	34 20 101	36 10 157	43 15 203	41 44 240	38 29 298	23 46 320
51	37 48 026	34 41 102	36 18 158	43 07 204	41 25 241	38 10 298	23 32 321
52	37 58 026	35 02 103	36 26 159	42 58 205	41 06 242	37 51 299	23 19 321
53	38 07 027	35 23 104	36 34 161	42 48 207	40 47 243	37 33 300	23 06 322
54	38 17 028	35 44 105	36 41 162	42 38 208	40 28 244	37 14 301	22 53 323
55	38 27 028	36 05 106	36 47 163	42 28 209	40 08 245	36 56 302	22 40 324
56	38 38 029	36 25 107	36 53 164	42 18 210	39 49 246	36 38 302	22 27 325
57	38 48 030	36 46 108	36 59 165	42 07 211	39 29 247	36 20 303	22 15 325
58	38 59 030	37 06 109	37 04 167	41 55 213	39 09 248	36 02 304	22 03 326
59	39 10 031	37 26 110	37 09 168	41 43 214	38 49 250	35 44 305	21 51 327

LHA ♈	Alioth	◆ POLLUX	ALDEBARAN	◆ Hamal	Alpheratz	DENEB	◆ VEGA
60	39 21 032	37 46 111	37 13 169	41 31 215	38 29 251	35 26 306	21 39 328
61	39 32 032	38 06 112	37 17 170	41 19 216	38 08 252	35 09 306	21 28 329
62	39 44 033	38 26 113	37 21 171	41 06 217	37 48 253	34 52 307	21 17 329
63	39 56 034	38 46 114	37 24 173	40 52 219	37 27 254	34 35 308	21 06 330
64	40 08 034	39 05 115	37 26 174	40 39 220	37 07 255	34 18 309	20 56 331
65	40 20 035	39 25 116	37 28 175	40 25 221	36 46 256	34 01 309	20 45 332
66	40 33 036	39 44 118	37 30 176	40 11 222	36 25 257	33 45 310	20 35 333
67	40 45 036	40 03 119	37 31 177	39 56 223	36 04 258	33 28 311	20 26 334
68	40 58 037	40 22 120	37 32 179	39 41 224	35 43 259	33 12 312	20 16 334
69	41 11 038	40 40 121	37 32 180	39 26 226	35 22 260	32 56 313	20 07 335
70	41 24 038	40 58 122	37 32 181	39 10 227	35 01 261	32 41 313	19 58 336
71	41 38 039	41 17 123	37 32 182	38 55 228	34 40 262	32 25 314	19 50 337
72	41 52 040	41 35 124	37 31 183	38 39 229	34 18 262	32 10 315	19 41 338
73	42 06 041	41 52 125	37 29 185	38 22 230	33 57 263	31 55 316	19 33 338
74	42 20 041	42 10 126	37 27 186	38 06 231	33 36 264	31 40 316	19 26 339

LHA ♈	Alioth	◆ REGULUS	PROCYON	◆ ALDEBARAN	Hamal	Alpheratz	◆ DENEB
75	42 34 042	15 38 098	20 58 137	37 25 187	37 49 232	33 14 265	31 25 317
76	42 48 043	16 00 099	21 12 138	37 22 188	37 32 233	32 53 266	31 10 318
77	43 03 043	16 21 099	21 26 139	37 19 189	37 14 235	32 31 267	30 56 319
78	43 18 044	16 42 100	21 40 140	37 15 191	36 57 236	32 10 268	30 42 320
79	43 33 045	17 03 101	21 54 141	37 11 192	36 39 237	31 48 269	30 28 320
80	43 48 045	17 24 102	22 08 142	37 06 193	36 21 238	31 27 270	30 15 321
81	44 03 046	17 45 103	22 21 143	37 01 194	36 02 239	31 05 271	30 01 322
82	44 19 047	18 06 104	22 34 144	36 55 195	35 44 240	30 44 272	29 48 323
83	44 35 047	18 27 105	22 46 145	36 49 197	35 25 241	30 22 273	29 35 323
84	44 51 048	18 47 106	22 58 146	36 43 198	35 06 242	30 01 274	29 23 324
85	45 07 049	19 08 107	23 10 147	36 36 199	34 47 243	29 39 275	29 10 325
86	45 23 050	19 29 108	23 21 148	36 29 200	34 28 244	29 18 276	28 58 326
87	45 40 050	19 49 109	23 33 149	36 22 201	34 08 245	28 57 277	28 46 327
88	45 56 051	20 09 110	23 43 150	36 13 203	33 49 246	28 35 277	28 34 327
89	46 13 052	20 29 111	23 54 151	36 05 204	33 29 247	28 14 278	28 23 328

LHA ♈	Alioth	◆ REGULUS	PROCYON	BETELGEUSE	◆ ALDEBARAN	Hamal	◆ DENEB
	Hc Zn	Hc Zn	Hc Zn	Hc Zn	Hc Zn	Hc Zn	Hc Zn
90	46 30 052	20 49 112	24 04 153	28 24 181	35 56 205	33 09 248	28 11 329
91	46 47 053	21 09 113	24 14 154	28 24 182	35 47 206	32 49 249	28 00 330
92	47 04 054	21 29 114	24 23 155	28 23 183	35 37 207	32 29 250	27 50 330
93	47 22 054	21 48 115	24 32 156	28 21 185	35 27 208	32 09 251	27 39 331
94	47 39 055	22 08 116	24 41 157	28 19 186	35 17 210	31 48 252	27 29 332
95	47 57 056	22 27 117	24 49 158	28 17 187	35 06 211	31 28 253	27 19 333
96	48 15 057	22 46 118	24 57 159	28 14 188	34 55 212	31 07 254	27 09 333
97	48 33 057	23 05 119	25 04 160	28 11 189	34 43 213	30 46 255	27 00 334
98	48 51 058	23 24 120	25 11 161	28 07 190	34 32 214	30 26 256	26 50 335
99	49 09 059	23 42 121	25 18 162	28 03 191	34 19 215	30 05 257	26 41 336
100	49 28 059	24 01 122	25 25 163	27 59 192	34 07 216	29 44 258	26 33 337
101	49 46 060	24 19 123	25 31 164	27 54 193	33 54 217	29 23 259	26 24 337
102	50 05 061	24 37 124	25 36 166	27 49 195	33 41 219	29 01 260	26 16 338
103	50 24 062	24 54 125	25 41 167	27 43 196	33 27 220	28 40 261	26 08 339
104	50 43 062	25 12 126	25 46 168	27 37 197	33 13 221	28 19 262	26 01 340

LHA ♈	Alioth	◆ REGULUS	PROCYON	BETELGEUSE	◆ CAPELLA	Hamal	◆ DENEB
105	51 02 063	25 29 127	25 50 169	27 31 198	63 40 222	27 58 263	25 53 340
106	51 21 064	25 46 128	25 54 170	27 24 199	63 25 224	27 36 264	25 46 341
107	51 41 065	26 03 129	25 58 171	27 17 200	63 10 225	27 15 265	25 39 342
108	52 00 065	26 19 130	26 01 172	27 09 201	62 55 227	26 53 266	25 33 343
109	52 20 066	26 36 131	26 04 173	27 01 202	62 39 228	26 32 267	25 26 343
110	52 39 067	26 52 132	26 06 174	26 53 203	62 23 230	26 10 268	25 20 344
111	52 59 068	27 07 133	26 08 176	26 44 205	62 06 231	25 49 269	25 15 345
112	53 19 068	27 23 135	26 09 177	26 35 206	61 49 232	25 27 270	25 09 346
113	53 39 069	27 38 136	26 10 178	26 25 207	61 32 234	25 06 271	25 04 347
114	53 59 070	27 53 137	26 11 179	26 16 208	61 15 235	24 44 272	24 59 347
115	54 20 071	28 07 138	26 11 180	26 05 209	60 57 236	24 23 272	24 55 348
116	54 40 071	28 22 139	26 11 181	25 55 210	60 39 238	24 01 273	24 50 349
117	55 00 072	28 36 140	26 10 182	25 44 211	60 21 239	23 40 274	24 46 350
118	55 21 073	28 49 141	26 09 183	25 33 212	60 02 240	23 19 275	24 43 350
119	55 41 074	29 03 142	26 08 184	25 21 213	59 43 241	22 57 276	24 39 351

LHA ♈	◆ VEGA	ARCTURUS	◆ REGULUS	PROCYON	◆ CAPELLA	Schedar	DENEB
120	18 53 017	16 21 079	29 16 143	26 06 186	59 24 243	45 30 312	24 36 352
121	18 59 018	16 42 080	29 29 144	26 04 187	59 05 244	45 14 313	24 33 353
122	19 06 019	17 03 081	29 41 145	26 01 188	58 46 245	44 59 314	24 30 353
123	19 13 019	17 24 082	29 53 146	25 58 189	58 26 246	44 43 314	24 28 354
124	19 20 020	17 46 083	30 05 148	25 54 190	58 07 247	44 28 315	24 26 355
125	19 28 021	18 07 084	30 16 149	25 50 191	57 47 248	44 13 316	24 24 356
126	19 35 022	18 28 085	30 27 150	25 46 192	57 27 250	43 58 316	24 23 357
127	19 44 023	18 50 086	30 38 151	25 41 193	57 06 251	43 43 317	24 22 357
128	19 52 023	19 11 087	30 48 152	25 36 194	56 46 252	43 29 318	24 21 358
129	20 01 024	19 33 087	30 58 153	25 31 195	56 26 253	43 14 318	24 20 359
130	20 10 025	19 54 088	31 07 154	25 25 197	56 05 254	43 00 319	24 20 000
131	20 19 026	20 16 089	31 16 155	25 19 198	55 44 255	42 46 320	24 20 000
132	20 28 027	20 37 090	31 25 157	25 12 199	55 23 256	42 32 321	24 20 001
133	20 38 027	20 59 091	31 34 158	25 05 200	55 02 257	42 19 321	24 21 002
134	20 48 028	21 20 092	31 42 159	24 57 201	54 41 258	42 05 322	24 22 003

LHA ♈	DENEB	◆ VEGA	ARCTURUS	◆ REGULUS	PROCYON	◆ CAPELLA	Schedar
135	24 23 003	20 59 029	21 42 093	31 49 160	24 49 202	54 20 259	41 52 323
136	24 24 004	21 09 030	22 03 094	31 56 161	24 41 203	53 59 260	41 39 323
137	24 26 005	21 20 031	22 25 095	32 03 162	24 32 204	53 38 261	41 26 324
138	24 28 006	21 31 032	22 46 096	32 09 163	24 23 205	53 17 262	41 14 325
139	24 31 007	21 43 032	23 07 097	32 15 165	24 14 206	52 55 263	41 02 325
140	24 33 007	21 54 033	23 29 098	32 21 166	24 04 207	52 34 264	40 49 326
141	24 36 008	22 06 034	23 50 099	32 26 167	23 54 209	52 13 265	40 37 327
142	24 39 009	22 18 035	24 11 100	32 31 168	23 44 210	51 51 266	40 26 327
143	24 43 010	22 31 036	24 32 101	32 35 169	23 33 211	51 30 267	40 14 328
144	24 46 010	22 43 036	24 53 102	32 39 170	23 22 212	51 08 268	40 03 329
145	24 50 011	22 56 037	25 14 103	32 42 172	23 10 213	50 47 269	39 52 329
146	24 55 012	23 09 038	25 35 104	32 45 173	22 59 214	50 25 270	39 41 330
147	24 59 013	23 23 039	25 56 105	32 47 174	22 47 215	50 04 271	39 30 331
148	25 04 014	23 36 040	26 17 106	32 50 175	22 34 216	49 42 272	39 20 331
149	25 09 014	23 50 040	26 38 107	32 51 176	22 21 217	49 21 273	39 10 332

LHA ♈	DENEB	◆ VEGA	ARCTURUS	◆ REGULUS	PROCYON	◆ CAPELLA	Schedar
150	25 15 015	24 04 041	26 58 108	32 52 177	22 08 218	48 59 274	39 00 333
151	25 21 016	24 18 042	27 19 109	32 53 178	21 55 219	48 38 275	38 50 333
152	25 27 017	24 33 043	27 39 109	32 54 180	21 41 220	48 16 275	38 41 334
153	25 33 017	24 48 044	27 59 110	32 53 181	21 27 221	47 55 276	38 31 335
154	25 39 018	25 03 045	28 19 112	32 53 182	21 13 222	47 34 277	38 22 335
155	25 46 019	25 18 045	28 39 113	32 52 183	20 58 223	47 12 278	38 13 336
156	25 53 020	25 33 046	28 59 114	32 51 184	20 43 224	46 51 279	38 05 337
157	26 01 020	25 49 047	29 19 115	32 49 185	20 28 225	46 30 280	37 56 337
158	26 08 021	26 05 048	29 38 116	32 46 187	20 13 226	46 09 281	37 48 338
159	26 16 022	26 21 049	29 58 117	32 44 188	19 57 227	45 48 282	37 40 339
160	26 24 023	26 37 049	30 17 118	32 41 189	19 41 228	45 27 282	37 33 339
161	26 33 024	26 53 050	30 36 119	32 37 190	19 25 229	45 06 283	37 25 340
162	26 42 024	27 10 051	30 54 120	32 33 191	19 08 230	44 45 284	37 18 341
163	26 51 025	27 27 052	31 13 121	32 29 192	18 52 231	44 24 285	37 11 342
164	27 00 026	27 44 053	31 31 122	32 24 194	18 35 232	44 03 286	37 05 342

LHA ♈	DENEB	◆ VEGA	ARCTURUS	◆ REGULUS	POLLUX	◆ CAPELLA	Schedar
165	27 09 027	28 01 054	31 50 123	32 19 195	40 24 240	43 43 287	36 58 343
166	27 19 027	28 18 054	32 07 124	32 13 196	40 05 241	43 22 288	36 52 344
167	27 29 028	28 36 055	32 25 125	32 07 197	39 46 242	43 02 288	36 46 344
168	27 39 029	28 54 056	32 43 126	32 00 198	39 27 243	42 41 289	36 40 345
169	27 50 030	29 12 057	33 00 127	31 53 199	39 08 244	42 21 290	36 35 346
170	28 01 030	29 30 058	33 17 128	31 46 200	38 48 246	42 01 291	36 29 346
171	28 12 031	29 48 058	33 34 129	31 38 202	38 28 247	41 41 292	36 24 347
172	28 23 032	30 06 059	33 50 130	31 30 203	38 09 248	41 21 292	36 20 348
173	28 34 033	30 25 060	34 07 131	31 22 204	37 49 249	41 01 293	36 15 348
174	28 46 034	30 44 061	34 23 133	31 13 205	37 29 250	40 41 294	36 11 349
175	28 58 034	31 03 062	34 38 134	31 03 206	37 08 251	40 22 295	36 07 350
176	29 10 035	31 22 063	34 54 135	30 54 207	36 48 252	40 02 296	36 03 350
177	29 23 036	31 41 063	35 09 136	30 44 208	36 27 253	39 43 296	36 00 351
178	29 36 037	32 00 064	35 24 137	30 33 210	36 07 254	39 24 297	35 56 352
179	29 49 037	32 20 065	35 38 138	30 23 211	35 46 255	39 05 298	35 53 352

 LAT 69°N

LHA ♈	Hc	Zn	Hc	Zn	Hc	Zn	Hc	Zn	Hc	Zn	Hc	Zn	Hc	Zn
	◆DENEB		VEGA		◆ARCTURUS		REGULUS		◆POLLUX		CAPELLA		Schedar	
180	30 02	038	32 39	066	35 52	139	30 11	212	35 25	256	38 46	299	35 51	353
181	30 15	039	32 59	067	36 06	140	30 00	213	35 05	257	38 27	300	35 48	354
182	30 29	040	33 19	068	36 20	141	29 48	214	34 44	258	38 09	300	35 46	354
183	30 43	040	33 39	068	36 33	143	29 36	215	34 23	259	37 50	301	35 44	355
184	30 57	041	33 59	069	36 46	144	29 23	216	34 01	260	37 32	302	35 42	356
185	31 11	042	34 19	070	36 59	145	29 10	217	33 40	261	37 14	303	35 41	356
186	31 25	043	34 39	071	37 11	146	28 57	218	33 19	262	36 56	304	35 40	357
187	31 40	044	34 59	072	37 23	147	28 44	219	32 58	263	36 38	304	35 39	358
188	31 55	044	35 20	073	37 34	148	28 30	221	32 36	264	36 20	305	35 38	358
189	32 10	045	35 41	074	37 45	150	28 16	222	32 15	265	36 03	306	35 37	359
190	32 25	046	36 01	074	37 56	151	28 01	223	31 53	265	35 45	307	35 37	000
191	32 41	047	36 22	075	38 06	152	27 47	224	31 32	266	35 28	308	35 37	000
192	32 57	047	36 43	076	38 16	153	27 32	225	31 11	267	35 11	308	35 38	001
193	33 13	048	37 04	077	38 26	154	27 16	226	30 49	268	34 54	309	35 38	002
194	33 29	049	37 25	078	38 35	155	27 01	227	30 28	269	34 38	310	35 39	002
	Schedar		◆DENEB		VEGA		◆ARCTURUS		REGULUS		◆POLLUX		CAPELLA	
195	35 40	003	33 45	050	37 46	079	38 43	157	26 45	228	30 06	270	34 21	311
196	35 41	004	34 02	051	38 07	080	38 52	158	26 29	229	29 45	271	34 05	311
197	35 43	005	34 18	051	38 28	081	39 00	159	26 12	230	29 23	272	33 49	312
198	35 45	005	34 35	052	38 49	081	39 07	160	25 56	231	29 02	273	33 33	313
199	35 47	006	34 52	053	39 11	082	39 14	161	25 39	232	28 40	274	33 18	314
200	35 49	007	35 09	054	39 32	083	39 21	163	25 22	233	28 19	275	33 02	314
201	35 52	007	35 27	054	39 53	084	39 27	164	25 05	234	27 57	276	32 47	315
202	35 54	008	35 44	055	40 15	085	39 33	165	24 47	235	27 36	277	32 32	316
203	35 57	009	36 02	056	40 36	086	39 38	166	24 29	236	27 15	278	32 17	317
204	36 01	009	36 20	057	40 58	087	39 43	168	24 11	237	26 53	278	32 03	318
205	36 04	010	36 38	058	41 19	088	39 47	169	23 53	238	26 32	279	31 48	318
206	36 08	011	36 56	058	41 41	089	39 51	170	23 35	239	26 11	280	31 34	319
207	36 12	011	37 15	059	42 02	090	39 55	171	23 16	240	25 50	281	31 20	320
208	36 17	012	37 33	060	42 24	091	39 58	172	22 57	241	25 29	282	31 06	321
209	36 21	013	37 52	061	42 45	092	40 00	174	22 38	242	25 08	283	30 53	321
	Schedar		◆DENEB		VEGA		◆ARCTURUS		REGULUS		◆POLLUX		CAPELLA	
210	36 26	013	38 11	062	43 07	093	40 02	175	22 19	243	24 47	284	30 39	322
211	36 31	014	38 30	062	43 28	093	40 04	176	22 00	244	24 26	285	30 26	323
212	36 36	015	38 49	063	43 50	094	40 05	177	21 40	245	24 05	286	30 13	324
213	36 42	015	39 08	064	44 11	095	40 06	179	21 21	246	23 45	287	30 01	324
214	36 48	016	39 28	065	44 32	096	40 06	180	21 01	247	23 24	287	29 48	325
215	36 54	017	39 47	066	44 54	097	40 06	181	20 41	248	23 04	288	29 36	326
216	37 00	017	40 07	066	45 15	098	40 05	182	20 21	249	22 43	289	29 24	327
217	37 07	018	40 26	067	45 36	099	40 04	184	20 01	250	22 23	290	29 13	328
218	37 13	019	40 46	068	45 57	100	40 03	185	19 40	251	22 03	291	29 01	328
219	37 20	019	41 06	069	46 19	101	40 01	186	19 20	252	21 43	292	28 50	329
220	37 28	020	41 26	070	46 40	102	39 58	187	18 59	253	21 23	293	28 39	330
221	37 35	021	41 47	070	47 01	103	39 55	189	18 39	254	21 03	294	28 28	331
222	37 43	021	42 07	071	47 21	104	39 52	190	18 18	255	20 43	294	28 18	331
223	37 51	022	42 27	072	47 42	105	39 48	191	17 57	256	20 24	295	28 08	332
224	37 59	023	42 48	073	48 03	106	39 44	192	17 36	257	20 05	296	27 58	333
	Schedar		◆DENEB		VEGA		◆ARCTURUS		REGULUS		◆POLLUX		CAPELLA	
225	38 08	023	43 09	074	48 23	107	39 39	193	17 15	258	19 45	297	27 48	334
226	38 16	024	43 29	075	48 44	109	39 34	195	16 54	259	19 26	298	27 39	334
227	38 25	025	43 50	076	49 04	110	39 28	196	16 33	260	19 07	299	27 30	335
228	38 34	025	44 11	076	49 24	111	39 22	197	16 12	261	18 49	300	27 21	336
229	38 44	026	44 32	077	49 44	112	39 15	198	15 51	262	18 30	301	27 12	337
230	38 53	027	44 53	078	50 04	113	39 08	200	15 29	263	18 12	301	27 04	337
231	39 03	027	45 14	079	50 24	114	39 01	201	15 08	264	17 53	302	26 56	338
232	39 13	028	45 35	080	50 44	115	38 53	202	14 47	265	17 35	303	26 48	339
233	39 23	029	45 56	081	51 03	116	38 45	203	14 25	266	17 17	304	26 40	340
234	39 34	030	46 17	082	51 22	117	38 36	204	14 04	267	17 00	305	26 33	341
235	39 44	030	46 39	082	51 41	118	38 27	206	13 42	268	16 42	306	26 26	341
236	39 55	031	47 00	083	52 00	120	38 18	207	13 21	268	16 25	307	26 19	342
237	40 07	032	47 21	084	52 19	121	38 08	208	12 59	269	16 08	308	26 13	343
238	40 18	032	47 43	085	52 37	122	37 58	209	12 38	270	15 51	308	26 06	344
239	40 29	033	48 04	086	52 55	123	37 47	210	12 16	271	15 34	309	26 00	344
	Alpheratz		◆DENEB		VEGA		Rasalhague		◆ARCTURUS		Alioth		◆CAPELLA	
240	16 44	050	48 26	087	53 13	124	31 31	152	37 36	211	65 44	261	25 55	345
241	17 01	051	48 47	088	53 31	126	31 40	153	37 25	213	65 23	262	25 49	346
242	17 18	052	49 09	089	53 48	127	31 50	155	37 13	214	65 02	263	25 44	347
243	17 35	053	49 30	090	54 05	128	31 59	156	37 01	215	64 40	264	25 39	347
244	17 52	054	49 52	091	54 22	129	32 07	157	36 48	216	64 19	265	25 35	348
245	18 09	055	50 13	092	54 38	131	32 16	158	36 35	217	63 58	266	25 31	349
246	18 27	056	50 35	093	54 55	132	32 24	159	36 22	218	63 36	267	25 27	350
247	18 45	056	50 56	093	55 10	133	32 31	160	36 09	219	63 15	268	25 23	350
248	19 03	057	51 18	094	55 26	134	32 38	161	35 55	221	62 53	269	25 20	351
249	19 21	058	51 39	095	55 41	136	32 45	163	35 41	222	62 32	270	25 16	352
250	19 39	059	52 00	096	55 56	137	32 51	164	35 26	223	62 10	271	25 14	353
251	19 58	060	52 22	097	56 10	138	32 57	165	35 11	224	61 49	272	25 11	354
252	20 17	061	52 43	098	56 25	140	33 02	166	34 56	225	61 27	273	25 09	354
253	20 35	062	53 04	099	56 38	141	33 07	167	34 41	226	61 06	274	25 07	355
254	20 54	063	53 26	100	56 52	142	33 12	168	34 25	227	60 44	274	25 05	356
	Alpheratz		◆DENEB		ALTAIR		Rasalhague		◆ARCTURUS		Alioth		◆CAPELLA	
255	21 14	063	53 47	101	23 50	133	33 16	170	34 09	228	60 23	275	25 04	357
256	21 33	064	54 08	102	24 05	134	33 19	171	33 53	229	60 01	276	25 02	357
257	21 52	065	54 29	103	24 21	135	33 23	172	33 37	231	59 40	277	25 02	358
258	22 12	066	54 49	105	24 36	136	33 25	173	33 20	232	59 19	278	25 01	359
259	22 32	067	55 10	106	24 51	137	33 28	174	33 03	233	58 57	279	25 01	000
260	22 52	068	55 31	107	25 05	138	33 30	175	32 46	234	58 36	280	25 01	000
261	23 11	069	55 51	108	25 20	139	33 31	177	32 28	235	58 15	280	25 01	001
262	23 32	070	56 12	109	25 34	140	33 32	178	32 11	236	57 54	281	25 02	002
263	23 52	070	56 32	110	25 47	141	33 33	179	31 53	237	57 33	282	25 03	003
264	24 12	071	56 52	111	26 01	142	33 33	180	31 35	238	57 12	283	25 04	003
265	24 33	072	57 12	112	26 14	143	33 33	181	31 16	239	56 51	284	25 05	004
266	24 53	073	57 32	113	26 26	144	33 32	182	30 58	240	56 30	284	25 07	005
267	25 14	074	57 52	115	26 39	145	33 31	184	30 39	241	56 09	285	25 09	006
268	25 34	075	58 11	116	26 51	147	33 29	185	30 20	242	55 49	286	25 11	007
269	25 55	076	58 30	117	27 02	148	33 27	186	30 01	243	55 28	287	25 14	007

LHA ♈	Hc	Zn	Hc	Zn	Hc	Zn	Hc	Zn	Hc	Zn	Hc	Zn	Hc	Zn
	◆CAPELLA		Alpheratz		◆DENEB		ALTAIR		Rasalhague		◆ARCTURUS		Alioth	
270	25 17	008	26 16	077	58 49	118	27 14	149	33 25	187	29 42	244	55 07	288
271	25 20	009	26 37	078	59 08	119	27 25	150	33 22	188	29 22	245	54 47	288
272	25 23	010	26 58	078	59 27	121	27 35	151	33 19	189	29 02	246	54 27	289
273	25 27	010	27 19	079	59 45	122	27 46	152	33 15	191	28 43	247	54 06	290
274	25 31	011	27 40	080	60 03	123	27 56	153	33 11	192	28 23	248	53 46	291
275	25 35	012	28 02	081	60 21	124	28 05	154	33 06	193	28 03	249	53 26	291
276	25 40	013	28 23	082	60 39	126	28 14	155	33 01	194	27 43	250	53 06	292
277	25 45	013	28 44	083	60 56	127	28 23	156	32 56	195	27 22	251	52 46	293
278	25 50	014	29 05	084	61 13	128	28 31	158	32 50	196	27 02	252	52 26	294
279	25 55	015	29 27	085	61 30	130	28 39	159	32 43	198	26 41	253	52 07	294
280	26 01	016	29 48	086	61 46	131	28 47	160	32 37	199	26 21	254	51 47	295
281	26 07	017	30 10	087	62 02	132	28 54	161	32 30	200	26 00	255	51 28	296
282	26 13	017	30 31	088	62 18	134	29 01	162	32 22	201	25 39	256	51 09	297
283	26 20	018	30 53	088	62 33	135	29 08	163	32 14	202	25 18	257	50 50	297
284	26 27	019	31 14	089	62 48	137	29 14	164	32 06	203	24 57	258	50 30	298
	◆CAPELLA		Hamal		Alpheratz		◆DENEB		VEGA		◆ARCTURUS		Alioth	
285	26 34	020	16 04	066	31 36	090	63 03	138	59 39	189	24 36	259	50 12	299
286	26 41	020	16 23	067	31 57	091	63 17	140	59 35	190	24 15	260	49 53	300
287	26 49	021	16 43	068	32 19	092	63 31	141	59 31	192	23 54	261	49 34	300
288	26 56	022	17 03	069	32 40	093	63 44	143	59 26	193	23 32	262	49 16	301
289	27 05	023	17 23	069	33 02	094	63 57	144	59 21	195	23 11	263	48 57	302
290	27 13	023	17 43	070	33 23	095	64 09	146	59 15	196	22 50	264	48 39	302
291	27 22	024	18 04	071	33 44	096	64 21	147	59 09	198	22 28	265	48 21	303
292	27 31	025	18 24	072	34 06	097	64 33	149	59 02	199	22 07	266	48 03	304
293	27 40	026	18 45	073	34 27	098	64 43	150	58 55	201	21 45	267	47 45	305
294	27 49	026	19 05	074	34 48	099	64 54	152	58 47	202	21 24	268	47 28	305
295	27 59	027	19 26	075	35 10	100	65 04	154	58 38	204	21 02	269	47 10	306
296	28 09	028	19 47	076	35 31	101	65 13	155	58 30	205	20 41	270	46 53	307
297	28 19	029	20 08	077	35 52	102	65 22	157	58 20	207	20 19	271	46 36	307
298	28 30	030	20 29	077	36 13	103	65 30	159	58 10	208	19 58	271	46 19	308
299	28 40	030	20 50	078	36 34	104	65 37	160	58 00	210	19 36	272	46 02	309
	◆CAPELLA		Hamal		Alpheratz		◆DENEB		VEGA		◆ARCTURUS		Dubhe	
300	28 51	031	21 11	079	36 55	105	65 44	162	57 49	211	19 15	273	44 45	331
301	29 02	032	21 32	080	37 15	106	65 51	164	57 38	212	18 54	274	44 35	332
302	29 14	033	21 53	081	37 36	107	65 57	165	57 26	214	18 32	275	44 24	332
303	29 26	033	22 14	082	37 57	108	66 02	167	57 14	215	18 11	276	44 15	333
304	29 38	034	22 36	083	38 17	109	66 06	169	57 01	217	17 49	277	44 05	334
305	29 50	035	22 57	084	38 37	110	66 10	170	56 48	218	17 28	278	43 56	334
306	30 02	036	23 18	085	38 57	111	66 13	172	56 35	219	17 07	279	43 46	335
307	30 15	036	23 40	086	39 17	112	66 16	174	56 21	221	16 46	280	43 37	336
308	30 28	037	24 01	087	39 37	113	66 18	176	56 06	222	16 24	281	43 29	336
309	30 41	038	24 23	088	39 57	114	66 19	177	55 52	223	16 03	282	43 20	337
310	30 54	039	24 44	088	40 17	115	66 20	179	55 37	225	15 42	282	43 12	337
311	31 08	039	25 06	089	40 36	116	66 20	181	55 22	226	15 21	283	43 03	338
312	31 21	040	25 27	090	40 55	117	66 19	183	55 06	227	15 00	284	42 56	339
313	31 35	041	25 49	091	41 14	118	66 18	184	54 50	229	14 40	285	42 48	339
314	31 50	042	26 10	092	41 33	119	66 16	186	54 34	230	14 19	286	42 40	340
	◆CAPELLA		Hamal		Alpheratz		◆DENEB		VEGA		◆Alphecca		Dubhe	
315	32 04	043	26 32	093	41 52	121	66 13	188	54 17	231	27 55	272	42 33	341
316	32 19	043	26 53	094	42 10	122	66 10	190	54 00	232	27 33	273	42 26	341
317	32 33	044	27 15	095	42 28	123	66 06	191	53 43	234	27 12	274	42 19	342
318	32 49	045	27 36	096	42 46	124	66 02	193	53 26	235	26 50	275	42 13	342
319	33 04	046	27 57	097	43 04	125	65 56	195	53 08	236	26 29	276	42 06	343
320	33 19	046	28 19	098	43 21	126	65 51	196	52 50	237	26 08	277	42 00	344
321	33 35	047	28 40	099	43 39	127	65 44	198	52 32	238	25 46	278	41 54	344
322	33 51	048	29 01	100	43 56	128	65 37	200	52 14	240	25 25	279	41 48	345
323	34 07	049	29 22	101	44 12	130	65 30	202	51 55	241	25 04	279	41 43	346
324	34 23	049	29 43	102	44 29	131	65 21	203	51 36	242	24 43	280	41 38	346
325	34 39	050	30 04	103	44 45	132	65 13	205	51 17	243	24 21	281	41 33	347
326	34 56	051	30 25	104	45 01	133	65 03	206	50 58	244	24 00	282	41 28	347
327	35 13	052	30 46	105	45 16	134	64 54	208	50 38	245	23 39	283	41 23	348
328	35 30	053	31 07	106	45 32	135	64 43	210	50 19	246	23 19	284	41 19	349
329	35 47	053	31 28	107	45 47	137	64 32	211	49 59	247	22 58	285	41 15	349
	CAPELLA		◆Hamal		Alpheratz		◆ALTAIR		VEGA		Alphecca		◆Alioth	
330	36 04	054	31 48	108	46 01	138	26 23	216	49 39	249	22 37	286	38 52	330
331	36 22	055	32 09	109	46 16	139	26 10	217	49 19	250	22 16	287	38 41	331
332	36 40	056	32 29	110	46 29	140	25 57	218	48 59	251	21 56	288	38 31	332
333	36 57	056	32 49	111	46 43	141	25 44	219	48 38	252	21 35	288	38 21	332
334	37 15	057	33 09	112	46 56	143	25 30	220	48 18	253	21 15	289	38 11	333
335	37 34	058	33 29	113	47 09	144	25 16	221	47 57	254	20 55	290	38 01	334
336	37 52	059	33 49	114	47 22	145	25 02	222	47 37	255	20 35	291	37 52	334
337	38 10	060	34 08	115	47 34	146	24 47	223	47 16	256	20 15	292	37 42	335
338	38 29	060	34 28	116	47 45	148	24 32	224	46 55	257	19 55	293	37 33	336
339	38 48	061	34 47	117	47 57	149	24 17	225	46 34	258	19 35	294	37 25	336
340	39 07	062	35 06	118	48 07	150	24 02	227	46 13	259	19 15	295	37 16	337
341	39 26	063	35 25	119	48 18	152	23 46	228	45 52	260	18 56	295	37 08	338
342	39 45	064	35 44	120	48 28	153	23 30	229	45 30	261	18 37	296	37 00	338
343	40 04	064	36 02	121	48 38	154	23 14	230	45 09	262	18 17	297	36 52	339
344	40 24	065	36 20	122	48 47	155	22 57	231	44 48	263	17 58	298	36 44	340
	◆POLLUX		CAPELLA		Hamal		◆Alpheratz		ALTAIR		◆VEGA		Alioth	
345	13 11	043	40 43	066	36 39	123	48 55	157	22 40	232	44 26	264	36 37	340
346	13 26	044	41 03	067	36 56	124	49 04	158	22 23	233	44 05	265	36 30	341
347	13 41	044	41 23	068	37 14	125	49 12	159	22 06	234	43 44	266	36 23	342
348	13 56	045	41 43	068	37 31	127	49 19	161	21 49	235	43 22	267	36 17	342
349	14 12	046	42 03	069	37 49	128	49 26	162	21 31	236	43 01	268	36 10	343
350	14 27	047	42 23	070	38 05	129	49 32	163	21 13	237	42 39	269	36 04	344
351	14 43	048	42 43	071	38 22	130	49 38	165	20 55	238	42 18	270	35 58	345
352	14 59	049	43 04	072	38 38	131	49 43	166	20 37	239	41 56	271	35 53	345
353	15 16	050	43 24	073	38 54	132	49 48	167	20 18	240	41 35	272	35 47	346
354	15 32	051	43 45	073	39 10	133	49 53	169	20 00	241	41 13	272	35 42	347
355	15 49	051	44 05	074	39 26	134	49 57	170	19 41	242	40 52	273	35 37	347
356	16 06	052	44 26	075	39 41	136	50 00	171	19 22	243	40 30	274	35 33	348
357	16 23	053	44 47	076	39 56	137	50 03	173	19 03	244	40 09	275	35 28	349
358	16 40	054	45 08	077	40 11	138	50 06	174	18 43	245	39 47	276	35 24	349
359	16 58	055	45 29	078	40 25	139	50 08	176	18 24	246	39 26	277	35 20	350

LAT 68°N

LAT 68°N

LHA ♈	◆POLLUX Hc	Zn	CAPELLA Hc	Zn	Hamal Hc	Zn	◆Alpheratz Hc	Zn	DENEB Hc	Zn	◆VEGA Hc	Zn	Alioth Hc	Zn
0	16 42	056	45 37	077	41 25	140	51 09	177	56 08	254	38 56	279	34 17	351
1	17 00	056	45 59	078	41 39	141	51 10	178	55 47	255	38 34	280	34 14	351
2	17 19	057	46 21	079	41 53	142	51 10	180	55 25	256	38 12	280	34 11	352
3	17 38	058	46 43	080	42 07	143	51 10	181	55 03	257	37 50	281	34 08	353
4	17 57	059	47 06	081	42 20	144	51 10	182	54 41	258	37 28	282	34 05	353
5	18 17	060	47 28	082	42 33	146	51 08	184	54 19	259	37 06	283	34 03	354
6	18 36	061	47 50	083	42 45	147	51 07	185	53 57	260	36 44	284	34 01	355
7	18 56	062	48 12	084	42 57	148	51 04	187	53 35	261	36 22	285	33 59	355
8	19 16	062	48 35	084	43 09	149	51 02	188	53 13	262	36 00	286	33 57	356
9	19 36	063	48 57	085	43 20	150	50 58	189	52 51	263	35 39	286	33 56	357
10	19 56	064	49 19	086	43 31	152	50 54	191	52 28	264	35 17	287	33 55	358
11	20 16	065	49 42	087	43 42	153	50 50	192	52 06	265	34 56	288	33 54	358
12	20 37	066	50 04	088	43 52	154	50 45	193	51 43	266	34 35	289	33 53	359
13	20 57	067	50 27	089	44 01	155	50 39	195	51 21	267	34 13	290	33 53	000
14	21 18	068	50 49	090	44 10	157	50 33	196	50 59	268	33 52	291	33 53	000

LHA ♈	Alioth Hc	Zn	◆POLLUX Hc	Zn	CAPELLA Hc	Zn	Hamal Hc	Zn	◆Alpheratz Hc	Zn	DENEB Hc	Zn	◆VEGA Hc	Zn
15	33 53	001	21 39	069	51 12	091	44 19	158	50 27	198	50 36	269	33 31	292
16	33 53	002	22 00	069	51 34	092	44 27	159	50 20	199	50 14	270	33 11	292
17	33 54	002	22 21	070	51 57	093	44 35	161	50 12	200	49 51	271	32 50	293
18	33 55	003	22 42	071	52 19	094	44 42	162	50 04	202	49 29	272	32 29	294
19	33 56	004	23 03	072	52 42	095	44 49	163	49 56	203	49 06	272	32 09	295
20	33 58	004	23 25	073	53 04	096	44 55	164	49 47	204	48 44	273	31 48	296
21	34 00	005	23 46	074	53 26	096	45 01	166	49 37	206	48 21	274	31 28	296
22	34 02	006	24 08	075	53 49	097	45 06	167	49 27	207	47 59	275	31 08	297
23	34 04	006	24 30	076	54 11	098	45 11	168	49 17	208	47 37	276	30 48	298
24	34 07	007	24 51	076	54 33	099	45 16	170	49 06	210	47 14	277	30 29	299
25	34 10	008	25 13	077	54 55	101	45 19	171	48 55	211	46 52	278	30 09	300
26	34 13	008	25 35	078	55 17	102	45 23	172	48 43	212	46 30	279	29 50	301
27	34 16	009	25 57	079	55 39	103	45 26	173	48 31	213	46 07	280	29 30	301
28	34 20	010	26 19	080	56 01	104	45 28	175	48 18	215	45 45	280	29 11	302
29	34 24	010	26 42	081	56 23	105	45 30	176	48 05	216	45 23	281	28 52	303

LHA ♈	Alioth Hc	Zn	◆POLLUX Hc	Zn	ALDEBARAN Hc	Zn	◆Hamal Hc	Zn	Alpheratz Hc	Zn	DENEB Hc	Zn	◆VEGA Hc	Zn
30	34 28	011	27 04	082	32 50	134	45 31	177	47 52	217	45 01	282	28 34	304
31	34 32	012	27 26	083	33 06	135	45 32	179	47 38	218	44 39	283	28 15	305
32	34 37	012	27 48	084	33 22	136	45 32	180	47 24	220	44 17	284	27 57	305
33	34 42	013	28 11	085	33 37	137	45 32	181	47 09	221	43 56	285	27 38	306
34	34 47	014	28 33	085	33 53	138	45 31	183	46 54	222	43 34	285	27 20	307
35	34 53	014	28 56	086	34 07	139	45 30	184	46 39	223	43 12	286	27 02	308
36	34 58	015	29 18	087	34 22	141	45 28	185	46 23	225	42 51	287	26 45	309
37	35 04	016	29 41	088	34 36	142	45 26	187	46 07	226	42 29	288	26 27	310
38	35 11	016	30 03	089	34 50	143	45 23	188	45 51	227	42 08	289	26 10	310
39	35 17	017	30 25	090	35 03	144	45 19	189	45 35	228	41 47	290	25 53	311
40	35 24	018	30 48	091	35 16	145	45 16	190	45 18	229	41 26	290	25 36	312
41	35 31	018	31 10	092	35 29	146	45 11	192	45 00	231	41 05	291	25 20	313
42	35 38	019	31 33	093	35 41	147	45 06	193	44 43	232	40 44	292	25 03	314
43	35 46	020	31 55	094	35 53	149	45 01	194	44 25	233	40 23	293	24 47	314
44	35 53	020	32 18	095	36 05	150	44 55	196	44 07	234	40 02	294	24 31	315

LHA ♈	Alioth Hc	Zn	◆POLLUX Hc	Zn	ALDEBARAN Hc	Zn	◆Hamal Hc	Zn	Alpheratz Hc	Zn	DENEB Hc	Zn	◆VEGA Hc	Zn
45	36 01	021	32 40	096	36 16	151	44 49	197	43 49	235	39 42	294	24 15	316
46	36 09	022	33 02	097	36 27	152	44 42	198	43 30	236	39 21	295	24 00	317
47	36 18	022	33 25	098	36 37	153	44 35	199	43 11	237	39 01	296	23 45	318
48	36 27	023	33 47	099	36 47	154	44 27	201	42 52	239	38 41	297	23 30	318
49	36 36	024	34 09	100	36 56	156	44 19	202	42 33	240	38 21	298	23 15	319
50	36 45	025	34 31	100	37 05	157	44 10	203	42 14	241	38 01	298	23 00	320
51	36 54	025	34 53	101	37 14	158	44 01	205	41 54	242	37 41	299	22 46	321
52	37 04	026	35 15	102	37 22	159	43 52	206	41 34	243	37 22	300	22 32	322
53	37 14	027	35 37	103	37 30	160	43 42	207	41 14	244	37 02	301	22 18	322
54	37 24	027	35 59	104	37 37	162	43 31	208	40 54	245	36 43	301	22 05	323
55	37 34	028	36 21	105	37 44	163	43 21	210	40 33	246	36 24	302	21 51	324
56	37 45	029	36 42	106	37 51	164	43 09	211	40 12	247	36 05	303	21 38	325
57	37 56	029	37 04	107	37 57	165	42 58	212	39 52	248	35 46	304	21 25	326
58	38 07	030	37 25	108	38 02	166	42 45	213	39 31	249	35 28	305	21 13	326
59	38 18	031	37 47	109	38 07	168	42 33	214	39 10	250	35 09	305	21 00	327

LHA ♈	Alioth Hc	Zn	◆POLLUX Hc	Zn	ALDEBARAN Hc	Zn	◆Hamal Hc	Zn	Alpheratz Hc	Zn	DENEB Hc	Zn	◆VEGA Hc	Zn
60	38 30	031	38 08	110	38 12	169	42 20	216	38 48	251	34 51	306	20 48	328
61	38 42	032	38 29	112	38 16	170	42 07	217	38 27	252	34 33	307	20 37	329
62	38 54	033	38 50	113	38 20	171	41 53	218	38 06	253	34 15	308	20 25	330
63	39 06	033	39 10	114	38 23	172	41 39	219	37 44	254	33 58	308	20 14	330
64	39 18	034	39 31	115	38 26	174	41 25	220	37 22	255	33 40	309	20 03	331
65	39 31	035	39 51	116	38 28	175	41 10	222	37 01	256	33 23	310	19 52	332
66	39 44	035	40 11	117	38 30	176	40 55	223	36 39	257	33 06	311	19 42	333
67	39 57	036	40 31	118	38 31	177	40 40	224	36 17	258	32 49	312	19 32	334
68	40 10	037	40 51	119	38 32	179	40 24	225	35 55	259	32 32	312	19 22	335
69	40 24	037	41 10	120	38 32	180	40 08	226	35 32	260	32 16	313	19 13	335
70	40 37	038	41 30	121	38 32	181	39 51	227	35 10	261	31 59	314	19 03	336
71	40 51	039	41 49	122	38 32	182	39 35	228	34 48	262	31 43	315	18 54	337
72	41 05	039	42 08	123	38 30	183	39 18	230	34 26	263	31 27	315	18 46	338
73	41 20	040	42 27	124	38 29	185	39 00	231	34 03	264	31 11	316	18 37	339
74	41 34	041	42 45	126	38 27	186	38 43	232	33 41	265	30 56	317	18 29	339

LHA ♈	Alioth Hc	Zn	◆REGULUS Hc	Zn	PROCYON Hc	Zn	◆ALDEBARAN Hc	Zn	Hamal Hc	Zn	Alpheratz Hc	Zn	◆DENEB Hc	Zn
75	41 49	041	15 46	097	21 41	136	38 24	187	38 25	233	33 19	266	30 41	318
76	42 04	042	16 08	098	21 56	137	38 21	188	38 07	234	32 56	267	30 26	318
77	42 19	043	16 30	099	22 11	139	38 18	190	37 49	235	32 34	268	30 11	319
78	42 34	043	16 53	100	22 26	140	38 14	191	37 30	236	32 11	269	29 56	320
79	42 50	044	17 15	101	22 41	141	38 09	192	37 11	237	31 49	270	29 42	321
80	43 06	045	17 37	102	22 55	142	38 04	193	36 52	238	31 26	271	29 28	321
81	43 22	045	17 59	103	23 09	143	37 59	194	36 33	239	31 04	272	29 14	322
82	43 38	046	18 21	104	23 22	144	37 53	196	36 14	241	30 41	273	29 00	323
83	43 54	047	18 42	105	23 35	145	37 47	197	35 54	242	30 19	273	28 47	324
84	44 10	047	19 04	106	23 48	146	37 40	198	35 34	243	29 57	274	28 34	325
85	44 27	048	19 26	107	24 00	147	37 33	199	35 14	244	29 34	275	28 21	325
86	44 44	049	19 47	108	24 12	148	37 25	200	34 54	245	29 12	276	28 08	326
87	45 01	049	20 08	109	24 24	149	37 17	202	34 33	246	28 49	277	27 56	327
88	45 18	050	20 30	110	24 35	150	37 09	203	34 13	247	28 27	278	27 44	328
89	45 35	051	20 51	111	24 46	151	37 00	204	33 52	248	28 05	279	27 32	328

LHA ♈	Alioth Hc	Zn	◆REGULUS Hc	Zn	PROCYON Hc	Zn	BETELGEUSE Hc	Zn	◆ALDEBARAN Hc	Zn	Hamal Hc	Zn	◆DENEB Hc	Zn
90	45 53	052	21 12	112	24 57	152	29 24	181	36 51	205	33 31	249	27 20	329
91	46 11	052	21 32	113	25 07	153	29 24	182	36 41	206	33 10	250	27 09	330
92	46 28	053	21 53	114	25 17	154	29 23	183	36 31	208	32 49	251	26 57	331
93	46 46	054	22 14	115	25 27	156	29 21	185	36 20	209	32 28	252	26 46	331
94	47 05	054	22 34	116	25 36	157	29 19	186	36 09	210	32 06	253	26 36	332
95	47 23	055	22 54	117	25 45	158	29 16	187	35 58	211	31 45	254	26 25	333
96	47 41	056	23 14	118	25 53	159	29 14	188	35 46	212	31 23	255	26 15	334
97	48 00	056	23 34	119	26 01	160	29 10	189	35 34	213	31 01	256	26 05	334
98	48 19	057	23 54	120	26 08	161	29 06	190	35 21	214	30 40	257	25 56	335
99	48 38	058	24 13	121	26 15	162	29 02	191	35 08	216	30 18	258	25 47	336
100	48 57	058	24 32	122	26 22	163	28 58	192	34 55	217	29 56	259	25 38	337
101	49 16	059	24 51	123	26 28	164	28 53	194	34 41	218	29 34	260	25 29	337
102	49 35	060	25 10	124	26 34	165	28 47	195	34 27	219	29 11	261	25 20	338
103	49 55	061	25 29	125	26 40	167	28 41	196	34 13	220	28 49	262	25 12	339
104	50 15	061	25 47	126	26 45	168	28 35	197	33 58	221	28 27	263	25 04	340

LHA ♈	Alioth Hc	Zn	◆REGULUS Hc	Zn	PROCYON Hc	Zn	BETELGEUSE Hc	Zn	◆CAPELLA Hc	Zn	Hamal Hc	Zn	◆DENEB Hc	Zn
105	50 34	062	26 05	127	26 49	169	28 28	198	64 24	224	28 05	264	24 57	341
106	50 54	063	26 23	128	26 53	170	28 21	199	64 08	225	27 42	265	24 49	341
107	51 14	063	26 41	129	26 57	171	28 13	200	63 52	227	27 20	265	24 42	342
108	51 35	064	26 58	130	27 00	172	28 05	201	63 35	228	26 57	266	24 35	343
109	51 55	065	27 15	131	27 03	173	27 57	203	63 18	230	26 35	267	24 29	344
110	52 15	066	27 32	132	27 06	174	27 48	204	63 01	231	26 13	268	24 23	344
111	52 36	066	27 48	133	27 08	175	27 39	205	62 43	232	25 50	269	24 17	345
112	52 56	067	28 05	134	27 09	177	27 29	206	62 25	234	25 28	270	24 11	346
113	53 17	068	28 21	135	27 10	178	27 19	207	62 07	235	25 05	271	24 06	347
114	53 38	069	28 36	136	27 11	179	27 09	208	61 49	236	24 43	272	24 01	347
115	53 59	069	28 52	137	27 11	180	26 58	209	61 30	238	24 20	273	23 56	348
116	54 20	070	29 07	138	27 11	181	26 47	210	61 10	239	23 58	274	23 51	349
117	54 41	071	29 22	140	27 10	182	26 35	211	60 51	240	23 35	275	23 47	350
118	55 03	072	29 36	141	27 09	183	26 23	212	60 31	242	23 13	276	23 43	350
119	55 24	072	29 50	142	27 08	184	26 11	214	60 12	243	22 51	277	23 40	351

LHA ♈	◆VEGA Hc	Zn	ARCTURUS Hc	Zn	◆REGULUS Hc	Zn	PROCYON Hc	Zn	◆CAPELLA Hc	Zn	Schedar Hc	Zn	DENEB Hc	Zn
120	17 55	017	16 09	079	30 04	143	27 06	186	59 51	244	44 49	313	23 37	352
121	18 02	018	16 31	080	30 17	144	27 03	187	59 31	245	44 33	314	23 34	353
122	18 09	018	16 54	081	30 30	145	27 00	188	59 11	246	44 17	314	23 31	354
123	18 16	019	17 16	082	30 43	146	26 57	189	58 50	248	44 01	315	23 28	354
124	18 24	020	17 38	083	30 55	147	26 53	190	58 29	249	43 45	316	23 26	355
125	18 32	021	18 00	083	31 07	148	26 49	191	58 08	250	43 29	316	23 25	356
126	18 40	022	18 23	084	31 19	150	26 45	192	57 47	251	43 14	317	23 23	357
127	18 48	022	18 45	085	31 30	151	26 40	193	57 26	252	42 59	318	23 22	357
128	18 57	023	19 07	086	31 41	152	26 34	194	57 04	253	42 44	318	23 21	358
129	19 06	024	19 30	087	31 51	153	26 29	196	56 42	254	42 29	319	23 20	359
130	19 15	025	19 52	088	32 01	154	26 22	197	56 21	255	42 14	320	23 20	000
131	19 25	026	20 15	089	32 11	155	26 16	198	55 59	256	42 00	320	23 20	000
132	19 35	026	20 37	090	32 20	156	26 09	199	55 37	258	41 46	321	23 20	001
133	19 45	027	21 00	091	32 29	157	26 01	200	55 15	259	41 32	322	23 21	002
134	19 55	028	21 22	092	32 37	159	25 53	201	54 53	260	41 18	322	23 22	003

LHA ♈	DENEB Hc	Zn	◆VEGA Hc	Zn	ARCTURUS Hc	Zn	◆REGULUS Hc	Zn	PROCYON Hc	Zn	◆CAPELLA Hc	Zn	Schedar Hc	Zn
135	23 23	003	20 06	029	21 45	093	32 45	160	25 45	202	54 31	261	41 04	323
136	23 25	004	20 17	030	22 07	094	32 53	161	25 36	203	54 09	262	40 51	324
137	23 26	005	20 28	031	22 30	095	33 00	162	25 27	204	53 46	263	40 38	324
138	23 29	006	20 40	031	22 52	095	33 07	163	25 18	205	53 24	264	40 25	325
139	23 31	007	20 52	032	23 14	096	33 13	164	25 08	207	53 02	265	40 12	326
140	23 34	007	21 04	033	23 37	097	33 19	166	24 58	208	52 39	266	40 00	326
141	23 37	008	21 16	034	23 59	098	33 24	167	24 47	209	52 17	267	39 47	327
142	23 40	009	21 29	035	24 21	099	33 29	168	24 36	210	51 54	267	39 35	328
143	23 44	010	21 42	035	24 43	100	33 34	169	24 25	211	51 32	268	39 23	328
144	23 47	010	21 55	036	25 05	101	33 38	170	24 13	212	51 10	269	39 12	329
145	23 52	011	22 08	037	25 27	102	33 41	171	24 01	213	50 47	270	39 00	330
146	23 56	012	22 22	038	25 49	103	33 44	173	23 48	214	50 25	271	38 49	330
147	24 01	013	22 36	039	26 11	104	33 47	174	23 36	215	50 02	272	38 38	331
148	24 06	013	22 50	039	26 33	105	33 49	175	23 23	216	49 40	273	38 27	332
149	24 11	014	23 04	040	26 55	106	33 51	176	23 09	217	49 17	274	38 17	332

LHA ♈	DENEB Hc	Zn	◆VEGA Hc	Zn	ARCTURUS Hc	Zn	◆REGULUS Hc	Zn	PROCYON Hc	Zn	◆CAPELLA Hc	Zn	Schedar Hc	Zn
150	24 17	015	23 19	041	27 16	107	33 52	177	22 55	218	48 55	275	38 06	333
151	24 23	016	23 34	042	27 38	108	33 53	178	22 41	219	48 32	276	37 56	334
152	24 29	016	23 49	043	27 59	109	33 54	180	22 27	220	48 10	277	37 47	334
153	24 36	017	24 04	043	28 20	110	33 53	181	22 12	221	47 48	277	37 37	335
154	24 42	018	24 20	044	28 41	111	33 53	182	21 57	222	47 26	278	37 28	336
155	24 49	019	24 36	045	29 02	112	33 52	183	21 42	224	47 03	279	37 19	336
156	24 57	020	24 52	046	29 23	113	33 50	184	21 26	225	46 41	280	37 10	337
157	25 04	020	25 08	047	29 43	114	33 48	186	21 10	226	46 19	281	37 01	338
158	25 12	021	25 24	047	30 04	115	33 46	187	20 54	227	45 57	282	36 53	338
159	25 21	022	25 41	048	30 24	116	33 43	188	20 38	228	45 35	283	36 44	339
160	25 29	023	25 58	049	30 44	117	33 40	189	20 21	229	45 13	283	36 37	340
161	25 38	023	26 15	050	31 04	118	33 36	190	20 04	230	44 51	284	36 29	340
162	25 47	024	26 32	051	31 24	119	33 32	191	19 47	231	44 30	285	36 21	341
163	25 56	025	26 50	051	31 43	120	33 27	193	19 29	232	44 08	286	36 14	342
164	26 06	026	27 07	052	32 03	121	33 22	194	19 11	233	43 46	287	36 07	342

LHA ♈	DENEB Hc	Zn	◆VEGA Hc	Zn	ARCTURUS Hc	Zn	◆REGULUS Hc	Zn	POLLUX Hc	Zn	◆CAPELLA Hc	Zn	Schedar Hc	Zn
165	26 16	026	27 25	053	32 22	122	33 17	195	40 53	241	43 25	288	36 01	343
166	26 26	027	27 43	054	32 41	123	33 11	196	40 33	242	43 04	288	35 54	344
167	26 36	028	28 02	055	32 59	124	33 04	197	40 14	243	42 42	289	35 48	344
168	26 47	029	28 20	056	33 18	125	32 57	198	39 53	244	42 21	290	35 42	345
169	26 58	029	28 39	056	33 36	127	32 50	200	39 33	245	42 00	291	35 37	346
170	27 09	030	28 57	057	33 54	128	32 42	201	39 13	246	41 39	292	35 31	346
171	27 20	031	29 16	058	34 12	129	32 34	202	38 52	247	41 18	292	35 26	347
172	27 32	032	29 36	059	34 29	130	32 25	203	38 31	248	40 58	293	35 21	348
173	27 44	032	29 55	060	34 46	131	32 16	204	38 10	249	40 37	294	35 16	348
174	27 56	033	30 14	060	35 03	132	32 07	205	37 49	250	40 16	295	35 12	349
175	28 09	034	30 34	061	35 20	133	31 57	206	37 28	251	39 56	296	35 08	350
176	28 21	035	30 54	062	35 36	134	31 47	208	37 06	252	39 36	296	35 04	350
177	28 34	036	31 14	063	35 52	135	31 36	209	36 45	253	39 16	297	35 00	351
178	28 47	036	31 34	064	36 07	136	31 25	210	36 23	254	38 56	298	34 57	352
179	29 01	037	31 54	065	36 23	138	31 14	211	36 02	255	38 36	299	34 54	352

LHA ♈	◆ DENEB Hc Zn	VEGA Hc Zn	◆ ARCTURUS Hc Zn	REGULUS Hc Zn	◆ POLLUX Hc Zn	CAPELLA Hc Zn	Schedar Hc Zn
180	29 14 038	32 14 065	36 38 139	31 02 212	35 40 256	38 17 300	34 51 353
181	29 28 039	32 35 066	36 52 140	30 50 213	35 18 257	37 57 300	34 49 354
182	29 42 039	32 56 067	37 07 141	30 38 214	34 56 258	37 38 301	34 46 354
183	29 57 040	33 16 068	37 21 142	30 25 215	34 34 259	37 19 302	34 44 355
184	30 11 041	33 37 069	37 34 143	30 12 217	34 12 260	37 00 303	34 42 356
185	30 26 042	33 58 070	37 48 144	29 58 218	33 50 261	36 41 303	34 41 356
186	30 41 042	34 19 070	38 00 146	29 44 219	33 27 262	36 22 304	34 40 357
187	30 56 043	34 41 071	38 13 147	29 30 220	33 05 263	36 04 305	34 39 358
188	31 12 044	35 02 072	38 25 148	29 15 221	32 43 264	35 45 306	34 38 358
189	31 28 045	35 23 073	38 37 149	29 01 222	32 20 265	35 27 307	34 37 359
190	31 43 045	35 45 074	38 48 150	28 45 223	31 58 266	35 09 307	34 37 000
191	32 00 046	36 06 075	38 59 152	28 30 224	31 35 267	34 51 308	34 37 000
192	32 16 047	36 28 075	39 09 153	28 14 225	31 13 268	34 34 309	34 38 001
193	32 32 048	36 50 076	39 20 154	27 58 226	30 51 269	34 16 310	34 38 002
194	32 49 048	37 12 077	39 29 155	27 42 227	30 28 270	33 59 310	34 39 002

LHA ♈	Schedar Hc Zn	◆ DENEB Hc Zn	VEGA Hc Zn	◆ ARCTURUS Hc Zn	REGULUS Hc Zn	◆ POLLUX Hc Zn	CAPELLA Hc Zn
195	34 40 003	33 06 049	37 34 078	39 38 156	27 25 228	30 06 271	33 42 311
196	34 41 004	33 23 050	37 56 079	39 47 158	27 08 229	29 43 272	33 25 312
197	34 43 004	33 41 051	38 18 080	39 56 159	26 51 230	29 21 273	33 09 313
198	34 45 005	33 58 052	38 40 081	40 04 160	26 33 232	28 58 274	32 52 313
199	34 47 006	34 16 052	39 02 082	40 11 161	26 16 233	28 36 274	32 36 314
200	34 49 006	34 34 053	39 25 082	40 18 162	25 58 234	28 13 275	32 20 315
201	34 52 007	34 52 054	39 47 083	40 25 164	25 39 235	27 51 276	32 04 316
202	34 55 008	35 10 055	40 09 084	40 31 165	25 21 236	27 29 277	31 49 316
203	34 58 008	35 28 055	40 32 085	40 36 166	25 02 237	27 06 278	31 33 317
204	35 02 009	35 47 056	40 54 086	40 41 167	24 43 238	26 44 279	31 18 318
205	35 05 010	36 06 057	41 16 087	40 46 169	24 24 239	26 22 280	31 03 319
206	35 09 010	36 25 058	41 39 088	40 50 170	24 05 240	26 00 281	30 48 319
207	35 13 011	36 44 059	42 01 089	40 54 171	23 45 241	25 38 282	30 34 320
208	35 18 012	37 03 059	42 24 090	40 57 172	23 26 242	25 16 283	30 20 321
209	35 23 012	37 22 060	42 46 091	41 00 174	23 06 243	24 54 283	30 06 322

LHA ♈	Schedar Hc Zn	◆ DENEB Hc Zn	VEGA Hc Zn	◆ ARCTURUS Hc Zn	REGULUS Hc Zn	◆ POLLUX Hc Zn	CAPELLA Hc Zn
210	35 28 013	37 42 061	43 09 092	41 02 175	22 46 244	24 32 284	29 52 323
211	35 33 014	38 02 062	43 31 093	41 04 176	22 26 245	24 10 285	29 38 323
212	35 38 014	38 21 062	43 54 093	41 05 177	22 05 246	23 49 286	29 25 324
213	35 44 015	38 41 063	44 16 094	41 06 179	21 45 247	23 27 287	29 12 325
214	35 50 016	39 02 064	44 38 095	41 06 180	21 24 248	23 06 288	28 59 326
215	35 56 016	39 22 065	45 01 096	41 06 181	21 03 249	22 44 289	28 46 326
216	36 03 017	39 42 066	45 23 097	41 05 182	20 42 250	22 23 290	28 34 327
217	36 10 018	40 03 066	45 45 098	41 04 184	20 21 251	22 02 290	28 22 328
218	36 17 018	40 24 067	46 08 099	41 03 185	20 00 252	21 41 291	28 10 329
219	36 24 019	40 44 068	46 30 100	41 00 186	19 38 253	21 20 292	27 59 329
220	36 31 020	41 05 069	46 52 101	40 58 187	19 17 254	20 59 293	27 47 330
221	36 39 020	41 26 070	47 14 102	40 55 189	18 55 255	20 39 294	27 36 331
222	36 47 021	41 47 070	47 36 103	40 51 190	18 33 255	20 18 295	27 25 332
223	36 55 022	42 09 071	47 58 104	40 47 191	18 11 256	19 58 296	27 15 332
224	37 04 022	42 30 072	48 19 105	40 42 192	17 50 257	19 38 297	27 04 333

LHA ♈	Schedar Hc Zn	◆ DENEB Hc Zn	VEGA Hc Zn	◆ ARCTURUS Hc Zn	REGULUS Hc Zn	◆ POLLUX Hc Zn	CAPELLA Hc Zn
225	37 12 023	42 51 073	48 41 106	40 37 194	17 28 258	19 18 297	26 54 334
226	37 21 024	43 13 074	49 02 107	40 32 195	17 06 259	18 58 298	26 45 335
227	37 31 024	43 35 075	49 24 109	40 26 196	16 43 260	18 38 299	26 35 335
228	37 40 025	43 56 075	49 45 110	40 19 197	16 21 261	18 19 300	26 26 336
229	37 50 026	44 18 076	50 06 111	40 12 199	15 59 262	17 59 301	26 17 337
230	38 00 026	44 40 077	50 27 112	40 05 200	15 37 263	17 40 302	26 08 338
231	38 10 027	45 02 078	50 48 113	39 57 201	15 14 264	17 21 303	26 00 338
232	38 20 028	45 24 079	51 09 114	39 49 202	14 52 265	17 02 303	25 52 339
233	38 31 028	45 46 080	51 29 115	39 40 203	14 30 266	16 44 304	25 44 340
234	38 41 029	46 08 081	51 49 116	39 31 205	14 07 267	16 25 305	25 36 341
235	38 52 030	46 30 081	52 09 117	39 21 206	13 45 268	16 07 306	25 29 341
236	39 04 030	46 53 082	52 29 119	39 11 207	13 22 269	15 49 307	25 22 342
237	39 15 031	47 15 083	52 49 120	39 01 208	13 00 270	15 31 308	25 15 343
238	39 27 032	47 37 084	53 08 121	38 50 209	12 37 271	15 13 309	25 09 344
239	39 39 032	48 00 085	53 27 122	38 39 211	12 15 271	14 56 310	25 03 344

LHA ♈	Alpheratz Hc Zn	◆ DENEB Hc Zn	VEGA Hc Zn	Rasalhague Hc Zn	◆ ARCTURUS Hc Zn	Alioth Hc Zn	◆ CAPELLA Hc Zn
240	16 06 050	48 22 086	53 46 123	32 24 152	38 27 212	65 53 263	24 57 345
241	16 23 051	48 44 087	54 05 124	32 34 153	38 15 213	65 30 264	24 51 346
242	16 41 052	49 07 088	54 23 126	32 44 154	38 03 214	65 08 265	24 46 347
243	16 58 053	49 29 089	54 42 127	32 53 155	37 50 215	64 46 266	24 41 347
244	17 16 054	49 52 089	54 59 128	33 03 157	37 37 217	64 23 267	24 36 348
245	17 35 054	50 14 090	55 17 129	33 11 158	37 23 218	64 01 268	24 32 349
246	17 53 055	50 37 091	55 34 131	33 20 159	37 09 219	63 38 269	24 28 350
247	18 12 056	50 59 092	55 51 132	33 27 160	36 55 220	63 16 270	24 24 351
248	18 30 057	51 22 093	56 07 133	33 35 161	36 40 221	62 53 271	24 20 351
249	18 49 058	51 44 094	56 24 135	33 42 162	36 25 222	62 31 272	24 17 352
250	19 08 059	52 06 095	56 39 136	33 48 164	36 10 223	62 08 273	24 14 353
251	19 28 060	52 29 096	56 55 137	33 55 165	35 54 224	61 46 274	24 11 354
252	19 47 060	52 51 097	57 10 139	34 00 166	35 39 226	61 23 274	24 09 354
253	20 07 061	53 13 098	57 25 140	34 06 167	35 22 227	61 01 275	24 07 355
254	20 27 062	53 36 099	57 39 141	34 10 168	35 06 228	60 39 276	24 05 356

LHA ♈	Alpheratz Hc Zn	◆ DENEB Hc Zn	ALTAIR Hc Zn	Rasalhague Hc Zn	◆ ARCTURUS Hc Zn	Alioth Hc Zn	◆ CAPELLA Hc Zn
255	20 47 063	53 58 100	24 30 132	34 15 169	34 49 229	60 16 277	24 04 357
256	21 07 064	54 20 101	24 47 133	34 19 171	34 32 230	59 54 278	24 02 357
257	21 27 065	54 42 102	25 03 134	34 22 172	34 15 231	59 32 279	24 02 358
258	21 47 066	55 04 103	25 19 136	34 25 173	33 57 232	59 10 280	24 01 359
259	22 08 067	55 26 104	25 34 137	34 27 174	33 39 233	58 47 280	24 01 000
260	22 29 067	55 47 105	25 50 138	34 29 175	33 21 234	58 25 281	24 01 000
261	22 49 068	56 09 106	26 05 139	34 31 177	33 03 235	58 03 282	24 01 001
262	23 10 069	56 31 107	26 19 140	34 32 178	32 44 236	57 41 283	24 02 002
263	23 31 070	56 52 109	26 34 141	34 33 179	32 25 238	57 20 284	24 03 003
264	23 53 071	57 13 110	26 48 142	34 33 180	32 06 239	56 58 284	24 04 003
265	24 14 072	57 34 111	27 02 143	34 33 181	31 47 240	56 36 285	24 05 004
266	24 35 073	57 55 112	27 15 144	34 32 182	31 27 241	56 14 286	24 07 005
267	24 57 074	58 16 113	27 28 145	34 31 184	31 08 242	55 53 287	24 09 006
268	25 18 074	58 37 114	27 41 146	34 29 185	30 48 243	55 31 287	24 12 006
269	25 40 075	58 57 115	27 53 147	34 27 186	30 28 244	55 10 288	24 14 007

LAT 68°N

LHA ♈	◆ CAPELLA Hc Zn	Alpheratz Hc Zn	◆ DENEB Hc Zn	ALTAIR Hc Zn	Rasalhague Hc Zn	◆ ARCTURUS Hc Zn	Alioth Hc Zn
270	24 17 008	26 02 076	59 17 117	28 05 148	34 24 187	30 07 245	54 49 289
271	24 21 009	26 24 077	59 37 118	28 16 150	34 21 188	29 47 246	54 27 290
272	24 24 010	26 46 078	59 57 119	28 28 151	34 18 190	29 26 247	54 06 290
273	24 28 010	27 08 079	60 16 120	28 38 152	34 14 191	29 06 248	53 45 291
274	24 32 011	27 30 080	60 36 122	28 49 153	34 09 192	28 45 249	53 24 292
275	24 37 012	27 52 081	60 55 123	28 59 154	34 05 193	28 24 250	53 04 293
276	24 41 013	28 14 081	61 13 124	29 09 155	33 59 194	28 03 251	52 43 293
277	24 46 013	28 36 082	61 32 126	29 18 156	33 53 195	27 41 252	52 22 294
278	24 52 014	28 59 083	61 50 127	29 27 157	33 47 197	27 20 253	52 02 295
279	24 57 015	29 21 084	62 08 128	29 35 158	33 41 198	26 58 254	51 41 296
280	25 03 016	29 43 085	62 25 130	29 43 160	33 34 199	26 37 255	51 21 296
281	25 09 016	30 06 086	62 42 131	29 51 161	33 26 200	26 15 256	51 01 297
282	25 16 017	30 28 087	62 59 132	29 58 162	33 18 201	25 53 257	50 41 298
283	25 23 018	30 51 088	63 16 134	30 05 163	33 10 202	25 31 258	50 21 298
284	25 30 019	31 13 089	63 32 135	30 11 164	33 01 204	25 09 259	50 02 299

LHA ♈	◆ CAPELLA Hc Zn	Hamal Hc Zn	Alpheratz Hc Zn	◆ DENEB Hc Zn	VEGA Hc Zn	◆ ARCTURUS Hc Zn	Alioth Hc Zn
285	25 37 019	15 39 066	31 36 090	63 47 137	60 38 189	24 47 260	49 42 300
286	25 45 020	16 00 066	31 58 091	64 02 138	60 34 191	24 25 261	49 23 301
287	25 53 021	16 20 067	32 21 092	64 17 140	60 30 192	24 03 262	49 03 301
288	26 01 022	16 41 068	32 43 092	64 31 141	60 25 194	23 40 262	48 44 302
289	26 09 022	17 02 069	33 06 093	64 45 143	60 19 195	23 18 263	48 25 303
290	26 18 023	17 23 070	33 28 [illegible]	64 58 144	60 13 197	22 56 264	48 06 303
291	26 27 024	17 44 071	33 50 095	65 11 146	60 06 198	22 33 265	47 48 304
292	26 36 025	18 05 072	34 13 096	65 24 148	59 59 200	22 11 266	47 29 305
293	26 46 025	18 27 073	34 35 097	65 35 149	59 51 201	21 49 267	47 11 305
294	26 55 026	18 48 074	34 57 098	65 47 151	59 42 203	21 26 268	46 53 306
295	27 06 027	19 10 074	35 20 099	65 57 153	59 33 204	21 04 269	46 35 307
296	27 16 028	19 32 075	35 42 100	66 07 154	59 24 206	20 41 270	46 17 308
297	27 26 028	19 53 076	36 04 101	66 17 156	59 14 207	20 19 271	45 59 308
298	27 37 029	20 15 077	36 26 102	66 26 158	59 03 209	19 56 272	45 41 309
299	27 48 030	20 37 078	36 48 103	66 34 159	58 52 210	19 34 273	45 24 310

LHA ♈	◆ CAPELLA Hc Zn	Hamal Hc Zn	Alpheratz Hc Zn	◆ DENEB Hc Zn	VEGA Hc Zn	◆ ARCTURUS Hc Zn	Dubhe Hc Zn
300	28 00 031	20 59 079	37 10 104	66 41 161	58 40 212	19 11 274	43 52 332
301	28 11 032	21 21 080	37 31 105	66 48 163	58 28 213	18 49 275	43 42 332
302	28 23 032	21 44 081	37 53 106	66 55 165	58 15 215	18 27 275	43 31 333
303	28 35 033	22 06 082	38 15 107	67 00 166	58 02 216	18 04 276	43 21 333
304	28 48 034	22 28 083	38 36 108	67 05 168	57 49 218	17 42 277	43 11 334
305	29 00 035	22 50 083	38 57 109	67 09 170	57 35 219	17 20 278	43 01 335
306	29 13 035	23 13 084	39 18 110	67 13 172	57 21 220	16 57 279	42 52 335
307	29 26 036	23 35 085	39 39 111	67 16 174	57 06 222	16 35 280	42 43 336
308	29 40 037	23 57 086	40 00 112	67 18 175	56 51 223	16 13 281	42 34 337
309	29 53 038	24 20 087	40 21 113	67 19 177	56 35 224	15 51 282	42 25 337
310	30 07 038	24 42 088	40 42 114	67 20 179	56 19 226	15 29 283	42 16 338
311	30 21 039	25 05 089	41 02 115	67 20 181	56 03 227	15 07 284	42 08 338
312	30 35 040	25 27 090	41 22 116	67 19 183	55 46 228	14 45 285	42 00 339
313	30 50 041	25 50 091	41 42 118	67 18 185	55 29 230	14 24 285	41 52 340
314	31 05 041	26 12 092	42 02 119	67 16 186	55 12 231	14 02 286	41 44 340

LHA ♈	◆ CAPELLA Hc Zn	Hamal Hc Zn	Alpheratz Hc Zn	◆ DENEB Hc Zn	VEGA Hc Zn	◆ Alphecca Hc Zn	Dubhe Hc Zn
315	31 20 042	26 35 093	42 22 120	67 13 188	54 54 232	27 52 273	41 36 341
316	31 35 043	26 57 094	42 41 121	67 09 190	54 37 233	27 30 274	41 29 341
317	31 50 044	27 20 095	43 00 122	67 05 192	54 18 235	27 07 274	41 22 342
318	32 06 044	27 42 095	43 19 123	67 00 194	54 00 236	26 45 275	41 15 343
319	32 22 045	28 04 096	43 38 124	66 54 195	53 41 237	26 23 276	41 09 343
320	32 38 046	28 27 097	43 56 125	66 48 197	53 22 238	26 00 277	41 02 344
321	32 54 047	28 49 098	44 15 126	66 41 199	53 03 239	25 38 278	40 56 345
322	33 10 047	29 11 099	44 33 128	66 34 201	52 43 241	25 16 279	40 50 345
323	33 27 048	29 33 100	44 50 129	66 25 202	52 24 242	24 54 280	40 45 346
324	33 44 049	29 55 101	45 08 130	66 16 204	52 04 243	24 32 281	40 39 346
325	34 01 050	30 17 102	45 25 131	66 07 206	51 44 244	24 10 282	40 34 347
326	34 18 050	30 39 103	45 42 132	65 57 207	51 23 245	23 48 283	40 29 348
327	34 36 051	31 01 104	45 58 133	65 46 209	51 03 246	23 26 283	40 24 348
328	34 53 052	31 23 105	46 14 135	65 35 211	50 42 247	23 04 284	40 20 349
329	35 11 053	31 45 106	46 30 136	65 23 212	50 21 249	22 42 285	40 16 349

LHA ♈	CAPELLA Hc Zn	◆ Hamal Hc Zn	Alpheratz Hc Zn	◆ ALTAIR Hc Zn	VEGA Hc Zn	Alphecca Hc Zn	◆ Alioth Hc Zn
330	35 29 054	32 06 107	46 45 137	27 12 216	50 00 250	22 20 286	38 00 331
331	35 47 054	32 27 108	47 01 138	26 58 217	49 39 251	21 59 287	37 49 331
332	36 05 055	32 49 109	47 15 140	26 44 218	49 18 252	21 37 288	37 38 332
333	36 24 056	33 10 110	47 30 141	26 30 219	48 57 253	21 16 289	37 28 333
334	36 43 057	33 31 111	47 44 142	26 16 220	48 35 254	20 55 290	37 17 333
335	37 02 057	33 52 112	47 57 143	26 01 222	48 13 255	20 34 291	37 07 334
336	37 21 058	34 13 113	48 11 145	25 46 223	47 52 256	20 13 291	36 58 335
337	37 40 059	34 33 114	48 23 146	25 31 224	47 30 257	19 52 292	36 48 335
338	37 59 060	34 54 115	48 36 147	25 15 225	47 08 258	19 31 293	36 39 336
339	38 19 061	35 14 116	48 48 148	24 59 226	46 46 259	19 11 294	36 30 337
340	38 38 061	35 34 117	48 59 150	24 43 227	46 24 260	18 50 295	36 21 337
341	38 58 062	35 54 118	49 11 151	24 26 228	46 02 261	18 30 296	36 12 338
342	39 18 063	36 13 119	49 21 152	24 10 229	45 39 262	18 10 297	36 04 339
343	39 38 064	36 33 121	49 31 154	23 52 230	45 17 263	17 50 298	35 56 339
344	39 58 064	36 52 122	49 41 155	23 35 231	44 55 264	17 30 298	35 48 340

LHA ♈	◆ POLLUX Hc Zn	CAPELLA Hc Zn	Hamal Hc Zn	◆ Alpheratz Hc Zn	ALTAIR Hc Zn	◆ VEGA Hc Zn	Alioth Hc Zn
345	12 27 043	40 19 065	37 11 123	49 50 156	23 18 232	44 32 265	35 41 341
346	12 43 043	40 39 066	37 30 124	49 59 158	23 00 233	44 10 266	35 33 341
347	12 58 044	41 00 067	37 49 125	50 08 159	22 42 234	43 47 267	35 26 342
348	13 14 045	41 20 068	38 07 126	50 15 160	22 23 235	43 25 268	35 19 343
349	13 30 046	41 41 068	38 25 127	50 23 162	22 05 236	43 03 269	35 13 343
350	13 46 047	42 02 069	38 43 128	50 30 163	21 46 237	42 40 270	35 06 344
351	14 03 048	42 23 070	39 00 129	50 36 164	21 27 238	42 18 271	35 00 345
352	14 20 049	42 44 071	39 18 130	50 42 166	21 08 239	41 55 271	34 55 345
353	14 37 050	43 06 072	39 35 132	50 47 167	20 48 240	41 33 272	34 49 346
354	14 54 050	43 27 072	39 51 133	50 52 168	20 29 241	41 10 273	34 44 347
355	15 11 051	43 49 073	40 08 134	50 56 170	20 09 242	40 48 274	34 39 347
356	15 29 052	44 10 074	40 24 135	51 00 171	19 49 243	40 25 275	34 34 348
357	15 47 053	44 32 075	40 39 136	51 03 173	19 29 244	40 03 276	34 29 349
358	16 05 054	44 54 076	40 55 137	51 05 174	19 09 245	39 41 277	34 25 349
359	16 23 055	45 15 077	41 10 138	51 07 175	18 48 246	39 18 278	34 21 350

LHA ♈	Hc	Zn	Hc	Zn	Hc	Zn	Hc	Zn	Hc	Zn	Hc	Zn	Hc	Zn
	◆ POLLUX		CAPELLA		Hamal		◆ Alpheratz		DENEB		◆ VEGA		Alioth	
0	16 07	055	45 24	076	42 10	139	52 09	177	56 25	255	38 47	279	33 18	351
1	16 27	056	45 47	077	42 25	140	52 10	178	56 02	256	38 24	280	33 15	352
2	16 46	057	46 09	078	42 40	141	52 10	180	55 39	257	38 01	281	33 11	352
3	17 06	058	46 32	079	42 55	143	52 10	181	55 16	258	37 38	282	33 08	353
4	17 26	059	46 56	080	43 09	144	52 10	182	54 53	259	37 15	283	33 05	354
5	17 46	060	47 19	081	43 22	145	52 08	184	54 30	260	36 52	284	33 03	354
6	18 07	060	47 42	082	43 35	146	52 06	185	54 07	261	36 29	285	33 01	355
7	18 27	061	48 05	082	43 48	148	52 04	187	53 44	262	36 07	285	32 59	356
8	18 48	062	48 28	083	44 01	149	52 01	188	53 20	263	35 44	286	32 57	356
9	19 09	063	48 52	084	44 13	150	51 57	190	52 57	264	35 22	287	32 56	357
10	19 29	064	49 15	085	44 24	151	51 53	191	52 34	265	34 59	288	32 55	358
11	19 51	065	49 38	086	44 35	153	51 48	192	52 10	266	34 37	289	32 54	358
12	20 12	066	50 02	087	44 46	154	51 43	194	51 47	267	34 15	290	32 53	359
13	20 33	066	50 25	088	44 56	155	51 37	195	51 24	268	33 53	290	32 53	000
14	20 55	067	50 48	089	45 05	156	51 31	197	51 00	269	33 31	291	32 53	000
	Alioth		◆ POLLUX		CAPELLA		Hamal		◆ Alpheratz		DENEB		◆ VEGA	
15	32 53	001	21 17	068	51 12	090	45 15	158	51 24	198	50 37	270	33 09	292
16	32 53	002	21 38	069	51 35	090	45 23	159	51 16	199	50 13	271	32 47	293
17	32 54	002	22 00	070	51 59	091	45 31	160	51 08	201	49 50	272	32 26	294
18	32 55	003	22 22	071	52 22	092	45 39	161	51 00	202	49 26	273	32 05	295
19	32 57	004	22 45	072	52 46	093	45 46	163	50 51	203	49 03	274	31 43	295
20	32 58	004	23 07	073	53 09	094	45 53	164	50 41	205	48 40	274	31 22	296
21	33 00	005	23 29	073	53 32	095	45 59	165	50 31	206	48 16	275	31 01	297
22	33 02	006	23 52	074	53 56	096	46 05	167	50 21	207	47 53	276	30 40	298
23	33 05	006	24 14	075	54 19	097	46 10	168	50 10	209	47 30	277	30 20	299
24	33 07	007	24 37	076	54 42	098	46 15	169	49 58	210	47 06	278	29 59	299
25	33 10	008	25 00	077	55 05	099	46 19	171	49 46	211	46 43	279	29 39	300
26	33 13	008	25 23	078	55 29	100	46 22	172	49 34	213	46 20	280	29 19	301
27	33 17	009	25 46	079	55 52	101	46 25	173	49 21	214	45 57	281	28 59	302
28	33 21	010	26 09	080	56 15	102	46 28	175	49 07	215	45 34	281	28 39	303
29	33 25	010	26 32	080	56 37	103	46 30	176	48 53	217	45 11	282	28 19	304
	Alioth		◆ POLLUX		ALDEBARAN		◆ Hamal		Alpheratz		DENEB		◆ VEGA	
30	33 29	011	26 55	081	33 32	133	46 31	177	48 39	218	44 48	283	28 00	304
31	33 34	012	27 18	082	33 48	134	46 32	179	48 25	219	44 25	284	27 41	305
32	33 38	012	27 42	083	34 05	136	46 32	180	48 10	220	44 03	285	27 22	306
33	33 44	013	28 05	084	34 21	137	46 32	181	47 54	222	43 40	286	27 03	307
34	33 49	014	28 28	085	34 37	138	46 31	183	47 38	223	43 17	286	26 44	308
35	33 55	014	28 52	086	34 53	139	46 30	184	47 22	224	42 55	287	26 25	308
36	34 00	015	29 15	087	35 08	140	46 28	185	47 06	225	42 33	288	26 07	309
37	34 07	016	29 38	088	35 23	141	46 25	187	46 49	227	42 10	289	25 49	310
38	34 13	016	30 02	089	35 37	142	46 22	188	46 32	228	41 48	290	25 31	311
39	34 20	017	30 25	089	35 51	143	46 19	189	46 14	229	41 26	290	25 14	312
40	34 27	018	30 49	090	36 05	145	46 15	191	45 56	230	41 04	291	24 56	312
41	34 34	018	31 12	091	36 19	146	46 10	192	45 38	231	40 43	292	24 39	313
42	34 41	019	31 35	092	36 32	147	46 05	193	45 20	233	40 21	293	24 22	314
43	34 49	020	31 59	093	36 44	148	45 59	195	45 01	234	39 59	294	24 05	315
44	34 57	020	32 22	094	36 56	149	45 53	196	44 42	235	39 38	294	23 49	316
	Alioth		◆ POLLUX		ALDEBARAN		◆ Hamal		Alpheratz		DENEB		◆ VEGA	
45	35 05	021	32 46	095	37 08	150	45 46	197	44 23	236	39 17	295	23 32	316
46	35 14	022	33 09	096	37 19	152	45 39	198	44 03	237	38 55	296	23 16	317
47	35 22	022	33 32	097	37 30	153	45 32	200	43 43	238	38 34	297	23 00	318
48	35 31	023	33 56	098	37 41	154	45 23	201	43 23	239	38 14	297	22 45	319
49	35 41	024	34 19	099	37 51	155	45 15	202	43 03	240	37 53	298	22 29	319
50	35 50	024	34 42	100	38 00	156	45 06	204	42 43	242	37 32	299	22 14	320
51	36 00	025	35 05	101	38 10	158	44 56	205	42 22	243	37 12	300	21 59	321
52	36 10	026	35 28	102	38 18	159	44 46	206	42 01	244	36 52	301	21 45	322
53	36 20	026	35 51	103	38 27	160	44 35	207	41 40	245	36 31	301	21 30	323
54	36 31	027	36 14	104	38 34	161	44 24	209	41 18	246	36 12	302	21 16	323
55	36 41	028	36 36	105	38 42	162	44 13	210	40 57	247	35 52	303	21 03	324
56	36 52	028	36 59	106	38 48	164	44 01	211	40 35	248	35 32	304	20 49	325
57	37 03	029	37 22	107	38 55	165	43 48	212	40 14	249	35 13	304	20 36	326
58	37 15	029	37 44	108	39 01	166	43 36	214	39 52	250	34 53	305	20 23	327
59	37 26	030	38 06	109	39 06	167	43 22	215	39 30	251	34 34	306	20 10	327
	Alioth		◆ POLLUX		ALDEBARAN		◆ Hamal		Alpheratz		DENEB		◆ VEGA	
60	37 38	031	38 28	110	39 11	169	43 09	216	39 07	252	34 16	307	19 57	328
61	37 51	031	38 50	111	39 15	170	42 55	217	38 45	253	33 57	307	19 45	329
62	38 03	032	39 12	112	39 19	171	42 40	219	38 22	254	33 38	308	19 33	330
63	38 15	033	39 34	113	39 23	172	42 25	220	38 00	255	33 20	309	19 22	331
64	38 28	033	39 55	114	39 25	174	42 10	221	37 37	256	33 02	310	19 10	331
65	38 41	034	40 17	115	39 28	175	41 55	222	37 14	257	32 44	311	18 59	332
66	38 55	035	40 38	116	39 30	176	41 39	223	36 51	258	32 26	311	18 49	333
67	39 08	035	40 59	117	39 31	177	41 23	224	36 28	259	32 09	312	18 38	334
68	39 22	036	41 20	118	39 32	179	41 06	226	36 05	260	31 51	313	18 28	335
69	39 36	037	41 40	119	39 32	180	40 49	227	35 42	261	31 34	314	18 18	335
70	39 50	037	42 01	120	39 32	181	40 32	228	35 19	262	31 17	314	18 09	336
71	40 04	038	42 21	121	39 31	182	40 14	229	34 56	263	31 01	315	17 59	337
72	40 19	039	42 41	123	39 30	183	39 56	230	34 33	264	30 44	316	17 50	338
73	40 34	039	43 00	124	39 29	185	39 38	231	34 09	265	30 28	317	17 42	339
74	40 49	040	43 20	125	39 26	186	39 20	232	33 46	266	30 12	317	17 33	340
	Alioth		◆ REGULUS		PROCYON		◆ ALDEBARAN		Hamal		Alpheratz		◆ DENEB	
75	41 04	041	15 53	097	22 24	136	39 24	187	39 01	234	33 22	267	29 56	318
76	41 19	041	16 17	098	22 41	137	39 21	188	38 42	235	32 59	268	29 41	319
77	41 35	042	16 40	099	22 56	138	39 17	190	38 23	236	32 36	269	29 25	320
78	41 51	043	17 03	100	23 12	139	39 13	191	38 03	237	32 12	269	29 10	320
79	42 07	043	17 26	101	23 27	140	39 08	192	37 44	238	31 49	270	28 55	321
80	42 23	044	17 49	102	23 42	141	39 03	193	37 24	239	31 25	271	28 41	322
81	42 39	045	18 12	103	23 56	142	38 57	195	37 03	240	31 02	272	28 26	323
82	42 56	045	18 35	104	24 10	143	38 51	196	36 43	241	30 38	273	28 12	323
83	43 13	046	18 58	105	24 24	145	38 44	197	36 22	242	30 15	274	27 58	324
84	43 30	047	19 20	106	24 37	146	38 37	198	36 01	243	29 52	275	27 45	325
85	43 47	047	19 43	106	24 51	147	38 30	199	35 40	244	29 28	276	27 31	326
86	44 04	048	20 05	107	25 03	148	38 22	201	35 19	245	29 05	277	27 18	326
87	44 22	049	20 27	108	25 16	149	38 13	202	34 58	246	28 42	278	27 05	327
88	44 39	049	20 50	109	25 27	150	38 04	203	34 36	247	28 19	279	26 53	328
89	44 57	050	21 12	110	25 39	151	37 55	204	34 14	248	27 55	279	26 40	329

LHA ♈	Hc	Zn	Hc	Zn	Hc	Zn	Hc	Zn	Hc	Zn	Hc	Zn	Hc	Zn
	Alioth		◆ REGULUS		PROCYON		BETELGEUSE		◆ ALDEBARAN		Hamal		◆ DENEB	
90	45 15	051	21 34	111	25 50	152	30 24	181	37 45	206	33 53	249	26 28	329
91	45 33	051	21 55	112	26 01	153	30 24	182	37 34	207	33 31	250	26 17	330
92	45 52	052	22 17	113	26 11	154	30 22	183	37 24	208	33 08	251	26 05	331
93	46 10	053	22 38	114	26 21	155	30 21	185	37 13	209	32 46	252	25 54	332
94	46 29	053	23 00	115	26 31	156	30 19	186	37 01	210	32 24	253	25 43	332
95	46 48	054	23 21	116	26 40	158	30 16	187	36 49	211	32 01	254	25 32	333
96	47 07	055	23 42	117	26 49	159	30 13	188	36 37	213	31 38	255	25 22	334
97	47 26	055	24 03	118	26 57	160	30 09	189	36 24	214	31 16	256	25 11	335
98	47 46	056	24 23	119	27 05	161	30 06	190	36 10	215	30 53	257	25 01	335
99	48 05	057	24 43	120	27 12	162	30 01	191	35 57	216	30 30	258	24 52	336
100	48 25	058	25 04	121	27 19	163	29 56	193	35 43	217	30 07	259	24 42	337
101	48 45	058	25 24	122	27 26	164	29 51	194	35 29	218	29 44	260	24 33	338
102	49 05	059	25 43	123	27 32	165	29 45	195	35 14	219	29 21	261	24 25	338
103	49 25	060	26 03	124	27 38	166	29 39	196	34 59	221	28 58	262	24 16	339
104	49 45	060	26 22	125	27 43	168	29 32	197	34 43	222	28 34	263	24 08	340
	Alioth		◆ REGULUS		PROCYON		BETELGEUSE		◆ CAPELLA		Hamal		◆ DENEB	
105	50 06	061	26 41	126	27 48	169	29 25	198	65 07	225	28 11	264	24 00	341
106	50 26	062	27 00	127	27 52	170	29 17	199	64 50	227	27 48	265	23 52	341
107	50 47	062	27 18	128	27 56	171	29 09	201	64 32	228	27 24	266	23 45	342
108	51 08	063	27 36	130	28 00	172	29 01	202	64 15	230	27 01	267	23 38	343
109	51 29	064	27 54	131	28 03	173	28 52	203	63 57	231	26 38	268	23 31	344
110	51 50	064	28 12	132	28 05	174	28 43	204	63 38	233	26 14	269	23 25	344
111	52 11	065	28 29	133	28 07	175	28 33	205	63 19	234	25 51	270	23 19	345
112	52 32	066	28 46	134	28 09	177	28 23	206	63 00	235	25 27	271	23 13	346
113	52 54	067	29 03	135	28 10	178	28 12	207	62 41	237	25 04	272	23 07	347
114	53 15	067	29 20	136	28 11	179	28 01	208	62 21	238	24 40	272	23 02	347
115	53 37	068	29 36	137	28 11	180	27 50	209	62 01	239	24 17	273	22 57	348
116	53 59	069	29 52	138	28 11	181	27 38	211	61 41	241	23 54	274	22 53	349
117	54 21	069	30 07	139	28 10	182	27 26	212	61 20	242	23 30	275	22 48	350
118	54 43	070	30 22	140	28 09	183	27 14	213	60 59	243	23 07	276	22 44	351
119	55 05	071	30 37	141	28 07	184	27 01	214	60 38	244	22 44	277	22 41	351
	◆ VEGA		ARCTURUS		◆ REGULUS		PROCYON		◆ CAPELLA		Schedar		DENEB	
120	16 58	017	15 58	079	30 51	142	28 05	186	60 17	246	44 08	314	22 37	352
121	17 05	017	16 21	080	31 06	144	28 03	187	59 56	247	43 51	314	22 34	353
122	17 12	018	16 44	080	31 19	145	28 00	188	59 34	248	43 35	315	22 31	354
123	17 20	019	17 07	081	31 33	146	27 56	189	59 12	249	43 18	316	22 29	354
124	17 27	020	17 30	082	31 46	147	27 53	190	58 50	250	43 02	316	22 27	355
125	17 36	021	17 53	083	31 58	148	27 48	191	58 28	251	42 46	317	22 25	356
126	17 44	022	18 17	084	32 10	149	27 43	192	58 06	253	42 30	318	22 23	357
127	17 53	022	18 40	085	32 22	150	27 38	193	57 43	254	42 14	318	22 22	357
128	18 02	023	19 03	086	32 34	151	27 32	195	57 21	255	41 59	319	22 21	358
129	18 11	024	19 27	087	32 45	153	27 26	196	56 58	256	41 43	320	22 20	359
130	18 21	025	19 50	088	32 55	154	27 20	197	56 35	257	41 28	320	22 20	000
131	18 31	026	20 14	089	33 05	155	27 13	198	56 12	258	41 14	321	22 20	000
132	18 41	026	20 37	090	33 15	156	27 05	199	55 49	259	40 59	322	22 20	001
133	18 52	027	21 00	090	33 24	157	26 57	200	55 26	260	40 44	322	22 21	002
134	19 02	028	21 24	091	33 33	158	26 49	201	55 03	261	40 30	323	22 22	003
	DENEB		◆ VEGA		ARCTURUS		◆ REGULUS		PROCYON		◆ CAPELLA		Schedar	
135	22 23	003	19 14	029	21 47	092	33 42	160	26 40	202	54 40	262	40 16	324
136	22 25	004	19 25	030	22 11	093	33 50	161	26 31	203	54 17	263	40 02	324
137	22 27	005	19 37	030	22 34	094	33 57	162	26 22	205	53 53	264	39 49	325
138	22 29	006	19 49	031	22 57	095	34 04	163	26 12	206	53 30	265	39 35	326
139	22 31	006	20 01	032	23 21	096	34 11	164	26 01	207	53 07	266	39 22	326
140	22 34	007	20 13	033	23 44	097	34 17	165	25 51	208	52 43	267	39 09	327
141	22 37	008	20 26	034	24 07	098	34 23	167	25 40	209	52 20	268	38 57	328
142	22 41	009	20 39	034	24 31	099	34 28	168	25 28	210	51 56	269	38 44	328
143	22 44	010	20 53	035	24 54	100	34 33	169	25 16	211	51 33	270	38 32	329
144	22 48	010	21 06	036	25 17	101	34 37	170	25 04	212	51 10	271	38 20	330
145	22 53	011	21 20	037	25 40	102	34 41	171	24 51	213	50 46	271	38 08	330
146	22 57	012	21 34	038	26 03	103	34 44	173	24 38	214	50 23	272	37 57	331
147	23 02	013	21 49	038	26 26	104	34 47	174	24 25	215	49 59	273	37 45	331
148	23 08	013	22 03	039	26 48	105	34 49	175	24 11	216	49 36	274	37 34	332
149	23 13	014	22 18	040	27 11	106	34 51	176	23 57	218	49 13	275	37 23	333
	DENEB		◆ VEGA		ARCTURUS		◆ REGULUS		PROCYON		◆ CAPELLA		Schedar	
150	23 19	015	22 34	041	27 33	107	34 52	177	23 42	219	48 49	276	37 13	333
151	23 25	016	22 49	042	27 56	108	34 53	178	23 28	220	48 26	277	37 02	334
152	23 32	016	23 05	042	28 18	108	34 54	180	23 12	221	48 03	278	36 52	335
153	23 38	017	23 21	043	28 40	109	34 53	181	22 57	222	47 39	279	36 42	335
154	23 45	018	23 37	044	29 02	110	34 53	182	22 41	223	47 16	279	36 33	336
155	23 53	019	23 53	045	29 24	111	34 52	183	22 25	224	46 53	280	36 23	337
156	24 00	019	24 10	046	29 46	112	34 50	184	22 09	225	46 30	281	36 14	337
157	24 08	020	24 27	046	30 08	113	34 48	186	21 52	226	46 07	282	36 05	338
158	24 16	021	24 44	047	30 29	115	34 46	187	21 35	227	45 44	283	35 57	339
159	24 25	022	25 01	048	30 50	116	34 43	188	21 18	228	45 21	284	35 48	339
160	24 34	022	25 18	049	31 11	117	34 39	189	21 00	229	44 59	284	35 40	340
161	24 43	023	25 36	050	31 32	118	34 35	190	20 43	230	44 36	285	35 32	341
162	24 52	024	25 54	050	31 53	119	34 31	192	20 24	231	44 13	286	35 25	341
163	25 02	025	26 12	051	32 13	120	34 26	193	20 06	232	43 51	287	35 17	342
164	25 12	025	26 31	052	32 34	121	34 20	194	19 47	233	43 29	288	35 10	343
	DENEB		◆ VEGA		ARCTURUS		◆ REGULUS		POLLUX		◆ CAPELLA		Schedar	
165	25 22	026	26 49	053	32 54	122	34 15	195	41 22	242	43 06	288	35 03	343
166	25 32	027	27 08	054	33 13	123	34 08	196	41 01	243	42 44	289	34 57	344
167	25 43	028	27 27	054	33 33	124	34 01	197	40 40	244	42 22	290	34 50	345
168	25 54	028	27 46	055	33 52	125	33 54	199	40 19	245	42 00	291	34 44	345
169	26 05	029	28 05	056	34 11	126	33 46	200	39 58	246	41 38	292	34 38	346
170	26 17	030	28 25	057	34 30	127	33 38	201	39 36	247	41 17	292	34 33	347
171	26 29	031	28 44	058	34 49	128	33 30	202	39 15	248	40 55	293	34 27	347
172	26 41	031	29 04	058	35 07	129	33 21	203	38 53	249	40 33	294	34 22	348
173	26 53	032	29 24	059	35 25	130	33 11	204	38 31	250	40 12	295	34 18	349
174	27 06	033	29 45	060	35 43	131	33 01	206	38 09	251	39 51	296	34 13	349
175	27 19	034	30 05	061	36 00	133	32 51	207	37 47	252	39 30	296	34 09	350
176	27 32	034	30 25	062	36 17	134	32 40	208	37 24	253	39 09	297	34 05	351
177	27 45	035	30 46	062	36 34	135	32 29	209	37 02	254	38 48	298	34 01	351
178	27 59	036	31 07	063	36 51	136	32 17	210	36 39	255	38 27	299	33 58	352
179	28 13	037	31 28	064	37 07	137	32 05	211	36 16	256	38 07	299	33 55	353

LHA ♈	Hc	Zn	Hc	Zn	Hc	Zn	Hc	Zn	Hc	Zn	Hc	Zn	Hc	Zn
	◆DENEB		VEGA		◆ARCTURUS		REGULUS		◆POLLUX		CAPELLA		Schedar	
180	28 27	037	31 49	065	37 23	138	31 53	212	35 54	257	37 47	300	33 52	353
181	28 41	038	32 10	066	37 38	139	31 40	214	35 31	258	37 26	301	33 49	354
182	28 56	039	32 32	066	37 53	141	31 27	215	35 08	259	37 06	302	33 47	354
183	29 11	040	32 53	067	38 08	142	31 14	216	34 45	260	36 47	303	33 44	355
184	29 26	040	33 15	068	38 22	143	31 00	217	34 21	261	36 27	303	33 43	356
185	29 41	041	33 37	069	38 36	144	30 46	218	33 58	262	36 07	304	33 41	356
186	29 57	042	33 59	070	38 50	145	30 31	219	33 35	263	35 48	305	33 40	357
187	30 12	043	34 21	071	39 03	146	30 16	220	33 12	264	35 29	306	33 39	358
188	30 28	043	34 43	071	39 16	148	30 01	221	32 48	265	35 10	306	33 38	358
189	30 45	044	35 05	072	39 28	149	29 45	222	32 25	266	34 51	307	33 37	359
190	31 01	045	35 28	073	39 40	150	29 29	223	32 02	267	34 33	308	33 37	000
191	31 18	046	35 50	074	39 52	151	29 13	225	31 38	268	34 14	309	33 37	000
192	31 35	046	36 13	075	40 03	152	28 56	226	31 15	269	33 56	309	33 38	001
193	31 52	047	36 35	076	40 13	154	28 39	227	30 51	270	33 38	310	33 38	002
194	32 09	048	36 58	076	40 24	155	28 22	228	30 28	270	33 20	311	33 39	002
	Schedar		◆DENEB		VEGA		◆ARCTURUS		REGULUS		◆POLLUX		CAPELLA	
195	33 40	003	32 27	049	37 21	077	40 33	156	28 05	229	30 04	271	33 02	312
196	33 41	004	32 44	050	37 44	078	40 43	157	27 47	230	29 41	272	32 45	312
197	33 43	004	33 02	050	38 07	079	40 52	158	27 29	231	29 18	273	32 28	313
198	33 45	005	33 21	051	38 30	080	41 00	160	27 10	232	28 54	274	32 11	314
199	33 47	006	33 39	052	38 53	081	41 08	161	26 52	233	28 31	275	31 54	315
200	33 50	006	33 57	053	39 16	082	41 15	162	26 33	234	28 08	276	31 37	315
201	33 52	007	34 16	053	39 39	083	41 22	163	26 14	235	27 44	277	31 21	316
202	33 56	008	34 35	054	40 03	083	41 29	165	25 55	236	27 21	278	31 05	317
203	33 59	008	34 54	055	40 26	084	41 34	166	25 35	237	26 58	279	30 49	318
204	34 02	009	35 13	056	40 49	085	41 40	167	25 15	238	26 35	279	30 33	318
205	34 06	010	35 33	056	41 13	086	41 45	168	24 55	239	26 11	280	30 18	319
206	34 10	010	35 52	057	41 36	087	41 49	170	24 35	240	25 48	281	30 03	320
207	34 15	011	36 12	058	42 00	088	41 53	171	24 15	241	25 26	282	29 48	321
208	34 19	012	36 32	059	42 23	089	41 57	172	23 54	242	25 03	283	29 33	321
209	34 24	012	36 52	059	42 46	090	42 00	174	23 33	243	24 40	284	29 18	322
	Schedar		◆DENEB		VEGA		◆ARCTURUS		REGULUS		◆POLLUX		CAPELLA	
210	34 29	013	37 12	060	43 10	091	42 02	175	23 12	244	24 17	285	29 04	323
211	34 35	014	37 33	061	43 33	092	42 04	176	22 51	245	23 54	286	28 50	324
212	34 40	014	37 53	062	43 57	092	42 05	177	22 30	246	23 32	287	28 36	324
213	34 46	015	38 14	063	44 20	093	42 06	179	22 08	247	23 10	287	28 23	325
214	34 52	016	38 35	063	44 44	094	42 06	180	21 46	248	22 47	288	28 10	326
215	34 59	016	38 56	064	45 07	095	42 06	181	21 25	249	22 25	289	27 56	327
216	35 05	017	39 17	065	45 30	096	42 05	182	21 03	250	22 03	290	27 44	327
217	35 12	018	39 38	066	45 54	097	42 04	184	20 40	251	21 41	291	27 31	328
218	35 20	018	40 00	066	46 17	098	42 02	185	20 18	252	21 19	292	27 19	329
219	35 27	019	40 21	067	46 40	099	42 00	186	19 56	253	20 57	293	27 07	330
220	35 35	020	40 43	068	47 03	100	41 57	188	19 33	254	20 36	293	26 55	330
221	35 43	020	41 05	069	47 26	101	41 54	189	19 11	255	20 14	294	26 44	331
222	35 51	021	41 27	070	47 49	102	41 50	190	18 48	256	19 53	295	26 33	332
223	35 59	022	41 49	070	48 12	103	41 46	191	18 25	257	19 32	296	26 22	333
224	36 08	022	42 11	071	48 35	104	41 41	193	18 03	258	19 11	297	26 11	333
	Schedar		◆DENEB		VEGA		◆ARCTURUS		REGULUS		◆POLLUX		CAPELLA	
225	36 17	023	42 33	072	48 57	105	41 35	194	17 40	259	18 50	298	26 01	334
226	36 26	023	42 56	073	49 20	106	41 30	195	17 17	260	18 29	299	25 50	335
227	36 36	024	43 18	074	49 42	107	41 23	196	16 53	261	18 09	299	25 41	336
228	36 46	025	43 41	074	50 05	108	41 16	198	16 30	261	17 49	300	25 31	336
229	36 56	025	44 03	075	50 27	110	41 09	199	16 07	262	17 28	301	25 22	337
230	37 06	026	44 26	076	50 49	111	41 01	200	15 44	263	17 08	302	25 13	338
231	37 16	027	44 49	077	51 11	112	40 53	201	15 21	264	16 49	303	25 04	339
232	37 27	027	45 12	078	51 32	113	40 44	203	14 57	265	16 29	304	24 56	339
233	37 38	028	45 35	079	51 54	114	40 35	204	14 34	266	16 10	305	24 48	340
234	37 49	029	45 58	079	52 15	115	40 25	205	14 10	267	15 51	305	24 40	341
235	38 00	029	46 21	080	52 36	116	40 15	206	13 47	268	15 32	306	24 32	342
236	38 12	030	46 44	081	52 57	117	40 05	207	13 24	269	15 13	307	24 25	342
237	38 24	031	47 07	082	53 18	119	39 54	209	13 00	270	14 54	308	24 18	343
238	38 36	031	47 30	083	53 39	120	39 42	210	12 37	271	14 36	309	24 11	344
239	38 48	032	47 54	084	53 59	121	39 30	211	12 13	272	14 18	310	24 05	345
	Alpheratz		◆DENEB		VEGA		Rasalhague		◆ARCTURUS		Alioth		◆CAPELLA	
240	15 27	050	48 17	085	54 19	122	33 17	152	39 18	212	65 59	265	23 59	345
241	15 45	051	48 40	086	54 38	123	33 28	153	39 05	213	65 35	266	23 53	346
242	16 04	052	49 04	086	54 58	125	33 38	154	38 52	215	65 12	267	23 47	347
243	16 22	053	49 27	087	55 17	126	33 48	155	38 39	216	64 48	268	23 42	348
244	16 41	053	49 51	088	55 36	127	33 58	156	38 25	217	64 25	269	23 37	348
245	17 00	054	50 14	089	55 55	128	34 07	158	38 10	218	64 02	270	23 33	349
246	17 19	055	50 37	090	56 13	130	34 16	159	37 56	219	63 38	271	23 29	350
247	17 38	056	51 01	091	56 31	131	34 24	160	37 41	220	63 15	272	23 25	351
248	17 58	057	51 24	092	56 48	132	34 32	161	37 25	222	62 51	273	23 21	351
249	18 17	058	51 48	093	57 05	134	34 39	162	37 10	223	62 28	274	23 18	352
250	18 37	058	52 11	094	57 22	135	34 46	163	36 53	224	62 04	275	23 14	353
251	18 57	059	52 34	095	57 39	136	34 52	165	36 37	225	61 41	275	23 12	354
252	19 18	060	52 58	096	57 55	138	34 58	166	36 20	226	61 18	276	23 09	354
253	19 38	061	53 21	097	58 10	139	35 04	167	36 03	227	60 55	277	23 07	355
254	19 59	062	53 44	098	58 25	140	35 09	168	35 46	228	60 31	278	23 05	356
	Alpheratz		◆DENEB		ALTAIR		Rasalhague		◆ARCTURUS		Alioth		◆CAPELLA	
255	20 19	063	54 08	099	25 11	132	35 14	169	35 28	229	60 08	279	23 04	357
256	20 40	064	54 31	100	25 28	133	35 18	171	35 10	231	59 45	280	23 03	357
257	21 01	064	54 54	101	25 45	134	35 21	172	34 52	232	59 22	280	23 02	358
258	21 23	065	55 17	102	26 02	135	35 24	173	34 34	233	58 59	281	23 01	359
259	21 44	066	55 40	103	26 18	136	35 27	174	34 15	234	58 36	282	23 01	000
260	22 05	067	56 03	104	26 34	137	35 29	175	33 56	235	58 13	283	23 01	000
261	22 27	068	56 25	105	26 50	138	35 31	177	33 36	236	57 50	284	23 01	001
262	22 49	069	56 48	106	27 05	139	35 32	178	33 17	237	57 27	284	23 02	002
263	23 11	070	57 10	107	27 20	141	35 33	179	32 57	238	57 05	285	23 03	003
264	23 33	070	57 33	108	27 35	142	35 33	180	32 37	239	56 42	286	23 04	003
265	23 55	071	57 55	109	27 49	143	35 33	181	32 17	240	56 20	287	23 05	004
266	24 17	072	58 17	110	28 03	144	35 32	183	31 56	241	55 57	287	23 07	005
267	24 40	073	58 39	112	28 17	145	35 31	184	31 36	242	55 35	288	23 09	006
268	25 02	074	59 00	113	28 30	146	35 29	185	31 15	243	55 13	289	23 12	006
269	25 25	075	59 22	114	28 43	147	35 27	186	30 54	244	54 50	290	23 15	007

LAT 67°N

LHA ♈	Hc	Zn	Hc	Zn	Hc	Zn	Hc	Zn	Hc	Zn	Hc	Zn	Hc	Zn
	◆CAPELLA		Alpheratz		◆DENEB		ALTAIR		Rasalhague		◆ARCTURUS		Alioth	
270	23 18	008	25 47	076	59 43	115	28 56	148	35 24	187	30 33	245	54 28	290
271	23 21	009	26 10	077	60 04	116	29 08	149	35 21	188	30 11	246	54 06	291
272	23 25	009	26 33	077	60 25	118	29 20	150	35 17	190	29 50	247	53 45	292
273	23 29	010	26 56	078	60 46	119	29 31	151	35 13	191	29 28	248	53 23	292
274	23 33	011	27 19	079	61 06	120	29 42	153	35 08	192	29 06	249	53 01	293
275	23 38	012	27 42	080	61 27	121	29 53	154	35 03	193	28 44	250	52 40	294
276	23 43	012	28 05	081	61 46	123	30 03	155	34 57	194	28 22	251	52 18	295
277	23 48	013	28 28	082	62 06	124	30 13	156	34 51	196	28 00	252	51 57	295
278	23 54	014	28 51	083	62 25	125	30 22	157	34 45	197	27 37	253	51 36	296
279	23 59	015	29 15	084	62 44	127	30 31	158	34 38	198	27 15	254	51 15	297
280	24 05	015	29 38	085	63 03	128	30 40	159	34 30	199	26 52	255	50 54	297
281	24 12	016	30 01	085	63 21	130	30 48	160	34 22	200	26 29	256	50 33	298
282	24 19	017	30 25	086	63 39	131	30 55	162	34 14	202	26 07	257	50 13	299
283	24 26	018	30 48	087	63 57	132	31 02	163	34 05	203	25 44	258	49 52	300
284	24 33	018	31 12	088	64 14	134	31 09	164	33 56	204	25 21	259	49 32	300
	◆CAPELLA		Hamal		Alpheratz		◆DENEB		VEGA		◆ARCTURUS		Alioth	
285	24 40	019	15 14	065	31 35	089	64 30	135	61 37	189	24 58	260	49 12	301
286	24 48	020	15 35	066	31 59	090	64 47	137	61 33	191	24 35	261	48 52	302
287	24 56	021	15 57	067	32 22	091	65 02	138	61 28	193	24 11	262	48 32	302
288	25 05	021	16 19	068	32 45	092	65 18	140	61 23	194	23 48	263	48 12	303
289	25 14	022	16 40	069	33 09	093	65 33	142	61 17	196	23 25	264	47 53	304
290	25 23	023	17 02	070	33 32	094	65 47	143	61 10	197	23 02	265	47 33	304
291	25 32	024	17 24	071	33 56	095	66 01	145	61 03	199	22 38	266	47 14	305
292	25 42	024	17 47	071	34 19	096	66 14	146	60 55	201	22 15	267	46 55	306
293	25 51	025	18 09	072	34 42	097	66 27	148	60 46	202	21 51	268	46 36	306
294	26 02	026	18 31	073	35 06	098	66 39	150	60 37	204	21 28	268	46 17	307
295	26 12	027	18 54	074	35 29	098	66 50	152	60 28	205	21 04	269	45 58	308
296	26 23	027	19 16	075	35 52	099	67 01	153	60 17	207	20 41	270	45 40	308
297	26 34	028	19 39	076	36 15	100	67 11	155	60 07	208	20 18	271	45 21	309
298	26 45	029	20 02	077	36 38	101	67 21	157	59 55	210	19 54	272	45 03	310
299	26 56	030	20 25	078	37 01	102	67 30	159	59 43	211	19 31	273	44 45	310
	◆CAPELLA		Hamal		Alpheratz		◆DENEB		VEGA		◆ARCTURUS		Dubhe	
300	27 08	030	20 48	079	37 24	103	67 38	160	59 31	213	19 07	274	42 59	332
301	27 20	031	21 11	079	37 47	104	67 46	162	59 18	214	18 44	275	42 48	333
302	27 32	032	21 34	080	38 09	105	67 52	164	59 04	216	18 21	276	42 38	333
303	27 45	033	21 57	081	38 32	106	67 58	166	58 50	217	17 57	277	42 27	334
304	27 58	033	22 20	082	38 54	107	68 04	168	58 36	219	17 34	278	42 17	334
305	28 11	034	22 43	083	39 17	108	68 08	170	58 21	220	17 11	279	42 07	335
306	28 24	035	23 07	084	39 39	109	68 12	171	58 06	221	16 48	279	41 57	336
307	28 38	036	23 30	085	40 01	110	68 15	173	57 50	223	16 25	280	41 48	336
308	28 52	036	23 53	086	40 23	111	68 18	175	57 34	224	16 02	281	41 38	337
309	29 06	037	24 17	087	40 44	113	68 19	177	57 18	226	15 39	282	41 29	338
310	29 20	038	24 40	088	41 06	114	68 20	179	57 01	227	15 16	283	41 21	338
311	29 34	039	25 03	088	41 27	115	68 20	181	56 43	228	14 53	284	41 12	339
312	29 49	039	25 27	089	41 49	116	68 19	183	56 26	229	14 30	285	41 03	339
313	30 04	040	25 50	090	42 10	117	68 18	185	56 08	231	14 08	286	40 55	340
314	30 19	041	26 14	091	42 30	118	68 15	187	55 49	232	13 45	287	40 47	341
	◆CAPELLA		Hamal		Alpheratz		◆DENEB		VEGA		◆Alphecca		Dubhe	
315	30 35	042	26 37	092	42 51	119	68 12	189	55 31	233	27 49	273	40 40	341
316	30 51	042	27 01	093	43 12	120	68 08	190	55 12	235	27 26	274	40 32	342
317	31 07	043	27 24	094	43 32	121	68 04	192	54 53	236	27 02	275	40 25	342
318	31 23	044	27 47	095	43 52	122	67 58	194	54 33	237	26 39	276	40 18	343
319	31 39	045	28 11	096	44 11	123	67 52	196	54 13	238	26 16	277	40 11	344
320	31 56	045	28 34	097	44 31	125	67 45	198	53 53	239	25 53	278	40 05	344
321	32 13	046	28 57	098	44 50	126	67 38	200	53 33	241	25 29	279	39 58	345
322	32 30	047	29 21	099	45 09	127	67 30	202	53 12	242	25 06	279	39 52	345
323	32 47	048	29 44	100	45 28	128	67 21	203	52 52	243	24 43	280	39 47	346
324	33 04	048	30 07	101	45 46	129	67 11	205	52 31	244	24 20	281	39 41	347
325	33 22	049	30 30	102	46 04	130	67 01	207	52 09	245	23 57	282	39 36	347
326	33 40	050	30 53	103	46 22	132	66 50	209	51 48	246	23 34	283	39 31	348
327	33 58	051	31 15	104	46 39	133	66 38	210	51 26	247	23 11	284	39 26	348
328	34 16	051	31 38	105	46 56	134	66 26	212	51 05	249	22 49	285	39 21	349
329	34 34	052	32 01	106	47 13	135	66 14	214	50 43	250	22 26	286	39 17	350
	CAPELLA		◆Hamal		Alpheratz		◆ALTAIR		VEGA		Alphecca		◆Alioth	
330	34 53	053	32 23	107	47 29	136	28 00	217	50 21	251	22 04	287	37 07	331
331	35 12	054	32 46	108	47 45	138	27 46	218	49 58	252	21 41	287	36 56	332
332	35 31	054	33 08	109	48 01	139	27 31	219	49 36	253	21 19	288	36 45	332
333	35 50	055	33 30	110	48 16	140	27 17	220	49 14	254	20 57	289	36 34	333
334	36 09	056	33 52	111	48 31	141	27 01	221	48 51	255	20 35	290	36 24	334
335	36 29	057	34 14	112	48 45	143	26 46	222	48 28	256	20 13	291	36 13	334
336	36 49	058	34 36	113	48 59	144	26 30	223	48 06	257	19 51	292	36 03	335
337	37 08	058	34 57	114	49 13	145	26 14	224	47 43	258	19 29	293	35 53	336
338	37 29	059	35 19	115	49 26	146	25 58	225	47 20	259	19 07	293	35 44	336
339	37 49	060	35 40	116	49 39	148	25 41	226	46 57	260	18 46	294	35 35	337
340	38 09	061	36 01	117	49 51	149	25 24	227	46 34	261	18 25	295	35 25	338
341	38 30	061	36 22	118	50 03	150	25 06	228	46 10	262	18 04	296	35 17	338
342	38 50	062	36 43	119	50 14	152	24 49	229	45 47	263	17 43	297	35 08	339
343	39 11	063	37 03	120	50 25	153	24 31	230	45 24	264	17 22	298	35 00	340
344	39 32	064	37 23	121	50 35	154	24 13	231	45 00	265	17 01	299	34 52	340
	◆POLLUX		CAPELLA		Hamal		◆Alpheratz		ALTAIR		◆VEGA		Alioth	
345	11 43	042	39 53	064	37 43	122	50 45	156	23 54	232	44 37	266	34 44	341
346	11 59	043	40 14	065	38 03	123	50 55	157	23 36	233	44 14	267	34 36	342
347	12 15	044	40 36	066	38 23	124	51 04	159	23 17	234	43 50	268	34 29	342
348	12 32	045	40 57	067	38 42	125	51 12	160	22 57	235	43 27	269	34 22	343
349	12 48	046	41 19	068	39 01	126	51 20	161	22 38	236	43 03	270	34 15	344
350	13 05	047	41 40	068	39 20	128	51 27	163	22 18	237	42 40	271	34 09	344
351	13 23	048	42 02	069	39 38	129	51 34	164	21 59	238	42 17	271	34 03	345
352	13 40	048	42 24	070	39 56	130	51 40	165	21 38	239	41 53	272	33 57	346
353	13 58	049	42 46	071	40 14	131	51 45	167	21 18	240	41 30	273	33 51	346
354	14 16	050	43 09	072	40 32	132	51 50	168	20 58	241	41 06	274	33 45	347
355	14 34	051	43 31	072	40 49	133	51 55	170	20 37	242	40 43	275	33 40	348
356	14 52	052	43 53	073	41 06	134	51 59	171	20 16	243	40 20	276	33 35	348
357	15 11	053	44 16	074	41 22	136	52 02	172	19 55	244	39 56	277	33 31	349
358	15 29	054	44 38	075	41 39	137	52 05	174	19 34	245	39 33	278	33 26	350
359	15 48	054	45 01	076	41 55	138	52 07	175	19 12	246	39 10	279	33 22	350

LAT 66°N

LHA ♈	Hc	Zn	Hc	Zn	Hc	Zn	Hc	Zn	Hc	Zn	Hc	Zn	Hc	Zn
	◆ POLLUX		CAPELLA		Hamal		◆ Alpheratz		DENEB		◆ VEGA		Alioth	
0	15 33	055	45 09	076	42 55	138	53 09	177	56 39	257	38 36	280	32 19	351
1	15 53	056	45 33	076	43 11	140	53 10	178	56 15	258	38 12	281	32 15	352
2	16 14	057	45 57	077	43 27	141	53 10	180	55 52	259	37 49	282	32 12	352
3	16 34	058	46 20	078	43 42	142	53 10	181	55 28	260	37 25	283	32 09	353
4	16 55	058	46 44	079	43 57	143	53 09	182	55 04	261	37 01	284	32 06	354
5	17 16	059	47 08	080	44 11	145	53 08	184	54 39	262	36 37	284	32 03	354
6	17 37	060	47 32	080	44 25	146	53 06	185	54 15	263	36 14	285	32 01	355
7	17 58	061	47 56	081	44 39	147	53 04	187	53 51	264	35 50	286	31 59	356
8	18 20	062	48 21	082	44 52	148	53 00	188	53 27	265	35 27	287	31 57	356
9	18 41	063	48 45	083	45 04	150	52 56	190	53 02	266	35 04	288	31 56	357
10	19 03	064	49 09	084	45 17	151	52 52	191	52 38	267	34 40	289	31 55	358
11	19 25	064	49 33	085	45 28	152	52 47	193	52 14	267	34 17	289	31 54	358
12	19 47	065	49 58	086	45 39	153	52 41	194	51 49	268	33 54	290	31 53	359
13	20 09	066	50 22	086	45 50	155	52 35	195	51 25	269	33 31	291	31 53	000
14	20 32	067	50 46	087	46 00	156	52 28	197	51 01	270	33 09	292	31 53	000
	Alioth		◆ POLLUX		CAPELLA		Hamal		◆ Alpheratz		DENEB		◆ VEGA	
15	31 53	001	20 54	068	51 11	088	46 10	157	52 21	198	50 36	271	32 46	293
16	31 53	002	21 17	069	51 35	089	46 19	159	52 13	200	50 12	272	32 24	294
17	31 54	002	21 40	070	52 00	090	46 28	160	52 04	201	49 47	273	32 01	294
18	31 55	003	22 02	070	52 24	091	46 36	161	51 55	203	49 23	274	31 39	295
19	31 57	004	22 26	071	52 48	092	46 44	162	51 46	204	48 59	275	31 17	296
20	31 58	004	22 49	072	53 13	093	46 51	164	51 36	205	48 34	276	30 55	297
21	32 00	005	23 12	073	53 37	094	46 57	165	51 25	207	48 10	276	30 34	298
22	32 02	006	23 35	074	54 01	095	47 03	166	51 14	208	47 46	277	30 12	298
23	32 05	006	23 59	075	54 26	096	47 09	168	51 02	209	47 22	278	29 51	299
24	32 08	007	24 22	076	54 50	097	47 14	169	50 50	211	46 58	279	29 30	300
25	32 11	007	24 46	076	55 14	098	47 18	171	50 37	212	46 34	280	29 08	301
26	32 14	008	25 10	077	55 38	099	47 22	172	50 24	213	46 09	281	28 48	302
27	32 18	009	25 34	078	56 02	100	47 25	173	50 10	215	45 46	282	28 27	302
28	32 22	009	25 58	079	56 26	101	47 27	175	49 56	216	45 22	282	28 06	303
29	32 26	010	26 22	080	56 50	102	47 29	176	49 41	217	44 58	283	27 46	304
	Alioth		◆ POLLUX		ALDEBARAN		◆ Hamal		Alpheratz		DENEB		◆ VEGA	
30	32 30	011	26 46	081	34 13	133	47 31	177	49 26	219	44 34	284	27 26	305
31	32 35	011	27 10	082	34 30	134	47 32	179	49 11	220	44 11	285	27 06	306
32	32 40	012	27 34	083	34 48	135	47 32	180	48 55	221	43 47	286	26 46	306
33	32 45	013	27 58	083	35 05	136	47 32	181	48 39	222	43 24	286	26 27	307
34	32 51	013	28 23	084	35 21	137	47 31	183	48 22	224	43 00	287	26 07	308
35	32 56	014	28 47	085	35 38	138	47 29	184	48 05	225	42 37	288	25 48	309
36	33 02	015	29 11	086	35 54	140	47 27	185	47 48	226	42 14	289	25 29	309
37	33 09	015	29 36	087	36 09	141	47 25	187	47 30	227	41 51	290	25 10	310
38	33 15	016	30 00	088	36 25	142	47 22	188	47 12	229	41 28	290	24 52	311
39	33 22	017	30 24	089	36 40	143	47 18	189	46 53	230	41 05	291	24 34	312
40	33 29	017	30 49	090	36 54	144	47 14	191	46 34	231	40 42	292	24 16	313
41	33 37	018	31 13	091	37 08	145	47 09	192	46 15	232	40 20	293	23 58	313
42	33 44	019	31 38	092	37 22	147	47 03	194	45 56	233	39 57	294	23 40	314
43	33 52	019	32 02	093	37 35	148	46 57	195	45 36	234	39 35	294	23 23	315
44	34 01	020	32 26	093	37 48	149	46 51	196	45 16	236	39 13	295	23 06	316
	Alioth		◆ POLLUX		ALDEBARAN		◆ Hamal		Alpheratz		DENEB		◆ VEGA	
45	34 09	021	32 51	094	38 00	150	46 44	198	44 56	237	38 51	296	22 49	317
46	34 18	021	33 15	095	38 12	151	46 36	199	44 35	238	38 29	297	22 32	317
47	34 27	022	33 39	096	38 24	152	46 28	200	44 15	239	38 07	297	22 16	318
48	34 36	023	34 03	097	38 35	154	46 19	201	43 54	240	37 46	298	22 00	319
49	34 46	023	34 28	098	38 45	155	46 10	203	43 32	241	37 24	299	21 44	320
50	34 55	024	34 52	099	38 55	156	46 00	204	43 11	242	37 03	300	21 28	321
51	35 05	025	35 16	100	39 05	157	45 50	205	42 49	243	36 42	300	21 13	321
52	35 16	025	35 40	101	39 14	159	45 40	207	42 27	245	36 21	301	20 58	322
53	35 26	026	36 04	102	39 23	160	45 28	208	42 05	246	36 00	302	20 43	323
54	35 37	027	36 28	103	39 31	161	45 17	209	41 43	247	35 39	303	20 28	324
55	35 48	027	36 51	104	39 39	162	45 05	210	41 20	248	35 19	303	20 14	324
56	35 59	028	37 15	105	39 46	163	44 52	212	40 58	249	34 59	304	20 00	325
57	36 11	028	37 38	106	39 53	165	44 39	213	40 35	250	34 39	305	19 46	326
58	36 23	029	38 02	107	39 59	166	44 25	214	40 12	251	34 19	306	19 32	327
59	36 35	030	38 25	108	40 05	167	44 11	215	39 49	252	33 59	306	19 19	328
	Alioth		◆ POLLUX		ALDEBARAN		◆ Hamal		Alpheratz		DENEB		◆ VEGA	
60	36 47	030	38 48	109	40 10	168	43 57	217	39 25	253	33 39	307	19 06	328
61	36 59	031	39 11	110	40 14	170	43 42	218	39 02	254	33 20	308	18 54	329
62	37 12	032	39 34	111	40 18	171	43 27	219	38 38	255	33 01	309	18 41	330
63	37 25	032	39 57	112	40 22	172	43 11	220	38 15	256	32 42	309	18 29	331
64	37 38	033	40 19	113	40 25	173	42 55	222	37 51	257	32 23	310	18 18	332
65	37 52	034	40 42	114	40 28	175	42 39	223	37 27	258	32 05	311	18 06	332
66	38 05	034	41 04	115	40 30	176	42 22	224	37 03	259	31 46	312	17 55	333
67	38 19	035	41 26	116	40 31	177	42 05	225	36 39	260	31 28	312	17 44	334
68	38 33	036	41 48	117	40 32	178	41 48	226	36 15	261	31 10	313	17 34	335
69	38 47	036	42 09	118	40 32	180	41 30	227	35 51	262	30 53	314	17 23	336
70	39 02	037	42 30	120	40 32	181	41 12	229	35 27	263	30 35	315	17 14	336
71	39 17	038	42 52	121	40 31	182	40 53	230	35 03	264	30 18	315	17 04	337
72	39 32	038	43 12	122	40 30	184	40 34	231	34 39	265	30 01	316	16 55	338
73	39 47	039	43 33	123	40 28	185	40 15	232	34 14	265	29 44	317	16 46	339
74	40 02	040	43 53	124	40 26	186	39 56	233	33 50	266	29 28	318	16 37	340
	Alioth		◆ REGULUS		PROCYON		◆ ALDEBARAN		Hamal		Alpheratz		◆ DENEB	
75	40 18	040	16 01	097	23 08	136	40 23	187	39 36	234	33 26	267	29 11	318
76	40 34	041	16 25	098	23 24	137	40 20	189	39 16	235	33 01	268	28 55	319
77	40 50	041	16 49	099	23 41	138	40 16	190	38 56	236	32 37	269	28 40	320
78	41 06	042	17 13	100	23 57	139	40 12	191	38 36	238	32 12	270	28 24	321
79	41 23	043	17 37	100	24 13	140	40 07	192	38 15	239	31 48	271	28 09	321
80	41 39	043	18 01	101	24 28	141	40 01	194	37 54	240	31 24	272	27 54	322
81	41 56	044	18 25	102	24 44	142	39 55	195	37 33	241	30 59	273	27 39	323
82	42 13	045	18 49	103	24 58	143	39 49	196	37 11	242	30 35	274	27 24	324
83	42 31	045	19 13	104	25 13	144	39 42	197	36 50	243	30 11	275	27 10	324
84	42 48	046	19 36	105	25 27	145	39 34	199	36 28	244	29 46	276	26 56	325
85	43 06	047	20 00	106	25 41	146	39 26	200	36 06	245	29 22	276	26 42	326
86	43 24	047	20 23	107	25 54	148	39 18	201	35 44	246	28 58	277	26 28	327
87	43 42	048	20 46	108	26 07	149	39 09	202	35 21	247	28 34	278	26 15	327
88	44 00	049	21 09	109	26 19	150	38 59	203	34 59	248	28 09	279	26 02	328
89	44 18	049	21 32	110	26 31	151	38 49	205	34 36	249	27 45	280	25 49	329

LHA ♈	Hc	Zn	Hc	Zn	Hc	Zn	Hc	Zn	Hc	Zn	Hc	Zn	Hc	Zn
	Alioth		◆ REGULUS		PROCYON		BETELGEUSE		◆ ALDEBARAN		Hamal		◆ DENEB	
90	44 37	050	21 55	111	26 43	152	31 24	181	38 39	206	34 13	250	25 37	330
91	44 56	051	22 18	112	26 54	153	31 24	182	38 28	207	33 50	251	25 24	330
92	45 15	051	22 41	113	27 05	154	31 22	183	38 17	208	33 27	252	25 13	331
93	45 34	052	23 03	114	27 16	155	31 21	185	38 05	209	33 04	253	25 01	332
94	45 53	053	23 25	115	27 26	156	31 18	186	37 53	211	32 40	254	24 50	333
95	46 13	053	23 47	116	27 35	157	31 16	187	37 40	212	32 17	255	24 38	333
96	46 32	054	24 09	117	27 45	158	31 12	188	37 27	213	31 53	256	24 28	334
97	46 52	055	24 31	118	27 53	160	31 09	189	37 13	214	31 30	257	24 17	335
98	47 12	055	24 52	119	28 02	161	31 05	190	37 00	215	31 06	258	24 07	336
99	47 32	056	25 14	120	28 09	162	31 00	192	36 45	216	30 42	259	23 57	336
100	47 52	057	25 35	121	28 17	163	30 55	193	36 31	218	30 18	260	23 47	337
101	48 13	057	25 55	122	28 24	164	30 49	194	36 15	219	29 54	261	23 38	338
102	48 33	058	26 16	123	28 30	165	30 43	195	36 00	220	29 30	262	23 29	339
103	48 54	059	26 36	124	28 36	166	30 36	196	35 44	221	29 05	263	23 20	339
104	49 15	059	26 56	125	28 42	167	30 29	197	35 28	222	28 41	264	23 12	340
	Alioth		◆ REGULUS		PROCYON		BETELGEUSE		◆ CAPELLA		Hamal		◆ DENEB	
105	49 36	060	27 16	126	28 47	169	30 22	198	65 48	227	28 17	265	23 03	341
106	49 57	061	27 36	127	28 51	170	30 14	200	65 30	228	27 53	266	22 56	342
107	50 19	061	27 55	128	28 56	171	30 06	201	65 12	230	27 28	266	22 48	342
108	50 40	062	28 14	129	28 59	172	29 57	202	64 53	231	27 04	267	22 41	343
109	51 02	063	28 33	130	29 02	173	29 47	203	64 33	233	26 40	268	22 34	344
110	51 24	063	28 52	131	29 05	174	29 38	204	64 14	234	26 15	269	22 27	345
111	51 45	064	29 10	132	29 07	175	29 27	205	63 54	236	25 51	270	22 21	345
112	52 07	065	29 28	133	29 09	177	29 17	206	63 34	237	25 26	271	22 15	346
113	52 29	065	29 45	134	29 10	178	29 06	207	63 13	238	25 02	272	22 09	347
114	52 52	066	30 03	136	29 11	179	28 54	209	62 52	240	24 38	273	22 04	348
115	53 14	067	30 20	137	29 11	180	28 42	210	62 31	241	24 13	274	21 58	348
116	53 37	067	30 36	138	29 11	181	28 30	211	62 09	242	23 49	275	21 54	349
117	53 59	068	30 52	139	29 10	182	28 17	212	61 48	244	23 25	276	21 49	350
118	54 22	069	31 08	140	29 09	183	28 04	213	61 26	245	23 00	276	21 45	351
119	54 45	070	31 24	141	29 07	185	27 51	214	61 03	246	22 36	277	21 41	351
	◆ VEGA		ARCTURUS		◆ REGULUS		PROCYON		◆ CAPELLA		Schedar		DENEB	
120	16 00	017	15 46	078	31 39	142	29 05	186	60 41	247	43 26	314	21 38	352
121	16 08	017	16 10	079	31 54	143	29 02	187	60 18	248	43 09	315	21 35	353
122	16 15	018	16 34	080	32 08	144	28 59	188	59 56	250	42 52	316	21 32	354
123	16 23	019	16 58	081	32 22	145	28 56	189	59 33	251	42 35	316	21 29	354
124	16 31	020	17 22	082	32 36	147	28 52	190	59 10	252	42 18	317	21 27	355
125	16 39	021	17 46	083	32 49	148	28 47	191	58 46	253	42 02	318	21 25	356
126	16 48	021	18 10	084	33 02	149	28 42	192	58 23	254	41 45	318	21 23	357
127	16 57	022	18 34	085	33 14	150	28 36	194	57 59	255	41 29	319	21 22	357
128	17 07	023	18 59	085	33 26	151	28 31	195	57 36	256	41 13	320	21 21	358
129	17 16	024	19 23	086	33 38	152	28 24	196	57 12	257	40 58	320	21 20	359
130	17 26	025	19 47	087	33 49	153	28 17	197	56 48	258	40 42	321	21 20	000
131	17 37	025	20 12	088	34 00	155	28 10	198	56 24	259	40 27	322	21 20	000
132	17 47	026	20 36	089	34 10	156	28 02	199	56 00	260	40 12	322	21 20	001
133	17 58	027	21 01	090	34 20	157	27 54	200	55 36	261	39 57	323	21 21	002
134	18 09	028	21 25	091	34 29	158	27 45	201	55 12	262	39 42	323	21 22	003
	DENEB		◆ VEGA		ARCTURUS		◆ REGULUS		PROCYON		◆ CAPELLA		Schedar	
135	21 23	003	18 21	029	21 49	092	34 38	159	27 36	203	54 48	263	39 28	324
136	21 25	004	18 33	029	22 14	093	34 46	160	27 26	204	54 23	264	39 14	325
137	21 27	005	18 45	030	22 38	094	34 54	162	27 16	205	53 59	265	39 00	325
138	21 29	006	18 57	031	23 03	095	35 02	163	27 06	206	53 35	266	38 46	326
139	21 32	006	19 10	032	23 27	096	35 09	164	26 55	207	53 10	267	38 32	327
140	21 35	007	19 23	033	23 51	097	35 15	165	26 44	208	52 46	268	38 19	327
141	21 38	008	19 36	033	24 15	097	35 21	166	26 32	209	52 22	269	38 06	328
142	21 41	009	19 50	034	24 40	098	35 27	168	26 20	210	51 57	270	37 53	329
143	21 45	009	20 04	035	25 04	099	35 31	169	26 07	211	51 33	271	37 41	329
144	21 49	010	20 18	036	25 28	100	35 36	170	25 54	212	51 08	272	37 28	330
145	21 54	011	20 32	037	25 52	101	35 40	171	25 41	214	50 44	273	37 16	331
146	21 59	012	20 47	037	26 16	102	35 43	172	25 28	215	50 20	274	37 04	331
147	22 04	012	21 02	038	26 39	103	35 46	174	25 13	216	49 55	274	36 53	332
148	22 09	013	21 17	039	27 03	104	35 49	175	24 59	217	49 31	275	36 41	332
149	22 15	014	21 32	040	27 27	105	35 51	176	24 44	218	49 07	276	36 30	333
	DENEB		◆ VEGA		ARCTURUS		◆ REGULUS		PROCYON		◆ CAPELLA		Schedar	
150	22 21	015	21 48	040	27 50	106	35 52	177	24 29	219	48 42	277	36 19	334
151	22 27	015	22 04	041	28 14	107	35 53	178	24 14	220	48 18	278	36 08	334
152	22 34	016	22 20	042	28 37	108	35 54	180	23 58	221	47 54	279	35 58	335
153	22 41	017	22 37	043	29 00	109	35 53	181	23 42	222	47 30	280	35 48	336
154	22 48	018	22 53	044	29 23	110	35 53	182	23 25	223	47 06	280	35 38	336
155	22 56	018	23 10	044	29 46	111	35 52	183	23 08	224	46 42	281	35 28	337
156	23 04	019	23 28	045	30 09	112	35 50	184	22 51	225	46 18	282	35 19	338
157	23 12	020	23 45	046	30 31	113	35 48	186	22 34	226	45 54	283	35 10	338
158	23 20	021	24 03	047	30 54	114	35 45	187	22 16	227	45 31	284	35 01	339
159	23 29	021	24 21	048	31 16	115	35 42	188	21 58	228	45 07	285	34 52	340
160	23 38	022	24 39	048	31 38	116	35 38	189	21 40	229	44 43	285	34 44	340
161	23 47	023	24 57	049	32 00	117	35 34	190	21 21	230	44 20	286	34 36	341
162	23 57	024	25 16	050	32 21	118	35 29	192	21 02	231	43 56	287	34 28	342
163	24 07	024	25 34	051	32 43	119	35 24	193	20 43	232	43 33	288	34 20	342
164	24 17	025	25 53	052	33 04	120	35 19	194	20 23	233	43 10	289	34 13	343
	DENEB		◆ VEGA		ARCTURUS		◆ REGULUS		POLLUX		◆ CAPELLA		Schedar	
165	24 28	026	26 13	052	33 25	121	35 12	195	41 50	242	42 47	289	34 06	343
166	24 39	027	26 32	053	33 46	122	35 06	196	41 28	244	42 24	290	33 59	344
167	24 50	027	26 52	054	34 06	123	34 59	198	41 06	245	42 01	291	33 52	345
168	25 01	028	27 11	055	34 26	124	34 51	199	40 44	246	41 38	292	33 46	345
169	25 13	029	27 31	055	34 47	125	34 43	200	40 22	247	41 16	292	33 40	346
170	25 25	030	27 52	056	35 06	127	34 34	201	39 59	248	40 53	293	33 34	347
171	25 37	030	28 12	057	35 26	128	34 25	202	39 37	249	40 31	294	33 29	347
172	25 50	031	28 33	058	35 45	129	34 16	204	39 14	250	40 09	295	33 24	348
173	26 02	032	28 53	059	36 04	130	34 06	205	38 51	251	39 47	296	33 19	349
174	26 15	033	29 14	059	36 22	131	33 55	206	38 28	252	39 25	296	33 14	349
175	26 29	033	29 35	060	36 41	132	33 44	207	38 05	253	39 03	297	33 10	350
176	26 42	034	29 57	061	36 59	133	33 33	208	37 41	254	38 41	298	33 06	351
177	26 56	035	30 18	062	37 16	134	33 21	209	37 18	255	38 20	299	33 02	351
178	27 10	036	30 40	063	37 34	135	33 09	210	36 54	256	37 58	299	32 58	352
179	27 25	036	31 01	063	37 51	137	32 57	212	36 30	257	37 37	300	32 55	353

 LAT 66°N

LHA ♈	Hc	Zn	Hc	Zn	Hc	Zn	Hc	Zn	Hc	Zn	Hc	Zn	Hc	Zn
	◆ DENEB		VEGA		◆ ARCTURUS		REGULUS		◆ POLLUX		CAPELLA		Schedar	
180	27 39	037	31 23	064	38 07	138	32 44	213	36 06	258	37 16	301	32 52	353
181	27 54	038	31 45	065	38 23	139	32 30	214	35 43	259	36 55	302	32 49	354
182	28 09	039	32 08	066	38 39	140	32 16	215	35 19	260	36 35	302	32 47	355
183	28 24	039	32 30	067	38 55	141	32 02	216	34 55	261	36 14	303	32 45	355
184	28 40	040	32 52	068	39 10	142	31 48	217	34 30	262	35 54	304	32 43	356
185	28 56	041	33 15	068	39 25	144	31 33	218	34 06	263	35 34	305	32 41	357
186	29 12	042	33 38	069	39 39	145	31 17	219	33 42	264	35 14	305	32 40	357
187	29 28	042	34 01	070	39 53	146	31 02	221	33 18	265	34 54	306	32 39	358
188	29 45	043	34 24	071	40 06	147	30 46	222	32 53	266	34 34	307	32 38	358
189	30 02	044	34 47	072	40 19	148	30 29	223	32 29	266	34 15	308	32 37	359
190	30 19	045	35 10	072	40 32	150	30 13	224	32 05	267	33 56	308	32 37	000
191	30 36	045	35 33	073	40 44	151	29 55	225	31 40	268	33 37	309	32 37	000
192	30 53	046	35 57	074	40 56	152	29 38	226	31 16	269	33 18	310	32 38	001
193	31 11	047	36 20	075	41 07	153	29 20	227	30 52	270	32 59	311	32 38	002
194	31 29	048	36 44	076	41 18	154	29 02	228	30 27	271	32 41	311	32 39	002
	Schedar		◆ DENEB		VEGA		◆ ARCTURUS		REGULUS		◆ POLLUX		CAPELLA	
195	32 40	003	31 47	048	37 07	077	41 28	156	28 44	229	30 03	272	32 22	312
196	32 42	004	32 05	049	37 31	077	41 38	157	28 25	230	29 38	273	32 04	313
197	32 43	004	32 24	050	37 55	078	41 47	158	28 06	231	29 14	274	31 47	314
198	32 45	005	32 43	051	38 19	079	41 56	159	27 47	232	28 50	275	31 29	314
199	32 48	006	33 02	051	38 43	080	42 04	161	27 28	233	28 25	276	31 12	315
200	32 50	006	33 21	052	39 07	081	42 12	162	27 08	234	28 01	276	30 55	316
201	32 53	007	33 40	053	39 31	082	42 20	163	26 48	235	27 37	277	30 38	317
202	32 56	008	34 00	054	39 55	083	42 26	164	26 28	236	27 13	278	30 21	317
203	32 59	008	34 19	054	40 20	083	42 33	166	26 07	238	26 49	279	30 05	318
204	33 03	009	34 39	055	40 44	084	42 38	167	25 47	239	26 24	280	29 48	319
205	33 07	010	34 59	056	41 08	085	42 44	168	25 26	240	26 00	281	29 32	319
206	33 11	010	35 19	057	41 33	086	42 48	170	25 05	241	25 37	282	29 17	320
207	33 16	011	35 40	057	41 57	087	42 52	171	24 43	242	25 13	283	29 01	321
208	33 20	012	36 01	058	42 21	088	42 56	172	24 22	243	24 49	283	28 46	322
209	33 25	012	36 21	059	42 46	089	42 59	173	24 00	244	24 25	284	28 31	322
	Schedar		◆ DENEB		VEGA		◆ ARCTURUS		REGULUS		◆ POLLUX		CAPELLA	
210	33 31	013	36 42	060	43 10	090	43 02	175	23 38	245	24 02	285	28 16	323
211	33 36	013	37 03	060	43 34	091	43 04	176	23 16	246	23 38	286	28 02	324
212	33 42	014	37 25	061	43 59	092	43 05	177	22 54	247	23 15	287	27 47	325
213	33 48	015	37 46	062	44 23	092	43 06	179	22 31	247	22 51	288	27 34	325
214	33 54	015	38 08	063	44 48	093	43 06	180	22 09	248	22 28	289	27 20	326
215	34 01	016	38 29	063	45 12	094	43 06	181	21 46	249	22 05	289	27 06	327
216	34 08	017	38 51	064	45 36	095	43 05	182	21 23	250	21 42	290	26 53	328
217	34 15	017	39 13	065	46 01	096	43 04	184	21 00	251	21 19	291	26 40	328
218	34 23	018	39 36	066	46 25	097	43 02	185	20 37	252	20 57	292	26 28	329
219	34 30	019	39 58	066	46 49	098	43 00	186	20 13	253	20 34	293	26 15	330
220	34 38	019	40 20	067	47 13	099	42 57	188	19 50	254	20 12	294	26 03	331
221	34 46	020	40 43	068	47 37	100	42 53	189	19 26	255	19 50	295	25 51	331
222	34 55	021	41 06	069	48 01	101	42 49	190	19 03	256	19 27	295	25 40	332
223	35 04	021	41 28	070	48 25	102	42 45	191	18 39	257	19 05	296	25 28	333
224	35 13	022	41 51	070	48 49	103	42 39	193	18 15	258	18 44	297	25 17	334
	Schedar		◆ DENEB		VEGA		◆ ARCTURUS		REGULUS		◆ POLLUX		CAPELLA	
225	35 22	023	42 14	071	49 13	104	42 34	194	17 51	259	18 22	298	25 07	334
226	35 31	023	42 38	072	49 36	105	42 28	195	17 27	260	18 01	299	24 56	335
227	35 41	024	43 01	073	50 00	106	42 21	197	17 03	261	17 39	300	24 46	336
228	35 51	025	43 24	074	50 23	107	42 14	198	16 39	262	17 18	301	24 36	337
229	36 01	025	43 48	074	50 46	108	42 06	199	16 15	263	16 57	301	24 26	337
230	36 12	026	44 11	075	51 09	109	41 58	200	15 51	264	16 37	302	24 17	338
231	36 23	026	44 35	076	51 32	111	41 49	202	15 26	265	16 16	303	24 08	339
232	36 34	027	44 59	077	51 55	112	41 40	203	15 02	265	15 56	304	23 59	339
233	36 45	028	45 22	078	52 18	113	41 30	204	14 38	266	15 36	305	23 51	340
234	36 56	028	45 46	078	52 40	114	41 20	205	14 13	267	15 16	306	23 43	341
235	37 08	029	46 10	079	53 02	115	41 09	207	13 49	268	14 56	307	23 35	342
236	37 20	030	46 34	080	53 24	116	40 58	208	13 25	269	14 36	307	23 28	342
237	37 32	030	46 58	081	53 46	117	40 46	209	13 00	270	14 17	308	23 20	343
238	37 45	031	47 22	082	54 08	118	40 34	210	12 36	271	13 58	309	23 14	344
239	37 57	032	47 47	083	54 29	120	40 22	211	12 11	272	13 39	310	23 07	345
	Alpheratz		◆ DENEB		VEGA		Rasalhague		◆ ARCTURUS		Alioth		◆ CAPELLA	
240	14 48	050	48 11	084	54 50	121	34 09	151	40 09	213	66 02	268	23 01	345
241	15 07	051	48 35	084	55 11	122	34 21	153	39 55	214	65 38	269	22 55	346
242	15 26	051	48 59	085	55 31	123	34 32	154	39 41	215	65 14	269	22 49	347
243	15 45	052	49 24	086	55 52	125	34 42	155	39 27	216	64 49	270	22 44	348
244	16 05	053	49 48	087	56 12	126	34 53	156	39 12	217	64 25	271	22 39	348
245	16 24	054	50 12	088	56 31	127	35 02	157	38 57	219	64 00	272	22 34	349
246	16 44	055	50 37	089	56 51	128	35 11	158	38 42	220	63 36	273	22 29	350
247	17 04	056	51 01	090	57 09	130	35 20	160	38 26	221	63 12	274	22 25	351
248	17 25	057	51 26	091	57 28	131	35 28	161	38 10	222	62 47	275	22 22	351
249	17 45	057	51 50	092	57 46	132	35 36	162	37 53	223	62 23	276	22 18	352
250	18 06	058	52 14	093	58 04	134	35 43	163	37 37	224	61 59	276	22 15	353
251	18 27	059	52 39	093	58 22	135	35 50	164	37 19	226	61 35	277	22 12	354
252	18 48	060	53 03	094	58 39	137	35 57	166	37 02	227	61 10	278	22 10	354
253	19 09	061	53 27	095	58 55	138	36 02	167	36 44	228	60 46	279	22 07	355
254	19 30	062	53 52	096	59 11	139	36 08	168	36 26	229	60 22	280	22 05	356
	Alpheratz		◆ DENEB		ALTAIR		Rasalhague		◆ ARCTURUS		Alioth		◆ CAPELLA	
255	19 52	062	54 16	097	25 51	132	36 13	169	36 07	230	59 58	280	22 04	357
256	20 13	063	54 40	098	26 09	133	36 17	170	35 48	231	59 34	281	22 03	357
257	20 35	064	55 04	099	26 27	134	36 21	172	35 29	232	59 10	282	22 02	358
258	20 57	065	55 28	100	26 44	135	36 24	173	35 10	233	58 46	283	22 01	359
259	21 20	066	55 52	101	27 01	136	36 27	174	34 50	234	58 23	284	22 01	000
260	21 42	067	56 16	102	27 18	137	36 29	175	34 30	235	57 59	284	22 01	000
261	22 04	068	56 40	103	27 34	138	36 31	176	34 10	237	57 35	285	22 01	001
262	22 27	068	57 04	105	27 51	139	36 32	178	33 49	238	57 12	286	22 02	002
263	22 50	069	57 27	106	28 06	140	36 33	179	33 29	239	56 48	287	22 03	003
264	23 13	070	57 51	107	28 22	141	36 33	180	33 08	240	56 25	287	22 04	003
265	23 36	071	58 14	108	28 37	142	36 33	181	32 46	241	56 02	288	22 06	004
266	23 59	072	58 37	109	28 52	143	36 32	183	32 25	242	55 39	289	22 08	005
267	24 22	073	59 00	110	29 06	145	36 31	184	32 03	243	55 16	289	22 10	006
268	24 45	073	59 23	111	29 20	146	36 29	185	31 42	244	54 53	290	22 12	006
269	25 09	074	59 46	112	29 34	147	36 26	186	31 20	245	54 30	291	22 15	007

LHA ♈	Hc	Zn	Hc	Zn	Hc	Zn	Hc	Zn	Hc	Zn	Hc	Zn	Hc	Zn
	◆ CAPELLA		Alpheratz		◆ DENEB		ALTAIR		Rasalhague		◆ ARCTURUS		Alioth	
270	22 18	008	25 32	075	60 08	114	29 47	148	36 23	187	30 57	246	54 07	292
271	22 22	009	25 56	076	60 30	115	30 00	149	36 20	189	30 35	247	53 44	292
272	22 26	009	26 20	077	60 52	116	30 12	150	36 16	190	30 13	248	53 22	293
273	22 30	010	26 43	078	61 14	117	30 24	151	36 12	191	29 50	249	52 59	294
274	22 34	011	27 07	079	61 36	119	30 35	152	36 07	192	29 27	250	52 37	294
275	22 39	012	27 31	080	61 57	120	30 47	153	36 01	193	29 04	251	52 15	295
276	22 44	012	27 55	080	62 18	121	30 57	155	35 55	195	28 41	252	51 53	296
277	22 50	013	28 19	081	62 39	122	31 08	156	35 49	196	28 18	253	51 31	296
278	22 55	014	28 44	082	62 59	124	31 17	157	35 42	197	27 54	254	51 09	297
279	23 01	015	29 08	083	63 19	125	31 27	158	35 35	198	27 31	255	50 48	298
280	23 08	015	29 32	084	63 39	127	31 36	159	35 27	199	27 07	256	50 26	298
281	23 14	016	29 56	085	63 59	128	31 44	160	35 19	201	26 43	257	50 05	299
282	23 21	017	30 21	086	64 18	129	31 52	161	35 10	202	26 20	258	49 43	300
283	23 28	018	30 45	087	64 36	131	32 00	163	35 00	203	25 56	259	49 22	301
284	23 36	018	31 09	088	64 55	132	32 07	164	34 51	204	25 32	260	49 01	301
	◆ CAPELLA		Hamal		Alpheratz		◆ ALTAIR		VEGA		◆ ARCTURUS		Alioth	
285	23 44	019	14 49	065	31 34	088	32 13	165	62 36	190	25 08	261	48 41	302
286	23 52	020	15 11	066	31 58	089	32 19	166	62 32	191	24 44	261	48 20	303
287	24 00	021	15 33	067	32 23	090	32 25	167	62 27	193	24 20	262	47 59	303
288	24 09	021	15 56	068	32 47	091	32 30	168	62 21	195	23 55	263	47 39	304
289	24 18	022	16 19	069	33 11	092	32 35	170	62 15	196	23 31	264	47 19	305
290	24 27	023	16 41	069	33 36	093	32 39	171	62 07	198	23 07	265	46 59	305
291	24 37	024	17 04	070	34 00	094	32 43	172	62 00	200	22 42	266	46 39	306
292	24 47	024	17 27	071	34 24	095	32 46	173	61 51	201	22 18	267	46 19	307
293	24 57	025	17 50	072	34 49	096	32 49	174	61 42	203	21 54	268	46 00	307
294	25 08	026	18 14	073	35 13	097	32 51	175	61 32	204	21 29	269	45 40	308
295	25 18	027	18 37	074	35 37	098	32 52	177	61 22	206	21 05	270	45 21	308
296	25 29	027	19 01	075	36 01	099	32 54	178	61 11	208	20 40	271	45 02	309
297	25 41	028	19 24	076	36 25	100	32 54	179	60 59	209	20 16	272	44 43	310
298	25 52	029	19 48	076	36 49	101	32 55	180	60 47	211	19 52	273	44 25	310
299	26 04	029	20 12	077	37 13	102	32 54	181	60 34	212	19 27	273	44 06	311
	◆ CAPELLA		Hamal		Alpheratz		◆ ALTAIR		VEGA		◆ ARCTURUS		Dubhe	
300	26 16	030	20 35	078	37 37	103	32 53	182	60 21	214	19 03	274	42 06	333
301	26 29	031	20 59	079	38 01	104	32 52	184	60 07	215	18 39	275	41 55	333
302	26 41	032	21 23	080	38 25	105	32 50	185	59 53	217	18 14	276	41 44	334
303	26 54	032	21 47	081	38 48	106	32 48	186	59 38	218	17 50	277	41 33	334
304	27 08	033	22 12	082	39 12	107	32 45	187	59 23	220	17 26	278	41 23	335
305	27 21	034	22 36	083	39 35	108	32 42	188	59 07	221	17 02	279	41 13	335
306	27 35	035	23 00	084	39 58	109	32 38	190	58 51	222	16 38	280	41 03	336
307	27 49	035	23 24	084	40 21	110	32 34	191	58 34	224	16 14	281	40 53	337
308	28 03	036	23 49	085	40 44	111	32 29	192	58 17	225	15 50	282	40 43	337
309	28 18	037	24 13	086	41 07	112	32 24	193	57 59	227	15 26	282	40 34	338
310	28 32	038	24 37	087	41 30	113	32 18	194	57 41	228	15 02	283	40 25	338
311	28 47	038	25 02	088	41 52	114	32 12	195	57 23	229	14 38	284	40 16	339
312	29 03	039	25 26	089	42 14	115	32 05	197	57 04	231	14 15	285	40 07	340
313	29 18	040	25 50	090	42 36	116	31 58	198	56 45	232	13 51	286	39 59	340
314	29 34	041	26 15	091	42 58	117	31 50	199	56 26	233	13 28	287	39 51	341
	CAPELLA		◆ Hamal		Alpheratz		◆ ALTAIR		VEGA		Alphecca		◆ Dubhe	
315	29 50	041	26 39	092	43 20	118	31 42	200	56 06	235	27 46	274	39 43	341
316	30 06	042	27 04	093	43 41	119	31 34	201	55 46	236	27 21	275	39 35	342
317	30 23	043	27 28	094	44 02	120	31 25	202	55 26	237	26 57	275	39 28	343
318	30 39	044	27 52	094	44 23	121	31 15	203	55 05	238	26 33	276	39 21	343
319	30 56	044	28 17	095	44 44	123	31 05	205	54 44	239	26 08	277	39 14	344
320	31 13	045	28 41	096	45 04	124	30 55	206	54 23	241	25 44	278	39 07	344
321	31 31	046	29 05	097	45 25	125	30 44	207	54 02	242	25 20	279	39 00	345
322	31 48	046	29 29	098	45 44	126	30 33	208	53 40	243	24 56	280	38 54	346
323	32 06	047	29 53	099	46 04	127	30 21	209	53 18	244	24 32	281	38 48	346
324	32 24	048	30 18	100	46 23	128	30 09	210	52 56	245	24 08	282	38 43	347
325	32 42	049	30 42	101	46 42	130	29 57	211	52 34	246	23 44	283	38 37	347
326	33 01	049	31 05	102	47 01	131	29 44	212	52 11	248	23 21	283	38 32	348
327	33 20	050	31 29	103	47 19	132	29 30	214	51 49	249	22 57	284	38 27	349
328	33 38	051	31 53	104	47 37	133	29 17	215	51 26	250	22 33	285	38 22	349
329	33 57	052	32 17	105	47 55	134	29 03	216	51 03	251	22 10	286	38 18	350
	CAPELLA		◆ Hamal		Alpheratz		◆ ALTAIR		VEGA		Alphecca		◆ Alioth	
330	34 17	052	32 40	106	48 12	136	28 48	217	50 40	252	21 46	287	36 15	331
331	34 36	053	33 04	107	48 29	137	28 33	218	50 17	253	21 23	288	36 03	332
332	34 56	054	33 27	108	48 46	138	28 18	219	49 53	254	21 00	289	35 52	333
333	35 16	055	33 50	109	49 02	139	28 03	220	49 30	255	20 37	290	35 41	333
334	35 36	055	34 13	110	49 17	141	27 47	221	49 06	256	20 14	290	35 30	334
335	35 56	056	34 36	111	49 33	142	27 30	222	48 42	257	19 51	291	35 19	335
336	36 16	057	34 59	112	49 48	143	27 14	223	48 18	258	19 28	292	35 09	335
337	36 37	058	35 21	113	50 02	144	26 57	224	47 55	259	19 06	293	34 59	336
338	36 57	058	35 44	114	50 16	146	26 40	225	47 31	260	18 43	294	34 49	337
339	37 18	059	36 06	115	50 29	147	26 22	226	47 06	261	18 21	295	34 39	337
340	37 39	060	36 28	116	50 42	148	26 04	228	46 42	262	17 59	296	34 30	338
341	38 00	061	36 50	117	50 55	150	25 46	229	46 18	263	17 37	296	34 21	338
342	38 22	061	37 11	118	51 07	151	25 28	230	45 54	264	17 15	297	34 12	339
343	38 43	062	37 33	119	51 18	153	25 09	231	45 30	265	16 54	298	34 04	340
344	39 05	063	37 54	120	51 29	154	24 50	232	45 05	266	16 32	299	33 55	340
	◆ POLLUX		CAPELLA		Hamal		◆ Alpheratz		ALTAIR		◆ VEGA		Alioth	
345	10 59	042	39 27	064	38 15	121	51 40	155	24 31	233	44 41	267	33 47	341
346	11 15	043	39 49	064	38 36	122	51 50	157	24 11	234	44 17	268	33 39	342
347	11 32	044	40 11	065	38 56	124	51 59	158	23 51	235	43 52	269	33 32	342
348	11 49	045	40 33	066	39 16	125	52 08	159	23 31	236	43 28	270	33 25	343
349	12 07	046	40 55	067	39 36	126	52 16	161	23 11	237	43 03	271	33 18	344
350	12 24	047	41 18	068	39 56	127	52 24	162	22 51	238	42 39	271	33 11	344
351	12 42	047	41 41	068	40 15	128	52 31	164	22 30	239	42 15	272	33 05	345
352	13 00	048	42 03	069	40 34	129	52 38	165	22 09	240	41 50	273	32 58	346
353	13 18	049	42 26	070	40 53	130	52 44	167	21 48	241	41 26	274	32 53	346
354	13 37	050	42 49	071	41 12	131	52 49	168	21 26	242	41 01	275	32 47	347
355	13 56	051	43 12	072	41 30	133	52 54	169	21 05	243	40 37	276	32 42	348
356	14 15	052	43 35	072	41 47	134	52 58	171	20 43	244	40 13	277	32 36	348
357	14 34	053	43 59	073	42 05	135	53 02	172	20 21	245	39 49	278	32 32	349
358	14 54	053	44 22	074	42 22	136	53 05	174	19 59	246	39 25	279	32 27	350
359	15 13	054	44 46	075	42 39	137	53 07	175	19 36	247	39 00	279	32 23	350

LHA ♈	Hc Zn	Hc Zn	Hc Zn	Hc Zn	Hc Zn	Hc Zn	Hc Zn
	◆POLLUX	CAPELLA	Hamal	◆Alpheratz	DENEB	◆VEGA	Alioth
0	14 59 055	44 54 075	43 40 138	54 09 177	56 52 258	38 25 281	31 20 351
1	15 20 056	45 18 075	43 57 139	54 10 178	56 28 259	38 00 282	31 16 352
2	15 41 057	45 43 076	44 13 140	54 10 180	56 03 260	37 36 283	31 12 352
3	16 02 057	46 07 077	44 29 141	54 10 181	55 38 261	37 11 284	31 09 353
4	16 23 058	46 32 078	44 45 143	54 09 183	55 13 262	36 46 284	31 06 354
5	16 45 059	46 57 079	45 00 144	54 08 184	54 47 263	36 22 285	31 04 354
6	17 07 060	47 22 079	45 15 145	54 06 186	54 22 264	35 57 286	31 01 355
7	17 29 061	47 47 080	45 29 146	54 03 187	53 57 265	35 33 287	30 59 356
8	17 51 062	48 12 081	45 43 148	54 00 188	53 32 266	35 09 288	30 57 356
9	18 14 062	48 37 082	45 56 149	53 56 190	53 06 267	34 45 288	30 56 357
10	18 36 063	49 02 083	46 09 150	53 51 191	52 41 268	34 21 289	30 55 358
11	18 59 064	49 27 084	46 21 152	53 46 193	52 16 269	33 57 290	30 54 358
12	19 22 065	49 52 084	46 33 153	53 40 194	51 50 270	33 33 291	30 53 359
13	19 45 066	50 18 085	46 44 154	53 33 196	51 25 271	33 10 292	30 53 000
14	20 08 067	50 43 086	46 55 155	53 26 197	51 00 271	32 46 293	30 53 000
	Alioth	◆POLLUX	CAPELLA	Hamal	◆Alpheratz	DENEB	◆VEGA
15	30 53 001	20 31 067	51 08 087	47 05 157	53 18 199	50 34 272	32 23 293
16	30 54 002	20 55 068	51 34 088	47 15 158	53 09 200	50 09 273	32 00 294
17	30 54 002	21 18 069	51 59 089	47 24 159	53 00 202	49 44 274	31 36 295
18	30 55 003	21 42 070	52 24 090	47 33 161	52 51 203	49 18 275	31 14 296
19	30 57 003	22 06 071	52 50 091	47 41 162	52 41 204	48 53 276	30 51 296
20	30 59 004	22 30 072	53 15 092	47 48 164	52 30 206	48 28 277	30 28 297
21	31 00 005	22 54 073	53 40 092	47 55 165	52 18 207	48 03 278	30 06 298
22	31 03 005	23 18 073	54 06 093	48 02 166	52 07 209	47 38 278	29 43 299
23	31 05 006	23 43 074	54 31 094	48 07 168	51 54 210	47 13 279	29 21 300
24	31 08 007	24 07 075	54 56 095	48 12 169	51 41 211	46 48 280	28 59 300
25	31 11 007	24 32 076	55 22 096	48 17 170	51 28 213	46 23 281	28 38 301
26	31 15 008	24 57 077	55 47 097	48 21 172	51 14 214	45 58 282	28 16 302
27	31 18 009	25 21 078	56 12 098	48 24 173	50 59 215	45 33 283	27 55 303
28	31 22 009	25 46 079	56 37 099	48 27 174	50 44 217	45 08 283	27 33 304
29	31 27 010	26 11 079	57 02 100	48 29 176	50 29 218	44 44 284	27 12 304
	Alioth	◆POLLUX	ALDEBARAN	◆Hamal	Alpheratz	DENEB	◆VEGA
30	31 31 011	26 36 080	34 53 132	48 31 177	50 13 219	44 19 285	26 51 305
31	31 36 011	27 01 081	35 12 133	48 32 179	49 57 221	43 55 286	26 31 306
32	31 41 012	27 26 082	35 30 135	48 32 180	49 40 222	43 30 287	26 10 307
33	31 46 013	27 51 083	35 48 136	48 32 181	49 23 223	43 06 287	25 50 308
34	31 52 013	28 16 084	36 05 137	48 31 183	49 05 224	42 42 288	25 30 308
35	31 58 014	28 42 085	36 23 138	48 29 184	48 47 226	42 18 289	25 10 309
36	32 04 015	29 07 086	36 39 139	48 27 186	48 29 227	41 54 290	24 51 310
37	32 11 015	29 32 086	36 56 140	48 24 187	48 10 228	41 30 290	24 31 311
38	32 18 016	29 57 087	37 12 141	48 21 188	47 51 229	41 06 291	24 12 311
39	32 25 017	30 23 088	37 27 143	48 17 190	47 32 231	40 43 292	23 53 312
40	32 32 017	30 48 089	37 43 144	48 12 191	47 12 232	40 19 293	23 35 313
41	32 40 018	31 14 090	37 57 145	48 07 192	46 52 233	39 56 294	23 16 314
42	32 48 018	31 39 091	38 12 146	48 02 194	46 31 234	39 33 294	22 58 315
43	32 56 019	32 04 092	38 26 147	47 55 195	46 11 235	39 10 295	22 40 315
44	33 04 020	32 30 093	38 39 148	47 48 196	45 50 236	38 47 296	22 22 316
	Alioth	◆POLLUX	ALDEBARAN	◆Hamal	Alpheratz	DENEB	◆VEGA
45	33 13 020	32 55 094	38 52 150	47 41 198	45 28 238	38 24 297	22 05 317
46	33 22 021	33 20 095	39 05 151	47 33 199	45 07 239	38 02 297	21 48 318
47	33 31 022	33 45 096	39 17 152	47 24 201	44 45 240	37 39 298	21 31 318
48	33 41 022	34 11 097	39 28 153	47 15 202	44 23 241	37 17 299	21 14 319
49	33 50 023	34 36 097	39 40 155	47 05 203	44 01 242	36 55 300	20 58 320
50	34 00 024	35 01 098	39 50 156	46 55 204	43 38 243	36 33 300	20 42 321
51	34 11 024	35 26 099	40 00 157	46 44 206	43 15 244	36 11 301	20 26 322
52	34 21 025	35 51 100	40 10 158	46 33 207	42 53 245	35 49 302	20 10 322
53	34 32 026	36 16 101	40 19 159	46 21 208	42 29 246	35 28 303	19 55 323
54	34 43 026	36 41 102	40 28 161	46 09 210	42 06 247	35 07 303	19 40 324
55	34 55 027	37 05 103	40 36 162	45 56 211	41 43 249	34 46 304	19 25 325
56	35 06 027	37 30 104	40 43 163	45 43 212	41 19 250	34 25 305	19 10 325
57	35 18 028	37 55 105	40 51 164	45 29 214	40 55 251	34 04 306	18 56 326
58	35 30 029	38 19 106	40 57 166	45 15 215	40 31 252	33 43 306	18 42 327
59	35 42 029	38 43 107	41 03 167	45 00 216	40 07 253	33 23 307	18 29 328
	Alioth	◆POLLUX	ALDEBARAN	◆Hamal	Alpheratz	DENEB	◆VEGA
60	35 55 030	39 07 108	41 08 168	44 45 217	39 43 254	33 03 308	18 15 329
61	36 08 031	39 31 109	41 13 170	44 29 219	39 18 255	32 43 309	18 02 329
62	36 21 031	39 55 110	41 18 171	44 13 220	38 54 256	32 23 309	17 49 330
63	36 34 032	40 19 111	41 21 172	43 57 221	38 29 257	32 04 310	17 37 331
64	36 48 033	40 43 112	41 25 173	43 40 222	38 04 258	31 44 311	17 25 332
65	37 01 033	41 06 113	41 27 175	43 23 223	37 40 259	31 25 311	17 13 333
66	37 15 034	41 29 114	41 29 176	43 05 225	37 15 260	31 06 312	17 01 333
67	37 30 035	41 52 116	41 31 177	42 47 226	36 50 261	30 48 313	16 50 334
68	37 44 035	42 15 117	41 32 178	42 29 227	36 25 261	30 29 314	16 39 335
69	37 59 036	42 37 118	41 32 180	42 10 228	36 00 262	30 11 314	16 29 336
70	38 14 036	43 00 119	41 32 181	41 51 229	35 34 263	29 53 315	16 19 337
71	38 29 037	43 22 120	41 31 182	41 32 230	35 09 264	29 35 316	16 09 337
72	38 45 038	43 44 121	41 30 184	41 12 232	34 44 265	29 18 317	15 59 338
73	39 00 038	44 05 122	41 28 185	40 52 233	34 19 266	29 00 317	15 50 339
74	39 16 039	44 27 123	41 26 186	40 32 234	33 53 267	28 43 318	15 41 340
	Alioth	◆REGULUS	PROCYON	◆ALDEBARAN	Hamal	Alpheratz	◆DENEB
75	39 32 040	16 08 096	23 51 136	41 23 187	40 11 235	33 28 268	28 26 319
76	39 48 040	16 33 097	24 08 137	41 19 189	39 50 236	33 03 269	28 10 320
77	40 05 041	16 58 098	24 25 138	41 15 190	39 29 237	32 37 270	27 54 320
78	40 22 042	17 23 099	24 42 139	41 10 191	39 08 238	32 12 271	27 37 321
79	40 39 042	17 48 100	24 59 140	41 05 193	38 46 239	31 47 272	27 22 322
80	40 56 043	18 13 101	25 15 141	40 59 194	38 24 240	31 21 273	27 06 322
81	41 13 043	18 38 102	25 31 142	40 53 195	38 02 241	30 56 273	26 51 323
82	41 31 044	19 02 103	25 46 143	40 46 196	37 40 243	30 31 274	26 36 324
83	41 48 045	19 27 104	26 01 144	40 39 198	37 17 244	30 05 275	26 21 325
84	42 06 045	19 52 105	26 16 145	40 31 199	36 54 245	29 40 276	26 06 325
85	42 24 046	20 16 106	26 31 146	40 23 200	36 31 246	29 15 277	25 52 326
86	42 43 047	20 40 107	26 44 147	40 14 201	36 08 247	28 50 278	25 38 327
87	43 01 047	21 05 108	26 58 148	40 04 203	35 45 248	28 25 279	25 24 328
88	43 20 048	21 29 109	27 11 149	39 54 204	35 21 249	28 00 280	25 11 328
89	43 39 049	21 53 110	27 24 151	39 44 205	34 57 250	27 35 280	24 58 329

LHA ♈	Hc Zn	Hc Zn	Hc Zn	Hc Zn	Hc Zn	Hc Zn	Hc Zn
	Alioth	◆REGULUS	PROCYON	BETELGEUSE	◆ALDEBARAN	Hamal	◆DENEB
90	43 58 049	22 17 111	27 36 152	32 24 181	39 33 206	34 33 251	24 45 330
91	44 17 050	22 40 112	27 48 153	32 23 182	39 21 207	34 09 252	24 32 331
92	44 37 051	23 04 113	27 59 154	32 22 184	39 09 209	33 45 253	24 20 331
93	44 57 051	23 27 113	28 10 155	32 20 185	38 57 210	33 21 254	24 08 332
94	45 16 052	23 50 114	28 21 156	32 18 186	38 44 211	32 57 255	23 56 333
95	45 36 052	24 13 115	28 31 157	32 15 187	38 31 212	32 32 256	23 45 334
96	45 57 053	24 36 116	28 40 158	32 12 188	38 17 213	32 07 257	23 34 334
97	46 17 054	24 59 117	28 50 159	32 08 189	38 03 215	31 43 258	23 23 335
98	46 37 054	25 21 118	28 58 161	32 04 191	37 48 216	31 18 259	23 12 336
99	46 58 055	25 43 119	29 06 162	31 59 192	37 33 217	30 53 260	23 02 336
100	47 19 056	26 05 120	29 14 163	31 53 193	37 18 218	30 28 260	22 52 337
101	47 40 056	26 27 121	29 21 164	31 47 194	37 02 219	30 03 261	22 42 338
102	48 01 057	26 48 122	29 28 165	31 41 195	36 46 220	29 38 262	22 33 339
103	48 23 058	27 10 124	29 35 166	31 34 196	36 29 222	29 13 263	22 24 339
104	48 44 058	27 31 125	29 40 167	31 27 198	36 12 223	28 48 264	22 15 340
	Alioth	◆REGULUS	PROCYON	BETELGEUSE	◆CAPELLA	Hamal	◆DENEB
105	49 06 059	27 51 126	29 46 168	31 19 199	66 28 229	28 22 265	22 07 341
106	49 27 060	28 12 127	29 50 170	31 10 200	66 09 230	27 57 266	21 59 342
107	49 49 060	28 32 128	29 55 171	31 02 201	65 50 232	27 32 267	21 51 342
108	50 11 061	28 52 129	29 59 172	30 52 202	65 29 233	27 06 268	21 43 343
109	50 34 062	29 12 130	30 02 173	30 43 203	65 09 235	26 41 269	21 36 344
110	50 56 062	29 31 131	30 05 174	30 32 204	64 48 236	26 16 270	21 29 345
111	51 19 063	29 50 132	30 07 175	30 22 206	64 27 237	25 50 271	21 23 345
112	51 41 064	30 09 133	30 09 177	30 10 207	64 05 239	25 25 272	21 16 346
113	52 04 064	30 27 134	30 10 178	29 59 208	63 44 240	25 00 272	21 11 347
114	52 27 065	30 45 135	30 11 179	29 47 209	63 21 241	24 34 273	21 05 348
115	52 50 066	31 03 136	30 11 180	29 34 210	62 59 243	24 09 274	21 00 348
116	53 13 066	31 20 137	30 11 181	29 21 211	62 36 244	23 44 275	20 55 349
117	53 36 067	31 37 138	30 10 182	29 08 212	62 13 245	23 18 276	20 50 350
118	54 00 068	31 54 140	30 09 183	28 54 213	61 50 246	22 53 277	20 46 351
119	54 23 068	32 10 141	30 07 185	28 40 214	61 27 248	22 28 278	20 42 351
	◆VEGA	ARCTURUS	◆REGULUS	PROCYON	◆CAPELLA	Schedar	DENEB
120	15 03 017	15 33 078	32 26 142	30 05 186	61 03 249	42 44 315	20 38 352
121	15 10 017	15 58 079	32 42 143	30 02 187	60 40 250	42 26 316	20 35 353
122	15 18 018	16 23 080	32 57 144	29 59 188	60 16 251	42 09 316	20 32 354
123	15 26 019	16 48 081	33 12 145	29 55 189	59 52 252	41 51 317	20 29 354
124	15 34 020	17 13 082	33 26 146	29 51 190	59 27 253	41 34 318	20 27 355
125	15 43 021	17 38 082	33 40 147	29 46 191	59 03 255	41 17 318	20 25 356
126	15 52 021	18 03 083	33 53 149	29 41 193	58 38 256	41 00 319	20 23 357
127	16 02 022	18 29 084	34 06 150	29 35 194	58 14 257	40 44 320	20 22 357
128	16 11 023	18 54 085	34 19 151	29 29 195	57 49 258	40 27 320	20 21 358
129	16 21 024	19 19 086	34 31 152	29 22 196	57 24 259	40 11 321	20 20 359
130	16 32 024	19 44 087	34 43 153	29 15 197	56 59 260	39 55 321	20 20 000
131	16 42 025	20 10 088	34 54 154	29 07 198	56 34 261	39 40 322	20 20 000
132	16 53 026	20 35 089	35 05 156	28 59 199	56 09 262	39 24 323	20 20 001
133	17 05 027	21 01 090	35 15 157	28 50 201	55 44 263	39 09 323	20 21 002
134	17 16 028	21 26 091	35 25 158	28 41 202	55 19 264	38 54 324	20 22 003
	DENEB	◆VEGA	ARCTURUS	◆REGULUS	PROCYON	◆CAPELLA	Schedar
135	20 23 003	17 28 028	21 51 091	35 34 159	28 31 203	54 54 265	38 39 325
136	20 25 004	17 40 029	22 17 092	35 43 160	28 21 204	54 28 266	38 24 325
137	20 27 005	17 53 030	22 42 093	35 51 161	28 11 205	54 03 267	38 10 326
138	20 29 006	18 06 031	23 07 094	35 59 163	28 00 206	53 38 268	37 56 326
139	20 32 006	18 19 032	23 32 095	36 06 164	27 48 207	53 13 269	37 42 327
140	20 35 007	18 32 032	23 58 096	36 13 165	27 37 208	52 47 269	37 28 328
141	20 38 008	18 46 033	24 23 097	36 19 166	27 24 209	52 22 270	37 15 328
142	20 42 009	19 00 034	24 48 098	36 25 167	27 12 211	51 56 271	37 02 329
143	20 46 009	19 14 035	25 13 099	36 30 169	26 59 212	51 31 272	36 49 330
144	20 50 010	19 29 036	25 38 100	36 35 170	26 45 213	51 06 273	36 36 330
145	20 55 011	19 44 036	26 03 101	36 39 171	26 31 214	50 40 274	36 24 331
146	21 00 012	19 59 037	26 28 102	36 43 172	26 17 215	50 15 275	36 12 332
147	21 05 012	20 14 038	26 53 103	36 46 174	26 02 216	49 50 276	36 00 332
148	21 11 013	20 30 039	27 17 104	36 49 175	25 47 217	49 25 277	35 48 333
149	21 17 014	20 46 039	27 42 105	36 51 176	25 32 218	49 00 277	35 36 333
	DENEB	◆VEGA	ARCTURUS	◆REGULUS	PROCYON	◆CAPELLA	Schedar
150	21 23 015	21 02 040	28 07 106	36 52 177	25 16 219	48 34 278	35 25 334
151	21 29 015	21 19 041	28 31 106	36 53 178	25 00 220	48 09 279	35 14 335
152	21 36 016	21 36 042	28 55 107	36 54 180	24 43 221	47 44 280	35 04 335
153	21 43 017	21 53 043	29 19 108	36 53 181	24 26 222	47 19 281	34 53 336
154	21 51 018	22 10 043	29 43 109	36 53 182	24 09 223	46 55 282	34 43 337
155	21 59 018	22 27 044	30 07 110	36 52 183	23 51 224	46 30 282	34 33 337
156	22 07 019	22 45 045	30 31 111	36 50 185	23 33 225	46 05 283	34 23 338
157	22 15 020	23 03 046	30 54 112	36 48 186	23 15 226	45 40 284	34 14 339
158	22 24 021	23 21 046	31 18 113	36 45 187	22 57 227	45 16 285	34 05 339
159	22 33 021	23 40 047	31 41 114	36 41 188	22 38 229	44 51 286	33 56 340
160	22 43 022	23 59 048	32 04 115	36 38 189	22 19 230	44 27 286	33 47 340
161	22 52 023	24 18 049	32 27 116	36 33 191	21 59 231	44 03 287	33 39 341
162	23 02 024	24 37 050	32 49 117	36 28 192	21 40 232	43 38 288	33 31 342
163	23 12 024	24 56 050	33 12 119	36 23 193	21 20 233	43 14 289	33 23 342
164	23 23 025	25 16 051	33 34 120	36 17 194	20 59 234	42 50 289	33 16 343
	DENEB	◆VEGA	ARCTURUS	◆REGULUS	POLLUX	◆CAPELLA	Schedar
165	23 34 026	25 36 052	33 56 121	36 10 195	42 17 243	42 27 290	33 08 344
166	23 45 026	25 56 053	34 17 122	36 03 197	41 55 244	42 03 291	33 01 344
167	23 57 027	26 16 053	34 39 123	35 56 198	41 32 245	41 39 292	32 55 345
168	24 08 028	26 37 054	35 00 124	35 48 199	41 09 246	41 16 293	32 48 346
169	24 20 029	26 57 055	35 21 125	35 39 200	40 45 248	40 52 293	32 42 346
170	24 33 029	27 18 056	35 42 126	35 30 201	40 22 249	40 29 294	32 36 347
171	24 45 030	27 39 057	36 02 127	35 21 203	39 58 250	40 06 295	32 30 348
172	24 58 031	28 00 057	36 22 128	35 11 204	39 34 251	39 43 296	32 25 348
173	25 11 032	28 22 058	36 42 129	35 00 205	39 10 252	39 20 296	32 20 349
174	25 25 032	28 44 059	37 01 130	34 49 206	38 46 253	38 58 297	32 15 349
175	25 38 033	29 05 060	37 21 131	34 38 207	38 22 254	38 35 298	32 11 350
176	25 52 034	29 27 061	37 39 133	34 26 208	37 57 255	38 13 299	32 06 351
177	26 07 035	29 50 061	37 58 134	34 14 210	37 33 256	37 51 299	32 03 351
178	26 21 035	30 12 062	38 16 135	34 01 211	37 08 257	37 29 300	31 59 352
179	26 36 036	30 34 063	38 34 136	33 48 212	36 44 258	37 07 301	31 56 353

LHA ♈	Hc	Zn	Hc	Zn	Hc	Zn	Hc	Zn	Hc	Zn	Hc	Zn	Hc	Zn
	DENEB		◆ VEGA		ARCTURUS		◆ Denebola		REGULUS		POLLUX		◆ CAPELLA	
180	26 51	037	30 57	064	38 51	137	39 27	183	33 34	213	36 19	259	36 45	302
181	27 06	038	31 20	065	39 08	138	39 26	184	33 20	214	35 54	260	36 24	302
182	27 22	038	31 43	065	39 25	139	39 24	186	33 05	215	35 29	261	36 02	303
183	27 38	039	32 06	066	39 41	141	39 21	187	32 51	216	35 04	261	35 41	304
184	27 54	040	32 29	067	39 57	142	39 17	188	32 35	218	34 39	262	35 20	305
185	28 10	040	32 53	068	40 13	143	39 14	189	32 20	219	34 14	263	34 59	305
186	28 27	041	33 16	069	40 28	144	39 09	191	32 04	220	33 48	264	34 39	306
187	28 44	042	33 40	069	40 42	145	39 04	192	31 47	221	33 23	265	34 18	307
188	29 01	043	34 04	070	40 57	147	38 59	193	31 30	222	32 58	266	33 58	307
189	29 18	043	34 27	071	41 10	148	38 53	194	31 13	223	32 32	267	33 38	308
190	29 36	044	34 51	072	41 24	149	38 46	196	30 56	224	32 07	268	33 18	309
191	29 53	045	35 16	073	41 36	150	38 39	197	30 38	225	31 42	269	32 58	310
192	30 11	046	35 40	073	41 49	152	38 31	198	30 20	226	31 16	270	32 39	310
193	30 30	046	36 04	074	42 00	153	38 23	199	30 01	227	30 51	271	32 20	311
194	30 48	047	36 29	075	42 12	154	38 14	201	29 42	229	30 26	272	32 01	312
	DENEB		◆ VEGA		ARCTURUS		◆ Denebola		REGULUS		POLLUX		◆ CAPELLA	
195	31 07	048	36 53	076	42 23	155	38 05	202	29 23	230	30 00	273	31 42	313
196	31 26	049	37 18	077	42 33	157	37 56	203	29 04	231	29 35	273	31 23	313
197	31 45	049	37 43	078	42 43	158	37 46	204	28 44	232	29 10	274	31 05	314
198	32 04	050	38 07	078	42 52	159	37 35	205	28 24	233	28 45	275	30 47	315
199	32 24	051	38 32	079	43 01	160	37 24	207	28 03	234	28 19	276	30 29	315
200	32 44	052	38 57	080	43 09	162	37 12	208	27 43	235	27 54	277	30 11	316
201	33 03	052	39 22	081	43 17	163	37 00	209	27 22	236	27 29	278	29 54	317
202	33 24	053	39 47	082	43 24	164	36 48	210	27 01	237	27 04	279	29 37	318
203	33 44	054	40 12	083	43 31	165	36 35	211	26 40	238	26 39	280	29 20	318
204	34 05	054	40 38	083	43 37	167	36 21	212	26 18	239	26 14	280	29 03	319
205	34 25	055	41 03	084	43 42	168	36 07	214	25 56	240	25 49	281	28 47	320
206	34 46	056	41 28	085	43 47	169	35 53	215	25 34	241	25 24	282	28 30	321
207	35 07	057	41 53	086	43 52	171	35 39	216	25 12	242	24 59	283	28 14	321
208	35 29	057	42 19	087	43 56	172	35 23	217	24 49	243	24 35	284	27 59	322
209	35 50	058	42 44	088	43 59	173	35 08	218	24 27	244	24 10	285	27 43	323
	DENEB		◆ VEGA		ARCTURUS		◆ Denebola		REGULUS		POLLUX		◆ CAPELLA	
210	36 12	059	43 09	089	44 01	175	34 52	219	24 04	245	23 46	286	27 28	324
211	36 33	060	43 35	090	44 04	176	34 36	221	23 41	246	23 21	286	27 13	324
212	36 55	060	44 00	091	44 05	177	34 19	222	23 17	247	22 57	287	26 58	325
213	37 18	061	44 25	091	44 06	179	34 02	223	22 54	248	22 33	288	26 44	326
214	37 40	062	44 51	092	44 06	180	33 45	224	22 30	249	22 09	289	26 30	326
215	38 02	063	45 16	093	44 06	181	33 27	225	22 07	250	21 45	290	26 16	327
216	38 25	063	45 41	094	44 05	183	33 09	226	21 43	251	21 21	291	26 02	328
217	38 48	064	46 07	095	44 04	184	32 50	227	21 19	252	20 58	292	25 49	329
218	39 11	065	46 32	096	44 02	185	32 32	228	20 55	253	20 34	292	25 36	329
219	39 34	066	46 57	097	43 59	186	32 12	229	20 30	254	20 11	293	25 23	330
220	39 57	066	47 22	098	43 56	188	31 53	230	20 06	255	19 47	294	25 11	331
221	40 20	067	47 47	099	43 52	189	31 33	232	19 41	256	19 24	295	24 58	332
222	40 44	068	48 12	100	43 48	190	31 13	233	19 17	256	19 01	296	24 47	332
223	41 07	069	48 37	101	43 43	192	30 53	234	18 52	257	18 39	297	24 35	333
224	41 31	070	49 02	102	43 38	193	30 33	235	18 27	258	18 16	297	24 23	334
	◆ DENEB		VEGA		Rasalhague		◆ ARCTURUS		Denebola		Dubhe		◆ CAPELLA	
225	41 55	070	49 27	103	31 12	134	43 32	194	30 12	236	64 22	290	24 12	334
226	42 19	071	49 51	104	31 30	135	43 25	196	29 51	237	63 58	291	24 02	335
227	42 43	072	50 16	105	31 47	136	43 18	197	29 29	238	63 34	291	23 51	336
228	43 07	073	50 40	106	32 05	137	43 11	198	29 08	239	63 11	292	23 41	337
229	43 31	073	51 05	107	32 22	139	43 02	199	28 46	240	62 47	293	23 31	337
230	43 55	074	51 29	108	32 38	140	42 54	201	28 24	241	62 24	293	23 22	338
231	44 20	075	51 53	109	32 54	141	42 45	202	28 02	242	62 01	294	23 12	339
232	44 44	076	52 17	110	33 10	142	42 35	203	27 39	243	61 37	294	23 03	340
233	45 09	077	52 40	112	33 26	143	42 25	205	27 16	244	61 14	295	22 55	340
234	45 34	077	53 04	113	33 41	144	42 14	206	26 54	245	60 51	296	22 46	341
235	45 59	078	53 27	114	33 55	145	42 02	207	26 30	246	60 29	296	22 38	342
236	46 23	079	53 50	115	34 09	146	41 51	208	26 07	247	60 06	297	22 30	343
237	46 48	080	54 13	116	34 23	148	41 38	209	25 44	248	59 43	297	22 23	343
238	47 13	081	54 36	117	34 37	149	41 26	211	25 20	249	59 21	298	22 16	344
239	47 38	082	54 58	118	34 50	150	41 13	212	24 57	250	58 58	298	22 09	345
	Alpheratz		◆ DENEB		VEGA		Rasalhague		◆ ARCTURUS		Alioth		◆ CAPELLA	
240	14 10	050	48 03	082	55 20	120	35 02	151	40 59	213	66 04	270	22 03	346
241	14 29	050	48 29	083	55 42	121	35 14	152	40 45	214	65 38	271	21 56	346
242	14 49	051	48 54	084	56 04	122	35 26	153	40 30	216	65 13	272	21 51	347
243	15 09	052	49 19	085	56 25	123	35 37	155	40 15	217	64 48	272	21 45	348
244	15 29	053	49 44	086	56 46	125	35 47	156	40 00	218	64 22	273	21 40	349
245	15 49	054	50 10	087	57 07	126	35 57	157	39 44	219	63 57	274	21 35	349
246	16 10	055	50 35	088	57 27	127	36 07	158	39 28	220	63 32	275	21 30	350
247	16 30	055	51 00	089	57 47	129	36 16	159	39 11	221	63 07	276	21 26	351
248	16 51	056	51 26	089	58 07	130	36 25	161	38 54	223	62 41	277	21 22	351
249	17 13	057	51 51	090	58 26	131	36 33	162	38 37	224	62 16	277	21 19	352
250	17 34	058	52 16	091	58 45	133	36 41	163	38 19	225	61 51	278	21 15	353
251	17 56	059	52 42	092	59 04	134	36 48	164	38 01	226	61 26	279	21 12	354
252	18 17	060	53 07	093	59 22	135	36 55	165	37 43	227	61 01	280	21 10	354
253	18 39	060	53 32	094	59 39	137	37 01	167	37 24	228	60 36	281	21 08	355
254	19 01	061	53 58	095	59 56	138	37 06	168	37 05	229	60 11	281	21 06	356
	Alpheratz		◆ DENEB		ALTAIR		Rasalhague		◆ ARCTURUS		Alioth		◆ CAPELLA	
255	19 24	062	54 23	096	26 30	131	37 11	169	36 45	231	59 46	282	21 04	357
256	19 46	063	54 48	097	26 49	132	37 16	170	36 26	232	59 22	283	21 03	357
257	20 09	064	55 13	098	27 08	133	37 20	172	36 06	233	58 57	284	21 02	358
258	20 32	065	55 38	099	27 26	134	37 24	173	35 45	234	58 32	284	21 01	359
259	20 55	065	56 03	100	27 44	136	37 26	174	35 25	235	58 08	285	21 01	000
260	21 18	066	56 28	101	28 02	137	37 29	175	35 04	236	57 43	286	21 01	000
261	21 41	067	56 53	102	28 19	138	37 31	176	34 43	237	57 19	287	21 01	001
262	22 05	068	57 18	103	28 36	139	37 32	178	34 21	238	56 55	287	21 02	002
263	22 28	069	57 43	104	28 52	140	37 33	179	34 00	239	56 31	288	21 03	003
264	22 52	070	58 07	105	29 09	141	37 33	180	33 38	240	56 06	289	21 04	003
265	23 16	071	58 32	106	29 24	142	37 33	181	33 15	241	55 43	289	21 06	004
266	23 40	071	58 56	107	29 40	143	37 32	183	32 53	242	55 19	290	21 08	005
267	24 04	072	59 20	108	29 55	144	37 30	184	32 31	243	54 55	291	21 10	006
268	24 28	073	59 44	110	30 09	145	37 28	185	32 08	244	54 31	291	21 13	006
269	24 52	074	60 08	111	30 24	146	37 26	186	31 45	245	54 08	292	21 16	007

LHA ♈	Hc	Zn	Hc	Zn	Hc	Zn	Hc	Zn	Hc	Zn	Hc	Zn	Hc	Zn
	◆ CAPELLA		Alpheratz		◆ DENEB		ALTAIR		Rasalhague		◆ ARCTURUS		Alioth	
270	21 19	008	25 17	075	60 31	112	30 37	148	37 23	187	31 22	246	53 44	293
271	21 23	009	25 41	076	60 55	113	30 51	149	37 19	189	30 58	247	53 21	294
272	21 27	009	26 06	076	61 18	114	31 04	150	37 15	190	30 35	248	52 58	294
273	21 31	010	26 31	077	61 41	116	31 16	151	37 11	191	30 11	249	52 35	295
274	21 35	011	26 55	078	62 04	117	31 29	152	37 05	192	29 47	250	52 12	296
275	21 40	012	27 20	079	62 26	118	31 40	153	37 00	194	29 23	251	51 49	296
276	21 46	012	27 45	080	62 48	119	31 51	154	36 53	195	28 59	252	51 26	297
277	21 51	013	28 10	081	63 10	121	32 02	155	36 47	196	28 35	253	51 04	298
278	21 57	014	28 35	082	63 32	122	32 12	157	36 39	197	28 11	254	50 41	298
279	22 03	015	29 00	083	63 53	123	32 22	158	36 32	198	27 46	255	50 19	299
280	22 10	015	29 25	083	64 14	125	32 32	159	36 23	200	27 22	256	49 57	300
281	22 17	016	29 51	084	64 35	126	32 41	160	36 15	201	26 57	257	49 35	300
282	22 24	017	30 16	085	64 55	128	32 49	161	36 05	202	26 32	258	49 13	301
283	22 31	017	30 41	086	65 15	129	32 57	162	35 56	203	26 07	259	48 51	302
284	22 39	018	31 07	087	65 34	131	33 04	164	35 45	204	25 42	260	48 30	302
	◆ CAPELLA		Alpheratz		Enif		◆ ALTAIR		VEGA		◆ ARCTURUS		Alioth	
285	22 47	019	31 32	088	28 00	133	33 11	165	63 36	190	25 17	261	48 08	303
286	22 55	020	31 57	089	28 19	134	33 18	166	63 31	192	24 52	262	47 47	303
287	23 04	020	32 23	090	28 37	135	33 24	167	63 25	193	24 27	263	47 26	304
288	23 13	021	32 48	091	28 55	136	33 29	168	63 19	195	24 02	264	47 05	305
289	23 22	022	33 13	091	29 12	137	33 34	169	63 12	197	23 37	265	46 45	305
290	23 32	023	33 39	092	29 29	138	33 38	171	63 04	199	23 12	266	46 24	306
291	23 42	023	34 04	093	29 46	139	33 42	172	62 56	200	22 46	267	46 04	307
292	23 52	024	34 29	094	30 03	140	33 45	173	62 47	202	22 21	267	45 43	307
293	24 03	025	34 55	095	30 19	141	33 48	174	62 37	204	21 56	268	45 23	308
294	24 14	026	35 20	096	30 34	142	33 51	175	62 27	205	21 30	269	45 03	309
295	24 25	026	35 45	097	30 50	144	33 52	177	62 15	207	21 05	270	44 44	309
296	24 36	027	36 10	098	31 05	145	33 54	178	62 04	208	20 40	271	44 24	310
297	24 48	028	36 35	099	31 19	146	33 54	179	61 51	210	20 14	272	44 05	311
298	25 00	029	37 00	100	31 33	147	33 55	180	61 38	212	19 49	273	43 45	311
299	25 12	029	37 25	101	31 47	148	33 54	181	61 25	213	19 24	274	43 27	312
	◆ CAPELLA		Alpheratz		Enif		◆ ALTAIR		VEGA		◆ ARCTURUS		Alioth	
300	25 24	030	37 50	102	32 00	149	33 53	183	61 11	215	18 58	275	43 08	312
301	25 37	031	38 15	103	32 13	150	33 52	184	60 56	216	18 33	276	42 49	313
302	25 50	031	38 39	104	32 25	151	33 50	185	60 41	218	18 08	276	42 31	314
303	26 04	032	39 04	105	32 37	153	33 48	186	60 25	219	17 43	277	42 12	314
304	26 17	033	39 28	106	32 49	154	33 45	187	60 09	221	17 17	278	41 54	315
305	26 31	034	39 53	107	33 00	155	33 41	188	59 52	222	16 52	279	41 37	316
306	26 45	034	40 17	108	33 10	156	33 37	190	59 34	224	16 27	280	41 19	316
307	27 00	035	40 41	109	33 20	157	33 33	191	59 17	225	16 02	281	41 02	317
308	27 15	036	41 05	110	33 30	158	33 28	192	58 59	226	15 38	282	40 44	318
309	27 30	037	41 29	111	33 39	159	33 22	193	58 40	228	15 13	283	40 27	318
310	27 45	037	41 52	112	33 48	161	33 16	194	58 21	229	14 48	284	40 11	319
311	28 00	038	42 16	113	33 56	162	33 10	196	58 02	231	14 24	284	39 54	319
312	28 16	039	42 39	114	34 03	163	33 03	197	57 42	232	13 59	285	39 38	320
313	28 32	039	43 02	115	34 11	164	32 55	198	57 22	233	13 35	286	39 21	321
314	28 48	040	43 25	116	34 17	165	32 47	199	57 01	234	13 10	287	39 06	321
	CAPELLA		◆ Hamal		Alpheratz		Enif		◆ ALTAIR		VEGA		◆ Alioth	
315	29 05	041	26 41	091	43 48	117	34 23	167	32 38	200	56 40	236	38 50	322
316	29 22	042	27 06	092	44 10	118	34 29	168	32 29	201	56 19	237	38 34	323
317	29 39	042	27 31	093	44 32	119	34 34	169	32 20	203	55 58	238	38 19	323
318	29 56	043	27 57	094	44 54	121	34 39	170	32 10	204	55 36	239	38 04	324
319	30 13	044	28 22	095	45 16	122	34 43	171	32 00	205	55 14	241	37 49	325
320	30 31	045	28 47	096	45 37	123	34 46	173	31 49	206	54 52	242	37 35	325
321	30 49	045	29 12	097	45 59	124	34 49	174	31 37	207	54 30	243	37 20	326
322	31 07	046	29 38	098	46 19	125	34 52	175	31 26	208	54 07	244	37 06	327
323	31 25	047	30 03	099	46 40	126	34 54	176	31 13	209	53 44	245	36 52	327
324	31 44	048	30 28	100	47 00	127	34 55	177	31 01	210	53 21	247	36 39	328
325	32 03	048	30 53	100	47 20	129	34 56	179	30 48	212	52 57	248	36 25	328
326	32 22	049	31 18	101	47 40	130	34 57	180	30 34	213	52 34	249	36 12	329
327	32 41	050	31 42	102	47 59	131	34 57	181	30 20	214	52 10	250	35 59	330
328	33 00	050	32 07	103	48 18	132	34 56	182	30 06	215	51 46	251	35 47	330
329	33 20	051	32 32	104	48 37	134	34 55	183	29 51	216	51 22	252	35 34	331
	CAPELLA		◆ Hamal		Alpheratz		Enif		◆ ALTAIR		VEGA		◆ Alioth	
330	33 40	052	32 56	105	48 55	135	34 53	185	29 36	217	50 58	253	35 22	332
331	34 00	053	33 21	106	49 13	136	34 51	186	29 21	218	50 34	254	35 10	332
332	34 20	053	33 45	107	49 30	137	34 48	187	29 05	219	50 09	255	34 58	333
333	34 41	054	34 09	108	49 47	139	34 45	188	28 48	220	49 45	256	34 47	334
334	35 01	055	34 33	109	50 04	140	34 41	189	28 32	222	49 20	257	34 36	334
335	35 22	056	34 57	110	50 20	141	34 36	191	28 15	223	48 55	258	34 25	335
336	35 43	056	35 21	111	50 35	142	34 31	192	27 57	224	48 30	259	34 14	336
337	36 04	057	35 44	112	50 51	144	34 26	193	27 40	225	48 05	260	34 04	336
338	36 26	058	36 08	113	51 05	145	34 20	194	27 22	226	47 40	261	33 54	337
339	36 47	059	36 31	114	51 20	146	34 14	195	27 03	227	47 15	262	33 44	337
340	37 09	059	36 54	115	51 33	148	34 07	196	26 45	228	46 50	263	33 34	338
341	37 31	060	37 17	116	51 47	149	33 59	198	26 26	229	46 25	264	33 25	339
342	37 53	061	37 39	117	51 59	151	33 51	199	26 07	230	46 00	265	33 16	339
343	38 15	061	38 02	119	52 12	152	33 43	200	25 47	231	45 34	266	33 07	340
344	38 37	062	38 24	120	52 23	153	33 34	201	25 27	232	45 09	267	32 59	341
	CAPELLA		ALDEBARAN		◆ Hamal		Alpheratz		◆ ALTAIR		VEGA		◆ Alioth	
345	39 00	063	17 24	088	38 46	121	52 34	155	25 07	233	44 44	268	32 50	341
346	39 23	064	17 49	089	39 07	122	52 45	156	24 47	234	44 18	269	32 42	342
347	39 45	064	18 14	090	39 29	123	52 55	158	24 26	235	43 53	270	32 35	343
348	40 08	065	18 40	091	39 50	124	53 04	159	24 05	236	43 28	271	32 27	343
349	40 31	066	19 05	092	40 11	125	53 13	160	23 44	237	43 02	271	32 20	344
350	40 55	067	19 30	093	40 32	126	53 21	162	23 22	238	42 37	272	32 13	345
351	41 18	068	19 56	094	40 52	127	53 29	163	23 01	239	42 12	273	32 07	345
352	41 42	068	20 21	094	41 12	128	53 36	165	22 39	240	41 46	274	32 00	346
353	42 05	069	20 46	095	41 32	130	53 42	166	22 17	241	41 21	275	31 54	347
354	42 29	070	21 12	096	41 51	131	53 48	168	21 54	242	40 56	276	31 48	347
355	42 53	071	21 37	097	42 10	132	53 53	169	21 32	243	40 31	277	31 43	348
356	43 17	071	22 02	098	42 29	133	53 57	171	21 09	244	40 05	278	31 38	348
357	43 41	072	22 27	099	42 47	134	54 01	172	20 46	245	39 40	278	31 33	349
358	44 05	073	22 52	100	43 05	135	54 04	174	20 23	246	39 15	279	31 28	350
359	44 29	074	23 17	101	43 23	137	54 07	175	20 00	247	38 50	280	31 24	350

 LAT 64°N

LHA ♈	Hc	Zn	Hc	Zn	Hc	Zn	Hc	Zn	Hc	Zn	Hc	Zn	Hc	Zn
	◆POLLUX		CAPELLA		Hamal		◆Alpheratz		DENEB		◆VEGA		Alioth	
0	14 24	055	44 37	074	44 24	137	55 09	176	57 04	260	38 13	282	30 20	351
1	14 46	055	45 03	074	44 42	138	55 10	178	56 38	261	37 48	283	30 17	352
2	15 07	056	45 28	075	44 59	140	55 10	180	56 12	262	37 22	283	30 13	352
3	15 29	057	45 53	076	45 16	141	55 10	181	55 46	263	36 57	284	30 10	353
4	15 52	058	46 19	077	45 32	142	55 09	183	55 20	264	36 31	285	30 07	354
5	16 14	059	46 45	078	45 48	143	55 08	184	54 54	265	36 06	286	30 04	354
6	16 37	060	47 10	078	46 04	145	55 06	186	54 28	265	35 41	287	30 01	355
7	16 59	060	47 36	079	46 19	146	55 03	187	54 01	266	35 15	288	29 59	356
8	17 22	061	48 02	080	46 33	147	54 59	189	53 35	267	34 50	288	29 57	356
9	17 46	062	48 28	081	46 47	148	54 55	190	53 09	268	34 25	289	29 56	357
10	18 09	063	48 54	082	47 01	150	54 50	192	52 43	269	34 01	290	29 55	358
11	18 32	064	49 20	082	47 14	151	54 44	193	52 16	270	33 36	291	29 54	358
12	18 56	065	49 46	083	47 26	152	54 38	195	51 50	271	33 12	292	29 53	359
13	19 20	065	50 12	084	47 38	154	54 31	196	51 24	272	32 47	292	29 53	000
14	19 44	066	50 38	085	47 49	155	54 23	198	50 57	273	32 23	293	29 53	000
	Alioth		◆POLLUX		CAPELLA		Hamal		◆Alpheratz		DENEB		◆VEGA	
15	29 53	001	20 08	067	51 05	086	48 00	156	54 15	199	50 31	274	31 59	294
16	29 54	002	20 32	068	51 31	087	48 11	158	54 06	201	50 05	274	31 35	295
17	29 54	002	20 57	069	51 57	088	48 20	159	53 56	202	49 39	275	31 11	295
18	29 55	003	21 21	070	52 23	088	48 29	160	53 46	204	49 13	276	30 47	296
19	29 57	003	21 46	070	52 50	089	48 38	162	53 35	205	48 46	277	30 24	297
20	29 59	004	22 11	071	53 16	090	48 46	163	53 24	206	48 20	278	30 00	298
21	30 01	005	22 36	072	53 42	091	48 53	165	53 12	208	47 54	279	29 37	299
22	30 03	005	23 01	073	54 09	092	49 00	166	52 59	209	47 28	279	29 14	299
23	30 06	006	23 26	074	54 35	093	49 06	167	52 46	211	47 02	280	28 51	300
24	30 09	007	23 52	075	55 01	094	49 11	169	52 32	212	46 37	281	28 29	301
25	30 12	007	24 17	076	55 27	095	49 16	170	52 18	213	46 11	282	28 06	302
26	30 15	008	24 43	076	55 53	096	49 20	172	52 03	215	45 45	283	27 44	302
27	30 19	009	25 08	077	56 20	097	49 24	173	51 48	216	45 20	284	27 22	303
28	30 23	009	25 34	078	56 46	098	49 27	174	51 32	218	44 54	284	27 00	304
29	30 28	010	26 00	079	57 12	099	49 29	176	51 16	219	44 29	285	26 38	305
	Alioth		◆POLLUX		ALDEBARAN		◆Hamal		Alpheratz		DENEB		◆VEGA	
30	30 32	011	26 26	080	35 33	132	49 31	177	50 59	220	44 03	286	26 17	306
31	30 37	011	26 51	081	35 53	133	49 32	179	50 42	221	43 38	287	25 55	306
32	30 42	012	27 17	082	36 12	134	49 32	180	50 24	223	43 13	287	25 34	307
33	30 48	012	27 44	082	36 31	135	49 32	181	50 06	224	42 48	288	25 14	308
34	30 54	013	28 10	083	36 49	136	49 31	183	49 48	225	42 23	289	24 53	309
35	31 00	014	28 36	084	37 07	137	49 29	184	49 29	227	41 58	290	24 32	309
36	31 06	014	29 02	085	37 25	139	49 27	186	49 10	228	41 33	291	24 12	310
37	31 13	015	29 28	086	37 42	140	49 24	187	48 50	229	41 09	291	23 52	311
38	31 20	016	29 54	087	37 59	141	49 20	188	48 30	230	40 44	292	23 33	312
39	31 27	016	30 21	088	38 15	142	49 16	190	48 09	231	40 20	293	23 13	313
40	31 35	017	30 47	089	38 31	143	49 11	191	47 49	233	39 56	294	22 54	313
41	31 43	018	31 13	089	38 46	144	49 06	193	47 28	234	39 32	294	22 35	314
42	31 51	018	31 40	090	39 01	146	49 00	194	47 06	235	39 08	295	22 16	315
43	31 59	019	32 06	091	39 16	147	48 53	195	46 44	236	38 44	296	21 57	316
44	32 08	020	32 32	092	39 30	148	48 46	197	46 22	237	38 21	297	21 39	316
	Alioth		◆POLLUX		ALDEBARAN		◆Hamal		Alpheratz		DENEB		◆VEGA	
45	32 17	020	32 58	093	39 44	149	48 38	198	46 00	238	37 57	297	21 21	317
46	32 26	021	33 25	094	39 57	150	48 29	200	45 38	240	37 34	298	21 03	318
47	32 35	021	33 51	095	40 10	152	48 20	201	45 15	241	37 11	299	20 46	319
48	32 45	022	34 17	096	40 22	153	48 11	202	44 52	242	36 48	300	20 29	319
49	32 55	023	34 43	097	40 34	154	48 00	204	44 28	243	36 25	300	20 12	320
50	33 05	023	35 09	098	40 45	155	47 50	205	44 05	244	36 02	301	19 55	321
51	33 16	024	35 35	099	40 55	157	47 38	206	43 41	245	35 40	302	19 39	322
52	33 27	025	36 01	100	41 06	158	47 26	208	43 17	246	35 17	302	19 22	323
53	33 38	025	36 27	101	41 15	159	47 14	209	42 53	247	34 55	303	19 07	323
54	33 49	026	36 53	102	41 24	160	47 01	210	42 29	248	34 33	304	18 51	324
55	34 01	027	37 19	103	41 33	162	46 47	212	42 04	249	34 12	305	18 36	325
56	34 13	027	37 44	103	41 41	163	46 33	213	41 39	250	33 50	305	18 21	326
57	34 25	028	38 10	104	41 48	164	46 19	214	41 15	251	33 29	306	18 06	326
58	34 37	028	38 35	105	41 55	166	46 04	215	40 50	252	33 08	307	17 52	327
59	34 50	029	39 01	106	42 01	167	45 48	217	40 24	253	32 47	308	17 38	328
	Alioth		◆POLLUX		ALDEBARAN		◆Hamal		Alpheratz		DENEB		◆VEGA	
60	35 03	030	39 26	107	42 07	168	45 32	218	39 59	254	32 26	308	17 24	329
61	35 16	030	39 51	108	42 12	169	45 16	219	39 34	255	32 05	309	17 10	330
62	35 29	031	40 16	109	42 17	171	44 59	220	39 08	256	31 45	310	16 57	330
63	35 43	032	40 40	111	42 21	172	44 42	222	38 43	257	31 25	310	16 44	331
64	35 57	032	41 05	112	42 24	173	44 24	223	38 17	258	31 05	311	16 32	332
65	36 11	033	41 29	113	42 27	175	44 06	224	37 51	259	30 45	312	16 20	333
66	36 26	033	41 54	114	42 29	176	43 48	225	37 25	260	30 26	313	16 08	334
67	36 40	034	42 18	115	42 31	177	43 29	226	36 59	261	30 07	313	15 56	334
68	36 55	035	42 41	116	42 32	178	43 10	228	36 33	262	29 48	314	15 45	335
69	37 10	035	43 05	117	42 32	180	42 50	229	36 07	263	29 29	315	15 34	336
70	37 26	036	43 28	118	42 32	181	42 30	230	35 41	264	29 10	316	15 23	337
71	37 41	037	43 51	119	42 31	182	42 10	231	35 15	265	28 52	316	15 13	337
72	37 57	037	44 14	120	42 30	184	41 49	232	34 49	266	28 34	317	15 03	338
73	38 13	038	44 37	121	42 28	185	41 28	233	34 22	267	28 16	318	14 54	339
74	38 29	039	44 59	122	42 25	186	41 07	235	33 56	268	27 59	318	14 44	340
	Alioth		◆REGULUS		PROCYON		◆ALDEBARAN		Hamal		Alpheratz		◆DENEB	
75	38 46	039	16 14	096	24 33	135	42 22	188	40 45	236	33 30	269	27 41	319
76	39 02	040	16 40	097	24 52	136	42 19	189	40 23	237	33 04	270	27 24	320
77	39 19	040	17 06	098	25 10	137	42 14	190	40 01	238	32 37	270	27 07	321
78	39 37	041	17 32	099	25 27	138	42 09	191	39 39	239	32 11	271	26 51	321
79	39 54	042	17 58	100	25 45	139	42 04	193	39 16	240	31 45	272	26 34	322
80	40 11	042	18 24	101	26 01	141	41 58	194	38 53	241	31 18	273	26 18	323
81	40 29	043	18 50	102	26 18	142	41 51	195	38 30	242	30 52	274	26 03	323
82	40 47	044	19 16	103	26 34	143	41 44	197	38 07	243	30 26	275	25 47	324
83	41 05	044	19 41	104	26 50	144	41 36	198	37 43	244	30 00	276	25 32	325
84	41 24	045	20 07	104	27 05	145	41 28	199	37 20	245	29 34	277	25 17	326
85	41 43	045	20 32	105	27 20	146	41 19	200	36 56	246	29 07	278	25 02	326
86	42 01	046	20 58	106	27 35	147	41 09	202	36 31	247	28 41	278	24 48	327
87	42 20	047	21 23	107	27 49	148	41 00	203	36 07	248	28 15	279	24 34	328
88	42 40	047	21 48	108	28 03	149	40 49	204	35 42	249	27 49	280	24 20	329
89	42 59	048	22 13	109	28 16	150	40 38	205	35 18	250	27 24	281	24 06	329

LHA ♈	Hc	Zn	Hc	Zn	Hc	Zn	Hc	Zn	Hc	Zn	Hc	Zn	Hc	Zn
	Alioth		◆REGULUS		PROCYON		BETELGEUSE		◆ALDEBARAN		Hamal		◆DENEB	
90	43 19	049	22 37	110	28 29	151	33 24	181	40 27	207	34 53	251	23 53	330
91	43 38	049	23 02	111	28 41	152	33 23	182	40 15	208	34 28	252	23 40	331
92	43 58	050	23 27	112	28 53	154	33 22	184	40 02	209	34 03	253	23 27	332
93	44 19	050	23 51	113	29 05	155	33 20	185	39 49	210	33 37	254	23 15	332
94	44 39	051	24 15	114	29 16	156	33 18	186	39 36	211	33 12	255	23 03	333
95	44 59	052	24 39	115	29 26	157	33 15	187	39 22	213	32 47	256	22 51	334
96	45 20	052	25 03	116	29 36	158	33 11	188	39 07	214	32 21	257	22 40	334
97	45 41	053	25 26	117	29 46	159	33 07	189	38 52	215	31 55	258	22 28	335
98	46 02	054	25 49	118	29 55	160	33 03	191	38 37	216	31 29	259	22 17	336
99	46 23	054	26 13	119	30 03	161	32 57	192	38 21	217	31 04	260	22 07	337
100	46 45	055	26 35	120	30 11	163	32 52	193	38 05	219	30 38	261	21 57	337
101	47 06	055	26 58	121	30 19	164	32 46	194	37 48	220	30 12	262	21 47	338
102	47 28	056	27 20	122	30 26	165	32 39	195	37 31	221	29 46	263	21 37	339
103	47 50	057	27 43	123	30 33	166	32 32	197	37 14	222	29 19	264	21 28	340
104	48 12	057	28 05	124	30 39	167	32 24	198	36 56	223	28 53	265	21 19	340
	Alioth		◆REGULUS		PROCYON		BETELGEUSE		◆CAPELLA		Hamal		◆DENEB	
105	48 34	058	28 26	125	30 44	168	32 16	199	67 07	230	28 27	266	21 10	341
106	48 57	059	28 48	126	30 49	170	32 07	200	66 47	232	28 01	267	21 02	342
107	49 19	059	29 09	127	30 54	171	31 58	201	66 26	233	27 35	268	20 54	343
108	49 42	060	29 29	128	30 58	172	31 48	202	66 05	235	27 08	268	20 46	343
109	50 05	060	29 50	129	31 01	173	31 38	203	65 43	236	26 42	269	20 38	344
110	50 28	061	30 10	130	31 04	174	31 27	205	65 21	238	26 16	270	20 31	345
111	50 51	062	30 30	131	31 07	175	31 16	206	64 58	239	25 49	271	20 25	346
112	51 14	062	30 50	133	31 09	176	31 04	207	64 36	241	25 23	272	20 18	346
113	51 37	063	31 09	134	31 10	178	30 52	208	64 13	242	24 57	273	20 12	347
114	52 01	064	31 28	135	31 11	179	30 39	209	63 49	243	24 31	274	20 06	348
115	52 24	064	31 46	136	31 11	180	30 26	210	63 26	245	24 04	275	20 01	348
116	52 48	065	32 04	137	31 11	181	30 13	211	63 02	246	23 38	276	19 56	349
117	53 12	066	32 22	138	31 10	182	29 59	213	62 38	247	23 12	276	19 51	350
118	53 36	066	32 40	139	31 09	183	29 44	214	62 13	248	22 46	277	19 47	351
119	54 00	067	32 57	140	31 07	185	29 30	215	61 49	249	22 20	278	19 43	351
	◆VEGA		ARCTURUS		◆REGULUS		PROCYON		◆CAPELLA		Schedar		DENEB	
120	14 05	016	15 21	078	33 13	141	31 05	186	61 24	251	42 01	316	19 39	352
121	14 13	017	15 47	079	33 29	142	31 02	187	60 59	252	41 43	316	19 35	353
122	14 21	018	16 12	080	33 45	144	30 58	188	60 34	253	41 25	317	19 32	354
123	14 29	019	16 38	080	34 01	145	30 54	189	60 09	254	41 07	318	19 30	354
124	14 38	020	17 04	081	34 16	146	30 50	190	59 44	255	40 49	318	19 27	355
125	14 47	020	17 30	082	34 30	147	30 45	192	59 18	256	40 32	319	19 25	356
126	14 56	021	17 56	083	34 44	148	30 39	193	58 53	257	40 15	319	19 24	357
127	15 06	022	18 22	084	34 58	149	30 33	194	58 27	258	39 58	320	19 22	357
128	15 16	023	18 49	085	35 11	150	30 26	195	58 01	259	39 41	321	19 21	358
129	15 26	024	19 15	086	35 24	152	30 19	196	57 35	260	39 25	321	19 20	359
130	15 37	024	19 41	087	35 36	153	30 12	197	57 09	261	39 08	322	19 20	000
131	15 48	025	20 07	087	35 48	154	30 04	198	56 43	262	38 52	323	19 20	000
132	15 59	026	20 34	088	35 59	155	29 55	200	56 17	263	38 36	323	19 20	001
133	16 11	027	21 00	089	36 10	156	29 46	201	55 51	264	38 21	324	19 21	002
134	16 23	027	21 26	090	36 20	158	29 37	202	55 25	265	38 05	324	19 22	003
	DENEB		◆VEGA		ARCTURUS		◆REGULUS		PROCYON		◆CAPELLA		Schedar	
135	19 24	003	16 35	028	21 53	091	36 30	159	29 27	203	54 58	266	37 50	325
136	19 25	004	16 48	029	22 19	092	36 39	160	29 16	204	54 32	267	37 35	326
137	19 27	005	17 01	030	22 45	093	36 48	161	29 05	205	54 06	268	37 20	326
138	19 30	006	17 14	031	23 11	094	36 56	162	28 54	206	53 40	269	37 06	327
139	19 32	006	17 28	031	23 38	095	37 04	164	28 42	207	53 13	270	36 52	328
140	19 36	007	17 42	032	24 04	096	37 11	165	28 29	209	52 47	271	36 38	328
141	19 39	008	17 56	033	24 30	097	37 18	166	28 16	210	52 21	272	36 24	329
142	19 43	009	18 10	034	24 56	097	37 24	167	28 03	211	51 54	273	36 10	329
143	19 47	009	18 25	035	25 22	098	37 29	169	27 50	212	51 28	273	35 57	330
144	19 51	010	18 40	035	25 48	099	37 34	170	27 35	213	51 02	274	35 44	331
145	19 56	011	18 55	036	26 14	100	37 39	171	27 21	214	50 36	275	35 31	331
146	20 01	012	19 11	037	26 40	101	37 42	172	27 06	215	50 10	276	35 19	332
147	20 06	012	19 27	038	27 06	102	37 46	173	26 51	216	49 43	277	35 06	333
148	20 12	013	19 43	038	27 31	103	37 48	175	26 35	217	49 17	278	34 54	333
149	20 18	014	20 00	039	27 57	104	37 51	176	26 19	218	48 51	279	34 43	334
	DENEB		◆VEGA		ARCTURUS		◆REGULUS		PROCYON		◆CAPELLA		Schedar	
150	20 25	015	20 16	040	28 22	105	37 52	177	26 02	219	48 25	279	34 31	334
151	20 32	015	20 33	041	28 48	106	37 53	178	25 45	221	47 59	280	34 20	335
152	20 39	016	20 51	042	29 13	107	37 54	180	25 28	222	47 33	281	34 09	336
153	20 46	017	21 08	042	29 38	108	37 53	181	25 10	223	47 08	282	33 58	336
154	20 54	017	21 26	043	30 03	109	37 53	182	24 52	224	46 42	283	33 48	337
155	21 02	018	21 44	044	30 28	110	37 52	183	24 34	225	46 16	283	33 38	338
156	21 10	019	22 03	045	30 52	111	37 50	185	24 15	226	45 51	284	33 28	338
157	21 19	020	22 21	045	31 17	112	37 47	186	23 56	227	45 25	285	33 18	339
158	21 28	020	22 40	046	31 41	113	37 44	187	23 37	228	45 00	286	33 09	339
159	21 37	021	22 59	047	32 05	114	37 41	188	23 17	229	44 35	286	33 00	340
160	21 47	022	23 18	048	32 29	115	37 37	190	22 57	230	44 10	287	32 51	341
161	21 57	023	23 38	048	32 53	116	37 32	191	22 37	231	43 44	288	32 42	341
162	22 07	023	23 58	049	33 17	117	37 27	192	22 17	232	43 20	289	32 34	342
163	22 18	024	24 18	050	33 40	118	37 21	193	21 56	233	42 55	290	32 26	343
164	22 29	025	24 38	051	34 03	119	37 15	194	21 35	234	42 30	290	32 18	343
	DENEB		◆VEGA		ARCTURUS		◆REGULUS		POLLUX		◆CAPELLA		Schedar	
165	22 40	026	24 59	052	34 26	120	37 08	196	42 44	244	42 05	291	32 11	344
166	22 51	026	25 19	052	34 49	121	37 01	197	42 20	245	41 41	292	32 03	344
167	23 03	027	25 40	053	35 11	122	36 53	198	41 56	246	41 17	293	31 57	345
168	23 15	028	26 01	054	35 33	123	36 44	199	41 32	247	40 52	293	31 50	346
169	23 28	029	26 23	055	35 55	124	36 35	201	41 08	248	40 28	294	31 44	346
170	23 40	029	26 44	055	36 17	125	36 26	202	40 43	249	40 04	295	31 38	347
171	23 53	030	27 06	056	36 38	126	36 16	203	40 19	250	39 40	296	31 32	348
172	24 07	031	27 28	057	36 59	128	36 05	204	39 54	251	39 17	296	31 26	348
173	24 20	031	27 50	058	37 20	129	35 54	205	39 29	252	38 53	297	31 21	349
174	24 34	032	28 12	059	37 40	130	35 43	206	39 04	253	38 30	298	31 16	350
175	24 48	033	28 35	059	38 00	131	35 31	208	38 38	254	38 07	299	31 12	350
176	25 03	034	28 58	060	38 20	132	35 19	209	38 13	255	37 44	299	31 07	351
177	25 17	034	29 21	061	38 39	133	35 06	210	37 47	256	37 21	300	31 03	351
178	25 32	035	29 44	062	38 58	134	34 52	211	37 22	257	36 58	301	30 59	352
179	25 48	036	30 07	062	39 17	135	34 38	212	36 56	258	36 36	301	30 56	353

LAT 64°N

LHA ♈	Hc	Zn	Hc	Zn	Hc	Zn	Hc	Zn	Hc	Zn	Hc	Zn	Hc	Zn
	DENEB		◆VEGA		ARCTURUS		◆Denebola		REGULUS		POLLUX		◆CAPELLA	
180	26 03	037	30 30	063	39 35	137	40 27	183	34 24	213	36 30	259	36 13	302
181	26 19	037	30 54	064	39 53	138	40 26	185	34 09	215	36 04	260	35 51	303
182	26 35	038	31 17	065	40 11	139	40 23	186	33 54	216	35 38	261	35 29	304
183	26 51	039	31 41	066	40 28	140	40 20	187	33 39	217	35 12	262	35 07	304
184	27 08	039	32 05	066	40 44	141	40 17	188	33 23	218	34 46	263	34 46	305
185	27 25	040	32 30	067	41 00	143	40 13	190	33 06	219	34 20	264	34 24	306
186	27 42	041	32 54	068	41 16	144	40 08	191	32 50	220	33 54	265	34 03	307
187	27 59	042	33 18	069	41 32	145	40 03	192	32 32	221	33 28	266	33 42	307
188	28 17	042	33 43	069	41 46	146	39 57	193	32 15	222	33 01	267	33 21	308
189	28 34	043	34 08	070	42 01	147	39 51	195	31 57	224	32 35	268	33 01	309
190	28 53	044	34 32	071	42 15	149	39 44	196	31 38	225	32 09	269	32 40	309
191	29 11	044	34 57	072	42 28	150	39 36	197	31 20	226	31 43	270	32 20	310
192	29 29	045	35 22	073	42 41	151	39 28	198	31 01	227	31 16	270	32 00	311
193	29 48	046	35 48	074	42 54	152	39 20	200	30 41	228	30 50	271	31 40	312
194	30 07	047	36 13	074	43 06	154	39 11	201	30 22	229	30 24	272	31 21	312
	DENEB		◆VEGA		ARCTURUS		◆Denebola		REGULUS		POLLUX		◆CAPELLA	
195	30 26	047	36 38	075	43 17	155	39 01	202	30 02	230	29 57	273	31 01	313
196	30 46	048	37 04	076	43 28	156	38 51	203	29 41	231	29 31	274	30 42	314
197	31 06	049	37 29	077	43 38	157	38 40	205	29 21	232	29 05	275	30 23	314
198	31 26	050	37 55	078	43 48	159	38 29	206	29 00	233	28 39	276	30 05	315
199	31 46	050	38 21	078	43 57	160	38 17	207	28 39	234	28 13	277	29 46	316
200	32 06	051	38 46	079	44 06	161	38 05	208	28 17	235	27 47	277	29 28	317
201	32 27	052	39 12	080	44 14	163	37 53	209	27 55	236	27 20	278	29 10	317
202	32 47	052	39 38	081	44 22	164	37 39	211	27 33	237	26 55	279	28 52	318
203	33 08	053	40 04	082	44 29	165	37 26	212	27 11	238	26 29	280	28 35	319
204	33 29	054	40 30	083	44 35	167	37 12	213	26 49	239	26 03	281	28 18	319
205	33 51	055	40 56	083	44 41	168	36 57	214	26 26	240	25 37	282	28 01	320
206	34 12	055	41 23	084	44 46	169	36 42	215	26 03	241	25 11	283	27 44	321
207	34 34	056	41 49	085	44 51	171	36 27	216	25 40	242	24 46	283	27 28	322
208	34 56	057	42 15	086	44 55	172	36 11	218	25 16	243	24 20	284	27 11	322
209	35 18	058	42 41	087	44 58	173	35 55	219	24 53	244	23 55	285	26 55	323
	DENEB		◆VEGA		ARCTURUS		◆Denebola		REGULUS		POLLUX		◆CAPELLA	
210	35 40	058	43 07	088	45 01	175	35 38	220	24 29	245	23 29	286	26 40	324
211	36 03	059	43 34	089	45 03	176	35 21	221	24 05	246	23 04	287	26 24	325
212	36 25	060	44 00	090	45 05	177	35 04	222	23 41	247	22 39	288	26 09	325
213	36 48	061	44 26	090	45 06	179	34 46	223	23 16	248	22 14	289	25 54	326
214	37 11	061	44 53	091	45 06	180	34 28	224	22 52	249	21 49	289	25 40	327
215	37 34	062	45 19	092	45 06	181	34 09	225	22 27	250	21 24	290	25 25	327
216	37 58	063	45 45	093	45 05	183	33 50	227	22 02	251	21 00	291	25 11	328
217	38 21	063	46 11	094	45 04	184	33 31	228	21 37	252	20 35	292	24 58	329
218	38 45	064	46 38	095	45 02	185	33 11	229	21 12	253	20 11	293	24 44	330
219	39 09	065	47 04	096	44 59	187	32 51	230	20 47	254	19 47	294	24 31	330
220	39 32	066	47 30	097	44 56	188	32 31	231	20 22	255	19 23	294	24 18	331
221	39 57	066	47 56	098	44 52	189	32 10	232	19 56	256	18 59	295	24 06	332
222	40 21	067	48 22	099	44 47	191	31 50	233	19 31	257	18 35	296	23 53	332
223	40 45	068	48 48	100	44 42	192	31 28	234	19 05	258	18 12	297	23 41	333
224	41 09	069	49 14	101	44 36	193	31 07	235	18 39	259	17 48	298	23 30	334
	◆DENEB		VEGA		Rasalhague		◆ARCTURUS		Denebola		Dubhe		◆CAPELLA	
225	41 34	069	49 40	102	31 53	134	44 30	195	30 45	236	64 00	292	23 18	335
226	41 59	070	50 05	103	32 12	135	44 23	196	30 23	237	63 36	293	23 07	335
227	42 24	071	50 31	104	32 31	136	44 16	197	30 01	238	63 11	293	22 56	336
228	42 48	072	50 56	105	32 49	137	44 08	198	29 39	239	62 47	294	22 46	337
229	43 14	073	51 22	106	33 06	138	43 59	200	29 16	240	62 23	294	22 36	338
230	43 39	073	51 47	107	33 24	139	43 50	201	28 53	241	61 59	295	22 26	338
231	44 04	074	52 12	108	33 41	140	43 40	202	28 30	242	61 36	295	22 16	339
232	44 29	075	52 37	109	33 57	142	43 30	204	28 06	243	61 12	296	22 07	340
233	44 55	076	53 02	110	34 13	143	43 19	205	27 43	244	60 48	297	21 58	341
234	45 20	076	53 26	111	34 29	144	43 08	206	27 19	245	60 25	297	21 49	341
235	45 46	077	53 51	113	34 45	145	42 56	207	26 55	246	60 01	298	21 41	342
236	46 12	078	54 15	114	34 59	146	42 43	209	26 31	247	59 38	298	21 33	343
237	46 37	079	54 39	115	35 14	147	42 31	210	26 06	248	59 15	299	21 26	343
238	47 03	080	55 03	116	35 28	148	42 17	211	25 42	249	58 52	299	21 18	344
239	47 29	081	55 26	117	35 41	150	42 03	212	25 17	250	58 29	300	21 11	345
	Alpheratz		◆DENEB		VEGA		Rasalhague		◆ARCTURUS		Alioth		◆CAPELLA	
240	13 31	049	47 55	081	55 49	118	35 54	151	41 49	214	66 03	272	21 04	346
241	13 51	050	48 21	082	56 12	120	36 07	152	41 34	215	65 36	273	20 58	346
242	14 11	051	48 47	083	56 35	121	36 19	153	41 19	216	65 10	274	20 52	347
243	14 32	052	49 13	084	56 58	122	36 31	154	41 03	217	64 44	275	20 46	348
244	14 52	053	49 39	085	57 20	123	36 42	156	40 47	218	64 18	275	20 41	349
245	15 14	054	50 06	086	57 42	125	36 53	157	40 30	220	63 52	276	20 36	349
246	15 35	054	50 32	086	58 03	126	37 03	158	40 13	221	63 25	277	20 31	350
247	15 56	055	50 58	087	58 24	127	37 12	159	39 56	222	62 59	278	20 27	351
248	16 18	056	51 24	088	58 45	129	37 22	160	39 38	223	62 33	279	20 23	352
249	16 40	057	51 51	089	59 05	130	37 30	162	39 20	224	62 07	279	20 19	352
250	17 02	058	52 17	090	59 25	131	37 38	163	39 01	226	61 41	280	20 16	353
251	17 24	058	52 43	091	59 45	133	37 46	164	38 43	227	61 16	281	20 13	354
252	17 47	059	53 10	092	60 04	134	37 53	165	38 23	228	60 50	282	20 10	354
253	18 10	060	53 36	093	60 23	136	37 59	166	38 04	229	60 24	282	20 08	355
254	18 32	061	54 02	094	60 41	137	38 05	168	37 44	230	59 58	283	20 06	356
	Alpheratz		◆DENEB		ALTAIR		Rasalhague		◆ARCTURUS		Alioth		◆CAPELLA	
255	18 56	062	54 28	095	27 10	131	38 10	169	37 23	231	59 33	284	20 04	357
256	19 19	063	54 55	096	27 30	132	38 15	170	37 03	232	59 07	285	20 03	357
257	19 42	063	55 21	096	27 49	133	38 19	171	36 42	233	58 42	285	20 02	358
258	20 06	064	55 47	097	28 08	134	38 23	173	36 20	234	58 17	286	20 01	359
259	20 30	065	56 13	098	28 27	135	38 26	174	35 59	236	57 51	287	20 01	000
260	20 54	066	56 39	099	28 45	136	38 29	175	35 37	237	57 26	287	20 01	000
261	21 18	067	57 05	100	29 03	137	38 31	176	35 15	238	57 01	288	20 01	001
262	21 42	068	57 31	101	29 21	138	38 32	178	34 53	239	56 36	289	20 02	002
263	22 06	068	57 56	103	29 38	139	38 33	179	34 30	240	56 11	289	20 03	003
264	22 31	069	58 22	104	29 55	141	38 33	180	34 07	241	55 47	290	20 04	003
265	22 56	070	58 48	105	30 12	142	38 33	181	33 44	242	55 22	291	20 06	004
266	23 20	071	59 13	106	30 28	143	38 32	183	33 21	243	54 57	291	20 08	005
267	23 45	072	59 38	107	30 43	144	38 30	184	32 57	244	54 33	292	20 10	006
268	24 10	073	60 03	108	30 59	145	38 28	185	32 33	245	54 09	293	20 13	006
269	24 35	073	60 28	109	31 14	146	38 26	186	32 10	246	53 44	293	20 16	007

LHA ♈	Hc	Zn	Hc	Zn	Hc	Zn	Hc	Zn	Hc	Zn	Hc	Zn	Hc	Zn
	◆CAPELLA		Alpheratz		◆DENEB		ALTAIR		Rasalhague		◆ARCTURUS		Alioth	
270	20 20	008	25 01	074	60 53	110	31 28	147	38 22	188	31 45	247	53 20	294
271	20 23	009	25 26	075	61 17	111	31 42	148	38 19	189	31 21	248	52 56	295
272	20 27	009	25 52	076	61 42	113	31 56	149	38 14	190	30 57	249	52 33	295
273	20 32	010	26 17	077	62 06	114	32 09	151	38 09	191	30 32	250	52 09	296
274	20 36	011	26 43	078	62 30	115	32 21	152	38 04	193	30 07	251	51 45	297
275	20 42	011	27 09	079	62 54	116	32 34	153	37 58	194	29 42	252	51 22	297
276	20 47	012	27 34	079	63 17	118	32 45	154	37 51	195	29 17	253	50 59	298
277	20 53	013	28 00	080	63 40	119	32 57	155	37 44	196	28 52	254	50 35	299
278	20 59	014	28 26	081	64 03	120	33 07	156	37 37	197	28 27	255	50 12	299
279	21 05	014	28 52	082	64 26	122	33 18	158	37 29	199	28 01	256	49 50	300
280	21 12	015	29 18	083	64 48	123	33 28	159	37 20	200	27 36	257	49 27	301
281	21 19	016	29 44	084	65 10	125	33 37	160	37 11	201	27 10	258	49 04	301
282	21 26	017	30 11	085	65 31	126	33 46	161	37 01	202	26 44	259	48 42	302
283	21 34	017	30 37	085	65 52	127	33 54	162	36 51	204	26 19	260	48 20	302
284	21 42	018	31 03	086	66 13	129	34 02	163	36 40	205	25 53	261	47 57	303
	◆CAPELLA		Alpheratz		Enif		◆ALTAIR		VEGA		◆ARCTURUS		Alioth	
285	21 50	019	31 29	087	28 41	132	34 09	165	64 35	190	25 27	261	47 36	304
286	21 59	020	31 56	088	29 00	133	34 16	166	64 30	192	25 01	262	47 14	304
287	22 08	020	32 22	089	29 19	134	34 22	167	64 24	194	24 34	263	46 52	305
288	22 17	021	32 48	090	29 38	135	34 28	168	64 17	196	24 08	264	46 31	306
289	22 27	022	33 14	091	29 56	137	34 33	169	64 09	197	23 42	265	46 09	306
290	22 37	022	33 41	092	30 14	138	34 37	171	64 01	199	23 16	266	45 48	307
291	22 47	023	34 07	093	30 31	139	34 41	172	63 52	201	22 50	267	45 27	308
292	22 57	024	34 33	094	30 49	140	34 45	173	63 42	203	22 23	268	45 07	308
293	23 08	025	35 00	094	31 05	141	34 48	174	63 32	204	21 57	269	44 46	309
294	23 19	025	35 26	095	31 22	142	34 50	175	63 21	206	21 31	270	44 26	309
295	23 31	026	35 52	096	31 38	143	34 52	177	63 09	208	21 05	271	44 05	310
296	23 43	027	36 18	097	31 53	144	34 54	178	62 56	209	20 38	271	43 45	311
297	23 55	028	36 44	098	32 09	145	34 54	179	62 43	211	20 12	272	43 25	311
298	24 07	028	37 10	099	32 23	147	34 55	180	62 29	213	19 46	273	43 06	312
299	24 19	029	37 36	100	32 38	148	34 54	181	62 15	214	19 19	274	42 46	313
	◆CAPELLA		Alpheratz		Enif		◆ALTAIR		VEGA		◆ARCTURUS		Alioth	
300	24 32	030	38 02	101	32 51	149	34 53	183	62 00	216	18 53	275	42 27	313
301	24 46	030	38 28	102	33 05	150	34 52	184	61 44	217	18 27	276	42 08	314
302	24 59	031	38 53	103	33 18	151	34 50	185	61 28	219	18 01	277	41 49	314
303	25 13	032	39 19	104	33 30	152	34 47	186	61 11	220	17 35	278	41 30	315
304	25 27	033	39 44	105	33 42	153	34 44	187	60 54	222	17 09	279	41 12	316
305	25 41	033	40 10	106	33 54	155	34 41	189	60 36	223	16 43	279	40 53	316
306	25 56	034	40 35	107	34 05	156	34 36	190	60 17	225	16 17	280	40 35	317
307	26 11	035	41 00	108	34 15	157	34 32	191	59 59	226	15 51	281	40 18	318
308	26 26	036	41 25	109	34 25	158	34 26	192	59 39	228	15 25	282	40 00	318
309	26 41	036	41 50	110	34 35	159	34 21	193	59 20	229	15 00	283	39 42	319
310	26 57	037	42 14	111	34 44	160	34 14	195	59 00	230	14 34	284	39 25	319
311	27 13	038	42 39	112	34 53	162	34 07	196	58 39	232	14 08	285	39 08	320
312	27 29	038	43 03	113	35 01	163	34 00	197	58 18	233	13 43	286	38 51	321
313	27 46	039	43 27	114	35 08	164	33 52	198	57 57	234	13 18	286	38 35	321
314	28 02	040	43 51	115	35 15	165	33 44	199	57 36	236	12 53	287	38 19	322
	CAPELLA		◆Hamal		Alpheratz		Enif		◆ALTAIR		VEGA		◆Alioth	
315	28 19	041	26 42	091	44 15	116	35 22	166	33 35	200	57 14	237	38 02	323
316	28 37	041	27 08	092	44 38	118	35 28	168	33 25	202	56 51	238	37 47	323
317	28 54	042	27 34	092	45 01	119	35 33	169	33 15	203	56 29	240	37 31	324
318	29 12	043	28 01	093	45 24	120	35 38	170	33 05	204	56 06	241	37 15	324
319	29 30	043	28 27	094	45 47	121	35 42	171	32 54	205	55 43	242	37 00	325
320	29 48	044	28 53	095	46 10	122	35 46	172	32 43	206	55 20	243	36 45	326
321	30 06	045	29 19	096	46 32	123	35 49	174	32 31	207	54 56	244	36 31	326
322	30 25	046	29 45	097	46 54	124	35 52	175	32 18	209	54 32	245	36 16	327
323	30 44	046	30 11	098	47 15	125	35 54	176	32 06	210	54 08	247	36 02	328
324	31 03	047	30 37	099	47 36	127	35 55	177	31 52	211	53 44	248	35 48	328
325	31 23	048	31 03	100	47 57	128	35 56	179	31 39	212	53 20	249	35 34	329
326	31 42	048	31 29	101	48 18	129	35 57	180	31 25	213	52 55	250	35 21	329
327	32 02	049	31 55	102	48 38	130	35 56	181	31 10	214	52 30	251	35 07	330
328	32 22	050	32 21	103	48 58	131	35 56	182	30 55	215	52 05	252	34 54	331
329	32 42	051	32 46	104	49 18	133	35 55	183	30 40	216	51 40	253	34 42	331
	CAPELLA		◆Hamal		Alpheratz		Enif		◆ALTAIR		VEGA		◆Alioth	
330	33 03	051	33 12	105	49 37	134	35 53	185	30 24	218	51 15	254	34 29	332
331	33 23	052	33 37	106	49 56	135	35 50	186	30 08	219	50 49	255	34 17	333
332	33 44	053	34 02	107	50 14	136	35 47	187	29 51	220	50 24	256	34 05	333
333	34 05	054	34 28	108	50 32	138	35 44	188	29 34	221	49 58	257	33 53	334
334	34 26	054	34 53	109	50 49	139	35 40	189	29 17	222	49 33	258	33 42	335
335	34 48	055	35 17	110	51 06	140	35 35	191	28 59	223	49 07	259	33 31	335
336	35 10	056	35 42	111	51 23	142	35 30	192	28 41	224	48 41	260	33 20	336
337	35 31	056	36 07	112	51 39	143	35 24	193	28 22	225	48 15	261	33 09	336
338	35 53	057	36 31	113	51 54	144	35 18	194	28 03	226	47 49	262	32 59	337
339	36 16	058	36 55	114	52 09	146	35 12	195	27 44	227	47 23	263	32 48	338
340	36 38	059	37 19	115	52 24	147	35 04	197	27 25	228	46 57	264	32 39	338
341	37 00	059	37 43	116	52 38	149	34 56	198	27 05	229	46 30	265	32 29	339
342	37 23	060	38 07	117	52 51	150	34 48	199	26 45	230	46 04	266	32 20	340
343	37 46	061	38 30	118	53 04	151	34 39	200	26 25	231	45 38	267	32 11	340
344	38 09	062	38 53	119	53 17	153	34 30	201	26 04	232	45 12	268	32 02	341
	CAPELLA		ALDEBARAN		◆Hamal		Alpheratz		◆ALTAIR		VEGA		◆Alioth	
345	38 32	062	17 21	088	39 16	120	53 28	154	25 43	233	44 45	269	31 54	342
346	38 56	063	17 48	089	39 39	121	53 40	156	25 22	234	44 19	270	31 45	342
347	39 19	064	18 14	090	40 01	122	53 50	157	25 00	236	43 53	271	31 37	343
348	39 43	064	18 40	090	40 23	123	54 00	158	24 38	237	43 26	272	31 30	343
349	40 07	065	19 07	091	40 45	124	54 09	160	24 16	238	43 00	272	31 22	344
350	40 31	066	19 33	092	41 07	125	54 18	161	23 54	239	42 34	273	31 15	345
351	40 55	067	19 59	093	41 28	127	54 26	163	23 31	240	42 08	274	31 09	345
352	41 19	067	20 25	094	41 49	128	54 34	164	23 09	241	41 41	275	31 02	346
353	41 43	068	20 52	095	42 10	129	54 40	166	22 45	242	41 15	276	30 56	347
354	42 08	069	21 18	096	42 30	130	54 46	167	22 22	242	40 49	277	30 50	347
355	42 32	070	21 44	097	42 50	131	54 52	169	21 59	243	40 23	278	30 44	348
356	42 57	071	22 10	098	43 09	132	54 57	170	21 35	244	39 57	278	30 39	349
357	43 22	071	22 36	099	43 29	134	55 01	172	21 11	245	39 31	279	30 34	349
358	43 47	072	23 02	100	43 48	135	55 04	173	20 47	246	39 05	280	30 29	350
359	44 12	073	23 28	100	44 06	136	55 07	175	20 23	247	38 39	281	30 25	351

LHA ♈	Hc	Zn	Hc	Zn	Hc	Zn	Hc	Zn	Hc	Zn	Hc	Zn	Hc	Zn
	◆POLLUX		CAPELLA		Hamal		◆Alpheratz		DENEB		◆VEGA		Alioth	
0	13 49	054	44 20	073	45 08	136	56 08	176	57 14	261	38 01	283	29 21	351
1	14 12	055	44 46	073	45 26	138	56 10	178	56 47	262	37 34	283	29 17	352
2	14 34	056	45 12	074	45 45	139	56 10	180	56 20	263	37 08	284	29 13	353
3	14 57	057	45 38	075	46 02	140	56 10	181	55 53	264	36 41	285	29 10	353
4	15 20	058	46 05	076	46 19	141	56 09	183	55 26	265	36 15	286	29 07	354
5	15 43	059	46 31	076	46 36	143	56 08	184	54 59	266	35 49	287	29 04	354
6	16 06	059	46 58	077	46 52	144	56 05	186	54 32	267	35 23	287	29 02	355
7	16 30	060	47 24	078	47 08	145	56 02	187	54 04	268	34 57	288	28 59	356
8	16 53	061	47 51	079	47 23	147	55 58	189	53 37	269	34 31	289	28 58	356
9	17 17	062	48 18	080	47 38	148	55 54	190	53 10	270	34 06	290	28 56	357
10	17 42	063	48 44	080	47 52	149	55 48	192	52 43	270	33 40	291	28 55	358
11	18 06	064	49 11	081	48 06	151	55 42	194	52 16	271	33 15	291	28 54	358
12	18 30	064	49 38	082	48 19	152	55 36	195	51 48	272	32 49	292	28 53	359
13	18 55	065	50 05	083	48 32	153	55 28	197	51 21	273	32 24	293	28 53	000
14	19 20	066	50 32	084	48 44	155	55 20	198	50 54	274	31 59	294	28 53	000
	Alioth		◆POLLUX		CAPELLA		Hamal		◆Alpheratz		DENEB		◆VEGA	
15	28 53	001	19 45	067	50 59	085	48 55	156	55 11	200	50 27	275	31 34	294
16	28 54	001	20 10	068	51 27	085	49 06	157	55 02	201	50 00	276	31 09	295
17	28 54	002	20 35	068	51 54	086	49 16	159	54 52	203	49 33	276	30 45	296
18	28 56	003	21 00	069	52 21	087	49 26	160	54 41	204	49 06	277	30 20	297
19	28 57	003	21 26	070	52 48	088	49 35	161	54 29	206	48 39	278	29 56	298
20	28 59	004	21 52	071	53 15	089	49 43	163	54 17	207	48 12	279	29 32	298
21	29 01	005	22 17	072	53 43	090	49 51	164	54 04	209	47 45	280	29 08	299
22	29 03	005	22 43	073	54 10	091	49 58	166	53 51	210	47 18	281	28 45	300
23	29 06	006	23 09	073	54 37	092	50 04	167	53 37	211	46 51	281	28 21	301
24	29 09	007	23 36	074	55 04	092	50 10	169	53 23	213	46 24	282	27 58	301
25	29 12	007	24 02	075	55 32	093	50 15	170	53 08	214	45 58	283	27 35	302
26	29 16	008	24 28	076	55 59	094	50 20	171	52 52	216	45 31	284	27 12	303
27	29 20	009	24 55	077	56 26	095	50 23	173	52 36	217	45 05	285	26 49	304
28	29 24	009	25 21	078	56 53	096	50 26	174	52 19	218	44 39	285	26 26	304
29	29 28	010	25 48	078	57 20	097	50 29	176	52 02	220	44 12	286	26 04	305
	Alioth		◆POLLUX		ALDEBARAN		◆Hamal		Alpheratz		DENEB		◆VEGA	
30	29 33	010	26 15	079	36 13	131	50 31	177	51 45	221	43 46	287	25 42	306
31	29 38	011	26 42	080	36 34	132	50 32	179	51 27	222	43 20	288	25 20	307
32	29 44	012	27 08	081	36 54	134	50 32	180	51 08	224	42 54	288	24 58	307
33	29 49	012	27 35	082	37 13	135	50 32	181	50 49	225	42 29	289	24 37	308
34	29 55	013	28 02	083	37 32	136	50 31	183	50 30	226	42 03	290	24 15	309
35	30 02	014	28 29	084	37 51	137	50 29	184	50 10	227	41 37	291	23 54	310
36	30 08	014	28 56	084	38 09	138	50 26	186	49 50	229	41 12	291	23 33	311
37	30 15	015	29 24	085	38 27	139	50 23	187	49 29	230	40 47	292	23 13	311
38	30 22	016	29 51	086	38 45	140	50 20	189	49 08	231	40 21	293	22 52	312
39	30 30	016	30 18	087	39 02	142	50 15	190	48 46	232	39 56	294	22 32	313
40	30 37	017	30 45	088	39 19	143	50 10	191	48 25	234	39 31	294	22 13	314
41	30 45	017	31 12	089	39 35	144	50 04	193	48 03	235	39 07	295	21 53	314
42	30 54	018	31 40	090	39 51	145	49 58	194	47 40	236	38 42	296	21 34	315
43	31 02	019	32 07	091	40 06	146	49 51	196	47 17	237	38 18	297	21 14	316
44	31 11	019	32 34	092	40 21	148	49 43	197	46 54	238	37 53	297	20 56	317
	Alioth		◆POLLUX		ALDEBARAN		◆Hamal		Alpheratz		DENEB		◆VEGA	
45	31 20	020	33 01	092	40 35	149	49 35	199	46 31	239	37 29	298	20 37	317
46	31 30	021	33 29	093	40 49	150	49 26	200	46 08	241	37 05	299	20 19	318
47	31 39	021	33 56	094	41 02	151	49 16	201	45 44	242	36 41	299	20 01	319
48	31 49	022	34 23	095	41 15	153	49 06	203	45 20	243	36 18	300	19 43	320
49	32 00	022	34 50	096	41 28	154	48 55	204	44 55	244	35 54	301	19 26	320
50	32 10	023	35 17	097	41 39	155	48 44	205	44 31	245	35 31	302	19 08	321
51	32 21	024	35 44	098	41 51	156	48 32	207	44 06	246	35 08	302	18 51	322
52	32 32	024	36 11	099	42 01	158	48 19	208	43 41	247	34 45	303	18 35	323
53	32 44	025	36 38	100	42 11	159	48 06	209	43 16	248	34 22	304	18 18	324
54	32 55	026	37 05	101	42 21	160	47 53	211	42 50	249	34 00	304	18 02	324
55	33 07	026	37 31	102	42 30	161	47 38	212	42 25	250	33 37	305	17 47	325
56	33 19	027	37 58	103	42 38	163	47 24	213	41 59	251	33 15	306	17 31	326
57	33 32	027	38 25	104	42 46	164	47 08	215	41 33	252	32 53	307	17 16	327
58	33 44	028	38 51	105	42 53	165	46 53	216	41 07	253	32 31	307	17 01	327
59	33 57	029	39 17	106	43 00	167	46 36	217	40 41	254	32 10	308	16 47	328
	Alioth		◆POLLUX		ALDEBARAN		◆Hamal		Alpheratz		DENEB		◆VEGA	
60	34 11	029	39 43	107	43 06	168	46 20	219	40 15	255	31 49	309	16 33	329
61	34 24	030	40 09	108	43 11	169	46 02	220	39 48	256	31 27	309	16 19	330
62	34 38	031	40 35	109	43 16	171	45 45	221	39 22	257	31 07	310	16 05	331
63	34 52	031	41 01	110	43 20	172	45 27	222	38 55	258	30 46	311	15 52	331
64	35 06	032	41 27	111	43 24	173	45 08	224	38 29	259	30 25	312	15 39	332
65	35 21	032	41 52	112	43 27	174	44 49	225	38 02	260	30 05	312	15 26	333
66	35 35	033	42 17	113	43 29	176	44 30	226	37 35	261	29 45	313	15 14	334
67	35 50	034	42 42	114	43 31	177	44 10	227	37 08	262	29 25	314	15 02	334
68	36 06	034	43 07	115	43 32	178	43 50	228	36 41	263	29 06	314	14 51	335
69	36 21	035	43 32	116	43 32	180	43 29	229	36 14	264	28 46	315	14 39	336
70	36 37	036	43 56	117	43 32	181	43 08	231	35 47	265	28 27	316	14 28	337
71	36 53	036	44 20	118	43 31	182	42 47	232	35 20	266	28 09	317	14 18	338
72	37 09	037	44 44	119	43 30	184	42 26	233	34 53	267	27 50	317	14 08	338
73	37 25	037	45 08	120	43 28	185	42 04	234	34 25	268	27 32	318	13 58	339
74	37 42	038	45 31	122	43 25	186	41 41	235	33 58	268	27 14	319	13 48	340
	Alioth		◆REGULUS		PROCYON		◆ALDEBARAN		Hamal		Alpheratz		◆DENEB	
75	37 59	039	16 20	096	25 16	135	43 22	188	41 19	236	33 31	269	26 56	319
76	38 16	039	16 48	097	25 35	136	43 18	189	40 56	237	33 04	270	26 38	320
77	38 33	040	17 15	098	25 54	137	43 13	190	40 33	239	32 36	271	26 21	321
78	38 51	040	17 42	099	26 12	138	43 08	192	40 10	240	32 09	272	26 04	322
79	39 09	041	18 08	100	26 30	139	43 02	193	39 46	241	31 42	273	25 47	322
80	39 27	042	18 35	100	26 48	140	42 56	194	39 22	242	31 15	274	25 31	323
81	39 45	042	19 02	101	27 05	141	42 49	196	38 58	243	30 48	275	25 14	324
82	40 04	043	19 29	102	27 22	142	42 41	197	38 34	244	30 20	275	24 58	325
83	40 22	044	19 55	103	27 38	143	42 33	198	38 09	245	29 53	276	24 43	325
84	40 41	044	20 22	104	27 54	144	42 24	199	37 44	246	29 26	277	24 27	326
85	41 00	045	20 48	105	28 10	146	42 15	201	37 19	247	28 59	278	24 12	327
86	41 19	045	21 14	106	28 25	147	42 05	202	36 54	248	28 32	279	23 57	327
87	41 39	046	21 40	107	28 40	148	41 55	203	36 29	249	28 05	280	23 43	328
88	41 59	047	22 06	108	28 54	149	41 44	204	36 03	250	27 39	281	23 29	329
89	42 19	047	22 32	109	29 08	150	41 32	206	35 38	251	27 12	281	23 15	330

LAT 63°N

LHA ♈	Hc	Zn	Hc	Zn	Hc	Zn	Hc	Zn	Hc	Zn	Hc	Zn	Hc	Zn
	Alioth		◆REGULUS		PROCYON		BETELGEUSE		◆ALDEBARAN		Hamal		◆DENEB	
90	42 39	048	22 58	110	29 21	151	34 24	181	41 20	207	35 12	252	23 01	330
91	42 59	048	23 24	111	29 34	152	34 23	182	41 07	208	34 46	253	22 48	331
92	43 19	049	23 49	112	29 47	153	34 22	184	40 54	209	34 20	254	22 35	332
93	43 40	050	24 14	113	29 59	154	34 20	185	40 41	211	33 53	255	22 22	332
94	44 01	050	24 39	114	30 10	156	34 17	186	40 27	212	33 27	256	22 09	333
95	44 22	051	25 04	115	30 21	157	34 14	187	40 12	213	33 00	257	21 57	334
96	44 43	051	25 29	116	30 32	158	34 11	188	39 57	214	32 34	258	21 45	335
97	45 05	052	25 53	117	30 42	159	34 06	190	39 41	216	32 07	259	21 34	335
98	45 26	053	26 17	118	30 51	160	34 01	191	39 25	217	31 40	260	21 23	336
99	45 48	053	26 41	119	31 00	161	33 56	192	39 09	218	31 14	261	21 12	337
100	46 10	054	27 05	120	31 09	162	33 50	193	38 52	219	30 47	262	21 01	338
101	46 32	055	27 29	121	31 17	164	33 44	194	38 34	220	30 20	263	20 51	338
102	46 54	055	27 52	122	31 24	165	33 37	196	38 16	221	29 53	263	20 41	339
103	47 17	056	28 15	123	31 31	166	33 29	197	37 58	223	29 26	264	20 31	340
104	47 39	056	28 38	124	31 37	167	33 21	198	37 40	224	28 58	265	20 22	340
	Alioth		◆REGULUS		PROCYON		BETELGEUSE		◆CAPELLA		Hamal		◆DENEB	
105	48 02	057	29 01	125	31 43	168	33 12	199	67 45	232	28 31	266	20 13	341
106	48 25	058	29 23	126	31 48	169	33 03	200	67 23	234	28 04	267	20 05	342
107	48 48	058	29 45	127	31 53	171	32 53	201	67 01	235	27 37	268	19 56	343
108	49 11	059	30 06	128	31 57	172	32 43	203	66 38	237	27 10	269	19 48	343
109	49 35	059	30 28	129	32 01	173	32 33	204	66 15	238	26 42	270	19 41	344
110	49 58	060	30 49	130	32 04	174	32 21	205	65 52	240	26 15	271	19 33	345
111	50 22	061	31 10	131	32 07	175	32 10	206	65 28	241	25 48	272	19 26	346
112	50 46	061	31 30	132	32 09	176	31 57	207	65 04	242	25 21	272	19 20	346
113	51 10	062	31 50	133	32 10	178	31 45	208	64 40	244	24 54	273	19 14	347
114	51 34	063	32 10	134	32 11	179	31 32	209	64 15	245	24 26	274	19 08	348
115	51 58	063	32 29	135	32 11	180	31 18	211	63 51	246	23 59	275	19 02	349
116	52 22	064	32 48	136	32 11	181	31 04	212	63 26	248	23 32	276	18 57	349
117	52 47	064	33 07	138	32 10	182	30 49	213	63 00	249	23 05	277	18 52	350
118	53 12	065	33 25	139	32 09	184	30 34	214	62 35	250	22 38	278	18 47	351
119	53 36	066	33 42	140	32 07	185	30 19	215	62 09	251	22 11	279	18 43	352
	◆VEGA		ARCTURUS		◆REGULUS		PROCYON		◆CAPELLA		Schedar		DENEB	
120	13 08	016	15 08	078	34 00	141	32 04	186	61 43	252	41 18	316	18 39	352
121	13 16	017	15 35	078	34 17	142	32 01	187	61 17	253	40 59	317	18 36	353
122	13 24	018	16 01	079	34 33	143	31 58	188	60 51	255	40 41	318	18 33	354
123	13 33	019	16 28	080	34 49	144	31 53	189	60 25	256	40 23	318	18 30	354
124	13 41	020	16 55	081	35 05	145	31 49	191	59 58	257	40 04	319	18 27	355
125	13 51	020	17 22	082	35 20	147	31 43	192	59 32	258	39 47	319	18 25	356
126	14 00	021	17 49	083	35 35	148	31 38	193	59 05	259	39 29	320	18 24	357
127	14 10	022	18 16	084	35 49	149	31 31	194	58 38	260	39 12	321	18 22	357
128	14 21	023	18 43	084	36 03	150	31 24	195	58 11	261	38 54	321	18 21	358
129	14 31	023	19 10	085	36 17	151	31 17	196	57 44	262	38 38	322	18 20	359
130	14 42	024	19 37	086	36 29	153	31 09	198	57 17	263	38 21	322	18 20	000
131	14 54	025	20 05	087	36 42	154	31 01	199	56 50	264	38 04	323	18 20	000
132	15 05	026	20 32	088	36 53	155	30 52	200	56 23	265	37 48	324	18 20	001
133	15 17	027	20 59	089	37 05	156	30 42	201	55 56	266	37 32	324	18 21	002
134	15 30	027	21 26	090	37 16	157	30 32	202	55 29	267	37 16	325	18 22	003
	DENEB		◆VEGA		ARCTURUS		◆REGULUS		PROCYON		◆CAPELLA		Schedar	
135	18 24	003	15 42	028	21 53	091	37 26	159	30 22	203	55 02	268	37 01	325
136	18 25	004	15 55	029	22 21	092	37 36	160	30 11	204	54 34	269	36 45	326
137	18 28	005	16 09	030	22 48	092	37 45	161	29 59	205	54 07	269	36 30	327
138	18 30	006	16 22	030	23 15	093	37 53	162	29 47	207	53 40	270	36 15	327
139	18 33	006	16 36	031	23 42	094	38 01	163	29 35	208	53 13	271	36 01	328
140	18 36	007	16 51	032	24 09	095	38 09	165	29 22	209	52 45	272	35 47	329
141	18 39	008	17 05	033	24 37	096	38 16	166	29 09	210	52 18	273	35 32	329
142	18 43	009	17 20	034	25 04	097	38 22	167	28 55	211	51 51	274	35 19	330
143	18 48	009	17 35	034	25 31	098	38 28	168	28 40	212	51 24	275	35 05	330
144	18 52	010	17 51	035	25 58	099	38 33	170	28 26	213	50 57	276	34 52	331
145	18 57	011	18 07	036	26 24	100	38 38	171	28 11	214	50 30	276	34 39	332
146	19 02	011	18 23	037	26 51	101	38 42	172	27 55	215	50 03	277	34 26	332
147	19 08	012	18 39	037	27 18	102	38 45	173	27 39	217	49 36	278	34 13	333
148	19 14	013	18 56	038	27 45	103	38 48	175	27 23	218	49 09	279	34 01	333
149	19 20	014	19 13	039	28 11	104	38 50	176	27 06	219	48 42	280	33 49	334
	DENEB		◆VEGA		ARCTURUS		◆REGULUS		PROCYON		◆CAPELLA		Schedar	
150	19 27	014	19 30	040	28 38	104	38 52	177	26 48	220	48 15	280	33 37	335
151	19 34	015	19 48	041	29 04	105	38 53	178	26 31	221	47 48	281	33 25	335
152	19 41	016	20 06	041	29 30	106	38 54	180	26 13	222	47 22	282	33 14	336
153	19 49	017	20 24	042	29 56	107	38 53	181	25 54	223	46 55	283	33 03	337
154	19 57	017	20 42	043	30 22	108	38 53	182	25 36	224	46 28	284	32 53	337
155	20 05	018	21 01	044	30 48	109	38 51	183	25 17	225	46 02	284	32 42	338
156	20 13	019	21 20	044	31 14	110	38 49	185	24 57	226	45 36	285	32 32	338
157	20 22	020	21 39	045	31 39	111	38 47	186	24 37	227	45 09	286	32 22	339
158	20 32	020	21 58	046	32 04	112	38 44	187	24 17	228	44 43	287	32 12	340
159	20 41	021	22 18	047	32 29	113	38 40	188	23 57	229	44 17	287	32 03	340
160	20 51	022	22 38	047	32 54	114	38 36	190	23 36	230	43 51	288	31 54	341
161	21 01	022	22 58	048	33 19	115	38 31	191	23 15	231	43 25	289	31 45	342
162	21 12	023	23 18	049	33 44	116	38 26	192	22 54	232	43 00	290	31 37	342
163	21 23	024	23 39	050	34 08	117	38 20	193	22 32	233	42 34	290	31 29	343
164	21 34	025	24 00	050	34 32	118	38 13	195	22 10	234	42 09	291	31 21	343
	DENEB		◆VEGA		ARCTURUS		◆REGULUS		POLLUX		◆CAPELLA		Schedar	
165	21 46	025	24 21	051	34 56	119	38 06	196	43 10	245	41 43	292	31 13	344
166	21 58	026	24 42	052	35 19	120	37 58	197	42 45	246	41 18	293	31 06	345
167	22 10	027	25 04	053	35 43	122	37 50	198	42 20	247	40 53	293	30 59	345
168	22 22	028	25 26	053	36 06	123	37 41	200	41 55	248	40 28	294	30 52	346
169	22 35	028	25 48	054	36 29	124	37 32	201	41 30	249	40 03	295	30 45	347
170	22 48	029	26 10	055	36 51	125	37 22	202	41 04	250	39 39	296	30 39	347
171	23 01	030	26 32	056	37 13	126	37 11	203	40 38	251	39 14	296	30 33	348
172	23 15	030	26 55	057	37 35	127	37 00	204	40 12	252	38 50	297	30 28	348
173	23 29	031	27 18	057	37 57	128	36 49	206	39 46	253	38 26	298	30 22	349
174	23 43	032	27 41	058	38 18	129	36 37	207	39 20	254	38 02	298	30 17	350
175	23 58	033	28 04	059	38 39	130	36 24	208	38 54	255	37 38	299	30 12	350
176	24 13	033	28 28	060	39 00	131	36 11	209	38 28	256	37 14	300	30 08	351
177	24 28	034	28 51	060	39 20	133	35 58	210	38 01	257	36 51	301	30 04	352
178	24 43	035	29 15	061	39 40	134	35 44	212	37 34	258	36 27	301	30 00	352
179	24 59	036	29 39	062	39 59	135	35 29	213	37 08	259	36 04	302	29 56	353

LAT 63°N

LHA ♈	Hc	Zn	Hc	Zn	Hc	Zn	Hc	Zn	Hc	Zn	Hc	Zn	Hc	Zn
	DENEB		◆VEGA		ARCTURUS		◆Denebola		REGULUS		POLLUX		◆CAPELLA	
180	25 15	036	30 03	063	40 19	136	41 27	183	35 14	214	36 41	260	35 41	303
181	25 31	037	30 27	063	40 37	137	41 25	185	34 59	215	36 14	261	35 18	304
182	25 47	038	30 52	064	40 56	138	41 23	186	34 43	216	35 47	262	34 56	304
183	26 04	038	31 16	065	41 13	140	41 20	187	34 27	217	35 20	263	34 33	305
184	26 21	039	31 41	066	41 31	141	41 16	188	34 10	218	34 53	264	34 11	306
185	26 39	040	32 06	067	41 48	142	41 12	190	33 53	220	34 26	265	33 49	306
186	26 56	041	32 31	067	42 04	143	41 07	191	33 35	221	33 59	266	33 27	307
187	27 14	041	32 56	068	42 21	144	41 01	192	33 17	222	33 32	267	33 06	308
188	27 32	042	33 22	069	42 36	146	40 55	194	32 59	223	33 05	267	32 44	308
189	27 50	043	33 47	070	42 51	147	40 49	195	32 40	224	32 37	268	32 23	309
190	28 09	043	34 13	070	43 06	148	40 41	196	32 21	225	32 10	269	32 02	310
191	28 28	044	34 38	071	43 20	149	40 34	197	32 02	226	31 43	270	31 41	311
192	28 47	045	35 04	072	43 34	151	40 25	199	31 42	227	31 16	271	31 21	311
193	29 06	046	35 30	073	43 47	152	40 16	200	31 21	228	30 48	272	31 00	312
194	29 26	046	35 56	074	43 59	153	40 07	201	31 01	229	30 21	273	30 40	313
	DENEB		◆VEGA		ARCTURUS		◆Denebola		REGULUS		POLLUX		◆CAPELLA	
195	29 46	047	36 22	074	44 11	154	39 57	202	30 40	230	29 54	274	30 20	313
196	30 06	048	36 49	075	44 23	156	39 46	204	30 19	232	29 27	275	30 01	314
197	30 26	048	37 15	076	44 34	157	39 35	205	29 57	233	29 00	275	29 41	315
198	30 46	049	37 42	077	44 44	158	39 23	206	29 36	234	28 33	276	29 22	316
199	31 07	050	38 08	078	44 54	160	39 11	207	29 14	235	28 05	277	29 03	316
200	31 28	051	38 35	078	45 03	161	38 58	209	28 51	236	27 38	278	28 44	317
201	31 49	051	39 02	079	45 12	162	38 45	210	28 29	237	27 12	279	28 26	318
202	32 11	052	39 28	080	45 19	164	38 31	211	28 06	238	26 45	280	28 08	318
203	32 32	053	39 55	081	45 27	165	38 17	212	27 42	239	26 18	281	27 50	319
204	32 54	053	40 22	082	45 34	166	38 02	213	27 19	240	25 51	281	27 32	320
205	33 16	054	40 49	083	45 40	168	37 47	215	26 55	241	25 24	282	27 14	321
206	33 38	055	41 16	083	45 45	169	37 31	216	26 31	242	24 58	283	26 57	321
207	34 00	056	41 43	084	45 50	170	37 15	217	26 07	243	24 31	284	26 40	322
208	34 23	056	42 10	085	45 54	172	36 59	218	25 43	244	24 05	285	26 24	323
209	34 46	057	42 38	086	45 58	173	36 42	219	25 18	245	23 39	286	26 07	323
	DENEB		◆VEGA		ARCTURUS		◆Denebola		REGULUS		POLLUX		◆CAPELLA	
210	35 09	058	43 05	087	46 01	174	36 24	220	24 54	246	23 13	286	25 51	324
211	35 32	058	43 32	088	46 03	176	36 06	221	24 29	247	22 46	287	25 35	325
212	35 55	059	43 59	089	46 05	177	35 48	223	24 04	248	22 20	288	25 20	326
213	36 18	060	44 26	090	46 06	179	35 29	224	23 38	249	21 55	289	25 05	326
214	36 42	061	44 54	090	46 06	180	35 10	225	23 13	250	21 29	290	24 50	327
215	37 06	061	45 21	091	46 06	181	34 51	226	22 47	251	21 03	291	24 35	328
216	37 30	062	45 48	092	46 05	183	34 31	227	22 22	252	20 38	291	24 20	328
217	37 54	063	46 15	093	46 04	184	34 11	228	21 56	253	20 13	292	24 06	329
218	38 18	064	46 42	094	46 01	185	33 51	229	21 30	253	19 48	293	23 52	330
219	38 43	064	47 10	095	45 58	187	33 30	230	21 03	254	19 23	294	23 39	331
220	39 07	065	47 37	096	45 55	188	33 09	231	20 37	255	18 58	295	23 26	331
221	39 32	066	48 04	097	45 51	189	32 47	233	20 11	256	18 33	296	23 13	332
222	39 57	066	48 31	098	45 46	191	32 25	234	19 44	257	18 09	296	23 00	333
223	40 22	067	48 58	099	45 41	192	32 03	235	19 18	258	17 44	297	22 48	333
224	40 47	068	49 25	100	45 35	193	31 41	236	18 51	259	17 20	298	22 36	334
	◆DENEB		VEGA		Rasalhague		◆ARCTURUS		Denebola		Dubhe		◆CAPELLA	
225	41 13	069	49 51	101	32 35	133	45 28	195	31 18	237	63 36	294	22 24	335
226	41 38	069	50 18	102	32 54	134	45 21	196	30 56	238	63 12	295	22 13	336
227	42 04	070	50 45	103	33 14	136	45 13	197	30 32	239	62 47	295	22 01	336
228	42 29	071	51 11	104	33 32	137	45 04	199	30 09	240	62 22	296	21 51	337
229	42 55	072	51 38	105	33 51	138	44 55	200	29 45	241	61 58	296	21 40	338
230	43 21	072	52 04	106	34 09	139	44 46	201	29 21	242	61 33	297	21 30	338
231	43 47	073	52 30	107	34 27	140	44 36	203	28 57	243	61 09	297	21 20	339
232	44 13	074	52 56	108	34 44	141	44 25	204	28 33	244	60 45	298	21 11	340
233	44 39	075	53 22	109	35 01	142	44 13	205	28 08	245	60 21	298	21 01	341
234	45 06	076	53 48	110	35 18	143	44 01	207	27 44	246	59 57	299	20 53	341
235	45 32	076	54 13	111	35 34	145	43 49	208	27 19	247	59 33	299	20 44	342
236	45 59	077	54 38	112	35 49	146	43 36	209	26 53	248	59 09	300	20 36	343
237	46 25	078	55 03	114	36 04	147	43 22	210	26 28	249	58 46	300	20 28	344
238	46 52	079	55 28	115	36 19	148	43 08	212	26 03	250	58 22	301	20 20	344
239	47 19	079	55 53	116	36 33	149	42 54	213	25 37	251	57 59	301	20 13	345
	Alpheratz		◆DENEB		VEGA		Rasalhague		◆ARCTURUS		Alioth		◆CAPELLA	
240	12 52	049	47 45	080	56 17	117	36 47	150	42 39	214	65 59	274	20 06	346
241	13 12	050	48 12	081	56 41	118	37 00	152	42 23	215	65 32	275	20 00	346
242	13 33	051	48 39	082	57 05	119	37 13	153	42 07	217	65 05	276	19 54	347
243	13 55	052	49 06	083	57 29	121	37 25	154	41 51	218	64 38	277	19 48	348
244	14 16	052	49 33	084	57 52	122	37 37	155	41 34	219	64 11	277	19 42	349
245	14 38	053	50 00	084	58 15	123	37 48	156	41 16	220	63 44	278	19 37	349
246	15 00	054	50 28	085	58 38	125	37 58	158	40 59	221	63 17	279	19 32	350
247	15 22	055	50 55	086	59 00	126	38 08	159	40 40	223	62 50	280	19 28	351
248	15 44	056	51 22	087	59 22	127	38 18	160	40 22	224	62 23	280	19 24	352
249	16 07	057	51 49	088	59 43	129	38 27	161	40 03	225	61 57	281	19 20	352
250	16 30	057	52 16	089	60 04	130	38 35	163	39 43	226	61 30	282	19 16	353
251	16 53	058	52 44	090	60 25	131	38 43	164	39 23	227	61 03	283	19 13	354
252	17 16	059	53 11	090	60 45	133	38 51	165	39 03	228	60 37	283	19 10	355
253	17 40	060	53 38	091	61 05	134	38 57	166	38 43	230	60 10	284	19 08	355
254	18 03	061	54 05	092	61 24	136	39 04	168	38 22	231	59 44	285	19 06	356
	Alpheratz		◆DENEB		ALTAIR		Rasalhague		◆ARCTURUS		Alioth		◆CAPELLA	
255	18 27	062	54 32	093	27 49	131	39 09	169	38 01	232	59 18	285	19 04	357
256	18 51	062	55 00	094	28 10	132	39 14	170	37 39	233	58 51	286	19 03	357
257	19 15	063	55 27	095	28 30	133	39 19	171	37 17	234	58 25	287	19 02	358
258	19 40	064	55 54	096	28 50	134	39 23	173	36 55	235	57 59	287	19 01	359
259	20 04	065	56 21	097	29 09	135	39 26	174	36 33	236	57 33	288	19 01	000
260	20 29	066	56 48	098	29 28	136	39 28	175	36 10	237	57 08	289	19 01	000
261	20 54	066	57 15	099	29 47	137	39 30	176	35 47	238	56 42	289	19 01	001
262	21 19	067	57 42	100	30 06	138	39 32	178	35 23	239	56 16	290	19 02	002
263	21 44	068	58 09	101	30 24	139	39 33	179	35 00	240	55 51	291	19 03	003
264	22 09	069	58 35	102	30 41	140	39 33	180	34 36	241	55 26	291	19 04	003
265	22 35	070	59 02	103	30 58	141	39 33	181	34 12	242	55 00	292	19 06	004
266	23 01	071	59 28	104	31 15	142	39 32	183	33 48	244	54 35	293	19 08	005
267	23 26	071	59 55	105	31 32	143	39 30	184	33 23	245	54 10	293	19 11	006
268	23 52	072	60 21	106	31 48	145	39 28	185	32 59	246	53 45	294	19 13	006
269	24 18	073	60 47	107	32 03	146	39 25	186	32 34	247	53 20	295	19 17	007

LHA ♈	Hc	Zn	Hc	Zn	Hc	Zn	Hc	Zn	Hc	Zn	Hc	Zn	Hc	Zn
	◆CAPELLA		Alpheratz		◆DENEB		ALTAIR		Rasalhague		◆ARCTURUS		Alioth	
270	19 20	008	24 44	074	61 13	109	32 18	147	39 22	188	32 09	248	52 55	295
271	19 24	008	25 11	075	61 39	110	32 33	148	39 18	189	31 43	249	52 31	296
272	19 28	009	25 37	076	62 04	111	32 47	149	39 13	190	31 18	250	52 06	297
273	19 33	010	26 03	076	62 29	112	33 01	150	39 08	191	30 52	251	51 42	297
274	19 38	011	26 30	077	62 55	113	33 14	151	39 03	193	30 27	252	51 18	298
275	19 43	011	26 56	078	63 19	115	33 27	153	38 56	194	30 01	252	50 54	298
276	19 48	012	27 23	079	63 44	116	33 39	154	38 49	195	29 35	253	50 30	299
277	19 54	013	27 50	080	64 08	117	33 51	155	38 42	196	29 08	254	50 06	300
278	20 00	014	28 17	081	64 33	119	34 02	156	38 34	198	28 42	255	49 43	300
279	20 07	014	28 44	081	64 56	120	34 13	157	38 25	199	28 16	256	49 19	301
280	20 14	015	29 11	082	65 20	121	34 23	158	38 16	200	27 49	257	48 56	302
281	20 21	016	29 38	083	65 43	123	34 33	160	38 07	201	27 23	258	48 33	302
282	20 29	017	30 05	084	66 06	124	34 42	161	37 56	203	26 56	259	48 10	303
283	20 37	017	30 32	085	66 28	126	34 51	162	37 46	204	26 29	260	47 47	303
284	20 45	018	30 59	086	66 50	127	34 59	163	37 34	205	26 02	261	47 24	304
	◆CAPELLA		Alpheratz		Enif		◆ALTAIR		VEGA		◆ARCTURUS		Alioth	
285	20 53	019	31 26	087	29 21	132	35 07	164	65 34	191	25 35	262	47 02	305
286	21 02	019	31 53	088	29 41	133	35 14	166	65 28	193	25 08	263	46 39	305
287	21 12	020	32 21	088	30 01	134	35 20	167	65 22	194	24 41	264	46 17	306
288	21 21	021	32 48	089	30 20	135	35 26	168	65 15	196	24 14	265	45 55	306
289	21 31	022	33 15	090	30 39	136	35 32	169	65 07	198	23 47	266	45 34	307
290	21 41	022	33 42	091	30 58	137	35 37	170	64 58	200	23 20	266	45 12	308
291	21 52	023	34 09	092	31 16	138	35 41	172	64 48	202	22 53	267	44 50	308
292	22 03	024	34 37	093	31 34	139	35 45	173	64 38	203	22 25	268	44 29	309
293	22 14	024	35 04	094	31 52	141	35 48	174	64 26	205	21 58	269	44 08	310
294	22 25	025	35 31	095	32 09	142	35 50	175	64 14	207	21 31	270	43 47	310
295	22 37	026	35 58	096	32 26	143	35 52	176	64 02	209	21 04	271	43 26	311
296	22 49	027	36 25	097	32 42	144	35 54	178	63 48	210	20 36	272	43 06	311
297	23 01	027	36 52	097	32 58	145	35 54	179	63 34	212	20 09	273	42 46	312
298	23 14	028	37 19	098	33 13	146	35 55	180	63 19	214	19 42	274	42 25	313
299	23 27	029	37 46	099	33 28	147	35 54	181	63 04	215	19 15	274	42 05	313
	◆CAPELLA		Alpheratz		◆Enif		ALTAIR		VEGA		◆ARCTURUS		Alioth	
300	23 40	030	38 13	100	33 43	148	35 53	183	62 48	217	18 48	275	41 46	314
301	23 54	030	38 40	101	33 57	150	35 52	184	62 31	219	18 21	276	41 26	314
302	24 08	031	39 06	102	34 10	151	35 50	185	62 14	220	17 54	277	41 07	315
303	24 22	032	39 33	103	34 23	152	35 47	186	61 56	222	17 27	278	40 48	316
304	24 36	032	39 59	104	34 36	153	35 44	187	61 38	223	17 00	279	40 29	316
305	24 51	033	40 26	105	34 48	154	35 40	189	61 19	225	16 33	280	40 10	317
306	25 06	034	40 52	106	34 59	155	35 35	190	61 00	226	16 06	281	39 51	317
307	25 21	035	41 18	107	35 11	157	35 31	191	60 40	228	15 39	281	39 33	318
308	25 37	035	41 44	108	35 21	158	35 25	192	60 19	229	15 13	282	39 15	319
309	25 53	036	42 10	109	35 31	159	35 19	194	59 59	230	14 46	283	38 57	319
310	26 09	037	42 36	110	35 41	160	35 12	195	59 37	232	14 20	284	38 39	320
311	26 25	037	43 01	111	35 50	161	35 05	196	59 16	233	13 53	285	38 22	321
312	26 42	038	43 26	112	35 58	163	34 57	197	58 54	234	13 27	286	38 05	321
313	26 59	039	43 51	113	36 06	164	34 49	198	58 31	236	13 01	287	37 48	322
314	27 16	040	44 16	114	36 13	165	34 40	199	58 09	237	12 35	288	37 31	322
	CAPELLA		◆Hamal		Alpheratz		Enif		◆ALTAIR		VEGA		◆Alioth	
315	27 34	040	26 42	090	44 41	116	36 20	166	34 31	201	57 46	238	37 15	323
316	27 51	041	27 09	091	45 05	117	36 26	167	34 21	202	57 22	240	36 58	324
317	28 09	042	27 37	092	45 30	118	36 32	169	34 11	203	56 59	241	36 42	324
318	28 28	042	28 04	093	45 54	119	36 37	170	34 00	204	56 35	242	36 27	325
319	28 46	043	28 31	094	46 17	120	36 41	171	33 48	205	56 11	243	36 11	325
320	29 05	044	28 58	095	46 41	121	36 45	172	33 36	207	55 46	244	35 56	326
321	29 24	044	29 25	096	47 04	122	36 49	174	33 24	208	55 21	246	35 41	327
322	29 43	045	29 52	096	47 27	123	36 51	175	33 11	209	54 57	247	35 26	327
323	30 02	046	30 19	097	47 50	125	36 54	176	32 58	210	54 31	248	35 11	328
324	30 22	047	30 46	098	48 12	126	36 55	177	32 44	211	54 06	249	34 57	329
325	30 42	047	31 13	099	48 34	127	36 56	178	32 30	212	53 41	250	34 43	329
326	31 02	048	31 40	100	48 55	128	36 57	180	32 15	213	53 15	251	34 29	330
327	31 23	049	32 07	101	49 17	129	36 56	181	32 00	215	52 49	252	34 15	330
328	31 43	049	32 34	102	49 38	131	36 56	182	31 44	216	52 23	253	34 02	331
329	32 04	050	33 00	103	49 58	132	36 54	183	31 28	217	51 57	254	33 49	332
	CAPELLA		◆Hamal		Alpheratz		Enif		◆ALTAIR		VEGA		◆Alioth	
330	32 25	051	33 27	104	50 18	133	36 53	185	31 11	218	51 30	255	33 36	332
331	32 46	052	33 53	105	50 38	134	36 50	186	30 54	219	51 04	257	33 24	333
332	33 08	052	34 19	106	50 57	136	36 47	187	30 37	220	50 37	258	33 11	334
333	33 29	053	34 45	107	51 16	137	36 43	188	30 19	221	50 11	259	32 59	334
334	33 51	054	35 11	108	51 34	138	36 39	190	30 01	222	49 44	260	32 48	335
335	34 13	054	35 37	109	51 52	140	36 34	191	29 43	223	49 17	261	32 36	335
336	34 36	055	36 03	110	52 10	141	36 29	192	29 24	224	48 50	261	32 25	336
337	34 58	056	36 28	111	52 26	142	36 23	193	29 04	225	48 23	262	32 14	337
338	35 21	057	36 54	112	52 43	144	36 16	194	28 45	227	47 56	263	32 03	337
339	35 43	057	37 19	113	52 59	145	36 09	196	28 25	228	47 29	264	31 53	338
340	36 06	058	37 44	114	53 14	146	36 02	197	28 05	229	47 02	265	31 43	339
341	36 30	059	38 09	115	53 29	148	35 54	198	27 44	230	46 35	266	31 33	339
342	36 53	059	38 33	116	53 43	149	35 45	199	27 23	231	46 08	267	31 23	340
343	37 17	060	38 58	117	53 57	151	35 36	200	27 02	232	45 41	268	31 14	340
344	37 40	061	39 22	118	54 10	152	35 26	202	26 40	233	45 13	269	31 05	341
	CAPELLA		ALDEBARAN		◆Hamal		Alpheratz		◆ALTAIR		VEGA		◆Alioth	
345	38 04	062	17 19	087	39 46	119	54 22	154	26 18	234	44 46	270	30 57	342
346	38 28	063	17 46	088	40 09	120	54 34	155	25 56	235	44 19	271	30 48	342
347	38 52	063	18 13	089	40 33	121	54 45	156	25 34	236	43 52	272	30 40	343
348	39 17	064	18 41	090	40 56	123	54 56	158	25 11	237	43 24	272	30 32	344
349	39 41	064	19 08	091	41 19	124	55 06	159	24 48	238	42 57	273	30 25	344
350	40 06	065	19 35	092	41 41	125	55 15	161	24 25	239	42 30	274	30 17	345
351	40 31	066	20 02	093	42 03	126	55 23	162	24 02	240	42 03	275	30 10	346
352	40 56	067	20 30	094	42 25	127	55 31	164	23 38	241	41 36	276	30 04	346
353	41 21	067	20 57	095	42 47	128	55 38	166	23 14	242	41 09	277	29 57	347
354	41 46	068	21 24	095	43 08	129	55 45	167	22 50	243	40 42	278	29 51	347
355	42 11	069	21 51	096	43 29	130	55 51	169	22 25	244	40 15	278	29 46	348
356	42 37	070	22 18	097	43 50	132	55 56	170	22 01	245	39 48	279	29 40	349
357	43 02	070	22 45	098	44 10	133	56 00	172	21 36	246	39 21	280	29 35	349
358	43 28	071	23 12	099	44 29	134	56 04	173	21 11	247	38 54	281	29 30	350
359	43 54	072	23 39	100	44 49	135	56 06	175	20 46	248	38 27	282	29 25	351

LAT 62°N

LHA ♈	Hc	Zn	Hc	Zn	Hc	Zn	Hc	Zn	Hc	Zn	Hc	Zn	Hc	Zn
	◆ POLLUX		CAPELLA		Hamal		◆ Alpheratz		DENEB		◆ VEGA		Alioth	
0	13 14	054	44 01	072	45 51	136	57 08	176	57 23	263	37 47	283	28 22	351
1	13 37	055	44 28	072	46 11	137	57 10	178	56 55	264	37 20	284	28 18	352
2	14 01	056	44 55	073	46 30	138	57 10	180	56 27	265	36 53	285	28 14	353
3	14 24	057	45 22	074	46 48	140	57 10	181	55 59	266	36 26	286	28 10	353
4	14 48	058	45 49	075	47 06	141	57 09	183	55 31	266	35 58	287	28 07	354
5	15 11	058	46 17	075	47 24	142	57 07	184	55 02	267	35 32	287	28 04	354
6	15 36	059	46 44	076	47 41	143	57 05	186	54 34	268	35 05	288	28 02	355
7	16 00	060	47 11	077	47 57	145	57 02	188	54 06	269	34 38	289	28 00	356
8	16 24	061	47 39	078	48 13	146	56 58	189	53 38	270	34 11	290	27 58	356
9	16 49	062	48 06	079	48 29	147	56 53	191	53 10	271	33 45	290	27 56	357
10	17 14	062	48 34	079	48 44	149	56 47	192	52 42	272	33 19	291	27 55	358
11	17 39	063	49 02	080	48 58	150	56 41	194	52 13	273	32 52	292	27 54	358
12	18 04	064	49 29	081	49 12	151	56 33	195	51 45	274	32 26	293	27 53	359
13	18 30	065	49 57	082	49 25	153	56 26	197	51 17	274	32 00	293	27 53	000
14	18 55	066	50 25	083	49 38	154	56 17	199	50 49	275	31 35	294	27 53	000
	Alioth		◆ POLLUX		CAPELLA		Hamal		◆ Alpheratz		DENEB		◆ VEGA	
15	27 53	001	19 21	066	50 53	083	49 50	155	56 08	200	50 21	276	31 09	295
16	27 54	001	19 47	067	51 21	084	50 01	157	55 58	202	49 53	277	30 44	296
17	27 54	002	20 13	068	51 49	085	50 12	158	55 47	203	49 25	278	30 18	297
18	27 56	003	20 39	069	52 17	086	50 22	160	55 35	205	48 57	278	29 53	297
19	27 57	003	21 05	070	52 45	087	50 32	161	55 23	206	48 29	279	29 28	298
20	27 59	004	21 32	071	53 14	088	50 40	162	55 10	208	48 02	280	29 03	299
21	28 01	005	21 59	071	53 42	088	50 49	164	54 57	209	47 34	281	28 39	300
22	28 04	005	22 25	072	54 10	089	50 56	165	54 43	211	47 06	282	28 14	300
23	28 06	006	22 52	073	54 38	090	51 03	167	54 28	212	46 39	282	27 50	301
24	28 09	007	23 19	074	55 06	091	51 09	168	54 13	214	46 11	283	27 26	302
25	28 13	007	23 46	075	55 34	092	51 14	170	53 57	215	45 44	284	27 02	303
26	28 16	008	24 14	076	56 02	093	51 19	171	53 41	216	45 17	285	26 39	303
27	28 20	008	24 41	076	56 31	094	51 23	173	53 24	218	44 49	285	26 15	304
28	28 25	009	25 08	077	56 59	095	51 26	174	53 06	219	44 22	286	25 52	305
29	28 29	010	25 36	078	57 27	096	51 29	176	52 48	220	43 55	287	25 29	306
	Alioth		◆ POLLUX		ALDEBARAN		◆ Hamal		Alpheratz		DENEB		◆ VEGA	
30	28 34	010	26 03	079	36 53	131	51 31	177	52 30	222	43 28	288	25 06	306
31	28 39	011	26 31	080	37 14	132	51 32	179	52 11	223	43 02	288	24 44	307
32	28 45	012	26 59	081	37 35	133	51 32	180	51 51	224	42 35	289	24 21	308
33	28 51	012	27 27	081	37 55	134	51 32	181	51 31	226	42 09	290	23 59	309
34	28 57	013	27 55	082	38 15	135	51 31	183	51 11	227	41 42	291	23 37	309
35	29 03	013	28 22	083	38 35	136	51 29	184	50 50	228	41 16	291	23 16	310
36	29 10	014	28 50	084	38 54	138	51 26	186	50 29	230	40 50	292	22 54	311
37	29 17	015	29 18	085	39 13	139	51 23	187	50 07	231	40 24	293	22 33	312
38	29 24	015	29 47	086	39 31	140	51 19	189	49 45	232	39 58	294	22 12	312
39	29 32	016	30 15	087	39 49	141	51 14	190	49 23	233	39 32	294	21 51	313
40	29 40	017	30 43	087	40 06	142	51 09	192	49 00	234	39 06	295	21 31	314
41	29 48	017	31 11	088	40 23	144	51 03	193	48 37	236	38 41	296	21 11	315
42	29 57	018	31 39	089	40 40	145	50 56	195	48 13	237	38 16	296	20 51	315
43	30 05	019	32 07	090	40 56	146	50 49	196	47 50	238	37 51	297	20 31	316
44	30 14	019	32 35	091	41 11	147	50 41	197	47 26	239	37 26	298	20 12	317
	Alioth		◆ POLLUX		ALDEBARAN		◆ Hamal		Alpheratz		DENEB		◆ VEGA	
45	30 24	020	33 04	092	41 26	148	50 32	199	47 01	240	37 01	299	19 53	318
46	30 34	020	33 32	093	41 41	150	50 22	200	46 37	241	36 36	299	19 34	318
47	30 43	021	34 00	094	41 55	151	50 12	202	46 12	243	36 12	300	19 15	319
48	30 54	022	34 28	095	42 08	152	50 01	203	45 47	244	35 47	301	18 57	320
49	31 04	022	34 56	095	42 21	153	49 50	205	45 21	245	35 23	301	18 39	321
50	31 15	023	35 24	096	42 34	155	49 38	206	44 56	246	34 59	302	18 21	321
51	31 26	023	35 52	097	42 45	156	49 25	207	44 30	247	34 36	303	18 04	322
52	31 38	024	36 20	098	42 57	157	49 12	209	44 04	248	34 12	304	17 47	323
53	31 49	025	36 48	099	43 07	159	48 58	210	43 38	249	33 49	304	17 30	324
54	32 01	025	37 16	100	43 17	160	48 44	211	43 11	250	33 26	305	17 14	325
55	32 13	026	37 43	101	43 27	161	48 29	213	42 45	251	33 03	306	16 57	325
56	32 26	027	38 11	102	43 35	162	48 14	214	42 18	252	32 40	306	16 42	326
57	32 38	027	38 38	103	43 44	164	47 57	215	41 51	253	32 17	307	16 26	327
58	32 52	028	39 06	104	43 51	165	47 41	217	41 24	254	31 55	308	16 11	328
59	33 05	028	39 33	105	43 58	166	47 24	218	40 57	255	31 33	309	15 56	328
	Alioth		◆ POLLUX		ALDEBARAN		◆ Hamal		Alpheratz		DENEB		◆ VEGA	
60	33 18	029	40 00	106	44 05	168	47 06	219	40 30	256	31 11	309	15 41	329
61	33 32	030	40 27	107	44 10	169	46 48	220	40 02	257	30 49	310	15 27	330
62	33 46	030	40 54	108	44 15	170	46 30	222	39 35	258	30 28	311	15 13	331
63	34 01	031	41 21	109	44 20	172	46 11	223	39 07	259	30 06	311	14 59	331
64	34 15	031	41 47	110	44 23	173	45 51	224	38 40	260	29 45	312	14 46	332
65	34 30	032	42 14	111	44 26	174	45 31	225	38 12	261	29 25	313	14 33	333
66	34 45	033	42 40	112	44 29	176	45 11	227	37 44	262	29 04	313	14 20	334
67	35 00	033	43 06	113	44 31	177	44 50	228	37 16	263	28 44	314	14 08	335
68	35 16	034	43 32	114	44 32	178	44 29	229	36 48	264	28 24	315	13 56	335
69	35 32	035	43 57	115	44 32	180	44 08	230	36 20	265	28 04	316	13 44	336
70	35 48	035	44 23	116	44 32	181	43 46	231	35 52	265	27 44	316	13 33	337
71	36 04	036	44 48	117	44 31	182	43 24	233	35 24	266	27 25	317	13 22	338
72	36 21	036	45 13	118	44 30	184	43 01	234	34 56	267	27 06	318	13 12	338
73	36 38	037	45 38	120	44 28	185	42 39	235	34 28	268	26 47	318	13 02	339
74	36 55	038	46 02	121	44 25	186	42 15	236	33 59	269	26 28	319	12 52	340
	Alioth		◆ REGULUS		PROCYON		◆ ALDEBARAN		Hamal		Alpheratz		◆ DENEB	
75	37 12	038	16 26	096	25 58	135	44 21	188	41 52	237	33 31	270	26 10	320
76	37 30	039	16 54	096	26 18	136	44 17	189	41 28	238	33 03	271	25 52	321
77	37 47	039	17 22	097	26 37	137	44 12	190	41 04	239	32 35	272	25 34	321
78	38 05	040	17 50	098	26 57	138	44 07	192	40 40	240	32 07	273	25 17	322
79	38 23	041	18 18	099	27 15	139	44 01	193	40 15	241	31 39	273	24 59	323
80	38 42	041	18 46	100	27 34	140	43 54	194	39 50	243	31 11	274	24 42	323
81	39 01	042	19 14	101	27 52	141	43 47	196	39 25	244	30 42	275	24 26	324
82	39 19	042	19 41	102	28 09	142	43 39	197	39 00	245	30 14	276	24 09	325
83	39 39	043	20 09	103	28 26	143	43 30	198	38 34	246	29 46	277	23 53	325
84	39 58	044	20 36	104	28 43	144	43 21	200	38 08	247	29 18	278	23 37	326
85	40 17	044	21 03	105	28 59	145	43 11	201	37 42	248	28 51	279	23 22	327
86	40 37	045	21 31	106	29 15	146	43 01	202	37 16	249	28 23	279	23 07	328
87	40 57	045	21 58	107	29 30	147	42 50	204	36 50	250	27 55	280	22 52	328
88	41 17	046	22 25	108	29 45	149	42 38	205	36 23	251	27 27	281	22 37	329
89	41 37	047	22 51	108	30 00	150	42 26	206	35 57	252	27 00	282	22 23	330

LHA ♈	Hc	Zn	Hc	Zn	Hc	Zn	Hc	Zn	Hc	Zn	Hc	Zn	Hc	Zn
	Alioth		◆ REGULUS		PROCYON		BETELGEUSE		◆ ALDEBARAN		Hamal		◆ DENEB	
90	41 58	047	23 18	109	30 14	151	35 24	181	42 13	207	35 30	253	22 09	330
91	42 19	048	23 45	110	30 27	152	35 23	182	42 00	209	35 03	254	21 55	331
92	42 40	048	24 11	111	30 40	153	35 22	184	41 47	210	34 36	255	21 42	332
93	43 01	049	24 37	112	30 53	154	35 20	185	41 32	211	34 09	256	21 29	333
94	43 22	050	25 03	113	31 05	155	35 17	186	41 17	212	33 41	257	21 16	333
95	43 44	050	25 29	114	31 16	156	35 14	187	41 02	214	33 14	258	21 03	334
96	44 05	051	25 54	115	31 27	158	35 10	189	40 46	215	32 46	259	20 51	335
97	44 27	051	26 20	116	31 38	159	35 05	190	40 30	216	32 19	259	20 39	336
98	44 49	052	26 45	117	31 48	160	35 00	191	40 13	217	31 51	260	20 28	336
99	45 12	053	27 10	118	31 57	161	34 55	192	39 56	218	31 23	261	20 17	337
100	45 34	053	27 35	119	32 06	162	34 49	193	39 38	220	30 55	262	20 06	338
101	45 57	054	27 59	120	32 14	163	34 42	195	39 20	221	30 27	263	19 55	338
102	46 19	054	28 23	121	32 22	165	34 34	196	39 01	222	29 59	264	19 45	339
103	46 42	055	28 47	122	32 29	166	34 27	197	38 42	223	29 31	265	19 35	340
104	47 06	055	29 11	123	32 36	167	34 18	198	38 23	224	29 03	266	19 26	341
	Alioth		◆ REGULUS		PROCYON		BETELGEUSE		◆ CAPELLA		Hamal		◆ DENEB	
105	47 29	056	29 34	124	32 42	168	34 09	199	68 21	234	28 35	267	19 16	341
106	47 52	057	29 58	125	32 47	169	33 59	200	67 58	236	28 07	268	19 08	342
107	48 16	057	30 20	126	32 52	170	33 49	202	67 34	237	27 39	269	18 59	343
108	48 40	058	30 43	127	32 57	172	33 39	203	67 10	239	27 10	269	18 51	343
109	49 04	058	31 05	128	33 01	173	33 27	204	66 46	240	26 42	270	18 43	344
110	49 28	059	31 27	129	33 04	174	33 16	205	66 21	242	26 14	271	18 35	345
111	49 52	060	31 49	131	33 06	175	33 04	206	65 56	243	25 46	272	18 28	346
112	50 16	060	32 10	132	33 08	176	32 51	207	65 31	244	25 18	273	18 22	346
113	50 41	061	32 31	133	33 10	178	32 38	209	65 06	246	24 50	274	18 15	347
114	51 06	061	32 51	134	33 11	179	32 24	210	64 40	247	24 22	275	18 09	348
115	51 30	062	33 11	135	33 11	180	32 10	211	64 14	248	23 54	276	18 03	349
116	51 55	063	33 31	136	33 11	181	31 55	212	63 48	249	23 26	276	17 58	349
117	52 20	063	33 51	137	33 10	182	31 40	213	63 21	251	22 58	277	17 53	350
118	52 46	064	34 10	138	33 09	184	31 24	214	62 54	252	22 30	278	17 48	351
119	53 11	065	34 28	139	33 07	185	31 08	215	62 27	253	22 02	279	17 44	352
	◆ VEGA		ARCTURUS		◆ REGULUS		PROCYON		◆ CAPELLA		Schedar		DENEB	
120	12 10	016	14 55	077	34 46	140	33 04	186	62 00	254	40 34	317	17 40	352
121	12 18	017	15 22	078	35 04	142	33 01	187	61 33	255	40 15	318	17 36	353
122	12 27	018	15 50	079	35 21	143	32 57	188	61 06	256	39 56	318	17 33	354
123	12 36	019	16 18	080	35 38	144	32 53	189	60 39	257	39 38	319	17 30	354
124	12 45	019	16 45	081	35 54	145	32 48	191	60 11	258	39 19	319	17 28	355
125	12 54	020	17 13	082	36 10	146	32 42	192	59 43	260	39 01	320	17 26	356
126	13 04	021	17 41	082	36 26	147	32 36	193	59 16	261	38 43	321	17 24	357
127	13 15	022	18 09	083	36 41	149	32 29	194	58 48	262	38 25	321	17 22	357
128	13 25	023	18 37	084	36 55	150	32 22	195	58 20	263	38 08	322	17 21	358
129	13 36	023	19 05	085	37 09	151	32 15	197	57 52	264	37 50	322	17 20	359
130	13 48	024	19 33	086	37 22	152	32 06	198	57 24	264	37 33	323	17 20	000
131	13 59	025	20 01	087	37 35	153	31 57	199	56 56	265	37 16	324	17 20	000
132	14 11	026	20 29	088	37 48	155	31 48	200	56 28	266	37 00	324	17 20	001
133	14 24	026	20 58	089	38 00	156	31 38	201	56 00	267	36 43	325	17 21	002
134	14 36	027	21 26	089	38 11	157	31 28	202	55 31	268	36 27	325	17 22	003
	DENEB		◆ VEGA		ARCTURUS		◆ REGULUS		PROCYON		◆ CAPELLA		Schedar	
135	17 24	003	14 50	028	21 54	090	38 22	158	31 17	203	55 03	269	36 11	326
136	17 26	004	15 03	029	22 22	091	38 32	159	31 05	205	54 35	270	35 55	326
137	17 28	005	15 17	030	22 50	092	38 41	161	30 53	206	54 07	271	35 40	327
138	17 30	006	15 31	030	23 18	093	38 50	162	30 41	207	53 39	272	35 25	328
139	17 33	006	15 45	031	23 47	094	38 59	163	30 28	208	53 11	273	35 10	328
140	17 36	007	16 00	032	24 15	095	39 07	164	30 14	209	52 43	273	34 55	329
141	17 40	008	16 15	033	24 43	096	39 14	166	30 00	210	52 14	274	34 41	329
142	17 44	008	16 30	033	25 11	097	39 21	167	29 46	211	51 46	275	34 27	330
143	17 48	009	16 46	034	25 39	097	39 27	168	29 31	212	51 18	276	34 13	331
144	17 53	010	17 02	035	26 07	098	39 32	169	29 16	214	50 50	277	33 59	331
145	17 58	011	17 18	036	26 34	099	39 37	171	29 00	215	50 22	278	33 46	332
146	18 03	011	17 35	036	27 02	100	39 41	172	28 44	216	49 55	278	33 33	333
147	18 09	012	17 52	037	27 30	101	39 45	173	28 27	217	49 27	279	33 20	333
148	18 15	013	18 09	038	27 57	102	39 48	175	28 10	218	48 59	280	33 07	334
149	18 22	014	18 26	039	28 25	103	39 50	176	27 52	219	48 31	281	32 55	334
	DENEB		◆ VEGA		ARCTURUS		◆ REGULUS		PROCYON		◆ CAPELLA		Schedar	
150	18 29	014	18 44	040	28 52	104	39 52	177	27 34	220	48 04	282	32 43	335
151	18 36	015	19 02	040	29 20	105	39 53	178	27 16	221	47 36	282	32 31	336
152	18 43	016	19 21	041	29 47	106	39 54	180	26 57	222	47 09	283	32 19	336
153	18 51	017	19 39	042	30 14	107	39 53	181	26 38	223	46 41	284	32 08	337
154	18 59	017	19 58	043	30 41	108	39 53	182	26 19	224	46 14	285	31 57	337
155	19 08	018	20 17	043	31 07	109	39 51	183	25 59	225	45 47	285	31 47	338
156	19 17	019	20 37	044	31 34	110	39 49	185	25 39	226	45 19	286	31 36	339
157	19 26	019	20 56	045	32 00	111	39 47	186	25 18	227	44 52	287	31 26	339
158	19 35	020	21 16	046	32 27	112	39 43	187	24 57	228	44 26	288	31 16	340
159	19 45	021	21 37	046	32 53	113	39 40	189	24 36	230	43 59	288	31 07	340
160	19 55	022	21 57	047	33 19	114	39 35	190	24 14	231	43 32	289	30 57	341
161	20 06	022	22 18	048	33 44	115	39 30	191	23 52	232	43 06	290	30 48	342
162	20 17	023	22 39	049	34 10	116	39 24	192	23 30	233	42 39	291	30 40	342
163	20 28	024	23 00	049	34 35	117	39 18	194	23 08	234	42 13	291	30 31	343
164	20 40	025	23 22	050	35 00	118	39 11	195	22 45	235	41 47	292	30 23	344
	DENEB		◆ VEGA		ARCTURUS		◆ REGULUS		POLLUX		◆ CAPELLA		Schedar	
165	20 51	025	23 43	051	35 25	119	39 03	196	43 35	246	41 21	293	30 15	344
166	21 04	026	24 05	052	35 50	120	38 55	197	43 09	247	40 55	293	30 08	345
167	21 16	027	24 28	052	36 14	121	38 47	199	42 43	248	40 29	294	30 01	345
168	21 29	027	24 50	053	36 38	122	38 37	200	42 17	249	40 03	295	29 54	346
169	21 42	028	25 13	054	37 02	123	38 28	201	41 50	250	39 38	296	29 47	347
170	21 55	029	25 35	055	37 25	124	38 17	202	41 24	251	39 12	296	29 41	347
171	22 09	030	25 59	055	37 48	125	38 06	204	40 57	252	38 47	297	29 35	348
172	22 23	030	26 22	056	38 11	126	37 55	205	40 30	253	38 22	298	29 29	349
173	22 38	031	26 45	057	38 34	127	37 43	206	40 03	254	37 57	298	29 23	349
174	22 52	032	27 09	058	38 56	129	37 30	207	39 36	255	37 33	299	29 18	350
175	23 07	032	27 33	058	39 18	130	37 17	208	39 09	256	37 08	300	29 13	350
176	23 22	033	27 57	059	39 39	131	37 03	210	38 42	257	36 44	301	29 09	351
177	23 38	034	28 21	060	40 00	132	36 49	211	38 14	258	36 20	301	29 05	352
178	23 54	035	28 46	061	40 21	133	36 35	212	37 46	259	35 56	302	29 01	352
179	24 10	035	29 10	061	40 42	134	36 19	213	37 19	260	35 32	303	28 57	353

LAT 62°N

LHA ♈	Hc	Zn	Hc	Zn	Hc	Zn	Hc	Zn	Hc	Zn	Hc	Zn	Hc	Zn
	DENEB		◆ VEGA		ARCTURUS		◆ Denebola		REGULUS		POLLUX		◆ CAPELLA	
180	24 26	036	29 35	062	41 01	135	42 27	183	36 04	214	36 51	261	35 08	303
181	24 43	037	30 00	063	41 21	137	42 25	185	35 48	215	36 23	262	34 45	304
182	25 00	037	30 25	064	41 40	138	42 23	186	35 31	217	35 55	263	34 22	305
183	25 17	038	30 51	064	41 59	139	42 19	187	35 14	218	35 27	264	33 59	305
184	25 35	039	31 16	065	42 17	140	42 16	189	34 57	219	34 59	264	33 36	306
185	25 52	040	31 42	066	42 35	141	42 11	190	34 39	220	34 31	265	33 13	307
186	26 10	040	32 08	067	42 52	143	42 06	191	34 21	221	34 03	266	32 51	308
187	26 29	041	32 34	068	43 09	144	42 00	192	34 02	222	33 35	267	32 29	308
188	26 47	042	33 00	068	43 26	145	41 54	194	33 43	223	33 07	268	32 07	309
189	27 06	042	33 26	069	43 41	146	41 47	195	33 23	224	32 39	269	31 45	310
190	27 25	043	33 52	070	43 57	148	41 39	196	33 03	226	32 11	270	31 23	310
191	27 45	044	34 19	071	44 12	149	41 31	198	32 43	227	31 42	271	31 02	311
192	28 04	044	34 45	071	44 26	150	41 22	199	32 22	228	31 14	272	30 41	312
193	28 24	045	35 12	072	44 40	151	41 13	200	32 01	229	30 46	273	30 20	312
194	28 44	046	35 39	073	44 53	153	41 03	201	31 40	230	30 18	273	29 59	313
	DENEB		◆ VEGA		ARCTURUS		◆ Denebola		REGULUS		POLLUX		◆ CAPELLA	
195	29 05	047	36 06	074	45 05	154	40 52	203	31 18	231	29 50	274	29 39	314
196	29 25	047	36 33	075	45 17	155	40 41	204	30 56	232	29 22	275	29 19	315
197	29 46	048	37 00	075	45 29	157	40 29	205	30 34	233	28 54	276	28 59	315
198	30 07	049	37 28	076	45 40	158	40 17	206	30 11	234	28 26	277	28 39	316
199	30 28	049	37 55	077	45 50	159	40 04	208	29 48	235	27 58	278	28 19	317
200	30 50	050	38 22	078	46 00	161	39 51	209	29 25	236	27 30	279	28 00	317
201	31 11	051	38 50	078	46 09	162	39 37	210	29 01	237	27 02	279	27 41	318
202	31 33	051	39 18	079	46 17	163	39 22	211	28 37	238	26 34	280	27 23	319
203	31 56	052	39 45	080	46 25	165	39 07	213	28 13	239	26 07	281	27 04	319
204	32 18	053	40 13	081	46 32	166	38 52	214	27 49	240	25 39	282	26 46	320
205	32 40	054	40 41	082	46 38	167	38 36	215	27 24	241	25 11	283	26 28	321
206	33 03	054	41 09	083	46 44	169	38 20	216	27 00	242	24 44	284	26 10	322
207	33 26	055	41 37	083	46 49	170	38 03	217	26 35	243	24 17	284	25 53	322
208	33 49	056	42 05	084	46 54	172	37 46	218	26 09	244	23 49	285	25 36	323
209	34 13	056	42 33	085	46 57	173	37 28	220	25 44	245	23 22	286	25 19	324
	DENEB		◆ VEGA		ARCTURUS		◆ Denebola		REGULUS		POLLUX		◆ CAPELLA	
210	34 36	057	43 01	086	47 01	174	37 10	221	25 18	246	22 55	287	25 03	324
211	35 00	058	43 29	087	47 03	176	36 51	222	24 52	247	22 28	288	24 46	325
212	35 24	059	43 57	088	47 05	177	36 32	223	24 26	248	22 02	289	24 30	326
213	35 48	059	44 25	089	47 06	178	36 13	224	24 00	249	21 35	289	24 15	326
214	36 12	060	44 54	089	47 06	180	35 53	225	23 34	250	21 08	290	23 59	327
215	36 37	061	45 22	090	47 06	181	35 33	226	23 07	251	20 42	291	23 44	328
216	37 01	061	45 50	091	47 05	183	35 12	228	22 40	252	20 16	292	23 29	329
217	37 26	062	46 18	092	47 03	184	34 51	229	22 13	253	19 50	293	23 15	329
218	37 51	063	46 46	093	47 01	185	34 30	230	21 46	254	19 24	293	23 01	330
219	38 16	064	47 14	094	46 58	187	34 08	231	21 19	255	18 58	294	22 47	331
220	38 42	064	47 42	095	46 54	188	33 46	232	20 52	256	18 33	295	22 33	331
221	39 07	065	48 10	096	46 50	190	33 24	233	20 25	257	18 07	296	22 20	332
222	39 33	066	48 38	097	46 45	191	33 01	234	19 57	258	17 42	297	22 07	333
223	39 58	066	49 06	098	46 39	192	32 38	235	19 30	258	17 17	298	21 54	334
224	40 24	067	49 34	099	46 33	194	32 15	236	19 02	259	16 52	298	21 42	334
	◆ DENEB		VEGA		Rasalhague		◆ ARCTURUS		Denebola		Dubhe		◆ CAPELLA	
225	40 50	068	50 02	100	33 16	133	46 26	195	31 51	237	63 11	296	21 30	335
226	41 17	069	50 30	101	33 36	134	46 18	196	31 27	238	62 46	296	21 18	336
227	41 43	069	50 57	102	33 56	135	46 10	198	31 03	239	62 21	297	21 06	336
228	42 09	070	51 25	103	34 16	136	46 01	199	30 39	240	61 56	297	20 55	337
229	42 36	071	51 52	104	34 35	137	45 52	200	30 14	241	61 31	298	20 45	338
230	43 02	072	52 20	105	34 54	138	45 42	202	29 49	242	61 06	298	20 34	339
231	43 29	072	52 47	106	35 13	140	45 31	203	29 24	243	60 41	299	20 24	339
232	43 56	073	53 14	107	35 31	141	45 19	204	28 59	244	60 16	299	20 14	340
233	44 23	074	53 41	108	35 48	142	45 08	206	28 34	245	59 52	300	20 05	341
234	44 50	075	54 08	109	36 06	143	44 55	207	28 08	246	59 27	300	19 56	341
235	45 17	075	54 34	110	36 22	144	44 42	208	27 42	247	59 03	301	19 47	342
236	45 45	076	55 01	111	36 39	145	44 28	210	27 16	248	58 39	301	19 39	343
237	46 12	077	55 27	112	36 54	146	44 14	211	26 50	249	58 15	302	19 30	344
238	46 40	078	55 53	113	37 10	148	43 59	212	26 23	250	57 51	302	19 23	344
239	47 07	078	56 18	115	37 24	149	43 44	213	25 57	251	57 27	303	19 15	345
	Alpheratz		◆ DENEB		VEGA		Rasalhague		◆ ARCTURUS		Alioth		◆ CAPELLA	
240	12 12	049	47 35	079	56 44	116	37 39	150	43 28	215	65 54	277	19 08	346
241	12 34	050	48 02	080	57 09	117	37 53	151	43 12	216	65 26	277	19 01	347
242	12 55	051	48 30	081	57 34	118	38 06	152	42 55	217	64 58	278	18 55	347
243	13 17	051	48 58	082	57 59	119	38 19	154	42 38	218	64 30	279	18 49	348
244	13 39	052	49 26	082	58 23	121	38 31	155	42 20	220	64 02	280	18 43	349
245	14 02	053	49 54	083	58 47	122	38 43	156	42 02	221	63 34	280	18 38	349
246	14 24	054	50 22	084	59 11	123	38 54	157	41 43	222	63 07	281	18 33	350
247	14 47	055	50 50	085	59 35	125	39 04	159	41 24	223	62 39	282	18 28	351
248	15 10	056	51 18	086	59 58	126	39 14	160	41 05	224	62 12	282	18 24	352
249	15 34	056	51 46	087	60 20	127	39 24	161	40 45	226	61 44	283	18 20	352
250	15 57	057	52 14	087	60 42	129	39 33	162	40 25	227	61 17	284	18 17	353
251	16 21	058	52 42	088	61 04	130	39 41	164	40 04	228	60 49	284	18 14	354
252	16 45	059	53 11	089	61 25	132	39 49	165	39 43	229	60 22	285	18 11	355
253	17 09	060	53 39	090	61 46	133	39 56	166	39 21	230	59 55	286	18 08	355
254	17 34	060	54 07	091	62 07	134	40 02	167	39 00	231	59 28	286	18 06	356
	Alpheratz		◆ DENEB		ALTAIR		Rasalhague		◆ ARCTURUS		Alioth		◆ CAPELLA	
255	17 58	061	54 35	092	28 28	130	40 08	169	38 38	232	59 01	287	18 04	357
256	18 23	062	55 03	093	28 49	131	40 13	170	38 15	233	58 34	288	18 03	357
257	18 48	063	55 31	094	29 10	132	40 18	171	37 52	235	58 07	288	18 02	358
258	19 13	064	55 59	095	29 31	133	40 22	172	37 29	236	57 41	289	18 01	359
259	19 39	064	56 27	095	29 51	134	40 25	174	37 06	237	57 14	290	18 01	000
260	20 04	065	56 55	096	30 11	135	40 28	175	36 42	238	56 47	290	18 01	000
261	20 30	066	57 23	097	30 31	137	40 30	176	36 18	239	56 21	291	18 01	001
262	20 56	067	57 51	098	30 50	138	40 32	178	35 54	240	55 55	292	18 02	002
263	21 22	068	58 19	099	31 09	139	40 33	179	35 29	241	55 29	292	18 03	003
264	21 48	069	58 47	100	31 27	140	40 33	180	35 05	242	55 03	293	18 04	003
265	22 14	069	59 15	101	31 45	141	40 33	181	34 40	243	54 37	293	18 06	004
266	22 40	070	59 42	102	32 03	142	40 32	183	34 14	244	54 11	294	18 08	005
267	23 07	071	60 10	104	32 20	143	40 30	184	33 49	245	53 45	295	18 11	006
268	23 34	072	60 37	105	32 37	144	40 28	185	33 23	246	53 20	295	18 14	006
269	24 00	073	61 04	106	32 53	145	40 25	187	32 57	247	52 54	296	18 17	007

LHA ♈	Hc	Zn	Hc	Zn	Hc	Zn	Hc	Zn	Hc	Zn	Hc	Zn	Hc	Zn
	◆ CAPELLA		Alpheratz		◆ DENEB		ALTAIR		Rasalhague		◆ ARCTURUS		Alioth	
270	18 21	008	24 27	073	61 31	107	33 09	147	40 21	188	32 31	248	52 29	296
271	18 25	008	24 54	074	61 58	108	33 24	148	40 17	189	32 05	249	52 04	297
272	18 29	009	25 22	075	62 25	109	33 39	149	40 12	190	31 39	250	51 39	298
273	18 34	010	25 49	076	62 51	110	33 53	150	40 07	192	31 12	251	51 14	298
274	18 39	011	26 16	077	63 18	112	34 07	151	40 01	193	30 45	252	50 49	299
275	18 44	011	26 44	078	63 44	113	34 20	152	39 54	194	30 18	253	50 25	300
276	18 50	012	27 11	078	64 09	114	34 33	153	39 47	195	29 51	254	50 00	300
277	18 56	013	27 39	079	64 35	115	34 45	155	39 39	197	29 24	255	49 36	301
278	19 02	014	28 07	080	65 00	117	34 57	156	39 31	198	28 57	256	49 12	301
279	19 09	014	28 34	081	65 25	118	35 08	157	39 22	199	28 30	257	48 48	302
280	19 16	015	29 02	082	65 50	119	35 19	158	39 13	200	28 02	258	48 24	303
281	19 23	016	29 30	083	66 14	121	35 29	159	39 02	202	27 35	259	48 00	303
282	19 31	016	29 58	083	66 38	122	35 39	161	38 52	203	27 07	260	47 37	304
283	19 39	017	30 26	084	67 02	124	35 48	162	38 41	204	26 39	261	47 14	304
284	19 48	018	30 54	085	67 25	125	35 57	163	38 29	205	26 11	261	46 50	305
	◆ CAPELLA		Alpheratz		Enif		◆ ALTAIR		VEGA		◆ ARCTURUS		Alioth	
285	19 57	019	31 22	086	30 01	131	36 05	164	66 33	191	25 43	262	46 27	306
286	20 06	019	31 50	087	30 22	133	36 12	165	66 27	193	25 16	263	46 05	306
287	20 15	020	32 18	088	30 43	134	36 19	167	66 20	195	24 48	264	45 42	307
288	20 25	021	32 47	089	31 03	135	36 25	168	66 12	197	24 19	265	45 19	307
289	20 35	021	33 15	090	31 23	136	36 31	169	66 04	199	23 51	266	44 57	308
290	20 46	022	33 43	090	31 42	137	36 36	170	65 54	201	23 23	267	44 35	308
291	20 56	023	34 11	091	32 01	138	36 40	172	65 44	202	22 55	268	44 13	309
292	21 08	024	34 39	092	32 20	139	36 44	173	65 32	204	22 27	269	43 51	310
293	21 19	024	35 07	093	32 38	140	36 47	174	65 20	206	21 59	270	43 30	310
294	21 31	025	35 36	094	32 56	141	36 50	175	65 08	208	21 31	270	43 08	311
295	21 43	026	36 04	095	33 13	142	36 52	176	64 54	210	21 02	271	42 47	311
296	21 55	026	36 32	096	33 30	144	36 53	178	64 40	211	20 34	272	42 26	312
297	22 08	027	37 00	097	33 47	145	36 54	179	64 25	213	20 06	273	42 05	313
298	22 21	028	37 28	098	34 03	146	36 55	180	64 09	215	19 38	274	41 45	313
299	22 34	029	37 56	099	34 19	147	36 54	181	63 53	217	19 10	275	41 24	314
	◆ CAPELLA		Alpheratz		◆ Enif		ALTAIR		VEGA		◆ ARCTURUS		Alioth	
300	22 48	029	38 23	100	34 34	148	36 53	183	63 35	218	18 42	276	41 04	314
301	23 02	030	38 51	100	34 48	149	36 52	184	63 18	220	18 14	277	40 44	315
302	23 16	031	39 19	101	35 02	150	36 49	185	62 59	221	17 46	277	40 24	316
303	23 31	031	39 46	102	35 16	152	36 47	186	62 41	223	17 18	278	40 04	316
304	23 46	032	40 14	103	35 29	153	36 43	188	62 21	224	16 50	279	39 45	317
305	24 01	033	40 41	104	35 42	154	36 39	189	62 01	226	16 22	280	39 26	317
306	24 16	034	41 08	105	35 54	155	36 35	190	61 41	227	15 55	281	39 07	318
307	24 32	034	41 35	106	36 06	156	36 29	191	61 20	229	15 27	282	38 48	319
308	24 48	035	42 02	107	36 17	158	36 24	192	60 58	230	15 00	283	38 30	319
309	25 04	036	42 29	108	36 27	159	36 17	194	60 36	232	14 32	283	38 11	320
310	25 21	036	42 56	109	36 37	160	36 10	195	60 14	233	14 05	284	37 53	320
311	25 38	037	43 22	110	36 46	161	36 03	196	59 51	234	13 38	285	37 36	321
312	25 55	038	43 49	111	36 55	162	35 55	197	59 28	236	13 10	286	37 18	322
313	26 12	039	44 15	112	37 03	164	35 46	199	59 05	237	12 43	287	37 01	322
314	26 30	039	44 41	114	37 11	165	35 37	200	58 41	238	12 17	288	36 43	323
	CAPELLA		◆ Hamal		Alpheratz		Enif		◆ ALTAIR		VEGA		◆ Alioth	
315	26 48	040	26 42	090	45 06	115	37 18	166	35 27	201	58 17	240	36 27	323
316	27 06	041	27 10	091	45 32	116	37 25	167	35 17	202	57 52	241	36 10	324
317	27 24	041	27 38	091	45 57	117	37 31	169	35 06	203	57 27	242	35 53	325
318	27 43	042	28 06	092	46 22	118	37 36	170	34 54	204	57 02	243	35 37	325
319	28 02	043	28 35	093	46 47	119	37 41	171	34 42	206	56 37	245	35 21	326
320	28 21	043	29 03	094	47 11	120	37 45	172	34 30	207	56 11	246	35 06	326
321	28 41	044	29 31	095	47 36	121	37 48	173	34 17	208	55 46	247	34 50	327
322	29 01	045	29 59	096	48 00	122	37 51	175	34 04	209	55 20	248	34 35	328
323	29 21	046	30 27	097	48 23	124	37 53	176	33 50	210	54 53	249	34 20	328
324	29 41	046	30 55	098	48 46	125	37 55	177	33 35	211	54 27	250	34 05	329
325	30 01	047	31 23	099	49 09	126	37 56	178	33 20	213	54 00	251	33 51	330
326	30 22	048	31 50	100	49 32	127	37 57	180	33 05	214	53 33	253	33 37	330
327	30 43	048	32 18	101	49 54	128	37 56	181	32 49	215	53 07	254	33 23	331
328	31 04	049	32 46	101	50 16	130	37 56	182	32 33	216	52 39	255	33 09	331
329	31 25	050	33 13	102	50 38	131	37 54	183	32 16	217	52 12	256	32 56	332
	CAPELLA		◆ Hamal		Alpheratz		Enif		◆ ALTAIR		VEGA		◆ Alioth	
330	31 47	050	33 41	103	50 59	132	37 52	185	31 58	218	51 45	257	32 43	333
331	32 09	051	34 08	104	51 19	133	37 50	186	31 41	219	51 17	258	32 30	333
332	32 31	052	34 35	105	51 40	135	37 46	187	31 23	220	50 50	259	32 18	334
333	32 53	052	35 03	106	51 59	136	37 43	188	31 04	222	50 22	260	32 05	334
334	33 15	053	35 30	107	52 19	137	37 38	190	30 45	223	49 54	261	31 53	335
335	33 38	054	35 56	108	52 38	139	37 33	191	30 26	224	49 27	262	31 41	336
336	34 01	055	36 23	109	52 56	140	37 28	192	30 06	225	48 59	263	31 30	336
337	34 24	055	36 50	110	53 14	141	37 21	193	29 46	226	48 31	264	31 19	337
338	34 47	056	37 16	111	53 31	143	37 14	195	29 26	227	48 03	265	31 08	338
339	35 11	057	37 42	112	53 48	144	37 07	196	29 05	228	47 35	265	30 57	338
340	35 34	057	38 08	113	54 04	146	36 59	197	28 44	229	47 06	266	30 47	339
341	35 58	058	38 34	114	54 19	147	36 51	198	28 23	230	46 38	267	30 37	339
342	36 22	059	38 59	115	54 34	149	36 41	200	28 01	231	46 10	268	30 27	340
343	36 46	059	39 25	116	54 49	150	36 32	201	27 39	232	45 42	269	30 18	341
344	37 11	060	39 50	117	55 03	151	36 22	202	27 16	233	45 14	270	30 08	341
	CAPELLA		ALDEBARAN		◆ Hamal		Alpheratz		◆ ALTAIR		VEGA		◆ Alioth	
345	37 35	061	17 16	087	40 15	119	55 16	153	26 54	234	44 46	271	30 00	342
346	38 00	062	17 44	088	40 39	120	55 28	154	26 31	235	44 18	272	29 51	343
347	38 25	062	18 12	089	41 04	121	55 40	156	26 07	236	43 49	273	29 43	343
348	38 50	063	18 41	090	41 28	122	55 51	157	25 44	237	43 21	273	29 35	344
349	39 15	064	19 09	091	41 52	123	56 02	159	25 20	238	42 53	274	29 27	344
350	39 40	064	19 37	092	42 15	124	56 12	160	24 56	239	42 25	275	29 19	345
351	40 06	065	20 05	092	42 38	125	56 21	162	24 31	240	41 57	276	29 12	346
352	40 31	066	20 33	093	43 01	126	56 29	164	24 07	241	41 29	277	29 06	346
353	40 57	067	21 01	094	43 24	127	56 37	165	23 42	242	41 01	278	28 59	347
354	41 23	067	21 29	095	43 46	129	56 43	167	23 17	243	40 33	278	28 53	348
355	41 49	068	21 57	096	44 08	130	56 49	168	22 52	244	40 05	279	28 47	348
356	42 15	069	22 25	097	44 29	131	56 55	170	22 26	245	39 38	280	28 41	349
357	42 42	070	22 53	098	44 50	132	56 59	172	22 01	246	39 10	281	28 36	349
358	43 08	070	23 21	099	45 11	133	57 03	173	21 35	247	38 42	282	28 31	350
359	43 35	071	23 49	100	45 31	135	57 06	175	21 09	248	38 15	283	28 26	351

 LAT 61°N

LHA ♈	Hc	Zn	Hc	Zn	Hc	Zn	Hc	Zn	Hc	Zn	Hc	Zn	Hc	Zn
	◆POLLUX		CAPELLA		Hamal		◆Alpheratz		DENEB		◆VEGA		Alioth	
0	12 39	054	43 42	071	46 34	135	58 08	176	57 30	264	37 33	284	27 22	351
1	13 03	055	44 10	072	46 54	136	58 10	178	57 01	265	37 05	285	27 18	352
2	13 27	056	44 37	072	47 14	138	58 10	180	56 32	266	36 37	286	27 14	353
3	13 51	056	45 05	073	47 33	139	58 10	181	56 03	267	36 09	286	27 11	353
4	14 15	057	45 33	074	47 52	140	58 09	183	55 33	268	35 41	287	27 08	354
5	14 40	058	46 01	074	48 11	141	58 07	184	55 04	269	35 13	288	27 05	355
6	15 05	059	46 29	075	48 29	143	58 05	186	54 35	270	34 46	289	27 02	355
7	15 30	060	46 57	076	48 46	144	58 01	188	54 06	271	34 18	289	27 00	356
8	15 55	061	47 25	077	49 03	145	57 57	189	53 37	271	33 51	290	26 58	356
9	16 20	061	47 54	077	49 19	147	57 52	191	53 08	272	33 24	291	26 56	357
10	16 46	062	48 22	078	49 35	148	57 46	193	52 39	273	32 57	292	26 55	358
11	17 12	063	48 51	079	49 50	149	57 39	194	52 10	274	32 30	293	26 54	358
12	17 38	064	49 19	080	50 04	151	57 31	196	51 41	275	32 03	293	26 53	359
13	18 04	065	49 48	081	50 18	152	57 23	198	51 12	276	31 36	294	26 53	000
14	18 30	065	50 17	081	50 32	154	57 14	199	50 43	276	31 10	295	26 53	000
	Alioth		◆POLLUX		CAPELLA		Hamal		◆Alpheratz		DENEB		◆VEGA	
15	26 53	001	18 57	066	50 46	082	50 44	155	57 04	201	50 14	277	30 43	296
16	26 54	001	19 23	067	51 14	083	50 56	156	56 53	202	49 45	278	30 17	296
17	26 54	002	19 50	068	51 43	084	51 08	158	56 42	204	49 17	279	29 51	297
18	26 56	003	20 17	069	52 12	085	51 18	159	56 30	205	48 48	280	29 25	298
19	26 57	003	20 44	069	52 41	085	51 28	161	56 17	207	48 19	280	29 00	299
20	26 59	004	21 12	070	53 10	086	51 38	162	56 03	208	47 51	281	28 34	299
21	27 01	005	21 39	071	53 39	087	51 46	164	55 49	210	47 22	282	28 09	300
22	27 04	005	22 07	072	54 08	088	51 54	165	55 34	211	46 54	283	27 44	301
23	27 07	006	22 34	073	54 37	089	52 01	167	55 19	213	46 25	283	27 19	302
24	27 10	006	23 02	073	55 06	090	52 08	168	55 03	214	45 57	284	26 54	302
25	27 13	007	23 30	074	55 36	090	52 13	169	54 46	216	45 29	285	26 30	303
26	27 17	008	23 58	075	56 05	091	52 18	171	54 29	217	45 01	286	26 06	304
27	27 21	008	24 26	076	56 34	092	52 22	172	54 11	219	44 33	286	25 42	304
28	27 25	009	24 55	077	57 03	093	52 26	174	53 53	220	44 05	287	25 18	305
29	27 30	010	25 23	078	57 32	094	52 29	175	53 34	221	43 37	288	24 54	306
	Alioth		◆POLLUX		ALDEBARAN		◆Hamal		Alpheratz		DENEB		◆VEGA	
30	27 35	010	25 52	078	37 32	130	52 30	177	53 14	223	43 10	289	24 31	307
31	27 40	011	26 20	079	37 54	131	52 32	178	52 54	224	42 42	289	24 07	307
32	27 46	011	26 49	080	38 15	132	52 32	180	52 34	225	42 15	290	23 44	308
33	27 52	012	27 17	081	38 37	134	52 32	181	52 13	227	41 48	291	23 22	309
34	27 58	013	27 46	082	38 58	135	52 30	183	51 51	228	41 20	292	22 59	310
35	28 05	013	28 15	083	39 18	136	52 29	185	51 30	229	40 53	292	22 37	310
36	28 12	014	28 44	083	39 38	137	52 26	186	51 07	231	40 27	293	22 15	311
37	28 19	015	29 13	084	39 58	138	52 22	188	50 45	232	40 00	294	21 53	312
38	28 26	015	29 42	085	40 17	139	52 18	189	50 22	233	39 33	294	21 32	313
39	28 34	016	30 11	086	40 35	141	52 13	191	49 58	234	39 07	295	21 10	313
40	28 42	016	30 40	087	40 54	142	52 08	192	49 34	235	38 41	296	20 49	314
41	28 51	017	31 09	088	41 11	143	52 01	193	49 10	237	38 15	296	20 29	315
42	28 59	018	31 38	089	41 29	144	51 54	195	48 46	238	37 49	297	20 08	316
43	29 08	018	32 07	089	41 45	145	51 46	196	48 21	239	37 23	298	19 48	316
44	29 18	019	32 36	090	42 02	147	51 38	198	47 56	240	36 57	299	19 28	317
	Alioth		◆POLLUX		ALDEBARAN		◆Hamal		Alpheratz		DENEB		◆VEGA	
45	29 27	020	33 05	091	42 17	148	51 28	199	47 31	241	36 32	299	19 08	318
46	29 37	020	33 34	092	42 33	149	51 18	201	47 05	242	36 06	300	18 49	319
47	29 47	021	34 03	093	42 47	150	51 08	202	46 39	243	35 41	301	18 30	319
48	29 58	021	34 32	094	43 01	152	50 56	204	46 13	245	35 16	301	18 11	320
49	30 09	022	35 01	095	43 15	153	50 44	205	45 46	246	34 52	302	17 53	321
50	30 20	023	35 30	096	43 28	154	50 32	206	45 20	247	34 27	303	17 34	322
51	30 31	023	35 59	097	43 40	156	50 19	208	44 53	248	34 03	303	17 17	322
52	30 43	024	36 28	097	43 52	157	50 05	209	44 26	249	33 39	304	16 59	323
53	30 55	024	36 57	098	44 03	158	49 50	211	43 59	250	33 15	305	16 42	324
54	31 07	025	37 26	099	44 13	159	49 35	212	43 31	251	32 51	306	16 25	325
55	31 19	026	37 54	100	44 23	161	49 19	213	43 04	252	32 27	306	16 08	325
56	31 32	026	38 23	101	44 33	162	49 03	215	42 36	253	32 04	307	15 52	326
57	31 45	027	38 51	102	44 41	163	48 46	216	42 08	254	31 41	308	15 36	327
58	31 58	028	39 20	103	44 49	165	48 29	217	41 40	255	31 18	308	15 20	328
59	32 12	028	39 48	104	44 56	166	48 11	219	41 12	256	30 55	309	15 05	328
	Alioth		◆POLLUX		ALDEBARAN		◆Hamal		Alpheratz		DENEB		◆VEGA	
60	32 26	029	40 16	105	45 03	167	47 53	220	40 44	257	30 33	310	14 50	329
61	32 40	029	40 44	106	45 09	169	47 34	221	40 15	258	30 10	310	14 35	330
62	32 54	030	41 12	107	45 14	170	47 14	222	39 47	259	29 48	311	14 21	331
63	33 09	031	41 40	108	45 19	172	46 54	224	39 18	260	29 27	312	14 06	332
64	33 24	031	42 07	109	45 23	173	46 34	225	38 50	261	29 05	312	13 53	332
65	33 39	032	42 35	110	45 26	174	46 13	226	38 21	262	28 44	313	13 39	333
66	33 54	032	43 02	111	45 29	176	45 52	227	37 52	263	28 23	314	13 26	334
67	34 10	033	43 29	112	45 31	177	45 30	229	37 23	264	28 02	315	13 14	335
68	34 26	034	43 56	113	45 32	178	45 08	230	36 54	264	27 41	315	13 02	335
69	34 42	034	44 23	114	45 32	180	44 46	231	36 25	265	27 21	316	12 50	336
70	34 59	035	44 49	115	45 32	181	44 23	232	35 56	266	27 01	317	12 38	337
71	35 15	035	45 15	116	45 31	182	44 00	233	35 27	267	26 41	317	12 27	338
72	35 32	036	45 41	118	45 30	184	43 37	234	34 58	268	26 21	318	12 16	338
73	35 50	037	46 07	119	45 27	185	43 13	236	34 29	269	26 02	319	12 05	339
74	36 07	037	46 32	120	45 24	187	42 49	237	34 00	270	25 43	319	11 55	340
	Alioth		◆REGULUS		PROCYON		◆ALDEBARAN		Hamal		Alpheratz		◆DENEB	
75	36 25	038	16 32	095	26 40	134	45 21	188	42 24	238	33 31	271	25 24	320
76	36 43	038	17 01	096	27 01	135	45 16	189	41 59	239	33 02	272	25 06	321
77	37 01	039	17 30	097	27 21	136	45 11	191	41 34	240	32 33	272	24 47	322
78	37 19	039	17 59	098	27 41	137	45 06	192	41 09	241	32 04	273	24 29	322
79	37 38	040	18 28	099	28 00	138	44 59	193	40 43	242	31 35	274	24 12	323
80	37 57	041	18 56	100	28 19	140	44 52	195	40 17	243	31 06	275	23 54	324
81	38 16	041	19 25	101	28 38	141	44 44	196	39 51	244	30 37	276	23 37	324
82	38 35	042	19 53	102	28 56	142	44 36	197	39 25	245	30 08	277	23 20	325
83	38 54	042	20 22	102	29 14	143	44 27	199	38 58	246	29 39	277	23 04	326
84	39 14	043	20 50	103	29 32	144	44 17	200	38 32	247	29 10	278	22 48	326
85	39 34	044	21 18	104	29 48	145	44 07	201	38 05	248	28 41	279	22 32	327
86	39 54	044	21 47	105	30 05	146	43 56	203	37 38	249	28 13	280	22 16	328
87	40 15	045	22 15	106	30 21	147	43 45	204	37 10	250	27 44	281	22 01	329
88	40 35	045	22 42	107	30 36	148	43 33	205	36 43	251	27 16	282	21 46	329
89	40 56	046	23 10	108	30 52	149	43 20	207	36 15	252	26 47	282	21 31	330

LHA ♈	Hc	Zn	Hc	Zn	Hc	Zn	Hc	Zn	Hc	Zn	Hc	Zn	Hc	Zn
	Alioth		◆REGULUS		PROCYON		BETELGEUSE		◆ALDEBARAN		Hamal		◆DENEB	
90	41 17	046	23 38	109	31 06	151	36 24	181	43 07	208	35 47	253	21 17	331
91	41 38	047	24 05	110	31 20	152	36 23	182	42 53	209	35 19	254	21 02	331
92	42 00	048	24 32	111	31 34	153	36 22	184	42 38	210	34 51	255	20 49	332
93	42 21	048	25 00	112	31 47	154	36 20	185	42 23	212	34 23	256	20 35	333
94	42 43	049	25 26	113	31 59	155	36 17	186	42 08	213	33 55	257	20 22	334
95	43 05	049	25 53	114	32 11	156	36 13	187	41 52	214	33 26	258	20 09	334
96	43 27	050	26 20	115	32 23	157	36 09	189	41 35	215	32 58	259	19 57	335
97	43 50	051	26 46	116	32 34	159	36 05	190	41 18	217	32 29	260	19 45	336
98	44 12	051	27 12	117	32 44	160	35 59	191	41 01	218	32 00	261	19 33	336
99	44 35	052	27 38	118	32 54	161	35 53	192	40 43	219	31 32	262	19 21	337
100	44 58	052	28 04	119	33 03	162	35 47	193	40 24	220	31 03	263	19 10	338
101	45 21	053	28 29	120	33 12	163	35 40	195	40 05	221	30 34	264	18 59	339
102	45 44	053	28 54	121	33 20	164	35 32	196	39 46	223	30 05	265	18 49	339
103	46 08	054	29 19	122	33 27	166	35 24	197	39 26	224	29 36	266	18 39	340
104	46 31	055	29 44	123	33 34	167	35 15	198	39 06	225	29 07	266	18 29	341
	Alioth		◆REGULUS		PROCYON		BETELGEUSE		◆CAPELLA		Hamal		◆DENEB	
105	46 55	055	30 08	124	33 41	168	35 06	200	68 55	236	28 38	267	18 20	341
106	47 19	056	30 32	125	33 46	169	34 56	201	68 31	238	28 09	268	18 10	342
107	47 43	056	30 56	126	33 52	170	34 45	202	68 06	239	27 40	269	18 02	343
108	48 07	057	31 19	127	33 56	172	34 34	203	67 40	241	27 11	270	17 53	344
109	48 32	058	31 42	128	34 00	173	34 22	204	67 15	242	26 42	271	17 45	344
110	48 56	058	32 05	129	34 03	174	34 10	205	66 49	244	26 13	272	17 38	345
111	49 21	059	32 28	130	34 06	175	33 57	207	66 23	245	25 44	273	17 30	346
112	49 46	059	32 50	131	34 08	176	33 44	208	65 56	246	25 15	273	17 23	346
113	50 11	060	33 11	132	34 10	178	33 30	209	65 29	248	24 45	274	17 17	347
114	50 36	060	33 33	133	34 11	179	33 16	210	65 02	249	24 16	275	17 10	348
115	51 02	061	33 54	134	34 11	180	33 01	211	64 35	250	23 48	276	17 04	349
116	51 27	062	34 14	136	34 11	181	32 46	212	64 08	251	23 19	277	16 59	349
117	51 53	062	34 34	137	34 10	182	32 30	214	63 40	253	22 50	278	16 54	350
118	52 19	063	34 54	138	34 08	184	32 14	215	63 12	254	22 21	279	16 49	351
119	52 45	063	35 14	139	34 06	185	31 57	216	62 44	255	21 52	279	16 45	352
	◆VEGA		ARCTURUS		◆REGULUS		PROCYON		◆CAPELLA		Schedar		DENEB	
120	11 13	016	14 41	077	35 32	140	34 04	186	62 16	256	39 50	318	16 40	352
121	11 21	017	15 10	078	35 51	141	34 00	187	61 48	257	39 31	318	16 37	353
122	11 30	018	15 38	079	36 09	142	33 56	188	61 19	258	39 11	319	16 33	354
123	11 39	019	16 07	080	36 26	143	33 52	190	60 51	259	38 52	319	16 30	355
124	11 48	019	16 36	080	36 44	145	33 47	191	60 22	260	38 33	320	16 28	355
125	11 58	020	17 04	081	37 00	146	33 41	192	59 53	261	38 15	320	16 26	356
126	12 08	021	17 33	082	37 16	147	33 35	193	59 25	262	37 56	321	16 24	357
127	12 19	022	18 02	083	37 32	148	33 28	194	58 56	263	37 38	322	16 22	357
128	12 30	022	18 31	084	37 47	149	33 20	196	58 27	264	37 20	322	16 21	358
129	12 41	023	19 00	085	38 01	151	33 12	197	57 58	265	37 03	323	16 20	359
130	12 53	024	19 29	086	38 15	152	33 03	198	57 29	266	36 45	323	16 20	000
131	13 05	025	19 58	086	38 29	153	32 54	199	57 00	267	36 28	324	16 20	000
132	13 17	026	20 27	087	38 42	154	32 44	200	56 31	268	36 11	325	16 20	001
133	13 30	026	20 56	088	38 54	155	32 34	201	56 02	269	35 54	325	16 21	002
134	13 43	027	21 25	089	39 06	157	32 23	203	55 33	270	35 38	326	16 22	003
	DENEB		◆VEGA		ARCTURUS		◆REGULUS		PROCYON		◆CAPELLA		Schedar	
135	16 24	003	13 57	028	21 54	090	39 17	158	32 12	204	55 04	271	35 21	326
136	16 26	004	14 10	029	22 23	091	39 28	159	32 00	205	54 34	271	35 05	327
137	16 28	005	14 24	029	22 52	092	39 38	160	31 47	206	54 05	272	34 50	327
138	16 31	006	14 39	030	23 21	093	39 47	162	31 34	207	53 36	273	34 34	328
139	16 34	006	14 54	031	23 50	093	39 56	163	31 21	208	53 07	274	34 19	329
140	16 37	007	15 09	032	24 19	094	40 04	164	31 07	209	52 38	275	34 04	329
141	16 41	008	15 24	032	24 48	095	40 12	165	30 52	211	52 09	276	33 49	330
142	16 45	008	15 40	033	25 17	096	40 19	167	30 37	212	51 40	276	33 35	330
143	16 49	009	15 56	034	25 46	097	40 25	168	30 22	213	51 12	277	33 20	331
144	16 54	010	16 13	035	26 15	098	40 31	169	30 06	214	50 43	278	33 06	332
145	16 59	011	16 29	036	26 44	099	40 36	171	29 49	215	50 14	279	32 53	332
146	17 05	011	16 46	036	27 13	100	40 41	172	29 32	216	49 45	280	32 39	333
147	17 11	012	17 04	037	27 41	101	40 44	173	29 15	217	49 17	280	32 26	333
148	17 17	013	17 21	038	28 10	102	40 48	174	28 57	218	48 48	281	32 13	334
149	17 23	014	17 39	039	28 38	102	40 50	176	28 39	219	48 19	282	32 01	335
	DENEB		◆VEGA		ARCTURUS		◆REGULUS		PROCYON		◆CAPELLA		Schedar	
150	17 30	014	17 58	039	29 06	103	40 52	177	28 20	220	47 51	283	31 48	335
151	17 38	015	18 16	040	29 35	104	40 53	178	28 01	222	47 23	283	31 36	336
152	17 45	016	18 35	041	30 03	105	40 54	180	27 42	223	46 54	284	31 24	336
153	17 54	016	18 54	042	30 31	106	40 53	181	27 22	224	46 26	285	31 13	337
154	18 02	017	19 14	042	30 59	107	40 53	182	27 02	225	45 58	286	31 02	338
155	18 11	018	19 33	043	31 26	108	40 51	184	26 41	226	45 30	286	30 51	338
156	18 20	019	19 53	044	31 54	109	40 49	185	26 20	227	45 02	287	30 40	339
157	18 29	019	20 14	045	32 21	110	40 46	186	25 59	228	44 35	288	30 30	339
158	18 39	020	20 34	045	32 49	111	40 43	187	25 37	229	44 07	289	30 20	340
159	18 49	021	20 55	046	33 16	112	40 39	189	25 15	230	43 39	289	30 10	341
160	19 00	021	21 16	047	33 43	113	40 34	190	24 52	231	43 12	290	30 01	341
161	19 10	022	21 38	048	34 09	114	40 29	191	24 30	232	42 45	291	29 51	342
162	19 22	023	21 59	048	34 36	115	40 23	193	24 07	233	42 18	291	29 42	342
163	19 33	024	22 21	049	35 02	116	40 16	194	23 43	234	41 51	292	29 34	343
164	19 45	024	22 43	050	35 28	117	40 09	195	23 20	235	41 24	293	29 26	344
	DENEB		◆VEGA		ARCTURUS		◆REGULUS		POLLUX		◆CAPELLA		Schedar	
165	19 57	025	23 05	051	35 54	118	40 01	196	43 59	247	40 57	294	29 18	344
166	20 10	026	23 28	051	36 19	119	39 53	198	43 32	248	40 30	294	29 10	345
167	20 22	026	23 51	052	36 44	120	39 44	199	43 05	249	40 04	295	29 02	346
168	20 36	027	24 14	053	37 09	121	39 34	200	42 38	250	39 38	296	28 55	346
169	20 49	028	24 37	053	37 34	122	39 24	201	42 11	251	39 12	296	28 49	347
170	21 03	029	25 01	054	37 58	123	39 13	203	41 43	252	38 46	297	28 42	347
171	21 17	029	25 24	055	38 23	125	39 01	204	41 15	253	38 20	298	28 36	348
172	21 31	030	25 48	056	38 46	126	38 49	205	40 47	254	37 54	298	28 30	349
173	21 46	031	26 12	056	39 10	127	38 37	206	40 19	255	37 29	299	28 24	349
174	22 01	031	26 37	057	39 33	128	38 23	208	39 51	256	37 03	300	28 19	350
175	22 16	032	27 01	058	39 56	129	38 10	209	39 23	257	36 38	301	28 14	350
176	22 32	033	27 26	059	40 18	130	37 55	210	38 55	258	36 13	301	28 09	351
177	22 48	034	27 51	059	40 40	131	37 41	211	38 26	259	35 48	302	28 05	352
178	23 04	034	28 16	060	41 02	132	37 25	212	37 58	260	35 24	303	28 01	352
179	23 21	035	28 41	061	41 23	134	37 10	213	37 29	261	34 59	303	27 57	353

LAT 61°N

LHA ♈	Hc	Zn	Hc	Zn	Hc	Zn	Hc	Zn	Hc	Zn	Hc	Zn	Hc	Zn
	DENEB		◆VEGA		ARCTURUS		◆Denebola		REGULUS		POLLUX		◆CAPELLA	
180	23 38	036	29 07	062	41 44	135	43 27	183	36 53	215	37 00	262	34 35	304
181	23 55	036	29 33	062	42 04	136	43 25	185	36 36	216	36 31	262	34 11	305
182	24 12	037	29 58	063	42 24	137	43 22	186	36 19	217	36 03	263	33 47	305
183	24 30	038	30 24	064	42 44	138	43 19	187	36 01	218	35 34	264	33 24	306
184	24 48	039	30 51	065	43 03	140	43 15	189	35 43	219	35 05	265	33 00	307
185	25 06	039	31 17	065	43 22	141	43 10	190	35 25	220	34 36	266	32 37	307
186	25 25	040	31 44	066	43 40	142	43 05	191	35 06	222	34 07	267	32 14	308
187	25 43	041	32 10	067	43 57	143	42 59	193	34 46	223	33 38	268	31 51	309
188	26 02	041	32 37	068	44 15	145	42 52	194	34 26	224	33 08	269	31 29	309
189	26 22	042	33 04	068	44 31	146	42 45	195	34 06	225	32 39	270	31 06	310
190	26 41	043	33 31	069	44 47	147	42 37	197	33 45	226	32 10	271	30 44	311
191	27 01	043	33 58	070	45 03	148	42 28	198	33 24	227	31 41	271	30 22	312
192	27 21	044	34 26	071	45 18	150	42 19	199	33 02	228	31 12	272	30 01	312
193	27 42	045	34 53	071	45 32	151	42 09	200	32 40	229	30 43	273	29 39	313
194	28 02	045	35 21	072	45 46	152	41 58	202	32 18	230	30 14	274	29 18	314
	DENEB		◆VEGA		ARCTURUS		◆Denebola		REGULUS		POLLUX		◆CAPELLA	
195	28 23	046	35 49	073	45 59	154	41 47	203	31 56	231	29 45	275	28 57	314
196	28 44	047	36 17	074	46 12	155	41 36	204	31 33	233	29 16	276	28 36	315
197	29 06	048	36 45	075	46 24	156	41 23	206	31 10	234	28 47	277	28 16	316
198	29 27	048	37 13	075	46 35	158	41 10	207	30 46	235	28 18	277	27 56	316
199	29 49	049	37 41	076	46 46	159	40 57	208	30 22	236	27 49	278	27 36	317
200	30 11	050	38 09	077	46 56	160	40 43	209	29 58	237	27 21	279	27 16	318
201	30 33	050	38 38	078	47 06	162	40 29	211	29 34	238	26 52	280	26 57	318
202	30 56	051	39 06	079	47 14	163	40 14	212	29 09	239	26 23	281	26 37	319
203	31 19	052	39 35	079	47 23	164	39 58	213	28 44	240	25 55	282	26 18	320
204	31 41	052	40 03	080	47 30	166	39 42	214	28 19	241	25 26	282	26 00	320
205	32 05	053	40 32	081	47 37	167	39 25	215	27 53	242	24 58	283	25 41	321
206	32 28	054	41 01	082	47 43	169	39 08	217	27 27	243	24 30	284	25 23	322
207	32 52	054	41 29	083	47 48	170	38 51	218	27 01	244	24 02	285	25 05	323
208	33 15	055	41 58	083	47 53	171	38 32	219	26 35	245	23 34	286	24 48	323
209	33 39	056	42 27	084	47 57	173	38 14	220	26 09	246	23 06	286	24 31	324
	DENEB		◆VEGA		ARCTURUS		◆Denebola		REGULUS		POLLUX		◆CAPELLA	
210	34 03	057	42 56	085	48 00	174	37 55	221	25 42	247	22 38	287	24 14	325
211	34 28	057	43 25	086	48 03	176	37 36	222	25 15	248	22 10	288	23 57	325
212	34 52	058	43 54	087	48 05	177	37 16	224	24 48	249	21 42	289	23 41	326
213	35 17	059	44 23	088	48 06	178	36 55	225	24 21	250	21 15	290	23 25	327
214	35 42	059	44 52	088	48 06	180	36 35	226	23 54	250	20 48	291	23 09	327
215	36 07	060	45 21	089	48 06	181	36 14	227	23 26	251	20 20	291	22 53	328
216	36 32	061	45 51	090	48 05	183	35 52	228	22 59	252	19 53	292	22 38	329
217	36 58	061	46 20	091	48 03	184	35 30	229	22 31	253	19 27	293	22 23	330
218	37 24	062	46 49	092	48 01	186	35 08	230	22 03	254	19 00	294	22 09	330
219	37 49	063	47 18	093	47 58	187	34 46	231	21 35	255	18 33	295	21 54	331
220	38 15	064	47 47	094	47 54	188	34 23	232	21 07	256	18 07	295	21 40	332
221	38 41	064	48 16	095	47 49	190	33 59	234	20 38	257	17 41	296	21 27	332
222	39 08	065	48 45	096	47 44	191	33 36	235	20 10	258	17 15	297	21 13	333
223	39 34	066	49 14	096	47 38	193	33 12	236	19 42	259	16 49	298	21 00	334
224	40 01	066	49 43	097	47 31	194	32 48	237	19 13	260	16 23	299	20 48	334
	◆DENEB		VEGA		Rasalhague		◆ARCTURUS		Denebola		Dubhe		◆CAPELLA	
225	40 27	067	50 11	098	33 56	132	47 24	195	32 23	238	62 44	298	20 35	335
226	40 54	068	50 40	099	34 18	133	47 16	197	31 59	239	62 18	298	20 23	336
227	41 21	069	51 09	100	34 38	135	47 07	198	31 34	240	61 53	298	20 11	337
228	41 48	069	51 37	101	34 59	136	46 58	199	31 08	241	61 27	299	20 00	337
229	42 16	070	52 06	102	35 19	137	46 48	201	30 43	242	61 02	299	19 49	338
230	42 43	071	52 34	103	35 39	138	46 37	202	30 17	243	60 37	300	19 38	339
231	43 11	071	53 02	104	35 58	139	46 26	204	29 51	244	60 11	300	19 28	339
232	43 38	072	53 31	105	36 17	140	46 14	205	29 25	245	59 46	301	19 18	340
233	44 06	073	53 59	106	36 35	141	46 01	206	28 58	246	59 21	301	19 08	341
234	44 34	074	54 26	108	36 53	143	45 48	207	28 32	247	58 57	302	18 59	342
235	45 02	074	54 54	109	37 11	144	45 35	209	28 05	248	58 32	302	18 50	342
236	45 30	075	55 21	110	37 28	145	45 20	210	27 38	249	58 07	302	18 41	343
237	45 58	076	55 49	111	37 44	146	45 05	211	27 11	250	57 43	303	18 33	344
238	46 26	077	56 16	112	38 00	147	44 50	213	26 43	251	57 18	303	18 25	344
239	46 55	077	56 43	113	38 16	148	44 34	214	26 16	252	56 54	304	18 17	345
	Alpheratz		◆DENEB		VEGA		Rasalhague		◆ARCTURUS		Alioth		◆CAPELLA	
240	11 33	049	47 23	078	57 09	114	38 31	150	44 17	215	65 46	279	18 10	346
241	11 55	050	47 51	079	57 36	115	38 45	151	44 00	216	65 17	279	18 03	347
242	12 17	050	48 20	080	58 02	117	38 59	152	43 43	218	64 48	280	17 57	347
243	12 40	051	48 49	080	58 28	118	39 12	153	43 25	219	64 20	281	17 50	348
244	13 03	052	49 17	081	58 53	119	39 25	155	43 06	220	63 51	282	17 45	349
245	13 26	053	49 46	082	59 18	120	39 37	156	42 47	221	63 23	282	17 39	350
246	13 49	054	50 15	083	59 43	122	39 49	157	42 28	223	62 54	283	17 34	350
247	14 13	055	50 44	084	60 08	123	40 00	158	42 08	224	62 26	284	17 29	351
248	14 36	055	51 13	084	60 32	124	40 11	160	41 48	225	61 58	284	17 25	352
249	15 00	056	51 42	085	60 56	126	40 21	161	41 27	226	61 30	285	17 21	352
250	15 25	057	52 11	086	61 19	127	40 30	162	41 06	227	61 02	285	17 17	353
251	15 49	058	52 40	087	61 42	129	40 38	163	40 44	229	60 34	286	17 14	354
252	16 14	059	53 09	088	62 05	130	40 47	165	40 22	230	60 06	287	17 11	355
253	16 39	059	53 38	089	62 27	132	40 54	166	40 00	231	59 38	287	17 08	355
254	17 04	060	54 07	089	62 48	133	41 01	167	39 37	232	59 10	288	17 06	356
	Alpheratz		◆DENEB		ALTAIR		Rasalhague		◆ARCTURUS		Alioth		◆CAPELLA	
255	17 29	061	54 36	090	29 06	130	41 07	168	39 14	233	58 42	289	17 04	357
256	17 55	062	55 05	091	29 29	131	41 12	170	38 50	234	58 15	289	17 03	357
257	18 21	063	55 34	092	29 50	132	41 17	171	38 27	235	57 48	290	17 02	358
258	18 46	063	56 03	093	30 12	133	41 21	172	38 03	236	57 20	290	17 01	359
259	19 13	064	56 32	094	30 33	134	41 25	174	37 38	237	56 53	291	17 01	000
260	19 39	065	57 01	095	30 54	135	41 28	175	37 14	238	56 26	292	17 01	000
261	20 05	066	57 30	096	31 14	136	41 30	176	36 49	240	55 59	292	17 01	001
262	20 32	067	57 59	097	31 34	137	41 32	178	36 24	241	55 32	293	17 02	002
263	20 59	067	58 28	098	31 54	138	41 33	179	35 58	242	55 05	293	17 03	003
264	21 26	068	58 57	099	32 13	139	41 33	180	35 32	243	54 39	294	17 05	003
265	21 53	069	59 26	100	32 32	140	41 33	181	35 06	244	54 12	295	17 06	004
266	22 20	070	59 54	101	32 50	142	41 32	183	34 40	245	53 46	295	17 09	005
267	22 47	071	60 23	102	33 08	143	41 30	184	34 14	246	53 20	296	17 11	005
268	23 15	071	60 51	103	33 25	144	41 27	185	33 47	247	52 54	296	17 14	006
269	23 42	072	61 19	104	33 42	145	41 24	187	33 20	248	52 28	297	17 17	007

LHA ♈	Hc	Zn	Hc	Zn	Hc	Zn	Hc	Zn	Hc	Zn	Hc	Zn	Hc	Zn
	◆CAPELLA		Alpheratz		◆DENEB		ALTAIR		Rasalhague		◆ARCTURUS		Alioth	
270	17 21	008	24 10	073	61 48	105	33 58	146	41 21	188	32 53	249	52 02	298
271	17 25	008	24 38	074	62 16	106	34 14	147	41 16	189	32 26	250	51 36	298
272	17 30	009	25 06	075	62 44	107	34 30	148	41 11	191	31 59	251	51 11	299
273	17 34	010	25 34	075	63 11	108	34 45	150	41 06	192	31 31	252	50 45	299
274	17 40	011	26 02	076	63 39	110	34 59	151	41 00	193	31 04	253	50 20	300
275	17 45	011	26 31	077	64 06	111	35 13	152	40 53	194	30 36	254	49 55	301
276	17 51	012	26 59	078	64 33	112	35 27	153	40 45	196	30 08	255	49 30	301
277	17 57	013	27 27	079	65 00	113	35 40	154	40 37	197	29 40	255	49 05	302
278	18 04	013	27 56	080	65 26	115	35 52	156	40 28	198	29 11	256	48 40	302
279	18 11	014	28 25	080	65 53	116	36 04	157	40 19	199	28 43	257	48 16	303
280	18 18	015	28 53	081	66 19	117	36 15	158	40 09	201	28 15	258	47 51	303
281	18 26	016	29 22	082	66 44	119	36 26	159	39 58	202	27 46	259	47 27	304
282	18 34	016	29 51	083	67 10	120	36 36	160	39 47	203	27 17	260	47 03	305
283	18 42	017	30 20	084	67 35	122	36 45	162	39 35	204	26 49	261	46 39	305
284	18 51	018	30 49	085	67 59	123	36 54	163	39 23	206	26 20	262	46 16	306
	◆CAPELLA		Alpheratz		Enif		◆ALTAIR		VEGA		◆ARCTURUS		Alioth	
285	19 00	018	31 18	085	30 41	131	37 02	164	67 31	192	25 51	263	45 52	306
286	19 09	019	31 47	086	31 02	132	37 10	165	67 25	194	25 22	264	45 29	307
287	19 19	020	32 16	087	31 24	133	37 17	166	67 18	196	24 53	265	45 06	308
288	19 29	021	32 45	088	31 45	134	37 24	168	67 09	198	24 24	266	44 43	308
289	19 39	021	33 14	089	32 05	135	37 30	169	67 00	200	23 55	266	44 20	309
290	19 50	022	33 43	090	32 26	136	37 35	170	66 50	201	23 26	267	43 57	309
291	20 01	023	34 12	091	32 46	137	37 40	171	66 39	203	22 57	268	43 35	310
292	20 13	023	34 41	091	33 05	139	37 44	173	66 27	205	22 28	269	43 13	310
293	20 24	024	35 10	092	33 24	140	37 47	174	66 14	207	21 59	270	42 50	311
294	20 36	025	35 39	093	33 43	141	37 50	175	66 00	209	21 30	271	42 29	312
295	20 49	026	36 08	094	34 01	142	37 52	176	65 46	211	21 01	272	42 07	312
296	21 02	026	36 37	095	34 18	143	37 53	178	65 31	213	20 32	273	41 45	313
297	21 15	027	37 06	096	34 36	144	37 54	179	65 15	214	20 03	273	41 24	313
298	21 28	028	37 35	097	34 52	145	37 55	180	64 58	216	19 34	274	41 03	314
299	21 42	028	38 04	098	35 09	147	37 54	181	64 40	218	19 05	275	40 42	314
	◆CAPELLA		Alpheratz		◆Enif		ALTAIR		VEGA		◆ARCTURUS		Alioth	
300	21 56	029	38 33	099	35 24	148	37 53	183	64 22	219	18 36	276	40 22	315
301	22 10	030	39 02	100	35 40	149	37 51	184	64 03	221	18 07	277	40 01	316
302	22 25	031	39 30	101	35 55	150	37 49	185	63 44	223	17 38	278	39 41	316
303	22 40	031	39 59	102	36 09	151	37 46	186	63 24	224	17 09	279	39 21	317
304	22 55	032	40 27	103	36 23	152	37 43	188	63 03	226	16 41	279	39 01	317
305	23 10	033	40 56	103	36 36	154	37 38	189	62 42	227	16 12	280	38 42	318
306	23 26	033	41 24	104	36 48	155	37 34	190	62 21	229	15 43	281	38 22	319
307	23 42	034	41 52	105	37 00	156	37 28	191	61 59	230	15 15	282	38 03	319
308	23 59	035	42 20	106	37 12	157	37 22	193	61 36	232	14 46	283	37 44	320
309	24 15	035	42 48	107	37 23	158	37 16	194	61 13	233	14 18	284	37 25	320
310	24 32	036	43 15	108	37 33	160	37 08	195	60 49	235	13 50	285	37 07	321
311	24 50	037	43 43	109	37 43	161	37 00	196	60 25	236	13 22	285	36 49	322
312	25 07	038	44 10	111	37 52	162	36 52	198	60 01	237	12 54	286	36 31	322
313	25 25	038	44 37	112	38 01	163	36 43	199	59 37	239	12 26	287	36 13	323
314	25 43	039	45 04	113	38 09	165	36 33	200	59 12	240	11 58	288	35 56	323
	CAPELLA		◆Hamal		Alpheratz		Enif		◆ALTAIR		VEGA		◆Alioth	
315	26 02	040	26 41	089	45 31	114	38 16	166	36 23	201	58 46	241	35 38	324
316	26 20	040	27 10	090	45 58	115	38 23	167	36 12	202	58 21	242	35 21	324
317	26 39	041	27 40	091	46 24	116	38 29	168	36 01	204	57 55	244	35 04	325
318	26 58	042	28 09	092	46 50	117	38 35	170	35 49	205	57 28	245	34 48	326
319	27 18	042	28 38	093	47 16	118	38 40	171	35 36	206	57 02	246	34 32	326
320	27 38	043	29 07	094	47 41	119	38 44	172	35 23	207	56 35	247	34 16	327
321	27 58	044	29 36	094	48 06	120	38 48	173	35 10	208	56 08	248	34 00	327
322	28 18	044	30 05	095	48 31	122	38 51	175	34 56	210	55 41	249	33 44	328
323	28 38	045	30 34	096	48 56	123	38 53	176	34 41	211	55 14	251	33 29	329
324	28 59	046	31 03	097	49 20	124	38 55	177	34 26	212	54 46	252	33 14	329
325	29 20	046	31 31	098	49 44	125	38 56	178	34 11	213	54 19	253	32 59	330
326	29 41	047	32 00	099	50 08	126	38 57	180	33 55	214	53 51	254	32 45	330
327	30 03	048	32 29	100	50 31	127	38 56	181	33 38	215	53 23	255	32 31	331
328	30 24	049	32 57	101	50 54	129	38 56	182	33 21	216	52 55	256	32 17	332
329	30 46	049	33 26	102	51 17	130	38 54	184	33 03	218	52 26	257	32 03	332
	CAPELLA		◆Hamal		Alpheratz		Enif		◆ALTAIR		VEGA		◆Alioth	
330	31 08	050	33 54	103	51 39	131	38 52	185	32 45	219	51 58	258	31 50	333
331	31 31	051	34 23	104	52 00	133	38 49	186	32 27	220	51 29	259	31 36	333
332	31 53	051	34 51	105	52 22	134	38 46	187	32 08	221	51 01	260	31 24	334
333	32 16	052	35 19	106	52 42	135	38 42	189	31 49	222	50 32	261	31 11	335
334	32 39	053	35 47	107	53 03	137	38 37	190	31 29	223	50 03	262	30 59	335
335	33 03	053	36 15	108	53 22	138	38 32	191	31 09	224	49 35	263	30 47	336
336	33 26	054	36 42	109	53 42	139	38 26	192	30 49	225	49 06	264	30 35	337
337	33 50	055	37 10	110	54 00	141	38 20	194	30 28	226	48 37	265	30 24	337
338	34 13	055	37 37	111	54 18	142	38 13	195	30 07	227	48 08	266	30 12	338
339	34 37	056	38 04	112	54 36	143	38 05	196	29 45	228	47 39	267	30 02	338
340	35 02	057	38 31	113	54 53	145	37 56	197	29 23	230	47 10	267	29 51	339
341	35 26	057	38 58	114	55 10	146	37 47	199	29 01	231	46 41	268	29 41	340
342	35 51	058	39 25	115	55 25	148	37 38	200	28 38	232	46 12	269	29 31	340
343	36 16	059	39 51	116	55 41	149	37 28	201	28 15	233	45 43	270	29 21	341
344	36 41	060	40 17	117	55 55	151	37 17	202	27 52	234	45 13	271	29 12	341
	CAPELLA		ALDEBARAN		◆Hamal		Alpheratz		◆ALTAIR		VEGA		◆Alioth	
345	37 06	060	17 13	087	40 43	118	56 09	152	27 28	235	44 44	272	29 03	342
346	37 31	061	17 42	088	41 09	119	56 22	154	27 05	236	44 15	273	28 54	343
347	37 57	062	18 11	089	41 34	120	56 35	155	26 40	237	43 46	274	28 45	343
348	38 22	062	18 40	089	41 59	121	56 47	157	26 16	238	43 17	274	28 37	344
349	38 48	063	19 09	090	42 24	122	56 58	158	25 51	239	42 48	275	28 29	345
350	39 14	064	19 38	091	42 48	123	57 08	160	25 26	240	42 19	276	28 21	345
351	39 40	064	20 07	092	43 12	124	57 18	162	25 01	241	41 50	277	28 14	346
352	40 07	065	20 36	093	43 36	126	57 26	163	24 36	242	41 22	278	28 07	346
353	40 33	066	21 05	094	44 00	127	57 34	165	24 10	243	40 53	278	28 01	347
354	41 00	067	21 34	095	44 23	128	57 42	166	23 44	244	40 24	279	27 54	348
355	41 26	067	22 03	096	44 46	129	57 48	168	23 18	245	39 55	280	27 48	348
356	41 53	068	22 32	096	45 08	130	57 54	170	22 51	246	39 27	281	27 42	349
357	42 20	069	23 01	097	45 30	131	57 59	171	22 25	247	38 58	282	27 37	350
358	42 47	069	23 30	098	45 52	133	58 03	173	21 58	247	38 30	283	27 32	350
359	43 15	070	23 59	099	46 13	134	58 06	175	21 31	248	38 01	283	27 27	351

LHA ♈	Hc	Zn	Hc	Zn	Hc	Zn	Hc	Zn	Hc	Zn	Hc	Zn	Hc	Zn
	Dubhe		◆CAPELLA		ALDEBARAN		Hamal		◆Alpheratz		ALTAIR		◆VEGA	
0	32 08	008	43 22	070	24 38	100	47 16	134	59 08	176	21 25	250	37 18	285
1	32 12	008	43 50	071	25 07	101	47 37	136	59 10	178	20 57	251	36 49	286
2	32 17	009	44 19	071	25 37	101	47 58	137	59 10	180	20 28	252	36 20	286
3	32 21	009	44 47	072	26 06	102	48 18	138	59 10	181	20 00	253	35 52	287
4	32 26	010	45 16	073	26 35	103	48 38	139	59 09	183	19 31	253	35 23	288
5	32 32	010	45 44	073	27 05	104	48 57	141	59 07	185	19 02	254	34 55	289
6	32 37	011	46 13	074	27 34	105	49 16	142	59 04	186	18 33	255	34 26	289
7	32 43	012	46 42	075	28 02	106	49 34	143	59 01	188	18 04	256	33 58	290
8	32 49	012	47 11	076	28 31	107	49 52	145	58 56	190	17 35	257	33 30	291
9	32 56	013	47 40	076	29 00	108	50 09	146	58 50	191	17 06	258	33 02	292
10	33 03	013	48 09	077	29 28	109	50 26	147	58 44	193	16 36	259	32 34	292
11	33 10	014	48 39	078	29 57	110	50 41	149	58 37	195	16 07	260	32 06	293
12	33 17	014	49 08	079	30 25	111	50 57	150	58 29	196	15 37	261	31 39	294
13	33 24	015	49 38	079	30 53	112	51 11	152	58 20	198	15 08	262	31 12	295
14	33 32	015	50 07	080	31 20	113	51 25	153	58 10	200	14 38	262	30 44	295
	Dubhe		◆CAPELLA		ALDEBARAN		Hamal		◆Alpheratz		DENEB		◆VEGA	
15	33 40	016	50 37	081	31 48	114	51 39	154	58 00	201	50 06	278	30 17	296
16	33 49	017	51 06	082	32 15	115	51 51	156	57 49	203	49 36	279	29 50	297
17	33 57	017	51 36	082	32 42	116	52 03	157	57 37	204	49 07	280	29 24	298
18	34 06	018	52 06	083	33 09	117	52 14	159	57 24	206	48 37	281	28 57	298
19	34 16	018	52 36	084	33 36	118	52 25	160	57 10	208	48 08	281	28 31	299
20	34 25	019	53 05	085	34 02	119	52 35	162	56 56	209	47 39	282	28 05	300
21	34 35	019	53 35	086	34 28	120	52 44	163	56 41	211	47 09	283	27 39	300
22	34 45	020	54 05	086	34 54	121	52 52	165	56 25	212	46 40	284	27 13	301
23	34 55	020	54 35	087	35 20	122	52 59	166	56 09	214	46 11	284	26 48	302
24	35 06	021	55 05	088	35 45	123	53 06	168	55 52	215	45 42	285	26 22	303
25	35 16	021	55 35	089	36 10	124	53 12	169	55 35	217	45 13	286	25 57	303
26	35 27	022	56 05	090	36 35	125	53 17	171	55 16	218	44 44	287	25 32	304
27	35 39	022	56 35	091	36 59	126	53 22	172	54 58	219	44 16	287	25 07	305
28	35 50	023	57 05	092	37 23	127	53 25	174	54 38	221	43 47	288	24 43	306
29	36 02	024	57 35	092	37 47	128	53 28	175	54 18	222	43 19	289	24 19	306
	Dubhe		◆CAPELLA		ALDEBARAN		Hamal		◆Alpheratz		DENEB		◆VEGA	
30	36 14	024	58 05	093	38 10	130	53 30	177	53 58	224	42 50	290	23 55	307
31	36 27	025	58 35	094	38 33	131	53 32	178	53 37	225	42 22	290	23 31	308
32	36 39	025	59 05	095	38 56	132	53 32	180	53 15	226	41 54	291	23 07	309
33	36 52	026	59 35	096	39 18	133	53 32	182	52 54	228	41 26	292	22 44	309
34	37 05	026	60 05	097	39 40	134	53 30	183	52 31	229	40 58	292	22 21	310
35	37 19	027	60 34	098	40 01	135	53 28	185	52 08	230	40 30	293	21 58	311
36	37 32	027	61 04	099	40 22	136	53 26	186	51 45	232	40 03	294	21 35	311
37	37 46	028	61 34	100	40 42	138	53 22	188	51 21	233	39 35	294	21 13	312
38	38 00	028	62 03	101	41 02	139	53 18	189	50 57	234	39 08	295	20 51	313
39	38 14	029	62 32	102	41 22	140	53 12	191	50 33	235	38 41	296	20 29	314
40	38 29	029	63 02	103	41 41	141	53 06	192	50 08	236	38 14	296	20 07	314
41	38 44	030	63 31	104	41 59	142	53 00	194	49 43	238	37 47	297	19 46	315
42	38 59	030	64 00	106	42 17	144	52 52	195	49 17	239	37 21	298	19 25	316
43	39 14	031	64 29	107	42 35	145	52 44	197	48 52	240	36 54	299	19 04	317
44	39 30	031	64 57	108	42 52	146	52 35	198	48 25	241	36 28	299	18 44	317
	◆Dubhe		POLLUX		BETELGEUSE		◆ALDEBARAN		Hamal		Alpheratz		◆DENEB	
45	39 45	032	33 06	090	27 56	129	43 08	147	52 25	200	47 59	242	36 02	300
46	40 01	032	33 36	091	28 19	130	43 24	149	52 14	201	47 32	243	35 36	301
47	40 18	033	34 06	092	28 42	131	43 39	150	52 03	203	47 05	244	35 10	301
48	40 34	033	34 36	093	29 04	132	43 54	151	51 51	204	46 38	246	34 45	302
49	40 51	034	35 06	094	29 26	133	44 08	153	51 39	206	46 11	247	34 20	303
50	41 07	034	35 36	095	29 48	134	44 22	154	51 25	207	45 43	248	33 54	303
51	41 25	035	36 06	096	30 10	135	44 35	155	51 11	208	45 15	249	33 29	304
52	41 42	035	36 35	097	30 31	136	44 47	156	50 57	210	44 47	250	33 05	305
53	41 59	036	37 05	098	30 51	137	44 59	158	50 42	211	44 19	251	32 40	305
54	42 17	036	37 35	099	31 11	138	45 10	159	50 26	213	43 51	252	32 16	306
55	42 35	037	38 05	099	31 31	139	45 20	160	50 09	214	43 22	253	31 52	307
56	42 53	037	38 34	100	31 50	141	45 30	162	49 52	215	42 53	254	31 28	307
57	43 11	038	39 04	101	32 09	142	45 39	163	49 35	217	42 24	255	31 04	308
58	43 30	038	39 33	102	32 28	143	45 47	165	49 16	218	41 55	256	30 40	309
59	43 49	039	40 02	103	32 45	144	45 55	166	48 58	219	41 26	257	30 17	309
	◆Dubhe		POLLUX		BETELGEUSE		◆ALDEBARAN		Hamal		Alpheratz		◆DENEB	
60	44 08	039	40 31	104	33 03	145	46 02	167	48 38	221	40 57	258	29 54	310
61	44 27	040	41 00	105	33 20	146	46 08	169	48 19	222	40 28	259	29 31	311
62	44 46	040	41 29	106	33 36	147	46 13	170	47 58	223	39 58	260	29 09	312
63	45 06	041	41 58	107	33 52	148	46 18	171	47 37	224	39 28	261	28 46	312
64	45 25	041	42 27	108	34 08	150	46 22	173	47 16	226	38 59	262	28 24	313
65	45 45	042	42 55	109	34 23	151	46 26	174	46 55	227	38 29	262	28 02	314
66	46 05	042	43 23	110	34 37	152	46 29	176	46 32	228	37 59	263	27 41	314
67	46 26	043	43 51	111	34 51	153	46 31	177	46 10	229	37 30	264	27 19	315
68	46 46	043	44 19	112	35 04	154	46 32	178	45 47	231	37 00	265	26 58	316
69	47 07	044	44 47	113	35 17	155	46 32	180	45 23	232	36 30	266	26 37	316
70	47 28	044	45 14	114	35 29	157	46 32	181	45 00	233	36 00	267	26 17	317
71	47 49	045	45 41	116	35 41	158	46 31	183	44 36	234	35 30	268	25 57	318
72	48 10	045	46 08	117	35 52	159	46 29	184	44 11	235	35 00	269	25 36	318
73	48 31	046	46 35	118	36 02	160	46 27	185	43 46	236	34 30	270	25 17	319
74	48 53	046	47 01	119	36 12	161	46 24	187	43 21	238	34 00	270	24 57	320
	◆Dubhe		REGULUS		PROCYON		◆BETELGEUSE		ALDEBARAN		◆Alpheratz		DENEB	
75	49 15	047	16 38	095	27 22	134	36 21	163	46 20	188	33 30	271	24 38	320
76	49 37	047	17 07	096	27 43	135	36 30	164	46 15	189	33 00	272	24 19	321
77	49 59	048	17 37	097	28 04	136	36 38	165	46 10	191	32 30	273	24 00	322
78	50 21	048	18 07	098	28 25	137	36 45	166	46 04	192	32 00	274	23 42	322
79	50 43	048	18 37	099	28 45	138	36 52	168	45 57	194	31 30	275	23 24	323
80	51 06	049	19 06	099	29 05	139	36 58	169	45 50	195	31 00	276	23 06	324
81	51 28	049	19 36	100	29 24	140	37 04	170	45 42	196	30 30	276	22 48	325
82	51 51	050	20 05	101	29 43	141	37 09	171	45 33	198	30 01	277	22 31	325
83	52 14	050	20 35	102	30 02	142	37 13	173	45 24	199	29 31	278	22 14	326
84	52 37	051	21 04	103	30 20	144	37 16	174	45 14	200	29 01	279	21 57	327
85	53 01	051	21 33	104	30 38	145	37 19	175	45 03	202	28 32	280	21 41	327
86	53 24	052	22 02	105	30 55	146	37 22	176	44 52	203	28 02	281	21 25	328
87	53 48	052	22 31	106	31 11	147	37 23	178	44 40	204	27 33	281	21 09	329
88	54 12	053	23 00	107	31 27	148	37 24	179	44 27	206	27 03	282	20 54	329
89	54 35	053	23 29	108	31 43	149	37 25	180	44 14	207	26 34	283	20 39	330

LHA ♈	Hc	Zn	Hc	Zn	Hc	Zn	Hc	Zn	Hc	Zn	Hc	Zn	Hc	Zn
	Dubhe		◆REGULUS		PROCYON		BETELGEUSE		◆ALDEBARAN		Mirfak		◆DENEB	
90	54 59	053	23 57	109	31 58	150	37 24	181	44 00	208	66 04	262	20 24	331
91	55 24	054	24 25	110	32 13	151	37 23	183	43 45	210	65 34	263	20 10	332
92	55 48	054	24 54	110	32 27	153	37 22	184	43 30	211	65 04	264	19 56	332
93	56 12	055	25 22	111	32 41	154	37 19	185	43 14	212	64 35	265	19 42	333
94	56 37	055	25 50	112	32 54	155	37 16	186	42 58	213	64 05	266	19 28	334
95	57 02	056	26 17	113	33 06	156	37 13	187	42 41	215	63 35	267	19 15	334
96	57 26	056	26 45	114	33 18	157	37 09	189	42 24	216	63 05	268	19 02	335
97	57 51	056	27 12	115	33 29	158	37 04	190	42 06	217	62 35	269	18 50	336
98	58 16	057	27 39	116	33 40	159	36 58	191	41 48	218	62 05	270	18 38	337
99	58 42	057	28 06	117	33 50	161	36 52	192	41 29	219	61 35	271	18 26	337
100	59 07	058	28 32	118	34 00	162	36 45	194	41 10	221	61 05	272	18 15	338
101	59 32	058	28 59	119	34 09	163	36 38	195	40 50	222	60 35	273	18 03	339
102	59 58	059	29 25	120	34 18	164	36 30	196	40 30	223	60 05	273	17 53	339
103	60 24	059	29 50	121	34 25	165	36 21	197	40 09	224	59 35	274	17 42	340
104	60 49	059	30 16	122	34 33	167	36 12	199	39 48	225	59 05	275	17 32	341
	Alioth		◆REGULUS		PROCYON		BETELGEUSE		◆ALDEBARAN		Mirfak		◆DENEB	
105	46 20	054	30 41	123	34 39	168	36 02	200	39 26	227	58 35	276	17 23	342
106	46 45	055	31 06	124	34 45	169	35 52	201	39 04	228	58 05	277	17 13	342
107	47 09	055	31 31	125	34 51	170	35 41	202	38 42	229	57 35	277	17 04	343
108	47 34	056	31 55	126	34 55	171	35 29	203	38 19	230	57 06	278	16 56	344
109	47 59	057	32 19	127	35 00	173	35 17	205	37 56	231	56 36	279	16 47	344
110	48 24	057	32 43	129	35 03	174	35 04	206	37 32	232	56 06	280	16 40	345
111	48 50	058	33 06	130	35 06	175	34 51	207	37 09	233	55 37	280	16 32	346
112	49 15	058	33 29	131	35 08	176	34 37	208	36 44	234	55 07	281	16 25	347
113	49 41	059	33 51	132	35 10	178	34 23	209	36 20	235	54 38	282	16 18	347
114	50 06	059	34 14	133	35 11	179	34 08	210	35 55	237	54 09	282	16 12	348
115	50 32	060	34 35	134	35 11	180	33 52	212	35 30	238	53 39	283	16 06	349
116	50 58	060	34 57	135	35 11	181	33 36	213	35 04	239	53 10	284	16 00	349
117	51 24	061	35 18	136	35 10	182	33 20	214	34 39	240	52 41	285	15 55	350
118	51 51	062	35 38	137	35 08	184	33 03	215	34 13	241	52 12	285	15 50	351
119	52 17	062	35 59	138	35 06	185	32 45	216	33 46	242	51 43	286	15 45	352
	◆VEGA		ARCTURUS		◆REGULUS		PROCYON		BETELGEUSE		◆CAPELLA		DENEB	
120	10 15	016	14 28	077	36 18	140	35 03	186	32 27	217	62 30	258	15 41	352
121	10 24	017	14 57	078	36 37	141	35 00	187	32 09	218	62 00	259	15 37	353
122	10 33	018	15 26	078	36 56	142	34 56	188	31 50	219	61 31	260	15 34	354
123	10 42	019	15 56	079	37 15	143	34 51	190	31 31	221	61 01	261	15 31	355
124	10 52	019	16 25	080	37 32	144	34 46	191	31 11	222	60 31	262	15 28	355
125	11 02	020	16 55	081	37 50	145	34 40	192	30 51	223	60 02	263	15 26	356
126	11 12	021	17 25	082	38 06	147	34 33	193	30 30	224	59 32	264	15 24	357
127	11 23	022	17 54	083	38 23	148	34 26	195	30 09	225	59 02	265	15 22	357
128	11 34	022	18 24	083	38 38	149	34 18	196	29 48	226	58 32	266	15 21	358
129	11 46	023	18 54	084	38 54	150	34 09	197	29 26	227	58 02	267	15 20	359
130	11 58	024	19 24	085	39 08	151	34 00	198	29 04	228	57 32	268	15 20	000
131	12 10	025	19 54	086	39 22	153	33 51	199	28 42	229	57 02	268	15 20	000
132	12 23	025	20 24	087	39 36	154	33 41	200	28 19	230	56 32	269	15 21	001
133	12 36	026	20 54	088	39 49	155	33 30	202	27 55	231	56 02	270	15 21	002
134	12 50	027	21 24	089	40 01	156	33 19	203	27 32	232	55 32	271	15 22	003
	DENEB		◆VEGA		ARCTURUS		◆REGULUS		PROCYON		BETELGEUSE		◆CAPELLA	
135	15 24	003	13 03	028	21 54	089	40 13	158	33 07	204	27 08	233	55 02	272
136	15 26	004	13 18	029	22 24	090	40 24	159	32 54	205	26 44	234	54 32	273
137	15 28	005	13 32	029	22 54	091	40 34	160	32 41	206	26 19	235	54 02	274
138	15 31	005	13 47	030	23 24	092	40 44	161	32 28	207	25 55	236	53 32	274
139	15 34	006	14 02	031	23 54	093	40 54	163	32 14	209	25 29	237	53 03	275
140	15 37	007	14 18	032	24 24	094	41 02	164	31 59	210	25 04	238	52 33	276
141	15 41	008	14 34	032	24 53	095	41 10	165	31 44	211	24 38	239	52 03	277
142	15 45	008	14 50	033	25 23	096	41 17	167	31 28	212	24 12	240	51 33	278
143	15 50	009	15 06	034	25 53	096	41 24	168	31 12	213	23 46	241	51 03	278
144	15 55	010	15 23	035	26 23	097	41 30	169	30 55	214	23 20	242	50 34	279
145	16 00	011	15 40	035	26 53	098	41 35	170	30 38	215	22 53	243	50 04	280
146	16 06	011	15 58	036	27 22	099	41 40	172	30 21	216	22 26	244	49 35	281
147	16 12	012	16 16	037	27 52	100	41 44	173	30 03	218	21 59	245	49 05	281
148	16 18	013	16 34	038	28 21	101	41 47	174	29 44	219	21 32	246	48 36	282
149	16 25	013	16 52	038	28 51	102	41 50	176	29 25	220	21 04	247	48 07	283
	DENEB		◆VEGA		ARCTURUS		Denebola		◆REGULUS		POLLUX		◆CAPELLA	
150	16 32	014	17 11	039	29 20	103	40 16	144	41 52	177	50 47	230	47 37	284
151	16 40	015	17 30	040	29 49	104	40 33	145	41 53	178	50 24	232	47 08	284
152	16 48	016	17 50	040	30 18	105	40 50	147	41 54	180	50 00	233	46 39	285
153	16 56	016	18 09	041	30 47	106	41 06	148	41 53	181	49 36	234	46 10	286
154	17 05	017	18 29	042	31 16	107	41 21	149	41 53	182	49 12	235	45 42	287
155	17 14	018	18 50	043	31 45	108	41 37	150	41 51	184	48 47	236	45 13	287
156	17 23	018	19 10	044	32 13	109	41 51	152	41 49	185	48 22	238	44 44	288
157	17 33	019	19 31	044	32 42	110	42 05	153	41 46	186	47 56	239	44 16	289
158	17 43	020	19 52	045	33 10	110	42 18	154	41 42	187	47 31	240	43 47	289
159	17 53	021	20 13	046	33 38	111	42 31	155	41 38	189	47 05	241	43 19	290
160	18 04	021	20 35	047	34 06	112	42 43	157	41 33	190	46 38	242	42 51	291
161	18 15	022	20 57	047	34 33	113	42 55	158	41 28	191	46 11	243	42 23	292
162	18 26	023	21 19	048	35 01	114	43 06	159	41 21	193	45 45	244	41 55	292
163	18 38	024	21 41	049	35 28	115	43 16	161	41 14	194	45 17	245	41 28	293
164	18 50	024	22 04	049	35 55	117	43 26	162	41 07	195	44 50	247	41 00	294
	◆DENEB		VEGA		ARCTURUS		◆SPICA		REGULUS		◆POLLUX		CAPELLA	
165	19 03	025	22 27	050	36 22	118	13 02	143	40 59	197	44 22	248	40 33	294
166	19 16	026	22 50	051	36 48	119	13 20	144	40 50	198	43 55	249	40 05	295
167	19 29	026	23 14	052	37 14	120	13 37	145	40 40	199	43 26	250	39 38	296
168	19 42	027	23 37	052	37 40	121	13 54	146	40 30	200	42 58	251	39 11	296
169	19 56	028	24 01	053	38 06	122	14 10	147	40 19	202	42 30	252	38 45	297
170	20 10	028	24 25	054	38 31	123	14 26	148	40 08	203	42 01	253	38 18	298
171	20 25	029	24 50	055	38 56	124	14 42	149	39 56	204	41 33	254	37 51	298
172	20 39	030	25 14	055	39 21	125	14 57	150	39 43	205	41 04	255	37 25	299
173	20 54	031	25 39	056	39 45	126	15 12	151	39 30	207	40 35	256	36 59	300
174	21 10	031	26 04	057	40 10	127	15 26	152	39 17	208	40 06	257	36 33	300
175	21 26	032	26 29	058	40 33	128	15 40	153	39 02	209	39 36	258	36 07	301
176	21 42	033	26 55	058	40 57	129	15 54	154	38 47	210	39 07	259	35 42	302
177	21 58	033	27 20	059	41 20	131	16 07	155	38 32	212	38 38	259	35 16	303
178	22 15	034	27 46	060	41 42	132	16 19	156	38 16	213	38 08	260	34 51	303
179	22 32	035	28 12	060	42 04	133	16 31	157	38 00	214	37 38	261	34 26	304

LHA ♈	Hc	Zn	Hc	Zn	Hc	Zn	Hc	Zn	Hc	Zn	Hc	Zn	Hc	Zn
	◆ DENEB		VEGA		ARCTURUS		◆ SPICA		REGULUS		◆ POLLUX		CAPELLA	
180	22 49	035	28 38	061	42 26	134	16 43	158	37 43	215	37 09	262	34 01	305
181	23 06	036	29 05	062	42 47	135	16 54	159	37 25	216	36 39	263	33 37	305
182	23 24	037	29 31	063	43 08	137	17 04	160	37 07	217	36 09	264	33 12	306
183	23 42	038	29 58	063	43 29	138	17 14	161	36 49	219	35 39	265	32 48	307
184	24 01	038	30 25	064	43 49	139	17 24	162	36 30	220	35 09	266	32 24	307
185	24 19	039	30 52	065	44 08	140	17 33	163	36 10	221	34 39	267	32 00	308
186	24 38	040	31 19	066	44 27	141	17 41	164	35 50	222	34 09	268	31 37	309
187	24 58	040	31 46	066	44 45	143	17 49	165	35 30	223	33 39	269	31 13	309
188	25 17	041	32 14	067	45 03	144	17 57	166	35 09	224	33 09	269	30 50	310
189	25 37	042	32 42	068	45 21	145	18 04	167	34 48	225	32 39	270	30 27	311
190	25 57	042	33 10	069	45 37	147	18 10	168	34 26	227	32 09	271	30 05	311
191	26 17	043	33 38	069	45 54	148	18 16	169	34 04	228	31 39	272	29 42	312
192	26 38	044	34 06	070	46 09	149	18 21	170	33 42	229	31 10	273	29 20	313
193	26 59	044	34 34	071	46 25	150	18 26	171	33 19	230	30 40	274	28 58	313
194	27 20	045	35 02	072	46 39	152	18 30	172	32 56	231	30 10	275	28 36	314
	◆ DENEB		VEGA		Rasalhague		◆ ARCTURUS		REGULUS		◆ POLLUX		CAPELLA	
195	27 41	046	35 31	072	21 20	102	46 53	153	32 33	232	29 40	275	28 15	315
196	28 03	046	36 00	073	21 49	103	47 06	154	32 09	233	29 10	276	27 54	315
197	28 25	047	36 28	074	22 19	104	47 19	156	31 45	234	28 40	277	27 33	316
198	28 47	048	36 57	075	22 48	105	47 31	157	31 21	235	28 10	278	27 12	317
199	29 09	049	37 26	075	23 17	106	47 42	159	30 56	236	27 41	279	26 52	317
200	29 32	049	37 55	076	23 45	107	47 53	160	30 31	237	27 11	280	26 31	318
201	29 55	050	38 24	077	24 14	108	48 03	161	30 05	238	26 41	280	26 12	319
202	30 18	051	38 54	078	24 43	109	48 12	163	29 40	239	26 12	281	25 52	319
203	30 41	051	39 23	078	25 11	110	48 20	164	29 14	240	25 43	282	25 33	320
204	31 05	052	39 52	079	25 39	110	48 28	166	28 48	241	25 13	283	25 13	321
205	31 28	053	40 22	080	26 07	111	48 35	167	28 21	242	24 44	284	24 55	321
206	31 52	053	40 52	081	26 35	112	48 42	168	27 55	243	24 15	284	24 36	322
207	32 16	054	41 21	082	27 03	113	48 47	170	27 28	244	23 46	285	24 18	323
208	32 41	055	41 51	082	27 30	114	48 52	171	27 01	245	23 17	286	24 00	324
209	33 05	055	42 21	083	27 57	115	48 57	173	26 33	246	22 48	287	23 42	324
	◆ DENEB		VEGA		Rasalhague		◆ ARCTURUS		REGULUS		◆ POLLUX		CAPELLA	
210	33 30	056	42 51	084	28 24	116	49 00	174	26 06	247	22 20	288	23 25	325
211	33 55	057	43 20	085	28 51	117	49 03	176	25 38	248	21 51	288	23 08	326
212	34 20	057	43 50	086	29 18	118	49 05	177	25 10	249	21 23	289	22 51	326
213	34 46	058	44 20	087	29 44	119	49 06	178	24 42	250	20 55	290	22 34	327
214	35 11	059	44 50	087	30 10	120	49 06	180	24 14	251	20 26	291	22 18	328
215	35 37	059	45 20	088	30 36	121	49 06	181	23 45	252	19 58	292	22 02	328
216	36 03	060	45 50	089	31 01	122	49 05	183	23 17	253	19 31	292	21 47	329
217	36 29	061	46 20	090	31 26	123	49 03	184	22 48	254	19 03	293	21 31	330
218	36 55	061	46 50	091	31 51	124	49 01	186	22 19	255	18 36	294	21 16	330
219	37 22	062	47 20	092	32 16	125	48 57	187	21 50	256	18 08	295	21 02	331
220	37 48	063	47 50	093	32 40	126	48 53	189	21 21	256	17 41	296	20 47	332
221	38 15	064	48 20	094	33 04	128	48 48	190	20 52	257	17 14	296	20 33	333
222	38 42	064	48 50	094	33 28	129	48 43	191	20 22	258	16 47	297	20 20	333
223	39 09	065	49 20	095	33 51	130	48 36	193	19 53	259	16 21	298	20 06	334
224	39 36	066	49 50	096	34 14	131	48 29	194	19 24	260	15 54	299	19 53	335
	DENEB		◆ VEGA		Rasalhague		◆ ARCTURUS		Denebola		Dubhe		◆ CAPELLA	
225	40 04	066	50 20	097	34 37	132	48 22	196	32 55	238	62 16	299	19 41	335
226	40 31	067	50 49	098	34 59	133	48 13	197	32 29	239	61 50	300	19 28	336
227	40 59	068	51 19	099	35 20	134	48 04	198	32 03	240	61 24	300	19 16	337
228	41 27	068	51 49	100	35 42	135	47 54	200	31 37	241	60 58	300	19 05	337
229	41 55	069	52 18	101	36 03	136	47 44	201	31 11	242	60 32	301	18 53	338
230	42 23	070	52 47	102	36 23	137	47 33	203	30 44	243	60 06	301	18 42	339
231	42 51	071	53 17	103	36 43	139	47 21	204	30 17	244	59 41	302	18 32	340
232	43 19	071	53 46	104	37 03	140	47 08	205	29 50	245	59 15	302	18 21	340
233	43 48	072	54 15	105	37 22	141	46 55	207	29 23	246	58 50	303	18 11	341
234	44 16	073	54 44	106	37 41	142	46 41	208	28 55	247	58 24	303	18 02	342
235	44 45	073	55 12	107	37 59	143	46 27	209	28 27	248	57 59	303	17 53	342
236	45 14	074	55 41	108	38 17	144	46 12	211	27 59	249	57 34	304	17 44	343
237	45 43	075	56 09	109	38 34	146	45 56	212	27 31	250	57 10	304	17 35	344
238	46 12	076	56 38	111	38 51	147	45 40	213	27 03	251	56 45	305	17 27	345
239	46 41	076	57 06	112	39 07	148	45 24	215	26 34	252	56 20	305	17 19	345
	DENEB		◆ VEGA		Rasalhague		◆ ARCTURUS		Denebola		Dubhe		◆ CAPELLA	
240	47 10	077	57 33	113	39 22	149	45 06	216	26 06	253	55 56	306	17 12	346
241	47 39	078	58 01	114	39 37	150	44 48	217	25 37	254	55 31	306	17 05	347
242	48 09	079	58 28	115	39 52	152	44 30	218	25 08	255	55 07	306	16 58	347
243	48 38	079	58 55	116	40 06	153	44 11	220	24 39	256	54 43	307	16 52	348
244	49 08	080	59 22	118	40 19	154	43 52	221	24 10	257	54 19	307	16 46	349
245	49 37	081	59 48	119	40 32	155	43 32	222	23 41	258	53 55	308	16 40	350
246	50 07	082	60 14	120	40 44	157	43 12	223	23 11	259	53 32	308	16 35	350
247	50 37	082	60 40	122	40 56	158	42 51	224	22 42	260	53 08	309	16 30	351
248	51 06	083	61 05	123	41 07	159	42 30	226	22 12	260	52 45	309	16 25	352
249	51 36	084	61 30	124	41 17	160	42 08	227	21 43	261	52 22	310	16 21	352
250	52 06	085	61 55	126	41 27	162	41 46	228	21 13	262	51 59	310	16 18	353
251	52 36	086	62 19	127	41 36	163	41 23	229	20 43	263	51 36	310	16 14	354
252	53 06	086	62 43	129	41 44	164	41 01	230	20 13	264	51 13	311	16 11	355
253	53 36	087	63 06	130	41 52	166	40 37	231	19 44	265	50 50	311	16 09	355
254	54 06	088	63 29	132	41 59	167	40 14	233	19 14	266	50 28	312	16 06	356
	Schedar		DENEB		◆ ALTAIR		Rasalhague		◆ ARCTURUS		Dubhe		◆ CAPELLA	
255	37 16	039	54 36	089	29 45	129	42 06	168	39 50	234	50 06	312	16 04	357
256	37 34	039	55 06	090	30 08	130	42 11	170	39 25	235	49 44	313	16 03	358
257	37 53	040	55 36	091	30 30	131	42 17	171	39 01	236	49 22	313	16 02	358
258	38 13	040	56 06	092	30 53	132	42 21	172	38 36	237	49 00	314	16 01	359
259	38 32	041	56 36	092	31 15	134	42 25	174	38 10	238	48 38	314	16 01	000
260	38 52	041	57 06	093	31 36	135	42 28	175	37 45	239	48 17	315	16 01	000
261	39 12	042	57 36	094	31 57	136	42 30	176	37 19	240	47 56	315	16 01	001
262	39 32	043	58 06	095	32 18	137	42 32	177	36 53	241	47 34	316	16 02	002
263	39 53	043	58 35	096	32 38	138	42 33	179	36 26	242	47 14	316	16 03	003
264	40 13	044	59 05	097	32 58	139	42 33	180	36 00	243	46 53	317	16 05	003
265	40 34	044	59 35	098	33 18	140	42 33	181	35 33	244	46 32	317	16 07	004
266	40 55	045	60 05	099	33 37	141	42 31	183	35 05	245	46 12	318	16 09	005
267	41 17	045	60 34	100	33 55	142	42 30	184	34 38	246	45 52	318	16 11	005
268	41 38	046	61 04	101	34 13	143	42 27	185	34 11	247	45 32	318	16 15	006
269	42 00	047	61 33	102	34 31	145	42 24	187	33 43	248	45 12	319	16 18	007

LAT 60°N

LHA ♈	Hc	Zn	Hc	Zn	Hc	Zn	Hc	Zn	Hc	Zn	Hc	Zn	Hc	Zn
	◆ CAPELLA		Alpheratz		◆ ALTAIR		Rasalhague		◆ ARCTURUS		Alkaid		Dubhe	
270	16 22	008	23 52	073	34 48	146	42 20	188	33 15	249	53 33	282	44 52	319
271	16 26	008	24 21	073	35 05	147	42 16	189	32 47	250	53 03	283	44 33	320
272	16 30	009	24 50	074	35 21	148	42 10	191	32 18	251	52 34	283	44 14	320
273	16 35	010	25 19	075	35 37	149	42 04	192	31 50	252	52 05	284	43 55	321
274	16 41	010	25 48	076	35 52	150	41 58	193	31 21	253	51 36	285	43 36	321
275	16 46	011	26 17	077	36 06	152	41 51	195	30 52	254	51 07	285	43 17	322
276	16 52	012	26 46	077	36 20	153	41 43	196	30 23	255	50 38	286	42 59	322
277	16 59	013	27 15	078	36 34	154	41 34	197	29 54	256	50 09	287	42 41	323
278	17 05	013	27 45	079	36 46	155	41 25	198	29 25	257	49 41	287	42 23	323
279	17 13	014	28 14	080	36 59	156	41 15	200	28 56	258	49 12	288	42 05	324
280	17 20	015	28 44	081	37 10	158	41 05	201	28 27	259	48 44	289	41 47	324
281	17 28	016	29 14	081	37 22	159	40 54	202	27 57	260	48 15	290	41 30	325
282	17 36	016	29 43	082	37 32	160	40 42	204	27 27	261	47 47	290	41 13	325
283	17 45	017	30 13	083	37 42	161	40 30	205	26 58	262	47 19	291	40 56	326
284	17 54	018	30 43	084	37 51	163	40 17	206	26 28	262	46 51	292	40 39	326
	◆ CAPELLA		Alpheratz		◆ ALTAIR		Rasalhague		◆ ARCTURUS		Alkaid		Dubhe	
285	18 03	018	31 13	085	38 00	164	40 03	207	25 58	263	46 23	292	40 23	327
286	18 12	019	31 43	086	38 08	165	39 49	209	25 29	264	45 56	293	40 07	327
287	18 22	020	32 12	086	38 15	166	39 35	210	24 59	265	45 28	294	39 50	328
288	18 33	020	32 42	087	38 22	168	39 20	211	24 29	266	45 01	294	39 35	328
289	18 43	021	33 12	088	38 28	169	39 04	212	23 59	267	44 33	295	39 19	329
290	18 54	022	33 42	089	38 34	170	38 48	213	23 29	268	44 06	296	39 04	329
291	19 06	023	34 12	090	38 39	171	38 31	215	22 59	269	43 39	296	38 49	330
292	19 18	023	34 42	091	38 43	173	38 13	216	22 29	270	43 12	297	38 34	331
293	19 30	024	35 12	092	38 47	174	37 56	217	21 59	270	42 46	297	38 19	331
294	19 42	025	35 42	093	38 50	175	37 37	218	21 29	271	42 19	298	38 05	332
295	19 55	025	36 12	093	38 52	176	37 19	219	20 59	272	41 53	299	37 51	332
296	20 08	026	36 42	094	38 53	178	36 59	220	20 29	273	41 26	299	37 37	333
297	20 21	027	37 12	095	38 54	179	36 40	222	19 59	274	41 00	300	37 23	333
298	20 35	028	37 42	096	38 55	180	36 19	223	19 29	275	40 35	301	37 10	334
299	20 49	028	38 12	097	38 54	181	35 59	224	18 59	276	40 09	301	36 56	334
	CAPELLA		◆ Alpheratz		Enif		ALTAIR		◆ VEGA		ARCTURUS		◆ Dubhe	
300	21 03	029	38 42	098	36 15	147	38 53	183	65 08	221	18 29	276	36 43	335
301	21 18	030	39 11	099	36 31	149	38 51	184	64 48	222	18 00	277	36 31	335
302	21 33	030	39 41	100	36 46	150	38 49	185	64 28	224	17 30	278	36 18	336
303	21 48	031	40 10	101	37 01	151	38 46	186	64 06	226	17 00	279	36 06	336
304	22 04	032	40 40	102	37 16	152	38 42	188	63 45	227	16 31	280	35 54	337
305	22 20	032	41 09	103	37 29	153	38 38	189	63 22	229	16 01	281	35 43	337
306	22 36	033	41 38	104	37 43	154	38 33	190	63 00	230	15 32	281	35 31	338
307	22 52	034	42 07	105	37 55	156	38 27	192	62 36	232	15 02	282	35 20	338
308	23 09	034	42 36	106	38 07	157	38 21	193	62 12	233	14 33	283	35 09	339
309	23 26	035	43 05	107	38 19	158	38 14	194	61 48	235	14 04	284	34 58	340
310	23 44	036	43 34	108	38 30	159	38 06	195	61 24	236	13 35	285	34 48	340
311	24 02	037	44 02	109	38 40	161	37 58	197	60 58	237	13 06	286	34 38	341
312	24 20	037	44 31	110	38 49	162	37 49	198	60 33	239	12 37	286	34 28	341
313	24 38	038	44 59	111	38 58	163	37 40	199	60 07	240	12 08	287	34 19	342
314	24 56	039	45 27	112	39 07	164	37 30	200	59 41	241	11 40	288	34 09	342
	CAPELLA		◆ Hamal		Alpheratz		Enif		◆ ALTAIR		VEGA		◆ Alioth	
315	25 15	039	26 40	089	45 55	113	39 15	166	37 19	201	59 14	243	34 50	324
316	25 34	040	27 10	090	46 22	114	39 22	167	37 08	203	58 48	244	34 32	325
317	25 54	041	27 40	090	46 50	115	39 28	168	36 56	204	58 21	245	34 15	325
318	26 14	041	28 10	091	47 17	116	39 34	169	36 43	205	57 53	246	33 58	326
319	26 33	042	28 40	092	47 43	117	39 39	171	36 30	206	57 26	247	33 42	327
320	26 54	043	29 10	093	48 10	118	39 44	172	36 17	207	56 58	249	33 25	327
321	27 14	043	29 40	094	48 36	119	39 47	173	36 03	209	56 30	250	33 09	328
322	27 35	044	30 10	095	49 02	121	39 51	175	35 48	210	56 02	251	32 53	328
323	27 56	045	30 40	096	49 28	122	39 53	176	35 33	211	55 33	252	32 38	329
324	28 17	045	31 10	097	49 53	123	39 55	177	35 17	212	55 05	253	32 22	330
325	28 39	046	31 40	097	50 18	124	39 56	178	35 01	213	54 36	254	32 07	330
326	29 00	047	32 09	098	50 43	125	39 57	180	34 44	215	54 07	255	31 53	331
327	29 22	047	32 39	099	51 07	127	39 56	181	34 27	216	53 38	256	31 38	331
328	29 45	048	33 08	100	51 31	128	39 56	182	34 09	217	53 09	257	31 24	332
329	30 07	049	33 38	101	51 55	129	39 54	184	33 51	218	52 39	258	31 10	333
	CAPELLA		◆ Hamal		Alpheratz		Enif		◆ ALTAIR		VEGA		◆ Alioth	
330	30 30	049	34 07	102	52 18	130	39 52	185	33 32	219	52 10	259	30 56	333
331	30 53	050	34 37	103	52 41	132	39 49	186	33 13	220	51 40	260	30 43	334
332	31 16	051	35 06	104	53 03	133	39 45	187	32 53	221	51 11	261	30 30	334
333	31 39	051	35 35	105	53 24	134	39 41	189	32 33	222	50 41	262	30 17	335
334	32 03	052	36 04	106	53 46	136	39 36	190	32 13	224	50 11	263	30 04	336
335	32 26	053	36 33	107	54 06	137	39 31	191	31 52	225	49 42	264	29 52	336
336	32 50	054	37 01	108	54 27	138	39 25	192	31 31	226	49 12	265	29 40	337
337	33 15	054	37 30	109	54 46	140	39 18	194	31 09	227	48 42	266	29 28	337
338	33 39	055	37 58	110	55 05	141	39 10	195	30 47	228	48 12	267	29 17	338
339	34 04	056	38 26	111	55 24	143	39 02	196	30 25	229	47 42	268	29 06	339
340	34 29	056	38 54	112	55 42	144	38 54	198	30 02	230	47 12	269	28 55	339
341	34 54	057	39 22	113	55 59	145	38 44	199	29 39	231	46 42	269	28 44	340
342	35 19	058	39 49	114	56 16	147	38 34	200	29 15	232	46 12	270	28 34	340
343	35 44	058	40 17	115	56 32	148	38 24	201	28 52	233	45 42	271	28 24	341
344	36 10	059	40 44	116	56 47	150	38 13	202	28 27	234	45 12	272	28 15	342
	CAPELLA		ALDEBARAN		◆ Hamal		Alpheratz		◆ ALTAIR		VEGA		◆ Alioth	
345	36 36	060	17 09	086	41 11	117	57 02	152	28 03	235	44 42	273	28 05	342
346	37 02	060	17 39	087	41 37	118	57 16	153	27 38	236	44 12	274	27 56	343
347	37 28	061	18 09	088	42 04	119	57 29	155	27 13	237	43 42	274	27 48	343
348	37 54	062	18 39	089	42 30	120	57 42	156	26 48	238	43 12	275	27 39	344
349	38 21	062	19 09	090	42 55	121	57 53	158	26 22	239	42 42	276	27 31	345
350	38 47	063	19 39	091	43 21	122	58 04	159	25 56	240	42 12	277	27 23	345
351	39 14	064	20 09	092	43 46	124	58 14	161	25 30	241	41 43	278	27 16	346
352	39 41	064	20 39	093	44 11	125	58 24	163	25 04	242	41 13	279	27 09	347
353	40 08	065	21 09	093	44 35	126	58 32	164	24 37	243	40 43	279	27 02	347
354	40 35	066	21 39	094	44 59	127	58 40	166	24 10	244	40 14	280	26 56	348
355	41 03	066	22 09	095	45 23	128	58 47	168	23 43	245	39 44	281	26 49	348
356	41 30	067	22 39	096	45 47	129	58 53	169	23 16	246	39 15	282	26 43	349
357	41 58	068	23 09	097	46 10	131	58 58	171	22 48	247	38 46	283	26 38	350
358	42 26	069	23 39	098	46 32	132	59 02	173	22 21	248	38 16	283	26 33	350
359	42 54	069	24 08	099	46 54	133	59 06	174	21 53	249	37 47	284	26 28	351

 LAT 59°N

LHA ♈	Hc	Zn	Hc	Zn	Hc	Zn	Hc	Zn	Hc	Zn	Hc	Zn	Hc	Zn
	Dubhe		◆CAPELLA		ALDEBARAN		Hamal		◆Alpheratz		ALTAIR		◆VEGA	
0	31 09	008	43 01	069	24 48	099	47 58	133	60 08	176	21 45	250	37 02	286
1	31 13	008	43 30	070	25 18	100	48 20	135	60 10	178	21 16	251	36 33	286
2	31 17	009	43 59	070	25 48	101	48 41	136	60 10	179	20 47	252	36 03	287
3	31 22	009	44 28	071	26 19	102	49 03	137	60 10	181	20 18	253	35 34	288
4	31 27	010	44 57	072	26 49	103	49 23	139	60 09	183	19 48	254	35 04	289
5	31 33	010	45 27	072	27 19	104	49 44	140	60 07	185	19 18	255	34 35	289
6	31 38	011	45 56	073	27 49	105	50 03	141	60 04	186	18 48	256	34 06	290
7	31 44	011	46 26	074	28 19	106	50 22	143	60 00	188	18 18	256	33 37	291
8	31 51	012	46 56	075	28 49	107	50 41	144	59 55	190	17 48	257	33 08	291
9	31 57	013	47 26	075	29 18	107	50 59	145	59 49	192	17 18	258	32 39	292
10	32 04	013	47 56	076	29 47	108	51 16	147	59 43	193	16 48	259	32 11	293
11	32 11	014	48 26	077	30 17	109	51 33	148	59 35	195	16 17	260	31 43	294
12	32 19	014	48 56	077	30 46	110	51 49	150	59 26	197	15 47	261	31 14	294
13	32 26	015	49 26	078	31 15	111	52 04	151	59 17	199	15 16	262	30 46	295
14	32 34	015	49 56	079	31 43	112	52 19	152	59 07	200	14 46	263	30 18	296
	Dubhe		◆CAPELLA		ALDEBARAN		Hamal		◆Alpheratz		DENEB		◆VEGA	
15	32 43	016	50 27	080	32 12	113	52 33	154	58 56	202	49 57	280	29 51	297
16	32 51	016	50 57	080	32 40	114	52 46	155	58 44	203	49 26	280	29 23	297
17	33 00	017	51 28	081	33 08	115	52 58	157	58 31	205	48 56	281	28 56	298
18	33 09	017	51 58	082	33 36	116	53 10	158	58 18	207	48 26	282	28 29	299
19	33 19	018	52 29	083	34 04	117	53 21	160	58 03	208	47 55	283	28 02	299
20	33 28	018	52 59	084	34 31	118	53 32	161	57 48	210	47 25	283	27 35	300
21	33 38	019	53 30	084	34 58	119	53 41	163	57 32	211	46 55	284	27 08	301
22	33 48	020	54 01	085	35 25	120	53 50	164	57 16	213	46 25	285	26 42	302
23	33 59	020	54 32	086	35 51	121	53 58	166	56 59	215	45 55	285	26 16	302
24	34 10	021	55 03	087	36 18	122	54 05	167	56 41	216	45 26	286	25 50	303
25	34 21	021	55 33	088	36 44	124	54 11	169	56 22	217	44 56	287	25 24	304
26	34 32	022	56 04	088	37 09	125	54 17	171	56 03	219	44 27	288	24 58	305
27	34 43	022	56 35	089	37 34	126	54 21	172	55 44	220	43 57	288	24 33	305
28	34 55	023	57 06	090	37 59	127	54 25	174	55 23	222	43 28	289	24 08	306
29	35 07	023	57 37	091	38 24	128	54 28	175	55 02	223	42 59	290	23 43	307
	Dubhe		◆CAPELLA		ALDEBARAN		Hamal		◆Alpheratz		DENEB		◆VEGA	
30	35 19	024	58 08	092	38 48	129	54 30	177	54 41	225	42 30	290	23 18	307
31	35 32	024	58 39	093	39 12	130	54 32	178	54 19	226	42 01	291	22 54	308
32	35 45	025	59 10	094	39 35	131	54 32	180	53 57	227	41 32	292	22 30	309
33	35 58	025	59 40	094	39 58	132	54 32	182	53 34	229	41 03	292	22 06	310
34	36 11	026	60 11	095	40 21	134	54 30	183	53 10	230	40 35	293	21 42	310
35	36 25	026	60 42	096	40 43	135	54 28	185	52 46	231	40 07	294	21 19	311
36	36 39	027	61 13	097	41 05	136	54 25	186	52 22	233	39 38	294	20 55	312
37	36 53	027	61 43	098	41 26	137	54 21	188	51 57	234	39 10	295	20 32	312
38	37 07	028	62 14	099	41 47	138	54 17	189	51 32	235	38 42	296	20 10	313
39	37 22	028	62 44	100	42 07	139	54 11	191	51 07	236	38 15	297	19 47	314
40	37 37	029	63 15	101	42 27	141	54 05	193	50 41	237	37 47	297	19 25	315
41	37 52	029	63 45	102	42 47	142	53 58	194	50 15	239	37 20	298	19 03	315
42	38 07	030	64 15	104	43 05	143	53 50	196	49 48	240	36 52	299	18 42	316
43	38 23	030	64 45	105	43 24	144	53 41	197	49 21	241	36 25	299	18 21	317
44	38 38	031	65 15	106	43 41	146	53 32	199	48 54	242	35 59	300	18 00	318
	◆Dubhe		POLLUX		BETELGEUSE		◆ALDEBARAN		Hamal		Alpheratz		◆DENEB	
45	38 54	031	33 06	090	28 33	128	43 59	147	53 21	200	48 26	243	35 32	301
46	39 11	032	33 37	091	28 57	129	44 15	148	53 10	202	47 59	244	35 05	301
47	39 27	032	34 08	092	29 21	130	44 31	149	52 58	203	47 31	245	34 39	302
48	39 44	033	34 39	092	29 44	131	44 47	151	52 46	205	47 03	247	34 13	303
49	40 01	033	35 10	093	30 07	133	45 01	152	52 33	206	46 34	248	33 47	303
50	40 18	034	35 41	094	30 30	134	45 15	153	52 19	208	46 05	249	33 21	304
51	40 35	034	36 11	095	30 52	135	45 29	155	52 04	209	45 37	250	32 56	305
52	40 53	035	36 42	096	31 14	136	45 42	156	51 49	210	45 07	251	32 30	305
53	41 11	035	37 13	097	31 35	137	45 54	157	51 33	212	44 38	252	32 05	306
54	41 29	036	37 43	098	31 56	138	46 06	159	51 16	213	44 09	253	31 40	307
55	41 47	036	38 14	099	32 16	139	46 16	160	50 59	215	43 39	254	31 16	307
56	42 05	037	38 45	100	32 36	140	46 27	161	50 41	216	43 09	255	30 51	308
57	42 24	037	39 15	101	32 56	141	46 36	163	50 22	217	42 40	256	30 27	309
58	42 43	038	39 45	101	33 15	142	46 45	164	50 03	219	42 10	257	30 03	309
59	43 02	038	40 16	102	33 34	143	46 53	166	49 44	220	41 39	258	29 39	310
	◆Dubhe		POLLUX		BETELGEUSE		◆ALDEBARAN		Hamal		Alpheratz		◆DENEB	
60	43 21	039	40 46	103	33 52	145	47 00	167	49 24	221	41 09	259	29 15	311
61	43 41	039	41 16	104	34 10	146	47 07	168	49 03	223	40 39	260	28 52	311
62	44 00	040	41 46	105	34 27	147	47 13	170	48 42	224	40 08	260	28 29	312
63	44 20	040	42 15	106	34 43	148	47 18	171	48 20	225	39 38	261	28 06	313
64	44 40	041	42 45	107	34 59	149	47 22	173	47 58	227	39 07	262	27 43	313
65	45 00	041	43 14	108	35 15	150	47 26	174	47 35	228	38 37	263	27 21	314
66	45 21	042	43 44	109	35 30	152	47 28	175	47 12	229	38 06	264	26 59	315
67	45 42	042	44 13	110	35 44	153	47 30	177	46 49	230	37 35	265	26 37	315
68	46 02	043	44 41	111	35 58	154	47 32	178	46 25	231	37 04	266	26 15	316
69	46 23	043	45 10	112	36 11	155	47 32	180	46 00	233	36 34	267	25 54	317
70	46 45	044	45 39	113	36 24	156	47 32	181	45 36	234	36 03	268	25 33	317
71	47 06	044	46 07	115	36 36	158	47 31	183	45 10	235	35 32	269	25 12	318
72	47 27	044	46 35	116	36 48	159	47 29	184	44 45	236	35 01	269	24 52	319
73	47 49	045	47 03	117	36 59	160	47 27	185	44 19	237	34 30	270	24 31	319
74	48 11	045	47 30	118	37 09	161	47 23	187	43 53	238	33 59	271	24 11	320
	◆Dubhe		REGULUS		PROCYON		◆SIRIUS		ALDEBARAN		◆Alpheratz		DENEB	
75	48 33	046	16 43	095	28 03	133	11 14	154	47 19	188	33 28	272	23 52	321
76	48 55	046	17 13	096	28 25	135	11 27	155	47 15	190	32 57	273	23 32	321
77	49 18	047	17 44	096	28 47	136	11 40	156	47 09	191	32 26	274	23 13	322
78	49 40	047	18 15	097	29 09	137	11 52	157	47 03	192	31 56	274	22 54	323
79	50 03	048	18 45	098	29 30	138	12 04	158	46 56	194	31 25	275	22 36	323
80	50 26	048	19 16	099	29 50	139	12 15	159	46 48	195	30 54	276	22 17	324
81	50 49	048	19 46	100	30 10	140	12 26	160	46 40	197	30 23	277	21 59	325
82	51 12	049	20 17	101	30 30	141	12 36	161	46 30	198	29 53	278	21 42	325
83	51 36	049	20 47	102	30 49	142	12 46	162	46 20	199	29 22	279	21 24	326
84	51 59	050	21 17	103	31 08	143	12 55	163	46 10	201	28 52	279	21 07	327
85	52 23	050	21 47	104	31 26	144	13 04	164	45 59	202	28 21	280	20 51	328
86	52 47	051	22 17	104	31 44	145	13 13	165	45 47	203	27 51	281	20 34	328
87	53 10	051	22 47	105	32 01	147	13 20	166	45 34	205	27 21	282	20 18	329
88	53 35	051	23 17	106	32 18	148	13 28	167	45 21	206	26 50	283	20 02	330
89	53 59	052	23 47	107	32 35	149	13 35	168	45 07	207	26 20	283	19 47	330

LHA ♈	Hc	Zn	Hc	Zn	Hc	Zn	Hc	Zn	Hc	Zn	Hc	Zn	Hc	Zn
	Dubhe		◆REGULUS		PROCYON		SIRIUS		◆ALDEBARAN		Mirfak		◆DENEB	
90	54 23	052	24 16	108	32 50	150	13 41	169	44 52	209	66 11	265	19 32	331
91	54 48	053	24 45	109	33 05	151	13 47	170	44 37	210	65 40	266	19 17	332
92	55 12	053	25 14	110	33 20	152	13 52	171	44 21	211	65 09	267	19 02	332
93	55 37	054	25 43	111	33 34	153	13 57	172	44 05	213	64 38	268	18 48	333
94	56 02	054	26 12	112	33 48	155	14 01	173	43 48	214	64 07	268	18 34	334
95	56 27	054	26 41	113	34 01	156	14 05	174	43 31	215	63 36	269	18 21	335
96	56 52	055	27 09	114	34 13	157	14 08	175	43 13	216	63 06	270	18 08	335
97	57 18	055	27 37	115	34 25	158	14 10	176	42 54	218	62 35	271	17 55	336
98	57 43	056	28 05	116	34 36	159	14 13	177	42 35	219	62 04	272	17 43	337
99	58 09	056	28 33	117	34 47	160	14 14	178	42 15	220	61 33	273	17 31	337
100	58 34	056	29 00	118	34 57	162	14 15	179	41 55	221	61 02	273	17 19	338
101	59 00	057	29 28	119	35 06	163	14 16	180	41 34	222	60 31	274	17 08	339
102	59 26	057	29 55	120	35 15	164	14 16	181	41 13	224	60 00	275	16 57	339
103	59 52	058	30 21	121	35 23	165	14 15	182	40 52	225	59 30	276	16 46	340
104	60 18	058	30 48	122	35 31	166	14 14	183	40 30	226	58 59	277	16 36	341
	Alioth		◆REGULUS		PROCYON		BETELGEUSE		◆ALDEBARAN		Mirfak		◆DENEB	
105	45 45	053	31 14	123	35 38	168	36 59	200	40 07	227	58 28	277	16 26	342
106	46 10	054	31 40	124	35 44	169	36 48	201	39 44	228	57 58	278	16 16	342
107	46 35	055	32 05	125	35 50	170	36 36	202	39 21	229	57 27	279	16 07	343
108	47 00	055	32 30	126	35 55	171	36 24	204	38 58	231	56 57	280	15 58	344
109	47 26	056	32 55	127	35 59	173	36 11	205	38 33	232	56 26	280	15 50	344
110	47 51	056	33 20	128	36 03	174	35 58	206	38 09	233	55 56	281	15 42	345
111	48 17	057	33 44	129	36 06	175	35 44	207	37 44	234	55 25	282	15 34	346
112	48 43	057	34 08	130	36 08	176	35 30	208	37 19	235	54 55	282	15 27	347
113	49 09	058	34 31	131	36 10	178	35 15	210	36 54	236	54 25	283	15 20	347
114	49 35	058	34 54	132	36 11	179	34 59	211	36 28	237	53 55	284	15 13	348
115	50 02	059	35 17	133	36 11	180	34 43	212	36 02	238	53 25	284	15 07	349
116	50 28	059	35 39	135	36 11	181	34 27	213	35 35	239	52 55	285	15 01	350
117	50 55	060	36 01	136	36 10	182	34 09	214	35 09	240	52 25	286	14 56	350
118	51 22	061	36 22	137	36 08	184	33 52	215	34 42	241	51 56	287	14 50	351
119	51 49	061	36 43	138	36 06	185	33 34	217	34 14	242	51 26	287	14 46	352
	◆Kochab		ARCTURUS		◆REGULUS		PROCYON		BETELGEUSE		◆CAPELLA		DENEB	
120	52 30	026	14 14	076	37 04	139	36 03	186	33 15	218	62 41	260	14 42	352
121	52 44	026	14 44	077	37 24	140	35 59	187	32 56	219	62 11	261	14 38	353
122	52 58	027	15 14	078	37 43	141	35 55	189	32 36	220	61 40	262	14 34	354
123	53 11	027	15 45	079	38 02	143	35 50	190	32 16	221	61 10	263	14 31	355
124	53 25	027	16 15	080	38 21	144	35 44	191	31 56	222	60 39	264	14 28	355
125	53 40	027	16 45	081	38 39	145	35 38	192	31 35	223	60 08	265	14 26	356
126	53 54	028	17 16	081	38 56	146	35 31	193	31 14	224	59 37	266	14 24	357
127	54 08	028	17 47	082	39 13	147	35 24	195	30 52	225	59 07	267	14 22	357
128	54 23	028	18 17	083	39 30	149	35 16	196	30 30	226	58 36	267	14 21	358
129	54 37	028	18 48	084	39 46	150	35 07	197	30 07	227	58 05	268	14 21	359
130	54 52	028	19 19	085	40 01	151	34 57	198	29 44	229	57 34	269	14 20	000
131	55 07	029	19 49	086	40 15	152	34 47	200	29 21	230	57 03	270	14 20	000
132	55 21	029	20 20	087	40 30	153	34 37	201	28 57	231	56 32	271	14 21	001
133	55 36	029	20 51	087	40 43	155	34 26	202	28 33	232	56 01	272	14 21	002
134	55 51	029	21 22	088	40 56	156	34 14	203	28 08	233	55 30	273	14 22	003
	DENEB		◆VEGA		ARCTURUS		◆REGULUS		PROCYON		BETELGEUSE		◆CAPELLA	
135	14 24	003	12 10	028	21 53	089	41 08	157	34 01	204	27 44	234	54 59	273
136	14 26	004	12 25	028	22 24	090	41 20	159	33 48	205	27 19	235	54 29	274
137	14 28	005	12 40	029	22 55	091	41 31	160	33 35	207	26 53	236	53 58	275
138	14 31	005	12 55	030	23 26	092	41 41	161	33 21	208	26 28	237	53 27	276
139	14 34	006	13 11	031	23 56	093	41 51	162	33 06	209	26 02	238	52 56	277
140	14 38	007	13 27	031	24 27	093	42 00	164	32 51	210	25 35	239	52 26	277
141	14 42	008	13 43	032	24 58	094	42 08	165	32 35	211	25 09	240	51 55	278
142	14 46	008	14 00	033	25 29	095	42 16	166	32 19	212	24 42	241	51 24	279
143	14 51	009	14 17	034	26 00	096	42 23	168	32 02	213	24 15	242	50 54	280
144	14 56	010	14 34	034	26 30	097	42 29	169	31 45	215	23 48	243	50 24	280
145	15 01	011	14 52	035	27 01	098	42 35	170	31 27	216	23 20	244	49 53	281
146	15 07	011	15 09	036	27 32	099	42 39	172	31 09	217	22 52	245	49 23	282
147	15 13	012	15 28	037	28 02	100	42 44	173	30 50	218	22 24	245	48 53	283
148	15 20	013	15 46	037	28 33	100	42 47	174	30 31	219	21 56	246	48 23	283
149	15 27	013	16 05	038	29 03	101	42 50	176	30 11	220	21 28	247	47 53	284
	DENEB		◆VEGA		ARCTURUS		Denebola		◆REGULUS		POLLUX		◆CAPELLA	
150	15 34	014	16 25	039	29 33	102	41 04	144	42 52	177	51 25	231	47 23	285
151	15 42	015	16 44	040	30 03	103	41 22	145	42 53	178	51 01	233	46 53	285
152	15 50	016	17 04	040	30 33	104	41 40	146	42 54	180	50 36	234	46 23	286
153	15 58	016	17 24	041	31 03	105	41 56	147	42 53	181	50 11	235	45 53	287
154	16 07	017	17 45	042	31 33	106	42 13	149	42 53	182	49 46	236	45 24	288
155	16 16	018	18 05	043	32 03	107	42 29	150	42 51	184	49 20	237	44 54	288
156	16 26	018	18 27	043	32 32	108	42 44	151	42 49	185	48 54	239	44 25	289
157	16 36	019	18 48	044	33 01	109	42 58	152	42 46	186	48 27	240	43 56	290
158	16 46	020	19 10	045	33 31	110	43 12	154	42 42	188	48 00	241	43 27	290
159	16 57	021	19 31	046	34 00	111	43 26	155	42 37	189	47 33	242	42 58	291
160	17 08	021	19 54	046	34 28	112	43 38	156	42 32	190	47 06	243	42 29	292
161	17 19	022	20 16	047	34 57	113	43 51	158	42 26	192	46 38	244	42 01	292
162	17 31	023	20 39	048	35 25	114	44 02	159	42 20	193	46 10	245	41 32	293
163	17 43	023	21 02	048	35 53	115	44 13	160	42 13	194	45 42	246	41 04	294
164	17 56	024	21 25	049	36 21	116	44 23	162	42 05	196	45 13	247	40 36	294
	◆DENEB		VEGA		ARCTURUS		◆SPICA		REGULUS		◆POLLUX		CAPELLA	
165	18 08	025	21 49	050	36 49	117	13 50	143	41 56	197	44 45	248	40 08	295
166	18 21	025	22 12	051	37 17	118	14 08	144	41 47	198	44 16	250	39 40	296
167	18 35	026	22 36	051	37 44	119	14 26	145	41 37	199	43 47	251	39 12	296
168	18 49	027	23 01	052	38 11	120	14 44	146	41 26	201	43 18	252	38 44	297
169	19 03	028	23 25	053	38 37	121	15 01	147	41 15	202	42 48	253	38 17	298
170	19 17	028	23 50	053	39 04	122	15 17	148	41 03	203	42 19	254	37 50	298
171	19 32	029	24 15	054	39 30	123	15 33	149	40 51	205	41 49	255	37 23	299
172	19 47	030	24 40	055	39 55	124	15 49	150	40 38	206	41 19	256	36 56	300
173	20 03	030	25 05	056	40 21	125	16 04	151	40 24	207	40 49	256	36 29	300
174	20 19	031	25 31	056	40 46	127	16 19	152	40 09	208	40 19	257	36 02	301
175	20 35	032	25 57	057	41 10	128	16 34	153	39 55	210	39 49	258	35 36	302
176	20 51	032	26 23	058	41 34	129	16 48	154	39 39	211	39 18	259	35 10	302
177	21 08	033	26 49	059	41 58	130	17 01	155	39 23	212	38 48	260	34 44	303
178	21 25	034	27 16	059	42 21	131	17 14	156	39 06	213	38 18	261	34 18	304
179	21 42	035	27 42	060	42 45	132	17 26	157	38 49	214	37 47	262	33 52	304

LAT 59°N

LHA ♈	Hc	Zn	Hc	Zn	Hc	Zn	Hc	Zn	Hc	Zn	Hc	Zn	Hc	Zn
	◆ DENEB		VEGA		ARCTURUS		◆ SPICA		REGULUS		◆ POLLUX		CAPELLA	
180	22 00	035	28 09	061	43 08	133	17 38	158	38 31	216	37 16	263	33 27	305
181	22 18	036	28 36	061	43 30	135	17 50	159	38 13	217	36 46	264	33 02	306
182	22 36	037	29 03	062	43 52	136	18 00	160	37 54	218	36 15	265	32 37	306
183	22 55	037	29 31	063	44 13	137	18 11	161	37 35	219	35 44	266	32 12	307
184	23 14	038	29 58	064	44 34	138	18 21	162	37 16	220	35 13	267	31 48	308
185	23 33	039	30 26	064	44 54	140	18 30	163	36 55	221	34 42	267	31 23	308
186	23 52	039	30 54	065	45 14	141	18 39	164	36 35	223	34 12	268	30 59	309
187	24 12	040	31 22	066	45 33	142	18 47	165	36 14	224	33 41	269	30 35	310
188	24 32	041	31 50	067	45 52	143	18 55	166	35 52	225	33 10	270	30 12	310
189	24 52	041	32 19	067	46 10	145	19 02	167	35 30	226	32 39	271	29 48	311
190	25 13	042	32 47	068	46 27	146	19 09	168	35 08	227	32 08	272	29 25	312
191	25 34	043	33 16	069	46 44	147	19 15	169	34 45	228	31 37	273	29 02	312
192	25 55	043	33 45	069	47 01	149	19 20	170	34 22	229	31 06	273	28 39	313
193	26 16	044	34 14	070	47 17	150	19 25	171	33 58	230	30 35	274	28 17	314
194	26 38	045	34 43	071	47 32	151	19 30	172	33 34	231	30 05	275	27 55	314
	◆ DENEB		VEGA		Rasalhague		◆ ARCTURUS		REGULUS		◆ POLLUX		CAPELLA	
195	26 59	045	35 12	072	21 32	102	47 46	153	33 10	232	29 34	276	27 33	315
196	27 22	046	35 42	072	22 03	103	48 00	154	32 45	234	29 03	277	27 11	316
197	27 44	047	36 11	073	22 33	104	48 13	155	32 20	235	28 32	278	26 50	316
198	28 07	047	36 41	074	23 03	104	48 26	157	31 55	236	28 02	278	26 28	317
199	28 29	048	37 11	075	23 33	105	48 38	158	31 29	237	27 31	279	26 07	318
200	28 53	049	37 41	075	24 02	106	48 49	160	31 03	238	27 01	280	25 47	318
201	29 16	049	38 10	076	24 32	107	48 59	161	30 37	239	26 30	281	25 26	319
202	29 40	050	38 41	077	25 01	108	49 09	162	30 10	240	26 00	282	25 06	320
203	30 03	051	39 11	078	25 31	109	49 18	164	29 43	241	25 30	282	24 46	320
204	30 27	051	39 41	078	26 00	110	49 26	165	29 16	242	25 00	283	24 27	321
205	30 52	052	40 11	079	26 29	111	49 34	167	28 49	243	24 30	284	24 08	322
206	31 16	053	40 42	080	26 58	112	49 40	168	28 21	244	24 00	285	23 49	322
207	31 41	053	41 12	081	27 26	113	49 46	170	27 54	245	23 30	286	23 30	323
208	32 06	054	41 43	082	27 54	114	49 52	171	27 26	246	23 00	286	23 11	324
209	32 31	055	42 13	082	28 23	115	49 56	173	26 57	247	22 31	287	22 53	324
	◆ DENEB		VEGA		Rasalhague		◆ ARCTURUS		REGULUS		◆ POLLUX		CAPELLA	
210	32 56	055	42 44	083	28 51	116	50 00	174	26 29	248	22 01	288	22 36	325
211	33 22	056	43 15	084	29 18	117	50 03	175	26 00	248	21 32	289	22 18	326
212	33 48	057	43 45	085	29 46	118	50 05	177	25 31	249	21 03	290	22 01	327
213	34 14	057	44 16	086	30 13	119	50 06	178	25 02	250	20 34	290	21 44	327
214	34 40	058	44 47	086	30 40	120	50 06	180	24 33	251	20 05	291	21 27	328
215	35 06	059	45 18	087	31 07	121	50 06	181	24 04	252	19 36	292	21 11	329
216	35 33	059	45 49	088	31 33	122	50 05	183	23 34	253	19 08	293	20 55	329
217	35 59	060	46 20	089	31 59	123	50 03	184	23 05	254	18 39	294	20 39	330
218	36 26	061	46 51	090	32 25	124	50 00	186	22 35	255	18 11	294	20 24	331
219	36 53	061	47 21	091	32 50	125	49 57	187	22 05	256	17 43	295	20 09	331
220	37 20	062	47 52	092	33 16	126	49 52	189	21 35	257	17 15	296	19 54	332
221	37 48	063	48 23	092	33 41	127	49 47	190	21 05	258	16 47	297	19 40	333
222	38 15	063	48 54	093	34 05	128	49 42	192	20 35	259	16 20	298	19 26	333
223	38 43	064	49 25	094	34 29	129	49 35	193	20 04	260	15 52	298	19 12	334
224	39 11	065	49 56	095	34 53	130	49 28	194	19 34	260	15 25	299	18 59	335
	DENEB		◆ VEGA		Rasalhague		◆ ARCTURUS		Denebola		Dubhe		◆ CAPELLA	
225	39 39	066	50 26	096	35 16	131	49 19	196	33 26	239	61 46	301	18 46	335
226	40 07	066	50 57	097	35 39	132	49 11	197	33 00	240	61 19	301	18 33	336
227	40 36	067	51 28	098	36 02	134	49 01	199	32 33	241	60 53	302	18 21	337
228	41 04	068	51 58	099	36 24	135	48 51	200	32 06	242	60 26	302	18 09	338
229	41 33	068	52 29	100	36 46	136	48 40	202	31 38	243	60 00	302	17 58	338
230	42 02	069	52 59	101	37 07	137	48 28	203	31 11	244	59 34	303	17 46	339
231	42 31	070	53 30	102	37 28	138	48 16	204	30 43	245	59 08	303	17 35	340
232	43 00	070	54 00	103	37 49	139	48 02	206	30 15	246	58 43	304	17 25	340
233	43 29	071	54 30	104	38 08	140	47 49	207	29 46	247	58 17	304	17 15	341
234	43 58	072	55 00	105	38 28	142	47 34	208	29 18	248	57 51	304	17 05	342
235	44 27	072	55 30	106	38 47	143	47 19	210	28 49	249	57 26	305	16 55	343
236	44 57	073	55 59	107	39 05	144	47 04	211	28 20	250	57 00	305	16 46	343
237	45 27	074	56 29	108	39 23	145	46 47	213	27 51	251	56 35	306	16 38	344
238	45 56	075	56 58	109	39 41	146	46 30	214	27 22	252	56 10	306	16 29	345
239	46 26	075	57 27	110	39 57	148	46 13	215	26 53	253	55 45	306	16 21	345
	DENEB		◆ VEGA		Rasalhague		◆ ARCTURUS		Denebola		Dubhe		◆ CAPELLA	
240	46 56	076	57 56	111	40 14	149	45 55	216	26 23	254	55 20	307	16 14	346
241	47 26	077	58 25	113	40 30	150	45 36	218	25 53	254	54 56	307	16 06	347
242	47 56	077	58 53	114	40 45	151	45 17	219	25 23	255	54 31	308	15 59	347
243	48 26	078	59 21	115	40 59	153	44 57	220	24 53	256	54 07	308	15 53	348
244	48 57	079	59 49	116	41 13	154	44 37	221	24 23	257	53 42	308	15 47	349
245	49 27	080	60 17	117	41 27	155	44 16	223	23 53	258	53 18	309	15 41	350
246	49 58	080	60 44	119	41 39	156	43 55	224	23 23	259	52 54	309	15 36	350
247	50 28	081	61 11	120	41 51	158	43 34	225	22 52	260	52 30	310	15 31	351
248	50 59	082	61 37	121	42 03	159	43 11	226	22 22	261	52 07	310	15 26	352
249	51 29	083	62 04	123	42 14	160	42 49	227	21 51	262	51 43	311	15 22	352
250	52 00	084	62 29	124	42 24	161	42 26	229	21 21	263	51 20	311	15 18	353
251	52 31	084	62 55	126	42 33	163	42 02	230	20 50	263	50 56	311	15 15	354
252	53 01	085	63 20	127	42 42	164	41 39	231	20 19	264	50 33	312	15 11	355
253	53 32	086	63 44	129	42 50	165	41 14	232	19 49	265	50 10	312	15 09	355
254	54 03	087	64 08	130	42 58	167	40 50	233	19 18	266	49 48	313	15 06	356
	Schedar		DENEB		◆ ALTAIR		Rasalhague		◆ ARCTURUS		Dubhe		◆ CAPELLA	
255	36 29	038	54 34	088	30 22	129	43 04	168	40 25	234	49 25	313	15 05	357
256	36 48	039	55 05	088	30 46	130	43 10	169	40 00	235	49 02	314	15 03	358
257	37 07	039	55 36	089	31 10	131	43 16	171	39 34	237	48 40	314	15 02	358
258	37 27	040	56 07	090	31 33	132	43 20	172	39 08	238	48 18	315	15 01	359
259	37 47	040	56 38	091	31 56	133	43 24	173	38 42	239	47 56	315	15 01	000
260	38 07	041	57 08	092	32 18	134	43 27	175	38 15	240	47 34	315	15 01	000
261	38 27	042	57 39	093	32 40	135	43 30	176	37 48	241	47 13	316	15 01	001
262	38 48	042	58 10	094	33 02	136	43 32	177	37 21	242	46 51	316	15 02	002
263	39 09	043	58 41	095	33 23	137	43 33	179	36 54	243	46 30	317	15 03	003
264	39 30	043	59 12	095	33 43	139	43 33	180	36 26	244	46 09	317	15 05	003
265	39 51	044	59 42	096	34 04	140	43 33	181	35 58	245	45 48	318	15 07	004
266	40 13	044	60 13	097	34 23	141	43 31	183	35 30	246	45 27	318	15 09	005
267	40 34	045	60 44	098	34 43	142	43 30	184	35 02	247	45 07	319	15 12	005
268	40 56	045	61 14	099	35 02	143	43 27	186	34 33	248	44 47	319	15 15	006
269	41 18	046	61 45	100	35 20	144	43 24	187	34 05	249	44 27	320	15 18	007

LHA ♈	Hc	Zn	Hc	Zn	Hc	Zn	Hc	Zn	Hc	Zn	Hc	Zn	Hc	Zn
	◆ CAPELLA		Alpheratz		◆ ALTAIR		Rasalhague		◆ ARCTURUS		Alkaid		Dubhe	
270	15 22	008	23 34	072	35 38	145	43 20	188	33 36	250	53 20	283	44 07	320
271	15 27	008	24 04	073	35 55	147	43 15	190	33 07	251	52 50	284	43 47	321
272	15 31	009	24 33	074	36 12	148	43 09	191	32 37	252	52 20	285	43 27	321
273	15 36	010	25 03	075	36 28	149	43 03	192	32 08	253	51 50	285	43 08	322
274	15 42	010	25 33	075	36 44	150	42 56	194	31 38	254	51 20	286	42 49	322
275	15 47	011	26 03	076	36 59	151	42 49	195	31 08	255	50 50	287	42 30	322
276	15 54	012	26 33	077	37 13	152	42 40	196	30 39	256	50 21	287	42 11	323
277	16 00	013	27 03	078	37 27	154	42 32	197	30 09	257	49 51	288	41 53	323
278	16 07	013	27 33	079	37 41	155	42 22	199	29 38	258	49 22	289	41 34	324
279	16 14	014	28 03	079	37 54	156	42 12	200	29 08	258	48 53	289	41 16	324
280	16 22	015	28 34	080	38 06	157	42 01	201	28 38	259	48 24	290	40 58	325
281	16 30	015	29 04	081	38 17	159	41 49	203	28 07	260	47 55	291	40 41	325
282	16 38	016	29 35	082	38 28	160	41 37	204	27 37	261	47 26	291	40 23	326
283	16 47	017	30 06	083	38 39	161	41 24	205	27 06	262	46 57	292	40 06	326
284	16 56	018	30 36	083	38 48	162	41 11	206	26 36	263	46 29	293	39 49	327
	◆ CAPELLA		Alpheratz		◆ ALTAIR		Rasalhague		◆ ARCTURUS		Alkaid		Dubhe	
285	17 06	018	31 07	084	38 58	164	40 57	208	26 05	264	46 00	293	39 32	327
286	17 16	019	31 38	085	39 06	165	40 42	209	25 34	265	45 32	294	39 16	328
287	17 26	020	32 08	086	39 14	166	40 27	210	25 03	266	45 04	294	39 00	328
288	17 37	020	32 39	087	39 21	167	40 11	211	24 33	266	44 35	295	38 43	329
289	17 47	021	33 10	088	39 27	169	39 54	213	24 02	267	44 08	296	38 28	329
290	17 59	022	33 41	088	39 33	170	39 37	214	23 31	268	43 40	296	38 12	330
291	18 10	022	34 12	089	39 38	171	39 20	215	23 00	269	43 12	297	37 57	330
292	18 22	023	34 43	090	39 43	172	39 02	216	22 29	270	42 45	298	37 41	331
293	18 35	024	35 14	091	39 46	174	38 43	217	21 58	271	42 17	298	37 27	331
294	18 47	025	35 45	092	39 49	175	38 24	219	21 27	272	41 50	299	37 12	332
295	19 00	025	36 16	093	39 52	176	38 05	220	20 56	272	41 23	300	36 57	332
296	19 14	026	36 46	094	39 53	178	37 45	221	20 26	273	40 57	300	36 43	333
297	19 28	027	37 17	094	39 54	179	37 24	222	19 55	274	40 30	301	36 29	333
298	19 42	027	37 48	095	39 55	180	37 03	223	19 24	275	40 04	301	36 16	334
299	19 56	028	38 19	096	39 54	181	36 42	224	18 53	276	39 37	302	36 02	335
	CAPELLA		◆ Alpheratz		Enif		ALTAIR		◆ VEGA		Alphecca		◆ Dubhe	
300	20 11	029	38 49	097	37 05	147	39 53	183	65 53	222	34 48	265	35 49	335
301	20 26	029	39 20	098	37 22	148	39 51	184	65 32	224	34 17	265	35 36	336
302	20 41	030	39 51	099	37 38	149	39 49	185	65 10	226	33 46	266	35 24	336
303	20 57	031	40 21	100	37 54	151	39 45	187	64 48	227	33 15	267	35 11	337
304	21 13	032	40 52	101	38 09	152	39 42	188	64 25	229	32 44	268	34 59	337
305	21 29	032	41 22	102	38 23	153	39 37	189	64 01	230	32 13	269	34 47	338
306	21 46	033	41 52	103	38 37	154	39 32	190	63 37	232	31 43	270	34 35	338
307	22 03	034	42 22	104	38 50	155	39 26	192	63 13	233	31 12	271	34 24	339
308	22 20	034	42 52	105	39 02	157	39 19	193	62 48	235	30 41	271	34 13	339
309	22 37	035	43 22	106	39 14	158	39 12	194	62 22	236	30 10	272	34 02	340
310	22 55	036	43 52	107	39 26	159	39 04	195	61 56	238	29 39	273	33 52	340
311	23 13	036	44 21	108	39 36	160	38 55	197	61 30	239	29 08	274	33 41	341
312	23 32	037	44 50	109	39 46	162	38 46	198	61 03	240	28 37	275	33 31	341
313	23 50	038	45 20	110	39 56	163	38 36	199	60 36	242	28 07	276	33 22	342
314	24 09	038	45 49	111	40 05	164	38 26	200	60 09	243	27 36	277	33 12	342
	CAPELLA		◆ Hamal		Alpheratz		Enif		◆ ALTAIR		VEGA		◆ Alioth	
315	24 29	039	26 39	088	46 17	112	40 13	165	38 15	202	59 41	244	34 01	325
316	24 48	040	27 09	089	46 46	113	40 20	167	38 03	203	59 13	245	33 43	325
317	25 08	040	27 40	090	47 14	114	40 27	168	37 51	204	58 45	247	33 26	326
318	25 28	041	28 11	091	47 42	115	40 33	169	37 38	205	58 17	248	33 08	326
319	25 49	042	28 42	092	48 10	116	40 38	171	37 24	207	57 48	249	32 51	327
320	26 09	042	29 13	092	48 38	117	40 43	172	37 10	208	57 19	250	32 35	328
321	26 30	043	29 44	093	49 05	118	40 47	173	36 55	209	56 50	251	32 18	328
322	26 52	044	30 15	094	49 32	120	40 50	174	36 40	210	56 21	252	32 02	329
323	27 13	044	30 46	095	49 59	121	40 53	176	36 24	211	55 51	253	31 46	329
324	27 35	045	31 16	096	50 25	122	40 55	177	36 08	213	55 21	254	31 31	330
325	27 57	046	31 47	097	50 52	123	40 56	178	35 51	214	54 52	255	31 15	330
326	28 19	046	32 18	098	51 17	124	40 57	180	35 33	215	54 22	257	31 00	331
327	28 42	047	32 48	099	51 43	126	40 56	181	35 15	216	53 51	258	30 45	332
328	29 04	048	33 19	100	52 08	127	40 56	182	34 57	217	53 21	259	30 31	332
329	29 27	048	33 49	100	52 32	128	40 54	184	34 38	218	52 51	260	30 16	333
	CAPELLA		◆ Hamal		Alpheratz		Enif		◆ ALTAIR		VEGA		◆ Alioth	
330	29 51	049	34 20	101	52 56	129	40 52	185	34 19	219	52 20	260	30 03	333
331	30 14	050	34 50	102	53 20	131	40 49	186	33 59	221	51 50	261	29 49	334
332	30 38	050	35 20	103	53 43	132	40 45	188	33 38	222	51 19	262	29 35	335
333	31 02	051	35 50	104	54 06	133	40 41	189	33 18	223	50 49	263	29 22	335
334	31 26	052	36 20	105	54 28	135	40 36	190	32 56	224	50 18	264	29 10	336
335	31 50	052	36 50	106	54 50	136	40 30	191	32 35	225	49 47	265	28 57	336
336	32 15	053	37 19	107	55 11	137	40 23	193	32 13	226	49 16	266	28 45	337
337	32 39	054	37 49	108	55 32	139	40 16	194	31 50	227	48 46	267	28 33	338
338	33 04	054	38 18	109	55 52	140	40 08	195	31 27	228	48 15	268	28 21	338
339	33 30	055	38 47	110	56 11	142	40 00	197	31 04	229	47 44	269	28 10	339
340	33 55	056	39 16	111	56 30	143	39 51	198	30 40	230	47 13	270	27 59	339
341	34 21	056	39 45	112	56 48	145	39 41	199	30 16	231	46 42	270	27 48	340
342	34 46	057	40 13	113	57 06	146	39 31	200	29 52	232	46 11	271	27 38	341
343	35 12	058	40 42	114	57 23	148	39 20	202	29 27	234	45 40	272	27 28	341
344	35 39	058	41 10	115	57 39	149	39 08	203	29 02	235	45 09	273	27 18	342
	CAPELLA		ALDEBARAN		◆ Hamal		Alpheratz		◆ ALTAIR		VEGA		◆ Alioth	
345	36 05	059	17 06	086	41 37	116	57 55	151	28 37	236	44 38	274	27 08	342
346	36 32	060	17 36	087	42 05	117	58 09	152	28 11	237	44 08	275	26 59	343
347	36 58	060	18 07	088	42 32	118	58 23	154	27 46	238	43 37	275	26 50	344
348	37 25	061	18 38	089	42 59	119	58 36	156	27 19	239	43 06	276	26 42	344
349	37 52	062	19 09	090	43 26	121	58 49	157	26 53	240	42 35	277	26 33	345
350	38 20	062	19 40	090	43 53	122	59 00	159	26 26	241	42 05	278	26 25	345
351	38 47	063	20 11	091	44 19	123	59 11	161	25 59	242	41 34	279	26 18	346
352	39 15	064	20 42	092	44 45	124	59 21	162	25 32	243	41 04	279	26 11	347
353	39 42	064	21 13	093	45 10	125	59 30	164	25 04	243	40 33	280	26 04	347
354	40 10	065	21 44	094	45 35	126	59 38	166	24 36	244	40 03	281	25 57	348
355	40 38	066	22 14	095	46 00	127	59 45	167	24 08	245	39 33	282	25 51	348
356	41 07	066	22 45	096	46 24	129	59 52	169	23 40	246	39 02	283	25 45	349
357	41 35	067	23 16	097	46 48	130	59 57	171	23 12	247	38 32	283	25 39	350
358	42 04	068	23 46	097	47 12	131	60 02	172	22 43	248	38 02	284	25 34	350
359	42 32	068	24 17	098	47 35	132	60 05	174	22 14	249	37 32	285	25 29	351

LAT 58°N

LHA ♈	Dubhe Hc Zn	◆CAPELLA Hc Zn	ALDEBARAN Hc Zn	Hamal Hc Zn	◆Alpheratz Hc Zn	ALTAIR Hc Zn	◆VEGA Hc Zn
0	30 09 008	42 39 068	24 57 099	48 39 133	61 08 176	22 06 250	36 46 286
1	30 13 008	43 09 069	25 28 100	49 02 134	61 10 178	21 36 251	36 16 287
2	30 18 009	43 38 070	26 00 101	49 24 135	61 10 179	21 05 252	35 45 288
3	30 23 009	44 08 070	26 31 101	49 46 136	61 10 181	20 35 253	35 15 288
4	30 28 010	44 38 071	27 02 102	50 08 138	61 09 183	20 05 254	34 45 289
5	30 34 010	45 08 072	27 33 103	50 29 139	61 07 185	19 34 255	34 15 290
6	30 40 011	45 39 072	28 04 104	50 50 140	61 03 187	19 03 256	33 45 291
7	30 46 011	46 09 073	28 35 105	51 10 142	60 59 188	18 32 257	33 15 291
8	30 52 012	46 39 074	29 05 106	51 29 143	60 54 190	18 01 258	32 46 292
9	30 59 012	47 10 074	29 36 107	51 48 145	60 48 192	17 30 259	32 16 293
10	31 06 013	47 41 075	30 06 108	52 06 146	60 41 194	16 59 259	31 47 294
11	31 13 013	48 11 076	30 36 109	52 23 147	60 33 196	16 28 260	31 18 294
12	31 21 014	48 42 076	31 06 110	52 40 149	60 24 197	15 56 261	30 49 295
13	31 28 015	49 13 077	31 36 111	52 56 150	60 14 199	15 25 262	30 21 296
14	31 36 015	49 44 078	32 06 112	53 12 152	60 03 201	14 53 263	29 52 296

LHA ♈	Dubhe	◆CAPELLA	ALDEBARAN	Hamal	◆Alpheratz	DENEB	◆VEGA
15	31 45 016	50 15 079	32 35 113	53 26 153	59 51 202	49 46 281	29 24 297
16	31 54 016	50 46 079	33 04 114	53 40 155	59 39 204	49 15 281	28 55 298
17	32 03 017	51 18 080	33 34 115	53 53 156	59 25 206	48 44 282	28 27 299
18	32 12 017	51 49 081	34 02 116	54 06 158	59 11 207	48 13 283	27 59 299
19	32 21 018	52 20 081	34 31 117	54 17 159	58 56 209	47 42 284	27 32 300
20	32 31 018	52 52 082	34 59 118	54 28 161	58 40 211	47 11 284	27 04 301
21	32 41 019	53 23 083	35 27 119	54 38 162	58 23 212	46 40 285	26 37 301
22	32 52 019	53 55 084	35 55 120	54 47 164	58 06 214	46 10 286	26 10 302
23	33 02 020	54 27 084	36 22 121	54 56 166	57 48 215	45 39 286	25 43 303
24	33 13 020	54 58 085	36 50 122	55 03 167	57 29 217	45 09 287	25 17 303
25	33 24 021	55 30 086	37 16 123	55 10 169	57 10 218	44 38 288	24 50 304
26	33 36 021	56 02 087	37 43 124	55 16 170	56 50 220	44 08 289	24 24 305
27	33 48 022	56 34 088	38 09 125	55 21 172	56 29 221	43 38 289	23 58 306
28	34 00 022	57 05 089	38 35 126	55 25 174	56 08 223	43 08 290	23 32 306
29	34 12 023	57 37 089	39 00 127	55 28 175	55 46 224	42 38 291	23 07 307

LHA ♈	Dubhe	◆CAPELLA	ALDEBARAN	Hamal	◆Alpheratz	DENEB	◆VEGA
30	34 25 023	58 09 090	39 26 128	55 30 177	55 23 226	42 08 291	22 42 308
31	34 37 024	58 41 091	39 50 129	55 32 178	55 00 227	41 39 292	22 17 308
32	34 50 025	59 12 092	40 15 131	55 32 180	54 37 228	41 09 293	21 52 309
33	35 04 025	59 44 093	40 39 132	55 32 182	54 12 230	40 40 293	21 27 310
34	35 17 026	60 16 094	41 02 133	55 30 183	53 48 231	40 11 294	21 03 311
35	35 31 026	60 48 095	41 25 134	55 28 185	53 23 232	39 42 295	20 39 311
36	35 45 027	61 19 096	41 48 135	55 25 186	52 58 234	39 13 295	20 15 312
37	36 00 027	61 51 096	42 10 136	55 21 188	52 32 235	38 44 296	19 52 313
38	36 14 028	62 23 097	42 32 138	55 16 190	52 06 236	38 16 297	19 29 313
39	36 29 028	62 54 098	42 53 139	55 10 191	51 39 237	37 48 297	19 06 314
40	36 44 029	63 25 099	43 13 140	55 03 193	51 13 238	37 19 298	18 43 315
41	36 59 029	63 57 100	43 34 141	54 56 194	50 45 240	36 51 299	18 21 316
42	37 15 030	64 28 102	43 53 143	54 48 196	50 18 241	36 24 299	17 59 316
43	37 31 030	64 59 103	44 12 144	54 38 198	49 50 242	35 56 300	17 37 317
44	37 47 031	65 30 104	44 31 145	54 28 199	49 22 243	35 28 301	17 15 318

LHA ♈	◆Dubhe	POLLUX	BETELGEUSE	◆ALDEBARAN	Hamal	Alpheratz	◆DENEB
45	38 03 031	33 06 089	29 10 128	44 49 146	54 18 201	48 53 244	35 01 301
46	38 20 032	33 37 090	29 35 129	45 06 148	54 06 202	48 24 245	34 34 302
47	38 36 032	34 09 091	30 00 130	45 23 149	53 54 204	47 55 246	34 07 302
48	38 53 033	34 41 092	30 24 131	45 39 150	53 40 205	47 26 248	33 40 303
49	39 10 033	35 13 093	30 48 132	45 54 152	53 26 207	46 57 249	33 14 304
50	39 28 033	35 45 093	31 11 133	46 09 153	53 12 208	46 27 250	32 47 304
51	39 46 034	36 16 094	31 34 134	46 23 154	52 56 210	45 57 251	32 21 305
52	40 03 034	36 48 095	31 56 135	46 37 156	52 40 211	45 27 252	31 55 306
53	40 22 035	37 20 096	32 19 136	46 49 157	52 23 213	44 57 253	31 30 306
54	40 40 035	37 51 097	32 40 137	47 01 158	52 06 214	44 26 254	31 04 307
55	40 58 036	38 23 098	33 02 139	47 13 160	51 48 215	43 56 255	30 39 308
56	41 17 036	38 54 099	33 22 140	47 23 161	51 29 217	43 25 256	30 14 308
57	41 36 037	39 26 100	33 43 141	47 33 163	51 10 218	42 54 257	29 49 309
58	41 55 037	39 57 101	34 03 142	47 43 164	50 50 220	42 23 258	29 25 310
59	42 15 038	40 28 102	34 22 143	47 51 165	50 29 221	41 52 259	29 00 310

LHA ♈	◆Dubhe	POLLUX	BETELGEUSE	◆ALDEBARAN	Hamal	Alpheratz	◆DENEB
60	42 34 038	40 59 103	34 41 144	47 59 167	50 08 222	41 21 259	28 36 311
61	42 54 039	41 30 104	34 59 145	48 05 168	49 47 223	40 49 260	28 12 312
62	43 14 039	42 01 104	35 17 147	48 12 170	49 25 225	40 18 261	27 49 312
63	43 34 040	42 32 105	35 34 148	48 17 171	49 02 226	39 46 262	27 25 313
64	43 54 040	43 02 106	35 51 149	48 21 172	48 39 227	39 15 263	27 02 314
65	44 15 041	43 33 107	36 07 150	48 25 174	48 15 229	38 43 264	26 39 314
66	44 36 041	44 03 108	36 23 151	48 28 175	47 51 230	38 12 265	26 17 315
67	44 57 041	44 33 109	36 38 152	48 30 177	47 27 231	37 40 266	25 54 316
68	45 18 042	45 03 110	36 52 154	48 32 178	47 02 232	37 08 267	25 32 316
69	45 39 042	45 33 111	37 06 155	48 32 180	46 36 233	36 36 268	25 10 317
70	46 01 043	46 02 113	37 19 156	48 32 181	46 11 235	36 05 268	24 49 318
71	46 22 043	46 31 114	37 32 157	48 31 183	45 45 236	35 33 269	24 27 318
72	46 44 044	47 00 115	37 44 159	48 29 184	45 18 237	35 01 270	24 06 319
73	47 06 044	47 29 116	37 55 160	48 26 186	44 51 238	34 29 271	23 46 320
74	47 29 045	47 58 117	38 06 161	48 23 187	44 24 239	33 58 272	23 25 320

LHA ♈	◆Dubhe	REGULUS	PROCYON	◆SIRIUS	ALDEBARAN	◆Alpheratz	DENEB
75	47 51 045	16 47 094	28 44 133	12 08 154	48 19 188	33 26 273	23 05 321
76	48 14 045	17 19 095	29 07 134	12 21 155	48 14 190	32 54 273	22 45 322
77	48 36 046	17 51 096	29 30 135	12 35 156	48 08 191	32 22 274	22 26 322
78	48 59 046	18 22 097	29 52 136	12 47 157	48 01 193	31 51 275	22 06 323
79	49 22 047	18 54 098	30 14 137	12 59 158	47 54 194	31 19 276	21 47 324
80	49 45 047	19 25 099	30 35 138	13 11 159	47 46 196	30 47 277	21 29 324
81	50 09 048	19 57 100	30 56 139	13 22 160	47 37 197	30 16 278	21 10 325
82	50 32 048	20 28 100	31 17 141	13 33 161	47 27 198	29 44 278	20 52 326
83	50 56 048	20 59 101	31 36 142	13 43 162	47 17 200	29 13 279	20 35 326
84	51 20 049	21 30 102	31 56 143	13 53 163	47 06 201	28 42 280	20 17 327
85	51 44 049	22 01 103	32 15 144	14 02 164	46 54 202	28 10 281	20 00 328
86	52 08 050	22 32 104	32 33 145	14 11 165	46 42 204	27 39 282	19 43 328
87	52 32 050	23 03 105	32 51 146	14 19 166	46 28 205	27 08 282	19 27 329
88	52 57 050	23 34 106	33 09 147	14 26 167	46 15 207	26 37 283	19 10 330
89	53 21 051	24 04 107	33 26 148	14 33 168	46 00 208	26 06 284	18 55 331

LHA ♈	Dubhe	◆REGULUS	PROCYON	SIRIUS	◆ALDEBARAN	Mirfak	◆DENEB
90	53 46 051	24 34 108	33 42 150	14 40 169	45 45 209	66 15 267	18 39 331
91	54 11 052	25 05 109	33 58 151	14 46 170	45 29 211	65 43 268	18 24 332
92	54 36 052	25 35 110	34 13 152	14 51 171	45 13 212	65 12 269	18 09 333
93	55 01 052	26 05 110	34 28 153	14 56 172	44 56 213	64 40 270	17 55 333
94	55 26 053	26 34 111	34 42 154	15 00 173	44 38 214	64 08 270	17 41 334
95	55 52 053	27 04 112	34 55 155	15 04 174	44 20 216	63 36 271	17 27 335
96	56 17 054	27 33 113	35 08 157	15 08 175	44 01 217	63 04 272	17 13 335
97	56 43 054	28 02 114	35 21 158	15 10 176	43 41 218	62 33 273	17 00 336
98	57 09 054	28 31 115	35 32 159	15 12 177	43 21 219	62 01 274	16 48 337
99	57 34 055	29 00 116	35 44 160	15 14 178	43 01 221	61 29 275	16 35 337
100	58 00 055	29 28 117	35 54 161	15 15 179	42 40 222	60 57 275	16 23 338
101	58 27 055	29 56 118	36 04 163	15 16 180	42 19 223	60 26 276	16 12 339
102	58 53 056	30 24 119	36 13 164	15 16 181	41 57 224	59 54 277	16 00 340
103	59 19 056	30 52 120	36 21 165	15 15 182	41 34 225	59 23 278	15 49 340
104	59 46 056	31 19 121	36 29 166	15 14 183	41 11 227	58 51 278	15 39 341

LHA ♈	Alioth	◆REGULUS	PROCYON	BETELGEUSE	◆ALDEBARAN	Mirfak	◆DENEB
105	45 09 053	31 46 122	36 37 168	37 55 200	40 48 228	58 20 279	15 29 342
106	45 34 053	32 13 123	36 43 169	37 44 202	40 24 229	57 48 280	15 19 342
107	46 00 054	32 39 124	36 49 170	37 32 203	40 00 230	57 17 280	15 10 343
108	46 26 054	33 05 125	36 54 171	37 19 204	39 35 231	56 46 281	15 00 344
109	46 51 055	33 31 126	36 59 172	37 06 205	39 10 232	56 15 282	14 52 345
110	47 18 055	33 57 127	37 02 174	36 52 206	38 45 233	55 44 282	14 44 345
111	47 44 056	34 22 129	37 06 175	36 37 208	38 19 235	55 13 283	14 36 346
112	48 10 056	34 46 130	37 08 176	36 22 209	37 53 236	54 42 284	14 28 347
113	48 37 057	35 11 131	37 10 177	36 07 210	37 27 237	54 11 284	14 21 347
114	49 03 057	35 34 132	37 11 179	35 51 211	37 00 238	53 40 285	14 14 348
115	49 30 058	35 58 133	37 11 180	35 34 212	36 33 239	53 09 286	14 08 349
116	49 57 058	36 21 134	37 11 181	35 17 213	36 06 240	52 39 286	14 02 350
117	50 24 059	36 44 135	37 10 182	34 59 215	35 38 241	52 08 287	13 56 350
118	50 52 059	37 06 136	37 08 184	34 41 216	35 10 242	51 38 288	13 51 351
119	51 19 060	37 28 137	37 06 185	34 22 217	34 42 243	51 08 288	13 46 352

LHA ♈	◆Kochab	ARCTURUS	◆REGULUS	PROCYON	BETELGEUSE	◆CAPELLA	DENEB
120	51 36 025	14 00 076	37 49 139	37 03 186	34 02 218	62 51 262	13 42 352
121	51 50 026	14 31 077	38 10 140	36 59 187	33 43 219	62 19 263	13 38 353
122	52 04 026	15 02 078	38 30 141	36 54 189	33 22 220	61 48 264	13 34 354
123	52 18 026	15 33 079	38 50 142	36 49 190	33 01 221	61 16 265	13 31 355
124	52 32 026	16 04 080	39 09 143	36 43 191	32 40 223	60 45 265	13 28 355
125	52 46 027	16 35 080	39 28 144	36 37 192	32 18 224	60 13 266	13 26 356
126	53 00 027	17 07 081	39 46 146	36 30 194	31 56 225	59 41 267	13 24 357
127	53 15 027	17 38 082	40 04 147	36 22 195	31 34 226	59 09 268	13 23 357
128	53 29 027	18 10 083	40 21 148	36 13 196	31 11 227	58 38 269	13 21 358
129	53 44 028	18 41 084	40 37 149	36 04 197	30 47 228	58 06 270	13 21 359
130	53 59 028	19 13 084	40 53 151	35 54 199	30 24 229	57 34 271	13 20 000
131	54 14 028	19 45 085	41 08 152	35 44 200	29 59 230	57 02 272	13 20 000
132	54 29 028	20 16 086	41 23 153	35 33 201	29 35 231	56 30 272	13 21 001
133	54 44 028	20 48 087	41 37 154	35 21 202	29 10 232	55 59 273	13 21 002
134	54 59 029	21 20 088	41 51 156	35 09 203	28 45 233	55 27 274	13 23 003

LHA ♈	DENEB	◆VEGA	ARCTURUS	◆REGULUS	PROCYON	BETELGEUSE	◆CAPELLA
135	13 24 003	11 17 028	21 52 089	42 03 157	34 56 205	28 19 234	54 55 275
136	13 26 004	11 32 028	22 23 090	42 16 158	34 43 206	27 53 235	54 24 276
137	13 29 005	11 47 029	22 55 090	42 27 160	34 28 207	27 27 236	53 52 276
138	13 31 005	12 03 030	23 27 091	42 38 161	34 14 208	27 00 237	53 20 277
139	13 35 006	12 19 031	23 59 092	42 48 162	33 59 209	26 33 238	52 49 278
140	13 38 007	12 35 031	24 31 093	42 57 163	33 43 210	26 06 239	52 17 279
141	13 42 008	12 52 032	25 02 094	43 06 165	33 26 212	25 39 240	51 46 279
142	13 47 008	13 09 033	25 34 095	43 14 166	33 10 213	25 11 241	51 15 280
143	13 51 009	13 27 034	26 06 096	43 21 167	32 52 214	24 43 242	50 43 281
144	13 57 010	13 44 034	26 37 096	43 28 169	32 34 215	24 15 243	50 12 282
145	14 02 010	14 02 035	27 09 097	43 34 170	32 16 216	23 47 244	49 41 282
146	14 08 011	14 21 036	27 40 098	43 39 171	31 57 217	23 18 245	49 10 283
147	14 14 012	14 40 037	28 12 099	43 43 173	31 37 218	22 49 246	48 39 284
148	14 21 013	14 59 037	28 43 100	43 47 174	31 17 219	22 20 247	48 08 284
149	14 28 013	15 18 038	29 15 101	43 50 176	30 57 220	21 51 248	47 37 285

LHA ♈	DENEB	◆VEGA	ARCTURUS	Denebola	◆REGULUS	POLLUX	◆CAPELLA
150	14 36 014	15 38 039	29 46 102	41 52 143	43 52 177	52 02 232	47 07 286
151	14 44 015	15 58 039	30 17 103	42 11 144	43 53 178	51 37 234	46 36 286
152	14 52 015	16 18 040	30 48 104	42 29 146	43 54 180	51 11 235	46 06 287
153	15 01 016	16 39 041	31 19 105	42 47 147	43 53 181	50 45 236	45 36 288
154	15 10 017	17 00 042	31 49 105	43 04 148	43 53 182	50 19 237	45 05 289
155	15 19 018	17 21 042	32 20 106	43 20 149	43 51 184	49 52 238	44 35 289
156	15 29 018	17 43 043	32 50 107	43 36 151	43 48 185	49 24 240	44 05 290
157	15 39 019	18 05 044	33 21 108	43 52 152	43 45 186	48 57 241	43 35 291
158	15 50 020	18 27 045	33 51 109	44 06 153	43 41 188	48 29 242	43 06 291
159	16 01 020	18 49 045	34 21 110	44 20 155	43 37 189	48 01 243	42 36 292
160	16 12 021	19 12 046	34 50 111	44 33 156	43 31 190	47 32 244	42 07 293
161	16 24 022	19 35 047	35 20 112	44 46 157	43 25 192	47 04 245	41 37 293
162	16 36 023	19 58 047	35 49 113	44 58 159	43 18 193	46 35 246	41 08 294
163	16 48 023	20 22 048	36 18 114	45 09 160	43 11 194	46 05 247	40 39 295
164	17 01 024	20 46 049	36 47 115	45 20 161	43 03 196	45 36 248	40 10 295

LHA ♈	◆DENEB	VEGA	ARCTURUS	◆SPICA	REGULUS	◆POLLUX	CAPELLA
165	17 14 025	21 10 050	37 16 116	14 38 143	42 54 197	45 06 249	39 42 296
166	17 27 025	21 34 050	37 44 117	14 57 144	42 44 198	44 36 250	39 13 297
167	17 41 026	21 59 051	38 12 118	15 15 145	42 33 200	44 06 251	38 45 297
168	17 55 027	22 23 052	38 40 119	15 33 146	42 22 201	43 36 252	38 17 298
169	18 10 027	22 49 052	39 08 120	15 51 147	42 11 202	43 06 253	37 49 298
170	18 24 028	23 14 053	39 35 121	16 08 148	41 58 204	42 35 254	37 21 299
171	18 40 029	23 39 054	40 02 123	16 25 149	41 45 205	42 05 255	36 53 300
172	18 55 030	24 05 055	40 29 124	16 41 150	41 31 206	41 34 256	36 26 300
173	19 11 030	24 31 055	40 55 125	16 57 151	41 17 207	41 03 257	35 58 301
174	19 27 031	24 58 056	41 21 126	17 12 152	41 02 209	40 32 258	35 31 302
175	19 44 032	25 24 057	41 47 127	17 27 153	40 47 210	40 00 259	35 04 302
176	20 00 032	25 51 057	42 12 128	17 41 154	40 30 211	39 29 260	34 37 303
177	20 17 033	26 18 058	42 37 129	17 55 155	40 14 212	38 58 261	34 11 304
178	20 35 034	26 45 059	43 01 130	18 09 156	39 56 214	38 26 262	33 44 304
179	20 53 034	27 12 060	43 25 132	18 21 157	39 39 215	37 55 263	33 18 305

LAT 58°N

LHA ♈	Hc Zn	Hc Zn	Hc Zn	Hc Zn	Hc Zn	Hc Zn	Hc Zn
	◆DENEB	VEGA	ARCTURUS	◆SPICA	REGULUS	◆POLLUX	CAPELLA
180	21 11 035	27 39 060	43 49 133	18 34 158	39 20 216	37 23 264	32 52 306
181	21 29 036	28 07 061	44 12 134	18 45 159	39 01 217	36 52 265	32 27 306
182	21 48 036	28 35 062	44 34 135	18 57 160	38 42 218	36 20 266	32 01 307
183	22 07 037	29 03 062	44 56 136	19 07 161	38 22 220	35 48 266	31 36 308
184	22 26 038	29 31 063	45 18 138	19 18 162	38 01 221	35 16 267	31 11 308
185	22 46 038	30 00 064	45 39 139	19 27 163	37 40 222	34 45 268	30 46 309
186	23 06 039	30 28 065	46 00 140	19 36 164	37 19 223	34 13 269	30 21 310
187	23 26 040	30 57 065	46 20 141	19 45 165	36 57 224	33 41 270	29 57 310
188	23 46 040	31 26 066	46 40 143	19 53 166	36 34 225	33 09 271	29 33 311
189	24 07 041	31 55 067	46 59 144	20 00 167	36 12 226	32 38 272	29 09 311
190	24 28 042	32 25 067	47 17 145	20 07 168	35 48 228	32 06 272	28 45 312
191	24 49 042	32 54 068	47 35 147	20 14 169	35 25 229	31 34 273	28 21 313
192	25 11 043	33 24 069	47 52 148	20 19 170	35 01 230	31 02 274	27 58 313
193	25 33 044	33 53 070	48 08 149	20 25 171	34 36 231	30 31 275	27 35 314
194	25 55 044	34 23 070	48 24 151	20 29 172	34 11 232	29 59 276	27 13 315
	◆DENEB	VEGA	Rasalhague	◆ARCTURUS	REGULUS	◆POLLUX	CAPELLA
195	26 17 045	34 53 071	21 44 101	48 39 152	33 46 233	29 27 277	26 50 315
196	26 40 046	35 23 072	22 16 102	48 54 153	33 20 234	28 56 277	26 28 316
197	27 03 046	35 54 072	22 47 103	49 08 155	32 55 235	28 24 278	26 06 317
198	27 26 047	36 24 073	23 18 104	49 21 156	32 28 236	27 53 279	25 44 317
199	27 49 048	36 54 074	23 48 105	49 33 158	32 02 237	27 21 280	25 23 318
200	28 13 048	37 25 075	24 19 106	49 45 159	31 35 238	26 50 281	25 02 319
201	28 37 049	37 56 075	24 49 107	49 56 161	31 08 239	26 19 281	24 41 319
202	29 01 050	38 27 076	25 20 108	50 06 162	30 40 240	25 48 282	24 20 320
203	29 25 050	38 57 077	25 50 109	50 16 163	30 13 241	25 17 283	24 00 321
204	29 50 051	39 29 078	26 20 110	50 24 165	29 45 242	24 46 284	23 40 321
205	30 15 052	40 00 078	26 50 110	50 32 166	29 16 243	24 15 285	23 20 322
206	30 40 052	40 31 079	27 20 111	50 39 168	28 48 244	23 44 285	23 01 323
207	31 05 053	41 02 080	27 49 112	50 45 169	28 19 245	23 14 286	22 42 323
208	31 30 054	41 33 081	28 18 113	50 51 171	27 50 246	22 43 287	22 23 324
209	31 56 054	42 05 081	28 48 114	50 56 172	27 21 247	22 13 288	22 04 325
	◆DENEB	VEGA	Rasalhague	◆ARCTURUS	REGULUS	◆POLLUX	CAPELLA
210	32 22 055	42 36 082	29 16 115	50 59 174	26 52 248	21 43 288	21 46 325
211	32 48 056	43 08 083	29 45 116	51 02 175	26 22 249	21 12 289	21 28 326
212	33 15 056	43 39 084	30 13 117	51 04 177	25 52 250	20 42 290	21 11 327
213	33 41 057	44 11 085	30 42 118	51 06 178	25 22 251	20 13 291	20 53 327
214	34 08 058	44 43 085	31 09 119	51 06 180	24 52 252	19 43 292	20 36 328
215	34 35 058	45 14 086	31 37 120	51 06 181	24 22 253	19 14 292	20 20 329
216	35 02 059	45 46 087	32 04 121	51 05 183	23 51 254	18 44 293	20 03 329
217	35 29 060	46 18 088	32 31 122	51 03 184	23 21 255	18 15 294	19 47 330
218	35 57 060	46 50 089	32 58 123	51 00 186	22 50 255	17 46 295	19 32 331
219	36 24 061	47 22 090	33 25 124	50 56 187	22 19 256	17 17 295	19 16 331
220	36 52 061	47 53 090	33 51 125	50 52 189	21 48 257	16 49 296	19 01 332
221	37 20 062	48 25 091	34 16 126	50 46 190	21 17 258	16 20 297	18 47 333
222	37 48 063	48 57 092	34 42 128	50 40 192	20 46 259	15 52 298	18 32 334
223	38 17 063	49 29 093	35 07 129	50 33 193	20 15 260	15 24 299	18 18 334
224	38 45 064	50 00 094	35 31 130	50 26 195	19 44 261	14 56 299	18 05 335
	DENEB	◆VEGA	Rasalhague	◆ARCTURUS	Denebola	Dubhe	◆CAPELLA
225	39 14 065	50 32 095	35 56 131	50 17 196	33 57 239	61 14 302	17 52 336
226	39 43 065	51 04 096	36 20 132	50 08 198	33 30 240	60 47 303	17 39 336
227	40 12 066	51 35 097	36 43 133	49 58 199	33 02 241	60 21 303	17 26 337
228	40 41 067	52 07 098	37 06 134	49 47 201	32 34 242	59 54 303	17 14 338
229	41 10 067	52 38 098	37 29 135	49 35 202	32 05 243	59 28 304	17 02 338
230	41 40 068	53 10 099	37 51 136	49 23 203	31 37 244	59 01 304	16 50 339
231	42 09 069	53 41 100	38 13 138	49 10 205	31 08 245	58 35 305	16 39 340
232	42 39 069	54 12 101	38 34 139	48 56 206	30 39 246	58 09 305	16 28 340
233	43 09 070	54 43 102	38 55 140	48 42 208	30 10 247	57 43 305	16 18 341
234	43 39 071	55 14 103	39 15 141	48 27 209	29 40 248	57 17 306	16 08 342
235	44 09 072	55 45 104	39 34 142	48 11 210	29 11 249	56 51 306	15 58 343
236	44 39 072	56 16 106	39 54 143	47 55 212	28 41 250	56 25 306	15 49 343
237	45 09 073	56 47 107	40 12 145	47 38 213	28 11 251	56 00 307	15 40 344
238	45 40 074	57 17 108	40 30 146	47 20 214	27 41 252	55 34 307	15 31 345
239	46 10 074	57 47 109	40 48 147	47 02 216	27 10 253	55 09 307	15 23 345
	DENEB	◆VEGA	Rasalhague	◆ARCTURUS	Denebola	Dubhe	◆CAPELLA
240	46 41 075	58 17 110	41 05 148	46 43 217	26 40 254	54 44 308	15 15 346
241	47 12 076	58 47 111	41 21 150	46 23 218	26 09 255	54 19 308	15 08 347
242	47 43 076	59 16 112	41 37 151	46 03 220	25 38 256	53 54 309	15 01 348
243	48 14 077	59 46 113	41 52 152	45 43 221	25 07 257	53 29 309	14 54 348
244	48 45 078	60 15 115	42 07 153	45 22 222	24 36 258	53 05 309	14 48 349
245	49 16 079	60 44 116	42 21 155	45 00 223	24 05 259	52 40 310	14 42 350
246	49 47 079	61 12 117	42 34 156	44 38 225	23 34 259	52 16 310	14 37 350
247	50 18 080	61 40 118	42 47 157	44 16 226	23 03 260	51 52 311	14 31 351
248	50 50 081	62 08 120	42 59 159	43 53 227	22 31 261	51 28 311	14 27 352
249	51 21 082	62 35 121	43 10 160	43 29 228	22 00 262	51 04 311	14 22 353
250	51 53 082	63 02 123	43 21 161	43 05 229	21 28 263	50 40 312	14 18 353
251	52 24 083	63 29 124	43 31 163	42 41 231	20 57 264	50 16 312	14 15 354
252	52 56 084	63 55 125	43 40 164	42 16 232	20 25 265	49 53 313	14 12 355
253	53 27 085	64 21 127	43 48 165	41 51 233	19 54 266	49 30 313	14 09 355
254	53 59 085	64 46 128	43 56 167	41 25 234	19 22 266	49 07 314	14 07 356
	Schedar	DENEB	◆ALTAIR	Rasalhague	◆ARCTURUS	Dubhe	◆CAPELLA
255	35 41 038	54 31 086	31 00 128	44 03 168	41 00 235	48 44 314	14 05 357
256	36 01 038	55 02 087	31 24 129	44 09 169	40 33 236	48 21 314	14 03 358
257	36 21 039	55 34 088	31 49 130	44 15 171	40 07 237	47 58 315	14 02 358
258	36 41 039	56 06 089	32 13 132	44 20 172	39 40 238	47 36 315	14 01 359
259	37 01 040	56 38 089	32 36 133	44 24 173	39 13 239	47 13 316	14 01 000
260	37 21 040	57 09 090	33 00 134	44 27 175	38 45 240	46 51 316	14 01 000
261	37 42 041	57 41 091	33 22 135	44 30 176	38 17 242	46 29 317	14 01 001
262	38 03 042	58 13 092	33 45 136	44 32 177	37 49 243	46 08 317	14 02 002
263	38 24 042	58 45 093	34 07 137	44 33 179	37 21 244	45 46 318	14 03 003
264	38 46 043	59 17 094	34 28 138	44 33 180	36 52 245	45 25 318	14 05 003
265	39 07 043	59 48 095	34 49 139	44 33 181	36 23 246	45 04 318	14 07 004
266	39 29 044	60 20 096	35 10 140	44 31 183	35 54 247	44 43 319	14 09 005
267	39 51 044	60 52 097	35 30 141	44 29 184	35 25 248	44 22 319	14 12 005
268	40 14 045	61 23 098	35 49 143	44 27 186	34 55 249	44 01 320	14 15 006
269	40 36 045	61 55 099	36 08 144	44 23 187	34 26 250	43 41 320	14 19 007

LHA ♈	Hc Zn	Hc Zn	Hc Zn	Hc Zn	Hc Zn	Hc Zn	Hc Zn
	◆CAPELLA	Alpheratz	◆ALTAIR	Rasalhague	◆ARCTURUS	Alkaid	Dubhe
270	14 23 008	23 16 072	36 27 145	44 19 188	33 56 251	53 05 284	43 20 321
271	14 27 008	23 46 073	36 45 146	44 14 190	33 26 252	52 35 285	43 00 321
272	14 32 009	24 16 073	37 02 147	44 08 191	32 56 253	52 04 286	42 40 322
273	14 37 010	24 47 074	37 19 148	44 02 192	32 25 253	51 34 286	42 21 322
274	14 43 010	25 17 075	37 36 150	43 55 194	31 55 254	51 03 287	42 01 323
275	14 49 011	25 48 076	37 51 151	43 47 195	31 24 255	50 33 288	41 42 323
276	14 55 012	26 19 076	38 07 152	43 38 196	30 53 256	50 03 288	41 23 323
277	15 02 013	26 50 077	38 21 153	43 29 198	30 22 257	49 32 289	41 04 324
278	15 09 013	27 21 078	38 35 155	43 19 199	29 51 258	49 02 290	40 46 324
279	15 16 014	27 52 079	38 48 156	43 08 200	29 20 259	48 33 290	40 27 325
280	15 24 015	28 23 080	39 01 157	42 57 202	28 49 260	48 03 291	40 09 325
281	15 32 015	28 55 080	39 13 158	42 44 203	28 17 261	47 33 292	39 51 326
282	15 41 016	29 26 081	39 25 160	42 32 204	27 46 262	47 04 292	39 34 326
283	15 50 017	29 57 082	39 35 161	42 18 206	27 14 263	46 34 293	39 16 327
284	15 59 017	30 29 083	39 46 162	42 04 207	26 43 263	46 05 293	38 59 327
	◆CAPELLA	Alpheratz	◆ALTAIR	Rasalhague	◆ARCTURUS	Alkaid	Dubhe
285	16 09 018	31 01 084	39 55 163	41 50 208	26 11 264	45 36 294	38 42 328
286	16 19 019	31 32 084	40 04 165	41 34 209	25 40 265	45 07 295	38 25 328
287	16 29 020	32 04 085	40 12 166	41 18 211	25 08 266	44 38 295	38 08 329
288	16 40 020	32 36 086	40 19 167	41 02 212	24 36 267	44 10 296	37 52 329
289	16 51 021	33 07 087	40 26 168	40 45 213	24 04 268	43 41 297	37 36 330
290	17 03 022	33 39 088	40 32 170	40 27 214	23 33 269	43 13 297	37 20 330
291	17 15 022	34 11 089	40 37 171	40 09 216	23 01 270	42 45 298	37 04 331
292	17 27 023	34 43 089	40 42 172	39 50 217	22 29 270	42 17 298	36 49 331
293	17 40 024	35 14 090	40 46 174	39 31 218	21 57 271	41 49 299	36 34 332
294	17 53 024	35 46 091	40 49 175	39 11 219	21 25 272	41 21 300	36 19 332
295	18 06 025	36 18 092	40 52 176	38 51 220	20 54 273	40 53 300	36 04 333
296	18 20 026	36 50 093	40 53 178	38 30 222	20 22 274	40 26 301	35 50 333
297	18 34 027	37 21 094	40 54 179	38 09 223	19 50 275	39 59 302	35 36 334
298	18 48 027	37 53 095	40 55 180	37 47 224	19 19 275	39 32 302	35 22 334
299	19 03 028	38 25 095	40 54 181	37 25 225	18 47 276	39 05 303	35 08 335
	CAPELLA	◆Alpheratz	Enif	ALTAIR	◆VEGA	Alphecca	◆Dubhe
300	19 18 029	38 56 096	37 56 147	40 53 183	66 37 224	34 53 265	34 55 335
301	19 33 029	39 28 097	38 13 148	40 51 184	66 15 226	34 21 266	34 41 336
302	19 49 030	40 00 098	38 30 149	40 48 185	65 52 227	33 50 267	34 29 336
303	20 05 031	40 31 099	38 46 150	40 45 187	65 28 229	33 18 268	34 16 337
304	20 21 031	41 02 100	39 01 151	40 41 188	65 04 230	32 46 269	34 04 337
305	20 38 032	41 34 101	39 16 153	40 36 189	64 39 232	32 14 270	33 52 338
306	20 55 033	42 05 102	39 31 154	40 31 191	64 14 233	31 42 270	33 40 338
307	21 12 033	42 36 103	39 44 155	40 25 192	63 48 235	31 11 271	33 28 339
308	21 30 034	43 07 104	39 57 156	40 18 193	63 22 236	30 39 272	33 17 339
309	21 48 035	43 38 105	40 10 158	40 10 194	62 55 238	30 07 273	33 06 340
310	22 06 035	44 08 106	40 22 159	40 02 196	62 28 239	29 35 274	32 55 341
311	22 25 036	44 39 107	40 33 160	39 53 197	62 00 241	29 04 275	32 45 341
312	22 44 037	45 09 108	40 43 161	39 43 198	61 32 242	28 32 275	32 34 342
313	23 03 037	45 39 109	40 53 163	39 33 200	61 04 243	28 00 276	32 25 342
314	23 22 038	46 09 110	41 02 164	39 22 201	60 36 244	27 29 277	32 15 343
	CAPELLA	◆Hamal	Alpheratz	Enif	◆ALTAIR	VEGA	◆Alioth
315	23 42 039	26 36 088	46 39 111	41 11 165	39 10 202	60 07 246	33 12 325
316	24 02 039	27 08 088	47 09 112	41 18 167	38 58 203	59 38 247	32 54 326
317	24 22 040	27 40 089	47 38 113	41 26 168	38 45 205	59 08 248	32 36 326
318	24 43 041	28 12 090	48 07 114	41 32 169	38 32 206	58 39 249	32 18 327
319	25 04 041	28 43 091	48 36 115	41 38 170	38 18 207	58 09 250	32 01 327
320	25 25 042	29 15 092	49 05 116	41 42 172	38 03 208	57 39 252	31 44 328
321	25 46 043	29 47 093	49 33 117	41 47 173	37 48 209	57 09 253	31 27 328
322	26 08 043	30 19 094	50 01 118	41 50 174	37 32 211	56 38 254	31 11 329
323	26 30 044	30 51 094	50 29 120	41 53 176	37 15 212	56 08 255	30 54 330
324	26 52 045	31 22 095	50 57 121	41 55 177	36 58 213	55 37 256	30 39 330
325	27 15 045	31 54 096	51 24 122	41 56 178	36 41 214	55 06 257	30 23 331
326	27 38 046	32 25 097	51 51 123	41 57 180	36 22 215	54 35 258	30 08 331
327	28 01 047	32 57 098	52 17 124	41 56 181	36 04 216	54 04 259	29 52 332
328	28 24 047	33 28 099	52 43 126	41 56 182	35 45 218	53 32 260	29 38 333
329	28 47 048	34 00 100	53 09 127	41 54 184	35 25 219	53 01 261	29 23 333
	CAPELLA	◆Hamal	Alpheratz	Enif	◆ALTAIR	VEGA	◆Alioth
330	29 11 049	34 31 101	53 34 128	41 51 185	35 05 220	52 30 262	29 09 334
331	29 35 049	35 02 102	53 59 130	41 48 186	34 44 221	51 58 263	28 55 334
332	29 59 050	35 33 103	54 23 131	41 44 188	34 23 222	51 27 264	28 41 335
333	30 24 051	36 04 104	54 47 132	41 40 189	34 01 223	50 55 265	28 28 335
334	30 48 051	36 35 104	55 10 134	41 35 190	33 39 224	50 23 265	28 15 336
335	31 13 052	37 06 105	55 33 135	41 29 192	33 17 225	49 52 266	28 02 337
336	31 38 053	37 36 106	55 55 136	41 22 193	32 54 227	49 20 267	27 49 337
337	32 04 053	38 07 107	56 17 138	41 14 194	32 31 228	48 48 268	27 37 338
338	32 29 054	38 37 108	56 38 139	41 06 195	32 07 229	48 16 269	27 25 338
339	32 55 054	39 07 109	56 58 141	40 57 197	31 43 230	47 45 270	27 14 339
340	33 21 055	39 37 110	57 18 142	40 48 198	31 19 231	47 13 271	27 03 340
341	33 47 056	40 07 111	57 37 144	40 38 199	30 54 232	46 41 272	26 52 340
342	34 13 056	40 36 112	57 56 145	40 27 201	30 28 233	46 09 272	26 41 341
343	34 40 057	41 06 113	58 13 147	40 15 202	30 03 234	45 37 273	26 31 341
344	35 07 058	41 35 114	58 30 148	40 03 203	29 37 235	45 06 274	26 21 342
	CAPELLA	ALDEBARAN	◆Hamal	Alpheratz	◆ALTAIR	VEGA	◆Alioth
345	35 34 058	17 01 086	42 04 115	58 47 150	29 11 236	44 34 275	26 11 343
346	36 01 059	17 33 087	42 32 116	59 02 152	28 44 237	44 02 276	26 02 343
347	36 28 060	18 05 088	43 01 118	59 17 153	28 17 238	43 31 276	25 53 344
348	36 56 060	18 37 088	43 29 119	59 31 155	27 50 239	42 59 277	25 44 344
349	37 24 061	19 09 089	43 56 120	59 44 157	27 23 240	42 28 278	25 35 345
350	37 51 062	19 40 090	44 24 121	59 56 158	26 55 241	41 56 279	25 27 346
351	38 19 062	20 12 091	44 51 122	60 08 160	26 27 242	41 25 280	25 20 346
352	38 48 063	20 44 092	45 18 123	60 18 162	25 59 243	40 53 280	25 12 347
353	39 16 064	21 16 093	45 44 124	60 28 163	25 31 244	40 22 281	25 05 347
354	39 45 064	21 47 094	46 10 125	60 36 165	25 02 245	39 51 282	24 58 348
355	40 13 065	22 19 094	46 36 127	60 44 167	24 33 246	39 20 283	24 52 349
356	40 42 066	22 51 095	47 01 128	60 51 169	24 04 247	38 49 283	24 46 349
357	41 11 066	23 22 096	47 26 129	60 56 170	23 35 248	38 18 284	24 40 350
358	41 40 067	23 54 097	47 51 130	61 01 172	23 05 249	37 47 285	24 34 350
359	42 10 068	24 26 098	48 15 131	61 05 174	22 36 250	37 17 286	24 29 351

LHA ♈	Hc	Zn	Hc	Zn	Hc	Zn	Hc	Zn	Hc	Zn	Hc	Zn	Hc	Zn
	Dubhe		◆CAPELLA		ALDEBARAN		Hamal		◆Alpheratz		ALTAIR		◆VEGA	
0	29 10	007	42 16	067	25 06	098	49 19	132	62 08	176	22 26	251	36 29	287
1	29 14	008	42 47	068	25 38	099	49 43	133	62 10	178	21 55	252	35 58	288
2	29 19	009	43 17	069	26 10	100	50 07	134	62 10	179	21 23	253	35 27	288
3	29 24	009	43 47	069	26 43	101	50 30	136	62 10	181	20 52	254	34 56	289
4	29 29	010	44 18	070	27 15	102	50 52	137	62 09	183	20 21	254	34 25	290
5	29 35	010	44 49	071	27 47	103	51 14	138	62 06	185	19 49	255	33 54	291
6	29 41	011	45 20	071	28 18	104	51 36	140	62 03	187	19 18	256	33 24	291
7	29 47	011	45 51	072	28 50	105	51 57	141	61 59	189	18 46	257	32 53	292
8	29 53	012	46 22	073	29 22	105	52 17	142	61 53	191	18 14	258	32 23	293
9	30 00	012	46 53	073	29 53	106	52 36	144	61 47	192	17 42	259	31 53	293
10	30 07	013	47 24	074	30 24	107	52 55	145	61 39	194	17 10	260	31 23	294
11	30 15	013	47 56	075	30 55	108	53 14	147	61 30	196	16 37	261	30 53	295
12	30 22	014	48 27	075	31 26	109	53 31	148	61 21	198	16 05	261	30 24	296
13	30 30	014	48 59	076	31 57	110	53 48	150	61 10	200	15 33	262	29 54	296
14	30 39	015	49 31	077	32 28	111	54 04	151	60 59	201	15 00	263	29 25	297
	Dubhe		◆CAPELLA		ALDEBARAN		Hamal		◆Alpheratz		DENEB		◆VEGA	
15	30 47	015	50 03	077	32 58	112	54 20	153	60 47	203	49 34	282	28 56	298
16	30 56	016	50 35	078	33 28	113	54 34	154	60 33	205	49 02	283	28 27	298
17	31 05	017	51 07	079	33 58	114	54 48	156	60 19	207	48 31	283	27 58	299
18	31 15	017	51 39	079	34 28	115	55 01	157	60 04	208	47 59	284	27 30	300
19	31 24	018	52 11	080	34 57	116	55 13	159	59 48	210	47 27	285	27 02	300
20	31 34	018	52 43	081	35 27	117	55 25	160	59 31	212	46 56	285	26 34	301
21	31 44	019	53 15	082	35 56	118	55 35	162	59 14	213	46 24	286	26 06	302
22	31 55	019	53 48	082	36 24	119	55 45	164	58 56	215	45 53	287	25 38	302
23	32 06	020	54 20	083	36 53	120	55 54	165	58 37	216	45 22	287	25 11	303
24	32 17	020	54 53	084	37 21	121	56 02	167	58 17	218	44 50	288	24 43	304
25	32 28	021	55 25	085	37 49	122	56 09	168	57 56	219	44 19	289	24 16	305
26	32 40	021	55 58	085	38 16	123	56 15	170	57 35	221	43 49	289	23 50	305
27	32 52	022	56 30	086	38 43	124	56 20	172	57 14	222	43 18	290	23 23	306
28	33 04	022	57 03	087	39 10	125	56 24	173	56 51	224	42 47	291	22 57	307
29	33 17	023	57 36	088	39 37	127	56 28	175	56 28	225	42 17	291	22 31	307
	Dubhe		◆CAPELLA		ALDEBARAN		Hamal		◆Alpheratz		DENEB		◆VEGA	
30	33 29	023	58 08	089	40 03	128	56 30	177	56 05	227	41 46	292	22 05	308
31	33 42	024	58 41	089	40 28	129	56 31	178	55 41	228	41 16	293	21 39	309
32	33 56	024	59 14	090	40 53	130	56 32	180	55 16	229	40 46	293	21 14	309
33	34 09	025	59 46	091	41 18	131	56 31	182	54 51	231	40 16	294	20 49	310
34	34 23	025	60 19	092	41 43	132	56 30	183	54 26	232	39 46	295	20 24	311
35	34 37	026	60 52	093	42 07	133	56 28	185	54 00	233	39 17	295	19 59	312
36	34 51	026	61 24	094	42 30	135	56 24	187	53 33	235	38 47	296	19 35	312
37	35 06	027	61 57	095	42 53	136	56 20	188	53 06	236	38 18	297	19 11	313
38	35 21	027	62 29	096	43 16	137	56 15	190	52 39	237	37 49	297	18 47	314
39	35 36	028	63 02	097	43 38	138	56 09	192	52 11	238	37 20	298	18 24	314
40	35 51	028	63 34	097	43 59	139	56 02	193	51 43	240	36 51	299	18 01	315
41	36 07	029	64 07	098	44 20	141	55 54	195	51 15	241	36 22	299	17 38	316
42	36 23	029	64 39	099	44 41	142	55 45	196	50 46	242	35 54	300	17 15	317
43	36 39	030	65 11	101	45 01	143	55 36	198	50 17	243	35 26	300	16 53	317
44	36 55	030	65 43	102	45 20	145	55 25	200	49 48	244	34 58	301	16 31	318
	◆Dubhe		POLLUX		BETELGEUSE		◆ALDEBARAN		Hamal		Alpheratz		◆DENEB	
45	37 12	031	33 04	089	29 47	127	45 38	146	55 14	201	49 19	245	34 30	302
46	37 28	031	33 37	089	30 13	129	45 57	147	55 01	203	48 49	246	34 02	302
47	37 45	032	34 10	090	30 38	130	46 14	148	54 48	204	48 19	247	33 35	303
48	38 03	032	34 42	091	31 03	131	46 31	150	54 34	206	47 48	249	33 07	304
49	38 20	033	35 15	092	31 28	132	46 47	151	54 20	207	47 18	250	32 40	304
50	38 38	033	35 48	093	31 52	133	47 02	152	54 04	209	46 47	251	32 13	305
51	38 56	034	36 20	094	32 16	134	47 17	154	53 48	210	46 16	252	31 47	306
52	39 14	034	36 53	094	32 39	135	47 31	155	53 31	212	45 45	253	31 20	306
53	39 32	034	37 26	095	33 02	136	47 44	157	53 14	213	45 14	254	30 54	307
54	39 51	035	37 58	096	33 24	137	47 57	158	52 56	215	44 42	255	30 28	308
55	40 10	035	38 31	097	33 46	138	48 09	159	52 37	216	44 11	256	30 02	308
56	40 29	036	39 03	098	34 08	139	48 20	161	52 17	218	43 39	257	29 37	309
57	40 48	036	39 35	099	34 29	140	48 31	162	51 57	219	43 07	258	29 11	309
58	41 07	037	40 08	100	34 50	142	48 40	164	51 36	220	42 35	258	28 46	310
59	41 27	037	40 40	101	35 10	143	48 49	165	51 15	222	42 03	259	28 21	311
	◆Dubhe		POLLUX		BETELGEUSE		◆ALDEBARAN		Hamal		Alpheratz		◆DENEB	
60	41 47	038	41 12	102	35 29	144	48 57	167	50 53	223	41 31	260	27 57	311
61	42 07	038	41 44	103	35 48	145	49 04	168	50 30	224	40 59	261	27 32	312
62	42 27	039	42 15	104	36 07	146	49 11	169	50 07	226	40 27	262	27 08	313
63	42 48	039	42 47	105	36 25	147	49 16	171	49 43	227	39 54	263	26 44	313
64	43 08	039	43 19	106	36 42	148	49 21	172	49 19	228	39 22	264	26 21	314
65	43 29	040	43 50	106	36 59	150	49 25	174	48 55	229	38 49	265	25 57	315
66	43 50	040	44 21	107	37 15	151	49 28	175	48 29	231	38 17	266	25 34	315
67	44 12	041	44 52	108	37 31	152	49 30	177	48 04	232	37 44	267	25 11	316
68	44 33	041	45 23	110	37 46	153	49 32	178	47 38	233	37 11	267	24 49	317
69	44 55	042	45 54	111	38 00	155	49 32	180	47 12	234	36 39	268	24 26	317
70	45 16	042	46 25	112	38 14	156	49 32	181	46 45	235	36 06	269	24 04	318
71	45 38	043	46 55	113	38 27	157	49 31	183	46 18	237	35 33	270	23 43	319
72	46 01	043	47 25	114	38 39	158	49 29	184	45 50	238	35 01	271	23 21	319
73	46 23	043	47 55	115	38 51	159	49 26	186	45 23	239	34 28	272	23 00	320
74	46 46	044	48 24	116	39 02	161	49 23	187	44 55	240	33 55	272	22 39	321
	◆Dubhe		REGULUS		PROCYON		◆SIRIUS		ALDEBARAN		◆Alpheratz		DENEB	
75	47 08	044	16 52	094	29 25	133	13 02	154	49 18	189	33 23	273	22 18	321
76	47 31	045	17 24	095	29 49	134	13 16	155	49 13	190	32 50	274	21 58	322
77	47 54	045	17 57	096	30 12	135	13 29	156	49 07	191	32 17	275	21 38	323
78	48 17	045	18 29	097	30 35	136	13 42	157	49 00	193	31 45	276	21 18	323
79	48 41	046	19 02	098	30 58	137	13 55	158	48 52	194	31 12	277	20 59	324
80	49 04	046	19 34	098	31 20	138	14 07	159	48 44	196	30 40	277	20 40	325
81	49 28	047	20 06	099	31 42	139	14 19	160	48 34	197	30 08	278	20 21	325
82	49 52	047	20 39	100	32 03	140	14 30	161	48 24	199	29 35	279	20 03	326
83	50 16	047	21 11	101	32 23	141	14 40	162	48 13	200	29 03	280	19 44	327
84	50 40	048	21 43	102	32 44	142	14 50	163	48 02	201	28 31	280	19 27	327
85	51 04	048	22 15	103	33 03	144	15 00	164	47 50	203	27 59	281	19 09	328
86	51 29	049	22 47	104	33 22	145	15 08	165	47 36	204	27 27	282	18 52	329
87	51 53	049	23 18	105	33 41	146	15 17	166	47 23	206	26 55	283	18 35	329
88	52 18	049	23 50	105	33 59	147	15 25	167	47 08	207	26 23	284	18 19	330
89	52 43	050	24 21	106	34 17	148	15 32	168	46 53	208	25 51	284	18 02	331

LHA ♈	Hc	Zn	Hc	Zn	Hc	Zn	Hc	Zn	Hc	Zn	Hc	Zn	Hc	Zn
	Dubhe		◆REGULUS		PROCYON		SIRIUS		◆ALDEBARAN		Mirfak		◆DENEB	
90	53 08	050	24 53	107	34 34	149	15 39	169	46 37	210	66 17	269	17 47	331
91	53 33	051	25 24	108	34 50	150	15 45	170	46 21	211	65 44	270	17 31	332
92	53 59	051	25 55	109	35 06	152	15 50	171	46 03	212	65 12	271	17 16	333
93	54 24	051	26 25	110	35 21	153	15 55	172	45 46	214	64 39	272	17 01	333
94	54 50	052	26 56	111	35 36	154	16 00	173	45 27	215	64 06	273	16 47	334
95	55 15	052	27 26	112	35 50	155	16 04	174	45 08	216	63 34	273	16 33	335
96	55 41	052	27 57	113	36 03	156	16 07	175	44 49	218	63 01	274	16 19	335
97	56 07	053	28 27	114	36 16	158	16 10	176	44 28	219	62 29	275	16 05	336
98	56 33	053	28 56	115	36 28	159	16 12	177	44 08	220	61 56	276	15 52	337
99	56 59	053	29 26	116	36 40	160	16 14	178	43 46	221	61 23	276	15 40	338
100	57 25	054	29 55	117	36 51	161	16 15	179	43 24	223	60 51	277	15 28	338
101	57 52	054	30 24	118	37 01	162	16 16	180	43 02	224	60 19	278	15 16	339
102	58 18	054	30 53	119	37 11	164	16 16	181	42 39	225	59 46	278	15 04	340
103	58 45	055	31 22	120	37 19	165	16 15	182	42 16	226	59 14	279	14 53	340
104	59 12	055	31 50	121	37 28	166	16 14	183	41 52	227	58 42	280	14 42	341
	Alioth		◆REGULUS		PROCYON		BETELGEUSE		◆ALDEBARAN		Mirfak		◆DENEB	
105	44 32	052	32 18	122	37 35	167	38 51	201	41 28	228	58 10	281	14 32	342
106	44 58	052	32 46	123	37 42	169	38 39	202	41 03	230	57 37	281	14 22	342
107	45 24	053	33 13	124	37 48	170	38 27	203	40 38	231	57 05	282	14 12	343
108	45 50	053	33 40	125	37 53	171	38 14	204	40 13	232	56 34	283	14 03	344
109	46 17	054	34 06	126	37 58	172	38 00	205	39 47	233	56 02	283	13 54	345
110	46 43	054	34 33	127	38 02	174	37 46	207	39 20	234	55 30	284	13 46	345
111	47 10	055	34 59	128	38 05	175	37 31	208	38 54	235	54 58	285	13 37	346
112	47 36	055	35 24	129	38 08	176	37 15	209	38 27	236	54 27	285	13 30	347
113	48 03	056	35 49	130	38 10	177	36 59	210	37 59	237	53 55	286	13 22	347
114	48 31	056	36 14	131	38 11	179	36 42	212	37 32	238	53 24	286	13 16	348
115	48 58	057	36 39	132	38 11	180	36 25	213	37 04	239	52 52	287	13 09	349
116	49 25	057	37 03	133	38 11	181	36 07	214	36 36	241	52 21	288	13 03	350
117	49 53	058	37 26	135	38 10	183	35 48	215	36 07	242	51 50	288	12 57	350
118	50 21	058	37 49	136	38 08	184	35 29	216	35 38	243	51 19	289	12 52	351
119	50 49	059	38 12	137	38 05	185	35 10	217	35 09	244	50 48	290	12 47	352
	◆Kochab		ARCTURUS		◆REGULUS		PROCYON		BETELGEUSE		◆CAPELLA		DENEB	
120	50 42	025	13 45	076	38 34	138	38 02	186	34 50	218	62 59	264	12 43	352
121	50 56	025	14 17	077	38 55	139	37 58	188	34 29	220	62 26	265	12 39	353
122	51 10	025	14 49	078	39 16	140	37 54	189	34 08	221	61 54	265	12 35	354
123	51 24	026	15 21	078	39 37	142	37 48	190	33 46	222	61 21	266	12 32	355
124	51 38	026	15 53	079	39 57	143	37 42	191	33 24	223	60 48	267	12 29	355
125	51 52	026	16 25	080	40 17	144	37 35	193	33 02	224	60 16	268	12 26	356
126	52 07	026	16 58	081	40 35	145	37 28	194	32 39	225	59 43	269	12 24	357
127	52 21	027	17 30	082	40 54	146	37 20	195	32 15	226	59 10	270	12 23	357
128	52 36	027	18 02	082	41 12	148	37 11	196	31 52	227	58 38	271	12 21	358
129	52 51	027	18 35	083	41 29	149	37 01	198	31 27	228	58 05	272	12 21	359
130	53 06	027	19 07	084	41 45	150	36 51	199	31 03	229	57 32	272	12 20	000
131	53 21	027	19 40	085	42 01	151	36 40	200	30 38	230	57 00	273	12 20	000
132	53 36	027	20 12	086	42 17	153	36 29	201	30 12	232	56 27	274	12 21	001
133	53 51	028	20 45	087	42 31	154	36 17	202	29 47	233	55 54	275	12 21	002
134	54 06	028	21 17	087	42 45	155	36 04	204	29 21	234	55 22	275	12 23	003
	DENEB		◆VEGA		ARCTURUS		◆REGULUS		PROCYON		BETELGEUSE		◆CAPELLA	
135	12 24	003	10 24	027	21 50	088	42 59	157	35 51	205	28 54	235	54 49	276
136	12 26	004	10 39	028	22 23	089	43 11	158	35 37	206	28 27	236	54 17	277
137	12 29	005	10 55	029	22 55	090	43 23	159	35 22	207	28 00	237	53 45	278
138	12 32	005	11 11	030	23 28	091	43 34	161	35 07	208	27 33	238	53 12	278
139	12 35	006	11 27	030	24 01	092	43 45	162	34 51	210	27 05	239	52 40	279
140	12 39	007	11 44	031	24 33	092	43 55	163	34 34	211	26 37	240	52 08	280
141	12 43	008	12 01	032	25 06	093	44 04	165	34 17	212	26 09	241	51 36	281
142	12 47	008	12 19	033	25 39	094	44 12	166	34 00	213	25 40	241	51 03	281
143	12 52	009	12 37	033	26 11	095	44 20	167	33 42	214	25 11	242	50 31	282
144	12 57	010	12 55	034	26 44	096	44 27	169	33 23	215	24 42	243	50 00	283
145	13 03	010	13 13	035	27 16	097	44 33	170	33 04	216	24 13	244	49 28	283
146	13 09	011	13 32	036	27 49	098	44 38	171	32 44	218	23 43	245	48 56	284
147	13 16	012	13 51	036	28 21	099	44 43	173	32 24	219	23 13	246	48 24	285
148	13 23	013	14 11	037	28 53	099	44 46	174	32 04	220	22 43	247	47 53	285
149	13 30	013	14 31	038	29 26	100	44 49	175	31 42	221	22 13	248	47 21	286
	DENEB		◆VEGA		ARCTURUS		Denebola		◆REGULUS		POLLUX		◆CAPELLA	
150	13 38	014	14 51	039	29 58	101	42 40	143	44 52	177	52 39	233	46 50	287
151	13 46	015	15 12	039	30 30	102	43 00	144	44 53	178	52 13	235	46 19	287
152	13 54	015	15 32	040	31 02	103	43 19	145	44 54	180	51 46	236	45 48	288
153	14 03	016	15 54	041	31 33	104	43 37	146	44 53	181	51 18	237	45 17	289
154	14 12	017	16 15	041	32 05	105	43 55	148	44 52	182	50 51	238	44 46	289
155	14 22	018	16 37	042	32 36	106	44 12	149	44 51	184	50 23	239	44 15	290
156	14 32	018	16 59	043	33 08	107	44 28	150	44 48	185	49 54	241	43 44	291
157	14 42	019	17 21	044	33 39	108	44 44	152	44 45	186	49 26	242	43 14	291
158	14 53	020	17 44	044	34 10	109	45 00	153	44 41	188	48 57	243	42 44	292
159	15 04	020	18 07	045	34 41	110	45 14	154	44 36	189	48 28	244	42 13	293
160	15 16	021	18 30	046	35 12	111	45 28	156	44 30	191	47 58	245	41 43	293
161	15 28	022	18 54	046	35 42	112	45 41	157	44 24	192	47 28	246	41 13	294
162	15 40	022	19 18	047	36 13	112	45 54	158	44 17	193	46 58	247	40 44	295
163	15 53	023	19 42	048	36 43	113	46 05	160	44 09	195	46 28	248	40 14	295
164	16 06	024	20 06	049	37 12	114	46 16	161	44 00	196	45 58	249	39 45	296
	◆DENEB		VEGA		ARCTURUS		◆SPICA		REGULUS		◆POLLUX		CAPELLA	
165	16 19	025	20 31	049	37 42	116	15 25	143	43 51	197	45 27	250	39 15	297
166	16 33	025	20 56	050	38 11	117	15 45	144	43 41	199	44 56	251	38 46	297
167	16 47	026	21 21	051	38 41	118	16 04	145	43 30	200	44 25	252	38 17	298
168	17 02	027	21 46	051	39 09	119	16 23	146	43 18	201	43 54	253	37 48	299
169	17 16	027	22 12	052	39 38	120	16 41	147	43 06	203	43 22	254	37 20	299
170	17 31	028	22 38	053	40 06	121	16 59	148	42 53	204	42 51	255	36 51	300
171	17 47	029	23 04	054	40 34	122	17 16	149	42 40	205	42 19	256	36 23	300
172	18 03	029	23 30	054	41 02	123	17 33	150	42 25	207	41 47	257	35 55	301
173	18 19	030	23 57	055	41 29	124	17 49	151	42 10	208	41 15	258	35 27	302
174	18 36	031	24 24	056	41 56	125	18 05	152	41 55	209	40 43	259	34 59	302
175	18 52	031	24 51	056	42 22	126	18 20	153	41 39	210	40 11	260	34 32	303
176	19 10	032	25 18	057	42 49	127	18 35	154	41 22	212	39 39	261	34 04	304
177	19 27	033	25 46	058	43 14	129	18 49	155	41 04	213	39 07	262	33 37	304
178	19 45	033	26 13	058	43 40	130	19 03	156	40 46	214	38 34	263	33 10	305
179	20 03	034	26 41	059	44 05	131	19 16	157	40 28	215	38 02	264	32 44	305

LAT 57°N

LHA ♈	Hc	Zn	Hc	Zn	Hc	Zn	Hc	Zn	Hc	Zn	Hc	Zn	Hc	Zn
	◆ DENEB		VEGA		ARCTURUS		◆ SPICA		REGULUS		◆ POLLUX		CAPELLA	
180	20 22	035	27 09	060	44 29	132	19 29	158	40 08	217	37 29	265	32 17	306
181	20 40	035	27 38	060	44 53	133	19 41	159	39 49	218	36 57	265	31 51	307
182	20 59	036	28 06	061	45 17	134	19 53	160	39 29	219	36 24	266	31 25	307
183	21 19	037	28 35	062	45 40	136	20 04	161	39 08	220	35 52	267	30 59	308
184	21 39	037	29 04	063	46 02	137	20 15	162	38 46	221	35 19	268	30 33	309
185	21 59	038	29 33	063	46 24	138	20 25	163	38 25	222	34 46	269	30 08	309
186	22 19	039	30 02	064	46 46	140	20 34	164	38 02	224	34 14	270	29 43	310
187	22 40	039	30 32	065	47 07	141	20 43	165	37 40	225	33 41	271	29 18	311
188	23 01	040	31 01	065	47 27	142	20 51	166	37 16	226	33 08	271	28 53	311
189	23 22	041	31 31	066	47 47	143	20 59	167	36 53	227	32 36	272	28 29	312
190	23 43	041	32 01	067	48 06	145	21 06	168	36 29	228	32 03	273	28 05	313
191	24 05	042	32 31	068	48 25	146	21 13	169	36 04	229	31 30	274	27 41	313
192	24 27	043	33 02	068	48 43	147	21 19	170	35 39	230	30 58	275	27 17	314
193	24 49	043	33 32	069	49 00	149	21 24	171	35 14	231	30 25	275	26 53	314
194	25 12	044	34 03	070	49 16	150	21 29	172	34 48	232	29 53	276	26 30	315
	◆ DENEB		VEGA		Rasalhague		◆ ARCTURUS		REGULUS		◆ POLLUX		CAPELLA	
195	25 35	045	34 33	070	21 56	101	49 32	152	34 22	234	29 20	277	26 07	316
196	25 58	045	35 04	071	22 28	102	49 48	153	33 55	235	28 48	278	25 45	316
197	26 21	046	35 35	072	23 00	103	50 02	154	33 29	236	28 15	279	25 22	317
198	26 45	047	36 06	072	23 32	104	50 16	156	33 02	237	27 43	279	25 00	318
199	27 09	047	36 37	073	24 04	105	50 29	157	32 34	238	27 11	280	24 38	318
200	27 33	048	37 09	074	24 35	105	50 41	159	32 06	239	26 39	281	24 17	319
201	27 57	049	37 40	075	25 07	106	50 52	160	31 38	240	26 07	282	23 55	320
202	28 22	049	38 12	075	25 38	107	51 03	162	31 10	241	25 35	283	23 34	320
203	28 47	050	38 43	076	26 09	108	51 13	163	30 41	242	25 03	283	23 14	321
204	29 12	051	39 15	077	26 40	109	51 22	165	30 12	243	24 31	284	22 53	322
205	29 37	051	39 47	078	27 11	110	51 30	166	29 43	244	24 00	285	22 33	322
206	30 03	052	40 19	078	27 41	111	51 38	168	29 14	245	23 28	286	22 13	323
207	30 29	052	40 51	079	28 12	112	51 44	169	28 44	246	22 57	286	21 54	324
208	30 55	053	41 23	080	28 42	113	51 50	171	28 14	247	22 26	287	21 34	324
209	31 21	054	41 55	081	29 12	114	51 55	172	27 44	248	21 54	288	21 15	325
	◆ DENEB		VEGA		Rasalhague		◆ ARCTURUS		REGULUS		◆ POLLUX		CAPELLA	
210	31 47	054	42 28	081	29 42	115	51 59	174	27 14	248	21 23	289	20 57	326
211	32 14	055	43 00	082	30 11	116	52 02	175	26 43	249	20 53	290	20 38	326
212	32 41	056	43 32	083	30 41	117	52 04	177	26 13	250	20 22	290	20 20	327
213	33 08	056	44 05	084	31 10	118	52 06	178	25 42	251	19 51	291	20 03	328
214	33 35	057	44 37	084	31 39	119	52 06	180	25 11	252	19 21	292	19 45	328
215	34 03	058	45 10	085	32 07	120	52 06	181	24 40	253	18 51	293	19 28	329
216	34 31	058	45 43	086	32 35	121	52 05	183	24 08	254	18 21	293	19 12	330
217	34 58	059	46 15	087	33 03	122	52 03	184	23 37	255	17 51	294	18 55	330
218	35 27	060	46 48	088	33 31	123	52 00	186	23 05	256	17 21	295	18 39	331
219	35 55	060	47 20	088	33 58	124	51 56	188	22 33	257	16 51	296	18 24	332
220	36 23	061	47 53	089	34 25	125	51 51	189	22 01	258	16 22	296	18 08	332
221	36 52	061	48 26	090	34 52	126	51 45	191	21 30	258	15 53	297	17 53	333
222	37 21	062	48 59	091	35 18	127	51 39	192	20 57	259	15 24	298	17 39	334
223	37 50	063	49 31	092	35 44	128	51 32	194	20 25	260	14 55	299	17 24	334
224	38 19	063	50 04	093	36 10	129	51 24	195	19 53	261	14 27	300	17 10	335
	DENEB		◆ VEGA		Rasalhague		◆ ARCTURUS		Denebola		Dubhe		◆ CAPELLA	
225	38 48	064	50 36	094	36 35	130	51 15	197	34 27	240	60 41	304	16 57	336
226	39 18	065	51 09	094	36 59	131	51 05	198	33 59	241	60 14	304	16 44	336
227	39 47	065	51 42	095	37 24	132	50 54	200	33 30	242	59 47	305	16 31	337
228	40 17	066	52 14	096	37 48	134	50 43	201	33 01	243	59 20	305	16 18	338
229	40 47	067	52 47	097	38 11	135	50 31	202	32 32	244	58 54	305	16 06	339
230	41 17	067	53 19	098	38 34	136	50 18	204	32 02	245	58 27	306	15 54	339
231	41 47	068	53 51	099	38 57	137	50 04	205	31 33	246	58 00	306	15 43	340
232	42 17	069	54 23	100	39 19	138	49 50	207	31 03	247	57 34	306	15 32	341
233	42 48	069	54 56	101	39 40	139	49 35	208	30 32	248	57 08	307	15 21	341
234	43 19	070	55 28	102	40 01	141	49 19	210	30 02	249	56 41	307	15 11	342
235	43 49	071	56 00	103	40 22	142	49 03	211	29 32	250	56 15	307	15 01	343
236	44 20	071	56 31	104	40 42	143	48 46	212	29 01	251	55 49	308	14 51	343
237	44 51	072	57 03	105	41 01	144	48 28	214	28 30	252	55 23	308	14 42	344
238	45 22	073	57 34	106	41 20	145	48 09	215	27 59	253	54 58	308	14 33	345
239	45 54	073	58 06	107	41 38	147	47 50	216	27 27	254	54 32	309	14 25	345
	DENEB		◆ VEGA		Rasalhague		◆ ARCTURUS		Denebola		Dubhe		◆ CAPELLA	
240	46 25	074	58 37	108	41 56	148	47 31	218	26 56	255	54 07	309	14 17	346
241	46 56	075	59 08	109	42 13	149	47 10	219	26 24	255	53 41	309	14 09	347
242	47 28	075	59 38	111	42 29	150	46 49	220	25 53	256	53 16	310	14 02	348
243	48 00	076	60 09	112	42 45	152	46 28	222	25 21	257	52 51	310	13 55	348
244	48 31	077	60 39	113	43 00	153	46 06	223	24 49	258	52 26	310	13 49	349
245	49 03	077	61 09	114	43 15	154	45 44	224	24 17	259	52 01	311	13 43	350
246	49 35	078	61 39	116	43 29	156	45 21	225	23 45	260	51 37	311	13 37	350
247	50 07	079	62 08	117	43 42	157	44 57	227	23 13	261	51 12	312	13 32	351
248	50 39	080	62 37	118	43 54	158	44 33	228	22 40	262	50 48	312	13 27	352
249	51 12	080	63 06	119	44 06	160	44 09	229	22 08	263	50 24	312	13 23	353
250	51 44	081	63 34	121	44 17	161	43 44	230	21 36	263	50 00	313	13 19	353
251	52 16	082	64 02	122	44 28	162	43 19	231	21 03	264	49 36	313	13 15	354
252	52 48	082	64 29	124	44 37	164	42 53	232	20 31	265	49 12	314	13 12	355
253	53 21	083	64 56	125	44 46	165	42 27	234	19 58	266	48 48	314	13 09	355
254	53 53	084	65 22	127	44 54	166	42 00	235	19 25	267	48 25	314	13 07	356
	Schedar		DENEB		◆ ALTAIR		Rasalhague		◆ ARCTURUS		Dubhe		◆ CAPELLA	
255	34 54	037	54 26	085	31 37	128	45 02	168	41 34	236	48 02	315	13 05	357
256	35 14	038	54 58	086	32 02	129	45 08	169	41 06	237	47 38	315	13 03	358
257	35 34	038	55 31	086	32 28	130	45 14	170	40 39	238	47 16	316	13 02	358
258	35 54	039	56 04	087	32 52	131	45 19	172	40 11	239	46 53	316	13 01	359
259	36 15	039	56 36	088	33 17	132	45 23	173	39 43	240	46 30	316	13 01	000
260	36 36	040	57 09	089	33 41	133	45 27	175	39 14	241	46 08	317	13 01	000
261	36 57	041	57 42	090	34 05	134	45 30	176	38 46	242	45 46	317	13 01	001
262	37 18	041	58 14	090	34 28	135	45 32	177	38 16	243	45 24	318	13 02	002
263	37 40	042	58 47	091	34 50	137	45 33	179	37 47	244	45 02	318	13 03	003
264	38 01	042	59 20	092	35 13	138	45 33	180	37 18	245	44 40	319	13 05	003
265	38 24	043	59 52	093	35 34	139	45 33	182	36 48	246	44 18	319	13 07	004
266	38 46	043	60 25	094	35 56	140	45 31	183	36 18	247	43 57	319	13 09	005
267	39 08	044	60 57	095	36 17	141	45 29	184	35 47	248	43 36	320	13 12	005
268	39 31	044	61 30	096	36 37	142	45 26	186	35 17	249	43 15	320	13 16	006
269	39 54	045	62 03	097	36 57	143	45 23	187	34 46	250	42 54	321	13 19	007

LHA ♈	Hc	Zn	Hc	Zn	Hc	Zn	Hc	Zn	Hc	Zn	Hc	Zn	Hc	Zn
	◆ CAPELLA		Alpheratz		◆ ALTAIR		Rasalhague		◆ ARCTURUS		Alkaid		Dubhe	
270	13 23	008	22 57	071	37 16	145	45 18	188	34 15	251	52 50	286	42 34	321
271	13 28	008	23 28	072	37 35	146	45 13	190	33 44	252	52 18	286	42 13	322
272	13 33	009	23 59	073	37 53	147	45 07	191	33 13	253	51 47	287	41 53	322
273	13 38	010	24 30	074	38 10	148	45 00	193	32 42	254	51 16	288	41 33	323
274	13 44	010	25 01	074	38 27	149	44 53	194	32 10	255	50 45	288	41 14	323
275	13 50	011	25 33	075	38 44	151	44 45	195	31 39	256	50 14	289	40 54	324
276	13 56	012	26 05	076	38 59	152	44 36	197	31 07	257	49 43	290	40 35	324
277	14 03	012	26 36	077	39 15	153	44 26	198	30 35	258	49 12	290	40 16	324
278	14 10	013	27 08	077	39 29	154	44 15	199	30 03	259	48 42	291	39 57	325
279	14 18	014	27 40	078	39 43	155	44 04	201	29 31	260	48 11	291	39 38	325
280	14 26	015	28 12	079	39 56	157	43 52	202	28 59	260	47 41	292	39 20	326
281	14 34	015	28 44	080	40 09	158	43 40	203	28 27	261	47 11	293	39 01	326
282	14 43	016	29 17	081	40 21	159	43 26	205	27 54	262	46 40	293	38 43	327
283	14 52	017	29 49	081	40 32	161	43 12	206	27 22	263	46 11	294	38 26	327
284	15 02	017	30 21	082	40 43	162	42 58	207	26 49	264	45 41	294	38 08	328
	◆ CAPELLA		Alpheratz		◆ ALTAIR		Rasalhague		◆ ARCTURUS		Alkaid		Dubhe	
285	15 12	018	30 54	083	40 53	163	42 42	209	26 17	265	45 11	295	37 51	328
286	15 22	019	31 26	084	41 02	164	42 26	210	25 44	266	44 41	296	37 34	329
287	15 33	019	31 59	085	41 10	166	42 10	211	25 12	267	44 12	296	37 17	329
288	15 44	020	32 31	085	41 18	167	41 53	212	24 39	267	43 43	297	37 00	330
289	15 55	021	33 04	086	41 25	168	41 35	214	24 06	268	43 14	297	36 44	330
290	16 07	022	33 36	087	41 31	170	41 17	215	23 34	269	42 45	298	36 28	331
291	16 19	022	34 09	088	41 37	171	40 58	216	23 01	270	42 16	299	36 12	331
292	16 32	023	34 42	089	41 41	172	40 38	217	22 28	271	41 48	299	35 56	332
293	16 45	024	35 14	090	41 46	174	40 18	218	21 56	272	41 19	300	35 41	332
294	16 58	024	35 47	090	41 49	175	39 57	220	21 23	272	40 51	300	35 26	333
295	17 12	025	36 20	091	41 51	176	39 36	221	20 50	273	40 23	301	35 11	333
296	17 26	026	36 52	092	41 53	178	39 15	222	20 18	274	39 55	302	34 56	334
297	17 40	026	37 25	093	41 54	179	38 53	223	19 45	275	39 27	302	34 42	334
298	17 55	027	37 58	094	41 55	180	38 30	224	19 13	276	39 00	303	34 28	335
299	18 10	028	38 30	095	41 54	181	38 07	225	18 40	277	38 32	303	34 14	335
	CAPELLA		◆ Alpheratz		Enif		ALTAIR		◆ VEGA		Alphecca		◆ Dubhe	
300	18 25	028	39 03	096	38 46	146	41 53	183	67 20	225	34 58	266	34 00	336
301	18 41	029	39 35	096	39 03	147	41 51	184	66 56	227	34 25	267	33 47	336
302	18 57	030	40 08	097	39 21	148	41 48	185	66 32	229	33 52	268	33 34	337
303	19 13	030	40 40	098	39 38	150	41 45	187	66 07	231	33 20	268	33 21	337
304	19 30	031	41 12	099	39 54	151	41 40	188	65 41	232	32 47	269	33 08	338
305	19 47	032	41 45	100	40 09	152	41 35	189	65 15	234	32 14	270	32 56	338
306	20 05	032	42 17	101	40 24	153	41 30	191	64 49	235	31 42	271	32 44	339
307	20 22	033	42 49	102	40 39	155	41 23	192	64 22	237	31 09	272	32 32	339
308	20 40	034	43 21	103	40 52	156	41 16	193	63 54	238	30 36	273	32 21	340
309	20 59	034	43 52	104	41 05	157	41 08	195	63 26	240	30 04	273	32 09	340
310	21 17	035	44 24	105	41 18	159	41 00	196	62 58	241	29 31	274	31 58	341
311	21 36	036	44 56	106	41 29	160	40 50	197	62 29	242	28 59	275	31 48	341
312	21 56	036	45 27	107	41 40	161	40 40	199	62 00	244	28 26	276	31 37	342
313	22 15	037	45 58	108	41 50	162	40 29	200	61 31	245	27 54	277	31 27	342
314	22 35	038	46 29	109	42 00	164	40 18	201	61 01	246	27 21	278	31 18	343
	CAPELLA		◆ Hamal		Alpheratz		Enif		◆ ALTAIR		VEGA		◆ Alioth	
315	22 55	038	26 34	087	47 00	110	42 09	165	40 06	202	60 31	247	32 22	325
316	23 16	039	27 06	088	47 31	111	42 17	166	39 53	204	60 00	248	32 04	326
317	23 36	040	27 39	089	48 01	112	42 24	168	39 40	205	59 30	250	31 46	327
318	23 57	040	28 12	090	48 31	113	42 31	169	39 26	206	58 59	251	31 28	327
319	24 19	041	28 44	090	49 01	114	42 37	170	39 11	207	58 28	252	31 10	328
320	24 40	042	29 17	091	49 31	115	42 42	172	38 56	209	57 57	253	30 53	328
321	25 02	042	29 50	092	50 00	116	42 46	173	38 40	210	57 26	254	30 36	329
322	25 24	043	30 22	093	50 30	117	42 50	174	38 23	211	56 54	255	30 19	329
323	25 47	044	30 55	094	50 58	119	42 53	176	38 06	212	56 23	256	30 03	330
324	26 10	044	31 27	095	51 27	120	42 55	177	37 48	213	55 51	257	29 46	330
325	26 32	045	32 00	096	51 55	121	42 56	178	37 30	215	55 19	258	29 30	331
326	26 56	046	32 33	096	52 23	122	42 57	180	37 11	216	54 47	259	29 15	332
327	27 19	046	33 05	097	52 50	123	42 56	181	36 52	217	54 15	260	28 59	332
328	27 43	047	33 37	098	53 18	125	42 55	182	36 32	218	53 42	261	28 44	333
329	28 07	048	34 10	099	53 44	126	42 54	184	36 12	219	53 10	262	28 29	333
	CAPELLA		◆ Hamal		Alpheratz		Enif		◆ ALTAIR		VEGA		◆ Alioth	
330	28 31	048	34 42	100	54 11	127	42 51	185	35 51	220	52 38	263	28 15	334
331	28 56	049	35 14	101	54 36	128	42 48	186	35 29	222	52 05	264	28 01	334
332	29 20	049	35 46	102	55 02	130	42 44	188	35 07	223	51 33	265	27 47	335
333	29 45	050	36 18	103	55 27	131	42 39	189	34 45	224	51 00	266	27 33	336
334	30 10	051	36 50	104	55 51	133	42 34	190	34 22	225	50 27	267	27 20	336
335	30 36	051	37 21	105	56 15	134	42 27	192	33 59	226	49 55	268	27 07	337
336	31 02	052	37 53	106	56 38	135	42 20	193	33 35	227	49 22	268	26 54	337
337	31 27	053	38 24	107	57 01	137	42 13	194	33 11	228	48 49	269	26 42	338
338	31 54	053	38 56	108	57 23	138	42 04	196	32 46	229	48 17	270	26 30	339
339	32 20	054	39 27	109	57 44	140	41 55	197	32 22	230	47 44	271	26 18	339
340	32 46	055	39 58	110	58 05	141	41 45	198	31 56	231	47 11	272	26 06	340
341	33 13	055	40 28	110	58 25	143	41 34	200	31 30	232	46 39	273	25 55	340
342	33 40	056	40 59	112	58 45	144	41 23	201	31 04	233	46 06	273	25 44	341
343	34 07	056	41 29	113	59 03	146	41 11	202	30 38	234	45 34	274	25 34	342
344	34 34	057	41 59	114	59 21	147	40 58	203	30 11	235	45 01	275	25 24	342
	CAPELLA		ALDEBARAN		◆ Hamal		Alpheratz		◆ ALTAIR		VEGA		◆ Alioth	
345	35 02	058	16 57	086	42 29	115	59 38	149	29 44	236	44 28	276	25 14	343
346	35 30	058	17 30	086	42 59	116	59 55	151	29 17	237	43 56	277	25 04	343
347	35 58	059	18 02	087	43 28	117	60 10	152	28 49	238	43 24	277	24 55	344
348	36 26	060	18 35	088	43 57	118	60 25	154	28 21	239	42 51	278	24 46	344
349	36 54	060	19 08	089	44 26	119	60 39	156	27 53	240	42 19	279	24 37	345
350	37 23	061	19 40	090	44 54	120	60 52	158	27 24	241	41 47	280	24 29	346
351	37 51	062	20 13	091	45 22	121	61 04	159	26 55	242	41 14	280	24 21	346
352	38 20	062	20 46	091	45 50	122	61 15	161	26 26	243	40 42	281	24 14	347
353	38 49	063	21 18	092	46 18	123	61 25	163	25 57	244	40 10	282	24 06	347
354	39 18	063	21 51	093	46 45	125	61 34	165	25 27	245	39 38	283	24 00	348
355	39 47	064	22 23	094	47 11	126	61 42	166	24 58	246	39 06	283	23 53	349
356	40 17	065	22 56	095	47 38	127	61 49	168	24 28	247	38 35	284	23 47	349
357	40 47	065	23 29	096	48 04	128	61 56	170	23 57	248	38 03	285	23 41	350
358	41 16	066	24 01	097	48 29	129	62 01	172	23 27	249	37 32	286	23 35	350
359	41 46	067	24 34	097	48 54	131	62 05	174	22 56	250	37 00	286	23 30	351

LAT 56°N

LHA ♈	Hc	Zn	Hc	Zn	Hc	Zn	Hc	Zn	Hc	Zn	Hc	Zn	Hc	Zn
	Dubhe		◆ CAPELLA		ALDEBARAN		Hamal		◆ Alpheratz		ALTAIR		◆ VEGA	
0	28 10	007	41 53	066	25 14	098	49 59	131	63 07	176	22 45	251	36 11	288
1	28 15	008	42 24	067	25 48	099	50 24	132	63 09	178	22 13	252	35 39	288
2	28 19	008	42 55	068	26 21	100	50 48	133	63 10	179	21 41	253	35 07	289
3	28 25	009	43 26	068	26 54	100	51 12	135	63 10	181	21 09	254	34 36	290
4	28 30	010	43 57	069	27 27	101	51 36	136	63 09	183	20 37	255	34 04	290
5	28 36	010	44 28	070	27 59	102	51 59	137	63 06	185	20 04	256	33 33	291
6	28 42	011	45 00	070	28 32	103	52 21	139	63 03	187	19 32	257	33 02	292
7	28 48	011	45 32	071	29 05	104	52 43	140	62 58	189	18 59	257	32 30	293
8	28 55	012	46 03	072	29 37	105	53 04	142	62 52	191	18 26	258	32 00	293
9	29 01	012	46 35	072	30 10	106	53 25	143	62 45	193	17 53	259	31 29	294
10	29 09	013	47 07	073	30 42	107	53 44	144	62 37	195	17 20	260	30 58	295
11	29 16	013	47 39	074	31 14	108	54 04	146	62 28	197	16 47	261	30 28	295
12	29 24	014	48 12	074	31 46	109	54 22	147	62 18	198	16 14	262	29 58	296
13	29 32	014	48 44	075	32 18	110	54 40	149	62 07	200	15 41	263	29 28	297
14	29 41	015	49 16	076	32 49	111	54 57	150	61 55	202	15 07	263	28 58	297
	Dubhe		◆ CAPELLA		ALDEBARAN		Hamal		◆ Alpheratz		DENEB		◆ VEGA	
15	29 49	015	49 49	076	33 20	111	55 13	152	61 42	204	49 21	283	28 28	298
16	29 58	016	50 22	077	33 51	112	55 28	154	61 27	206	48 49	284	27 58	299
17	30 08	016	50 54	078	34 22	113	55 43	155	61 12	207	48 16	284	27 29	299
18	30 17	017	51 27	078	34 53	114	55 56	157	60 57	209	47 44	285	27 00	300
19	30 27	017	52 00	079	35 23	115	56 09	158	60 40	211	47 11	286	26 31	301
20	30 37	018	52 33	080	35 54	116	56 21	160	60 22	212	46 39	286	26 02	302
21	30 48	018	53 06	080	36 24	117	56 32	161	60 04	214	46 07	287	25 34	302
22	30 58	019	53 39	081	36 53	118	56 43	163	59 45	216	45 35	288	25 06	303
23	31 09	019	54 12	082	37 23	119	56 52	165	59 25	217	45 03	288	24 38	304
24	31 21	020	54 46	082	37 52	121	57 00	166	59 04	219	44 31	289	24 10	304
25	31 32	020	55 19	083	38 20	122	57 08	168	58 42	220	44 00	290	23 42	305
26	31 44	021	55 52	084	38 49	123	57 14	170	58 20	222	43 28	290	23 15	306
27	31 56	021	56 26	085	39 17	124	57 19	171	57 58	223	42 57	291	22 48	306
28	32 09	022	56 59	085	39 45	125	57 24	173	57 34	225	42 25	292	22 21	307
29	32 21	022	57 32	086	40 12	126	57 27	175	57 10	226	41 54	292	21 54	308
	Dubhe		◆ CAPELLA		ALDEBARAN		Hamal		◆ Alpheratz		DENEB		◆ VEGA	
30	32 34	023	58 06	087	40 39	127	57 30	177	56 46	228	41 23	293	21 28	308
31	32 47	023	58 39	088	41 06	128	57 31	178	56 20	229	40 53	294	21 01	309
32	33 01	024	59 13	089	41 32	129	57 32	180	55 55	231	40 22	294	20 36	310
33	33 15	024	59 47	089	41 58	130	57 31	182	55 29	232	39 51	295	20 10	310
34	33 29	025	60 20	090	42 23	132	57 30	183	55 02	233	39 21	295	19 44	311
35	33 43	025	60 54	091	42 48	133	57 27	185	54 35	235	38 51	296	19 19	312
36	33 58	026	61 27	092	43 12	134	57 24	187	54 07	236	38 21	297	18 55	313
37	34 12	026	62 01	093	43 36	135	57 20	189	53 39	237	37 51	297	18 30	313
38	34 27	027	62 34	094	43 59	136	57 14	190	53 11	238	37 21	298	18 06	314
39	34 43	027	63 08	095	44 22	138	57 08	192	52 42	239	36 51	299	17 42	315
40	34 58	028	63 41	095	44 45	139	57 00	194	52 13	241	36 22	299	17 18	315
41	35 14	028	64 14	096	45 06	140	56 52	195	51 44	242	35 53	300	16 55	316
42	35 30	029	64 48	097	45 28	141	56 43	197	51 14	243	35 24	300	16 31	317
43	35 46	029	65 21	098	45 48	143	56 33	198	50 44	244	34 55	301	16 09	318
44	36 03	030	65 54	099	46 08	144	56 21	200	50 14	245	34 26	302	15 46	318
	◆ Dubhe		POLLUX		BETELGEUSE		◆ ALDEBARAN		Hamal		Alpheratz		◆ DENEB	
45	36 20	030	33 03	088	30 23	127	46 28	145	56 09	202	49 43	246	33 58	302
46	36 37	031	33 36	089	30 50	128	46 47	147	55 57	203	49 12	247	33 30	303
47	36 54	031	34 10	090	31 16	129	47 05	148	55 43	205	48 41	249	33 02	304
48	37 12	032	34 43	090	31 42	130	47 22	149	55 28	206	48 10	250	32 34	304
49	37 29	032	35 17	091	32 07	131	47 39	151	55 13	208	47 38	251	32 06	305
50	37 47	033	35 50	092	32 32	132	47 55	152	54 57	210	47 07	252	31 39	305
51	38 05	033	36 24	093	32 57	133	48 11	153	54 40	211	46 35	253	31 11	306
52	38 24	034	36 57	094	33 21	134	48 26	155	54 22	213	46 03	254	30 44	307
53	38 43	034	37 31	095	33 45	135	48 39	156	54 04	214	45 30	255	30 18	307
54	39 01	034	38 04	095	34 08	137	48 53	158	53 45	215	44 58	256	29 51	308
55	39 21	035	38 38	096	34 31	138	49 05	159	53 25	217	44 25	257	29 25	309
56	39 40	035	39 11	097	34 53	139	49 17	160	53 04	218	43 53	258	28 59	309
57	39 59	036	39 44	098	35 15	140	49 28	162	52 43	220	43 20	258	28 33	310
58	40 19	036	40 17	099	35 36	141	49 38	163	52 21	221	42 47	259	28 07	311
59	40 39	037	40 50	100	35 57	142	49 47	165	51 59	223	42 14	260	27 42	311
	◆ Dubhe		POLLUX		BETELGEUSE		◆ ALDEBARAN		Hamal		Alpheratz		◆ DENEB	
60	40 59	037	41 23	101	36 18	143	49 55	166	51 36	224	41 41	261	27 17	312
61	41 20	038	41 56	102	36 37	145	50 03	168	51 13	225	41 08	262	26 52	312
62	41 40	038	42 29	103	36 57	146	50 10	169	50 48	226	40 34	263	26 27	313
63	42 01	038	43 02	104	37 15	147	50 15	171	50 24	228	40 01	264	26 03	314
64	42 22	039	43 34	105	37 33	148	50 20	172	49 59	229	39 28	265	25 39	314
65	42 43	039	44 07	106	37 51	149	50 25	174	49 33	230	38 54	266	25 15	315
66	43 04	040	44 39	107	38 07	150	50 28	175	49 07	232	38 21	266	24 51	316
67	43 26	040	45 11	108	38 24	152	50 30	177	48 41	233	37 47	267	24 28	316
68	43 48	041	45 43	109	38 39	153	50 32	178	48 14	234	37 14	268	24 05	317
69	44 10	041	46 15	110	38 54	154	50 32	180	47 46	235	36 40	269	23 42	318
70	44 32	041	46 46	111	39 08	155	50 32	181	47 19	236	36 07	270	23 20	318
71	44 54	042	47 17	112	39 22	157	50 31	183	46 51	238	35 33	271	22 57	319
72	45 16	042	47 49	113	39 35	158	50 29	184	46 22	239	34 59	272	22 35	320
73	45 39	043	48 19	114	39 47	159	50 26	186	45 53	240	34 26	272	22 14	320
74	46 02	043	48 50	115	39 59	160	50 22	187	45 24	241	33 52	273	21 53	321
	◆ Dubhe		REGULUS		PROCYON		◆ SIRIUS		ALDEBARAN		◆ Alpheratz		DENEB	
75	46 25	043	16 56	094	30 06	132	13 56	154	50 17	189	33 19	274	21 31	321
76	46 48	044	17 29	095	30 30	133	14 10	155	50 12	190	32 45	275	21 11	322
77	47 11	044	18 03	095	30 54	134	14 24	156	50 06	192	32 12	276	20 50	323
78	47 35	045	18 36	096	31 18	135	14 38	157	49 58	193	31 39	276	20 30	323
79	47 59	045	19 09	097	31 42	137	14 51	158	49 50	195	31 05	277	20 10	324
80	48 23	045	19 43	098	32 04	138	15 03	159	49 41	196	30 32	278	19 51	325
81	48 47	046	20 16	099	32 27	139	15 15	160	49 32	198	29 59	279	19 32	325
82	49 11	046	20 49	100	32 49	140	15 26	161	49 21	199	29 26	279	19 13	326
83	49 35	047	21 22	101	33 10	141	15 37	162	49 10	200	28 53	280	18 54	327
84	49 59	047	21 55	101	33 31	142	15 47	163	48 58	202	28 20	281	18 36	327
85	50 24	047	22 28	102	33 51	143	15 57	164	48 45	203	27 47	282	18 18	328
86	50 49	048	23 01	103	34 11	144	16 06	165	48 31	205	27 14	283	18 01	329
87	51 14	048	23 33	104	34 31	145	16 15	166	48 17	206	26 41	283	17 43	329
88	51 39	048	24 06	105	34 49	147	16 23	167	48 02	208	26 09	284	17 27	330
89	52 04	049	24 38	106	35 08	148	16 30	168	47 46	209	25 36	285	17 10	331

LHA ♈	Hc	Zn	Hc	Zn	Hc	Zn	Hc	Zn	Hc	Zn	Hc	Zn	Hc	Zn
	Dubhe		◆ REGULUS		PROCYON		SIRIUS		◆ ALDEBARAN		Mirfak		◆ DENEB	
90	52 29	049	25 10	107	35 25	149	16 37	169	47 29	210	66 17	272	16 54	332
91	52 55	050	25 42	108	35 42	150	16 44	170	47 12	212	65 43	272	16 38	332
92	53 20	050	26 14	109	35 59	151	16 50	171	46 54	213	65 10	273	16 23	333
93	53 46	050	26 46	110	36 15	152	16 55	172	46 35	214	64 36	274	16 07	334
94	54 12	051	27 17	110	36 30	154	16 59	173	46 16	216	64 03	275	15 53	334
95	54 38	051	27 49	111	36 44	155	17 04	174	45 56	217	63 29	275	15 38	335
96	55 04	051	28 20	112	36 58	156	17 07	175	45 36	218	62 56	276	15 24	336
97	55 30	052	28 51	113	37 12	157	17 10	176	45 15	219	62 22	277	15 11	336
98	55 56	052	29 21	114	37 24	158	17 12	177	44 53	221	61 49	277	14 57	337
99	56 23	052	29 52	115	37 36	160	17 14	178	44 31	222	61 16	278	14 44	338
100	56 49	052	30 22	116	37 48	161	17 15	179	44 08	223	60 43	279	14 32	338
101	57 16	053	30 52	117	37 58	162	17 16	180	43 45	224	60 10	280	14 20	339
102	57 43	053	31 22	118	38 08	163	17 16	181	43 22	226	59 37	280	14 08	340
103	58 10	053	31 51	119	38 17	165	17 15	182	42 57	227	59 04	281	13 56	340
104	58 37	054	32 20	120	38 26	166	17 14	183	42 33	228	58 31	281	13 45	341
	Alioth		◆ REGULUS		PROCYON		BETELGEUSE		◆ ALDEBARAN		Mirfak		◆ DENEB	
105	43 55	051	32 49	121	38 34	167	39 47	201	42 07	229	57 58	282	13 35	342
106	44 21	052	33 18	122	38 41	168	39 35	202	41 42	230	57 25	283	13 25	343
107	44 48	052	33 46	123	38 47	170	39 22	203	41 16	231	56 52	283	13 15	343
108	45 14	053	34 14	124	38 53	171	39 08	205	40 49	233	56 20	284	13 05	344
109	45 41	053	34 41	125	38 58	172	38 54	206	40 23	234	55 47	285	12 56	345
110	46 08	054	35 09	126	39 02	174	38 39	207	39 55	235	55 15	285	12 47	345
111	46 35	054	35 35	127	39 05	175	38 23	208	39 28	236	54 42	286	12 39	346
112	47 02	055	36 02	129	39 08	176	38 07	210	39 00	237	54 10	286	12 31	347
113	47 29	055	36 28	130	39 10	177	37 50	211	38 32	238	53 38	287	12 24	348
114	47 57	055	36 54	131	39 11	179	37 33	212	38 03	239	53 06	288	12 17	348
115	48 25	056	37 19	132	39 11	180	37 15	213	37 34	240	52 34	288	12 10	349
116	48 53	056	37 44	133	39 11	181	36 56	214	37 05	241	52 02	289	12 04	350
117	49 21	057	38 08	134	39 10	183	36 37	215	36 35	242	51 31	289	11 58	350
118	49 49	057	38 32	135	39 08	184	36 17	217	36 05	243	50 59	290	11 53	351
119	50 17	058	38 55	136	39 05	185	35 57	218	35 35	244	50 28	291	11 48	352
	◆ Kochab		ARCTURUS		◆ REGULUS		PROCYON		BETELGEUSE		◆ CAPELLA		DENEB	
120	49 47	024	13 31	076	39 18	138	39 02	186	35 36	219	63 04	266	11 43	352
121	50 01	025	14 03	077	39 41	139	38 58	188	35 15	220	62 31	266	11 39	353
122	50 15	025	14 36	077	40 02	140	38 53	189	34 53	221	61 57	267	11 35	354
123	50 30	025	15 09	078	40 24	141	38 47	190	34 31	222	61 24	268	11 32	355
124	50 44	025	15 42	079	40 45	142	38 41	191	34 08	223	60 50	269	11 29	355
125	50 58	026	16 15	080	41 05	143	38 34	193	33 45	225	60 17	270	11 26	356
126	51 13	026	16 48	081	41 25	145	38 26	194	33 21	226	59 43	271	11 24	357
127	51 28	026	17 21	081	41 44	146	38 18	195	32 57	227	59 10	272	11 23	358
128	51 42	026	17 54	082	42 02	147	38 08	197	32 32	228	58 36	272	11 21	358
129	51 57	026	18 27	083	42 20	148	37 59	198	32 07	229	58 03	273	11 21	359
130	52 12	027	19 01	084	42 37	150	37 48	199	31 42	230	57 29	274	11 20	000
131	52 27	027	19 34	085	42 54	151	37 37	200	31 16	231	56 56	275	11 20	000
132	52 42	027	20 08	085	43 10	152	37 25	201	30 50	232	56 22	275	11 21	001
133	52 57	027	20 41	086	43 25	154	37 12	203	30 23	233	55 49	276	11 21	002
134	53 13	027	21 15	087	43 40	155	36 59	204	29 56	234	55 15	277	11 23	003
	DENEB		◆ Kochab		ARCTURUS		◆ REGULUS		PROCYON		BETELGEUSE		◆ CAPELLA	
135	11 24	003	53 28	027	21 48	088	43 54	156	36 45	205	29 29	235	54 42	278
136	11 26	004	53 44	028	22 22	089	44 07	158	36 30	206	29 01	236	54 09	278
137	11 29	005	53 59	028	22 55	090	44 19	159	36 15	208	28 33	237	53 36	279
138	11 32	005	54 15	028	23 29	090	44 31	160	35 59	209	28 05	238	53 03	280
139	11 35	006	54 30	028	24 02	091	44 42	162	35 43	210	27 36	239	52 30	280
140	11 39	007	54 46	028	24 36	092	44 52	163	35 26	211	27 07	240	51 57	281
141	11 43	008	55 02	028	25 09	093	45 02	164	35 08	212	26 38	241	51 24	282
142	11 48	008	55 18	028	25 43	094	45 10	166	34 50	213	26 09	242	50 51	283
143	11 53	009	55 34	028	26 16	095	45 18	167	34 31	215	25 39	243	50 18	283
144	11 58	010	55 50	029	26 50	095	45 25	168	34 12	216	25 09	244	49 46	284
145	12 04	010	56 06	029	27 23	096	45 32	170	33 52	217	24 39	245	49 13	285
146	12 10	011	56 22	029	27 56	097	45 37	171	33 32	218	24 08	246	48 41	285
147	12 17	012	56 38	029	28 30	098	45 42	173	33 11	219	23 37	247	48 08	286
148	12 24	013	56 55	029	29 03	099	45 46	174	32 50	220	23 06	248	47 36	287
149	12 32	013	57 11	029	29 36	100	45 49	175	32 28	221	22 35	248	47 04	287
	DENEB		◆ VEGA		ARCTURUS		Denebola		◆ REGULUS		POLLUX		◆ CAPELLA	
150	12 39	014	14 04	038	30 09	101	43 28	142	45 51	177	53 14	234	46 32	288
151	12 48	015	14 25	039	30 42	102	43 48	143	45 53	178	52 47	236	46 00	288
152	12 56	015	14 46	040	31 15	102	44 08	145	45 54	180	52 19	237	45 28	289
153	13 05	016	15 08	041	31 47	103	44 27	146	45 53	181	51 50	238	44 57	290
154	13 15	017	15 30	041	32 20	104	44 45	147	45 52	182	51 22	239	44 25	290
155	13 25	017	15 52	042	32 52	105	45 03	148	45 51	184	50 53	240	43 54	291
156	13 35	018	16 15	043	33 25	106	45 20	150	45 48	185	50 23	242	43 23	292
157	13 46	019	16 38	043	33 57	107	45 37	151	45 44	187	49 54	243	42 52	292
158	13 57	020	17 01	044	34 29	108	45 53	152	45 40	188	49 24	244	42 21	293
159	14 08	020	17 24	045	35 01	109	46 08	154	45 35	189	48 53	245	41 50	294
160	14 20	021	17 48	046	35 32	110	46 23	155	45 29	191	48 23	246	41 19	294
161	14 32	022	18 12	046	36 04	111	46 36	156	45 23	192	47 52	247	40 49	295
162	14 45	022	18 37	047	36 35	112	46 49	158	45 15	194	47 21	248	40 18	295
163	14 58	023	19 01	048	37 06	113	47 02	159	45 07	195	46 50	249	39 48	296
164	15 11	024	19 26	048	37 37	114	47 13	161	44 58	196	46 18	250	39 18	297
	◆ DENEB		VEGA		ARCTURUS		◆ SPICA		REGULUS		◆ POLLUX		CAPELLA	
165	15 25	024	19 51	049	38 08	115	16 13	143	44 48	198	45 47	251	38 48	297
166	15 39	025	20 17	050	38 38	116	16 33	144	44 37	199	45 15	252	38 18	298
167	15 53	026	20 43	050	39 08	117	16 53	145	44 26	200	44 43	253	37 49	299
168	16 08	026	21 09	051	39 38	118	17 12	145	44 14	202	44 10	254	37 19	299
169	16 23	027	21 35	052	40 07	119	17 31	146	44 01	203	43 38	255	36 50	300
170	16 38	028	22 01	052	40 36	120	17 49	147	43 48	204	43 06	256	36 21	300
171	16 54	029	22 28	053	41 05	121	18 07	148	43 34	206	42 33	257	35 52	301
172	17 10	029	22 55	054	41 34	122	18 25	149	43 19	207	42 00	258	35 24	302
173	17 27	030	23 22	055	42 02	123	18 41	150	43 03	208	41 27	259	34 55	302
174	17 44	031	23 50	055	42 30	124	18 58	151	42 47	210	40 54	260	34 27	303
175	18 01	031	24 17	056	42 58	126	19 13	152	42 30	211	40 21	261	33 59	304
176	18 19	032	24 45	057	43 25	127	19 29	153	42 13	212	39 48	262	33 31	304
177	18 37	033	25 13	057	43 51	128	19 44	154	41 55	213	39 15	263	33 03	305
178	18 55	033	25 42	058	44 18	129	19 58	155	41 36	215	38 41	264	32 36	305
179	19 13	034	26 10	059	44 44	130	20 11	156	41 16	216	38 08	264	32 09	306

 LAT 56°N

LHA ♈	Hc	Zn	Hc	Zn	Hc	Zn	Hc	Zn	Hc	Zn	Hc	Zn	Hc	Zn
	◆ DENEB		VEGA		ARCTURUS		◆ SPICA		REGULUS		◆ POLLUX		CAPELLA	
180	19 32	035	26 39	059	45 09	131	20 25	157	40 57	217	37 35	265	31 42	307
181	19 51	035	27 08	060	45 34	133	20 37	158	40 36	218	37 01	266	31 15	307
182	20 11	036	27 37	061	45 58	134	20 49	159	40 15	219	36 28	267	30 48	308
183	20 31	037	28 07	061	46 22	135	21 01	161	39 53	221	35 54	268	30 22	309
184	20 51	037	28 36	062	46 46	136	21 12	162	39 31	222	35 21	269	29 56	309
185	21 11	038	29 06	063	47 09	138	21 22	163	39 09	223	34 47	270	29 30	310
186	21 32	039	29 36	063	47 31	139	21 32	164	38 46	224	34 14	270	29 04	310
187	21 53	039	30 06	064	47 53	140	21 41	165	38 22	225	33 40	271	28 39	311
188	22 14	040	30 36	065	48 14	141	21 49	166	37 58	226	33 06	272	28 13	312
189	22 36	040	31 07	066	48 35	143	21 57	167	37 33	228	32 33	273	27 49	312
190	22 58	041	31 37	066	48 55	144	22 05	168	37 08	229	31 59	274	27 24	313
191	23 20	042	32 08	067	49 14	145	22 12	169	36 43	230	31 26	274	26 59	314
192	23 43	042	32 39	068	49 33	147	22 18	170	36 17	231	30 53	275	26 35	314
193	24 06	043	33 10	068	49 51	148	22 23	171	35 51	232	30 19	276	26 11	315
194	24 29	044	33 41	069	50 08	150	22 28	172	35 24	233	29 46	277	25 48	315
	◆ DENEB		VEGA		Rasalhague		◆ ARCTURUS		REGULUS		◆ POLLUX		CAPELLA	
195	24 52	044	34 13	070	22 07	101	50 25	151	34 57	234	29 13	278	25 24	316
196	25 16	045	34 44	070	22 40	101	50 41	152	34 30	235	28 39	278	25 01	317
197	25 39	046	35 16	071	23 13	102	50 56	154	34 02	236	28 06	279	24 38	317
198	26 04	046	35 48	072	23 46	103	51 10	155	33 34	237	27 33	280	24 16	318
199	26 28	047	36 20	073	24 18	104	51 24	157	33 06	238	27 00	281	23 53	319
200	26 53	048	36 52	073	24 51	105	51 37	158	32 37	239	26 27	282	23 31	319
201	27 17	048	37 24	074	25 23	106	51 49	160	32 08	240	25 54	282	23 09	320
202	27 43	049	37 56	075	25 55	107	52 00	161	31 39	241	25 22	283	22 48	321
203	28 08	049	38 29	075	26 27	108	52 10	163	31 09	242	24 49	284	22 27	321
204	28 34	050	39 01	076	26 59	109	52 20	164	30 40	243	24 16	285	22 06	322
205	28 59	051	39 34	077	27 31	110	52 29	166	30 09	244	23 44	285	21 45	323
206	29 26	051	40 07	078	28 03	110	52 36	167	29 39	245	23 12	286	21 25	323
207	29 52	052	40 39	078	28 34	111	52 43	169	29 09	246	22 40	287	21 05	324
208	30 18	053	41 12	079	29 05	112	52 49	170	28 38	247	22 08	288	20 46	324
209	30 45	053	41 45	080	29 36	113	52 54	172	28 07	248	21 36	288	20 26	325
	◆ DENEB		VEGA		Rasalhague		◆ ARCTURUS		REGULUS		◆ POLLUX		CAPELLA	
210	31 12	054	42 18	080	30 07	114	52 59	174	27 36	249	21 04	289	20 07	326
211	31 39	055	42 51	081	30 37	115	53 02	175	27 04	250	20 32	290	19 49	326
212	32 07	055	43 25	082	31 07	116	53 04	177	26 33	251	20 01	291	19 30	327
213	32 35	056	43 58	083	31 37	117	53 06	178	26 01	252	19 29	291	19 12	328
214	33 02	056	44 31	083	32 07	118	53 06	180	25 29	253	18 58	292	18 54	328
215	33 30	057	45 04	084	32 37	119	53 06	181	24 57	254	18 27	293	18 37	329
216	33 59	058	45 38	085	33 06	120	53 05	183	24 24	254	17 57	294	18 20	330
217	34 27	058	46 11	086	33 35	121	53 02	185	23 52	255	17 26	294	18 03	330
218	34 56	059	46 45	087	34 03	122	52 59	186	23 20	256	16 55	295	17 47	331
219	35 25	060	47 18	087	34 31	123	52 55	188	22 47	257	16 25	296	17 31	332
220	35 54	060	47 52	088	34 59	124	52 50	189	22 14	258	15 55	297	17 15	332
221	36 23	061	48 25	089	35 27	125	52 44	191	21 41	259	15 25	297	17 00	333
222	36 52	061	48 59	090	35 54	126	52 38	192	21 08	260	14 56	298	16 45	334
223	37 22	062	49 32	091	36 21	127	52 30	194	20 35	261	14 26	299	16 30	335
224	37 52	063	50 06	092	36 47	129	52 22	195	20 02	261	13 57	300	16 16	335
	DENEB		◆ VEGA		Rasalhague		◆ ARCTURUS		Denebola		Dubhe		◆ CAPELLA	
225	38 21	063	50 40	092	37 13	130	52 12	197	34 57	241	60 07	305	16 02	336
226	38 52	064	51 13	093	37 39	131	52 02	198	34 28	242	59 40	306	15 49	337
227	39 22	065	51 47	094	38 04	132	51 51	200	33 58	243	59 13	306	15 35	337
228	39 52	065	52 20	095	38 29	133	51 39	201	33 28	244	58 45	306	15 23	338
229	40 23	066	52 53	096	38 53	134	51 26	203	32 58	245	58 18	307	15 10	339
230	40 53	067	53 27	097	39 17	135	51 13	204	32 27	246	57 52	307	14 58	339
231	41 24	067	54 00	098	39 40	136	50 59	206	31 57	247	57 25	307	14 46	340
232	41 55	068	54 33	099	40 03	138	50 44	207	31 26	248	56 58	307	14 35	341
233	42 26	068	55 06	100	40 26	139	50 28	209	30 55	249	56 31	308	14 24	341
234	42 58	069	55 39	101	40 47	140	50 11	210	30 23	249	56 05	308	14 14	342
235	43 29	070	56 12	102	41 09	141	49 54	212	29 52	250	55 39	308	14 04	343
236	44 01	070	56 45	103	41 29	142	49 36	213	29 20	251	55 12	309	13 54	343
237	44 32	071	57 18	104	41 50	144	49 18	214	28 48	252	54 46	309	13 44	344
238	45 04	072	57 50	105	42 09	145	48 58	216	28 16	253	54 20	309	13 36	345
239	45 36	072	58 23	106	42 28	146	48 38	217	27 44	254	53 54	310	13 27	346
	DENEB		◆ VEGA		Rasalhague		◆ ARCTURUS		Denebola		Dubhe		◆ CAPELLA	
240	46 08	073	58 55	107	42 47	147	48 18	218	27 12	255	53 29	310	13 19	346
241	46 40	074	59 27	108	43 04	149	47 57	220	26 39	256	53 03	310	13 11	347
242	47 12	074	59 59	109	43 22	150	47 35	221	26 07	257	52 37	311	13 04	348
243	47 45	075	60 30	110	43 38	151	47 13	222	25 34	258	52 12	311	12 57	348
244	48 17	076	61 02	111	43 54	153	46 50	224	25 01	259	51 47	311	12 50	349
245	48 50	076	61 33	113	44 09	154	46 27	225	24 28	259	51 22	312	12 44	350
246	49 22	077	62 04	114	44 23	155	46 03	226	23 55	260	50 57	312	12 38	350
247	49 55	078	62 34	115	44 37	156	45 38	227	23 22	261	50 32	313	12 33	351
248	50 28	078	63 04	116	44 50	158	45 13	228	22 49	262	50 07	313	12 28	352
249	51 01	079	63 34	118	45 02	159	44 48	230	22 16	263	49 43	313	12 23	353
250	51 34	080	64 04	119	45 14	161	44 22	231	21 42	264	49 18	314	12 19	353
251	52 07	080	64 33	121	45 25	162	43 56	232	21 09	265	48 54	314	12 16	354
252	52 40	081	65 02	122	45 35	163	43 29	233	20 35	265	48 30	314	12 12	355
253	53 13	082	65 30	123	45 44	165	43 02	234	20 02	266	48 06	315	12 09	355
254	53 46	083	65 58	125	45 53	166	42 35	235	19 28	267	47 43	315	12 07	356
	Schedar		DENEB		◆ ALTAIR		Rasalhague		◆ ARCTURUS		Dubhe		◆ CAPELLA	
255	34 06	037	54 20	083	32 13	127	46 00	167	42 07	237	47 19	316	12 05	357
256	34 26	037	54 53	084	32 40	128	46 07	169	41 39	238	46 56	316	12 03	358
257	34 47	038	55 26	085	33 06	129	46 13	170	41 10	239	46 32	316	12 02	358
258	35 07	038	56 00	086	33 32	131	46 19	172	40 42	240	46 09	317	12 01	359
259	35 28	039	56 33	086	33 57	132	46 23	173	40 12	241	45 46	317	12 01	000
260	35 50	040	57 07	087	34 22	133	46 27	174	39 43	242	45 24	318	12 01	000
261	36 11	040	57 40	088	34 46	134	46 29	176	39 13	243	45 01	318	12 01	001
262	36 33	041	58 14	089	35 10	135	46 31	177	38 43	244	44 39	318	12 02	002
263	36 55	041	58 47	090	35 34	136	46 33	179	38 13	245	44 17	319	12 03	003
264	37 17	042	59 21	090	35 57	137	46 33	180	37 42	246	43 55	319	12 05	003
265	37 39	042	59 54	091	36 19	138	46 33	182	37 12	247	43 33	320	12 07	004
266	38 02	043	60 28	092	36 41	139	46 31	183	36 41	248	43 11	320	12 10	005
267	38 25	043	61 02	093	37 03	141	46 29	184	36 09	249	42 50	321	12 13	005
268	38 48	044	61 35	094	37 24	142	46 26	186	35 38	250	42 29	321	12 16	006
269	39 11	044	62 08	095	37 45	143	46 22	187	35 06	251	42 08	321	12 20	007

LHA ♈	Hc	Zn	Hc	Zn	Hc	Zn	Hc	Zn	Hc	Zn	Hc	Zn	Hc	Zn
	◆ CAPELLA		Alpheratz		◆ ALTAIR		Rasalhague		◆ ARCTURUS		Alkaid		Dubhe	
270	12 24	007	22 37	071	38 05	144	46 18	189	34 34	252	52 33	287	41 47	322
271	12 28	008	23 09	072	38 24	145	46 12	190	34 02	253	52 01	288	41 26	322
272	12 33	009	23 41	072	38 43	146	46 06	191	33 30	254	51 29	288	41 06	323
273	12 39	010	24 13	073	39 01	148	45 59	193	32 58	255	50 57	289	40 45	323
274	12 45	010	24 45	074	39 19	149	45 51	194	32 26	256	50 26	289	40 25	324
275	12 51	011	25 17	075	39 36	150	45 42	196	31 53	257	49 54	290	40 06	324
276	12 57	012	25 50	075	39 52	151	45 33	197	31 20	257	49 22	291	39 46	324
277	13 04	012	26 22	076	40 08	153	45 23	198	30 48	258	48 51	291	39 27	325
278	13 12	013	26 55	077	40 23	154	45 12	200	30 15	259	48 20	292	39 08	325
279	13 20	014	27 28	078	40 38	155	45 00	201	29 42	260	47 49	292	38 49	326
280	13 28	015	28 01	079	40 51	156	44 48	202	29 09	261	47 18	293	38 30	326
281	13 36	015	28 33	079	41 04	158	44 35	204	28 35	262	46 47	294	38 11	327
282	13 45	016	29 06	080	41 17	159	44 21	205	28 02	263	46 16	294	37 53	327
283	13 55	017	29 40	081	41 29	160	44 06	206	27 29	264	45 46	295	37 35	328
284	14 05	017	30 13	082	41 40	162	43 51	208	26 55	264	45 15	295	37 17	328
	◆ CAPELLA		Alpheratz		◆ ALTAIR		Rasalhague		◆ ARCTURUS		Alkaid		Dubhe	
285	14 15	018	30 46	082	41 50	163	43 35	209	26 22	265	44 45	296	37 00	329
286	14 25	019	31 19	083	41 59	164	43 18	210	25 49	266	44 15	297	36 42	329
287	14 36	019	31 53	084	42 08	165	43 01	212	25 15	267	43 45	297	36 25	330
288	14 48	020	32 26	085	42 16	167	42 43	213	24 42	268	43 15	298	36 08	330
289	14 59	021	32 59	086	42 24	168	42 25	214	24 08	269	42 46	298	35 52	331
290	15 11	021	33 33	086	42 30	169	42 06	215	23 34	270	42 16	299	35 35	331
291	15 24	022	34 06	087	42 36	171	41 46	217	23 01	270	41 47	299	35 19	331
292	15 37	023	34 40	088	42 41	172	41 26	218	22 27	271	41 18	300	35 03	332
293	15 50	024	35 13	089	42 45	173	41 05	219	21 54	272	40 49	301	34 48	332
294	16 03	024	35 47	090	42 49	175	40 43	220	21 20	273	40 20	301	34 32	333
295	16 17	025	36 21	090	42 51	176	40 21	221	20 47	274	39 52	302	34 17	333
296	16 32	026	36 54	091	42 53	177	39 59	223	20 13	274	39 23	302	34 02	334
297	16 46	026	37 28	092	42 54	179	39 36	224	19 40	275	38 55	303	33 48	334
298	17 01	027	38 01	093	42 55	180	39 13	225	19 07	276	38 27	304	33 33	335
299	17 17	028	38 35	094	42 54	182	38 49	226	18 33	277	37 59	304	33 19	335
	CAPELLA		◆ Alpheratz		Enif		ALTAIR		◆ VEGA		Alphecca		◆ Dubhe	
300	17 32	028	39 08	095	39 35	146	42 53	183	68 01	227	35 02	267	33 05	336
301	17 48	029	39 41	096	39 54	147	42 51	184	67 36	229	34 28	267	32 52	336
302	18 05	030	40 15	096	40 12	148	42 48	186	67 10	231	33 55	268	32 38	337
303	18 22	030	40 48	097	40 29	149	42 44	187	66 44	232	33 21	269	32 25	337
304	18 39	031	41 21	098	40 46	151	42 40	188	66 17	234	32 47	270	32 13	338
305	18 56	032	41 55	099	41 02	152	42 35	190	65 50	235	32 14	271	32 00	338
306	19 14	032	42 28	100	41 18	153	42 29	191	65 22	237	31 40	272	31 48	339
307	19 32	033	43 01	101	41 33	154	42 22	192	64 54	238	31 07	272	31 36	339
308	19 50	034	43 34	102	41 47	156	42 14	194	64 25	240	30 33	273	31 24	340
309	20 09	034	44 06	103	42 01	157	42 06	195	63 56	241	30 00	274	31 13	340
310	20 28	035	44 39	104	42 13	158	41 57	196	63 26	243	29 26	275	31 02	341
311	20 48	036	45 11	105	42 25	159	41 47	198	62 56	244	28 53	276	30 51	341
312	21 07	036	45 44	106	42 37	161	41 37	199	62 26	245	28 20	276	30 40	342
313	21 27	037	46 16	107	42 48	162	41 26	200	61 55	247	27 46	277	30 30	342
314	21 47	038	46 48	108	42 57	163	41 14	201	61 24	248	27 13	278	30 20	343
	CAPELLA		◆ Hamal		Alpheratz		Enif		◆ ALTAIR		VEGA		◆ Alioth	
315	22 08	038	26 30	087	47 20	109	43 07	165	41 01	203	60 53	249	31 33	326
316	22 29	039	27 04	087	47 52	110	43 15	166	40 48	204	60 22	250	31 14	326
317	22 50	039	27 37	088	48 23	111	43 23	167	40 34	205	59 50	251	30 56	327
318	23 12	040	28 11	089	48 54	112	43 30	169	40 19	206	59 18	252	30 38	327
319	23 33	041	28 44	090	49 25	113	43 36	170	40 04	208	58 46	254	30 20	328
320	23 55	041	29 18	091	49 56	114	43 41	171	39 48	209	58 14	255	30 02	329
321	24 18	042	29 52	092	50 26	115	43 46	173	39 32	210	57 41	256	29 45	329
322	24 40	043	30 25	092	50 57	116	43 50	174	39 15	211	57 09	257	29 27	330
323	25 03	043	30 59	093	51 27	117	43 52	176	38 57	213	56 36	258	29 11	330
324	25 26	044	31 32	094	51 56	119	43 55	177	38 38	214	56 03	259	28 54	331
325	25 50	045	32 06	095	52 26	120	43 56	178	38 19	215	55 30	260	28 38	331
326	26 14	045	32 39	096	52 54	121	43 57	180	38 00	216	54 57	261	28 22	332
327	26 38	046	33 12	097	53 23	122	43 56	181	37 40	217	54 24	262	28 06	332
328	27 02	047	33 46	098	53 51	123	43 55	182	37 19	219	53 51	263	27 51	333
329	27 26	047	34 19	098	54 19	125	43 54	184	36 58	220	53 18	263	27 36	334
	CAPELLA		◆ Hamal		Alpheratz		Enif		◆ ALTAIR		VEGA		◆ Alioth	
330	27 51	048	34 52	099	54 46	126	43 51	185	36 36	221	52 44	264	27 21	334
331	28 16	048	35 25	100	55 13	127	43 48	187	36 14	222	52 11	265	27 07	335
332	28 41	049	35 58	101	55 40	129	43 43	188	35 51	223	51 37	266	26 52	335
333	29 07	050	36 31	102	56 06	130	43 38	189	35 28	224	51 04	267	26 38	336
334	29 32	050	37 04	103	56 31	131	43 33	191	35 04	225	50 30	268	26 25	336
335	29 58	051	37 36	104	56 56	133	43 26	192	34 40	226	49 57	269	26 12	337
336	30 24	052	38 09	105	57 20	134	43 19	193	34 16	228	49 23	270	25 59	338
337	30 51	052	38 41	106	57 44	136	43 11	195	33 51	229	48 50	270	25 46	338
338	31 17	053	39 13	107	58 07	137	43 02	196	33 25	230	48 16	271	25 34	339
339	31 44	053	39 45	108	58 30	139	42 52	197	33 00	231	47 43	272	25 22	339
340	32 11	054	40 17	109	58 51	140	42 42	199	32 33	232	47 09	273	25 10	340
341	32 39	055	40 49	110	59 13	142	42 31	200	32 07	233	46 36	274	24 59	340
342	33 06	055	41 20	111	59 33	143	42 19	201	31 40	234	46 02	274	24 48	341
343	33 34	056	41 52	112	59 53	145	42 07	203	31 13	235	45 29	275	24 37	342
344	34 02	057	42 23	113	60 12	147	41 53	204	30 45	236	44 55	276	24 27	342
	CAPELLA		ALDEBARAN		◆ Hamal		Alpheratz		◆ ALTAIR		VEGA		◆ Alioth	
345	34 30	057	16 52	085	42 54	114	60 30	148	30 17	237	44 22	277	24 16	343
346	34 58	058	17 26	086	43 24	115	60 47	150	29 49	238	43 49	277	24 07	343
347	35 27	058	17 59	087	43 54	116	61 03	152	29 20	239	43 15	278	23 57	344
348	35 55	059	18 33	088	44 24	117	61 19	153	28 51	240	42 42	279	23 48	345
349	36 24	060	19 06	089	44 54	118	61 33	155	28 22	241	42 09	280	23 39	345
350	36 53	060	19 40	089	45 24	119	61 47	157	27 53	242	41 36	280	23 31	346
351	37 22	061	20 13	090	45 53	120	62 00	159	27 23	243	41 03	281	23 23	346
352	37 52	062	20 47	091	46 22	121	62 12	160	26 53	244	40 30	282	23 15	347
353	38 21	062	21 20	092	46 50	122	62 22	162	26 23	245	39 58	283	23 08	348
354	38 51	063	21 54	093	47 18	124	62 32	164	25 52	246	39 25	283	23 01	348
355	39 21	063	22 27	094	47 46	125	62 41	166	25 22	247	38 52	284	22 54	349
356	39 51	064	23 01	094	48 13	126	62 48	168	24 51	248	38 20	285	22 48	349
357	40 21	065	23 34	095	48 40	127	62 55	170	24 20	249	37 47	286	22 42	350
358	40 52	065	24 08	096	49 07	128	63 00	172	23 48	249	37 15	286	22 36	351
359	41 22	066	24 41	097	49 33	130	63 04	174	23 17	250	36 43	287	22 31	351

LHA ♈	Hc	Zn	Hc	Zn	Hc	Zn	Hc	Zn	Hc	Zn	Hc	Zn	Hc	Zn
	◆ CAPELLA		ALDEBARAN		Hamal		◆ Alpheratz		ALTAIR		◆ VEGA		Alioth	
0	41 29	066	25 22	097	50 37	130	64 07	175	23 04	252	35 52	288	21 26	352
1	42 00	066	25 56	098	51 04	131	64 09	177	22 31	253	35 20	289	21 22	352
2	42 32	067	26 30	099	51 29	133	64 10	179	21 58	253	34 47	290	21 17	353
3	43 03	068	27 04	100	51 54	134	64 10	181	21 25	254	34 15	290	21 13	354
4	43 35	068	27 38	101	52 19	135	64 09	183	20 52	255	33 43	291	21 10	354
5	44 07	069	28 12	102	52 43	137	64 06	185	20 19	256	33 11	292	21 06	355
6	44 39	069	28 46	103	53 06	138	64 02	187	19 45	257	32 39	292	21 03	355
7	45 12	070	29 19	103	53 29	139	63 57	189	19 12	258	32 07	293	21 01	356
8	45 44	071	29 52	104	53 51	141	63 51	191	18 38	259	31 36	294	20 59	357
9	46 17	071	30 26	105	54 12	142	63 44	193	18 04	260	31 04	295	20 57	357
10	46 49	072	30 59	106	54 33	144	63 35	195	17 30	260	30 33	295	20 55	358
11	47 22	072	31 32	107	54 53	145	63 25	197	16 56	261	30 02	296	20 54	358
12	47 55	073	32 05	108	55 12	147	63 15	199	16 22	262	29 31	297	20 53	359
13	48 28	074	32 37	109	55 31	148	63 03	201	15 48	263	29 00	297	20 53	000
14	49 01	074	33 10	110	55 49	150	62 50	203	15 14	264	28 30	298	20 53	000
	Dubhe		◆ CAPELLA		ALDEBARAN		Hamal		◆ Alpheratz		DENEB		◆ VEGA	
15	28 51	015	49 34	075	33 42	111	56 06	151	62 36	205	49 07	284	28 00	299
16	29 00	016	50 07	076	34 14	112	56 22	153	62 21	206	48 34	285	27 29	299
17	29 10	016	50 41	076	34 46	113	56 37	154	62 06	208	48 01	285	26 59	300
18	29 20	017	51 14	077	35 18	114	56 51	156	61 49	210	47 28	286	26 30	301
19	29 30	017	51 48	078	35 49	115	57 05	158	61 31	212	46 55	287	26 00	301
20	29 40	018	52 21	078	36 20	116	57 18	159	61 13	213	46 22	287	25 31	302
21	29 51	018	52 55	079	36 51	117	57 29	161	60 53	215	45 49	288	25 02	303
22	30 02	019	53 29	080	37 21	118	57 40	163	60 33	217	45 16	289	24 33	303
23	30 13	019	54 03	080	37 52	119	57 50	164	60 12	218	44 44	289	24 04	304
24	30 24	020	54 37	081	38 22	120	57 58	166	59 50	220	44 11	290	23 36	305
25	30 36	020	55 11	082	38 51	121	58 06	168	59 28	222	43 39	291	23 08	305
26	30 48	021	55 45	082	39 21	122	58 13	170	59 05	223	43 07	291	22 40	306
27	31 00	021	56 19	083	39 50	123	58 19	171	58 41	225	42 35	292	22 12	307
28	31 13	022	56 53	084	40 19	124	58 24	173	58 16	226	42 03	292	21 44	307
29	31 26	022	57 28	085	40 47	125	58 27	175	57 51	228	41 31	293	21 17	308
	Dubhe		◆ POLLUX		BETELGEUSE		RIGEL		◆ Hamal		Alpheratz		◆ DENEB	
30	31 39	023	24 31	076	23 29	112	14 54	130	58 30	176	57 25	229	41 00	294
31	31 52	023	25 04	076	24 01	113	15 21	130	58 31	178	56 59	230	40 28	294
32	32 06	024	25 37	077	24 33	114	15 47	131	58 32	180	56 32	232	39 57	295
33	32 20	024	26 11	078	25 04	115	16 12	132	58 31	182	56 05	233	39 26	296
34	32 34	025	26 45	079	25 35	116	16 38	133	58 30	184	55 37	234	38 55	296
35	32 49	025	27 19	079	26 06	117	17 02	134	58 27	185	55 09	236	38 24	297
36	33 04	026	27 52	080	26 37	118	17 27	135	58 24	187	54 41	237	37 53	297
37	33 19	026	28 26	081	27 07	119	17 51	136	58 19	189	54 12	238	37 23	298
38	33 34	027	29 00	082	27 37	120	18 15	137	58 13	190	53 42	239	36 53	299
39	33 49	027	29 34	083	28 07	121	18 38	138	58 06	192	53 12	241	36 22	299
40	34 05	028	30 09	083	28 36	122	19 01	139	57 59	194	52 42	242	35 53	300
41	34 21	028	30 43	084	29 06	123	19 23	140	57 50	196	52 12	243	35 23	300
42	34 37	029	31 17	085	29 35	124	19 45	141	57 40	197	51 41	244	34 53	301
43	34 54	029	31 51	086	30 03	125	20 06	142	57 29	199	51 10	245	34 24	302
44	35 11	029	32 26	086	30 31	126	20 27	143	57 18	201	50 38	246	33 55	302
	Dubhe		◆ POLLUX		BETELGEUSE		RIGEL		◆ Hamal		Alpheratz		◆ DENEB	
45	35 28	030	33 00	087	30 59	127	20 48	144	57 05	202	50 07	247	33 26	303
46	35 45	030	33 34	088	31 27	128	21 08	145	56 52	204	49 35	249	32 57	304
47	36 03	031	34 09	089	31 54	129	21 27	146	56 37	206	49 03	250	32 28	304
48	36 20	031	34 43	090	32 20	130	21 46	147	56 22	207	48 30	251	32 00	305
49	36 38	032	35 18	090	32 47	131	22 05	148	56 06	209	47 58	252	31 32	305
50	36 57	032	35 52	091	33 12	132	22 23	149	55 49	210	47 25	253	31 04	306
51	37 15	033	36 26	092	33 38	133	22 41	150	55 31	212	46 52	254	30 36	307
52	37 34	033	37 01	093	34 03	134	22 57	151	55 13	213	46 19	255	30 08	307
53	37 53	034	37 35	094	34 28	135	23 14	152	54 53	215	45 46	256	29 41	308
54	38 12	034	38 10	095	34 52	136	23 30	153	54 33	216	45 12	257	29 14	308
55	38 31	034	38 44	096	35 15	137	23 45	154	54 13	218	44 39	258	28 47	309
56	38 51	035	39 18	096	35 38	138	24 00	155	53 51	219	44 05	258	28 21	310
57	39 11	035	39 52	097	36 01	139	24 14	156	53 29	221	43 31	259	27 54	310
58	39 31	036	40 26	098	36 23	141	24 28	157	53 06	222	42 57	260	27 28	311
59	39 51	036	41 00	099	36 45	142	24 41	158	52 43	223	42 24	261	27 02	312
	◆ Dubhe		POLLUX		SIRIUS		◆ RIGEL		Hamal		◆ Alpheratz		DENEB	
60	40 11	037	41 34	100	10 07	140	24 53	159	52 19	225	41 49	262	26 37	312
61	40 32	037	42 08	101	10 29	141	25 05	160	51 55	226	41 15	263	26 11	313
62	40 53	037	42 42	102	10 51	142	25 16	162	51 29	227	40 41	264	25 46	313
63	41 14	038	43 15	103	11 12	143	25 27	163	51 04	229	40 07	265	25 21	314
64	41 35	038	43 49	104	11 33	144	25 37	164	50 38	230	39 33	266	24 57	315
65	41 56	039	44 22	105	11 53	144	25 46	165	50 11	231	38 58	266	24 32	315
66	42 18	039	44 56	106	12 13	145	25 55	166	49 44	232	38 24	267	24 08	316
67	42 40	040	45 29	107	12 32	146	26 03	167	49 17	234	37 50	268	23 44	317
68	43 02	040	46 02	108	12 51	147	26 10	168	48 49	235	37 15	269	23 21	317
69	43 24	040	46 34	109	13 09	148	26 17	169	48 20	236	36 41	270	22 58	318
70	43 47	041	47 07	110	13 27	149	26 23	170	47 52	237	36 06	271	22 35	319
71	44 09	041	47 39	111	13 45	150	26 29	171	47 22	238	35 32	271	22 12	319
72	44 32	042	48 11	112	14 02	151	26 33	172	46 53	240	34 57	272	21 50	320
73	44 55	042	48 43	113	14 18	152	26 38	174	46 23	241	34 23	273	21 28	320
74	45 18	042	49 15	114	14 34	153	26 41	175	45 53	242	33 49	274	21 06	321
	Dubhe		◆ REGULUS		PROCYON		SIRIUS		◆ RIGEL		Hamal		◆ DENEB	
75	45 41	043	17 00	093	30 46	132	14 49	154	26 44	176	45 22	243	20 44	322
76	46 05	043	17 34	094	31 11	133	15 04	155	26 46	177	44 52	244	20 23	322
77	46 28	044	18 08	095	31 36	134	15 19	156	26 48	178	44 21	245	20 02	323
78	46 52	044	18 43	096	32 01	135	15 33	157	26 49	179	43 49	246	19 42	323
79	47 16	044	19 17	097	32 25	136	15 46	158	26 49	180	43 18	247	19 22	324
80	47 40	045	19 51	098	32 49	137	15 59	159	26 48	181	42 46	248	19 02	325
81	48 04	045	20 25	099	33 12	138	16 11	160	26 47	182	42 14	249	18 42	326
82	48 29	045	20 59	099	33 34	139	16 23	161	26 46	184	41 42	250	18 23	326
83	48 53	046	21 33	100	33 57	140	16 34	162	26 43	185	41 09	251	18 04	327
84	49 18	046	22 07	101	34 18	142	16 45	163	26 40	186	40 36	252	17 45	328
85	49 43	046	22 40	102	34 39	143	16 55	164	26 36	187	40 04	253	17 27	328
86	50 08	047	23 14	103	35 00	144	17 04	165	26 32	188	39 31	254	17 09	329
87	50 33	047	23 48	104	35 20	145	17 13	166	26 27	189	38 57	255	16 52	330
88	50 59	048	24 21	105	35 39	146	17 21	167	26 21	190	38 24	256	16 34	330
89	51 24	048	24 54	105	35 58	147	17 29	167	26 15	191	37 51	257	16 18	331

LHA ♈	Hc	Zn	Hc	Zn	Hc	Zn	Hc	Zn	Hc	Zn	Hc	Zn	Hc	Zn
	Dubhe		◆ REGULUS		PROCYON		SIRIUS		◆ RIGEL		Mirfak		◆ DENEB	
90	51 50	048	25 27	106	36 16	149	17 36	168	26 07	192	66 14	274	16 01	332
91	52 15	049	26 00	107	36 34	150	17 43	169	26 00	193	65 39	275	15 45	332
92	52 41	049	26 33	108	36 51	151	17 49	170	25 51	195	65 05	275	15 29	333
93	53 07	049	27 06	109	37 08	152	17 54	171	25 43	196	64 31	276	15 14	334
94	53 33	050	27 38	110	37 23	153	17 59	172	25 33	197	63 57	277	14 59	334
95	54 00	050	28 10	111	37 39	154	18 03	174	25 23	198	63 23	277	14 44	335
96	54 26	050	28 42	112	37 53	156	18 07	175	25 12	199	62 48	278	14 30	336
97	54 52	050	29 14	113	38 07	157	18 10	176	25 00	200	62 14	279	14 16	336
98	55 19	051	29 46	114	38 20	158	18 12	177	24 48	201	61 40	279	14 02	337
99	55 46	051	30 17	115	38 32	159	18 14	178	24 36	202	61 06	280	13 49	338
100	56 12	051	30 48	116	38 44	161	18 15	179	24 23	203	60 33	281	13 36	338
101	56 39	052	31 19	117	38 55	162	18 16	180	24 09	204	59 59	281	13 24	339
102	57 06	052	31 50	118	39 06	163	18 16	181	23 54	205	59 25	282	13 11	340
103	57 33	052	32 20	119	39 15	164	18 15	182	23 39	206	58 51	282	13 00	341
104	58 01	052	32 50	120	39 24	166	18 14	183	23 24	207	58 18	283	12 49	341
	◆ Dubhe		Denebola		REGULUS		◆ SIRIUS		RIGEL		ALDEBARAN		◆ Mirfak	
105	58 28	053	21 52	096	33 20	121	18 12	184	23 08	208	42 46	230	57 44	284
106	58 55	053	22 26	097	33 49	122	18 09	185	22 51	209	42 20	231	57 11	284
107	59 23	053	23 00	098	34 19	123	18 06	186	22 34	210	41 53	232	56 38	285
108	59 50	053	23 34	098	34 47	124	18 03	187	22 16	211	41 26	233	56 04	285
109	60 18	054	24 08	099	35 16	125	17 59	188	21 58	212	40 58	234	55 31	286
110	60 46	054	24 42	100	35 44	126	17 54	189	21 39	213	40 30	235	54 58	287
111	61 14	054	25 16	101	36 12	127	17 48	190	21 20	214	40 01	237	54 25	287
112	61 42	054	25 49	102	36 39	128	17 42	191	21 01	215	39 32	238	53 53	288
113	62 09	054	26 23	103	37 06	129	17 36	192	20 40	216	39 03	239	53 20	288
114	62 38	055	26 57	104	37 32	130	17 28	193	20 20	217	38 33	240	52 47	289
115	63 06	055	27 30	105	37 59	131	17 21	194	19 58	218	38 04	241	52 15	290
116	63 34	055	28 03	105	38 24	132	17 12	195	19 37	219	37 33	242	51 42	290
117	64 02	055	28 36	106	38 49	133	17 03	196	19 15	220	37 03	243	51 10	291
118	64 30	055	29 09	107	39 14	135	16 54	197	18 52	221	36 32	244	50 38	291
119	64 58	055	29 42	108	39 38	136	16 44	198	18 29	222	36 01	245	50 06	292
	Kochab		◆ ARCTURUS		REGULUS		◆ SIRIUS		BETELGEUSE		CAPELLA		◆ Schedar	
120	48 53	024	13 16	076	40 02	137	16 33	199	36 23	219	63 08	268	35 18	321
121	49 07	024	13 49	076	40 25	138	16 22	200	36 01	221	62 34	268	34 56	321
122	49 21	024	14 23	077	40 48	139	16 10	200	35 38	222	61 59	269	34 35	322
123	49 35	025	14 56	078	41 10	141	15 58	201	35 15	223	61 25	270	34 14	322
124	49 50	025	15 30	079	41 32	142	15 45	202	34 51	224	60 50	271	33 53	323
125	50 04	025	16 04	079	41 53	143	15 31	203	34 27	225	60 16	272	33 32	323
126	50 19	025	16 38	080	42 13	144	15 17	204	34 03	226	59 41	272	33 11	324
127	50 33	025	17 12	081	42 33	145	15 03	205	33 38	227	59 07	273	32 51	324
128	50 48	026	17 46	082	42 52	147	14 48	206	33 12	228	58 33	274	32 31	325
129	51 03	026	18 20	083	43 11	148	14 33	207	32 46	229	57 58	275	32 11	325
130	51 18	026	18 54	083	43 29	149	14 17	208	32 20	230	57 24	275	31 52	326
131	51 33	026	19 28	084	43 46	151	14 00	209	31 53	231	56 50	276	31 32	326
132	51 49	026	20 03	085	44 03	152	13 43	210	31 26	232	56 16	277	31 13	327
133	52 04	026	20 37	086	44 19	153	13 26	211	30 59	233	55 42	278	30 55	327
134	52 19	027	21 11	087	44 34	154	13 08	212	30 31	234	55 08	278	30 36	328
	Kochab		◆ ARCTURUS		REGULUS		◆ POLLUX		BETELGEUSE		CAPELLA		◆ Schedar	
135	52 35	027	21 46	087	44 48	156	59 52	214	30 03	236	54 34	279	30 18	328
136	52 50	027	22 20	088	45 02	157	59 33	215	29 34	237	54 00	280	30 00	329
137	53 06	027	22 54	089	45 15	158	59 12	217	29 05	237	53 26	280	29 43	329
138	53 22	027	23 29	090	45 27	160	58 51	219	28 36	238	52 52	281	29 25	330
139	53 37	027	24 03	091	45 39	161	58 29	220	28 07	239	52 18	282	29 08	331
140	53 53	027	24 38	092	45 50	163	58 07	222	27 37	240	51 44	282	28 51	331
141	54 09	028	25 12	092	45 59	164	57 44	223	27 07	241	51 11	283	28 35	332
142	54 25	028	25 46	093	46 08	165	57 20	225	26 37	242	50 37	284	28 19	332
143	54 41	028	26 21	094	46 17	167	56 55	226	26 06	243	50 04	284	28 03	333
144	54 57	028	26 55	095	46 24	168	56 30	228	25 35	244	49 31	285	27 47	333
145	55 13	028	27 29	096	46 31	170	56 05	229	25 04	245	48 58	286	27 32	334
146	55 29	028	28 04	097	46 37	171	55 38	230	24 33	246	48 24	286	27 17	334
147	55 46	028	28 38	097	46 42	172	55 12	232	24 01	247	47 51	287	27 02	335
148	56 02	028	29 12	098	46 46	174	54 44	233	23 29	248	47 19	288	26 48	335
149	56 18	028	29 46	099	46 49	175	54 17	234	22 57	249	46 46	288	26 33	336
	◆ VEGA		ARCTURUS		SPICA		◆ REGULUS		POLLUX		◆ CAPELLA		Schedar	
150	13 17	038	30 20	100	10 59	129	46 51	177	53 49	236	46 13	289	26 20	337
151	13 38	039	30 54	101	11 26	129	46 53	178	53 20	237	45 41	289	26 06	337
152	14 00	040	31 27	102	11 52	130	46 54	180	52 51	238	45 08	290	25 53	338
153	14 22	040	32 01	103	12 18	131	46 53	181	52 22	239	44 36	291	25 40	338
154	14 45	041	32 34	104	12 44	132	46 52	182	51 52	240	44 04	291	25 27	339
155	15 08	042	33 08	105	13 09	133	46 50	184	51 22	242	43 32	292	25 15	339
156	15 31	042	33 41	105	13 34	134	46 48	185	50 51	243	43 00	293	25 03	340
157	15 54	043	34 14	106	13 59	135	46 44	187	50 21	244	42 28	293	24 52	341
158	16 18	044	34 47	107	14 23	136	46 40	188	49 50	245	41 57	294	24 40	341
159	16 42	045	35 20	108	14 47	137	46 34	190	49 18	246	41 25	294	24 29	342
160	17 06	045	35 52	109	15 10	138	46 28	191	48 47	247	40 54	295	24 19	342
161	17 31	046	36 25	110	15 33	139	46 21	192	48 15	248	40 23	296	24 08	343
162	17 56	047	36 57	111	15 56	140	46 13	194	47 43	249	39 52	296	23 58	343
163	18 21	047	37 29	112	16 18	140	46 05	195	47 11	250	39 21	297	23 49	344
164	18 46	048	38 01	113	16 40	141	45 55	197	46 38	251	38 51	297	23 39	345
	◆ DENEB		VEGA		ARCTURUS		◆ SPICA		REGULUS		◆ POLLUX		CAPELLA	
165	14 30	024	19 12	049	38 32	114	17 01	142	45 45	198	46 05	252	38 20	298
166	14 44	025	19 38	049	39 04	115	17 22	143	45 34	199	45 32	253	37 50	299
167	14 59	026	20 04	050	39 35	116	17 42	144	45 22	201	44 59	254	37 20	299
168	15 14	026	20 31	051	40 05	117	18 02	145	45 10	202	44 26	255	36 50	300
169	15 30	027	20 58	051	40 36	118	18 21	146	44 57	203	43 53	256	36 20	300
170	15 45	028	21 25	052	41 06	119	18 40	147	44 42	205	43 19	257	35 50	301
171	16 02	028	21 52	053	41 36	120	18 58	148	44 28	206	42 46	258	35 21	302
172	16 18	029	22 20	054	42 06	121	19 16	149	44 12	207	42 12	259	34 52	302
173	16 35	030	22 47	054	42 35	123	19 33	150	43 56	209	41 38	260	34 23	303
174	16 52	030	23 15	055	43 04	124	19 50	151	43 39	210	41 04	261	33 54	303
175	17 10	031	23 44	056	43 32	125	20 07	152	43 22	211	40 30	262	33 25	304
176	17 28	032	24 12	056	44 00	126	20 22	153	43 03	213	39 56	263	32 57	305
177	17 46	032	24 41	057	44 28	127	20 38	154	42 45	214	39 22	263	32 29	305
178	18 05	033	25 10	058	44 55	128	20 52	155	42 25	215	38 48	264	32 01	306
179	18 23	034	25 39	058	45 22	129	21 06	156	42 05	216	38 14	265	31 33	307

LHA ♈	Hc	Zn	Hc	Zn	Hc	Zn	Hc	Zn	Hc	Zn	Hc	Zn	Hc	Zn
	DENEB		◆VEGA		ARCTURUS		◆SPICA		REGULUS		POLLUX		◆CAPELLA	
180	18 43	034	26 08	059	45 48	131	21 20	157	41 44	218	37 39	266	31 06	307
181	19 02	035	26 38	060	46 14	132	21 33	158	41 23	219	37 05	267	30 38	308
182	19 22	036	27 08	060	46 40	133	21 45	159	41 01	220	36 30	268	30 11	308
183	19 42	036	27 38	061	47 05	134	21 57	160	40 39	221	35 56	269	29 44	309
184	20 03	037	28 08	062	47 29	135	22 08	161	40 16	222	35 22	269	29 18	310
185	20 24	038	28 38	062	47 53	137	22 19	162	39 52	224	34 47	270	28 51	310
186	20 45	038	29 09	063	48 16	138	22 29	164	39 28	225	34 13	271	28 25	311
187	21 07	039	29 40	064	48 39	139	22 39	165	39 04	226	33 38	272	27 59	311
188	21 28	040	30 10	064	49 01	141	22 48	166	38 39	227	33 04	273	27 33	312
189	21 50	040	30 42	065	49 22	142	22 56	167	38 14	228	32 30	273	27 08	313
190	22 13	041	31 13	066	49 43	143	23 03	168	37 48	229	31 55	274	26 43	313
191	22 35	042	31 44	066	50 03	145	23 10	169	37 22	230	31 21	275	26 18	314
192	22 58	042	32 16	067	50 23	146	23 17	170	36 55	231	30 47	276	25 53	315
193	23 22	043	32 48	068	50 42	148	23 22	171	36 28	233	30 13	277	25 29	315
194	23 45	043	33 20	068	51 00	149	23 28	172	36 00	234	29 38	277	25 05	316
	◆DENEB		VEGA		Rasalhague		◆ARCTURUS		REGULUS		◆POLLUX		CAPELLA	
195	24 09	044	33 52	069	22 18	100	51 17	150	35 32	235	29 04	278	24 41	316
196	24 33	045	34 24	070	22 52	101	51 34	152	35 04	236	28 30	279	24 17	317
197	24 57	045	34 56	070	23 26	102	51 50	153	34 35	237	27 56	280	23 54	318
198	25 22	046	35 29	071	23 59	103	52 05	155	34 07	238	27 22	280	23 31	318
199	25 47	047	36 01	072	24 33	104	52 19	156	33 37	239	26 49	281	23 08	319
200	26 12	047	36 34	072	25 06	105	52 32	158	33 08	240	26 15	282	22 46	320
201	26 37	048	37 07	073	25 39	105	52 45	159	32 38	241	25 41	283	22 23	320
202	27 03	048	37 40	074	26 12	106	52 57	161	32 08	242	25 08	284	22 02	321
203	27 29	049	38 13	075	26 45	107	53 08	162	31 37	243	24 34	284	21 40	321
204	27 55	050	38 46	075	27 18	108	53 18	164	31 06	244	24 01	285	21 19	322
205	28 21	050	39 20	076	27 51	109	53 27	165	30 35	245	23 28	286	20 58	323
206	28 48	051	39 53	077	28 23	110	53 35	167	30 04	246	22 55	287	20 37	323
207	29 15	052	40 27	077	28 56	111	53 42	169	29 33	247	22 22	287	20 17	324
208	29 42	052	41 00	078	29 28	112	53 48	170	29 01	248	21 49	288	19 57	325
209	30 09	053	41 34	079	29 59	113	53 54	172	28 29	249	21 17	289	19 37	325
	◆DENEB		VEGA		Rasalhague		◆ARCTURUS		REGULUS		◆POLLUX		CAPELLA	
210	30 37	053	42 08	080	30 31	114	53 58	173	27 57	249	20 44	290	19 18	326
211	31 04	054	42 42	080	31 02	115	54 02	175	27 25	250	20 12	290	18 58	327
212	31 32	055	43 16	081	31 34	116	54 04	177	26 52	251	19 39	291	18 40	327
213	32 01	055	43 50	082	32 05	117	54 06	178	26 19	252	19 07	292	18 21	328
214	32 29	056	44 24	083	32 35	118	54 06	180	25 47	253	18 36	293	18 03	329
215	32 58	057	44 58	083	33 06	119	54 06	181	25 14	254	18 04	293	17 45	329
216	33 26	057	45 32	084	33 36	120	54 05	183	24 40	255	17 32	294	17 28	330
217	33 55	058	46 06	085	34 05	121	54 02	185	24 07	256	17 01	295	17 11	331
218	34 25	058	46 41	086	34 35	122	53 59	186	23 34	257	16 30	295	16 54	331
219	34 54	059	47 15	086	35 04	123	53 55	188	23 00	258	15 59	296	16 38	332
220	35 24	060	47 49	087	35 33	124	53 49	189	22 26	258	15 28	297	16 22	333
221	35 53	060	48 24	088	36 01	125	53 43	191	21 53	259	14 57	298	16 06	333
222	36 23	061	48 58	089	36 29	126	53 36	193	21 19	260	14 27	298	15 51	334
223	36 53	061	49 33	089	36 57	127	53 28	194	20 45	261	13 57	299	15 36	335
224	37 24	062	50 07	090	37 24	128	53 19	196	20 11	262	13 27	300	15 22	335
	◆DENEB		VEGA		Rasalhague		◆ARCTURUS		REGULUS		Dubhe		◆CAPELLA	
225	37 54	063	50 41	091	37 51	129	53 09	197	19 37	263	59 32	307	15 07	336
226	38 25	063	51 16	092	38 18	130	52 59	199	19 03	264	59 04	307	14 53	337
227	38 56	064	51 50	093	38 44	131	52 47	200	18 28	264	58 37	307	14 40	337
228	39 27	064	52 25	094	39 10	132	52 35	202	17 54	265	58 09	308	14 27	338
229	39 58	065	52 59	095	39 35	134	52 21	203	17 20	266	57 42	308	14 14	339
230	40 29	066	53 33	095	39 59	135	52 07	205	16 45	267	57 15	308	14 02	339
231	41 01	066	54 07	096	40 24	136	51 52	206	16 11	268	56 48	308	13 50	340
232	41 32	067	54 42	097	40 47	137	51 37	208	15 37	269	56 21	309	13 39	341
233	42 04	068	55 16	098	41 11	138	51 20	209	15 02	269	55 54	309	13 27	341
234	42 36	068	55 50	099	41 33	139	51 03	211	14 28	270	55 27	309	13 17	342
235	43 08	069	56 24	100	41 55	141	50 45	212	13 53	271	55 01	309	13 06	343
236	43 40	069	56 57	101	42 17	142	50 26	214	13 19	272	54 34	310	12 56	344
237	44 12	070	57 31	102	42 38	143	50 07	215	12 45	273	54 08	310	12 47	344
238	44 45	071	58 05	103	42 58	144	49 47	216	12 10	273	53 42	310	12 38	345
239	45 17	071	58 38	104	43 18	146	49 26	218	11 36	274	53 16	311	12 29	346
	Schedar		◆DENEB		VEGA		Rasalhague		◆ARCTURUS		Denebola		◆Dubhe	
240	28 40	029	45 50	072	59 11	105	43 37	147	49 05	219	27 27	256	52 50	311
241	28 57	029	46 23	073	59 45	106	43 55	148	48 43	220	26 54	256	52 24	311
242	29 14	030	46 56	073	60 18	107	44 13	149	48 20	222	26 20	257	51 58	312
243	29 31	030	47 29	074	60 50	109	44 30	151	47 57	223	25 47	258	51 32	312
244	29 48	031	48 02	075	61 23	110	44 47	152	47 33	224	25 13	259	51 07	312
245	30 06	031	48 35	075	61 55	111	45 03	153	47 09	226	24 39	260	50 41	313
246	30 24	032	49 08	076	62 27	112	45 18	155	46 44	227	24 05	261	50 16	313
247	30 42	032	49 42	077	62 59	113	45 32	156	46 19	228	23 31	262	49 51	313
248	31 01	033	50 15	077	63 30	115	45 46	157	45 53	229	22 57	262	49 26	314
249	31 19	033	50 49	078	64 01	116	45 58	159	45 27	230	22 23	263	49 01	314
250	31 38	034	51 22	079	64 32	117	46 10	160	45 00	232	21 49	264	48 37	314
251	31 58	034	51 56	079	65 03	119	46 22	162	44 33	233	21 14	265	48 12	315
252	32 17	035	52 30	080	65 33	120	46 32	163	44 05	234	20 40	266	47 48	315
253	32 37	035	53 04	081	66 02	122	46 42	164	43 37	235	20 06	267	47 24	316
254	32 57	036	53 38	081	66 31	123	46 51	166	43 09	236	19 31	268	47 00	316
	Schedar		DENEB		◆ALTAIR		Rasalhague		◆ARCTURUS		Alkaid		◆CAPELLA	
255	33 18	037	54 12	082	32 50	127	46 59	167	42 40	237	60 36	279	11 05	357
256	33 38	037	54 46	083	33 17	128	47 06	169	42 11	238	60 02	280	11 03	358
257	33 59	038	55 20	083	33 44	129	47 12	170	41 41	239	59 28	280	11 02	358
258	34 20	038	55 54	084	34 10	130	47 18	171	41 11	241	58 54	281	11 01	359
259	34 42	039	56 29	085	34 37	131	47 23	173	40 41	242	58 20	282	11 01	000
260	35 03	039	57 03	086	35 02	132	47 26	174	40 11	243	57 47	282	11 01	000
261	35 25	040	57 37	086	35 28	133	47 29	176	39 40	244	57 13	283	11 01	001
262	35 47	040	58 12	087	35 52	134	47 31	177	39 09	245	56 40	283	11 02	002
263	36 09	041	58 46	088	36 17	136	47 33	179	38 38	246	56 06	284	11 03	003
264	36 32	041	59 20	089	36 41	137	47 33	180	38 06	247	55 33	285	11 05	003
265	36 54	042	59 55	090	37 04	138	47 32	182	37 35	248	55 00	285	11 07	004
266	37 17	042	60 29	090	37 27	139	47 31	183	37 03	249	54 26	286	11 10	005
267	37 41	043	61 04	091	37 49	140	47 29	184	36 30	250	53 53	286	11 13	005
268	38 04	043	61 38	092	38 11	141	47 26	186	35 58	251	53 20	287	11 16	006
269	38 28	044	62 12	093	38 32	142	47 22	187	35 26	252	52 48	288	11 20	007

LHA ♈	Hc	Zn	Hc	Zn	Hc	Zn	Hc	Zn	Hc	Zn	Hc	Zn	Hc	Zn
	◆CAPELLA		Alpheratz		◆ALTAIR		Rasalhague		◆ARCTURUS		Alkaid		Kochab	
270	11 24	007	22 17	071	38 53	144	47 17	189	34 53	253	52 15	288	63 25	333
271	11 29	008	22 50	071	39 13	145	47 11	190	34 20	253	51 42	289	63 10	333
272	11 34	009	23 23	072	39 33	146	47 05	192	33 47	254	51 10	289	62 54	333
273	11 40	010	23 55	073	39 52	147	46 57	193	33 14	255	50 37	290	62 38	333
274	11 46	010	24 28	074	40 10	148	46 49	194	32 40	256	50 05	291	62 23	333
275	11 52	011	25 01	074	40 28	150	46 40	196	32 07	257	49 33	291	62 07	332
276	11 59	012	25 34	075	40 45	151	46 30	197	31 33	258	49 01	292	61 51	332
277	12 06	012	26 08	076	41 01	152	46 20	199	30 59	259	48 29	292	61 35	332
278	12 13	013	26 41	077	41 17	153	46 08	200	30 26	260	47 57	293	61 18	332
279	12 21	014	27 15	077	41 32	155	45 56	201	29 52	261	47 25	293	61 02	332
280	12 30	014	27 48	078	41 46	156	45 43	203	29 18	262	46 54	294	60 46	332
281	12 39	015	28 22	079	42 00	157	45 29	204	28 44	262	46 23	295	60 30	332
282	12 48	016	28 56	080	42 13	159	45 15	206	28 09	263	45 51	295	60 13	332
283	12 57	017	29 30	080	42 25	160	45 00	207	27 35	264	45 20	296	59 57	332
284	13 07	017	30 04	081	42 36	161	44 44	208	27 01	265	44 49	296	59 41	332
	◆CAPELLA		Alpheratz		◆ALTAIR		Rasalhague		◆ARCTURUS		Alkaid		Kochab	
285	13 18	018	30 38	082	42 47	163	44 27	209	26 27	266	44 19	297	59 24	332
286	13 28	019	31 12	083	42 57	164	44 10	211	25 52	267	43 48	297	59 08	331
287	13 40	019	31 46	083	43 06	165	43 52	212	25 18	267	43 17	298	58 51	331
288	13 51	020	32 20	084	43 15	167	43 34	213	24 44	268	42 47	299	58 35	331
289	14 03	021	32 54	085	43 22	168	43 14	215	24 09	269	42 17	299	58 19	331
290	14 16	021	33 29	086	43 29	169	42 54	216	23 35	270	41 47	300	58 02	331
291	14 28	022	34 03	087	43 35	171	42 34	217	23 00	271	41 17	300	57 46	331
292	14 41	023	34 37	087	43 40	172	42 13	218	22 26	272	40 47	301	57 29	332
293	14 55	023	35 12	088	43 45	173	41 51	220	21 52	272	40 18	301	57 13	332
294	15 09	024	35 46	089	43 48	175	41 29	221	21 17	273	39 49	302	56 56	332
295	15 23	025	36 21	090	43 51	176	41 06	222	20 43	274	39 20	302	56 40	332
296	15 38	025	36 55	091	43 53	177	40 43	223	20 09	275	38 51	303	56 24	332
297	15 53	026	37 29	091	43 54	179	40 19	224	19 34	276	38 22	304	56 07	332
298	16 08	027	38 04	092	43 55	180	39 55	226	19 00	276	37 53	304	55 51	332
299	16 24	027	38 38	093	43 54	182	39 30	227	18 26	277	37 25	305	55 35	332
	CAPELLA		◆Alpheratz		Enif		ALTAIR		◆VEGA		Alphecca		◆Alioth	
300	16 40	028	39 13	094	40 25	145	43 53	183	68 41	229	35 05	267	36 00	318
301	16 56	029	39 47	095	40 44	146	43 51	184	68 15	231	34 30	268	35 37	319
302	17 13	029	40 21	096	41 03	148	43 48	186	67 48	233	33 56	269	35 14	319
303	17 30	030	40 55	097	41 21	149	43 44	187	67 20	234	33 22	270	34 52	320
304	17 47	031	41 30	097	41 38	150	43 39	188	66 52	236	32 47	271	34 30	320
305	18 05	031	42 04	098	41 55	151	43 34	190	66 23	237	32 13	271	34 08	321
306	18 23	032	42 38	099	42 11	153	43 28	191	65 54	239	31 38	272	33 46	321
307	18 42	033	43 12	100	42 27	154	43 21	192	65 24	240	31 04	273	33 25	322
308	19 00	033	43 45	101	42 42	155	43 13	194	64 54	242	30 30	274	33 04	322
309	19 19	034	44 19	102	42 56	157	43 04	195	64 24	243	29 55	275	32 43	323
310	19 39	035	44 53	103	43 09	158	42 55	196	63 53	244	29 21	275	32 22	323
311	19 59	035	45 26	104	43 22	159	42 45	198	63 22	246	28 47	276	32 02	324
312	20 19	036	46 00	105	43 33	160	42 34	199	62 50	247	28 13	277	31 42	325
313	20 39	037	46 33	106	43 45	162	42 22	200	62 18	248	27 38	278	31 22	325
314	21 00	037	47 06	107	43 55	163	42 10	202	61 46	249	27 04	279	31 03	326
	CAPELLA		◆Hamal		Alpheratz		Enif		◆ALTAIR		VEGA		◆Alioth	
315	21 21	038	26 27	086	47 39	108	44 05	165	41 57	203	61 14	251	30 43	326
316	21 42	039	27 01	087	48 11	109	44 13	166	41 43	204	60 41	252	30 24	327
317	22 04	039	27 35	088	48 44	110	44 21	167	41 28	206	60 08	253	30 05	327
318	22 26	040	28 10	089	49 16	111	44 29	169	41 13	207	59 35	254	29 47	328
319	22 48	041	28 44	089	49 48	112	44 35	170	40 57	208	59 02	255	29 29	328
320	23 10	041	29 19	090	50 20	113	44 40	171	40 41	209	58 29	256	29 11	329
321	23 33	042	29 53	091	50 52	114	44 45	173	40 23	211	57 55	257	28 53	329
322	23 56	042	30 27	092	51 23	115	44 49	174	40 06	212	57 22	258	28 36	330
323	24 19	043	31 02	093	51 54	116	44 52	176	39 47	213	56 48	259	28 19	330
324	24 43	044	31 36	094	52 24	118	44 55	177	39 28	214	56 14	260	28 02	331
325	25 07	044	32 10	094	52 55	119	44 56	178	39 08	215	55 40	261	27 45	332
326	25 31	045	32 45	095	53 25	120	44 57	180	38 48	217	55 06	262	27 29	332
327	25 56	046	33 19	096	53 55	121	44 56	181	38 27	218	54 32	263	27 13	333
328	26 20	046	33 53	097	54 24	122	44 55	182	38 06	219	53 58	264	26 57	333
329	26 45	047	34 27	098	54 53	124	44 53	184	37 44	220	53 24	265	26 42	334
	CAPELLA		◆Hamal		Alpheratz		Enif		◆ALTAIR		VEGA		◆Alioth	
330	27 11	047	35 01	099	55 21	125	44 51	185	37 21	221	52 49	266	26 27	334
331	27 36	048	35 35	100	55 49	126	44 47	187	36 58	223	52 15	267	26 12	335
332	28 02	049	36 09	100	56 17	128	44 43	188	36 35	224	51 41	267	25 58	335
333	28 28	049	36 43	101	56 44	129	44 38	189	36 11	225	51 06	268	25 44	336
334	28 54	050	37 17	102	57 10	130	44 32	191	35 46	226	50 32	269	25 30	337
335	29 20	050	37 50	103	57 36	132	44 25	192	35 21	227	49 57	270	25 16	337
336	29 47	051	38 24	104	58 02	133	44 17	194	34 56	228	49 23	271	25 03	338
337	30 14	052	38 57	105	58 27	135	44 09	195	34 30	229	48 49	272	24 50	338
338	30 41	052	39 30	106	58 51	136	43 59	196	34 04	230	48 14	272	24 38	339
339	31 08	053	40 03	107	59 14	138	43 49	198	33 37	231	47 40	273	24 26	339
340	31 36	054	40 36	108	59 37	139	43 39	199	33 10	232	47 06	274	24 14	340
341	32 04	054	41 09	109	59 59	141	43 27	200	32 43	233	46 31	275	24 02	341
342	32 32	055	41 41	110	60 21	142	43 15	202	32 15	234	45 57	275	23 51	341
343	33 00	055	42 13	111	60 41	144	43 02	203	31 47	235	45 23	276	23 40	342
344	33 28	056	42 45	112	61 01	146	42 48	204	31 18	236	44 49	277	23 29	342
	◆CAPELLA		ALDEBARAN		◆Diphda		Enif		ALTAIR		◆VEGA		Alioth	
345	33 57	057	16 47	085	13 47	154	42 34	205	30 50	237	44 14	278	23 19	343
346	34 26	057	17 21	086	14 02	155	42 19	207	30 20	238	43 40	278	23 09	344
347	34 55	058	17 56	087	14 16	156	42 03	208	29 51	239	43 06	279	23 00	344
348	35 24	058	18 30	087	14 30	157	41 46	209	29 21	240	42 32	280	22 50	345
349	35 53	059	19 05	088	14 43	158	41 29	211	28 51	241	41 58	281	22 41	345
350	36 23	060	19 39	089	14 55	159	41 11	212	28 21	242	41 25	281	22 33	346
351	36 53	060	20 13	090	15 07	160	40 53	213	27 50	243	40 51	282	22 25	346
352	37 23	061	20 48	091	15 18	161	40 34	214	27 19	244	40 17	283	22 17	347
353	37 53	061	21 22	091	15 29	162	40 14	216	26 48	245	39 44	284	22 09	348
354	38 23	062	21 57	092	15 39	163	39 54	217	26 17	246	39 10	284	22 02	348
355	38 54	063	22 31	093	15 49	164	39 33	218	25 45	247	38 37	285	21 55	349
356	39 24	063	23 05	094	15 58	165	39 11	219	25 13	248	38 04	286	21 49	349
357	39 55	064	23 40	095	16 07	166	38 49	220	24 41	249	37 31	286	21 43	350
358	40 26	064	24 14	096	16 15	167	38 27	221	24 09	250	36 58	287	21 37	351
359	40 57	065	24 48	097	16 22	168	38 04	223	23 37	251	36 25	288	21 31	351

LHA ♈	Hc	Zn	Hc	Zn	Hc	Zn	Hc	Zn	Hc	Zn	Hc	Zn	Hc	Zn
	◆CAPELLA		ALDEBARAN		Hamal		◆Alpheratz		ALTAIR		◆VEGA		Alioth	
0	41 03	065	25 30	097	51 16	129	65 07	175	23 23	252	35 33	289	20 27	352
1	41 35	065	26 05	098	51 43	130	65 09	177	22 49	253	35 00	290	20 22	352
2	42 08	066	26 40	099	52 09	132	65 10	179	22 15	254	34 27	290	20 18	353
3	42 40	067	27 14	099	52 35	133	65 10	181	21 41	255	33 54	291	20 14	354
4	43 12	067	27 49	100	53 01	134	65 09	184	21 07	256	33 21	292	20 10	354
5	43 45	068	28 24	101	53 26	136	65 06	186	20 33	256	32 48	292	20 07	355
6	44 18	068	28 58	102	53 50	137	65 02	188	19 59	257	32 16	293	20 04	355
7	44 51	069	29 33	103	54 14	138	64 56	190	19 24	258	31 43	294	20 01	356
8	45 24	070	30 07	104	54 37	140	64 50	192	18 50	259	31 11	294	19 59	357
9	45 57	070	30 41	105	54 59	141	64 42	194	18 15	260	30 39	295	19 57	357
10	46 30	071	31 15	106	55 21	143	64 33	196	17 40	261	30 07	296	19 55	358
11	47 03	071	31 49	107	55 42	144	64 23	198	17 05	262	29 36	296	19 54	358
12	47 37	072	32 23	107	56 02	146	64 11	200	16 31	262	29 04	297	19 53	359
13	48 10	073	32 56	108	56 22	147	63 59	202	15 56	263	28 33	298	19 53	000
14	48 44	073	33 30	109	56 40	149	63 45	204	15 21	264	28 02	298	19 53	000
	Dubhe		◆CAPELLA		ALDEBARAN		Hamal		◆Alpheratz		DENEB		◆VEGA	
15	27 53	015	49 18	074	34 03	110	56 58	151	63 31	206	48 52	285	27 31	299
16	28 03	016	49 52	075	34 36	111	57 15	152	63 15	207	48 18	286	27 00	300
17	28 12	016	50 26	075	35 09	112	57 31	154	62 58	209	47 44	287	26 29	300
18	28 22	017	51 00	076	35 41	113	57 46	155	62 40	211	47 10	287	25 59	301
19	28 32	017	51 34	076	36 14	114	58 00	157	62 22	213	46 37	288	25 29	302
20	28 43	018	52 09	077	36 46	115	58 14	159	62 02	215	46 03	288	24 59	302
21	28 54	018	52 43	078	37 18	116	58 26	160	61 42	216	45 30	289	24 29	303
22	29 05	019	53 18	078	37 49	117	58 37	162	61 21	218	44 57	290	24 00	304
23	29 16	019	53 52	079	38 20	118	58 47	164	60 59	220	44 23	290	23 31	304
24	29 28	020	54 27	080	38 51	119	58 57	166	60 36	221	43 50	291	23 02	305
25	29 40	020	55 02	080	39 22	120	59 05	167	60 12	223	43 18	291	22 33	306
26	29 52	021	55 36	081	39 52	121	59 12	169	59 48	224	42 45	292	22 04	306
27	30 04	021	56 11	082	40 22	122	59 18	171	59 23	226	42 12	293	21 36	307
28	30 17	022	56 46	082	40 52	123	59 23	173	58 57	227	41 40	293	21 08	308
29	30 30	022	57 21	083	41 21	124	59 27	175	58 31	229	41 07	294	20 40	308
	Dubhe		◆POLLUX		BETELGEUSE		RIGEL		◆Hamal		Alpheratz		◆DENEB	
30	30 44	022	24 15	075	23 52	112	15 32	129	59 30	176	58 04	230	40 35	294
31	30 57	023	24 50	076	24 24	113	16 00	130	59 31	178	57 37	232	40 03	295
32	31 11	023	25 24	077	24 57	113	16 26	131	59 32	180	57 09	233	39 31	296
33	31 25	024	25 58	077	25 29	114	16 53	132	59 31	182	56 41	234	39 00	296
34	31 40	024	26 33	078	26 01	115	17 19	133	59 30	184	56 12	236	38 28	297
35	31 54	025	27 07	079	26 33	116	17 44	134	59 27	185	55 43	237	37 57	297
36	32 09	025	27 42	080	27 04	117	18 09	135	59 23	187	55 13	238	37 25	298
37	32 25	026	28 17	080	27 36	118	18 34	136	59 18	189	54 43	239	36 54	299
38	32 40	026	28 51	081	28 07	119	18 58	137	59 12	191	54 12	241	36 24	299
39	32 56	027	29 26	082	28 37	120	19 22	138	59 05	193	53 41	242	35 53	300
40	33 12	027	30 01	083	29 08	121	19 46	139	58 57	194	53 10	243	35 22	300
41	33 28	028	30 36	083	29 38	122	20 09	140	58 48	196	52 38	244	34 52	301
42	33 45	028	31 11	084	30 07	123	20 31	141	58 37	198	52 07	245	34 22	302
43	34 01	029	31 46	085	30 37	124	20 54	142	58 26	200	51 34	246	33 52	302
44	34 18	029	32 22	086	31 06	125	21 15	143	58 14	201	51 02	247	33 22	303
	Dubhe		◆POLLUX		BETELGEUSE		RIGEL		◆Hamal		Alpheratz		◆DENEB	
45	34 36	030	32 57	087	31 35	126	21 36	144	58 00	203	50 29	249	32 53	303
46	34 53	030	33 32	087	32 03	127	21 57	145	57 46	205	49 56	250	32 23	304
47	35 11	030	34 07	088	32 31	128	22 17	146	57 31	206	49 23	251	31 54	305
48	35 29	031	34 43	089	32 58	129	22 37	147	57 15	208	48 50	252	31 25	305
49	35 47	031	35 18	090	33 26	130	22 56	148	56 58	209	48 16	253	30 57	306
50	36 06	032	35 53	091	33 52	131	23 14	149	56 40	211	47 42	254	30 28	306
51	36 24	032	36 28	091	34 19	132	23 32	150	56 22	213	47 08	255	30 00	307
52	36 43	033	37 04	092	34 44	133	23 50	151	56 02	214	46 34	256	29 32	308
53	37 03	033	37 39	093	35 10	135	24 07	152	55 42	216	46 00	257	29 04	308
54	37 22	034	38 14	094	35 35	136	24 23	153	55 21	217	45 26	258	28 37	309
55	37 42	034	38 49	095	35 59	137	24 39	154	55 00	219	44 51	258	28 09	309
56	38 01	034	39 24	096	36 23	138	24 54	155	54 37	220	44 17	259	27 42	310
57	38 21	035	39 59	096	36 46	139	25 09	156	54 14	222	43 42	260	27 15	311
58	38 42	035	40 34	097	37 09	140	25 23	157	53 51	223	43 07	261	26 49	311
59	39 02	036	41 09	098	37 32	141	25 36	158	53 26	224	42 32	262	26 22	312
	◆Dubhe		POLLUX		SIRIUS		◆RIGEL		Hamal		◆Alpheratz		DENEB	
60	39 23	036	41 44	099	10 53	140	25 49	159	53 01	226	41 57	263	25 56	313
61	39 44	037	42 19	100	11 16	141	26 01	160	52 36	227	41 22	264	25 30	313
62	40 05	037	42 54	101	11 38	142	26 13	161	52 10	228	40 47	265	25 05	314
63	40 26	037	43 28	102	12 00	142	26 24	162	51 43	230	40 12	266	24 39	314
64	40 48	038	44 03	103	12 21	143	26 34	164	51 16	231	39 37	266	24 14	315
65	41 09	038	44 37	104	12 42	144	26 44	165	50 48	232	39 02	267	23 50	316
66	41 31	039	45 11	105	13 02	145	26 53	166	50 20	233	38 26	268	23 25	316
67	41 53	039	45 45	106	13 22	146	27 01	167	49 52	235	37 51	269	23 01	317
68	42 16	039	46 19	107	13 41	147	27 09	168	49 23	236	37 16	270	22 37	318
69	42 38	040	46 53	108	14 00	148	27 16	169	48 53	237	36 41	271	22 13	318
70	43 01	040	47 26	109	14 19	149	27 22	170	48 24	238	36 05	271	21 50	319
71	43 24	041	48 00	110	14 37	150	27 28	171	47 53	239	35 30	272	21 27	319
72	43 47	041	48 33	111	14 54	151	27 33	172	47 23	240	34 55	273	21 04	320
73	44 10	041	49 06	112	15 11	152	27 37	174	46 52	242	34 20	274	20 41	321
74	44 33	042	49 38	113	15 27	153	27 41	175	46 21	243	33 44	274	20 19	321
	Dubhe		◆REGULUS		PROCYON		SIRIUS		◆RIGEL		Hamal		◆DENEB	
75	44 57	042	17 03	093	31 26	131	15 43	154	27 44	176	45 49	244	19 57	322
76	45 21	042	17 38	094	31 52	132	15 59	155	27 46	177	45 18	245	19 36	323
77	45 45	043	18 14	095	32 18	133	16 13	156	27 48	178	44 45	246	19 14	323
78	46 09	043	18 49	096	32 43	135	16 28	157	27 49	179	44 13	247	18 53	324
79	46 33	044	19 24	096	33 08	136	16 42	158	27 49	180	43 41	248	18 33	325
80	46 57	044	19 59	097	33 32	137	16 55	159	27 48	181	43 08	249	18 13	325
81	47 22	044	20 34	098	33 56	138	17 07	160	27 47	182	42 35	250	17 53	326
82	47 46	045	21 09	099	34 20	139	17 19	160	27 45	184	42 02	251	17 33	326
83	48 11	045	21 43	100	34 43	140	17 31	161	27 43	185	41 28	252	17 14	327
84	48 36	045	22 18	101	35 05	141	17 42	162	27 40	186	40 54	253	16 55	328
85	49 01	046	22 53	102	35 27	142	17 52	163	27 36	187	40 21	254	16 36	328
86	49 27	046	23 27	102	35 48	143	18 02	164	27 31	188	39 47	255	16 18	329
87	49 52	046	24 02	103	36 09	145	18 11	165	27 26	189	39 13	256	16 00	330
88	50 18	047	24 36	104	36 29	146	18 20	166	27 20	190	38 38	257	15 42	330
89	50 43	047	25 10	105	36 49	147	18 28	167	27 13	191	38 04	258	15 25	331

LHA ♈	Hc	Zn	Hc	Zn	Hc	Zn	Hc	Zn	Hc	Zn	Hc	Zn	Hc	Zn
	Dubhe		◆REGULUS		PROCYON		SIRIUS		◆RIGEL		Mirfak		◆DENEB	
90	51 09	047	25 44	106	37 08	148	18 35	168	27 06	192	66 09	276	15 08	332
91	51 35	048	26 18	107	37 26	149	18 42	169	26 58	194	65 34	277	14 52	332
92	52 01	048	26 51	108	37 44	151	18 48	170	26 50	195	64 59	277	14 36	333
93	52 28	048	27 25	109	38 01	152	18 54	171	26 40	196	64 24	278	14 20	334
94	52 54	048	27 58	110	38 17	153	18 58	172	26 30	197	63 49	279	14 04	334
95	53 20	049	28 31	110	38 33	154	19 03	173	26 20	198	63 14	279	13 49	335
96	53 47	049	29 04	111	38 48	155	19 06	174	26 09	199	62 39	280	13 35	336
97	54 14	049	29 37	112	39 02	157	19 10	175	25 57	200	62 04	281	13 21	337
98	54 41	050	30 10	113	39 16	158	19 12	176	25 44	201	61 30	281	13 07	337
99	55 07	050	30 42	114	39 29	159	19 14	178	25 31	202	60 55	282	12 53	338
100	55 34	050	31 14	115	39 41	160	19 15	179	25 18	203	60 21	282	12 40	339
101	56 02	050	31 46	116	39 52	162	19 16	180	25 04	204	59 46	283	12 27	339
102	56 29	051	32 17	117	40 03	163	19 16	181	24 49	205	59 12	283	12 15	340
103	56 56	051	32 49	118	40 13	164	19 15	182	24 33	206	58 38	284	12 03	341
104	57 24	051	33 20	119	40 22	166	19 14	183	24 17	208	58 04	285	11 52	341
	◆Dubhe		Denebola		REGULUS		◆SIRIUS		RIGEL		ALDEBARAN		◆Mirfak	
105	57 51	051	21 58	096	33 50	120	19 12	184	24 01	209	43 25	231	57 29	285
106	58 19	052	22 33	096	34 21	121	19 09	185	23 43	210	42 57	232	56 55	286
107	58 46	052	23 08	097	34 51	122	19 06	186	23 26	211	42 30	233	56 22	286
108	59 14	052	23 43	098	35 20	123	19 02	187	23 08	212	42 01	234	55 48	287
109	59 42	052	24 17	099	35 50	124	18 58	188	22 49	213	41 33	235	55 14	287
110	60 10	052	24 52	100	36 19	125	18 53	189	22 29	214	41 03	236	54 40	288
111	60 38	053	25 27	101	36 47	126	18 47	190	22 10	215	40 34	237	54 07	289
112	61 06	053	26 02	101	37 16	127	18 41	191	21 49	216	40 04	238	53 34	289
113	61 34	053	26 36	102	37 43	128	18 34	192	21 28	217	39 34	239	53 00	290
114	62 02	053	27 11	103	38 11	130	18 27	193	21 07	218	39 03	240	52 27	290
115	62 30	053	27 45	104	38 38	131	18 19	194	20 45	219	38 33	241	51 54	291
116	62 59	053	28 19	105	39 04	132	18 10	195	20 23	220	38 01	243	51 21	291
117	63 27	053	28 53	106	39 31	133	18 01	196	20 00	221	37 30	244	50 48	292
118	63 55	054	29 27	107	39 56	134	17 51	197	19 37	222	36 58	245	50 16	292
119	64 24	054	30 00	108	40 21	135	17 41	198	19 14	223	36 26	246	49 43	293
	Kochab		◆ARCTURUS		REGULUS		◆SIRIUS		BETELGEUSE		CAPELLA		◆Schedar	
120	47 58	024	13 01	075	40 46	136	17 30	199	37 09	220	63 09	269	34 31	321
121	48 12	024	13 35	076	41 10	138	17 18	200	36 46	221	62 34	270	34 09	322
122	48 26	024	14 09	077	41 33	139	17 06	201	36 23	222	61 59	271	33 48	322
123	48 41	024	14 44	078	41 56	140	16 53	202	35 59	223	61 24	272	33 26	323
124	48 55	024	15 18	078	42 19	141	16 40	203	35 34	224	60 48	273	33 05	323
125	49 10	025	15 53	079	42 41	142	16 26	204	35 10	225	60 13	273	32 44	324
126	49 24	025	16 28	080	43 02	144	16 12	204	34 44	227	59 38	274	32 23	324
127	49 39	025	17 02	081	43 22	145	15 57	205	34 18	228	59 03	275	32 02	325
128	49 54	025	17 37	082	43 42	146	15 42	206	33 52	229	58 28	276	31 42	325
129	50 09	025	18 12	082	44 02	147	15 26	207	33 25	230	57 53	276	31 22	326
130	50 24	025	18 47	083	44 20	149	15 09	208	32 58	231	57 18	277	31 02	326
131	50 39	026	19 22	084	44 38	150	14 52	209	32 31	232	56 43	278	30 42	327
132	50 55	026	19 57	085	44 56	151	14 35	210	32 03	233	56 08	278	30 23	327
133	51 10	026	20 32	085	45 12	153	14 17	211	31 34	234	55 33	279	30 04	328
134	51 25	026	21 08	086	45 28	154	13 58	212	31 06	235	54 58	280	29 45	328
	Kochab		◆ARCTURUS		REGULUS		◆POLLUX		BETELGEUSE		CAPELLA		◆Schedar	
135	51 41	026	21 43	087	45 43	155	60 42	215	30 37	236	54 23	280	29 27	329
136	51 57	026	22 18	088	45 57	157	60 21	216	30 07	237	53 49	281	29 09	329
137	52 12	026	22 53	089	46 11	158	60 00	218	29 37	238	53 14	282	28 51	330
138	52 28	027	23 28	089	46 24	159	59 38	220	29 07	239	52 40	282	28 33	330
139	52 44	027	24 04	090	46 36	161	59 15	221	28 37	240	52 05	283	28 16	331
140	53 00	027	24 39	091	46 47	162	58 51	223	28 06	241	51 31	284	27 59	331
141	53 16	027	25 14	092	46 57	164	58 27	224	27 35	242	50 57	284	27 42	332
142	53 32	027	25 49	093	47 07	165	58 02	226	27 04	243	50 23	285	27 26	332
143	53 48	027	26 25	094	47 15	167	57 37	227	26 33	244	49 49	286	27 09	333
144	54 04	027	27 00	094	47 23	168	57 10	229	26 01	245	49 15	286	26 53	333
145	54 20	027	27 35	095	47 30	169	56 44	230	25 29	246	48 41	287	26 38	334
146	54 36	027	28 10	096	47 36	171	56 16	231	24 57	247	48 07	287	26 23	335
147	54 53	027	28 45	097	47 41	172	55 48	233	24 24	247	47 33	288	26 08	335
148	55 09	028	29 20	098	47 45	174	55 20	234	23 52	248	47 00	289	25 53	336
149	55 25	028	29 55	099	47 49	175	54 51	235	23 19	249	46 27	289	25 39	336
	◆VEGA		ARCTURUS		SPICA		◆REGULUS		POLLUX		◆CAPELLA		Schedar	
150	12 30	038	30 30	099	11 37	128	47 51	177	54 22	237	45 53	290	25 24	337
151	12 52	039	31 05	100	12 04	129	47 53	178	53 52	238	45 20	290	25 11	337
152	13 14	040	31 39	101	12 31	130	47 54	180	53 22	239	44 47	291	24 57	338
153	13 37	040	32 14	102	12 58	131	47 53	181	52 52	240	44 14	292	24 44	338
154	14 00	041	32 48	103	13 24	132	47 52	182	52 21	242	43 42	292	24 31	339
155	14 23	042	33 23	104	13 50	133	47 50	184	51 50	243	43 09	293	24 19	340
156	14 46	042	33 57	105	14 16	134	47 47	185	51 18	244	42 37	293	24 07	340
157	15 10	043	34 31	106	14 41	135	47 44	187	50 47	245	42 04	294	23 55	341
158	15 35	044	35 05	107	15 06	136	47 39	188	50 15	246	41 32	295	23 43	341
159	15 59	044	35 38	108	15 31	137	47 33	190	49 42	247	41 00	295	23 32	342
160	16 24	045	36 12	108	15 55	137	47 27	191	49 10	248	40 28	296	23 21	342
161	16 49	046	36 45	109	16 18	138	47 20	193	48 37	249	39 57	296	23 11	343
162	17 14	046	37 18	110	16 41	139	47 12	194	48 04	250	39 25	297	23 01	344
163	17 40	047	37 51	111	17 04	140	47 03	195	47 30	251	38 54	298	22 51	344
164	18 06	048	38 24	112	17 26	141	46 53	197	46 57	252	38 23	298	22 41	345
	◆DENEB		VEGA		ARCTURUS		◆SPICA		REGULUS		◆POLLUX		CAPELLA	
165	13 35	024	18 32	048	38 57	113	17 48	142	46 42	198	46 23	253	37 52	299
166	13 50	025	18 59	049	39 29	114	18 10	143	46 31	200	45 49	254	37 21	299
167	14 05	026	19 26	050	40 01	115	18 31	144	46 18	201	45 15	255	36 50	300
168	14 20	026	19 53	051	40 33	116	18 51	145	46 05	202	44 41	256	36 20	300
169	14 36	027	20 20	051	41 04	117	19 11	146	45 51	204	44 07	257	35 49	301
170	14 52	028	20 48	052	41 35	118	19 30	147	45 37	205	43 32	258	35 19	302
171	15 09	028	21 16	053	42 06	120	19 49	148	45 21	207	42 58	259	34 49	302
172	15 26	029	21 44	053	42 36	121	20 08	149	45 05	208	42 23	260	34 20	303
173	15 43	030	22 12	054	43 07	122	20 26	150	44 49	209	41 48	261	33 50	303
174	16 00	030	22 41	055	43 36	123	20 43	151	44 31	211	41 13	262	33 21	304
175	16 18	031	23 10	055	44 06	124	21 00	152	44 13	212	40 38	263	32 52	305
176	16 37	032	23 39	056	44 35	125	21 16	153	43 54	213	40 03	263	32 23	305
177	16 56	032	24 08	057	45 04	126	21 32	154	43 34	214	39 28	264	31 54	306
178	17 14	033	24 37	057	45 32	127	21 47	155	43 14	216	38 53	265	31 25	306
179	17 34	034	25 07	058	46 00	129	22 01	156	42 53	217	38 18	266	30 57	307

LHA ♈	Hc	Zn	Hc	Zn	Hc	Zn	Hc	Zn	Hc	Zn	Hc	Zn	Hc	Zn
	DENEB		◆VEGA		ARCTURUS		◆SPICA		REGULUS		POLLUX		◆CAPELLA	
180	17 53	034	25 37	059	46 27	130	22 15	157	42 32	218	37 43	267	30 29	308
181	18 13	035	26 07	059	46 54	131	22 29	158	42 10	219	37 08	268	30 01	308
182	18 33	035	26 38	060	47 20	132	22 42	159	41 47	221	36 32	268	29 34	309
183	18 54	036	27 08	061	47 46	133	22 54	160	41 24	222	35 57	269	29 06	309
184	19 15	037	27 39	061	48 11	135	23 05	161	41 00	223	35 22	270	28 39	310
185	19 36	037	28 10	062	48 36	136	23 16	162	40 36	224	34 47	271	28 12	311
186	19 58	038	28 41	062	49 00	137	23 27	163	40 11	225	34 11	272	27 46	311
187	20 20	039	29 13	063	49 24	139	23 36	164	39 46	226	33 36	273	27 19	312
188	20 42	039	29 44	064	49 47	140	23 46	166	39 20	228	33 01	273	26 53	312
189	21 04	040	30 16	064	50 09	141	23 54	167	38 53	229	32 26	274	26 27	313
190	21 27	041	30 48	065	50 31	143	24 02	168	38 27	230	31 51	275	26 02	314
191	21 50	041	31 20	066	50 52	144	24 09	169	38 00	231	31 15	276	25 36	314
192	22 14	042	31 52	066	51 13	145	24 16	170	37 32	232	30 40	276	25 11	315
193	22 37	043	32 25	067	51 32	147	24 22	171	37 04	233	30 05	277	24 46	315
194	23 01	043	32 57	068	51 51	148	24 27	172	36 36	234	29 30	278	24 22	316
	◆DENEB		VEGA		Rasalhague		◆ARCTURUS		REGULUS		◆POLLUX		CAPELLA	
195	23 26	044	33 30	068	22 28	100	52 09	150	36 07	235	28 56	279	23 57	317
196	23 50	044	34 03	069	23 03	101	52 27	151	35 38	236	28 21	279	23 33	317
197	24 15	045	34 36	070	23 38	101	52 43	153	35 08	237	27 46	280	23 09	318
198	24 40	046	35 09	070	24 12	102	52 59	154	34 38	238	27 11	281	22 46	319
199	25 05	046	35 42	071	24 47	103	53 14	156	34 08	239	26 37	282	22 23	319
200	25 31	047	36 16	072	25 21	104	53 28	157	33 38	240	26 02	282	22 00	320
201	25 57	047	36 49	072	25 55	105	53 41	159	33 07	241	25 28	283	21 37	320
202	26 23	048	37 23	073	26 29	106	53 53	160	32 36	242	24 54	284	21 15	321
203	26 49	049	37 57	074	27 03	107	54 05	162	32 04	243	24 19	285	20 53	322
204	27 16	049	38 31	075	27 37	108	54 15	164	31 33	244	23 45	285	20 31	322
205	27 43	050	39 05	075	28 10	109	54 25	165	31 01	245	23 11	286	20 10	323
206	28 10	051	39 39	076	28 44	109	54 33	167	30 29	246	22 38	287	19 49	324
207	28 37	051	40 13	077	29 17	110	54 41	168	29 56	247	22 04	288	19 28	324
208	29 05	052	40 48	077	29 50	111	54 48	170	29 24	248	21 30	288	19 08	325
209	29 33	052	41 22	078	30 22	112	54 53	172	28 51	249	20 57	289	18 48	326
	◆DENEB		VEGA		Rasalhague		◆ARCTURUS		REGULUS		◆POLLUX		CAPELLA	
210	30 01	053	41 57	079	30 55	113	54 58	173	28 18	250	20 24	290	18 28	326
211	30 29	054	42 31	079	31 27	114	55 01	175	27 44	251	19 51	291	18 08	327
212	30 58	054	43 06	080	31 59	115	55 04	177	27 11	252	19 18	291	17 49	327
213	31 26	055	43 41	081	32 31	116	55 06	178	26 37	253	18 45	292	17 30	328
214	31 55	055	44 15	082	33 03	117	55 06	180	26 04	254	18 12	293	17 12	329
215	32 24	056	44 50	082	33 34	118	55 06	182	25 30	254	17 40	294	16 54	329
216	32 54	057	45 25	083	34 05	119	55 04	183	24 56	255	17 08	294	16 36	330
217	33 23	057	46 00	084	34 36	120	55 02	185	24 22	256	16 36	295	16 19	331
218	33 53	058	46 35	084	35 06	121	54 59	186	23 47	257	16 04	296	16 02	331
219	34 23	058	47 11	085	35 36	122	54 54	188	23 13	258	15 32	296	15 45	332
220	34 53	059	47 46	086	36 06	123	54 49	190	22 38	259	15 01	297	15 29	333
221	35 23	060	48 21	087	36 35	124	54 42	191	22 04	260	14 29	298	15 13	333
222	35 54	060	48 56	088	37 04	125	54 35	193	21 29	261	13 58	299	14 57	334
223	36 24	061	49 31	088	37 33	126	54 26	195	20 54	261	13 28	299	14 42	335
224	36 55	061	50 07	089	38 01	127	54 17	196	20 19	262	12 57	300	14 27	335
	Schedar		◆DENEB		VEGA		Rasalhague		◆ARCTURUS		Denebola		◆Dubhe	
225	24 11	020	37 26	062	50 42	090	38 29	128	54 07	198	35 55	242	58 55	308
226	24 23	021	37 58	063	51 17	091	38 56	130	53 55	199	35 24	243	58 28	308
227	24 35	021	38 29	063	51 52	092	39 23	131	53 43	201	34 52	244	58 00	309
228	24 48	022	39 00	064	52 28	092	39 50	132	53 30	202	34 20	245	57 32	309
229	25 02	022	39 32	064	53 03	093	40 16	133	53 16	204	33 48	246	57 05	309
230	25 15	023	40 04	065	53 38	094	40 41	134	53 02	206	33 16	247	56 38	309
231	25 29	023	40 36	066	54 13	095	41 06	135	52 46	207	32 43	248	56 10	310
232	25 43	024	41 08	066	54 48	096	41 31	136	52 30	209	32 11	249	55 43	310
233	25 58	024	41 41	067	55 23	097	41 55	138	52 12	210	31 38	250	55 16	310
234	26 12	025	42 13	067	55 58	098	42 19	139	51 54	211	31 04	251	54 49	310
235	26 27	026	42 46	068	56 33	099	42 41	140	51 36	213	30 31	252	54 22	311
236	26 43	026	43 18	069	57 08	100	43 04	141	51 16	214	29 58	252	53 56	311
237	26 58	027	43 51	069	57 43	101	43 26	143	50 56	216	29 24	253	53 29	311
238	27 14	027	44 24	070	58 18	102	43 47	144	50 35	217	28 50	254	53 02	311
239	27 31	028	44 58	070	58 52	103	44 07	145	50 13	218	28 16	255	52 36	312
	Schedar		◆DENEB		VEGA		Rasalhague		◆ARCTURUS		Denebola		◆Dubhe	
240	27 47	028	45 31	071	59 26	104	44 27	146	49 51	220	27 42	256	52 10	312
241	28 04	029	46 04	072	60 01	105	44 46	148	49 28	221	27 08	257	51 44	312
242	28 21	029	46 38	072	60 35	106	45 05	149	49 05	222	26 33	258	51 18	313
243	28 39	030	47 11	073	61 08	107	45 23	150	48 40	224	25 59	259	50 52	313
244	28 56	030	47 45	073	61 42	108	45 40	152	48 16	225	25 24	259	50 26	313
245	29 14	031	48 19	074	62 16	109	45 56	153	47 51	226	24 49	260	50 00	314
246	29 33	031	48 53	075	62 49	110	46 12	154	47 25	228	24 14	261	49 35	314
247	29 51	032	49 27	075	63 22	111	46 27	156	46 58	229	23 40	262	49 10	314
248	30 10	033	50 01	076	63 54	113	46 41	157	46 32	230	23 05	263	48 44	315
249	30 29	033	50 35	077	64 27	114	46 54	158	46 04	231	22 30	264	48 19	315
250	30 49	034	51 10	077	64 59	115	47 07	160	45 37	232	21 54	265	47 54	315
251	31 08	034	51 44	078	65 31	117	47 19	161	45 09	234	21 19	265	47 30	316
252	31 28	035	52 19	079	66 02	118	47 30	163	44 40	235	20 44	266	47 05	316
253	31 48	035	52 53	079	66 33	120	47 40	164	44 11	236	20 09	267	46 41	316
254	32 09	036	53 28	080	67 03	121	47 49	166	43 42	237	19 34	268	46 16	317
	◆Schedar		DENEB		ALTAIR		◆Rasalhague		ARCTURUS		◆Alkaid		Kochab	
255	32 29	036	54 03	081	33 25	126	47 57	167	43 12	238	60 26	281	66 05	339
256	32 50	037	54 38	081	33 54	127	48 05	168	42 42	239	59 51	281	65 52	338
257	33 11	037	55 13	082	34 21	128	48 11	170	42 11	240	59 16	282	65 39	338
258	33 33	038	55 48	083	34 49	130	48 17	171	41 40	241	58 42	283	65 26	338
259	33 54	038	56 23	083	35 16	131	48 22	173	41 09	242	58 08	283	65 12	337
260	34 16	039	56 58	084	35 42	132	48 26	174	40 38	243	57 33	284	64 59	337
261	34 39	039	57 33	085	36 09	133	48 29	176	40 06	244	56 59	284	64 45	337
262	35 01	040	58 08	086	36 34	134	48 31	177	39 34	245	56 25	285	64 30	336
263	35 23	040	58 43	086	36 59	135	48 33	179	39 02	246	55 51	285	64 16	336
264	35 46	041	59 18	087	37 24	136	48 33	180	38 30	247	55 17	286	64 02	336
265	36 09	041	59 53	088	37 48	137	48 32	182	37 57	248	54 43	287	63 47	335
266	36 33	042	60 29	089	38 12	138	48 31	183	37 24	249	54 09	287	63 32	335
267	36 56	042	61 04	089	38 35	140	48 29	185	36 51	250	53 36	288	63 17	335
268	37 20	043	61 39	090	38 58	141	48 25	186	36 18	251	53 02	288	63 02	335
269	37 44	043	62 15	091	39 20	142	48 21	187	35 44	252	52 29	289	62 47	334

LAT 54°N

LHA ♈	Hc	Zn	Hc	Zn	Hc	Zn	Hc	Zn	Hc	Zn	Hc	Zn	Hc	Zn
	◆Mirfak		Alpheratz		◆ALTAIR		Rasalhague		◆ARCTURUS		Alkaid		Kochab	
270	18 52	025	21 57	070	39 41	143	48 16	189	35 10	253	51 55	289	62 32	334
271	19 07	026	22 30	071	40 02	144	48 10	190	34 37	254	51 22	290	62 16	334
272	19 23	026	23 04	072	40 22	146	48 03	192	34 03	255	50 49	291	62 01	334
273	19 38	027	23 37	072	40 42	147	47 56	193	33 28	256	50 16	291	61 45	334
274	19 55	028	24 11	073	41 01	148	47 47	195	32 54	257	49 43	292	61 29	333
275	20 11	028	24 45	074	41 19	149	47 38	196	32 20	258	49 11	292	61 13	333
276	20 28	029	25 19	075	41 37	150	47 28	198	31 45	259	48 38	293	60 57	333
277	20 45	030	25 53	075	41 54	152	47 17	199	31 11	260	48 06	293	60 41	333
278	21 03	030	26 27	076	42 10	153	47 05	200	30 36	260	47 33	294	60 25	333
279	21 21	031	27 01	077	42 26	154	46 52	202	30 01	261	47 01	294	60 09	333
280	21 39	031	27 36	078	42 41	156	46 38	203	29 26	262	46 29	295	59 53	333
281	21 57	032	28 10	078	42 55	157	46 24	205	28 51	263	45 57	296	59 37	333
282	22 16	033	28 45	079	43 09	158	46 09	206	28 16	264	45 25	296	59 20	332
283	22 35	033	29 19	080	43 21	160	45 53	207	27 41	265	44 54	297	59 04	332
284	22 55	034	29 54	080	43 33	161	45 37	209	27 06	265	44 22	297	58 48	332
	◆CAPELLA		Alpheratz		◆ALTAIR		Rasalhague		◆ARCTURUS		Alkaid		Kochab	
285	12 21	018	30 29	081	43 44	162	45 19	210	26 31	266	43 51	298	58 31	332
286	12 32	019	31 04	082	43 55	164	45 01	211	25 56	267	43 20	298	58 15	332
287	12 43	019	31 39	083	44 04	165	44 43	213	25 20	268	42 49	299	57 59	332
288	12 55	020	32 14	084	44 13	166	44 23	214	24 45	269	42 18	299	57 42	332
289	13 07	021	32 49	084	44 21	168	44 03	215	24 10	270	41 47	300	57 26	332
290	13 20	021	33 24	085	44 28	169	43 43	216	23 35	270	41 17	300	57 09	332
291	13 33	022	33 59	086	44 34	170	43 22	218	22 59	271	40 47	301	56 53	332
292	13 46	023	34 34	087	44 40	172	43 00	219	22 24	272	40 16	302	56 36	332
293	14 00	023	35 10	087	44 44	173	42 37	220	21 49	273	39 46	302	56 20	332
294	14 14	024	35 45	088	44 48	175	42 14	221	21 14	274	39 17	303	56 04	332
295	14 28	025	36 20	089	44 51	176	41 51	223	20 38	274	38 47	303	55 47	332
296	14 43	025	36 55	090	44 53	177	41 27	224	20 03	275	38 18	304	55 31	332
297	14 59	026	37 31	091	44 54	179	41 02	225	19 28	276	37 48	304	55 14	332
298	15 14	027	38 06	091	44 55	180	40 37	226	18 53	277	37 19	305	54 58	332
299	15 30	027	38 41	092	44 54	182	40 11	227	18 18	278	36 50	305	54 42	333
	CAPELLA		◆Alpheratz		Enif		ALTAIR		◆VEGA		Alphecca		◆Alioth	
300	15 47	028	39 16	093	41 14	145	44 53	183	69 20	231	35 07	268	35 15	319
301	16 03	029	39 51	094	41 34	146	44 50	184	68 52	233	34 32	269	34 51	319
302	16 20	029	40 27	095	41 53	147	44 47	186	68 23	235	33 57	270	34 29	320
303	16 38	030	41 02	096	42 12	148	44 43	187	67 54	236	33 21	270	34 06	320
304	16 56	031	41 37	097	42 30	150	44 38	189	67 25	238	32 46	271	33 43	321
305	17 14	031	42 12	097	42 48	151	44 33	190	66 55	239	32 11	272	33 21	321
306	17 32	032	42 47	098	43 04	152	44 26	191	66 24	241	31 36	273	32 59	322
307	17 51	033	43 22	099	43 21	154	44 19	193	65 53	242	31 00	274	32 38	322
308	18 10	033	43 56	100	43 36	155	44 11	194	65 22	244	30 25	274	32 16	323
309	18 30	034	44 31	101	43 51	156	44 02	195	64 50	245	29 50	275	31 55	323
310	18 50	035	45 06	102	44 04	157	43 52	197	64 18	246	29 15	276	31 34	324
311	19 10	035	45 40	103	44 18	159	43 42	198	63 45	248	28 40	277	31 13	324
312	19 30	036	46 14	104	44 30	160	43 30	199	63 13	249	28 05	278	30 53	325
313	19 51	036	46 49	105	44 42	162	43 18	201	62 40	250	27 30	278	30 33	325
314	20 12	037	47 23	106	44 52	163	43 05	202	62 06	251	26 55	279	30 13	326
	CAPELLA		◆Hamal		Alpheratz		Enif		◆ALTAIR		VEGA		◆Alioth	
315	20 33	038	26 22	086	47 56	107	45 02	164	42 52	203	61 33	252	29 53	326
316	20 55	038	26 57	086	48 30	108	45 11	166	42 37	205	60 59	254	29 34	327
317	21 17	039	27 33	087	49 04	109	45 20	167	42 22	206	60 25	255	29 15	328
318	21 40	040	28 08	088	49 37	110	45 27	168	42 07	207	59 51	256	28 56	328
319	22 02	040	28 43	089	50 10	111	45 34	170	41 50	209	59 17	257	28 38	329
320	22 25	041	29 18	090	50 43	112	45 40	171	41 33	210	58 42	258	28 19	329
321	22 48	041	29 54	090	51 15	113	45 45	173	41 15	211	58 08	259	28 01	330
322	23 12	042	30 29	091	51 48	114	45 49	174	40 56	212	57 33	260	27 44	330
323	23 36	043	31 04	092	52 20	115	45 52	175	40 37	214	56 59	261	27 26	331
324	24 00	043	31 39	093	52 52	116	45 54	177	40 17	215	56 24	262	27 09	331
325	24 24	044	32 15	094	53 23	118	45 56	178	39 57	216	55 49	263	26 52	332
326	24 49	045	32 50	095	53 54	119	45 57	180	39 36	217	55 14	263	26 36	332
327	25 14	045	33 25	095	54 25	120	45 56	181	39 14	218	54 39	264	26 20	333
328	25 39	046	34 00	096	54 55	121	45 55	183	38 52	220	54 04	265	26 04	333
329	26 04	046	34 35	097	55 25	122	45 53	184	38 30	221	53 28	266	25 48	334
	CAPELLA		◆Hamal		Alpheratz		Enif		◆ALTAIR		VEGA		◆Alioth	
330	26 30	047	35 10	098	55 55	124	45 50	185	38 06	222	52 53	267	25 33	335
331	26 56	048	35 45	099	56 24	125	45 47	187	37 42	223	52 18	268	25 18	335
332	27 22	048	36 20	100	56 53	126	45 42	188	37 18	224	51 43	269	25 03	336
333	27 48	049	36 54	101	57 21	128	45 37	190	36 53	225	51 07	269	24 49	336
334	28 15	049	37 29	102	57 49	129	45 30	191	36 28	226	50 32	270	24 35	337
335	28 42	050	38 04	102	58 16	130	45 23	192	36 02	228	49 57	271	24 21	337
336	29 09	051	38 38	103	58 42	132	45 15	194	35 36	229	49 22	272	24 08	338
337	29 36	051	39 12	104	59 08	133	45 07	195	35 09	230	48 46	273	23 55	339
338	30 04	052	39 46	105	59 33	135	44 57	196	34 42	231	48 11	273	23 42	339
339	30 32	052	40 20	106	59 58	136	44 47	198	34 15	232	47 36	274	23 29	340
340	31 00	053	40 54	107	60 22	138	44 35	199	33 47	233	47 01	275	23 17	340
341	31 28	054	41 28	108	60 45	140	44 23	201	33 18	234	46 26	276	23 05	341
342	31 57	054	42 01	109	61 08	141	44 11	202	32 50	235	45 51	276	22 54	341
343	32 26	055	42 34	110	61 30	143	43 57	203	32 21	236	45 16	277	22 43	342
344	32 55	055	43 07	111	61 51	144	43 43	205	31 51	237	44 41	278	22 32	343
	◆CAPELLA		ALDEBARAN		◆Diphda		Enif		ALTAIR		◆VEGA		Alioth	
345	33 24	056	16 42	085	14 42	154	43 28	206	31 22	238	44 06	279	22 22	343
346	33 53	057	17 17	085	14 57	155	43 12	207	30 52	239	43 31	279	22 12	344
347	34 23	057	17 52	086	15 11	156	42 56	208	30 21	240	42 56	280	22 02	344
348	34 52	058	18 27	087	15 25	157	42 38	210	29 51	241	42 22	281	21 52	345
349	35 22	058	19 02	088	15 38	158	42 20	211	29 20	242	41 47	282	21 43	345
350	35 52	059	19 38	089	15 51	159	42 02	212	28 48	243	41 12	282	21 35	346
351	36 23	060	20 13	089	16 03	160	41 43	214	28 17	244	40 38	283	21 26	347
352	36 53	060	20 48	090	16 15	161	41 23	215	27 45	245	40 04	284	21 18	347
353	37 24	061	21 23	091	16 26	162	41 03	216	27 13	246	39 29	284	21 11	348
354	37 55	061	21 59	092	16 37	163	40 41	217	26 41	247	38 55	285	21 03	348
355	38 26	062	22 34	093	16 47	164	40 20	218	26 08	248	38 21	286	20 56	349
356	38 57	063	23 09	094	16 56	165	39 58	220	25 36	248	37 47	286	20 50	350
357	39 28	063	23 44	094	17 05	166	39 35	221	25 03	249	37 14	287	20 44	350
358	40 00	064	24 20	095	17 13	167	39 12	222	24 30	250	36 40	288	20 38	351
359	40 32	064	24 55	096	17 21	168	38 48	223	23 56	251	36 06	288	20 32	351

 LAT 53°N

LHA ♈	Hc Zn	Hc Zn	Hc Zn	Hc Zn	Hc Zn	Hc Zn	Hc Zn
	◆CAPELLA	ALDEBARAN	Hamal	◆Alpheratz	ALTAIR	◆VEGA	Alioth
0	40 38 064	25 37 096	51 53 128	66 07 175	23 41 252	35 13 290	19 28 352
1	41 10 065	26 12 097	52 21 129	66 09 177	23 07 253	34 39 290	19 23 353
2	41 43 065	26 48 098	52 49 131	66 10 179	22 32 254	34 05 291	19 18 353
3	42 16 066	27 24 099	53 16 132	66 10 182	21 57 255	33 32 292	19 14 354
4	42 49 066	28 00 100	53 43 133	66 08 184	21 22 256	32 58 292	19 10 354
5	43 22 067	28 35 101	54 09 135	66 05 186	20 47 257	32 25 293	19 07 355
6	43 55 068	29 11 101	54 34 136	66 01 188	20 12 258	31 52 294	19 04 355
7	44 29 068	29 46 102	54 59 138	65 55 190	19 36 258	31 19 294	19 01 356
8	45 02 069	30 21 103	55 23 139	65 48 192	19 01 259	30 46 295	18 59 357
9	45 36 069	30 56 104	55 46 140	65 40 194	18 25 260	30 13 296	18 57 357
10	46 10 070	31 31 105	56 09 142	65 31 196	17 50 261	29 41 296	18 55 358
11	46 44 070	32 06 106	56 31 143	65 20 198	17 14 262	29 09 297	18 54 358
12	47 18 071	32 41 107	56 52 145	65 08 200	16 38 263	28 37 298	18 53 359
13	47 52 072	33 15 108	57 12 147	64 54 202	16 03 263	28 05 298	18 53 000
14	48 26 072	33 49 109	57 31 148	64 40 204	15 27 264	27 33 299	18 53 000
	Dubhe	◆CAPELLA	ALDEBARAN	Hamal	◆Alpheratz	DENEB	◆VEGA
15	26 55 015	49 01 073	34 23 110	57 50 150	64 25 206	48 36 286	27 01 299
16	27 05 015	49 35 073	34 57 111	58 08 151	64 08 208	48 01 287	26 30 300
17	27 15 016	50 10 074	35 31 111	58 25 153	63 50 210	47 27 288	25 59 301
18	27 25 016	50 45 075	36 05 112	58 41 155	63 32 212	46 52 288	25 28 301
19	27 35 017	51 20 075	36 38 113	58 55 156	63 12 214	46 18 289	24 57 302
20	27 46 017	51 55 076	37 11 114	59 09 158	62 51 216	45 44 289	24 27 303
21	27 57 018	52 30 076	37 44 115	59 22 160	62 30 217	45 10 290	23 56 303
22	28 08 018	53 05 077	38 16 116	59 34 162	62 08 219	44 36 291	23 26 304
23	28 19 019	53 40 078	38 48 117	59 45 163	61 44 221	44 02 291	22 57 305
24	28 31 019	54 15 078	39 20 118	59 55 165	61 21 222	43 29 292	22 27 305
25	28 43 020	54 51 079	39 52 119	60 03 167	60 56 224	42 55 292	21 58 306
26	28 56 020	55 26 080	40 23 121	60 11 169	60 30 225	42 22 293	21 29 307
27	29 08 021	56 02 080	40 54 122	60 17 171	60 04 227	41 49 293	21 00 307
28	29 21 021	56 37 081	41 25 123	60 23 173	59 38 229	41 16 294	20 31 308
29	29 35 022	57 13 082	41 55 124	60 27 174	59 10 230	40 43 295	20 03 309
	Dubhe	◆POLLUX	BETELGEUSE	RIGEL	◆Hamal	Alpheratz	◆DENEB
30	29 48 022	24 00 075	24 14 111	16 10 129	60 30 176	58 42 231	40 10 295
31	30 02 023	24 35 075	24 47 112	16 38 130	60 31 178	58 14 233	39 37 296
32	30 16 023	25 10 076	25 21 113	17 06 131	60 32 180	57 45 234	39 05 296
33	30 30 024	25 45 077	25 54 114	17 33 132	60 31 182	57 15 236	38 33 297
34	30 45 024	26 20 078	26 27 115	17 59 133	60 30 184	56 45 237	38 01 298
35	31 00 025	26 55 078	26 59 116	18 26 134	60 27 186	56 15 238	37 29 298
36	31 15 025	27 31 079	27 32 117	18 52 135	60 23 187	55 44 239	36 57 299
37	31 31 026	28 06 080	28 04 118	19 17 136	60 17 189	55 13 241	36 25 299
38	31 46 026	28 42 081	28 36 119	19 42 137	60 11 191	54 41 242	35 54 300
39	32 02 026	29 18 081	29 07 120	20 07 138	60 03 193	54 09 243	35 23 300
40	32 18 027	29 53 082	29 38 121	20 31 139	59 55 195	53 37 244	34 52 301
41	32 35 027	30 29 083	30 09 122	20 55 139	59 45 197	53 04 245	34 21 302
42	32 52 028	31 05 084	30 40 123	21 18 140	59 34 198	52 31 246	33 50 302
43	33 09 028	31 41 084	31 10 124	21 41 141	59 22 200	51 58 248	33 20 303
44	33 26 029	32 17 085	31 40 125	22 03 142	59 10 202	51 24 249	32 50 303
	Dubhe	◆POLLUX	BETELGEUSE	RIGEL	◆Hamal	Alpheratz	◆DENEB
45	33 43 029	32 53 086	32 10 126	22 25 143	58 56 204	50 51 250	32 19 304
46	34 01 030	33 29 087	32 39 127	22 46 144	58 41 205	50 17 251	31 50 305
47	34 19 030	34 05 088	33 08 128	23 07 145	58 25 207	49 42 252	31 20 305
48	34 37 031	34 41 088	33 36 129	23 27 146	58 08 209	49 08 253	30 51 306
49	34 56 031	35 17 089	34 04 130	23 46 147	57 50 210	48 33 254	30 21 306
50	35 15 031	35 53 090	34 32 131	24 06 148	57 32 212	47 59 255	29 52 307
51	35 34 032	36 29 091	34 59 132	24 24 150	57 12 213	47 24 256	29 24 308
52	35 53 032	37 06 091	35 25 133	24 42 151	56 52 215	46 49 257	28 55 308
53	36 12 033	37 42 092	35 52 134	25 00 152	56 31 217	46 13 258	28 27 309
54	36 32 033	38 18 093	36 17 135	25 17 153	56 09 218	45 38 259	27 59 309
55	36 52 034	38 54 094	36 43 136	25 33 154	55 46 220	45 03 259	27 31 310
56	37 12 034	39 30 095	37 07 137	25 49 155	55 23 221	44 27 260	27 03 310
57	37 32 034	40 06 096	37 32 139	26 04 156	54 59 222	43 52 261	26 36 311
58	37 53 035	40 42 096	37 55 140	26 18 157	54 34 224	43 16 262	26 09 312
59	38 13 035	41 17 097	38 18 141	26 32 158	54 09 225	42 40 263	25 42 312
	◆Dubhe	POLLUX	SIRIUS	◆RIGEL	Hamal	◆Alpheratz	DENEB
60	38 34 036	41 53 098	11 39 140	26 45 159	53 43 227	42 04 264	25 15 313
61	38 55 036	42 29 099	12 02 141	26 58 160	53 16 228	41 28 265	24 49 313
62	39 17 036	43 05 100	12 25 141	27 10 161	52 49 229	40 52 266	24 23 314
63	39 38 037	43 40 101	12 47 142	27 21 162	52 22 231	40 16 266	23 57 315
64	40 00 037	44 15 102	13 09 143	27 32 163	51 53 232	39 40 267	23 32 315
65	40 22 038	44 51 103	13 30 144	27 42 165	51 25 233	39 04 268	23 07 316
66	40 44 038	45 26 104	13 51 145	27 51 166	50 56 234	38 28 269	22 42 317
67	41 07 038	46 01 105	14 12 146	28 00 167	50 26 236	37 52 270	22 17 317
68	41 29 039	46 36 106	14 32 147	28 08 168	49 56 237	37 16 270	21 52 318
69	41 52 039	47 10 107	14 51 148	28 15 169	49 26 238	36 40 271	21 28 318
70	42 15 040	47 45 108	15 10 149	28 21 170	48 55 239	36 04 272	21 05 319
71	42 38 040	48 19 109	15 28 150	28 27 171	48 24 240	35 27 273	20 41 320
72	43 01 040	48 53 110	15 46 151	28 32 172	47 52 241	34 51 274	20 18 320
73	43 25 041	49 27 111	16 04 152	28 37 173	47 20 243	34 15 274	19 55 321
74	43 48 041	50 01 112	16 21 153	28 41 175	46 48 244	33 39 275	19 32 322
	Dubhe	◆REGULUS	PROCYON	SIRIUS	◆RIGEL	Hamal	◆DENEB
75	44 12 041	17 06 093	32 05 131	16 37 154	28 44 176	46 15 245	19 10 322
76	44 36 042	17 42 094	32 32 132	16 53 155	28 46 177	45 43 246	18 48 323
77	45 00 042	18 18 094	32 59 133	17 08 155	28 48 178	45 10 247	18 26 323
78	45 25 043	18 54 095	33 25 134	17 23 156	28 49 179	44 36 248	18 05 324
79	45 49 043	19 30 096	33 51 135	17 37 157	28 49 180	44 03 249	17 44 325
80	46 14 043	20 06 097	34 16 136	17 51 158	28 48 181	43 29 250	17 23 325
81	46 39 044	20 42 098	34 41 137	18 04 159	28 47 182	42 55 251	17 03 326
82	47 03 044	21 18 099	35 05 138	18 16 160	28 45 184	42 21 252	16 43 327
83	47 29 044	21 53 099	35 28 140	18 28 161	28 43 185	41 46 253	16 23 327
84	47 54 045	22 29 100	35 52 141	18 39 162	28 39 186	41 12 254	16 04 328
85	48 19 045	23 04 101	36 14 142	18 50 163	28 35 187	40 37 255	15 45 329
86	48 45 045	23 40 102	36 36 143	19 00 164	28 31 188	40 02 256	15 26 329
87	49 10 045	24 15 103	36 58 144	19 09 165	28 25 189	39 27 257	15 08 330
88	49 36 046	24 50 104	37 19 145	19 18 166	28 19 190	38 52 257	14 50 331
89	50 02 046	25 25 105	37 39 147	19 26 167	28 12 191	38 16 258	14 33 331

LHA ♈	Hc Zn	Hc Zn	Hc Zn	Hc Zn	Hc Zn	Hc Zn	Hc Zn
	◆Dubhe	REGULUS	PROCYON	◆SIRIUS	RIGEL	◆Hamal	Schedar
90	50 28 046	26 00 105	37 58 148	19 34 168	28 05 193	37 41 259	46 35 308
91	50 54 047	26 35 106	38 17 149	19 41 169	27 56 194	37 06 260	46 06 308
92	51 21 047	27 09 107	38 36 150	19 47 170	27 48 195	36 30 261	45 38 309
93	51 47 047	27 44 108	38 53 151	19 53 171	27 38 196	35 54 262	45 10 309
94	52 14 048	28 18 109	39 10 153	19 58 172	27 28 197	35 18 263	44 42 310
95	52 40 048	28 52 110	39 27 154	20 02 173	27 17 198	34 43 264	44 15 310
96	53 07 048	29 26 111	39 42 155	20 06 174	27 05 199	34 07 264	43 47 311
97	53 34 048	30 00 112	39 57 156	20 09 175	26 53 200	33 31 265	43 20 311
98	54 01 049	30 33 113	40 11 158	20 12 176	26 40 201	32 55 266	42 53 311
99	54 28 049	31 06 114	40 25 159	20 14 177	26 27 202	32 19 267	42 26 312
100	54 56 049	31 39 115	40 37 160	20 15 179	26 13 203	31 43 268	41 59 312
101	55 23 049	32 12 116	40 49 161	20 16 180	25 58 205	31 06 269	41 32 313
102	55 50 050	32 44 116	41 00 163	20 16 181	25 43 206	30 30 269	41 06 313
103	56 18 050	33 17 117	41 11 164	20 15 182	25 27 207	29 54 270	40 39 314
104	56 45 050	33 48 118	41 20 165	20 14 183	25 10 208	29 18 271	40 13 314
	◆Dubhe	Denebola	REGULUS	◆SIRIUS	RIGEL	ALDEBARAN	◆Mirfak
105	57 13 050	22 03 095	34 20 119	20 12 184	24 53 209	44 03 231	57 13 287
106	57 41 050	22 39 096	34 51 120	20 09 185	24 36 210	43 34 232	56 38 287
107	58 09 051	23 15 097	35 22 121	20 06 186	24 17 211	43 05 234	56 04 288
108	58 37 051	23 51 098	35 53 123	20 02 187	23 59 212	42 36 235	55 30 288
109	59 05 051	24 27 098	36 23 124	19 57 188	23 39 213	42 07 236	54 55 289
110	59 33 051	25 02 099	36 53 125	19 52 189	23 19 214	41 36 237	54 21 289
111	60 01 051	25 38 100	37 23 126	19 47 190	22 59 215	41 06 238	53 47 290
112	60 29 051	26 13 101	37 52 127	19 40 191	22 38 216	40 35 239	53 13 290
113	60 57 051	26 49 102	38 21 128	19 33 192	22 17 217	40 04 240	52 40 291
114	61 25 052	27 24 103	38 49 129	19 25 193	21 55 218	39 33 241	52 06 291
115	61 54 052	27 59 104	39 17 130	19 17 194	21 32 219	39 01 242	51 32 292
116	62 22 052	28 34 104	39 44 131	19 08 195	21 09 220	38 29 243	50 59 292
117	62 50 052	29 09 105	40 11 132	18 59 196	20 46 221	37 56 244	50 26 293
118	63 19 052	29 44 106	40 38 133	18 49 197	20 22 222	37 24 245	49 52 293
119	63 47 052	30 18 107	41 04 135	18 38 198	19 58 223	36 51 246	49 19 294
	Kochab	◆ARCTURUS	REGULUS	◆SIRIUS	BETELGEUSE	CAPELLA	◆Schedar
120	47 03 023	12 46 075	41 29 136	18 27 199	37 55 220	63 09 271	33 45 321
121	47 17 023	13 21 076	41 54 137	18 15 200	37 31 222	62 33 272	33 22 322
122	47 31 024	13 56 077	42 18 138	18 02 201	37 07 223	61 57 273	33 00 322
123	47 46 024	14 31 077	42 42 139	17 49 202	36 42 224	61 21 274	32 38 323
124	48 00 024	15 06 078	43 05 141	17 36 203	36 17 225	60 45 274	32 17 323
125	48 15 024	15 41 079	43 28 142	17 21 204	35 51 226	60 09 275	31 55 324
126	48 30 024	16 17 080	43 50 143	17 07 205	35 25 227	59 33 276	31 34 324
127	48 45 024	16 53 080	44 11 144	16 51 206	34 59 228	58 57 277	31 13 325
128	49 00 025	17 28 081	44 32 146	16 36 207	34 31 229	58 21 277	30 53 325
129	49 15 025	18 04 082	44 52 147	16 19 207	34 04 230	57 45 278	30 32 326
130	49 30 025	18 40 083	45 12 148	16 02 208	33 36 231	57 10 279	30 12 326
131	49 45 025	19 16 084	45 30 150	15 45 209	33 07 232	56 34 279	29 52 327
132	50 00 025	19 51 084	45 48 151	15 27 210	32 39 233	55 58 280	29 33 327
133	50 16 025	20 27 085	46 05 152	15 08 211	32 09 234	55 23 280	29 13 328
134	50 31 026	21 03 086	46 22 154	14 49 212	31 40 235	54 47 281	28 54 328
	Kochab	◆ARCTURUS	REGULUS	◆POLLUX	BETELGEUSE	CAPELLA	◆Schedar
135	50 47 026	21 39 087	46 37 155	61 31 216	31 10 236	54 12 282	28 36 329
136	51 03 026	22 15 087	46 52 156	61 09 218	30 40 237	53 37 282	28 17 329
137	51 18 026	22 52 088	47 06 158	60 47 219	30 09 238	53 01 283	27 59 330
138	51 34 026	23 28 089	47 20 159	60 24 221	29 38 239	52 26 284	27 41 331
139	51 50 026	24 04 090	47 32 161	60 00 222	29 07 240	51 51 284	27 23 331
140	52 06 026	24 40 091	47 44 162	59 35 224	28 35 241	51 16 285	27 06 332
141	52 22 026	25 16 091	47 55 163	59 10 225	28 04 242	50 41 285	26 49 332
142	52 38 026	25 52 092	48 04 165	58 44 227	27 31 243	50 07 286	26 32 333
143	52 54 027	26 28 093	48 13 166	58 17 228	26 59 244	49 32 287	26 16 333
144	53 10 027	27 04 094	48 22 168	57 50 230	26 26 245	48 57 287	26 00 334
145	53 27 027	27 40 095	48 29 169	57 22 231	25 53 246	48 23 288	25 44 334
146	53 43 027	28 16 096	48 35 171	56 53 233	25 20 247	47 49 288	25 28 335
147	53 59 027	28 52 096	48 41 172	56 24 234	24 47 248	47 14 289	25 13 335
148	54 16 027	29 28 097	48 45 174	55 55 235	24 13 249	46 40 290	24 58 336
149	54 32 027	30 04 098	48 49 175	55 25 237	23 40 250	46 06 290	24 44 336
	◆VEGA	ARCTURUS	SPICA	◆REGULUS	POLLUX	◆CAPELLA	Schedar
150	11 43 038	30 39 099	12 14 128	48 51 177	54 55 238	45 33 291	24 29 337
151	12 05 039	31 15 100	12 42 129	48 53 178	54 24 239	44 59 291	24 15 338
152	12 28 039	31 51 101	13 10 130	48 54 180	53 53 240	44 25 292	24 02 338
153	12 51 040	32 26 101	13 37 131	48 53 181	53 21 241	43 52 293	23 48 339
154	13 14 041	33 01 102	14 04 132	48 52 183	52 49 243	43 19 293	23 35 339
155	13 38 041	33 37 103	14 31 133	48 50 184	52 17 244	42 45 294	23 23 340
156	14 02 042	34 12 104	14 57 134	48 47 186	51 44 245	42 12 294	23 10 340
157	14 26 043	34 47 105	15 23 135	48 43 187	51 12 246	41 40 295	22 58 341
158	14 51 044	35 21 106	15 49 135	48 38 188	50 38 247	41 07 295	22 47 341
159	15 16 044	35 56 107	16 14 136	48 33 190	50 05 248	40 34 296	22 35 342
160	15 41 045	36 31 108	16 39 137	48 26 191	49 31 249	40 02 297	22 24 343
161	16 07 046	37 05 109	17 03 138	48 18 193	48 57 250	39 30 297	22 14 343
162	16 33 046	37 39 110	17 27 139	48 10 194	48 23 251	38 58 298	22 03 344
163	16 59 047	38 13 111	17 50 140	48 00 196	47 49 252	38 26 298	21 53 344
164	17 26 048	38 47 112	18 13 141	47 50 197	47 14 253	37 54 299	21 44 345
	DENEB	◆VEGA	ARCTURUS	◆SPICA	REGULUS	POLLUX	◆CAPELLA
165	12 40 024	17 52 048	39 20 113	18 36 142	47 39 199	46 40 254	37 23 299
166	12 55 025	18 20 049	39 53 114	18 58 143	47 27 200	46 05 255	36 51 300
167	13 11 025	18 47 050	40 26 115	19 19 144	47 14 201	45 30 256	36 20 301
168	13 26 026	19 15 050	40 59 116	19 40 145	47 01 203	44 55 257	35 49 301
169	13 43 027	19 42 051	41 31 117	20 01 146	46 46 204	44 20 258	35 18 302
170	13 59 027	20 11 052	42 03 118	20 21 147	46 31 206	43 44 259	34 47 302
171	14 16 028	20 39 052	42 35 119	20 40 148	46 15 207	43 09 260	34 17 303
172	14 33 029	21 08 053	43 07 120	20 59 149	45 58 208	42 33 261	33 47 303
173	14 51 029	21 37 054	43 38 121	21 17 150	45 41 210	41 57 262	33 17 304
174	15 08 030	22 06 054	44 09 122	21 35 151	45 23 211	41 22 263	32 47 305
175	15 27 031	22 35 055	44 39 123	21 53 152	45 04 212	40 46 263	32 17 305
176	15 45 031	23 05 056	45 09 124	22 09 153	44 44 214	40 10 264	31 48 306
177	16 04 032	23 35 056	45 39 125	22 26 154	44 24 215	39 34 265	31 19 306
178	16 24 033	24 05 057	46 08 127	22 41 155	44 03 216	38 58 266	30 50 307
179	16 43 033	24 35 057	46 37 128	22 56 156	43 41 217	38 22 267	30 21 307

 LAT 53°N

LHA ♈	Hc	Zn	Hc	Zn	Hc	Zn	Hc	Zn	Hc	Zn	Hc	Zn	Hc	Zn
	DENEB		◆VEGA		ARCTURUS		◆SPICA		REGULUS		POLLUX		◆CAPELLA	
180	17 03	034	25 06	058	47 05	129	23 11	157	43 19	219	37 46	268	29 52	308
181	17 24	035	25 36	059	47 33	130	23 24	158	42 56	220	37 10	268	29 24	309
182	17 45	035	26 07	059	48 00	131	23 38	159	42 32	221	36 34	269	28 56	309
183	18 06	036	26 39	060	48 27	133	23 50	160	42 08	222	35 58	270	28 28	310
184	18 27	037	27 10	061	48 53	134	24 02	161	41 44	224	35 21	271	28 00	310
185	18 49	037	27 42	061	49 19	135	24 13	162	41 19	225	34 45	272	27 33	311
186	19 11	038	28 13	062	49 44	137	24 24	163	40 53	226	34 09	272	27 06	312
187	19 33	038	28 45	063	50 09	138	24 34	164	40 27	227	33 33	273	26 39	312
188	19 55	039	29 18	063	50 33	139	24 44	165	40 00	228	32 57	274	26 12	313
189	20 18	040	29 50	064	50 56	141	24 52	166	39 33	229	32 21	275	25 46	313
190	20 42	040	30 22	065	51 19	142	25 01	168	39 05	230	31 45	275	25 20	314
191	21 05	041	30 55	065	51 41	143	25 08	169	38 37	232	31 09	276	24 54	315
192	21 29	042	31 28	066	52 02	145	25 15	170	38 09	233	30 33	277	24 29	315
193	21 53	042	32 01	067	52 22	146	25 21	171	37 40	234	29 58	278	24 03	316
194	22 18	043	32 34	067	52 42	148	25 26	172	37 10	235	29 22	279	23 38	316
	◆DENEB		VEGA		Rasalhague		◆ARCTURUS		REGULUS		◆POLLUX		CAPELLA	
195	22 42	043	33 08	068	22 38	099	53 01	149	36 41	236	28 46	279	23 13	317
196	23 07	044	33 41	068	23 14	100	53 19	151	36 11	237	28 11	280	22 49	318
197	23 32	045	34 15	069	23 49	101	53 36	152	35 40	238	27 35	281	22 25	318
198	23 58	045	34 49	070	24 25	102	53 53	154	35 09	239	27 00	281	22 01	319
199	24 24	046	35 23	070	25 00	103	54 08	155	34 38	240	26 24	282	21 37	319
200	24 50	047	35 57	071	25 35	104	54 23	157	34 07	241	25 49	283	21 14	320
201	25 16	047	36 31	072	26 10	104	54 37	158	33 35	242	25 14	284	20 51	321
202	25 43	048	37 05	072	26 45	105	54 50	160	33 03	243	24 39	284	20 28	321
203	26 10	048	37 40	073	27 20	106	55 02	162	32 31	244	24 04	285	20 06	322
204	26 37	049	38 14	074	27 55	107	55 13	163	31 58	245	23 29	286	19 44	323
205	27 04	050	38 49	074	28 29	108	55 23	165	31 26	246	22 54	287	19 22	323
206	27 32	050	39 24	075	29 03	109	55 32	166	30 52	247	22 20	287	19 00	324
207	28 00	051	39 59	076	29 37	110	55 40	168	30 19	248	21 46	288	18 39	324
208	28 28	051	40 34	076	30 11	111	55 47	170	29 46	249	21 11	289	18 18	325
209	28 56	052	41 09	077	30 45	112	55 53	171	29 12	250	20 37	290	17 58	326
	◆DENEB		VEGA		Rasalhague		◆ARCTURUS		REGULUS		◆POLLUX		CAPELLA	
210	29 24	053	41 44	078	31 18	113	55 57	173	28 38	250	20 03	290	17 38	326
211	29 53	053	42 20	078	31 51	114	56 01	175	28 04	251	19 29	291	17 18	327
212	30 22	054	42 55	079	32 24	115	56 04	176	27 30	252	18 56	292	16 59	328
213	30 51	054	43 31	080	32 57	115	56 06	178	26 55	253	18 22	292	16 39	328
214	31 21	055	44 06	081	33 30	116	56 06	180	26 20	254	17 49	293	16 21	329
215	31 50	055	44 42	081	34 02	117	56 06	182	25 46	255	17 16	294	16 02	330
216	32 20	056	45 18	082	34 34	118	56 04	183	25 11	256	16 43	295	15 44	330
217	32 50	057	45 53	083	35 05	119	56 02	185	24 36	257	16 10	295	15 26	331
218	33 21	057	46 29	083	35 37	120	55 58	187	24 00	258	15 38	296	15 09	332
219	33 51	058	47 05	084	36 08	121	55 53	188	23 25	258	15 05	297	14 52	332
220	34 22	058	47 41	085	36 38	122	55 48	190	22 50	259	14 33	297	14 35	333
221	34 53	059	48 17	086	37 09	124	55 41	192	22 14	260	14 01	298	14 19	334
222	35 24	060	48 53	086	37 38	125	55 33	193	21 39	261	13 29	299	14 03	334
223	35 55	060	49 29	087	38 08	126	55 24	195	21 03	262	12 58	300	13 48	335
224	36 26	061	50 05	088	38 37	127	55 15	197	20 27	263	12 27	300	13 32	336
	Schedar		◆DENEB		VEGA		Rasalhague		◆ARCTURUS		Denebola		◆Dubhe	
225	23 14	020	36 58	061	50 41	089	39 06	128	55 04	198	36 23	243	58 18	309
226	23 27	020	37 30	062	51 17	089	39 34	129	54 52	200	35 51	244	57 50	310
227	23 39	021	38 01	062	51 53	090	40 02	130	54 39	201	35 18	245	57 22	310
228	23 53	022	38 34	063	52 30	091	40 30	131	54 26	203	34 45	245	56 54	310
229	24 06	022	39 06	064	53 06	092	40 56	132	54 11	205	34 12	246	56 27	310
230	24 20	023	39 38	064	53 42	093	41 23	133	53 56	206	33 39	247	55 59	310
231	24 34	023	40 11	065	54 18	094	41 49	135	53 39	208	33 06	248	55 32	311
232	24 48	024	40 44	065	54 54	094	42 14	136	53 22	209	32 32	249	55 04	311
233	25 03	024	41 17	066	55 30	095	42 39	137	53 04	211	31 58	250	54 37	311
234	25 18	025	41 50	067	56 06	096	43 04	138	52 45	212	31 24	251	54 10	311
235	25 33	025	42 23	067	56 42	097	43 27	139	52 26	214	30 50	252	53 43	312
236	25 49	026	42 56	068	57 17	098	43 50	141	52 05	215	30 15	253	53 16	312
237	26 05	026	43 30	068	57 53	099	44 13	142	51 44	216	29 41	254	52 49	312
238	26 21	027	44 03	069	58 29	100	44 35	143	51 22	218	29 06	255	52 22	312
239	26 38	028	44 37	069	59 04	101	44 56	144	51 00	219	28 31	256	51 56	313
	◆Schedar		DENEB		VEGA		◆Rasalhague		ARCTURUS		◆Denebola		Dubhe	
240	26 54	028	45 11	070	59 40	102	45 17	146	50 37	221	27 56	257	51 29	313
241	27 12	029	45 45	071	60 15	103	45 37	147	50 13	222	27 21	257	51 03	313
242	27 29	029	46 19	071	60 50	104	45 56	148	49 49	223	26 46	258	50 37	314
243	27 47	030	46 53	072	61 25	105	46 15	150	49 23	225	26 10	259	50 10	314
244	28 05	030	47 28	072	62 00	106	46 32	151	48 58	226	25 35	260	49 45	314
245	28 23	031	48 02	073	62 34	107	46 50	152	48 32	227	24 59	261	49 19	314
246	28 41	031	48 37	074	63 09	108	47 06	154	48 05	228	24 23	262	48 53	315
247	29 00	032	49 11	074	63 43	110	47 21	155	47 38	230	23 48	262	48 27	315
248	29 19	032	49 46	075	64 17	111	47 36	157	47 10	231	23 12	263	48 02	315
249	29 39	033	50 21	075	64 50	112	47 50	158	46 42	232	22 36	264	47 37	316
250	29 58	033	50 56	076	65 24	113	48 03	159	46 13	233	22 00	265	47 11	316
251	30 18	034	51 31	077	65 57	115	48 15	161	45 44	234	21 24	266	46 46	316
252	30 39	034	52 06	077	66 29	116	48 27	162	45 14	236	20 48	267	46 22	317
253	30 59	035	52 42	078	67 01	118	48 37	164	44 44	237	20 12	267	45 57	317
254	31 20	035	53 17	079	67 33	119	48 47	165	44 14	238	19 36	268	45 32	317
	◆Schedar		DENEB		ALTAIR		◆Rasalhague		ARCTURUS		◆Alkaid		Kochab	
255	31 41	036	53 52	079	34 01	126	48 56	167	43 43	239	60 14	282	65 09	340
256	32 02	036	54 28	080	34 30	127	49 04	168	43 12	240	59 38	283	64 56	339
257	32 23	037	55 03	081	34 59	128	49 10	170	42 41	241	59 03	284	64 43	339
258	32 45	037	55 39	081	35 27	129	49 17	171	42 09	242	58 28	284	64 30	338
259	33 07	038	56 15	082	35 55	130	49 22	173	41 37	243	57 53	285	64 17	338
260	33 29	038	56 51	083	36 22	131	49 26	174	41 04	244	57 18	285	64 03	338
261	33 52	039	57 26	083	36 49	132	49 29	176	40 32	245	56 44	286	63 49	337
262	34 15	039	58 02	084	37 16	133	49 31	177	39 59	246	56 09	286	63 35	337
263	34 37	040	58 38	085	37 42	134	49 33	179	39 26	247	55 34	287	63 21	337
264	35 01	040	59 14	085	38 07	136	49 33	180	38 52	248	55 00	287	63 07	336
265	35 24	041	59 50	086	38 32	137	49 32	182	38 19	249	54 25	288	62 52	336
266	35 48	041	60 26	087	38 57	138	49 31	183	37 45	250	53 51	288	62 38	336
267	36 11	042	61 02	088	39 21	139	49 28	185	37 11	251	53 17	289	62 23	336
268	36 36	042	61 38	088	39 44	140	49 25	186	36 36	252	52 43	290	62 08	335
269	37 00	042	62 15	089	40 07	141	49 21	188	36 02	253	52 09	290	61 53	335

LHA ♈	Hc	Zn	Hc	Zn	Hc	Zn	Hc	Zn	Hc	Zn	Hc	Zn	Hc	Zn
	◆Mirfak		Alpheratz		◆ALTAIR		Rasalhague		◆ARCTURUS		Alkaid		Kochab	
270	17 58	025	21 37	070	40 29	143	49 15	189	35 27	254	51 35	291	61 37	335
271	18 13	026	22 11	071	40 51	144	49 09	191	34 53	255	51 01	291	61 22	335
272	18 29	026	22 45	071	41 12	145	49 02	192	34 18	256	50 28	292	61 07	335
273	18 45	027	23 19	072	41 32	146	48 54	194	33 43	257	49 54	292	60 51	334
274	19 01	027	23 53	073	41 52	148	48 45	195	33 08	257	49 21	293	60 35	334
275	19 18	028	24 28	073	42 11	149	48 35	196	32 32	258	48 47	293	60 20	334
276	19 35	029	25 03	074	42 29	150	48 25	198	31 57	259	48 14	294	60 04	334
277	19 53	029	25 37	075	42 47	151	48 13	199	31 21	260	47 41	294	59 48	334
278	20 11	030	26 12	076	43 04	153	48 01	201	30 46	261	47 09	295	59 32	334
279	20 29	031	26 47	076	43 20	154	47 48	202	30 10	262	46 36	295	59 16	333
280	20 48	031	27 22	077	43 36	155	47 33	204	29 34	263	46 03	296	58 59	333
281	21 06	032	27 58	078	43 50	157	47 19	205	28 58	264	45 31	296	58 43	333
282	21 26	032	28 33	078	44 04	158	47 03	206	28 22	264	44 59	297	58 27	333
283	21 45	033	29 08	079	44 17	159	46 46	208	27 46	265	44 27	297	58 11	333
284	22 05	034	29 44	080	44 30	161	46 29	209	27 10	266	43 55	298	57 54	333
	◆Mirfak		Alpheratz		◆ALTAIR		Rasalhague		◆ARCTURUS		Alkaid		Kochab	
285	22 25	034	30 19	081	44 41	162	46 11	210	26 34	267	43 23	299	57 38	333
286	22 45	035	30 55	081	44 52	163	45 53	212	25 58	268	42 51	299	57 22	333
287	23 06	035	31 31	082	45 02	165	45 33	213	25 22	268	42 20	300	57 05	333
288	23 27	036	32 07	083	45 11	166	45 13	214	24 46	269	41 48	300	56 49	333
289	23 48	036	32 43	084	45 20	167	44 52	216	24 10	270	41 17	301	56 32	333
290	24 10	037	33 18	084	45 27	169	44 31	217	23 34	271	40 46	301	56 16	333
291	24 32	038	33 54	085	45 33	170	44 09	218	22 58	272	40 15	302	56 00	333
292	24 54	038	34 30	086	45 39	172	43 46	220	22 22	272	39 45	302	55 43	333
293	25 17	039	35 06	087	45 44	173	43 23	221	21 46	273	39 14	303	55 27	333
294	25 39	039	35 43	087	45 48	174	42 59	222	21 10	274	38 44	303	55 10	333
295	26 02	040	36 19	088	45 51	176	42 35	223	20 34	275	38 14	304	54 54	333
296	26 26	041	36 55	089	45 53	177	42 10	224	19 58	276	37 44	304	54 37	333
297	26 49	041	37 31	090	45 54	179	41 44	226	19 22	276	37 14	305	54 21	333
298	27 13	042	38 07	091	45 55	180	41 18	227	18 46	277	36 45	305	54 05	333
299	27 37	042	38 43	091	45 54	182	40 52	228	18 10	278	36 15	306	53 48	333
	CAPELLA		◆Alpheratz		Enif		ALTAIR		◆VEGA		Alphecca		◆Alioth	
300	14 54	028	39 19	092	42 02	144	45 53	183	69 56	233	35 09	269	34 29	319
301	15 11	029	39 55	093	42 23	145	45 50	184	69 27	235	34 33	270	34 06	320
302	15 28	029	40 31	094	42 43	147	45 47	186	68 57	237	33 57	270	33 43	320
303	15 46	030	41 07	095	43 03	148	45 43	187	68 27	238	33 21	271	33 20	321
304	16 04	030	41 43	096	43 22	149	45 38	189	67 56	240	32 45	272	32 57	321
305	16 22	031	42 19	096	43 40	150	45 32	190	67 24	241	32 08	273	32 34	322
306	16 41	032	42 55	097	43 57	152	45 25	191	66 53	243	31 32	273	32 12	322
307	17 00	032	43 31	098	44 14	153	45 18	193	66 20	244	30 56	274	31 50	323
308	17 20	033	44 06	099	44 30	154	45 09	194	65 47	246	30 20	275	31 28	323
309	17 40	034	44 42	100	44 45	156	45 00	196	65 14	247	29 44	276	31 07	324
310	18 00	034	45 18	101	45 00	157	44 50	197	64 41	248	29 09	277	30 46	324
311	18 21	035	45 53	102	45 13	158	44 39	198	64 07	250	28 33	277	30 25	325
312	18 41	036	46 28	103	45 26	160	44 27	200	63 33	251	27 57	278	30 04	325
313	19 03	036	47 03	104	45 38	161	44 14	201	62 59	252	27 21	279	29 43	326
314	19 24	037	47 38	105	45 50	163	44 01	202	62 25	253	26 46	280	29 23	326
	CAPELLA		◆Hamal		Alpheratz		Enif		◆ALTAIR		VEGA		◆Alioth	
315	19 46	037	26 17	085	48 13	106	46 00	164	43 47	204	61 50	254	29 03	327
316	20 08	038	26 53	086	48 48	107	46 10	165	43 32	205	61 15	255	28 44	327
317	20 30	039	27 30	087	49 22	108	46 18	167	43 16	206	60 40	256	28 24	328
318	20 53	039	28 06	087	49 57	109	46 26	168	43 00	208	60 05	257	28 05	328
319	21 16	040	28 42	088	50 31	110	46 33	170	42 43	209	59 30	258	27 46	329
320	21 40	041	29 18	089	51 05	111	46 39	171	42 25	210	58 54	259	27 28	329
321	22 03	041	29 54	090	51 38	112	46 44	172	42 06	212	58 19	260	27 09	330
322	22 27	042	30 30	091	52 12	113	46 49	174	41 47	213	57 43	261	26 52	330
323	22 51	042	31 06	091	52 45	114	46 52	175	41 27	214	57 07	262	26 34	331
324	23 16	043	31 42	092	53 18	115	46 54	177	41 07	215	56 32	263	26 16	332
325	23 41	044	32 18	093	53 50	116	46 56	178	40 45	216	55 56	264	25 59	332
326	24 06	044	32 54	094	54 22	117	46 57	180	40 24	218	55 20	265	25 43	333
327	24 31	045	33 30	095	54 54	119	46 56	181	40 01	219	54 44	266	25 26	333
328	24 57	045	34 06	096	55 26	120	46 55	183	39 38	220	54 08	267	25 10	334
329	25 23	046	34 42	096	55 57	121	46 53	184	39 15	221	53 32	267	24 54	334
	CAPELLA		◆Hamal		Alpheratz		Enif		◆ALTAIR		VEGA		◆Alioth	
330	25 49	047	35 18	097	56 28	122	46 50	185	38 51	222	52 56	268	24 39	335
331	26 15	047	35 54	098	56 58	124	46 46	187	38 26	224	52 20	269	24 23	335
332	26 42	048	36 30	099	57 28	125	46 42	188	38 01	225	51 43	270	24 08	336
333	27 09	048	37 05	100	57 57	126	46 36	190	37 35	226	51 07	271	23 54	336
334	27 36	049	37 41	101	58 26	128	46 29	191	37 09	227	50 31	272	23 40	337
335	28 03	050	38 16	102	58 54	129	46 22	193	36 43	228	49 55	272	23 26	338
336	28 31	050	38 51	103	59 22	131	46 14	194	36 15	229	49 19	273	23 12	338
337	28 59	051	39 27	103	59 49	132	46 05	195	35 48	230	48 43	274	22 59	339
338	29 27	051	40 02	104	60 15	134	45 55	197	35 20	231	48 07	275	22 46	339
339	29 55	052	40 37	105	60 41	135	45 44	198	34 52	232	47 31	275	22 33	340
340	30 24	053	41 11	106	61 06	137	45 32	200	34 23	233	46 55	276	22 21	340
341	30 53	053	41 46	107	61 31	138	45 19	201	33 54	234	46 19	277	22 09	341
342	31 22	054	42 20	108	61 54	140	45 06	202	33 24	235	45 43	277	21 57	341
343	31 51	054	42 54	109	62 17	142	44 52	204	32 54	236	45 08	278	21 46	342
344	32 20	055	43 28	110	62 39	143	44 37	205	32 24	237	44 32	279	21 35	343
	◆CAPELLA		ALDEBARAN		◆Diphda		Enif		ALTAIR		◆VEGA		Alioth	
345	32 50	055	16 36	084	15 36	154	44 22	206	31 53	238	43 56	280	21 24	343
346	33 20	056	17 12	085	15 51	155	44 05	208	31 22	239	43 21	280	21 14	344
347	33 50	057	17 48	086	16 06	156	43 48	209	30 51	240	42 45	281	21 04	344
348	34 20	057	18 24	087	16 20	157	43 30	210	30 19	241	42 10	282	20 55	345
349	34 51	058	19 00	088	16 34	158	43 12	212	29 48	242	41 35	282	20 45	345
350	35 21	058	19 36	088	16 47	159	42 53	213	29 15	243	40 59	283	20 36	346
351	35 52	059	20 12	089	17 00	160	42 33	214	28 43	244	40 24	284	20 28	347
352	36 23	060	20 48	090	17 12	161	42 12	215	28 10	245	39 49	284	20 20	347
353	36 54	060	21 24	091	17 23	162	41 51	217	27 37	246	39 14	285	20 12	348
354	37 26	061	22 01	092	17 34	163	41 29	218	27 04	247	38 39	286	20 05	348
355	37 57	061	22 37	092	17 44	164	41 07	219	26 31	248	38 05	286	19 57	349
356	38 29	062	23 13	093	17 54	165	40 44	220	25 57	249	37 30	287	19 51	350
357	39 01	062	23 49	094	18 03	166	40 20	221	25 24	250	36 56	288	19 44	350
358	39 33	063	24 25	095	18 12	167	39 56	223	24 50	251	36 21	288	19 38	351
359	40 05	064	25 01	096	18 20	168	39 31	224	24 15	252	35 47	289	19 33	351

LHA ♈	Hc	Zn	Hc	Zn	Hc	Zn	Hc	Zn	Hc	Zn	Hc	Zn	Hc	Zn
	◆ CAPELLA		ALDEBARAN		Hamal		◆ Alpheratz		ALTAIR		◆ VEGA		Alioth	
0	40 11	063	25 43	096	52 30	127	67 07	175	23 59	253	34 53	290	18 28	352
1	40 44	064	26 20	097	52 59	128	67 09	177	23 24	254	34 18	291	18 23	353
2	41 17	064	26 56	098	53 28	130	67 10	179	22 48	255	33 44	292	18 19	353
3	41 51	065	27 33	098	53 56	131	67 10	182	22 12	255	33 09	292	18 14	354
4	42 24	066	28 09	099	54 23	132	67 08	184	21 36	256	32 35	293	18 10	354
5	42 58	066	28 46	100	54 50	134	67 05	186	21 01	257	32 01	294	18 07	355
6	43 32	067	29 22	101	55 17	135	67 00	188	20 24	258	31 28	294	18 04	355
7	44 06	067	29 58	102	55 43	137	66 54	191	19 48	259	30 54	295	18 01	356
8	44 40	068	30 35	103	56 08	138	66 47	193	19 12	260	30 21	295	17 59	357
9	45 14	068	31 11	104	56 32	139	66 38	195	18 36	260	29 47	296	17 57	357
10	45 49	069	31 46	104	56 56	141	66 28	197	17 59	261	29 14	297	17 55	358
11	46 23	069	32 22	105	57 18	143	66 16	199	17 23	262	28 41	297	17 54	358
12	46 58	070	32 58	106	57 41	144	66 04	201	16 46	263	28 09	298	17 53	359
13	47 33	071	33 33	107	58 02	146	65 50	203	16 09	264	27 36	299	17 53	000
14	48 08	071	34 08	108	58 22	147	65 34	205	15 32	265	27 04	299	17 53	000
	Dubhe		◆ CAPELLA		ALDEBARAN		Hamal		◆ Alpheratz		DENEB		◆ VEGA	
15	25 57	015	48 43	072	34 43	109	58 42	149	65 18	207	48 18	287	26 32	300
16	26 07	015	49 18	072	35 18	110	59 00	151	65 00	209	47 43	288	26 00	301
17	26 17	016	49 53	073	35 53	111	59 18	152	64 42	211	47 08	289	25 28	301
18	26 27	016	50 28	073	36 27	112	59 35	154	64 22	213	46 33	289	24 56	302
19	26 38	017	51 04	074	37 01	113	59 50	156	64 02	215	45 58	290	24 25	302
20	26 48	017	51 39	075	37 35	114	60 05	158	63 40	217	45 23	290	23 54	303
21	26 59	018	52 15	075	38 09	115	60 19	159	63 17	219	44 49	291	23 23	304
22	27 11	018	52 51	076	38 42	116	60 31	161	62 54	220	44 14	291	22 53	304
23	27 22	019	53 27	076	39 16	117	60 42	163	62 30	222	43 40	292	22 22	305
24	27 34	019	54 03	077	39 48	118	60 53	165	62 04	224	43 06	293	21 52	306
25	27 47	020	54 39	078	40 21	119	61 02	167	61 39	225	42 32	293	21 22	306
26	27 59	020	55 15	078	40 53	120	61 10	169	61 12	227	41 58	294	20 53	307
27	28 12	021	55 51	079	41 25	121	61 17	170	60 45	228	41 24	294	20 23	308
28	28 25	021	56 27	079	41 57	122	61 22	172	60 17	230	40 51	295	19 54	308
29	28 39	022	57 03	080	42 28	123	61 26	174	59 48	231	40 17	295	19 25	309
	Dubhe		◆ POLLUX		BETELGEUSE		RIGEL		◆ Hamal		Alpheratz		◆ DENEB	
30	28 52	022	23 44	074	24 35	111	16 48	129	61 29	176	59 19	233	39 44	296
31	29 06	023	24 20	075	25 10	112	17 17	130	61 31	178	58 50	234	39 11	297
32	29 21	023	24 55	076	25 44	113	17 45	131	61 32	180	58 19	235	38 38	297
33	29 35	023	25 31	076	26 18	114	18 13	132	61 31	182	57 49	237	38 05	298
34	29 50	024	26 07	077	26 52	114	18 40	133	61 29	184	57 18	238	37 33	298
35	30 05	024	26 43	078	27 25	115	19 07	134	61 26	186	56 46	239	37 00	299
36	30 21	025	27 19	079	27 58	116	19 34	134	61 22	188	56 14	241	36 28	299
37	30 36	025	27 56	079	28 31	117	20 00	135	61 17	190	55 42	242	35 56	300
38	30 52	026	28 32	080	29 04	118	20 26	136	61 10	191	55 09	243	35 24	301
39	31 08	026	29 08	081	29 37	119	20 51	137	61 02	193	54 36	244	34 52	301
40	31 25	027	29 45	082	30 09	120	21 16	138	60 53	195	54 02	245	34 20	302
41	31 42	027	30 21	082	30 40	121	21 40	139	60 43	197	53 29	247	33 49	302
42	31 59	028	30 58	083	31 12	122	22 04	140	60 31	199	52 54	248	33 18	303
43	32 16	028	31 35	084	31 43	123	22 27	141	60 19	201	52 20	249	32 47	303
44	32 33	028	32 12	085	32 14	124	22 50	142	60 05	202	51 46	250	32 16	304
	Dubhe		◆ POLLUX		BETELGEUSE		RIGEL		◆ Hamal		Alpheratz		◆ DENEB	
45	32 51	029	32 48	085	32 44	125	23 13	143	59 50	204	51 11	251	31 46	304
46	33 09	029	33 25	086	33 14	126	23 35	144	59 35	206	50 36	252	31 15	305
47	33 27	030	34 02	087	33 44	127	23 56	145	59 18	208	50 01	253	30 45	306
48	33 46	030	34 39	088	34 13	128	24 17	146	59 00	209	49 25	254	30 15	306
49	34 04	031	35 16	088	34 42	129	24 37	147	58 42	211	48 50	255	29 46	307
50	34 23	031	35 53	089	35 11	130	24 57	148	58 22	213	48 14	256	29 16	307
51	34 43	032	36 30	090	35 39	131	25 16	149	58 02	214	47 38	257	28 47	308
52	35 02	032	37 07	091	36 06	132	25 34	150	57 41	216	47 02	258	28 18	309
53	35 22	032	37 44	092	36 33	133	25 52	151	57 19	217	46 26	259	27 49	309
54	35 42	033	38 21	092	37 00	135	26 10	152	56 56	219	45 50	260	27 21	310
55	36 02	033	38 57	093	37 26	136	26 27	153	56 32	221	45 13	260	26 52	310
56	36 22	034	39 34	094	37 51	137	26 43	155	56 08	222	44 37	261	26 24	311
57	36 42	034	40 11	095	38 16	138	26 58	156	55 43	223	44 00	262	25 56	311
58	37 03	034	40 48	095	38 41	139	27 13	157	55 17	225	43 24	263	25 29	312
59	37 24	035	41 25	096	39 05	140	27 28	158	54 51	226	42 47	264	25 02	313
	◆ Dubhe		POLLUX		SIRIUS		◆ RIGEL		Hamal		◆ Alpheratz		DENEB	
60	37 45	035	42 01	097	12 25	140	27 41	159	54 24	228	42 10	265	24 34	313
61	38 07	036	42 38	098	12 49	140	27 54	160	53 56	229	41 33	266	24 08	314
62	38 28	036	43 14	099	13 12	141	28 07	161	53 28	230	40 56	266	23 41	314
63	38 50	036	43 51	100	13 35	142	28 18	162	52 59	232	40 19	267	23 15	315
64	39 12	037	44 27	101	13 57	143	28 29	163	52 30	233	39 43	268	22 49	316
65	39 34	037	45 03	102	14 19	144	28 39	164	52 00	234	39 06	269	22 23	316
66	39 57	038	45 40	103	14 40	145	28 49	165	51 30	235	38 29	270	21 58	317
67	40 19	038	46 16	104	15 01	146	28 58	167	50 59	237	37 52	270	21 33	317
68	40 42	038	46 51	105	15 22	147	29 06	168	50 28	238	37 15	271	21 08	318
69	41 05	039	47 27	105	15 42	148	29 14	169	49 57	239	36 38	272	20 43	319
70	41 28	039	48 03	106	16 01	149	29 20	170	49 25	240	36 01	273	20 19	319
71	41 52	039	48 38	107	16 20	150	29 26	171	48 53	241	35 24	274	19 55	320
72	42 15	040	49 13	108	16 39	151	29 32	172	48 20	242	34 47	274	19 32	321
73	42 39	040	49 48	109	16 57	152	29 36	173	47 47	244	34 10	275	19 08	321
74	43 03	040	50 23	111	17 14	152	29 40	175	47 14	245	33 34	276	18 45	322
	Dubhe		◆ REGULUS		PROCYON		SIRIUS		◆ RIGEL		Hamal		◆ DENEB	
75	43 27	041	17 09	093	32 44	130	17 31	153	29 44	176	46 41	246	18 22	322
76	43 51	041	17 46	093	33 12	131	17 47	154	29 46	177	46 07	247	18 00	323
77	44 16	041	18 23	094	33 40	133	18 03	155	29 48	178	45 33	248	17 38	324
78	44 40	042	19 00	095	34 06	134	18 18	156	29 49	179	44 58	249	17 16	324
79	45 05	042	19 37	096	34 33	135	18 32	157	29 49	180	44 24	250	16 55	325
80	45 30	042	20 13	097	34 59	136	18 46	158	29 48	181	43 49	251	16 34	326
81	45 55	043	20 50	097	35 25	137	19 00	159	29 47	182	43 14	252	16 13	326
82	46 20	043	21 27	098	35 50	138	19 12	160	29 45	184	42 39	253	15 53	327
83	46 45	043	22 03	099	36 14	139	19 25	161	29 42	185	42 04	254	15 33	327
84	47 11	044	22 39	100	36 38	140	19 36	162	29 39	186	41 28	255	15 13	328
85	47 36	044	23 16	101	37 01	141	19 47	163	29 35	187	40 52	256	14 54	329
86	48 02	044	23 52	102	37 24	143	19 57	164	29 30	188	40 16	256	14 35	329
87	48 28	045	24 28	102	37 46	144	20 07	165	29 24	189	39 41	257	14 16	330
88	48 54	045	25 04	103	38 08	145	20 16	166	29 18	190	39 04	258	13 58	331
89	49 20	045	25 40	104	38 29	146	20 25	167	29 11	192	38 28	259	13 40	331

LHA ♈	Hc	Zn	Hc	Zn	Hc	Zn	Hc	Zn	Hc	Zn	Hc	Zn	Hc	Zn
	◆ Dubhe		REGULUS		PROCYON		◆ SIRIUS		RIGEL		◆ Hamal		Schedar	
90	49 47	046	26 16	105	38 49	147	20 33	168	29 03	193	37 52	260	45 57	309
91	50 13	046	26 51	106	39 09	148	20 40	169	28 55	194	37 15	261	45 29	309
92	50 39	046	27 27	107	39 28	150	20 46	170	28 46	195	36 39	262	45 00	310
93	51 06	046	28 02	108	39 46	151	20 52	171	28 36	196	36 02	263	44 32	310
94	51 33	047	28 37	108	40 03	152	20 57	172	28 25	197	35 26	263	44 04	310
95	52 00	047	29 12	109	40 20	153	21 02	173	28 14	198	34 49	264	43 36	311
96	52 27	047	29 47	110	40 36	155	21 06	174	28 02	199	34 12	265	43 08	311
97	52 54	047	30 22	111	40 52	156	21 09	175	27 49	200	33 35	266	42 40	312
98	53 21	048	30 56	112	41 07	157	21 12	176	27 36	202	32 58	267	42 13	312
99	53 48	048	31 30	113	41 20	159	21 14	177	27 22	203	32 22	268	41 45	312
100	54 16	048	32 04	114	41 34	160	21 15	179	27 08	204	31 45	268	41 18	313
101	54 43	048	32 38	115	41 46	161	21 16	180	26 53	205	31 08	269	40 51	313
102	55 11	048	33 11	116	41 58	162	21 16	181	26 37	206	30 31	270	40 24	314
103	55 39	049	33 44	117	42 08	164	21 15	182	26 20	207	29 54	271	39 58	314
104	56 06	049	34 17	118	42 18	165	21 14	183	26 03	208	29 17	271	39 31	315
	◆ Dubhe		Denebola		REGULUS		◆ SIRIUS		RIGEL		ALDEBARAN		◆ Mirfak	
105	56 34	049	22 08	095	34 49	119	21 12	184	25 46	209	44 40	232	56 55	288
106	57 02	049	22 45	096	35 21	120	21 09	185	25 28	210	44 11	233	56 20	289
107	57 30	049	23 22	096	35 53	121	21 06	186	25 09	211	43 41	234	55 45	289
108	57 58	049	23 58	097	36 25	122	21 02	187	24 49	212	43 11	235	55 10	290
109	58 26	050	24 35	098	36 56	123	20 57	188	24 30	213	42 40	237	54 35	290
110	58 54	050	25 12	099	37 27	124	20 52	189	24 09	214	42 09	238	54 01	291
111	59 23	050	25 48	100	37 57	125	20 46	190	23 48	215	41 38	239	53 26	291
112	59 51	050	26 24	100	38 27	126	20 39	191	23 26	216	41 06	240	52 52	292
113	60 19	050	27 01	101	38 57	127	20 32	192	23 04	217	40 34	241	52 18	292
114	60 48	050	27 37	102	39 26	128	20 24	193	22 42	218	40 01	242	51 43	293
115	61 16	050	28 13	103	39 55	129	20 15	194	22 19	219	39 29	243	51 09	293
116	61 44	050	28 49	104	40 23	130	20 06	195	21 55	220	38 55	244	50 35	294
117	62 13	050	29 25	105	40 51	132	19 57	196	21 31	221	38 22	245	50 02	294
118	62 41	050	30 00	106	41 19	133	19 46	197	21 07	222	37 49	246	49 28	295
119	63 10	050	30 36	107	41 45	134	19 35	198	20 42	223	37 15	247	48 54	295
	Kochab		◆ ARCTURUS		REGULUS		◆ SIRIUS		BETELGEUSE		CAPELLA		◆ Schedar	
120	46 07	023	12 30	075	42 12	135	19 23	199	38 41	221	63 06	273	32 58	322
121	46 22	023	13 06	076	42 38	136	19 11	200	38 16	222	62 30	274	32 35	322
122	46 36	023	13 42	076	43 03	138	18 58	201	37 51	223	61 53	275	32 12	323
123	46 51	023	14 18	077	43 27	139	18 45	202	37 26	224	61 16	276	31 50	323
124	47 05	023	14 54	078	43 52	140	18 31	203	36 59	225	60 39	276	31 28	324
125	47 20	024	15 30	079	44 15	141	18 16	204	36 33	227	60 03	277	31 07	324
126	47 35	024	16 06	079	44 38	142	18 01	205	36 06	228	59 26	278	30 45	325
127	47 50	024	16 42	080	45 00	144	17 45	206	35 38	229	58 49	278	30 24	325
128	48 05	024	17 19	081	45 21	145	17 29	207	35 10	230	58 13	279	30 03	326
129	48 20	024	17 55	082	45 42	146	17 12	208	34 42	231	57 36	279	29 42	326
130	48 35	024	18 32	082	46 02	148	16 55	209	34 13	232	57 00	280	29 22	327
131	48 51	025	19 09	083	46 22	149	16 37	210	33 44	233	56 24	281	29 02	327
132	49 06	025	19 45	084	46 40	150	16 19	210	33 14	234	55 47	281	28 42	328
133	49 22	025	20 22	085	46 58	152	16 00	211	32 44	235	55 11	282	28 22	328
134	49 37	025	20 59	085	47 15	153	15 40	212	32 14	236	54 35	283	28 03	329
	Kochab		◆ ARCTURUS		REGULUS		◆ POLLUX		BETELGEUSE		CAPELLA		◆ Schedar	
135	49 53	025	21 36	086	47 32	154	62 19	217	31 43	237	53 59	283	27 44	329
136	50 09	025	22 13	087	47 47	156	61 56	219	31 12	238	53 23	284	27 25	330
137	50 24	025	22 50	088	48 02	157	61 33	220	30 40	239	52 47	284	27 07	330
138	50 40	026	23 26	089	48 16	159	61 09	222	30 08	240	52 11	285	26 49	331
139	50 56	026	24 03	089	48 29	160	60 44	224	29 36	241	51 36	285	26 31	331
140	51 12	026	24 40	090	48 41	162	60 18	225	29 04	242	51 00	286	26 13	332
141	51 28	026	25 17	091	48 52	163	59 51	227	28 31	243	50 25	287	25 56	332
142	51 44	026	25 54	092	49 02	165	59 24	228	27 58	244	49 49	287	25 39	333
143	52 00	026	26 31	093	49 12	166	58 56	230	27 25	245	49 14	288	25 22	333
144	52 17	026	27 08	093	49 20	167	58 28	231	26 51	246	48 39	288	25 06	334
145	52 33	026	27 45	094	49 28	169	57 59	232	26 18	246	48 04	289	24 50	334
146	52 49	026	28 22	095	49 34	170	57 29	234	25 44	247	47 29	289	24 34	335
147	53 06	026	28 58	096	49 40	172	56 59	235	25 09	248	46 54	290	24 19	336
148	53 22	026	29 35	097	49 45	173	56 28	237	24 35	249	46 20	291	24 03	336
149	53 38	026	30 12	097	49 48	175	55 57	238	24 00	250	45 45	291	23 49	337
	◆ Kochab		ARCTURUS		◆ SPICA		REGULUS		◆ POLLUX		CAPELLA		Schedar	
150	53 55	026	30 48	098	12 51	128	49 51	177	55 26	239	45 11	292	23 34	337
151	54 11	026	31 25	099	13 20	129	49 53	178	54 54	240	44 37	292	23 20	338
152	54 28	026	32 01	100	13 48	130	49 54	180	54 22	242	44 02	293	23 06	338
153	54 44	026	32 38	101	14 16	131	49 53	181	53 49	243	43 29	293	22 52	339
154	55 00	026	33 14	102	14 44	132	49 52	183	53 16	244	42 55	294	22 39	339
155	55 17	026	33 50	103	15 12	133	49 50	184	52 43	245	42 21	294	22 26	340
156	55 33	026	34 26	103	15 39	133	49 47	186	52 09	246	41 47	295	22 14	340
157	55 50	026	35 02	104	16 05	134	49 43	187	51 35	247	41 14	296	22 02	341
158	56 06	026	35 38	105	16 32	135	49 38	189	51 01	248	40 41	296	21 50	342
159	56 23	026	36 13	106	16 57	136	49 32	190	50 27	249	40 08	297	21 38	342
160	56 39	026	36 49	107	17 23	137	49 25	192	49 52	250	39 35	297	21 27	343
161	56 55	026	37 24	108	17 48	138	49 17	193	49 17	251	39 02	298	21 16	343
162	57 12	026	37 59	109	18 12	139	49 08	195	48 42	252	38 29	298	21 06	344
163	57 28	026	38 34	110	18 36	140	48 58	196	48 07	253	37 57	299	20 55	344
164	57 44	026	39 08	111	19 00	141	48 47	198	47 31	254	37 25	299	20 46	345
	DENEB		◆ VEGA		ARCTURUS		◆ SPICA		REGULUS		POLLUX		◆ CAPELLA	
165	11 46	024	17 12	048	39 43	112	19 23	142	48 36	199	46 55	255	36 53	300
166	12 01	025	17 40	049	40 17	113	19 45	143	48 23	200	46 20	256	36 21	301
167	12 17	025	18 08	049	40 51	114	20 08	144	48 10	202	45 44	257	35 49	301
168	12 33	026	18 36	050	41 24	115	20 29	145	47 56	203	45 08	258	35 18	302
169	12 49	027	19 04	051	41 58	116	20 50	146	47 41	205	44 32	259	34 46	302
170	13 06	027	19 33	051	42 31	117	21 11	147	47 25	206	43 55	260	34 15	303
171	13 23	028	20 02	052	43 04	118	21 31	148	47 08	207	43 19	261	33 44	303
172	13 40	029	20 31	053	43 36	119	21 50	149	46 51	209	42 42	262	33 14	304
173	13 58	029	21 01	053	44 08	120	22 09	150	46 33	210	42 06	263	32 43	305
174	14 17	030	21 31	054	44 40	121	22 28	151	46 14	212	41 29	263	32 13	305
175	14 35	031	22 00	055	45 11	122	22 45	152	45 54	213	40 52	264	31 43	306
176	14 54	031	22 31	055	45 43	123	23 03	153	45 34	214	40 15	265	31 13	306
177	15 14	032	23 01	056	46 13	125	23 19	154	45 13	215	39 39	266	30 43	307
178	15 33	033	23 32	056	46 43	126	23 35	155	44 51	217	39 02	267	30 13	307
179	15 53	033	24 03	057	47 13	127	23 51	156	44 28	218	38 25	268	29 44	308

 LAT 52°N

LHA ♈	Hc	Zn	Hc	Zn	Hc	Zn	Hc	Zn	Hc	Zn	Hc	Zn	Hc	Zn
	DENEB		◆ VEGA		ARCTURUS		◆ SPICA		REGULUS		POLLUX		◆ CAPELLA	
180	16 14	034	24 34	058	47 42	128	24 06	157	44 05	219	37 48	268	29 15	309
181	16 34	034	25 05	058	48 11	129	24 20	158	43 42	221	37 11	269	28 46	309
182	16 55	035	25 37	059	48 40	131	24 34	159	43 17	222	36 34	270	28 18	310
183	17 17	036	26 08	060	49 07	132	24 47	160	42 52	223	35 57	271	27 50	310
184	17 39	036	26 40	060	49 35	133	24 59	161	42 27	224	35 20	272	27 21	311
185	18 01	037	27 13	061	50 01	134	25 11	162	42 01	225	34 43	272	26 54	311
186	18 23	038	27 45	062	50 27	136	25 22	163	41 34	227	34 06	273	26 26	312
187	18 46	038	28 18	062	50 53	137	25 32	164	41 07	228	33 29	274	25 59	313
188	19 09	039	28 50	063	51 18	138	25 42	165	40 40	229	32 53	275	25 32	313
189	19 32	040	29 23	063	51 42	140	25 51	166	40 12	230	32 16	275	25 05	314
190	19 56	040	29 56	064	52 06	141	25 59	167	39 43	231	31 39	276	24 38	314
191	20 20	041	30 30	065	52 28	143	26 07	169	39 14	232	31 02	277	24 12	315
192	20 44	041	31 03	065	52 51	144	26 14	170	38 45	233	30 26	278	23 46	316
193	21 09	042	31 37	066	53 12	145	26 20	171	38 15	234	29 49	278	23 20	316
194	21 33	043	32 11	067	53 32	147	26 26	172	37 45	235	29 13	279	22 55	317
	◆ DENEB		VEGA		Rasalhague		◆ ARCTURUS		REGULUS		◆ POLLUX		CAPELLA	
195	21 59	043	32 45	067	22 48	099	53 52	148	37 14	236	28 36	280	22 29	317
196	22 24	044	33 19	068	23 24	100	54 11	150	36 43	238	28 00	281	22 05	318
197	22 50	044	33 53	069	24 01	101	54 29	151	36 12	239	27 24	281	21 40	319
198	23 16	045	34 28	069	24 37	101	54 46	153	35 40	240	26 47	282	21 16	319
199	23 42	046	35 02	070	25 13	102	55 03	155	35 08	241	26 11	283	20 52	320
200	24 08	046	35 37	070	25 49	103	55 18	156	34 36	242	25 35	283	20 28	320
201	24 35	047	36 12	071	26 25	104	55 33	158	34 03	243	24 59	284	20 04	321
202	25 02	047	36 47	072	27 01	105	55 46	159	33 30	244	24 24	285	19 41	322
203	25 30	048	37 22	072	27 36	106	55 59	161	32 57	244	23 48	286	19 18	322
204	25 57	049	37 57	073	28 12	107	56 10	163	32 24	245	23 13	286	18 56	323
205	26 25	049	38 33	074	28 47	107	56 21	164	31 50	246	22 37	287	18 34	323
206	26 53	050	39 08	074	29 22	108	56 30	166	31 16	247	22 02	288	18 12	324
207	27 21	050	39 44	075	29 57	109	56 38	168	30 42	248	21 27	288	17 50	325
208	27 50	051	40 19	076	30 32	110	56 46	169	30 07	249	20 52	289	17 29	325
209	28 19	051	40 55	076	31 07	111	56 52	171	29 33	250	20 17	290	17 08	326
	◆ DENEB		VEGA		Rasalhague		◆ ARCTURUS		REGULUS		◆ POLLUX		CAPELLA	
210	28 48	052	41 31	077	31 41	112	56 57	173	28 58	251	19 42	291	16 48	327
211	29 17	053	42 07	078	32 15	113	57 01	175	28 23	252	19 08	291	16 28	327
212	29 46	053	42 43	078	32 49	114	57 04	176	27 48	253	18 33	292	16 08	328
213	30 16	054	43 20	079	33 23	115	57 06	178	27 12	254	17 59	293	15 48	328
214	30 46	054	43 56	080	33 56	116	57 06	180	26 37	255	17 25	293	15 29	329
215	31 16	055	44 32	080	34 29	117	57 06	182	26 01	255	16 51	294	15 10	330
216	31 47	056	45 09	081	35 02	118	57 04	183	25 25	256	16 18	295	14 52	330
217	32 17	056	45 45	082	35 35	119	57 02	185	24 49	257	15 44	296	14 34	331
218	32 48	057	46 22	082	36 07	120	56 58	187	24 13	258	15 11	296	14 16	332
219	33 19	057	46 58	083	36 39	121	56 53	189	23 37	259	14 38	297	13 59	332
220	33 50	058	47 35	084	37 10	122	56 47	190	23 01	260	14 05	298	13 42	333
221	34 21	058	48 12	085	37 41	123	56 40	192	22 24	260	13 33	298	13 25	334
222	34 53	059	48 49	085	38 12	124	56 31	194	21 48	261	13 00	299	13 09	334
223	35 25	060	49 25	086	38 43	125	56 22	195	21 11	262	12 28	300	12 53	335
224	35 57	060	50 02	087	39 13	126	56 12	197	20 35	263	11 56	301	12 38	336
	Schedar		◆ DENEB		VEGA		Rasalhague		◆ ARCTURUS		Denebola		◆ Dubhe	
225	22 18	020	36 29	061	50 39	087	39 42	127	56 01	199	36 50	243	57 39	311
226	22 30	020	37 01	061	51 16	088	40 12	128	55 48	200	36 17	244	57 11	311
227	22 43	021	37 33	062	51 53	089	40 40	129	55 35	202	35 44	245	56 43	311
228	22 57	021	38 06	062	52 30	090	41 09	131	55 21	204	35 10	246	56 15	311
229	23 10	022	38 39	063	53 07	091	41 37	132	55 06	205	34 36	247	55 47	311
230	23 24	022	39 12	063	53 44	091	42 04	133	54 49	207	34 02	248	55 20	312
231	23 39	023	39 45	064	54 21	092	42 31	134	54 32	208	33 28	249	54 52	312
232	23 53	024	40 18	065	54 58	093	42 57	135	54 14	210	32 53	250	54 25	312
233	24 08	024	40 52	065	55 35	094	43 23	136	53 55	211	32 18	251	53 57	312
234	24 23	025	41 25	066	56 11	095	43 48	138	53 36	213	31 43	252	53 30	312
235	24 39	025	41 59	066	56 48	096	44 13	139	53 15	214	31 08	253	53 03	313
236	24 55	026	42 33	067	57 25	096	44 37	140	52 54	216	30 33	254	52 35	313
237	25 11	026	43 07	067	58 02	097	45 00	141	52 32	217	29 57	254	52 08	313
238	25 28	027	43 41	068	58 38	098	45 23	143	52 10	219	29 22	255	51 42	313
239	25 44	027	44 15	069	59 15	099	45 45	144	51 46	220	28 46	256	51 15	314
	◆ Schedar		DENEB		VEGA		◆ Rasalhague		ARCTURUS		◆ Denebola		Dubhe	
240	26 01	028	44 50	069	59 51	100	46 06	145	51 22	221	28 10	257	50 48	314
241	26 19	028	45 24	070	60 27	101	46 27	147	50 57	223	27 34	258	50 21	314
242	26 36	029	45 59	070	61 04	102	46 47	148	50 32	224	26 58	259	49 55	314
243	26 54	029	46 34	071	61 40	103	47 06	149	50 06	225	26 21	260	49 29	315
244	27 13	030	47 09	071	62 15	104	47 25	151	49 39	227	25 45	260	49 02	315
245	27 31	030	47 44	072	62 51	105	47 43	152	49 12	228	25 08	261	48 36	315
246	27 50	031	48 19	073	63 27	107	48 00	153	48 44	229	24 32	262	48 10	316
247	28 09	031	48 54	073	64 02	108	48 16	155	48 16	230	23 55	263	47 45	316
248	28 29	032	49 30	074	64 37	109	48 31	156	47 47	232	23 19	264	47 19	316
249	28 48	032	50 05	074	65 12	110	48 46	158	47 18	233	22 42	265	46 53	316
250	29 08	033	50 41	075	65 46	111	48 59	159	46 49	234	22 05	265	46 28	317
251	29 28	033	51 17	076	66 21	113	49 12	161	46 18	235	21 28	266	46 03	317
252	29 49	034	51 53	076	66 55	114	49 24	162	45 48	236	20 51	267	45 38	317
253	30 10	034	52 28	077	67 28	115	49 35	163	45 17	238	20 14	268	45 13	318
254	30 31	035	53 04	077	68 01	117	49 45	165	44 46	239	19 37	269	44 48	318
	◆ Schedar		DENEB		ALTAIR		◆ Rasalhague		ARCTURUS		◆ Alkaid		Kochab	
255	30 52	035	53 41	078	34 36	125	49 54	166	44 14	240	60 00	284	64 13	340
256	31 13	036	54 17	079	35 06	126	50 02	168	43 42	241	59 24	285	64 00	340
257	31 35	036	54 53	079	35 35	127	50 10	169	43 09	242	58 48	285	63 47	340
258	31 57	037	55 29	080	36 04	128	50 16	171	42 37	243	58 13	286	63 34	339
259	32 20	037	56 06	080	36 33	129	50 21	172	42 04	244	57 37	286	63 21	339
260	32 42	038	56 42	081	37 01	131	50 25	174	41 30	245	57 02	287	63 08	338
261	33 05	038	57 19	082	37 29	132	50 29	176	40 57	246	56 27	287	62 54	338
262	33 28	039	57 55	082	37 57	133	50 31	177	40 23	247	55 51	288	62 40	338
263	33 51	039	58 32	083	38 23	134	50 33	179	39 49	248	55 16	288	62 26	337
264	34 15	040	59 09	084	38 50	135	50 33	180	39 14	249	54 41	289	62 12	337
265	34 38	040	59 45	084	39 16	136	50 32	182	38 40	250	54 06	289	61 57	337
266	35 02	041	60 22	085	39 41	137	50 31	183	38 05	251	53 31	290	61 43	337
267	35 26	041	60 59	086	40 06	138	50 28	185	37 30	252	52 57	290	61 28	336
268	35 51	042	61 36	086	40 30	140	50 25	186	36 55	253	52 22	291	61 13	336
269	36 15	042	62 13	087	40 53	141	50 20	188	36 19	254	51 48	291	60 58	336

LHA ♈	Hc	Zn	Hc	Zn	Hc	Zn	Hc	Zn	Hc	Zn	Hc	Zn	Hc	Zn
	◆ Mirfak		Alpheratz		◆ ALTAIR		Rasalhague		◆ ARCTURUS		Alkaid		Kochab	
270	17 03	025	21 16	069	41 17	142	50 15	189	35 44	255	51 13	292	60 43	336
271	17 19	025	21 50	070	41 39	143	50 08	191	35 08	255	50 39	292	60 28	335
272	17 35	026	22 25	071	42 01	145	50 01	192	34 32	256	50 05	293	60 12	335
273	17 51	027	23 00	072	42 22	146	49 52	194	33 56	257	49 31	293	59 57	335
274	18 08	027	23 35	072	42 42	147	49 43	195	33 20	258	48 57	294	59 41	335
275	18 25	028	24 10	073	43 02	148	49 33	197	32 44	259	48 23	294	59 25	335
276	18 43	029	24 46	074	43 21	150	49 22	198	32 08	260	47 50	295	59 10	335
277	19 01	029	25 21	074	43 39	151	49 10	200	31 31	261	47 16	295	58 54	334
278	19 19	030	25 57	075	43 57	152	48 57	201	30 55	262	46 43	296	58 38	334
279	19 37	030	26 33	076	44 14	154	48 43	203	30 18	262	46 10	296	58 22	334
280	19 56	031	27 09	076	44 30	155	48 28	204	29 42	263	45 37	297	58 06	334
281	20 15	032	27 45	077	44 45	156	48 13	206	29 05	264	45 04	297	57 49	334
282	20 35	032	28 21	078	45 00	158	47 57	207	28 28	265	44 31	298	57 33	334
283	20 55	033	28 57	079	45 13	159	47 39	208	27 51	266	43 58	298	57 17	334
284	21 15	033	29 33	079	45 26	160	47 22	210	27 14	267	43 26	299	57 01	334
	◆ Mirfak		Alpheratz		◆ ALTAIR		Rasalhague		◆ ARCTURUS		Alkaid		Kochab	
285	21 35	034	30 09	080	45 38	162	47 03	211	26 37	267	42 54	299	56 44	334
286	21 56	034	30 46	081	45 50	163	46 43	212	26 01	268	42 22	300	56 28	334
287	22 17	035	31 22	082	46 00	164	46 23	214	25 24	269	41 50	300	56 12	334
288	22 38	036	31 59	082	46 09	166	46 02	215	24 47	270	41 18	301	55 55	334
289	23 00	036	32 36	083	46 18	167	45 41	216	24 10	270	40 46	301	55 39	334
290	23 22	037	33 12	084	46 26	169	45 19	218	23 33	271	40 15	302	55 22	334
291	23 44	037	33 49	085	46 33	170	44 56	219	22 56	272	39 44	302	55 06	334
292	24 07	038	34 26	085	46 38	172	44 32	220	22 19	273	39 12	303	54 49	334
293	24 30	039	35 03	086	46 43	173	44 08	221	21 42	274	38 42	303	54 33	334
294	24 53	039	35 40	087	46 48	174	43 43	223	21 05	274	38 11	304	54 17	334
295	25 16	040	36 16	088	46 51	176	43 18	224	20 28	275	37 40	304	54 00	334
296	25 40	040	36 53	088	46 53	177	42 52	225	19 52	276	37 10	305	53 44	334
297	26 04	041	37 30	089	46 54	179	42 26	226	19 15	277	36 40	306	53 27	334
298	26 28	041	38 07	090	46 55	180	41 59	227	18 38	277	36 10	306	53 11	334
299	26 53	042	38 44	091	46 54	182	41 31	229	18 02	278	35 40	307	52 55	334
	◆ CAPELLA		Alpheratz		◆ Enif		ALTAIR		Rasalhague		◆ Alphecca		Alioth	
300	14 01	028	39 21	091	42 51	144	46 52	183	41 04	230	35 10	269	33 44	320
301	14 18	028	39 58	092	43 12	145	46 50	185	40 35	231	34 33	270	33 20	320
302	14 36	029	40 35	093	43 33	146	46 47	186	40 06	232	33 56	271	32 56	321
303	14 54	030	41 12	094	43 54	147	46 42	187	39 37	233	33 19	272	32 33	321
304	15 12	030	41 49	095	44 13	149	46 37	189	39 07	234	32 42	273	32 10	322
305	15 31	031	42 25	096	44 32	150	46 31	190	38 37	235	32 05	273	31 47	322
306	15 50	032	43 02	096	44 50	151	46 24	192	38 07	236	31 28	274	31 25	323
307	16 10	032	43 39	097	45 08	153	46 16	193	37 36	237	30 52	275	31 02	323
308	16 30	033	44 15	098	45 24	154	46 07	195	37 04	238	30 15	276	30 40	324
309	16 50	034	44 52	099	45 40	155	45 58	196	36 33	239	29 38	276	30 18	324
310	17 10	034	45 28	100	45 55	157	45 47	197	36 01	240	29 01	277	29 57	325
311	17 31	035	46 05	101	46 09	158	45 36	199	35 29	241	28 25	278	29 35	325
312	17 53	035	46 41	102	46 23	159	45 23	200	34 56	242	27 48	279	29 14	326
313	18 14	036	47 17	103	46 35	161	45 10	201	34 23	243	27 12	279	28 54	326
314	18 36	037	47 53	104	46 47	162	44 56	203	33 50	244	26 35	280	28 33	327
	CAPELLA		◆ Hamal		Alpheratz		Enif		◆ ALTAIR		VEGA		◆ Alioth	
315	18 58	037	26 12	085	48 29	105	46 58	164	44 42	204	62 06	256	28 13	327
316	19 21	038	26 49	085	49 05	106	47 08	165	44 26	205	61 30	257	27 53	328
317	19 44	039	27 26	086	49 40	107	47 17	167	44 10	207	60 54	258	27 33	328
318	20 07	039	28 03	087	50 15	108	47 25	168	43 53	208	60 17	259	27 14	329
319	20 30	040	28 40	088	50 50	109	47 32	169	43 35	209	59 41	260	26 55	329
320	20 54	040	29 17	089	51 25	110	47 38	171	43 16	211	59 05	261	26 36	330
321	21 18	041	29 53	089	52 00	111	47 44	172	42 57	212	58 28	262	26 17	330
322	21 42	042	30 30	090	52 35	112	47 48	174	42 37	213	57 51	263	25 59	331
323	22 07	042	31 07	091	53 09	113	47 52	175	42 17	215	57 15	264	25 41	331
324	22 32	043	31 44	092	53 43	114	47 54	177	41 55	216	56 38	265	25 24	332
325	22 57	043	32 21	092	54 16	115	47 56	178	41 34	217	56 01	266	25 06	332
326	23 23	044	32 58	093	54 50	116	47 57	180	41 11	218	55 24	266	24 49	333
327	23 48	045	33 35	094	55 23	117	47 56	181	40 48	219	54 47	267	24 33	333
328	24 15	045	34 12	095	55 55	119	47 55	183	40 24	221	54 11	268	24 16	334
329	24 41	046	34 49	096	56 27	120	47 53	184	40 00	222	53 34	269	24 00	334
	CAPELLA		◆ Hamal		Alpheratz		Enif		◆ ALTAIR		VEGA		◆ Alioth	
330	25 07	046	35 25	097	56 59	121	47 50	186	39 35	223	52 57	270	23 44	335
331	25 34	047	36 02	097	57 31	122	47 46	187	39 09	224	52 20	270	23 29	336
332	26 01	048	36 39	098	58 02	124	47 41	188	38 43	225	51 43	271	23 14	336
333	26 29	048	37 15	099	58 32	125	47 35	190	38 17	226	51 06	272	22 59	337
334	26 56	049	37 51	100	59 02	126	47 28	191	37 50	228	50 29	273	22 44	337
335	27 24	049	38 28	101	59 31	128	47 20	193	37 22	229	49 52	273	22 30	338
336	27 52	050	39 04	102	60 00	129	47 12	194	36 54	230	49 15	274	22 16	338
337	28 21	050	39 40	103	60 29	131	47 02	196	36 26	231	48 38	275	22 03	339
338	28 49	051	40 16	104	60 56	132	46 52	197	35 57	232	48 02	276	21 50	339
339	29 18	052	40 52	104	61 23	134	46 41	198	35 28	233	47 25	276	21 37	340
340	29 47	052	41 28	105	61 49	135	46 28	200	34 58	234	46 48	277	21 24	340
341	30 16	053	42 03	106	62 15	137	46 15	201	34 28	235	46 12	278	21 12	341
342	30 46	053	42 39	107	62 40	139	46 02	203	33 58	236	45 35	279	21 00	342
343	31 16	054	43 14	108	63 04	140	45 47	204	33 27	237	44 59	279	20 49	342
344	31 46	054	43 49	109	63 27	142	45 32	205	32 56	238	44 22	280	20 38	343
	◆ CAPELLA		ALDEBARAN		◆ Diphda		Enif		ALTAIR		◆ VEGA		Alioth	
345	32 16	055	16 30	084	16 30	154	45 15	207	32 24	239	43 46	281	20 27	343
346	32 46	056	17 07	085	16 45	155	44 58	208	31 52	240	43 10	281	20 16	344
347	33 17	056	17 44	086	17 01	156	44 41	209	31 20	241	42 33	282	20 06	344
348	33 47	057	18 20	086	17 15	157	44 22	211	30 48	242	41 57	283	19 57	345
349	34 18	057	18 57	087	17 30	158	44 03	212	30 15	243	41 21	283	19 47	346
350	34 49	058	19 34	088	17 43	159	43 43	213	29 42	244	40 45	284	19 38	346
351	35 21	058	20 11	089	17 56	160	43 22	215	29 09	245	40 10	285	19 30	347
352	35 52	059	20 48	090	18 09	161	43 01	216	28 35	246	39 34	285	19 21	347
353	36 24	059	21 25	090	18 20	162	42 39	217	28 01	247	38 58	286	19 13	348
354	36 56	060	22 02	091	18 32	163	42 16	218	27 27	248	38 23	287	19 06	348
355	37 28	061	22 39	092	18 42	164	41 53	220	26 53	248	37 47	287	18 59	349
356	38 00	061	23 16	093	18 52	165	41 29	221	26 19	249	37 12	288	18 52	350
357	38 33	062	23 53	093	19 01	166	41 05	222	25 44	250	36 37	288	18 45	350
358	39 05	062	24 29	094	19 10	167	40 40	223	25 09	251	36 02	289	18 39	351
359	39 38	063	25 06	095	19 18	168	40 14	224	24 34	252	35 27	290	18 33	351

 LAT 51°N

LHA ♈	Hc	Zn	Hc	Zn	Hc	Zn	Hc	Zn	Hc	Zn	Hc	Zn	Hc	Zn
	◆ CAPELLA		ALDEBARAN		Hamal		◆ Alpheratz		ALTAIR		◆ VEGA		Alioth	
0	39 44	063	25 49	095	53 05	126	68 06	175	24 16	253	34 31	291	17 29	352
1	40 17	063	26 27	096	53 36	127	68 09	177	23 40	254	33 56	292	17 24	353
2	40 51	064	27 04	097	54 05	129	68 10	179	23 04	255	33 21	292	17 19	353
3	41 25	064	27 42	098	54 35	130	68 10	182	22 27	256	32 46	293	17 15	354
4	41 59	065	28 19	099	55 03	131	68 08	184	21 50	257	32 12	294	17 11	354
5	42 33	065	28 56	100	55 31	133	68 05	186	21 14	258	31 37	294	17 07	355
6	43 08	066	29 33	100	55 59	134	68 00	189	20 37	258	31 03	295	17 04	356
7	43 42	066	30 10	101	56 26	136	67 53	191	20 00	259	30 28	295	17 01	356
8	44 17	067	30 47	102	56 52	137	67 45	193	19 23	260	29 54	296	16 59	357
9	44 52	067	31 24	103	57 17	138	67 36	196	18 45	261	29 21	297	16 57	357
10	45 27	068	32 01	104	57 42	140	67 25	198	18 08	262	28 47	297	16 55	358
11	46 02	068	32 38	105	58 06	142	67 13	200	17 31	262	28 13	298	16 54	358
12	46 37	069	33 14	106	58 29	143	66 59	202	16 53	263	27 40	298	16 53	359
13	47 12	070	33 50	106	58 51	145	66 45	204	16 16	264	27 07	299	16 53	000
14	47 48	070	34 26	107	59 12	146	66 28	206	15 38	265	26 34	300	16 53	000
	Dubhe		◆ CAPELLA		ALDEBARAN		Hamal		◆ Alpheratz		DENEB		◆ VEGA	
15	24 59	015	48 23	071	35 02	108	59 33	148	66 11	208	48 00	289	26 01	300
16	25 09	015	48 59	071	35 38	109	59 52	150	65 53	210	47 24	289	25 29	301
17	25 19	016	49 35	072	36 14	110	60 11	151	65 33	212	46 48	290	24 57	302
18	25 29	016	50 11	072	36 49	111	60 28	153	65 12	214	46 13	290	24 25	302
19	25 40	017	50 47	073	37 24	112	60 45	155	64 50	216	45 37	291	23 53	303
20	25 51	017	51 23	073	37 59	113	61 00	157	64 28	218	45 02	291	23 21	303
21	26 02	018	51 59	074	38 34	114	61 15	159	64 04	220	44 27	292	22 50	304
22	26 14	018	52 35	074	39 08	115	61 28	161	63 39	222	43 52	292	22 19	305
23	26 26	019	53 12	075	39 42	116	61 40	162	63 14	223	43 17	293	21 48	305
24	26 38	019	53 48	076	40 16	117	61 51	164	62 47	225	42 42	293	21 17	306
25	26 50	019	54 25	076	40 50	118	62 00	166	62 20	227	42 08	294	20 47	307
26	27 03	020	55 02	077	41 23	119	62 09	168	61 53	228	41 34	295	20 16	307
27	27 16	020	55 38	077	41 56	120	62 16	170	61 24	230	40 59	295	19 47	308
28	27 29	021	56 15	078	42 28	121	62 21	172	60 55	231	40 25	296	19 17	309
29	27 43	021	56 52	078	43 00	122	62 26	174	60 25	233	39 51	296	18 47	309
	Dubhe		◆ POLLUX		BETELGEUSE		RIGEL		◆ Hamal		Alpheratz		◆ DENEB	
30	27 57	022	23 27	074	24 56	110	17 26	129	62 29	176	59 55	234	39 17	297
31	28 11	022	24 04	075	25 32	111	17 55	130	62 31	178	59 24	235	38 44	297
32	28 26	023	24 40	075	26 07	112	18 24	130	62 32	180	58 53	237	38 10	298
33	28 40	023	25 17	076	26 42	113	18 53	131	62 31	182	58 21	238	37 37	298
34	28 55	024	25 54	077	27 16	114	19 21	132	62 29	184	57 49	239	37 04	299
35	29 11	024	26 30	077	27 51	115	19 48	133	62 26	186	57 16	241	36 31	299
36	29 26	025	27 07	078	28 25	116	20 16	134	62 22	188	56 43	242	35 58	300
37	29 42	025	27 44	079	28 59	117	20 42	135	62 16	190	56 09	243	35 25	301
38	29 58	026	28 21	080	29 32	118	21 09	136	62 09	192	55 35	244	34 53	301
39	30 15	026	28 59	080	30 06	119	21 35	137	62 00	194	55 01	246	34 21	302
40	30 31	026	29 36	081	30 38	120	22 00	138	61 51	196	54 27	247	33 49	302
41	30 48	027	30 13	082	31 11	121	22 25	139	61 40	198	53 52	248	33 17	303
42	31 05	027	30 51	082	31 44	122	22 50	140	61 28	199	53 17	249	32 45	303
43	31 23	028	31 28	083	32 16	122	23 14	141	61 15	201	52 41	250	32 14	304
44	31 40	028	32 06	084	32 47	123	23 38	142	61 00	203	52 06	251	31 43	304
	Dubhe		◆ POLLUX		BETELGEUSE		RIGEL		◆ Hamal		Alpheratz		◆ DENEB	
45	31 58	029	32 43	085	33 19	124	24 01	143	60 45	205	51 30	252	31 12	305
46	32 17	029	33 21	085	33 49	126	24 23	144	60 29	207	50 54	253	30 41	306
47	32 35	029	33 58	086	34 20	127	24 45	145	60 11	208	50 18	254	30 10	306
48	32 54	030	34 36	087	34 50	128	25 06	146	59 53	210	49 41	255	29 40	307
49	33 13	030	35 14	088	35 20	129	25 27	147	59 33	212	49 05	256	29 10	307
50	33 32	031	35 52	088	35 49	130	25 48	148	59 13	214	48 28	257	28 40	308
51	33 51	031	36 29	089	36 18	131	26 07	149	58 51	215	47 51	258	28 10	308
52	34 11	032	37 07	090	36 46	132	26 26	150	58 29	217	47 14	259	27 40	309
53	34 31	032	37 45	091	37 14	133	26 45	151	58 06	218	46 37	260	27 11	310
54	34 51	032	38 23	092	37 42	134	27 03	152	57 42	220	46 00	261	26 42	310
55	35 11	033	39 00	092	38 09	135	27 20	153	57 17	222	45 23	261	26 13	311
56	35 32	033	39 38	093	38 35	136	27 37	154	56 52	223	44 45	262	25 45	311
57	35 53	034	40 16	094	39 01	137	27 53	155	56 26	224	44 08	263	25 17	312
58	36 14	034	40 53	095	39 26	139	28 08	156	55 59	226	43 30	264	24 49	312
59	36 35	034	41 31	096	39 51	140	28 23	158	55 32	227	42 53	265	24 21	313
	◆ Dubhe		POLLUX		SIRIUS		◆ RIGEL		Hamal		◆ Alpheratz		DENEB	
60	36 56	035	42 08	096	13 10	139	28 37	159	55 04	229	42 15	266	23 53	314
61	37 18	035	42 46	097	13 35	140	28 51	160	54 35	230	41 37	266	23 26	314
62	37 40	036	43 23	098	13 59	141	29 03	161	54 06	231	41 00	267	22 59	315
63	38 02	036	44 01	099	14 22	142	29 15	162	53 36	233	40 22	268	22 32	315
64	38 24	036	44 38	100	14 45	143	29 27	163	53 06	234	39 44	269	22 06	316
65	38 46	037	45 15	101	15 08	144	29 37	164	52 35	235	39 06	270	21 40	317
66	39 09	037	45 52	102	15 30	145	29 47	165	52 04	236	38 29	270	21 14	317
67	39 32	037	46 29	103	15 51	146	29 56	166	51 32	238	37 51	271	20 48	318
68	39 55	038	47 06	103	16 12	147	30 05	168	51 00	239	37 13	272	20 23	318
69	40 18	038	47 43	104	16 33	148	30 13	169	50 27	240	36 35	273	19 58	319
70	40 42	038	48 19	105	16 53	149	30 20	170	49 54	241	35 58	273	19 34	320
71	41 05	039	48 55	106	17 12	149	30 26	171	49 21	242	35 20	274	19 09	320
72	41 29	039	49 31	107	17 31	150	30 31	172	48 48	243	34 42	275	18 45	321
73	41 53	040	50 07	108	17 49	151	30 36	173	48 14	245	34 05	276	18 21	321
74	42 17	040	50 43	109	18 07	152	30 40	174	47 39	246	33 27	276	17 58	322
	Dubhe		◆ REGULUS		PROCYON		SIRIUS		◆ RIGEL		Hamal		◆ DENEB	
75	42 41	040	17 12	092	33 23	130	18 24	153	30 43	176	47 05	247	17 35	323
76	43 06	041	17 49	093	33 52	131	18 41	154	30 46	177	46 30	248	17 12	323
77	43 30	041	18 27	094	34 20	132	18 57	155	30 48	178	45 55	249	16 50	324
78	43 55	041	19 05	095	34 48	133	19 13	156	30 49	179	45 20	250	16 28	324
79	44 20	042	19 42	095	35 15	134	19 28	157	30 49	180	44 44	251	16 06	325
80	44 45	042	20 20	096	35 42	135	19 42	158	30 48	181	44 08	252	15 44	326
81	45 10	042	20 57	097	36 08	136	19 56	159	30 47	183	43 32	253	15 23	326
82	45 36	042	21 35	098	36 34	137	20 09	160	30 45	184	42 56	254	15 02	327
83	46 01	043	22 12	099	36 59	139	20 21	161	30 42	185	42 20	255	14 42	328
84	46 27	043	22 50	099	37 24	140	20 33	162	30 39	186	41 44	255	14 22	328
85	46 53	043	23 27	100	37 48	141	20 45	163	30 34	187	41 07	256	14 02	329
86	47 19	044	24 04	101	38 11	142	20 55	164	30 29	188	40 30	257	13 43	330
87	47 45	044	24 41	102	38 34	143	21 05	165	30 24	189	39 53	258	13 24	330
88	48 11	044	25 18	103	38 57	144	21 15	166	30 17	191	39 16	259	13 05	331
89	48 38	044	25 54	104	39 18	146	21 23	167	30 10	192	38 39	260	12 47	331

LHA ♈	Hc	Zn	Hc	Zn	Hc	Zn	Hc	Zn	Hc	Zn	Hc	Zn	Hc	Zn
	◆ Dubhe		REGULUS		PROCYON		◆ SIRIUS		RIGEL		◆ Hamal		Schedar	
90	49 04	045	26 31	104	39 39	147	21 31	168	30 02	193	38 02	261	45 19	310
91	49 31	045	27 08	105	40 00	148	21 39	169	29 53	194	37 25	262	44 50	310
92	49 58	045	27 44	106	40 19	149	21 45	170	29 44	195	36 47	262	44 22	310
93	50 24	045	28 20	107	40 38	151	21 51	171	29 33	196	36 10	263	43 53	311
94	50 51	046	28 56	108	40 56	152	21 57	172	29 22	197	35 32	264	43 24	311
95	51 18	046	29 32	109	41 14	153	22 02	173	29 11	198	34 55	265	42 56	312
96	51 46	046	30 08	110	41 31	154	22 06	174	28 59	200	34 17	266	42 28	312
97	52 13	046	30 43	111	41 47	156	22 09	175	28 46	201	33 39	267	42 00	312
98	52 40	047	31 18	112	42 02	157	22 12	176	28 32	202	33 02	267	41 32	313
99	53 08	047	31 53	112	42 16	158	22 14	177	28 18	203	32 24	268	41 05	313
100	53 35	047	32 28	113	42 30	160	22 15	178	28 03	204	31 46	269	40 37	314
101	54 03	047	33 03	114	42 43	161	22 16	180	27 47	205	31 08	270	40 10	314
102	54 31	047	33 37	115	42 55	162	22 16	181	27 31	206	30 31	270	39 43	314
103	54 59	048	34 11	116	43 06	163	22 15	182	27 14	207	29 53	271	39 16	315
104	55 26	048	34 45	117	43 16	165	22 14	183	26 56	208	29 15	272	38 49	315
	◆ Dubhe		Denebola		REGULUS		◆ SIRIUS		RIGEL		ALDEBARAN		◆ Mirfak	
105	55 54	048	22 13	094	35 18	118	22 11	184	26 38	209	45 17	233	56 36	290
106	56 22	048	22 51	095	35 51	119	22 09	185	26 19	210	44 46	234	56 00	290
107	56 50	048	23 28	096	36 24	120	22 05	186	26 00	211	44 15	235	55 25	291
108	57 19	048	24 06	097	36 56	121	22 01	187	25 40	212	43 44	236	54 49	291
109	57 47	048	24 43	098	37 28	122	21 56	188	25 20	213	43 13	237	54 14	291
110	58 15	049	25 21	098	38 00	123	21 51	189	24 59	214	42 41	238	53 39	292
111	58 43	049	25 58	099	38 31	124	21 45	190	24 37	215	42 08	240	53 04	292
112	59 12	049	26 35	100	39 02	125	21 38	191	24 15	216	41 36	241	52 29	293
113	59 40	049	27 12	101	39 33	127	21 31	192	23 52	217	41 03	242	51 54	293
114	60 09	049	27 49	102	40 03	128	21 22	193	23 29	218	40 29	243	51 20	294
115	60 37	049	28 26	103	40 33	129	21 14	194	23 05	219	39 55	244	50 45	294
116	61 05	049	29 03	103	41 02	130	21 04	195	22 41	220	39 21	245	50 11	295
117	61 34	049	29 40	104	41 31	131	20 54	196	22 16	221	38 47	246	49 37	295
118	62 02	049	30 16	105	41 59	132	20 44	197	21 51	222	38 13	247	49 03	296
119	62 31	049	30 53	106	42 27	133	20 32	198	21 25	223	37 38	248	48 29	296
	Kochab		◆ ARCTURUS		REGULUS		◆ SIRIUS		BETELGEUSE		CAPELLA		◆ Schedar	
120	45 12	022	12 14	075	42 54	134	20 20	199	39 26	221	63 02	275	32 10	322
121	45 26	022	12 51	075	43 21	136	20 08	200	39 00	223	62 24	276	31 47	323
122	45 41	023	13 27	076	43 47	137	19 54	201	38 35	224	61 47	277	31 25	323
123	45 55	023	14 04	077	44 12	138	19 41	202	38 08	225	61 09	277	31 02	324
124	46 10	023	14 41	078	44 37	139	19 26	203	37 41	226	60 32	278	30 40	324
125	46 25	023	15 18	078	45 02	141	19 11	204	37 14	227	59 54	279	30 18	325
126	46 40	023	15 55	079	45 25	142	18 56	205	36 46	228	59 17	279	29 56	325
127	46 55	024	16 32	080	45 48	143	18 39	206	36 18	229	58 40	280	29 35	326
128	47 10	024	17 09	081	46 10	144	18 23	207	35 49	230	58 03	280	29 13	326
129	47 25	024	17 47	081	46 32	146	18 05	208	35 20	231	57 26	281	28 52	327
130	47 41	024	18 24	082	46 53	147	17 48	209	34 50	232	56 49	282	28 32	327
131	47 56	024	19 01	083	47 13	148	17 29	210	34 20	233	56 12	282	28 11	328
132	48 11	024	19 39	084	47 32	150	17 10	211	33 49	234	55 35	283	27 51	328
133	48 27	024	20 16	084	47 51	151	16 51	212	33 18	236	54 58	283	27 31	329
134	48 43	025	20 54	085	48 09	153	16 31	213	32 47	237	54 21	284	27 12	329
	Kochab		◆ ARCTURUS		REGULUS		◆ POLLUX		BETELGEUSE		CAPELLA		◆ Schedar	
135	48 58	025	21 32	086	48 26	154	63 07	218	32 15	238	53 45	284	26 52	330
136	49 14	025	22 09	087	48 42	155	62 43	220	31 43	239	53 08	285	26 33	330
137	49 30	025	22 47	087	48 57	157	62 18	222	31 11	239	52 32	286	26 15	331
138	49 46	025	23 25	088	49 12	158	61 53	223	30 38	240	51 55	286	25 56	331
139	50 02	025	24 02	089	49 25	160	61 27	225	30 05	241	51 19	287	25 38	332
140	50 18	025	24 40	090	49 38	161	61 00	226	29 32	242	50 43	287	25 20	332
141	50 34	025	25 18	090	49 49	163	60 32	228	28 58	243	50 07	288	25 03	333
142	50 50	025	25 56	091	50 00	164	60 04	229	28 24	244	49 31	288	24 46	333
143	51 06	025	26 34	092	50 10	166	59 34	231	27 50	245	48 55	289	24 29	334
144	51 23	025	27 11	093	50 19	167	59 05	232	27 16	246	48 20	289	24 12	334
145	51 39	026	27 49	094	50 27	169	58 35	234	26 41	247	47 44	290	23 56	335
146	51 55	026	28 27	094	50 33	170	58 04	235	26 06	248	47 09	290	23 40	335
147	52 12	026	29 04	095	50 39	172	57 33	236	25 31	249	46 33	291	23 24	336
148	52 28	026	29 42	096	50 44	173	57 01	238	24 56	250	45 58	292	23 09	336
149	52 44	026	30 19	097	50 48	175	56 29	239	24 21	250	45 23	292	22 53	337
	◆ Kochab		ARCTURUS		◆ SPICA		REGULUS		◆ POLLUX		CAPELLA		Schedar	
150	53 01	026	30 57	098	13 28	128	50 51	176	55 56	240	44 48	293	22 39	337
151	53 17	026	31 34	099	13 57	129	50 53	178	55 23	242	44 13	293	22 24	338
152	53 34	026	32 11	099	14 27	130	50 54	180	54 50	243	43 39	294	22 10	338
153	53 50	026	32 49	100	14 56	131	50 53	181	54 16	244	43 04	294	21 57	339
154	54 07	026	33 26	101	15 24	131	50 52	183	53 42	245	42 30	295	21 43	339
155	54 23	026	34 03	102	15 52	132	50 50	184	53 08	246	41 56	295	21 30	340
156	54 39	026	34 40	103	16 20	133	50 47	186	52 33	247	41 22	296	21 17	341
157	54 56	026	35 16	104	16 47	134	50 42	187	51 58	248	40 48	296	21 05	341
158	55 12	026	35 53	105	17 14	135	50 37	189	51 23	249	40 14	297	20 53	342
159	55 29	026	36 29	105	17 41	136	50 31	190	50 47	250	39 40	297	20 41	342
160	55 45	026	37 06	106	18 07	137	50 23	192	50 12	252	39 07	298	20 30	343
161	56 01	026	37 42	107	18 32	138	50 15	193	49 36	253	38 34	299	20 19	343
162	56 18	026	38 18	108	18 57	139	50 06	195	49 00	254	38 01	299	20 08	344
163	56 34	025	38 54	109	19 22	140	49 56	196	48 23	254	37 28	300	19 58	344
164	56 50	025	39 29	110	19 46	141	49 45	198	47 47	255	36 55	300	19 48	345
	DENEB		◆ VEGA		ARCTURUS		◆ SPICA		REGULUS		POLLUX		◆ CAPELLA	
165	10 51	024	16 32	048	40 05	111	20 10	142	49 33	199	47 10	256	36 22	301
166	11 06	025	17 00	048	40 40	112	20 33	143	49 20	201	46 33	257	35 50	301
167	11 22	025	17 29	049	41 15	113	20 56	144	49 06	202	45 56	258	35 18	302
168	11 39	026	17 57	050	41 49	114	21 18	144	48 51	204	45 19	259	34 46	302
169	11 55	027	18 26	050	42 24	115	21 40	145	48 35	205	44 42	260	34 14	303
170	12 12	027	18 56	051	42 58	116	22 01	146	48 19	207	44 05	261	33 42	303
171	12 30	028	19 25	052	43 31	117	22 21	147	48 02	208	43 28	262	33 11	304
172	12 48	029	19 55	052	44 05	118	22 42	148	47 43	209	42 50	263	32 40	304
173	13 06	029	20 25	053	44 38	119	23 01	149	47 24	211	42 13	263	32 09	305
174	13 25	030	20 55	054	45 11	120	23 20	150	47 05	212	41 35	264	31 38	306
175	13 44	030	21 26	054	45 43	121	23 38	151	46 44	213	40 58	265	31 07	306
176	14 03	031	21 56	055	46 15	123	23 56	152	46 23	215	40 20	266	30 37	307
177	14 23	032	22 27	055	46 47	124	24 13	154	46 01	216	39 42	267	30 07	307
178	14 43	032	22 58	056	47 18	125	24 30	155	45 39	217	39 05	268	29 37	308
179	15 03	033	23 30	057	47 49	126	24 46	156	45 15	219	38 27	268	29 07	308

LAT 51°N

LHA ♈	Hc	Zn	Hc	Zn	Hc	Zn	Hc	Zn	Hc	Zn	Hc	Zn	Hc	Zn
	DENEB		◆VEGA		ARCTURUS		◆SPICA		REGULUS		POLLUX		◆CAPELLA	
180	15 24	034	24 02	057	48 19	127	25 01	157	44 52	220	37 49	269	28 38	309
181	15 45	034	24 34	058	48 49	128	25 16	158	44 27	221	37 11	270	28 08	309
182	16 06	035	25 06	059	49 18	130	25 30	159	44 02	222	36 34	271	27 39	310
183	16 28	036	25 38	059	49 47	131	25 43	160	43 36	224	35 56	271	27 11	311
184	16 50	036	26 11	060	50 15	132	25 56	161	43 10	225	35 18	272	26 42	311
185	17 13	037	26 43	060	50 43	133	26 08	162	42 43	226	34 40	273	26 14	312
186	17 36	037	27 16	061	51 10	135	26 19	163	42 15	227	34 03	274	25 46	312
187	17 59	038	27 49	062	51 37	136	26 30	164	41 47	228	33 25	275	25 18	313
188	18 22	039	28 23	062	52 02	138	26 40	165	41 19	229	32 47	275	24 50	313
189	18 46	039	28 56	063	52 28	139	26 49	166	40 50	231	32 10	276	24 23	314
190	19 10	040	29 30	064	52 52	140	26 58	167	40 21	232	31 32	277	23 56	315
191	19 34	040	30 04	064	53 16	142	27 06	168	39 51	233	30 55	277	23 29	315
192	19 59	041	30 38	065	53 39	143	27 13	170	39 20	234	30 17	278	23 03	316
193	20 24	042	31 12	065	54 01	145	27 19	171	38 50	235	29 40	279	22 37	316
194	20 49	042	31 47	066	54 22	146	27 25	172	38 19	236	29 03	280	22 11	317
	◆DENEB		VEGA		Rasalhague		◆ARCTURUS		REGULUS		◆POLLUX		CAPELLA	
195	21 15	043	32 21	067	22 57	099	54 43	148	37 47	237	28 26	280	21 45	318
196	21 41	044	32 56	067	23 34	099	55 03	149	37 15	238	27 49	281	21 20	318
197	22 07	044	33 31	068	24 12	100	55 22	151	36 43	239	27 12	282	20 55	319
198	22 33	045	34 06	069	24 49	101	55 40	152	36 10	240	26 35	282	20 30	319
199	23 00	045	34 41	069	25 26	102	55 57	154	35 37	241	25 58	283	20 06	320
200	23 27	046	35 16	070	26 03	103	56 13	156	35 04	242	25 21	284	19 42	321
201	23 54	046	35 52	070	26 39	104	56 28	157	34 31	243	24 45	285	19 18	321
202	24 22	047	36 28	071	27 16	104	56 42	159	33 57	244	24 08	285	18 54	322
203	24 49	048	37 03	072	27 52	105	56 55	161	33 23	245	23 32	286	18 31	322
204	25 17	048	37 39	072	28 29	106	57 07	162	32 48	246	22 55	287	18 08	323
205	25 46	049	38 15	073	29 05	107	57 18	164	32 14	247	22 19	287	17 46	324
206	26 14	049	38 51	074	29 41	108	57 28	166	31 39	248	21 43	288	17 23	324
207	26 43	050	39 28	074	30 17	109	57 37	167	31 04	249	21 08	289	17 01	325
208	27 12	051	40 04	075	30 53	110	57 45	169	30 28	250	20 32	290	16 40	325
209	27 41	051	40 41	075	31 28	111	57 51	171	29 53	251	19 56	290	16 19	326
	◆DENEB		VEGA		Rasalhague		◆ARCTURUS		REGULUS		◆POLLUX		CAPELLA	
210	28 11	052	41 17	076	32 03	111	57 56	173	29 17	252	19 21	291	15 58	327
211	28 40	052	41 54	077	32 38	112	58 01	174	28 41	252	18 46	292	15 37	327
212	29 10	053	42 31	077	33 13	113	58 04	176	28 05	253	18 11	292	15 17	328
213	29 41	053	43 08	078	33 48	114	58 06	178	27 29	254	17 36	293	14 57	329
214	30 11	054	43 45	079	34 22	115	58 06	180	26 52	255	17 01	294	14 38	329
215	30 42	054	44 22	079	34 56	116	58 06	182	26 16	256	16 27	294	14 18	330
216	31 12	055	44 59	080	35 30	117	58 04	183	25 39	257	15 53	295	14 00	331
217	31 43	056	45 36	081	36 03	118	58 01	185	25 02	258	15 18	296	13 41	331
218	32 15	056	46 13	081	36 36	119	57 57	187	24 26	258	14 45	296	13 23	332
219	32 46	057	46 51	082	37 09	120	57 52	189	23 48	259	14 11	297	13 06	332
220	33 18	057	47 28	083	37 42	121	57 46	191	23 11	260	13 37	298	12 48	333
221	33 50	058	48 06	083	38 14	122	57 38	192	22 34	261	13 04	299	12 31	334
222	34 22	058	48 43	084	38 45	123	57 30	194	21 57	262	12 31	299	12 15	334
223	34 54	059	49 21	085	39 17	124	57 20	196	21 19	263	11 58	300	11 59	335
224	35 26	059	49 58	086	39 48	125	57 09	197	20 42	263	11 26	301	11 43	336
	Schedar		◆DENEB		VEGA		Rasalhague		◆ARCTURUS		Denebola		◆Dubhe	
225	21 21	020	35 59	060	50 36	086	40 18	126	56 57	199	37 17	244	57 00	312
226	21 34	020	36 32	061	51 14	087	40 49	128	56 45	201	36 43	245	56 31	312
227	21 47	021	37 05	061	51 51	088	41 18	129	56 31	203	36 08	246	56 03	312
228	22 01	021	37 38	062	52 29	088	41 47	130	56 16	204	35 34	247	55 35	312
229	22 15	022	38 11	062	53 07	089	42 16	131	56 00	206	34 59	248	55 07	312
230	22 29	022	38 45	063	53 45	090	42 44	132	55 43	207	34 24	249	54 40	313
231	22 43	023	39 18	063	54 22	091	43 12	133	55 25	209	33 49	250	54 12	313
232	22 58	023	39 52	064	55 00	092	43 39	135	55 06	211	33 13	251	53 44	313
233	23 13	024	40 26	064	55 38	092	44 06	136	54 47	212	32 38	251	53 17	313
234	23 29	024	41 00	065	56 16	093	44 32	137	54 26	214	32 02	252	52 49	313
235	23 45	025	41 34	065	56 53	094	44 58	138	54 05	215	31 26	253	52 22	314
236	24 01	026	42 09	066	57 31	095	45 22	139	53 43	217	30 49	254	51 54	314
237	24 17	026	42 43	067	58 08	096	45 47	141	53 20	218	30 13	255	51 27	314
238	24 34	027	43 18	067	58 46	097	46 10	142	52 56	219	29 36	256	51 00	314
239	24 51	027	43 53	068	59 23	098	46 33	143	52 32	221	29 00	257	50 33	314
	◆Schedar		DENEB		VEGA		◆Rasalhague		ARCTURUS		◆Denebola		Dubhe	
240	25 08	028	44 28	068	60 01	099	46 55	145	52 07	222	28 23	258	50 06	315
241	25 26	028	45 03	069	60 38	099	47 17	146	51 41	224	27 46	258	49 39	315
242	25 44	029	45 38	069	61 15	100	47 38	147	51 15	225	27 09	259	49 13	315
243	26 02	029	46 14	070	61 52	101	47 58	149	50 48	226	26 32	260	48 46	315
244	26 21	030	46 49	070	62 29	102	48 17	150	50 20	228	25 55	261	48 20	316
245	26 39	030	47 25	071	63 06	104	48 35	151	49 52	229	25 17	262	47 53	316
246	26 59	031	48 01	071	63 43	105	48 53	153	49 23	230	24 40	263	47 27	316
247	27 18	031	48 37	072	64 19	106	49 10	154	48 54	231	24 02	263	47 01	317
248	27 38	032	49 13	073	64 55	107	49 26	156	48 24	233	23 25	264	46 35	317
249	27 58	032	49 49	073	65 32	108	49 41	157	47 54	234	22 47	265	46 10	317
250	28 18	033	50 25	074	66 07	109	49 55	159	47 23	235	22 10	266	45 44	317
251	28 38	033	51 01	074	66 43	111	50 08	160	46 52	236	21 32	267	45 19	318
252	28 59	034	51 38	075	67 18	112	50 21	162	46 21	237	20 54	267	44 53	318
253	29 20	034	52 14	075	67 53	113	50 32	163	45 49	238	20 17	268	44 28	318
254	29 41	035	52 51	076	68 27	115	50 43	165	45 16	239	19 39	269	44 03	319
	◆Schedar		DENEB		ALTAIR		◆Rasalhague		ARCTURUS		◆Alkaid		Kochab	
255	30 03	035	53 27	077	35 10	125	50 52	166	44 44	241	59 44	286	63 16	341
256	30 25	036	54 04	077	35 41	126	51 01	168	44 11	242	59 08	286	63 04	341
257	30 47	036	54 41	078	36 11	127	51 08	169	43 37	243	58 32	287	62 51	340
258	31 09	036	55 18	078	36 41	128	51 15	171	43 03	244	57 56	287	62 38	340
259	31 32	037	55 55	079	37 11	129	51 20	172	42 29	245	57 20	288	62 25	339
260	31 55	037	56 32	080	37 40	130	51 25	174	41 55	246	56 44	288	62 12	339
261	32 18	038	57 09	080	38 09	131	51 29	175	41 21	247	56 08	289	61 58	339
262	32 41	038	57 46	081	38 37	132	51 31	177	40 46	248	55 32	289	61 44	338
263	33 04	039	58 24	081	39 05	133	51 33	179	40 11	249	54 57	290	61 30	338
264	33 28	039	59 01	082	39 32	134	51 33	180	39 35	250	54 21	290	61 16	338
265	33 52	040	59 38	083	39 59	136	51 32	182	39 00	251	53 46	291	61 02	338
266	34 17	040	60 16	083	40 25	137	51 31	183	38 24	252	53 10	291	60 47	337
267	34 41	041	60 53	084	40 50	138	51 28	185	37 48	253	52 35	292	60 33	337
268	35 06	041	61 31	085	41 15	139	51 24	186	37 12	253	52 00	292	60 18	337
269	35 31	042	62 09	085	41 40	140	51 20	188	36 36	254	51 25	292	60 03	337

LHA ♈	Hc	Zn	Hc	Zn	Hc	Zn	Hc	Zn	Hc	Zn	Hc	Zn	Hc	Zn
	◆Mirfak		Alpheratz		◆ALTAIR		Rasalhague		◆ARCTURUS		Alkaid		Kochab	
270	16 09	025	20 54	069	42 04	142	51 14	190	35 59	255	50 50	293	59 48	336
271	16 25	025	21 30	070	42 27	143	51 07	191	35 23	256	50 16	293	59 33	336
272	16 41	026	22 05	070	42 49	144	50 59	193	34 46	257	49 41	294	59 18	336
273	16 58	027	22 41	071	43 11	145	50 51	194	34 09	258	49 07	294	59 02	336
274	17 15	027	23 17	072	43 32	147	50 41	196	33 32	259	48 32	295	58 47	336
275	17 32	028	23 53	073	43 53	148	50 30	197	32 55	260	47 58	295	58 31	335
276	17 50	028	24 29	073	44 13	149	50 19	199	32 18	260	47 24	296	58 15	335
277	18 08	029	25 05	074	44 32	150	50 06	200	31 41	261	46 50	296	57 59	335
278	18 27	030	25 41	075	44 50	152	49 53	202	31 03	262	46 16	297	57 44	335
279	18 45	030	26 18	075	45 07	153	49 38	203	30 26	263	45 43	297	57 28	335
280	19 05	031	26 54	076	45 24	154	49 23	205	29 48	264	45 09	298	57 12	335
281	19 24	031	27 31	077	45 40	156	49 07	206	29 11	265	44 36	298	56 55	335
282	19 44	032	28 08	077	45 55	157	48 50	207	28 33	265	44 03	299	56 39	335
283	20 04	033	28 45	078	46 09	159	48 32	209	27 55	266	43 30	299	56 23	335
284	20 25	033	29 22	079	46 23	160	48 14	210	27 18	267	42 57	300	56 07	334
	◆Mirfak		Alpheratz		◆ALTAIR		Rasalhague		◆ARCTURUS		Alkaid		Kochab	
285	20 45	034	29 59	080	46 35	161	47 54	212	26 40	268	42 24	300	55 50	334
286	21 06	034	30 36	080	46 47	163	47 34	213	26 02	269	41 51	301	55 34	334
287	21 28	035	31 13	081	46 58	164	47 13	214	25 25	269	41 19	301	55 18	334
288	21 50	035	31 51	082	47 08	166	46 51	216	24 47	270	40 47	302	55 01	334
289	22 12	036	32 28	082	47 17	167	46 29	217	24 09	271	40 15	302	54 45	334
290	22 34	037	33 05	083	47 25	168	46 06	218	23 31	272	39 43	303	54 29	334
291	22 57	037	33 43	084	47 32	170	45 42	220	22 54	272	39 11	303	54 12	334
292	23 19	038	34 21	085	47 38	171	45 18	221	22 16	273	38 40	304	53 56	334
293	23 43	038	34 58	085	47 43	173	44 53	222	21 38	274	38 08	304	53 39	334
294	24 06	039	35 36	086	47 47	174	44 27	223	21 00	275	37 37	305	53 23	334
295	24 30	039	36 13	087	47 51	176	44 01	225	20 23	276	37 06	305	53 06	334
296	24 54	040	36 51	088	47 53	177	43 34	226	19 45	276	36 35	306	52 50	334
297	25 18	040	37 29	088	47 54	179	43 07	227	19 08	277	36 05	306	52 33	334
298	25 43	041	38 07	089	47 55	180	42 39	228	18 30	278	35 34	307	52 17	334
299	26 08	042	38 44	090	47 54	182	42 11	229	17 53	279	35 04	307	52 01	334
	◆CAPELLA		Alpheratz		◆Enif		ALTAIR		Rasalhague		◆Alphecca		Alioth	
300	13 07	028	39 22	091	43 39	143	47 52	183	41 42	230	35 10	270	32 58	320
301	13 25	028	40 00	091	44 01	144	47 50	185	41 13	231	34 32	271	32 34	321
302	13 43	029	40 38	092	44 23	146	47 46	186	40 43	233	33 55	272	32 10	321
303	14 02	030	41 15	093	44 44	147	47 42	188	40 13	234	33 17	272	31 46	321
304	14 20	030	41 53	094	45 04	148	47 36	189	39 42	235	32 39	273	31 23	322
305	14 40	031	42 31	095	45 24	149	47 30	190	39 11	236	32 01	274	31 00	322
306	14 59	031	43 08	095	45 43	151	47 23	192	38 40	237	31 24	275	30 37	323
307	15 19	032	43 46	096	46 01	152	47 14	193	38 08	238	30 46	275	30 14	323
308	15 39	033	44 23	097	46 18	154	47 05	195	37 36	239	30 09	276	29 52	324
309	16 00	033	45 01	098	46 34	155	46 55	196	37 03	240	29 31	277	29 30	324
310	16 21	034	45 38	099	46 50	156	46 44	198	36 30	241	28 54	278	29 08	325
311	16 42	035	46 15	100	47 05	158	46 32	199	35 57	242	28 16	278	28 46	325
312	17 04	035	46 53	101	47 19	159	46 20	200	35 24	243	27 39	279	28 25	326
313	17 26	036	47 30	102	47 32	160	46 06	202	34 50	244	27 02	280	28 04	326
314	17 48	036	48 07	103	47 44	162	45 52	203	34 16	245	26 25	281	27 43	327
	CAPELLA		◆Hamal		Alpheratz		Enif		◆ALTAIR		VEGA		◆Alioth	
315	18 10	037	26 06	084	48 43	103	47 55	163	45 36	205	62 19	258	27 22	327
316	18 33	038	26 44	085	49 20	104	48 06	165	45 20	206	61 42	259	27 02	328
317	18 57	038	27 22	086	49 56	105	48 15	166	45 03	207	61 05	260	26 42	328
318	19 20	039	27 59	086	50 33	106	48 23	168	44 46	209	60 28	261	26 23	329
319	19 44	039	28 37	087	51 09	107	48 31	169	44 27	210	59 51	262	26 03	329
320	20 08	040	29 15	088	51 45	108	48 38	171	44 08	211	59 13	263	25 44	330
321	20 33	041	29 52	089	52 21	109	48 43	172	43 48	213	58 36	264	25 25	330
322	20 57	041	30 30	089	52 56	110	48 48	174	43 27	214	57 58	264	25 07	331
323	21 22	042	31 08	090	53 31	112	48 52	175	43 06	215	57 20	265	24 49	331
324	21 48	042	31 46	091	54 06	113	48 54	177	42 44	216	56 43	266	24 31	332
325	22 13	043	32 23	092	54 41	114	48 56	178	42 21	218	56 05	267	24 13	332
326	22 39	044	33 01	093	55 15	115	48 57	180	41 58	219	55 27	268	23 56	333
327	23 06	044	33 39	093	55 50	116	48 56	181	41 34	220	54 50	269	23 39	334
328	23 32	045	34 17	094	56 23	117	48 55	183	41 09	221	54 12	269	23 22	334
329	23 59	045	34 54	095	56 57	119	48 53	184	40 44	222	53 34	270	23 06	335
	CAPELLA		◆Hamal		Alpheratz		Enif		◆ALTAIR		VEGA		◆Alioth	
330	24 26	046	35 32	096	57 30	120	48 50	186	40 19	224	52 56	271	22 50	335
331	24 53	047	36 09	097	58 02	121	48 45	187	39 52	225	52 19	272	22 34	336
332	25 21	047	36 47	098	58 34	122	48 40	189	39 25	226	51 41	272	22 19	336
333	25 49	048	37 24	098	59 06	124	48 34	190	38 58	227	51 03	273	22 04	337
334	26 17	048	38 01	099	59 37	125	48 27	192	38 30	228	50 26	274	21 49	337
335	26 45	049	38 39	100	60 08	127	48 19	193	38 02	229	49 48	275	21 35	338
336	27 13	049	39 16	101	60 38	128	48 10	195	37 33	230	49 10	275	21 21	338
337	27 42	050	39 53	102	61 07	129	48 00	196	37 04	231	48 33	276	21 07	339
338	28 11	051	40 30	103	61 36	131	47 49	197	36 34	232	47 55	277	20 53	340
339	28 41	051	41 06	104	62 04	133	47 37	199	36 04	233	47 18	277	20 40	340
340	29 10	052	41 43	105	62 32	134	47 25	200	35 33	235	46 40	278	20 28	341
341	29 40	052	42 20	105	62 58	136	47 11	202	35 02	236	46 03	279	20 15	341
342	30 10	053	42 56	106	63 24	137	46 57	203	34 31	237	45 26	280	20 03	342
343	30 40	053	43 32	107	63 50	139	46 42	204	33 59	238	44 48	280	19 52	342
344	31 10	054	44 08	108	64 14	141	46 26	206	33 27	239	44 11	281	19 40	343
	◆CAPELLA		ALDEBARAN		◆Diphda		Enif		ALTAIR		◆VEGA		Alioth	
345	31 41	054	16 24	084	17 24	154	46 09	207	32 55	240	43 34	282	19 29	343
346	32 12	055	17 01	085	17 40	155	45 51	209	32 22	241	42 57	282	19 19	344
347	32 43	056	17 39	085	17 56	156	45 33	210	31 49	242	42 20	283	19 09	345
348	33 14	056	18 16	086	18 11	157	45 13	211	31 16	242	41 44	283	18 59	345
349	33 46	057	18 54	087	18 25	158	44 53	213	30 42	243	41 07	284	18 49	346
350	34 17	057	19 32	088	18 39	159	44 33	214	30 08	244	40 30	285	18 40	346
351	34 49	058	20 10	088	18 52	160	44 11	215	29 34	245	39 54	285	18 31	347
352	35 21	058	20 47	089	19 05	161	43 49	216	29 00	246	39 18	286	18 23	347
353	35 53	059	21 25	090	19 17	162	43 27	218	28 25	247	38 41	287	18 15	348
354	36 26	059	22 03	091	19 29	163	43 03	219	27 50	248	38 05	287	18 07	349
355	36 58	060	22 41	091	19 40	164	42 39	220	27 15	249	37 29	288	18 00	349
356	37 31	060	23 18	092	19 50	165	42 15	221	26 40	250	36 53	289	17 53	350
357	38 04	061	23 56	093	20 00	166	41 49	223	26 04	251	36 18	289	17 46	350
358	38 37	062	24 34	094	20 09	167	41 23	224	25 28	252	35 42	290	17 40	351
359	39 10	062	25 11	095	20 17	168	40 57	225	24 52	252	35 07	290	17 34	351

LAT 50°N
LAT 50°N

LHA ♈	Hc	Zn	Hc	Zn	Hc	Zn	Hc	Zn	Hc	Zn	Hc	Zn	Hc	Zn
	◆CAPELLA		ALDEBARAN		Hamal		◆Alpheratz		ALTAIR		◆VEGA		Kochab	
0	39 16	062	25 54	095	53 40	125	69 06	174	24 33	254	34 09	292	37 23	346
1	39 50	062	26 33	096	54 12	126	69 09	177	23 56	255	33 34	292	37 14	347
2	40 24	063	27 11	097	54 42	127	69 10	179	23 19	255	32 58	293	37 06	347
3	40 59	063	27 49	097	55 13	129	69 10	182	22 42	256	32 23	293	36 57	347
4	41 33	064	28 28	098	55 42	130	69 08	184	22 04	257	31 47	294	36 49	348
5	42 08	064	29 06	099	56 12	132	69 04	187	21 26	258	31 12	295	36 40	348
6	42 43	065	29 44	100	56 40	133	68 59	189	20 49	259	30 37	295	36 33	348
7	43 18	065	30 22	101	57 08	134	68 52	191	20 11	260	30 03	296	36 25	349
8	43 53	066	31 00	101	57 35	136	68 44	194	19 33	260	29 28	297	36 17	349
9	44 28	067	31 37	102	58 02	137	68 34	196	18 55	261	28 53	297	36 10	349
10	45 04	067	32 15	103	58 27	139	68 22	199	18 17	262	28 19	298	36 03	349
11	45 39	068	32 52	104	58 52	141	68 09	201	17 38	263	27 45	298	35 56	350
12	46 15	068	33 30	105	59 16	142	67 55	203	17 00	264	27 11	299	35 49	350
13	46 51	069	34 07	106	59 40	144	67 39	205	16 22	264	26 38	300	35 42	350
14	47 27	069	34 44	107	60 02	145	67 22	207	15 43	265	26 04	300	35 36	351
	◆CAPELLA		ALDEBARAN		Hamal		◆Diphda		Alpheratz		◆DENEB		Kochab	
15	48 03	070	35 21	108	60 23	147	22 00	184	67 04	210	47 40	290	35 30	351
16	48 39	070	35 58	109	60 44	149	21 57	185	66 44	212	47 04	290	35 24	351
17	49 15	071	36 34	109	61 03	151	21 54	186	66 23	214	46 28	291	35 18	352
18	49 52	071	37 10	110	61 22	152	21 49	187	66 01	216	45 52	291	35 13	352
19	50 28	072	37 46	111	61 39	154	21 44	188	65 38	217	45 16	292	35 08	352
20	51 05	072	38 22	112	61 55	156	21 38	189	65 14	219	44 40	292	35 02	353
21	51 42	073	38 58	113	62 10	158	21 32	190	64 49	221	44 04	293	34 58	353
22	52 19	073	39 33	114	62 24	160	21 25	191	64 24	223	43 29	293	34 53	353
23	52 56	074	40 08	115	62 37	162	21 17	192	63 57	225	42 53	294	34 49	354
24	53 33	074	40 43	116	62 48	164	21 09	193	63 29	226	42 18	294	34 44	354
25	54 10	075	41 17	117	62 58	166	20 59	194	63 01	228	41 43	295	34 40	354
26	54 47	075	41 51	118	63 07	168	20 50	195	62 32	230	41 08	295	34 36	355
27	55 25	076	42 25	119	63 15	170	20 39	196	62 02	231	40 33	296	34 33	355
28	56 02	076	42 59	120	63 21	172	20 28	197	61 32	233	39 59	296	34 30	355
29	56 40	077	43 32	121	63 26	174	20 16	198	61 01	234	39 24	297	34 26	355
	CAPELLA		◆BETELGEUSE		RIGEL		Hamal		◆Alpheratz		DENEB		◆Kochab	
30	57 17	078	25 17	110	18 03	128	63 29	176	60 30	236	38 50	297	34 23	356
31	57 55	078	25 53	111	18 33	129	63 31	178	59 58	237	38 16	298	34 21	356
32	58 33	079	26 29	112	19 03	130	63 32	180	59 25	238	37 42	299	34 18	356
33	59 10	079	27 05	113	19 32	131	63 31	182	58 52	240	37 08	299	34 16	357
34	59 48	080	27 40	113	20 01	132	63 29	184	58 18	241	36 34	300	34 14	357
35	60 26	080	28 16	114	20 29	133	63 26	186	57 45	242	36 01	300	34 12	357
36	61 04	081	28 51	115	20 57	134	63 21	188	57 10	243	35 28	301	34 11	358
37	61 43	082	29 25	116	21 25	135	63 15	190	56 36	245	34 55	301	34 09	358
38	62 21	082	30 00	117	21 52	136	63 07	192	56 01	246	34 22	302	34 08	358
39	62 59	083	30 34	118	22 19	137	62 58	194	55 25	247	33 49	302	34 07	359
40	63 37	083	31 08	119	22 45	138	62 48	196	54 50	248	33 17	303	34 06	359
41	64 16	084	31 41	120	23 11	139	62 37	198	54 14	249	32 44	303	34 06	359
42	64 54	085	32 15	121	23 36	140	62 24	200	53 38	250	32 12	304	34 06	000
43	65 32	085	32 48	122	24 00	141	62 10	202	53 01	251	31 40	304	34 06	000
44	66 11	086	33 20	123	24 25	142	61 55	204	52 25	252	31 08	305	34 06	000
	◆Dubhe		POLLUX		BETELGEUSE		◆RIGEL		Hamal		◆Alpheratz		DENEB	
45	31 06	028	32 37	084	33 52	124	24 48	143	61 39	206	51 48	253	30 37	305
46	31 24	029	33 16	085	34 24	125	25 11	144	61 22	208	51 11	254	30 06	306
47	31 43	029	33 54	085	34 56	126	25 34	145	61 04	209	50 34	255	29 35	307
48	32 02	030	34 32	086	35 27	127	25 56	146	60 44	211	49 56	256	29 04	307
49	32 21	030	35 11	087	35 57	128	26 18	147	60 24	213	49 19	257	28 33	308
50	32 40	030	35 49	088	36 27	129	26 38	148	60 02	215	48 41	258	28 03	308
51	33 00	031	36 28	088	36 57	130	26 59	149	59 40	216	48 03	259	27 32	309
52	33 20	031	37 07	089	37 26	131	27 18	150	59 17	218	47 25	260	27 02	309
53	33 40	032	37 45	090	37 55	132	27 37	151	58 53	219	46 47	261	26 33	310
54	34 00	032	38 24	091	38 23	133	27 56	152	58 28	221	46 09	262	26 03	310
55	34 21	032	39 02	092	38 51	135	28 14	153	58 02	223	45 31	262	25 34	311
56	34 42	033	39 41	092	39 18	136	28 31	154	57 36	224	44 53	263	25 05	312
57	35 03	033	40 19	093	39 45	137	28 47	155	57 08	226	44 14	264	24 36	312
58	35 24	034	40 58	094	40 11	138	29 03	156	56 41	227	43 36	265	24 08	313
59	35 45	034	41 36	095	40 36	139	29 18	157	56 12	228	42 58	266	23 40	313
	◆Dubhe		POLLUX		SIRIUS		◆RIGEL		Hamal		◆Alpheratz		DENEB	
60	36 07	034	42 15	096	13 56	139	29 33	158	55 43	230	42 19	267	23 12	314
61	36 29	035	42 53	096	14 21	140	29 47	160	55 13	231	41 41	267	22 44	314
62	36 51	035	43 31	097	14 45	141	30 00	161	54 43	233	41 02	268	22 17	315
63	37 13	035	44 10	098	15 09	142	30 12	162	54 12	234	40 23	269	21 50	316
64	37 36	036	44 48	099	15 33	143	30 24	163	53 40	235	39 45	270	21 23	316
65	37 58	036	45 26	100	15 56	144	30 35	164	53 09	236	39 06	270	20 56	317
66	38 21	037	46 04	101	16 19	145	30 45	165	52 36	238	38 28	271	20 30	317
67	38 44	037	46 42	102	16 41	146	30 55	166	52 04	239	37 49	272	20 04	318
68	39 07	037	47 19	102	17 02	146	31 03	167	51 30	240	37 11	273	19 38	319
69	39 31	038	47 57	103	17 23	147	31 11	169	50 57	241	36 32	273	19 13	319
70	39 54	038	48 34	104	17 44	148	31 19	170	50 23	242	35 54	274	18 48	320
71	40 18	038	49 12	105	18 04	149	31 25	171	49 49	243	35 15	275	18 23	320
72	40 42	039	49 49	106	18 23	150	31 31	172	49 14	244	34 37	276	17 59	321
73	41 06	039	50 26	107	18 42	151	31 36	173	48 39	246	33 59	276	17 34	322
74	41 31	039	51 02	108	19 00	152	31 40	174	48 04	247	33 20	277	17 11	322
	◆Dubhe		REGULUS		PROCYON		◆SIRIUS		RIGEL		◆Hamal		DENEB	
75	41 55	040	17 14	092	34 01	129	19 18	153	31 43	176	47 28	248	16 47	323
76	42 20	040	17 52	093	34 31	130	19 35	154	31 46	177	46 52	249	16 24	323
77	42 45	040	18 31	093	35 00	132	19 52	155	31 48	178	46 16	250	16 01	324
78	43 10	041	19 09	094	35 28	133	20 08	156	31 49	179	45 40	251	15 39	325
79	43 35	041	19 48	095	35 57	134	20 23	157	31 49	180	45 03	252	15 17	325
80	44 00	041	20 26	096	36 24	135	20 38	158	31 48	181	44 27	253	14 55	326
81	44 26	041	21 05	097	36 51	136	20 52	159	31 47	183	43 50	254	14 33	326
82	44 51	042	21 43	097	37 18	137	21 05	160	31 45	184	43 13	254	14 12	327
83	45 17	042	22 21	098	37 44	138	21 18	161	31 42	185	42 36	255	13 51	328
84	45 43	042	22 59	099	38 09	139	21 30	162	31 38	186	41 58	256	13 31	328
85	46 09	043	23 37	100	38 34	140	21 42	163	31 34	187	41 21	257	13 11	329
86	46 35	043	24 15	101	38 59	142	21 53	164	31 29	188	40 43	258	12 51	330
87	47 02	043	24 53	101	39 22	143	22 03	165	31 23	190	40 05	259	12 32	330
88	47 28	043	25 31	102	39 45	144	22 13	166	31 16	191	39 27	260	12 13	331
89	47 55	044	26 08	103	40 08	145	22 22	167	31 08	192	38 49	261	11 54	332

LHA ♈	Hc	Zn	Hc	Zn	Hc	Zn	Hc	Zn	Hc	Zn	Hc	Zn	Hc	Zn
	◆Dubhe		REGULUS		PROCYON		◆SIRIUS		RIGEL		ALDEBARAN		◆Mirfak	
90	48 21	044	26 46	104	40 29	146	22 30	168	31 00	193	52 34	214	65 25	285
91	48 48	044	27 23	105	40 50	148	22 38	169	30 51	194	52 12	216	64 48	285
92	49 15	044	28 00	106	41 11	149	22 45	170	30 41	195	51 49	217	64 10	286
93	49 42	045	28 37	107	41 30	150	22 51	171	30 31	196	51 26	218	63 33	286
94	50 09	045	29 14	107	41 49	151	22 56	172	30 20	197	51 01	220	62 56	286
95	50 36	045	29 51	108	42 07	153	23 01	173	30 08	199	50 36	221	62 19	287
96	51 04	045	30 28	109	42 25	154	23 05	174	29 55	200	50 11	222	61 43	287
97	51 31	045	31 04	110	42 41	155	23 09	175	29 42	201	49 44	224	61 06	288
98	51 59	046	31 40	111	42 57	157	23 12	176	29 28	202	49 17	225	60 29	288
99	52 26	046	32 16	112	43 12	158	23 14	177	29 13	203	48 50	226	59 52	289
100	52 54	046	32 52	113	43 26	159	23 15	178	28 58	204	48 22	228	59 16	289
101	53 22	046	33 27	114	43 39	161	23 16	180	28 41	205	47 53	229	58 39	289
102	53 50	046	34 02	115	43 52	162	23 16	181	28 25	206	47 23	230	58 03	290
103	54 18	047	34 37	116	44 03	163	23 15	182	28 07	207	46 54	231	57 27	290
104	54 46	047	35 12	117	44 14	165	23 13	183	27 49	208	46 23	232	56 51	291
	◆Dubhe		Denebola		REGULUS		◆SIRIUS		RIGEL		ALDEBARAN		◆Mirfak	
105	55 14	047	22 17	094	35 46	118	23 11	184	27 31	210	45 52	234	56 15	291
106	55 42	047	22 56	095	36 20	119	23 08	185	27 11	211	45 21	235	55 39	291
107	56 10	047	23 34	095	36 54	120	23 05	186	26 51	212	44 49	236	55 03	292
108	56 38	047	24 12	096	37 27	121	23 01	187	26 31	213	44 17	237	54 27	292
109	57 07	047	24 51	097	38 00	122	22 56	188	26 10	214	43 45	238	53 52	293
110	57 35	047	25 29	098	38 33	123	22 50	189	25 48	215	43 12	239	53 16	293
111	58 03	047	26 07	099	39 05	124	22 44	190	25 26	216	42 38	240	52 41	294
112	58 32	047	26 45	099	39 37	125	22 37	191	25 03	217	42 05	241	52 05	294
113	59 00	048	27 23	100	40 08	126	22 29	192	24 40	218	41 31	242	51 30	294
114	59 29	048	28 01	101	40 39	127	22 21	193	24 16	219	40 56	243	50 55	295
115	59 57	048	28 39	102	41 10	128	22 12	194	23 51	220	40 22	244	50 20	295
116	60 26	048	29 17	103	41 40	129	22 02	195	23 27	221	39 47	245	49 45	296
117	60 54	048	29 54	104	42 10	130	21 52	196	23 01	222	39 12	246	49 11	296
118	61 22	048	30 32	105	42 39	131	21 41	197	22 35	223	38 36	247	48 36	297
119	61 51	048	31 09	105	43 08	133	21 29	198	22 09	224	38 00	248	48 02	297
	◆Kochab		Denebola		◆REGULUS		SIRIUS		RIGEL		◆ALDEBARAN		CAPELLA	
120	44 16	022	31 46	106	43 36	134	21 17	199	21 42	225	37 24	249	62 55	277
121	44 31	022	32 23	107	44 03	135	21 04	200	21 15	225	36 48	250	62 17	278
122	44 45	022	33 00	108	44 30	136	20 50	201	20 47	226	36 12	251	61 39	279
123	45 00	022	33 36	109	44 57	137	20 36	202	20 19	227	35 35	252	61 01	279
124	45 15	023	34 13	110	45 23	139	20 21	203	19 50	228	34 58	253	60 23	280
125	45 30	023	34 49	111	45 48	140	20 06	204	19 21	229	34 22	254	59 45	280
126	45 45	023	35 25	112	46 12	141	19 50	205	18 52	230	33 44	255	59 07	281
127	46 00	023	36 00	113	46 36	143	19 33	206	18 22	231	33 07	256	58 29	281
128	46 15	023	36 36	114	46 59	144	19 16	207	17 52	232	32 30	256	57 51	282
129	46 30	023	37 11	115	47 21	145	18 58	208	17 21	233	31 52	257	57 13	283
130	46 46	024	37 46	116	47 43	147	18 40	209	16 51	234	31 14	258	56 36	283
131	47 01	024	38 21	117	48 04	148	18 21	210	16 19	235	30 37	259	55 58	284
132	47 17	024	38 55	118	48 24	149	18 02	211	15 48	235	29 59	260	55 21	284
133	47 32	024	39 29	119	48 43	151	17 42	212	15 16	236	29 21	261	54 43	285
134	47 48	024	40 03	120	49 02	152	17 21	213	14 44	237	28 43	261	54 06	285
	◆Kochab		ARCTURUS		Denebola		◆REGULUS		SIRIUS		BETELGEUSE		◆CAPELLA	
135	48 04	024	21 27	085	40 36	121	49 20	153	17 00	214	32 47	238	53 29	286
136	48 20	024	22 06	086	41 09	122	49 36	155	16 39	215	32 14	239	52 52	286
137	48 36	024	22 44	087	41 42	123	49 52	156	16 16	215	31 41	240	52 15	287
138	48 51	025	23 23	088	42 14	124	50 07	158	15 54	216	31 08	241	51 38	287
139	49 08	025	24 01	088	42 46	125	50 21	159	15 31	217	30 34	242	51 01	288
140	49 24	025	24 40	089	43 17	126	50 34	161	15 07	218	30 00	243	50 25	288
141	49 40	025	25 18	090	43 48	127	50 47	162	14 43	219	29 25	244	49 48	289
142	49 56	025	25 57	091	44 19	128	50 58	164	14 18	220	28 50	245	49 12	289
143	50 12	025	26 35	092	44 49	129	51 08	165	13 53	221	28 15	246	48 35	290
144	50 28	025	27 14	092	45 18	131	51 17	167	13 28	222	27 40	247	47 59	290
145	50 45	025	27 52	093	45 47	132	51 25	169	13 02	223	27 05	247	47 23	291
146	51 01	025	28 31	094	46 16	133	51 33	170	12 36	223	26 29	248	46 47	291
147	51 17	025	29 09	095	46 44	134	51 39	172	12 09	224	25 53	249	46 11	292
148	51 34	025	29 48	095	47 11	136	51 44	173	11 42	225	25 17	250	45 36	293
149	51 50	025	30 26	096	47 38	137	51 48	175	11 14	226	24 40	251	45 00	293
	◆Kochab		ARCTURUS		◆SPICA		REGULUS		PROCYON		◆BETELGEUSE		CAPELLA	
150	52 07	025	31 05	097	14 05	128	51 51	176	36 25	225	24 04	252	44 25	294
151	52 23	025	31 43	098	14 35	129	51 53	178	35 58	226	23 27	253	43 49	294
152	52 39	025	32 21	099	15 05	129	51 54	180	35 30	227	22 50	253	43 14	295
153	52 56	025	32 59	100	15 34	130	51 53	181	35 01	228	22 13	254	42 39	295
154	53 12	025	33 37	100	16 04	131	51 52	183	34 32	230	21 36	255	42 04	296
155	53 29	025	34 15	101	16 32	132	51 50	184	34 02	231	20 59	256	41 30	296
156	53 45	025	34 53	102	17 01	133	51 46	186	33 32	232	20 21	257	40 55	297
157	54 02	025	35 30	103	17 29	134	51 42	187	33 02	233	19 44	258	40 21	297
158	54 18	025	36 08	104	17 56	135	51 36	189	32 31	234	19 06	258	39 47	298
159	54 34	025	36 45	105	18 24	136	51 30	191	32 00	235	18 28	259	39 12	298
160	54 51	025	37 22	106	18 50	137	51 22	192	31 28	236	17 50	260	38 39	299
161	55 07	025	37 59	107	19 17	138	51 14	194	30 56	237	17 12	261	38 05	299
162	55 23	025	38 36	107	19 42	138	51 04	195	30 24	238	16 34	262	37 31	300
163	55 39	025	39 13	108	20 08	139	50 53	197	29 51	239	15 56	262	36 58	300
164	55 56	025	39 49	109	20 33	140	50 42	198	29 18	239	15 17	263	36 25	301
	◆VEGA		ARCTURUS		◆SPICA		REGULUS		PROCYON		◆POLLUX		CAPELLA	
165	15 52	048	40 26	110	20 57	141	50 29	200	28 45	240	47 24	257	35 52	301
166	16 20	048	41 02	111	21 21	142	50 16	201	28 11	241	46 46	258	35 19	302
167	16 49	049	41 38	112	21 44	143	50 01	203	27 37	242	46 08	259	34 46	302
168	17 18	049	42 13	113	22 07	144	49 46	204	27 03	243	45 30	260	34 14	303
169	17 48	050	42 49	114	22 29	145	49 29	206	26 28	244	44 52	261	33 41	303
170	18 18	051	43 24	115	22 51	146	49 12	207	25 53	245	44 14	262	33 09	304
171	18 48	051	43 58	116	23 12	147	48 54	209	25 18	246	43 36	263	32 37	304
172	19 18	052	44 33	117	23 33	148	48 36	210	24 43	247	42 58	264	32 06	305
173	19 48	053	45 07	118	23 53	149	48 16	211	24 07	248	42 19	264	31 34	306
174	20 19	053	45 41	119	24 12	150	47 55	213	23 31	249	41 41	265	31 03	306
175	20 50	054	46 14	121	24 31	151	47 34	214	22 55	249	41 02	266	30 32	307
176	21 22	055	46 47	122	24 49	152	47 12	215	22 19	250	40 24	267	30 01	307
177	21 53	055	47 20	123	25 07	153	46 50	217	21 43	251	39 45	268	29 30	308
178	22 25	056	47 52	124	25 24	154	46 26	218	21 06	252	39 07	268	29 00	308
179	22 57	056	48 24	125	25 40	155	46 02	219	20 30	253	38 28	269	28 30	309

LHA ♈	Hc	Zn	Hc	Zn	Hc	Zn	Hc	Zn	Hc	Zn	Hc	Zn	Hc	Zn
	◆ DENEB		VEGA		ARCTURUS		◆ SPICA		REGULUS		◆ POLLUX		CAPELLA	
180	14 34	034	23 29	057	48 55	126	25 56	156	45 37	221	37 50	270	28 00	309
181	14 55	034	24 02	058	49 26	128	26 11	157	45 12	222	37 11	271	27 30	310
182	15 17	035	24 34	058	49 56	129	26 25	159	44 46	223	36 33	271	27 01	310
183	15 39	035	25 07	059	50 26	130	26 39	160	44 19	224	35 54	272	26 31	311
184	16 02	036	25 40	059	50 55	131	26 52	161	43 52	226	35 15	273	26 02	312
185	16 25	037	26 13	060	51 24	133	27 05	162	43 24	227	34 37	274	25 34	312
186	16 48	037	26 47	061	51 52	134	27 16	163	42 56	228	33 58	274	25 05	313
187	17 11	038	27 21	061	52 20	135	27 27	164	42 27	229	33 20	275	24 37	313
188	17 35	038	27 55	062	52 46	137	27 38	165	41 58	230	32 42	276	24 09	314
189	17 59	039	28 29	062	53 12	138	27 47	166	41 28	231	32 03	277	23 41	314
190	18 24	040	29 03	063	53 38	139	27 56	167	40 57	232	31 25	277	23 14	315
191	18 49	040	29 37	064	54 03	141	28 04	168	40 27	234	30 47	278	22 47	316
192	19 14	041	30 12	064	54 27	142	28 12	169	39 55	235	30 09	279	22 20	316
193	19 39	041	30 47	065	54 50	144	28 19	171	39 24	236	29 31	279	21 53	317
194	20 05	042	31 22	065	55 12	145	28 25	172	38 52	237	28 53	280	21 27	317
	◆ DENEB		VEGA		Rasalhague		◆ ARCTURUS		REGULUS		◆ POLLUX		CAPELLA	
195	20 31	043	31 57	066	23 06	098	55 34	147	38 19	238	28 15	281	21 01	318
196	20 57	043	32 32	067	23 44	099	55 54	148	37 46	239	27 37	282	20 35	318
197	21 24	044	33 08	067	24 22	100	56 14	150	37 13	240	26 59	282	20 10	319
198	21 50	044	33 44	068	25 00	101	56 33	152	36 40	241	26 21	283	19 45	320
199	22 18	045	34 19	068	25 38	101	56 51	153	36 06	242	25 44	284	19 20	320
200	22 45	046	34 55	069	26 15	102	57 07	155	35 32	243	25 06	284	18 55	321
201	23 13	046	35 31	070	26 53	103	57 23	157	34 57	244	24 29	285	18 31	321
202	23 41	047	36 08	070	27 31	104	57 38	158	34 23	245	23 52	286	18 07	322
203	24 09	047	36 44	071	28 08	105	57 52	160	33 48	246	23 15	286	17 43	323
204	24 37	048	37 21	072	28 45	106	58 04	162	33 12	247	22 38	287	17 20	323
205	25 06	048	37 57	072	29 22	106	58 16	164	32 37	248	22 01	288	16 57	324
206	25 35	049	38 34	073	29 59	107	58 26	165	32 01	248	21 25	288	16 35	324
207	26 04	050	39 11	073	30 36	108	58 35	167	31 25	249	20 48	289	16 12	325
208	26 34	050	39 48	074	31 12	109	58 43	169	30 49	250	20 12	290	15 50	326
209	27 03	051	40 25	075	31 49	110	58 50	171	30 12	251	19 36	291	15 29	326
	◆ DENEB		VEGA		Rasalhague		◆ ARCTURUS		REGULUS		◆ POLLUX		CAPELLA	
210	27 33	051	41 02	075	32 25	111	58 56	173	29 36	252	18 59	291	15 08	327
211	28 03	052	41 40	076	33 01	112	59 00	174	28 59	253	18 24	292	14 47	327
212	28 34	052	42 17	076	33 37	113	59 04	176	28 22	254	17 48	293	14 26	328
213	29 05	053	42 55	077	34 12	114	59 06	178	27 45	255	17 12	293	14 06	329
214	29 35	053	43 32	078	34 47	115	59 06	180	27 08	256	16 37	294	13 46	329
215	30 06	054	44 10	078	35 22	116	59 06	182	26 30	256	16 02	295	13 27	330
216	30 38	055	44 48	079	35 57	117	59 04	184	25 53	257	15 27	295	13 07	331
217	31 09	055	45 26	080	36 31	118	59 01	185	25 15	258	14 52	296	12 49	331
218	31 41	056	46 04	080	37 05	118	58 57	187	24 37	259	14 18	297	12 30	332
219	32 13	056	46 42	081	37 39	120	58 51	189	23 59	260	13 43	297	12 12	333
220	32 45	057	47 20	082	38 12	121	58 45	191	23 21	260	13 09	298	11 55	333
221	33 17	057	47 58	082	38 45	122	58 37	193	22 43	261	12 35	299	11 38	334
222	33 50	058	48 36	083	39 18	123	58 28	194	22 05	262	12 02	300	11 21	334
223	34 23	058	49 15	084	39 50	124	58 18	196	21 27	263	11 28	300	11 04	335
224	34 56	059	49 53	084	40 22	125	58 06	198	20 49	264	10 55	301	10 48	336
	DENEB		◆ VEGA		Rasalhague		ANTARES		◆ ARCTURUS		Denebola		◆ Dubhe	
225	35 29	059	50 31	085	40 54	126	10 57	160	57 54	200	37 43	245	56 19	313
226	36 02	060	51 10	086	41 25	127	11 10	160	57 40	201	37 08	246	55 51	313
227	36 35	060	51 48	086	41 55	128	11 23	161	57 26	203	36 33	246	55 23	313
228	37 09	061	52 27	087	42 26	129	11 35	162	57 10	205	35 57	247	54 55	313
229	37 43	062	53 05	088	42 55	130	11 46	163	56 54	206	35 22	248	54 27	313
230	38 17	062	53 44	089	43 24	131	11 57	164	56 36	208	34 46	249	53 59	314
231	38 51	063	54 22	089	43 53	133	12 08	165	56 17	210	34 09	250	53 31	314
232	39 25	063	55 01	090	44 21	134	12 18	166	55 58	211	33 33	251	53 03	314
233	40 00	064	55 40	091	44 49	135	12 27	167	55 37	213	32 56	252	52 35	314
234	40 34	064	56 18	092	45 16	136	12 35	168	55 16	214	32 20	253	52 08	314
235	41 09	065	56 57	093	45 42	137	12 43	168	54 54	216	31 43	254	51 40	314
236	41 44	065	57 35	093	46 08	139	12 51	169	54 31	217	31 06	255	51 12	315
237	42 19	066	58 14	094	46 33	140	12 58	170	54 07	219	30 28	256	50 45	315
238	42 54	066	58 52	095	46 57	141	13 04	171	53 42	220	29 51	256	50 18	315
239	43 30	067	59 31	096	47 21	143	13 09	172	53 17	222	29 13	257	49 51	315
	◆ DENEB		ALTAIR		Rasalhague		◆ ANTARES		ARCTURUS		Denebola		◆ Dubhe	
240	44 05	067	27 09	110	47 44	144	13 14	173	52 51	223	28 36	258	49 24	316
241	44 41	068	27 45	111	48 06	145	13 19	174	52 24	225	27 58	259	48 57	316
242	45 17	068	28 21	112	48 28	147	13 23	175	51 57	226	27 20	260	48 30	316
243	45 53	069	28 56	112	48 49	148	13 26	176	51 29	227	26 42	261	48 03	316
244	46 29	069	29 32	113	49 09	149	13 28	177	51 00	228	26 04	261	47 36	317
245	47 05	070	30 07	114	49 28	151	13 30	178	50 31	230	25 26	262	47 10	317
246	47 41	070	30 42	115	49 46	152	13 31	179	50 01	231	24 47	263	46 44	317
247	48 18	071	31 17	116	50 04	154	13 32	179	49 31	232	24 09	264	46 17	317
248	48 54	072	31 52	117	50 20	155	13 32	180	49 00	233	23 31	265	45 51	318
249	49 31	072	32 26	118	50 36	157	13 32	181	48 29	235	22 52	265	45 25	318
250	50 07	073	33 00	119	50 51	158	13 30	182	47 57	236	22 14	266	45 00	318
251	50 44	073	33 33	120	51 05	160	13 29	183	47 25	237	21 35	267	44 34	318
252	51 21	074	34 06	121	51 18	161	13 26	184	46 53	238	20 57	268	44 08	319
253	51 58	074	34 39	122	51 30	163	13 23	185	46 20	239	20 18	269	43 43	319
254	52 35	075	35 12	123	51 41	164	13 19	186	45 46	240	19 40	269	43 18	319
	◆ Schedar		DENEB		ALTAIR		◆ Rasalhague		ARCTURUS		◆ Alkaid		Kochab	
255	29 14	035	53 13	075	35 44	124	51 51	166	45 13	241	59 27	287	62 19	342
256	29 36	035	53 50	076	36 16	125	51 59	167	44 39	243	58 51	288	62 07	341
257	29 58	036	54 28	076	36 47	126	52 07	169	44 04	244	58 14	288	61 54	341
258	30 21	036	55 05	077	37 18	127	52 14	171	43 30	245	57 37	289	61 42	340
259	30 44	037	55 43	078	37 48	128	52 20	172	42 55	246	57 01	289	61 29	340
260	31 07	037	56 20	078	38 18	129	52 25	174	42 19	247	56 24	290	61 15	340
261	31 30	038	56 58	079	38 48	130	52 28	175	41 44	248	55 48	290	61 02	339
262	31 54	038	57 36	079	39 17	132	52 31	177	41 08	249	55 12	290	60 48	339
263	32 18	038	58 14	080	39 46	133	52 33	179	40 32	250	54 36	291	60 35	339
264	32 42	039	58 52	080	40 14	134	52 33	180	39 56	251	54 00	291	60 21	339
265	33 06	039	59 30	081	40 41	135	52 32	182	39 19	251	53 24	292	60 06	338
266	33 31	040	60 08	082	41 08	136	52 31	183	38 43	252	52 48	292	59 52	338
267	33 55	040	60 46	082	41 35	137	52 28	185	38 06	253	52 13	293	59 37	338
268	34 20	041	61 24	083	42 01	139	52 24	187	37 29	254	51 37	293	59 23	338
269	34 46	041	62 03	083	42 26	140	52 19	188	36 52	255	51 02	294	59 08	337

LAT 50°N

LHA ♈	Hc	Zn	Hc	Zn	Hc	Zn	Hc	Zn	Hc	Zn	Hc	Zn	Hc	Zn
	◆ Mirfak		Alpheratz		◆ ALTAIR		Rasalhague		◆ ARCTURUS		Alkaid		Kochab	
270	15 14	025	20 33	069	42 50	141	52 13	190	36 14	256	50 26	294	58 53	337
271	15 30	025	21 09	069	43 14	142	52 06	191	35 37	257	49 51	295	58 38	337
272	15 47	026	21 45	070	43 38	143	51 58	193	34 59	258	49 16	295	58 23	337
273	16 04	026	22 21	071	44 00	145	51 49	194	34 21	259	48 41	295	58 07	336
274	16 21	027	22 58	071	44 22	146	51 39	196	33 44	259	48 07	296	57 52	336
275	16 39	028	23 34	072	44 44	147	51 28	198	33 06	260	47 32	296	57 36	336
276	16 57	028	24 11	073	45 04	149	51 15	199	32 27	261	46 57	297	57 21	336
277	17 16	029	24 48	073	45 24	150	51 02	201	31 49	262	46 23	297	57 05	336
278	17 34	029	25 25	074	45 43	151	50 48	202	31 11	263	45 49	298	56 49	336
279	17 54	030	26 02	075	46 01	153	50 33	204	30 33	264	45 15	298	56 33	336
280	18 13	031	26 40	076	46 18	154	50 17	205	29 54	264	44 41	299	56 17	335
281	18 33	031	27 17	076	46 35	155	50 01	207	29 16	265	44 07	299	56 01	335
282	18 53	032	27 54	077	46 50	157	49 43	208	28 38	266	43 33	300	55 45	335
283	19 13	032	28 32	078	47 05	158	49 25	209	27 59	267	43 00	300	55 29	335
284	19 34	033	29 10	078	47 19	160	49 05	211	27 21	268	42 27	300	55 12	335
	◆ Mirfak		Alpheratz		◆ ALTAIR		Rasalhague		◆ ARCTURUS		Alkaid		Kochab	
285	19 55	033	29 48	079	47 32	161	48 45	212	26 42	268	41 53	301	54 56	335
286	20 17	034	30 26	080	47 44	162	48 24	214	26 04	269	41 20	301	54 40	335
287	20 39	035	31 04	080	47 55	164	48 02	215	25 25	270	40 48	302	54 24	335
288	21 01	035	31 42	081	48 06	165	47 40	216	24 46	271	40 15	302	54 07	335
289	21 23	036	32 20	082	48 15	167	47 17	218	24 08	271	39 42	303	53 51	335
290	21 46	036	32 58	082	48 23	168	46 53	219	23 29	272	39 10	303	53 34	335
291	22 09	037	33 36	083	48 31	170	46 28	220	22 51	273	38 38	304	53 18	335
292	22 32	037	34 14	084	48 37	171	46 03	221	22 12	274	38 06	304	53 01	335
293	22 55	038	34 53	085	48 43	173	45 37	223	21 34	274	37 34	305	52 45	335
294	23 19	039	35 31	085	48 47	174	45 11	224	20 55	275	37 03	305	52 29	335
295	23 44	039	36 10	086	48 50	176	44 44	225	20 17	276	36 31	306	52 12	335
296	24 08	040	36 48	087	48 53	177	44 16	226	19 39	277	36 00	306	51 56	335
297	24 33	040	37 27	088	48 54	179	43 48	228	19 00	277	35 29	307	51 39	335
298	24 58	041	38 05	088	48 55	180	43 19	229	18 22	278	34 58	307	51 23	335
299	25 23	041	38 44	089	48 54	182	42 50	230	17 44	279	34 28	308	51 07	335
	CAPELLA		◆ Alpheratz		Enif		ALTAIR		◆ Rasalhague		Alphecca		◆ Kochab	
300	12 14	028	39 22	090	44 27	142	48 52	183	42 20	231	35 10	271	50 50	335
301	12 32	028	40 01	091	44 50	144	48 50	185	41 50	232	34 31	272	50 34	335
302	12 51	029	40 40	091	45 12	145	48 46	186	41 19	233	33 53	272	50 18	335
303	13 09	029	41 18	092	45 34	146	48 41	188	40 48	234	33 14	273	50 01	335
304	13 28	030	41 57	093	45 55	148	48 36	189	40 16	235	32 36	274	49 45	335
305	13 48	031	42 35	094	46 15	149	48 29	191	39 44	237	31 57	275	49 29	335
306	14 08	031	43 14	095	46 35	150	48 21	192	39 12	238	31 19	275	49 13	335
307	14 28	032	43 52	095	46 54	152	48 13	194	38 39	239	30 40	276	48 57	335
308	14 49	033	44 30	096	47 12	153	48 03	195	38 06	240	30 02	277	48 41	336
309	15 10	033	45 09	097	47 29	154	47 53	197	37 33	241	29 24	277	48 25	336
310	15 31	034	45 47	098	47 45	156	47 41	198	36 59	242	28 45	278	48 09	336
311	15 53	034	46 25	099	48 00	157	47 29	199	36 25	243	28 07	279	47 53	336
312	16 15	035	47 03	100	48 15	159	47 16	201	35 50	244	27 29	280	47 38	336
313	16 37	036	47 41	100	48 28	160	47 02	202	35 16	245	26 51	280	47 22	336
314	17 00	036	48 19	101	48 41	162	46 47	204	34 41	246	26 13	281	47 06	336
	CAPELLA		◆ Hamal		Alpheratz		Enif		◆ ALTAIR		VEGA		◆ Kochab	
315	17 22	037	26 00	084	48 57	102	48 53	163	46 31	205	62 31	260	46 51	336
316	17 46	037	26 38	084	49 34	103	49 03	165	46 14	206	61 53	261	46 36	337
317	18 09	038	27 17	085	50 12	104	49 13	166	45 56	208	61 15	262	46 20	337
318	18 33	039	27 55	086	50 49	105	49 22	167	45 38	209	60 37	263	46 05	337
319	18 58	039	28 34	087	51 26	106	49 30	169	45 19	210	59 58	263	45 50	337
320	19 22	040	29 12	087	52 03	107	49 37	171	44 59	212	59 20	264	45 35	337
321	19 47	040	29 51	088	52 40	108	49 43	172	44 38	213	58 42	265	45 20	337
322	20 12	041	30 29	089	53 16	109	49 47	174	44 17	214	58 03	266	45 05	337
323	20 38	042	31 08	090	53 53	110	49 51	175	43 55	216	57 25	267	44 50	338
324	21 03	042	31 46	090	54 29	111	49 54	177	43 32	217	56 46	268	44 36	338
325	21 30	043	32 25	091	55 05	112	49 56	178	43 09	218	56 07	268	44 21	338
326	21 56	043	33 04	092	55 40	114	49 57	180	42 45	219	55 29	269	44 07	338
327	22 23	044	33 42	093	56 15	115	49 56	181	42 20	221	54 50	270	43 53	338
328	22 49	045	34 21	094	56 50	116	49 55	183	41 54	222	54 12	271	43 38	339
329	23 17	045	34 59	094	57 25	117	49 53	184	41 28	223	53 33	272	43 24	339
	CAPELLA		◆ Hamal		Diphda		Enif		◆ ALTAIR		VEGA		◆ Kochab	
330	23 44	046	35 38	095	13 02	140	49 49	186	41 02	224	52 55	272	43 11	339
331	24 12	046	36 16	096	13 27	141	49 45	187	40 35	225	52 16	273	42 57	339
332	24 40	047	36 54	097	13 51	142	49 40	189	40 07	226	51 38	274	42 43	339
333	25 08	047	37 32	098	14 14	143	49 33	190	39 39	228	50 59	274	42 30	340
334	25 37	048	38 11	098	14 37	144	49 26	192	39 10	229	50 21	275	42 16	340
335	26 05	048	38 49	099	15 00	145	49 17	193	38 41	230	49 42	276	42 03	340
336	26 34	049	39 27	100	15 22	145	49 08	195	38 11	231	49 04	277	41 50	340
337	27 04	050	40 05	101	15 44	146	48 58	196	37 41	232	48 26	277	41 37	340
338	27 33	050	40 43	102	16 05	147	48 46	198	37 10	233	47 48	278	41 24	341
339	28 03	051	41 20	103	16 25	148	48 34	199	36 39	234	47 09	279	41 11	341
340	28 33	051	41 58	104	16 45	149	48 21	201	36 08	235	46 31	279	40 59	341
341	29 03	052	42 35	105	17 05	150	48 07	202	35 36	236	45 53	280	40 47	341
342	29 33	052	43 12	105	17 24	151	47 52	204	35 04	237	45 15	281	40 34	342
343	30 04	053	43 49	106	17 42	152	47 36	205	34 31	238	44 37	281	40 22	342
344	30 35	053	44 26	107	18 00	153	47 20	206	33 58	239	44 00	282	40 10	342
	◆ CAPELLA		ALDEBARAN		◆ Diphda		Enif		ALTAIR		◆ VEGA		Kochab	
345	31 06	054	16 17	083	18 17	154	47 02	208	33 25	240	43 22	282	39 59	342
346	31 37	055	16 55	084	18 34	155	46 44	209	32 51	241	42 44	283	39 47	343
347	32 09	055	17 34	085	18 50	156	46 25	210	32 18	242	42 07	284	39 36	343
348	32 40	056	18 12	086	19 06	157	46 05	212	31 43	243	41 29	284	39 24	343
349	33 12	056	18 51	086	19 21	158	45 44	213	31 09	244	40 52	285	39 13	343
350	33 44	057	19 29	087	19 35	159	45 22	214	30 34	245	40 15	286	39 03	344
351	34 17	057	20 08	088	19 49	160	45 00	216	29 59	246	39 38	286	38 52	344
352	34 49	058	20 46	089	20 02	161	44 37	217	29 24	247	39 01	287	38 41	344
353	35 22	058	21 25	090	20 14	162	44 14	218	28 48	248	38 24	287	38 31	345
354	35 55	059	22 03	090	20 26	163	43 50	220	28 12	249	37 47	288	38 21	345
355	36 28	059	22 42	091	20 37	164	43 25	221	27 36	249	37 10	289	38 11	345
356	37 01	060	23 20	092	20 48	165	42 59	222	27 00	250	36 34	289	38 01	345
357	37 35	060	23 59	093	20 58	166	42 33	223	26 24	251	35 58	290	37 51	346
358	38 08	061	24 38	093	21 07	167	42 07	224	25 47	252	35 21	290	37 42	346
359	38 42	061	25 16	094	21 16	168	41 39	226	25 10	253	34 45	291	37 32	346

 LAT 49°N

LHA ♈	Hc	Zn	Hc	Zn	Hc	Zn	Hc	Zn	Hc	Zn	Hc	Zn	Hc	Zn
	◆ CAPELLA		ALDEBARAN		Hamal		◆ Diphda		ALTAIR		◆ VEGA		Kochab	
0	38 47	061	25 59	094	54 14	124	22 22	169	24 50	254	33 47	292	36 25	347
1	39 22	062	26 39	095	54 46	125	22 30	170	24 12	255	33 11	293	36 16	347
2	39 56	062	27 18	096	55 18	126	22 37	171	23 34	256	32 34	293	36 07	347
3	40 31	063	27 57	097	55 50	128	22 43	172	22 56	257	31 58	294	35 58	348
4	41 06	063	28 36	098	56 21	129	22 48	173	22 17	258	31 23	295	35 50	348
5	41 42	064	29 15	098	56 51	130	22 53	174	21 39	258	30 47	295	35 42	348
6	42 17	064	29 54	099	57 21	132	22 57	175	21 00	259	30 11	296	35 34	348
7	42 52	065	30 33	100	57 50	133	23 00	176	20 21	260	29 36	296	35 26	349
8	43 28	065	31 11	101	58 18	135	23 02	177	19 43	261	29 01	297	35 18	349
9	44 04	066	31 50	102	58 46	136	23 04	178	19 04	262	28 26	298	35 11	349
10	44 40	066	32 28	103	59 12	138	23 05	179	18 25	262	27 51	298	35 04	350
11	45 16	067	33 07	103	59 38	139	23 06	180	17 46	263	27 17	299	34 57	350
12	45 52	067	33 45	104	60 04	141	23 05	181	17 07	264	26 42	299	34 50	350
13	46 28	068	34 23	105	60 28	143	23 04	182	16 27	265	26 08	300	34 43	351
14	47 05	068	35 01	106	60 51	144	23 03	183	15 48	265	25 34	301	34 37	351
	◆ CAPELLA		ALDEBARAN		Hamal		◆ Diphda		Alpheratz		◆ DENEB		Kochab	
15	47 41	069	35 39	107	61 14	146	23 00	184	67 55	211	47 20	291	34 31	351
16	48 18	069	36 16	108	61 35	148	22 57	185	67 35	213	46 43	291	34 25	351
17	48 55	070	36 54	109	61 55	150	22 53	186	67 13	215	46 06	292	34 19	352
18	49 32	070	37 31	110	62 15	152	22 49	187	66 50	217	45 30	292	34 13	352
19	50 09	071	38 08	111	62 33	153	22 44	188	66 25	219	44 53	293	34 08	352
20	50 46	071	38 45	112	62 50	155	22 38	189	66 00	221	44 17	293	34 03	353
21	51 23	072	39 21	112	63 06	157	22 31	190	65 34	223	43 41	294	33 58	353
22	52 01	072	39 57	113	63 20	159	22 24	191	65 07	224	43 05	294	33 53	353
23	52 38	073	40 33	114	63 34	161	22 16	192	64 39	226	42 29	295	33 49	354
24	53 16	073	41 09	115	63 46	163	22 07	193	64 10	228	41 53	295	33 45	354
25	53 54	074	41 44	116	63 56	165	21 58	194	63 41	229	41 18	296	33 41	354
26	54 31	074	42 19	117	64 06	167	21 48	195	63 10	231	40 42	296	33 37	355
27	55 09	075	42 54	118	64 14	169	21 37	196	62 39	233	40 07	297	33 33	355
28	55 47	075	43 29	120	64 20	171	21 25	197	62 08	234	39 32	297	33 30	355
29	56 25	076	44 03	121	64 25	174	21 13	198	61 36	236	38 57	298	33 27	356
	CAPELLA		◆ BETELGEUSE		RIGEL		Hamal		◆ Alpheratz		DENEB		◆ Kochab	
30	57 03	076	25 37	109	18 40	128	64 29	176	61 03	237	38 22	298	33 24	356
31	57 42	077	26 14	110	19 11	129	64 31	178	60 30	238	37 47	299	33 21	356
32	58 20	077	26 51	111	19 41	130	64 32	180	59 56	240	37 13	299	33 18	357
33	58 58	078	27 28	112	20 11	131	64 31	182	59 22	241	36 39	300	33 16	357
34	59 37	078	28 04	113	20 41	132	64 29	184	58 47	242	36 05	300	33 14	357
35	60 15	079	28 40	114	21 10	133	64 25	186	58 12	244	35 31	301	33 12	357
36	60 54	079	29 16	115	21 39	134	64 20	188	57 37	245	34 57	301	33 11	358
37	61 33	080	29 52	116	22 07	135	64 14	191	57 01	246	34 23	302	33 09	358
38	62 12	080	30 27	117	22 35	136	64 06	193	56 25	247	33 50	302	33 08	358
39	62 50	081	31 02	118	23 02	136	63 57	195	55 48	248	33 17	303	33 07	359
40	63 29	081	31 37	119	23 29	137	63 46	197	55 12	249	32 44	303	33 06	359
41	64 08	082	32 11	119	23 56	138	63 34	199	54 35	250	32 11	304	33 06	359
42	64 47	082	32 45	120	24 21	139	63 21	201	53 57	251	31 38	304	33 06	000
43	65 26	083	33 19	121	24 47	140	63 06	203	53 20	252	31 06	305	33 06	000
44	66 05	084	33 52	122	25 12	141	62 50	205	52 42	253	30 34	305	33 06	000
	◆ Dubhe		POLLUX		BETELGEUSE		◆ RIGEL		Hamal		◆ Alpheratz		DENEB	
45	30 13	028	32 31	083	34 26	123	25 36	142	62 33	207	52 04	254	30 02	306
46	30 31	028	33 10	084	34 58	124	26 00	143	62 15	208	51 26	255	29 30	306
47	30 50	029	33 49	085	35 31	125	26 23	144	61 56	210	50 48	256	28 59	307
48	31 09	029	34 28	086	36 02	126	26 46	145	61 35	212	50 10	257	28 27	308
49	31 29	030	35 07	086	36 34	127	27 08	146	61 14	214	49 31	258	27 56	308
50	31 48	030	35 47	087	37 05	129	27 29	147	60 51	216	48 53	259	27 25	309
51	32 08	030	36 26	088	37 35	130	27 50	149	60 28	217	48 14	260	26 55	309
52	32 28	031	37 05	088	38 06	131	28 10	150	60 04	219	47 35	261	26 24	310
53	32 49	031	37 45	089	38 35	132	28 30	151	59 39	221	46 56	262	25 54	310
54	33 09	032	38 24	090	39 04	133	28 49	152	59 13	222	46 17	263	25 24	311
55	33 30	032	39 03	091	39 33	134	29 07	153	58 46	224	45 38	263	24 55	311
56	33 51	032	39 43	091	40 01	135	29 25	154	58 18	225	44 59	264	24 25	312
57	34 12	033	40 22	092	40 28	136	29 42	155	57 50	227	44 20	265	23 56	312
58	34 34	033	41 01	093	40 55	137	29 58	156	57 21	228	43 41	266	23 27	313
59	34 55	034	41 41	094	41 21	139	30 14	157	56 51	230	43 01	267	22 58	314
	◆ Dubhe		POLLUX		SIRIUS		◆ RIGEL		Hamal		◆ Alpheratz		DENEB	
60	35 17	034	42 20	095	14 41	139	30 29	158	56 21	231	42 22	267	22 30	314
61	35 39	034	42 59	095	15 07	140	30 43	159	55 50	232	41 43	268	22 02	315
62	36 02	035	43 38	096	15 32	141	30 56	160	55 19	234	41 03	269	21 34	315
63	36 24	035	44 17	097	15 57	142	31 09	162	54 47	235	40 24	270	21 07	316
64	36 47	035	44 57	098	16 21	143	31 21	163	54 14	236	39 45	271	20 39	316
65	37 10	036	45 35	099	16 44	144	31 33	164	53 41	237	39 05	271	20 12	317
66	37 33	036	46 14	100	17 07	144	31 43	165	53 08	239	38 26	272	19 46	318
67	37 56	036	46 53	100	17 30	145	31 53	166	52 34	240	37 47	273	19 19	318
68	38 20	037	47 32	101	17 52	146	32 02	167	52 00	241	37 07	274	18 53	319
69	38 43	037	48 10	102	18 14	147	32 10	169	51 25	242	36 28	274	18 27	319
70	39 07	037	48 49	103	18 35	148	32 18	170	50 50	243	35 49	275	18 02	320
71	39 31	038	49 27	104	18 55	149	32 24	171	50 15	244	35 10	276	17 37	321
72	39 55	038	50 05	105	19 15	150	32 30	172	49 39	246	34 31	276	17 12	321
73	40 20	038	50 43	106	19 34	151	32 35	173	49 03	247	33 51	277	16 47	322
74	40 44	039	51 21	107	19 53	152	32 40	174	48 27	248	33 12	278	16 23	322
	◆ Dubhe		REGULUS		PROCYON		◆ SIRIUS		RIGEL		◆ Hamal		DENEB	
75	41 09	039	17 16	092	34 39	129	20 11	153	32 43	176	47 50	249	15 59	323
76	41 34	039	17 55	092	35 09	130	20 29	154	32 46	177	47 14	250	15 36	324
77	41 59	040	18 34	093	35 39	131	20 46	155	32 48	178	46 37	251	15 13	324
78	42 24	040	19 14	094	36 09	132	21 02	156	32 49	179	45 59	252	14 50	325
79	42 49	040	19 53	095	36 38	133	21 18	157	32 49	180	45 22	253	14 27	325
80	43 15	041	20 32	095	37 06	134	21 33	158	32 48	181	44 44	254	14 05	326
81	43 41	041	21 11	096	37 34	135	21 48	159	32 47	183	44 06	254	13 43	327
82	44 06	041	21 50	097	38 02	136	22 02	160	32 45	184	43 28	255	13 22	327
83	44 32	041	22 29	098	38 29	138	22 15	161	32 42	185	42 50	256	13 01	328
84	44 58	042	23 08	099	38 55	139	22 27	162	32 38	186	42 12	257	12 40	328
85	45 25	042	23 47	099	39 20	140	22 39	163	32 33	187	41 33	258	12 19	329
86	45 51	042	24 26	100	39 45	141	22 51	164	32 28	188	40 55	259	11 59	330
87	46 17	042	25 05	101	40 10	142	23 01	165	32 22	190	40 16	260	11 40	330
88	46 44	043	25 43	102	40 34	143	23 11	166	32 15	191	39 37	261	11 21	331
89	47 11	043	26 22	103	40 57	145	23 20	167	32 07	192	38 59	261	11 02	332

LHA ♈	Hc	Zn	Hc	Zn	Hc	Zn	Hc	Zn	Hc	Zn	Hc	Zn	Hc	Zn
	◆ Dubhe		REGULUS		PROCYON		◆ SIRIUS		RIGEL		ALDEBARAN		◆ Mirfak	
90	47 38	043	27 00	104	41 19	146	23 29	168	31 59	193	53 24	215	65 08	287
91	48 05	043	27 38	104	41 41	147	23 37	169	31 49	194	53 01	216	64 31	287
92	48 32	044	28 16	105	42 02	148	23 44	170	31 39	195	52 37	218	63 53	288
93	48 59	044	28 54	106	42 22	150	23 50	171	31 28	197	52 13	219	63 16	288
94	49 26	044	29 32	107	42 42	151	23 56	172	31 17	198	51 47	221	62 38	288
95	49 54	044	30 10	108	43 00	152	24 01	173	31 05	199	51 21	222	62 01	289
96	50 21	044	30 47	109	43 18	154	24 05	174	30 52	200	50 55	223	61 24	289
97	50 49	045	31 24	110	43 36	155	24 09	175	30 38	201	50 27	225	60 47	289
98	51 16	045	32 01	110	43 52	156	24 11	176	30 23	202	49 59	226	60 10	290
99	51 44	045	32 38	111	44 07	157	24 14	177	30 08	203	49 31	227	59 33	290
100	52 12	045	33 15	112	44 22	159	24 15	178	29 52	204	49 02	228	58 56	291
101	52 40	045	33 51	113	44 36	160	24 16	180	29 36	205	48 32	230	58 19	291
102	53 08	045	34 27	114	44 49	162	24 16	181	29 18	207	48 02	231	57 42	291
103	53 36	046	35 03	115	45 01	163	24 15	182	29 00	208	47 31	232	57 05	292
104	54 04	046	35 38	116	45 12	164	24 13	183	28 42	209	46 59	233	56 29	292
	◆ Dubhe		Denebola		REGULUS		◆ SIRIUS		RIGEL		ALDEBARAN		◆ Mirfak	
105	54 32	046	22 21	093	36 14	117	24 11	184	28 23	210	46 28	235	55 52	292
106	55 00	046	23 00	094	36 48	118	24 08	185	28 03	211	45 55	236	55 16	293
107	55 29	046	23 40	095	37 23	119	24 05	186	27 42	212	45 23	237	54 40	293
108	55 57	046	24 19	096	37 57	120	24 00	187	27 21	213	44 49	238	54 04	294
109	56 25	046	24 58	097	38 31	121	23 55	188	27 00	214	44 16	239	53 28	294
110	56 54	046	25 37	097	39 05	122	23 49	189	26 37	215	43 42	240	52 52	294
111	57 22	046	26 16	098	39 38	123	23 43	190	26 14	216	43 08	241	52 16	295
112	57 51	046	26 55	099	40 11	124	23 36	191	25 51	217	42 33	242	51 40	295
113	58 19	046	27 34	100	40 43	125	23 28	192	25 27	218	41 58	243	51 05	296
114	58 48	046	28 12	101	41 15	126	23 19	193	25 03	219	41 23	244	50 29	296
115	59 16	046	28 51	101	41 47	127	23 10	194	24 37	220	40 47	245	49 54	296
116	59 45	046	29 30	102	42 18	128	23 00	195	24 12	221	40 11	246	49 19	297
117	60 13	046	30 08	103	42 48	130	22 50	196	23 46	222	39 35	247	48 44	297
118	60 41	046	30 46	104	43 18	131	22 38	197	23 19	223	38 59	248	48 09	298
119	61 10	046	31 24	105	43 48	132	22 26	198	22 52	224	38 22	249	47 34	298
	◆ Kochab		Denebola		◆ REGULUS		SIRIUS		RIGEL		◆ ALDEBARAN		CAPELLA	
120	43 21	022	32 02	106	44 17	133	22 14	199	22 25	225	37 45	250	62 46	279
121	43 35	022	32 40	107	44 46	134	22 00	200	21 57	226	37 08	251	62 08	280
122	43 50	022	33 18	107	45 13	136	21 46	201	21 28	227	36 31	252	61 29	280
123	44 05	022	33 55	108	45 41	137	21 32	202	20 59	228	35 53	253	60 50	281
124	44 19	022	34 33	109	46 07	138	21 17	203	20 30	229	35 16	254	60 12	281
125	44 34	022	35 10	110	46 33	139	21 01	204	20 00	229	34 38	255	59 33	282
126	44 49	023	35 47	111	46 59	141	20 44	205	19 30	230	34 00	255	58 55	282
127	45 05	023	36 23	112	47 23	142	20 27	206	19 00	231	33 22	256	58 16	283
128	45 20	023	37 00	113	47 47	143	20 10	207	18 29	232	32 43	257	57 38	284
129	45 35	023	37 36	114	48 11	145	19 51	208	17 58	233	32 05	258	57 00	284
130	45 51	023	38 12	115	48 33	146	19 33	209	17 26	234	31 26	259	56 21	285
131	46 06	023	38 47	116	48 55	147	19 13	210	16 54	235	30 48	260	55 43	285
132	46 22	023	39 22	117	49 16	149	18 53	211	16 22	236	30 09	260	55 05	286
133	46 37	024	39 57	118	49 36	150	18 33	212	15 49	237	29 30	261	54 28	286
134	46 53	024	40 32	119	49 55	152	18 12	213	15 16	237	28 51	262	53 50	287
	◆ Kochab		ARCTURUS		Denebola		◆ REGULUS		SIRIUS		BETELGEUSE		◆ CAPELLA	
135	47 09	024	21 22	085	41 06	120	50 13	153	17 50	214	33 19	239	53 12	287
136	47 25	024	22 01	086	41 40	121	50 31	154	17 28	215	32 45	240	52 35	288
137	47 41	024	22 41	087	42 14	122	50 47	156	17 05	216	32 11	241	51 57	288
138	47 57	024	23 20	087	42 47	123	51 03	157	16 42	217	31 36	242	51 20	289
139	48 13	024	23 59	088	43 20	124	51 17	159	16 18	217	31 02	242	50 42	289
140	48 29	024	24 39	089	43 52	125	51 31	160	15 54	218	30 27	243	50 05	290
141	48 45	024	25 18	090	44 24	126	51 44	162	15 30	219	29 51	244	49 28	290
142	49 01	024	25 57	090	44 56	128	51 55	164	15 04	220	29 16	245	48 51	290
143	49 18	024	26 37	091	45 27	129	52 06	165	14 39	221	28 40	246	48 14	291
144	49 34	024	27 16	092	45 57	130	52 16	167	14 13	222	28 04	247	47 38	291
145	49 50	025	27 55	093	46 27	131	52 24	168	13 46	223	27 27	248	47 01	292
146	50 07	025	28 35	093	46 57	132	52 32	170	13 19	224	26 51	249	46 25	292
147	50 23	025	29 14	094	47 25	134	52 38	171	12 52	225	26 14	250	45 48	293
148	50 39	025	29 53	095	47 54	135	52 43	173	12 24	225	25 37	251	45 12	293
149	50 56	025	30 32	096	48 21	136	52 48	175	11 56	226	25 00	251	44 36	294
	◆ Kochab		ARCTURUS		◆ SPICA		REGULUS		PROCYON		◆ BETELGEUSE		CAPELLA	
150	51 12	025	31 12	097	14 41	127	52 51	176	37 08	226	24 22	252	44 00	294
151	51 29	025	31 51	097	15 12	128	52 53	178	36 39	227	23 45	253	43 25	295
152	51 45	025	32 30	098	15 43	129	52 54	180	36 10	228	23 07	254	42 49	295
153	52 02	025	33 09	099	16 13	130	52 53	181	35 41	229	22 29	255	42 13	296
154	52 18	025	33 47	100	16 43	131	52 52	183	35 11	230	21 51	256	41 38	296
155	52 34	025	34 26	101	17 13	132	52 50	184	34 40	231	21 13	256	41 03	297
156	52 51	025	35 05	101	17 42	133	52 46	186	34 09	232	20 35	257	40 28	297
157	53 07	025	35 43	102	18 10	134	52 41	188	33 38	233	19 56	258	39 53	298
158	53 24	025	36 22	103	18 39	135	52 36	189	33 07	234	19 18	259	39 18	298
159	53 40	024	37 00	104	19 06	135	52 29	191	32 34	235	18 39	260	38 44	299
160	53 56	024	37 38	105	19 34	136	52 21	192	32 02	236	18 00	260	38 09	299
161	54 12	024	38 16	106	20 01	137	52 12	194	31 29	237	17 21	261	37 35	300
162	54 29	024	38 54	107	20 27	138	52 02	196	30 56	238	16 42	262	37 01	300
163	54 45	024	39 32	108	20 53	139	51 51	197	30 22	239	16 03	263	36 27	301
164	55 01	024	40 09	109	21 19	140	51 39	199	29 48	240	15 24	264	35 54	301
	◆ VEGA		ARCTURUS		◆ SPICA		REGULUS		PROCYON		◆ POLLUX		CAPELLA	
165	15 11	047	40 46	109	21 44	141	51 25	200	29 14	241	47 36	259	35 20	302
166	15 40	048	41 23	110	22 08	142	51 11	202	28 39	242	46 58	259	34 47	302
167	16 10	049	42 00	111	22 32	143	50 56	203	28 05	243	46 19	260	34 14	303
168	16 39	049	42 36	112	22 55	144	50 40	205	27 29	244	45 40	261	33 41	303
169	17 09	050	43 13	113	23 18	145	50 23	206	26 54	245	45 01	262	33 08	304
170	17 40	051	43 49	114	23 41	146	50 06	208	26 18	245	44 22	263	32 35	304
171	18 10	051	44 24	115	24 02	147	49 47	209	25 42	246	43 43	264	32 03	305
172	18 41	052	45 00	116	24 24	148	49 27	211	25 06	247	43 04	264	31 31	306
173	19 12	052	45 35	117	24 44	149	49 07	212	24 30	248	42 25	265	30 59	306
174	19 43	053	46 10	119	25 04	150	48 46	213	23 53	249	41 46	266	30 27	307
175	20 15	054	46 44	120	25 23	151	48 24	215	23 16	250	41 06	267	29 56	307
176	20 47	054	47 18	121	25 42	152	48 01	216	22 39	251	40 27	268	29 24	308
177	21 19	055	47 52	122	26 00	153	47 37	217	22 02	252	39 47	268	28 53	308
178	21 51	055	48 25	123	26 18	154	47 13	219	21 25	252	39 08	269	28 23	309
179	22 23	056	48 58	124	26 35	155	46 48	220	20 47	253	38 29	270	27 52	309

LHA ♈	Hc	Zn	Hc	Zn	Hc	Zn	Hc	Zn	Hc	Zn	Hc	Zn	Hc	Zn
	◆DENEB		VEGA		ARCTURUS		◆SPICA		REGULUS		◆POLLUX		CAPELLA	
180	13 44	033	22 56	057	49 30	125	26 51	156	46 23	221	37 49	271	27 22	310
181	14 06	034	23 29	057	50 02	127	27 06	157	45 56	223	37 10	271	26 51	310
182	14 28	035	24 02	058	50 33	128	27 21	158	45 29	224	36 31	272	26 22	311
183	14 50	035	24 36	058	51 04	129	27 35	159	45 02	225	35 51	273	25 52	311
184	15 13	036	25 09	059	51 34	130	27 49	161	44 34	226	35 12	274	25 22	312
185	15 36	036	25 43	060	52 04	132	28 02	162	44 05	227	34 33	274	24 53	312
186	16 00	037	26 17	060	52 33	133	28 14	163	43 36	229	33 53	275	24 24	313
187	16 24	038	26 52	061	53 02	134	28 25	164	43 06	230	33 14	276	23 56	314
188	16 48	038	27 26	061	53 30	136	28 36	165	42 36	231	32 35	277	23 27	314
189	17 13	039	28 01	062	53 57	137	28 46	166	42 05	232	31 56	277	22 59	315
190	17 38	039	28 36	063	54 23	139	28 55	167	41 34	233	31 17	278	22 31	315
191	18 03	040	29 11	063	54 49	140	29 03	168	41 02	234	30 38	279	22 04	316
192	18 28	041	29 46	064	55 14	141	29 11	169	40 30	235	29 59	279	21 37	316
193	18 54	041	30 21	064	55 38	143	29 18	170	39 57	236	29 20	280	21 10	317
194	19 20	042	30 57	065	56 01	145	29 24	172	39 24	237	28 42	281	20 43	318
	◆DENEB		VEGA		Rasalhague		◆ARCTURUS		REGULUS		◆POLLUX		CAPELLA	
195	19 46	042	31 33	066	23 14	098	56 24	146	38 51	238	28 03	281	20 16	318
196	20 13	043	32 08	066	23 53	098	56 45	148	38 17	239	27 25	282	19 50	319
197	20 40	044	32 44	067	24 32	099	57 06	149	37 43	240	26 46	283	19 24	319
198	21 07	044	33 21	067	25 11	100	57 25	151	37 09	241	26 08	283	18 59	320
199	21 35	045	33 57	068	25 49	101	57 44	153	36 34	242	25 30	284	18 34	320
200	22 03	045	34 34	068	26 28	102	58 02	154	35 59	243	24 51	285	18 09	321
201	22 31	046	35 10	069	27 06	103	58 18	156	35 24	244	24 13	285	17 44	322
202	22 59	046	35 47	070	27 45	103	58 34	158	34 48	245	23 36	286	17 20	322
203	23 28	047	36 24	070	28 23	104	58 48	159	34 12	246	22 58	287	16 56	323
204	23 57	048	37 01	071	29 01	105	59 01	161	33 36	247	22 20	288	16 32	323
205	24 26	048	37 38	071	29 39	106	59 13	163	32 59	248	21 43	288	16 09	324
206	24 55	049	38 16	072	30 17	107	59 24	165	32 23	249	21 05	289	15 46	325
207	25 25	049	38 53	073	30 54	108	59 34	167	31 46	250	20 28	290	15 23	325
208	25 55	050	39 31	073	31 32	108	59 42	169	31 09	251	19 51	290	15 01	326
209	26 25	050	40 09	074	32 09	109	59 50	170	30 32	252	19 14	291	14 39	326
	DENEB		◆VEGA		Rasalhague		◆ARCTURUS		Denebola		REGULUS		◆Dubhe	
210	26 56	051	40 47	074	32 46	110	59 55	172	46 24	229	29 54	253	62 44	314
211	27 26	051	41 25	075	33 23	111	60 00	174	45 54	230	29 16	253	62 16	314
212	27 57	052	42 03	076	33 59	112	60 03	176	45 24	231	28 39	254	61 47	314
213	28 28	052	42 41	076	34 36	113	60 06	178	44 53	233	28 01	255	61 19	314
214	28 59	053	43 19	077	35 12	114	60 06	180	44 21	234	27 23	256	60 51	314
215	29 31	054	43 57	077	35 48	115	60 06	182	43 49	235	26 44	257	60 22	314
216	30 03	054	44 36	078	36 23	116	60 04	184	43 17	236	26 06	258	59 54	314
217	30 35	055	45 14	079	36 59	117	60 01	186	42 44	237	25 27	258	59 25	314
218	31 07	055	45 53	079	37 34	118	59 56	187	42 11	238	24 49	259	58 57	314
219	31 39	056	46 32	080	38 08	119	59 51	189	41 37	239	24 10	260	58 28	314
220	32 12	056	47 11	081	38 43	120	59 44	191	41 03	240	23 31	261	58 00	314
221	32 45	057	47 49	081	39 16	121	59 35	193	40 29	241	22 52	262	57 31	314
222	33 18	057	48 28	082	39 50	122	59 26	195	39 54	242	22 13	262	57 03	314
223	33 51	058	49 07	083	40 23	123	59 15	197	39 19	243	21 34	263	56 35	314
224	34 24	058	49 46	083	40 56	124	59 03	198	38 44	244	20 55	264	56 06	314
	DENEB		◆VEGA		Rasalhague		ANTARES		◆ARCTURUS		Denebola		◆Dubhe	
225	34 58	059	50 26	084	41 29	125	11 53	159	58 50	200	38 08	245	55 38	314
226	35 32	059	51 05	085	42 01	126	12 07	160	58 36	202	37 33	246	55 10	314
227	36 06	060	51 44	085	42 32	127	12 20	161	58 21	204	36 56	247	54 41	314
228	36 40	060	52 23	086	43 03	128	12 32	162	58 05	205	36 20	248	54 13	314
229	37 14	061	53 02	087	43 34	130	12 44	163	57 47	207	35 43	249	53 45	314
230	37 48	061	53 42	087	44 04	131	12 55	164	57 29	209	35 06	250	53 17	315
231	38 23	062	54 21	088	44 33	132	13 06	165	57 09	210	34 29	251	52 49	315
232	38 58	062	55 00	089	45 02	133	13 16	166	56 49	212	33 52	252	52 21	315
233	39 33	063	55 40	089	45 31	134	13 25	167	56 27	214	33 15	253	51 53	315
234	40 08	063	56 19	090	45 59	136	13 34	168	56 05	215	32 37	254	51 25	315
235	40 43	064	56 59	091	46 26	137	13 42	168	55 42	217	31 59	254	50 58	315
236	41 19	064	57 38	092	46 53	138	13 50	169	55 18	218	31 21	255	50 30	316
237	41 54	065	58 17	093	47 19	139	13 57	170	54 53	220	30 43	256	50 02	316
238	42 30	065	58 57	093	47 44	141	14 03	171	54 28	221	30 05	257	49 35	316
239	43 06	066	59 36	094	48 09	142	14 09	172	54 01	223	29 26	258	49 08	316
	◆DENEB		ALTAIR		Rasalhague		◆ANTARES		ARCTURUS		Denebola		◆Dubhe	
240	43 42	066	27 29	109	48 32	143	14 14	173	53 34	224	28 48	259	48 40	316
241	44 18	067	28 06	110	48 56	145	14 18	174	53 07	225	28 09	259	48 13	317
242	44 54	067	28 43	111	49 18	146	14 22	175	52 38	227	27 30	260	47 46	317
243	45 31	068	29 19	112	49 40	147	14 25	176	52 09	228	26 51	261	47 19	317
244	46 07	068	29 56	113	50 00	149	14 28	177	51 40	229	26 13	262	46 53	317
245	46 44	069	30 32	114	50 20	150	14 30	178	51 09	231	25 34	263	46 26	318
246	47 21	069	31 08	115	50 39	152	14 31	179	50 39	232	24 54	263	45 59	318
247	47 57	070	31 43	116	50 58	153	14 32	179	50 07	233	24 15	264	45 33	318
248	48 34	070	32 19	117	51 15	155	14 32	180	49 36	234	23 36	265	45 07	318
249	49 12	071	32 54	118	51 31	156	14 32	181	49 03	236	22 57	266	44 41	319
250	49 49	071	33 29	119	51 47	158	14 30	182	48 31	237	22 18	267	44 15	319
251	50 26	072	34 03	120	52 01	159	14 28	183	47 58	238	21 38	267	43 49	319
252	51 04	072	34 37	120	52 14	161	14 26	184	47 24	239	20 59	268	43 23	319
253	51 41	073	35 11	121	52 27	162	14 23	185	46 50	240	20 20	269	42 58	320
254	52 19	073	35 44	122	52 38	164	14 19	186	46 16	241	19 40	270	42 32	320
	◆Schedar		DENEB		ALTAIR		◆Rasalhague		ARCTURUS		◆Alkaid		Kochab	
255	28 24	034	52 57	074	36 17	123	52 49	166	45 41	242	59 09	289	61 22	342
256	28 47	035	53 35	075	36 50	125	52 58	167	45 06	243	58 31	289	61 10	342
257	29 09	035	54 13	075	37 22	126	53 06	169	44 31	244	57 54	290	60 58	341
258	29 32	036	54 51	076	37 54	127	53 13	170	43 55	245	57 17	290	60 45	341
259	29 55	036	55 29	076	38 25	128	53 19	172	43 19	246	56 40	291	60 32	341
260	30 19	037	56 07	077	38 56	129	53 24	174	42 43	247	56 04	291	60 19	340
261	30 42	037	56 46	077	39 27	130	53 28	175	42 06	248	55 27	291	60 06	340
262	31 06	038	57 24	078	39 57	131	53 31	177	41 30	249	54 50	292	59 52	340
263	31 30	038	58 02	078	40 26	132	53 33	179	40 53	250	54 14	292	59 38	339
264	31 55	038	58 41	079	40 55	133	53 33	180	40 15	251	53 37	293	59 25	339
265	32 19	039	59 20	079	41 23	134	53 32	182	39 38	252	53 01	293	59 10	339
266	32 44	039	59 58	080	41 51	136	53 31	183	39 00	253	52 25	293	58 56	339
267	33 09	040	60 37	080	42 19	137	53 28	185	38 23	254	51 49	294	58 42	338
268	33 35	040	61 16	081	42 45	138	53 24	187	37 45	255	51 13	294	58 27	338
269	34 00	041	61 55	082	43 11	139	53 18	188	37 07	256	50 37	295	58 12	338

LAT 49°N

LHA ♈	Hc	Zn	Hc	Zn	Hc	Zn	Hc	Zn	Hc	Zn	Hc	Zn	Hc	Zn
	◆Mirfak		Alpheratz		◆ALTAIR		Rasalhague		◆ARCTURUS		Alkaid		Kochab	
270	14 20	025	20 11	068	43 37	140	53 12	190	36 28	257	50 02	295	57 58	338
271	14 36	025	20 48	069	44 02	142	53 05	192	35 50	258	49 26	296	57 43	337
272	14 53	026	21 24	070	44 26	143	52 56	193	35 12	258	48 50	296	57 27	337
273	15 10	026	22 01	070	44 49	144	52 47	195	34 33	259	48 15	296	57 12	337
274	15 28	027	22 38	071	45 12	145	52 36	196	33 54	260	47 40	297	56 57	337
275	15 46	028	23 16	072	45 34	147	52 25	198	33 15	261	47 05	297	56 41	337
276	16 04	028	23 53	072	45 55	148	52 12	199	32 36	262	46 30	298	56 26	337
277	16 23	029	24 31	073	46 15	149	51 58	201	31 57	263	45 55	298	56 10	336
278	16 42	029	25 09	074	46 35	151	51 44	203	31 18	263	45 21	299	55 54	336
279	17 02	030	25 46	074	46 54	152	51 28	204	30 39	264	44 46	299	55 38	336
280	17 21	030	26 24	075	47 12	153	51 12	206	30 00	265	44 12	299	55 22	336
281	17 41	031	27 02	076	47 29	155	50 54	207	29 21	266	43 38	300	55 06	336
282	18 02	032	27 41	076	47 45	156	50 36	209	28 42	267	43 04	300	54 50	336
283	18 23	032	28 19	077	48 01	158	50 17	210	28 02	267	42 30	301	54 34	336
284	18 44	033	28 57	078	48 15	159	49 57	211	27 23	268	41 56	301	54 18	336
	◆Mirfak		Alpheratz		◆ALTAIR		Rasalhague		◆ARCTURUS		Alkaid		Kochab	
285	19 05	033	29 36	078	48 29	161	49 36	213	26 44	269	41 22	302	54 02	336
286	19 27	034	30 14	079	48 41	162	49 14	214	26 04	270	40 49	302	53 45	336
287	19 49	034	30 53	080	48 53	164	48 51	216	25 25	270	40 16	303	53 29	335
288	20 11	035	31 32	080	49 04	165	48 28	217	24 45	271	39 43	303	53 13	335
289	20 34	036	32 11	081	49 13	166	48 04	218	24 06	272	39 10	304	52 56	335
290	20 57	036	32 50	082	49 22	168	47 39	220	23 27	273	38 37	304	52 40	335
291	21 21	037	33 29	083	49 30	170	47 14	221	22 47	273	38 04	304	52 24	335
292	21 44	037	34 08	083	49 36	171	46 48	222	22 08	274	37 32	305	52 07	335
293	22 08	038	34 47	084	49 42	173	46 21	223	21 29	275	37 00	305	51 51	335
294	22 32	038	35 26	085	49 47	174	45 54	225	20 50	276	36 28	306	51 34	335
295	22 57	039	36 05	085	49 50	176	45 26	226	20 11	276	35 56	306	51 18	335
296	23 22	039	36 45	086	49 53	177	44 57	227	19 31	277	35 24	307	51 01	335
297	23 47	040	37 24	087	49 54	179	44 28	228	18 52	278	34 53	307	50 45	335
298	24 12	040	38 03	088	49 55	180	43 58	229	18 13	278	34 22	308	50 28	335
299	24 38	041	38 42	088	49 54	182	43 28	231	17 35	279	33 51	308	50 12	335
	CAPELLA		◆Alpheratz		Enif		ALTAIR		◆Rasalhague		Alphecca		◆Kochab	
300	11 21	027	39 22	089	45 14	142	49 52	183	42 58	232	35 08	272	49 56	335
301	11 39	028	40 01	090	45 38	143	49 49	185	42 26	233	34 29	272	49 39	336
302	11 58	029	40 41	091	46 01	144	49 46	186	41 55	234	33 50	273	49 23	336
303	12 17	029	41 20	091	46 24	146	49 41	188	41 23	235	33 10	274	49 07	336
304	12 37	030	41 59	092	46 46	147	49 35	189	40 50	236	32 31	274	48 51	336
305	12 56	031	42 39	093	47 07	148	49 28	191	40 17	237	31 52	275	48 34	336
306	13 17	031	43 18	094	47 27	150	49 20	192	39 44	238	31 13	276	48 18	336
307	13 37	032	43 57	094	47 46	151	49 11	194	39 10	239	30 34	277	48 02	336
308	13 58	032	44 36	095	48 05	153	49 01	195	38 36	240	29 55	277	47 46	336
309	14 19	033	45 16	096	48 23	154	48 50	197	38 02	241	29 16	278	47 30	336
310	14 41	034	45 55	097	48 39	155	48 38	198	37 27	242	28 37	279	47 14	336
311	15 03	034	46 34	098	48 55	157	48 26	200	36 52	243	27 58	279	46 58	336
312	15 25	035	47 13	099	49 10	158	48 12	201	36 17	244	27 19	280	46 43	336
313	15 48	035	47 52	099	49 25	160	47 57	203	35 41	245	26 40	281	46 27	337
314	16 11	036	48 30	100	49 38	161	47 42	204	35 05	246	26 02	282	46 11	337
	CAPELLA		◆Hamal		Alpheratz		Enif		◆ALTAIR		VEGA		◆Kochab	
315	16 34	037	25 53	083	49 09	101	49 50	163	47 25	205	62 41	262	45 56	337
316	16 58	037	26 32	084	49 48	102	50 01	164	47 08	207	62 02	263	45 40	337
317	17 22	038	27 11	085	50 26	103	50 11	166	46 49	208	61 23	263	45 25	337
318	17 46	038	27 51	085	51 04	104	50 21	167	46 30	210	60 43	264	45 10	337
319	18 11	039	28 30	086	51 42	105	50 29	169	46 11	211	60 04	265	44 55	337
320	18 36	040	29 09	087	52 20	106	50 36	170	45 50	212	59 25	266	44 39	338
321	19 01	040	29 49	088	52 58	107	50 42	172	45 29	214	58 46	267	44 24	338
322	19 27	041	30 28	088	53 36	108	50 47	173	45 06	215	58 06	268	44 10	338
323	19 53	041	31 07	089	54 13	109	50 51	175	44 44	216	57 27	268	43 55	338
324	20 19	042	31 47	090	54 50	110	50 54	177	44 20	217	56 48	269	43 40	338
325	20 45	043	32 26	091	55 27	111	50 56	178	43 56	219	56 08	270	43 26	338
326	21 12	043	33 05	091	56 03	112	50 57	180	43 31	220	55 29	271	43 11	339
327	21 39	044	33 45	092	56 40	113	50 56	181	43 05	221	54 50	271	42 57	339
328	22 07	044	34 24	093	57 16	115	50 55	183	42 39	222	54 10	272	42 43	339
329	22 34	045	35 03	094	57 51	116	50 53	184	42 12	224	53 31	273	42 28	339
	CAPELLA		◆Hamal		Diphda		Enif		◆ALTAIR		VEGA		◆Kochab	
330	23 02	045	35 43	094	13 48	140	50 49	186	41 45	225	52 52	274	42 14	339
331	23 30	046	36 22	095	14 13	141	50 44	187	41 17	226	52 12	274	42 01	340
332	23 59	046	37 01	096	14 38	142	50 39	189	40 48	227	51 33	275	41 47	340
333	24 27	047	37 40	097	15 02	143	50 32	191	40 19	228	50 54	276	41 33	340
334	24 56	048	38 19	098	15 26	143	50 24	192	39 49	229	50 15	276	41 20	340
335	25 25	048	38 58	098	15 49	144	50 16	194	39 19	230	49 36	277	41 07	340
336	25 55	049	39 37	099	16 11	145	50 06	195	38 49	232	48 57	278	40 53	341
337	26 25	049	40 16	100	16 34	146	49 55	197	38 18	233	48 18	278	40 40	341
338	26 54	050	40 54	101	16 55	147	49 43	198	37 46	234	47 39	279	40 27	341
339	27 25	050	41 33	102	17 16	148	49 31	200	37 14	235	47 00	280	40 15	341
340	27 55	051	42 11	103	17 37	149	49 17	201	36 42	236	46 21	280	40 02	341
341	28 26	051	42 50	104	17 57	150	49 02	203	36 09	237	45 42	281	39 50	342
342	28 57	052	43 28	105	18 16	151	48 47	204	35 36	238	45 04	281	39 37	342
343	29 28	052	44 06	106	18 35	152	48 31	205	35 03	239	44 25	282	39 25	342
344	29 59	053	44 44	106	18 54	153	48 13	207	34 29	240	43 47	283	39 13	342
	◆CAPELLA		ALDEBARAN		◆Diphda		Enif		ALTAIR		◆VEGA		Kochab	
345	30 30	053	16 10	083	19 11	154	47 55	208	33 55	241	43 08	283	39 01	343
346	31 02	054	16 49	084	19 28	155	47 36	210	33 20	242	42 30	284	38 50	343
347	31 34	055	17 28	085	19 45	156	47 16	211	32 45	243	41 52	285	38 38	343
348	32 06	055	18 08	085	20 01	157	46 55	212	32 10	244	41 14	285	38 27	343
349	32 39	056	18 47	086	20 16	158	46 34	214	31 35	245	40 36	286	38 16	344
350	33 11	056	19 26	087	20 31	159	46 12	215	30 59	245	39 58	286	38 05	344
351	33 44	057	20 05	088	20 45	160	45 49	216	30 23	246	39 21	287	37 54	344
352	34 17	057	20 45	088	20 58	161	45 25	218	29 47	247	38 43	288	37 43	344
353	34 50	058	21 24	089	21 11	162	45 01	219	29 11	248	38 06	288	37 33	345
354	35 23	058	22 03	090	21 23	163	44 36	220	28 34	249	37 28	289	37 23	345
355	35 57	059	22 43	091	21 35	164	44 10	221	27 57	250	36 51	289	37 13	345
356	36 31	059	23 22	091	21 46	165	43 44	223	27 20	251	36 14	290	37 03	346
357	37 05	060	24 01	092	21 56	166	43 17	224	26 43	252	35 37	291	36 53	346
358	37 39	060	24 41	093	22 05	167	42 49	225	26 05	253	35 00	291	36 43	346
359	38 13	061	25 20	094	22 14	168	42 21	226	25 28	253	34 24	292	36 34	346

LAT 48°N

LHA ♈	Hc	Zn	Hc	Zn	Hc	Zn	Hc	Zn	Hc	Zn	Hc	Zn	Hc	Zn
	◆ CAPELLA		ALDEBARAN		Hamal		◆ Diphda		ALTAIR		◆ VEGA		Kochab	
0	38 18	060	26 04	094	54 47	123	23 21	169	25 06	255	33 24	293	35 26	347
1	38 53	061	26 44	095	55 20	124	23 29	170	24 27	255	32 47	293	35 17	347
2	39 28	061	27 24	096	55 53	125	23 36	171	23 48	256	32 10	294	35 09	347
3	40 03	062	28 04	096	56 26	126	23 42	172	23 09	257	31 34	295	35 00	348
4	40 39	062	28 44	097	56 58	128	23 47	173	22 30	258	30 57	295	34 51	348
5	41 15	063	29 23	098	57 29	129	23 52	174	21 51	259	30 21	296	34 43	348
6	41 50	063	30 03	099	58 00	131	23 56	175	21 11	259	29 45	296	34 35	349
7	42 26	064	30 43	099	58 30	132	24 00	176	20 32	260	29 09	297	34 27	349
8	43 02	064	31 22	100	59 00	134	24 02	177	19 52	261	28 33	297	34 19	349
9	43 39	065	32 02	101	59 28	135	24 04	178	19 12	262	27 58	298	34 12	349
10	44 15	065	32 41	102	59 56	137	24 05	179	18 33	263	27 23	299	34 05	350
11	44 52	066	33 20	103	60 24	138	24 06	180	17 53	263	26 47	299	33 58	350
12	45 28	066	33 59	104	60 50	140	24 05	181	17 13	264	26 13	300	33 51	350
13	46 05	067	34 38	104	61 15	142	24 04	182	16 33	265	25 38	300	33 44	351
14	46 42	067	35 17	105	61 40	143	24 03	183	15 53	266	25 03	301	33 38	351
	◆ CAPELLA		ALDEBARAN		Hamal		◆ Diphda		Alpheratz		◆ DENEB		Kochab	
15	47 19	068	35 56	106	62 03	145	24 00	184	68 47	212	46 58	292	33 31	351
16	47 56	068	36 34	107	62 26	147	23 57	185	68 25	214	46 21	292	33 25	352
17	48 33	068	37 13	108	62 47	149	23 53	186	68 02	216	45 44	293	33 20	352
18	49 11	069	37 51	109	63 07	151	23 48	187	67 37	218	45 06	293	33 14	352
19	49 48	069	38 29	110	63 26	153	23 43	188	67 12	220	44 30	294	33 09	352
20	50 26	070	39 06	111	63 44	154	23 37	189	66 45	222	43 53	294	33 03	353
21	51 04	070	39 44	112	64 01	156	23 30	190	66 18	224	43 16	294	32 58	353
22	51 42	071	40 21	113	64 16	158	23 22	191	65 49	226	42 40	295	32 54	353
23	52 20	071	40 58	114	64 30	161	23 14	192	65 20	228	42 03	295	32 49	354
24	52 58	072	41 34	115	64 43	163	23 05	193	64 50	229	41 27	296	32 45	354
25	53 36	072	42 11	116	64 54	165	22 56	194	64 19	231	40 51	296	32 41	354
26	54 14	073	42 47	117	65 04	167	22 45	195	63 47	233	40 15	297	32 37	355
27	54 53	073	43 22	118	65 13	169	22 34	196	63 15	234	39 40	297	32 33	355
28	55 31	074	43 58	119	65 20	171	22 23	197	62 42	236	39 04	298	32 30	355
29	56 10	074	44 33	120	65 25	173	22 10	198	62 09	237	38 29	298	32 27	356
	CAPELLA		◆ BETELGEUSE		RIGEL		Hamal		◆ Alpheratz		DENEB		◆ Kochab	
30	56 48	075	25 57	109	19 17	128	65 29	176	61 35	239	37 53	299	32 24	356
31	57 27	075	26 35	110	19 49	129	65 31	178	61 00	240	37 18	299	32 21	356
32	58 06	075	27 13	111	20 20	130	65 32	180	60 25	241	36 43	300	32 19	357
33	58 45	076	27 50	112	20 51	131	65 31	182	59 50	243	36 09	300	32 16	357
34	59 24	076	28 27	112	21 21	131	65 29	184	59 14	244	35 34	301	32 14	357
35	60 03	077	29 04	113	21 51	132	65 25	187	58 38	245	35 00	301	32 12	358
36	60 42	077	29 41	114	22 20	133	65 20	189	58 01	246	34 26	302	32 11	358
37	61 21	078	30 17	115	22 49	134	65 13	191	57 25	247	33 52	302	32 09	358
38	62 00	078	30 54	116	23 18	135	65 04	193	56 47	249	33 18	303	32 08	358
39	62 40	079	31 30	117	23 46	136	64 55	195	56 10	250	32 44	303	32 07	359
40	63 19	079	32 05	118	24 13	137	64 43	197	55 32	251	32 11	304	32 06	359
41	63 59	080	32 40	119	24 40	138	64 31	199	54 54	252	31 37	304	32 06	359
42	64 38	080	33 15	120	25 07	139	64 17	202	54 16	253	31 04	305	32 06	000
43	65 18	081	33 50	121	25 33	140	64 01	204	53 37	254	30 31	305	32 06	000
44	65 58	081	34 24	122	25 58	141	63 44	206	52 59	255	29 59	306	32 06	000
	◆ Dubhe		POLLUX		BETELGEUSE		◆ RIGEL		Hamal		◆ Alpheratz		DENEB	
45	29 20	028	32 23	083	34 58	123	26 23	142	63 27	207	52 20	256	29 26	306
46	29 39	028	33 03	083	35 32	124	26 48	143	63 07	209	51 41	257	28 54	307
47	29 58	029	33 43	084	36 05	125	27 12	144	62 47	211	51 02	258	28 22	307
48	30 17	029	34 23	085	36 38	126	27 35	145	62 26	213	50 23	259	27 51	308
49	30 37	029	35 03	086	37 10	127	27 58	146	62 03	215	49 43	259	27 19	309
50	30 56	030	35 43	086	37 42	128	28 20	147	61 40	217	49 04	260	26 48	309
51	31 16	030	36 23	087	38 13	129	28 41	148	61 15	218	48 24	261	26 17	310
52	31 37	031	37 03	088	38 44	130	29 02	149	60 50	220	47 44	262	25 46	310
53	31 57	031	37 43	088	39 15	131	29 22	150	60 24	222	47 04	263	25 15	311
54	32 18	031	38 24	089	39 45	132	29 42	151	59 57	223	46 25	264	24 45	311
55	32 39	032	39 04	090	40 14	133	30 00	153	59 29	225	45 45	264	24 15	312
56	33 00	032	39 44	091	40 43	135	30 19	154	59 00	226	45 05	265	23 45	312
57	33 22	032	40 24	091	41 11	136	30 36	155	58 31	228	44 25	266	23 15	313
58	33 43	033	41 04	092	41 39	137	30 53	156	58 01	229	43 45	267	22 46	313
59	34 05	033	41 44	093	42 06	138	31 09	157	57 30	231	43 04	268	22 17	314
	◆ Dubhe		POLLUX		SIRIUS		◆ RIGEL		Hamal		◆ Alpheratz		DENEB	
60	34 27	034	42 24	094	15 26	139	31 24	158	56 58	232	42 24	268	21 48	314
61	34 50	034	43 04	094	15 53	140	31 39	159	56 26	234	41 44	269	21 20	315
62	35 12	034	43 44	095	16 18	141	31 53	160	55 54	235	41 04	270	20 51	316
63	35 35	035	44 24	096	16 44	142	32 06	161	55 21	236	40 24	271	20 23	316
64	35 58	035	45 04	097	17 08	142	32 19	163	54 47	237	39 44	271	19 56	317
65	36 21	035	45 44	098	17 32	143	32 30	164	54 13	239	39 04	272	19 28	317
66	36 44	036	46 24	099	17 56	144	32 41	165	53 39	240	38 24	273	19 01	318
67	37 08	036	47 03	099	18 19	145	32 51	166	53 04	241	37 43	274	18 35	318
68	37 31	036	47 43	100	18 42	146	33 00	167	52 28	242	37 03	274	18 08	319
69	37 55	037	48 22	101	19 04	147	33 09	168	51 53	243	36 23	275	17 42	320
70	38 19	037	49 02	102	19 26	148	33 17	170	51 17	244	35 43	276	17 16	320
71	38 43	037	49 41	103	19 47	149	33 23	171	50 40	246	35 03	276	16 50	321
72	39 08	038	50 20	104	20 07	150	33 30	172	50 04	247	34 24	277	16 25	321
73	39 32	038	50 59	105	20 27	151	33 35	173	49 27	248	33 44	278	16 00	322
74	39 57	038	51 38	106	20 46	152	33 39	174	48 49	249	33 04	278	15 36	323
	◆ Dubhe		REGULUS		PROCYON		◆ SIRIUS		RIGEL		◆ Hamal		Schedar	
75	40 22	039	17 17	091	35 16	128	21 05	153	33 43	175	48 12	250	51 05	308
76	40 47	039	17 57	092	35 48	129	21 23	154	33 46	177	47 34	251	50 34	308
77	41 12	039	18 38	093	36 19	130	21 40	155	33 48	178	46 56	252	50 02	308
78	41 38	039	19 18	094	36 49	131	21 57	156	33 49	179	46 18	253	49 30	308
79	42 03	040	19 58	094	37 19	133	22 13	157	33 49	180	45 39	254	48 59	309
80	42 29	040	20 38	095	37 48	134	22 29	158	33 48	181	45 01	255	48 28	309
81	42 55	040	21 18	096	38 17	135	22 44	159	33 47	183	44 22	255	47 57	309
82	43 21	040	21 58	097	38 45	136	22 58	160	33 45	184	43 43	256	47 26	309
83	43 47	041	22 37	097	39 13	137	23 12	161	33 42	185	43 04	257	46 55	310
84	44 13	041	23 17	098	39 40	138	23 24	162	33 38	186	42 25	258	46 24	310
85	44 40	041	23 57	099	40 06	139	23 37	163	33 33	187	41 45	259	45 53	310
86	45 06	041	24 37	100	40 32	141	23 48	164	33 27	189	41 06	260	45 23	311
87	45 33	042	25 16	101	40 57	142	23 59	165	33 21	190	40 26	261	44 52	311
88	46 00	042	25 55	101	41 22	143	24 09	166	33 14	191	39 47	261	44 22	311
89	46 27	042	26 35	102	41 46	144	24 19	167	33 06	192	39 07	262	43 52	312

LHA ♈	Hc	Zn	Hc	Zn	Hc	Zn	Hc	Zn	Hc	Zn	Hc	Zn	Hc	Zn
	◆ Dubhe		REGULUS		PROCYON		◆ SIRIUS		RIGEL		ALDEBARAN		◆ Mirfak	
90	46 54	042	27 14	103	42 09	145	24 27	168	32 57	193	54 13	216	64 50	289
91	47 21	043	27 53	104	42 31	147	24 35	169	32 48	194	53 49	217	64 12	289
92	47 48	043	28 32	105	42 53	148	24 43	170	32 37	196	53 24	219	63 34	290
93	48 15	043	29 11	106	43 14	149	24 49	171	32 26	197	52 59	220	62 56	290
94	48 43	043	29 49	106	43 34	150	24 55	172	32 14	198	52 33	221	62 19	290
95	49 10	043	30 28	107	43 53	152	25 00	173	32 01	199	52 06	223	61 41	290
96	49 38	044	31 06	108	44 12	153	25 05	174	31 48	200	51 38	224	61 03	291
97	50 06	044	31 44	109	44 30	154	25 08	175	31 34	201	51 10	225	60 26	291
98	50 33	044	32 22	110	44 47	156	25 11	176	31 19	202	50 41	227	59 48	291
99	51 01	044	33 00	111	45 03	157	25 14	177	31 03	203	50 11	228	59 11	292
100	51 29	044	33 37	112	45 18	158	25 15	178	30 47	205	49 41	229	58 34	292
101	51 57	044	34 14	113	45 32	160	25 16	180	30 30	206	49 10	231	57 57	292
102	52 25	044	34 51	113	45 46	161	25 16	181	30 12	207	48 39	232	57 20	293
103	52 54	045	35 28	114	45 58	163	25 15	182	29 54	208	48 07	233	56 43	293
104	53 22	045	36 04	115	46 10	164	25 13	183	29 34	209	47 35	234	56 06	293
	◆ Dubhe		Denebola		REGULUS		◆ SIRIUS		RIGEL		ALDEBARAN		◆ Mirfak	
105	53 50	045	22 25	093	36 40	116	25 11	184	29 15	210	47 02	235	55 29	294
106	54 18	045	23 05	094	37 16	117	25 08	185	28 54	211	46 29	237	54 52	294
107	54 47	045	23 45	095	37 52	118	25 04	186	28 33	212	45 55	238	54 16	294
108	55 15	045	24 25	095	38 27	119	25 00	187	28 12	213	45 21	239	53 39	295
109	55 43	045	25 05	096	39 02	120	24 55	188	27 49	214	44 47	240	53 03	295
110	56 12	045	25 44	097	39 36	121	24 49	189	27 26	215	44 12	241	52 27	296
111	56 40	045	26 24	098	40 10	122	24 42	190	27 03	216	43 36	242	51 50	296
112	57 09	045	27 04	098	40 44	123	24 35	191	26 39	217	43 01	243	51 14	296
113	57 37	045	27 44	099	41 18	124	24 27	192	26 14	218	42 25	244	50 38	297
114	58 06	045	28 23	100	41 50	126	24 18	193	25 49	219	41 49	245	50 03	297
115	58 34	045	29 03	101	42 23	127	24 08	194	25 23	220	41 12	246	49 27	297
116	59 03	045	29 42	102	42 55	128	23 58	195	24 57	221	40 35	247	48 51	298
117	59 31	045	30 21	103	43 26	129	23 47	196	24 30	222	39 58	248	48 16	298
118	59 59	045	31 00	103	43 57	130	23 36	197	24 03	223	39 21	249	47 41	299
119	60 28	045	31 39	104	44 28	131	23 23	198	23 35	224	38 43	250	47 05	299
	◆ Kochab		Denebola		◆ REGULUS		SIRIUS		RIGEL		◆ ALDEBARAN		CAPELLA	
120	42 25	021	32 18	105	44 58	132	23 10	199	23 07	225	38 05	251	62 36	281
121	42 39	021	32 57	106	45 27	134	22 57	200	22 38	226	37 27	252	61 56	282
122	42 54	022	33 36	107	45 56	135	22 42	201	22 09	227	36 49	253	61 17	282
123	43 09	022	34 14	108	46 24	136	22 27	202	21 40	228	36 11	253	60 38	283
124	43 24	022	34 52	109	46 52	137	22 12	203	21 10	229	35 32	254	59 59	283
125	43 39	022	35 30	109	47 19	139	21 56	204	20 39	230	34 54	255	59 20	284
126	43 54	022	36 08	110	47 45	140	21 39	205	20 08	231	34 15	256	58 41	284
127	44 09	022	36 45	111	48 10	141	21 21	206	19 37	232	33 36	257	58 02	285
128	44 24	022	37 23	112	48 35	143	21 03	207	19 06	232	32 57	258	57 23	285
129	44 40	023	38 00	113	48 59	144	20 44	208	18 34	233	32 17	259	56 44	286
130	44 55	023	38 36	114	49 22	145	20 25	209	18 01	234	31 38	259	56 06	286
131	45 11	023	39 13	115	49 45	147	20 05	210	17 28	235	30 58	260	55 27	286
132	45 27	023	39 49	116	50 07	148	19 45	211	16 55	236	30 19	261	54 49	287
133	45 42	023	40 25	117	50 27	149	19 24	212	16 22	237	29 39	262	54 10	287
134	45 58	023	41 01	118	50 47	151	19 02	213	15 48	238	28 59	263	53 32	288
	◆ Kochab		ARCTURUS		Denebola		◆ REGULUS		SIRIUS		BETELGEUSE		◆ CAPELLA	
135	46 14	023	21 17	085	41 36	119	51 06	152	18 40	214	33 50	239	52 54	288
136	46 30	023	21 57	085	42 11	120	51 25	154	18 17	215	33 15	240	52 16	289
137	46 46	024	22 37	086	42 45	121	51 42	155	17 54	216	32 40	241	51 38	289
138	47 02	024	23 17	087	43 19	122	51 58	157	17 30	217	32 05	242	51 00	290
139	47 18	024	23 57	088	43 53	123	52 13	158	17 06	218	31 29	243	50 22	290
140	47 34	024	24 37	088	44 27	124	52 28	160	16 41	219	30 53	244	49 45	291
141	47 50	024	25 17	089	44 59	126	52 41	162	16 16	219	30 17	245	49 07	291
142	48 07	024	25 57	090	45 32	127	52 53	163	15 50	220	29 41	246	48 30	292
143	48 23	024	26 38	091	46 04	128	53 04	165	15 24	221	29 04	247	47 52	292
144	48 39	024	27 18	091	46 35	129	53 14	166	14 57	222	28 27	248	47 15	292
145	48 56	024	27 58	092	47 06	130	53 23	168	14 30	223	27 50	248	46 38	293
146	49 12	024	28 38	093	47 37	131	53 31	170	14 03	224	27 12	249	46 01	293
147	49 28	024	29 18	094	48 06	133	53 37	171	13 35	225	26 35	250	45 25	294
148	49 45	024	29 58	094	48 36	134	53 43	173	13 06	226	25 57	251	44 48	294
149	50 01	024	30 38	095	49 04	135	53 47	175	12 37	226	25 19	252	44 11	295
	◆ Kochab		ARCTURUS		◆ SPICA		REGULUS		PROCYON		◆ BETELGEUSE		CAPELLA	
150	50 18	024	31 18	096	15 18	127	53 51	176	37 49	226	24 41	253	43 35	295
151	50 34	024	31 58	097	15 49	128	53 53	178	37 20	227	24 02	253	42 59	296
152	50 50	024	32 38	097	16 21	129	53 54	180	36 50	228	23 24	254	42 23	296
153	51 07	024	33 18	098	16 52	130	53 53	181	36 20	230	22 45	255	41 47	297
154	51 23	024	33 57	099	17 22	131	53 52	183	35 49	231	22 06	256	41 11	297
155	51 40	024	34 37	100	17 53	132	53 49	184	35 18	232	21 27	257	40 35	298
156	51 56	024	35 16	101	18 22	133	53 46	186	34 46	233	20 48	258	40 00	298
157	52 13	024	35 56	102	18 52	133	53 41	188	34 14	234	20 09	258	39 25	299
158	52 29	024	36 35	102	19 21	134	53 35	189	33 41	235	19 29	259	38 49	299
159	52 45	024	37 14	103	19 49	135	53 28	191	33 08	236	18 50	260	38 14	300
160	53 01	024	37 53	104	20 17	136	53 19	193	32 35	237	18 10	261	37 40	300
161	53 18	024	38 32	105	20 45	137	53 10	194	32 01	238	17 30	261	37 05	301
162	53 34	024	39 11	106	21 12	138	52 59	196	31 27	239	16 51	262	36 30	301
163	53 50	024	39 49	107	21 39	139	52 48	197	30 53	240	16 11	263	35 56	302
164	54 06	024	40 28	108	22 05	140	52 35	199	30 18	240	15 31	264	35 22	302
	◆ VEGA		ARCTURUS		◆ SPICA		REGULUS		PROCYON		◆ POLLUX		CAPELLA	
165	14 31	047	41 06	109	22 30	141	52 22	201	29 43	241	47 48	260	34 48	303
166	15 00	048	41 44	110	22 55	142	52 07	202	29 08	242	47 08	260	34 14	303
167	15 30	048	42 21	111	23 20	143	51 51	204	28 32	243	46 28	261	33 41	304
168	16 00	049	42 59	111	23 44	144	51 35	205	27 56	244	45 49	262	33 07	304
169	16 31	050	43 36	112	24 07	145	51 17	207	27 20	245	45 09	263	32 34	305
170	17 01	050	44 13	113	24 30	146	50 59	208	26 43	246	44 29	264	32 01	305
171	17 32	051	44 50	114	24 53	147	50 39	210	26 06	247	43 49	265	31 28	306
172	18 04	051	45 26	116	25 14	148	50 19	211	25 29	248	43 09	265	30 56	306
173	18 35	052	46 02	117	25 35	149	49 58	213	24 52	249	42 29	266	30 23	307
174	19 07	053	46 38	118	25 56	150	49 36	214	24 15	249	41 49	267	29 51	307
175	19 39	053	47 13	119	26 16	151	49 13	215	23 37	250	41 09	268	29 19	308
176	20 11	054	47 48	120	26 35	152	48 49	217	22 59	251	40 29	269	28 48	308
177	20 44	054	48 23	121	26 54	153	48 25	218	22 21	252	39 49	269	28 16	309
178	21 17	055	48 57	122	27 12	154	48 00	219	21 43	253	39 08	270	27 45	309
179	21 50	056	49 31	123	27 29	155	47 34	221	21 04	254	38 28	271	27 14	310

LHA ♈	Hc	Zn	Hc	Zn	Hc	Zn	Hc	Zn	Hc	Zn	Hc	Zn	Hc	Zn
	◆DENEB		VEGA		ARCTURUS		◆SPICA		REGULUS		◆POLLUX		CAPELLA	
180	12 54	033	22 23	056	50 04	124	27 46	156	47 08	222	37 48	271	26 43	310
181	13 16	034	22 57	057	50 37	126	28 02	157	46 40	223	37 08	272	26 12	311
182	13 38	034	23 30	057	51 10	127	28 17	158	46 13	224	36 28	273	25 42	311
183	14 01	035	24 04	058	51 42	128	28 32	159	45 44	226	35 48	274	25 12	312
184	14 25	036	24 38	059	52 13	129	28 45	160	45 15	227	35 08	274	24 42	312
185	14 48	036	25 13	059	52 44	131	28 59	161	44 45	228	34 28	275	24 13	313
186	15 12	037	25 47	060	53 14	132	29 11	163	44 15	229	33 48	276	23 43	313
187	15 36	037	26 22	060	53 43	133	29 23	164	43 45	230	33 08	276	23 14	314
188	16 01	038	26 57	061	54 12	135	29 34	165	43 13	232	32 28	277	22 45	314
189	16 26	039	27 32	062	54 40	136	29 44	166	42 42	233	31 48	278	22 17	315
190	16 51	039	28 08	062	55 08	138	29 53	167	42 09	234	31 08	279	21 49	316
191	17 17	040	28 43	063	55 35	139	30 02	168	41 37	235	30 29	279	21 21	316
192	17 43	040	29 19	063	56 00	141	30 10	169	41 04	236	29 49	280	20 53	317
193	18 09	041	29 55	064	56 26	142	30 17	170	40 30	237	29 10	281	20 26	317
194	18 35	042	30 31	064	56 50	144	30 23	171	39 56	238	28 30	281	19 58	318
	◆DENEB		VEGA		Rasalhague		◆ARCTURUS		REGULUS		◆POLLUX		CAPELLA	
195	19 02	042	31 07	065	23 22	097	57 13	145	39 22	239	27 51	282	19 32	318
196	19 29	043	31 44	066	24 01	098	57 36	147	38 47	240	27 12	283	19 05	319
197	19 57	043	32 20	066	24 41	099	57 57	148	38 12	241	26 33	283	18 39	319
198	20 24	044	32 57	067	25 21	100	58 18	150	37 37	242	25 54	284	18 13	320
199	20 52	044	33 34	067	26 00	100	58 37	152	37 01	243	25 15	285	17 47	321
200	21 20	045	34 11	068	26 40	101	58 56	154	36 25	244	24 36	285	17 22	321
201	21 49	046	34 49	068	27 19	102	59 13	155	35 49	245	23 57	286	16 57	322
202	22 18	046	35 26	069	27 58	103	59 29	157	35 13	246	23 19	287	16 32	322
203	22 47	047	36 03	070	28 37	104	59 44	159	34 36	247	22 40	287	16 08	323
204	23 16	047	36 41	070	29 16	104	59 58	161	33 59	248	22 02	288	15 44	324
205	23 46	048	37 19	071	29 55	105	60 11	163	33 21	249	21 24	289	15 20	324
206	24 16	048	37 57	071	30 34	106	60 22	164	32 44	250	20 46	289	14 57	325
207	24 46	049	38 35	072	31 12	107	60 32	166	32 06	251	20 08	290	14 34	325
208	25 16	049	39 13	072	31 51	108	60 41	168	31 28	251	19 30	291	14 11	326
209	25 47	050	39 52	073	32 29	109	60 49	170	30 50	252	18 53	291	13 49	327
	DENEB		◆VEGA		Rasalhague		◆ARCTURUS		Denebola		REGULUS		◆Dubhe	
210	26 17	050	40 30	074	33 07	110	60 55	172	47 03	230	30 12	253	62 02	316
211	26 49	051	41 09	074	33 44	111	61 00	174	46 33	231	29 33	254	61 33	315
212	27 20	052	41 47	075	34 22	111	61 03	176	46 01	232	28 55	255	61 05	315
213	27 51	052	42 26	075	34 59	112	61 05	178	45 29	233	28 16	256	60 37	315
214	28 23	053	43 05	076	35 36	113	61 06	180	44 57	235	27 37	257	60 09	315
215	28 55	053	43 44	077	36 13	114	61 06	182	44 24	236	26 58	257	59 40	315
216	29 27	054	44 23	077	36 49	115	61 04	184	43 50	237	26 18	258	59 12	315
217	30 00	054	45 02	078	37 25	116	61 00	186	43 17	238	25 39	259	58 43	315
218	30 32	055	45 41	078	38 01	117	60 56	188	42 42	239	25 00	260	58 15	315
219	31 05	055	46 21	079	38 37	118	60 50	190	42 08	240	24 20	261	57 46	315
220	31 38	056	47 00	080	39 12	119	60 43	191	41 33	241	23 40	261	57 18	315
221	32 12	056	47 40	080	39 47	120	60 34	193	40 58	242	23 01	262	56 49	315
222	32 45	057	48 19	081	40 21	121	60 24	195	40 22	243	22 21	263	56 21	315
223	33 19	057	48 59	081	40 56	122	60 13	197	39 46	244	21 41	264	55 53	315
224	33 52	058	49 39	082	41 29	123	60 00	199	39 10	245	21 01	264	55 24	315
	DENEB		◆VEGA		Rasalhague		ANTARES		◆ARCTURUS		Denebola		◆Dubhe	
225	34 26	058	50 19	083	42 03	124	12 49	159	59 47	201	38 33	246	54 56	315
226	35 01	059	50 58	083	42 36	125	13 03	160	59 32	203	37 56	247	54 27	315
227	35 35	059	51 38	084	43 08	127	13 16	161	59 16	204	37 19	248	53 59	315
228	36 10	060	52 18	085	43 40	128	13 29	162	58 59	206	36 42	249	53 31	315
229	36 44	060	52 58	085	44 12	129	13 41	163	58 40	208	36 04	250	53 03	315
230	37 19	061	53 38	086	44 43	130	13 53	164	58 21	210	35 27	251	52 34	316
231	37 54	061	54 18	087	45 13	131	14 04	165	58 01	211	34 49	252	52 06	316
232	38 30	062	54 58	087	45 43	132	14 14	166	57 39	213	34 11	252	51 38	316
233	39 05	062	55 38	088	46 13	134	14 23	167	57 17	215	33 32	253	51 10	316
234	39 41	063	56 19	089	46 41	135	14 33	167	56 54	216	32 54	254	50 42	316
235	40 16	063	56 59	089	47 10	136	14 41	168	56 30	218	32 15	255	50 15	316
236	40 52	064	57 39	090	47 37	137	14 49	169	56 05	219	31 36	256	49 47	316
237	41 28	064	58 19	091	48 04	139	14 56	170	55 39	221	30 57	257	49 19	317
238	42 04	065	58 59	092	48 30	140	15 02	171	55 12	222	30 18	258	48 52	317
239	42 41	065	59 39	093	48 56	141	15 08	172	54 45	224	29 39	258	48 24	317
	◆DENEB		ALTAIR		Rasalhague		◆ANTARES		ARCTURUS		Denebola		◆Dubhe	
240	43 17	066	27 49	109	49 20	143	15 13	173	54 17	225	28 59	259	47 57	317
241	43 54	066	28 27	110	49 44	144	15 18	174	53 48	226	28 20	260	47 30	317
242	44 31	067	29 04	111	50 08	145	15 22	175	53 19	228	27 40	261	47 02	318
243	45 08	067	29 42	112	50 30	147	15 25	176	52 49	229	27 01	262	46 35	318
244	45 45	067	30 19	112	50 52	148	15 28	177	52 18	230	26 21	262	46 08	318
245	46 22	068	30 56	113	51 12	150	15 30	178	51 47	232	25 41	263	45 42	318
246	46 59	068	31 33	114	51 32	151	15 31	179	51 15	233	25 01	264	45 15	318
247	47 36	069	32 09	115	51 51	153	15 32	179	50 43	234	24 21	265	44 48	319
248	48 14	069	32 45	116	52 09	154	15 32	180	50 10	235	23 41	265	44 22	319
249	48 52	070	33 21	117	52 26	156	15 32	181	49 37	237	23 01	266	43 56	319
250	49 29	070	33 57	118	52 42	157	15 30	182	49 03	238	22 21	267	43 29	319
251	50 07	071	34 32	119	52 57	159	15 28	183	48 29	239	21 41	268	43 03	320
252	50 45	071	35 07	120	53 11	160	15 26	184	47 54	240	21 01	269	42 37	320
253	51 23	072	35 42	121	53 24	162	15 23	185	47 19	241	20 21	269	42 12	320
254	52 01	072	36 16	122	53 36	164	15 19	186	46 44	242	19 40	270	41 46	321
	◆Schedar		DENEB		ALTAIR		◆Rasalhague		ARCTURUS		◆Alkaid		Kochab	
255	27 35	034	52 40	073	36 50	123	53 47	165	46 08	243	58 48	291	60 25	343
256	27 57	035	53 18	073	37 24	124	53 56	167	45 32	244	58 11	291	60 13	342
257	28 20	035	53 57	074	37 57	125	54 05	168	44 56	245	57 33	291	60 01	342
258	28 43	035	54 35	074	38 29	126	54 13	170	44 19	246	56 56	292	59 48	342
259	29 07	036	55 14	075	39 02	127	54 19	172	43 43	247	56 19	292	59 35	341
260	29 31	036	55 53	075	39 34	128	54 24	173	43 05	248	55 41	292	59 22	341
261	29 55	037	56 31	076	40 05	129	54 28	175	42 28	249	55 04	293	59 09	341
262	30 19	037	57 10	076	40 36	130	54 31	177	41 50	250	54 27	293	58 56	340
263	30 43	038	57 49	077	41 06	131	54 33	178	41 12	251	53 51	294	58 42	340
264	31 08	038	58 28	077	41 36	133	54 33	180	40 34	252	53 14	294	58 28	340
265	31 33	039	59 08	078	42 05	134	54 32	182	39 56	253	52 37	294	58 14	339
266	31 58	039	59 47	078	42 34	135	54 30	184	39 17	254	52 01	295	58 00	339
267	32 23	039	60 26	079	43 02	136	54 27	185	38 39	255	51 24	295	57 46	339
268	32 49	040	61 06	079	43 30	137	54 23	187	38 00	256	50 48	295	57 31	339
269	33 14	040	61 45	080	43 57	138	54 18	189	37 21	257	50 12	296	57 17	338

LHA ♈	Hc	Zn	Hc	Zn	Hc	Zn	Hc	Zn	Hc	Zn	Hc	Zn	Hc	Zn
	◆Mirfak		Alpheratz		◆ALTAIR		Rasalhague		◆ARCTURUS		Alkaid		Kochab	
270	13 25	024	19 49	068	44 23	140	54 11	190	36 42	257	49 36	296	57 02	338
271	13 42	025	20 26	069	44 48	141	54 04	192	36 03	258	49 00	297	56 47	338
272	13 59	026	21 03	069	45 13	142	53 55	193	35 23	259	48 24	297	56 32	338
273	14 17	026	21 41	070	45 38	144	53 45	195	34 44	260	47 48	297	56 17	338
274	14 34	027	22 19	071	46 01	145	53 34	197	34 04	261	47 12	298	56 01	337
275	14 53	027	22 57	071	46 24	146	53 22	198	33 24	262	46 37	298	55 46	337
276	15 11	028	23 35	072	46 46	147	53 09	200	32 45	262	46 02	299	55 30	337
277	15 30	029	24 13	073	47 07	149	52 54	202	32 05	263	45 27	299	55 15	337
278	15 50	029	24 51	073	47 27	150	52 39	203	31 25	264	44 51	299	54 59	337
279	16 09	030	25 30	074	47 47	152	52 23	205	30 45	265	44 17	300	54 43	337
280	16 30	030	26 09	075	48 06	153	52 06	206	30 05	266	43 42	300	54 27	337
281	16 50	031	26 47	075	48 23	154	51 48	208	29 25	266	43 07	301	54 11	337
282	17 11	031	27 26	076	48 40	156	51 28	209	28 45	267	42 33	301	53 55	336
283	17 32	032	28 05	077	48 56	157	51 08	211	28 05	268	41 59	302	53 39	336
284	17 53	033	28 44	077	49 11	159	50 48	212	27 25	269	41 24	302	53 23	336
	◆Mirfak		Alpheratz		◆ALTAIR		Rasalhague		◆ARCTURUS		Alkaid		Kochab	
285	18 15	033	29 23	078	49 25	160	50 26	213	26 45	269	40 50	302	53 07	336
286	18 37	034	30 03	079	49 38	162	50 03	215	26 04	270	40 17	303	52 51	336
287	19 00	034	30 42	079	49 50	163	49 40	216	25 24	271	39 43	303	52 34	336
288	19 22	035	31 22	080	50 02	165	49 16	218	24 44	272	39 10	304	52 18	336
289	19 45	035	32 01	081	50 12	166	48 51	219	24 04	272	38 36	304	52 02	336
290	20 09	036	32 41	081	50 21	168	48 25	220	23 24	273	38 03	305	51 45	336
291	20 32	036	33 21	082	50 29	169	47 59	222	22 44	274	37 30	305	51 29	336
292	20 56	037	34 00	083	50 36	171	47 32	223	22 04	274	36 57	306	51 12	336
293	21 21	037	34 40	083	50 42	172	47 04	224	21 24	275	36 25	306	50 56	336
294	21 45	038	35 20	084	50 46	174	46 36	225	20 44	276	35 52	306	50 40	336
295	22 10	039	36 00	085	50 50	175	46 07	227	20 04	277	35 20	307	50 23	336
296	22 35	039	36 40	085	50 53	177	45 38	228	19 24	277	34 48	307	50 07	336
297	23 01	040	37 20	086	50 54	179	45 08	229	18 44	278	34 16	308	49 50	336
298	23 26	040	38 00	087	50 55	180	44 37	230	18 05	279	33 45	308	49 34	336
299	23 52	041	38 40	087	50 54	182	44 06	231	17 25	279	33 13	309	49 17	336
	Mirfak		◆Alpheratz		Enif		ALTAIR		◆Rasalhague		Alphecca		◆Kochab	
300	24 19	041	39 20	088	46 01	141	50 52	183	43 34	233	35 06	272	49 01	336
301	24 45	042	40 00	089	46 26	142	50 49	185	43 02	234	34 26	273	48 45	336
302	25 12	042	40 41	090	46 50	144	50 45	186	42 30	235	33 46	274	48 28	336
303	25 39	043	41 21	090	47 13	145	50 40	188	41 57	236	33 06	274	48 12	336
304	26 06	043	42 01	091	47 36	146	50 34	190	41 23	237	32 26	275	47 56	336
305	26 34	044	42 41	092	47 58	148	50 27	191	40 49	238	31 46	276	47 40	336
306	27 02	044	43 21	093	48 19	149	50 19	193	40 15	239	31 06	277	47 23	336
307	27 30	045	44 01	093	48 39	151	50 09	194	39 41	240	30 26	277	47 07	336
308	27 58	045	44 41	094	48 58	152	49 59	196	39 06	241	29 47	278	46 51	336
309	28 27	046	45 21	095	49 16	153	49 48	197	38 30	242	29 07	279	46 35	337
310	28 56	046	46 01	096	49 34	155	49 35	199	37 55	243	28 27	279	46 19	337
311	29 25	047	46 41	097	49 50	156	49 22	200	37 19	244	27 48	280	46 03	337
312	29 54	047	47 21	097	50 06	158	49 08	202	36 42	245	27 08	281	45 48	337
313	30 24	048	48 01	098	50 21	159	48 52	203	36 06	246	26 29	281	45 32	337
314	30 54	048	48 40	099	50 34	161	48 36	205	35 29	247	25 49	282	45 16	337
	CAPELLA		◆Hamal		Alpheratz		Enif		◆ALTAIR		VEGA		◆Kochab	
315	15 46	037	25 46	083	49 20	100	50 47	162	48 19	206	62 48	264	45 01	337
316	16 10	037	26 26	083	50 00	101	50 59	164	48 01	207	62 08	264	44 45	337
317	16 35	038	27 06	084	50 39	102	51 09	165	47 42	209	61 28	265	44 30	337
318	16 59	038	27 46	085	51 18	103	51 19	167	47 22	210	60 48	266	44 14	338
319	17 24	039	28 26	086	51 57	104	51 28	169	47 02	211	60 08	267	43 59	338
320	17 50	039	29 06	086	52 36	105	51 35	170	46 41	213	59 28	268	43 44	338
321	18 15	040	29 46	087	53 15	106	51 41	172	46 18	214	58 48	268	43 29	338
322	18 41	041	30 26	088	53 53	107	51 47	173	45 55	215	58 08	269	43 14	338
323	19 08	041	31 06	088	54 32	108	51 51	175	45 32	217	57 28	270	42 59	338
324	19 34	042	31 46	089	55 10	109	51 54	176	45 07	218	56 48	271	42 44	339
325	20 01	042	32 26	090	55 48	110	51 56	178	44 42	219	56 08	271	42 30	339
326	20 28	043	33 06	091	56 26	111	51 57	180	44 17	221	55 27	272	42 15	339
327	20 56	043	33 46	091	57 03	112	51 56	181	43 50	222	54 47	273	42 01	339
328	21 23	044	34 27	092	57 40	113	51 55	183	43 23	223	54 07	274	41 47	339
329	21 51	045	35 07	093	58 17	114	51 52	184	42 55	224	53 27	274	41 32	339
	CAPELLA		◆Hamal		Diphda		Enif		◆ALTAIR		VEGA		◆Kochab	
330	22 20	045	35 47	094	14 34	140	51 49	186	42 27	225	52 47	275	41 18	340
331	22 48	046	36 27	094	15 00	141	51 44	188	41 58	227	52 07	276	41 04	340
332	23 17	046	37 07	095	15 25	142	51 38	189	41 29	228	51 27	276	40 51	340
333	23 46	047	37 47	096	15 49	142	51 31	191	40 59	229	50 47	277	40 37	340
334	24 16	047	38 27	097	16 14	143	51 23	192	40 28	230	50 08	278	40 23	340
335	24 45	048	39 07	098	16 37	144	51 14	194	39 57	231	49 28	278	40 10	341
336	25 15	048	39 46	099	17 01	145	51 04	195	39 26	232	48 48	279	39 57	341
337	25 45	049	40 26	099	17 23	146	50 53	197	38 54	233	48 08	279	39 44	341
338	26 16	049	41 05	100	17 46	147	50 40	198	38 22	234	47 29	280	39 31	341
339	26 46	050	41 45	101	18 07	148	50 27	200	37 49	235	46 49	281	39 18	341
340	27 17	050	42 24	102	18 28	149	50 13	201	37 16	236	46 10	281	39 05	342
341	27 48	051	43 04	103	18 49	150	49 58	203	36 42	237	45 31	282	38 53	342
342	28 19	051	43 43	104	19 09	151	49 42	204	36 08	238	44 51	282	38 40	342
343	28 51	052	44 22	105	19 28	152	49 25	206	35 34	239	44 12	283	38 28	342
344	29 23	053	45 00	105	19 47	153	49 07	207	34 59	240	43 33	284	38 16	343
	◆CAPELLA		ALDEBARAN		◆Diphda		Enif		ALTAIR		◆VEGA		Kochab	
345	29 55	053	16 03	083	20 05	154	48 48	209	34 24	241	42 54	284	38 04	343
346	30 27	054	16 43	084	20 23	155	48 28	210	33 48	242	42 15	285	37 52	343
347	30 59	054	17 23	084	20 40	155	48 07	212	33 13	243	41 37	285	37 41	343
348	31 32	055	18 03	085	20 56	156	47 46	213	32 37	244	40 58	286	37 29	344
349	32 05	055	18 43	086	21 12	157	47 24	214	32 00	245	40 19	287	37 18	344
350	32 38	056	19 23	087	21 27	158	47 01	216	31 24	246	39 41	287	37 07	344
351	33 11	056	20 03	087	21 41	159	46 37	217	30 47	247	39 03	288	36 56	344
352	33 44	057	20 43	088	21 55	160	46 13	218	30 10	248	38 24	288	36 46	345
353	34 18	057	21 23	089	22 08	161	45 47	220	29 33	249	37 46	289	36 35	345
354	34 51	058	22 03	089	22 21	162	45 21	221	28 55	250	37 09	289	36 25	345
355	35 25	058	22 43	090	22 32	163	44 55	222	28 17	250	36 31	290	36 15	345
356	36 00	059	23 23	091	22 44	164	44 28	223	27 40	251	35 53	291	36 05	346
357	36 34	059	24 04	092	22 54	165	44 00	224	27 01	252	35 16	291	35 55	346
358	37 08	059	24 44	092	23 04	166	43 31	226	26 23	253	34 38	292	35 45	346
359	37 43	060	25 24	093	23 13	167	43 02	227	25 45	254	34 01	292	35 36	347

LHA ♈	Hc Zn	Hc Zn	Hc Zn	Hc Zn	Hc Zn	Hc Zn	Hc Zn
	◆CAPELLA	ALDEBARAN	Hamal	◆Diphda	ALTAIR	◆VEGA	Kochab
0	37 48 060	26 08 094	55 19 121	24 20 168	25 22 255	33 00 294	34 28 347
1	38 23 060	26 49 094	55 53 123	24 28 169	24 42 256	32 23 294	34 19 347
2	38 59 061	27 29 095	56 28 124	24 35 170	24 02 257	31 46 295	34 10 348
3	39 35 061	28 10 096	57 01 125	24 41 172	23 22 258	31 08 295	34 01 348
4	40 11 062	28 51 097	57 34 127	24 47 173	22 42 258	30 32 296	33 53 348
5	40 47 062	29 31 097	58 07 128	24 52 174	22 02 259	29 55 296	33 44 348
6	41 23 063	30 12 098	58 39 129	24 56 175	21 22 260	29 18 297	33 36 349
7	41 59 063	30 52 099	59 10 131	24 59 176	20 42 261	28 42 297	33 28 349
8	42 36 063	31 33 100	59 41 132	25 02 177	20 01 261	28 06 298	33 21 349
9	43 13 064	32 13 101	60 11 134	25 04 178	19 21 262	27 29 299	33 13 350
10	43 50 064	32 53 101	60 40 135	25 05 179	18 40 263	26 54 299	33 06 350
11	44 26 065	33 33 102	61 08 137	25 06 180	18 00 264	26 18 300	32 59 350
12	45 04 065	34 13 103	61 35 139	25 05 181	17 19 264	25 42 300	32 52 350
13	45 41 066	34 53 104	62 02 140	25 04 182	16 38 265	25 07 301	32 45 351
14	46 18 066	35 33 105	62 27 142	25 03 183	15 57 266	24 32 301	32 38 351
	◆CAPELLA	ALDEBARAN	Hamal	◆Diphda	Alpheratz	◆DENEB	Kochab
15	46 56 067	36 12 106	62 52 144	25 00 184	69 37 213	46 35 293	32 32 351
16	47 33 067	36 52 106	63 16 146	24 57 185	69 14 216	45 58 293	32 26 352
17	48 11 067	37 31 107	63 38 148	24 53 186	68 49 218	45 20 293	32 20 352
18	48 49 068	38 10 108	63 59 150	24 48 187	68 24 220	44 43 294	32 15 352
19	49 27 068	38 48 109	64 19 152	24 42 188	67 57 222	44 05 294	32 09 353
20	50 05 069	39 27 110	64 38 154	24 36 189	67 29 224	43 28 295	32 04 353
21	50 43 069	40 05 111	64 56 156	24 29 190	67 00 226	42 51 295	31 59 353
22	51 21 070	40 43 112	65 12 158	24 21 191	66 30 228	42 14 296	31 54 353
23	52 00 070	41 21 113	65 27 160	24 13 192	66 00 229	41 37 296	31 50 354
24	52 38 070	41 59 114	65 40 162	24 04 193	65 28 231	41 01 297	31 45 354
25	53 17 071	42 36 115	65 52 164	23 54 194	64 56 233	40 24 297	31 41 354
26	53 56 071	43 13 116	66 03 166	23 43 196	64 23 234	39 48 298	31 37 355
27	54 34 072	43 50 117	66 12 169	23 32 197	63 50 236	39 12 298	31 34 355
28	55 13 072	44 26 118	66 19 171	23 20 198	63 15 237	38 36 299	31 30 355
29	55 52 073	45 02 119	66 25 173	23 07 199	62 41 239	38 00 299	31 27 356
	CAPELLA	◆BETELGEUSE	RIGEL	Hamal	◆Alpheratz	DENEB	◆Kochab
30	56 31 073	26 16 109	19 54 128	66 29 175	62 06 240	37 24 300	31 24 356
31	57 11 074	26 55 109	20 26 128	66 31 178	61 30 242	36 49 300	31 21 356
32	57 50 074	27 34 110	20 58 129	66 32 180	60 54 243	36 13 300	31 19 357
33	58 29 074	28 12 111	21 30 130	66 31 182	60 17 244	35 38 301	31 16 357
34	59 09 075	28 50 112	22 01 131	66 29 185	59 40 245	35 03 301	31 14 357
35	59 48 075	29 28 113	22 31 132	66 25 187	59 03 247	34 28 302	31 12 358
36	60 28 076	30 05 114	23 01 133	66 19 189	58 25 248	33 54 302	31 11 358
37	61 08 076	30 43 115	23 31 134	66 12 191	57 47 249	33 19 303	31 09 358
38	61 47 077	31 20 116	24 00 135	66 03 194	57 09 250	32 45 303	31 08 359
39	62 27 077	31 57 116	24 29 136	65 52 196	56 30 251	32 11 304	31 07 359
40	63 07 077	32 33 117	24 57 137	65 40 198	55 51 252	31 37 304	31 06 359
41	63 47 078	33 09 118	25 25 138	65 27 200	55 12 253	31 03 305	31 06 359
42	64 27 078	33 45 119	25 52 139	65 12 202	54 33 254	30 30 305	31 06 000
43	65 07 079	34 21 120	26 19 140	64 56 204	53 53 255	29 57 306	31 06 000
44	65 47 079	34 56 121	26 45 141	64 38 206	53 14 256	29 23 306	31 06 000
	◆Dubhe	POLLUX	BETELGEUSE	◆RIGEL	Hamal	◆Alpheratz	DENEB
45	28 27 028	32 15 082	35 31 122	27 11 142	64 20 208	52 34 257	28 51 307
46	28 46 028	32 56 083	36 05 123	27 36 143	63 59 210	51 54 258	28 18 307
47	29 05 028	33 37 083	36 39 124	28 00 144	63 38 212	51 14 259	27 46 308
48	29 24 029	34 17 084	37 13 125	28 24 145	63 16 214	50 34 260	27 13 308
49	29 44 029	34 58 085	37 46 126	28 47 146	62 52 216	49 54 261	26 41 309
50	30 04 029	35 39 086	38 19 127	29 10 147	62 28 218	49 13 261	26 10 309
51	30 25 030	36 20 086	38 51 128	29 32 148	62 02 220	48 33 262	25 38 310
52	30 45 030	37 01 087	39 23 129	29 53 149	61 36 221	47 52 263	25 07 310
53	31 06 031	37 41 088	39 54 131	30 14 150	61 08 223	47 11 264	24 36 311
54	31 27 031	38 22 088	40 25 132	30 34 151	60 40 224	46 31 265	24 05 312
55	31 48 031	39 03 089	40 55 133	30 54 152	60 11 226	45 50 266	23 35 312
56	32 09 032	39 44 090	41 25 134	31 12 153	59 41 228	45 09 266	23 04 313
57	32 31 032	40 25 091	41 54 135	31 30 154	59 10 229	44 28 267	22 34 313
58	32 53 032	41 06 091	42 23 136	31 48 156	58 39 231	43 47 268	22 05 314
59	33 15 033	41 47 092	42 51 137	32 04 157	58 07 232	43 06 269	21 35 314
	◆Dubhe	POLLUX	SIRIUS	◆RIGEL	Hamal	◆Alpheratz	DENEB
60	33 37 033	42 28 093	16 12 139	32 20 158	57 35 233	42 26 269	21 06 315
61	34 00 034	43 09 094	16 38 140	32 35 159	57 02 235	41 45 270	20 37 315
62	34 22 034	43 49 094	17 05 140	32 49 160	56 28 236	41 04 271	20 08 316
63	34 45 034	44 30 095	17 30 141	33 03 161	55 54 237	40 23 272	19 40 316
64	35 08 035	45 11 096	17 56 142	33 16 162	55 19 239	39 42 272	19 12 317
65	35 32 035	45 52 097	18 21 143	33 28 164	54 44 240	39 01 273	18 44 318
66	35 55 035	46 32 098	18 45 144	33 39 165	54 08 241	38 20 274	18 17 318
67	36 19 036	47 13 098	19 09 145	33 49 166	53 32 242	37 39 274	17 50 319
68	36 43 036	47 53 099	19 32 146	33 59 167	52 56 243	36 59 275	17 23 319
69	37 07 036	48 34 100	19 54 147	34 08 168	52 19 244	36 18 276	16 56 320
70	37 31 037	49 14 101	20 16 148	34 16 169	51 42 246	35 37 276	16 30 320
71	37 56 037	49 54 102	20 38 149	34 23 171	51 05 247	34 56 277	16 04 321
72	38 20 037	50 34 103	20 59 150	34 29 172	50 27 248	34 16 278	15 38 322
73	38 45 037	51 14 104	21 19 151	34 34 173	49 49 249	33 35 278	15 13 322
74	39 10 038	51 53 105	21 39 152	34 39 174	49 11 250	32 55 279	14 48 323
	◆Dubhe	REGULUS	PROCYON	◆SIRIUS	RIGEL	◆Hamal	Schedar
75	39 35 038	17 19 091	35 53 128	21 58 153	34 43 175	48 32 251	50 28 309
76	40 00 038	17 59 092	36 26 129	22 17 154	34 45 177	47 53 252	49 56 309
77	40 26 039	18 40 092	36 57 130	22 35 155	34 47 178	47 14 253	49 25 309
78	40 51 039	19 21 093	37 28 131	22 52 156	34 49 179	46 35 254	48 53 309
79	41 17 039	20 02 094	37 59 132	23 08 157	34 49 180	45 56 255	48 21 310
80	41 43 039	20 43 095	38 29 133	23 24 158	34 48 181	45 16 255	47 50 310
81	42 09 040	21 24 095	38 59 134	23 40 159	34 47 183	44 37 256	47 18 310
82	42 35 040	22 04 096	39 28 135	23 54 160	34 45 184	43 57 257	46 47 310
83	43 01 040	22 45 097	39 56 136	24 08 161	34 41 185	43 17 258	46 16 311
84	43 28 040	23 26 098	40 24 138	24 21 162	34 37 186	42 37 259	45 45 311
85	43 54 041	24 06 099	40 51 139	24 34 163	34 32 187	41 56 260	45 14 311
86	44 21 041	24 46 099	41 18 140	24 46 164	34 27 189	41 16 261	44 43 311
87	44 48 041	25 27 100	41 44 141	24 57 165	34 20 190	40 36 261	44 13 312
88	45 15 041	26 07 101	42 09 142	25 07 166	34 13 191	39 55 262	43 42 312
89	45 42 041	26 47 102	42 34 144	25 17 167	34 05 192	39 15 263	43 12 312

LAT 47°N

LHA ♈	Hc Zn	Hc Zn	Hc Zn	Hc Zn	Hc Zn	Hc Zn	Hc Zn
	◆Dubhe	REGULUS	PROCYON	◆SIRIUS	RIGEL	ALDEBARAN	◆Mirfak
90	46 09 042	27 27 103	42 58 145	25 26 168	33 55 193	55 01 216	64 29 291
91	46 36 042	28 07 103	43 21 146	25 34 169	33 46 195	54 36 218	63 51 291
92	47 04 042	28 47 104	43 44 147	25 42 170	33 35 196	54 11 219	63 13 291
93	47 31 042	29 26 105	44 05 149	25 49 171	33 23 197	53 44 221	62 35 292
94	47 59 042	30 06 106	44 26 150	25 55 172	33 11 198	53 17 222	61 57 292
95	48 26 043	30 45 107	44 46 151	26 00 173	32 58 199	52 49 224	61 19 292
96	48 54 043	31 24 107	45 05 153	26 04 174	32 44 200	52 21 225	60 41 292
97	49 22 043	32 03 108	45 24 154	26 08 175	32 30 201	51 52 226	60 04 293
98	49 50 043	32 42 109	45 41 155	26 11 176	32 14 203	51 22 228	59 26 293
99	50 18 043	33 20 110	45 58 157	26 13 177	31 58 204	50 51 229	58 48 293
100	50 46 043	33 59 111	46 14 158	26 15 178	31 41 205	50 20 230	58 11 294
101	51 14 043	34 37 112	46 28 159	26 16 180	31 24 206	49 48 232	57 33 294
102	51 42 044	35 15 113	46 42 161	26 16 181	31 05 207	49 16 233	56 56 294
103	52 10 044	35 52 114	46 55 162	26 15 182	30 47 208	48 43 234	56 18 294
104	52 39 044	36 30 115	47 07 164	26 13 183	30 27 209	48 10 235	55 41 295
	◆Dubhe	Denebola	REGULUS	◆SIRIUS	RIGEL	ALDEBARAN	◆Mirfak
105	53 07 044	22 28 093	37 07 116	26 11 184	30 07 210	47 36 236	55 04 295
106	53 35 044	23 08 093	37 43 117	26 08 185	29 46 211	47 02 237	54 27 295
107	54 04 044	23 49 094	38 20 118	26 04 186	29 24 212	46 27 239	53 50 296
108	54 32 044	24 30 095	38 56 119	25 59 187	29 02 214	45 52 240	53 13 296
109	55 01 044	25 11 096	39 32 120	25 54 188	28 39 215	45 16 241	52 37 296
110	55 29 044	25 51 096	40 07 121	25 48 189	28 15 216	44 40 242	52 00 297
111	55 58 044	26 32 097	40 42 122	25 41 190	27 51 217	44 04 243	51 24 297
112	56 26 044	27 13 098	41 17 123	25 34 191	27 26 218	43 28 244	50 47 297
113	56 55 044	27 53 099	41 51 124	25 25 192	27 01 219	42 51 245	50 11 298
114	57 23 044	28 34 100	42 25 125	25 16 193	26 35 220	42 14 246	49 35 298
115	57 51 044	29 14 100	42 58 126	25 06 194	26 09 221	41 36 247	48 59 298
116	58 20 044	29 54 101	43 31 127	24 56 195	25 42 222	40 58 248	48 23 299
117	58 48 044	30 34 102	44 04 128	24 45 196	25 15 223	40 20 249	47 47 299
118	59 17 044	31 14 103	44 36 129	24 33 197	24 47 224	39 42 250	47 11 300
119	59 45 044	31 54 104	45 07 130	24 20 198	24 18 224	39 04 251	46 36 300
	◆Kochab	Denebola	◆REGULUS	SIRIUS	RIGEL	◆ALDEBARAN	CAPELLA
120	41 29 021	32 34 104	45 38 132	24 07 199	23 49 225	38 25 251	62 23 283
121	41 43 021	33 13 105	46 08 133	23 53 201	23 20 226	37 46 252	61 43 283
122	41 58 021	33 53 106	46 38 134	23 38 202	22 50 227	37 07 253	61 04 284
123	42 13 021	34 32 107	47 07 135	23 23 203	22 20 228	36 28 254	60 24 284
124	42 28 022	35 11 108	47 36 137	23 07 204	21 49 229	35 48 255	59 44 285
125	42 43 022	35 50 109	48 03 138	22 50 205	21 18 230	35 09 256	59 05 285
126	42 58 022	36 28 110	48 30 139	22 33 206	20 46 231	34 29 257	58 25 286
127	43 14 022	37 07 111	48 57 140	22 15 207	20 14 232	33 49 258	57 46 286
128	43 29 022	37 45 111	49 23 142	21 56 207	19 42 233	33 09 258	57 07 287
129	43 44 022	38 23 112	49 47 143	21 37 208	19 09 234	32 29 259	56 28 287
130	44 00 022	39 01 113	50 12 145	21 17 209	18 36 234	31 49 260	55 48 287
131	44 16 022	39 38 114	50 35 146	20 57 210	18 03 235	31 08 261	55 09 288
132	44 31 023	40 15 115	50 57 147	20 36 211	17 29 236	30 28 262	54 31 288
133	44 47 023	40 52 116	51 19 149	20 14 212	16 55 237	29 47 262	53 52 289
134	45 03 023	41 28 117	51 40 150	19 52 213	16 20 238	29 07 263	53 13 289
	◆Kochab	ARCTURUS	Denebola	◆REGULUS	SIRIUS	BETELGEUSE	◆CAPELLA
135	45 19 023	21 11 084	42 05 118	51 59 152	19 30 214	34 20 240	52 34 290
136	45 35 023	21 52 085	42 41 119	52 18 153	19 06 215	33 45 241	51 56 290
137	45 51 023	22 33 086	43 16 120	52 36 155	18 43 216	33 09 242	51 18 290
138	46 07 023	23 13 086	43 51 121	52 53 156	18 18 217	32 33 243	50 39 291
139	46 23 023	23 54 087	44 26 123	53 09 158	17 53 218	31 56 244	50 01 291
140	46 39 023	24 35 088	45 00 124	53 24 160	17 28 219	31 19 244	49 23 292
141	46 55 023	25 16 089	45 34 125	53 38 161	17 02 220	30 42 245	48 45 292
142	47 12 023	25 57 089	46 07 126	53 50 163	16 36 221	30 05 246	48 07 293
143	47 28 024	26 38 090	46 40 127	54 02 164	16 09 221	29 27 247	47 29 293
144	47 44 024	27 19 091	47 13 128	54 12 166	15 42 222	28 50 248	46 52 293
145	48 01 024	28 00 092	47 45 129	54 22 168	15 14 223	28 12 249	46 14 294
146	48 17 024	28 41 092	48 16 131	54 30 169	14 46 224	27 33 250	45 37 294
147	48 33 024	29 22 093	48 47 132	54 37 171	14 17 225	26 55 251	45 00 295
148	48 50 024	30 02 094	49 17 133	54 42 173	13 48 226	26 16 251	44 23 295
149	49 06 024	30 43 095	49 46 134	54 47 174	13 19 227	25 37 252	43 46 296
	◆Kochab	ARCTURUS	◆SPICA	REGULUS	PROCYON	◆BETELGEUSE	CAPELLA
150	49 23 024	31 24 095	15 54 127	54 50 176	38 30 227	24 58 253	43 09 296
151	49 39 024	32 05 096	16 26 128	54 53 178	38 00 228	24 19 254	42 32 297
152	49 56 024	32 45 097	16 58 129	54 54 180	37 30 229	23 40 255	41 56 297
153	50 12 024	33 26 098	17 30 130	54 53 181	36 59 230	23 00 256	41 19 298
154	50 28 024	34 06 098	18 01 130	54 52 183	36 27 231	22 20 256	40 43 298
155	50 45 024	34 47 099	18 32 131	54 49 185	35 55 232	21 40 257	40 07 298
156	51 01 024	35 27 100	19 03 132	54 45 186	35 22 233	21 01 258	39 31 299
157	51 18 024	36 07 101	19 33 133	54 40 188	34 49 234	20 20 259	38 56 299
158	51 34 023	36 48 102	20 02 134	54 34 190	34 16 235	19 40 259	38 20 300
159	51 50 023	37 28 103	20 32 135	54 26 191	33 42 236	19 00 260	37 45 300
160	52 06 023	38 07 103	21 00 136	54 18 193	33 08 237	18 20 261	37 09 301
161	52 23 023	38 47 104	21 29 137	54 08 195	32 33 238	17 39 262	36 34 301
162	52 39 023	39 27 105	21 56 138	53 57 196	31 58 239	16 59 263	35 59 302
163	52 55 023	40 06 106	22 24 139	53 45 198	31 23 240	16 18 263	35 25 302
164	53 11 023	40 45 107	22 50 140	53 32 200	30 47 241	15 37 264	34 50 303
	◆VEGA	ARCTURUS	◆SPICA	REGULUS	PROCYON	◆POLLUX	CAPELLA
165	13 50 047	41 25 108	23 17 141	53 18 201	30 11 242	47 58 261	34 16 303
166	14 20 048	42 03 109	23 42 142	53 03 203	29 35 243	47 17 262	33 41 304
167	14 50 048	42 42 110	24 08 143	52 46 204	28 59 244	46 37 262	33 07 304
168	15 21 049	43 20 111	24 32 143	52 29 206	28 22 245	45 56 263	32 34 305
169	15 52 049	43 59 112	24 56 144	52 11 207	27 45 246	45 16 264	32 00 305
170	16 23 050	44 37 113	25 20 145	51 51 209	27 07 246	44 35 265	31 27 306
171	16 54 051	45 14 114	25 43 146	51 31 210	26 30 247	43 54 266	30 53 306
172	17 26 051	45 52 115	26 05 147	51 10 212	25 52 248	43 13 266	30 20 306
173	17 58 052	46 29 116	26 27 148	50 48 213	25 14 249	42 32 267	29 48 307
174	18 31 052	47 05 117	26 48 150	50 25 215	24 35 250	41 52 268	29 15 307
175	19 03 053	47 42 118	27 08 151	50 02 216	23 57 251	41 11 269	28 43 308
176	19 36 054	48 18 119	27 28 152	49 37 217	23 18 251	40 30 269	28 10 308
177	20 09 054	48 53 120	27 47 153	49 12 219	22 39 252	39 49 270	27 39 309
178	20 42 055	49 29 121	28 06 154	48 46 220	22 00 253	39 08 271	27 07 310
179	21 16 055	50 04 122	28 23 155	48 19 221	21 21 254	38 27 272	26 35 310

 LAT 47°N

LHA ♈	Hc	Zn	Hc	Zn	Hc	Zn	Hc	Zn	Hc	Zn	Hc	Zn	Hc	Zn
	◆DENEB		VEGA		ARCTURUS		◆SPICA		REGULUS		◆POLLUX		CAPELLA	
180	12 03	033	21 50	056	50 38	123	28 41	156	47 52	223	37 46	272	26 04	311
181	12 26	034	22 24	057	51 12	125	28 57	157	47 24	224	37 05	273	25 33	311
182	12 49	034	22 58	057	51 45	126	29 13	158	46 55	225	36 24	274	25 02	312
183	13 12	035	23 32	058	52 18	127	29 28	159	46 26	226	35 44	274	24 32	312
184	13 36	036	24 07	058	52 51	128	29 42	160	45 56	228	35 03	275	24 02	313
185	14 00	036	24 42	059	53 22	130	29 55	161	45 25	229	34 22	276	23 32	313
186	14 24	037	25 17	059	53 54	131	30 08	162	44 54	230	33 41	276	23 02	314
187	14 49	037	25 52	060	54 24	132	30 20	163	44 22	231	33 01	277	22 33	314
188	15 14	038	26 28	060	54 54	134	30 31	165	43 50	232	32 20	278	22 03	315
189	15 39	039	27 03	061	55 23	135	30 42	166	43 18	233	31 40	278	21 34	315
190	16 05	039	27 39	062	55 52	137	30 52	167	42 45	235	30 59	279	21 06	316
191	16 31	040	28 16	062	56 19	138	31 01	168	42 11	236	30 19	280	20 37	316
192	16 57	040	28 52	063	56 46	140	31 09	169	41 37	237	29 39	280	20 09	317
193	17 23	041	29 28	063	57 13	141	31 16	170	41 03	238	28 58	281	19 41	317
194	17 50	041	30 05	064	57 38	143	31 23	171	40 28	239	28 18	282	19 14	318
	◆DENEB		VEGA		Rasalhague		◆ARCTURUS		REGULUS		◆POLLUX		CAPELLA	
195	18 18	042	30 42	064	23 29	097	58 02	144	39 53	240	27 38	282	18 47	319
196	18 45	043	31 19	065	24 10	098	58 26	146	39 17	241	26 58	283	18 20	319
197	19 13	043	31 56	066	24 50	098	58 48	148	38 41	242	26 19	284	17 53	320
198	19 41	044	32 33	066	25 31	099	59 09	149	38 05	243	25 39	284	17 27	320
199	20 09	044	33 11	067	26 11	100	59 30	151	37 28	244	24 59	285	17 01	321
200	20 38	045	33 48	067	26 51	101	59 49	153	36 51	245	24 20	286	16 35	321
201	21 07	045	34 26	068	27 31	102	60 07	155	36 14	246	23 41	286	16 10	322
202	21 36	046	35 04	068	28 11	102	60 24	156	35 37	247	23 01	287	15 45	323
203	22 06	046	35 42	069	28 51	103	60 40	158	34 59	248	22 22	288	15 20	323
204	22 35	047	36 20	069	29 31	104	60 55	160	34 21	248	21 43	288	14 56	324
205	23 05	047	36 59	070	30 11	105	61 08	162	33 43	249	21 05	289	14 32	324
206	23 36	048	37 37	071	30 50	106	61 20	164	33 05	250	20 26	290	14 08	325
207	24 06	048	38 16	071	31 30	106	61 30	166	32 26	251	19 47	290	13 44	325
208	24 37	049	38 55	072	32 09	107	61 40	168	31 47	252	19 09	291	13 21	326
209	25 08	050	39 34	072	32 48	108	61 48	170	31 08	253	18 31	292	12 59	327
	DENEB		◆VEGA		Rasalhague		◆ARCTURUS		Denebola		REGULUS		◆Dubhe	
210	25 39	050	40 13	073	33 26	109	61 54	172	47 42	231	30 29	254	61 18	317
211	26 11	051	40 52	073	34 05	110	61 59	174	47 10	232	29 50	255	60 50	317
212	26 42	051	41 31	074	34 43	111	62 03	176	46 37	233	29 10	255	60 22	316
213	27 14	052	42 10	074	35 22	112	62 05	178	46 04	234	28 30	256	59 54	316
214	27 46	052	42 50	075	35 59	113	62 06	180	45 31	235	27 51	257	59 26	316
215	28 19	053	43 29	076	36 37	114	62 06	182	44 57	236	27 11	258	58 57	316
216	28 52	053	44 09	076	37 14	115	62 04	184	44 23	238	26 31	259	58 29	316
217	29 24	054	44 49	077	37 51	115	62 00	186	43 48	239	25 50	259	58 01	316
218	29 57	054	45 29	077	38 28	116	61 55	188	43 13	240	25 10	260	57 32	316
219	30 31	055	46 09	078	39 05	117	61 49	190	42 37	241	24 30	261	57 04	316
220	31 04	055	46 49	078	39 41	118	61 41	192	42 02	242	23 49	262	56 35	316
221	31 38	056	47 29	079	40 17	119	61 32	194	41 25	243	23 09	263	56 07	316
222	32 12	056	48 09	080	40 52	120	61 22	196	40 49	244	22 28	263	55 38	316
223	32 46	057	48 49	080	41 27	121	61 10	198	40 12	245	21 47	264	55 10	316
224	33 20	057	49 30	081	42 02	123	60 57	200	39 35	246	21 07	265	54 41	316
	DENEB		◆VEGA		Rasalhague		ANTARES		◆ARCTURUS		Denebola		◆Dubhe	
225	33 55	058	50 10	081	42 36	124	13 45	159	60 43	201	38 57	247	54 13	316
226	34 29	058	50 51	082	43 10	125	14 00	160	60 27	203	38 20	248	53 45	316
227	35 04	059	51 31	083	43 44	126	14 13	161	60 10	205	37 42	249	53 16	316
228	35 39	059	52 12	083	44 17	127	14 26	162	59 52	207	37 03	250	52 48	316
229	36 14	060	52 53	084	44 49	128	14 39	163	59 33	209	36 25	250	52 20	316
230	36 50	060	53 33	085	45 21	129	14 50	164	59 13	210	35 46	251	51 51	316
231	37 25	060	54 14	085	45 52	130	15 01	165	58 52	212	35 07	252	51 23	317
232	38 01	061	54 55	086	46 23	132	15 12	166	58 30	214	34 28	253	50 55	317
233	38 37	061	55 36	087	46 53	133	15 22	166	58 06	215	33 49	254	50 27	317
234	39 13	062	56 17	087	47 23	134	15 31	167	57 42	217	33 10	255	49 59	317
235	39 49	062	56 57	088	47 52	135	15 40	168	57 17	219	32 30	256	49 31	317
236	40 25	063	57 38	089	48 21	137	15 48	169	56 51	220	31 50	256	49 03	317
237	41 02	063	58 19	089	48 49	138	15 55	170	56 24	222	31 11	257	48 35	317
238	41 38	064	59 00	090	49 16	139	16 02	171	55 57	223	30 31	258	48 08	318
239	42 15	064	59 41	091	49 42	141	16 08	172	55 28	225	29 50	259	47 40	318
	◆DENEB		ALTAIR		Rasalhague		◆ANTARES		ARCTURUS		Denebola		◆Dubhe	
240	42 52	065	28 08	108	50 08	142	16 13	173	54 59	226	29 10	260	47 13	318
241	43 29	065	28 47	109	50 33	143	16 18	174	54 29	227	28 30	261	46 45	318
242	44 06	066	29 25	110	50 57	145	16 22	175	53 59	229	27 50	261	46 18	318
243	44 44	066	30 04	111	51 20	146	16 25	176	53 28	230	27 09	262	45 51	318
244	45 21	067	30 42	112	51 42	148	16 28	177	52 56	231	26 28	263	45 24	319
245	45 59	067	31 19	113	52 04	149	16 30	178	52 24	233	25 48	264	44 57	319
246	46 36	067	31 57	114	52 24	151	16 31	179	51 51	234	25 07	264	44 30	319
247	47 14	068	32 34	115	52 44	152	16 32	179	51 18	235	24 26	265	44 03	319
248	47 52	068	33 12	115	53 03	154	16 32	180	50 44	236	23 46	266	43 36	320
249	48 30	069	33 48	116	53 21	155	16 31	181	50 09	238	23 05	267	43 10	320
250	49 09	069	34 25	117	53 37	157	16 30	182	49 35	239	22 24	267	42 44	320
251	49 47	070	35 01	118	53 53	158	16 28	183	49 00	240	21 43	268	42 17	320
252	50 25	070	35 37	119	54 07	160	16 26	184	48 24	241	21 02	269	41 51	321
253	51 04	071	36 12	120	54 21	162	16 22	185	47 48	242	20 21	270	41 25	321
254	51 42	071	36 48	121	54 33	163	16 18	186	47 12	243	19 40	270	41 00	321
	◆Schedar		DENEB		ALTAIR		◆Rasalhague		ARCTURUS		◆Alkaid		Kochab	
255	26 45	034	52 21	072	37 22	122	54 45	165	46 35	244	58 26	292	59 28	343
256	27 08	034	53 00	072	37 57	123	54 55	166	45 58	245	57 49	292	59 16	343
257	27 31	035	53 39	072	38 31	124	55 04	168	45 21	246	57 11	293	59 04	343
258	27 55	035	54 18	073	39 04	125	55 12	170	44 43	247	56 33	293	58 51	342
259	28 18	036	54 57	073	39 38	126	55 18	172	44 05	248	55 55	293	58 38	342
260	28 42	036	55 37	074	40 10	127	55 24	173	43 27	249	55 18	294	58 26	341
261	29 06	036	56 16	074	40 43	129	55 28	175	42 49	250	54 41	294	58 13	341
262	29 31	037	56 55	075	41 14	130	55 31	177	42 10	251	54 03	294	57 59	341
263	29 55	037	57 35	075	41 46	131	55 32	178	41 31	252	53 26	295	57 46	341
264	30 20	038	58 14	076	42 16	132	55 33	180	40 52	253	52 49	295	57 32	340
265	30 46	038	58 54	076	42 46	133	55 32	182	40 13	254	52 12	295	57 18	340
266	31 11	039	59 34	076	43 16	134	55 30	184	39 34	255	51 35	296	57 04	340
267	31 37	039	60 14	077	43 45	135	55 27	185	38 54	256	50 58	296	56 50	340
268	32 02	039	60 54	077	44 13	137	55 23	187	38 14	256	50 22	297	56 35	339
269	32 28	040	61 33	078	44 41	138	55 17	189	37 34	257	49 45	297	56 21	339

LHA ♈	Hc	Zn	Hc	Zn	Hc	Zn	Hc	Zn	Hc	Zn	Hc	Zn	Hc	Zn
	◆Mirfak		Alpheratz		◆ALTAIR		Rasalhague		◆ARCTURUS		Alkaid		Kochab	
270	12 30	024	19 26	068	45 08	139	55 10	190	36 55	258	49 09	297	56 06	339
271	12 47	025	20 04	068	45 35	140	55 02	192	36 14	259	48 32	298	55 51	339
272	13 05	026	20 42	069	46 01	142	54 53	194	35 34	260	47 56	298	55 36	338
273	13 23	026	21 20	070	46 26	143	54 43	195	34 54	261	47 20	298	55 21	338
274	13 41	027	21 59	070	46 50	144	54 31	197	34 13	261	46 44	299	55 06	338
275	13 59	027	22 37	071	47 13	146	54 19	199	33 33	262	46 08	299	54 51	338
276	14 18	028	23 16	072	47 36	147	54 05	200	32 52	263	45 33	300	54 35	338
277	14 38	028	23 55	072	47 58	148	53 50	202	32 12	264	44 57	300	54 20	338
278	14 57	029	24 34	073	48 19	150	53 34	204	31 31	265	44 22	300	54 04	337
279	15 17	030	25 13	073	48 40	151	53 17	205	30 50	265	43 46	301	53 48	337
280	15 38	030	25 52	074	48 59	152	52 59	207	30 09	266	43 11	301	53 32	337
281	15 58	031	26 32	075	49 17	154	52 41	208	29 29	267	42 36	302	53 16	337
282	16 19	031	27 11	075	49 35	155	52 21	210	28 48	268	42 01	302	53 00	337
283	16 41	032	27 51	076	49 51	157	52 00	211	28 07	268	41 27	302	52 44	337
284	17 03	032	28 31	077	50 07	158	51 38	213	27 26	269	40 52	303	52 28	337
	◆Mirfak		Alpheratz		◆ALTAIR		Rasalhague		◆ARCTURUS		Alkaid		Kochab	
285	17 25	033	29 11	077	50 22	160	51 16	214	26 45	270	40 18	303	52 12	337
286	17 47	033	29 51	078	50 35	161	50 52	216	26 04	271	39 44	304	51 56	337
287	18 10	034	30 31	079	50 48	163	50 28	217	25 23	271	39 10	304	51 39	337
288	18 33	035	31 11	079	50 59	164	50 03	218	24 42	272	38 36	304	51 23	336
289	18 56	035	31 51	080	51 10	166	49 37	220	24 01	273	38 02	305	51 07	336
290	19 20	036	32 31	081	51 19	167	49 11	221	23 21	273	37 29	305	50 50	336
291	19 44	036	33 12	081	51 28	169	48 44	222	22 40	274	36 55	306	50 34	336
292	20 08	037	33 52	082	51 35	171	48 16	224	21 59	275	36 22	306	50 18	336
293	20 33	037	34 33	083	51 41	172	47 47	225	21 18	276	35 49	307	50 01	336
294	20 58	038	35 13	083	51 46	174	47 18	226	20 37	276	35 17	307	49 45	336
295	21 23	038	35 54	084	51 50	175	46 48	227	19 57	277	34 44	307	49 28	336
296	21 49	039	36 35	085	51 53	177	46 18	229	19 16	278	34 12	308	49 12	336
297	22 14	039	37 16	085	51 54	179	45 47	230	18 36	278	33 39	308	48 55	336
298	22 40	040	37 56	086	51 55	180	45 15	231	17 55	279	33 07	309	48 39	336
299	23 07	040	38 37	087	51 54	182	44 43	232	17 15	280	32 36	309	48 23	336
	Mirfak		◆Alpheratz		Enif		ALTAIR		◆Rasalhague		Alphecca		◆Kochab	
300	23 33	041	39 18	087	46 48	141	51 52	183	44 11	233	35 04	273	48 06	336
301	24 00	041	39 59	088	47 13	142	51 49	185	43 37	234	34 23	274	47 50	336
302	24 27	042	40 40	089	47 38	143	51 45	187	43 04	236	33 42	274	47 33	336
303	24 55	042	41 21	090	48 02	144	51 40	188	42 30	237	33 01	275	47 17	337
304	25 23	043	42 02	090	48 26	146	51 33	190	41 56	238	32 21	276	47 01	337
305	25 51	043	42 43	091	48 48	147	51 26	191	41 21	239	31 40	276	46 45	337
306	26 19	044	43 23	092	49 10	149	51 17	193	40 46	240	30 59	277	46 28	337
307	26 47	044	44 04	092	49 31	150	51 07	194	40 10	241	30 19	278	46 12	337
308	27 16	045	44 45	093	49 51	151	50 57	196	39 34	242	29 38	278	45 56	337
309	27 45	045	45 26	094	50 10	153	50 45	198	38 58	243	28 58	279	45 40	337
310	28 14	046	46 07	095	50 28	154	50 32	199	38 22	244	28 17	280	45 24	337
311	28 44	046	46 48	096	50 45	156	50 18	201	37 45	245	27 37	280	45 08	337
312	29 13	047	47 28	096	51 02	157	50 03	202	37 08	246	26 57	281	44 52	337
313	29 43	047	48 09	097	51 17	159	49 47	204	36 30	247	26 17	282	44 37	337
314	30 13	048	48 49	098	51 31	160	49 31	205	35 52	248	25 37	282	44 21	337
	CAPELLA		◆Hamal		Alpheratz		Enif		◆ALTAIR		VEGA		◆Kochab	
315	14 58	036	25 38	082	49 30	099	51 44	162	49 13	206	62 54	265	44 05	338
316	15 22	037	26 19	083	50 10	100	51 56	164	48 54	208	62 13	266	43 50	338
317	15 47	038	26 59	084	50 51	101	52 07	165	48 35	209	61 32	267	43 34	338
318	16 12	038	27 40	084	51 31	102	52 17	167	48 14	211	60 52	268	43 19	338
319	16 38	039	28 21	085	52 11	102	52 26	168	47 53	212	60 11	269	43 03	338
320	17 03	039	29 01	086	52 51	103	52 34	170	47 31	213	59 30	269	42 48	338
321	17 29	040	29 42	086	53 30	104	52 41	171	47 08	215	58 49	270	42 33	338
322	17 56	040	30 23	087	54 10	105	52 46	173	46 44	216	58 08	271	42 18	339
323	18 22	041	31 04	088	54 49	106	52 51	175	46 20	217	57 27	272	42 03	339
324	18 49	041	31 45	089	55 28	107	52 54	176	45 54	219	56 46	272	41 48	339
325	19 17	042	32 26	089	56 07	108	52 56	178	45 29	220	56 05	273	41 34	339
326	19 44	043	33 07	090	56 46	109	52 57	180	45 02	221	55 24	274	41 19	339
327	20 12	043	33 48	091	57 25	111	52 56	181	44 35	222	54 44	274	41 05	339
328	20 40	044	34 29	091	58 03	112	52 55	183	44 07	224	54 03	275	40 50	340
329	21 09	044	35 09	092	58 41	113	52 52	185	43 38	225	53 22	276	40 36	340
	CAPELLA		◆Hamal		Diphda		Enif		◆ALTAIR		VEGA		◆Kochab	
330	21 37	045	35 50	093	15 20	140	52 48	186	43 09	226	52 41	276	40 22	340
331	22 06	045	36 31	094	15 46	140	52 43	188	42 39	227	52 01	277	40 08	340
332	22 35	046	37 12	095	16 12	141	52 37	189	42 09	228	51 20	277	39 54	340
333	23 05	046	37 53	095	16 37	142	52 30	191	41 38	230	50 40	278	39 40	340
334	23 35	047	38 33	096	17 02	143	52 22	193	41 07	231	49 59	279	39 27	341
335	24 05	047	39 14	097	17 26	144	52 12	194	40 35	232	49 19	279	39 13	341
336	24 35	048	39 55	098	17 50	145	52 02	196	40 02	233	48 38	280	39 00	341
337	25 06	048	40 35	098	18 13	146	51 50	197	39 30	234	47 58	281	38 47	341
338	25 36	049	41 16	099	18 36	147	51 37	199	38 56	235	47 18	281	38 34	342
339	26 07	050	41 56	100	18 58	148	51 24	200	38 23	236	46 38	282	38 21	342
340	26 39	050	42 36	101	19 20	149	51 09	202	37 48	237	45 58	282	38 08	342
341	27 10	051	43 16	102	19 41	150	50 53	203	37 14	238	45 18	283	37 56	342
342	27 42	051	43 56	103	20 01	151	50 36	205	36 39	239	44 38	283	37 43	342
343	28 14	052	44 36	104	20 21	151	50 18	206	36 04	240	43 58	284	37 31	343
344	28 46	052	45 16	105	20 40	152	50 00	208	35 28	241	43 18	285	37 19	343
	◆CAPELLA		ALDEBARAN		◆Diphda		Enif		ALTAIR		◆VEGA		Kochab	
345	29 18	053	15 55	083	20 59	153	49 40	209	34 52	242	42 39	285	37 07	343
346	29 51	053	16 36	083	21 17	154	49 20	211	34 16	243	41 59	286	36 55	343
347	30 24	054	17 17	084	21 34	155	48 58	212	33 39	244	41 20	286	36 43	344
348	30 57	054	17 57	085	21 51	156	48 36	214	33 03	245	40 41	287	36 32	344
349	31 30	055	18 38	085	22 07	157	48 13	215	32 25	246	40 02	287	36 21	344
350	32 03	055	19 19	086	22 23	158	47 49	216	31 48	247	39 23	288	36 09	344
351	32 37	056	20 00	087	22 37	159	47 25	218	31 10	247	38 44	289	35 59	345
352	33 11	056	20 41	088	22 52	160	46 59	219	30 32	248	38 05	289	35 48	345
353	33 45	056	21 21	088	23 05	161	46 33	220	29 54	249	37 27	290	35 37	345
354	34 19	057	22 02	089	23 18	162	46 07	221	29 16	250	36 48	290	35 27	345
355	34 53	057	22 43	090	23 30	163	45 39	223	28 37	251	36 10	291	35 16	346
356	35 28	058	23 24	091	23 41	164	45 11	224	27 59	252	35 32	291	35 06	346
357	36 03	058	24 05	091	23 52	165	44 42	225	27 20	253	34 54	292	34 56	346
358	36 38	059	24 46	092	24 02	166	44 13	226	26 40	253	34 16	292	34 47	346
359	37 13	059	25 27	093	24 11	167	43 43	228	26 01	254	33 38	293	34 37	347

LHA ♈	Hc	Zn	Hc	Zn	Hc	Zn	Hc	Zn	Hc	Zn	Hc	Zn	Hc	Zn
	◆CAPELLA		ALDEBARAN		Hamal		◆Diphda		ALTAIR		◆VEGA		Kochab	
0	37 18	059	26 11	093	55 49	120	25 19	168	25 37	256	32 36	294	33 30	347
1	37 53	060	26 53	094	56 25	121	25 27	169	24 56	256	31 58	295	33 20	347
2	38 29	060	27 34	094	57 00	123	25 34	170	24 16	257	31 20	295	33 11	348
3	39 06	060	28 16	095	57 35	124	25 41	171	23 35	258	30 43	296	33 03	348
4	39 42	061	28 57	096	58 10	125	25 46	173	22 54	259	30 05	296	32 54	348
5	40 18	061	29 39	097	58 43	127	25 51	174	22 13	259	29 28	297	32 46	349
6	40 55	062	30 20	098	59 16	128	25 56	175	21 32	260	28 51	297	32 37	349
7	41 32	062	31 01	098	59 49	130	25 59	176	20 51	261	28 14	298	32 29	349
8	42 09	063	31 43	099	60 21	131	26 02	177	20 10	262	27 37	298	32 22	349
9	42 46	063	32 24	100	60 52	133	26 04	178	19 29	263	27 01	299	32 14	350
10	43 23	063	33 05	101	61 22	134	26 05	179	18 47	263	26 24	300	32 07	350
11	44 00	064	33 46	101	61 51	136	26 06	180	18 06	264	25 48	300	31 59	350
12	44 38	064	34 26	102	62 20	138	26 05	181	17 24	265	25 12	301	31 52	351
13	45 16	065	35 07	103	62 48	139	26 04	182	16 43	266	24 36	301	31 46	351
14	45 53	065	35 48	104	63 14	141	26 02	183	16 01	266	24 01	302	31 39	351
	◆CAPELLA		ALDEBARAN		Hamal		◆Diphda		Enif		◆DENEB		Kochab	
15	46 31	066	36 28	105	63 40	143	26 00	184	35 07	245	46 12	294	31 33	351
16	47 09	066	37 08	106	64 05	145	25 56	185	34 29	246	45 34	294	31 27	352
17	47 47	066	37 48	107	64 28	147	25 52	186	33 51	247	44 56	294	31 21	352
18	48 26	067	38 28	107	64 51	149	25 47	187	33 12	248	44 18	295	31 15	352
19	49 04	067	39 08	108	65 12	151	25 42	188	32 34	249	43 40	295	31 10	353
20	49 43	068	39 47	109	65 32	153	25 35	189	31 55	249	43 02	296	31 04	353
21	50 21	068	40 26	110	65 50	155	25 28	190	31 16	250	42 25	296	30 59	353
22	51 00	068	41 05	111	66 07	157	25 20	191	30 36	251	41 48	297	30 55	354
23	51 39	069	41 44	112	66 23	159	25 11	193	29 57	252	41 10	297	30 50	354
24	52 18	069	42 23	113	66 37	161	25 02	194	29 17	253	40 33	297	30 46	354
25	52 57	070	43 01	114	66 50	163	24 52	195	28 37	254	39 56	298	30 41	354
26	53 36	070	43 39	115	67 01	166	24 41	196	27 57	254	39 20	298	30 38	355
27	54 15	070	44 17	116	67 10	168	24 29	197	27 17	255	38 43	299	30 34	355
28	54 54	071	44 54	117	67 18	170	24 17	198	26 36	256	38 07	299	30 30	355
29	55 34	071	45 31	118	67 24	173	24 04	199	25 56	257	37 30	300	30 27	356
	CAPELLA		◆BETELGEUSE		RIGEL		Hamal		◆Alpheratz		DENEB		◆Kochab	
30	56 13	072	26 35	108	20 31	127	67 28	175	62 35	242	36 54	300	30 24	356
31	56 53	072	27 15	109	21 03	128	67 31	178	61 58	243	36 18	301	30 21	356
32	57 33	072	27 54	110	21 36	129	67 32	180	61 20	244	35 43	301	30 19	357
33	58 12	073	28 33	111	22 08	130	67 31	182	60 42	246	35 07	302	30 16	357
34	58 52	073	29 12	111	22 40	131	67 28	185	60 04	247	34 32	302	30 14	357
35	59 32	074	29 51	112	23 11	132	67 24	187	59 26	248	33 56	302	30 12	358
36	60 12	074	30 29	113	23 42	133	67 18	190	58 47	249	33 21	303	30 11	358
37	60 52	074	31 07	114	24 12	134	67 10	192	58 08	250	32 46	303	30 09	358
38	61 32	075	31 45	115	24 42	135	67 01	194	57 28	251	32 12	304	30 08	359
39	62 13	075	32 23	116	25 12	136	66 50	196	56 49	252	31 37	304	30 07	359
40	62 53	076	33 00	117	25 41	136	66 37	199	56 09	253	31 03	305	30 06	359
41	63 33	076	33 37	118	26 09	137	66 23	201	55 29	254	30 29	305	30 06	359
42	64 14	076	34 14	119	26 37	138	66 08	203	54 49	255	29 55	306	30 06	000
43	64 54	077	34 51	120	27 04	139	65 50	205	54 08	256	29 21	306	30 06	000
44	65 35	077	35 27	121	27 31	140	65 32	207	53 28	257	28 48	307	30 06	000
	◆Dubhe		POLLUX		BETELGEUSE		◆RIGEL		Hamal		◆Alpheratz		DENEB	
45	27 33	027	32 07	082	36 02	122	27 58	141	65 12	209	52 47	258	28 14	307
46	27 53	028	32 48	082	36 38	123	28 23	142	64 51	211	52 06	259	27 41	308
47	28 12	028	33 30	083	37 12	124	28 48	143	64 29	213	51 25	260	27 09	308
48	28 32	028	34 11	083	37 47	125	29 13	144	64 05	215	50 44	261	26 36	309
49	28 52	029	34 52	084	38 21	126	29 37	146	63 40	217	50 03	262	26 04	309
50	29 12	029	35 34	085	38 55	127	30 00	147	63 15	219	49 21	263	25 31	310
51	29 32	030	36 15	086	39 28	128	30 23	148	62 48	221	48 40	263	25 00	310
52	29 53	030	36 57	086	40 01	129	30 45	149	62 20	222	47 59	264	24 28	311
53	30 14	030	37 39	087	40 33	130	31 06	150	61 52	224	47 17	265	23 56	311
54	30 35	031	38 20	088	41 05	131	31 27	151	61 22	226	46 36	266	23 25	312
55	30 57	031	39 02	088	41 36	132	31 47	152	60 52	227	45 54	267	22 54	312
56	31 18	031	39 43	089	42 06	133	32 06	153	60 21	229	45 12	267	22 24	313
57	31 40	032	40 25	090	42 36	134	32 24	154	59 49	230	44 31	268	21 53	313
58	32 02	032	41 07	090	43 06	136	32 42	155	59 17	232	43 49	269	21 23	314
59	32 24	032	41 49	091	43 35	137	32 59	156	58 44	233	43 07	270	20 53	314
	◆Dubhe		POLLUX		SIRIUS		◆RIGEL		Hamal		◆Alpheratz		DENEB	
60	32 47	033	42 30	092	16 57	138	33 16	158	58 10	235	42 26	270	20 24	315
61	33 10	033	43 12	093	17 24	139	33 31	159	57 36	236	41 44	271	19 54	316
62	33 32	034	43 53	093	17 51	140	33 46	160	57 01	237	41 02	272	19 25	316
63	33 56	034	44 35	094	18 17	141	34 00	161	56 25	239	40 21	272	18 57	317
64	34 19	034	45 17	095	18 43	142	34 13	162	55 50	240	39 39	273	18 28	317
65	34 42	034	45 58	096	19 09	143	34 25	163	55 13	241	38 57	274	18 00	318
66	35 06	035	46 40	096	19 33	144	34 37	165	54 37	242	38 16	274	17 32	318
67	35 30	035	47 21	097	19 58	145	34 48	166	54 00	243	37 34	275	17 04	319
68	35 54	035	48 02	098	20 21	146	34 57	167	53 22	245	36 53	276	16 37	319
69	36 18	036	48 43	099	20 45	147	35 06	168	52 44	246	36 11	276	16 10	320
70	36 43	036	49 25	100	21 07	148	35 15	169	52 06	247	35 30	277	15 44	321
71	37 07	036	50 06	101	21 29	149	35 22	171	51 28	248	34 49	278	15 17	321
72	37 32	037	50 46	102	21 51	150	35 28	172	50 49	249	34 07	278	14 51	322
73	37 57	037	51 27	102	22 12	150	35 34	173	50 10	250	33 26	279	14 26	322
74	38 22	037	52 08	103	22 32	151	35 39	174	49 31	251	32 45	280	14 00	323
	◆Dubhe		REGULUS		PROCYON		◆SIRIUS		RIGEL		◆Hamal		Schedar	
75	38 48	037	17 19	091	36 30	127	22 51	152	35 42	175	48 51	252	49 50	310
76	39 13	038	18 01	091	37 03	128	23 10	153	35 45	177	48 12	253	49 18	310
77	39 39	038	18 43	092	37 35	129	23 29	154	35 47	178	47 32	254	48 46	310
78	40 04	038	19 24	093	38 07	130	23 46	155	35 49	179	46 52	255	48 14	310
79	40 30	039	20 06	094	38 39	131	24 03	156	35 49	180	46 11	256	47 43	310
80	40 56	039	20 48	094	39 10	133	24 20	157	35 48	181	45 31	256	47 11	311
81	41 23	039	21 29	095	39 40	134	24 35	158	35 47	183	44 50	257	46 39	311
82	41 49	039	22 11	096	40 10	135	24 50	159	35 44	184	44 09	258	46 08	311
83	42 15	040	22 52	097	40 40	136	25 05	160	35 41	185	43 29	259	45 37	311
84	42 42	040	23 33	097	41 08	137	25 18	161	35 37	186	42 48	260	45 05	312
85	43 09	040	24 15	098	41 36	138	25 31	163	35 32	188	42 07	261	44 34	312
86	43 36	040	24 56	099	42 04	139	25 43	164	35 26	189	41 25	262	44 03	312
87	44 02	040	25 37	100	42 31	141	25 55	165	35 19	190	40 44	262	43 32	312
88	44 30	041	26 18	100	42 57	142	26 06	166	35 12	191	40 03	263	43 02	313
89	44 57	041	26 59	101	43 22	143	26 15	167	35 03	192	39 21	264	42 31	313

LHA ♈	Hc	Zn	Hc	Zn	Hc	Zn	Hc	Zn	Hc	Zn	Hc	Zn	Hc	Zn
	◆Dubhe		REGULUS		PROCYON		◆SIRIUS		RIGEL		ALDEBARAN		◆Mirfak	
90	45 24	041	27 40	102	43 47	144	26 25	168	34 54	194	55 49	217	64 07	293
91	45 51	041	28 21	103	44 11	146	26 33	169	34 44	195	55 23	219	63 29	293
92	46 19	041	29 01	104	44 34	147	26 41	170	34 33	196	54 57	220	62 50	293
93	46 47	042	29 42	104	44 56	148	26 48	171	34 21	197	54 30	222	62 12	293
94	47 14	042	30 22	105	45 18	149	26 54	172	34 08	198	54 01	223	61 34	294
95	47 42	042	31 02	106	45 39	151	26 59	173	33 55	199	53 32	225	60 56	294
96	48 10	042	31 42	107	45 59	152	27 04	174	33 40	201	53 03	226	60 18	294
97	48 38	042	32 22	108	46 18	154	27 08	175	33 25	202	52 33	227	59 40	294
98	49 06	042	33 01	109	46 36	155	27 11	176	33 10	203	52 02	229	59 02	295
99	49 34	042	33 41	109	46 53	156	27 13	177	32 53	204	51 30	230	58 24	295
100	50 02	043	34 20	110	47 09	158	27 15	178	32 36	205	50 58	231	57 46	295
101	50 30	043	34 59	111	47 25	159	27 16	180	32 18	206	50 25	232	57 08	295
102	50 58	043	35 38	112	47 39	161	27 16	181	31 59	207	49 52	234	56 31	296
103	51 27	043	36 16	113	47 52	162	27 15	182	31 39	208	49 18	235	55 53	296
104	51 55	043	36 54	114	48 05	163	27 13	183	31 19	210	48 44	236	55 16	296
	◆Dubhe		Denebola		REGULUS		◆SIRIUS		RIGEL		ALDEBARAN		◆Mirfak	
105	52 23	043	22 30	092	37 32	115	27 11	184	30 58	211	48 09	237	54 38	296
106	52 52	043	23 12	093	38 10	116	27 08	185	30 37	212	47 33	238	54 01	297
107	53 20	043	23 53	094	38 47	117	27 04	186	30 14	213	46 58	239	53 24	297
108	53 49	043	24 35	094	39 24	118	26 59	187	29 52	214	46 22	241	52 46	297
109	54 17	043	25 16	095	40 01	119	26 53	188	29 28	215	45 45	242	52 09	298
110	54 46	043	25 58	096	40 37	120	26 47	189	29 04	216	45 08	243	51 33	298
111	55 14	043	26 39	097	41 13	121	26 40	190	28 39	217	44 31	244	50 56	298
112	55 43	043	27 21	097	41 49	122	26 32	191	28 14	218	43 54	245	50 19	298
113	56 11	043	28 02	098	42 24	123	26 24	192	27 48	219	43 16	246	49 42	299
114	56 40	043	28 43	099	42 59	124	26 15	193	27 21	220	42 38	247	49 06	299
115	57 08	043	29 24	100	43 33	125	26 05	194	26 54	221	41 59	248	48 30	299
116	57 36	043	30 05	101	44 07	126	25 54	196	26 27	222	41 21	249	47 53	300
117	58 05	043	30 46	101	44 40	127	25 42	197	25 59	223	40 42	250	47 17	300
118	58 33	043	31 27	102	45 13	128	25 30	198	25 30	224	40 03	250	46 41	300
119	59 01	043	32 08	103	45 46	130	25 17	199	25 01	225	39 23	251	46 05	301
	◆Kochab		Denebola		◆REGULUS		SIRIUS		RIGEL		◆ALDEBARAN		CAPELLA	
120	40 33	021	32 48	104	46 17	131	25 03	200	24 31	226	38 44	252	62 09	285
121	40 47	021	33 29	105	46 49	132	24 49	201	24 01	227	38 04	253	61 28	285
122	41 02	021	34 09	105	47 19	133	24 34	202	23 31	228	37 24	254	60 48	286
123	41 17	021	34 49	106	47 49	135	24 18	203	23 00	229	36 44	255	60 08	286
124	41 32	021	35 29	107	48 19	136	24 02	204	22 28	229	36 03	256	59 28	286
125	41 47	021	36 09	108	48 48	137	23 45	205	21 56	230	35 23	257	58 48	287
126	42 03	022	36 48	109	49 16	138	23 27	206	21 24	231	34 42	257	58 08	287
127	42 18	022	37 27	110	49 43	140	23 09	207	20 51	232	34 02	258	57 29	288
128	42 33	022	38 07	111	50 09	141	22 50	208	20 18	233	33 21	259	56 49	288
129	42 49	022	38 45	112	50 35	142	22 30	209	19 45	234	32 40	260	56 09	288
130	43 04	022	39 24	113	51 00	144	22 10	210	19 11	235	31 59	261	55 30	289
131	43 20	022	40 02	114	51 24	145	21 49	211	18 37	236	31 18	261	54 50	289
132	43 36	022	40 40	115	51 48	147	21 27	212	18 02	236	30 36	262	54 11	290
133	43 52	022	41 18	115	52 10	148	21 05	212	17 27	237	29 55	263	53 32	290
134	44 07	022	41 56	116	52 32	150	20 42	213	16 52	238	29 14	264	52 53	290
	◆Kochab		ARCTURUS		Denebola		◆REGULUS		SIRIUS		BETELGEUSE		◆CAPELLA	
135	44 23	023	21 05	084	42 33	117	52 52	151	20 19	214	34 50	240	52 14	291
136	44 39	023	21 46	085	43 10	119	53 12	153	19 55	215	34 14	241	51 35	291
137	44 55	023	22 28	085	43 46	120	53 30	154	19 31	216	33 37	242	50 56	292
138	45 12	023	23 10	086	44 22	121	53 48	156	19 06	217	33 00	243	50 17	292
139	45 28	023	23 51	087	44 58	122	54 04	157	18 41	218	32 23	244	49 39	292
140	45 44	023	24 33	087	45 33	123	54 20	159	18 15	219	31 45	245	49 00	293
141	46 00	023	25 14	088	46 08	124	54 34	161	17 48	220	31 07	246	48 22	293
142	46 17	023	25 56	089	46 42	125	54 47	162	17 21	221	30 29	247	47 44	294
143	46 33	023	26 38	090	47 16	126	55 00	164	16 54	222	29 51	248	47 05	294
144	46 49	023	27 19	090	47 49	127	55 10	166	16 26	222	29 12	249	46 27	294
145	47 06	023	28 01	091	48 22	129	55 20	167	15 58	223	28 33	249	45 50	295
146	47 22	023	28 43	092	48 55	130	55 29	169	15 29	224	27 54	250	45 12	295
147	47 38	023	29 24	092	49 26	131	55 36	171	15 00	225	27 15	251	44 34	296
148	47 55	023	30 06	093	49 58	132	55 42	173	14 30	226	26 35	252	43 57	296
149	48 11	023	30 48	094	50 28	134	55 47	174	14 00	227	25 55	253	43 19	297
	◆Kochab		ARCTURUS		◆SPICA		REGULUS		PROCYON		◆BETELGEUSE		CAPELLA	
150	48 28	023	31 29	095	16 30	127	55 50	176	39 11	227	25 15	254	42 42	297
151	48 44	023	32 11	095	17 03	128	55 53	178	38 40	229	24 35	254	42 05	297
152	49 01	023	32 52	096	17 36	129	55 54	179	38 09	230	23 55	255	41 28	298
153	49 17	023	33 34	097	18 08	129	55 53	181	37 37	231	23 15	256	40 51	298
154	49 33	023	34 15	098	18 40	130	55 52	183	37 04	232	22 34	257	40 15	299
155	49 50	023	34 56	099	19 12	131	55 49	185	36 31	233	21 54	258	39 38	299
156	50 06	023	35 37	099	19 43	132	55 45	186	35 58	234	21 13	258	39 02	300
157	50 22	023	36 18	100	20 14	133	55 40	188	35 24	235	20 32	259	38 26	300
158	50 39	023	36 59	101	20 44	134	55 33	190	34 50	236	19 51	260	37 50	300
159	50 55	023	37 40	102	21 14	135	55 25	192	34 15	237	19 10	261	37 14	301
160	51 11	023	38 21	103	21 43	136	55 16	193	33 40	238	18 29	261	36 38	301
161	51 27	023	39 02	103	22 12	137	55 06	195	33 05	239	17 48	262	36 03	302
162	51 44	023	39 42	104	22 41	137	54 55	197	32 29	240	17 06	263	35 27	302
163	52 00	023	40 22	105	23 09	138	54 42	198	31 53	241	16 25	264	34 52	303
164	52 16	022	41 02	106	23 36	139	54 28	200	31 16	242	15 43	264	34 17	303
	◆VEGA		ARCTURUS		◆SPICA		REGULUS		PROCYON		◆POLLUX		CAPELLA	
165	13 09	047	41 42	107	24 03	140	54 14	202	30 39	242	48 07	262	33 43	304
166	13 39	047	42 22	108	24 29	141	53 58	203	30 02	243	47 26	263	33 08	304
167	14 10	048	43 02	109	24 55	142	53 41	205	29 25	244	46 44	263	32 34	305
168	14 41	049	43 41	110	25 20	143	53 23	206	28 47	245	46 03	264	31 59	305
169	15 13	049	44 20	111	25 45	144	53 04	208	28 09	246	45 21	265	31 25	306
170	15 44	050	44 59	112	26 09	145	52 44	209	27 31	247	44 40	266	30 52	306
171	16 16	050	45 38	113	26 33	146	52 23	211	26 53	248	43 58	267	30 18	306
172	16 49	051	46 16	114	26 55	147	52 01	212	26 14	249	43 17	267	29 44	307
173	17 21	052	46 54	115	27 18	148	51 38	214	25 35	249	42 35	268	29 11	307
174	17 54	052	47 32	116	27 39	149	51 14	215	24 56	250	41 53	269	28 38	308
175	18 27	053	48 09	117	28 00	150	50 50	217	24 17	251	41 12	270	28 06	308
176	19 00	053	48 46	118	28 21	151	50 25	218	23 37	252	40 30	270	27 33	309
177	19 34	054	49 23	119	28 40	152	49 59	219	22 57	253	39 48	271	27 01	309
178	20 08	054	49 59	120	28 59	153	49 32	221	22 18	254	39 07	272	26 29	310
179	20 42	055	50 35	121	29 18	155	49 04	222	21 37	254	38 25	272	25 57	310

 LAT 46°N

LHA ♈	Hc	Zn	Hc	Zn	Hc	Zn	Hc	Zn	Hc	Zn	Hc	Zn	Hc	Zn
	◆DENEB		VEGA		ARCTURUS		◆SPICA		REGULUS		◆POLLUX		CAPELLA	
180	11 13	033	21 16	056	51 10	122	29 35	156	48 36	223	37 43	273	25 25	311
181	11 36	034	21 50	056	51 45	124	29 52	157	48 07	225	37 02	274	24 54	311
182	11 59	034	22 25	057	52 20	125	30 08	158	47 37	226	36 20	274	24 23	312
183	12 23	035	23 00	057	52 54	126	30 24	159	47 07	227	35 39	275	23 52	312
184	12 47	035	23 35	058	53 27	127	30 38	160	46 36	228	34 57	276	23 21	313
185	13 11	036	24 11	058	54 00	129	30 52	161	46 04	230	34 16	276	22 51	313
186	13 36	037	24 46	059	54 32	130	31 05	162	45 32	231	33 34	277	22 20	314
187	14 01	037	25 22	060	55 04	131	31 18	163	45 00	232	32 53	278	21 51	314
188	14 26	038	25 58	060	55 35	133	31 29	164	44 27	233	32 12	278	21 21	315
189	14 52	038	26 34	061	56 05	134	31 40	166	43 53	234	31 31	279	20 52	316
190	15 18	039	27 11	061	56 35	136	31 50	167	43 19	235	30 49	280	20 23	316
191	15 44	039	27 47	062	57 04	137	31 59	168	42 44	236	30 08	280	19 54	317
192	16 11	040	28 24	062	57 32	139	32 08	169	42 10	237	29 27	281	19 25	317
193	16 38	041	29 01	063	57 59	140	32 15	170	41 34	239	28 47	282	18 57	318
194	17 05	041	29 38	063	58 25	142	32 22	171	40 58	240	28 06	282	18 29	318
	◆DENEB		VEGA		Rasalhague		◆ARCTURUS		REGULUS		◆POLLUX		CAPELLA	
195	17 33	042	30 16	064	23 36	096	58 51	143	40 22	241	27 25	283	18 02	319
196	18 01	042	30 53	064	24 17	097	59 15	145	39 46	242	26 45	284	17 34	319
197	18 29	043	31 31	065	24 59	098	59 38	147	39 09	243	26 04	284	17 07	320
198	18 57	043	32 09	066	25 40	099	60 01	148	38 32	244	25 24	285	16 41	320
199	19 26	044	32 47	066	26 21	099	60 22	150	37 54	245	24 44	285	16 14	321
200	19 55	044	33 25	067	27 02	100	60 42	152	37 17	245	24 03	286	15 48	322
201	20 25	045	34 03	067	27 43	101	61 01	154	36 39	246	23 23	287	15 22	322
202	20 54	046	34 42	068	28 24	102	61 19	156	36 00	247	22 44	287	14 57	323
203	21 24	046	35 20	068	29 05	103	61 36	158	35 22	248	22 04	288	14 32	323
204	21 54	047	35 59	069	29 45	103	61 51	159	34 43	249	21 24	289	14 07	324
205	22 25	047	36 38	069	30 26	104	62 05	161	34 04	250	20 45	289	13 43	324
206	22 55	048	37 17	070	31 06	105	62 17	163	33 24	251	20 06	290	13 19	325
207	23 26	048	37 56	070	31 46	106	62 29	165	32 45	252	19 27	291	12 55	326
208	23 57	049	38 35	071	32 26	107	62 38	167	32 05	253	18 48	291	12 32	326
209	24 29	049	39 15	071	33 06	108	62 47	169	31 25	253	18 09	292	12 09	327
	DENEB		◆VEGA		Rasalhague		◆ARCTURUS		Denebola		REGULUS		◆Dubhe	
210	25 00	050	39 54	072	33 46	108	62 54	172	48 19	232	30 45	254	60 34	318
211	25 32	050	40 34	072	34 25	109	62 59	174	47 47	233	30 05	255	60 06	318
212	26 05	051	41 14	073	35 04	110	63 03	176	47 13	234	29 25	256	59 38	318
213	26 37	051	41 54	074	35 43	111	63 05	178	46 39	235	28 44	257	59 10	318
214	27 09	052	42 34	074	36 22	112	63 06	180	46 05	236	28 04	258	58 42	317
215	27 42	052	43 14	075	37 01	113	63 06	182	45 30	237	27 23	258	58 14	317
216	28 15	053	43 54	075	37 39	114	63 04	184	44 55	238	26 42	259	57 45	317
217	28 49	053	44 35	076	38 17	115	63 00	186	44 19	239	26 01	260	57 17	317
218	29 22	054	45 15	076	38 55	116	62 55	188	43 43	241	25 20	261	56 49	317
219	29 56	054	45 56	077	39 32	117	62 48	190	43 06	242	24 39	261	56 20	317
220	30 30	055	46 36	077	40 09	118	62 40	192	42 30	243	23 58	262	55 52	317
221	31 04	055	47 17	078	40 46	119	62 30	194	41 52	244	23 16	263	55 23	317
222	31 38	056	47 58	079	41 22	120	62 19	196	41 15	245	22 35	264	54 55	317
223	32 13	056	48 39	079	41 58	121	62 07	198	40 37	246	21 53	264	54 26	317
224	32 47	057	49 20	080	42 34	122	61 53	200	39 59	247	21 12	265	53 58	317
	DENEB		◆VEGA		Rasalhague		ANTARES		◆ARCTURUS		Denebola		◆Dubhe	
225	33 22	057	50 01	080	43 09	123	14 42	159	61 38	202	39 21	247	53 29	317
226	33 57	058	50 42	081	43 44	124	14 56	160	61 22	204	38 42	248	53 01	317
227	34 33	058	51 23	081	44 18	125	15 10	161	61 04	206	38 03	249	52 33	317
228	35 08	058	52 04	082	44 52	126	15 23	162	60 46	208	37 24	250	52 04	317
229	35 44	059	52 46	083	45 26	127	15 36	163	60 26	210	36 45	251	51 36	317
230	36 19	059	53 27	083	45 59	128	15 48	164	60 05	211	36 05	252	51 08	317
231	36 55	060	54 08	084	46 31	130	15 59	165	59 42	213	35 25	253	50 39	317
232	37 31	060	54 50	084	47 03	131	16 10	166	59 19	215	34 45	254	50 11	317
233	38 08	061	55 31	085	47 34	132	16 20	166	58 55	216	34 05	255	49 43	318
234	38 44	061	56 13	086	48 05	133	16 30	167	58 30	218	33 25	255	49 15	318
235	39 21	062	56 54	086	48 35	135	16 38	168	58 04	220	32 45	256	48 47	318
236	39 57	062	57 36	087	49 04	136	16 47	169	57 37	221	32 04	257	48 19	318
237	40 34	063	58 18	088	49 33	137	16 54	170	57 09	223	31 23	258	47 51	318
238	41 11	063	58 59	088	50 01	138	17 01	171	56 40	224	30 43	259	47 23	318
239	41 49	063	59 41	089	50 28	140	17 07	172	56 11	226	30 02	259	46 55	318
	◆DENEB		ALTAIR		Rasalhague		◆ANTARES		ARCTURUS		Denebola		◆Dubhe	
240	42 26	064	28 27	108	50 55	141	17 13	173	55 40	227	29 21	260	46 28	319
241	43 03	064	29 06	109	51 21	143	17 17	174	55 10	228	28 40	261	46 00	319
242	43 41	065	29 46	110	51 45	144	17 22	175	54 38	230	27 58	262	45 33	319
243	44 19	065	30 25	110	52 10	145	17 25	176	54 06	231	27 17	263	45 05	319
244	44 57	066	31 04	111	52 33	147	17 28	177	53 33	232	26 36	263	44 38	319
245	45 35	066	31 42	112	52 55	148	17 30	178	53 00	234	25 54	264	44 11	320
246	46 13	066	32 21	113	53 17	150	17 31	179	52 26	235	25 13	265	43 44	320
247	46 51	067	32 59	114	53 37	151	17 32	179	51 51	236	24 31	266	43 17	320
248	47 30	067	33 37	115	53 56	153	17 32	180	51 17	237	23 50	266	42 51	320
249	48 08	068	34 15	116	54 15	155	17 31	181	50 41	239	23 08	267	42 24	320
250	48 47	068	34 52	117	54 32	156	17 30	182	50 05	240	22 26	268	41 57	321
251	49 26	069	35 29	118	54 49	158	17 28	183	49 29	241	21 45	269	41 31	321
252	50 04	069	36 06	119	55 04	159	17 25	184	48 53	242	21 03	269	41 05	321
253	50 43	069	36 42	120	55 18	161	17 22	185	48 16	243	20 21	270	40 39	321
254	51 22	070	37 18	121	55 31	163	17 18	186	47 38	244	19 40	271	40 13	322
	◆Schedar		DENEB		ALTAIR		◆Rasalhague		ARCTURUS		◆Alkaid		Kochab	
255	25 55	034	52 02	070	37 54	122	55 43	164	47 01	245	58 03	294	58 30	344
256	26 18	034	52 41	071	38 29	123	55 53	166	46 23	246	57 25	294	58 18	343
257	26 42	034	53 20	071	39 04	124	56 03	168	45 44	247	56 47	294	58 06	343
258	27 05	035	54 00	072	39 39	125	56 11	170	45 06	248	56 09	294	57 54	343
259	27 29	035	54 39	072	40 13	126	56 18	171	44 27	249	55 31	295	57 41	342
260	27 54	036	55 19	072	40 46	127	56 23	173	43 48	250	54 53	295	57 29	342
261	28 18	036	55 59	073	41 20	128	56 28	175	43 09	251	54 15	295	57 16	342
262	28 43	037	56 39	073	41 52	129	56 31	177	42 29	252	53 38	296	57 02	341
263	29 08	037	57 19	074	42 24	130	56 32	178	41 49	253	53 00	296	56 49	341
264	29 33	037	57 59	074	42 56	131	56 33	180	41 09	254	52 23	296	56 35	341
265	29 58	038	58 39	074	43 27	132	56 32	182	40 29	255	51 46	297	56 22	341
266	30 24	038	59 19	075	43 58	134	56 30	184	39 49	256	51 08	297	56 08	340
267	30 50	039	59 59	075	44 28	135	56 27	185	39 09	256	50 31	297	55 53	340
268	31 16	039	60 40	076	44 57	136	56 22	187	38 28	257	49 54	298	55 39	340
269	31 42	039	61 20	076	45 26	137	56 16	189	37 47	258	49 17	298	55 25	340

LHA ♈	Hc	Zn	Hc	Zn	Hc	Zn	Hc	Zn	Hc	Zn	Hc	Zn	Hc	Zn
	◆Mirfak		Alpheratz		◆ALTAIR		Rasalhague		◆ARCTURUS		Alkaid		Kochab	
270	11 36	024	19 03	067	45 54	138	56 09	191	37 06	259	48 41	298	55 10	339
271	11 53	025	19 42	068	46 21	140	56 01	192	36 25	260	48 04	299	54 55	339
272	12 11	025	20 20	069	46 47	141	55 51	194	35 44	261	47 27	299	54 40	339
273	12 29	026	20 59	069	47 13	142	55 40	196	35 03	261	46 51	299	54 25	339
274	12 47	027	21 38	070	47 38	144	55 28	198	34 22	262	46 15	300	54 10	339
275	13 06	027	22 17	070	48 03	145	55 15	199	33 41	263	45 39	300	53 55	338
276	13 25	028	22 57	071	48 26	146	55 01	201	32 59	264	45 03	300	53 39	338
277	13 45	028	23 36	072	48 49	148	54 46	203	32 18	264	44 27	301	53 24	338
278	14 05	029	24 16	072	49 11	149	54 29	204	31 36	265	43 51	301	53 08	338
279	14 25	029	24 56	073	49 32	150	54 12	206	30 55	266	43 15	302	52 53	338
280	14 46	030	25 36	074	49 52	152	53 53	207	30 13	267	42 40	302	52 37	338
281	15 07	031	26 16	074	50 11	153	53 33	209	29 32	267	42 05	302	52 21	338
282	15 28	031	26 56	075	50 29	155	53 13	210	28 50	268	41 29	303	52 05	337
283	15 50	032	27 36	075	50 46	156	52 51	212	28 08	269	40 54	303	51 49	337
284	16 12	032	28 17	076	51 03	158	52 29	213	27 27	270	40 20	303	51 33	337
	◆Mirfak		Alpheratz		◆ALTAIR		Rasalhague		◆ARCTURUS		Alkaid		Kochab	
285	16 34	033	28 57	077	51 18	159	52 05	215	26 45	270	39 45	304	51 17	337
286	16 57	033	29 38	077	51 32	161	51 41	216	26 03	271	39 10	304	51 01	337
287	17 20	034	30 18	078	51 45	162	51 16	218	25 22	272	38 36	305	50 44	337
288	17 43	034	30 59	079	51 57	164	50 50	219	24 40	272	38 02	305	50 28	337
289	18 07	035	31 40	079	52 08	166	50 23	220	23 58	273	37 28	305	50 12	337
290	18 31	035	32 21	080	52 18	167	49 56	222	23 17	274	36 54	306	49 55	337
291	18 55	036	33 02	081	52 27	169	49 28	223	22 35	275	36 20	306	49 39	337
292	19 20	037	33 43	081	52 34	170	48 59	224	21 54	275	35 47	307	49 23	337
293	19 45	037	34 25	082	52 40	172	48 29	226	21 12	276	35 13	307	49 06	337
294	20 10	038	35 06	083	52 46	174	47 59	227	20 31	277	34 40	308	48 50	337
295	20 36	038	35 47	083	52 50	175	47 28	228	19 49	277	34 07	308	48 33	337
296	21 02	039	36 29	084	52 52	177	46 57	229	19 08	278	33 35	308	48 17	337
297	21 28	039	37 10	085	52 54	179	46 25	231	18 27	279	33 02	309	48 00	337
298	21 54	040	37 52	085	52 55	180	45 53	232	17 46	279	32 30	309	47 44	337
299	22 21	040	38 33	086	52 54	182	45 20	233	17 05	280	31 57	310	47 28	337
	Mirfak		◆Alpheratz		Enif		ALTAIR		◆Rasalhague		Alphecca		◆Kochab	
300	22 48	041	39 15	087	47 34	140	52 52	183	44 46	234	35 00	274	47 11	337
301	23 15	041	39 56	087	48 00	141	52 49	185	44 12	235	34 19	274	46 55	337
302	23 43	042	40 38	088	48 26	142	52 44	187	43 38	236	33 37	275	46 38	337
303	24 10	042	41 20	089	48 51	144	52 39	188	43 03	237	32 56	276	46 22	337
304	24 39	043	42 01	089	49 15	145	52 32	190	42 27	238	32 14	276	46 06	337
305	25 07	043	42 43	090	49 38	147	52 25	192	41 52	239	31 33	277	45 49	337
306	25 35	044	43 25	091	50 01	148	52 16	193	41 16	241	30 51	278	45 33	337
307	26 04	044	44 06	092	50 23	149	52 06	195	40 39	242	30 10	278	45 17	337
308	26 33	044	44 48	092	50 43	151	51 54	196	40 02	243	29 29	279	45 01	337
309	27 03	045	45 30	093	51 03	152	51 42	198	39 25	243	28 48	280	44 45	337
310	27 32	045	46 11	094	51 22	154	51 29	199	38 48	244	28 07	280	44 29	337
311	28 02	046	46 53	095	51 40	155	51 14	201	38 10	245	27 26	281	44 13	338
312	28 32	046	47 34	095	51 57	157	50 59	203	37 32	246	26 45	282	43 57	338
313	29 02	047	48 16	096	52 13	158	50 42	204	36 54	247	26 04	282	43 41	338
314	29 33	047	48 57	097	52 28	160	50 25	205	36 15	248	25 24	283	43 25	338
	CAPELLA		◆Hamal		Alpheratz		Enif		◆ALTAIR		VEGA		◆Kochab	
315	14 10	036	25 30	082	49 39	098	52 41	162	50 07	207	62 58	267	43 10	338
316	14 34	037	26 11	082	50 20	099	52 54	163	49 47	208	62 16	268	42 54	338
317	15 00	037	26 52	083	51 01	099	53 05	165	49 27	210	61 34	269	42 39	338
318	15 25	038	27 34	084	51 42	100	53 16	166	49 06	211	60 53	270	42 23	338
319	15 51	038	28 15	084	52 23	101	53 25	168	48 44	213	60 11	270	42 08	338
320	16 17	039	28 57	085	53 04	102	53 33	170	48 21	214	59 29	271	41 52	339
321	16 43	040	29 38	086	53 45	103	53 40	171	47 57	215	58 48	272	41 37	339
322	17 10	040	30 20	087	54 25	104	53 46	173	47 32	217	58 06	272	41 22	339
323	17 37	041	31 01	087	55 05	105	53 50	175	47 07	218	57 25	273	41 07	339
324	18 04	041	31 43	088	55 46	106	53 54	176	46 41	219	56 43	274	40 52	339
325	18 32	042	32 25	089	56 26	107	53 56	178	46 14	221	56 01	274	40 38	339
326	19 00	042	33 06	089	57 05	108	53 57	180	45 47	222	55 20	275	40 23	340
327	19 28	043	33 48	090	57 45	109	53 56	181	45 19	223	54 38	276	40 08	340
328	19 57	043	34 30	091	58 24	110	53 55	183	44 50	224	53 57	276	39 54	340
329	20 26	044	35 11	092	59 03	111	53 52	185	44 20	226	53 15	277	39 40	340
	CAPELLA		◆Hamal		Diphda		Enif		◆ALTAIR		VEGA		◆Kochab	
330	20 55	045	35 53	092	16 05	139	53 48	186	43 50	227	52 34	278	39 26	340
331	21 24	045	36 35	093	16 32	140	53 43	188	43 20	228	51 53	278	39 12	340
332	21 54	046	37 16	094	16 58	141	53 36	190	42 48	229	51 12	279	38 58	341
333	22 23	046	37 58	095	17 24	142	53 29	191	42 17	230	50 30	279	38 44	341
334	22 54	047	38 39	095	17 50	143	53 20	193	41 44	231	49 49	280	38 30	341
335	23 24	047	39 21	096	18 15	144	53 10	195	41 12	232	49 08	280	38 17	341
336	23 55	048	40 02	097	18 39	145	52 59	196	40 38	233	48 27	281	38 03	341
337	24 26	048	40 44	098	19 03	146	52 47	198	40 05	235	47 46	282	37 50	342
338	24 57	049	41 25	098	19 26	147	52 34	199	39 30	236	47 06	282	37 37	342
339	25 28	049	42 06	099	19 49	148	52 20	201	38 56	237	46 25	283	37 24	342
340	26 00	050	42 47	100	20 11	148	52 04	202	38 21	238	45 44	283	37 11	342
341	26 32	050	43 28	101	20 32	149	51 48	204	37 45	239	45 04	284	36 58	342
342	27 04	051	44 09	102	20 53	150	51 30	205	37 10	240	44 23	284	36 46	343
343	27 36	051	44 50	103	21 14	151	51 12	207	36 34	241	43 43	285	36 34	343
344	28 09	052	45 30	104	21 33	152	50 53	208	35 57	242	43 03	285	36 21	343
	◆CAPELLA		ALDEBARAN		◆Diphda		Enif		ALTAIR		◆VEGA		Kochab	
345	28 42	052	15 47	082	21 52	153	50 32	210	35 20	243	42 23	286	36 09	343
346	29 15	053	16 29	083	22 11	154	50 11	211	34 43	243	41 43	287	35 57	344
347	29 48	053	17 10	084	22 29	155	49 49	213	34 06	244	41 03	287	35 46	344
348	30 21	054	17 52	084	22 46	156	49 26	214	33 28	245	40 23	288	35 34	344
349	30 55	054	18 33	085	23 02	157	49 02	216	32 50	246	39 43	288	35 23	344
350	31 29	055	19 15	086	23 18	158	48 38	217	32 12	247	39 04	289	35 12	345
351	32 03	055	19 56	087	23 33	159	48 12	218	31 33	248	38 25	289	35 01	345
352	32 37	055	20 38	087	23 48	160	47 46	220	30 54	249	37 45	290	34 50	345
353	33 11	056	21 19	088	24 02	161	47 19	221	30 15	250	37 06	290	34 39	345
354	33 46	056	22 01	089	24 15	162	46 51	222	29 36	251	36 27	291	34 29	346
355	34 21	057	22 43	089	24 27	163	46 23	223	28 57	251	35 48	291	34 18	346
356	34 56	057	23 25	090	24 39	164	45 54	225	28 17	252	35 10	292	34 08	346
357	35 31	058	24 06	091	24 50	165	45 25	226	27 37	253	34 31	292	33 58	346
358	36 06	058	24 48	092	25 00	166	44 54	227	26 57	254	33 52	293	33 48	347
359	36 42	059	25 30	092	25 10	167	44 23	228	26 17	255	33 14	294	33 39	347

LHA ♈	◆ CAPELLA Hc	Zn	ALDEBARAN Hc	Zn	Hamal Hc	Zn	◆ Diphda Hc	Zn	ALTAIR Hc	Zn	◆ VEGA Hc	Zn	Kochab Hc	Zn
0	36 46	058	26 14	093	56 19	119	26 17	168	25 52	256	32 11	295	32 31	347
1	37 23	059	26 56	093	56 56	120	26 26	169	25 10	257	31 33	295	32 22	348
2	37 59	059	27 39	094	57 32	121	26 33	170	24 29	258	30 55	296	32 13	348
3	38 36	060	28 21	095	58 08	123	26 40	171	23 47	258	30 16	296	32 04	348
4	39 12	060	29 03	095	58 44	124	26 46	172	23 06	259	29 38	297	31 55	348
5	39 49	061	29 46	096	59 19	125	26 51	174	22 24	260	29 01	297	31 47	349
6	40 26	061	30 28	097	59 53	127	26 56	175	21 42	261	28 23	298	31 38	349
7	41 04	061	31 10	098	60 27	128	26 59	176	21 00	261	27 46	298	31 30	349
8	41 41	062	31 52	098	61 00	130	27 02	177	20 18	262	27 08	299	31 23	349
9	42 18	062	32 34	099	61 32	131	27 04	178	19 36	263	26 31	299	31 15	350
10	42 56	063	33 16	100	62 03	133	27 05	179	18 54	264	25 54	300	31 07	350
11	43 34	063	33 57	101	62 34	134	27 06	180	18 12	264	25 18	300	31 00	350
12	44 12	063	34 39	102	63 04	136	27 05	181	17 30	265	24 41	301	30 53	351
13	44 50	064	35 20	102	63 33	138	27 04	182	16 47	266	24 05	302	30 46	351
14	45 28	064	36 02	103	64 01	140	27 02	183	16 05	267	23 29	302	30 40	351

LHA ♈	◆ CAPELLA Hc	Zn	BETELGEUSE Hc	Zn	RIGEL Hc	Zn	◆ Diphda Hc	Zn	Enif Hc	Zn	◆ DENEB Hc	Zn	Kochab Hc	Zn
15	46 06	065	16 32	096	12 01	115	27 00	184	35 32	246	45 47	294	30 33	352
16	46 44	065	17 14	097	12 39	116	26 56	185	34 53	246	45 09	295	30 27	352
17	47 23	065	17 56	098	13 17	116	26 52	186	34 14	247	44 30	295	30 21	352
18	48 02	066	18 38	098	13 55	117	26 47	187	33 35	248	43 52	296	30 16	352
19	48 40	066	19 20	099	14 33	118	26 41	188	32 55	249	43 14	296	30 10	353
20	49 19	067	20 02	100	15 10	119	26 34	189	32 16	250	42 36	297	30 05	353
21	49 58	067	20 44	101	15 47	119	26 27	191	31 36	251	41 58	297	30 00	353
22	50 37	067	21 25	101	16 24	120	26 19	192	30 55	252	41 20	297	29 55	354
23	51 17	068	22 07	102	17 01	121	26 10	193	30 15	253	40 43	298	29 50	354
24	51 56	068	22 48	103	17 37	122	26 00	194	29 35	253	40 05	298	29 46	354
25	52 35	068	23 29	104	18 13	123	25 50	195	28 54	254	39 28	299	29 42	355
26	53 15	069	24 11	104	18 48	124	25 39	196	28 13	255	38 51	299	29 38	355
27	53 54	069	24 52	105	19 23	124	25 27	197	27 32	256	38 14	300	29 34	355
28	54 34	070	25 33	106	19 58	125	25 14	198	26 51	257	37 37	300	29 31	355
29	55 14	070	26 13	107	20 33	126	25 01	199	26 09	257	37 00	300	29 27	356

LHA ♈	◆ CAPELLA Hc	Zn	BETELGEUSE Hc	Zn	RIGEL Hc	Zn	◆ Diphda Hc	Zn	Alpheratz Hc	Zn	◆ DENEB Hc	Zn	Kochab Hc	Zn
30	55 54	070	26 54	108	21 07	127	24 47	200	63 02	244	36 24	301	29 24	356
31	56 34	071	27 34	108	21 40	128	24 32	201	62 24	245	35 47	301	29 21	356
32	57 14	071	28 14	109	22 14	129	24 17	202	61 45	246	35 11	302	29 19	357
33	57 54	071	28 54	110	22 47	130	24 00	203	61 06	247	34 35	302	29 16	357
34	58 34	072	29 34	111	23 19	131	23 44	204	60 27	249	33 59	303	29 14	357
35	59 14	072	30 13	112	23 51	131	23 26	205	59 47	250	33 24	303	29 12	358
36	59 55	072	30 53	113	24 23	132	23 08	206	59 07	251	32 48	304	29 11	358
37	60 35	073	31 32	114	24 54	133	22 49	207	58 27	252	32 13	304	29 09	358
38	61 16	073	32 10	114	25 24	134	22 30	208	57 47	253	31 38	304	29 08	359
39	61 56	073	32 49	115	25 55	135	22 10	209	57 06	254	31 03	305	29 07	359
40	62 37	074	33 27	116	26 24	136	21 49	210	56 25	255	30 28	305	29 06	359
41	63 18	074	34 05	117	26 53	137	21 28	211	55 44	256	29 54	306	29 06	359
42	63 59	074	34 43	118	27 22	138	21 06	212	55 03	257	29 20	306	29 06	000
43	64 40	075	35 20	119	27 50	139	20 43	213	54 22	258	28 45	307	29 06	000
44	65 20	075	35 57	120	28 17	140	20 20	213	53 40	259	28 12	307	29 06	000

LHA ♈	◆ Dubhe Hc	Zn	POLLUX Hc	Zn	BETELGEUSE Hc	Zn	◆ RIGEL Hc	Zn	Diphda Hc	Zn	◆ Alpheratz Hc	Zn	DENEB Hc	Zn
45	26 40	027	31 58	081	36 33	121	28 44	141	19 56	214	52 58	260	27 38	308
46	26 59	027	32 40	082	37 10	122	29 11	142	19 32	215	52 17	260	27 04	308
47	27 19	028	33 22	082	37 45	123	29 37	143	19 07	216	51 35	261	26 31	309
48	27 39	028	34 04	083	38 21	124	30 02	144	18 42	217	50 53	262	25 58	309
49	27 59	029	34 46	083	38 56	125	30 26	145	18 16	218	50 11	263	25 25	310
50	28 20	029	35 28	084	39 30	126	30 50	146	17 50	219	49 29	264	24 53	310
51	28 40	029	36 10	085	40 04	127	31 13	147	17 23	220	48 46	265	24 21	311
52	29 01	030	36 53	085	40 38	128	31 36	148	16 55	221	48 04	265	23 49	311
53	29 22	030	37 35	086	41 11	129	31 58	149	16 27	222	47 22	266	23 17	312
54	29 44	030	38 17	087	41 44	130	32 19	151	15 59	222	46 39	267	22 45	312
55	30 05	031	39 00	087	42 16	131	32 40	152	15 30	223	45 57	268	22 14	313
56	30 27	031	39 42	088	42 47	133	32 59	153	15 01	224	45 15	268	21 43	313
57	30 49	031	40 24	089	43 18	134	33 18	154	14 31	225	44 32	269	21 12	314
58	31 11	032	41 07	090	43 49	135	33 37	155	14 01	226	43 50	270	20 41	314
59	31 34	032	41 49	090	44 18	136	33 54	156	13 31	227	43 07	270	20 11	315

LHA ♈	◆ Dubhe Hc	Zn	POLLUX Hc	Zn	PROCYON Hc	Zn	◆ SIRIUS Hc	Zn	RIGEL Hc	Zn	◆ Hamal Hc	Zn	DENEB Hc	Zn
60	31 56	032	42 32	091	27 53	113	17 41	138	34 11	157	58 44	236	19 41	315
61	32 19	033	43 14	092	28 32	113	18 09	139	34 27	158	58 09	237	19 11	316
62	32 42	033	43 56	092	29 11	114	18 37	140	34 42	160	57 33	239	18 42	316
63	33 06	033	44 39	093	29 49	115	19 04	141	34 56	161	56 56	240	18 13	317
64	33 29	034	45 21	094	30 27	116	19 30	142	35 10	162	56 19	241	17 44	317
65	33 53	034	46 04	095	31 05	117	19 56	143	35 23	163	55 42	242	17 15	318
66	34 17	034	46 46	095	31 43	118	20 22	144	35 35	164	55 04	244	16 47	318
67	34 41	035	47 28	096	32 20	119	20 47	145	35 46	166	54 26	245	16 19	319
68	35 05	035	48 10	097	32 57	120	21 11	146	35 56	167	53 47	246	15 52	320
69	35 30	035	48 52	098	33 34	121	21 35	146	36 05	168	53 08	247	15 24	320
70	35 54	036	49 34	099	34 10	122	21 58	147	36 14	169	52 29	248	14 57	321
71	36 19	036	50 16	099	34 46	123	22 20	148	36 21	170	51 50	249	14 31	321
72	36 44	036	50 58	100	35 22	124	22 42	149	36 28	172	51 10	250	14 04	322
73	37 09	036	51 40	101	35 57	125	23 04	150	36 33	173	50 30	251	13 38	322
74	37 34	037	52 21	102	36 32	126	23 24	151	36 38	174	49 50	252	13 12	323

LHA ♈	◆ Dubhe Hc	Zn	REGULUS Hc	Zn	PROCYON Hc	Zn	◆ SIRIUS Hc	Zn	RIGEL Hc	Zn	◆ Hamal Hc	Zn	Schedar Hc	Zn
75	38 00	037	17 20	090	37 06	127	23 45	152	36 42	175	49 09	253	49 12	310
76	38 25	037	18 02	091	37 40	128	24 04	153	36 45	177	48 29	254	48 40	311
77	38 51	038	18 45	092	38 13	129	24 23	154	36 47	178	47 48	255	48 08	311
78	39 17	038	19 27	093	38 46	130	24 41	155	36 49	179	47 07	256	47 35	311
79	39 43	038	20 10	093	39 18	131	24 58	156	36 49	180	46 26	257	47 03	311
80	40 09	038	20 52	094	39 50	132	25 15	157	36 48	181	45 44	257	46 32	311
81	40 36	039	21 34	095	40 22	133	25 31	158	36 47	183	45 03	258	46 00	312
82	41 02	039	22 17	095	40 52	134	25 47	159	36 44	184	44 21	259	45 28	312
83	41 29	039	22 59	096	41 22	135	26 01	160	36 41	185	43 40	260	44 57	312
84	41 56	039	23 41	097	41 52	136	26 15	161	36 37	186	42 58	261	44 25	312
85	42 23	039	24 23	098	42 21	138	26 28	162	36 31	188	42 16	262	43 54	313
86	42 49	040	25 05	098	42 49	139	26 41	163	36 25	189	41 34	262	43 23	313
87	43 17	040	25 47	099	43 17	140	26 53	164	36 18	190	40 52	263	42 52	313
88	43 44	040	26 29	100	43 44	141	27 04	166	36 11	191	40 10	264	42 21	313
89	44 11	040	27 10	101	44 10	142	27 14	167	36 02	192	39 27	265	41 50	314

LHA ♈	◆ Dubhe Hc	Zn	REGULUS Hc	Zn	PROCYON Hc	Zn	◆ SIRIUS Hc	Zn	RIGEL Hc	Zn	ALDEBARAN Hc	Zn	◆ Mirfak Hc	Zn
90	44 39	040	27 52	101	44 35	144	27 23	168	35 52	194	56 37	218	63 43	295
91	45 06	041	28 34	102	45 00	145	27 32	169	35 42	195	56 10	220	63 04	295
92	45 34	041	29 15	103	45 24	146	27 40	170	35 30	196	55 42	221	62 26	295
93	46 01	041	29 56	104	45 47	148	27 47	171	35 18	197	55 14	223	61 47	295
94	46 29	041	30 37	105	46 09	149	27 53	172	35 05	198	54 45	224	61 09	295
95	46 57	041	31 18	105	46 31	150	27 59	173	34 51	200	54 15	226	60 31	295
96	47 25	041	31 59	106	46 52	152	28 04	174	34 37	201	53 44	227	59 52	296
97	47 53	041	32 40	107	47 11	153	28 08	175	34 21	202	53 13	228	59 14	296
98	48 21	042	33 20	108	47 30	154	28 11	176	34 05	203	52 41	230	58 36	296
99	48 49	042	34 01	109	47 48	156	28 13	177	33 48	204	52 08	231	57 58	296
100	49 18	042	34 41	110	48 05	157	28 15	178	33 30	205	51 35	232	57 20	296
101	49 46	042	35 20	111	48 21	159	28 16	180	33 11	207	51 01	233	56 42	297
102	50 14	042	36 00	111	48 35	160	28 16	181	32 52	208	50 27	235	56 04	297
103	50 42	042	36 39	112	48 49	162	28 15	182	32 32	209	49 52	236	55 26	297
104	51 11	042	37 18	113	49 02	163	28 13	183	32 11	210	49 17	237	54 49	297

LHA ♈	◆ Dubhe Hc	Zn	Denebola Hc	Zn	REGULUS Hc	Zn	◆ SIRIUS Hc	Zn	RIGEL Hc	Zn	ALDEBARAN Hc	Zn	◆ Mirfak Hc	Zn
105	51 39	042	22 32	092	37 57	114	28 11	184	31 50	211	48 41	238	54 11	298
106	52 08	042	23 15	093	38 36	115	28 07	185	31 28	212	48 05	239	53 33	298
107	52 36	042	23 57	093	39 14	116	28 03	186	31 05	213	47 28	240	52 56	298
108	53 05	042	24 39	094	39 52	117	27 59	187	30 41	214	46 51	241	52 18	298
109	53 33	042	25 22	095	40 30	118	27 53	188	30 17	215	46 13	242	51 41	299
110	54 02	042	26 04	095	41 07	119	27 46	189	29 52	216	45 36	244	51 04	299
111	54 30	042	26 46	096	41 44	120	27 39	190	29 27	217	44 57	245	50 27	299
112	54 58	042	27 28	097	42 20	121	27 31	191	29 01	218	44 19	246	49 50	300
113	55 27	042	28 10	098	42 56	122	27 22	192	28 34	219	43 40	247	49 13	300
114	55 55	042	28 52	098	43 32	123	27 13	194	28 07	220	43 01	248	48 36	300
115	56 24	042	29 34	099	44 07	124	27 03	195	27 40	221	42 22	248	48 00	300
116	56 52	042	30 16	100	44 42	125	26 52	196	27 11	222	41 42	249	47 23	301
117	57 20	042	30 58	101	45 16	127	26 40	197	26 43	223	41 02	250	46 47	301
118	57 48	042	31 39	102	45 50	128	26 27	198	26 13	224	40 22	251	46 11	301
119	58 16	041	32 21	102	46 24	129	26 14	199	25 43	225	39 42	252	45 34	302

LHA ♈	◆ Kochab Hc	Zn	Denebola Hc	Zn	◆ REGULUS Hc	Zn	SIRIUS Hc	Zn	RIGEL Hc	Zn	◆ ALDEBARAN Hc	Zn	CAPELLA Hc	Zn
120	39 36	020	33 02	103	46 56	130	26 00	200	25 13	226	39 02	253	61 52	287
121	39 51	020	33 44	104	47 29	131	25 45	201	24 42	227	38 21	254	61 12	287
122	40 06	021	34 25	105	48 00	132	25 30	202	24 11	228	37 40	255	60 31	287
123	40 21	021	35 06	106	48 31	134	25 14	203	23 39	229	36 59	256	59 51	288
124	40 36	021	35 46	107	49 02	135	24 57	204	23 07	230	36 18	256	59 10	288
125	40 51	021	36 27	107	49 31	136	24 39	205	22 34	231	35 37	257	58 30	288
126	41 07	021	37 07	108	50 00	138	24 21	206	22 01	232	34 55	258	57 50	289
127	41 22	021	37 47	109	50 28	139	24 02	207	21 28	232	34 14	259	57 10	289
128	41 38	021	38 27	110	50 56	140	23 43	208	20 54	233	33 32	260	56 30	289
129	41 53	022	39 07	111	51 23	142	23 22	209	20 20	234	32 50	260	55 50	290
130	42 09	022	39 47	112	51 48	143	23 02	210	19 45	235	32 08	261	55 10	290
131	42 24	022	40 26	113	52 14	145	22 40	211	19 10	236	31 26	262	54 30	291
132	42 40	022	41 05	114	52 38	146	22 18	212	18 35	237	30 44	263	53 50	291
133	42 56	022	41 44	115	53 01	147	21 56	213	18 00	238	30 02	264	53 11	291
134	43 12	022	42 22	116	53 23	149	21 32	214	17 24	238	29 20	264	52 31	292

LHA ♈	◆ Kochab Hc	Zn	ARCTURUS Hc	Zn	Denebola Hc	Zn	◆ REGULUS Hc	Zn	SIRIUS Hc	Zn	BETELGEUSE Hc	Zn	◆ CAPELLA Hc	Zn
135	43 28	022	20 58	084	43 00	117	53 46	151	21 09	215	35 20	241	51 52	292
136	43 44	022	21 41	084	43 38	118	54 05	152	20 44	215	34 42	242	51 13	292
137	44 00	022	22 23	085	44 15	119	54 24	154	20 19	216	34 05	243	50 33	293
138	44 16	022	23 05	086	44 52	120	54 43	155	19 54	217	33 27	244	49 54	293
139	44 32	022	23 47	086	45 29	121	55 00	157	19 28	218	32 49	245	49 15	293
140	44 49	023	24 30	087	46 05	122	55 16	159	19 01	219	32 10	246	48 36	294
141	45 05	023	25 12	088	46 41	123	55 31	160	18 34	220	31 31	246	47 58	294
142	45 21	023	25 55	088	47 16	124	55 45	162	18 07	221	30 52	247	47 19	295
143	45 38	023	26 37	089	47 51	125	55 57	164	17 39	222	30 13	248	46 41	295
144	45 54	023	27 19	090	48 26	126	56 09	165	17 10	223	29 34	249	46 02	295
145	46 10	023	28 02	090	48 59	128	56 19	167	16 41	224	28 54	250	45 24	296
146	46 27	023	28 44	091	49 33	129	56 28	169	16 12	224	28 14	251	44 46	296
147	46 43	023	29 27	092	50 05	130	56 35	171	15 42	225	27 34	252	44 08	297
148	47 00	023	30 09	093	50 38	131	56 41	172	15 12	226	26 53	252	43 30	297
149	47 16	023	30 51	093	51 09	133	56 46	174	14 41	227	26 13	253	42 52	297

LHA ♈	◆ Kochab Hc	Zn	ARCTURUS Hc	Zn	◆ SPICA Hc	Zn	REGULUS Hc	Zn	PROCYON Hc	Zn	◆ POLLUX Hc	Zn	CAPELLA Hc	Zn
150	47 32	023	31 34	094	17 06	127	56 50	176	39 52	228	58 32	249	42 15	298
151	47 49	023	32 16	095	17 40	127	56 52	178	39 20	229	57 52	250	41 37	298
152	48 05	023	32 58	096	18 13	128	56 54	179	38 47	230	57 12	251	41 00	299
153	48 22	023	33 41	096	18 46	129	56 53	181	38 15	231	56 32	252	40 23	299
154	48 38	023	34 23	097	19 19	130	56 52	183	37 41	232	55 51	253	39 46	299
155	48 55	023	35 05	098	19 51	131	56 49	185	37 07	233	55 11	254	39 09	300
156	49 11	023	35 47	099	20 23	132	56 45	187	36 33	234	54 30	255	38 32	300
157	49 27	023	36 29	099	20 55	133	56 39	188	35 58	235	53 49	256	37 55	301
158	49 43	023	37 10	100	21 26	133	56 32	190	35 23	236	53 07	257	37 19	301
159	50 00	022	37 52	101	21 56	134	56 24	192	34 48	237	52 26	258	36 43	302
160	50 16	022	38 34	102	22 26	135	56 15	194	34 12	238	51 44	259	36 07	302
161	50 32	022	39 15	103	22 56	136	56 04	195	33 36	239	51 03	260	35 31	302
162	50 48	022	39 56	104	23 25	137	55 52	197	32 59	240	50 21	260	34 55	303
163	51 04	022	40 38	104	23 53	138	55 39	199	32 22	241	49 39	261	34 20	303
164	51 20	022	41 19	105	24 21	139	55 25	200	31 45	242	48 57	262	33 44	304

LHA ♈	◆ Kochab Hc	Zn	ARCTURUS Hc	Zn	◆ SPICA Hc	Zn	REGULUS Hc	Zn	PROCYON Hc	Zn	◆ POLLUX Hc	Zn	CAPELLA Hc	Zn
165	51 36	022	42 00	106	24 49	140	55 09	202	31 07	243	48 15	263	33 09	304
166	51 52	022	42 40	107	25 16	141	54 53	204	30 29	244	47 33	264	32 34	305
167	52 07	022	43 21	108	25 42	142	54 35	205	29 51	245	46 51	264	31 59	305
168	52 23	021	44 01	109	26 08	143	54 16	207	29 12	246	46 08	265	31 25	306
169	52 38	021	44 41	110	26 34	144	53 57	209	28 33	247	45 26	266	30 50	306
170	52 54	021	45 21	111	26 58	145	53 36	210	27 54	247	44 44	267	30 16	306
171	53 09	021	46 00	112	27 22	146	53 14	212	27 15	248	44 01	268	29 42	307
172	53 24	021	46 40	113	27 46	147	52 51	213	26 36	249	43 19	268	29 08	307
173	53 39	021	47 19	114	28 09	148	52 28	215	25 56	250	42 37	269	28 35	308
174	53 54	020	47 57	115	28 31	149	52 03	216	25 16	251	41 54	270	28 01	308
175	54 09	020	48 36	116	28 52	150	51 38	217	24 36	252	41 12	270	27 28	309
176	54 23	020	49 14	117	29 13	151	51 12	219	23 56	252	40 29	271	26 55	309
177	54 38	020	49 51	118	29 33	152	50 45	220	23 15	253	39 47	272	26 22	310
178	54 52	020	50 29	119	29 53	153	50 17	222	22 34	254	39 05	272	25 50	310
179	55 06	019	51 06	120	30 12	154	49 48	223	21 54	255	38 22	273	25 18	311

LHA ♈	Hc Zn	Hc Zn	Hc Zn	Hc Zn	Hc Zn	Hc Zn	Hc Zn
	Kochab	**◆VEGA**	**ARCTURUS**	**◆SPICA**	**REGULUS**	**◆POLLUX**	**CAPELLA**
180	55 20 019	20 42 055	51 42 121	30 30 155	49 19 224	37 40 274	24 46 311
181	55 34 019	21 17 056	52 18 122	30 47 156	48 49 226	36 57 274	24 14 312
182	55 48 019	21 52 056	52 54 124	31 04 158	48 18 227	36 15 275	23 42 312
183	56 01 018	22 27 057	53 29 125	31 20 159	47 47 228	35 33 276	23 11 313
184	56 14 018	23 03 057	54 03 126	31 35 160	47 15 229	34 51 276	22 40 313
185	56 27 018	23 39 058	54 37 127	31 49 161	46 43 230	34 09 277	22 09 314
186	56 40 017	24 15 059	55 11 129	32 02 162	46 10 232	33 27 278	21 39 314
187	56 52 017	24 51 059	55 43 130	32 15 163	45 36 233	32 45 278	21 08 315
188	57 05 017	25 28 060	56 15 132	32 27 164	45 02 234	32 03 279	20 38 315
189	57 17 016	26 05 060	56 47 133	32 38 165	44 28 235	31 21 280	20 09 316
190	57 29 016	26 42 061	57 17 134	32 48 167	43 53 236	30 39 280	19 39 316
191	57 40 016	27 19 061	57 47 136	32 58 168	43 17 237	29 57 281	19 10 317
192	57 51 015	27 56 062	58 16 137	33 06 169	42 41 238	29 16 282	18 41 317
193	58 02 015	28 33 062	58 45 139	33 14 170	42 05 239	28 34 282	18 13 318
194	58 13 014	29 11 063	59 12 141	33 21 171	41 28 240	27 53 283	17 44 318
	◆VEGA	**Rasalhague**	**ARCTURUS**	**◆SPICA**	**REGULUS**	**◆POLLUX**	**Dubhe**
195	29 49 063	23 42 096	59 38 142	33 27 172	40 51 241	27 11 283	66 24 325
196	30 27 064	24 25 097	60 04 144	33 32 174	40 14 242	26 30 284	65 59 325
197	31 05 064	25 07 097	60 28 146	33 37 175	39 36 243	25 49 285	65 35 324
198	31 43 065	25 49 098	60 52 147	33 40 176	38 58 244	25 08 285	65 10 323
199	32 22 065	26 31 099	61 14 149	33 43 177	38 20 245	24 27 286	64 44 323
200	33 01 066	27 12 100	61 35 151	33 45 178	37 41 246	23 47 287	64 18 322
201	33 39 067	27 54 100	61 55 153	33 46 179	37 02 247	23 06 287	63 52 322
202	34 18 067	28 36 101	62 13 155	33 46 181	36 23 248	22 25 288	63 26 322
203	34 58 068	29 17 102	62 31 157	33 45 182	35 44 249	21 45 288	63 00 321
204	35 37 068	29 59 103	62 47 159	33 43 183	35 04 250	21 05 289	62 33 321
205	36 16 069	30 40 104	63 02 161	33 40 184	34 24 251	20 25 290	62 06 321
206	36 56 069	31 21 104	63 15 163	33 37 185	33 44 252	19 45 290	61 39 320
207	37 36 070	32 02 105	63 27 165	33 32 186	33 03 252	19 05 291	61 12 320
208	38 15 070	32 43 106	63 37 167	33 27 188	32 23 253	18 26 291	60 44 320
209	38 55 071	33 24 107	63 46 169	33 21 189	31 42 254	17 46 292	60 17 319
	◆DENEB	**VEGA**	**Rasalhague**	**ANTARES**	**◆ARCTURUS**	**REGULUS**	**◆Dubhe**
210	24 22 049	39 35 071	34 04 108	10 45 146	63 53 171	31 01 255	59 49 319
211	24 54 050	40 16 072	34 45 109	11 08 147	63 59 173	30 20 256	59 21 319
212	25 26 050	40 56 072	35 25 110	11 31 148	64 03 175	29 39 256	58 53 319
213	25 59 051	41 36 073	36 05 110	11 53 149	64 05 178	28 58 257	58 25 319
214	26 32 051	42 17 073	36 44 111	12 15 150	64 06 180	28 16 258	57 57 318
215	27 05 052	42 58 074	37 24 112	12 36 150	64 06 182	27 35 259	57 29 318
216	27 39 052	43 38 074	38 03 113	12 57 151	64 03 184	26 53 260	57 01 318
217	28 13 053	44 19 075	38 42 114	13 17 152	64 00 186	26 11 260	56 33 318
218	28 46 053	45 00 075	39 20 115	13 37 153	63 54 188	25 30 261	56 04 318
219	29 21 054	45 41 076	39 59 116	13 56 154	63 47 191	24 48 262	55 36 318
220	29 55 054	46 23 076	40 37 117	14 14 155	63 39 193	24 06 263	55 08 318
221	30 29 055	47 04 077	41 14 118	14 32 156	63 28 195	23 23 263	54 39 318
222	31 04 055	47 45 077	41 52 119	14 49 156	63 17 197	22 41 264	54 11 318
223	31 39 056	48 27 078	42 29 120	15 06 157	63 04 199	21 59 265	53 42 318
224	32 14 056	49 08 079	43 05 121	15 22 158	62 50 201	21 17 266	53 14 318
	DENEB	**◆ALTAIR**	**Rasalhague**	**ANTARES**	**◆ARCTURUS**	**Denebola**	**◆Dubhe**
225	32 49 057	18 22 096	43 41 122	15 38 159	62 34 203	39 43 248	52 45 318
226	33 25 057	19 04 097	44 17 123	15 52 160	62 17 205	39 04 249	52 17 318
227	34 00 057	19 47 097	44 52 124	16 07 161	61 58 207	38 24 250	51 48 318
228	34 36 058	20 29 098	45 27 125	16 20 162	61 38 209	37 44 251	51 20 318
229	35 12 058	21 11 099	46 02 126	16 33 163	61 18 210	37 04 252	50 52 318
230	35 48 059	21 52 100	46 36 128	16 45 164	60 56 212	36 23 253	50 23 318
231	36 25 059	22 34 100	47 09 129	16 57 165	60 32 214	35 43 254	49 55 318
232	37 01 060	23 16 101	47 42 130	17 08 165	60 08 216	35 02 254	49 27 318
233	37 38 060	23 58 102	48 14 131	17 18 166	59 43 217	34 21 255	48 58 318
234	38 15 060	24 39 103	48 46 132	17 28 167	59 17 219	33 40 256	48 30 318
235	38 52 061	25 20 103	49 17 134	17 37 168	58 49 221	32 59 257	48 02 319
236	39 29 061	26 02 104	49 47 135	17 46 169	58 21 222	32 17 258	47 34 319
237	40 06 062	26 43 105	50 17 136	17 53 170	57 52 224	31 36 258	47 06 319
238	40 44 062	27 24 106	50 46 138	18 00 171	57 23 225	30 54 259	46 38 319
239	41 21 063	28 04 107	51 14 139	18 06 172	56 52 227	30 12 260	46 10 319
	◆DENEB	**ALTAIR**	**Rasalhague**	**◆ANTARES**	**ARCTURUS**	**Denebola**	**◆Dubhe**
240	41 59 063	28 45 107	51 41 140	18 12 173	56 21 228	29 31 261	45 43 319
241	42 37 063	29 25 108	52 08 142	18 17 174	55 49 230	28 49 262	45 15 319
242	43 15 064	30 05 109	52 34 143	18 21 175	55 16 231	28 07 262	44 47 320
243	43 53 064	30 45 110	52 59 145	18 25 176	54 43 232	27 25 263	44 20 320
244	44 32 065	31 25 111	53 23 146	18 28 177	54 09 234	26 42 264	43 53 320
245	45 10 065	32 05 112	53 46 148	18 30 178	53 35 235	26 00 265	43 25 320
246	45 49 066	32 44 112	54 08 149	18 31 179	53 00 236	25 18 265	42 58 320
247	46 27 066	33 23 113	54 29 151	18 32 179	52 24 237	24 36 266	42 31 321
248	47 06 066	34 02 114	54 50 152	18 32 180	51 48 239	23 53 267	42 04 321
249	47 45 067	34 41 115	55 09 154	18 31 181	51 12 240	23 11 268	41 37 321
250	48 24 067	35 19 116	55 27 156	18 30 182	50 35 241	22 28 268	41 11 321
251	49 03 068	35 57 117	55 44 157	18 28 183	49 58 242	21 46 269	40 44 321
252	49 42 068	36 34 118	56 00 159	18 25 184	49 20 243	21 04 270	40 18 322
253	50 22 068	37 12 119	56 15 161	18 22 185	48 42 244	20 21 270	39 52 322
254	51 01 069	37 49 120	56 28 162	18 18 186	48 04 245	19 39 271	39 25 322
	◆DENEB	**ALTAIR**	**Nunki**	**◆ANTARES**	**ARCTURUS**	**◆Alkaid**	**Kochab**
255	51 41 069	38 25 121	13 58 153	18 13 187	47 25 246	57 38 295	57 32 344
256	52 20 069	39 01 122	14 16 154	18 07 188	46 46 247	57 00 295	57 21 344
257	53 00 070	39 37 123	14 34 155	18 01 189	46 07 248	56 22 296	57 09 343
258	53 40 070	40 13 124	14 52 156	17 54 190	45 28 249	55 43 296	56 57 343
259	54 20 071	40 48 125	15 09 157	17 47 191	44 48 250	55 05 296	56 44 343
260	55 00 071	41 22 126	15 25 158	17 39 192	44 08 251	54 27 296	56 31 342
261	55 40 071	41 56 127	15 41 159	17 30 193	43 28 252	53 49 297	56 19 342
262	56 21 072	42 30 128	15 56 160	17 20 194	42 47 253	53 11 297	56 05 342
263	57 01 072	43 03 129	16 11 160	17 10 194	42 07 254	52 33 297	55 52 342
264	57 41 073	43 35 131	16 25 161	16 59 195	41 26 255	51 56 297	55 39 341
265	58 22 073	44 07 132	16 38 162	16 47 196	40 45 255	51 18 298	55 25 341
266	59 02 073	44 39 133	16 51 163	16 35 197	40 04 256	50 41 298	55 11 341
267	59 43 074	45 10 134	17 03 164	16 22 198	39 22 257	50 03 298	54 57 341
268	60 24 074	45 40 135	17 14 165	16 09 199	38 41 258	49 26 299	54 43 340
269	61 05 074	46 09 136	17 25 166	15 55 200	37 59 259	48 49 299	54 28 340

LHA ♈	Hc Zn	Hc Zn	Hc Zn	Hc Zn	Hc Zn	Hc Zn	Hc Zn
	◆Alpheratz	**ALTAIR**	**Nunki**	**◆ANTARES**	**ARCTURUS**	**◆Alkaid**	**Kochab**
270	18 40 067	46 38 138	17 35 167	15 40 201	37 18 260	48 12 299	54 14 340
271	19 19 068	47 06 139	17 44 168	15 25 202	36 36 260	47 35 300	53 59 340
272	19 58 068	47 34 140	17 53 169	15 09 203	35 54 261	46 58 300	53 44 339
273	20 38 069	48 01 142	18 01 170	14 52 203	35 12 262	46 21 300	53 29 339
274	21 17 070	48 27 143	18 08 171	14 35 204	34 30 263	45 45 301	53 14 339
275	21 57 070	48 52 144	18 15 171	14 17 205	33 48 264	45 08 301	52 59 339
276	22 37 071	49 16 146	18 21 172	13 59 206	33 06 264	44 32 301	52 44 339
277	23 17 071	49 40 147	18 26 173	13 40 207	32 23 265	43 56 302	52 28 339
278	23 58 072	50 02 148	18 31 174	13 21 208	31 41 266	43 20 302	52 13 338
279	24 38 073	50 24 150	18 34 175	13 01 209	30 59 267	42 44 302	51 57 338
280	25 19 073	50 45 151	18 38 176	12 40 209	30 16 267	42 08 303	51 41 338
281	25 59 074	51 05 153	18 40 177	12 19 210	29 34 268	41 32 303	51 25 338
282	26 40 074	51 23 154	18 42 178	11 57 211	28 52 269	40 57 303	51 09 338
283	27 21 075	51 41 156	18 43 179	11 35 212	28 09 269	40 21 304	50 54 338
284	28 02 076	51 58 157	18 43 180	11 12 213	27 27 270	39 46 304	50 37 338
	◆Mirfak	**Alpheratz**	**◆ALTAIR**	**Rasalhague**	**◆ARCTURUS**	**Alkaid**	**Kochab**
285	15 44 033	28 43 076	52 14 159	52 54 216	26 44 271	39 11 305	50 21 338
286	16 07 033	29 24 077	52 29 160	52 29 217	26 02 272	38 36 305	50 05 338
287	16 30 034	30 06 077	52 42 162	52 03 219	25 19 272	38 02 305	49 49 337
288	16 54 034	30 47 078	52 55 164	51 36 220	24 37 273	37 27 306	49 33 337
289	17 18 035	31 29 079	53 06 165	51 09 221	23 55 274	36 53 306	49 16 337
290	17 42 035	32 10 079	53 16 167	50 40 223	23 12 274	36 18 306	49 00 337
291	18 07 036	32 52 080	53 25 169	50 11 224	22 30 275	35 44 307	48 44 337
292	18 32 036	33 34 081	53 33 170	49 41 225	21 48 276	35 11 307	48 27 337
293	18 57 037	34 16 081	53 40 172	49 11 227	21 06 276	34 37 308	48 11 337
294	19 23 037	34 58 082	53 45 174	48 40 228	20 24 277	34 03 308	47 54 337
295	19 49 038	35 40 082	53 49 175	48 08 229	19 41 278	33 30 309	47 38 337
296	20 15 038	36 22 083	53 52 177	47 36 230	18 59 278	32 57 309	47 22 337
297	20 41 039	37 04 084	53 54 179	47 03 231	18 18 279	32 24 309	47 05 337
298	21 08 039	37 46 084	53 55 180	46 29 233	17 36 280	31 51 310	46 49 337
299	21 35 040	38 29 085	53 54 182	45 55 234	16 54 280	31 19 310	46 32 337
	Mirfak	**◆Alpheratz**	**Enif**	**◆ALTAIR**	**Rasalhague**	**Alphecca**	**◆Kochab**
300	22 02 040	39 11 086	48 19 139	53 52 184	45 21 235	34 56 274	46 16 337
301	22 30 041	39 53 086	48 47 140	53 48 185	44 46 236	34 14 275	45 59 337
302	22 58 041	40 35 087	49 13 142	53 44 187	44 11 237	33 32 276	45 43 337
303	23 26 042	41 18 088	49 39 143	53 38 189	43 35 238	32 49 276	45 27 337
304	23 54 042	42 00 088	50 04 145	53 31 190	42 58 239	32 07 277	45 10 337
305	24 23 043	42 43 089	50 28 146	53 23 192	42 22 240	31 25 278	44 54 337
306	24 52 043	43 25 090	50 52 147	53 14 193	41 45 241	30 43 278	44 38 338
307	25 21 044	44 08 091	51 14 149	53 03 195	41 07 242	30 01 279	44 22 338
308	25 50 044	44 50 091	51 36 150	52 52 197	40 30 243	29 19 280	44 06 338
309	26 20 045	45 32 092	51 56 152	52 39 198	39 52 244	28 38 280	43 49 338
310	26 50 045	46 15 093	52 16 153	52 25 200	39 13 245	27 56 281	43 33 338
311	27 20 045	46 57 093	52 34 155	52 10 201	38 35 246	27 14 281	43 17 338
312	27 50 046	47 39 094	52 52 156	51 54 203	37 56 247	26 33 282	43 01 338
313	28 21 046	48 22 095	53 08 158	51 37 205	37 16 248	25 51 283	42 46 338
314	28 52 047	49 04 096	53 24 160	51 19 206	36 37 249	25 10 283	42 30 338
	CAPELLA	**◆Alpheratz**	**Enif**	**◆ALTAIR**	**Rasalhague**	**VEGA**	**◆Kochab**
315	13 21 036	49 46 097	53 38 161	51 00 208	35 57 250	62 59 269	42 14 338
316	13 46 037	50 28 097	53 51 163	50 40 209	35 17 251	62 17 270	41 58 338
317	14 12 037	51 10 098	54 03 164	50 19 211	34 37 252	61 35 271	41 43 339
318	14 38 038	51 52 099	54 14 166	49 57 212	33 57 252	60 52 271	41 27 339
319	15 04 038	52 34 100	54 24 168	49 34 213	33 16 253	60 10 272	41 12 339
320	15 30 039	53 16 101	54 32 169	49 10 215	32 36 254	59 27 273	40 57 339
321	15 57 039	53 57 102	54 39 171	48 46 216	31 55 255	58 45 273	40 41 339
322	16 24 040	54 39 103	54 45 173	48 20 217	31 14 256	58 03 274	40 26 339
323	16 52 041	55 20 104	54 50 174	47 54 219	30 33 257	57 20 275	40 11 339
324	17 19 041	56 01 104	54 54 176	47 27 220	29 51 257	56 38 275	39 56 339
325	17 47 042	56 42 105	54 56 178	47 00 221	29 10 258	55 56 276	39 41 340
326	18 16 042	57 23 106	54 57 180	46 31 223	28 28 259	55 14 277	39 27 340
327	18 44 043	58 04 108	54 56 181	46 02 224	27 47 260	54 32 277	39 12 340
328	19 13 043	58 44 109	54 55 183	45 32 225	27 05 260	53 50 278	38 58 340
329	19 42 044	59 24 110	54 52 185	45 02 226	26 23 261	53 08 278	38 43 340
	◆CAPELLA	**Hamal**	**Diphda**	**◆FOMALHAUT**	**ALTAIR**	**◆VEGA**	**Kochab**
330	20 12 044	35 55 092	16 51 139	14 17 167	44 31 227	52 26 279	38 29 340
331	20 41 045	36 37 092	17 18 140	14 26 168	44 00 229	51 44 279	38 15 341
332	21 11 045	37 20 093	17 45 141	14 35 169	43 27 230	51 02 280	38 01 341
333	21 42 046	38 02 094	18 12 142	14 43 170	42 55 231	50 20 281	37 47 341
334	22 12 046	38 45 094	18 38 143	14 50 170	42 22 232	49 38 281	37 33 341
335	22 43 047	39 27 095	19 03 144	14 57 171	41 48 233	48 57 282	37 20 341
336	23 14 047	40 09 096	19 28 145	15 03 172	41 14 234	48 15 282	37 06 342
337	23 45 048	40 51 097	19 52 145	15 08 173	40 39 235	47 34 283	36 53 342
338	24 17 048	41 33 098	20 16 146	15 13 174	40 04 236	46 52 283	36 40 342
339	24 49 049	42 15 098	20 39 147	15 17 175	39 29 237	46 11 284	36 27 342
340	25 21 049	42 57 099	21 02 148	15 20 176	38 53 238	45 30 284	36 14 342
341	25 53 050	43 39 100	21 24 149	15 23 177	38 16 239	44 49 285	36 01 343
342	26 26 050	44 21 101	21 45 150	15 25 178	37 40 240	44 08 285	35 49 343
343	26 58 051	45 02 102	22 06 151	15 27 179	37 03 241	43 27 286	35 36 343
344	27 31 051	45 44 103	22 26 152	15 27 179	36 25 242	42 46 286	35 24 343
	◆CAPELLA	**ALDEBARAN**	**Diphda**	**◆FOMALHAUT**	**ALTAIR**	**◆VEGA**	**Kochab**
345	28 05 052	15 39 082	22 46 153	15 27 180	35 48 243	42 06 287	35 12 344
346	28 38 052	16 21 083	23 05 154	15 27 181	35 10 244	41 25 287	35 00 344
347	29 12 053	17 03 083	23 23 155	15 26 182	34 31 245	40 45 288	34 48 344
348	29 45 053	17 46 084	23 41 156	15 24 183	33 53 246	40 05 288	34 37 344
349	30 19 054	18 28 085	23 58 157	15 21 184	33 14 247	39 24 289	34 25 344
350	30 54 054	19 10 085	24 14 158	15 18 185	32 35 248	38 44 289	34 14 345
351	31 28 054	19 52 086	24 29 159	15 14 186	31 55 249	38 04 290	34 03 345
352	32 03 055	20 35 087	24 44 160	15 09 187	31 16 249	37 25 291	33 52 345
353	32 38 055	21 17 088	24 59 161	15 04 188	30 36 250	36 45 291	33 41 345
354	33 13 056	22 00 088	25 12 162	14 58 188	29 56 251	36 05 292	33 30 346
355	33 48 056	22 42 089	25 25 163	14 52 189	29 15 252	35 26 292	33 20 346
356	34 23 057	23 24 090	25 37 164	14 44 190	28 35 253	34 47 293	33 10 346
357	34 59 057	24 07 090	25 48 165	14 37 191	27 54 254	34 08 293	33 00 346
358	35 34 058	24 49 091	25 59 166	14 28 192	27 14 254	33 29 294	32 50 347
359	36 10 058	25 32 092	26 08 167	14 19 193	26 33 255	32 50 294	32 40 347

LAT 44°N

LHA ♈	Hc	Zn	Hc	Zn	Hc	Zn	Hc	Zn	Hc	Zn	Hc	Zn	Hc	Zn
	◆ CAPELLA		ALDEBARAN		◆ Diphda		FOMALHAUT		ALTAIR		◆ VEGA		Kochab	
0	36 15	058	26 16	092	27 16	168	15 07	194	26 06	257	31 46	295	31 32	347
1	36 51	058	27 00	093	27 25	169	14 57	195	25 24	257	31 07	296	31 23	348
2	37 28	059	27 43	093	27 32	170	14 45	196	24 42	258	30 28	296	31 14	348
3	38 05	059	28 26	094	27 39	171	14 34	196	23 59	259	29 50	297	31 05	348
4	38 42	059	29 09	095	27 45	172	14 21	197	23 17	260	29 11	297	30 56	348
5	39 20	060	29 52	096	27 51	173	14 08	198	22 34	260	28 33	298	30 48	349
6	39 57	060	30 35	096	27 55	175	13 54	199	21 52	261	27 55	298	30 40	349
7	40 34	061	31 18	097	27 59	176	13 40	200	21 09	262	27 17	299	30 31	349
8	41 12	061	32 00	098	28 02	177	13 25	201	20 26	263	26 39	299	30 24	350
9	41 50	061	32 43	099	28 04	178	13 09	202	19 44	263	26 02	300	30 16	350
10	42 28	062	33 26	099	28 05	179	12 53	202	19 01	264	25 24	300	30 08	350
11	43 06	062	34 08	100	28 06	180	12 36	203	18 18	265	24 47	301	30 01	350
12	43 44	063	34 51	101	28 05	181	12 19	204	17 35	265	24 10	301	29 54	351
13	44 23	063	35 33	102	28 04	182	12 01	205	16 52	266	23 34	302	29 47	351
14	45 01	063	36 15	103	28 02	183	11 42	206	16 09	267	22 57	302	29 41	351
	◆ CAPELLA		BETELGEUSE		RIGEL		◆ Diphda		Enif		◆ DENEB		Kochab	
15	45 40	064	16 38	096	12 26	115	28 00	184	35 56	246	45 22	295	29 34	352
16	46 19	064	17 21	097	13 05	115	27 56	185	35 17	247	44 43	296	29 28	352
17	46 58	064	18 04	097	13 44	116	27 52	186	34 37	248	44 04	296	29 22	352
18	47 37	065	18 47	098	14 23	117	27 46	187	33 57	249	43 26	297	29 16	352
19	48 16	065	19 29	099	15 01	118	27 40	189	33 16	250	42 47	297	29 11	353
20	48 55	066	20 12	099	15 39	118	27 34	190	32 36	251	42 09	297	29 05	353
21	49 34	066	20 54	100	16 17	119	27 26	191	31 55	251	41 31	298	29 00	353
22	50 14	066	21 37	101	16 54	120	27 18	192	31 14	252	40 52	298	28 55	354
23	50 53	067	22 19	102	17 32	121	27 09	193	30 33	253	40 14	299	28 51	354
24	51 33	067	23 01	102	18 09	122	26 59	194	29 51	254	39 37	299	28 46	354
25	52 13	067	23 43	103	18 45	122	26 48	195	29 10	255	38 59	299	28 42	355
26	52 52	068	24 25	104	19 21	123	26 36	196	28 28	255	38 21	300	28 38	355
27	53 32	068	25 07	105	19 57	124	26 24	197	27 46	256	37 44	300	28 34	355
28	54 12	068	25 49	106	20 33	125	26 11	198	27 04	257	37 07	301	28 31	355
29	54 53	069	26 30	106	21 08	126	25 58	199	26 22	258	36 30	301	28 27	356
	◆ CAPELLA		BETELGEUSE		RIGEL		◆ Diphda		Alpheratz		◆ DENEB		Kochab	
30	55 33	069	27 12	107	21 43	127	25 43	200	63 28	245	35 53	301	28 24	356
31	56 13	069	27 53	108	22 17	128	25 28	201	62 49	247	35 16	302	28 22	356
32	56 53	069	28 34	109	22 51	128	25 12	202	62 09	248	34 39	302	28 19	357
33	57 34	070	29 15	110	23 25	129	24 56	203	61 29	249	34 03	303	28 17	357
34	58 14	070	29 55	110	23 58	130	24 38	204	60 48	250	33 27	303	28 14	357
35	58 55	070	30 35	111	24 31	131	24 21	205	60 07	251	32 51	304	28 13	358
36	59 36	071	31 16	112	25 03	132	24 02	206	59 26	252	32 15	304	28 11	358
37	60 17	071	31 55	113	25 35	133	23 43	207	58 45	253	31 39	304	28 09	358
38	60 57	071	32 35	114	26 06	134	23 23	208	58 04	254	31 04	305	28 08	359
39	61 38	072	33 14	115	26 37	135	23 02	209	57 22	255	30 29	305	28 07	359
40	62 19	072	33 53	116	27 07	136	22 41	210	56 40	256	29 53	306	28 06	359
41	63 00	072	34 32	117	27 37	137	22 19	211	55 58	257	29 19	306	28 06	359
42	63 41	072	35 11	117	28 06	138	21 57	212	55 16	258	28 44	307	28 06	000
43	64 23	073	35 49	118	28 35	139	21 34	213	54 34	259	28 09	307	28 06	000
44	65 04	073	36 27	119	29 03	140	21 10	214	53 51	260	27 35	308	28 06	000
	◆ Dubhe		POLLUX		BETELGEUSE		◆ RIGEL		Diphda		◆ Alpheratz		DENEB	
45	25 46	027	31 48	080	37 04	120	29 31	141	20 46	215	53 09	261	27 01	308
46	26 06	027	32 31	081	37 41	121	29 58	142	20 21	216	52 26	262	26 27	309
47	26 26	028	33 13	082	38 18	122	30 24	143	19 56	216	51 43	263	25 54	309
48	26 46	028	33 56	082	38 54	123	30 50	144	19 30	217	51 00	263	25 20	310
49	27 06	028	34 39	083	39 30	124	31 15	145	19 03	218	50 17	264	24 47	310
50	27 27	029	35 22	083	40 05	125	31 40	146	18 36	219	49 35	265	24 14	311
51	27 48	029	36 04	084	40 40	126	32 04	147	18 09	220	48 51	266	23 41	311
52	28 09	029	36 47	085	41 15	127	32 27	148	17 41	221	48 08	266	23 09	311
53	28 30	030	37 30	085	41 49	129	32 49	149	17 12	222	47 25	267	22 37	312
54	28 52	030	38 13	086	42 22	130	33 11	150	16 43	223	46 42	268	22 05	312
55	29 13	030	38 57	087	42 55	131	33 32	151	16 14	223	45 59	269	21 33	313
56	29 35	031	39 40	087	43 28	132	33 53	152	15 44	224	45 16	269	21 02	313
57	29 58	031	40 23	088	43 59	133	34 12	154	15 14	225	44 33	270	20 30	314
58	30 20	031	41 06	089	44 31	134	34 31	155	14 43	226	43 50	271	19 59	314
59	30 43	032	41 49	089	45 01	135	34 49	156	14 12	227	43 06	271	19 29	315
	◆ Dubhe		POLLUX		PROCYON		◆ SIRIUS		RIGEL		◆ Hamal		DENEB	
60	31 06	032	42 32	090	28 16	112	18 26	138	35 06	157	59 17	237	18 58	316
61	31 29	032	43 15	091	28 55	113	18 55	139	35 23	158	58 40	239	18 28	316
62	31 52	033	43 59	091	29 35	114	19 23	140	35 38	159	58 03	240	17 59	317
63	32 15	033	44 42	092	30 14	115	19 50	141	35 53	161	57 26	241	17 29	317
64	32 39	033	45 25	093	30 53	116	20 18	142	36 07	162	56 48	242	17 00	318
65	33 03	034	46 08	094	31 32	116	20 44	143	36 20	163	56 09	244	16 31	318
66	33 27	034	46 51	094	32 11	117	21 10	143	36 32	164	55 30	245	16 02	319
67	33 51	034	47 34	095	32 49	118	21 35	144	36 44	165	54 51	246	15 34	319
68	34 16	035	48 17	096	33 27	119	22 00	145	36 54	167	54 11	247	15 06	320
69	34 40	035	49 00	097	34 04	120	22 25	146	37 04	168	53 31	248	14 38	320
70	35 05	035	49 43	097	34 42	121	22 48	147	37 12	169	52 51	249	14 11	321
71	35 30	035	50 25	098	35 18	122	23 11	148	37 20	170	52 11	250	13 44	321
72	35 55	036	51 08	099	35 55	123	23 34	149	37 27	171	51 30	251	13 17	322
73	36 21	036	51 51	100	36 31	124	23 56	150	37 33	173	50 49	252	12 50	323
74	36 46	036	52 33	101	37 06	125	24 17	151	37 38	174	50 08	253	12 24	323
	◆ Dubhe		REGULUS		PROCYON		◆ SIRIUS		RIGEL		◆ Hamal		Schedar	
75	37 12	037	17 20	090	37 41	126	24 38	152	37 42	175	49 26	254	48 33	311
76	37 38	037	18 03	091	38 16	127	24 57	153	37 45	176	48 45	255	48 00	311
77	38 03	037	18 47	091	38 50	128	25 17	154	37 47	178	48 03	256	47 28	312
78	38 30	037	19 30	092	39 24	129	25 35	155	37 49	179	47 21	257	46 56	312
79	38 56	038	20 13	093	39 57	130	25 53	156	37 49	180	46 39	258	46 24	312
80	39 22	038	20 56	094	40 30	131	26 10	157	37 48	181	45 57	258	45 52	312
81	39 49	038	21 39	094	41 02	132	26 27	158	37 47	183	45 15	259	45 20	312
82	40 15	038	22 22	095	41 34	134	26 43	159	37 44	184	44 32	260	44 48	313
83	40 42	038	23 05	096	42 05	135	26 58	160	37 41	185	43 49	261	44 16	313
84	41 09	039	23 48	096	42 35	136	27 12	161	37 36	186	43 07	262	43 45	313
85	41 36	039	24 31	097	43 05	137	27 26	162	37 31	188	42 24	263	43 13	313
86	42 03	039	25 14	098	43 34	138	27 38	163	37 25	189	41 41	263	42 42	314
87	42 30	039	25 56	099	44 03	139	27 50	164	37 17	190	40 58	264	42 10	314
88	42 58	039	26 39	099	44 30	141	28 02	165	37 09	191	40 15	265	41 39	314
89	43 25	040	27 21	100	44 57	142	28 12	166	37 00	193	39 32	266	41 08	314

LHA ♈	Hc	Zn	Hc	Zn	Hc	Zn	Hc	Zn	Hc	Zn	Hc	Zn	Hc	Zn
	◆ Dubhe		REGULUS		PROCYON		◆ SIRIUS		RIGEL		ALDEBARAN		◆ Mirfak	
90	43 53	040	28 04	101	45 24	143	28 22	168	36 50	194	57 23	219	63 17	297
91	44 20	040	28 46	102	45 49	144	28 31	169	36 40	195	56 56	221	62 38	297
92	44 48	040	29 28	103	46 14	146	28 39	170	36 28	196	56 27	222	62 00	297
93	45 16	040	30 10	103	46 38	147	28 46	171	36 15	198	55 58	224	61 21	297
94	45 44	040	30 52	104	47 01	148	28 53	172	36 02	199	55 27	225	60 43	297
95	46 12	040	31 34	105	47 23	150	28 59	173	35 48	200	54 56	227	60 04	297
96	46 40	041	32 16	106	47 44	151	29 03	174	35 33	201	54 25	228	59 26	297
97	47 08	041	32 57	107	48 05	153	29 08	175	35 17	202	53 52	229	58 47	297
98	47 36	041	33 38	107	48 24	154	29 11	176	35 00	203	53 19	231	58 09	297
99	48 04	041	34 20	108	48 42	155	29 13	177	34 42	205	52 46	232	57 31	298
100	48 32	041	35 00	109	49 00	157	29 15	178	34 24	206	52 11	233	56 53	298
101	49 01	041	35 41	110	49 16	158	29 16	180	34 05	207	51 36	234	56 14	298
102	49 29	041	36 22	111	49 32	160	29 16	181	33 45	208	51 01	236	55 36	298
103	49 58	041	37 02	112	49 46	161	29 15	182	33 25	209	50 25	237	54 58	298
104	50 26	041	37 42	113	50 00	163	29 13	183	33 03	210	49 49	238	54 20	299
	Dubhe		◆ Denebola		REGULUS		◆ SIRIUS		RIGEL		ALDEBARAN		◆ Mirfak	
105	50 54	041	22 34	091	38 22	114	29 11	184	32 41	211	49 12	239	53 43	299
106	51 23	041	23 17	092	39 01	114	29 07	185	32 18	212	48 35	240	53 05	299
107	51 51	041	24 00	093	39 40	115	29 03	186	31 55	213	47 57	241	52 27	299
108	52 20	041	24 43	093	40 19	116	28 58	187	31 31	214	47 19	242	51 49	300
109	52 48	041	25 26	094	40 57	117	28 52	188	31 06	216	46 41	243	51 12	300
110	53 17	041	26 09	095	41 36	118	28 46	189	30 41	217	46 02	244	50 35	300
111	53 45	041	26 52	096	42 13	119	28 38	190	30 15	218	45 23	245	49 57	300
112	54 14	041	27 35	096	42 51	120	28 30	192	29 48	219	44 43	246	49 20	301
113	54 42	041	28 18	097	43 28	121	28 21	193	29 21	220	44 04	247	48 43	301
114	55 10	041	29 01	098	44 05	122	28 11	194	28 53	221	43 24	248	48 06	301
115	55 39	041	29 44	099	44 41	124	28 01	195	28 25	222	42 43	249	47 29	301
116	56 07	041	30 26	099	45 17	125	27 49	196	27 56	223	42 03	250	46 52	302
117	56 35	041	31 09	100	45 52	126	27 37	197	27 26	224	41 22	251	46 15	302
118	57 03	041	31 51	101	46 27	127	27 24	198	26 56	225	40 41	252	45 39	302
119	57 31	040	32 33	102	47 01	128	27 11	199	26 26	225	40 00	253	45 02	303
	◆ Kochab		Denebola		◆ REGULUS		SIRIUS		RIGEL		◆ ALDEBARAN		CAPELLA	
120	38 40	020	33 16	103	47 35	129	26 56	200	25 55	226	39 19	254	61 34	288
121	38 55	020	33 58	103	48 08	130	26 41	201	25 23	227	38 37	255	60 53	289
122	39 10	020	34 40	104	48 40	132	26 25	202	24 51	228	37 55	255	60 12	289
123	39 25	020	35 21	105	49 12	133	26 09	203	24 19	229	37 14	256	59 32	289
124	39 40	021	36 03	106	49 44	134	25 52	204	23 46	230	36 32	257	58 51	290
125	39 55	021	36 44	107	50 14	135	25 34	205	23 12	231	35 49	258	58 10	290
126	40 11	021	37 26	108	50 44	137	25 15	206	22 39	232	35 07	259	57 30	290
127	40 26	021	38 07	108	51 13	138	24 56	207	22 04	233	34 25	260	56 49	291
128	40 42	021	38 48	109	51 42	139	24 36	208	21 30	234	33 42	260	56 09	291
129	40 57	021	39 28	110	52 09	141	24 15	209	20 55	234	33 00	261	55 29	291
130	41 13	021	40 09	111	52 36	142	23 54	210	20 20	235	32 17	262	54 49	291
131	41 29	021	40 49	112	53 02	144	23 32	211	19 44	236	31 34	263	54 08	292
132	41 44	022	41 29	113	53 27	145	23 09	212	19 08	237	30 51	263	53 28	292
133	42 00	022	42 08	114	53 51	147	22 46	213	18 32	238	30 09	264	52 48	292
134	42 16	022	42 48	115	54 15	148	22 22	214	17 55	239	29 26	265	52 09	293
	◆ Kochab		ARCTURUS		Denebola		◆ REGULUS		SIRIUS		BETELGEUSE		◆ CAPELLA	
135	42 32	022	20 51	083	43 27	116	54 37	150	21 58	215	35 48	242	51 29	293
136	42 48	022	21 34	084	44 05	117	54 58	151	21 33	216	35 10	243	50 49	293
137	43 04	022	22 17	084	44 44	118	55 18	153	21 08	217	34 32	243	50 10	294
138	43 21	022	23 00	085	45 22	119	55 37	155	20 42	218	33 53	244	49 30	294
139	43 37	022	23 43	086	45 59	120	55 55	156	20 15	218	33 14	245	48 51	295
140	43 53	022	24 26	087	46 36	121	56 12	158	19 48	219	32 35	246	48 12	295
141	44 09	022	25 09	087	47 13	122	56 27	160	19 20	220	31 55	247	47 33	295
142	44 26	022	25 53	088	47 50	123	56 42	161	18 52	221	31 15	248	46 54	296
143	44 42	022	26 36	089	48 25	124	56 55	163	18 23	222	30 35	249	46 15	296
144	44 58	022	27 19	089	49 01	126	57 07	165	17 54	223	29 55	250	45 36	296
145	45 15	022	28 02	090	49 36	127	57 17	167	17 25	224	29 14	250	44 57	297
146	45 31	022	28 45	091	50 10	128	57 26	169	16 55	225	28 33	251	44 19	297
147	45 48	022	29 28	091	50 44	129	57 34	170	16 24	225	27 52	252	43 41	297
148	46 04	022	30 11	092	51 17	130	57 41	172	15 53	226	27 11	253	43 02	298
149	46 21	022	30 55	093	51 49	132	57 46	174	15 22	227	26 30	254	42 24	298
	◆ Kochab		ARCTURUS		◆ SPICA		REGULUS		PROCYON		◆ POLLUX		CAPELLA	
150	46 37	022	31 38	093	17 41	126	57 50	176	40 31	229	58 53	250	41 46	299
151	46 54	022	32 21	094	18 16	127	57 52	178	39 59	230	58 12	251	41 08	299
152	47 10	022	33 04	095	18 50	128	57 54	179	39 26	231	57 31	252	40 31	299
153	47 26	022	33 47	096	19 24	129	57 53	181	38 52	232	56 49	253	39 53	300
154	47 43	022	34 30	096	19 57	130	57 52	183	38 18	233	56 08	254	39 16	300
155	47 59	022	35 13	097	20 30	131	57 49	185	37 43	234	55 26	255	38 39	301
156	48 15	022	35 55	098	21 03	131	57 44	187	37 08	235	54 44	256	38 01	301
157	48 32	022	36 38	099	21 35	132	57 38	189	36 32	236	54 02	257	37 25	301
158	48 48	022	37 21	099	22 07	133	57 31	190	35 56	237	53 20	258	36 48	302
159	49 04	022	38 03	100	22 38	134	57 23	192	35 20	238	52 38	259	36 11	302
160	49 20	022	38 46	101	23 09	135	57 13	194	34 43	239	51 56	260	35 35	303
161	49 36	022	39 28	102	23 39	136	57 02	196	34 06	240	51 13	261	34 58	303
162	49 52	022	40 10	103	24 09	137	56 49	198	33 28	241	50 30	262	34 22	303
163	50 08	022	40 52	104	24 38	138	56 36	199	32 51	242	49 48	262	33 46	304
164	50 24	022	41 34	104	25 07	139	56 21	201	32 12	243	49 05	263	33 11	304
	◆ Kochab		ARCTURUS		◆ SPICA		REGULUS		PROCYON		◆ POLLUX		CAPELLA	
165	50 40	021	42 16	105	25 35	140	56 05	203	31 34	244	48 22	264	32 35	305
166	50 56	021	42 57	106	26 03	141	55 48	204	30 55	244	47 39	265	32 00	305
167	51 11	021	43 39	107	26 30	142	55 29	206	30 16	245	46 56	266	31 25	306
168	51 27	021	44 20	108	26 56	143	55 10	208	29 37	246	46 13	266	30 50	306
169	51 42	021	45 01	109	27 22	144	54 49	209	28 57	247	45 30	267	30 15	306
170	51 58	021	45 42	110	27 47	145	54 28	211	28 17	248	44 47	268	29 40	307
171	52 13	021	46 22	111	28 12	146	54 05	212	27 37	249	44 04	268	29 06	307
172	52 28	020	47 02	112	28 36	147	53 41	214	26 57	250	43 20	269	28 32	308
173	52 43	020	47 42	113	28 59	148	53 17	215	26 16	250	42 37	270	27 58	308
174	52 58	020	48 22	114	29 22	149	52 51	217	25 36	251	41 54	271	27 24	309
175	53 13	020	49 01	115	29 44	150	52 25	218	24 55	252	41 11	271	26 50	309
176	53 27	020	49 40	116	30 06	151	51 58	220	24 14	253	40 28	272	26 17	310
177	53 41	019	50 19	117	30 26	152	51 30	221	23 32	254	39 45	273	25 44	310
178	53 56	019	50 57	118	30 46	153	51 01	222	22 51	254	39 02	273	25 11	311
179	54 10	019	51 35	119	31 06	154	50 32	224	22 09	255	38 18	274	24 38	311

LHA ♈	Hc	Zn	Hc	Zn	Hc	Zn	Hc	Zn	Hc	Zn	Hc	Zn	Hc	Zn
	Kochab		◆VEGA		ARCTURUS		◆SPICA		REGULUS		◆POLLUX		CAPELLA	
180	54 23	019	20 07	055	52 13	120	31 24	155	50 02	225	37 35	275	24 06	312
181	54 37	018	20 43	056	52 50	121	31 42	156	49 31	226	36 52	275	23 34	312
182	54 51	018	21 19	056	53 27	123	31 59	157	48 59	228	36 09	276	23 02	313
183	55 04	018	21 55	057	54 03	124	32 15	158	48 27	229	35 27	277	22 30	313
184	55 17	017	22 31	057	54 38	125	32 31	160	47 54	230	34 44	277	21 59	314
185	55 30	017	23 07	058	55 13	126	32 46	161	47 21	231	34 01	278	21 28	314
186	55 43	017	23 44	058	55 48	128	32 59	162	46 47	232	33 18	278	20 57	315
187	55 55	017	24 20	059	56 22	129	33 13	163	46 12	234	32 35	279	20 26	315
188	56 07	016	24 57	059	56 55	130	33 25	164	45 37	235	31 53	280	19 56	316
189	56 19	016	25 35	060	57 27	132	33 36	165	45 02	236	31 10	280	19 26	316
190	56 31	016	26 12	060	57 59	133	33 47	166	44 26	237	30 28	281	18 56	317
191	56 42	015	26 50	061	58 30	135	33 56	168	43 49	238	29 46	281	18 26	317
192	56 53	015	27 27	061	59 00	136	34 05	169	43 13	239	29 03	282	17 57	318
193	57 04	014	28 05	062	59 30	138	34 13	170	42 35	240	28 21	283	17 28	318
194	57 15	014	28 43	062	59 58	140	34 20	171	41 58	241	27 39	283	16 59	319
	◆VEGA		Rasalhague		ARCTURUS		◆SPICA		REGULUS		◆POLLUX		Dubhe	
195	29 22	063	23 48	096	60 26	141	34 27	172	41 20	242	26 57	284	65 34	326
196	30 00	063	24 31	096	60 52	143	34 32	173	40 42	243	26 15	285	65 10	326
197	30 39	064	25 14	097	61 18	145	34 37	175	40 03	244	25 34	285	64 46	325
198	31 18	064	25 57	098	61 42	146	34 40	176	39 24	245	24 52	286	64 21	325
199	31 57	065	26 40	098	62 05	148	34 43	177	38 45	246	24 11	286	63 56	324
200	32 36	065	27 22	099	62 27	150	34 45	178	38 05	247	23 29	287	63 30	324
201	33 15	066	28 05	100	62 48	152	34 46	179	37 25	248	22 48	288	63 05	323
202	33 55	066	28 47	101	63 08	154	34 46	181	36 45	249	22 07	288	62 39	323
203	34 34	067	29 30	101	63 26	156	34 45	182	36 05	250	21 26	289	62 13	322
204	35 14	067	30 12	102	63 43	158	34 43	183	35 24	250	20 45	289	61 46	322
205	35 54	068	30 54	103	63 58	160	34 40	184	34 44	251	20 05	290	61 19	322
206	36 34	068	31 36	104	64 12	162	34 37	185	34 03	252	19 24	291	60 53	321
207	37 14	069	32 18	105	64 24	164	34 32	187	33 21	253	18 44	291	60 26	321
208	37 55	069	33 00	105	64 35	166	34 27	188	32 40	254	18 04	292	59 58	321
209	38 35	070	33 41	106	64 45	169	34 20	189	31 58	255	17 24	292	59 31	321
	◆DENEB		VEGA		Rasalhague		ANTARES		◆ARCTURUS		REGULUS		◆Dubhe	
210	23 42	049	39 16	070	34 22	107	11 35	146	64 52	171	31 17	255	59 03	320
211	24 15	050	39 56	071	35 04	108	11 59	147	64 58	173	30 35	256	58 36	320
212	24 48	050	40 37	071	35 44	109	12 22	148	65 03	175	29 53	257	58 08	320
213	25 21	050	41 18	072	36 25	110	12 45	149	65 05	178	29 11	258	57 40	320
214	25 55	051	41 59	072	37 06	111	13 07	149	65 06	180	28 29	259	57 12	320
215	26 28	051	42 40	073	37 46	111	13 29	150	65 06	182	27 46	259	56 44	319
216	27 02	052	43 22	073	38 26	112	13 50	151	65 03	184	27 04	260	56 16	319
217	27 36	052	44 03	074	39 06	113	14 10	152	64 59	187	26 21	261	55 48	319
218	28 10	053	44 45	074	39 45	114	14 30	153	64 53	189	25 38	262	55 19	319
219	28 45	053	45 26	075	40 25	115	14 50	154	64 46	191	24 56	262	54 51	319
220	29 20	054	46 08	075	41 03	116	15 09	155	64 37	193	24 13	263	54 23	319
221	29 54	054	46 50	076	41 42	117	15 27	155	64 26	195	23 30	264	53 54	319
222	30 30	055	47 32	076	42 20	118	15 44	156	64 14	197	22 47	265	53 26	319
223	31 05	055	48 14	077	42 58	119	16 01	157	64 01	200	22 04	265	52 57	319
224	31 40	056	48 56	077	43 36	120	16 18	158	63 45	202	21 21	266	52 29	319
	DENEB		◆ALTAIR		Rasalhague		ANTARES		◆ARCTURUS		Denebola		◆Dubhe	
225	32 16	056	18 28	095	44 13	121	16 34	159	63 29	204	40 05	249	52 00	319
226	32 52	056	19 11	096	44 49	122	16 49	160	63 11	206	39 25	250	51 32	319
227	33 28	057	19 54	097	45 26	123	17 03	161	62 52	208	38 44	251	51 04	319
228	34 04	057	20 37	098	46 02	124	17 17	162	62 31	209	38 03	252	50 35	319
229	34 41	058	21 20	098	46 37	126	17 30	163	62 09	211	37 22	253	50 07	319
230	35 17	058	22 02	099	47 12	127	17 43	164	61 46	213	36 41	253	49 38	319
231	35 54	059	22 45	100	47 46	128	17 55	164	61 22	215	35 59	254	49 10	319
232	36 31	059	23 27	101	48 20	129	18 06	165	60 57	217	35 18	255	48 42	319
233	37 08	059	24 10	101	48 53	130	18 17	166	60 30	218	34 36	256	48 13	319
234	37 45	060	24 52	102	49 26	132	18 27	167	60 03	220	33 54	257	47 45	319
235	38 22	060	25 34	103	49 58	133	18 36	168	59 35	222	33 12	258	47 17	319
236	39 00	061	26 16	104	50 29	134	18 44	169	59 05	223	32 30	258	46 49	319
237	39 38	061	26 58	104	51 00	135	18 52	170	58 35	225	31 47	259	46 21	320
238	40 15	061	27 40	105	51 30	137	18 59	171	58 04	226	31 05	260	45 53	320
239	40 53	062	28 21	106	51 59	138	19 06	172	57 33	228	30 22	261	45 25	320
	◆DENEB		ALTAIR		Rasalhague		◆ANTARES		ARCTURUS		Denebola		◆Dubhe	
240	41 32	062	29 02	107	52 27	140	19 12	173	57 00	229	29 40	261	44 57	320
241	42 10	063	29 44	108	52 55	141	19 17	174	56 27	231	28 57	262	44 29	320
242	42 48	063	30 25	108	53 22	142	19 21	175	55 54	232	28 14	263	44 01	320
243	43 27	063	31 06	109	53 47	144	19 25	176	55 19	233	27 31	264	43 34	320
244	44 05	064	31 46	110	54 12	145	19 28	177	54 44	235	26 49	264	43 06	321
245	44 44	064	32 27	111	54 36	147	19 30	178	54 09	236	26 06	265	42 39	321
246	45 23	065	33 07	112	55 00	148	19 31	178	53 33	237	25 23	266	42 12	321
247	46 02	065	33 47	113	55 22	150	19 32	179	52 56	238	24 39	267	41 45	321
248	46 41	065	34 26	114	55 43	152	19 32	180	52 19	240	23 56	267	41 18	321
249	47 21	066	35 06	115	56 03	153	19 31	181	51 42	241	23 13	268	40 51	321
250	48 00	066	35 45	115	56 21	155	19 30	182	51 04	242	22 30	269	40 24	322
251	48 40	066	36 24	116	56 39	157	19 28	183	50 26	243	21 47	269	39 57	322
252	49 19	067	37 02	117	56 56	158	19 25	184	49 47	244	21 04	270	39 31	322
253	49 59	067	37 40	118	57 11	160	19 22	185	49 08	245	20 21	271	39 04	322
254	50 39	068	38 18	119	57 25	162	19 17	186	48 29	246	19 37	271	38 38	323
	◆DENEB		ALTAIR		Nunki		◆ANTARES		ARCTURUS		◆Alkaid		Kochab	
255	51 19	068	38 56	120	14 51	153	19 13	187	47 49	247	57 12	296	56 35	345
256	51 59	068	39 33	121	15 10	154	19 07	188	47 09	248	56 34	297	56 23	344
257	52 39	069	40 10	122	15 29	155	19 01	189	46 29	249	55 55	297	56 11	344
258	53 19	069	40 46	123	15 47	156	18 54	190	45 49	250	55 17	297	55 59	344
259	54 00	069	41 22	124	16 04	157	18 46	191	45 08	251	54 38	297	55 47	343
260	54 40	070	41 57	125	16 21	158	18 37	192	44 27	252	54 00	298	55 34	343
261	55 21	070	42 32	126	16 37	159	18 28	193	43 46	253	53 22	298	55 21	343
262	56 01	070	43 07	128	16 53	159	18 18	194	43 04	254	52 44	298	55 08	342
263	56 42	071	43 41	129	17 07	160	18 08	195	42 23	255	52 06	298	54 55	342
264	57 23	071	44 14	130	17 22	161	17 57	195	41 41	255	51 28	299	54 42	342
265	58 03	071	44 47	131	17 35	162	17 45	196	40 59	256	50 50	299	54 28	341
266	58 44	072	45 19	132	17 48	163	17 33	197	40 17	257	50 12	299	54 14	341
267	59 25	072	45 51	133	18 00	164	17 19	198	39 35	258	49 34	299	54 00	341
268	60 06	072	46 22	135	18 12	165	17 06	199	38 53	259	48 57	300	53 46	341
269	60 48	073	46 52	136	18 23	166	16 51	200	38 11	260	48 19	300	53 32	341

LHA ♈	Hc	Zn	Hc	Zn	Hc	Zn	Hc	Zn	Hc	Zn	Hc	Zn	Hc	Zn
	◆Alpheratz		ALTAIR		Nunki		◆ANTARES		ARCTURUS		◆Alkaid		Kochab	
270	18 16	067	47 22	137	18 33	167	16 36	201	37 28	260	47 42	300	53 17	340
271	18 56	067	47 51	138	18 43	168	16 20	202	36 45	261	47 05	301	53 03	340
272	19 36	068	48 20	140	18 52	169	16 04	203	36 03	262	46 28	301	52 48	340
273	20 16	069	48 47	141	19 00	170	15 47	204	35 20	263	45 51	301	52 33	340
274	20 56	069	49 14	142	19 07	170	15 30	204	34 37	263	45 14	301	52 18	340
275	21 37	070	49 40	144	19 14	171	15 12	205	33 54	264	44 37	302	52 03	339
276	22 17	070	50 05	145	19 20	172	14 53	206	33 11	265	44 00	302	51 48	339
277	22 58	071	50 30	146	19 26	173	14 34	207	32 28	266	43 24	302	51 32	339
278	23 39	072	50 53	148	19 30	174	14 14	208	31 45	266	42 47	303	51 17	339
279	24 20	072	51 16	149	19 34	175	13 53	209	31 02	267	42 11	303	51 01	339
280	25 01	073	51 37	151	19 38	176	13 32	210	30 19	268	41 35	303	50 45	339
281	25 42	073	51 58	152	19 40	177	13 11	210	29 36	269	40 59	304	50 30	338
282	26 24	074	52 17	154	19 42	178	12 48	211	28 53	269	40 23	304	50 14	338
283	27 05	074	52 36	155	19 43	179	12 26	212	28 09	270	39 48	304	49 58	338
284	27 47	075	52 53	157	19 43	180	12 03	213	27 26	271	39 12	305	49 42	338
	◆Mirfak		Alpheratz		◆ALTAIR		Rasalhague		◆ARCTURUS		Alkaid		Kochab	
285	14 53	032	28 29	076	53 10	158	53 43	216	26 43	271	38 37	305	49 26	338
286	15 17	033	29 10	076	53 25	160	53 17	218	26 00	272	38 02	306	49 10	338
287	15 40	034	29 52	077	53 39	162	52 50	219	25 17	273	37 27	306	48 53	338
288	16 04	034	30 34	077	53 52	163	52 22	221	24 34	273	36 52	306	48 37	338
289	16 29	035	31 17	078	54 04	165	51 53	222	23 51	274	36 17	307	48 21	338
290	16 53	035	31 59	079	54 15	167	51 24	223	23 08	275	35 43	307	48 05	338
291	17 18	036	32 41	079	54 24	168	50 54	225	22 25	275	35 08	307	47 48	338
292	17 43	036	33 24	080	54 32	170	50 23	226	21 42	276	34 34	308	47 32	338
293	18 09	037	34 06	081	54 39	172	49 52	227	20 59	277	34 00	308	47 15	338
294	18 35	037	34 49	081	54 45	173	49 20	229	20 16	277	33 26	309	46 59	338
295	19 01	038	35 32	082	54 49	175	48 47	230	19 33	278	32 53	309	46 43	338
296	19 28	038	36 14	082	54 52	177	48 14	231	18 51	279	32 19	309	46 26	338
297	19 54	039	36 57	083	54 54	178	47 40	232	18 08	279	31 46	310	46 10	338
298	20 21	039	37 40	084	54 55	180	47 05	233	17 25	280	31 13	310	45 53	338
299	20 49	040	38 23	084	54 54	182	46 30	235	16 43	281	30 40	311	45 37	338
	Mirfak		◆Alpheratz		Enif		◆ALTAIR		Rasalhague		Alphecca		◆Kochab	
300	21 16	040	39 06	085	49 04	138	54 52	184	45 55	236	34 51	275	45 20	338
301	21 44	041	39 49	086	49 33	140	54 48	185	45 19	237	34 08	276	45 04	338
302	22 13	041	40 32	086	50 00	141	54 44	187	44 43	238	33 25	276	44 48	338
303	22 41	041	41 15	087	50 27	142	54 38	189	44 06	239	32 42	277	44 31	338
304	23 10	042	41 58	088	50 53	144	54 30	190	43 29	240	32 00	278	44 15	338
305	23 39	042	42 41	088	51 18	145	54 22	192	42 51	241	31 17	278	43 59	338
306	24 08	043	43 24	089	51 42	147	54 12	194	42 13	242	30 34	279	43 42	338
307	24 37	043	44 08	090	52 05	148	54 01	195	41 35	243	29 52	279	43 26	338
308	25 07	044	44 51	090	52 28	150	53 49	197	40 56	244	29 09	280	43 10	338
309	25 37	044	45 34	091	52 49	151	53 36	199	40 17	245	28 27	281	42 54	338
310	26 07	045	46 17	092	53 09	153	53 22	200	39 38	246	27 44	281	42 38	338
311	26 38	045	47 00	092	53 29	154	53 06	202	38 59	247	27 02	282	42 22	338
312	27 09	046	47 43	093	53 47	156	52 49	204	38 19	248	26 20	283	42 06	338
313	27 39	046	48 26	094	54 04	157	52 32	205	37 39	249	25 38	283	41 50	338
314	28 11	046	49 09	095	54 20	159	52 13	207	36 58	250	24 56	284	41 34	339
	CAPELLA		◆Alpheratz		FOMALHAUT		◆ALTAIR		Rasalhague		VEGA		◆Kochab	
315	12 33	036	49 52	095	11 38	154	51 53	208	36 18	250	62 59	271	41 18	339
316	12 58	036	50 35	096	11 56	155	51 32	210	35 37	251	62 16	272	41 03	339
317	13 24	037	51 18	097	12 14	156	51 10	211	34 56	252	61 33	273	40 47	339
318	13 50	038	52 01	098	12 32	156	50 48	213	34 15	253	60 50	273	40 31	339
319	14 17	038	52 44	099	12 49	157	50 24	214	33 33	254	60 07	274	40 16	339
320	14 43	039	53 26	099	13 05	158	49 59	215	32 52	255	59 24	274	40 01	339
321	15 11	039	54 09	100	13 21	159	49 34	217	32 10	255	58 41	275	39 45	339
322	15 38	040	54 51	101	13 36	160	49 08	218	31 28	256	57 58	276	39 30	339
323	16 06	040	55 34	102	13 51	161	48 41	219	30 46	257	57 15	276	39 15	340
324	16 34	041	56 16	103	14 05	162	48 13	221	30 04	258	56 32	277	39 00	340
325	17 02	041	56 58	104	14 18	162	47 44	222	29 22	259	55 49	277	38 45	340
326	17 31	042	57 39	105	14 31	163	47 15	223	28 40	259	55 06	278	38 30	340
327	18 00	042	58 21	106	14 43	164	46 45	225	27 57	260	54 23	278	38 16	340
328	18 29	043	59 02	107	14 54	165	46 15	226	27 14	261	53 41	279	38 01	340
329	18 59	043	59 44	108	15 05	166	45 43	227	26 32	262	52 58	280	37 47	341
	◆CAPELLA		Hamal		Diphda		◆FOMALHAUT		ALTAIR		◆VEGA		Kochab	
330	19 29	044	35 56	091	17 36	139	15 15	167	45 11	228	52 16	280	37 32	341
331	19 59	045	36 39	092	18 04	140	15 25	168	44 39	229	51 33	281	37 18	341
332	20 29	045	37 23	092	18 32	141	15 33	169	44 06	231	50 51	281	37 04	341
333	21 00	046	38 06	093	18 59	142	15 42	170	43 32	232	50 09	282	36 50	341
334	21 31	046	38 49	094	19 25	143	15 49	170	42 58	233	49 26	282	36 37	341
335	22 02	047	39 32	094	19 51	143	15 56	171	42 24	234	48 44	283	36 23	342
336	22 33	047	40 15	095	20 17	144	16 02	172	41 49	235	48 02	283	36 09	342
337	23 05	047	40 58	096	20 42	145	16 08	173	41 13	236	47 20	284	35 56	342
338	23 37	048	41 41	097	21 06	146	16 13	174	40 37	237	46 38	284	35 43	342
339	24 09	048	42 24	097	21 30	147	16 17	175	40 01	238	45 56	285	35 30	342
340	24 42	049	43 06	098	21 53	148	16 20	176	39 24	239	45 15	285	35 17	343
341	25 14	049	43 49	099	22 15	149	16 23	177	38 47	240	44 33	286	35 04	343
342	25 47	050	44 32	100	22 37	150	16 25	178	38 09	241	43 52	286	34 51	343
343	26 20	050	45 14	101	22 59	151	16 27	179	37 31	242	43 10	287	34 39	343
344	26 54	051	45 56	102	23 19	152	16 27	179	36 53	243	42 29	287	34 26	344
	◆CAPELLA		ALDEBARAN		Diphda		◆FOMALHAUT		ALTAIR		◆VEGA		Kochab	
345	27 27	051	15 31	082	23 39	153	16 27	180	36 14	244	41 48	288	34 14	344
346	28 01	052	16 14	082	23 59	154	16 27	181	35 35	245	41 07	288	34 02	344
347	28 35	052	16 56	083	24 17	155	16 26	182	34 56	246	40 26	289	33 50	344
348	29 09	053	17 39	084	24 35	156	16 24	183	34 17	247	39 45	289	33 39	344
349	29 44	053	18 22	084	24 53	157	16 21	184	33 37	247	39 04	290	33 27	345
350	30 18	054	19 05	085	25 09	158	16 18	185	32 57	248	38 24	290	33 16	345
351	30 53	054	19 48	086	25 25	159	16 14	186	32 17	249	37 43	291	33 05	345
352	31 28	054	20 31	086	25 41	160	16 09	187	31 36	250	37 03	291	32 54	345
353	32 03	055	21 14	087	25 55	161	16 04	188	30 56	251	36 23	292	32 43	346
354	32 39	055	21 58	088	26 09	162	15 57	188	30 15	252	35 43	292	32 32	346
355	33 14	056	22 41	089	26 22	163	15 51	189	29 34	253	35 03	293	32 22	346
356	33 50	056	23 24	089	26 34	164	15 43	190	28 52	253	34 23	293	32 12	346
357	34 26	057	24 07	090	26 46	165	15 35	191	28 11	254	33 44	294	32 02	347
358	35 02	057	24 50	091	26 57	166	15 27	192	27 29	255	33 04	294	31 52	347
359	35 38	057	25 33	091	27 07	167	15 17	193	26 48	256	32 25	295	31 42	347

LHA ♈	Hc	Zn	Hc	Zn	Hc	Zn	Hc	Zn	Hc	Zn	Hc	Zn	Hc	Zn
	◆ CAPELLA		ALDEBARAN		◆ Diphda		FOMALHAUT		ALTAIR		◆ VEGA		Kochab	
0	35 43	057	26 18	092	28 15	168	16 06	194	26 20	257	31 20	296	30 34	348
1	36 20	058	27 02	092	28 24	169	15 55	195	25 37	258	30 41	296	30 25	348
2	36 57	058	27 46	093	28 31	170	15 43	196	24 54	259	30 01	297	30 15	348
3	37 34	058	28 30	094	28 39	171	15 31	197	24 11	259	29 22	297	30 06	348
4	38 11	059	29 14	094	28 45	172	15 18	197	23 28	260	28 43	298	29 58	349
5	38 49	059	29 57	095	28 50	173	15 05	198	22 44	261	28 05	298	29 49	349
6	39 27	060	30 41	096	28 55	174	14 51	199	22 01	261	27 26	299	29 41	349
7	40 05	060	31 25	097	28 59	176	14 36	200	21 18	262	26 48	299	29 32	349
8	40 43	060	32 08	097	29 02	177	14 21	201	20 34	263	26 10	300	29 25	350
9	41 21	061	32 52	098	29 04	178	14 05	202	19 50	264	25 32	300	29 17	350
10	41 59	061	33 35	099	29 05	179	13 48	203	19 07	264	24 54	301	29 09	350
11	42 38	061	34 18	100	29 06	180	13 31	203	18 23	265	24 16	301	29 02	351
12	43 16	062	35 02	100	29 05	181	13 13	204	17 39	266	23 39	302	28 55	351
13	43 55	062	35 45	101	29 04	182	12 55	205	16 56	266	23 02	302	28 48	351
14	44 34	062	36 28	102	29 02	183	12 36	206	16 12	267	22 25	303	28 41	351
	◆ CAPELLA		BETELGEUSE		RIGEL		◆ Diphda		Enif		◆ DENEB		Kochab	
15	45 13	063	16 44	096	12 51	114	28 59	184	36 20	247	44 56	296	28 35	352
16	45 52	063	17 28	096	13 31	115	28 56	185	35 40	248	44 17	297	28 29	352
17	46 31	063	18 11	097	14 10	116	28 51	186	34 59	249	43 38	297	28 22	352
18	47 11	064	18 55	098	14 50	117	28 46	188	34 18	249	42 59	297	28 17	353
19	47 50	064	19 38	098	15 29	117	28 40	189	33 37	250	42 20	298	28 11	353
20	48 30	064	20 22	099	16 08	118	28 33	190	32 55	251	41 41	298	28 06	353
21	49 09	065	21 05	100	16 46	119	28 25	191	32 14	252	41 02	299	28 01	353
22	49 49	065	21 48	101	17 24	120	28 16	192	31 32	253	40 24	299	27 56	354
23	50 29	065	22 31	101	18 02	121	28 07	193	30 50	254	39 45	299	27 51	354
24	51 09	066	23 14	102	18 40	121	27 57	194	30 08	254	39 07	300	27 46	354
25	51 49	066	23 57	103	19 17	122	27 46	195	29 25	255	38 29	300	27 42	355
26	52 29	066	24 40	104	19 54	123	27 34	196	28 43	256	37 51	300	27 38	355
27	53 09	067	25 22	104	20 31	124	27 22	197	28 00	257	37 14	301	27 34	355
28	53 50	067	26 05	105	21 07	125	27 08	198	27 18	258	36 36	301	27 31	356
29	54 30	067	26 47	106	21 43	126	26 54	199	26 35	258	35 58	302	27 28	356
	◆ CAPELLA		BETELGEUSE		RIGEL		◆ Diphda		Alpheratz		◆ DENEB		Kochab	
30	55 10	068	27 29	107	22 18	126	26 40	200	63 52	247	35 21	302	27 25	356
31	55 51	068	28 11	107	22 54	127	26 24	201	63 12	248	34 44	302	27 22	356
32	56 32	068	28 53	108	23 28	128	26 08	202	62 31	250	34 07	303	27 19	357
33	57 13	068	29 34	109	24 03	129	25 51	203	61 49	251	33 30	303	27 17	357
34	57 53	069	30 16	110	24 37	130	25 33	204	61 08	252	32 54	304	27 14	357
35	58 34	069	30 57	111	25 10	131	25 15	205	60 26	253	32 17	304	27 13	358
36	59 15	069	31 38	112	25 43	132	24 56	206	59 44	254	31 41	305	27 11	358
37	59 56	069	32 19	112	26 16	133	24 36	207	59 02	255	31 05	305	27 09	358
38	60 37	070	32 59	113	26 48	134	24 16	208	58 19	256	30 29	305	27 08	359
39	61 18	070	33 39	114	27 19	134	23 55	209	57 36	257	29 54	306	27 07	359
40	62 00	070	34 19	115	27 50	135	23 33	210	56 54	258	29 18	306	27 06	359
41	62 41	070	34 59	116	28 21	136	23 11	211	56 11	259	28 43	307	27 06	359
42	63 22	070	35 38	117	28 51	137	22 48	212	55 27	260	28 08	307	27 06	000
43	64 04	071	36 17	118	29 20	138	22 24	213	54 44	261	27 33	308	27 06	000
44	64 45	071	36 56	119	29 49	139	22 00	214	54 01	261	26 58	308	27 06	000
	◆ Dubhe		POLLUX		BETELGEUSE		◆ RIGEL		Diphda		◆ Alpheratz		DENEB	
45	24 53	027	31 38	080	37 34	120	30 17	140	21 35	215	53 17	262	26 24	309
46	25 13	027	32 21	080	38 12	121	30 45	141	21 10	216	52 34	263	25 50	309
47	25 33	027	33 04	081	38 49	122	31 12	142	20 44	217	51 50	264	25 16	309
48	25 53	028	33 47	081	39 27	123	31 39	143	20 17	218	51 07	265	24 42	310
49	26 13	028	34 31	082	40 03	124	32 04	144	19 50	218	50 23	265	24 08	310
50	26 34	028	35 14	083	40 40	125	32 29	146	19 23	219	49 39	266	23 35	311
51	26 55	029	35 58	083	41 16	126	32 54	147	18 55	220	48 55	267	23 02	311
52	27 17	029	36 41	084	41 51	127	33 18	148	18 26	221	48 12	268	22 29	312
53	27 38	030	37 25	085	42 26	128	33 41	149	17 57	222	47 28	268	21 56	312
54	28 00	030	38 09	085	43 00	129	34 03	150	17 28	223	46 44	269	21 24	313
55	28 22	030	38 53	086	43 34	130	34 25	151	16 57	224	46 00	270	20 52	313
56	28 44	031	39 36	086	44 07	131	34 46	152	16 27	224	45 16	270	20 20	314
57	29 06	031	40 20	087	44 40	132	35 06	153	15 56	225	44 32	271	19 49	314
58	29 29	031	41 04	088	45 12	134	35 25	154	15 25	226	43 48	272	19 17	315
59	29 52	032	41 48	088	45 44	135	35 44	156	14 53	227	43 05	272	18 46	315
	◆ Dubhe		POLLUX		PROCYON		◆ SIRIUS		RIGEL		◆ Hamal		DENEB	
60	30 15	032	42 32	089	28 38	112	19 11	138	36 01	157	59 49	239	18 16	316
61	30 38	032	43 16	090	29 19	112	19 40	139	36 18	158	59 11	240	17 45	316
62	31 01	032	44 00	090	29 59	113	20 09	140	36 34	159	58 33	241	17 15	317
63	31 25	033	44 43	091	30 39	114	20 37	140	36 50	160	57 54	243	16 45	317
64	31 49	033	45 27	092	31 19	115	21 04	141	37 04	162	57 15	244	16 15	318
65	32 13	033	46 11	093	31 59	116	21 32	142	37 17	163	56 35	245	15 46	318
66	32 37	034	46 55	093	32 38	117	21 58	143	37 30	164	55 55	246	15 17	319
67	33 02	034	47 39	094	33 17	118	22 24	144	37 42	165	55 15	247	14 48	319
68	33 26	034	48 22	095	33 56	119	22 50	145	37 53	166	54 34	248	14 20	320
69	33 51	035	49 06	096	34 34	120	23 14	146	38 02	168	53 53	249	13 52	320
70	34 16	035	49 50	096	35 12	120	23 39	147	38 11	169	53 12	250	13 24	321
71	34 41	035	50 33	097	35 50	121	24 02	148	38 19	170	52 31	251	12 57	322
72	35 07	035	51 17	098	36 27	122	24 25	149	38 26	171	51 49	252	12 30	322
73	35 32	036	52 00	099	37 04	123	24 48	150	38 32	173	51 07	253	12 03	323
74	35 58	036	52 44	100	37 40	124	25 09	151	38 38	174	50 25	254	11 36	323
	◆ Dubhe		REGULUS		PROCYON		◆ SIRIUS		RIGEL		◆ Hamal		Schedar	
75	36 23	036	17 20	090	38 16	125	25 30	152	38 42	175	49 42	255	47 53	312
76	36 49	036	18 04	090	38 52	126	25 51	153	38 45	176	49 00	256	47 20	312
77	37 15	037	18 48	091	39 27	127	26 11	154	38 47	178	48 17	257	46 48	312
78	37 42	037	19 32	092	40 02	128	26 30	155	38 49	179	47 34	258	46 15	313
79	38 08	037	20 16	093	40 36	130	26 48	156	38 49	180	46 51	259	45 43	313
80	38 35	037	20 59	093	41 09	131	27 06	157	38 48	182	46 08	259	45 11	313
81	39 01	037	21 43	094	41 42	132	27 22	158	38 47	183	45 25	260	44 39	313
82	39 28	038	22 27	095	42 15	133	27 39	159	38 44	184	44 42	261	44 07	313
83	39 55	038	23 11	095	42 47	134	27 54	160	38 40	185	43 58	262	43 35	314
84	40 22	038	23 54	096	43 18	135	28 09	161	38 36	187	43 15	263	43 03	314
85	40 49	038	24 38	097	43 49	136	28 23	162	38 30	188	42 31	263	42 32	314
86	41 16	038	25 22	097	44 19	138	28 36	163	38 24	189	41 48	264	42 00	314
87	41 44	039	26 05	098	44 48	139	28 48	164	38 16	190	41 04	265	41 29	314
88	42 11	039	26 48	099	45 16	140	29 00	165	38 08	192	40 20	266	40 57	315
89	42 39	039	27 32	100	45 44	141	29 11	166	37 59	193	39 37	266	40 26	315

LAT 43°N

LHA ♈	Hc	Zn	Hc	Zn	Hc	Zn	Hc	Zn	Hc	Zn	Hc	Zn	Hc	Zn
	◆ Dubhe		REGULUS		PROCYON		◆ SIRIUS		RIGEL		ALDEBARAN		◆ Mirfak	
90	43 06	039	28 15	100	46 11	143	29 20	167	37 49	194	58 10	220	62 49	298
91	43 34	039	28 58	101	46 38	144	29 30	168	37 38	195	57 41	222	62 11	298
92	44 02	039	29 41	102	47 03	145	29 38	170	37 25	197	57 11	223	61 32	298
93	44 30	040	30 24	103	47 28	146	29 46	171	37 13	198	56 41	225	60 53	298
94	44 58	040	31 07	104	47 52	148	29 52	172	36 59	199	56 09	226	60 15	298
95	45 26	040	31 49	104	48 15	149	29 58	173	36 44	200	55 37	228	59 36	299
96	45 54	040	32 32	105	48 37	151	30 03	174	36 29	201	55 04	229	58 58	299
97	46 22	040	33 14	106	48 58	152	30 07	175	36 12	203	54 31	230	58 19	299
98	46 50	040	33 56	107	49 18	153	30 11	176	35 55	204	53 57	232	57 41	299
99	47 19	040	34 38	108	49 37	155	30 13	177	35 37	205	53 22	233	57 02	299
100	47 47	040	35 20	108	49 55	156	30 15	178	35 18	206	52 47	234	56 24	299
101	48 15	040	36 01	109	50 12	158	30 16	179	34 58	207	52 11	235	55 46	299
102	48 44	040	36 43	110	50 28	159	30 16	181	34 38	208	51 35	237	55 07	299
103	49 12	040	37 24	111	50 43	161	30 15	182	34 17	209	50 58	238	54 29	300
104	49 41	040	38 05	112	50 57	162	30 13	183	33 55	211	50 20	239	53 51	300
	Dubhe		◆ Denebola		REGULUS		◆ SIRIUS		RIGEL		ALDEBARAN		◆ Mirfak	
105	50 09	040	22 35	091	38 45	113	30 10	184	33 32	212	49 42	240	53 13	300
106	50 37	040	23 19	092	39 25	114	30 07	185	33 09	213	49 04	241	52 35	300
107	51 06	040	24 03	092	40 05	115	30 03	186	32 45	214	48 25	242	51 57	300
108	51 34	040	24 47	093	40 45	116	29 58	187	32 20	215	47 46	243	51 19	301
109	52 03	040	25 31	094	41 25	117	29 52	188	31 55	216	47 07	244	50 42	301
110	52 31	040	26 14	094	42 04	118	29 45	189	31 29	217	46 27	245	50 04	301
111	53 00	040	26 58	095	42 42	119	29 37	191	31 02	218	45 47	246	49 26	301
112	53 28	040	27 42	096	43 21	120	29 29	192	30 35	219	45 07	247	48 49	302
113	53 56	040	28 25	097	43 59	121	29 20	193	30 07	220	44 26	248	48 12	302
114	54 25	040	29 09	097	44 36	122	29 10	194	29 38	221	43 45	249	47 34	302
115	54 53	040	29 52	098	45 14	123	28 59	195	29 09	222	43 04	250	46 57	302
116	55 21	040	30 36	099	45 50	124	28 47	196	28 40	223	42 23	251	46 20	303
117	55 49	040	31 19	100	46 27	125	28 35	197	28 09	224	41 41	252	45 43	303
118	56 17	040	32 02	100	47 02	126	28 21	198	27 39	225	40 59	253	45 06	303
119	56 45	039	32 45	101	47 38	127	28 07	199	27 08	226	40 17	254	44 30	303
	◆ Kochab		Denebola		◆ REGULUS		SIRIUS		RIGEL		◆ ALDEBARAN		CAPELLA	
120	37 44	020	33 28	102	48 12	128	27 53	200	26 36	227	39 35	255	61 14	290
121	37 59	020	34 11	103	48 46	130	27 37	201	26 04	228	38 53	255	60 33	290
122	38 14	020	34 54	103	49 20	131	27 21	202	25 31	229	38 10	256	59 52	291
123	38 29	020	35 37	104	49 53	132	27 04	203	24 58	230	37 27	257	59 11	291
124	38 44	020	36 19	105	50 25	133	26 46	204	24 24	230	36 45	258	58 30	291
125	38 59	020	37 01	106	50 57	135	26 28	205	23 50	231	36 02	259	57 49	291
126	39 15	021	37 43	107	51 28	136	26 09	206	23 16	232	35 19	259	57 08	292
127	39 30	021	38 25	108	51 58	137	25 49	207	22 41	233	34 35	260	56 28	292
128	39 46	021	39 07	109	52 27	139	25 28	208	22 05	234	33 52	261	55 47	292
129	40 01	021	39 49	109	52 56	140	25 07	209	21 30	235	33 09	262	55 06	292
130	40 17	021	40 30	110	53 23	142	24 46	210	20 54	236	32 25	262	54 26	293
131	40 33	021	41 11	111	53 50	143	24 23	211	20 17	236	31 42	263	53 46	293
132	40 49	021	41 52	112	54 16	144	24 00	212	19 41	237	30 58	264	53 05	293
133	41 04	021	42 32	113	54 41	146	23 36	213	19 03	238	30 14	265	52 25	294
134	41 20	021	43 12	114	55 05	148	23 12	214	18 26	239	29 31	265	51 45	294
	◆ Kochab		ARCTURUS		Denebola		◆ REGULUS		SIRIUS		BETELGEUSE		◆ CAPELLA	
135	41 37	021	20 44	083	43 52	115	55 28	149	22 47	215	36 17	242	51 05	294
136	41 53	022	21 28	083	44 32	116	55 50	151	22 22	216	35 38	243	50 25	295
137	42 09	022	22 11	084	45 11	117	56 11	152	21 56	217	34 58	244	49 45	295
138	42 25	022	22 55	085	45 50	118	56 31	154	21 29	218	34 19	245	49 05	295
139	42 41	022	23 39	085	46 29	119	56 50	156	21 02	219	33 39	246	48 26	296
140	42 57	022	24 22	086	47 07	120	57 07	157	20 34	220	32 59	247	47 46	296
141	43 14	022	25 06	087	47 45	121	57 23	159	20 06	220	32 18	248	47 07	296
142	43 30	022	25 50	087	48 22	122	57 38	161	19 37	221	31 38	248	46 27	297
143	43 47	022	26 34	088	48 59	123	57 52	163	19 08	222	30 57	249	45 48	297
144	44 03	022	27 18	089	49 35	125	58 04	165	18 38	223	30 15	250	45 09	297
145	44 19	022	28 02	089	50 11	126	58 15	166	18 08	224	29 34	251	44 30	298
146	44 36	022	28 46	090	50 46	127	58 25	168	17 37	225	28 52	252	43 51	298
147	44 52	022	29 29	091	51 21	128	58 33	170	17 06	226	28 11	253	43 12	298
148	45 09	022	30 13	091	51 55	129	58 40	172	16 35	226	27 29	253	42 34	299
149	45 25	022	30 57	092	52 29	131	58 46	174	16 02	227	26 47	254	41 55	299
	◆ Kochab		ARCTURUS		◆ SPICA		REGULUS		PROCYON		◆ POLLUX		CAPELLA	
150	45 42	022	31 41	093	18 17	126	58 50	176	41 11	229	59 12	252	41 17	299
151	45 58	022	32 25	094	18 52	127	58 52	178	40 37	230	58 30	253	40 39	300
152	46 14	022	33 09	094	19 27	128	58 54	179	40 03	232	57 48	254	40 01	300
153	46 31	022	33 52	095	20 01	129	58 53	181	39 29	233	57 06	255	39 23	300
154	46 47	022	34 36	096	20 36	129	58 51	183	38 54	234	56 23	256	38 45	301
155	47 03	022	35 20	096	21 09	130	58 48	185	38 18	235	55 41	257	38 08	301
156	47 20	022	36 03	097	21 43	131	58 44	187	37 42	236	54 58	258	37 30	302
157	47 36	022	36 47	098	22 15	132	58 38	189	37 06	237	54 15	259	36 53	302
158	47 52	022	37 30	099	22 48	133	58 30	191	36 29	238	53 32	260	36 16	302
159	48 08	022	38 13	099	23 20	134	58 21	193	35 51	239	52 49	260	35 39	303
160	48 25	022	38 57	100	23 51	135	58 11	194	35 14	240	52 05	261	35 02	303
161	48 41	021	39 40	101	24 22	136	57 59	196	34 36	240	51 22	262	34 25	304
162	48 57	021	40 23	102	24 52	137	57 46	198	33 57	241	50 38	263	33 49	304
163	49 13	021	41 06	103	25 22	137	57 32	200	33 19	242	49 55	264	33 13	304
164	49 28	021	41 48	104	25 52	138	57 17	202	32 40	243	49 11	264	32 37	305
	◆ Kochab		ARCTURUS		◆ SPICA		REGULUS		PROCYON		◆ POLLUX		CAPELLA	
165	49 44	021	42 31	104	26 21	139	57 00	203	32 00	244	48 28	265	32 01	305
166	50 00	021	43 13	105	26 49	140	56 42	205	31 21	245	47 44	266	31 25	306
167	50 15	021	43 56	106	27 17	141	56 23	207	30 41	246	47 00	267	30 49	306
168	50 31	021	44 38	107	27 44	142	56 03	208	30 01	247	46 16	267	30 14	307
169	50 46	020	45 20	108	28 10	143	55 41	210	29 20	248	45 32	268	29 39	307
170	51 02	020	46 01	109	28 36	144	55 19	212	28 40	248	44 48	269	29 04	307
171	51 17	020	46 43	110	29 01	145	54 55	213	27 59	249	44 05	269	28 29	308
172	51 32	020	47 24	111	29 26	146	54 31	215	27 18	250	43 21	270	27 55	308
173	51 47	020	48 05	112	29 50	147	54 06	216	26 36	251	42 37	271	27 20	309
174	52 01	020	48 46	113	30 13	148	53 39	218	25 55	252	41 53	271	26 46	309
175	52 16	019	49 26	114	30 36	149	53 12	219	25 13	252	41 09	272	26 12	310
176	52 30	019	50 06	115	30 58	151	52 44	221	24 31	253	40 25	273	25 39	310
177	52 45	019	50 46	116	31 19	152	52 15	222	23 49	254	39 41	273	25 05	311
178	52 59	019	51 25	117	31 40	153	51 45	223	23 07	255	38 58	274	24 32	311
179	53 13	018	52 04	118	32 00	154	51 15	225	22 24	255	38 14	275	23 59	311

LHA ♈	Hc	Zn	Hc	Zn	Hc	Zn	Hc	Zn	Hc	Zn	Hc	Zn	Hc	Zn
	Kochab		◆VEGA		ARCTURUS		◆SPICA		REGULUS		◆POLLUX		CAPELLA	
180	53 27	018	19 33	055	52 42	119	32 19	155	50 44	226	37 30	275	23 26	312
181	53 40	018	20 09	055	53 21	120	32 37	156	50 12	227	36 47	276	22 53	312
182	53 54	018	20 45	056	53 58	121	32 54	157	49 39	229	36 03	277	22 21	313
183	54 07	017	21 21	056	54 35	123	33 11	158	49 06	230	35 19	277	21 49	313
184	54 20	017	21 58	057	55 12	124	33 27	159	48 32	231	34 36	278	21 17	314
185	54 33	017	22 35	057	55 48	125	33 42	160	47 58	232	33 52	278	20 46	314
186	54 45	016	23 12	058	56 24	126	33 56	162	47 23	233	33 09	279	20 15	315
187	54 57	016	23 49	058	56 59	128	34 10	163	46 48	234	32 26	280	19 44	315
188	55 09	016	24 27	059	57 33	129	34 22	164	46 12	236	31 43	280	19 13	316
189	55 21	016	25 04	059	58 07	131	34 34	165	45 35	237	30 59	281	18 42	316
190	55 33	015	25 42	060	58 40	132	34 45	166	44 58	238	30 16	281	18 12	317
191	55 44	015	26 20	060	59 12	134	34 55	167	44 21	239	29 33	282	17 42	317
192	55 55	014	26 58	061	59 43	135	35 04	169	43 43	240	28 51	283	17 13	318
193	56 06	014	27 37	061	60 14	137	35 12	170	43 05	241	28 08	283	16 43	318
194	56 17	014	28 15	062	60 43	138	35 20	171	42 26	242	27 25	284	16 14	319
	◆VEGA		Rasalhague		ARCTURUS		◆SPICA		REGULUS		◆POLLUX		Dubhe	
195	28 54	062	23 54	095	61 12	140	35 26	172	41 48	243	26 43	284	64 44	328
196	29 33	063	24 38	096	61 40	142	35 32	173	41 08	244	26 00	285	64 20	327
197	30 12	063	25 21	096	62 06	144	35 36	175	40 29	245	25 18	286	63 56	326
198	30 52	064	26 05	097	62 32	145	35 40	176	39 49	246	24 36	286	63 32	326
199	31 31	064	26 48	098	62 56	147	35 43	177	39 09	247	23 53	287	63 07	325
200	32 11	065	27 32	099	63 19	149	35 45	178	38 28	248	23 12	287	62 42	325
201	32 50	065	28 15	099	63 41	151	35 46	179	37 48	248	22 30	288	62 16	324
202	33 30	066	28 58	100	64 01	153	35 46	181	37 07	249	21 48	289	61 51	324
203	34 11	066	29 41	101	64 20	155	35 45	182	36 25	250	21 07	289	61 25	324
204	34 51	067	30 24	102	64 38	157	35 43	183	35 44	251	20 25	290	60 58	323
205	35 31	067	31 07	102	64 54	159	35 40	184	35 02	252	19 44	290	60 32	323
206	36 12	068	31 50	103	65 09	162	35 36	185	34 21	253	19 03	291	60 05	322
207	36 52	068	32 33	104	65 22	164	35 32	187	33 39	254	18 22	292	59 39	322
208	37 33	069	33 15	105	65 34	166	35 26	188	32 56	254	17 41	292	59 11	322
209	38 14	069	33 58	106	65 43	168	35 20	189	32 14	255	17 01	293	58 44	322
	◆DENEB		VEGA		Rasalhague		ANTARES		◆ARCTURUS		REGULUS		◆Dubhe	
210	23 03	049	38 55	070	34 40	106	12 25	146	65 51	171	31 32	256	58 17	321
211	23 36	049	39 36	070	35 22	107	12 49	147	65 58	173	30 49	257	57 49	321
212	24 09	050	40 18	071	36 03	108	13 13	148	66 02	175	30 06	258	57 22	321
213	24 43	050	40 59	071	36 45	109	13 36	148	66 05	177	29 23	258	56 54	321
214	25 17	051	41 41	072	37 26	110	13 59	149	66 06	180	28 40	259	56 26	320
215	25 51	051	42 22	072	38 08	111	14 21	150	66 06	182	27 57	260	55 58	320
216	26 25	051	43 04	072	38 49	112	14 42	151	66 03	184	27 14	261	55 30	320
217	26 59	052	43 46	073	39 29	113	15 03	152	65 59	187	26 30	261	55 02	320
218	27 34	052	44 28	073	40 10	113	15 24	153	65 53	189	25 47	262	54 34	320
219	28 09	053	45 10	074	40 50	114	15 43	154	65 45	191	25 03	263	54 06	320
220	28 44	053	45 52	074	41 30	115	16 03	154	65 35	194	24 20	264	53 37	320
221	29 19	054	46 35	075	42 09	116	16 21	155	65 24	196	23 36	264	53 09	320
222	29 55	054	47 17	075	42 48	117	16 39	156	65 11	198	22 53	265	52 40	320
223	30 30	055	48 00	076	43 27	118	16 57	157	64 57	200	22 09	266	52 12	320
224	31 06	055	48 42	076	44 05	119	17 13	158	64 41	202	21 25	266	51 44	320
	DENEB		◆ALTAIR		Rasalhague		ANTARES		◆ARCTURUS		Denebola		◆Dubhe	
225	31 42	055	18 34	095	44 43	120	17 30	159	64 24	204	40 26	250	51 15	320
226	32 18	056	19 17	096	45 21	121	17 45	160	64 05	207	39 45	251	50 47	320
227	32 55	056	20 01	097	45 58	122	18 00	161	63 45	209	39 03	252	50 18	320
228	33 31	057	20 45	097	46 35	124	18 14	162	63 23	210	38 22	252	49 50	320
229	34 08	057	21 28	098	47 11	125	18 28	162	63 00	212	37 40	253	49 21	320
230	34 45	058	22 11	099	47 47	126	18 41	163	62 36	214	36 58	254	48 53	320
231	35 22	058	22 55	099	48 23	127	18 53	164	62 11	216	36 15	255	48 24	320
232	36 00	058	23 38	100	48 57	128	19 04	165	61 44	218	35 33	256	47 56	320
233	36 37	059	24 21	101	49 32	129	19 15	166	61 17	220	34 50	257	47 28	320
234	37 15	059	25 04	102	50 05	131	19 25	167	60 48	221	34 07	257	46 59	320
235	37 52	060	25 47	102	50 38	132	19 35	168	60 19	223	33 25	258	46 31	320
236	38 30	060	26 30	103	51 10	133	19 43	169	59 49	225	32 42	259	46 03	320
237	39 08	060	27 13	104	51 42	135	19 51	170	59 17	226	31 58	260	45 35	320
238	39 46	061	27 55	105	52 13	136	19 59	171	58 45	228	31 15	260	45 07	320
239	40 25	061	28 37	106	52 43	137	20 05	172	58 13	229	30 32	261	44 39	320
	◆DENEB		ALTAIR		Rasalhague		◆ANTARES		ARCTURUS		Denebola		◆Dubhe	
240	41 03	061	29 20	106	53 13	139	20 11	173	57 39	231	29 49	262	44 11	321
241	41 42	062	30 02	107	53 41	140	20 16	174	57 05	232	29 05	263	43 43	321
242	42 21	062	30 43	108	54 09	142	20 21	175	56 30	233	28 21	263	43 15	321
243	43 00	063	31 25	109	54 36	143	20 24	176	55 55	235	27 38	264	42 47	321
244	43 39	063	32 07	110	55 02	145	20 27	177	55 18	236	26 54	265	42 20	321
245	44 18	063	32 48	110	55 27	146	20 30	178	54 42	237	26 10	266	41 52	321
246	44 57	064	33 29	111	55 50	148	20 31	178	54 05	238	25 27	266	41 25	321
247	45 36	064	34 10	112	56 13	149	20 32	179	53 27	240	24 43	267	40 58	322
248	46 16	064	34 50	113	56 35	151	20 32	180	52 49	241	23 59	268	40 31	322
249	46 56	065	35 30	114	56 56	153	20 31	181	52 11	242	23 15	268	40 04	322
250	47 35	065	36 10	115	57 16	154	20 30	182	51 32	243	22 31	269	39 37	322
251	48 15	065	36 50	116	57 34	156	20 28	183	50 52	244	21 47	270	39 10	322
252	48 55	066	37 29	117	57 51	158	20 25	184	50 13	245	21 04	270	38 43	323
253	49 35	066	38 08	118	58 07	160	20 21	185	49 33	246	20 20	271	38 17	323
254	50 15	066	38 47	119	58 22	161	20 17	186	48 53	247	19 36	272	37 50	323
	◆DENEB		ALTAIR		Nunki		◆ANTARES		ARCTURUS		◆Alkaid		Kochab	
255	50 56	067	39 26	120	15 45	153	20 12	187	48 12	248	56 45	298	55 37	345
256	51 36	067	40 04	120	16 04	154	20 06	188	47 31	249	56 06	298	55 25	345
257	52 17	067	40 41	121	16 23	155	20 00	189	46 50	250	55 28	298	55 14	344
258	52 57	068	41 18	123	16 42	156	19 53	190	46 09	251	54 49	298	55 02	344
259	53 38	068	41 55	124	16 59	157	19 45	191	45 27	252	54 10	299	54 49	344
260	54 19	068	42 32	125	17 16	158	19 36	192	44 45	253	53 32	299	54 37	343
261	54 59	069	43 07	126	17 33	158	19 27	193	44 03	254	52 53	299	54 24	343
262	55 40	069	43 43	127	17 49	159	19 17	194	43 21	255	52 15	299	54 11	343
263	56 21	069	44 18	128	18 04	160	19 06	195	42 38	256	51 37	299	53 58	342
264	57 02	070	44 52	129	18 18	161	18 55	196	41 56	256	50 58	300	53 45	342
265	57 43	070	45 26	130	18 32	162	18 43	196	41 13	257	50 20	300	53 31	342
266	58 25	070	45 59	131	18 46	163	18 30	197	40 30	258	49 42	300	53 17	342
267	59 06	070	46 32	133	18 58	164	18 16	198	39 47	259	49 04	300	53 04	341
268	59 47	071	47 04	134	19 10	165	18 02	199	39 04	260	48 27	301	52 49	341
269	60 29	071	47 35	135	19 21	166	17 48	200	38 21	260	47 49	301	52 35	341

LHA ♈	Hc	Zn	Hc	Zn	Hc	Zn	Hc	Zn	Hc	Zn	Hc	Zn	Hc	Zn
	◆Alpheratz		ALTAIR		Nunki		◆ANTARES		ARCTURUS		◆Alkaid		Kochab	
270	17 52	066	48 06	136	19 32	167	17 32	201	37 38	261	47 11	301	52 21	341
271	18 33	067	48 36	138	19 41	168	17 16	202	36 54	262	46 34	301	52 06	341
272	19 13	068	49 05	139	19 50	169	17 00	203	36 11	263	45 56	302	51 52	340
273	19 54	068	49 34	140	19 59	169	16 42	204	35 27	263	45 19	302	51 37	340
274	20 35	069	50 01	142	20 06	170	16 24	205	34 44	264	44 42	302	51 22	340
275	21 16	069	50 28	143	20 13	171	16 06	205	34 00	265	44 05	303	51 07	340
276	21 57	070	50 54	144	20 20	172	15 47	206	33 16	266	43 28	303	50 51	340
277	22 38	071	51 20	146	20 25	173	15 27	207	32 32	266	42 51	303	50 36	339
278	23 20	071	51 44	147	20 30	174	15 07	208	31 49	267	42 15	304	50 21	339
279	24 01	072	52 07	149	20 34	175	14 46	209	31 05	268	41 38	304	50 05	339
280	24 43	072	52 29	150	20 37	176	14 24	210	30 21	268	41 02	304	49 50	339
281	25 25	073	52 51	152	20 40	177	14 02	211	29 37	269	40 25	304	49 34	339
282	26 07	073	53 11	153	20 42	178	13 40	211	28 53	270	39 49	305	49 18	339
283	26 49	074	53 30	155	20 43	179	13 17	212	28 09	270	39 13	305	49 02	339
284	27 31	075	53 49	156	20 43	180	12 53	213	27 25	271	38 38	305	48 46	339
	◆Mirfak		Alpheratz		◆ALTAIR		Rasalhague		◆ARCTURUS		Alkaid		Kochab	
285	14 03	032	28 13	075	54 06	158	54 31	217	26 42	272	38 02	306	48 30	339
286	14 26	033	28 56	076	54 21	160	54 04	219	25 58	273	37 26	306	48 14	338
287	14 50	033	29 39	076	54 36	161	53 36	220	25 14	273	36 51	307	47 58	338
288	15 14	034	30 21	077	54 50	163	53 07	222	24 30	274	36 16	307	47 42	338
289	15 39	034	31 04	078	55 02	165	52 38	223	23 46	274	35 41	307	47 25	338
290	16 04	035	31 47	078	55 13	166	52 07	224	23 03	275	35 06	308	47 09	338
291	16 29	035	32 30	079	55 23	168	51 36	226	22 19	276	34 31	308	46 53	338
292	16 55	036	33 13	079	55 31	170	51 05	227	21 35	276	33 57	308	46 36	338
293	17 21	036	33 56	080	55 39	171	50 32	228	20 52	277	33 23	309	46 20	338
294	17 47	037	34 39	080	55 44	173	49 59	230	20 08	278	32 49	309	46 03	338
295	18 13	037	35 23	081	55 49	175	49 25	231	19 25	278	32 15	310	45 47	338
296	18 40	038	36 06	082	55 52	177	48 51	232	18 41	279	31 41	310	45 31	338
297	19 07	038	36 49	082	55 54	178	48 16	233	17 58	280	31 07	310	45 14	338
298	19 35	039	37 33	083	55 55	180	47 41	234	17 15	280	30 34	311	44 58	338
299	20 02	039	38 17	084	55 54	182	47 05	235	16 32	281	30 01	311	44 41	338
	Mirfak		◆Alpheratz		Enif		◆ALTAIR		Rasalhague		Alphecca		◆Kochab	
300	20 30	040	39 00	084	49 49	138	55 51	184	46 28	237	34 46	276	44 25	338
301	20 59	040	39 44	085	50 18	139	55 48	185	45 52	238	34 02	276	44 08	338
302	21 27	041	40 28	085	50 47	140	55 43	187	45 14	239	33 18	277	43 52	338
303	21 56	041	41 11	086	51 14	142	55 37	189	44 37	240	32 35	278	43 36	338
304	22 25	042	41 55	087	51 41	143	55 29	191	43 58	241	31 51	278	43 19	338
305	22 54	042	42 39	087	52 07	144	55 21	192	43 20	242	31 08	279	43 03	338
306	23 24	043	43 23	088	52 32	146	55 11	194	42 41	243	30 25	279	42 47	338
307	23 54	043	44 07	089	52 56	147	54 59	196	42 02	244	29 41	280	42 30	338
308	24 24	043	44 51	089	53 19	149	54 47	198	41 22	245	28 58	281	42 14	338
309	24 54	044	45 34	090	53 41	150	54 33	199	40 42	246	28 15	281	41 58	338
310	25 25	044	46 18	091	54 02	152	54 18	201	40 02	247	27 32	282	41 42	338
311	25 55	045	47 02	091	54 22	154	54 02	202	39 22	248	26 49	282	41 26	339
312	26 26	045	47 46	092	54 41	155	53 44	204	38 41	249	26 06	283	41 10	339
313	26 58	046	48 30	093	54 59	157	53 26	206	38 00	249	25 24	284	40 54	339
314	27 29	046	49 14	093	55 16	159	53 06	207	37 19	250	24 41	284	40 38	339
	CAPELLA		◆Alpheratz		FOMALHAUT		◆ALTAIR		Rasalhague		VEGA		◆Kochab	
315	11 44	036	49 57	094	12 31	154	52 46	209	36 37	251	62 57	273	40 22	339
316	12 10	036	50 41	095	12 51	155	52 24	210	35 56	252	62 13	274	40 07	339
317	12 36	037	51 25	096	13 09	156	52 02	212	35 14	253	61 29	274	39 51	339
318	13 03	037	52 09	097	13 27	156	51 38	213	34 32	254	60 45	275	39 35	339
319	13 29	038	52 52	097	13 44	157	51 13	215	33 50	254	60 02	276	39 20	339
320	13 57	039	53 36	098	14 01	158	50 48	216	33 07	255	59 18	276	39 04	340
321	14 24	039	54 19	099	14 17	159	50 22	217	32 25	256	58 34	277	38 49	340
322	14 52	040	55 02	100	14 32	160	49 55	219	31 42	257	57 51	277	38 34	340
323	15 20	040	55 45	101	14 47	161	49 27	220	30 59	258	57 07	278	38 19	340
324	15 48	041	56 28	101	15 02	162	48 58	221	30 16	258	56 24	278	38 04	340
325	16 17	041	57 11	102	15 15	162	48 29	223	29 33	259	55 41	279	37 49	340
326	16 46	042	57 54	103	15 28	163	47 59	224	28 50	260	54 57	279	37 34	340
327	17 16	042	58 37	104	15 40	164	47 28	225	28 07	261	54 14	280	37 19	340
328	17 45	043	59 19	105	15 52	165	46 56	227	27 24	261	53 31	280	37 05	341
329	18 15	043	60 01	106	16 03	166	46 24	228	26 40	262	52 48	281	36 50	341
	◆CAPELLA		Hamal		Diphda		◆FOMALHAUT		ALTAIR		◆VEGA		Kochab	
330	18 45	044	35 57	090	18 21	139	16 13	167	45 51	229	52 05	281	36 36	341
331	19 16	044	36 41	091	18 50	140	16 23	168	45 18	230	51 22	282	36 22	341
332	19 47	045	37 25	091	19 18	141	16 32	169	44 44	231	50 39	282	36 07	341
333	20 18	045	38 08	092	19 46	141	16 41	169	44 09	232	49 56	283	35 53	342
334	20 49	046	38 52	093	20 13	142	16 48	170	43 34	233	49 13	283	35 40	342
335	21 21	046	39 36	094	20 39	143	16 55	171	42 59	235	48 30	284	35 26	342
336	21 52	047	40 20	094	21 05	144	17 02	172	42 23	236	47 48	284	35 12	342
337	22 24	047	41 04	095	21 31	145	17 07	173	41 46	237	47 05	285	34 59	342
338	22 57	048	41 47	096	21 56	146	17 12	174	41 09	238	46 23	285	34 46	342
339	23 29	048	42 31	097	22 20	147	17 16	175	40 32	239	45 41	286	34 32	343
340	24 02	049	43 14	097	22 44	148	17 20	176	39 54	240	44 59	286	34 19	343
341	24 35	049	43 58	098	23 07	149	17 23	177	39 16	241	44 16	287	34 07	343
342	25 08	050	44 41	099	23 29	150	17 25	178	38 38	242	43 34	287	33 54	343
343	25 42	050	45 25	100	23 51	151	17 27	179	37 59	243	42 53	288	33 41	343
344	26 16	050	46 08	101	24 12	152	17 27	179	37 20	244	42 11	288	33 29	344
	◆CAPELLA		ALDEBARAN		Diphda		◆FOMALHAUT		ALTAIR		◆VEGA		Kochab	
345	26 50	051	15 22	082	24 33	153	17 27	180	36 40	245	41 29	289	33 17	344
346	27 24	051	16 06	082	24 52	154	17 27	181	36 01	245	40 48	289	33 05	344
347	27 58	052	16 49	083	25 12	155	17 25	182	35 21	246	40 06	290	32 53	344
348	28 33	052	17 33	083	25 30	156	17 23	183	34 40	247	39 25	290	32 41	345
349	29 07	053	18 16	084	25 48	157	17 21	184	34 00	248	38 44	291	32 29	345
350	29 42	053	19 00	085	26 05	158	17 17	185	33 19	249	38 03	291	32 18	345
351	30 18	054	19 44	085	26 21	159	17 13	186	32 38	250	37 22	291	32 07	345
352	30 53	054	20 27	086	26 37	160	17 08	187	31 57	251	36 41	292	31 56	346
353	31 29	054	21 11	087	26 52	161	17 03	188	31 15	251	36 00	292	31 45	346
354	32 04	055	21 55	087	27 06	162	16 57	189	30 33	252	35 20	293	31 34	346
355	32 40	055	22 39	088	27 19	163	16 50	189	29 51	253	34 40	293	31 24	346
356	33 16	056	23 23	089	27 32	164	16 42	190	29 09	254	33 59	294	31 13	347
357	33 53	056	24 07	089	27 44	165	16 34	191	28 27	255	33 19	294	31 03	347
358	34 29	056	24 51	090	27 55	166	16 25	192	27 45	255	32 39	295	30 53	347
359	35 06	057	25 34	091	28 05	167	16 16	193	27 02	256	32 00	295	30 43	347

LAT 42°N

LHA ♈	Hc	Zn	Hc	Zn	Hc	Zn	Hc	Zn	Hc	Zn	Hc	Zn	Hc	Zn
	◆ CAPELLA		ALDEBARAN		◆ Diphda		FOMALHAUT		ALTAIR		◆ VEGA		Kochab	
0	35 10	057	26 20	091	29 14	168	17 04	194	26 33	257	30 54	296	29 35	348
1	35 47	057	27 04	092	29 22	169	16 53	195	25 49	258	30 14	297	29 26	348
2	36 25	057	27 49	092	29 31	170	16 41	196	25 06	259	29 34	297	29 17	348
3	37 02	058	28 33	093	29 38	171	16 29	197	24 22	260	28 55	298	29 08	348
4	37 40	058	29 18	094	29 44	172	16 15	198	23 38	260	28 15	298	28 59	349
5	38 18	058	30 02	094	29 50	173	16 02	198	22 54	261	27 36	299	28 50	349
6	38 56	059	30 47	095	29 55	174	15 47	199	22 10	262	26 57	299	28 42	349
7	39 34	059	31 31	096	29 59	176	15 32	200	21 25	263	26 18	300	28 34	350
8	40 13	060	32 15	097	30 02	177	15 17	201	20 41	263	25 40	300	28 25	350
9	40 51	060	33 00	097	30 04	178	15 00	202	19 57	264	25 01	301	28 18	350
10	41 30	060	33 44	098	30 05	179	14 44	203	19 13	265	24 23	301	28 10	350
11	42 09	061	34 28	099	30 06	180	14 26	204	18 28	265	23 45	302	28 03	351
12	42 48	061	35 12	100	30 05	181	14 08	204	17 44	266	23 07	302	27 56	351
13	43 27	061	35 56	100	30 04	182	13 49	205	16 59	267	22 29	303	27 49	351
14	44 06	062	36 40	101	30 02	183	13 30	206	16 15	267	21 52	303	27 42	351
	◆ CAPELLA		BETELGEUSE		RIGEL		◆ Diphda		Enif		◆ DENEB		Kochab	
15	44 45	062	16 50	095	13 15	114	29 59	184	36 44	248	44 29	297	27 35	352
16	45 24	062	17 34	096	13 56	115	29 55	185	36 02	248	43 49	298	27 29	352
17	46 04	063	18 18	097	14 36	116	29 51	186	35 21	249	43 10	298	27 23	352
18	46 44	063	19 02	097	15 16	116	29 45	188	34 39	250	42 31	298	27 17	353
19	47 23	063	19 47	098	15 56	117	29 39	189	33 57	251	41 51	299	27 12	353
20	48 03	063	20 31	099	16 36	118	29 32	190	33 15	252	41 12	299	27 06	353
21	48 43	064	21 15	099	17 15	119	29 24	191	32 32	253	40 33	299	27 01	353
22	49 23	064	21 59	100	17 54	119	29 15	192	31 49	253	39 54	300	26 56	354
23	50 03	064	22 43	101	18 33	120	29 05	193	31 07	254	39 16	300	26 51	354
24	50 44	065	23 26	102	19 11	121	28 55	194	30 24	255	38 37	300	26 47	354
25	51 24	065	24 10	102	19 49	122	28 44	195	29 40	256	37 59	301	26 43	355
26	52 04	065	24 53	103	20 27	123	28 32	196	28 57	257	37 21	301	26 38	355
27	52 45	065	25 37	104	21 04	124	28 19	197	28 14	257	36 42	301	26 35	355
28	53 25	066	26 20	105	21 41	124	28 05	198	27 30	258	36 05	302	26 31	356
29	54 06	066	27 03	105	22 18	125	27 51	199	26 47	259	35 27	302	26 28	356
	◆ CAPELLA		BETELGEUSE		RIGEL		◆ Diphda		Alpheratz		◆ DENEB		Kochab	
30	54 47	066	27 46	106	22 54	126	27 36	200	64 15	249	34 49	303	26 25	356
31	55 28	066	28 29	107	23 30	127	27 20	201	63 33	250	34 12	303	26 22	356
32	56 09	067	29 11	108	24 05	128	27 03	202	62 51	251	33 34	303	26 19	357
33	56 50	067	29 54	109	24 40	129	26 46	203	62 08	253	32 57	304	26 17	357
34	57 31	067	30 36	109	25 15	130	26 28	204	61 25	254	32 20	304	26 15	357
35	58 12	067	31 18	110	25 49	130	26 09	205	60 43	255	31 44	305	26 13	358
36	58 53	068	32 00	111	26 23	131	25 50	206	59 59	256	31 07	305	26 11	358
37	59 34	068	32 41	112	26 56	132	25 29	207	59 16	257	30 31	305	26 09	358
38	60 16	068	33 22	113	27 29	133	25 08	208	58 33	258	29 54	306	26 08	359
39	60 57	068	34 03	114	28 01	134	24 47	209	57 49	259	29 18	306	26 07	359
40	61 38	068	34 44	114	28 33	135	24 25	210	57 05	259	28 42	307	26 06	359
41	62 20	068	35 25	115	29 04	136	24 02	211	56 21	260	28 07	307	26 06	359
42	63 01	069	36 05	116	29 35	137	23 38	212	55 37	261	27 31	308	26 06	000
43	63 43	069	36 45	117	30 05	138	23 14	213	54 53	262	26 56	308	26 06	000
44	64 24	069	37 24	118	30 34	139	22 50	214	54 09	263	26 21	308	26 06	000
	◆ Dubhe		POLLUX		BETELGEUSE		◆ RIGEL		Diphda		◆ Alpheratz		DENEB	
45	23 59	026	31 26	079	38 03	119	31 03	140	22 24	215	53 25	264	25 46	309
46	24 19	027	32 10	080	38 42	120	31 32	141	21 58	216	52 41	264	25 12	309
47	24 39	027	32 54	080	39 21	121	31 59	142	21 32	217	51 56	265	24 37	310
48	25 00	027	33 38	081	39 59	122	32 27	143	21 05	218	51 12	266	24 03	310
49	25 20	028	34 22	081	40 36	123	32 53	144	20 37	219	50 27	267	23 29	311
50	25 41	028	35 06	082	41 14	124	33 19	145	20 09	220	49 43	267	22 56	311
51	26 03	029	35 51	083	41 50	125	33 44	146	19 40	220	48 58	268	22 22	312
52	26 24	029	36 35	083	42 27	126	34 08	147	19 11	221	48 14	269	21 49	312
53	26 46	029	37 19	084	43 02	127	34 32	148	18 42	222	47 29	269	21 16	313
54	27 08	030	38 03	084	43 38	128	34 55	150	18 11	223	46 44	270	20 43	313
55	27 30	030	38 48	085	44 12	129	35 17	151	17 41	224	46 00	271	20 11	314
56	27 52	030	39 32	086	44 47	130	35 39	152	17 10	225	45 15	271	19 39	314
57	28 15	031	40 17	086	45 20	132	35 59	153	16 38	226	44 31	272	19 07	314
58	28 37	031	41 01	087	45 53	133	36 19	154	16 06	226	43 46	273	18 35	315
59	29 00	031	41 46	088	46 26	134	36 38	155	15 34	227	43 02	273	18 04	315
	◆ Dubhe		POLLUX		PROCYON		◆ SIRIUS		RIGEL		◆ Hamal		Schedar	
60	29 24	032	42 30	088	29 00	111	19 55	138	36 56	156	60 19	240	55 26	312
61	29 47	032	43 15	089	29 41	112	20 25	138	37 14	158	59 40	242	54 53	312
62	30 11	032	44 00	090	30 23	113	20 54	139	37 30	159	59 01	243	54 20	312
63	30 35	032	44 44	090	31 03	114	21 23	140	37 46	160	58 21	244	53 47	312
64	30 59	033	45 29	091	31 44	114	21 51	141	38 01	161	57 40	245	53 14	312
65	31 23	033	46 13	092	32 25	115	22 19	142	38 15	162	57 00	246	52 41	312
66	31 47	033	46 58	092	33 05	116	22 46	143	38 28	164	56 19	248	52 08	312
67	32 12	034	47 42	093	33 45	117	23 13	144	38 40	165	55 37	249	51 35	312
68	32 37	034	48 27	094	34 24	118	23 39	145	38 51	166	54 56	250	51 02	312
69	33 02	034	49 11	094	35 03	119	24 04	146	39 01	167	54 14	251	50 29	312
70	33 27	034	49 56	095	35 42	120	24 29	147	39 10	169	53 31	252	49 56	312
71	33 52	035	50 40	096	36 21	121	24 53	148	39 18	170	52 49	253	49 23	313
72	34 17	035	51 24	097	36 59	122	25 17	149	39 26	171	52 06	254	48 50	313
73	34 43	035	52 09	097	37 37	123	25 39	150	39 32	173	51 23	255	48 18	313
74	35 09	035	52 53	098	38 14	124	26 02	151	39 37	174	50 40	255	47 45	313
	◆ Dubhe		REGULUS		PROCYON		◆ SIRIUS		RIGEL		◆ Hamal		Schedar	
75	35 35	036	17 20	089	38 51	125	26 23	152	39 42	175	49 57	256	47 12	313
76	36 01	036	18 04	090	39 27	126	26 44	153	39 45	176	49 14	257	46 40	313
77	36 27	036	18 49	091	40 03	127	27 04	154	39 47	178	48 30	258	46 07	313
78	36 54	036	19 34	091	40 39	128	27 24	155	39 49	179	47 46	259	45 35	313
79	37 20	037	20 18	092	41 14	129	27 43	156	39 49	180	47 03	260	45 02	314
80	37 47	037	21 03	093	41 48	130	28 01	157	39 48	182	46 19	261	44 30	314
81	38 13	037	21 47	094	42 22	131	28 18	158	39 46	183	45 35	261	43 58	314
82	38 40	037	22 32	094	42 55	132	28 35	159	39 44	184	44 51	262	43 26	314
83	39 07	037	23 16	095	43 28	133	28 50	160	39 40	185	44 06	263	42 54	314
84	39 35	038	24 00	096	44 00	134	29 05	161	39 35	187	43 22	264	42 22	314
85	40 02	038	24 45	096	44 32	136	29 20	162	39 30	188	42 38	264	41 50	315
86	40 29	038	25 29	097	45 03	137	29 33	163	39 23	189	41 53	265	41 18	315
87	40 57	038	26 13	098	45 33	138	29 46	164	39 15	190	41 09	266	40 47	315
88	41 24	038	26 58	098	46 02	139	29 58	165	39 07	192	40 24	267	40 15	315
89	41 52	038	27 42	099	46 31	141	30 09	166	38 57	193	39 40	267	39 44	315

LHA ♈	Hc	Zn	Hc	Zn	Hc	Zn	Hc	Zn	Hc	Zn	Hc	Zn	Hc	Zn
	◆ Dubhe		REGULUS		PROCYON		◆ SIRIUS		RIGEL		ALDEBARAN		◆ Mirfak	
90	42 20	039	28 26	100	46 59	142	30 19	167	38 47	194	58 55	221	62 20	300
91	42 47	039	29 09	101	47 26	143	30 28	168	38 35	196	58 25	223	61 41	300
92	43 15	039	29 53	101	47 52	145	30 37	169	38 23	197	57 54	224	61 03	300
93	43 43	039	30 37	102	48 18	146	30 45	171	38 10	198	57 23	226	60 24	300
94	44 11	039	31 20	103	48 42	147	30 52	172	37 55	199	56 50	227	59 45	300
95	44 39	039	32 04	104	49 06	149	30 58	173	37 40	200	56 17	229	59 07	300
96	45 08	039	32 47	104	49 29	150	31 03	174	37 24	202	55 43	230	58 28	300
97	45 36	039	33 30	105	49 51	151	31 07	175	37 08	203	55 09	231	57 50	300
98	46 04	039	34 13	106	50 11	153	31 11	176	36 50	204	54 34	233	57 11	300
99	46 32	039	34 56	107	50 31	154	31 13	177	36 31	205	53 58	234	56 33	300
100	47 01	040	35 38	108	50 50	156	31 15	178	36 12	206	53 21	235	55 54	300
101	47 29	040	36 21	109	51 08	157	31 16	179	35 52	207	52 44	237	55 16	301
102	47 58	040	37 03	109	51 24	159	31 16	181	35 31	209	52 07	238	54 37	301
103	48 26	040	37 45	110	51 40	160	31 15	182	35 09	210	51 29	239	53 59	301
104	48 55	040	38 27	111	51 54	162	31 13	183	34 47	211	50 51	240	53 21	301
	Dubhe		◆ Denebola		REGULUS		◆ SIRIUS		RIGEL		ALDEBARAN		◆ Mirfak	
105	49 23	040	22 36	091	39 08	112	31 10	184	34 23	212	50 12	241	52 43	301
106	49 52	040	23 21	091	39 49	113	31 07	185	33 59	213	49 33	242	52 04	301
107	50 20	040	24 05	092	40 30	114	31 02	186	33 35	214	48 53	243	51 26	301
108	50 48	040	24 50	093	41 11	115	30 57	187	33 09	215	48 13	244	50 48	302
109	51 17	040	25 34	093	41 51	116	30 51	188	32 43	216	47 32	245	50 10	302
110	51 45	040	26 19	094	42 31	117	30 44	190	32 17	217	46 52	246	49 33	302
111	52 14	039	27 03	095	43 11	118	30 36	191	31 49	218	46 11	247	48 55	302
112	52 42	039	27 48	095	43 50	119	30 28	192	31 21	219	45 29	248	48 17	302
113	53 10	039	28 32	096	44 29	120	30 18	193	30 53	220	44 48	249	47 40	303
114	53 39	039	29 16	097	45 07	121	30 08	194	30 24	221	44 06	250	47 02	303
115	54 07	039	30 01	098	45 46	122	29 57	195	29 54	222	43 24	251	46 25	303
116	54 35	039	30 45	098	46 23	123	29 45	196	29 23	223	42 42	252	45 48	303
117	55 03	039	31 29	099	47 00	124	29 32	197	28 53	224	41 59	253	45 10	304
118	55 31	039	32 13	100	47 37	125	29 18	198	28 21	225	41 17	254	44 33	304
119	55 58	038	32 57	101	48 13	126	29 04	199	27 49	226	40 34	255	43 56	304
	◆ Kochab		Denebola		◆ REGULUS		SIRIUS		RIGEL		◆ ALDEBARAN		CAPELLA	
120	36 47	020	33 40	101	48 49	127	28 49	200	27 17	227	39 51	255	60 53	292
121	37 02	020	34 24	102	49 24	129	28 33	201	26 44	228	39 07	256	60 11	292
122	37 17	020	35 08	103	49 59	130	28 16	202	26 10	229	38 24	257	59 30	292
123	37 32	020	35 51	104	50 33	131	27 59	203	25 36	230	37 40	258	58 49	292
124	37 48	020	36 34	104	51 06	132	27 41	204	25 02	231	36 57	259	58 08	293
125	38 03	020	37 17	105	51 38	134	27 22	206	24 27	232	36 13	259	57 27	293
126	38 18	020	38 00	106	52 10	135	27 02	207	23 52	233	35 29	260	56 46	293
127	38 34	020	38 43	107	52 41	136	26 42	208	23 17	233	34 45	261	56 05	293
128	38 49	021	39 26	108	53 12	138	26 21	209	22 41	234	34 01	262	55 24	294
129	39 05	021	40 08	109	53 41	139	26 00	210	22 04	235	33 17	262	54 43	294
130	39 21	021	40 50	109	54 10	141	25 37	211	21 27	236	32 33	263	54 02	294
131	39 37	021	41 32	110	54 38	142	25 14	211	20 50	237	31 48	264	53 21	294
132	39 53	021	42 14	111	55 05	144	24 51	212	20 13	238	31 04	265	52 41	295
133	40 09	021	42 55	112	55 31	145	24 27	213	19 35	238	30 20	265	52 00	295
134	40 25	021	43 36	113	55 56	147	24 02	214	18 57	239	29 35	266	51 20	295
	◆ Kochab		ARCTURUS		Denebola		◆ REGULUS		SIRIUS		BETELGEUSE		◆ CAPELLA	
135	40 41	021	20 36	082	44 17	114	56 20	148	23 36	215	36 44	243	50 40	295
136	40 57	021	21 21	083	44 58	115	56 43	150	23 10	216	36 04	244	49 59	296
137	41 13	021	22 05	084	45 38	116	57 04	152	22 44	217	35 24	245	49 19	296
138	41 29	021	22 49	084	46 18	117	57 25	153	22 16	218	34 44	246	48 39	296
139	41 45	021	23 34	085	46 57	118	57 44	155	21 49	219	34 03	246	47 59	297
140	42 02	021	24 18	086	47 37	119	58 02	157	21 20	220	33 22	247	47 19	297
141	42 18	022	25 03	086	48 15	120	58 19	159	20 51	221	32 41	248	46 40	297
142	42 34	022	25 47	087	48 54	121	58 35	160	20 22	222	31 59	249	46 00	297
143	42 51	022	26 32	088	49 31	122	58 49	162	19 52	222	31 18	250	45 21	298
144	43 07	022	27 16	088	50 09	124	59 02	164	19 22	223	30 36	251	44 41	298
145	43 24	022	28 01	089	50 46	125	59 14	166	18 51	224	29 53	251	44 02	298
146	43 40	022	28 45	090	51 22	126	59 24	168	18 20	225	29 11	252	43 23	299
147	43 56	022	29 30	090	51 58	127	59 32	170	17 48	226	28 28	253	42 44	299
148	44 13	022	30 15	091	52 33	128	59 40	172	17 16	227	27 46	254	42 05	299
149	44 29	022	30 59	092	53 08	130	59 45	174	16 43	228	27 03	255	41 26	300
	◆ Kochab		ARCTURUS		◆ SPICA		REGULUS		PROCYON		◆ POLLUX		CAPELLA	
150	44 46	022	31 44	092	18 52	126	59 50	176	41 50	230	59 30	253	40 47	300
151	45 02	022	32 28	093	19 28	127	59 52	177	41 15	231	58 47	254	40 09	300
152	45 19	022	33 13	094	20 04	127	59 54	179	40 40	232	58 04	255	39 31	301
153	45 35	022	33 57	094	20 39	128	59 53	181	40 05	233	57 21	256	38 52	301
154	45 51	022	34 42	095	21 14	129	59 51	183	39 29	234	56 37	257	38 14	302
155	46 08	021	35 26	096	21 48	130	59 48	185	38 52	235	55 54	258	37 36	302
156	46 24	021	36 10	096	22 22	131	59 43	187	38 16	236	55 10	259	36 59	302
157	46 40	021	36 55	097	22 55	132	59 37	189	37 38	237	54 26	260	36 21	303
158	46 56	021	37 39	098	23 28	133	59 29	191	37 01	238	53 42	261	35 43	303
159	47 13	021	38 23	099	24 01	133	59 20	193	36 22	239	52 58	262	35 06	303
160	47 29	021	39 07	099	24 33	134	59 09	195	35 44	240	52 14	262	34 29	304
161	47 45	021	39 51	100	25 05	135	58 57	197	35 05	241	51 30	263	33 52	304
162	48 01	021	40 35	101	25 36	136	58 43	199	34 26	242	50 45	264	33 15	305
163	48 17	021	41 18	102	26 06	137	58 29	200	33 46	243	50 01	265	32 39	305
164	48 32	021	42 02	103	26 36	138	58 12	202	33 07	244	49 17	266	32 02	305
	◆ Kochab		ARCTURUS		◆ SPICA		REGULUS		PROCYON		◆ POLLUX		CAPELLA	
165	48 48	021	42 45	103	27 06	139	57 55	204	32 26	245	48 32	266	31 26	306
166	49 04	020	43 29	104	27 35	140	57 36	206	31 46	246	47 48	267	30 50	306
167	49 19	020	44 12	105	28 03	141	57 16	207	31 05	246	47 03	268	30 14	307
168	49 35	020	44 55	106	28 31	142	56 55	209	30 24	247	46 18	268	29 38	307
169	49 50	020	45 38	107	28 58	143	56 33	211	29 43	248	45 34	269	29 03	307
170	50 05	020	46 20	108	29 25	144	56 10	212	29 02	249	44 49	270	28 27	308
171	50 20	020	47 02	109	29 51	145	55 46	214	28 20	250	44 05	270	27 52	308
172	50 35	020	47 45	110	30 16	146	55 20	215	27 38	250	43 20	271	27 17	309
173	50 50	019	48 26	111	30 41	147	54 54	217	26 56	251	42 36	272	26 43	309
174	51 05	019	49 08	112	31 04	148	54 26	218	26 13	252	41 51	272	26 08	310
175	51 19	019	49 49	113	31 28	149	53 58	220	25 31	253	41 06	273	25 34	310
176	51 34	019	50 30	114	31 50	150	53 29	221	24 48	254	40 22	274	25 00	310
177	51 48	018	51 11	115	32 12	151	52 59	223	24 05	254	39 37	274	24 26	311
178	52 02	018	51 51	116	32 33	152	52 29	224	23 22	255	38 53	275	23 52	311
179	52 16	018	52 31	117	32 53	153	51 57	226	22 39	256	38 09	276	23 19	312

LHA ♈	Hc	Zn	Hc	Zn	Hc	Zn	Hc	Zn	Hc	Zn	Hc	Zn	Hc	Zn
	Kochab		◆VEGA		ARCTURUS		◆SPICA		REGULUS		◆POLLUX		CAPELLA	
180	52 29	018	18 58	054	53 11	118	33 13	155	51 25	227	37 24	276	22 46	312
181	52 43	018	19 34	054	53 50	119	33 32	156	50 52	228	36 40	277	22 13	313
182	52 56	017	20 11	055	54 29	120	33 50	157	50 19	229	35 56	277	21 40	313
183	53 09	017	20 48	056	55 07	121	34 07	158	49 44	231	35 11	278	21 08	314
184	53 22	017	21 25	056	55 45	123	34 23	159	49 10	232	34 27	279	20 36	314
185	53 35	016	22 02	057	56 22	124	34 39	160	48 34	233	33 43	279	20 04	315
186	53 47	016	22 40	057	56 59	125	34 53	161	47 58	234	32 59	280	19 32	315
187	54 00	016	23 17	058	57 35	127	35 07	163	47 22	235	32 15	280	19 01	316
188	54 12	015	23 55	058	58 11	128	35 20	164	46 45	236	31 32	281	18 30	316
189	54 23	015	24 33	059	58 45	129	35 32	165	46 08	238	30 48	281	17 59	317
190	54 35	015	25 12	059	59 20	131	35 43	166	45 30	239	30 04	282	17 28	317
191	54 46	014	25 50	060	59 53	132	35 54	167	44 52	240	29 21	283	16 58	318
192	54 57	014	26 29	060	60 25	134	36 03	168	44 13	241	28 37	283	16 28	318
193	55 08	014	27 08	061	60 57	136	36 11	170	43 34	242	27 54	284	15 58	319
194	55 18	013	27 47	061	61 28	137	36 19	171	42 54	243	27 10	284	15 29	319
	◆VEGA		Rasalhague		ARCTURUS		◆SPICA		REGULUS		◆POLLUX		Dubhe	
195	28 26	062	23 59	095	61 58	139	36 26	172	42 15	244	26 27	285	63 53	329
196	29 06	062	24 43	095	62 26	141	36 31	173	41 34	245	25 44	285	63 30	328
197	29 45	063	25 28	096	62 54	142	36 36	175	40 54	246	25 01	286	63 06	327
198	30 25	063	26 12	097	63 21	144	36 40	176	40 13	247	24 19	287	62 42	327
199	31 05	064	26 56	097	63 46	146	36 43	177	39 32	247	23 36	287	62 17	326
200	31 45	064	27 40	098	64 10	148	36 45	178	38 51	248	22 53	288	61 52	326
201	32 25	065	28 25	099	64 33	150	36 46	179	38 09	249	22 11	288	61 27	325
202	33 06	065	29 09	100	64 55	152	36 46	181	37 27	250	21 29	289	61 02	325
203	33 46	066	29 52	100	65 15	154	36 45	182	36 45	251	20 47	289	60 36	325
204	34 27	066	30 36	101	65 33	156	36 43	183	36 03	252	20 05	290	60 10	324
205	35 08	067	31 20	102	65 50	159	36 40	184	35 21	253	19 23	291	59 44	324
206	35 49	067	32 04	103	66 06	161	36 36	186	34 38	253	18 41	291	59 17	323
207	36 30	068	32 47	103	66 20	163	36 31	187	33 55	254	18 00	292	58 51	323
208	37 11	068	33 30	104	66 32	165	36 26	188	33 12	255	17 18	292	58 24	323
209	37 52	068	34 13	105	66 42	168	36 19	189	32 29	256	16 37	293	57 57	323
	◆DENEB		VEGA		Rasalhague		ANTARES		◆ARCTURUS		REGULUS		◆Dubhe	
210	22 23	048	38 34	069	34 56	106	13 14	146	66 51	170	31 46	257	57 30	322
211	22 57	049	39 16	069	35 39	107	13 39	147	66 57	173	31 02	257	57 02	322
212	23 30	049	39 57	070	36 22	107	14 03	148	67 02	175	30 19	258	56 35	322
213	24 04	050	40 39	070	37 04	108	14 27	148	67 05	177	29 35	259	56 07	322
214	24 38	050	41 21	071	37 46	109	14 50	149	67 06	180	28 51	260	55 40	321
215	25 13	051	42 03	071	38 29	110	15 13	150	67 06	182	28 07	260	55 12	321
216	25 47	051	42 46	072	39 10	111	15 35	151	67 03	185	27 23	261	54 44	321
217	26 22	052	43 28	072	39 52	112	15 56	152	66 58	187	26 39	262	54 16	321
218	26 57	052	44 10	072	40 33	113	16 17	153	66 52	189	25 55	263	53 48	321
219	27 32	052	44 53	073	41 14	114	16 37	153	66 44	192	25 11	263	53 19	321
220	28 08	053	45 36	073	41 55	115	16 57	154	66 34	194	24 26	264	52 51	321
221	28 43	053	46 19	074	42 35	115	17 16	155	66 22	196	23 42	265	52 23	321
222	29 19	054	47 01	074	43 15	116	17 34	156	66 08	199	22 58	265	51 54	320
223	29 55	054	47 44	075	43 55	117	17 52	157	65 53	201	22 13	266	51 26	320
224	30 32	055	48 27	075	44 34	118	18 09	158	65 36	203	21 29	267	50 58	320
	DENEB		◆ALTAIR		Rasalhague		ANTARES		◆ARCTURUS		Denebola		◆Dubhe	
225	31 08	055	18 39	095	45 13	119	18 26	159	65 18	205	40 47	251	50 29	320
226	31 45	055	19 23	096	45 52	121	18 41	160	64 58	207	40 04	251	50 01	320
227	32 21	056	20 08	096	46 30	122	18 57	161	64 37	210	39 22	252	49 32	320
228	32 58	056	20 52	097	47 08	123	19 11	161	64 14	212	38 39	253	49 04	320
229	33 35	057	21 36	098	47 45	124	19 25	162	63 50	213	37 57	254	48 35	320
230	34 13	057	22 20	098	48 22	125	19 38	163	63 25	215	37 14	255	48 07	320
231	34 50	057	23 04	099	48 58	126	19 50	164	62 59	217	36 31	256	47 38	320
232	35 28	058	23 48	100	49 34	127	20 02	165	62 31	219	35 47	256	47 10	320
233	36 06	058	24 32	100	50 09	129	20 13	166	62 03	221	35 04	257	46 42	320
234	36 44	059	25 16	101	50 44	130	20 24	167	61 33	222	34 20	258	46 13	321
235	37 22	059	26 00	102	51 18	131	20 33	168	61 02	224	33 37	259	45 45	321
236	38 00	059	26 43	103	51 51	132	20 42	169	60 31	226	32 53	260	45 17	321
237	38 38	060	27 27	103	52 24	134	20 50	170	59 59	227	32 09	260	44 48	321
238	39 17	060	28 10	104	52 56	135	20 58	171	59 25	229	31 25	261	44 20	321
239	39 56	060	28 53	105	53 27	136	21 05	172	58 51	230	30 41	262	43 52	321
	◆DENEB		ALTAIR		Rasalhague		◆ANTARES		ARCTURUS		Denebola		◆Dubhe	
240	40 34	061	29 36	106	53 57	138	21 11	173	58 17	232	29 57	263	43 24	321
241	41 13	061	30 19	107	54 27	139	21 16	174	57 41	233	29 12	263	42 56	321
242	41 52	061	31 02	107	54 56	141	21 21	175	57 05	235	28 28	264	42 28	321
243	42 32	062	31 44	108	55 23	142	21 24	176	56 29	236	27 44	265	42 01	322
244	43 11	062	32 26	109	55 50	144	21 27	177	55 52	237	26 59	265	41 33	322
245	43 50	062	33 08	110	56 16	145	21 30	178	55 14	238	26 15	266	41 05	322
246	44 30	063	33 50	111	56 41	147	21 31	178	54 36	240	25 30	267	40 38	322
247	45 10	063	34 32	112	57 05	149	21 32	179	53 57	241	24 46	267	40 11	322
248	45 50	063	35 13	112	57 28	150	21 32	180	53 18	242	24 01	268	39 43	322
249	46 30	064	35 54	113	57 49	152	21 31	181	52 38	243	23 17	269	39 16	323
250	47 10	064	36 35	114	58 10	154	21 30	182	51 58	244	22 32	269	38 49	323
251	47 50	064	37 16	115	58 29	155	21 28	183	51 18	245	21 47	270	38 22	323
252	48 30	065	37 56	116	58 47	157	21 25	184	50 37	246	21 03	271	37 55	323
253	49 10	065	38 36	117	59 03	159	21 21	185	49 57	247	20 18	271	37 29	323
254	49 51	065	39 16	118	59 19	161	21 17	186	49 15	248	19 34	272	37 02	324
	◆DENEB		ALTAIR		Nunki		◆ANTARES		ARCTURUS		◆Alkaid		Kochab	
255	50 31	066	39 55	119	16 38	153	21 12	187	48 34	249	56 16	299	54 39	345
256	51 12	066	40 34	120	16 58	154	21 06	188	47 52	250	55 37	299	54 27	345
257	51 53	066	41 12	121	17 18	155	20 59	189	47 10	251	54 59	299	54 16	345
258	52 34	067	41 50	122	17 36	156	20 52	190	46 27	252	54 20	300	54 04	344
259	53 15	067	42 28	123	17 54	156	20 44	191	45 45	253	53 41	300	53 52	344
260	53 56	067	43 05	124	18 12	157	20 35	192	45 02	254	53 02	300	53 39	344
261	54 37	067	43 42	125	18 29	158	20 25	193	44 19	255	52 24	300	53 27	343
262	55 18	068	44 18	126	18 45	159	20 15	194	43 36	256	51 45	300	53 14	343
263	55 59	068	44 54	127	19 00	160	20 04	195	42 53	256	51 07	300	53 01	343
264	56 41	068	45 30	128	19 15	161	19 52	196	42 10	257	50 28	301	52 48	343
265	57 22	068	46 04	129	19 29	162	19 40	197	41 26	258	49 50	301	52 34	342
266	58 04	069	46 38	131	19 43	163	19 27	197	40 42	259	49 12	301	52 20	342
267	58 45	069	47 12	132	19 56	164	19 13	198	39 59	260	48 34	301	52 07	342
268	59 27	069	47 45	133	20 08	165	18 59	199	39 15	260	47 56	302	51 53	342
269	60 08	069	48 17	134	20 19	166	18 44	200	38 31	261	47 18	302	51 38	341

LHA ♈	Hc	Zn	Hc	Zn	Hc	Zn	Hc	Zn	Hc	Zn	Hc	Zn	Hc	Zn
	◆Alpheratz		ALTAIR		Nunki		◆ANTARES		ARCTURUS		◆Alkaid		Kochab	
270	17 28	066	48 49	135	20 30	167	18 28	201	37 46	262	46 40	302	51 24	341
271	18 09	067	49 20	137	20 40	168	18 12	202	37 02	263	46 02	302	51 10	341
272	18 50	067	49 50	138	20 49	168	17 55	203	36 18	263	45 25	303	50 55	341
273	19 31	068	50 19	139	20 58	169	17 37	204	35 34	264	44 47	303	50 40	341
274	20 13	068	50 48	141	21 06	170	17 19	205	34 49	265	44 10	303	50 25	340
275	20 54	069	51 16	142	21 13	171	17 00	206	34 05	266	43 32	303	50 10	340
276	21 36	070	51 43	144	21 19	172	16 40	206	33 20	266	42 55	304	49 55	340
277	22 18	070	52 09	145	21 25	173	16 20	207	32 36	267	42 18	304	49 40	340
278	23 00	071	52 34	146	21 30	174	16 00	208	31 51	268	41 41	304	49 24	340
279	23 42	071	52 58	148	21 34	175	15 38	209	31 07	268	41 04	305	49 09	340
280	24 24	072	53 21	149	21 37	176	15 16	210	30 22	269	40 28	305	48 53	339
281	25 07	072	53 43	151	21 40	177	14 54	211	29 38	270	39 51	305	48 38	339
282	25 49	073	54 05	153	21 42	178	14 31	212	28 53	270	39 15	305	48 22	339
283	26 32	074	54 25	154	21 43	179	14 07	212	28 08	271	38 39	306	48 06	339
284	27 15	074	54 43	156	21 43	180	13 43	213	27 24	272	38 03	306	47 50	339
	◆Mirfak		Alpheratz		◆ALTAIR		Rasalhague		◆ARCTURUS		Alkaid		Kochab	
285	13 12	032	27 58	075	55 01	157	55 18	218	26 39	272	37 27	306	47 34	339
286	13 36	033	28 41	075	55 18	159	54 50	220	25 55	273	36 51	307	47 18	339
287	14 00	033	29 24	076	55 33	161	54 21	221	25 10	274	36 15	307	47 02	339
288	14 25	034	30 07	076	55 47	162	53 52	223	24 26	274	35 40	307	46 46	339
289	14 49	034	30 51	077	56 00	164	53 21	224	23 41	275	35 04	308	46 29	339
290	15 15	035	31 34	077	56 11	166	52 50	225	22 57	276	34 29	308	46 13	339
291	15 40	035	32 18	078	56 21	168	52 18	227	22 13	276	33 54	309	45 57	339
292	16 06	036	33 01	079	56 30	169	51 45	228	21 28	277	33 20	309	45 41	338
293	16 32	036	33 45	079	56 38	171	51 12	229	20 44	277	32 45	309	45 24	338
294	16 59	037	34 29	080	56 44	173	50 38	230	20 00	278	32 10	310	45 08	338
295	17 26	037	35 13	080	56 49	175	50 03	232	19 16	279	31 36	310	44 51	338
296	17 53	038	35 57	081	56 52	177	49 28	233	18 32	279	31 02	310	44 35	338
297	18 20	038	36 41	082	56 54	178	48 52	234	17 48	280	30 28	311	44 18	338
298	18 48	039	37 25	082	56 55	180	48 15	235	17 04	281	29 55	311	44 02	338
299	19 16	039	38 09	083	56 54	182	47 38	236	16 20	281	29 21	312	43 46	338
	Mirfak		◆Alpheratz		Enif		◆ALTAIR		Rasalhague		Alphecca		◆Kochab	
300	19 44	040	38 54	083	50 33	137	56 51	184	47 01	238	34 39	276	43 29	338
301	20 13	040	39 38	084	51 03	138	56 48	186	46 23	239	33 55	277	43 13	338
302	20 42	041	40 22	085	51 32	139	56 43	187	45 45	240	33 11	278	42 56	338
303	21 11	041	41 07	085	52 01	141	56 36	189	45 06	241	32 27	278	42 40	338
304	21 40	041	41 51	086	52 29	142	56 28	191	44 27	242	31 42	279	42 24	338
305	22 10	042	42 36	086	52 56	144	56 19	193	43 48	243	30 58	279	42 07	339
306	22 40	042	43 20	087	53 21	145	56 09	195	43 08	244	30 14	280	41 51	339
307	23 10	043	44 05	088	53 46	147	55 57	196	42 28	245	29 31	281	41 35	339
308	23 40	043	44 49	088	54 10	148	55 44	198	41 47	246	28 47	281	41 18	339
309	24 11	044	45 34	089	54 33	150	55 29	200	41 07	247	28 03	282	41 02	339
310	24 42	044	46 18	090	54 55	151	55 14	201	40 26	247	27 20	282	40 46	339
311	25 13	044	47 03	090	55 16	153	54 57	203	39 44	248	26 36	283	40 30	339
312	25 44	045	47 48	091	55 36	155	54 39	205	39 03	249	25 53	284	40 14	339
313	26 16	045	48 32	092	55 54	156	54 20	206	38 21	250	25 09	284	39 58	339
314	26 47	046	49 17	092	56 12	158	54 00	208	37 39	251	24 26	285	39 42	339
	CAPELLA		◆Alpheratz		FOMALHAUT		◆ALTAIR		Rasalhague		VEGA		◆Kochab	
315	10 55	036	50 01	093	13 25	154	53 38	209	36 56	252	62 52	275	39 26	339
316	11 21	036	50 46	094	13 45	155	53 16	211	36 14	253	62 08	276	39 10	339
317	11 48	037	51 30	094	14 04	155	52 52	212	35 31	254	61 23	276	38 55	339
318	12 15	037	52 15	095	14 22	156	52 28	214	34 48	254	60 39	277	38 39	340
319	12 42	038	52 59	096	14 39	157	52 03	215	34 05	255	59 55	277	38 24	340
320	13 10	038	53 43	097	14 56	158	51 36	217	33 22	256	59 11	278	38 08	340
321	13 37	039	54 28	098	15 13	159	51 09	218	32 39	257	58 27	278	37 53	340
322	14 06	039	55 12	098	15 29	160	50 41	220	31 55	257	57 42	279	37 37	340
323	14 34	040	55 56	099	15 44	161	50 12	221	31 12	258	56 58	279	37 22	340
324	15 03	040	56 40	100	15 58	161	49 43	222	30 28	259	56 14	280	37 07	340
325	15 32	041	57 24	101	16 12	162	49 12	224	29 44	260	55 31	280	36 52	340
326	16 01	042	58 07	102	16 26	163	48 41	225	29 00	261	54 47	281	36 37	341
327	16 31	042	58 51	103	16 38	164	48 10	226	28 16	261	54 03	281	36 23	341
328	17 01	043	59 34	104	16 50	165	47 37	227	27 32	262	53 19	282	36 08	341
329	17 31	043	60 17	105	17 01	166	47 04	229	26 48	263	52 36	282	35 53	341
	◆CAPELLA		Hamal		Diphda		◆FOMALHAUT		ALTAIR		◆VEGA		Kochab	
330	18 02	044	35 57	089	19 06	139	17 12	167	46 30	230	51 52	283	35 39	341
331	18 33	044	36 41	090	19 36	139	17 22	168	45 56	231	51 09	283	35 25	341
332	19 04	045	37 26	091	20 04	140	17 31	169	45 21	232	50 25	284	35 11	342
333	19 35	045	38 10	091	20 32	141	17 40	169	44 46	233	49 42	284	34 57	342
334	20 07	045	38 55	092	21 00	142	17 47	170	44 10	234	48 59	284	34 43	342
335	20 39	046	39 39	093	21 27	143	17 55	171	43 33	235	48 16	285	34 29	342
336	21 11	046	40 24	093	21 54	144	18 01	172	42 56	236	47 32	285	34 15	342
337	21 44	047	41 08	094	22 20	145	18 07	173	42 19	237	46 50	286	34 02	342
338	22 16	047	41 53	095	22 45	146	18 12	174	41 41	238	46 07	286	33 48	343
339	22 49	048	42 37	096	23 10	147	18 16	175	41 03	239	45 24	287	33 35	343
340	23 22	048	43 22	096	23 34	148	18 20	176	40 24	240	44 41	287	33 22	343
341	23 56	049	44 06	097	23 58	149	18 23	177	39 45	241	43 59	288	33 09	343
342	24 29	049	44 50	098	24 21	149	18 25	178	39 06	242	43 16	288	32 56	343
343	25 03	050	45 34	098	24 43	150	18 27	179	38 26	243	42 34	289	32 44	344
344	25 37	050	46 18	099	25 05	151	18 27	179	37 46	244	41 52	289	32 31	344
	◆CAPELLA		ALDEBARAN		Diphda		◆FOMALHAUT		ALTAIR		◆VEGA		Kochab	
345	26 12	051	15 13	081	25 26	152	18 27	180	37 06	245	41 10	289	32 19	344
346	26 46	051	15 57	082	25 46	153	18 27	181	36 25	246	40 28	290	32 07	344
347	27 21	051	16 41	083	26 06	154	18 25	182	35 44	247	39 46	290	31 55	345
348	27 56	052	17 26	083	26 25	155	18 23	183	35 03	248	39 04	291	31 43	345
349	28 31	052	18 10	084	26 43	156	18 21	184	34 22	249	38 22	291	31 31	345
350	29 06	053	18 54	084	27 00	157	18 17	185	33 40	250	37 41	292	31 20	345
351	29 42	053	19 39	085	27 17	158	18 13	186	32 58	250	37 00	292	31 09	345
352	30 17	053	20 23	086	27 33	159	18 08	187	32 16	251	36 18	293	30 58	346
353	30 53	054	21 08	086	27 48	160	18 02	188	31 34	252	35 37	293	30 47	346
354	31 29	054	21 52	087	28 03	162	17 56	189	30 51	253	34 56	294	30 36	346
355	32 06	055	22 37	088	28 17	163	17 49	189	30 09	254	34 16	294	30 25	346
356	32 42	055	23 21	088	28 30	164	17 41	190	29 26	254	33 35	294	30 15	347
357	33 19	055	24 06	089	28 42	165	17 33	191	28 43	255	32 54	295	30 05	347
358	33 56	056	24 50	090	28 53	166	17 24	192	28 00	256	32 14	295	29 55	347
359	34 33	056	25 35	090	29 04	167	17 14	193	27 16	257	31 34	296	29 45	347

LHA ♈	Hc Zn	Hc Zn	Hc Zn	Hc Zn	Hc Zn	Hc Zn	Hc Zn
	◆ CAPELLA	ALDEBARAN	◆ Diphda	FOMALHAUT	ALTAIR	◆ VEGA	Kochab
0	34 37 056	26 20 091	30 12 168	18 02 194	26 46 258	30 27 297	28 37 348
1	35 14 056	27 06 091	30 21 169	17 51 195	26 01 259	29 47 297	28 27 348
2	35 52 057	27 51 092	30 30 170	17 39 196	25 17 259	29 06 298	28 18 348
3	36 30 057	28 36 093	30 37 171	17 26 197	24 32 260	28 26 298	28 09 349
4	37 08 057	29 21 093	30 44 172	17 13 198	23 48 261	27 47 299	28 00 349
5	37 46 058	30 07 094	30 50 173	16 59 198	23 03 262	27 07 299	27 51 349
6	38 25 058	30 52 095	30 54 174	16 44 199	22 18 262	26 28 300	27 43 349
7	39 03 059	31 37 095	30 58 175	16 29 200	21 33 263	25 48 300	27 35 350
8	39 42 059	32 22 096	31 02 177	16 13 201	20 48 264	25 09 301	27 26 350
9	40 21 059	33 07 097	31 04 178	15 56 202	20 03 264	24 30 301	27 19 350
10	41 00 060	33 52 097	31 05 179	15 39 203	19 18 265	23 52 302	27 11 350
11	41 39 060	34 37 098	31 06 180	15 21 204	18 33 266	23 13 302	27 04 351
12	42 18 060	35 22 099	31 05 181	15 03 204	17 48 266	22 35 303	26 56 351
13	42 57 060	36 06 100	31 04 182	14 44 205	17 02 267	21 57 303	26 49 351
14	43 37 061	36 51 100	31 02 183	14 24 206	16 17 268	21 19 304	26 43 352
	◆ CAPELLA	BETELGEUSE	RIGEL	◆ Diphda	Enif	◆ DENEB	Kochab
15	44 16 061	16 55 095	13 40 114	30 59 184	37 06 248	44 01 298	26 36 352
16	44 56 061	17 40 096	14 21 115	30 55 185	36 24 249	43 21 298	26 30 352
17	45 36 062	18 25 096	15 02 115	30 50 187	35 42 250	42 41 299	26 24 352
18	46 16 062	19 10 097	15 43 116	30 45 188	34 59 251	42 02 299	26 18 353
19	46 56 062	19 55 098	16 23 117	30 38 189	34 16 252	41 22 299	26 12 353
20	47 36 062	20 40 098	17 04 118	30 31 190	33 33 252	40 43 300	26 07 353
21	48 16 063	21 24 099	17 44 118	30 23 191	32 50 253	40 04 300	26 01 354
22	48 56 063	22 09 100	18 23 119	30 14 192	32 06 254	39 24 300	25 56 354
23	49 37 063	22 54 100	19 03 120	30 04 193	31 23 255	38 45 301	25 52 354
24	50 17 064	23 38 101	19 42 121	29 53 194	30 39 256	38 07 301	25 47 354
25	50 58 064	24 23 102	20 21 122	29 42 195	29 55 256	37 28 301	25 43 355
26	51 39 064	25 07 103	20 59 122	29 29 196	29 11 257	36 49 302	25 39 355
27	52 19 064	25 51 103	21 37 123	29 16 197	28 27 258	36 11 302	25 35 355
28	53 00 065	26 35 104	22 15 124	29 02 198	27 42 259	35 33 302	25 31 356
29	53 41 065	27 19 105	22 52 125	28 48 200	26 58 259	34 54 303	25 28 356
	◆ CAPELLA	BETELGEUSE	RIGEL	◆ Diphda	Alpheratz	◆ DENEB	Kochab
30	54 22 065	28 02 106	23 29 126	28 32 201	64 35 251	34 16 303	25 25 356
31	55 03 065	28 46 106	24 06 127	28 16 202	63 52 252	33 39 304	25 22 356
32	55 44 065	29 29 107	24 42 127	27 59 203	63 09 253	33 01 304	25 19 357
33	56 25 066	30 12 108	25 18 128	27 41 204	62 25 254	32 24 304	25 17 357
34	57 07 066	30 55 109	25 53 129	27 22 205	61 42 255	31 46 305	25 15 357
35	57 48 066	31 38 110	26 28 130	27 03 206	60 58 256	31 09 305	25 13 358
36	58 29 066	32 21 110	27 02 131	26 43 207	60 13 257	30 32 306	25 11 358
37	59 11 066	33 03 111	27 36 132	26 23 208	59 29 258	29 55 306	25 09 358
38	59 52 066	33 45 112	28 10 133	26 01 209	58 45 259	29 19 306	25 08 359
39	60 34 066	34 27 113	28 43 134	25 39 210	58 00 260	28 43 307	25 07 359
40	61 15 067	35 09 114	29 15 135	25 16 211	57 16 261	28 06 307	25 07 359
41	61 57 067	35 50 115	29 47 136	24 53 212	56 31 262	27 30 308	25 06 359
42	62 38 067	36 31 116	30 18 137	24 29 212	55 46 263	26 55 308	25 06 000
43	63 20 067	37 12 116	30 49 138	24 04 213	55 01 263	26 19 308	25 06 000
44	64 02 067	37 52 117	31 20 139	23 39 214	54 16 264	25 44 309	25 06 000
	◆ Dubhe	POLLUX	BETELGEUSE	◆ RIGEL	Diphda	◆ Alpheratz	DENEB
45	23 05 026	31 15 078	38 32 118	31 49 140	23 13 215	53 31 265	25 08 309
46	23 25 027	31 59 079	39 12 119	32 18 141	22 47 216	52 46 266	24 34 310
47	23 46 027	32 44 080	39 51 120	32 47 142	22 20 217	52 01 266	23 59 310
48	24 06 027	33 28 080	40 30 121	33 14 143	21 52 218	51 15 267	23 24 311
49	24 27 028	34 13 081	41 09 122	33 42 144	21 24 219	50 30 268	22 50 311
50	24 48 028	34 58 081	41 47 123	34 08 145	20 55 220	49 45 268	22 16 311
51	25 10 028	35 42 082	42 24 124	34 34 146	20 26 221	49 00 269	21 42 312
52	25 31 029	36 27 082	43 02 125	34 59 147	19 56 222	48 14 270	21 09 312
53	25 53 029	37 12 083	43 38 126	35 23 148	19 26 222	47 29 270	20 35 313
54	26 15 029	37 57 084	44 15 127	35 47 149	18 55 223	46 44 271	20 02 313
55	26 38 030	38 42 084	44 50 129	36 09 150	18 24 224	45 59 272	19 29 314
56	27 00 030	39 27 085	45 25 130	36 31 151	17 52 225	45 13 272	18 57 314
57	27 23 030	40 12 085	46 00 131	36 53 153	17 20 226	44 28 273	18 25 315
58	27 46 031	40 58 086	46 34 132	37 13 154	16 47 227	43 43 274	17 53 315
59	28 09 031	41 43 087	47 07 133	37 33 155	16 14 227	42 58 274	17 21 316
	◆ Dubhe	POLLUX	PROCYON	◆ SIRIUS	RIGEL	◆ Hamal	Schedar
60	28 33 031	42 28 087	29 21 111	20 39 137	37 51 156	60 48 242	54 45 313
61	28 56 032	43 13 088	30 03 111	21 10 138	38 09 157	60 08 243	54 12 313
62	29 20 032	43 58 089	30 45 112	21 40 139	38 26 159	59 27 244	53 39 313
63	29 44 032	44 44 089	31 27 113	22 09 140	38 42 160	58 46 246	53 06 313
64	30 08 032	45 29 090	32 09 114	22 38 141	38 58 161	58 05 247	52 33 313
65	30 32 033	46 14 090	32 50 115	23 06 142	39 12 162	57 23 248	52 00 313
66	30 57 033	47 00 091	33 31 116	23 34 143	39 25 163	56 41 249	51 27 313
67	31 22 033	47 45 092	34 12 116	24 01 144	39 38 165	55 58 250	50 54 313
68	31 47 034	48 30 093	34 52 117	24 28 145	39 49 166	55 16 251	50 21 313
69	32 12 034	49 15 093	35 32 118	24 54 145	40 00 167	54 33 252	49 48 313
70	32 37 034	50 01 094	36 12 119	25 19 146	40 09 169	53 50 253	49 15 313
71	33 03 034	50 46 095	36 51 120	25 44 147	40 17 170	53 06 254	48 42 313
72	33 28 035	51 31 095	37 30 121	26 08 148	40 25 171	52 23 255	48 09 313
73	33 54 035	52 16 096	38 09 122	26 31 149	40 31 172	51 39 256	47 36 314
74	34 20 035	53 01 097	38 47 123	26 54 150	40 37 174	50 55 257	47 04 314
	◆ Dubhe	REGULUS	PROCYON	◆ SIRIUS	RIGEL	◆ Hamal	Schedar
75	34 46 035	17 19 089	39 25 124	27 16 151	40 41 175	50 11 257	46 31 314
76	35 12 036	18 04 090	40 02 125	27 37 152	40 45 176	49 26 258	45 58 314
77	35 39 036	18 50 090	40 39 126	27 58 153	40 47 178	48 42 259	45 26 314
78	36 05 036	19 35 091	41 15 127	28 18 154	40 49 179	47 58 260	44 53 314
79	36 32 036	20 20 092	41 51 128	28 37 155	40 49 180	47 13 261	44 21 314
80	36 58 036	21 05 092	42 26 129	28 56 156	40 48 182	46 28 262	43 48 314
81	37 25 037	21 51 093	43 01 130	29 13 157	40 46 183	45 43 262	43 16 315
82	37 52 037	22 36 094	43 35 131	29 30 159	40 44 184	44 58 263	42 44 315
83	38 20 037	23 21 094	44 09 133	29 47 160	40 40 185	44 13 264	42 11 315
84	38 47 037	24 06 095	44 42 134	30 02 161	40 35 187	43 28 265	41 39 315
85	39 14 037	24 51 096	45 14 135	30 17 162	40 29 188	42 43 265	41 07 315
86	39 42 037	25 36 097	45 46 136	30 31 163	40 22 189	41 58 266	40 36 315
87	40 09 038	26 21 097	46 17 137	30 44 164	40 14 191	41 13 267	40 04 316
88	40 37 038	27 06 098	46 47 139	30 56 165	40 06 192	40 28 267	39 32 316
89	41 05 038	27 51 099	47 17 140	31 07 166	39 56 193	39 42 268	39 01 316

LHA ♈	Hc Zn	Hc Zn	Hc Zn	Hc Zn	Hc Zn	Hc Zn	Hc Zn
	◆ Dubhe	REGULUS	PROCYON	◆ SIRIUS	RIGEL	ALDEBARAN	◆ Mirfak
90	41 32 038	28 36 099	47 46 141	31 18 167	39 45 194	59 40 222	61 49 302
91	42 00 038	29 20 100	48 14 143	31 27 168	39 33 196	59 09 224	61 11 302
92	42 28 038	30 05 101	48 41 144	31 36 169	39 20 197	58 37 226	60 32 301
93	42 56 038	30 49 102	49 07 145	31 44 170	39 07 198	58 04 227	59 53 301
94	43 25 038	31 33 102	49 33 147	31 51 172	38 52 199	57 31 228	59 15 301
95	43 53 039	32 18 103	49 57 148	31 57 173	38 37 201	56 56 230	58 36 301
96	44 21 039	33 02 104	50 21 149	32 02 174	38 20 202	56 21 231	57 58 301
97	44 49 039	33 46 105	50 43 151	32 07 175	38 03 203	55 46 233	57 19 301
98	45 18 039	34 29 105	51 05 152	32 10 176	37 45 204	55 09 234	56 40 302
99	45 46 039	35 13 106	51 25 154	32 13 177	37 26 205	54 33 235	56 02 302
100	46 14 039	35 56 107	51 45 155	32 15 178	37 06 207	53 55 236	55 23 302
101	46 43 039	36 39 108	52 03 157	32 16 179	36 45 208	53 17 238	54 45 302
102	47 11 039	37 22 109	52 20 158	32 16 181	36 23 209	52 39 239	54 06 302
103	47 40 039	38 05 110	52 36 160	32 15 182	36 01 210	52 00 240	53 28 302
104	48 08 039	38 48 110	52 51 162	32 13 183	35 38 211	51 20 241	52 49 302
	Dubhe	◆ Denebola	REGULUS	◆ SIRIUS	RIGEL	ALDEBARAN	◆ Mirfak
105	48 37 039	22 36 090	39 30 111	32 10 184	35 14 212	50 40 242	52 11 302
106	49 05 039	23 22 091	40 12 112	32 06 185	34 50 213	50 00 243	51 33 302
107	49 34 039	24 07 091	40 54 113	32 02 186	34 24 215	49 19 244	50 55 303
108	50 02 039	24 52 092	41 36 114	31 57 187	33 58 216	48 38 245	50 16 303
109	50 30 039	25 37 093	42 17 115	31 50 189	33 32 217	47 57 246	49 38 303
110	50 59 039	26 23 094	42 58 116	31 43 190	33 04 218	47 15 247	49 00 303
111	51 27 039	27 08 094	43 38 117	31 35 191	32 36 219	46 33 248	48 22 303
112	51 55 039	27 53 095	44 18 118	31 26 192	32 08 220	45 51 249	47 45 303
113	52 24 038	28 38 096	44 58 119	31 17 193	31 38 221	45 09 250	47 07 304
114	52 52 038	29 23 096	45 38 120	31 06 194	31 08 222	44 26 251	46 29 304
115	53 20 038	30 08 097	46 17 121	30 55 195	30 38 223	43 43 252	45 52 304
116	53 48 038	30 53 098	46 55 122	30 42 196	30 07 224	43 00 253	45 14 304
117	54 16 038	31 38 098	47 34 123	30 29 197	29 35 225	42 17 254	44 37 305
118	54 43 038	32 23 099	48 11 124	30 15 198	29 03 226	41 33 255	44 00 305
119	55 11 038	33 07 100	48 49 125	30 01 199	28 31 227	40 49 255	43 22 305
	◆ Kochab	Denebola	◆ REGULUS	SIRIUS	RIGEL	◆ ALDEBARAN	CAPELLA
120	35 51 019	33 52 101	49 25 127	29 45 201	27 57 228	40 05 256	60 30 294
121	36 06 019	34 36 101	50 01 128	29 29 202	27 24 228	39 21 257	59 48 294
122	36 21 020	35 21 102	50 37 129	29 12 203	26 50 229	38 37 258	59 07 294
123	36 36 020	36 05 103	51 12 130	28 54 204	26 15 230	37 53 259	58 25 294
124	36 51 020	36 49 104	51 46 131	28 35 205	25 40 231	37 08 259	57 44 294
125	37 07 020	37 33 104	52 20 133	28 16 206	25 04 232	36 24 260	57 03 294
126	37 22 020	38 17 105	52 52 134	27 56 207	24 28 233	35 39 261	56 21 294
127	37 38 020	39 00 106	53 25 135	27 35 208	23 52 234	34 54 262	55 40 295
128	37 53 020	39 44 107	53 56 137	27 14 209	23 15 235	34 10 262	54 59 295
129	38 09 020	40 27 108	54 27 138	26 52 210	22 38 235	33 25 263	54 18 295
130	38 25 020	41 10 109	54 56 140	26 29 211	22 01 236	32 40 264	53 37 295
131	38 41 021	41 53 110	55 25 141	26 05 212	21 23 237	31 55 264	52 56 296
132	38 56 021	42 35 110	55 53 143	25 41 213	20 45 238	31 10 265	52 15 296
133	39 12 021	43 17 111	56 20 144	25 17 214	20 06 239	30 24 266	51 35 296
134	39 29 021	44 00 112	56 46 146	24 51 215	19 27 240	29 39 267	50 54 296
	◆ Kochab	ARCTURUS	Denebola	◆ REGULUS	SIRIUS	BETELGEUSE	◆ CAPELLA
135	39 45 021	20 28 082	44 41 113	57 11 148	24 25 216	37 11 244	50 13 296
136	40 01 021	21 13 083	45 23 114	57 34 149	23 59 216	36 31 244	49 33 297
137	40 17 021	21 58 083	46 04 115	57 57 151	23 31 217	35 50 245	48 52 297
138	40 33 021	22 43 084	46 45 116	58 18 153	23 04 218	35 08 246	48 12 297
139	40 49 021	23 28 085	47 25 117	58 39 154	22 35 219	34 27 247	47 32 298
140	41 06 021	24 13 085	48 05 118	58 57 156	22 06 220	33 45 248	46 52 298
141	41 22 021	24 58 086	48 45 119	59 15 158	21 37 221	33 03 249	46 12 298
142	41 39 021	25 44 086	49 24 120	59 31 160	21 07 222	32 20 250	45 32 298
143	41 55 021	26 29 087	50 03 121	59 46 162	20 36 223	31 38 250	44 52 299
144	42 11 021	27 14 088	50 42 123	60 00 164	20 05 224	30 55 251	44 12 299
145	42 28 021	27 59 088	51 20 124	60 12 166	19 34 224	30 12 252	43 33 299
146	42 44 021	28 45 089	51 57 125	60 22 167	19 02 225	29 29 253	42 53 300
147	43 01 021	29 30 090	52 34 126	60 31 169	18 30 226	28 46 254	42 14 300
148	43 17 021	30 15 090	53 10 127	60 39 171	17 57 227	28 02 254	41 35 300
149	43 34 021	31 00 091	53 46 129	60 45 173	17 23 228	27 18 255	40 56 301
	◆ Kochab	ARCTURUS	◆ SPICA	REGULUS	PROCYON	◆ POLLUX	CAPELLA
150	43 50 021	31 46 092	19 27 126	60 49 175	42 28 231	59 46 255	40 17 301
151	44 06 021	32 31 092	20 04 126	60 52 177	41 53 232	59 02 256	39 38 301
152	44 23 021	33 16 093	20 40 127	60 54 179	41 17 233	58 18 257	38 59 302
153	44 39 021	34 01 094	21 16 128	60 53 181	40 40 234	57 34 258	38 21 302
154	44 55 021	34 47 094	21 51 129	60 51 183	40 04 235	56 50 259	37 43 302
155	45 12 021	35 32 095	22 26 130	60 48 185	39 26 236	56 05 260	37 04 303
156	45 28 021	36 17 096	23 01 130	60 43 187	38 49 237	55 20 261	36 26 303
157	45 44 021	37 02 096	23 35 131	60 36 189	38 10 238	54 36 261	35 48 303
158	46 00 021	37 47 097	24 09 132	60 28 191	37 32 239	53 51 262	35 10 304
159	46 17 021	38 32 098	24 42 133	60 18 193	36 53 240	53 06 263	34 33 304
160	46 33 021	39 16 099	25 15 134	60 07 195	36 14 241	52 21 264	33 55 304
161	46 49 021	40 01 099	25 47 135	59 54 197	35 34 242	51 36 265	33 18 305
162	47 05 021	40 46 100	26 19 136	59 40 199	34 54 243	50 51 265	32 41 305
163	47 20 020	41 30 101	26 50 137	59 25 201	34 13 243	50 06 266	32 04 305
164	47 36 020	42 15 102	27 21 138	59 08 203	33 33 244	49 21 267	31 27 306
	◆ Kochab	ARCTURUS	◆ SPICA	REGULUS	PROCYON	◆ POLLUX	CAPELLA
165	47 52 020	42 59 103	27 51 139	58 50 205	32 52 245	48 35 267	30 51 306
166	48 07 020	43 43 103	28 21 140	58 30 206	32 11 246	47 50 268	30 14 307
167	48 23 020	44 27 104	28 50 141	58 10 208	31 29 247	47 05 269	29 38 307
168	48 38 020	45 11 105	29 18 142	57 48 210	30 47 248	46 20 269	29 02 307
169	48 54 020	45 55 106	29 46 143	57 25 211	30 05 249	45 34 270	28 26 308
170	49 09 019	46 38 107	30 13 144	57 00 213	29 23 249	44 49 271	27 50 308
171	49 24 019	47 21 108	30 40 145	56 35 215	28 40 250	44 04 271	27 15 309
172	49 39 019	48 04 109	31 06 146	56 09 216	27 58 251	43 18 272	26 40 309
173	49 53 019	48 47 110	31 31 147	55 41 218	27 15 252	42 33 273	26 05 309
174	50 08 019	49 30 110	31 55 148	55 13 219	26 32 253	41 48 273	25 30 310
175	50 22 019	50 12 111	32 19 149	54 44 221	25 48 253	41 03 274	24 55 310
176	50 37 018	50 54 112	32 42 150	54 14 222	25 05 254	40 18 274	24 21 311
177	50 51 018	51 36 113	33 04 151	53 43 224	24 21 255	39 33 275	23 47 311
178	51 05 018	52 17 115	33 26 152	53 11 225	23 38 256	38 47 276	23 13 312
179	51 19 018	52 58 116	33 47 153	52 39 226	22 54 256	38 02 276	22 39 312

LAT 41°N

LHA ♈	Hc	Zn	Hc	Zn	Hc	Zn	Hc	Zn	Hc	Zn	Hc	Zn	Hc	Zn
	Kochab		◆VEGA		ARCTURUS		◆SPICA		REGULUS		◆POLLUX		CAPELLA	
180	51 32	017	18 23	054	53 39	117	34 07	154	52 06	228	37 17	277	22 05	313
181	51 46	017	19 00	055	54 19	118	34 26	155	51 32	229	36 32	277	21 32	313
182	51 59	017	19 37	055	54 59	119	34 45	157	50 57	230	35 48	278	20 59	313
183	52 12	017	20 14	056	55 38	120	35 02	158	50 22	232	35 03	279	20 26	314
184	52 25	016	20 52	056	56 17	121	35 19	159	49 46	233	34 18	279	19 54	314
185	52 37	016	21 29	057	56 55	123	35 35	160	49 10	234	33 33	280	19 22	315
186	52 50	016	22 07	057	57 33	124	35 50	161	48 33	235	32 49	280	18 50	315
187	53 02	015	22 45	058	58 10	125	36 04	162	47 56	236	32 04	281	18 18	316
188	53 14	015	23 24	058	58 47	127	36 18	164	47 18	237	31 20	281	17 46	316
189	53 26	015	24 02	059	59 23	128	36 30	165	46 39	238	30 36	282	17 15	317
190	53 37	014	24 41	059	59 58	130	36 42	166	46 01	240	29 51	283	16 44	317
191	53 48	014	25 20	060	60 33	131	36 52	167	45 21	241	29 07	283	16 14	318
192	53 59	014	25 59	060	61 07	133	37 02	168	44 42	242	28 23	284	15 43	318
193	54 10	013	26 38	060	61 39	134	37 10	170	44 02	243	27 39	284	15 13	319
194	54 20	013	27 18	061	62 11	136	37 18	171	43 21	244	26 55	285	14 44	319
	◆VEGA		Rasalhague		ARCTURUS		◆SPICA		REGULUS		◆POLLUX		Dubhe	
195	27 58	061	24 03	094	62 42	138	37 25	172	42 41	245	26 12	285	63 02	330
196	28 37	062	24 49	095	63 12	139	37 31	173	42 00	245	25 28	286	62 38	329
197	29 17	062	25 34	096	63 41	141	37 36	174	41 18	246	24 45	287	62 15	329
198	29 58	063	26 19	096	64 09	143	37 40	176	40 37	247	24 01	287	61 51	328
199	30 38	063	27 04	097	64 36	145	37 43	177	39 55	248	23 18	288	61 27	327
200	31 19	064	27 49	098	65 01	147	37 45	178	39 13	249	22 35	288	61 02	327
201	31 59	064	28 34	098	65 25	149	37 46	179	38 30	250	21 52	289	60 38	326
202	32 40	065	29 18	099	65 47	151	37 46	181	37 47	251	21 09	289	60 12	326
203	33 21	065	30 03	100	66 09	153	37 45	182	37 05	252	20 26	290	59 47	326
204	34 02	065	30 48	101	66 28	156	37 43	183	36 22	252	19 44	290	59 21	325
205	34 43	066	31 32	101	66 46	158	37 40	184	35 38	253	19 02	291	58 55	325
206	35 25	066	32 16	102	67 02	160	37 36	186	34 55	254	18 19	292	58 29	324
207	36 06	067	33 01	103	67 17	162	37 31	187	34 11	255	17 37	292	58 03	324
208	36 48	067	33 45	104	67 30	165	37 25	188	33 27	256	16 55	293	57 36	324
209	37 30	068	34 29	104	67 41	167	37 18	189	32 43	256	16 14	293	57 09	323
	◆DENEB		VEGA		Rasalhague		ANTARES		◆ARCTURUS		REGULUS		◆Dubhe	
210	21 43	048	38 12	068	35 12	105	14 04	146	67 50	170	31 59	257	56 42	323
211	22 17	049	38 54	069	35 56	106	14 29	147	67 57	172	31 15	258	56 15	323
212	22 51	049	39 36	069	36 39	107	14 54	147	68 02	175	30 31	259	55 47	323
213	23 25	049	40 19	069	37 23	108	15 18	148	68 05	177	29 46	259	55 20	323
214	24 00	050	41 01	070	38 06	108	15 42	149	68 06	180	29 02	260	54 52	322
215	24 35	050	41 44	070	38 49	109	16 05	150	68 05	182	28 17	261	54 25	322
216	25 09	051	42 26	071	39 31	110	16 27	151	68 03	185	27 32	262	53 57	322
217	25 45	051	43 09	071	40 14	111	16 49	152	67 58	187	26 47	262	53 29	322
218	26 20	052	43 52	072	40 56	112	17 10	152	67 51	190	26 02	263	53 01	322
219	26 56	052	44 35	072	41 38	113	17 31	153	67 42	192	25 18	264	52 33	322
220	27 31	052	45 18	072	42 19	114	17 51	154	67 32	195	24 32	264	52 04	321
221	28 07	053	46 01	073	43 01	115	18 10	155	67 19	197	23 47	265	51 36	321
222	28 44	053	46 45	073	43 42	116	18 29	156	67 05	200	23 02	266	51 08	321
223	29 20	054	47 28	074	44 22	117	18 47	157	66 49	202	22 17	266	50 40	321
224	29 57	054	48 12	074	45 03	118	19 05	158	66 31	204	21 32	267	50 11	321
	DENEB		◆ALTAIR		Rasalhague		ANTARES		◆ARCTURUS		Denebola		◆Dubhe	
225	30 33	054	18 44	094	45 43	119	19 21	159	66 12	206	41 06	251	49 43	321
226	31 10	055	19 29	095	46 22	120	19 38	160	65 51	208	40 23	252	49 14	321
227	31 47	055	20 14	096	47 01	121	19 53	160	65 29	211	39 40	253	48 46	321
228	32 25	056	20 59	097	47 40	122	20 08	161	65 05	213	38 56	254	48 17	321
229	33 02	056	21 44	097	48 18	123	20 22	162	64 40	215	38 13	255	47 49	321
230	33 40	056	22 29	098	48 56	124	20 35	163	64 14	217	37 29	256	47 20	321
231	34 18	057	23 14	099	49 33	125	20 48	164	63 46	218	36 45	256	46 52	321
232	34 55	057	23 58	099	50 10	126	21 00	165	63 17	220	36 01	257	46 23	321
233	35 34	058	24 43	100	50 46	128	21 12	166	62 48	222	35 17	258	45 55	321
234	36 12	058	25 28	101	51 22	129	21 22	167	62 17	224	34 32	259	45 27	321
235	36 50	058	26 12	101	51 57	130	21 32	168	61 45	225	33 48	259	44 58	321
236	37 29	059	26 56	102	52 31	131	21 41	169	61 12	227	33 03	260	44 30	321
237	38 08	059	27 40	103	53 05	133	21 49	170	60 39	229	32 19	261	44 02	321
238	38 46	059	28 25	104	53 38	134	21 57	171	60 04	230	31 34	262	43 34	322
239	39 26	060	29 08	104	54 10	135	22 04	172	59 29	232	30 49	262	43 05	322
	◆DENEB		ALTAIR		Rasalhague		◆ANTARES		ARCTURUS		Denebola		◆Dubhe	
240	40 05	060	29 52	105	54 41	137	22 10	173	58 53	233	30 04	263	42 37	322
241	40 44	060	30 36	106	55 12	138	22 16	174	58 17	234	29 19	264	42 09	322
242	41 23	061	31 19	107	55 42	140	22 20	175	57 40	236	28 34	264	41 41	322
243	42 03	061	32 03	108	56 10	141	22 24	176	57 02	237	27 49	265	41 14	322
244	42 43	061	32 46	108	56 38	143	22 27	177	56 24	238	27 04	266	40 46	322
245	43 22	062	33 29	109	57 05	144	22 30	177	55 45	240	26 19	267	40 18	322
246	44 02	062	34 11	110	57 31	146	22 31	178	55 06	241	25 33	267	39 50	323
247	44 42	062	34 54	111	57 56	148	22 32	179	54 26	242	24 48	268	39 23	323
248	45 22	063	35 36	112	58 19	149	22 32	180	53 46	243	24 03	269	38 56	323
249	46 03	063	36 18	113	58 42	151	22 31	181	53 05	244	23 18	269	38 28	323
250	46 43	063	36 59	113	59 03	153	22 30	182	52 24	245	22 32	270	38 01	323
251	47 23	063	37 41	114	59 23	155	22 28	183	51 43	246	21 47	271	37 34	323
252	48 04	064	38 22	115	59 42	156	22 25	184	51 01	247	21 02	271	37 07	324
253	48 45	064	39 03	116	59 59	158	22 21	185	50 19	248	20 17	272	36 40	324
254	49 25	064	39 43	117	60 15	160	22 16	186	49 37	249	19 31	272	36 14	324
	◆DENEB		ALTAIR		Nunki		◆ANTARES		ARCTURUS		◆Alkaid		Kochab	
255	50 06	065	40 23	118	17 32	153	22 11	187	48 54	250	55 47	300	53 41	346
256	50 47	065	41 03	119	17 52	154	22 05	188	48 12	251	55 08	301	53 29	345
257	51 28	065	41 43	120	18 12	155	21 58	189	47 29	252	54 29	301	53 18	345
258	52 09	065	42 22	121	18 31	155	21 51	190	46 45	253	53 50	301	53 06	345
259	52 51	066	43 00	122	18 49	156	21 43	191	46 02	254	53 11	301	52 54	344
260	53 32	066	43 38	123	19 07	157	21 34	192	45 18	255	52 32	301	52 42	344
261	54 13	066	44 16	124	19 24	158	21 24	193	44 35	256	51 53	301	52 29	344
262	54 55	066	44 53	125	19 41	159	21 13	194	43 51	256	51 14	301	52 16	344
263	55 36	067	45 30	126	19 57	160	21 02	195	43 07	257	50 36	302	52 03	343
264	56 18	067	46 06	127	20 12	161	20 50	196	42 22	258	49 57	302	51 50	343
265	56 59	067	46 42	129	20 26	162	20 38	197	41 38	259	49 19	302	51 37	343
266	57 41	067	47 17	130	20 40	163	20 24	198	40 53	260	48 40	302	51 23	342
267	58 23	067	47 52	131	20 53	164	20 10	198	40 09	260	48 02	302	51 10	342
268	59 05	067	48 26	132	21 06	165	19 56	199	39 24	261	47 24	303	50 56	342
269	59 46	068	48 59	133	21 17	166	19 40	200	38 39	262	46 46	303	50 42	342

LHA ♈	Hc	Zn	Hc	Zn	Hc	Zn	Hc	Zn	Hc	Zn	Hc	Zn	Hc	Zn
	◆Alpheratz		ALTAIR		Nunki		◆ANTARES		ARCTURUS		◆Alkaid		Kochab	
270	17 04	066	49 31	135	21 28	166	19 24	201	37 55	263	46 08	303	50 27	342
271	17 45	066	50 03	136	21 39	167	19 07	202	37 10	263	45 30	303	50 13	341
272	18 27	067	50 34	137	21 48	168	18 50	203	36 25	264	44 52	303	49 58	341
273	19 09	068	51 05	139	21 57	169	18 32	204	35 39	265	44 14	304	49 44	341
274	19 51	068	51 34	140	22 05	170	18 13	205	34 54	266	43 36	304	49 29	341
275	20 33	069	52 03	141	22 12	171	17 54	206	34 09	266	42 59	304	49 14	341
276	21 15	069	52 31	143	22 19	172	17 34	207	33 24	267	42 22	304	48 59	340
277	21 57	070	52 58	144	22 24	173	17 14	207	32 39	268	41 44	305	48 43	340
278	22 40	070	53 24	146	22 29	174	16 52	208	31 53	268	41 07	305	48 28	340
279	23 23	071	53 49	147	22 34	175	16 31	209	31 08	269	40 30	305	48 13	340
280	24 05	071	54 13	149	22 37	176	16 08	210	30 23	270	39 53	306	47 57	340
281	24 48	072	54 36	150	22 40	177	15 45	211	29 38	270	39 16	306	47 41	340
282	25 32	073	54 58	152	22 42	178	15 22	212	28 52	271	38 40	306	47 26	340
283	26 15	073	55 18	154	22 43	179	14 58	212	28 07	272	38 03	306	47 10	339
284	26 58	074	55 38	155	22 43	180	14 33	213	27 22	272	37 27	307	46 54	339
	◆Mirfak		Alpheratz		◆ALTAIR		Rasalhague		◆ARCTURUS		Alkaid		Kochab	
285	12 21	032	27 42	074	55 56	157	56 05	219	26 37	273	36 51	307	46 38	339
286	12 45	033	28 25	075	56 14	159	55 36	221	25 51	273	36 15	307	46 22	339
287	13 10	033	29 09	075	56 29	160	55 06	222	25 06	274	35 39	308	46 06	339
288	13 35	034	29 53	076	56 44	162	54 36	223	24 21	275	35 03	308	45 50	339
289	14 00	034	30 37	076	56 57	164	54 04	225	23 36	275	34 27	308	45 34	339
290	14 25	035	31 21	077	57 09	166	53 32	226	22 51	276	33 52	309	45 17	339
291	14 51	035	32 05	077	57 20	167	52 59	228	22 06	277	33 17	309	45 01	339
292	15 17	036	32 49	078	57 29	169	52 25	229	21 21	277	32 42	309	44 45	339
293	15 44	036	33 34	079	57 37	171	51 50	230	20 36	278	32 07	310	44 28	339
294	16 11	037	34 18	079	57 44	173	51 15	231	19 51	278	31 32	310	44 12	339
295	16 38	037	35 03	080	57 48	175	50 40	233	19 06	279	30 57	310	43 56	339
296	17 05	038	35 47	080	57 52	177	50 03	234	18 22	280	30 23	311	43 39	339
297	17 33	038	36 32	081	57 54	178	49 26	235	17 37	280	29 49	311	43 23	339
298	18 01	038	37 17	081	57 55	180	48 49	236	16 53	281	29 15	312	43 06	339
299	18 29	039	38 01	082	57 54	182	48 11	237	16 08	282	28 41	312	42 50	339
	Mirfak		◆Alpheratz		Enif		◆ALTAIR		Rasalhague		Alphecca		◆Kochab	
300	18 58	039	38 46	083	51 16	136	57 51	184	47 33	238	34 32	277	42 33	339
301	19 27	040	39 31	083	51 47	137	57 47	186	46 54	239	33 47	278	42 17	339
302	19 56	040	40 16	084	52 18	139	57 42	188	46 15	241	33 02	278	42 00	339
303	20 25	041	41 01	084	52 47	140	57 35	189	45 35	242	32 18	279	41 44	339
304	20 55	041	41 46	085	53 16	141	57 27	191	44 55	243	31 33	279	41 28	339
305	21 25	042	42 31	085	53 44	143	57 18	193	44 15	244	30 48	280	41 11	339
306	21 55	042	43 17	086	54 10	144	57 07	195	43 34	245	30 04	281	40 55	339
307	22 26	042	44 02	087	54 36	146	56 54	197	42 53	246	29 19	281	40 39	339
308	22 56	043	44 47	087	55 01	147	56 41	198	42 12	246	28 35	282	40 22	339
309	23 27	043	45 32	088	55 25	149	56 26	200	41 30	247	27 51	282	40 06	339
310	23 58	044	46 17	089	55 48	151	56 10	202	40 48	248	27 06	283	39 50	339
311	24 30	044	47 03	089	56 09	152	55 52	204	40 06	249	26 22	283	39 34	339
312	25 01	045	47 48	090	56 30	154	55 33	205	39 23	250	25 38	284	39 18	339
313	25 33	045	48 33	090	56 49	156	55 13	207	38 41	251	24 54	285	39 02	339
314	26 05	045	49 19	091	57 07	157	54 52	208	37 58	252	24 11	285	38 46	339
	CAPELLA		◆Alpheratz		FOMALHAUT		◆ALTAIR		Rasalhague		VEGA		◆Kochab	
315	10 07	036	50 04	092	14 19	154	54 30	210	37 15	253	62 46	277	38 30	340
316	10 33	036	50 49	093	14 39	154	54 07	212	36 31	253	62 01	278	38 14	340
317	11 00	037	51 34	093	14 58	155	53 43	213	35 48	254	61 16	278	37 59	340
318	11 27	037	52 19	094	15 17	156	53 18	215	35 04	255	60 31	279	37 43	340
319	11 55	038	53 05	095	15 35	157	52 51	216	34 20	256	59 46	279	37 27	340
320	12 23	038	53 50	095	15 52	158	52 24	218	33 37	257	59 02	279	37 12	340
321	12 51	039	54 35	096	16 09	159	51 56	219	32 52	257	58 17	280	36 56	340
322	13 19	039	55 20	097	16 25	160	51 27	220	32 08	258	57 32	280	36 41	340
323	13 48	040	56 05	098	16 40	160	50 57	222	31 24	259	56 48	281	36 26	340
324	14 17	040	56 50	099	16 55	161	50 27	223	30 39	260	56 03	281	36 11	341
325	14 47	041	57 34	099	17 09	162	49 56	224	29 55	260	55 19	282	35 56	341
326	15 16	041	58 19	100	17 23	163	49 24	226	29 10	261	54 35	282	35 41	341
327	15 46	042	59 03	101	17 36	164	48 51	227	28 25	262	53 51	283	35 26	341
328	16 17	042	59 48	102	17 48	165	48 17	228	27 40	262	53 06	283	35 11	341
329	16 47	043	60 32	103	17 59	166	47 43	229	26 55	263	52 22	283	34 57	341
	◆CAPELLA		Hamal		Diphda		◆FOMALHAUT		ALTAIR		◆VEGA		Kochab	
330	17 18	043	35 56	089	19 51	138	18 10	167	47 09	231	51 38	284	34 42	341
331	17 50	044	36 41	089	20 21	139	18 20	168	46 33	232	50 54	284	34 28	342
332	18 21	044	37 26	090	20 50	140	18 30	168	45 58	233	50 11	285	34 14	342
333	18 53	045	38 11	091	21 19	141	18 39	169	45 21	234	49 27	285	34 00	342
334	19 25	045	38 57	091	21 47	142	18 47	170	44 44	235	48 43	286	33 46	342
335	19 57	046	39 42	092	22 15	143	18 54	171	44 07	236	48 00	286	33 32	342
336	20 30	046	40 27	093	22 42	144	19 00	172	43 29	237	47 16	286	33 18	342
337	21 02	047	41 12	093	23 09	145	19 06	173	42 51	238	46 33	287	33 04	343
338	21 35	047	41 58	094	23 35	145	19 12	174	42 12	239	45 49	287	32 51	343
339	22 09	048	42 43	095	24 00	146	19 16	175	41 33	240	45 06	288	32 38	343
340	22 42	048	43 28	095	24 25	147	19 20	176	40 54	241	44 23	288	32 25	343
341	23 16	048	44 13	096	24 49	148	19 23	177	40 14	242	43 40	289	32 12	343
342	23 50	049	44 58	097	25 12	149	19 25	178	39 33	243	42 57	289	31 59	344
343	24 24	049	45 43	098	25 35	150	19 26	179	38 53	244	42 14	289	31 46	344
344	24 59	050	46 28	098	25 57	151	19 27	179	38 12	245	41 32	290	31 34	344
	◆CAPELLA		ALDEBARAN		Diphda		◆FOMALHAUT		ALTAIR		◆VEGA		Kochab	
345	25 33	050	15 04	081	26 19	152	19 27	180	37 31	246	40 49	290	31 21	344
346	26 08	051	15 49	082	26 40	153	19 27	181	36 49	247	40 07	291	31 09	344
347	26 43	051	16 34	082	27 00	154	19 25	182	36 08	248	39 25	291	30 57	345
348	27 18	051	17 18	083	27 19	155	19 23	183	35 26	248	38 42	292	30 45	345
349	27 54	052	18 03	083	27 38	156	19 20	184	34 43	249	38 00	292	30 33	345
350	28 30	052	18 48	084	27 56	157	19 17	185	34 01	250	37 18	292	30 22	345
351	29 05	053	19 33	085	28 13	158	19 13	186	33 18	251	36 37	293	30 11	346
352	29 42	053	20 19	085	28 29	159	19 08	187	32 35	252	35 55	293	29 59	346
353	30 18	053	21 04	086	28 45	160	19 02	188	31 52	253	35 13	294	29 48	346
354	30 54	054	21 49	087	29 00	161	18 55	189	31 09	253	34 32	294	29 38	346
355	31 31	054	22 34	087	29 14	162	18 48	190	30 25	254	33 51	295	29 27	347
356	32 08	055	23 19	088	29 27	163	18 40	190	29 42	255	33 10	295	29 17	347
357	32 45	055	24 05	089	29 40	165	18 32	191	28 58	256	32 29	296	29 06	347
358	33 22	055	24 50	089	29 51	166	18 23	192	28 14	256	31 48	296	28 56	347
359	33 59	056	25 35	090	30 02	167	18 13	193	27 30	257	31 07	296	28 46	348

LAT 40°N

LHA ♈	Hc	Zn	Hc	Zn	Hc	Zn	Hc	Zn	Hc	Zn	Hc	Zn	Hc	Zn
	◆ CAPELLA		ALDEBARAN		◆ Diphda		FOMALHAUT		ALTAIR		◆ VEGA		Kochab	
0	34 03	055	26 21	090	31 11	168	19 00	194	26 58	258	30 00	297	27 38	348
1	34 41	056	27 07	091	31 20	169	18 49	195	26 13	259	29 19	298	27 28	348
2	35 19	056	27 53	091	31 29	170	18 36	196	25 28	260	28 38	298	27 19	348
3	35 57	057	28 39	092	31 36	171	18 24	197	24 42	261	27 58	299	27 10	349
4	36 36	057	29 25	093	31 43	172	18 10	198	23 57	261	27 18	299	27 01	349
5	37 14	057	30 10	093	31 49	173	17 56	199	23 11	262	26 38	300	26 52	349
6	37 53	058	30 56	094	31 54	174	17 41	199	22 26	263	25 58	300	26 44	349
7	38 32	058	31 42	095	31 58	175	17 25	200	21 40	263	25 18	301	26 35	350
8	39 11	058	32 28	095	32 01	177	17 09	201	20 55	264	24 39	301	26 27	350
9	39 50	058	33 14	096	32 04	178	16 52	202	20 09	265	23 59	301	26 19	350
10	40 29	059	33 59	097	32 05	179	16 34	203	19 23	265	23 20	302	26 12	351
11	41 08	059	34 45	097	32 06	180	16 16	204	18 37	266	22 41	302	26 04	351
12	41 48	059	35 31	098	32 05	181	15 57	205	17 51	267	22 02	303	25 57	351
13	42 27	060	36 16	099	32 04	182	15 38	205	17 05	267	21 24	303	25 50	351
14	43 07	060	37 01	100	32 02	183	15 18	206	16 19	268	20 46	304	25 43	352
	◆ CAPELLA		BETELGEUSE		RIGEL		◆ Diphda		Enif		◆ DENEB		Kochab	
15	43 47	060	17 00	095	14 04	114	31 59	184	37 28	249	43 32	299	25 37	352
16	44 27	060	17 46	095	14 46	114	31 55	186	36 45	250	42 52	299	25 30	352
17	45 07	061	18 31	096	15 28	115	31 50	187	36 02	251	42 12	299	25 24	352
18	45 47	061	19 17	097	16 09	116	31 44	188	35 18	251	41 32	300	25 18	353
19	46 27	061	20 03	097	16 50	117	31 38	189	34 35	252	40 52	300	25 12	353
20	47 08	062	20 48	098	17 31	117	31 30	190	33 51	253	40 13	300	25 07	353
21	47 48	062	21 34	099	18 12	118	31 22	191	33 07	254	39 33	301	25 02	354
22	48 29	062	22 19	099	18 52	119	31 12	192	32 22	255	38 54	301	24 57	354
23	49 09	062	23 04	100	19 33	120	31 02	193	31 38	255	38 14	301	24 52	354
24	49 50	062	23 50	101	20 12	120	30 51	194	30 54	256	37 35	302	24 47	354
25	50 31	063	24 35	101	20 52	121	30 40	195	30 09	257	36 56	302	24 43	355
26	51 12	063	25 20	102	21 31	122	30 27	197	29 24	258	36 17	302	24 39	355
27	51 53	063	26 05	103	22 10	123	30 13	198	28 39	258	35 39	303	24 35	355
28	52 34	063	26 49	104	22 48	124	29 59	199	27 54	259	35 00	303	24 31	356
29	53 15	064	27 34	104	23 26	124	29 44	200	27 09	260	34 22	303	24 28	356
	◆ CAPELLA		BETELGEUSE		RIGEL		◆ Diphda		Alpheratz		◆ DENEB		Kochab	
30	53 56	064	28 18	105	24 04	125	29 28	201	64 53	253	33 43	304	24 25	356
31	54 37	064	29 03	106	24 41	126	29 12	202	64 09	254	33 05	304	24 22	357
32	55 19	064	29 47	107	25 18	127	28 54	203	63 25	255	32 27	305	24 19	357
33	56 00	064	30 31	107	25 55	128	28 36	204	62 40	256	31 49	305	24 17	357
34	56 41	064	31 14	108	26 31	129	28 17	205	61 56	257	31 12	305	24 15	357
35	57 23	064	31 58	109	27 06	130	27 57	206	61 11	258	30 34	306	24 13	358
36	58 04	065	32 41	110	27 41	131	27 37	207	60 26	259	29 57	306	24 11	358
37	58 46	065	33 25	111	28 16	131	27 16	208	59 41	260	29 20	306	24 10	358
38	59 27	065	34 07	111	28 50	132	26 54	209	58 55	261	28 43	307	24 08	359
39	60 09	065	34 50	112	29 24	133	26 31	210	58 10	262	28 06	307	24 07	359
40	60 51	065	35 33	113	29 57	134	26 08	211	57 24	262	27 30	308	24 07	359
41	61 32	065	36 15	114	30 30	135	25 44	212	56 39	263	26 54	308	24 06	359
42	62 14	065	36 57	115	31 02	136	25 20	213	55 53	264	26 17	308	24 06	000
43	62 56	065	37 38	116	31 33	137	24 54	214	55 07	265	25 42	309	24 06	000
44	63 37	065	38 19	117	32 04	138	24 29	215	54 21	266	25 06	309	24 06	000
	◆ Dubhe		POLLUX		SIRIUS		◆ RIGEL		Diphda		◆ Alpheratz		DENEB	
45	22 11	026	31 02	078	12 44	125	32 35	139	24 02	216	53 36	266	24 30	310
46	22 32	026	31 47	078	13 21	126	33 04	140	23 35	216	52 50	267	23 55	310
47	22 52	027	32 33	079	13 58	127	33 34	141	23 08	217	52 04	268	23 20	310
48	23 13	027	33 18	080	14 35	127	34 02	142	22 39	218	51 18	268	22 45	311
49	23 34	027	34 03	080	15 11	128	34 30	143	22 11	219	50 32	269	22 11	311
50	23 55	028	34 48	081	15 47	129	34 57	144	21 41	220	49 46	270	21 36	312
51	24 17	028	35 34	081	16 23	130	35 23	145	21 12	221	49 00	270	21 02	312
52	24 39	028	36 19	082	16 58	130	35 49	147	20 41	222	48 14	271	20 28	313
53	25 01	029	37 05	082	17 33	131	36 14	148	20 10	223	47 28	272	19 54	313
54	25 23	029	37 50	083	18 07	132	36 38	149	19 39	223	46 42	272	19 21	314
55	25 45	029	38 36	083	18 41	133	37 01	150	19 07	224	45 56	273	18 48	314
56	26 08	030	39 21	084	19 14	134	37 24	151	18 35	225	45 10	273	18 15	315
57	26 31	030	40 07	085	19 47	135	37 46	152	18 02	226	44 24	274	17 42	315
58	26 54	030	40 53	085	20 20	135	38 07	153	17 29	227	43 39	275	17 10	315
59	27 18	031	41 39	086	20 52	136	38 27	155	16 55	228	42 53	275	16 38	316
	◆ Dubhe		POLLUX		PROCYON		◆ SIRIUS		RIGEL		◆ Hamal		Schedar	
60	27 41	031	42 25	086	29 42	110	21 23	137	38 46	156	61 16	244	54 03	314
61	28 05	031	43 11	087	30 25	111	21 54	138	39 05	157	60 34	245	53 30	314
62	28 29	032	43 56	088	31 08	112	22 25	139	39 22	158	59 52	246	52 58	314
63	28 53	032	44 42	088	31 50	112	22 55	140	39 39	159	59 10	247	52 25	314
64	29 17	032	45 28	089	32 33	113	23 24	141	39 54	161	58 28	248	51 52	314
65	29 42	032	46 14	089	33 15	114	23 53	142	40 09	162	57 45	249	51 19	314
66	30 07	033	47 00	090	33 57	115	24 22	142	40 23	163	57 02	250	50 46	314
67	30 32	033	47 46	091	34 38	116	24 49	143	40 35	165	56 18	251	50 13	314
68	30 57	033	48 32	091	35 19	117	25 16	144	40 47	166	55 35	252	49 40	314
69	31 22	033	49 18	092	36 00	118	25 43	145	40 58	167	54 51	253	49 07	314
70	31 47	034	50 04	093	36 41	119	26 09	146	41 08	168	54 07	254	48 34	314
71	32 13	034	50 50	093	37 21	119	26 34	147	41 17	170	53 22	255	48 01	314
72	32 39	034	51 36	094	38 01	120	26 59	148	41 24	171	52 38	256	47 28	314
73	33 05	034	52 22	095	38 40	121	27 23	149	41 31	172	51 53	257	46 55	314
74	33 31	035	53 07	096	39 19	122	27 46	150	41 37	174	51 08	258	46 22	314
	◆ Dubhe		POLLUX		PROCYON		◆ SIRIUS		RIGEL		◆ Hamal		Schedar	
75	33 57	035	53 53	096	39 58	123	28 09	151	41 41	175	50 23	259	45 49	314
76	34 23	035	54 39	097	40 36	124	28 30	152	41 45	176	49 38	259	45 16	315
77	34 50	035	55 24	098	41 14	125	28 52	153	41 47	178	48 53	260	44 44	315
78	35 16	036	56 10	099	41 51	126	29 12	154	41 49	179	48 07	261	44 11	315
79	35 43	036	56 55	100	42 28	127	29 32	155	41 49	180	47 22	262	43 38	315
80	36 10	036	57 40	100	43 04	129	29 51	156	41 48	182	46 36	263	43 06	315
81	36 37	036	58 26	101	43 40	130	30 09	157	41 46	183	45 51	263	42 34	315
82	37 04	036	59 11	102	44 15	131	30 26	158	41 43	184	45 05	264	42 01	315
83	37 31	036	59 55	103	44 49	132	30 43	159	41 40	186	44 19	265	41 29	315
84	37 59	037	60 40	104	45 23	133	30 59	160	41 35	187	43 34	265	40 57	316
85	38 26	037	61 25	105	45 57	134	31 14	162	41 29	188	42 48	266	40 25	316
86	38 54	037	62 09	106	46 29	135	31 28	163	41 22	189	42 02	267	39 53	316
87	39 21	037	62 53	107	47 01	137	31 41	164	41 13	191	41 16	268	39 21	316
88	39 49	037	63 37	108	47 32	138	31 54	165	41 04	192	40 30	268	38 49	316
89	40 17	037	64 20	109	48 03	139	32 05	166	40 54	193	39 44	269	38 17	317

LAT 40°N

LHA ♈	Hc	Zn	Hc	Zn	Hc	Zn	Hc	Zn	Hc	Zn	Hc	Zn	Hc	Zn
	◆ Dubhe		REGULUS		PROCYON		◆ SIRIUS		RIGEL		ALDEBARAN		◆ Mirfak	
90	40 45	037	28 45	099	48 32	140	32 16	167	40 43	195	60 24	224	61 17	303
91	41 13	038	29 30	100	49 01	142	32 26	168	40 31	196	59 52	225	60 39	303
92	41 41	038	30 16	100	49 29	143	32 35	169	40 18	197	59 18	227	60 00	303
93	42 09	038	31 01	101	49 56	145	32 43	170	40 04	198	58 45	228	59 22	303
94	42 37	038	31 46	102	50 22	146	32 50	171	39 49	200	58 10	230	58 43	303
95	43 06	038	32 31	102	50 48	147	32 57	173	39 33	201	57 35	231	58 04	303
96	43 34	038	33 16	103	51 12	149	33 02	174	39 16	202	56 58	232	57 26	303
97	44 02	038	34 00	104	51 35	150	33 07	175	38 58	203	56 22	234	56 47	303
98	44 31	038	34 45	105	51 58	152	33 10	176	38 39	205	55 44	235	56 08	303
99	44 59	038	35 29	106	52 19	153	33 13	177	38 20	206	55 06	236	55 30	303
100	45 27	038	36 13	106	52 39	155	33 15	178	37 59	207	54 28	238	54 51	303
101	45 56	038	36 57	107	52 58	156	33 16	179	37 38	208	53 49	239	54 13	303
102	46 24	038	37 41	108	53 16	158	33 16	181	37 16	209	53 09	240	53 34	303
103	46 53	038	38 25	109	53 32	160	33 15	182	36 53	210	52 29	241	52 56	303
104	47 21	038	39 08	110	53 48	161	33 13	183	36 29	212	51 49	242	52 17	303
	◆ Kochab		Denebola		◆ REGULUS		SIRIUS		RIGEL		◆ ALDEBARAN		Mirfak	
105	31 23	017	22 36	090	39 52	110	33 10	184	36 05	213	51 08	243	51 39	303
106	31 36	017	23 22	090	40 34	111	33 06	185	35 40	214	50 26	244	51 00	303
107	31 49	017	24 08	091	41 17	112	33 02	186	35 14	215	49 45	245	50 22	304
108	32 03	017	24 54	092	42 00	113	32 56	187	34 47	216	49 03	246	49 43	304
109	32 16	017	25 40	092	42 42	114	32 50	189	34 20	217	48 21	247	49 05	304
110	32 30	017	26 26	093	43 23	115	32 42	190	33 52	218	47 38	248	48 27	304
111	32 44	018	27 12	094	44 05	116	32 34	191	33 23	219	46 55	249	47 49	304
112	32 58	018	27 58	094	44 46	117	32 25	192	32 54	220	46 12	250	47 11	304
113	33 12	018	28 44	095	45 27	118	32 15	193	32 24	221	45 29	251	46 33	305
114	33 26	018	29 29	096	46 07	119	32 04	194	31 53	222	44 45	252	45 55	305
115	33 40	018	30 15	096	46 47	120	31 52	195	31 22	223	44 01	253	45 18	305
116	33 55	018	31 01	097	47 27	121	31 40	196	30 50	224	43 17	254	44 40	305
117	34 09	019	31 46	098	48 06	122	31 26	198	30 18	225	42 33	255	44 02	305
118	34 24	019	32 32	099	48 45	123	31 12	199	29 45	226	41 49	255	43 25	306
119	34 39	019	33 17	099	49 23	124	30 57	200	29 12	227	41 04	256	42 48	306
	◆ Kochab		Denebola		◆ REGULUS		SIRIUS		RIGEL		◆ ALDEBARAN		CAPELLA	
120	34 54	019	34 03	100	50 00	126	30 41	201	28 38	228	40 19	257	60 05	295
121	35 09	019	34 48	101	50 38	127	30 25	202	28 03	229	39 34	258	59 23	295
122	35 24	019	35 33	101	51 14	128	30 07	203	27 28	230	38 49	259	58 42	295
123	35 39	019	36 18	102	51 50	129	29 49	204	26 53	231	38 04	259	58 00	295
124	35 55	020	37 03	103	52 25	130	29 30	205	26 17	232	37 19	260	57 19	296
125	36 10	020	37 47	104	53 00	132	29 10	206	25 41	232	36 34	261	56 37	296
126	36 26	020	38 32	105	53 34	133	28 50	207	25 05	233	35 48	262	55 56	296
127	36 41	020	39 16	105	54 07	134	28 28	208	24 27	234	35 03	262	55 14	296
128	36 57	020	40 01	106	54 39	136	28 06	209	23 50	235	34 17	263	54 33	296
129	37 13	020	40 45	107	55 11	137	27 44	210	23 12	236	33 32	264	53 52	296
130	37 28	020	41 29	108	55 42	139	27 20	211	22 34	237	32 46	264	53 11	297
131	37 44	020	42 12	109	56 12	140	26 56	212	21 55	237	32 00	265	52 30	297
132	38 00	020	42 56	110	56 40	142	26 32	213	21 16	238	31 14	266	51 49	297
133	38 16	020	43 39	110	57 08	143	26 06	214	20 37	239	30 28	266	51 08	297
134	38 32	021	44 22	111	57 35	145	25 40	215	19 58	240	29 43	267	50 27	297
	Kochab		◆ ARCTURUS		SPICA		REGULUS		◆ SIRIUS		BETELGEUSE		◆ CAPELLA	
135	38 48	021	20 20	082	10 02	114	58 01	147	25 14	216	37 38	244	49 46	298
136	39 05	021	21 05	082	10 44	115	58 26	148	24 47	217	36 56	245	49 05	298
137	39 21	021	21 51	083	11 26	115	58 49	150	24 19	218	36 14	246	48 25	298
138	39 37	021	22 37	083	12 07	116	59 11	152	23 51	219	35 32	247	47 44	298
139	39 53	021	23 22	084	12 49	117	59 32	154	23 22	219	34 50	248	47 04	298
140	40 10	021	24 08	085	13 29	118	59 52	155	22 52	220	34 07	249	46 23	299
141	40 26	021	24 54	085	14 10	118	60 11	157	22 22	221	33 24	249	45 43	299
142	40 43	021	25 40	086	14 50	119	60 28	159	21 52	222	32 41	250	45 03	299
143	40 59	021	26 25	087	15 30	120	60 43	161	21 20	223	31 58	251	44 23	300
144	41 15	021	27 11	087	16 10	121	60 57	163	20 49	224	31 14	252	43 43	300
145	41 32	021	27 57	088	16 50	121	61 10	165	20 17	225	30 30	253	43 03	300
146	41 48	021	28 43	088	17 29	122	61 21	167	19 44	226	29 46	253	42 23	300
147	42 05	021	29 29	089	18 07	123	61 30	169	19 11	226	29 02	254	41 44	301
148	42 21	021	30 15	090	18 46	124	61 38	171	18 38	227	28 18	255	41 04	301
149	42 38	021	31 01	090	19 24	124	61 45	173	18 04	228	27 34	256	40 25	301
	◆ Kochab		ARCTURUS		◆ SPICA		REGULUS		PROCYON		◆ POLLUX		CAPELLA	
150	42 54	021	31 47	091	20 02	125	61 49	175	43 06	231	60 01	257	39 46	302
151	43 10	021	32 33	092	20 39	126	61 52	177	42 29	233	59 16	258	39 07	302
152	43 27	021	33 19	092	21 16	127	61 54	179	41 53	234	58 31	259	38 28	302
153	43 43	021	34 05	093	21 53	128	61 53	181	41 15	235	57 46	260	37 49	303
154	43 59	021	34 51	094	22 29	129	61 51	184	40 38	236	57 00	260	37 10	303
155	44 16	021	35 37	094	23 05	129	61 48	186	40 00	237	56 15	261	36 32	303
156	44 32	021	36 22	095	23 40	130	61 42	188	39 21	238	55 30	262	35 53	304
157	44 48	021	37 08	096	24 15	131	61 35	190	38 42	239	54 44	263	35 15	304
158	45 04	021	37 54	096	24 49	132	61 27	192	38 03	240	53 58	264	34 37	304
159	45 20	020	38 39	097	25 23	133	61 17	194	37 23	240	53 13	264	33 59	305
160	45 36	020	39 25	098	25 57	134	61 05	196	36 43	241	52 27	265	33 21	305
161	45 52	020	40 11	099	26 30	135	60 52	198	36 02	242	51 41	266	32 44	305
162	46 08	020	40 56	099	27 02	136	60 37	200	35 21	243	50 55	266	32 06	306
163	46 24	020	41 41	100	27 34	136	60 21	202	34 40	244	50 09	267	31 29	306
164	46 40	020	42 26	101	28 05	137	60 03	203	33 58	245	49 23	268	30 52	306
	◆ Kochab		ARCTURUS		◆ SPICA		REGULUS		PROCYON		◆ POLLUX		CAPELLA	
165	46 55	020	43 12	102	28 36	138	59 44	205	33 17	246	48 37	269	30 15	307
166	47 11	020	43 56	102	29 06	139	59 24	207	32 35	247	47 52	269	29 38	307
167	47 26	020	44 41	103	29 36	140	59 02	209	31 52	247	47 06	270	29 02	307
168	47 42	019	45 26	104	30 05	141	58 39	211	31 10	248	46 20	270	28 25	308
169	47 57	019	46 10	105	30 34	142	58 15	212	30 27	249	45 34	271	27 49	308
170	48 12	019	46 55	106	31 01	143	57 50	214	29 44	250	44 48	272	27 13	309
171	48 27	019	47 39	107	31 29	144	57 24	216	29 01	251	44 02	272	26 37	309
172	48 42	019	48 23	108	31 55	145	56 57	217	28 17	251	43 16	273	26 02	309
173	48 57	019	49 07	108	32 21	146	56 29	219	27 33	252	42 30	274	25 26	310
174	49 11	018	49 50	109	32 46	147	55 59	220	26 49	253	41 44	274	24 51	310
175	49 25	018	50 33	110	33 10	148	55 29	222	26 05	254	40 58	275	24 16	311
176	49 40	018	51 16	111	33 34	150	54 58	223	25 21	255	40 13	275	23 41	311
177	49 54	018	51 59	112	33 57	151	54 26	225	24 37	255	39 27	276	23 07	312
178	50 08	017	52 41	113	34 19	152	53 53	226	23 52	256	38 41	276	22 33	312
179	50 21	017	53 23	114	34 40	153	53 20	227	23 08	257	37 55	277	21 59	312

LHA ♈	Hc	Zn	Hc	Zn	Hc	Zn	Hc	Zn	Hc	Zn	Hc	Zn	Hc	Zn
	◆ VEGA		Alphecca		ARCTURUS		◆ SPICA		REGULUS		◆ POLLUX		CAPELLA	
180	17 48	054	43 50	090	54 05	115	35 01	154	52 46	229	37 10	278	21 25	313
181	18 25	054	44 36	090	54 46	117	35 21	155	52 11	230	36 24	278	20 51	313
182	19 03	055	45 22	091	55 27	118	35 40	156	51 35	231	35 39	279	20 18	314
183	19 40	055	46 07	092	56 08	119	35 58	157	50 59	233	34 53	279	19 45	314
184	20 18	056	46 53	092	56 48	120	36 15	159	50 22	234	34 08	280	19 12	315
185	20 56	056	47 39	093	57 27	121	36 31	160	49 45	235	33 23	280	18 39	315
186	21 35	057	48 25	094	58 06	123	36 47	161	49 07	236	32 38	281	18 07	316
187	22 13	057	49 11	094	58 45	124	37 01	162	48 29	237	31 53	282	17 35	316
188	22 52	058	49 57	095	59 22	125	37 15	163	47 50	238	31 08	282	17 03	316
189	23 31	058	50 43	096	60 00	127	37 28	164	47 10	239	30 23	283	16 32	317
190	24 10	059	51 28	097	60 36	128	37 40	166	46 31	240	29 38	283	16 00	317
191	24 49	059	52 14	097	61 12	130	37 51	167	45 51	241	28 53	284	15 29	318
192	25 29	060	53 00	098	61 47	131	38 00	168	45 10	242	28 09	284	14 59	318
193	26 09	060	53 45	099	62 21	133	38 09	169	44 29	243	27 24	285	14 28	319
194	26 49	061	54 30	100	62 54	135	38 17	171	43 48	244	26 40	285	13 58	319
	DENEB		◆ VEGA		ARCTURUS		◆ SPICA		REGULUS		◆ POLLUX		Dubhe	
195	13 02	041	27 29	061	63 26	136	38 24	172	43 06	245	25 55	286	62 09	331
196	13 32	041	28 09	061	63 57	138	38 30	173	42 24	246	25 11	286	61 47	330
197	14 02	042	28 49	062	64 28	140	38 35	174	41 42	247	24 27	287	61 24	329
198	14 33	042	29 30	062	64 57	142	38 39	176	40 59	248	23 43	287	61 00	329
199	15 04	043	30 11	063	65 24	144	38 43	177	40 17	249	23 00	288	60 36	328
200	15 35	043	30 52	063	65 51	146	38 45	178	39 34	250	22 16	289	60 12	328
201	16 07	044	31 33	064	66 16	148	38 46	179	38 50	251	21 32	289	59 47	327
202	16 39	044	32 14	064	66 40	150	38 46	181	38 07	252	20 49	290	59 22	327
203	17 11	045	32 55	064	67 02	152	38 45	182	37 23	252	20 06	290	58 57	327
204	17 43	045	33 37	065	67 23	155	38 42	183	36 39	253	19 23	291	58 32	326
205	18 16	046	34 19	065	67 41	157	38 39	184	35 55	254	18 40	291	58 06	326
206	18 49	046	35 01	066	67 59	159	38 35	186	35 11	255	17 57	292	57 40	325
207	19 22	046	35 43	066	68 14	162	38 30	187	34 26	256	17 15	292	57 14	325
208	19 55	047	36 25	067	68 28	164	38 24	188	33 42	256	16 32	293	56 47	325
209	20 29	047	37 07	067	68 39	167	38 17	189	32 57	257	15 50	294	56 21	324
	DENEB		◆ VEGA		Rasalhague		ANTARES		◆ SPICA		REGULUS		◆ Dubhe	
210	21 03	048	37 49	067	35 28	104	14 54	146	38 09	191	32 12	258	55 54	324
211	21 37	048	38 32	068	36 12	105	15 19	146	38 00	192	31 27	259	55 27	324
212	22 11	049	39 14	068	36 56	106	15 44	147	37 50	193	30 42	259	54 59	324
213	22 46	049	39 57	069	37 40	107	16 09	148	37 40	194	29 57	260	54 32	323
214	23 21	050	40 40	069	38 24	108	16 33	149	37 28	196	29 12	261	54 05	323
215	23 56	050	41 23	069	39 08	108	16 56	150	37 15	197	28 26	261	53 37	323
216	24 31	050	42 06	070	39 52	109	17 19	151	37 01	198	27 41	262	53 09	323
217	25 07	051	42 49	070	40 35	110	17 42	151	36 47	199	26 55	263	52 41	323
218	25 43	051	43 33	071	41 18	111	18 03	152	36 31	200	26 09	264	52 13	322
219	26 18	052	44 16	071	42 01	112	18 24	153	36 15	201	25 24	264	51 45	322
220	26 55	052	45 00	071	42 43	113	18 45	154	35 58	203	24 38	265	51 17	322
221	27 31	052	45 43	072	43 25	114	19 05	155	35 40	204	23 52	266	50 49	322
222	28 07	053	46 27	072	44 07	115	19 24	156	35 21	205	23 06	266	50 21	322
223	28 44	053	47 11	073	44 49	116	19 42	157	35 01	206	22 21	267	49 53	322
224	29 21	054	47 55	073	45 30	117	20 00	158	34 40	207	21 35	268	49 24	322
	DENEB		◆ ALTAIR		Rasalhague		ANTARES		◆ SPICA		Denebola		◆ Dubhe	
225	29 58	054	18 48	094	46 11	118	20 17	158	34 19	208	41 25	252	48 56	322
226	30 35	054	19 34	095	46 51	119	20 34	159	33 57	209	40 41	253	48 27	322
227	31 13	055	20 20	095	47 31	120	20 50	160	33 34	210	39 57	254	47 59	322
228	31 51	055	21 06	096	48 11	121	21 05	161	33 10	212	39 12	255	47 30	322
229	32 28	055	21 51	097	48 50	122	21 19	162	32 46	213	38 28	256	47 02	322
230	33 06	056	22 37	098	49 29	123	21 33	163	32 21	214	37 43	256	46 33	322
231	33 44	056	23 22	098	50 07	124	21 46	164	31 55	215	36 59	257	46 05	322
232	34 23	057	24 08	099	50 45	125	21 58	165	31 28	216	36 14	258	45 37	322
233	35 01	057	24 53	100	51 22	127	22 10	166	31 01	217	35 29	259	45 08	322
234	35 40	057	25 39	100	51 59	128	22 21	167	30 33	218	34 44	259	44 40	322
235	36 18	058	26 24	101	52 35	129	22 31	168	30 05	219	33 59	260	44 11	322
236	36 57	058	27 09	102	53 10	130	22 40	169	29 36	220	33 13	261	43 43	322
237	37 36	058	27 54	102	53 45	132	22 49	170	29 06	221	32 28	262	43 15	322
238	38 16	059	28 39	103	54 19	133	22 56	171	28 36	222	31 42	262	42 46	322
239	38 55	059	29 23	104	54 52	134	23 03	172	28 05	223	30 57	263	42 18	322
	◆ DENEB		ALTAIR		Nunki		◆ ANTARES		ARCTURUS		◆ Alkaid		Kochab	
240	39 34	059	30 08	105	12 04	140	23 10	173	59 29	234	65 02	303	54 57	352
241	40 14	060	30 52	105	12 33	141	23 15	174	58 51	236	64 23	302	54 50	351
242	40 54	060	31 36	106	13 02	142	23 20	175	58 13	237	63 44	302	54 43	351
243	41 33	060	32 20	107	13 30	143	23 24	176	57 34	238	63 05	302	54 35	351
244	42 13	061	33 04	108	13 58	144	23 27	177	56 55	240	62 26	302	54 28	350
245	42 53	061	33 48	109	14 25	144	23 30	177	56 15	241	61 47	302	54 20	350
246	43 34	061	34 31	109	14 51	145	23 31	178	55 34	242	61 08	302	54 11	349
247	44 14	061	35 15	110	15 17	146	23 32	179	54 53	243	60 29	302	54 03	349
248	44 54	062	35 58	111	15 43	147	23 32	180	54 12	244	59 50	302	53 54	349
249	45 35	062	36 40	112	16 08	148	23 31	181	53 31	245	59 11	302	53 44	348
250	46 15	062	37 23	113	16 32	148	23 30	182	52 49	246	58 31	302	53 35	348
251	46 56	062	38 05	114	16 56	149	23 28	183	52 06	248	57 52	302	53 25	347
252	47 37	063	38 47	115	17 19	150	23 25	184	51 24	249	57 13	302	53 15	347
253	48 18	063	39 29	115	17 42	151	23 21	185	50 41	250	56 34	302	53 04	347
254	48 59	063	40 10	116	18 04	152	23 16	186	49 58	250	55 55	302	52 54	346
	◆ DENEB		ALTAIR		Nunki		◆ ANTARES		ARCTURUS		◆ Alkaid		Kochab	
255	49 40	063	40 51	117	18 25	153	23 11	187	49 14	251	55 16	302	52 43	346
256	50 21	064	41 32	118	18 46	154	23 05	188	48 30	252	54 37	302	52 31	346
257	51 02	064	42 12	119	19 06	154	22 58	189	47 47	253	53 57	302	52 20	345
258	51 44	064	42 52	120	19 25	155	22 50	190	47 02	254	53 18	302	52 08	345
259	52 25	064	43 32	121	19 44	156	22 41	191	46 18	255	52 39	302	51 56	345
260	53 07	065	44 11	122	20 02	157	22 32	192	45 34	256	52 00	302	51 44	344
261	53 48	065	44 49	123	20 20	158	22 22	193	44 49	257	51 22	302	51 31	344
262	54 30	065	45 28	124	20 37	159	22 12	194	44 04	257	50 43	302	51 19	344
263	55 12	065	46 05	125	20 53	160	22 00	195	43 19	258	50 04	303	51 06	344
264	55 53	065	46 42	127	21 09	161	21 48	196	42 34	259	49 25	303	50 53	343
265	56 35	066	47 19	128	21 23	162	21 35	197	41 49	260	48 47	303	50 39	343
266	57 17	066	47 55	129	21 37	163	21 21	198	41 04	261	48 08	303	50 26	343
267	57 59	066	48 31	130	21 51	164	21 07	199	40 18	261	47 30	303	50 12	343
268	58 41	066	49 05	131	22 03	164	20 52	200	39 33	262	46 51	303	49 59	342
269	59 23	066	49 40	133	22 15	165	20 36	200	38 47	263	46 13	304	49 45	342

LHA ♈	Hc	Zn	Hc	Zn	Hc	Zn	Hc	Zn	Hc	Zn	Hc	Zn	Hc	Zn
	◆ Alpheratz		ALTAIR		Nunki		◆ ANTARES		ARCTURUS		◆ Alkaid		Kochab	
270	16 39	066	50 13	134	22 27	166	20 20	201	38 02	263	45 35	304	49 30	342
271	17 21	066	50 46	135	22 37	167	20 03	202	37 16	264	44 56	304	49 16	342
272	18 03	067	51 18	136	22 47	168	19 45	203	36 30	265	44 18	304	49 01	342
273	18 46	067	51 49	138	22 56	169	19 27	204	35 44	266	43 40	304	48 47	341
274	19 28	068	52 20	139	23 04	170	19 08	205	34 59	266	43 03	305	48 32	341
275	20 11	068	52 50	141	23 11	171	18 48	206	34 13	267	42 25	305	48 17	341
276	20 53	069	53 18	142	23 18	172	18 28	207	33 27	268	41 47	305	48 02	341
277	21 36	069	53 46	143	23 24	173	18 07	208	32 41	268	41 10	305	47 47	341
278	22 19	070	54 13	145	23 29	174	17 45	208	31 55	269	40 32	306	47 32	341
279	23 03	070	54 39	146	23 33	175	17 23	209	31 09	270	39 55	306	47 16	340
280	23 46	071	55 04	148	23 37	176	17 00	210	30 23	270	39 18	306	47 01	340
281	24 30	072	55 28	150	23 40	177	16 37	211	29 37	271	38 41	306	46 45	340
282	25 13	072	55 50	151	23 42	178	16 13	212	28 51	271	38 04	307	46 29	340
283	25 57	073	56 12	153	23 43	179	15 49	213	28 05	272	37 27	307	46 14	340
284	26 41	073	56 32	155	23 43	180	15 23	213	27 19	273	36 51	307	45 58	340
	◆ Alpheratz		Enif		ALTAIR		◆ Rasalhague		ARCTURUS		Alkaid		◆ Kochab	
285	27 25	074	42 43	118	56 51	156	56 51	220	26 33	273	36 14	308	45 42	340
286	28 09	074	43 24	119	57 09	158	56 21	222	25 48	274	35 38	308	45 26	340
287	28 53	075	44 04	120	57 26	160	55 51	223	25 02	275	35 02	308	45 10	339
288	29 38	075	44 44	121	57 41	162	55 19	224	24 16	275	34 26	309	44 54	339
289	30 22	076	45 23	122	57 55	163	54 46	226	23 30	276	33 50	309	44 37	339
290	31 07	076	46 02	123	58 08	165	54 13	227	22 44	276	33 14	309	44 21	339
291	31 52	077	46 40	124	58 19	167	53 39	229	21 59	277	32 39	310	44 05	339
292	32 37	077	47 18	125	58 28	169	53 04	230	21 13	278	32 03	310	43 49	339
293	33 21	078	47 55	126	58 36	171	52 28	231	20 28	278	31 28	310	43 32	339
294	34 06	078	48 32	128	58 43	173	51 52	232	19 42	279	30 53	311	43 16	339
295	34 51	079	49 08	129	58 48	175	51 16	234	18 57	279	30 18	311	43 00	339
296	35 37	080	49 43	130	58 52	176	50 38	235	18 12	280	29 44	311	42 43	339
297	36 22	080	50 18	131	58 54	178	50 00	236	17 26	281	29 09	312	42 27	339
298	37 07	081	50 53	132	58 55	180	49 22	237	16 41	281	28 35	312	42 10	339
299	37 53	081	51 26	134	58 54	182	48 43	238	15 56	282	28 01	312	41 54	339
	◆ Mirfak		Alpheratz		◆ Enif		ALTAIR		Rasalhague		◆ Alphecca		Kochab	
300	18 11	039	38 38	082	51 59	135	58 51	184	48 04	239	34 24	278	41 37	339
301	18 41	040	39 24	082	52 31	136	58 47	186	47 24	240	33 39	278	41 21	339
302	19 10	040	40 09	083	53 02	138	58 42	188	46 44	241	32 53	279	41 04	339
303	19 40	040	40 55	083	53 33	139	58 35	190	46 03	242	32 08	279	40 48	339
304	20 10	041	41 40	084	54 03	141	58 26	192	45 22	243	31 23	280	40 32	339
305	20 40	041	42 26	085	54 31	142	58 16	193	44 41	244	30 38	281	40 15	339
306	21 10	042	43 12	085	54 59	144	58 05	195	43 59	245	29 52	281	39 59	339
307	21 41	042	43 58	086	55 26	145	57 52	197	43 18	246	29 07	282	39 43	339
308	22 12	043	44 44	086	55 52	147	57 38	199	42 35	247	28 22	282	39 26	339
309	22 43	043	45 29	087	56 16	148	57 22	201	41 53	248	27 38	283	39 10	339
310	23 15	043	46 15	088	56 40	150	57 05	202	41 10	249	26 53	283	38 54	339
311	23 47	044	47 01	088	57 02	152	56 47	204	40 27	250	26 08	284	38 38	339
312	24 18	044	47 47	089	57 24	153	56 27	206	39 44	251	25 24	284	38 22	340
313	24 51	045	48 33	089	57 44	155	56 07	208	39 00	252	24 39	285	38 06	340
314	25 23	045	49 19	090	58 02	157	55 45	209	38 16	253	23 55	286	37 50	340
	◆ Mirfak		Hamal		Diphda		◆ FOMALHAUT		ALTAIR		◆ VEGA		Kochab	
315	25 56	045	24 30	079	12 04	126	15 13	154	55 22	211	62 37	279	37 34	340
316	26 28	046	25 15	080	12 41	127	15 33	154	54 58	212	61 52	280	37 18	340
317	27 01	046	26 00	080	13 18	128	15 53	155	54 33	214	61 06	280	37 02	340
318	27 35	046	26 45	081	13 54	128	16 12	156	54 07	215	60 21	280	36 46	340
319	28 08	047	27 31	081	14 30	129	16 30	157	53 40	217	59 36	281	36 31	340
320	28 42	047	28 16	082	15 05	130	16 48	158	53 11	218	58 51	281	36 15	340
321	29 16	048	29 02	083	15 40	131	17 05	159	52 42	220	58 06	282	36 00	340
322	29 50	048	29 47	083	16 15	131	17 21	159	52 13	221	57 21	282	35 45	341
323	30 24	048	30 33	084	16 49	132	17 37	160	51 42	223	56 36	282	35 29	341
324	30 58	049	31 19	084	17 23	133	17 52	161	51 10	224	55 51	283	35 14	341
325	31 33	049	32 04	085	17 56	134	18 07	162	50 38	225	55 06	283	34 59	341
326	32 07	049	32 50	085	18 29	135	18 20	163	50 05	227	54 21	283	34 44	341
327	32 42	050	33 36	086	19 02	136	18 33	164	49 31	228	53 37	284	34 29	341
328	33 17	050	34 22	087	19 33	136	18 46	165	48 57	229	52 52	284	34 14	341
329	33 53	050	35 08	087	20 05	137	18 58	166	48 22	230	52 08	285	34 00	342
	◆ CAPELLA		Hamal		Diphda		◆ FOMALHAUT		ALTAIR		◆ VEGA		Kochab	
330	16 35	043	35 54	088	20 36	138	19 09	167	47 46	231	51 23	285	33 45	342
331	17 06	044	36 40	089	21 06	139	19 19	167	47 10	233	50 39	285	33 31	342
332	17 38	044	37 26	089	21 36	140	19 29	168	46 33	234	49 55	286	33 17	342
333	18 10	045	38 12	090	22 06	141	19 37	169	45 56	235	49 11	286	33 02	342
334	18 42	045	38 58	090	22 35	142	19 46	170	45 18	236	48 26	287	32 48	342
335	19 15	045	39 44	091	23 03	142	19 53	171	44 40	237	47 42	287	32 35	342
336	19 48	046	40 29	092	23 30	143	20 00	172	44 01	238	46 59	287	32 21	343
337	20 21	046	41 15	092	23 58	144	20 06	173	43 22	239	46 15	288	32 07	343
338	20 54	047	42 01	093	24 24	145	20 11	174	42 42	240	45 31	288	31 54	343
339	21 28	047	42 47	094	24 50	146	20 16	175	42 02	241	44 47	289	31 40	343
340	22 02	048	43 33	095	25 15	147	20 20	176	41 22	242	44 04	289	31 27	343
341	22 36	048	44 19	095	25 40	148	20 23	177	40 41	243	43 21	289	31 14	344
342	23 10	049	45 05	096	26 04	149	20 25	178	40 00	244	42 37	290	31 01	344
343	23 45	049	45 50	097	26 27	150	20 26	178	39 19	245	41 54	290	30 48	344
344	24 20	049	46 36	097	26 50	151	20 27	179	38 37	246	41 11	291	30 36	344
	◆ CAPELLA		ALDEBARAN		Diphda		◆ FOMALHAUT		ALTAIR		◆ VEGA		Kochab	
345	24 55	050	14 54	081	27 12	152	20 27	180	37 55	247	40 28	291	30 23	344
346	25 30	050	15 40	081	27 33	153	20 27	181	37 13	247	39 45	291	30 11	345
347	26 05	051	16 25	082	27 54	154	20 25	182	36 30	248	39 03	292	29 59	345
348	26 41	051	17 11	083	28 14	155	20 23	183	35 47	249	38 20	292	29 47	345
349	27 17	051	17 56	083	28 33	156	20 20	184	35 04	250	37 37	293	29 35	345
350	27 53	052	18 42	084	28 51	157	20 17	185	34 21	251	36 55	293	29 24	346
351	28 29	052	19 28	084	29 09	158	20 12	186	33 37	252	36 13	294	29 12	346
352	29 05	053	20 14	085	29 25	159	20 07	187	32 54	252	35 31	294	29 01	346
353	29 42	053	20 59	086	29 41	160	20 01	188	32 10	253	34 49	294	28 50	346
354	30 19	053	21 45	086	29 57	161	19 55	189	31 26	254	34 07	295	28 39	346
355	30 56	054	22 31	087	30 11	162	19 48	190	30 41	255	33 26	295	28 29	347
356	31 33	054	23 17	088	30 25	163	19 39	191	29 57	256	32 44	296	28 18	347
357	32 10	054	24 03	088	30 37	164	19 31	191	29 12	256	32 03	296	28 08	347
358	32 47	055	24 49	089	30 49	165	19 21	192	28 28	257	31 21	297	27 58	347
359	33 25	055	25 35	089	31 01	167	19 11	193	27 43	258	30 40	297	27 48	348

 LAT 39°N

LHA ♈	Hc	Zn	Hc	Zn	Hc	Zn	Hc	Zn	Hc	Zn	Hc	Zn	Hc	Zn
	◆ CAPELLA		ALDEBARAN		◆ Diphda		FOMALHAUT		ALTAIR		◆ VEGA		Kochab	
0	33 29	055	26 21	090	32 09	168	19 58	194	27 10	259	29 32	298	26 39	348
1	34 07	055	27 07	090	32 19	169	19 47	195	26 24	260	28 51	298	26 30	348
2	34 45	056	27 54	091	32 28	170	19 34	196	25 38	260	28 10	299	26 20	349
3	35 24	056	28 40	091	32 36	171	19 21	197	24 52	261	27 29	299	26 11	349
4	36 03	056	29 27	092	32 43	172	19 07	198	24 06	262	26 48	300	26 02	349
5	36 41	057	30 14	093	32 49	173	18 52	199	23 20	262	26 08	300	25 53	349
6	37 20	057	31 00	093	32 54	174	18 37	200	22 33	263	25 27	300	25 45	350
7	37 59	057	31 47	094	32 58	175	18 21	200	21 47	264	24 47	301	25 36	350
8	38 39	057	32 33	095	33 01	176	18 05	201	21 01	264	24 07	301	25 28	350
9	39 18	058	33 20	095	33 04	178	17 47	202	20 14	265	23 28	302	25 20	350
10	39 58	058	34 06	096	33 05	179	17 29	203	19 28	266	22 48	302	25 13	351
11	40 37	058	34 52	097	33 06	180	17 11	204	18 41	266	22 09	303	25 05	351
12	41 17	059	35 39	097	33 05	181	16 52	205	17 55	267	21 30	303	24 58	351
13	41 57	059	36 25	098	33 04	182	16 32	206	17 08	268	20 51	304	24 51	351
14	42 37	059	37 11	099	33 02	183	16 11	206	16 21	268	20 12	304	24 44	352
	◆ CAPELLA		BETELGEUSE		RIGEL		◆ Diphda		Enif		◆ DENEB		Kochab	
15	43 17	059	17 04	094	14 28	113	32 59	184	37 49	250	43 03	300	24 37	352
16	43 57	060	17 51	095	15 11	114	32 55	186	37 05	251	42 23	300	24 31	352
17	44 37	060	18 37	096	15 53	115	32 50	187	36 21	251	41 42	300	24 25	353
18	45 18	060	19 24	096	16 35	116	32 44	188	35 37	252	41 02	301	24 19	353
19	45 58	060	20 10	097	17 17	116	32 37	189	34 53	253	40 22	301	24 13	353
20	46 39	061	20 56	098	17 59	117	32 29	190	34 08	254	39 42	301	24 07	353
21	47 19	061	21 43	098	18 40	118	32 21	191	33 23	254	39 02	301	24 02	354
22	48 00	061	22 29	099	19 21	119	32 11	192	32 38	255	38 22	302	23 57	354
23	48 41	061	23 15	100	20 02	119	32 01	193	31 53	256	37 43	302	23 52	354
24	49 22	061	24 01	100	20 43	120	31 50	194	31 08	257	37 03	302	23 48	354
25	50 03	062	24 46	101	21 23	121	31 37	196	30 22	257	36 24	303	23 43	355
26	50 44	062	25 32	102	22 03	122	31 24	197	29 37	258	35 45	303	23 39	355
27	51 25	062	26 18	102	22 42	123	31 11	198	28 51	259	35 06	303	23 35	355
28	52 06	062	27 03	103	23 21	123	30 56	199	28 05	260	34 27	304	23 32	356
29	52 48	062	27 49	104	24 00	124	30 41	200	27 19	260	33 48	304	23 28	356
	◆ CAPELLA		BETELGEUSE		RIGEL		◆ Diphda		Alpheratz		◆ DENEB		Kochab	
30	53 29	062	28 34	105	24 38	125	30 24	201	65 10	255	33 10	304	23 25	356
31	54 10	063	29 19	105	25 16	126	30 07	202	64 25	256	32 31	305	23 22	357
32	54 52	063	30 04	106	25 54	127	29 49	203	63 39	257	31 53	305	23 19	357
33	55 33	063	30 48	107	26 31	128	29 31	204	62 54	258	31 15	305	23 17	357
34	56 15	063	31 33	108	27 08	128	29 11	205	62 08	259	30 37	306	23 15	357
35	56 56	063	32 17	108	27 44	129	28 51	206	61 22	260	29 59	306	23 13	358
36	57 38	063	33 01	109	28 20	130	28 30	207	60 36	261	29 22	306	23 11	358
37	58 19	063	33 45	110	28 56	131	28 09	208	59 50	262	28 44	307	23 10	358
38	59 01	063	34 29	111	29 31	132	27 46	209	59 04	262	28 07	307	23 08	359
39	59 43	063	35 13	112	30 05	133	27 23	210	58 18	263	27 30	308	23 07	359
40	60 24	063	35 56	112	30 39	134	26 59	211	57 31	264	26 53	308	23 07	359
41	61 06	063	36 39	113	31 12	135	26 35	212	56 45	265	26 17	308	23 06	000
42	61 48	063	37 21	114	31 45	136	26 10	213	55 58	265	25 40	309	23 06	000
43	62 29	063	38 04	115	32 17	137	25 44	214	55 12	266	25 04	309	23 06	000
44	63 11	063	38 46	116	32 49	138	25 18	215	54 25	267	24 28	310	23 06	000
	◆ Dubhe		POLLUX		SIRIUS		◆ RIGEL		Diphda		◆ Alpheratz		DENEB	
45	21 18	026	30 50	077	13 18	125	33 20	139	24 51	216	53 39	268	23 52	310
46	21 38	026	31 35	078	13 56	126	33 50	140	24 23	217	52 52	268	23 16	310
47	21 59	027	32 21	078	14 34	126	34 20	141	23 55	218	52 06	269	22 41	311
48	22 20	027	33 06	079	15 11	127	34 49	142	23 26	219	51 19	270	22 06	311
49	22 41	027	33 52	079	15 48	128	35 18	143	22 57	219	50 32	270	21 31	312
50	23 02	028	34 38	080	16 25	129	35 46	144	22 27	220	49 46	271	20 56	312
51	23 24	028	35 24	080	17 01	129	36 13	145	21 57	221	48 59	271	20 22	313
52	23 46	028	36 10	081	17 37	130	36 39	146	21 26	222	48 13	272	19 47	313
53	24 08	029	36 56	082	18 12	131	37 05	147	20 54	223	47 26	273	19 13	313
54	24 31	029	37 42	082	18 47	132	37 29	148	20 22	224	46 39	273	18 39	314
55	24 53	029	38 29	083	19 22	133	37 53	150	19 50	225	45 53	274	18 06	314
56	25 16	030	39 15	083	19 56	133	38 17	151	19 17	225	45 06	274	17 33	315
57	25 39	030	40 01	084	20 29	134	38 39	152	18 43	226	44 20	275	17 00	315
58	26 02	030	40 48	084	21 02	135	39 00	153	18 10	227	43 33	275	16 27	316
59	26 26	030	41 34	085	21 35	136	39 21	154	17 35	228	42 47	276	15 55	316
	◆ Dubhe		POLLUX		PROCYON		◆ SIRIUS		RIGEL		◆ Hamal		Schedar	
60	26 50	031	42 20	085	30 02	110	22 07	137	39 41	155	61 42	245	53 21	315
61	27 14	031	43 07	086	30 46	110	22 39	138	40 00	157	60 59	246	52 48	315
62	27 38	031	43 53	087	31 30	111	23 10	139	40 18	158	60 16	248	52 15	315
63	28 02	032	44 40	087	32 13	112	23 41	139	40 35	159	59 33	249	51 42	315
64	28 26	032	45 27	088	32 56	113	24 11	140	40 51	160	58 49	250	51 10	315
65	28 51	032	46 13	088	33 39	114	24 40	141	41 06	162	58 05	251	50 37	315
66	29 16	032	47 00	089	34 22	114	25 09	142	41 20	163	57 21	252	50 04	315
67	29 41	033	47 46	090	35 04	115	25 37	143	41 33	164	56 37	253	49 31	315
68	30 06	033	48 33	090	35 46	116	26 05	144	41 45	166	55 52	254	48 58	315
69	30 32	033	49 20	091	36 28	117	26 32	145	41 56	167	55 07	255	48 25	315
70	30 57	033	50 06	092	37 09	118	26 59	146	42 07	168	54 22	256	47 52	315
71	31 23	034	50 53	092	37 50	119	27 24	147	42 16	170	53 37	257	47 19	315
72	31 49	034	51 39	093	38 31	120	27 50	148	42 23	171	52 51	257	46 46	315
73	32 15	034	52 26	094	39 11	121	28 14	149	42 30	172	52 06	258	46 13	315
74	32 41	034	53 13	094	39 51	122	28 38	150	42 36	174	51 20	259	45 40	315
	◆ Dubhe		POLLUX		PROCYON		◆ SIRIUS		RIGEL		◆ Hamal		Schedar	
75	33 08	035	53 59	095	40 31	123	29 01	151	42 41	175	50 34	260	45 07	315
76	33 34	035	54 45	096	41 10	124	29 23	152	42 45	176	49 48	261	44 34	315
77	34 01	035	55 32	096	41 48	125	29 45	153	42 47	178	49 02	261	44 01	315
78	34 27	035	56 18	097	42 26	126	30 06	154	42 49	179	48 16	262	43 29	315
79	34 54	035	57 04	098	43 04	127	30 26	155	42 49	180	47 30	263	42 56	316
80	35 21	035	57 50	099	43 41	128	30 46	156	42 48	182	46 44	264	42 23	316
81	35 48	036	58 36	100	44 18	129	31 04	157	42 46	183	45 57	264	41 51	316
82	36 16	036	59 22	101	44 54	130	31 22	158	42 43	184	45 11	265	41 18	316
83	36 43	036	60 08	101	45 29	131	31 39	159	42 39	186	44 24	266	40 46	316
84	37 10	036	60 54	102	46 04	132	31 55	160	42 34	187	43 38	266	40 14	316
85	37 38	036	61 39	103	46 38	133	32 11	161	42 28	188	42 51	267	39 41	316
86	38 06	036	62 25	104	47 12	135	32 25	162	42 21	190	42 05	268	39 09	317
87	38 33	037	63 10	105	47 44	136	32 39	164	42 12	191	41 18	268	38 37	317
88	39 01	037	63 55	106	48 17	137	32 52	165	42 03	192	40 31	269	38 05	317
89	39 29	037	64 39	107	48 48	138	33 03	166	41 52	194	39 45	270	37 34	317

LHA ♈	Hc	Zn	Hc	Zn	Hc	Zn	Hc	Zn	Hc	Zn	Hc	Zn	Hc	Zn
	◆ Dubhe		REGULUS		PROCYON		◆ SIRIUS		RIGEL		ALDEBARAN		◆ Mirfak	
90	39 57	037	28 54	098	49 18	140	33 14	167	41 41	195	61 07	225	60 44	305
91	40 25	037	29 40	099	49 48	141	33 25	168	41 29	196	60 33	226	60 05	305
92	40 53	037	30 26	100	50 17	142	33 34	169	41 15	197	59 59	228	59 27	304
93	41 22	037	31 12	100	50 45	144	33 42	170	41 01	199	59 24	229	58 48	304
94	41 50	037	31 58	101	51 12	145	33 50	171	40 45	200	58 48	231	58 10	304
95	42 18	037	32 44	102	51 38	147	33 56	173	40 29	201	58 12	232	57 31	304
96	42 46	037	33 29	103	52 03	148	34 02	174	40 11	203	57 34	234	56 53	304
97	43 15	038	34 15	103	52 27	150	34 06	175	39 53	204	56 57	235	56 14	304
98	43 43	038	35 00	104	52 50	151	34 10	176	39 34	205	56 18	236	55 35	304
99	44 12	038	35 45	105	53 12	153	34 13	177	39 14	206	55 39	238	54 57	304
100	44 40	038	36 30	106	53 33	154	34 15	178	38 53	207	54 59	239	54 18	304
101	45 09	038	37 15	106	53 53	156	34 16	179	38 31	209	54 19	240	53 39	304
102	45 37	038	37 59	107	54 11	157	34 16	181	38 08	210	53 39	241	53 01	304
103	46 06	038	38 44	108	54 29	159	34 15	182	37 45	211	52 57	242	52 22	304
104	46 34	038	39 28	109	54 45	161	34 13	183	37 20	212	52 16	243	51 44	304
	◆ Kochab		Denebola		◆ REGULUS		SIRIUS		RIGEL		◆ ALDEBARAN		CAPELLA	
105	30 25	016	22 36	089	40 12	110	34 10	184	36 55	213	51 34	244	70 00	299
106	30 38	017	23 22	090	40 56	111	34 06	185	36 29	214	50 52	245	69 20	298
107	30 52	017	24 09	091	41 39	111	34 01	186	36 03	215	50 09	247	68 38	298
108	31 05	017	24 56	091	42 23	112	33 56	188	35 35	216	49 26	247	67 57	298
109	31 19	017	25 42	092	43 06	113	33 49	189	35 07	217	48 43	248	67 16	298
110	31 33	017	26 29	093	43 48	114	33 41	190	34 39	219	48 00	249	66 35	297
111	31 46	017	27 16	093	44 31	115	33 33	191	34 09	220	47 16	250	65 53	297
112	32 01	018	28 02	094	45 13	116	33 24	192	33 39	221	46 32	251	65 12	297
113	32 15	018	28 49	094	45 55	117	33 13	193	33 09	222	45 48	252	64 30	297
114	32 29	018	29 35	095	46 36	118	33 02	194	32 37	223	45 03	253	63 49	297
115	32 43	018	30 21	096	47 17	119	32 50	195	32 05	224	44 18	254	63 07	297
116	32 58	018	31 08	096	47 57	120	32 37	197	31 33	225	43 33	255	62 25	297
117	33 13	018	31 54	097	48 37	121	32 24	198	31 00	226	42 48	255	61 44	297
118	33 27	019	32 40	098	49 17	122	32 09	199	30 26	227	42 03	256	61 02	297
119	33 42	019	33 26	099	49 56	123	31 54	200	29 52	227	41 18	257	60 20	297
	◆ Kochab		Denebola		◆ REGULUS		SIRIUS		RIGEL		◆ ALDEBARAN		CAPELLA	
120	33 57	019	34 13	099	50 35	125	31 37	201	29 18	228	40 32	258	59 39	297
121	34 12	019	34 59	100	51 13	126	31 20	202	28 43	229	39 47	259	58 57	297
122	34 27	019	35 44	101	51 51	127	31 02	203	28 07	230	39 01	259	58 15	297
123	34 43	019	36 30	101	52 28	128	30 44	204	27 31	231	38 15	260	57 34	297
124	34 58	019	37 16	102	53 04	129	30 24	205	26 55	232	37 29	261	56 52	297
125	35 14	019	38 01	103	53 40	131	30 04	206	26 18	233	36 43	262	56 11	297
126	35 29	020	38 47	104	54 14	132	29 43	207	25 40	234	35 57	262	55 29	297
127	35 45	020	39 32	105	54 49	133	29 21	208	25 02	235	35 11	263	54 48	297
128	36 00	020	40 17	105	55 22	135	28 59	209	24 24	235	34 24	264	54 06	297
129	36 16	020	41 02	106	55 55	136	28 36	210	23 46	236	33 38	264	53 25	298
130	36 32	020	41 46	107	56 27	138	28 12	211	23 07	237	32 51	265	52 43	298
131	36 48	020	42 31	108	56 57	139	27 47	212	22 28	238	32 05	266	52 02	298
132	37 04	020	43 15	109	57 27	141	27 22	213	21 48	239	31 18	266	51 21	298
133	37 20	020	43 59	110	57 56	142	26 56	214	21 08	239	30 32	267	50 40	298
134	37 36	020	44 43	110	58 24	144	26 30	215	20 28	240	29 45	268	49 59	298
	Kochab		◆ ARCTURUS		SPICA		REGULUS		◆ SIRIUS		BETELGEUSE		◆ CAPELLA	
135	37 52	020	20 11	081	10 27	114	58 51	146	26 02	216	38 03	245	49 18	299
136	38 08	020	20 57	082	11 09	115	59 16	148	25 35	217	37 21	246	48 37	299
137	38 25	020	21 43	082	11 52	115	59 41	149	25 06	218	36 38	247	47 56	299
138	38 41	020	22 30	083	12 34	116	60 04	151	24 37	219	35 55	248	47 15	299
139	38 57	021	23 16	084	13 16	117	60 26	153	24 08	220	35 12	248	46 35	299
140	39 14	021	24 02	084	13 57	117	60 47	155	23 38	221	34 29	249	45 54	300
141	39 30	021	24 49	085	14 38	118	61 06	157	23 07	222	33 45	250	45 14	300
142	39 46	021	25 35	085	15 19	119	61 24	159	22 36	222	33 01	251	44 33	300
143	40 03	021	26 22	086	16 00	120	61 40	161	22 04	223	32 17	252	43 53	300
144	40 19	021	27 08	087	16 40	120	61 55	163	21 32	224	31 33	252	43 13	301
145	40 36	021	27 55	087	17 21	121	62 08	165	20 59	225	30 48	253	42 33	301
146	40 52	021	28 41	088	18 00	122	62 19	167	20 26	226	30 03	254	41 53	301
147	41 09	021	29 28	088	18 40	123	62 29	169	19 52	227	29 18	255	41 13	301
148	41 25	021	30 14	089	19 19	123	62 38	171	19 18	227	28 33	255	40 33	302
149	41 41	021	31 01	090	19 58	124	62 44	173	18 44	228	27 48	256	39 54	302
	◆ Kochab		ARCTURUS		◆ SPICA		REGULUS		PROCYON		◆ POLLUX		CAPELLA	
150	41 58	021	31 48	090	20 36	125	62 49	175	43 43	232	60 13	259	39 14	302
151	42 14	021	32 34	091	21 14	126	62 52	177	43 06	233	59 28	259	38 35	303
152	42 31	021	33 21	092	21 52	127	62 54	179	42 28	234	58 42	260	37 56	303
153	42 47	020	34 08	092	22 29	127	62 53	182	41 50	235	57 56	261	37 16	303
154	43 03	020	34 54	093	23 06	128	62 51	184	41 11	236	57 10	262	36 37	303
155	43 20	020	35 41	094	23 42	129	62 47	186	40 32	237	56 23	263	35 59	304
156	43 36	020	36 27	094	24 18	130	62 42	188	39 53	238	55 37	263	35 20	304
157	43 52	020	37 14	095	24 54	131	62 34	190	39 13	239	54 51	264	34 41	304
158	44 08	020	38 00	096	25 29	132	62 25	192	38 33	240	54 04	265	34 03	305
159	44 24	020	38 47	096	26 04	132	62 15	194	37 52	241	53 18	266	33 25	305
160	44 40	020	39 33	097	26 38	133	62 03	196	37 11	242	52 31	266	32 47	305
161	44 56	020	40 19	098	27 12	134	61 49	198	36 30	243	51 45	267	32 09	306
162	45 12	020	41 05	098	27 45	135	61 33	200	35 48	244	50 58	268	31 31	306
163	45 28	020	41 51	099	28 17	136	61 16	202	35 06	245	50 12	268	30 53	306
164	45 43	020	42 37	100	28 49	137	60 58	204	34 24	246	49 25	269	30 16	307
	◆ Kochab		ARCTURUS		◆ SPICA		REGULUS		PROCYON		◆ POLLUX		CAPELLA	
165	45 59	019	43 23	101	29 21	138	60 38	206	33 41	246	48 38	270	29 39	307
166	46 14	019	44 09	101	29 52	139	60 17	208	32 58	247	47 52	270	29 02	308
167	46 30	019	44 55	102	30 22	140	59 55	210	32 15	248	47 05	271	28 25	308
168	46 45	019	45 40	103	30 52	141	59 31	211	31 32	249	46 19	272	27 48	308
169	47 00	019	46 25	104	31 21	142	59 06	213	30 48	250	45 32	272	27 12	309
170	47 15	019	47 11	105	31 49	143	58 40	215	30 04	250	44 45	273	26 35	309
171	47 30	019	47 56	106	32 17	144	58 13	217	29 20	251	43 59	273	25 59	309
172	47 45	018	48 40	106	32 44	145	57 44	218	28 36	252	43 12	274	25 23	310
173	48 00	018	49 25	107	33 11	146	57 15	220	27 51	253	42 26	274	24 48	310
174	48 14	018	50 09	108	33 36	147	56 45	221	27 07	254	41 39	275	24 12	311
175	48 28	018	50 54	109	34 01	148	56 13	223	26 22	254	40 53	276	23 37	311
176	48 43	018	51 37	110	34 26	149	55 41	224	25 37	255	40 07	276	23 02	311
177	48 57	017	52 21	111	34 49	150	55 08	226	24 52	256	39 20	277	22 27	312
178	49 10	017	53 04	112	35 12	151	54 35	227	24 07	256	38 34	277	21 52	312
179	49 24	017	53 48	113	35 34	153	54 00	228	23 21	257	37 48	278	21 18	313

LAT 39°N

LHA ♈	Hc	Zn	Hc	Zn	Hc	Zn	Hc	Zn	Hc	Zn	Hc	Zn	Hc	Zn
	◆VEGA		Alphecca		ARCTURUS		◆SPICA		REGULUS		◆POLLUX		CAPELLA	
180	17 12	054	43 49	089	54 30	114	35 55	154	53 25	230	37 02	278	20 44	313
181	17 50	054	44 35	089	55 13	115	36 15	155	52 49	231	36 15	279	20 10	314
182	18 28	055	45 22	090	55 55	116	36 35	156	52 12	232	35 29	279	19 36	314
183	19 06	055	46 09	091	56 36	118	36 53	157	51 35	234	34 43	280	19 03	314
184	19 44	056	46 55	091	57 17	119	37 11	158	50 57	235	33 58	281	18 30	315
185	20 23	056	47 42	092	57 58	120	37 28	159	50 19	236	33 12	281	17 57	315
186	21 02	056	48 28	092	58 38	121	37 44	161	49 40	237	32 26	282	17 24	316
187	21 41	057	49 15	093	59 17	123	37 58	162	49 01	238	31 40	282	16 52	316
188	22 20	057	50 02	094	59 56	124	38 13	163	48 21	239	30 55	283	16 19	317
189	22 59	058	50 48	095	60 35	125	38 26	164	47 41	240	30 09	283	15 48	317
190	23 39	058	51 34	095	61 13	127	38 38	166	47 00	241	29 24	284	15 16	318
191	24 18	059	52 21	096	61 49	128	38 49	167	46 19	242	28 39	284	14 45	318
192	24 58	059	53 07	097	62 26	130	38 59	168	45 37	243	27 54	285	14 14	319
193	25 39	060	53 54	097	63 01	131	39 08	169	44 55	244	27 09	285	13 43	319
194	26 19	060	54 40	098	63 36	133	39 17	170	44 13	245	26 24	286	13 13	320
	DENEB		◆VEGA		Alphecca		◆SPICA		REGULUS		◆POLLUX		Dubhe	
195	12 16	040	26 59	061	55 26	099	39 24	172	43 31	246	25 39	286	61 17	332
196	12 47	041	27 40	061	56 12	100	39 30	173	42 48	247	24 54	287	60 55	331
197	13 17	041	28 21	061	56 58	101	39 35	174	42 05	248	24 10	287	60 32	330
198	13 48	042	29 02	062	57 43	102	39 39	176	41 21	249	23 25	288	60 08	330
199	14 20	042	29 43	062	58 29	102	39 42	177	40 38	250	22 41	288	59 45	329
200	14 51	043	30 24	063	59 14	103	39 44	178	39 54	251	21 57	289	59 21	329
201	15 23	043	31 06	063	60 00	104	39 46	179	39 10	251	21 13	289	58 56	328
202	15 55	044	31 48	063	60 45	105	39 46	181	38 25	252	20 29	290	58 32	328
203	16 28	044	32 29	064	61 30	106	39 44	182	37 41	253	19 45	291	58 07	327
204	17 01	045	33 11	064	62 14	107	39 42	183	36 56	254	19 01	291	57 42	327
205	17 34	045	33 53	065	62 59	108	39 39	184	36 11	255	18 18	292	57 16	327
206	18 07	046	34 36	065	63 43	110	39 35	186	35 26	255	17 35	292	56 50	326
207	18 40	046	35 18	066	64 27	111	39 30	187	34 41	256	16 52	293	56 24	326
208	19 14	047	36 00	066	65 10	112	39 24	188	33 56	257	16 09	293	55 58	326
209	19 48	047	36 43	066	65 53	113	39 17	190	33 10	258	15 26	294	55 31	325
	DENEB		◆VEGA		Rasalhague		ANTARES		◆SPICA		REGULUS		◆Dubhe	
210	20 22	048	37 26	067	35 42	104	15 43	145	39 08	191	32 25	258	55 05	325
211	20 57	048	38 09	067	36 28	105	16 09	146	38 59	192	31 39	259	54 38	325
212	21 32	048	38 52	067	37 13	105	16 35	147	38 49	193	30 53	260	54 11	324
213	22 07	049	39 35	068	37 57	106	17 00	148	38 38	195	30 07	261	53 44	324
214	22 42	049	40 18	068	38 42	107	17 24	149	38 26	196	29 21	261	53 16	324
215	23 17	050	41 01	069	39 27	108	17 48	150	38 12	197	28 35	262	52 49	324
216	23 53	050	41 45	069	40 11	109	18 12	150	37 58	198	27 49	263	52 21	324
217	24 29	050	42 29	069	40 55	109	18 34	151	37 43	199	27 02	263	51 53	323
218	25 05	051	43 12	070	41 39	110	18 56	152	37 27	201	26 16	264	51 26	323
219	25 41	051	43 56	070	42 23	111	19 18	153	37 11	202	25 30	265	50 58	323
220	26 18	052	44 40	071	43 06	112	19 39	154	36 53	203	24 43	265	50 30	323
221	26 54	052	45 24	071	43 49	113	19 59	155	36 34	204	23 57	266	50 01	323
222	27 31	052	46 08	071	44 32	114	20 18	156	36 15	205	23 10	267	49 33	323
223	28 08	053	46 52	072	45 14	115	20 37	157	35 55	206	22 24	267	49 05	323
224	28 45	053	47 37	072	45 57	116	20 56	157	35 34	207	21 37	268	48 37	323
	DENEB		◆ALTAIR		Rasalhague		ANTARES		◆SPICA		Denebola		◆Dubhe	
225	29 23	054	18 52	094	46 38	117	21 13	158	35 12	209	41 43	253	48 08	323
226	30 00	054	19 39	094	47 20	118	21 30	159	34 49	210	40 58	254	47 40	322
227	30 38	054	20 25	095	48 01	119	21 46	160	34 25	211	40 13	255	47 12	322
228	31 16	055	21 12	096	48 41	120	22 02	161	34 01	212	39 28	256	46 43	322
229	31 54	055	21 58	096	49 22	121	22 16	162	33 36	213	38 43	256	46 15	322
230	32 32	055	22 44	097	50 01	122	22 30	163	33 10	214	37 57	257	45 46	322
231	33 11	056	23 31	098	50 41	123	22 44	164	32 44	215	37 12	258	45 18	322
232	33 49	056	24 17	098	51 20	124	22 56	165	32 17	216	36 26	259	44 49	322
233	34 28	056	25 03	099	51 58	126	23 08	166	31 49	217	35 40	259	44 21	322
234	35 07	057	25 49	100	52 35	127	23 19	167	31 21	218	34 54	260	43 52	322
235	35 46	057	26 35	101	53 12	128	23 29	168	30 52	219	34 08	261	43 24	322
236	36 25	057	27 21	101	53 49	129	23 39	169	30 22	220	33 22	261	42 56	323
237	37 05	058	28 06	102	54 25	131	23 48	170	29 52	221	32 36	262	42 27	323
238	37 44	058	28 52	103	55 00	132	23 56	171	29 21	222	31 50	263	41 59	323
239	38 24	058	29 37	103	55 34	133	24 03	172	28 49	223	31 04	264	41 31	323
	◆DENEB		ALTAIR		Nunki		◆ANTARES		ARCTURUS		◆Alkaid		Kochab	
240	39 03	059	30 23	104	12 50	140	24 09	173	60 03	236	64 28	304	53 57	352
241	39 43	059	31 08	105	13 20	141	24 15	174	59 24	237	63 50	304	53 51	352
242	40 23	059	31 53	106	13 49	142	24 20	175	58 45	238	63 11	304	53 44	351
243	41 03	059	32 38	106	14 18	143	24 24	175	58 05	240	62 32	304	53 36	351
244	41 43	060	33 22	107	14 46	143	24 27	176	57 24	241	61 54	304	53 29	350
245	42 24	060	34 07	108	15 13	144	24 29	177	56 43	242	61 15	303	53 21	350
246	43 04	060	34 51	109	15 40	145	24 31	178	56 02	243	60 36	303	53 12	350
247	43 45	061	35 35	110	16 07	146	24 32	179	55 20	245	59 57	303	53 04	349
248	44 25	061	36 19	110	16 33	147	24 32	180	54 38	246	59 18	303	52 55	349
249	45 06	061	37 02	111	16 58	147	24 31	181	53 55	247	58 39	303	52 46	348
250	45 47	061	37 46	112	17 23	148	24 30	182	53 12	248	57 59	303	52 36	348
251	46 28	062	38 29	113	17 47	149	24 27	183	52 29	249	57 20	303	52 26	348
252	47 09	062	39 12	114	18 11	150	24 24	184	51 45	250	56 41	303	52 16	347
253	47 50	062	39 54	115	18 34	151	24 20	185	51 01	251	56 02	303	52 06	347
254	48 31	062	40 36	116	18 56	152	24 16	186	50 17	252	55 23	303	51 55	347
	◆DENEB		ALTAIR		Nunki		◆ANTARES		ARCTURUS		◆Alkaid		Kochab	
255	49 13	062	41 18	117	19 18	153	24 10	187	49 33	253	54 44	303	51 44	346
256	49 54	063	42 00	117	19 39	153	24 04	188	48 48	253	54 04	303	51 33	346
257	50 36	063	42 41	118	20 00	154	23 57	189	48 03	254	53 25	303	51 22	346
258	51 17	063	43 22	119	20 20	155	23 49	190	47 18	255	52 46	303	51 10	345
259	51 59	063	44 02	120	20 39	156	23 40	191	46 33	256	52 07	303	50 58	345
260	52 40	063	44 42	121	20 58	157	23 31	192	45 48	257	51 28	303	50 46	345
261	53 22	064	45 22	122	21 16	158	23 21	193	45 02	258	50 49	303	50 34	344
262	54 04	064	46 01	124	21 33	159	23 10	194	44 17	258	50 10	303	50 21	344
263	54 46	064	46 40	125	21 49	160	22 58	195	43 31	259	49 31	304	50 08	344
264	55 28	064	47 18	126	22 05	161	22 46	196	42 45	260	48 52	304	49 55	344
265	56 10	064	47 55	127	22 20	162	22 33	197	41 59	261	48 14	304	49 42	343
266	56 52	064	48 32	128	22 35	162	22 19	198	41 13	261	47 35	304	49 29	343
267	57 34	064	49 09	129	22 48	163	22 04	199	40 27	262	46 56	304	49 15	343
268	58 16	064	49 45	130	23 01	164	21 49	200	39 41	263	46 18	304	49 01	343
269	58 58	065	50 20	132	23 13	165	21 33	201	38 55	264	45 39	304	48 47	342

LHA ♈	Hc	Zn	Hc	Zn	Hc	Zn	Hc	Zn	Hc	Zn	Hc	Zn	Hc	Zn
	◆Alpheratz		ALTAIR		Nunki		◆ANTARES		ARCTURUS		◆Alkaid		Kochab	
270	16 14	065	50 54	133	23 25	166	21 16	201	38 08	264	45 01	305	48 33	342
271	16 57	066	51 28	134	23 36	167	20 58	202	37 22	265	44 23	305	48 19	342
272	17 39	066	52 01	136	23 46	168	20 40	203	36 35	266	43 44	305	48 05	342
273	18 22	067	52 34	137	23 55	169	20 22	204	35 49	266	43 06	305	47 50	342
274	19 05	067	53 05	138	24 03	170	20 02	205	35 02	267	42 28	305	47 35	342
275	19 48	068	53 36	140	24 11	171	19 42	206	34 16	268	41 50	306	47 20	341
276	20 32	068	54 05	141	24 17	172	19 21	207	33 29	268	41 12	306	47 05	341
277	21 15	069	54 34	143	24 23	173	19 00	208	32 42	269	40 35	306	46 50	341
278	21 59	070	55 02	144	24 29	174	18 38	209	31 56	270	39 57	306	46 35	341
279	22 42	070	55 29	146	24 33	175	18 15	209	31 09	270	39 20	307	46 20	341
280	23 26	071	55 55	147	24 37	176	17 52	210	30 23	271	38 42	307	46 04	341
281	24 10	071	56 19	149	24 40	177	17 28	211	29 36	271	38 05	307	45 49	340
282	24 55	072	56 43	150	24 42	178	17 04	212	28 49	272	37 28	307	45 33	340
283	25 39	072	57 05	152	24 43	179	16 39	213	28 03	273	36 51	308	45 17	340
284	26 23	073	57 26	154	24 43	180	16 13	214	27 16	273	36 14	308	45 01	340
	◆Alpheratz		Enif		ALTAIR		◆Rasalhague		ARCTURUS		Alkaid		◆Kochab	
285	27 08	073	43 11	117	57 46	156	57 37	221	26 30	274	35 37	308	44 46	340
286	27 53	074	43 52	118	58 05	157	57 06	223	25 43	274	35 01	309	44 30	340
287	28 37	074	44 33	119	58 22	159	56 34	224	24 57	275	34 24	309	44 14	340
288	29 22	075	45 14	120	58 38	161	56 01	225	24 10	276	33 48	309	43 57	340
289	30 07	075	45 54	121	58 52	163	55 28	227	23 24	276	33 12	309	43 41	340
290	30 52	076	46 34	122	59 05	165	54 53	228	22 38	277	32 36	310	43 25	340
291	31 38	076	47 13	123	59 17	167	54 18	230	21 51	277	32 00	310	43 09	340
292	32 23	077	47 52	124	59 27	169	53 42	231	21 05	278	31 25	310	42 53	340
293	33 09	077	48 30	125	59 36	170	53 06	232	20 19	279	30 49	311	42 36	339
294	33 54	078	49 08	127	59 43	172	52 28	233	19 33	279	30 14	311	42 20	339
295	34 40	078	49 45	128	59 48	174	51 51	235	18 47	280	29 39	311	42 03	339
296	35 25	079	50 21	129	59 52	176	51 12	236	18 01	280	29 04	312	41 47	339
297	36 11	079	50 57	130	59 54	178	50 34	237	17 15	281	28 29	312	41 31	339
298	36 57	080	51 33	131	59 55	180	49 54	238	16 29	282	27 55	312	41 14	339
299	37 43	080	52 07	133	59 54	182	49 14	239	15 44	282	27 20	313	40 58	339
	◆Mirfak		Alpheratz		◆Enif		ALTAIR		Rasalhague		◆Alphecca		Kochab	
300	17 25	039	38 29	081	52 41	134	59 51	184	48 34	240	34 16	278	40 41	339
301	17 54	039	39 15	081	53 14	135	59 47	186	47 53	241	33 30	279	40 25	339
302	18 24	040	40 01	082	53 47	137	59 41	188	47 12	242	32 44	280	40 08	339
303	18 54	040	40 47	083	54 18	138	59 34	190	46 31	243	31 58	280	39 52	339
304	19 24	041	41 34	083	54 49	140	59 25	192	45 49	244	31 12	281	39 36	339
305	19 55	041	42 20	084	55 18	141	59 14	194	45 07	245	30 26	281	39 19	339
306	20 26	042	43 06	084	55 47	143	59 02	196	44 24	246	29 41	282	39 03	339
307	20 57	042	43 53	085	56 15	144	58 49	198	43 41	247	28 55	282	38 47	340
308	21 28	042	44 39	085	56 41	146	58 34	199	42 58	248	28 09	283	38 30	340
309	21 59	043	45 26	086	57 07	147	58 18	201	42 15	249	27 24	283	38 14	340
310	22 31	043	46 12	086	57 32	149	58 00	203	41 31	250	26 39	284	37 58	340
311	23 03	044	46 59	087	57 55	151	57 41	205	40 47	251	25 53	284	37 42	340
312	23 35	044	47 45	088	58 17	153	57 21	207	40 03	252	25 08	285	37 25	340
313	24 08	044	48 32	088	58 38	154	57 00	208	39 19	252	24 23	285	37 09	340
314	24 40	045	49 19	089	58 57	156	56 37	210	38 34	253	23 38	286	36 53	340
	◆Mirfak		Hamal		Diphda		◆FOMALHAUT		ALTAIR		◆VEGA		Kochab	
315	25 13	045	24 18	079	12 40	126	16 07	153	56 13	212	62 27	281	36 37	340
316	25 46	045	25 04	079	13 17	127	16 27	154	55 48	213	61 41	281	36 22	340
317	26 20	046	25 49	080	13 54	127	16 47	155	55 22	215	60 55	282	36 06	340
318	26 53	046	26 35	080	14 31	128	17 06	156	54 55	216	60 10	282	35 50	340
319	27 27	046	27 21	081	15 08	129	17 25	157	54 27	218	59 24	282	35 34	340
320	28 01	047	28 07	081	15 44	130	17 43	158	53 58	219	58 38	283	35 19	341
321	28 35	047	28 54	082	16 19	130	18 01	158	53 28	221	57 53	283	35 03	341
322	29 09	048	29 40	083	16 55	131	18 17	159	52 57	222	57 08	283	34 48	341
323	29 44	048	30 26	083	17 29	132	18 33	160	52 26	223	56 22	284	34 33	341
324	30 18	048	31 12	084	18 04	133	18 49	161	51 53	225	55 37	284	34 17	341
325	30 53	048	31 59	084	18 38	134	19 04	162	51 20	226	54 52	284	34 02	341
326	31 28	049	32 45	085	19 11	134	19 18	163	50 46	227	54 07	285	33 47	341
327	32 03	049	33 32	085	19 44	135	19 31	164	50 11	229	53 22	285	33 32	341
328	32 39	049	34 18	086	20 17	136	19 44	165	49 36	230	52 37	286	33 18	342
329	33 14	050	35 05	087	20 49	137	19 56	166	49 00	231	51 52	286	33 03	342
	◆CAPELLA		Hamal		Diphda		◆FOMALHAUT		ALTAIR		◆VEGA		Kochab	
330	15 51	043	35 51	087	21 20	138	20 07	166	48 24	232	51 07	286	32 48	342
331	16 23	043	36 38	088	21 52	139	20 18	167	47 46	233	50 22	287	32 34	342
332	16 55	044	37 24	088	22 22	140	20 27	168	47 09	235	49 38	287	32 20	342
333	17 27	044	38 11	089	22 52	140	20 36	169	46 30	236	48 53	287	32 05	342
334	18 00	045	38 58	090	23 21	141	20 45	170	45 52	237	48 09	288	31 51	343
335	18 33	045	39 44	090	23 50	142	20 52	171	45 12	238	47 24	288	31 37	343
336	19 06	046	40 31	091	24 19	143	20 59	172	44 33	239	46 40	288	31 23	343
337	19 40	046	41 18	092	24 46	144	21 05	173	43 53	240	45 56	289	31 10	343
338	20 13	047	42 04	092	25 13	145	21 11	174	43 12	241	45 12	289	30 56	343
339	20 47	047	42 51	093	25 40	146	21 15	175	42 31	242	44 28	290	30 43	343
340	21 21	047	43 37	094	26 06	147	21 19	176	41 50	243	43 44	290	30 30	344
341	21 56	048	44 24	094	26 31	148	21 22	177	41 08	244	43 00	290	30 17	344
342	22 30	048	45 10	095	26 55	149	21 25	178	40 26	245	42 17	291	30 04	344
343	23 05	049	45 57	096	27 19	150	21 26	178	39 44	246	41 33	291	29 51	344
344	23 40	049	46 43	096	27 42	151	21 27	179	39 01	246	40 49	291	29 38	344
	◆CAPELLA		ALDEBARAN		Diphda		◆FOMALHAUT		ALTAIR		◆VEGA		Kochab	
345	24 16	049	14 45	080	28 05	152	21 27	180	38 18	247	40 06	292	29 26	345
346	24 51	050	15 31	081	28 27	153	21 27	181	37 35	248	39 23	292	29 13	345
347	25 27	050	16 17	082	28 48	154	21 25	182	36 52	249	38 40	293	29 01	345
348	26 03	051	17 03	082	29 08	155	21 23	183	36 08	250	37 57	293	28 49	345
349	26 39	051	17 49	083	29 27	156	21 20	184	35 24	251	37 14	293	28 37	345
350	27 15	051	18 35	083	29 46	157	21 16	185	34 40	251	36 31	294	28 26	346
351	27 52	052	19 22	084	30 04	158	21 12	186	33 56	252	35 49	294	28 14	346
352	28 29	052	20 08	085	30 21	159	21 07	187	33 11	253	35 06	295	28 03	346
353	29 05	052	20 55	085	30 38	160	21 01	188	32 27	254	34 24	295	27 52	346
354	29 43	053	21 41	086	30 53	161	20 54	189	31 42	255	33 42	295	27 41	347
355	30 20	053	22 28	086	31 08	162	20 47	190	30 57	255	33 00	296	27 30	347
356	30 57	054	23 14	087	31 22	163	20 38	191	30 12	256	32 18	296	27 20	347
357	31 35	054	24 01	088	31 35	164	20 30	191	29 26	257	31 36	297	27 09	347
358	32 13	054	24 47	088	31 48	165	20 20	192	28 41	258	30 54	297	26 59	348
359	32 51	055	25 34	089	31 59	166	20 10	193	27 55	258	30 13	297	26 49	348

LAT 38°N

LHA ♈	Hc Zn	Hc Zn	Hc Zn	Hc Zn	Hc Zn	Hc Zn	Hc Zn
	◆ CAPELLA	ALDEBARAN	◆ Diphda	FOMALHAUT	ALTAIR	◆ VEGA	Kochab
0	32 54 054	26 20 089	33 08 167	20 57 194	27 21 259	29 03 298	25 41 348
1	33 32 055	27 07 090	33 18 169	20 45 195	26 34 260	28 22 299	25 31 348
2	34 11 055	27 54 090	33 27 170	20 32 196	25 48 261	27 40 299	25 22 349
3	34 50 055	28 42 091	33 35 171	20 18 197	25 01 262	26 59 300	25 12 349
4	35 29 056	29 29 092	33 42 172	20 04 198	24 14 262	26 18 300	25 03 349
5	36 08 056	30 16 092	33 48 173	19 49 199	23 27 263	25 37 300	24 54 349
6	36 47 056	31 03 093	33 53 174	19 34 200	22 40 263	24 57 301	24 46 350
7	37 27 057	31 51 093	33 58 175	19 17 201	21 53 264	24 16 301	24 37 350
8	38 06 057	32 38 094	34 01 176	19 00 201	21 06 265	23 36 302	24 29 350
9	38 46 057	33 25 095	34 04 178	18 43 202	20 19 265	22 56 302	24 21 350
10	39 25 057	34 12 095	34 05 179	18 25 203	19 32 266	22 16 303	24 13 351
11	40 05 058	34 59 096	34 06 180	18 06 204	18 45 267	21 36 303	24 06 351
12	40 45 058	35 46 097	34 05 181	17 46 205	17 58 267	20 57 304	23 58 351
13	41 25 058	36 33 097	34 04 182	17 26 206	17 10 268	20 17 304	23 51 351
14	42 06 058	37 20 098	34 02 183	17 05 207	16 23 269	19 38 304	23 44 352
	◆ CAPELLA	BETELGEUSE	RIGEL	◆ Diphda	Enif	◆ DENEB	Kochab
15	42 46 059	17 09 094	14 52 113	33 58 184	38 10 250	42 33 301	23 38 352
16	43 26 059	17 56 095	15 35 114	33 54 186	37 25 251	41 52 301	23 31 352
17	44 07 059	18 43 095	16 18 115	33 49 187	36 40 252	41 12 301	23 25 353
18	44 47 059	19 30 096	17 01 115	33 43 188	35 55 253	40 31 301	23 19 353
19	45 28 059	20 17 097	17 44 116	33 36 189	35 10 254	39 51 302	23 13 353
20	46 09 060	21 04 097	18 26 117	33 28 190	34 24 254	39 11 302	23 08 353
21	46 50 060	21 51 098	19 08 118	33 19 191	33 39 255	38 31 302	23 02 354
22	47 31 060	22 38 099	19 50 118	33 10 192	32 53 256	37 51 302	22 57 354
23	48 12 060	23 24 099	20 31 119	32 59 194	32 07 257	37 11 303	22 53 354
24	48 53 060	24 11 100	21 13 120	32 48 195	31 21 257	36 31 303	22 48 355
25	49 34 061	24 58 101	21 53 121	32 35 196	30 35 258	35 51 303	22 44 355
26	50 15 061	25 44 101	22 34 121	32 22 197	29 49 259	35 12 304	22 39 355
27	50 56 061	26 30 102	23 14 122	32 08 198	29 02 259	34 33 304	22 35 355
28	51 38 061	27 17 103	23 54 123	31 53 199	28 16 260	33 54 304	22 32 356
29	52 19 061	28 03 103	24 34 124	31 37 200	27 29 261	33 15 305	22 28 356
	◆ CAPELLA	BETELGEUSE	RIGEL	◆ Diphda	Alpheratz	◆ DENEB	Kochab
30	53 01 061	28 49 104	25 13 125	31 20 201	65 24 257	32 36 305	22 25 356
31	53 42 061	29 34 105	25 51 125	31 03 202	64 38 258	31 57 305	22 22 357
32	54 24 061	30 20 106	26 30 126	30 45 203	63 52 259	31 18 306	22 20 357
33	55 05 062	31 05 106	27 08 127	30 25 204	63 05 260	30 40 306	22 17 357
34	55 47 062	31 51 107	27 45 128	30 06 205	62 18 261	30 02 306	22 15 357
35	56 28 062	32 36 108	28 22 129	29 45 206	61 32 262	29 24 307	22 13 358
36	57 10 062	33 21 109	28 59 130	29 24 207	60 45 263	28 46 307	22 11 358
37	57 52 062	34 06 109	29 35 131	29 01 208	59 58 263	28 08 307	22 10 358
38	58 33 062	34 50 110	30 11 132	28 39 209	59 11 264	27 31 308	22 08 359
39	59 15 062	35 34 111	30 46 132	28 15 210	58 24 265	26 53 308	22 07 359
40	59 57 062	36 18 112	31 20 133	27 51 211	57 37 266	26 16 308	22 07 359
41	60 38 062	37 02 113	31 54 134	27 26 212	56 50 266	25 39 309	22 06 000
42	61 20 062	37 46 113	32 28 135	27 00 213	56 02 267	25 02 309	22 06 000
43	62 02 062	38 29 114	33 01 136	26 34 214	55 15 268	24 26 310	22 06 000
44	62 43 062	39 12 115	33 33 137	26 07 215	54 28 268	23 49 310	22 06 000
	◆ Dubhe	POLLUX	SIRIUS	◆ RIGEL	Diphda	◆ Alpheratz	DENEB
45	20 23 026	30 36 077	13 52 125	34 05 138	25 39 216	53 41 269	23 13 310
46	20 44 026	31 22 077	14 31 125	34 36 139	25 11 217	52 53 270	22 37 311
47	21 05 026	32 08 078	15 09 126	35 07 140	24 43 218	52 06 270	22 02 311
48	21 26 027	32 55 078	15 47 127	35 36 141	24 13 219	51 19 271	21 26 312
49	21 47 027	33 41 079	16 25 128	36 06 142	23 43 220	50 32 271	20 51 312
50	22 09 027	34 27 079	17 02 128	36 34 144	23 13 221	49 44 272	20 16 312
51	22 31 028	35 14 080	17 39 129	37 02 145	22 42 221	48 57 273	19 41 313
52	22 53 028	36 00 080	18 15 130	37 29 146	22 10 222	48 10 273	19 06 313
53	23 15 028	36 47 081	18 51 131	37 55 147	21 38 223	47 23 274	18 32 314
54	23 38 029	37 34 081	19 27 132	38 20 148	21 06 224	46 35 274	17 58 314
55	24 01 029	38 20 082	20 02 132	38 45 149	20 33 225	45 48 275	17 24 315
56	24 24 029	39 07 082	20 37 133	39 09 150	19 59 226	45 01 275	16 50 315
57	24 47 030	39 54 083	21 11 134	39 32 152	19 25 226	44 14 276	16 17 315
58	25 10 030	40 41 083	21 45 135	39 54 153	18 50 227	43 27 276	15 44 316
59	25 34 030	41 28 084	22 18 136	40 15 154	18 16 228	42 40 277	15 11 316
	◆ Dubhe	POLLUX	PROCYON	◆ SIRIUS	RIGEL	◆ Hamal	Schedar
60	25 58 030	42 15 085	30 22 109	22 51 137	40 35 155	62 06 247	52 38 316
61	26 22 031	43 02 085	31 07 110	23 23 137	40 55 156	61 22 248	52 05 316
62	26 46 031	43 49 086	31 51 111	23 55 138	41 13 158	60 38 249	51 32 316
63	27 11 031	44 37 086	32 35 111	24 26 139	41 31 159	59 54 250	51 00 316
64	27 35 032	45 24 087	33 19 112	24 57 140	41 47 160	59 09 251	50 27 316
65	28 00 032	46 11 087	34 03 113	25 27 141	42 03 161	58 24 252	49 54 316
66	28 25 032	46 58 088	34 46 114	25 56 142	42 17 163	57 39 253	49 21 316
67	28 50 032	47 45 089	35 29 115	26 25 143	42 31 164	56 54 254	48 48 316
68	29 16 033	48 33 089	36 12 115	26 54 144	42 43 165	56 08 255	48 15 316
69	29 41 033	49 20 090	36 55 116	27 21 145	42 55 167	55 22 256	47 42 316
70	30 07 033	50 07 090	37 37 117	27 48 146	43 05 168	54 36 257	47 09 316
71	30 33 033	50 55 091	38 19 118	28 15 147	43 15 169	53 50 258	46 36 316
72	30 59 034	51 42 092	39 00 119	28 40 148	43 23 171	53 04 259	46 03 316
73	31 25 034	52 29 092	39 41 120	29 05 149	43 30 172	52 17 260	45 30 316
74	31 52 034	53 16 093	40 22 121	29 30 150	43 36 173	51 31 260	44 57 316
	◆ Dubhe	POLLUX	PROCYON	◆ SIRIUS	RIGEL	◆ Hamal	Schedar
75	32 18 034	54 04 094	41 03 122	29 53 151	43 41 175	50 44 261	44 24 316
76	32 45 034	54 51 094	41 43 123	30 16 152	43 44 176	49 57 262	43 51 316
77	33 11 035	55 38 095	42 22 124	30 38 153	43 47 178	49 11 263	43 18 316
78	33 38 035	56 25 096	43 01 125	31 00 154	43 49 179	48 24 263	42 46 316
79	34 05 035	57 12 096	43 40 126	31 20 155	43 49 180	47 37 264	42 13 316
80	34 32 035	57 59 097	44 18 127	31 40 156	43 48 182	46 50 265	41 40 316
81	35 00 035	58 46 098	44 55 128	31 59 157	43 46 183	46 03 265	41 07 316
82	35 27 035	59 32 099	45 32 129	32 18 158	43 43 184	45 15 266	40 35 317
83	35 54 036	60 19 100	46 08 130	32 35 159	43 39 186	44 28 267	40 02 317
84	36 22 036	61 06 101	46 44 132	32 52 160	43 34 187	43 41 267	39 30 317
85	36 50 036	61 52 101	47 19 133	33 07 161	43 27 188	42 54 268	38 58 317
86	37 17 036	62 38 102	47 54 134	33 22 162	43 20 190	42 06 269	38 26 317
87	37 45 036	63 24 103	48 27 135	33 36 163	43 11 191	41 19 269	37 53 317
88	38 13 036	64 10 104	49 00 136	33 49 164	43 02 192	40 32 270	37 21 317
89	38 41 036	64 56 105	49 32 138	34 02 166	42 51 194	39 45 271	36 49 318

LHA ♈	Hc Zn	Hc Zn	Hc Zn	Hc Zn	Hc Zn	Hc Zn	Hc Zn
	◆ Dubhe	REGULUS	PROCYON	◆ SIRIUS	RIGEL	ALDEBARAN	◆ Mirfak
90	39 09 036	29 02 098	50 04 139	34 13 167	42 39 195	61 49 226	60 09 306
91	39 37 037	29 49 098	50 35 140	34 23 168	42 26 196	61 14 228	59 31 306
92	40 05 037	30 36 099	51 04 142	34 33 169	42 12 198	60 39 229	58 52 306
93	40 34 037	31 23 100	51 33 143	34 41 170	41 57 199	60 03 231	58 14 306
94	41 02 037	32 09 100	52 01 145	34 49 171	41 41 200	59 26 232	57 35 306
95	41 30 037	32 56 101	52 28 146	34 56 172	41 24 202	58 48 234	56 57 305
96	41 59 037	33 42 102	52 54 147	35 01 174	41 07 203	58 09 235	56 18 305
97	42 27 037	34 28 103	53 19 149	35 06 175	40 48 204	57 30 236	55 40 305
98	42 55 037	35 14 103	53 43 150	35 10 176	40 28 205	56 51 238	55 01 305
99	43 24 037	36 00 104	54 05 152	35 13 177	40 07 207	56 11 239	54 23 305
100	43 52 037	36 46 105	54 27 154	35 15 178	39 46 208	55 30 240	53 44 305
101	44 21 037	37 31 106	54 47 155	35 16 179	39 23 209	54 49 241	53 05 305
102	44 49 037	38 17 106	55 07 157	35 16 181	39 00 210	54 07 242	52 27 305
103	45 18 037	39 02 107	55 24 159	35 15 182	38 36 211	53 25 243	51 48 305
104	45 46 037	39 47 108	55 41 160	35 13 183	38 11 212	52 42 245	51 09 305
	◆ Kochab	Denebola	◆ REGULUS	SIRIUS	RIGEL	◆ ALDEBARAN	CAPELLA
105	29 28 016	22 35 089	40 32 109	35 10 184	37 45 214	51 59 246	69 30 301
106	29 41 016	23 22 090	41 17 110	35 06 185	37 19 215	51 16 247	68 50 301
107	29 54 017	24 09 090	42 01 111	35 01 186	36 52 216	50 33 248	68 09 300
108	30 08 017	24 57 091	42 45 111	34 55 188	36 24 217	49 49 249	67 28 300
109	30 21 017	25 44 091	43 29 112	34 48 189	35 55 218	49 05 250	66 47 300
110	30 35 017	26 31 092	44 13 113	34 41 190	35 25 219	48 20 250	66 06 299
111	30 49 017	27 19 093	44 56 114	34 32 191	34 55 220	47 35 251	65 25 299
112	31 03 017	28 06 093	45 39 115	34 22 192	34 25 221	46 51 252	64 44 299
113	31 18 018	28 53 094	46 21 116	34 12 193	33 53 222	46 05 253	64 02 299
114	31 32 018	29 40 095	47 04 117	34 00 195	33 21 223	45 20 254	63 21 299
115	31 46 018	30 27 095	47 46 118	33 48 196	32 49 224	44 35 255	62 39 298
116	32 01 018	31 14 096	48 27 119	33 35 197	32 16 225	43 49 256	61 58 298
117	32 16 018	32 01 097	49 08 120	33 21 198	31 42 226	43 03 256	61 16 298
118	32 30 018	32 48 097	49 49 121	33 06 199	31 08 227	42 17 257	60 34 298
119	32 45 018	33 35 098	50 29 122	32 50 200	30 33 228	41 31 258	59 53 298
	◆ Kochab	Denebola	◆ REGULUS	SIRIUS	RIGEL	◆ ALDEBARAN	CAPELLA
120	33 00 019	34 22 099	51 09 124	32 33 201	29 57 229	40 45 259	59 11 298
121	33 15 019	35 09 099	51 48 125	32 16 202	29 22 230	39 58 259	58 29 298
122	33 31 019	35 55 100	52 26 126	31 58 203	28 45 231	39 12 260	57 48 298
123	33 46 019	36 42 101	53 04 127	31 38 204	28 09 231	38 25 261	57 06 298
124	34 01 019	37 28 101	53 42 128	31 18 205	27 31 232	37 38 262	56 24 298
125	34 17 019	38 14 102	54 18 130	30 58 206	26 54 233	36 51 262	55 43 298
126	34 33 019	39 01 103	54 54 131	30 36 208	26 16 234	36 04 263	55 01 298
127	34 48 019	39 47 104	55 30 132	30 14 209	25 37 235	35 18 264	54 20 299
128	35 04 019	40 32 105	56 04 134	29 51 210	24 58 236	34 31 264	53 38 299
129	35 20 020	41 18 105	56 38 135	29 27 211	24 19 237	33 43 265	52 57 299
130	35 36 020	42 04 106	57 11 137	29 03 212	23 39 237	32 56 266	52 15 299
131	35 52 020	42 49 107	57 43 138	28 38 213	22 59 238	32 09 266	51 34 299
132	36 08 020	43 34 108	58 13 140	28 12 214	22 19 239	31 22 267	50 52 299
133	36 24 020	44 19 109	58 43 141	27 46 214	21 38 240	30 35 268	50 11 299
134	36 40 020	45 04 109	59 12 143	27 19 215	20 57 240	29 47 268	49 30 299
	Kochab	◆ ARCTURUS	SPICA	REGULUS	◆ SIRIUS	BETELGEUSE	◆ CAPELLA
135	36 56 020	20 02 081	10 51 114	59 40 145	26 51 216	38 29 246	48 49 300
136	37 12 020	20 48 082	11 34 114	60 07 147	26 23 217	37 45 247	48 08 300
137	37 28 020	21 35 082	12 17 115	60 32 148	25 54 218	37 02 247	47 27 300
138	37 45 020	22 22 083	13 00 116	60 56 150	25 24 219	36 18 248	46 46 300
139	38 01 020	23 09 083	13 42 116	61 19 152	24 54 220	35 34 249	46 05 300
140	38 17 020	23 56 084	14 25 117	61 41 154	24 23 221	34 50 250	45 24 301
141	38 34 020	24 43 084	15 06 118	62 01 156	23 52 222	34 05 251	44 43 301
142	38 50 020	25 30 085	15 48 119	62 19 158	23 20 223	33 20 251	44 03 301
143	39 07 020	26 17 086	16 30 119	62 36 160	22 48 224	32 36 252	43 22 301
144	39 23 020	27 04 086	17 11 120	62 52 162	22 15 224	31 50 253	42 42 301
145	39 40 020	27 52 087	17 51 121	63 06 164	21 42 225	31 05 254	42 02 302
146	39 56 020	28 39 087	18 32 122	63 18 166	21 08 226	30 20 254	41 21 302
147	40 12 020	29 26 088	19 12 122	63 28 168	20 34 227	29 34 255	40 41 302
148	40 29 020	30 13 089	19 52 123	63 37 171	19 59 228	28 48 256	40 01 302
149	40 45 020	31 01 089	20 31 124	63 44 173	19 24 229	28 02 257	39 22 303
	◆ Kochab	ARCTURUS	◆ SPICA	REGULUS	PROCYON	◆ POLLUX	CAPELLA
150	41 02 020	31 48 090	21 10 125	63 49 175	44 19 233	60 25 260	38 42 303
151	41 18 020	32 35 090	21 49 125	63 52 177	43 41 234	59 38 261	38 02 303
152	41 34 020	33 22 091	22 27 126	63 54 179	43 03 235	58 51 262	37 23 304
153	41 51 020	34 10 092	23 05 127	63 53 182	42 24 236	58 04 263	36 43 304
154	42 07 020	34 57 092	23 43 128	63 51 184	41 44 237	57 17 263	36 04 304
155	42 23 020	35 44 093	24 20 129	63 47 186	41 04 238	56 30 264	35 25 304
156	42 39 020	36 31 094	24 57 130	63 41 188	40 24 239	55 43 265	34 46 305
157	42 56 020	37 19 094	25 33 130	63 33 190	39 43 240	54 56 266	34 07 305
158	43 12 020	38 06 095	26 09 131	63 24 193	39 02 241	54 09 266	33 29 305
159	43 28 020	38 53 096	26 44 132	63 13 195	38 21 242	53 22 267	32 50 306
160	43 44 020	39 40 096	27 19 133	63 00 197	37 39 243	52 35 268	32 12 306
161	44 00 020	40 27 097	27 53 134	62 46 199	36 57 244	51 47 268	31 34 306
162	44 15 019	41 14 098	28 27 135	62 29 201	36 14 245	51 00 269	30 56 307
163	44 31 019	42 00 098	29 00 136	62 12 203	35 31 245	50 13 270	30 18 307
164	44 47 019	42 47 099	29 33 137	61 53 205	34 48 246	49 25 270	29 40 307
	◆ Kochab	ARCTURUS	◆ SPICA	REGULUS	PROCYON	◆ POLLUX	CAPELLA
165	45 02 019	43 34 100	30 05 138	61 32 207	34 05 247	48 38 271	29 02 308
166	45 18 019	44 20 101	30 37 139	61 10 209	33 21 248	47 51 271	28 25 308
167	45 33 019	45 07 101	31 08 140	60 47 211	32 37 249	47 04 272	27 48 308
168	45 48 019	45 53 102	31 38 141	60 22 212	31 53 249	46 16 273	27 11 309
169	46 03 019	46 39 103	32 08 142	59 56 214	31 09 250	45 29 273	26 34 309
170	46 18 018	47 25 104	32 37 143	59 29 216	30 24 251	44 42 274	25 57 309
171	46 33 018	48 11 105	33 06 144	59 00 218	29 39 252	43 55 274	25 21 310
172	46 48 018	48 57 105	33 33 145	58 31 219	28 54 253	43 08 275	24 45 310
173	47 03 018	49 42 106	34 00 146	58 01 221	28 09 253	42 21 275	24 09 311
174	47 17 018	50 28 107	34 27 147	57 29 222	27 24 254	41 34 276	23 33 311
175	47 31 017	51 13 108	34 52 148	56 57 224	26 38 255	40 47 276	22 57 311
176	47 45 017	51 58 109	35 17 149	56 24 225	25 52 255	40 00 277	22 22 312
177	47 59 017	52 42 110	35 41 150	55 50 227	25 07 256	39 13 278	21 47 312
178	48 13 017	53 26 111	36 04 151	55 15 228	24 21 257	38 26 278	21 12 313
179	48 27 017	54 10 112	36 27 152	54 39 229	23 34 258	37 39 279	20 37 313

LAT 38°N

LHA ♈	Hc	Zn	Hc	Zn	Hc	Zn	Hc	Zn	Hc	Zn	Hc	Zn	Hc	Zn
	◆ VEGA		Alphecca		ARCTURUS		◆ SPICA		REGULUS		◆ POLLUX		CAPELLA	
180	16 37	053	43 47	088	54 54	113	36 49	153	54 03	231	36 52	279	20 03	313
181	17 15	054	44 34	088	55 38	114	37 09	154	53 26	232	36 06	280	19 28	314
182	17 53	054	45 21	089	56 21	115	37 29	156	52 49	233	35 19	280	18 54	314
183	18 31	055	46 09	089	57 03	116	37 48	157	52 10	235	34 33	281	18 21	315
184	19 10	055	46 56	090	57 45	117	38 06	158	51 32	236	33 46	281	17 47	315
185	19 49	056	47 43	091	58 27	119	38 24	159	50 52	237	33 00	282	17 14	316
186	20 28	056	48 30	091	59 08	120	38 40	160	50 12	238	32 14	282	16 41	316
187	21 08	057	49 18	092	59 49	121	38 55	162	49 32	239	31 27	283	16 08	316
188	21 47	057	50 05	093	60 29	122	39 10	163	48 51	240	30 41	283	15 36	317
189	22 27	057	50 52	093	61 09	124	39 23	164	48 10	241	29 55	284	15 04	317
190	23 07	058	51 39	094	61 48	125	39 36	165	47 28	242	29 10	284	14 32	318
191	23 47	058	52 26	095	62 26	127	39 47	167	46 46	243	28 24	285	14 00	318
192	24 27	059	53 14	095	63 04	128	39 58	168	46 04	244	27 38	285	13 29	319
193	25 08	059	54 01	096	63 40	130	40 07	169	45 21	245	26 53	286	12 58	319
194	25 49	060	54 48	097	64 16	132	40 16	170	44 38	246	26 07	286	12 27	320
	DENEB		◆ VEGA		Alphecca		◆ SPICA		REGULUS		◆ POLLUX		Dubhe	
195	11 31	040	26 30	060	55 34	098	40 23	172	43 54	247	25 22	287	60 24	332
196	12 01	041	27 11	060	56 21	098	40 30	173	43 11	248	24 37	287	60 02	332
197	12 32	041	27 52	061	57 08	099	40 35	174	42 27	249	23 51	288	59 39	331
198	13 04	042	28 33	061	57 55	100	40 39	175	41 43	250	23 07	288	59 16	331
199	13 35	042	29 15	062	58 41	101	40 42	177	40 58	251	22 22	289	58 53	330
200	14 07	043	29 57	062	59 28	102	40 44	178	40 13	251	21 37	289	58 29	330
201	14 40	043	30 38	063	60 14	103	40 46	179	39 28	252	20 52	290	58 05	329
202	15 12	044	31 20	063	61 00	104	40 46	181	38 43	253	20 08	290	57 41	329
203	15 45	044	32 03	063	61 46	105	40 44	182	37 58	254	19 24	291	57 16	328
204	16 18	045	32 45	064	62 31	106	40 42	183	37 12	255	18 40	291	56 51	328
205	16 51	045	33 27	064	63 17	107	40 39	185	36 27	255	17 56	292	56 26	327
206	17 25	046	34 10	064	64 02	108	40 35	186	35 41	256	17 12	292	56 00	327
207	17 59	046	34 53	065	64 47	109	40 30	187	34 55	257	16 28	293	55 34	327
208	18 33	046	35 36	065	65 31	110	40 23	188	34 09	258	15 45	293	55 08	326
209	19 07	047	36 19	066	66 16	111	40 16	190	33 23	258	15 02	294	54 42	326
	DENEB		◆ VEGA		Rasalhague		ANTARES		◆ SPICA		REGULUS		◆ Dubhe	
210	19 42	047	37 02	066	35 56	103	16 32	145	40 07	191	32 36	259	54 15	326
211	20 17	048	37 45	066	36 42	104	16 59	146	39 58	192	31 50	260	53 49	325
212	20 52	048	38 28	067	37 28	105	17 25	147	39 47	193	31 03	260	53 22	325
213	21 27	048	39 12	067	38 14	105	17 51	148	39 36	195	30 17	261	52 55	325
214	22 03	049	39 56	067	38 59	106	18 16	149	39 23	196	29 30	262	52 28	325
215	22 38	049	40 39	068	39 45	107	18 40	149	39 10	197	28 43	263	52 00	325
216	23 14	050	41 23	068	40 30	108	19 04	150	38 55	198	27 56	263	51 33	324
217	23 50	050	42 07	069	41 15	109	19 27	151	38 40	200	27 09	264	51 05	324
218	24 27	050	42 51	069	41 59	109	19 49	152	38 24	201	26 22	265	50 37	324
219	25 03	051	43 35	069	42 44	110	20 11	153	38 06	202	25 35	265	50 09	324
220	25 40	051	44 20	070	43 28	111	20 33	154	37 48	203	24 48	266	49 41	324
221	26 17	052	45 04	070	44 12	112	20 53	155	37 29	204	24 01	266	49 13	324
222	26 54	052	45 48	070	44 56	113	21 13	156	37 09	206	23 13	267	48 45	323
223	27 32	052	46 33	071	45 39	114	21 32	156	36 48	207	22 26	268	48 17	323
224	28 09	053	47 18	071	46 22	115	21 51	157	36 27	208	21 39	268	47 49	323
	DENEB		◆ ALTAIR		Rasalhague		ANTARES		◆ SPICA		Denebola		◆ Dubhe	
225	28 47	053	18 56	093	47 05	116	22 09	158	36 04	209	42 00	254	47 21	323
226	29 25	053	19 43	094	47 47	117	22 26	159	35 41	210	41 14	255	46 52	323
227	30 03	054	20 31	095	48 29	118	22 43	160	35 17	211	40 28	256	46 24	323
228	30 41	054	21 18	095	49 11	119	22 58	161	34 52	212	39 42	256	45 55	323
229	31 19	054	22 05	096	49 52	120	23 13	162	34 26	213	38 56	257	45 27	323
230	31 58	055	22 52	097	50 33	121	23 28	163	34 00	214	38 10	258	44 58	323
231	32 37	055	23 39	097	51 13	122	23 41	164	33 33	215	37 24	259	44 30	323
232	33 16	055	24 25	098	51 53	123	23 54	165	33 05	216	36 38	259	44 02	323
233	33 55	056	25 12	099	52 32	124	24 06	166	32 37	217	35 51	260	43 33	323
234	34 34	056	25 59	099	53 11	126	24 17	167	32 08	218	35 04	261	43 05	323
235	35 13	056	26 46	100	53 49	127	24 28	168	31 38	219	34 18	261	42 36	323
236	35 53	057	27 32	101	54 26	128	24 38	169	31 08	220	33 31	262	42 08	323
237	36 32	057	28 18	101	55 03	130	24 47	170	30 37	221	32 44	263	41 39	323
238	37 12	057	29 05	102	55 39	131	24 55	171	30 05	222	31 57	264	41 11	323
239	37 52	058	29 51	103	56 15	132	25 02	172	29 33	223	31 10	264	40 43	323
	◆ DENEB		ALTAIR		Nunki		◆ ANTARES		ARCTURUS		◆ Alkaid		Kochab	
240	38 32	058	30 37	104	13 37	140	25 09	173	60 36	237	63 54	306	52 58	352
241	39 12	058	31 23	104	14 07	141	25 14	173	59 56	239	63 15	306	52 51	352
242	39 52	058	32 09	105	14 36	142	25 19	174	59 16	240	62 37	306	52 44	351
243	40 32	059	32 54	106	15 05	142	25 24	175	58 34	241	61 58	305	52 37	351
244	41 13	059	33 40	107	15 34	143	25 27	176	57 53	242	61 20	305	52 29	351
245	41 53	059	34 25	107	16 02	144	25 29	177	57 11	244	60 41	305	52 22	350
246	42 34	059	35 10	108	16 29	145	25 31	178	56 28	245	60 02	305	52 13	350
247	43 15	060	35 55	109	16 56	146	25 32	179	55 45	246	59 23	305	52 05	349
248	43 56	060	36 39	110	17 23	146	25 32	180	55 02	247	58 44	304	51 56	349
249	44 37	060	37 24	110	17 49	147	25 31	181	54 18	248	58 05	304	51 47	349
250	45 18	060	38 08	111	18 14	148	25 30	182	53 34	249	57 26	304	51 37	348
251	45 59	061	38 52	112	18 39	149	25 27	183	52 50	250	56 47	304	51 28	348
252	46 40	061	39 36	113	19 03	150	25 24	184	52 05	251	56 08	304	51 18	348
253	47 22	061	40 19	114	19 26	151	25 20	185	51 20	252	55 29	304	51 07	347
254	48 03	061	41 02	115	19 49	151	25 15	186	50 35	253	54 50	304	50 57	347
	◆ DENEB		ALTAIR		Nunki		◆ ANTARES		ARCTURUS		◆ Alkaid		Kochab	
255	48 44	061	41 45	116	20 11	152	25 10	187	49 50	254	54 11	304	50 46	347
256	49 26	062	42 27	117	20 33	153	25 03	188	49 05	255	53 31	304	50 35	346
257	50 08	062	43 09	118	20 54	154	24 56	189	48 19	255	52 52	304	50 24	346
258	50 49	062	43 51	119	21 14	155	24 48	190	47 33	256	52 13	304	50 12	346
259	51 31	062	44 32	120	21 34	156	24 39	191	46 47	257	51 34	304	50 00	345
260	52 13	062	45 13	121	21 53	157	24 30	192	46 01	258	50 55	304	49 48	345
261	52 55	062	45 54	122	22 11	158	24 19	193	45 15	259	50 16	304	49 36	345
262	53 37	063	46 34	123	22 29	159	24 08	194	44 28	259	49 37	304	49 23	345
263	54 19	063	47 13	124	22 46	160	23 56	195	43 42	260	48 58	305	49 11	344
264	55 01	063	47 52	125	23 02	160	23 43	196	42 55	261	48 19	305	48 58	344
265	55 43	063	48 31	126	23 17	161	23 30	197	42 09	262	47 40	305	48 44	344
266	56 25	063	49 09	127	23 32	162	23 16	198	41 22	262	47 01	305	48 31	344
267	57 07	063	49 46	128	23 46	163	23 01	199	40 35	263	46 22	305	48 18	343
268	57 49	063	50 23	129	23 59	164	22 45	200	39 48	264	45 44	305	48 04	343
269	58 31	063	50 59	131	24 12	165	22 29	201	39 01	264	45 05	305	47 50	343

LHA ♈	Hc	Zn	Hc	Zn	Hc	Zn	Hc	Zn	Hc	Zn	Hc	Zn	Hc	Zn
	◆ Alpheratz		ALTAIR		Nunki		◆ ANTARES		ARCTURUS		◆ Alkaid		Kochab	
270	15 49	065	51 35	132	24 23	166	22 12	202	38 14	265	44 26	305	47 36	343
271	16 32	066	52 10	133	24 34	167	21 54	203	37 27	266	43 48	306	47 22	342
272	17 15	066	52 44	135	24 44	168	21 35	203	36 39	266	43 10	306	47 07	342
273	17 59	067	53 17	136	24 54	169	21 16	204	35 52	267	42 31	306	46 53	342
274	18 42	067	53 49	137	25 02	170	20 56	205	35 05	268	41 53	306	46 38	342
275	19 26	068	54 21	139	25 10	171	20 36	206	34 18	268	41 15	306	46 23	342
276	20 09	068	54 52	140	25 17	172	20 15	207	33 31	269	40 37	307	46 09	342
277	20 53	069	55 22	142	25 23	173	19 53	208	32 43	270	39 59	307	45 53	341
278	21 38	069	55 50	143	25 28	174	19 31	209	31 56	270	39 21	307	45 38	341
279	22 22	070	56 18	145	25 33	175	19 08	210	31 09	271	38 44	307	45 23	341
280	23 06	070	56 45	146	25 37	176	18 44	210	30 21	271	38 06	308	45 08	341
281	23 51	071	57 10	148	25 40	177	18 20	211	29 34	272	37 29	308	44 52	341
282	24 35	071	57 35	150	25 42	178	17 55	212	28 47	273	36 51	308	44 36	341
283	25 20	072	57 58	151	25 43	179	17 29	213	28 00	273	36 14	308	44 21	341
284	26 05	072	58 20	153	25 43	180	17 03	214	27 13	274	35 37	309	44 05	340
	Alpheratz		◆ Enif		ALTAIR		◆ Rasalhague		ARCTURUS		Alkaid		◆ Kochab	
285	26 50	073	43 38	116	58 41	155	58 22	222	26 25	274	35 00	309	43 49	340
286	27 35	073	44 20	117	59 00	157	57 50	224	25 38	275	34 23	309	43 33	340
287	28 21	074	45 02	118	59 18	159	57 17	225	24 51	276	33 47	309	43 17	340
288	29 06	074	45 44	119	59 35	160	56 43	227	24 04	276	33 10	310	43 01	340
289	29 52	075	46 25	120	59 50	162	56 08	228	23 17	277	32 34	310	42 45	340
290	30 37	075	47 05	121	60 03	164	55 33	229	22 30	277	31 58	310	42 29	340
291	31 23	076	47 46	122	60 15	166	54 56	231	21 43	278	31 22	311	42 13	340
292	32 09	076	48 25	123	60 26	168	54 20	232	20 56	278	30 46	311	41 56	340
293	32 55	077	49 04	125	60 35	170	53 42	233	20 10	279	30 10	311	41 40	340
294	33 41	077	49 43	126	60 42	172	53 04	235	19 23	280	29 34	311	41 24	340
295	34 27	078	50 21	127	60 48	174	52 25	236	18 36	280	28 59	312	41 07	340
296	35 13	078	50 59	128	60 52	176	51 46	237	17 50	281	28 24	312	40 51	340
297	36 00	079	51 36	129	60 54	178	51 06	238	17 04	281	27 49	312	40 34	340
298	36 46	079	52 12	131	60 55	180	50 25	239	16 17	282	27 14	313	40 18	340
299	37 33	080	52 48	132	60 53	182	49 45	240	15 31	282	26 39	313	40 02	340
	◆ Mirfak		Alpheratz		◆ FOMALHAUT		ALTAIR		Rasalhague		◆ Alphecca		Kochab	
300	16 38	039	38 19	080	10 38	142	60 51	184	49 03	241	34 07	279	39 45	340
301	17 08	039	39 06	081	11 07	142	60 46	186	48 22	242	33 20	280	39 29	340
302	17 38	040	39 52	081	11 35	143	60 40	188	47 39	243	32 34	280	39 12	340
303	18 08	040	40 39	082	12 04	144	60 33	190	46 57	244	31 47	281	38 56	340
304	18 39	040	41 26	082	12 31	145	60 23	192	46 14	245	31 01	281	38 39	340
305	19 09	041	42 13	083	12 58	145	60 13	194	45 31	246	30 14	282	38 23	340
306	19 41	041	43 00	083	13 25	146	60 00	196	44 48	247	29 28	282	38 07	340
307	20 12	042	43 47	084	13 51	147	59 46	198	44 04	248	28 42	283	37 50	340
308	20 43	042	44 34	084	14 17	148	59 31	200	43 20	249	27 56	283	37 34	340
309	21 15	042	45 21	085	14 42	148	59 14	202	42 36	250	27 10	284	37 18	340
310	21 47	043	46 08	085	15 06	149	58 55	204	41 51	251	26 24	284	37 01	340
311	22 19	043	46 55	086	15 30	150	58 36	205	41 06	252	25 38	285	36 45	340
312	22 52	044	47 42	087	15 54	151	58 15	207	40 21	252	24 53	285	36 29	340
313	23 25	044	48 30	087	16 16	152	57 53	209	39 36	253	24 07	286	36 13	340
314	23 58	044	49 17	088	16 39	152	57 29	211	38 51	254	23 22	286	35 57	340
	◆ Mirfak		Hamal		Diphda		◆ FOMALHAUT		ALTAIR		◆ VEGA		Kochab	
315	24 31	045	24 06	078	13 15	126	17 00	153	57 04	212	62 14	283	35 41	340
316	25 04	045	24 52	079	13 53	127	17 21	154	56 38	214	61 28	283	35 25	340
317	25 38	045	25 38	079	14 31	127	17 41	155	56 11	216	60 42	283	35 09	340
318	26 11	046	26 25	080	15 08	128	18 01	156	55 43	217	59 56	284	34 53	341
319	26 45	046	27 12	080	15 45	129	18 20	157	55 14	219	59 10	284	34 38	341
320	27 20	046	27 58	081	16 22	129	18 39	158	54 44	220	58 24	284	34 22	341
321	27 54	047	28 45	081	16 58	130	18 56	158	54 13	222	57 39	285	34 07	341
322	28 29	047	29 32	082	17 34	131	19 13	159	53 42	223	56 53	285	33 51	341
323	29 03	047	30 19	083	18 09	132	19 30	160	53 09	224	56 07	285	33 36	341
324	29 38	048	31 05	083	18 45	133	19 46	161	52 36	226	55 22	286	33 21	341
325	30 13	048	31 52	084	19 19	133	20 01	162	52 01	227	54 36	286	33 05	341
326	30 48	048	32 39	084	19 53	134	20 15	163	51 26	228	53 51	286	32 50	341
327	31 24	049	33 26	085	20 27	135	20 29	164	50 51	230	53 05	286	32 35	342
328	31 59	049	34 14	085	21 00	136	20 42	165	50 14	231	52 20	287	32 21	342
329	32 35	049	35 01	086	21 33	137	20 54	165	49 37	232	51 35	287	32 06	342
	◆ CAPELLA		Hamal		Diphda		◆ FOMALHAUT		ALTAIR		◆ VEGA		Kochab	
330	15 07	043	35 48	086	22 05	138	21 05	166	49 00	233	50 50	287	31 51	342
331	15 39	043	36 35	087	22 36	138	21 16	167	48 22	234	50 05	288	31 37	342
332	16 11	044	37 22	088	23 08	139	21 26	168	47 43	235	49 20	288	31 22	342
333	16 44	044	38 10	088	23 38	140	21 35	169	47 04	237	48 35	288	31 08	343
334	17 17	045	38 57	089	24 08	141	21 44	170	46 24	238	47 50	289	30 54	343
335	17 51	045	39 44	089	24 38	142	21 52	171	45 44	239	47 05	289	30 40	343
336	18 24	045	40 31	090	25 06	143	21 59	172	45 03	240	46 21	289	30 26	343
337	18 58	046	41 19	091	25 35	144	22 05	173	44 22	241	45 36	290	30 12	343
338	19 32	046	42 06	091	26 02	145	22 10	174	43 41	242	44 52	290	29 59	343
339	20 06	047	42 53	092	26 29	146	22 15	175	42 59	243	44 07	290	29 45	344
340	20 41	047	43 40	093	26 56	147	22 19	176	42 17	244	43 23	291	29 32	344
341	21 15	047	44 28	093	27 21	148	22 22	177	41 34	245	42 39	291	29 19	344
342	21 50	048	45 15	094	27 47	148	22 25	178	40 52	245	41 55	292	29 06	344
343	22 26	048	46 02	095	28 11	149	22 26	178	40 08	246	41 11	292	28 53	344
344	23 01	049	46 49	095	28 35	150	22 27	179	39 25	247	40 27	292	28 40	345
	◆ CAPELLA		ALDEBARAN		Diphda		◆ FOMALHAUT		ALTAIR		◆ VEGA		Kochab	
345	23 37	049	14 34	080	28 58	151	22 27	180	38 41	248	39 43	293	28 28	345
346	24 12	049	15 21	081	29 20	152	22 27	181	37 57	249	39 00	293	28 15	345
347	24 48	050	16 08	081	29 41	153	22 25	182	37 13	250	38 16	293	28 03	345
348	25 25	050	16 55	082	30 02	154	22 23	183	36 29	251	37 33	294	27 51	345
349	26 01	051	17 41	083	30 22	156	22 20	184	35 44	251	36 50	294	27 39	346
350	26 38	051	18 28	083	30 41	157	22 16	185	34 59	252	36 07	294	27 28	346
351	27 15	051	19 15	084	31 00	158	22 12	186	34 14	253	35 24	295	27 16	346
352	27 52	052	20 02	084	31 17	159	22 06	187	33 29	254	34 41	295	27 05	346
353	28 29	052	20 49	085	31 34	160	22 00	188	32 43	254	33 58	296	26 54	346
354	29 06	052	21 37	085	31 50	161	21 53	189	31 58	255	33 16	296	26 43	347
355	29 44	053	22 24	086	32 05	162	21 46	190	31 12	256	32 33	296	26 32	347
356	30 21	053	23 11	087	32 20	163	21 37	191	30 26	257	31 51	297	26 21	347
357	30 59	053	23 58	087	32 33	164	21 28	192	29 40	257	31 09	297	26 11	347
358	31 37	054	24 45	088	32 46	165	21 19	192	28 54	258	30 27	298	26 01	348
359	32 16	054	25 33	088	32 57	166	21 08	193	28 07	259	29 45	298	25 50	348

LAT 37°N

LHA ♈	Hc	Zn	Hc	Zn	Hc	Zn	Hc	Zn	Hc	Zn	Hc	Zn	Hc	Zn
	◆ CAPELLA		ALDEBARAN		◆ Diphda		FOMALHAUT		ALTAIR		◆ VEGA		Kochab	
0	32 19	054	26 19	089	34 07	167	21 55	194	27 32	260	28 35	299	24 42	348
1	32 58	054	27 07	089	34 17	168	21 42	195	26 44	261	27 53	299	24 32	348
2	33 37	054	27 54	090	34 26	170	21 29	196	25 57	261	27 11	300	24 23	349
3	34 16	055	28 42	090	34 34	171	21 16	197	25 10	262	26 29	300	24 13	349
4	34 55	055	29 30	091	34 41	172	21 01	198	24 22	263	25 48	300	24 04	349
5	35 34	055	30 18	092	34 48	173	20 46	199	23 34	263	25 07	301	23 55	349
6	36 14	056	31 06	092	34 53	174	20 30	200	22 47	264	24 26	301	23 47	350
7	36 53	056	31 54	093	34 58	175	20 14	201	21 59	265	23 45	302	23 38	350
8	37 33	056	32 42	093	35 01	176	19 56	202	21 11	265	23 04	302	23 30	350
9	38 13	056	33 30	094	35 04	178	19 38	202	20 24	266	22 24	303	23 22	350
10	38 53	057	34 17	095	35 05	179	19 20	203	19 36	266	21 44	303	23 14	351
11	39 33	057	35 05	095	35 06	180	19 01	204	18 48	267	21 03	303	23 07	351
12	40 13	057	35 53	096	35 05	181	18 41	205	18 00	268	20 24	304	22 59	351
13	40 53	057	36 40	097	35 04	182	18 20	206	17 12	268	19 44	304	22 52	352
14	41 34	058	37 28	097	35 02	183	17 59	207	16 24	269	19 04	305	22 45	352
	◆ CAPELLA		BETELGEUSE		RIGEL		◆ Diphda		Enif		◆ DENEB		Kochab	
15	42 14	058	17 13	094	15 15	113	34 58	185	38 29	251	42 02	301	22 38	352
16	42 55	058	18 01	094	15 59	114	34 54	186	37 44	252	41 21	302	22 32	352
17	43 36	058	18 48	095	16 43	114	34 49	187	36 58	253	40 40	302	22 26	353
18	44 16	058	19 36	096	17 27	115	34 43	188	36 12	254	40 00	302	22 20	353
19	44 57	059	20 24	096	18 10	116	34 35	189	35 26	254	39 19	302	22 14	353
20	45 38	059	21 11	097	18 53	116	34 27	190	34 40	255	38 39	303	22 08	353
21	46 19	059	21 59	097	19 36	117	34 18	191	33 54	256	37 58	303	22 03	354
22	47 00	059	22 46	098	20 18	118	34 08	193	33 07	256	37 18	303	21 58	354
23	47 42	059	23 34	099	21 00	119	33 57	194	32 21	257	36 38	303	21 53	354
24	48 23	059	24 21	099	21 42	119	33 46	195	31 34	258	35 58	304	21 48	355
25	49 04	060	25 08	100	22 24	120	33 33	196	30 47	259	35 18	304	21 44	355
26	49 45	060	25 56	101	23 05	121	33 19	197	30 00	259	34 39	304	21 40	355
27	50 27	060	26 43	101	23 46	122	33 05	198	29 13	260	33 59	304	21 36	355
28	51 08	060	27 29	102	24 27	123	32 49	199	28 26	261	33 20	305	21 32	356
29	51 50	060	28 16	103	25 07	123	32 33	200	27 38	261	32 40	305	21 29	356
	◆ CAPELLA		BETELGEUSE		RIGEL		◆ Diphda		Alpheratz		◆ DENEB		Kochab	
30	52 31	060	29 03	104	25 47	124	32 16	201	65 36	259	32 01	305	21 25	356
31	53 13	060	29 49	104	26 26	125	31 58	202	64 49	260	31 22	306	21 22	357
32	53 55	060	30 36	105	27 05	126	31 40	204	64 02	261	30 43	306	21 20	357
33	54 36	060	31 22	106	27 44	127	31 20	205	63 14	262	30 05	306	21 17	357
34	55 18	060	32 08	106	28 22	128	31 00	206	62 27	263	29 26	307	21 15	357
35	55 59	060	32 54	107	29 00	128	30 39	207	61 39	264	28 48	307	21 13	358
36	56 41	060	33 40	108	29 37	129	30 17	208	60 52	264	28 10	307	21 11	358
37	57 23	060	34 25	109	30 14	130	29 54	209	60 04	265	27 32	308	21 10	358
38	58 04	060	35 10	109	30 50	131	29 31	210	59 16	266	26 54	308	21 08	359
39	58 46	060	35 55	110	31 26	132	29 07	211	58 28	266	26 16	308	21 07	359
40	59 28	060	36 40	111	32 01	133	28 42	212	57 41	267	25 39	309	21 07	359
41	60 09	060	37 25	112	32 36	134	28 16	213	56 53	268	25 01	309	21 06	000
42	60 51	060	38 09	113	33 10	135	27 50	214	56 05	268	24 24	309	21 06	000
43	61 32	060	38 53	114	33 44	136	27 23	215	55 17	269	23 47	310	21 06	000
44	62 14	060	39 37	114	34 17	137	26 56	215	54 29	270	23 11	310	21 06	000
	◆ Dubhe		POLLUX		SIRIUS		◆ RIGEL		Diphda		◆ Alpheratz		DENEB	
45	19 29	026	30 22	076	14 26	124	34 50	138	26 28	216	53 41	270	22 34	311
46	19 50	026	31 09	077	15 06	125	35 21	139	25 59	217	52 53	271	21 58	311
47	20 11	026	31 55	077	15 45	126	35 53	140	25 30	218	52 05	271	21 22	311
48	20 32	027	32 42	078	16 23	127	36 23	141	25 00	219	51 17	272	20 46	312
49	20 54	027	33 29	078	17 01	127	36 53	142	24 29	220	50 29	273	20 11	312
50	21 16	027	34 16	079	17 39	128	37 22	143	23 58	221	49 42	273	19 35	313
51	21 38	028	35 03	079	18 17	129	37 51	144	23 27	222	48 54	274	19 00	313
52	22 00	028	35 50	080	18 54	130	38 18	145	22 55	223	48 06	274	18 25	313
53	22 23	028	36 37	080	19 30	131	38 45	146	22 22	223	47 18	275	17 50	314
54	22 45	028	37 24	081	20 07	131	39 11	148	21 49	224	46 30	275	17 16	314
55	23 08	029	38 12	081	20 42	132	39 36	149	21 15	225	45 43	276	16 42	315
56	23 31	029	38 59	082	21 18	133	40 01	150	20 41	226	44 55	276	16 08	315
57	23 55	029	39 46	082	21 53	134	40 24	151	20 06	227	44 08	277	15 34	316
58	24 18	030	40 34	083	22 27	135	40 47	152	19 31	228	43 20	277	15 01	316
59	24 42	030	41 21	083	23 01	135	41 09	154	18 56	228	42 32	278	14 28	316
	◆ Dubhe		POLLUX		PROCYON		◆ SIRIUS		RIGEL		◆ Hamal		Schedar	
60	25 06	030	42 09	084	30 41	108	23 34	136	41 30	155	62 29	249	51 54	317
61	25 30	030	42 57	084	31 27	109	24 07	137	41 50	156	61 44	250	51 22	317
62	25 55	031	43 44	085	32 12	110	24 40	138	42 09	157	60 59	251	50 49	317
63	26 19	031	44 32	085	32 57	111	25 11	139	42 27	159	60 13	252	50 16	317
64	26 44	031	45 20	086	33 41	111	25 43	140	42 44	160	59 28	253	49 43	317
65	27 09	032	46 08	086	34 26	112	26 13	141	43 00	161	58 42	254	49 11	317
66	27 34	032	46 55	087	35 10	113	26 43	142	43 15	162	57 56	255	48 38	317
67	28 00	032	47 43	087	35 54	114	27 13	142	43 29	164	57 09	256	48 05	317
68	28 25	032	48 31	088	36 38	115	27 42	143	43 41	165	56 23	257	47 32	316
69	28 51	033	49 19	089	37 21	116	28 10	144	43 53	166	55 36	258	46 59	316
70	29 17	033	50 07	089	38 04	117	28 38	145	44 04	168	54 49	258	46 26	316
71	29 43	033	50 55	090	38 47	117	29 05	146	44 13	169	54 02	259	45 53	316
72	30 09	033	51 43	090	39 29	118	29 31	147	44 22	171	53 15	260	45 20	316
73	30 35	033	52 31	091	40 11	119	29 56	148	44 29	172	52 28	261	44 47	316
74	31 02	034	53 19	092	40 53	120	30 21	149	44 35	173	51 40	262	44 14	317
	◆ Dubhe		POLLUX		PROCYON		◆ SIRIUS		RIGEL		◆ Hamal		Schedar	
75	31 28	034	54 07	092	41 34	121	30 45	150	44 40	175	50 53	262	43 41	317
76	31 55	034	54 54	093	42 15	122	31 09	151	44 44	176	50 05	263	43 08	317
77	32 22	034	55 42	094	42 55	123	31 32	152	44 47	177	49 18	264	42 35	317
78	32 49	034	56 30	094	43 35	124	31 53	153	44 48	179	48 30	264	42 02	317
79	33 16	035	57 18	095	44 14	125	32 15	154	44 49	180	47 42	265	41 29	317
80	33 43	035	58 06	096	44 53	126	32 35	155	44 48	182	46 55	266	40 56	317
81	34 10	035	58 53	096	45 32	127	32 54	157	44 46	183	46 07	266	40 24	317
82	34 38	035	59 41	097	46 10	128	33 13	158	44 43	184	45 19	267	39 51	317
83	35 05	035	60 28	098	46 47	130	33 31	159	44 39	186	44 31	268	39 19	317
84	35 33	035	61 16	099	47 24	131	33 48	160	44 33	187	43 43	268	38 46	317
85	36 01	035	62 03	100	48 00	132	34 04	161	44 27	189	42 55	269	38 14	318
86	36 29	036	62 50	100	48 35	133	34 19	162	44 19	190	42 07	270	37 41	318
87	36 57	036	63 37	101	49 09	134	34 34	163	44 10	191	41 19	270	37 09	318
88	37 25	036	64 24	102	49 43	136	34 47	164	44 00	193	40 32	271	36 37	318
89	37 53	036	65 11	103	50 17	137	35 00	165	43 49	194	39 44	271	36 05	318

LHA ♈	Hc	Zn	Hc	Zn	Hc	Zn	Hc	Zn	Hc	Zn	Hc	Zn	Hc	Zn
	◆ Dubhe		REGULUS		PROCYON		◆ SIRIUS		RIGEL		ALDEBARAN		◆ Mirfak	
90	38 21	036	29 10	097	50 49	138	35 11	167	43 37	195	62 30	228	59 33	307
91	38 49	036	29 58	098	51 20	140	35 22	168	43 24	197	61 54	229	58 55	307
92	39 17	036	30 45	099	51 51	141	35 32	169	43 09	198	61 17	231	58 17	307
93	39 45	036	31 32	099	52 21	142	35 40	170	42 54	199	60 40	232	57 38	307
94	40 14	036	32 20	100	52 50	144	35 48	171	42 38	201	60 02	234	57 00	307
95	40 42	036	33 07	101	53 18	145	35 55	172	42 20	202	59 23	235	56 22	307
96	41 10	036	33 54	101	53 44	147	36 01	174	42 02	203	58 43	236	55 43	307
97	41 39	036	34 41	102	54 10	148	36 06	175	41 42	204	58 03	238	55 05	306
98	42 07	036	35 28	103	54 35	150	36 10	176	41 22	206	57 22	239	54 26	306
99	42 36	036	36 14	103	54 58	151	36 13	177	41 01	207	56 41	240	53 48	306
100	43 04	036	37 01	104	55 21	153	36 15	178	40 39	208	55 59	241	53 09	306
101	43 33	036	37 47	105	55 42	155	36 16	179	40 16	209	55 17	243	52 30	306
102	44 01	036	38 33	106	56 02	156	36 16	181	39 52	211	54 34	244	51 52	306
103	44 30	036	39 19	106	56 20	158	36 15	182	39 27	212	53 51	245	51 13	306
104	44 58	036	40 05	107	56 38	160	36 13	183	39 02	213	53 07	246	50 34	306
	Kochab		◆ Denebola		REGULUS		◆ SIRIUS		RIGEL		ALDEBARAN		◆ CAPELLA	
105	28 30	016	22 34	089	40 51	108	36 09	184	38 35	214	52 24	247	68 58	303
106	28 43	016	23 21	089	41 36	109	36 05	185	38 08	215	51 39	248	68 18	303
107	28 57	016	24 09	090	42 22	110	36 00	187	37 40	216	50 55	249	67 38	302
108	29 10	017	24 57	090	43 07	111	35 55	188	37 11	217	50 10	250	66 57	302
109	29 24	017	25 45	091	43 51	111	35 48	189	36 42	218	49 25	251	66 17	302
110	29 38	017	26 33	092	44 36	112	35 40	190	36 12	219	48 40	252	65 36	301
111	29 52	017	27 21	092	45 20	113	35 31	191	35 41	220	47 54	252	64 55	301
112	30 06	017	28 09	093	46 04	114	35 21	192	35 10	222	47 08	253	64 14	301
113	30 20	017	28 57	093	46 47	115	35 10	194	34 38	223	46 22	254	63 32	301
114	30 35	018	29 45	094	47 31	116	34 58	195	34 05	224	45 36	255	62 51	300
115	30 49	018	30 32	095	48 13	117	34 46	196	33 32	225	44 50	256	62 10	300
116	31 04	018	31 20	095	48 56	118	34 32	197	32 58	225	44 03	257	61 28	300
117	31 19	018	32 08	096	49 38	119	34 18	198	32 23	226	43 17	257	60 47	300
118	31 33	018	32 55	097	50 19	120	34 03	199	31 48	227	42 30	258	60 05	300
119	31 48	018	33 43	097	51 01	121	33 46	200	31 13	228	41 43	259	59 24	300
	◆ Kochab		Denebola		◆ REGULUS		SIRIUS		RIGEL		◆ ALDEBARAN		CAPELLA	
120	32 03	018	34 30	098	51 41	123	33 29	201	30 37	229	40 56	260	58 42	300
121	32 19	019	35 18	099	52 21	124	33 11	203	30 00	230	40 09	260	58 00	300
122	32 34	019	36 05	099	53 01	125	32 53	204	29 23	231	39 21	261	57 19	300
123	32 49	019	36 52	100	53 40	126	32 33	205	28 46	232	38 34	262	56 37	300
124	33 05	019	37 40	101	54 18	127	32 13	206	28 08	233	37 47	262	55 55	300
125	33 20	019	38 27	101	54 56	129	31 51	207	27 29	234	36 59	263	55 14	300
126	33 36	019	39 14	102	55 33	130	31 29	208	26 51	234	36 11	264	54 32	300
127	33 52	019	40 00	103	56 10	131	31 07	209	26 11	235	35 24	264	53 50	300
128	34 07	019	40 47	104	56 45	133	30 43	210	25 32	236	34 36	265	53 09	300
129	34 23	019	41 33	104	57 20	134	30 19	211	24 52	237	33 48	266	52 27	300
130	34 39	019	42 20	105	57 54	136	29 54	212	24 12	238	33 01	266	51 46	300
131	34 55	020	43 06	106	58 27	137	29 28	213	23 31	239	32 13	267	51 04	300
132	35 11	020	43 52	107	58 59	139	29 02	214	22 50	239	31 25	268	50 23	300
133	35 27	020	44 38	108	59 30	140	28 35	215	22 08	240	30 37	268	49 41	300
134	35 43	020	45 23	109	60 00	142	28 07	216	21 27	241	29 49	269	49 00	300
	Kochab		◆ ARCTURUS		SPICA		REGULUS		◆ SIRIUS		BETELGEUSE		◆ CAPELLA	
135	36 00	020	19 52	081	11 15	113	60 29	144	27 39	217	38 53	246	48 19	301
136	36 16	020	20 39	081	11 59	114	60 57	146	27 10	218	38 09	247	47 37	301
137	36 32	020	21 27	082	12 42	115	61 23	147	26 41	219	37 25	248	46 56	301
138	36 48	020	22 14	082	13 26	116	61 48	149	26 10	219	36 40	249	46 15	301
139	37 05	020	23 02	083	14 09	116	62 12	151	25 40	220	35 55	250	45 34	301
140	37 21	020	23 49	083	14 52	117	62 34	153	25 08	221	35 10	251	44 53	301
141	37 37	020	24 37	084	15 34	118	62 55	155	24 37	222	34 25	251	44 12	302
142	37 54	020	25 25	085	16 17	118	63 15	157	24 04	223	33 39	252	43 32	302
143	38 10	020	26 12	085	16 59	119	63 33	159	23 31	224	32 54	253	42 51	302
144	38 27	020	27 00	086	17 41	120	63 49	161	22 58	225	32 08	254	42 10	302
145	38 43	020	27 48	086	18 22	120	64 03	164	22 24	226	31 22	254	41 30	302
146	39 00	020	28 36	087	19 03	121	64 16	166	21 49	226	30 35	255	40 49	303
147	39 16	020	29 24	087	19 44	122	64 27	168	21 14	227	29 49	256	40 09	303
148	39 33	020	30 11	088	20 24	123	64 36	170	20 39	228	29 03	256	39 29	303
149	39 49	020	30 59	089	21 05	124	64 43	172	20 03	229	28 16	257	38 49	303
	◆ Kochab		ARCTURUS		◆ SPICA		REGULUS		PROCYON		◆ POLLUX		CAPELLA	
150	40 05	020	31 47	089	21 44	124	64 49	175	44 55	234	60 34	262	38 09	304
151	40 22	020	32 35	090	22 24	125	64 52	177	44 16	235	59 46	263	37 29	304
152	40 38	020	33 23	090	23 03	126	64 54	179	43 37	236	58 59	264	36 49	304
153	40 54	020	34 11	091	23 41	127	64 53	182	42 57	237	58 11	264	36 10	304
154	41 11	020	34 59	092	24 20	127	64 51	184	42 17	238	57 23	265	35 30	305
155	41 27	020	35 47	092	24 57	128	64 47	186	41 36	239	56 36	266	34 51	305
156	41 43	020	36 35	093	25 35	129	64 40	189	40 55	240	55 48	266	34 12	305
157	41 59	020	37 22	093	26 12	130	64 32	191	40 13	241	55 00	267	33 33	306
158	42 15	020	38 10	094	26 48	131	64 23	193	39 31	242	54 12	268	32 54	306
159	42 31	019	38 58	095	27 24	132	64 11	195	38 49	243	53 24	268	32 15	306
160	42 47	019	39 46	095	28 00	133	63 57	197	38 06	243	52 36	269	31 36	306
161	43 03	019	40 33	096	28 35	134	63 42	200	37 23	244	51 48	270	30 58	307
162	43 19	019	41 21	097	29 09	134	63 25	202	36 40	245	51 01	270	30 20	307
163	43 34	019	42 09	097	29 43	135	63 07	204	35 56	246	50 13	271	29 41	307
164	43 50	019	42 56	098	30 17	136	62 47	206	35 12	247	49 25	271	29 03	308
	◆ Kochab		ARCTURUS		◆ SPICA		REGULUS		PROCYON		◆ POLLUX		CAPELLA	
165	44 06	019	43 44	099	30 49	137	62 25	208	34 28	248	48 37	272	28 26	308
166	44 21	019	44 31	100	31 22	138	62 02	210	33 43	248	47 49	272	27 48	308
167	44 36	019	45 18	100	31 53	139	61 38	212	32 59	249	47 01	273	27 10	309
168	44 51	018	46 05	101	32 24	140	61 12	213	32 14	250	46 13	274	26 33	309
169	45 07	018	46 52	102	32 55	141	60 45	215	31 29	251	45 25	274	25 56	309
170	45 21	018	47 39	103	33 25	142	60 17	217	30 43	252	44 38	275	25 19	310
171	45 36	018	48 26	103	33 54	143	59 48	219	29 58	252	43 50	275	24 42	310
172	45 51	018	49 12	104	34 22	144	59 17	220	29 12	253	43 02	276	24 06	311
173	46 05	018	49 59	105	34 50	145	58 46	222	28 26	254	42 15	276	23 30	311
174	46 20	017	50 45	106	35 17	146	58 13	223	27 40	254	41 27	277	22 54	311
175	46 34	017	51 31	107	35 43	147	57 40	225	26 54	255	40 39	277	22 18	312
176	46 48	017	52 16	108	36 08	148	57 06	226	26 07	256	39 52	278	21 42	312
177	47 02	017	53 02	109	36 33	150	56 31	228	25 21	257	39 04	278	21 06	312
178	47 16	016	53 47	110	36 57	151	55 55	229	24 34	257	38 17	279	20 31	313
179	47 29	016	54 32	111	37 20	152	55 18	231	23 47	258	37 30	279	19 56	313

 LAT 37°N

LHA ♈	Hc	Zn	Hc	Zn	Hc	Zn	Hc	Zn	Hc	Zn	Hc	Zn	Hc	Zn
	◆ VEGA		Alphecca		ARCTURUS		◆ SPICA		REGULUS		◆ POLLUX		CAPELLA	
180	16 01	053	43 44	087	55 17	112	37 42	153	54 41	232	36 42	280	19 21	314
181	16 39	054	44 32	087	56 01	113	38 03	154	54 03	233	35 55	280	18 47	314
182	17 18	054	45 20	088	56 45	114	38 24	155	53 24	234	35 08	281	18 12	314
183	17 57	055	46 08	088	57 29	115	38 43	156	52 45	236	34 21	281	17 38	315
184	18 36	055	46 55	089	58 12	116	39 02	158	52 05	237	33 34	282	17 05	315
185	19 15	055	47 43	090	58 55	117	39 20	159	51 24	238	32 47	282	16 31	316
186	19 55	056	48 31	090	59 38	118	39 37	160	50 44	239	32 01	283	15 58	316
187	20 35	056	49 19	091	60 20	120	39 52	161	50 02	240	31 14	283	15 25	317
188	21 14	057	50 07	091	61 01	121	40 07	163	49 20	241	30 27	284	14 52	317
189	21 55	057	50 55	092	61 42	122	40 21	164	48 38	242	29 41	284	14 19	318
190	22 35	058	51 43	093	62 22	124	40 34	165	47 56	243	28 55	285	13 47	318
191	23 16	058	52 31	093	63 01	125	40 46	166	47 13	244	28 08	285	13 15	318
192	23 56	058	53 19	094	63 40	127	40 56	168	46 29	245	27 22	286	12 44	319
193	24 37	059	54 06	095	64 18	128	41 06	169	45 46	246	26 36	286	12 12	319
194	25 18	059	54 54	095	64 55	130	41 15	170	45 02	247	25 50	287	11 41	320
	DENEB		◆ VEGA		Alphecca		◆ SPICA		REGULUS		◆ POLLUX		Dubhe	
195	10 45	040	25 59	060	55 42	096	41 23	171	44 17	248	25 04	287	59 31	333
196	11 16	041	26 41	060	56 29	097	41 29	173	43 33	249	24 19	288	59 09	333
197	11 47	041	27 23	060	57 17	098	41 35	174	42 48	250	23 33	288	58 47	332
198	12 19	042	28 04	061	58 04	098	41 39	175	42 03	251	22 47	289	58 24	331
199	12 51	042	28 46	061	58 52	099	41 42	177	41 18	251	22 02	289	58 01	331
200	13 23	043	29 28	062	59 39	100	41 44	178	40 32	252	21 17	290	57 37	330
201	13 56	043	30 11	062	60 26	101	41 46	179	39 46	253	20 32	290	57 13	330
202	14 29	044	30 53	062	61 13	102	41 46	181	39 00	254	19 47	291	56 49	329
203	15 02	044	31 35	063	62 00	103	41 44	182	38 14	255	19 02	291	56 25	329
204	15 35	044	32 18	063	62 46	104	41 42	183	37 28	255	18 18	292	56 00	329
205	16 09	045	33 01	064	63 33	105	41 39	185	36 42	256	17 33	292	55 35	328
206	16 43	045	33 44	064	64 19	106	41 35	186	35 55	257	16 49	293	55 10	328
207	17 17	046	34 27	064	65 05	107	41 29	187	35 08	258	16 05	293	54 44	327
208	17 51	046	35 10	065	65 51	108	41 22	189	34 21	258	15 21	294	54 18	327
209	18 26	047	35 54	065	66 36	109	41 15	190	33 34	259	14 37	294	53 52	327
	DENEB		◆ VEGA		Rasalhague		ANTARES		◆ SPICA		REGULUS		◆ Dubhe	
210	19 01	047	36 37	065	36 09	102	17 22	145	41 06	191	32 47	260	53 26	327
211	19 36	047	37 21	066	36 56	103	17 49	146	40 56	192	32 00	260	52 59	326
212	20 12	048	38 04	066	37 43	104	18 15	147	40 46	194	31 13	261	52 32	326
213	20 47	048	38 48	066	38 29	105	18 41	148	40 34	195	30 25	262	52 05	326
214	21 23	049	39 32	067	39 16	105	19 07	148	40 21	196	29 38	262	51 38	325
215	21 59	049	40 16	067	40 02	106	19 32	149	40 07	197	28 50	263	51 11	325
216	22 35	049	41 00	067	40 48	107	19 56	150	39 52	199	28 03	264	50 44	325
217	23 12	050	41 45	068	41 33	108	20 19	151	39 36	200	27 15	264	50 16	325
218	23 48	050	42 29	068	42 19	109	20 42	152	39 20	201	26 27	265	49 49	325
219	24 25	051	43 14	068	43 04	109	21 05	153	39 02	202	25 40	266	49 21	325
220	25 02	051	43 58	069	43 49	110	21 26	154	38 43	204	24 52	266	48 53	324
221	25 40	051	44 43	069	44 34	111	21 47	154	38 24	205	24 04	267	48 25	324
222	26 17	052	45 28	069	45 19	112	22 08	155	38 03	206	23 16	268	47 57	324
223	26 55	052	46 13	070	46 03	113	22 27	156	37 42	207	22 28	268	47 29	324
224	27 33	052	46 58	070	46 47	114	22 46	157	37 20	208	21 40	269	47 01	324
	DENEB		◆ ALTAIR		Rasalhague		ANTARES		◆ SPICA		Denebola		◆ Dubhe	
225	28 11	053	19 00	093	47 31	115	23 05	158	36 57	209	42 16	255	46 32	324
226	28 49	053	19 48	094	48 14	116	23 22	159	36 33	210	41 29	256	46 04	324
227	29 27	053	20 35	094	48 57	117	23 39	160	36 08	212	40 43	256	45 36	324
228	30 06	054	21 23	095	49 39	118	23 55	161	35 43	213	39 56	257	45 07	324
229	30 44	054	22 11	096	50 22	119	24 10	162	35 16	214	39 09	258	44 39	324
230	31 23	054	22 58	096	51 03	120	24 25	163	34 50	215	38 23	259	44 10	324
231	32 02	055	23 46	097	51 45	121	24 39	164	34 22	216	37 35	259	43 42	324
232	32 41	055	24 34	098	52 25	122	24 52	165	33 53	217	36 48	260	43 13	324
233	33 21	055	25 21	098	53 06	123	25 04	166	33 24	218	36 01	261	42 45	324
234	34 00	056	26 08	099	53 45	125	25 16	167	32 55	219	35 14	261	42 17	324
235	34 40	056	26 56	100	54 25	126	25 26	168	32 24	220	34 26	262	41 48	324
236	35 19	056	27 43	100	55 03	127	25 36	169	31 53	221	33 39	263	41 20	324
237	35 59	056	28 30	101	55 41	128	25 46	169	31 21	222	32 51	263	40 51	324
238	36 39	057	29 17	102	56 18	130	25 54	170	30 49	223	32 04	264	40 23	324
239	37 19	057	30 04	102	56 55	131	26 01	171	30 16	224	31 16	265	39 54	324
	◆ DENEB		ALTAIR		Nunki		◆ ANTARES		ARCTURUS		◆ Alkaid		Kochab	
240	38 00	057	30 51	103	14 23	140	26 08	172	61 08	239	63 18	308	51 58	352
241	38 40	057	31 37	104	14 53	141	26 14	173	60 27	240	62 40	307	51 52	352
242	39 20	058	32 24	104	15 23	141	26 19	174	59 45	241	62 01	307	51 45	352
243	40 01	058	33 10	105	15 53	142	26 23	175	59 03	243	61 23	307	51 38	351
244	40 42	058	33 56	106	16 22	143	26 27	176	58 20	244	60 45	307	51 30	351
245	41 22	058	34 42	107	16 50	144	26 29	177	57 37	245	60 06	306	51 22	350
246	42 03	059	35 28	107	17 18	145	26 31	178	56 53	246	59 27	306	51 14	350
247	42 44	059	36 14	108	17 46	145	26 32	179	56 09	247	58 49	306	51 06	350
248	43 25	059	36 59	109	18 13	146	26 32	180	55 25	248	58 10	306	50 57	349
249	44 07	059	37 44	110	18 39	147	26 31	181	54 40	249	57 31	306	50 48	349
250	44 48	060	38 29	111	19 05	148	26 30	182	53 55	250	56 52	305	50 39	349
251	45 29	060	39 14	111	19 30	149	26 27	183	53 10	251	56 13	305	50 29	348
252	46 11	060	39 59	112	19 55	150	26 24	184	52 24	252	55 34	305	50 19	348
253	46 52	060	40 43	113	20 19	150	26 20	185	51 39	253	54 55	305	50 09	348
254	47 34	060	41 27	114	20 42	151	26 15	186	50 53	254	54 16	305	49 58	347
	◆ DENEB		ALTAIR		Nunki		◆ ANTARES		ARCTURUS		◆ Alkaid		Kochab	
255	48 15	060	42 10	115	21 05	152	26 09	187	50 07	255	53 36	305	49 48	347
256	48 57	061	42 54	116	21 27	153	26 03	188	49 20	256	52 57	305	49 37	347
257	49 39	061	43 37	117	21 48	154	25 55	189	48 34	256	52 18	305	49 25	346
258	50 21	061	44 19	118	22 09	155	25 47	190	47 47	257	51 39	305	49 14	346
259	51 03	061	45 02	119	22 29	156	25 38	191	47 00	258	51 00	305	49 02	346
260	51 45	061	45 43	120	22 48	157	25 28	192	46 13	259	50 21	305	48 50	345
261	52 27	061	46 25	121	23 07	158	25 18	193	45 26	260	49 41	305	48 38	345
262	53 09	061	47 06	122	23 25	158	25 06	194	44 39	260	49 02	305	48 25	345
263	53 51	061	47 46	123	23 42	159	24 54	195	43 52	261	48 23	305	48 13	345
264	54 33	062	48 26	124	23 58	160	24 41	196	43 04	262	47 44	306	48 00	344
265	55 15	062	49 06	125	24 14	161	24 27	197	42 17	262	47 05	306	47 47	344
266	55 57	062	49 45	126	24 29	162	24 13	198	41 29	263	46 26	306	47 34	344
267	56 39	062	50 23	127	24 43	163	23 58	199	40 42	264	45 48	306	47 20	344
268	57 21	062	51 01	129	24 57	164	23 42	200	39 54	264	45 09	306	47 07	343
269	58 04	062	51 38	130	25 10	165	23 25	201	39 06	265	44 30	306	46 53	343

LHA ♈	Hc	Zn	Hc	Zn	Hc	Zn	Hc	Zn	Hc	Zn	Hc	Zn	Hc	Zn
	◆ DENEB		ALTAIR		Nunki		◆ ANTARES		ARCTURUS		◆ Alkaid		Kochab	
270	58 46	062	52 15	131	25 21	166	23 07	202	38 19	266	43 51	306	46 39	343
271	59 28	062	52 50	132	25 33	167	22 49	203	37 31	266	43 13	306	46 25	343
272	60 10	062	53 26	134	25 43	168	22 30	204	36 43	267	42 34	307	46 10	343
273	60 52	061	54 00	135	25 52	169	22 11	205	35 55	268	41 56	307	45 56	342
274	61 34	061	54 33	136	26 01	170	21 51	205	35 07	268	41 17	307	45 41	342
275	62 16	061	55 06	138	26 09	171	21 30	206	34 19	269	40 39	307	45 26	342
276	62 58	061	55 38	139	26 16	172	21 08	207	33 31	270	40 01	307	45 12	342
277	63 40	061	56 08	141	26 23	173	20 46	208	32 43	270	39 23	307	44 57	342
278	64 22	061	56 38	142	26 28	174	20 23	209	31 56	271	38 45	308	44 41	342
279	65 04	061	57 07	144	26 33	175	20 00	210	31 08	271	38 07	308	44 26	341
280	65 46	060	57 35	146	26 37	176	19 36	211	30 20	272	37 29	308	44 11	341
281	66 27	060	58 01	147	26 39	177	19 11	211	29 32	273	36 52	308	43 55	341
282	67 09	060	58 26	149	26 42	178	18 46	212	28 44	273	36 14	309	43 40	341
283	67 50	059	58 51	151	26 43	179	18 20	213	27 56	274	35 37	309	43 24	341
284	68 31	059	59 13	152	26 43	180	17 53	214	27 08	274	34 59	309	43 08	341
	Alpheratz		◆ Enif		ALTAIR		◆ Rasalhague		ARCTURUS		Alkaid		◆ Kochab	
285	26 32	072	44 04	115	59 35	154	59 06	223	26 21	275	34 22	309	42 53	341
286	27 18	073	44 47	116	59 55	156	58 33	225	25 33	275	33 45	310	42 37	341
287	28 04	073	45 30	117	60 14	158	57 59	226	24 45	276	33 08	310	42 21	340
288	28 50	074	46 12	118	60 31	160	57 24	228	23 58	277	32 32	310	42 05	340
289	29 36	074	46 54	119	60 47	162	56 48	229	23 10	277	31 55	310	41 48	340
290	30 22	075	47 36	120	61 01	164	56 11	230	22 22	278	31 19	311	41 32	340
291	31 08	075	48 17	121	61 14	166	55 34	232	21 35	278	30 42	311	41 16	340
292	31 54	076	48 58	122	61 24	168	54 56	233	20 48	279	30 06	311	41 00	340
293	32 41	076	49 38	124	61 34	170	54 17	234	20 00	279	29 30	312	40 44	340
294	33 27	076	50 18	125	61 41	172	53 38	236	19 13	280	28 55	312	40 27	340
295	34 14	077	50 57	126	61 47	174	52 58	237	18 26	280	28 19	312	40 11	340
296	35 01	077	51 35	127	61 51	176	52 18	238	17 39	281	27 44	312	39 54	340
297	35 48	078	52 13	128	61 54	178	51 37	239	16 52	282	27 08	313	39 38	340
298	36 34	078	52 51	130	61 55	180	50 56	240	16 05	282	26 33	313	39 22	340
299	37 21	079	53 27	131	61 53	182	50 14	241	15 18	283	25 58	313	39 05	340
	◆ Mirfak		Alpheratz		◆ FOMALHAUT		ALTAIR		Rasalhague		◆ Alphecca		Kochab	
300	15 51	039	38 08	079	11 25	141	61 51	184	49 32	242	33 57	280	38 49	340
301	16 21	039	38 56	080	11 54	142	61 46	187	48 49	243	33 10	280	38 32	340
302	16 52	039	39 43	080	12 23	143	61 40	189	48 06	244	32 23	281	38 16	340
303	17 22	040	40 30	081	12 52	144	61 32	191	47 23	245	31 36	281	37 59	340
304	17 53	040	41 17	081	13 20	144	61 22	193	46 39	246	30 49	282	37 43	340
305	18 24	041	42 05	082	13 48	145	61 11	195	45 55	247	30 02	282	37 27	340
306	18 55	041	42 52	082	14 15	146	60 58	197	45 10	248	29 15	283	37 10	340
307	19 27	041	43 40	083	14 41	147	60 43	199	44 26	249	28 28	283	36 54	340
308	19 59	042	44 27	083	15 08	147	60 27	201	43 41	250	27 42	284	36 38	340
309	20 31	042	45 15	084	15 33	148	60 09	203	42 56	251	26 55	284	36 21	340
310	21 03	043	46 03	084	15 58	149	59 50	204	42 10	252	26 09	285	36 05	340
311	21 36	043	46 50	085	16 22	150	59 30	206	41 25	252	25 23	285	35 49	340
312	22 08	043	47 38	085	16 46	151	59 08	208	40 39	253	24 36	286	35 33	340
313	22 41	044	48 26	086	17 09	151	58 45	210	39 53	254	23 50	286	35 17	340
314	23 15	044	49 14	087	17 32	152	58 20	212	39 07	255	23 04	287	35 00	340
	◆ Mirfak		Hamal		Diphda		◆ FOMALHAUT		ALTAIR		◆ VEGA		Kochab	
315	23 48	044	23 53	078	13 50	126	17 54	153	57 55	213	62 00	285	34 44	340
316	24 22	045	24 40	078	14 28	126	18 15	154	57 28	215	61 14	285	34 29	341
317	24 55	045	25 27	079	15 07	127	18 36	155	57 00	216	60 27	285	34 13	341
318	25 29	045	26 14	079	15 45	128	18 56	156	56 31	218	59 41	285	33 57	341
319	26 04	046	27 01	080	16 23	129	19 15	157	56 01	220	58 55	286	33 41	341
320	26 38	046	27 48	080	17 00	129	19 34	157	55 30	221	58 09	286	33 26	341
321	27 13	046	28 36	081	17 37	130	19 52	158	54 58	223	57 23	286	33 10	341
322	27 48	047	29 23	081	18 13	131	20 10	159	54 25	224	56 37	286	32 54	341
323	28 22	047	30 10	082	18 49	132	20 26	160	53 52	225	55 51	287	32 39	341
324	28 58	047	30 58	082	19 25	132	20 42	161	53 17	227	55 05	287	32 24	341
325	29 33	048	31 45	083	20 00	133	20 58	162	52 42	228	54 19	287	32 09	342
326	30 08	048	32 33	084	20 35	134	21 12	163	52 06	229	53 33	287	31 53	342
327	30 44	048	33 21	084	21 09	135	21 26	164	51 29	231	52 48	288	31 38	342
328	31 20	048	34 08	085	21 43	136	21 39	164	50 52	232	52 02	288	31 24	342
329	31 56	049	34 56	085	22 16	136	21 52	165	50 14	233	51 17	288	31 09	342
	◆ CAPELLA		Hamal		Diphda		◆ FOMALHAUT		ALTAIR		◆ VEGA		Kochab	
330	14 23	043	35 44	086	22 49	137	22 04	166	49 35	234	50 31	289	30 54	342
331	14 55	043	36 32	086	23 21	138	22 15	167	48 56	235	49 46	289	30 40	342
332	15 28	043	37 19	087	23 53	139	22 25	168	48 17	236	49 00	289	30 25	343
333	16 01	044	38 07	087	24 24	140	22 34	169	47 36	237	48 15	290	30 11	343
334	16 34	044	38 55	088	24 55	141	22 43	170	46 56	239	47 30	290	29 57	343
335	17 08	045	39 43	089	25 25	142	22 51	171	46 15	240	46 45	290	29 43	343
336	17 42	045	40 31	089	25 54	143	22 58	172	45 33	241	46 00	290	29 29	343
337	18 16	046	41 19	090	26 23	143	23 04	173	44 51	242	45 15	291	29 15	343
338	18 50	046	42 07	090	26 51	144	23 10	174	44 09	243	44 31	291	29 01	344
339	19 25	046	42 55	091	27 19	145	23 15	175	43 26	243	43 46	291	28 48	344
340	20 00	047	43 43	092	27 46	146	23 19	176	42 43	244	43 01	292	28 34	344
341	20 35	047	44 31	092	28 12	147	23 22	177	42 00	245	42 17	292	28 21	344
342	21 10	048	45 18	093	28 38	148	23 25	178	41 16	246	41 32	292	28 08	344
343	21 45	048	46 06	094	29 03	149	23 26	178	40 32	247	40 48	293	27 55	344
344	22 21	048	46 54	094	29 27	150	23 27	179	39 48	248	40 04	293	27 42	345
	◆ CAPELLA		ALDEBARAN		Diphda		◆ FOMALHAUT		ALTAIR		◆ VEGA		Kochab	
345	22 57	049	14 24	080	29 50	151	23 27	180	39 03	249	39 20	293	27 30	345
346	23 33	049	15 11	081	30 13	152	23 27	181	38 19	250	38 36	294	27 17	345
347	24 10	050	15 59	081	30 35	153	23 25	182	37 33	250	37 52	294	27 05	345
348	24 46	050	16 46	082	30 56	154	23 23	183	36 48	251	37 09	294	26 53	345
349	25 23	050	17 34	082	31 17	155	23 20	184	36 03	252	36 25	295	26 41	346
350	26 00	051	18 21	083	31 36	156	23 16	185	35 17	253	35 42	295	26 29	346
351	26 37	051	19 09	083	31 55	157	23 11	186	34 31	254	34 58	295	26 18	346
352	27 14	051	19 56	084	32 13	158	23 06	187	33 45	254	34 15	296	26 06	346
353	27 52	052	20 44	084	32 30	159	23 00	188	32 59	255	33 32	296	25 55	347
354	28 29	052	21 32	085	32 47	161	22 53	189	32 13	256	32 49	297	25 44	347
355	29 07	052	22 19	086	33 02	162	22 45	190	31 26	257	32 06	297	25 33	347
356	29 45	053	23 07	086	33 17	163	22 36	191	30 39	257	31 24	297	25 23	347
357	30 23	053	23 55	087	33 31	164	22 27	192	29 53	258	30 41	298	25 12	347
358	31 02	053	24 43	087	33 44	165	22 17	193	29 06	259	29 59	298	25 02	348
359	31 40	054	25 31	088	33 55	166	22 06	193	28 19	259	29 17	298	24 52	348

LAT 36°N

LHA ♈	Hc	Zn	Hc	Zn	Hc	Zn	Hc	Zn	Hc	Zn	Hc	Zn	Hc	Zn
	◆ CAPELLA		ALDEBARAN		◆ Diphda		FOMALHAUT		ALTAIR		◆ VEGA		Kochab	
0	31 43	053	26 17	088	35 05	167	22 53	195	27 42	260	28 05	299	23 43	348
1	32 22	054	27 05	089	35 15	168	22 40	195	26 54	261	27 23	300	23 33	349
2	33 01	054	27 54	089	35 25	169	22 27	196	26 06	262	26 41	300	23 24	349
3	33 41	054	28 42	090	35 33	171	22 13	197	25 18	262	25 59	300	23 15	349
4	34 20	054	29 31	090	35 41	172	21 58	198	24 30	263	25 17	301	23 05	349
5	35 00	055	30 20	091	35 47	173	21 43	199	23 41	264	24 36	301	22 56	350
6	35 40	055	31 08	092	35 53	174	21 27	200	22 53	264	23 54	302	22 48	350
7	36 19	055	31 57	092	35 57	175	21 10	201	22 05	265	23 13	302	22 39	350
8	36 59	056	32 45	093	36 01	176	20 52	202	21 16	266	22 32	302	22 31	350
9	37 39	056	33 34	093	36 04	178	20 34	203	20 28	266	21 51	303	22 23	351
10	38 20	056	34 22	094	36 05	179	20 15	203	19 39	267	21 11	303	22 15	351
11	39 00	056	35 10	095	36 06	180	19 55	204	18 51	267	20 30	304	22 07	351
12	39 40	056	35 59	095	36 05	181	19 35	205	18 02	268	19 50	304	22 00	351
13	40 21	057	36 47	096	36 04	182	19 14	206	17 14	269	19 10	305	21 53	352
14	41 01	057	37 35	097	36 01	183	18 52	207	16 25	269	18 30	305	21 46	352
	◆ CAPELLA		BETELGEUSE		RIGEL		◆ Diphda		Enif		◆ DENEB		Kochab	
15	41 42	057	17 17	093	15 39	113	35 58	185	38 48	252	41 31	302	21 39	352
16	42 23	057	18 05	094	16 23	113	35 54	186	38 02	253	40 50	302	21 32	352
17	43 04	057	18 53	095	17 08	114	35 48	187	37 16	253	40 09	302	21 26	353
18	43 45	058	19 42	095	17 52	115	35 42	188	36 29	254	39 28	303	21 20	353
19	44 26	058	20 30	096	18 36	115	35 35	189	35 42	255	38 47	303	21 14	353
20	45 07	058	21 18	096	19 20	116	35 26	190	34 55	256	38 06	303	21 09	353
21	45 48	058	22 07	097	20 03	117	35 17	192	34 08	256	37 26	303	21 03	354
22	46 29	058	22 55	098	20 46	118	35 07	193	33 21	257	36 45	304	20 58	354
23	47 10	058	23 43	098	21 29	118	34 56	194	32 34	258	36 05	304	20 53	354
24	47 52	058	24 31	099	22 12	119	34 44	195	31 46	259	35 25	304	20 48	355
25	48 33	059	25 19	100	22 54	120	34 31	196	30 59	259	34 45	304	20 44	355
26	49 15	059	26 06	100	23 36	121	34 17	197	30 11	260	34 05	305	20 40	355
27	49 56	059	26 54	101	24 17	121	34 02	198	29 23	261	33 25	305	20 36	355
28	50 38	059	27 42	102	24 59	122	33 46	199	28 35	261	32 45	305	20 32	356
29	51 19	059	28 29	102	25 40	123	33 29	201	27 47	262	32 06	306	20 29	356
	◆ CAPELLA		BETELGEUSE		RIGEL		◆ Diphda		Alpheratz		◆ DENEB		Kochab	
30	52 01	059	29 17	103	26 20	124	33 12	202	65 46	262	31 26	306	20 25	356
31	52 43	059	30 04	104	27 00	125	32 54	203	64 58	262	30 47	306	20 22	357
32	53 24	059	30 51	104	27 40	125	32 35	204	64 10	263	30 08	306	20 20	357
33	54 06	059	31 38	105	28 19	126	32 15	205	63 22	264	29 29	307	20 17	357
34	54 48	059	32 25	106	28 58	127	31 54	206	62 33	265	28 50	307	20 15	357
35	55 29	059	33 11	107	29 37	128	31 32	207	61 45	265	28 11	307	20 13	358
36	56 11	059	33 58	107	30 15	129	31 10	208	60 57	266	27 33	308	20 11	358
37	56 53	059	34 44	108	30 52	130	30 47	209	60 08	267	26 55	308	20 10	358
38	57 34	059	35 30	109	31 29	131	30 23	210	59 20	267	26 17	308	20 08	359
39	58 16	059	36 16	110	32 06	132	29 58	211	58 31	268	25 39	309	20 07	359
40	58 57	059	37 02	110	32 42	132	29 33	212	57 43	269	25 01	309	20 07	359
41	59 39	059	37 47	111	33 18	133	29 07	213	56 54	269	24 23	309	20 06	000
42	60 20	059	38 32	112	33 53	134	28 40	214	56 06	270	23 46	310	20 06	000
43	61 02	058	39 17	113	34 27	135	28 13	215	55 17	271	23 09	310	20 06	000
44	61 43	058	40 01	114	35 01	136	27 45	216	54 29	271	22 32	311	20 06	000
	◆ Dubhe		POLLUX		SIRIUS		◆ RIGEL		Diphda		◆ Alpheratz		DENEB	
45	18 35	025	30 07	076	15 00	124	35 34	137	27 16	217	53 40	272	21 55	311
46	18 56	026	30 54	076	15 40	125	36 06	138	26 47	218	52 51	272	21 19	311
47	19 17	026	31 42	077	16 20	126	36 38	139	26 17	219	52 03	273	20 42	312
48	19 39	026	32 29	077	16 59	126	37 10	140	25 46	219	51 15	273	20 06	312
49	20 00	027	33 16	077	17 38	127	37 40	142	25 15	220	50 26	274	19 30	312
50	20 22	027	34 04	078	18 16	128	38 10	143	24 44	221	49 38	274	18 54	313
51	20 45	027	34 51	078	18 54	129	38 39	144	24 11	222	48 49	275	18 19	313
52	21 07	028	35 39	079	19 32	129	39 07	145	23 39	223	48 01	275	17 44	314
53	21 30	028	36 26	079	20 09	130	39 35	146	23 05	224	47 13	276	17 09	314
54	21 52	028	37 14	080	20 46	131	40 02	147	22 32	225	46 24	276	16 34	315
55	22 16	029	38 02	080	21 23	132	40 28	148	21 57	225	45 36	277	16 00	315
56	22 39	029	38 50	081	21 59	133	40 53	149	21 22	226	44 48	277	15 25	315
57	23 02	029	39 38	081	22 34	133	41 17	151	20 47	227	44 00	278	14 51	316
58	23 26	029	40 26	082	23 09	134	41 40	152	20 12	228	43 12	278	14 18	316
59	23 50	030	41 14	082	23 44	135	42 03	153	19 35	229	42 24	279	13 44	317
	◆ Dubhe		POLLUX		PROCYON		◆ SIRIUS		RIGEL		◆ Hamal		Schedar	
60	24 14	030	42 02	083	31 00	108	24 18	136	42 24	154	62 50	250	51 10	318
61	24 39	030	42 50	083	31 46	109	24 51	137	42 44	156	62 04	252	50 37	318
62	25 03	031	43 38	084	32 32	109	25 24	138	43 04	157	61 18	253	50 05	318
63	25 28	031	44 27	084	33 18	110	25 56	139	43 23	158	60 31	254	49 32	318
64	25 53	031	45 15	085	34 03	111	26 28	139	43 40	160	59 44	255	48 59	318
65	26 18	031	46 03	085	34 48	112	27 00	140	43 56	161	58 58	256	48 27	317
66	26 43	032	46 52	086	35 33	112	27 30	141	44 12	162	58 10	256	47 54	317
67	27 09	032	47 40	086	36 18	113	28 00	142	44 26	164	57 23	257	47 21	317
68	27 34	032	48 29	087	37 02	114	28 30	143	44 39	165	56 36	258	46 48	317
69	28 00	032	49 17	087	37 47	115	28 59	144	44 52	166	55 48	259	46 15	317
70	28 26	032	50 06	088	38 31	116	29 27	145	45 03	168	55 00	260	45 42	317
71	28 52	033	50 54	089	39 14	117	29 54	146	45 12	169	54 13	261	45 09	317
72	29 19	033	51 43	089	39 57	118	30 21	147	45 21	170	53 25	261	44 36	317
73	29 45	033	52 31	090	40 40	118	30 47	148	45 29	172	52 37	262	44 03	317
74	30 12	033	53 20	090	41 23	119	31 13	149	45 35	173	51 49	263	43 30	317
	◆ Dubhe		POLLUX		PROCYON		◆ SIRIUS		RIGEL		◆ Hamal		Schedar	
75	30 38	033	54 08	091	42 05	120	31 37	150	45 40	175	51 00	264	42 57	317
76	31 05	034	54 57	091	42 46	121	32 01	151	45 44	176	50 12	264	42 24	317
77	31 32	034	55 45	092	43 28	122	32 25	152	45 47	177	49 24	265	41 51	317
78	31 59	034	56 34	093	44 08	123	32 47	153	45 48	179	48 35	266	41 18	317
79	32 26	034	57 22	093	44 49	124	33 09	154	45 49	180	47 47	266	40 45	317
80	32 54	034	58 11	094	45 29	125	33 29	155	45 48	182	46 59	267	40 12	318
81	33 21	034	58 59	095	46 08	126	33 49	156	45 46	183	46 10	267	39 40	318
82	33 49	035	59 47	095	46 47	128	34 09	157	45 43	185	45 22	268	39 07	318
83	34 16	035	60 36	096	47 25	129	34 27	158	45 38	186	44 33	269	38 34	318
84	34 44	035	61 24	097	48 02	130	34 44	160	45 33	187	43 44	269	38 02	318
85	35 12	035	62 12	098	48 39	131	35 01	161	45 26	189	42 56	270	37 29	318
86	35 40	035	63 00	099	49 16	132	35 16	162	45 18	190	42 07	270	36 57	318
87	36 08	035	63 48	099	49 51	133	35 31	163	45 09	192	41 19	271	36 25	318
88	36 36	035	64 36	100	50 26	135	35 45	164	44 59	193	40 30	272	35 52	318
89	37 04	035	65 24	101	51 00	136	35 58	165	44 47	194	39 42	272	35 20	319

LHA ♈	Hc	Zn	Hc	Zn	Hc	Zn	Hc	Zn	Hc	Zn	Hc	Zn	Hc	Zn
	◆ Dubhe		REGULUS		PROCYON		◆ SIRIUS		RIGEL		ALDEBARAN		◆ Mirfak	
90	37 32	036	29 17	097	51 33	137	36 10	166	44 35	196	63 10	229	58 56	309
91	38 00	036	30 06	097	52 06	139	36 21	168	44 21	197	62 33	231	58 18	309
92	38 29	036	30 54	098	52 37	140	36 31	169	44 06	198	61 55	232	57 40	308
93	38 57	036	31 42	099	53 08	142	36 40	170	43 51	200	61 16	234	57 02	308
94	39 25	036	32 30	099	53 38	143	36 48	171	43 34	201	60 37	235	56 24	308
95	39 54	036	33 18	100	54 07	144	36 55	172	43 16	202	59 57	236	55 45	308
96	40 22	036	34 05	101	54 34	146	37 01	173	42 57	204	59 16	238	55 07	308
97	40 50	036	34 53	101	55 01	147	37 06	175	42 37	205	58 35	239	54 29	308
98	41 19	036	35 40	102	55 26	149	37 10	176	42 16	206	57 53	240	53 50	307
99	41 47	036	36 28	103	55 51	151	37 13	177	41 54	207	57 10	242	53 12	307
100	42 16	036	37 15	103	56 14	152	37 15	178	41 32	209	56 27	243	52 33	307
101	42 44	036	38 02	104	56 36	154	37 16	179	41 08	210	55 44	244	51 54	307
102	43 13	036	38 49	105	56 56	156	37 16	181	40 43	211	55 00	245	51 16	307
103	43 41	036	39 36	106	57 16	157	37 15	182	40 18	212	54 16	246	50 37	307
104	44 10	036	40 23	106	57 34	159	37 12	183	39 52	213	53 32	247	49 58	307
	Kochab		◆ Denebola		REGULUS		◆ SIRIUS		RIGEL		ALDEBARAN		◆ CAPELLA	
105	27 32	016	22 32	088	41 09	107	37 09	184	39 25	214	52 47	248	68 24	306
106	27 46	016	23 20	089	41 55	108	37 05	185	38 57	216	52 02	249	67 45	305
107	27 59	016	24 09	089	42 42	109	37 00	187	38 28	217	51 16	250	67 05	304
108	28 13	016	24 57	090	43 27	110	36 54	188	37 59	218	50 30	251	66 25	304
109	28 27	017	25 46	090	44 13	111	36 47	189	37 29	219	49 44	252	65 44	304
110	28 40	017	26 34	091	44 58	111	36 39	190	36 58	220	48 58	253	65 04	303
111	28 55	017	27 23	092	45 43	112	36 30	191	36 27	221	48 12	253	64 23	303
112	29 09	017	28 12	092	46 28	113	36 20	193	35 54	222	47 25	254	63 42	302
113	29 23	017	29 00	093	47 12	114	36 08	194	35 22	223	46 38	255	63 01	302
114	29 37	017	29 48	093	47 57	115	35 56	195	34 48	224	45 51	256	62 20	302
115	29 52	018	30 37	094	48 40	116	35 44	196	34 14	225	45 04	257	61 39	302
116	30 07	018	31 25	095	49 24	117	35 30	197	33 40	226	44 17	257	60 58	302
117	30 21	018	32 14	095	50 07	118	35 15	198	33 05	227	43 29	258	60 16	301
118	30 36	018	33 02	096	50 49	119	34 59	199	32 29	228	42 42	259	59 35	301
119	30 51	018	33 50	097	51 31	120	34 43	201	31 53	229	41 54	260	58 53	301
	◆ Kochab		Denebola		◆ REGULUS		SIRIUS		RIGEL		◆ ALDEBARAN		CAPELLA	
120	31 06	018	34 38	097	52 13	121	34 25	202	31 16	230	41 06	260	58 12	301
121	31 22	018	35 27	098	52 54	123	34 07	203	30 39	231	40 18	261	57 30	301
122	31 37	018	36 15	099	53 35	124	33 48	204	30 01	231	39 30	262	56 48	301
123	31 52	019	37 03	099	54 15	125	33 27	205	29 23	232	38 42	262	56 07	301
124	32 08	019	37 50	100	54 54	126	33 07	206	28 44	233	37 54	263	55 25	301
125	32 23	019	38 38	101	55 33	128	32 45	207	28 05	234	37 06	264	54 43	301
126	32 39	019	39 26	101	56 11	129	32 22	208	27 25	235	36 18	264	54 02	301
127	32 55	019	40 13	102	56 49	130	31 59	209	26 45	236	35 29	265	53 20	301
128	33 11	019	41 01	103	57 26	132	31 35	210	26 05	237	34 41	266	52 38	301
129	33 27	019	41 48	104	58 01	133	31 10	211	25 24	237	33 53	266	51 57	301
130	33 42	019	42 35	104	58 36	135	30 45	212	24 43	238	33 04	267	51 15	301
131	33 58	019	43 22	105	59 11	136	30 19	213	24 02	239	32 16	268	50 34	301
132	34 15	019	44 09	106	59 44	138	29 52	214	23 20	240	31 27	268	49 52	301
133	34 31	019	44 55	107	60 16	139	29 24	215	22 38	240	30 39	269	49 11	301
134	34 47	019	45 42	108	60 47	141	28 56	216	21 56	241	29 50	269	48 29	301
	Kochab		◆ ARCTURUS		SPICA		REGULUS		◆ SIRIUS		BETELGEUSE		◆ CAPELLA	
135	35 03	020	19 42	080	11 39	113	61 17	143	28 27	217	39 17	247	47 48	302
136	35 19	020	20 30	081	12 23	114	61 46	145	27 58	218	38 32	248	47 06	302
137	35 36	020	21 18	081	13 08	115	62 13	146	27 27	219	37 47	249	46 25	302
138	35 52	020	22 06	082	13 52	115	62 40	148	26 57	220	37 01	250	45 44	302
139	36 08	020	22 54	082	14 35	116	63 04	150	26 25	221	36 16	250	45 03	302
140	36 25	020	23 42	083	15 19	117	63 28	152	25 53	222	35 30	251	44 22	302
141	36 41	020	24 30	083	16 02	117	63 50	154	25 21	222	34 44	252	43 41	302
142	36 57	020	25 19	084	16 45	118	64 10	156	24 48	223	33 57	253	43 00	303
143	37 14	020	26 07	085	17 28	119	64 29	158	24 14	224	33 11	253	42 19	303
144	37 30	020	26 55	085	18 10	119	64 45	161	23 40	225	32 24	254	41 38	303
145	37 47	020	27 44	086	18 52	120	65 01	163	23 06	226	31 38	255	40 57	303
146	38 03	020	28 32	086	19 34	121	65 14	165	22 31	227	30 51	256	40 17	303
147	38 20	020	29 20	087	20 16	122	65 25	167	21 55	227	30 03	256	39 36	304
148	38 36	020	30 09	087	20 57	122	65 35	170	21 19	228	29 16	257	38 56	304
149	38 53	020	30 57	088	21 38	123	65 43	172	20 43	229	28 29	258	38 16	304
	◆ Kochab		ARCTURUS		◆ SPICA		REGULUS		PROCYON		◆ POLLUX		CAPELLA	
150	39 09	020	31 46	089	22 18	124	65 48	175	45 30	235	60 41	264	37 35	304
151	39 25	020	32 35	089	22 58	125	65 52	177	44 50	236	59 53	264	36 55	305
152	39 42	020	33 23	090	23 38	126	65 54	179	44 10	237	59 05	265	36 15	305
153	39 58	020	34 12	090	24 17	126	65 53	182	43 29	238	58 16	266	35 36	305
154	40 14	020	35 00	091	24 56	127	65 51	184	42 48	239	57 28	267	34 56	305
155	40 30	019	35 49	091	25 34	128	65 46	186	42 06	240	56 39	267	34 16	306
156	40 46	019	36 37	092	26 13	129	65 40	189	41 24	241	55 51	268	33 37	306
157	41 03	019	37 26	093	26 50	130	65 31	191	40 42	241	55 02	268	32 58	306
158	41 19	019	38 14	093	27 27	130	65 21	193	39 59	242	54 14	269	32 18	306
159	41 35	019	39 03	094	28 04	131	65 09	196	39 16	243	53 25	270	31 39	307
160	41 51	019	39 51	095	28 40	132	64 55	198	38 32	244	52 37	270	31 00	307
161	42 06	019	40 39	095	29 16	133	64 39	200	37 49	245	51 48	271	30 22	307
162	42 22	019	41 28	096	29 51	134	64 21	202	37 04	246	51 00	271	29 43	308
163	42 38	019	42 16	097	30 26	135	64 02	205	36 20	247	50 11	272	29 05	308
164	42 53	019	43 04	097	31 00	136	63 41	207	35 35	248	49 23	273	28 27	308
	◆ Kochab		ARCTURUS		◆ SPICA		REGULUS		PROCYON		◆ POLLUX		CAPELLA	
165	43 09	019	43 52	098	31 33	137	63 18	209	34 50	248	48 34	273	27 48	308
166	43 24	018	44 40	099	32 06	138	62 54	211	34 05	249	47 46	274	27 11	309
167	43 39	018	45 28	099	32 39	139	62 29	213	33 20	250	46 57	274	26 33	309
168	43 54	018	46 16	100	33 10	140	62 02	214	32 34	251	46 09	275	25 55	309
169	44 09	018	47 04	101	33 41	141	61 34	216	31 48	251	45 21	275	25 18	310
170	44 24	018	47 51	102	34 12	142	61 05	218	31 02	252	44 32	276	24 41	310
171	44 39	018	48 39	102	34 42	143	60 34	220	30 16	253	43 44	276	24 04	311
172	44 54	017	49 26	103	35 11	144	60 03	221	29 29	254	42 56	277	23 27	311
173	45 08	017	50 14	104	35 39	145	59 30	223	28 42	254	42 07	277	22 50	311
174	45 22	017	51 01	105	36 06	146	58 57	225	27 56	255	41 19	278	22 14	312
175	45 37	017	51 47	106	36 33	147	58 22	226	27 09	256	40 31	278	21 38	312
176	45 51	017	52 34	106	36 59	148	57 47	228	26 22	256	39 43	279	21 02	312
177	46 04	016	53 20	107	37 25	149	57 10	229	25 34	257	38 55	279	20 26	313
178	46 18	016	54 07	108	37 49	150	56 33	230	24 47	258	38 07	280	19 50	313
179	46 31	016	54 53	109	38 13	151	55 56	232	23 59	258	37 20	280	19 15	313

 LAT 36°N

LHA ♈	Hc Zn	Hc Zn	Hc Zn	Hc Zn	Hc Zn	Hc Zn	Hc Zn
	◆ VEGA	Alphecca	ARCTURUS	◆ SPICA	REGULUS	◆ POLLUX	Dubhe
180	15 25 053	43 40 086	55 38 110	38 35 153	55 17 233	36 32 281	62 54 346
181	16 03 053	44 28 086	56 24 111	38 57 154	54 38 234	35 44 281	62 41 345
182	16 43 054	45 17 087	57 09 112	39 18 155	53 58 236	34 57 282	62 28 344
183	17 22 054	46 05 087	57 54 113	39 38 156	53 18 237	34 09 282	62 14 343
184	18 01 055	46 54 088	58 38 114	39 57 157	52 37 238	33 22 282	61 59 342
185	18 41 055	47 42 089	59 22 116	40 16 159	51 56 239	32 34 283	61 44 341
186	19 21 056	48 31 089	60 05 117	40 33 160	51 14 240	31 47 283	61 28 340
187	20 01 056	49 19 090	60 48 118	40 49 161	50 32 241	31 00 284	61 11 339
188	20 41 056	50 08 090	61 31 119	41 04 162	49 49 242	30 13 284	60 54 339
189	21 22 057	50 57 091	62 13 121	41 19 164	49 06 243	29 26 285	60 36 338
190	22 03 057	51 45 091	62 54 122	41 32 165	48 22 244	28 39 285	60 17 337
191	22 44 058	52 34 092	63 35 124	41 44 166	47 38 245	27 52 286	59 58 337
192	23 25 058	53 22 093	64 15 125	41 55 167	46 54 246	27 06 286	59 39 336
193	24 06 058	54 11 093	64 55 127	42 05 169	46 09 247	26 19 287	59 19 335
194	24 47 059	54 59 094	65 33 128	42 14 170	45 25 248	25 33 287	58 58 335
	Kochab	◆ VEGA	Alphecca	◆ SPICA	REGULUS	◆ POLLUX	Dubhe
195	49 37 011	25 29 059	55 47 095	42 22 171	44 39 249	24 46 288	58 37 334
196	49 46 011	26 11 060	56 36 095	42 29 173	43 54 250	24 00 288	58 15 333
197	49 55 011	26 53 060	57 24 096	42 34 174	43 08 251	23 14 289	57 53 333
198	50 04 010	27 35 060	58 12 097	42 39 175	42 22 251	22 28 289	57 31 332
199	50 12 010	28 17 061	59 00 098	42 42 177	41 36 252	21 42 290	57 08 332
200	50 21 010	29 00 061	59 48 098	42 44 178	40 50 253	20 57 290	56 45 331
201	50 28 009	29 42 061	60 36 099	42 46 179	40 03 254	20 11 291	56 21 331
202	50 36 009	30 25 062	61 24 100	42 46 181	39 17 255	19 26 291	55 57 330
203	50 43 008	31 08 062	62 12 101	42 44 182	38 30 255	18 40 292	55 33 330
204	50 50 008	31 51 063	63 00 102	42 42 183	37 43 256	17 55 292	55 09 329
205	50 57 008	32 34 063	63 47 103	42 39 185	36 56 257	17 10 292	54 44 329
206	51 03 007	33 17 063	64 34 104	42 34 186	36 08 258	16 26 293	54 19 329
207	51 09 007	34 01 064	65 21 105	42 29 187	35 21 258	15 41 293	53 53 328
208	51 14 006	34 44 064	66 08 106	42 22 189	34 33 259	14 57 294	53 27 328
209	51 20 006	35 28 064	66 55 107	42 14 190	33 45 260	14 12 294	53 01 328
	DENEB	◆ VEGA	Rasalhague	ANTARES	◆ SPICA	REGULUS	◆ Dubhe
210	18 20 047	36 12 065	36 22 102	18 11 145	42 05 191	32 58 260	52 35 327
211	18 55 047	36 56 065	37 09 102	18 38 146	41 55 193	32 10 261	52 09 327
212	19 31 048	37 40 065	37 57 103	19 05 147	41 44 194	31 22 262	51 42 327
213	20 07 048	38 24 066	38 44 104	19 32 147	41 32 195	30 34 262	51 16 326
214	20 43 048	39 08 066	39 31 105	19 58 148	41 19 196	29 46 263	50 49 326
215	21 20 049	39 52 066	40 18 105	20 23 149	41 04 198	28 57 264	50 22 326
216	21 56 049	40 37 067	41 05 106	20 48 150	40 49 199	28 09 264	49 54 326
217	22 33 049	41 22 067	41 51 107	21 12 151	40 33 200	27 21 265	49 27 326
218	23 10 050	42 06 067	42 38 108	21 35 152	40 16 201	26 32 266	48 59 325
219	23 47 050	42 51 068	43 24 108	21 58 152	39 57 203	25 44 266	48 32 325
220	24 24 051	43 36 068	44 10 109	22 20 153	39 38 204	24 56 267	48 04 325
221	25 02 051	44 21 068	44 55 110	22 41 154	39 18 205	24 07 267	47 36 325
222	25 40 051	45 06 068	45 41 111	23 02 155	38 57 206	23 19 268	47 08 325
223	26 18 052	45 51 069	46 26 112	23 22 156	38 35 207	22 30 269	46 40 325
224	26 56 052	46 36 069	47 11 113	23 42 157	38 12 209	21 41 269	46 12 325
	DENEB	◆ ALTAIR	Rasalhague	ANTARES	◆ SPICA	Denebola	◆ Dubhe
225	27 34 052	19 03 093	47 55 114	24 00 158	37 49 210	42 31 256	45 44 324
226	28 13 053	19 51 093	48 40 115	24 18 159	37 24 211	41 44 256	45 15 324
227	28 51 053	20 40 094	49 23 116	24 35 160	36 59 212	40 57 257	44 47 324
228	29 30 053	21 28 095	50 07 117	24 52 161	36 33 213	40 09 258	44 19 324
229	30 09 054	22 16 095	50 50 118	25 07 162	36 06 214	39 22 259	43 50 324
230	30 48 054	23 05 096	51 33 119	25 22 163	35 39 215	38 34 259	43 22 324
231	31 27 054	23 53 096	52 15 120	25 36 164	35 10 216	37 46 260	42 53 324
232	32 07 054	24 41 097	52 57 121	25 50 165	34 41 217	36 58 261	42 25 324
233	32 46 055	25 29 098	53 38 122	26 02 165	34 12 218	36 10 261	41 57 324
234	33 26 055	26 17 098	54 19 123	26 14 166	33 41 219	35 22 262	41 28 324
235	34 06 055	27 05 099	54 59 125	26 25 167	33 10 220	34 34 263	41 00 324
236	34 46 056	27 53 100	55 39 126	26 35 168	32 38 221	33 46 263	40 31 324
237	35 26 056	28 41 100	56 18 127	26 45 169	32 06 222	32 58 264	40 03 324
238	36 06 056	29 29 101	56 56 129	26 53 170	31 33 223	32 09 265	39 34 324
239	36 46 056	30 16 102	57 34 130	27 01 171	31 00 224	31 21 265	39 06 324
	◆ DENEB	ALTAIR	Nunki	◆ ANTARES	ARCTURUS	◆ Alkaid	Kochab
240	37 27 057	31 04 102	15 08 140	27 08 172	61 38 240	62 40 309	50 59 353
241	38 07 057	31 51 103	15 39 141	27 14 173	60 56 242	62 02 309	50 52 352
242	38 48 057	32 38 104	16 10 141	27 19 174	60 13 243	61 25 309	50 46 352
243	39 29 057	33 26 104	16 40 142	27 23 175	59 29 244	60 47 308	50 38 351
244	40 10 058	34 12 105	17 10 143	27 27 176	58 46 245	60 08 308	50 31 351
245	40 51 058	34 59 106	17 39 144	27 29 177	58 01 246	59 30 308	50 23 351
246	41 32 058	35 46 107	18 07 144	27 31 178	57 17 248	58 52 307	50 15 350
247	42 13 058	36 32 107	18 35 145	27 32 179	56 32 249	58 13 307	50 07 350
248	42 54 058	37 18 108	19 03 146	27 32 180	55 46 250	57 34 307	49 58 349
249	43 36 059	38 04 109	19 29 147	27 31 181	55 01 251	56 55 307	49 49 349
250	44 17 059	38 50 110	19 56 148	27 30 182	54 15 252	56 17 307	49 40 349
251	44 59 059	39 36 111	20 21 149	27 27 183	53 28 252	55 38 307	49 30 348
252	45 40 059	40 21 111	20 46 149	27 24 184	52 42 253	54 59 306	49 20 348
253	46 22 059	41 06 112	21 11 150	27 20 185	51 55 254	54 20 306	49 10 348
254	47 04 059	41 51 113	21 34 151	27 15 186	51 09 255	53 41 306	49 00 347
	◆ DENEB	ALTAIR	Nunki	◆ ANTARES	ARCTURUS	◆ Alkaid	Kochab
255	47 45 059	42 35 114	21 58 152	27 09 187	50 22 256	53 01 306	48 49 347
256	48 27 060	43 19 115	22 20 153	27 02 188	49 34 257	52 22 306	48 38 347
257	49 09 060	44 03 116	22 42 154	26 54 189	48 47 258	51 43 306	48 27 347
258	49 51 060	44 47 117	23 03 155	26 46 190	48 00 258	51 04 306	48 16 346
259	50 33 060	45 30 118	23 23 156	26 37 191	47 12 259	50 25 306	48 04 346
260	51 15 060	46 13 119	23 43 156	26 27 192	46 24 260	49 46 306	47 52 346
261	51 57 060	46 55 120	24 02 157	26 16 193	45 37 261	49 06 306	47 40 345
262	52 39 060	47 37 121	24 20 158	26 04 194	44 49 261	48 27 306	47 27 345
263	53 21 060	48 18 122	24 38 159	25 52 195	44 01 262	47 48 306	47 15 345
264	54 04 060	48 59 123	24 55 160	25 39 196	43 12 263	47 09 306	47 02 345
265	54 46 060	49 40 124	25 11 161	25 25 197	42 24 263	46 30 306	46 49 344
266	55 28 060	50 20 125	25 26 162	25 10 198	41 36 264	45 51 307	46 36 344
267	56 10 060	50 59 126	25 41 163	24 54 199	40 48 265	45 12 307	46 23 344
268	56 52 060	51 38 128	25 54 164	24 38 200	39 59 265	44 33 307	46 09 344
269	57 34 060	52 16 129	26 07 165	24 21 201	39 11 266	43 54 307	45 55 343

LHA ♈	Hc Zn	Hc Zn	Hc Zn	Hc Zn	Hc Zn	Hc Zn	Hc Zn
	◆ DENEB	ALTAIR	Nunki	◆ ANTARES	ARCTURUS	◆ Alkaid	Kochab
270	58 17 060	52 54 130	26 20 166	24 03 202	38 23 267	43 15 307	45 41 343
271	58 59 060	53 30 131	26 31 167	23 45 203	37 34 267	42 37 307	45 27 343
272	59 41 060	54 07 133	26 42 168	23 25 204	36 46 268	41 58 307	45 13 343
273	60 23 060	54 42 134	26 51 169	23 05 205	35 57 268	41 19 307	44 59 343
274	61 05 060	55 16 135	27 00 170	22 45 206	35 09 269	40 41 308	44 44 342
275	61 47 060	55 50 137	27 08 171	22 24 206	34 20 270	40 03 308	44 29 342
276	62 29 059	56 23 138	27 16 172	22 02 207	33 31 270	39 24 308	44 15 342
277	63 10 059	56 55 140	27 22 173	21 39 208	32 43 271	38 46 308	44 00 342
278	63 52 059	57 25 141	27 28 174	21 16 209	31 54 271	38 08 308	43 44 342
279	64 34 059	57 55 143	27 32 175	20 52 210	31 06 272	37 30 309	43 29 342
280	65 15 058	58 24 145	27 36 176	20 27 211	30 17 273	36 52 309	43 14 342
281	65 56 058	58 51 146	27 39 177	20 02 212	29 29 273	36 14 309	42 59 341
282	66 37 058	59 18 148	27 42 178	19 36 212	28 40 274	35 36 309	42 43 341
283	67 18 057	59 43 150	27 43 179	19 10 213	27 52 274	34 59 309	42 27 341
284	67 59 057	60 06 152	27 43 180	18 43 214	27 04 275	34 21 310	42 12 341
	Alpheratz	◆ Enif	ALTAIR	◆ Rasalhague	ARCTURUS	Alkaid	◆ Kochab
285	26 14 072	44 29 114	60 29 153	59 50 224	26 15 275	33 44 310	41 56 341
286	27 00 072	45 13 115	60 50 155	59 15 226	25 27 276	33 07 310	41 40 341
287	27 46 073	45 57 116	61 09 157	58 40 227	24 39 276	32 30 310	41 24 341
288	28 32 073	46 40 117	61 27 159	58 04 229	23 50 277	31 53 311	41 08 341
289	29 19 074	47 23 118	61 44 161	57 27 230	23 02 278	31 16 311	40 52 341
290	30 05 074	48 06 119	61 58 163	56 49 232	22 14 278	30 39 311	40 36 341
291	30 52 074	48 48 120	62 12 165	56 11 233	21 26 279	30 03 311	40 20 340
292	31 39 075	49 30 121	62 23 167	55 32 234	20 38 279	29 27 312	40 03 340
293	32 26 075	50 11 123	62 33 169	54 52 236	19 50 280	28 50 312	39 47 340
294	33 13 076	50 51 124	62 41 172	54 11 237	19 03 280	28 14 312	39 31 340
295	34 00 076	51 32 125	62 47 174	53 31 238	18 15 281	27 39 313	39 14 340
296	34 47 077	52 11 126	62 51 176	52 49 239	17 27 281	27 03 313	38 58 340
297	35 35 077	52 50 127	62 54 178	52 07 240	16 40 282	26 27 313	38 42 340
298	36 22 078	53 28 128	62 55 180	51 25 241	15 52 282	25 52 313	38 25 340
299	37 09 078	54 06 130	62 53 182	50 42 242	15 05 283	25 17 314	38 09 340
	◆ Mirfak	Alpheratz	◆ FOMALHAUT	ALTAIR	Rasalhague	◆ Alphecca	Kochab
300	15 04 038	37 57 079	12 11 141	62 50 185	49 59 243	33 46 280	37 52 340
301	15 35 039	38 45 079	12 42 142	62 46 187	49 15 244	32 59 281	37 36 340
302	16 05 039	39 32 080	13 11 143	62 39 189	48 31 245	32 11 281	37 19 340
303	16 36 040	40 20 080	13 40 144	62 31 191	47 47 246	31 23 282	37 03 340
304	17 07 040	41 08 080	14 09 144	62 20 193	47 02 247	30 36 282	36 47 340
305	17 38 040	41 56 081	14 37 145	62 09 195	46 18 248	29 49 283	36 30 340
306	18 10 041	42 44 081	15 05 146	61 55 197	45 32 249	29 01 283	36 14 340
307	18 42 041	43 32 082	15 32 147	61 40 199	44 47 250	28 14 284	35 57 340
308	19 14 042	44 20 082	15 58 147	61 23 201	44 01 251	27 27 284	35 41 340
309	19 46 042	45 08 083	16 24 148	61 05 203	43 15 252	26 40 285	35 25 340
310	20 19 042	45 56 083	16 49 149	60 45 205	42 29 252	25 53 285	35 09 340
311	20 52 043	46 44 084	17 14 150	60 23 207	41 43 253	25 07 286	34 52 340
312	21 25 043	47 33 084	17 38 151	60 01 209	40 56 254	24 20 286	34 36 341
313	21 58 043	48 21 085	18 02 151	59 37 211	40 09 255	23 33 287	34 20 341
314	22 31 044	49 09 085	18 25 152	59 11 212	39 22 256	22 47 287	34 04 341
	◆ Mirfak	Hamal	Diphda	◆ FOMALHAUT	ALTAIR	◆ VEGA	Kochab
315	23 05 044	23 40 077	14 25 125	18 47 153	58 45 214	61 44 287	33 48 341
316	23 39 044	24 28 078	15 04 126	19 09 154	58 17 216	60 57 287	33 32 341
317	24 13 045	25 15 078	15 43 127	19 30 155	57 48 217	60 11 287	33 16 341
318	24 47 045	26 03 079	16 22 128	19 50 156	57 18 219	59 24 287	33 00 341
319	25 22 045	26 50 079	17 00 128	20 10 156	56 47 221	58 38 287	32 44 341
320	25 56 046	27 38 080	17 38 129	20 29 157	56 15 222	57 52 287	32 29 341
321	26 31 046	28 26 080	18 15 130	20 48 158	55 42 224	57 05 288	32 13 341
322	27 06 046	29 14 081	18 52 131	21 06 159	55 08 225	56 19 288	31 58 341
323	27 41 047	30 02 081	19 29 131	21 23 160	54 33 226	55 33 288	31 42 342
324	28 17 047	30 50 082	20 05 132	21 39 161	53 58 228	54 47 288	31 27 342
325	28 52 047	31 38 082	20 41 133	21 55 162	53 22 229	54 01 289	31 12 342
326	29 28 047	32 26 083	21 16 134	22 10 163	52 45 230	53 15 289	30 56 342
327	30 04 048	33 14 083	21 51 134	22 24 163	52 07 232	52 29 289	30 41 342
328	30 40 048	34 02 084	22 26 135	22 37 164	51 29 233	51 43 289	30 26 342
329	31 16 048	34 51 085	23 00 136	22 50 165	50 50 234	50 57 289	30 12 342
	◆ CAPELLA	Hamal	Diphda	◆ FOMALHAUT	ALTAIR	◆ VEGA	Kochab
330	13 38 042	35 39 085	23 33 137	23 02 166	50 10 235	50 11 290	29 57 342
331	14 11 043	36 27 086	24 06 138	23 13 167	49 30 236	49 26 290	29 42 343
332	14 44 043	37 16 086	24 38 139	23 24 168	48 49 237	48 40 290	29 28 343
333	15 18 044	38 04 087	25 10 140	23 33 169	48 08 238	47 55 291	29 14 343
334	15 51 044	38 53 087	25 41 140	23 42 170	47 27 239	47 09 291	28 59 343
335	16 25 045	39 41 088	26 12 141	23 50 171	46 45 240	46 24 291	28 45 343
336	16 59 045	40 30 088	26 42 142	23 57 172	46 02 241	45 39 291	28 31 343
337	17 34 045	41 18 089	27 11 143	24 04 173	45 19 242	44 54 292	28 17 344
338	18 08 046	42 07 090	27 40 144	24 10 174	44 36 243	44 09 292	28 04 344
339	18 43 046	42 55 090	28 08 145	24 15 175	43 53 244	43 24 292	27 50 344
340	19 18 047	43 44 091	28 36 146	24 19 176	43 09 245	42 39 293	27 37 344
341	19 54 047	44 32 091	29 02 147	24 22 177	42 25 246	41 54 293	27 23 344
342	20 29 047	45 21 092	29 29 148	24 25 177	41 40 247	41 09 293	27 10 344
343	21 05 048	46 09 093	29 54 149	24 26 178	40 55 248	40 25 293	26 57 345
344	21 41 048	46 58 093	30 19 150	24 27 179	40 10 249	39 40 294	26 45 345
	◆ CAPELLA	ALDEBARAN	Diphda	◆ FOMALHAUT	ALTAIR	◆ VEGA	Kochab
345	22 17 048	14 14 080	30 43 151	24 27 180	39 25 250	38 56 294	26 32 345
346	22 54 049	15 01 080	31 06 152	24 27 181	38 39 250	38 12 294	26 19 345
347	23 31 049	15 49 081	31 28 153	24 25 182	37 53 251	37 27 295	26 07 345
348	24 07 050	16 37 081	31 50 154	24 23 183	37 07 252	36 43 295	25 55 346
349	24 44 050	17 25 082	32 11 155	24 20 184	36 21 253	36 00 295	25 43 346
350	25 22 050	18 13 082	32 31 156	24 16 185	35 34 253	35 16 296	25 31 346
351	25 59 051	19 01 083	32 50 157	24 11 186	34 48 254	34 32 296	25 20 346
352	26 37 051	19 50 084	33 09 158	24 05 187	34 01 255	33 49 296	25 08 346
353	27 14 051	20 38 084	33 27 159	23 59 188	33 14 256	33 05 297	24 57 347
354	27 52 052	21 26 085	33 43 160	23 52 189	32 27 256	32 22 297	24 46 347
355	28 30 052	22 15 085	33 59 161	23 44 190	31 40 257	31 39 298	24 35 347
356	29 09 052	23 03 086	34 14 163	23 35 191	30 52 258	30 56 298	24 24 347
357	29 47 052	23 51 086	34 28 164	23 26 192	30 05 258	30 13 298	24 14 348
358	30 26 053	24 40 087	34 41 165	23 16 193	29 17 259	29 30 299	24 03 348
359	31 04 053	25 28 087	34 54 166	23 05 194	28 30 260	28 48 299	23 53 348

LHA ♈	Hc	Zn	Hc	Zn	Hc	Zn	Hc	Zn	Hc	Zn	Hc	Zn	Hc	Zn
	◆ CAPELLA		ALDEBARAN		Diphda		◆ FOMALHAUT		ALTAIR		◆ VEGA		Kochab	
0	31 07	053	26 15	088	36 03	167	23 51	195	27 51	261	27 36	300	22 44	348
1	31 47	053	27 04	088	36 14	168	23 38	196	27 03	262	26 53	300	22 35	349
2	32 26	053	27 53	089	36 24	169	23 25	196	26 14	262	26 11	301	22 25	349
3	33 05	054	28 42	089	36 32	170	23 10	197	25 25	263	25 29	301	22 16	349
4	33 45	054	29 31	090	36 40	172	22 55	198	24 37	264	24 46	301	22 06	349
5	34 25	054	30 20	090	36 47	173	22 39	199	23 48	264	24 05	302	21 57	350
6	35 05	054	31 09	091	36 53	174	22 23	200	22 59	265	23 23	302	21 49	350
7	35 45	055	31 59	092	36 57	175	22 06	201	22 10	265	22 41	302	21 40	350
8	36 25	055	32 48	092	37 01	176	21 48	202	21 21	266	22 00	303	21 32	350
9	37 05	055	33 37	093	37 04	178	21 29	203	20 32	267	21 19	303	21 24	351
10	37 46	055	34 26	093	37 05	179	21 10	204	19 43	267	20 38	304	21 16	351
11	38 26	056	35 15	094	37 06	180	20 50	204	18 54	268	19 57	304	21 08	351
12	39 07	056	36 04	095	37 05	181	20 29	205	18 04	268	19 16	304	21 01	351
13	39 47	056	36 53	095	37 04	182	20 08	206	17 15	269	18 36	305	20 53	352
14	40 28	056	37 42	096	37 01	183	19 46	207	16 26	269	17 55	305	20 46	352
	◆ CAPELLA		RIGEL		◆ Diphda		FOMALHAUT		Enif		◆ DENEB		Kochab	
15	41 09	056	16 02	112	36 58	185	19 23	208	39 07	253	40 58	303	20 39	352
16	41 50	056	16 47	113	36 53	186	19 00	209	38 20	253	40 17	303	20 33	352
17	42 31	057	17 32	114	36 48	187	18 36	209	37 32	254	39 36	303	20 27	353
18	43 12	057	18 17	114	36 41	188	18 12	210	36 45	255	38 55	303	20 20	353
19	43 53	057	19 02	115	36 34	189	17 47	211	35 58	256	38 14	304	20 15	353
20	44 35	057	19 46	116	36 25	191	17 21	212	35 10	256	37 33	304	20 09	354
21	45 16	057	20 30	117	36 16	192	16 55	213	34 22	257	36 52	304	20 04	354
22	45 57	057	21 14	117	36 05	193	16 28	213	33 34	258	36 12	304	19 58	354
23	46 39	057	21 57	118	35 54	194	16 01	214	32 46	258	35 31	305	19 53	354
24	47 20	058	22 41	119	35 42	195	15 33	215	31 58	259	34 51	305	19 49	355
25	48 02	058	23 24	119	35 28	196	15 04	216	31 09	260	34 10	305	19 44	355
26	48 43	058	24 06	120	35 14	197	14 35	216	30 21	260	33 30	305	19 40	355
27	49 25	058	24 48	121	34 59	199	14 06	217	29 32	261	32 50	306	19 36	355
28	50 06	058	25 30	122	34 43	200	13 36	218	28 44	262	32 10	306	19 32	356
29	50 48	058	26 12	123	34 26	201	13 06	219	27 55	262	31 30	306	19 29	356
	◆ CAPELLA		BETELGEUSE		RIGEL		◆ Diphda		Alpheratz		◆ DENEB		Kochab	
30	51 30	058	29 30	102	26 53	123	34 08	202	65 54	264	30 51	306	19 26	356
31	52 11	058	30 18	103	27 34	124	33 49	203	65 05	265	30 11	307	19 23	357
32	52 53	058	31 06	104	28 15	125	33 29	204	64 16	265	29 32	307	19 20	357
33	53 35	058	31 53	104	28 55	126	33 09	205	63 27	266	28 53	307	19 17	357
34	54 16	058	32 41	105	29 34	127	32 48	206	62 38	267	28 14	308	19 15	357
35	54 58	058	33 28	106	30 14	128	32 26	207	61 49	267	27 35	308	19 13	358
36	55 40	058	34 15	107	30 52	128	32 03	208	61 00	268	26 56	308	19 11	358
37	56 21	058	35 02	107	31 31	129	31 39	209	60 11	269	26 18	308	19 10	358
38	57 03	058	35 49	108	32 08	130	31 15	210	59 21	269	25 39	309	19 08	359
39	57 44	058	36 36	109	32 46	131	30 50	211	58 32	270	25 01	309	19 07	359
40	58 26	057	37 22	110	33 22	132	30 24	212	57 43	270	24 23	309	19 07	359
41	59 07	057	38 08	110	33 59	133	29 57	213	56 54	271	23 45	310	19 06	000
42	59 48	057	38 54	111	34 34	134	29 30	214	56 05	271	23 07	310	19 06	000
43	60 30	057	39 40	112	35 09	135	29 02	215	55 16	272	22 30	311	19 06	000
44	61 11	057	40 25	113	35 44	136	28 33	216	54 27	273	21 53	311	19 06	000
	◆ Dubhe		POLLUX		SIRIUS		◆ RIGEL		Diphda		◆ Alpheratz		Schedar	
45	17 41	025	29 52	075	15 34	124	36 18	137	28 04	217	53 38	273	58 11	324
46	18 02	026	30 40	075	16 14	125	36 51	138	27 34	218	52 48	274	57 41	323
47	18 23	026	31 27	076	16 55	125	37 24	139	27 04	219	51 59	274	57 12	323
48	18 45	026	32 15	076	17 34	126	37 56	140	26 33	220	51 10	275	56 42	322
49	19 07	027	33 03	077	18 14	127	38 27	141	26 01	221	50 21	275	56 11	322
50	19 29	027	33 51	077	18 53	128	38 57	142	25 29	221	49 33	276	55 41	321
51	19 51	027	34 39	078	19 32	128	39 27	143	24 56	222	48 44	276	55 10	321
52	20 14	027	35 27	078	20 10	129	39 56	144	24 23	223	47 55	276	54 39	321
53	20 37	028	36 15	079	20 48	130	40 24	146	23 49	224	47 06	277	54 08	320
54	21 00	028	37 03	079	21 25	131	40 52	147	23 14	225	46 17	277	53 37	320
55	21 23	028	37 51	080	22 02	132	41 18	148	22 39	226	45 28	278	53 05	320
56	21 46	029	38 40	080	22 39	132	41 44	149	22 04	226	44 40	278	52 33	320
57	22 10	029	39 28	080	23 15	133	42 09	150	21 28	227	43 51	279	52 02	319
58	22 34	029	40 17	081	23 51	134	42 33	151	20 52	228	43 03	279	51 30	319
59	22 58	030	41 05	081	24 26	135	42 56	153	20 15	229	42 14	280	50 57	319
	◆ Dubhe		POLLUX		PROCYON		◆ SIRIUS		RIGEL		◆ Hamal		Schedar	
60	23 22	030	41 54	082	31 18	107	25 01	136	43 18	154	63 09	252	50 25	319
61	23 47	030	42 43	082	32 05	108	25 35	136	43 39	155	62 22	253	49 53	319
62	24 11	030	43 31	083	32 51	109	26 08	137	43 59	157	61 35	254	49 20	319
63	24 36	031	44 20	083	33 38	109	26 41	138	44 18	158	60 47	255	48 48	318
64	25 01	031	45 09	084	34 24	110	27 14	139	44 36	159	60 00	256	48 15	318
65	25 27	031	45 58	084	35 10	111	27 46	140	44 53	161	59 12	257	47 42	318
66	25 52	031	46 47	085	35 56	112	28 17	141	45 09	162	58 24	258	47 09	318
67	26 18	032	47 36	085	36 41	113	28 48	142	45 24	163	57 36	259	46 36	318
68	26 43	032	48 25	086	37 27	113	29 18	143	45 37	165	56 47	260	46 04	318
69	27 09	032	49 14	086	38 12	114	29 47	144	45 50	166	55 59	260	45 31	318
70	27 35	032	50 03	087	38 56	115	30 16	145	46 01	167	55 10	261	44 58	318
71	28 02	032	50 52	087	39 41	116	30 44	146	46 11	169	54 22	262	44 25	318
72	28 28	033	51 41	088	40 25	117	31 11	147	46 20	170	53 33	263	43 52	318
73	28 55	033	52 30	088	41 08	118	31 38	148	46 28	172	52 44	263	43 19	318
74	29 21	033	53 19	089	41 52	119	32 04	149	46 35	173	51 55	264	42 46	318
	◆ Dubhe		POLLUX		PROCYON		◆ SIRIUS		RIGEL		◆ Hamal		Mirfak	
75	29 48	033	54 08	089	42 35	120	32 29	150	46 40	174	51 06	265	67 13	318
76	30 15	033	54 58	090	43 17	121	32 54	151	46 44	176	50 17	265	66 40	317
77	30 42	033	55 47	091	43 59	122	33 18	152	46 47	177	49 28	266	66 07	317
78	31 09	034	56 36	091	44 41	123	33 40	153	46 48	179	48 39	267	65 33	316
79	31 37	034	57 25	092	45 22	124	34 03	154	46 49	180	47 50	267	64 58	315
80	32 04	034	58 14	092	46 03	125	34 24	155	46 48	182	47 01	268	64 23	314
81	32 32	034	59 03	093	46 43	126	34 44	156	46 46	183	46 12	269	63 48	314
82	32 59	034	59 52	094	47 23	127	35 04	157	46 43	185	45 23	269	63 12	313
83	33 27	034	60 41	094	48 02	128	35 23	158	46 38	186	44 34	270	62 36	313
84	33 55	035	61 30	095	48 40	129	35 40	159	46 32	187	43 45	270	62 00	312
85	34 23	035	62 19	096	49 18	130	35 57	160	46 25	189	42 56	271	61 24	312
86	34 50	035	63 08	097	49 56	131	36 13	162	46 17	190	42 06	271	60 47	311
87	35 19	035	63 57	097	50 32	133	36 28	163	46 08	192	41 17	272	60 10	311
88	35 47	035	64 45	098	51 08	134	36 42	164	45 57	193	40 28	272	59 33	311
89	36 15	035	65 34	099	51 43	135	36 56	165	45 45	195	39 39	273	58 55	310

LAT 35°N

LHA ♈	Hc	Zn	Hc	Zn	Hc	Zn	Hc	Zn	Hc	Zn	Hc	Zn	Hc	Zn
	◆ Dubhe		REGULUS		PROCYON		◆ SIRIUS		RIGEL		ALDEBARAN		◆ Mirfak	
90	36 43	035	29 24	096	52 17	136	37 08	166	45 32	196	63 49	230	58 18	310
91	37 11	035	30 13	097	52 51	138	37 19	167	45 18	197	63 10	232	57 40	310
92	37 40	035	31 02	097	53 23	139	37 29	169	45 03	199	62 31	234	57 02	310
93	38 08	035	31 50	098	53 55	141	37 39	170	44 47	200	61 51	235	56 24	309
94	38 36	035	32 39	099	54 25	142	37 47	171	44 30	201	61 10	237	55 46	309
95	39 05	035	33 28	099	54 55	144	37 54	172	44 11	203	60 29	238	55 08	309
96	39 33	035	34 16	100	55 24	145	38 00	173	43 52	204	59 47	239	54 30	309
97	40 02	035	35 04	101	55 51	147	38 05	175	43 31	205	59 05	240	53 52	309
98	40 30	035	35 53	101	56 18	148	38 10	176	43 10	206	58 22	242	53 13	309
99	40 59	035	36 41	102	56 43	150	38 13	177	42 48	208	57 38	243	52 35	308
100	41 27	035	37 29	103	57 07	152	38 15	178	42 24	209	56 54	244	51 56	308
101	41 56	035	38 17	103	57 30	153	38 16	179	42 00	210	56 10	245	51 18	308
102	42 24	035	39 04	104	57 51	155	38 16	181	41 35	211	55 25	246	50 39	308
103	42 52	035	39 52	105	58 11	157	38 14	182	41 09	213	54 40	247	50 00	308
104	43 21	035	40 39	106	58 30	159	38 12	183	40 42	214	53 54	248	49 22	308
	◆ Alkaid		REGULUS		Alphard		◆ SIRIUS		RIGEL		ALDEBARAN		◆ CAPELLA	
105	18 50	042	41 27	106	33 59	134	38 09	184	40 14	215	53 09	249	67 49	308
106	19 24	043	42 14	107	34 34	135	38 05	186	39 46	216	52 22	250	67 10	307
107	19 57	043	43 00	108	35 08	136	38 00	187	39 16	217	51 36	251	66 30	306
108	20 31	044	43 47	109	35 42	137	37 53	188	38 46	218	50 50	252	65 50	306
109	21 05	044	44 34	110	36 15	138	37 46	189	38 15	219	50 03	253	65 10	305
110	21 39	044	45 20	111	36 48	139	37 38	190	37 44	220	49 16	254	64 30	305
111	22 13	045	46 06	111	37 20	140	37 28	192	37 12	221	48 28	255	63 50	305
112	22 48	045	46 51	112	37 51	141	37 18	193	36 39	222	47 41	255	63 09	304
113	23 23	045	47 37	113	38 22	142	37 07	194	36 05	223	46 53	256	62 29	304
114	23 58	046	48 22	114	38 51	143	36 54	195	35 31	224	46 05	257	61 48	304
115	24 33	046	49 06	115	39 20	144	36 41	196	34 57	225	45 17	258	61 07	303
116	25 08	046	49 51	116	39 49	146	36 27	197	34 21	226	44 29	258	60 25	303
117	25 44	046	50 35	117	40 16	147	36 12	199	33 45	227	43 41	259	59 44	303
118	26 20	047	51 18	118	40 42	148	35 56	200	33 09	228	42 53	260	59 03	303
119	26 55	047	52 01	119	41 08	149	35 39	201	32 32	229	42 04	261	58 22	303
	◆ Alkaid		REGULUS		◆ Alphard		SIRIUS		RIGEL		ALDEBARAN		◆ CAPELLA	
120	27 31	047	52 44	120	41 33	150	35 21	202	31 54	230	41 16	261	57 40	302
121	28 08	048	53 26	121	41 57	151	35 02	203	31 16	231	40 27	262	56 59	302
122	28 44	048	54 08	123	42 20	153	34 42	204	30 38	232	39 39	263	56 17	302
123	29 21	048	54 49	124	42 42	154	34 22	205	29 59	233	38 50	263	55 35	302
124	29 57	048	55 29	125	43 03	155	34 00	206	29 20	234	38 01	264	54 54	302
125	30 34	049	56 09	126	43 23	156	33 38	207	28 40	234	37 12	265	54 12	302
126	31 11	049	56 49	128	43 43	158	33 15	208	28 00	235	36 23	265	53 30	302
127	31 48	049	57 27	129	44 01	159	32 52	209	27 19	236	35 34	266	52 49	302
128	32 26	049	58 05	130	44 18	160	32 27	210	26 38	237	34 45	266	52 07	302
129	33 03	050	58 42	132	44 34	162	32 02	211	25 57	238	33 56	267	51 25	302
130	33 40	050	59 18	133	44 49	163	31 36	212	25 15	239	33 07	268	50 44	302
131	34 18	050	59 53	135	45 02	164	31 09	213	24 33	239	32 18	268	50 02	302
132	34 56	050	60 28	136	45 15	166	30 41	214	23 50	240	31 29	269	49 21	302
133	35 34	051	61 01	138	45 26	167	30 13	215	23 08	241	30 40	269	48 39	302
134	36 12	051	61 33	140	45 37	169	29 44	216	22 25	242	29 50	270	47 57	302
	◆ Alkaid		ARCTURUS		SPICA		◆ Alphard		SIRIUS		BETELGEUSE		◆ CAPELLA	
135	36 50	051	19 32	080	12 03	113	45 46	170	29 15	217	39 39	249	47 16	302
136	37 28	051	20 20	080	12 48	114	45 54	171	28 45	218	38 54	249	46 34	303
137	38 06	051	21 09	081	13 32	114	46 01	173	28 14	219	38 08	250	45 53	303
138	38 45	051	21 57	081	14 17	115	46 06	174	27 43	220	37 22	250	45 12	303
139	39 23	052	22 46	082	15 02	116	46 11	176	27 11	221	36 35	251	44 30	303
140	40 02	052	23 35	083	15 46	116	46 14	177	26 38	222	35 49	252	43 49	303
141	40 40	052	24 23	083	16 30	117	46 16	178	26 05	223	35 02	253	43 08	303
142	41 19	052	25 12	084	17 13	118	46 17	180	25 31	224	34 15	253	42 27	303
143	41 58	052	26 01	084	17 57	118	46 16	181	24 57	224	33 28	254	41 46	304
144	42 37	052	26 50	085	18 40	119	46 14	183	24 23	225	32 40	255	41 05	304
145	43 15	052	27 39	085	19 22	120	46 11	184	23 47	226	31 53	256	40 24	304
146	43 54	052	28 28	086	20 05	121	46 07	186	23 12	227	31 05	256	39 43	304
147	44 33	053	29 17	086	20 47	121	46 02	187	22 36	228	30 17	257	39 03	304
148	45 12	053	30 06	087	21 29	122	45 55	188	21 59	229	29 29	258	38 22	304
149	45 51	053	30 55	087	22 10	123	45 47	190	21 22	229	28 41	258	37 42	305
	Alkaid		◆ ARCTURUS		SPICA		◆ Alphard		PROCYON		BETELGEUSE		◆ CAPELLA	
150	46 31	053	31 44	088	22 51	124	45 38	191	46 05	235	27 53	259	37 01	305
151	47 10	053	32 33	088	23 32	124	45 28	193	45 24	236	27 05	260	36 21	305
152	47 49	053	33 22	089	24 12	125	45 17	194	44 43	237	26 17	260	35 41	305
153	48 28	053	34 12	090	24 52	126	45 04	195	44 01	238	25 28	261	35 01	306
154	49 07	053	35 01	090	25 32	127	44 51	197	43 19	239	24 40	261	34 21	306
155	49 46	053	35 50	091	26 11	128	44 36	198	42 36	240	23 51	262	33 41	306
156	50 26	053	36 39	091	26 50	128	44 20	199	41 54	241	23 02	263	33 01	306
157	51 05	053	37 28	092	27 28	129	44 03	201	41 10	242	22 13	263	32 22	307
158	51 44	053	38 17	093	28 06	130	43 46	202	40 27	243	21 25	264	31 43	307
159	52 23	053	39 06	093	28 43	131	43 27	203	39 43	244	20 36	265	31 03	307
160	53 02	053	39 55	094	29 20	132	43 07	205	38 58	245	19 47	265	30 24	307
161	53 41	053	40 44	094	29 57	133	42 46	206	38 14	246	18 58	266	29 45	308
162	54 20	052	41 33	095	30 33	134	42 24	207	37 29	247	18 09	266	29 06	308
163	54 59	052	42 22	096	31 08	134	42 01	208	36 43	247	17 20	267	28 28	308
164	55 38	052	43 11	096	31 43	135	41 37	210	35 58	248	16 30	268	27 49	309
	◆ Dubhe		Alkaid		◆ ARCTURUS		SPICA		REGULUS		◆ PROCYON		CAPELLA	
165	63 19	001	56 16	052	44 00	097	32 17	136	64 11	210	35 12	249	27 11	309
166	63 20	000	56 55	052	44 49	098	32 51	137	63 46	212	34 26	250	26 33	309
167	63 19	359	57 34	052	45 37	098	33 24	138	63 19	214	33 40	251	25 55	310
168	63 18	358	58 12	051	46 26	099	33 56	139	62 51	215	32 53	251	25 17	310
169	63 16	357	58 50	051	47 15	100	34 28	140	62 22	217	32 07	252	24 39	310
170	63 13	356	59 28	051	48 03	100	34 59	141	61 52	219	31 20	253	24 02	311
171	63 09	355	60 06	050	48 51	101	35 29	142	61 20	221	30 33	253	23 25	311
172	63 04	354	60 44	050	49 39	102	35 59	143	60 47	223	29 46	254	22 47	311
173	62 59	353	61 22	050	50 27	103	36 28	144	60 14	224	28 58	255	22 11	312
174	62 52	352	61 59	049	51 15	104	36 56	145	59 39	226	28 11	256	21 34	312
175	62 45	351	62 36	049	52 03	104	37 23	147	59 03	227	27 23	256	20 57	312
176	62 37	350	63 13	048	52 50	105	37 50	148	58 27	229	26 35	257	20 21	313
177	62 27	349	63 50	048	53 38	106	38 16	149	57 49	230	25 48	258	19 45	313
178	62 18	348	64 26	047	54 25	107	38 41	150	57 11	232	24 59	258	19 09	313
179	62 07	347	65 02	047	55 12	108	39 05	151	56 32	233	24 11	259	18 34	314

LHA ♈	Hc	Zn	Hc	Zn	Hc	Zn	Hc	Zn	Hc	Zn	Hc	Zn	Hc	Zn
	◆ VEGA		Alphecca		ARCTURUS		◆ SPICA		REGULUS		◆ POLLUX		Dubhe	
180	14 48	053	43 35	085	55 58	109	39 29	152	55 53	234	36 20	281	61 55	346
181	15 28	053	44 24	085	56 45	110	39 51	153	55 13	235	35 32	282	61 43	345
182	16 07	054	45 13	086	57 31	111	40 13	155	54 32	237	34 44	282	61 30	344
183	16 47	054	46 02	086	58 17	112	40 33	156	53 50	238	33 56	283	61 17	343
184	17 27	054	46 51	087	59 02	113	40 53	157	53 09	239	33 08	283	61 02	343
185	18 07	055	47 40	087	59 47	114	41 11	158	52 26	240	32 20	284	60 47	342
186	18 47	055	48 29	088	60 32	115	41 29	160	51 43	241	31 33	284	60 31	341
187	19 27	056	49 18	089	61 16	116	41 46	161	51 00	242	30 45	284	60 15	340
188	20 08	056	50 08	089	62 00	118	42 02	162	50 16	243	29 58	285	59 58	339
189	20 49	056	50 57	090	62 43	119	42 16	163	49 32	244	29 10	285	59 40	339
190	21 30	057	51 46	090	63 26	120	42 30	165	48 48	245	28 23	286	59 22	338
191	22 11	057	52 35	091	64 08	122	42 42	166	48 03	246	27 36	286	59 03	337
192	22 53	058	53 24	091	64 49	123	42 54	167	47 18	247	26 48	287	58 44	337
193	23 34	058	54 13	092	65 30	125	43 04	169	46 32	248	26 01	287	58 24	336
194	24 16	058	55 02	093	66 10	127	43 13	170	45 47	249	25 15	288	58 04	335
	◆ Kochab		VEGA		Rasalhague		◆ ANTARES		SPICA		◆ REGULUS		Dubhe	
195	48 38	011	24 58	059	24 21	091	10 57	134	43 21	171	45 01	250	57 43	335
196	48 47	011	25 40	059	25 10	092	11 32	134	43 28	173	44 14	251	57 22	334
197	48 56	010	26 23	060	25 59	093	12 07	135	43 34	174	43 28	252	57 00	333
198	49 05	010	27 05	060	26 49	093	12 42	136	43 39	175	42 41	252	56 38	333
199	49 13	010	27 48	060	27 38	094	13 16	136	43 42	177	41 54	253	56 15	332
200	49 21	009	28 30	061	28 27	094	13 50	137	43 44	178	41 07	254	55 52	332
201	49 29	009	29 13	061	29 16	095	14 23	138	43 46	179	40 20	255	55 29	331
202	49 37	009	29 56	061	30 05	096	14 56	139	43 46	181	39 32	255	55 05	331
203	49 44	008	30 40	062	30 53	096	15 28	139	43 44	182	38 45	256	54 41	331
204	49 51	008	31 23	062	31 42	097	16 00	140	43 42	183	37 57	257	54 17	330
205	49 57	007	32 06	062	32 31	098	16 31	141	43 39	185	37 09	258	53 52	330
206	50 03	007	32 50	063	33 20	098	17 02	142	43 34	186	36 21	258	53 27	329
207	50 09	007	33 34	063	34 08	099	17 32	142	43 28	187	35 33	259	53 02	329
208	50 15	006	34 18	063	34 57	100	18 02	143	43 21	189	34 44	260	52 36	329
209	50 20	006	35 02	064	35 45	100	18 31	144	43 13	190	33 56	260	52 11	328
	◆ Kochab		VEGA		Rasalhague		◆ ANTARES		SPICA		◆ REGULUS		Dubhe	
210	50 25	005	35 46	064	36 34	101	19 00	145	43 04	191	33 07	261	51 45	328
211	50 29	005	36 30	064	37 22	102	19 28	146	42 54	193	32 19	262	51 18	328
212	50 33	005	37 14	065	38 10	102	19 55	146	42 42	194	31 30	262	50 52	327
213	50 37	004	37 59	065	38 58	103	20 22	147	42 30	195	30 41	263	50 25	327
214	50 40	004	38 43	065	39 46	104	20 49	148	42 16	197	29 53	264	49 59	327
215	50 43	003	39 28	066	40 33	104	21 14	149	42 01	198	29 04	264	49 32	327
216	50 46	003	40 13	066	41 21	105	21 40	150	41 46	199	28 15	265	49 05	326
217	50 48	002	40 58	066	42 08	106	22 04	151	41 29	200	27 26	265	48 37	326
218	50 50	002	41 43	066	42 55	107	22 28	151	41 11	202	26 37	266	48 10	326
219	50 52	002	42 28	067	43 42	108	22 51	152	40 53	203	25 48	267	47 42	326
220	50 53	001	43 13	067	44 29	108	23 14	153	40 33	204	24 59	267	47 15	326
221	50 54	001	43 58	067	45 15	109	23 35	154	40 12	205	24 10	268	46 47	325
222	50 54	000	44 44	067	46 02	110	23 57	155	39 51	207	23 20	268	46 19	325
223	50 54	000	45 29	068	46 48	111	24 17	156	39 28	208	22 31	269	45 51	325
224	50 54	359	46 14	068	47 34	112	24 37	157	39 05	209	21 42	270	45 23	325
	DENEB		VEGA		◆ ALTAIR		ANTARES		◆ SPICA		Denebola		◆ Dubhe	
225	26 57	052	47 00	068	19 05	092	24 56	158	38 41	210	42 45	257	44 55	325
226	27 36	052	47 46	068	19 55	093	25 14	159	38 16	211	41 57	257	44 27	325
227	28 15	052	48 32	069	20 44	094	25 31	160	37 50	212	41 09	258	43 58	325
228	28 54	053	49 17	069	21 33	094	25 48	161	37 23	213	40 21	259	43 30	325
229	29 33	053	50 03	069	22 22	095	26 04	161	36 56	215	39 33	260	43 02	325
230	30 12	053	50 49	069	23 11	095	26 19	162	36 28	216	38 45	260	42 33	325
231	30 52	054	51 35	070	24 00	096	26 34	163	35 59	217	37 56	261	42 05	325
232	31 32	054	52 21	070	24 48	097	26 48	164	35 29	218	37 08	262	41 36	325
233	32 11	054	53 08	070	25 37	097	27 00	165	34 59	219	36 19	262	41 08	325
234	32 51	054	53 54	070	26 26	098	27 12	166	34 27	220	35 30	263	40 39	325
235	33 31	055	54 40	070	27 15	099	27 24	167	33 56	221	34 41	263	40 11	325
236	34 11	055	55 26	071	28 03	099	27 34	168	33 23	222	33 52	264	39 42	325
237	34 52	055	56 13	071	28 52	100	27 44	169	32 50	223	33 04	265	39 14	325
238	35 32	055	56 59	071	29 40	100	27 52	170	32 17	224	32 15	265	38 45	325
239	36 13	056	57 46	071	30 28	101	28 00	171	31 42	225	31 26	266	38 17	325
	◆ DENEB		ALTAIR		Nunki		◆ ANTARES		SPICA		ARCTURUS		◆ Alkaid	
240	36 53	056	31 16	102	15 54	140	28 07	172	31 08	226	62 07	242	62 02	311
241	37 34	056	32 04	102	16 26	140	28 13	173	30 32	226	61 24	243	61 24	310
242	38 15	056	32 52	103	16 57	141	28 19	174	29 56	227	60 39	245	60 47	310
243	38 56	057	33 40	104	17 27	142	28 23	175	29 20	228	59 55	246	60 09	310
244	39 37	057	34 28	105	17 58	143	28 27	176	28 43	229	59 10	247	59 31	309
245	40 18	057	35 15	105	18 27	143	28 29	177	28 06	230	58 25	248	58 53	309
246	41 00	057	36 03	106	18 56	144	28 31	178	27 28	231	57 39	249	58 15	309
247	41 41	057	36 50	107	19 25	145	28 32	179	26 50	232	56 53	250	57 36	308
248	42 22	058	37 37	108	19 52	146	28 32	180	26 11	232	56 06	251	56 58	308
249	43 04	058	38 24	108	20 20	147	28 31	181	25 32	233	55 20	252	56 19	308
250	43 46	058	39 10	109	20 46	148	28 30	182	24 52	234	54 33	253	55 40	308
251	44 27	058	39 56	110	21 12	148	28 27	183	24 12	235	53 46	254	55 01	308
252	45 09	058	40 43	111	21 38	149	28 24	184	23 32	236	52 59	255	54 22	308
253	45 51	058	41 28	112	22 03	150	28 19	186	22 51	236	52 11	255	53 44	307
254	46 33	058	42 14	112	22 27	151	28 14	187	22 10	237	51 23	256	53 05	307
	◆ DENEB		ALTAIR		Nunki		◆ ANTARES		ARCTURUS		◆ Alkaid		Kochab	
255	47 14	059	42 59	113	22 50	152	28 08	188	50 36	257	52 25	307	47 51	347
256	47 56	059	43 44	114	23 13	153	28 01	189	49 48	258	51 46	307	47 40	347
257	48 38	059	44 29	115	23 36	154	27 54	190	49 00	259	51 07	307	47 29	347
258	49 20	059	45 13	116	23 57	154	27 45	191	48 11	259	50 28	307	47 17	346
259	50 03	059	45 57	117	24 18	155	27 36	192	47 23	260	49 49	307	47 06	346
260	50 45	059	46 41	118	24 38	156	27 25	193	46 34	261	49 10	307	46 54	346
261	51 27	059	47 24	119	24 57	157	27 14	194	45 46	262	48 31	307	46 42	346
262	52 09	059	48 07	120	25 16	158	27 02	194	44 57	262	47 51	307	46 29	345
263	52 51	059	48 50	121	25 34	159	26 50	195	44 08	263	47 12	307	46 17	345
264	53 33	059	49 32	122	25 51	160	26 36	196	43 20	264	46 33	307	46 04	345
265	54 15	059	50 13	123	26 08	161	26 22	197	42 31	264	45 54	307	45 51	345
266	54 58	059	50 54	124	26 23	162	26 07	198	41 42	265	45 15	307	45 38	344
267	55 40	059	51 34	125	26 38	163	25 51	199	40 53	266	44 36	307	45 25	344
268	56 22	059	52 14	127	26 52	164	25 34	200	40 04	266	43 57	308	45 11	344
269	57 04	059	52 53	128	27 05	165	25 17	201	39 15	267	43 18	308	44 58	344

LAT 35°N

LHA ♈	Hc	Zn	Hc	Zn	Hc	Zn	Hc	Zn	Hc	Zn	Hc	Zn	Hc	Zn
	◆ DENEB		ALTAIR		◆ Nunki		ANTARES		ARCTURUS		◆ Alkaid		Kochab	
270	57 46	059	53 32	129	27 18	166	24 59	202	38 26	267	42 39	308	44 44	344
271	58 28	059	54 10	130	27 29	167	24 40	203	37 37	268	42 00	308	44 30	343
272	59 10	059	54 47	132	27 40	168	24 20	204	36 47	269	41 21	308	44 16	343
273	59 52	058	55 23	133	27 50	169	24 00	205	35 58	269	40 43	308	44 01	343
274	60 34	058	55 59	134	27 59	170	23 39	206	35 09	270	40 04	308	43 47	343
275	61 16	058	56 33	136	28 08	171	23 17	207	34 20	270	39 26	308	43 32	343
276	61 57	058	57 07	137	28 15	172	22 55	208	33 31	271	38 47	309	43 17	342
277	62 39	058	57 40	139	28 22	173	22 32	208	32 42	271	38 09	309	43 02	342
278	63 20	057	58 12	140	28 27	174	22 08	209	31 53	272	37 30	309	42 47	342
279	64 02	057	58 43	142	28 32	175	21 44	210	31 03	273	36 52	309	42 32	342
280	64 43	057	59 12	144	28 36	176	21 19	211	30 14	273	36 14	309	42 17	342
281	65 24	056	59 41	145	28 39	177	20 53	212	29 25	274	35 36	309	42 02	342
282	66 04	056	60 08	147	28 42	178	20 27	213	28 36	274	34 58	310	41 46	342
283	66 45	055	60 34	149	28 43	179	20 00	214	27 47	275	34 21	310	41 31	341
284	67 25	055	60 59	151	28 43	180	19 33	214	26 58	275	33 43	310	41 15	341
	◆ Alpheratz		Enif		ALTAIR		◆ ANTARES		ARCTURUS		◆ Alkaid		Kochab	
285	25 55	071	44 54	114	61 22	153	19 05	215	26 09	276	33 05	310	40 59	341
286	26 41	072	45 39	114	61 44	155	18 36	216	25 21	276	32 28	311	40 43	341
287	27 28	072	46 23	115	62 04	157	18 07	217	24 32	277	31 51	311	40 27	341
288	28 15	073	47 08	116	62 23	159	17 37	218	23 43	277	31 14	311	40 11	341
289	29 02	073	47 51	117	62 40	161	17 07	218	22 54	278	30 37	311	39 55	341
290	29 49	073	48 35	118	62 56	163	16 36	219	22 06	278	30 00	312	39 39	341
291	30 36	074	49 18	119	63 10	165	16 05	220	21 17	279	29 23	312	39 23	341
292	31 23	074	50 00	120	63 22	167	15 33	221	20 29	280	28 46	312	39 07	341
293	32 11	075	50 43	122	63 32	169	15 01	221	19 40	280	28 10	312	38 51	341
294	32 58	075	51 24	123	63 40	171	14 28	222	18 52	281	27 34	313	38 34	341
295	33 46	076	52 05	124	63 47	174	13 55	223	18 03	281	26 58	313	38 18	341
296	34 33	076	52 46	125	63 51	176	13 22	223	17 15	282	26 22	313	38 02	341
297	35 21	077	53 26	126	63 54	178	12 48	224	16 27	282	25 46	314	37 45	341
298	36 09	077	54 05	127	63 55	180	12 13	225	15 39	283	25 11	314	37 29	340
299	36 57	077	54 44	129	63 53	183	11 38	226	14 51	283	24 35	314	37 12	340
	◆ Mirfak		Alpheratz		◆ FOMALHAUT		ALTAIR		Rasalhague		◆ Alphecca		Kochab	
300	14 17	038	37 45	078	12 58	141	63 50	185	50 25	244	33 35	281	36 56	340
301	14 48	039	38 33	078	13 29	142	63 45	187	49 41	245	32 47	282	36 39	340
302	15 19	039	39 21	079	13 59	143	63 38	189	48 56	246	31 59	282	36 23	340
303	15 50	039	40 09	079	14 28	143	63 29	191	48 11	247	31 11	283	36 07	340
304	16 21	040	40 58	080	14 58	144	63 19	194	47 25	248	30 23	283	35 50	340
305	16 53	040	41 46	080	15 26	145	63 06	196	46 39	249	29 35	283	35 34	340
306	17 25	041	42 34	081	15 54	146	62 52	198	45 53	250	28 47	284	35 17	341
307	17 57	041	43 23	081	16 22	146	62 36	200	45 07	251	28 00	284	35 01	341
308	18 29	041	44 11	081	16 49	147	62 19	202	44 20	252	27 12	285	34 45	341
309	19 02	042	45 00	082	17 15	148	62 00	204	43 34	253	26 25	285	34 28	341
310	19 34	042	45 49	082	17 41	149	61 39	206	42 47	253	25 37	286	34 12	341
311	20 07	042	46 37	083	18 06	150	61 17	208	41 59	254	24 50	286	33 56	341
312	20 41	043	47 26	083	18 30	150	60 53	210	41 12	255	24 03	287	33 39	341
313	21 14	043	48 15	084	18 54	151	60 28	212	40 25	256	23 16	287	33 23	341
314	21 48	043	49 04	084	19 18	152	60 02	213	39 37	256	22 29	288	33 07	341
	◆ Mirfak		Hamal		Diphda		◆ FOMALHAUT		ALTAIR		◆ VEGA		Kochab	
315	22 22	044	23 27	077	14 59	125	19 41	153	59 34	215	61 26	288	32 51	341
316	22 56	044	24 15	077	15 39	126	20 03	154	59 05	217	60 39	288	32 35	341
317	23 30	044	25 03	078	16 19	127	20 24	155	58 35	218	59 53	289	32 19	341
318	24 05	045	25 51	078	16 58	127	20 45	155	58 04	220	59 06	289	32 03	341
319	24 39	045	26 39	079	17 37	128	21 05	156	57 32	222	58 19	289	31 48	341
320	25 14	045	27 27	079	18 16	129	21 25	157	56 59	223	57 33	289	31 32	341
321	25 49	046	28 16	080	18 54	130	21 43	158	56 25	225	56 46	289	31 16	342
322	26 25	046	29 04	080	19 31	130	22 02	159	55 50	226	56 00	289	31 01	342
323	27 00	046	29 52	081	20 09	131	22 19	160	55 14	227	55 14	289	30 45	342
324	27 36	047	30 41	081	20 45	132	22 36	161	54 38	229	54 27	290	30 30	342
325	28 11	047	31 30	082	21 22	133	22 52	162	54 01	230	53 41	290	30 15	342
326	28 47	047	32 18	082	21 58	133	23 07	162	53 23	231	52 55	290	29 59	342
327	29 23	047	33 07	083	22 33	134	23 21	163	52 44	233	52 09	290	29 44	342
328	30 00	048	33 56	083	23 08	135	23 35	164	52 04	234	51 23	290	29 29	342
329	30 36	048	34 45	084	23 43	136	23 48	165	51 25	235	50 37	291	29 14	342
	◆ CAPELLA		Hamal		Diphda		◆ FOMALHAUT		ALTAIR		◆ VEGA		Kochab	
330	12 54	042	35 34	084	24 17	137	24 00	166	50 44	236	49 51	291	29 00	343
331	13 27	043	36 22	085	24 50	138	24 12	167	50 03	237	49 05	291	28 45	343
332	14 01	043	37 11	085	25 23	138	24 22	168	49 21	238	48 19	291	28 31	343
333	14 34	043	38 00	086	25 55	139	24 32	169	48 39	239	47 33	292	28 16	343
334	15 08	044	38 49	086	26 27	140	24 41	170	47 57	240	46 47	292	28 02	343
335	15 42	044	39 39	087	26 58	141	24 49	171	47 14	241	46 02	292	27 48	343
336	16 17	045	40 28	088	27 29	142	24 57	172	46 31	242	45 16	292	27 34	344
337	16 52	045	41 17	088	27 59	143	25 04	173	45 47	243	44 31	293	27 20	344
338	17 27	046	42 06	089	28 28	144	25 09	174	45 03	244	43 46	293	27 06	344
339	18 02	046	42 55	089	28 57	145	25 14	175	44 18	245	43 00	293	26 52	344
340	18 37	046	43 44	090	29 25	146	25 19	176	43 33	246	42 15	293	26 39	344
341	19 13	047	44 33	090	29 53	147	25 22	177	42 48	247	41 30	294	26 26	344
342	19 49	047	45 22	091	30 19	148	25 25	177	42 03	248	40 45	294	26 13	345
343	20 25	047	46 12	091	30 45	149	25 26	178	41 17	249	40 00	294	26 00	345
344	21 01	048	47 01	092	31 11	150	25 27	179	40 31	250	39 16	295	25 47	345
	◆ CAPELLA		ALDEBARAN		Diphda		◆ FOMALHAUT		ALTAIR		◆ VEGA		Kochab	
345	21 38	048	14 03	079	31 35	151	25 27	180	39 45	250	38 31	295	25 34	345
346	22 14	049	14 51	080	31 59	152	25 27	181	38 59	251	37 46	295	25 21	345
347	22 51	049	15 40	081	32 22	153	25 25	182	38 12	252	37 02	295	25 09	346
348	23 28	049	16 28	081	32 44	154	25 23	183	37 25	253	36 18	296	24 57	346
349	24 06	050	17 17	082	33 05	155	25 20	184	36 38	253	35 33	296	24 45	346
350	24 43	050	18 05	082	33 26	156	25 16	185	35 51	254	34 49	296	24 33	346
351	25 21	050	18 54	083	33 46	157	25 11	186	35 04	255	34 05	297	24 21	346
352	25 59	051	19 43	083	34 05	158	25 05	187	34 16	256	33 22	297	24 10	347
353	26 37	051	20 32	084	34 23	159	24 59	188	33 29	256	32 38	297	23 58	347
354	27 15	051	21 20	084	34 40	160	24 51	189	32 41	257	31 54	298	23 47	347
355	27 53	051	22 09	085	34 56	161	24 43	190	31 53	258	31 11	298	23 36	347
356	28 32	052	22 58	085	35 11	162	24 34	191	31 05	258	30 28	298	23 26	347
357	29 10	052	23 47	086	35 26	163	24 25	192	30 17	259	29 44	299	23 15	348
358	29 49	052	24 36	086	35 39	165	24 14	193	29 28	260	29 01	299	23 05	348
359	30 28	053	25 25	087	35 52	166	24 03	194	28 40	260	28 19	299	22 54	348

LAT 34°N

LHA ♈	Hc Zn	Hc Zn	Hc Zn	Hc Zn	Hc Zn	Hc Zn	Hc Zn
	◆ CAPELLA	ALDEBARAN	Diphda	◆ FOMALHAUT	ALTAIR	◆ DENEB	Kochab
0	30 31 052	26 12 087	37 02 167	24 49 195	28 00 262	50 54 302	21 46 348
1	31 10 053	27 01 088	37 13 168	24 36 196	27 11 262	50 12 302	21 36 349
2	31 50 053	27 51 088	37 23 169	24 22 197	26 22 263	49 30 302	21 26 349
3	32 30 053	28 41 089	37 32 170	24 08 197	25 32 263	48 48 302	21 17 349
4	33 10 053	29 31 089	37 39 171	23 52 198	24 43 264	48 06 302	21 07 349
5	33 50 054	30 20 090	37 46 173	23 36 199	23 54 265	47 24 302	20 58 350
6	34 30 054	31 10 090	37 52 174	23 19 200	23 04 265	46 42 302	20 50 350
7	35 10 054	32 00 091	37 57 175	23 02 201	22 14 266	46 00 302	20 41 350
8	35 50 054	32 50 092	38 01 176	22 44 202	21 25 266	45 18 303	20 33 350
9	36 31 055	33 39 092	38 03 177	22 25 203	20 35 267	44 36 303	20 24 351
10	37 11 055	34 29 093	38 05 179	22 05 204	19 45 267	43 54 303	20 16 351
11	37 52 055	35 19 093	38 06 180	21 45 205	18 56 268	43 12 303	20 09 351
12	38 33 055	36 08 094	38 05 181	21 23 205	18 06 269	42 30 303	20 01 351
13	39 14 055	36 58 094	38 04 182	21 02 206	17 16 269	41 49 303	19 54 352
14	39 54 055	37 48 095	38 01 184	20 39 207	16 27 270	41 07 303	19 47 352
	◆ CAPELLA	RIGEL	◆ Diphda	FOMALHAUT	Enif	◆ DENEB	Kochab
15	40 35 056	16 25 112	37 58 185	20 16 208	39 24 253	40 26 304	19 40 352
16	41 17 056	17 10 113	37 53 186	19 53 209	38 36 254	39 44 304	19 33 352
17	41 58 056	17 56 114	37 47 187	19 28 210	37 48 255	39 03 304	19 27 353
18	42 39 056	18 42 114	37 41 188	19 04 210	37 00 256	38 22 304	19 21 353
19	43 20 056	19 27 115	37 33 190	18 38 211	36 12 256	37 40 304	19 15 353
20	44 02 056	20 12 116	37 24 191	18 12 212	35 24 257	36 59 304	19 09 354
21	44 43 056	20 57 116	37 15 192	17 45 213	34 35 258	36 18 305	19 04 354
22	45 24 056	21 41 117	37 04 193	17 18 214	33 46 258	35 38 305	18 59 354
23	46 06 057	22 25 118	36 52 194	16 50 214	32 58 259	34 57 305	18 54 354
24	46 47 057	23 09 118	36 39 195	16 22 215	32 09 260	34 16 305	18 49 355
25	47 29 057	23 53 119	36 26 197	15 53 216	31 20 260	33 36 306	18 44 355
26	48 11 057	24 36 120	36 11 198	15 24 217	30 31 261	32 55 306	18 40 355
27	48 52 057	25 19 121	35 56 199	14 54 217	29 41 262	32 15 306	18 36 356
28	49 34 057	26 02 121	35 39 200	14 23 218	28 52 262	31 35 306	18 32 356
29	50 16 057	26 44 122	35 22 201	13 52 219	28 03 263	30 55 307	18 29 356
	CAPELLA	BETELGEUSE	◆ RIGEL	Diphda	◆ Alpheratz	DENEB	◆ Kochab
30	50 57 057	29 42 102	27 26 123	35 03 202	65 59 266	30 15 307	18 26 356
31	51 39 057	30 31 103	28 08 124	34 44 203	65 09 267	29 35 307	18 23 357
32	52 21 057	31 20 103	28 49 125	34 24 204	64 20 267	28 56 307	18 20 357
33	53 02 057	32 08 104	29 30 125	34 03 205	63 30 268	28 16 308	18 17 357
34	53 44 057	32 56 105	30 10 126	33 41 206	62 40 269	27 37 308	18 15 358
35	54 25 057	33 44 105	30 50 127	33 19 207	61 51 269	26 58 308	18 13 358
36	55 07 057	34 32 106	31 29 128	32 56 209	61 01 270	26 19 309	18 11 358
37	55 49 057	35 20 107	32 08 129	32 31 210	60 11 270	25 40 309	18 10 358
38	56 30 056	36 07 107	32 47 130	32 07 211	59 21 271	25 01 309	18 08 359
39	57 11 056	36 55 108	33 25 131	31 41 212	58 32 271	24 23 310	18 07 359
40	57 53 056	37 42 109	34 02 132	31 14 213	57 42 272	23 45 310	18 07 359
41	58 34 056	38 29 110	34 39 132	30 47 214	56 52 272	23 07 310	18 06 000
42	59 15 056	39 16 111	35 16 133	30 19 214	56 03 273	22 29 310	18 06 000
43	59 56 055	40 02 111	35 52 134	29 51 215	55 13 273	21 51 311	18 06 000
44	60 37 055	40 48 112	36 27 135	29 22 216	54 23 274	21 13 311	18 06 000
	◆ Dubhe	POLLUX	SIRIUS	◆ RIGEL	Diphda	◆ Alpheratz	Schedar
45	16 47 025	29 36 074	16 07 124	37 02 136	28 52 217	53 34 274	57 22 325
46	17 08 025	30 24 075	16 49 125	37 36 137	28 21 218	52 44 275	56 53 324
47	17 29 026	31 12 075	17 29 125	38 09 138	27 50 219	51 55 275	56 24 324
48	17 51 026	32 01 076	18 10 126	38 42 139	27 19 220	51 05 276	55 54 323
49	18 13 026	32 49 076	18 50 127	39 13 141	26 46 221	50 16 276	55 24 323
50	18 35 027	33 37 077	19 30 127	39 45 142	26 14 222	49 26 277	54 54 322
51	18 58 027	34 26 077	20 09 128	40 15 143	25 40 223	48 37 277	54 23 322
52	19 20 027	35 14 077	20 48 129	40 45 144	25 06 223	47 47 278	53 53 322
53	19 43 028	36 03 078	21 26 130	41 14 145	24 32 224	46 58 278	53 22 321
54	20 07 028	36 51 078	22 04 130	41 42 146	23 57 225	46 09 278	52 50 321
55	20 30 028	37 40 079	22 42 131	42 09 147	23 21 226	45 20 279	52 19 321
56	20 54 028	38 29 079	23 19 132	42 36 149	22 45 227	44 31 279	51 47 320
57	21 17 029	39 18 080	23 56 133	43 01 150	22 09 228	43 42 280	51 16 320
58	21 41 029	40 07 080	24 32 134	43 26 151	21 32 228	42 53 280	50 44 320
59	22 06 029	40 56 081	25 08 134	43 49 152	20 54 229	42 04 281	50 12 320
	◆ Dubhe	POLLUX	PROCYON	◆ SIRIUS	RIGEL	◆ Hamal	Schedar
60	22 30 030	41 45 081	31 35 107	25 43 135	44 12 154	63 26 254	49 40 320
61	22 55 030	42 34 081	32 23 107	26 18 136	44 33 155	62 38 255	49 07 319
62	23 20 030	43 23 082	33 10 108	26 52 137	44 54 156	61 50 256	48 35 319
63	23 45 030	44 13 082	33 58 109	27 26 138	45 14 157	61 02 257	48 02 319
64	24 10 031	45 02 083	34 45 110	27 59 139	45 32 159	60 13 258	47 30 319
65	24 35 031	45 51 083	35 31 110	28 32 140	45 50 160	59 24 259	46 57 319
66	25 01 031	46 41 084	36 18 111	29 03 141	46 06 162	58 35 260	46 24 319
67	25 26 031	47 30 084	37 04 112	29 35 141	46 21 163	57 46 260	45 52 319
68	25 52 031	48 20 085	37 50 113	30 05 142	46 35 164	56 57 261	45 19 319
69	26 18 032	49 09 085	38 36 114	30 35 143	46 48 166	56 08 262	44 46 319
70	26 45 032	49 59 086	39 21 114	31 05 144	47 00 167	55 19 263	44 13 319
71	27 11 032	50 48 086	40 07 115	31 33 145	47 10 169	54 29 263	43 40 318
72	27 37 032	51 38 087	40 51 116	32 01 146	47 19 170	53 40 264	43 07 318
73	28 04 032	52 28 087	41 36 117	32 29 147	47 27 171	52 50 265	42 34 318
74	28 31 033	53 17 088	42 20 118	32 55 148	47 34 173	52 01 265	42 01 318
	◆ Dubhe	POLLUX	PROCYON	◆ SIRIUS	RIGEL	◆ Hamal	Mirfak
75	28 58 033	54 07 088	43 04 119	33 21 149	47 40 174	51 11 266	66 28 320
76	29 25 033	54 57 089	43 47 120	33 46 150	47 44 176	50 22 267	65 56 319
77	29 52 033	55 47 089	44 30 121	34 10 151	47 47 177	49 32 267	65 23 318
78	30 19 033	56 36 090	45 13 122	34 34 152	47 48 179	48 42 268	64 49 317
79	30 47 033	57 26 090	45 55 123	34 56 154	47 49 180	47 53 268	64 15 317
80	31 14 034	58 16 091	46 37 124	35 18 155	47 48 182	47 03 269	63 41 316
81	31 42 034	59 06 091	47 18 125	35 39 156	47 46 183	46 13 270	63 06 315
82	32 09 034	59 55 092	47 58 126	35 59 157	47 42 185	45 23 270	62 31 315
83	32 37 034	60 45 093	48 38 127	36 18 158	47 38 186	44 34 271	61 55 314
84	33 05 034	61 35 093	49 18 128	36 36 159	47 32 188	43 44 271	61 19 314
85	33 33 034	62 24 094	49 57 129	36 54 160	47 25 189	42 54 272	60 43 313
86	34 01 034	63 14 095	50 35 130	37 10 161	47 16 191	42 04 272	60 07 313
87	34 29 034	64 03 095	51 12 132	37 26 162	47 06 192	41 15 273	59 30 312
88	34 57 035	64 53 096	51 49 133	37 40 164	46 55 193	40 25 273	58 53 312
89	35 26 035	65 42 097	52 25 134	37 54 165	46 43 195	39 35 274	58 16 312

LHA ♈	Hc Zn	Hc Zn	Hc Zn	Hc Zn	Hc Zn	Hc Zn	Hc Zn
	◆ Dubhe	REGULUS	PROCYON	◆ SIRIUS	RIGEL	ALDEBARAN	◆ Mirfak
90	35 54 035	29 30 096	53 00 136	38 06 166	46 30 196	64 26 232	57 39 311
91	36 22 035	30 20 096	53 35 137	38 18 167	46 16 198	63 46 234	57 01 311
92	36 50 035	31 09 097	54 08 138	38 28 168	46 00 199	63 06 235	56 24 311
93	37 19 035	31 58 097	54 41 140	38 38 170	45 43 200	62 25 237	55 46 310
94	37 47 035	32 48 098	55 13 141	38 46 171	45 25 202	61 43 238	55 08 310
95	38 16 035	33 37 099	55 43 143	38 53 172	45 07 203	61 00 239	54 30 310
96	38 44 035	34 26 099	56 13 144	39 00 173	44 47 204	60 17 241	53 52 310
97	39 13 035	35 15 100	56 41 146	39 05 175	44 26 206	59 34 242	53 14 310
98	39 41 035	36 04 101	57 09 147	39 09 176	44 04 207	58 49 243	52 35 310
99	40 10 035	36 53 101	57 35 149	39 13 177	43 41 208	58 05 244	51 57 309
100	40 38 035	37 42 102	57 59 151	39 15 178	43 17 209	57 20 245	51 18 309
101	41 07 035	38 30 103	58 23 153	39 16 179	42 52 211	56 34 247	50 40 309
102	41 35 035	39 19 103	58 45 154	39 16 181	42 26 212	55 49 248	50 01 309
103	42 03 035	40 07 104	59 06 156	39 14 182	41 59 213	55 02 249	49 23 309
104	42 32 035	40 55 105	59 25 158	39 12 183	41 32 214	54 16 250	48 44 309
	◆ Alkaid	REGULUS	Alphard	◆ SIRIUS	RIGEL	ALDEBARAN	◆ CAPELLA
105	18 06 042	41 43 106	34 41 134	39 09 184	41 03 215	53 29 250	67 11 309
106	18 40 043	42 31 106	35 16 135	39 05 186	40 34 217	52 42 251	66 33 309
107	19 13 043	43 19 107	35 51 135	38 59 187	40 04 218	51 55 252	65 54 308
108	19 47 043	44 06 108	36 26 136	38 53 188	39 33 219	51 07 253	65 15 308
109	20 22 044	44 53 109	37 00 138	38 45 189	39 02 220	50 20 254	64 35 307
110	20 56 044	45 40 110	37 33 139	38 37 190	38 29 221	49 32 255	63 55 307
111	21 31 044	46 27 110	38 06 140	38 27 192	37 57 222	48 44 256	63 15 306
112	22 05 045	47 13 111	38 38 141	38 17 193	37 23 223	47 55 256	62 35 306
113	22 40 045	48 00 112	39 09 142	38 05 194	36 49 224	47 07 257	61 54 305
114	23 16 045	48 46 113	39 39 143	37 52 195	36 14 225	46 18 258	61 14 305
115	23 51 046	49 31 114	40 09 144	37 39 196	35 38 226	45 30 259	60 33 305
116	24 27 046	50 16 115	40 38 145	37 24 198	35 02 227	44 41 259	59 52 305
117	25 02 046	51 01 116	41 06 146	37 09 199	34 26 228	43 52 260	59 11 304
118	25 38 046	51 46 117	41 33 147	36 52 200	33 49 229	43 03 261	58 30 304
119	26 14 047	52 30 118	42 00 149	36 35 201	33 11 230	42 14 261	57 49 304
	◆ Alkaid	REGULUS	◆ Alphard	SIRIUS	RIGEL	ALDEBARAN	◆ CAPELLA
120	26 51 047	53 14 119	42 25 150	36 16 202	32 33 231	41 25 262	57 07 304
121	27 27 047	53 57 120	42 50 151	35 57 203	31 54 232	40 35 263	56 26 304
122	28 04 047	54 40 121	43 13 152	35 37 204	31 15 232	39 46 263	55 44 303
123	28 40 048	55 22 123	43 36 154	35 16 206	30 35 233	38 56 264	55 03 303
124	29 17 048	56 03 124	43 58 155	34 54 207	29 55 234	38 07 265	54 21 303
125	29 54 048	56 44 125	44 18 156	34 31 208	29 15 235	37 17 265	53 40 303
126	30 32 048	57 25 126	44 38 157	34 08 209	28 34 236	36 28 266	52 58 303
127	31 09 049	58 04 128	44 57 159	33 44 210	27 52 237	35 38 266	52 16 303
128	31 46 049	58 43 129	45 14 160	33 19 211	27 11 237	34 48 267	51 35 303
129	32 24 049	59 21 131	45 31 161	32 53 212	26 29 238	33 59 268	50 53 303
130	33 02 049	59 59 132	45 46 163	32 26 213	25 46 239	33 09 268	50 11 303
131	33 39 050	60 35 134	46 00 164	31 59 214	25 03 240	32 19 269	49 30 303
132	34 17 050	61 11 135	46 13 166	31 31 215	24 20 240	31 30 269	48 48 303
133	34 55 050	61 45 137	46 25 167	31 02 216	23 37 241	30 40 270	48 07 303
134	35 33 050	62 19 139	46 36 168	30 33 217	22 53 242	29 50 271	47 25 303
	◆ Alkaid	ARCTURUS	SPICA	◆ Alphard	SIRIUS	BETELGEUSE	◆ CAPELLA
135	36 12 050	19 21 080	12 26 113	46 45 170	30 02 218	40 02 249	46 43 303
136	36 50 050	20 10 080	13 12 114	46 53 171	29 32 219	39 15 249	46 02 303
137	37 28 051	20 59 081	13 57 114	47 00 173	29 00 220	38 28 250	45 20 304
138	38 07 051	21 48 081	14 42 115	47 06 174	28 28 220	37 42 251	44 39 304
139	38 46 051	22 37 082	15 27 115	47 11 176	27 56 221	36 54 252	43 57 304
140	39 24 051	23 26 082	16 12 116	47 14 177	27 23 222	36 07 253	43 16 304
141	40 03 051	24 16 083	16 57 117	47 16 178	26 49 223	35 19 253	42 35 304
142	40 42 051	25 05 083	17 41 118	47 17 180	26 15 224	34 32 254	41 54 304
143	41 21 051	25 55 084	18 25 118	47 16 181	25 40 225	33 44 255	41 12 304
144	41 59 052	26 44 084	19 09 119	47 14 183	25 05 226	32 56 255	40 31 304
145	42 38 052	27 34 085	19 52 120	47 11 184	24 29 226	32 08 256	39 50 305
146	43 17 052	28 23 085	20 35 120	47 07 186	23 53 227	31 19 257	39 09 305
147	43 57 052	29 13 086	21 18 121	47 01 187	23 16 228	30 31 257	38 29 305
148	44 36 052	30 02 086	22 00 122	46 54 189	22 39 229	29 42 258	37 48 305
149	45 15 052	30 52 087	22 43 122	46 46 190	22 01 230	28 53 259	37 07 305
	Alkaid	◆ ARCTURUS	SPICA	◆ Alphard	PROCYON	BETELGEUSE	◆ CAPELLA
150	45 54 052	31 42 087	23 24 123	46 37 191	46 38 236	28 04 259	36 27 306
151	46 33 052	32 31 088	24 06 124	46 27 193	45 57 237	27 16 260	35 46 306
152	47 12 052	33 21 088	24 47 125	46 15 194	45 15 238	26 27 261	35 06 306
153	47 51 052	34 11 089	25 27 126	46 02 196	44 32 239	25 37 261	34 26 306
154	48 31 052	35 00 089	26 08 126	45 48 197	43 49 240	24 48 262	33 46 306
155	49 10 052	35 50 090	26 48 127	45 33 198	43 06 241	23 59 263	33 06 307
156	49 49 052	36 40 091	27 27 128	45 17 200	42 22 242	23 10 263	32 26 307
157	50 28 052	37 30 091	28 06 129	45 00 201	41 38 243	22 20 264	31 46 307
158	51 07 052	38 19 092	28 45 130	44 41 202	40 53 244	21 31 264	31 06 307
159	51 46 052	39 09 092	29 23 131	44 22 204	40 08 245	20 41 265	30 27 308
160	52 25 052	39 59 093	30 00 131	44 01 205	39 23 246	19 52 266	29 48 308
161	53 04 051	40 48 093	30 37 132	43 40 206	38 38 246	19 02 266	29 08 308
162	53 43 051	41 38 094	31 14 133	43 17 208	37 52 247	18 12 267	28 29 308
163	54 22 051	42 28 095	31 50 134	42 54 209	37 06 248	17 23 267	27 50 309
164	55 00 051	43 17 095	32 25 135	42 29 210	36 20 249	16 33 268	27 12 309
	◆ Dubhe	Alkaid	◆ ARCTURUS	SPICA	REGULUS	◆ PROCYON	CAPELLA
165	62 19 001	55 39 051	44 07 096	33 00 136	65 02 211	35 33 250	26 33 309
166	62 20 000	56 17 051	44 56 097	33 35 137	64 36 213	34 47 250	25 55 310
167	62 19 359	56 56 050	45 46 097	34 08 138	64 09 215	34 00 251	25 16 310
168	62 18 358	57 34 050	46 35 098	34 41 139	63 40 217	33 12 252	24 38 311
169	62 16 357	58 12 050	47 24 099	35 14 140	63 09 219	32 25 253	24 00 311
170	62 13 356	58 50 049	48 13 099	35 45 141	62 38 220	31 38 253	23 23 311
171	62 09 355	59 28 049	49 02 100	36 16 142	62 05 222	30 50 254	22 45 311
172	62 05 354	60 05 049	49 51 101	36 47 143	61 31 224	30 02 255	22 08 311
173	61 59 353	60 42 048	50 40 102	37 16 144	60 56 225	29 14 255	21 31 312
174	61 53 352	61 19 048	51 29 102	37 45 145	60 20 227	28 26 256	20 54 312
175	61 46 351	61 56 047	52 17 103	38 13 146	59 43 229	27 37 257	20 17 313
176	61 37 350	62 33 047	53 06 104	38 41 147	59 06 230	26 49 257	19 40 313
177	61 29 349	63 09 046	53 54 105	39 07 148	58 27 231	26 00 258	19 04 313
178	61 19 348	63 45 046	54 42 106	39 33 150	57 48 233	25 12 259	18 28 314
179	61 08 347	64 20 045	55 30 107	39 58 151	57 08 234	24 23 259	17 52 314

 LAT 34°N

LHA ♈	Hc Zn	Hc Zn	Hc Zn	Hc Zn	Hc Zn	Hc Zn	Hc Zn
	◆VEGA	Alphecca	ARCTURUS	◆SPICA	REGULUS	◆POLLUX	Dubhe
180	14 12 052	43 29 084	56 17 107	40 22 152	56 27 235	36 08 282	60 57 346
181	14 51 053	44 19 084	57 04 108	40 45 153	55 46 237	35 20 282	60 45 346
182	15 31 053	45 08 085	57 52 109	41 07 154	55 04 238	34 31 283	60 32 345
183	16 11 054	45 58 085	58 38 110	41 28 155	54 22 239	33 43 283	60 19 344
184	16 51 054	46 47 086	59 25 111	41 48 157	53 39 240	32 54 284	60 05 343
185	17 32 055	47 37 086	60 11 113	42 07 158	52 56 241	32 06 284	59 50 342
186	18 13 055	48 27 087	60 57 114	42 25 159	52 12 242	31 18 285	59 34 341
187	18 53 055	49 16 087	61 42 115	42 42 160	51 27 243	30 30 285	59 18 341
188	19 34 056	50 06 088	62 27 116	42 59 162	50 43 244	29 42 285	59 02 340
189	20 16 056	50 56 088	63 11 117	43 14 163	49 58 245	28 54 286	58 44 339
190	20 57 057	51 45 089	63 55 119	43 28 164	49 12 246	28 06 286	58 26 339
191	21 39 057	52 35 089	64 39 120	43 40 166	48 27 247	27 19 287	58 08 338
192	22 20 057	53 25 090	65 21 122	43 52 167	47 41 248	26 31 287	57 49 337
193	23 02 058	54 15 091	66 03 123	44 03 168	46 54 249	25 43 288	57 29 337
194	23 45 058	55 04 091	66 45 125	44 12 170	46 08 250	24 56 288	57 09 336
	◆Kochab	VEGA	Rasalhague	◆ANTARES	SPICA	◆REGULUS	Dubhe
195	47 39 011	24 27 058	24 23 091	11 38 133	44 20 171	45 21 251	56 48 335
196	47 48 011	25 09 059	25 12 092	12 14 134	44 28 172	44 34 252	56 27 335
197	47 57 010	25 52 059	26 02 092	12 50 135	44 34 174	43 46 252	56 06 334
198	48 06 010	26 35 059	26 52 093	13 25 136	44 38 175	42 59 253	55 44 334
199	48 14 010	27 18 060	27 41 093	13 59 136	44 42 177	42 11 254	55 22 333
200	48 22 009	28 01 060	28 31 094	14 34 137	44 44 178	41 23 255	54 59 333
201	48 30 009	28 44 061	29 21 095	15 07 138	44 46 179	40 35 255	54 36 332
202	48 37 008	29 27 061	30 10 095	15 41 138	44 45 181	39 47 256	54 12 332
203	48 44 008	30 11 061	31 00 096	16 13 139	44 44 182	38 59 257	53 49 331
204	48 51 008	30 54 062	31 49 096	16 46 140	44 42 183	38 10 258	53 25 331
205	48 58 007	31 38 062	32 39 097	17 18 141	44 38 185	37 21 258	53 00 330
206	49 04 007	32 22 062	33 28 098	17 49 141	44 34 186	36 33 259	52 35 330
207	49 10 006	33 06 062	34 17 098	18 20 142	44 28 188	35 44 260	52 10 330
208	49 15 006	33 50 063	35 06 099	18 50 143	44 20 189	34 55 260	51 45 329
209	49 20 006	34 35 063	35 56 099	19 20 144	44 12 190	34 06 261	51 19 329
	◆Kochab	VEGA	Rasalhague	◆ANTARES	SPICA	◆REGULUS	Dubhe
210	49 25 005	35 19 063	36 45 100	19 49 145	44 03 192	33 16 262	50 54 329
211	49 29 005	36 04 064	37 33 101	20 17 145	43 52 193	32 27 262	50 28 328
212	49 33 004	36 48 064	38 22 102	20 45 146	43 40 194	31 38 263	50 01 328
213	49 37 004	37 33 064	39 11 102	21 13 147	43 27 196	30 48 264	49 35 328
214	49 41 004	38 18 065	39 59 103	21 40 148	43 13 197	29 59 264	49 08 327
215	49 44 003	39 03 065	40 48 104	22 06 149	42 58 198	29 09 265	48 41 327
216	49 46 003	39 48 065	41 36 104	22 31 149	42 42 200	28 20 265	48 14 327
217	49 48 002	40 33 065	42 24 105	22 56 150	42 25 201	27 30 266	47 47 327
218	49 50 002	41 18 066	43 12 106	23 21 151	42 07 202	26 41 267	47 20 327
219	49 52 002	42 04 066	44 00 107	23 44 152	41 48 203	25 51 267	46 52 326
220	49 53 001	42 49 066	44 47 107	24 07 153	41 28 205	25 01 268	46 25 326
221	49 54 001	43 34 066	45 35 108	24 29 154	41 07 206	24 12 268	45 57 326
222	49 54 000	44 20 067	46 22 109	24 51 155	40 44 207	23 22 269	45 29 326
223	49 54 000	45 06 067	47 09 110	25 12 156	40 21 208	22 32 269	45 01 326
224	49 54 359	45 52 067	47 55 111	25 32 157	39 58 209	21 42 270	44 33 326
	DENEB	VEGA	◆ALTAIR	ANTARES	◆SPICA	Denebola	◆Dubhe
225	26 20 051	46 37 067	19 08 092	25 51 158	39 33 210	42 59 258	44 05 326
226	26 59 052	47 23 067	19 58 093	26 10 158	39 07 212	42 10 258	43 37 325
227	27 38 052	48 09 068	20 47 093	26 28 159	38 41 213	41 21 259	43 09 325
228	28 17 052	48 55 068	21 37 094	26 45 160	38 13 214	40 32 260	42 41 325
229	28 57 053	49 41 068	22 26 094	27 01 161	37 45 215	39 43 260	42 12 325
230	29 36 053	50 28 068	23 16 095	27 17 162	37 16 216	38 54 261	41 44 325
231	30 16 053	51 14 068	24 06 096	27 31 163	36 47 217	38 05 262	41 16 325
232	30 56 053	52 00 069	24 55 096	27 45 164	36 16 218	37 16 262	40 47 325
233	31 36 054	52 46 069	25 44 097	27 58 165	35 45 219	36 27 263	40 19 325
234	32 16 054	53 33 069	26 34 097	28 11 166	35 13 220	35 37 264	39 50 325
235	32 56 054	54 19 069	27 23 098	28 22 167	34 41 221	34 48 264	39 22 325
236	33 37 054	55 06 069	28 12 099	28 33 168	34 08 222	33 58 265	38 53 325
237	34 17 055	55 52 069	29 01 099	28 42 169	33 34 223	33 09 265	38 25 325
238	34 58 055	56 39 070	29 51 100	28 51 170	33 00 224	32 19 266	37 56 325
239	35 39 055	57 26 070	30 40 101	28 59 171	32 25 225	31 29 267	37 28 325
	◆DENEB	ALTAIR	Nunki	◆ANTARES	SPICA	ARCTURUS	◆Alkaid
240	36 20 055	31 28 101	16 40 139	29 07 172	31 50 226	62 35 244	61 22 312
241	37 01 056	32 17 102	17 12 140	29 13 173	31 14 227	61 50 245	60 45 312
242	37 42 056	33 06 103	17 44 141	29 18 174	30 37 228	61 05 246	60 08 311
243	38 23 056	33 54 103	18 15 142	29 23 175	30 00 229	60 19 247	59 30 311
244	39 04 056	34 43 104	18 45 142	29 26 176	29 22 230	59 33 248	58 52 311
245	39 45 056	35 31 105	19 15 143	29 29 177	28 44 230	58 46 249	58 15 310
246	40 27 056	36 19 105	19 45 144	29 31 178	28 06 231	58 00 250	57 36 310
247	41 08 057	37 07 106	20 14 145	29 32 179	27 27 232	57 13 251	56 58 310
248	41 50 057	37 54 107	20 42 146	29 32 180	26 47 233	56 25 252	56 20 309
249	42 32 057	38 42 108	21 10 146	29 31 181	26 07 234	55 38 253	55 41 309
250	43 13 057	39 29 108	21 37 147	29 30 182	25 27 234	54 50 254	55 03 309
251	43 55 057	40 16 109	22 03 148	29 27 184	24 47 235	54 02 255	54 24 309
252	44 37 057	41 03 110	22 29 149	29 23 185	24 05 236	53 14 256	53 45 309
253	45 19 057	41 50 111	22 55 150	29 19 186	23 24 237	52 26 257	53 07 309
254	46 01 058	42 36 112	23 19 151	29 14 187	22 42 238	51 37 258	52 28 308
	◆DENEB	ALTAIR	Nunki	◆ANTARES	ARCTURUS	◆Alkaid	Kochab
255	46 43 058	43 23 112	23 43 152	29 08 188	50 48 258	51 49 308	46 52 348
256	47 25 058	44 08 113	24 07 152	29 01 189	50 00 259	51 10 308	46 41 347
257	48 07 058	44 54 114	24 29 153	28 53 190	49 11 260	50 31 308	46 30 347
258	48 49 058	45 39 115	24 51 154	28 44 191	48 22 261	49 51 308	46 19 347
259	49 31 058	46 24 116	25 12 155	28 34 192	47 33 261	49 12 308	46 07 346
260	50 13 058	47 09 117	25 33 156	28 24 193	46 43 262	48 33 308	45 56 346
261	50 55 058	47 53 118	25 53 157	28 13 194	45 54 263	47 54 308	45 44 346
262	51 38 058	48 37 119	26 12 158	28 00 195	45 05 263	47 15 308	45 31 346
263	52 20 058	49 20 120	26 30 159	27 48 196	44 15 264	46 36 308	45 19 345
264	53 02 058	50 03 121	26 48 160	27 34 197	43 26 265	45 56 308	45 06 345
265	53 44 058	50 45 122	27 04 161	27 19 198	42 36 265	45 17 308	44 53 345
266	54 26 058	51 27 123	27 20 162	27 04 199	41 47 266	44 38 308	44 40 345
267	55 08 058	52 09 124	27 35 163	26 48 199	40 57 266	43 59 308	44 27 344
268	55 50 058	52 49 125	27 50 164	26 31 200	40 07 267	43 20 308	44 14 344
269	56 32 058	53 30 127	28 03 165	26 13 201	39 18 268	42 41 308	44 00 344

LHA ♈	Hc Zn	Hc Zn	Hc Zn	Hc Zn	Hc Zn	Hc Zn	Hc Zn
	◆DENEB	ALTAIR	◆Nunki	ANTARES	ARCTURUS	◆Alkaid	Kochab
270	57 14 058	54 09 128	28 16 166	25 54 202	38 28 268	42 02 309	43 46 344
271	57 56 057	54 48 129	28 28 167	25 35 203	37 38 269	41 23 309	43 32 344
272	58 38 057	55 26 131	28 39 168	25 15 204	36 49 269	40 44 309	43 18 343
273	59 20 057	56 04 132	28 49 169	24 54 205	35 59 270	40 05 309	43 04 343
274	60 02 057	56 40 133	28 58 170	24 33 206	35 09 270	39 27 309	42 49 343
275	60 43 057	57 16 135	29 07 171	24 11 207	34 19 271	38 48 309	42 35 343
276	61 25 056	57 51 136	29 14 172	23 48 208	33 30 272	38 09 309	42 20 343
277	62 06 056	58 25 138	29 21 173	23 24 209	32 40 272	37 31 309	42 05 343
278	62 47 056	58 58 139	29 27 174	23 00 209	31 50 273	36 52 310	41 50 342
279	63 28 055	59 30 141	29 32 175	22 35 210	31 00 273	36 14 310	41 35 342
280	64 09 055	60 00 143	29 36 176	22 10 211	30 11 274	35 36 310	41 20 342
281	64 49 054	60 30 144	29 39 177	21 44 212	29 21 274	34 58 310	41 05 342
282	65 30 054	60 58 146	29 42 178	21 17 213	28 32 275	34 20 310	40 49 342
283	66 10 053	61 25 148	29 43 179	20 50 214	27 42 275	33 42 310	40 34 342
284	66 50 053	61 51 150	29 43 180	20 22 215	26 53 276	33 04 311	40 18 342
	◆Alpheratz	Enif	ALTAIR	◆ANTARES	ARCTURUS	◆Alkaid	Kochab
285	25 35 071	45 17 113	62 15 152	19 54 215	26 03 276	32 26 311	40 02 342
286	26 22 071	46 03 114	62 38 154	19 24 216	25 14 277	31 49 311	39 46 341
287	27 09 072	46 49 114	62 59 156	18 55 217	24 24 277	31 11 311	39 31 341
288	27 56 072	47 34 115	63 19 158	18 25 218	23 35 278	30 34 312	39 15 341
289	28 44 072	48 19 116	63 37 160	17 54 218	22 46 278	29 57 312	38 59 341
290	29 31 073	49 03 117	63 53 162	17 23 219	21 57 279	29 20 312	38 42 341
291	30 19 073	49 47 118	64 07 164	16 51 220	21 07 279	28 43 312	38 26 341
292	31 07 074	50 30 119	64 20 166	16 19 221	20 18 280	28 06 312	38 10 341
293	31 54 074	51 14 120	64 31 169	15 46 221	19 29 280	27 29 313	37 54 341
294	32 42 075	51 56 122	64 39 171	15 13 222	18 41 281	26 53 313	37 38 341
295	33 30 075	52 38 123	64 46 173	14 39 223	17 52 281	26 17 313	37 21 341
296	34 18 075	53 20 124	64 51 176	14 05 224	17 03 282	25 41 314	37 05 341
297	35 07 076	54 01 125	64 54 178	13 31 224	16 14 282	25 05 314	36 49 341
298	35 55 076	54 41 126	64 55 180	12 56 225	15 26 283	24 29 314	36 32 341
299	36 43 077	55 21 128	64 53 183	12 20 226	14 37 283	23 53 314	36 16 341
	◆Mirfak	Alpheratz	◆FOMALHAUT	ALTAIR	Rasalhague	◆Alphecca	Kochab
300	13 30 038	37 32 077	13 45 141	64 50 185	50 51 246	33 23 282	35 59 341
301	14 01 038	38 20 078	14 16 142	64 45 187	50 05 247	32 35 282	35 43 341
302	14 32 039	39 09 078	14 47 142	64 37 190	49 19 247	31 46 283	35 26 341
303	15 03 039	39 58 078	15 17 143	64 28 192	48 33 248	30 57 283	35 10 341
304	15 35 040	40 46 079	15 46 144	64 17 194	47 47 249	30 09 284	34 54 341
305	16 07 040	41 35 079	16 15 145	64 04 196	47 00 250	29 21 284	34 37 341
306	16 39 040	42 24 080	16 44 145	63 49 198	46 13 251	28 33 284	34 21 341
307	17 11 041	43 13 080	17 12 146	63 33 201	45 26 252	27 44 285	34 04 341
308	17 44 041	44 02 080	17 39 147	63 14 203	44 39 253	26 56 285	33 48 341
309	18 17 041	44 51 081	18 06 148	62 54 205	43 51 253	26 08 286	33 32 341
310	18 50 042	45 40 081	18 32 149	62 33 207	43 03 254	25 21 286	33 15 341
311	19 23 042	46 29 082	18 58 149	62 10 209	42 15 255	24 33 287	32 59 341
312	19 57 043	47 19 082	19 23 150	61 45 211	41 27 256	23 45 287	32 43 341
313	20 30 043	48 08 083	19 47 151	61 19 212	40 39 256	22 58 288	32 27 341
314	21 04 043	48 57 083	20 11 152	60 52 214	39 51 257	22 11 288	32 10 341
	◆Mirfak	Hamal	Diphda	◆FOMALHAUT	ALTAIR	◆VEGA	Kochab
315	21 38 044	23 13 076	15 34 125	20 34 153	60 23 216	61 06 290	31 54 341
316	22 13 044	24 01 077	16 14 126	20 56 154	59 53 218	60 19 290	31 38 341
317	22 47 044	24 50 077	16 54 126	21 18 154	59 22 219	59 33 290	31 22 341
318	23 22 044	25 38 078	17 34 127	21 40 155	58 50 221	58 46 290	31 07 341
319	23 57 045	26 27 078	18 14 128	22 00 156	58 17 223	57 59 290	30 51 342
320	24 32 045	27 16 079	18 53 129	22 20 157	57 43 224	57 13 290	30 35 342
321	25 07 045	28 05 079	19 32 129	22 39 158	57 07 226	56 26 291	30 19 342
322	25 43 046	28 54 080	20 10 130	22 57 159	56 31 227	55 40 291	30 04 342
323	26 18 046	29 43 080	20 48 131	23 15 160	55 55 228	54 53 291	29 48 342
324	26 54 046	30 32 081	21 25 132	23 32 160	55 17 230	54 07 291	29 33 342
325	27 30 046	31 21 081	22 02 132	23 48 161	54 39 231	53 20 291	29 18 342
326	28 06 047	32 10 082	22 39 133	24 04 162	54 00 232	52 34 291	29 02 342
327	28 43 047	32 59 082	23 15 134	24 19 163	53 20 234	51 47 291	28 47 342
328	29 19 047	33 48 083	23 51 135	24 33 164	52 40 235	51 01 292	28 32 342
329	29 56 047	34 38 083	24 26 136	24 46 165	51 59 236	50 15 292	28 17 343
	◆CAPELLA	Hamal	Diphda	◆FOMALHAUT	ALTAIR	◆VEGA	Kochab
330	12 09 042	35 27 084	25 00 136	24 58 166	51 17 237	49 29 292	28 02 343
331	12 43 042	36 17 084	25 34 137	25 10 167	50 35 238	48 43 292	27 48 343
332	13 17 043	37 06 085	26 08 138	25 21 168	49 52 239	47 57 292	27 33 343
333	13 51 043	37 56 085	26 41 139	25 31 169	49 09 240	47 11 293	27 19 343
334	14 25 044	38 45 086	27 13 140	25 40 170	48 26 241	46 25 293	27 04 343
335	14 59 044	39 35 086	27 45 141	25 49 171	47 42 242	45 39 293	26 50 343
336	15 34 045	40 25 087	28 16 142	25 56 172	46 58 243	44 53 293	26 36 344
337	16 09 045	41 14 087	28 47 143	26 03 173	46 13 244	44 07 293	26 22 344
338	16 44 045	42 04 088	29 17 143	26 09 174	45 28 245	43 22 294	26 08 344
339	17 20 046	42 54 088	29 46 144	26 14 175	44 43 246	42 36 294	25 55 344
340	17 56 046	43 43 089	30 15 145	26 18 176	43 57 247	41 51 294	25 41 344
341	18 32 046	44 33 089	30 43 146	26 22 176	43 11 248	41 06 294	25 28 345
342	19 08 047	45 23 090	31 10 147	26 25 177	42 25 249	40 20 295	25 15 345
343	19 44 047	46 13 090	31 36 148	26 26 178	41 39 250	39 35 295	25 02 345
344	20 21 048	47 02 091	32 02 149	26 27 179	40 52 250	38 50 295	24 49 345
	◆CAPELLA	ALDEBARAN	Diphda	◆FOMALHAUT	ALTAIR	◆VEGA	Kochab
345	20 57 048	13 52 079	32 27 150	26 27 180	40 05 251	38 05 296	24 36 345
346	21 34 048	14 41 080	32 51 151	26 27 181	39 18 252	37 21 296	24 23 345
347	22 11 049	15 29 080	33 15 152	26 25 182	38 30 253	36 36 296	24 11 346
348	22 49 049	16 19 081	33 38 153	26 23 183	37 43 253	35 51 296	23 59 346
349	23 26 049	17 08 081	34 00 154	26 19 184	36 55 254	35 07 297	23 47 346
350	24 04 050	17 57 082	34 21 156	26 15 185	36 07 255	34 22 297	23 35 346
351	24 42 050	18 46 082	34 41 157	26 10 186	35 19 256	33 38 297	23 23 346
352	25 20 050	19 35 083	35 00 158	26 05 187	34 31 256	32 54 298	23 11 347
353	25 59 050	20 25 083	35 19 159	25 58 188	33 42 257	32 10 298	23 00 347
354	26 37 051	21 14 084	35 36 160	25 51 189	32 54 258	31 26 298	22 49 347
355	27 16 051	22 04 084	35 53 161	25 42 190	32 05 258	30 42 299	22 38 347
356	27 54 051	22 53 085	36 09 162	25 33 191	31 17 259	29 59 299	22 27 348
357	28 33 052	23 43 085	36 23 163	25 23 192	30 28 260	29 15 299	22 16 348
358	29 12 052	24 32 086	36 37 164	25 13 193	29 39 260	28 32 300	22 06 348
359	29 51 052	25 22 087	36 50 166	25 01 194	28 50 261	27 49 300	21 56 348

LAT 33°N

LHA ♈	Hc Zn	Hc Zn	Hc Zn	Hc Zn	Hc Zn	Hc Zn	Hc Zn
	◆CAPELLA	ALDEBARAN	Diphda	◆FOMALHAUT	ALTAIR	◆DENEB	Kochab
0	29 54 052	26 08 087	38 00 167	25 47 195	28 09 262	50 22 303	20 47 349
1	30 34 052	26 59 087	38 11 168	25 34 196	27 19 263	49 40 303	20 37 349
2	31 14 052	27 49 088	38 22 169	25 20 197	26 29 263	48 58 303	20 27 349
3	31 54 053	28 39 088	38 31 170	25 05 198	25 39 264	48 15 303	20 18 349
4	32 34 053	29 30 089	38 39 171	24 49 199	24 49 264	47 33 303	20 08 349
5	33 14 053	30 20 089	38 46 173	24 33 199	23 59 265	46 51 303	19 59 350
6	33 54 053	31 10 090	38 52 174	24 16 200	23 09 266	46 09 303	19 51 350
7	34 35 054	32 01 090	38 57 175	23 58 201	22 19 266	45 27 303	19 42 350
8	35 15 054	32 51 091	39 01 176	23 39 202	21 28 267	44 45 303	19 33 350
9	35 56 054	33 41 091	39 03 177	23 20 203	20 38 267	44 03 303	19 25 351
10	36 36 054	34 31 092	39 05 179	23 00 204	19 48 268	43 21 304	19 17 351
11	37 17 054	35 22 093	39 06 180	22 39 205	18 58 268	42 39 304	19 09 351
12	37 58 054	36 12 093	39 05 181	22 18 206	18 07 269	41 57 304	19 02 351
13	38 39 055	37 02 094	39 04 182	21 56 206	17 17 270	41 16 304	18 55 352
14	39 20 055	37 52 094	39 01 184	21 33 207	16 27 270	40 34 304	18 47 352
	◆CAPELLA	RIGEL	◆Diphda	FOMALHAUT	Enif	◆DENEB	Kochab
15	40 01 055	16 47 112	38 57 185	21 09 208	39 41 254	39 52 304	18 41 352
16	40 42 055	17 34 113	38 53 186	20 45 209	38 52 255	39 11 304	18 34 353
17	41 24 055	18 20 113	38 47 187	20 21 210	38 04 256	38 29 305	18 28 353
18	42 05 055	19 06 114	38 40 188	19 55 211	37 15 256	37 48 305	18 21 353
19	42 46 055	19 52 115	38 32 190	19 29 211	36 26 257	37 06 305	18 15 353
20	43 28 055	20 38 115	38 23 191	19 03 212	35 37 258	36 25 305	18 10 354
21	44 09 056	21 23 116	38 13 192	18 36 213	34 47 258	35 44 305	18 04 354
22	44 51 056	22 08 117	38 02 193	18 08 214	33 58 259	35 03 305	17 59 354
23	45 33 056	22 53 117	37 50 194	17 40 215	33 09 260	34 22 306	17 54 354
24	46 14 056	23 38 118	37 37 196	17 11 215	32 19 260	33 41 306	17 49 355
25	46 56 056	24 22 119	37 23 197	16 42 216	31 29 261	33 01 306	17 45 355
26	47 37 056	25 06 119	37 08 198	16 12 217	30 40 262	32 20 306	17 40 355
27	48 19 056	25 50 120	36 52 199	15 41 218	29 50 262	31 39 307	17 36 356
28	49 01 056	26 33 121	36 35 200	15 10 218	29 00 263	30 59 307	17 33 356
29	49 42 056	27 16 122	36 18 201	14 39 219	28 10 263	30 19 307	17 29 356
	CAPELLA	BETELGEUSE	◆RIGEL	Diphda	◆Alpheratz	DENEB	◆Kochab
30	50 24 056	29 55 101	27 59 122	35 59 202	66 02 268	29 39 307	17 26 356
31	51 06 056	30 44 102	28 41 123	35 39 204	65 12 269	28 59 308	17 23 357
32	51 47 056	31 33 103	29 23 124	35 19 205	64 21 269	28 19 308	17 20 357
33	52 29 056	32 22 103	30 04 125	34 57 206	63 31 270	27 39 308	17 17 357
34	53 11 056	33 11 104	30 45 126	34 35 207	62 41 271	27 00 308	17 15 358
35	53 52 056	34 00 105	31 26 127	34 12 208	61 51 271	26 20 309	17 13 358
36	54 34 055	34 48 105	32 06 127	33 48 209	61 00 272	25 41 309	17 11 358
37	55 15 055	35 37 106	32 46 128	33 24 210	60 10 272	25 02 309	17 10 358
38	55 56 055	36 25 107	33 25 129	32 58 211	59 20 273	24 23 310	17 08 359
39	56 38 055	37 13 107	34 04 130	32 32 212	58 29 273	23 45 310	17 07 359
40	57 19 055	38 01 108	34 42 131	32 05 213	57 39 273	23 06 310	17 07 359
41	58 00 055	38 49 109	35 20 132	31 37 214	56 49 274	22 28 310	17 06 000
42	58 41 054	39 36 110	35 57 133	31 09 215	55 59 274	21 50 311	17 06 000
43	59 22 054	40 23 111	36 33 134	30 40 216	55 09 275	21 12 311	17 06 000
44	60 02 054	41 10 111	37 09 135	30 10 217	54 18 275	20 34 311	17 06 000
	◆Dubhe	POLLUX	SIRIUS	◆RIGEL	Diphda	◆Alpheratz	Schedar
45	15 52 025	29 20 074	16 41 124	37 45 136	29 40 218	53 28 276	56 33 325
46	16 14 025	30 08 074	17 22 124	38 19 137	29 08 219	52 38 276	56 04 325
47	16 35 026	30 57 075	18 04 125	38 54 138	28 37 219	51 48 277	55 35 324
48	16 57 026	31 45 075	18 45 126	39 27 139	28 05 220	50 58 277	55 06 324
49	17 19 026	32 34 076	19 26 126	40 00 140	27 32 221	50 08 277	54 36 324
50	17 42 027	33 23 076	20 06 127	40 32 141	26 58 222	49 19 278	54 06 323
51	18 04 027	34 12 076	20 46 128	41 03 142	26 24 223	48 29 278	53 36 323
52	18 27 027	35 01 077	21 25 129	41 33 143	25 50 224	47 39 279	53 05 322
53	18 50 027	35 50 077	22 05 129	42 03 145	25 14 225	46 49 279	52 34 322
54	19 14 028	36 39 078	22 43 130	42 32 146	24 39 225	46 00 279	52 03 322
55	19 37 028	37 28 078	23 21 131	43 00 147	24 03 226	45 10 280	51 32 322
56	20 01 028	38 17 078	23 59 132	43 27 148	23 26 227	44 20 280	51 01 321
57	20 25 029	39 07 079	24 37 132	43 53 149	22 49 228	43 31 281	50 29 321
58	20 49 029	39 56 079	25 14 133	44 18 151	22 11 229	42 42 281	49 58 321
59	21 13 029	40 46 080	25 50 134	44 42 152	21 33 229	41 52 281	49 26 321
	◆Dubhe	POLLUX	PROCYON	◆SIRIUS	RIGEL	◆Hamal	Schedar
60	21 38 029	41 35 080	31 52 106	26 26 135	45 05 153	63 41 256	48 54 320
61	22 03 030	42 25 081	32 41 107	27 01 136	45 28 154	62 52 257	48 22 320
62	22 28 030	43 14 081	33 29 107	27 36 137	45 49 156	62 03 258	47 49 320
63	22 53 030	44 04 081	34 17 108	28 10 138	46 09 157	61 14 259	47 17 320
64	23 18 030	44 54 082	35 04 109	28 44 138	46 28 158	60 25 260	46 44 320
65	23 44 031	45 44 082	35 52 110	29 17 139	46 46 160	59 35 260	46 12 320
66	24 09 031	46 34 083	36 39 110	29 50 140	47 03 161	58 45 261	45 39 319
67	24 35 031	47 23 083	37 26 111	30 22 141	47 18 163	57 56 262	45 06 319
68	25 01 031	48 13 084	38 13 112	30 53 142	47 33 164	57 06 263	44 34 319
69	25 27 031	49 03 084	38 59 113	31 23 143	47 46 165	56 16 263	44 01 319
70	25 54 032	49 54 084	39 46 114	31 53 144	47 58 167	55 26 264	43 28 319
71	26 20 032	50 44 085	40 32 114	32 23 145	48 09 168	54 36 265	42 55 319
72	26 47 032	51 34 085	41 17 115	32 51 146	48 18 170	53 46 265	42 22 319
73	27 13 032	52 24 086	42 03 116	33 19 147	48 27 171	52 55 266	41 49 319
74	27 40 032	53 14 086	42 48 117	33 46 148	48 34 173	52 05 267	41 16 319
	◆Dubhe	POLLUX	PROCYON	◆SIRIUS	RIGEL	◆Hamal	Mirfak
75	28 07 033	54 04 087	43 32 118	34 12 149	48 39 174	51 15 267	65 42 321
76	28 34 033	54 55 087	44 17 119	34 38 150	48 44 176	50 25 268	65 10 320
77	29 02 033	55 45 088	45 00 120	35 03 151	48 47 177	49 34 268	64 38 319
78	29 29 033	56 35 088	45 44 121	35 27 152	48 48 179	48 44 269	64 05 319
79	29 57 033	57 25 089	46 27 122	35 50 153	48 49 180	47 54 270	63 31 318
80	30 24 033	58 16 089	47 09 123	36 12 154	48 48 182	47 03 270	62 57 317
81	30 52 033	59 06 090	47 52 124	36 34 155	48 46 183	46 13 271	62 23 317
82	31 20 034	59 56 090	48 33 125	36 54 156	48 42 185	45 23 271	61 48 316
83	31 47 034	60 47 091	49 14 126	37 14 158	48 37 186	44 32 272	61 13 315
84	32 15 034	61 37 091	49 54 127	37 32 159	48 31 188	43 42 272	60 37 315
85	32 43 034	62 27 092	50 34 128	37 50 160	48 24 189	42 52 273	60 02 314
86	33 11 034	63 18 093	51 13 130	38 07 161	48 15 191	42 02 273	59 25 314
87	33 40 034	64 08 093	51 52 131	38 23 162	48 05 192	41 11 274	58 49 314
88	34 08 034	64 58 094	52 30 132	38 38 163	47 54 194	40 21 274	58 13 313
89	34 36 034	65 48 095	53 07 133	38 51 165	47 41 195	39 31 275	57 36 313

LHA ♈	Hc Zn	Hc Zn	Hc Zn	Hc Zn	Hc Zn	Hc Zn	Hc Zn
	◆Dubhe	REGULUS	PROCYON	◆SIRIUS	RIGEL	ALDEBARAN	◆Mirfak
90	35 04 034	29 36 095	53 43 135	39 04 166	47 28 196	65 02 234	56 59 312
91	35 33 034	30 26 096	54 18 136	39 16 167	47 13 198	64 21 235	56 21 312
92	36 01 034	31 16 096	54 53 137	39 27 168	46 57 199	63 40 237	55 44 312
93	36 29 034	32 06 097	55 26 139	39 37 169	46 39 201	62 57 238	55 06 312
94	36 58 034	32 56 097	55 59 140	39 45 171	46 21 202	62 14 240	54 29 311
95	37 26 034	33 46 098	56 31 142	39 53 172	46 02 203	61 30 241	53 51 311
96	37 55 034	34 35 099	57 01 143	39 59 173	45 41 205	60 46 242	53 13 311
97	38 23 034	35 25 099	57 31 145	40 05 174	45 20 206	60 01 243	52 35 311
98	38 52 034	36 15 100	57 59 146	40 09 176	44 57 207	59 16 245	51 57 311
99	39 20 034	37 04 101	58 26 148	40 12 177	44 33 209	58 30 246	51 18 310
100	39 49 034	37 54 101	58 52 150	40 15 178	44 09 210	57 44 247	50 40 310
101	40 17 034	38 43 102	59 16 152	40 16 179	43 43 211	56 58 248	50 02 310
102	40 46 034	39 32 103	59 39 154	40 16 181	43 17 212	56 11 249	49 23 310
103	41 14 034	40 21 103	60 01 155	40 14 182	42 49 214	55 24 250	48 45 310
104	41 42 034	41 10 104	60 21 157	40 12 183	42 21 215	54 36 251	48 06 310
	◆Alkaid	REGULUS	Alphard	◆SIRIUS	RIGEL	ALDEBARAN	◆CAPELLA
105	17 22 042	41 59 105	35 22 133	40 09 184	41 52 216	53 49 252	66 33 311
106	17 55 042	42 47 105	35 58 134	40 04 186	41 22 217	53 01 253	65 55 310
107	18 29 043	43 36 106	36 34 135	39 59 187	40 51 218	52 13 254	65 16 310
108	19 04 043	44 24 107	37 09 136	39 52 188	40 20 219	51 24 254	64 37 309
109	19 38 043	45 12 108	37 44 137	39 45 189	39 48 220	50 36 255	63 58 309
110	20 13 044	46 00 109	38 18 138	39 36 191	39 15 221	49 47 256	63 19 308
111	20 48 044	46 47 109	38 51 139	39 26 192	38 41 222	48 58 257	62 39 308
112	21 23 044	47 35 110	39 24 140	39 15 193	38 07 224	48 09 258	61 59 307
113	21 58 045	48 22 111	39 56 141	39 03 194	37 32 225	47 20 258	61 19 307
114	22 33 045	49 09 112	40 27 142	38 50 195	36 56 226	46 30 259	60 39 307
115	23 09 045	49 55 113	40 57 143	38 36 197	36 20 227	45 41 260	59 58 306
116	23 45 045	50 41 114	41 27 145	38 21 198	35 43 227	44 51 260	59 17 306
117	24 21 046	51 27 115	41 56 146	38 05 199	35 06 228	44 02 261	58 37 306
118	24 57 046	52 13 116	42 24 147	37 49 200	34 28 229	43 12 262	57 56 305
119	25 33 046	52 58 117	42 51 148	37 31 201	33 49 230	42 22 262	57 15 305
	◆Alkaid	REGULUS	◆Alphard	SIRIUS	RIGEL	ALDEBARAN	◆CAPELLA
120	26 10 047	53 42 118	43 17 149	37 12 202	33 11 231	41 32 263	56 33 305
121	26 46 047	54 27 119	43 42 151	36 52 204	32 31 232	40 42 264	55 52 305
122	27 23 047	55 10 120	44 06 152	36 32 205	31 51 233	39 52 264	55 11 305
123	28 00 047	55 53 121	44 30 153	36 10 206	31 11 234	39 02 265	54 29 305
124	28 37 048	56 36 123	44 52 154	35 48 207	30 30 235	38 12 265	53 48 304
125	29 14 048	57 18 124	45 13 156	35 25 208	29 49 235	37 22 266	53 06 304
126	29 52 048	58 00 125	45 33 157	35 01 209	29 07 236	36 32 267	52 25 304
127	30 29 048	58 41 126	45 52 158	34 36 210	28 25 237	35 41 267	51 43 304
128	31 07 048	59 21 128	46 10 160	34 10 211	27 43 238	34 51 268	51 02 304
129	31 44 049	60 00 129	46 27 161	33 44 212	27 00 239	34 01 268	50 20 304
130	32 22 049	60 39 131	46 43 162	33 16 213	26 17 239	33 11 269	49 38 304
131	33 00 049	61 16 132	46 58 164	32 49 214	25 33 240	32 20 269	48 57 304
132	33 38 049	61 53 134	47 11 165	32 20 215	24 50 241	31 30 270	48 15 304
133	34 16 049	62 29 136	47 23 167	31 51 216	24 06 242	30 40 271	47 33 304
134	34 55 050	63 03 137	47 34 168	31 21 217	23 21 242	29 49 271	46 52 304
	◆Alkaid	ARCTURUS	SPICA	◆Alphard	SIRIUS	BETELGEUSE	◆CAPELLA
135	35 33 050	19 10 079	12 49 113	47 44 170	30 50 218	40 23 249	46 10 304
136	36 12 050	19 59 080	13 36 113	47 53 171	30 19 219	39 36 250	45 28 304
137	36 50 050	20 49 080	14 22 114	48 00 172	29 47 220	38 48 251	44 47 304
138	37 29 050	21 39 081	15 08 115	48 06 174	29 14 221	38 01 252	44 05 304
139	38 07 050	22 28 081	15 53 115	48 10 175	28 41 222	37 13 253	43 24 305
140	38 46 050	23 18 082	16 39 116	48 14 177	28 07 223	36 25 253	42 42 305
141	39 25 051	24 08 082	17 24 117	48 16 178	27 33 223	35 36 254	42 01 305
142	40 04 051	24 58 083	18 09 117	48 17 180	26 58 224	34 48 255	41 20 305
143	40 43 051	25 48 083	18 53 118	48 16 181	26 22 225	33 59 255	40 38 305
144	41 22 051	26 38 084	19 38 119	48 14 183	25 46 226	33 11 256	39 57 305
145	42 01 051	27 28 084	20 22 119	48 11 184	25 10 227	32 22 257	39 16 305
146	42 40 051	28 18 085	21 05 120	48 07 186	24 33 228	31 33 257	38 35 305
147	43 19 051	29 08 085	21 49 121	48 01 187	23 56 228	30 43 258	37 54 306
148	43 58 051	29 58 086	22 32 121	47 54 189	23 18 229	29 54 259	37 13 306
149	44 37 051	30 48 086	23 15 122	47 46 190	22 40 230	29 05 259	36 32 306
	Alkaid	◆ARCTURUS	SPICA	◆Alphard	PROCYON	BETELGEUSE	◆CAPELLA
150	45 17 051	31 38 087	23 57 123	47 36 192	47 11 237	28 15 260	35 52 306
151	45 56 051	32 29 087	24 39 124	47 25 193	46 29 238	27 26 261	35 11 306
152	46 35 051	33 19 088	25 21 124	47 13 195	45 46 239	26 36 261	34 30 306
153	47 14 051	34 09 088	26 02 125	47 00 196	45 02 240	25 46 262	33 50 307
154	47 53 051	35 00 089	26 43 126	46 46 197	44 19 241	24 56 262	33 10 307
155	48 32 051	35 50 089	27 24 127	46 30 199	43 34 242	24 06 263	32 30 307
156	49 11 051	36 40 090	28 04 128	46 13 200	42 50 243	23 16 264	31 50 307
157	49 51 051	37 30 090	28 43 128	45 55 201	42 05 244	22 26 264	31 10 308
158	50 30 051	38 21 091	29 23 129	45 36 203	41 19 245	21 36 265	30 30 308
159	51 08 051	39 11 091	30 01 130	45 16 204	40 34 246	20 46 265	29 50 308
160	51 47 051	40 01 092	30 40 131	44 55 205	39 48 246	19 56 266	29 11 308
161	52 26 050	40 52 093	31 17 132	44 33 207	39 01 247	19 06 266	28 31 309
162	53 05 050	41 42 093	31 55 133	44 10 208	38 15 248	18 16 267	27 52 309
163	53 44 050	42 32 094	32 31 134	43 46 209	37 28 249	17 25 268	27 13 309
164	54 22 050	43 22 094	33 08 135	43 21 210	36 41 250	16 35 268	26 34 309
	◆Dubhe	Alkaid	◆ARCTURUS	SPICA	REGULUS	◆PROCYON	CAPELLA
165	61 19 001	55 01 050	44 12 095	33 43 135	65 54 212	35 54 250	25 55 310
166	61 20 000	55 39 049	45 03 096	34 18 136	65 26 214	35 06 251	25 16 310
167	61 20 359	56 17 049	45 53 096	34 53 137	64 58 216	34 19 252	24 38 310
168	61 18 358	56 55 049	46 43 097	35 26 138	64 27 218	33 31 252	23 59 311
169	61 16 357	57 33 049	47 33 098	35 59 139	63 56 220	32 43 253	23 21 311
170	61 13 356	58 10 048	48 22 098	36 32 140	63 23 222	31 54 254	22 43 311
171	61 10 355	58 48 048	49 12 099	37 04 141	62 49 223	31 06 255	22 06 311
172	61 05 354	59 25 047	50 02 100	37 35 142	62 14 225	30 17 255	21 28 312
173	61 00 353	60 02 047	50 51 100	38 05 144	61 38 227	29 29 256	20 51 312
174	60 53 352	60 39 047	51 40 101	38 34 145	61 02 229	28 40 257	20 13 312
175	60 46 351	61 15 046	52 30 102	39 03 146	60 23 230	27 51 257	19 36 313
176	60 38 350	61 51 046	53 19 103	39 31 147	59 44 231	27 02 258	18 59 313
177	60 30 350	62 27 045	54 08 103	39 58 148	59 04 233	26 12 258	18 23 313
178	60 20 349	63 02 044	54 57 104	40 24 149	58 24 234	25 23 259	17 46 314
179	60 10 348	63 37 044	55 46 105	40 50 150	57 43 235	24 34 260	17 10 314

LAT 33°N

LHA ♈	Hc Zn	Hc Zn	Hc Zn	Hc Zn	Hc Zn	Hc Zn	Hc Zn
	◆VEGA	Alphecca	ARCTURUS	◆SPICA	REGULUS	◆POLLUX	Dubhe
180	13 35 052	43 22 083	56 34 106	41 14 151	57 01 237	35 55 283	59 59 347
181	14 15 053	44 12 083	57 23 107	41 38 153	56 19 238	35 06 283	59 47 346
182	14 55 053	45 02 084	58 11 108	42 01 154	55 36 239	34 17 284	59 34 345
183	15 36 054	45 52 084	58 58 109	42 22 155	54 52 240	33 29 284	59 21 344
184	16 16 054	46 42 085	59 46 110	42 43 156	54 08 241	32 40 284	59 07 344
185	16 57 054	47 33 085	60 33 111	43 03 158	53 24 242	31 51 285	58 53 343
186	17 38 055	48 23 086	61 20 112	43 21 159	52 39 244	31 02 285	58 37 342
187	18 19 055	49 13 086	62 06 113	43 39 160	51 54 245	30 14 286	58 22 341
188	19 01 055	50 03 087	62 52 114	43 56 161	51 08 246	29 26 286	58 05 340
189	19 42 056	50 53 087	63 38 116	44 11 163	50 22 246	28 37 286	57 48 340
190	20 24 056	51 44 088	64 23 117	44 25 164	49 36 247	27 49 287	57 30 339
191	21 06 057	52 34 088	65 08 118	44 38 165	48 49 248	27 01 287	57 12 338
192	21 48 057	53 24 089	65 52 120	44 51 167	48 02 249	26 13 288	56 53 338
193	22 30 057	54 15 089	66 35 121	45 01 168	47 15 250	25 25 288	56 34 337
194	23 13 058	55 05 090	67 18 123	45 11 170	46 28 251	24 37 289	56 14 336
	◆Kochab	VEGA	Rasalhague	◆ANTARES	SPICA	◆REGULUS	Dubhe
195	46 40 011	23 55 058	24 23 091	12 20 133	45 20 171	45 40 252	55 54 336
196	46 49 010	24 38 058	25 14 091	12 56 134	45 27 172	44 52 253	55 33 335
197	46 58 010	25 21 059	26 04 092	13 32 135	45 33 174	44 04 253	55 12 335
198	47 07 010	26 04 059	26 54 092	14 08 135	45 38 175	43 16 254	54 50 334
199	47 15 009	26 47 059	27 45 093	14 43 136	45 42 176	42 27 255	54 28 334
200	47 23 009	27 31 060	28 35 093	15 17 137	45 44 178	41 39 256	54 06 333
201	47 31 009	28 14 060	29 25 094	15 52 137	45 45 179	40 50 256	53 43 333
202	47 38 008	28 58 060	30 15 095	16 25 138	45 45 181	40 01 257	53 20 332
203	47 45 008	29 42 061	31 05 095	16 59 139	45 44 182	39 12 258	52 56 332
204	47 52 008	30 26 061	31 55 096	17 32 140	45 42 184	38 22 258	52 32 331
205	47 58 007	31 10 061	32 46 096	18 04 140	45 38 185	37 33 259	52 08 331
206	48 04 007	31 54 062	33 36 097	18 36 141	45 33 186	36 44 260	51 43 331
207	48 10 006	32 38 062	34 25 098	19 07 142	45 27 188	35 54 260	51 18 330
208	48 15 006	33 23 062	35 15 098	19 38 143	45 20 189	35 04 261	50 53 330
209	48 20 006	34 07 062	36 05 099	20 08 144	45 11 190	34 15 262	50 28 330
	◆Kochab	VEGA	Rasalhague	◆ANTARES	SPICA	◆REGULUS	Dubhe
210	48 25 005	34 52 063	36 55 099	20 38 144	45 01 192	33 25 262	50 02 329
211	48 30 005	35 37 063	37 44 100	21 07 145	44 50 193	32 35 263	49 36 329
212	48 34 004	36 22 063	38 34 101	21 35 146	44 38 195	31 45 264	49 10 329
213	48 37 004	37 07 064	39 23 101	22 03 147	44 25 196	30 55 264	48 44 328
214	48 41 004	37 52 064	40 12 102	22 30 148	44 11 197	30 05 265	48 18 328
215	48 44 003	38 37 064	41 02 103	22 57 148	43 55 199	29 15 265	47 51 328
216	48 46 003	39 23 064	41 51 104	23 23 149	43 39 200	28 25 266	47 24 328
217	48 48 002	40 08 065	42 39 104	23 48 150	43 21 201	27 34 266	46 57 327
218	48 50 002	40 53 065	43 28 105	24 13 151	43 03 202	26 44 267	46 30 327
219	48 52 002	41 39 065	44 17 106	24 37 152	42 43 204	25 54 268	46 02 327
220	48 53 001	42 24 065	45 05 107	25 00 153	42 22 205	25 04 268	45 35 327
221	48 54 001	43 10 065	45 53 107	25 23 154	42 00 206	24 13 269	45 07 327
222	48 54 000	43 56 066	46 41 108	25 45 155	41 38 207	23 23 269	44 40 326
223	48 54 000	44 42 066	47 29 109	26 06 155	41 14 209	22 33 270	44 12 326
224	48 54 359	45 28 066	48 16 110	26 27 156	40 50 210	21 42 270	43 44 326
	DENEB	VEGA	◆ALTAIR	ANTARES	◆SPICA	Denebola	◆Dubhe
225	25 42 051	46 14 066	19 10 092	26 47 157	40 24 211	43 11 258	43 16 326
226	26 22 051	47 00 066	20 00 092	27 06 158	39 58 212	42 22 259	42 48 326
227	27 01 052	47 46 067	20 50 093	27 24 159	39 31 213	41 32 260	42 19 326
228	27 41 052	48 32 067	21 41 093	27 41 160	39 03 214	40 42 260	41 51 326
229	28 20 052	49 19 067	22 31 094	27 58 161	38 34 215	39 53 261	41 23 326
230	29 00 052	50 05 067	23 21 095	28 14 162	38 05 216	39 03 262	40 55 326
231	29 40 053	50 51 067	24 11 095	28 29 163	37 34 218	38 14 262	40 26 326
232	30 20 053	51 38 067	25 01 096	28 43 164	37 03 219	37 24 263	39 58 326
233	31 00 053	52 24 068	25 51 096	28 56 165	36 32 220	36 34 264	39 29 326
234	31 41 053	53 11 068	26 41 097	29 09 166	35 59 221	35 44 264	39 01 326
235	32 21 054	53 57 068	27 31 097	29 21 167	35 26 222	34 53 265	38 32 326
236	33 02 054	54 44 068	28 21 098	29 31 168	34 52 223	34 03 265	38 04 326
237	33 42 054	55 31 068	29 11 099	29 41 169	34 18 224	33 13 266	37 36 326
238	34 23 054	56 17 068	30 01 099	29 50 170	33 43 225	32 23 267	37 07 326
239	35 04 055	57 04 068	30 50 100	29 59 171	33 07 225	31 33 267	36 39 326
	◆DENEB	ALTAIR	Nunki	◆ANTARES	SPICA	ARCTURUS	◆Alkaid
240	35 45 055	31 40 101	17 25 139	30 06 172	32 31 226	63 00 245	60 41 313
241	36 26 055	32 29 101	17 58 140	30 12 173	31 54 227	62 14 247	60 04 313
242	37 08 055	33 18 102	18 30 141	30 18 174	31 17 228	61 28 248	59 27 313
243	37 49 055	34 08 103	19 02 141	30 23 175	30 39 229	60 41 249	58 50 312
244	38 30 055	34 57 103	19 33 142	30 26 176	30 01 230	59 54 250	58 13 312
245	39 12 056	35 46 104	20 03 143	30 29 177	29 22 231	59 07 251	57 35 311
246	39 53 056	36 34 105	20 33 144	30 31 178	28 43 232	58 19 252	56 57 311
247	40 35 056	37 23 105	21 03 145	30 32 179	28 03 232	57 31 253	56 20 311
248	41 17 056	38 11 106	21 31 145	30 32 180	27 23 233	56 43 254	55 41 311
249	41 58 056	39 00 107	22 00 146	30 31 181	26 43 234	55 54 255	55 03 310
250	42 40 056	39 48 107	22 27 147	30 29 183	26 02 235	55 06 256	54 25 310
251	43 22 056	40 36 108	22 54 148	30 27 184	25 21 236	54 17 256	53 46 310
252	44 04 057	41 23 109	23 21 149	30 23 185	24 39 236	53 28 257	53 07 310
253	44 46 057	42 11 110	23 47 150	30 19 186	23 57 237	52 39 258	52 29 310
254	45 28 057	42 58 111	24 12 151	30 13 187	23 14 238	51 49 259	51 50 309
	◆DENEB	ALTAIR	Nunki	◆ANTARES	ARCTURUS	◆Alkaid	Kochab
255	46 10 057	43 45 111	24 36 151	30 07 188	51 00 260	51 11 309	45 53 348
256	46 52 057	44 32 112	25 00 152	30 00 189	50 10 260	50 32 309	45 43 348
257	47 34 057	45 18 113	25 23 153	29 52 190	49 21 261	49 53 309	45 32 347
258	48 17 057	46 04 114	25 45 154	29 43 191	48 31 262	49 14 309	45 20 347
259	48 59 057	46 50 115	26 07 155	29 33 192	47 41 262	48 35 309	45 09 347
260	49 41 057	47 35 116	26 28 156	29 22 193	46 51 263	47 56 309	44 57 346
261	50 23 057	48 20 117	26 48 157	29 11 194	46 01 264	47 17 309	44 45 346
262	51 05 057	49 05 118	27 07 158	28 59 195	45 11 264	46 37 309	44 33 346
263	51 47 057	49 49 119	27 26 159	28 45 196	44 21 265	45 58 309	44 21 346
264	52 30 057	50 33 120	27 44 160	28 31 197	43 31 265	45 19 309	44 08 345
265	53 12 057	51 17 121	28 01 161	28 16 198	42 41 266	44 40 309	43 55 345
266	53 54 057	52 00 122	28 17 162	28 01 199	41 51 267	44 01 309	43 42 345
267	54 36 057	52 42 123	28 33 163	27 44 200	41 00 267	43 22 309	43 29 345
268	55 18 057	53 24 124	28 47 164	27 27 201	40 10 268	42 43 309	43 16 344
269	56 00 056	54 05 126	29 01 165	27 09 202	39 20 268	42 03 309	43 02 344

LHA ♈	Hc Zn	Hc Zn	Hc Zn	Hc Zn	Hc Zn	Hc Zn	Hc Zn
	◆DENEB	ALTAIR	◆Nunki	ANTARES	ARCTURUS	◆Alkaid	Kochab
270	56 42 056	54 46 127	29 14 166	26 50 202	38 29 269	41 24 309	42 49 344
271	57 23 056	55 26 128	29 26 167	26 30 203	37 39 270	40 45 309	42 35 344
272	58 05 056	56 05 129	29 38 168	26 10 204	36 49 270	40 06 309	42 21 344
273	58 47 056	56 43 131	29 48 169	25 49 205	35 59 271	39 28 309	42 06 343
274	59 28 055	57 21 132	29 57 170	25 27 206	35 08 271	38 49 310	41 52 343
275	60 10 055	57 58 134	30 06 171	25 04 207	34 18 272	38 10 310	41 37 343
276	60 51 055	58 34 135	30 14 172	24 41 208	33 28 272	37 31 310	41 23 343
277	61 32 054	59 09 137	30 21 173	24 17 209	32 37 273	36 53 310	41 08 343
278	62 13 054	59 43 138	30 27 174	23 52 210	31 47 273	36 14 310	40 53 343
279	62 53 054	60 16 140	30 32 175	23 27 211	30 57 274	35 36 310	40 38 343
280	63 34 053	60 48 142	30 36 176	23 01 211	30 07 274	34 57 310	40 23 342
281	64 14 053	61 18 143	30 39 177	22 35 212	29 17 275	34 19 311	40 07 342
282	64 54 052	61 48 145	30 41 178	22 08 213	28 26 275	33 41 311	39 52 342
283	65 33 052	62 16 147	30 43 179	21 40 214	27 36 276	33 03 311	39 37 342
284	66 13 051	62 43 149	30 43 180	21 11 215	26 46 276	32 25 311	39 21 342
	◆Alpheratz	Enif	ALTAIR	◆ANTARES	ARCTURUS	◆Alkaid	Kochab
285	25 15 070	45 40 112	63 08 151	20 42 216	25 56 277	31 47 311	39 05 342
286	26 02 071	46 27 113	63 32 153	20 13 216	25 06 277	31 09 312	38 50 342
287	26 50 071	47 13 113	63 54 155	19 43 217	24 16 278	30 32 312	38 34 342
288	27 38 072	47 59 114	64 14 157	19 12 218	23 27 278	29 54 312	38 18 341
289	28 26 072	48 45 115	64 33 159	18 41 219	22 37 279	29 17 312	38 02 341
290	29 13 072	49 30 116	64 50 161	18 09 219	21 47 279	28 39 312	37 46 341
291	30 01 073	50 15 117	65 05 164	17 37 220	20 58 280	28 02 313	37 30 341
292	30 50 073	50 59 118	65 18 166	17 04 221	20 08 280	27 25 313	37 13 341
293	31 38 074	51 43 119	65 29 168	16 31 222	19 18 281	26 49 313	36 57 341
294	32 26 074	52 27 120	65 39 171	15 57 222	18 29 281	26 12 313	36 41 341
295	33 15 074	53 10 122	65 46 173	15 23 223	17 40 282	25 35 314	36 25 341
296	34 03 075	53 53 123	65 51 175	14 48 224	16 51 282	24 59 314	36 08 341
297	34 52 075	54 35 124	65 54 178	14 13 225	16 01 283	24 23 314	35 52 341
298	35 40 076	55 16 125	65 55 180	13 38 225	15 12 283	23 47 314	35 35 341
299	36 29 076	55 57 126	65 53 183	13 02 226	14 23 284	23 11 315	35 19 341
	◆Mirfak	Alpheratz	◆FOMALHAUT	ALTAIR	Rasalhague	◆Alphecca	Kochab
300	12 43 038	37 18 076	14 32 141	65 50 185	51 15 247	33 11 282	35 03 341
301	13 14 038	38 07 077	15 03 142	65 44 188	50 28 248	32 22 283	34 46 341
302	13 45 039	38 56 077	15 34 142	65 37 190	49 42 249	31 33 283	34 30 341
303	14 17 039	39 45 078	16 05 143	65 27 192	48 55 249	30 44 284	34 13 341
304	14 49 039	40 34 078	16 35 144	65 15 195	48 08 250	29 55 284	33 57 341
305	15 21 040	41 23 078	17 04 145	65 02 197	47 20 251	29 06 285	33 40 341
306	15 53 040	42 13 079	17 33 145	64 46 199	46 32 252	28 17 285	33 24 341
307	16 26 041	43 02 079	18 01 146	64 29 201	45 44 253	27 29 285	33 08 341
308	16 59 041	43 52 080	18 29 147	64 10 203	44 56 254	26 40 286	32 51 341
309	17 32 041	44 41 080	18 56 148	63 49 206	44 08 254	25 52 286	32 35 341
310	18 05 042	45 31 080	19 23 148	63 26 208	43 19 255	25 04 287	32 19 341
311	18 39 042	46 20 081	19 49 149	63 02 210	42 30 256	24 16 287	32 02 341
312	19 12 042	47 10 081	20 15 150	62 36 212	41 42 257	23 27 288	31 46 341
313	19 46 043	48 00 082	20 39 151	62 09 213	40 53 257	22 40 288	31 30 341
314	20 20 043	48 50 082	21 04 152	61 41 215	40 03 258	21 52 288	31 14 341
	◆Mirfak	Hamal	Diphda	◆FOMALHAUT	ALTAIR	◆VEGA	Kochab
315	20 55 043	22 59 076	16 08 125	21 27 152	61 11 217	60 45 292	30 58 341
316	21 29 044	23 47 076	16 49 125	21 50 153	60 40 219	59 58 292	30 42 341
317	22 04 044	24 36 077	17 30 126	22 12 154	60 08 221	59 11 292	30 26 342
318	22 39 044	25 26 077	18 10 127	22 34 155	59 35 222	58 25 292	30 10 342
319	23 14 044	26 15 078	18 50 128	22 55 156	59 00 224	57 38 292	29 54 342
320	23 50 045	27 04 078	19 30 128	23 15 157	58 25 225	56 51 292	29 38 342
321	24 25 045	27 53 079	20 10 129	23 35 158	57 49 227	56 04 292	29 22 342
322	25 01 045	28 43 079	20 48 130	23 53 159	57 12 228	55 18 292	29 07 342
323	25 37 046	29 32 080	21 27 130	24 11 159	56 34 230	54 31 292	28 51 342
324	26 13 046	30 22 080	22 05 131	24 29 160	55 55 231	53 44 292	28 36 342
325	26 49 046	31 11 081	22 43 132	24 45 161	55 16 232	52 58 292	28 20 342
326	27 25 046	32 01 081	23 20 133	25 01 162	54 36 233	52 11 292	28 05 342
327	28 01 047	32 51 082	23 56 134	25 16 163	53 55 235	51 25 293	27 50 343
328	28 38 047	33 40 082	24 33 134	25 30 164	53 14 236	50 38 293	27 35 343
329	29 15 047	34 30 082	25 08 135	25 44 165	52 32 237	49 52 293	27 20 343
	◆Mirfak	Hamal	Diphda	◆FOMALHAUT	ALTAIR	◆VEGA	Kochab
330	29 52 047	35 20 083	25 44 136	25 57 166	51 49 238	49 06 293	27 05 343
331	30 29 047	36 10 083	26 18 137	26 08 167	51 06 239	48 19 293	26 50 343
332	31 06 048	37 00 084	26 52 138	26 20 168	50 23 240	47 33 293	26 36 343
333	31 43 048	37 50 084	27 26 139	26 30 169	49 39 241	46 47 294	26 21 343
334	32 20 048	38 40 085	27 59 139	26 39 170	48 54 242	46 01 294	26 07 343
335	32 58 048	39 30 085	28 31 140	26 48 171	48 10 243	45 15 294	25 53 344
336	33 36 048	40 21 086	29 03 141	26 56 172	47 24 244	44 29 294	25 39 344
337	34 13 049	41 11 086	29 34 142	27 03 173	46 39 245	43 43 294	25 25 344
338	34 51 049	42 01 087	30 05 143	27 09 174	45 53 246	42 57 295	25 11 344
339	35 29 049	42 51 087	30 35 144	27 14 175	45 07 247	42 12 295	24 57 344
340	36 07 049	43 42 088	31 04 145	27 18 175	44 20 248	41 26 295	24 43 344
341	36 45 049	44 32 088	31 32 146	27 22 176	43 34 249	40 40 295	24 30 345
342	37 23 049	45 22 089	32 00 147	27 25 177	42 47 250	39 55 296	24 17 345
343	38 01 049	46 12 089	32 27 148	27 26 178	41 59 250	39 10 296	24 04 345
344	38 39 050	47 03 090	32 54 149	27 27 179	41 12 251	38 24 296	23 51 345
	◆CAPELLA	ALDEBARAN	Diphda	◆FOMALHAUT	ALTAIR	◆VEGA	Kochab
345	20 17 048	13 40 079	33 19 150	27 27 180	40 24 252	37 39 296	23 38 345
346	20 54 048	14 30 079	33 44 151	27 27 181	39 36 253	36 54 297	23 25 346
347	21 32 048	15 19 080	34 08 152	27 25 182	38 48 253	36 09 297	23 13 346
348	22 09 049	16 09 080	34 31 153	27 23 183	38 00 254	35 24 297	23 01 346
349	22 47 049	16 58 081	34 54 154	27 19 184	37 11 255	34 40 297	22 48 346
350	23 25 049	17 48 081	35 15 155	27 15 185	36 23 256	33 55 298	22 36 346
351	24 03 049	18 38 082	35 36 156	27 10 186	35 34 256	33 10 298	22 25 347
352	24 42 050	19 28 083	35 56 157	27 04 187	34 45 257	32 26 298	22 13 347
353	25 20 050	20 18 083	36 14 159	26 57 188	33 56 258	31 42 298	22 02 347
354	25 59 050	21 08 084	36 32 160	26 50 189	33 06 258	30 57 299	21 50 347
355	26 38 051	21 58 084	36 49 161	26 41 190	32 17 259	30 13 299	21 39 347
356	27 17 051	22 48 085	37 06 162	26 32 191	31 28 260	29 30 299	21 28 348
357	27 56 051	23 38 085	37 21 163	26 22 192	30 38 260	28 46 300	21 18 348
358	28 35 051	24 28 086	37 35 164	26 11 193	29 49 261	28 02 300	21 07 348
359	29 14 052	25 18 086	37 48 165	25 59 194	28 59 261	27 19 300	20 57 348

LHA ♈	Hc	Zn	Hc	Zn	Hc	Zn	Hc	Zn	Hc	Zn	Hc	Zn	Hc	Zn
	◆CAPELLA		ALDEBARAN		Diphda		◆FOMALHAUT		ALTAIR		◆DENEB		Kochab	
0	29 17	052	26 05	086	38 59	166	26 45	195	28 17	263	49 49	304	19 48	349
1	29 57	052	26 55	087	39 10	168	26 31	196	27 26	263	49 07	304	19 38	349
2	30 37	052	27 46	087	39 20	169	26 17	197	26 36	264	48 24	304	19 28	349
3	31 17	052	28 37	088	39 30	170	26 02	198	25 45	264	47 42	304	19 19	349
4	31 57	052	29 28	088	39 38	171	25 46	199	24 55	265	47 00	304	19 09	350
5	32 38	053	30 19	089	39 45	172	25 29	200	24 04	265	46 18	304	19 00	350
6	33 18	053	31 10	089	39 51	174	25 12	201	23 13	266	45 36	304	18 51	350
7	33 59	053	32 01	090	39 57	175	24 54	201	22 22	267	44 54	304	18 43	350
8	34 39	053	32 51	090	40 00	176	24 35	202	21 32	267	44 12	304	18 34	351
9	35 20	053	33 42	091	40 03	177	24 15	203	20 41	268	43 30	304	18 26	351
10	36 01	054	34 33	091	40 05	179	23 55	204	19 50	268	42 47	304	18 18	351
11	36 42	054	35 24	092	40 06	180	23 33	205	18 59	269	42 06	304	18 10	351
12	37 23	054	36 15	092	40 05	181	23 12	206	18 08	269	41 24	305	18 03	352
13	38 04	054	37 06	093	40 04	182	22 49	207	17 17	270	40 42	305	17 55	352
14	38 45	054	37 57	094	40 01	184	22 26	208	16 26	270	40 00	305	17 48	352
	◆CAPELLA		RIGEL		◆Diphda		FOMALHAUT		Enif		◆DENEB		Kochab	
15	39 27	054	17 09	112	39 57	185	22 02	208	39 57	255	39 18	305	17 41	352
16	40 08	054	17 57	112	39 52	186	21 38	209	39 07	256	38 36	305	17 34	353
17	40 49	054	18 43	113	39 46	187	21 13	210	38 18	256	37 55	305	17 28	353
18	41 31	055	19 30	114	39 39	189	20 47	211	37 29	257	37 13	305	17 22	353
19	42 12	055	20 17	114	39 31	190	20 20	212	36 39	258	36 32	306	17 16	353
20	42 54	055	21 03	115	39 22	191	19 54	212	35 49	258	35 50	306	17 10	354
21	43 35	055	21 49	116	39 12	192	19 26	213	34 59	259	35 09	306	17 05	354
22	44 17	055	22 35	116	39 01	193	18 58	214	34 09	260	34 28	306	16 59	354
23	44 58	055	23 20	117	38 48	195	18 29	215	33 19	260	33 47	306	16 54	354
24	45 40	055	24 06	118	38 35	196	18 00	215	32 29	261	33 06	306	16 49	355
25	46 22	055	24 51	118	38 21	197	17 30	216	31 39	262	32 25	307	16 45	355
26	47 03	055	25 35	119	38 05	198	17 00	217	30 48	262	31 44	307	16 41	355
27	47 45	055	26 20	120	37 49	199	16 29	218	29 58	263	31 04	307	16 37	356
28	48 27	055	27 04	121	37 32	200	15 58	218	29 07	263	30 23	307	16 33	356
29	49 08	055	27 47	121	37 13	202	15 26	219	28 17	264	29 43	308	16 29	356
	CAPELLA		BETELGEUSE		◆RIGEL		Diphda		◆Alpheratz		DENEB		◆Kochab	
30	49 50	055	30 06	101	28 31	122	36 54	203	66 03	271	29 02	308	16 26	356
31	50 32	055	30 56	101	29 13	123	36 34	204	65 12	271	28 22	308	16 23	357
32	51 13	055	31 46	102	29 56	124	36 13	205	64 21	272	27 42	308	16 20	357
33	51 55	055	32 35	103	30 38	124	35 51	206	63 30	272	27 02	309	16 17	357
34	52 36	055	33 25	103	31 20	125	35 29	207	62 39	272	26 22	309	16 15	358
35	53 18	054	34 15	104	32 01	126	35 05	208	61 48	273	25 43	309	16 13	358
36	53 59	054	35 04	105	32 42	127	34 41	209	60 58	273	25 03	309	16 11	358
37	54 40	054	35 53	105	33 23	128	34 15	210	60 07	274	24 24	310	16 10	358
38	55 22	054	36 42	106	34 03	129	33 49	211	59 16	274	23 45	310	16 08	359
39	56 03	054	37 31	107	34 42	130	33 23	212	58 25	275	23 06	310	16 07	359
40	56 44	054	38 19	107	35 21	130	32 55	213	57 35	275	22 27	310	16 07	359
41	57 24	053	39 08	108	36 00	131	32 27	214	56 44	275	21 49	311	16 06	000
42	58 05	053	39 56	109	36 37	132	31 58	215	55 53	276	21 10	311	16 06	000
43	58 46	053	40 44	110	37 15	133	31 28	216	55 03	276	20 32	311	16 06	000
44	59 26	052	41 32	111	37 51	134	30 58	217	54 12	277	19 54	312	16 06	000
	◆Dubhe		POLLUX		SIRIUS		◆RIGEL		Diphda		◆Alpheratz		Schedar	
45	14 58	025	29 03	073	17 14	123	38 28	135	30 27	218	53 22	277	55 43	326
46	15 19	025	29 52	074	17 56	124	39 03	136	29 55	219	52 31	277	55 15	326
47	15 41	025	30 41	074	18 38	125	39 38	137	29 23	220	51 41	278	54 46	325
48	16 03	026	31 30	075	19 20	125	40 12	138	28 50	221	50 50	278	54 17	325
49	16 25	026	32 19	075	20 01	126	40 45	139	28 17	222	50 00	279	53 47	324
50	16 48	026	33 08	075	20 42	127	41 18	141	27 43	222	49 10	279	53 18	324
51	17 11	027	33 57	076	21 23	128	41 50	142	27 08	223	48 20	279	52 48	324
52	17 34	027	34 47	076	22 03	128	42 21	143	26 33	224	47 29	280	52 17	323
53	17 57	027	35 36	077	22 42	129	42 52	144	25 57	225	46 39	280	51 47	323
54	18 20	028	36 26	077	23 22	130	43 21	145	25 21	226	45 49	280	51 16	323
55	18 44	028	37 15	077	24 01	131	43 50	146	24 44	227	44 59	281	50 45	322
56	19 08	028	38 05	078	24 39	131	44 17	148	24 07	227	44 09	281	50 14	322
57	19 32	028	38 55	078	25 17	132	44 44	149	23 29	228	43 19	282	49 42	322
58	19 56	029	39 44	078	25 55	133	45 10	150	22 51	229	42 30	282	49 11	322
59	20 21	029	40 34	079	26 32	134	45 35	151	22 12	230	41 40	282	48 39	321
	◆Dubhe		POLLUX		PROCYON		◆SIRIUS		RIGEL		◆Hamal		Schedar	
60	20 46	029	41 24	079	32 09	105	27 08	135	45 59	153	63 55	258	48 07	321
61	21 10	029	42 14	080	32 58	106	27 44	135	46 22	154	63 05	259	47 35	321
62	21 36	030	43 04	080	33 46	107	28 19	136	46 44	155	62 15	260	47 03	321
63	22 01	030	43 55	080	34 35	108	28 54	137	47 04	157	61 25	261	46 31	321
64	22 26	030	44 45	081	35 23	108	29 29	138	47 24	158	60 34	261	45 58	320
65	22 52	030	45 35	081	36 12	109	30 02	139	47 42	159	59 44	262	45 26	320
66	23 18	031	46 25	082	37 00	110	30 36	140	48 00	161	58 54	263	44 53	320
67	23 44	031	47 16	082	37 47	110	31 08	141	48 16	162	58 03	264	44 21	320
68	24 10	031	48 06	082	38 35	111	31 40	142	48 31	164	57 13	264	43 48	320
69	24 36	031	48 57	083	39 22	112	32 11	143	48 44	165	56 22	265	43 15	320
70	25 02	031	49 47	083	40 09	113	32 42	144	48 57	167	55 31	266	42 42	320
71	25 29	032	50 38	084	40 56	114	33 12	145	49 08	168	54 40	266	42 09	320
72	25 56	032	51 28	084	41 43	114	33 41	146	49 17	170	53 50	267	41 36	320
73	26 23	032	52 19	084	42 29	115	34 09	147	49 26	171	52 59	267	41 03	320
74	26 50	032	53 10	085	43 15	116	34 37	148	49 33	173	52 08	268	40 30	320
	◆Dubhe		POLLUX		PROCYON		◆SIRIUS		RIGEL		◆Hamal		Mirfak	
75	27 17	032	54 00	085	44 00	117	35 04	149	49 39	174	51 17	268	64 55	322
76	27 44	032	54 51	086	44 45	118	35 30	150	49 43	176	50 26	269	64 23	322
77	28 11	033	55 42	086	45 30	119	35 55	151	49 47	177	49 35	270	63 52	321
78	28 39	033	56 32	087	46 14	120	36 20	152	49 48	179	48 45	270	63 19	320
79	29 06	033	57 23	087	46 58	121	36 43	153	49 49	180	47 54	271	62 46	319
80	29 34	033	58 14	088	47 42	122	37 06	154	49 48	182	47 03	271	62 13	319
81	30 02	033	59 05	088	48 25	123	37 28	155	49 46	183	46 12	272	61 39	318
82	30 29	033	59 56	089	49 07	124	37 49	156	49 42	185	45 21	272	61 04	317
83	30 57	033	60 47	089	49 49	125	38 09	157	49 37	186	44 30	273	60 30	317
84	31 25	033	61 38	090	50 30	126	38 28	158	49 31	188	43 39	273	59 55	316
85	31 53	034	62 28	090	51 11	127	38 46	160	49 23	189	42 49	274	59 19	316
86	32 22	034	63 19	091	51 51	129	39 04	161	49 14	191	41 58	274	58 43	315
87	32 50	034	64 10	091	52 31	130	39 20	162	49 04	192	41 07	275	58 07	315
88	33 18	034	65 01	092	53 09	131	39 35	163	48 52	194	40 16	275	57 31	314
89	33 46	034	65 52	092	53 47	132	39 49	164	48 39	195	39 26	275	56 55	314

LAT 32°N

LHA ♈	Hc	Zn	Hc	Zn	Hc	Zn	Hc	Zn	Hc	Zn	Hc	Zn	Hc	Zn
	◆Dubhe		REGULUS		PROCYON		◆SIRIUS		RIGEL		ALDEBARAN		◆Mirfak	
90	34 15	034	29 40	094	54 25	134	40 02	166	48 25	197	65 37	236	56 18	314
91	34 43	034	30 31	095	55 01	135	40 15	167	48 10	198	64 55	237	55 41	313
92	35 11	034	31 22	096	55 37	136	40 26	168	47 53	200	64 12	239	55 04	313
93	35 40	034	32 12	096	56 11	138	40 36	169	47 36	201	63 28	240	54 26	313
94	36 08	034	33 03	097	56 45	139	40 44	171	47 17	202	62 43	241	53 49	312
95	36 37	034	33 53	097	57 17	141	40 52	172	46 57	204	61 59	243	53 11	312
96	37 05	034	34 44	098	57 49	142	40 59	173	46 36	205	61 13	244	52 33	312
97	37 34	034	35 34	099	58 19	144	41 05	174	46 13	207	60 27	245	51 55	312
98	38 02	034	36 25	099	58 49	146	41 09	176	45 50	208	59 41	246	51 17	312
99	38 31	034	37 15	100	59 17	147	41 12	177	45 26	209	58 54	247	50 39	311
100	38 59	034	38 05	100	59 43	149	41 15	178	45 01	210	58 07	248	50 01	311
101	39 27	034	38 55	101	60 09	151	41 16	179	44 34	212	57 19	249	49 23	311
102	39 56	034	39 45	102	60 33	153	41 16	181	44 07	213	56 32	250	48 44	311
103	40 24	034	40 34	102	60 55	155	41 14	182	43 39	214	55 44	251	48 06	311
104	40 52	034	41 24	103	61 16	157	41 12	183	43 10	215	54 55	252	47 27	311
	◆Alkaid		REGULUS		Alphard		◆SIRIUS		RIGEL		ALDEBARAN		◆CAPELLA	
105	16 37	042	42 14	104	36 02	133	41 09	185	42 40	216	54 07	253	65 52	313
106	17 11	042	43 03	105	36 40	133	41 04	186	42 10	218	53 18	254	65 15	312
107	17 45	042	43 52	105	37 16	134	40 58	187	41 38	219	52 29	255	64 37	311
108	18 20	043	44 41	106	37 52	135	40 52	188	41 06	220	51 40	256	63 59	311
109	18 54	043	45 30	107	38 28	136	40 44	190	40 33	221	50 50	256	63 20	310
110	19 29	043	46 18	108	39 02	137	40 35	191	39 59	222	50 01	257	62 41	310
111	20 04	044	47 07	108	39 36	139	40 25	192	39 25	223	49 11	258	62 02	309
112	20 40	044	47 55	109	40 10	140	40 13	193	38 50	224	48 21	259	61 22	309
113	21 15	044	48 43	110	40 42	141	40 01	194	38 14	225	47 31	259	60 42	308
114	21 51	045	49 31	111	41 14	142	39 48	196	37 38	226	46 41	260	60 02	308
115	22 26	045	50 18	112	41 45	143	39 34	197	37 01	227	45 51	261	59 22	308
116	23 03	045	51 05	113	42 16	144	39 18	198	36 23	228	45 01	261	58 42	307
117	23 39	045	51 52	114	42 45	145	39 02	199	35 45	229	44 11	262	58 01	307
118	24 15	046	52 38	115	43 14	146	38 45	200	35 07	230	43 20	263	57 20	307
119	24 52	046	53 24	116	43 41	148	38 26	202	34 28	231	42 30	263	56 40	306
	◆Alkaid		REGULUS		◆Alphard		SIRIUS		RIGEL		ALDEBARAN		◆CAPELLA	
120	25 28	046	54 10	117	44 08	149	38 07	203	33 48	232	41 39	264	55 59	306
121	26 05	046	54 55	118	44 34	150	37 47	204	33 08	233	40 49	264	55 17	306
122	26 42	047	55 40	119	44 59	151	37 26	205	32 27	233	39 58	265	54 36	306
123	27 19	047	56 24	120	45 23	153	37 04	206	31 46	234	39 07	266	53 55	306
124	27 56	047	57 08	121	45 46	154	36 41	207	31 05	235	38 16	266	53 14	306
125	28 34	047	57 51	123	46 08	155	36 17	208	30 23	236	37 26	267	52 32	305
126	29 11	048	58 34	124	46 28	157	35 53	209	29 40	237	36 35	267	51 51	305
127	29 49	048	59 16	125	46 48	158	35 27	210	28 58	237	35 44	268	51 09	305
128	30 27	048	59 57	126	47 07	159	35 01	212	28 15	238	34 53	268	50 27	305
129	31 05	048	60 37	128	47 24	161	34 34	213	27 31	239	34 02	269	49 46	305
130	31 43	048	61 17	129	47 40	162	34 07	214	26 47	240	33 11	270	49 04	305
131	32 21	049	61 56	131	47 55	164	33 38	215	26 03	241	32 20	270	48 23	305
132	32 59	049	62 34	133	48 09	165	33 09	216	25 19	241	31 30	271	47 41	305
133	33 37	049	63 11	134	48 22	166	32 39	217	24 34	242	30 39	271	46 59	305
134	34 16	049	63 47	136	48 33	168	32 08	217	23 49	243	29 48	272	46 18	305
	◆Alkaid		ARCTURUS		SPICA		◆Alphard		SIRIUS		BETELGEUSE		◆CAPELLA	
135	34 54	049	18 59	079	13 12	113	48 43	169	31 37	218	40 44	250	45 36	305
136	35 33	049	19 48	079	13 59	113	48 52	171	31 05	219	39 56	251	44 54	305
137	36 11	049	20 39	080	14 46	114	48 59	172	30 32	220	39 07	252	44 13	305
138	36 50	050	21 29	080	15 32	114	49 05	174	29 59	221	38 19	253	43 31	305
139	37 29	050	22 19	081	16 19	115	49 10	175	29 25	222	37 30	253	42 49	305
140	38 08	050	23 09	081	17 05	116	49 14	177	28 51	223	36 42	254	42 08	305
141	38 47	050	23 59	082	17 50	116	49 16	178	28 16	224	35 53	255	41 26	305
142	39 26	050	24 50	082	18 36	117	49 17	180	27 41	225	35 03	255	40 45	306
143	40 05	050	25 40	083	19 21	118	49 16	181	27 05	226	34 14	256	40 04	306
144	40 44	050	26 31	083	20 06	118	49 14	183	26 28	226	33 25	257	39 22	306
145	41 23	050	27 21	084	20 51	119	49 11	184	25 51	227	32 35	257	38 41	306
146	42 02	050	28 12	084	21 35	120	49 06	186	25 13	228	31 45	258	38 00	306
147	42 41	050	29 02	085	22 19	120	49 00	187	24 35	229	30 56	259	37 19	306
148	43 20	050	29 53	085	23 03	121	48 53	189	23 57	230	30 06	259	36 38	306
149	43 59	050	30 44	086	23 46	122	48 45	190	23 18	230	29 16	260	35 57	307
	Alkaid		◆ARCTURUS		SPICA		◆Alphard		PROCYON		BETELGEUSE		◆CAPELLA	
150	44 39	050	31 35	086	24 29	122	48 35	192	47 43	238	28 25	260	35 16	307
151	45 18	050	32 25	087	25 12	123	48 24	193	47 00	239	27 35	261	34 35	307
152	45 57	050	33 16	087	25 55	124	48 11	195	46 16	240	26 45	262	33 55	307
153	46 36	050	34 07	088	26 37	125	47 58	196	45 32	241	25 55	262	33 14	307
154	47 15	050	34 58	088	27 18	126	47 43	198	44 47	242	25 04	263	32 34	307
155	47 54	050	35 49	089	27 59	126	47 27	199	44 02	243	24 14	263	31 53	308
156	48 33	050	36 40	089	28 40	127	47 10	200	43 17	244	23 23	264	31 13	308
157	49 12	050	37 30	090	29 21	128	46 51	202	42 31	245	22 32	265	30 33	308
158	49 51	050	38 21	090	30 00	129	46 32	203	41 45	245	21 42	265	29 53	308
159	50 30	050	39 12	091	30 40	130	46 11	205	40 58	246	20 51	266	29 13	309
160	51 09	050	40 03	091	31 19	130	45 49	206	40 11	247	20 00	266	28 33	309
161	51 48	049	40 54	092	31 57	131	45 27	207	39 24	248	19 09	267	27 54	309
162	52 26	049	41 45	092	32 35	132	45 03	208	38 37	249	18 19	267	27 14	309
163	53 05	049	42 36	093	33 13	133	44 38	210	37 50	249	17 28	268	26 35	309
164	53 43	049	43 26	093	33 49	134	44 12	211	37 02	250	16 37	268	25 56	310
	Dubhe		◆Alkaid		ARCTURUS		◆SPICA		REGULUS		◆PROCYON		CAPELLA	
165	60 19	001	54 21	049	44 17	094	34 26	135	66 44	213	36 14	251	25 17	310
166	60 20	000	54 59	048	45 08	095	35 01	136	66 16	215	35 26	252	24 38	310
167	60 20	359	55 37	048	45 59	095	35 37	137	65 46	217	34 37	252	23 59	311
168	60 18	358	56 15	048	46 49	096	36 11	138	65 14	219	33 49	253	23 20	311
169	60 16	357	56 53	047	47 40	096	36 45	139	64 42	221	33 00	254	22 42	311
170	60 14	356	57 30	047	48 30	097	37 18	140	64 07	223	32 11	254	22 04	311
171	60 10	355	58 07	047	49 21	098	37 50	141	63 32	225	31 22	255	21 26	312
172	60 05	354	58 44	046	50 11	098	38 22	142	62 56	226	30 32	256	20 48	312
173	60 00	354	59 21	046	51 02	099	38 53	143	62 18	228	29 43	256	20 10	312
174	59 54	353	59 57	045	51 52	100	39 23	144	61 40	230	28 54	257	19 33	313
175	59 47	352	60 33	045	52 42	101	39 53	145	61 01	231	28 04	258	18 55	313
176	59 39	351	61 09	044	53 32	101	40 21	146	60 21	233	27 14	258	18 18	313
177	59 31	350	61 44	044	54 22	102	40 49	147	59 40	234	26 24	259	17 41	314
178	59 21	349	62 19	043	55 11	103	41 16	149	58 58	235	25 34	260	17 05	314
179	59 11	348	62 53	042	56 01	104	41 42	150	58 16	237	24 44	260	16 28	314

LAT 32°N

LHA ♈	Hc	Zn	Hc	Zn	Hc	Zn	Hc	Zn	Hc	Zn	Hc	Zn	Hc	Zn
	◆VEGA		Alphecca		ARCTURUS		◆SPICA		REGULUS		◆POLLUX		Dubhe	
180	12 58	052	43 15	082	56 50	105	42 07	151	57 33	238	35 42	283	59 00	347
181	13 39	053	44 05	082	57 39	105	42 31	152	56 50	239	34 52	284	58 49	346
182	14 19	053	44 55	083	58 28	106	42 54	153	56 06	240	34 03	284	58 36	346
183	15 00	053	45 46	083	59 17	107	43 17	155	55 21	242	33 14	285	58 23	345
184	15 41	054	46 36	084	60 05	108	43 38	156	54 36	243	32 25	285	58 10	344
185	16 22	054	47 27	084	60 54	109	43 58	157	53 51	244	31 35	285	57 55	343
186	17 03	054	48 18	085	61 42	110	44 17	159	53 05	245	30 46	286	57 40	342
187	17 45	055	49 08	085	62 29	111	44 35	160	52 19	246	29 58	286	57 25	342
188	18 26	055	49 59	085	63 16	113	44 52	161	51 32	247	29 09	287	57 08	341
189	19 08	056	50 50	086	64 03	114	45 08	162	50 46	248	28 20	287	56 52	340
190	19 50	056	51 41	086	64 49	115	45 23	164	49 58	249	27 31	287	56 34	340
191	20 33	056	52 31	087	65 35	116	45 37	165	49 11	249	26 43	288	56 16	339
192	21 15	057	53 22	087	66 21	118	45 49	167	48 23	250	25 54	288	55 58	338
193	21 58	057	54 13	088	67 05	119	46 00	168	47 35	251	25 06	289	55 39	338
194	22 40	057	55 04	088	67 50	121	46 10	169	46 47	252	24 18	289	55 19	337
	◆Kochab		VEGA		Rasalhague		◆ANTARES		SPICA		◆REGULUS		Dubhe	
195	45 41	010	23 23	058	24 24	090	13 01	133	46 19	171	45 58	253	54 59	336
196	45 50	010	24 06	058	25 15	091	13 38	134	46 27	172	45 10	254	54 38	336
197	45 59	010	24 50	058	26 06	091	14 14	134	46 33	174	44 21	254	54 17	335
198	46 07	009	25 33	059	26 56	092	14 50	135	46 38	175	43 32	255	53 56	335
199	46 16	009	26 17	059	27 47	092	15 26	136	46 42	176	42 42	256	53 34	334
200	46 24	009	27 00	059	28 38	093	16 01	137	46 44	178	41 53	256	53 12	334
201	46 31	008	27 44	060	29 29	093	16 36	137	46 45	179	41 03	257	52 49	333
202	46 39	008	28 28	060	30 20	094	17 10	138	46 45	181	40 14	258	52 26	333
203	46 46	008	29 12	060	31 10	095	17 44	139	46 44	182	39 24	259	52 03	332
204	46 52	007	29 56	060	32 01	095	18 17	139	46 42	184	38 34	259	51 39	332
205	46 59	007	30 41	061	32 52	096	18 50	140	46 38	185	37 44	260	51 15	332
206	47 05	007	31 25	061	33 42	096	19 22	141	46 33	186	36 54	260	50 51	331
207	47 10	006	32 10	061	34 33	097	19 54	142	46 26	188	36 04	261	50 26	331
208	47 16	006	32 54	062	35 23	097	20 25	143	46 19	189	35 13	262	50 01	330
209	47 21	005	33 39	062	36 14	098	20 56	143	46 10	191	34 23	262	49 36	330
	◆Kochab		VEGA		Rasalhague		◆ANTARES		SPICA		◆REGULUS		Dubhe	
210	47 25	005	34 24	062	37 04	099	21 26	144	46 00	192	33 33	263	49 11	330
211	47 30	005	35 09	062	37 54	099	21 56	145	45 49	193	32 42	264	48 45	330
212	47 34	004	35 54	063	38 45	100	22 25	146	45 36	195	31 51	264	48 19	329
213	47 37	004	36 40	063	39 35	101	22 53	147	45 23	196	31 01	265	47 53	329
214	47 41	004	37 25	063	40 25	101	23 21	147	45 08	198	30 10	265	47 26	329
215	47 44	003	38 10	063	41 14	102	23 48	148	44 52	199	29 19	266	47 00	328
216	47 46	003	38 56	064	42 04	103	24 15	149	44 35	200	28 29	266	46 33	328
217	47 49	002	39 41	064	42 54	103	24 40	150	44 17	201	27 38	267	46 06	328
218	47 50	002	40 27	064	43 43	104	25 06	151	43 58	203	26 47	268	45 39	328
219	47 52	001	41 13	064	44 32	105	25 30	152	43 38	204	25 56	268	45 12	328
220	47 53	001	41 59	064	45 22	106	25 54	153	43 16	205	25 05	269	44 44	327
221	47 54	001	42 45	065	46 11	106	26 17	153	42 54	207	24 14	269	44 17	327
222	47 54	000	43 31	065	46 59	107	26 39	154	42 31	208	23 23	270	43 49	327
223	47 54	000	44 17	065	47 48	108	27 01	155	42 07	209	22 33	270	43 22	327
224	47 54	359	45 03	065	48 36	109	27 22	156	41 42	210	21 42	271	42 54	327
	DENEB		VEGA		◆ALTAIR		ANTARES		◆SPICA		Denebola		◆Dubhe	
225	25 05	051	45 49	065	19 11	091	27 42	157	41 16	211	43 23	259	42 26	327
226	25 44	051	46 35	066	20 02	092	28 01	158	40 49	213	42 33	260	41 58	327
227	26 24	051	47 22	066	20 53	092	28 20	159	40 21	214	41 43	261	41 30	326
228	27 03	051	48 08	066	21 44	093	28 38	160	39 52	215	40 52	261	41 01	326
229	27 43	052	48 55	066	22 35	094	28 55	161	39 23	216	40 02	262	40 33	326
230	28 23	052	49 41	066	23 26	094	29 11	162	38 53	217	39 11	263	40 05	326
231	29 03	052	50 28	066	24 16	095	29 26	163	38 22	218	38 21	263	39 37	326
232	29 44	052	51 14	066	25 07	095	29 41	164	37 50	219	37 30	264	39 08	326
233	30 24	053	52 01	066	25 58	096	29 54	165	37 18	220	36 40	264	38 40	326
234	31 05	053	52 47	066	26 48	096	30 07	166	36 44	221	35 49	265	38 11	326
235	31 45	053	53 34	067	27 39	097	30 19	167	36 11	222	34 58	266	37 43	326
236	32 26	053	54 21	067	28 29	098	30 30	168	35 36	223	34 08	266	37 14	326
237	33 07	054	55 08	067	29 20	098	30 40	169	35 01	224	33 17	267	36 46	326
238	33 48	054	55 54	067	30 10	099	30 50	170	34 25	225	32 26	267	36 17	326
239	34 29	054	56 41	067	31 00	099	30 58	171	33 49	226	31 35	268	35 49	326
	◆DENEB		ALTAIR		Nunki		◆ANTARES		SPICA		ARCTURUS		◆Alkaid	
240	35 10	054	31 50	100	18 11	139	31 05	172	33 12	227	63 24	247	59 59	315
241	35 52	054	32 40	101	18 44	140	31 12	173	32 35	228	62 37	248	59 23	314
242	36 33	054	33 30	101	19 16	140	31 18	174	31 57	229	61 50	250	58 46	314
243	37 14	055	34 20	102	19 48	141	31 22	175	31 19	230	61 02	251	58 10	313
244	37 56	055	35 10	103	20 20	142	31 26	176	30 40	230	60 14	252	57 32	313
245	38 38	055	36 00	103	20 51	143	31 29	177	30 00	231	59 25	253	56 55	313
246	39 19	055	36 49	104	21 22	144	31 31	178	29 20	232	58 37	254	56 18	312
247	40 01	055	37 38	105	21 51	144	31 32	179	28 40	233	57 48	254	55 40	312
248	40 43	055	38 28	105	22 21	145	31 32	180	27 59	234	56 59	255	55 02	312
249	41 25	055	39 17	106	22 50	146	31 31	181	27 18	234	56 09	256	54 24	311
250	42 07	056	40 05	107	23 18	147	31 29	183	26 36	235	55 20	257	53 46	311
251	42 49	056	40 54	107	23 45	148	31 27	184	25 54	236	54 30	258	53 07	311
252	43 31	056	41 42	108	24 12	149	31 23	185	25 12	237	53 40	259	52 29	311
253	44 13	056	42 31	109	24 38	149	31 18	186	24 29	238	52 50	259	51 50	311
254	44 55	056	43 19	110	25 04	150	31 13	187	23 46	238	52 00	260	51 11	310
	◆DENEB		ALTAIR		Nunki		◆ANTARES		ARCTURUS		◆Alkaid		Kochab	
255	45 37	056	44 06	111	25 29	151	31 07	188	51 10	261	50 33	310	44 55	348
256	46 19	056	44 54	111	25 53	152	30 59	189	50 20	261	49 54	310	44 44	348
257	47 01	056	45 41	112	26 16	153	30 51	190	49 30	262	49 15	310	44 33	347
258	47 43	056	46 28	113	26 39	154	30 42	191	48 39	263	48 36	310	44 22	347
259	48 26	056	47 15	114	27 01	155	30 32	192	47 49	263	47 57	310	44 11	347
260	49 08	056	48 01	115	27 22	156	30 21	193	46 58	264	47 18	310	43 59	347
261	49 50	056	48 47	116	27 43	157	30 09	194	46 07	265	46 39	310	43 47	346
262	50 32	056	49 33	117	28 03	158	29 57	195	45 17	265	45 59	310	43 35	346
263	51 14	056	50 18	118	28 22	159	29 43	196	44 26	266	45 20	310	43 23	346
264	51 56	056	51 03	119	28 40	159	29 29	197	43 35	266	44 41	310	43 10	346
265	52 38	056	51 47	120	28 58	160	29 13	198	42 44	267	44 02	310	42 57	345
266	53 20	056	52 31	121	29 14	161	28 57	199	41 54	268	43 23	310	42 44	345
267	54 02	055	53 14	122	29 30	162	28 41	200	41 03	268	42 44	310	42 31	345
268	54 44	055	53 57	123	29 45	163	28 23	201	40 12	269	42 04	310	42 18	345
269	55 26	055	54 39	124	29 59	164	28 04	202	39 21	269	41 25	310	42 05	345

LHA ♈	Hc	Zn	Hc	Zn	Hc	Zn	Hc	Zn	Hc	Zn	Hc	Zn	Hc	Zn
	◆DENEB		ALTAIR		◆Nunki		ANTARES		ARCTURUS		◆Alkaid		Kochab	
270	56 08	055	55 21	126	30 12	165	27 45	203	38 30	270	40 46	310	41 51	344
271	56 49	055	56 02	127	30 25	166	27 25	204	37 39	270	40 07	310	41 37	344
272	57 31	055	56 42	128	30 36	167	27 04	205	36 48	271	39 28	310	41 23	344
273	58 12	054	57 22	130	30 47	168	26 43	205	35 58	271	38 49	310	41 09	344
274	58 54	054	58 01	131	30 56	169	26 21	206	35 07	272	38 10	310	40 54	344
275	59 35	054	58 39	132	31 05	171	25 58	207	34 16	272	37 31	310	40 40	343
276	60 16	053	59 16	134	31 13	172	25 34	208	33 25	273	36 53	310	40 25	343
277	60 56	053	59 52	135	31 20	173	25 10	209	32 34	273	36 14	310	40 11	343
278	61 37	053	60 27	137	31 26	174	24 45	210	31 43	274	35 35	311	39 56	343
279	62 17	052	61 01	139	31 31	175	24 19	211	30 53	274	34 57	311	39 41	343
280	62 57	052	61 34	140	31 36	176	23 52	212	30 02	275	34 18	311	39 26	343
281	63 37	051	62 06	142	31 39	177	23 25	213	29 11	275	33 40	311	39 10	342
282	64 16	051	62 37	144	31 41	178	22 58	213	28 21	276	33 01	311	38 55	342
283	64 55	050	63 06	146	31 43	179	22 29	214	27 30	276	32 23	311	38 39	342
284	65 34	049	63 34	148	31 43	180	22 01	215	26 39	277	31 45	312	38 24	342
	◆Alpheratz		Enif		ALTAIR		◆ANTARES		ARCTURUS		◆Alkaid		Kochab	
285	24 55	070	46 02	111	64 00	150	21 31	216	25 49	277	31 07	312	38 08	342
286	25 42	070	46 49	112	64 25	152	21 01	217	24 58	278	30 29	312	37 53	342
287	26 30	071	47 36	112	64 48	154	20 31	217	24 08	278	29 51	312	37 37	342
288	27 19	071	48 23	113	65 09	156	19 59	218	23 18	279	29 14	312	37 21	342
289	28 07	071	49 10	114	65 29	158	19 28	219	22 27	279	28 36	313	37 05	342
290	28 55	072	49 56	115	65 47	161	18 55	220	21 37	280	27 59	313	36 49	342
291	29 43	072	50 42	116	66 03	163	18 23	220	20 47	280	27 22	313	36 33	342
292	30 32	073	51 27	117	66 16	165	17 49	221	19 57	281	26 44	313	36 17	341
293	31 21	073	52 12	118	66 28	168	17 16	222	19 07	281	26 07	313	36 00	341
294	32 09	073	52 57	119	66 38	170	16 42	223	18 17	282	25 31	314	35 44	341
295	32 58	074	53 41	120	66 45	173	16 07	223	17 27	282	24 54	314	35 28	341
296	33 47	074	54 25	122	66 51	175	15 32	224	16 38	282	24 17	314	35 11	341
297	34 36	075	55 08	123	66 54	178	14 56	225	15 48	283	23 41	315	34 55	341
298	35 25	075	55 50	124	66 55	180	14 20	225	14 59	283	23 05	315	34 39	341
299	36 14	075	56 32	125	66 53	183	13 44	226	14 09	284	22 29	315	34 22	341
	◆Mirfak		Alpheratz		◆FOMALHAUT		ALTAIR		Rasalhague		◆Alphecca		Kochab	
300	11 55	038	37 03	076	15 18	141	66 50	185	51 38	248	32 57	283	34 06	341
301	12 27	038	37 53	076	15 50	141	66 44	188	50 51	249	32 08	283	33 49	341
302	12 58	039	38 42	076	16 21	142	66 36	190	50 03	250	31 18	284	33 33	341
303	13 30	039	39 32	077	16 52	143	66 26	193	49 15	251	30 29	284	33 17	341
304	14 02	039	40 21	077	17 23	144	66 13	195	48 27	251	29 40	285	33 00	341
305	14 35	040	41 11	077	17 53	144	65 59	198	47 39	252	28 51	285	32 44	341
306	15 07	040	42 01	078	18 22	145	65 43	200	46 50	253	28 02	285	32 27	341
307	15 40	040	42 50	078	18 51	146	65 24	202	46 01	254	27 13	286	32 11	341
308	16 13	041	43 40	079	19 19	147	65 04	204	45 13	255	26 24	286	31 54	341
309	16 47	041	44 30	079	19 47	147	64 43	206	44 23	255	25 35	287	31 38	341
310	17 20	041	45 20	079	20 14	148	64 19	209	43 34	256	24 46	287	31 22	341
311	17 54	042	46 10	080	20 41	149	63 54	211	42 45	257	23 58	288	31 05	341
312	18 28	042	47 00	080	21 07	150	63 27	213	41 55	257	23 09	288	30 49	341
313	19 02	042	47 50	080	21 32	151	62 59	215	41 05	258	22 21	288	30 33	341
314	19 36	043	48 41	081	21 56	151	62 29	216	40 15	259	21 33	289	30 17	342
	◆Mirfak		Hamal		Diphda		◆FOMALHAUT		ALTAIR		◆VEGA		Kochab	
315	20 11	043	22 44	076	16 42	124	22 20	152	61 59	218	60 22	293	30 01	342
316	20 46	043	23 33	076	17 24	125	22 44	153	61 26	220	59 35	293	29 45	342
317	21 21	044	24 23	076	18 05	126	23 06	154	60 53	222	58 48	293	29 29	342
318	21 56	044	25 12	077	18 46	127	23 28	155	60 19	223	58 02	293	29 13	342
319	22 31	044	26 02	077	19 27	127	23 50	156	59 43	225	57 15	293	28 57	342
320	23 07	044	26 51	078	20 07	128	24 10	157	59 07	226	56 28	293	28 41	342
321	23 43	045	27 41	078	20 47	129	24 30	157	58 30	228	55 41	293	28 25	342
322	24 18	045	28 31	079	21 27	129	24 49	158	57 51	229	54 55	293	28 10	342
323	24 54	045	29 21	079	22 06	130	25 08	159	57 12	231	54 08	293	27 54	342
324	25 31	045	30 11	080	22 44	131	25 25	160	56 33	232	53 21	293	27 39	342
325	26 07	046	31 01	080	23 23	132	25 42	161	55 52	233	52 35	294	27 23	342
326	26 43	046	31 51	080	24 00	132	25 58	162	55 11	235	51 48	294	27 08	343
327	27 20	046	32 41	081	24 38	133	26 14	163	54 29	236	51 01	294	26 53	343
328	27 57	046	33 32	081	25 15	134	26 28	164	53 47	237	50 15	294	26 38	343
329	28 34	047	34 22	082	25 51	135	26 42	165	53 04	238	49 28	294	26 23	343
	◆Mirfak		Hamal		Diphda		◆FOMALHAUT		ALTAIR		◆VEGA		Kochab	
330	29 11	047	35 12	082	26 27	136	26 55	166	52 20	239	48 42	294	26 08	343
331	29 48	047	36 03	083	27 02	137	27 07	167	51 36	240	47 55	294	25 53	343
332	30 25	047	36 53	083	27 37	137	27 18	168	50 52	241	47 09	294	25 38	343
333	31 03	047	37 44	084	28 11	138	27 29	169	50 07	242	46 23	295	25 24	343
334	31 40	048	38 35	084	28 44	139	27 38	170	49 22	243	45 36	295	25 09	344
335	32 18	048	39 25	085	29 17	140	27 47	171	48 36	244	44 50	295	24 55	344
336	32 55	048	40 16	085	29 50	141	27 55	172	47 50	245	44 04	295	24 41	344
337	33 33	048	41 07	085	30 22	142	28 02	172	47 04	246	43 18	295	24 27	344
338	34 11	048	41 57	086	30 53	143	28 08	173	46 17	247	42 32	295	24 13	344
339	34 49	048	42 48	086	31 23	144	28 14	174	45 30	248	41 46	296	23 59	344
340	35 27	049	43 39	087	31 53	145	28 18	175	44 42	249	41 00	296	23 46	345
341	36 05	049	44 30	087	32 22	146	28 22	176	43 55	250	40 14	296	23 32	345
342	36 44	049	45 20	088	32 50	147	28 24	177	43 07	250	39 29	296	23 19	345
343	37 22	049	46 11	088	33 18	148	28 26	178	42 19	251	38 43	296	23 06	345
344	38 00	049	47 02	089	33 45	149	28 27	179	41 31	252	37 58	297	22 53	345
	◆CAPELLA		ALDEBARAN		Diphda		◆FOMALHAUT		ALTAIR		◆VEGA		Kochab	
345	19 36	047	13 29	079	34 11	150	28 27	180	40 42	253	37 12	297	22 40	345
346	20 14	048	14 19	079	34 36	151	28 27	181	39 54	253	36 27	297	22 27	346
347	20 52	048	15 09	080	35 01	152	28 25	182	39 05	254	35 42	297	22 15	346
348	21 29	048	15 59	080	35 25	153	28 22	183	38 16	255	34 57	298	22 02	346
349	22 08	049	16 49	081	35 48	154	28 19	184	37 26	256	34 12	298	21 50	346
350	22 46	049	17 39	081	36 10	155	28 15	185	36 37	256	33 27	298	21 38	346
351	23 24	049	18 29	082	36 31	156	28 10	186	35 48	257	32 42	298	21 26	347
352	24 03	049	19 20	082	36 51	157	28 04	187	34 58	258	31 57	299	21 15	347
353	24 42	050	20 10	083	37 10	158	27 57	188	34 08	258	31 13	299	21 03	347
354	25 20	050	21 01	083	37 29	159	27 49	189	33 18	259	30 28	299	20 52	347
355	25 59	050	21 51	084	37 46	161	27 40	190	32 28	260	29 44	300	20 41	347
356	26 39	051	22 42	084	38 03	162	27 31	191	31 38	260	29 00	300	20 30	348
357	27 18	051	23 33	085	38 18	163	27 21	192	30 48	261	28 16	300	20 19	348
358	27 58	051	24 23	085	38 33	164	27 10	193	29 58	261	27 32	300	20 09	348
359	28 37	051	25 14	086	38 46	165	26 58	194	29 07	262	26 48	301	19 58	348

LAT 31°N

LHA ♈	Hc	Zn	Hc	Zn	Hc	Zn	Hc	Zn	Hc	Zn	Hc	Zn	Hc	Zn
	◆ CAPELLA		ALDEBARAN		Diphda		◆ FOMALHAUT		ALTAIR		◆ DENEB		Kochab	
0	28 39	051	26 00	086	39 57	166	27 43	195	28 24	263	49 15	305	18 49	349
1	29 19	051	26 52	086	40 09	167	27 29	196	27 33	264	48 33	305	18 39	349
2	30 00	052	27 43	087	40 19	169	27 14	197	26 42	264	47 51	305	18 29	349
3	30 40	052	28 34	087	40 29	170	26 59	198	25 51	265	47 08	305	18 20	349
4	31 20	052	29 26	088	40 37	171	26 43	199	25 00	265	46 26	305	18 10	350
5	32 01	052	30 17	088	40 45	172	26 26	200	24 08	266	45 44	305	18 01	350
6	32 42	052	31 08	089	40 51	174	26 08	201	23 17	266	45 02	305	17 52	350
7	33 22	052	32 00	089	40 56	175	25 49	202	22 26	267	44 20	305	17 44	350
8	34 03	053	32 51	090	41 00	176	25 30	202	21 34	268	43 38	305	17 35	351
9	34 44	053	33 43	090	41 03	177	25 10	203	20 43	268	42 55	305	17 27	351
10	35 25	053	34 34	091	41 05	179	24 49	204	19 52	269	42 13	305	17 19	351
11	36 06	053	35 26	091	41 06	180	24 28	205	19 00	269	41 31	305	17 11	351
12	36 47	053	36 17	092	41 05	181	24 06	206	18 09	270	40 49	305	17 03	352
13	37 29	053	37 08	092	41 04	182	23 43	207	17 17	270	40 07	305	16 56	352
14	38 10	053	38 00	093	41 01	184	23 19	208	16 26	271	39 25	305	16 49	352
	◆ CAPELLA		RIGEL		◆ Diphda		FOMALHAUT		Enif		◆ DENEB		Kochab	
15	38 51	054	17 31	111	40 57	185	22 55	209	40 12	256	38 43	306	16 42	352
16	39 33	054	18 19	112	40 52	186	22 30	209	39 22	257	38 02	306	16 35	353
17	40 14	054	19 07	113	40 46	187	22 05	210	38 32	257	37 20	306	16 28	353
18	40 56	054	19 54	113	40 39	189	21 38	211	37 42	258	36 38	306	16 22	353
19	41 37	054	20 41	114	40 30	190	21 12	212	36 51	259	35 57	306	16 16	353
20	42 19	054	21 28	115	40 21	191	20 44	213	36 01	259	35 15	306	16 10	354
21	43 00	054	22 15	115	40 11	192	20 16	213	35 10	260	34 34	306	16 05	354
22	43 42	054	23 01	116	39 59	194	19 48	214	34 19	260	33 52	307	16 00	354
23	44 24	054	23 47	117	39 46	195	19 18	215	33 29	261	33 11	307	15 55	354
24	45 05	054	24 33	117	39 33	196	18 49	216	32 38	262	32 30	307	15 50	355
25	45 47	054	25 19	118	39 18	197	18 18	216	31 47	262	31 49	307	15 45	355
26	46 29	054	26 04	119	39 02	198	17 48	217	30 56	263	31 08	307	15 41	355
27	47 10	054	26 49	119	38 46	200	17 16	218	30 05	263	30 27	308	15 37	356
28	47 52	054	27 34	120	38 28	201	16 44	219	29 14	264	29 46	308	15 33	356
29	48 33	054	28 18	121	38 09	202	16 12	219	28 23	265	29 06	308	15 29	356
	CAPELLA		BETELGEUSE		◆ RIGEL		Diphda		◆ Alpheratz		DENEB		◆ Kochab	
30	49 15	054	30 17	100	29 02	122	37 50	203	66 01	273	28 25	308	15 26	356
31	49 57	054	31 07	101	29 46	122	37 29	204	65 10	273	27 45	308	15 23	357
32	50 38	054	31 58	101	30 29	123	37 08	205	64 18	274	27 05	309	15 20	357
33	51 20	054	32 48	102	31 12	124	36 45	206	63 27	274	26 25	309	15 18	357
34	52 01	054	33 39	103	31 54	125	36 22	207	62 36	274	25 45	309	15 15	358
35	52 42	053	34 29	103	32 36	126	35 58	208	61 44	275	25 05	309	15 13	358
36	53 24	053	35 19	104	33 18	126	35 33	210	60 53	275	24 25	310	15 11	358
37	54 05	053	36 08	105	33 59	127	35 07	211	60 02	276	23 46	310	15 10	358
38	54 46	053	36 58	105	34 40	128	34 41	212	59 11	276	23 06	310	15 08	359
39	55 27	053	37 48	106	35 20	129	34 13	213	58 20	276	22 27	311	15 07	359
40	56 07	052	38 37	107	36 00	130	33 45	214	57 29	277	21 48	311	15 07	359
41	56 48	052	39 26	107	36 39	131	33 16	215	56 38	277	21 09	311	15 06	000
42	57 29	052	40 15	108	37 18	132	32 47	216	55 46	277	20 31	311	15 06	000
43	58 09	051	41 04	109	37 56	133	32 17	217	54 55	278	19 52	312	15 06	000
44	58 49	051	41 52	110	38 33	134	31 46	217	54 05	278	19 14	312	15 06	000
	◆ Dubhe		POLLUX		SIRIUS		◆ RIGEL		Diphda		◆ Alpheratz		Schedar	
45	14 03	025	28 46	073	17 47	123	39 10	135	31 14	218	53 14	278	54 53	327
46	14 25	025	29 35	073	18 30	124	39 46	136	30 42	219	52 23	279	54 25	327
47	14 47	025	30 24	074	19 12	124	40 22	137	30 09	220	51 32	279	53 56	326
48	15 09	026	31 14	074	19 54	125	40 57	138	29 35	221	50 41	279	53 28	326
49	15 32	026	32 03	074	20 36	126	41 31	139	29 01	222	49 51	280	52 58	325
50	15 54	026	32 53	075	21 18	127	42 04	140	28 27	223	49 00	280	52 29	325
51	16 17	027	33 42	075	21 59	127	42 37	141	27 51	224	48 09	280	51 59	324
52	16 40	027	34 32	075	22 40	128	43 09	142	27 16	225	47 19	281	51 29	324
53	17 04	027	35 22	076	23 20	129	43 40	143	26 39	225	46 28	281	50 59	324
54	17 27	027	36 12	076	24 00	129	44 10	145	26 02	226	45 38	281	50 28	323
55	17 51	028	37 02	077	24 39	130	44 39	146	25 25	227	44 47	282	49 57	323
56	18 15	028	37 52	077	25 19	131	45 08	147	24 47	228	43 57	282	49 26	323
57	18 39	028	38 42	077	25 57	132	45 35	148	24 09	229	43 07	283	48 55	322
58	19 04	028	39 32	078	26 35	133	46 02	150	23 30	229	42 17	283	48 24	322
59	19 28	029	40 22	078	27 13	133	46 27	151	22 51	230	41 27	283	47 52	322
	◆ Dubhe		POLLUX		PROCYON		◆ SIRIUS		RIGEL		◆ Hamal		Schedar	
60	19 53	029	41 13	078	32 24	105	27 50	134	46 52	152	64 06	260	47 20	322
61	20 18	029	42 03	079	33 14	106	28 27	135	47 16	154	63 15	261	46 48	322
62	20 43	029	42 54	079	34 04	106	29 03	136	47 38	155	62 24	262	46 16	321
63	21 09	030	43 44	079	34 53	107	29 38	137	47 59	156	61 34	262	45 44	321
64	21 34	030	44 35	080	35 42	108	30 13	138	48 19	158	60 43	263	45 12	321
65	22 00	030	45 25	080	36 31	108	30 48	139	48 38	159	59 51	264	44 40	321
66	22 26	030	46 16	081	37 20	109	31 21	139	48 56	160	59 00	265	44 07	321
67	22 52	031	47 07	081	38 08	110	31 54	140	49 13	162	58 09	265	43 34	321
68	23 18	031	47 58	081	38 56	110	32 27	141	49 28	163	57 18	266	43 02	321
69	23 45	031	48 48	082	39 44	111	32 59	142	49 42	165	56 26	266	42 29	320
70	24 11	031	49 39	082	40 32	112	33 30	143	49 55	166	55 35	267	41 56	320
71	24 38	031	50 30	082	41 20	113	34 00	144	50 06	168	54 44	268	41 23	320
72	25 05	032	51 21	083	42 07	114	34 30	145	50 16	169	53 52	268	40 50	320
73	25 32	032	52 12	083	42 54	114	34 59	146	50 25	171	53 01	269	40 18	320
74	25 59	032	53 03	084	43 41	115	35 27	147	50 33	172	52 10	269	39 45	320
	◆ Dubhe		POLLUX		PROCYON		◆ SIRIUS		RIGEL		◆ Hamal		Mirfak	
75	26 26	032	53 55	084	44 27	116	35 55	148	50 39	174	51 18	270	64 07	324
76	26 53	032	54 46	084	45 13	117	36 22	149	50 43	176	50 27	270	63 36	323
77	27 21	032	55 37	085	45 59	118	36 47	150	50 47	177	49 35	271	63 05	322
78	27 48	032	56 28	085	46 44	119	37 13	151	50 48	179	48 44	271	62 33	321
79	28 16	033	57 19	086	47 29	120	37 37	153	50 49	180	47 52	272	62 00	320
80	28 43	033	58 11	086	48 13	121	38 00	154	50 48	182	47 01	272	61 27	320
81	29 11	033	59 02	086	48 57	122	38 22	155	50 46	183	46 10	273	60 54	319
82	29 39	033	59 53	087	49 40	123	38 44	156	50 42	185	45 18	273	60 20	318
83	30 07	033	60 45	087	50 23	124	39 04	157	50 37	187	44 27	274	59 46	318
84	30 35	033	61 36	088	51 05	125	39 24	158	50 30	188	43 36	274	59 11	317
85	31 03	033	62 28	088	51 47	126	39 43	159	50 22	190	42 44	275	58 36	317
86	31 31	033	63 19	089	52 28	128	40 00	161	50 13	191	41 53	275	58 00	316
87	32 00	033	64 10	089	53 09	129	40 17	162	50 02	193	41 02	275	57 25	316
88	32 28	033	65 02	090	53 48	130	40 33	163	49 50	194	40 11	276	56 49	315
89	32 56	033	65 53	090	54 27	131	40 47	164	49 37	196	39 20	276	56 13	315

LHA ♈	Hc	Zn	Hc	Zn	Hc	Zn	Hc	Zn	Hc	Zn	Hc	Zn	Hc	Zn
	◆ Dubhe		REGULUS		PROCYON		◆ SIRIUS		RIGEL		ALDEBARAN		◆ Mirfak	
90	33 25	034	29 45	094	55 06	133	41 01	165	49 23	197	66 10	237	55 36	315
91	33 53	034	30 36	094	55 43	134	41 13	167	49 07	199	65 26	239	54 59	314
92	34 22	034	31 27	095	56 20	135	41 24	168	48 50	200	64 42	240	54 22	314
93	34 50	034	32 18	095	56 55	137	41 35	169	48 31	201	63 57	242	53 45	314
94	35 18	034	33 10	096	57 30	138	41 44	170	48 12	203	63 11	243	53 08	313
95	35 47	034	34 01	097	58 04	140	41 52	172	47 51	204	62 25	244	52 30	313
96	36 15	034	34 52	097	58 36	141	41 59	173	47 30	206	61 39	246	51 53	313
97	36 44	034	35 43	098	59 08	143	42 04	174	47 07	207	60 52	247	51 15	313
98	37 12	034	36 34	098	59 38	145	42 09	176	46 43	208	60 04	248	50 37	312
99	37 41	034	37 25	099	60 07	147	42 12	177	46 18	210	59 16	249	49 59	312
100	38 09	034	38 15	100	60 35	148	42 15	178	45 52	211	58 28	250	49 21	312
101	38 38	033	39 06	100	61 01	150	42 16	179	45 25	212	57 40	251	48 43	312
102	39 06	033	39 57	101	61 26	152	42 16	181	44 57	213	56 51	252	48 05	312
103	39 34	033	40 47	102	61 49	154	42 14	182	44 29	215	56 02	253	47 26	312
104	40 02	033	41 37	102	62 11	156	42 12	183	43 59	216	55 13	254	46 48	312
	◆ Alkaid		REGULUS		Alphard		◆ SIRIUS		RIGEL		ALDEBARAN		◆ CAPELLA	
105	15 52	042	42 27	103	36 43	132	42 08	185	43 28	217	54 24	254	65 11	314
106	16 26	042	43 18	104	37 21	133	42 04	186	42 57	218	53 34	255	64 34	314
107	17 01	042	44 07	104	37 58	134	41 58	187	42 25	219	52 44	256	63 57	313
108	17 36	043	44 57	105	38 35	135	41 51	188	41 52	220	51 54	257	63 19	312
109	18 10	043	45 47	106	39 11	136	41 43	190	41 18	221	51 04	258	62 41	312
110	18 46	043	46 36	107	39 46	137	41 34	191	40 44	223	50 14	258	62 02	311
111	19 21	043	47 25	107	40 21	138	41 23	192	40 09	224	49 23	259	61 23	311
112	19 56	044	48 14	108	40 55	139	41 12	193	39 33	225	48 33	260	60 44	310
113	20 32	044	49 03	109	41 29	140	40 59	195	38 56	226	47 42	260	60 05	310
114	21 08	044	49 52	110	42 01	141	40 46	196	38 19	227	46 51	261	59 25	309
115	21 44	045	50 40	111	42 33	142	40 31	197	37 42	228	46 00	262	58 45	309
116	22 20	045	51 28	112	43 04	143	40 15	198	37 03	229	45 10	262	58 05	309
117	22 56	045	52 15	113	43 34	145	39 59	200	36 25	229	44 19	263	57 25	308
118	23 33	045	53 03	114	44 04	146	39 41	201	35 45	230	43 27	264	56 44	308
119	24 10	046	53 50	114	44 32	147	39 22	202	35 05	231	42 36	264	56 03	308
	◆ Alkaid		REGULUS		◆ Alphard		SIRIUS		RIGEL		ALDEBARAN		◆ CAPELLA	
120	24 47	046	54 36	116	44 59	148	39 03	203	34 25	232	41 45	265	55 23	307
121	25 24	046	55 23	117	45 26	150	38 42	204	33 44	233	40 54	265	54 42	307
122	26 01	046	56 08	118	45 52	151	38 20	205	33 03	234	40 03	266	54 01	307
123	26 38	047	56 54	119	46 16	152	37 58	206	32 21	235	39 11	266	53 19	307
124	27 15	047	57 38	120	46 40	153	37 34	208	31 39	236	38 20	267	52 38	307
125	27 53	047	58 23	121	47 02	155	37 10	209	30 56	236	37 29	268	51 57	306
126	28 31	047	59 06	122	47 23	156	36 45	210	30 13	237	36 37	268	51 15	306
127	29 09	047	59 50	124	47 44	158	36 19	211	29 30	238	35 46	269	50 34	306
128	29 46	048	60 32	125	48 03	159	35 52	212	28 46	239	34 54	269	49 52	306
129	30 24	048	61 14	126	48 21	160	35 25	213	28 02	239	34 03	270	49 11	306
130	31 03	048	61 55	128	48 37	162	34 56	214	27 17	240	33 11	270	48 29	306
131	31 41	048	62 35	130	48 53	163	34 27	215	26 33	241	32 20	271	47 48	306
132	32 19	048	63 14	131	49 07	165	33 58	216	25 47	242	31 29	271	47 06	306
133	32 58	048	63 52	133	49 20	166	33 27	217	25 02	242	30 37	272	46 24	306
134	33 36	049	64 30	135	49 32	168	32 56	218	24 16	243	29 46	272	45 43	306
	◆ Alkaid		ARCTURUS		SPICA		◆ Alphard		SIRIUS		BETELGEUSE		◆ CAPELLA	
135	34 15	049	18 47	079	13 35	112	49 42	169	32 24	219	41 04	251	45 01	306
136	34 53	049	19 37	079	14 23	113	49 51	171	31 51	220	40 15	252	44 19	306
137	35 32	049	20 28	079	15 10	113	49 59	172	31 18	221	39 26	253	43 38	306
138	36 11	049	21 18	080	15 57	114	50 05	174	30 44	222	38 37	253	42 56	306
139	36 50	049	22 09	080	16 44	115	50 10	175	30 10	222	37 47	254	42 14	306
140	37 29	049	23 00	081	17 30	115	50 14	177	29 35	223	36 58	255	41 33	306
141	38 08	049	23 50	081	18 17	116	50 16	178	28 59	224	36 08	255	40 51	306
142	38 47	049	24 41	082	19 03	117	50 17	180	28 23	225	35 18	256	40 10	306
143	39 26	049	25 32	082	19 49	117	50 16	181	27 47	226	34 28	257	39 28	306
144	40 05	050	26 23	083	20 34	118	50 14	183	27 09	227	33 38	257	38 47	306
145	40 44	050	27 14	083	21 20	119	50 11	185	26 32	228	32 48	258	38 06	307
146	41 23	050	28 05	084	22 05	119	50 06	186	25 53	228	31 58	259	37 24	307
147	42 02	050	28 57	084	22 49	120	50 00	188	25 15	229	31 07	259	36 43	307
148	42 42	050	29 48	084	23 34	121	49 52	189	24 36	230	30 16	260	36 02	307
149	43 21	050	30 39	085	24 18	121	49 44	191	23 56	231	29 26	260	35 21	307
	Alkaid		◆ ARCTURUS		SPICA		◆ Alphard		PROCYON		BETELGEUSE		◆ CAPELLA	
150	44 00	050	31 30	085	25 02	122	49 33	192	48 15	239	28 35	261	34 40	307
151	44 39	050	32 21	086	25 45	123	49 22	194	47 30	240	27 44	262	33 59	307
152	45 18	050	33 13	086	26 28	124	49 09	195	46 46	241	26 53	262	33 18	308
153	45 57	049	34 04	087	27 11	124	48 55	197	46 00	242	26 02	263	32 38	308
154	46 36	049	34 55	087	27 53	125	48 40	198	45 15	243	25 11	263	31 57	308
155	47 15	049	35 47	088	28 35	126	48 23	199	44 29	244	24 20	264	31 16	308
156	47 54	049	36 38	088	29 16	127	48 06	201	43 43	245	23 29	264	30 36	308
157	48 33	049	37 30	089	29 57	127	47 47	202	42 56	245	22 38	265	29 56	309
158	49 12	049	38 21	089	30 38	128	47 27	204	42 09	246	21 47	266	29 15	309
159	49 51	049	39 12	090	31 18	129	47 06	205	41 22	247	20 55	266	28 35	309
160	50 30	049	40 04	090	31 58	130	46 43	206	40 34	248	20 04	267	27 55	309
161	51 08	048	40 55	091	32 37	131	46 20	208	39 47	249	19 13	267	27 16	309
162	51 47	048	41 47	091	33 15	132	45 56	209	38 58	249	18 21	268	26 36	310
163	52 25	048	42 38	092	33 53	133	45 30	210	38 10	250	17 30	268	25 56	310
164	53 03	048	43 30	093	34 31	134	45 04	211	37 22	251	16 38	269	25 17	310
	Dubhe		◆ Alkaid		ARCTURUS		◆ SPICA		REGULUS		◆ PROCYON		CAPELLA	
165	59 19	001	53 41	048	44 21	093	35 08	134	67 34	214	36 33	252	24 38	310
166	59 20	000	54 19	047	45 12	094	35 44	135	67 05	217	35 44	252	23 59	311
167	59 20	359	54 57	047	46 04	094	36 20	136	66 33	219	34 55	253	23 20	311
168	59 18	358	55 34	047	46 55	095	36 55	137	66 00	221	34 06	254	22 41	311
169	59 16	357	56 12	046	47 46	095	37 30	138	65 26	223	33 16	254	22 02	311
170	59 14	356	56 49	046	48 37	096	38 04	139	64 51	224	32 27	255	21 24	312
171	59 10	356	57 26	046	49 28	097	38 37	140	64 14	226	31 37	256	20 46	312
172	59 06	355	58 02	045	50 19	097	39 09	141	63 37	228	30 47	256	20 08	312
173	59 00	354	58 38	045	51 10	098	39 41	143	62 58	230	29 57	257	19 30	313
174	58 54	353	59 14	044	52 01	099	40 12	144	62 18	231	29 07	258	18 52	313
175	58 48	352	59 50	044	52 52	099	40 42	145	61 38	233	28 16	258	18 14	313
176	58 40	351	60 25	043	53 43	100	41 11	146	60 57	234	27 26	259	17 37	314
177	58 31	350	61 00	042	54 33	101	41 39	147	60 14	235	26 35	259	17 00	314
178	58 22	349	61 34	042	55 24	101	42 07	148	59 32	237	25 45	260	16 23	314
179	58 12	348	62 08	041	56 14	102	42 34	149	58 48	238	24 54	261	15 46	315

 LAT 31°N

LHA ♈	Hc	Zn	Hc	Zn	Hc	Zn	Hc	Zn	Hc	Zn	Hc	Zn	Hc	Zn
	◆ VEGA		Alphecca		ARCTURUS		◆ SPICA		REGULUS		◆ POLLUX		Dubhe	
180	12 22	052	43 06	081	57 04	103	42 59	151	58 04	239	35 28	284	58 02	348
181	13 02	052	43 57	081	57 54	104	43 24	152	57 20	241	34 38	285	57 50	347
182	13 43	053	44 47	082	58 44	105	43 48	153	56 35	242	33 48	285	57 38	346
183	14 24	053	45 38	082	59 34	106	44 11	154	55 49	243	32 58	285	57 25	345
184	15 05	053	46 29	083	60 23	107	44 33	156	55 03	244	32 09	286	57 12	344
185	15 47	054	47 20	083	61 13	107	44 53	157	54 17	245	31 19	286	56 58	344
186	16 28	054	48 11	083	62 01	108	45 13	158	53 30	246	30 30	286	56 43	343
187	17 10	055	49 03	084	62 50	110	45 32	159	52 43	247	29 41	287	56 28	342
188	17 52	055	49 54	084	63 38	111	45 49	161	51 56	248	28 51	287	56 12	342
189	18 34	055	50 45	085	64 26	112	46 05	162	51 08	249	28 02	287	55 55	341
190	19 17	056	51 36	085	65 14	113	46 21	164	50 20	250	27 13	288	55 38	340
191	19 59	056	52 27	086	66 01	114	46 35	165	49 31	251	26 24	288	55 20	339
192	20 42	056	53 19	086	66 48	116	46 47	166	48 43	251	25 36	289	55 02	339
193	21 25	057	54 10	086	67 34	117	46 59	168	47 54	252	24 47	289	54 43	338
194	22 08	057	55 01	087	68 19	119	47 09	169	47 05	253	23 58	289	54 24	338
	◆ Kochab		VEGA		Rasalhague		◆ ANTARES		SPICA		◆ REGULUS		Dubhe	
195	44 42	010	22 51	057	24 24	090	13 42	133	47 18	171	46 16	254	54 04	337
196	44 51	010	23 34	058	25 15	090	14 19	134	47 26	172	45 26	254	53 44	336
197	45 00	010	24 18	058	26 07	091	14 56	134	47 32	173	44 37	255	53 23	336
198	45 08	009	25 02	058	26 58	091	15 33	135	47 38	175	43 47	256	53 02	335
199	45 16	009	25 45	059	27 49	092	16 09	136	47 42	176	42 57	257	52 40	335
200	45 24	009	26 29	059	28 41	092	16 45	136	47 44	178	42 07	257	52 18	334
201	45 32	008	27 13	059	29 32	093	17 20	137	47 45	179	41 16	258	51 56	334
202	45 39	008	27 58	059	30 23	093	17 55	138	47 45	181	40 26	259	51 33	333
203	45 46	008	28 42	060	31 15	094	18 29	139	47 44	182	39 36	259	51 10	333
204	45 53	007	29 26	060	32 06	094	19 03	139	47 42	184	38 45	260	50 46	333
205	45 59	007	30 11	060	32 57	095	19 36	140	47 38	185	37 54	261	50 22	332
206	46 05	007	30 56	061	33 49	096	20 09	141	47 32	187	37 03	261	49 58	332
207	46 11	006	31 41	061	34 40	096	20 41	142	47 26	188	36 13	262	49 34	331
208	46 16	006	32 26	061	35 31	097	21 13	142	47 18	189	35 22	262	49 09	331
209	46 21	005	33 11	061	36 22	097	21 44	143	47 09	191	34 31	263	48 44	331
	◆ Kochab		VEGA		Rasalhague		◆ ANTARES		SPICA		◆ REGULUS		Dubhe	
210	46 26	005	33 56	062	37 13	098	22 15	144	46 59	192	33 40	264	48 19	330
211	46 30	005	34 41	062	38 04	099	22 45	145	46 47	194	32 48	264	47 53	330
212	46 34	004	35 26	062	38 55	099	23 14	145	46 34	195	31 57	265	47 27	330
213	46 38	004	36 12	062	39 45	100	23 43	146	46 20	196	31 06	265	47 01	329
214	46 41	003	36 57	062	40 36	100	24 11	147	46 05	198	30 15	266	46 35	329
215	46 44	003	37 43	063	41 26	101	24 39	148	45 49	199	29 23	266	46 09	329
216	46 46	003	38 29	063	42 17	102	25 06	149	45 31	201	28 32	267	45 42	329
217	46 49	002	39 15	063	43 07	102	25 32	150	45 13	202	27 41	267	45 15	328
218	46 50	002	40 00	063	43 57	103	25 58	151	44 53	203	26 49	268	44 48	328
219	46 52	001	40 46	063	44 47	104	26 23	151	44 32	204	25 58	269	44 21	328
220	46 53	001	41 32	064	45 37	105	26 47	152	44 11	206	25 06	269	43 54	328
221	46 54	001	42 19	064	46 27	105	27 11	153	43 48	207	24 15	270	43 26	328
222	46 54	000	43 05	064	47 16	106	27 33	154	43 24	208	23 24	270	42 59	328
223	46 54	000	43 51	064	48 06	107	27 55	155	42 59	209	22 32	271	42 31	327
224	46 54	359	44 37	064	48 55	108	28 17	156	42 33	211	21 41	271	42 03	327
	DENEB		VEGA		◆ ALTAIR		ANTARES		◆ SPICA		Denebola		◆ Dubhe	
225	24 26	050	45 24	064	19 13	091	28 37	157	42 07	212	43 33	260	41 36	327
226	25 06	051	46 10	065	20 04	092	28 57	158	41 39	213	42 43	261	41 08	327
227	25 46	051	46 57	065	20 56	092	29 16	159	41 11	214	41 52	262	40 40	327
228	26 26	051	47 43	065	21 47	093	29 34	160	40 42	215	41 01	262	40 11	327
229	27 06	051	48 30	065	22 38	093	29 51	161	40 11	216	40 10	263	39 43	327
230	27 46	052	49 16	065	23 30	094	30 08	162	39 41	217	39 19	263	39 15	327
231	28 26	052	50 03	065	24 21	094	30 24	163	39 09	219	38 28	264	38 47	327
232	29 07	052	50 50	065	25 12	095	30 38	164	38 36	220	37 37	265	38 18	327
233	29 48	052	51 36	065	26 03	095	30 52	165	38 03	221	36 45	265	37 50	326
234	30 28	052	52 23	065	26 55	096	31 05	166	37 30	222	35 54	266	37 21	326
235	31 09	053	53 10	065	27 46	096	31 18	167	36 55	223	35 03	266	36 53	326
236	31 50	053	53 56	065	28 37	097	31 29	168	36 20	224	34 11	267	36 25	326
237	32 31	053	54 43	065	29 28	098	31 39	169	35 44	225	33 20	267	35 56	326
238	33 12	053	55 30	065	30 19	098	31 49	170	35 08	226	32 29	268	35 28	326
239	33 54	053	56 17	065	31 10	099	31 57	171	34 31	226	31 37	268	34 59	326
	◆ DENEB		ALTAIR		Nunki		◆ ANTARES		SPICA		ARCTURUS		◆ Alkaid	
240	34 35	054	32 00	099	18 56	139	32 05	172	33 53	227	63 47	249	59 17	316
241	35 16	054	32 51	100	19 29	140	32 12	173	33 15	228	62 58	250	58 41	315
242	35 58	054	33 42	101	20 03	140	32 17	174	32 36	229	62 10	251	58 04	315
243	36 39	054	34 32	101	20 35	141	32 22	175	31 57	230	61 21	252	57 28	315
244	37 21	054	35 23	102	21 07	142	32 26	176	31 18	231	60 32	253	56 51	314
245	38 03	054	36 13	102	21 39	143	32 29	177	30 38	232	59 42	254	56 14	314
246	38 45	054	37 03	103	22 10	143	32 31	178	29 57	233	58 53	255	55 37	313
247	39 27	055	37 53	104	22 40	144	32 32	179	29 16	233	58 03	256	54 59	313
248	40 08	055	38 43	104	23 10	145	32 32	180	28 34	234	57 13	257	54 22	313
249	40 50	055	39 33	105	23 39	146	32 31	182	27 53	235	56 23	258	53 44	312
250	41 32	055	40 22	106	24 08	147	32 29	183	27 10	236	55 33	258	53 06	312
251	42 14	055	41 12	107	24 36	147	32 27	184	26 28	236	54 42	259	52 27	312
252	42 57	055	42 01	107	25 03	148	32 23	185	25 45	237	53 52	260	51 49	312
253	43 39	055	42 50	108	25 30	149	32 18	186	25 01	238	53 01	261	51 11	312
254	44 21	055	43 39	109	25 56	150	32 13	187	24 17	239	52 10	261	50 32	311
	◆ DENEB		ALTAIR		Nunki		◆ ANTARES		ARCTURUS		◆ Alkaid		Kochab	
255	45 03	055	44 27	110	26 21	151	32 06	188	51 19	262	49 53	311	43 56	348
256	45 45	055	45 15	110	26 46	152	31 59	189	50 28	263	49 15	311	43 45	348
257	46 27	055	46 03	111	27 10	153	31 50	190	49 37	263	48 36	311	43 35	348
258	47 10	055	46 51	112	27 33	154	31 41	191	48 46	264	47 57	311	43 23	347
259	47 52	055	47 39	113	27 55	155	31 31	192	47 55	265	47 18	311	43 12	347
260	48 34	055	48 26	114	28 17	155	31 19	193	47 04	265	46 39	311	43 01	347
261	49 16	055	49 13	115	28 38	156	31 07	194	46 12	266	46 00	311	42 49	347
262	49 58	055	49 59	116	28 58	157	30 54	195	45 21	266	45 21	310	42 37	346
263	50 40	055	50 45	117	29 18	158	30 41	196	44 30	267	44 42	310	42 24	346
264	51 22	055	51 31	118	29 36	159	30 26	197	43 38	267	44 03	310	42 12	346
265	52 04	055	52 16	119	29 54	160	30 11	198	42 47	268	43 23	310	41 59	346
266	52 46	055	53 01	120	30 11	161	29 54	199	41 56	268	42 44	310	41 46	345
267	53 28	054	53 46	121	30 27	162	29 37	200	41 04	269	42 05	310	41 33	345
268	54 10	054	54 29	122	30 42	163	29 19	201	40 13	270	41 26	310	41 20	345
269	54 51	054	55 13	123	30 57	164	29 00	202	39 21	270	40 47	310	41 07	345

LHA ♈	Hc	Zn	Hc	Zn	Hc	Zn	Hc	Zn	Hc	Zn	Hc	Zn	Hc	Zn
	◆ DENEB		ALTAIR		◆ Nunki		ANTARES		ARCTURUS		◆ Alkaid		Kochab	
270	55 33	054	55 55	124	31 10	165	28 40	203	38 30	271	40 08	310	40 53	345
271	56 14	054	56 38	126	31 23	166	28 20	204	37 39	271	39 28	311	40 39	344
272	56 56	053	57 19	127	31 35	167	27 59	205	36 47	272	38 49	311	40 25	344
273	57 37	053	58 00	128	31 45	168	27 37	206	35 56	272	38 10	311	40 11	344
274	58 18	053	58 40	130	31 55	169	27 14	207	35 04	273	37 31	311	39 57	344
275	58 59	052	59 19	131	32 04	170	26 51	208	34 13	273	36 52	311	39 42	344
276	59 39	052	59 57	133	32 13	171	26 27	208	33 22	274	36 14	311	39 28	343
277	60 20	052	60 34	134	32 20	173	26 02	209	32 30	274	35 35	311	39 13	343
278	61 00	051	61 11	136	32 26	174	25 36	210	31 39	274	34 56	311	38 58	343
279	61 40	051	61 46	137	32 31	175	25 10	211	30 48	275	34 17	311	38 43	343
280	62 19	050	62 20	139	32 36	176	24 43	212	29 57	275	33 39	311	38 28	343
281	62 59	050	62 53	141	32 39	177	24 16	213	29 05	276	33 00	312	38 13	343
282	63 38	049	63 25	143	32 41	178	23 48	214	28 14	276	32 22	312	37 58	343
283	64 16	048	63 55	145	32 43	179	23 19	214	27 23	277	31 43	312	37 42	342
284	64 54	048	64 24	147	32 43	180	22 50	215	26 32	277	31 05	312	37 27	342
	◆ Alpheratz		Enif		ALTAIR		◆ ANTARES		ARCTURUS		◆ Alkaid		Kochab	
285	24 34	069	46 23	110	64 52	149	22 20	216	25 41	278	30 27	312	37 11	342
286	25 22	070	47 11	111	65 18	151	21 49	217	24 50	278	29 49	312	36 55	342
287	26 10	070	47 59	111	65 42	153	21 18	218	23 59	279	29 11	313	36 40	342
288	26 59	071	48 47	112	66 04	155	20 46	218	23 08	279	28 33	313	36 24	342
289	27 47	071	49 34	113	66 25	158	20 14	219	22 18	280	27 55	313	36 08	342
290	28 36	071	50 21	114	66 43	160	19 42	220	21 27	280	27 18	313	35 52	342
291	29 25	072	51 08	115	67 00	162	19 08	221	20 36	280	26 40	313	35 36	342
292	30 14	072	51 54	116	67 14	165	18 35	221	19 46	281	26 03	314	35 20	342
293	31 03	072	52 40	117	67 27	167	18 00	222	18 55	281	25 26	314	35 03	342
294	31 52	073	53 26	118	67 37	170	17 26	223	18 05	282	24 49	314	34 47	342
295	32 41	073	54 11	119	67 45	172	16 50	224	17 15	282	24 12	314	34 31	342
296	33 30	073	54 56	120	67 50	175	16 15	224	16 25	283	23 35	315	34 15	341
297	34 20	074	55 40	121	67 54	178	15 39	225	15 34	283	22 59	315	33 58	341
298	35 09	074	56 23	123	67 55	180	15 02	226	14 44	284	22 22	315	33 42	341
299	35 59	075	57 06	124	67 53	183	14 25	226	13 55	284	21 46	315	33 25	341
	◆ Mirfak		Alpheratz		◆ FOMALHAUT		ALTAIR		Rasalhague		◆ Alphecca		Kochab	
300	11 08	038	36 48	075	16 04	141	67 49	186	52 00	249	32 44	284	33 09	341
301	11 40	038	37 38	075	16 37	141	67 43	188	51 12	250	31 54	284	32 53	341
302	12 11	038	38 28	076	17 09	142	67 35	191	50 23	251	31 04	284	32 36	341
303	12 43	039	39 17	076	17 40	143	67 24	193	49 35	252	30 14	285	32 20	341
304	13 16	039	40 07	076	18 11	143	67 11	196	48 46	252	29 24	285	32 03	341
305	13 48	040	40 57	077	18 42	144	66 56	198	47 57	253	28 35	286	31 47	341
306	14 21	040	41 47	077	19 11	145	66 39	201	47 07	254	27 45	286	31 30	341
307	14 54	040	42 38	077	19 41	146	66 20	203	46 18	255	26 56	286	31 14	341
308	15 28	041	43 28	078	20 09	146	65 59	205	45 28	256	26 07	287	30 58	341
309	16 01	041	44 18	078	20 38	147	65 36	207	44 38	256	25 17	287	30 41	341
310	16 35	041	45 08	078	21 05	148	65 11	210	43 48	257	24 28	288	30 25	341
311	17 09	042	45 59	079	21 32	149	64 45	212	42 58	258	23 39	288	30 09	342
312	17 43	042	46 49	079	21 58	150	64 17	214	42 08	258	22 50	288	29 52	342
313	18 18	042	47 40	079	22 24	150	63 48	216	41 17	259	22 02	289	29 36	342
314	18 52	042	48 30	080	22 49	151	63 17	218	40 27	260	21 13	289	29 20	342
	◆ Mirfak		Hamal		Diphda		◆ FOMALHAUT		ALTAIR		◆ VEGA		Kochab	
315	19 27	043	22 29	075	17 16	124	23 13	152	62 45	219	59 57	295	29 04	342
316	20 02	043	23 19	076	17 58	125	23 37	153	62 12	221	59 11	295	28 48	342
317	20 37	043	24 08	076	18 40	126	24 00	154	61 38	223	58 24	295	28 32	342
318	21 13	044	24 58	076	19 22	126	24 23	155	61 02	225	57 37	295	28 16	342
319	21 48	044	25 48	077	20 03	127	24 44	156	60 25	226	56 50	295	28 00	342
320	22 24	044	26 39	077	20 44	128	25 05	156	59 48	228	56 04	295	27 44	342
321	23 00	044	27 29	078	21 25	128	25 25	157	59 09	229	55 17	295	27 28	342
322	23 36	045	28 19	078	22 05	129	25 45	158	58 30	231	54 30	295	27 13	342
323	24 12	045	29 09	079	22 44	130	26 04	159	57 50	232	53 43	295	26 57	342
324	24 48	045	30 00	079	23 24	131	26 22	160	57 09	233	52 57	295	26 41	342
325	25 25	045	30 50	079	24 02	131	26 39	161	56 27	235	52 10	295	26 26	343
326	26 02	046	31 41	080	24 41	132	26 55	162	55 45	236	51 23	295	26 11	343
327	26 38	046	32 32	080	25 19	133	27 11	163	55 02	237	50 37	295	25 55	343
328	27 15	046	33 22	081	25 56	134	27 26	164	54 19	238	49 50	295	25 40	343
329	27 52	046	34 13	081	26 33	135	27 40	165	53 35	239	49 03	295	25 25	343
	◆ Mirfak		Hamal		Diphda		◆ FOMALHAUT		ALTAIR		◆ VEGA		Kochab	
330	28 30	046	35 04	082	27 09	135	27 53	166	52 50	240	48 17	295	25 10	343
331	29 07	047	35 55	082	27 45	136	28 05	167	52 05	241	47 30	295	24 56	343
332	29 44	047	36 46	082	28 21	137	28 17	168	51 20	242	46 44	295	24 41	343
333	30 22	047	37 37	083	28 55	138	28 27	169	50 34	243	45 57	295	24 26	344
334	31 00	047	38 28	083	29 30	139	28 37	169	49 48	244	45 11	296	24 12	344
335	31 37	047	39 19	084	30 03	140	28 46	170	49 01	245	44 24	296	23 57	344
336	32 15	047	40 10	084	30 36	141	28 54	171	48 15	246	43 38	296	23 43	344
337	32 53	048	41 01	085	31 09	141	29 02	172	47 27	247	42 52	296	23 29	344
338	33 31	048	41 52	085	31 40	142	29 08	173	46 40	248	42 06	296	23 15	344
339	34 09	048	42 44	085	32 11	143	29 13	174	45 52	249	41 20	296	23 01	345
340	34 47	048	43 35	086	32 42	144	29 18	175	45 04	250	40 34	297	22 48	345
341	35 26	048	44 26	086	33 11	145	29 22	176	44 15	251	39 48	297	22 34	345
342	36 04	048	45 18	087	33 40	146	29 24	177	43 27	251	39 02	297	22 21	345
343	36 42	048	46 09	087	34 09	147	29 26	178	42 38	252	38 16	297	22 08	345
344	37 21	048	47 00	088	34 36	148	29 27	179	41 49	253	37 30	297	21 55	345
	◆ CAPELLA		ALDEBARAN		Diphda		◆ FOMALHAUT		ALTAIR		◆ VEGA		Kochab	
345	18 56	047	13 17	078	35 03	149	29 27	180	41 00	254	36 45	298	21 42	346
346	19 33	047	14 07	079	35 29	150	29 27	181	40 10	254	35 59	298	21 29	346
347	20 11	048	14 58	079	35 54	151	29 25	182	39 21	255	35 14	298	21 16	346
348	20 49	048	15 48	080	36 18	152	29 22	183	38 31	256	34 29	298	21 04	346
349	21 28	048	16 39	080	36 41	154	29 19	184	37 41	256	33 43	299	20 52	346
350	22 06	049	17 30	081	37 04	155	29 14	185	36 51	257	32 58	299	20 40	347
351	22 45	049	18 21	081	37 25	156	29 09	186	36 01	258	32 13	299	20 28	347
352	23 24	049	19 11	082	37 46	157	29 03	187	35 10	258	31 28	299	20 16	347
353	24 03	049	20 02	082	38 06	158	28 56	188	34 20	259	30 43	300	20 05	347
354	24 42	050	20 53	083	38 25	159	28 48	189	33 29	260	29 59	300	19 53	347
355	25 21	050	21 44	083	38 43	160	28 39	190	32 39	260	29 14	300	19 42	348
356	26 00	050	22 36	084	39 00	161	28 30	191	31 48	261	28 30	300	19 31	348
357	26 40	050	23 27	084	39 15	163	28 19	192	30 57	261	27 45	301	19 20	348
358	27 20	051	24 18	085	39 30	164	28 08	193	30 06	262	27 01	301	19 10	348
359	27 59	051	25 09	085	39 44	165	27 56	194	29 15	263	26 17	301	18 59	348

LHA ♈	Hc	Zn	Hc	Zn	Hc	Zn	Hc	Zn	Hc	Zn	Hc	Zn	Hc	Zn
	Schedar		◆ CAPELLA		ALDEBARAN		◆ Diphda		FOMALHAUT		ALTAIR		◆ DENEB	
0	62 24	012	28 02	051	25 56	085	40 55	166	28 41	195	28 31	264	48 40	306
1	62 35	011	28 42	051	26 47	086	41 07	167	28 27	196	27 40	264	47 58	306
2	62 45	010	29 22	051	27 39	086	41 18	168	28 12	197	26 48	265	47 16	306
3	62 53	009	30 03	051	28 31	087	41 28	170	27 56	198	25 56	265	46 34	306
4	63 01	008	30 43	051	29 23	087	41 37	171	27 40	199	25 04	266	45 51	306
5	63 07	007	31 24	052	30 15	087	41 44	172	27 22	200	24 13	266	45 09	306
6	63 12	005	32 05	052	31 07	088	41 51	173	27 04	201	23 21	267	44 27	306
7	63 17	004	32 46	052	31 59	088	41 56	175	26 45	202	22 29	267	43 45	306
8	63 20	003	33 26	052	32 51	089	42 00	176	26 26	203	21 37	268	43 03	306
9	63 22	002	34 08	052	33 43	089	42 03	177	26 05	204	20 45	268	42 21	306
10	63 23	000	34 49	052	34 34	090	42 05	179	25 44	204	19 53	269	41 38	306
11	63 23	359	35 30	053	35 26	090	42 06	180	25 22	205	19 01	269	40 56	306
12	63 21	358	36 11	053	36 18	091	42 05	181	25 00	206	18 09	270	40 14	306
13	63 19	357	36 52	053	37 10	091	42 04	182	24 36	207	17 17	270	39 32	306
14	63 15	356	37 34	053	38 02	092	42 01	184	24 12	208	16 25	271	38 50	306
	◆ CAPELLA		ALDEBARAN		RIGEL		◆ Diphda		FOMALHAUT		Enif		◆ DENEB	
15	38 15	053	38 54	092	17 53	111	41 57	185	23 48	209	40 26	257	38 08	306
16	38 57	053	39 46	093	18 41	112	41 52	186	23 22	210	39 35	257	37 26	306
17	39 38	053	40 38	094	19 30	112	41 45	188	22 56	210	38 45	258	36 45	306
18	40 20	053	41 30	094	20 18	113	41 38	189	22 30	211	37 54	259	36 03	307
19	41 01	053	42 22	095	21 05	114	41 30	190	22 02	212	37 03	259	35 21	307
20	41 43	053	43 13	095	21 53	114	41 20	191	21 35	213	36 12	260	34 39	307
21	42 25	053	44 05	096	22 40	115	41 09	193	21 06	214	35 20	261	33 58	307
22	43 06	053	44 57	096	23 27	115	40 57	194	20 37	214	34 29	261	33 16	307
23	43 48	053	45 48	097	24 14	116	40 44	195	20 08	215	33 38	262	32 35	307
24	44 30	053	46 40	098	25 00	117	40 30	196	19 37	216	32 46	262	31 54	307
25	45 11	053	47 31	098	25 47	117	40 15	197	19 07	217	31 55	263	31 13	308
26	45 53	053	48 23	099	26 33	118	39 59	199	18 35	217	31 03	263	30 31	308
27	46 35	053	49 14	100	27 18	119	39 42	200	18 04	218	30 12	264	29 50	308
28	47 16	053	50 05	100	28 04	120	39 24	201	17 31	219	29 20	265	29 10	308
29	47 58	053	50 56	101	28 49	120	39 05	202	16 58	220	28 28	265	28 29	308
	CAPELLA		◆ ALDEBARAN		RIGEL		◆ Diphda		Alpheratz		DENEB		◆ Kochab	
30	48 39	053	51 47	102	29 33	121	38 45	203	65 57	275	27 48	309	14 26	356
31	49 21	053	52 38	102	30 18	122	38 24	204	65 05	275	27 08	309	14 23	357
32	50 02	053	53 29	103	31 02	123	38 02	206	64 13	276	26 27	309	14 20	357
33	50 44	053	54 19	104	31 45	123	37 39	207	63 22	276	25 47	309	14 18	357
34	51 25	053	55 10	105	32 28	124	37 15	208	62 30	276	25 07	310	14 15	358
35	52 06	052	56 00	106	33 11	125	36 51	209	61 38	277	24 27	310	14 13	358
36	52 47	052	56 50	106	33 53	126	36 25	210	60 47	277	23 47	310	14 11	358
37	53 28	052	57 39	107	34 35	127	35 59	211	59 55	277	23 07	310	14 10	358
38	54 09	052	58 29	108	35 17	128	35 32	212	59 04	278	22 28	311	14 08	359
39	54 50	051	59 18	109	35 58	128	35 04	213	58 12	278	21 48	311	14 07	359
40	55 30	051	60 07	110	36 38	129	34 35	214	57 21	278	21 09	311	14 07	359
41	56 11	051	60 56	111	37 18	130	34 06	215	56 29	278	20 30	311	14 06	000
42	56 51	051	61 44	112	37 57	131	33 36	216	55 38	279	19 51	312	14 06	000
43	57 31	050	62 32	113	38 36	132	33 05	217	54 47	279	19 12	312	14 06	000
44	58 11	050	63 19	115	39 14	133	32 33	218	53 55	279	18 34	312	14 06	000
	◆ CAPELLA		PROCYON		SIRIUS		◆ RIGEL		Acamar		Diphda		◆ Alpheratz	
45	58 50	049	19 52	096	18 19	123	39 52	134	19 45	180	32 01	219	53 04	280
46	59 30	049	20 44	096	19 03	123	40 29	135	19 45	181	31 28	220	52 13	280
47	60 09	048	21 35	097	19 46	124	41 05	136	19 43	182	30 55	221	51 22	280
48	60 47	048	22 27	097	20 29	125	41 41	137	19 41	183	30 21	221	50 31	281
49	61 26	047	23 19	098	21 11	125	42 16	138	19 39	183	29 46	222	49 40	281
50	62 04	047	24 10	098	21 53	126	42 50	139	19 35	184	29 11	223	48 49	281
51	62 42	046	25 01	099	22 35	127	43 23	141	19 31	185	28 35	224	47 58	282
52	63 19	045	25 53	099	23 16	128	43 56	142	19 26	186	27 58	225	47 07	282
53	63 56	045	26 44	100	23 57	128	44 28	143	19 20	187	27 21	226	46 16	282
54	64 32	044	27 35	101	24 38	129	44 59	144	19 14	188	26 44	227	45 25	282
55	65 08	043	28 26	101	25 18	130	45 29	145	19 07	188	26 06	227	44 35	283
56	65 43	042	29 17	102	25 58	131	45 58	146	18 59	189	25 28	228	43 44	283
57	66 18	041	30 08	102	26 37	131	46 26	148	18 50	190	24 49	229	42 53	283
58	66 52	040	30 58	103	27 16	132	46 54	149	18 41	191	24 09	230	42 03	284
59	67 25	039	31 49	104	27 54	133	47 20	150	18 31	191	23 30	230	41 12	284
	◆ Dubhe		PROCYON		SIRIUS		◆ RIGEL		Diphda		◆ Hamal		Mirfak	
60	19 01	029	32 39	104	28 32	134	47 45	152	22 49	231	64 15	262	69 03	344
61	19 26	029	33 30	105	29 09	135	48 09	153	22 09	232	63 24	263	68 48	343
62	19 51	029	34 20	106	29 46	135	48 32	154	21 28	233	62 32	264	68 32	341
63	20 17	030	35 10	106	30 22	136	48 54	156	20 46	233	61 40	264	68 14	339
64	20 42	030	36 00	107	30 57	137	49 15	157	20 04	234	60 49	265	67 55	338
65	21 08	030	36 49	108	31 32	138	49 34	159	19 22	235	59 57	266	67 35	337
66	21 34	030	37 39	108	32 07	139	49 53	160	18 40	235	59 05	266	67 14	335
67	22 00	030	38 28	109	32 40	140	50 10	162	17 57	236	58 13	267	66 51	334
68	22 27	031	39 17	110	33 14	141	50 25	163	17 14	237	57 21	267	66 28	332
69	22 53	031	40 06	110	33 46	142	50 40	165	16 30	237	56 29	268	66 03	331
70	23 20	031	40 54	111	34 18	143	50 53	166	15 46	238	55 38	268	65 38	330
71	23 47	031	41 43	112	34 49	144	51 05	168	15 02	238	54 46	269	65 12	329
72	24 13	031	42 31	113	35 19	145	51 15	169	14 18	239	53 54	269	64 44	328
73	24 40	031	43 18	114	35 49	146	51 24	171	13 33	240	53 02	270	64 16	327
74	25 08	032	44 06	114	36 18	147	51 32	172	12 48	240	52 10	270	63 48	326
	◆ Dubhe		POLLUX		PROCYON		◆ SIRIUS		RIGEL		◆ Hamal		Mirfak	
75	25 35	032	53 48	083	44 53	115	36 46	148	51 38	174	51 18	271	63 18	325
76	26 02	032	54 39	083	45 40	116	37 13	149	51 43	175	50 26	271	62 48	324
77	26 30	032	55 31	083	46 26	117	37 40	150	51 46	177	49 34	272	62 17	323
78	26 57	032	56 22	084	47 12	118	38 05	151	51 48	179	48 42	272	61 46	322
79	27 25	032	57 14	084	47 58	119	38 30	152	51 49	180	47 50	273	61 14	322
80	27 53	032	58 06	084	48 43	120	38 54	153	51 48	182	46 58	273	60 41	321
81	28 21	032	58 57	085	49 28	121	39 17	154	51 45	183	46 06	274	60 08	320
82	28 49	033	59 49	085	50 12	122	39 39	156	51 42	185	45 14	274	59 35	320
83	29 17	033	60 41	085	50 56	123	40 00	157	51 36	187	44 23	275	59 01	319
84	29 45	033	61 33	086	51 39	124	40 20	158	51 29	188	43 31	275	58 26	318
85	30 13	033	62 25	086	52 22	125	40 39	159	51 21	190	42 39	275	57 52	318
86	30 41	033	63 16	087	53 04	126	40 57	160	51 12	191	41 47	276	57 17	317
87	31 09	033	64 08	087	53 46	128	41 14	161	51 01	193	40 56	276	56 41	317
88	31 38	033	65 00	087	54 26	129	41 30	163	50 48	194	40 04	277	56 06	316
89	32 06	033	65 52	088	55 07	130	41 45	164	50 35	196	39 13	277	55 30	316

LAT 30°N

LHA ♈	Hc	Zn	Hc	Zn	Hc	Zn	Hc	Zn	Hc	Zn	Hc	Zn	Hc	Zn
	Dubhe		◆ REGULUS		PROCYON		SIRIUS		◆ RIGEL		ALDEBARAN		◆ Mirfak	
90	32 35	033	29 48	093	55 46	132	41 59	165	50 20	198	66 42	239	54 54	316
91	33 03	033	30 40	094	56 24	133	42 11	166	50 04	199	65 57	241	54 17	315
92	33 31	033	31 32	094	57 02	134	42 23	168	49 46	200	65 11	242	53 40	315
93	34 00	033	32 24	095	57 39	136	42 33	169	49 27	202	64 25	244	53 03	315
94	34 28	033	33 16	095	58 14	137	42 43	170	49 07	203	63 38	245	52 26	314
95	34 57	033	34 07	096	58 49	139	42 51	172	48 46	205	62 50	246	51 49	314
96	35 25	033	34 59	097	59 23	140	42 58	173	48 24	206	62 03	247	51 12	314
97	35 54	033	35 51	097	59 55	142	43 04	174	48 00	207	61 15	248	50 34	314
98	36 22	033	36 42	098	60 27	144	43 09	175	47 36	209	60 26	249	49 56	313
99	36 51	033	37 34	098	60 57	146	43 12	177	47 10	210	59 37	250	49 18	313
100	37 19	033	38 25	099	61 26	147	43 14	178	46 44	211	58 48	251	48 40	313
101	37 47	033	39 16	099	61 53	149	43 16	179	46 16	213	57 59	252	48 02	313
102	38 16	033	40 07	100	62 19	151	43 16	181	45 47	214	57 09	253	47 24	313
103	38 44	033	40 59	101	62 43	153	43 14	182	45 18	215	56 19	254	46 46	313
104	39 12	033	41 50	101	63 06	155	43 12	183	44 47	216	55 29	255	46 08	312
	◆ Dubhe		REGULUS		◆ Alphard		SIRIUS		RIGEL		◆ ALDEBARAN		CAPELLA	
105	39 40	033	42 40	102	37 23	131	43 08	185	44 16	218	54 39	256	64 28	316
106	40 08	033	43 31	103	38 01	132	43 03	186	43 44	219	53 49	257	63 52	315
107	40 36	032	44 22	103	38 39	133	42 57	187	43 11	220	52 58	257	63 15	314
108	41 04	032	45 12	104	39 17	134	42 50	189	42 37	221	52 07	258	62 38	314
109	41 32	032	46 03	105	39 54	135	42 42	190	42 03	222	51 16	259	62 00	313
110	41 59	032	46 53	106	40 30	136	42 33	191	41 28	223	50 25	259	61 22	313
111	42 27	032	47 43	106	41 06	137	42 22	192	40 52	224	49 34	260	60 44	312
112	42 54	032	48 32	107	41 40	138	42 10	194	40 15	225	48 43	261	60 05	311
113	43 21	031	49 22	108	42 14	140	41 57	195	39 38	226	47 52	261	59 26	311
114	43 48	031	50 11	109	42 48	141	41 43	196	39 00	227	47 00	262	58 46	311
115	44 15	031	51 00	110	43 20	142	41 28	197	38 22	228	46 09	263	58 07	310
116	44 42	031	51 49	110	43 52	143	41 12	199	37 43	229	45 17	263	57 27	310
117	45 09	031	52 38	111	44 23	144	40 55	200	37 03	230	44 25	264	56 47	309
118	45 35	030	53 26	112	44 53	145	40 37	201	36 23	231	43 34	265	56 07	309
119	46 01	030	54 14	113	45 22	147	40 18	202	35 43	232	42 42	265	55 26	309
	◆ Dubhe		REGULUS		◆ Alphard		SIRIUS		RIGEL		◆ ALDEBARAN		CAPELLA	
120	46 27	030	55 02	114	45 50	148	39 58	203	35 01	233	41 50	266	54 46	309
121	46 53	029	55 49	115	46 18	149	39 37	205	34 20	234	40 58	266	54 05	308
122	47 18	029	56 36	116	46 44	150	39 14	206	33 38	234	40 06	267	53 24	308
123	47 43	029	57 22	117	47 09	152	38 51	207	32 55	235	39 15	267	52 43	308
124	48 08	029	58 08	119	47 33	153	38 28	208	32 12	236	38 23	268	52 02	308
125	48 33	028	58 53	120	47 56	154	38 03	209	31 29	237	37 31	268	51 21	307
126	48 57	028	59 38	121	48 18	156	37 37	210	30 45	238	36 39	269	50 40	307
127	49 21	027	60 22	122	48 39	157	37 11	211	30 01	238	35 47	269	49 58	307
128	49 45	027	61 06	124	48 59	159	36 43	212	29 17	239	34 55	270	49 17	307
129	50 09	027	61 49	125	49 17	160	36 15	213	28 32	240	34 03	270	48 35	307
130	50 32	026	62 31	126	49 34	161	35 46	214	27 47	241	33 11	271	47 54	307
131	50 54	026	63 12	128	49 50	163	35 16	215	27 01	241	32 19	271	47 12	307
132	51 17	025	63 53	130	50 05	164	34 46	216	26 16	242	31 27	272	46 30	307
133	51 39	025	64 32	131	50 18	166	34 15	217	25 30	243	30 35	272	45 49	307
134	52 00	024	65 11	133	50 30	167	33 43	218	24 43	243	29 43	273	45 07	307
	Dubhe		◆ ARCTURUS		SPICA		Alphard		◆ SIRIUS		BETELGEUSE		◆ CAPELLA	
135	52 21	024	18 35	078	13 58	112	50 41	169	33 10	219	41 23	252	44 26	307
136	52 42	023	19 26	079	14 46	113	50 50	170	32 37	220	40 33	253	43 44	307
137	53 02	023	20 17	079	15 34	113	50 58	172	32 03	221	39 43	253	43 02	307
138	53 22	022	21 08	080	16 21	114	51 05	174	31 29	222	38 53	254	42 21	307
139	53 41	021	21 59	080	17 09	114	51 10	175	30 54	223	38 03	255	41 39	307
140	54 00	021	22 50	080	17 56	115	51 13	177	30 18	224	37 13	255	40 57	307
141	54 18	020	23 41	081	18 43	116	51 16	178	29 42	225	36 23	256	40 16	307
142	54 36	020	24 32	081	19 30	116	51 17	180	29 05	225	35 32	257	39 34	307
143	54 53	019	25 24	082	20 16	117	51 16	181	28 28	226	34 42	257	38 53	307
144	55 09	018	26 15	082	21 02	118	51 14	183	27 50	227	33 51	258	38 11	307
145	55 25	018	27 07	083	21 48	118	51 10	185	27 12	228	33 00	259	37 30	307
146	55 41	017	27 58	083	22 34	119	51 06	186	26 33	229	32 09	259	36 48	307
147	55 56	016	28 50	083	23 19	120	50 59	188	25 54	229	31 18	260	36 07	307
148	56 10	015	29 42	084	24 04	120	50 52	189	25 14	230	30 27	260	35 26	308
149	56 23	015	30 33	084	24 49	121	50 42	191	24 34	231	29 36	261	34 45	308
	Dubhe		◆ ARCTURUS		SPICA		◆ Alphard		SIRIUS		POLLUX		◆ CAPELLA	
150	56 36	014	31 25	085	25 33	122	50 32	192	23 54	232	60 47	274	34 03	308
151	56 48	013	32 17	085	26 17	122	50 20	194	23 13	232	59 55	275	33 22	308
152	57 00	012	33 09	086	27 01	123	50 07	195	22 31	233	59 03	275	32 41	308
153	57 10	011	34 00	086	27 44	124	49 53	197	21 49	234	58 12	276	32 01	308
154	57 20	011	34 52	087	28 27	125	49 37	198	21 07	235	57 20	276	31 20	308
155	57 30	010	35 44	087	29 10	125	49 20	200	20 25	235	56 28	276	30 39	309
156	57 38	009	36 36	088	29 52	126	49 02	201	19 42	236	55 37	277	29 59	309
157	57 46	008	37 28	088	30 34	127	48 42	203	18 59	237	54 45	277	29 18	309
158	57 53	007	38 20	089	31 15	128	48 22	204	18 15	237	53 54	277	28 38	309
159	57 59	006	39 12	089	31 56	129	48 00	205	17 31	238	53 02	278	27 58	309
160	58 04	006	40 04	090	32 36	130	47 37	207	16 47	239	52 11	278	27 17	310
161	58 09	005	40 56	090	33 16	130	47 13	208	16 02	239	51 19	278	26 37	310
162	58 13	004	41 48	091	33 55	131	46 48	209	15 18	240	50 28	279	25 58	310
163	58 16	003	42 40	091	34 34	132	46 22	211	14 33	240	49 36	279	25 18	310
164	58 18	002	43 32	092	35 12	133	45 55	212	13 47	241	48 45	279	24 38	310
	Dubhe		◆ Alkaid		ARCTURUS		◆ SPICA		Alphard		◆ PROCYON		POLLUX	
165	58 19	001	53 00	047	44 24	092	35 50	134	45 27	213	36 51	252	47 54	280
166	58 20	000	53 38	046	45 16	093	36 27	135	44 58	214	36 02	253	47 03	280
167	58 20	359	54 16	046	46 07	093	37 03	136	44 28	216	35 12	254	46 12	280
168	58 18	358	54 53	046	46 59	094	37 39	137	43 57	217	34 22	254	45 21	281
169	58 17	357	55 30	045	47 51	094	38 14	138	43 26	218	33 32	255	44 29	281
170	58 14	357	56 07	045	48 43	095	38 49	139	42 53	219	32 42	256	43 39	281
171	58 10	356	56 43	044	49 35	095	39 23	140	42 20	220	31 51	256	42 48	282
172	58 06	355	57 19	044	50 26	096	39 56	141	41 46	221	31 01	257	41 57	282
173	58 01	354	57 55	043	51 18	097	40 28	142	41 11	222	30 10	258	41 06	282
174	57 55	353	58 31	043	52 10	097	41 00	143	40 36	223	29 19	258	40 15	283
175	57 48	352	59 06	042	53 01	098	41 31	144	40 00	225	28 28	259	39 25	283
176	57 41	351	59 41	042	53 53	099	42 01	145	39 23	226	27 37	259	38 34	283
177	57 32	350	60 15	041	54 44	099	42 30	147	38 46	227	26 46	260	37 44	284
178	57 23	350	60 49	041	55 35	100	42 58	148	38 08	227	25 55	261	36 53	284
179	57 14	349	61 23	040	56 26	101	43 25	149	37 29	228	25 04	261	36 03	284

LHA ♈	Hc	Zn	Hc	Zn	Hc	Zn	Hc	Zn	Hc	Zn	Hc	Zn	Hc	Zn
	◆VEGA		Alphecca		◆SPICA		Gienah		REGULUS		◆POLLUX		Dubhe	
180	11 45	052	42 56	080	43 52	150	42 12	175	58 34	241	35 13	285	57 03	348
181	12 25	052	43 47	081	44 17	151	42 17	176	57 49	242	34 22	285	56 52	347
182	13 07	053	44 38	081	44 41	153	42 20	177	57 03	243	33 32	286	56 40	346
183	13 48	053	45 30	081	45 05	154	42 22	179	56 16	244	32 42	286	56 27	346
184	14 29	053	46 21	082	45 27	155	42 22	180	55 29	245	31 52	286	56 14	345
185	15 11	054	47 13	082	45 48	156	42 22	181	54 42	246	31 02	287	56 00	344
186	15 53	054	48 04	082	46 09	158	42 20	182	53 54	247	30 13	287	55 46	343
187	16 35	054	48 56	083	46 28	159	42 18	184	53 06	248	29 23	287	55 30	343
188	17 18	055	49 47	083	46 46	160	42 14	185	52 18	249	28 33	288	55 15	342
189	18 00	055	50 39	084	47 02	162	42 09	186	51 29	250	27 44	288	54 58	341
190	18 43	055	51 30	084	47 18	163	42 03	188	50 40	251	26 55	288	54 41	341
191	19 26	056	52 22	084	47 32	165	41 55	189	49 51	252	26 05	289	54 24	340
192	20 09	056	53 14	085	47 46	166	41 47	190	49 01	252	25 16	289	54 06	339
193	20 52	056	54 06	085	47 57	168	41 37	191	48 12	253	24 27	289	53 47	339
194	21 35	057	54 57	085	48 08	169	41 26	193	47 22	254	23 38	290	53 28	338
	◆Kochab		VEGA		Rasalhague		◆ANTARES		SPICA		◆REGULUS		Dubhe	
195	43 43	010	22 19	057	24 23	089	14 22	133	48 17	170	46 32	255	53 08	338
196	43 52	010	23 02	057	25 15	090	15 00	133	48 25	172	45 42	255	52 48	337
197	44 01	010	23 46	058	26 07	090	15 38	134	48 32	173	44 51	256	52 28	336
198	44 09	009	24 30	058	26 59	091	16 15	135	48 37	175	44 01	257	52 07	336
199	44 17	009	25 14	058	27 51	091	16 52	135	48 41	176	43 10	258	51 46	335
200	44 25	009	25 58	058	28 43	092	17 28	136	48 44	178	42 19	258	51 24	335
201	44 32	008	26 42	059	29 35	092	18 04	137	48 45	179	41 28	259	51 02	334
202	44 40	008	27 27	059	30 27	093	18 39	138	48 45	181	40 37	260	50 39	334
203	44 47	007	28 12	059	31 19	093	19 14	138	48 44	182	39 46	260	50 16	334
204	44 53	007	28 56	060	32 10	094	19 48	139	48 41	184	38 55	261	49 53	333
205	44 59	007	29 41	060	33 02	094	20 22	140	48 37	185	38 04	261	49 29	333
206	45 05	006	30 26	060	33 54	095	20 55	140	48 32	187	37 12	262	49 05	332
207	45 11	006	31 11	060	34 46	095	21 28	141	48 25	188	36 21	263	48 41	332
208	45 16	006	31 56	060	35 38	096	22 00	142	48 17	190	35 29	263	48 16	332
209	45 21	005	32 42	061	36 29	097	22 32	143	48 08	191	34 38	264	47 51	331
	Kochab		◆VEGA		Rasalhague		ANTARES		◆SPICA		REGULUS		◆Dubhe	
210	45 26	005	33 27	061	37 21	097	23 03	144	47 57	193	33 46	264	47 26	331
211	45 30	005	34 12	061	38 12	098	23 34	144	47 45	194	32 54	265	47 01	331
212	45 34	004	34 58	061	39 04	098	24 04	145	47 32	195	32 02	265	46 35	330
213	45 38	004	35 44	062	39 55	099	24 33	146	47 18	197	31 11	266	46 09	330
214	45 41	003	36 29	062	40 46	100	25 02	147	47 02	198	30 19	266	45 43	330
215	45 44	003	37 15	062	41 38	100	25 30	148	46 46	200	29 27	267	45 17	329
216	45 46	003	38 01	062	42 29	101	25 57	149	46 28	201	28 35	268	44 51	329
217	45 49	002	38 47	062	43 20	102	26 24	149	46 09	202	27 43	268	44 24	329
218	45 50	002	39 33	063	44 10	102	26 50	150	45 48	204	26 51	269	43 57	329
219	45 52	001	40 19	063	45 01	103	27 15	151	45 27	205	25 59	269	43 30	329
220	45 53	001	41 05	063	45 52	104	27 40	152	45 05	206	25 07	270	43 03	328
221	45 54	001	41 52	063	46 42	104	28 04	153	44 41	207	24 15	270	42 36	328
222	45 54	000	42 38	063	47 32	105	28 27	154	44 17	209	23 23	271	42 08	328
223	45 54	000	43 24	063	48 23	106	28 50	155	43 51	210	22 31	271	41 41	328
224	45 54	359	44 11	063	49 12	107	29 11	156	43 25	211	21 39	272	41 13	328
	VEGA		◆ALTAIR		Nunki		ANTARES		◆SPICA		Denebola		◆Alkaid	
225	44 57	064	19 14	091	10 15	129	29 32	157	42 58	212	43 43	261	66 26	330
226	45 44	064	20 06	091	10 56	129	29 52	158	42 29	213	42 52	262	65 59	329
227	46 30	064	20 58	092	11 36	130	30 12	159	42 00	215	42 00	262	65 32	327
228	47 17	064	21 49	092	12 16	130	30 30	160	41 30	216	41 09	263	65 03	326
229	48 04	064	22 41	093	12 55	131	30 48	161	41 00	217	40 17	264	64 34	325
230	48 50	064	23 33	093	13 34	132	31 05	162	40 28	218	39 25	264	64 04	324
231	49 37	064	24 25	094	14 13	132	31 21	163	39 56	219	38 34	265	63 34	323
232	50 24	064	25 17	094	14 51	133	31 36	164	39 23	220	37 42	265	63 02	323
233	51 11	064	26 09	095	15 29	134	31 50	165	38 49	221	36 50	266	62 30	322
234	51 57	064	27 00	095	16 06	134	32 03	166	38 14	222	35 58	266	61 58	321
235	52 44	064	27 52	096	16 43	135	32 16	167	37 39	223	35 06	267	61 25	320
236	53 31	064	28 44	096	17 19	136	32 27	168	37 03	224	34 14	268	60 51	320
237	54 18	064	29 35	097	17 55	136	32 38	169	36 27	225	33 22	268	60 18	319
238	55 04	064	30 27	098	18 31	137	32 48	170	35 50	226	32 30	269	59 43	318
239	55 51	064	31 18	098	19 06	138	32 56	171	35 12	227	31 39	269	59 08	318
	◆VEGA		ALTAIR		Nunki		◆ANTARES		SPICA		ARCTURUS		◆Alkaid	
240	56 38	064	32 10	099	19 41	139	33 04	172	34 34	228	64 07	251	58 33	317
241	57 24	064	33 01	099	20 15	139	33 11	173	33 55	229	63 18	252	57 58	317
242	58 11	064	33 52	100	20 49	140	33 17	174	33 15	230	62 28	253	57 22	316
243	58 58	064	34 44	101	21 22	141	33 22	175	32 36	230	61 38	254	56 45	316
244	59 44	064	35 35	101	21 54	142	33 26	176	31 55	231	60 48	255	56 09	315
245	60 31	063	36 26	102	22 26	142	33 29	177	31 15	232	59 58	256	55 32	315
246	61 17	063	37 16	102	22 58	143	33 31	178	30 33	233	59 07	257	54 55	314
247	62 03	063	38 07	103	23 29	144	33 32	179	29 52	234	58 17	258	54 18	314
248	62 50	063	38 58	104	23 59	145	33 32	180	29 09	235	57 26	258	53 40	314
249	63 36	062	39 48	104	24 29	146	33 31	182	28 27	235	56 35	259	53 03	313
250	64 22	062	40 38	105	24 58	146	33 29	183	27 44	236	55 44	260	52 25	313
251	65 07	062	41 28	106	25 26	147	33 26	184	27 01	237	54 53	261	51 47	313
252	65 53	061	42 18	106	25 54	148	33 23	185	26 17	238	54 01	261	51 09	313
253	66 39	061	43 08	107	26 21	149	33 18	186	25 33	238	53 10	262	50 31	312
254	67 24	060	43 58	108	26 48	150	33 12	187	24 49	239	52 19	263	49 52	312
	◆DENEB		ALTAIR		Nunki		◆ANTARES		SPICA		ARCTURUS		◆Alkaid	
255	44 28	054	44 47	109	27 14	151	33 05	188	24 04	240	51 27	263	49 14	312
256	45 10	054	45 36	110	27 39	152	32 58	189	23 19	240	50 35	264	48 35	312
257	45 53	054	46 25	110	28 03	152	32 49	190	22 33	241	49 44	264	47 56	312
258	46 35	054	47 13	111	28 27	153	32 40	191	21 48	242	48 52	265	47 17	312
259	47 17	054	48 02	112	28 50	154	32 29	192	21 02	242	48 00	266	46 39	311
260	47 59	054	48 50	113	29 12	155	32 18	193	20 16	243	47 08	266	46 00	311
261	48 41	054	49 37	114	29 33	156	32 06	194	19 29	244	46 16	267	45 21	311
262	49 23	054	50 25	115	29 54	157	31 52	195	18 43	244	45 25	267	44 42	311
263	50 05	054	51 12	116	30 13	158	31 38	196	17 56	245	44 33	268	44 02	311
264	50 47	054	51 59	117	30 32	159	31 23	197	17 08	246	43 41	268	43 23	311
265	51 29	054	52 45	118	30 50	160	31 08	198	16 21	246	42 49	269	42 44	311
266	52 11	053	53 31	119	31 08	161	30 51	199	15 33	247	41 57	269	42 05	311
267	52 52	053	54 16	120	31 24	162	30 33	200	14 46	247	41 05	270	41 26	311
268	53 34	053	55 01	121	31 40	163	30 15	201	13 57	248	40 13	270	40 47	311
269	54 16	053	55 45	122	31 54	164	29 56	202	13 09	249	39 21	271	40 08	311

LHA ♈	Hc	Zn	Hc	Zn	Hc	Zn	Hc	Zn	Hc	Zn	Hc	Zn	Hc	Zn
	◆DENEB		ALTAIR		◆Nunki		ANTARES		◆ARCTURUS		Alkaid		Kochab	
270	54 57	053	56 29	123	32 08	165	29 36	203	38 29	271	39 28	311	39 55	345
271	55 38	052	57 12	124	32 21	166	29 15	204	37 37	272	38 49	311	39 41	345
272	56 19	052	57 55	126	32 33	167	28 53	205	36 45	272	38 10	311	39 28	344
273	57 00	052	58 36	127	32 44	168	28 31	206	35 53	273	37 31	311	39 13	344
274	57 41	051	59 17	128	32 54	169	28 08	207	35 01	273	36 52	311	38 59	344
275	58 21	051	59 58	130	33 04	170	27 44	208	34 09	274	36 13	311	38 45	344
276	59 02	051	60 37	131	33 12	171	27 20	209	33 18	274	35 34	311	38 30	344
277	59 42	050	61 16	133	33 19	172	26 54	210	32 26	275	34 55	312	38 16	344
278	60 22	050	61 53	135	33 26	173	26 28	210	31 34	275	34 16	312	38 01	343
279	61 01	049	62 30	136	33 31	175	26 02	211	30 42	276	33 37	312	37 46	343
280	61 40	049	63 05	138	33 35	176	25 34	212	29 51	276	32 59	312	37 31	343
281	62 19	048	63 39	140	33 39	177	25 06	213	28 59	276	32 20	312	37 16	343
282	62 58	048	64 12	142	33 41	178	24 38	214	28 07	277	31 42	312	37 00	343
283	63 36	047	64 44	144	33 43	179	24 09	215	27 16	277	31 03	312	36 45	343
284	64 13	046	65 14	146	33 43	180	23 39	215	26 24	278	30 25	312	36 30	343
	◆Alpheratz		Enif		ALTAIR		◆ANTARES		ARCTURUS		◆Alkaid		Kochab	
285	24 13	069	46 42	109	65 43	148	23 08	216	25 33	278	29 46	313	36 14	342
286	25 01	069	47 32	110	66 10	150	22 37	217	24 41	279	29 08	313	35 58	342
287	25 50	070	48 20	110	66 35	152	22 06	218	23 50	279	28 30	313	35 43	342
288	26 39	070	49 09	111	66 58	154	21 33	219	22 59	280	27 52	313	35 27	342
289	27 28	070	49 57	112	67 20	157	21 01	219	22 08	280	27 14	313	35 11	342
290	28 17	071	50 45	113	67 39	159	20 28	220	21 16	280	26 37	314	34 55	342
291	29 06	071	51 33	114	67 57	162	19 54	221	20 25	281	25 59	314	34 39	342
292	29 55	072	52 20	115	68 12	164	19 20	222	19 34	281	25 22	314	34 23	342
293	30 44	072	53 07	116	68 25	167	18 45	222	18 43	282	24 44	314	34 06	342
294	31 34	072	53 54	117	68 36	169	18 10	223	17 53	282	24 07	314	33 50	342
295	32 23	073	54 40	118	68 44	172	17 34	224	17 02	283	23 30	315	33 34	342
296	33 13	073	55 25	119	68 50	175	16 58	224	16 11	283	22 53	315	33 18	342
297	34 03	073	56 10	120	68 54	178	16 21	225	15 21	284	22 16	315	33 01	342
298	34 52	074	56 55	121	68 55	180	15 44	226	14 30	284	21 40	315	32 45	342
299	35 42	074	57 39	123	68 53	183	15 07	226	13 40	284	21 03	316	32 29	342
	◆Schedar		Alpheratz		◆FOMALHAUT		ALTAIR		Rasalhague		◆Alphecca		Kochab	
300	35 18	039	36 32	074	16 51	140	68 49	186	52 21	250	32 29	284	32 12	342
301	35 51	039	37 22	074	17 24	141	68 42	189	51 32	251	31 39	285	31 56	342
302	36 24	039	38 12	075	17 56	142	68 34	191	50 43	252	30 49	285	31 39	342
303	36 57	039	39 02	075	18 28	142	68 22	194	49 53	253	29 58	285	31 23	342
304	37 30	039	39 53	075	18 59	143	68 09	196	49 03	254	29 08	286	31 06	342
305	38 03	039	40 43	076	19 30	144	67 53	199	48 13	254	28 18	286	30 50	342
306	38 36	039	41 33	076	20 00	145	67 35	201	47 23	255	27 29	286	30 34	342
307	39 09	039	42 24	076	20 30	145	67 15	204	46 33	256	26 39	287	30 17	342
308	39 42	039	43 14	077	20 59	146	66 53	206	45 42	257	25 49	287	30 01	342
309	40 15	039	44 05	077	21 28	147	66 29	209	44 52	257	24 59	288	29 44	342
310	40 47	039	44 56	077	21 56	148	66 03	211	44 01	258	24 10	288	29 28	342
311	41 20	039	45 46	078	22 23	149	65 36	213	43 10	259	23 21	288	29 12	342
312	41 53	039	46 37	078	22 50	149	65 07	215	42 19	259	22 31	289	28 55	342
313	42 26	039	47 28	078	23 16	150	64 36	217	41 28	260	21 42	289	28 39	342
314	42 58	039	48 19	079	23 42	151	64 04	219	40 37	261	20 53	290	28 23	342
	◆Mirfak		Hamal		Diphda		◆FOMALHAUT		ALTAIR		◆VEGA		Kochab	
315	18 43	043	22 13	075	17 49	124	24 06	152	63 31	221	59 31	296	28 07	342
316	19 18	043	23 03	075	18 32	125	24 31	153	62 57	222	58 45	296	27 51	342
317	19 53	043	23 54	076	19 15	125	24 54	154	62 21	224	57 58	296	27 35	342
318	20 29	043	24 44	076	19 57	126	25 17	154	61 44	226	57 12	296	27 19	342
319	21 05	044	25 35	076	20 39	127	25 39	155	61 06	227	56 25	296	27 03	342
320	21 41	044	26 25	077	21 21	127	26 00	156	60 28	229	55 38	296	26 47	342
321	22 17	044	27 16	077	22 02	128	26 21	157	59 48	230	54 51	296	26 31	342
322	22 53	044	28 06	078	22 42	129	26 41	158	59 08	232	54 05	296	26 15	342
323	23 29	045	28 57	078	23 23	130	27 00	159	58 26	233	53 18	296	26 00	343
324	24 06	045	29 48	078	24 03	130	27 18	160	57 44	235	52 31	296	25 44	343
325	24 43	045	30 39	079	24 42	131	27 35	161	57 02	236	51 44	296	25 29	343
326	25 19	045	31 30	079	25 21	132	27 52	162	56 18	237	50 58	296	25 13	343
327	25 56	045	32 21	080	25 59	133	28 08	163	55 34	238	50 11	296	24 58	343
328	26 34	046	33 12	080	26 37	133	28 23	164	54 50	239	49 24	296	24 43	343
329	27 11	046	34 03	080	27 15	134	28 38	165	54 05	241	48 37	296	24 28	343
	◆Mirfak		Hamal		Diphda		◆FOMALHAUT		ALTAIR		◆VEGA		Kochab	
330	27 48	046	34 55	081	27 52	135	28 51	165	53 20	242	47 51	296	24 13	343
331	28 26	046	35 46	081	28 29	136	29 04	166	52 34	243	47 04	296	23 58	343
332	29 03	046	36 37	082	29 04	137	29 15	167	51 47	244	46 18	296	23 43	344
333	29 41	047	37 29	082	29 40	138	29 26	168	51 01	245	45 31	296	23 29	344
334	30 19	047	38 20	082	30 15	138	29 36	169	50 13	246	44 44	297	23 14	344
335	30 56	047	39 12	083	30 49	139	29 45	170	49 26	246	43 58	297	23 00	344
336	31 34	047	40 04	083	31 22	140	29 54	171	48 38	247	43 12	297	22 46	344
337	32 12	047	40 55	084	31 55	141	30 01	172	47 50	248	42 25	297	22 31	344
338	32 51	047	41 47	084	32 28	142	30 07	173	47 02	249	41 39	297	22 17	344
339	33 29	047	42 39	085	32 59	143	30 13	174	46 13	250	40 53	297	22 04	345
340	34 07	047	43 30	085	33 30	144	30 18	175	45 24	251	40 06	297	21 50	345
341	34 45	048	44 22	085	34 01	145	30 21	176	44 35	251	39 20	298	21 36	345
342	35 24	048	45 14	086	34 30	146	30 24	177	43 46	252	38 34	298	21 23	345
343	36 02	048	46 06	086	34 59	147	30 26	178	42 56	253	37 48	298	21 10	345
344	36 41	048	46 58	087	35 27	148	30 27	179	42 06	254	37 02	298	20 57	345
	◆CAPELLA		ALDEBARAN		Diphda		◆FOMALHAUT		ALTAIR		◆VEGA		Kochab	
345	18 15	047	13 05	078	35 54	149	30 27	180	41 16	254	36 17	298	20 44	346
346	18 53	047	13 56	079	36 21	150	30 27	181	40 26	255	35 31	298	20 31	346
347	19 31	047	14 47	079	36 46	151	30 25	182	39 36	256	34 45	299	20 18	346
348	20 09	048	15 38	080	37 11	152	30 22	183	38 45	256	34 00	299	20 06	346
349	20 48	048	16 29	080	37 35	153	30 19	184	37 55	257	33 14	299	19 54	346
350	21 26	048	17 20	081	37 58	154	30 14	185	37 04	258	32 29	299	19 41	347
351	22 05	049	18 11	081	38 20	155	30 09	186	36 13	258	31 44	300	19 29	347
352	22 44	049	19 03	081	38 41	157	30 03	187	35 22	259	30 59	300	19 18	347
353	23 23	049	19 54	082	39 01	158	29 55	188	34 31	260	30 14	300	19 06	347
354	24 03	049	20 46	082	39 21	159	29 47	189	33 40	260	29 29	300	18 55	347
355	24 42	050	21 37	083	39 39	160	29 38	190	32 49	261	28 44	301	18 44	348
356	25 22	050	22 29	083	39 56	161	29 29	191	31 57	261	27 59	301	18 32	348
357	26 02	050	23 20	084	40 13	162	29 18	192	31 06	262	27 15	301	18 22	348
358	26 41	050	24 12	084	40 28	164	29 06	193	30 15	263	26 30	301	18 11	348
359	27 21	050	25 04	085	40 42	165	28 54	194	29 23	263	25 46	302	18 01	349

LAT 29°N

LHA ♈	Schedar Hc Zn	◆ CAPELLA Hc Zn	ALDEBARAN Hc Zn	◆ Diphda Hc Zn	FOMALHAUT Hc Zn	ALTAIR Hc Zn	◆ DENEB Hc Zn
0	61 26 012	27 23 050	25 50 085	41 53 166	29 39 195	28 38 264	48 04 307
1	61 36 011	28 04 050	26 42 085	42 06 167	29 24 196	27 45 265	47 22 307
2	61 45 010	28 44 051	27 35 086	42 17 168	29 09 197	26 53 265	46 40 307
3	61 54 009	29 25 051	28 27 086	42 27 170	28 53 198	26 01 266	45 58 307
4	62 01 007	30 06 051	29 19 086	42 36 171	28 36 199	25 08 266	45 16 307
5	62 07 006	30 46 051	30 12 087	42 44 172	28 19 200	24 16 267	44 34 307
6	62 13 005	31 27 051	31 04 087	42 50 173	28 00 201	23 24 267	43 52 307
7	62 17 004	32 08 051	31 57 088	42 56 175	27 41 202	22 31 268	43 10 307
8	62 20 003	32 49 052	32 49 088	43 00 176	27 21 203	21 39 268	42 27 307
9	62 22 002	33 31 052	33 42 089	43 03 177	27 00 204	20 46 269	41 45 307
10	62 23 000	34 12 052	34 34 089	43 05 179	26 39 205	19 54 269	41 03 307
11	62 23 359	34 53 052	35 27 090	43 06 180	26 16 206	19 01 270	40 21 307
12	62 21 358	35 34 052	36 19 090	43 05 181	25 53 206	18 09 270	39 39 307
13	62 19 357	36 16 052	37 11 091	43 04 182	25 30 207	17 16 271	38 57 307
14	62 16 356	36 57 052	38 04 091	43 01 184	25 05 208	16 24 271	38 15 307

LHA ♈	◆ CAPELLA	ALDEBARAN	RIGEL	◆ Diphda	FOMALHAUT	Enif	◆ DENEB
15	37 39 052	38 56 092	18 14 111	42 57 185	24 40 209	40 39 258	37 33 307
16	38 20 052	39 49 092	19 03 111	42 51 186	24 14 210	39 48 258	36 51 307
17	39 02 052	40 41 093	19 52 112	42 45 188	23 48 211	38 57 259	36 09 307
18	39 44 052	41 34 093	20 41 113	42 37 189	23 21 211	38 05 259	35 27 307
19	40 25 053	42 26 094	21 29 113	42 29 190	22 53 212	37 13 260	34 45 307
20	41 07 053	43 18 094	22 17 114	42 19 192	22 25 213	36 22 261	34 03 307
21	41 49 053	44 11 095	23 05 114	42 08 193	21 56 214	35 30 261	33 22 307
22	42 30 053	45 03 095	23 53 115	41 56 194	21 27 215	34 38 262	32 40 308
23	43 12 053	45 55 096	24 40 116	41 42 195	20 57 215	33 46 262	31 58 308
24	43 54 053	46 47 097	25 27 116	41 28 196	20 26 216	32 54 263	31 17 308
25	44 35 053	47 39 097	26 14 117	41 12 198	19 55 217	32 02 263	30 36 308
26	45 17 052	48 31 098	27 01 118	40 56 199	19 23 218	31 10 264	29 54 308
27	45 58 052	49 23 098	27 47 118	40 38 200	18 51 218	30 18 265	29 13 308
28	46 40 052	50 15 099	28 33 119	40 20 201	18 18 219	29 25 265	28 32 309
29	47 21 052	51 07 100	29 19 120	40 00 202	17 45 220	28 33 266	27 51 309

LHA ♈	CAPELLA	◆ ALDEBARAN	RIGEL	◆ Diphda	Alpheratz	DENEB	◆ Kochab
30	48 03 052	51 59 100	30 04 121	39 40 204	65 51 277	27 10 309	13 26 356
31	48 44 052	52 50 101	30 49 121	39 18 205	64 58 277	26 30 309	13 23 357
32	49 26 052	53 42 102	31 34 122	38 56 206	64 06 278	25 49 309	13 20 357
33	50 07 052	54 33 103	32 18 123	38 32 207	63 14 278	25 09 310	13 18 357
34	50 48 052	55 24 103	33 02 124	38 08 208	62 23 278	24 28 310	13 15 358
35	51 29 051	56 15 104	33 45 124	37 43 209	61 31 278	23 48 310	13 13 358
36	52 10 051	57 06 105	34 28 125	37 17 210	60 39 279	23 08 310	13 11 358
37	52 51 051	57 57 106	35 11 126	36 50 211	59 47 279	22 28 311	13 10 358
38	53 31 051	58 47 107	35 53 127	36 23 212	58 55 279	21 48 311	13 08 359
39	54 12 050	59 37 108	36 35 128	35 54 213	58 03 279	21 09 311	13 07 359
40	54 52 050	60 27 109	37 16 129	35 25 214	57 12 280	20 29 311	13 07 359
41	55 32 050	61 17 110	37 57 130	34 55 215	56 20 280	19 50 312	13 06 000
42	56 12 049	62 06 111	38 37 131	34 24 216	55 28 280	19 11 312	13 06 000
43	56 52 049	62 55 112	39 16 132	33 53 217	54 37 280	18 32 312	13 06 000
44	57 32 049	63 43 113	39 55 133	33 20 218	53 45 281	17 53 312	13 06 000

LHA ♈	◆ CAPELLA	PROCYON	SIRIUS	◆ RIGEL	Acamar	Diphda	◆ Alpheratz
45	58 11 048	19 58 095	18 52 122	40 34 134	20 45 180	32 48 219	52 53 281
46	58 50 048	20 50 096	19 36 123	41 11 135	20 45 181	32 14 220	52 02 281
47	59 28 047	21 42 096	20 19 124	41 48 136	20 43 182	31 40 221	51 10 282
48	60 07 047	22 34 097	21 03 124	42 25 137	20 41 183	31 05 222	50 19 282
49	60 45 046	23 26 097	21 46 125	43 00 138	20 38 184	30 30 223	49 28 282
50	61 22 045	24 18 098	22 29 126	43 35 139	20 35 184	29 54 224	48 36 282
51	62 00 045	25 10 098	23 11 127	44 10 140	20 31 185	29 18 224	47 45 283
52	62 36 044	26 02 099	23 53 127	44 43 141	20 25 186	28 41 225	46 54 283
53	63 13 043	26 54 100	24 35 128	45 16 142	20 20 187	28 03 226	46 03 283
54	63 48 043	27 46 100	25 16 129	45 47 143	20 13 188	27 25 227	45 12 283
55	64 24 042	28 37 101	25 56 129	46 18 145	20 06 188	26 47 228	44 21 284
56	64 58 041	29 29 101	26 37 130	46 48 146	19 58 189	26 07 228	43 30 284
57	65 32 040	30 20 102	27 16 131	47 17 147	19 49 190	25 28 229	42 39 284
58	66 05 039	31 12 102	27 56 132	47 45 148	19 40 191	24 48 230	41 48 285
59	66 38 038	32 03 103	28 35 133	48 12 150	19 30 192	24 08 231	40 57 285

LHA ♈	◆ Dubhe	PROCYON	SIRIUS	◆ RIGEL	Diphda	◆ Hamal	Mirfak
60	18 08 029	32 54 104	29 13 133	48 38 151	23 27 231	64 22 264	68 05 345
61	18 33 029	33 45 104	29 51 134	49 02 152	22 46 232	63 30 265	67 51 343
62	18 59 029	34 36 105	30 28 135	49 26 154	22 04 233	62 38 266	67 35 342
63	19 24 029	35 26 106	31 05 136	49 49 155	21 22 234	61 45 266	67 18 340
64	19 50 030	36 17 106	31 41 137	50 10 157	20 40 234	60 53 267	67 00 339
65	20 16 030	37 07 107	32 17 138	50 30 158	19 57 235	60 01 267	66 40 337
66	20 42 030	37 57 108	32 52 139	50 49 160	19 14 236	59 08 268	66 19 336
67	21 08 030	38 47 108	33 26 140	51 07 161	18 30 236	58 16 268	65 57 335
68	21 35 030	39 37 109	34 00 140	51 23 163	17 46 237	57 23 269	65 35 333
69	22 01 031	40 26 110	34 33 141	51 38 164	17 02 237	56 31 269	65 11 332
70	22 28 031	41 16 110	35 05 142	51 51 166	16 18 238	55 38 270	64 46 331
71	22 55 031	42 05 111	35 37 143	52 04 167	15 33 239	54 46 270	64 20 330
72	23 22 031	42 54 112	36 08 144	52 14 169	14 48 239	53 53 271	63 53 329
73	23 49 031	43 42 113	36 38 145	52 24 171	14 03 240	53 01 271	63 26 328
74	24 16 031	44 30 114	37 08 146	52 32 172	13 17 241	52 09 272	62 58 327

LHA ♈	◆ Dubhe	POLLUX	PROCYON	◆ SIRIUS	RIGEL	◆ Hamal	Mirfak
75	24 44 031	53 39 081	45 18 114	37 36 147	52 38 174	51 16 272	62 29 326
76	25 11 032	54 31 082	46 06 115	38 04 148	52 43 175	50 24 273	61 59 325
77	25 39 032	55 23 082	46 53 116	38 31 150	52 46 177	49 31 273	61 29 324
78	26 06 032	56 15 082	47 40 117	38 57 151	52 48 179	48 39 274	60 58 323
79	26 34 032	57 07 082	48 27 118	39 23 152	52 49 180	47 46 274	60 26 323
80	27 02 032	57 59 083	49 13 119	39 47 153	52 48 182	46 54 274	59 54 322
81	27 30 032	58 51 083	49 58 120	40 11 154	52 45 184	46 02 275	59 22 321
82	27 58 032	59 43 083	50 44 121	40 33 155	52 41 185	45 10 275	58 49 321
83	28 26 032	60 35 084	51 28 122	40 55 156	52 36 187	44 17 276	58 15 320
84	28 54 032	61 28 084	52 13 123	41 15 158	52 29 188	43 25 276	57 41 319
85	29 23 033	62 20 084	52 56 124	41 35 159	52 20 190	42 33 276	57 07 319
86	29 51 033	63 12 085	53 39 125	41 53 160	52 10 192	41 41 277	56 32 318
87	30 19 033	64 04 085	54 22 127	42 11 161	51 59 193	40 49 277	55 57 318
88	30 47 033	64 57 085	55 04 128	42 27 162	51 46 195	39 57 278	55 22 317
89	31 16 033	65 49 086	55 45 129	42 42 164	51 32 196	39 05 278	54 46 317

LHA ♈	Dubhe	◆ REGULUS	PROCYON	SIRIUS	◆ RIGEL	ALDEBARAN	◆ Mirfak
90	31 44 033	29 51 093	56 25 130	42 57 165	51 17 198	67 11 241	54 10 317
91	32 13 033	30 44 093	57 05 132	43 10 166	51 00 199	66 25 243	53 34 316
92	32 41 033	31 36 094	57 43 133	43 22 168	50 42 201	65 38 244	52 58 316
93	33 10 033	32 29 094	58 21 135	43 32 169	50 23 202	64 50 246	52 21 316
94	33 38 033	33 21 095	58 58 136	43 42 170	50 02 204	64 02 247	51 44 315
95	34 07 033	34 13 095	59 34 138	43 50 171	49 40 205	63 14 248	51 07 315
96	34 35 033	35 05 096	60 09 139	43 58 173	49 17 207	62 25 249	50 30 315
97	35 03 033	35 58 096	60 42 141	44 04 174	48 53 208	61 36 250	49 52 314
98	35 32 033	36 50 097	61 15 143	44 08 175	48 28 209	60 46 251	49 15 314
99	36 00 033	37 42 098	61 46 144	44 12 177	48 02 211	59 57 252	48 37 314
100	36 29 033	38 34 098	62 16 146	44 14 178	47 35 212	59 07 253	47 59 314
101	36 57 033	39 26 099	62 44 148	44 16 179	47 06 213	58 16 254	47 21 314
102	37 25 033	40 18 099	63 11 150	44 16 181	46 37 215	57 26 255	46 43 313
103	37 53 032	41 09 100	63 36 152	44 14 182	46 07 216	56 35 256	46 05 313
104	38 21 032	42 01 100	64 00 154	44 12 183	45 36 217	55 44 256	45 27 313

LHA ♈	◆ Dubhe	REGULUS	◆ Alphard	SIRIUS	RIGEL	◆ ALDEBARAN	CAPELLA
105	38 50 032	42 52 101	38 02 131	44 08 185	45 04 218	54 53 257	63 45 317
106	39 17 032	43 44 102	38 42 132	44 03 186	44 31 219	54 02 258	63 09 317
107	39 45 032	44 35 102	39 20 133	43 57 187	43 57 220	53 10 259	62 33 316
108	40 13 032	45 26 103	39 59 134	43 50 189	43 23 222	52 19 259	61 56 315
109	40 41 032	46 17 104	40 36 135	43 41 190	42 47 223	51 27 260	61 19 314
110	41 08 032	47 08 105	41 13 136	43 31 191	42 11 224	50 36 261	60 41 314
111	41 36 031	47 59 105	41 49 137	43 20 193	41 35 225	49 44 261	60 03 313
112	42 03 031	48 50 106	42 25 138	43 08 194	40 57 226	48 52 262	59 25 313
113	42 30 031	49 40 107	43 00 139	42 55 195	40 19 227	48 00 263	58 46 312
114	42 57 031	50 30 108	43 34 140	42 41 196	39 41 228	47 08 263	58 07 312
115	43 24 031	51 20 108	44 07 141	42 26 198	39 02 229	46 16 264	57 28 311
116	43 50 030	52 10 109	44 40 142	42 09 199	38 22 230	45 23 264	56 48 311
117	44 17 030	52 59 110	45 11 144	41 52 200	37 42 231	44 31 265	56 08 311
118	44 43 030	53 48 111	45 42 145	41 33 201	37 01 232	43 39 265	55 28 310
119	45 09 030	54 37 112	46 12 146	41 13 203	36 19 232	42 47 266	54 48 310

LHA ♈	◆ Dubhe	REGULUS	◆ Alphard	SIRIUS	RIGEL	◆ ALDEBARAN	CAPELLA
120	45 35 029	55 26 113	46 41 147	40 53 204	35 38 233	41 54 267	54 08 310
121	46 00 029	56 14 114	47 09 148	40 31 205	34 55 234	41 02 267	53 27 309
122	46 26 029	57 01 115	47 36 150	40 08 206	34 13 235	40 09 268	52 47 309
123	46 51 028	57 49 116	48 02 151	39 45 207	33 29 236	39 17 268	52 06 309
124	47 15 028	58 36 117	48 26 152	39 20 208	32 46 237	38 24 269	51 25 309
125	47 40 028	59 22 118	48 50 154	38 55 209	32 02 237	37 32 269	50 44 308
126	48 04 027	60 08 119	49 13 155	38 29 211	31 17 238	36 40 270	50 03 308
127	48 28 027	60 54 121	49 34 157	38 02 212	30 33 239	35 47 270	49 21 308
128	48 52 026	61 38 122	49 54 158	37 34 213	29 47 240	34 55 271	48 40 308
129	49 15 026	62 23 123	50 13 160	37 05 214	29 02 240	34 02 271	47 59 308
130	49 38 026	63 06 125	50 31 161	36 36 215	28 16 241	33 10 272	47 17 308
131	50 00 025	63 49 126	50 47 163	36 05 216	27 30 242	32 17 272	46 36 308
132	50 22 025	64 30 128	51 03 164	35 34 217	26 44 243	31 25 272	45 54 308
133	50 44 024	65 11 130	51 16 166	35 02 218	25 57 243	30 32 273	45 13 308
134	51 05 024	65 51 131	51 29 167	34 30 219	25 10 244	29 40 273	44 31 307

LHA ♈	Dubhe	◆ ARCTURUS	SPICA	Alphard	◆ SIRIUS	BETELGEUSE	◆ CAPELLA
135	51 26 023	18 22 078	14 20 112	51 40 169	33 57 220	41 41 253	43 49 307
136	51 47 023	19 14 078	15 09 112	51 49 170	33 23 221	40 51 253	43 08 307
137	52 07 022	20 05 079	15 57 113	51 58 172	32 49 221	40 00 254	42 26 307
138	52 26 022	20 56 079	16 45 114	52 04 173	32 14 222	39 10 255	41 44 307
139	52 45 021	21 48 080	17 33 114	52 10 175	31 38 223	38 19 256	41 03 307
140	53 04 020	22 40 080	18 21 115	52 13 177	31 02 224	37 28 256	40 21 307
141	53 22 020	23 31 080	19 09 115	52 16 178	30 25 225	36 37 257	39 39 308
142	53 39 019	24 23 081	19 56 116	52 17 180	29 47 226	35 46 257	38 58 308
143	53 56 018	25 15 081	20 43 117	52 16 181	29 09 227	34 54 258	38 16 308
144	54 12 018	26 07 082	21 30 117	52 14 183	28 31 227	34 03 259	37 35 308
145	54 28 017	26 59 082	22 16 118	52 10 185	27 52 228	33 12 259	36 53 308
146	54 43 016	27 51 083	23 03 119	52 05 186	27 13 229	32 20 260	36 12 308
147	54 58 016	28 43 083	23 49 119	51 59 188	26 33 230	31 28 260	35 30 308
148	55 12 015	29 35 083	24 34 120	51 51 189	25 53 231	30 36 261	34 49 308
149	55 25 014	30 27 084	25 20 121	51 41 191	25 12 231	29 45 262	34 08 308

LHA ♈	Dubhe	◆ ARCTURUS	SPICA	◆ Alphard	SIRIUS	POLLUX	◆ CAPELLA
150	55 38 014	31 19 084	26 05 121	51 31 193	24 31 232	60 41 276	33 26 308
151	55 50 013	32 12 085	26 49 122	51 18 194	23 49 233	59 49 277	32 45 308
152	56 01 012	33 04 085	27 34 123	51 05 196	23 07 234	58 57 277	32 04 309
153	56 11 011	33 56 086	28 18 123	50 50 197	22 25 234	58 05 277	31 23 309
154	56 21 010	34 48 086	29 01 124	50 34 199	21 42 235	57 13 277	30 42 309
155	56 30 010	35 41 086	29 44 125	50 16 200	20 59 236	56 21 278	30 02 309
156	56 39 009	36 33 087	30 27 126	49 58 202	20 15 236	55 29 278	29 21 309
157	56 46 008	37 26 087	31 10 127	49 38 203	19 31 237	54 37 278	28 40 309
158	56 53 007	38 18 088	31 51 127	49 16 205	18 47 238	53 45 279	28 00 310
159	56 59 006	39 10 088	32 33 128	48 54 206	18 03 238	52 53 279	27 19 310
160	57 05 005	40 03 089	33 14 129	48 30 207	17 18 239	52 02 279	26 39 310
161	57 09 005	40 55 089	33 54 130	48 06 209	16 33 239	51 10 280	25 59 310
162	57 13 004	41 48 090	34 34 131	47 40 210	15 48 240	50 18 280	25 19 310
163	57 16 003	42 40 090	35 14 132	47 13 211	15 02 241	49 26 280	24 39 311
164	57 18 002	43 33 091	35 53 133	46 46 213	14 16 241	48 35 281	23 59 311

LHA ♈	Dubhe	◆ Alkaid	ARCTURUS	◆ SPICA	Alphard	◆ PROCYON	POLLUX
165	57 19 001	52 19 046	44 25 091	36 31 133	46 17 214	37 09 253	47 43 281
166	57 20 000	52 56 045	45 18 092	37 09 134	45 47 215	36 19 254	46 52 281
167	57 20 359	53 33 045	46 10 092	37 46 135	45 16 216	35 28 254	46 00 281
168	57 18 358	54 10 045	47 03 093	38 23 136	44 45 217	34 38 255	45 09 282
169	57 17 358	54 47 044	47 55 093	38 59 137	44 13 219	33 47 256	44 17 282
170	57 14 357	55 24 044	48 47 094	39 34 138	43 39 220	32 56 256	43 26 282
171	57 10 356	56 00 043	49 40 094	40 09 139	43 05 221	32 05 257	42 35 283
172	57 06 355	56 36 043	50 32 095	40 42 140	42 31 222	31 14 258	41 44 283
173	57 01 354	57 11 042	51 24 095	41 15 142	41 55 223	30 23 258	40 53 283
174	56 55 353	57 46 042	52 17 096	41 48 143	41 19 224	29 31 259	40 02 284
175	56 49 352	58 21 041	53 09 097	42 19 144	40 42 225	28 40 259	39 11 284
176	56 41 352	58 56 041	54 01 097	42 50 145	40 05 226	27 48 260	38 20 284
177	56 33 351	59 30 040	54 53 098	43 20 146	39 27 227	26 56 260	37 29 285
178	56 24 350	60 03 039	55 45 099	43 48 147	38 48 228	26 05 261	36 38 285
179	56 15 349	60 36 039	56 37 099	44 16 148	38 09 229	25 13 262	35 47 285

LAT 29°N

LHA ♈	Hc	Zn	Hc	Zn	Hc	Zn	Hc	Zn	Hc	Zn	Hc	Zn	Hc	Zn
	◆VEGA		Alphecca		◆SPICA		Gienah		REGULUS		◆POLLUX		Dubhe	
180	11 07	052	42 45	079	44 43	150	43 12	175	59 03	242	34 57	286	56 04	348
181	11 49	052	43 37	080	45 09	151	43 17	176	58 16	243	34 06	286	55 53	347
182	12 30	052	44 28	080	45 35	152	43 20	177	57 29	244	33 16	286	55 42	347
183	13 12	053	45 20	080	45 59	153	43 22	178	56 42	246	32 26	286	55 29	346
184	13 53	053	46 12	081	46 21	155	43 22	180	55 54	247	31 35	287	55 16	345
185	14 36	053	47 04	081	46 43	156	43 22	181	55 05	248	30 45	287	55 02	344
186	15 18	054	47 56	081	47 04	157	43 20	182	54 17	248	29 55	287	54 48	344
187	16 00	054	48 47	082	47 24	159	43 18	184	53 28	249	29 05	288	54 33	343
188	16 43	054	49 39	082	47 42	160	43 14	185	52 39	250	28 15	288	54 18	342
189	17 26	055	50 31	082	47 59	162	43 08	186	51 49	251	27 25	288	54 01	342
190	18 08	055	51 23	083	48 15	163	43 02	188	50 59	252	26 35	289	53 45	341
191	18 52	055	52 15	083	48 30	164	42 54	189	50 09	253	25 46	289	53 27	340
192	19 35	056	53 08	083	48 44	166	42 46	190	49 19	254	24 56	290	53 10	340
193	20 18	056	54 00	084	48 56	167	42 36	191	48 29	254	24 07	290	52 51	339
194	21 02	056	54 52	084	49 07	169	42 25	193	47 38	255	23 18	290	52 32	339
	◆Kochab		VEGA		Rasalhague		◆ANTARES		SPICA		◆REGULUS		Dubhe	
195	42 44	010	21 46	057	24 22	089	15 03	133	49 16	170	46 47	256	52 13	338
196	42 53	010	22 30	057	25 14	089	15 42	133	49 25	172	45 56	256	51 53	338
197	43 01	009	23 14	057	26 07	090	16 20	134	49 32	173	45 05	257	51 33	337
198	43 10	009	23 58	057	26 59	090	16 57	135	49 37	175	44 14	258	51 12	336
199	43 18	009	24 42	058	27 52	091	17 34	135	49 41	176	43 23	258	50 51	336
200	43 26	008	25 27	058	28 44	091	18 11	136	49 44	178	42 31	259	50 29	335
201	43 33	008	26 11	058	29 37	092	18 47	137	49 45	179	41 39	260	50 07	335
202	43 40	008	26 56	059	30 29	092	19 23	137	49 45	181	40 48	260	49 45	335
203	43 47	007	27 41	059	31 22	093	19 59	138	49 44	182	39 56	261	49 22	334
204	43 54	007	28 26	059	32 14	093	20 33	139	49 41	184	39 04	262	48 59	334
205	44 00	007	29 11	059	33 06	094	21 08	140	49 37	185	38 12	262	48 36	333
206	44 06	006	29 56	060	33 59	094	21 42	140	49 32	187	37 20	263	48 12	333
207	44 11	006	30 41	060	34 51	095	22 15	141	49 25	188	36 28	263	47 48	332
208	44 17	006	31 26	060	35 43	095	22 48	142	49 16	190	35 36	264	47 23	332
209	44 22	005	32 12	060	36 36	096	23 20	143	49 07	191	34 44	264	46 59	332
	Kochab		◆VEGA		Rasalhague		ANTARES		◆SPICA		REGULUS		◆Dubhe	
210	44 26	005	32 57	060	37 28	096	23 51	143	48 56	193	33 51	265	46 34	331
211	44 30	004	33 43	061	38 20	097	24 22	144	48 44	194	32 59	265	46 08	331
212	44 34	004	34 29	061	39 12	098	24 53	145	48 30	196	32 07	266	45 43	331
213	44 38	004	35 15	061	40 04	098	25 23	146	48 15	197	31 15	267	45 17	331
214	44 41	003	36 01	061	40 56	099	25 52	147	47 59	198	30 22	267	44 51	330
215	44 44	003	36 47	061	41 48	099	26 20	147	47 42	200	29 30	268	44 25	330
216	44 46	003	37 33	061	42 39	100	26 48	148	47 24	201	28 37	268	43 59	330
217	44 49	002	38 19	062	43 31	101	27 16	149	47 04	203	27 45	269	43 32	329
218	44 50	002	39 05	062	44 23	101	27 42	150	46 43	204	26 52	269	43 06	329
219	44 52	001	39 51	062	45 14	102	28 08	151	46 21	205	26 00	270	42 39	329
220	44 53	001	40 38	062	46 05	103	28 33	152	45 58	207	25 07	270	42 12	329
221	44 54	001	41 24	062	46 56	103	28 57	153	45 34	208	24 15	271	41 44	329
222	44 54	000	42 11	062	47 47	104	29 21	154	45 09	209	23 22	271	41 17	328
223	44 54	000	42 57	062	48 38	105	29 44	155	44 43	210	22 30	271	40 50	328
224	44 54	359	43 44	063	49 29	105	30 06	156	44 16	212	21 38	272	40 22	328
	VEGA		◆ALTAIR		Nunki		ANTARES		◆SPICA		Denebola		◆Alkaid	
225	44 30	063	19 14	090	10 53	128	30 27	156	43 48	213	43 52	262	65 34	331
226	45 17	063	20 07	091	11 34	129	30 48	157	43 19	214	43 00	263	65 08	330
227	46 03	063	20 59	091	12 14	130	31 08	158	42 50	215	42 08	263	64 41	329
228	46 50	063	21 52	092	12 54	130	31 27	159	42 19	216	41 15	264	64 13	328
229	47 37	063	22 44	092	13 34	131	31 45	160	41 47	217	40 23	264	63 44	326
230	48 24	063	23 36	093	14 14	132	32 02	161	41 15	219	39 31	265	63 15	326
231	49 10	063	24 29	093	14 53	132	32 18	162	40 42	220	38 39	266	62 45	325
232	49 57	063	25 21	094	15 32	133	32 33	163	40 08	221	37 46	266	62 14	324
233	50 44	063	26 14	094	16 10	133	32 48	164	39 34	222	36 54	267	61 43	323
234	51 31	063	27 06	095	16 48	134	33 02	165	38 58	223	36 01	267	61 11	322
235	52 17	063	27 58	095	17 25	135	33 14	167	38 23	224	35 09	268	60 38	321
236	53 04	063	28 50	096	18 02	135	33 26	168	37 46	225	34 17	268	60 05	321
237	53 51	063	29 43	096	18 39	136	33 37	169	37 09	226	33 24	269	59 32	320
238	54 37	063	30 35	097	19 15	137	33 47	170	36 31	227	32 32	269	58 58	319
239	55 24	063	31 27	098	19 51	138	33 56	171	35 53	227	31 39	270	58 24	319
	◆VEGA		ALTAIR		Nunki		◆ANTARES		SPICA		ARCTURUS		◆Alkaid	
240	56 11	063	32 19	098	20 26	138	34 04	172	35 14	228	64 26	253	57 49	318
241	56 57	063	33 11	099	21 00	139	34 11	173	34 34	229	63 35	254	57 14	318
242	57 44	062	34 02	099	21 35	140	34 17	174	33 54	230	62 45	255	56 38	317
243	58 30	062	34 54	100	22 08	141	34 22	175	33 14	231	61 54	256	56 02	317
244	59 17	062	35 46	100	22 41	141	34 26	176	32 33	232	61 03	257	55 26	316
245	60 03	062	36 37	101	23 14	142	34 29	177	31 51	233	60 12	258	54 50	316
246	60 49	062	37 29	102	23 46	143	34 31	178	31 09	233	59 20	258	54 13	315
247	61 35	061	38 20	102	24 17	144	34 32	179	30 27	234	58 29	259	53 36	315
248	62 21	061	39 11	103	24 48	144	34 32	180	29 44	235	57 37	260	52 59	315
249	63 07	061	40 02	104	25 18	145	34 31	182	29 01	236	56 46	261	52 21	314
250	63 53	060	40 53	104	25 48	146	34 29	183	28 17	237	55 54	261	51 44	314
251	64 38	060	41 44	105	26 17	147	34 26	184	27 33	237	55 02	262	51 06	314
252	65 23	059	42 35	106	26 45	148	34 22	185	26 49	238	54 10	263	50 28	314
253	66 08	059	43 25	106	27 13	149	34 18	186	26 04	239	53 18	263	49 50	313
254	66 53	058	44 16	107	27 40	150	34 12	187	25 19	239	52 26	264	49 12	313
	◆DENEB		ALTAIR		Nunki		◆ANTARES		SPICA		ARCTURUS		◆Alkaid	
255	43 53	053	45 06	108	28 06	150	34 05	188	24 34	240	51 33	264	48 33	313
256	44 35	053	45 55	109	28 31	151	33 57	189	23 48	241	50 41	265	47 55	313
257	45 17	053	46 45	109	28 56	152	33 48	190	23 02	241	49 49	266	47 16	313
258	45 59	053	47 35	110	29 20	153	33 39	191	22 16	242	48 56	266	46 37	312
259	46 41	053	48 24	111	29 44	154	33 28	192	21 30	243	48 04	267	45 59	312
260	47 24	053	49 13	112	30 06	155	33 16	193	20 43	243	47 12	267	45 20	312
261	48 06	053	50 01	113	30 28	156	33 04	194	19 56	244	46 19	268	44 41	312
262	48 47	053	50 49	114	30 49	157	32 50	195	19 08	245	45 27	268	44 02	312
263	49 29	053	51 37	115	31 09	158	32 36	196	18 21	245	44 34	269	43 23	312
264	50 11	053	52 25	115	31 28	159	32 21	197	17 33	246	43 42	269	42 44	312
265	50 53	053	53 12	116	31 47	160	32 04	198	16 45	246	42 49	270	42 04	312
266	51 35	052	53 59	117	32 04	161	31 47	199	15 57	247	41 57	270	41 25	312
267	52 16	052	54 45	119	32 21	162	31 30	200	15 08	248	41 04	271	40 46	312
268	52 58	052	55 31	120	32 37	163	31 11	201	14 20	248	40 12	271	40 07	312
269	53 39	052	56 16	121	32 52	164	30 51	202	13 31	249	39 20	272	39 28	312

LHA ♈	Hc	Zn	Hc	Zn	Hc	Zn	Hc	Zn	Hc	Zn	Hc	Zn	Hc	Zn
	◆DENEB		ALTAIR		◆Nunki		ANTARES		◆ARCTURUS		Alkaid		Kochab	
270	54 20	052	57 01	122	33 06	165	30 31	203	38 27	272	38 49	312	38 57	345
271	55 01	051	57 45	123	33 19	166	30 10	204	37 35	273	38 09	312	38 44	345
272	55 42	051	58 29	124	33 32	167	29 48	205	36 42	273	37 30	312	38 30	345
273	56 22	051	59 12	126	33 43	168	29 25	206	35 50	274	36 51	312	38 16	344
274	57 03	050	59 54	127	33 53	169	29 01	207	34 57	274	36 12	312	38 02	344
275	57 43	050	60 36	129	34 03	170	28 37	208	34 05	274	35 33	312	37 47	344
276	58 23	049	61 16	130	34 11	171	28 12	209	33 13	275	34 54	312	37 33	344
277	59 03	049	61 56	132	34 19	172	27 46	210	32 21	275	34 15	312	37 18	344
278	59 42	048	62 35	133	34 25	173	27 20	211	31 28	276	33 36	312	37 03	344
279	60 21	048	63 13	135	34 31	175	26 53	212	30 36	276	32 57	312	36 48	343
280	61 00	047	63 49	137	34 35	176	26 25	212	29 44	277	32 19	312	36 33	343
281	61 39	047	64 25	138	34 39	177	25 57	213	28 52	277	31 40	313	36 18	343
282	62 17	046	64 59	140	34 41	178	25 28	214	28 00	277	31 01	313	36 03	343
283	62 54	045	65 32	142	34 43	179	24 58	215	27 08	278	30 23	313	35 48	343
284	63 31	045	66 03	144	34 43	180	24 27	216	26 16	278	29 44	313	35 32	343
	◆Alpheratz		Enif		ALTAIR		◆ANTARES		ARCTURUS		◆Alkaid		Kochab	
285	23 51	069	47 01	108	66 33	146	23 57	217	25 24	279	29 06	313	35 17	343
286	24 40	069	47 51	109	67 01	149	23 25	217	24 32	279	28 27	313	35 01	343
287	25 29	069	48 41	109	67 28	151	22 53	218	23 40	280	27 49	313	34 45	343
288	26 18	070	49 30	110	67 52	153	22 20	219	22 49	280	27 11	314	34 30	342
289	27 07	070	50 19	111	68 15	156	21 47	220	21 57	280	26 33	314	34 14	342
290	27 57	070	51 08	112	68 35	158	21 13	220	21 05	281	25 55	314	33 58	342
291	28 46	071	51 57	113	68 54	161	20 39	221	20 14	281	25 18	314	33 42	342
292	29 36	071	52 45	114	69 10	163	20 04	222	19 22	282	24 40	314	33 26	342
293	30 25	071	53 33	115	69 24	166	19 29	223	18 31	282	24 02	315	33 09	342
294	31 15	072	54 20	116	69 35	169	18 53	223	17 40	282	23 25	315	32 53	342
295	32 05	072	55 07	117	69 44	172	18 17	224	16 49	283	22 48	315	32 37	342
296	32 55	072	55 54	118	69 50	175	17 40	225	15 57	283	22 11	315	32 21	342
297	33 45	073	56 40	119	69 54	177	17 03	225	15 06	284	21 34	315	32 04	342
298	34 35	073	57 26	120	69 55	180	16 26	226	14 16	284	20 57	316	31 48	342
299	35 25	073	58 11	121	69 53	183	15 48	227	13 25	285	20 20	316	31 32	342
	◆Schedar		Alpheratz		◆FOMALHAUT		ALTAIR		Rasalhague		◆Alphecca		Kochab	
300	34 31	039	36 15	073	17 37	140	69 49	186	52 41	252	32 14	285	31 15	342
301	35 04	039	37 06	074	18 10	141	69 42	189	51 51	252	31 23	285	30 59	342
302	35 37	039	37 56	074	18 43	142	69 32	192	51 01	253	30 33	286	30 42	342
303	36 10	039	38 47	074	19 15	142	69 20	194	50 10	254	29 42	286	30 26	342
304	36 43	039	39 37	075	19 47	143	69 06	197	49 20	255	28 52	286	30 09	342
305	37 16	039	40 28	075	20 19	144	68 50	200	48 29	255	28 01	287	29 53	342
306	37 49	039	41 19	075	20 49	144	68 31	202	47 38	256	27 11	287	29 37	342
307	38 22	039	42 09	076	21 20	145	68 10	205	46 47	257	26 21	287	29 20	342
308	38 55	039	43 00	076	21 49	146	67 46	207	45 56	258	25 31	288	29 04	342
309	39 28	039	43 51	076	22 18	147	67 21	210	45 05	258	24 41	288	28 47	342
310	40 01	039	44 42	076	22 47	148	66 55	212	44 13	259	23 51	288	28 31	342
311	40 33	039	45 33	077	23 14	148	66 26	214	43 22	260	23 02	289	28 15	342
312	41 06	038	46 24	077	23 42	149	65 56	216	42 30	260	22 12	289	27 58	342
313	41 39	038	47 15	077	24 08	150	65 24	218	41 38	261	21 22	290	27 42	342
314	42 11	038	48 07	077	24 34	151	64 51	220	40 46	261	20 33	290	27 26	342
	◆Mirfak		Hamal		Diphda		◆FOMALHAUT		ALTAIR		◆VEGA		Kochab	
315	17 59	042	21 57	074	18 23	124	24 59	152	64 16	222	59 04	298	27 10	342
316	18 34	043	22 48	075	19 06	124	25 24	153	63 40	224	58 17	298	26 54	342
317	19 10	043	23 39	075	19 49	125	25 48	153	63 04	226	57 31	298	26 37	342
318	19 45	043	24 29	076	20 32	126	26 11	154	62 26	227	56 44	297	26 21	342
319	20 21	043	25 20	076	21 15	126	26 33	155	61 47	229	55 58	297	26 06	342
320	20 57	044	26 11	076	21 57	127	26 55	156	61 07	230	55 11	297	25 50	342
321	21 34	044	27 02	077	22 39	128	27 16	157	60 26	232	54 25	297	25 34	343
322	22 10	044	27 53	077	23 20	128	27 36	158	59 44	233	53 38	297	25 18	343
323	22 47	044	28 45	077	24 01	129	27 56	159	59 02	235	52 51	297	25 02	343
324	23 23	044	29 36	078	24 41	130	28 14	160	58 19	236	52 04	297	24 47	343
325	24 00	045	30 27	078	25 21	131	28 32	161	57 35	237	51 18	297	24 31	343
326	24 37	045	31 19	079	26 01	131	28 49	162	56 50	238	50 31	297	24 16	343
327	25 14	045	32 10	079	26 40	132	29 05	162	56 05	240	49 44	297	24 01	343
328	25 51	045	33 02	079	27 19	133	29 21	163	55 20	241	48 57	297	23 45	343
329	26 29	045	33 53	080	27 57	134	29 35	164	54 34	242	48 11	297	23 30	343
	◆Mirfak		Hamal		Diphda		◆FOMALHAUT		ALTAIR		◆VEGA		Kochab	
330	27 06	046	34 45	080	28 34	135	29 49	165	53 48	243	47 24	297	23 15	343
331	27 44	046	35 37	081	29 11	135	30 02	166	53 01	244	46 37	297	23 00	344
332	28 22	046	36 28	081	29 48	136	30 14	167	52 13	245	45 51	297	22 46	344
333	28 59	046	37 20	081	30 24	137	30 25	168	51 26	246	45 04	297	22 31	344
334	29 37	046	38 12	082	30 59	138	30 35	169	50 38	247	44 17	297	22 17	344
335	30 15	046	39 04	082	31 34	139	30 45	170	49 49	248	43 31	297	22 02	344
336	30 53	047	39 56	082	32 08	140	30 53	171	49 01	248	42 44	298	21 48	344
337	31 31	047	40 48	083	32 42	141	31 00	172	48 12	249	41 58	298	21 34	344
338	32 10	047	41 40	083	33 15	142	31 07	173	47 23	250	41 11	298	21 20	345
339	32 48	047	42 32	084	33 47	143	31 13	174	46 33	251	40 25	298	21 06	345
340	33 26	047	43 25	084	34 19	144	31 18	175	45 43	252	39 39	298	20 52	345
341	34 05	047	44 17	084	34 50	144	31 21	176	44 54	252	38 52	298	20 38	345
342	34 43	047	45 09	085	35 20	145	31 24	177	44 03	253	38 06	298	20 25	345
343	35 22	047	46 01	085	35 49	146	31 26	178	43 13	254	37 20	299	20 12	345
344	36 00	047	46 54	086	36 18	147	31 27	179	42 23	255	36 34	299	19 59	346
	◆CAPELLA		ALDEBARAN		Diphda		◆FOMALHAUT		ALTAIR		◆VEGA		Kochab	
345	17 34	047	12 52	078	36 46	149	31 27	180	41 32	255	35 48	299	19 46	346
346	18 12	047	13 44	078	37 12	150	31 27	181	40 41	256	35 02	299	19 33	346
347	18 50	047	14 35	079	37 39	151	31 25	182	39 50	257	34 16	299	19 20	346
348	19 29	047	15 27	079	38 04	152	31 22	183	38 59	257	33 31	299	19 08	346
349	20 07	048	16 18	080	38 28	153	31 19	184	38 08	258	32 45	300	18 55	347
350	20 46	048	17 10	080	38 52	154	31 14	185	37 16	259	31 59	300	18 43	347
351	21 25	048	18 02	081	39 15	155	31 08	186	36 25	259	31 14	300	18 31	347
352	22 05	048	18 54	081	39 36	156	31 02	187	35 33	260	30 29	300	18 19	347
353	22 44	049	19 46	082	39 57	157	30 55	188	34 42	260	29 43	301	18 08	347
354	23 23	049	20 37	082	40 17	159	30 47	190	33 50	261	28 58	301	17 56	348
355	24 03	049	21 29	082	40 35	160	30 37	190	32 58	261	28 13	301	17 45	348
356	24 43	049	22 22	083	40 53	161	30 27	191	32 06	262	27 28	301	17 34	348
357	25 23	050	23 14	083	41 10	162	30 17	192	31 14	263	26 43	301	17 23	348
358	26 03	050	24 06	084	41 25	163	30 05	193	30 22	263	25 59	302	17 12	348
359	26 43	050	24 58	084	41 40	165	29 52	194	29 30	264	25 14	302	17 02	349

LHA ♈	Hc Zn	Hc Zn	Hc Zn	Hc Zn	Hc Zn	Hc Zn	Hc Zn
	Schedar	◆CAPELLA	ALDEBARAN	◆Diphda	FOMALHAUT	ALTAIR	◆DENEB
0	60 27 012	26 45 050	25 44 084	42 51 166	30 36 196	28 43 265	47 28 308
1	60 37 010	27 25 050	26 37 085	43 04 167	30 22 197	27 51 265	46 46 308
2	60 46 009	28 06 050	27 30 085	43 16 168	30 06 197	26 58 266	46 04 308
3	60 54 008	28 47 050	28 23 085	43 26 169	29 50 198	26 05 266	45 22 307
4	61 02 007	29 28 051	29 15 086	43 35 171	29 33 199	25 12 267	44 40 307
5	61 08 006	30 09 051	30 08 086	43 43 172	29 15 200	24 19 267	43 58 307
6	61 13 005	30 50 051	31 01 087	43 50 173	28 56 201	23 26 268	43 16 307
7	61 17 004	31 31 051	31 54 087	43 56 175	28 36 202	22 33 268	42 34 307
8	61 20 003	32 12 051	32 47 088	44 00 176	28 16 203	21 40 269	41 51 307
9	61 22 002	32 53 051	33 40 088	44 03 177	27 55 204	20 47 269	41 09 307
10	61 23 000	33 35 051	34 33 089	44 05 179	27 33 205	19 54 270	40 27 307
11	61 23 359	34 16 051	35 26 089	44 06 180	27 10 206	19 01 270	39 45 307
12	61 21 358	34 57 051	36 19 089	44 05 181	26 47 207	18 08 271	39 03 307
13	61 19 357	35 39 052	37 12 090	44 03 183	26 23 207	17 16 271	38 21 307
14	61 16 356	36 20 052	38 05 090	44 01 184	25 58 208	16 23 272	37 38 307
	◆CAPELLA	ALDEBARAN	RIGEL	◆Diphda	FOMALHAUT	Enif	◆DENEB
15	37 02 052	38 58 091	18 35 110	43 56 185	25 33 209	40 52 258	36 56 307
16	37 43 052	39 51 091	19 25 111	43 51 186	25 06 210	40 00 259	36 14 308
17	38 25 052	40 44 092	20 14 112	43 44 188	24 40 211	39 08 260	35 32 308
18	39 07 052	41 37 092	21 04 112	43 37 189	24 12 212	38 16 260	34 50 308
19	39 48 052	42 30 093	21 52 113	43 28 190	23 44 212	37 23 261	34 08 308
20	40 30 052	43 22 093	22 41 113	43 17 192	23 15 213	36 31 261	33 27 308
21	41 12 052	44 15 094	23 30 114	43 06 193	22 46 214	35 39 262	32 45 308
22	41 53 052	45 08 094	24 18 115	42 54 194	22 16 215	34 46 262	32 03 308
23	42 35 052	46 01 095	25 06 115	42 40 195	21 45 216	33 54 263	31 22 308
24	43 17 052	46 54 096	25 54 116	42 25 197	21 14 216	33 01 264	30 40 308
25	43 58 052	47 46 096	26 41 117	42 10 198	20 43 217	32 08 264	29 59 309
26	44 40 052	48 39 097	27 29 117	41 53 199	20 11 218	31 16 265	29 17 309
27	45 21 052	49 32 097	28 15 118	41 35 200	19 38 219	30 23 265	28 36 309
28	46 03 051	50 24 098	29 02 119	41 16 202	19 05 219	29 30 266	27 55 309
29	46 44 051	51 17 098	29 48 119	40 56 203	18 31 220	28 37 266	27 14 309
	CAPELLA	◆ALDEBARAN	RIGEL	◆Diphda	Alpheratz	DENEB	◆Kochab
30	47 26 051	52 09 099	30 34 120	40 35 204	65 42 279	26 33 309	12 26 356
31	48 07 051	53 01 100	31 20 121	40 13 205	64 50 280	25 52 310	12 23 357
32	48 48 051	53 53 100	32 05 122	39 50 206	63 57 280	25 11 310	12 20 357
33	49 29 051	54 45 101	32 50 122	39 26 207	63 05 280	24 30 310	12 18 357
34	50 10 051	55 37 102	33 35 123	39 01 208	62 13 280	23 50 310	12 15 358
35	50 51 050	56 29 103	34 19 124	38 35 210	61 21 280	23 09 310	12 13 358
36	51 32 050	57 21 103	35 03 125	38 09 211	60 29 280	22 29 311	12 11 358
37	52 13 050	58 12 104	35 46 126	37 41 212	59 37 281	21 49 311	12 10 358
38	52 53 050	59 03 105	36 29 126	37 13 213	58 45 281	21 09 311	12 08 359
39	53 33 049	59 54 106	37 11 127	36 44 214	57 53 281	20 29 311	12 07 359
40	54 13 049	60 45 107	37 53 128	36 14 215	57 01 281	19 50 312	12 07 359
41	54 53 049	61 36 108	38 35 129	35 44 216	56 09 281	19 10 312	12 06 000
42	55 33 048	62 26 109	39 16 130	35 12 217	55 17 282	18 31 312	12 06 000
43	56 12 048	63 16 110	39 56 131	34 40 218	54 25 282	17 52 312	12 06 000
44	56 51 047	64 06 111	40 36 132	34 07 219	53 33 282	17 13 313	12 06 000
	◆CAPELLA	PROCYON	SIRIUS	◆RIGEL	Acamar	Diphda	◆Alpheratz
45	57 30 047	20 03 095	19 24 122	41 15 133	21 45 180	33 34 220	52 41 282
46	58 09 047	20 56 095	20 08 123	41 53 134	21 45 181	33 00 220	51 50 283
47	58 47 046	21 49 096	20 53 123	42 31 135	21 43 182	32 25 221	50 58 283
48	59 25 045	22 41 096	21 37 124	43 08 136	21 41 183	31 50 222	50 06 283
49	60 03 045	23 34 097	22 20 125	43 45 137	21 38 184	31 14 223	49 15 283
50	60 40 044	24 26 097	23 04 126	44 20 138	21 35 184	30 37 224	48 23 283
51	61 17 044	25 19 098	23 47 126	44 55 139	21 30 185	30 00 225	47 32 284
52	61 53 043	26 11 098	24 29 127	45 29 140	21 25 186	29 23 226	46 40 284
53	62 28 042	27 04 099	25 11 128	46 03 142	21 19 187	28 45 226	45 49 284
54	63 04 041	27 56 100	25 53 128	46 35 143	21 13 188	28 06 227	44 57 284
55	63 38 040	28 48 100	26 34 129	47 07 144	21 05 188	27 27 228	44 06 285
56	64 12 039	29 40 101	27 15 130	47 37 145	20 57 189	26 47 229	43 15 285
57	64 46 038	30 32 101	27 56 131	48 07 147	20 48 190	26 07 230	42 24 285
58	65 18 037	31 24 102	28 36 131	48 36 148	20 39 191	25 26 230	41 33 285
59	65 50 036	32 16 102	29 15 132	49 03 149	20 28 192	24 46 231	40 42 286
	◆Dubhe	PROCYON	SIRIUS	◆RIGEL	Diphda	◆Hamal	Mirfak
60	17 15 029	33 08 103	29 54 133	49 30 151	24 04 232	64 27 266	67 07 346
61	17 41 029	33 59 104	30 33 134	49 56 152	23 22 232	63 34 267	66 53 344
62	18 06 029	34 51 104	31 11 135	50 20 153	22 40 233	62 41 267	66 38 343
63	18 32 029	35 42 105	31 48 136	50 43 155	21 57 234	61 49 268	66 21 341
64	18 58 029	36 33 105	32 25 136	51 05 156	21 15 235	60 56 269	66 03 340
65	19 24 030	37 24 106	33 01 137	51 26 158	20 31 235	60 03 269	65 44 338
66	19 50 030	38 15 107	33 37 138	51 45 159	19 48 236	59 10 270	65 24 337
67	20 17 030	39 06 107	34 12 139	52 03 161	19 04 236	58 17 270	65 03 336
68	20 43 030	39 56 108	34 46 140	52 20 162	18 19 237	57 24 270	64 41 334
69	21 10 030	40 46 109	35 20 141	52 35 164	17 35 238	56 31 271	64 17 333
70	21 37 030	41 36 110	35 53 142	52 49 165	16 50 238	55 38 271	63 53 332
71	22 04 031	42 26 110	36 25 143	53 02 167	16 04 239	54 45 272	63 28 331
72	22 31 031	43 16 111	36 57 144	53 13 169	15 19 240	53 52 272	63 02 330
73	22 58 031	44 05 112	37 28 145	53 23 170	14 33 240	52 59 273	62 35 329
74	23 25 031	44 54 113	37 58 146	53 31 172	13 47 241	52 06 273	62 07 328
	◆Dubhe	POLLUX	PROCYON	◆SIRIUS	RIGEL	◆Hamal	Mirfak
75	23 53 031	53 29 080	45 43 113	38 27 147	53 38 174	51 13 273	61 39 327
76	24 20 031	54 22 080	46 31 114	38 55 148	53 43 175	50 20 274	61 09 326
77	24 48 032	55 14 080	47 19 115	39 23 149	53 46 177	49 27 274	60 40 325
78	25 15 032	56 06 081	48 07 116	39 50 150	53 48 179	48 35 274	60 09 325
79	25 43 032	56 58 081	48 54 117	40 16 151	53 49 180	47 42 275	59 38 324
80	26 11 032	57 51 081	49 41 118	40 40 152	53 48 182	46 49 275	59 06 323
81	26 39 032	58 43 081	50 28 119	41 04 154	53 45 184	45 56 276	58 34 322
82	27 07 032	59 35 082	51 14 120	41 27 155	53 41 185	45 04 276	58 02 322
83	27 35 032	60 28 082	52 00 121	41 50 156	53 35 187	44 11 277	57 29 321
84	28 04 032	61 20 082	52 45 122	42 11 157	53 28 189	43 18 277	56 55 320
85	28 32 032	62 13 082	53 30 123	42 31 158	53 19 190	42 26 277	56 21 320
86	29 00 032	63 05 083	54 14 124	42 50 160	53 09 192	41 33 278	55 47 319
87	29 28 032	63 58 083	54 57 125	43 07 161	52 58 194	40 41 278	55 12 319
88	29 57 032	64 51 083	55 40 127	43 24 162	52 44 195	39 48 278	54 37 318
89	30 25 032	65 43 083	56 22 128	43 40 163	52 30 197	38 56 279	54 02 318

LHA ♈	Hc Zn	Hc Zn	Hc Zn	Hc Zn	Hc Zn	Hc Zn	Hc Zn
	Dubhe	◆REGULUS	PROCYON	SIRIUS	◆RIGEL	ALDEBARAN	◆Mirfak
90	30 54 032	29 54 092	57 04 129	43 54 165	52 14 198	67 39 244	53 26 318
91	31 22 032	30 47 093	57 44 131	44 08 166	51 57 200	66 51 245	52 50 317
92	31 51 033	31 40 093	58 24 132	44 20 167	51 38 201	66 03 246	52 14 317
93	32 19 033	32 33 094	59 03 133	44 31 169	51 18 203	65 14 247	51 38 316
94	32 48 033	33 26 094	59 41 135	44 41 170	50 57 204	64 25 249	51 01 316
95	33 16 032	34 18 095	60 18 137	44 50 171	50 35 206	63 36 250	50 24 316
96	33 44 032	35 11 095	60 54 138	44 57 173	50 11 207	62 46 251	49 47 315
97	34 13 032	36 04 096	61 29 140	45 03 174	49 46 209	61 56 252	49 10 315
98	34 41 032	36 57 096	62 02 142	45 08 175	49 20 210	61 05 253	48 33 315
99	35 10 032	37 49 097	62 34 143	45 12 177	48 53 211	60 14 254	47 55 315
100	35 38 032	38 42 097	63 05 145	45 14 178	48 25 213	59 23 255	47 17 315
101	36 06 032	39 34 098	63 35 147	45 16 179	47 56 214	58 32 255	46 40 314
102	36 34 032	40 27 098	64 03 149	45 16 181	47 26 215	57 41 256	46 02 314
103	37 03 032	41 19 099	64 29 151	45 14 182	46 55 216	56 49 257	45 24 314
104	37 31 032	42 11 100	64 54 153	45 12 183	46 23 218	55 58 258	44 46 314
	◆Dubhe	REGULUS	◆Alphard	SIRIUS	RIGEL	◆ALDEBARAN	CAPELLA
105	37 59 032	43 04 100	38 41 130	45 08 185	45 51 219	55 06 259	63 00 319
106	38 27 032	43 56 101	39 21 131	45 03 186	45 17 220	54 14 259	62 25 318
107	38 54 032	44 48 101	40 01 132	44 56 188	44 42 221	53 22 260	61 49 317
108	39 22 031	45 40 102	40 40 133	44 49 189	44 07 222	52 29 261	61 13 316
109	39 50 031	46 31 103	41 18 134	44 40 190	43 31 223	51 37 261	60 36 316
110	40 17 031	47 23 103	41 56 135	44 30 192	42 54 224	50 45 262	59 59 315
111	40 44 031	48 14 104	42 33 136	44 19 193	42 17 225	49 52 262	59 21 315
112	41 11 031	49 06 105	43 09 137	44 07 194	41 39 226	49 00 263	58 43 314
113	41 38 031	49 57 106	43 45 138	43 53 195	41 00 227	48 07 264	58 05 313
114	42 05 030	50 48 106	44 20 139	43 38 197	40 21 228	47 14 264	57 26 313
115	42 32 030	51 38 107	44 54 141	43 23 198	39 41 229	46 22 265	56 48 312
116	42 58 030	52 29 108	45 27 142	43 06 199	39 00 230	45 29 265	56 08 312
117	43 25 030	53 19 109	45 59 143	42 48 200	38 19 231	44 36 266	55 29 312
118	43 51 029	54 09 110	46 31 144	42 29 202	37 38 232	43 43 266	54 49 311
119	44 17 029	54 59 111	47 02 145	42 09 203	36 56 233	42 50 267	54 09 311
	◆Dubhe	REGULUS	◆Alphard	SIRIUS	RIGEL	◆ALDEBARAN	CAPELLA
120	44 42 029	55 48 112	47 31 147	41 47 204	36 13 234	41 57 267	53 29 311
121	45 08 028	56 37 113	48 00 148	41 25 205	35 30 235	41 04 268	52 49 310
122	45 33 028	57 26 114	48 27 149	41 02 206	34 47 236	40 11 268	52 08 310
123	45 58 028	58 14 115	48 54 151	40 38 208	34 03 236	39 18 269	51 28 310
124	46 22 027	59 02 116	49 20 152	40 13 209	33 18 237	38 26 269	50 47 310
125	46 47 027	59 50 117	49 44 153	39 47 210	32 34 238	37 33 270	50 06 309
126	47 11 027	60 37 118	50 07 155	39 20 211	31 49 239	36 40 270	49 25 309
127	47 34 026	61 24 119	50 29 156	38 53 212	31 03 239	35 47 271	48 44 309
128	47 58 026	62 10 120	50 50 158	38 24 213	30 17 240	34 54 271	48 03 309
129	48 21 026	62 55 122	51 09 159	37 55 214	29 31 241	34 01 272	47 22 309
130	48 43 025	63 40 123	51 28 161	37 25 215	28 45 242	33 08 272	46 40 309
131	49 06 025	64 24 125	51 45 162	36 54 216	27 58 242	32 15 273	45 59 308
132	49 28 024	65 07 126	52 00 164	36 22 217	27 11 243	31 22 273	45 17 308
133	49 49 024	65 49 128	52 14 165	35 50 218	26 24 244	30 29 274	44 36 308
134	50 10 023	66 30 130	52 27 167	35 17 219	25 36 244	29 36 274	43 54 308
	Dubhe	◆ARCTURUS	SPICA	Alphard	◆SIRIUS	BETELGEUSE	◆CAPELLA
135	50 31 023	18 09 078	14 42 112	52 39 168	34 43 220	41 58 254	43 13 308
136	50 51 022	19 01 078	15 32 112	52 48 170	34 08 221	41 07 254	42 31 308
137	51 11 022	19 53 078	16 21 113	52 57 172	33 33 222	40 16 255	41 49 308
138	51 30 021	20 45 079	17 09 113	53 04 173	32 58 223	39 25 256	41 08 308
139	51 49 021	21 37 079	17 58 114	53 09 175	32 21 224	38 33 256	40 26 308
140	52 07 020	22 29 080	18 46 114	53 13 177	31 44 225	37 42 257	39 44 308
141	52 25 019	23 21 080	19 34 115	53 16 178	31 07 225	36 50 258	39 03 308
142	52 42 019	24 13 080	20 22 116	53 17 180	30 29 226	35 58 258	38 21 308
143	52 59 018	25 06 081	21 10 116	53 16 182	29 50 227	35 07 259	37 39 308
144	53 15 017	25 58 081	21 57 117	53 14 183	29 11 228	34 15 259	36 58 308
145	53 31 017	26 50 082	22 44 118	53 10 185	28 32 229	33 22 260	36 16 308
146	53 46 016	27 43 082	23 31 118	53 05 186	27 52 229	32 30 260	35 35 308
147	54 00 015	28 35 082	24 18 119	52 58 188	27 11 230	31 38 261	34 53 309
148	54 14 015	29 28 083	25 04 119	52 50 190	26 30 231	30 46 262	34 12 309
149	54 27 014	30 20 083	25 50 120	52 40 191	25 49 232	29 53 262	33 30 309
	Dubhe	◆ARCTURUS	SPICA	◆Alphard	SIRIUS	POLLUX	◆CAPELLA
150	54 39 013	31 13 084	26 36 121	52 29 193	25 07 232	60 34 278	32 49 309
151	54 51 012	32 06 084	27 21 122	52 17 195	24 25 233	59 41 278	32 08 309
152	55 02 012	32 58 084	28 06 122	52 03 196	23 43 234	58 49 279	31 27 309
153	55 13 011	33 51 085	28 50 123	51 47 198	23 00 235	57 57 279	30 46 309
154	55 22 010	34 44 085	29 35 124	51 31 199	22 16 235	57 04 279	30 05 309
155	55 31 009	35 37 086	30 19 125	51 13 201	21 33 236	56 12 279	29 24 309
156	55 39 009	36 30 086	31 02 125	50 53 202	20 48 237	55 20 280	28 43 310
157	55 47 008	37 22 087	31 45 126	50 33 204	20 04 237	54 28 280	28 02 310
158	55 54 007	38 15 087	32 28 127	50 11 205	19 19 238	53 35 280	27 21 310
159	56 00 006	39 08 087	33 10 128	49 48 206	18 34 238	52 43 280	26 41 310
160	56 05 005	40 01 088	33 51 129	49 24 208	17 49 239	51 51 281	26 00 310
161	56 09 004	40 54 088	34 33 129	48 58 209	17 03 240	50 59 281	25 20 311
162	56 13 004	41 47 089	35 13 130	48 32 211	16 18 240	50 07 281	24 40 311
163	56 16 003	42 40 089	35 54 131	48 04 212	15 31 241	49 15 281	24 00 311
164	56 18 002	43 33 090	36 33 132	47 36 213	14 45 241	48 23 282	23 20 311
	Dubhe	◆Alkaid	ARCTURUS	◆SPICA	Alphard	◆PROCYON	POLLUX
165	56 19 001	51 37 045	44 26 090	37 12 133	47 06 214	37 26 254	47 31 282
166	56 20 000	52 14 044	45 19 091	37 51 134	46 36 216	36 35 254	46 40 282
167	56 20 359	52 51 044	46 12 091	38 29 135	46 05 217	35 44 255	45 48 282
168	56 18 358	53 27 044	47 05 092	39 06 136	45 32 218	34 53 256	44 56 283
169	56 17 358	54 04 043	47 58 092	39 43 137	44 59 219	34 02 256	44 04 283
170	56 14 357	54 40 043	48 51 093	40 19 138	44 25 220	33 10 257	43 13 283
171	56 11 356	55 16 042	49 44 093	40 54 139	43 51 222	32 18 258	42 21 284
172	56 06 355	55 51 042	50 37 094	41 28 140	43 15 223	31 26 258	41 30 284
173	56 01 354	56 27 041	51 29 094	42 02 141	42 39 224	30 35 259	40 38 284
174	55 56 353	57 01 041	52 22 095	42 35 142	42 02 225	29 43 259	39 47 284
175	55 49 353	57 36 040	53 15 095	43 07 143	41 24 226	28 50 260	38 56 285
176	55 42 352	58 10 040	54 08 096	43 39 144	40 46 227	27 58 260	38 05 285
177	55 34 351	58 43 039	55 00 096	44 09 145	40 07 228	27 06 261	37 13 285
178	55 25 350	59 17 038	55 53 097	44 39 147	39 28 229	26 14 261	36 22 286
179	55 16 349	59 49 038	56 45 098	45 07 148	38 48 230	25 21 262	35 31 286

LAT 28°N

LHA ♈	Hc Zn	Hc Zn	Hc Zn	Hc Zn	Hc Zn	Hc Zn	Hc Zn
	◆ VEGA	Alphecca	◆ SPICA	Gienah	REGULUS	◆ POLLUX	Dubhe
180	10 30 051	42 34 078	45 35 149	44 12 174	59 30 244	34 40 286	55 06 349
181	11 12 052	43 25 079	46 02 150	44 16 176	58 43 245	33 50 286	54 55 348
182	11 53 052	44 17 079	46 27 152	44 20 177	57 54 246	32 59 287	54 43 347
183	12 35 053	45 09 079	46 52 153	44 22 178	57 06 247	32 08 287	54 31 346
184	13 17 053	46 02 080	47 16 154	44 22 180	56 17 248	31 18 287	54 18 346
185	14 00 053	46 54 080	47 38 156	44 22 181	55 28 249	30 27 288	54 05 345
186	14 42 054	47 46 080	47 59 157	44 20 182	54 38 250	29 37 288	53 50 344
187	15 25 054	48 38 080	48 20 158	44 17 184	53 48 251	28 46 288	53 36 343
188	16 08 054	49 30 081	48 39 160	44 13 185	52 58 252	27 56 289	53 20 343
189	16 51 055	50 23 081	48 56 161	44 08 186	52 08 252	27 06 289	53 04 342
190	17 34 055	51 15 081	49 13 163	44 01 188	51 17 253	26 16 289	52 48 342
191	18 17 055	52 07 082	49 28 164	43 54 189	50 26 254	25 26 290	52 31 341
192	19 01 055	53 00 082	49 42 166	43 45 190	49 35 255	24 36 290	52 13 340
193	19 45 056	53 52 082	49 54 167	43 35 192	48 44 255	23 46 290	51 55 340
194	20 29 056	54 45 083	50 06 168	43 23 193	47 53 256	22 57 291	51 36 339
	◆ Kochab	VEGA	Rasalhague	◆ ANTARES	SPICA	◆ REGULUS	Dubhe
195	41 45 010	21 13 056	24 20 088	15 44 132	50 16 170	47 01 257	51 17 339
196	41 54 010	21 57 057	25 13 089	16 23 133	50 24 172	46 10 257	50 58 338
197	42 02 009	22 41 057	26 06 089	17 01 134	50 31 173	45 18 258	50 37 337
198	42 10 009	23 25 057	26 59 090	17 39 134	50 37 175	44 26 259	50 17 337
199	42 18 009	24 10 057	27 52 090	18 17 135	50 41 176	43 34 259	49 56 336
200	42 26 008	24 55 058	28 45 091	18 54 136	50 44 178	42 42 260	49 35 336
201	42 34 008	25 39 058	29 38 091	19 31 136	50 45 179	41 50 261	49 13 335
202	42 41 008	26 24 058	30 31 092	20 07 137	50 45 181	40 57 261	48 51 335
203	42 48 007	27 09 058	31 24 092	20 43 138	50 44 182	40 05 262	48 28 335
204	42 54 007	27 55 059	32 17 093	21 18 139	50 41 184	39 13 262	48 05 334
205	43 00 007	28 40 059	33 10 093	21 53 139	50 37 185	38 20 263	47 42 334
206	43 06 006	29 25 059	34 03 094	22 28 140	50 31 187	37 27 263	47 18 333
207	43 12 006	30 11 059	34 56 094	23 01 141	50 24 188	36 35 264	46 54 333
208	43 17 005	30 56 059	35 49 095	23 35 142	50 16 190	35 42 265	46 30 333
209	43 22 005	31 42 060	36 41 095	24 07 142	50 06 192	34 49 265	46 06 332
	Kochab	◆ VEGA	Rasalhague	ANTARES	◆ SPICA	REGULUS	◆ Dubhe
210	43 26 005	32 28 060	37 34 096	24 39 143	49 54 193	33 56 266	45 41 332
211	43 31 004	33 13 060	38 27 096	25 11 144	49 42 194	33 04 266	45 16 332
212	43 34 004	33 59 060	39 19 097	25 42 145	49 28 196	32 11 267	44 50 331
213	43 38 004	34 45 060	40 12 097	26 12 146	49 13 197	31 18 267	44 25 331
214	43 41 003	35 31 061	41 05 098	26 42 146	48 56 199	30 25 268	43 59 331
215	43 44 003	36 18 061	41 57 098	27 11 147	48 38 200	29 32 268	43 33 330
216	43 47 003	37 04 061	42 49 099	27 39 148	48 19 202	28 39 269	43 07 330
217	43 49 002	37 50 061	43 42 100	28 07 149	47 59 203	27 46 269	42 41 330
218	43 51 002	38 36 061	44 34 100	28 34 150	47 38 204	26 53 270	42 14 330
219	43 52 001	39 23 061	45 26 101	29 00 151	47 15 206	26 00 270	41 47 330
220	43 53 001	40 09 061	46 18 102	29 26 152	46 52 207	25 07 270	41 20 329
221	43 54 001	40 56 061	47 10 102	29 51 152	46 27 208	24 14 271	40 53 329
222	43 54 000	41 42 062	48 01 103	30 15 153	46 02 210	23 21 271	40 26 329
223	43 54 000	42 29 062	48 53 104	30 38 154	45 35 211	22 28 272	39 58 329
224	43 54 359	43 16 062	49 44 104	31 01 155	45 07 212	21 35 272	39 31 329
	VEGA	◆ ALTAIR	Nunki	ANTARES	◆ SPICA	Denebola	◆ Alkaid
225	44 02 062	19 14 090	11 30 128	31 22 156	44 38 213	43 59 263	64 41 332
226	44 49 062	20 07 090	12 11 129	31 43 157	44 09 215	43 07 264	64 16 331
227	45 36 062	21 00 091	12 52 129	32 03 158	43 38 216	42 14 264	63 49 330
228	46 22 062	21 53 091	13 33 130	32 23 159	43 07 217	41 21 265	63 22 329
229	47 09 062	22 46 092	14 13 131	32 41 160	42 35 218	40 28 265	62 54 328
230	47 56 062	23 39 092	14 53 131	32 59 161	42 02 219	39 36 266	62 25 327
231	48 43 062	24 32 093	15 33 132	33 15 162	41 28 220	38 43 266	61 56 326
232	49 29 062	25 25 093	16 12 133	33 31 163	40 54 221	37 50 267	61 26 325
233	50 16 062	26 18 094	16 51 133	33 46 164	40 18 222	36 57 267	60 55 324
234	51 03 062	27 11 094	17 29 134	34 00 165	39 42 223	36 04 268	60 23 323
235	51 50 062	28 03 095	18 07 135	34 13 166	39 06 224	35 11 268	59 51 322
236	52 36 062	28 56 095	18 45 135	34 25 167	38 28 225	34 18 269	59 19 322
237	53 23 062	29 49 096	19 22 136	34 36 168	37 51 226	33 25 269	58 46 321
238	54 10 062	30 42 096	19 59 137	34 46 170	37 12 227	32 32 270	58 12 320
239	54 56 061	31 34 097	20 35 137	34 55 171	36 33 228	31 39 270	57 38 320
	◆ VEGA	ALTAIR	Nunki	◆ ANTARES	SPICA	ARCTURUS	◆ Alkaid
240	55 43 061	32 27 097	21 10 138	35 03 172	35 53 229	64 42 255	57 04 319
241	56 29 061	33 19 098	21 46 139	35 10 173	35 13 230	63 51 256	56 29 319
242	57 15 061	34 12 099	22 20 140	35 16 174	34 32 231	62 59 257	55 54 318
243	58 02 061	35 04 099	22 54 140	35 21 175	33 51 232	62 08 258	55 18 318
244	58 48 061	35 56 100	23 28 141	35 26 176	33 09 232	61 16 259	54 42 317
245	59 34 060	36 48 100	24 01 142	35 29 177	32 27 233	60 24 259	54 06 317
246	60 20 060	37 41 101	24 34 143	35 31 178	31 45 234	59 32 260	53 30 316
247	61 06 060	38 33 101	25 05 143	35 32 179	31 02 235	58 39 261	52 53 316
248	61 51 059	39 24 102	25 37 144	35 32 180	30 18 235	57 47 261	52 16 316
249	62 37 059	40 16 103	26 07 145	35 31 182	29 34 236	56 55 262	51 39 315
250	63 22 058	41 08 103	26 37 146	35 29 183	28 50 237	56 02 263	51 02 315
251	64 07 058	41 59 104	27 07 147	35 26 184	28 06 238	55 09 263	50 24 315
252	64 52 057	42 51 105	27 36 148	35 22 185	27 21 238	54 17 264	49 46 314
253	65 36 057	43 42 105	28 04 148	35 17 186	26 35 239	53 24 265	49 08 314
254	66 21 056	44 33 106	28 31 149	35 11 187	25 50 240	52 31 265	48 30 314
	◆ DENEB	ALTAIR	Nunki	◆ ANTARES	SPICA	ARCTURUS	◆ Alkaid
255	43 17 053	45 23 107	28 58 150	35 04 188	25 04 241	51 39 266	47 52 314
256	43 59 053	46 14 108	29 24 151	34 56 189	24 17 241	50 46 266	47 14 314
257	44 41 053	47 04 108	29 49 152	34 47 190	23 31 242	49 53 267	46 35 313
258	45 23 053	47 55 109	30 14 153	34 37 191	22 44 242	49 00 267	45 57 313
259	46 05 052	48 45 110	30 37 154	34 27 192	21 57 243	48 07 268	45 18 313
260	46 47 052	49 34 111	31 00 155	34 15 193	21 09 244	47 14 268	44 39 313
261	47 29 052	50 24 112	31 23 156	34 02 195	20 22 244	46 21 269	44 00 313
262	48 11 052	51 13 112	31 44 157	33 48 196	19 34 245	45 28 269	43 21 313
263	48 53 052	52 02 113	32 05 158	33 33 197	18 46 246	44 35 270	42 42 313
264	49 35 052	52 50 114	32 24 159	33 18 198	17 58 246	43 42 270	42 03 313
265	50 16 052	53 38 115	32 43 160	33 01 199	17 09 247	42 49 271	41 24 312
266	50 58 051	54 26 116	33 01 161	32 44 200	16 20 247	41 56 271	40 45 312
267	51 39 051	55 13 117	33 18 162	32 26 201	15 31 248	41 03 272	40 06 312
268	52 20 051	56 00 118	33 34 163	32 07 202	14 42 248	40 10 272	39 27 312
269	53 01 051	56 46 119	33 50 164	31 47 203	13 53 249	39 17 273	38 48 312

LHA ♈	Hc Zn	Hc Zn	Hc Zn	Hc Zn	Hc Zn	Hc Zn	Hc Zn
	◆ DENEB	ALTAIR	◆ Nunki	ANTARES	◆ ARCTURUS	Alkaid	Kochab
270	53 42 050	57 32 121	34 04 165	31 26 204	38 24 273	38 08 312	37 59 345
271	54 23 050	58 18 122	34 18 166	31 04 205	37 32 273	37 29 312	37 46 345
272	55 04 050	59 02 123	34 30 167	30 42 205	36 39 274	36 50 312	37 32 345
273	55 44 049	59 46 124	34 42 168	30 19 206	35 46 274	36 11 312	37 18 345
274	56 24 049	60 30 126	34 52 169	29 55 207	34 53 275	35 32 312	37 04 344
275	57 04 049	61 12 127	35 02 170	29 30 208	34 00 275	34 53 312	36 49 344
276	57 44 048	61 54 129	35 10 171	29 05 209	33 07 275	34 14 313	36 35 344
277	58 23 048	62 35 130	35 18 172	28 38 210	32 15 276	33 35 313	36 20 344
278	59 02 047	63 15 132	35 25 173	28 11 211	31 22 276	32 56 313	36 06 344
279	59 41 047	63 54 133	35 30 174	27 44 212	30 29 277	32 17 313	35 51 344
280	60 19 046	64 32 135	35 35 176	27 16 213	29 37 277	31 38 313	35 36 344
281	60 57 045	65 09 137	35 39 177	26 47 214	28 44 278	30 59 313	35 21 343
282	61 34 045	65 45 139	35 41 178	26 17 214	27 52 278	30 20 313	35 06 343
283	62 12 044	66 19 141	35 43 179	25 47 215	26 59 278	29 42 313	34 50 343
284	62 48 043	66 51 143	35 43 180	25 16 216	26 07 279	29 03 313	34 35 343
	◆ Alpheratz	Enif	Nunki	◆ ANTARES	ARCTURUS	◆ Alkaid	Kochab
285	23 29 068	47 19 107	35 43 181	24 45 217	25 15 279	28 25 313	34 19 343
286	24 18 069	48 10 107	35 41 182	24 13 218	24 22 280	27 46 314	34 04 343
287	25 07 069	49 00 108	35 39 183	23 40 218	23 30 280	27 08 314	33 48 343
288	25 57 069	49 50 109	35 35 184	23 07 219	22 38 280	26 30 314	33 32 343
289	26 47 070	50 40 110	35 31 185	22 33 220	21 46 281	25 52 314	33 16 343
290	27 36 070	51 30 111	35 25 187	21 59 221	20 54 281	25 14 314	33 00 342
291	28 26 070	52 19 112	35 19 188	21 24 221	20 02 282	24 36 314	32 44 342
292	29 16 070	53 08 113	35 11 189	20 49 222	19 10 282	23 58 315	32 28 342
293	30 06 071	53 57 113	35 03 190	20 13 223	18 18 282	23 20 315	32 12 342
294	30 56 071	54 46 114	34 53 191	19 37 224	17 27 283	22 43 315	31 56 342
295	31 46 071	55 34 115	34 43 192	19 00 224	16 35 283	22 05 315	31 40 342
296	32 36 072	56 21 116	34 31 193	18 23 225	15 43 284	21 28 315	31 24 342
297	33 27 072	57 08 118	34 19 194	17 45 226	14 52 284	20 51 316	31 07 342
298	34 17 072	57 55 119	34 05 195	17 07 226	14 01 284	20 14 316	30 51 342
299	35 07 072	58 41 120	33 51 196	16 29 227	13 09 285	19 37 316	30 35 342
	Schedar	◆ Alpheratz	FOMALHAUT	◆ Nunki	Rasalhague	◆ VEGA	Kochab
300	33 45 039	35 58 073	18 23 140	33 36 197	52 59 253	69 44 308	30 18 342
301	34 18 039	36 49 073	18 57 141	33 20 198	52 08 254	69 02 307	30 02 342
302	34 51 039	37 39 073	19 30 141	33 03 199	51 17 254	68 19 306	29 45 342
303	35 24 039	38 30 074	20 03 142	32 45 200	50 26 255	67 36 305	29 29 342
304	35 57 038	39 21 074	20 35 143	32 26 201	49 35 256	66 52 304	29 12 342
305	36 29 038	40 12 074	21 07 144	32 07 202	48 43 257	66 08 304	28 56 342
306	37 02 038	41 03 074	21 38 144	31 46 203	47 52 257	65 24 303	28 40 342
307	37 35 038	41 54 075	22 09 145	31 25 204	47 00 258	64 40 302	28 23 342
308	38 08 038	42 45 075	22 39 146	31 03 205	46 08 259	63 55 302	28 07 342
309	38 41 038	43 36 075	23 08 147	30 40 206	45 16 259	63 10 301	27 50 342
310	39 14 038	44 27 075	23 37 147	30 16 207	44 24 260	62 24 301	27 34 342
311	39 46 038	45 19 076	24 05 148	29 52 208	43 32 260	61 39 301	27 18 342
312	40 19 038	46 10 076	24 33 149	29 26 209	42 40 261	60 53 300	27 01 342
313	40 51 038	47 02 076	25 00 150	29 00 210	41 47 262	60 07 300	26 45 342
314	41 24 038	47 53 076	25 26 151	28 34 211	40 55 262	59 21 300	26 29 342
	◆ Mirfak	Hamal	Diphda	◆ FOMALHAUT	ALTAIR	◆ VEGA	Kochab
315	17 14 042	21 41 074	18 56 123	25 52 151	65 00 223	58 35 299	26 13 342
316	17 50 042	22 32 074	19 40 124	26 17 152	64 23 225	57 49 299	25 56 342
317	18 25 043	23 23 075	20 24 125	26 41 153	63 45 227	57 03 299	25 40 342
318	19 01 043	24 14 075	21 07 125	27 05 154	63 06 229	56 16 299	25 24 342
319	19 38 043	25 05 076	21 50 126	27 28 155	62 25 230	55 30 299	25 08 342
320	20 14 043	25 57 076	22 33 127	27 50 156	61 44 232	54 43 298	24 52 343
321	20 50 044	26 48 076	23 15 127	28 11 157	61 02 233	53 57 298	24 37 343
322	21 27 044	27 40 077	23 57 128	28 32 158	60 19 235	53 10 298	24 21 343
323	22 03 044	28 31 077	24 38 129	28 51 159	59 36 236	52 23 298	24 05 343
324	22 40 044	29 23 077	25 20 130	29 10 159	58 52 237	51 37 298	23 50 343
325	23 17 044	30 15 078	26 00 130	29 29 160	58 07 238	50 50 298	23 34 343
326	23 54 045	31 06 078	26 40 131	29 46 161	57 21 240	50 03 298	23 19 343
327	24 32 045	31 58 078	27 20 132	30 03 162	56 35 241	49 16 298	23 03 343
328	25 09 045	32 50 079	27 59 133	30 18 163	55 49 242	48 30 298	22 48 343
329	25 47 045	33 42 079	28 38 133	30 33 164	55 02 243	47 43 298	22 33 343
	◆ Mirfak	Hamal	Diphda	◆ FOMALHAUT	ALTAIR	◆ VEGA	Kochab
330	26 24 045	34 34 079	29 16 134	30 47 165	54 14 244	46 56 298	22 18 344
331	27 02 045	35 26 080	29 54 135	31 00 166	53 27 245	46 09 298	22 03 344
332	27 40 046	36 19 080	30 31 136	31 12 167	52 38 246	45 23 298	21 48 344
333	28 18 046	37 11 081	31 08 137	31 24 168	51 50 247	44 36 298	21 33 344
334	28 56 046	38 03 081	31 44 138	31 34 169	51 01 248	43 49 298	21 19 344
335	29 34 046	38 55 081	32 19 138	31 44 170	50 12 249	43 03 298	21 04 344
336	30 12 046	39 48 082	32 54 139	31 52 171	49 22 249	42 16 298	20 50 344
337	30 50 046	40 40 082	33 28 140	32 00 172	48 33 250	41 29 298	20 36 345
338	31 28 046	41 33 082	34 02 141	32 07 173	47 43 251	40 43 299	20 22 345
339	32 07 046	42 25 083	34 35 142	32 12 174	46 52 252	39 56 299	20 08 345
340	32 45 047	43 18 083	35 07 143	32 17 175	46 02 253	39 10 299	19 54 345
341	33 24 047	44 10 083	35 38 144	32 21 176	45 11 253	38 24 299	19 40 345
342	34 02 047	45 03 084	36 09 145	32 24 177	44 20 254	37 37 299	19 27 345
343	34 41 047	45 56 084	36 39 146	32 26 178	43 29 255	36 51 299	19 14 345
344	35 19 047	46 48 085	37 08 147	32 27 179	42 38 255	36 05 299	19 00 346
	◆ CAPELLA	ALDEBARAN	Diphda	◆ FOMALHAUT	ALTAIR	◆ VEGA	Kochab
345	16 52 046	12 40 078	37 37 148	32 27 180	41 47 256	35 19 300	18 47 346
346	17 31 047	13 32 078	38 04 149	32 27 181	40 55 257	34 33 300	18 34 346
347	18 09 047	14 24 079	38 31 150	32 25 182	40 04 257	33 47 300	18 22 346
348	18 48 047	15 16 079	38 57 151	32 22 183	39 12 258	33 01 300	18 09 346
349	19 27 047	16 08 080	39 22 152	32 18 185	38 20 259	32 15 300	17 57 347
350	20 06 048	17 00 080	39 46 154	32 14 186	37 28 259	31 29 300	17 45 347
351	20 45 048	17 52 080	40 09 155	32 08 187	36 36 260	30 44 301	17 33 347
352	21 25 048	18 44 081	40 31 156	32 02 188	35 44 260	29 58 301	17 21 347
353	22 04 048	19 37 081	40 52 157	31 54 189	34 51 261	29 13 301	17 09 347
354	22 44 049	20 29 082	41 12 158	31 46 190	33 59 262	28 27 301	16 58 348
355	23 24 049	21 21 082	41 32 159	31 36 191	33 07 262	27 42 301	16 46 348
356	24 04 049	22 14 082	41 50 161	31 26 192	32 14 263	26 57 302	16 35 348
357	24 44 049	23 06 083	42 07 162	31 15 193	31 21 263	26 12 302	16 24 348
358	25 24 049	23 59 083	42 23 163	31 03 194	30 29 264	25 27 302	16 13 348
359	26 04 050	24 52 084	42 38 164	30 50 195	29 36 264	24 42 302	16 03 349

LHA ♈	Hc	Zn	Hc	Zn	Hc	Zn	Hc	Zn	Hc	Zn	Hc	Zn	Hc	Zn
	Schedar		◆CAPELLA		ALDEBARAN		◆Diphda		FOMALHAUT		ALTAIR		◆DENEB	
0	59 28	011	26 06	049	25 38	084	43 50	165	31 34	196	28 49	265	46 51	309
1	59 38	010	26 47	050	26 31	084	44 03	167	31 19	197	27 55	266	46 09	308
2	59 47	009	27 27	050	27 24	085	44 14	168	31 04	198	27 02	266	45 27	308
3	59 55	008	28 08	050	28 18	085	44 25	169	30 47	199	26 09	267	44 45	308
4	60 02	007	28 49	050	29 11	085	44 34	171	30 29	200	25 15	267	44 03	308
5	60 08	006	29 30	050	30 04	086	44 43	172	30 11	201	24 22	268	43 21	308
6	60 13	005	30 12	050	30 57	086	44 50	173	29 52	201	23 28	268	42 39	308
7	60 17	004	30 53	050	31 51	087	44 55	175	29 32	202	22 35	269	41 57	308
8	60 20	003	31 34	051	32 44	087	45 00	176	29 11	203	21 42	269	41 15	308
9	60 22	001	32 15	051	33 38	087	45 03	177	28 50	204	20 48	270	40 33	308
10	60 23	000	32 57	051	34 31	088	45 05	179	28 27	205	19 55	270	39 50	308
11	60 23	359	33 38	051	35 24	088	45 06	180	28 04	206	19 01	270	39 08	308
12	60 21	358	34 20	051	36 18	089	45 05	181	27 41	207	18 08	271	38 26	308
13	60 19	357	35 01	051	37 11	089	45 03	183	27 16	208	17 14	271	37 44	308
14	60 16	356	35 43	051	38 05	090	45 00	184	26 51	209	16 21	272	37 02	308
	◆CAPELLA		ALDEBARAN		RIGEL		◆Diphda		FOMALHAUT		Enif		◆DENEB	
15	36 24	051	38 58	090	18 56	110	44 56	185	26 25	209	41 04	259	36 20	308
16	37 06	051	39 52	091	19 46	111	44 51	187	25 58	210	40 11	260	35 38	308
17	37 48	051	40 45	091	20 36	111	44 44	188	25 31	211	39 18	260	34 55	308
18	38 29	051	41 39	091	21 26	112	44 36	189	25 03	212	38 26	261	34 13	308
19	39 11	051	42 32	092	22 16	112	44 27	191	24 35	213	37 33	262	33 32	308
20	39 53	051	43 25	092	23 05	113	44 16	192	24 05	213	36 40	262	32 50	308
21	40 34	051	44 19	093	23 54	114	44 05	193	23 36	214	35 47	263	32 08	309
22	41 16	051	45 12	093	24 43	114	43 52	194	23 05	215	34 54	263	31 26	309
23	41 58	051	46 06	094	25 31	115	43 38	196	22 34	216	34 01	264	30 44	309
24	42 39	051	46 59	094	26 20	115	43 23	197	22 03	217	33 07	264	30 03	309
25	43 21	051	47 52	095	27 08	116	43 07	198	21 31	217	32 14	265	29 21	309
26	44 02	051	48 45	096	27 56	117	42 49	200	20 58	218	31 21	265	28 39	309
27	44 44	051	49 39	096	28 43	117	42 31	201	20 25	219	30 28	266	27 58	309
28	45 25	051	50 32	097	29 31	118	42 11	202	19 51	219	29 34	266	27 17	309
29	46 07	051	51 25	097	30 18	119	41 51	203	19 17	220	28 41	267	26 35	310
	CAPELLA		◆ALDEBARAN		RIGEL		◆Diphda		Alpheratz		DENEB		◆Kochab	
30	46 48	050	52 18	098	31 04	120	41 29	204	65 31	282	25 54	310	11 26	356
31	47 29	050	53 11	098	31 51	120	41 07	205	64 39	282	25 13	310	11 23	357
32	48 10	050	54 04	099	32 37	121	40 43	207	63 46	282	24 32	310	11 20	357
33	48 51	050	54 56	100	33 22	122	40 19	208	62 54	282	23 52	310	11 18	357
34	49 32	050	55 49	100	34 07	123	39 54	209	62 02	282	23 11	311	11 15	358
35	50 13	049	56 41	101	34 52	123	39 27	210	61 09	282	22 30	311	11 13	358
36	50 53	049	57 34	102	35 37	124	39 00	211	60 17	282	21 50	311	11 11	358
37	51 33	049	58 26	103	36 21	125	38 32	212	59 25	282	21 10	311	11 10	358
38	52 14	049	59 18	103	37 04	126	38 03	213	58 32	282	20 29	311	11 08	359
39	52 54	048	60 10	104	37 47	127	37 34	214	57 40	283	19 49	312	11 07	359
40	53 34	048	61 02	105	38 30	128	37 03	215	56 48	283	19 10	312	11 07	359
41	54 13	048	61 53	106	39 12	128	36 32	216	55 56	283	18 30	312	11 06	000
42	54 53	047	62 45	107	39 54	129	36 00	217	55 04	283	17 50	312	11 06	000
43	55 32	047	63 36	108	40 35	130	35 28	218	54 12	283	17 11	313	11 06	000
44	56 10	046	64 26	109	41 15	131	34 54	219	53 20	283	16 32	313	11 06	000
	◆CAPELLA		PROCYON		SIRIUS		◆RIGEL		Acamar		Diphda		◆Alpheratz	
45	56 49	046	20 08	095	19 56	122	41 55	132	22 45	180	34 20	220	52 28	284
46	57 27	045	21 01	095	20 41	123	42 35	133	22 45	181	33 45	221	51 36	284
47	58 05	045	21 55	095	21 26	123	43 13	134	22 43	182	33 10	222	50 44	284
48	58 43	044	22 48	096	22 10	124	43 51	135	22 41	183	32 34	223	49 52	284
49	59 20	044	23 41	096	22 54	124	44 28	136	22 38	184	31 58	224	49 00	284
50	59 56	043	24 34	097	23 38	125	45 05	137	22 34	184	31 20	224	48 09	285
51	60 33	042	25 27	097	24 22	126	45 41	139	22 30	185	30 43	225	47 17	285
52	61 08	042	26 20	098	25 05	127	46 15	140	22 25	186	30 05	226	46 25	285
53	61 43	041	27 13	099	25 48	127	46 50	141	22 19	187	29 26	227	45 34	285
54	62 18	040	28 06	099	26 30	128	47 23	142	22 12	188	28 47	228	44 42	285
55	62 52	039	28 58	100	27 12	129	47 55	143	22 05	188	28 07	228	43 50	286
56	63 25	038	29 51	100	27 54	129	48 27	145	21 56	189	27 27	229	42 59	286
57	63 58	037	30 44	101	28 35	130	48 57	146	21 47	190	26 46	230	42 08	286
58	64 30	036	31 36	101	29 15	131	49 26	147	21 38	191	26 05	231	41 16	286
59	65 01	035	32 29	102	29 55	132	49 55	149	21 27	192	25 23	231	40 25	287
	◆Dubhe		PROCYON		SIRIUS		◆RIGEL		Diphda		◆Hamal		Mirfak	
60	16 23	028	33 21	102	30 35	133	50 22	150	24 41	232	64 30	268	66 09	346
61	16 48	029	34 13	103	31 14	133	50 48	151	23 59	233	63 37	269	65 55	345
62	17 14	029	35 05	104	31 53	134	51 13	153	23 16	234	62 43	269	65 40	343
63	17 40	029	35 57	104	32 31	135	51 37	154	22 33	234	61 50	270	65 24	342
64	18 06	029	36 49	105	33 08	136	52 00	156	21 49	235	60 56	270	65 07	340
65	18 32	029	37 40	105	33 45	137	52 21	157	21 05	236	60 03	271	64 49	339
66	18 58	030	38 32	106	34 21	138	52 41	159	20 21	236	59 09	271	64 29	338
67	19 25	030	39 23	107	34 57	139	53 00	160	19 37	237	58 16	272	64 08	337
68	19 51	030	40 14	107	35 32	140	53 17	162	18 52	237	57 22	272	63 46	335
69	20 18	030	41 05	108	36 06	141	53 33	164	18 06	238	56 29	272	63 23	334
70	20 45	030	41 56	109	36 40	141	53 48	165	17 21	239	55 36	273	63 00	333
71	21 12	030	42 46	109	37 13	142	54 00	167	16 35	239	54 42	273	62 35	332
72	21 39	031	43 37	110	37 45	143	54 12	168	15 49	240	53 49	274	62 09	331
73	22 06	031	44 27	111	38 17	144	54 22	170	15 03	240	52 55	274	61 43	330
74	22 34	031	45 17	112	38 47	146	54 30	172	14 16	241	52 02	274	61 16	329
	◆Dubhe		POLLUX		PROCYON		◆SIRIUS		RIGEL		◆Hamal		Mirfak	
75	23 01	031	53 18	079	46 06	113	39 17	147	54 37	173	51 09	275	60 48	328
76	23 29	031	54 11	079	46 55	113	39 46	148	54 43	175	50 16	275	60 19	327
77	23 57	031	55 03	079	47 44	114	40 14	149	54 46	177	49 22	275	59 50	326
78	24 24	031	55 56	079	48 33	115	40 42	150	54 48	179	48 29	276	59 20	326
79	24 52	031	56 48	079	49 21	116	41 08	151	54 49	180	47 36	276	58 49	325
80	25 20	032	57 41	080	50 09	117	41 34	152	54 48	182	46 43	276	58 18	324
81	25 48	032	58 33	080	50 56	118	41 58	153	54 45	184	45 50	277	57 47	323
82	26 16	032	59 26	080	51 44	119	42 22	154	54 41	185	44 57	277	57 14	323
83	26 45	032	60 19	080	52 30	120	42 44	156	54 35	187	44 04	277	56 42	322
84	27 13	032	61 11	080	53 16	121	43 06	157	54 27	189	43 11	278	56 09	321
85	27 41	032	62 04	081	54 02	122	43 26	158	54 18	191	42 18	278	55 35	321
86	28 09	032	62 57	081	54 47	123	43 46	159	54 08	192	41 25	279	55 01	320
87	28 38	032	63 50	081	55 31	124	44 04	161	53 56	194	40 32	279	54 27	320
88	29 06	032	64 42	081	56 15	125	44 21	162	53 42	195	39 39	279	53 52	319
89	29 35	032	65 35	081	56 59	127	44 37	163	53 27	197	38 46	280	53 17	319

LAT 27°N

LHA ♈	Hc	Zn	Hc	Zn	Hc	Zn	Hc	Zn	Hc	Zn	Hc	Zn	Hc	Zn
	Dubhe		◆REGULUS		PROCYON		SIRIUS		◆RIGEL		ALDEBARAN		◆Mirfak	
90	30 03	032	29 56	092	57 41	128	44 52	164	53 11	199	68 05	246	52 42	318
91	30 31	032	30 49	092	58 23	129	45 06	166	52 53	200	67 16	247	52 06	318
92	31 00	032	31 43	092	59 04	131	45 19	167	52 34	202	66 26	248	51 30	318
93	31 28	032	32 36	093	59 44	132	45 30	168	52 13	203	65 36	250	50 54	317
94	31 57	032	33 29	093	60 23	134	45 40	170	51 52	205	64 46	251	50 18	317
95	32 25	032	34 23	094	61 01	135	45 49	171	51 29	206	63 55	252	49 41	317
96	32 54	032	35 16	094	61 38	137	45 57	172	51 04	208	63 05	253	49 04	316
97	33 22	032	36 09	095	62 14	139	46 03	174	50 39	209	62 13	254	48 27	316
98	33 51	032	37 03	095	62 49	140	46 08	175	50 12	211	61 22	255	47 50	316
99	34 19	032	37 56	096	63 22	142	46 12	177	49 44	212	60 30	255	47 13	316
100	34 47	032	38 49	096	63 54	144	46 14	178	49 16	213	59 38	256	46 35	315
101	35 15	032	39 42	097	64 25	146	46 16	179	48 46	215	58 46	257	45 57	315
102	35 44	032	40 35	098	64 54	148	46 16	181	48 15	216	57 54	258	45 20	315
103	36 12	032	41 28	098	65 21	150	46 14	182	47 43	217	57 02	259	44 42	315
104	36 40	032	42 21	099	65 47	152	46 12	184	47 11	218	56 09	259	44 04	315
	Dubhe		◆REGULUS		Alphard		SIRIUS		◆RIGEL		ALDEBARAN		◆CAPELLA	
105	37 08	031	43 14	099	39 20	130	46 08	185	46 37	219	55 17	260	62 15	320
106	37 35	031	44 06	100	40 01	131	46 02	186	46 03	221	54 24	261	61 40	319
107	38 03	031	44 59	100	40 41	131	45 56	188	45 27	222	53 31	261	61 05	318
108	38 31	031	45 52	101	41 21	132	45 48	189	44 51	223	52 39	262	60 29	318
109	38 58	031	46 44	102	42 00	133	45 39	190	44 15	224	51 46	263	59 53	317
110	39 26	031	47 36	102	42 38	134	45 29	192	43 37	225	50 53	263	59 16	316
111	39 53	031	48 28	103	43 16	136	45 17	193	42 59	226	49 59	264	58 39	316
112	40 20	030	49 20	104	43 53	137	45 05	194	42 20	227	49 06	264	58 01	315
113	40 47	030	50 12	104	44 30	138	44 51	196	41 41	228	48 13	265	57 23	315
114	41 13	030	51 04	105	45 05	139	44 36	197	41 00	229	47 20	265	56 45	314
115	41 40	030	51 55	106	45 40	140	44 20	198	40 20	230	46 26	266	56 07	314
116	42 06	029	52 47	107	46 14	141	44 02	200	39 39	231	45 33	266	55 28	313
117	42 32	029	53 38	108	46 47	142	43 44	201	38 57	232	44 40	267	54 49	313
118	42 58	029	54 29	108	47 19	143	43 24	202	38 14	233	43 46	267	54 09	312
119	43 24	029	55 19	109	47 51	145	43 04	203	37 32	234	42 53	268	53 30	312
	◆Dubhe		REGULUS		◆Alphard		SIRIUS		RIGEL		◆ALDEBARAN		CAPELLA	
120	43 50	028	56 10	110	48 21	146	42 42	204	36 48	234	42 00	268	52 50	312
121	44 15	028	57 00	111	48 50	147	42 19	206	36 05	235	41 06	269	52 10	311
122	44 40	028	57 49	112	49 19	149	41 56	207	35 20	236	40 13	269	51 29	311
123	45 05	027	58 39	113	49 46	150	41 31	208	34 36	237	39 19	270	50 49	311
124	45 29	027	59 28	114	50 12	151	41 06	209	33 51	238	38 26	270	50 08	311
125	45 53	027	60 16	115	50 37	153	40 39	210	33 05	238	37 32	271	49 28	310
126	46 17	026	61 04	116	51 01	154	40 12	211	32 20	239	36 39	271	48 47	310
127	46 40	026	61 52	118	51 24	156	39 43	212	31 34	240	35 45	272	48 06	310
128	47 04	025	62 39	119	51 45	157	39 14	214	30 47	241	34 52	272	47 25	310
129	47 26	025	63 26	120	52 05	159	38 44	215	30 00	241	33 58	272	46 44	310
130	47 49	025	64 12	121	52 24	160	38 14	216	29 13	242	33 05	273	46 02	309
131	48 11	024	64 57	123	52 42	162	37 42	217	28 26	243	32 12	273	45 21	309
132	48 33	024	65 41	124	52 58	163	37 10	218	27 38	243	31 18	274	44 40	309
133	48 54	023	66 25	126	53 12	165	36 37	219	26 50	244	30 25	274	43 58	309
134	49 15	023	67 08	128	53 26	167	36 03	220	26 02	245	29 32	275	43 17	309
	Dubhe		◆ARCTURUS		SPICA		Alphard		◆SIRIUS		BETELGEUSE		◆CAPELLA	
135	49 35	022	17 56	077	15 04	111	53 37	168	35 29	221	42 15	255	42 35	309
136	49 55	022	18 48	078	15 54	112	53 48	170	34 54	221	41 23	255	41 54	309
137	50 15	021	19 41	078	16 44	112	53 56	171	34 18	222	40 31	256	41 12	309
138	50 34	021	20 33	078	17 33	113	54 03	173	33 42	223	39 39	256	40 30	309
139	50 53	020	21 25	079	18 22	114	54 09	175	33 05	224	38 47	257	39 49	309
140	51 11	019	22 18	079	19 11	114	54 13	176	32 27	225	37 55	258	39 07	309
141	51 28	019	23 10	080	20 00	115	54 16	178	31 49	226	37 03	258	38 25	309
142	51 45	018	24 03	080	20 48	115	54 17	180	31 10	227	36 10	259	37 44	309
143	52 02	018	24 56	080	21 36	116	54 16	182	30 31	228	35 18	259	37 02	309
144	52 18	017	25 48	081	22 24	117	54 14	183	29 52	228	34 25	260	36 20	309
145	52 33	016	26 41	081	23 12	117	54 10	185	29 11	229	33 33	261	35 39	309
146	52 48	016	27 34	081	23 59	118	54 04	187	28 31	230	32 40	261	34 57	309
147	53 02	015	28 27	082	24 46	118	53 58	188	27 50	231	31 47	262	34 16	309
148	53 16	014	29 20	082	25 33	119	53 49	190	27 08	231	30 54	262	33 34	309
149	53 29	014	30 13	083	26 20	120	53 39	192	26 26	232	30 01	263	32 53	309
	Dubhe		◆ARCTURUS		SPICA		◆Alphard		SIRIUS		POLLUX		◆CAPELLA	
150	53 41	013	31 06	083	27 06	120	53 28	193	25 44	233	60 25	280	32 11	309
151	53 52	012	31 59	083	27 52	121	53 15	195	25 01	234	59 32	280	31 30	309
152	54 03	011	32 52	084	28 38	122	53 00	196	24 18	234	58 39	280	30 49	310
153	54 14	011	33 45	084	29 23	123	52 44	198	23 34	235	57 47	280	30 07	310
154	54 23	010	34 39	085	30 08	123	52 27	200	22 50	236	56 54	281	29 26	310
155	54 32	009	35 32	085	30 52	124	52 09	201	22 06	236	56 02	281	28 45	310
156	54 40	008	36 25	085	31 36	125	51 49	203	21 21	237	55 09	281	28 04	310
157	54 47	008	37 18	086	32 20	126	51 27	204	20 36	238	54 17	281	27 23	310
158	54 54	007	38 12	086	33 03	126	51 05	206	19 51	238	53 24	281	26 43	310
159	55 00	006	39 05	087	33 46	127	50 41	207	19 06	239	52 32	282	26 02	311
160	55 05	005	39 58	087	34 29	128	50 16	208	18 20	239	51 39	282	25 21	311
161	55 09	004	40 52	087	35 11	129	49 50	210	17 34	240	50 47	282	24 41	311
162	55 13	003	41 45	088	35 52	130	49 23	211	16 47	241	49 55	282	24 01	311
163	55 16	003	42 39	088	36 33	131	48 55	212	16 00	241	49 03	283	23 20	311
164	55 18	002	43 32	089	37 13	131	48 26	214	15 14	242	48 11	283	22 40	311
	◆Dubhe		Alkaid		ARCTURUS		◆SPICA		Alphard		◆PROCYON		POLLUX	
165	55 19	001	50 54	044	44 26	089	37 53	132	47 56	215	37 43	255	47 18	283
166	55 20	000	51 31	044	45 19	090	38 32	133	47 25	216	36 51	255	46 26	283
167	55 20	359	52 07	043	46 12	090	39 11	134	46 52	218	35 59	256	45 34	283
168	55 18	358	52 44	043	47 06	090	39 49	135	46 19	219	35 07	256	44 42	284
169	55 17	358	53 20	042	47 59	091	40 26	136	45 46	220	34 15	257	43 50	284
170	55 14	357	53 56	042	48 53	091	41 03	137	45 11	221	33 23	258	42 59	284
171	55 11	356	54 31	041	49 46	092	41 39	138	44 35	222	32 31	258	42 07	284
172	55 07	355	55 06	041	50 40	092	42 14	139	43 59	223	31 38	259	41 15	285
173	55 02	354	55 41	040	51 33	093	42 49	140	43 22	224	30 46	259	40 23	285
174	54 56	354	56 16	040	52 26	093	43 22	141	42 44	225	29 53	260	39 32	285
175	54 50	353	56 50	039	53 20	094	43 55	143	42 06	226	29 01	260	38 40	285
176	54 43	352	57 23	039	54 13	095	44 27	144	41 27	227	28 08	261	37 49	286
177	54 35	351	57 56	038	55 06	095	44 58	145	40 47	228	27 15	261	36 57	286
178	54 26	350	58 29	037	56 00	096	45 29	146	40 07	229	26 22	262	36 06	286
179	54 17	350	59 01	037	56 53	096	45 58	147	39 26	230	25 29	262	35 15	287

LHA ♈	Hc	Zn	Hc	Zn	Hc	Zn	Hc	Zn	Hc	Zn	Hc	Zn	Hc	Zn
	◆ Alkaid		Alphecca		◆ SPICA		Gienah		REGULUS		◆ POLLUX		Dubhe	
180	59 33	036	42 21	077	46 26	149	45 12	174	59 56	245	34 23	287	54 07	349
181	60 04	035	43 13	078	46 54	150	45 16	176	59 07	246	33 32	287	53 56	348
182	60 34	034	44 05	078	47 20	151	45 20	177	58 18	247	32 41	287	53 45	347
183	61 04	033	44 58	078	47 45	152	45 22	178	57 29	248	31 50	288	53 33	347
184	61 33	032	45 50	079	48 10	154	45 22	180	56 39	249	30 59	288	53 20	346
185	62 01	031	46 43	079	48 33	155	45 22	181	55 49	250	30 09	288	53 07	345
186	62 29	030	47 35	079	48 55	157	45 20	183	54 58	251	29 18	289	52 53	345
187	62 56	029	48 28	079	49 15	158	45 17	184	54 08	252	28 27	289	52 38	344
188	63 21	028	49 20	080	49 35	159	45 13	185	53 17	253	27 37	289	52 23	343
189	63 46	027	50 13	080	49 53	161	45 08	187	52 25	254	26 46	289	52 07	343
190	64 10	026	51 05	080	50 10	162	45 01	188	51 34	254	25 56	290	51 51	342
191	64 33	025	51 58	080	50 26	164	44 53	189	50 42	255	25 06	290	51 34	341
192	64 55	024	52 51	081	50 40	165	44 44	191	49 51	256	24 15	290	51 17	341
193	65 16	022	53 44	081	50 53	167	44 33	192	48 59	257	23 25	291	50 59	340
194	65 36	021	54 36	081	51 04	168	44 22	193	48 07	257	22 35	291	50 40	340
	◆ Kochab		VEGA		Rasalhague		◆ ANTARES		SPICA		◆ REGULUS		Dubhe	
195	40 46	010	20 39	056	24 18	088	16 24	132	51 15	170	47 15	258	50 21	339
196	40 54	009	21 23	056	25 12	088	17 03	133	51 23	171	46 22	259	50 02	338
197	41 03	009	22 08	057	26 05	089	17 42	133	51 31	173	45 30	259	49 42	338
198	41 11	009	22 53	057	26 59	089	18 21	134	51 37	174	44 37	260	49 22	337
199	41 19	008	23 37	057	27 52	090	18 59	135	51 41	176	43 45	260	49 01	337
200	41 27	008	24 22	057	28 46	090	19 37	135	51 44	178	42 52	261	48 40	336
201	41 34	008	25 07	057	29 39	091	20 14	136	51 45	179	41 59	262	48 18	336
202	41 41	007	25 52	058	30 33	091	20 51	137	51 45	181	41 06	262	47 56	335
203	41 48	007	26 38	058	31 26	091	21 27	138	51 44	182	40 13	263	47 34	335
204	41 55	007	27 23	058	32 19	092	22 03	138	51 41	184	39 20	263	47 11	335
205	42 01	006	28 08	058	33 13	092	22 39	139	51 37	186	38 27	264	46 48	334
206	42 06	006	28 54	059	34 06	093	23 13	140	51 31	187	37 34	264	46 25	334
207	42 12	006	29 40	059	35 00	093	23 48	140	51 23	189	36 41	265	46 01	333
208	42 17	005	30 25	059	35 53	094	24 21	141	51 15	190	35 47	265	45 37	333
209	42 22	005	31 11	059	36 46	094	24 55	142	51 04	192	34 54	266	45 12	333
	Kochab		◆ VEGA		Rasalhague		ANTARES		◆ SPICA		REGULUS		◆ Dubhe	
210	42 27	005	31 57	059	37 40	095	25 27	143	50 53	193	34 01	266	44 48	332
211	42 31	004	32 43	059	38 33	095	25 59	144	50 40	195	33 07	267	44 23	332
212	42 35	004	33 29	060	39 26	096	26 31	144	50 25	196	32 14	267	43 58	332
213	42 38	004	34 15	060	40 19	096	27 02	145	50 10	198	31 21	268	43 32	331
214	42 41	003	35 02	060	41 12	097	27 32	146	49 53	199	30 27	268	43 07	331
215	42 44	003	35 48	060	42 05	098	28 01	147	49 35	201	29 34	269	42 41	331
216	42 47	002	36 34	060	42 58	098	28 30	148	49 15	202	28 40	269	42 15	331
217	42 49	002	37 21	060	43 51	099	28 58	149	48 54	204	27 47	270	41 48	330
218	42 51	002	38 07	060	44 44	099	29 26	150	48 32	205	26 53	270	41 22	330
219	42 52	001	38 54	060	45 37	100	29 53	150	48 09	206	26 00	271	40 55	330
220	42 53	001	39 40	061	46 29	101	30 19	151	47 45	208	25 06	271	40 28	330
221	42 54	001	40 27	061	47 22	101	30 44	152	47 20	209	24 13	271	40 01	330
222	42 54	000	41 13	061	48 14	102	31 08	153	46 54	210	23 19	272	39 34	329
223	42 54	000	42 00	061	49 07	102	31 32	154	46 26	211	22 26	272	39 07	329
224	42 54	000	42 47	061	49 59	103	31 55	155	45 58	213	21 33	273	38 40	329
	VEGA		◆ ALTAIR		Nunki		ANTARES		◆ SPICA		Denebola		◆ Alkaid	
225	43 33	061	19 14	090	12 07	128	32 17	156	45 28	214	44 06	264	63 48	333
226	44 20	061	20 08	090	12 49	129	32 39	157	44 58	215	43 13	265	63 23	332
227	45 07	061	21 01	091	13 30	129	32 59	158	44 27	216	42 20	265	62 57	331
228	45 54	061	21 54	091	14 12	130	33 19	159	43 55	217	41 26	266	62 31	330
229	46 40	061	22 48	091	14 52	130	33 37	160	43 22	219	40 33	266	62 03	329
230	47 27	061	23 41	092	15 33	131	33 55	161	42 48	220	39 40	267	61 35	328
231	48 14	061	24 35	092	16 13	132	34 12	162	42 14	221	38 46	267	61 06	327
232	49 01	061	25 28	093	16 53	132	34 28	163	41 39	222	37 53	268	60 36	326
233	49 47	061	26 22	093	17 32	133	34 43	164	41 03	223	36 59	268	60 06	325
234	50 34	061	27 15	094	18 11	134	34 58	165	40 26	224	36 06	269	59 35	324
235	51 21	061	28 08	094	18 49	134	35 11	166	39 49	225	35 12	269	59 03	323
236	52 07	061	29 02	095	19 27	135	35 23	167	39 11	226	34 19	270	58 31	323
237	52 54	061	29 55	095	20 05	136	35 34	168	38 32	227	33 26	270	57 59	322
238	53 40	060	30 48	096	20 42	136	35 45	169	37 53	228	32 32	270	57 26	321
239	54 27	060	31 41	096	21 19	137	35 54	171	37 13	229	31 39	271	56 52	321
	◆ VEGA		ALTAIR		Nunki		◆ ANTARES		SPICA		ARCTURUS		◆ Alkaid	
240	55 13	060	32 34	097	21 55	138	36 02	172	36 33	229	64 56	257	56 18	320
241	55 59	060	33 27	097	22 31	139	36 10	173	35 52	230	64 04	258	55 43	320
242	56 46	060	34 20	098	23 06	139	36 16	174	35 10	231	63 12	259	55 09	319
243	57 32	059	35 13	098	23 40	140	36 21	175	34 28	232	62 19	260	54 33	319
244	58 18	059	36 06	099	24 15	141	36 25	176	33 46	233	61 27	260	53 58	318
245	59 04	059	36 59	100	24 48	142	36 29	177	33 03	234	60 34	261	53 22	318
246	59 49	058	37 52	100	25 21	142	36 31	178	32 20	234	59 41	262	52 46	317
247	60 35	058	38 44	101	25 53	143	36 32	179	31 36	235	58 48	262	52 10	317
248	61 20	058	39 37	101	26 25	144	36 32	180	30 52	236	57 55	263	51 33	316
249	62 05	057	40 29	102	26 56	145	36 31	182	30 07	237	57 02	264	50 56	316
250	62 50	057	41 21	103	27 27	146	36 29	183	29 23	237	56 09	264	50 19	316
251	63 35	056	42 13	103	27 57	146	36 26	184	28 37	238	55 16	265	49 41	316
252	64 19	056	43 05	104	28 26	147	36 22	185	27 52	239	54 22	265	49 04	315
253	65 03	055	43 57	104	28 55	148	36 17	186	27 06	240	53 29	266	48 26	315
254	65 47	054	44 49	105	29 23	149	36 11	187	26 20	240	52 36	266	47 48	315
	◆ DENEB		ALTAIR		Nunki		◆ ANTARES		SPICA		ARCTURUS		◆ Alkaid	
255	42 40	052	45 40	106	29 50	150	36 04	188	25 33	241	51 42	267	47 10	314
256	43 22	052	46 32	107	30 16	151	35 56	189	24 46	242	50 49	267	46 32	314
257	44 04	052	47 23	107	30 42	152	35 46	190	23 59	242	49 56	268	45 54	314
258	44 46	052	48 14	108	31 07	153	35 36	191	23 12	243	49 02	268	45 15	314
259	45 28	052	49 04	109	31 31	154	35 25	193	22 24	243	48 09	269	44 37	314
260	46 10	052	49 55	110	31 55	155	35 13	194	21 36	244	47 15	269	43 58	314
261	46 52	051	50 45	110	32 17	155	35 00	195	20 48	245	46 22	270	43 19	313
262	47 34	051	51 35	111	32 39	156	34 46	196	19 59	245	45 28	270	42 40	313
263	48 16	051	52 25	112	33 00	157	34 31	197	19 11	246	44 35	271	42 01	313
264	48 57	051	53 14	113	33 20	158	34 15	198	18 22	246	43 41	271	41 23	313
265	49 39	051	54 03	114	33 39	159	33 58	199	17 33	247	42 48	272	40 43	313
266	50 20	051	54 52	115	33 58	160	33 40	200	16 43	248	41 54	272	40 04	313
267	51 01	050	55 40	116	34 15	161	33 22	201	15 54	248	41 01	273	39 25	313
268	51 42	050	56 28	117	34 32	162	33 02	202	15 04	249	40 08	273	38 46	313
269	52 23	050	57 15	118	34 47	164	32 42	203	14 14	249	39 14	273	38 07	313

LHA ♈	Hc	Zn	Hc	Zn	Hc	Zn	Hc	Zn	Hc	Zn	Hc	Zn	Hc	Zn
	◆ DENEB		ALTAIR		◆ Nunki		ANTARES		◆ ARCTURUS		Alkaid		Kochab	
270	53 04	049	58 02	119	35 02	165	32 21	204	38 21	274	37 28	313	37 01	345
271	53 44	049	58 49	120	35 16	166	31 59	205	37 28	274	36 49	313	36 48	345
272	54 24	049	59 34	122	35 29	167	31 36	206	36 34	275	36 10	313	36 34	345
273	55 04	048	60 20	123	35 40	168	31 12	207	35 41	275	35 30	313	36 20	345
274	55 44	048	61 04	124	35 51	169	30 48	208	34 48	275	34 51	313	36 06	345
275	56 24	048	61 48	126	36 01	170	30 23	209	33 55	276	34 12	313	35 52	344
276	57 03	047	62 31	127	36 10	171	29 57	209	33 01	276	33 33	313	35 37	344
277	57 42	047	63 13	129	36 18	172	29 30	210	32 08	277	32 54	313	35 23	344
278	58 21	046	63 55	130	36 24	173	29 03	211	31 15	277	32 15	313	35 08	344
279	58 59	045	64 35	132	36 30	174	28 35	212	30 22	277	31 36	313	34 53	344
280	59 37	045	65 14	134	36 35	175	28 06	213	29 29	278	30 57	313	34 38	344
281	60 14	044	65 52	135	36 39	177	27 37	214	28 36	278	30 18	313	34 23	344
282	60 51	044	66 29	137	36 41	178	27 07	215	27 43	278	29 39	313	34 08	343
283	61 28	043	67 05	139	36 43	179	26 36	215	26 50	279	29 00	314	33 53	343
284	62 04	042	67 39	141	36 43	180	26 05	216	25 58	279	28 22	314	33 38	343
	◆ Alpheratz		Enif		Nunki		◆ ANTARES		ARCTURUS		◆ Alkaid		Kochab	
285	23 06	068	47 36	106	36 43	181	25 33	217	25 05	280	27 43	314	33 22	343
286	23 56	068	48 27	106	36 41	182	25 00	218	24 12	280	27 05	314	33 06	343
287	24 46	068	49 18	107	36 39	183	24 27	219	23 20	280	26 26	314	32 51	343
288	25 35	069	50 09	108	36 35	184	23 53	219	22 27	281	25 48	314	32 35	343
289	26 25	069	51 00	109	36 31	186	23 19	220	21 35	281	25 10	314	32 19	343
290	27 15	069	51 51	110	36 25	187	22 44	221	20 42	282	24 32	315	32 03	343
291	28 05	070	52 41	110	36 18	188	22 09	222	19 50	282	23 53	315	31 47	343
292	28 55	070	53 31	111	36 11	189	21 33	222	18 57	282	23 16	315	31 31	342
293	29 46	070	54 20	112	36 02	190	20 57	223	18 05	283	22 38	315	31 15	342
294	30 36	070	55 10	113	35 52	191	20 20	224	17 13	283	22 00	315	30 59	342
295	31 27	071	55 59	114	35 41	192	19 43	224	16 21	283	21 23	316	30 43	342
296	32 17	071	56 47	115	35 30	193	19 05	225	15 29	284	20 45	316	30 26	342
297	33 08	071	57 36	116	35 17	194	18 27	226	14 37	284	20 08	316	30 10	342
298	33 58	072	58 23	117	35 03	195	17 49	226	13 46	285	19 31	316	29 54	342
299	34 49	072	59 11	118	34 49	196	17 10	227	12 54	285	18 54	316	29 37	342
	Schedar		◆ Alpheratz		FOMALHAUT		◆ Nunki		Rasalhague		◆ VEGA		Kochab	
300	32 57	038	35 40	072	19 09	140	34 33	197	53 16	254	69 07	310	29 21	342
301	33 30	038	36 31	072	19 43	140	34 17	198	52 25	255	68 26	309	29 05	342
302	34 03	038	37 22	073	20 17	141	33 59	199	51 33	256	67 43	308	28 48	342
303	34 36	038	38 13	073	20 50	142	33 41	200	50 41	256	67 01	307	28 32	342
304	35 09	038	39 04	073	21 23	143	33 22	201	49 49	257	66 18	306	28 15	342
305	35 42	038	39 55	073	21 55	143	33 02	202	48 57	258	65 35	305	27 59	342
306	36 15	038	40 46	074	22 27	144	32 41	203	48 05	258	64 51	305	27 42	342
307	36 48	038	41 38	074	22 58	145	32 19	204	47 12	259	64 07	304	27 26	342
308	37 21	038	42 29	074	23 28	146	31 57	205	46 20	260	63 22	304	27 10	342
309	37 54	038	43 20	074	23 58	146	31 34	206	45 27	260	62 38	303	26 53	342
310	38 26	038	44 12	074	24 28	147	31 09	207	44 34	261	61 53	303	26 37	342
311	38 59	038	45 03	075	24 56	148	30 45	208	43 41	261	61 07	302	26 20	342
312	39 31	037	45 55	075	25 24	149	30 19	209	42 49	262	60 22	302	26 04	342
313	40 04	037	46 47	075	25 52	150	29 52	210	41 56	263	59 37	301	25 48	342
314	40 36	037	47 38	075	26 19	150	29 25	211	41 03	263	58 51	301	25 32	342
	◆ Mirfak		Hamal		Diphda		◆ FOMALHAUT		ALTAIR		◆ VEGA		Kochab	
315	16 29	042	21 24	074	19 29	123	26 45	151	65 43	225	58 05	301	25 15	342
316	17 05	042	22 16	074	20 13	124	27 10	152	65 05	227	57 19	301	24 59	342
317	17 41	042	23 07	074	20 58	124	27 35	153	64 25	229	56 33	300	24 43	342
318	18 17	043	23 59	075	21 42	125	27 59	154	63 45	230	55 47	300	24 27	343
319	18 54	043	24 50	075	22 25	126	28 22	155	63 03	232	55 00	300	24 11	343
320	19 30	043	25 42	075	23 09	126	28 44	156	62 21	233	54 14	300	23 55	343
321	20 07	043	26 34	076	23 51	127	29 06	156	61 38	235	53 28	300	23 39	343
322	20 43	044	27 26	076	24 34	128	29 27	157	60 54	236	52 41	299	23 24	343
323	21 20	044	28 17	076	25 16	128	29 47	158	60 09	237	51 55	299	23 08	343
324	21 57	044	29 09	077	25 58	129	30 07	159	59 23	239	51 08	299	22 52	343
325	22 34	044	30 02	077	26 39	130	30 25	160	58 37	240	50 21	299	22 37	343
326	23 12	044	30 54	077	27 20	131	30 43	161	57 51	241	49 34	299	22 21	343
327	23 49	044	31 46	078	28 00	131	31 00	162	57 04	242	48 48	299	22 06	343
328	24 27	045	32 38	078	28 40	132	31 16	163	56 16	243	48 01	299	21 51	343
329	25 04	045	33 31	078	29 19	133	31 31	164	55 28	244	47 14	299	21 35	344
	◆ Mirfak		Hamal		Diphda		◆ FOMALHAUT		ALTAIR		◆ VEGA		Kochab	
330	25 42	045	34 23	079	29 58	134	31 45	165	54 40	245	46 27	299	21 20	344
331	26 20	045	35 15	079	30 36	135	31 58	166	53 51	246	45 41	299	21 05	344
332	26 58	045	36 08	079	31 14	135	32 11	167	53 02	247	44 54	299	20 50	344
333	27 36	045	37 01	080	31 51	136	32 22	168	52 13	248	44 07	299	20 36	344
334	28 14	045	37 53	080	32 28	137	32 33	169	51 23	249	43 20	299	20 21	344
335	28 52	046	38 46	080	33 04	138	32 43	170	50 33	250	42 34	299	20 07	344
336	29 30	046	39 39	081	33 39	139	32 52	171	49 43	251	41 47	299	19 52	344
337	30 08	046	40 31	081	34 14	140	32 59	172	48 52	251	41 00	299	19 38	345
338	30 47	046	41 24	081	34 48	141	33 06	173	48 01	252	40 14	299	19 24	345
339	31 25	046	42 17	082	35 22	142	33 12	174	47 10	253	39 27	299	19 10	345
340	32 04	046	43 10	082	35 55	143	33 17	175	46 19	254	38 41	300	18 56	345
341	32 42	046	44 03	082	36 27	144	33 21	176	45 28	254	37 54	300	18 42	345
342	33 21	046	44 56	083	36 58	145	33 24	177	44 36	255	37 08	300	18 29	345
343	33 59	046	45 49	083	37 29	146	33 26	178	43 45	256	36 21	300	18 15	346
344	34 38	046	46 42	084	37 58	147	33 27	179	42 53	256	35 35	300	18 02	346
	◆ CAPELLA		ALDEBARAN		Diphda		◆ FOMALHAUT		ALTAIR		◆ VEGA		Kochab	
345	16 11	046	12 27	078	38 27	148	33 27	180	42 01	257	34 49	300	17 49	346
346	16 49	046	13 19	078	38 56	149	33 27	181	41 09	258	34 03	300	17 36	346
347	17 28	047	14 12	078	39 23	150	33 25	182	40 16	258	33 16	300	17 23	346
348	18 07	047	15 04	079	39 49	151	33 22	184	39 24	259	32 30	301	17 11	346
349	18 46	047	15 57	079	40 15	152	33 18	185	38 31	259	31 44	301	16 58	347
350	19 26	047	16 49	080	40 39	153	33 13	186	37 39	260	30 59	301	16 46	347
351	20 05	048	17 42	080	41 03	154	33 08	187	36 46	261	30 13	301	16 34	347
352	20 45	048	18 34	080	41 26	155	33 01	188	35 53	261	29 27	301	16 22	347
353	21 24	048	19 27	081	41 47	157	32 53	189	35 00	262	28 41	302	16 10	347
354	22 04	048	20 20	081	42 08	158	32 45	190	34 07	262	27 56	302	15 59	348
355	22 44	049	21 13	082	42 28	159	32 35	191	33 14	263	27 10	302	15 48	348
356	23 24	049	22 06	082	42 46	160	32 25	192	32 21	263	26 25	302	15 36	348
357	24 04	049	22 59	082	43 04	162	32 14	193	31 28	264	25 40	302	15 25	348
358	24 45	049	23 52	083	43 20	163	32 01	194	30 35	264	24 55	303	15 15	348
359	25 25	049	24 45	083	43 35	164	31 48	195	29 42	265	24 10	303	15 04	349

LHA ♈	Hc	Zn	Hc	Zn	Hc	Zn	Hc	Zn	Hc	Zn	Hc	Zn	Hc	Zn
	Schedar		◆ CAPELLA		ALDEBARAN		◆ Diphda		FOMALHAUT		ALTAIR		◆ DENEB	
0	58 29	011	25 27	049	25 31	083	44 48	165	32 32	196	28 53	266	46 13	309
1	58 39	010	26 08	049	26 25	084	45 01	166	32 17	197	27 59	266	45 31	309
2	58 48	009	26 49	049	27 18	084	45 13	168	32 01	198	27 06	267	44 50	309
3	58 56	008	27 30	050	28 12	084	45 24	169	31 44	199	26 12	267	44 08	309
4	59 03	007	28 11	050	29 06	085	45 34	170	31 26	200	25 18	268	43 26	309
5	59 08	006	28 52	050	29 59	085	45 42	172	31 07	201	24 24	268	42 44	309
6	59 13	005	29 33	050	30 53	086	45 49	173	30 48	202	23 30	269	42 02	309
7	59 17	004	30 14	050	31 47	086	45 55	174	30 27	203	22 36	269	41 20	309
8	59 20	003	30 56	050	32 41	086	46 00	176	30 06	204	21 42	270	40 38	309
9	59 22	001	31 37	050	33 35	087	46 03	177	29 44	204	20 48	270	39 55	309
10	59 23	000	32 19	050	34 28	087	46 05	179	29 22	205	19 54	270	39 13	309
11	59 23	359	33 00	050	35 22	088	46 06	180	28 58	206	19 00	271	38 31	309
12	59 21	358	33 42	050	36 16	088	46 05	181	28 34	207	18 07	271	37 49	309
13	59 19	357	34 23	050	37 10	088	46 03	183	28 09	208	17 13	272	37 07	309
14	59 16	356	35 05	051	38 04	089	46 00	184	27 43	209	16 19	272	36 25	309
	◆ CAPELLA		ALDEBARAN		RIGEL		◆ Diphda		FOMALHAUT		Enif		◆ DENEB	
15	35 47	051	38 58	089	19 17	110	45 56	185	27 17	210	41 14	260	35 42	309
16	36 28	051	39 52	090	20 07	110	45 50	187	26 50	211	40 21	261	35 00	309
17	37 10	051	40 46	090	20 58	111	45 43	188	26 22	211	39 28	261	34 18	309
18	37 52	051	41 40	091	21 48	111	45 35	189	25 54	212	38 35	262	33 36	309
19	38 33	051	42 34	091	22 38	112	45 26	191	25 25	213	37 41	262	32 54	309
20	39 15	051	43 28	091	23 28	113	45 15	192	24 55	214	36 48	263	32 12	309
21	39 57	051	44 21	092	24 18	113	45 03	193	24 25	215	35 54	263	31 30	309
22	40 38	050	45 15	092	25 07	114	44 50	195	23 54	215	35 01	264	30 48	309
23	41 20	050	46 09	093	25 56	114	44 36	196	23 23	216	34 07	264	30 06	309
24	42 01	050	47 03	093	26 45	115	44 20	197	22 51	217	33 13	265	29 25	309
25	42 43	050	47 57	094	27 34	116	44 04	199	22 18	218	32 19	265	28 43	309
26	43 24	050	48 51	094	28 23	116	43 46	200	21 45	218	31 26	266	28 01	310
27	44 06	050	49 44	095	29 11	117	43 27	201	21 11	219	30 32	266	27 20	310
28	44 47	050	50 38	095	29 59	118	43 07	202	20 37	220	29 38	267	26 38	310
29	45 28	050	51 32	096	30 46	118	42 46	203	20 03	220	28 44	267	25 57	310
	CAPELLA		◆ ALDEBARAN		RIGEL		◆ Diphda		Alpheratz		DENEB		◆ Kochab	
30	46 09	050	52 25	097	31 34	119	42 24	205	65 18	284	25 16	310	10 27	356
31	46 50	049	53 19	097	32 21	120	42 01	206	64 25	284	24 35	310	10 23	357
32	47 31	049	54 12	098	33 07	120	41 37	207	63 33	284	23 54	310	10 21	357
33	48 12	049	55 06	098	33 54	121	41 12	208	62 41	284	23 13	311	10 18	357
34	48 53	049	55 59	099	34 40	122	40 46	209	61 48	284	22 32	311	10 15	358
35	49 33	049	56 52	100	35 25	123	40 19	210	60 56	284	21 51	311	10 13	358
36	50 14	048	57 45	100	36 10	124	39 52	211	60 03	284	21 10	311	10 11	358
37	50 54	048	58 38	101	36 55	124	39 23	213	59 11	284	20 30	311	10 10	358
38	51 34	048	59 31	102	37 39	125	38 54	214	58 19	284	19 50	312	10 09	359
39	52 13	047	60 24	103	38 23	126	38 23	215	57 26	284	19 09	312	10 07	359
40	52 53	047	61 16	103	39 06	127	37 52	216	56 34	284	18 29	312	10 07	359
41	53 32	047	62 09	104	39 49	128	37 20	217	55 42	284	17 49	312	10 06	000
42	54 11	046	63 01	105	40 32	129	36 48	218	54 50	284	17 10	313	10 06	000
43	54 50	046	63 53	106	41 13	130	36 15	219	53 57	285	16 30	313	10 06	000
44	55 29	045	64 45	107	41 55	131	35 41	220	53 05	285	15 51	313	10 06	000
	◆ CAPELLA		PROCYON		SIRIUS		◆ RIGEL		Acamar		Diphda		◆ Alpheratz	
45	56 07	045	20 13	094	20 27	122	42 35	132	23 45	180	35 06	220	52 13	285
46	56 45	044	21 06	095	21 13	122	43 15	133	23 45	181	34 31	221	51 21	285
47	57 22	044	22 00	095	21 58	123	43 55	134	23 43	182	33 55	222	50 29	285
48	57 59	043	22 54	096	22 43	123	44 33	135	23 41	183	33 18	223	49 37	285
49	58 36	042	23 47	096	23 28	124	45 12	136	23 38	184	32 41	224	48 45	285
50	59 12	042	24 41	097	24 13	125	45 49	137	23 34	184	32 03	225	47 53	286
51	59 48	041	25 35	097	24 57	125	46 25	138	23 30	185	31 25	226	47 01	286
52	60 23	040	26 28	097	25 41	126	47 01	139	23 24	186	30 46	226	46 09	286
53	60 58	040	27 21	098	26 24	127	47 36	140	23 18	187	30 07	227	45 17	286
54	61 32	039	28 15	099	27 07	128	48 10	141	23 12	188	29 27	228	44 26	286
55	62 05	038	29 08	099	27 49	128	48 43	143	23 04	189	28 46	229	43 34	287
56	62 38	037	30 01	100	28 32	129	49 15	144	22 56	189	28 06	230	42 42	287
57	63 10	036	30 55	100	29 13	130	49 47	145	22 46	190	27 24	230	41 51	287
58	63 41	035	31 48	101	29 54	131	50 17	147	22 37	191	26 43	231	40 59	287
59	64 12	034	32 41	101	30 35	131	50 46	148	22 26	192	26 00	232	40 07	287
	◆ Dubhe		PROCYON		SIRIUS		◆ RIGEL		Diphda		◆ Hamal		Mirfak	
60	15 30	028	33 33	102	31 15	132	51 14	149	25 18	232	64 31	271	65 10	347
61	15 55	028	34 26	102	31 55	133	51 41	151	24 35	233	63 37	271	64 57	345
62	16 21	029	35 19	103	32 34	134	52 07	152	23 51	234	62 43	271	64 43	344
63	16 47	029	36 11	103	33 13	135	52 31	154	23 08	235	61 49	272	64 27	342
64	17 13	029	37 04	104	33 51	135	52 54	155	22 24	235	60 55	272	64 10	341
65	17 39	029	37 56	105	34 29	136	53 16	157	21 39	236	60 01	272	63 52	340
66	18 06	029	38 48	105	35 06	137	53 37	158	20 54	236	59 07	273	63 33	339
67	18 32	030	39 40	106	35 42	138	53 56	160	20 09	237	58 13	273	63 13	337
68	18 59	030	40 32	107	36 17	139	54 14	161	19 24	238	57 19	274	62 52	336
69	19 26	030	41 23	107	36 52	140	54 31	163	18 38	238	56 26	274	62 29	335
70	19 53	030	42 15	108	37 27	141	54 45	165	17 52	239	55 32	274	62 06	334
71	20 20	030	43 06	109	38 00	142	54 59	166	17 06	239	54 38	275	61 42	333
72	20 47	030	43 57	109	38 33	143	55 11	168	16 19	240	53 44	275	61 17	332
73	21 15	031	44 48	110	39 05	144	55 21	170	15 32	241	52 51	275	60 51	331
74	21 42	031	45 38	111	39 37	145	55 30	172	14 45	241	51 57	276	60 24	330
	◆ Dubhe		POLLUX		PROCYON		◆ SIRIUS		RIGEL		◆ Hamal		Mirfak	
75	22 10	031	53 06	077	46 29	112	40 07	146	55 37	173	51 03	276	59 57	329
76	22 37	031	53 58	077	47 19	112	40 37	147	55 42	175	50 10	276	59 29	328
77	23 05	031	54 51	078	48 08	113	41 06	148	55 46	177	49 16	277	59 00	327
78	23 33	031	55 44	078	48 58	114	41 33	149	55 48	179	48 23	277	58 30	326
79	24 01	031	56 36	078	49 47	115	42 00	151	55 49	180	47 29	277	58 00	326
80	24 29	031	57 29	078	50 36	116	42 27	152	55 48	182	46 36	278	57 29	325
81	24 57	031	58 22	078	51 24	117	42 52	153	55 45	184	45 42	278	56 58	324
82	25 25	032	59 15	078	52 12	118	43 16	154	55 40	186	44 49	278	56 26	324
83	25 53	032	60 08	079	52 59	119	43 39	155	55 34	187	43 55	278	55 54	323
84	26 22	032	61 00	079	53 47	120	44 01	156	55 27	189	43 02	279	55 21	322
85	26 50	032	61 53	079	54 33	121	44 22	158	55 17	191	42 09	279	54 48	322
86	27 18	032	62 46	079	55 19	122	44 42	159	55 07	192	41 16	279	54 15	321
87	27 47	032	63 39	079	56 05	123	45 01	160	54 54	194	40 22	280	53 41	321
88	28 15	032	64 32	079	56 50	124	45 18	162	54 40	196	39 29	280	53 06	320
89	28 44	032	65 25	079	57 34	125	45 35	163	54 25	198	38 36	280	52 32	320

LHA ♈	Hc	Zn	Hc	Zn	Hc	Zn	Hc	Zn	Hc	Zn	Hc	Zn	Hc	Zn
	Dubhe		◆ REGULUS		PROCYON		SIRIUS		◆ RIGEL		ALDEBARAN		◆ Mirfak	
90	29 12	032	29 57	091	58 17	127	45 50	164	54 08	199	68 28	248	51 57	319
91	29 41	032	30 51	091	59 00	128	46 04	165	53 49	201	67 38	249	51 21	319
92	30 09	032	31 45	092	59 42	129	46 17	167	53 30	202	66 47	251	50 46	318
93	30 38	032	32 39	092	60 24	131	46 29	168	53 08	204	65 56	252	50 10	318
94	31 06	032	33 33	093	61 04	132	46 39	170	52 46	205	65 05	253	49 34	318
95	31 34	032	34 27	093	61 43	134	46 48	171	52 22	207	64 13	254	48 57	317
96	32 03	032	35 20	094	62 21	136	46 56	172	51 57	208	63 21	255	48 21	317
97	32 31	032	36 14	094	62 59	137	47 03	174	51 31	210	62 29	255	47 44	317
98	33 00	032	37 08	095	63 35	139	47 08	175	51 04	211	61 37	256	47 07	317
99	33 28	032	38 02	095	64 09	141	47 12	177	50 35	213	60 45	257	46 30	316
100	33 56	032	38 55	096	64 43	143	47 14	178	50 06	214	59 52	258	45 52	316
101	34 24	031	39 49	096	65 14	145	47 16	179	49 35	215	58 59	259	45 15	316
102	34 52	031	40 43	097	65 45	147	47 16	181	49 03	216	58 06	259	44 37	316
103	35 20	031	41 36	097	66 13	149	47 14	182	48 31	218	57 13	260	43 59	315
104	35 48	031	42 30	098	66 40	151	47 11	184	47 57	219	56 20	261	43 21	315
	Dubhe		◆ REGULUS		Alphard		SIRIUS		◆ RIGEL		ALDEBARAN		◆ CAPELLA	
105	36 16	031	43 23	098	39 58	129	47 07	185	47 23	220	55 27	261	61 28	321
106	36 44	031	44 16	099	40 39	130	47 02	186	46 48	221	54 33	262	60 54	320
107	37 12	031	45 10	100	41 20	131	46 55	188	46 12	222	53 40	263	60 19	320
108	37 39	031	46 03	100	42 01	132	46 47	189	45 35	224	52 46	263	59 44	319
109	38 07	030	46 56	101	42 41	133	46 38	191	44 58	225	51 53	264	59 08	318
110	38 34	030	47 49	101	43 20	134	46 28	192	44 19	226	50 59	264	58 32	317
111	39 01	030	48 41	102	43 59	135	46 16	193	43 40	227	50 05	265	57 55	317
112	39 28	030	49 34	103	44 36	136	46 03	195	43 01	228	49 12	265	57 18	316
113	39 55	030	50 27	103	45 14	137	45 49	196	42 20	229	48 18	266	56 41	316
114	40 21	029	51 19	104	45 50	138	45 33	197	41 39	230	47 24	266	56 03	315
115	40 48	029	52 11	105	46 26	139	45 17	199	40 58	231	46 30	267	55 25	315
116	41 14	029	53 03	105	47 00	140	44 59	200	40 16	232	45 36	267	54 46	314
117	41 40	029	53 55	106	47 34	142	44 40	201	39 33	233	44 43	268	54 07	314
118	42 06	028	54 47	107	48 07	143	44 20	202	38 50	233	43 49	268	53 28	313
119	42 31	028	55 38	108	48 40	144	43 59	204	38 07	234	42 55	269	52 49	313
	◆ Dubhe		REGULUS		◆ Alphard		SIRIUS		RIGEL		◆ ALDEBARAN		CAPELLA	
120	42 57	028	56 30	109	49 11	145	43 37	205	37 23	235	42 01	269	52 09	313
121	43 22	028	57 20	110	49 41	147	43 13	206	36 38	236	41 07	270	51 30	312
122	43 47	027	58 11	111	50 10	148	42 49	207	35 54	237	40 13	270	50 50	312
123	44 11	027	59 01	112	50 38	149	42 24	208	35 08	238	39 19	271	50 10	312
124	44 35	027	59 51	113	51 05	151	41 58	210	34 23	238	38 25	271	49 29	311
125	44 59	026	60 41	114	51 31	152	41 31	211	33 36	239	37 31	271	48 49	311
126	45 23	026	61 30	115	51 55	154	41 03	212	32 50	240	36 37	272	48 08	311
127	45 46	025	62 19	116	52 18	155	40 34	213	32 03	241	35 43	272	47 27	311
128	46 09	025	63 07	117	52 40	157	40 04	214	31 16	241	34 49	273	46 46	311
129	46 32	025	63 55	118	53 01	158	39 34	215	30 29	242	33 56	273	46 05	310
130	46 54	024	64 42	120	53 21	160	39 02	216	29 41	243	33 02	273	45 24	310
131	47 16	024	65 29	121	53 39	161	38 30	217	28 53	243	32 08	274	44 43	310
132	47 38	023	66 15	123	53 55	163	37 57	218	28 05	244	31 14	274	44 01	310
133	47 59	023	67 00	124	54 10	165	37 23	219	27 16	245	30 20	275	43 20	310
134	48 20	022	67 44	126	54 24	166	36 49	220	26 27	245	29 27	275	42 39	310
	Dubhe		◆ ARCTURUS		SPICA		Alphard		◆ SIRIUS		BETELGEUSE		◆ CAPELLA	
135	48 40	022	17 43	077	15 26	111	54 36	168	36 14	221	42 30	255	41 57	310
136	49 00	021	18 35	077	16 16	112	54 47	170	35 38	222	41 38	256	41 16	310
137	49 19	021	19 28	078	17 06	112	54 56	171	35 02	223	40 46	257	40 34	310
138	49 38	020	20 21	078	17 56	113	55 03	173	34 25	224	39 53	257	39 52	309
139	49 56	020	21 14	078	18 46	113	55 09	175	33 47	225	39 00	258	39 11	309
140	50 14	019	22 06	079	19 35	114	55 13	176	33 09	225	38 08	258	38 29	309
141	50 32	019	22 59	079	20 24	114	55 16	178	32 31	226	37 15	259	37 47	309
142	50 48	018	23 52	079	21 14	115	55 17	180	31 51	227	36 22	260	37 06	309
143	51 05	017	24 45	080	22 02	116	55 16	182	31 12	228	35 29	260	36 24	309
144	51 20	017	25 39	080	22 51	116	55 14	183	30 31	229	34 35	261	35 42	309
145	51 36	016	26 32	081	23 39	117	55 10	185	29 50	230	33 42	261	35 01	309
146	51 50	015	27 25	081	24 27	117	55 04	187	29 09	230	32 49	262	34 19	310
147	52 04	015	28 18	081	25 15	118	54 57	188	28 28	231	31 55	262	33 38	310
148	52 18	014	29 12	082	26 02	119	54 48	190	27 45	232	31 02	263	32 56	310
149	52 30	013	30 05	082	26 49	119	54 38	192	27 03	232	30 08	263	32 15	310
	Dubhe		◆ ARCTURUS		SPICA		◆ Alphard		SIRIUS		POLLUX		◆ CAPELLA	
150	52 42	013	30 58	082	27 36	120	54 26	194	26 20	233	60 14	281	31 33	310
151	52 54	012	31 52	083	28 23	121	54 13	195	25 36	234	59 21	282	30 52	310
152	53 05	011	32 45	083	29 09	121	53 58	197	24 53	235	58 28	282	30 10	310
153	53 15	010	33 39	084	29 55	122	53 41	198	24 09	235	57 35	282	29 29	310
154	53 24	010	34 33	084	30 41	123	53 24	200	23 24	236	56 42	282	28 48	310
155	53 33	009	35 26	084	31 26	124	53 04	202	22 39	237	55 50	282	28 07	310
156	53 41	008	36 20	085	32 10	124	52 44	203	21 54	237	54 57	282	27 26	310
157	53 48	007	37 14	085	32 55	125	52 22	205	21 09	238	54 04	283	26 45	311
158	53 54	007	38 07	085	33 39	126	51 59	206	20 23	238	53 12	283	26 04	311
159	54 00	006	39 01	086	34 22	127	51 35	208	19 37	239	52 19	283	25 23	311
160	54 05	005	39 55	086	35 05	127	51 09	209	18 50	240	51 27	283	24 42	311
161	54 10	004	40 49	087	35 48	128	50 42	210	18 03	240	50 34	283	24 01	311
162	54 13	003	41 43	087	36 30	129	50 15	212	17 17	241	49 42	283	23 21	311
163	54 16	003	42 36	087	37 12	130	49 46	213	16 29	241	48 49	284	22 41	312
164	54 18	002	43 30	088	37 53	131	49 16	214	15 42	242	47 57	284	22 00	312
	◆ Dubhe		Alkaid		ARCTURUS		◆ SPICA		Alphard		◆ PROCYON		POLLUX	
165	54 19	001	50 10	043	44 24	088	38 33	132	48 45	216	37 58	255	47 04	284
166	54 20	000	50 47	043	45 18	089	39 13	133	48 13	217	37 06	256	46 12	284
167	54 20	359	51 23	042	46 12	089	39 52	134	47 40	218	36 14	257	45 20	284
168	54 19	359	51 59	042	47 06	089	40 31	135	47 06	219	35 21	257	44 28	285
169	54 17	358	52 35	041	48 00	090	41 09	136	46 31	221	34 28	258	43 36	285
170	54 14	357	53 11	041	48 54	090	41 47	137	45 56	222	33 36	258	42 43	285
171	54 11	356	53 46	041	49 48	091	42 23	138	45 20	223	32 43	259	41 51	285
172	54 07	355	54 21	040	50 42	091	42 59	139	44 43	224	31 50	259	40 59	286
173	54 02	354	54 55	039	51 36	092	43 35	140	44 05	225	30 57	260	40 07	286
174	53 56	354	55 29	039	52 29	092	44 09	141	43 26	226	30 04	260	39 16	286
175	53 50	353	56 03	038	53 23	093	44 43	142	42 47	227	29 10	261	38 24	286
176	53 43	352	56 36	038	54 17	093	45 15	143	42 07	228	28 17	261	37 32	286
177	53 35	351	57 09	037	55 11	094	45 47	144	41 27	229	27 24	262	36 40	287
178	53 27	351	57 41	036	56 05	094	46 18	146	40 46	230	26 30	262	35 49	287
179	53 18	350	58 13	036	56 59	095	46 48	147	40 04	231	25 37	263	34 57	287

LHA ♈	Hc	Zn	Hc	Zn	Hc	Zn	Hc	Zn	Hc	Zn	Hc	Zn	Hc	Zn
	◆ Alkaid		Alphecca		◆ SPICA		Gienah		REGULUS		◆ POLLUX		Dubhe	
180	58 44	035	42 08	077	47 17	148	46 11	174	60 21	247	34 06	287	53 08	349
181	59 14	034	43 00	077	47 45	149	46 16	176	59 31	248	33 14	288	52 57	348
182	59 44	033	43 53	077	48 12	151	46 20	177	58 41	249	32 23	288	52 46	348
183	60 14	032	44 45	077	48 38	152	46 22	178	57 50	250	31 32	288	52 34	347
184	60 42	031	45 38	078	49 03	153	46 22	180	56 59	251	30 41	289	52 22	346
185	61 10	031	46 30	078	49 27	155	46 22	181	56 08	252	29 50	289	52 09	346
186	61 37	030	47 23	078	49 49	156	46 20	183	55 17	252	28 59	289	51 55	345
187	62 03	029	48 16	078	50 11	157	46 17	184	54 25	253	28 08	289	51 40	344
188	62 28	027	49 09	079	50 31	159	46 13	185	53 34	254	27 17	290	51 25	344
189	62 53	026	50 02	079	50 50	160	46 07	187	52 42	255	26 26	290	51 10	343
190	63 16	025	50 55	079	51 07	162	46 00	188	51 50	256	25 35	290	50 54	342
191	63 39	024	51 48	079	51 23	163	45 52	189	50 57	256	24 45	290	50 37	342
192	64 00	023	52 41	079	51 38	165	45 43	191	50 05	257	23 54	291	50 20	341
193	64 20	021	53 34	080	51 51	166	45 32	192	49 12	258	23 04	291	50 02	341
194	64 39	020	54 27	080	52 03	168	45 20	193	48 20	258	22 14	291	49 44	340
	◆ Kochab		VEGA		Rasalhague		◆ ANTARES		SPICA		◆ REGULUS		Dubhe	
195	39 46	010	20 05	056	24 16	087	17 04	132	52 14	170	47 27	259	49 25	339
196	39 55	009	20 50	056	25 10	088	17 44	133	52 23	171	46 34	260	49 06	339
197	40 04	009	21 35	056	26 04	088	18 24	133	52 30	173	45 41	260	48 46	338
198	40 12	009	22 20	056	26 58	089	19 03	134	52 36	174	44 47	261	48 26	338
199	40 20	008	23 05	057	27 52	089	19 41	135	52 41	176	43 54	261	48 06	337
200	40 27	008	23 50	057	28 45	090	20 20	135	52 44	178	43 01	262	47 45	337
201	40 35	008	24 35	057	29 39	090	20 57	136	52 45	179	42 07	262	47 23	336
202	40 42	007	25 20	057	30 33	090	21 35	137	52 45	181	41 14	263	47 01	336
203	40 49	007	26 06	057	31 27	091	22 12	137	52 44	182	40 20	263	46 39	336
204	40 55	007	26 51	058	32 21	091	22 48	138	52 41	184	39 27	264	46 17	335
205	41 01	006	27 37	058	33 15	092	23 24	139	52 36	186	38 33	265	45 54	335
206	41 07	006	28 23	058	34 09	092	23 59	139	52 30	187	37 39	265	45 31	334
207	41 12	006	29 08	058	35 03	093	24 34	140	52 23	189	36 46	266	45 07	334
208	41 17	005	29 54	058	35 57	093	25 08	141	52 14	190	35 52	266	44 43	334
209	41 22	005	30 40	059	36 51	094	25 42	142	52 03	192	34 58	266	44 19	333
	Kochab		◆ VEGA		Rasalhague		ANTARES		◆ SPICA		REGULUS		◆ Dubhe	
210	41 27	005	31 26	059	37 44	094	26 15	142	51 51	194	34 04	267	43 55	333
211	41 31	004	32 12	059	38 38	095	26 48	143	51 38	195	33 10	267	43 30	333
212	41 35	004	32 59	059	39 32	095	27 19	144	51 23	197	32 16	268	43 05	332
213	41 38	004	33 45	059	40 26	096	27 51	145	51 07	198	31 23	268	42 40	332
214	41 41	003	34 31	059	41 19	096	28 21	146	50 49	200	30 29	269	42 14	332
215	41 44	003	35 18	059	42 13	097	28 51	147	50 31	201	29 35	269	41 48	331
216	41 47	002	36 04	060	43 06	097	29 21	147	50 11	203	28 41	270	41 22	331
217	41 49	002	36 51	060	44 00	098	29 49	148	49 49	204	27 47	270	40 56	331
218	41 51	002	37 37	060	44 53	098	30 17	149	49 27	205	26 53	271	40 30	331
219	41 52	001	38 24	060	45 47	099	30 45	150	49 03	207	25 59	271	40 03	330
220	41 53	001	39 10	060	46 40	099	31 11	151	48 38	208	25 05	271	39 36	330
221	41 54	001	39 57	060	47 33	100	31 37	152	48 12	209	24 11	272	39 10	330
222	41 54	000	40 44	060	48 26	101	32 02	153	47 45	211	23 17	272	38 43	330
223	41 54	000	41 30	060	49 19	101	32 26	154	47 17	212	22 23	273	38 15	330
224	41 54	000	42 17	060	50 12	102	32 49	155	46 48	213	21 30	273	37 48	329
	VEGA		◆ ALTAIR		Nunki		ANTARES		◆ SPICA		Denebola		◆ Alkaid	
225	43 04	060	19 14	089	12 44	128	33 12	156	46 18	214	44 12	265	62 54	334
226	43 51	060	20 07	090	13 26	129	33 34	157	45 47	216	43 18	266	62 30	333
227	44 37	060	21 01	090	14 08	129	33 55	158	45 15	217	42 24	266	62 05	332
228	45 24	060	21 55	091	14 50	130	34 15	159	44 42	218	41 30	267	61 39	331
229	46 11	060	22 49	091	15 31	130	34 34	160	44 09	219	40 36	267	61 12	330
230	46 58	060	23 43	091	16 12	131	34 52	161	43 34	220	39 43	268	60 44	329
231	47 44	060	24 37	092	16 53	132	35 09	162	42 59	221	38 49	268	60 15	328
232	48 31	060	25 31	092	17 33	132	35 26	163	42 23	222	37 55	268	59 46	327
233	49 18	060	26 25	093	18 13	133	35 41	164	41 46	223	37 01	269	59 16	326
234	50 04	060	27 19	093	18 52	133	35 56	165	41 09	224	36 07	269	58 46	325
235	50 51	060	28 13	094	19 31	134	36 09	166	40 31	225	35 13	270	58 15	324
236	51 37	060	29 06	094	20 10	135	36 22	167	39 52	226	34 19	270	57 43	324
237	52 24	059	30 00	095	20 48	135	36 33	168	39 13	227	33 25	271	57 11	323
238	53 10	059	30 54	095	21 25	136	36 44	169	38 33	228	32 31	271	56 38	322
239	53 57	059	31 47	096	22 03	137	36 53	170	37 52	229	31 37	272	56 05	322
	◆ VEGA		ALTAIR		Nunki		◆ ANTARES		SPICA		ARCTURUS		◆ Alkaid	
240	54 43	059	32 41	096	22 39	138	37 02	171	37 11	230	65 09	259	55 32	321
241	55 29	059	33 35	097	23 15	138	37 09	173	36 30	231	64 16	260	54 57	321
242	56 15	058	34 28	097	23 51	139	37 16	174	35 48	232	63 22	261	54 23	320
243	57 01	058	35 22	098	24 26	140	37 21	175	35 05	233	62 29	261	53 48	320
244	57 46	058	36 15	098	25 01	140	37 25	176	34 22	233	61 36	262	53 13	319
245	58 32	057	37 08	099	25 35	141	37 29	177	33 38	234	60 42	263	52 37	319
246	59 17	057	38 02	099	26 08	142	37 31	178	32 54	235	59 49	263	52 02	318
247	60 02	057	38 55	100	26 41	143	37 32	179	32 10	236	58 55	264	51 25	318
248	60 47	056	39 48	100	27 14	144	37 32	180	31 25	236	58 02	265	50 49	317
249	61 32	056	40 41	101	27 45	144	37 31	182	30 40	237	57 08	265	50 12	317
250	62 16	055	41 34	102	28 16	145	37 29	183	29 55	238	56 14	266	49 36	317
251	63 01	055	42 27	102	28 47	146	37 26	184	29 09	239	55 20	266	48 58	316
252	63 44	054	43 19	103	29 17	147	37 22	185	28 23	239	54 26	267	48 21	316
253	64 28	053	44 12	104	29 46	148	37 17	186	27 36	240	53 33	267	47 44	316
254	65 11	053	45 04	104	30 14	149	37 10	187	26 49	241	52 39	268	47 06	315
	◆ DENEB		ALTAIR		Nunki		◆ ANTARES		SPICA		ARCTURUS		◆ Alkaid	
255	42 03	051	45 56	105	30 42	150	37 03	188	26 02	241	51 45	268	46 28	315
256	42 45	051	46 48	106	31 09	150	36 55	189	25 14	242	50 51	269	45 50	315
257	43 27	051	47 40	106	31 35	151	36 45	191	24 27	243	49 57	269	45 12	315
258	44 09	051	48 32	107	32 00	152	36 35	192	23 39	243	49 03	270	44 33	315
259	44 51	051	49 23	108	32 25	153	36 24	193	22 50	244	48 09	270	43 55	314
260	45 33	051	50 15	108	32 49	154	36 11	194	22 02	244	47 15	271	43 16	314
261	46 14	051	51 06	109	33 12	155	35 58	195	21 13	245	46 21	271	42 38	314
262	46 56	050	51 56	110	33 34	156	35 44	196	20 24	246	45 27	271	41 59	314
263	47 37	050	52 47	111	33 55	157	35 28	197	19 35	246	44 33	272	41 20	314
264	48 19	050	53 37	112	34 16	158	35 12	198	18 45	247	43 40	272	40 41	314
265	49 00	050	54 27	113	34 35	159	34 55	199	17 56	247	42 46	273	40 02	314
266	49 41	050	55 17	114	34 54	160	34 37	200	17 06	248	41 52	273	39 23	314
267	50 22	049	56 06	115	35 12	161	34 18	201	16 16	248	40 58	273	38 44	314
268	51 03	049	56 55	116	35 29	162	33 58	202	15 26	249	40 04	274	38 05	314
269	51 44	049	57 43	117	35 45	163	33 37	203	14 35	249	39 10	274	37 26	313

LHA ♈	Hc	Zn	Hc	Zn	Hc	Zn	Hc	Zn	Hc	Zn	Hc	Zn	Hc	Zn
	◆ DENEB		ALTAIR		◆ Nunki		ANTARES		◆ ARCTURUS		Alkaid		Kochab	
270	52 24	048	58 31	118	36 00	164	33 16	204	38 17	275	36 47	313	36 03	346
271	53 04	048	59 18	119	36 14	165	32 53	205	37 23	275	36 08	313	35 50	345
272	53 44	048	60 05	120	36 27	167	32 30	206	36 29	275	35 28	313	35 36	345
273	54 24	047	60 52	121	36 39	168	32 06	207	35 35	276	34 49	313	35 22	345
274	55 04	047	61 37	123	36 50	169	31 41	208	34 42	276	34 10	313	35 08	345
275	55 43	046	62 22	124	37 00	170	31 15	209	33 48	276	33 31	313	34 54	345
276	56 22	046	63 07	126	37 09	171	30 49	210	32 55	277	32 52	313	34 40	344
277	57 00	045	63 50	127	37 17	172	30 22	211	32 01	277	32 13	314	34 25	344
278	57 39	045	64 33	129	37 24	173	29 54	212	31 08	278	31 34	314	34 10	344
279	58 16	044	65 14	130	37 30	174	29 26	212	30 14	278	30 55	314	33 56	344
280	58 54	044	65 55	132	37 35	175	28 56	213	29 21	278	30 16	314	33 41	344
281	59 31	043	66 35	134	37 38	177	28 26	214	28 27	279	29 37	314	33 26	344
282	60 07	042	67 13	136	37 41	178	27 56	215	27 34	279	28 58	314	33 11	344
283	60 44	042	67 50	138	37 43	179	27 25	216	26 41	279	28 19	314	32 55	344
284	61 19	041	68 25	140	37 43	180	26 53	217	25 48	280	27 40	314	32 40	343
	DENEB		◆ Alpheratz		Enif		◆ Nunki		ANTARES		◆ ARCTURUS		Kochab	
285	61 54	040	22 44	067	47 52	105	37 43	181	26 20	217	24 55	280	32 25	343
286	62 28	039	23 33	068	48 44	105	37 41	182	25 47	218	24 02	280	32 09	343
287	63 02	038	24 23	068	49 36	106	37 39	183	25 14	219	23 09	281	31 53	343
288	63 35	037	25 13	068	50 27	107	37 35	184	24 40	220	22 16	281	31 38	343
289	64 07	036	26 04	069	51 19	108	37 30	186	24 05	220	21 23	282	31 22	343
290	64 38	035	26 54	069	52 10	108	37 25	187	23 30	221	20 30	282	31 06	343
291	65 09	034	27 44	069	53 01	109	37 18	188	22 54	222	19 37	282	30 50	343
292	65 39	033	28 35	069	53 52	110	37 10	189	22 18	223	18 45	283	30 34	343
293	66 07	031	29 25	070	54 43	111	37 01	190	21 41	223	17 52	283	30 18	343
294	66 35	030	30 16	070	55 33	112	36 51	191	21 04	224	16 59	283	30 02	343
295	67 01	029	31 06	070	56 23	113	36 40	192	20 26	225	16 07	284	29 46	342
296	67 27	027	31 57	070	57 12	114	36 28	193	19 48	225	15 15	284	29 29	342
297	67 51	026	32 48	071	58 01	115	36 15	194	19 09	226	14 22	285	29 13	342
298	68 14	024	33 39	071	58 50	116	36 01	196	18 30	227	13 30	285	28 57	342
299	68 35	023	34 30	071	59 38	117	35 46	197	17 51	227	12 38	285	28 40	342
	Schedar		◆ Alpheratz		FOMALHAUT		◆ Nunki		Rasalhague		◆ VEGA		Kochab	
300	32 10	038	35 21	071	19 54	139	35 30	198	53 32	255	68 28	312	28 24	342
301	32 43	038	36 12	072	20 29	140	35 14	199	52 40	256	67 47	311	28 08	342
302	33 16	038	37 03	072	21 03	141	34 56	200	51 47	257	67 06	310	27 51	342
303	33 49	038	37 55	072	21 37	142	34 37	201	50 55	257	66 24	309	27 35	342
304	34 22	038	38 46	072	22 10	142	34 18	202	50 02	258	65 42	308	27 18	342
305	34 55	038	39 37	073	22 43	143	33 57	203	49 09	259	64 59	307	27 02	342
306	35 28	038	40 29	073	23 15	144	33 36	204	48 16	259	64 16	306	26 45	342
307	36 01	037	41 20	073	23 47	145	33 14	205	47 23	260	63 32	306	26 29	342
308	36 33	037	42 12	073	24 18	145	32 51	206	46 30	261	62 48	305	26 13	342
309	37 06	037	43 04	073	24 48	146	32 27	207	45 37	261	62 04	305	25 56	342
310	37 39	037	43 55	074	25 18	147	32 03	208	44 43	262	61 20	304	25 40	342
311	38 11	037	44 47	074	25 47	148	31 37	209	43 50	262	60 35	304	25 23	342
312	38 44	037	45 39	074	26 16	148	31 11	209	42 56	263	59 50	303	25 07	342
313	39 16	037	46 31	074	26 44	149	30 44	210	42 03	263	59 05	303	24 51	342
314	39 48	037	47 23	074	27 11	150	30 17	211	41 09	264	58 19	302	24 34	342
	◆ Mirfak		Hamal		Diphda		◆ FOMALHAUT		ALTAIR		◆ VEGA		Kochab	
315	15 45	042	21 07	073	20 02	123	27 37	151	66 25	227	57 34	302	24 18	343
316	16 21	042	21 59	074	20 47	123	28 03	152	65 45	228	56 48	302	24 02	343
317	16 57	042	22 51	074	21 32	124	28 28	153	65 04	230	56 02	302	23 46	343
318	17 33	042	23 43	074	22 16	125	28 53	154	64 22	232	55 16	301	23 30	343
319	18 10	043	24 34	075	23 00	125	29 16	154	63 40	233	54 30	301	23 14	343
320	18 46	043	25 27	075	23 44	126	29 39	155	62 56	235	53 44	301	22 58	343
321	19 23	043	26 19	075	24 27	127	30 01	156	62 12	236	52 57	301	22 42	343
322	20 00	043	27 11	076	25 10	127	30 22	157	61 26	238	52 11	301	22 26	343
323	20 37	043	28 03	076	25 53	128	30 43	158	60 40	239	51 25	300	22 10	343
324	21 14	044	28 55	076	26 35	129	31 03	159	59 54	240	50 38	300	21 55	343
325	21 51	044	29 48	077	27 17	130	31 22	160	59 07	241	49 51	300	21 39	343
326	22 29	044	30 40	077	27 59	130	31 40	161	58 19	242	49 05	300	21 24	343
327	23 06	044	31 33	077	28 39	131	31 57	162	57 31	244	48 18	300	21 08	343
328	23 44	044	32 25	077	29 20	132	32 13	163	56 43	245	47 31	300	20 53	344
329	24 21	044	33 18	078	30 00	133	32 28	164	55 54	246	46 45	300	20 38	344
	◆ Mirfak		Hamal		Diphda		◆ FOMALHAUT		ALTAIR		◆ VEGA		Kochab	
330	24 59	045	34 11	078	30 39	133	32 43	165	55 05	247	45 58	300	20 23	344
331	25 37	045	35 04	078	31 18	134	32 57	166	54 15	248	45 11	300	20 08	344
332	26 15	045	35 57	079	31 57	135	33 09	167	53 25	248	44 24	300	19 53	344
333	26 53	045	36 50	079	32 35	136	33 21	168	52 35	249	43 38	300	19 38	344
334	27 31	045	37 42	079	33 12	137	33 32	169	51 44	250	42 51	300	19 23	344
335	28 10	045	38 36	080	33 48	138	33 42	170	50 53	251	42 04	300	19 09	344
336	28 48	045	39 29	080	34 25	138	33 51	171	50 02	252	41 17	300	18 54	345
337	29 26	045	40 22	080	35 00	139	33 59	172	49 11	252	40 31	300	18 40	345
338	30 05	045	41 15	081	35 35	140	34 06	173	48 19	253	39 44	300	18 26	345
339	30 43	046	42 08	081	36 09	141	34 12	174	47 28	254	38 57	300	18 12	345
340	31 22	046	43 01	081	36 42	142	34 17	175	46 36	255	38 11	300	17 58	345
341	32 00	046	43 55	082	37 15	143	34 21	176	45 44	255	37 24	300	17 44	345
342	32 39	046	44 48	082	37 47	144	34 24	177	44 51	256	36 38	300	17 31	345
343	33 18	046	45 41	082	38 18	145	34 26	178	43 59	257	35 51	301	17 17	346
344	33 56	046	46 35	082	38 48	146	34 27	179	43 06	257	35 05	301	17 04	346
	◆ CAPELLA		ALDEBARAN		Diphda		◆ FOMALHAUT		ALTAIR		◆ VEGA		Kochab	
345	15 29	046	12 14	077	39 18	147	34 27	180	42 14	258	34 18	301	16 51	346
346	16 08	046	13 07	078	39 47	148	34 27	181	41 21	258	33 32	301	16 38	346
347	16 47	046	14 00	078	40 15	149	34 25	183	40 28	259	32 46	301	16 25	346
348	17 26	047	14 52	079	40 42	151	34 22	184	39 35	260	32 00	301	16 13	347
349	18 05	047	15 45	079	41 08	152	34 18	185	38 42	260	31 14	301	16 00	347
350	18 45	047	16 38	079	41 33	153	34 13	186	37 49	261	30 27	301	15 48	347
351	19 24	047	17 31	080	41 57	154	34 07	187	36 55	261	29 42	302	15 36	347
352	20 04	048	18 24	080	42 20	155	34 01	188	36 02	262	28 56	302	15 24	347
353	20 44	048	19 17	081	42 42	156	33 53	189	35 09	262	28 10	302	15 12	347
354	21 24	048	20 11	081	43 04	158	33 44	190	34 15	263	27 24	302	15 00	348
355	22 04	048	21 04	081	43 24	159	33 34	191	33 22	263	26 39	302	14 49	348
356	22 45	048	21 57	082	43 43	160	33 24	192	32 28	264	25 53	303	14 38	348
357	23 25	049	22 51	082	44 01	161	33 12	193	31 34	264	25 08	303	14 27	348
358	24 06	049	23 44	082	44 17	162	33 00	194	30 41	265	24 22	303	14 16	349
359	24 46	049	24 38	083	44 33	164	32 46	195	29 47	265	23 37	303	14 05	349

LHA ♈	Hc	Zn	Hc	Zn	Hc	Zn	Hc	Zn	Hc	Zn	Hc	Zn	Hc	Zn
	Schedar		◆ CAPELLA		ALDEBARAN		◆ Diphda		FOMALHAUT		◆ ALTAIR		DENEB	
0	57 30	011	24 47	049	25 24	083	45 45	165	33 30	196	28 57	266	45 35	310
1	57 40	010	25 28	049	26 18	083	45 59	166	33 14	197	28 03	267	44 53	310
2	57 49	009	26 09	049	27 12	083	46 12	167	32 58	198	27 09	267	44 11	310
3	57 56	008	26 51	049	28 06	084	46 23	169	32 40	199	26 14	268	43 30	310
4	58 03	007	27 32	049	29 00	084	46 33	170	32 22	200	25 20	268	42 48	310
5	58 09	006	28 13	049	29 54	085	46 41	172	32 03	201	24 26	269	42 06	310
6	58 13	005	28 54	050	30 48	085	46 49	173	31 43	202	23 31	269	41 24	309
7	58 17	003	29 36	050	31 42	085	46 55	174	31 23	203	22 37	269	40 42	309
8	58 20	002	30 17	050	32 37	086	46 59	176	31 01	204	21 43	270	40 00	309
9	58 22	001	30 59	050	33 31	086	47 03	177	30 39	205	20 48	270	39 18	309
10	58 23	000	31 40	050	34 25	086	47 05	178	30 16	206	19 54	271	38 36	309
11	58 23	359	32 22	050	35 19	087	47 06	180	29 52	206	18 59	271	37 53	309
12	58 21	358	33 03	050	36 14	087	47 05	181	29 27	207	18 05	272	37 11	309
13	58 19	357	33 45	050	37 08	088	47 03	183	29 02	208	17 11	272	36 29	309
14	58 16	356	34 27	050	38 02	088	47 00	184	28 36	209	16 16	272	35 47	309
	◆ CAPELLA		ALDEBARAN		RIGEL		◆ Diphda		FOMALHAUT		Enif		◆ DENEB	
15	35 08	050	38 57	088	19 37	109	46 56	185	28 09	210	41 24	261	35 05	309
16	35 50	050	39 51	089	20 28	110	46 50	187	27 42	211	40 30	262	34 23	309
17	36 32	050	40 45	089	21 19	111	46 43	188	27 14	212	39 37	262	33 40	309
18	37 13	050	41 40	090	22 10	111	46 34	190	26 45	212	38 43	263	32 58	309
19	37 55	050	42 34	090	23 01	112	46 25	191	26 15	213	37 49	263	32 16	309
20	38 37	050	43 29	091	23 51	112	46 14	192	25 45	214	36 55	264	31 34	309
21	39 18	050	44 23	091	24 41	113	46 01	194	25 14	215	36 01	264	30 52	309
22	40 00	050	45 17	091	25 31	113	45 48	195	24 43	216	35 07	265	30 10	310
23	40 41	050	46 12	092	26 21	114	45 33	196	24 11	216	34 12	265	29 28	310
24	41 23	050	47 06	092	27 11	115	45 17	198	23 39	217	33 18	266	28 47	310
25	42 04	050	48 00	093	28 00	115	45 00	199	23 06	218	32 24	266	28 05	310
26	42 46	049	48 55	093	28 49	116	44 42	200	22 32	219	31 30	266	27 23	310
27	43 27	049	49 49	094	29 38	116	44 23	201	21 58	219	30 35	267	26 41	310
28	44 08	049	50 43	094	30 26	117	44 02	203	21 23	220	29 41	267	26 00	310
29	44 49	049	51 37	095	31 15	118	43 41	204	20 48	221	28 47	268	25 18	310
	CAPELLA		◆ ALDEBARAN		RIGEL		Acamar		◆ Diphda		Alpheratz		◆ DENEB	
30	45 30	049	52 32	095	32 03	119	23 20	168	43 18	205	65 02	286	24 37	311
31	46 11	049	53 26	096	32 50	119	23 31	169	42 55	206	64 10	286	23 56	311
32	46 52	048	54 20	096	33 37	120	23 41	169	42 30	207	63 18	286	23 14	311
33	47 32	048	55 14	097	34 24	121	23 51	170	42 05	209	62 25	286	22 33	311
34	48 13	048	56 08	098	35 11	121	24 00	171	41 38	210	61 33	286	21 52	311
35	48 53	048	57 02	098	35 57	122	24 08	172	41 11	211	60 41	286	21 11	311
36	49 33	047	57 55	099	36 43	123	24 15	173	40 43	212	59 48	286	20 31	312
37	50 13	047	58 49	099	37 29	124	24 22	174	40 13	213	58 56	286	19 50	312
38	50 53	047	59 43	100	38 14	125	24 27	174	39 43	214	58 03	286	19 10	312
39	51 32	046	60 36	101	38 58	125	24 32	175	39 13	215	57 11	286	18 29	312
40	52 12	046	61 29	102	39 42	126	24 36	176	38 41	216	56 19	286	17 49	312
41	52 51	046	62 23	102	40 26	127	24 40	177	38 08	217	55 26	286	17 09	313
42	53 29	045	63 16	103	41 09	128	24 42	178	37 35	218	54 34	286	16 29	313
43	54 08	045	64 09	104	41 51	129	24 44	179	37 01	219	53 42	286	15 49	313
44	54 46	044	65 01	105	42 33	130	24 45	179	36 27	220	52 49	286	15 10	313
	CAPELLA		◆ POLLUX		PROCYON		SIRIUS		◆ Acamar		Diphda		◆ Alpheratz	
45	55 24	044	26 50	070	20 17	094	20 58	121	24 45	180	35 51	221	51 57	286
46	56 01	043	27 42	070	21 11	094	21 45	122	24 45	181	35 15	222	51 05	286
47	56 38	043	28 33	070	22 05	095	22 31	122	24 43	182	34 39	223	50 13	286
48	57 15	042	29 24	071	22 59	095	23 16	123	24 41	183	34 02	224	49 20	286
49	57 51	041	30 15	071	23 53	096	24 02	124	24 38	184	33 24	224	48 28	287
50	58 27	041	31 07	071	24 48	096	24 47	124	24 34	184	32 46	225	47 36	287
51	59 02	040	31 58	071	25 42	097	25 32	125	24 30	185	32 07	226	46 44	287
52	59 37	039	32 50	072	26 36	097	26 16	126	24 24	186	31 27	227	45 52	287
53	60 11	038	33 41	072	27 30	097	27 00	126	24 18	187	30 47	228	45 00	287
54	60 45	038	34 33	072	28 23	098	27 43	127	24 11	188	30 07	229	44 08	287
55	61 17	037	35 25	072	29 17	098	28 26	128	24 03	189	29 26	229	43 16	287
56	61 50	036	36 17	073	30 11	099	29 09	129	23 55	189	28 44	230	42 24	288
57	62 21	035	37 09	073	31 05	099	29 51	129	23 45	190	28 02	231	41 33	288
58	62 52	034	38 01	073	31 58	100	30 33	130	23 35	191	27 20	231	40 41	288
59	63 22	033	38 53	073	32 52	101	31 15	131	23 25	192	26 37	232	39 49	288
	◆ CAPELLA		PROCYON		◆ SIRIUS		RIGEL		Diphda		◆ Hamal		Mirfak	
60	63 51	032	33 45	101	31 55	132	52 05	149	25 54	233	64 29	273	64 12	347
61	64 19	030	34 39	102	32 36	132	52 33	150	25 11	234	63 35	273	63 59	346
62	64 46	029	35 32	102	33 16	133	53 00	152	24 27	234	62 40	273	63 45	344
63	65 12	028	36 25	103	33 55	134	53 25	153	23 42	235	61 46	274	63 30	343
64	65 37	027	37 18	103	34 34	135	53 49	155	22 58	236	60 52	274	63 13	342
65	66 00	025	38 11	104	35 12	136	54 11	156	22 13	236	59 58	274	62 56	340
66	66 23	024	39 03	104	35 49	137	54 33	158	21 27	237	59 03	275	62 37	339
67	66 44	022	39 56	105	36 26	138	54 53	159	20 42	237	58 09	275	62 17	338
68	67 04	021	40 48	106	37 03	139	55 11	161	19 56	238	57 15	275	61 57	337
69	67 23	019	41 41	106	37 38	140	55 28	163	19 09	239	56 21	275	61 35	336
70	67 40	017	42 33	107	38 13	141	55 43	164	18 23	239	55 27	276	61 12	335
71	67 55	016	43 25	108	38 47	141	55 57	166	17 36	240	54 33	276	60 48	334
72	68 09	014	44 16	108	39 21	142	56 09	168	16 49	240	53 38	276	60 24	333
73	68 22	012	45 08	109	39 54	144	56 20	170	16 02	241	52 44	277	59 58	332
74	68 32	010	45 59	110	40 26	145	56 29	171	15 14	241	51 50	277	59 32	331
	CAPELLA		◆ Dubhe		POLLUX		PROCYON		◆ SIRIUS		RIGEL		◆ Hamal	
75	68 41	009	21 18	031	52 52	076	46 50	111	40 57	146	56 36	173	50 56	277
76	68 48	007	21 46	031	53 45	076	47 41	111	41 27	147	56 42	175	50 03	277
77	68 54	005	22 14	031	54 37	076	48 31	112	41 56	148	56 46	177	49 09	278
78	68 57	003	22 42	031	55 30	076	49 22	113	42 25	149	56 48	179	48 15	278
79	68 59	001	23 10	031	56 23	076	50 12	114	42 53	150	56 49	180	47 21	278
80	68 59	359	23 38	031	57 16	077	51 01	115	43 19	151	56 48	182	46 27	279
81	68 57	357	24 06	031	58 09	077	51 50	116	43 45	152	56 45	184	45 33	279
82	68 53	355	24 34	031	59 02	077	52 39	117	44 10	154	56 40	186	44 40	279
83	68 48	353	25 02	031	59 55	077	53 28	118	44 33	155	56 34	188	43 46	279
84	68 40	351	25 31	031	60 48	077	54 16	119	44 56	156	56 26	189	42 52	280
85	68 31	349	25 59	031	61 41	077	55 03	120	45 17	157	56 16	191	41 59	280
86	68 20	348	26 27	031	62 34	077	55 50	121	45 38	159	56 05	193	41 05	280
87	68 08	346	26 56	032	63 27	077	56 37	122	45 57	160	55 52	195	40 12	281
88	67 54	344	27 24	032	64 20	077	57 23	123	46 15	161	55 38	196	39 18	281
89	67 38	342	27 53	032	65 13	077	58 08	124	46 32	163	55 22	198	38 25	281

LAT 25°N

LHA ♈	Hc	Zn	Hc	Zn	Hc	Zn	Hc	Zn	Hc	Zn	Hc	Zn	Hc	Zn
	Dubhe		◆ REGULUS		Alphard		SIRIUS		◆ RIGEL		ALDEBARAN		◆ CAPELLA	
90	28 21	032	29 58	090	29 06	117	46 48	164	55 04	200	68 49	250	67 21	341
91	28 50	032	30 52	091	29 55	117	47 02	165	54 45	201	67 58	252	67 02	339
92	29 18	032	31 47	091	30 43	118	47 15	167	54 25	203	67 06	253	66 42	338
93	29 46	032	32 41	092	31 31	119	47 27	168	54 03	204	66 14	254	66 21	336
94	30 15	032	33 35	092	32 18	120	47 38	169	53 40	206	65 22	255	65 58	335
95	30 43	031	34 30	093	33 05	120	47 47	171	53 16	207	64 29	256	65 34	333
96	31 12	031	35 24	093	33 52	121	47 56	172	52 50	209	63 36	257	65 09	332
97	31 40	031	36 18	093	34 38	122	48 02	174	52 23	210	62 43	257	64 43	331
98	32 08	031	37 12	094	35 25	122	48 08	175	51 55	212	61 50	258	64 16	329
99	32 37	031	38 07	094	36 10	123	48 12	176	51 26	213	60 57	259	63 48	328
100	33 05	031	39 01	095	36 56	124	48 14	178	50 55	215	60 04	260	63 19	327
101	33 33	031	39 55	095	37 40	125	48 16	179	50 24	216	59 10	260	62 49	326
102	34 01	031	40 49	096	38 25	126	48 16	181	49 52	217	58 16	261	62 18	325
103	34 29	031	41 43	096	39 09	127	48 14	182	49 18	218	57 23	262	61 46	324
104	34 57	031	42 37	097	39 52	127	48 11	184	48 44	220	56 29	262	61 14	323
	Dubhe		◆ REGULUS		Alphard		SIRIUS		◆ RIGEL		ALDEBARAN		◆ CAPELLA	
105	35 25	031	43 31	097	40 35	128	48 07	185	48 09	221	55 35	263	60 41	322
106	35 52	031	44 25	098	41 17	129	48 02	187	47 33	222	54 41	263	60 08	321
107	36 20	030	45 19	099	41 59	130	47 55	188	46 56	223	53 47	264	59 33	321
108	36 47	030	46 13	099	42 41	131	47 47	189	46 18	224	52 53	265	58 59	320
109	37 15	030	47 06	100	43 21	132	47 37	191	45 40	225	51 59	265	58 23	319
110	37 42	030	48 00	100	44 01	133	47 26	192	45 01	226	51 04	266	57 48	319
111	38 09	030	48 53	101	44 41	134	47 14	194	44 21	228	50 10	266	57 11	318
112	38 36	029	49 47	101	45 19	135	47 01	195	43 41	229	49 16	267	56 35	317
113	39 02	029	50 40	102	45 57	136	46 46	196	43 00	229	48 22	267	55 58	317
114	39 29	029	51 33	103	46 34	137	46 30	198	42 18	230	47 27	268	55 20	316
115	39 55	029	52 26	103	47 11	139	46 13	199	41 36	231	46 33	268	54 42	316
116	40 21	029	53 19	104	47 46	140	45 55	200	40 53	232	45 39	268	54 04	315
117	40 47	028	54 11	105	48 21	141	45 36	202	40 10	233	44 44	269	53 26	315
118	41 13	028	55 04	106	48 55	142	45 15	203	39 26	234	43 50	269	52 47	314
119	41 38	028	55 56	106	49 28	143	44 54	204	38 42	235	42 55	270	52 08	314
	◆ Dubhe		REGULUS		◆ Alphard		SIRIUS		RIGEL		◆ ALDEBARAN		CAPELLA	
120	42 04	027	56 48	107	50 00	145	44 31	205	37 57	236	42 01	270	51 29	314
121	42 28	027	57 40	108	50 31	146	44 07	207	37 12	237	41 07	271	50 49	313
122	42 53	027	58 31	109	51 01	147	43 42	208	36 26	237	40 12	271	50 09	313
123	43 18	026	59 23	110	51 29	149	43 17	209	35 40	238	39 18	271	49 29	313
124	43 42	026	60 14	111	51 57	150	42 50	210	34 54	239	38 24	272	48 49	312
125	44 05	026	61 04	112	52 24	152	42 22	211	34 07	240	37 29	272	48 09	312
126	44 29	025	61 55	113	52 49	153	41 54	212	33 20	240	36 35	273	47 28	312
127	44 52	025	62 44	114	53 13	155	41 24	213	32 33	241	35 41	273	46 48	312
128	45 15	025	63 34	115	53 35	156	40 54	214	31 45	242	34 46	273	46 07	311
129	45 37	024	64 23	117	53 57	158	40 23	216	30 57	242	33 52	274	45 26	311
130	46 00	024	65 11	118	54 17	159	39 51	217	30 08	243	32 58	274	44 45	311
131	46 21	023	65 59	119	54 35	161	39 18	218	29 20	244	32 04	275	44 04	311
132	46 43	023	66 46	121	54 52	163	38 44	219	28 31	244	31 09	275	43 23	311
133	47 03	022	67 32	122	55 08	164	38 10	220	27 42	245	30 15	275	42 41	311
134	47 24	022	68 18	124	55 22	166	37 35	221	26 52	246	29 21	276	42 00	310
	Dubhe		◆ ARCTURUS		SPICA		◆ Alphard		SIRIUS		BETELGEUSE		◆ CAPELLA	
135	47 44	021	17 29	077	15 48	111	55 35	168	36 59	221	42 45	256	41 19	310
136	48 04	021	18 22	077	16 38	111	55 46	169	36 23	222	41 52	257	40 37	310
137	48 23	020	19 15	077	17 29	112	55 55	171	35 46	223	40 59	257	39 56	310
138	48 42	020	20 08	078	18 19	112	56 03	173	35 08	224	40 06	258	39 14	310
139	49 00	019	21 01	078	19 09	113	56 09	175	34 30	225	39 13	259	38 32	310
140	49 17	019	21 55	078	19 59	113	56 13	176	33 51	226	38 19	259	37 51	310
141	49 35	018	22 48	079	20 49	114	56 16	178	33 12	227	37 26	260	37 09	310
142	49 51	018	23 41	079	21 39	115	56 17	180	32 32	228	36 32	260	36 27	310
143	50 07	017	24 35	079	22 28	115	56 16	182	31 52	228	35 38	261	35 46	310
144	50 23	016	25 28	080	23 17	116	56 13	183	31 11	229	34 45	261	35 04	310
145	50 38	016	26 22	080	24 06	116	56 09	185	30 29	230	33 51	262	34 22	310
146	50 52	015	27 15	080	24 55	117	56 04	187	29 47	231	32 57	262	33 41	310
147	51 06	014	28 09	081	25 43	118	55 56	189	29 05	231	32 03	263	32 59	310
148	51 19	014	29 03	081	26 31	118	55 47	190	28 22	232	31 09	263	32 18	310
149	51 32	013	29 56	081	27 19	119	55 36	192	27 39	233	30 15	264	31 36	310
	Dubhe		◆ ARCTURUS		SPICA		◆ Alphard		SIRIUS		POLLUX		◆ CAPELLA	
150	51 44	012	30 50	082	28 06	120	55 24	194	26 56	234	60 01	283	30 54	310
151	51 55	012	31 44	082	28 53	120	55 10	196	26 12	234	59 08	283	30 13	310
152	52 06	011	32 38	083	29 40	121	54 55	197	25 27	235	58 15	283	29 32	310
153	52 16	010	33 32	083	30 27	122	54 38	199	24 43	236	57 22	283	28 50	311
154	52 25	009	34 26	083	31 13	122	54 20	200	23 57	236	56 29	284	28 09	311
155	52 33	009	35 20	084	31 59	123	54 00	202	23 12	237	55 36	284	27 28	311
156	52 41	008	36 14	084	32 44	124	53 39	204	22 26	238	54 43	284	26 46	311
157	52 48	007	37 08	084	33 29	124	53 17	205	21 40	238	53 51	284	26 05	311
158	52 55	006	38 02	085	34 14	125	52 53	207	20 54	239	52 58	284	25 24	311
159	53 01	006	38 56	085	34 58	126	52 28	208	20 07	239	52 05	284	24 43	311
160	53 06	005	39 50	085	35 42	127	52 01	210	19 20	240	51 12	284	24 03	311
161	53 10	004	40 45	086	36 25	128	51 34	211	18 33	241	50 20	284	23 22	312
162	53 13	003	41 39	086	37 08	129	51 05	212	17 46	241	49 27	285	22 41	312
163	53 16	003	42 33	086	37 50	129	50 36	214	16 58	242	48 34	285	22 01	312
164	53 18	002	43 27	087	38 32	130	50 05	215	16 10	242	47 42	285	21 20	312
	◆ Dubhe		Alkaid		ARCTURUS		◆ SPICA		Alphard		◆ PROCYON		POLLUX	
165	53 19	001	49 26	042	44 22	087	39 13	131	49 33	216	38 13	256	46 49	285
166	53 20	000	50 02	042	45 16	088	39 54	132	49 00	218	37 20	257	45 57	285
167	53 20	359	50 38	041	46 10	088	40 34	133	48 27	219	36 27	257	45 04	285
168	53 19	359	51 14	041	47 05	088	41 13	134	47 52	220	35 34	258	44 12	286
169	53 17	358	51 50	041	47 59	089	41 52	135	47 17	221	34 41	258	43 20	286
170	53 14	357	52 25	040	48 53	089	42 30	136	46 40	222	33 48	259	42 27	286
171	53 11	356	53 00	040	49 48	090	43 07	137	46 03	224	32 54	259	41 35	286
172	53 07	355	53 35	039	50 42	090	43 44	138	45 26	225	32 01	260	40 43	286
173	53 02	355	54 09	039	51 37	090	44 20	139	44 47	226	31 07	261	39 51	287
174	52 57	354	54 42	038	52 31	091	44 55	140	44 08	227	30 13	261	38 59	287
175	52 51	353	55 16	037	53 25	091	45 30	141	43 28	228	29 20	262	38 07	287
176	52 44	352	55 48	037	54 20	092	46 03	143	42 47	229	28 26	262	37 15	287
177	52 36	352	56 21	036	55 14	092	46 36	144	42 06	230	27 32	262	36 23	287
178	52 28	351	56 53	035	56 08	093	47 08	145	41 24	231	26 38	263	35 31	288
179	52 19	350	57 24	035	57 03	093	47 38	146	40 42	232	25 44	263	34 39	288

LAT 25°N

LHA ♈	Hc	Zn	Hc	Zn	Hc	Zn	Hc	Zn	Hc	Zn	Hc	Zn	Hc	Zn
	◆ Alkaid		Alphecca		◆ SPICA		Gienah		REGULUS		◆ POLLUX		Dubhe	
180	57 54	034	41 53	076	48 08	147	47 11	174	60 43	248	33 47	288	52 09	349
181	58 25	033	42 46	076	48 37	149	47 16	176	59 53	249	32 56	288	51 59	349
182	58 54	032	43 39	076	49 05	150	47 19	177	59 01	250	32 04	289	51 47	348
183	59 23	031	44 31	076	49 31	151	47 22	178	58 10	251	31 13	289	51 36	347
184	59 51	031	45 24	077	49 57	153	47 22	180	57 18	252	30 21	289	51 23	347
185	60 18	030	46 17	077	50 21	154	47 22	181	56 27	253	29 30	289	51 10	346
186	60 44	029	47 10	077	50 44	156	47 20	183	55 34	254	28 39	290	50 57	345
187	61 10	028	48 03	077	51 06	157	47 17	184	54 42	255	27 47	290	50 43	345
188	61 35	027	48 56	077	51 27	158	47 13	185	53 50	255	26 56	290	50 28	344
189	61 59	025	49 49	078	51 46	160	47 07	187	52 57	256	26 05	290	50 12	343
190	62 22	024	50 42	078	52 04	161	47 00	188	52 04	257	25 14	291	49 57	343
191	62 44	023	51 36	078	52 21	163	46 51	190	51 11	257	24 24	291	49 40	342
192	63 04	022	52 29	078	52 36	165	46 42	191	50 18	258	23 33	291	49 23	341
193	63 24	021	53 22	078	52 50	166	46 31	192	49 25	259	22 42	291	49 05	341
194	63 43	019	54 15	078	53 02	168	46 18	194	48 31	259	21 52	292	48 47	340
	◆ Kochab		VEGA		Rasalhague		◆ ANTARES		SPICA		◆ REGULUS		Dubhe	
195	38 47	009	19 31	055	24 13	087	17 44	132	53 13	169	47 38	260	48 29	340
196	38 56	009	20 16	056	25 07	087	18 25	132	53 22	171	46 44	261	48 10	339
197	39 04	009	21 01	056	26 02	088	19 05	133	53 30	173	45 50	261	47 50	339
198	39 13	008	21 46	056	26 56	088	19 44	134	53 36	174	44 57	262	47 30	338
199	39 20	008	22 31	056	27 50	089	20 23	134	53 41	176	44 03	262	47 10	338
200	39 28	008	23 17	056	28 45	089	21 02	135	53 44	178	43 09	263	46 49	337
201	39 35	008	24 02	057	29 39	089	21 40	136	53 45	179	42 15	263	46 28	337
202	39 42	007	24 48	057	30 33	090	22 18	136	53 45	181	41 21	264	46 07	336
203	39 49	007	25 33	057	31 28	090	22 56	137	53 44	182	40 27	264	45 45	336
204	39 55	007	26 19	057	32 22	091	23 32	138	53 41	184	39 33	265	45 22	336
205	40 01	006	27 05	057	33 17	091	24 09	138	53 36	186	38 38	265	44 59	335
206	40 07	006	27 51	058	34 11	092	24 45	139	53 30	187	37 44	266	44 36	335
207	40 13	006	28 37	058	35 05	092	25 20	140	53 22	189	36 50	266	44 13	334
208	40 18	005	29 23	058	36 00	092	25 55	141	53 13	191	35 56	267	43 49	334
209	40 22	005	30 09	058	36 54	093	26 29	141	53 02	192	35 01	267	43 25	334
	◆ Kochab		VEGA		Rasalhague		◆ ANTARES		SPICA		◆ REGULUS		Dubhe	
210	40 27	005	30 55	058	37 48	093	27 02	142	52 49	194	34 07	268	43 01	333
211	40 31	004	31 41	058	38 43	094	27 36	143	52 36	195	33 13	268	42 36	333
212	40 35	004	32 27	058	39 37	094	28 08	144	52 20	197	32 18	269	42 12	333
213	40 38	003	33 14	059	40 31	095	28 40	145	52 04	199	31 24	269	41 46	332
214	40 41	003	34 00	059	41 25	095	29 11	145	51 46	200	30 30	269	41 21	332
215	40 44	003	34 47	059	42 19	096	29 41	146	51 27	202	29 35	270	40 56	332
216	40 47	002	35 33	059	43 13	096	30 11	147	51 06	203	28 41	270	40 30	332
217	40 49	002	36 20	059	44 07	097	30 40	148	50 44	204	27 46	271	40 04	331
218	40 51	002	37 07	059	45 01	097	31 09	149	50 21	206	26 52	271	39 37	331
219	40 52	001	37 53	059	45 55	098	31 37	150	49 57	207	25 58	271	39 11	331
220	40 53	001	38 40	059	46 49	098	32 04	151	49 31	209	25 03	272	38 44	331
221	40 54	001	39 27	059	47 43	099	32 30	152	49 04	210	24 09	272	38 18	330
222	40 54	000	40 13	059	48 37	100	32 55	153	48 37	211	23 15	273	37 51	330
223	40 54	000	41 00	059	49 30	100	33 20	154	48 08	213	22 20	273	37 23	330
224	40 54	000	41 47	059	50 24	101	33 44	154	47 38	214	21 26	274	36 56	330
	VEGA		◆ ALTAIR		Nunki		ANTARES		◆ SPICA		Denebola		◆ Alkaid	
225	42 34	059	19 13	089	13 21	128	34 07	155	47 07	215	44 16	266	62 00	335
226	43 20	059	20 07	089	14 04	128	34 29	156	46 36	216	43 22	267	61 36	333
227	44 07	059	21 01	090	14 46	129	34 50	157	46 03	217	42 28	267	61 12	332
228	44 54	059	21 56	090	15 28	129	35 11	158	45 29	219	41 33	267	60 46	331
229	45 41	059	22 50	091	16 10	130	35 30	159	44 55	220	40 39	268	60 20	330
230	46 27	059	23 45	091	16 52	131	35 49	161	44 20	221	39 45	268	59 53	329
231	47 14	059	24 39	091	17 33	131	36 06	162	43 44	222	38 50	269	59 25	329
232	48 01	059	25 33	092	18 13	132	36 23	163	43 07	223	37 56	269	58 56	328
233	48 47	059	26 28	092	18 54	133	36 39	164	42 30	224	37 02	270	58 26	327
234	49 34	059	27 22	093	19 33	133	36 54	165	41 52	225	36 07	270	57 56	326
235	50 20	059	28 16	093	20 13	134	37 07	166	41 13	226	35 13	271	57 26	325
236	51 07	058	29 10	094	20 52	134	37 20	167	40 33	227	34 18	271	56 55	325
237	51 53	058	30 05	094	21 30	135	37 32	168	39 53	228	33 24	271	56 23	324
238	52 39	058	30 59	095	22 09	136	37 43	169	39 13	229	32 30	272	55 51	323
239	53 25	058	31 53	095	22 46	137	37 52	170	38 31	230	31 35	272	55 18	323
	◆ VEGA		ALTAIR		Nunki		◆ ANTARES		SPICA		ARCTURUS		◆ Alkaid	
240	54 11	058	32 47	096	23 23	137	38 01	171	37 50	231	65 19	261	54 45	322
241	54 57	057	33 41	096	24 00	138	38 09	173	37 07	231	64 25	262	54 11	321
242	55 43	057	34 35	097	24 36	139	38 15	174	36 25	232	63 31	263	53 37	321
243	56 28	057	35 29	097	25 12	139	38 21	175	35 41	233	62 37	263	53 02	320
244	57 14	056	36 23	098	25 47	140	38 25	176	34 57	234	61 43	264	52 27	320
245	57 59	056	37 17	098	26 22	141	38 29	177	34 13	235	60 49	265	51 52	319
246	58 44	056	38 11	099	26 56	142	38 31	178	33 29	236	59 55	265	51 17	319
247	59 29	055	39 05	099	27 29	142	38 32	179	32 44	236	59 01	266	50 41	319
248	60 13	055	39 58	100	28 02	143	38 32	180	31 58	237	58 06	266	50 05	318
249	60 58	054	40 52	100	28 34	144	38 31	182	31 12	238	57 12	267	49 28	318
250	61 41	054	41 45	101	29 06	145	38 29	183	30 26	238	56 18	267	48 52	317
251	62 25	053	42 39	101	29 37	146	38 26	184	29 40	239	55 23	268	48 15	317
252	63 08	052	43 32	102	30 07	147	38 22	185	28 53	240	54 29	268	47 38	317
253	63 51	052	44 25	103	30 36	147	38 16	186	28 06	240	53 35	269	47 00	317
254	64 34	051	45 18	103	31 05	148	38 10	187	27 18	241	52 40	269	46 23	316
	◆ DENEB		ALTAIR		◆ Nunki		ANTARES		SPICA		◆ ARCTURUS		Alkaid	
255	41 25	051	46 11	104	31 33	149	38 02	188	26 31	242	51 46	270	45 45	316
256	42 07	050	47 04	104	32 01	150	37 54	190	25 42	242	50 52	270	45 07	316
257	42 49	050	47 56	105	32 27	151	37 44	191	24 54	243	49 57	270	44 29	316
258	43 31	050	48 49	106	32 53	152	37 34	192	24 06	244	49 03	271	43 51	315
259	44 13	050	49 41	107	33 18	153	37 22	193	23 17	244	48 08	271	43 13	315
260	44 54	050	50 33	107	33 43	154	37 10	194	22 28	245	47 14	272	42 34	315
261	45 36	050	51 25	108	34 06	155	36 56	195	21 38	245	46 20	272	41 56	315
262	46 17	050	52 16	109	34 29	156	36 41	196	20 49	246	45 25	272	41 17	315
263	46 59	049	53 08	110	34 51	157	36 26	197	19 59	247	44 31	273	40 38	315
264	47 40	049	53 59	111	35 11	158	36 09	198	19 09	247	43 37	273	39 59	314
265	48 21	049	54 50	111	35 32	159	35 52	199	18 19	248	42 43	273	39 21	314
266	49 02	049	55 40	112	35 51	160	35 33	200	17 28	248	41 48	274	38 42	314
267	49 43	048	56 30	113	36 09	161	35 14	201	16 38	249	40 54	274	38 03	314
268	50 23	048	57 20	114	36 26	162	34 54	202	15 47	249	40 00	275	37 24	314
269	51 04	048	58 09	115	36 42	163	34 32	203	14 56	250	39 06	275	36 44	314

LHA ♈	Hc	Zn	Hc	Zn	Hc	Zn	Hc	Zn	Hc	Zn	Hc	Zn	Hc	Zn
	◆ DENEB		Enif		◆ Nunki		ANTARES		◆ ARCTURUS		Alkaid		Kochab	
270	51 44	047	34 42	095	36 58	164	34 10	204	38 11	275	36 05	314	35 05	346
271	52 24	047	35 36	096	37 12	165	33 48	205	37 17	276	35 26	314	34 52	346
272	53 04	047	36 30	096	37 25	166	33 24	206	36 23	276	34 47	314	34 38	345
273	53 43	046	37 24	097	37 38	167	32 59	207	35 29	276	34 08	314	34 24	345
274	54 22	046	38 18	097	37 49	169	32 34	208	34 35	277	33 29	314	34 10	345
275	55 01	045	39 12	098	37 59	170	32 08	209	33 41	277	32 50	314	33 56	345
276	55 40	045	40 06	098	38 08	171	31 41	210	32 47	277	32 10	314	33 42	345
277	56 18	044	40 59	099	38 16	172	31 13	211	31 53	278	31 31	314	33 27	345
278	56 56	044	41 53	099	38 24	173	30 45	212	30 59	278	30 52	314	33 13	344
279	57 33	043	42 47	100	38 30	174	30 16	213	30 06	278	30 13	314	32 58	344
280	58 10	043	43 40	100	38 34	175	29 46	214	29 12	279	29 34	314	32 43	344
281	58 47	042	44 34	101	38 38	176	29 16	214	28 18	279	28 55	314	32 28	344
282	59 23	041	45 27	102	38 41	178	28 45	215	27 25	279	28 16	314	32 13	344
283	59 58	040	46 20	102	38 43	179	28 13	216	26 31	280	27 37	314	31 58	344
284	60 33	040	47 13	103	38 43	180	27 41	217	25 37	280	26 58	314	31 43	344
	DENEB		◆ Alpheratz		FOMALHAUT		◆ Nunki		ANTARES		◆ ARCTURUS		Kochab	
285	61 08	039	22 20	067	10 59	130	38 43	181	27 08	218	24 44	281	31 27	343
286	61 41	038	23 10	067	11 40	131	38 41	182	26 34	218	23 50	281	31 12	343
287	62 14	037	24 01	068	12 21	131	38 39	183	26 00	219	22 57	281	30 56	343
288	62 47	036	24 51	068	13 02	132	38 35	185	25 26	220	22 04	282	30 40	343
289	63 18	035	25 41	068	13 42	132	38 30	186	24 50	221	21 11	282	30 24	343
290	63 49	034	26 32	068	14 22	133	38 24	187	24 15	221	20 17	282	30 09	343
291	64 19	033	27 23	069	15 02	134	38 17	188	23 38	222	19 24	283	29 53	343
292	64 48	032	28 13	069	15 41	134	38 09	189	23 02	223	18 31	283	29 37	343
293	65 16	030	29 04	069	16 20	135	38 00	190	22 24	224	17 38	283	29 21	343
294	65 43	029	29 55	069	16 58	135	37 50	191	21 47	224	16 45	284	29 04	343
295	66 09	028	30 46	070	17 36	136	37 39	192	21 08	225	15 53	284	28 48	343
296	66 33	026	31 37	070	18 14	137	37 26	194	20 30	226	15 00	284	28 32	343
297	66 57	025	32 28	070	18 51	137	37 13	195	19 51	226	14 07	285	28 16	343
298	67 19	023	33 19	070	19 28	138	36 59	196	19 11	227	13 15	285	27 59	343
299	67 39	022	34 10	071	20 04	139	36 44	197	18 31	228	12 22	286	27 43	342
	◆ DENEB		Schedar		Alpheratz		◆ FOMALHAUT		Nunki		◆ Rasalhague		VEGA	
300	67 59	020	31 23	037	35 02	071	20 40	139	36 28	198	53 46	257	67 47	313
301	68 16	018	31 56	037	35 53	071	21 15	140	36 10	199	52 53	257	67 08	312
302	68 33	016	32 29	037	36 44	071	21 50	141	35 52	200	52 00	258	66 27	311
303	68 47	015	33 01	037	37 36	071	22 24	141	35 33	201	51 07	259	65 46	310
304	69 00	013	33 34	037	38 27	072	22 58	142	35 13	202	50 14	259	65 04	310
305	69 11	011	34 07	037	39 19	072	23 31	143	34 53	203	49 20	260	64 22	309
306	69 21	009	34 40	037	40 11	072	24 04	144	34 31	204	48 27	261	63 40	308
307	69 28	007	35 13	037	41 02	072	24 36	144	34 08	205	47 33	261	62 57	307
308	69 34	005	35 46	037	41 54	072	25 07	145	33 45	206	46 39	262	62 13	307
309	69 38	003	36 18	037	42 46	072	25 38	146	33 21	207	45 45	262	61 29	306
310	69 40	001	36 51	037	43 38	073	26 08	147	32 56	208	44 51	263	60 45	306
311	69 40	359	37 23	037	44 30	073	26 38	147	32 30	209	43 57	263	60 01	305
312	69 38	357	37 55	036	45 22	073	27 07	148	32 03	210	43 03	264	59 16	305
313	69 34	355	38 28	036	46 14	073	27 35	149	31 36	211	42 09	264	58 31	304
314	69 28	353	39 00	036	47 06	073	28 03	150	31 08	212	41 15	265	57 46	304
	◆ Alpheratz		Diphda		◆ FOMALHAUT		ALTAIR		Rasalhague		◆ VEGA		DENEB	
315	47 58	073	20 34	122	28 30	151	67 06	228	40 21	265	57 01	303	69 21	351
316	48 50	074	21 20	123	28 56	152	66 24	230	39 27	266	56 16	303	69 11	349
317	49 42	074	22 05	124	29 21	152	65 42	232	38 33	266	55 30	303	69 00	347
318	50 34	074	22 50	124	29 46	153	64 59	233	37 38	267	54 44	303	68 47	345
319	51 27	074	23 35	125	30 10	154	64 15	235	36 44	267	53 58	302	68 32	343
320	52 19	074	24 19	126	30 34	155	63 30	236	35 50	268	53 12	302	68 16	342
321	53 11	074	25 03	126	30 56	156	62 44	238	34 55	268	52 26	302	67 58	340
322	54 03	074	25 47	127	31 18	157	61 58	239	34 01	269	51 40	302	67 39	338
323	54 56	074	26 30	128	31 39	158	61 11	240	33 07	269	50 54	301	67 18	337
324	55 48	074	27 13	128	31 59	159	60 23	242	32 12	269	50 07	301	66 56	335
325	56 41	074	27 55	129	32 18	160	59 35	243	31 18	270	49 21	301	66 32	334
326	57 33	074	28 37	130	32 36	161	58 46	244	30 23	270	48 34	301	66 08	332
327	58 25	074	29 19	131	32 54	162	57 57	245	29 29	271	47 48	301	65 42	331
328	59 18	074	30 00	131	33 10	163	57 08	246	28 35	271	47 01	301	65 15	330
329	60 10	074	30 40	132	33 26	164	56 18	247	27 40	272	46 14	301	64 47	328
	◆ Mirfak		Hamal		Diphda		◆ FOMALHAUT		ALTAIR		◆ VEGA		DENEB	
330	24 16	044	33 58	077	31 20	133	33 41	165	55 28	248	45 28	301	64 18	327
331	24 54	044	34 51	078	32 00	134	33 55	166	54 37	249	44 41	301	63 48	326
332	25 33	045	35 45	078	32 39	135	34 08	167	53 46	250	43 54	301	63 17	325
333	26 11	045	36 38	078	33 17	135	34 20	168	52 55	251	43 07	301	62 46	324
334	26 49	045	37 31	079	33 55	136	34 31	169	52 04	251	42 21	301	62 13	323
335	27 27	045	38 24	079	34 33	137	34 41	170	51 12	252	41 34	301	61 40	322
336	28 06	045	39 18	079	35 09	138	34 50	171	50 20	253	40 47	301	61 07	321
337	28 44	045	40 11	079	35 45	139	34 58	172	49 28	254	40 00	301	60 32	320
338	29 23	045	41 05	080	36 21	140	35 05	173	48 36	254	39 14	301	59 57	320
339	30 01	045	41 58	080	36 55	141	35 11	174	47 44	255	38 27	301	59 22	319
340	30 40	045	42 52	080	37 29	142	35 17	175	46 51	256	37 40	301	58 46	318
341	31 18	045	43 45	081	38 03	143	35 21	176	45 58	256	36 54	301	58 09	317
342	31 57	045	44 39	081	38 35	144	35 24	177	45 05	257	36 07	301	57 32	317
343	32 35	045	45 33	081	39 07	145	35 26	178	44 12	258	35 20	301	56 55	316
344	33 14	045	46 27	081	39 38	146	35 27	179	43 19	258	34 34	301	56 17	316
	Schedar		CAPELLA		◆ ALDEBARAN		Diphda		◆ FOMALHAUT		ALTAIR		◆ DENEB	
345	53 28	023	14 47	046	12 01	077	40 08	147	35 27	180	42 26	259	55 39	315
346	53 50	023	15 26	046	12 54	078	40 38	148	35 26	181	41 32	259	55 00	315
347	54 10	022	16 05	046	13 47	078	41 06	149	35 25	183	40 39	260	54 21	314
348	54 30	021	16 45	046	14 40	078	41 34	150	35 22	184	39 45	260	53 42	314
349	54 49	020	17 24	047	15 34	079	42 00	151	35 18	185	38 52	261	53 03	313
350	55 08	020	18 04	047	16 27	079	42 26	152	35 13	186	37 58	262	52 23	313
351	55 26	019	18 44	047	17 20	079	42 51	154	35 07	187	37 04	262	51 43	313
352	55 43	018	19 24	047	18 14	080	43 15	155	35 00	188	36 10	263	51 03	312
353	55 59	017	20 04	048	19 07	080	43 37	156	34 52	189	35 16	263	50 22	312
354	56 15	016	20 44	048	20 01	081	43 59	157	34 43	190	34 22	264	49 42	312
355	56 29	015	21 24	048	20 55	081	44 19	158	34 33	191	33 28	264	49 01	311
356	56 43	014	22 05	048	21 48	081	44 39	160	34 22	192	32 34	265	48 20	311
357	56 56	013	22 45	048	22 42	082	44 57	161	34 11	193	31 40	265	47 39	311
358	57 09	013	23 26	048	23 36	082	45 15	162	33 58	194	30 46	265	46 58	311
359	57 20	012	24 07	049	24 30	082	45 31	163	33 44	195	29 52	266	46 16	310

LHA ♈	Hc Zn	Hc Zn	Hc Zn	Hc Zn	Hc Zn	Hc Zn	Hc Zn
	Schedar	◆CAPELLA	ALDEBARAN	◆Diphda	FOMALHAUT	◆ALTAIR	DENEB
0	56 31 010	24 08 048	25 16 082	46 43 165	34 27 196	29 01 267	44 56 311
1	56 41 009	24 49 049	26 10 083	46 57 166	34 12 197	28 06 267	44 14 311
2	56 49 008	25 30 049	27 05 083	47 10 167	33 55 198	27 11 268	43 33 311
3	56 57 007	26 11 049	27 59 083	47 22 169	33 37 199	26 16 268	42 51 310
4	57 03 006	26 52 049	28 54 084	47 32 170	33 19 200	25 22 269	42 09 310
5	57 09 005	27 34 049	29 48 084	47 41 171	32 59 201	24 27 269	41 27 310
6	57 14 004	28 15 049	30 43 084	47 48 173	32 39 202	23 32 269	40 46 310
7	57 17 003	28 57 049	31 37 085	47 54 174	32 18 203	22 37 270	40 04 310
8	57 20 002	29 38 049	32 32 085	47 59 176	31 56 204	21 42 270	39 22 310
9	57 22 001	30 20 049	33 26 085	48 03 177	31 33 205	20 48 271	38 40 310
10	57 23 000	31 01 049	34 21 086	48 05 178	31 10 206	19 53 271	37 57 310
11	57 23 359	31 43 049	35 16 086	48 06 180	30 46 207	18 58 272	37 15 310
12	57 21 358	32 25 049	36 10 087	48 05 181	30 21 208	18 03 272	36 33 310
13	57 19 357	33 06 049	37 05 087	48 03 183	29 55 208	17 08 272	35 51 310
14	57 16 356	33 48 049	38 00 087	48 00 184	29 28 209	16 14 273	35 09 310
	◆CAPELLA	ALDEBARAN	RIGEL	◆Diphda	FOMALHAUT	Enif	◆DENEB
15	34 29 049	38 55 088	19 57 109	47 55 186	29 01 210	41 33 262	34 27 310
16	35 11 049	39 49 088	20 48 110	47 49 187	28 33 211	40 39 262	33 45 310
17	35 53 049	40 44 088	21 40 110	47 42 188	28 05 212	39 44 263	33 02 310
18	36 34 049	41 39 089	22 31 111	47 33 190	27 35 213	38 50 263	32 20 310
19	37 16 049	42 34 089	23 22 111	47 23 191	27 05 213	37 56 264	31 38 310
20	37 58 049	43 29 090	24 13 112	47 12 193	26 35 214	37 01 264	30 56 310
21	38 39 049	44 23 090	25 04 112	47 00 194	26 04 215	36 07 265	30 14 310
22	39 21 049	45 18 090	25 55 113	46 46 195	25 32 216	35 12 265	29 32 310
23	40 02 049	46 13 091	26 45 114	46 31 197	24 59 217	34 17 266	28 50 310
24	40 44 049	47 08 091	27 35 114	46 15 198	24 27 217	33 23 266	28 08 310
25	41 25 049	48 03 092	28 25 115	45 57 199	23 53 218	32 28 267	27 26 310
26	42 06 049	48 57 092	29 15 115	45 38 201	23 19 219	31 33 267	26 44 310
27	42 47 049	49 52 093	30 04 116	45 19 202	22 44 219	30 38 267	26 03 310
28	43 29 048	50 47 093	30 53 117	44 58 203	22 09 220	29 44 268	25 21 311
29	44 09 048	51 42 093	31 42 117	44 36 204	21 34 221	28 49 268	24 39 311
	CAPELLA	◆ALDEBARAN	RIGEL	Acamar	◆Diphda	Alpheratz	◆DENEB
30	44 50 048	52 36 094	32 31 118	24 19 168	44 13 205	64 45 288	23 58 311
31	45 31 048	53 31 094	33 19 119	24 30 169	43 49 207	63 53 288	23 16 311
32	46 12 048	54 26 095	34 07 119	24 40 169	43 24 208	63 01 288	22 35 311
33	46 52 047	55 20 096	34 55 120	24 50 170	42 57 209	62 08 287	21 54 311
34	47 32 047	56 15 096	35 42 121	24 59 171	42 30 210	61 16 287	21 13 311
35	48 12 047	57 09 097	36 29 122	25 07 172	42 02 211	60 24 287	20 32 312
36	48 52 047	58 04 097	37 15 122	25 15 173	41 33 212	59 31 287	19 51 312
37	49 32 046	58 58 098	38 02 123	25 21 173	41 04 213	58 39 287	19 10 312
38	50 12 046	59 52 098	38 47 124	25 27 174	40 33 215	57 47 287	18 29 312
39	50 51 046	60 46 099	39 33 125	25 32 175	40 01 216	56 54 287	17 49 312
40	51 30 045	61 41 100	40 17 126	25 36 176	39 29 217	56 02 287	17 08 313
41	52 08 045	62 34 100	41 02 126	25 40 177	38 56 218	55 09 287	16 28 313
42	52 47 044	63 28 101	41 46 127	25 42 178	38 22 219	54 17 287	15 48 313
43	53 25 044	64 22 102	42 29 128	25 44 179	37 48 220	53 25 287	15 08 313
44	54 03 043	65 16 103	43 12 129	25 45 179	37 13 220	52 32 287	14 28 314
	CAPELLA	◆POLLUX	PROCYON	SIRIUS	◆Acamar	Diphda	◆Alpheratz
45	54 40 043	26 30 069	20 20 093	21 29 121	25 45 180	36 37 221	51 40 287
46	55 17 042	27 21 070	21 15 094	22 16 122	25 45 181	36 00 222	50 48 287
47	55 54 042	28 12 070	22 10 094	23 03 122	25 43 182	35 23 223	49 55 287
48	56 30 041	29 04 070	23 04 095	23 49 123	25 41 183	34 45 224	49 03 288
49	57 06 040	29 55 070	23 59 095	24 35 123	25 38 184	34 07 225	48 11 288
50	57 41 040	30 47 071	24 54 096	25 21 124	25 34 184	33 28 226	47 19 288
51	58 16 039	31 39 071	25 48 096	26 06 125	25 29 185	32 48 227	46 26 288
52	58 50 038	32 31 071	26 43 097	26 51 125	25 24 186	32 08 227	45 34 288
53	59 24 037	33 22 071	27 37 097	27 35 126	25 18 187	31 27 228	44 42 288
54	59 57 037	34 14 071	28 32 097	28 19 127	25 10 188	30 46 229	43 50 288
55	60 29 036	35 06 072	29 26 098	29 03 127	25 03 189	30 05 230	42 58 288
56	61 01 035	35 58 072	30 20 098	29 46 128	24 54 189	29 23 230	42 06 288
57	61 31 034	36 51 072	31 14 099	30 29 129	24 45 190	28 40 231	41 14 289
58	62 02 033	37 43 072	32 08 099	31 12 130	24 34 191	27 57 232	40 22 289
59	62 31 032	38 35 072	33 02 100	31 54 130	24 23 192	27 14 233	39 30 289
	◆CAPELLA	PROCYON	◆SIRIUS	RIGEL	Diphda	◆Hamal	Mirfak
60	62 59 031	33 56 100	32 35 131	52 56 148	26 30 233	64 25 275	63 13 348
61	63 27 029	34 50 101	33 16 132	53 25 149	25 46 234	63 30 275	63 01 346
62	63 53 028	35 44 101	33 57 133	53 52 151	25 02 235	62 36 275	62 47 345
63	64 18 027	36 38 102	34 37 134	54 18 152	24 17 235	61 41 275	62 32 344
64	64 43 026	37 31 103	35 16 135	54 43 154	23 32 236	60 47 276	62 16 342
65	65 06 024	38 25 103	35 55 135	55 06 156	22 46 237	59 52 276	61 59 341
66	65 28 023	39 18 104	36 33 136	55 28 157	22 00 237	58 58 276	61 41 340
67	65 49 021	40 11 104	37 11 137	55 49 159	21 14 238	58 03 276	61 22 339
68	66 08 020	41 04 105	37 47 138	56 08 161	20 27 238	57 09 277	61 01 338
69	66 26 018	41 57 105	38 24 139	56 25 162	19 41 239	56 14 277	60 40 337
70	66 42 017	42 50 106	38 59 140	56 41 164	18 54 239	55 20 277	60 18 335
71	66 57 015	43 42 107	39 34 141	56 55 166	18 06 240	54 26 277	59 54 334
72	67 11 013	44 35 107	40 08 142	57 08 168	17 19 241	53 31 278	59 30 333
73	67 23 012	45 27 108	40 42 143	57 19 169	16 31 241	52 37 278	59 05 332
74	67 33 010	46 19 109	41 14 144	57 28 171	15 43 242	51 43 278	58 40 332
	CAPELLA	◆Dubhe	POLLUX	PROCYON	◆SIRIUS	RIGEL	◆Hamal
75	67 42 008	20 26 030	52 37 075	47 11 110	41 46 145	57 36 173	50 48 278
76	67 49 006	20 54 031	53 29 075	48 02 110	42 17 146	57 42 175	49 54 279
77	67 54 005	21 22 031	54 22 075	48 54 111	42 47 147	57 46 177	49 00 279
78	67 57 003	21 50 031	55 15 075	49 45 112	43 16 148	57 48 178	48 06 279
79	67 59 001	22 18 031	56 08 075	50 35 113	43 44 150	57 49 180	47 12 279
80	67 59 359	22 46 031	57 01 075	51 26 114	44 12 151	57 48 182	46 18 280
81	67 57 357	23 14 031	57 54 075	52 16 114	44 38 152	57 45 184	45 24 280
82	67 54 355	23 43 031	58 47 075	53 06 115	45 03 153	57 40 186	44 30 280
83	67 48 353	24 11 031	59 40 075	53 55 116	45 27 154	57 33 188	43 36 280
84	67 41 352	24 39 031	60 33 075	54 44 117	45 51 156	57 25 190	42 42 281
85	67 32 350	25 08 031	61 26 075	55 32 118	46 13 157	57 15 191	41 48 281
86	67 22 348	25 36 031	62 19 075	56 20 119	46 34 158	57 04 193	40 54 281
87	67 10 346	26 05 031	63 12 075	57 08 120	46 53 160	56 50 195	40 00 281
88	66 56 345	26 33 031	64 05 075	57 55 122	47 12 161	56 35 197	39 07 282
89	66 41 343	27 01 031	64 58 075	58 41 123	47 29 162	56 19 198	38 13 282

LAT 24°N

LHA ♈	Hc Zn	Hc Zn	Hc Zn	Hc Zn	Hc Zn	Hc Zn	Hc Zn
	Dubhe	◆REGULUS	Alphard	SIRIUS	◆RIGEL	ALDEBARAN	◆CAPELLA
90	27 30 031	29 58 090	29 33 116	47 45 164	56 01 200	69 08 253	66 24 341
91	27 58 031	30 53 090	30 22 117	48 00 165	55 41 202	68 16 254	66 06 340
92	28 27 031	31 48 091	31 11 118	48 14 166	55 20 203	67 23 255	65 47 338
93	28 55 031	32 42 091	31 59 118	48 26 168	54 58 205	66 30 256	65 26 337
94	29 24 031	33 37 091	32 47 119	48 37 169	54 34 207	65 36 257	65 04 336
95	29 52 031	34 32 092	33 35 120	48 47 171	54 09 208	64 43 258	64 40 334
96	30 20 031	35 27 092	34 23 120	48 55 172	53 42 210	63 49 258	64 16 333
97	30 49 031	36 21 093	35 10 121	49 02 173	53 14 211	62 56 259	63 50 332
98	31 17 031	37 16 093	35 57 122	49 07 175	52 46 213	62 02 260	63 24 330
99	31 45 031	38 11 094	36 43 123	49 12 176	52 16 214	61 08 261	62 56 329
100	32 13 031	39 06 094	37 29 123	49 14 178	51 44 215	60 14 261	62 28 328
101	32 42 031	40 00 095	38 14 124	49 16 179	51 12 217	59 19 262	61 59 327
102	33 10 031	40 55 095	38 59 125	49 16 181	50 39 218	58 25 263	61 28 326
103	33 38 031	41 49 095	39 44 126	49 14 182	50 05 219	57 31 263	60 57 325
104	34 05 030	42 44 096	40 28 127	49 11 184	49 30 220	56 36 264	60 26 324
	Dubhe	◆REGULUS	Alphard	SIRIUS	◆RIGEL	ALDEBARAN	◆CAPELLA
105	34 33 030	43 38 096	41 12 128	49 07 185	48 54 222	55 42 264	59 53 323
106	35 01 030	44 33 097	41 55 129	49 01 187	48 17 223	54 47 265	59 20 323
107	35 28 030	45 27 098	42 38 129	48 54 188	47 39 224	53 52 265	58 47 322
108	35 55 030	46 22 098	43 20 130	48 46 190	47 01 225	52 58 266	58 12 321
109	36 23 030	47 16 099	44 01 131	48 36 191	46 22 226	52 03 266	57 38 320
110	36 50 030	48 10 099	44 42 132	48 25 192	45 42 227	51 08 267	57 02 320
111	37 17 029	49 04 100	45 22 133	48 13 194	45 01 228	50 14 267	56 26 319
112	37 43 029	49 58 100	46 02 134	47 59 195	44 20 229	49 19 268	55 50 318
113	38 10 029	50 52 101	46 40 136	47 44 197	43 38 230	48 24 268	55 14 318
114	38 36 029	51 46 102	47 18 137	47 28 198	42 56 231	47 29 269	54 36 317
115	39 03 028	52 39 102	47 56 138	47 10 199	42 13 232	46 35 269	53 59 317
116	39 29 028	53 33 103	48 32 139	46 51 201	41 29 233	45 40 269	53 21 316
117	39 54 028	54 26 104	49 08 140	46 32 202	40 45 234	44 45 270	52 43 316
118	40 20 028	55 19 104	49 42 141	46 11 203	40 01 235	43 50 270	52 05 315
119	40 45 027	56 12 105	50 16 143	45 48 204	39 16 236	42 55 271	51 26 315
	◆Dubhe	REGULUS	◆Alphard	SIRIUS	RIGEL	◆ALDEBARAN	CAPELLA
120	41 10 027	57 05 106	50 49 144	45 25 206	38 30 236	42 00 271	50 47 314
121	41 35 027	57 58 107	51 20 145	45 01 207	37 45 237	41 06 271	50 08 314
122	42 00 026	58 50 107	51 51 147	44 35 208	36 58 238	40 11 272	49 28 314
123	42 24 026	59 42 108	52 21 148	44 09 209	36 12 239	39 16 272	48 48 313
124	42 48 026	60 34 109	52 49 149	43 42 211	35 25 239	38 21 273	48 08 313
125	43 11 025	61 26 110	53 16 151	43 13 212	34 37 240	37 27 273	47 28 313
126	43 35 025	62 17 111	53 42 152	42 44 213	33 49 241	36 32 273	46 48 313
127	43 58 025	63 08 112	54 07 154	42 14 214	33 01 242	35 37 274	46 08 312
128	44 20 024	63 59 113	54 30 156	41 43 215	32 13 242	34 42 274	45 27 312
129	44 43 024	64 49 115	54 52 157	41 11 216	31 24 243	33 48 274	44 46 312
130	45 05 023	65 38 116	55 13 159	40 39 217	30 35 244	32 53 275	44 05 312
131	45 26 023	66 27 117	55 32 160	40 05 218	29 46 244	31 59 275	43 24 312
132	45 47 022	67 16 119	55 50 162	39 31 219	28 57 245	31 04 275	42 43 311
133	46 08 022	68 03 120	56 06 164	38 56 220	28 07 246	30 09 276	42 02 311
134	46 28 022	68 50 122	56 20 165	38 20 221	27 17 246	29 15 276	41 21 311
	Dubhe	◆ARCTURUS	SPICA	◆Alphard	SIRIUS	BETELGEUSE	◆CAPELLA
135	46 48 021	17 15 076	16 09 111	56 33 167	37 44 222	42 59 257	40 40 311
136	47 08 021	18 08 077	17 00 111	56 44 169	37 07 223	42 05 258	39 58 311
137	47 27 020	19 02 077	17 51 112	56 54 171	36 29 224	41 11 258	39 17 311
138	47 45 019	19 55 077	18 42 112	57 02 173	35 51 225	40 18 259	38 35 311
139	48 03 019	20 49 078	19 33 113	57 08 174	35 12 226	39 24 259	37 54 311
140	48 21 018	21 42 078	20 23 113	57 13 176	34 33 226	38 30 260	37 12 311
141	48 38 018	22 36 078	21 13 114	57 16 178	33 53 227	37 36 261	36 30 311
142	48 54 017	23 30 079	22 03 114	57 17 180	33 12 228	36 42 261	35 49 311
143	49 10 017	24 23 079	22 53 115	57 16 182	32 31 229	35 48 262	35 07 311
144	49 25 016	25 17 079	23 43 115	57 13 184	31 50 229	34 53 262	34 25 311
145	49 40 015	26 11 080	24 32 116	57 09 185	31 08 230	33 59 263	33 44 311
146	49 54 015	27 05 080	25 22 117	57 03 187	30 25 231	33 05 263	33 02 311
147	50 08 014	27 59 080	26 10 117	56 55 189	29 42 232	32 10 263	32 20 311
148	50 21 013	28 53 081	26 59 118	56 46 191	28 59 233	31 16 264	31 39 311
149	50 33 013	29 47 081	27 47 118	56 35 192	28 15 233	30 21 264	30 57 311
	Dubhe	◆ARCTURUS	SPICA	◆Alphard	SIRIUS	POLLUX	◆CAPELLA
150	50 45 012	30 41 081	28 35 119	56 22 194	27 31 234	59 46 285	30 16 311
151	50 56 011	31 35 082	29 23 120	56 08 196	26 46 235	58 53 285	29 34 311
152	51 07 011	32 30 082	30 11 120	55 52 198	26 02 235	58 00 285	28 52 311
153	51 17 010	33 24 082	30 58 121	55 35 199	25 16 236	57 07 285	28 11 311
154	51 26 009	34 18 083	31 45 122	55 16 201	24 31 237	56 14 285	27 30 311
155	51 34 008	35 13 083	32 31 122	54 56 203	23 45 237	55 21 285	26 48 311
156	51 42 008	36 07 083	33 17 123	54 34 204	22 58 238	54 29 285	26 07 311
157	51 49 007	37 02 084	34 03 124	54 11 206	22 12 239	53 36 285	25 26 311
158	51 55 006	37 56 084	34 48 125	53 46 207	21 25 239	52 43 285	24 45 311
159	52 01 006	38 51 084	35 33 125	53 20 209	20 38 240	51 50 285	24 04 312
160	52 06 005	39 45 085	36 17 126	52 53 210	19 50 240	50 57 285	23 23 312
161	52 10 004	40 40 085	37 01 127	52 25 212	19 02 241	50 04 286	22 42 312
162	52 13 003	41 34 085	37 45 128	51 56 213	18 14 241	49 11 286	22 01 312
163	52 16 002	42 29 086	38 28 129	51 25 214	17 26 242	48 19 286	21 20 312
164	52 18 002	43 24 086	39 10 130	50 54 216	16 38 242	47 26 286	20 40 312
	◆Dubhe	Alkaid	ARCTURUS	◆SPICA	Alphard	◆PROCYON	POLLUX
165	52 19 001	48 41 041	44 18 086	39 52 131	50 21 217	38 27 257	46 33 286
166	52 20 000	49 17 041	45 13 087	40 34 131	49 48 218	37 34 257	45 41 286
167	52 20 359	49 53 041	46 08 087	41 14 132	49 13 220	36 40 258	44 48 286
168	52 19 359	50 29 040	47 02 087	41 54 133	48 38 221	35 46 259	43 55 287
169	52 17 358	51 04 040	47 57 088	42 34 134	48 02 222	34 53 259	43 03 287
170	52 14 357	51 39 039	48 52 088	43 13 135	47 24 223	33 59 260	42 10 287
171	52 11 356	52 14 039	49 47 088	43 51 136	46 47 224	33 05 260	41 18 287
172	52 07 355	52 48 038	50 42 089	44 29 137	46 08 225	32 11 261	40 26 287
173	52 03 355	53 21 038	51 36 089	45 05 138	45 29 226	31 17 261	39 33 287
174	51 57 354	53 55 037	52 31 090	45 41 140	44 49 227	30 22 262	38 41 288
175	51 51 353	54 28 037	53 26 090	46 16 141	44 08 228	29 28 262	37 49 288
176	51 44 352	55 00 036	54 21 090	46 51 142	43 27 229	28 34 263	36 57 288
177	51 37 352	55 32 035	55 16 091	47 24 143	42 45 230	27 39 263	36 04 288
178	51 28 351	56 03 035	56 10 091	47 56 144	42 02 231	26 45 263	35 12 288
179	51 20 350	56 34 034	57 05 092	48 28 146	41 19 232	25 51 264	34 20 289

LAT 24°N

LHA ♈	Hc	Zn	Hc	Zn	Hc	Zn	Hc	Zn	Hc	Zn	Hc	Zn	Hc	Zn
	◆ Alkaid		Alphecca		◆ SPICA		Gienah		REGULUS		◆ POLLUX		Dubhe	
180	57 04	033	41 38	075	48 59	147	48 11	174	61 04	250	33 28	289	51 10	350
181	57 34	032	42 31	075	49 28	148	48 16	175	60 13	251	32 37	289	51 00	349
182	58 03	031	43 24	075	49 56	149	48 19	177	59 21	252	31 45	289	50 49	348
183	58 31	031	44 17	075	50 24	151	48 22	178	58 29	253	30 53	289	50 37	347
184	58 59	030	45 10	076	50 50	152	48 22	180	57 36	254	30 01	290	50 25	347
185	59 26	029	46 03	076	51 15	154	48 22	181	56 43	255	29 10	290	50 12	346
186	59 52	028	46 56	076	51 39	155	48 20	183	55 50	255	28 18	290	49 59	345
187	60 17	027	47 49	076	52 01	156	48 17	184	54 57	256	27 27	290	49 45	345
188	60 41	026	48 43	076	52 22	158	48 12	186	54 04	257	26 35	291	49 30	344
189	61 04	025	49 36	076	52 42	159	48 06	187	53 11	257	25 44	291	49 15	344
190	61 27	024	50 29	077	53 01	161	47 59	188	52 17	258	24 53	291	48 59	343
191	61 48	022	51 22	077	53 18	163	47 50	190	51 23	259	24 02	291	48 43	342
192	62 09	021	52 16	077	53 34	164	47 40	191	50 30	259	23 11	292	48 26	342
193	62 28	020	53 09	077	53 48	166	47 29	193	49 36	260	22 20	292	48 09	341
194	62 46	019	54 03	077	54 00	167	47 17	194	48 42	261	21 29	292	47 51	341
	◆ Kochab		VEGA		Rasalhague		◆ ANTARES		SPICA		◆ REGULUS		Dubhe	
195	37 48	009	18 57	055	24 10	087	18 24	131	54 12	169	47 48	261	47 33	340
196	37 57	009	19 42	055	25 04	087	19 05	132	54 21	171	46 53	262	47 14	340
197	38 05	009	20 27	056	25 59	087	19 45	133	54 29	172	45 59	262	46 54	339
198	38 13	008	21 13	056	26 54	088	20 25	133	54 36	174	45 05	263	46 35	339
199	38 21	008	21 58	056	27 49	088	21 05	134	54 41	176	44 10	263	46 15	338
200	38 29	008	22 43	056	28 43	088	21 44	135	54 44	177	43 16	264	45 54	338
201	38 36	007	23 29	056	29 38	089	22 23	135	54 45	179	42 21	264	45 33	337
202	38 43	007	24 15	057	30 33	089	23 01	136	54 45	181	41 27	265	45 11	337
203	38 49	007	25 00	057	31 28	090	23 39	137	54 44	183	40 32	265	44 50	336
204	38 56	006	25 46	057	32 23	090	24 17	137	54 41	184	39 38	266	44 27	336
205	39 02	006	26 32	057	33 17	090	24 54	138	54 36	186	38 43	266	44 05	336
206	39 07	006	27 18	057	34 12	091	25 30	139	54 29	188	37 48	267	43 42	335
207	39 13	005	28 04	057	35 07	091	26 06	140	54 21	189	36 53	267	43 19	335
208	39 18	005	28 51	057	36 02	092	26 41	140	54 12	191	35 59	267	42 55	334
209	39 23	005	29 37	058	36 57	092	27 16	141	54 00	193	35 04	268	42 31	334
	◆ Kochab		VEGA		Rasalhague		◆ ANTARES		SPICA		◆ REGULUS		Dubhe	
210	39 27	004	30 23	058	37 51	093	27 50	142	53 48	194	34 09	268	42 07	334
211	39 31	004	31 09	058	38 46	093	28 23	143	53 33	196	33 14	269	41 43	333
212	39 35	004	31 56	058	39 41	093	28 56	143	53 18	197	32 20	269	41 18	333
213	39 38	003	32 42	058	40 36	094	29 29	144	53 01	199	31 25	270	40 53	333
214	39 42	003	33 29	058	41 30	094	30 00	145	52 42	201	30 30	270	40 28	332
215	39 44	003	34 15	058	42 25	095	30 31	146	52 22	202	29 35	270	40 03	332
216	39 47	002	35 02	058	43 19	095	31 02	147	52 01	204	28 40	271	39 37	332
217	39 49	002	35 49	058	44 14	096	31 31	148	51 39	205	27 46	271	39 11	332
218	39 51	002	36 35	058	45 08	096	32 00	149	51 15	206	26 51	272	38 45	331
219	39 52	001	37 22	058	46 03	097	32 28	149	50 50	208	25 56	272	38 18	331
220	39 53	001	38 09	059	46 57	097	32 56	150	50 24	209	25 01	272	37 52	331
221	39 54	001	38 56	059	47 52	098	33 22	151	49 56	211	24 06	273	37 25	331
222	39 54	000	39 42	059	48 46	098	33 48	152	49 28	212	23 12	273	36 58	331
223	39 54	000	40 29	059	49 40	099	34 13	153	48 58	213	22 17	274	36 31	330
224	39 54	000	41 16	059	50 34	100	34 38	154	48 28	214	21 22	274	36 04	330
	VEGA		◆ ALTAIR		Nunki		ANTARES		◆ SPICA		Denebola		◆ Alkaid	
225	42 03	059	19 11	089	13 58	128	35 01	155	47 56	216	44 20	267	61 06	335
226	42 49	058	20 06	089	14 41	128	35 24	156	47 24	217	43 25	267	60 43	334
227	43 36	058	21 01	089	15 24	129	35 45	157	46 50	218	42 30	268	60 18	333
228	44 23	058	21 56	090	16 06	129	36 06	158	46 16	219	41 36	268	59 53	332
229	45 09	058	22 51	090	16 49	130	36 26	159	45 41	220	40 41	269	59 27	331
230	45 56	058	23 45	091	17 31	130	36 45	160	45 05	222	39 46	269	59 01	330
231	46 43	058	24 40	091	18 12	131	37 03	161	44 28	223	38 51	270	58 33	329
232	47 29	058	25 35	091	18 53	132	37 20	162	43 51	224	37 56	270	58 05	329
233	48 16	058	26 30	092	19 34	132	37 36	163	43 13	225	37 02	270	57 36	328
234	49 02	058	27 25	092	20 14	133	37 51	165	42 34	226	36 07	271	57 06	327
235	49 48	058	28 19	093	20 54	134	38 05	166	41 54	227	35 12	271	56 36	326
236	50 35	057	29 14	093	21 34	134	38 19	167	41 14	228	34 17	272	56 05	325
237	51 21	057	30 09	094	22 13	135	38 31	168	40 33	229	33 22	272	55 34	325
238	52 07	057	31 03	094	22 52	136	38 42	169	39 52	229	32 28	272	55 02	324
239	52 53	057	31 58	094	23 30	136	38 52	170	39 10	230	31 33	273	54 30	323
	◆ VEGA		ALTAIR		Nunki		◆ ANTARES		SPICA		ARCTURUS		◆ Alkaid	
240	53 38	056	32 53	095	24 07	137	39 00	171	38 27	231	65 27	264	53 57	323
241	54 24	056	33 47	095	24 45	138	39 08	172	37 44	232	64 32	264	53 24	322
242	55 10	056	34 42	096	25 21	138	39 15	174	37 01	233	63 38	265	52 50	322
243	55 55	056	35 36	096	25 57	139	39 21	175	36 17	234	62 43	265	52 16	321
244	56 40	055	36 31	097	26 33	140	39 25	176	35 33	235	61 48	266	51 41	321
245	57 25	055	37 25	097	27 08	141	39 28	177	34 48	235	60 54	266	51 06	320
246	58 09	054	38 20	098	27 43	141	39 31	178	34 02	236	59 59	267	50 31	320
247	58 54	054	39 14	098	28 17	142	39 32	179	33 17	237	59 04	267	49 56	319
248	59 38	053	40 08	099	28 50	143	39 32	180	32 31	238	58 09	268	49 20	319
249	60 22	053	41 02	099	29 23	144	39 31	182	31 44	238	57 15	268	48 44	319
250	61 05	052	41 56	100	29 55	145	39 29	183	30 57	239	56 20	269	48 07	318
251	61 48	052	42 50	100	30 26	145	39 26	184	30 10	240	55 25	269	47 30	318
252	62 31	051	43 44	101	30 57	146	39 21	185	29 23	240	54 30	270	46 54	318
253	63 14	050	44 38	102	31 27	147	39 16	186	28 35	241	53 35	270	46 16	317
254	63 55	049	45 31	102	31 56	148	39 09	187	27 47	242	52 41	270	45 39	317
	◆ DENEB		ALTAIR		◆ Nunki		ANTARES		SPICA		◆ ARCTURUS		Alkaid	
255	40 47	050	46 25	103	32 25	149	39 02	189	26 59	242	51 46	271	45 02	317
256	41 29	050	47 18	103	32 53	150	38 53	190	26 10	243	50 51	271	44 24	316
257	42 11	050	48 12	104	33 20	151	38 43	191	25 21	243	49 56	272	43 46	316
258	42 52	050	49 05	105	33 46	152	38 32	192	24 32	244	49 01	272	43 08	316
259	43 34	049	49 58	105	34 12	153	38 21	193	23 43	245	48 07	272	42 30	316
260	44 15	049	50 50	106	34 37	154	38 08	194	22 53	245	47 12	273	41 52	316
261	44 57	049	51 43	107	35 00	155	37 54	195	22 03	246	46 17	273	41 13	315
262	45 38	049	52 35	108	35 24	156	37 39	196	21 13	246	45 22	273	40 35	315
263	46 19	049	53 27	108	35 46	157	37 23	197	20 23	247	44 28	274	39 56	315
264	47 00	048	54 19	109	36 07	158	37 06	198	19 32	247	43 33	274	39 17	315
265	47 41	048	55 11	110	36 27	159	36 48	200	18 42	248	42 38	274	38 38	315
266	48 22	048	56 02	111	36 47	160	36 29	201	17 51	248	41 44	275	38 00	315
267	49 03	048	56 53	112	37 05	161	36 10	202	17 00	249	40 49	275	37 21	315
268	49 43	047	57 44	113	37 23	162	35 49	203	16 08	249	39 55	275	36 42	315
269	50 23	047	58 34	114	37 40	163	35 27	204	15 17	250	39 00	276	36 03	315

LHA ♈	Hc	Zn	Hc	Zn	Hc	Zn	Hc	Zn	Hc	Zn	Hc	Zn	Hc	Zn
	◆ DENEB		Enif		◆ Nunki		ANTARES		◆ ARCTURUS		Alkaid		Kochab	
270	51 03	047	34 47	095	37 55	164	35 05	205	38 05	276	35 24	314	34 07	346
271	51 43	046	35 41	095	38 10	165	34 42	206	37 11	276	34 44	314	33 53	346
272	52 22	046	36 36	095	38 23	166	34 18	207	36 17	277	34 05	314	33 40	346
273	53 01	045	37 30	096	38 36	167	33 53	208	35 22	277	33 26	314	33 26	345
274	53 40	045	38 25	096	38 48	168	33 27	209	34 28	277	32 47	314	33 12	345
275	54 19	044	39 19	097	38 58	170	33 00	209	33 33	278	32 08	314	32 58	345
276	54 57	044	40 14	097	39 07	171	32 33	210	32 39	278	31 29	314	32 44	345
277	55 35	043	41 08	098	39 16	172	32 05	211	31 45	278	30 49	314	32 29	345
278	56 12	043	42 02	098	39 23	173	31 36	212	30 51	279	30 10	314	32 15	345
279	56 49	042	42 57	099	39 29	174	31 07	213	29 57	279	29 31	314	32 00	344
280	57 26	041	43 51	100	39 34	175	30 36	214	29 02	279	28 52	315	31 45	344
281	58 02	041	44 45	100	39 38	176	30 05	215	28 08	280	28 13	315	31 30	344
282	58 37	040	45 39	101	39 41	178	29 34	216	27 14	280	27 34	315	31 15	344
283	59 12	039	46 32	101	39 43	179	29 02	216	26 20	280	26 55	315	31 00	344
284	59 47	039	47 26	102	39 43	180	28 29	217	25 26	281	26 16	315	30 45	344
	DENEB		◆ Alpheratz		FOMALHAUT		◆ Nunki		ANTARES		◆ Alphecca		Kochab	
285	60 20	038	21 57	067	11 37	130	39 43	181	27 55	218	43 59	285	30 30	344
286	60 54	037	22 47	067	12 19	131	39 41	182	27 21	219	43 06	285	30 14	344
287	61 26	036	23 38	067	13 00	131	39 39	183	26 47	220	42 13	285	29 58	343
288	61 58	035	24 28	067	13 42	132	39 35	185	26 12	220	41 20	285	29 43	343
289	62 29	034	25 19	068	14 22	132	39 30	186	25 36	221	40 27	285	29 27	343
290	62 59	033	26 10	068	15 03	133	39 24	187	25 00	222	39 34	286	29 11	343
291	63 28	032	27 00	068	15 43	133	39 17	188	24 23	222	38 42	286	28 55	343
292	63 56	030	27 51	068	16 23	134	39 08	189	23 45	223	37 49	286	28 39	343
293	64 24	029	28 42	069	17 02	134	38 59	190	23 08	224	36 56	286	28 23	343
294	64 50	028	29 33	069	17 41	135	38 49	191	22 29	225	36 04	286	28 07	343
295	65 15	027	30 25	069	18 19	136	38 37	193	21 51	225	35 11	287	27 51	343
296	65 39	025	31 16	069	18 57	136	38 25	194	21 12	226	34 19	287	27 35	343
297	66 02	024	32 07	069	19 35	137	38 11	195	20 32	227	33 26	287	27 19	343
298	66 23	022	32 59	070	20 12	138	37 57	196	19 52	227	32 34	287	27 02	343
299	66 43	021	33 50	070	20 49	138	37 41	197	19 12	228	31 42	288	26 46	343
	◆ DENEB		Schedar		Alpheratz		◆ FOMALHAUT		Nunki		◆ Rasalhague		VEGA	
300	67 02	019	30 35	037	34 41	070	21 25	139	37 25	198	54 00	258	67 06	315
301	67 19	017	31 08	037	35 33	070	22 01	140	37 07	199	53 06	259	66 27	314
302	67 35	016	31 41	037	36 25	070	22 36	140	36 49	200	52 12	259	65 47	313
303	67 49	014	32 14	037	37 16	071	23 11	141	36 29	201	51 18	260	65 06	312
304	68 02	012	32 46	037	38 08	071	23 45	142	36 09	202	50 24	260	64 25	311
305	68 12	010	33 19	037	39 00	071	24 19	143	35 48	203	49 30	261	63 44	310
306	68 21	009	33 52	037	39 52	071	24 52	143	35 26	204	48 36	262	63 02	310
307	68 29	007	34 25	037	40 44	071	25 24	144	35 03	205	47 42	262	62 19	309
308	68 34	005	34 57	036	41 36	071	25 56	145	34 39	206	46 47	263	61 37	308
309	68 38	003	35 30	036	42 28	072	26 27	146	34 14	207	45 53	263	60 53	308
310	68 40	001	36 02	036	43 20	072	26 58	146	33 49	208	44 58	264	60 10	307
311	68 40	359	36 35	036	44 12	072	27 28	147	33 22	209	44 04	264	59 26	307
312	68 38	357	37 07	036	45 04	072	27 58	148	32 55	210	43 09	265	58 42	306
313	68 34	355	37 39	036	45 56	072	28 26	149	32 28	211	42 15	265	57 57	306
314	68 29	353	38 11	036	46 48	072	28 55	150	31 59	212	41 20	266	57 12	305
	◆ Alpheratz		Diphda		◆ FOMALHAUT		ALTAIR		Rasalhague		◆ VEGA		DENEB	
315	47 40	072	21 06	122	29 22	150	67 45	230	40 25	266	56 28	305	68 21	351
316	48 33	072	21 52	123	29 49	151	67 02	232	39 31	267	55 42	304	68 12	350
317	49 25	073	22 38	123	30 15	152	66 18	234	38 36	267	54 57	304	68 01	348
318	50 17	073	23 24	124	30 40	153	65 34	235	37 41	268	54 12	304	67 49	346
319	51 09	073	24 09	125	31 04	154	64 48	237	36 46	268	53 26	303	67 35	344
320	52 02	073	24 54	125	31 28	155	64 02	238	35 52	268	52 40	303	67 19	342
321	52 54	073	25 38	126	31 51	156	63 15	240	34 57	269	51 54	303	67 02	341
322	53 46	073	26 23	127	32 13	157	62 28	241	34 02	269	51 08	303	66 43	339
323	54 39	073	27 06	127	32 34	158	61 40	242	33 07	270	50 22	303	66 23	338
324	55 31	073	27 50	128	32 55	159	60 51	243	32 12	270	49 36	302	66 01	336
325	56 24	073	28 33	129	33 14	160	60 02	244	31 18	270	48 49	302	65 38	335
326	57 16	073	29 15	129	33 33	161	59 12	245	30 23	271	48 03	302	65 14	333
327	58 08	073	29 58	130	33 51	162	58 22	246	29 28	271	47 16	302	64 49	332
328	59 01	073	30 39	131	34 08	163	57 32	247	28 33	272	46 30	302	64 23	331
329	59 53	073	31 20	132	34 24	164	56 41	248	27 38	272	45 43	302	63 56	329
	◆ Mirfak		Hamal		Diphda		◆ FOMALHAUT		ALTAIR		◆ VEGA		DENEB	
330	23 33	044	33 45	077	32 01	132	34 39	165	55 50	249	44 57	302	63 27	328
331	24 12	044	34 38	077	32 41	133	34 53	166	54 58	250	44 10	302	62 58	327
332	24 50	044	35 32	077	33 21	134	35 06	167	54 07	251	43 23	302	62 28	326
333	25 28	044	36 25	078	34 00	135	35 18	168	53 15	252	42 36	301	61 57	325
334	26 06	044	37 19	078	34 38	136	35 30	169	52 22	253	41 50	301	61 25	324
335	26 45	044	38 12	078	35 16	137	35 40	170	51 30	253	41 03	301	60 53	323
336	27 23	045	39 06	078	35 54	138	35 49	171	50 37	254	40 16	301	60 19	322
337	28 02	045	40 00	079	36 30	138	35 58	172	49 45	255	39 29	301	59 46	321
338	28 40	045	40 54	079	37 06	139	36 05	173	48 52	255	38 43	301	59 11	321
339	29 19	045	41 47	079	37 42	140	36 11	174	47 59	256	37 56	302	58 36	320
340	29 57	045	42 41	079	38 16	141	36 16	175	47 05	257	37 09	302	58 01	319
341	30 36	045	43 35	080	38 50	142	36 21	176	46 12	257	36 23	302	57 25	318
342	31 14	045	44 29	080	39 24	143	36 24	177	45 18	258	35 36	302	56 48	318
343	31 53	045	45 23	080	39 56	144	36 26	178	44 25	259	34 49	302	56 11	317
344	32 32	045	46 17	080	40 28	145	36 27	179	43 31	259	34 03	302	55 34	317
	Schedar		◆ CAPELLA		ALDEBARAN		Diphda		◆ FOMALHAUT		ALTAIR		◆ DENEB	
345	52 33	023	14 05	046	11 47	077	40 58	146	36 27	180	42 37	260	54 56	316
346	52 54	022	14 44	046	12 41	077	41 28	147	36 26	181	41 43	260	54 18	316
347	53 14	021	15 24	046	13 34	078	41 57	149	36 25	183	40 49	261	53 39	315
348	53 34	021	16 03	046	14 28	078	42 26	150	36 22	184	39 55	261	53 00	315
349	53 53	020	16 43	046	15 22	078	42 53	151	36 18	185	39 01	262	52 21	314
350	54 11	019	17 23	047	16 15	079	43 19	152	36 13	186	38 06	262	51 42	314
351	54 29	018	18 03	047	17 09	079	43 44	153	36 06	187	37 12	263	51 02	313
352	54 46	017	18 43	047	18 03	079	44 09	154	35 59	188	36 18	263	50 22	313
353	55 02	017	19 23	047	18 57	080	44 32	156	35 51	189	35 23	264	49 42	313
354	55 17	016	20 03	047	19 51	080	44 54	157	35 42	190	34 29	264	49 02	312
355	55 31	015	20 44	048	20 45	081	45 15	158	35 32	191	33 34	265	48 21	312
356	55 45	014	21 25	048	21 39	081	45 35	159	35 21	192	32 40	265	47 40	312
357	55 58	013	22 05	048	22 33	081	45 54	161	35 09	193	31 45	266	46 59	312
358	56 10	012	22 46	048	23 27	082	46 12	162	34 56	194	30 50	266	46 18	311
359	56 21	011	23 27	048	24 22	082	46 28	163	34 42	195	29 56	267	45 37	311

LHA ♈	Hc	Zn	Hc	Zn	Hc	Zn	Hc	Zn	Hc	Zn	Hc	Zn	Hc	Zn
	Schedar		◆ CAPELLA		ALDEBARAN		◆ Diphda		FOMALHAUT		◆ ALTAIR		DENEB	
0	55 32	010	23 28	048	25 08	082	47 41	164	35 25	196	29 04	268	44 16	312
1	55 42	009	24 09	048	26 02	082	47 55	166	35 09	197	28 08	268	43 35	312
2	55 50	008	24 50	048	26 57	082	48 09	167	34 52	198	27 13	268	42 53	311
3	55 57	007	25 32	048	27 52	083	48 20	168	34 34	199	26 18	269	42 12	311
4	56 04	006	26 13	049	28 47	083	48 31	170	34 15	200	25 23	269	41 30	311
5	56 09	005	26 54	049	29 42	083	48 40	171	33 55	201	24 28	270	40 49	311
6	56 14	004	27 36	049	30 36	084	48 48	173	33 35	202	23 32	270	40 07	311
7	56 17	003	28 17	049	31 31	084	48 54	174	33 13	203	22 37	270	39 25	311
8	56 20	002	28 59	049	32 26	084	48 59	176	32 51	204	21 42	271	38 43	311
9	56 22	001	29 40	049	33 21	085	49 03	177	32 28	205	20 47	271	38 01	310
10	56 23	000	30 22	049	34 16	085	49 05	178	32 04	206	19 52	271	37 19	310
11	56 23	359	31 04	049	35 11	085	49 06	180	31 39	207	18 56	272	36 37	310
12	56 22	358	31 45	049	36 06	086	49 05	181	31 14	208	18 01	272	35 55	310
13	56 19	357	32 27	049	37 02	086	49 03	183	30 48	209	17 06	273	35 12	310
14	56 16	356	33 09	049	37 57	086	49 00	184	30 21	210	16 11	273	34 30	310
	◆ CAPELLA		ALDEBARAN		RIGEL		◆ Diphda		FOMALHAUT		Enif		◆ DENEB	
15	33 50	049	38 52	087	20 16	109	48 55	186	29 53	210	41 41	263	33 48	310
16	34 32	049	39 47	087	21 08	109	48 49	187	29 25	211	40 46	263	33 06	310
17	35 14	049	40 42	088	22 00	110	48 41	189	28 55	212	39 52	264	32 24	310
18	35 55	049	41 37	088	22 52	110	48 32	190	28 26	213	38 57	264	31 42	310
19	36 37	049	42 32	088	23 44	111	48 22	191	27 55	214	38 02	265	30 59	310
20	37 18	049	43 28	089	24 36	111	48 11	193	27 24	215	37 07	265	30 17	310
21	38 00	049	44 23	089	25 27	112	47 58	194	26 53	215	36 12	266	29 35	310
22	38 41	049	45 18	089	26 18	112	47 44	196	26 20	216	35 17	266	28 53	310
23	39 23	048	46 13	090	27 09	113	47 28	197	25 48	217	34 21	266	28 11	310
24	40 04	048	47 09	090	28 00	114	47 12	198	25 14	218	33 26	267	27 29	311
25	40 45	048	48 04	091	28 50	114	46 54	200	24 40	218	32 31	267	26 47	311
26	41 26	048	48 59	091	29 40	115	46 35	201	24 06	219	31 36	268	26 05	311
27	42 07	048	49 54	091	30 30	115	46 14	202	23 31	220	30 41	268	25 23	311
28	42 48	048	50 49	092	31 20	116	45 53	203	22 55	220	29 46	268	24 42	311
29	43 29	048	51 45	092	32 10	117	45 30	205	22 19	221	28 50	269	24 00	311
	CAPELLA		◆ ALDEBARAN		RIGEL		Acamar		◆ Diphda		Alpheratz		◆ DENEB	
30	44 10	047	52 40	093	32 59	117	25 17	168	45 07	206	64 26	290	23 18	311
31	44 51	047	53 35	093	33 48	118	25 29	168	44 42	207	63 34	290	22 37	311
32	45 31	047	54 30	094	34 36	119	25 39	169	44 16	208	62 42	289	21 55	311
33	46 11	047	55 25	094	35 25	119	25 49	170	43 50	209	61 49	289	21 14	312
34	46 51	046	56 20	095	36 12	120	25 58	171	43 22	211	60 57	289	20 33	312
35	47 31	046	57 15	095	37 00	121	26 07	172	42 53	212	60 05	289	19 52	312
36	48 11	046	58 10	096	37 47	122	26 14	173	42 24	213	59 13	289	19 11	312
37	48 50	045	59 05	096	38 34	122	26 21	173	41 54	214	58 20	289	18 30	312
38	49 29	045	60 00	097	39 20	123	26 27	174	41 22	215	57 28	289	17 49	312
39	50 08	045	60 55	097	40 06	124	26 32	175	40 50	216	56 36	289	17 08	313
40	50 47	044	61 50	098	40 52	125	26 36	176	40 17	217	55 43	289	16 28	313
41	51 26	044	62 44	099	41 37	126	26 40	177	39 43	218	54 51	288	15 47	313
42	52 04	043	63 39	099	42 22	127	26 42	178	39 09	219	53 59	288	15 07	313
43	52 41	043	64 33	100	43 06	128	26 44	179	38 34	220	53 06	288	14 27	314
44	53 19	042	65 28	101	43 49	128	26 45	179	37 58	221	52 14	288	13 47	314
	CAPELLA		◆ POLLUX		PROCYON		SIRIUS		◆ Acamar		Diphda		◆ Alpheratz	
45	53 56	042	26 08	069	20 24	093	22 00	121	26 45	180	37 21	222	51 21	288
46	54 32	041	27 00	069	21 19	093	22 47	121	26 45	181	36 44	223	50 29	289
47	55 09	041	27 51	069	22 14	094	23 35	122	26 43	182	36 06	224	49 37	289
48	55 45	040	28 43	070	23 09	094	24 21	122	26 41	183	35 28	225	48 44	289
49	56 20	039	29 35	070	24 04	095	25 08	123	26 38	184	34 49	225	47 52	289
50	56 55	039	30 27	070	24 59	095	25 54	124	26 34	185	34 09	226	47 00	289
51	57 29	038	31 19	070	25 54	096	26 40	124	26 29	185	33 29	227	46 07	289
52	58 03	037	32 11	070	26 49	096	27 25	125	26 23	186	32 48	228	45 15	289
53	58 36	036	33 03	071	27 44	096	28 10	126	26 17	187	32 07	229	44 23	289
54	59 08	036	33 55	071	28 39	097	28 55	126	26 10	188	31 25	229	43 31	289
55	59 40	035	34 47	071	29 34	097	29 39	127	26 02	189	30 43	230	42 39	289
56	60 11	034	35 39	071	30 29	098	30 23	128	25 53	190	30 01	231	41 46	289
57	60 41	033	36 32	071	31 23	098	31 07	128	25 44	190	29 18	232	40 54	289
58	61 11	032	37 24	072	32 18	099	31 50	129	25 33	191	28 34	232	40 02	290
59	61 40	031	38 16	072	33 12	099	32 32	130	25 22	192	27 50	233	39 10	290
	◆ CAPELLA		PROCYON		◆ SIRIUS		RIGEL		Diphda		◆ Hamal		Mirfak	
60	62 07	030	34 07	100	33 14	131	53 47	147	27 06	234	64 19	277	62 15	348
61	62 34	028	35 01	100	33 56	132	54 16	149	26 21	234	63 24	277	62 03	347
62	63 00	027	35 56	101	34 37	132	54 44	150	25 36	235	62 29	277	61 49	345
63	63 25	026	36 50	101	35 18	133	55 11	152	24 51	236	61 35	277	61 35	344
64	63 49	025	37 44	102	35 58	134	55 37	153	24 05	236	60 40	277	61 19	343
65	64 11	023	38 38	102	36 37	135	56 01	155	23 19	237	59 45	278	61 02	342
66	64 32	022	39 32	103	37 16	136	56 23	157	22 33	237	58 50	278	60 44	341
67	64 53	021	40 26	103	37 54	137	56 44	158	21 46	238	57 56	278	60 26	339
68	65 11	019	41 19	104	38 32	138	57 04	160	20 59	239	57 01	278	60 06	338
69	65 29	018	42 13	105	39 09	139	57 22	162	20 11	239	56 06	278	59 45	337
70	65 45	016	43 06	105	39 45	139	57 39	164	19 24	240	55 12	279	59 23	336
71	65 59	015	43 59	106	40 21	140	57 53	165	18 36	240	54 17	279	59 00	335
72	66 13	013	44 52	107	40 55	141	58 07	167	17 48	241	53 23	279	58 36	334
73	66 24	011	45 45	107	41 29	142	58 18	169	17 00	241	52 28	279	58 12	333
74	66 34	010	46 38	108	42 03	144	58 28	171	16 11	242	51 33	279	57 47	332
	CAPELLA		◆ Dubhe		POLLUX		PROCYON		◆ SIRIUS		RIGEL		◆ Hamal	
75	66 42	008	19 35	030	52 20	073	47 30	109	42 35	145	58 36	173	50 39	280
76	66 49	006	20 03	030	53 13	074	48 23	109	43 07	146	58 42	175	49 45	280
77	66 54	004	20 30	030	54 06	074	49 15	110	43 37	147	58 46	177	48 50	280
78	66 57	003	20 58	031	54 59	074	50 06	111	44 07	148	58 48	178	47 56	280
79	66 59	001	21 27	031	55 52	074	50 58	112	44 36	149	58 49	180	47 01	280
80	66 59	359	21 55	031	56 45	074	51 49	112	45 04	150	58 48	182	46 07	281
81	66 57	357	22 23	031	57 38	074	52 40	113	45 31	151	58 44	184	45 13	281
82	66 54	355	22 51	031	58 31	074	53 31	114	45 57	153	58 40	186	44 19	281
83	66 49	354	23 20	031	59 24	074	54 21	115	46 21	154	58 33	188	43 24	281
84	66 42	352	23 48	031	60 17	073	55 11	116	46 45	155	58 24	190	42 30	281
85	66 33	350	24 16	031	61 10	073	56 00	117	47 08	157	58 14	192	41 36	282
86	66 23	349	24 45	031	62 03	073	56 49	118	47 29	158	58 02	194	40 42	282
87	66 11	347	25 13	031	62 56	073	57 38	119	47 49	159	57 48	195	39 48	282
88	65 58	345	25 42	031	63 48	073	58 26	120	48 08	160	57 33	197	38 54	282
89	65 43	344	26 10	031	64 41	073	59 13	121	48 26	162	57 16	199	38 00	283

LAT 23°N

LHA ♈	Hc	Zn	Hc	Zn	Hc	Zn	Hc	Zn	Hc	Zn	Hc	Zn	Hc	Zn
	Dubhe		◆ REGULUS		Alphard		SIRIUS		◆ RIGEL		ALDEBARAN		◆ CAPELLA	
90	26 39	031	29 57	089	30 00	116	48 43	163	56 57	201	69 25	255	65 27	342
91	27 07	031	30 53	090	30 49	116	48 58	165	56 37	202	68 31	256	65 10	341
92	27 35	031	31 48	090	31 38	117	49 12	166	56 15	204	67 37	257	64 51	339
93	28 04	031	32 43	090	32 27	118	49 25	168	55 52	206	66 43	258	64 30	338
94	28 32	031	33 38	091	33 16	118	49 36	169	55 27	207	65 49	259	64 09	336
95	29 01	031	34 34	091	34 05	119	49 46	170	55 01	209	64 55	260	63 46	335
96	29 29	031	35 29	092	34 53	120	49 54	172	54 34	210	64 00	261	63 22	334
97	29 57	031	36 24	092	35 41	121	50 01	173	54 06	212	63 06	261	62 57	333
98	30 26	031	37 19	092	36 28	121	50 07	175	53 36	213	62 11	262	62 31	331
99	30 54	031	38 14	093	37 15	122	50 11	176	53 05	215	61 16	262	62 05	330
100	31 22	031	39 09	093	38 02	123	50 14	178	52 33	216	60 22	263	61 37	329
101	31 50	030	40 05	094	38 48	124	50 16	179	52 00	217	59 27	264	61 08	328
102	32 18	030	41 00	094	39 34	124	50 16	181	51 26	219	58 32	264	60 38	327
103	32 46	030	41 55	095	40 19	125	50 14	182	50 51	220	57 37	265	60 08	326
104	33 14	030	42 50	095	41 04	126	50 11	184	50 15	221	56 42	265	59 37	325
	Dubhe		◆ REGULUS		Alphard		SIRIUS		◆ RIGEL		ALDEBARAN		◆ CAPELLA	
105	33 41	030	43 45	096	41 48	127	50 07	185	49 38	222	55 47	266	59 05	324
106	34 09	030	44 40	096	42 32	128	50 01	187	49 01	224	54 52	266	58 32	324
107	34 36	030	45 35	097	43 16	129	49 54	188	48 22	225	53 57	267	57 59	323
108	35 03	030	46 29	097	43 58	130	49 45	190	47 43	226	53 01	267	57 25	322
109	35 30	029	47 24	098	44 41	131	49 35	191	47 03	227	52 06	268	56 51	321
110	35 57	029	48 19	098	45 22	132	49 24	193	46 22	228	51 11	268	56 16	321
111	36 24	029	49 14	099	46 03	133	49 11	194	45 41	229	50 16	268	55 41	320
112	36 51	029	50 08	099	46 43	134	48 57	195	44 59	230	49 21	269	55 05	319
113	37 17	029	51 03	100	47 23	135	48 41	197	44 16	231	48 25	269	54 29	319
114	37 44	028	51 57	100	48 02	136	48 25	198	43 33	232	47 30	270	53 52	318
115	38 10	028	52 51	101	48 40	137	48 07	200	42 49	233	46 35	270	53 15	318
116	38 36	028	53 46	102	49 17	138	47 48	201	42 05	234	45 40	270	52 38	317
117	39 01	028	54 40	102	49 53	139	47 27	202	41 20	235	44 45	271	52 00	317
118	39 27	027	55 33	103	50 29	141	47 06	204	40 35	235	43 49	271	51 22	316
119	39 52	027	56 27	104	51 03	142	46 43	205	39 49	236	42 54	272	50 43	316
	◆ Dubhe		Denebola		◆ Alphard		SIRIUS		RIGEL		◆ ALDEBARAN		CAPELLA	
120	40 17	027	35 15	088	51 37	143	46 19	206	39 03	237	41 59	272	50 05	315
121	40 41	026	36 10	088	52 09	145	45 54	207	38 17	238	41 04	272	49 26	315
122	41 06	026	37 06	089	52 41	146	45 28	209	37 30	239	40 09	273	48 46	315
123	41 30	026	38 01	089	53 11	147	45 01	210	36 42	239	39 13	273	48 07	314
124	41 54	025	38 56	090	53 40	149	44 33	211	35 55	240	38 18	273	47 27	314
125	42 17	025	39 51	090	54 08	150	44 04	212	35 07	241	37 23	274	46 47	314
126	42 40	025	40 47	090	54 35	152	43 35	213	34 18	242	36 28	274	46 07	313
127	43 03	024	41 42	091	55 01	153	43 04	214	33 30	242	35 33	274	45 27	313
128	43 25	024	42 37	091	55 25	155	42 32	216	32 41	243	34 38	275	44 46	313
129	43 48	023	43 32	092	55 47	157	42 00	217	31 51	244	33 43	275	44 06	313
130	44 09	023	44 27	092	56 09	158	41 26	218	31 02	244	32 48	275	43 25	312
131	44 31	023	45 23	092	56 28	160	40 52	219	30 12	245	31 53	276	42 44	312
132	44 52	022	46 18	093	56 47	162	40 17	220	29 22	245	30 58	276	42 03	312
133	45 12	022	47 13	093	57 03	163	39 42	221	28 32	246	30 03	276	41 22	312
134	45 32	021	48 08	094	57 18	165	39 05	222	27 41	247	29 08	277	40 41	312
	Dubhe		◆ ARCTURUS		SPICA		◆ Alphard		SIRIUS		BETELGEUSE		◆ CAPELLA	
135	45 52	021	17 01	076	16 30	110	57 32	167	38 28	223	43 11	258	40 00	312
136	46 11	020	17 54	076	17 21	111	57 43	169	37 51	223	42 17	259	39 19	312
137	46 30	020	18 48	077	18 13	111	57 53	171	37 12	224	41 23	259	38 37	311
138	46 48	019	19 42	077	19 04	112	58 02	172	36 34	225	40 29	260	37 56	311
139	47 06	019	20 36	077	19 55	112	58 08	174	35 54	226	39 34	260	37 14	311
140	47 24	018	21 30	078	20 47	113	58 13	176	35 14	227	38 40	261	36 33	311
141	47 40	017	22 24	078	21 37	113	58 15	178	34 33	228	37 45	261	35 51	311
142	47 57	017	23 18	078	22 28	114	58 17	180	33 52	229	36 51	262	35 09	311
143	48 12	016	24 12	079	23 18	114	58 16	182	33 10	229	35 56	262	34 28	311
144	48 28	016	25 06	079	24 09	115	58 13	184	32 28	230	35 01	263	33 46	311
145	48 42	015	26 00	079	24 58	116	58 09	185	31 46	231	34 07	263	33 04	311
146	48 56	014	26 54	079	25 48	116	58 03	187	31 03	232	33 12	264	32 23	311
147	49 10	014	27 49	080	26 38	117	57 55	189	30 19	232	32 17	264	31 41	311
148	49 23	013	28 43	080	27 27	117	57 45	191	29 35	233	31 22	265	30 59	311
149	49 35	012	29 37	080	28 16	118	57 34	193	28 51	234	30 27	265	30 18	311
	Dubhe		◆ ARCTURUS		SPICA		◆ Alphard		SIRIUS		POLLUX		◆ CAPELLA	
150	49 46	012	30 32	081	29 04	119	57 21	195	28 06	234	59 30	286	29 36	311
151	49 57	011	31 26	081	29 53	119	57 06	196	27 21	235	58 37	286	28 55	311
152	50 08	010	32 21	081	30 41	120	56 49	198	26 35	236	57 44	286	28 13	311
153	50 17	010	33 16	082	31 29	121	56 31	200	25 50	236	56 51	286	27 32	311
154	50 26	009	34 10	082	32 16	121	56 12	202	25 03	237	55 58	286	26 50	311
155	50 35	008	35 05	082	33 03	122	55 51	203	24 17	238	55 05	286	26 09	311
156	50 42	008	36 00	082	33 50	123	55 28	205	23 30	238	54 12	286	25 27	312
157	50 49	007	36 54	083	34 36	123	55 05	206	22 43	239	53 19	286	24 46	312
158	50 56	006	37 49	083	35 22	124	54 39	208	21 56	239	52 26	287	24 05	312
159	51 01	005	38 44	083	36 07	125	54 13	209	21 08	240	51 33	287	23 24	312
160	51 06	005	39 39	084	36 53	126	53 45	211	20 20	241	50 40	287	22 43	312
161	51 10	004	40 34	084	37 37	126	53 16	212	19 32	241	49 48	287	22 02	312
162	51 13	003	41 29	084	38 21	127	52 46	214	18 43	242	48 55	287	21 21	312
163	51 16	002	42 24	085	39 05	128	52 15	215	17 54	242	48 02	287	20 40	312
164	51 18	002	43 19	085	39 48	129	51 42	217	17 05	243	47 09	287	19 59	313
	◆ Dubhe		Alkaid		ARCTURUS		◆ SPICA		Alphard		◆ PROCYON		POLLUX	
165	51 19	001	47 56	041	44 14	085	40 31	130	51 09	218	38 40	258	46 16	287
166	51 20	000	48 32	040	45 09	086	41 13	131	50 34	219	37 46	258	45 23	287
167	51 20	359	49 07	040	46 04	086	41 55	132	49 59	220	36 52	259	44 31	287
168	51 19	359	49 43	039	46 59	086	42 35	133	49 23	222	35 58	259	43 38	287
169	51 17	358	50 18	039	47 54	087	43 16	134	48 46	223	35 04	260	42 45	288
170	51 14	357	50 52	039	48 49	087	43 55	135	48 08	224	34 09	260	41 53	288
171	51 11	356	51 27	038	49 44	087	44 34	136	47 29	225	33 15	261	41 00	288
172	51 07	356	52 00	038	50 40	088	45 13	137	46 50	226	32 20	261	40 07	288
173	51 03	355	52 34	037	51 35	088	45 50	138	46 10	227	31 26	262	39 15	288
174	50 57	354	53 07	036	52 30	088	46 27	139	45 29	228	30 31	262	38 22	288
175	50 51	353	53 39	036	53 25	089	47 03	140	44 47	229	29 36	263	37 30	288
176	50 45	353	54 11	035	54 20	089	47 38	141	44 05	230	28 41	263	36 38	289
177	50 37	352	54 43	034	55 16	089	48 12	142	43 23	231	27 47	264	35 45	289
178	50 29	351	55 14	034	56 11	090	48 45	144	42 39	232	26 52	264	34 53	289
179	50 20	350	55 44	033	57 06	090	49 17	145	41 55	233	25 57	264	34 01	289

 LAT 23°N

LHA ♈	Hc	Zn	Hc	Zn	Hc	Zn	Hc	Zn	Hc	Zn	Hc	Zn	Hc	Zn
	◆ Alkaid		Alphecca		◆ SPICA		Gienah		REGULUS		◆ POLLUX		Dubhe	
180	56 14	032	41 22	074	49 49	146	49 10	174	61 24	252	33 09	289	50 11	350
181	56 43	031	42 15	074	50 19	147	49 16	175	60 31	253	32 17	290	50 01	349
182	57 12	031	43 08	074	50 48	149	49 19	177	59 38	254	31 25	290	49 50	348
183	57 39	030	44 01	074	51 16	150	49 22	178	58 45	254	30 33	290	49 39	348
184	58 07	029	44 54	075	51 43	152	49 22	180	57 52	255	29 41	290	49 27	347
185	58 33	028	45 48	075	52 09	153	49 22	181	56 59	256	28 49	290	49 14	346
186	58 58	027	46 41	075	52 33	154	49 20	183	56 05	257	27 57	291	49 01	346
187	59 23	026	47 34	075	52 56	156	49 17	184	55 11	257	27 06	291	48 47	345
188	59 47	025	48 28	075	53 18	157	49 12	186	54 17	258	26 14	291	48 32	345
189	60 10	024	49 21	075	53 38	159	49 06	187	53 23	259	25 23	291	48 17	344
190	60 32	023	50 15	075	53 57	161	48 58	189	52 29	259	24 31	292	48 02	343
191	60 53	022	51 08	076	54 15	162	48 50	190	51 34	260	23 40	292	47 46	343
192	61 13	021	52 02	076	54 31	164	48 39	191	50 40	261	22 49	292	47 29	342
193	61 31	019	52 55	076	54 46	165	48 28	193	49 46	261	21 57	292	47 12	342
194	61 49	018	53 49	076	54 59	167	48 15	194	48 51	262	21 06	292	46 54	341
	◆ Kochab		VEGA		Rasalhague		◆ ANTARES		SPICA		◆ REGULUS		Dubhe	
195	36 49	009	18 23	055	24 06	086	19 04	131	55 10	169	47 56	262	46 36	341
196	36 57	009	19 08	055	25 01	086	19 45	132	55 20	170	47 01	263	46 17	340
197	37 06	009	19 53	055	25 56	087	20 26	132	55 29	172	46 07	263	45 58	340
198	37 14	008	20 39	055	26 51	087	21 07	133	55 35	174	45 12	264	45 39	339
199	37 22	008	21 24	056	27 46	088	21 47	134	55 40	176	44 17	264	45 19	339
200	37 29	008	22 10	056	28 41	088	22 26	134	55 44	177	43 22	265	44 58	338
201	37 36	007	22 56	056	29 37	088	23 06	135	55 45	179	42 27	265	44 37	338
202	37 43	007	23 41	056	30 32	089	23 44	136	55 45	181	41 32	266	44 16	337
203	37 50	007	24 27	056	31 27	089	24 23	136	55 44	183	40 37	266	43 55	337
204	37 56	006	25 13	056	32 22	089	25 01	137	55 40	184	39 42	266	43 33	336
205	38 02	006	25 59	057	33 18	090	25 38	138	55 35	186	38 47	267	43 10	336
206	38 08	006	26 46	057	34 13	090	26 15	139	55 29	188	37 51	267	42 48	336
207	38 13	005	27 32	057	35 08	091	26 51	139	55 20	190	36 56	268	42 25	335
208	38 18	005	28 18	057	36 03	091	27 27	140	55 10	191	36 01	268	42 01	335
209	38 23	005	29 04	057	36 58	091	28 02	141	54 59	193	35 06	269	41 37	334
	◆ Kochab		VEGA		Rasalhague		◆ ANTARES		SPICA		◆ REGULUS		Dubhe	
210	38 27	004	29 51	057	37 54	092	28 37	142	54 46	195	34 11	269	41 13	334
211	38 31	004	30 37	057	38 49	092	29 11	142	54 31	196	33 15	269	40 49	334
212	38 35	004	31 24	057	39 44	093	29 44	143	54 15	198	32 20	270	40 25	333
213	38 39	003	32 10	058	40 39	093	30 17	144	53 57	199	31 25	270	40 00	333
214	38 42	003	32 57	058	41 34	093	30 49	145	53 38	201	30 30	271	39 35	333
215	38 44	003	33 44	058	42 29	094	31 21	146	53 18	203	29 34	271	39 09	333
216	38 47	002	34 30	058	43 25	094	31 52	146	52 56	204	28 39	271	38 44	332
217	38 49	002	35 17	058	44 20	095	32 22	147	52 33	206	27 44	272	38 18	332
218	38 51	002	36 04	058	45 15	095	32 51	148	52 08	207	26 49	272	37 52	332
219	38 52	001	36 50	058	46 10	096	33 20	149	51 43	208	25 54	272	37 26	332
220	38 53	001	37 37	058	47 04	096	33 48	150	51 16	210	24 58	273	36 59	331
221	38 54	001	38 24	058	47 59	097	34 15	151	50 48	211	24 03	273	36 33	331
222	38 54	000	39 11	058	48 54	097	34 41	152	50 19	213	23 08	274	36 06	331
223	38 54	000	39 57	058	49 49	098	35 07	153	49 48	214	22 13	274	35 39	331
224	38 54	000	40 44	058	50 44	098	35 32	154	49 17	215	21 18	274	35 12	331
	VEGA		◆ ALTAIR		Nunki		ANTARES		◆ SPICA		Denebola		◆ Alkaid	
225	41 31	058	19 10	088	14 34	127	35 56	155	48 45	216	44 23	268	60 11	336
226	42 18	058	20 05	089	15 18	128	36 19	156	48 12	218	43 27	268	59 48	335
227	43 04	058	21 00	089	16 01	128	36 41	157	47 37	219	42 32	269	59 25	334
228	43 51	058	21 55	089	16 44	129	37 02	158	47 02	220	41 37	269	59 00	333
229	44 38	057	22 51	090	17 27	130	37 22	159	46 26	221	40 42	270	58 35	332
230	45 24	057	23 46	090	18 09	130	37 42	160	45 50	222	39 46	270	58 08	331
231	46 11	057	24 41	091	18 51	131	38 00	161	45 12	223	38 51	270	57 41	330
232	46 57	057	25 36	091	19 33	131	38 17	162	44 34	224	37 56	271	57 13	329
233	47 43	057	26 31	091	20 14	132	38 34	163	43 55	225	37 01	271	56 45	329
234	48 30	057	27 27	092	20 55	133	38 49	164	43 15	226	36 06	272	56 16	328
235	49 16	057	28 22	092	21 36	133	39 04	165	42 35	227	35 10	272	55 46	327
236	50 02	056	29 17	093	22 16	134	39 17	167	41 54	228	34 15	272	55 16	326
237	50 48	056	30 12	093	22 55	135	39 29	168	41 13	229	33 20	273	54 45	326
238	51 34	056	31 07	093	23 34	135	39 40	169	40 31	230	32 25	273	54 13	325
239	52 19	056	32 02	094	24 13	136	39 51	170	39 48	231	31 30	273	53 41	324
	◆ VEGA		ALTAIR		Nunki		◆ ANTARES		SPICA		ARCTURUS		◆ Alkaid	
240	53 05	055	32 58	094	24 51	137	40 00	171	39 05	232	65 32	266	53 09	324
241	53 50	055	33 53	095	25 29	137	40 08	172	38 21	233	64 37	266	52 36	323
242	54 35	055	34 48	095	26 06	138	40 15	173	37 37	234	63 42	267	52 03	323
243	55 20	054	35 43	096	26 43	139	40 20	175	36 52	234	62 47	267	51 29	322
244	56 05	054	36 38	096	27 19	140	40 25	176	36 07	235	61 52	268	50 55	321
245	56 50	054	37 32	097	27 54	140	40 28	177	35 22	236	60 57	268	50 20	321
246	57 34	053	38 27	097	28 29	141	40 31	178	34 36	237	60 01	269	49 45	321
247	58 18	053	39 22	098	29 04	142	40 32	179	33 49	237	59 06	269	49 10	320
248	59 02	052	40 17	098	29 38	143	40 32	180	33 03	238	58 11	269	48 34	320
249	59 45	051	41 12	099	30 11	143	40 31	182	32 16	239	57 16	270	47 58	319
250	60 28	051	42 06	099	30 43	144	40 29	183	31 28	239	56 20	270	47 22	319
251	61 11	050	43 01	100	31 15	145	40 26	184	30 40	240	55 25	271	46 46	319
252	61 53	049	43 55	100	31 47	146	40 21	185	29 52	241	54 30	271	46 09	318
253	62 35	049	44 49	101	32 17	147	40 16	186	29 04	241	53 35	271	45 32	318
254	63 16	048	45 44	101	32 47	148	40 09	188	28 15	242	52 40	272	44 55	318
	◆ DENEB		ALTAIR		◆ Nunki		ANTARES		SPICA		◆ ARCTURUS		Alkaid	
255	40 08	049	46 38	102	33 16	149	40 01	189	27 26	243	51 44	272	44 18	317
256	40 50	049	47 32	102	33 45	150	39 52	190	26 37	243	50 49	272	43 40	317
257	41 31	049	48 26	103	34 12	150	39 42	191	25 48	244	49 54	273	43 03	317
258	42 13	049	49 19	104	34 39	151	39 31	192	24 58	244	48 59	273	42 25	317
259	42 55	049	50 13	104	35 05	152	39 19	193	24 08	245	48 04	273	41 47	316
260	43 36	048	51 06	105	35 30	153	39 06	194	23 18	246	47 09	274	41 08	316
261	44 17	048	52 00	106	35 55	154	38 52	195	22 28	246	46 13	274	40 30	316
262	44 58	048	52 53	106	36 18	155	38 36	197	21 37	247	45 18	274	39 52	316
263	45 39	048	53 46	107	36 41	156	38 20	198	20 46	247	44 23	275	39 13	316
264	46 20	048	54 38	108	37 02	157	38 03	199	19 55	248	43 28	275	38 35	316
265	47 01	047	55 31	109	37 23	158	37 45	200	19 04	248	42 33	275	37 56	315
266	47 42	047	56 23	110	37 43	159	37 25	201	18 13	249	41 38	276	37 17	315
267	48 22	047	57 15	110	38 02	161	37 05	202	17 21	249	40 43	276	36 38	315
268	49 02	046	58 06	111	38 20	162	36 44	203	16 29	250	39 48	276	35 59	315
269	49 42	046	58 58	112	38 37	163	36 22	204	15 37	250	38 54	277	35 20	315

LHA ♈	Hc	Zn	Hc	Zn	Hc	Zn	Hc	Zn	Hc	Zn	Hc	Zn	Hc	Zn
	◆ DENEB		Enif		◆ Nunki		ANTARES		◆ ARCTURUS		Alkaid		Kochab	
270	50 21	046	34 51	094	38 53	164	35 59	205	37 59	277	34 41	315	33 09	346
271	51 01	045	35 46	094	39 08	165	35 36	206	37 04	277	34 02	315	32 55	346
272	51 40	045	36 41	095	39 22	166	35 11	207	36 09	277	33 23	315	32 42	346
273	52 19	044	37 36	095	39 35	167	34 46	208	35 14	278	32 44	315	32 28	346
274	52 57	044	38 31	096	39 46	168	34 19	209	34 20	278	32 05	315	32 14	345
275	53 35	043	39 26	096	39 57	169	33 52	210	33 25	278	31 26	315	32 00	345
276	54 13	043	40 21	097	40 07	171	33 25	211	32 30	279	30 46	315	31 46	345
277	54 51	042	41 16	097	40 15	172	32 56	212	31 36	279	30 07	315	31 32	345
278	55 28	042	42 11	098	40 23	173	32 27	212	30 41	279	29 28	315	31 17	345
279	56 04	041	43 05	098	40 29	174	31 57	213	29 47	280	28 49	315	31 02	345
280	56 40	040	44 00	099	40 34	175	31 26	214	28 52	280	28 10	315	30 48	344
281	57 16	040	44 55	099	40 38	176	30 55	215	27 58	280	27 31	315	30 33	344
282	57 51	039	45 49	100	40 41	178	30 23	216	27 04	281	26 52	315	30 18	344
283	58 25	038	46 44	100	40 43	179	29 50	217	26 09	281	26 13	315	30 03	344
284	58 59	037	47 38	101	40 43	180	29 16	218	25 15	281	25 34	315	29 47	344
	DENEB		◆ Alpheratz		FOMALHAUT		◆ Nunki		ANTARES		◆ Alphecca		Kochab	
285	59 33	037	21 33	066	12 16	130	40 43	181	28 43	218	43 43	286	29 32	344
286	60 05	036	22 23	067	12 58	130	40 41	182	28 08	219	42 50	286	29 16	344
287	60 37	035	23 14	067	13 40	131	40 38	183	27 33	220	41 57	286	29 01	344
288	61 08	034	24 05	067	14 21	131	40 35	185	26 57	221	41 04	286	28 45	343
289	61 39	033	24 56	067	15 03	132	40 29	186	26 21	221	40 11	286	28 30	343
290	62 08	032	25 47	067	15 44	133	40 23	187	25 44	222	39 18	286	28 14	343
291	62 37	031	26 38	068	16 24	133	40 16	188	25 07	223	38 25	287	27 58	343
292	63 04	029	27 29	068	17 04	134	40 08	189	24 29	224	37 32	287	27 42	343
293	63 31	028	28 20	068	17 44	134	39 58	190	23 51	224	36 39	287	27 26	343
294	63 57	027	29 12	068	18 23	135	39 47	192	23 12	225	35 46	287	27 10	343
295	64 21	026	30 03	069	19 02	135	39 36	193	22 33	226	34 54	287	26 54	343
296	64 45	024	30 54	069	19 41	136	39 23	194	21 53	226	34 01	288	26 37	343
297	65 07	023	31 46	069	20 19	137	39 09	195	21 13	227	33 08	288	26 21	343
298	65 28	021	32 37	069	20 56	137	38 54	196	20 33	227	32 16	288	26 05	343
299	65 47	020	33 29	069	21 34	138	38 39	197	19 52	228	31 23	288	25 49	343
	◆ DENEB		Schedar		Alpheratz		◆ FOMALHAUT		Nunki		◆ Rasalhague		VEGA	
300	66 05	018	29 47	037	34 21	069	22 10	139	38 22	198	54 11	259	66 22	317
301	66 22	017	30 20	037	35 12	070	22 46	139	38 04	199	53 17	260	65 44	316
302	66 37	015	30 53	037	36 04	070	23 22	140	37 45	200	52 23	261	65 05	315
303	66 51	013	31 25	037	36 56	070	23 57	141	37 25	202	51 28	261	64 26	314
304	67 03	012	31 58	036	37 48	070	24 32	141	37 05	203	50 34	262	63 45	313
305	67 13	010	32 31	036	38 40	070	25 06	142	36 43	204	49 39	262	63 04	312
306	67 22	008	33 04	036	39 32	070	25 40	143	36 20	205	48 44	263	62 23	311
307	67 29	006	33 36	036	40 24	070	26 13	144	35 57	206	47 49	263	61 41	310
308	67 34	005	34 09	036	41 16	071	26 45	144	35 33	207	46 54	264	60 59	310
309	67 38	003	34 42	036	42 08	071	27 17	145	35 08	208	45 59	264	60 16	309
310	67 40	001	35 14	036	43 00	071	27 48	146	34 42	209	45 04	265	59 33	308
311	67 40	359	35 46	036	43 52	071	28 19	147	34 15	209	44 09	265	58 50	308
312	67 38	357	36 18	036	44 45	071	28 48	148	33 47	210	43 14	266	58 06	307
313	67 34	355	36 50	035	45 37	071	29 18	148	33 19	211	42 19	266	57 22	307
314	67 29	354	37 22	035	46 29	071	29 46	149	32 50	212	41 24	267	56 37	306
	◆ Alpheratz		Diphda		◆ FOMALHAUT		ALTAIR		Rasalhague		◆ VEGA		DENEB	
315	47 22	071	21 38	122	30 14	150	68 22	232	40 29	267	55 53	306	67 22	352
316	48 14	071	22 25	122	30 41	151	67 38	234	39 34	267	55 08	306	67 13	350
317	49 06	071	23 11	123	31 08	152	66 53	236	38 39	268	54 23	305	67 03	348
318	49 59	071	23 57	124	31 33	153	66 07	237	37 43	268	53 38	305	66 51	346
319	50 51	071	24 43	124	31 58	154	65 21	239	36 48	269	52 52	305	66 37	345
320	51 43	072	25 28	125	32 22	155	64 33	240	35 53	269	52 07	304	66 22	343
321	52 36	072	26 14	126	32 45	156	63 45	241	34 58	269	51 21	304	66 05	342
322	53 28	072	26 58	126	33 08	156	62 56	243	34 03	270	50 35	304	65 47	340
323	54 20	072	27 43	127	33 30	157	62 07	244	33 07	270	49 49	304	65 27	338
324	55 13	072	28 27	128	33 50	158	61 17	245	32 12	271	49 03	303	65 06	337
325	56 05	071	29 10	128	34 10	159	60 27	246	31 17	271	48 17	303	64 44	336
326	56 58	071	29 53	129	34 29	160	59 36	247	30 22	271	47 31	303	64 21	334
327	57 50	071	30 36	130	34 48	161	58 45	248	29 26	272	46 44	303	63 56	333
328	58 42	071	31 18	130	35 05	162	57 54	249	28 31	272	45 58	303	63 30	332
329	59 35	071	32 00	131	35 21	163	57 02	250	27 36	273	45 11	303	63 04	330
	◆ Mirfak		Hamal		Diphda		◆ FOMALHAUT		ALTAIR		◆ VEGA		DENEB	
330	22 50	044	33 31	076	32 41	132	35 37	164	56 10	251	44 25	302	62 36	329
331	23 28	044	34 25	076	33 22	133	35 51	165	55 18	251	43 38	302	62 07	328
332	24 07	044	35 18	077	34 02	134	36 04	166	54 26	252	42 51	302	61 38	327
333	24 45	044	36 12	077	34 42	134	36 17	167	53 33	253	42 05	302	61 07	326
334	25 23	044	37 06	077	35 21	135	36 28	168	52 40	254	41 18	302	60 36	325
335	26 02	044	38 00	077	36 00	136	36 39	170	51 47	255	40 31	302	60 04	324
336	26 40	044	38 54	078	36 38	137	36 48	171	50 53	255	39 45	302	59 32	323
337	27 19	044	39 48	078	37 15	138	36 57	172	50 00	256	38 58	302	58 58	322
338	27 57	044	40 42	078	37 52	139	37 04	173	49 06	257	38 11	302	58 24	322
339	28 36	044	41 36	078	38 28	140	37 11	174	48 13	257	37 24	302	57 50	321
340	29 14	044	42 30	078	39 03	141	37 16	175	47 19	258	36 38	302	57 15	320
341	29 53	044	43 24	079	39 38	142	37 21	176	46 25	258	35 51	302	56 39	320
342	30 32	044	44 18	079	40 11	143	37 24	177	45 30	259	35 04	302	56 03	319
343	31 10	044	45 12	079	40 45	144	37 26	178	44 36	259	34 17	302	55 27	318
344	31 49	044	46 07	079	41 17	145	37 27	179	43 42	260	33 31	302	54 50	318
	Schedar		◆ CAPELLA		ALDEBARAN		Diphda		◆ FOMALHAUT		ALTAIR		◆ DENEB	
345	51 38	022	13 23	045	11 34	077	41 48	146	37 27	180	42 47	261	54 12	317
346	51 58	022	14 03	046	12 28	077	42 19	147	37 26	182	41 53	261	53 34	317
347	52 18	021	14 42	046	13 22	077	42 48	148	37 24	183	40 58	262	52 56	316
348	52 38	020	15 22	046	14 15	078	43 17	149	37 21	184	40 04	262	52 18	316
349	52 56	019	16 02	046	15 09	078	43 45	150	37 17	185	39 09	263	51 39	315
350	53 14	019	16 42	046	16 04	078	44 12	151	37 12	186	38 14	263	51 00	315
351	53 32	018	17 22	047	16 58	079	44 38	153	37 06	187	37 19	264	50 20	314
352	53 48	017	18 02	047	17 52	079	45 03	154	36 59	188	36 24	264	49 41	314
353	54 04	016	18 42	047	18 46	079	45 26	155	36 51	189	35 29	264	49 01	314
354	54 19	015	19 23	047	19 41	080	45 49	156	36 41	190	34 34	265	48 21	313
355	54 33	015	20 03	047	20 35	080	46 11	158	36 31	191	33 39	265	47 40	313
356	54 47	014	20 44	048	21 29	080	46 31	159	36 20	192	32 44	266	47 00	313
357	54 59	013	21 25	048	22 24	081	46 51	160	36 08	193	31 49	266	46 19	312
358	55 11	012	22 06	048	23 18	081	47 09	162	35 54	194	30 54	267	45 38	312
359	55 22	011	22 47	048	24 13	081	47 25	163	35 40	195	29 59	267	44 57	312

LHA ♈	Hc	Zn	Hc	Zn	Hc	Zn	Hc	Zn	Hc	Zn	Hc	Zn	Hc	Zn
	Schedar		◆CAPELLA		ALDEBARAN		◆Diphda		FOMALHAUT		◆ALTAIR		DENEB	
0	54 33	010	22 48	048	24 59	081	48 39	164	36 22	197	29 06	268	43 36	312
1	54 42	009	23 29	048	25 54	082	48 54	165	36 06	198	28 10	268	42 55	312
2	54 50	008	24 10	048	26 49	082	49 07	167	35 49	199	27 15	269	42 14	312
3	54 58	007	24 52	048	27 44	082	49 19	168	35 30	200	26 19	269	41 32	312
4	55 04	006	25 33	048	28 39	083	49 30	170	35 11	201	25 24	270	40 51	312
5	55 09	005	26 14	048	29 34	083	49 39	171	34 51	202	24 28	270	40 09	312
6	55 14	004	26 56	048	30 30	083	49 47	172	34 30	203	23 32	270	39 27	311
7	55 18	003	27 38	048	31 25	084	49 54	174	34 08	204	22 37	271	38 45	311
8	55 20	002	28 19	048	32 20	084	49 59	175	33 46	205	21 41	271	38 04	311
9	55 22	001	29 01	048	33 15	084	50 03	177	33 22	205	20 45	271	37 22	311
10	55 23	000	29 42	048	34 11	084	50 05	178	32 58	206	19 50	272	36 40	311
11	55 23	359	30 24	048	35 06	085	50 06	180	32 33	207	18 54	272	35 58	311
12	55 22	358	31 06	049	36 02	085	50 05	181	32 07	208	17 59	273	35 16	311
13	55 20	357	31 47	049	36 57	085	50 03	183	31 40	209	17 03	273	34 33	311
14	55 17	356	32 29	048	37 53	086	50 00	184	31 13	210	16 07	273	33 51	311
	◆CAPELLA		ALDEBARAN		RIGEL		◆Diphda		FOMALHAUT		Enif		◆DENEB	
15	33 11	048	38 48	086	20 35	108	49 55	186	30 45	211	41 48	264	33 09	311
16	33 52	048	39 44	086	21 28	109	49 48	187	30 16	212	40 53	264	32 27	311
17	34 34	048	40 39	087	22 21	109	49 41	189	29 46	212	39 58	265	31 45	311
18	35 16	048	41 35	087	23 13	110	49 32	190	29 16	213	39 02	265	31 03	311
19	35 57	048	42 30	087	24 05	110	49 21	192	28 45	214	38 07	265	30 21	311
20	36 39	048	43 26	088	24 57	111	49 09	193	28 14	215	37 11	266	29 38	311
21	37 20	048	44 21	088	25 49	111	48 56	194	27 42	216	36 16	266	28 56	311
22	38 01	048	45 17	088	26 41	112	48 41	196	27 09	216	35 20	267	28 14	311
23	38 43	048	46 13	089	27 32	113	48 26	197	26 35	217	34 25	267	27 32	311
24	39 24	048	47 08	089	28 23	113	48 08	199	26 02	218	33 29	267	26 50	311
25	40 05	048	48 04	089	29 15	114	47 50	200	25 27	219	32 34	268	26 08	311
26	40 46	047	48 59	090	30 05	114	47 31	201	24 52	219	31 38	268	25 26	311
27	41 27	047	49 55	090	30 56	115	47 10	203	24 17	220	30 42	269	24 44	311
28	42 08	047	50 51	091	31 46	116	46 48	204	23 41	221	29 47	269	24 02	311
29	42 49	047	51 46	091	32 36	116	46 25	205	23 04	221	28 51	269	23 21	311
	CAPELLA		◆ALDEBARAN		RIGEL		Acamar		◆Diphda		Alpheratz		◆DENEB	
30	43 29	047	52 42	091	33 26	117	26 16	168	46 01	206	64 04	292	22 39	311
31	44 09	046	53 38	092	34 16	117	26 27	168	45 35	208	63 13	291	21 57	312
32	44 50	046	54 33	092	35 05	118	26 38	169	45 09	209	62 21	291	21 16	312
33	45 30	046	55 29	093	35 54	119	26 48	170	44 42	210	61 29	291	20 34	312
34	46 10	046	56 24	093	36 42	120	26 58	171	44 14	211	60 37	291	19 53	312
35	46 49	045	57 20	094	37 31	120	27 06	172	43 44	212	59 45	291	19 12	312
36	47 29	045	58 15	094	38 18	121	27 14	173	43 14	213	58 53	290	18 30	312
37	48 08	045	59 11	094	39 06	122	27 21	173	42 43	214	58 00	290	17 49	313
38	48 47	044	60 06	095	39 53	123	27 27	174	42 11	216	57 08	290	17 08	313
39	49 25	044	61 02	096	40 40	123	27 32	175	41 38	217	56 16	290	16 28	313
40	50 04	043	61 57	096	41 26	124	27 36	176	41 05	218	55 24	290	15 47	313
41	50 42	043	62 52	097	42 12	125	27 40	177	40 31	219	54 31	290	15 06	313
42	51 20	043	63 48	097	42 57	126	27 42	178	39 55	220	53 39	290	14 26	313
43	51 57	042	64 43	098	43 42	127	27 44	179	39 20	221	52 47	290	13 46	314
44	52 34	042	65 38	099	44 26	128	27 45	179	38 43	222	51 54	290	13 05	314
	CAPELLA		◆POLLUX		PROCYON		SIRIUS		◆Acamar		Diphda		◆Alpheratz	
45	53 11	041	25 46	068	20 27	093	22 30	120	27 45	180	38 06	222	51 02	290
46	53 47	040	26 38	069	21 22	093	23 18	121	27 45	181	37 28	223	50 09	290
47	54 23	040	27 30	069	22 18	093	24 06	121	27 43	182	36 50	224	49 17	290
48	54 58	039	28 22	069	23 13	094	24 53	122	27 41	183	36 10	225	48 25	290
49	55 33	038	29 14	069	24 09	094	25 40	123	27 38	184	35 31	226	47 32	290
50	56 08	038	30 06	069	25 04	095	26 27	123	27 34	185	34 51	227	46 40	290
51	56 41	037	30 58	070	26 00	095	27 13	124	27 29	185	34 10	228	45 48	290
52	57 15	036	31 50	070	26 55	095	27 59	125	27 23	186	33 28	228	44 55	290
53	57 47	035	32 43	070	27 51	096	28 45	125	27 17	187	32 47	229	44 03	290
54	58 19	035	33 35	070	28 46	096	29 30	126	27 09	188	32 04	230	43 11	290
55	58 50	034	34 27	070	29 41	097	30 15	127	27 01	189	31 22	231	42 18	290
56	59 21	033	35 20	070	30 36	097	31 00	127	26 52	190	30 38	231	41 26	290
57	59 51	032	36 12	071	31 32	098	31 44	128	26 43	190	29 55	232	40 34	290
58	60 20	031	37 05	071	32 27	098	32 28	129	26 32	191	29 11	233	39 42	290
59	60 48	030	37 57	071	33 22	099	33 11	129	26 21	192	28 26	233	38 50	290
	◆CAPELLA		PROCYON		◆SIRIUS		RIGEL		Diphda		◆Hamal		Mirfak	
60	61 15	029	34 17	099	33 53	130	54 37	147	27 41	234	64 11	279	61 16	348
61	61 41	028	35 12	100	34 36	131	55 07	148	26 56	235	63 16	279	61 04	347
62	62 06	026	36 06	100	35 17	132	55 36	150	26 10	235	62 21	279	60 51	346
63	62 31	025	37 01	101	35 59	133	56 04	151	25 24	236	61 26	279	60 37	345
64	62 54	024	37 56	101	36 39	133	56 30	153	24 38	237	60 31	279	60 22	343
65	63 16	023	38 50	102	37 19	134	56 55	154	23 52	237	59 36	279	60 05	342
66	63 37	021	39 45	102	37 59	135	57 18	156	23 05	238	58 41	279	59 48	341
67	63 56	020	40 39	103	38 38	136	57 40	158	22 17	238	57 46	280	59 29	340
68	64 15	018	41 33	103	39 16	137	58 00	159	21 30	239	56 52	280	59 10	339
69	64 32	017	42 27	104	39 54	138	58 19	161	20 42	240	55 57	280	58 49	338
70	64 47	016	43 21	104	40 31	139	58 36	163	19 54	240	55 02	280	58 28	337
71	65 01	014	44 15	105	41 07	140	58 51	165	19 06	241	54 07	280	58 05	336
72	65 14	012	45 09	106	41 42	141	59 05	167	18 17	241	53 12	280	57 42	335
73	65 25	011	46 02	106	42 17	142	59 17	169	17 28	242	52 18	280	57 18	334
74	65 35	009	46 56	107	42 51	143	59 27	171	16 39	242	51 23	281	56 53	333
	CAPELLA		◆Dubhe		POLLUX		PROCYON		◆SIRIUS		RIGEL		◆Hamal	
75	65 43	008	18 43	030	52 02	072	47 49	107	43 24	144	59 35	173	50 28	281
76	65 49	006	19 11	030	52 55	072	48 42	108	43 56	145	59 41	174	49 34	281
77	65 54	004	19 39	030	53 48	072	49 35	109	44 27	146	59 46	176	48 39	281
78	65 58	002	20 07	030	54 41	072	50 27	110	44 58	147	59 48	178	47 45	281
79	65 59	001	20 35	030	55 34	072	51 19	110	45 27	149	59 49	180	46 50	281
80	65 59	359	21 03	030	56 27	072	52 11	111	45 56	150	59 48	182	45 56	282
81	65 57	357	21 31	031	57 20	072	53 03	112	46 23	151	59 44	184	45 01	282
82	65 54	356	22 00	031	58 13	072	53 55	113	46 50	152	59 39	186	44 07	282
83	65 49	354	22 28	031	59 06	072	54 46	114	47 15	153	59 32	188	43 12	282
84	65 42	352	22 56	031	59 59	072	55 36	115	47 40	155	59 23	190	42 18	282
85	65 34	351	23 25	031	60 52	072	56 27	116	48 03	156	59 13	192	41 24	283
86	65 24	349	23 53	031	61 45	071	57 17	117	48 25	157	59 00	194	40 29	283
87	65 13	347	24 22	031	62 37	071	58 06	118	48 45	159	58 46	196	39 35	283
88	65 00	346	24 50	031	63 30	071	58 55	119	49 05	160	58 30	198	38 41	283
89	64 46	344	25 19	031	64 23	071	59 44	120	49 23	162	58 12	199	37 47	283

LAT 22°N

LHA ♈	Hc	Zn	Hc	Zn	Hc	Zn	Hc	Zn	Hc	Zn	Hc	Zn	Hc	Zn
	Dubhe		◆REGULUS		Alphard		SIRIUS		◆RIGEL		ALDEBARAN		◆CAPELLA	
90	25 47	031	29 56	089	30 25	115	49 40	163	57 53	201	69 38	258	64 30	343
91	26 16	031	30 52	089	31 16	116	49 56	164	57 32	203	68 44	259	64 13	341
92	26 44	031	31 47	089	32 05	117	50 10	166	57 10	205	67 49	260	63 54	340
93	27 12	031	32 43	090	32 55	117	50 23	167	56 46	206	66 54	261	63 35	339
94	27 41	031	33 39	090	33 44	118	50 35	169	56 21	208	65 59	261	63 14	337
95	28 09	031	34 34	090	34 34	118	50 45	170	55 54	209	65 04	262	62 52	336
96	28 37	031	35 30	091	35 22	119	50 54	172	55 26	211	64 09	263	62 28	335
97	29 06	031	36 26	091	36 11	120	51 01	173	54 56	213	63 14	263	62 04	333
98	29 34	030	37 21	092	36 59	121	51 07	175	54 26	214	62 19	264	61 39	332
99	30 02	030	38 17	092	37 46	121	51 11	176	53 54	215	61 23	264	61 12	331
100	30 30	030	39 12	092	38 34	122	51 14	178	53 21	217	60 28	265	60 45	330
101	30 58	030	40 08	093	39 21	123	51 16	179	52 48	218	59 33	265	60 17	329
102	31 26	030	41 04	093	40 07	124	51 16	181	52 13	219	58 37	266	59 48	328
103	31 54	030	41 59	094	40 53	124	51 14	182	51 37	221	57 42	266	59 18	327
104	32 22	030	42 55	094	41 39	125	51 11	184	51 00	222	56 46	267	58 47	326
	Dubhe		◆REGULUS		Alphard		SIRIUS		◆RIGEL		ALDEBARAN		◆CAPELLA	
105	32 49	030	43 50	095	42 24	126	51 06	185	50 22	223	55 51	267	58 16	325
106	33 17	029	44 45	095	43 09	127	51 00	187	49 44	224	54 55	268	57 44	324
107	33 44	029	45 41	095	43 53	128	50 53	188	49 05	226	53 59	268	57 11	324
108	34 11	029	46 36	096	44 36	129	50 44	190	48 25	227	53 04	268	56 38	323
109	34 38	029	47 32	096	45 19	130	50 34	191	47 44	228	52 08	269	56 04	322
110	35 05	029	48 27	097	46 02	131	50 22	193	47 02	229	51 12	269	55 30	321
111	35 32	029	49 22	097	46 43	132	50 09	194	46 20	230	50 17	270	54 55	321
112	35 58	028	50 17	098	47 25	133	49 55	196	45 37	231	49 21	270	54 19	320
113	36 25	028	51 12	098	48 05	134	49 39	197	44 54	232	48 26	270	53 43	320
114	36 51	028	52 07	099	48 45	135	49 22	199	44 10	233	47 30	271	53 07	319
115	37 17	028	53 02	100	49 23	136	49 03	200	43 25	234	46 34	271	52 30	318
116	37 42	027	53 57	100	50 01	137	48 44	201	42 40	234	45 39	271	51 53	318
117	38 08	027	54 52	101	50 39	139	48 23	203	41 55	235	44 43	272	51 16	317
118	38 33	027	55 46	101	51 15	140	48 01	204	41 09	236	43 48	272	50 38	317
119	38 58	027	56 41	102	51 50	141	47 37	205	40 22	237	42 52	273	50 00	317
	◆Dubhe		Denebola		◆Alphard		SIRIUS		RIGEL		◆ALDEBARAN		CAPELLA	
120	39 23	026	35 13	087	52 25	142	47 13	207	39 36	238	41 56	273	49 22	316
121	39 47	026	36 08	088	52 58	144	46 47	208	38 48	239	41 01	273	48 43	316
122	40 12	026	37 04	088	53 30	145	46 21	209	38 01	239	40 05	274	48 04	315
123	40 36	025	38 00	088	54 02	147	45 53	210	37 13	240	39 10	274	47 25	315
124	40 59	025	38 55	089	54 32	148	45 25	212	36 24	241	38 14	274	46 45	315
125	41 23	025	39 51	089	55 00	150	44 55	213	35 36	241	37 19	274	46 06	314
126	41 46	024	40 46	090	55 28	151	44 24	214	34 47	242	36 23	275	45 26	314
127	42 08	024	41 42	090	55 54	153	43 53	215	33 57	243	35 28	275	44 46	314
128	42 31	023	42 38	090	56 19	154	43 21	216	33 08	243	34 33	275	44 05	314
129	42 52	023	43 33	091	56 42	156	42 48	217	32 18	244	33 37	276	43 25	313
130	43 14	023	44 29	091	57 04	158	42 14	218	31 28	245	32 42	276	42 44	313
131	43 35	022	45 25	091	57 25	159	41 39	219	30 37	245	31 47	276	42 04	313
132	43 56	022	46 20	092	57 43	161	41 03	220	29 47	246	30 51	277	41 23	313
133	44 16	021	47 16	092	58 01	163	40 27	221	28 56	247	29 56	277	40 42	313
134	44 36	021	48 11	093	58 16	165	39 50	222	28 04	247	29 01	277	40 01	312
	Dubhe		◆ARCTURUS		SPICA		◆Alphard		SIRIUS		BETELGEUSE		◆CAPELLA	
135	44 56	020	16 46	076	16 50	110	58 30	167	39 12	223	43 23	259	39 20	312
136	45 15	020	17 40	076	17 42	110	58 42	168	38 34	224	42 29	260	38 39	312
137	45 34	019	18 34	076	18 35	111	58 52	170	37 55	225	41 34	260	37 57	312
138	45 52	019	19 28	077	19 26	111	59 01	172	37 16	226	40 39	261	37 16	312
139	46 09	018	20 22	077	20 18	112	59 08	174	36 35	227	39 44	261	36 34	312
140	46 26	018	21 16	077	21 10	112	59 12	176	35 55	227	38 49	262	35 53	312
141	46 43	017	22 11	077	22 01	113	59 15	178	35 13	228	37 54	262	35 11	312
142	46 59	017	23 05	078	22 52	113	59 17	180	34 32	229	36 59	263	34 30	312
143	47 15	016	23 59	078	23 43	114	59 16	182	33 49	230	36 04	263	33 48	312
144	47 30	015	24 54	078	24 34	115	59 13	184	33 07	231	35 09	263	33 07	312
145	47 44	015	25 48	079	25 24	115	59 09	186	32 23	231	34 13	264	32 25	312
146	47 58	014	26 43	079	26 14	116	59 02	188	31 40	232	33 18	264	31 43	311
147	48 11	014	27 38	079	27 04	116	58 54	189	30 56	233	32 23	265	31 02	311
148	48 24	013	28 32	080	27 54	117	58 44	191	30 11	234	31 27	265	30 20	312
149	48 36	012	29 27	080	28 44	117	58 32	193	29 26	234	30 32	266	29 38	312
	Dubhe		◆ARCTURUS		SPICA		◆Alphard		SIRIUS		POLLUX		◆CAPELLA	
150	48 48	012	30 22	080	29 33	118	58 19	195	28 41	235	59 12	288	28 57	312
151	48 58	011	31 17	080	30 22	119	58 03	197	27 55	236	58 19	288	28 15	312
152	49 09	010	32 11	081	31 10	119	57 46	199	27 09	236	57 26	288	27 33	312
153	49 18	010	33 06	081	31 59	120	57 28	200	26 23	237	56 33	288	26 52	312
154	49 27	009	34 01	081	32 47	121	57 08	202	25 36	237	55 41	288	26 10	312
155	49 35	008	34 56	081	33 34	121	56 46	204	24 49	238	54 48	288	25 29	312
156	49 43	007	35 51	082	34 22	122	56 23	205	24 01	239	53 55	288	24 47	312
157	49 50	007	36 46	082	35 09	123	55 58	207	23 14	239	53 02	288	24 06	312
158	49 56	006	37 42	082	35 55	124	55 32	209	22 26	240	52 09	288	23 25	312
159	50 01	005	38 37	083	36 42	124	55 05	210	21 38	240	51 16	288	22 44	312
160	50 06	005	39 32	083	37 27	125	54 36	212	20 49	241	50 23	288	22 02	312
161	50 10	004	40 27	083	38 13	126	54 07	213	20 00	241	49 30	288	21 21	312
162	50 14	003	41 22	083	38 57	127	53 36	215	19 11	242	48 37	288	20 40	313
163	50 16	002	42 18	084	39 42	127	53 03	216	18 22	243	47 44	288	19 59	313
164	50 18	002	43 13	084	40 26	128	52 30	217	17 33	243	46 51	288	19 19	313
	◆Dubhe		Alkaid		ARCTURUS		◆SPICA		Alphard		◆PROCYON		POLLUX	
165	50 19	001	47 10	040	44 08	084	41 09	129	51 56	219	38 53	258	45 58	288
166	50 20	000	47 46	040	45 04	085	41 52	130	51 21	220	37 58	259	45 05	288
167	50 20	359	48 21	039	45 59	085	42 34	131	50 45	221	37 03	259	44 12	288
168	50 19	359	48 56	039	46 54	085	43 16	132	50 08	222	36 09	260	43 19	288
169	50 17	358	49 31	038	47 50	085	43 57	133	49 30	224	35 14	260	42 27	288
170	50 14	357	50 05	038	48 45	086	44 37	134	48 51	225	34 19	261	41 34	289
171	50 11	356	50 39	037	49 41	086	45 17	135	48 11	226	33 24	261	40 41	289
172	50 08	356	51 13	037	50 36	086	45 56	136	47 31	227	32 29	262	39 49	289
173	50 03	355	51 46	036	51 32	087	46 34	137	46 50	228	31 34	262	38 56	289
174	49 58	354	52 18	036	52 27	087	47 12	138	46 09	229	30 39	263	38 03	289
175	49 52	354	52 50	035	53 23	087	47 48	139	45 26	230	29 44	263	37 11	289
176	49 45	353	53 22	034	54 19	088	48 24	141	44 43	231	28 48	264	36 18	289
177	49 38	352	53 53	034	55 14	088	48 59	142	44 00	232	27 53	264	35 26	289
178	49 30	351	54 24	033	56 10	088	49 33	143	43 16	233	26 58	264	34 33	290
179	49 21	351	54 54	032	57 05	089	50 06	144	42 31	234	26 02	265	33 41	290

 LAT 22°N

LHA ♈	Hc Zn	Hc Zn	Hc Zn	Hc Zn	Hc Zn	Hc Zn	Hc Zn
	◆ Alkaid	Alphecca	◆ SPICA	Gienah	REGULUS	◆ POLLUX	Dubhe
180	55 23 031	41 05 073	50 38 145	50 10 174	61 42 254	32 49 290	49 12 350
181	55 52 031	41 58 073	51 09 147	50 15 175	60 48 254	31 56 290	49 02 349
182	56 20 030	42 51 073	51 39 148	50 19 177	59 55 255	31 04 290	48 51 349
183	56 47 029	43 45 074	52 08 150	50 22 178	59 01 256	30 12 291	48 40 348
184	57 14 028	44 38 074	52 35 151	50 22 180	58 07 257	29 20 291	48 28 347
185	57 40 027	45 31 074	53 02 152	50 22 181	57 12 257	28 28 291	48 16 347
186	58 05 026	46 25 074	53 27 154	50 20 183	56 18 258	27 36 291	48 02 346
187	58 29 025	47 18 074	53 51 155	50 17 184	55 23 259	26 44 291	47 49 345
188	58 52 024	48 12 074	54 13 157	50 12 186	54 29 259	25 52 292	47 34 345
189	59 15 023	49 05 074	54 34 159	50 05 187	53 34 260	25 01 292	47 20 344
190	59 36 022	49 59 074	54 54 160	49 58 189	52 39 261	24 09 292	47 04 344
191	59 57 021	50 52 074	55 12 162	49 49 190	51 44 261	23 17 292	46 48 343
192	60 16 020	51 46 074	55 29 163	49 38 192	50 49 262	22 26 292	46 32 343
193	60 35 019	52 40 074	55 44 165	49 26 193	49 54 262	21 35 293	46 15 342
194	60 52 018	53 33 074	55 57 167	49 13 194	48 59 263	20 43 293	45 57 341
	◆ Kochab	VEGA	Rasalhague	◆ ANTARES	SPICA	◆ REGULUS	Dubhe
195	35 49 009	17 48 055	24 01 086	19 43 131	56 09 169	48 04 263	45 39 341
196	35 58 009	18 33 055	24 57 086	20 25 132	56 20 170	47 09 264	45 21 340
197	36 06 008	19 19 055	25 52 086	21 06 132	56 28 172	46 13 264	45 02 340
198	36 14 008	20 05 055	26 48 087	21 47 133	56 35 174	45 18 265	44 43 339
199	36 22 008	20 50 055	27 43 087	22 28 133	56 40 176	44 22 265	44 23 339
200	36 30 008	21 36 055	28 39 087	23 08 134	56 44 177	43 27 266	44 03 338
201	36 37 007	22 22 056	29 35 088	23 48 135	56 45 179	42 32 266	43 42 338
202	36 44 007	23 08 056	30 30 088	24 27 135	56 45 181	41 36 266	43 21 338
203	36 50 007	23 54 056	31 26 088	25 06 136	56 44 183	40 40 267	42 59 337
204	36 56 006	24 40 056	32 21 089	25 45 137	56 40 184	39 45 267	42 38 337
205	37 02 006	25 26 056	33 17 089	26 22 137	56 35 186	38 49 268	42 15 336
206	37 08 006	26 12 056	34 13 090	27 00 138	56 28 188	37 54 268	41 53 336
207	37 13 005	26 59 056	35 08 090	27 37 139	56 20 190	36 58 269	41 30 336
208	37 18 005	27 45 057	36 04 090	28 13 140	56 09 192	36 03 269	41 07 335
209	37 23 005	28 32 057	36 59 091	28 49 140	55 57 193	35 07 269	40 43 335
	◆ Kochab	VEGA	Rasalhague	◆ ANTARES	SPICA	◆ REGULUS	Dubhe
210	37 27 004	29 18 057	37 55 091	29 24 141	55 44 195	34 11 270	40 19 334
211	37 32 004	30 05 057	38 51 091	29 58 142	55 29 197	33 16 270	39 55 334
212	37 35 004	30 51 057	39 46 092	30 32 143	55 12 198	32 20 270	39 31 334
213	37 39 003	31 38 057	40 42 092	31 06 144	54 54 200	31 24 271	39 06 334
214	37 42 003	32 25 057	41 38 093	31 38 144	54 34 201	30 29 271	38 41 333
215	37 44 003	33 11 057	42 33 093	32 10 145	54 13 203	29 33 272	38 16 333
216	37 47 002	33 58 057	43 29 093	32 42 146	53 51 205	28 38 272	37 51 333
217	37 49 002	34 45 057	44 24 094	33 12 147	53 27 206	27 42 272	37 25 332
218	37 51 002	35 31 057	45 20 094	33 42 148	53 02 208	26 46 273	36 59 332
219	37 52 001	36 18 057	46 15 095	34 11 149	52 35 209	25 51 273	36 33 332
220	37 53 001	37 05 057	47 11 095	34 40 150	52 08 210	24 55 273	36 07 332
221	37 54 001	37 52 057	48 06 096	35 07 151	51 39 212	24 00 274	35 40 331
222	37 54 000	38 38 057	49 01 096	35 34 152	51 09 213	23 04 274	35 14 331
223	37 54 000	39 25 057	49 56 097	36 00 153	50 38 215	22 09 274	34 47 331
224	37 54 000	40 12 057	50 52 097	36 25 154	50 06 216	21 13 275	34 20 331
	VEGA	◆ ALTAIR	Nunki	ANTARES	◆ SPICA	Denebola	◆ Alkaid
225	40 59 057	19 08 088	15 10 127	36 50 155	49 33 217	44 24 269	59 16 337
226	41 45 057	20 03 088	15 55 128	37 13 156	48 59 218	43 28 269	58 54 336
227	42 32 057	20 59 089	16 38 128	37 36 157	48 24 219	42 33 270	58 31 335
228	43 18 057	21 55 089	17 22 129	37 57 158	47 48 221	41 37 270	58 06 334
229	44 05 057	22 50 089	18 05 129	38 18 159	47 11 222	40 42 270	57 41 333
230	44 51 057	23 46 090	18 48 130	38 38 160	46 34 223	39 46 271	57 15 332
231	45 38 056	24 41 090	19 30 131	38 57 161	45 56 224	38 50 271	56 49 331
232	46 24 056	25 37 090	20 13 131	39 14 162	45 17 225	37 55 272	56 22 330
233	47 10 056	26 33 091	20 54 132	39 31 163	44 37 226	36 59 272	55 54 329
234	47 56 056	27 28 091	21 36 132	39 47 164	43 57 227	36 04 272	55 25 329
235	48 42 056	28 24 092	22 17 133	40 02 165	43 16 228	35 08 273	54 56 328
236	49 28 055	29 19 092	22 57 134	40 15 166	42 34 229	34 12 273	54 26 327
237	50 14 055	30 15 092	23 37 134	40 28 168	41 52 230	33 17 273	53 55 326
238	51 00 055	31 11 093	24 17 135	40 39 169	41 09 231	32 21 274	53 24 326
239	51 45 055	32 06 093	24 56 136	40 50 170	40 25 232	31 26 274	52 52 325
	◆ VEGA	ALTAIR	Nunki	◆ ANTARES	SPICA	ARCTURUS	◆ Alkaid
240	52 30 054	33 02 094	25 35 136	40 59 171	39 42 233	65 36 268	52 20 324
241	53 15 054	33 57 094	26 13 137	41 07 172	38 57 233	64 40 268	51 48 324
242	54 00 054	34 53 094	26 50 138	41 14 173	38 12 234	63 44 269	51 15 323
243	54 45 053	35 48 095	27 28 138	41 20 175	37 27 235	62 49 269	50 41 323
244	55 29 053	36 44 095	28 04 139	41 25 176	36 41 236	61 53 270	50 07 322
245	56 13 052	37 39 096	28 40 140	41 28 177	35 55 236	60 57 270	49 33 322
246	56 57 052	38 34 096	29 16 141	41 31 178	35 08 237	60 02 270	48 58 321
247	57 41 051	39 30 097	29 51 141	41 32 179	34 21 238	59 06 271	48 23 321
248	58 24 051	40 25 097	30 25 142	41 32 180	33 34 239	58 11 271	47 48 320
249	59 07 050	41 20 098	30 59 143	41 31 182	32 46 239	57 15 271	47 13 320
250	59 50 049	42 15 098	31 32 144	41 29 183	31 58 240	56 19 272	46 37 320
251	60 32 049	43 10 099	32 04 145	41 25 184	31 10 241	55 24 272	46 01 319
252	61 13 048	44 05 099	32 36 146	41 21 185	30 21 241	54 28 272	45 24 319
253	61 54 047	45 00 100	33 07 146	41 15 186	29 33 242	53 33 273	44 47 319
254	62 35 046	45 55 100	33 38 147	41 08 188	28 43 243	52 37 273	44 10 318
	◆ DENEB	ALTAIR	◆ Nunki	ANTARES	SPICA	◆ ARCTURUS	Alkaid
255	39 28 049	46 49 101	34 07 148	41 00 189	27 54 243	51 42 273	43 33 318
256	40 10 048	47 44 101	34 36 149	40 51 190	27 04 244	50 46 274	42 56 318
257	40 52 048	48 39 102	35 04 150	40 41 191	26 14 244	49 50 274	42 19 317
258	41 33 048	49 33 102	35 32 151	40 30 192	25 24 245	48 55 274	41 41 317
259	42 15 048	50 27 103	35 58 152	40 17 193	24 33 245	48 00 275	41 03 317
260	42 56 048	51 21 104	36 24 153	40 04 195	23 43 246	47 04 275	40 25 317
261	43 37 048	52 15 104	36 49 154	39 49 196	22 52 247	46 09 275	39 47 317
262	44 18 047	53 09 105	37 13 155	39 34 197	22 01 247	45 13 275	39 09 316
263	44 59 047	54 03 106	37 36 156	39 17 198	21 09 248	44 18 276	38 30 316
264	45 40 047	54 56 107	37 58 157	39 00 199	20 18 248	43 23 276	37 52 316
265	46 20 047	55 49 107	38 19 158	38 41 200	19 26 249	42 27 276	37 13 316
266	47 00 046	56 42 108	38 39 159	38 21 201	18 34 249	41 32 277	36 34 316
267	47 40 046	57 35 109	38 59 160	38 01 202	17 42 250	40 37 277	35 55 316
268	48 20 046	58 27 110	39 17 161	37 39 203	16 50 250	39 41 277	35 17 316
269	49 00 045	59 20 111	39 34 162	37 17 204	15 58 250	38 46 277	34 38 316

LHA ♈	Hc Zn	Hc Zn	Hc Zn	Hc Zn	Hc Zn	Hc Zn	Hc Zn
	◆ DENEB	Enif	◆ Nunki	ANTARES	◆ ARCTURUS	Alkaid	Kochab
270	49 39 045	34 55 093	39 50 164	36 54 205	37 51 278	33 59 315	32 10 346
271	50 18 044	35 50 094	40 06 165	36 30 206	36 56 278	33 20 315	31 57 346
272	50 57 044	36 46 094	40 20 166	36 05 207	36 01 278	32 41 315	31 44 346
273	51 36 044	37 41 094	40 33 167	35 39 208	35 06 278	32 01 315	31 30 346
274	52 14 043	38 37 095	40 45 168	35 12 209	34 11 279	31 22 315	31 16 346
275	52 52 043	39 32 095	40 56 169	34 44 210	33 16 279	30 43 315	31 02 345
276	53 29 042	40 28 096	41 06 170	34 16 211	32 21 279	30 04 315	30 48 345
277	54 06 041	41 23 096	41 15 172	33 47 212	31 26 280	29 25 315	30 34 345
278	54 42 041	42 18 097	41 22 173	33 17 213	30 31 280	28 46 315	30 19 345
279	55 19 040	43 13 097	41 29 174	32 47 214	29 36 280	28 06 315	30 05 345
280	55 54 040	44 09 098	41 34 175	32 16 215	28 42 280	27 27 315	29 50 345
281	56 29 039	45 04 098	41 38 176	31 44 215	27 47 281	26 48 315	29 35 344
282	57 04 038	45 59 099	41 41 178	31 11 216	26 52 281	26 09 315	29 20 344
283	57 38 037	46 54 099	41 43 179	30 38 217	25 58 281	25 30 315	29 05 344
284	58 11 036	47 49 100	41 43 180	30 04 218	25 03 282	24 51 315	28 50 344
	DENEB	◆ Alpheratz	FOMALHAUT	◆ Nunki	ANTARES	◆ Alphecca	Kochab
285	58 44 036	21 09 066	12 54 130	41 43 181	29 29 219	43 27 286	28 34 344
286	59 16 035	21 59 066	13 37 130	41 41 182	28 54 219	42 33 287	28 19 344
287	59 48 034	22 50 066	14 19 131	41 38 184	28 19 220	41 40 287	28 03 344
288	60 18 033	23 41 067	15 01 131	41 34 185	27 43 221	40 47 287	27 48 344
289	60 48 032	24 33 067	15 43 132	41 29 186	27 06 222	39 54 287	27 32 344
290	61 17 031	25 24 067	16 24 132	41 23 187	26 29 222	39 00 287	27 16 343
291	61 45 030	26 15 067	17 05 133	41 15 188	25 51 223	38 07 287	27 00 343
292	62 12 029	27 06 067	17 46 133	41 07 189	25 13 224	37 14 288	26 44 343
293	62 38 027	27 58 068	18 26 134	40 57 191	24 34 225	36 21 288	26 28 343
294	63 03 026	28 49 068	19 06 135	40 46 192	23 55 225	35 28 288	26 12 343
295	63 27 025	29 41 068	19 45 135	40 34 193	23 15 226	34 35 288	25 56 343
296	63 50 023	30 32 068	20 24 136	40 21 194	22 35 226	33 42 288	25 40 343
297	64 11 022	31 24 068	21 02 136	40 07 195	21 54 227	32 50 288	25 24 343
298	64 32 021	32 16 068	21 40 137	39 52 196	21 13 228	31 57 289	25 08 343
299	64 51 019	33 07 069	22 18 138	39 36 197	20 32 228	31 04 289	24 51 343
	◆ DENEB	Schedar	Alpheratz	◆ FOMALHAUT	Nunki	◆ Rasalhague	VEGA
300	65 08 018	28 58 036	33 59 069	22 55 138	39 19 199	54 22 261	65 38 318
301	65 24 016	29 31 036	34 51 069	23 32 139	39 00 200	53 27 261	65 01 317
302	65 39 015	30 04 036	35 43 069	24 08 140	38 41 201	52 32 262	64 23 316
303	65 52 013	30 37 036	36 35 069	24 44 140	38 21 202	51 37 262	63 44 315
304	66 04 011	31 10 036	37 27 069	25 19 141	38 00 203	50 42 263	63 04 314
305	66 14 010	31 43 036	38 19 069	25 53 142	37 38 204	49 46 263	62 24 313
306	66 23 008	32 15 036	39 11 070	26 27 143	37 15 205	48 51 264	61 43 312
307	66 30 006	32 48 036	40 04 070	27 01 143	36 51 206	47 56 264	61 02 312
308	66 35 004	33 20 036	40 56 070	27 34 144	36 26 207	47 00 265	60 20 311
309	66 38 003	33 53 036	41 48 070	28 06 145	36 01 208	46 05 265	59 38 310
310	66 40 001	34 25 035	42 40 070	28 38 146	35 34 209	45 09 266	58 55 310
311	66 40 359	34 57 035	43 32 070	29 09 147	35 07 210	44 14 266	58 12 309
312	66 38 357	35 29 035	44 25 070	29 39 147	34 39 211	43 18 267	57 29 309
313	66 34 356	36 01 035	45 17 070	30 09 148	34 10 212	42 23 267	56 45 308
314	66 29 354	36 33 035	46 09 070	30 38 149	33 41 213	41 27 267	56 01 308
	◆ Alpheratz	Diphda	◆ FOMALHAUT	ALTAIR	Rasalhague	◆ VEGA	DENEB
315	47 02 070	22 09 122	31 06 150	68 58 234	40 32 268	55 17 307	66 22 352
316	47 54 070	22 57 122	31 34 151	68 13 236	39 36 268	54 33 307	66 14 350
317	48 47 070	23 44 123	32 00 152	67 26 238	38 40 269	53 48 306	66 04 349
318	49 39 070	24 30 123	32 26 152	66 39 239	37 45 269	53 03 306	65 52 347
319	50 31 070	25 17 124	32 52 153	65 51 240	36 49 269	52 18 306	65 39 345
320	51 24 070	26 03 125	33 16 154	65 02 242	35 54 270	51 33 305	65 24 344
321	52 16 070	26 48 125	33 40 155	64 13 243	34 58 270	50 47 305	65 08 342
322	53 08 070	27 34 126	34 03 156	63 23 244	34 02 271	50 01 305	64 50 341
323	54 01 070	28 19 126	34 25 157	62 33 245	33 07 271	49 16 305	64 31 339
324	54 53 070	29 03 127	34 46 158	61 42 247	32 11 271	48 30 304	64 11 338
325	55 45 070	29 47 128	35 06 159	60 51 248	31 15 272	47 44 304	63 49 336
326	56 38 070	30 31 129	35 26 160	59 59 249	30 20 272	46 58 304	63 26 335
327	57 30 070	31 14 129	35 44 161	59 07 250	29 24 272	46 11 304	63 02 334
328	58 22 070	31 57 130	36 02 162	58 15 250	28 29 273	45 25 304	62 37 333
329	59 14 070	32 39 131	36 19 163	57 22 251	27 33 273	44 39 303	62 11 331
	◆ Mirfak	Hamal	Diphda	◆ FOMALHAUT	ALTAIR	◆ VEGA	DENEB
330	22 07 043	33 16 076	33 21 132	36 34 164	56 29 252	43 52 303	61 44 330
331	22 45 044	34 10 076	34 03 132	36 49 165	55 36 253	43 06 303	61 16 329
332	23 23 044	35 04 076	34 44 133	37 03 166	54 43 254	42 19 303	60 47 328
333	24 02 044	35 58 076	35 24 134	37 15 167	53 50 254	41 32 303	60 17 327
334	24 40 044	36 52 076	36 04 135	37 27 168	52 56 255	40 46 303	59 47 326
335	25 19 044	37 46 077	36 43 136	37 38 169	52 02 256	39 59 303	59 15 325
336	25 57 044	38 40 077	37 22 137	37 48 171	51 08 256	39 12 303	58 43 324
337	26 36 044	39 34 077	37 59 137	37 56 172	50 14 257	38 26 303	58 10 323
338	27 14 044	40 29 077	38 37 138	38 04 173	49 20 258	37 39 303	57 37 323
339	27 53 044	41 23 077	39 13 139	38 10 174	48 25 258	36 52 303	57 03 322
340	28 31 044	42 17 078	39 49 140	38 16 175	47 31 259	36 05 303	56 28 321
341	29 10 044	43 12 078	40 25 141	38 20 176	46 36 259	35 19 303	55 53 320
342	29 49 044	44 06 078	40 59 142	38 24 177	45 41 260	34 32 303	55 18 320
343	30 27 044	45 00 078	41 33 143	38 26 178	44 47 260	33 45 303	54 41 319
344	31 06 044	45 55 078	42 06 144	38 27 179	43 52 261	32 58 303	54 05 319
	Schedar	◆ CAPELLA	ALDEBARAN	Diphda	◆ FOMALHAUT	ALTAIR	◆ DENEB
345	50 42 022	12 41 045	11 20 077	42 38 145	38 27 180	42 57 261	53 28 318
346	51 02 021	13 21 045	12 14 077	43 09 146	38 26 182	42 02 262	52 50 317
347	51 22 020	14 00 046	13 08 077	43 39 148	38 24 183	41 07 262	52 13 317
348	51 41 020	14 40 046	14 03 078	44 09 149	38 21 184	40 11 263	51 35 316
349	52 00 019	15 20 046	14 57 078	44 37 150	38 17 185	39 16 263	50 56 316
350	52 17 018	16 00 046	15 51 078	45 05 151	38 12 186	38 21 264	50 17 316
351	52 35 017	16 40 046	16 46 079	45 31 152	38 06 187	37 26 264	49 38 315
352	52 51 017	17 21 047	17 40 079	45 56 153	37 58 188	36 30 265	48 59 315
353	53 06 016	18 01 047	18 35 079	46 21 155	37 50 189	35 35 265	48 19 314
354	53 21 015	18 42 047	19 30 079	46 44 156	37 40 190	34 39 266	47 39 314
355	53 35 014	19 23 047	20 24 080	47 06 157	37 30 191	33 44 266	46 59 314
356	53 48 013	20 04 047	21 19 080	47 27 159	37 18 192	32 48 266	46 19 313
357	54 01 012	20 44 047	22 14 080	47 47 160	37 06 194	31 53 267	45 38 313
358	54 13 012	21 25 048	23 09 081	48 05 161	36 52 195	30 57 267	44 58 313
359	54 23 011	22 06 048	24 04 081	48 23 163	36 38 196	30 02 268	44 17 313

LAT 21°N

LAT 21°N

LHA ♈	Hc	Zn	Hc	Zn	Hc	Zn	Hc	Zn	Hc	Zn	Hc	Zn	Hc	Zn
	Schedar		◆CAPELLA		ALDEBARAN		◆Diphda		FOMALHAUT		◆ALTAIR		DENEB	
0	53 34	010	22 07	047	24 50	081	49 36	164	37 20	197	29 08	269	42 55	313
1	53 43	009	22 49	048	25 45	081	49 52	165	37 03	198	28 12	269	42 14	313
2	53 51	008	23 30	048	26 40	081	50 05	166	36 45	199	27 16	269	41 33	313
3	53 58	007	24 11	048	27 36	082	50 18	168	36 27	200	26 20	270	40 52	312
4	54 04	006	24 53	048	28 31	082	50 29	169	36 07	201	25 24	270	40 10	312
5	54 10	005	25 34	048	29 27	082	50 38	171	35 47	202	24 28	270	39 29	312
6	54 14	004	26 16	048	30 22	083	50 47	172	35 25	203	23 32	271	38 47	312
7	54 18	003	26 58	048	31 18	083	50 53	174	35 03	204	22 36	271	38 06	312
8	54 20	002	27 39	048	32 13	083	50 59	175	34 40	205	21 40	271	37 24	312
9	54 22	001	28 21	048	33 09	083	51 03	177	34 16	206	20 44	272	36 42	312
10	54 23	000	29 02	048	34 05	084	51 05	178	33 51	207	19 48	272	36 00	312
11	54 23	359	29 44	048	35 00	084	51 06	180	33 26	208	18 52	273	35 18	311
12	54 22	358	30 26	048	35 56	084	51 05	181	32 59	208	17 56	273	34 36	311
13	54 20	357	31 07	048	36 52	085	51 03	183	32 32	209	17 00	273	33 54	311
14	54 17	357	31 49	048	37 48	085	50 59	184	32 05	210	16 04	274	33 12	311
	◆CAPELLA		ALDEBARAN		RIGEL		◆ACHERNAR		FOMALHAUT		Enif		◆DENEB	
15	32 31	048	38 43	085	20 54	108	11 26	175	31 36	211	41 55	264	32 30	311
16	33 12	048	39 39	086	21 47	109	11 31	175	31 07	212	40 59	265	31 48	311
17	33 54	048	40 35	086	22 40	109	11 35	176	30 37	213	40 03	265	31 06	311
18	34 35	048	41 31	086	23 33	109	11 39	176	30 06	214	39 07	266	30 23	311
19	35 17	048	42 27	086	24 26	110	11 42	177	29 35	214	38 11	266	29 41	311
20	35 58	048	43 23	087	25 18	110	11 45	177	29 03	215	37 15	267	28 59	311
21	36 40	048	44 19	087	26 11	111	11 47	178	28 30	216	36 19	267	28 17	311
22	37 21	047	45 15	087	27 03	112	11 49	179	27 57	217	35 23	267	27 35	311
23	38 02	047	46 11	088	27 55	112	11 50	179	27 23	217	34 28	268	26 53	311
24	38 43	047	47 07	088	28 47	113	11 50	180	26 49	218	33 32	268	26 11	311
25	39 24	047	48 03	088	29 38	113	11 50	180	26 14	219	32 36	269	25 28	311
26	40 05	047	48 59	089	30 30	114	11 50	181	25 38	220	31 40	269	24 46	311
27	40 46	047	49 55	089	31 21	114	11 49	181	25 02	220	30 44	269	24 04	312
28	41 27	046	50 51	089	32 12	115	11 47	182	24 26	221	29 48	270	23 23	312
29	42 07	046	51 47	090	33 02	116	11 45	182	23 49	222	28 52	270	22 41	312
	◆CAPELLA		ALDEBARAN		RIGEL		◆ACHERNAR		FOMALHAUT		◆Alpheratz		DENEB	
30	42 48	046	52 43	090	33 53	116	11 42	183	23 11	222	63 41	294	21 59	312
31	43 28	046	53 39	090	34 43	117	11 39	184	22 33	223	62 50	293	21 17	312
32	44 08	045	54 35	091	35 33	117	11 35	184	21 55	224	61 58	293	20 36	312
33	44 48	045	55 31	091	36 22	118	11 31	185	21 16	224	61 07	293	19 54	312
34	45 27	045	56 27	092	37 12	119	11 26	185	20 37	225	60 15	292	19 13	312
35	46 07	045	57 23	092	38 00	120	11 21	186	19 57	225	59 23	292	18 31	312
36	46 46	044	58 19	092	38 49	120	11 15	186	19 17	226	58 31	292	17 50	313
37	47 25	044	59 15	093	39 37	121	11 09	187	18 36	227	57 39	292	17 09	313
38	48 03	043	60 11	093	40 25	122	11 02	187	17 56	227	56 47	292	16 28	313
39	48 42	043	61 06	094	41 12	123	10 54	188	17 14	228	55 55	291	15 47	313
40	49 20	043	62 02	094	41 59	123	10 46	188	16 33	228	55 03	291	15 06	313
41	49 58	042	62 58	095	42 46	124	10 38	189	15 51	229	54 10	291	14 25	313
42	50 35	042	63 54	095	43 32	125	10 29	190	15 08	229	53 18	291	13 44	314
43	51 12	041	64 50	096	44 18	126	10 19	190	14 26	230	52 26	291	13 04	314
44	51 49	041	65 46	096	45 03	127	10 09	191	13 43	230	51 33	291	12 24	314
	CAPELLA		◆POLLUX		PROCYON		SIRIUS		◆Acamar		Diphda		◆Alpheratz	
45	52 25	040	25 24	068	20 29	092	23 00	120	28 45	180	38 50	223	50 41	291
46	53 01	040	26 16	068	21 25	093	23 49	120	28 45	181	38 11	224	49 49	291
47	53 37	039	27 08	068	22 21	093	24 37	121	28 43	182	37 32	225	48 56	291
48	54 11	038	28 00	069	23 17	093	25 25	122	28 41	183	36 53	226	48 04	291
49	54 46	038	28 52	069	24 13	094	26 12	122	28 37	184	36 12	226	47 12	291
50	55 20	037	29 45	069	25 09	094	27 00	123	28 33	185	35 31	227	46 19	291
51	55 53	036	30 37	069	26 05	095	27 47	123	28 28	185	34 50	228	45 27	291
52	56 26	035	31 29	069	27 01	095	28 33	124	28 23	186	34 08	229	44 34	291
53	56 58	035	32 22	069	27 57	095	29 19	125	28 16	187	33 26	230	43 42	291
54	57 29	034	33 14	070	28 52	096	30 05	125	28 09	188	32 43	230	42 50	291
55	58 00	033	34 07	070	29 48	096	30 51	126	28 00	189	31 59	231	41 57	291
56	58 30	032	34 59	070	30 44	097	31 36	127	27 51	190	31 16	232	41 05	291
57	58 59	031	35 52	070	31 39	097	32 21	127	27 42	191	30 31	233	40 13	291
58	59 28	030	36 45	070	32 35	097	33 05	128	27 31	191	29 47	233	39 21	291
59	59 55	029	37 37	070	33 30	098	33 49	129	27 19	192	29 02	234	38 28	291
	◆CAPELLA		PROCYON		◆SIRIUS		RIGEL		Diphda		◆Hamal		Mirfak	
60	60 22	028	34 26	098	34 32	130	55 27	146	28 16	235	64 01	281	60 17	349
61	60 48	027	35 21	099	35 15	130	55 58	147	27 30	235	63 06	281	60 06	347
62	61 13	026	36 16	099	35 57	131	56 28	149	26 44	236	62 11	281	59 53	346
63	61 36	024	37 12	100	36 39	132	56 56	150	25 58	236	61 16	281	59 39	345
64	61 59	023	38 07	100	37 20	133	57 23	152	25 11	237	60 21	281	59 24	344
65	62 20	022	39 02	101	38 01	134	57 49	154	24 24	238	59 26	281	59 08	343
66	62 41	021	39 57	101	38 41	135	58 13	155	23 36	238	58 31	281	58 51	342
67	63 00	019	40 52	102	39 21	136	58 35	157	22 49	239	57 36	281	58 33	341
68	63 18	018	41 47	102	40 00	136	58 56	159	22 01	239	56 41	281	58 14	339
69	63 34	016	42 41	103	40 38	137	59 16	161	21 12	240	55 46	281	57 54	338
70	63 49	015	43 36	103	41 16	138	59 33	163	20 24	240	54 51	281	57 33	337
71	64 03	013	44 30	104	41 52	139	59 49	164	19 35	241	53 56	282	57 11	336
72	64 15	012	45 25	105	42 29	140	60 03	166	18 46	241	53 01	282	56 48	336
73	64 26	010	46 19	105	43 04	141	60 16	168	17 57	242	52 06	282	56 24	335
74	64 36	009	47 13	106	43 39	142	60 26	170	17 07	242	51 11	282	56 00	334
	CAPELLA		◆Dubhe		POLLUX		PROCYON		◆SIRIUS		RIGEL		◆Hamal	
75	64 43	007	17 51	030	51 44	071	48 06	106	44 12	143	60 34	172	50 17	282
76	64 50	006	18 19	030	52 37	071	49 00	107	44 45	145	60 41	174	49 22	282
77	64 54	004	18 47	030	53 29	071	49 54	108	45 17	146	60 46	176	48 27	282
78	64 58	002	19 15	030	54 22	071	50 47	108	45 48	147	60 48	178	47 32	282
79	64 59	001	19 43	030	55 15	071	51 40	109	46 18	148	60 49	180	46 38	283
80	64 59	359	20 11	030	56 08	071	52 33	110	46 48	149	60 47	182	45 43	283
81	64 57	357	20 40	030	57 01	071	53 25	111	47 16	150	60 44	184	44 48	283
82	64 54	356	21 08	030	57 54	070	54 17	112	47 43	152	60 39	186	43 54	283
83	64 49	354	21 36	030	58 47	070	55 09	112	48 09	153	60 32	188	42 59	283
84	64 43	353	22 05	030	59 39	070	56 01	113	48 34	154	60 22	190	42 05	283
85	64 35	351	22 33	031	60 32	070	56 52	114	48 57	156	60 11	192	41 10	283
86	64 25	349	23 02	031	61 25	070	57 43	115	49 20	157	59 58	194	40 16	284
87	64 14	348	23 30	031	62 17	070	58 33	116	49 41	158	59 44	196	39 21	284
88	64 02	346	23 59	031	63 10	069	59 23	117	50 01	160	59 27	198	38 27	284
89	63 48	345	24 27	031	64 02	069	60 13	118	50 20	161	59 09	200	37 32	284

LHA ♈	Hc	Zn	Hc	Zn	Hc	Zn	Hc	Zn	Hc	Zn	Hc	Zn	Hc	Zn
	Dubhe		◆REGULUS		Alphard		SIRIUS		◆RIGEL		ALDEBARAN		◆CAPELLA	
90	24 55	031	29 55	088	30 51	115	50 38	163	58 49	202	69 49	261	63 33	343
91	25 24	031	30 50	088	31 42	115	50 54	164	58 27	204	68 54	262	63 16	342
92	25 52	030	31 46	089	32 32	116	51 08	165	58 04	205	67 58	262	62 58	341
93	26 21	030	32 42	089	33 22	117	51 22	167	57 39	207	67 03	263	62 39	339
94	26 49	030	33 39	089	34 12	117	51 34	168	57 13	209	66 07	263	62 18	338
95	27 17	030	34 35	090	35 02	118	51 44	170	56 46	210	65 12	264	61 57	337
96	27 46	030	35 31	090	35 51	119	51 53	172	56 17	212	64 16	265	61 34	335
97	28 14	030	36 27	091	36 40	119	52 01	173	55 47	213	63 20	265	61 10	334
98	28 42	030	37 23	091	37 29	120	52 07	175	55 15	215	62 24	266	60 45	333
99	29 10	030	38 19	091	38 17	121	52 11	176	54 43	216	61 28	266	60 19	332
100	29 38	030	39 15	092	39 05	121	52 14	178	54 09	218	60 32	267	59 53	331
101	30 06	030	40 11	092	39 53	122	52 16	179	53 35	219	59 37	267	59 25	330
102	30 34	030	41 07	092	40 40	123	52 16	181	52 59	220	58 41	267	58 57	329
103	31 02	030	42 02	093	41 27	124	52 14	182	52 22	222	57 45	268	58 27	328
104	31 29	029	42 58	093	42 13	125	52 11	184	51 44	223	56 49	268	57 57	327
	Dubhe		◆REGULUS		Alphard		SIRIUS		◆RIGEL		ALDEBARAN		◆CAPELLA	
105	31 57	029	43 54	094	42 59	125	52 06	186	51 06	224	55 53	269	57 26	326
106	32 24	029	44 50	094	43 45	126	52 00	187	50 26	225	54 57	269	56 55	325
107	32 51	029	45 46	094	44 29	127	51 52	189	49 46	226	54 01	269	56 23	325
108	33 19	029	46 42	095	45 14	128	51 43	190	49 05	227	53 05	270	55 50	324
109	33 46	029	47 38	095	45 58	129	51 33	192	48 24	229	52 09	270	55 16	323
110	34 12	028	48 33	096	46 41	130	51 21	193	47 41	230	51 13	271	54 42	322
111	34 39	028	49 29	096	47 23	131	51 07	195	46 58	231	50 17	271	54 08	322
112	35 05	028	50 25	097	48 05	132	50 52	196	46 15	232	49 21	271	53 33	321
113	35 32	028	51 20	097	48 46	133	50 36	198	45 31	233	48 25	272	52 58	320
114	35 58	028	52 16	098	49 27	134	50 18	199	44 46	233	47 29	272	52 22	320
115	36 23	027	53 11	098	50 06	135	49 59	200	44 01	234	46 33	272	51 45	319
116	36 49	027	54 07	099	50 45	137	49 39	202	43 15	235	45 37	273	51 09	319
117	37 14	027	55 02	099	51 23	138	49 18	203	42 29	236	44 41	273	50 31	318
118	37 40	027	55 57	100	52 01	139	48 55	205	41 42	237	43 45	273	49 54	318
119	38 04	026	56 52	101	52 37	140	48 31	206	40 55	238	42 49	273	49 16	317
	◆Dubhe		Denebola		◆Alphard		SIRIUS		RIGEL		◆ALDEBARAN		CAPELLA	
120	38 29	026	35 10	087	53 12	142	48 06	207	40 07	238	41 53	274	48 38	317
121	38 53	026	36 06	087	53 46	143	47 40	208	39 19	239	40 57	274	48 00	317
122	39 18	025	37 02	087	54 19	144	47 13	210	38 31	240	40 01	274	47 21	316
123	39 41	025	37 58	088	54 51	146	46 45	211	37 42	241	39 05	275	46 42	316
124	40 05	025	38 54	088	55 22	147	46 16	212	36 53	241	38 10	275	46 03	315
125	40 28	024	39 50	088	55 52	149	45 45	213	36 04	242	37 14	275	45 23	315
126	40 51	024	40 46	089	56 20	150	45 14	214	35 14	243	36 18	276	44 44	315
127	41 13	023	41 42	089	56 47	152	44 42	216	34 24	243	35 22	276	44 04	315
128	41 35	023	42 38	089	57 13	154	44 09	217	33 34	244	34 27	276	43 24	314
129	41 57	023	43 34	090	57 37	155	43 35	218	32 44	245	33 31	276	42 44	314
130	42 19	022	44 30	090	58 00	157	43 01	219	31 53	245	32 35	277	42 03	314
131	42 40	022	45 26	090	58 21	159	42 25	220	31 02	246	31 40	277	41 23	314
132	43 00	021	46 22	091	58 40	161	41 49	221	30 11	246	30 44	277	40 42	313
133	43 20	021	47 18	091	58 58	162	41 12	222	29 19	247	29 48	278	40 01	313
134	43 40	020	48 14	092	59 14	164	40 34	223	28 28	248	28 53	278	39 20	313
	Dubhe		◆ARCTURUS		SPICA		◆Alphard		SIRIUS		BETELGEUSE		◆CAPELLA	
135	44 00	020	16 31	075	17 11	110	59 28	166	39 56	224	43 34	260	38 39	313
136	44 18	019	17 25	076	18 03	110	59 41	168	39 17	225	42 39	260	37 58	313
137	44 37	019	18 20	076	18 56	111	59 52	170	38 37	225	41 44	261	37 17	313
138	44 55	018	19 14	076	19 48	111	60 00	172	37 57	226	40 49	261	36 36	312
139	45 12	018	20 08	077	20 40	112	60 07	174	37 16	227	39 53	262	35 54	312
140	45 29	017	21 03	077	21 32	112	60 12	176	36 35	228	38 58	262	35 13	312
141	45 46	017	21 58	077	22 24	113	60 15	178	35 53	229	38 02	263	34 31	312
142	46 02	016	22 52	077	23 16	113	60 17	180	35 11	230	37 06	263	33 50	312
143	46 17	016	23 47	078	24 07	114	60 16	182	34 28	230	36 11	264	33 08	312
144	46 32	015	24 42	078	24 58	114	60 13	184	33 44	231	35 15	264	32 27	312
145	46 46	014	25 36	078	25 49	115	60 08	186	33 01	232	34 19	265	31 45	312
146	47 00	014	26 31	078	26 40	115	60 02	188	32 16	233	33 24	265	31 03	312
147	47 13	013	27 26	079	27 31	116	59 53	190	31 32	233	32 28	265	30 22	312
148	47 26	013	28 21	079	28 21	116	59 43	192	30 46	234	31 32	266	29 40	312
149	47 38	012	29 16	079	29 11	117	59 30	194	30 01	235	30 36	266	28 58	312
	Dubhe		◆ARCTURUS		SPICA		◆Alphard		SIRIUS		POLLUX		◆CAPELLA	
150	47 49	011	30 11	079	30 01	118	59 16	195	29 15	235	58 53	290	28 17	312
151	48 00	011	31 06	080	30 50	118	59 01	197	28 29	236	58 00	290	27 35	312
152	48 10	010	32 01	080	31 40	119	58 43	199	27 42	237	57 07	289	26 53	312
153	48 19	009	32 57	080	32 29	119	58 24	201	26 55	237	56 14	289	26 12	312
154	48 28	009	33 52	081	33 17	120	58 03	203	26 08	238	55 21	289	25 30	312
155	48 36	008	34 47	081	34 05	121	57 41	204	25 20	238	54 29	289	24 49	312
156	48 43	007	35 42	081	34 53	121	57 17	206	24 32	239	53 36	289	24 07	312
157	48 50	007	36 38	081	35 41	122	56 51	208	23 44	240	52 43	289	23 26	312
158	48 56	006	37 33	082	36 28	123	56 25	209	22 56	240	51 50	289	22 44	312
159	49 02	005	38 29	082	37 15	124	55 57	211	22 07	241	50 57	289	22 03	313
160	49 06	004	39 24	082	38 01	124	55 27	212	21 18	241	50 04	289	21 22	313
161	49 10	004	40 20	082	38 47	125	54 57	214	20 29	242	49 11	289	20 41	313
162	49 14	003	41 15	083	39 33	126	54 25	215	19 39	242	48 18	289	20 00	313
163	49 16	002	42 11	083	40 18	127	53 52	217	18 50	243	47 25	289	19 19	313
164	49 18	002	43 06	083	41 03	128	53 18	218	18 00	243	46 32	289	18 38	313
	◆Dubhe		Alkaid		ARCTURUS		◆SPICA		Alphard		◆PROCYON		POLLUX	
165	49 19	001	46 24	039	44 02	083	41 47	129	52 43	219	39 04	259	45 39	289
166	49 20	000	46 59	039	44 57	084	42 30	129	52 07	221	38 09	260	44 46	289
167	49 20	359	47 34	038	45 53	084	43 13	130	51 29	222	37 14	260	43 53	289
168	49 19	359	48 09	038	46 49	084	43 56	131	50 52	223	36 19	261	43 00	289
169	49 17	358	48 44	038	47 45	084	44 37	132	50 13	224	35 24	261	42 07	289
170	49 15	357	49 17	037	48 40	085	45 19	133	49 33	226	34 28	262	41 14	289
171	49 11	356	49 51	037	49 36	085	45 59	134	48 53	227	33 33	262	40 22	289
172	49 08	356	50 24	036	50 32	085	46 39	135	48 12	228	32 37	262	39 29	290
173	49 03	355	50 57	035	51 28	085	47 18	136	47 30	229	31 42	263	38 36	290
174	48 58	354	51 29	035	52 24	086	47 56	137	46 48	230	30 46	263	37 43	290
175	48 52	354	52 01	034	53 19	086	48 34	139	46 05	231	29 50	264	36 51	290
176	48 46	353	52 32	034	54 15	086	49 10	140	45 21	232	28 55	264	35 58	290
177	48 38	352	53 03	033	55 11	086	49 46	141	44 37	233	27 59	265	35 05	290
178	48 31	352	53 33	032	56 07	087	50 21	142	43 52	234	27 03	265	34 13	290
179	48 22	351	54 03	032	57 03	087	50 55	143	43 07	234	26 07	265	33 20	290

 LAT 21°N

LHA ♈	Hc	Zn	Hc	Zn	Hc	Zn	Hc	Zn	Hc	Zn	Hc	Zn	Hc	Zn
	◆ Alkaid		Alphecca		◆ SPICA		Gienah		REGULUS		◆ POLLUX		Dubhe	
180	54 32	031	40 47	072	51 27	145	51 10	174	61 58	255	32 28	291	48 13	350
181	55 00	030	41 40	072	51 59	146	51 15	175	61 03	256	31 35	291	48 03	350
182	55 28	029	42 34	073	52 30	147	51 19	177	60 09	257	30 43	291	47 52	349
183	55 55	028	43 27	073	52 59	149	51 22	178	59 14	258	29 51	291	47 41	348
184	56 21	027	44 21	073	53 28	150	51 22	180	58 20	258	28 59	291	47 29	348
185	56 46	027	45 14	073	53 55	152	51 22	181	57 25	259	28 06	291	47 17	347
186	57 11	026	46 08	073	54 21	153	51 20	183	56 30	260	27 14	292	47 04	346
187	57 35	025	47 01	073	54 45	155	51 16	184	55 34	260	26 22	292	46 51	346
188	57 57	024	47 55	073	55 08	156	51 11	186	54 39	261	25 30	292	46 37	345
189	58 20	023	48 48	073	55 30	158	51 05	187	53 44	261	24 38	292	46 22	345
190	58 41	022	49 42	073	55 50	160	50 57	189	52 48	262	23 46	292	46 07	344
191	59 01	021	50 36	073	56 09	161	50 48	190	51 53	262	22 55	293	45 51	343
192	59 20	019	51 29	073	56 26	163	50 37	192	50 57	263	22 03	293	45 35	343
193	59 38	018	52 23	073	56 42	165	50 25	193	50 02	263	21 11	293	45 18	342
194	59 55	017	53 16	073	56 56	166	50 11	195	49 06	264	20 20	293	45 00	342
	◆ Kochab		VEGA		Rasalhague		◆ ANTARES		SPICA		◆ REGULUS		Dubhe	
195	34 50	009	17 13	054	23 57	085	20 22	131	57 08	168	48 10	264	44 43	341
196	34 59	009	17 59	054	24 52	085	21 05	131	57 19	170	47 15	265	44 24	341
197	35 07	008	18 44	055	25 48	086	21 47	132	57 28	172	46 19	265	44 06	340
198	35 15	008	19 30	055	26 44	086	22 28	132	57 35	174	45 23	266	43 46	340
199	35 23	008	20 16	055	27 40	086	23 09	133	57 40	175	44 27	266	43 27	339
200	35 30	007	21 02	055	28 36	087	23 50	134	57 44	177	43 31	267	43 07	339
201	35 37	007	21 48	055	29 32	087	24 30	134	57 45	179	42 35	267	42 46	338
202	35 44	007	22 34	055	30 28	087	25 10	135	57 45	181	41 39	267	42 25	338
203	35 51	007	23 20	056	31 24	088	25 49	136	57 44	183	40 43	268	42 04	337
204	35 57	006	24 06	056	32 20	088	26 28	136	57 40	185	39 47	268	41 42	337
205	36 03	006	24 53	056	33 16	088	27 06	137	57 35	186	38 51	269	41 20	337
206	36 08	006	25 39	056	34 12	089	27 44	138	57 28	188	37 55	269	40 58	336
207	36 14	005	26 25	056	35 08	089	28 22	139	57 19	190	36 59	269	40 35	336
208	36 19	005	27 12	056	36 04	090	28 58	139	57 08	192	36 03	270	40 12	336
209	36 23	005	27 58	056	37 00	090	29 35	140	56 56	194	35 07	270	39 49	335
	◆ Kochab		VEGA		Rasalhague		◆ ANTARES		SPICA		◆ REGULUS		Dubhe	
210	36 28	004	28 45	056	37 56	090	30 10	141	56 42	195	34 11	270	39 25	335
211	36 32	004	29 32	056	38 52	091	30 45	142	56 26	197	33 15	271	39 01	334
212	36 35	004	30 18	056	39 48	091	31 20	142	56 09	199	32 19	271	38 37	334
213	36 39	003	31 05	056	40 44	091	31 54	143	55 50	200	31 23	271	38 12	334
214	36 42	003	31 52	057	41 40	092	32 27	144	55 30	202	30 27	272	37 48	334
215	36 45	003	32 38	057	42 36	092	33 00	145	55 08	204	29 31	272	37 23	333
216	36 47	002	33 25	057	43 32	092	33 31	146	54 45	205	28 35	272	36 57	333
217	36 49	002	34 12	057	44 28	093	34 03	147	54 21	207	27 39	273	36 32	333
218	36 51	002	34 59	057	45 24	093	34 33	148	53 55	208	26 43	273	36 06	332
219	36 52	001	35 45	057	46 20	094	35 03	148	53 28	210	25 47	273	35 40	332
220	36 53	001	36 32	057	47 15	094	35 32	149	52 59	211	24 52	274	35 14	332
221	36 54	001	37 19	057	48 11	095	36 00	150	52 30	213	23 56	274	34 47	332
222	36 54	000	38 06	057	49 07	095	36 27	151	51 59	214	23 00	274	34 21	332
223	36 54	000	38 52	056	50 03	095	36 53	152	51 27	215	22 04	275	33 54	331
224	36 54	000	39 39	056	50 59	096	37 19	153	50 54	217	21 08	275	33 27	331
	VEGA		◆ ALTAIR		Nunki		ANTARES		◆ SPICA		Denebola		◆ Alkaid	
225	40 26	056	19 05	088	15 47	127	37 44	154	50 20	218	44 25	270	58 21	337
226	41 12	056	20 01	088	16 31	127	38 08	155	49 46	219	43 29	270	57 59	336
227	41 59	056	20 57	088	17 15	128	38 31	156	49 10	220	42 33	271	57 36	335
228	42 45	056	21 53	089	17 59	129	38 53	157	48 33	221	41 37	271	57 12	334
229	43 32	056	22 49	089	18 43	129	39 14	158	47 56	223	40 41	271	56 48	334
230	44 18	056	23 45	089	19 26	130	39 34	159	47 18	224	39 45	272	56 22	333
231	45 04	056	24 41	090	20 09	130	39 53	161	46 39	225	38 49	272	55 56	332
232	45 50	055	25 37	090	20 52	131	40 11	162	45 59	226	37 53	272	55 29	331
233	46 36	055	26 33	090	21 34	131	40 29	163	45 18	227	36 57	273	55 02	330
234	47 22	055	27 29	091	22 16	132	40 45	164	44 37	228	36 01	273	54 33	329
235	48 08	055	28 25	091	22 57	133	41 00	165	43 55	229	35 05	273	54 05	329
236	48 54	054	29 21	091	23 38	133	41 14	166	43 13	230	34 09	274	53 35	328
237	49 39	054	30 17	092	24 19	134	41 26	167	42 30	231	33 13	274	53 05	327
238	50 25	054	31 13	092	24 59	135	41 38	168	41 46	231	32 17	274	52 34	326
239	51 10	054	32 09	093	25 39	135	41 49	170	41 02	232	31 21	275	52 03	326
	◆ VEGA		ALTAIR		Nunki		◆ ANTARES		SPICA		ARCTURUS		◆ Alkaid	
240	51 55	053	33 05	093	26 18	136	41 58	171	40 18	233	65 37	270	51 31	325
241	52 40	053	34 01	093	26 57	137	42 07	172	39 33	234	64 41	270	50 59	325
242	53 24	052	34 57	094	27 35	137	42 14	173	38 47	235	63 45	271	50 26	324
243	54 09	052	35 53	094	28 12	138	42 20	174	38 01	236	62 49	271	49 53	323
244	54 53	052	36 49	095	28 50	139	42 25	176	37 15	236	61 53	271	49 20	323
245	55 36	051	37 45	095	29 26	140	42 28	177	36 28	237	60 57	272	48 46	322
246	56 20	051	38 40	095	30 02	140	42 31	178	35 41	238	60 01	272	48 11	322
247	57 03	050	39 36	096	30 38	141	42 32	179	34 53	239	59 05	272	47 37	322
248	57 46	049	40 32	096	31 13	142	42 32	181	34 05	239	58 09	273	47 02	321
249	58 28	049	41 27	097	31 47	143	42 31	182	33 17	240	57 13	273	46 26	321
250	59 10	048	42 23	097	32 20	144	42 29	183	32 28	241	56 17	273	45 51	320
251	59 52	048	43 19	098	32 53	144	42 25	184	31 39	241	55 21	274	45 15	320
252	60 33	047	44 14	098	33 26	145	42 21	185	30 50	242	54 25	274	44 39	320
253	61 13	046	45 09	099	33 57	146	42 15	187	30 01	242	53 29	274	44 02	319
254	61 53	045	46 05	099	34 28	147	42 08	188	29 11	243	52 33	274	43 25	319
	◆ DENEB		ALTAIR		◆ Nunki		ANTARES		SPICA		◆ ARCTURUS		Alkaid	
255	38 49	048	47 00	100	34 58	148	42 00	189	28 21	244	51 37	275	42 49	319
256	39 30	048	47 55	100	35 28	149	41 50	190	27 30	244	50 42	275	42 11	318
257	40 12	048	48 50	101	35 56	150	41 40	191	26 40	245	49 46	275	41 34	318
258	40 53	048	49 45	101	36 24	151	41 28	192	25 49	245	48 50	275	40 57	318
259	41 34	047	50 40	102	36 51	152	41 16	194	24 58	246	47 54	276	40 19	318
260	42 15	047	51 35	103	37 17	153	41 02	195	24 07	246	46 58	276	39 41	317
261	42 56	047	52 30	103	37 42	154	40 47	196	23 15	247	46 03	276	39 03	317
262	43 37	047	53 24	104	38 07	155	40 31	197	22 24	247	45 07	276	38 25	317
263	44 18	046	54 18	104	38 30	156	40 14	198	21 32	248	44 11	277	37 47	317
264	44 58	046	55 12	105	38 53	157	39 56	199	20 40	248	43 16	277	37 08	317
265	45 39	046	56 06	106	39 15	158	39 37	200	19 48	249	42 20	277	36 30	316
266	46 19	045	57 00	107	39 35	159	39 17	201	18 55	249	41 25	277	35 51	316
267	46 58	045	57 54	107	39 55	160	38 56	202	18 03	250	40 29	278	35 12	316
268	47 38	045	58 47	108	40 14	161	38 35	204	17 10	250	39 34	278	34 34	316
269	48 17	044	59 40	109	40 31	162	38 12	205	16 17	251	38 38	278	33 55	316

LHA ♈	Hc	Zn	Hc	Zn	Hc	Zn	Hc	Zn	Hc	Zn	Hc	Zn	Hc	Zn
	◆ DENEB		Enif		◆ Nunki		ANTARES		◆ ARCTURUS		Alkaid		Kochab	
270	48 56	044	34 58	092	40 48	163	37 48	206	37 43	278	33 16	316	31 12	346
271	49 35	044	35 54	093	41 04	164	37 23	207	36 47	279	32 37	316	30 59	346
272	50 14	043	36 50	093	41 18	166	36 58	208	35 52	279	31 58	316	30 45	346
273	50 52	043	37 45	094	41 31	167	36 31	209	34 57	279	31 19	316	30 32	346
274	51 30	042	38 41	094	41 44	168	36 04	210	34 01	279	30 40	316	30 18	346
275	52 07	042	39 37	094	41 55	169	35 36	210	33 06	280	30 00	316	30 04	345
276	52 44	041	40 33	095	42 05	170	35 07	211	32 11	280	29 21	316	29 50	345
277	53 21	041	41 29	095	42 14	171	34 38	212	31 16	280	28 42	316	29 36	345
278	53 57	040	42 25	096	42 22	173	34 08	213	30 21	280	28 03	316	29 21	345
279	54 32	039	43 20	096	42 28	174	33 37	214	29 26	281	27 24	316	29 07	345
280	55 08	039	44 16	097	42 34	175	33 05	215	28 31	281	26 45	316	28 52	345
281	55 42	038	45 12	097	42 38	176	32 32	216	27 36	281	26 05	316	28 37	345
282	56 16	037	46 07	098	42 41	178	31 59	217	26 41	282	25 26	316	28 22	344
283	56 50	036	47 03	098	42 43	179	31 26	217	25 46	282	24 47	316	28 07	344
284	57 23	036	47 58	099	42 43	180	30 51	218	24 51	282	24 08	316	27 52	344
	DENEB		◆ Alpheratz		FOMALHAUT		◆ Nunki		ANTARES		◆ Alphecca		Kochab	
285	57 55	035	20 44	066	13 32	129	42 43	181	30 16	219	43 09	287	27 37	344
286	58 27	034	21 35	066	14 15	130	42 41	182	29 41	220	42 16	287	27 21	344
287	58 57	033	22 26	066	14 58	130	42 38	184	29 04	221	41 22	288	27 06	344
288	59 28	032	23 17	066	15 40	131	42 34	185	28 28	221	40 29	288	26 50	344
289	59 57	031	24 09	066	16 23	132	42 29	186	27 51	222	39 36	288	26 34	344
290	60 25	030	25 00	067	17 04	132	42 22	187	27 13	223	38 42	288	26 19	344
291	60 53	029	25 52	067	17 46	133	42 15	188	26 34	223	37 49	288	26 03	344
292	61 19	028	26 43	067	18 27	133	42 06	190	25 56	224	36 56	288	25 47	343
293	61 45	026	27 35	067	19 07	134	41 56	191	25 16	225	36 03	288	25 31	343
294	62 09	025	28 26	067	19 48	134	41 45	192	24 37	226	35 09	289	25 15	343
295	62 32	024	29 18	067	20 27	135	41 33	193	23 57	226	34 16	289	24 59	343
296	62 55	023	30 10	068	21 07	136	41 19	194	23 16	227	33 23	289	24 43	343
297	63 16	021	31 02	068	21 46	136	41 05	195	22 35	227	32 30	289	24 26	343
298	63 35	020	31 53	068	22 24	137	40 50	197	21 53	228	31 37	289	24 10	343
299	63 54	019	32 45	068	23 02	137	40 33	198	21 12	229	30 45	289	23 54	343
	◆ DENEB		Schedar		Alpheratz		◆ FOMALHAUT		Nunki		◆ Rasalhague		VEGA	
300	64 11	017	28 10	036	33 37	068	23 40	138	40 15	199	54 31	262	64 53	320
301	64 27	016	28 43	036	34 29	068	24 17	139	39 57	200	53 35	263	64 16	319
302	64 41	014	29 16	036	35 21	068	24 54	140	39 37	201	52 40	263	63 39	317
303	64 54	012	29 49	036	36 14	069	25 30	140	39 17	202	51 44	264	63 01	316
304	65 05	011	30 21	036	37 06	069	26 06	141	38 55	203	50 48	264	62 22	316
305	65 15	009	30 54	036	37 58	069	26 41	142	38 33	204	49 53	265	61 42	315
306	65 23	008	31 27	036	38 50	069	27 15	142	38 09	205	48 57	265	61 02	314
307	65 30	006	31 59	035	39 42	069	27 49	143	37 45	206	48 01	265	60 21	313
308	65 35	004	32 32	035	40 35	069	28 22	144	37 20	207	47 05	266	59 40	312
309	65 38	003	33 04	035	41 27	069	28 55	145	36 54	208	46 09	266	58 59	312
310	65 40	001	33 36	035	42 19	069	29 27	145	36 27	209	45 13	267	58 16	311
311	65 40	359	34 08	035	43 12	069	29 59	146	35 59	210	44 17	267	57 34	310
312	65 38	357	34 40	035	44 04	069	30 29	147	35 30	211	43 21	268	56 51	310
313	65 35	356	35 12	035	44 56	069	31 00	148	35 01	212	42 25	268	56 08	309
314	65 30	354	35 44	034	45 49	069	31 29	149	34 31	213	41 29	268	55 24	309
	◆ Alpheratz		Diphda		◆ FOMALHAUT		ALTAIR		Rasalhague		◆ VEGA		DENEB	
315	46 41	069	22 40	121	31 58	150	69 33	236	40 33	269	54 40	308	65 23	352
316	47 33	069	23 28	122	32 26	150	68 46	238	39 37	269	53 56	308	65 15	351
317	48 26	069	24 16	122	32 53	151	67 58	240	38 41	269	53 12	307	65 05	349
318	49 18	069	25 03	123	33 20	152	67 09	241	37 45	270	52 27	307	64 54	347
319	50 11	069	25 50	123	33 45	153	66 20	242	36 49	270	51 42	307	64 41	346
320	51 03	069	26 36	124	34 10	154	65 30	244	35 53	271	50 57	306	64 26	344
321	51 55	069	27 23	125	34 34	155	64 39	245	34 57	271	50 12	306	64 11	343
322	52 48	069	28 08	125	34 58	156	63 48	246	34 01	271	49 27	306	63 53	341
323	53 40	069	28 54	126	35 20	157	62 57	247	33 05	272	48 41	305	63 35	340
324	54 32	069	29 39	127	35 42	158	62 05	248	32 09	272	47 56	305	63 15	339
325	55 24	069	30 24	127	36 02	159	61 13	249	31 13	272	47 10	305	62 54	337
326	56 17	069	31 08	128	36 22	160	60 20	250	30 17	273	46 24	305	62 32	336
327	57 09	068	31 52	129	36 41	161	59 27	251	29 22	273	45 38	305	62 08	335
328	58 01	068	32 35	130	36 59	162	58 34	252	28 26	273	44 51	304	61 44	333
329	58 53	068	33 18	130	37 16	163	57 41	253	27 30	274	44 05	304	61 18	332
	◆ Mirfak		Hamal		Diphda		◆ FOMALHAUT		ALTAIR		◆ VEGA		DENEB	
330	21 23	043	33 01	075	34 01	131	37 32	164	56 47	254	43 19	304	60 52	331
331	22 01	043	33 55	075	34 43	132	37 47	165	55 53	254	42 32	304	60 24	330
332	22 40	043	34 49	075	35 24	133	38 01	166	54 59	255	41 46	304	59 56	329
333	23 18	043	35 43	075	36 05	133	38 14	167	54 05	256	40 59	304	59 27	328
334	23 57	043	36 38	076	36 46	134	38 26	168	53 11	256	40 13	304	58 57	327
335	24 35	043	37 32	076	37 26	135	38 37	169	52 16	257	39 26	304	58 26	326
336	25 14	044	38 26	076	38 05	136	38 47	170	51 22	258	38 39	304	57 54	325
337	25 52	044	39 21	076	38 43	137	38 56	171	50 27	258	37 53	303	57 22	324
338	26 31	044	40 15	076	39 21	138	39 03	173	49 32	259	37 06	303	56 49	324
339	27 10	044	41 09	077	39 59	139	39 10	174	48 37	259	36 19	303	56 15	323
340	27 48	044	42 04	077	40 35	140	39 16	175	47 42	260	35 33	303	55 41	322
341	28 27	044	42 59	077	41 11	141	39 20	176	46 47	260	34 46	303	55 07	321
342	29 05	044	43 53	077	41 46	142	39 24	177	45 51	261	33 59	303	54 31	321
343	29 44	044	44 48	077	42 21	143	39 26	178	44 56	261	33 12	303	53 56	320
344	30 23	044	45 42	077	42 54	144	39 27	179	44 01	262	32 26	303	53 20	319
	Schedar		◆ CAPELLA		ALDEBARAN		Diphda		◆ FOMALHAUT		ALTAIR		◆ DENEB	
345	49 46	021	11 59	045	11 06	076	43 27	145	39 27	180	43 05	262	52 43	319
346	50 06	021	12 38	045	12 00	077	43 59	146	39 26	182	42 10	263	52 06	318
347	50 26	020	13 18	045	12 55	077	44 30	147	39 24	183	41 14	263	51 28	318
348	50 45	019	13 58	046	13 50	077	45 00	148	39 21	184	40 18	264	50 51	317
349	51 03	019	14 38	046	14 44	078	45 29	149	39 17	185	39 23	264	50 13	317
350	51 20	018	15 19	046	15 39	078	45 57	151	39 12	186	38 27	265	49 34	316
351	51 37	017	15 59	046	16 34	078	46 24	152	39 05	187	37 31	265	48 55	316
352	51 53	016	16 40	046	17 29	079	46 50	153	38 58	188	36 35	266	48 16	316
353	52 09	016	17 20	047	18 24	079	47 15	154	38 49	189	35 39	266	47 37	315
354	52 23	015	18 01	047	19 19	079	47 39	155	38 39	190	34 43	266	46 57	315
355	52 37	014	18 42	047	20 14	079	48 01	157	38 29	192	33 48	267	46 17	315
356	52 50	013	19 23	047	21 09	080	48 23	158	38 17	193	32 52	267	45 37	314
357	53 02	012	20 04	047	22 04	080	48 43	159	38 04	194	31 56	267	44 57	314
358	53 14	011	20 45	047	22 59	080	49 02	161	37 50	195	31 00	268	44 17	314
359	53 24	010	21 26	047	23 54	081	49 20	162	37 36	196	30 04	268	43 36	313

LAT 20°N

LHA ♈	Hc	Zn	Hc	Zn	Hc	Zn	Hc	Zn	Hc	Zn	Hc	Zn	Hc	Zn
	Schedar		CAPELLA		◆ALDEBARAN		Diphda		◆FOMALHAUT		ALTAIR		◆DENEB	
0	52 35	009	21 27	047	24 40	080	50 34	163	38 17	197	29 09	269	42 14	314
1	52 44	008	22 08	047	25 36	081	50 49	165	38 00	198	28 13	270	41 33	314
2	52 52	008	22 49	047	26 31	081	51 04	166	37 42	199	27 16	270	40 52	313
3	52 59	007	23 31	047	27 27	081	51 16	168	37 23	200	26 20	270	40 11	313
4	53 05	006	24 12	047	28 23	082	51 28	169	37 03	201	25 23	271	39 30	313
5	53 10	005	24 54	048	29 18	082	51 38	171	36 42	202	24 27	271	38 48	313
6	53 14	004	25 36	048	30 14	082	51 46	172	36 21	203	23 31	271	38 07	313
7	53 18	003	26 17	048	31 10	082	51 53	174	35 58	204	22 34	272	37 25	312
8	53 20	002	26 59	048	32 06	083	51 58	175	35 34	205	21 38	272	36 44	312
9	53 22	001	27 41	048	33 02	083	52 02	177	35 10	206	20 42	272	36 02	312
10	53 23	000	28 22	048	33 58	083	52 05	178	34 45	207	19 45	273	35 20	312
11	53 23	359	29 04	048	34 54	083	52 06	180	34 19	208	18 49	273	34 38	312
12	53 22	358	29 46	048	35 50	084	52 05	181	33 52	209	17 53	273	33 56	312
13	53 20	358	30 27	048	36 46	084	52 03	183	33 25	210	16 56	274	33 14	312
14	53 17	357	31 09	048	37 42	084	51 59	185	32 56	211	16 00	274	32 32	312
	CAPELLA		◆ALDEBARAN		RIGEL		ACHERNAR		◆FOMALHAUT		Enif		◆DENEB	
15	31 50	048	38 38	084	21 12	108	12 25	175	32 27	211	42 00	265	31 50	312
16	32 32	047	39 34	085	22 06	108	12 30	175	31 57	212	41 04	266	31 08	312
17	33 14	047	40 30	085	23 00	109	12 35	176	31 27	213	40 07	266	30 26	312
18	33 55	047	41 27	085	23 53	109	12 39	176	30 56	214	39 11	267	29 44	312
19	34 36	047	42 23	086	24 46	110	12 42	177	30 24	215	38 15	267	29 02	312
20	35 18	047	43 19	086	25 39	110	12 45	177	29 52	216	37 19	267	28 19	312
21	35 59	047	44 15	086	26 32	111	12 47	178	29 19	216	36 22	268	27 37	312
22	36 40	047	45 11	086	27 25	111	12 49	179	28 45	217	35 26	268	26 55	312
23	37 21	047	46 08	087	28 17	112	12 50	179	28 11	218	34 30	268	26 13	312
24	38 02	047	47 04	087	29 10	112	12 50	180	27 36	219	33 33	269	25 31	312
25	38 43	046	48 00	087	30 02	113	12 50	180	27 00	219	32 37	269	24 49	312
26	39 24	046	48 57	088	30 54	113	12 50	181	26 25	220	31 40	270	24 07	312
27	40 05	046	49 53	088	31 45	114	12 49	181	25 48	221	30 44	270	23 25	312
28	40 45	046	50 49	088	32 37	114	12 47	182	25 11	221	29 48	270	22 43	312
29	41 25	046	51 46	088	33 28	115	12 45	182	24 34	222	28 51	271	22 01	312
	Mirfak		CAPELLA		◆ALDEBARAN		RIGEL		ACHERNAR		◆FOMALHAUT		◆DENEB	
30	55 37	025	42 06	045	52 42	089	34 19	116	12 42	183	23 56	223	21 19	312
31	56 00	024	42 46	045	53 38	089	35 10	116	12 39	184	23 17	223	20 37	312
32	56 22	023	43 26	045	54 35	089	36 00	117	12 35	184	22 38	224	19 55	312
33	56 43	022	44 05	044	55 31	090	36 50	118	12 31	185	21 59	225	19 14	312
34	57 04	021	44 45	044	56 28	090	37 40	118	12 26	185	21 19	225	18 32	313
35	57 23	020	45 24	044	57 24	090	38 30	119	12 21	186	20 39	226	17 51	313
36	57 42	019	46 03	043	58 20	091	39 19	120	12 15	186	19 59	226	17 09	313
37	57 59	018	46 41	043	59 17	091	40 08	120	12 08	187	19 18	227	16 28	313
38	58 15	016	47 20	043	60 13	091	40 56	121	12 01	187	18 36	227	15 47	313
39	58 31	015	47 58	042	61 09	092	41 44	122	11 54	188	17 54	228	15 06	313
40	58 45	014	48 36	042	62 06	092	42 32	123	11 46	188	17 12	229	14 25	313
41	58 58	013	49 13	041	63 02	093	43 19	123	11 37	189	16 30	229	13 44	314
42	59 11	012	49 50	041	63 58	093	44 06	124	11 28	190	15 47	230	13 03	314
43	59 21	011	50 27	040	64 55	094	44 52	125	11 18	190	15 04	230	12 22	314
44	59 31	009	51 03	040	65 51	094	45 38	126	11 08	191	14 21	231	11 42	314
	CAPELLA		◆POLLUX		PROCYON		SIRIUS		◆Acamar		Diphda		◆Alpheratz	
45	51 39	039	25 01	068	20 32	092	23 30	120	29 45	180	39 34	224	50 19	292
46	52 15	039	25 54	068	21 28	092	24 19	120	29 45	181	38 55	224	49 27	292
47	52 50	038	26 46	068	22 24	093	25 08	121	29 43	182	38 15	225	48 35	292
48	53 24	037	27 38	068	23 21	093	25 56	121	29 41	183	37 34	226	47 42	292
49	53 58	037	28 30	068	24 17	093	26 44	122	29 37	184	36 53	227	46 50	292
50	54 32	036	29 23	068	25 13	094	27 32	122	29 33	185	36 12	228	45 57	292
51	55 04	035	30 15	069	26 09	094	28 20	123	29 28	186	35 30	229	45 05	292
52	55 37	035	31 08	069	27 06	094	29 07	124	29 22	186	34 47	229	44 13	292
53	56 08	034	32 00	069	28 02	095	29 53	124	29 16	187	34 04	230	43 20	292
54	56 39	033	32 53	069	28 58	095	30 40	125	29 08	188	33 21	231	42 28	292
55	57 10	032	33 46	069	29 54	096	31 26	126	29 00	189	32 37	232	41 36	292
56	57 39	031	34 38	069	30 50	096	32 12	126	28 51	190	31 53	232	40 43	292
57	58 08	030	35 31	069	31 46	096	32 57	127	28 41	191	31 08	233	39 51	292
58	58 36	029	36 24	069	32 42	097	33 42	128	28 30	192	30 23	234	38 59	292
59	59 03	028	37 17	069	33 38	097	34 26	128	28 18	192	29 37	234	38 06	292
	◆CAPELLA		POLLUX		PROCYON		◆SIRIUS		CANOPUS		Diphda		◆Hamal	
60	59 29	027	38 09	070	34 34	098	35 10	129	10 51	159	28 51	235	63 48	283
61	59 54	026	39 02	070	35 30	098	35 54	130	11 11	159	28 05	236	62 53	283
62	60 18	025	39 55	070	36 26	099	36 37	131	11 31	160	27 18	236	61 58	283
63	60 41	024	40 48	070	37 22	099	37 19	132	11 50	160	26 31	237	61 03	283
64	61 04	022	41 41	070	38 17	099	38 01	132	12 09	161	25 43	237	60 08	283
65	61 25	021	42 34	070	39 13	100	38 42	133	12 27	161	24 56	238	59 13	283
66	61 44	020	43 27	070	40 08	100	39 23	134	12 45	162	24 08	239	58 18	283
67	62 03	019	44 20	070	41 04	101	40 03	135	13 02	162	23 20	239	57 23	283
68	62 20	017	45 13	070	41 59	101	40 43	136	13 19	163	22 31	240	56 28	283
69	62 36	016	46 06	070	42 54	102	41 22	137	13 35	164	21 42	240	55 33	283
70	62 51	014	46 59	070	43 49	102	42 00	138	13 51	164	20 53	241	54 38	283
71	63 05	013	47 52	070	44 44	103	42 38	139	14 06	165	20 04	241	53 43	283
72	63 17	012	48 45	070	45 39	104	43 15	140	14 21	165	19 14	242	52 48	283
73	63 27	010	49 38	070	46 34	104	43 51	141	14 35	166	18 25	242	51 53	283
74	63 36	009	50 31	070	47 28	105	44 26	142	14 48	166	17 35	243	50 58	283
	CAPELLA		◆POLLUX		PROCYON		SIRIUS		◆RIGEL		Menkar		◆Hamal	
75	63 44	007	51 23	070	48 23	105	45 00	143	61 34	172	57 25	245	50 04	283
76	63 50	005	52 16	070	49 17	106	45 34	144	61 41	174	56 34	246	49 09	283
77	63 55	004	53 09	070	50 11	107	46 07	145	61 45	176	55 42	247	48 14	283
78	63 58	002	54 02	070	51 05	107	46 38	146	61 48	178	54 50	247	47 19	283
79	63 59	001	54 55	069	51 59	108	47 09	147	61 49	180	53 58	248	46 24	284
80	63 59	359	55 48	069	52 52	109	47 39	149	61 47	182	53 05	249	45 29	284
81	63 57	358	56 40	069	53 46	110	48 08	150	61 44	185	52 13	250	44 35	284
82	63 54	356	57 33	069	54 39	110	48 36	151	61 38	187	51 20	251	43 40	284
83	63 50	354	58 26	069	55 31	111	49 02	152	61 31	189	50 26	251	42 45	284
84	63 43	353	59 18	069	56 24	112	49 28	154	61 21	191	49 33	252	41 50	284
85	63 35	351	60 11	068	57 16	113	49 52	155	61 10	193	48 39	253	40 56	284
86	63 26	350	61 03	068	58 08	114	50 15	156	60 56	195	47 45	253	40 01	284
87	63 16	348	61 55	068	58 59	115	50 37	158	60 41	197	46 51	254	39 06	285
88	63 03	347	62 47	067	59 50	116	50 58	159	60 24	199	45 57	255	38 12	285
89	62 50	345	63 39	067	60 41	117	51 17	161	60 05	201	45 02	255	37 17	285

LHA ♈	Hc	Zn	Hc	Zn	Hc	Zn	Hc	Zn	Hc	Zn	Hc	Zn	Hc	Zn
	Dubhe		◆REGULUS		Alphard		SIRIUS		◆RIGEL		ALDEBARAN		◆CAPELLA	
90	24 04	030	29 52	087	31 16	114	51 35	162	59 44	202	69 57	263	62 35	344
91	24 32	030	30 49	088	32 07	115	51 51	164	59 22	204	69 01	264	62 19	343
92	25 01	030	31 45	088	32 58	115	52 06	165	58 58	206	68 05	265	62 01	341
93	25 29	030	32 41	088	33 49	116	52 20	167	58 33	208	67 09	265	61 42	340
94	25 57	030	33 38	089	34 39	117	52 32	168	58 06	209	66 13	266	61 22	339
95	26 26	030	34 34	089	35 30	117	52 43	170	57 37	211	65 17	266	61 01	337
96	26 54	030	35 30	089	36 20	118	52 52	171	57 08	213	64 20	267	60 39	336
97	27 22	030	36 27	090	37 09	119	53 00	173	56 37	214	63 24	267	60 16	335
98	27 50	030	37 23	090	37 59	119	53 06	174	56 04	216	62 28	268	59 52	334
99	28 18	030	38 19	090	38 48	120	53 11	176	55 31	217	61 31	268	59 26	333
100	28 46	030	39 16	091	39 36	121	53 14	178	54 56	219	60 35	268	59 00	332
101	29 14	030	40 12	091	40 25	121	53 16	179	54 21	220	59 39	269	58 33	331
102	29 42	029	41 09	092	41 12	122	53 16	181	53 44	221	58 42	269	58 05	330
103	30 10	029	42 05	092	42 00	123	53 14	182	53 07	222	57 46	269	57 36	329
104	30 37	029	43 01	092	42 47	124	53 11	184	52 28	224	56 50	270	57 07	328
	Dubhe		◆REGULUS		Alphard		SIRIUS		◆RIGEL		ALDEBARAN		◆CAPELLA	
105	31 04	029	43 58	093	43 34	125	53 06	186	51 49	225	55 53	270	56 36	327
106	31 32	029	44 54	093	44 20	126	53 00	187	51 08	226	54 57	270	56 05	326
107	31 59	029	45 50	093	45 05	126	52 52	189	50 27	227	54 01	271	55 33	325
108	32 26	029	46 46	094	45 50	127	52 42	190	49 46	228	53 04	271	55 01	325
109	32 53	028	47 43	094	46 35	128	52 31	192	49 03	229	52 08	271	54 28	324
110	33 19	028	48 39	095	47 19	129	52 19	193	48 20	230	51 11	272	53 55	323
111	33 46	028	49 35	095	48 02	130	52 05	195	47 36	231	50 15	272	53 21	323
112	34 12	028	50 31	096	48 45	131	51 50	196	46 52	232	49 19	272	52 46	322
113	34 38	027	51 27	096	49 27	132	51 33	198	46 07	233	48 22	273	52 11	321
114	35 04	027	52 23	096	50 08	133	51 15	199	45 21	234	47 26	273	51 35	321
115	35 30	027	53 19	097	50 49	135	50 56	201	44 35	235	46 30	273	51 00	320
116	35 56	027	54 15	097	51 29	136	50 35	202	43 49	236	45 33	274	50 23	320
117	36 21	026	55 11	098	52 08	137	50 13	204	43 02	237	44 37	274	49 46	319
118	36 46	026	56 07	099	52 46	138	49 50	205	42 14	238	43 41	274	49 09	319
119	37 11	026	57 03	099	53 23	139	49 25	206	41 27	238	42 45	274	48 32	318
	Dubhe		◆Denebola		Alphard		◆SIRIUS		RIGEL		ALDEBARAN		◆CAPELLA	
120	37 35	026	35 06	086	53 59	141	49 00	208	40 38	239	41 49	275	47 54	318
121	37 59	025	36 02	086	54 34	142	48 33	209	39 50	240	40 52	275	47 16	317
122	38 23	025	36 58	087	55 08	144	48 05	210	39 01	241	39 56	275	46 37	317
123	38 47	025	37 55	087	55 41	145	47 36	211	38 11	241	39 00	275	45 59	316
124	39 10	024	38 51	087	56 13	147	47 06	213	37 22	242	38 04	276	45 20	316
125	39 33	024	39 47	088	56 43	148	46 35	214	36 32	243	37 08	276	44 41	316
126	39 56	024	40 44	088	57 12	150	46 04	215	35 42	243	36 12	276	44 01	315
127	40 18	023	41 40	088	57 40	151	45 31	216	34 51	244	35 16	277	43 22	315
128	40 40	023	42 36	088	58 06	153	44 57	217	34 00	245	34 20	277	42 42	315
129	41 02	022	43 33	089	58 31	155	44 23	218	33 09	245	33 24	277	42 02	315
130	41 23	022	44 29	089	58 55	156	43 47	219	32 18	246	32 28	277	41 21	314
131	41 44	021	45 26	089	59 16	158	43 11	220	31 26	246	31 32	278	40 41	314
132	42 04	021	46 22	090	59 37	160	42 34	221	30 34	247	30 36	278	40 01	314
133	42 24	021	47 18	090	59 55	162	41 57	222	29 42	248	29 40	278	39 20	314
134	42 44	020	48 15	090	60 12	164	41 18	223	28 50	248	28 44	278	38 39	314
	Dubhe		◆ARCTURUS		SPICA		◆Alphard		SIRIUS		BETELGEUSE		◆CAPELLA	
135	43 03	020	16 16	075	17 31	109	60 27	166	40 39	224	43 44	261	37 58	313
136	43 22	019	17 10	075	18 24	110	60 40	168	40 00	225	42 49	261	37 17	313
137	43 40	019	18 05	076	19 17	110	60 51	170	39 19	226	41 53	262	36 36	313
138	43 58	018	19 00	076	20 10	111	61 00	172	38 38	227	40 57	262	35 55	313
139	44 15	018	19 54	076	21 02	111	61 07	174	37 57	228	40 01	263	35 14	313
140	44 32	017	20 49	076	21 55	112	61 12	176	37 15	229	39 05	263	34 32	313
141	44 48	017	21 44	077	22 47	112	61 15	178	36 32	229	38 09	264	33 51	313
142	45 04	016	22 39	077	23 39	113	61 17	180	35 49	230	37 13	264	33 09	313
143	45 19	015	23 34	077	24 31	113	61 16	182	35 06	231	36 17	264	32 28	313
144	45 34	015	24 29	077	25 23	114	61 13	184	34 22	232	35 21	265	31 46	312
145	45 48	014	25 24	078	26 14	114	61 08	186	33 37	232	34 25	265	31 05	312
146	46 02	014	26 19	078	27 06	115	61 01	188	32 53	233	33 28	266	30 23	312
147	46 15	013	27 14	078	27 57	115	60 52	190	32 07	234	32 32	266	29 41	312
148	46 27	012	28 09	078	28 47	116	60 41	192	31 22	234	31 36	266	29 00	312
149	46 39	012	29 05	079	29 38	116	60 29	194	30 35	235	30 40	267	28 18	312
	Dubhe		◆ARCTURUS		SPICA		◆Alphard		SIRIUS		BETELGEUSE		◆CAPELLA	
150	46 50	011	30 00	079	30 28	117	60 14	196	29 49	236	29 43	267	27 36	312
151	47 01	010	30 55	079	31 18	118	59 58	198	29 02	236	28 47	268	26 55	312
152	47 11	010	31 51	079	32 08	118	59 40	200	28 15	237	27 51	268	26 13	312
153	47 20	009	32 46	080	32 58	119	59 20	202	27 28	238	26 54	268	25 31	312
154	47 28	009	33 42	080	33 47	120	58 58	203	26 40	238	25 58	269	24 50	312
155	47 37	008	34 37	080	34 36	120	58 35	205	25 52	239	25 02	269	24 08	313
156	47 44	007	35 33	080	35 24	121	58 11	207	25 03	239	24 05	269	23 27	313
157	47 51	006	36 28	081	36 13	122	57 44	208	24 14	240	23 09	270	22 45	313
158	47 57	006	37 24	081	37 01	122	57 17	210	23 26	241	22 13	270	22 04	313
159	48 02	005	38 20	081	37 48	123	56 48	212	22 36	241	21 16	270	21 22	313
160	48 07	004	39 15	081	38 35	124	56 18	213	21 47	242	20 20	271	20 41	313
161	48 10	004	40 11	081	39 22	125	55 46	215	20 57	242	19 23	271	20 00	313
162	48 14	003	41 07	082	40 08	125	55 13	216	20 07	243	18 27	271	19 19	313
163	48 16	002	42 03	082	40 54	126	54 40	218	19 17	243	17 31	272	18 38	313
164	48 18	002	42 58	082	41 39	127	54 05	219	18 27	244	16 34	272	17 57	313
	◆Dubhe		Alkaid		ARCTURUS		◆SPICA		Suhail		◆PROCYON		POLLUX	
165	48 19	001	45 37	039	43 54	082	42 24	128	21 33	201	39 15	260	45 19	290
166	48 20	000	46 13	038	44 50	083	43 08	129	21 12	202	38 20	260	44 26	290
167	48 20	359	46 47	038	45 46	083	43 52	130	20 50	203	37 24	261	43 33	290
168	48 19	359	47 22	037	46 42	083	44 35	131	20 28	203	36 28	261	42 40	290
169	48 17	358	47 56	037	47 38	083	45 18	131	20 06	204	35 32	262	41 47	290
170	48 15	357	48 29	036	48 34	083	45 59	132	19 42	205	34 37	262	40 54	290
171	48 12	357	49 03	036	49 30	084	46 41	133	19 19	205	33 41	263	40 01	290
172	48 08	356	49 35	035	50 26	084	47 21	135	18 54	206	32 45	263	39 08	290
173	48 03	355	50 08	035	51 22	084	48 01	136	18 29	207	31 49	264	38 15	290
174	47 58	354	50 40	034	52 18	084	48 40	137	18 04	207	30 53	264	37 23	291
175	47 53	354	51 11	034	53 14	085	49 18	138	17 38	208	29 57	264	36 30	291
176	47 46	353	51 42	033	54 11	085	49 56	139	17 11	208	29 00	265	35 37	291
177	47 39	352	52 12	032	55 07	085	50 32	140	16 44	209	28 04	265	34 44	291
178	47 31	352	52 42	032	56 03	085	51 08	141	16 16	210	27 08	266	33 52	291
179	47 23	351	53 11	031	56 59	085	51 43	143	15 48	210	26 12	266	32 59	291

 LAT 20°N

LHA ♈	Hc	Zn	Hc	Zn	Hc	Zn	Hc	Zn	Hc	Zn	Hc	Zn	Hc	Zn
	◆ Alkaid		ANTARES		◆ SPICA		Gienah		◆ REGULUS		POLLUX		Dubhe	
180	53 40	030	09 42	123	52 16	144	52 09	174	62 12	257	32 06	291	47 14	350
181	54 08	029	10 29	123	52 49	145	52 15	175	61 17	258	31 14	291	47 04	350
182	54 35	028	11 16	124	53 20	147	52 19	177	60 22	259	30 21	291	46 53	349
183	55 02	028	12 03	124	53 51	148	52 21	178	59 26	259	29 29	292	46 42	348
184	55 27	027	12 49	125	54 20	150	52 22	180	58 31	260	28 37	292	46 31	348
185	55 52	026	13 35	125	54 48	151	52 22	181	57 35	261	27 44	292	46 19	347
186	56 17	025	14 21	126	55 14	153	52 20	183	56 40	261	26 52	292	46 06	347
187	56 40	024	15 07	126	55 39	154	52 16	184	55 44	262	26 00	292	45 52	346
188	57 02	023	15 52	127	56 03	156	52 11	186	54 48	262	25 08	292	45 39	345
189	57 24	022	16 37	127	56 26	157	52 04	188	53 52	263	24 15	293	45 24	345
190	57 45	021	17 22	128	56 46	159	51 56	189	52 56	263	23 23	293	45 09	344
191	58 04	020	18 07	128	57 06	161	51 47	191	52 00	264	22 31	293	44 53	344
192	58 23	019	18 51	129	57 24	163	51 36	192	51 04	264	21 40	293	44 37	343
193	58 41	018	19 35	129	57 40	164	51 23	194	50 08	265	20 48	293	44 21	343
194	58 57	017	20 18	130	57 54	166	51 09	195	49 12	265	19 56	294	44 03	342
	Kochab		◆ VEGA		Rasalhague		ANTARES		◆ SPICA		◆ REGULUS		Dubhe	
195	33 51	009	16 38	054	23 51	085	21 01	130	58 07	168	48 16	265	43 46	342
196	33 59	009	17 24	054	24 47	085	21 44	131	58 18	170	47 19	266	43 28	341
197	34 08	008	18 10	054	25 44	085	22 26	132	58 27	172	46 23	266	43 09	341
198	34 16	008	18 55	055	26 40	086	23 08	132	58 34	173	45 27	267	42 50	340
199	34 23	008	19 41	055	27 36	086	23 50	133	58 40	175	44 31	267	42 31	340
200	34 31	007	20 27	055	28 32	086	24 31	133	58 44	177	43 34	268	42 11	339
201	34 38	007	21 14	055	29 29	087	25 12	134	58 45	179	42 38	268	41 50	339
202	34 45	007	22 00	055	30 25	087	25 52	135	58 45	181	41 42	268	41 30	338
203	34 51	006	22 46	055	31 21	087	26 32	135	58 44	183	40 45	269	41 09	338
204	34 57	006	23 32	055	32 17	088	27 11	136	58 40	185	39 49	269	40 47	337
205	35 03	006	24 19	055	33 14	088	27 50	137	58 34	187	38 52	269	40 25	337
206	35 09	006	25 05	056	34 10	088	28 29	137	58 27	188	37 56	270	40 03	337
207	35 14	005	25 52	056	35 06	088	29 07	138	58 18	190	37 00	270	39 40	336
208	35 19	005	26 38	056	36 03	089	29 44	139	58 07	192	36 03	270	39 18	336
209	35 23	005	27 25	056	36 59	089	30 21	140	57 54	194	35 07	271	38 54	336
	Kochab		◆ VEGA		Rasalhague		◆ ANTARES		SPICA		◆ REGULUS		Dubhe	
210	35 28	004	28 12	056	37 56	089	30 57	140	57 40	196	34 11	271	38 31	335
211	35 32	004	28 58	056	38 52	090	31 32	141	57 23	197	33 14	271	38 07	335
212	35 35	004	29 45	056	39 48	090	32 07	142	57 06	199	32 18	272	37 43	335
213	35 39	003	30 32	056	40 45	090	32 42	143	56 46	201	31 21	272	37 18	334
214	35 42	003	31 18	056	41 41	091	33 15	144	56 25	203	30 25	272	36 54	334
215	35 45	003	32 05	056	42 37	091	33 48	145	56 03	204	29 29	273	36 29	334
216	35 47	002	32 52	056	43 34	092	34 21	145	55 39	206	28 32	273	36 04	333
217	35 49	002	33 39	056	44 30	092	34 53	146	55 14	207	27 36	273	35 38	333
218	35 51	002	34 25	056	45 27	092	35 23	147	54 47	209	26 40	274	35 13	333
219	35 52	001	35 12	056	46 23	093	35 54	148	54 19	210	25 44	274	34 47	333
220	35 53	001	35 59	056	47 19	093	36 23	149	53 50	212	24 47	274	34 21	332
221	35 54	001	36 46	056	48 15	093	36 52	150	53 20	213	23 51	275	33 54	332
222	35 54	000	37 32	056	49 12	094	37 20	151	52 49	215	22 55	275	33 28	332
223	35 54	000	38 19	056	50 08	094	37 47	152	52 16	216	21 59	275	33 01	332
224	35 54	000	39 06	056	51 04	095	38 13	153	51 42	217	21 03	275	32 35	332
	VEGA		◆ ALTAIR		Nunki		ANTARES		◆ SPICA		Denebola		◆ Alkaid	
225	39 52	056	19 03	087	16 23	127	38 38	154	51 08	219	44 24	271	57 25	338
226	40 39	056	19 59	088	17 08	127	39 02	155	50 32	220	43 28	271	57 04	337
227	41 25	055	20 55	088	17 52	128	39 26	156	49 55	221	42 31	272	56 41	336
228	42 11	055	21 52	088	18 37	128	39 48	157	49 18	222	41 35	272	56 18	335
229	42 58	055	22 48	089	19 21	129	40 10	158	48 40	223	40 39	272	55 54	334
230	43 44	055	23 44	089	20 05	129	40 30	159	48 01	224	39 42	273	55 29	333
231	44 30	055	24 41	089	20 48	130	40 50	160	47 21	225	38 46	273	55 03	332
232	45 16	055	25 37	090	21 31	131	41 08	161	46 40	227	37 50	273	54 37	332
233	46 02	054	26 33	090	22 14	131	41 26	163	45 59	228	36 54	273	54 10	331
234	46 48	054	27 30	090	22 56	132	41 42	164	45 17	229	35 57	274	53 42	330
235	47 33	054	28 26	091	23 38	132	41 58	165	44 35	229	35 01	274	53 13	329
236	48 19	054	29 23	091	24 19	133	42 12	166	43 52	230	34 05	274	52 44	329
237	49 04	053	30 19	091	25 00	134	42 25	167	43 08	231	33 09	275	52 14	328
238	49 49	053	31 15	092	25 41	134	42 37	168	42 23	232	32 12	275	51 44	327
239	50 34	053	32 12	092	26 21	135	42 48	170	41 39	233	31 16	275	51 13	327
	◆ VEGA		ALTAIR		Nunki		◆ ANTARES		SPICA		◆ ARCTURUS		Alkaid	
240	51 19	052	33 08	092	27 01	136	42 57	171	40 53	234	65 35	272	50 42	326
241	52 03	052	34 04	093	27 40	136	43 06	172	40 08	235	64 39	273	50 10	325
242	52 47	051	35 01	093	28 19	137	43 13	173	39 21	235	63 43	273	49 38	325
243	53 31	051	35 57	093	28 57	138	43 19	174	38 35	236	62 46	273	49 05	324
244	54 15	051	36 53	094	29 35	138	43 24	176	37 48	237	61 50	273	48 32	324
245	54 58	050	37 49	094	30 12	139	43 28	177	37 00	238	60 54	274	47 58	323
246	55 41	049	38 46	095	30 48	140	43 31	178	36 12	238	59 58	274	47 24	323
247	56 24	049	39 42	095	31 24	141	43 32	179	35 24	239	59 01	274	46 50	322
248	57 06	048	40 38	095	32 00	142	43 32	181	34 36	240	58 05	274	46 15	322
249	57 48	048	41 34	096	32 34	142	43 31	182	33 47	240	57 09	274	45 40	321
250	58 30	047	42 30	096	33 09	143	43 29	183	32 57	241	56 13	275	45 04	321
251	59 11	046	43 26	097	33 42	144	43 25	184	32 08	242	55 16	275	44 29	321
252	59 51	045	44 22	097	34 15	145	43 20	185	31 18	242	54 20	275	43 53	320
253	60 31	045	45 18	098	34 47	146	43 14	187	30 28	243	53 24	275	43 17	320
254	61 10	044	46 14	098	35 18	147	43 07	188	29 38	244	52 28	276	42 40	320
	◆ DENEB		ALTAIR		◆ Nunki		ANTARES		SPICA		◆ ARCTURUS		Alkaid	
255	38 08	047	47 10	099	35 49	148	42 59	189	28 47	244	51 32	276	42 03	319
256	38 50	047	48 05	099	36 19	148	42 49	190	27 56	245	50 36	276	41 26	319
257	39 31	047	49 01	100	36 48	149	42 39	191	27 05	245	49 40	276	40 49	319
258	40 12	047	49 57	100	37 16	150	42 27	193	26 14	246	48 44	277	40 11	318
259	40 53	047	50 52	101	37 44	151	42 14	194	25 22	246	47 48	277	39 34	318
260	41 34	046	51 47	101	38 10	152	42 00	195	24 31	247	46 52	277	38 57	318
261	42 15	046	52 43	102	38 36	153	41 45	196	23 39	247	45 56	277	38 19	318
262	42 56	046	53 38	102	39 01	154	41 29	197	22 47	248	45 00	277	37 41	318
263	43 36	046	54 33	103	39 25	155	41 11	198	21 54	248	44 04	278	37 03	317
264	44 16	045	55 27	104	39 48	156	40 53	200	21 02	249	43 08	278	36 24	317
265	44 56	045	56 22	104	40 10	157	40 34	201	20 09	249	42 12	278	35 46	317
266	45 36	045	57 17	105	40 31	159	40 13	202	19 16	250	41 16	278	35 07	317
267	46 16	044	58 11	106	40 51	160	39 52	203	18 23	250	40 21	279	34 29	317
268	46 55	044	59 05	107	41 10	161	39 29	204	17 30	251	39 25	279	33 50	317
269	47 34	044	59 59	107	41 28	162	39 06	205	16 37	251	38 29	279	33 11	316

LHA ♈	Hc	Zn	Hc	Zn	Hc	Zn	Hc	Zn	Hc	Zn	Hc	Zn	Hc	Zn
	◆ DENEB		Enif		◆ Nunki		ANTARES		◆ ARCTURUS		Alkaid		Kochab	
270	48 13	043	35 00	092	41 45	163	38 42	206	37 34	279	32 32	316	30 14	347
271	48 51	043	35 56	092	42 01	164	38 17	207	36 38	279	31 54	316	30 01	346
272	49 30	042	36 53	092	42 16	165	37 51	208	35 42	280	31 15	316	29 47	346
273	50 07	042	37 49	093	42 30	167	37 24	209	34 47	280	30 36	316	29 34	346
274	50 45	041	38 45	093	42 42	168	36 56	210	33 51	280	29 56	316	29 20	346
275	51 22	041	39 41	094	42 54	169	36 28	211	32 56	280	29 17	316	29 06	346
276	51 58	040	40 38	094	43 04	170	35 59	212	32 00	281	28 38	316	28 52	345
277	52 35	040	41 34	094	43 13	171	35 28	213	31 05	281	27 59	316	28 38	345
278	53 10	039	42 30	095	43 21	173	34 58	214	30 10	281	27 20	316	28 23	345
279	53 46	038	43 26	095	43 28	174	34 26	214	29 14	281	26 41	316	28 09	345
280	54 20	038	44 22	096	43 33	175	33 54	215	28 19	282	26 02	316	27 54	345
281	54 55	037	45 19	096	43 38	176	33 21	216	27 24	282	25 22	316	27 39	345
282	55 28	036	46 15	097	43 41	177	32 47	217	26 29	282	24 43	316	27 24	345
283	56 01	035	47 11	097	43 43	179	32 13	218	25 33	282	24 04	316	27 09	344
284	56 34	035	48 06	098	43 43	180	31 38	219	24 38	282	23 25	316	26 54	344
	◆ DENEB		Alpheratz		◆ FOMALHAUT		Nunki		ANTARES		◆ Rasalhague		Kochab	
285	57 06	034	20 19	065	14 10	129	43 43	181	31 03	219	68 27	253	26 39	344
286	57 37	033	21 10	065	14 54	130	43 41	182	30 27	220	67 33	254	26 24	344
287	58 07	032	22 02	066	15 37	130	43 38	184	29 50	221	66 39	255	26 08	344
288	58 36	031	22 53	066	16 20	131	43 34	185	29 13	222	65 44	256	25 53	344
289	59 05	030	23 44	066	17 02	131	43 28	186	28 35	222	64 49	257	25 37	344
290	59 33	029	24 36	066	17 44	132	43 22	187	27 57	223	63 54	257	25 21	344
291	60 00	028	25 28	066	18 26	132	43 14	189	27 18	224	62 59	258	25 05	344
292	60 26	027	26 19	067	19 08	133	43 05	190	26 39	225	62 04	259	24 49	344
293	60 51	026	27 11	067	19 49	134	42 55	191	25 59	225	61 09	260	24 33	344
294	61 15	024	28 03	067	20 29	134	42 44	192	25 19	226	60 13	260	24 17	343
295	61 37	023	28 55	067	21 10	135	42 31	193	24 38	226	59 18	261	24 01	343
296	61 59	022	29 47	067	21 50	135	42 18	195	23 57	227	58 22	261	23 45	343
297	62 20	021	30 39	067	22 29	136	42 03	196	23 15	228	57 26	262	23 29	343
298	62 39	019	31 31	067	23 08	137	41 47	197	22 33	228	56 30	262	23 13	343
299	62 57	018	32 23	067	23 47	137	41 30	198	21 51	229	55 34	263	22 56	343
	◆ DENEB		Schedar		Alpheratz		◆ FOMALHAUT		Nunki		◆ Rasalhague		VEGA	
300	63 14	016	27 21	036	33 15	068	24 25	138	41 12	199	54 38	263	64 07	321
301	63 29	015	27 54	036	34 07	068	25 02	139	40 53	200	53 42	264	63 31	320
302	63 43	014	28 27	036	34 59	068	25 39	139	40 33	201	52 46	264	62 54	319
303	63 55	012	29 00	035	35 51	068	26 16	140	40 12	202	51 50	265	62 17	318
304	64 06	010	29 33	035	36 43	068	26 52	141	39 50	203	50 54	265	61 38	317
305	64 16	009	30 05	035	37 36	068	27 27	141	39 27	205	49 58	266	61 00	316
306	64 24	007	30 38	035	38 28	068	28 02	142	39 03	206	49 01	266	60 20	315
307	64 30	006	31 10	035	39 20	068	28 37	143	38 39	207	48 05	267	59 40	314
308	64 35	004	31 42	035	40 13	068	29 11	144	38 13	208	47 09	267	58 59	314
309	64 38	002	32 15	035	41 05	068	29 44	144	37 46	209	46 12	267	58 18	313
310	64 40	001	32 47	035	41 57	068	30 16	145	37 19	210	45 16	268	57 37	312
311	64 40	359	33 19	034	42 50	068	30 48	146	36 51	211	44 20	268	56 55	312
312	64 38	358	33 51	034	43 42	068	31 20	147	36 22	211	43 23	269	56 12	311
313	64 35	356	34 22	034	44 35	068	31 50	148	35 52	212	42 27	269	55 29	310
314	64 30	354	34 54	034	45 27	068	32 20	148	35 21	213	41 31	269	54 46	310
	◆ Alpheratz		Diphda		◆ FOMALHAUT		Nunki		Rasalhague		◆ VEGA		DENEB	
315	46 19	068	23 11	121	32 49	149	34 50	214	40 34	270	54 03	309	64 24	353
316	47 12	068	24 00	121	33 18	150	34 18	215	39 38	270	53 19	309	64 16	351
317	48 04	068	24 48	122	33 46	151	33 45	216	38 42	270	52 35	308	64 06	349
318	48 56	068	25 35	122	34 13	152	33 12	217	37 45	271	51 51	308	63 55	348
319	49 49	068	26 23	123	34 39	153	32 38	218	36 49	271	51 06	308	63 42	346
320	50 41	068	27 10	124	35 04	154	32 03	218	35 52	271	50 21	307	63 28	345
321	51 33	068	27 57	124	35 29	155	31 28	219	34 56	272	49 36	307	63 13	343
322	52 26	068	28 43	125	35 52	156	30 52	220	34 00	272	48 51	307	62 56	342
323	53 18	068	29 29	126	36 15	157	30 15	221	33 03	272	48 06	306	62 38	341
324	54 10	068	30 15	126	36 37	158	29 38	221	32 07	273	47 21	306	62 19	339
325	55 02	067	31 00	127	36 58	159	29 01	222	31 11	273	46 35	306	61 59	338
326	55 54	067	31 45	128	37 18	160	28 22	223	30 14	273	45 49	306	61 37	337
327	56 46	067	32 29	128	37 38	161	27 44	224	29 18	273	45 03	305	61 14	335
328	57 38	067	33 13	129	37 56	162	27 05	224	28 22	274	44 17	305	60 50	334
329	58 29	066	33 57	130	38 13	163	26 25	225	27 26	274	43 31	305	60 25	333
	◆ Mirfak		Hamal		Diphda		◆ FOMALHAUT		ALTAIR		◆ VEGA		DENEB	
330	20 39	043	32 45	074	34 40	131	38 30	164	57 03	255	42 45	305	59 59	332
331	21 17	043	33 39	074	35 23	131	38 45	165	56 09	256	41 59	305	59 32	331
332	21 56	043	34 34	075	36 05	132	38 59	166	55 14	256	41 12	305	59 04	330
333	22 34	043	35 28	075	36 46	133	39 12	167	54 19	257	40 26	304	58 36	329
334	23 13	043	36 22	075	37 27	134	39 25	168	53 24	258	39 39	304	58 06	328
335	23 51	043	37 17	075	38 08	135	39 36	169	52 29	258	38 53	304	57 36	327
336	24 30	043	38 11	075	38 48	135	39 46	170	51 34	259	38 06	304	57 05	326
337	25 09	043	39 06	075	39 27	136	39 55	171	50 39	259	37 19	304	56 33	325
338	25 47	043	40 00	076	40 06	137	40 03	172	49 43	260	36 33	304	56 00	324
339	26 26	043	40 55	076	40 44	138	40 10	174	48 47	260	35 46	304	55 27	324
340	27 05	043	41 50	076	41 21	139	40 15	175	47 52	261	34 59	304	54 54	323
341	27 43	043	42 44	076	41 57	140	40 20	176	46 56	261	34 12	304	54 20	322
342	28 22	043	43 39	076	42 33	141	40 24	177	46 00	262	33 26	304	53 45	322
343	29 00	043	44 34	076	43 08	142	40 26	178	45 04	262	32 39	304	53 09	321
344	29 39	043	45 29	076	43 42	143	40 27	179	44 09	263	31 52	304	52 34	320
	Schedar		Mirfak		◆ ALDEBARAN		Diphda		◆ FOMALHAUT		ALTAIR		◆ DENEB	
345	48 50	021	30 18	043	10 52	076	44 16	144	40 27	180	43 13	263	51 57	320
346	49 10	020	30 56	043	11 47	076	44 48	145	40 26	182	42 17	264	51 21	319
347	49 29	020	31 34	043	12 41	077	45 20	146	40 24	183	41 20	264	50 44	319
348	49 48	019	32 13	043	13 36	077	45 51	148	40 21	184	40 24	265	50 06	318
349	50 06	018	32 51	043	14 31	077	46 20	149	40 17	185	39 28	265	49 28	318
350	50 23	017	33 29	043	15 26	078	46 49	150	40 11	186	38 32	265	48 50	317
351	50 40	017	34 08	043	16 21	078	47 17	151	40 05	187	37 36	266	48 12	317
352	50 56	016	34 46	042	17 17	078	47 43	152	39 57	188	36 40	266	47 33	316
353	51 11	015	35 24	042	18 12	079	48 09	154	39 48	190	35 43	267	46 54	316
354	51 25	014	36 01	042	19 07	079	48 33	155	39 38	191	34 47	267	46 15	316
355	51 39	014	36 39	042	20 02	079	48 56	156	39 27	192	33 51	267	45 35	315
356	51 52	013	37 17	042	20 58	079	49 18	158	39 15	193	32 54	268	44 55	315
357	52 04	012	37 54	042	21 53	080	49 39	159	39 02	194	31 58	268	44 15	315
358	52 15	011	38 32	041	22 49	080	49 59	160	38 48	195	31 02	268	43 35	314
359	52 25	010	39 09	041	23 44	080	50 17	162	38 33	196	30 05	269	42 55	314

LHA ♈	Hc	Zn	Hc	Zn	Hc	Zn	Hc	Zn	Hc	Zn	Hc	Zn	Hc	Zn
	Schedar		CAPELLA		◆ALDEBARAN		ACHERNAR		◆FOMALHAUT		ALTAIR		◆DENEB	
0	51 36	009	20 46	047	24 30	080	11 07	167	39 15	197	29 09	270	41 32	314
1	51 44	008	21 27	047	25 26	080	11 20	167	38 57	198	28 13	270	40 52	314
2	51 52	007	22 09	047	26 21	080	11 32	168	38 39	199	27 16	270	40 11	314
3	51 59	007	22 50	047	27 17	081	11 44	168	38 19	200	26 19	271	39 30	314
4	52 05	006	23 32	047	28 13	081	11 55	169	37 59	201	25 23	271	38 49	314
5	52 10	005	24 13	047	29 10	081	12 06	169	37 38	202	24 26	271	38 08	313
6	52 14	004	24 55	047	30 06	081	12 16	170	37 16	203	23 29	272	37 26	313
7	52 18	003	25 37	047	31 02	082	12 26	170	36 53	204	22 32	272	36 45	313
8	52 20	002	26 18	047	31 58	082	12 35	171	36 29	205	21 36	272	36 03	313
9	52 22	001	27 00	047	32 54	082	12 44	171	36 04	206	20 39	273	35 22	313
10	52 23	000	27 42	047	33 50	082	12 52	172	35 38	207	19 42	273	34 40	313
11	52 23	359	28 23	047	34 47	083	13 00	172	35 12	208	18 46	273	33 58	312
12	52 22	359	29 05	047	35 43	083	13 07	173	34 45	209	17 49	274	33 16	312
13	52 20	358	29 47	047	36 39	083	13 14	174	34 17	210	16 52	274	32 34	312
14	52 17	357	30 28	047	37 35	083	13 20	174	33 48	211	15 56	274	31 52	312
	CAPELLA		◆ALDEBARAN		RIGEL		ACHERNAR		◆FOMALHAUT		Enif		◆DENEB	
15	31 10	047	38 32	084	21 30	107	13 25	175	33 18	212	42 04	266	31 10	312
16	31 51	047	39 28	084	22 25	108	13 30	175	32 48	213	41 08	267	30 28	312
17	32 33	047	40 25	084	23 19	108	13 35	176	32 17	213	40 11	267	29 46	312
18	33 14	047	41 21	084	24 12	109	13 38	176	31 46	214	39 14	267	29 04	312
19	33 55	047	42 18	085	25 06	109	13 42	177	31 13	215	38 18	268	28 22	312
20	34 37	047	43 14	085	26 00	110	13 45	177	30 40	216	37 21	268	27 39	312
21	35 18	046	44 11	085	26 53	110	13 47	178	30 07	217	36 24	268	26 57	312
22	35 59	046	45 07	085	27 46	111	13 49	179	29 33	217	35 28	269	26 15	312
23	36 40	046	46 04	086	28 39	111	13 50	179	28 58	218	34 31	269	25 33	312
24	37 21	046	47 00	086	29 32	112	13 50	180	28 23	219	33 34	269	24 51	312
25	38 02	046	47 57	086	30 25	112	13 50	180	27 47	220	32 37	270	24 09	312
26	38 42	046	48 53	086	31 17	113	13 50	181	27 10	220	31 41	270	23 26	312
27	39 23	045	49 50	087	32 09	113	13 49	181	26 33	221	30 44	270	22 44	312
28	40 03	045	50 47	087	33 01	114	13 47	182	25 56	222	29 47	271	22 02	312
29	40 43	045	51 43	087	33 53	114	13 45	182	25 18	222	28 50	271	21 20	312
	Mirfak		◆CAPELLA		ALDEBARAN		RIGEL		◆ACHERNAR		FOMALHAUT		◆Alpheratz	
30	54 42	024	41 23	045	52 40	087	34 45	115	13 42	183	24 40	223	62 49	297
31	55 05	023	42 03	044	53 37	088	35 36	116	13 39	184	24 01	224	61 59	297
32	55 27	022	42 43	044	54 33	088	36 27	116	13 35	184	23 21	224	61 08	296
33	55 47	021	43 22	044	55 30	088	37 18	117	13 31	185	22 42	225	60 17	296
34	56 07	020	44 01	043	56 27	089	38 08	118	13 26	185	22 01	225	59 26	296
35	56 26	019	44 40	043	57 24	089	38 58	118	13 20	186	21 21	226	58 35	295
36	56 45	018	45 19	043	58 20	089	39 48	119	13 14	186	20 40	227	57 43	295
37	57 02	017	45 57	042	59 17	089	40 38	120	13 08	187	19 58	227	56 52	295
38	57 18	016	46 35	042	60 14	090	41 27	120	13 01	187	19 17	228	56 00	294
39	57 33	015	47 13	042	61 10	090	42 16	121	12 53	188	18 34	228	55 08	294
40	57 47	014	47 51	041	62 07	090	43 04	122	12 45	189	17 52	229	54 17	294
41	58 00	013	48 28	041	63 04	091	43 52	123	12 36	189	17 09	229	53 25	294
42	58 12	011	49 04	040	64 01	091	44 40	124	12 27	190	16 26	230	52 33	293
43	58 22	010	49 41	040	64 57	091	45 27	124	12 18	190	15 42	230	51 41	293
44	58 32	009	50 17	039	65 54	092	46 13	125	12 07	191	14 59	231	50 48	293
	CAPELLA		◆POLLUX		PROCYON		SIRIUS		◆Acamar		Diphda		◆Alpheratz	
45	50 52	039	24 38	067	20 33	092	24 00	119	30 45	180	40 17	224	49 56	293
46	51 27	038	25 31	067	21 30	092	24 49	120	30 45	181	39 37	225	49 04	293
47	52 02	037	26 23	067	22 27	092	25 38	120	30 43	182	38 57	226	48 12	293
48	52 36	037	27 16	068	23 24	093	26 27	121	30 41	183	38 16	227	47 19	293
49	53 10	036	28 08	068	24 20	093	27 16	121	30 37	184	37 34	228	46 27	293
50	53 43	035	29 01	068	25 17	093	28 04	122	30 33	185	36 52	228	45 35	293
51	54 15	034	29 53	068	26 14	094	28 52	123	30 28	186	36 09	229	44 42	293
52	54 47	034	30 46	068	27 10	094	29 40	123	30 22	186	35 26	230	43 50	293
53	55 18	033	31 38	068	28 07	094	30 27	124	30 15	187	34 43	231	42 58	293
54	55 49	032	32 31	068	29 03	095	31 14	124	30 08	188	33 59	231	42 05	293
55	56 18	031	33 24	068	30 00	095	32 01	125	29 59	189	33 14	232	41 13	293
56	56 47	030	34 17	069	30 56	095	32 47	126	29 50	190	32 29	233	40 21	293
57	57 16	029	35 09	069	31 53	096	33 33	126	29 39	191	31 44	233	39 28	293
58	57 43	028	36 02	069	32 49	096	34 18	127	29 28	192	30 58	234	38 36	293
59	58 10	027	36 55	069	33 46	097	35 03	128	29 17	192	30 12	235	37 43	293
	CAPELLA		◆POLLUX		PROCYON		SIRIUS		◆CANOPUS		Diphda		◆Hamal	
60	58 35	026	37 48	069	34 42	097	35 48	129	11 47	159	29 25	235	63 34	285
61	59 00	025	38 41	069	35 38	097	36 32	129	12 07	159	28 38	236	62 39	285
62	59 24	024	39 34	069	36 34	098	37 15	130	12 27	160	27 51	237	61 44	285
63	59 46	023	40 27	069	37 31	098	37 59	131	12 46	160	27 03	237	60 49	284
64	60 08	022	41 20	069	38 27	099	38 41	132	13 05	161	26 16	238	59 54	284
65	60 28	021	42 13	069	39 23	099	39 23	133	13 24	161	25 27	238	58 59	284
66	60 48	019	43 06	069	40 19	100	40 05	133	13 42	162	24 39	239	58 04	284
67	61 06	018	43 59	069	41 15	100	40 46	134	13 59	162	23 50	239	57 09	284
68	61 23	017	44 52	069	42 10	101	41 26	135	14 16	163	23 01	240	56 14	284
69	61 39	015	45 45	069	43 06	101	42 05	136	14 33	163	22 12	241	55 19	284
70	61 53	014	46 38	069	44 02	102	42 44	137	14 49	164	21 22	241	54 24	284
71	62 06	013	47 31	069	44 57	102	43 23	138	15 04	165	20 33	242	53 29	284
72	62 18	011	48 24	069	45 53	103	44 00	139	15 19	165	19 43	242	52 34	284
73	62 28	010	49 16	069	46 48	103	44 37	140	15 33	166	18 52	243	51 39	284
74	62 37	008	50 09	069	47 43	104	45 13	141	15 47	166	18 02	243	50 44	284
	CAPELLA		◆POLLUX		PROCYON		SIRIUS		◆RIGEL		Menkar		◆Hamal	
75	62 44	007	51 02	069	48 38	104	45 48	142	62 33	172	57 50	246	49 49	284
76	62 50	005	51 55	069	49 33	105	46 22	143	62 40	174	56 58	247	48 54	284
77	62 55	004	52 48	068	50 28	105	46 56	145	62 45	176	56 05	248	47 59	284
78	62 58	002	53 41	068	51 22	106	47 28	146	62 48	178	55 13	249	47 04	284
79	62 59	001	54 33	068	52 17	107	48 00	147	62 49	180	54 20	250	46 10	285
80	62 59	359	55 26	068	53 11	107	48 30	148	62 47	183	53 26	250	45 15	285
81	62 57	358	56 18	068	54 05	108	49 00	149	62 44	185	52 33	251	44 20	285
82	62 54	356	57 11	068	54 59	109	49 28	151	62 38	187	51 39	252	43 25	285
83	62 50	355	58 03	067	55 52	110	49 55	152	62 30	189	50 45	253	42 30	285
84	62 44	353	58 56	067	56 46	111	50 21	153	62 20	191	49 51	253	41 35	285
85	62 36	352	59 48	067	57 39	111	50 46	155	62 08	193	48 56	254	40 40	285
86	62 27	350	60 40	066	58 31	112	51 10	156	61 54	195	48 02	254	39 46	285
87	62 17	349	61 32	066	59 24	113	51 32	157	61 39	197	47 07	255	38 51	285
88	62 05	347	62 24	066	60 16	114	51 54	159	61 21	199	46 12	256	37 56	285
89	61 52	346	63 15	065	61 07	115	52 13	160	61 01	201	45 17	256	37 02	286

LHA ♈	Hc	Zn	Hc	Zn	Hc	Zn	Hc	Zn	Hc	Zn	Hc	Zn	Hc	Zn
	Dubhe		◆REGULUS		Alphard		SIRIUS		◆RIGEL		ALDEBARAN		◆CAPELLA	
90	23 12	030	29 49	087	31 40	114	52 32	162	60 40	203	70 03	266	61 37	344
91	23 40	030	30 46	087	32 32	114	52 49	163	60 17	205	69 06	267	61 21	343
92	24 09	030	31 43	088	33 23	115	53 04	165	59 52	207	68 10	267	61 04	342
93	24 37	030	32 39	088	34 15	115	53 19	166	59 26	208	67 13	268	60 46	341
94	25 05	030	33 36	088	35 06	116	53 31	168	58 58	210	66 16	268	60 26	339
95	25 34	030	34 33	088	35 57	117	53 42	170	58 29	212	65 20	268	60 06	338
96	26 02	030	35 29	089	36 47	117	53 52	171	57 58	213	64 23	269	59 44	337
97	26 30	030	36 26	089	37 38	118	54 00	173	57 26	215	63 26	269	59 21	336
98	26 58	030	37 23	089	38 28	119	54 06	174	56 53	217	62 29	269	58 58	335
99	27 26	030	38 20	090	39 17	119	54 11	176	56 19	218	61 33	270	58 33	334
100	27 54	029	39 16	090	40 07	120	54 14	178	55 43	219	60 36	270	58 07	333
101	28 22	029	40 13	090	40 56	121	54 16	179	55 07	221	59 39	270	57 40	332
102	28 50	029	41 10	091	41 44	121	54 15	181	54 29	222	58 42	271	57 13	331
103	29 17	029	42 06	091	42 32	122	54 14	183	53 50	223	57 46	271	56 45	330
104	29 45	029	43 03	091	43 20	123	54 10	184	53 11	225	56 49	271	56 15	329
	Dubhe		◆REGULUS		Alphard		SIRIUS		◆RIGEL		ALDEBARAN		◆CAPELLA	
105	30 12	029	44 00	092	44 07	124	54 06	186	52 31	226	55 52	272	55 46	328
106	30 39	029	44 57	092	44 54	125	53 59	187	51 50	227	54 56	272	55 15	327
107	31 06	028	45 53	092	45 41	126	53 51	189	51 08	228	53 59	272	54 44	326
108	31 33	028	46 50	093	46 27	127	53 41	191	50 25	229	53 02	272	54 12	325
109	32 00	028	47 47	093	47 12	127	53 30	192	49 42	230	52 06	273	53 39	325
110	32 26	028	48 43	094	47 57	128	53 17	194	48 58	231	51 09	273	53 06	324
111	32 53	028	49 40	094	48 41	129	53 03	195	48 13	232	50 12	273	52 33	323
112	33 19	027	50 36	094	49 24	130	52 47	197	47 28	233	49 16	274	51 59	323
113	33 45	027	51 33	095	50 07	131	52 30	198	46 42	234	48 19	274	51 24	322
114	34 11	027	52 30	095	50 49	133	52 12	200	45 56	235	47 22	274	50 49	321
115	34 37	027	53 26	096	51 31	134	51 52	201	45 09	236	46 26	274	50 13	321
116	35 02	026	54 22	096	52 11	135	51 30	203	44 22	237	45 29	275	49 37	320
117	35 27	026	55 19	097	52 51	136	51 08	204	43 34	238	44 33	275	49 01	320
118	35 52	026	56 15	097	53 30	137	50 44	206	42 46	238	43 36	275	48 24	319
119	36 17	026	57 11	098	54 08	139	50 19	207	41 58	239	42 40	275	47 47	319
	Dubhe		◆Denebola		Alphard		◆SIRIUS		RIGEL		ALDEBARAN		◆CAPELLA	
120	36 41	025	35 01	085	54 45	140	49 53	208	41 09	240	41 43	276	47 09	318
121	37 05	025	35 58	086	55 21	141	49 25	210	40 19	241	40 47	276	46 32	318
122	37 29	025	36 55	086	55 56	143	48 57	211	39 30	241	39 50	276	45 53	318
123	37 52	024	37 51	086	56 30	144	48 27	212	38 40	242	38 54	276	45 15	317
124	38 15	024	38 48	086	57 02	146	47 57	213	37 50	243	37 58	277	44 36	317
125	38 38	024	39 44	087	57 34	147	47 25	214	36 59	243	37 01	277	43 57	316
126	39 01	023	40 41	087	58 04	149	46 52	216	36 08	244	36 05	277	43 18	316
127	39 23	023	41 38	087	58 32	150	46 19	217	35 17	245	35 09	277	42 39	316
128	39 45	022	42 34	088	59 00	152	45 45	218	34 26	245	34 12	277	41 59	316
129	40 06	022	43 31	088	59 25	154	45 09	219	33 34	246	33 16	278	41 19	315
130	40 27	022	44 28	088	59 50	156	44 33	220	32 42	246	32 20	278	40 39	315
131	40 48	021	45 24	088	60 12	158	43 57	221	31 50	247	31 24	278	39 59	315
132	41 08	021	46 21	089	60 33	159	43 19	222	30 58	248	30 28	278	39 19	315
133	41 28	020	47 18	089	60 52	161	42 41	223	30 05	248	29 31	279	38 38	314
134	41 48	020	48 15	089	61 09	163	42 02	224	29 12	249	28 35	279	37 58	314
	Dubhe		◆ARCTURUS		SPICA		◆Alphard		SIRIUS		BETELGEUSE		◆CAPELLA	
135	42 06	019	16 00	075	17 51	109	61 25	165	41 22	225	43 53	262	37 17	314
136	42 25	019	16 55	075	18 44	110	61 38	167	40 42	226	42 57	262	36 36	314
137	42 43	018	17 50	075	19 37	110	61 50	169	40 01	227	42 01	263	35 55	314
138	43 01	018	18 45	076	20 31	110	61 59	171	39 19	227	41 05	263	35 14	314
139	43 18	017	19 40	076	21 24	111	62 07	173	38 37	228	40 08	264	34 33	313
140	43 35	017	20 35	076	22 17	111	62 12	176	37 54	229	39 12	264	33 51	313
141	43 51	016	21 30	076	23 09	112	62 15	178	37 11	230	38 15	264	33 10	313
142	44 06	016	22 25	077	24 02	112	62 17	180	36 28	231	37 19	265	32 29	313
143	44 21	015	23 20	077	24 54	113	62 16	182	35 43	231	36 22	265	31 47	313
144	44 36	015	24 16	077	25 47	113	62 13	184	34 59	232	35 26	266	31 06	313
145	44 50	014	25 11	077	26 39	114	62 08	186	34 14	233	34 29	266	30 24	313
146	45 03	013	26 06	077	27 30	114	62 00	188	33 28	234	33 33	266	29 42	313
147	45 16	013	27 02	078	28 22	115	61 51	190	32 42	234	32 36	267	29 01	313
148	45 28	012	27 57	078	29 13	115	61 40	192	31 56	235	31 39	267	28 19	313
149	45 40	012	28 53	078	30 05	116	61 27	194	31 09	236	30 43	267	27 37	313
	Dubhe		◆ARCTURUS		SPICA		◆Alphard		SIRIUS		BETELGEUSE		◆CAPELLA	
150	45 51	011	29 48	078	30 55	117	61 12	196	30 22	236	29 46	268	26 56	313
151	46 02	010	30 44	079	31 46	117	60 55	198	29 35	237	28 49	268	26 14	313
152	46 11	010	31 39	079	32 36	118	60 36	200	28 47	238	27 53	268	25 32	313
153	46 21	009	32 35	079	33 27	118	60 16	202	27 59	238	26 56	269	24 51	313
154	46 29	008	33 31	079	34 16	119	59 53	204	27 11	239	25 59	269	24 09	313
155	46 37	008	34 26	079	35 06	120	59 29	206	26 22	239	25 03	269	23 28	313
156	46 44	007	35 22	080	35 55	120	59 04	208	25 33	240	24 06	270	22 46	313
157	46 51	006	36 18	080	36 44	121	58 37	209	24 44	240	23 09	270	22 04	313
158	46 57	006	37 14	080	37 32	122	58 09	211	23 55	241	22 12	270	21 23	313
159	47 02	005	38 10	080	38 20	122	57 39	213	23 05	241	21 16	271	20 42	313
160	47 07	004	39 06	080	39 08	123	57 08	214	22 15	242	20 19	271	20 00	313
161	47 11	004	40 02	081	39 55	124	56 35	216	21 25	242	19 22	271	19 19	313
162	47 14	003	40 58	081	40 42	125	56 02	217	20 35	243	18 25	272	18 38	313
163	47 16	002	41 54	081	41 29	125	55 27	218	19 44	243	17 29	272	17 56	313
164	47 18	002	42 50	081	42 15	126	54 51	220	18 53	244	16 32	272	17 15	314
	◆Dubhe		Alkaid		ARCTURUS		◆SPICA		Suhail		◆PROCYON		POLLUX	
165	47 19	001	44 50	038	43 46	081	43 00	127	22 29	202	39 25	261	44 58	291
166	47 20	000	45 25	038	44 42	082	43 45	128	22 08	202	38 29	261	44 05	291
167	47 20	359	46 00	037	45 38	082	44 30	129	21 46	203	37 33	262	43 12	291
168	47 19	359	46 34	037	46 34	082	45 14	130	21 23	204	36 37	262	42 19	291
169	47 17	358	47 08	036	47 30	082	45 57	131	21 00	204	35 41	263	41 26	291
170	47 15	357	47 41	036	48 27	082	46 40	132	20 37	205	34 44	263	40 33	291
171	47 12	357	48 14	035	49 23	083	47 22	133	20 13	206	33 48	263	39 40	291
172	47 08	356	48 46	035	50 19	083	48 03	134	19 48	206	32 52	264	38 47	291
173	47 04	355	49 18	034	51 15	083	48 44	135	19 23	207	31 55	264	37 54	291
174	46 59	355	49 50	033	52 12	083	49 23	136	18 57	207	30 59	265	37 01	291
175	46 53	354	50 21	033	53 08	083	50 03	137	18 31	208	30 02	265	36 08	291
176	46 47	353	50 51	032	54 04	083	50 41	138	18 04	209	29 06	265	35 16	291
177	46 39	353	51 21	032	55 01	084	51 18	139	17 36	209	28 09	266	34 23	291
178	46 32	352	51 51	031	55 57	084	51 55	141	17 08	210	27 13	266	33 30	292
179	46 23	351	52 20	030	56 54	084	52 30	142	16 40	210	26 16	266	32 37	292

LAT 19°N

LHA ♈	Hc	Zn	Hc	Zn	Hc	Zn	Hc	Zn	Hc	Zn	Hc	Zn	Hc	Zn
	◆Alkaid		ANTARES		◆SPICA		Gienah		◆REGULUS		POLLUX		Dubhe	
180	52 48	029	10 14	123	53 05	143	53 09	173	62 24	259	31 44	292	46 14	351
181	53 15	029	11 02	123	53 38	145	53 15	175	61 28	260	30 52	292	46 05	350
182	53 42	028	11 49	124	54 10	146	53 19	177	60 32	260	29 59	292	45 55	349
183	54 08	027	12 36	124	54 41	147	53 21	178	59 36	261	29 07	292	45 44	349
184	54 34	026	13 23	125	55 11	149	53 22	180	58 40	262	28 14	292	45 32	348
185	54 58	025	14 10	125	55 40	150	53 22	181	57 44	262	27 22	292	45 20	347
186	55 22	024	14 56	125	56 07	152	53 20	183	56 48	263	26 29	293	45 07	347
187	55 45	023	15 42	126	56 33	154	53 16	185	55 52	263	25 37	293	44 54	346
188	56 07	022	16 28	126	56 58	155	53 11	186	54 55	264	24 44	293	44 40	346
189	56 28	021	17 14	127	57 21	157	53 04	188	53 59	264	23 52	293	44 26	345
190	56 49	020	17 59	127	57 42	159	52 56	189	53 03	265	23 00	293	44 11	344
191	57 08	019	18 44	128	58 02	160	52 46	191	52 06	265	22 08	293	43 56	344
192	57 26	018	19 28	128	58 21	162	52 34	192	51 09	265	21 16	293	43 40	343
193	57 44	017	20 13	129	58 37	164	52 21	194	50 13	266	20 24	294	43 23	343
194	58 00	016	20 57	130	58 52	166	52 07	195	49 16	266	19 32	294	43 06	342
	Kochab		◆VEGA		Rasalhague		ANTARES		◆SPICA		◆REGULUS		Dubhe	
195	32 52	009	16 03	054	23 45	084	21 40	130	59 05	168	48 20	267	42 49	342
196	33 00	008	16 49	054	24 42	085	22 23	131	59 17	169	47 23	267	42 31	341
197	33 08	008	17 34	054	25 38	085	23 06	131	59 26	171	46 26	267	42 12	341
198	33 16	008	18 20	054	26 35	085	23 49	132	59 34	173	45 30	268	41 54	340
199	33 24	008	19 07	054	27 31	085	24 31	132	59 40	175	44 33	268	41 34	340
200	33 31	007	19 53	055	28 28	086	25 12	133	59 43	177	43 36	268	41 15	339
201	33 38	007	20 39	055	29 25	086	25 54	134	59 45	179	42 40	269	40 54	339
202	33 45	007	21 25	055	30 21	086	26 34	134	59 45	181	41 43	269	40 34	339
203	33 51	006	22 12	055	31 18	087	27 15	135	59 43	183	40 46	269	40 13	338
204	33 58	006	22 58	055	32 15	087	27 55	136	59 40	185	39 49	270	39 52	338
205	34 03	006	23 45	055	33 11	087	28 34	136	59 34	187	38 53	270	39 30	337
206	34 09	005	24 31	055	34 08	087	29 13	137	59 26	189	37 56	270	39 08	337
207	34 14	005	25 18	055	35 05	088	29 51	138	59 17	191	36 59	271	38 45	337
208	34 19	005	26 04	055	36 01	088	30 29	139	59 05	192	36 03	271	38 23	336
209	34 24	005	26 51	055	36 58	088	31 06	139	58 52	194	35 06	271	38 00	336
	Kochab		◆VEGA		Rasalhague		◆ANTARES		SPICA		◆REGULUS		Dubhe	
210	34 28	004	27 38	055	37 55	089	31 43	140	58 37	196	34 09	272	37 36	335
211	34 32	004	28 24	055	38 51	089	32 19	141	58 21	198	33 12	272	37 13	335
212	34 36	004	29 11	055	39 48	089	32 55	142	58 02	200	32 16	272	36 49	335
213	34 39	003	29 58	055	40 45	090	33 29	142	57 42	201	31 19	273	36 24	335
214	34 42	003	30 45	056	41 42	090	34 04	143	57 21	203	30 22	273	36 00	334
215	34 45	003	31 31	056	42 38	090	34 37	144	56 58	205	29 26	273	35 35	334
216	34 47	002	32 18	056	43 35	091	35 10	145	56 33	206	28 29	274	35 10	334
217	34 49	002	33 05	055	44 32	091	35 42	146	56 07	208	27 32	274	34 45	333
218	34 51	002	33 52	055	45 28	091	36 14	147	55 40	210	26 36	274	34 19	333
219	34 52	001	34 38	055	46 25	092	36 44	148	55 11	211	25 39	274	33 53	333
220	34 53	001	35 25	055	47 22	092	37 14	149	54 41	213	24 43	275	33 27	333
221	34 54	001	36 12	055	48 19	092	37 44	150	54 10	214	23 46	275	33 01	332
222	34 54	000	36 58	055	49 15	093	38 12	151	53 38	215	22 50	275	32 35	332
223	34 54	000	37 45	055	50 12	093	38 39	152	53 04	217	21 53	276	32 08	332
224	34 54	000	38 31	055	51 09	094	39 06	153	52 30	218	20 57	276	31 42	332
	VEGA		◆ALTAIR		Nunki		ANTARES		◆SPICA		Denebola		◆Alkaid	
225	39 18	055	18 59	087	16 58	126	39 32	154	51 54	219	44 23	272	56 30	339
226	40 04	055	19 56	087	17 44	127	39 57	155	51 18	221	43 26	272	56 08	338
227	40 51	055	20 53	087	18 29	128	40 20	156	50 40	222	42 29	272	55 46	337
228	41 37	055	21 49	088	19 14	128	40 43	157	50 02	223	41 33	273	55 24	336
229	42 23	054	22 46	088	19 58	129	41 05	158	49 23	224	40 36	273	55 00	335
230	43 09	054	23 43	088	20 43	129	41 26	159	48 43	225	39 39	273	54 35	334
231	43 55	054	24 40	089	21 26	130	41 46	160	48 03	226	38 43	274	54 10	333
232	44 41	054	25 36	089	22 10	130	42 05	161	47 21	227	37 46	274	53 44	332
233	45 26	054	26 33	089	22 53	131	42 23	162	46 39	228	36 50	274	53 17	331
234	46 12	053	27 30	090	23 36	131	42 40	163	45 57	229	35 53	274	52 50	331
235	46 57	053	28 26	090	24 18	132	42 55	165	45 13	230	34 56	275	52 21	330
236	47 43	053	29 23	090	25 00	133	43 10	166	44 29	231	34 00	275	51 53	329
237	48 28	052	30 20	091	25 42	133	43 23	167	43 45	232	33 03	275	51 23	328
238	49 12	052	31 17	091	26 23	134	43 36	168	43 00	233	32 07	276	50 53	328
239	49 57	052	32 13	091	27 03	135	43 47	169	42 14	234	31 10	276	50 23	327
	◆VEGA		ALTAIR		Nunki		◆ANTARES		SPICA		◆ARCTURUS		Alkaid	
240	50 41	051	33 10	092	27 44	135	43 57	171	41 28	235	65 32	275	49 52	327
241	51 26	051	34 07	092	28 23	136	44 05	172	40 42	235	64 35	275	49 20	326
242	52 09	050	35 03	092	29 02	137	44 13	173	39 55	236	63 39	275	48 48	325
243	52 53	050	36 00	093	29 41	137	44 19	174	39 08	237	62 42	275	48 16	325
244	53 36	049	36 57	093	30 19	138	44 24	176	38 20	238	61 46	275	47 43	324
245	54 19	049	37 53	093	30 57	139	44 28	177	37 32	238	60 49	275	47 10	324
246	55 02	048	38 50	094	31 34	140	44 31	178	36 43	239	59 53	276	46 36	323
247	55 44	048	39 47	094	32 11	140	44 32	179	35 55	240	58 56	276	46 02	323
248	56 26	047	40 43	095	32 46	141	44 32	181	35 05	240	58 00	276	45 27	322
249	57 07	047	41 40	095	33 22	142	44 31	182	34 16	241	57 03	276	44 53	322
250	57 48	046	42 36	095	33 56	143	44 29	183	33 26	242	56 07	276	44 18	322
251	58 29	045	43 33	096	34 30	144	44 25	184	32 36	242	55 11	276	43 42	321
252	59 09	044	44 29	096	35 04	144	44 20	186	31 46	243	54 14	277	43 06	321
253	59 48	043	45 25	097	35 36	145	44 14	187	30 55	243	53 18	277	42 30	320
254	60 27	043	46 22	097	36 08	146	44 07	188	30 04	244	52 21	277	41 54	320
	◆DENEB		ALTAIR		◆Nunki		ANTARES		SPICA		◆ARCTURUS		Alkaid	
255	37 27	047	47 18	098	36 39	147	43 58	189	29 13	245	51 25	277	41 18	320
256	38 09	047	48 14	098	37 10	148	43 48	190	28 22	245	50 29	277	40 41	319
257	38 50	046	49 10	099	37 39	149	43 38	192	27 30	246	49 33	277	40 04	319
258	39 31	046	50 07	099	38 08	150	43 25	193	26 38	246	48 36	278	39 27	319
259	40 12	046	51 02	100	38 36	151	43 12	194	25 46	247	47 40	278	38 50	319
260	40 53	046	51 58	100	39 03	152	42 58	195	24 54	247	46 44	278	38 12	318
261	41 33	046	52 54	101	39 30	153	42 42	196	24 02	248	45 48	278	37 34	318
262	42 14	045	53 50	101	39 55	154	42 26	198	23 09	248	44 52	278	36 56	318
263	42 54	045	54 46	102	40 19	155	42 08	199	22 16	249	43 56	279	36 18	318
264	43 34	045	55 41	102	40 43	156	41 49	200	21 23	249	42 59	279	35 40	318
265	44 14	044	56 36	103	41 05	157	41 30	201	20 30	250	42 03	279	35 02	317
266	44 53	044	57 32	104	41 27	158	41 09	202	19 37	250	41 07	279	34 24	317
267	45 33	044	58 27	104	41 48	159	40 47	203	18 44	250	40 11	279	33 45	317
268	46 12	043	59 21	105	42 07	160	40 24	204	17 50	251	39 15	280	33 06	317
269	46 51	043	60 16	106	42 25	162	40 01	205	16 56	251	38 19	280	32 28	317

LHA ♈	Hc	Zn	Hc	Zn	Hc	Zn	Hc	Zn	Hc	Zn	Hc	Zn	Hc	Zn
	◆DENEB		Enif		◆Nunki		ANTARES		◆ARCTURUS		Alkaid		Kochab	
270	47 29	042	35 01	091	42 43	163	39 36	206	37 24	280	31 49	317	29 15	347
271	48 07	042	35 58	091	42 59	164	39 10	207	36 28	280	31 10	317	29 02	346
272	48 45	042	36 55	092	43 14	165	38 44	208	35 32	280	30 31	317	28 49	346
273	49 22	041	37 51	092	43 28	166	38 16	209	34 36	281	29 52	317	28 35	346
274	49 59	041	38 48	092	43 41	168	37 48	210	33 40	281	29 13	316	28 22	346
275	50 36	040	39 45	093	43 53	169	37 19	211	32 45	281	28 34	316	28 08	346
276	51 12	039	40 41	093	44 03	170	36 49	212	31 49	281	27 55	316	27 54	346
277	51 48	039	41 38	094	44 13	171	36 19	213	30 53	281	27 16	316	27 40	345
278	52 24	038	42 35	094	44 21	172	35 48	214	29 58	282	26 37	316	27 25	345
279	52 58	038	43 31	094	44 28	174	35 15	215	29 02	282	25 57	316	27 11	345
280	53 33	037	44 28	095	44 33	175	34 43	216	28 07	282	25 18	316	26 56	345
281	54 07	036	45 24	095	44 38	176	34 09	217	27 11	282	24 39	316	26 41	345
282	54 40	035	46 21	096	44 41	177	33 35	217	26 16	282	24 00	316	26 26	345
283	55 12	035	47 17	096	44 43	179	33 00	218	25 20	283	23 21	316	26 11	345
284	55 44	034	48 14	096	44 43	180	32 25	219	24 25	283	22 42	316	25 56	344
	◆DENEB		Alpheratz		◆FOMALHAUT		Nunki		ANTARES		◆Rasalhague		VEGA	
285	56 15	033	19 54	065	14 48	129	44 43	181	31 49	220	68 43	255	69 36	347
286	56 46	032	20 45	065	15 32	130	44 41	182	31 12	221	67 48	256	69 23	345
287	57 16	031	21 37	065	16 16	130	44 38	184	30 35	221	66 53	257	69 07	343
288	57 45	030	22 28	065	16 59	131	44 34	185	29 57	222	65 58	258	68 50	341
289	58 13	029	23 20	066	17 42	131	44 28	186	29 19	223	65 02	259	68 31	339
290	58 40	028	24 12	066	18 24	132	44 21	187	28 40	223	64 06	259	68 10	337
291	59 07	027	25 03	066	19 07	132	44 13	189	28 01	224	63 11	260	67 47	335
292	59 32	026	25 55	066	19 49	133	44 04	190	27 21	225	62 15	261	67 22	334
293	59 56	025	26 47	066	20 30	133	43 54	191	26 41	226	61 19	261	66 57	332
294	60 20	024	27 39	066	21 11	134	43 42	192	26 00	226	60 22	262	66 29	330
295	60 42	023	28 31	066	21 52	134	43 29	194	25 19	227	59 26	262	66 01	329
296	61 03	021	29 23	067	22 32	135	43 16	195	24 38	227	58 30	263	65 31	327
297	61 23	020	30 15	067	23 12	136	43 01	196	23 56	228	57 34	263	65 00	326
298	61 42	019	31 07	067	23 51	136	42 44	197	23 13	229	56 37	264	64 27	325
299	62 00	017	31 59	067	24 30	137	42 27	198	22 30	229	55 41	264	63 54	323
	◆DENEB		Schedar		Alpheratz		◆FOMALHAUT		Nunki		◆Rasalhague		VEGA	
300	62 16	016	26 33	035	32 52	067	25 09	138	42 09	199	54 44	265	63 20	322
301	62 31	015	27 05	035	33 44	067	25 47	138	41 49	201	53 48	265	62 45	321
302	62 44	013	27 38	035	34 36	067	26 25	139	41 29	202	52 51	266	62 09	320
303	62 57	012	28 11	035	35 28	067	27 02	140	41 08	203	51 55	266	61 32	319
304	63 07	010	28 44	035	36 21	067	27 38	140	40 45	204	50 58	267	60 54	318
305	63 16	009	29 16	035	37 13	067	28 14	141	40 22	205	50 01	267	60 16	317
306	63 24	007	29 49	035	38 05	067	28 50	142	39 57	206	49 05	267	59 37	316
307	63 30	005	30 21	035	38 58	067	29 25	142	39 32	207	48 08	268	58 58	315
308	63 35	004	30 53	035	39 50	067	29 59	143	39 06	208	47 11	268	58 18	315
309	63 38	002	31 25	034	40 42	067	30 32	144	38 39	209	46 15	268	57 37	314
310	63 40	001	31 57	034	41 35	067	31 06	145	38 11	210	45 18	269	56 56	313
311	63 40	359	32 29	034	42 27	067	31 38	146	37 42	211	44 21	269	56 14	313
312	63 38	358	33 01	034	43 20	067	32 10	146	37 13	212	43 25	269	55 32	312
313	63 35	356	33 33	034	44 12	067	32 41	147	36 42	213	42 28	270	54 50	311
314	63 30	354	34 04	034	45 04	067	33 11	148	36 11	214	41 31	270	54 07	311
	◆Alpheratz		Diphda		◆FOMALHAUT		Nunki		◆Rasalhague		VEGA		DENEB	
315	45 57	067	23 42	120	33 41	149	35 40	215	40 34	270	53 24	310	63 24	353
316	46 49	067	24 31	121	34 10	150	35 07	215	39 38	271	52 41	310	63 16	351
317	47 41	067	25 19	122	34 38	151	34 34	216	38 41	271	51 57	309	63 07	350
318	48 34	067	26 07	122	35 05	152	34 00	217	37 44	271	51 13	309	62 56	348
319	49 26	067	26 55	123	35 32	152	33 25	218	36 47	272	50 29	309	62 44	347
320	50 18	067	27 43	123	35 58	153	32 50	219	35 51	272	49 45	308	62 30	345
321	51 10	067	28 30	124	36 23	154	32 14	220	34 54	272	49 00	308	62 16	344
322	52 02	067	29 17	124	36 47	155	31 38	220	33 57	273	48 15	308	61 59	343
323	52 54	066	30 04	125	37 10	156	31 01	221	33 01	273	47 30	307	61 42	341
324	53 46	066	30 50	126	37 33	157	30 23	222	32 04	273	46 45	307	61 23	340
325	54 38	066	31 36	126	37 54	158	29 45	223	31 07	273	45 59	307	61 03	339
326	55 30	066	32 21	127	38 15	159	29 06	223	30 11	274	45 14	306	60 42	337
327	56 22	066	33 06	128	38 34	160	28 27	224	29 14	274	44 28	306	60 19	336
328	57 13	065	33 51	128	38 53	161	27 47	225	28 18	274	43 42	306	59 56	335
329	58 05	065	34 35	129	39 10	162	27 07	225	27 21	275	42 56	306	59 31	334
	◆Mirfak		Hamal		Diphda		◆FOMALHAUT		ALTAIR		◆VEGA		DENEB	
330	19 55	043	32 28	074	35 19	130	39 27	163	57 18	257	42 10	306	59 06	333
331	20 33	043	33 23	074	36 02	131	39 43	165	56 23	257	41 24	305	58 39	332
332	21 12	043	34 17	074	36 45	132	39 57	166	55 28	258	40 38	305	58 12	331
333	21 50	043	35 12	074	37 27	132	40 11	167	54 32	258	39 51	305	57 44	330
334	22 29	043	36 06	074	38 09	133	40 23	168	53 36	259	39 05	305	57 15	329
335	23 08	043	37 01	074	38 50	134	40 35	169	52 41	260	38 19	305	56 45	328
336	23 46	043	37 56	075	39 30	135	40 45	170	51 45	260	37 32	305	56 15	327
337	24 25	043	38 50	075	40 10	136	40 54	171	50 49	261	36 45	305	55 43	326
338	25 03	043	39 45	075	40 50	137	41 02	172	49 53	261	35 59	305	55 11	325
339	25 42	043	40 40	075	41 28	138	41 09	174	48 57	262	35 12	305	54 39	325
340	26 21	043	41 35	075	42 06	139	41 15	175	48 01	262	34 25	305	54 06	324
341	26 59	043	42 29	075	42 43	140	41 20	176	47 04	263	33 39	305	53 32	323
342	27 38	043	43 24	075	43 20	141	41 24	177	46 08	263	32 52	305	52 57	322
343	28 17	043	44 19	075	43 55	142	41 26	178	45 12	263	32 05	304	52 23	322
344	28 55	043	45 14	075	44 30	143	41 27	179	44 15	264	31 18	304	51 47	321
	Schedar		◆Mirfak		ALDEBARAN		Diphda		◆FOMALHAUT		ALTAIR		◆DENEB	
345	47 54	021	29 34	043	10 37	076	45 04	144	41 27	180	43 19	264	51 11	321
346	48 14	020	30 12	043	11 32	076	45 37	145	41 26	182	42 23	265	50 35	320
347	48 33	019	30 50	043	12 28	077	46 10	146	41 24	183	41 26	265	49 58	319
348	48 51	019	31 29	042	13 23	077	46 41	147	41 21	184	40 30	265	49 21	319
349	49 09	018	32 07	042	14 18	077	47 11	148	41 16	185	39 33	266	48 44	318
350	49 26	017	32 45	042	15 13	077	47 41	149	41 11	186	38 36	266	48 06	318
351	49 42	016	33 23	042	16 09	078	48 09	151	41 04	187	37 40	267	47 28	318
352	49 58	016	34 01	042	17 04	078	48 36	152	40 56	189	36 43	267	46 49	317
353	50 13	015	34 39	042	18 00	078	49 02	153	40 47	190	35 46	267	46 11	317
354	50 27	014	35 17	042	18 55	078	49 27	155	40 37	191	34 50	268	45 32	316
355	50 40	013	35 54	041	19 51	079	49 51	156	40 26	192	33 53	268	44 52	316
356	50 53	012	36 32	041	20 47	079	50 14	157	40 14	193	32 56	268	44 13	316
357	51 05	012	37 09	041	21 42	079	50 35	159	40 01	194	32 00	269	43 33	315
358	51 16	011	37 46	041	22 38	079	50 55	160	39 46	195	31 03	269	42 53	315
359	51 26	010	38 23	041	23 34	080	51 14	161	39 31	196	30 06	269	42 13	315

LHA ♈	Hc	Zn	Hc	Zn	Hc	Zn	Hc	Zn	Hc	Zn	Hc	Zn	Hc	Zn
	Schedar		CAPELLA		◆ ALDEBARAN		ACHERNAR		◆ FOMALHAUT		ALTAIR		◆ DENEB	
0	50 36	009	20 05	047	24 19	080	12 05	167	40 12	198	29 09	270	40 50	315
1	50 45	008	20 46	047	25 15	080	12 18	167	39 54	199	28 12	271	40 10	315
2	50 53	007	21 28	047	26 11	080	12 31	168	39 35	200	27 15	271	39 29	315
3	50 59	006	22 09	047	27 08	080	12 43	168	39 16	201	26 18	271	38 48	314
4	51 05	006	22 51	047	28 04	080	12 54	169	38 55	202	25 21	272	38 07	314
5	51 10	005	23 32	047	29 00	081	13 05	169	38 33	203	24 24	272	37 26	314
6	51 15	004	24 14	047	29 56	081	13 15	170	38 11	204	23 27	272	36 45	314
7	51 18	003	24 56	047	30 53	081	13 25	170	37 47	205	22 30	272	36 04	314
8	51 20	002	25 37	047	31 49	081	13 34	171	37 23	206	21 33	273	35 22	313
9	51 22	001	26 19	047	32 46	082	13 43	171	36 58	207	20 36	273	34 41	313
10	51 23	000	27 01	047	33 42	082	13 52	172	36 32	208	19 39	273	33 59	313
11	51 23	359	27 42	047	34 39	082	13 59	172	36 05	209	18 42	274	33 17	313
12	51 22	359	28 24	047	35 35	082	14 06	173	35 37	209	17 45	274	32 35	313
13	51 20	358	29 06	047	36 32	082	14 13	174	35 08	210	16 48	274	31 54	313
14	51 17	357	29 47	047	37 28	083	14 19	174	34 39	211	15 51	274	31 12	313
	CAPELLA		◆ ALDEBARAN		RIGEL		ACHERNAR		◆ FOMALHAUT		Enif		◆ DENEB	
15	30 29	047	38 25	083	21 48	107	14 25	175	34 09	212	42 08	267	30 30	313
16	31 10	047	39 21	083	22 43	107	14 30	175	33 39	213	41 11	268	29 48	313
17	31 52	046	40 18	083	23 37	108	14 34	176	33 07	214	40 14	268	29 06	312
18	32 33	046	41 15	084	24 31	108	14 38	176	32 35	215	39 17	268	28 23	312
19	33 14	046	42 11	084	25 25	109	14 42	177	32 02	215	38 20	269	27 41	312
20	33 55	046	43 08	084	26 19	109	14 45	177	31 29	216	37 23	269	26 59	312
21	34 36	046	44 05	084	27 13	110	14 47	178	30 55	217	36 25	269	26 17	312
22	35 17	046	45 02	084	28 07	110	14 49	179	30 20	218	35 28	270	25 35	312
23	35 58	046	45 59	085	29 00	111	14 50	179	29 45	218	34 31	270	24 53	312
24	36 39	045	46 55	085	29 54	111	14 50	180	29 09	219	33 34	270	24 10	312
25	37 20	045	47 52	085	30 47	112	14 50	180	28 33	220	32 37	270	23 28	312
26	38 00	045	48 49	085	31 40	112	14 50	181	27 56	221	31 40	271	22 46	312
27	38 40	045	49 46	085	32 33	113	14 49	181	27 19	221	30 43	271	22 04	312
28	39 21	045	50 43	086	33 25	113	14 47	182	26 41	222	29 46	271	21 22	313
29	40 01	044	51 40	086	34 18	114	14 45	182	26 02	223	28 49	272	20 40	313
	Mirfak		◆ CAPELLA		ALDEBARAN		RIGEL		◆ ACHERNAR		FOMALHAUT		◆ Alpheratz	
30	53 47	023	40 40	044	52 37	086	35 10	114	14 42	183	25 23	223	62 21	299
31	54 09	022	41 20	044	53 34	086	36 02	115	14 39	184	24 44	224	61 31	298
32	54 31	022	41 59	044	54 31	087	36 53	116	14 35	184	24 04	225	60 41	298
33	54 51	021	42 39	043	55 28	087	37 45	116	14 31	185	23 24	225	59 50	297
34	55 11	020	43 17	043	56 25	087	38 36	117	14 26	185	22 43	226	59 00	297
35	55 30	019	43 56	042	57 21	087	39 26	117	14 20	186	22 02	226	58 09	297
36	55 48	018	44 35	042	58 19	088	40 17	118	14 14	186	21 21	227	57 17	296
37	56 04	017	45 13	042	59 16	088	41 07	119	14 07	187	20 39	227	56 26	296
38	56 20	016	45 50	041	60 13	088	41 57	120	14 00	187	19 57	228	55 35	296
39	56 35	014	46 28	041	61 10	088	42 46	120	13 53	188	19 14	229	54 43	295
40	56 49	013	47 05	040	62 07	089	43 35	121	13 44	189	18 31	229	53 52	295
41	57 01	012	47 42	040	63 04	089	44 24	122	13 36	189	17 48	230	53 00	295
42	57 13	011	48 18	039	64 01	089	45 12	123	13 26	190	17 05	230	52 08	295
43	57 23	010	48 54	039	64 58	089	46 00	124	13 17	190	16 21	231	51 16	294
44	57 33	009	49 30	038	65 55	090	46 47	124	13 06	191	15 36	231	50 24	294
	CAPELLA		◆ POLLUX		PROCYON		SIRIUS		◆ Acamar		Diphda		◆ Alpheratz	
45	50 05	038	24 15	067	20 35	091	24 29	119	31 45	180	41 00	225	49 32	294
46	50 40	037	25 07	067	21 32	091	25 19	119	31 45	181	40 19	226	48 40	294
47	51 14	037	26 00	067	22 29	092	26 08	120	31 43	182	39 38	226	47 48	294
48	51 48	036	26 52	067	23 26	092	26 58	120	31 40	183	38 57	227	46 56	294
49	52 21	035	27 45	067	24 23	092	27 47	121	31 37	184	38 14	228	46 04	294
50	52 54	034	28 38	067	25 20	093	28 35	121	31 33	185	37 32	229	45 11	294
51	53 26	034	29 30	067	26 17	093	29 24	122	31 28	186	36 48	230	44 19	294
52	53 57	033	30 23	068	27 14	093	30 12	123	31 22	187	36 05	230	43 27	293
53	54 28	032	31 16	068	28 11	094	31 00	123	31 15	187	35 20	231	42 34	293
54	54 58	031	32 09	068	29 08	094	31 48	124	31 07	188	34 36	232	41 42	293
55	55 27	030	33 01	068	30 05	094	32 35	125	30 58	189	33 51	233	40 50	293
56	55 55	030	33 54	068	31 02	095	33 22	125	30 49	190	33 05	233	39 57	293
57	56 23	029	34 47	068	31 58	095	34 08	126	30 38	191	32 19	234	39 05	293
58	56 50	028	35 40	068	32 55	096	34 54	127	30 27	192	31 33	235	38 12	293
59	57 16	027	36 33	068	33 52	096	35 40	127	30 15	193	30 46	235	37 20	293
	CAPELLA		◆ POLLUX		PROCYON		SIRIUS		◆ CANOPUS		Diphda		◆ Hamal	
60	57 41	026	37 26	068	34 49	096	36 25	128	12 42	159	29 59	236	63 18	287
61	58 06	025	38 19	068	35 46	097	37 10	129	13 03	159	29 12	237	62 23	287
62	58 29	023	39 12	068	36 42	097	37 54	130	13 23	160	28 24	237	61 28	286
63	58 51	022	40 05	068	37 39	098	38 38	130	13 43	160	27 36	238	60 33	286
64	59 12	021	40 58	068	38 35	098	39 21	131	14 02	161	26 47	238	59 39	286
65	59 32	020	41 51	068	39 32	098	40 04	132	14 21	161	25 59	239	58 44	286
66	59 51	019	42 44	068	40 28	099	40 46	133	14 39	162	25 10	239	57 49	286
67	60 09	018	43 37	068	41 25	099	41 27	134	14 57	162	24 21	240	56 54	286
68	60 25	016	44 30	068	42 21	100	42 08	135	15 14	163	23 31	240	55 59	286
69	60 41	015	45 23	068	43 17	100	42 48	136	15 30	163	22 41	241	55 04	286
70	60 55	014	46 16	068	44 13	101	43 28	136	15 46	164	21 51	241	54 09	285
71	61 08	012	47 09	068	45 09	101	44 07	137	16 02	165	21 01	242	53 14	285
72	61 19	011	48 01	068	46 05	102	44 45	138	16 17	165	20 11	242	52 19	285
73	61 29	009	48 54	068	47 01	102	45 23	139	16 31	166	19 20	243	51 24	285
74	61 38	008	49 47	068	47 57	103	45 59	141	16 45	166	18 29	243	50 29	285
	CAPELLA		◆ POLLUX		PROCYON		SIRIUS		◆ RIGEL		Menkar		◆ Hamal	
75	61 45	007	50 40	068	48 52	103	46 35	142	63 33	171	58 13	248	49 34	285
76	61 51	005	51 33	067	49 48	104	47 10	143	63 40	174	57 20	249	48 39	285
77	61 55	004	52 25	067	50 43	104	47 44	144	63 45	176	56 27	249	47 44	285
78	61 58	002	53 18	067	51 39	105	48 17	145	63 48	178	55 34	250	46 49	286
79	61 59	001	54 10	067	52 34	106	48 50	146	63 49	180	54 40	251	45 54	286
80	61 59	359	55 03	067	53 28	106	49 21	147	63 47	183	53 46	252	44 59	286
81	61 58	358	55 55	066	54 23	107	49 51	149	63 44	185	52 51	252	44 04	286
82	61 55	356	56 47	066	55 18	108	50 20	150	63 38	187	51 57	253	43 09	286
83	61 50	355	57 39	066	56 12	108	50 48	151	63 29	189	51 02	254	42 14	286
84	61 44	353	58 31	066	57 06	109	51 15	153	63 19	191	50 07	254	41 19	286
85	61 37	352	59 23	065	58 00	110	51 40	154	63 07	194	49 12	255	40 24	286
86	61 28	350	60 15	065	58 53	111	52 05	155	62 52	196	48 17	256	39 30	286
87	61 18	349	61 07	064	59 47	112	52 28	157	62 36	198	47 22	256	38 35	286
88	61 06	348	61 58	064	60 39	113	52 49	158	62 17	200	46 27	257	37 40	286
89	60 53	346	62 49	063	61 32	114	53 10	160	61 57	202	45 31	257	36 45	286

LAT 18°N

LHA ♈	Hc	Zn	Hc	Zn	Hc	Zn	Hc	Zn	Hc	Zn	Hc	Zn	Hc	Zn
	Dubhe		◆ REGULUS		Alphard		SIRIUS		◆ RIGEL		ALDEBARAN		◆ CAPELLA	
90	22 20	030	29 46	086	32 04	113	53 29	161	61 35	204	70 05	269	60 39	345
91	22 48	030	30 43	087	32 56	114	53 46	163	61 11	206	69 08	269	60 24	344
92	23 17	030	31 40	087	33 48	114	54 02	164	60 45	208	68 11	270	60 07	342
93	23 45	030	32 37	087	34 40	115	54 17	166	60 18	209	67 14	270	59 49	341
94	24 13	030	33 34	087	35 32	115	54 30	168	59 50	211	66 17	270	59 30	340
95	24 42	030	34 31	088	36 23	116	54 41	169	59 19	213	65 20	271	59 10	339
96	25 10	030	35 28	088	37 15	117	54 51	171	58 48	214	64 23	271	58 49	338
97	25 38	029	36 25	088	38 05	117	54 59	173	58 15	216	63 26	271	58 26	336
98	26 06	029	37 22	089	38 56	118	55 06	174	57 41	217	62 29	271	58 03	335
99	26 34	029	38 19	089	39 46	119	55 11	176	57 06	219	61 32	272	57 39	334
100	27 02	029	39 16	089	40 36	119	55 14	178	56 29	220	60 35	272	57 14	333
101	27 29	029	40 13	089	41 26	120	55 16	179	55 52	222	59 38	272	56 47	332
102	27 57	029	41 10	090	42 15	121	55 15	181	55 13	223	58 41	272	56 20	331
103	28 25	029	42 07	090	43 04	121	55 14	183	54 34	224	57 44	273	55 53	330
104	28 52	029	43 04	090	43 52	122	55 10	184	53 53	226	56 47	273	55 24	329
	Dubhe		◆ REGULUS		Alphard		SIRIUS		◆ RIGEL		ALDEBARAN		◆ CAPELLA	
105	29 19	028	44 01	091	44 41	123	55 05	186	53 12	227	55 50	273	54 55	329
106	29 46	028	44 58	091	45 28	124	54 59	188	52 30	228	54 53	273	54 25	328
107	30 13	028	45 55	091	46 15	125	54 50	189	51 47	229	53 56	274	53 54	327
108	30 40	028	46 52	092	47 02	126	54 40	191	51 04	230	52 59	274	53 22	326
109	31 07	028	47 49	092	47 48	127	54 29	193	50 20	231	52 02	274	52 50	325
110	31 33	028	48 46	092	48 34	128	54 15	194	49 35	232	51 05	274	52 18	325
111	32 00	027	49 43	093	49 18	128	54 01	196	48 50	233	50 08	274	51 44	324
112	32 26	027	50 40	093	50 03	130	53 45	197	48 04	234	49 11	275	51 11	323
113	32 52	027	51 37	094	50 47	131	53 27	199	47 17	235	48 14	275	50 36	323
114	33 17	027	52 34	094	51 30	132	53 08	200	46 30	236	47 18	275	50 02	322
115	33 43	026	53 31	094	52 12	133	52 47	202	45 43	237	46 21	275	49 26	322
116	34 08	026	54 28	095	52 53	134	52 26	203	44 55	238	45 24	276	48 51	321
117	34 33	026	55 25	095	53 34	135	52 02	205	44 06	238	44 27	276	48 15	321
118	34 58	026	56 22	096	54 14	136	51 38	206	43 17	239	43 30	276	47 38	320
119	35 22	025	57 19	096	54 53	138	51 12	207	42 28	240	42 34	276	47 01	320
	Dubhe		◆ Denebola		Alphard		◆ SIRIUS		RIGEL		ALDEBARAN		◆ CAPELLA	
120	35 47	025	34 56	085	55 31	139	50 45	209	41 38	241	41 37	276	46 24	319
121	36 10	025	35 53	085	56 08	140	50 17	210	40 49	241	40 40	277	45 47	319
122	36 34	024	36 50	085	56 43	142	49 48	211	39 58	242	39 44	277	45 09	318
123	36 57	024	37 47	085	57 18	143	49 18	213	39 08	243	38 47	277	44 31	318
124	37 20	024	38 44	086	57 52	145	48 47	214	38 17	243	37 50	277	43 52	317
125	37 43	023	39 40	086	58 24	146	48 14	215	37 26	244	36 54	277	43 14	317
126	38 06	023	40 37	086	58 55	148	47 41	216	36 34	245	35 57	278	42 35	317
127	38 28	023	41 34	086	59 24	150	47 07	217	35 42	245	35 01	278	41 55	316
128	38 49	022	42 31	087	59 53	151	46 32	218	34 50	246	34 04	278	41 16	316
129	39 10	022	43 28	087	60 19	153	45 56	220	33 58	246	33 08	278	40 36	316
130	39 31	021	44 25	087	60 44	155	45 19	221	33 06	247	32 11	279	39 57	316
131	39 52	021	45 22	087	61 07	157	44 42	222	32 13	248	31 15	279	39 17	315
132	40 12	020	46 19	088	61 29	159	44 03	223	31 20	248	30 18	279	38 36	315
133	40 32	020	47 16	088	61 49	161	43 24	224	30 27	249	29 22	279	37 56	315
134	40 51	020	48 13	088	62 07	163	42 45	225	29 34	249	28 26	279	37 16	315
	Dubhe		◆ ARCTURUS		SPICA		◆ Alphard		SIRIUS		BETELGEUSE		◆ CAPELLA	
135	41 10	019	15 44	075	18 10	109	62 23	165	42 04	225	44 01	263	36 35	315
136	41 28	019	16 39	075	19 04	109	62 37	167	41 23	226	43 05	263	35 54	314
137	41 46	018	17 35	075	19 58	110	62 49	169	40 42	227	42 08	264	35 13	314
138	42 04	018	18 30	075	20 51	110	62 58	171	40 00	228	41 11	264	34 32	314
139	42 21	017	19 25	076	21 45	111	63 06	173	39 17	229	40 15	264	33 51	314
140	42 37	017	20 20	076	22 38	111	63 12	175	38 33	230	39 18	265	33 10	314
141	42 53	016	21 16	076	23 32	111	63 15	178	37 50	231	38 21	265	32 29	314
142	43 08	015	22 11	076	24 25	112	63 17	180	37 05	231	37 24	266	31 47	314
143	43 23	015	23 06	076	25 17	112	63 16	182	36 21	232	36 27	266	31 06	313
144	43 38	014	24 02	077	26 10	113	63 13	184	35 35	233	35 30	266	30 25	313
145	43 52	014	24 57	077	27 03	113	63 07	186	34 50	233	34 33	267	29 43	313
146	44 05	013	25 53	077	27 55	114	63 00	189	34 04	234	33 36	267	29 01	313
147	44 18	013	26 49	077	28 47	114	62 50	191	33 17	235	32 39	267	28 20	313
148	44 30	012	27 44	077	29 39	115	62 39	193	32 30	236	31 42	268	27 38	313
149	44 41	011	28 40	078	30 31	115	62 25	195	31 43	236	30 45	268	26 57	313
	Dubhe		◆ ARCTURUS		SPICA		◆ Alphard		SIRIUS		BETELGEUSE		◆ CAPELLA	
150	44 52	011	29 36	078	31 22	116	62 09	197	30 56	237	29 48	268	26 15	313
151	45 03	010	30 32	078	32 13	117	61 52	199	30 08	237	28 51	269	25 33	313
152	45 12	009	31 27	078	33 04	117	61 32	201	29 19	238	27 54	269	24 52	313
153	45 21	009	32 23	078	33 55	118	61 11	203	28 31	239	26 57	269	24 10	313
154	45 30	008	33 19	079	34 45	118	60 48	205	27 42	239	26 00	270	23 28	313
155	45 38	008	34 15	079	35 35	119	60 23	207	26 53	240	25 03	270	22 47	313
156	45 45	007	35 11	079	36 25	120	59 57	208	26 03	240	24 06	270	22 05	313
157	45 51	006	36 07	079	37 14	120	59 29	210	25 14	241	23 09	270	21 23	313
158	45 57	006	37 03	079	38 03	121	59 00	212	24 24	241	22 12	271	20 42	313
159	46 02	005	37 59	079	38 52	122	58 29	213	23 34	242	21 15	271	20 00	313
160	46 07	004	38 55	080	39 41	122	57 57	215	22 43	242	20 18	271	19 19	313
161	46 11	004	39 52	080	40 29	123	57 24	216	21 53	243	19 21	272	18 38	314
162	46 14	003	40 48	080	41 16	124	56 49	218	21 02	243	18 24	272	17 56	314
163	46 16	002	41 44	080	42 03	125	56 13	219	20 11	244	17 27	272	17 15	314
164	46 18	001	42 40	080	42 50	125	55 37	221	19 19	244	16 30	273	16 34	314
	◆ Dubhe		Alkaid		ARCTURUS		◆ SPICA		Suhail		◆ PROCYON		POLLUX	
165	46 19	001	44 03	037	43 36	080	43 36	126	23 24	202	39 34	262	44 36	292
166	46 20	000	44 38	037	44 33	081	44 22	127	23 03	202	38 38	262	43 43	292
167	46 20	359	45 12	037	45 29	081	45 07	128	22 41	203	37 41	262	42 50	292
168	46 19	359	45 46	036	46 25	081	45 52	129	22 18	204	36 45	263	41 57	292
169	46 17	358	46 19	036	47 22	081	46 36	130	21 55	204	35 48	263	41 04	292
170	46 15	357	46 52	035	48 18	081	47 19	131	21 31	205	34 51	264	40 11	292
171	46 12	357	47 25	035	49 14	081	48 02	132	21 07	206	33 55	264	39 18	292
172	46 08	356	47 57	034	50 11	082	48 44	133	20 42	206	32 58	264	38 25	292
173	46 04	355	48 28	033	51 07	082	49 26	134	20 16	207	32 01	265	37 32	292
174	45 59	355	49 00	033	52 04	082	50 06	135	19 50	208	31 04	265	36 39	292
175	45 53	354	49 30	032	53 00	082	50 46	136	19 23	208	30 07	265	35 46	292
176	45 47	353	50 01	032	53 57	082	51 25	137	18 56	209	29 10	266	34 53	292
177	45 40	353	50 30	031	54 53	082	52 03	139	18 29	209	28 13	266	34 00	292
178	45 32	352	50 59	030	55 50	082	52 41	140	18 00	210	27 16	267	33 08	292
179	45 24	351	51 28	030	56 46	082	53 17	141	17 32	211	26 19	267	32 15	292

 LAT 18°N

LHA ♈	Hc Zn	Hc Zn	Hc Zn	Hc Zn	Hc Zn	Hc Zn	Hc Zn
	◆ Alkaid	ANTARES	◆ SPICA	Gienah	◆ REGULUS	POLLUX	Dubhe
180	51 55 029	10 47 123	53 52 142	54 09 173	62 34 261	31 22 292	45 15 351
181	52 22 028	11 35 123	54 27 144	54 14 175	61 38 262	30 29 292	45 06 350
182	52 49 027	12 22 123	55 00 145	54 19 176	60 42 262	29 36 293	44 56 349
183	53 15 026	13 10 124	55 32 147	54 21 178	59 45 263	28 44 293	44 45 349
184	53 40 026	13 57 124	56 02 148	54 22 180	58 48 263	27 51 293	44 33 348
185	54 04 025	14 44 125	56 32 150	54 22 181	57 52 264	26 59 293	44 22 348
186	54 27 024	15 31 125	57 00 151	54 20 183	56 55 264	26 06 293	44 09 347
187	54 50 023	16 17 126	57 27 153	54 16 185	55 58 265	25 13 293	43 56 346
188	55 12 022	17 04 126	57 52 155	54 10 186	55 01 265	24 21 293	43 42 346
189	55 32 021	17 49 127	58 16 156	54 03 188	54 04 265	23 29 293	43 28 345
190	55 52 020	18 35 127	58 38 158	53 55 190	53 08 266	22 36 294	43 13 345
191	56 11 019	19 20 128	58 59 160	53 45 191	52 11 266	21 44 294	42 58 344
192	56 29 018	20 05 128	59 18 162	53 33 193	51 14 267	20 52 294	42 42 344
193	56 46 017	20 50 129	59 35 163	53 20 194	50 17 267	20 00 294	42 26 343
194	57 02 016	21 35 129	59 50 165	53 05 196	49 20 267	19 07 294	42 09 343
	Kochab	◆ VEGA	Rasalhague	ANTARES	◆ SPICA	◆ REGULUS	Dubhe
195	31 52 009	15 27 054	23 39 084	22 19 130	60 04 167	48 23 268	41 52 342
196	32 01 008	16 13 054	24 36 084	23 02 130	60 16 169	47 26 268	41 34 342
197	32 09 008	16 59 054	25 33 084	23 46 131	60 26 171	46 29 268	41 16 341
198	32 17 008	17 45 054	26 30 085	24 29 132	60 33 173	45 32 269	40 57 341
199	32 24 007	18 32 054	27 26 085	25 11 132	60 39 175	44 35 269	40 38 340
200	32 32 007	19 18 054	28 23 085	25 53 133	60 43 177	43 37 269	40 18 340
201	32 39 007	20 04 054	29 20 085	26 35 133	60 45 179	42 40 270	39 58 339
202	32 45 007	20 51 054	30 17 086	27 16 134	60 45 181	41 43 270	39 38 339
203	32 52 006	21 37 055	31 14 086	27 57 135	60 43 183	40 46 270	39 17 338
204	32 58 006	22 24 055	32 11 086	28 37 135	60 39 185	39 49 271	38 56 338
205	33 04 006	23 10 055	33 08 087	29 17 136	60 33 187	38 52 271	38 35 338
206	33 09 005	23 57 055	34 05 087	29 57 137	60 25 189	37 55 271	38 13 337
207	33 14 005	24 43 055	35 02 087	30 35 137	60 16 191	36 58 272	37 50 337
208	33 19 005	25 30 055	35 59 087	31 14 138	60 04 193	36 01 272	37 28 336
209	33 24 004	26 17 055	36 56 088	31 52 139	59 50 195	35 04 272	37 05 336
	Kochab	◆ VEGA	Rasalhague	◆ ANTARES	SPICA	◆ REGULUS	Dubhe
210	33 28 004	27 03 055	37 53 088	32 29 140	59 35 197	34 07 272	36 42 336
211	33 32 004	27 50 055	38 50 088	33 05 140	59 18 198	33 10 273	36 18 335
212	33 36 003	28 37 055	39 47 088	33 41 141	58 59 200	32 13 273	35 54 335
213	33 39 003	29 24 055	40 44 089	34 17 142	58 38 202	31 16 273	35 30 335
214	33 42 003	30 10 055	41 41 089	34 52 143	58 16 204	30 19 273	35 06 335
215	33 45 003	30 57 055	42 38 089	35 26 144	57 52 206	29 22 274	34 41 334
216	33 47 002	31 44 055	43 35 090	35 59 145	57 27 207	28 25 274	34 16 334
217	33 49 002	32 31 055	44 32 090	36 32 145	57 00 209	27 28 274	33 51 334
218	33 51 002	33 17 055	45 29 090	37 04 146	56 32 210	26 31 275	33 26 333
219	33 52 001	34 04 055	46 26 091	37 35 147	56 02 212	25 34 275	33 00 333
220	33 53 001	34 51 055	47 23 091	38 06 148	55 31 213	24 38 275	32 34 333
221	33 54 001	35 37 055	48 20 091	38 35 149	54 59 215	23 41 275	32 08 333
222	33 54 000	36 24 055	49 17 092	39 04 150	54 26 216	22 44 276	31 42 333
223	33 54 000	37 10 055	50 14 092	39 32 151	53 52 218	21 47 276	31 15 332
224	33 54 000	37 57 054	51 12 092	39 59 152	53 17 219	20 50 276	30 49 332
	VEGA	◆ ALTAIR	Nunki	ANTARES	◆ SPICA	Denebola	◆ Alkaid
225	38 43 054	18 56 087	17 34 126	40 25 153	52 40 220	44 20 273	55 34 339
226	39 29 054	19 53 087	18 20 127	40 51 154	52 03 221	43 23 273	55 13 338
227	40 16 054	20 50 087	19 05 127	41 15 155	51 25 223	42 26 273	54 51 337
228	41 02 054	21 47 087	19 51 128	41 38 156	50 46 224	41 29 274	54 29 336
229	41 48 054	22 44 088	20 36 128	42 01 157	50 06 225	40 32 274	54 05 335
230	42 34 053	23 41 088	21 20 129	42 22 159	49 25 226	39 35 274	53 41 335
231	43 19 053	24 38 088	22 05 129	42 43 160	48 44 227	38 39 274	53 16 334
232	44 05 053	25 35 089	22 48 130	43 02 161	48 02 228	37 42 275	52 51 333
233	44 50 053	26 32 089	23 32 130	43 20 162	47 19 229	36 45 275	52 24 332
234	45 36 052	27 29 089	24 15 131	43 37 163	46 35 230	35 48 275	51 57 331
235	46 21 052	28 26 089	24 58 132	43 53 164	45 51 231	34 51 275	51 29 331
236	47 06 052	29 23 090	25 41 132	44 08 165	45 07 232	33 54 276	51 01 330
237	47 51 051	30 20 090	26 23 133	44 22 167	44 22 233	32 58 276	50 32 329
238	48 35 051	31 17 090	27 04 134	44 34 168	43 36 234	32 01 276	50 02 328
239	49 19 051	32 14 091	27 45 134	44 46 169	42 50 235	31 04 276	49 32 328
	◆ VEGA	ALTAIR	Nunki	◆ ANTARES	SPICA	◆ ARCTURUS	Alkaid
240	50 03 050	33 12 091	28 26 135	44 56 170	42 03 235	65 26 277	49 02 327
241	50 47 050	34 09 091	29 06 136	45 05 172	41 16 236	64 29 277	48 30 327
242	51 31 049	35 06 092	29 46 136	45 12 173	40 28 237	63 32 277	47 59 326
243	52 14 049	36 03 092	30 25 137	45 19 174	39 40 238	62 36 277	47 27 325
244	52 57 048	37 00 092	31 04 138	45 24 175	38 52 238	61 39 277	46 54 325
245	53 39 048	37 57 093	31 42 138	45 28 177	38 03 239	60 43 277	46 21 324
246	54 22 047	38 54 093	32 20 139	45 31 178	37 14 240	59 46 277	45 48 324
247	55 03 047	39 51 093	32 57 140	45 32 179	36 25 240	58 49 277	45 14 323
248	55 45 046	40 48 094	33 33 141	45 32 181	35 35 241	57 53 277	44 40 323
249	56 26 045	41 45 094	34 09 142	45 31 182	34 45 242	56 56 278	44 05 323
250	57 06 045	42 41 094	34 44 142	45 28 183	33 54 242	56 00 278	43 30 322
251	57 46 044	43 38 095	35 19 143	45 25 184	33 04 243	55 03 278	42 55 322
252	58 25 043	44 35 095	35 52 144	45 20 186	32 13 243	54 07 278	42 20 321
253	59 04 042	45 32 096	36 26 145	45 14 187	31 22 244	53 10 278	41 44 321
254	59 42 041	46 29 096	36 58 146	45 06 188	30 30 245	52 14 278	41 08 321
	◆ VEGA	ALTAIR	◆ Nunki	ANTARES	SPICA	◆ ARCTURUS	Alkaid
255	60 19 040	47 25 096	37 30 147	44 57 189	29 39 245	51 17 278	40 32 320
256	60 56 040	48 22 097	38 01 148	44 47 191	28 47 246	50 21 278	39 55 320
257	61 32 038	49 19 097	38 31 149	44 36 192	27 55 246	49 24 279	39 18 320
258	62 07 037	50 15 098	39 00 150	44 24 193	27 02 247	48 28 279	38 41 319
259	62 41 036	51 12 098	39 29 151	44 10 194	26 10 247	47 31 279	38 04 319
260	63 15 035	52 08 099	39 56 152	43 56 196	25 17 248	46 35 279	37 27 319
261	63 47 034	53 05 099	40 23 153	43 40 197	24 24 248	45 39 279	36 49 319
262	64 18 032	54 01 100	40 49 154	43 23 198	23 31 249	44 42 279	36 12 319
263	64 48 031	54 57 100	41 14 155	43 05 199	22 38 249	43 46 280	35 34 318
264	65 17 030	55 53 101	41 38 156	42 46 200	21 45 249	42 50 280	34 56 318
265	65 44 028	56 49 101	42 01 157	42 26 201	20 51 250	41 54 280	34 18 318
266	66 10 026	57 45 102	42 23 158	42 04 202	19 57 250	40 57 280	33 39 318
267	66 35 025	58 41 103	42 44 159	41 42 203	19 04 251	40 01 280	33 01 318
268	66 58 023	59 36 103	43 03 160	41 19 205	18 10 251	39 05 280	32 22 317
269	67 20 021	60 32 104	43 22 161	40 55 206	17 16 252	38 09 281	31 44 317

LHA ♈	Hc Zn	Hc Zn	Hc Zn	Hc Zn	Hc Zn	Hc Zn	Hc Zn
	VEGA	◆ DENEB	Enif	◆ Nunki	ANTARES	◆ ARCTURUS	Alkaid
270	67 40 019	46 44 042	35 02 090	43 40 162	40 30 207	37 13 281	31 05 317
271	67 58 018	47 22 041	35 59 091	43 57 164	40 03 208	36 17 281	30 26 317
272	68 14 016	48 00 041	36 56 091	44 12 165	39 37 209	35 21 281	29 47 317
273	68 29 014	48 37 040	37 53 091	44 26 166	39 09 210	34 25 281	29 08 317
274	68 41 012	49 14 040	38 50 092	44 40 167	38 40 211	33 29 281	28 29 317
275	68 51 009	49 50 039	39 47 092	44 52 169	38 10 212	32 33 282	27 50 317
276	69 00 007	50 26 039	40 44 092	45 02 170	37 40 213	31 37 282	27 11 317
277	69 06 005	51 01 038	41 41 093	45 12 171	37 09 213	30 41 282	26 32 317
278	69 10 003	51 36 037	42 38 093	45 20 172	36 37 214	29 45 282	25 53 317
279	69 12 001	52 11 037	43 35 093	45 27 174	36 05 215	28 50 282	25 14 317
280	69 12 359	52 45 036	44 32 094	45 33 175	35 31 216	27 54 283	24 35 317
281	69 09 356	53 18 035	45 29 094	45 37 176	34 57 217	26 58 283	23 56 317
282	69 05 354	53 51 035	46 26 094	45 41 177	34 23 218	26 03 283	23 16 317
283	68 58 352	54 23 034	47 23 095	45 43 179	33 47 219	25 07 283	22 37 317
284	68 49 350	54 54 033	48 20 095	45 43 180	33 11 219	24 11 283	21 58 317
	◆ DENEB	Alpheratz	◆ FOMALHAUT	Nunki	ANTARES	◆ Rasalhague	VEGA
285	55 25 032	19 28 065	15 26 129	45 43 181	32 35 220	68 57 258	68 38 348
286	55 55 031	20 20 065	16 10 129	45 41 183	31 58 221	68 01 259	68 25 346
287	56 24 030	21 11 065	16 54 130	45 38 184	31 20 222	67 05 260	68 10 344
288	56 53 029	22 03 065	17 38 130	45 33 185	30 42 222	66 09 260	67 53 342
289	57 20 028	22 55 065	18 21 131	45 28 186	30 03 223	65 13 261	67 34 340
290	57 47 027	23 47 065	19 04 131	45 21 188	29 24 224	64 16 261	67 14 338
291	58 13 026	24 39 065	19 47 132	45 13 189	28 44 225	63 20 262	66 52 336
292	58 38 025	25 31 066	20 29 132	45 03 190	28 04 225	62 23 263	66 28 335
293	59 02 024	26 23 066	21 11 133	44 53 191	27 23 226	61 27 263	66 03 333
294	59 25 023	27 15 066	21 53 134	44 41 193	26 42 227	60 30 264	65 37 332
295	59 47 022	28 07 066	22 34 134	44 28 194	26 00 227	59 33 264	65 09 330
296	60 07 021	28 59 066	23 14 135	44 14 195	25 18 228	58 36 265	64 40 329
297	60 27 019	29 51 066	23 55 135	43 58 196	24 36 228	57 40 265	64 09 327
298	60 45 018	30 43 066	24 35 136	43 42 197	23 53 229	56 43 265	63 38 326
299	61 02 017	31 35 066	25 14 137	43 24 199	23 09 230	55 46 266	63 05 325
	◆ DENEB	Schedar	Alpheratz	◆ FOMALHAUT	Nunki	◆ Rasalhague	VEGA
300	61 18 015	25 44 035	32 28 066	25 53 137	43 05 200	54 49 266	62 32 323
301	61 33 014	26 16 035	33 20 066	26 32 138	42 46 201	53 52 267	61 57 322
302	61 46 013	26 49 035	34 12 066	27 10 139	42 25 202	52 55 267	61 22 321
303	61 58 011	27 22 035	35 05 066	27 47 139	42 03 203	51 58 267	60 46 320
304	62 08 010	27 54 035	35 57 067	28 24 140	41 40 204	51 01 268	60 09 319
305	62 17 008	28 27 035	36 49 067	29 01 141	41 16 205	50 04 268	59 32 318
306	62 25 007	28 59 035	37 42 067	29 37 141	40 51 206	49 07 268	58 53 317
307	62 31 005	29 32 034	38 34 067	30 12 142	40 26 207	48 10 269	58 14 317
308	62 35 004	30 04 034	39 27 067	30 47 143	39 59 208	47 13 269	57 35 316
309	62 38 002	30 36 034	40 19 067	31 21 144	39 31 209	46 16 269	56 55 315
310	62 40 001	31 08 034	41 11 067	31 54 144	39 03 210	45 19 270	56 14 314
311	62 40 359	31 40 034	42 04 067	32 27 145	38 34 211	44 22 270	55 33 314
312	62 38 358	32 11 034	42 56 067	33 00 146	38 04 212	43 25 270	54 52 313
313	62 35 356	32 43 033	43 48 067	33 31 147	37 33 213	42 28 271	54 10 312
314	62 31 355	33 14 033	44 41 066	34 02 148	37 01 214	41 30 271	53 28 312
	◆ Alpheratz	Diphda	◆ FOMALHAUT	Nunki	◆ Rasalhague	VEGA	DENEB
315	45 33 066	24 12 120	34 32 149	36 29 215	40 33 271	52 45 311	62 24 353
316	46 25 066	25 01 121	35 02 149	35 56 216	39 36 272	52 02 311	62 17 352
317	47 18 066	25 50 121	35 30 150	35 22 217	38 39 272	51 19 310	62 08 350
318	48 10 066	26 39 122	35 58 151	34 47 218	37 42 272	50 35 310	61 57 349
319	49 02 066	27 28 122	36 25 152	34 12 218	36 45 272	49 51 310	61 46 347
320	49 54 066	28 16 123	36 51 153	33 37 219	35 48 273	49 07 309	61 32 346
321	50 46 066	29 03 123	37 17 154	33 00 220	34 51 273	48 23 309	61 18 345
322	51 38 065	29 51 124	37 41 155	32 23 221	33 54 273	47 38 308	61 02 343
323	52 30 065	30 38 125	38 05 156	31 46 222	32 57 274	46 53 308	60 45 342
324	53 22 065	31 25 125	38 28 157	31 08 222	32 00 274	46 08 308	60 26 341
325	54 13 065	32 11 126	38 50 158	30 29 223	31 03 274	45 23 307	60 07 339
326	55 05 065	32 57 127	39 11 159	29 50 224	30 07 274	44 38 307	59 46 338
327	55 56 064	33 43 127	39 31 160	29 10 224	29 10 275	43 52 307	59 24 337
328	56 48 064	34 28 128	39 50 161	28 30 225	28 13 275	43 07 307	59 01 336
329	57 39 064	35 13 129	40 08 162	27 49 226	27 16 275	42 21 307	58 37 335
	◆ Mirfak	Hamal	Diphda	◆ FOMALHAUT	ALTAIR	◆ VEGA	DENEB
330	19 11 042	32 11 073	35 57 129	40 25 163	57 31 258	41 35 306	58 12 334
331	19 49 042	33 06 073	36 41 130	40 41 164	56 36 259	40 49 306	57 46 332
332	20 28 042	34 00 073	37 24 131	40 55 165	55 40 259	40 03 306	57 20 331
333	21 06 043	34 55 073	38 07 132	41 09 167	54 43 260	39 17 306	56 52 330
334	21 45 043	35 50 074	38 50 133	41 22 168	53 47 260	38 30 306	56 23 330
335	22 24 043	36 45 074	39 31 133	41 34 169	52 51 261	37 44 306	55 54 329
336	23 02 043	37 39 074	40 12 134	41 44 170	51 55 261	36 57 305	55 24 328
337	23 41 043	38 34 074	40 53 135	41 54 171	50 58 262	36 11 305	54 53 327
338	24 19 043	39 29 074	41 33 136	42 02 172	50 02 262	35 24 305	54 22 326
339	24 58 043	40 24 074	42 12 137	42 09 173	49 05 263	34 38 305	53 50 325
340	25 37 043	41 19 074	42 51 138	42 15 175	48 08 263	33 51 305	53 17 325
341	26 15 043	42 14 074	43 29 139	42 20 176	47 12 264	33 04 305	52 44 324
342	26 54 043	43 08 074	44 06 140	42 23 177	46 15 264	32 18 305	52 10 323
343	27 32 042	44 03 074	44 42 141	42 26 178	45 18 264	31 31 305	51 35 323
344	28 11 042	44 58 074	45 18 142	42 27 179	44 21 265	30 44 305	51 00 322
	Schedar	◆ Mirfak	ALDEBARAN	Diphda	◆ FOMALHAUT	ALTAIR	◆ DENEB
345	46 58 020	28 49 042	10 23 076	45 52 143	42 27 180	43 25 265	50 25 321
346	47 17 020	29 28 042	11 18 076	46 26 144	42 26 182	42 28 266	49 49 321
347	47 36 019	30 06 042	12 14 076	46 59 145	42 24 183	41 31 266	49 13 320
348	47 54 018	30 44 042	13 09 077	47 31 146	42 21 184	40 34 266	48 36 320
349	48 12 017	31 22 042	14 05 077	48 02 148	42 16 185	39 37 267	47 59 319
350	48 29 017	32 01 042	15 00 077	48 32 149	42 11 186	38 40 267	47 21 319
351	48 45 016	32 39 042	15 56 077	49 01 150	42 04 187	37 43 267	46 43 318
352	49 00 015	33 16 041	16 52 078	49 29 151	41 56 189	36 46 268	46 05 318
353	49 15 015	33 54 041	17 47 078	49 56 153	41 47 190	35 49 268	45 27 317
354	49 29 014	34 32 041	18 43 078	50 22 154	41 36 191	34 52 268	44 48 317
355	49 42 013	35 09 041	19 39 078	50 46 155	41 25 192	33 55 269	44 09 317
356	49 54 012	35 47 041	20 35 079	51 09 157	41 12 193	32 58 269	43 30 316
357	50 06 011	36 24 041	21 31 079	51 31 158	40 59 194	32 01 269	42 50 316
358	50 17 011	37 01 040	22 27 079	51 52 160	40 44 195	31 04 270	42 10 316
359	50 27 010	37 38 040	23 23 079	52 11 161	40 29 197	30 06 270	41 30 315

LAT 17°N

LHA ♈	Hc	Zn	Hc	Zn	Hc	Zn	Hc	Zn	Hc	Zn	Hc	Zn	Hc	Zn
	Schedar		CAPELLA		◆ ALDEBARAN		ACHERNAR		◆ FOMALHAUT		ALTAIR		◆ DENEB	
0	49 37	009	19 23	046	24 08	079	13 04	167	41 09	198	29 09	271	40 07	316
1	49 45	008	20 05	046	25 04	079	13 17	167	40 51	199	28 11	271	39 27	315
2	49 53	007	20 46	046	26 01	080	13 29	168	40 32	200	27 14	271	38 47	315
3	50 00	006	21 28	047	26 57	080	13 41	168	40 12	201	26 17	272	38 06	315
4	50 06	005	22 10	047	27 54	080	13 53	169	39 51	202	25 19	272	37 25	315
5	50 11	005	22 51	047	28 50	080	14 04	169	39 28	203	24 22	272	36 44	314
6	50 15	004	23 33	047	29 47	080	14 14	170	39 05	204	23 25	273	36 03	314
7	50 18	003	24 15	047	30 43	081	14 24	170	38 42	205	22 27	273	35 22	314
8	50 20	002	24 56	047	31 40	081	14 34	171	38 17	206	21 30	273	34 41	314
9	50 22	001	25 38	047	32 36	081	14 43	171	37 51	207	20 33	273	33 59	314
10	50 23	000	26 20	047	33 33	081	14 51	172	37 25	208	19 36	274	33 18	314
11	50 23	359	27 01	046	34 30	081	14 59	172	36 57	209	18 38	274	32 36	313
12	50 22	359	27 43	046	35 27	082	15 06	173	36 29	210	17 41	274	31 55	313
13	50 20	358	28 24	046	36 23	082	15 13	174	36 00	211	16 44	274	31 13	313
14	50 17	357	29 06	046	37 20	082	15 19	174	35 30	212	15 47	275	30 31	313
	CAPELLA		◆ ALDEBARAN		RIGEL		ACHERNAR		◆ FOMALHAUT		Enif		◆ DENEB	
15	29 47	046	38 17	082	22 05	107	15 25	175	35 00	212	42 10	268	29 49	313
16	30 29	046	39 14	082	23 00	107	15 30	175	34 29	213	41 13	268	29 07	313
17	31 10	046	40 11	082	23 55	107	15 34	176	33 57	214	40 15	269	28 25	313
18	31 51	046	41 08	083	24 50	108	15 38	176	33 24	215	39 18	269	27 43	313
19	32 32	046	42 04	083	25 44	108	15 42	177	32 51	216	38 21	269	27 01	313
20	33 14	046	43 01	083	26 39	109	15 44	177	32 17	217	37 23	270	26 19	313
21	33 55	045	43 58	083	27 33	109	15 47	178	31 43	217	36 26	270	25 36	313
22	34 35	045	44 55	083	28 27	110	15 48	179	31 08	218	35 29	270	24 54	313
23	35 16	045	45 52	084	29 21	110	15 50	179	30 32	219	34 31	271	24 12	313
24	35 57	045	46 49	084	30 15	111	15 50	180	29 56	220	33 34	271	23 30	313
25	36 37	045	47 46	084	31 09	111	15 50	180	29 19	220	32 36	271	22 48	313
26	37 18	045	48 43	084	32 02	112	15 50	181	28 42	221	31 39	271	22 06	313
27	37 58	044	49 41	084	32 56	112	15 49	181	28 04	222	30 42	272	21 23	313
28	38 38	044	50 38	084	33 49	113	15 47	182	27 25	222	29 44	272	20 41	313
29	39 17	044	51 35	085	34 41	113	15 45	182	26 46	223	28 47	272	19 59	313
	Mirfak		◆ CAPELLA		ALDEBARAN		RIGEL		◆ ACHERNAR		FOMALHAUT		◆ Alpheratz	
30	52 52	023	39 57	044	52 32	085	35 34	114	15 42	183	26 07	224	61 51	301
31	53 14	022	40 36	043	53 29	085	36 27	114	15 39	184	25 27	224	61 02	300
32	53 35	021	41 16	043	54 26	085	37 19	115	15 35	184	24 47	225	60 12	299
33	53 55	020	41 55	043	55 23	085	38 11	115	15 30	185	24 06	225	59 22	299
34	54 14	019	42 33	042	56 21	086	39 02	116	15 25	185	23 25	226	58 32	298
35	54 33	018	43 12	042	57 18	086	39 54	117	15 20	186	22 44	227	57 41	298
36	54 50	017	43 50	041	58 15	086	40 45	117	15 14	186	22 02	227	56 50	298
37	55 07	016	44 28	041	59 12	086	41 36	118	15 07	187	21 20	228	55 59	297
38	55 22	015	45 05	041	60 10	086	42 26	119	15 00	187	20 37	228	55 08	297
39	55 37	014	45 42	040	61 07	086	43 16	119	14 52	188	19 54	229	54 17	297
40	55 50	013	46 19	040	62 04	087	44 06	120	14 44	189	19 11	229	53 26	296
41	56 03	012	46 56	039	63 01	087	44 55	121	14 35	189	18 27	230	52 34	296
42	56 14	011	47 32	039	63 59	087	45 44	122	14 26	190	17 43	230	51 43	296
43	56 24	010	48 07	038	64 56	087	46 33	123	14 16	190	16 59	231	50 51	296
44	56 33	009	48 43	038	65 53	087	47 21	123	14 05	191	16 14	231	49 59	295
	CAPELLA		◆ POLLUX		PROCYON		SIRIUS		◆ Acamar		Diphda		◆ Alpheratz	
45	49 18	037	23 51	066	20 36	091	24 57	118	32 45	180	41 42	225	49 07	295
46	49 52	036	24 44	066	21 33	091	25 48	119	32 45	181	41 01	226	48 15	295
47	50 26	036	25 36	067	22 31	091	26 38	119	32 43	182	40 19	227	47 23	295
48	50 59	035	26 29	067	23 28	092	27 28	120	32 40	183	39 37	228	46 31	295
49	51 32	034	27 22	067	24 25	092	28 17	120	32 37	184	38 54	229	45 39	295
50	52 04	034	28 14	067	25 23	092	29 07	121	32 33	185	38 11	230	44 47	295
51	52 35	033	29 07	067	26 20	093	29 56	122	32 27	186	37 27	230	43 55	294
52	53 06	032	30 00	067	27 17	093	30 44	122	32 21	187	36 43	231	43 02	294
53	53 37	031	30 53	067	28 15	093	31 33	123	32 14	187	35 58	232	42 10	294
54	54 06	031	31 46	067	29 12	094	32 21	123	32 06	188	35 13	232	41 18	294
55	54 35	030	32 39	067	30 09	094	33 09	124	31 57	189	34 27	233	40 25	294
56	55 03	029	33 31	067	31 06	094	33 56	125	31 48	190	33 41	234	39 33	294
57	55 30	028	34 24	067	32 04	095	34 43	125	31 37	191	32 54	234	38 41	294
58	55 57	027	35 17	067	33 01	095	35 30	126	31 26	192	32 07	235	37 48	294
59	56 22	026	36 10	067	33 58	095	36 16	127	31 14	193	31 20	236	36 56	294
	CAPELLA		◆ POLLUX		PROCYON		SIRIUS		◆ CANOPUS		Diphda		◆ Hamal	
60	56 47	025	37 03	067	34 55	096	37 02	127	13 38	158	30 32	236	62 59	289
61	57 11	024	37 56	067	35 52	096	37 47	128	13 59	159	29 44	237	62 05	288
62	57 34	023	38 49	067	36 49	096	38 32	129	14 19	159	28 56	238	61 10	288
63	57 55	022	39 42	067	37 46	097	39 16	130	14 39	160	28 08	238	60 16	288
64	58 16	021	40 35	067	38 43	097	40 00	131	14 59	161	27 19	239	59 21	288
65	58 36	019	41 28	067	39 40	098	40 43	131	15 17	161	26 30	239	58 26	287
66	58 54	018	42 21	067	40 37	098	41 26	132	15 36	162	25 40	240	57 32	287
67	59 12	017	43 14	067	41 34	098	42 08	133	15 54	162	24 50	240	56 37	287
68	59 28	016	44 07	067	42 30	099	42 50	134	16 11	163	24 01	241	55 42	287
69	59 43	014	45 00	067	43 27	099	43 31	135	16 28	163	23 10	241	54 47	287
70	59 56	013	45 53	067	44 24	100	44 11	136	16 44	164	22 20	242	53 52	287
71	60 09	012	46 46	067	45 20	100	44 51	137	17 00	164	21 29	242	52 57	287
72	60 20	010	47 38	067	46 17	101	45 30	138	17 15	165	20 38	243	52 02	287
73	60 30	009	48 31	067	47 13	101	46 08	139	17 29	166	19 47	243	51 07	287
74	60 38	008	49 24	067	48 09	102	46 45	140	17 43	166	18 56	244	50 12	287
	CAPELLA		◆ POLLUX		PROCYON		SIRIUS		◆ RIGEL		Menkar		◆ Hamal	
75	60 45	006	50 16	066	49 06	102	47 22	141	64 32	171	58 35	249	49 17	287
76	60 51	005	51 09	066	50 02	103	47 58	142	64 40	173	57 42	250	48 22	287
77	60 55	004	52 01	066	50 58	103	48 33	143	64 45	176	56 48	251	47 27	287
78	60 58	002	52 54	066	51 53	104	49 06	144	64 48	178	55 53	252	46 32	287
79	60 59	001	53 46	066	52 49	104	49 39	146	64 49	180	54 59	252	45 37	287
80	60 59	359	54 38	065	53 45	105	50 11	147	64 47	183	54 04	253	44 42	287
81	60 58	358	55 30	065	54 40	106	50 42	148	64 43	185	53 09	254	43 47	287
82	60 55	356	56 22	065	55 35	106	51 12	149	64 37	187	52 14	254	42 52	287
83	60 50	355	57 14	064	56 30	107	51 40	151	64 29	190	51 19	255	41 57	287
84	60 45	354	58 06	064	57 25	108	52 08	152	64 18	192	50 23	255	41 02	287
85	60 37	352	58 57	064	58 19	108	52 34	153	64 05	194	49 28	256	40 08	287
86	60 29	351	59 49	063	59 14	109	52 59	155	63 50	196	48 32	257	39 13	287
87	60 19	349	60 40	063	60 08	110	53 23	156	63 33	198	47 36	257	38 18	287
88	60 08	348	61 31	062	61 02	111	53 45	158	63 14	201	46 40	258	37 23	287
89	59 55	347	62 21	062	61 55	112	54 06	159	62 53	203	45 44	258	36 28	287

LHA ♈	Hc	Zn	Hc	Zn	Hc	Zn	Hc	Zn	Hc	Zn	Hc	Zn	Hc	Zn
	Dubhe		◆ REGULUS		Alphard		SIRIUS		◆ RIGEL		ALDEBARAN		◆ CAPELLA	
90	21 28	030	29 42	086	32 27	112	54 26	161	62 30	205	70 05	272	59 41	345
91	21 56	030	30 39	086	33 20	113	54 44	162	62 05	207	69 08	272	59 26	344
92	22 25	030	31 36	086	34 13	114	55 00	164	61 38	208	68 10	272	59 10	343
93	22 53	030	32 33	087	35 05	114	55 15	166	61 10	210	67 13	272	58 52	342
94	23 21	029	33 31	087	35 57	115	55 28	167	60 41	212	66 16	273	58 34	340
95	23 49	029	34 28	087	36 49	115	55 40	169	60 10	214	65 18	273	58 14	339
96	24 17	029	35 25	087	37 41	116	55 50	171	59 37	215	64 21	273	57 53	338
97	24 46	029	36 23	088	38 33	117	55 59	172	59 03	217	63 24	273	57 31	337
98	25 14	029	37 20	088	39 24	117	56 05	174	58 28	218	62 26	273	57 09	336
99	25 41	029	38 17	088	40 15	118	56 11	176	57 52	220	61 29	273	56 45	335
100	26 09	029	39 15	088	41 05	118	56 14	177	57 15	221	60 32	274	56 20	334
101	26 37	029	40 12	089	41 55	119	56 16	179	56 36	223	59 35	274	55 54	333
102	27 04	029	41 09	089	42 45	120	56 15	181	55 57	224	58 37	274	55 28	332
103	27 32	029	42 07	089	43 35	121	56 14	183	55 16	225	57 40	274	55 00	331
104	27 59	028	43 04	089	44 24	121	56 10	184	54 35	227	56 43	274	54 32	330
	Dubhe		◆ REGULUS		Alphard		SIRIUS		◆ RIGEL		ALDEBARAN		◆ CAPELLA	
105	28 26	028	44 01	090	45 13	122	56 05	186	53 53	228	55 46	275	54 03	329
106	28 54	028	44 59	090	46 01	123	55 58	188	53 10	229	54 49	275	53 34	328
107	29 20	028	45 56	090	46 49	124	55 49	189	52 26	230	53 51	275	53 03	328
108	29 47	028	46 54	091	47 36	125	55 39	191	51 42	231	52 54	275	52 32	327
109	30 14	027	47 51	091	48 23	126	55 27	193	50 57	232	51 57	275	52 01	326
110	30 40	027	48 48	091	49 10	127	55 14	194	50 11	233	51 00	275	51 28	325
111	31 06	027	49 46	092	49 55	128	54 59	196	49 25	234	50 03	276	50 56	325
112	31 32	027	50 43	092	50 41	129	54 42	198	48 38	235	49 06	276	50 22	324
113	31 58	027	51 40	092	51 25	130	54 24	199	47 51	236	48 09	276	49 48	324
114	32 24	026	52 38	093	52 09	131	54 04	201	47 03	237	47 12	276	49 14	323
115	32 49	026	53 35	093	52 52	132	53 43	202	46 15	238	46 15	276	48 39	322
116	33 14	026	54 32	093	53 35	133	53 21	204	45 26	238	45 18	277	48 04	322
117	33 39	026	55 30	094	54 16	134	52 57	205	44 37	239	44 21	277	47 28	321
118	34 04	025	56 27	094	54 57	135	52 32	207	43 48	240	43 24	277	46 52	321
119	34 28	025	57 24	094	55 37	137	52 05	208	42 58	241	42 27	277	46 16	320
	Dubhe		◆ Denebola		Alphard		◆ SIRIUS		RIGEL		ALDEBARAN		◆ CAPELLA	
120	34 52	025	34 50	084	56 16	138	51 38	209	42 07	241	41 30	277	45 39	320
121	35 16	024	35 47	084	56 53	139	51 09	211	41 17	242	40 33	277	45 01	319
122	35 39	024	36 44	084	57 30	141	50 39	212	40 26	243	39 36	278	44 24	319
123	36 03	024	37 41	085	58 06	142	50 08	213	39 35	244	38 39	278	43 46	319
124	36 25	023	38 39	085	58 40	144	49 36	215	38 43	244	37 42	278	43 08	318
125	36 48	023	39 36	085	59 14	145	49 03	216	37 51	245	36 46	278	42 29	318
126	37 10	023	40 33	085	59 45	147	48 29	217	36 59	245	35 49	278	41 51	317
127	37 32	022	41 30	085	60 16	149	47 54	218	36 07	246	34 52	279	41 12	317
128	37 54	022	42 27	086	60 45	151	47 19	219	35 15	247	33 55	279	40 33	317
129	38 15	021	43 25	086	61 12	152	46 42	220	34 22	247	32 59	279	39 53	316
130	38 35	021	44 22	086	61 38	154	46 04	221	33 29	248	32 02	279	39 14	316
131	38 56	021	45 19	086	62 02	156	45 26	222	32 36	248	31 05	279	38 34	316
132	39 16	020	46 16	087	62 25	158	44 47	223	31 42	249	30 09	280	37 54	316
133	39 35	020	47 14	087	62 45	160	44 08	224	30 49	249	29 12	280	37 14	315
134	39 54	019	48 11	087	63 04	162	43 27	225	29 55	250	28 16	280	36 33	315
	Dubhe		◆ ARCTURUS		SPICA		◆ Alphard		SIRIUS		BETELGEUSE		◆ CAPELLA	
135	40 13	019	15 28	074	18 29	108	63 20	164	42 46	226	44 08	264	35 53	315
136	40 31	018	16 24	075	19 24	109	63 35	166	42 04	227	43 11	264	35 12	315
137	40 49	018	17 19	075	20 18	109	63 47	169	41 22	228	42 14	265	34 31	315
138	41 06	017	18 14	075	21 12	110	63 58	171	40 39	229	41 17	265	33 50	314
139	41 23	017	19 10	075	22 06	110	64 06	173	39 56	230	40 20	265	33 09	314
140	41 39	016	20 05	075	23 00	111	64 12	175	39 12	230	39 23	266	32 28	314
141	41 55	016	21 01	076	23 53	111	64 15	178	38 28	231	38 26	266	31 47	314
142	42 11	015	21 56	076	24 47	111	64 17	180	37 43	232	37 28	266	31 06	314
143	42 25	015	22 52	076	25 40	112	64 16	182	36 57	233	36 31	267	30 25	314
144	42 40	014	23 48	076	26 33	112	64 12	184	36 11	233	35 34	267	29 43	314
145	42 53	014	24 43	076	27 26	113	64 07	187	35 25	234	34 36	267	29 02	314
146	43 06	013	25 39	077	28 19	113	63 59	189	34 39	235	33 39	268	28 20	314
147	43 19	012	26 35	077	29 12	114	63 49	191	33 52	235	32 42	268	27 39	314
148	43 31	012	27 31	077	30 04	114	63 37	193	33 04	236	31 44	268	26 57	314
149	43 42	011	28 27	077	30 56	115	63 23	195	32 16	237	30 47	269	26 15	313
	Dubhe		◆ ARCTURUS		SPICA		◆ Alphard		SIRIUS		BETELGEUSE		◆ CAPELLA	
150	43 53	011	29 23	077	31 48	115	63 07	198	31 28	237	29 50	269	25 34	313
151	44 03	010	30 19	077	32 40	116	62 48	200	30 40	238	28 52	269	24 52	313
152	44 13	009	31 15	078	33 31	117	62 28	202	29 51	238	27 55	269	24 10	313
153	44 22	009	32 11	078	34 22	117	62 06	204	29 02	239	26 58	270	23 29	313
154	44 30	008	33 07	078	35 13	118	61 42	206	28 13	240	26 00	270	22 47	313
155	44 38	007	34 03	078	36 04	118	61 17	207	27 23	240	25 03	270	22 05	313
156	44 45	007	34 59	078	36 54	119	60 50	209	26 33	241	24 05	271	21 24	313
157	44 51	006	35 55	078	37 44	120	60 21	211	25 43	241	23 08	271	20 42	314
158	44 57	005	36 52	079	38 34	120	59 51	213	24 52	242	22 11	271	20 01	314
159	45 03	005	37 48	079	39 23	121	59 19	214	24 02	242	21 13	271	19 19	314
160	45 07	004	38 44	079	40 12	122	58 46	216	23 11	243	20 16	272	18 38	314
161	45 11	003	39 40	079	41 01	122	58 12	217	22 20	243	19 19	272	17 56	314
162	45 14	003	40 37	079	41 49	123	57 36	219	21 28	244	18 21	272	17 15	314
163	45 16	002	41 33	079	42 37	124	56 59	220	20 37	244	17 24	273	16 33	314
164	45 18	001	42 30	079	43 24	125	56 22	222	19 45	245	16 27	273	15 52	314
	◆ Dubhe		Alkaid		ARCTURUS		◆ SPICA		Suhail		◆ PROCYON		POLLUX	
165	45 19	001	43 15	037	43 26	080	44 11	126	24 20	202	39 43	262	44 13	293
166	45 20	000	43 49	036	44 22	080	44 58	126	23 59	203	38 46	263	43 20	293
167	45 20	359	44 23	036	45 19	080	45 44	127	23 36	203	37 49	263	42 27	293
168	45 19	359	44 57	036	46 15	080	46 29	128	23 13	204	36 52	264	41 34	293
169	45 17	358	45 30	035	47 12	080	47 14	129	22 50	204	35 55	264	40 41	293
170	45 15	357	46 03	035	48 08	080	47 58	130	22 26	205	34 58	264	39 48	293
171	45 12	357	46 35	034	49 05	080	48 42	131	22 01	206	34 00	265	38 55	293
172	45 08	356	47 07	033	50 01	080	49 25	132	21 36	206	33 03	265	38 02	293
173	45 04	355	47 38	033	50 58	080	50 07	133	21 10	207	32 06	265	37 09	293
174	44 59	355	48 09	032	51 55	081	50 48	134	20 43	208	31 09	266	36 16	293
175	44 54	354	48 39	032	52 51	081	51 29	135	20 16	208	30 12	266	35 24	293
176	44 47	353	49 09	031	53 48	081	52 09	137	19 49	209	29 14	266	34 31	293
177	44 40	353	49 38	030	54 44	081	52 48	138	19 21	210	28 17	267	33 38	293
178	44 33	352	50 07	030	55 41	081	53 26	139	18 52	210	27 20	267	32 45	293
179	44 25	352	50 35	029	56 38	081	54 03	140	18 23	211	26 23	267	31 52	293

LAT 17°N

LHA ♈	◆ Alkaid Hc Zn	ANTARES Hc Zn	◆ SPICA Hc Zn	Gienah Hc Zn	◆ REGULUS Hc Zn	POLLUX Hc Zn	Dubhe Hc Zn
180	51 03 028	11 19 122	54 40 142	55 08 173	62 43 263	30 59 293	44 16 351
181	51 29 027	12 07 123	55 15 143	55 14 175	61 46 263	30 06 293	44 07 350
182	51 55 027	12 55 123	55 49 144	55 19 176	60 49 264	29 13 293	43 57 350
183	52 21 026	13 43 124	56 22 146	55 21 178	59 52 264	28 20 293	43 46 349
184	52 45 025	14 31 124	56 53 147	55 22 180	58 55 265	27 28 293	43 35 348
185	53 09 024	15 18 125	57 23 149	55 22 181	57 57 265	26 35 293	43 23 348
186	53 32 023	16 05 125	57 52 150	55 20 183	57 00 266	25 42 293	43 11 347
187	53 54 022	16 52 125	58 20 152	55 16 185	56 03 266	24 50 294	42 58 347
188	54 16 021	17 39 126	58 46 154	55 10 186	55 06 266	23 57 294	42 44 346
189	54 36 020	18 25 126	59 11 156	55 03 188	54 08 267	23 05 294	42 30 346
190	54 56 019	19 11 127	59 34 157	54 54 190	53 11 267	22 12 294	42 15 345
191	55 14 018	19 57 127	59 55 159	54 43 191	52 14 268	21 20 294	42 00 344
192	55 32 017	20 42 128	60 14 161	54 31 193	51 17 268	20 27 294	41 45 344
193	55 49 016	21 28 128	60 32 163	54 18 195	50 19 268	19 35 294	41 28 343
194	56 04 015	22 12 129	60 48 165	54 02 196	49 22 269	18 43 294	41 12 343

LHA ♈	Kochab	◆ VEGA	Rasalhague	ANTARES	◆ SPICA	◆ REGULUS	Dubhe
195	30 53 009	14 51 053	23 33 083	22 57 129	61 02 167	48 24 269	40 55 342
196	31 01 008	15 38 053	24 30 084	23 41 130	61 15 169	47 27 269	40 37 342
197	31 09 008	16 24 054	25 27 084	24 25 131	61 25 171	46 30 269	40 19 341
198	31 17 008	17 10 054	26 24 084	25 08 131	61 33 173	45 32 270	40 00 341
199	31 25 007	17 56 054	27 21 084	25 51 132	61 39 175	44 35 270	39 41 340
200	31 32 007	18 43 054	28 18 085	26 34 132	61 43 177	43 38 270	39 22 340
201	31 39 007	19 29 054	29 15 085	27 16 133	61 45 179	42 40 271	39 02 340
202	31 46 007	20 16 054	30 12 085	27 58 134	61 45 181	41 43 271	38 42 339
203	31 52 006	21 02 054	31 09 085	28 39 134	61 43 183	40 45 271	38 21 339
204	31 58 006	21 49 054	32 07 086	29 20 135	61 39 185	39 48 271	38 00 338
205	32 04 006	22 35 054	33 04 086	30 00 136	61 33 187	38 51 272	37 39 338
206	32 09 005	23 22 054	34 01 086	30 40 136	61 25 189	37 53 272	37 17 338
207	32 15 005	24 09 054	34 58 086	31 19 137	61 14 191	36 56 272	36 55 337
208	32 19 005	24 55 055	35 56 087	31 58 138	61 02 193	35 59 273	36 33 337
209	32 24 004	25 42 055	36 53 087	32 37 138	60 48 195	35 01 273	36 10 336

LHA ♈	Kochab	◆ VEGA	Rasalhague	◆ ANTARES	SPICA	◆ REGULUS	Dubhe
210	32 28 004	26 29 055	37 50 087	33 14 139	60 32 197	34 04 273	35 47 336
211	32 32 004	27 16 055	38 48 087	33 52 140	60 14 199	33 07 273	35 23 336
212	32 36 003	28 02 055	39 45 088	34 28 141	59 55 201	32 10 274	35 00 335
213	32 39 003	28 49 055	40 42 088	35 04 142	59 33 203	31 12 274	34 36 335
214	32 42 003	29 36 055	41 40 088	35 39 142	59 10 204	30 15 274	34 11 335
215	32 45 002	30 23 055	42 37 088	36 14 143	58 46 206	29 18 274	33 47 335
216	32 47 002	31 09 054	43 34 089	36 48 144	58 20 208	28 21 275	33 22 334
217	32 49 002	31 56 054	44 32 089	37 21 145	57 52 210	27 23 275	32 57 334
218	32 51 002	32 43 054	45 29 089	37 54 146	57 23 211	26 26 275	32 32 334
219	32 52 001	33 29 054	46 26 090	38 25 147	56 53 213	25 29 275	32 06 333
220	32 53 001	34 16 054	47 24 090	38 56 148	56 21 214	24 32 276	31 41 333
221	32 54 001	35 02 054	48 21 090	39 27 149	55 48 216	23 35 276	31 15 333
222	32 54 000	35 49 054	49 18 090	39 56 150	55 14 217	22 38 276	30 49 333
223	32 54 000	36 35 054	50 16 091	40 24 151	54 39 218	21 41 276	30 22 333
224	32 54 000	37 22 054	51 13 091	40 52 152	54 03 220	20 44 277	29 56 332

LHA ♈	VEGA	◆ ALTAIR	Nunki	ANTARES	◆ SPICA	Denebola	◆ Alkaid
225	38 08 054	18 52 086	18 09 126	41 19 153	53 26 221	44 17 274	54 38 340
226	38 54 053	19 49 086	18 56 126	41 45 154	52 48 222	43 19 274	54 17 339
227	39 40 053	20 47 087	19 42 127	42 09 155	52 09 223	42 22 274	53 56 338
228	40 26 053	21 44 087	20 27 127	42 33 156	51 29 225	41 25 275	53 34 337
229	41 12 053	22 41 087	21 13 128	42 56 157	50 48 226	40 28 275	53 11 336
230	41 58 053	23 39 088	21 58 128	43 18 158	50 07 227	39 31 275	52 47 335
231	42 43 052	24 36 088	22 42 129	43 39 159	49 24 228	38 34 275	52 22 334
232	43 28 052	25 33 088	23 27 130	43 58 160	48 41 229	37 36 275	51 57 333
233	44 14 052	26 31 088	24 11 130	44 17 162	47 58 230	36 39 276	51 31 333
234	44 59 052	27 28 089	24 55 131	44 35 163	47 14 231	35 42 276	51 04 332
235	45 44 051	28 25 089	25 38 131	44 51 164	46 29 232	34 45 276	50 37 331
236	46 28 051	29 23 089	26 21 132	45 06 165	45 43 233	33 48 276	50 09 330
237	47 13 051	30 20 090	27 03 133	45 20 166	44 57 234	32 51 277	49 40 330
238	47 57 050	31 17 090	27 45 133	45 33 168	44 11 234	31 54 277	49 11 329
239	48 41 050	32 15 090	28 27 134	45 45 169	43 24 235	30 57 277	48 41 328

LHA ♈	◆ VEGA	ALTAIR	Nunki	◆ ANTARES	SPICA	◆ ARCTURUS	Alkaid
240	49 25 049	33 12 090	29 08 134	45 55 170	42 37 236	65 18 279	48 11 328
241	50 08 049	34 10 091	29 49 135	46 04 171	41 49 237	64 21 279	47 40 327
242	50 51 049	35 07 091	30 29 136	46 12 173	41 01 238	63 24 279	47 09 327
243	51 34 048	36 04 091	31 09 137	46 19 174	40 12 238	62 28 279	46 37 326
244	52 17 047	37 02 092	31 48 137	46 24 175	39 23 239	61 31 279	46 05 326
245	52 59 047	37 59 092	32 27 138	46 28 177	38 34 240	60 34 279	45 32 325
246	53 41 046	38 56 092	33 05 139	46 31 178	37 44 240	59 38 279	44 59 325
247	54 22 046	39 54 093	33 42 140	46 32 179	36 54 241	58 41 279	44 26 324
248	55 03 045	40 51 093	34 19 140	46 32 181	36 04 242	57 44 279	43 52 324
249	55 43 044	41 48 093	34 56 141	46 31 182	35 13 242	56 48 279	43 17 323
250	56 23 044	42 46 094	35 31 142	46 28 183	34 22 243	55 51 279	42 43 323
251	57 02 043	43 43 094	36 07 143	46 25 184	33 31 243	54 54 279	42 08 322
252	57 41 042	44 40 094	36 41 144	46 19 186	32 39 244	53 58 279	41 33 322
253	58 19 041	45 37 095	37 15 144	46 13 187	31 48 245	53 01 279	40 57 322
254	58 57 040	46 34 095	37 48 145	46 05 188	30 56 245	52 04 279	40 21 321

LHA ♈	◆ VEGA	ALTAIR	◆ Nunki	ANTARES	SPICA	◆ ARCTURUS	Alkaid
255	59 33 039	47 32 095	38 20 146	45 57 190	30 04 246	51 08 280	39 45 321
256	60 09 038	48 29 096	38 51 147	45 46 191	29 11 246	50 11 280	39 09 321
257	60 45 037	49 26 096	39 22 148	45 35 192	28 19 247	49 15 280	38 33 320
258	61 19 036	50 23 097	39 52 149	45 22 193	27 26 247	48 18 280	37 56 320
259	61 53 035	51 20 097	40 21 150	45 09 195	26 33 248	47 22 280	37 19 320
260	62 25 034	52 17 098	40 49 151	44 54 196	25 40 248	46 25 280	36 41 319
261	62 57 033	53 14 098	41 16 152	44 37 197	24 46 249	45 29 280	36 04 319
262	63 27 031	54 10 098	41 42 153	44 20 198	23 53 249	44 32 280	35 26 319
263	63 56 030	55 07 099	42 08 154	44 02 199	22 59 249	43 36 280	34 49 319
264	64 24 029	56 04 099	42 32 155	43 42 200	22 05 250	42 39 281	34 11 319
265	64 51 027	57 00 100	42 56 156	43 21 202	21 11 250	41 43 281	33 33 318
266	65 16 026	57 57 101	43 18 158	43 00 203	20 17 251	40 47 281	32 55 318
267	65 40 024	58 53 101	43 40 159	42 37 204	19 23 251	39 50 281	32 16 318
268	66 03 022	59 49 102	44 00 160	42 13 205	18 29 252	38 54 281	31 38 318
269	66 24 020	60 45 102	44 19 161	41 49 206	17 34 252	37 58 281	30 59 318

LHA ♈	VEGA	◆ DENEB	Enif	◆ Nunki	ANTARES	◆ ARCTURUS	Alkaid
270	66 43 019	45 59 041	35 02 090	44 37 162	41 23 207	37 01 281	30 21 318
271	67 01 017	46 37 041	35 59 090	44 54 163	40 57 208	36 05 282	29 42 318
272	67 16 015	47 14 040	36 57 090	45 10 165	40 29 209	35 09 282	29 03 317
273	67 30 013	47 51 040	37 54 091	45 25 166	40 01 210	34 13 282	28 24 317
274	67 42 011	48 27 039	38 52 091	45 38 167	39 31 211	33 17 282	27 46 317
275	67 52 009	49 03 039	39 49 091	45 50 168	39 01 212	32 21 282	27 07 317
276	68 00 007	49 39 038	40 46 091	46 01 170	38 31 213	31 24 282	26 27 317
277	68 06 005	50 14 037	41 44 092	46 11 171	37 59 214	30 28 283	25 48 317
278	68 10 003	50 48 037	42 41 092	46 20 172	37 27 215	29 32 283	25 09 317
279	68 12 001	51 22 036	43 38 092	46 27 173	36 53 216	28 37 283	24 30 317
280	68 12 359	51 56 035	44 36 093	46 33 175	36 20 217	27 41 283	23 51 317
281	68 09 357	52 29 035	45 33 093	46 37 176	35 45 217	26 45 283	23 12 317
282	68 05 354	53 01 034	46 30 093	46 41 177	35 10 218	25 49 283	22 33 317
283	67 58 352	53 33 033	47 28 094	46 43 179	34 34 219	24 53 284	21 53 317
284	67 50 350	54 04 032	48 25 094	46 43 180	33 58 220	23 57 284	21 14 317

LHA ♈	◆ DENEB	Alpheratz	◆ FOMALHAUT	Nunki	ANTARES	◆ Rasalhague	VEGA
285	54 34 031	19 02 064	16 03 129	46 43 181	33 21 221	69 08 261	67 39 348
286	55 03 031	19 54 064	16 48 129	46 41 183	32 43 221	68 12 261	67 27 346
287	55 32 030	20 46 065	17 33 130	46 38 184	32 05 222	67 15 262	67 12 344
288	56 00 029	21 38 065	18 17 130	46 33 185	31 26 223	66 18 262	66 56 343
289	56 27 028	22 30 065	19 00 131	46 27 186	30 47 224	65 21 263	66 38 341
290	56 54 027	23 22 065	19 44 131	46 20 188	30 07 224	64 24 264	66 18 339
291	57 19 026	24 14 065	20 27 132	46 12 189	29 27 225	63 27 264	65 57 337
292	57 44 025	25 06 065	21 09 132	46 02 190	28 46 226	62 30 265	65 34 336
293	58 07 024	25 58 065	21 52 133	45 51 192	28 05 226	61 33 265	65 10 334
294	58 29 022	26 50 065	22 34 133	45 39 193	27 23 227	60 36 265	64 44 333
295	58 51 021	27 42 065	23 15 134	45 26 194	26 41 228	59 39 266	64 17 331
296	59 11 020	28 34 066	23 57 134	45 11 195	25 58 228	58 41 266	63 48 330
297	59 30 019	29 27 066	24 37 135	44 56 196	25 15 229	57 44 267	63 19 328
298	59 48 018	30 19 066	25 18 136	44 39 198	24 32 229	56 47 267	62 48 327
299	60 05 016	31 11 066	25 58 136	44 21 199	23 48 230	55 49 267	62 16 326

LHA ♈	◆ DENEB	Schedar	Alpheratz	◆ FOMALHAUT	Nunki	◆ Rasalhague	VEGA
300	60 20 015	24 54 035	32 03 066	26 37 137	44 02 200	54 52 268	61 43 325
301	60 35 014	25 27 035	32 56 066	27 16 138	43 42 201	53 55 268	61 10 323
302	60 47 012	26 00 035	33 48 066	27 55 138	43 20 202	52 57 268	60 35 322
303	60 59 011	26 32 035	34 41 066	28 33 139	42 58 203	52 00 269	60 00 321
304	61 09 009	27 05 034	35 33 066	29 10 140	42 35 205	51 03 269	59 23 320
305	61 18 008	27 37 034	36 25 066	29 47 140	42 10 206	50 05 269	58 46 319
306	61 25 007	28 10 034	37 18 066	30 23 141	41 45 207	49 08 270	58 09 319
307	61 31 005	28 42 034	38 10 066	30 59 142	41 19 208	48 11 270	57 30 318
308	61 35 004	29 14 034	39 02 066	31 34 142	40 52 209	47 13 270	56 51 317
309	61 38 002	29 46 034	39 55 066	32 09 143	40 24 210	46 16 271	56 12 316
310	61 40 001	30 18 034	40 47 066	32 43 144	39 55 211	45 18 271	55 32 315
311	61 40 359	30 50 033	41 40 066	33 16 145	39 25 212	44 21 271	54 51 315
312	61 38 358	31 21 033	42 32 066	33 49 146	38 54 213	43 24 271	54 10 314
313	61 35 356	31 53 033	43 24 066	34 21 146	38 23 214	42 26 272	53 29 313
314	61 31 355	32 24 033	44 16 066	34 53 147	37 51 215	41 29 272	52 47 313

LHA ♈	◆ Alpheratz	Diphda	◆ FOMALHAUT	Nunki	◆ Rasalhague	VEGA	DENEB
315	45 09 065	24 42 120	35 23 148	37 18 215	40 32 272	52 05 312	61 25 353
316	46 01 065	25 32 120	35 53 149	36 44 216	39 34 272	51 22 312	61 18 352
317	46 53 065	26 21 121	36 22 150	36 10 217	38 37 273	50 40 311	61 09 350
318	47 45 065	27 10 121	36 51 151	35 35 218	37 40 273	49 56 311	60 59 349
319	48 37 065	27 59 122	37 18 152	34 59 219	36 42 273	49 13 310	60 47 348
320	49 29 065	28 48 122	37 45 153	34 23 220	35 45 273	48 29 310	60 34 346
321	50 21 065	29 36 123	38 11 154	33 46 220	34 48 274	47 45 310	60 20 345
322	51 12 064	30 24 124	38 36 155	33 09 221	33 51 274	47 01 309	60 04 344
323	52 04 064	31 12 124	39 00 156	32 30 222	32 53 274	46 16 309	59 48 342
324	52 56 064	31 59 125	39 23 157	31 52 223	31 56 274	45 31 309	59 30 341
325	53 47 064	32 46 125	39 45 158	31 13 223	30 59 275	44 46 308	59 11 340
326	54 38 063	33 33 126	40 07 159	30 33 224	30 02 275	44 01 308	58 50 339
327	55 30 063	34 19 127	40 27 160	29 53 225	29 05 275	43 16 308	58 29 338
328	56 21 063	35 05 127	40 46 161	29 12 225	28 07 275	42 31 307	58 06 336
329	57 11 062	35 50 128	41 05 162	28 31 226	27 10 276	41 45 307	57 43 335

LHA ♈	◆ Mirfak	Hamal	Diphda	◆ FOMALHAUT	ALTAIR	◆ VEGA	DENEB
330	18 26 042	31 53 072	36 35 129	41 22 163	57 43 260	40 59 307	57 18 334
331	19 05 042	32 48 073	37 20 130	41 38 164	56 47 260	40 13 307	56 53 333
332	19 43 042	33 43 073	38 03 130	41 53 165	55 50 261	39 27 307	56 27 332
333	20 22 042	34 38 073	38 47 131	42 08 166	54 53 261	38 41 306	56 00 331
334	21 01 042	35 32 073	39 30 132	42 21 167	53 57 262	37 55 306	55 31 330
335	21 39 042	36 27 073	40 12 133	42 32 169	53 00 262	37 09 306	55 03 329
336	22 18 042	37 22 073	40 54 134	42 43 170	52 03 263	36 22 306	54 33 329
337	22 57 042	38 17 073	41 35 135	42 53 171	51 06 263	35 36 306	54 03 328
338	23 35 042	39 12 073	42 16 135	43 01 172	50 09 263	34 50 306	53 32 327
339	24 14 042	40 07 073	42 56 136	43 09 173	49 12 264	34 03 306	53 00 326
340	24 52 042	41 02 073	43 35 137	43 15 174	48 15 264	33 16 306	52 28 325
341	25 31 042	41 57 073	44 14 138	43 20 176	47 18 265	32 30 306	51 55 325
342	26 09 042	42 52 073	44 51 139	43 23 177	46 21 265	31 43 306	51 21 324
343	26 48 042	43 47 073	45 29 140	43 26 178	45 23 265	30 56 305	50 47 323
344	27 26 042	44 42 073	46 05 141	43 27 179	44 26 266	30 10 305	50 13 323

LHA ♈	Schedar	◆ Mirfak	ALDEBARAN	Diphda	◆ FOMALHAUT	ALTAIR	◆ DENEB
345	46 02 020	28 05 042	10 08 076	46 40 142	43 27 180	43 29 266	49 38 322
346	46 21 019	28 43 042	11 04 076	47 15 144	43 26 182	42 32 267	49 02 321
347	46 39 019	29 21 042	11 59 076	47 48 145	43 24 183	41 34 267	48 26 321
348	46 57 018	30 00 042	12 55 076	48 21 146	43 21 184	40 37 267	47 50 320
349	47 14 017	30 38 042	13 51 077	48 53 147	43 16 185	39 40 268	47 13 320
350	47 31 016	31 16 041	14 47 077	49 24 148	43 10 186	38 43 268	46 36 319
351	47 47 016	31 54 041	15 43 077	49 53 150	43 03 188	37 45 268	45 58 319
352	48 02 015	32 31 041	16 39 077	50 22 151	42 55 189	36 48 268	45 21 318
353	48 17 014	33 09 041	17 35 078	50 49 152	42 46 190	35 50 269	44 42 318
354	48 30 014	33 46 041	18 31 078	51 15 153	42 35 191	34 53 269	44 04 318
355	48 43 013	34 24 041	19 27 078	51 40 155	42 24 192	33 56 269	43 25 317
356	48 56 012	35 01 040	20 23 078	52 04 156	42 11 193	32 58 270	42 46 317
357	49 07 011	35 38 040	21 19 078	52 27 158	41 57 195	32 01 270	42 07 317
358	49 18 010	36 15 040	22 15 079	52 48 159	41 42 196	31 04 270	41 27 316
359	49 28 010	36 52 040	23 12 079	53 07 161	41 26 197	30 06 271	40 47 316

LAT 16°N

LHA ♈	Hc	Zn	Hc	Zn	Hc	Zn	Hc	Zn	Hc	Zn	Hc	Zn	Hc	Zn
	Schedar		CAPELLA		◆ALDEBARAN		ACHERNAR		◆FOMALHAUT		ALTAIR		◆DENEB	
0	48 38	009	18 42	046	23 56	079	14 02	167	42 06	198	29 08	271	39 24	316
1	48 46	008	19 23	046	24 53	079	14 15	167	41 48	199	28 10	272	38 44	316
2	48 53	007	20 05	046	25 49	079	14 28	168	41 28	200	27 12	272	38 04	316
3	49 00	006	20 47	046	26 46	079	14 40	168	41 08	201	26 15	272	37 24	315
4	49 06	005	21 28	046	27 43	079	14 52	169	40 46	202	25 17	272	36 43	315
5	49 11	004	22 10	046	28 40	080	15 03	169	40 24	203	24 19	273	36 02	315
6	49 15	004	22 52	046	29 36	080	15 13	170	40 00	204	23 22	273	35 21	315
7	49 18	003	23 33	046	30 33	080	15 23	170	39 36	205	22 24	273	34 40	315
8	49 21	002	24 15	046	31 30	080	15 33	171	39 11	206	21 27	273	33 59	314
9	49 22	001	24 57	046	32 27	080	15 42	171	38 44	207	20 29	274	33 18	314
10	49 23	000	25 38	046	33 24	080	15 50	172	38 17	208	19 32	274	32 36	314
11	49 23	359	26 20	046	34 20	081	15 58	172	37 50	209	18 34	274	31 55	314
12	49 22	359	27 01	046	35 17	081	16 06	173	37 21	210	17 37	274	31 13	314
13	49 20	358	27 43	046	36 14	081	16 12	173	36 52	211	16 39	275	30 31	314
14	49 17	357	28 24	046	37 11	081	16 19	174	36 21	212	15 42	275	29 50	314
	CAPELLA		◆ALDEBARAN		RIGEL		ACHERNAR		◆FOMALHAUT		Enif		◆DENEB	
15	29 06	046	38 08	081	22 22	106	16 24	175	35 50	213	42 12	269	29 08	313
16	29 47	046	39 05	081	23 18	107	16 29	175	35 19	214	41 14	269	28 26	313
17	30 28	046	40 02	082	24 13	107	16 34	176	34 46	215	40 16	270	27 44	313
18	31 09	045	40 59	082	25 08	107	16 38	176	34 13	215	39 19	270	27 02	313
19	31 50	045	41 56	082	26 03	108	16 42	177	33 40	216	38 21	270	26 20	313
20	32 31	045	42 54	082	26 58	108	16 44	177	33 05	217	37 23	270	25 38	313
21	33 12	045	43 51	082	27 53	109	16 47	178	32 30	218	36 26	271	24 56	313
22	33 53	045	44 48	082	28 47	109	16 48	179	31 55	218	35 28	271	24 13	313
23	34 34	045	45 45	083	29 42	110	16 50	179	31 19	219	34 30	271	23 31	313
24	35 14	044	46 42	083	30 36	110	16 50	180	30 42	220	33 33	271	22 49	313
25	35 54	044	47 39	083	31 30	110	16 50	180	30 05	221	32 35	272	22 07	313
26	36 35	044	48 37	083	32 24	111	16 50	181	29 27	221	31 37	272	21 25	313
27	37 15	044	49 34	083	33 18	111	16 49	181	28 48	222	30 40	272	20 43	313
28	37 54	044	50 31	083	34 11	112	16 47	182	28 10	223	29 42	272	20 00	313
29	38 34	043	51 29	083	35 05	112	16 45	183	27 30	223	28 44	273	19 18	313
	Mirfak		◆CAPELLA		ALDEBARAN		RIGEL		◆ACHERNAR		FOMALHAUT		◆Alpheratz	
30	51 57	022	39 13	043	52 26	084	35 58	113	16 42	183	26 50	224	61 20	302
31	52 18	021	39 53	043	53 23	084	36 51	114	16 39	184	26 10	225	60 31	302
32	52 39	021	40 31	042	54 20	084	37 44	114	16 35	184	25 29	225	59 42	301
33	52 59	020	41 10	042	55 18	084	38 36	115	16 30	185	24 48	226	58 52	300
34	53 18	019	41 49	042	56 15	084	39 28	115	16 25	185	24 07	226	58 02	300
35	53 36	018	42 27	041	57 13	084	40 20	116	16 19	186	23 25	227	57 12	299
36	53 53	017	43 05	041	58 10	084	41 12	117	16 13	186	22 43	227	56 22	299
37	54 09	016	43 42	040	59 07	084	42 04	117	16 07	187	22 00	228	55 31	299
38	54 24	015	44 19	040	60 05	085	42 55	118	15 59	188	21 17	229	54 41	298
39	54 39	014	44 56	040	61 02	085	43 45	119	15 51	188	20 33	229	53 50	298
40	54 52	013	45 33	039	62 00	085	44 36	119	15 43	189	19 50	230	52 59	298
41	55 04	012	46 09	039	62 57	085	45 26	120	15 34	189	19 06	230	52 07	297
42	55 15	011	46 45	038	63 54	085	46 16	121	15 25	190	18 21	231	51 16	297
43	55 25	009	47 20	038	64 52	085	47 05	122	15 15	190	17 37	231	50 24	297
44	55 34	008	47 55	037	65 49	085	47 54	123	15 04	191	16 52	231	49 33	296
	CAPELLA		◆POLLUX		PROCYON		SIRIUS		◆Acamar		Diphda		◆Alpheratz	
45	48 29	036	23 27	066	20 37	090	25 26	118	33 45	180	42 24	226	48 41	296
46	49 03	036	24 19	066	21 34	091	26 16	118	33 45	181	41 42	227	47 49	296
47	49 37	035	25 12	066	22 32	091	27 07	119	33 43	182	41 00	228	46 58	296
48	50 10	034	26 05	066	23 30	091	27 57	119	33 40	183	40 17	229	46 06	296
49	50 42	034	26 58	066	24 27	092	28 47	120	33 37	184	39 34	229	45 14	296
50	51 14	033	27 51	066	25 25	092	29 37	121	33 32	185	38 50	230	44 22	295
51	51 45	032	28 43	066	26 23	092	30 27	121	33 27	186	38 05	231	43 29	295
52	52 15	032	29 36	067	27 20	092	31 16	122	33 21	187	37 20	232	42 37	295
53	52 45	031	30 29	067	28 18	093	32 05	122	33 14	188	36 35	232	41 45	295
54	53 14	030	31 22	067	29 15	093	32 54	123	33 06	188	35 49	233	40 53	295
55	53 43	029	32 15	067	30 13	093	33 42	123	32 57	189	35 03	234	40 00	295
56	54 10	028	33 08	067	31 11	094	34 30	124	32 47	190	34 16	234	39 08	295
57	54 37	027	34 01	067	32 08	094	35 17	125	32 36	191	33 29	235	38 16	295
58	55 03	026	34 54	067	33 06	094	36 05	125	32 25	192	32 41	236	37 23	295
59	55 28	025	35 47	067	34 03	095	36 51	126	32 12	193	31 54	236	36 31	295
	CAPELLA		◆POLLUX		PROCYON		SIRIUS		◆CANOPUS		Diphda		◆Hamal	
60	55 53	024	36 40	067	35 01	095	37 38	127	14 34	158	31 05	237	62 39	290
61	56 16	023	37 33	067	35 58	095	38 24	128	14 55	159	30 17	237	61 45	290
62	56 38	022	38 26	067	36 55	096	39 09	128	15 16	159	29 28	238	60 51	290
63	57 00	021	39 19	067	37 53	096	39 54	129	15 36	160	28 39	239	59 57	289
64	57 20	020	40 12	067	38 50	096	40 39	130	15 55	160	27 50	239	59 02	289
65	57 39	019	41 05	067	39 47	097	41 23	131	16 14	161	27 00	240	58 08	289
66	57 57	018	41 58	067	40 45	097	42 06	132	16 33	162	26 10	240	57 13	289
67	58 14	017	42 51	066	41 42	097	42 49	132	16 51	162	25 20	241	56 19	289
68	58 30	015	43 43	066	42 39	098	43 31	133	17 08	163	24 30	241	55 24	288
69	58 45	014	44 36	066	43 36	098	44 13	134	17 25	163	23 39	242	54 29	288
70	58 58	013	45 29	066	44 33	099	44 54	135	17 42	164	22 48	242	53 34	288
71	59 10	011	46 22	066	45 30	099	45 35	136	17 57	164	21 57	243	52 39	288
72	59 21	010	47 14	066	46 27	100	46 14	137	18 13	165	21 06	243	51 45	288
73	59 30	009	48 07	066	47 24	100	46 53	138	18 27	166	20 14	243	50 50	288
74	59 39	007	48 59	066	48 21	100	47 31	139	18 42	166	19 22	244	49 55	288
	CAPELLA		◆POLLUX		PROCYON		SIRIUS		◆RIGEL		Menkar		◆Hamal	
75	59 46	006	49 52	065	49 17	101	48 08	140	65 31	171	58 56	251	49 00	288
76	59 51	005	50 44	065	50 14	101	48 45	141	65 39	173	58 01	252	48 05	288
77	59 55	003	51 37	065	51 11	102	49 20	143	65 45	176	57 07	252	47 10	288
78	59 58	002	52 29	065	52 07	102	49 55	144	65 48	178	56 12	253	46 15	288
79	59 59	001	53 21	064	53 03	103	50 29	145	65 49	180	55 16	254	45 20	288
80	59 59	359	54 13	064	53 59	104	51 01	146	65 47	183	54 21	254	44 25	287
81	59 58	358	55 05	064	54 55	104	51 33	147	65 43	185	53 25	255	43 30	287
82	59 55	356	55 56	063	55 51	105	52 03	149	65 37	188	52 30	256	42 35	287
83	59 51	355	56 48	063	56 47	105	52 33	150	65 28	190	51 34	256	41 40	288
84	59 45	354	57 39	063	57 42	106	53 01	151	65 17	192	50 38	257	40 45	288
85	59 38	352	58 30	062	58 38	107	53 28	153	65 03	195	49 41	257	39 50	288
86	59 30	351	59 21	062	59 33	108	53 53	154	64 47	197	48 45	258	38 55	288
87	59 20	350	60 12	061	60 28	108	54 18	156	64 30	199	47 49	258	38 00	288
88	59 09	348	61 02	061	61 22	109	54 41	157	64 10	201	46 52	259	37 05	288
89	58 57	347	61 52	060	62 17	110	55 02	159	63 48	203	45 56	259	36 10	288

LHA ♈	Hc	Zn	Hc	Zn	Hc	Zn	Hc	Zn	Hc	Zn	Hc	Zn	Hc	Zn
	Dubhe		◆REGULUS		Alphard		SIRIUS		◆RIGEL		ALDEBARAN		◆CAPELLA	
90	20 36	029	29 37	085	32 50	112	55 22	160	63 24	205	70 02	274	58 43	346
91	21 04	029	30 34	085	33 43	112	55 41	162	62 58	207	69 04	275	58 28	345
92	21 32	029	31 32	086	34 36	113	55 58	164	62 31	209	68 07	275	58 13	343
93	22 01	029	32 29	086	35 29	113	56 13	165	62 02	211	67 09	275	57 55	342
94	22 29	029	33 27	086	36 22	114	56 27	167	61 31	213	66 12	275	57 37	341
95	22 57	029	34 24	086	37 15	115	56 39	169	60 59	215	65 14	275	57 18	340
96	23 25	029	35 22	087	38 07	115	56 49	170	60 26	216	64 17	275	56 57	339
97	23 53	029	36 20	087	38 59	116	56 58	172	59 51	218	63 19	275	56 36	338
98	24 21	029	37 17	087	39 51	116	57 05	174	59 15	220	62 22	275	56 14	337
99	24 49	029	38 15	087	40 42	117	57 10	176	58 38	221	61 25	275	55 50	336
100	25 17	029	39 12	088	41 33	118	57 14	177	57 59	222	60 27	275	55 26	335
101	25 44	029	40 10	088	42 24	118	57 16	179	57 20	224	59 30	276	55 01	334
102	26 12	028	41 08	088	43 15	119	57 15	181	56 39	225	58 32	276	54 35	333
103	26 39	028	42 05	088	44 05	120	57 14	183	55 58	226	57 35	276	54 08	332
104	27 06	028	43 03	089	44 55	121	57 10	185	55 16	228	56 38	276	53 40	331
	Dubhe		◆REGULUS		Alphard		SIRIUS		◆RIGEL		ALDEBARAN		◆CAPELLA	
105	27 34	028	44 01	089	45 44	121	57 05	186	54 33	229	55 40	276	53 11	330
106	28 01	028	44 58	089	46 34	122	56 57	188	53 49	230	54 43	276	52 42	329
107	28 27	028	45 56	089	47 22	123	56 48	190	53 04	231	53 46	276	52 12	328
108	28 54	027	46 54	090	48 10	124	56 38	191	52 19	232	52 48	276	51 42	328
109	29 20	027	47 51	090	48 58	125	56 26	193	51 33	233	51 51	277	51 11	327
110	29 47	027	48 49	090	49 45	126	56 12	195	50 47	234	50 54	277	50 39	326
111	30 13	027	49 47	090	50 32	127	55 56	196	50 00	235	49 56	277	50 06	325
112	30 39	027	50 44	091	51 18	128	55 39	198	49 12	236	48 59	277	49 33	325
113	31 04	026	51 42	091	52 03	129	55 20	200	48 24	237	48 02	277	49 00	324
114	31 30	026	52 40	091	52 48	130	55 00	201	47 36	238	47 05	277	48 26	324
115	31 55	026	53 37	092	53 32	131	54 38	203	46 47	239	46 07	277	47 51	323
116	32 20	026	54 35	092	54 15	132	54 15	204	45 57	239	45 10	278	47 17	322
117	32 45	025	55 33	092	54 58	133	53 51	206	45 07	240	44 13	278	46 41	322
118	33 09	025	56 30	093	55 39	134	53 25	207	44 17	241	43 16	278	46 05	321
119	33 34	025	57 28	093	56 20	136	52 58	209	43 27	242	42 19	278	45 29	321
	Dubhe		◆Denebola		Alphard		◆SIRIUS		RIGEL		ALDEBARAN		◆CAPELLA	
120	33 57	024	34 43	083	57 00	137	52 30	210	42 36	242	41 22	278	44 53	320
121	34 21	024	35 41	083	57 39	138	52 00	211	41 45	243	40 25	278	44 16	320
122	34 44	024	36 38	084	58 16	140	51 30	213	40 53	244	39 28	278	43 38	320
123	35 08	023	37 35	084	58 53	141	50 58	214	40 01	244	38 31	279	43 01	319
124	35 30	023	38 33	084	59 29	143	50 25	215	39 09	245	37 34	279	42 23	319
125	35 53	023	39 30	084	60 03	144	49 52	216	38 17	245	36 37	279	41 45	318
126	36 15	022	40 27	084	60 36	146	49 17	218	37 24	246	35 40	279	41 06	318
127	36 36	022	41 25	085	61 07	148	48 41	219	36 31	247	34 43	279	40 28	318
128	36 58	022	42 22	085	61 37	150	48 05	220	35 38	247	33 46	279	39 49	317
129	37 19	021	43 20	085	62 05	151	47 28	221	34 45	248	32 49	280	39 09	317
130	37 39	021	44 17	085	62 32	153	46 49	222	33 52	248	31 52	280	38 30	317
131	38 00	020	45 15	085	62 57	155	46 10	223	32 58	249	30 55	280	37 50	316
132	38 19	020	46 12	086	63 20	157	45 31	224	32 04	249	29 58	280	37 11	316
133	38 39	019	47 10	086	63 42	159	44 50	225	31 10	250	29 02	280	36 31	316
134	38 58	019	48 07	086	64 01	162	44 09	226	30 16	250	28 05	281	35 50	316
	Dubhe		◆ARCTURUS		SPICA		◆Alphard		SIRIUS		BETELGEUSE		◆CAPELLA	
135	39 16	018	15 12	074	18 48	108	64 18	164	43 27	227	44 14	265	35 10	316
136	39 34	018	16 07	074	19 43	109	64 33	166	42 45	228	43 17	265	34 30	315
137	39 52	018	17 03	074	20 37	109	64 46	168	42 02	229	42 19	265	33 49	315
138	40 09	017	17 59	075	21 32	109	64 57	170	41 19	229	41 22	266	33 08	315
139	40 26	017	18 54	075	22 26	110	65 05	173	40 35	230	40 24	266	32 27	315
140	40 42	016	19 50	075	23 20	110	65 11	175	39 50	231	39 27	266	31 46	315
141	40 58	015	20 46	075	24 15	111	65 15	177	39 05	232	38 29	267	31 05	315
142	41 13	015	21 41	075	25 08	111	65 17	180	38 19	233	37 32	267	30 24	314
143	41 27	014	22 37	076	26 02	111	65 16	182	37 33	233	36 34	267	29 43	314
144	41 41	014	23 33	076	26 56	112	65 12	185	36 47	234	35 37	268	29 02	314
145	41 55	013	24 29	076	27 49	112	65 06	187	36 00	235	34 39	268	28 20	314
146	42 08	013	25 25	076	28 42	113	64 58	189	35 13	235	33 41	268	27 39	314
147	42 20	012	26 21	076	29 36	113	64 48	191	34 25	236	32 44	269	26 57	314
148	42 32	012	27 17	076	30 28	114	64 35	194	33 37	237	31 46	269	26 16	314
149	42 44	011	28 13	077	31 21	114	64 21	196	32 49	237	30 48	269	25 34	314
	Dubhe		◆ARCTURUS		SPICA		◆Alphard		SIRIUS		BETELGEUSE		◆CAPELLA	
150	42 54	010	29 09	077	32 14	115	64 04	198	32 00	238	29 51	269	24 52	314
151	43 04	010	30 05	077	33 06	115	63 45	200	31 11	238	28 53	270	24 11	314
152	43 14	009	31 02	077	33 58	116	63 24	202	30 22	239	27 55	270	23 29	314
153	43 23	009	31 58	077	34 49	117	63 01	204	29 33	240	26 58	270	22 47	314
154	43 31	008	32 54	077	35 41	117	62 36	206	28 43	240	26 00	271	22 06	314
155	43 39	007	33 50	077	36 32	118	62 10	208	27 53	241	25 02	271	21 24	314
156	43 46	007	34 47	078	37 23	118	61 42	210	27 02	241	24 05	271	20 42	314
157	43 52	006	35 43	078	38 14	119	61 12	212	26 12	242	23 07	271	20 01	314
158	43 58	005	36 39	078	39 04	120	60 41	214	25 21	242	22 09	272	19 19	314
159	44 03	005	37 36	078	39 54	120	60 08	215	24 30	243	21 12	272	18 38	314
160	44 07	004	38 32	078	40 44	121	59 34	217	23 38	243	20 14	272	17 56	314
161	44 11	003	39 29	078	41 33	122	58 59	218	22 47	244	19 16	272	17 15	314
162	44 14	003	40 25	078	42 22	122	58 22	220	21 55	244	18 19	273	16 33	314
163	44 16	002	41 22	078	43 10	123	57 45	221	21 03	244	17 21	273	15 52	314
164	44 18	001	42 18	078	43 58	124	57 06	223	20 11	245	16 23	273	15 10	314
	◆Dubhe		Alkaid		ARCTURUS		◆SPICA		Suhail		◆PROCYON		POLLUX	
165	44 19	001	42 27	036	43 15	079	44 46	125	25 16	202	39 50	263	43 49	294
166	44 20	000	43 01	036	44 11	079	45 33	126	24 54	203	38 53	264	42 57	294
167	44 20	359	43 35	035	45 08	079	46 20	126	24 31	203	37 55	264	42 04	294
168	44 19	359	44 08	035	46 04	079	47 06	127	24 08	204	36 58	264	41 11	293
169	44 17	358	44 41	034	47 01	079	47 51	128	23 44	205	36 01	265	40 18	293
170	44 15	357	45 13	034	47 57	079	48 36	129	23 20	205	35 03	265	39 25	293
171	44 12	357	45 45	033	48 54	079	49 21	130	22 55	206	34 06	265	38 32	293
172	44 08	356	46 17	033	49 51	079	50 05	131	22 29	207	33 08	266	37 39	293
173	44 04	355	46 48	032	50 47	079	50 48	132	22 03	207	32 11	266	36 46	293
174	43 59	355	47 18	032	51 44	079	51 30	133	21 36	208	31 13	266	35 53	293
175	43 54	354	47 48	031	52 41	079	52 12	134	21 09	209	30 15	267	35 00	293
176	43 48	354	48 18	030	53 37	079	52 52	136	20 41	209	29 18	267	34 07	293
177	43 41	353	48 47	030	54 34	079	53 32	137	20 13	210	28 20	267	33 14	293
178	43 33	352	49 15	029	55 31	079	54 11	138	19 44	210	27 23	268	32 21	293
179	43 25	352	49 42	028	56 27	079	54 49	139	19 15	211	26 25	268	31 28	293

LAT 16°N

LHA ♈	Hc	Zn	Hc	Zn	Hc	Zn	Hc	Zn	Hc	Zn	Hc	Zn	Hc	Zn
	◆ Alkaid		ANTARES		◆ SPICA		Gienah		◆ REGULUS		POLLUX		Dubhe	
180	50 10	028	11 51	122	55 26	141	56 08	173	62 49	265	30 35	293	43 17	351
181	50 36	027	12 40	123	56 02	142	56 14	175	61 52	265	29 42	293	43 07	350
182	51 02	026	13 28	123	56 37	143	56 19	176	60 54	266	28 50	294	42 58	350
183	51 27	025	14 16	123	57 11	145	56 21	178	59 57	266	27 57	294	42 47	349
184	51 51	024	15 04	124	57 43	146	56 22	180	58 59	267	27 04	294	42 36	349
185	52 14	024	15 52	124	58 15	148	56 22	181	58 02	267	26 11	294	42 24	348
186	52 37	023	16 40	125	58 44	150	56 20	183	57 04	267	25 18	294	42 12	347
187	52 59	022	17 27	125	59 13	151	56 15	185	56 06	268	24 26	294	41 59	347
188	53 20	021	18 14	126	59 40	153	56 10	187	55 09	268	23 33	294	41 46	346
189	53 40	020	19 01	126	60 05	155	56 02	188	54 11	268	22 40	294	41 32	346
190	53 59	019	19 47	127	60 29	157	55 53	190	53 13	269	21 48	294	41 17	345
191	54 17	018	20 33	127	60 51	158	55 42	192	52 16	269	20 55	294	41 02	345
192	54 35	017	21 19	128	61 11	160	55 30	193	51 18	269	20 03	295	40 47	344
193	54 51	016	22 05	128	61 30	162	55 16	195	50 20	269	19 10	295	40 31	344
194	55 06	015	22 50	129	61 46	164	55 00	197	49 23	270	18 18	295	40 14	343
	Kochab		◆ VEGA		Rasalhague		ANTARES		◆ SPICA		◆ REGULUS		Dubhe	
195	29 54	008	14 16	053	23 26	083	23 35	129	62 01	166	48 25	270	39 57	343
196	30 02	008	15 02	053	24 23	083	24 19	130	62 13	168	47 27	270	39 40	342
197	30 10	008	15 48	053	25 20	083	25 04	130	62 24	170	46 30	271	39 22	342
198	30 18	008	16 34	054	26 17	084	25 47	131	62 33	173	45 32	271	39 04	341
199	30 25	007	17 21	054	27 15	084	26 31	131	62 39	175	44 34	271	38 45	341
200	30 33	007	18 07	054	28 12	084	27 14	132	62 43	177	43 37	271	38 26	340
201	30 39	007	18 54	054	29 09	084	27 57	133	62 45	179	42 39	272	38 06	340
202	30 46	006	19 40	054	30 07	085	28 39	133	62 45	181	41 41	272	37 46	339
203	30 52	006	20 27	054	31 04	085	29 21	134	62 43	183	40 44	272	37 25	339
204	30 58	006	21 14	054	32 02	085	30 02	135	62 39	185	39 46	272	37 05	339
205	31 04	006	22 00	054	32 59	085	30 43	135	62 32	187	38 48	273	36 43	338
206	31 10	005	22 47	054	33 57	085	31 23	136	62 24	190	37 51	273	36 22	338
207	31 15	005	23 34	054	34 54	086	32 03	137	62 13	192	36 53	273	36 00	337
208	31 20	005	24 20	054	35 52	086	32 43	137	62 01	194	35 56	273	35 37	337
209	31 24	004	25 07	054	36 49	086	33 21	138	61 46	196	34 58	274	35 15	337
	Kochab		◆ VEGA		Rasalhague		◆ ANTARES		SPICA		◆ REGULUS		Dubhe	
210	31 28	004	25 54	054	37 47	086	34 00	139	61 29	198	34 01	274	34 52	336
211	31 32	004	26 41	054	38 44	087	34 37	140	61 11	200	33 03	274	34 29	336
212	31 36	003	27 27	054	39 42	087	35 14	140	60 51	202	32 05	274	34 05	336
213	31 39	003	28 14	054	40 40	087	35 51	141	60 29	203	31 08	274	33 41	335
214	31 42	003	29 01	054	41 37	087	36 27	142	60 05	205	30 10	275	33 17	335
215	31 45	002	29 48	054	42 35	088	37 02	143	59 40	207	29 13	275	32 53	335
216	31 47	002	30 34	054	43 32	088	37 36	144	59 13	209	28 16	275	32 28	335
217	31 49	002	31 21	054	44 30	088	38 10	145	58 44	210	27 18	275	32 03	334
218	31 51	002	32 07	054	45 28	088	38 43	145	58 14	212	26 21	276	31 38	334
219	31 52	001	32 54	054	46 25	088	39 16	146	57 43	214	25 23	276	31 13	334
220	31 53	001	33 41	054	47 23	089	39 47	147	57 11	215	24 26	276	30 47	334
221	31 54	001	34 27	054	48 21	089	40 18	148	56 37	217	23 29	276	30 21	333
222	31 54	000	35 13	053	49 18	089	40 48	149	56 02	218	22 31	276	29 55	333
223	31 54	000	36 00	053	50 16	090	41 17	150	55 26	219	21 34	277	29 29	333
224	31 54	000	36 46	053	51 14	090	41 45	151	54 49	221	20 37	277	29 02	333
	VEGA		◆ ALTAIR		Nunki		ANTARES		◆ SPICA		Denebola		◆ Alkaid	
225	37 32	053	18 48	086	18 44	126	42 12	152	54 11	222	44 12	275	53 41	340
226	38 18	053	19 46	086	19 31	126	42 38	153	53 32	223	43 15	275	53 21	339
227	39 04	053	20 43	086	20 18	127	43 04	154	52 52	224	42 17	275	53 00	338
228	39 50	052	21 41	087	21 04	127	43 28	156	52 11	226	41 20	275	52 38	337
229	40 35	052	22 38	087	21 49	128	43 51	157	51 30	227	40 22	276	52 16	336
230	41 21	052	23 36	087	22 35	128	44 14	158	50 47	228	39 25	276	51 52	336
231	42 06	052	24 33	087	23 20	129	44 35	159	50 04	229	38 28	276	51 28	335
232	42 51	051	25 31	088	24 05	129	44 55	160	49 21	230	37 30	276	51 03	334
233	43 36	051	26 29	088	24 49	130	45 14	161	48 36	231	36 33	276	50 38	333
234	44 21	051	27 26	088	25 34	130	45 32	163	47 51	232	35 36	277	50 11	332
235	45 06	051	28 24	088	26 17	131	45 49	164	47 06	233	34 38	277	49 44	332
236	45 50	050	29 22	089	27 01	132	46 04	165	46 19	234	33 41	277	49 17	331
237	46 34	050	30 19	089	27 44	132	46 18	166	45 33	234	32 44	277	48 48	330
238	47 18	049	31 17	089	28 26	133	46 32	167	44 46	235	31 47	277	48 20	330
239	48 02	049	32 15	089	29 08	133	46 43	169	43 58	236	30 50	278	47 50	329
	◆ VEGA		ALTAIR		Nunki		◆ ANTARES		SPICA		◆ ARCTURUS		Alkaid	
240	48 45	049	33 12	090	29 50	134	46 54	170	43 10	237	65 07	281	47 20	328
241	49 29	048	34 10	090	30 31	135	47 03	171	42 21	238	64 11	281	46 50	328
242	50 11	048	35 08	090	31 12	135	47 11	173	41 33	238	63 14	281	46 19	327
243	50 54	047	36 05	091	31 52	136	47 18	174	40 43	239	62 17	281	45 47	327
244	51 36	047	37 03	091	32 32	137	47 24	175	39 54	240	61 21	281	45 15	326
245	52 18	046	38 01	091	33 11	138	47 28	177	39 04	240	60 24	281	44 43	326
246	52 59	045	38 58	091	33 50	138	47 30	178	38 13	241	59 27	281	44 10	325
247	53 40	045	39 56	092	34 28	139	47 32	179	37 23	242	58 31	281	43 37	325
248	54 20	044	40 54	092	35 05	140	47 32	181	36 32	242	57 34	281	43 03	324
249	55 00	043	41 51	092	35 42	141	47 31	182	35 41	243	56 37	281	42 29	324
250	55 39	043	42 49	093	36 19	141	47 28	183	34 49	243	55 41	281	41 55	323
251	56 18	042	43 46	093	36 54	142	47 24	185	33 57	244	54 44	281	41 20	323
252	56 56	041	44 44	093	37 29	143	47 19	186	33 05	245	53 47	281	40 45	322
253	57 34	040	45 42	094	38 03	144	47 13	187	32 13	245	52 51	281	40 10	322
254	58 11	039	46 39	094	38 37	145	47 05	188	31 21	246	51 54	281	39 34	322
	◆ VEGA		ALTAIR		◆ Nunki		ANTARES		SPICA		◆ ARCTURUS		Alkaid	
255	58 47	038	47 37	094	39 10	146	46 56	190	30 28	246	50 57	281	38 59	321
256	59 22	037	48 34	095	39 42	147	46 45	191	29 35	247	50 01	281	38 22	321
257	59 57	036	49 32	095	40 13	148	46 34	192	28 42	247	49 04	281	37 46	321
258	60 30	035	50 29	095	40 43	149	46 21	194	27 49	248	48 07	281	37 10	320
259	61 03	034	51 27	096	41 13	150	46 07	195	26 55	248	47 11	281	36 33	320
260	61 35	033	52 24	096	41 41	151	45 51	196	26 02	249	46 14	281	35 56	320
261	62 06	032	53 21	097	42 09	152	45 35	197	25 08	249	45 17	281	35 18	320
262	62 35	030	54 18	097	42 36	153	45 17	198	24 14	249	44 21	281	34 41	319
263	63 04	029	55 16	098	43 02	154	44 58	200	23 20	250	43 24	281	34 03	319
264	63 31	028	56 13	098	43 27	155	44 38	201	22 26	250	42 28	281	33 26	319
265	63 57	026	57 10	098	43 51	156	44 17	202	21 32	251	41 31	282	32 48	319
266	64 22	025	58 07	099	44 14	157	43 55	203	20 37	251	40 35	282	32 10	319
267	64 45	023	59 04	100	44 35	158	43 32	204	19 42	251	39 38	282	31 32	318
268	65 07	021	60 01	100	44 56	160	43 08	205	18 48	252	38 42	282	30 53	318
269	65 27	020	60 57	101	45 16	161	42 43	206	17 53	252	37 45	282	30 15	318

LHA ♈	Hc	Zn	Hc	Zn	Hc	Zn	Hc	Zn	Hc	Zn	Hc	Zn	Hc	Zn
	VEGA		◆ DENEB		Enif		◆ Nunki		ANTARES		◆ ARCTURUS		Alkaid	
270	65 46	018	45 14	040	35 01	089	45 34	162	42 16	207	36 49	282	29 36	318
271	66 03	016	45 51	040	35 59	089	45 52	163	41 49	209	35 53	282	28 58	318
272	66 18	014	46 28	039	36 57	089	46 08	164	41 21	210	34 56	282	28 19	318
273	66 32	013	47 04	039	37 54	090	46 23	166	40 52	211	34 00	283	27 40	318
274	66 43	011	47 40	038	38 52	090	46 37	167	40 23	212	33 04	283	27 01	318
275	66 53	009	48 16	038	39 50	090	46 49	168	39 52	212	32 08	283	26 22	318
276	67 01	007	48 51	037	40 47	091	47 00	169	39 21	213	31 11	283	25 43	317
277	67 06	005	49 26	037	41 45	091	47 10	171	38 49	214	30 15	283	25 04	317
278	67 10	003	50 00	036	42 43	091	47 19	172	38 16	215	29 19	283	24 25	317
279	67 12	001	50 34	035	43 40	091	47 26	173	37 42	216	28 23	283	23 46	317
280	67 12	359	51 07	035	44 38	092	47 32	175	37 08	217	27 27	284	23 07	317
281	67 09	357	51 39	034	45 36	092	47 37	176	36 33	218	26 31	284	22 28	317
282	67 05	355	52 11	033	46 33	092	47 41	177	35 57	219	25 35	284	21 49	317
283	66 59	353	52 42	032	47 31	093	47 43	179	35 21	219	24 39	284	21 10	317
284	66 50	351	53 13	032	48 29	093	47 43	180	34 44	220	23 43	284	20 30	317
	◆ DENEB		Alpheratz		◆ FOMALHAUT		Nunki		ANTARES		◆ Rasalhague		VEGA	
285	53 43	031	18 36	064	16 41	128	47 43	181	34 06	221	69 17	263	66 40	349
286	54 12	030	19 28	064	17 26	129	47 41	183	33 28	222	68 20	264	66 28	347
287	54 40	029	20 20	064	18 11	129	47 38	184	32 49	223	67 22	264	66 14	345
288	55 07	028	21 12	064	18 55	130	47 33	185	32 10	223	66 25	265	65 59	343
289	55 34	027	22 04	064	19 39	130	47 27	187	31 30	224	65 27	265	65 41	342
290	56 00	026	22 56	065	20 23	131	47 20	188	30 50	225	64 30	266	65 22	340
291	56 25	025	23 48	065	21 07	131	47 11	189	30 09	225	63 32	266	65 01	338
292	56 49	024	24 40	065	21 50	132	47 01	190	29 28	226	62 35	266	64 39	337
293	57 12	023	25 32	065	22 32	132	46 50	192	28 46	227	61 37	267	64 15	335
294	57 34	022	26 25	065	23 15	133	46 38	193	28 04	227	60 40	267	63 50	333
295	57 55	021	27 17	065	23 57	134	46 24	194	27 21	228	59 42	268	63 24	332
296	58 15	020	28 09	065	24 38	134	46 09	196	26 38	229	58 44	268	62 56	331
297	58 33	018	29 02	065	25 20	135	45 53	197	25 55	229	57 47	268	62 27	329
298	58 51	017	29 54	065	26 00	135	45 36	198	25 11	230	56 49	269	61 57	328
299	59 07	016	30 46	065	26 41	136	45 18	199	24 27	230	55 51	269	61 26	327
	◆ DENEB		Schedar		Alpheratz		◆ FOMALHAUT		Nunki		◆ Rasalhague		VEGA	
300	59 22	015	24 05	035	31 39	065	27 21	137	44 58	200	54 54	269	60 54	326
301	59 36	013	24 38	034	32 31	065	28 00	137	44 37	202	53 56	269	60 21	324
302	59 49	012	25 10	034	33 23	065	28 39	138	44 16	203	52 58	270	59 47	323
303	60 00	011	25 43	034	34 16	065	29 18	139	43 53	204	52 01	270	59 12	322
304	60 10	009	26 15	034	35 08	065	29 56	139	43 29	205	51 03	270	58 37	321
305	60 18	008	26 48	034	36 00	065	30 33	140	43 04	206	50 05	271	58 00	320
306	60 25	006	27 20	034	36 53	065	31 10	141	42 39	207	49 08	271	57 23	320
307	60 31	005	27 52	034	37 45	065	31 46	141	42 12	208	48 10	271	56 46	319
308	60 35	004	28 24	034	38 38	065	32 22	142	41 44	209	47 12	271	56 07	318
309	60 38	002	28 56	033	39 30	065	32 57	143	41 16	210	46 15	272	55 28	317
310	60 40	001	29 28	033	40 22	065	33 32	144	40 46	211	45 17	272	54 49	316
311	60 40	359	29 59	033	41 15	065	34 05	144	40 16	212	44 19	272	54 09	316
312	60 38	358	30 31	033	42 07	065	34 39	145	39 45	213	43 22	272	53 28	315
313	60 35	356	31 02	033	42 59	065	35 11	146	39 13	214	42 24	273	52 47	314
314	60 31	355	31 33	033	43 51	065	35 43	147	38 40	215	41 27	273	52 06	314
	◆ Alpheratz		Diphda		◆ FOMALHAUT		Nunki		◆ Rasalhague		VEGA		DENEB	
315	44 43	065	25 11	119	36 14	148	38 07	216	40 29	273	51 24	313	60 25	354
316	45 35	064	26 02	120	36 44	149	37 32	217	39 31	273	50 42	313	60 18	352
317	46 27	064	26 52	120	37 14	150	36 58	218	38 34	273	50 00	312	60 10	351
318	47 19	064	27 41	121	37 43	150	36 22	218	37 36	274	49 17	312	60 00	349
319	48 11	064	28 31	121	38 11	151	35 46	219	36 39	274	48 34	311	59 48	348
320	49 03	064	29 20	122	38 38	152	35 09	220	35 41	274	47 50	311	59 36	347
321	49 54	063	30 09	122	39 04	153	34 32	221	34 44	274	47 06	310	59 22	345
322	50 46	063	30 57	123	39 30	154	33 54	222	33 46	275	46 22	310	59 07	344
323	51 37	063	31 45	124	39 54	155	33 15	222	32 49	275	45 38	310	58 50	343
324	52 29	063	32 33	124	40 18	156	32 36	223	31 51	275	44 54	309	58 33	342
325	53 20	062	33 21	125	40 41	157	31 56	224	30 54	275	44 09	309	58 14	340
326	54 11	062	34 08	126	41 03	158	31 16	225	29 56	275	43 24	309	57 54	339
327	55 02	062	34 55	126	41 23	159	30 35	225	28 59	276	42 39	308	57 33	338
328	55 52	061	35 41	127	41 43	161	29 54	226	28 02	276	41 54	308	57 11	337
329	56 43	061	36 27	128	42 02	162	29 12	227	27 04	276	41 08	308	56 48	336
	◆ Mirfak		Hamal		Diphda		◆ FOMALHAUT		ALTAIR		◆ VEGA		DENEB	
330	17 42	042	31 35	072	37 12	128	42 19	163	57 53	261	40 23	308	56 24	335
331	18 20	042	32 30	072	37 58	129	42 36	164	56 56	262	39 37	308	55 59	334
332	18 59	042	33 25	072	38 42	130	42 51	165	55 59	262	38 51	307	55 33	333
333	19 38	042	34 20	072	39 26	131	43 06	166	55 02	263	38 05	307	55 07	332
334	20 16	042	35 14	072	40 10	131	43 19	167	54 05	263	37 19	307	54 39	331
335	20 55	042	36 09	072	40 53	132	43 31	168	53 07	263	36 33	307	54 11	330
336	21 33	042	37 04	072	41 35	133	43 42	170	52 10	264	35 47	307	53 42	329
337	22 12	042	37 59	072	42 17	134	43 52	171	51 13	264	35 01	307	53 12	328
338	22 51	042	38 54	072	42 58	135	44 01	172	50 15	265	34 14	306	52 41	328
339	23 29	042	39 49	072	43 39	136	44 08	173	49 18	265	33 28	306	52 10	327
340	24 08	042	40 44	072	44 19	137	44 14	174	48 20	265	32 41	306	51 38	326
341	24 46	042	41 39	072	44 58	138	44 19	176	47 23	266	31 55	306	51 06	325
342	25 25	042	42 34	073	45 37	139	44 23	177	46 25	266	31 08	306	50 33	325
343	26 03	042	43 29	073	46 14	140	44 26	178	45 28	266	30 21	306	49 59	324
344	26 42	042	44 24	073	46 51	141	44 27	179	44 30	267	29 35	306	49 25	323
	Schedar		◆ Mirfak		ALDEBARAN		Diphda		◆ FOMALHAUT		ALTAIR		◆ DENEB	
345	45 05	019	27 20	042	09 53	075	47 28	142	44 27	180	43 33	267	48 50	323
346	45 24	019	27 58	042	10 49	076	48 03	143	44 26	182	42 35	267	48 15	322
347	45 42	018	28 37	041	11 45	076	48 37	144	44 24	183	41 37	268	47 39	322
348	46 00	018	29 15	041	12 41	076	49 11	145	44 20	184	40 40	268	47 03	321
349	46 17	017	29 53	041	13 37	076	49 43	146	44 16	185	39 42	268	46 27	321
350	46 33	016	30 30	041	14 33	077	50 14	148	44 10	187	38 44	269	45 50	320
351	46 49	015	31 08	041	15 29	077	50 45	149	44 03	188	37 47	269	45 13	320
352	47 04	015	31 46	041	16 25	077	51 14	150	43 54	189	36 49	269	44 35	319
353	47 18	014	32 23	040	17 21	077	51 42	152	43 45	190	35 51	270	43 57	319
354	47 32	013	33 01	040	18 18	077	52 09	153	43 34	191	34 54	270	43 19	318
355	47 45	013	33 38	040	19 14	078	52 35	154	43 22	192	33 56	270	42 41	318
356	47 57	012	34 15	040	20 10	078	52 59	156	43 09	194	32 58	270	42 02	318
357	48 08	011	34 52	040	21 07	078	53 22	157	42 55	195	32 01	271	41 23	317
358	48 19	010	35 29	039	22 03	078	53 44	159	42 40	196	31 03	271	40 44	317
359	48 29	009	36 05	039	23 00	078	54 04	160	42 23	197	30 05	271	40 04	317

LAT 15°N

LHA ♈	Hc	Zn	Hc	Zn	Hc	Zn	Hc	Zn	Hc	Zn	Hc	Zn	Hc	Zn
	CAPELLA		◆ ALDEBARAN		Acamar		ACHERNAR		◆ FOMALHAUT		ALTAIR		◆ DENEB	
0	18 00	046	23 44	078	20 54	145	15 00	167	43 03	198	29 06	272	38 41	317
1	18 42	046	24 41	078	21 27	145	15 14	167	42 44	200	28 08	272	38 01	316
2	19 23	046	25 38	079	22 00	146	15 26	168	42 24	201	27 10	272	37 21	316
3	20 05	046	26 35	079	22 32	147	15 39	168	42 03	202	26 12	273	36 41	316
4	20 47	046	27 31	079	23 04	147	15 50	169	41 41	203	25 14	273	36 00	316
5	21 28	046	28 28	079	23 35	148	16 02	169	41 19	204	24 16	273	35 20	315
6	22 10	046	29 25	079	24 05	148	16 12	170	40 55	205	23 19	273	34 39	315
7	22 52	046	30 22	079	24 35	149	16 22	170	40 30	206	22 21	274	33 58	315
8	23 33	046	31 19	080	25 05	150	16 32	171	40 04	207	21 23	274	33 17	315
9	24 15	046	32 16	080	25 34	150	16 41	171	39 38	208	20 25	274	32 36	315
10	24 57	046	33 13	080	26 02	151	16 50	172	39 10	209	19 27	274	31 54	314
11	25 38	046	34 10	080	26 30	152	16 58	172	38 42	210	18 29	275	31 13	314
12	26 20	046	35 07	080	26 57	152	17 05	173	38 13	211	17 32	275	30 32	314
13	27 01	046	36 04	080	27 23	153	17 12	173	37 43	212	16 34	275	29 50	314
14	27 42	046	37 02	080	27 49	154	17 18	174	37 12	212	15 36	275	29 08	314
	CAPELLA		◆ ALDEBARAN		RIGEL		ACHERNAR		◆ FOMALHAUT		Enif		◆ DENEB	
15	28 24	045	37 59	081	22 39	106	17 24	175	36 41	213	42 12	270	28 26	314
16	29 05	045	38 56	081	23 35	106	17 29	175	36 09	214	41 14	270	27 45	314
17	29 46	045	39 53	081	24 30	107	17 34	176	35 36	215	40 16	270	27 03	314
18	30 27	045	40 50	081	25 26	107	17 38	176	35 02	216	39 18	271	26 21	314
19	31 08	045	41 48	081	26 21	107	17 41	177	34 28	217	38 20	271	25 39	313
20	31 49	045	42 45	081	27 16	108	17 44	177	33 53	217	37 22	271	24 57	313
21	32 30	045	43 42	081	28 11	108	17 47	178	33 18	218	36 25	271	24 14	313
22	33 10	044	44 39	081	29 06	109	17 48	179	32 42	219	35 27	272	23 32	313
23	33 51	044	45 37	082	30 01	109	17 50	179	32 05	220	34 29	272	22 50	313
24	34 31	044	46 34	082	30 56	109	17 50	180	31 28	220	33 31	272	22 08	313
25	35 11	044	47 31	082	31 51	110	17 50	180	30 50	221	32 33	272	21 26	313
26	35 51	044	48 29	082	32 45	110	17 50	181	30 12	222	31 35	273	20 44	313
27	36 31	043	49 26	082	33 39	111	17 49	181	29 33	222	30 37	273	20 01	313
28	37 11	043	50 24	082	34 33	111	17 47	182	28 53	223	29 39	273	19 19	313
29	37 50	043	51 21	082	35 27	112	17 45	183	28 14	224	28 41	273	18 37	313
	Mirfak		◆ CAPELLA		ALDEBARAN		RIGEL		◆ ACHERNAR		FOMALHAUT		◆ Alpheratz	
30	51 01	022	38 29	042	52 18	082	36 21	112	17 42	183	27 33	224	60 47	304
31	51 22	021	39 08	042	53 16	082	37 15	113	17 38	184	26 53	225	59 59	303
32	51 43	020	39 47	042	54 13	082	38 08	113	17 34	184	26 12	226	59 10	302
33	52 02	019	40 25	041	55 11	082	39 01	114	17 30	185	25 30	226	58 21	302
34	52 21	018	41 04	041	56 08	083	39 54	115	17 25	185	24 48	227	57 32	301
35	52 39	017	41 41	041	57 06	083	40 46	115	17 19	186	24 06	227	56 42	301
36	52 55	016	42 19	040	58 03	083	41 39	116	17 13	186	23 23	228	55 52	300
37	53 11	015	42 56	040	59 01	083	42 31	116	17 06	187	22 40	228	55 02	300
38	53 26	014	43 33	039	59 58	083	43 22	117	16 59	188	21 56	229	54 12	299
39	53 40	013	44 10	039	60 56	083	44 14	118	16 51	188	21 13	229	53 21	299
40	53 53	012	44 46	038	61 53	083	45 05	119	16 42	189	20 29	230	52 30	299
41	54 05	011	45 22	038	62 51	083	45 56	119	16 33	189	19 44	230	51 39	298
42	54 16	010	45 57	037	63 48	083	46 46	120	16 24	190	18 59	231	50 48	298
43	54 26	009	46 32	037	64 46	083	47 36	121	16 14	190	18 14	231	49 57	298
44	54 35	008	47 07	036	65 43	083	48 26	122	16 03	191	17 29	232	49 06	297
	CAPELLA		◆ POLLUX		PROCYON		SIRIUS		◆ ACHERNAR		Diphda		◆ Alpheratz	
45	47 41	036	23 02	066	20 37	090	25 53	117	15 52	191	43 06	227	48 14	297
46	48 14	035	23 55	066	21 35	090	26 45	118	15 40	192	42 23	228	47 23	297
47	48 47	034	24 48	066	22 33	091	27 36	118	15 28	192	41 40	228	46 31	297
48	49 20	034	25 41	066	23 31	091	28 27	119	15 15	193	40 57	229	45 39	297
49	49 52	033	26 33	066	24 29	091	29 17	119	15 02	193	40 13	230	44 47	296
50	50 23	032	27 26	066	25 27	091	30 08	120	14 48	194	39 28	231	43 55	296
51	50 54	032	28 19	066	26 25	092	30 58	121	14 34	194	38 43	231	43 03	296
52	51 24	031	29 12	066	27 22	092	31 47	121	14 20	195	37 57	232	42 11	296
53	51 53	030	30 05	066	28 20	092	32 37	122	14 04	195	37 11	233	41 19	296
54	52 22	029	30 58	066	29 18	092	33 26	122	13 49	196	36 25	234	40 27	296
55	52 50	028	31 51	066	30 16	093	34 15	123	13 33	196	35 38	234	39 35	296
56	53 17	028	32 44	066	31 14	093	35 03	124	13 16	197	34 51	235	38 43	296
57	53 44	027	33 37	066	32 12	093	35 51	124	12 59	197	34 03	236	37 50	296
58	54 09	026	34 30	066	33 10	094	36 39	125	12 41	198	33 15	236	36 58	295
59	54 34	025	35 23	066	34 08	094	37 27	125	12 23	198	32 27	237	36 06	295
	CAPELLA		◆ POLLUX		PROCYON		SIRIUS		◆ CANOPUS		Diphda		◆ Hamal	
60	54 58	024	36 16	066	35 05	094	38 14	126	15 30	158	31 38	237	62 17	292
61	55 21	023	37 09	066	36 03	095	39 00	127	15 51	159	30 49	238	61 24	292
62	55 43	022	38 02	066	37 01	095	39 46	128	16 12	159	30 00	239	60 30	291
63	56 03	021	38 55	066	37 59	095	40 32	128	16 32	160	29 10	239	59 36	291
64	56 23	020	39 48	066	38 56	096	41 17	129	16 52	160	28 20	240	58 42	291
65	56 42	018	40 40	066	39 54	096	42 02	130	17 11	161	27 30	240	57 47	290
66	57 00	017	41 33	066	40 52	096	42 46	131	17 30	161	26 40	241	56 53	290
67	57 17	016	42 26	066	41 49	097	43 29	132	17 48	162	25 49	241	55 59	290
68	57 32	015	43 19	065	42 47	097	44 12	133	18 05	163	24 58	242	55 04	290
69	57 46	014	44 12	065	43 44	097	44 55	133	18 23	163	24 07	242	54 10	290
70	57 59	012	45 04	065	44 42	098	45 36	134	18 39	164	23 16	243	53 15	289
71	58 11	011	45 57	065	45 39	098	46 17	135	18 55	164	22 24	243	52 20	289
72	58 22	010	46 49	065	46 37	098	46 58	136	19 11	165	21 33	243	51 26	289
73	58 31	009	47 42	065	47 34	099	47 37	137	19 26	165	20 41	244	50 31	289
74	58 39	007	48 34	064	48 31	099	48 16	138	19 40	166	19 49	244	49 36	289
	CAPELLA		◆ POLLUX		PROCYON		SIRIUS		◆ CANOPUS		Acamar		◆ Hamal	
75	58 46	006	49 26	064	49 28	100	48 54	140	19 54	167	28 00	206	48 41	289
76	58 51	005	50 18	064	50 25	100	49 31	141	20 07	167	27 34	207	47 46	289
77	58 55	003	51 11	064	51 22	101	50 08	142	20 19	168	27 08	207	46 51	289
78	58 58	002	52 02	063	52 19	101	50 43	143	20 31	168	26 41	208	45 56	289
79	58 59	001	52 54	063	53 16	102	51 18	144	20 42	169	26 14	209	45 01	288
80	58 59	359	53 46	063	54 13	102	51 51	145	20 53	170	25 45	209	44 06	288
81	58 58	358	54 37	062	55 09	103	52 23	147	21 03	170	25 17	210	43 11	288
82	58 55	357	55 29	062	56 06	103	52 54	148	21 13	171	24 48	211	42 16	288
83	58 51	355	56 20	062	57 02	104	53 25	149	21 22	172	24 18	211	41 21	288
84	58 45	354	57 11	061	57 58	105	53 53	151	21 30	172	23 47	212	40 26	288
85	58 38	353	58 01	061	58 54	105	54 21	152	21 37	173	23 17	213	39 31	288
86	58 30	351	58 52	060	59 50	106	54 47	154	21 44	173	22 45	213	38 36	288
87	58 21	350	59 42	060	60 46	107	55 12	155	21 51	174	22 13	214	37 41	288
88	58 10	349	60 32	059	61 41	107	55 36	157	21 56	175	21 41	214	36 46	288
89	57 58	347	61 22	058	62 36	108	55 58	158	22 01	175	21 08	215	35 51	288

LHA ♈	Hc	Zn	Hc	Zn	Hc	Zn	Hc	Zn	Hc	Zn	Hc	Zn	Hc	Zn
	Dubhe		◆ REGULUS		Suhail		SIRIUS		◆ RIGEL		ALDEBARAN		◆ CAPELLA	
90	19 43	029	29 32	085	17 22	146	56 19	160	64 18	206	69 56	277	57 45	346
91	20 12	029	30 29	085	17 54	147	56 38	162	63 51	208	68 58	277	57 31	345
92	20 40	029	31 27	085	18 26	147	56 55	163	63 23	210	68 01	277	57 15	344
93	21 08	029	32 25	085	18 57	148	57 11	165	62 53	212	67 03	277	56 58	343
94	21 36	029	33 23	085	19 28	148	57 25	167	62 21	214	66 06	277	56 40	341
95	22 05	029	34 20	086	19 58	149	57 38	168	61 48	216	65 08	277	56 21	340
96	22 33	029	35 18	086	20 28	149	57 49	170	61 14	217	64 11	277	56 01	339
97	23 01	029	36 16	086	20 57	150	57 58	172	60 38	219	63 13	277	55 40	338
98	23 28	029	37 14	086	21 26	151	58 05	174	60 01	221	62 16	277	55 18	337
99	23 56	029	38 12	087	21 54	151	58 10	176	59 22	222	61 18	277	54 55	336
100	24 24	028	39 09	087	22 22	152	58 14	177	58 43	224	60 21	277	54 32	335
101	24 52	028	40 07	087	22 49	152	58 16	179	58 03	225	59 23	277	54 07	334
102	25 19	028	41 05	087	23 16	153	58 15	181	57 21	226	58 26	277	53 41	333
103	25 46	028	42 03	087	23 42	154	58 14	183	56 39	228	57 28	277	53 15	332
104	26 13	028	43 01	088	24 07	154	58 10	185	55 56	229	56 31	277	52 47	331
	Dubhe		◆ REGULUS		Suhail		◆ SIRIUS		RIGEL		ALDEBARAN		◆ CAPELLA	
105	26 40	028	43 59	088	24 32	155	58 04	186	55 12	230	55 33	277	52 19	331
106	27 07	028	44 57	088	24 56	156	57 57	188	54 27	231	54 36	278	51 51	330
107	27 34	027	45 55	088	25 20	156	57 48	190	53 42	232	53 38	278	51 21	329
108	28 01	027	46 53	089	25 43	157	57 37	192	52 56	233	52 41	278	50 51	328
109	28 27	027	47 51	089	26 05	158	57 24	194	52 09	234	51 43	278	50 20	328
110	28 53	027	48 49	089	26 27	158	57 10	195	51 22	235	50 46	278	49 49	327
111	29 19	027	49 46	089	26 48	159	56 54	197	50 34	236	49 49	278	49 17	326
112	29 45	026	50 44	089	27 09	160	56 36	199	49 45	237	48 51	278	48 44	325
113	30 11	026	51 42	090	27 28	160	56 17	200	48 57	238	47 54	278	48 11	325
114	30 36	026	52 40	090	27 47	161	55 56	202	48 07	239	46 57	278	47 37	324
115	31 01	026	53 38	090	28 06	162	55 34	203	47 18	239	45 59	278	47 03	324
116	31 26	025	54 36	091	28 23	163	55 10	205	46 27	240	45 02	279	46 29	323
117	31 51	025	55 34	091	28 40	163	54 45	206	45 37	241	44 05	279	45 54	323
118	32 15	025	56 32	091	28 56	164	54 18	208	44 46	242	43 07	279	45 18	322
119	32 39	024	57 30	091	29 12	165	53 51	209	43 55	242	42 10	279	44 42	322
	Dubhe		◆ Denebola		Suhail		◆ SIRIUS		RIGEL		ALDEBARAN		◆ CAPELLA	
120	33 03	024	34 36	083	29 26	166	53 22	211	43 03	243	41 13	279	44 06	321
121	33 26	024	35 33	083	29 40	167	52 52	212	42 11	244	40 16	279	43 30	321
122	33 50	023	36 31	083	29 53	167	52 20	213	41 19	244	39 18	279	42 53	320
123	34 12	023	37 28	083	30 05	168	51 48	215	40 27	245	38 21	279	42 15	320
124	34 35	023	38 26	083	30 17	169	51 14	216	39 34	246	37 24	280	41 38	319
125	34 57	022	39 24	083	30 28	170	50 40	217	38 41	246	36 27	280	41 00	319
126	35 19	022	40 21	084	30 37	171	50 04	218	37 48	247	35 30	280	40 22	319
127	35 41	022	41 19	084	30 46	171	49 28	219	36 55	247	34 33	280	39 43	318
128	36 02	021	42 16	084	30 55	172	48 51	221	36 01	248	33 36	280	39 04	318
129	36 23	021	43 14	084	31 02	173	48 13	222	35 07	248	32 39	280	38 25	318
130	36 43	020	44 12	084	31 09	174	47 34	223	34 13	249	31 42	280	37 46	317
131	37 03	020	45 09	084	31 14	175	46 54	224	33 19	249	30 45	281	37 07	317
132	37 23	020	46 07	085	31 19	176	46 14	225	32 25	250	29 48	281	36 27	317
133	37 42	019	47 05	085	31 23	176	45 32	226	31 30	250	28 51	281	35 47	316
134	38 01	019	48 02	085	31 26	177	44 51	227	30 36	251	27 54	281	35 07	316
	Dubhe		◆ ARCTURUS		SPICA		◆ Suhail		SIRIUS		BETELGEUSE		◆ CAPELLA	
135	38 19	018	14 55	074	19 07	108	31 28	178	44 08	228	44 19	266	34 27	316
136	38 37	018	15 51	074	20 02	108	31 30	179	43 25	228	43 22	266	33 47	316
137	38 55	017	16 47	074	20 57	109	31 30	180	42 42	229	42 24	266	33 06	316
138	39 12	017	17 43	074	21 52	109	31 30	181	41 57	230	41 26	267	32 26	315
139	39 28	016	18 38	075	22 46	109	31 29	182	41 13	231	40 28	267	31 45	315
140	39 44	016	19 34	075	23 41	110	31 27	182	40 28	232	39 30	267	31 04	315
141	40 00	015	20 30	075	24 35	110	31 24	183	39 42	232	38 32	268	30 23	315
142	40 15	015	21 26	075	25 30	111	31 20	184	38 56	233	37 34	268	29 42	315
143	40 29	014	22 22	075	26 24	111	31 16	185	38 09	234	36 36	268	29 01	315
144	40 43	014	23 18	075	27 18	111	31 10	186	37 22	235	35 39	268	28 20	315
145	40 57	013	24 14	075	28 12	112	31 04	187	36 35	235	34 41	269	27 38	314
146	41 09	013	25 10	076	29 06	112	30 57	187	35 47	236	33 43	269	26 57	314
147	41 22	012	26 07	076	29 59	113	30 49	188	34 59	237	32 45	269	26 15	314
148	41 33	011	27 03	076	30 52	113	30 40	189	34 10	237	31 47	269	25 34	314
149	41 45	011	27 59	076	31 46	114	30 30	190	33 21	238	30 49	270	24 52	314
	◆ Dubhe		Alkaid		ARCTURUS		◆ SPICA		Suhail		◆ SIRIUS		POLLUX	
150	41 55	010	32 38	041	28 55	076	32 38	114	30 20	191	32 32	238	56 26	298
151	42 05	010	33 15	040	29 51	076	33 31	115	30 09	192	31 43	239	55 35	298
152	42 15	009	33 53	040	30 48	076	34 24	115	29 57	192	30 53	239	54 43	298
153	42 23	008	34 30	040	31 44	077	35 16	116	29 44	193	30 03	240	53 52	297
154	42 32	008	35 07	040	32 41	077	36 08	116	29 30	194	29 12	241	53 00	297
155	42 39	007	35 44	039	33 37	077	37 00	117	29 16	195	28 22	241	52 08	297
156	42 46	007	36 21	039	34 33	077	37 51	118	29 01	196	27 31	242	51 17	296
157	42 52	006	36 57	039	35 30	077	38 42	118	28 45	196	26 40	242	50 25	296
158	42 58	005	37 33	038	36 26	077	39 33	119	28 28	197	25 49	243	49 32	296
159	43 03	005	38 09	038	37 23	077	40 24	120	28 11	198	24 57	243	48 40	296
160	43 07	004	38 45	038	38 19	077	41 14	120	27 52	199	24 05	243	47 48	295
161	43 11	003	39 20	037	39 16	077	42 04	121	27 34	199	23 13	244	46 55	295
162	43 14	003	39 55	037	40 12	077	42 54	122	27 14	200	22 21	244	46 03	295
163	43 17	002	40 30	037	41 09	078	43 43	122	26 54	201	21 29	245	45 10	295
164	43 18	001	41 04	036	42 06	078	44 31	123	26 33	201	20 36	245	44 18	295
	◆ Dubhe		ARCTURUS		◆ SPICA		ACRUX		Suhail		◆ PROCYON		POLLUX	
165	43 19	001	43 02	078	45 20	124	09 59	170	26 11	202	39 57	264	43 25	295
166	43 20	000	43 59	078	46 08	125	10 09	171	25 49	203	38 59	264	42 32	294
167	43 20	359	44 55	078	46 55	126	10 18	171	25 26	204	38 01	265	41 39	294
168	43 19	359	45 52	078	47 42	126	10 27	171	25 03	204	37 03	265	40 47	294
169	43 17	358	46 49	078	48 28	127	10 35	172	24 39	205	36 06	265	39 54	294
170	43 15	357	47 45	078	49 14	128	10 43	172	24 14	206	35 08	266	39 01	294
171	43 12	357	48 42	078	49 59	129	10 51	173	23 49	206	34 10	266	38 08	294
172	43 09	356	49 39	078	50 44	130	10 58	173	23 23	207	33 12	266	37 15	294
173	43 04	356	50 36	078	51 28	131	11 05	174	22 56	207	32 14	267	36 22	294
174	43 00	355	51 32	078	52 11	132	11 11	174	22 29	208	31 17	267	35 29	294
175	42 54	354	52 29	078	52 53	134	11 16	175	22 02	209	30 19	267	34 36	294
176	42 48	354	53 26	078	53 35	135	11 22	175	21 34	209	29 21	268	33 43	294
177	42 41	353	54 22	078	54 16	136	11 26	175	21 05	210	28 23	268	32 50	294
178	42 34	352	55 19	078	54 56	137	11 31	176	20 36	210	27 25	268	31 57	294
179	42 26	352	56 16	078	55 34	138	11 35	176	20 06	211	26 27	268	31 04	294

LHA ♈	Hc	Zn	Hc	Zn	Hc	Zn	Hc	Zn	Hc	Zn	Hc	Zn	Hc	Zn
	Alkaid		◆ Alphecca		ANTARES		◆ ACRUX		REGULUS		◆ POLLUX		Dubhe	
180	49 16	027	38 44	068	12 23	122	11 38	177	62 54	267	30 11	294	42 17	351
181	49 42	026	39 37	068	13 12	122	11 41	177	61 56	267	29 18	294	42 08	351
182	50 08	026	40 31	068	14 01	123	11 44	178	60 58	268	28 25	294	41 58	350
183	50 32	025	41 24	067	14 49	123	11 46	178	60 00	268	27 32	294	41 48	349
184	50 56	024	42 18	067	15 38	124	11 47	179	59 02	268	26 40	294	41 37	349
185	51 19	023	43 11	067	16 26	124	11 48	179	58 04	268	25 47	294	41 26	348
186	51 41	022	44 05	067	17 14	124	11 49	180	57 06	269	24 54	294	41 13	348
187	52 03	021	44 58	067	18 01	125	11 49	180	56 08	269	24 01	294	41 01	347
188	52 24	020	45 51	067	18 49	125	11 49	181	55 10	269	23 08	294	40 47	347
189	52 43	019	46 45	067	19 36	126	11 48	181	54 12	270	22 15	295	40 34	346
190	53 02	019	47 38	067	20 23	126	11 47	181	53 14	270	21 23	295	40 19	345
191	53 20	018	48 31	067	21 09	127	11 45	182	52 16	270	20 30	295	40 05	345
192	53 37	017	49 24	066	21 56	127	11 43	182	51 18	270	19 37	295	39 49	344
193	53 53	016	50 17	066	22 42	128	11 40	183	50 20	271	18 45	295	39 33	344
194	54 08	015	51 10	066	23 27	128	11 37	183	49 22	271	17 52	295	39 17	343
	◆ VEGA		Rasalhague		ANTARES		◆ RIGIL KENT		Gienah		◆ REGULUS		Dubhe	
195	13 40	053	23 18	083	24 13	129	11 29	168	55 40	199	48 24	271	39 00	343
196	14 26	053	24 15	083	24 58	129	11 41	168	55 21	200	47 27	271	38 43	342
197	15 12	053	25 13	083	25 42	130	11 53	169	55 00	202	46 29	272	38 25	342
198	15 59	053	26 11	083	26 27	130	12 04	169	54 38	203	45 31	272	38 07	341
199	16 45	053	27 08	083	27 10	131	12 14	170	54 14	205	44 33	272	37 48	341
200	17 32	053	28 06	084	27 54	132	12 25	170	53 49	206	43 35	272	37 29	341
201	18 18	054	29 03	084	28 37	132	12 34	171	53 23	208	42 37	272	37 10	340
202	19 05	054	30 01	084	29 20	133	12 44	171	52 56	209	41 39	273	36 50	340
203	19 51	054	30 59	084	30 02	133	12 52	172	52 27	210	40 41	273	36 29	339
204	20 38	054	31 56	084	30 44	134	13 01	172	51 57	212	39 43	273	36 09	339
205	21 25	054	32 54	085	31 25	135	13 08	172	51 26	213	38 45	273	35 48	338
206	22 12	054	33 52	085	32 06	135	13 16	173	50 54	214	37 48	274	35 26	338
207	22 58	054	34 49	085	32 47	136	13 23	173	50 21	215	36 50	274	35 04	338
208	23 45	054	35 47	085	33 27	137	13 29	174	49 47	217	35 52	274	34 42	337
209	24 32	054	36 45	085	34 06	138	13 35	174	49 12	218	34 54	274	34 20	337
	◆ VEGA		Rasalhague		ANTARES		◆ RIGIL KENT		SPICA		◆ REGULUS		Dubhe	
210	25 19	054	37 43	086	34 45	138	13 40	175	62 27	198	33 56	274	33 57	337
211	26 05	054	38 40	086	35 23	139	13 45	175	62 07	200	32 59	275	33 34	336
212	26 52	054	39 38	086	36 01	140	13 49	176	61 46	202	32 01	275	33 10	336
213	27 39	054	40 36	086	36 38	141	13 53	176	61 24	204	31 03	275	32 47	336
214	28 25	054	41 34	086	37 14	142	13 57	177	60 59	206	30 05	275	32 23	335
215	29 12	054	42 32	087	37 50	142	14 00	177	60 33	208	29 08	275	31 58	335
216	29 59	054	43 30	087	38 25	143	14 02	178	60 05	210	28 10	276	31 34	335
217	30 45	053	44 27	087	38 59	144	14 04	178	59 36	211	27 12	276	31 09	335
218	31 32	053	45 25	087	39 33	145	14 05	179	59 05	213	26 15	276	30 44	334
219	32 18	053	46 23	087	40 05	146	14 06	179	58 33	214	25 17	276	30 19	334
220	33 05	053	47 21	088	40 37	147	14 06	180	58 00	216	24 19	276	29 53	334
221	33 51	053	48 19	088	41 09	148	14 06	180	57 25	217	23 22	277	29 27	334
222	34 37	053	49 17	088	41 39	149	14 05	181	56 49	219	22 24	277	29 02	333
223	35 24	053	50 15	088	42 09	150	14 04	181	56 12	220	21 27	277	28 35	333
224	36 10	053	51 13	089	42 37	151	14 03	182	55 34	222	20 29	277	28 09	333
	◆ VEGA		ALTAIR		ANTARES		◆ RIGIL KENT		SPICA		◆ Denebola		Alkaid	
225	36 56	052	18 43	085	43 05	152	14 00	182	54 55	223	44 07	276	52 45	341
226	37 42	052	19 41	086	43 32	153	13 58	183	54 15	224	43 09	276	52 25	340
227	38 27	052	20 39	086	43 58	154	13 54	183	53 35	225	42 11	276	52 04	339
228	39 13	052	21 37	086	44 23	155	13 51	184	52 53	226	41 14	276	51 43	338
229	39 58	052	22 35	086	44 46	156	13 46	184	52 10	228	40 16	276	51 21	337
230	40 44	051	23 33	087	45 09	157	13 42	185	51 27	229	39 19	277	50 58	336
231	41 29	051	24 30	087	45 31	159	13 37	185	50 43	230	38 21	277	50 34	335
232	42 14	051	25 28	087	45 51	160	13 31	186	49 59	231	37 23	277	50 09	335
233	42 59	050	26 26	087	46 11	161	13 25	186	49 14	232	36 26	277	49 44	334
234	43 43	050	27 24	088	46 29	162	13 18	187	48 28	233	35 28	277	49 18	333
235	44 27	050	28 22	088	46 46	163	13 11	187	47 42	234	34 31	277	48 51	332
236	45 12	049	29 20	088	47 02	165	13 03	188	46 55	234	33 33	278	48 24	332
237	45 55	049	30 18	088	47 17	166	12 55	188	46 07	235	32 36	278	47 56	331
238	46 39	049	31 16	089	47 30	167	12 46	189	45 19	236	31 39	278	47 28	330
239	47 22	048	32 14	089	47 42	169	12 37	189	44 31	237	30 41	278	46 59	330
	◆ VEGA		ALTAIR		Nunki		◆ ANTARES		SPICA		◆ ARCTURUS		Alkaid	
240	48 05	048	33 12	089	30 32	134	47 53	170	43 42	238	64 55	283	46 29	329
241	48 48	047	34 10	089	31 13	134	48 03	171	42 53	238	63 58	283	45 59	328
242	49 31	047	35 08	090	31 55	135	48 11	172	42 04	239	63 02	283	45 28	328
243	50 13	046	36 06	090	32 35	136	48 18	174	41 14	240	62 05	283	44 57	327
244	50 54	046	37 03	090	33 16	136	48 23	175	40 24	240	61 09	282	44 25	327
245	51 35	045	38 01	090	33 55	137	48 28	177	39 33	241	60 12	282	43 53	326
246	52 16	044	38 59	091	34 34	138	48 30	178	38 42	242	59 15	282	43 21	326
247	52 57	044	39 57	091	35 13	139	48 32	179	37 51	242	58 19	282	42 48	325
248	53 37	043	40 55	091	35 51	139	48 32	181	36 59	243	57 22	282	42 14	325
249	54 16	042	41 53	091	36 29	140	48 31	182	36 08	244	56 25	282	41 41	324
250	54 55	042	42 51	092	37 05	141	48 28	183	35 16	244	55 29	282	41 07	324
251	55 33	041	43 49	092	37 41	142	48 24	185	34 23	245	54 32	282	40 32	323
252	56 11	040	44 47	092	38 17	143	48 19	186	33 31	245	53 35	282	39 58	323
253	56 48	039	45 45	093	38 52	144	48 12	187	32 38	246	52 39	282	39 22	323
254	57 24	038	46 43	093	39 26	144	48 04	189	31 45	246	51 42	282	38 47	322
	◆ VEGA		ALTAIR		◆ Nunki		ANTARES		SPICA		◆ ARCTURUS		Alkaid	
255	57 59	037	47 41	093	39 59	145	47 55	190	30 52	247	50 45	282	38 12	322
256	58 34	036	48 39	094	40 32	146	47 44	191	29 59	247	49 49	282	37 36	322
257	59 08	035	49 36	094	41 03	147	47 32	193	29 05	248	48 52	282	36 59	321
258	59 41	034	50 34	094	41 34	148	47 19	194	28 11	248	47 55	282	36 23	321
259	60 13	033	51 32	095	42 04	149	47 05	195	27 18	249	46 59	282	35 46	321
260	60 44	032	52 30	095	42 34	150	46 49	196	26 24	249	46 02	282	35 10	320
261	61 14	031	53 27	095	43 02	151	46 32	198	25 29	249	45 05	282	34 33	320
262	61 43	029	54 25	096	43 29	152	46 14	199	24 35	250	44 09	282	33 55	320
263	62 11	028	55 23	096	43 56	153	45 55	200	23 41	250	43 12	282	33 18	320
264	62 38	027	56 20	096	44 21	155	45 34	201	22 46	251	42 15	282	32 40	319
265	63 03	025	57 18	097	44 45	156	45 13	202	21 51	251	41 19	282	32 03	319
266	63 27	024	58 15	097	45 09	157	44 50	204	20 56	251	40 22	283	31 25	319
267	63 50	022	59 13	098	45 31	158	44 27	205	20 01	252	39 26	283	30 47	319
268	64 11	021	60 10	098	45 52	159	44 02	206	19 06	252	38 29	283	30 08	319
269	64 31	019	61 08	099	46 12	160	43 36	207	18 11	253	37 33	283	29 30	319

LHA ♈	Hc	Zn	Hc	Zn	Hc	Zn	Hc	Zn	Hc	Zn	Hc	Zn	Hc	Zn
	VEGA		◆ DENEB		Enif		◆ Nunki		ANTARES		◆ ARCTURUS		Alkaid	
270	64 49	017	44 28	040	35 00	088	46 31	162	43 10	208	36 36	283	28 52	318
271	65 05	016	45 05	039	35 58	088	46 49	163	42 42	209	35 40	283	28 13	318
272	65 20	014	45 41	039	36 56	089	47 06	164	42 13	210	34 43	283	27 34	318
273	65 33	012	46 18	038	37 54	089	47 21	165	41 44	211	33 47	283	26 56	318
274	65 44	010	46 53	038	38 52	089	47 35	167	41 14	212	32 50	283	26 17	318
275	65 54	008	47 28	037	39 50	089	47 48	168	40 43	213	31 54	283	25 38	318
276	66 01	006	48 03	037	40 48	090	47 59	169	40 11	214	30 58	284	24 59	318
277	66 07	005	48 37	036	41 45	090	48 09	171	39 38	215	30 01	284	24 20	318
278	66 10	003	49 11	035	42 43	090	48 18	172	39 05	216	29 05	284	23 41	318
279	66 12	001	49 44	035	43 41	090	48 26	173	38 30	217	28 09	284	23 02	318
280	66 12	359	50 17	034	44 39	091	48 32	175	37 55	217	27 12	284	22 23	318
281	66 09	357	50 49	033	45 37	091	48 37	176	37 20	218	26 16	284	21 44	318
282	66 05	355	51 21	032	46 35	091	48 41	177	36 44	219	25 20	284	21 05	317
283	65 59	353	51 51	032	47 33	092	48 43	179	36 07	220	24 24	285	20 25	317
284	65 51	351	52 21	031	48 31	092	48 43	180	35 29	221	23 28	285	19 46	317
	◆ DENEB		Alpheratz		◆ FOMALHAUT		Nunki		ANTARES		◆ Rasalhague		VEGA	
285	52 51	030	18 10	064	17 18	128	48 43	181	34 51	222	69 23	266	65 41	349
286	53 19	029	19 02	064	18 03	129	48 41	183	34 12	222	68 25	266	65 30	347
287	53 47	028	19 54	064	18 49	129	48 37	184	33 33	223	67 27	267	65 16	346
288	54 14	027	20 46	064	19 33	130	48 33	185	32 53	224	66 29	267	65 01	344
289	54 41	026	21 38	064	20 18	130	48 27	187	32 13	224	65 31	267	64 44	342
290	55 06	025	22 30	064	21 02	131	48 19	188	31 32	225	64 33	268	64 26	341
291	55 30	024	23 22	064	21 46	131	48 10	189	30 51	226	63 35	268	64 05	339
292	55 54	023	24 14	064	22 30	132	48 00	191	30 09	226	62 37	268	63 44	337
293	56 17	022	25 07	064	23 13	132	47 49	192	29 27	227	61 40	269	63 21	336
294	56 38	021	25 59	064	23 56	133	47 36	193	28 44	228	60 42	269	62 56	334
295	56 59	020	26 51	065	24 38	133	47 22	195	28 01	228	59 44	269	62 31	333
296	57 18	019	27 44	065	25 20	134	47 07	196	27 18	229	58 46	270	62 04	332
297	57 36	018	28 36	065	26 02	134	46 51	197	26 34	229	57 48	270	61 36	330
298	57 53	017	29 28	065	26 43	135	46 33	198	25 50	230	56 50	270	61 06	329
299	58 09	015	30 21	065	27 24	136	46 14	200	25 05	231	55 52	270	60 36	328
	◆ DENEB		Alpheratz		◆ FOMALHAUT		Peacock		◆ ANTARES		Rasalhague		VEGA	
300	58 24	014	31 13	065	28 04	136	18 06	176	24 20	231	54 54	271	60 04	327
301	58 38	013	32 06	065	28 44	137	18 09	177	23 35	232	53 56	271	59 32	325
302	58 50	012	32 58	065	29 23	137	18 12	177	22 49	232	52 58	271	58 59	324
303	59 01	010	33 50	065	30 02	138	18 15	178	22 03	233	52 00	271	58 25	323
304	59 11	009	34 43	065	30 41	139	18 17	178	21 17	233	51 02	272	57 50	322
305	59 19	008	35 35	065	31 19	140	18 18	179	20 30	234	50 04	272	57 14	321
306	59 26	006	36 27	065	31 56	140	18 19	180	19 44	234	49 06	272	56 37	321
307	59 31	005	37 20	065	32 33	141	18 19	180	18 57	235	48 08	272	56 00	320
308	59 36	003	38 12	064	33 09	142	18 18	181	18 09	235	47 10	272	55 22	319
309	59 38	002	39 04	064	33 45	142	18 17	181	17 22	235	46 12	273	54 44	318
310	59 40	001	39 57	064	34 20	143	18 16	182	16 34	236	45 15	273	54 05	317
311	59 40	359	40 49	064	34 54	144	18 13	182	15 46	236	44 17	273	53 26	317
312	59 38	358	41 41	064	35 28	145	18 11	183	14 57	237	43 19	273	52 46	316
313	59 35	357	42 33	064	36 01	146	18 07	184	14 09	237	42 21	273	52 05	315
314	59 31	355	43 25	064	36 33	147	18 03	184	13 20	237	41 23	274	51 24	315
	Alpheratz		◆ Diphda		FOMALHAUT		◆ Nunki		Rasalhague		VEGA		◆ DENEB	
315	44 17	064	25 41	119	37 05	147	38 55	216	40 25	274	50 43	314	59 26	354
316	45 09	064	26 31	119	37 36	148	38 20	217	39 28	274	50 01	314	59 19	352
317	46 01	063	27 22	120	38 06	149	37 45	218	38 30	274	49 19	313	59 10	351
318	46 52	063	28 12	120	38 35	150	37 09	219	37 32	274	48 36	313	59 01	350
319	47 44	063	29 02	121	39 04	151	36 32	220	36 34	275	47 54	312	58 50	348
320	48 36	063	29 51	121	39 31	152	35 55	221	35 36	275	47 10	312	58 37	347
321	49 27	062	30 41	122	39 58	153	35 17	221	34 39	275	46 27	311	58 24	346
322	50 18	062	31 30	123	40 24	154	34 38	222	33 41	275	45 43	311	58 09	345
323	51 10	062	32 18	123	40 49	155	33 59	223	32 43	275	44 59	310	57 53	343
324	52 01	062	33 07	124	41 13	156	33 19	224	31 46	276	44 15	310	57 36	342
325	52 51	061	33 55	124	41 36	157	32 39	224	30 48	276	43 31	310	57 17	341
326	53 42	061	34 42	125	41 58	158	31 59	225	29 50	276	42 46	309	56 58	340
327	54 33	060	35 30	126	42 19	159	31 17	226	28 53	276	42 01	309	56 37	339
328	55 23	060	36 17	126	42 40	160	30 36	226	27 55	276	41 16	309	56 16	338
329	56 13	060	37 03	127	42 59	161	29 54	227	26 57	277	40 31	309	55 53	337
	◆ Alpheratz		Diphda		◆ FOMALHAUT		Peacock		ALTAIR		◆ VEGA		DENEB	
330	57 03	059	37 49	128	43 17	162	15 43	193	58 01	263	39 46	308	55 30	336
331	57 52	059	38 35	128	43 34	164	15 30	194	57 04	263	39 00	308	55 05	335
332	58 42	058	39 20	129	43 49	165	15 16	194	56 06	264	38 15	308	54 40	334
333	59 31	057	40 05	130	44 04	166	15 02	195	55 09	264	37 29	308	54 14	333
334	60 19	057	40 49	131	44 18	167	14 47	195	54 11	264	36 43	308	53 47	332
335	61 08	056	41 33	132	44 30	168	14 32	196	53 13	265	35 57	307	53 19	331
336	61 55	055	42 16	132	44 41	169	14 16	196	52 16	265	35 11	307	52 50	330
337	62 43	054	42 58	133	44 51	171	14 00	197	51 18	266	34 25	307	52 21	329
338	63 30	054	43 40	134	45 00	172	13 43	197	50 20	266	33 38	307	51 50	328
339	64 16	053	44 22	135	45 08	173	13 25	198	49 22	266	32 52	307	51 20	328
340	65 02	052	45 02	136	45 14	174	13 08	198	48 24	267	32 06	307	50 48	327
341	65 47	051	45 42	137	45 19	176	12 50	199	47 27	267	31 19	307	50 16	326
342	66 31	049	46 21	138	45 23	177	12 31	199	46 29	267	30 32	307	49 43	325
343	67 15	048	47 00	139	45 26	178	12 12	199	45 31	267	29 46	306	49 10	325
344	67 58	047	47 38	140	45 27	179	11 52	200	44 33	268	28 59	306	48 36	324
	Schedar		◆ Mirfak		Hamal		◆ ACHERNAR		FOMALHAUT		◆ ALTAIR		DENEB	
345	44 08	019	26 35	041	45 01	072	10 44	159	45 27	180	43 35	268	48 02	323
346	44 27	019	27 13	041	45 56	071	11 04	160	45 26	182	42 37	268	47 27	323
347	44 45	018	27 51	041	46 51	071	11 24	160	45 24	183	41 39	269	46 52	322
348	45 03	017	28 29	041	47 46	071	11 44	161	45 20	184	40 41	269	46 17	322
349	45 20	017	29 07	041	48 40	071	12 02	161	45 15	185	39 43	269	45 40	321
350	45 36	016	29 45	041	49 35	071	12 21	162	45 09	187	38 45	269	45 04	321
351	45 51	015	30 23	040	50 30	071	12 39	162	45 02	188	37 47	270	44 27	320
352	46 06	014	31 00	040	51 25	071	12 57	163	44 53	189	36 49	270	43 50	320
353	46 20	014	31 38	040	52 20	071	13 14	163	44 44	190	35 51	270	43 12	319
354	46 34	013	32 15	040	53 14	071	13 30	164	44 33	191	34 54	270	42 34	319
355	46 46	012	32 52	040	54 09	070	13 47	164	44 21	193	33 56	271	41 56	319
356	46 58	012	33 29	039	55 04	070	14 02	164	44 07	194	32 58	271	41 17	318
357	47 09	011	34 06	039	55 58	070	14 18	165	43 53	195	32 00	271	40 39	318
358	47 20	010	34 42	039	56 52	070	14 32	165	43 37	196	31 02	271	40 00	317
359	47 30	009	35 18	039	57 47	070	14 47	166	43 21	197	30 04	272	39 20	317

LAT 14°N

LHA ♈	Hc	Zn	Hc	Zn	Hc	Zn	Hc	Zn	Hc	Zn	Hc	Zn	Hc	Zn
	CAPELLA		◆ ALDEBARAN		Acamar		ACHERNAR		◆ FOMALHAUT		ALTAIR		◆ DENEB	
0	17 18	046	23 32	078	21 43	145	15 59	166	44 00	199	29 04	273	37 57	317
1	18 00	046	24 29	078	22 17	145	16 12	167	43 41	200	28 05	273	37 17	317
2	18 42	046	25 26	078	22 50	146	16 25	167	43 20	201	27 07	273	36 37	317
3	19 23	046	26 23	078	23 22	146	16 37	168	42 59	202	26 09	273	35 57	316
4	20 05	046	27 20	078	23 54	147	16 49	169	42 37	203	25 11	273	35 17	316
5	20 47	046	28 17	079	24 25	148	17 01	169	42 13	204	24 13	274	34 37	316
6	21 28	046	29 14	079	24 56	148	17 11	170	41 49	205	23 15	274	33 56	316
7	22 10	046	30 11	079	25 27	149	17 22	170	41 24	206	22 17	274	33 15	315
8	22 51	046	31 08	079	25 56	150	17 31	171	40 58	207	21 19	274	32 35	315
9	23 33	046	32 05	079	26 26	150	17 40	171	40 31	208	20 21	274	31 53	315
10	24 15	045	33 02	079	26 54	151	17 49	172	40 03	209	19 23	275	31 12	315
11	24 56	045	34 00	079	27 22	152	17 57	172	39 34	210	18 25	275	30 31	315
12	25 38	045	34 57	079	27 50	152	18 05	173	39 04	211	17 27	275	29 50	315
13	26 19	045	35 54	080	28 17	153	18 12	173	38 34	212	16 29	275	29 08	314
14	27 00	045	36 51	080	28 43	154	18 18	174	38 03	213	15 31	276	28 26	314
	CAPELLA		◆ ALDEBARAN		RIGEL		ACHERNAR		◆ FOMALHAUT		Enif		◆ DENEB	
15	27 41	045	37 48	080	22 55	105	18 24	175	37 31	214	42 12	271	27 45	314
16	28 23	045	38 46	080	23 51	106	18 29	175	36 58	215	41 14	271	27 03	314
17	29 04	045	39 43	080	24 47	106	18 34	176	36 25	215	40 15	271	26 21	314
18	29 45	045	40 40	080	25 43	106	18 38	176	35 51	216	39 17	271	25 39	314
19	30 25	044	41 38	080	26 39	107	18 41	177	35 16	217	38 19	272	24 57	314
20	31 06	044	42 35	080	27 34	107	18 44	177	34 41	218	37 21	272	24 15	314
21	31 47	044	43 33	080	28 30	108	18 47	178	34 05	219	36 23	272	23 33	314
22	32 27	044	44 30	080	29 25	108	18 48	179	33 28	219	35 24	272	22 51	314
23	33 08	044	45 27	081	30 21	108	18 50	179	32 51	220	34 26	273	22 09	314
24	33 48	043	46 25	081	31 16	109	18 50	180	32 13	221	33 28	273	21 27	314
25	34 28	043	47 22	081	32 11	109	18 50	180	31 35	221	32 30	273	20 45	314
26	35 08	043	48 20	081	33 06	110	18 50	181	30 56	222	31 32	273	20 02	314
27	35 47	043	49 17	081	34 00	110	18 49	181	30 17	223	30 34	273	19 20	314
28	36 27	042	50 15	081	34 55	111	18 47	182	29 37	223	29 36	274	18 38	314
29	37 06	042	51 12	081	35 49	111	18 45	183	28 57	224	28 38	274	17 56	314
	Mirfak		◆ CAPELLA		ALDEBARAN		RIGEL		◆ ACHERNAR		FOMALHAUT		◆ Alpheratz	
30	50 05	021	37 45	042	52 10	081	36 44	112	18 42	183	28 16	225	60 14	305
31	50 26	021	38 23	042	53 07	081	37 38	112	18 38	184	27 35	225	59 26	304
32	50 46	020	39 02	041	54 05	081	38 31	113	18 34	184	26 54	226	58 38	304
33	51 05	019	39 40	041	55 02	081	39 25	113	18 30	185	26 12	226	57 49	303
34	51 24	018	40 18	040	56 00	081	40 18	114	18 25	185	25 29	227	57 00	303
35	51 41	017	40 56	040	56 57	081	41 11	114	18 19	186	24 46	228	56 11	302
36	51 58	016	41 33	040	57 55	081	42 04	115	18 12	186	24 03	228	55 21	302
37	52 13	015	42 10	039	58 52	081	42 57	116	18 06	187	23 20	229	54 32	301
38	52 28	014	42 47	039	59 50	081	43 49	116	17 58	188	22 36	229	53 42	301
39	52 42	013	43 23	038	60 47	081	44 41	117	17 50	188	21 52	230	52 51	300
40	52 55	012	43 59	038	61 45	081	45 33	118	17 42	189	21 07	230	52 01	300
41	53 06	011	44 34	037	62 42	081	46 25	118	17 33	189	20 22	231	51 10	299
42	53 17	010	45 09	037	63 40	081	47 16	119	17 23	190	19 37	231	50 20	299
43	53 27	009	45 44	036	64 37	081	48 06	120	17 13	190	18 52	232	49 29	299
44	53 35	008	46 18	036	65 35	081	48 57	121	17 02	191	18 06	232	48 38	298
	CAPELLA		◆ POLLUX		PROCYON		SIRIUS		◆ ACHERNAR		Diphda		◆ Alpheratz	
45	46 52	035	22 37	065	20 37	090	26 21	117	16 51	191	43 47	227	47 46	298
46	47 25	034	23 30	065	21 35	090	27 13	118	16 39	192	43 03	228	46 55	298
47	47 58	034	24 23	065	22 33	090	28 04	118	16 27	192	42 20	229	46 03	298
48	48 30	033	25 16	065	23 31	090	28 55	118	16 14	193	41 36	230	45 12	298
49	49 01	032	26 09	065	24 30	091	29 46	119	16 01	193	40 51	231	44 20	297
50	49 32	032	27 02	065	25 28	091	30 37	120	15 47	194	40 06	231	43 28	297
51	50 03	031	27 54	065	26 26	091	31 28	120	15 32	195	39 20	232	42 37	297
52	50 32	030	28 47	065	27 24	091	32 18	121	15 18	195	38 34	233	41 45	297
53	51 01	029	29 40	066	28 22	092	33 08	121	15 02	196	37 47	234	40 53	297
54	51 30	029	30 33	066	29 21	092	33 58	122	14 46	196	37 00	234	40 01	297
55	51 57	028	31 26	066	30 19	092	34 47	122	14 30	196	36 13	235	39 08	296
56	52 24	027	32 19	066	31 17	092	35 36	123	14 13	197	35 25	236	38 16	296
57	52 50	026	33 12	065	32 15	093	36 25	124	13 56	197	34 37	236	37 24	296
58	53 15	025	34 05	065	33 13	093	37 13	124	13 38	198	33 48	237	36 32	296
59	53 39	024	34 58	065	34 11	093	38 01	125	13 20	198	32 59	237	35 40	296
	CAPELLA		◆ POLLUX		PROCYON		SIRIUS		◆ CANOPUS		Diphda		◆ Hamal	
60	54 03	023	35 51	065	35 09	094	38 49	126	16 26	158	32 10	238	61 54	294
61	54 25	022	36 44	065	36 08	094	39 36	126	16 47	159	31 21	238	61 01	294
62	54 47	021	37 37	065	37 06	094	40 23	127	17 08	159	30 31	239	60 07	293
63	55 07	020	38 30	065	38 04	094	41 09	128	17 28	160	29 41	240	59 13	293
64	55 27	019	39 23	065	39 02	095	41 55	129	17 48	160	28 50	240	58 20	292
65	55 45	018	40 15	065	40 00	095	42 40	129	18 08	161	28 00	241	57 26	292
66	56 03	017	41 08	065	40 58	095	43 25	130	18 27	161	27 09	241	56 32	292
67	56 19	016	42 01	065	41 56	096	44 09	131	18 45	162	26 18	242	55 37	291
68	56 34	014	42 54	065	42 54	096	44 53	132	19 03	162	25 27	242	54 43	291
69	56 48	013	43 46	064	43 51	096	45 36	133	19 20	163	24 35	242	53 49	291
70	57 01	012	44 39	064	44 49	097	46 18	134	19 37	164	23 43	243	52 54	291
71	57 12	011	45 31	064	45 47	097	47 00	135	19 53	164	22 52	243	52 00	290
72	57 23	010	46 23	064	46 45	097	47 41	136	20 09	165	21 59	244	51 05	290
73	57 32	008	47 16	064	47 43	098	48 21	137	20 24	165	21 07	244	50 11	290
74	57 40	007	48 08	063	48 40	098	49 01	138	20 38	166	20 15	245	49 16	290
	CAPELLA		◆ POLLUX		PROCYON		SIRIUS		◆ CANOPUS		Acamar		◆ Hamal	
75	57 46	006	49 00	063	49 38	099	49 40	139	20 52	167	28 54	206	48 21	290
76	57 51	005	49 52	063	50 35	099	50 18	140	21 05	167	28 28	207	47 26	290
77	57 55	003	50 44	063	51 33	099	50 55	141	21 18	168	28 01	208	46 32	290
78	57 58	002	51 35	062	52 30	100	51 31	142	21 30	168	27 34	208	45 37	289
79	57 59	001	52 27	062	53 28	100	52 06	143	21 41	169	27 06	209	44 42	289
80	57 59	359	53 18	062	54 25	101	52 40	145	21 52	170	26 38	210	43 47	289
81	57 58	358	54 09	061	55 22	101	53 13	146	22 02	170	26 09	210	42 52	289
82	57 55	357	55 00	061	56 19	102	53 45	147	22 12	171	25 39	211	41 57	289
83	57 51	355	55 51	060	57 16	102	54 16	149	22 21	171	25 09	212	41 02	289
84	57 46	354	56 41	060	58 13	103	54 46	150	22 29	172	24 38	212	40 07	289
85	57 39	353	57 32	059	59 09	104	55 14	152	22 37	173	24 07	213	39 12	289
86	57 31	352	58 21	059	60 06	104	55 41	153	22 44	173	23 35	213	38 17	289
87	57 22	350	59 11	058	61 02	105	56 07	155	22 50	174	23 03	214	37 22	289
88	57 11	349	60 01	058	61 58	106	56 31	156	22 56	175	22 30	215	36 27	289
89	57 00	348	60 49	057	62 54	106	56 54	158	23 01	175	21 57	215	35 32	289

LHA ♈	Hc	Zn	Hc	Zn	Hc	Zn	Hc	Zn	Hc	Zn	Hc	Zn	Hc	Zn
	Dubhe		◆ REGULUS		Suhail		SIRIUS		◆ RIGEL		ALDEBARAN		◆ CAPELLA	
90	18 51	029	29 26	084	18 12	146	57 15	159	65 12	207	69 47	280	56 47	347
91	19 19	029	30 24	084	18 44	146	57 35	161	64 44	209	68 49	280	56 33	345
92	19 48	029	31 22	084	19 16	147	57 53	163	64 15	211	67 52	280	56 17	344
93	20 16	029	32 19	085	19 48	148	58 09	165	63 44	213	66 55	279	56 01	343
94	20 44	029	33 17	085	20 19	148	58 24	166	63 11	215	65 57	279	55 43	342
95	21 12	029	34 15	085	20 49	149	58 37	168	62 37	217	65 00	279	55 25	341
96	21 40	029	35 13	085	21 19	149	58 48	170	62 01	219	64 02	279	55 05	340
97	22 08	029	36 11	085	21 49	150	58 57	172	61 24	220	63 05	279	54 45	339
98	22 36	028	37 09	086	22 18	150	59 04	174	60 46	222	62 07	279	54 23	338
99	23 04	028	38 08	086	22 47	151	59 10	175	60 07	223	61 10	279	54 00	337
100	23 31	028	39 06	086	23 15	152	59 14	177	59 26	225	60 12	279	53 37	336
101	23 59	028	40 04	086	23 42	152	59 16	179	58 45	226	59 15	279	53 13	335
102	24 26	028	41 02	086	24 09	153	59 15	181	58 02	227	58 17	279	52 47	334
103	24 53	028	42 00	086	24 35	153	59 13	183	57 19	229	57 20	279	52 21	333
104	25 20	028	42 58	087	25 01	154	59 10	185	56 35	230	56 22	279	51 54	332
	Dubhe		◆ REGULUS		Suhail		◆ SIRIUS		RIGEL		ALDEBARAN		◆ CAPELLA	
105	25 47	027	43 56	087	25 26	155	59 04	187	55 50	231	55 25	279	51 27	331
106	26 14	027	44 54	087	25 51	155	58 56	188	55 04	232	54 27	279	50 59	330
107	26 41	027	45 52	087	26 15	156	58 47	190	54 18	233	53 30	279	50 29	330
108	27 07	027	46 51	087	26 38	157	58 35	192	53 31	234	52 32	279	50 00	329
109	27 33	027	47 49	088	27 01	157	58 22	194	52 44	235	51 35	279	49 29	328
110	28 00	027	48 47	088	27 23	158	58 07	196	51 55	236	50 37	279	48 58	327
111	28 25	026	49 45	088	27 44	159	57 51	197	51 07	237	49 40	279	48 27	327
112	28 51	026	50 43	088	28 05	160	57 33	199	50 18	238	48 42	279	47 55	326
113	29 17	026	51 41	088	28 25	160	57 13	201	49 28	239	47 45	279	47 22	325
114	29 42	026	52 40	089	28 44	161	56 52	202	48 38	240	46 47	279	46 49	325
115	30 07	025	53 38	089	29 03	162	56 29	204	47 48	240	45 50	279	46 15	324
116	30 32	025	54 36	089	29 21	163	56 04	206	46 57	241	44 52	280	45 41	324
117	30 56	025	55 34	089	29 38	163	55 38	207	46 06	242	43 55	280	45 06	323
118	31 20	024	56 32	090	29 54	164	55 11	209	45 14	243	42 58	280	44 31	323
119	31 44	024	57 31	090	30 10	165	54 43	210	44 22	243	42 00	280	43 55	322
	Dubhe		◆ Denebola		Suhail		◆ SIRIUS		RIGEL		ALDEBARAN		◆ CAPELLA	
120	32 08	024	34 28	082	30 24	166	54 13	211	43 30	244	41 03	280	43 19	322
121	32 31	024	35 26	082	30 38	166	53 42	213	42 38	245	40 06	280	42 43	321
122	32 54	023	36 23	082	30 52	167	53 10	214	41 45	245	39 08	280	42 06	321
123	33 17	023	37 21	082	31 04	168	52 37	215	40 52	246	38 11	280	41 29	320
124	33 40	023	38 19	082	31 16	169	52 03	217	39 59	246	37 14	280	40 52	320
125	34 02	022	39 16	083	31 27	170	51 27	218	39 05	247	36 16	280	40 14	319
126	34 23	022	40 14	083	31 37	171	50 51	219	38 11	247	35 19	281	39 36	319
127	34 45	021	41 12	083	31 46	171	50 14	220	37 18	248	34 22	281	38 58	319
128	35 06	021	42 10	083	31 54	172	49 36	221	36 23	249	33 25	281	38 20	318
129	35 27	021	43 07	083	32 02	173	48 57	222	35 29	249	32 28	281	37 41	318
130	35 47	020	44 05	083	32 08	174	48 18	223	34 35	250	31 30	281	37 02	318
131	36 07	020	45 03	083	32 14	175	47 37	224	33 40	250	30 33	281	36 23	318
132	36 26	019	46 01	084	32 19	176	46 56	225	32 45	250	29 36	281	35 43	317
133	36 45	019	46 59	084	32 23	176	46 14	226	31 50	251	28 39	281	35 04	317
134	37 04	018	47 57	084	32 26	177	45 32	227	30 55	251	27 42	282	34 24	317
	Dubhe		◆ ARCTURUS		SPICA		◆ Suhail		SIRIUS		BETELGEUSE		◆ CAPELLA	
135	37 22	018	14 38	074	19 25	108	32 28	178	44 49	228	44 23	267	33 44	316
136	37 40	018	15 34	074	20 20	108	32 30	179	44 05	229	43 25	267	33 04	316
137	37 57	017	16 30	074	21 16	108	32 30	180	43 20	230	42 27	267	32 23	316
138	38 14	017	17 26	074	22 11	109	32 30	181	42 36	231	41 29	268	31 43	316
139	38 30	016	18 22	074	23 06	109	32 29	182	41 50	232	40 31	268	31 02	316
140	38 46	016	19 18	074	24 01	109	32 27	182	41 04	232	39 33	268	30 21	316
141	39 02	015	20 14	074	24 56	110	32 24	183	40 18	233	38 34	268	29 41	315
142	39 17	015	21 10	075	25 51	110	32 20	184	39 31	234	37 36	269	29 00	315
143	39 31	014	22 07	075	26 45	111	32 15	185	38 44	235	36 38	269	28 18	315
144	39 45	013	23 03	075	27 40	111	32 10	186	37 57	235	35 40	269	27 37	315
145	39 58	013	23 59	075	28 34	111	32 03	187	37 09	236	34 42	269	26 56	315
146	40 11	012	24 55	075	29 28	112	31 56	188	36 20	237	33 43	270	26 15	315
147	40 23	012	25 52	075	30 22	112	31 48	188	35 31	237	32 45	270	25 33	315
148	40 35	011	26 48	075	31 16	113	31 39	189	34 42	238	31 47	270	24 52	315
149	40 46	011	27 44	076	32 09	113	31 29	190	33 53	238	30 49	270	24 10	314
	◆ Dubhe		Alkaid		ARCTURUS		◆ SPICA		Suhail		◆ SIRIUS		POLLUX	
150	40 56	010	31 52	040	28 41	076	33 03	114	31 19	191	33 03	239	55 57	300
151	41 06	009	32 30	040	29 37	076	33 56	114	31 07	192	32 13	239	55 06	299
152	41 15	009	33 07	040	30 33	076	34 49	115	30 55	193	31 23	240	54 15	299
153	41 24	008	33 44	039	31 30	076	35 42	115	30 42	193	30 32	241	53 24	298
154	41 32	008	34 21	039	32 26	076	36 34	116	30 28	194	29 42	241	52 33	298
155	41 40	007	34 58	039	33 23	076	37 27	116	30 14	195	28 51	242	51 41	298
156	41 46	006	35 34	039	34 19	076	38 19	117	29 58	196	27 59	242	50 49	297
157	41 53	006	36 10	038	35 16	076	39 10	118	29 42	196	27 08	243	49 58	297
158	41 58	005	36 46	038	36 13	076	40 02	118	29 25	197	26 16	243	49 06	297
159	42 03	005	37 22	037	37 09	076	40 53	119	29 08	198	25 24	243	48 14	297
160	42 07	004	37 57	037	38 06	077	41 44	119	28 49	199	24 32	244	47 22	296
161	42 11	003	38 32	037	39 02	077	42 35	120	28 30	200	23 39	244	46 29	296
162	42 14	003	39 07	037	39 59	077	43 25	121	28 10	200	22 47	245	45 37	296
163	42 17	002	39 42	036	40 56	077	44 14	122	27 50	201	21 54	245	44 45	296
164	42 18	001	40 16	036	41 52	077	45 04	122	27 29	202	21 01	246	43 52	296
	◆ Dubhe		ARCTURUS		◆ SPICA		ACRUX		Suhail		◆ PROCYON		POLLUX	
165	42 19	001	42 49	077	45 53	123	10 58	170	27 07	202	40 02	265	43 00	295
166	42 20	000	43 46	077	46 41	124	11 08	171	26 44	203	39 04	265	42 07	295
167	42 20	359	44 42	077	47 30	125	11 18	171	26 21	204	38 06	266	41 14	295
168	42 19	359	45 39	077	48 17	126	11 26	171	25 58	204	37 08	266	40 22	295
169	42 17	358	46 36	077	49 04	126	11 35	172	25 33	205	36 10	266	39 29	295
170	42 15	358	47 32	077	49 51	127	11 43	172	25 08	206	35 12	266	38 36	295
171	42 12	357	48 29	077	50 37	128	11 50	173	24 42	206	34 14	267	37 43	295
172	42 09	356	49 26	077	51 22	129	11 58	173	24 16	207	33 16	267	36 50	295
173	42 05	356	50 22	077	52 07	130	12 04	174	23 50	208	32 18	267	35 57	295
174	42 00	355	51 19	077	52 51	131	12 10	174	23 22	208	31 19	268	35 04	295
175	41 54	354	52 16	077	53 34	133	12 16	175	22 54	209	30 21	268	34 11	295
176	41 48	354	53 12	077	54 17	134	12 21	175	22 26	210	29 23	268	33 18	295
177	41 42	353	54 09	077	54 58	135	12 26	175	21 57	210	28 25	268	32 26	294
178	41 35	353	55 06	077	55 39	136	12 31	176	21 28	211	27 27	269	31 33	294
179	41 27	352	56 02	076	56 19	137	12 35	176	20 58	211	26 28	269	30 40	294

LHA ♈	Hc	Zn	Hc	Zn	Hc	Zn	Hc	Zn	Hc	Zn	Hc	Zn	Hc	Zn
	Alkaid		◆ Alphecca		ANTARES		◆ ACRUX		REGULUS		◆ POLLUX		Dubhe	
180	48 23	027	38 20	067	12 55	122	12 38	177	62 56	269	29 47	294	41 18	351
181	48 48	026	39 14	067	13 44	122	12 41	177	61 58	269	28 54	295	41 09	351
182	49 13	025	40 07	067	14 33	123	12 44	178	60 59	269	28 01	295	40 59	350
183	49 38	024	41 01	067	15 22	123	12 46	178	60 01	270	27 08	295	40 49	350
184	50 01	023	41 54	067	16 11	123	12 47	179	59 03	270	26 15	295	40 38	349
185	50 24	023	42 48	066	16 59	124	12 48	179	58 05	270	25 22	295	40 27	348
186	50 46	022	43 41	066	17 48	124	12 49	180	57 07	270	24 29	295	40 15	348
187	51 07	021	44 34	066	18 36	125	12 49	180	56 08	271	23 36	295	40 02	347
188	51 27	020	45 28	066	19 23	125	12 49	181	55 10	271	22 43	295	39 49	347
189	51 47	019	46 21	066	20 11	126	12 48	181	54 12	271	21 50	295	39 35	346
190	52 05	018	47 14	066	20 58	126	12 47	181	53 14	271	20 58	295	39 21	346
191	52 23	017	48 07	065	21 45	126	12 45	182	52 15	271	20 05	295	39 07	345
192	52 40	016	49 00	065	22 32	127	12 43	182	51 17	272	19 12	295	38 51	345
193	52 56	015	49 53	065	23 18	127	12 40	183	50 19	272	18 19	295	38 36	344
194	53 10	014	50 45	065	24 04	128	12 37	183	49 21	272	17 27	295	38 19	344
	◆ VEGA		Rasalhague		ANTARES		◆ RIGIL KENT		Gienah		◆ REGULUS		Dubhe	
195	13 03	053	23 10	082	24 50	128	12 28	168	56 37	199	48 23	272	38 03	343
196	13 50	053	24 08	082	25 35	129	12 40	168	56 17	201	47 25	272	37 46	343
197	14 36	053	25 05	082	26 21	129	12 52	169	55 56	202	46 26	273	37 28	342
198	15 23	053	26 03	083	27 05	130	13 03	169	55 33	204	45 28	273	37 10	342
199	16 09	053	27 01	083	27 50	131	13 13	170	55 09	205	44 30	273	36 51	341
200	16 56	053	27 59	083	28 34	131	13 24	170	54 43	207	43 32	273	36 32	341
201	17 42	053	28 56	083	29 17	132	13 33	171	54 16	208	42 34	273	36 13	340
202	18 29	053	29 54	083	30 00	132	13 43	171	53 48	210	41 36	274	35 53	340
203	19 16	053	30 52	084	30 43	133	13 52	172	53 19	211	40 38	274	35 33	340
204	20 02	053	31 50	084	31 26	134	14 00	172	52 48	212	39 40	274	35 13	339
205	20 49	053	32 48	084	32 07	134	14 08	172	52 16	214	38 41	274	34 52	339
206	21 36	053	33 46	084	32 49	135	14 15	173	51 43	215	37 43	274	34 30	338
207	22 23	053	34 44	084	33 30	136	14 22	173	51 10	216	36 45	275	34 09	338
208	23 09	053	35 42	084	34 10	136	14 29	174	50 35	217	35 47	275	33 47	338
209	23 56	053	36 40	085	34 50	137	14 35	174	49 59	219	34 49	275	33 24	337
	◆ VEGA		Rasalhague		ANTARES		◆ RIGIL KENT		SPICA		◆ REGULUS		Dubhe	
210	24 43	053	37 38	085	35 29	138	14 40	175	63 23	199	33 51	275	33 02	337
211	25 30	053	38 36	085	36 08	139	14 45	175	63 04	201	32 53	275	32 39	337
212	26 16	053	39 34	085	36 46	139	14 49	176	62 42	203	31 55	275	32 15	336
213	27 03	053	40 32	085	37 24	140	14 53	176	62 18	205	30 57	276	31 52	336
214	27 50	053	41 30	086	38 01	141	14 57	177	61 53	207	30 00	276	31 28	336
215	28 36	053	42 28	086	38 37	142	14 59	177	61 26	209	29 02	276	31 04	335
216	29 23	053	43 26	086	39 13	143	15 02	178	60 57	210	28 04	276	30 39	335
217	30 09	053	44 24	086	39 47	144	15 04	178	60 27	212	27 06	276	30 15	335
218	30 56	053	45 22	086	40 22	145	15 05	179	59 55	214	26 08	277	29 50	335
219	31 42	053	46 20	086	40 55	145	15 06	179	59 22	215	25 10	277	29 25	334
220	32 29	053	47 18	087	41 28	146	15 06	180	58 48	217	24 12	277	28 59	334
221	33 15	053	48 16	087	41 59	147	15 06	180	58 12	218	23 15	277	28 34	334
222	34 01	052	49 14	087	42 30	148	15 05	181	57 35	220	22 17	277	28 08	334
223	34 47	052	50 12	087	43 00	149	15 04	181	56 58	221	21 19	278	27 42	333
224	35 33	052	51 11	087	43 30	150	15 02	182	56 19	223	20 21	278	27 16	333
	◆ VEGA		ALTAIR		ANTARES		◆ RIGIL KENT		SPICA		◆ Denebola		Alkaid	
225	36 19	052	18 39	085	43 58	151	15 00	182	55 39	224	44 00	277	51 48	341
226	37 04	052	19 37	085	44 25	153	14 58	183	54 58	225	43 02	277	51 29	340
227	37 50	051	20 35	086	44 52	154	14 54	183	54 16	226	42 04	277	51 08	339
228	38 35	051	21 33	086	45 17	155	14 51	184	53 34	227	41 07	277	50 47	338
229	39 21	051	22 31	086	45 41	156	14 46	184	52 51	229	40 09	277	50 25	337
230	40 06	051	23 29	086	46 04	157	14 42	185	52 07	230	39 11	277	50 03	337
231	40 51	050	24 27	086	46 27	158	14 36	185	51 22	231	38 13	278	49 39	336
232	41 35	050	25 25	087	46 48	159	14 31	186	50 36	232	37 16	278	49 15	335
233	42 20	050	26 23	087	47 07	161	14 24	186	49 50	233	36 18	278	48 50	334
234	43 04	049	27 21	087	47 26	162	14 18	187	49 04	234	35 20	278	48 24	334
235	43 48	049	28 19	087	47 44	163	14 10	187	48 17	234	34 23	278	47 58	333
236	44 32	049	29 18	088	48 00	164	14 03	188	47 29	235	33 25	278	47 31	332
237	45 16	048	30 16	088	48 15	166	13 54	188	46 41	236	32 28	278	47 04	331
238	45 59	048	31 14	088	48 29	167	13 46	189	45 53	237	31 30	279	46 35	331
239	46 42	047	32 12	088	48 41	168	13 37	189	45 04	238	30 32	279	46 07	330
	◆ VEGA		ALTAIR		Nunki		◆ ANTARES		SPICA		◆ ARCTURUS		Alkaid	
240	47 25	047	33 10	088	31 13	133	48 52	170	44 14	238	64 40	285	45 37	329
241	48 07	046	34 09	089	31 55	134	49 02	171	43 24	239	63 44	285	45 08	329
242	48 49	046	35 07	089	32 37	135	49 10	172	42 34	240	62 48	285	44 37	328
243	49 31	045	36 05	089	33 18	135	49 17	174	41 44	241	61 51	284	44 06	328
244	50 12	045	37 03	089	33 59	136	49 23	175	40 53	241	60 55	284	43 35	327
245	50 53	044	38 01	090	34 39	137	49 27	176	40 02	242	59 58	284	43 03	327
246	51 33	044	39 00	090	35 19	137	49 30	178	39 10	242	59 02	284	42 31	326
247	52 13	043	39 58	090	35 58	138	49 32	179	38 18	243	58 05	284	41 58	326
248	52 52	042	40 56	090	36 36	139	49 32	181	37 26	244	57 09	284	41 25	325
249	53 31	041	41 54	091	37 14	140	49 31	182	36 34	244	56 12	284	40 52	325
250	54 10	041	42 52	091	37 52	141	49 28	183	35 41	245	55 16	283	40 18	324
251	54 47	040	43 51	091	38 28	141	49 24	185	34 49	245	54 19	283	39 44	324
252	55 24	039	44 49	091	39 04	142	49 19	186	33 56	246	53 22	283	39 09	323
253	56 01	038	45 47	092	39 40	143	49 12	187	33 02	246	52 26	283	38 35	323
254	56 36	037	46 45	092	40 14	144	49 03	189	32 09	247	51 29	283	38 00	323
	◆ VEGA		ALTAIR		◆ Nunki		ANTARES		SPICA		◆ ARCTURUS		Alkaid	
255	57 11	036	47 43	092	40 48	145	48 54	190	31 15	247	50 32	283	37 24	322
256	57 45	035	48 42	092	41 21	146	48 43	191	30 22	248	49 36	283	36 48	322
257	58 19	034	49 40	093	41 54	147	48 31	193	29 28	248	48 39	283	36 13	322
258	58 51	033	50 38	093	42 25	148	48 17	194	28 34	249	47 42	283	35 36	321
259	59 23	032	51 36	093	42 56	149	48 02	195	27 39	249	46 46	283	35 00	321
260	59 53	031	52 34	094	43 26	150	47 46	197	26 45	249	45 49	283	34 23	321
261	60 23	030	53 32	094	43 54	151	47 29	198	25 50	250	44 52	283	33 46	321
262	60 51	029	54 30	094	44 22	152	47 11	199	24 55	250	43 55	283	33 09	320
263	61 18	027	55 28	095	44 49	153	46 51	200	24 01	251	42 59	283	32 32	320
264	61 44	026	56 26	095	45 15	154	46 30	202	23 06	251	42 02	283	31 55	320
265	62 09	024	57 24	095	45 40	155	46 08	203	22 10	251	41 05	283	31 17	320
266	62 32	023	58 22	096	46 04	156	45 45	204	21 15	252	40 09	283	30 39	319
267	62 54	021	59 20	096	46 27	158	45 21	205	20 20	252	39 12	283	30 01	319
268	63 15	020	60 18	097	46 48	159	44 56	206	19 24	252	38 16	283	29 23	319
269	63 34	018	61 16	097	47 09	160	44 30	207	18 29	253	37 19	284	28 45	319

LHA ♈	Hc	Zn	Hc	Zn	Hc	Zn	Hc	Zn	Hc	Zn	Hc	Zn	Hc	Zn
	VEGA		◆ DENEB		Enif		◆ Nunki		ANTARES		◆ ARCTURUS		Alkaid	
270	63 52	017	43 42	039	34 58	088	47 28	161	44 02	208	36 22	284	28 07	319
271	64 08	015	44 18	039	35 56	088	47 46	162	43 34	209	35 26	284	27 28	319
272	64 22	013	44 54	038	36 54	088	48 03	164	43 05	210	34 29	284	26 50	318
273	64 34	012	45 30	038	37 52	088	48 19	165	42 35	211	33 33	284	26 11	318
274	64 45	010	46 06	037	38 50	088	48 33	166	42 05	212	32 36	284	25 32	318
275	64 54	008	46 40	036	39 49	089	48 46	168	41 33	213	31 40	284	24 53	318
276	65 01	006	47 15	036	40 47	089	48 58	169	41 00	214	30 43	284	24 15	318
277	65 07	004	47 49	035	41 45	089	49 09	170	40 27	215	29 47	284	23 36	318
278	65 10	003	48 22	035	42 43	089	49 18	172	39 53	216	28 50	284	22 57	318
279	65 12	001	48 55	034	43 41	090	49 25	173	39 18	217	27 54	284	22 18	318
280	65 12	359	49 27	033	44 40	090	49 32	174	38 43	218	26 58	285	21 39	318
281	65 10	357	49 59	033	45 38	090	49 37	176	38 07	219	26 01	285	20 59	318
282	65 06	355	50 30	032	46 36	090	49 40	177	37 30	220	25 05	285	20 20	318
283	65 00	353	51 00	031	47 34	091	49 43	179	36 53	220	24 09	285	19 41	318
284	64 52	351	51 30	030	48 32	091	49 43	180	36 14	221	23 12	285	19 02	318
	◆ DENEB		Alpheratz		◆ FOMALHAUT		Nunki		ANTARES		◆ Rasalhague		VEGA	
285	51 59	029	17 43	063	17 55	128	49 43	181	35 36	222	69 26	268	64 42	350
286	52 27	029	18 35	064	18 41	128	49 41	183	34 57	223	68 27	269	64 31	348
287	52 54	028	19 27	064	19 26	129	49 37	184	34 17	223	67 29	269	64 18	346
288	53 21	027	20 19	064	20 12	129	49 32	185	33 36	224	66 31	269	64 03	344
289	53 47	026	21 12	064	20 56	130	49 26	187	32 56	225	65 33	270	63 47	343
290	54 12	025	22 04	064	21 41	130	49 19	188	32 14	226	64 35	270	63 29	341
291	54 36	024	22 56	064	22 25	131	49 10	190	31 33	226	63 36	270	63 09	340
292	54 59	023	23 48	064	23 09	131	48 59	191	30 50	227	62 38	270	62 48	338
293	55 21	022	24 41	064	23 53	132	48 48	192	30 08	227	61 40	271	62 26	337
294	55 42	021	25 33	064	24 36	132	48 35	194	29 24	228	60 42	271	62 02	335
295	56 02	020	26 25	064	25 19	133	48 20	195	28 41	229	59 43	271	61 37	334
296	56 21	019	27 18	064	26 01	133	48 05	196	27 57	229	58 45	271	61 11	332
297	56 39	017	28 10	064	26 44	134	47 48	197	27 13	230	57 47	271	60 43	331
298	56 56	016	29 02	064	27 25	135	47 30	199	26 28	230	56 49	272	60 15	330
299	57 11	015	29 55	064	28 06	135	47 11	200	25 43	231	55 51	272	59 45	329
	◆ DENEB		Alpheratz		◆ FOMALHAUT		Peacock		◆ ANTARES		Rasalhague		VEGA	
300	57 26	014	30 47	064	28 47	136	19 06	176	24 58	231	54 53	272	59 14	328
301	57 39	013	31 40	064	29 28	136	19 09	177	24 12	232	53 54	272	58 42	326
302	57 51	011	32 32	064	30 08	137	19 12	177	23 26	233	52 56	272	58 10	325
303	58 02	010	33 24	064	30 47	138	19 15	178	22 39	233	51 58	273	57 36	324
304	58 11	009	34 17	064	31 26	138	19 17	178	21 53	233	51 00	273	57 02	323
305	58 19	007	35 09	064	32 04	139	19 18	179	21 06	234	50 02	273	56 27	322
306	58 26	006	36 01	064	32 42	140	19 19	180	20 19	234	49 04	273	55 51	322
307	58 32	005	36 54	064	33 19	141	19 19	180	19 31	235	48 05	273	55 14	321
308	58 36	003	37 46	064	33 56	141	19 18	181	18 43	235	47 07	273	54 37	320
309	58 38	002	38 38	064	34 32	142	19 17	181	17 55	236	46 09	274	53 59	319
310	58 40	001	39 30	064	35 08	143	19 16	182	17 07	236	45 11	274	53 21	318
311	58 40	359	40 22	063	35 43	144	19 13	182	16 19	237	44 13	274	52 42	318
312	58 38	358	41 14	063	36 17	144	19 11	183	15 30	237	43 15	274	52 02	317
313	58 36	357	42 06	063	36 50	145	19 07	184	14 41	237	42 17	274	51 22	316
314	58 31	355	42 58	063	37 23	146	19 03	184	13 52	238	41 19	275	50 42	316
	Alpheratz		◆ Diphda		FOMALHAUT		◆ Nunki		Rasalhague		VEGA		◆ DENEB	
315	43 50	063	26 09	118	37 55	147	39 43	217	40 21	275	50 01	315	58 26	354
316	44 42	063	27 00	119	38 27	148	39 08	218	39 23	275	49 19	314	58 19	353
317	45 33	062	27 51	119	38 57	149	38 32	219	38 25	275	48 38	314	58 11	351
318	46 25	062	28 42	120	39 27	150	37 55	219	37 27	275	47 55	313	58 02	350
319	47 16	062	29 32	120	39 56	151	37 18	220	36 29	275	47 13	313	57 51	349
320	48 08	062	30 22	121	40 24	152	36 40	221	35 31	276	46 30	312	57 39	347
321	48 59	061	31 12	121	40 51	153	36 02	222	34 33	276	45 47	312	57 26	346
322	49 50	061	32 02	122	41 18	154	35 23	223	33 35	276	45 04	312	57 11	345
323	50 41	061	32 51	123	41 43	155	34 43	223	32 37	276	44 20	311	56 55	344
324	51 31	060	33 40	123	42 08	156	34 03	224	31 39	276	43 36	311	56 39	343
325	52 22	060	34 28	124	42 31	157	33 22	225	30 41	276	42 52	311	56 21	341
326	53 12	060	35 17	124	42 54	158	32 41	225	29 44	277	42 08	310	56 02	340
327	54 02	059	36 04	125	43 15	159	31 59	226	28 46	277	41 23	310	55 41	339
328	54 52	059	36 52	126	43 36	160	31 17	227	27 48	277	40 38	310	55 20	338
329	55 42	058	37 39	126	43 55	161	30 34	227	26 50	277	39 53	309	54 58	337
	◆ Alpheratz		Diphda		◆ FOMALHAUT		Peacock		ALTAIR		◆ VEGA		DENEB	
330	56 31	058	38 26	127	44 14	162	16 42	193	58 08	264	39 08	309	54 35	336
331	57 20	057	39 12	128	44 31	163	16 28	194	57 10	265	38 23	309	54 11	335
332	58 09	057	39 58	128	44 47	164	16 14	194	56 12	265	37 37	309	53 46	334
333	58 58	056	40 43	129	45 02	166	16 00	195	55 14	265	36 52	308	53 20	333
334	59 46	055	41 28	130	45 16	167	15 45	195	54 16	266	36 06	308	52 54	332
335	60 33	055	42 12	131	45 29	168	15 29	196	53 18	266	35 20	308	52 26	331
336	61 21	054	42 56	132	45 40	169	15 13	196	52 20	266	34 34	308	51 58	331
337	62 07	053	43 39	133	45 50	170	14 57	197	51 22	267	33 48	308	51 29	330
338	62 53	052	44 22	133	45 59	172	14 40	197	50 24	267	33 02	307	50 59	329
339	63 39	051	45 04	134	46 07	173	14 23	198	49 26	267	32 16	307	50 29	328
340	64 24	050	45 45	135	46 14	174	14 05	198	48 28	268	31 29	307	49 58	327
341	65 08	049	46 26	136	46 19	175	13 46	199	47 29	268	30 43	307	49 26	327
342	65 52	048	47 06	137	46 23	177	13 28	199	46 31	268	29 57	307	48 54	326
343	66 34	047	47 45	138	46 26	178	13 09	200	45 33	269	29 10	307	48 21	325
344	67 16	045	48 23	139	46 27	179	12 49	200	44 35	269	28 23	307	47 48	325
	Schedar		◆ Mirfak		Hamal		◆ ACHERNAR		FOMALHAUT		◆ ALTAIR		DENEB	
345	43 12	019	25 50	041	44 41	071	11 40	159	46 27	180	43 37	269	47 14	324
346	43 30	018	26 28	041	45 36	071	12 01	160	46 26	182	42 38	269	46 39	323
347	43 48	018	27 06	041	46 31	070	12 21	160	46 24	183	41 40	270	46 05	323
348	44 05	017	27 44	041	47 26	070	12 40	161	46 20	184	40 42	270	45 29	322
349	44 22	016	28 22	040	48 21	070	12 59	161	46 15	186	39 44	270	44 53	322
350	44 38	016	28 59	040	49 15	070	13 18	162	46 09	187	38 45	270	44 17	321
351	44 53	015	29 37	040	50 10	070	13 36	162	46 01	188	37 47	270	43 41	321
352	45 08	014	30 14	040	51 05	070	13 54	162	45 53	189	36 49	271	43 04	320
353	45 22	013	30 52	040	51 59	070	14 11	163	45 43	190	35 51	271	42 26	320
354	45 35	013	31 29	039	52 54	069	14 28	163	45 32	192	34 53	271	41 49	320
355	45 48	012	32 06	039	53 48	069	14 44	164	45 19	193	33 54	271	41 11	319
356	45 59	011	32 42	039	54 43	069	15 00	164	45 06	194	32 56	272	40 33	319
357	46 11	011	33 19	039	55 37	069	15 16	165	44 51	195	31 58	272	39 54	318
358	46 21	010	33 55	039	56 31	068	15 30	165	44 35	196	31 00	272	39 15	318
359	46 30	009	34 31	038	57 25	068	15 45	166	44 18	198	30 02	272	38 36	318

LHA ♈	Hc	Zn	Hc	Zn	Hc	Zn	Hc	Zn	Hc	Zn	Hc	Zn	Hc	Zn
	CAPELLA		◆ ALDEBARAN		Acamar		ACHERNAR		◆ FOMALHAUT		ALTAIR		◆ DENEB	
0	16 36	045	23 19	077	22 32	144	16 57	166	44 57	199	29 01	273	37 12	318
1	17 18	045	24 16	078	23 06	145	17 11	167	44 37	200	28 02	273	36 33	318
2	18 00	045	25 13	078	23 39	146	17 24	167	44 16	201	27 04	273	35 53	317
3	18 41	045	26 10	078	24 12	146	17 36	168	43 55	202	26 05	274	35 14	317
4	19 23	045	27 07	078	24 44	147	17 48	168	43 32	203	25 07	274	34 34	317
5	20 05	045	28 05	078	25 16	147	17 59	169	43 08	205	24 09	274	33 53	316
6	20 46	045	29 02	078	25 47	148	18 10	170	42 43	206	23 11	274	33 13	316
7	21 28	045	29 59	078	26 18	149	18 21	170	42 18	207	22 12	274	32 32	316
8	22 09	045	30 56	078	26 48	149	18 31	171	41 51	208	21 14	275	31 52	316
9	22 51	045	31 53	078	27 18	150	18 40	171	41 23	209	20 16	275	31 11	316
10	23 32	045	32 51	079	27 47	151	18 48	172	40 55	210	19 17	275	30 30	315
11	24 14	045	33 48	079	28 15	151	18 57	172	40 26	211	18 19	275	29 49	315
12	24 55	045	34 45	079	28 43	152	19 04	173	39 56	211	17 21	275	29 07	315
13	25 37	045	35 43	079	29 10	153	19 11	173	39 25	212	16 23	276	28 26	315
14	26 18	045	36 40	079	29 37	153	19 18	174	38 53	213	15 25	276	27 44	315
	CAPELLA		◆ ALDEBARAN		RIGEL		ACHERNAR		◆ FOMALHAUT		Enif		◆ DENEB	
15	26 59	045	37 37	079	23 11	105	19 24	175	38 21	214	42 11	272	27 03	315
16	27 40	045	38 35	079	24 07	105	19 29	175	37 47	215	41 12	272	26 21	314
17	28 21	044	39 32	079	25 03	106	19 34	176	37 14	216	40 14	272	25 39	314
18	29 02	044	40 30	079	26 00	106	19 38	176	36 39	217	39 15	272	24 57	314
19	29 43	044	41 27	079	26 56	106	19 41	177	36 04	217	38 17	272	24 16	314
20	30 23	044	42 25	079	27 52	107	19 44	177	35 28	218	37 18	273	23 34	314
21	31 04	044	43 22	079	28 48	107	19 47	178	34 52	219	36 20	273	22 52	314
22	31 44	043	44 19	079	29 44	107	19 48	179	34 14	220	35 22	273	22 10	314
23	32 24	043	45 17	080	30 39	108	19 50	179	33 37	220	34 23	273	21 27	314
24	33 04	043	46 14	080	31 35	108	19 50	180	32 59	221	33 25	273	20 45	314
25	33 44	043	47 12	080	32 30	109	19 50	180	32 20	222	32 27	274	20 03	314
26	34 23	043	48 09	080	33 26	109	19 50	181	31 41	223	31 28	274	19 21	314
27	35 03	042	49 07	080	34 21	110	19 49	181	31 01	223	30 30	274	18 39	314
28	35 42	042	50 04	080	35 16	110	19 47	182	30 21	224	29 32	274	17 57	314
29	36 21	042	51 02	080	36 11	110	19 45	183	29 40	224	28 33	274	17 14	314
	Mirfak		◆ CAPELLA		ALDEBARAN		RIGEL		◆ ACHERNAR		FOMALHAUT		◆ Alpheratz	
30	49 09	021	37 00	041	52 00	080	37 05	111	19 42	183	28 59	225	59 38	307
31	49 30	020	37 38	041	52 57	080	38 00	111	19 38	184	28 17	226	58 51	306
32	49 50	019	38 17	041	53 55	080	38 54	112	19 34	184	27 35	226	58 04	305
33	50 09	018	38 55	040	54 52	080	39 48	112	19 29	185	26 53	227	57 16	304
34	50 27	018	39 32	040	55 50	080	40 42	113	19 24	185	26 10	227	56 27	304
35	50 44	017	40 10	040	56 47	080	41 36	114	19 18	186	25 27	228	55 38	303
36	51 00	016	40 47	039	57 45	080	42 29	114	19 12	187	24 43	228	54 49	303
37	51 15	015	41 23	039	58 42	079	43 23	115	19 05	187	23 59	229	54 00	302
38	51 30	014	42 00	038	59 40	079	44 15	115	18 58	188	23 15	229	53 11	302
39	51 43	013	42 36	038	60 37	079	45 08	116	18 50	188	22 30	230	52 21	301
40	51 56	012	43 11	037	61 34	079	46 01	117	18 41	189	21 45	230	51 31	301
41	52 07	011	43 46	037	62 32	079	46 53	117	18 32	189	21 00	231	50 40	301
42	52 18	010	44 21	036	63 29	079	47 44	118	18 22	190	20 15	231	49 50	300
43	52 27	009	44 55	036	64 27	079	48 36	119	18 12	190	19 29	232	48 59	300
44	52 36	008	45 29	035	65 24	079	49 27	120	18 01	191	18 43	232	48 08	299
	CAPELLA		◆ POLLUX		PROCYON		SIRIUS		◆ ACHERNAR		Diphda		◆ Alpheratz	
45	46 03	034	22 12	065	20 36	089	26 48	117	17 50	191	44 27	228	47 17	299
46	46 35	034	23 05	065	21 35	090	27 40	117	17 38	192	43 43	229	46 26	299
47	47 08	033	23 58	065	22 33	090	28 32	118	17 25	193	42 59	230	45 35	299
48	47 40	033	24 50	065	23 32	090	29 24	118	17 12	193	42 14	231	44 44	298
49	48 11	032	25 43	065	24 30	090	30 15	118	16 59	194	41 29	231	43 52	298
50	48 41	031	26 36	065	25 28	090	31 07	119	16 45	194	40 43	232	43 01	298
51	49 11	030	27 29	065	26 27	091	31 58	119	16 30	195	39 56	233	42 09	298
52	49 40	030	28 22	065	27 25	091	32 48	120	16 15	195	39 10	233	41 17	298
53	50 09	029	29 15	065	28 24	091	33 39	121	16 00	196	38 22	234	40 25	297
54	50 37	028	30 08	065	29 22	091	34 29	121	15 44	196	37 35	235	39 33	297
55	51 04	027	31 01	065	30 21	092	35 19	122	15 28	197	36 47	235	38 41	297
56	51 30	026	31 54	065	31 19	092	36 08	122	15 11	197	35 59	236	37 49	297
57	51 56	025	32 47	065	32 18	092	36 58	123	14 53	198	35 10	237	36 57	297
58	52 21	025	33 40	065	33 16	092	37 47	124	14 36	198	34 21	237	36 05	297
59	52 44	024	34 33	065	34 14	093	38 35	124	14 17	198	33 31	238	35 13	297
	CAPELLA		◆ POLLUX		PROCYON		SIRIUS		◆ CANOPUS		Diphda		◆ Hamal	
60	53 07	023	35 26	065	35 13	093	39 23	125	17 21	158	32 42	238	61 29	296
61	53 30	022	36 19	065	36 11	093	40 11	126	17 43	159	31 52	239	60 36	295
62	53 51	021	37 12	065	37 10	093	40 58	126	18 04	159	31 01	240	59 43	295
63	54 11	020	38 04	064	38 08	094	41 45	127	18 25	160	30 11	240	58 50	294
64	54 30	019	38 57	064	39 06	094	42 32	128	18 45	160	29 20	241	57 56	294
65	54 48	017	39 50	064	40 05	094	43 18	129	19 04	161	28 29	241	57 03	293
66	55 05	016	40 42	064	41 03	094	44 03	129	19 23	161	27 38	242	56 09	293
67	55 21	015	41 35	064	42 01	095	44 48	130	19 42	162	26 46	242	55 15	293
68	55 36	014	42 27	064	42 59	095	45 32	131	20 00	162	25 55	242	54 21	292
69	55 50	013	43 20	064	43 58	095	46 16	132	20 17	163	25 03	243	53 27	292
70	56 02	012	44 12	063	44 56	096	46 59	133	20 34	163	24 11	243	52 33	292
71	56 13	011	45 04	063	45 54	096	47 42	134	20 51	164	23 18	244	51 38	292
72	56 24	009	45 57	063	46 52	096	48 24	135	21 06	165	22 26	244	50 44	291
73	56 32	008	46 49	063	47 50	097	49 05	136	21 22	165	21 33	245	49 50	291
74	56 40	007	47 41	062	48 48	097	49 45	137	21 36	166	20 40	245	48 55	291
	CAPELLA		◆ POLLUX		PROCYON		SIRIUS		◆ CANOPUS		Acamar		◆ Hamal	
75	56 46	006	48 32	062	49 46	097	50 25	138	21 50	166	29 47	206	48 00	291
76	56 52	004	49 24	062	50 44	098	51 03	139	22 04	167	29 21	207	47 06	291
77	56 55	003	50 15	062	51 42	098	51 41	140	22 16	168	28 54	208	46 11	291
78	56 58	002	51 07	061	52 40	099	52 18	141	22 29	168	28 27	208	45 16	290
79	56 59	001	51 58	061	53 38	099	52 54	143	22 40	169	27 59	209	44 21	290
80	56 59	359	52 49	060	54 35	099	53 29	144	22 51	170	27 30	210	43 27	290
81	56 58	358	53 40	060	55 33	100	54 03	145	23 02	170	27 00	210	42 32	290
82	56 55	357	54 30	060	56 30	100	54 36	147	23 11	171	26 31	211	41 37	290
83	56 51	355	55 21	059	57 28	101	55 07	148	23 20	171	26 00	212	40 42	290
84	56 46	354	56 11	059	58 25	101	55 37	149	23 29	172	25 29	212	39 47	290
85	56 39	353	57 00	058	59 23	102	56 07	151	23 36	173	24 57	213	38 52	290
86	56 32	352	57 50	057	60 20	103	56 34	152	23 44	173	24 25	214	37 57	290
87	56 23	351	58 39	057	61 17	103	57 01	154	23 50	174	23 53	214	37 02	290
88	56 12	349	59 28	056	62 13	104	57 26	156	23 56	175	23 20	215	36 07	290
89	56 01	348	60 16	055	63 10	105	57 49	157	24 01	175	22 46	215	35 12	290

LAT 13°N

LHA ♈	Hc	Zn	Hc	Zn	Hc	Zn	Hc	Zn	Hc	Zn	Hc	Zn	Hc	Zn
	Dubhe		◆ REGULUS		Suhail		SIRIUS		◆ RIGEL		ALDEBARAN		◆ CAPELLA	
90	17 59	029	29 19	084	19 02	146	58 11	159	66 05	208	69 35	283	55 48	347
91	18 27	029	30 17	084	19 34	146	58 31	161	65 36	210	68 38	282	55 34	346
92	18 55	029	31 15	084	20 07	147	58 50	162	65 06	212	67 41	282	55 19	345
93	19 23	029	32 14	084	20 38	147	59 07	164	64 33	214	66 44	282	55 03	343
94	19 51	029	33 12	084	21 10	148	59 22	166	64 00	216	65 46	281	54 46	342
95	20 19	029	34 10	084	21 40	148	59 35	168	63 24	218	64 49	281	54 28	341
96	20 47	029	35 08	084	22 11	149	59 47	170	62 48	220	63 52	281	54 09	340
97	21 15	028	36 06	085	22 41	150	59 56	171	62 10	221	62 54	281	53 49	339
98	21 43	028	37 04	085	23 10	150	60 04	173	61 30	223	61 57	281	53 27	338
99	22 11	028	38 03	085	23 39	151	60 10	175	60 50	224	60 59	281	53 05	337
100	22 38	028	39 01	085	24 07	151	60 14	177	60 08	226	60 02	281	52 42	336
101	23 06	028	39 59	085	24 35	152	60 16	179	59 26	227	59 05	281	52 18	335
102	23 33	028	40 57	085	25 02	153	60 15	181	58 42	229	58 07	280	51 53	334
103	24 00	028	41 56	086	25 29	153	60 13	183	57 58	230	57 10	280	51 28	334
104	24 27	027	42 54	086	25 55	154	60 09	185	57 13	231	56 12	280	51 01	333
	Dubhe		◆ REGULUS		Suhail		◆ SIRIUS		RIGEL		ALDEBARAN		◆ CAPELLA	
105	24 54	027	43 52	086	26 20	154	60 03	187	56 27	232	55 15	280	50 34	332
106	25 21	027	44 51	086	26 45	155	59 55	189	55 41	233	54 17	280	50 06	331
107	25 47	027	45 49	086	27 10	156	59 46	191	54 53	234	53 20	280	49 38	330
108	26 14	027	46 47	086	27 33	157	59 34	192	54 06	235	52 22	280	49 08	330
109	26 40	026	47 46	087	27 56	157	59 20	194	53 17	236	51 25	280	48 38	329
110	27 06	026	48 44	087	28 19	158	59 05	196	52 28	237	50 27	280	48 08	328
111	27 32	026	49 42	087	28 40	159	58 48	198	51 39	238	49 29	280	47 36	327
112	27 57	026	50 41	087	29 01	159	58 29	200	50 49	239	48 32	280	47 05	327
113	28 23	026	51 39	087	29 21	160	58 09	201	49 59	240	47 34	280	46 32	326
114	28 48	025	52 38	087	29 41	161	57 47	203	49 08	241	46 37	280	45 59	325
115	29 13	025	53 36	088	30 00	162	57 23	205	48 17	241	45 39	280	45 26	325
116	29 37	025	54 34	088	30 18	162	56 58	206	47 25	242	44 42	281	44 52	324
117	30 02	024	55 33	088	30 35	163	56 32	208	46 33	243	43 45	281	44 18	324
118	30 26	024	56 31	088	30 52	164	56 04	209	45 41	244	42 47	281	43 43	323
119	30 49	024	57 30	088	31 08	165	55 35	211	44 49	244	41 50	281	43 08	323
	Dubhe		◆ Denebola		Suhail		◆ SIRIUS		RIGEL		ALDEBARAN		◆ CAPELLA	
120	31 13	024	34 19	081	31 23	166	55 04	212	43 56	245	40 52	281	42 32	322
121	31 36	023	35 17	081	31 37	166	54 32	214	43 03	245	39 55	281	41 56	322
122	31 59	023	36 15	081	31 50	167	54 00	215	42 10	246	38 57	281	41 20	321
123	32 22	023	37 12	082	32 03	168	53 26	216	41 16	247	38 00	281	40 43	321
124	32 44	022	38 10	082	32 15	169	52 51	217	40 22	247	37 03	281	40 06	320
125	33 06	022	39 08	082	32 26	170	52 15	219	39 28	248	36 05	281	39 28	320
126	33 28	022	40 06	082	32 36	170	51 38	220	38 34	248	35 08	281	38 51	320
127	33 49	021	41 04	082	32 45	171	51 00	221	37 40	249	34 10	281	38 13	319
128	34 10	021	42 02	082	32 54	172	50 21	222	36 45	249	33 13	281	37 35	319
129	34 30	020	43 00	082	33 01	173	49 41	223	35 50	250	32 16	282	36 56	319
130	34 51	020	43 58	082	33 08	174	49 01	224	34 55	250	31 19	282	36 17	318
131	35 10	020	44 56	082	33 14	175	48 20	225	34 00	251	30 21	282	35 38	318
132	35 30	019	45 53	082	33 19	176	47 38	226	33 05	251	29 24	282	34 59	318
133	35 49	019	46 51	083	33 23	177	46 55	227	32 10	251	28 27	282	34 20	317
134	36 07	018	47 49	083	33 26	177	46 12	228	31 14	252	27 30	282	33 40	317
	Dubhe		◆ ARCTURUS		SPICA		◆ Suhail		SIRIUS		BETELGEUSE		◆ CAPELLA	
135	36 25	018	14 21	073	19 43	107	33 28	178	45 28	229	44 26	268	33 00	317
136	36 43	017	15 17	073	20 39	108	33 30	179	44 44	230	43 28	268	32 20	317
137	37 00	017	16 13	074	21 34	108	33 30	180	43 59	231	42 30	268	31 40	316
138	37 17	016	17 10	074	22 30	108	33 30	181	43 13	231	41 31	268	31 00	316
139	37 33	016	18 06	074	23 25	109	33 29	182	42 27	232	40 33	269	30 19	316
140	37 49	015	19 02	074	24 21	109	33 27	182	41 41	233	39 34	269	29 38	316
141	38 04	015	19 58	074	25 16	109	33 24	183	40 54	234	38 36	269	28 58	316
142	38 19	014	20 54	074	26 11	110	33 20	184	40 07	234	37 37	269	28 17	316
143	38 33	014	21 51	074	27 06	110	33 15	185	39 19	235	36 39	270	27 36	315
144	38 46	013	22 47	074	28 01	110	33 10	186	38 31	236	35 40	270	26 55	315
145	39 00	013	23 43	075	28 56	111	33 03	187	37 42	236	34 42	270	26 14	315
146	39 12	012	24 40	075	29 50	111	32 56	188	36 53	237	33 43	270	25 32	315
147	39 24	012	25 36	075	30 45	112	32 47	189	36 04	238	32 45	271	24 51	315
148	39 36	011	26 32	075	31 39	112	32 38	189	35 14	238	31 47	271	24 10	315
149	39 47	010	27 29	075	32 33	113	32 29	190	34 24	239	30 48	271	23 28	315
	◆ Dubhe		Alkaid		ARCTURUS		◆ SPICA		Suhail		◆ SIRIUS		POLLUX	
150	39 57	010	31 06	040	28 25	075	33 27	113	32 18	191	33 34	239	55 26	301
151	40 07	009	31 43	040	29 22	075	34 20	114	32 06	192	32 44	240	54 36	300
152	40 16	009	32 21	039	30 18	075	35 14	114	31 54	193	31 53	241	53 46	300
153	40 25	008	32 57	039	31 15	075	36 07	115	31 41	193	31 02	241	52 55	300
154	40 33	008	33 34	039	32 12	075	37 00	115	31 27	194	30 10	242	52 04	299
155	40 40	007	34 11	038	33 08	075	37 53	116	31 12	195	29 19	242	51 13	299
156	40 47	006	34 47	038	34 05	076	38 46	116	30 56	196	28 27	243	50 21	298
157	40 53	006	35 23	038	35 01	076	39 38	117	30 40	197	27 35	243	49 30	298
158	40 58	005	35 59	038	35 58	076	40 30	117	30 23	197	26 43	243	48 38	298
159	41 03	004	36 34	037	36 55	076	41 22	118	30 05	198	25 51	244	47 47	298
160	41 08	004	37 09	037	37 51	076	42 13	119	29 46	199	24 58	244	46 55	297
161	41 11	003	37 44	036	38 48	076	43 04	119	29 27	200	24 05	245	46 03	297
162	41 14	003	38 19	036	39 45	076	43 55	120	29 07	200	23 12	245	45 10	297
163	41 17	002	38 53	036	40 41	076	44 46	121	28 46	201	22 19	246	44 18	297
164	41 18	001	39 27	035	41 38	076	45 36	121	28 25	202	21 26	246	43 26	296
	◆ Dubhe		ARCTURUS		◆ SPICA		ACRUX		Suhail		◆ PROCYON		POLLUX	
165	41 19	001	42 35	076	46 25	122	11 58	170	28 02	203	40 07	266	42 34	296
166	41 20	000	43 31	076	47 15	123	12 07	171	27 40	203	39 09	266	41 41	296
167	41 20	359	44 28	076	48 03	124	12 17	171	27 16	204	38 10	266	40 48	296
168	41 19	359	45 25	076	48 52	125	12 26	171	26 52	205	37 12	267	39 56	296
169	41 17	358	46 22	076	49 40	126	12 34	172	26 27	205	36 14	267	39 03	296
170	41 15	358	47 18	076	50 27	126	12 42	172	26 02	206	35 15	267	38 10	296
171	41 12	357	48 15	076	51 14	127	12 50	173	25 36	207	34 17	267	37 18	295
172	41 09	356	49 12	076	52 00	128	12 57	173	25 10	207	33 19	268	36 25	295
173	41 05	356	50 08	076	52 45	129	13 04	174	24 43	208	32 20	268	35 32	295
174	41 00	355	51 05	076	53 30	130	13 10	174	24 15	209	31 22	268	34 39	295
175	40 55	354	52 01	076	54 14	132	13 16	175	23 47	209	30 23	268	33 46	295
176	40 49	354	52 58	075	54 58	133	13 21	175	23 18	210	29 25	269	32 53	295
177	40 42	353	53 55	075	55 40	134	13 26	175	22 49	210	28 26	269	32 00	295
178	40 35	353	54 51	075	56 22	135	13 31	176	22 19	211	27 28	269	31 07	295
179	40 27	352	55 48	075	57 03	136	13 34	176	21 49	211	26 29	269	30 14	295

LAT 13°N

LHA ♈	Hc	Zn	Hc	Zn	Hc	Zn	Hc	Zn	Hc	Zn	Hc	Zn	Hc	Zn
	Alkaid		◆ Alphecca		ANTARES		◆ ACRUX		REGULUS		◆ POLLUX		Dubhe	
180	47 29	026	37 56	066	13 26	122	13 38	177	62 56	271	29 21	295	40 19	351
181	47 54	025	38 50	066	14 16	122	13 41	177	61 58	271	28 28	295	40 10	351
182	48 19	025	39 43	066	15 05	122	13 43	178	60 59	271	27 35	295	40 00	350
183	48 43	024	40 37	066	15 55	123	13 46	178	60 01	271	26 43	295	39 50	350
184	49 06	023	41 30	066	16 44	123	13 47	179	59 02	272	25 50	295	39 39	349
185	49 28	022	42 23	066	17 33	124	13 48	179	58 04	272	24 57	295	39 28	349
186	49 50	021	43 16	065	18 21	124	13 49	180	57 05	272	24 04	295	39 16	348
187	50 11	020	44 10	065	19 10	124	13 49	180	56 07	272	23 11	295	39 04	347
188	50 31	020	45 03	065	19 58	125	13 49	181	55 09	272	22 18	295	38 51	347
189	50 50	019	45 56	065	20 46	125	13 48	181	54 10	272	21 25	295	38 37	346
190	51 08	018	46 49	065	21 33	126	13 47	181	53 12	273	20 32	295	38 23	346
191	51 26	017	47 41	064	22 21	126	13 45	182	52 13	273	19 39	295	38 09	345
192	51 42	016	48 34	064	23 08	127	13 43	182	51 15	273	18 46	295	37 53	345
193	51 58	015	49 27	064	23 54	127	13 40	183	50 17	273	17 54	296	37 38	344
194	52 12	014	50 19	064	24 41	128	13 37	183	49 18	273	17 01	296	37 22	344
	◆ VEGA		Rasalhague		ANTARES		◆ RIGIL KENT		Gienah		◆ REGULUS		Dubhe	
195	12 27	053	23 02	082	25 27	128	13 26	168	57 33	200	48 20	273	37 05	343
196	13 13	053	23 59	082	26 13	129	13 39	168	57 13	201	47 21	274	36 48	343
197	14 00	053	24 57	082	26 59	129	13 50	169	56 51	203	46 23	274	36 31	342
198	14 46	053	25 55	082	27 44	130	14 02	169	56 28	204	45 25	274	36 13	342
199	15 33	053	26 53	082	28 29	130	14 12	170	56 03	206	44 26	274	35 55	341
200	16 20	053	27 51	083	29 13	131	14 23	170	55 36	207	43 28	274	35 36	341
201	17 06	053	28 49	083	29 57	131	14 33	171	55 09	209	42 30	274	35 17	341
202	17 53	053	29 47	083	30 41	132	14 42	171	54 40	210	41 31	274	34 57	340
203	18 40	053	30 45	083	31 24	133	14 51	171	54 10	212	40 33	275	34 37	340
204	19 27	053	31 43	083	32 07	133	14 59	172	53 38	213	39 35	275	34 17	339
205	20 13	053	32 41	083	32 49	134	15 07	172	53 06	214	38 37	275	33 56	339
206	21 00	053	33 39	083	33 31	135	15 15	173	52 32	216	37 38	275	33 35	339
207	21 47	053	34 37	084	34 13	135	15 22	173	51 58	217	36 40	275	33 13	338
208	22 34	053	35 35	084	34 53	136	15 28	174	51 22	218	35 42	275	32 51	338
209	23 20	053	36 34	084	35 34	137	15 34	174	50 46	219	34 44	276	32 29	338
	◆ VEGA		Rasalhague		ANTARES		◆ RIGIL KENT		SPICA		◆ REGULUS		Dubhe	
210	24 07	053	37 32	084	36 14	137	15 40	175	64 20	200	33 46	276	32 06	337
211	24 54	053	38 30	084	36 53	138	15 45	175	63 59	202	32 48	276	31 44	337
212	25 40	053	39 28	084	37 32	139	15 49	176	63 37	204	31 49	276	31 20	337
213	26 27	053	40 26	084	38 10	140	15 53	176	63 12	206	30 51	276	30 57	336
214	27 14	053	41 24	085	38 47	141	15 56	177	62 46	208	29 53	276	30 33	336
215	28 00	053	42 23	085	39 24	141	15 59	177	62 18	210	28 55	277	30 09	336
216	28 47	053	43 21	085	40 00	142	16 02	178	61 49	211	27 57	277	29 45	335
217	29 33	053	44 19	085	40 36	143	16 04	178	61 17	213	26 59	277	29 20	335
218	30 20	052	45 17	085	41 10	144	16 05	179	60 45	215	26 01	277	28 56	335
219	31 06	052	46 16	085	41 44	145	16 06	179	60 11	216	25 03	277	28 31	335
220	31 52	052	47 14	085	42 17	146	16 06	180	59 35	218	24 05	277	28 05	334
221	32 38	052	48 12	086	42 50	147	16 06	180	58 59	219	23 07	278	27 40	334
222	33 24	052	49 10	086	43 21	148	16 05	181	58 21	221	22 09	278	27 14	334
223	34 10	052	50 09	086	43 52	149	16 04	181	57 42	222	21 11	278	26 48	334
224	34 56	051	51 07	086	44 22	150	16 02	182	57 03	224	20 13	278	26 22	333
	◆ VEGA		ALTAIR		ANTARES		◆ RIGIL KENT		SPICA		◆ Denebola		Alkaid	
225	35 41	051	18 33	085	44 50	151	16 00	182	56 22	225	43 52	278	50 51	341
226	36 27	051	19 32	085	45 18	152	15 57	183	55 40	226	42 55	278	50 32	340
227	37 12	051	20 30	085	45 45	153	15 54	183	54 57	227	41 57	278	50 12	340
228	37 58	051	21 28	085	46 11	154	15 50	184	54 14	228	40 59	278	49 51	339
229	38 43	050	22 26	086	46 36	155	15 46	184	53 30	230	40 01	278	49 30	338
230	39 28	050	23 25	086	47 00	157	15 41	185	52 45	231	39 03	278	49 07	337
231	40 12	050	24 23	086	47 22	158	15 36	185	51 59	232	38 05	278	48 44	336
232	40 57	049	25 21	086	47 44	159	15 30	186	51 13	233	37 07	278	48 20	336
233	41 41	049	26 20	086	48 04	160	15 24	186	50 27	234	36 10	279	47 56	335
234	42 25	049	27 18	087	48 23	162	15 17	187	49 39	234	35 12	279	47 31	334
235	43 09	048	28 16	087	48 41	163	15 10	187	48 51	235	34 14	279	47 05	333
236	43 52	048	29 15	087	48 58	164	15 02	188	48 03	236	33 16	279	46 38	333
237	44 36	048	30 13	087	49 13	165	14 54	188	47 14	237	32 18	279	46 11	332
238	45 19	047	31 12	087	49 27	167	14 45	189	46 25	238	31 21	279	45 43	331
239	46 01	047	32 10	088	49 40	168	14 36	189	45 35	239	30 23	279	45 15	331
	◆ VEGA		ALTAIR		Nunki		◆ ANTARES		SPICA		◆ ARCTURUS		Alkaid	
240	46 43	046	33 08	088	31 54	133	49 51	169	44 45	239	64 23	287	44 46	330
241	47 25	046	34 07	088	32 36	133	50 01	171	43 55	240	63 27	287	44 16	329
242	48 07	045	35 05	088	33 19	134	50 10	172	43 04	241	62 31	287	43 46	329
243	48 48	045	36 04	088	34 00	135	50 17	174	42 13	241	61 35	286	43 15	328
244	49 29	044	37 02	089	34 42	135	50 23	175	41 21	242	60 39	286	42 44	328
245	50 09	043	38 01	089	35 22	136	50 27	176	40 30	243	59 43	286	42 13	327
246	50 49	043	38 59	089	36 03	137	50 30	178	39 37	243	58 47	285	41 41	327
247	51 29	042	39 57	089	36 42	138	50 32	179	38 45	244	57 50	285	41 09	326
248	52 08	041	40 56	089	37 22	138	50 32	181	37 53	244	56 54	285	40 36	326
249	52 46	041	41 54	090	38 00	139	50 31	182	37 00	245	55 57	285	40 03	325
250	53 24	040	42 53	090	38 38	140	50 28	183	36 07	245	55 01	285	39 29	325
251	54 01	039	43 51	090	39 15	141	50 24	185	35 13	246	54 04	285	38 55	324
252	54 37	038	44 50	090	39 52	142	50 18	186	34 20	246	53 08	285	38 21	324
253	55 13	037	45 48	091	40 28	143	50 11	188	33 26	247	52 11	285	37 47	324
254	55 48	036	46 47	091	41 03	143	50 03	189	32 32	247	51 15	284	37 12	323
	◆ VEGA		ALTAIR		◆ Nunki		ANTARES		SPICA		◆ ARCTURUS		Alkaid	
255	56 23	035	47 45	091	41 37	144	49 53	190	31 38	248	50 18	284	36 36	323
256	56 56	035	48 44	091	42 11	145	49 42	192	30 44	248	49 21	284	36 01	322
257	57 29	033	49 42	092	42 44	146	49 29	193	29 50	249	48 25	284	35 25	322
258	58 01	032	50 40	092	43 16	147	49 15	194	28 55	249	47 28	284	34 49	322
259	58 32	031	51 39	092	43 47	148	49 00	196	28 00	250	46 31	284	34 13	322
260	59 01	030	52 37	092	44 17	149	48 44	197	27 06	250	45 35	284	33 37	321
261	59 30	029	53 36	093	44 47	150	48 26	198	26 11	250	44 38	284	33 00	321
262	59 58	028	54 34	093	45 15	151	48 07	200	25 16	251	43 41	284	32 23	321
263	60 25	026	55 32	093	45 43	153	47 47	201	24 20	251	42 45	284	31 46	320
264	60 50	025	56 31	093	46 09	154	47 26	202	23 25	251	41 48	284	31 09	320
265	61 14	024	57 29	094	46 34	155	47 03	203	22 29	252	40 51	284	30 31	320
266	61 37	022	58 27	094	46 59	156	46 40	204	21 34	252	39 55	284	29 53	320
267	61 58	021	59 26	094	47 22	157	46 15	205	20 38	253	38 58	284	29 16	320
268	62 18	019	60 24	095	47 44	158	45 50	207	19 42	253	38 01	284	28 38	319
269	62 37	018	61 22	095	48 05	160	45 23	208	18 46	253	37 04	284	28 00	319

LHA ♈	Hc	Zn	Hc	Zn	Hc	Zn	Hc	Zn	Hc	Zn	Hc	Zn	Hc	Zn
	VEGA		◆ DENEB		Enif		◆ Nunki		ANTARES		◆ ARCTURUS		Alkaid	
270	62 54	016	42 55	039	34 55	087	48 25	161	44 55	209	36 08	284	27 21	319
271	63 10	015	43 31	038	35 53	087	48 43	162	44 26	210	35 11	284	26 43	319
272	63 23	013	44 07	038	36 51	087	49 01	163	43 57	211	34 15	284	26 05	319
273	63 36	011	44 43	037	37 50	087	49 17	165	43 26	212	33 18	284	25 26	319
274	63 46	009	45 17	036	38 48	088	49 32	166	42 55	213	32 21	285	24 47	319
275	63 55	008	45 52	036	39 47	088	49 45	167	42 23	214	31 25	285	24 09	318
276	64 02	006	46 26	035	40 45	088	49 57	169	41 50	215	30 28	285	23 30	318
277	64 07	004	46 59	035	41 44	088	50 08	170	41 16	216	29 32	285	22 51	318
278	64 10	002	47 32	034	42 42	088	50 17	171	40 41	217	28 35	285	22 12	318
279	64 12	001	48 05	033	43 40	089	50 25	173	40 06	218	27 39	285	21 33	318
280	64 12	359	48 37	033	44 39	089	50 32	174	39 30	218	26 42	285	20 54	318
281	64 10	357	49 08	032	45 37	089	50 37	176	38 53	219	25 46	285	20 15	318
282	64 06	355	49 39	031	46 36	089	50 40	177	38 16	220	24 49	285	19 36	318
283	64 00	354	50 08	030	47 34	089	50 43	179	37 38	221	23 53	285	18 57	318
284	63 53	352	50 38	030	48 33	090	50 43	180	36 59	222	22 57	285	18 17	318
	◆ DENEB		Alpheratz		◆ FOMALHAUT		Nunki		ANTARES		◆ Rasalhague		VEGA	
285	51 06	029	17 16	063	18 32	128	50 43	181	36 20	222	69 26	271	63 43	350
286	51 34	028	18 08	063	19 18	128	50 41	183	35 40	223	68 27	271	63 32	348
287	52 01	027	19 00	063	20 04	129	50 37	184	35 00	224	67 29	271	63 20	347
288	52 27	026	19 53	063	20 49	129	50 32	186	34 19	225	66 31	272	63 05	345
289	52 53	025	20 45	063	21 35	129	50 26	187	33 38	225	65 32	272	62 49	343
290	53 17	024	21 37	063	22 20	130	50 18	188	32 56	226	64 34	272	62 32	342
291	53 41	023	22 29	064	23 04	130	50 09	190	32 14	227	63 35	272	62 13	340
292	54 03	022	23 22	064	23 49	131	49 58	191	31 31	227	62 37	272	61 53	339
293	54 25	021	24 14	064	24 33	131	49 46	192	30 48	228	61 38	272	61 31	337
294	54 46	020	25 07	064	25 16	132	49 33	194	30 04	229	60 40	273	61 08	336
295	55 06	019	25 59	064	26 00	132	49 18	195	29 20	229	59 42	273	60 43	335
296	55 24	018	26 51	064	26 43	133	49 02	196	28 36	230	58 43	273	60 17	333
297	55 42	017	27 44	064	27 25	134	48 45	198	27 51	230	57 45	273	59 50	332
298	55 58	016	28 36	064	28 07	134	48 27	199	27 06	231	56 46	273	59 22	331
299	56 13	015	29 28	064	28 49	135	48 07	200	26 21	231	55 48	273	58 53	330
	◆ DENEB		Alpheratz		◆ FOMALHAUT		Peacock		◆ ANTARES		Rasalhague		VEGA	
300	56 28	013	30 21	064	29 30	135	20 05	176	25 35	232	54 50	273	58 23	328
301	56 41	012	31 13	064	30 11	136	20 09	177	24 49	232	53 51	274	57 52	327
302	56 52	011	32 06	064	30 51	137	20 12	177	24 02	233	52 53	274	57 20	326
303	57 03	010	32 58	063	31 31	137	20 15	178	23 15	233	51 55	274	56 47	325
304	57 12	008	33 50	063	32 11	138	20 17	178	22 28	234	50 56	274	56 13	324
305	57 20	007	34 42	063	32 49	139	20 18	179	21 41	234	49 58	274	55 39	323
306	57 26	006	35 35	063	33 28	139	20 19	180	20 53	235	49 00	274	55 03	322
307	57 32	005	36 27	063	34 06	140	20 19	180	20 06	235	48 01	274	54 27	322
308	57 36	003	37 19	063	34 43	141	20 18	181	19 17	236	47 03	275	53 51	321
309	57 38	002	38 11	063	35 19	142	20 17	181	18 29	236	46 05	275	53 13	320
310	57 40	001	39 03	063	35 55	142	20 16	182	17 41	236	45 07	275	52 35	319
311	57 40	359	39 55	063	36 31	143	20 13	183	16 52	237	44 08	275	51 57	318
312	57 38	358	40 47	063	37 05	144	20 10	183	16 03	237	43 10	275	51 18	318
313	57 36	357	41 39	062	37 39	145	20 07	184	15 14	238	42 12	275	50 38	317
314	57 32	355	42 31	062	38 13	146	20 03	184	14 24	238	41 14	275	49 58	316
	Alpheratz		◆ Diphda		FOMALHAUT		◆ Nunki		Rasalhague		VEGA		◆ DENEB	
315	43 22	062	26 38	118	38 45	147	40 31	217	40 15	276	49 18	316	57 26	354
316	44 14	062	27 29	118	39 17	147	39 55	218	39 17	276	48 37	315	57 20	353
317	45 05	062	28 20	119	39 48	148	39 19	219	38 19	276	47 56	315	57 12	352
318	45 56	061	29 11	119	40 19	149	38 42	220	37 21	276	47 14	314	57 02	350
319	46 48	061	30 02	120	40 48	150	38 04	221	36 23	276	46 32	314	56 52	349
320	47 39	061	30 53	120	41 17	151	37 25	222	35 25	276	45 49	313	56 40	348
321	48 30	060	31 43	121	41 44	152	36 46	222	34 27	276	45 07	313	56 27	347
322	49 20	060	32 33	121	42 11	153	36 07	223	33 29	277	44 24	312	56 13	345
323	50 11	060	33 23	122	42 37	154	35 26	224	32 30	277	43 40	312	55 58	344
324	51 01	059	34 12	123	43 02	155	34 46	224	31 32	277	42 57	312	55 41	343
325	51 52	059	35 01	123	43 26	156	34 04	225	30 34	277	42 13	311	55 24	342
326	52 42	059	35 50	124	43 49	157	33 23	226	29 36	277	41 29	311	55 05	341
327	53 31	058	36 39	124	44 11	158	32 41	227	28 38	277	40 44	311	54 45	340
328	54 21	058	37 27	125	44 32	160	31 58	227	27 40	278	40 00	310	54 25	339
329	55 10	057	38 14	126	44 52	161	31 15	228	26 42	278	39 15	310	54 03	338
	◆ Alpheratz		Diphda		◆ FOMALHAUT		Peacock		ALTAIR		◆ VEGA		DENEB	
330	55 59	056	39 02	126	45 11	162	17 40	193	58 13	266	38 30	310	53 40	337
331	56 47	056	39 48	127	45 28	163	17 27	194	57 15	266	37 45	309	53 16	336
332	57 36	055	40 35	128	45 45	164	17 13	194	56 17	267	37 00	309	52 52	335
333	58 23	055	41 21	129	46 00	165	16 58	195	55 18	267	36 14	309	52 27	334
334	59 11	054	42 06	129	46 14	167	16 43	195	54 20	267	35 29	309	52 00	333
335	59 58	053	42 51	130	46 27	168	16 27	196	53 22	267	34 43	308	51 33	332
336	60 44	052	43 36	131	46 39	169	16 11	196	52 23	268	33 57	308	51 05	331
337	61 30	051	44 20	132	46 50	170	15 54	197	51 25	268	33 11	308	50 37	330
338	62 16	051	45 03	133	46 59	172	15 37	197	50 26	268	32 25	308	50 08	330
339	63 01	050	45 46	134	47 07	173	15 20	198	49 28	269	31 39	308	49 38	329
340	63 45	048	46 28	135	47 13	174	15 02	198	48 29	269	30 53	308	49 07	328
341	64 28	047	47 09	135	47 19	175	14 43	199	47 31	269	30 07	308	48 36	327
342	65 11	046	47 50	136	47 23	177	14 24	199	46 32	269	29 20	307	48 04	327
343	65 52	045	48 29	137	47 26	178	14 05	200	45 34	270	28 34	307	47 32	326
344	66 33	044	49 09	139	47 27	179	13 45	200	44 36	270	27 47	307	46 59	325
	Schedar		◆ Mirfak		Hamal		◆ ACHERNAR		FOMALHAUT		◆ ALTAIR		DENEB	
345	42 15	019	25 04	041	44 21	070	12 37	159	47 27	180	43 37	270	46 25	325
346	42 33	018	25 42	041	45 16	070	12 57	160	47 26	182	42 39	270	45 51	324
347	42 51	017	26 20	040	46 10	069	13 17	160	47 24	183	41 40	270	45 16	324
348	43 08	017	26 58	040	47 05	069	13 37	161	47 20	184	40 42	271	44 42	323
349	43 24	016	27 36	040	48 00	069	13 56	161	47 15	186	39 43	271	44 06	322
350	43 40	015	28 13	040	48 54	069	14 15	161	47 09	187	38 45	271	43 30	322
351	43 55	015	28 51	040	49 49	069	14 33	162	47 01	188	37 46	271	42 54	321
352	44 10	014	29 28	040	50 43	069	14 51	162	46 52	189	36 48	271	42 17	321
353	44 24	013	30 05	039	51 38	068	15 08	163	46 42	191	35 49	272	41 40	321
354	44 37	013	30 42	039	52 32	068	15 25	163	46 30	192	34 51	272	41 03	320
355	44 49	012	31 19	039	53 26	068	15 42	164	46 18	193	33 53	272	40 25	320
356	45 01	011	31 56	039	54 20	068	15 58	164	46 04	194	32 54	272	39 47	319
357	45 12	010	32 32	038	55 14	067	16 13	165	45 49	196	31 56	272	39 09	319
358	45 22	010	33 08	038	56 08	067	16 28	165	45 33	197	30 57	273	38 30	319
359	45 31	009	33 44	038	57 02	067	16 43	166	45 15	198	29 59	273	37 52	318

LAT 12°N

LHA ♈	Hc	Zn	Hc	Zn	Hc	Zn	Hc	Zn	Hc	Zn	Hc	Zn	Hc	Zn
	CAPELLA		◆ ALDEBARAN		Acamar		ACHERNAR		◆ FOMALHAUT		ALTAIR		◆ DENEB	
0	15 54	045	23 06	077	23 21	144	17 55	166	45 53	199	28 57	274	36 28	318
1	16 36	045	24 03	077	23 55	145	18 09	167	45 33	201	27 59	274	35 49	318
2	17 17	045	25 00	077	24 29	145	18 22	167	45 12	202	27 00	274	35 09	318
3	17 59	045	25 57	077	25 02	146	18 35	168	44 50	203	26 01	274	34 30	317
4	18 41	045	26 54	077	25 34	147	18 47	168	44 27	204	25 03	274	33 50	317
5	19 22	045	27 52	077	26 06	147	18 58	169	44 03	205	24 04	274	33 10	317
6	20 04	045	28 49	078	26 38	148	19 09	169	43 37	206	23 06	275	32 30	317
7	20 46	045	29 46	078	27 09	148	19 20	170	43 11	207	22 07	275	31 49	316
8	21 27	045	30 44	078	27 40	149	19 30	171	42 44	208	21 09	275	31 09	316
9	22 09	045	31 41	078	28 10	150	19 39	171	42 16	209	20 10	275	30 28	316
10	22 50	045	32 38	078	28 39	150	19 48	172	41 47	210	19 12	275	29 47	316
11	23 31	045	33 36	078	29 08	151	19 56	172	41 17	211	18 14	276	29 06	316
12	24 13	045	34 33	078	29 36	152	20 04	173	40 47	212	17 15	276	28 25	315
13	24 54	045	35 31	078	30 03	152	20 11	173	40 15	213	16 17	276	27 43	315
14	25 35	044	36 28	078	30 30	153	20 17	174	39 43	214	15 18	276	27 02	315
	CAPELLA		◆ ALDEBARAN		RIGEL		ACHERNAR		◆ FOMALHAUT		Enif		◆ DENEB	
15	26 16	044	37 26	078	23 26	105	20 23	174	39 10	215	42 08	273	26 21	315
16	26 57	044	38 23	078	24 23	105	20 29	175	38 36	215	41 10	273	25 39	315
17	27 38	044	39 21	078	25 19	105	20 33	176	38 02	216	40 11	273	24 57	315
18	28 19	044	40 18	078	26 16	105	20 38	176	37 27	217	39 12	273	24 15	315
19	28 59	044	41 16	078	27 12	106	20 41	177	36 51	218	38 14	273	23 34	314
20	29 40	043	42 13	078	28 09	106	20 44	177	36 15	219	37 15	273	22 52	314
21	30 20	043	43 11	078	29 05	107	20 47	178	35 38	219	36 17	274	22 10	314
22	31 00	043	44 08	079	30 01	107	20 48	179	35 00	220	35 18	274	21 28	314
23	31 40	043	45 06	079	30 57	107	20 50	179	34 22	221	34 20	274	20 46	314
24	32 20	043	46 03	079	31 53	108	20 50	180	33 44	222	33 21	274	20 04	314
25	33 00	042	47 01	079	32 49	108	20 50	180	33 04	222	32 22	274	19 21	314
26	33 39	042	47 58	079	33 45	108	20 50	181	32 25	223	31 24	274	18 39	314
27	34 18	042	48 56	079	34 41	109	20 49	181	31 44	224	30 25	275	17 57	314
28	34 57	042	49 53	078	35 36	109	20 47	182	31 04	224	29 27	275	17 15	314
29	35 36	041	50 51	078	36 31	110	20 45	183	30 23	225	28 28	275	16 33	314
	Mirfak		◆ CAPELLA		ALDEBARAN		RIGEL		◆ ACHERNAR		FOMALHAUT		◆ Alpheratz	
30	48 13	021	36 15	041	51 48	078	37 26	110	20 42	183	29 41	225	59 02	308
31	48 33	020	36 53	041	52 46	078	38 21	111	20 38	184	28 59	226	58 16	307
32	48 53	019	37 31	040	53 43	078	39 16	111	20 34	184	28 16	227	57 28	306
33	49 12	018	38 09	040	54 41	078	40 11	112	20 29	185	27 34	227	56 41	306
34	49 29	017	38 46	039	55 38	078	41 05	112	20 24	185	26 50	228	55 53	305
35	49 46	016	39 23	039	56 35	078	41 59	113	20 18	186	26 07	228	55 05	304
36	50 02	015	40 00	039	57 33	078	42 53	113	20 12	187	25 23	229	54 16	304
37	50 17	014	40 36	038	58 30	078	43 47	114	20 05	187	24 38	229	53 28	303
38	50 32	014	41 12	038	59 28	078	44 41	115	19 57	188	23 54	230	52 38	303
39	50 45	013	41 48	037	60 25	078	45 34	115	19 49	188	23 09	230	51 49	302
40	50 57	012	42 23	037	61 22	077	46 27	116	19 40	189	22 24	231	50 59	302
41	51 08	011	42 58	036	62 20	077	47 20	116	19 31	189	21 38	231	50 09	302
42	51 19	010	43 33	036	63 17	077	48 12	117	19 21	190	20 52	232	49 19	301
43	51 28	009	44 07	035	64 14	077	49 04	118	19 11	190	20 06	232	48 29	301
44	51 36	008	44 40	034	65 11	076	49 56	119	19 00	191	19 19	233	47 38	300
	CAPELLA		◆ POLLUX		PROCYON		SIRIUS		◆ ACHERNAR		Diphda		◆ Alpheratz	
45	45 13	034	21 46	064	20 35	089	27 15	116	18 48	192	45 07	229	46 48	300
46	45 46	033	22 39	064	21 34	089	28 07	117	18 36	192	44 22	230	45 57	300
47	46 17	033	23 32	064	22 33	089	29 00	117	18 24	193	43 37	230	45 06	300
48	46 49	032	24 25	065	23 31	090	29 52	117	18 11	193	42 52	231	44 15	299
49	47 20	031	25 18	065	24 30	090	30 44	118	17 57	194	42 06	232	43 24	299
50	47 50	031	26 11	065	25 29	090	31 35	118	17 43	194	41 19	233	42 32	299
51	48 19	030	27 04	065	26 27	090	32 27	119	17 29	195	40 32	233	41 41	299
52	48 48	029	27 57	065	27 26	090	33 18	119	17 13	195	39 45	234	40 49	298
53	49 16	028	28 50	064	28 25	091	34 09	120	16 58	196	38 57	235	39 57	298
54	49 44	027	29 43	064	29 23	091	35 00	121	16 42	196	38 09	235	39 06	298
55	50 10	027	30 36	064	30 22	091	35 50	121	16 25	197	37 21	236	38 14	298
56	50 36	026	31 29	064	31 21	091	36 40	122	16 08	197	36 32	237	37 22	298
57	51 02	025	32 21	064	32 19	091	37 30	122	15 51	198	35 42	237	36 30	298
58	51 26	024	33 14	064	33 18	092	38 20	123	15 33	198	34 53	238	35 38	297
59	51 49	023	34 07	064	34 17	092	39 09	124	15 14	199	34 03	238	34 46	297
	CAPELLA		◆ POLLUX		PROCYON		SIRIUS		◆ CANOPUS		Diphda		◆ Hamal	
60	52 12	022	35 00	064	35 15	092	39 57	124	18 17	158	33 13	239	61 02	297
61	52 34	021	35 53	064	36 14	092	40 46	125	18 39	158	32 22	240	60 10	297
62	52 54	020	36 45	064	37 13	093	41 34	126	19 00	159	31 32	240	59 17	296
63	53 14	019	37 38	064	38 11	093	42 21	126	19 21	159	30 41	241	58 24	296
64	53 33	018	38 31	064	39 10	093	43 08	127	19 41	160	29 49	241	57 31	295
65	53 51	017	39 23	063	40 08	093	43 55	128	20 01	161	28 58	242	56 38	295
66	54 07	016	40 16	063	41 07	094	44 41	129	20 20	161	28 06	242	55 45	294
67	54 23	015	41 08	063	42 06	094	45 26	129	20 39	162	27 14	242	54 51	294
68	54 38	014	42 01	063	43 04	094	46 11	130	20 57	162	26 22	243	53 57	294
69	54 51	013	42 53	063	44 03	094	46 56	131	21 15	163	25 30	243	53 04	293
70	55 03	011	43 45	063	45 01	095	47 40	132	21 32	163	24 37	244	52 10	293
71	55 14	010	44 37	062	46 00	095	48 23	133	21 48	164	23 45	244	51 16	293
72	55 24	009	45 29	062	46 58	095	49 06	134	22 04	165	22 52	244	50 22	293
73	55 33	008	46 21	062	47 57	096	49 47	135	22 20	165	21 59	245	49 27	292
74	55 41	007	47 12	062	48 55	096	50 29	136	22 34	166	21 06	245	48 33	292
	CAPELLA		◆ POLLUX		PROCYON		SIRIUS		◆ CANOPUS		Acamar		◆ Hamal	
75	55 47	005	48 04	061	49 53	096	51 09	137	22 49	166	30 41	207	47 39	292
76	55 52	004	48 55	061	50 52	097	51 48	138	23 02	167	30 15	207	46 44	292
77	55 55	003	49 46	061	51 50	097	52 27	139	23 15	168	29 47	208	45 49	292
78	55 58	002	50 37	060	52 48	097	53 05	141	23 27	168	29 19	209	44 55	291
79	55 59	001	51 28	060	53 46	098	53 41	142	23 39	169	28 51	209	44 00	291
80	55 59	359	52 19	059	54 44	098	54 17	143	23 50	169	28 22	210	43 05	291
81	55 58	358	53 09	059	55 43	098	54 52	144	24 01	170	27 52	211	42 11	291
82	55 55	357	53 59	058	56 41	099	55 25	146	24 10	171	27 22	211	41 16	291
83	55 51	356	54 49	058	57 39	099	55 58	147	24 20	171	26 51	212	40 21	291
84	55 46	354	55 39	057	58 36	100	56 29	149	24 28	172	26 20	213	39 26	291
85	55 40	353	56 28	057	59 34	100	56 59	150	24 36	173	25 48	213	38 31	291
86	55 32	352	57 17	056	60 32	101	57 27	152	24 43	173	25 15	214	37 36	291
87	55 23	351	58 06	056	61 29	101	57 54	153	24 50	174	24 42	214	36 41	291
88	55 13	350	58 54	055	62 27	102	58 20	155	24 55	175	24 09	215	35 46	290
89	55 02	348	59 41	054	63 24	103	58 44	157	25 01	175	23 35	216	34 51	290

LHA ♈	Hc	Zn	Hc	Zn	Hc	Zn	Hc	Zn	Hc	Zn	Hc	Zn	Hc	Zn
	Dubhe		◆ REGULUS		Suhail		SIRIUS		◆ RIGEL		ALDEBARAN		◆ CAPELLA	
90	17 06	029	29 12	083	19 51	146	59 07	158	66 57	209	69 21	285	54 50	347
91	17 34	029	30 10	083	20 24	146	59 28	160	66 27	212	68 24	285	54 36	346
92	18 02	029	31 09	083	20 57	147	59 47	162	65 56	214	67 27	284	54 22	345
93	18 31	029	32 07	083	21 29	147	60 04	164	65 23	216	66 30	284	54 06	344
94	18 59	029	33 05	084	22 00	148	60 20	165	64 48	218	65 33	284	53 49	343
95	19 27	028	34 04	084	22 32	148	60 34	167	64 11	219	64 36	283	53 31	342
96	19 55	028	35 02	084	23 02	149	60 46	169	63 33	221	63 39	283	53 12	341
97	20 22	028	36 00	084	23 32	149	60 56	171	62 54	223	62 42	283	52 52	340
98	20 50	028	36 59	084	24 02	150	61 04	173	62 14	224	61 45	283	52 32	339
99	21 18	028	37 57	084	24 31	151	61 10	175	61 32	226	60 47	282	52 10	338
100	21 45	028	38 55	084	25 00	151	61 14	177	60 50	227	59 50	282	51 47	337
101	22 13	028	39 54	084	25 28	152	61 16	179	60 06	229	58 53	282	51 24	336
102	22 40	028	40 52	085	25 55	152	61 15	181	59 22	230	57 55	282	50 59	335
103	23 07	027	41 51	085	26 22	153	61 13	183	58 36	231	56 58	282	50 34	334
104	23 34	027	42 49	085	26 49	154	61 09	185	57 50	232	56 01	282	50 08	333
	Dubhe		◆ REGULUS		Suhail		◆ SIRIUS		RIGEL		ALDEBARAN		◆ CAPELLA	
105	24 01	027	43 48	085	27 15	154	61 03	187	57 03	233	55 03	282	49 41	332
106	24 27	027	44 46	085	27 40	155	60 55	189	56 16	235	54 06	282	49 14	332
107	24 54	027	45 44	085	28 04	156	60 45	191	55 28	236	53 08	282	48 45	331
108	25 20	026	46 43	085	28 28	156	60 33	193	54 39	237	52 11	282	48 16	330
109	25 46	026	47 41	085	28 51	157	60 19	195	53 50	237	51 13	282	47 47	329
110	26 12	026	48 40	086	29 14	158	60 03	197	53 00	238	50 16	282	47 17	329
111	26 38	026	49 38	086	29 36	158	59 45	198	52 10	239	49 18	281	46 46	328
112	27 03	026	50 37	086	29 57	159	59 26	200	51 19	240	48 21	281	46 14	327
113	27 28	025	51 36	086	30 18	160	59 05	202	50 28	241	47 23	281	45 42	327
114	27 53	025	52 34	086	30 38	161	58 42	204	49 37	242	46 26	281	45 10	326
115	28 18	025	53 33	086	30 57	161	58 18	205	48 45	242	45 28	281	44 37	325
116	28 43	025	54 31	086	31 15	162	57 52	207	47 53	243	44 31	281	44 03	325
117	29 07	024	55 30	086	31 33	163	57 25	208	47 00	244	43 33	282	43 29	324
118	29 31	024	56 28	087	31 49	164	56 56	210	46 07	244	42 36	282	42 55	324
119	29 55	024	57 27	087	32 05	165	56 26	211	45 14	245	41 38	282	42 20	323
	Dubhe		◆ Denebola		Suhail		◆ SIRIUS		RIGEL		ALDEBARAN		◆ CAPELLA	
120	30 18	023	34 09	081	32 21	165	55 55	213	44 21	246	40 41	282	41 45	323
121	30 41	023	35 07	081	32 35	166	55 22	214	43 27	246	39 43	282	41 09	322
122	31 04	023	36 05	081	32 49	167	54 49	216	42 34	247	38 46	282	40 33	322
123	31 26	022	37 03	081	33 02	168	54 14	217	41 39	247	37 48	282	39 56	321
124	31 49	022	38 01	081	33 13	169	53 38	218	40 45	248	36 51	282	39 19	321
125	32 10	022	38 59	081	33 25	169	53 01	219	39 51	248	35 53	282	38 42	321
126	32 32	021	39 57	081	33 35	170	52 23	221	38 56	249	34 56	282	38 05	320
127	32 53	021	40 55	081	33 44	171	51 45	222	38 01	249	33 58	282	37 27	320
128	33 14	021	41 53	081	33 53	172	51 05	223	37 06	250	33 01	282	36 49	319
129	33 34	020	42 51	081	34 01	173	50 25	224	36 11	250	32 04	282	36 11	319
130	33 54	020	43 49	081	34 07	174	49 43	225	35 15	251	31 06	282	35 32	319
131	34 14	019	44 47	081	34 13	175	49 02	226	34 20	251	30 09	282	34 53	318
132	34 33	019	45 45	081	34 19	175	48 19	227	33 24	252	29 12	282	34 14	318
133	34 52	018	46 43	082	34 23	176	47 36	228	32 29	252	28 14	282	33 35	318
134	35 10	018	47 41	082	34 26	177	46 52	229	31 33	252	27 17	283	32 56	318
	Dubhe		◆ ARCTURUS		SPICA		◆ Suhail		SIRIUS		BETELGEUSE		◆ CAPELLA	
135	35 28	018	14 04	073	20 00	107	34 28	178	46 07	230	44 28	269	32 16	317
136	35 45	017	15 00	073	20 56	107	34 30	179	45 22	231	43 30	269	31 36	317
137	36 02	017	15 56	073	21 52	107	34 30	180	44 37	231	42 31	269	30 56	317
138	36 19	016	16 53	073	22 48	108	34 30	181	43 50	232	41 32	269	30 16	317
139	36 35	016	17 49	074	23 44	108	34 29	182	43 04	233	40 34	270	29 36	316
140	36 51	015	18 45	074	24 40	108	34 27	183	42 17	234	39 35	270	28 55	316
141	37 06	015	19 41	074	25 36	109	34 24	183	41 29	234	38 36	270	28 15	316
142	37 20	014	20 38	074	26 31	109	34 20	184	40 41	235	37 38	270	27 34	316
143	37 34	014	21 34	074	27 26	110	34 15	185	39 53	236	36 39	270	26 53	316
144	37 48	013	22 31	074	28 22	110	34 09	186	39 04	237	35 40	271	26 12	316
145	38 01	013	23 27	074	29 17	110	34 03	187	38 15	237	34 42	271	25 31	316
146	38 14	012	24 24	074	30 12	111	33 55	188	37 25	238	33 43	271	24 50	315
147	38 25	011	25 20	074	31 06	111	33 47	189	36 36	238	32 44	271	24 09	315
148	38 37	011	26 17	074	32 01	112	33 38	189	35 45	239	31 45	271	23 27	315
149	38 48	010	27 13	075	32 56	112	33 28	190	34 55	240	30 47	272	22 46	315
	◆ Dubhe		Alkaid		ARCTURUS		◆ SPICA		Suhail		◆ SIRIUS		POLLUX	
150	38 58	010	30 20	039	28 10	075	33 50	112	33 17	191	34 04	240	54 55	302
151	39 08	009	30 57	039	29 06	075	34 44	113	33 05	192	33 13	241	54 05	302
152	39 17	009	31 34	039	30 03	075	35 38	113	32 52	193	32 22	241	53 15	301
153	39 25	008	32 11	039	31 00	075	36 32	114	32 39	194	31 31	242	52 25	301
154	39 33	007	32 47	038	31 56	075	37 25	114	32 25	194	30 39	242	51 34	300
155	39 40	007	33 24	038	32 53	075	38 19	115	32 10	195	29 47	243	50 43	300
156	39 47	006	34 00	038	33 49	075	39 12	115	31 54	196	28 55	243	49 52	299
157	39 53	006	34 35	037	34 46	075	40 05	116	31 37	197	28 02	243	49 01	299
158	39 59	005	35 11	037	35 43	075	40 57	117	31 20	198	27 10	244	48 10	299
159	40 04	004	35 46	037	36 40	075	41 49	117	31 02	198	26 17	244	47 18	299
160	40 08	004	36 21	036	37 36	075	42 42	118	30 43	199	25 24	245	46 27	298
161	40 11	003	36 56	036	38 33	075	43 33	118	30 23	200	24 31	245	45 35	298
162	40 14	003	37 30	036	39 30	075	44 25	119	30 03	201	23 37	246	44 43	298
163	40 17	002	38 04	035	40 26	075	45 16	120	29 42	201	22 44	246	43 51	297
164	40 18	001	38 38	035	41 23	075	46 06	121	29 20	202	21 50	246	42 59	297
	◆ Dubhe		ARCTURUS		◆ SPICA		ACRUX		Suhail		◆ PROCYON		POLLUX	
165	40 19	001	42 20	075	46 57	121	12 57	170	28 58	203	40 11	267	42 07	297
166	40 20	000	43 16	075	47 47	122	13 07	171	28 35	204	39 12	267	41 14	297
167	40 20	359	44 13	075	48 36	123	13 16	171	28 11	204	38 14	267	40 22	297
168	40 19	359	45 10	075	49 25	124	13 25	171	27 47	205	37 15	267	39 29	297
169	40 17	358	46 06	075	50 14	125	13 34	172	27 22	206	36 17	268	38 37	296
170	40 15	358	47 03	075	51 02	125	13 42	172	26 56	206	35 18	268	37 44	296
171	40 12	357	48 00	075	51 50	126	13 49	173	26 30	207	34 19	268	36 52	296
172	40 09	356	48 56	075	52 37	127	13 57	173	26 03	207	33 21	268	35 59	296
173	40 05	356	49 53	075	53 23	128	14 03	174	25 36	208	32 22	269	35 06	296
174	40 00	355	50 49	074	54 09	129	14 10	174	25 08	209	31 23	269	34 13	296
175	39 55	355	51 46	074	54 54	130	14 16	175	24 39	209	30 25	269	33 20	296
176	39 49	354	52 42	074	55 38	132	14 21	175	24 10	210	29 26	269	32 28	296
177	39 43	353	53 39	074	56 21	133	14 26	175	23 41	211	28 27	269	31 35	296
178	39 36	353	54 35	074	57 04	134	14 30	176	23 11	211	27 29	270	30 42	296
179	39 28	352	55 31	074	57 46	135	14 34	176	22 40	212	26 30	270	29 49	296

LHA ♈	Hc Zn	Hc Zn	Hc Zn	Hc Zn	Hc Zn	Hc Zn	Hc Zn
	Alkaid	◆Alphecca	ANTARES	◆ACRUX	REGULUS	◆POLLUX	Dubhe
180	46 35 026	37 32 065	13 58 121	14 38 177	62 54 273	28 56 296	39 19 352
181	47 00 025	38 25 065	14 48 122	14 41 177	61 56 273	28 03 295	39 11 351
182	47 24 024	39 19 065	15 37 122	14 43 178	60 57 273	27 10 295	39 01 350
183	47 48 023	40 12 065	16 27 123	14 46 178	59 58 273	26 17 295	38 51 350
184	48 11 023	41 05 065	17 16 123	14 47 179	59 00 273	25 24 295	38 40 349
185	48 33 022	41 58 065	18 06 123	14 48 179	58 01 273	24 31 295	38 29 349
186	48 54 021	42 51 065	18 55 124	14 49 180	57 03 273	23 38 296	38 17 348
187	49 15 020	43 44 064	19 43 124	14 49 180	56 04 274	22 45 296	38 05 348
188	49 34 019	44 37 064	20 32 124	14 49 181	55 05 274	21 52 296	37 52 347
189	49 53 018	45 30 064	21 20 125	14 48 181	54 07 274	20 59 296	37 39 347
190	50 11 017	46 23 064	22 08 125	14 47 181	53 08 274	20 06 296	37 25 346
191	50 28 016	47 15 064	22 56 126	14 45 182	52 10 274	19 13 296	37 10 346
192	50 44 016	48 08 063	23 43 126	14 43 182	51 11 274	18 20 296	36 56 345
193	51 00 015	49 00 063	24 30 127	14 40 183	50 13 274	17 28 296	36 40 345
194	51 14 014	49 52 063	25 17 127	14 37 183	49 14 274	16 35 296	36 24 344
	◆VEGA	Rasalhague	ANTARES	◆RIGIL KENT	Gienah	◆REGULUS	Dubhe
195	11 50 052	22 53 081	26 04 128	14 25 168	58 30 200	48 16 274	36 08 344
196	12 37 052	23 51 081	26 50 128	14 37 168	58 09 202	47 17 275	35 51 343
197	13 23 053	24 49 082	27 36 129	14 49 169	57 46 203	46 19 275	35 34 343
198	14 10 053	25 47 082	28 22 129	15 01 169	57 22 205	45 20 275	35 16 342
199	14 57 053	26 45 082	29 07 130	15 11 170	56 57 207	44 22 275	34 58 342
200	15 43 053	27 43 082	29 52 130	15 22 170	56 30 208	43 23 275	34 39 341
201	16 30 053	28 41 082	30 37 131	15 32 170	56 01 210	42 25 275	34 20 341
202	17 17 053	29 39 082	31 21 132	15 41 171	55 32 211	41 26 275	34 00 340
203	18 04 053	30 37 082	32 04 132	15 50 171	55 01 212	40 28 275	33 41 340
204	18 50 053	31 36 083	32 48 133	15 59 172	54 28 214	39 30 276	33 20 340
205	19 37 053	32 34 083	33 31 133	16 07 172	53 55 215	38 31 276	33 00 339
206	20 24 053	33 32 083	34 13 134	16 14 173	53 21 216	37 33 276	32 39 339
207	21 11 053	34 30 083	34 55 135	16 21 173	52 45 218	36 34 276	32 17 338
208	21 57 053	35 29 083	35 36 135	16 28 174	52 09 219	35 36 276	31 56 338
209	22 44 053	36 27 083	36 17 136	16 34 174	51 32 220	34 38 276	31 34 338
	◆VEGA	Rasalhague	ANTARES	◆RIGIL KENT	SPICA	◆REGULUS	Dubhe
210	23 31 053	37 25 083	36 58 137	16 39 175	65 16 200	33 39 276	31 11 337
211	24 17 053	38 23 083	37 38 138	16 44 175	64 55 202	32 41 277	30 48 337
212	25 04 053	39 22 084	38 17 138	16 49 176	64 32 205	31 43 277	30 25 337
213	25 51 052	40 20 084	38 55 139	16 53 176	64 06 207	30 44 277	30 02 336
214	26 37 052	41 18 084	39 33 140	16 56 177	63 39 209	29 46 277	29 38 336
215	27 24 052	42 17 084	40 11 141	16 59 177	63 10 210	28 48 277	29 15 336
216	28 10 052	43 15 084	40 47 142	17 02 178	62 40 212	27 50 277	28 50 336
217	28 56 052	44 13 084	41 23 143	17 04 178	62 07 214	26 51 277	28 26 335
218	29 43 052	45 12 084	41 59 144	17 05 179	61 34 216	25 53 278	28 01 335
219	30 29 052	46 10 084	42 33 144	17 06 179	60 59 217	24 55 278	27 36 335
220	31 15 052	47 09 084	43 07 145	17 06 180	60 22 219	23 57 278	27 11 334
221	32 01 051	48 07 085	43 40 146	17 06 180	59 45 221	22 59 278	26 46 334
222	32 47 051	49 05 085	44 12 147	17 05 181	59 06 222	22 01 278	26 20 334
223	33 33 051	50 04 085	44 43 148	17 04 181	58 26 223	21 03 278	25 54 334
224	34 18 051	51 02 085	45 13 149	17 02 182	57 46 225	20 05 278	25 28 334
	◆VEGA	ALTAIR	ANTARES	◆RIGIL KENT	SPICA	◆Denebola	Alkaid
225	35 04 051	18 28 084	45 43 151	17 00 182	57 04 226	43 44 279	49 54 342
226	35 49 050	19 26 085	46 11 152	16 57 183	56 21 227	42 46 279	49 36 341
227	36 34 050	20 25 085	46 39 153	16 54 183	55 38 228	41 48 279	49 16 340
228	37 19 050	21 23 085	47 05 154	16 50 184	54 53 230	40 50 279	48 55 339
229	38 04 050	22 22 085	47 30 155	16 46 184	54 08 231	39 52 279	48 34 338
230	38 49 049	23 20 085	47 55 156	16 41 185	53 23 232	38 54 279	48 12 338
231	39 33 049	24 19 086	48 18 157	16 36 185	52 36 233	37 56 279	47 49 337
232	40 17 049	25 17 086	48 40 159	16 30 186	51 49 234	36 58 279	47 26 336
233	41 01 048	26 16 086	49 00 160	16 24 186	51 02 235	36 00 279	47 01 335
234	41 45 048	27 14 086	49 20 161	16 17 187	50 14 235	35 02 279	46 37 334
235	42 29 048	28 13 086	49 38 162	16 09 187	49 25 236	34 04 279	46 11 334
236	43 12 047	29 11 086	49 55 164	16 01 188	48 36 237	33 06 280	45 45 333
237	43 55 047	30 10 087	50 11 165	15 53 188	47 46 238	32 09 280	45 18 332
238	44 37 046	31 08 087	50 25 166	15 44 189	46 56 239	31 11 280	44 50 332
239	45 20 046	32 07 087	50 38 168	15 35 189	46 06 239	30 13 280	44 22 331
	◆VEGA	ALTAIR	Nunki	◆ANTARES	SPICA	◆ARCTURUS	Alkaid
240	46 02 045	33 06 087	32 34 132	50 50 169	45 15 240	64 05 289	43 53 330
241	46 43 045	34 04 087	33 17 133	51 00 171	44 24 241	63 09 289	43 24 330
242	47 24 044	35 03 087	34 00 134	51 09 172	43 33 242	62 14 288	42 55 329
243	48 05 044	36 02 088	34 43 134	51 17 173	42 41 242	61 18 288	42 24 329
244	48 46 043	37 00 088	35 24 135	51 23 175	41 49 243	60 22 288	41 54 328
245	49 26 043	37 59 088	36 06 136	51 27 176	40 57 243	59 26 287	41 22 328
246	50 05 042	38 57 088	36 46 136	51 30 178	40 04 244	58 30 287	40 51 327
247	50 44 041	39 56 088	37 27 137	51 32 179	39 11 245	57 34 287	40 19 327
248	51 22 041	40 55 089	38 06 138	51 32 181	38 18 245	56 37 287	39 46 326
249	52 00 040	41 53 089	38 45 139	51 31 182	37 25 246	55 41 286	39 13 326
250	52 37 039	42 52 089	39 24 139	51 28 183	36 31 246	54 45 286	38 40 325
251	53 14 038	43 51 089	40 02 140	51 24 185	35 38 247	53 48 286	38 06 325
252	53 50 037	44 50 089	40 39 141	51 18 186	34 44 247	52 52 286	37 32 324
253	54 25 036	45 48 090	41 15 142	51 11 188	33 50 248	51 56 286	36 58 324
254	55 00 036	46 47 090	41 51 143	51 02 189	32 55 248	50 59 286	36 23 324
	◆VEGA	ALTAIR	◆Nunki	ANTARES	SPICA	◆ARCTURUS	Alkaid
255	55 34 035	47 46 090	42 26 144	50 52 191	32 01 248	50 03 286	35 49 323
256	56 07 034	48 44 090	43 00 145	50 41 192	31 06 249	49 06 285	35 13 323
257	56 39 033	49 43 090	43 34 146	50 28 193	30 11 249	48 09 285	34 38 323
258	57 10 032	50 42 091	44 06 147	50 14 195	29 16 250	47 13 285	34 02 322
259	57 40 030	51 40 091	44 38 148	49 58 196	28 21 250	46 16 285	33 26 322
260	58 09 029	52 39 091	45 09 149	49 41 197	27 26 250	45 19 285	32 50 322
261	58 38 028	53 38 091	45 39 150	49 23 199	26 31 251	44 23 285	32 13 321
262	59 05 027	54 36 091	46 08 151	49 04 200	25 35 251	43 26 285	31 36 321
263	59 31 026	55 35 092	46 36 152	48 43 201	24 39 252	42 29 285	30 59 321
264	59 55 024	56 34 092	47 03 153	48 21 202	23 44 252	41 33 285	30 22 321
265	60 19 023	57 32 092	47 29 154	47 58 204	22 48 252	40 36 285	29 45 320
266	60 41 022	58 31 093	47 53 156	47 34 205	21 52 253	39 39 285	29 07 320
267	61 02 020	59 30 093	48 17 157	47 09 206	20 56 253	38 43 285	28 30 320
268	61 22 019	60 28 093	48 40 158	46 43 207	20 00 253	37 46 285	27 52 320
269	61 40 017	61 27 093	49 01 159	46 16 208	19 04 253	36 49 285	27 14 320

LAT 12°N

LHA ♈	Hc Zn	Hc Zn	Hc Zn	Hc Zn	Hc Zn	Hc Zn	Hc Zn
	VEGA	◆DENEB	Enif	◆Nunki	ANTARES	◆ARCTURUS	Alkaid
270	61 56 016	42 08 038	34 51 086	49 21 160	45 48 209	35 53 285	26 36 319
271	62 11 014	42 44 037	35 50 086	49 40 162	45 18 210	34 56 285	25 58 319
272	62 25 012	43 19 037	36 48 086	49 58 163	44 48 211	33 59 285	25 19 319
273	62 37 011	43 54 036	37 47 087	50 15 164	44 17 212	33 03 285	24 41 319
274	62 47 009	44 29 036	38 45 087	50 30 166	43 45 213	32 06 285	24 02 319
275	62 55 007	45 03 035	39 44 087	50 43 167	43 12 214	31 09 285	23 24 319
276	63 02 006	45 37 035	40 43 087	50 56 169	42 39 215	30 13 285	22 45 319
277	63 07 004	46 10 034	41 41 087	51 07 170	42 04 216	29 16 285	22 06 319
278	63 10 002	46 43 033	42 40 087	51 16 171	41 29 217	28 20 285	21 27 318
279	63 12 001	47 15 033	43 38 088	51 25 173	40 53 218	27 23 285	20 48 318
280	63 12 359	47 46 032	44 37 088	51 31 174	40 17 219	26 26 286	20 09 318
281	63 10 357	48 17 031	45 36 088	51 37 176	39 40 220	25 30 286	19 30 318
282	63 06 355	48 47 031	46 34 088	51 40 177	39 02 221	24 33 286	18 51 318
283	63 00 354	49 17 030	47 33 088	51 43 178	38 23 221	23 37 286	18 12 318
284	62 53 352	49 45 029	48 32 089	51 43 180	37 44 222	22 40 286	17 33 318
	◆DENEB	Alpheratz	◆FOMALHAUT	Nunki	ANTARES	◆Rasalhague	VEGA
285	50 14 028	16 49 063	19 08 127	51 43 181	37 04 223	69 23 274	62 44 350
286	50 41 027	17 41 063	19 55 128	51 41 183	36 24 224	68 25 274	62 34 349
287	51 07 027	18 33 063	20 41 128	51 37 184	35 43 224	67 26 274	62 21 347
288	51 33 026	19 26 063	21 27 129	51 32 186	35 02 225	66 28 274	62 07 346
289	51 58 025	20 18 063	22 13 129	51 25 187	34 20 226	65 29 274	61 52 344
290	52 22 024	21 10 063	22 58 130	51 17 189	33 38 226	64 31 274	61 35 342
291	52 46 023	22 03 063	23 43 130	51 08 190	32 55 227	63 32 274	61 16 341
292	53 08 022	22 55 063	24 28 131	50 57 191	32 12 228	62 33 274	60 57 339
293	53 29 021	23 47 063	25 12 131	50 45 193	31 28 228	61 35 274	60 35 338
294	53 49 020	24 40 063	25 56 132	50 31 194	30 44 229	60 36 274	60 13 337
295	54 09 019	25 32 063	26 40 132	50 16 195	29 59 230	59 38 274	59 49 335
296	54 27 018	26 24 063	27 23 133	50 00 197	29 15 230	58 39 274	59 24 334
297	54 44 016	27 17 063	28 06 133	49 42 198	28 29 231	57 41 275	58 57 333
298	55 00 015	28 09 063	28 49 134	49 23 199	27 44 231	56 42 275	58 30 332
299	55 15 014	29 02 063	29 31 134	49 03 201	26 58 232	55 44 275	58 01 330
	◆DENEB	Alpheratz	◆FOMALHAUT	Peacock	◆ANTARES	Rasalhague	VEGA
300	55 29 013	29 54 063	30 13 135	21 05 176	26 12 232	54 45 275	57 32 329
301	55 42 012	30 46 063	30 54 136	21 09 177	25 25 233	53 47 275	57 01 328
302	55 53 011	31 39 063	31 35 136	21 12 177	24 38 233	52 48 275	56 30 327
303	56 04 009	32 31 063	32 15 137	21 15 178	23 51 234	51 50 275	55 58 326
304	56 13 008	33 23 063	32 55 138	21 17 178	23 04 234	50 52 275	55 24 325
305	56 20 007	34 15 063	33 34 138	21 18 179	22 16 235	49 53 275	54 50 324
306	56 27 006	35 07 063	34 13 139	21 19 180	21 28 235	48 55 275	54 16 323
307	56 32 004	35 59 063	34 51 140	21 19 180	20 40 235	47 56 276	53 40 322
308	56 36 003	36 51 062	35 29 140	21 18 181	19 51 236	46 58 276	53 04 322
309	56 38 002	37 43 062	36 06 141	21 17 181	19 03 236	45 59 276	52 27 321
310	56 40 001	38 35 062	36 43 142	21 16 182	18 14 237	45 01 276	51 50 320
311	56 40 359	39 27 062	37 19 143	21 13 183	17 25 237	44 03 276	51 12 319
312	56 38 358	40 19 062	37 54 144	21 10 183	16 35 237	43 04 276	50 33 319
313	56 36 357	41 11 062	38 28 144	21 07 184	15 46 238	42 06 276	49 54 318
314	56 32 356	42 02 061	39 02 145	21 03 184	14 56 238	41 08 276	49 15 317
	Alpheratz	◆Diphda	FOMALHAUT	◆Nunki	Rasalhague	VEGA	◆DENEB
315	42 54 061	27 05 118	39 35 146	41 19 218	40 09 276	48 35 317	56 27 354
316	43 45 061	27 57 118	40 08 147	40 42 219	39 11 277	47 54 316	56 20 353
317	44 36 061	28 49 118	40 39 148	40 05 220	38 13 277	47 13 316	56 12 352
318	45 27 060	29 41 119	41 10 149	39 27 220	37 14 277	46 32 315	56 03 351
319	46 18 060	30 32 119	41 40 150	38 49 221	36 16 277	45 50 314	55 53 349
320	47 09 060	31 23 120	42 09 151	38 10 222	35 18 277	45 08 314	55 42 348
321	48 00 059	32 14 120	42 37 152	37 30 223	34 20 277	44 26 314	55 29 347
322	48 50 059	33 04 121	43 05 153	36 50 224	33 21 277	43 43 313	55 15 346
323	49 40 059	33 54 121	43 31 154	36 10 224	32 23 277	43 00 313	55 00 345
324	50 30 058	34 44 122	43 57 155	35 28 225	31 25 277	42 17 312	54 44 343
325	51 20 058	35 34 123	44 21 156	34 47 226	30 27 278	41 33 312	54 27 342
326	52 10 057	36 23 123	44 45 157	34 04 226	29 29 278	40 49 312	54 08 341
327	52 59 057	37 12 124	45 07 158	33 22 227	28 30 278	40 05 311	53 49 340
328	53 48 056	38 01 124	45 28 159	32 39 228	27 32 278	39 21 311	53 29 339
329	54 37 056	38 49 125	45 49 160	31 55 228	26 34 278	38 36 311	53 07 338
	◆Alpheratz	Diphda	◆FOMALHAUT	Peacock	ALTAIR	◆VEGA	DENEB
330	55 25 055	39 37 126	46 08 162	18 39 193	58 17 268	37 52 310	52 45 337
331	56 13 055	40 24 126	46 26 163	18 25 194	57 18 268	37 07 310	52 22 336
332	57 01 054	41 11 127	46 43 164	18 11 194	56 19 268	36 22 310	51 58 335
333	57 48 053	41 58 128	46 58 165	17 56 195	55 21 268	35 37 309	51 33 334
334	58 35 053	42 44 129	47 13 166	17 41 195	54 22 269	34 51 309	51 07 333
335	59 21 052	43 30 129	47 26 168	17 25 196	53 23 269	34 06 309	50 40 333
336	60 07 051	44 15 130	47 38 169	17 09 196	52 25 269	33 20 309	50 13 332
337	60 52 050	44 59 131	47 49 170	16 52 197	51 26 269	32 34 309	49 45 331
338	61 37 049	45 43 132	47 58 171	16 35 197	50 27 269	31 48 308	49 16 330
339	62 21 048	46 27 133	48 06 173	16 17 198	49 29 270	31 02 308	48 46 329
340	63 04 047	47 09 134	48 13 174	15 59 198	48 30 270	30 16 308	48 16 329
341	63 47 046	47 51 135	48 19 175	15 40 199	47 31 270	29 30 308	47 45 328
342	64 29 045	48 33 136	48 23 177	15 21 199	46 33 270	28 44 308	47 14 327
343	65 09 043	49 13 137	48 26 178	15 02 200	45 34 271	27 57 308	46 42 327
344	65 49 042	49 53 138	48 27 179	14 42 200	44 35 271	27 11 308	46 09 326
	Schedar	◆Mirfak	Hamal	◆ACHERNAR	FOMALHAUT	◆ALTAIR	DENEB
345	41 18 018	24 19 040	44 00 069	13 33 159	48 27 180	43 37 271	45 36 325
346	41 36 018	24 57 040	44 54 069	13 53 160	48 26 182	42 38 271	45 02 325
347	41 54 017	25 35 040	45 49 068	14 14 160	48 24 183	41 39 271	44 28 324
348	42 10 016	26 12 040	46 43 068	14 33 161	48 20 184	40 41 271	43 53 324
349	42 27 016	26 50 040	47 38 068	14 53 161	48 15 186	39 42 272	43 18 323
350	42 42 015	27 27 040	48 32 068	15 12 161	48 08 187	38 43 272	42 43 323
351	42 57 014	28 05 039	49 27 068	15 30 162	48 00 188	37 45 272	42 07 322
352	43 12 014	28 42 039	50 21 067	15 48 162	47 51 190	36 46 272	41 31 322
353	43 25 013	29 19 039	51 15 067	16 06 163	47 41 191	35 47 272	40 54 321
354	43 38 012	29 56 039	52 09 067	16 23 163	47 29 192	34 49 273	40 17 321
355	43 50 012	30 32 038	53 03 067	16 40 164	47 16 193	33 50 273	39 39 320
356	44 02 011	31 09 038	53 57 066	16 56 164	47 02 195	32 51 273	39 02 320
357	44 12 010	31 45 038	54 51 066	17 11 165	46 47 196	31 53 273	38 24 319
358	44 22 009	32 21 038	55 44 066	17 26 165	46 30 197	30 54 273	37 45 319
359	44 32 009	32 57 037	56 37 065	17 41 166	46 12 198	29 56 273	37 07 319

LHA ♈	Hc	Zn	Hc	Zn	Hc	Zn	Hc	Zn	Hc	Zn	Hc	Zn	Hc	Zn
	CAPELLA		◆ ALDEBARAN		Acamar		ACHERNAR		◆ FOMALHAUT		ALTAIR		◆ DENEB	
0	15 12	045	22 52	077	24 09	144	18 54	166	46 50	200	28 53	274	35 43	319
1	15 53	045	23 49	077	24 44	145	19 07	167	46 29	201	27 54	274	35 04	318
2	16 35	045	24 46	077	25 18	145	19 21	167	46 08	202	26 56	274	34 25	318
3	17 17	045	25 44	077	25 51	146	19 33	168	45 45	203	25 57	275	33 45	318
4	17 58	045	26 41	077	26 24	146	19 46	168	45 22	204	24 58	275	33 06	318
5	18 40	045	27 38	077	26 57	147	19 57	169	44 57	205	23 59	275	32 26	317
6	19 22	045	28 36	077	27 29	147	20 08	169	44 31	206	23 01	275	31 46	317
7	20 03	045	29 33	077	28 00	148	20 19	170	44 04	207	22 02	275	31 06	317
8	20 45	045	30 31	077	28 31	149	20 29	170	43 37	208	21 03	275	30 25	317
9	21 26	045	31 28	077	29 01	149	20 38	171	43 08	209	20 05	276	29 45	316
10	22 07	045	32 26	077	29 31	150	20 47	172	42 39	210	19 06	276	29 04	316
11	22 49	044	33 23	077	30 00	151	20 55	172	42 09	211	18 08	276	28 23	316
12	23 30	044	34 21	077	30 29	151	21 03	173	41 37	212	17 09	276	27 42	316
13	24 11	044	35 18	077	30 56	152	21 10	173	41 06	213	16 10	276	27 01	316
14	24 52	044	36 15	077	31 24	153	21 17	174	40 33	214	15 12	276	26 19	315
	CAPELLA		◆ ALDEBARAN		RIGEL		ACHERNAR		◆ FOMALHAUT		Enif		◆ DENEB	
15	25 33	044	37 13	077	23 41	104	21 23	174	39 59	215	42 05	274	25 38	315
16	26 14	044	38 10	078	24 38	104	21 28	175	39 25	216	41 06	274	24 57	315
17	26 55	044	39 08	078	25 35	105	21 33	176	38 50	217	40 07	274	24 15	315
18	27 35	043	40 06	078	26 32	105	21 37	176	38 15	218	39 09	274	23 33	315
19	28 16	043	41 03	078	27 29	105	21 41	177	37 39	218	38 10	274	22 52	315
20	28 56	043	42 01	078	28 25	106	21 44	177	37 02	219	37 11	274	22 10	315
21	29 36	043	42 58	078	29 22	106	21 47	178	36 24	220	36 12	274	21 28	315
22	30 16	043	43 56	078	30 18	106	21 48	179	35 46	221	35 14	274	20 46	315
23	30 56	042	44 53	078	31 15	107	21 50	179	35 08	221	34 15	275	20 04	314
24	31 36	042	45 51	078	32 11	107	21 50	180	34 28	222	33 16	275	19 22	314
25	32 15	042	46 48	077	33 08	107	21 50	180	33 49	223	32 18	275	18 40	314
26	32 54	042	47 46	077	34 04	108	21 50	181	33 08	223	31 19	275	17 57	314
27	33 33	041	48 43	077	35 00	108	21 49	181	32 28	224	30 20	275	17 15	314
28	34 12	041	49 41	077	35 56	109	21 47	182	31 47	225	29 22	275	16 33	314
29	34 51	041	50 38	077	36 51	109	21 44	183	31 05	225	28 23	275	15 51	314
	Mirfak		◆ CAPELLA		ALDEBARAN		RIGEL		◆ ACHERNAR		FOMALHAUT		◆ Alpheratz	
30	47 17	020	35 29	040	51 35	077	37 47	110	21 41	183	30 23	226	58 25	309
31	47 37	019	36 07	040	52 33	077	38 42	110	21 38	184	29 40	226	57 39	308
32	47 56	019	36 45	040	53 30	077	39 38	110	21 34	184	28 58	227	56 52	308
33	48 14	018	37 22	039	54 28	077	40 33	111	21 29	185	28 14	228	56 06	307
34	48 32	017	38 00	039	55 25	077	41 28	111	21 24	185	27 31	228	55 18	306
35	48 49	016	38 36	038	56 22	077	42 22	112	21 18	186	26 47	229	54 31	306
36	49 04	015	39 13	038	57 20	076	43 17	112	21 11	187	26 02	229	53 42	305
37	49 19	014	39 49	038	58 17	076	44 11	113	21 04	187	25 17	230	52 54	304
38	49 33	013	40 25	037	59 14	076	45 05	114	20 57	188	24 32	230	52 05	304
39	49 46	012	41 00	037	60 11	076	45 59	114	20 48	188	23 47	231	51 16	303
40	49 58	011	41 35	036	61 08	076	46 53	115	20 40	189	23 01	231	50 27	303
41	50 09	010	42 10	036	62 05	075	47 46	115	20 30	189	22 15	232	49 38	303
42	50 20	009	42 44	035	63 02	075	48 39	116	20 20	190	21 29	232	48 48	302
43	50 29	008	43 17	035	63 59	075	49 32	117	20 10	191	20 43	232	47 58	302
44	50 37	007	43 50	034	64 56	074	50 24	118	19 59	191	19 56	233	47 08	301
	CAPELLA		◆ POLLUX		PROCYON		SIRIUS		◆ ACHERNAR		Diphda		◆ Alpheratz	
45	44 23	033	21 20	064	20 34	089	27 41	116	19 47	192	45 46	230	46 17	301
46	44 55	033	22 13	064	21 33	089	28 34	116	19 35	192	45 01	230	45 27	301
47	45 27	032	23 06	064	22 32	089	29 27	117	19 22	193	44 15	231	44 36	300
48	45 58	031	23 59	064	23 31	089	30 19	117	19 09	193	43 29	232	43 45	300
49	46 28	031	24 52	064	24 29	089	31 12	117	18 56	194	42 43	233	42 54	300
50	46 58	030	25 45	064	25 28	089	32 04	118	18 41	194	41 55	233	42 03	300
51	47 27	029	26 38	064	26 27	090	32 56	118	18 27	195	41 08	234	41 12	299
52	47 56	029	27 31	064	27 26	090	33 47	119	18 11	195	40 20	235	40 20	299
53	48 23	028	28 24	064	28 25	090	34 39	119	17 56	196	39 32	235	39 29	299
54	48 50	027	29 17	064	29 24	090	35 30	120	17 39	196	38 43	236	38 37	299
55	49 17	026	30 09	064	30 23	090	36 21	120	17 23	197	37 54	237	37 45	299
56	49 42	025	31 02	064	31 22	091	37 12	121	17 05	197	37 04	237	36 54	298
57	50 07	024	31 55	064	32 21	091	38 02	122	16 48	198	36 15	238	36 02	298
58	50 31	024	32 48	064	33 19	091	38 52	122	16 30	198	35 25	239	35 10	298
59	50 54	023	33 41	064	34 18	091	39 41	123	16 11	199	34 34	239	34 18	298
	CAPELLA		◆ POLLUX		PROCYON		SIRIUS		◆ CANOPUS		Diphda		◆ Hamal	
60	51 16	022	34 33	063	35 17	091	40 31	124	19 12	158	33 43	240	60 34	299
61	51 38	021	35 26	063	36 16	092	41 20	124	19 34	158	32 53	240	59 42	298
62	51 58	020	36 19	063	37 15	092	42 08	125	19 56	159	32 01	241	58 50	298
63	52 17	019	37 11	063	38 14	092	42 56	126	20 17	159	31 10	241	57 58	297
64	52 36	018	38 04	063	39 13	092	43 44	126	20 37	160	30 18	242	57 05	297
65	52 53	017	38 56	063	40 12	093	44 31	127	20 57	160	29 26	242	56 12	296
66	53 10	016	39 49	063	41 10	093	45 18	128	21 17	161	28 34	242	55 19	296
67	53 25	015	40 41	062	42 09	093	46 04	129	21 36	162	27 42	243	54 26	295
68	53 39	013	41 33	062	43 08	093	46 50	129	21 54	162	26 49	243	53 33	295
69	53 52	012	42 25	062	44 07	093	47 35	130	22 12	163	25 57	244	52 39	295
70	54 04	011	43 17	062	45 06	094	48 20	131	22 29	163	25 04	244	51 46	294
71	54 15	010	44 09	061	46 04	094	49 04	132	22 46	164	24 11	244	50 52	294
72	54 25	009	45 00	061	47 03	094	49 47	133	23 02	164	23 17	245	49 58	294
73	54 34	008	45 52	061	48 02	094	50 30	134	23 18	165	22 24	245	49 04	293
74	54 41	007	46 43	061	49 01	095	51 11	135	23 32	166	21 31	246	48 10	293
	CAPELLA		◆ POLLUX		PROCYON		SIRIUS		◆ CANOPUS		Acamar		◆ Hamal	
75	54 47	005	47 35	060	49 59	095	51 53	136	23 47	166	31 35	207	47 16	293
76	54 52	004	48 26	060	50 58	095	52 33	137	24 01	167	31 08	208	46 21	293
77	54 56	003	49 16	060	51 57	096	53 12	139	24 14	167	30 40	208	45 27	292
78	54 58	002	50 07	059	52 55	096	53 51	140	24 26	168	30 12	209	44 33	292
79	54 59	001	50 58	059	53 54	096	54 28	141	24 38	169	29 43	210	43 38	292
80	54 59	359	51 48	058	54 52	097	55 05	142	24 49	169	29 14	210	42 43	292
81	54 58	358	52 38	058	55 51	097	55 40	144	25 00	170	28 44	211	41 49	292
82	54 55	357	53 27	057	56 49	097	56 15	145	25 10	171	28 13	212	40 54	292
83	54 51	356	54 17	057	57 47	098	56 48	146	25 19	171	27 42	212	39 59	292
84	54 46	355	55 06	056	58 46	098	57 20	148	25 27	172	27 10	213	39 05	291
85	54 40	353	55 55	056	59 44	099	57 51	149	25 35	173	26 38	214	38 10	291
86	54 33	352	56 43	055	60 42	099	58 20	151	25 43	173	26 05	214	37 15	291
87	54 24	351	57 31	054	61 40	100	58 48	153	25 49	174	25 32	215	36 20	291
88	54 14	350	58 19	053	62 38	100	59 14	154	25 55	175	24 58	215	35 25	291
89	54 03	349	59 06	053	63 36	101	59 39	156	26 00	175	24 24	216	34 30	291

LHA ♈	Hc	Zn	Hc	Zn	Hc	Zn	Hc	Zn	Hc	Zn	Hc	Zn	Hc	Zn
	Dubhe		◆ REGULUS		Suhail		SIRIUS		◆ RIGEL		ALDEBARAN		◆ CAPELLA	
90	16 13	029	29 04	082	20 41	145	60 02	158	67 49	211	69 04	288	53 51	348
91	16 42	029	30 03	083	21 14	146	60 24	159	67 18	213	68 08	287	53 38	346
92	17 10	029	31 01	083	21 47	146	60 44	161	66 45	215	67 11	287	53 24	345
93	17 38	028	32 00	083	22 19	147	61 02	163	66 11	217	66 15	286	53 08	344
94	18 06	028	32 58	083	22 51	147	61 18	165	65 35	219	65 18	286	52 52	343
95	18 34	028	33 57	083	23 22	148	61 32	167	64 57	221	64 21	285	52 34	342
96	19 02	028	34 55	083	23 53	149	61 45	169	64 18	222	63 25	285	52 16	341
97	19 30	028	35 53	083	24 24	149	61 55	171	63 38	224	62 28	285	51 56	340
98	19 57	028	36 52	083	24 54	150	62 03	173	62 56	226	61 31	284	51 36	339
99	20 25	028	37 50	083	25 23	150	62 09	175	62 14	227	60 34	284	51 14	338
100	20 52	028	38 49	084	25 52	151	62 14	177	61 30	229	59 36	284	50 52	337
101	21 19	028	39 48	084	26 21	151	62 16	179	60 45	230	58 39	284	50 29	336
102	21 47	027	40 46	084	26 49	152	62 15	181	60 00	231	57 42	284	50 05	335
103	22 14	027	41 45	084	27 16	153	62 13	183	59 13	232	56 45	283	49 40	335
104	22 40	027	42 43	084	27 43	153	62 09	185	58 26	234	55 47	283	49 14	334
	Dubhe		◆ REGULUS		Suhail		◆ SIRIUS		RIGEL		ALDEBARAN		◆ CAPELLA	
105	23 07	027	43 42	084	28 09	154	62 02	187	57 39	235	54 50	283	48 48	333
106	23 34	027	44 40	084	28 34	155	61 54	189	56 50	236	53 53	283	48 21	332
107	24 00	026	45 39	084	28 59	155	61 44	191	56 01	237	52 55	283	47 53	331
108	24 26	026	46 38	084	29 23	156	61 31	193	55 12	238	51 58	283	47 24	331
109	24 52	026	47 36	084	29 47	157	61 17	195	54 22	239	51 01	283	46 55	330
110	25 18	026	48 35	084	30 10	157	61 00	197	53 31	240	50 03	283	46 25	329
111	25 44	026	49 33	085	30 32	158	60 42	199	52 40	240	49 06	283	45 55	329
112	26 09	025	50 32	085	30 53	159	60 22	201	51 49	241	48 08	283	45 24	328
113	26 34	025	51 31	085	31 14	160	60 00	203	50 57	242	47 11	283	44 52	327
114	26 59	025	52 29	085	31 34	160	59 37	204	50 05	243	46 13	282	44 20	327
115	27 24	025	53 28	085	31 53	161	59 12	206	49 12	243	45 16	282	43 47	326
116	27 48	024	54 27	085	32 12	162	58 45	208	48 19	244	44 18	282	43 14	325
117	28 12	024	55 25	085	32 30	163	58 17	209	47 26	245	43 21	282	42 40	325
118	28 36	024	56 24	085	32 47	164	57 48	211	46 33	245	42 23	282	42 06	324
119	29 00	023	57 23	085	33 03	164	57 17	212	45 39	246	41 26	282	41 32	324
	Dubhe		◆ Denebola		Suhail		◆ SIRIUS		RIGEL		ALDEBARAN		◆ CAPELLA	
120	29 23	023	33 59	080	33 19	165	56 45	214	44 45	247	40 28	282	40 57	323
121	29 46	023	34 57	080	33 33	166	56 12	215	43 51	247	39 31	282	40 21	323
122	30 09	022	35 55	080	33 47	167	55 37	217	42 57	248	38 33	282	39 45	322
123	30 31	022	36 53	080	34 00	168	55 01	218	42 02	248	37 35	282	39 09	322
124	30 53	022	37 51	080	34 12	169	54 25	219	41 07	249	36 38	283	38 33	321
125	31 15	021	38 49	080	34 24	169	53 47	220	40 12	249	35 41	283	37 56	321
126	31 36	021	39 47	080	34 34	170	53 09	222	39 17	250	34 43	283	37 19	321
127	31 57	021	40 45	080	34 44	171	52 29	223	38 22	250	33 46	283	36 41	320
128	32 18	020	41 43	080	34 52	172	51 49	224	37 26	251	32 48	283	36 03	320
129	32 38	020	42 41	080	35 00	173	51 07	225	36 31	251	31 51	283	35 25	320
130	32 58	019	43 40	080	35 07	174	50 26	226	35 35	251	30 53	283	34 47	319
131	33 17	019	44 38	080	35 13	175	49 43	227	34 39	252	29 56	283	34 08	319
132	33 36	019	45 36	080	35 18	175	49 00	228	33 43	252	28 58	283	33 30	319
133	33 55	018	46 34	080	35 23	176	48 16	229	32 47	253	28 01	283	32 51	318
134	34 13	018	47 32	080	35 26	177	47 31	230	31 50	253	27 04	283	32 11	318
	Dubhe		◆ ARCTURUS		SPICA		◆ Suhail		SIRIUS		BETELGEUSE		◆ CAPELLA	
135	34 31	017	13 46	073	20 17	106	35 28	178	46 46	231	44 29	270	31 32	318
136	34 48	017	14 43	073	21 14	107	35 30	179	46 00	231	43 30	270	30 52	318
137	35 05	016	15 39	073	22 10	107	35 30	180	45 14	232	42 31	270	30 12	317
138	35 21	016	16 35	073	23 06	107	35 30	181	44 27	233	41 33	270	29 32	317
139	35 37	015	17 32	073	24 03	108	35 29	182	43 39	234	40 34	270	28 52	317
140	35 53	015	18 28	073	24 59	108	35 27	183	42 52	235	39 35	271	28 12	317
141	36 08	014	19 25	073	25 55	108	35 24	183	42 04	235	38 36	271	27 31	316
142	36 22	014	20 21	074	26 50	109	35 20	184	41 15	236	37 37	271	26 51	316
143	36 36	013	21 17	074	27 46	109	35 15	185	40 26	237	36 38	271	26 10	316
144	36 50	013	22 14	074	28 42	109	35 09	186	39 37	237	35 39	271	25 29	316
145	37 02	012	23 11	074	29 37	110	35 02	187	38 47	238	34 40	271	24 48	316
146	37 15	012	24 07	074	30 33	110	34 55	188	37 57	238	33 41	272	24 07	316
147	37 27	011	25 04	074	31 28	111	34 46	189	37 07	239	32 43	272	23 26	316
148	37 38	011	26 00	074	32 23	111	34 37	190	36 16	240	31 44	272	22 45	316
149	37 49	010	26 57	074	33 18	111	34 27	190	35 25	240	30 45	272	22 03	315
	◆ Dubhe		Alkaid		ARCTURUS		◆ SPICA		Suhail		◆ SIRIUS		POLLUX	
150	37 59	010	29 33	039	27 54	074	34 13	112	34 15	191	34 34	241	54 23	303
151	38 08	009	30 10	039	28 50	074	35 07	112	34 04	192	33 42	241	53 33	303
152	38 17	009	30 47	039	29 47	074	36 02	113	33 51	193	32 51	242	52 44	302
153	38 26	008	31 24	038	30 43	074	36 56	113	33 37	194	31 59	242	51 54	302
154	38 34	007	32 00	038	31 40	074	37 50	114	33 23	195	31 07	243	51 03	301
155	38 41	007	32 36	038	32 37	074	38 44	114	33 07	195	30 14	243	50 13	301
156	38 47	006	33 12	037	33 34	074	39 37	115	32 51	196	29 22	244	49 22	301
157	38 53	006	33 48	037	34 30	074	40 31	115	32 35	197	28 29	244	48 32	300
158	38 59	005	34 23	037	35 27	074	41 24	116	32 17	198	27 36	244	47 40	300
159	39 04	004	34 58	036	36 24	074	42 17	116	31 59	199	26 43	245	46 49	299
160	39 08	004	35 33	036	37 20	074	43 09	117	31 39	199	25 49	245	45 58	299
161	39 11	003	36 07	036	38 17	074	44 01	118	31 20	200	24 56	246	45 06	299
162	39 14	003	36 41	035	39 14	074	44 54	118	30 59	201	24 02	246	44 15	299
163	39 17	002	37 15	035	40 10	074	45 45	119	30 38	202	23 08	246	43 23	298
164	39 18	001	37 48	034	41 07	074	46 37	120	30 16	202	22 14	247	42 31	298
	◆ Dubhe		ARCTURUS		◆ SPICA		ACRUX		Suhail		◆ PROCYON		POLLUX	
165	39 19	001	42 04	074	47 28	120	13 56	170	29 53	203	40 14	267	41 39	298
166	39 20	000	43 00	074	48 18	121	14 06	170	29 30	204	39 15	268	40 47	298
167	39 20	359	43 57	074	49 08	122	14 15	171	29 06	204	38 16	268	39 55	297
168	39 19	359	44 54	074	49 58	123	14 24	171	28 41	205	37 18	268	39 02	297
169	39 17	358	45 50	074	50 48	124	14 33	172	28 16	206	36 19	268	38 10	297
170	39 15	358	46 47	074	51 36	124	14 41	172	27 50	206	35 20	269	37 17	297
171	39 12	357	47 43	074	52 25	125	14 49	173	27 23	207	34 21	269	36 25	297
172	39 09	356	48 40	074	53 13	126	14 56	173	26 56	208	33 22	269	35 32	297
173	39 05	356	49 36	073	54 00	127	15 03	174	26 28	208	32 23	269	34 40	297
174	39 01	355	50 33	073	54 46	128	15 09	174	26 00	209	31 24	269	33 47	296
175	38 55	355	51 29	073	55 32	129	15 15	174	25 31	210	30 25	270	32 54	296
176	38 49	354	52 25	073	56 17	130	15 21	175	25 02	210	29 26	270	32 01	296
177	38 43	353	53 22	073	57 02	132	15 26	175	24 32	211	28 28	270	31 08	296
178	38 36	353	54 18	072	57 45	133	15 30	176	24 02	211	27 29	270	30 16	296
179	38 28	352	55 14	072	58 28	134	15 34	176	23 31	212	26 30	270	29 23	296

LAT 11°N

LHA ♈	Alkaid Hc	Zn	◆Alphecca Hc	Zn	ANTARES Hc	Zn	◆ACRUX Hc	Zn	REGULUS Hc	Zn	◆POLLUX Hc	Zn	Dubhe Hc	Zn
180	45 41	025	37 07	065	14 29	121	15 38	177	62 50	275	28 30	296	38 20	352
181	46 05	024	38 00	065	15 19	122	15 41	177	61 52	275	27 37	296	38 11	351
182	46 29	024	38 53	064	16 09	122	15 43	178	60 53	275	26 44	296	38 02	351
183	46 53	023	39 46	064	16 59	122	15 45	178	59 54	275	25 51	296	37 52	350
184	47 15	022	40 39	064	17 49	123	15 47	179	58 56	275	24 58	296	37 41	349
185	47 37	021	41 32	064	18 38	123	15 48	179	57 57	275	24 05	296	37 30	349
186	47 58	020	42 25	064	19 28	123	15 49	180	56 58	275	23 12	296	37 19	348
187	48 18	020	43 18	064	20 17	124	15 49	180	56 00	275	22 19	296	37 06	348
188	48 38	019	44 11	063	21 06	124	15 49	181	55 01	275	21 26	296	36 54	347
189	48 56	018	45 03	063	21 54	125	15 48	181	54 02	275	20 33	296	36 40	347
190	49 14	017	45 56	063	22 43	125	15 47	181	53 04	275	19 40	296	36 27	346
191	49 31	016	46 48	063	23 31	125	15 45	182	52 05	275	18 47	296	36 12	346
192	49 46	015	47 40	062	24 19	126	15 43	182	51 06	275	17 54	296	35 58	345
193	50 01	014	48 32	062	25 06	126	15 40	183	50 08	275	17 01	296	35 42	345
194	50 15	013	49 24	062	25 53	127	15 37	183	49 09	276	16 09	296	35 26	344

LHA ♈	◆VEGA Hc	Zn	Rasalhague Hc	Zn	ANTARES Hc	Zn	◆RIGIL KENT Hc	Zn	Gienah Hc	Zn	◆REGULUS Hc	Zn	Dubhe Hc	Zn
195	11 14	052	22 43	081	26 40	127	15 24	168	59 26	201	48 10	276	35 10	344
196	12 00	052	23 42	081	27 27	128	15 36	168	59 04	202	47 12	276	34 54	343
197	12 47	052	24 40	081	28 14	128	15 48	169	58 41	204	46 13	276	34 36	343
198	13 34	052	25 38	081	29 00	129	15 59	169	58 16	206	45 15	276	34 19	342
199	14 20	052	26 36	081	29 45	129	16 10	169	57 50	207	44 16	276	34 01	342
200	15 07	053	27 34	081	30 31	130	16 21	170	57 22	209	43 17	276	33 42	341
201	15 54	053	28 33	082	31 16	130	16 31	170	56 53	210	42 19	276	33 23	341
202	16 41	053	29 31	082	32 00	131	16 41	171	56 23	212	41 20	276	33 04	341
203	17 27	053	30 29	082	32 45	132	16 50	171	55 51	213	40 22	276	32 44	340
204	18 14	053	31 28	082	33 28	132	16 58	172	55 18	215	39 23	276	32 24	340
205	19 01	053	32 26	082	34 12	133	17 06	172	54 44	216	38 25	277	32 04	339
206	19 48	053	33 24	082	34 55	134	17 14	173	54 09	217	37 26	277	31 43	339
207	20 34	052	34 23	082	35 37	134	17 21	173	53 33	219	36 28	277	31 21	339
208	21 21	052	35 21	082	36 19	135	17 28	174	52 56	220	35 29	277	31 00	338
209	22 08	052	36 19	082	37 00	136	17 34	174	52 17	221	34 31	277	30 38	338

LHA ♈	◆VEGA Hc	Zn	Rasalhague Hc	Zn	ANTARES Hc	Zn	◆RIGIL KENT Hc	Zn	SPICA Hc	Zn	◆REGULUS Hc	Zn	Dubhe Hc	Zn
210	22 54	052	37 18	083	37 41	136	17 39	175	66 13	201	33 32	277	30 16	338
211	23 41	052	38 16	083	38 22	137	17 44	175	65 50	203	32 34	277	29 53	337
212	24 27	052	39 14	083	39 01	138	17 49	176	65 26	205	31 35	277	29 30	337
213	25 14	052	40 13	083	39 41	139	17 53	176	65 00	208	30 37	277	29 07	337
214	26 00	052	41 11	083	40 19	139	17 56	177	64 32	210	29 39	278	28 44	336
215	26 47	052	42 10	083	40 57	140	17 59	177	64 02	212	28 40	278	28 20	336
216	27 33	052	43 08	083	41 34	141	18 02	178	63 30	213	27 42	278	27 56	336
217	28 19	052	44 07	083	42 11	142	18 04	178	62 57	215	26 43	278	27 31	335
218	29 06	052	45 05	083	42 47	143	18 05	179	62 22	217	25 45	278	27 07	335
219	29 52	051	46 04	083	43 22	144	18 06	179	61 46	219	24 47	278	26 42	335
220	30 38	051	47 02	083	43 56	145	18 06	180	61 09	220	23 49	278	26 17	335
221	31 23	051	48 01	083	44 30	146	18 06	180	60 30	222	22 50	278	25 52	334
222	32 09	051	48 59	083	45 02	147	18 05	181	59 50	223	21 52	279	25 26	334
223	32 55	051	49 58	084	45 34	148	18 04	181	59 10	225	20 54	279	25 01	334
224	33 40	050	50 56	084	46 05	149	18 02	182	58 28	226	19 56	279	24 35	334

LHA ♈	◆VEGA Hc	Zn	ALTAIR Hc	Zn	ANTARES Hc	Zn	◆RIGIL KENT Hc	Zn	SPICA Hc	Zn	◆Denebola Hc	Zn	Alkaid Hc	Zn
225	34 25	050	18 22	084	46 35	150	18 00	182	57 45	227	43 34	280	48 57	342
226	35 11	050	19 20	084	47 04	151	17 57	183	57 01	228	42 36	280	48 39	341
227	35 56	050	20 19	084	47 32	152	17 54	183	56 17	230	41 38	280	48 19	340
228	36 40	049	21 18	085	47 59	153	17 50	184	55 32	231	40 40	280	47 59	340
229	37 25	049	22 16	085	48 25	155	17 46	185	54 46	232	39 42	280	47 38	339
230	38 09	049	23 15	085	48 49	156	17 41	185	53 59	233	38 44	280	47 17	338
231	38 54	048	24 14	085	49 13	157	17 35	186	53 12	234	37 46	280	46 54	337
232	39 38	048	25 12	085	49 35	158	17 30	186	52 24	235	36 48	280	46 31	336
233	40 21	048	26 11	085	49 57	159	17 23	187	51 36	236	35 50	280	46 07	336
234	41 05	047	27 10	086	50 17	161	17 16	187	50 47	236	34 52	280	45 42	335
235	41 48	047	28 08	086	50 35	162	17 09	187	49 58	237	33 54	280	45 17	334
236	42 31	047	29 07	086	50 53	163	17 01	188	49 08	238	32 56	280	44 51	334
237	43 13	046	30 06	086	51 09	165	16 52	188	48 18	239	31 58	280	44 24	333
238	43 56	046	31 05	086	51 24	166	16 44	189	47 27	240	31 00	280	43 57	332
239	44 38	045	32 04	086	51 37	168	16 34	189	46 36	240	30 02	280	43 29	332

LHA ♈	◆VEGA Hc	Zn	ALTAIR Hc	Zn	Nunki Hc	Zn	◆ANTARES Hc	Zn	SPICA Hc	Zn	◆ARCTURUS Hc	Zn	Alkaid Hc	Zn
240	45 19	045	33 02	086	33 14	132	51 49	169	45 45	241	63 44	291	43 01	331
241	46 00	044	34 01	087	33 58	132	52 00	170	44 53	242	62 49	291	42 32	330
242	46 41	044	35 00	087	34 41	133	52 09	172	44 01	242	61 54	290	42 03	330
243	47 22	043	35 59	087	35 24	134	52 16	173	43 09	243	60 58	290	41 33	329
244	48 02	042	36 57	087	36 06	134	52 22	175	42 16	244	60 03	289	41 02	329
245	48 41	042	37 56	087	36 48	135	52 27	176	41 23	244	59 07	289	40 32	328
246	49 20	041	38 55	087	37 30	136	52 30	178	40 30	245	58 11	289	40 00	328
247	49 59	040	39 54	088	38 10	137	52 32	179	39 37	245	57 16	288	39 28	327
248	50 36	040	40 53	088	38 51	137	52 32	181	38 43	246	56 20	288	38 56	327
249	51 14	039	41 52	088	39 30	138	52 31	182	37 49	246	55 24	288	38 24	326
250	51 51	038	42 51	088	40 09	139	52 28	184	36 55	247	54 27	288	37 51	326
251	52 27	037	43 49	088	40 47	140	52 23	185	36 01	247	53 31	287	37 17	325
252	53 02	037	44 48	088	41 25	141	52 17	186	35 07	248	52 35	287	36 44	325
253	53 37	036	45 47	088	42 02	141	52 10	188	34 12	248	51 39	287	36 09	324
254	54 11	035	46 46	089	42 39	142	52 01	189	33 17	249	50 42	287	35 35	324

LHA ♈	◆VEGA Hc	Zn	ALTAIR Hc	Zn	◆Nunki Hc	Zn	ANTARES Hc	Zn	SPICA Hc	Zn	◆ARCTURUS Hc	Zn	Alkaid Hc	Zn
255	54 44	034	47 45	089	43 14	143	51 51	191	32 22	249	49 46	287	35 00	324
256	55 16	033	48 44	089	43 49	144	51 39	192	31 27	249	48 49	287	34 25	323
257	55 48	032	49 43	089	44 23	145	51 26	194	30 32	250	47 53	286	33 50	323
258	56 19	031	50 42	089	44 56	146	51 12	195	29 37	250	46 56	286	33 14	323
259	56 48	030	51 40	090	45 28	147	50 56	196	28 41	251	46 00	286	32 39	322
260	57 17	029	52 39	090	46 00	148	50 38	198	27 46	251	45 03	286	32 02	322
261	57 44	027	53 38	090	46 30	149	50 20	199	26 50	251	44 07	286	31 26	322
262	58 11	026	54 37	090	47 00	150	50 00	200	25 54	252	43 10	286	30 50	321
263	58 36	025	55 36	090	47 29	152	49 39	202	24 58	252	42 13	286	30 13	321
264	59 01	024	56 35	090	47 56	153	49 17	203	24 02	252	41 17	286	29 36	321
265	59 24	022	57 34	091	48 23	154	48 53	204	23 06	253	40 20	286	28 59	321
266	59 45	021	58 33	091	48 48	155	48 29	205	22 10	253	39 23	286	28 21	321
267	60 06	020	59 32	091	49 12	156	48 03	206	21 13	253	38 27	286	27 44	320
268	60 25	018	60 31	091	49 35	158	47 36	208	20 17	254	37 30	286	27 06	320
269	60 42	017	61 29	092	49 57	159	47 09	209	19 21	254	36 33	286	26 28	320

LHA ♈	VEGA Hc	Zn	◆DENEB Hc	Zn	Enif Hc	Zn	◆Nunki Hc	Zn	ANTARES Hc	Zn	◆ARCTURUS Hc	Zn	Alkaid Hc	Zn
270	60 58	015	41 20	037	34 47	085	50 18	160	46 40	210	35 37	286	25 50	320
271	61 13	014	41 56	037	35 45	086	50 37	161	46 10	211	34 40	286	25 12	320
272	61 26	012	42 31	036	36 44	086	50 56	163	45 39	212	33 43	286	24 34	319
273	61 38	010	43 06	036	37 43	086	51 12	164	45 08	213	32 47	286	23 56	319
274	61 48	009	43 40	035	38 42	086	51 28	165	44 35	214	31 50	286	23 17	319
275	61 56	007	44 14	035	39 40	086	51 42	167	44 02	215	30 53	286	22 38	319
276	62 02	006	44 47	034	40 39	086	51 55	168	43 28	216	29 57	286	22 00	319
277	62 07	004	45 20	033	41 38	086	52 06	170	42 53	217	29 00	286	21 21	319
278	62 11	002	45 52	033	42 37	087	52 16	171	42 17	218	28 03	286	20 42	319
279	62 12	001	46 24	032	43 35	087	52 24	173	41 40	219	27 07	286	20 03	319
280	62 12	359	46 55	031	44 34	087	52 31	174	41 03	220	26 10	286	19 24	319
281	62 10	357	47 25	031	45 33	087	52 36	175	40 26	220	25 13	286	18 45	318
282	62 06	356	47 55	030	46 32	087	52 40	177	39 47	221	24 17	286	18 06	318
283	62 01	354	48 24	029	47 31	087	52 43	178	39 08	222	23 20	286	17 27	318
284	61 54	352	48 53	028	48 30	087	52 43	180	38 28	223	22 24	286	16 48	318

LHA ♈	◆DENEB Hc	Zn	Alpheratz Hc	Zn	◆FOMALHAUT Hc	Zn	Nunki Hc	Zn	ANTARES Hc	Zn	◆Rasalhague Hc	Zn	VEGA Hc	Zn
285	49 21	028	16 21	063	19 45	127	52 43	181	37 48	224	69 18	276	61 45	351
286	49 47	027	17 14	063	20 32	128	52 40	183	37 07	224	68 19	276	61 35	349
287	50 14	026	18 06	063	21 18	128	52 37	184	36 26	225	67 21	276	61 23	348
288	50 39	025	18 58	063	22 04	128	52 32	186	35 44	226	66 22	276	61 09	346
289	51 04	024	19 51	063	22 50	129	52 25	187	35 02	226	65 24	276	60 54	344
290	51 27	023	20 43	063	23 36	129	52 17	189	34 19	227	64 25	276	60 38	343
291	51 50	022	21 35	063	24 22	130	52 07	190	33 36	228	63 27	276	60 20	341
292	52 12	021	22 28	063	25 07	130	51 56	192	32 52	228	62 28	276	60 00	340
293	52 33	020	23 20	063	25 52	131	51 43	193	32 08	229	61 30	276	59 39	339
294	52 53	019	24 12	063	26 36	131	51 29	194	31 23	229	60 31	276	59 17	337
295	53 12	018	25 05	063	27 20	132	51 14	196	30 38	230	59 32	276	58 54	336
296	53 30	017	25 57	063	28 04	132	50 57	197	29 53	231	58 34	276	58 29	335
297	53 47	016	26 50	063	28 47	133	50 39	198	29 07	231	57 35	276	58 04	333
298	54 02	015	27 42	063	29 30	133	50 20	200	28 21	232	56 37	276	57 37	332
299	54 17	014	28 34	063	30 13	134	49 59	201	27 35	232	55 38	276	57 09	331

LHA ♈	◆DENEB Hc	Zn	Alpheratz Hc	Zn	◆FOMALHAUT Hc	Zn	Peacock Hc	Zn	◆ANTARES Hc	Zn	Rasalhague Hc	Zn	VEGA Hc	Zn
300	54 31	013	29 27	063	30 55	135	22 05	176	26 48	233	54 40	276	56 40	330
301	54 43	012	30 19	063	31 37	135	22 09	177	26 01	233	53 41	276	56 10	329
302	54 54	010	31 11	062	32 18	136	22 12	177	25 14	234	52 42	276	55 39	328
303	55 04	009	32 03	062	32 59	136	22 15	178	24 26	234	51 44	276	55 08	327
304	55 13	008	32 55	062	33 39	137	22 17	178	23 39	235	50 45	276	54 35	326
305	55 21	007	33 47	062	34 19	138	22 18	179	22 51	235	49 47	276	54 01	325
306	55 27	006	34 39	062	34 58	138	22 19	180	22 02	235	48 48	277	53 27	324
307	55 32	004	35 31	062	35 37	139	22 19	180	21 14	236	47 50	277	52 52	323
308	55 36	003	36 23	062	36 15	140	22 18	181	20 25	236	46 51	277	52 17	322
309	55 39	002	37 15	062	36 53	141	22 17	181	19 36	237	45 53	277	51 40	322
310	55 40	001	38 07	061	37 30	141	22 16	182	18 47	237	44 54	277	51 04	321
311	55 40	359	38 59	061	38 06	142	22 13	183	17 57	237	43 56	277	50 26	320
312	55 38	358	39 50	061	38 42	143	22 10	183	17 07	238	42 57	277	49 48	319
313	55 36	357	40 42	061	39 17	144	22 07	184	16 18	238	41 59	277	49 09	319
314	55 32	356	41 33	061	39 51	145	22 03	184	15 27	238	41 01	277	48 30	318

LHA ♈	Alpheratz Hc	Zn	◆Diphda Hc	Zn	FOMALHAUT Hc	Zn	◆Nunki Hc	Zn	Rasalhague Hc	Zn	VEGA Hc	Zn	◆DENEB Hc	Zn
315	42 24	060	27 33	117	40 25	146	42 06	218	40 02	277	47 51	317	55 27	354
316	43 15	060	28 25	117	40 58	147	41 29	219	39 04	277	47 11	317	55 21	353
317	44 06	060	29 17	118	41 30	147	40 51	220	38 05	277	46 30	316	55 13	352
318	44 57	059	30 09	118	42 01	148	40 13	221	37 07	277	45 49	316	55 04	351
319	45 48	059	31 01	119	42 32	149	39 34	222	36 08	278	45 08	315	54 54	350
320	46 38	059	31 53	119	43 01	150	38 54	223	35 10	278	44 26	315	54 43	348
321	47 29	058	32 44	120	43 30	151	38 14	223	34 12	278	43 44	314	54 30	347
322	48 19	058	33 35	120	43 58	152	37 34	224	33 13	278	43 02	314	54 17	346
323	49 09	058	34 26	121	44 25	153	36 52	225	32 15	278	42 19	313	54 02	345
324	49 58	057	35 16	121	44 51	154	36 11	226	31 17	278	41 36	313	53 46	344
325	50 48	057	36 06	122	45 16	155	35 28	226	30 18	278	40 53	313	53 29	343
326	51 37	056	36 56	123	45 40	157	34 46	227	29 20	278	40 09	312	53 11	342
327	52 26	056	37 45	123	46 03	158	34 02	228	28 22	278	39 25	312	52 52	341
328	53 14	055	38 34	124	46 24	159	33 19	228	27 24	279	38 41	311	52 32	340
329	54 03	055	39 23	124	46 45	160	32 35	229	26 25	279	37 57	311	52 11	339

LHA ♈	◆Alpheratz Hc	Zn	Diphda Hc	Zn	◆FOMALHAUT Hc	Zn	Peacock Hc	Zn	ALTAIR Hc	Zn	◆VEGA Hc	Zn	DENEB Hc	Zn
330	54 50	054	40 12	125	47 05	161	19 37	193	58 18	269	37 13	311	51 49	338
331	55 38	053	41 00	126	47 23	162	19 23	194	57 20	269	36 28	311	51 27	337
332	56 25	053	41 47	126	47 40	164	19 09	194	56 21	270	35 43	310	51 03	336
333	57 12	052	42 34	127	47 56	165	18 54	195	55 22	270	34 58	310	50 38	335
334	57 58	051	43 21	128	48 11	166	18 39	195	54 23	270	34 13	310	50 13	334
335	58 44	050	44 07	129	48 25	167	18 23	196	53 24	270	33 28	310	49 47	333
336	59 29	050	44 53	129	48 37	169	18 06	196	52 25	270	32 42	309	49 20	332
337	60 13	049	45 38	130	48 48	170	17 49	197	51 26	271	31 56	309	48 52	332
338	60 57	048	46 23	131	48 57	171	17 32	197	50 27	271	31 11	309	48 24	331
339	61 40	047	47 07	132	49 06	173	17 14	198	49 28	271	30 25	309	47 54	330
340	62 23	046	47 50	133	49 13	174	16 56	198	48 30	271	29 39	309	47 25	329
341	63 05	044	48 33	134	49 18	175	16 37	199	47 31	271	28 53	308	46 54	329
342	63 45	043	49 15	135	49 23	176	16 18	199	46 32	271	28 07	308	46 23	328
343	64 25	042	49 57	136	49 26	178	15 58	200	45 33	272	27 20	308	45 51	327
344	65 04	041	50 37	137	49 27	179	15 38	200	44 34	272	26 34	308	45 19	326

LHA ♈	Schedar Hc	Zn	◆Mirfak Hc	Zn	Hamal Hc	Zn	◆ACHERNAR Hc	Zn	FOMALHAUT Hc	Zn	◆ALTAIR Hc	Zn	DENEB Hc	Zn
345	40 21	018	23 33	040	43 37	068	14 29	159	49 27	181	43 35	272	44 46	326
346	40 39	017	24 11	040	44 32	068	14 50	160	49 26	182	42 36	272	44 13	325
347	40 56	017	24 49	040	45 26	068	15 10	160	49 24	183	41 37	272	43 39	325
348	41 13	016	25 27	039	46 21	067	15 30	160	49 20	185	40 39	272	43 05	324
349	41 29	016	26 04	039	47 15	067	15 49	161	49 14	186	39 40	273	42 30	324
350	41 44	015	26 41	039	48 09	067	16 09	161	49 08	187	38 41	273	41 55	323
351	41 59	014	27 18	039	49 03	067	16 27	162	49 00	188	37 42	273	41 19	323
352	42 13	014	27 55	039	49 57	066	16 45	162	48 50	190	36 43	273	40 43	322
353	42 27	013	28 32	039	50 51	066	17 03	163	48 40	191	35 44	273	40 07	322
354	42 39	012	29 09	038	51 45	066	17 20	163	48 28	192	34 46	273	39 30	321
355	42 51	011	29 45	038	52 39	065	17 37	164	48 14	194	33 47	273	38 53	321
356	43 03	011	30 21	038	53 32	065	17 53	164	48 00	195	32 48	274	38 16	320
357	43 13	010	30 57	038	54 26	065	18 09	165	47 44	196	31 49	274	37 38	320
358	43 23	009	31 33	037	55 19	064	18 25	165	47 27	197	30 50	274	37 00	320
359	43 32	009	32 09	037	56 12	064	18 39	166	47 09	199	29 52	274	36 21	319

 LAT 10°N

LHA ♈	Hc	Zn	Hc	Zn	Hc	Zn	Hc	Zn	Hc	Zn	Hc	Zn	Hc	Zn
	◆ CAPELLA		ALDEBARAN		Acamar		◆ ACHERNAR		FOMALHAUT		◆ ALTAIR		DENEB	
0	14 29	045	22 38	076	24 58	144	19 52	166	47 46	200	28 48	275	34 57	319
1	15 11	045	23 35	076	25 33	144	20 06	167	47 25	201	27 49	275	34 19	319
2	15 53	045	24 32	076	26 07	145	20 19	167	47 03	202	26 51	275	33 40	319
3	16 34	045	25 30	076	26 41	145	20 32	168	46 40	204	25 52	275	33 01	318
4	17 16	045	26 27	076	27 14	146	20 44	168	46 16	205	24 53	275	32 21	318
5	17 57	045	27 25	076	27 47	147	20 56	169	45 51	206	23 54	275	31 42	318
6	18 39	045	28 22	077	28 19	147	21 07	169	45 25	207	22 55	276	31 02	317
7	19 20	045	29 20	077	28 51	148	21 18	170	44 58	208	21 56	276	30 22	317
8	20 02	044	30 17	077	29 22	148	21 28	170	44 29	209	20 58	276	29 41	317
9	20 43	044	31 15	077	29 53	149	21 38	171	44 00	210	19 59	276	29 01	317
10	21 25	044	32 12	077	30 23	150	21 47	172	43 30	211	19 00	276	28 20	317
11	22 06	044	33 10	077	30 52	150	21 55	172	43 00	212	18 01	276	27 40	316
12	22 47	044	34 07	077	31 21	151	22 03	173	42 28	213	17 03	276	26 59	316
13	23 28	044	35 05	077	31 49	152	22 10	173	41 56	214	16 04	276	26 18	316
14	24 09	044	36 02	077	32 17	153	22 17	174	41 22	215	15 05	277	25 37	316
	CAPELLA		◆ ALDEBARAN		RIGEL		ACHERNAR		◆ FOMALHAUT		Enif		◆ DENEB	
15	24 50	044	37 00	077	23 55	104	22 23	174	40 48	216	42 01	274	24 55	316
16	25 31	044	37 57	077	24 52	104	22 28	175	40 14	216	41 02	275	24 14	315
17	26 11	043	38 55	077	25 50	104	22 33	176	39 38	217	40 03	275	23 32	315
18	26 52	043	39 52	077	26 47	105	22 37	176	39 02	218	39 04	275	22 51	315
19	27 32	043	40 50	077	27 44	105	22 41	177	38 25	219	38 05	275	22 09	315
20	28 12	043	41 47	077	28 41	105	22 44	177	37 48	220	37 06	275	21 27	315
21	28 52	043	42 45	077	29 38	105	22 46	178	37 10	220	36 08	275	20 46	315
22	29 32	042	43 42	077	30 35	106	22 48	178	36 32	221	35 09	275	20 04	315
23	30 12	042	44 40	077	31 32	106	22 50	179	35 52	222	34 10	275	19 22	315
24	30 51	042	45 37	077	32 29	106	22 50	180	35 13	223	33 11	275	18 40	315
25	31 30	042	46 35	076	33 25	107	22 50	180	34 33	223	32 12	276	17 58	315
26	32 09	041	47 32	076	34 22	107	22 50	181	33 52	224	31 13	276	17 15	315
27	32 48	041	48 29	076	35 18	108	22 49	181	33 11	224	30 15	276	16 33	315
28	33 27	041	49 27	076	36 14	108	22 47	182	32 29	225	29 16	276	15 51	314
29	34 05	040	50 24	076	37 11	108	22 44	183	31 47	226	28 17	276	15 09	314
	Mirfak		CAPELLA		◆ ALDEBARAN		RIGEL		◆ ACHERNAR		FOMALHAUT		◆ Alpheratz	
30	46 21	020	34 43	040	51 22	076	38 07	109	22 41	183	31 05	226	57 46	310
31	46 40	019	35 21	040	52 19	076	39 02	109	22 38	184	30 22	227	57 01	310
32	46 59	018	35 59	039	53 16	076	39 58	110	22 34	184	29 38	227	56 15	309
33	47 17	017	36 36	039	54 13	076	40 54	110	22 29	185	28 55	228	55 29	308
34	47 34	017	37 13	038	55 11	075	41 49	111	22 23	186	28 10	229	54 42	307
35	47 51	016	37 49	038	56 08	075	42 44	111	22 17	186	27 26	229	53 55	307
36	48 06	015	38 25	038	57 05	075	43 39	112	22 11	187	26 41	230	53 08	306
37	48 21	014	39 01	037	58 02	075	44 34	112	22 04	187	25 56	230	52 20	306
38	48 35	013	39 37	037	58 59	074	45 29	113	21 56	188	25 11	230	51 31	305
39	48 48	012	40 12	036	59 56	074	46 23	113	21 48	188	24 25	231	50 43	304
40	48 59	011	40 46	036	60 53	074	47 17	114	21 39	189	23 39	231	49 54	304
41	49 10	010	41 21	035	61 49	074	48 11	114	21 29	189	22 53	232	49 05	304
42	49 20	009	41 54	035	62 46	073	49 05	115	21 19	190	22 06	232	48 16	303
43	49 29	008	42 28	034	63 42	073	49 58	116	21 09	191	21 19	233	47 26	303
44	49 37	007	43 01	033	64 39	072	50 51	116	20 58	191	20 32	233	46 36	302
	◆ CAPELLA		PROCYON		SIRIUS		◆ CANOPUS		ACHERNAR		Diphda		◆ Alpheratz	
45	43 33	033	20 32	088	28 07	115	13 42	151	20 46	192	46 25	230	45 46	302
46	44 05	032	21 31	088	29 00	116	14 10	151	20 34	192	45 39	231	44 56	302
47	44 36	032	22 30	088	29 53	116	14 39	152	20 21	193	44 53	232	44 05	301
48	45 06	031	23 29	089	30 46	116	15 06	152	20 08	193	44 06	233	43 15	301
49	45 36	030	24 28	089	31 39	117	15 34	153	19 54	194	43 19	233	42 24	301
50	46 06	030	25 27	089	32 32	117	16 01	153	19 39	194	42 31	234	41 33	300
51	46 35	029	26 27	089	33 24	118	16 27	153	19 25	195	41 43	235	40 42	300
52	47 03	028	27 26	089	34 16	118	16 54	154	19 09	195	40 54	236	39 51	300
53	47 30	027	28 25	089	35 08	119	17 19	154	18 53	196	40 05	236	38 59	300
54	47 57	026	29 24	090	36 00	119	17 45	155	18 37	196	39 16	237	38 08	299
55	48 23	026	30 23	090	36 51	120	18 10	155	18 20	197	38 26	237	37 16	299
56	48 48	025	31 22	090	37 42	120	18 34	156	18 03	197	37 36	238	36 25	299
57	49 12	024	32 21	090	38 33	121	18 58	156	17 45	198	36 46	239	35 33	299
58	49 36	023	33 20	090	39 24	122	19 22	157	17 27	198	35 56	239	34 41	299
59	49 59	022	34 19	091	40 14	122	19 45	157	17 08	199	35 05	240	33 49	299
	◆ CAPELLA		POLLUX		PROCYON		◆ SIRIUS		CANOPUS		◆ Diphda		Alpheratz	
60	50 21	021	34 06	063	35 18	091	41 04	123	20 08	158	34 14	240	32 57	298
61	50 41	020	34 59	063	36 17	091	41 53	123	20 30	158	33 22	241	32 05	298
62	51 02	019	35 51	063	37 17	091	42 42	124	20 52	159	32 31	241	31 13	298
63	51 21	018	36 44	062	38 16	091	43 31	125	21 13	159	31 39	242	30 21	298
64	51 39	017	37 36	062	39 15	091	44 19	126	21 34	160	30 47	242	29 29	298
65	51 56	016	38 28	062	40 14	092	45 07	126	21 54	160	29 54	243	28 37	298
66	52 12	015	39 21	062	41 13	092	45 54	127	22 14	161	29 02	243	27 45	298
67	52 27	014	40 13	062	42 12	092	46 41	128	22 33	161	28 09	243	26 52	298
68	52 41	013	41 05	061	43 11	092	47 28	129	22 51	162	27 16	244	26 00	298
69	52 54	012	41 56	061	44 10	092	48 14	130	23 09	163	26 23	244	25 08	298
70	53 06	011	42 48	061	45 09	093	48 59	130	23 27	163	25 30	245	24 15	298
71	53 16	010	43 40	061	46 08	093	49 44	131	23 44	164	24 36	245	23 23	298
72	53 26	009	44 31	060	47 07	093	50 28	132	24 00	164	23 43	245	22 31	298
73	53 34	008	45 22	060	48 06	093	51 11	133	24 16	165	22 49	246	21 38	298
74	53 41	006	46 13	060	49 05	094	51 54	134	24 31	166	21 55	246	20 46	298
	CAPELLA		◆ POLLUX		PROCYON		SIRIUS		◆ CANOPUS		Acamar		◆ Hamal	
75	53 47	005	47 04	059	50 04	094	52 36	135	24 45	166	32 28	207	46 52	294
76	53 52	004	47 55	059	51 03	094	53 17	137	24 59	167	32 01	208	45 58	294
77	53 56	003	48 46	059	52 02	094	53 57	138	25 12	167	31 33	209	45 04	293
78	53 58	002	49 36	058	53 01	095	54 36	139	25 25	168	31 04	209	44 09	293
79	53 59	001	50 26	058	54 00	095	55 15	140	25 37	169	30 35	210	43 15	293
80	53 59	359	51 16	057	54 58	095	55 52	141	25 48	169	30 05	211	42 21	293
81	53 58	358	52 05	057	55 57	096	56 28	143	25 59	170	29 35	211	41 26	293
82	53 55	357	52 55	056	56 56	096	57 04	144	26 09	171	29 04	212	40 31	292
83	53 52	356	53 43	056	57 55	096	57 38	146	26 18	171	28 32	213	39 37	292
84	53 47	355	54 32	055	58 54	097	58 10	147	26 27	172	28 00	213	38 42	292
85	53 41	353	55 20	054	59 52	097	58 42	149	26 35	173	27 28	214	37 47	292
86	53 33	352	56 08	054	60 51	097	59 12	150	26 42	173	26 55	214	36 53	292
87	53 25	351	56 55	053	61 49	098	59 41	152	26 49	174	26 21	215	35 58	292
88	53 15	350	57 42	052	62 48	098	60 08	153	26 55	175	25 47	216	35 03	292
89	53 04	349	58 29	051	63 46	099	60 34	155	27 00	175	25 12	216	34 08	292

LHA ♈	Hc	Zn	Hc	Zn	Hc	Zn	Hc	Zn	Hc	Zn	Hc	Zn	Hc	Zn
	◆ POLLUX		REGULUS		Suhail		◆ CANOPUS		RIGEL		◆ ALDEBARAN		CAPELLA	
90	59 15	051	28 56	082	21 30	145	27 05	176	68 41	212	68 44	290	52 53	348
91	60 00	050	29 55	082	22 03	146	27 09	177	68 08	214	67 49	289	52 40	347
92	60 45	049	30 53	082	22 37	146	27 12	177	67 34	216	66 53	289	52 25	346
93	61 29	048	31 52	082	23 09	147	27 14	178	66 58	218	65 57	288	52 10	345
94	62 12	047	32 50	082	23 42	147	27 16	179	66 21	220	65 01	288	51 54	344
95	62 55	045	33 49	082	24 13	148	27 17	179	65 42	222	64 04	287	51 37	343
96	63 36	044	34 47	082	24 45	148	27 18	180	65 02	224	63 08	287	51 19	342
97	64 17	043	35 46	082	25 15	149	27 17	181	64 20	226	62 11	287	51 00	341
98	64 57	042	36 45	083	25 46	149	27 16	181	63 38	227	61 15	286	50 39	340
99	65 35	040	37 43	083	26 15	150	27 15	182	62 54	229	60 18	286	50 18	339
100	66 13	039	38 42	083	26 45	151	27 12	183	62 09	230	59 21	286	49 56	338
101	66 49	037	39 40	083	27 13	151	27 09	183	61 23	231	58 24	285	49 34	337
102	67 24	035	40 39	083	27 42	152	27 05	184	60 37	233	57 27	285	49 10	336
103	67 57	033	41 38	083	28 09	153	27 01	185	59 49	234	56 30	285	48 45	335
104	68 29	032	42 36	083	28 36	153	26 56	185	59 01	235	55 33	285	48 20	334
	Dubhe		◆ REGULUS		Suhail		◆ CANOPUS		RIGEL		ALDEBARAN		◆ CAPELLA	
105	22 14	027	43 35	083	29 02	154	26 50	186	58 13	236	54 36	285	47 54	333
106	22 40	026	44 34	083	29 28	154	26 43	187	57 23	237	53 39	284	47 27	333
107	23 06	026	45 32	083	29 53	155	26 36	187	56 34	238	52 41	284	47 00	332
108	23 32	026	46 31	083	30 18	156	26 28	188	55 43	239	51 44	284	46 32	331
109	23 58	026	47 30	083	30 42	157	26 19	189	54 52	240	50 47	284	46 03	330
110	24 24	026	48 28	083	31 05	157	26 10	189	54 01	241	49 49	284	45 33	330
111	24 49	025	49 27	083	31 27	158	26 00	190	53 09	242	48 52	284	45 03	329
112	25 15	025	50 26	083	31 49	159	25 50	191	52 17	242	47 54	284	44 33	328
113	25 40	025	51 24	083	32 10	159	25 38	191	51 25	243	46 57	284	44 01	328
114	26 04	025	52 23	083	32 31	160	25 27	192	50 32	244	46 00	284	43 30	327
115	26 29	024	53 22	083	32 50	161	25 14	193	49 39	244	45 02	283	42 57	327
116	26 53	024	54 21	083	33 09	162	25 01	193	48 45	245	44 05	283	42 24	326
117	27 17	024	55 19	084	33 27	163	24 47	194	47 51	246	43 07	283	41 51	325
118	27 41	024	56 18	084	33 44	163	24 33	194	46 57	246	42 10	283	41 17	325
119	28 04	023	57 17	084	34 01	164	24 18	195	46 03	247	41 12	283	40 43	324
	Dubhe		◆ Denebola		Suhail		◆ SIRIUS		RIGEL		ALDEBARAN		◆ CAPELLA	
120	28 28	023	33 48	079	34 17	165	57 34	215	45 09	248	40 15	283	40 08	324
121	28 50	023	34 46	079	34 31	166	57 00	216	44 14	248	39 17	283	39 33	323
122	29 13	022	35 44	079	34 46	167	56 25	217	43 19	249	38 20	283	38 58	323
123	29 35	022	36 42	079	34 59	168	55 49	219	42 24	249	37 22	283	38 22	322
124	29 57	022	37 41	079	35 11	168	55 11	220	41 29	250	36 25	283	37 46	322
125	30 19	021	38 39	079	35 23	169	54 33	221	40 33	250	35 27	283	37 09	322
126	30 40	021	39 37	079	35 33	170	53 53	222	39 38	251	34 30	283	36 32	321
127	31 01	020	40 35	079	35 43	171	53 13	224	38 42	251	33 32	283	35 55	321
128	31 21	020	41 33	079	35 52	172	52 32	225	37 46	251	32 35	283	35 17	320
129	31 41	020	42 31	079	36 00	173	51 50	226	36 50	252	31 37	283	34 39	320
130	32 01	019	43 29	079	36 07	174	51 07	227	35 54	252	30 40	283	34 01	320
131	32 20	019	44 27	079	36 13	174	50 24	228	34 57	253	29 42	283	33 23	319
132	32 39	018	45 25	079	36 18	175	49 39	229	34 01	253	28 45	283	32 44	319
133	32 58	018	46 23	079	36 22	176	48 55	230	33 04	253	27 47	284	32 06	319
134	33 16	018	47 21	079	36 26	177	48 09	231	32 08	254	26 50	284	31 26	318
	Dubhe		◆ ARCTURUS		SPICA		◆ Suhail		SIRIUS		BETELGEUSE		◆ CAPELLA	
135	33 33	017	13 28	073	20 34	106	36 28	178	47 23	231	44 29	271	30 47	318
136	33 51	017	14 25	073	21 31	106	36 30	179	46 37	232	43 30	271	30 08	318
137	34 07	016	15 21	073	22 28	107	36 30	180	45 50	233	42 31	271	29 28	318
138	34 24	016	16 18	073	23 24	107	36 30	181	45 03	234	41 32	271	28 48	317
139	34 39	015	17 14	073	24 21	107	36 29	182	44 15	235	40 33	271	28 08	317
140	34 55	015	18 11	073	25 17	108	36 27	183	43 26	235	39 34	271	27 28	317
141	35 10	014	19 07	073	26 13	108	36 23	183	42 38	236	38 35	272	26 48	317
142	35 24	014	20 04	073	27 10	108	36 19	184	41 48	237	37 36	272	26 07	317
143	35 38	013	21 00	073	28 06	109	36 14	185	40 59	237	36 37	272	25 26	316
144	35 51	013	21 57	073	29 02	109	36 09	186	40 09	238	35 38	272	24 46	316
145	36 04	012	22 54	073	29 57	109	36 02	187	39 19	239	34 38	272	24 05	316
146	36 16	012	23 50	073	30 53	110	35 54	188	38 28	239	33 39	272	23 24	316
147	36 28	011	24 47	073	31 49	110	35 45	189	37 37	240	32 40	272	22 43	316
148	36 39	011	25 43	074	32 44	110	35 36	190	36 46	240	31 41	273	22 02	316
149	36 50	010	26 40	074	33 39	111	35 26	191	35 55	241	30 42	273	21 20	316
	Dubhe		◆ ARCTURUS		SPICA		ACRUX		◆ Suhail		SIRIUS		◆ POLLUX	
150	37 00	010	27 37	074	34 35	111	11 34	164	35 14	191	35 03	241	53 49	304
151	37 09	009	28 33	074	35 30	112	11 50	164	35 02	192	34 11	242	53 00	304
152	37 18	008	29 30	074	36 24	112	12 06	165	34 49	193	33 19	242	52 11	303
153	37 26	008	30 27	074	37 19	113	12 21	165	34 35	194	32 27	243	51 22	303
154	37 34	007	31 24	074	38 14	113	12 36	165	34 21	195	31 34	243	50 32	302
155	37 41	007	32 20	074	39 08	113	12 51	166	34 05	196	30 41	244	49 42	302
156	37 48	006	33 17	074	40 02	114	13 05	166	33 49	196	29 48	244	48 51	301
157	37 54	005	34 14	074	40 56	115	13 19	167	33 32	197	28 55	244	48 01	301
158	37 59	005	35 10	074	41 49	115	13 32	167	33 14	198	28 02	245	47 10	301
159	38 04	004	36 07	074	42 43	116	13 45	167	32 55	199	27 08	245	46 19	300
160	38 08	004	37 04	074	43 36	116	13 58	168	32 36	200	26 14	246	45 28	300
161	38 12	003	38 00	074	44 29	117	14 10	168	32 16	200	25 20	246	44 37	300
162	38 14	003	38 57	073	45 22	117	14 22	169	31 55	201	24 26	246	43 46	299
163	38 17	002	39 54	073	46 14	118	14 33	169	31 33	202	23 32	247	42 54	299
164	38 18	001	40 50	073	47 06	119	14 44	170	31 11	203	22 38	247	42 02	299
	Dubhe		◆ ARCTURUS		SPICA		◆ ACRUX		Suhail		PROCYON		◆ POLLUX	
165	38 19	001	41 47	073	47 57	119	14 55	170	30 48	203	40 16	268	41 11	299
166	38 20	000	42 43	073	48 49	120	15 05	170	30 25	204	39 17	269	40 19	298
167	38 20	359	43 40	073	49 40	121	15 15	171	30 00	205	38 18	269	39 27	298
168	38 19	359	44 36	073	50 30	122	15 24	171	29 35	205	37 19	269	38 34	298
169	38 17	358	45 33	073	51 20	122	15 32	172	29 10	206	36 20	269	37 42	298
170	38 15	358	46 29	073	52 10	123	15 41	172	28 43	207	35 21	269	36 50	298
171	38 13	357	47 26	073	52 59	124	15 48	173	28 17	207	34 22	269	35 58	297
172	38 09	356	48 22	072	53 48	125	15 56	173	27 49	208	33 23	270	35 05	297
173	38 05	356	49 18	072	54 36	126	16 03	174	27 21	209	32 24	270	34 13	297
174	38 01	355	50 15	072	55 23	127	16 09	174	26 53	209	31 25	270	33 20	297
175	37 56	355	51 11	072	56 10	128	16 15	174	26 24	210	30 25	270	32 27	297
176	37 50	354	52 07	072	56 56	129	16 21	175	25 54	210	29 26	270	31 35	297
177	37 43	354	53 03	071	57 41	130	16 26	175	25 24	211	28 27	271	30 42	297
178	37 36	353	53 59	071	58 26	132	16 30	176	24 53	212	27 28	271	29 49	297
179	37 29	352	54 55	071	59 09	133	16 34	176	24 22	212	26 29	271	28 56	297

LAT 10°N

LHA ♈	Hc	Zn	Hc	Zn	Hc	Zn	Hc	Zn	Hc	Zn	Hc	Zn	Hc	Zn
	◆Alphecca		ANTARES		RIGIL KENT		◆ACRUX		Suhail		◆REGULUS		Dubhe	
180	36 41	064	15 00	121	12 23	161	16 38	177	23 50	213	62 45	277	37 21	352
181	37 34	064	15 51	121	12 41	162	16 41	177	23 18	213	61 46	277	37 12	351
182	38 27	064	16 41	122	13 00	162	16 43	178	22 46	214	60 47	277	37 03	351
183	39 20	064	17 31	122	13 18	162	16 45	178	22 13	214	59 48	276	36 53	350
184	40 13	063	18 21	122	13 36	163	16 47	179	21 39	215	58 50	276	36 42	350
185	41 05	063	19 11	123	13 53	163	16 48	179	21 05	215	57 51	276	36 31	349
186	41 58	063	20 01	123	14 10	164	16 49	180	20 31	216	56 52	276	36 20	348
187	42 51	063	20 50	123	14 26	164	16 49	180	19 56	216	55 54	276	36 08	348
188	43 43	062	21 39	124	14 42	164	16 49	181	19 21	217	54 55	276	35 55	347
189	44 36	062	22 28	124	14 58	165	16 48	181	18 46	217	53 56	277	35 42	347
190	45 28	062	23 17	125	15 13	165	16 47	181	18 10	217	52 57	277	35 28	346
191	46 20	062	24 05	125	15 28	166	16 45	182	17 34	218	51 59	277	35 14	346
192	47 12	061	24 54	125	15 42	166	16 43	182	16 57	218	51 00	277	35 00	345
193	48 04	061	25 42	126	15 56	167	16 40	183	16 21	219	50 01	277	34 44	345
194	48 55	061	26 29	126	16 09	167	16 37	183	15 44	219	49 03	277	34 29	344
	◆VEGA		Rasalhague		ANTARES		◆RIGIL KENT		ACRUX		◆REGULUS		Dubhe	
195	10 37	052	22 34	080	27 17	127	16 22	168	16 33	184	48 04	277	34 13	344
196	11 24	052	23 32	081	28 04	127	16 35	168	16 29	184	47 05	277	33 56	343
197	12 10	052	24 30	081	28 51	128	16 47	168	16 24	185	46 07	277	33 39	343
198	12 57	052	25 29	081	29 37	128	16 58	169	16 19	185	45 08	277	33 21	343
199	13 44	052	26 27	081	30 23	129	17 09	169	16 13	186	44 09	277	33 04	342
200	14 30	052	27 25	081	31 09	129	17 20	170	16 07	186	43 11	277	32 45	342
201	15 17	052	28 24	081	31 54	130	17 30	170	16 01	187	42 12	277	32 26	341
202	16 04	052	29 22	081	32 40	131	17 40	171	15 54	187	41 13	277	32 07	341
203	16 51	052	30 20	081	33 24	131	17 49	171	15 46	187	40 15	277	31 48	340
204	17 37	052	31 19	081	34 09	132	17 58	172	15 38	188	39 16	277	31 28	340
205	18 24	052	32 17	081	34 52	132	18 06	172	15 30	188	38 17	277	31 07	340
206	19 11	052	33 16	081	35 36	133	18 13	173	15 21	189	37 19	277	30 47	339
207	19 58	052	34 14	082	36 19	134	18 21	173	15 12	189	36 20	277	30 26	339
208	20 44	052	35 13	082	37 01	134	18 27	174	15 02	190	35 22	278	30 04	339
209	21 31	052	36 11	082	37 43	135	18 33	174	14 52	190	34 23	278	29 42	338
	◆VEGA		Rasalhague		ANTARES		◆RIGIL KENT		SPICA		◆REGULUS		Dubhe	
210	22 18	052	37 09	082	38 25	136	18 39	175	67 08	202	33 25	278	29 20	338
211	23 04	052	38 08	082	39 05	137	18 44	175	66 45	204	32 26	278	28 58	338
212	23 51	052	39 06	082	39 46	137	18 49	176	66 20	206	31 27	278	28 35	337
213	24 37	052	40 05	082	40 26	138	18 53	176	65 53	209	30 29	278	28 12	337
214	25 23	052	41 03	082	41 05	139	18 56	177	65 23	211	29 30	278	27 49	337
215	26 10	052	42 02	082	41 43	140	18 59	177	64 52	213	28 32	278	27 25	336
216	26 56	051	43 00	082	42 21	141	19 02	178	64 20	215	27 33	278	27 01	336
217	27 42	051	43 59	082	42 58	142	19 04	178	63 45	216	26 35	278	26 37	336
218	28 28	051	44 58	082	43 35	142	19 05	179	63 10	218	25 37	278	26 12	335
219	29 14	051	45 56	082	44 10	143	19 06	179	62 33	220	24 38	279	25 48	335
220	30 00	051	46 55	082	44 45	144	19 06	180	61 54	221	23 40	279	25 23	335
221	30 45	051	47 53	082	45 19	145	19 06	180	61 14	223	22 41	279	24 58	335
222	31 31	050	48 52	082	45 52	146	19 05	181	60 34	224	21 43	279	24 32	334
223	32 16	050	49 50	082	46 25	147	19 04	181	59 52	226	20 45	279	24 07	334
224	33 02	050	50 49	082	46 56	148	19 02	182	59 09	227	19 46	279	23 41	334
	VEGA		◆ALTAIR		Nunki		ANTARES		RIGIL KENT		◆SPICA		◆Alkaid	
225	33 47	050	18 16	084	22 10	124	47 27	149	19 00	182	58 25	228	48 00	342
226	34 32	049	19 14	084	22 59	124	47 56	151	18 57	183	57 41	230	47 42	342
227	35 17	049	20 13	084	23 48	125	48 25	152	18 54	184	56 55	231	47 23	341
228	36 01	049	21 12	084	24 36	125	48 52	153	18 50	184	56 09	232	47 03	340
229	36 45	049	22 11	084	25 24	126	49 19	154	18 46	185	55 23	233	46 42	339
230	37 30	048	23 09	085	26 12	126	49 44	155	18 41	185	54 35	234	46 21	338
231	38 14	048	24 08	085	27 00	126	50 08	157	18 35	186	53 47	235	45 59	338
232	38 57	047	25 07	085	27 47	127	50 31	158	18 29	186	52 59	236	45 36	337
233	39 41	047	26 06	085	28 34	127	50 53	159	18 23	187	52 09	237	45 12	336
234	40 24	047	27 05	085	29 21	128	51 13	160	18 16	187	51 20	238	44 48	335
235	41 07	046	28 04	085	30 07	128	51 32	162	18 08	188	50 30	238	44 23	335
236	41 49	046	29 03	085	30 54	129	51 50	163	18 00	188	49 39	239	43 57	334
237	42 32	045	30 01	085	31 39	130	52 07	164	17 52	189	48 48	240	43 31	333
238	43 14	045	31 00	086	32 25	130	52 22	166	17 43	189	47 57	241	43 04	333
239	43 55	044	31 59	086	33 10	131	52 36	167	17 33	189	47 05	241	42 37	332
	◆VEGA		ALTAIR		Nunki		◆ANTARES		SPICA		◆ARCTURUS		Alkaid	
240	44 36	044	32 58	086	33 54	131	52 48	169	46 13	242	63 22	293	42 09	331
241	45 17	043	33 57	086	34 38	132	52 59	170	45 21	243	62 27	292	41 40	331
242	45 58	043	34 56	086	35 22	133	53 08	172	44 29	243	61 32	292	41 11	330
243	46 38	042	35 55	086	36 05	133	53 16	173	43 36	244	60 37	291	40 41	330
244	47 17	042	36 54	086	36 48	134	53 22	175	42 42	244	59 42	291	40 11	329
245	47 56	041	37 53	086	37 31	135	53 27	176	41 49	245	58 47	291	39 41	329
246	48 35	040	38 52	087	38 12	135	53 30	178	40 55	245	57 52	290	39 09	328
247	49 13	040	39 51	087	38 54	136	53 32	179	40 02	246	56 56	290	38 38	328
248	49 50	039	40 50	087	39 34	137	53 32	181	39 07	247	56 00	289	38 06	327
249	50 27	038	41 49	087	40 15	138	53 31	182	38 13	247	55 05	289	37 34	327
250	51 03	037	42 48	087	40 54	138	53 28	184	37 19	247	54 09	289	37 01	326
251	51 39	037	43 47	087	41 33	139	53 23	185	36 24	248	53 13	289	36 28	326
252	52 14	036	44 46	087	42 11	140	53 17	187	35 29	248	52 17	288	35 54	325
253	52 48	035	45 45	087	42 49	141	53 09	188	34 34	249	51 21	288	35 20	325
254	53 21	034	46 44	088	43 26	142	53 00	190	33 39	249	50 24	288	34 46	324
	VEGA		◆ALTAIR		Nunki		◆ANTARES		SPICA		ARCTURUS		◆Alkaid	
255	53 54	033	47 43	088	44 02	143	52 50	191	32 44	250	49 28	288	34 12	324
256	54 26	032	48 42	088	44 37	144	52 38	192	31 48	250	48 32	288	33 37	324
257	54 57	031	49 41	088	45 12	145	52 24	194	30 53	250	47 36	287	33 02	323
258	55 27	030	50 40	088	45 46	146	52 09	195	29 57	251	46 39	287	32 27	323
259	55 56	029	51 39	088	46 19	147	51 53	197	29 01	251	45 43	287	31 51	323
260	56 24	028	52 38	088	46 51	148	51 36	198	28 05	251	44 46	287	31 15	322
261	56 51	027	53 37	089	47 22	149	51 17	199	27 09	252	43 50	287	30 39	322
262	57 17	025	54 37	089	47 52	150	50 56	201	26 13	252	42 53	287	30 03	322
263	57 42	024	55 36	089	48 21	151	50 35	202	25 17	252	41 57	287	29 26	322
264	58 06	023	56 35	089	48 49	152	50 12	203	24 20	253	41 00	287	28 49	321
265	58 28	022	57 34	089	49 16	153	49 48	205	23 24	253	40 03	287	28 12	321
266	58 49	020	58 33	089	49 42	155	49 23	206	22 27	253	39 07	287	27 35	321
267	59 09	019	59 32	089	50 07	156	48 57	207	21 31	254	38 10	287	26 57	321
268	59 28	018	60 31	090	50 31	157	48 29	208	20 34	254	37 13	286	26 20	320
269	59 45	016	61 30	090	50 53	158	48 01	209	19 37	254	36 17	286	25 42	320

LHA ♈	Hc	Zn	Hc	Zn	Hc	Zn	Hc	Zn	Hc	Zn	Hc	Zn	Hc	Zn
	VEGA		◆DENEB		Enif		◆Nunki		Shaula		ANTARES		◆ARCTURUS	
270	60 00	015	40 33	037	34 42	085	51 14	160	42 31	187	47 32	210	35 20	286
271	60 15	013	41 08	036	35 40	085	51 34	161	42 23	188	47 01	211	34 23	286
272	60 27	012	41 43	036	36 39	085	51 53	162	42 14	189	46 30	213	33 27	286
273	60 39	010	42 17	035	37 38	085	52 10	164	42 05	190	45 58	214	32 30	286
274	60 48	009	42 51	035	38 37	085	52 26	165	41 54	191	45 25	215	31 33	286
275	60 56	007	43 25	034	39 36	085	52 40	167	41 42	192	44 51	216	30 37	286
276	61 03	005	43 57	034	40 35	085	52 53	168	41 29	193	44 16	217	29 40	286
277	61 07	004	44 30	033	41 34	086	53 05	169	41 15	194	43 40	217	28 43	286
278	61 11	002	45 02	032	42 33	086	53 15	171	41 00	195	43 04	218	27 47	286
279	61 12	001	45 33	032	43 32	086	53 24	172	40 44	196	42 27	219	26 50	286
280	61 12	359	46 04	031	44 30	086	53 31	174	40 27	197	41 49	220	25 53	286
281	61 10	357	46 34	030	45 29	086	53 36	175	40 09	198	41 11	221	24 57	287
282	61 06	356	47 03	029	46 28	086	53 40	177	39 50	199	40 32	222	24 00	287
283	61 01	354	47 32	029	47 27	086	53 43	178	39 31	200	39 52	223	23 03	287
284	60 54	353	48 00	028	48 26	086	53 43	180	39 10	201	39 12	223	22 07	287
	◆DENEB		Alpheratz		◆FOMALHAUT		Nunki		ANTARES		◆Rasalhague		VEGA	
285	48 27	027	15 53	062	20 21	127	53 43	181	38 31	224	69 10	279	60 46	351
286	48 54	026	16 46	062	21 08	127	53 40	183	37 50	225	68 12	279	60 36	349
287	49 20	025	17 38	062	21 55	128	53 37	184	37 08	225	67 13	279	60 24	348
288	49 45	025	18 31	062	22 42	128	53 31	186	36 26	226	66 15	278	60 11	346
289	50 09	024	19 23	062	23 28	128	53 24	187	35 43	227	65 16	278	59 56	345
290	50 32	023	20 15	062	24 14	129	53 16	189	35 00	227	64 18	278	59 40	343
291	50 54	022	21 08	062	25 00	129	53 06	190	34 16	228	63 19	278	59 23	342
292	51 16	021	22 00	062	25 45	130	52 55	192	33 32	229	62 21	278	59 04	341
293	51 37	020	22 52	062	26 31	130	52 42	193	32 47	229	61 22	278	58 43	339
294	51 56	019	23 45	062	27 15	131	52 27	195	32 02	230	60 24	278	58 22	338
295	52 15	018	24 37	062	28 00	131	52 12	196	31 17	230	59 25	278	57 59	337
296	52 32	017	25 30	062	28 44	132	51 55	198	30 31	231	58 27	278	57 35	335
297	52 49	016	26 22	062	29 28	132	51 36	199	29 45	232	57 28	278	57 10	334
298	53 04	015	27 14	062	30 11	133	51 16	200	28 58	232	56 29	278	56 44	333
299	53 19	014	28 06	062	30 54	134	50 55	202	28 12	233	55 31	278	56 16	332
	◆DENEB		Alpheratz		◆FOMALHAUT		Peacock		◆ANTARES		Rasalhague		VEGA	
300	53 32	012	28 59	062	31 37	134	23 05	176	27 24	233	54 32	278	55 48	331
301	53 44	011	29 51	062	32 19	135	23 09	177	26 37	234	53 34	278	55 19	330
302	53 55	010	30 43	062	33 01	135	23 12	177	25 49	234	52 35	278	54 48	329
303	54 05	009	31 35	062	33 42	136	23 15	178	25 01	234	51 37	278	54 17	328
304	54 14	008	32 27	062	34 23	137	23 17	178	24 13	235	50 38	278	53 45	327
305	54 21	007	33 19	062	35 03	137	23 18	179	23 25	235	49 40	278	53 12	326
306	54 27	005	34 11	061	35 43	138	23 19	180	22 36	236	48 41	278	52 38	325
307	54 32	004	35 03	061	36 22	139	23 19	180	21 47	236	47 42	278	52 04	324
308	54 36	003	35 55	061	37 01	139	23 18	181	20 58	236	46 44	278	51 29	323
309	54 39	002	36 46	061	37 39	140	23 17	181	20 09	237	45 45	278	50 53	322
310	54 40	001	37 38	061	38 17	141	23 16	182	19 19	237	44 47	278	50 17	322
311	54 40	359	38 29	061	38 53	142	23 13	183	18 29	238	43 48	278	49 40	321
312	54 38	358	39 21	060	39 30	143	23 10	183	17 39	238	42 50	278	49 02	320
313	54 36	357	40 12	060	40 05	143	23 07	184	16 49	238	41 51	278	48 24	319
314	54 32	356	41 03	060	40 40	144	23 02	184	15 59	239	40 53	278	47 45	319
	Alpheratz		◆Diphda		FOMALHAUT		◆Nunki		Rasalhague		VEGA		◆DENEB	
315	41 54	060	28 00	117	41 14	145	42 53	219	39 54	278	47 06	318	54 27	355
316	42 45	059	28 53	117	41 48	146	42 15	220	38 56	278	46 27	318	54 21	353
317	43 36	059	29 45	117	42 20	147	41 37	221	37 57	278	45 46	317	54 14	352
318	44 26	059	30 38	118	42 52	148	40 58	222	36 59	278	45 06	316	54 05	351
319	45 17	058	31 30	118	43 23	149	40 19	222	36 00	278	44 25	316	53 55	350
320	46 07	058	32 22	119	43 53	150	39 38	223	35 02	278	43 44	315	53 44	349
321	46 57	058	33 13	119	44 23	151	38 58	224	34 03	278	43 02	315	53 32	348
322	47 47	057	34 05	120	44 51	152	38 16	225	33 05	279	42 20	314	53 18	346
323	48 36	057	34 56	120	45 18	153	37 35	225	32 06	279	41 38	314	53 04	345
324	49 25	056	35 47	121	45 45	154	36 52	226	31 08	279	40 55	314	52 49	344
325	50 14	056	36 38	121	46 10	155	36 10	227	30 10	279	40 12	313	52 32	343
326	51 03	055	37 28	122	46 35	156	35 26	227	29 11	279	39 29	313	52 14	342
327	51 52	055	38 18	122	46 58	157	34 43	228	28 13	279	38 45	312	51 56	341
328	52 40	054	39 08	123	47 20	158	33 59	229	27 14	279	38 01	312	51 36	340
329	53 27	054	39 57	124	47 41	160	33 14	229	26 16	279	37 17	312	51 15	339
	◆Alpheratz		Diphda		◆FOMALHAUT		Peacock		ALTAIR		◆VEGA		DENEB	
330	54 15	053	40 46	124	48 01	161	20 35	193	58 18	271	36 33	311	50 54	338
331	55 02	052	41 34	125	48 20	162	20 21	194	57 19	271	35 49	311	50 31	337
332	55 48	052	42 23	126	48 38	163	20 07	194	56 20	271	35 04	311	50 08	336
333	56 34	051	43 10	126	48 54	165	19 52	195	55 21	271	34 19	311	49 44	335
334	57 20	050	43 58	127	49 09	166	19 36	196	54 22	271	33 34	310	49 19	335
335	58 05	049	44 45	128	49 23	167	19 20	196	53 23	272	32 49	310	48 53	334
336	58 49	048	45 31	129	49 36	168	19 04	197	52 24	272	32 04	310	48 26	333
337	59 33	047	46 17	130	49 47	170	18 47	197	51 25	272	31 18	310	47 59	332
338	60 16	046	47 02	130	49 57	171	18 29	198	50 26	272	30 33	309	47 31	331
339	60 59	045	47 47	131	50 05	172	18 11	198	49 27	272	29 47	309	47 02	331
340	61 40	044	48 31	132	50 12	174	17 53	198	48 28	272	29 01	309	46 33	330
341	62 21	043	49 15	133	50 18	175	17 34	199	47 29	272	28 15	309	46 03	329
342	63 01	042	49 57	134	50 23	176	17 14	199	46 30	272	27 29	309	45 32	328
343	63 40	041	50 40	135	50 26	178	16 54	200	45 31	273	26 43	309	45 01	328
344	64 18	039	51 21	136	50 27	179	16 34	200	44 32	273	25 57	308	44 29	327
	◆Mirfak		Hamal		Acamar		◆ACHERNAR		FOMALHAUT		◆ALTAIR		DENEB	
345	22 47	040	43 14	067	15 29	137	15 25	159	50 27	181	43 33	273	43 57	326
346	23 25	040	44 09	067	16 09	137	15 46	159	50 26	182	42 34	273	43 24	325
347	24 02	039	45 03	067	16 49	138	16 06	160	50 23	183	41 35	273	42 50	325
348	24 40	039	45 57	066	17 29	138	16 26	160	50 19	185	40 36	273	42 16	325
349	25 17	039	46 51	066	18 08	138	16 46	161	50 14	186	39 37	273	41 42	324
350	25 54	039	47 45	066	18 47	139	17 05	161	50 07	187	38 38	273	41 07	324
351	26 31	039	48 39	066	19 26	139	17 24	162	49 59	189	37 39	274	40 32	323
352	27 08	039	49 33	065	20 05	140	17 42	162	49 49	190	36 40	274	39 56	323
353	27 45	038	50 26	065	20 43	140	18 00	163	49 38	191	35 41	274	39 20	322
354	28 22	038	51 20	065	21 20	141	18 18	163	49 26	193	34 42	274	38 43	322
355	28 58	038	52 13	064	21 57	141	18 35	164	49 13	194	33 43	274	38 07	321
356	29 34	038	53 06	064	22 34	142	18 51	164	48 58	195	32 44	274	37 29	321
357	30 10	037	53 59	063	23 11	142	19 07	165	48 42	196	31 45	274	36 52	320
358	30 45	037	54 52	063	23 47	143	19 23	165	48 24	198	30 46	274	36 14	320
359	31 21	037	55 45	063	24 23	143	19 37	166	48 06	199	29 47	275	35 36	320

LAT 9°N

LHA ♈	Hc	Zn	Hc	Zn	Hc	Zn	Hc	Zn	Hc	Zn	Hc	Zn	Hc	Zn
	◆CAPELLA		ALDEBARAN		Acamar		◆ACHERNAR		FOMALHAUT		◆ALTAIR		DENEB	
0	13 47	045	22 23	076	25 46	143	20 50	166	48 43	200	28 43	275	34 12	320
1	14 28	045	23 21	076	26 21	144	21 04	167	48 21	202	27 44	275	33 33	319
2	15 10	045	24 18	076	26 56	145	21 18	167	47 59	203	26 45	275	32 55	319
3	15 52	045	25 15	076	27 30	145	21 31	168	47 35	204	25 46	276	32 16	319
4	16 33	045	26 13	076	28 04	146	21 43	168	47 11	205	24 47	276	31 37	318
5	17 15	044	27 10	076	28 37	146	21 55	169	46 45	206	23 48	276	30 57	318
6	17 56	044	28 08	076	29 10	147	22 06	169	46 18	207	22 49	276	30 17	318
7	18 38	044	29 05	076	29 42	147	22 17	170	45 51	208	21 50	276	29 38	318
8	19 19	044	30 03	076	30 13	148	22 27	170	45 22	209	20 51	276	28 57	317
9	20 00	044	31 00	076	30 44	149	22 37	171	44 52	210	19 52	276	28 17	317
10	20 42	044	31 58	076	31 15	149	22 46	171	44 22	211	18 54	276	27 37	317
11	21 23	044	32 55	076	31 44	150	22 54	172	43 50	212	17 55	277	26 56	317
12	22 04	044	33 53	076	32 14	151	23 02	173	43 18	213	16 56	277	26 15	316
13	22 45	044	34 50	076	32 42	152	23 10	173	42 45	214	15 57	277	25 35	316
14	23 26	044	35 48	076	33 10	152	23 16	174	42 12	215	14 58	277	24 54	316
	CAPELLA		◆ALDEBARAN		RIGEL		ACHERNAR		◆FOMALHAUT		Enif		◆DENEB	
15	24 06	043	36 45	076	24 09	103	23 22	174	41 37	216	41 56	275	24 12	316
16	24 47	043	37 43	076	25 07	103	23 28	175	41 02	217	40 57	275	23 31	316
17	25 27	043	38 41	076	26 04	104	23 33	176	40 26	218	39 58	275	22 50	316
18	26 08	043	39 38	076	27 02	104	23 37	176	39 49	219	38 59	276	22 08	315
19	26 48	043	40 35	076	27 59	104	23 41	177	39 12	219	38 00	276	21 27	315
20	27 28	042	41 33	076	28 57	105	23 44	177	38 34	220	37 01	276	20 45	315
21	28 08	042	42 30	076	29 54	105	23 46	178	37 56	221	36 02	276	20 03	315
22	28 47	042	43 28	076	30 51	105	23 48	178	37 17	222	35 03	276	19 21	315
23	29 27	042	44 25	076	31 48	106	23 50	179	36 37	222	34 04	276	18 39	315
24	30 06	041	45 23	076	32 45	106	23 50	180	35 57	223	33 05	276	17 57	315
25	30 45	041	46 20	075	33 42	106	23 50	180	35 16	224	32 06	276	17 15	315
26	31 24	041	47 17	075	34 39	107	23 50	181	34 35	224	31 07	276	16 33	315
27	32 03	041	48 15	075	35 36	107	23 49	181	33 53	225	30 08	276	15 51	315
28	32 41	040	49 12	075	36 33	107	23 47	182	33 11	226	29 09	276	15 09	315
29	33 19	040	50 09	075	37 29	108	23 44	183	32 29	226	28 10	277	14 27	315
	Mirfak		CAPELLA		◆ALDEBARAN		RIGEL		◆ACHERNAR		FOMALHAUT		◆Alpheratz	
30	45 24	020	33 57	040	51 06	075	38 25	108	23 41	183	31 46	227	57 07	312
31	45 44	019	34 35	039	52 04	075	39 22	108	23 38	184	31 02	227	56 22	311
32	46 02	018	35 12	039	53 01	074	40 18	109	23 33	184	30 19	228	55 37	310
33	46 20	017	35 49	038	53 58	074	41 14	109	23 29	185	29 35	228	54 51	309
34	46 37	016	36 26	038	54 55	074	42 10	110	23 23	186	28 50	229	54 05	309
35	46 53	015	37 02	038	55 52	074	43 05	110	23 17	186	28 05	229	53 19	308
36	47 08	015	37 38	037	56 48	073	44 01	111	23 11	187	27 20	230	52 32	307
37	47 23	014	38 13	037	57 45	073	44 56	111	23 03	187	26 35	230	51 44	307
38	47 36	013	38 48	036	58 42	073	45 52	112	22 55	188	25 49	231	50 57	306
39	47 49	012	39 23	036	59 39	073	46 46	112	22 47	188	25 03	231	50 08	305
40	48 01	011	39 58	035	60 35	072	47 41	113	22 38	189	24 16	232	49 20	305
41	48 11	010	40 31	035	61 31	072	48 36	113	22 29	190	23 30	232	48 31	304
42	48 21	009	41 05	034	62 28	071	49 30	114	22 18	190	22 43	233	47 42	304
43	48 30	008	41 38	034	63 24	071	50 24	115	22 08	191	21 55	233	46 53	304
44	48 38	007	42 10	033	64 20	070	51 18	115	21 56	191	21 08	233	46 04	303
	◆CAPELLA		PROCYON		SIRIUS		◆CANOPUS		ACHERNAR		Diphda		◆Alpheratz	
45	42 42	032	20 30	088	28 32	115	14 34	151	21 45	192	47 03	231	45 14	303
46	43 14	032	21 29	088	29 26	115	15 03	151	21 32	192	46 16	232	44 24	302
47	43 44	031	22 28	088	30 19	115	15 31	152	21 19	193	45 29	233	43 34	302
48	44 15	030	23 28	088	31 13	116	15 59	152	21 06	193	44 42	234	42 43	302
49	44 44	030	24 27	088	32 06	116	16 27	152	20 52	194	43 54	234	41 53	301
50	45 13	029	25 26	089	32 59	117	16 54	153	20 38	194	43 06	235	41 02	301
51	45 42	028	26 25	089	33 52	117	17 21	153	20 23	195	42 17	236	40 11	301
52	46 10	027	27 25	089	34 44	118	17 47	154	20 07	195	41 28	236	39 21	301
53	46 37	027	28 24	089	35 37	118	18 13	154	19 51	196	40 38	237	38 29	300
54	47 03	026	29 23	089	36 29	119	18 39	155	19 35	196	39 49	238	37 38	300
55	47 29	025	30 22	089	37 21	119	19 04	155	19 18	197	38 58	238	36 47	300
56	47 53	024	31 22	089	38 12	120	19 29	156	19 00	197	38 08	239	35 55	300
57	48 17	023	32 21	090	39 04	120	19 53	156	18 42	198	37 17	239	35 04	299
58	48 41	023	33 20	090	39 55	121	20 17	157	18 24	198	36 26	240	34 12	299
59	49 03	022	34 19	090	40 45	121	20 40	157	18 05	199	35 35	240	33 20	299
	◆CAPELLA		POLLUX		PROCYON		◆SIRIUS		CANOPUS		◆Diphda		Alpheratz	
60	49 25	021	33 39	062	35 19	090	41 36	122	21 03	158	34 43	241	32 29	299
61	49 45	020	34 31	062	36 18	090	42 26	123	21 26	158	33 51	241	31 37	299
62	50 05	019	35 24	062	37 17	090	43 15	123	21 48	159	32 59	242	30 45	299
63	50 24	018	36 16	062	38 17	090	44 05	124	22 09	159	32 07	242	29 53	299
64	50 41	017	37 08	062	39 16	091	44 54	125	22 30	160	31 14	243	29 01	298
65	50 58	016	38 00	061	40 15	091	45 42	125	22 50	160	30 22	243	28 09	298
66	51 14	015	38 52	061	41 14	091	46 30	126	23 10	161	29 29	243	27 16	298
67	51 29	014	39 44	061	42 14	091	47 18	127	23 30	161	28 36	244	26 24	298
68	51 42	013	40 36	061	43 13	091	48 05	128	23 48	162	27 42	244	25 32	298
69	51 55	012	41 27	060	44 12	092	48 52	129	24 06	162	26 49	245	24 40	298
70	52 07	011	42 19	060	45 11	092	49 38	130	24 24	163	25 55	245	23 47	298
71	52 17	010	43 10	060	46 10	092	50 23	130	24 41	164	25 02	245	22 55	298
72	52 26	008	44 01	059	47 10	092	51 08	131	24 58	164	24 08	246	22 03	298
73	52 35	007	44 52	059	48 09	092	51 52	132	25 13	165	23 14	246	21 10	298
74	52 42	006	45 43	059	49 08	092	52 35	133	25 29	165	22 19	246	20 18	298
	CAPELLA		◆POLLUX		PROCYON		SIRIUS		◆CANOPUS		Acamar		◆Hamal	
75	52 48	005	46 33	058	50 07	093	53 18	134	25 43	166	33 22	207	46 27	295
76	52 52	004	47 24	058	51 07	093	54 00	136	25 57	167	32 54	208	45 33	295
77	52 56	003	48 14	058	52 06	093	54 41	137	26 11	167	32 26	209	44 39	294
78	52 58	002	49 04	057	53 05	093	55 21	138	26 23	168	31 57	210	43 45	294
79	52 59	001	49 53	057	54 04	094	56 00	139	26 36	169	31 27	210	42 51	294
80	52 59	359	50 43	056	55 03	094	56 39	140	26 47	169	30 57	211	41 57	294
81	52 58	358	51 32	056	56 02	094	57 16	142	26 58	170	30 26	212	41 03	293
82	52 55	357	52 21	055	57 01	094	57 52	143	27 08	170	29 55	212	40 08	293
83	52 52	356	53 09	054	58 00	095	58 27	145	27 17	171	29 23	213	39 14	293
84	52 47	355	53 57	054	59 00	095	59 01	146	27 26	172	28 50	213	38 19	293
85	52 41	354	54 45	053	59 59	095	59 33	148	27 34	172	28 18	214	37 25	293
86	52 34	353	55 32	052	60 58	096	60 04	149	27 42	173	27 44	215	36 30	293
87	52 26	351	56 19	052	61 57	096	60 34	151	27 49	174	27 10	215	35 35	293
88	52 16	350	57 05	051	62 55	096	61 02	153	27 55	174	26 36	216	34 40	292
89	52 06	349	57 51	050	63 54	097	61 28	154	28 00	175	26 01	216	33 46	292

LHA ♈	Hc	Zn	Hc	Zn	Hc	Zn	Hc	Zn	Hc	Zn	Hc	Zn	Hc	Zn
	◆POLLUX		REGULUS		Suhail		◆CANOPUS		RIGEL		◆ALDEBARAN		CAPELLA	
90	58 36	049	28 47	081	22 19	145	28 05	176	69 31	213	68 23	292	51 54	348
91	59 21	048	29 46	081	22 53	145	28 09	177	68 58	216	67 28	292	51 41	347
92	60 05	047	30 45	081	23 26	146	28 12	177	68 22	218	66 32	291	51 27	346
93	60 48	046	31 43	082	23 59	146	28 14	178	67 45	220	65 37	290	51 12	345
94	61 30	045	32 42	082	24 32	147	28 16	179	67 06	222	64 41	290	50 57	344
95	62 12	044	33 41	082	25 04	147	28 17	179	66 26	224	63 46	289	50 40	343
96	62 53	043	34 39	082	25 36	148	28 18	180	65 45	225	62 50	289	50 22	342
97	63 33	042	35 38	082	26 07	149	28 17	181	65 02	227	61 53	288	50 03	341
98	64 11	040	36 36	082	26 37	149	28 16	181	64 18	229	60 57	288	49 43	340
99	64 49	039	37 35	082	27 07	150	28 15	182	63 33	230	60 01	288	49 22	339
100	65 25	037	38 34	082	27 37	150	28 12	183	62 47	231	59 04	287	49 01	338
101	66 01	036	39 32	082	28 06	151	28 09	183	62 00	233	58 07	287	48 38	337
102	66 34	034	40 31	082	28 34	152	28 05	184	61 13	234	57 11	287	48 15	336
103	67 07	032	41 30	082	29 02	152	28 01	185	60 24	235	56 14	286	47 51	336
104	67 38	030	42 29	082	29 30	153	27 55	185	59 35	236	55 17	286	47 26	335
	Dubhe		◆REGULUS		Suhail		◆CANOPUS		RIGEL		ALDEBARAN		◆CAPELLA	
105	21 20	027	43 27	082	29 56	154	27 49	186	58 46	237	54 20	286	47 00	334
106	21 46	026	44 26	082	30 22	154	27 43	187	57 56	238	53 23	286	46 34	333
107	22 13	026	45 25	082	30 48	155	27 36	187	57 05	239	52 26	285	46 07	332
108	22 38	026	46 23	082	31 13	156	27 27	188	56 14	240	51 29	285	45 39	332
109	23 04	026	47 22	082	31 37	156	27 19	189	55 22	241	50 32	285	45 11	331
110	23 30	025	48 21	082	32 00	157	27 09	189	54 30	242	49 34	285	44 41	330
111	23 55	025	49 19	082	32 23	158	26 59	190	53 37	243	48 37	285	44 12	330
112	24 20	025	50 18	082	32 45	159	26 49	191	52 44	243	47 40	285	43 41	329
113	24 45	025	51 17	082	33 06	159	26 37	191	51 51	244	46 42	285	43 11	328
114	25 10	024	52 16	082	33 27	160	26 25	192	50 58	245	45 45	285	42 39	328
115	25 34	024	53 14	082	33 47	161	26 13	193	50 04	246	44 48	284	42 07	327
116	25 58	024	54 13	082	34 06	162	25 59	193	49 10	246	43 50	284	41 35	326
117	26 22	024	55 12	082	34 24	162	25 45	194	48 16	247	42 53	284	41 02	326
118	26 46	023	56 10	082	34 42	163	25 31	195	47 21	247	41 55	284	40 28	325
119	27 09	023	57 09	082	34 59	164	25 16	195	46 26	248	40 58	284	39 54	325
	Dubhe		◆Denebola		Suhail		◆SIRIUS		RIGEL		ALDEBARAN		◆CAPELLA	
120	27 32	023	33 37	079	35 15	165	58 24	216	45 31	248	40 00	284	39 20	324
121	27 55	022	34 35	079	35 30	166	57 49	217	44 36	249	39 03	284	38 45	324
122	28 17	022	35 33	079	35 44	167	57 12	218	43 40	249	38 06	284	38 10	323
123	28 40	022	36 31	079	35 57	167	56 35	220	42 45	250	37 08	284	37 34	323
124	29 01	021	37 29	079	36 10	168	55 57	221	41 49	250	36 11	284	36 58	322
125	29 23	021	38 27	079	36 21	169	55 17	222	40 53	251	35 13	284	36 22	322
126	29 44	021	39 25	079	36 32	170	54 37	223	39 57	251	34 15	284	35 45	322
127	30 04	020	40 23	079	36 42	171	53 56	225	39 01	252	33 18	284	35 08	321
128	30 25	020	41 21	079	36 51	172	53 14	226	38 05	252	32 20	284	34 31	321
129	30 45	019	42 20	079	36 59	173	52 31	227	37 08	252	31 23	284	33 53	320
130	31 04	019	43 18	079	37 06	174	51 48	228	36 12	253	30 25	284	33 15	320
131	31 24	019	44 16	079	37 13	174	51 03	229	35 15	253	29 28	284	32 37	320
132	31 42	018	45 14	078	37 18	175	50 19	230	34 18	254	28 30	284	31 59	319
133	32 01	018	46 12	078	37 22	176	49 33	231	33 21	254	27 33	284	31 20	319
134	32 19	017	47 10	078	37 26	177	48 47	231	32 24	254	26 35	284	30 41	319
	Dubhe		◆ARCTURUS		SPICA		◆Suhail		SIRIUS		BETELGEUSE		◆CAPELLA	
135	32 36	017	13 10	072	20 51	106	37 28	178	48 00	232	44 28	272	30 02	319
136	32 53	016	14 07	072	21 48	106	37 30	179	47 13	233	43 29	272	29 23	318
137	33 10	016	15 03	073	22 45	106	37 30	180	46 26	234	42 30	272	28 44	318
138	33 26	016	16 00	073	23 42	107	37 30	181	45 38	235	41 30	272	28 04	318
139	33 42	015	16 56	073	24 38	107	37 29	182	44 49	235	40 31	272	27 24	318
140	33 57	015	17 53	073	25 35	107	37 27	183	44 00	236	39 32	272	26 44	317
141	34 11	014	18 50	073	26 32	107	37 23	184	43 11	237	38 33	272	26 04	317
142	34 26	014	19 46	073	27 28	108	37 19	184	42 21	237	37 33	272	25 23	317
143	34 39	013	20 43	073	28 24	108	37 14	185	41 31	238	36 34	273	24 43	317
144	34 52	013	21 40	073	29 21	108	37 08	186	40 40	239	35 35	273	24 02	317
145	35 05	012	22 36	073	30 17	109	37 01	187	39 50	239	34 36	273	23 21	316
146	35 17	012	23 33	073	31 13	109	36 53	188	38 59	240	33 37	273	22 41	316
147	35 29	011	24 30	073	32 09	109	36 45	189	38 07	240	32 38	273	22 00	316
148	35 40	010	25 26	073	33 05	110	36 35	190	37 16	241	31 38	273	21 19	316
149	35 50	010	26 23	073	34 00	110	36 25	191	36 24	241	30 39	273	20 37	316
	Dubhe		◆ARCTURUS		SPICA		ACRUX		◆Suhail		SIRIUS		◆POLLUX	
150	36 00	009	27 20	073	34 56	111	12 32	164	36 13	192	35 32	242	53 15	306
151	36 10	009	28 16	073	35 51	111	12 48	164	36 01	192	34 39	242	52 26	305
152	36 19	008	29 13	073	36 47	111	13 04	165	35 48	193	33 47	243	51 38	304
153	36 27	008	30 10	073	37 42	112	13 19	165	35 34	194	32 54	243	50 49	304
154	36 35	007	31 06	073	38 37	112	13 34	165	35 19	195	32 01	244	49 59	303
155	36 42	007	32 03	073	39 31	113	13 49	166	35 03	196	31 08	244	49 10	303
156	36 48	006	33 00	073	40 26	113	14 03	166	34 47	197	30 14	245	48 20	302
157	36 54	005	33 56	073	41 20	114	14 17	167	34 29	197	29 21	245	47 30	302
158	36 59	005	34 53	073	42 14	114	14 31	167	34 11	198	28 27	245	46 39	302
159	37 04	004	35 50	073	43 08	115	14 44	167	33 52	199	27 33	246	45 49	301
160	37 08	004	36 46	073	44 02	115	14 57	168	33 33	200	26 39	246	44 58	301
161	37 12	003	37 43	073	44 56	116	15 09	168	33 12	201	25 45	246	44 07	301
162	37 14	002	38 40	073	45 49	116	15 21	169	32 51	201	24 50	247	43 16	300
163	37 17	002	39 36	073	46 42	117	15 32	169	32 29	202	23 56	247	42 25	300
164	37 18	001	40 33	073	47 34	118	15 43	170	32 07	203	23 01	247	41 33	300
	Dubhe		◆ARCTURUS		SPICA		◆ACRUX		Suhail		PROCYON		◆POLLUX	
165	37 19	001	41 29	072	48 27	118	15 54	170	31 43	203	40 18	269	40 42	299
166	37 20	000	42 26	072	49 18	119	16 04	170	31 19	204	39 18	269	39 50	299
167	37 20	359	43 22	072	50 10	120	16 14	171	30 55	205	38 19	270	38 58	299
168	37 19	359	44 18	072	51 01	121	16 23	171	30 29	206	37 20	270	38 06	299
169	37 17	358	45 15	072	51 52	121	16 32	172	30 03	206	36 21	270	37 14	298
170	37 15	358	46 11	072	52 42	122	16 40	172	29 37	207	35 21	270	36 22	298
171	37 13	357	47 07	072	53 32	123	16 48	173	29 10	208	34 22	270	35 30	298
172	37 09	357	48 03	071	54 22	124	16 55	173	28 42	208	33 23	270	34 37	298
173	37 05	356	49 00	071	55 10	125	17 02	174	28 14	209	32 24	270	33 45	298
174	37 01	355	49 56	071	55 59	126	17 09	174	27 45	209	31 24	271	32 52	298
175	36 56	355	50 52	071	56 46	127	17 15	174	27 16	210	30 25	271	32 00	297
176	36 50	354	51 48	070	57 33	128	17 20	175	26 46	211	29 26	271	31 07	297
177	36 44	354	52 43	070	58 20	129	17 25	175	26 15	211	28 26	271	30 15	297
178	36 37	353	53 39	070	59 05	130	17 30	176	25 44	212	27 27	271	29 22	297
179	36 29	352	54 35	070	59 50	132	17 34	176	25 13	212	26 28	271	28 29	297

LHA ♈	Hc Zn	Hc Zn	Hc Zn	Hc Zn	Hc Zn	Hc Zn	Hc Zn
	◆ ARCTURUS	ANTARES	RIGIL KENT	◆ ACRUX	Suhail	◆ REGULUS	Dubhe
180	55 30 069	15 31 121	13 20 161	17 38 177	24 41 213	62 37 279	36 21 352
181	56 25 069	16 22 121	13 38 162	17 41 177	24 08 213	61 38 278	36 13 351
182	57 21 068	17 12 121	13 57 162	17 43 178	23 35 214	60 39 278	36 04 351
183	58 16 068	18 03 122	14 15 162	17 45 178	23 02 214	59 41 278	35 54 350
184	59 11 068	18 53 122	14 33 163	17 47 179	22 28 215	58 42 278	35 43 350
185	60 05 067	19 43 122	14 50 163	17 48 179	21 54 215	57 43 278	35 33 349
186	61 00 067	20 33 123	15 07 164	17 49 180	21 20 216	56 45 278	35 21 349
187	61 54 066	21 23 123	15 24 164	17 49 180	20 45 216	55 46 278	35 09 348
188	62 48 065	22 12 124	15 40 164	17 49 181	20 09 217	54 47 278	34 57 348
189	63 42 065	23 02 124	15 56 165	17 48 181	19 34 217	53 49 278	34 44 347
190	64 35 064	23 51 124	16 11 165	17 47 181	18 58 218	52 50 278	34 30 347
191	65 28 063	24 40 125	16 26 166	17 45 182	18 21 218	51 51 278	34 16 346
192	66 21 062	25 28 125	16 40 166	17 43 182	17 44 219	50 52 278	34 01 346
193	67 13 061	26 17 126	16 54 167	17 40 183	17 07 219	49 54 278	33 46 345
194	68 05 060	27 05 126	17 08 167	17 37 183	16 30 219	48 55 278	33 31 345
	◆ Alphecca	Rasalhague	ANTARES	◆ RIGIL KENT	ACRUX	◆ REGULUS	Dubhe
195	49 16 059	22 24 080	27 52 126	17 21 167	17 33 184	47 56 278	33 15 344
196	50 07 059	23 22 080	28 40 127	17 33 168	17 29 184	46 58 278	32 58 344
197	50 57 058	24 20 080	29 27 127	17 46 168	17 24 185	45 59 278	32 42 343
198	51 48 058	25 19 080	30 14 128	17 57 169	17 19 185	45 00 278	32 24 343
199	52 38 057	26 17 080	31 01 128	18 08 169	17 13 186	44 02 278	32 06 342
200	53 27 057	27 16 080	31 47 129	18 19 170	17 07 186	43 03 278	31 48 342
201	54 17 056	28 14 081	32 33 130	18 29 170	17 00 187	42 04 278	31 30 341
202	55 06 055	29 12 081	33 18 130	18 39 171	16 53 187	41 05 278	31 11 341
203	55 54 055	30 11 081	34 04 131	18 48 171	16 46 188	40 07 278	30 51 341
204	56 43 054	31 09 081	34 48 131	18 57 172	16 38 188	39 08 278	30 31 340
205	57 30 053	32 08 081	35 33 132	19 05 172	16 29 188	38 09 278	30 11 340
206	58 18 053	33 06 081	36 17 133	19 13 173	16 20 189	37 11 278	29 50 339
207	59 04 052	34 05 081	37 00 133	19 20 173	16 11 189	36 12 278	29 29 339
208	59 51 051	35 03 081	37 43 134	19 27 174	16 01 190	35 13 278	29 08 339
209	60 36 050	36 02 081	38 25 135	19 33 174	15 51 190	34 15 278	28 47 338
	◆ VEGA	Rasalhague	ANTARES	◆ RIGIL KENT	SPICA	◆ REGULUS	Dubhe
210	21 40 052	37 00 081	39 07 135	19 39 175	68 04 203	33 16 278	28 25 338
211	22 27 052	37 59 081	39 49 136	19 44 175	67 40 205	32 18 278	28 02 338
212	23 13 052	38 58 081	40 30 137	19 48 176	67 13 208	31 19 279	27 40 337
213	24 00 051	39 56 081	41 10 138	19 53 176	66 45 210	30 20 279	27 17 337
214	24 46 051	40 55 081	41 50 138	19 56 177	66 15 212	29 22 279	26 53 337
215	25 32 051	41 53 081	42 29 139	19 59 177	65 43 214	28 23 279	26 30 336
216	26 18 051	42 52 081	43 07 140	20 02 178	65 09 216	27 25 279	26 06 336
217	27 04 051	43 50 081	43 45 141	20 04 178	64 33 218	26 26 279	25 42 336
218	27 50 051	44 49 081	44 22 142	20 05 179	63 56 219	25 27 279	25 18 336
219	28 36 050	45 47 081	44 58 143	20 06 179	63 18 221	24 29 279	24 53 335
220	29 22 050	46 46 081	45 34 144	20 06 180	62 39 223	23 30 279	24 28 335
221	30 07 050	47 45 081	46 08 145	20 06 180	61 58 224	22 32 279	24 03 335
222	30 53 050	48 43 081	46 42 146	20 05 181	61 16 226	21 33 279	23 38 335
223	31 38 050	49 42 081	47 15 147	20 04 181	60 33 227	20 35 279	23 12 334
224	32 23 049	50 40 081	47 47 148	20 02 182	59 49 228	19 36 280	22 47 334
	VEGA	◆ ALTAIR	Nunki	ANTARES	RIGIL KENT	◆ SPICA	◆ Alkaid
225	33 08 049	18 09 084	22 43 124	48 18 149	20 00 183	59 05 230	47 03 343
226	33 52 049	19 08 084	23 33 124	48 48 150	19 57 183	58 19 231	46 45 342
227	34 37 049	20 07 084	24 22 124	49 17 151	19 54 184	57 33 232	46 26 341
228	35 21 048	21 06 084	25 10 125	49 46 152	19 50 184	56 46 233	46 07 340
229	36 05 048	22 05 084	25 59 125	50 13 154	19 45 185	55 58 234	45 46 340
230	36 49 048	23 04 084	26 47 126	50 38 155	19 40 185	55 10 235	45 25 339
231	37 33 047	24 02 084	27 35 126	51 03 156	19 35 186	54 21 236	45 03 338
232	38 16 047	25 01 084	28 23 127	51 27 157	19 29 186	53 32 237	44 41 337
233	39 00 047	26 00 084	29 11 127	51 49 159	19 22 187	52 42 238	44 17 336
234	39 42 046	26 59 085	29 58 127	52 10 160	19 15 187	51 52 239	43 53 336
235	40 25 046	27 58 085	30 45 128	52 29 161	19 08 188	51 01 239	43 29 335
236	41 07 045	28 57 085	31 31 129	52 48 163	19 00 188	50 10 240	43 03 334
237	41 49 045	29 56 085	32 17 129	53 05 164	18 51 189	49 18 241	42 37 334
238	42 31 044	30 55 085	33 03 130	53 20 166	18 42 189	48 26 242	42 11 333
239	43 12 044	31 54 085	33 49 130	53 34 167	18 32 190	47 34 242	41 44 332
	◆ VEGA	ALTAIR	Nunki	◆ ANTARES	SPICA	◆ ARCTURUS	Alkaid
240	43 53 043	32 54 085	34 34 131	53 47 168	46 41 243	62 57 295	41 16 332
241	44 33 043	33 53 085	35 18 131	53 58 170	45 48 244	62 03 294	40 48 331
242	45 13 042	34 52 085	36 03 132	54 07 171	44 55 244	61 09 294	40 19 331
243	45 53 042	35 51 085	36 46 133	54 15 173	44 02 245	60 15 293	39 49 330
244	46 32 041	36 50 086	37 30 133	54 22 174	43 08 245	59 20 292	39 20 329
245	47 11 040	37 49 086	38 13 134	54 27 176	42 14 246	58 25 292	38 49 329
246	47 49 040	38 48 086	38 55 135	54 30 178	41 20 246	57 30 292	38 18 328
247	48 26 039	39 47 086	39 37 135	54 32 179	40 26 247	56 35 291	37 47 328
248	49 03 038	40 46 086	40 18 136	54 32 181	39 31 247	55 40 291	37 16 327
249	49 40 037	41 45 086	40 59 137	54 31 182	38 36 248	54 44 290	36 43 327
250	50 15 037	42 44 086	41 39 138	54 27 184	37 41 248	53 49 290	36 11 327
251	50 50 036	43 44 086	42 18 139	54 23 185	36 46 249	52 53 290	35 38 326
252	51 25 035	44 43 086	42 57 139	54 17 187	35 51 249	51 57 290	35 05 326
253	51 58 034	45 42 086	43 35 140	54 09 188	34 56 249	51 01 289	34 31 325
254	52 31 033	46 41 087	44 13 141	54 00 190	34 00 250	50 05 289	33 57 325
	VEGA	◆ ALTAIR	Nunki	◆ ANTARES	SPICA	ARCTURUS	◆ Alkaid
255	53 03 032	47 40 087	44 50 142	53 49 191	33 04 250	49 09 289	33 23 324
256	53 35 031	48 39 087	45 26 143	53 36 193	32 08 251	48 13 289	32 49 324
257	54 05 030	49 38 087	46 01 144	53 23 194	31 13 251	47 17 288	32 14 324
258	54 35 029	50 38 087	46 35 145	53 07 196	30 16 251	46 21 288	31 38 323
259	55 03 028	51 37 087	47 09 146	52 51 197	29 20 252	45 25 288	31 03 323
260	55 31 027	52 36 087	47 41 147	52 32 198	28 24 252	44 28 288	30 27 323
261	55 57 026	53 35 087	48 13 148	52 13 200	27 28 252	43 32 288	29 51 322
262	56 23 025	54 34 087	48 44 149	51 52 201	26 31 253	42 35 288	29 15 322
263	56 47 024	55 34 087	49 13 150	51 30 202	25 35 253	41 39 288	28 39 322
264	57 10 022	56 33 087	49 42 152	51 07 204	24 38 253	40 42 288	28 02 322
265	57 32 021	57 32 088	50 10 153	50 43 205	23 41 253	39 46 287	27 25 321
266	57 53 020	58 31 088	50 36 154	50 17 206	22 44 254	38 49 287	26 48 321
267	58 12 018	59 30 088	51 02 155	49 50 207	21 47 254	37 53 287	26 11 321
268	58 30 017	60 30 088	51 26 157	49 22 209	20 50 254	36 56 287	25 34 321
269	58 47 016	61 29 088	51 49 158	48 53 210	19 53 255	35 59 287	24 56 321

LAT 9°N

LHA ♈	Hc Zn	Hc Zn	Hc Zn	Hc Zn	Hc Zn	Hc Zn	Hc Zn
	VEGA	◆ DENEB	Enif	◆ Nunki	Shaula	ANTARES	◆ ARCTURUS
270	59 02 014	39 45 036	34 36 084	52 10 159	43 30 187	48 23 211	35 03 287
271	59 16 013	40 19 036	35 35 084	52 31 161	43 23 188	47 52 212	34 06 287
272	59 29 011	40 54 035	36 34 084	52 50 162	43 14 189	47 20 213	33 10 287
273	59 40 010	41 28 035	37 33 084	53 08 163	43 04 190	46 48 214	32 13 287
274	59 49 008	42 02 034	38 32 084	53 24 165	42 53 191	46 14 215	31 16 287
275	59 57 007	42 35 034	39 31 084	53 39 166	42 41 192	45 39 216	30 19 287
276	60 03 005	43 07 033	40 30 085	53 52 168	42 27 193	45 04 217	29 23 287
277	60 08 004	43 39 032	41 29 085	54 04 169	42 13 194	44 28 218	28 26 287
278	60 11 002	44 11 032	42 28 085	54 14 171	41 58 195	43 51 219	27 29 287
279	60 12 001	44 42 031	43 27 085	54 23 172	41 42 196	43 13 220	26 33 287
280	60 12 359	45 12 030	44 26 085	54 30 174	41 24 197	42 35 221	25 36 287
281	60 10 357	45 42 030	45 25 085	54 36 175	41 06 198	41 56 222	24 39 287
282	60 06 356	46 11 029	46 24 085	54 40 177	40 47 199	41 17 222	23 43 287
283	60 01 354	46 39 028	47 23 085	54 43 178	40 27 200	40 36 223	22 46 287
284	59 55 353	47 07 027	48 22 085	54 43 180	40 06 201	39 56 224	21 49 287
	DENEB	◆ Alpheratz	FOMALHAUT	◆ Nunki	ANTARES	◆ Rasalhague	VEGA
285	47 34 027	15 25 062	20 57 127	54 43 181	39 14 225	68 59 282	59 47 351
286	48 00 026	16 18 062	21 44 127	54 40 183	38 32 225	68 01 281	59 37 350
287	48 25 025	17 10 062	22 31 127	54 36 185	37 50 226	67 03 281	59 25 348
288	48 50 024	18 03 062	23 18 128	54 31 186	37 07 227	66 05 281	59 13 347
289	49 14 023	18 55 062	24 05 128	54 24 188	36 24 227	65 06 280	58 58 345
290	49 37 022	19 47 062	24 52 129	54 15 189	35 40 228	64 08 280	58 43 344
291	49 59 021	20 40 062	25 38 129	54 05 191	34 56 229	63 10 280	58 25 343
292	50 20 020	21 32 062	26 24 129	53 53 192	34 11 229	62 11 280	58 07 341
293	50 40 019	22 25 062	27 09 130	53 40 194	33 26 230	61 13 280	57 47 340
294	50 59 018	23 17 062	27 54 130	53 25 195	32 40 230	60 15 280	57 26 339
295	51 18 017	24 09 062	28 39 131	53 09 197	31 55 231	59 16 279	57 04 337
296	51 35 016	25 01 062	29 24 131	52 52 198	31 08 231	58 18 279	56 40 336
297	51 51 015	25 54 062	30 08 132	52 33 199	30 22 232	57 19 279	56 16 335
298	52 06 014	26 46 062	30 52 133	52 13 201	29 35 233	56 21 279	55 50 334
299	52 20 013	27 38 062	31 36 133	51 51 202	28 48 233	55 22 279	55 23 333
	◆ DENEB	Alpheratz	◆ FOMALHAUT	Peacock	◆ ANTARES	Rasalhague	VEGA
300	52 34 012	28 30 062	32 19 134	24 05 176	28 00 233	54 24 279	54 55 331
301	52 45 011	29 22 061	33 01 134	24 09 177	27 13 234	53 25 279	54 27 330
302	52 56 010	30 15 061	33 43 135	24 12 177	26 25 234	52 27 279	53 57 329
303	53 06 009	31 06 061	34 25 136	24 15 178	25 36 235	51 28 279	53 26 328
304	53 14 008	31 58 061	35 06 136	24 17 178	24 48 235	50 29 279	52 55 327
305	53 22 006	32 50 061	35 47 137	24 18 179	23 59 236	49 31 279	52 22 326
306	53 28 005	33 42 061	36 27 138	24 19 180	23 10 236	48 32 279	51 49 326
307	53 32 004	34 34 061	37 07 138	24 19 180	22 21 236	47 34 279	51 15 325
308	53 36 003	35 25 060	37 46 139	24 18 181	21 31 237	46 35 279	50 41 324
309	53 39 002	36 17 060	38 25 140	24 17 181	20 41 237	45 37 279	50 05 323
310	53 40 001	37 08 060	39 03 140	24 15 182	19 51 238	44 38 279	49 30 322
311	53 40 359	38 00 060	39 40 141	24 13 183	19 01 238	43 40 279	48 53 322
312	53 39 358	38 51 060	40 17 142	24 10 183	18 11 238	42 41 279	48 16 321
313	53 36 357	39 42 059	40 53 143	24 07 184	17 21 239	41 42 279	47 38 320
314	53 32 356	40 33 059	41 29 144	24 02 184	16 30 239	40 44 279	47 00 319
	Alpheratz	◆ Diphda	FOMALHAUT	◆ Nunki	Rasalhague	VEGA	◆ DENEB
315	41 23 059	28 27 116	42 03 145	43 39 220	39 45 279	46 21 319	53 27 355
316	42 14 058	29 20 116	42 37 146	43 01 220	38 47 279	45 42 318	53 21 354
317	43 04 058	30 13 117	43 11 146	42 22 221	37 48 279	45 02 318	53 14 352
318	43 55 058	31 05 117	43 43 147	41 43 222	36 50 279	44 22 317	53 06 351
319	44 45 057	31 58 118	44 14 148	41 03 223	35 51 279	43 42 317	52 56 350
320	45 35 057	32 50 118	44 45 149	40 22 224	34 53 279	43 01 316	52 45 349
321	46 24 057	33 42 119	45 15 150	39 41 224	33 54 279	42 19 316	52 33 348
322	47 14 056	34 34 119	45 44 151	38 59 225	32 56 279	41 38 315	52 20 347
323	48 03 056	35 26 120	46 12 152	38 17 226	31 57 279	40 56 315	52 06 346
324	48 52 055	36 17 120	46 39 153	37 34 227	30 59 279	40 13 314	51 51 345
325	49 40 055	37 08 121	47 05 155	36 51 227	30 00 279	39 31 314	51 34 344
326	50 29 054	37 59 121	47 29 156	36 07 228	29 02 279	38 48 313	51 17 343
327	51 17 054	38 50 122	47 53 157	35 23 229	28 03 279	38 04 313	50 59 341
328	52 04 053	39 40 122	48 16 158	34 38 229	27 05 280	37 21 313	50 40 341
329	52 51 053	40 30 123	48 38 159	33 53 230	26 06 280	36 37 312	50 19 340
	◆ Alpheratz	Diphda	◆ FOMALHAUT	Peacock	ALTAIR	◆ VEGA	DENEB
330	53 38 052	41 19 124	48 58 160	21 34 194	58 17 272	35 53 312	49 58 339
331	54 25 051	42 09 124	49 17 162	21 20 194	57 18 272	35 09 312	49 36 338
332	55 11 050	42 57 125	49 35 163	21 05 195	56 18 273	34 25 311	49 13 337
333	55 56 050	43 46 126	49 52 164	20 50 195	55 19 273	33 40 311	48 49 336
334	56 41 049	44 34 126	50 07 166	20 34 196	54 20 273	32 55 311	48 25 335
335	57 25 048	45 21 127	50 22 167	20 18 196	53 21 273	32 10 311	47 59 334
336	58 09 047	46 08 128	50 34 168	20 01 197	52 22 273	31 25 310	47 33 333
337	58 52 046	46 55 129	50 46 169	19 44 197	51 22 273	30 40 310	47 06 333
338	59 35 045	47 41 130	50 56 171	19 26 198	50 23 273	29 55 310	46 38 332
339	60 16 044	48 26 130	51 05 172	19 08 198	49 24 273	29 09 310	46 10 331
340	60 57 043	49 11 131	51 12 174	18 50 199	48 25 273	28 23 309	45 41 330
341	61 37 042	49 55 132	51 18 175	18 30 199	47 26 273	27 38 309	45 11 330
342	62 16 041	50 39 133	51 23 176	18 11 200	46 27 273	26 52 309	44 41 329
343	62 54 039	51 22 134	51 26 178	17 51 200	45 27 274	26 06 309	44 10 328
344	63 31 038	52 04 135	51 27 179	17 30 200	44 28 274	25 19 309	43 38 328
	◆ Mirfak	Hamal	Acamar	◆ ACHERNAR	FOMALHAUT	◆ ALTAIR	DENEB
345	22 01 040	42 51 066	16 13 137	16 21 159	51 27 181	43 29 274	43 06 327
346	22 38 039	43 45 066	16 53 137	16 42 159	51 26 182	42 30 274	42 34 326
347	23 16 039	44 39 066	17 34 137	17 03 160	51 23 183	41 31 274	42 01 326
348	23 53 039	45 33 065	18 14 138	17 23 160	51 19 185	40 32 274	41 27 325
349	24 31 039	46 26 065	18 53 138	17 43 161	51 14 186	39 33 274	40 53 325
350	25 08 039	47 20 065	19 33 139	18 02 161	51 07 187	38 34 274	40 18 324
351	25 45 038	48 14 065	20 12 139	18 21 162	50 58 189	37 35 274	39 44 324
352	26 21 038	49 07 064	20 50 139	18 40 162	50 48 190	36 35 274	39 08 323
353	26 58 038	50 01 064	21 29 140	18 58 163	50 37 192	35 36 275	38 32 323
354	27 34 038	50 54 064	22 06 140	19 15 163	50 25 193	34 37 275	37 56 322
355	28 10 037	51 47 063	22 44 141	19 32 164	50 11 194	33 38 275	37 20 322
356	28 46 037	52 39 063	23 21 141	19 49 164	49 56 195	32 39 275	36 43 321
357	29 22 037	53 32 062	23 58 142	20 05 165	49 39 197	31 40 275	36 05 321
358	29 57 037	54 24 062	24 35 142	20 20 165	49 22 198	30 41 275	35 28 320
359	30 33 036	55 16 061	25 11 143	20 36 166	49 03 199	29 42 275	34 50 320

LHA ♈	Hc	Zn	Hc	Zn	Hc	Zn	Hc	Zn	Hc	Zn	Hc	Zn	Hc	Zn
	◆ CAPELLA		ALDEBARAN		RIGEL		◆ ACHERNAR		FOMALHAUT		◆ ALTAIR		DENEB	
0	13 04	045	22 08	075	09 48	100	21 48	166	49 39	201	28 37	276	33 26	320
1	13 46	044	23 06	075	10 47	100	22 02	166	49 17	202	27 38	276	32 48	320
2	14 27	044	24 03	075	11 45	100	22 16	167	48 54	203	26 39	276	32 09	319
3	15 09	044	25 01	075	12 44	100	22 29	168	48 30	204	25 40	276	31 30	319
4	15 50	044	25 58	075	13 42	101	22 42	168	48 05	206	24 41	276	30 51	319
5	16 32	044	26 56	075	14 41	101	22 54	169	47 39	207	23 42	276	30 12	319
6	17 13	044	27 53	075	15 39	101	23 05	169	47 11	208	22 43	276	29 33	318
7	17 55	044	28 51	075	16 37	101	23 16	170	46 43	209	21 44	276	28 53	318
8	18 36	044	29 48	075	17 36	101	23 26	170	46 14	210	20 45	277	28 13	318
9	19 17	044	30 46	075	18 34	101	23 36	171	45 44	211	19 46	277	27 33	317
10	19 58	044	31 43	075	19 32	102	23 45	171	45 13	212	18 47	277	26 53	317
11	20 39	044	32 41	075	20 30	102	23 54	172	44 41	213	17 48	277	26 12	317
12	21 20	044	33 38	075	21 28	102	24 02	173	44 08	214	16 49	277	25 32	317
13	22 01	043	34 36	075	22 27	102	24 09	173	43 35	215	15 50	277	24 51	317
14	22 42	043	35 33	075	23 25	103	24 16	174	43 00	216	14 51	277	24 10	316
	CAPELLA		◆ ALDEBARAN		RIGEL		ACHERNAR		◆ FOMALHAUT		Enif		◆ DENEB	
15	23 23	043	36 31	075	24 23	103	24 22	174	42 25	217	41 50	276	23 29	316
16	24 03	043	37 28	075	25 20	103	24 28	175	41 50	217	40 51	276	22 48	316
17	24 43	043	38 26	075	26 18	103	24 33	175	41 13	218	39 52	276	22 07	316
18	25 24	042	39 23	075	27 16	104	24 37	176	40 36	219	38 53	276	21 25	316
19	26 04	042	40 20	075	28 14	104	24 41	177	39 58	220	37 53	276	20 44	316
20	26 44	042	41 18	075	29 11	104	24 44	177	39 20	221	36 54	276	20 02	315
21	27 23	042	42 15	075	30 09	104	24 46	178	38 41	221	35 55	277	19 20	315
22	28 03	042	43 13	075	31 07	105	24 48	178	38 01	222	34 56	277	18 39	315
23	28 42	041	44 10	075	32 04	105	24 50	179	37 21	223	33 57	277	17 57	315
24	29 21	041	45 07	075	33 01	105	24 50	180	36 41	223	32 58	277	17 15	315
25	30 00	041	46 04	074	33 59	106	24 50	180	35 59	224	31 59	277	16 33	315
26	30 39	040	47 02	074	34 56	106	24 50	181	35 18	225	31 00	277	15 51	315
27	31 17	040	47 59	074	35 53	106	24 49	181	34 36	225	30 01	277	15 09	315
28	31 55	040	48 56	074	36 50	107	24 47	182	33 53	226	29 02	277	14 27	315
29	32 33	039	49 53	074	37 47	107	24 44	183	33 10	227	28 03	277	13 45	315
	Mirfak		CAPELLA		◆ ALDEBARAN		RIGEL		◆ ACHERNAR		FOMALHAUT		◆ Alpheratz	
30	44 28	019	33 11	039	50 50	074	38 44	107	24 41	183	32 27	227	56 27	313
31	44 47	018	33 48	039	51 47	073	39 40	108	24 38	184	31 43	228	55 43	312
32	45 05	018	34 25	038	52 44	073	40 37	108	24 33	184	30 59	228	54 58	311
33	45 23	017	35 02	038	53 41	073	41 33	108	24 28	185	30 14	229	54 13	310
34	45 39	016	35 38	038	54 37	073	42 30	109	24 23	186	29 29	229	53 28	310
35	45 55	015	36 14	037	55 34	072	43 26	109	24 17	186	28 44	230	52 42	309
36	46 10	014	36 50	037	56 31	072	44 22	110	24 10	187	27 59	230	51 55	308
37	46 24	013	37 25	036	57 27	072	45 18	110	24 03	187	27 13	231	51 08	308
38	46 38	013	38 00	036	58 23	071	46 13	111	23 55	188	26 26	231	50 21	307
39	46 50	012	38 34	035	59 20	071	47 09	111	23 46	188	25 40	232	49 33	306
40	47 02	011	39 08	035	60 16	071	48 04	112	23 37	189	24 53	232	48 45	306
41	47 12	010	39 42	034	61 12	070	48 59	112	23 28	190	24 06	233	47 57	305
42	47 22	009	40 15	034	62 08	070	49 54	113	23 17	190	23 19	233	47 08	305
43	47 31	008	40 48	033	63 03	069	50 48	114	23 07	191	22 31	233	46 19	304
44	47 38	007	41 20	032	63 58	068	51 43	114	22 55	191	21 44	234	45 30	304
	◆ CAPELLA		PROCYON		SIRIUS		◆ CANOPUS		ACHERNAR		Diphda		◆ Alpheratz	
45	41 51	032	20 28	087	28 57	114	15 27	151	22 43	192	47 40	232	44 41	304
46	42 22	031	21 27	088	29 51	115	15 56	151	22 31	192	46 53	233	43 51	303
47	42 53	031	22 26	088	30 45	115	16 24	151	22 18	193	46 05	234	43 02	303
48	43 23	030	23 26	088	31 39	115	16 52	152	22 04	193	45 17	234	42 12	302
49	43 52	029	24 25	088	32 32	116	17 20	152	21 50	194	44 29	235	41 21	302
50	44 21	029	25 24	088	33 26	116	17 48	153	21 36	195	43 40	236	40 31	302
51	44 49	028	26 24	088	34 19	117	18 15	153	21 21	195	42 50	236	39 40	302
52	45 16	027	27 23	088	35 12	117	18 41	154	21 05	196	42 01	237	38 50	301
53	45 43	026	28 23	088	36 05	118	19 07	154	20 49	196	41 11	238	37 59	301
54	46 09	026	29 22	089	36 57	118	19 33	154	20 32	197	40 20	238	37 08	301
55	46 34	025	30 21	089	37 50	119	19 59	155	20 15	197	39 30	239	36 17	300
56	46 59	024	31 21	089	38 42	119	20 24	155	19 57	198	38 39	239	35 25	300
57	47 22	023	32 20	089	39 33	120	20 48	156	19 39	198	37 48	240	34 34	300
58	47 45	022	33 20	089	40 25	120	21 12	156	19 21	198	36 56	240	33 43	300
59	48 07	021	34 19	089	41 16	121	21 36	157	19 02	199	36 04	241	32 51	300
	◆ CAPELLA		POLLUX		PROCYON		◆ SIRIUS		CANOPUS		◆ Diphda		Alpheratz	
60	48 28	020	33 11	062	35 18	089	42 07	121	21 59	157	35 12	241	31 59	300
61	48 49	019	34 03	062	36 18	089	42 58	122	22 21	158	34 20	242	31 08	299
62	49 08	019	34 55	061	37 17	090	43 48	123	22 44	158	33 27	242	30 16	299
63	49 26	018	35 47	061	38 17	090	44 38	123	23 05	159	32 35	243	29 24	299
64	49 44	017	36 39	061	39 16	090	45 28	124	23 26	159	31 42	243	28 32	299
65	50 00	016	37 31	061	40 15	090	46 17	125	23 47	160	30 49	244	27 40	299
66	50 16	015	38 23	060	41 15	090	47 05	125	24 07	161	29 55	244	26 48	299
67	50 30	014	39 14	060	42 14	090	47 54	126	24 26	161	29 02	244	25 56	299
68	50 44	013	40 06	060	43 14	090	48 41	127	24 45	162	28 08	245	25 03	299
69	50 56	012	40 57	060	44 13	091	49 29	128	25 04	162	27 15	245	24 11	298
70	51 08	010	41 48	059	45 13	091	50 15	129	25 21	163	26 21	245	23 19	298
71	51 18	009	42 39	059	46 12	091	51 01	129	25 39	163	25 26	246	22 27	298
72	51 27	008	43 30	059	47 11	091	51 47	130	25 55	164	24 32	246	21 34	298
73	51 35	007	44 21	058	48 11	091	52 32	131	26 11	165	23 38	246	20 42	298
74	51 42	006	45 11	058	49 10	091	53 16	132	26 27	165	22 43	247	19 50	298
	CAPELLA		◆ POLLUX		PROCYON		SIRIUS		◆ CANOPUS		Acamar		◆ Hamal	
75	51 48	005	46 02	058	50 10	091	54 00	133	26 42	166	34 15	208	46 01	296
76	51 52	004	46 52	057	51 09	092	54 42	135	26 56	167	33 47	208	45 08	295
77	51 56	003	47 41	057	52 08	092	55 24	136	27 09	167	33 18	209	44 14	295
78	51 58	002	48 31	056	53 08	092	56 05	137	27 22	168	32 49	210	43 20	295
79	51 59	001	49 20	056	54 07	092	56 45	138	27 34	168	32 19	211	42 26	295
80	51 59	359	50 09	055	55 06	092	57 25	139	27 46	169	31 48	211	41 32	294
81	51 58	358	50 58	055	56 06	093	58 03	141	27 57	170	31 17	212	40 38	294
82	51 55	357	51 46	054	57 05	093	58 40	142	28 07	170	30 45	213	39 44	294
83	51 52	356	52 34	053	58 04	093	59 15	144	28 17	171	30 13	213	38 50	294
84	51 47	355	53 21	053	59 04	093	59 50	145	28 26	172	29 40	214	37 55	294
85	51 41	354	54 08	052	60 03	094	60 23	147	28 34	172	29 07	214	37 01	294
86	51 34	353	54 55	051	61 02	094	60 55	148	28 41	173	28 33	215	36 06	293
87	51 26	352	55 41	051	62 02	094	61 26	150	28 48	174	27 59	216	35 12	293
88	51 17	350	56 27	050	63 01	094	61 55	152	28 54	174	27 24	216	34 17	293
89	51 07	349	57 12	049	64 00	095	62 22	154	29 00	175	26 49	217	33 23	293

LAT 8°N

LHA ♈	Hc	Zn	Hc	Zn	Hc	Zn	Hc	Zn	Hc	Zn	Hc	Zn	Hc	Zn
	◆ POLLUX		REGULUS		Suhail		◆ CANOPUS		Acamar		◆ ALDEBARAN		CAPELLA	
90	57 56	048	28 38	081	23 08	145	29 04	176	26 13	217	67 59	295	50 55	348
91	58 40	047	29 37	081	23 42	145	29 08	176	25 37	218	67 04	294	50 43	347
92	59 23	046	30 35	081	24 16	146	29 12	177	25 01	218	66 10	293	50 29	346
93	60 06	045	31 34	081	24 49	146	29 14	178	24 24	219	65 15	292	50 14	345
94	60 48	044	32 33	081	25 22	147	29 16	179	23 46	219	64 20	292	49 59	344
95	61 28	043	33 31	081	25 54	147	29 17	179	23 08	220	63 25	291	49 42	343
96	62 08	042	34 30	081	26 26	148	29 18	180	22 30	220	62 29	291	49 25	342
97	62 47	040	35 29	081	26 58	148	29 17	181	21 52	221	61 34	290	49 06	341
98	63 25	039	36 28	081	27 29	149	29 16	181	21 13	221	60 38	290	48 47	340
99	64 02	037	37 26	081	27 59	150	29 15	182	20 34	221	59 42	289	48 26	339
100	64 37	036	38 25	081	28 29	150	29 12	183	19 54	222	58 46	289	48 05	339
101	65 12	034	39 24	081	28 58	151	29 09	183	19 14	222	57 49	288	47 43	338
102	65 44	033	40 22	081	29 27	151	29 05	184	18 34	223	56 53	288	47 20	337
103	66 16	031	41 21	081	29 55	152	29 00	185	17 54	223	55 56	288	46 56	336
104	66 45	029	42 20	081	30 23	153	28 55	185	17 13	223	55 00	287	46 32	335
	Dubhe		◆ REGULUS		Suhail		◆ CANOPUS		RIGEL		ALDEBARAN		◆ CAPELLA	
105	20 26	026	43 18	081	30 50	153	28 49	186	59 17	239	54 03	287	46 06	334
106	20 53	026	44 17	081	31 16	154	28 42	187	58 26	240	53 06	287	45 40	334
107	21 19	026	45 16	081	31 42	155	28 35	188	57 35	241	52 09	287	45 14	333
108	21 44	026	46 15	081	32 07	155	28 27	188	56 43	242	51 12	286	44 46	332
109	22 10	026	47 13	081	32 32	156	28 18	189	55 50	242	50 15	286	44 18	331
110	22 36	025	48 12	081	32 55	157	28 09	190	54 57	243	49 18	286	43 49	331
111	23 01	025	49 11	081	33 18	158	27 58	190	54 04	244	48 21	286	43 20	330
112	23 26	025	50 09	081	33 41	158	27 48	191	53 11	245	47 24	286	42 50	329
113	23 51	025	51 08	081	34 02	159	27 36	191	52 17	245	46 27	286	42 19	329
114	24 15	024	52 07	081	34 23	160	27 24	192	51 23	246	45 30	285	41 48	328
115	24 40	024	53 05	081	34 44	161	27 11	193	50 28	247	44 32	285	41 17	328
116	25 04	024	54 04	081	35 03	161	26 58	193	49 34	247	43 35	285	40 44	327
117	25 27	023	55 03	081	35 21	162	26 44	194	48 39	248	42 38	285	40 12	326
118	25 51	023	56 01	081	35 39	163	26 29	195	47 44	248	41 40	285	39 39	326
119	26 14	023	57 00	080	35 56	164	26 14	195	46 48	249	40 43	285	39 05	325
	Dubhe		◆ Denebola		Suhail		◆ SIRIUS		RIGEL		ALDEBARAN		◆ CAPELLA	
120	26 37	023	33 24	078	36 12	165	59 12	217	45 53	249	39 45	285	38 31	325
121	27 00	022	34 23	078	36 28	165	58 36	218	44 57	250	38 48	285	37 56	324
122	27 22	022	35 21	078	36 42	166	57 59	219	44 01	250	37 51	285	37 21	324
123	27 44	022	36 19	078	36 56	167	57 21	221	43 05	251	36 53	285	36 46	323
124	28 05	021	37 17	078	37 09	168	56 42	222	42 09	251	35 56	285	36 10	323
125	28 27	021	38 15	078	37 20	169	56 01	223	41 12	252	34 58	285	35 34	322
126	28 48	020	39 13	078	37 31	170	55 20	224	40 16	252	34 01	285	34 58	322
127	29 08	020	40 11	078	37 41	171	54 38	226	39 19	252	33 03	285	34 21	322
128	29 28	020	41 09	078	37 51	172	53 55	227	38 23	253	32 06	285	33 44	321
129	29 48	019	42 07	078	37 59	173	53 12	228	37 26	253	31 08	285	33 07	321
130	30 08	019	43 05	078	38 06	173	52 28	229	36 29	254	30 11	285	32 29	321
131	30 27	018	44 03	078	38 12	174	51 43	230	35 32	254	29 13	285	31 51	320
132	30 45	018	45 01	077	38 18	175	50 57	231	34 35	254	28 16	285	31 13	320
133	31 03	018	45 59	077	38 22	176	50 11	231	33 38	255	27 18	285	30 35	320
134	31 21	017	46 57	077	38 26	177	49 24	232	32 40	255	26 21	285	29 56	319
	Dubhe		◆ ARCTURUS		SPICA		◆ Suhail		SIRIUS		BETELGEUSE		◆ CAPELLA	
135	31 39	017	12 52	072	21 07	105	38 28	178	48 37	233	44 26	273	29 17	319
136	31 56	016	13 49	072	22 04	106	38 30	179	47 49	234	43 27	273	28 38	319
137	32 12	016	14 45	072	23 01	106	38 30	180	47 01	235	42 27	273	27 59	318
138	32 28	015	15 42	072	23 58	106	38 30	181	46 12	235	41 28	273	27 19	318
139	32 44	015	16 38	072	24 55	106	38 29	182	45 23	236	40 28	273	26 40	318
140	32 59	014	17 35	072	25 52	107	38 26	183	44 33	237	39 29	273	26 00	318
141	33 13	014	18 32	072	26 49	107	38 23	184	43 43	238	38 30	273	25 20	318
142	33 27	013	19 28	072	27 46	107	38 19	184	42 53	238	37 30	273	24 39	317
143	33 41	013	20 25	073	28 43	108	38 14	185	42 02	239	36 31	273	23 59	317
144	33 54	012	21 22	073	29 39	108	38 08	186	41 11	239	35 32	273	23 18	317
145	34 06	012	22 18	073	30 36	108	38 01	187	40 20	240	34 33	274	22 38	317
146	34 18	011	23 15	073	31 32	108	37 53	188	39 29	240	33 33	274	21 57	317
147	34 30	011	24 12	073	32 29	109	37 44	189	38 37	241	32 34	274	21 16	316
148	34 41	010	25 08	073	33 25	109	37 34	190	37 45	242	31 35	274	20 35	316
149	34 51	010	26 05	073	34 21	110	37 23	191	36 52	242	30 35	274	19 54	316
	Dubhe		◆ ARCTURUS		SPICA		ACRUX		◆ Suhail		SIRIUS		◆ POLLUX	
150	35 01	009	27 02	073	35 17	110	13 29	164	37 12	192	36 00	243	52 39	307
151	35 11	009	27 59	073	36 13	110	13 46	164	36 59	193	35 07	243	51 51	306
152	35 19	008	28 55	073	37 08	111	14 02	165	36 46	193	34 14	243	51 03	305
153	35 27	008	29 52	073	38 04	111	14 17	165	36 32	194	33 21	244	50 15	305
154	35 35	007	30 49	072	38 59	112	14 32	165	36 17	195	32 27	244	49 26	304
155	35 42	006	31 45	072	39 54	112	14 47	166	36 01	196	31 33	245	48 37	304
156	35 48	006	32 42	072	40 49	112	15 02	166	35 44	197	30 40	245	47 47	303
157	35 54	005	33 39	072	41 44	113	15 16	167	35 26	198	29 46	245	46 57	303
158	36 00	005	34 35	072	42 39	113	15 29	167	35 08	198	28 52	246	46 07	303
159	36 04	004	35 32	072	43 33	114	15 43	167	34 49	199	27 57	246	45 17	302
160	36 08	004	36 28	072	44 27	114	15 55	168	34 29	200	27 03	247	44 27	302
161	36 12	003	37 25	072	45 21	115	16 08	168	34 08	201	26 08	247	43 36	301
162	36 15	002	38 21	072	46 15	116	16 20	169	33 47	202	25 14	247	42 45	301
163	36 17	002	39 18	072	47 09	116	16 31	169	33 25	202	24 19	248	41 54	301
164	36 18	001	40 14	072	48 02	117	16 42	169	33 02	203	23 24	248	41 03	300
	Dubhe		◆ ARCTURUS		SPICA		◆ ACRUX		Suhail		PROCYON		◆ POLLUX	
165	36 19	001	41 11	072	48 55	117	16 53	170	32 38	204	40 18	270	40 12	300
166	36 20	000	42 07	071	49 47	118	17 03	170	32 14	204	39 19	270	39 20	300
167	36 20	000	43 03	071	50 39	119	17 13	171	31 49	205	38 19	270	38 29	300
168	36 19	359	43 59	071	51 31	120	17 22	171	31 23	206	37 20	270	37 37	299
169	36 17	358	44 56	071	52 23	120	17 31	172	30 57	207	36 20	271	36 45	299
170	36 15	358	45 52	071	53 14	121	17 40	172	30 30	207	35 21	271	35 53	299
171	36 13	357	46 48	071	54 05	122	17 47	173	30 03	208	34 22	271	35 01	299
172	36 09	357	47 44	070	54 55	123	17 55	173	29 35	208	33 22	271	34 09	299
173	36 06	356	48 40	070	55 44	124	18 02	173	29 06	209	32 23	271	33 17	298
174	36 01	355	49 36	070	56 33	125	18 08	174	28 37	210	31 23	271	32 24	298
175	35 56	355	50 31	070	57 22	126	18 14	174	28 07	210	30 24	271	31 32	298
176	35 50	354	51 27	069	58 10	127	18 20	175	27 37	211	29 24	271	30 39	298
177	35 44	354	52 22	069	58 57	128	18 25	175	27 06	211	28 25	272	29 47	298
178	35 37	353	53 18	069	59 44	129	18 30	176	26 35	212	27 26	272	28 54	298
179	35 30	353	54 13	068	60 29	130	18 34	176	26 03	213	26 26	272	28 02	298

 LAT 8°N

LHA ♈	◆ARCTURUS Hc Zn	ANTARES Hc Zn	RIGIL KENT Hc Zn	◆ACRUX Hc Zn	Suhail Hc Zn	◆REGULUS Hc Zn	Dubhe Hc Zn
180	55 08 068	16 01 121	14 16 161	18 37 177	25 31 213	62 27 280	35 22 352
181	56 03 067	16 53 121	14 35 161	18 41 177	24 58 214	61 28 280	35 13 351
182	56 58 067	17 43 121	14 54 162	18 43 178	24 25 214	60 30 280	35 04 351
183	57 53 067	18 34 121	15 12 162	18 45 178	23 52 215	59 31 280	34 55 350
184	58 47 066	19 25 122	15 30 163	18 47 179	23 17 215	58 33 280	34 44 350
185	59 41 066	20 15 122	15 48 163	18 48 179	22 43 216	57 34 280	34 34 349
186	60 35 065	21 05 122	16 05 163	18 49 180	22 08 216	56 36 279	34 22 349
187	61 29 064	21 56 123	16 21 164	18 49 180	21 33 217	55 37 279	34 10 348
188	62 22 064	22 45 123	16 38 164	18 49 181	20 57 217	54 38 279	33 58 348
189	63 15 063	23 35 124	16 54 165	18 48 181	20 21 217	53 40 279	33 45 347
190	64 08 062	24 24 124	17 09 165	18 47 181	19 45 218	52 41 279	33 32 347
191	65 00 061	25 14 124	17 24 166	18 45 182	19 08 218	51 42 279	33 18 346
192	65 52 060	26 03 125	17 38 166	18 43 182	18 31 219	50 44 279	33 03 346
193	66 43 059	26 51 125	17 53 167	18 40 183	17 54 219	49 45 279	32 48 345
194	67 34 058	27 40 126	18 06 167	18 36 183	17 16 220	48 46 279	32 33 345

LHA	◆Alphecca	Rasalhague	ANTARES	◆RIGIL KENT	ACRUX	◆REGULUS	Dubhe
195	48 45 058	22 13 080	28 28 126	18 19 167	18 33 184	47 48 279	32 17 344
196	49 35 058	23 11 080	29 16 126	18 32 168	18 28 184	46 49 279	32 01 344
197	50 25 057	24 10 080	30 03 127	18 44 168	18 24 185	45 50 279	31 44 343
198	51 15 057	25 08 080	30 51 127	18 56 169	18 19 185	44 52 279	31 27 343
199	52 05 056	26 07 080	31 38 128	19 07 169	18 13 186	43 53 279	31 09 342
200	52 54 056	27 05 080	32 25 128	19 18 170	18 07 186	42 54 279	30 51 342
201	53 43 055	28 04 080	33 11 129	19 28 170	18 00 187	41 55 279	30 33 342
202	54 31 054	29 02 080	33 57 130	19 38 171	17 53 187	40 57 279	30 14 341
203	55 19 054	30 01 080	34 42 130	19 48 171	17 45 188	39 58 279	29 54 341
204	56 07 053	30 59 080	35 28 131	19 56 172	17 37 188	38 59 279	29 35 340
205	56 54 052	31 58 080	36 12 131	20 05 172	17 29 188	38 01 279	29 15 340
206	57 41 051	32 56 080	36 57 132	20 12 173	17 20 189	37 02 279	28 54 340
207	58 27 050	33 55 080	37 41 133	20 20 173	17 10 189	36 03 279	28 33 339
208	59 12 050	34 54 080	38 24 133	20 27 174	17 00 190	35 04 279	28 12 339
209	59 57 049	35 52 080	39 07 134	20 33 174	16 50 190	34 06 279	27 51 339

LHA	◆VEGA	Rasalhague	ANTARES	◆RIGIL KENT	SPICA	◆REGULUS	Dubhe
210	21 03 051	36 51 080	39 50 135	20 38 175	68 59 204	33 07 279	27 29 338
211	21 50 051	37 49 080	40 32 135	20 44 175	68 34 206	32 08 279	27 07 338
212	22 36 051	38 48 080	41 13 136	20 48 176	68 06 209	31 10 279	26 44 338
213	23 22 051	39 46 080	41 54 137	20 52 176	67 37 211	30 11 279	26 21 337
214	24 08 051	40 45 080	42 34 138	20 56 177	67 05 213	29 12 279	25 58 337
215	24 54 051	41 44 080	43 14 139	20 59 177	66 32 215	28 14 279	25 35 337
216	25 40 051	42 42 080	43 53 139	21 02 178	65 57 217	27 15 279	25 11 336
217	26 26 050	43 41 080	44 31 140	21 04 178	65 20 219	26 16 279	24 47 336
218	27 12 050	44 39 080	45 09 141	21 05 179	64 42 221	25 18 279	24 23 336
219	27 58 050	45 38 080	45 46 142	21 06 179	64 03 222	24 19 279	23 59 336
220	28 43 050	46 36 080	46 22 143	21 06 180	63 22 224	23 21 280	23 34 335
221	29 28 050	47 35 080	46 57 144	21 06 180	62 41 226	22 22 280	23 09 335
222	30 14 049	48 33 080	47 32 145	21 05 181	61 58 227	21 24 280	22 44 335
223	30 59 049	49 32 080	48 05 146	21 04 181	61 14 228	20 25 280	22 18 335
224	31 44 049	50 30 080	48 38 147	21 02 182	60 29 230	19 26 280	21 53 334

LHA	VEGA	◆ALTAIR	Nunki	ANTARES	RIGIL KENT	◆SPICA	◆Alkaid
225	32 28 049	18 02 083	23 16 123	49 09 148	21 00 183	59 43 231	46 05 343
226	33 13 048	19 01 083	24 06 124	49 40 149	20 57 183	58 57 232	45 48 342
227	33 57 048	20 00 083	24 55 124	50 10 151	20 54 184	58 09 233	45 29 341
228	34 41 048	20 59 083	25 44 124	50 39 152	20 50 184	57 22 234	45 10 341
229	35 25 047	21 58 084	26 33 125	51 06 153	20 45 185	56 33 235	44 50 340
230	36 09 047	22 57 084	27 22 125	51 33 154	20 40 185	55 44 236	44 29 339
231	36 52 047	23 56 084	28 10 126	51 58 156	20 35 186	54 54 237	44 07 338
232	37 35 046	24 55 084	28 59 126	52 22 157	20 29 186	54 04 238	43 45 338
233	38 18 046	25 54 084	29 47 127	52 45 158	20 22 187	53 13 239	43 22 337
234	39 01 046	26 53 084	30 34 127	53 06 160	20 15 187	52 22 240	42 58 336
235	39 43 045	27 53 084	31 21 128	53 26 161	20 07 188	51 31 240	42 34 335
236	40 25 045	28 52 084	32 08 128	53 45 162	19 59 188	50 39 241	42 09 335
237	41 06 044	29 51 084	32 55 129	54 02 164	19 50 189	49 47 242	41 43 334
238	41 48 044	30 50 084	33 41 129	54 18 165	19 41 189	48 54 243	41 17 333
239	42 29 043	31 49 084	34 27 130	54 33 167	19 32 190	48 01 243	40 50 333

LHA	◆VEGA	ALTAIR	Nunki	◆ANTARES	SPICA	◆ARCTURUS	Alkaid
240	43 09 043	32 48 085	35 13 130	54 46 168	47 08 244	62 31 296	40 23 332
241	43 49 042	33 47 085	35 58 131	54 57 170	46 15 244	61 38 296	39 55 332
242	44 29 042	34 46 085	36 43 131	55 07 171	45 21 245	60 44 295	39 26 331
243	45 08 041	35 46 085	37 27 132	55 15 173	44 27 246	59 50 295	38 57 330
244	45 46 040	36 45 085	38 11 133	55 22 174	43 33 246	58 56 294	38 28 330
245	46 25 040	37 44 085	38 54 133	55 27 176	42 38 247	58 02 294	37 58 329
246	47 02 039	38 43 085	39 37 134	55 30 177	41 44 247	57 07 293	37 27 329
247	47 39 038	39 42 085	40 19 135	55 32 179	40 49 248	56 13 293	36 56 328
248	48 16 038	40 42 085	41 01 136	55 32 181	39 54 248	55 18 292	36 25 328
249	48 52 037	41 41 085	41 42 136	55 31 182	38 59 248	54 23 292	35 53 327
250	49 27 036	42 40 085	42 23 137	55 27 184	38 03 249	53 27 291	35 21 327
251	50 02 035	43 39 085	43 03 138	55 23 185	37 08 249	52 32 291	34 48 326
252	50 35 034	44 38 085	43 43 139	55 16 187	36 12 250	51 36 291	34 15 326
253	51 09 033	45 38 085	44 21 140	55 08 189	35 16 250	50 41 290	33 42 326
254	51 41 033	46 37 085	44 59 141	54 59 190	34 20 250	49 45 290	33 08 325

LHA	VEGA	◆ALTAIR	Nunki	◆ANTARES	SPICA	ARCTURUS	◆Alkaid
255	52 13 032	47 36 086	45 37 142	54 48 192	33 24 251	48 49 290	32 34 325
256	52 43 031	48 35 086	46 13 142	54 35 193	32 28 251	47 53 290	32 00 324
257	53 13 030	49 35 086	46 49 143	54 21 195	31 32 252	46 58 289	31 25 324
258	53 42 029	50 34 086	47 24 144	54 05 196	30 35 252	46 01 289	30 50 324
259	54 10 028	51 33 086	47 58 145	53 48 197	29 39 252	45 05 289	30 15 323
260	54 37 027	52 32 086	48 32 147	53 29 199	28 42 252	44 09 289	29 39 323
261	55 03 025	53 32 086	49 04 148	53 09 200	27 46 253	43 13 289	29 04 323
262	55 28 024	54 31 086	49 35 149	52 48 202	26 49 253	42 17 289	28 28 323
263	55 52 023	55 30 086	50 06 150	52 26 203	25 52 253	41 20 288	27 51 322
264	56 15 022	56 29 086	50 35 151	52 02 204	24 55 254	40 24 288	27 15 322
265	56 36 021	57 29 086	51 03 152	51 37 206	23 58 254	39 28 288	26 38 322
266	56 56 019	58 28 086	51 30 153	51 11 207	23 01 254	38 31 288	26 01 321
267	57 15 018	59 27 086	51 56 155	50 43 208	22 04 254	37 35 288	25 24 321
268	57 33 017	60 26 086	52 21 156	50 15 209	21 06 255	36 38 288	24 47 321
269	57 49 015	61 26 086	52 44 157	49 45 210	20 09 255	35 41 288	24 10 321

LHA ♈	VEGA Hc Zn	◆DENEB Hc Zn	Enif Hc Zn	◆Nunki Hc Zn	Shaula Hc Zn	ANTARES Hc Zn	◆ARCTURUS Hc Zn
270	58 04 014	38 56 036	34 29 083	53 06 159	44 30 187	49 15 212	34 45 288
271	58 18 012	39 31 035	35 28 083	53 27 160	44 22 188	48 43 213	33 48 288
272	58 30 011	40 05 035	36 27 084	53 47 162	44 13 189	48 11 214	32 52 288
273	58 40 010	40 39 034	37 26 084	54 05 163	44 03 190	47 37 215	31 55 288
274	58 50 008	41 12 034	38 25 084	54 22 164	43 51 191	47 03 216	30 58 288
275	58 57 007	41 45 033	39 24 084	54 37 166	43 39 193	46 28 217	30 02 287
276	59 03 005	42 17 033	40 23 084	54 51 167	43 26 194	45 52 218	29 05 287
277	59 08 004	42 49 032	41 22 084	55 03 169	43 11 195	45 15 219	28 08 287
278	59 11 002	43 20 031	42 22 084	55 13 170	42 56 196	44 37 220	27 12 287
279	59 12 001	43 50 031	43 21 084	55 22 172	42 39 197	43 59 220	26 15 287
280	59 12 359	44 20 030	44 20 084	55 30 174	42 22 198	43 20 221	25 18 287
281	59 10 358	44 50 029	45 19 084	55 36 175	42 03 199	42 41 222	24 22 287
282	59 07 356	45 18 028	46 18 084	55 40 177	41 44 200	42 01 223	23 25 287
283	59 02 354	45 46 028	47 17 084	55 42 178	41 23 201	41 20 224	22 28 287
284	58 55 353	46 13 027	48 16 084	55 43 180	41 02 202	40 39 224	21 32 287

LHA	DENEB	◆Alpheratz	FOMALHAUT	◆Nunki	ANTARES	◆Rasalhague	VEGA
285	46 40 026	14 57 062	21 32 126	55 43 182	39 57 225	68 46 284	58 47 352
286	47 06 025	15 50 062	22 20 127	55 40 183	39 14 226	67 48 284	58 38 350
287	47 31 025	16 42 062	23 08 127	55 36 185	38 31 227	66 50 283	58 27 349
288	47 55 024	17 34 062	23 55 127	55 31 186	37 48 227	65 52 283	58 14 347
289	48 18 023	18 27 062	24 42 128	55 23 188	37 04 228	64 54 283	58 00 346
290	48 41 022	19 19 062	25 29 128	55 14 189	36 20 229	63 56 282	57 45 344
291	49 03 021	20 12 062	26 15 129	55 04 191	35 35 229	62 58 282	57 28 343
292	49 24 020	21 04 062	27 02 129	54 52 192	34 50 230	62 00 282	57 10 342
293	49 43 019	21 56 062	27 48 130	54 38 194	34 04 230	61 02 281	56 51 340
294	50 02 018	22 49 062	28 33 130	54 23 195	33 18 231	60 04 281	56 30 339
295	50 20 017	23 41 062	29 19 131	54 07 197	32 32 231	59 05 281	56 08 338
296	50 37 016	24 33 062	30 04 131	53 49 198	31 46 232	58 07 281	55 45 337
297	50 53 015	25 25 061	30 48 132	53 29 200	30 59 232	57 09 281	55 21 335
298	51 08 014	26 17 061	31 32 132	53 09 201	30 11 233	56 10 281	54 56 334
299	51 22 013	27 10 061	32 16 133	52 46 202	29 24 233	55 12 281	54 30 333

LHA	◆DENEB	Alpheratz	◆FOMALHAUT	Peacock	◆ANTARES	Rasalhague	VEGA
300	51 35 012	28 02 061	33 00 133	25 05 176	28 36 234	54 14 280	54 03 332
301	51 47 011	28 54 061	33 43 134	25 09 177	27 48 234	53 15 280	53 34 331
302	51 57 010	29 46 061	34 26 134	25 12 177	26 59 235	52 17 280	53 05 330
303	52 07 009	30 37 061	35 08 135	25 15 178	26 11 235	51 18 280	52 35 329
304	52 15 007	31 29 061	35 50 136	25 17 178	25 22 236	50 20 280	52 04 328
305	52 22 006	32 21 060	36 31 136	25 18 179	24 33 236	49 21 280	51 32 327
306	52 28 005	33 13 060	37 12 137	25 19 180	23 43 236	48 23 280	51 00 326
307	52 33 004	34 04 060	37 52 138	25 19 180	22 54 237	47 24 280	50 26 325
308	52 36 003	34 56 060	38 31 138	25 18 181	22 04 237	46 26 280	49 52 325
309	52 39 002	35 47 060	39 11 139	25 17 181	21 14 237	45 27 280	49 17 324
310	52 40 001	36 38 059	39 49 140	25 15 182	20 24 238	44 28 280	48 42 323
311	52 40 359	37 29 059	40 27 141	25 13 183	19 33 238	43 30 280	48 06 322
312	52 39 358	38 20 059	41 04 142	25 10 183	18 43 238	42 31 280	47 29 322
313	52 36 357	39 11 059	41 41 142	25 06 184	17 52 239	41 33 280	46 52 321
314	52 33 356	40 02 058	42 17 143	25 02 184	17 01 239	40 34 280	46 14 320

LHA	Alpheratz	◆Diphda	FOMALHAUT	◆Nunki	Rasalhague	VEGA	◆DENEB
315	40 52 058	28 53 116	42 52 144	44 25 220	39 36 280	45 36 320	52 28 355
316	41 42 058	29 46 116	43 27 145	43 46 221	38 37 280	44 57 319	52 22 354
317	42 32 057	30 40 116	44 00 146	43 07 222	37 38 280	44 18 318	52 15 353
318	43 22 057	31 33 117	44 33 147	42 27 223	36 40 280	43 38 318	52 06 351
319	44 12 057	32 26 117	45 05 148	41 46 224	35 41 280	42 58 317	51 57 350
320	45 02 056	33 18 118	45 37 149	41 05 224	34 43 280	42 17 317	51 46 349
321	45 51 056	34 11 118	46 07 150	40 23 225	33 44 280	41 36 316	51 34 348
322	46 40 055	35 03 119	46 36 151	39 41 226	32 46 280	40 55 316	51 22 347
323	47 29 055	35 55 119	47 05 152	38 58 226	31 47 280	40 13 315	51 08 346
324	48 17 054	36 47 120	47 32 153	38 15 227	30 49 280	39 31 315	50 53 345
325	49 05 054	37 39 120	47 59 154	37 31 228	29 50 280	38 49 314	50 37 344
326	49 53 053	38 30 121	48 24 155	36 47 228	28 52 280	38 06 314	50 20 343
327	50 41 053	39 21 121	48 48 156	36 02 229	27 53 280	37 23 314	50 02 342
328	51 28 052	40 12 122	49 12 158	35 17 230	26 55 280	36 40 313	49 43 341
329	52 14 052	41 02 122	49 34 159	34 32 230	25 56 280	35 57 313	49 23 340

LHA	◆Alpheratz	Diphda	◆FOMALHAUT	Peacock	ALTAIR	◆VEGA	DENEB
330	53 01 051	41 52 123	49 54 160	22 32 194	58 13 274	35 13 312	49 02 339
331	53 47 050	42 42 124	50 14 161	22 18 194	57 14 274	34 29 312	48 40 338
332	54 32 049	43 31 124	50 33 163	22 03 195	56 15 274	33 45 312	48 18 337
333	55 17 049	44 20 125	50 50 164	21 48 195	55 16 274	33 01 312	47 54 336
334	56 01 048	45 09 126	51 05 165	21 32 196	54 16 274	32 16 311	47 30 335
335	56 45 047	45 57 126	51 20 167	21 16 196	53 17 274	31 31 311	47 05 335
336	57 28 046	46 45 127	51 33 168	20 59 197	52 18 274	30 46 311	46 39 334
337	58 10 045	47 32 128	51 45 169	20 41 197	51 19 274	30 01 311	46 13 333
338	58 52 044	48 19 129	51 55 171	20 24 198	50 19 274	29 16 310	45 45 332
339	59 33 043	49 05 129	52 04 172	20 05 198	49 20 274	28 31 310	45 17 332
340	60 13 042	49 50 130	52 12 173	19 46 199	48 21 274	27 45 310	44 49 331
341	60 52 041	50 35 131	52 18 175	19 27 199	47 22 274	26 59 310	44 19 330
342	61 30 039	51 19 132	52 22 176	19 07 200	46 22 275	26 14 310	43 49 329
343	62 07 038	52 03 133	52 26 178	18 47 200	45 23 275	25 28 309	43 19 329
344	62 43 037	52 46 134	52 27 179	18 27 201	44 24 275	24 42 309	42 48 328

LHA	◆Mirfak	Hamal	Acamar	◆ACHERNAR	FOMALHAUT	◆ALTAIR	DENEB
345	21 14 039	42 26 065	16 56 136	17 17 159	52 27 181	43 25 275	42 16 327
346	21 52 039	43 20 065	17 37 137	17 38 159	52 26 182	42 26 275	41 44 327
347	22 29 039	44 14 065	18 18 137	17 59 160	52 23 183	41 28 275	41 11 326
348	23 07 039	45 07 065	18 58 138	18 19 160	52 19 185	40 27 275	40 38 326
349	23 44 039	46 01 064	19 38 138	18 39 161	52 13 186	39 28 275	40 04 325
350	24 21 038	46 54 064	20 17 138	18 59 161	52 06 188	38 29 275	39 30 325
351	24 57 038	47 48 064	20 57 139	19 18 161	51 58 189	37 30 275	38 55 324
352	25 34 038	48 41 063	21 36 139	19 37 162	51 47 190	36 30 275	38 20 324
353	26 10 038	49 34 063	22 14 140	19 55 162	51 36 192	35 31 275	37 45 323
354	26 47 037	50 26 062	22 53 140	20 13 163	51 23 193	34 32 275	37 09 323
355	27 23 037	51 19 062	23 31 141	20 30 163	51 09 194	33 33 275	36 32 322
356	27 58 037	52 11 062	24 08 141	20 46 164	50 54 196	32 34 275	35 56 322
357	28 34 037	53 03 061	24 45 142	21 03 164	50 37 197	31 35 276	35 19 321
358	29 09 036	53 55 061	25 22 142	21 18 165	50 19 198	30 36 276	34 41 321
359	29 44 036	54 47 060	25 58 143	21 34 165	49 59 200	29 36 276	34 04 321

LHA ♈	Hc	Zn	Hc	Zn	Hc	Zn	Hc	Zn	Hc	Zn	Hc	Zn	Hc	Zn
	◆ CAPELLA		ALDEBARAN		RIGEL		◆ ACHERNAR		FOMALHAUT		◆ ALTAIR		DENEB	
0	12 21	044	21 53	075	09 59	100	22 47	166	50 35	201	28 31	276	32 40	321
1	13 03	044	22 50	075	10 57	100	23 01	166	50 12	203	27 32	276	32 02	320
2	13 44	044	23 48	075	11 56	100	23 15	167	49 49	204	26 33	276	31 24	320
3	14 26	044	24 45	075	12 55	100	23 28	167	49 24	205	25 33	277	30 45	320
4	15 07	044	25 43	075	13 53	100	23 40	168	48 59	206	24 34	277	30 06	319
5	15 49	044	26 40	075	14 52	100	23 53	169	48 32	207	23 35	277	29 27	319
6	16 30	044	27 38	075	15 50	101	24 04	169	48 04	208	22 36	277	28 48	319
7	17 11	044	28 35	075	16 49	101	24 15	170	47 36	209	21 37	277	28 08	318
8	17 53	044	29 33	075	17 47	101	24 25	170	47 06	210	20 38	277	27 29	318
9	18 34	044	30 30	075	18 46	101	24 35	171	46 35	212	19 39	277	26 49	318
10	19 15	044	31 28	075	19 44	101	24 45	171	46 04	213	18 39	277	26 09	318
11	19 56	043	32 25	075	20 43	102	24 53	172	45 31	213	17 40	277	25 28	317
12	20 37	043	33 23	075	21 41	102	25 01	173	44 58	214	16 41	277	24 48	317
13	21 17	043	34 20	075	22 39	102	25 09	173	44 24	215	15 42	277	24 07	317
14	21 58	043	35 18	075	23 37	102	25 16	174	43 49	216	14 43	277	23 27	317
	CAPELLA		◆ ALDEBARAN		RIGEL		ACHERNAR		◆ FOMALHAUT		Enif		◆ DENEB	
15	22 39	043	36 15	075	24 36	102	25 22	174	43 13	217	41 43	277	22 46	317
16	23 19	043	37 12	075	25 34	103	25 27	175	42 37	218	40 44	277	22 05	316
17	23 59	042	38 10	074	26 32	103	25 32	175	42 00	219	39 45	277	21 23	316
18	24 39	042	39 07	074	27 30	103	25 37	176	41 22	220	38 45	277	20 42	316
19	25 19	042	40 05	074	28 28	103	25 41	177	40 44	220	37 46	277	20 01	316
20	25 59	042	41 02	074	29 26	104	25 44	177	40 05	221	36 47	277	19 19	316
21	26 38	041	41 59	074	30 24	104	25 46	178	39 26	222	35 48	277	18 38	316
22	27 18	041	42 56	074	31 21	104	25 48	178	38 46	223	34 49	277	17 56	316
23	27 57	041	43 54	074	32 19	104	25 50	179	38 05	223	33 50	277	17 14	315
24	28 36	041	44 51	074	33 17	105	25 50	180	37 24	224	32 51	277	16 32	315
25	29 14	040	45 48	073	34 14	105	25 50	180	36 42	225	31 52	277	15 50	315
26	29 53	040	46 45	073	35 12	105	25 50	181	36 00	225	30 53	277	15 09	315
27	30 31	040	47 42	073	36 09	106	25 48	181	35 18	226	29 54	277	14 26	315
28	31 09	039	48 39	073	37 07	106	25 47	182	34 35	227	28 55	278	13 44	315
29	31 47	039	49 36	073	38 04	106	25 44	183	33 51	227	27 56	278	13 02	315
	Mirfak		CAPELLA		◆ ALDEBARAN		RIGEL		◆ ACHERNAR		FOMALHAUT		◆ Alpheratz	
30	43 31	019	32 24	039	50 32	072	39 01	107	25 41	183	33 07	228	55 45	314
31	43 50	018	33 01	038	51 29	072	39 58	107	25 37	184	32 23	228	55 02	313
32	44 08	017	33 38	038	52 26	072	40 55	107	25 33	184	31 39	229	54 18	312
33	44 25	016	34 14	038	53 22	072	41 52	108	25 28	185	30 54	229	53 34	311
34	44 42	016	34 50	037	54 19	071	42 49	108	25 23	186	30 08	230	52 49	311
35	44 57	015	35 26	037	55 15	071	43 45	108	25 16	186	29 23	230	52 03	310
36	45 12	014	36 01	036	56 11	071	44 42	109	25 10	187	28 37	231	51 18	309
37	45 26	013	36 36	036	57 08	070	45 38	109	25 02	187	27 50	231	50 31	309
38	45 39	012	37 11	035	58 04	070	46 34	110	24 54	188	27 04	232	49 44	308
39	45 51	011	37 45	035	58 59	069	47 30	110	24 46	189	26 17	232	48 57	307
40	46 03	011	38 19	034	59 55	069	48 26	111	24 37	189	25 30	232	48 10	307
41	46 13	010	38 52	034	60 50	068	49 21	111	24 27	190	24 43	233	47 22	306
42	46 23	009	39 25	033	61 46	068	50 17	112	24 17	190	23 55	233	46 34	306
43	46 31	008	39 57	033	62 41	067	51 12	112	24 06	191	23 07	234	45 45	305
44	46 39	007	40 29	032	63 36	067	52 07	113	23 54	191	22 19	234	44 57	305
	◆ CAPELLA		PROCYON		SIRIUS		◆ CANOPUS		ACHERNAR		Diphda		◆ Alpheratz	
45	41 00	031	20 25	087	29 21	114	16 19	151	23 42	192	48 16	233	44 08	304
46	41 31	031	21 24	087	30 16	114	16 48	151	23 30	192	47 29	234	43 18	304
47	42 01	030	22 24	087	31 10	114	17 17	151	23 16	193	46 40	234	42 29	304
48	42 31	029	23 23	087	32 04	115	17 45	152	23 03	194	45 52	235	41 39	303
49	43 00	029	24 23	087	32 58	115	18 13	152	22 48	194	45 03	236	40 49	303
50	43 28	028	25 22	088	33 52	116	18 41	153	22 34	195	44 13	237	39 59	303
51	43 56	027	26 22	088	34 45	116	19 08	153	22 18	195	43 23	237	39 09	302
52	44 23	027	27 21	088	35 39	116	19 35	153	22 03	196	42 33	238	38 18	302
53	44 49	026	28 21	088	36 32	117	20 01	154	21 46	196	41 43	238	37 28	302
54	45 15	025	29 20	088	37 25	117	20 27	154	21 30	197	40 52	239	36 37	301
55	45 40	024	30 20	088	38 18	118	20 53	155	21 12	197	40 01	240	35 46	301
56	46 04	023	31 19	088	39 10	118	21 18	155	20 54	198	39 09	240	34 55	301
57	46 27	023	32 19	088	40 03	119	21 43	156	20 36	198	38 17	241	34 04	301
58	46 50	022	33 18	088	40 55	119	22 07	156	20 17	199	37 25	241	33 12	300
59	47 11	021	34 18	088	41 47	120	22 31	157	19 58	199	36 33	242	32 21	300
	◆ CAPELLA		POLLUX		PROCYON		◆ SIRIUS		CANOPUS		◆ Diphda		Alpheratz	
60	47 32	020	32 42	061	35 17	089	42 38	120	22 54	157	35 41	242	31 30	300
61	47 52	019	33 34	061	36 17	089	43 29	121	23 17	158	34 48	242	30 38	300
62	48 11	018	34 26	061	37 16	089	44 20	122	23 39	158	33 55	243	29 46	300
63	48 29	017	35 18	061	38 16	089	45 10	122	24 01	159	33 02	243	28 55	300
64	48 46	016	36 10	060	39 15	089	46 01	123	24 22	159	32 09	244	28 03	299
65	49 03	015	37 01	060	40 15	089	46 50	124	24 43	160	31 15	244	27 11	299
66	49 18	014	37 53	060	41 15	089	47 40	124	25 03	160	30 22	244	26 19	299
67	49 32	013	38 44	059	42 14	089	48 29	125	25 23	161	29 28	245	25 27	299
68	49 45	012	39 35	059	43 14	089	49 17	126	25 42	162	28 34	245	24 35	299
69	49 58	011	40 26	059	44 13	090	50 05	127	26 01	162	27 40	246	23 43	299
70	50 09	010	41 17	059	45 13	090	50 52	128	26 19	163	26 45	246	22 50	299
71	50 19	009	42 08	058	46 12	090	51 39	129	26 36	163	25 51	246	21 58	299
72	50 28	008	42 59	058	47 12	090	52 26	129	26 53	164	24 56	247	21 06	299
73	50 36	007	43 49	057	48 11	090	53 11	130	27 09	165	24 02	247	20 14	299
74	50 42	006	44 39	057	49 11	090	53 56	131	27 25	165	23 07	247	19 21	299
	CAPELLA		◆ POLLUX		PROCYON		SIRIUS		◆ CANOPUS		Acamar		◆ Hamal	
75	50 48	005	45 29	057	50 10	090	54 41	132	27 40	166	35 08	208	45 35	297
76	50 52	004	46 19	056	51 10	090	55 24	134	27 54	166	34 39	209	44 42	296
77	50 56	003	47 08	056	52 10	091	56 07	135	28 08	167	34 10	210	43 48	296
78	50 58	002	47 57	055	53 09	091	56 49	136	28 21	168	33 41	210	42 55	296
79	50 59	000	48 46	055	54 09	091	57 30	137	28 33	168	33 10	211	42 01	296
80	50 59	359	49 34	054	55 08	091	58 10	138	28 45	169	32 39	212	41 07	295
81	50 58	358	50 22	054	56 08	091	58 49	140	28 56	170	32 08	212	40 13	295
82	50 56	357	51 10	053	57 07	091	59 27	141	29 06	170	31 36	213	39 19	295
83	50 52	356	51 58	052	58 07	091	60 03	143	29 16	171	31 03	214	38 25	295
84	50 47	355	52 44	052	59 06	092	60 39	144	29 25	172	30 30	214	37 31	294
85	50 42	354	53 31	051	60 06	092	61 13	146	29 33	172	29 57	215	36 37	294
86	50 35	353	54 17	050	61 05	092	61 46	147	29 41	173	29 22	215	35 42	294
87	50 27	352	55 03	049	62 05	092	62 17	149	29 48	174	28 48	216	34 48	294
88	50 18	351	55 48	049	63 04	092	62 47	151	29 54	174	28 13	216	33 53	294
89	50 08	350	56 32	048	64 04	093	63 15	153	30 00	175	27 37	217	32 59	294

LHA ♈	Hc	Zn	Hc	Zn	Hc	Zn	Hc	Zn	Hc	Zn	Hc	Zn	Hc	Zn
	POLLUX		◆ REGULUS		Suhail		◆ CANOPUS		Acamar		◆ ALDEBARAN		CAPELLA	
90	57 16	047	28 28	080	23 57	144	30 04	176	27 01	218	67 32	297	49 56	349
91	57 59	046	29 27	080	24 31	145	30 08	176	26 24	218	66 39	296	49 44	348
92	58 41	045	30 26	080	25 05	145	30 12	177	25 48	219	65 45	295	49 31	347
93	59 23	044	31 24	080	25 39	146	30 14	178	25 10	219	64 51	294	49 16	346
94	60 04	043	32 23	080	26 12	146	30 16	179	24 33	219	63 57	294	49 01	345
95	60 44	042	33 22	080	26 45	147	30 17	179	23 54	220	63 02	293	48 45	344
96	61 23	040	34 20	080	27 17	148	30 18	180	23 16	220	62 07	292	48 27	343
97	62 01	039	35 19	080	27 49	148	30 17	181	22 37	221	61 12	292	48 09	342
98	62 38	038	36 18	080	28 20	149	30 16	181	21 58	221	60 17	291	47 50	341
99	63 14	036	37 17	080	28 51	149	30 15	182	21 19	222	59 21	291	47 30	340
100	63 48	035	38 15	080	29 21	150	30 12	183	20 39	222	58 25	290	47 09	339
101	64 22	033	39 14	080	29 51	150	30 09	183	19 59	223	57 29	290	46 47	338
102	64 54	032	40 13	080	30 20	151	30 05	184	19 18	223	56 33	290	46 25	337
103	65 24	030	41 11	080	30 48	152	30 00	185	18 38	223	55 37	289	46 01	336
104	65 53	028	42 10	080	31 16	152	29 55	186	17 57	224	54 41	289	45 37	336
	POLLUX		◆ REGULUS		Suhail		◆ CANOPUS		RIGEL		ALDEBARAN		◆ CAPELLA	
105	66 20	026	43 09	080	31 43	153	29 49	186	59 48	240	53 45	289	45 12	335
106	66 45	024	44 07	080	32 10	154	29 42	187	58 56	241	52 48	288	44 46	334
107	67 09	022	45 06	080	32 36	154	29 34	188	58 04	242	51 51	288	44 20	333
108	67 30	020	46 05	080	33 02	155	29 26	188	57 11	243	50 55	288	43 53	333
109	67 50	018	47 03	080	33 26	156	29 17	189	56 17	244	49 58	287	43 25	332
110	68 07	016	48 02	080	33 50	157	29 08	190	55 24	244	49 01	287	42 57	331
111	68 22	013	49 01	080	34 14	157	28 57	190	54 30	245	48 04	287	42 28	330
112	68 34	011	49 59	080	34 37	158	28 46	191	53 36	246	47 07	287	41 58	330
113	68 45	009	50 58	080	34 58	159	28 35	192	52 41	247	46 10	287	41 28	329
114	68 52	006	51 57	080	35 20	160	28 23	192	51 47	247	45 13	286	40 57	329
115	68 58	004	52 55	080	35 40	160	28 10	193	50 51	248	44 16	286	40 26	328
116	69 00	001	53 54	079	36 00	161	27 56	194	49 56	248	43 19	286	39 54	327
117	69 00	359	54 52	079	36 19	162	27 42	194	49 01	249	42 22	286	39 22	327
118	68 58	356	55 51	079	36 37	163	27 27	195	48 05	249	41 24	286	38 49	326
119	68 53	354	56 49	079	36 54	164	27 11	195	47 09	250	40 27	286	38 15	326
	Dubhe		◆ Denebola		Suhail		◆ SIRIUS		RIGEL		ALDEBARAN		◆ CAPELLA	
120	25 41	022	33 12	077	37 10	164	60 00	218	46 13	250	39 30	286	37 42	325
121	26 04	022	34 10	077	37 26	165	59 23	219	45 17	251	38 32	286	37 08	325
122	26 26	022	35 08	077	37 40	166	58 45	220	44 21	251	37 35	286	36 33	324
123	26 48	021	36 06	077	37 54	167	58 06	222	43 24	252	36 38	285	35 58	324
124	27 09	021	37 04	077	38 07	168	57 26	223	42 28	252	35 40	285	35 23	323
125	27 31	021	38 02	077	38 19	169	56 45	224	41 31	253	34 43	285	34 47	323
126	27 51	020	39 00	077	38 30	170	56 03	225	40 34	253	33 45	285	34 11	322
127	28 12	020	39 58	077	38 41	171	55 20	227	39 37	253	32 48	285	33 34	322
128	28 32	019	40 56	077	38 50	171	54 36	228	38 40	254	31 50	285	32 57	322
129	28 52	019	41 54	077	38 58	172	53 52	229	37 43	254	30 53	285	32 20	321
130	29 11	019	42 52	077	39 06	173	53 07	230	36 46	254	29 55	285	31 43	321
131	29 30	018	43 50	077	39 12	174	52 21	231	35 48	255	28 58	285	31 05	321
132	29 48	018	44 48	077	39 18	175	51 35	232	34 51	255	28 00	285	30 27	320
133	30 06	017	45 46	076	39 22	176	50 48	232	33 53	255	27 03	285	29 49	320
134	30 24	017	46 43	076	39 26	177	50 00	233	32 56	255	26 05	285	29 11	320
	Dubhe		◆ ARCTURUS		SPICA		◆ Suhail		SIRIUS		BETELGEUSE		◆ CAPELLA	
135	30 41	017	12 34	072	21 23	105	39 28	178	49 12	234	44 23	274	28 32	319
136	30 58	016	13 30	072	22 20	105	39 30	179	48 24	235	43 23	274	27 53	319
137	31 14	016	14 27	072	23 17	105	39 30	180	47 35	236	42 24	274	27 14	319
138	31 30	015	15 23	072	24 15	106	39 30	181	46 46	236	41 24	274	26 34	319
139	31 46	015	16 20	072	25 12	106	39 29	182	45 56	237	40 25	274	25 55	318
140	32 00	014	17 17	072	26 09	106	39 26	183	45 06	238	39 26	274	25 15	318
141	32 15	014	18 13	072	27 07	106	39 23	184	44 15	238	38 26	274	24 35	318
142	32 29	013	19 10	072	28 04	107	39 19	185	43 24	239	37 27	274	23 55	318
143	32 42	013	20 07	072	29 01	107	39 14	185	42 33	240	36 27	274	23 15	317
144	32 55	012	21 04	072	29 57	107	39 07	186	41 42	240	35 28	274	22 35	317
145	33 08	012	22 00	072	30 54	108	39 00	187	40 50	241	34 29	274	21 54	317
146	33 20	011	22 57	072	31 51	108	38 52	188	39 58	241	33 29	274	21 13	317
147	33 31	011	23 54	072	32 48	108	38 43	189	39 05	242	32 30	274	20 33	317
148	33 42	010	24 50	072	33 44	109	38 33	190	38 13	242	31 30	274	19 52	317
149	33 52	010	25 47	072	34 41	109	38 22	191	37 20	243	30 31	274	19 11	316
	Dubhe		◆ ARCTURUS		SPICA		ACRUX		◆ Suhail		SIRIUS		◆ POLLUX	
150	34 02	009	26 44	072	35 37	109	14 27	164	38 11	192	36 27	243	52 03	308
151	34 11	009	27 40	072	36 33	110	14 43	164	37 58	193	35 34	244	51 16	307
152	34 20	008	28 37	072	37 29	110	14 59	165	37 44	194	34 40	244	50 28	306
153	34 28	008	29 34	072	38 25	110	15 15	165	37 30	194	33 47	244	49 40	306
154	34 35	007	30 30	072	39 21	111	15 30	165	37 15	195	32 53	245	48 51	305
155	34 42	006	31 27	072	40 16	111	15 45	166	36 58	196	31 59	245	48 03	305
156	34 49	006	32 23	072	41 12	112	16 00	166	36 41	197	31 05	246	47 14	304
157	34 55	005	33 20	072	42 07	112	16 14	166	36 24	198	30 10	246	46 24	304
158	35 00	005	34 17	072	43 02	113	16 28	167	36 05	199	29 16	246	45 35	303
159	35 04	004	35 13	072	43 57	113	16 41	167	35 46	199	28 21	247	44 45	303
160	35 08	004	36 09	071	44 52	114	16 54	168	35 25	200	27 27	247	43 55	303
161	35 12	003	37 06	071	45 46	114	17 07	168	35 04	201	26 32	247	43 04	302
162	35 15	002	38 02	071	46 40	115	17 19	169	34 43	202	25 37	248	42 14	302
163	35 17	002	38 59	071	47 35	115	17 30	169	34 20	203	24 42	248	41 23	301
164	35 18	001	39 55	071	48 28	116	17 41	169	33 57	203	23 46	248	40 32	301
	Dubhe		◆ ARCTURUS		SPICA		◆ ACRUX		Suhail		PROCYON		◆ POLLUX	
165	35 19	001	40 51	071	49 22	116	17 52	170	33 33	204	40 18	271	39 41	301
166	35 20	000	41 47	071	50 15	117	18 02	170	33 09	205	39 18	271	38 50	301
167	35 20	000	42 44	070	51 08	118	18 12	171	32 43	205	38 18	271	37 59	300
168	35 19	359	43 40	070	52 00	118	18 22	171	32 17	206	37 19	271	37 07	300
169	35 17	358	44 36	070	52 53	119	18 31	172	31 51	207	36 19	271	36 16	300
170	35 15	358	45 32	070	53 44	120	18 39	172	31 24	207	35 20	271	35 24	300
171	35 13	357	46 27	070	54 36	121	18 47	173	30 56	208	34 20	272	34 32	299
172	35 10	357	47 23	069	55 27	122	18 54	173	30 28	209	33 21	272	33 40	299
173	35 06	356	48 19	069	56 17	123	19 02	173	29 59	209	32 21	272	32 48	299
174	35 01	355	49 14	069	57 07	123	19 08	174	29 29	210	31 22	272	31 56	299
175	34 56	355	50 10	068	57 56	124	19 14	174	28 59	211	30 22	272	31 03	299
176	34 51	354	51 05	068	58 45	126	19 20	175	28 29	211	29 23	272	30 11	298
177	34 45	354	52 00	068	59 33	127	19 25	175	27 57	212	28 23	272	29 19	298
178	34 38	353	52 55	067	60 21	128	19 30	176	27 26	212	27 24	272	28 26	298
179	34 30	353	53 50	067	61 08	129	19 34	176	26 54	213	26 24	272	27 34	298

LAT 7°N

LHA ♈	Hc	Zn	Hc	Zn	Hc	Zn	Hc	Zn	Hc	Zn	Hc	Zn	Hc	Zn
	◆ARCTURUS		ANTARES		RIGIL KENT		◆ACRUX		Suhail		◆REGULUS		Dubhe	
180	54 45	067	16 32	120	15 13	161	19 37	177	26 21	213	62 15	282	34 23	352
181	55 39	066	17 23	121	15 32	161	19 41	177	25 48	214	61 17	282	34 14	352
182	56 34	066	18 14	121	15 51	162	19 43	178	25 15	214	60 18	282	34 05	351
183	57 28	065	19 05	121	16 09	162	19 45	178	24 41	215	59 20	282	33 55	350
184	58 22	065	19 56	121	16 27	163	19 47	179	24 06	215	58 22	281	33 45	350
185	59 16	064	20 47	122	16 45	163	19 48	179	23 32	216	57 23	281	33 35	349
186	60 09	063	21 38	122	17 02	163	19 49	180	22 57	216	56 25	281	33 23	349
187	61 02	063	22 28	122	17 19	164	19 49	180	22 21	217	55 26	281	33 12	348
188	61 55	062	23 18	123	17 35	164	19 49	181	21 45	217	54 28	281	32 59	348
189	62 47	061	24 08	123	17 51	165	19 48	181	21 09	218	53 29	281	32 47	347
190	63 39	060	24 58	124	18 07	165	19 47	182	20 32	218	52 31	280	32 33	347
191	64 31	059	25 47	124	18 22	166	19 45	182	19 55	219	51 32	280	32 19	346
192	65 22	058	26 37	124	18 37	166	19 42	182	19 18	219	50 34	280	32 05	346
193	66 12	057	27 26	125	18 51	166	19 40	183	18 40	219	49 35	280	31 50	345
194	67 02	056	28 14	125	19 05	167	19 36	183	18 03	220	48 36	280	31 35	345
	◆Alphecca		Rasalhague		ANTARES		◆RIGIL KENT		ACRUX		◆REGULUS		Dubhe	
195	48 13	057	22 02	079	29 03	126	19 18	167	19 33	184	47 38	280	31 19	344
196	49 03	057	23 00	079	29 51	126	19 31	168	19 28	184	46 39	280	31 03	344
197	49 53	056	23 59	079	30 39	126	19 43	168	19 24	185	45 40	280	30 47	344
198	50 42	056	24 58	079	31 27	127	19 55	169	19 18	185	44 42	280	30 29	343
199	51 31	055	25 56	079	32 15	127	20 06	169	19 13	186	43 43	280	30 12	343
200	52 20	054	26 55	079	33 02	128	20 17	170	19 06	186	42 44	280	29 54	342
201	53 08	054	27 53	079	33 48	129	20 28	170	19 00	187	41 46	280	29 36	342
202	53 56	053	28 52	079	34 35	129	20 37	171	18 52	187	40 47	280	29 17	341
203	54 43	052	29 50	080	35 21	130	20 47	171	18 45	188	39 48	280	28 58	341
204	55 30	052	30 49	080	36 07	130	20 56	172	18 37	188	38 50	280	28 38	341
205	56 17	051	31 47	080	36 52	131	21 04	172	18 28	189	37 51	280	28 18	340
206	57 03	050	32 46	080	37 37	131	21 12	173	18 19	189	36 52	280	27 58	340
207	57 48	049	33 45	080	38 21	132	21 19	173	18 10	189	35 53	280	27 37	339
208	58 33	048	34 43	080	39 05	133	21 26	174	18 00	190	34 55	280	27 16	339
209	59 17	047	35 42	080	39 49	133	21 32	174	17 49	190	33 56	280	26 55	339
	◆VEGA		Rasalhague		ANTARES		◆RIGIL KENT		ACRUX		◆REGULUS		Dubhe	
210	20 26	051	36 40	080	40 32	134	21 38	175	17 38	191	32 57	280	26 33	338
211	21 12	051	37 39	080	41 14	135	21 43	175	17 27	191	31 59	280	26 11	338
212	21 58	051	38 37	080	41 56	136	21 48	176	17 15	192	31 00	280	25 49	338
213	22 44	051	39 36	079	42 38	136	21 52	176	17 03	192	30 01	280	25 26	337
214	23 30	051	40 34	079	43 19	137	21 56	177	16 51	192	29 03	280	25 03	337
215	24 16	050	41 33	079	43 59	138	21 59	177	16 37	193	28 04	280	24 40	337
216	25 02	050	42 32	079	44 38	139	22 02	178	16 24	193	27 05	280	24 16	337
217	25 48	050	43 30	079	45 17	140	22 04	178	16 10	194	26 06	280	23 52	336
218	26 33	050	44 29	079	45 55	141	22 05	179	15 56	194	25 08	280	23 28	336
219	27 19	050	45 27	079	46 33	141	22 06	179	15 41	194	24 09	280	23 04	336
220	28 04	049	46 26	079	47 10	142	22 06	180	15 26	195	23 10	280	22 39	335
221	28 49	049	47 24	079	47 45	143	22 06	180	15 11	195	22 12	280	22 15	335
222	29 34	049	48 22	079	48 21	144	22 05	181	14 55	196	21 13	280	21 49	335
223	30 19	049	49 21	079	48 55	145	22 04	181	14 39	196	20 15	280	21 24	335
224	31 04	048	50 19	079	49 28	147	22 02	182	14 22	196	19 16	280	20 59	335
	VEGA		◆ALTAIR		Nunki		ANTARES		RIGIL KENT		◆SPICA		◆Alkaid	
225	31 49	048	17 55	083	23 49	123	50 00	148	22 00	183	60 20	232	45 08	343
226	32 33	048	18 54	083	24 39	123	50 32	149	21 57	183	59 33	233	44 51	343
227	33 17	048	19 53	083	25 29	124	51 02	150	21 54	184	58 45	234	44 32	342
228	34 01	047	20 52	083	26 18	124	51 31	151	21 50	184	57 56	236	44 13	341
229	34 44	047	21 51	083	27 07	124	51 59	152	21 45	185	57 07	237	43 54	340
230	35 28	047	22 50	083	27 56	125	52 26	154	21 40	185	56 17	237	43 33	339
231	36 11	046	23 49	083	28 45	125	52 52	155	21 34	186	55 26	238	43 12	339
232	36 54	046	24 49	083	29 34	126	53 17	156	21 28	186	54 35	239	42 50	338
233	37 36	045	25 48	083	30 22	126	53 40	158	21 22	187	53 44	240	42 27	337
234	38 18	045	26 47	084	31 10	127	54 02	159	21 14	187	52 52	241	42 03	336
235	39 00	045	27 46	084	31 58	127	54 23	160	21 07	188	52 00	242	41 39	336
236	39 42	044	28 45	084	32 45	128	54 42	162	20 58	188	51 07	242	41 15	335
237	40 23	044	29 44	084	33 32	128	55 00	163	20 50	189	50 15	243	40 49	334
238	41 04	043	30 44	084	34 19	129	55 16	165	20 41	189	49 21	244	40 23	334
239	41 45	043	31 43	084	35 05	129	55 31	166	20 31	190	48 28	244	39 57	333
	VEGA		◆ALTAIR		Nunki		◆ANTARES		SPICA		◆ARCTURUS		Alkaid	
240	42 25	042	32 42	084	35 51	130	55 44	168	47 34	245	62 04	298	39 30	333
241	43 04	041	33 41	084	36 37	130	55 56	169	46 40	245	61 11	297	39 02	332
242	43 43	041	34 41	084	37 22	131	56 06	171	45 46	246	60 18	297	38 34	331
243	44 22	040	35 40	084	38 07	132	56 15	173	44 51	246	59 25	296	38 05	331
244	45 00	040	36 39	084	38 51	132	56 21	174	43 57	247	58 31	296	37 36	330
245	45 38	039	37 38	084	39 35	133	56 27	176	43 02	247	57 37	295	37 06	330
246	46 15	038	38 37	084	40 18	134	56 30	177	42 07	248	56 43	294	36 36	329
247	46 52	038	39 37	084	41 01	134	56 32	179	41 11	248	55 49	294	36 05	329
248	47 28	037	40 36	084	41 44	135	56 32	181	40 16	249	54 54	294	35 34	328
249	48 03	036	41 35	084	42 26	136	56 30	182	39 20	249	54 00	293	35 02	328
250	48 38	035	42 34	084	43 07	137	56 27	184	38 25	250	53 05	293	34 30	327
251	49 12	035	43 34	084	43 47	137	56 22	186	37 29	250	52 10	292	33 58	327
252	49 46	034	44 33	084	44 28	138	56 16	187	36 33	250	51 15	292	33 25	326
253	50 18	033	45 32	084	45 07	139	56 08	189	35 36	251	50 19	292	32 52	326
254	50 50	032	46 32	084	45 46	140	55 58	190	34 40	251	49 24	291	32 19	326
	VEGA		◆ALTAIR		Nunki		◆ANTARES		SPICA		ARCTURUS		◆Alkaid	
255	51 21	031	47 31	084	46 24	141	55 46	192	33 44	251	48 28	291	31 45	325
256	51 52	030	48 30	084	47 01	142	55 33	193	32 47	252	47 33	291	31 11	325
257	52 21	029	49 29	084	47 37	143	55 19	195	31 51	252	46 37	290	30 36	324
258	52 49	028	50 29	084	48 13	144	55 03	196	30 54	252	45 41	290	30 02	324
259	53 17	027	51 28	084	48 48	145	54 45	198	29 57	253	44 45	290	29 27	324
260	53 43	026	52 27	084	49 21	146	54 26	199	29 00	253	43 49	290	28 51	323
261	54 09	025	53 26	084	49 54	147	54 06	201	28 03	253	42 53	290	28 16	323
262	54 33	024	54 26	084	50 26	148	53 44	202	27 06	254	41 57	289	27 40	323
263	54 57	022	55 25	084	50 57	149	53 21	203	26 09	254	41 01	289	27 04	323
264	55 19	021	56 24	084	51 27	150	52 56	205	25 12	254	40 05	289	26 28	322
265	55 40	020	57 24	084	51 56	152	52 31	206	24 14	254	39 08	289	25 51	322
266	56 00	019	58 23	084	52 24	153	52 04	207	23 17	255	38 12	289	25 14	322
267	56 18	018	59 22	084	52 50	154	51 36	209	22 20	255	37 16	289	24 37	322
268	56 35	016	60 21	084	53 16	156	51 07	210	21 22	255	36 19	289	24 00	321
269	56 51	015	61 21	084	53 40	157	50 37	211	20 25	255	35 23	288	23 23	321

LHA ♈	Hc	Zn	Hc	Zn	Hc	Zn	Hc	Zn	Hc	Zn	Hc	Zn	Hc	Zn
	VEGA		◆DENEB		Enif		◆Nunki		Shaula		ANTARES		◆ARCTURUS	
270	57 06	013	38 07	035	34 22	083	54 02	158	45 29	187	50 06	212	34 26	288
271	57 19	012	38 42	035	35 21	083	54 24	160	45 21	188	49 33	213	33 30	288
272	57 31	011	39 16	034	36 20	083	54 44	161	45 12	189	49 00	214	32 33	288
273	57 41	009	39 49	034	37 19	083	55 02	163	45 02	191	48 26	215	31 37	288
274	57 50	008	40 22	033	38 18	083	55 19	164	44 50	192	47 51	216	30 40	288
275	57 58	006	40 54	033	39 17	083	55 35	166	44 38	193	47 16	217	29 43	288
276	58 03	005	41 26	032	40 16	083	55 49	167	44 24	194	46 39	218	28 47	288
277	58 08	003	41 58	031	41 16	083	56 02	169	44 09	195	46 02	219	27 50	288
278	58 11	002	42 28	031	42 15	083	56 13	170	43 53	196	45 24	220	26 53	288
279	58 12	001	42 58	030	43 14	083	56 22	172	43 37	197	44 45	221	25 57	288
280	58 12	359	43 28	029	44 13	083	56 30	173	43 19	198	44 05	222	25 00	288
281	58 10	358	43 57	029	45 12	083	56 36	175	43 00	199	43 25	223	24 03	288
282	58 07	356	44 25	028	46 11	083	56 40	177	42 40	200	42 44	224	23 07	288
283	58 02	355	44 53	027	47 10	083	56 42	178	42 19	201	42 03	224	22 10	288
284	57 56	353	45 20	026	48 09	083	56 43	180	41 58	202	41 21	225	21 13	288
	DENEB		◆Alpheratz		FOMALHAUT		◆Nunki		ANTARES		◆Rasalhague		VEGA	
285	45 46	026	14 29	062	22 07	126	56 43	182	40 39	226	68 30	287	57 48	352
286	46 11	025	15 21	062	22 56	126	56 40	183	39 56	227	67 33	286	57 39	350
287	46 36	024	16 14	062	23 44	127	56 36	185	39 12	227	66 35	286	57 28	349
288	47 00	023	17 06	062	24 31	127	56 30	186	38 28	228	65 38	285	57 16	348
289	47 23	022	17 58	062	25 19	127	56 23	188	37 44	228	64 40	285	57 02	346
290	47 45	021	18 51	062	26 06	128	56 14	190	36 59	229	63 43	284	56 47	345
291	48 07	021	19 43	061	26 53	128	56 03	191	36 14	230	62 45	284	56 31	343
292	48 27	020	20 35	061	27 39	129	55 50	193	35 28	230	61 47	284	56 13	342
293	48 47	019	21 28	061	28 26	129	55 36	194	34 42	231	60 49	283	55 54	341
294	49 05	018	22 20	061	29 12	130	55 21	196	33 56	231	59 51	283	55 34	340
295	49 23	017	23 12	061	29 57	130	55 04	197	33 09	232	58 53	283	55 13	338
296	49 40	016	24 04	061	30 43	131	54 46	199	32 22	232	57 55	282	54 50	337
297	49 55	015	24 56	061	31 28	131	54 26	200	31 35	233	56 57	282	54 27	336
298	50 10	014	25 48	061	32 13	132	54 04	202	30 47	233	55 59	282	54 02	335
299	50 24	013	26 40	061	32 57	132	53 42	203	29 59	234	55 00	282	53 36	334
	◆DENEB		Alpheratz		◆FOMALHAUT		Peacock		◆ANTARES		Rasalhague		VEGA	
300	50 36	012	27 32	061	33 41	133	26 05	176	29 11	234	54 02	282	53 09	333
301	50 48	011	28 24	061	34 24	133	26 09	177	28 23	235	53 04	282	52 42	332
302	50 58	009	29 16	060	35 07	134	26 12	177	27 34	235	52 05	281	52 13	331
303	51 07	008	30 08	060	35 50	135	26 14	178	26 45	236	51 07	281	51 43	330
304	51 15	007	30 59	060	36 32	135	26 17	178	25 55	236	50 09	281	51 13	329
305	51 22	006	31 51	060	37 14	136	26 18	179	25 06	236	49 10	281	50 41	328
306	51 28	005	32 43	060	37 55	137	26 19	180	24 16	237	48 12	281	50 09	327
307	51 33	004	33 34	059	38 36	137	26 19	180	23 26	237	47 13	281	49 37	326
308	51 36	003	34 25	059	39 16	138	26 18	181	22 36	237	46 15	281	49 03	325
309	51 39	002	35 16	059	39 56	139	26 17	181	21 46	238	45 16	281	48 29	324
310	51 40	001	36 07	059	40 35	139	26 15	182	20 55	238	44 18	281	47 54	324
311	51 40	359	36 58	059	41 13	140	26 13	183	20 05	238	43 19	281	47 18	323
312	51 39	358	37 49	058	41 51	141	26 10	183	19 14	239	42 21	281	46 42	322
313	51 36	357	38 39	058	42 28	142	26 06	184	18 23	239	41 22	281	46 05	322
314	51 33	356	39 30	058	43 05	143	26 02	184	17 32	239	40 24	281	45 28	321
	Alpheratz		◆Diphda		FOMALHAUT		◆Nunki		Rasalhague		VEGA		◆DENEB	
315	40 20	057	29 19	115	43 41	144	45 11	221	39 25	281	44 50	320	51 28	355
316	41 10	057	30 12	115	44 16	144	44 31	222	38 27	280	44 12	320	51 22	354
317	42 00	057	31 06	116	44 50	145	43 51	223	37 28	280	43 33	319	51 15	353
318	42 49	056	32 00	116	45 23	146	43 11	223	36 29	280	42 53	318	51 07	352
319	43 39	056	32 53	117	45 56	147	42 30	224	35 31	280	42 14	318	50 58	350
320	44 28	055	33 46	117	46 28	148	41 48	225	34 32	280	41 33	317	50 47	349
321	45 17	055	34 39	117	46 59	149	41 06	226	33 34	280	40 53	317	50 36	348
322	46 05	055	35 32	118	47 29	150	40 23	226	32 35	280	40 12	316	50 23	347
323	46 54	054	36 24	118	47 58	151	39 39	227	31 37	280	39 30	316	50 10	346
324	47 42	054	37 16	119	48 26	153	38 55	228	30 38	280	38 49	315	49 55	345
325	48 30	053	38 09	119	48 53	154	38 11	228	29 39	280	38 07	315	49 39	344
326	49 17	052	39 00	120	49 18	155	37 26	229	28 41	281	37 24	314	49 22	343
327	50 04	052	39 52	120	49 43	156	36 41	230	27 42	281	36 42	314	49 05	342
328	50 51	051	40 43	121	50 07	157	35 56	230	26 44	281	35 59	314	48 46	341
329	51 37	051	41 34	122	50 29	158	35 10	231	25 45	281	35 16	313	48 27	340
	◆Alpheratz		Diphda		◆FOMALHAUT		Peacock		ALTAIR		◆VEGA		DENEB	
330	52 22	050	42 25	122	50 51	160	23 30	194	58 08	276	34 32	313	48 06	339
331	53 08	049	43 15	123	51 11	161	23 16	194	57 09	276	33 49	313	47 45	339
332	53 52	048	44 05	123	51 30	162	23 01	195	56 10	276	33 05	312	47 22	338
333	54 37	048	44 54	124	51 47	164	22 46	195	55 11	276	32 21	312	46 59	337
334	55 20	047	45 43	125	52 03	165	22 30	196	54 11	276	31 36	312	46 35	336
335	56 03	046	46 32	125	52 18	166	22 13	196	53 12	276	30 52	311	46 11	335
336	56 46	045	47 20	126	52 32	168	21 56	197	52 13	276	30 07	311	45 45	334
337	57 27	044	48 08	127	52 44	169	21 39	197	51 14	276	29 22	311	45 19	333
338	58 08	043	48 56	128	52 54	170	21 21	198	50 14	276	28 37	311	44 52	333
339	58 48	042	49 42	129	53 04	172	21 02	198	49 15	276	27 52	310	44 25	332
340	59 28	041	50 29	129	53 11	173	20 43	199	48 16	276	27 06	310	43 56	331
341	60 06	039	51 14	130	53 18	175	20 24	199	47 16	276	26 21	310	43 27	331
342	60 43	038	51 59	131	53 22	176	20 04	200	46 17	276	25 35	310	42 58	330
343	61 20	037	52 44	132	53 25	178	19 44	200	45 18	276	24 49	310	42 27	329
344	61 55	036	53 28	133	53 27	179	19 23	201	44 19	276	24 04	310	41 57	329
	◆Mirfak		Hamal		Acamar		◆ACHERNAR		FOMALHAUT		◆ALTAIR		DENEB	
345	20 28	039	42 00	064	17 40	136	18 13	159	53 27	181	43 19	276	41 25	328
346	21 05	039	42 54	064	18 21	137	18 34	159	53 26	182	42 20	276	40 53	327
347	21 43	039	43 48	064	19 02	137	18 55	160	53 23	183	41 21	276	40 21	327
348	22 20	038	44 41	064	19 42	137	19 16	160	53 19	185	40 22	276	39 48	326
349	22 57	038	45 34	063	20 22	138	19 36	160	53 13	186	39 22	276	39 15	326
350	23 33	038	46 27	063	21 02	138	19 56	161	53 06	188	38 23	276	38 41	325
351	24 10	038	47 20	063	21 42	139	20 15	161	52 57	189	37 24	276	38 06	325
352	24 47	038	48 13	062	22 21	139	20 34	162	52 46	191	36 25	276	37 32	324
353	25 23	037	49 06	062	23 00	139	20 52	162	52 35	192	35 25	276	36 56	324
354	25 59	037	49 58	061	23 39	140	21 10	163	52 22	193	34 26	276	36 21	323
355	26 35	037	50 50	061	24 17	140	21 27	163	52 07	195	33 27	276	35 45	323
356	27 10	037	51 42	060	24 55	141	21 44	164	51 51	196	32 28	276	35 08	322
357	27 46	036	52 34	060	25 32	141	22 00	164	51 34	197	31 28	276	34 32	322
358	28 21	036	53 25	059	26 09	142	22 16	165	51 15	199	30 29	276	33 55	321
359	28 55	036	54 16	059	26 46	142	22 32	165	50 56	200	29 30	276	33 17	321

LHA ♈	Hc	Zn	Hc	Zn	Hc	Zn	Hc	Zn	Hc	Zn	Hc	Zn	Hc	Zn
	◆ CAPELLA		ALDEBARAN		RIGEL		◆ ACHERNAR		FOMALHAUT		◆ ALTAIR		DENEB	
0	11 38	044	21 37	075	10 08	099	23 45	166	51 30	202	28 24	277	31 53	321
1	12 20	044	22 34	075	11 07	100	23 59	166	51 08	203	27 25	277	31 16	321
2	13 01	044	23 32	075	12 06	100	24 13	167	50 44	204	26 26	277	30 38	320
3	13 43	044	24 29	075	13 05	100	24 26	167	50 19	205	25 26	277	29 59	320
4	14 24	044	25 27	075	14 04	100	24 39	168	49 53	207	24 27	277	29 21	320
5	15 06	044	26 24	074	15 02	100	24 51	168	49 25	208	23 28	277	28 42	319
6	15 47	044	27 22	074	16 01	100	25 03	169	48 57	209	22 29	277	28 03	319
7	16 28	044	28 19	074	17 00	100	25 14	170	48 28	210	21 29	277	27 23	319
8	17 09	044	29 17	074	17 59	101	25 25	170	47 57	211	20 30	277	26 44	318
9	17 50	043	30 14	074	18 57	101	25 35	171	47 26	212	19 31	277	26 04	318
10	18 31	043	31 12	074	19 56	101	25 44	171	46 54	213	18 32	277	25 24	318
11	19 12	043	32 09	074	20 54	101	25 53	172	46 21	214	17 33	277	24 44	318
12	19 53	043	33 07	074	21 53	101	26 01	172	45 47	215	16 34	278	24 04	317
13	20 34	043	34 04	074	22 51	102	26 08	173	45 13	216	15 34	278	23 23	317
14	21 14	043	35 01	074	23 50	102	26 15	174	44 37	217	14 35	278	22 43	317
	CAPELLA		◆ ALDEBARAN		RIGEL		ACHERNAR		◆ FOMALHAUT		Enif		◆ DENEB	
15	21 54	042	35 59	074	24 48	102	26 22	174	44 01	218	41 35	278	22 02	317
16	22 35	042	36 56	074	25 47	102	26 27	175	43 24	219	40 36	278	21 21	317
17	23 15	042	37 53	074	26 45	102	26 32	175	42 47	219	39 37	278	20 40	316
18	23 55	042	38 51	074	27 43	103	26 37	176	42 08	220	38 38	278	19 59	316
19	24 34	042	39 48	073	28 41	103	26 41	177	41 30	221	37 39	278	19 18	316
20	25 14	041	40 45	073	29 40	103	26 44	177	40 50	222	36 39	278	18 36	316
21	25 53	041	41 42	073	30 38	103	26 46	178	40 10	222	35 40	278	17 55	316
22	26 32	041	42 39	073	31 36	103	26 48	178	39 30	223	34 41	278	17 13	316
23	27 11	041	43 36	073	32 34	104	26 50	179	38 48	224	33 42	278	16 31	316
24	27 50	040	44 33	073	33 32	104	26 50	180	38 07	225	32 43	278	15 50	316
25	28 29	040	45 30	072	34 30	104	26 50	180	37 25	225	31 44	278	15 08	315
26	29 07	040	46 27	072	35 27	105	26 50	181	36 42	226	30 45	278	14 26	315
27	29 45	039	47 24	072	36 25	105	26 48	181	35 59	226	29 46	278	13 44	315
28	30 22	039	48 21	072	37 23	105	26 47	182	35 16	227	28 47	278	13 02	315
29	31 00	039	49 17	072	38 20	105	26 44	183	34 32	228	27 48	278	12 20	315
	Mirfak		CAPELLA		◆ ALDEBARAN		RIGEL		◆ ACHERNAR		FOMALHAUT		◆ Alpheratz	
30	42 34	019	31 37	038	50 14	071	39 18	106	26 41	183	33 48	228	55 04	315
31	42 53	018	32 14	038	51 10	071	40 15	106	26 37	184	33 03	229	54 21	314
32	43 10	017	32 50	038	52 07	071	41 12	106	26 33	184	32 18	229	53 38	313
33	43 27	016	33 27	037	53 03	070	42 10	107	26 28	185	31 33	230	52 54	312
34	43 44	015	34 02	037	53 59	070	43 07	107	26 22	186	30 47	230	52 09	312
35	43 59	015	34 38	036	54 55	070	44 04	108	26 16	186	30 01	231	51 25	311
36	44 14	014	35 13	036	55 51	069	45 01	108	26 09	187	29 14	231	50 39	310
37	44 28	013	35 48	035	56 47	069	45 57	108	26 02	187	28 28	232	49 53	309
38	44 40	012	36 22	035	57 42	068	46 54	109	25 54	188	27 41	232	49 07	309
39	44 53	011	36 56	034	58 37	068	47 50	109	25 45	189	26 54	232	48 20	308
40	45 04	010	37 29	034	59 33	067	48 47	110	25 36	189	26 06	233	47 33	308
41	45 14	009	38 02	033	60 28	067	49 43	110	25 26	190	25 19	233	46 46	307
42	45 23	009	38 35	033	61 22	066	50 39	111	25 16	190	24 31	234	45 58	307
43	45 32	008	39 07	032	62 17	065	51 34	111	25 05	191	23 42	234	45 10	306
44	45 39	007	39 38	032	63 11	065	52 30	112	24 53	191	22 54	234	44 22	306
	◆ CAPELLA		PROCYON		SIRIUS		◆ CANOPUS		ACHERNAR		Diphda		◆ Alpheratz	
45	40 09	031	20 21	087	29 45	113	17 11	150	24 41	192	48 52	234	43 33	305
46	40 39	030	21 21	087	30 40	114	17 41	151	24 28	193	48 04	235	42 44	305
47	41 09	030	22 21	087	31 34	114	18 09	151	24 15	193	47 15	235	41 55	304
48	41 38	029	23 20	087	32 29	114	18 38	152	24 01	194	46 26	236	41 06	304
49	42 07	028	24 20	087	33 23	115	19 06	152	23 47	194	45 36	237	40 16	304
50	42 35	028	25 19	087	34 17	115	19 34	152	23 32	195	44 46	237	39 26	303
51	43 02	027	26 19	087	35 11	115	20 01	153	23 16	195	43 56	238	38 36	303
52	43 29	026	27 18	087	36 05	116	20 29	153	23 00	196	43 05	239	37 46	303
53	43 55	025	28 18	087	36 59	116	20 55	154	22 44	196	42 14	239	36 56	302
54	44 20	025	29 18	087	37 52	117	21 21	154	22 27	197	41 22	240	36 05	302
55	44 45	024	30 17	087	38 46	117	21 47	155	22 10	197	40 31	240	35 15	302
56	45 09	023	31 17	088	39 39	118	22 13	155	21 52	198	39 39	241	34 24	301
57	45 32	022	32 17	088	40 31	118	22 37	156	21 33	198	38 47	241	33 33	301
58	45 54	021	33 16	088	41 24	119	23 02	156	21 14	199	37 54	242	32 42	301
59	46 15	021	34 16	088	42 16	119	23 26	157	20 55	199	37 01	242	31 51	301
	◆ CAPELLA		POLLUX		PROCYON		◆ SIRIUS		CANOPUS		◆ Diphda		Alpheratz	
60	46 36	020	32 13	061	35 15	088	43 08	120	23 49	157	36 09	243	30 59	301
61	46 55	019	33 05	060	36 15	088	44 00	120	24 12	158	35 15	243	30 08	300
62	47 14	018	33 56	060	37 15	088	44 51	121	24 35	158	34 22	243	29 16	300
63	47 32	017	34 48	060	38 14	088	45 42	121	24 57	159	33 29	244	28 25	300
64	47 49	016	35 40	060	39 14	088	46 33	122	25 18	159	32 35	244	27 33	300
65	48 05	015	36 31	059	40 14	088	47 23	123	25 39	160	31 41	245	26 41	300
66	48 20	014	37 22	059	41 13	088	48 13	124	26 00	160	30 47	245	25 49	300
67	48 34	013	38 13	059	42 13	088	49 03	124	26 20	161	29 53	245	24 57	299
68	48 47	012	39 04	059	43 13	089	49 52	125	26 39	161	28 59	246	24 05	299
69	48 59	011	39 55	058	44 12	089	50 40	126	26 58	162	28 04	246	23 13	299
70	49 10	010	40 46	058	45 12	089	51 29	127	27 16	163	27 10	246	22 21	299
71	49 19	009	41 36	057	46 11	089	52 16	128	27 34	163	26 15	247	21 29	299
72	49 28	008	42 26	057	47 11	089	53 03	128	27 51	164	25 20	247	20 37	299
73	49 36	007	43 16	057	48 11	089	53 50	129	28 07	164	24 25	247	19 45	299
74	49 43	006	44 06	056	49 10	089	54 35	130	28 23	165	23 30	247	18 52	299
	CAPELLA		◆ POLLUX		PROCYON		SIRIUS		◆ CANOPUS		Acamar		◆ Hamal	
75	49 48	005	44 56	056	50 10	089	55 21	131	28 38	166	36 01	208	45 08	298
76	49 53	004	45 45	055	51 10	089	56 05	132	28 52	166	35 32	209	44 15	297
77	49 56	003	46 34	055	52 09	089	56 49	134	29 06	167	35 02	210	43 21	297
78	49 58	002	47 22	054	53 09	089	57 31	135	29 19	168	34 32	211	42 28	297
79	49 59	000	48 11	054	54 09	089	58 13	136	29 32	168	34 02	211	41 35	296
80	49 59	359	48 59	053	55 08	090	58 54	137	29 44	169	33 31	212	40 41	296
81	49 58	358	49 46	053	56 08	090	59 34	139	29 55	170	32 59	213	39 48	296
82	49 56	357	50 34	052	57 08	090	60 13	140	30 05	170	32 26	213	38 54	296
83	49 52	356	51 20	051	58 07	090	60 51	142	30 15	171	31 53	214	38 00	295
84	49 48	355	52 07	051	59 07	090	61 27	143	30 24	172	31 20	214	37 06	295
85	49 42	354	52 53	050	60 07	090	62 03	145	30 33	172	30 46	215	36 12	295
86	49 35	353	53 38	049	61 07	090	62 36	146	30 41	173	30 11	216	35 18	295
87	49 27	352	54 23	048	62 06	090	63 09	148	30 47	174	29 36	216	34 23	294
88	49 19	351	55 08	048	63 06	090	63 39	150	30 54	174	29 01	217	33 29	294
89	49 09	350	55 51	047	64 06	090	64 09	152	30 59	175	28 25	217	32 35	294

LAT 6°N

LHA ♈	Hc	Zn	Hc	Zn	Hc	Zn	Hc	Zn	Hc	Zn	Hc	Zn	Hc	Zn
	POLLUX		◆ REGULUS		Suhail		◆ CANOPUS		Acamar		◆ ALDEBARAN		CAPELLA	
90	56 34	046	28 18	080	24 46	144	31 04	176	27 48	218	67 04	299	48 58	349
91	57 17	045	29 16	080	25 20	145	31 08	176	27 12	218	66 12	298	48 45	348
92	57 58	044	30 15	080	25 55	145	31 12	177	26 34	219	65 19	297	48 32	347
93	58 39	043	31 14	080	26 29	146	31 14	178	25 57	219	64 26	296	48 18	346
94	59 19	042	32 13	080	27 02	146	31 16	179	25 19	220	63 32	296	48 03	345
95	59 59	040	33 11	080	27 35	147	31 17	179	24 40	220	62 38	295	47 47	344
96	60 37	039	34 10	080	28 08	147	31 18	180	24 02	221	61 44	294	47 30	343
97	61 14	038	35 09	080	28 40	148	31 17	181	23 23	221	60 49	294	47 12	342
98	61 50	037	36 07	080	29 11	148	31 16	181	22 43	222	59 54	293	46 53	341
99	62 25	035	37 06	080	29 42	149	31 15	182	22 03	222	58 59	292	46 34	340
100	62 59	034	38 05	080	30 13	150	31 12	183	21 23	222	58 04	292	46 13	339
101	63 31	032	39 04	080	30 43	150	31 09	183	20 43	223	57 08	291	45 52	339
102	64 02	030	40 02	079	31 12	151	31 05	184	20 02	223	56 13	291	45 29	338
103	64 32	029	41 01	079	31 41	151	31 00	185	19 21	223	55 17	291	45 06	337
104	65 00	027	42 00	079	32 09	152	30 55	186	18 40	224	54 21	290	44 42	336
	POLLUX		◆ REGULUS		Suhail		◆ CANOPUS		RIGEL		ALDEBARAN		◆ CAPELLA	
105	65 26	025	42 58	079	32 37	153	30 48	186	60 17	242	53 25	290	44 18	335
106	65 50	023	43 57	079	33 04	153	30 42	187	59 24	243	52 29	289	43 52	334
107	66 13	021	44 55	079	33 30	154	30 34	188	58 31	244	51 32	289	43 26	334
108	66 34	019	45 54	079	33 56	155	30 26	188	57 37	244	50 36	289	43 00	333
109	66 52	017	46 53	079	34 21	156	30 17	189	56 43	245	49 39	289	42 32	332
110	67 09	015	47 51	079	34 45	156	30 07	190	55 49	246	48 43	288	42 04	332
111	67 23	013	48 50	079	35 09	157	29 56	190	54 55	247	47 46	288	41 35	331
112	67 35	011	49 48	079	35 32	158	29 45	191	54 00	247	46 49	288	41 06	330
113	67 45	008	50 47	079	35 54	159	29 34	192	53 05	248	45 52	288	40 36	330
114	67 53	006	51 45	078	36 16	159	29 21	192	52 09	248	44 56	287	40 06	329
115	67 58	004	52 44	078	36 37	160	29 08	193	51 14	249	43 59	287	39 35	328
116	68 00	001	53 42	078	36 56	161	28 54	194	50 18	249	43 02	287	39 03	328
117	68 00	359	54 40	078	37 16	162	28 40	194	49 22	250	42 05	287	38 31	327
118	67 58	357	55 39	078	37 34	163	28 25	195	48 26	250	41 07	287	37 59	327
119	67 53	354	56 37	077	37 51	163	28 09	196	47 29	251	40 10	287	37 26	326
	Dubhe		◆ Denebola		Suhail		◆ SIRIUS		RIGEL		ALDEBARAN		◆ CAPELLA	
120	24 46	022	32 58	077	38 08	164	60 47	219	46 33	251	39 13	286	36 52	326
121	25 08	022	33 56	077	38 24	165	60 09	220	45 36	252	38 16	286	36 18	325
122	25 30	021	34 54	077	38 39	166	59 30	221	44 40	252	37 19	286	35 44	325
123	25 52	021	35 52	076	38 53	167	58 50	223	43 43	253	36 21	286	35 09	324
124	26 13	021	36 50	076	39 06	168	58 09	224	42 46	253	35 24	286	34 34	324
125	26 34	020	37 48	076	39 18	169	57 27	225	41 49	253	34 27	286	33 59	323
126	26 55	020	38 46	076	39 29	170	56 44	227	40 51	254	33 29	286	33 23	323
127	27 15	020	39 44	076	39 40	170	56 01	228	39 54	254	32 32	286	32 47	322
128	27 35	019	40 42	076	39 49	171	55 16	229	38 57	254	31 34	286	32 10	322
129	27 55	019	41 40	076	39 58	172	54 31	230	37 59	255	30 37	286	31 33	322
130	28 14	019	42 38	076	40 05	173	53 45	231	37 01	255	29 39	286	30 56	321
131	28 33	018	43 35	076	40 12	174	52 59	232	36 04	255	28 42	286	30 19	321
132	28 51	018	44 33	076	40 17	175	52 12	233	35 06	256	27 44	286	29 41	321
133	29 09	017	45 31	075	40 22	176	51 24	233	34 08	256	26 47	286	29 03	320
134	29 27	017	46 29	075	40 25	177	50 36	234	33 10	256	25 49	285	28 25	320
	Dubhe		◆ ARCTURUS		SPICA		◆ Suhail		SIRIUS		BETELGEUSE		◆ CAPELLA	
135	29 44	016	12 15	072	21 38	105	40 28	178	49 47	235	44 18	275	27 46	320
136	30 00	016	13 11	072	22 36	105	40 30	179	48 58	236	43 19	275	27 07	319
137	30 16	016	14 08	072	23 33	105	40 30	180	48 08	237	42 20	275	26 29	319
138	30 32	015	15 05	072	24 31	105	40 30	181	47 18	237	41 20	275	25 49	319
139	30 48	015	16 02	072	25 28	105	40 29	182	46 28	238	40 21	275	25 10	319
140	31 02	014	16 58	072	26 26	106	40 26	183	45 37	239	39 21	275	24 30	318
141	31 17	014	17 55	072	27 23	106	40 23	184	44 46	239	38 22	275	23 51	318
142	31 30	013	18 52	072	28 21	106	40 19	185	43 55	240	37 22	275	23 11	318
143	31 44	013	19 48	072	29 18	106	40 13	186	43 03	240	36 23	275	22 31	318
144	31 57	012	20 45	072	30 15	107	40 07	187	42 11	241	35 23	275	21 50	317
145	32 09	012	21 42	072	31 12	107	40 00	187	41 19	241	34 24	275	21 10	317
146	32 21	011	22 38	072	32 09	107	39 52	188	40 26	242	33 24	275	20 30	317
147	32 32	011	23 35	072	33 06	108	39 42	189	39 34	242	32 25	275	19 49	317
148	32 43	010	24 32	072	34 03	108	39 32	190	38 41	243	31 25	275	19 08	317
149	32 53	010	25 28	072	35 00	108	39 21	191	37 47	243	30 26	275	18 27	317
	Dubhe		◆ ARCTURUS		SPICA		ACRUX		◆ Suhail		SIRIUS		◆ POLLUX	
150	33 03	009	26 25	072	35 56	109	15 25	164	39 09	192	36 54	244	51 26	309
151	33 12	009	27 22	072	36 53	109	15 41	164	38 56	193	36 00	244	50 39	308
152	33 20	008	28 18	072	37 49	109	15 57	164	38 43	194	35 06	245	49 52	307
153	33 28	007	29 15	071	38 45	110	16 13	165	38 28	195	34 12	245	49 04	307
154	33 36	007	30 11	071	39 42	110	16 29	165	38 12	196	33 18	245	48 16	306
155	33 43	006	31 08	071	40 38	110	16 44	166	37 56	196	32 24	246	47 28	306
156	33 49	006	32 04	071	41 33	111	16 58	166	37 39	197	31 29	246	46 39	305
157	33 55	005	33 01	071	42 29	111	17 12	166	37 21	198	30 35	247	45 51	305
158	34 00	005	33 57	071	43 25	112	17 26	167	37 02	199	29 40	247	45 01	304
159	34 04	004	34 54	071	44 20	112	17 40	167	36 42	200	28 45	247	44 12	304
160	34 08	004	35 50	071	45 15	113	17 53	168	36 22	200	27 50	247	43 22	303
161	34 12	003	36 46	071	46 10	113	18 05	168	36 00	201	26 55	248	42 32	303
162	34 15	002	37 43	070	47 05	114	18 17	168	35 38	202	25 59	248	41 42	303
163	34 17	002	38 39	070	48 00	114	18 29	169	35 16	203	25 04	248	40 52	302
164	34 18	001	39 35	070	48 54	115	18 40	169	34 52	204	24 08	249	40 01	302
	Dubhe		◆ ARCTURUS		SPICA		◆ ACRUX		Suhail		PROCYON		◆ POLLUX	
165	34 19	001	40 31	070	49 48	115	18 51	170	34 28	204	40 16	272	39 10	302
166	34 20	000	41 27	070	50 42	116	19 02	170	34 03	205	39 17	272	38 19	301
167	34 20	000	42 23	070	51 35	117	19 11	171	33 37	206	38 17	272	37 28	301
168	34 19	359	43 19	069	52 28	117	19 21	171	33 11	206	37 17	272	36 37	301
169	34 17	358	44 15	069	53 21	118	19 30	172	32 44	207	36 18	272	35 46	300
170	34 15	358	45 10	069	54 14	119	19 38	172	32 17	208	35 18	272	34 54	300
171	34 13	357	46 06	069	55 06	120	19 46	172	31 49	208	34 18	272	34 02	300
172	34 10	357	47 01	068	55 58	120	19 54	173	31 20	209	33 19	272	33 11	300
173	34 06	356	47 57	068	56 49	121	20 01	173	30 51	210	32 19	272	32 19	299
174	34 01	356	48 52	068	57 40	122	20 08	174	30 21	210	31 19	272	31 27	299
175	33 57	355	49 47	067	58 30	123	20 14	174	29 51	211	30 20	273	30 35	299
176	33 51	354	50 42	067	59 20	124	20 20	175	29 20	211	29 20	273	29 42	299
177	33 45	354	51 37	067	60 09	125	20 25	175	28 48	212	28 21	273	28 50	299
178	33 38	353	52 32	066	60 57	126	20 29	176	28 16	213	27 21	273	27 58	299
179	33 31	353	53 26	066	61 45	128	20 34	176	27 44	213	26 21	273	27 05	298

LAT 6°N

LHA ♈	Hc	Zn	Hc	Zn	Hc	Zn	Hc	Zn	Hc	Zn	Hc	Zn	Hc	Zn
	◆ ARCTURUS		ANTARES		RIGIL KENT		◆ ACRUX		Suhail		◆ REGULUS		Dubhe	
180	54 20	065	17 02	120	16 10	161	20 37	177	27 11	214	62 01	284	33 23	352
181	55 15	065	17 54	120	16 29	161	20 40	177	26 38	214	61 03	284	33 15	352
182	56 08	064	18 45	121	16 48	162	20 43	178	26 04	215	60 05	283	33 06	351
183	57 02	064	19 36	121	17 07	162	20 45	178	25 30	215	59 07	283	32 56	351
184	57 55	063	20 27	121	17 25	162	20 47	179	24 55	216	58 09	283	32 46	350
185	58 49	062	21 18	121	17 42	163	20 48	179	24 20	216	57 11	283	32 36	350
186	59 41	062	22 09	122	18 00	163	20 49	180	23 45	217	56 13	282	32 24	349
187	60 34	061	23 00	122	18 17	164	20 49	180	23 09	217	55 14	282	32 13	348
188	61 26	060	23 50	122	18 33	164	20 49	181	22 33	218	54 16	282	32 01	348
189	62 17	059	24 41	123	18 49	165	20 48	181	21 56	218	53 18	282	31 48	347
190	63 09	059	25 31	123	19 05	165	20 47	182	21 19	218	52 19	282	31 35	347
191	63 59	058	26 21	124	19 20	165	20 45	182	20 42	219	51 21	282	31 21	347
192	64 49	057	27 10	124	19 35	166	20 42	182	20 05	219	50 22	281	31 07	346
193	65 39	056	28 00	124	19 49	166	20 40	183	19 27	220	49 24	281	30 52	346
194	66 28	054	28 49	125	20 03	167	20 36	183	18 49	220	48 25	281	30 37	345
	◆ Alphecca		Rasalhague		ANTARES		◆ RIGIL KENT		ACRUX		◆ REGULUS		Dubhe	
195	47 40	056	21 51	079	29 38	125	20 16	167	20 32	184	47 27	281	30 22	345
196	48 30	056	22 49	079	30 26	126	20 29	168	20 28	184	46 28	281	30 06	344
197	49 19	055	23 48	079	31 15	126	20 42	168	20 23	185	45 30	281	29 49	344
198	50 08	055	24 46	079	32 03	126	20 54	169	20 18	185	44 31	281	29 32	343
199	50 56	054	25 45	079	32 51	127	21 05	169	20 12	186	43 32	281	29 15	343
200	51 44	053	26 43	079	33 38	127	21 16	170	20 06	186	42 34	281	28 57	342
201	52 32	053	27 42	079	34 26	128	21 27	170	19 59	187	41 35	281	28 39	342
202	53 19	052	28 40	079	35 12	129	21 37	171	19 52	187	40 36	281	28 20	342
203	54 06	051	29 39	079	35 59	129	21 46	171	19 44	188	39 38	280	28 01	341
204	54 52	051	30 38	079	36 45	130	21 55	172	19 36	188	38 39	280	27 42	341
205	55 38	050	31 36	079	37 31	130	22 04	172	19 27	189	37 40	280	27 22	340
206	56 24	049	32 35	079	38 16	131	22 12	173	19 18	189	36 42	280	27 02	340
207	57 08	048	33 33	079	39 01	131	22 19	173	19 09	189	35 43	280	26 41	340
208	57 52	047	34 32	079	39 46	132	22 26	174	18 59	190	34 44	280	26 20	339
209	58 36	046	35 30	079	40 30	133	22 32	174	18 48	190	33 46	280	25 59	339
	◆ VEGA		Rasalhague		ANTARES		◆ RIGIL KENT		ACRUX		◆ REGULUS		Dubhe	
210	19 48	051	36 29	079	41 13	133	22 38	175	18 37	191	32 47	280	25 37	339
211	20 34	051	37 27	079	41 56	134	22 43	175	18 26	191	31 48	280	25 15	338
212	21 20	051	38 26	079	42 39	135	22 48	176	18 14	192	30 50	280	24 53	338
213	22 06	050	39 25	079	43 21	136	22 52	176	18 02	192	29 51	280	24 31	338
214	22 52	050	40 23	079	44 02	136	22 56	177	17 49	192	28 52	280	24 08	337
215	23 38	050	41 22	079	44 43	137	22 59	177	17 36	193	27 53	280	23 45	337
216	24 24	050	42 20	078	45 23	138	23 01	178	17 22	193	26 55	280	23 21	337
217	25 09	050	43 18	078	46 03	139	23 04	178	17 09	194	25 56	280	22 57	336
218	25 55	050	44 17	078	46 41	140	23 05	179	16 54	194	24 57	280	22 33	336
219	26 40	049	45 15	078	47 20	141	23 06	179	16 39	195	23 59	280	22 09	336
220	27 25	049	46 14	078	47 57	142	23 06	180	16 24	195	23 00	280	21 45	336
221	28 10	049	47 12	078	48 33	143	23 06	180	16 09	195	22 01	280	21 20	335
222	28 55	049	48 10	078	49 09	144	23 05	181	15 53	196	21 03	280	20 55	335
223	29 40	048	49 09	078	49 44	145	23 04	182	15 37	196	20 04	280	20 30	335
224	30 24	048	50 07	078	50 18	146	23 02	182	15 20	196	19 05	281	20 04	335
	VEGA		◆ ALTAIR		Nunki		ANTARES		RIGIL KENT		◆ SPICA		◆ Alkaid	
225	31 08	048	17 47	083	24 21	122	50 51	147	23 00	183	60 57	234	44 10	344
226	31 52	047	18 46	083	25 11	123	51 23	148	22 57	183	60 08	235	43 53	343
227	32 36	047	19 45	083	26 02	123	51 54	149	22 53	184	59 19	236	43 35	342
228	33 20	047	20 45	083	26 51	124	52 24	151	22 49	184	58 29	237	43 17	341
229	34 03	046	21 44	083	27 41	124	52 52	152	22 45	185	57 39	238	42 57	341
230	34 46	046	22 43	083	28 30	124	53 20	153	22 40	185	56 48	239	42 37	340
231	35 29	046	23 42	083	29 20	125	53 46	154	22 34	186	55 57	240	42 16	339
232	36 12	045	24 41	083	30 09	125	54 12	156	22 28	186	55 06	240	41 54	338
233	36 54	045	25 41	083	30 57	126	54 36	157	22 21	187	54 13	241	41 32	338
234	37 36	044	26 40	083	31 46	126	54 58	159	22 14	187	53 21	242	41 08	337
235	38 17	044	27 39	083	32 34	127	55 19	160	22 06	188	52 28	243	40 45	336
236	38 59	043	28 38	083	33 21	127	55 39	161	21 58	188	51 35	243	40 20	335
237	39 40	043	29 38	083	34 09	128	55 57	163	21 49	189	50 41	244	39 55	335
238	40 20	043	30 37	083	34 56	128	56 14	164	21 40	189	49 48	245	39 29	334
239	41 00	042	31 36	083	35 43	129	56 29	166	21 30	190	48 53	245	39 03	334
	VEGA		◆ ALTAIR		Nunki		◆ ANTARES		SPICA		◆ ARCTURUS		Alkaid	
240	41 40	041	32 35	083	36 29	129	56 43	168	47 59	246	61 35	300	38 36	333
241	42 19	041	33 35	083	37 15	130	56 55	169	47 05	246	60 43	299	38 09	332
242	42 58	040	34 34	083	38 01	130	57 05	171	46 10	247	59 50	298	37 41	332
243	43 36	040	35 33	083	38 46	131	57 14	172	45 15	247	58 58	298	37 12	331
244	44 14	039	36 32	083	39 31	132	57 21	174	44 20	248	58 05	297	36 44	331
245	44 51	038	37 32	083	40 16	132	57 26	176	43 24	248	57 11	296	36 14	330
246	45 28	038	38 31	083	41 00	133	57 30	177	42 29	249	56 18	296	35 44	330
247	46 04	037	39 30	083	41 43	134	57 32	179	41 33	249	55 24	295	35 14	329
248	46 40	036	40 29	083	42 26	134	57 32	181	40 37	250	54 30	295	34 43	329
249	47 15	035	41 29	083	43 08	135	57 30	182	39 41	250	53 36	294	34 12	328
250	47 49	035	42 28	083	43 50	136	57 27	184	38 45	250	52 41	294	33 40	328
251	48 23	034	43 27	083	44 31	137	57 22	186	37 49	251	51 46	293	33 08	327
252	48 56	033	44 27	083	45 12	138	57 15	187	36 52	251	50 52	293	32 35	327
253	49 28	032	45 26	083	45 52	138	57 07	189	35 56	251	49 57	293	32 02	326
254	49 59	031	46 25	083	46 31	139	56 57	191	34 59	252	49 02	292	31 29	326
	VEGA		◆ ALTAIR		Nunki		◆ ANTARES		SPICA		ARCTURUS		◆ Alkaid	
255	50 30	030	47 24	083	47 10	140	56 45	192	34 02	252	48 06	292	30 56	326
256	50 59	029	48 24	083	47 48	141	56 32	194	33 06	252	47 11	292	30 22	325
257	51 28	028	49 23	083	48 25	142	56 17	195	32 09	253	46 15	291	29 47	325
258	51 56	027	50 22	083	49 01	143	56 00	197	31 12	253	45 20	291	29 13	324
259	52 23	026	51 21	083	49 36	144	55 42	198	30 15	253	44 24	291	28 38	324
260	52 49	025	52 21	083	50 11	145	55 23	200	29 17	254	43 28	291	28 03	324
261	53 14	024	53 20	083	50 44	146	55 02	201	28 20	254	42 33	291	27 28	323
262	53 38	023	54 19	083	51 17	147	54 39	203	27 23	254	41 37	290	26 52	323
263	54 01	022	55 18	083	51 49	149	54 16	204	26 25	254	40 41	290	26 16	323
264	54 23	021	56 18	083	52 19	150	53 51	205	25 28	255	39 45	290	25 40	323
265	54 43	020	57 17	083	52 49	151	53 25	207	24 30	255	38 48	290	25 04	322
266	55 03	018	58 16	083	53 17	152	52 57	208	23 33	255	37 52	290	24 27	322
267	55 21	017	59 15	083	53 44	154	52 29	209	22 35	255	36 56	289	23 50	322
268	55 38	016	60 14	083	54 10	155	51 59	210	21 37	255	36 00	289	23 13	322
269	55 53	014	61 14	082	54 35	156	51 28	212	20 40	256	35 03	289	22 36	321

LHA ♈	Hc	Zn	Hc	Zn	Hc	Zn	Hc	Zn	Hc	Zn	Hc	Zn	Hc	Zn
	VEGA		◆ DENEB		Enif		◆ Nunki		Shaula		ANTARES		◆ ARCTURUS	
270	56 08	013	37 18	035	34 14	082	54 58	158	46 29	187	50 56	213	34 07	289
271	56 20	012	37 52	034	35 13	082	55 20	159	46 21	188	50 23	214	33 11	289
272	56 32	010	38 26	034	36 12	082	55 40	161	46 11	190	49 50	215	32 14	289
273	56 42	009	38 59	033	37 11	082	55 59	162	46 01	191	49 15	216	31 18	289
274	56 51	008	39 32	033	38 10	082	56 17	164	45 49	192	48 39	217	30 21	289
275	56 58	006	40 04	032	39 09	082	56 33	165	45 36	193	48 03	218	29 25	289
276	57 04	005	40 35	032	40 09	082	56 48	167	45 22	194	47 26	219	28 28	289
277	57 08	003	41 06	031	41 08	082	57 00	168	45 07	195	46 48	220	27 31	288
278	57 11	002	41 37	030	42 07	082	57 12	170	44 51	196	46 09	221	26 35	288
279	57 12	001	42 06	030	43 06	082	57 21	172	44 34	197	45 30	222	25 38	288
280	57 12	359	42 36	029	44 05	082	57 29	173	44 16	198	44 50	223	24 42	288
281	57 10	358	43 04	028	45 04	082	57 35	175	43 57	199	44 09	223	23 45	288
282	57 07	356	43 32	028	46 03	082	57 40	177	43 36	200	43 28	224	22 48	288
283	57 02	355	43 59	027	47 02	082	57 42	178	43 15	201	42 46	225	21 51	288
284	56 56	353	44 26	026	48 01	082	57 43	180	42 53	202	42 03	226	20 55	288
	DENEB		Alpheratz		◆ FOMALHAUT		Nunki		◆ ANTARES		Rasalhague		◆ VEGA	
285	44 52	025	14 00	061	22 43	126	57 43	182	41 20	226	68 12	289	56 48	352
286	45 17	024	14 53	061	23 31	126	57 40	183	40 37	227	67 15	288	56 39	351
287	45 41	024	15 45	061	24 19	126	57 36	185	39 53	228	66 18	288	56 29	349
288	46 05	023	16 37	061	25 07	127	57 30	187	39 09	228	65 21	287	56 17	348
289	46 28	022	17 30	061	25 55	127	57 22	188	38 24	229	64 24	287	56 04	346
290	46 49	021	18 22	061	26 42	127	57 13	190	37 38	230	63 27	286	55 49	345
291	47 10	020	19 14	061	27 30	128	57 02	192	36 53	230	62 30	286	55 33	344
292	47 31	019	20 06	061	28 17	128	56 49	193	36 07	231	61 32	285	55 16	343
293	47 50	018	20 59	061	29 03	129	56 35	195	35 20	231	60 35	285	54 57	341
294	48 08	017	21 51	061	29 50	129	56 19	196	34 33	232	59 37	285	54 38	340
295	48 25	016	22 43	061	30 36	130	56 01	198	33 46	232	58 39	284	54 17	339
296	48 42	015	23 35	061	31 22	130	55 42	199	32 59	233	57 41	284	53 55	338
297	48 57	014	24 27	061	32 07	131	55 22	201	32 11	233	56 43	284	53 32	337
298	49 12	013	25 19	060	32 52	131	55 00	202	31 23	234	55 45	284	53 07	335
299	49 25	012	26 11	060	33 37	132	54 37	204	30 34	234	54 47	283	52 42	334
	◆ DENEB		Alpheratz		◆ FOMALHAUT		Peacock		◆ ANTARES		Rasalhague		VEGA	
300	49 37	011	27 03	060	34 21	132	27 04	176	29 46	235	53 49	283	52 16	333
301	49 49	010	27 55	060	35 05	133	27 08	176	28 57	235	52 51	283	51 49	332
302	49 59	009	28 46	060	35 49	133	27 12	177	28 08	236	51 53	283	51 20	331
303	50 08	008	29 38	060	36 32	134	27 14	178	27 18	236	50 55	283	50 51	330
304	50 16	007	30 29	060	37 15	135	27 17	178	26 29	236	49 56	282	50 21	329
305	50 23	006	31 21	059	37 57	135	27 18	179	25 39	237	48 58	282	49 51	328
306	50 28	005	32 12	059	38 39	136	27 19	180	24 49	237	48 00	282	49 19	328
307	50 33	004	33 03	059	39 20	137	27 19	180	23 59	238	47 01	282	48 47	327
308	50 36	003	33 54	059	40 01	137	27 18	181	23 08	238	46 03	282	48 13	326
309	50 39	002	34 45	058	40 41	138	27 17	181	22 18	238	45 05	282	47 40	325
310	50 40	001	35 36	058	41 20	139	27 15	182	21 27	238	44 06	282	47 05	324
311	50 40	359	36 26	058	41 59	140	27 13	183	20 36	239	43 08	282	46 30	324
312	50 39	358	37 17	058	42 38	140	27 10	183	19 45	239	42 09	282	45 54	323
313	50 36	357	38 07	057	43 15	141	27 06	184	18 54	239	41 11	281	45 18	322
314	50 33	356	38 57	057	43 52	142	27 02	184	18 02	240	40 12	281	44 41	321
	Alpheratz		◆ Diphda		FOMALHAUT		◆ Nunki		Rasalhague		VEGA		◆ DENEB	
315	39 47	057	29 44	115	44 29	143	45 56	222	39 14	281	44 04	321	50 28	355
316	40 37	056	30 38	115	45 04	144	45 16	222	38 15	281	43 26	320	50 22	354
317	41 26	056	31 32	115	45 39	145	44 35	223	37 17	281	42 47	320	50 16	353
318	42 16	055	32 26	116	46 13	146	43 54	224	36 18	281	42 08	319	50 08	352
319	43 05	055	33 20	116	46 46	147	43 12	225	35 20	281	41 29	318	49 58	351
320	43 54	055	34 13	116	47 19	148	42 30	226	34 21	281	40 49	318	49 48	350
321	44 42	054	35 06	117	47 50	149	41 47	226	33 22	281	40 09	317	49 37	349
322	45 30	054	35 59	117	48 21	150	41 04	227	32 24	281	39 28	317	49 25	348
323	46 18	053	36 52	118	48 50	151	40 20	228	31 25	281	38 47	316	49 11	347
324	47 06	053	37 45	118	49 19	152	39 36	228	30 27	281	38 06	316	48 57	346
325	47 53	052	38 38	119	49 46	153	38 51	229	29 28	281	37 24	315	48 41	345
326	48 40	051	39 30	119	50 13	154	38 06	230	28 30	281	36 42	315	48 25	344
327	49 26	051	40 22	120	50 38	155	37 20	230	27 31	281	36 00	315	48 08	343
328	50 13	050	41 14	120	51 02	157	36 34	231	26 33	281	35 17	314	47 49	342
329	50 58	050	42 05	121	51 25	158	35 47	231	25 34	281	34 34	314	47 30	341
	◆ Alpheratz		Diphda		◆ FOMALHAUT		Peacock		ALTAIR		◆ VEGA		DENEB	
330	51 43	049	42 56	121	51 47	159	24 29	194	58 02	277	33 51	313	47 10	340
331	52 28	048	43 47	122	52 08	161	24 14	194	57 03	277	33 08	313	46 49	339
332	53 12	047	44 37	123	52 27	162	23 59	195	56 03	277	32 24	313	46 27	338
333	53 56	047	45 27	123	52 45	163	23 44	195	55 04	277	31 40	312	46 04	337
334	54 39	046	46 17	124	53 01	165	23 27	196	54 05	277	30 56	312	45 41	336
335	55 21	045	47 07	125	53 17	166	23 11	196	53 06	277	30 12	312	45 16	336
336	56 03	044	47 55	125	53 30	167	22 54	197	52 06	277	29 27	312	44 51	335
337	56 44	043	48 44	126	53 43	169	22 36	197	51 07	277	28 43	311	44 25	334
338	57 24	042	49 32	127	53 54	170	22 18	198	50 08	277	27 58	311	43 59	333
339	58 03	041	50 19	128	54 03	172	21 59	198	49 09	277	27 13	311	43 31	332
340	58 42	040	51 06	129	54 11	173	21 40	199	48 09	277	26 27	311	43 03	332
341	59 19	038	51 53	129	54 17	175	21 20	199	47 10	277	25 42	310	42 35	331
342	59 56	037	52 39	130	54 22	176	21 00	200	46 11	277	24 57	310	42 06	330
343	60 31	036	53 24	131	54 25	178	20 40	200	45 11	277	24 11	310	41 36	330
344	61 06	035	54 08	132	54 27	179	20 19	201	44 12	277	23 25	310	41 05	329
	◆ Mirfak		Hamal		Acamar		◆ ACHERNAR		FOMALHAUT		◆ ALTAIR		DENEB	
345	19 41	039	41 34	064	18 23	136	19 09	159	54 27	181	43 13	277	40 34	328
346	20 18	039	42 28	063	19 04	136	19 30	159	54 26	182	42 14	277	40 03	328
347	20 56	038	43 21	063	19 45	137	19 51	159	54 23	184	41 14	277	39 31	327
348	21 33	038	44 14	063	20 26	137	20 12	160	54 19	185	40 15	277	38 58	327
349	22 09	038	45 07	062	21 07	137	20 32	160	54 13	187	39 16	277	38 25	326
350	22 46	038	46 00	062	21 47	138	20 52	161	54 05	188	38 17	277	37 51	325
351	23 23	038	46 52	062	22 27	138	21 12	161	53 56	189	37 17	277	37 17	325
352	23 59	037	47 45	061	23 06	139	21 31	162	53 45	191	36 18	277	36 43	324
353	24 35	037	48 37	061	23 45	139	21 49	162	53 33	192	35 19	277	36 08	324
354	25 11	037	49 29	060	24 24	140	22 07	163	53 20	194	34 19	277	35 33	323
355	25 46	037	50 21	060	25 03	140	22 25	163	53 05	195	33 20	277	34 57	323
356	26 22	036	51 12	059	25 41	140	22 42	164	52 49	197	32 21	277	34 21	323
357	26 57	036	52 03	059	26 19	141	22 58	164	52 31	198	31 22	277	33 45	322
358	27 32	036	52 54	058	26 56	141	23 14	165	52 12	199	30 22	277	33 08	322
359	28 07	035	53 45	058	27 33	142	23 30	165	51 52	200	29 23	277	32 31	321

LAT 5°N

LHA ♈	Hc	Zn	Hc	Zn	Hc	Zn	Hc	Zn	Hc	Zn	Hc	Zn	Hc	Zn
	◆ CAPELLA		ALDEBARAN		RIGEL		◆ ACHERNAR		FOMALHAUT		◆ ALTAIR		DENEB	
0	10 55	044	21 21	074	10 18	099	24 43	166	52 26	202	28 16	277	31 07	321
1	11 37	044	22 18	074	11 17	099	24 57	166	52 03	204	27 17	277	30 29	321
2	12 18	044	23 16	074	12 16	100	25 11	167	51 38	205	26 18	277	29 51	321
3	12 59	044	24 13	074	13 15	100	25 25	167	51 13	206	25 19	278	29 13	320
4	13 41	044	25 11	074	14 14	100	25 38	168	50 46	207	24 19	278	28 35	320
5	14 22	044	26 08	074	15 13	100	25 50	168	50 18	208	23 20	278	27 56	320
6	15 03	044	27 06	074	16 12	100	26 02	169	49 49	209	22 21	278	27 17	319
7	15 45	043	28 03	074	17 11	100	26 13	169	49 20	211	21 22	278	26 38	319
8	16 26	043	29 01	074	18 09	100	26 24	170	48 49	212	20 22	278	25 59	319
9	17 07	043	29 58	074	19 08	100	26 34	171	48 17	213	19 23	278	25 19	318
10	17 48	043	30 55	074	20 07	101	26 43	171	47 44	214	18 24	278	24 40	318
11	18 28	043	31 53	074	21 06	101	26 52	172	47 11	215	17 25	278	24 00	318
12	19 09	043	32 50	074	22 04	101	27 00	172	46 36	216	16 26	278	23 20	318
13	19 49	043	33 47	073	23 03	101	27 08	173	46 01	217	15 26	278	22 39	317
14	20 30	042	34 45	073	24 02	101	27 15	174	45 25	217	14 27	278	21 59	317
	CAPELLA		◆ ALDEBARAN		RIGEL		◆ ACHERNAR		FOMALHAUT		Enif		◆ DENEB	
15	21 10	042	35 42	073	25 00	101	27 21	174	44 48	218	41 26	279	21 18	317
16	21 50	042	36 39	073	25 59	102	27 27	175	44 11	219	40 27	279	20 37	317
17	22 30	042	37 36	073	26 57	102	27 32	175	43 33	220	39 28	279	19 57	317
18	23 10	042	38 33	073	27 56	102	27 37	176	42 54	221	38 29	279	19 15	317
19	23 49	041	39 30	073	28 54	102	27 40	177	42 15	222	37 30	279	18 34	316
20	24 29	041	40 27	072	29 53	102	27 44	177	41 35	222	36 31	279	17 53	316
21	25 08	041	41 24	072	30 51	103	27 46	178	40 54	223	35 32	279	17 12	316
22	25 47	041	42 21	072	31 49	103	27 48	178	40 13	224	34 33	279	16 30	316
23	26 26	040	43 18	072	32 48	103	27 50	179	39 32	224	33 33	279	15 48	316
24	27 04	040	44 15	072	33 46	103	27 50	180	38 49	225	32 34	279	15 07	316
25	27 42	040	45 12	071	34 44	104	27 50	180	38 07	226	31 35	279	14 25	316
26	28 21	039	46 08	071	35 42	104	27 50	181	37 24	226	30 36	279	13 43	316
27	28 58	039	47 05	071	36 40	104	27 48	181	36 40	227	29 37	279	13 01	315
28	29 36	039	48 01	071	37 38	104	27 47	182	35 56	228	28 38	279	12 19	315
29	30 13	038	48 58	070	38 36	105	27 44	183	35 12	228	27 39	279	11 37	315
	Mirfak		CAPELLA		◆ ALDEBARAN		RIGEL		◆ ACHERNAR		FOMALHAUT		◆ Alpheratz	
30	41 37	018	30 50	038	49 54	070	39 34	105	27 41	183	34 27	229	54 21	316
31	41 55	018	31 26	038	50 50	070	40 31	105	27 37	184	33 42	229	53 39	315
32	42 13	017	32 03	037	51 46	069	41 29	106	27 33	185	32 57	230	52 56	314
33	42 30	016	32 39	037	52 42	069	42 27	106	27 28	185	32 11	230	52 13	313
34	42 46	015	33 14	036	53 38	069	43 24	106	27 22	186	31 25	231	51 29	313
35	43 01	014	33 49	036	54 33	068	44 21	107	27 16	186	30 39	231	50 45	312
36	43 16	014	34 24	035	55 29	068	45 19	107	27 09	187	29 52	232	50 00	311
37	43 29	013	34 58	035	56 24	067	46 16	107	27 01	188	29 05	232	49 15	310
38	43 42	012	35 32	034	57 19	067	47 13	108	26 53	188	28 18	232	48 29	310
39	43 54	011	36 06	034	58 14	066	48 09	108	26 44	189	27 30	233	47 43	309
40	44 05	010	36 39	033	59 09	066	49 06	109	26 35	189	26 42	233	46 56	309
41	44 15	009	37 12	033	60 03	065	50 03	109	26 25	190	25 54	234	46 09	308
42	44 24	008	37 44	032	60 57	064	50 59	110	26 15	190	25 06	234	45 22	307
43	44 32	008	38 16	032	61 51	064	51 55	110	26 03	191	24 18	234	44 35	307
44	44 40	007	38 47	031	62 44	063	52 51	111	25 52	192	23 29	235	43 47	306
	CAPELLA		◆ PROCYON		SIRIUS		CANOPUS		◆ ACHERNAR		Diphda		◆ Alpheratz	
45	39 17	031	20 18	086	30 08	113	18 03	150	25 39	192	49 27	235	42 58	306
46	39 47	030	21 17	086	31 03	113	18 33	151	25 27	193	48 38	236	42 10	306
47	40 17	029	22 17	086	31 58	113	19 02	151	25 13	193	47 49	236	41 21	305
48	40 46	029	23 17	086	32 53	114	19 31	151	24 59	194	46 59	237	40 32	305
49	41 14	028	24 16	087	33 48	114	19 59	152	24 45	194	46 09	238	39 43	304
50	41 42	027	25 16	087	34 42	114	20 27	152	24 30	195	45 18	238	38 53	304
51	42 09	027	26 16	087	35 37	115	20 55	153	24 14	195	44 27	239	38 04	304
52	42 35	026	27 15	087	36 31	115	21 22	153	23 58	196	43 36	239	37 14	303
53	43 01	025	28 15	087	37 25	116	21 49	154	23 42	196	42 44	240	36 24	303
54	43 26	024	29 15	087	38 19	116	22 15	154	23 24	197	41 52	240	35 33	303
55	43 50	023	30 14	087	39 13	116	22 41	154	23 07	197	41 00	241	34 43	302
56	44 13	023	31 14	087	40 06	117	23 07	155	22 49	198	40 08	241	33 52	302
57	44 36	022	32 14	087	40 59	117	23 32	155	22 30	198	39 15	242	33 02	302
58	44 58	021	33 13	087	41 52	118	23 57	156	22 11	199	38 22	242	32 11	302
59	45 19	020	34 13	087	42 45	118	24 21	156	21 52	199	37 29	243	31 20	301
	◆ CAPELLA		PROCYON		◆ SIRIUS		CANOPUS		ACHERNAR		◆ Diphda		Alpheratz	
60	45 39	019	35 13	087	43 37	119	24 45	157	21 32	200	36 36	243	30 29	301
61	45 58	018	36 13	087	44 30	119	25 08	157	21 11	200	35 42	244	29 37	301
62	46 17	018	37 12	087	45 22	120	25 31	158	20 50	201	34 49	244	28 46	301
63	46 34	017	38 12	087	46 13	121	25 53	158	20 29	201	33 55	244	27 54	300
64	46 51	016	39 12	087	47 04	121	26 15	159	20 07	202	33 01	245	27 03	300
65	47 07	015	40 11	087	47 55	122	26 36	160	19 45	202	32 07	245	26 11	300
66	47 21	014	41 11	087	48 46	123	26 56	160	19 23	202	31 12	246	25 20	300
67	47 35	013	42 11	088	49 36	123	27 16	161	19 00	203	30 18	246	24 28	300
68	47 48	012	43 10	088	50 26	124	27 36	161	18 36	203	29 23	246	23 36	300
69	48 00	011	44 10	088	51 15	125	27 55	162	18 13	204	28 28	247	22 44	300
70	48 11	010	45 10	088	52 04	126	28 13	162	17 49	204	27 33	247	21 52	299
71	48 20	009	46 10	088	52 52	126	28 31	163	17 24	204	26 38	247	21 00	299
72	48 29	008	47 09	088	53 40	127	28 48	164	16 59	205	25 43	247	20 08	299
73	48 36	007	48 09	088	54 27	128	29 05	164	16 34	205	24 48	248	19 16	299
74	48 43	006	49 09	088	55 14	129	29 21	165	16 09	205	23 53	248	18 23	299
	CAPELLA		◆ POLLUX		PROCYON		SIRIUS		◆ CANOPUS		Acamar		◆ Hamal	
75	48 48	005	44 22	055	50 09	088	56 00	130	29 36	165	36 53	209	44 39	298
76	48 53	004	45 10	055	51 08	088	56 45	131	29 51	166	36 24	210	43 47	298
77	48 56	003	45 59	054	52 08	088	57 30	132	30 05	167	35 54	210	42 54	298
78	48 58	002	46 47	053	53 08	088	58 13	134	30 18	167	35 24	211	42 01	297
79	48 59	000	47 35	053	54 08	088	58 56	135	30 31	168	34 53	212	41 08	297
80	48 59	359	48 23	052	55 07	088	59 38	136	30 43	169	34 21	212	40 14	297
81	48 58	358	49 10	052	56 07	088	60 19	137	30 54	169	33 49	213	39 21	297
82	48 56	357	49 56	051	57 07	088	60 59	139	31 05	170	33 16	214	38 28	296
83	48 52	356	50 43	050	58 06	088	61 37	140	31 14	171	32 43	214	37 34	296
84	48 48	355	51 29	050	59 06	088	62 15	142	31 24	171	32 09	215	36 40	296
85	48 42	354	52 14	049	60 06	088	62 51	144	31 32	172	31 35	215	35 46	296
86	48 36	353	52 59	048	61 06	088	63 26	145	31 40	173	31 00	216	34 52	295
87	48 28	352	53 43	047	62 05	088	63 59	147	31 47	174	30 25	217	33 58	295
88	48 19	351	54 27	047	63 05	088	64 31	149	31 53	174	29 49	217	33 04	295
89	48 09	350	55 10	046	64 05	088	65 01	151	31 59	175	29 12	218	32 10	295

LHA ♈	Hc	Zn	Hc	Zn	Hc	Zn	Hc	Zn	Hc	Zn	Hc	Zn	Hc	Zn
	POLLUX		◆ REGULUS		Suhail		◆ CANOPUS		Acamar		◆ ALDEBARAN		CAPELLA	
90	55 52	045	28 07	079	25 34	144	32 04	176	28 36	218	66 34	301	47 59	349
91	56 34	044	29 05	079	26 09	144	32 08	176	27 59	219	65 43	300	47 47	348
92	57 15	043	30 04	079	26 44	145	32 12	177	27 21	219	64 51	299	47 34	347
93	57 55	042	31 03	079	27 18	145	32 14	178	26 43	220	63 58	298	47 20	346
94	58 34	041	32 02	079	27 52	146	32 16	179	26 05	220	63 05	297	47 05	345
95	59 13	039	33 00	079	28 25	146	32 17	179	25 26	221	62 12	297	46 49	344
96	59 50	038	33 59	079	28 58	147	32 18	180	24 47	221	61 18	296	46 33	343
97	60 26	037	34 58	079	29 30	147	32 17	181	24 08	221	60 24	295	46 15	342
98	61 02	035	35 56	079	30 02	148	32 16	181	23 28	222	59 30	294	45 56	341
99	61 36	034	36 55	079	30 34	149	32 15	182	22 48	222	58 35	294	45 37	341
100	62 08	033	37 54	079	31 04	149	32 12	183	22 08	223	57 41	293	45 17	340
101	62 40	031	38 52	079	31 35	150	32 09	184	21 27	223	56 46	293	44 56	339
102	63 10	029	39 51	079	32 04	150	32 05	184	20 46	223	55 51	292	44 34	338
103	63 39	028	40 49	079	32 34	151	32 00	185	20 05	224	54 55	292	44 11	337
104	64 06	026	41 48	079	33 02	152	31 54	186	19 23	224	54 00	291	43 47	336
	POLLUX		◆ REGULUS		Suhail		◆ CANOPUS		RIGEL		◆ ALDEBARAN		CAPELLA	
105	64 31	024	42 47	078	33 30	152	31 48	186	60 45	243	53 04	291	43 23	336
106	64 55	022	43 45	078	33 57	153	31 41	187	59 51	244	52 08	291	42 58	335
107	65 17	021	44 44	078	34 24	154	31 33	188	58 57	245	51 12	290	42 32	334
108	65 37	019	45 42	078	34 50	155	31 25	188	58 03	246	50 16	290	42 06	333
109	65 55	017	46 41	078	35 16	155	31 16	189	57 08	246	49 20	290	41 39	333
110	66 11	014	47 39	078	35 40	156	31 06	190	56 13	247	48 23	289	41 11	332
111	66 25	012	48 37	078	36 04	157	30 55	190	55 18	248	47 27	289	40 43	331
112	66 36	010	49 36	078	36 28	157	30 44	191	54 22	248	46 30	289	40 14	331
113	66 46	008	50 34	077	36 50	158	30 32	192	53 27	249	45 34	289	39 44	330
114	66 53	006	51 32	077	37 12	159	30 20	192	52 31	250	44 37	288	39 14	329
115	66 58	004	52 31	077	37 33	160	30 07	193	51 35	250	43 40	288	38 44	329
116	67 00	001	53 29	077	37 53	161	29 53	194	50 38	251	42 44	288	38 12	328
117	67 00	359	54 27	077	38 13	161	29 38	194	49 42	251	41 47	288	37 41	328
118	66 58	357	55 25	076	38 31	162	29 23	195	48 45	252	40 50	288	37 09	327
119	66 54	354	56 23	076	38 49	163	29 07	196	47 48	252	39 53	287	36 36	327
	Dubhe		◆ Denebola		Suhail		◆ CANOPUS		SIRIUS		BETELGEUSE		◆ CAPELLA	
120	23 50	022	32 44	076	39 06	164	28 51	196	61 34	220	59 05	276	36 03	326
121	24 13	022	33 42	076	39 22	165	28 33	197	60 55	221	58 06	276	35 29	326
122	24 34	021	34 40	076	39 37	166	28 16	198	60 15	223	57 07	276	34 55	325
123	24 56	021	35 38	076	39 51	167	27 58	198	59 34	224	56 07	276	34 21	325
124	25 17	021	36 36	076	40 04	168	27 39	199	58 52	225	55 08	276	33 46	324
125	25 38	020	37 33	076	40 17	168	27 19	199	58 09	226	54 08	276	33 11	324
126	25 59	020	38 31	075	40 28	169	26 59	200	57 25	228	53 09	276	32 35	323
127	26 19	020	39 29	075	40 39	170	26 39	200	56 41	229	52 09	276	31 59	323
128	26 39	019	40 27	075	40 49	171	26 18	201	55 55	230	51 10	276	31 23	322
129	26 58	019	41 25	075	40 57	172	25 56	201	55 09	231	50 10	276	30 46	322
130	27 17	018	42 22	075	41 05	173	25 34	202	54 23	232	49 11	276	30 09	322
131	27 36	018	43 20	075	41 11	174	25 11	203	53 36	233	48 11	276	29 32	321
132	27 54	018	44 18	075	41 17	175	24 48	203	52 48	234	47 12	276	28 55	321
133	28 12	017	45 15	074	41 22	176	24 24	204	51 59	234	46 12	275	28 17	321
134	28 29	017	46 13	074	41 25	177	24 00	204	51 10	235	45 13	275	27 39	320
	Dubhe		◆ SPICA		ACRUX		◆ CANOPUS		SIRIUS		BETELGEUSE		◆ CAPELLA	
135	28 46	016	21 53	104	11 31	159	23 36	205	50 21	236	44 13	275	27 00	320
136	29 03	016	22 51	104	11 53	159	23 11	205	49 31	237	43 14	275	26 22	320
137	29 19	015	23 49	105	12 14	159	22 45	205	48 41	237	42 14	275	25 43	319
138	29 34	015	24 46	105	12 35	160	22 19	206	47 51	238	41 15	275	25 04	319
139	29 49	014	25 44	105	12 56	160	21 53	206	47 00	239	40 15	275	24 25	319
140	30 04	014	26 42	105	13 16	160	21 26	207	46 08	239	39 16	275	23 45	319
141	30 18	014	27 40	105	13 36	161	20 59	207	45 17	240	38 16	276	23 06	318
142	30 32	013	28 37	106	13 56	161	20 31	208	44 25	241	37 17	276	22 26	318
143	30 45	013	29 35	106	14 15	161	20 03	208	43 32	241	36 17	276	21 46	318
144	30 58	012	30 32	106	14 35	162	19 35	209	42 40	242	35 18	276	21 06	318
145	31 10	012	31 29	106	14 53	162	19 06	209	41 47	242	34 18	276	20 26	318
146	31 22	011	32 27	107	15 12	162	18 37	209	40 54	243	33 19	276	19 45	317
147	31 33	011	33 24	107	15 30	163	18 08	210	40 01	243	32 19	276	19 05	317
148	31 44	010	34 21	107	15 48	163	17 38	210	39 07	244	31 20	276	18 24	317
149	31 54	009	35 18	108	16 05	163	17 08	210	38 14	244	30 20	276	17 43	317
	◆ Dubhe		ARCTURUS		◆ SPICA		ACRUX		◆ SIRIUS		PROCYON		POLLUX	
150	32 04	009	26 06	071	36 15	108	16 22	164	37 20	245	55 10	272	50 48	310
151	32 13	008	27 02	071	37 12	108	16 39	164	36 26	245	54 10	272	50 02	309
152	32 21	008	27 59	071	38 09	109	16 55	164	35 32	245	53 10	272	49 15	308
153	32 29	007	28 55	071	39 05	109	17 11	165	34 37	246	52 11	272	48 28	308
154	32 36	007	29 52	071	40 02	109	17 27	165	33 43	246	51 11	272	47 41	307
155	32 43	006	30 48	071	40 58	110	17 42	166	32 48	246	50 11	272	46 53	307
156	32 49	006	31 45	071	41 54	110	17 56	166	31 53	247	49 11	272	46 05	306
157	32 55	005	32 41	070	42 50	110	18 11	166	30 58	247	48 12	272	45 16	306
158	33 00	005	33 37	070	43 46	111	18 25	167	30 03	247	47 12	272	44 27	305
159	33 05	004	34 34	070	44 42	111	18 38	167	29 08	248	46 12	272	43 38	305
160	33 09	003	35 30	070	45 38	112	18 51	168	28 13	248	45 13	272	42 49	304
161	33 12	003	36 26	070	46 33	112	19 04	168	27 17	248	44 13	272	41 59	304
162	33 15	002	37 22	070	47 29	113	19 16	168	26 21	249	43 13	272	41 09	303
163	33 17	002	38 18	070	48 24	113	19 28	169	25 26	249	42 13	272	40 19	303
164	33 18	001	39 14	069	49 18	114	19 39	169	24 30	249	41 14	273	39 29	303
	Dubhe		◆ ARCTURUS		SPICA		◆ ACRUX		Suhail		PROCYON		◆ POLLUX	
165	33 19	001	40 10	069	50 13	114	19 50	170	35 22	205	40 14	273	38 39	302
166	33 20	000	41 06	069	51 07	115	20 01	170	34 57	205	39 14	273	37 48	302
167	33 20	000	42 02	069	52 02	115	20 11	171	34 31	206	38 15	273	36 57	302
168	33 19	359	42 57	068	52 55	116	20 20	171	34 05	207	37 15	273	36 06	301
169	33 17	358	43 53	068	53 49	117	20 29	172	33 38	207	36 15	273	35 15	301
170	33 15	358	44 48	068	54 42	118	20 38	172	33 10	208	35 15	273	34 24	301
171	33 13	357	45 44	068	55 35	118	20 46	172	32 41	209	34 16	273	33 32	300
172	33 10	357	46 39	067	56 27	119	20 54	173	32 12	209	33 16	273	32 41	300
173	33 06	356	47 34	067	57 19	120	21 01	173	31 43	210	32 16	273	31 49	300
174	33 02	356	48 29	067	58 11	121	21 07	174	31 13	211	31 17	273	30 57	300
175	32 57	355	49 24	066	59 02	122	21 14	174	30 42	211	30 17	273	30 05	300
176	32 51	354	50 18	066	59 53	123	21 19	175	30 11	212	29 17	273	29 13	299
177	32 45	354	51 13	065	60 43	124	21 25	175	29 39	212	28 18	273	28 21	299
178	32 39	353	52 07	065	61 32	125	21 29	176	29 07	213	27 18	273	27 29	299
179	32 31	353	53 01	065	62 21	126	21 33	176	28 34	213	26 18	273	26 36	299

 LAT 5°N

LHA ♈	Hc	Zn	Hc	Zn	Hc	Zn	Hc	Zn	Hc	Zn	Hc	Zn	Hc	Zn
	◆ARCTURUS		ANTARES		RIGIL KENT		◆ACRUX		Suhail		◆REGULUS		Dubhe	
180	53 55	064	17 32	120	17 06	161	21 37	177	28 01	214	61 46	286	32 24	352
181	54 48	064	18 24	120	17 26	161	21 40	177	27 27	215	60 48	286	32 15	352
182	55 42	063	19 15	120	17 45	162	21 43	178	26 53	215	59 51	285	32 06	351
183	56 35	062	20 07	121	18 04	162	21 45	178	26 19	216	58 53	285	31 57	351
184	57 28	062	20 58	121	18 22	162	21 47	179	25 44	216	57 55	284	31 47	350
185	58 20	061	21 50	121	18 40	163	21 48	179	25 09	216	56 57	284	31 37	350
186	59 12	060	22 41	121	18 57	163	21 49	180	24 33	217	55 59	284	31 26	349
187	60 04	060	23 32	122	19 14	164	21 49	180	23 57	217	55 01	284	31 14	349
188	60 55	059	24 22	122	19 31	164	21 49	181	23 20	218	54 03	283	31 02	348
189	61 46	058	25 13	122	19 47	164	21 48	181	22 43	218	53 05	283	30 49	348
190	62 37	057	26 03	123	20 03	165	21 47	182	22 06	219	52 07	283	30 36	347
191	63 26	056	26 54	123	20 18	165	21 45	182	21 29	219	51 08	283	30 23	347
192	64 16	055	27 43	123	20 33	166	21 42	182	20 51	219	50 10	283	30 09	346
193	65 04	054	28 33	124	20 48	166	21 40	183	20 13	220	49 12	282	29 54	346
194	65 52	053	29 23	124	21 01	167	21 36	183	19 35	220	48 13	282	29 39	345
	◆Alphecca		Rasalhague		ANTARES		◆RIGIL KENT		ACRUX		◆REGULUS		Dubhe	
195	47 06	055	21 39	078	30 12	125	21 15	167	21 32	184	47 15	282	29 24	345
196	47 55	055	22 37	078	31 01	125	21 28	168	21 28	184	46 16	282	29 08	344
197	48 44	054	23 36	078	31 50	126	21 41	168	21 23	185	45 18	282	28 51	344
198	49 33	054	24 34	078	32 38	126	21 53	169	21 18	185	44 19	282	28 35	343
199	50 20	053	25 33	078	33 27	126	22 04	169	21 12	186	43 21	282	28 17	343
200	51 08	052	26 32	078	34 15	127	22 15	170	21 06	186	42 22	282	28 00	343
201	51 55	052	27 30	078	35 02	127	22 26	170	20 59	187	41 24	281	27 42	342
202	52 42	051	28 29	078	35 50	128	22 36	171	20 52	187	40 25	281	27 23	342
203	53 28	050	29 27	078	36 37	128	22 45	171	20 44	188	39 26	281	27 04	341
204	54 14	050	30 26	078	37 23	129	22 54	172	20 35	188	38 28	281	26 45	341
205	54 59	049	31 24	078	38 09	130	23 03	172	20 27	189	37 29	281	26 25	341
206	55 44	048	32 23	078	38 55	130	23 11	173	20 18	189	36 31	281	26 05	340
207	56 28	047	33 21	078	39 41	131	23 18	173	20 08	190	35 32	281	25 45	340
208	57 11	046	34 20	078	40 26	131	23 25	174	19 58	190	34 33	281	25 24	339
209	57 54	045	35 18	078	41 10	132	23 32	174	19 47	190	33 35	281	25 03	339
	◆VEGA		Rasalhague		ANTARES		◆RIGIL KENT		ACRUX		◆REGULUS		Dubhe	
210	19 10	051	36 17	078	41 54	133	23 38	175	19 36	191	32 36	281	24 41	339
211	19 56	050	37 15	078	42 38	134	23 43	175	19 25	191	31 37	281	24 20	338
212	20 42	050	38 14	078	43 21	134	23 48	176	19 13	192	30 39	281	23 57	338
213	21 28	050	39 12	078	44 04	135	23 52	176	19 00	192	29 40	281	23 35	338
214	22 14	050	40 11	078	44 45	136	23 56	177	18 48	193	28 41	281	23 12	337
215	22 59	050	41 09	078	45 27	137	23 59	177	18 34	193	27 42	281	22 49	337
216	23 45	050	42 08	078	46 08	137	24 01	178	18 21	193	26 44	281	22 26	337
217	24 30	049	43 06	077	46 48	138	24 03	178	18 07	194	25 45	281	22 02	337
218	25 16	049	44 04	077	47 27	139	24 05	179	17 52	194	24 46	281	21 39	336
219	26 01	049	45 03	077	48 06	140	24 06	179	17 38	195	23 48	281	21 14	336
220	26 46	049	46 01	077	48 44	141	24 06	180	17 22	195	22 49	281	20 50	336
221	27 30	048	46 59	077	49 21	142	24 06	180	17 07	195	21 50	281	20 25	336
222	28 15	048	47 57	077	49 57	143	24 05	181	16 51	196	20 51	281	20 01	335
223	29 00	048	48 55	077	50 33	144	24 04	182	16 34	196	19 53	281	19 35	335
224	29 44	048	49 54	076	51 07	145	24 02	182	16 17	196	18 54	281	19 10	335
	VEGA		ALTAIR		◆Nunki		ANTARES		RIGIL KENT		◆SPICA		Alkaid	
225	30 28	047	17 39	082	24 53	122	51 41	146	24 00	183	61 32	235	43 13	344
226	31 12	047	18 38	082	25 44	122	52 14	147	23 57	183	60 42	236	42 56	343
227	31 55	047	19 38	082	26 34	123	52 45	149	23 53	184	59 52	237	42 38	342
228	32 39	046	20 37	082	27 24	123	53 16	150	23 49	184	59 02	238	42 20	342
229	33 22	046	21 36	082	28 14	123	53 45	151	23 45	185	58 11	239	42 00	341
230	34 04	046	22 35	082	29 04	124	54 13	152	23 39	185	57 19	240	41 40	340
231	34 47	045	23 35	082	29 54	124	54 40	154	23 34	186	56 27	241	41 20	339
232	35 29	045	24 34	082	30 43	125	55 06	155	23 28	186	55 35	242	40 58	339
233	36 11	044	25 33	083	31 32	125	55 31	157	23 21	187	54 42	242	40 36	338
234	36 53	044	26 32	083	32 21	126	55 54	158	23 13	187	53 49	243	40 13	337
235	37 34	043	27 32	083	33 09	126	56 15	159	23 06	188	52 55	244	39 50	337
236	38 15	043	28 31	083	33 57	126	56 36	161	22 57	188	52 01	245	39 25	336
237	38 55	042	29 30	083	34 45	127	56 55	162	22 48	189	51 07	245	39 01	335
238	39 36	042	30 29	083	35 33	127	57 12	164	22 39	189	50 13	246	38 35	335
239	40 15	041	31 29	083	36 20	128	57 27	166	22 29	190	49 18	246	38 09	334
	VEGA		◆ALTAIR		Nunki		◆ANTARES		SPICA		◆ARCTURUS		Alkaid	
240	40 55	041	32 28	083	37 07	129	57 41	167	48 23	247	61 04	301	37 43	333
241	41 34	040	33 27	083	37 54	129	57 54	169	47 28	247	60 13	301	37 16	333
242	42 12	040	34 27	083	38 40	130	58 04	171	46 33	248	59 21	300	36 48	332
243	42 50	039	35 26	083	39 25	130	58 13	172	45 37	248	58 29	299	36 20	332
244	43 27	038	36 25	083	40 11	131	58 21	174	44 42	249	57 37	298	35 51	331
245	44 04	038	37 24	083	40 56	132	58 26	176	43 46	249	56 44	298	35 22	330
246	44 40	037	38 24	083	41 40	132	58 30	177	42 50	250	55 51	297	34 52	330
247	45 16	036	39 23	083	42 24	133	58 32	179	41 54	250	54 58	297	34 22	329
248	45 51	036	40 22	083	43 08	134	58 32	181	40 58	250	54 04	296	33 51	329
249	46 26	035	41 21	083	43 51	134	58 30	182	40 01	251	53 10	296	33 20	328
250	47 00	034	42 21	082	44 33	135	58 27	184	39 05	251	52 16	295	32 49	328
251	47 33	033	43 20	082	45 15	136	58 22	186	38 08	251	51 22	295	32 17	328
252	48 05	032	44 19	082	45 56	137	58 15	188	37 11	252	50 28	294	31 45	327
253	48 37	032	45 18	082	46 37	138	58 06	189	36 15	252	49 33	294	31 12	327
254	49 08	031	46 18	082	47 16	139	57 56	191	35 18	252	48 38	293	30 39	326
	◆VEGA		ALTAIR		◆Nunki		ANTARES		◆SPICA		ARCTURUS		Alkaid	
255	49 38	030	47 17	082	47 56	139	57 44	192	34 21	253	47 43	293	30 06	326
256	50 07	029	48 16	082	48 34	140	57 30	194	33 24	253	46 48	293	29 32	326
257	50 35	028	49 15	082	49 12	141	57 14	196	32 26	253	45 53	292	28 58	325
258	51 03	027	50 15	082	49 49	142	56 57	197	31 29	254	44 58	292	28 24	325
259	51 29	026	51 14	082	50 25	143	56 39	199	30 32	254	44 02	292	27 49	324
260	51 55	025	52 13	082	51 00	145	56 19	200	29 34	254	43 07	292	27 15	324
261	52 19	024	53 12	082	51 34	146	55 57	202	28 37	254	42 11	291	26 39	324
262	52 43	023	54 11	082	52 07	147	55 35	203	27 39	255	41 15	291	26 04	323
263	53 05	021	55 10	082	52 40	148	55 10	205	26 41	255	40 20	291	25 28	323
264	53 27	020	56 09	081	53 11	149	54 45	206	25 44	255	39 24	291	24 52	323
265	53 47	019	57 09	081	53 41	150	54 18	207	24 46	255	38 28	290	24 16	323
266	54 06	018	58 08	081	54 10	152	53 50	209	23 48	255	37 32	290	23 40	322
267	54 23	017	59 07	081	54 38	153	53 21	210	22 50	256	36 36	290	23 03	322
268	54 40	015	60 06	081	55 04	154	52 50	211	21 52	256	35 40	290	22 26	322
269	54 55	014	61 05	081	55 29	156	52 19	212	20 54	256	34 43	290	21 49	322

LHA ♈	Hc	Zn	Hc	Zn	Hc	Zn	Hc	Zn	Hc	Zn	Hc	Zn	Hc	Zn
	VEGA		◆DENEB		FOMALHAUT		◆Peacock		Shaula		ANTARES		◆ARCTURUS	
270	55 09	013	36 29	035	10 46	121	21 27	159	47 28	187	51 46	213	33 47	290
271	55 22	012	37 03	034	11 37	122	21 48	160	47 20	189	51 13	215	32 51	290
272	55 33	010	37 36	034	12 28	122	22 09	160	47 10	190	50 39	216	31 54	289
273	55 43	009	38 09	033	13 19	122	22 29	161	47 00	191	50 03	217	30 58	289
274	55 51	007	38 41	032	14 10	122	22 48	161	46 48	192	49 27	218	30 02	289
275	55 58	006	39 13	032	15 00	122	23 07	162	46 35	193	48 50	219	29 05	289
276	56 04	005	39 44	031	15 51	123	23 26	162	46 20	194	48 12	220	28 09	289
277	56 08	003	40 15	031	16 41	123	23 44	163	46 05	195	47 34	221	27 12	289
278	56 11	002	40 45	030	17 31	123	24 01	163	45 49	196	46 54	222	26 16	289
279	56 12	001	41 14	029	18 21	123	24 18	164	45 31	198	46 14	222	25 19	289
280	56 12	359	41 43	029	19 11	124	24 35	164	45 13	199	45 34	223	24 22	289
281	56 10	358	42 11	028	20 00	124	24 51	165	44 53	200	44 52	224	23 26	289
282	56 07	356	42 39	027	20 50	124	25 06	165	44 33	201	44 10	225	22 29	289
283	56 02	355	43 06	026	21 39	125	25 21	166	44 11	202	43 28	226	21 33	289
284	55 56	354	43 32	026	22 28	125	25 35	166	43 49	203	42 45	226	20 36	289
	DENEB		Alpheratz		◆FOMALHAUT		Peacock		◆ANTARES		Rasalhague		◆VEGA	
285	43 57	025	13 31	061	23 17	125	25 49	167	42 02	227	67 51	291	55 49	352
286	44 22	024	14 24	061	24 06	126	26 02	168	41 18	228	66 55	291	55 40	351
287	44 46	023	15 16	061	24 55	126	26 15	168	40 33	228	65 59	290	55 30	349
288	45 09	022	16 08	061	25 43	126	26 27	169	39 48	229	65 03	289	55 18	348
289	45 32	022	17 01	061	26 31	127	26 38	169	39 03	230	64 06	289	55 05	347
290	45 53	021	17 53	061	27 19	127	26 49	170	38 17	230	63 09	288	54 51	346
291	46 14	020	18 45	061	28 06	127	27 00	170	37 31	231	62 12	288	54 35	344
292	46 34	019	19 37	061	28 54	128	27 09	171	36 44	231	61 15	287	54 19	343
293	46 53	018	20 29	061	29 41	128	27 18	172	35 57	232	60 18	287	54 01	342
294	47 11	017	21 22	061	30 27	129	27 27	172	35 10	232	59 21	286	53 41	341
295	47 28	016	22 14	060	31 14	129	27 35	173	34 22	233	58 23	286	53 21	339
296	47 44	015	23 06	060	32 00	130	27 42	173	33 35	233	57 26	286	52 59	338
297	47 59	014	23 58	060	32 46	130	27 48	174	32 46	234	56 28	285	52 36	337
298	48 13	013	24 49	060	33 32	131	27 54	175	31 58	234	55 31	285	52 13	336
299	48 26	012	25 41	060	34 17	131	28 00	175	31 09	235	54 33	285	51 48	335
	◆DENEB		Alpheratz		◆FOMALHAUT		Peacock		◆ANTARES		Rasalhague		VEGA	
300	48 38	011	26 33	060	35 01	132	28 04	176	30 20	235	53 35	284	51 22	334
301	48 50	010	27 24	060	35 46	132	28 08	176	29 31	236	52 37	284	50 55	333
302	48 59	009	28 16	059	36 30	133	28 12	177	28 41	236	51 39	284	50 28	332
303	49 08	008	29 07	059	37 13	133	28 14	178	27 52	236	50 41	284	49 59	331
304	49 16	007	29 59	059	37 57	134	28 16	178	27 02	237	49 43	284	49 30	330
305	49 23	006	30 50	059	38 39	135	28 18	179	26 12	237	48 45	283	48 59	329
306	49 29	005	31 41	059	39 22	135	28 19	180	25 21	238	47 47	283	48 28	328
307	49 33	004	32 32	058	40 03	136	28 19	180	24 31	238	46 48	283	47 56	327
308	49 36	003	33 23	058	40 44	137	28 18	181	23 40	238	45 50	283	47 24	327
309	49 39	002	34 13	058	41 25	137	28 17	181	22 49	239	44 52	283	46 50	326
310	49 40	001	35 04	058	42 05	138	28 15	182	21 58	239	43 53	283	46 16	325
311	49 40	359	35 54	057	42 45	139	28 13	183	21 07	239	42 55	283	45 42	324
312	49 39	358	36 44	057	43 24	140	28 10	183	20 15	239	41 57	282	45 06	323
313	49 36	357	37 34	057	44 02	141	28 06	184	19 24	240	40 58	282	44 30	323
314	49 33	356	38 24	056	44 39	141	28 02	185	18 32	240	40 00	282	43 54	322
	◆Alpheratz		◆FOMALHAUT		Peacock		Nunki		◆Rasalhague		VEGA		DENEB	
315	39 14	056	45 16	142	27 57	185	46 40	222	39 02	282	43 17	321	49 28	355
316	40 03	056	45 52	143	27 51	186	46 00	223	38 03	282	42 39	321	49 23	354
317	40 52	055	46 28	144	27 45	186	45 19	224	37 05	282	42 01	320	49 16	353
318	41 41	055	47 02	145	27 38	187	44 37	225	36 06	282	41 23	320	49 08	352
319	42 30	054	47 36	146	27 30	188	43 55	225	35 08	282	40 44	319	48 59	351
320	43 18	054	48 09	147	27 22	188	43 12	226	34 09	282	40 04	318	48 49	350
321	44 07	053	48 41	148	27 13	189	42 28	227	33 11	282	39 25	318	48 38	349
322	44 54	053	49 12	149	27 04	189	41 45	228	32 12	282	38 44	317	48 26	348
323	45 42	052	49 42	150	26 54	190	41 00	228	31 14	282	38 04	317	48 13	347
324	46 29	052	50 11	151	26 43	191	40 15	229	30 15	282	37 23	316	47 59	346
325	47 16	051	50 40	153	26 32	191	39 30	230	29 16	282	36 41	316	47 44	345
326	48 02	051	51 07	154	26 20	192	38 44	230	28 18	282	36 00	316	47 27	344
327	48 48	050	51 32	155	26 08	192	37 58	231	27 19	282	35 18	315	47 10	343
328	49 34	049	51 57	156	25 55	193	37 12	231	26 21	282	34 35	315	46 52	342
329	50 19	049	52 21	157	25 41	193	36 25	232	25 22	282	33 53	314	46 33	341
	◆Alpheratz		Diphda		◆FOMALHAUT		Peacock		◆ALTAIR		VEGA		DENEB	
330	51 03	048	43 27	121	52 43	159	25 27	194	57 53	279	33 10	314	46 13	340
331	51 48	047	44 18	121	53 04	160	25 12	194	56 54	279	32 27	314	45 53	339
332	52 31	046	45 09	122	53 24	161	24 57	195	55 55	279	31 43	313	45 31	338
333	53 14	046	46 00	122	53 42	163	24 41	196	54 56	278	31 00	313	45 09	338
334	53 56	045	46 50	123	53 59	164	24 25	196	53 57	278	30 16	313	44 46	337
335	54 38	044	47 40	124	54 15	166	24 08	197	52 58	278	29 32	312	44 22	336
336	55 19	043	48 30	124	54 29	167	23 51	197	51 59	278	28 47	312	43 57	335
337	55 59	042	49 19	125	54 42	168	23 33	198	50 59	278	28 03	312	43 31	334
338	56 39	041	50 08	126	54 53	170	23 15	198	50 00	278	27 18	312	43 05	334
339	57 17	040	50 56	127	55 02	171	22 56	199	49 01	278	26 33	311	42 38	333
340	57 55	039	51 43	128	55 10	173	22 37	199	48 02	278	25 48	311	42 11	332
341	58 32	037	52 31	128	55 17	174	22 17	200	47 03	278	25 03	311	41 42	331
342	59 08	036	53 17	129	55 22	176	21 57	200	46 03	278	24 18	311	41 13	331
343	59 43	035	54 03	130	55 25	178	21 36	200	45 04	278	23 32	310	40 44	330
344	60 16	034	54 48	131	55 27	179	21 15	201	44 05	278	22 47	310	40 14	329
	Alpheratz		◆Hamal		Acamar		◆ACHERNAR		FOMALHAUT		◆ALTAIR		DENEB	
345	60 49	032	41 07	063	19 06	136	20 04	158	55 27	181	43 06	278	39 43	329
346	61 20	031	42 00	063	19 48	136	20 26	159	55 26	182	42 06	277	39 12	328
347	61 50	029	42 53	062	20 29	136	20 47	159	55 23	184	41 07	277	38 40	328
348	62 18	028	43 46	062	21 10	137	21 08	160	55 18	185	40 08	277	38 08	327
349	62 45	026	44 39	062	21 51	137	21 29	160	55 12	187	39 08	277	37 35	326
350	63 10	024	45 31	061	22 31	138	21 49	161	55 04	188	38 09	277	37 02	326
351	63 34	023	46 23	061	23 11	138	22 09	161	54 55	190	37 10	277	36 28	325
352	63 56	021	47 15	060	23 51	138	22 28	162	54 44	191	36 11	277	35 54	325
353	64 17	019	48 07	060	24 31	139	22 46	162	54 32	193	35 11	277	35 19	324
354	64 35	017	48 59	059	25 10	139	23 04	163	54 18	194	34 12	277	34 44	324
355	64 52	015	49 50	059	25 49	140	23 22	163	54 03	195	33 13	277	34 09	323
356	65 06	013	50 41	058	26 27	140	23 39	164	53 46	197	32 14	277	33 33	323
357	65 19	011	51 32	058	27 05	141	23 56	164	53 28	198	31 14	277	32 57	323
358	65 29	009	52 22	057	27 43	141	24 12	165	53 09	200	30 15	277	32 21	322
359	65 38	007	53 12	056	28 20	142	24 28	165	52 48	201	29 16	277	31 44	322

LAT 4°N

LHA ♈	Hc	Zn	Hc	Zn	Hc	Zn	Hc	Zn	Hc	Zn	Hc	Zn	Hc	Zn
	Alpheratz		◆ Mirfak		ALDEBARAN		◆ ACHERNAR		FOMALHAUT		◆ ALTAIR		DENEB	
0	64 44	005	27 02	034	21 04	074	25 41	166	53 22	203	28 08	278	30 20	322
1	64 48	003	27 36	034	22 02	074	25 56	166	52 58	204	27 09	278	29 42	321
2	64 50	001	28 09	034	22 59	074	26 10	167	52 33	205	26 10	278	29 05	321
3	64 49	359	28 42	033	23 57	074	26 23	167	52 07	207	25 11	278	28 27	321
4	64 46	356	29 15	033	24 54	074	26 36	168	51 39	208	24 11	278	27 49	320
5	64 42	354	29 47	032	25 51	074	26 49	168	51 11	209	23 12	278	27 10	320
6	64 35	352	30 19	032	26 49	073	27 01	169	50 41	210	22 13	278	26 32	320
7	64 26	350	30 51	032	27 46	073	27 12	169	50 11	211	21 14	278	25 53	319
8	64 15	348	31 22	031	28 44	073	27 23	170	49 40	212	20 14	278	25 14	319
9	64 02	347	31 53	031	29 41	073	27 33	171	49 07	213	19 15	278	24 34	319
10	63 47	345	32 23	030	30 38	073	27 42	171	48 34	214	18 16	278	23 55	318
11	63 30	343	32 53	030	31 35	073	27 51	172	48 00	215	17 16	278	23 15	318
12	63 12	341	33 22	029	32 33	073	28 00	172	47 25	216	16 17	278	22 35	318
13	62 51	339	33 51	029	33 30	073	28 07	173	46 49	217	15 18	278	21 55	318
14	62 29	337	34 20	028	34 27	073	28 14	174	46 12	218	14 19	278	21 15	318
	CAPELLA		ALDEBARAN		◆ RIGEL		ACHERNAR		◆ FOMALHAUT		Enif		◆ Alpheratz	
15	20 26	042	35 24	073	25 12	101	28 21	174	45 35	219	41 16	280	62 05	336
16	21 06	042	36 21	072	26 11	101	28 27	175	44 57	220	40 17	280	61 40	334
17	21 45	042	37 18	072	27 09	101	28 32	175	44 19	221	39 18	280	61 13	333
18	22 25	041	38 15	072	28 08	101	28 36	176	43 39	221	38 19	280	60 45	331
19	23 04	041	39 12	072	29 07	102	28 40	177	42 59	222	37 20	279	60 15	330
20	23 43	041	40 09	072	30 05	102	28 44	177	42 19	223	36 21	279	59 44	328
21	24 22	041	41 06	071	31 04	102	28 46	178	41 38	224	35 22	279	59 12	327
22	25 01	040	42 02	071	32 02	102	28 48	178	40 56	224	34 23	279	58 39	326
23	25 40	040	42 59	071	33 01	102	28 50	179	40 14	225	33 24	279	58 05	324
24	26 18	040	43 56	071	33 59	103	28 50	180	39 32	226	32 25	279	57 29	323
25	26 56	039	44 52	071	34 58	103	28 50	180	38 48	226	31 26	279	56 53	322
26	27 34	039	45 49	070	35 56	103	28 50	181	38 05	227	30 27	279	56 15	321
27	28 12	039	46 45	070	36 54	103	28 48	182	37 21	228	29 28	279	55 37	320
28	28 49	038	47 41	070	37 52	104	28 47	182	36 37	228	28 29	279	54 58	319
29	29 26	038	48 37	069	38 51	104	28 44	183	35 52	229	27 30	279	54 18	318
	Mirfak		CAPELLA		◆ ALDEBARAN		RIGEL		◆ ACHERNAR		FOMALHAUT		◆ Alpheratz	
30	40 40	018	30 02	038	49 33	069	39 49	104	28 41	183	35 07	229	53 37	317
31	40 58	017	30 39	037	50 29	069	40 47	104	28 37	184	34 21	230	52 56	316
32	41 16	016	31 15	037	51 25	068	41 45	105	28 33	185	33 35	230	52 14	315
33	41 32	016	31 50	036	52 20	068	42 43	105	28 27	185	32 49	231	51 32	314
34	41 48	015	32 26	036	53 15	067	43 40	105	28 22	186	32 03	231	50 48	313
35	42 03	014	33 01	035	54 11	067	44 38	106	28 15	186	31 16	232	50 05	313
36	42 17	013	33 35	035	55 06	067	45 36	106	28 08	187	30 29	232	49 20	312
37	42 31	013	34 09	035	56 00	066	46 33	106	28 01	188	29 42	232	48 36	311
38	42 43	012	34 43	034	56 55	065	47 30	107	27 53	188	28 54	233	47 50	311
39	42 55	011	35 16	033	57 49	065	48 28	107	27 44	189	28 06	233	47 05	310
40	43 06	010	35 49	033	58 43	064	49 25	108	27 34	189	27 18	234	46 19	309
41	43 16	009	36 21	032	59 37	064	50 22	108	27 24	190	26 30	234	45 32	309
42	43 25	008	36 53	032	60 31	063	51 19	108	27 14	191	25 41	234	44 45	308
43	43 33	007	37 24	031	61 24	062	52 15	109	27 02	191	24 52	235	43 58	308
44	43 40	007	37 55	031	62 16	061	53 12	109	26 51	192	24 03	235	43 11	307
	CAPELLA		◆ PROCYON		SIRIUS		CANOPUS		◆ ACHERNAR		Diphda		◆ Alpheratz	
45	38 26	030	20 14	086	30 31	112	18 55	150	26 38	192	50 01	236	42 23	307
46	38 55	029	21 13	086	31 27	112	19 25	150	26 25	193	49 12	236	41 35	306
47	39 24	029	22 13	086	32 22	113	19 54	151	26 12	193	48 22	237	40 46	306
48	39 53	028	23 13	086	33 17	113	20 23	151	25 58	194	47 31	238	39 58	305
49	40 21	028	24 12	086	34 12	113	20 52	152	25 43	194	46 40	238	39 09	305
50	40 48	027	25 12	086	35 07	114	21 20	152	25 28	195	45 49	239	38 19	305
51	41 15	026	26 12	086	36 02	114	21 48	152	25 12	195	44 58	240	37 30	304
52	41 41	025	27 12	086	36 56	114	22 16	153	24 56	196	44 06	240	36 40	304
53	42 06	025	28 11	086	37 51	115	22 43	153	24 39	197	43 14	241	35 51	304
54	42 31	024	29 11	086	38 45	115	23 09	154	24 22	197	42 21	241	35 01	303
55	42 55	023	30 11	086	39 39	116	23 35	154	24 04	198	41 29	242	34 11	303
56	43 18	022	31 11	086	40 33	116	24 01	155	23 46	198	40 36	242	33 20	303
57	43 40	022	32 10	086	41 26	117	24 27	155	23 27	198	39 43	243	32 30	302
58	44 02	021	33 10	086	42 20	117	24 51	156	23 08	199	38 50	243	31 39	302
59	44 22	020	34 10	086	43 13	118	25 16	156	22 48	199	37 56	244	30 48	302
	◆ CAPELLA		PROCYON		◆ SIRIUS		CANOPUS		ACHERNAR		◆ Diphda		Alpheratz	
60	44 42	019	35 09	086	44 06	118	25 40	157	22 28	200	37 02	244	29 57	302
61	45 01	018	36 09	086	44 59	119	26 03	157	22 07	200	36 09	244	29 06	301
62	45 20	017	37 09	087	45 51	119	26 26	158	21 46	201	35 15	245	28 15	301
63	45 37	016	38 09	087	46 43	120	26 49	158	21 25	201	34 20	245	27 24	301
64	45 53	015	39 08	087	47 35	120	27 11	159	21 03	202	33 26	245	26 32	301
65	46 09	014	40 08	087	48 27	121	27 32	159	20 41	202	32 31	246	25 41	301
66	46 23	014	41 08	087	49 18	122	27 53	160	20 18	202	31 37	246	24 49	300
67	46 37	013	42 08	087	50 09	122	28 13	160	19 55	203	30 42	246	23 58	300
68	46 49	012	43 07	087	50 59	123	28 33	161	19 32	203	29 47	247	23 06	300
69	47 01	011	44 07	087	51 49	124	28 52	162	19 08	204	28 52	247	22 14	300
70	47 11	010	45 07	087	52 38	125	29 10	162	18 43	204	27 57	247	21 22	300
71	47 21	009	46 07	087	53 28	125	29 28	163	18 19	204	27 02	248	20 30	300
72	47 29	008	47 06	087	54 16	126	29 46	163	17 54	205	26 06	248	19 38	300
73	47 37	007	48 06	087	55 04	127	30 02	164	17 29	205	25 11	248	18 46	299
74	47 43	006	49 06	087	55 51	128	30 19	165	17 03	206	24 15	248	17 54	299
	CAPELLA		◆ POLLUX		PROCYON		SIRIUS		◆ CANOPUS		Acamar		◆ Hamal	
75	47 49	005	43 47	054	50 06	087	56 38	129	30 34	165	37 46	209	44 10	299
76	47 53	004	44 35	054	51 05	087	57 24	130	30 49	166	37 16	210	43 18	299
77	47 56	003	45 23	053	52 05	087	58 10	131	31 03	167	36 46	211	42 26	299
78	47 58	002	46 11	053	53 05	087	58 54	132	31 16	167	36 15	211	41 33	298
79	47 59	000	46 58	052	54 05	087	59 38	134	31 29	168	35 44	212	40 40	298
80	47 59	359	47 45	051	55 05	087	60 21	135	31 41	169	35 12	213	39 47	298
81	47 58	358	48 32	051	56 04	087	61 03	136	31 53	169	34 39	213	38 54	297
82	47 56	357	49 18	050	57 04	087	61 43	138	32 04	170	34 06	214	38 01	297
83	47 52	356	50 04	050	58 04	087	62 23	139	32 14	171	33 33	215	37 07	297
84	47 48	355	50 49	049	59 04	087	63 02	141	32 23	171	32 58	215	36 14	296
85	47 43	354	51 34	048	60 03	087	63 39	142	32 32	172	32 24	216	35 20	296
86	47 36	353	52 18	047	61 03	087	64 15	144	32 40	173	31 48	216	34 26	296
87	47 29	352	53 02	046	62 03	086	64 49	146	32 47	173	31 13	217	33 32	296
88	47 20	351	53 45	046	63 02	086	65 22	148	32 53	174	30 36	217	32 38	296
89	47 10	350	54 27	045	64 02	086	65 53	150	32 59	175	30 00	218	31 44	295

LHA ♈	Hc	Zn	Hc	Zn	Hc	Zn	Hc	Zn	Hc	Zn	Hc	Zn	Hc	Zn
	POLLUX		◆ REGULUS		Suhail		◆ CANOPUS		Acamar		◆ ALDEBARAN		CAPELLA	
90	55 09	044	27 55	079	26 23	144	33 04	176	29 23	219	66 02	303	47 00	349
91	55 50	043	28 54	079	26 58	144	33 08	176	28 45	219	65 12	302	46 48	348
92	56 30	042	29 53	079	27 33	145	33 11	177	28 07	219	64 21	301	46 35	347
93	57 10	041	30 51	079	28 07	145	33 14	178	27 29	220	63 29	300	46 22	346
94	57 48	039	31 50	078	28 41	146	33 16	178	26 51	220	62 37	299	46 07	345
95	58 26	038	32 49	078	29 15	146	33 17	179	26 12	221	61 44	298	45 52	344
96	59 02	037	33 47	078	29 48	147	33 18	180	25 32	221	60 51	297	45 35	344
97	59 38	036	34 46	078	30 21	147	33 17	181	24 53	222	59 58	297	45 18	343
98	60 12	034	35 44	078	30 53	148	33 16	181	24 13	222	59 04	296	45 00	342
99	60 46	033	36 43	078	31 25	148	33 14	182	23 32	223	58 10	295	44 40	341
100	61 18	032	37 42	078	31 56	149	33 12	183	22 52	223	57 16	295	44 20	340
101	61 48	030	38 40	078	32 26	150	33 09	184	22 11	223	56 22	294	44 00	339
102	62 18	029	39 39	078	32 57	150	33 04	184	21 30	224	55 27	294	43 38	338
103	62 45	027	40 37	078	33 26	151	33 00	185	20 48	224	54 32	293	43 16	338
104	63 12	025	41 36	078	33 55	151	32 54	186	20 06	224	53 37	293	42 52	337
	POLLUX		◆ REGULUS		Suhail		◆ CANOPUS		RIGEL		◆ ALDEBARAN		CAPELLA	
105	63 36	023	42 34	078	34 23	152	32 48	186	61 11	245	52 42	292	42 28	336
106	63 59	022	43 32	077	34 51	153	32 41	187	60 16	246	51 46	292	42 04	335
107	64 21	020	44 31	077	35 18	153	32 33	188	59 22	247	50 51	291	41 38	335
108	64 40	018	45 29	077	35 44	154	32 24	189	58 27	247	49 55	291	41 12	334
109	64 57	016	46 28	077	36 10	155	32 15	189	57 31	248	48 59	291	40 46	333
110	65 13	014	47 26	077	36 35	156	32 05	190	56 36	249	48 03	290	40 18	332
111	65 26	012	48 24	077	36 59	156	31 54	191	55 40	249	47 07	290	39 50	332
112	65 37	010	49 22	076	37 23	157	31 43	191	54 44	250	46 11	290	39 22	331
113	65 46	008	50 20	076	37 46	158	31 31	192	53 47	250	45 14	290	38 52	330
114	65 53	006	51 18	076	38 08	159	31 18	193	52 51	251	44 18	289	38 23	330
115	65 58	003	52 16	076	38 29	160	31 05	193	51 54	251	43 21	289	37 52	329
116	66 00	001	53 14	075	38 50	160	30 51	194	50 58	252	42 25	289	37 21	329
117	66 00	359	54 12	075	39 09	161	30 36	195	50 01	252	41 28	289	36 50	328
118	65 58	357	55 10	075	39 28	162	30 21	195	49 04	253	40 31	288	36 18	328
119	65 54	355	56 08	075	39 46	163	30 05	196	48 06	253	39 34	288	35 46	327
	Dubhe		◆ Denebola		Suhail		◆ CANOPUS		SIRIUS		BETELGEUSE		◆ CAPELLA	
120	22 55	022	32 29	075	40 03	164	29 48	196	62 19	221	58 58	278	35 13	326
121	23 17	021	33 27	075	40 20	165	29 31	197	61 40	222	57 59	278	34 39	326
122	23 38	021	34 25	075	40 35	166	29 13	198	60 59	224	57 00	277	34 06	325
123	24 00	021	35 22	075	40 50	166	28 55	198	60 17	225	56 00	277	33 32	325
124	24 21	020	36 20	075	41 03	167	28 35	199	59 34	226	55 01	277	32 57	325
125	24 42	020	37 18	075	41 16	168	28 16	199	58 50	228	54 01	277	32 22	324
126	25 02	020	38 16	075	41 27	169	27 56	200	58 05	229	53 02	277	31 47	324
127	25 22	019	39 14	075	41 38	170	27 35	201	57 20	230	52 03	277	31 11	323
128	25 42	019	40 11	074	41 48	171	27 14	201	56 34	231	51 03	277	30 35	323
129	26 01	019	41 09	074	41 57	172	26 52	202	55 47	232	50 04	277	29 59	322
130	26 20	018	42 06	074	42 04	173	26 29	202	54 59	233	49 04	277	29 22	322
131	26 39	018	43 04	074	42 11	174	26 07	203	54 11	234	48 05	277	28 45	322
132	26 57	017	44 01	074	42 17	175	25 43	203	53 23	235	47 05	277	28 08	321
133	27 14	017	44 59	073	42 22	176	25 19	204	52 34	236	46 06	277	27 30	321
134	27 32	017	45 56	073	42 25	177	24 55	204	51 44	236	45 07	276	26 52	321
	Dubhe		◆ SPICA		ACRUX		◆ CANOPUS		SIRIUS		BETELGEUSE		◆ CAPELLA	
135	27 48	016	22 07	104	12 27	159	24 30	205	50 54	237	44 07	276	26 14	320
136	28 05	016	23 06	104	12 49	159	24 05	205	50 04	238	43 08	276	25 36	320
137	28 21	015	24 04	104	13 10	159	23 39	206	49 13	238	42 08	276	24 57	320
138	28 36	015	25 02	104	13 31	160	23 13	206	48 22	239	41 09	276	24 19	319
139	28 51	014	26 00	105	13 52	160	22 46	207	47 30	240	40 09	276	23 40	319
140	29 06	014	26 57	105	14 13	160	22 19	207	46 38	240	39 10	276	23 00	319
141	29 20	013	27 55	105	14 33	160	21 52	207	45 46	241	38 10	276	22 21	319
142	29 34	013	28 53	105	14 53	161	21 24	208	44 54	241	37 11	276	21 41	318
143	29 47	012	29 51	105	15 12	161	20 56	208	44 01	242	36 11	276	21 02	318
144	29 59	012	30 49	106	15 31	161	20 27	209	43 08	243	35 12	276	20 22	318
145	30 11	011	31 46	106	15 50	162	19 59	209	42 15	243	34 12	276	19 41	318
146	30 23	011	32 44	106	16 09	162	19 29	209	41 21	244	33 13	276	19 01	318
147	30 34	010	33 41	106	16 27	162	19 00	210	40 28	244	32 13	276	18 21	317
148	30 45	010	34 39	107	16 45	163	18 30	210	39 34	244	31 14	276	17 40	317
149	30 55	009	35 36	107	17 02	163	17 59	211	38 40	245	30 14	276	17 00	317
	◆ Dubhe		ARCTURUS		◆ SPICA		ACRUX		◆ SIRIUS		PROCYON		POLLUX	
150	31 04	009	25 46	071	36 33	107	17 20	164	37 45	245	55 07	273	50 09	311
151	31 13	008	26 43	071	37 30	107	17 36	164	36 51	246	54 07	273	49 24	310
152	31 22	008	27 39	071	38 27	108	17 53	164	35 56	246	53 08	273	48 37	309
153	31 29	007	28 36	070	39 24	108	18 09	165	35 02	246	52 08	273	47 51	309
154	31 37	007	29 32	070	40 21	108	18 24	165	34 07	247	51 08	273	47 04	308
155	31 44	006	30 28	070	41 18	109	18 40	165	33 12	247	50 08	273	46 17	307
156	31 50	006	31 25	070	42 14	109	18 55	166	32 17	247	49 09	273	45 29	307
157	31 55	005	32 21	070	43 11	109	19 09	166	31 21	248	48 09	273	44 41	306
158	32 00	005	33 17	070	44 07	110	19 23	167	30 26	248	47 09	273	43 52	306
159	32 05	004	34 13	070	45 03	110	19 37	167	29 30	248	46 09	273	43 04	305
160	32 09	003	35 09	069	46 00	111	19 50	167	28 35	248	45 10	273	42 15	305
161	32 12	003	36 05	069	46 55	111	20 03	168	27 39	249	44 10	273	41 26	304
162	32 15	002	37 01	069	47 51	112	20 15	168	26 43	249	43 10	273	40 36	304
163	32 17	002	37 57	069	48 47	112	20 27	169	25 47	249	42 10	273	39 46	304
164	32 18	001	38 53	069	49 42	113	20 38	169	24 51	249	41 11	273	38 56	303
	Dubhe		◆ ARCTURUS		SPICA		◆ ACRUX		Suhail		PROCYON		◆ POLLUX	
165	32 19	001	39 48	068	50 37	113	20 49	170	36 17	205	40 11	273	38 06	303
166	32 20	000	40 44	068	51 32	114	21 00	170	35 51	206	39 11	273	37 16	303
167	32 20	000	41 39	068	52 27	114	21 10	171	35 25	206	38 11	273	36 25	302
168	32 19	359	42 35	068	53 21	115	21 19	171	34 58	207	37 12	273	35 35	302
169	32 17	358	43 30	067	54 15	116	21 29	171	34 31	208	36 12	274	34 44	302
170	32 15	358	44 25	067	55 09	116	21 37	172	34 03	208	35 12	274	33 53	301
171	32 13	357	45 20	067	56 03	117	21 45	172	33 34	209	34 12	274	33 01	301
172	32 10	357	46 15	066	56 56	118	21 53	173	33 05	210	33 13	274	32 10	301
173	32 06	356	47 10	066	57 49	119	22 00	173	32 35	210	32 13	274	31 19	301
174	32 02	356	48 04	066	58 41	119	22 07	174	32 04	211	31 13	274	30 27	300
175	31 57	355	48 59	065	59 33	120	22 13	174	31 33	212	30 13	274	29 35	300
176	31 52	355	49 53	065	60 24	121	22 19	175	31 02	212	29 14	274	28 43	300
177	31 46	354	50 47	064	61 15	122	22 24	175	30 30	213	28 14	274	27 51	300
178	31 39	353	51 41	064	62 06	123	22 29	176	29 57	213	27 14	274	26 59	299
179	31 32	353	52 35	063	62 55	124	22 33	176	29 24	214	26 14	274	26 07	299

LHA ♈	Hc Zn	Hc Zn	Hc Zn	Hc Zn	Hc Zn	Hc Zn	Hc Zn
	◆ARCTURUS	ANTARES	RIGIL KENT	◆ACRUX	Suhail	◆REGULUS	Dubhe
180	53 28 063	18 02 120	18 03 161	22 37 177	28 51 214	61 28 288	31 24 352
181	54 21 062	18 54 120	18 23 161	22 40 177	28 17 215	60 31 287	31 16 352
182	55 14 062	19 46 120	18 42 162	22 43 178	27 42 215	59 34 287	31 07 351
183	56 06 061	20 37 120	19 01 162	22 45 178	27 08 216	58 37 286	30 58 351
184	56 59 060	21 29 121	19 19 162	22 47 179	26 32 216	57 39 286	30 48 350
185	57 50 060	22 21 121	19 37 163	22 48 179	25 57 217	56 42 286	30 38 350
186	58 42 059	23 12 121	19 55 163	22 49 180	25 21 217	55 44 285	30 27 349
187	59 33 058	24 03 121	20 12 164	22 49 180	24 44 218	54 46 285	30 15 349
188	60 24 057	24 54 122	20 29 164	22 49 181	24 08 218	53 48 285	30 03 348
189	61 14 056	25 45 122	20 45 164	22 48 181	23 31 218	52 50 284	29 51 348
190	62 03 055	26 36 122	21 01 165	22 47 182	22 53 219	51 52 284	29 38 347
191	62 52 054	27 26 123	21 16 165	22 45 182	22 15 219	50 54 284	29 24 347
192	63 40 053	28 16 123	21 31 166	22 42 183	21 37 220	49 56 284	29 10 346
193	64 28 052	29 06 123	21 46 166	22 39 183	20 59 220	48 58 284	28 56 346
194	65 15 051	29 56 124	22 00 167	22 36 183	20 20 220	48 00 283	28 41 345
	◆Alphecca	Rasalhague	ANTARES	◆RIGIL KENT	ACRUX	◆REGULUS	Dubhe
195	46 32 055	21 27 078	30 46 124	22 13 167	22 32 184	47 02 283	28 26 345
196	47 21 054	22 25 078	31 35 125	22 27 167	22 28 184	46 03 283	28 10 344
197	48 09 053	23 24 078	32 25 125	22 39 168	22 23 185	45 05 283	27 54 344
198	48 57 053	24 22 078	33 13 125	22 51 169	22 18 185	44 07 283	27 37 344
199	49 44 052	25 21 078	34 02 126	23 03 169	22 12 186	43 08 283	27 20 343
200	50 31 051	26 19 078	34 50 126	23 14 169	22 05 186	42 10 282	27 02 343
201	51 18 051	27 18 078	35 38 127	23 25 170	21 58 187	41 11 282	26 44 342
202	52 04 050	28 16 078	36 26 127	23 35 170	21 51 187	40 13 282	26 26 342
203	52 50 049	29 15 078	37 14 128	23 45 171	21 43 188	39 14 282	26 07 342
204	53 35 048	30 13 078	38 01 128	23 54 171	21 35 188	38 16 282	25 48 341
205	54 19 048	31 12 078	38 47 129	24 02 172	21 26 189	37 17 282	25 29 341
206	55 03 047	32 10 078	39 34 130	24 11 173	21 17 189	36 19 282	25 09 340
207	55 46 046	33 09 078	40 20 130	24 18 173	21 07 190	35 20 282	24 48 340
208	56 29 045	34 07 078	41 05 131	24 25 174	20 57 190	34 21 282	24 28 340
209	57 11 044	35 06 077	41 50 131	24 32 174	20 46 190	33 23 282	24 07 339
	◆VEGA	Rasalhague	ANTARES	◆RIGIL KENT	ACRUX	◆REGULUS	Dubhe
210	18 32 050	36 04 077	42 35 132	24 37 175	20 35 191	32 24 282	23 45 339
211	19 18 050	37 03 077	43 19 133	24 43 175	20 24 191	31 26 282	23 24 339
212	20 03 050	38 01 077	44 03 134	24 48 176	20 12 192	30 27 281	23 02 338
213	20 49 050	38 59 077	44 46 134	24 52 176	19 59 192	29 28 281	22 39 338
214	21 35 050	39 58 077	45 28 135	24 56 177	19 46 193	28 30 281	22 17 338
215	22 20 049	40 56 077	46 10 136	24 59 177	19 33 193	27 31 281	21 54 337
216	23 06 049	41 54 077	46 52 137	25 01 178	19 19 193	26 32 281	21 31 337
217	23 51 049	42 52 077	47 32 138	25 03 178	19 05 194	25 33 281	21 07 337
218	24 36 049	43 51 076	48 12 138	25 05 179	18 51 194	24 35 281	20 44 336
219	25 21 049	44 49 076	48 52 139	25 06 179	18 36 195	23 36 281	20 20 336
220	26 06 048	45 47 076	49 30 140	25 06 180	18 20 195	22 37 281	19 55 336
221	26 51 048	46 45 076	50 08 141	25 06 180	18 04 195	21 39 281	19 31 336
222	27 35 048	47 43 076	50 45 142	25 05 181	17 48 196	20 40 281	19 06 335
223	28 19 047	48 41 076	51 21 143	25 04 182	17 32 196	19 41 281	18 41 335
224	29 03 047	49 39 075	51 56 144	25 02 182	17 15 197	18 43 281	18 16 335
	VEGA	ALTAIR	◆Nunki	ANTARES	RIGIL KENT	◆SPICA	◆Alkaid
225	29 47 047	17 31 082	25 25 122	52 31 146	25 00 183	62 05 237	42 15 344
226	30 31 047	18 30 082	26 16 122	53 04 147	24 57 183	61 15 238	41 58 343
227	31 14 046	19 29 082	27 06 122	53 36 148	24 53 184	60 24 239	41 41 343
228	31 57 046	20 29 082	27 57 123	54 07 149	24 49 184	59 33 240	41 23 342
229	32 40 045	21 28 082	28 47 123	54 38 150	24 44 185	58 41 241	41 04 341
230	33 22 045	22 27 082	29 37 123	55 06 152	24 39 185	57 48 241	40 44 340
231	34 04 045	23 26 082	30 27 124	55 34 153	24 33 186	56 56 242	40 23 340
232	34 46 044	24 26 082	31 17 124	56 01 155	24 27 186	56 02 243	40 02 339
233	35 28 044	25 25 082	32 06 125	56 26 156	24 20 187	55 09 244	39 40 338
234	36 09 043	26 24 082	32 55 125	56 49 157	24 13 187	54 15 244	39 18 338
235	36 50 043	27 24 082	33 44 125	57 12 159	24 05 188	53 21 245	38 55 337
236	37 31 042	28 23 082	34 33 126	57 32 160	23 57 188	52 26 246	38 31 336
237	38 11 042	29 22 082	35 21 126	57 52 162	23 48 189	51 32 246	38 06 336
238	38 51 041	30 21 082	36 09 127	58 09 164	23 38 189	50 37 247	37 41 335
239	39 30 041	31 21 082	36 57 127	58 25 165	23 28 190	49 42 247	37 15 334
	VEGA	◆ALTAIR	Nunki	◆ANTARES	SPICA	◆ARCTURUS	Alkaid
240	40 09 040	32 20 082	37 44 128	58 40 167	48 46 248	60 32 303	36 49 334
241	40 48 040	33 19 082	38 31 129	58 53 169	47 51 248	59 42 302	36 22 333
242	41 26 039	34 18 082	39 18 129	59 04 170	46 55 249	58 51 301	35 55 332
243	42 03 038	35 18 082	40 04 130	59 13 172	45 59 249	57 59 300	35 27 332
244	42 40 038	36 17 082	40 50 130	59 20 174	45 03 250	57 08 300	34 59 331
245	43 16 037	37 16 082	41 35 131	59 26 175	44 07 250	56 15 299	34 30 331
246	43 52 036	38 15 082	42 20 132	59 30 177	43 10 251	55 23 298	34 00 330
247	44 28 036	39 15 082	43 05 132	59 32 179	42 14 251	54 30 298	33 30 330
248	45 02 035	40 14 082	43 49 133	59 32 181	41 17 251	53 37 297	33 00 329
249	45 36 034	41 13 082	44 32 134	59 30 183	40 21 252	52 44 297	32 29 329
250	46 10 033	42 12 082	45 15 135	59 27 184	39 24 252	51 50 296	31 58 328
251	46 42 033	43 12 082	45 58 135	59 21 186	38 27 252	50 56 296	31 26 328
252	47 14 032	44 11 081	46 40 136	59 14 188	37 30 253	50 02 295	30 54 327
253	47 46 031	45 10 081	47 21 137	59 05 189	36 33 253	49 08 295	30 22 327
254	48 16 030	46 09 081	48 01 138	58 55 191	35 35 253	48 14 294	29 49 327
	◆VEGA	ALTAIR	◆Nunki	ANTARES	◆SPICA	ARCTURUS	Alkaid
255	48 46 029	47 08 081	48 41 139	58 42 193	34 38 253	47 19 294	29 16 326
256	49 14 028	48 07 081	49 20 140	58 28 195	33 41 254	46 25 294	28 43 326
257	49 42 027	49 07 081	49 58 141	58 12 196	32 43 254	45 30 293	28 09 325
258	50 09 026	50 06 081	50 36 142	57 55 198	31 46 254	44 35 293	27 35 325
259	50 35 025	51 05 081	51 13 143	57 36 199	30 48 254	43 40 293	27 00 325
260	51 00 024	52 04 081	51 49 144	57 15 201	29 50 255	42 44 292	26 26 324
261	51 24 023	53 03 080	52 23 145	56 53 202	28 53 255	41 49 292	25 51 324
262	51 47 022	54 02 080	52 57 146	56 30 204	27 55 255	40 53 292	25 16 324
263	52 09 021	55 01 080	53 30 147	56 05 205	26 57 255	39 58 292	24 40 323
264	52 30 020	56 00 080	54 02 148	55 39 207	25 59 255	39 02 291	24 04 323
265	52 50 019	56 59 080	54 33 150	55 11 208	25 01 256	38 06 291	23 28 323
266	53 08 017	57 58 080	55 03 151	54 42 209	24 03 256	37 11 291	22 52 323
267	53 26 016	58 56 079	55 31 152	54 13 211	23 05 256	36 15 291	22 16 322
268	53 42 015	59 55 079	55 58 154	53 42 212	22 07 256	35 19 291	21 39 322
269	53 57 014	60 54 079	56 24 155	53 09 213	21 09 256	34 23 290	21 02 322

LHA ♈	Hc Zn	Hc Zn	Hc Zn	Hc Zn	Hc Zn	Hc Zn	Hc Zn
	VEGA	◆DENEB	FOMALHAUT	◆Peacock	Shaula	ANTARES	◆ARCTURUS
270	54 11 013	35 40 034	11 17 121	22 24 159	48 28 188	52 36 214	33 27 290
271	54 23 011	36 13 034	12 09 121	22 45 160	48 19 189	52 02 215	32 30 290
272	54 34 010	36 46 033	13 00 122	23 05 160	48 10 190	51 27 216	31 34 290
273	54 43 009	37 18 033	13 51 122	23 25 161	47 59 191	50 51 217	30 38 290
274	54 52 007	37 50 032	14 41 122	23 45 161	47 46 192	50 14 219	29 42 290
275	54 59 006	38 22 031	15 32 122	24 04 162	47 33 193	49 37 220	28 45 290
276	55 04 005	38 53 031	16 23 122	24 23 162	47 19 195	48 58 220	27 49 290
277	55 08 003	39 23 030	17 13 123	24 41 163	47 03 196	48 19 221	26 52 289
278	55 11 002	39 53 029	18 04 123	24 59 163	46 46 197	47 39 222	25 56 289
279	55 12 000	40 22 029	18 54 123	25 16 164	46 28 198	46 58 223	25 00 289
280	55 12 359	40 50 028	19 44 123	25 32 164	46 10 199	46 17 224	24 03 289
281	55 10 358	41 18 027	20 34 124	25 49 165	45 50 200	45 35 225	23 06 289
282	55 07 356	41 45 027	21 24 124	26 04 165	45 29 201	44 53 226	22 10 289
283	55 03 355	42 12 026	22 13 124	26 19 166	45 07 202	44 10 226	21 13 289
284	54 57 354	42 38 025	23 02 125	26 34 166	44 44 203	43 26 227	20 17 289
	DENEB	Alpheratz	◆FOMALHAUT	Peacock	◆ANTARES	Rasalhague	◆VEGA
285	43 03 024	13 02 061	23 52 125	26 48 167	42 42 228	67 28 294	54 50 352
286	43 27 024	13 55 061	24 41 125	27 01 167	41 58 228	66 33 293	54 41 351
287	43 51 023	14 47 061	25 30 126	27 14 168	41 13 229	65 38 292	54 31 350
288	44 14 022	15 39 061	26 18 126	27 26 169	40 27 230	64 42 291	54 20 348
289	44 36 021	16 31 061	27 07 126	27 37 169	39 41 230	63 46 291	54 07 347
290	44 57 020	17 24 061	27 55 127	27 48 170	38 55 231	62 50 290	53 53 346
291	45 18 019	18 16 061	28 43 127	27 59 170	38 08 231	61 53 289	53 38 345
292	45 37 019	19 08 060	29 30 127	28 08 171	37 21 232	60 57 289	53 21 343
293	45 56 018	20 00 060	30 18 128	28 18 172	36 34 233	60 00 288	53 03 342
294	46 13 017	20 52 060	31 05 128	28 26 172	35 46 233	59 03 288	52 45 341
295	46 30 016	21 44 060	31 52 129	28 34 173	34 58 234	58 06 287	52 25 340
296	46 46 015	22 36 060	32 38 129	28 41 173	34 10 234	57 09 287	52 03 339
297	47 01 014	23 28 060	33 24 130	28 48 174	33 21 234	56 12 287	51 41 338
298	47 15 013	24 19 060	34 10 130	28 54 175	32 33 235	55 14 286	51 18 337
299	47 28 012	25 11 060	34 56 131	28 59 175	31 44 235	54 17 286	50 53 335
	◆DENEB	Alpheratz	◆FOMALHAUT	Peacock	◆ANTARES	Rasalhague	VEGA
300	47 40 011	26 02 059	35 41 131	29 04 176	30 54 236	53 19 286	50 28 334
301	47 50 010	26 54 059	36 26 132	29 08 176	30 05 236	52 22 285	50 02 333
302	48 00 009	27 45 059	37 10 132	29 12 177	29 15 237	51 24 285	49 35 332
303	48 09 008	28 36 059	37 55 133	29 14 178	28 25 237	50 26 285	49 06 331
304	48 17 007	29 28 059	38 38 134	29 16 178	27 34 237	49 28 285	48 37 331
305	48 23 006	30 19 058	39 21 134	29 18 179	26 44 238	48 30 284	48 08 330
306	48 29 005	31 09 058	40 04 135	29 19 180	25 53 238	47 32 284	47 37 329
307	48 33 004	32 00 058	40 46 135	29 19 180	25 02 238	46 34 284	47 06 328
308	48 36 003	32 51 058	41 28 136	29 18 181	24 11 239	45 36 284	46 33 327
309	48 39 002	33 41 057	42 09 137	29 17 181	23 20 239	44 38 284	46 01 326
310	48 40 001	34 31 057	42 50 138	29 15 182	22 29 239	43 40 284	45 27 326
311	48 40 359	35 22 057	43 30 138	29 13 183	21 38 239	42 42 283	44 53 325
312	48 39 358	36 11 056	44 09 139	29 10 183	20 46 240	41 43 283	44 18 324
313	48 36 357	37 01 056	44 48 140	29 06 184	19 54 240	40 45 283	43 42 323
314	48 33 356	37 51 056	45 26 141	29 01 185	19 02 240	39 47 283	43 06 323
	◆Alpheratz	◆FOMALHAUT	Peacock	Nunki	◆Rasalhague	VEGA	DENEB
315	38 40 055	46 04 142	28 56 185	47 25 223	38 49 283	42 30 322	48 29 355
316	39 29 055	46 40 143	28 51 186	46 44 224	37 50 283	41 53 321	48 23 354
317	40 18 054	47 16 144	28 44 186	46 02 225	36 52 283	41 15 321	48 16 353
318	41 06 054	47 51 144	28 37 187	45 19 225	35 53 283	40 37 320	48 09 352
319	41 55 054	48 26 145	28 30 188	44 37 226	34 55 283	39 58 320	48 00 351
320	42 43 053	48 59 146	28 21 188	43 53 227	33 57 282	39 19 319	47 50 350
321	43 30 053	49 32 148	28 12 189	43 09 228	32 58 282	38 40 318	47 39 349
322	44 18 052	50 04 149	28 03 189	42 25 228	32 00 282	38 00 318	47 27 348
323	45 05 052	50 34 150	27 53 190	41 40 229	31 01 282	37 20 317	47 14 347
324	45 52 051	51 04 151	27 42 191	40 54 230	30 03 282	36 39 317	47 00 346
325	46 38 050	51 33 152	27 31 191	40 09 230	29 04 282	35 58 316	46 46 345
326	47 24 050	52 00 153	27 19 192	39 22 231	28 06 282	35 17 316	46 30 344
327	48 09 049	52 27 154	27 06 192	38 36 231	27 07 282	34 35 316	46 13 343
328	48 54 048	52 52 156	26 53 193	37 49 232	26 09 282	33 53 315	45 55 342
329	49 39 048	53 16 157	26 39 193	37 01 233	25 10 282	33 11 315	45 36 341
	◆Alpheratz	Diphda	◆FOMALHAUT	Peacock	◆ALTAIR	VEGA	DENEB
330	50 23 047	43 57 120	53 39 158	26 25 194	57 43 280	32 28 314	45 17 341
331	51 06 046	44 49 120	54 00 160	26 10 195	56 44 280	31 45 314	44 57 340
332	51 49 045	45 40 121	54 21 161	25 55 195	55 46 280	31 02 314	44 35 339
333	52 32 045	46 32 121	54 39 162	25 39 196	54 47 280	30 18 313	44 13 338
334	53 13 044	47 23 122	54 57 164	25 23 196	53 48 280	29 35 313	43 50 337
335	53 54 043	48 13 123	55 13 165	25 06 197	52 49 279	28 51 313	43 27 336
336	54 35 042	49 03 123	55 27 167	24 48 197	51 49 279	28 07 312	43 02 336
337	55 14 041	49 53 124	55 40 168	24 30 198	50 50 279	27 23 312	42 37 335
338	55 53 040	50 42 125	55 52 170	24 12 198	49 51 279	26 38 312	42 11 334
339	56 31 039	51 31 126	56 02 171	23 53 199	48 52 279	25 54 312	41 45 333
340	57 08 038	52 20 126	56 10 173	23 33 199	47 53 279	25 09 311	41 17 333
341	57 44 036	53 07 127	56 17 174	23 14 200	46 54 279	24 24 311	40 49 332
342	58 19 035	53 55 128	56 22 176	22 53 200	45 55 279	23 39 311	40 21 331
343	58 53 034	54 41 129	56 25 177	22 32 201	44 56 279	22 53 311	39 52 331
344	59 26 033	55 27 130	56 27 179	22 11 201	43 56 279	22 08 311	39 22 330
	Alpheratz	◆Hamal	Acamar	◆ACHERNAR	FOMALHAUT	◆ALTAIR	DENEB
345	59 57 031	40 39 062	19 49 136	21 00 158	56 27 181	42 57 278	38 52 329
346	60 28 030	41 32 062	20 31 136	21 22 159	56 26 182	41 58 278	38 21 329
347	60 57 028	42 25 061	21 12 136	21 44 159	56 23 184	40 59 278	37 49 328
348	61 25 027	43 17 061	21 54 137	22 05 160	56 18 185	40 00 278	37 17 327
349	61 51 025	44 10 061	22 35 137	22 25 160	56 12 187	39 00 278	36 45 327
350	62 16 024	45 02 060	23 15 137	22 46 161	56 04 188	38 01 278	36 12 326
351	62 39 022	45 54 060	23 56 138	23 05 161	55 54 190	37 02 278	35 39 326
352	63 00 020	46 45 059	24 36 138	23 25 161	55 43 191	36 03 278	35 05 325
353	63 20 018	47 37 059	25 16 139	23 43 162	55 30 193	35 03 278	34 30 325
354	63 38 016	48 28 058	25 55 139	24 02 162	55 16 194	34 04 278	33 56 324
355	63 54 015	49 19 058	26 34 139	24 19 163	55 01 196	33 05 278	33 21 324
356	64 08 013	50 09 057	27 13 140	24 37 163	54 44 197	32 06 278	32 45 323
357	64 20 011	50 59 057	27 52 140	24 54 164	54 25 199	31 06 278	32 09 323
358	64 30 009	51 49 056	28 30 141	25 10 164	54 05 200	30 07 278	31 33 323
359	64 38 007	52 38 055	29 07 141	25 26 165	53 44 201	29 08 278	30 56 322

LAT 3°N

LHA ♈	Hc	Zn	Hc	Zn	Hc	Zn	Hc	Zn	Hc	Zn	Hc	Zn	Hc	Zn
	Alpheratz		◆ Mirfak		ALDEBARAN		◆ ACHERNAR		FOMALHAUT		◆ ALTAIR		DENEB	
0	63 44	005	26 13	034	20 47	073	26 39	165	54 17	203	28 00	278	29 32	322
1	63 48	003	26 46	034	21 45	073	26 54	166	53 52	205	27 01	278	28 55	322
2	63 50	001	27 19	033	22 42	073	27 08	166	53 27	206	26 01	278	28 18	321
3	63 49	359	27 52	033	23 40	073	27 22	167	53 00	207	25 02	278	27 40	321
4	63 47	357	28 24	033	24 37	073	27 35	168	52 32	208	24 03	278	27 03	321
5	63 42	355	28 56	032	25 34	073	27 48	168	52 03	210	23 04	278	26 24	320
6	63 35	353	29 28	032	26 32	073	28 00	169	51 33	211	22 04	278	25 46	320
7	63 27	351	30 00	031	27 29	073	28 11	169	51 02	212	21 05	278	25 07	320
8	63 16	349	30 30	031	28 26	073	28 22	170	50 30	213	20 06	278	24 28	319
9	63 04	347	31 01	030	29 23	073	28 32	170	49 57	214	19 06	278	23 49	319
10	62 49	345	31 31	030	30 20	073	28 42	171	49 23	215	18 07	278	23 10	319
11	62 33	343	32 01	029	31 18	072	28 51	172	48 49	216	17 08	278	22 30	319
12	62 15	342	32 30	029	32 15	072	28 59	172	48 13	217	16 09	278	21 50	318
13	61 55	340	32 59	028	33 12	072	29 07	173	47 37	218	15 09	278	21 11	318
14	61 34	338	33 27	028	34 09	072	29 14	173	46 59	219	14 10	278	20 30	318
	CAPELLA		ALDEBARAN		◆ RIGEL		ACHERNAR		◆ FOMALHAUT		Enif		◆ Alpheratz	
15	19 41	042	35 06	072	25 23	101	29 21	174	46 22	220	41 06	281	61 11	337
16	20 21	041	36 03	072	26 22	101	29 26	175	45 43	220	40 07	280	60 46	335
17	21 00	041	37 00	071	27 21	101	29 32	175	45 04	221	39 08	280	60 20	333
18	21 40	041	37 56	071	28 20	101	29 36	176	44 24	222	38 09	280	59 52	332
19	22 19	041	38 53	071	29 19	101	29 40	177	43 44	223	37 10	280	59 23	330
20	22 58	041	39 50	071	30 17	101	29 44	177	43 03	224	36 11	280	58 53	329
21	23 37	040	40 46	071	31 16	101	29 46	178	42 21	224	35 12	280	58 22	328
22	24 15	040	41 43	070	32 15	102	29 48	178	41 39	225	34 13	280	57 49	326
23	24 54	040	42 39	070	33 14	102	29 50	179	40 56	226	33 14	280	57 16	325
24	25 32	039	43 35	070	34 12	102	29 50	180	40 13	226	32 15	280	56 41	324
25	26 10	039	44 32	070	35 11	102	29 50	180	39 30	227	31 16	280	56 05	323
26	26 47	039	45 28	069	36 09	102	29 50	181	38 46	228	30 17	280	55 28	322
27	27 25	038	46 24	069	37 08	103	29 48	182	38 01	228	29 18	280	54 51	321
28	28 02	038	47 20	069	38 06	103	29 46	182	37 16	229	28 19	280	54 13	320
29	28 38	038	48 15	068	39 05	103	29 44	183	36 31	229	27 20	280	53 33	319
	Mirfak		CAPELLA		◆ ALDEBARAN		RIGEL		◆ ACHERNAR		FOMALHAUT		◆ Alpheratz	
30	39 43	018	29 15	037	49 11	068	40 03	103	29 41	183	35 46	230	52 53	318
31	40 01	017	29 51	037	50 06	068	41 01	104	29 37	184	35 00	230	52 13	317
32	40 18	016	30 27	036	51 02	067	41 59	104	29 32	185	34 14	231	51 31	316
33	40 34	015	31 02	036	51 57	067	42 58	104	29 27	185	33 27	231	50 49	315
34	40 50	015	31 37	036	52 52	066	43 56	104	29 21	186	32 40	232	50 07	314
35	41 05	014	32 12	035	53 47	066	44 54	105	29 15	186	31 53	232	49 24	314
36	41 19	013	32 46	035	54 41	065	45 52	105	29 08	187	31 06	233	48 40	313
37	41 32	012	33 20	034	55 35	065	46 49	105	29 00	188	30 18	233	47 56	312
38	41 44	011	33 53	034	56 29	064	47 47	106	28 52	188	29 30	233	47 11	311
39	41 56	011	34 26	033	57 23	063	48 45	106	28 43	189	28 42	234	46 26	311
40	42 06	010	34 58	033	58 17	063	49 42	106	28 33	189	27 53	234	45 40	310
41	42 16	009	35 30	032	59 10	062	50 40	107	28 23	190	27 05	234	44 54	310
42	42 25	008	36 02	031	60 02	061	51 37	107	28 13	191	26 16	235	44 08	309
43	42 33	007	36 33	031	60 55	061	52 34	108	28 01	191	25 27	235	43 21	308
44	42 40	006	37 04	030	61 47	060	53 31	108	27 49	192	24 38	235	42 34	308
	CAPELLA		◆ PROCYON		SIRIUS		CANOPUS		◆ ACHERNAR		Diphda		◆ Alpheratz	
45	37 34	030	20 09	086	30 54	112	19 47	150	27 37	192	50 35	237	41 47	307
46	38 03	029	21 09	086	31 49	112	20 17	150	27 24	193	49 44	237	40 59	307
47	38 32	028	22 09	086	32 45	112	20 47	151	27 10	193	48 54	238	40 11	306
48	39 00	028	23 08	086	33 40	112	21 16	151	26 56	194	48 03	239	39 23	306
49	39 28	027	24 08	086	34 36	113	21 45	151	26 41	195	47 11	239	38 34	306
50	39 55	026	25 08	086	35 31	113	22 13	152	26 26	195	46 20	240	37 45	305
51	40 21	026	26 08	086	36 26	113	22 41	152	26 10	196	45 28	241	36 56	305
52	40 47	025	27 07	086	37 21	114	23 09	153	25 54	196	44 35	241	36 07	304
53	41 12	024	28 07	086	38 15	114	23 36	153	25 37	197	43 43	242	35 17	304
54	41 36	024	29 07	086	39 10	114	24 03	154	25 19	197	42 50	242	34 28	304
55	41 59	023	30 07	086	40 05	115	24 29	154	25 01	198	41 57	243	33 38	303
56	42 22	022	31 06	086	40 59	115	24 55	155	24 43	198	41 04	243	32 48	303
57	42 44	021	32 06	086	41 53	116	25 21	155	24 24	199	40 10	243	31 57	303
58	43 06	020	33 06	086	42 47	116	25 46	155	24 05	199	39 16	244	31 07	303
59	43 26	020	34 06	086	43 40	117	26 11	156	23 45	200	38 23	244	30 16	302
	◆ CAPELLA		PROCYON		◆ SIRIUS		CANOPUS		ACHERNAR		◆ Diphda		Alpheratz	
60	43 46	019	35 05	086	44 34	117	26 35	156	23 24	200	37 28	245	29 26	302
61	44 04	018	36 05	086	45 27	118	26 58	157	23 04	200	36 34	245	28 35	302
62	44 22	017	37 05	086	46 20	118	27 22	158	22 43	201	35 40	245	27 44	302
63	44 39	016	38 05	086	47 13	119	27 44	158	22 21	201	34 45	246	26 53	301
64	44 55	015	39 04	086	48 05	119	28 06	159	21 59	202	33 51	246	26 02	301
65	45 11	014	40 04	086	48 57	120	28 28	159	21 36	202	32 56	246	25 10	301
66	45 25	013	41 04	086	49 49	121	28 49	160	21 14	203	32 01	247	24 19	301
67	45 38	012	42 04	086	50 40	121	29 10	160	20 50	203	31 06	247	23 27	301
68	45 50	011	43 03	086	51 31	122	29 29	161	20 27	203	30 11	247	22 36	300
69	46 02	010	44 03	086	52 22	123	29 49	161	20 03	204	29 15	248	21 44	300
70	46 12	009	45 03	086	53 12	123	30 08	162	19 38	204	28 20	248	20 52	300
71	46 22	009	46 03	086	54 02	124	30 26	163	19 13	205	27 24	248	20 00	300
72	46 30	008	47 02	086	54 51	125	30 43	163	18 48	205	26 29	248	19 08	300
73	46 37	007	48 02	086	55 40	126	31 00	164	18 23	205	25 33	249	18 17	300
74	46 44	006	49 02	086	56 28	127	31 16	165	17 57	206	24 37	249	17 24	300
	CAPELLA		◆ POLLUX		PROCYON		SIRIUS		◆ CANOPUS		Acamar		◆ Hamal	
75	46 49	005	43 11	053	50 02	086	57 16	128	31 32	165	38 38	210	43 41	300
76	46 53	004	43 59	053	51 01	085	58 02	129	31 47	166	38 08	210	42 49	300
77	46 56	002	44 47	052	52 01	085	58 49	130	32 01	166	37 38	211	41 56	299
78	46 58	001	45 34	052	53 01	085	59 34	131	32 15	167	37 07	212	41 04	299
79	46 59	000	46 21	051	54 01	085	60 19	132	32 28	168	36 35	212	40 12	299
80	46 59	359	47 08	051	55 00	085	61 03	134	32 40	169	36 02	213	39 19	298
81	46 58	358	47 54	050	56 00	085	61 46	135	32 52	169	35 29	214	38 26	298
82	46 56	357	48 40	049	57 00	085	62 27	136	33 03	170	34 56	214	37 33	298
83	46 53	356	49 25	049	57 59	085	63 08	138	33 13	171	34 22	215	36 40	297
84	46 48	355	50 09	048	58 59	085	63 48	139	33 22	171	33 47	216	35 47	297
85	46 43	354	50 54	047	59 59	085	64 26	141	33 31	172	33 12	216	34 53	297
86	46 37	353	51 37	046	60 58	085	65 03	143	33 39	173	32 37	217	34 00	297
87	46 29	352	52 20	045	61 58	085	65 39	145	33 46	173	32 00	217	33 06	296
88	46 21	351	53 03	045	62 58	084	66 12	146	33 53	174	31 24	218	32 12	296
89	46 11	350	53 44	044	63 57	084	66 45	148	33 59	175	30 47	218	31 18	296

LHA ♈	Hc	Zn	Hc	Zn	Hc	Zn	Hc	Zn	Hc	Zn	Hc	Zn	Hc	Zn
	POLLUX		◆ REGULUS		Suhail		◆ CANOPUS		Acamar		◆ ALDEBARAN		CAPELLA	
90	54 25	043	27 43	078	27 11	143	34 04	176	30 10	219	65 29	305	46 01	349
91	55 06	042	28 42	078	27 46	144	34 08	176	29 32	219	64 39	304	45 49	348
92	55 45	041	29 40	078	28 22	144	34 11	177	28 54	220	63 49	303	45 37	348
93	56 24	040	30 39	078	28 56	145	34 14	178	28 15	220	62 58	302	45 23	347
94	57 02	038	31 38	078	29 31	145	34 16	178	27 36	221	62 07	301	45 09	346
95	57 38	037	32 36	078	30 05	146	34 17	179	26 57	221	61 15	300	44 54	345
96	58 14	036	33 35	078	30 38	146	34 18	180	26 17	222	60 23	299	44 38	344
97	58 49	035	34 33	078	31 11	147	34 17	181	25 37	222	59 30	298	44 20	343
98	59 23	033	35 32	078	31 44	147	34 16	181	24 57	222	58 37	297	44 03	342
99	59 55	032	36 30	077	32 16	148	34 14	182	24 16	223	57 44	297	43 44	341
100	60 26	031	37 29	077	32 47	149	34 12	183	23 35	223	56 50	296	43 24	340
101	60 56	029	38 27	077	33 18	149	34 08	184	22 54	224	55 57	296	43 03	340
102	61 25	028	39 26	077	33 49	150	34 04	184	22 13	224	55 02	295	42 42	339
103	61 52	026	40 24	077	34 18	150	33 59	185	21 31	224	54 08	294	42 20	338
104	62 17	024	41 22	077	34 48	151	33 54	186	20 49	225	53 13	294	41 57	337
	POLLUX		◆ REGULUS		Suhail		◆ CANOPUS		RIGEL		◆ ALDEBARAN		CAPELLA	
105	62 41	023	42 21	077	35 16	152	33 47	186	61 35	247	52 18	293	41 34	336
106	63 03	021	43 19	076	35 44	152	33 40	187	60 40	247	51 23	293	41 09	336
107	63 24	019	44 17	076	36 12	153	33 32	188	59 45	248	50 28	293	40 44	335
108	63 43	017	45 15	076	36 38	154	33 24	189	58 49	249	49 33	292	40 18	334
109	63 59	015	46 13	076	37 04	155	33 14	189	57 53	249	48 37	292	39 52	333
110	64 14	013	47 12	076	37 30	155	33 04	190	56 57	250	47 42	291	39 25	333
111	64 27	011	48 10	075	37 54	156	32 53	191	56 00	251	46 46	291	38 57	332
112	64 38	009	49 08	075	38 18	157	32 42	191	55 04	251	45 50	291	38 29	331
113	64 47	007	50 05	075	38 41	158	32 30	192	54 07	252	44 54	290	38 00	331
114	64 54	005	51 03	075	39 04	158	32 17	193	53 10	252	43 57	290	37 31	330
115	64 58	003	52 01	074	39 25	159	32 03	193	52 13	253	43 01	290	37 01	330
116	65 00	001	52 59	074	39 46	160	31 49	194	51 16	253	42 05	290	36 30	329
117	65 00	359	53 56	074	40 06	161	31 34	195	50 18	253	41 08	289	35 59	328
118	64 58	357	54 54	073	40 25	162	31 19	195	49 21	254	40 12	289	35 27	328
119	64 54	355	55 51	073	40 44	163	31 02	196	48 23	254	39 15	289	34 55	327
	Dubhe		◆ Denebola		Suhail		◆ CANOPUS		SIRIUS		BETELGEUSE		◆ CAPELLA	
120	21 59	022	32 13	075	41 01	164	30 46	197	63 04	222	58 49	279	34 23	327
121	22 21	021	33 11	075	41 17	164	30 28	197	62 23	224	57 50	279	33 50	326
122	22 43	021	34 09	075	41 33	165	30 10	198	61 41	225	56 51	279	33 16	326
123	23 04	021	35 07	074	41 48	166	29 51	198	60 59	226	55 52	279	32 42	325
124	23 25	020	36 04	074	42 02	167	29 32	199	60 15	228	54 53	279	32 08	325
125	23 45	020	37 02	074	42 14	168	29 12	200	59 30	229	53 53	278	31 33	324
126	24 06	020	38 00	074	42 26	169	28 52	200	58 44	230	52 54	278	30 58	324
127	24 26	019	38 57	074	42 37	170	28 31	201	57 58	231	51 55	278	30 23	324
128	24 45	019	39 55	074	42 47	171	28 10	201	57 11	232	50 55	278	29 47	323
129	25 04	018	40 52	073	42 56	172	27 47	202	56 23	233	49 56	278	29 11	323
130	25 23	018	41 49	073	43 04	173	27 25	202	55 35	234	48 57	278	28 35	322
131	25 41	018	42 47	073	43 11	174	27 02	203	54 46	235	47 57	278	27 58	322
132	25 59	017	43 44	073	43 17	175	26 38	203	53 57	236	46 58	278	27 21	322
133	26 17	017	44 41	073	43 21	176	26 14	204	53 07	237	45 59	278	26 44	321
134	26 34	016	45 38	072	43 25	177	25 50	204	52 17	237	44 59	277	26 06	321
	Dubhe		◆ SPICA		ACRUX		◆ CANOPUS		SIRIUS		BETELGEUSE		◆ CAPELLA	
135	26 51	016	22 22	103	13 23	159	25 25	205	51 26	238	44 00	277	25 28	321
136	27 07	016	23 20	104	13 45	159	24 59	205	50 35	239	43 00	277	24 50	320
137	27 23	015	24 18	104	14 06	159	24 33	206	49 44	239	42 01	277	24 12	320
138	27 38	015	25 16	104	14 28	159	24 07	206	48 52	240	41 01	277	23 33	320
139	27 53	014	26 14	104	14 48	160	23 40	207	48 00	241	40 02	277	22 54	319
140	28 08	014	27 12	104	15 09	160	23 13	207	47 08	241	39 03	277	22 15	319
141	28 22	013	28 11	104	15 29	160	22 45	208	46 15	242	38 03	277	21 36	319
142	28 35	013	29 09	105	15 49	161	22 17	208	45 22	242	37 04	277	20 56	319
143	28 48	012	30 06	105	16 09	161	21 49	208	44 29	243	36 04	277	20 17	318
144	29 01	012	31 04	105	16 28	161	21 20	209	43 35	243	35 05	277	19 37	318
145	29 13	011	32 02	105	16 47	162	20 51	209	42 42	244	34 05	277	18 57	318
146	29 24	011	33 00	105	17 06	162	20 22	210	41 48	244	33 06	277	18 17	318
147	29 35	010	33 58	106	17 24	162	19 52	210	40 54	245	32 06	277	17 37	318
148	29 46	010	34 55	106	17 42	163	19 22	210	39 59	245	31 07	277	16 56	317
149	29 56	009	35 53	106	18 00	163	18 51	211	39 05	246	30 07	277	16 16	317
	◆ Dubhe		ARCTURUS		◆ SPICA		ACRUX		◆ SIRIUS		PROCYON		POLLUX	
150	30 05	009	25 26	070	36 50	106	18 17	163	38 10	246	55 03	275	49 30	311
151	30 14	008	26 23	070	37 48	107	18 34	164	37 15	246	54 03	275	48 45	311
152	30 22	008	27 19	070	38 45	107	18 51	164	36 21	247	53 03	275	47 59	310
153	30 30	007	28 15	070	39 42	107	19 07	165	35 25	247	52 04	275	47 13	309
154	30 37	007	29 11	070	40 40	108	19 22	165	34 30	247	51 04	275	46 27	309
155	30 44	006	30 08	070	41 37	108	19 38	165	33 35	248	50 04	274	45 40	308
156	30 50	006	31 04	069	42 34	108	19 53	166	32 39	248	49 04	274	44 53	308
157	30 56	005	32 00	069	43 30	109	20 07	166	31 44	248	48 05	274	44 05	307
158	31 01	005	32 56	069	44 27	109	20 21	167	30 48	248	47 05	274	43 17	307
159	31 05	004	33 52	069	45 24	109	20 35	167	29 52	249	46 05	274	42 29	306
160	31 09	003	34 48	069	46 20	110	20 48	167	28 57	249	45 06	274	41 40	306
161	31 12	003	35 43	069	47 17	110	21 01	168	28 01	249	44 06	274	40 51	305
162	31 15	002	36 39	068	48 13	111	21 14	168	27 04	249	43 06	274	40 02	305
163	31 17	002	37 35	068	49 09	111	21 26	169	26 08	250	42 06	274	39 13	304
164	31 18	001	38 30	068	50 05	112	21 37	169	25 12	250	41 07	274	38 23	304
	Dubhe		◆ ARCTURUS		SPICA		◆ ACRUX		Suhail		PROCYON		◆ POLLUX	
165	31 19	001	39 26	068	51 00	112	21 48	170	37 11	205	40 07	274	37 33	304
166	31 20	000	40 21	067	51 56	113	21 59	170	36 45	206	39 07	274	36 43	303
167	31 20	000	41 16	067	52 51	113	22 09	170	36 19	207	38 07	274	35 53	303
168	31 19	359	42 11	067	53 46	114	22 19	171	35 52	207	37 08	274	35 03	302
169	31 17	358	43 06	066	54 41	114	22 28	171	35 24	208	36 08	274	34 12	302
170	31 16	358	44 01	066	55 35	115	22 37	172	34 55	209	35 08	274	33 21	302
171	31 13	357	44 56	066	56 29	116	22 45	172	34 26	209	34 08	274	32 30	302
172	31 10	357	45 51	065	57 23	116	22 53	173	33 57	210	33 08	274	31 39	301
173	31 06	356	46 45	065	58 17	117	23 00	173	33 27	211	32 09	274	30 48	301
174	31 02	356	47 39	065	59 10	118	23 07	174	32 56	211	31 09	274	29 57	301
175	30 57	355	48 33	064	60 03	119	23 13	174	32 24	212	30 09	274	29 05	301
176	30 52	355	49 27	064	60 55	120	23 19	175	31 53	212	29 09	274	28 13	300
177	30 46	354	50 21	063	61 47	121	23 24	175	31 20	213	28 10	274	27 22	300
178	30 39	354	51 14	063	62 38	122	23 29	176	30 47	214	27 10	274	26 30	300
179	30 32	353	52 07	062	63 29	123	23 33	176	30 14	214	26 10	274	25 38	300

 LAT 3°N

LHA ♈	Hc	Zn	Hc	Zn	Hc	Zn	Hc	Zn	Hc	Zn	Hc	Zn	Hc	Zn
	◆ARCTURUS		ANTARES		RIGIL KENT		◆ACRUX		Suhail		◆REGULUS		Dubhe	
180	53 00	062	18 31	119	19 00	161	23 37	177	29 40	215	61 09	289	30 25	352
181	53 53	061	19 23	119	19 19	161	23 40	177	29 06	215	60 13	289	30 17	352
182	54 45	060	20 15	120	19 39	161	23 43	178	28 31	216	59 16	288	30 08	351
183	55 37	060	21 07	120	19 58	162	23 45	178	27 56	216	58 19	288	29 59	351
184	56 28	059	21 59	120	20 16	162	23 47	179	27 21	217	57 22	288	29 49	350
185	57 20	058	22 51	120	20 34	163	23 48	179	26 45	217	56 25	287	29 39	350
186	58 10	058	23 43	121	20 52	163	23 49	180	26 08	217	55 27	287	29 28	349
187	59 01	057	24 34	121	21 09	163	23 49	180	25 32	218	54 30	286	29 16	349
188	59 50	056	25 25	121	21 26	164	23 49	181	24 55	218	53 32	286	29 05	348
189	60 40	055	26 17	122	21 43	164	23 48	181	24 17	219	52 35	286	28 52	348
190	61 28	054	27 07	122	21 59	165	23 47	182	23 40	219	51 37	285	28 39	347
191	62 16	053	27 58	122	22 14	165	23 45	182	23 02	220	50 39	285	28 26	347
192	63 04	052	28 49	123	22 29	166	23 42	183	22 23	220	49 41	285	28 12	346
193	63 50	050	29 39	123	22 44	166	23 39	183	21 45	220	48 43	285	27 58	346
194	64 36	049	30 29	123	22 58	167	23 36	184	21 06	221	47 45	284	27 43	346
	◆Alphecca		Rasalhague		ANTARES		◆RIGIL KENT		ACRUX		◆REGULUS		Dubhe	
195	45 57	054	21 14	078	31 19	124	23 12	167	23 32	184	46 47	284	27 28	345
196	46 45	053	22 13	078	32 09	124	23 25	167	23 28	184	45 49	284	27 12	345
197	47 33	053	23 11	078	32 59	124	23 38	168	23 23	185	44 51	284	26 56	344
198	48 20	052	24 10	078	33 48	125	23 50	168	23 17	185	43 53	284	26 39	344
199	49 07	051	25 08	078	34 37	125	24 02	169	23 11	186	42 55	283	26 22	343
200	49 53	051	26 07	077	35 26	126	24 13	169	23 05	186	41 56	283	26 05	343
201	50 39	050	27 05	077	36 14	126	24 24	170	22 58	187	40 58	283	25 47	342
202	51 25	049	28 04	077	37 02	127	24 34	170	22 51	187	40 00	283	25 29	342
203	52 10	048	29 02	077	37 50	127	24 44	171	22 43	188	39 01	283	25 10	342
204	52 54	047	30 00	077	38 38	128	24 53	171	22 34	188	38 03	283	24 51	341
205	53 38	047	30 59	077	39 25	128	25 02	172	22 25	189	37 04	283	24 32	341
206	54 22	046	31 57	077	40 12	129	25 10	172	22 16	189	36 06	283	24 12	341
207	55 04	045	32 56	077	40 58	130	25 18	173	22 06	190	35 07	282	23 52	340
208	55 46	044	33 54	077	41 44	130	25 25	173	21 56	190	34 09	282	23 31	340
209	56 27	043	34 52	077	42 30	131	25 31	174	21 45	191	33 10	282	23 11	339
	◆VEGA		Rasalhague		ANTARES		◆RIGIL KENT		ACRUX		◆REGULUS		Dubhe	
210	17 53	050	35 51	077	43 15	131	25 37	175	21 34	191	32 12	282	22 49	339
211	18 39	050	36 49	077	43 59	132	25 43	175	21 22	191	31 13	282	22 28	339
212	19 25	050	37 47	076	44 44	133	25 47	176	21 10	192	30 15	282	22 06	338
213	20 10	050	38 45	076	45 27	134	25 52	176	20 58	192	29 16	282	21 44	338
214	20 56	049	39 44	076	46 10	134	25 56	177	20 45	193	28 17	282	21 21	338
215	21 41	049	40 42	076	46 53	135	25 59	177	20 31	193	27 19	282	20 59	338
216	22 26	049	41 40	076	47 35	136	26 01	178	20 18	194	26 20	282	20 35	337
217	23 12	049	42 38	076	48 16	137	26 03	178	20 03	194	25 21	282	20 12	337
218	23 57	048	43 36	075	48 57	138	26 05	179	19 49	194	24 23	282	19 48	337
219	24 41	048	44 34	075	49 37	139	26 06	179	19 34	195	23 24	282	19 25	336
220	25 26	048	45 32	075	50 16	140	26 06	180	19 18	195	22 25	282	19 00	336
221	26 10	048	46 30	075	50 55	141	26 06	180	19 02	196	21 27	282	18 36	336
222	26 54	047	47 28	075	51 32	142	26 05	181	18 46	196	20 28	282	18 11	336
223	27 38	047	48 25	074	52 09	143	26 04	182	18 29	196	19 29	282	17 47	335
224	28 22	047	49 23	074	52 45	144	26 02	182	18 12	197	18 31	282	17 21	335
	VEGA		ALTAIR		◆Nunki		ANTARES		RIGIL KENT		◆SPICA		◆Alkaid	
225	29 06	046	17 22	082	25 56	121	53 20	145	26 00	183	62 37	238	41 17	344
226	29 49	046	18 22	082	26 47	122	53 54	146	25 57	183	61 46	239	41 01	344
227	30 32	046	19 21	082	27 38	122	54 27	147	25 53	184	60 54	240	40 44	343
228	31 15	045	20 20	082	28 29	122	54 59	148	25 49	184	60 02	241	40 26	342
229	31 57	045	21 19	082	29 20	123	55 30	150	25 44	185	59 09	242	40 07	341
230	32 40	045	22 19	082	30 10	123	55 59	151	25 39	185	58 16	243	39 47	341
231	33 22	044	23 18	082	31 00	123	56 27	152	25 33	186	57 23	244	39 27	340
232	34 03	044	24 17	082	31 50	124	56 55	154	25 27	186	56 29	244	39 06	339
233	34 45	043	25 16	082	32 40	124	57 20	155	25 20	187	55 35	245	38 45	338
234	35 26	043	26 16	082	33 30	124	57 45	157	25 12	187	54 40	246	38 22	338
235	36 06	042	27 15	082	34 19	125	58 07	158	25 04	188	53 46	246	37 59	337
236	36 46	042	28 14	081	35 08	125	58 29	160	24 56	188	52 51	247	37 36	336
237	37 26	041	29 13	081	35 56	126	58 49	161	24 47	189	51 55	247	37 12	336
238	38 06	041	30 13	081	36 45	126	59 07	163	24 37	189	51 00	248	36 47	335
239	38 45	040	31 12	081	37 33	127	59 23	165	24 27	190	50 04	248	36 21	335
	VEGA		◆ALTAIR		Nunki		◆ANTARES		SPICA		◆ARCTURUS		Alkaid	
240	39 23	040	32 11	081	38 21	127	59 38	166	49 08	249	59 59	304	35 55	334
241	40 01	039	33 10	081	39 08	128	59 51	168	48 12	249	59 09	303	35 29	333
242	40 39	039	34 10	081	39 55	128	60 03	170	47 16	250	58 19	303	35 02	333
243	41 16	038	35 09	081	40 42	129	60 12	172	46 20	250	57 28	302	34 34	332
244	41 52	037	36 08	081	41 28	130	60 20	174	45 23	251	56 37	301	34 06	332
245	42 28	037	37 07	081	42 14	130	60 26	175	44 27	251	55 46	300	33 37	331
246	43 04	036	38 06	081	43 00	131	60 30	177	43 30	251	54 54	300	33 08	331
247	43 39	035	39 06	081	43 45	132	60 32	179	42 33	252	54 02	299	32 38	330
248	44 13	034	40 05	081	44 30	132	60 32	181	41 36	252	53 09	298	32 08	330
249	44 47	034	41 04	081	45 14	133	60 30	183	40 39	252	52 16	298	31 38	329
250	45 19	033	42 03	081	45 57	134	60 27	184	39 42	253	51 23	297	31 07	329
251	45 52	032	43 02	081	46 40	135	60 21	186	38 45	253	50 30	297	30 36	328
252	46 23	031	44 01	081	47 22	135	60 14	188	37 47	253	49 36	296	30 04	328
253	46 54	030	45 00	080	48 04	136	60 04	190	36 50	254	48 42	296	29 32	327
254	47 24	030	46 00	080	48 45	137	59 53	192	35 52	254	47 49	295	28 59	327
	◆VEGA		ALTAIR		◆Nunki		ANTARES		◆SPICA		ARCTURUS		Alkaid	
255	47 53	029	46 59	080	49 26	138	59 41	193	34 55	254	46 54	295	28 26	327
256	48 21	028	47 58	080	50 06	139	59 26	195	33 57	254	46 00	295	27 53	326
257	48 49	027	48 57	080	50 45	140	59 10	197	33 00	255	45 05	294	27 19	326
258	49 15	026	49 56	080	51 23	141	58 52	198	32 02	255	44 11	294	26 46	325
259	49 41	025	50 54	080	52 00	142	58 32	200	31 04	255	43 16	294	26 11	325
260	50 05	024	51 53	079	52 37	143	58 11	201	30 06	255	42 21	293	25 37	325
261	50 29	023	52 52	079	53 12	144	57 48	203	29 08	255	41 26	293	25 02	324
262	50 52	022	53 51	079	53 47	145	57 24	204	28 10	256	40 31	293	24 27	324
263	51 13	021	54 50	079	54 21	146	56 59	206	27 12	256	39 35	292	23 52	324
264	51 34	019	55 49	079	54 53	148	56 32	207	26 14	256	38 40	292	23 16	323
265	51 53	018	56 47	078	55 25	149	56 04	209	25 16	256	37 44	292	22 40	323
266	52 11	017	57 46	078	55 55	150	55 35	210	24 18	256	36 49	292	22 04	323
267	52 28	016	58 45	078	56 24	152	55 04	211	23 19	256	35 53	292	21 28	323
268	52 44	015	59 43	077	56 52	153	54 32	213	22 21	257	34 57	291	20 52	322
269	52 59	013	60 42	077	57 18	154	53 59	214	21 23	257	34 01	291	20 15	322

LHA ♈	Hc	Zn	Hc	Zn	Hc	Zn	Hc	Zn	Hc	Zn	Hc	Zn	Hc	Zn
	VEGA		◆DENEB		FOMALHAUT		◆Peacock		Shaula		ANTARES		◆ARCTURUS	
270	53 12	012	34 50	034	11 48	121	23 20	159	49 27	188	53 26	215	33 05	291
271	53 24	011	35 23	033	12 40	121	23 41	160	49 19	189	52 51	216	32 09	291
272	53 35	010	35 55	033	13 31	121	24 02	160	49 09	190	52 15	217	31 13	291
273	53 44	008	36 28	032	14 22	122	24 22	160	48 57	191	51 38	218	30 17	290
274	53 52	007	36 59	032	15 13	122	24 42	161	48 45	193	51 01	219	29 21	290
275	53 59	006	37 30	031	16 04	122	25 01	161	48 31	194	50 23	220	28 25	290
276	54 04	004	38 01	030	16 55	122	25 20	162	48 17	195	49 43	221	27 29	290
277	54 08	003	38 31	030	17 45	122	25 38	162	48 01	196	49 04	222	26 32	290
278	54 11	002	39 00	029	18 36	123	25 56	163	47 44	197	48 23	223	25 36	290
279	54 12	000	39 29	028	19 26	123	26 13	163	47 25	198	47 42	224	24 40	290
280	54 12	359	39 57	028	20 17	123	26 30	164	47 06	199	47 00	225	23 43	290
281	54 10	358	40 25	027	21 07	123	26 46	165	46 46	200	46 18	226	22 47	289
282	54 07	356	40 52	026	21 57	124	27 02	165	46 25	201	45 34	226	21 50	289
283	54 03	355	41 18	026	22 47	124	27 17	166	46 02	202	44 51	227	20 54	289
284	53 57	354	41 43	025	23 36	124	27 32	166	45 39	203	44 07	228	19 57	289
	DENEB		Alpheratz		◆FOMALHAUT		Peacock		◆ANTARES		Rasalhague		◆VEGA	
285	42 08	024	12 33	061	24 26	124	27 46	167	43 22	228	67 03	296	53 50	353
286	42 32	023	13 25	061	25 15	125	27 59	167	42 37	229	66 09	295	53 42	351
287	42 56	022	14 18	061	26 04	125	28 12	168	41 52	230	65 14	294	53 32	350
288	43 18	022	15 10	061	26 53	125	28 25	168	41 06	230	64 19	293	53 21	349
289	43 40	021	16 02	060	27 42	126	28 36	169	40 19	231	63 24	292	53 08	347
290	44 01	020	16 54	060	28 30	126	28 47	170	39 33	232	62 28	292	52 55	346
291	44 21	019	17 46	060	29 19	127	28 58	170	38 46	232	61 33	291	52 40	345
292	44 40	018	18 38	060	30 07	127	29 08	171	37 58	233	60 37	291	52 24	344
293	44 58	017	19 30	060	30 54	127	29 17	171	37 10	233	59 40	290	52 06	343
294	45 16	016	20 22	060	31 42	128	29 26	172	36 22	234	58 44	289	51 48	341
295	45 32	016	21 14	060	32 29	128	29 34	173	35 34	234	57 47	289	51 28	340
296	45 48	015	22 06	060	33 16	129	29 41	173	34 45	235	56 51	289	51 07	339
297	46 03	014	22 57	059	34 03	129	29 48	174	33 56	235	55 54	288	50 46	338
298	46 16	013	23 49	059	34 49	130	29 54	174	33 07	235	54 57	288	50 23	337
299	46 29	012	24 40	059	35 35	130	29 59	175	32 17	236	54 00	287	49 59	336
	◆DENEB		Alpheratz		◆FOMALHAUT		Peacock		◆ANTARES		Rasalhague		VEGA	
300	46 41	011	25 32	059	36 20	131	30 04	176	31 28	236	53 02	287	49 34	335
301	46 51	010	26 23	059	37 06	131	30 08	176	30 38	237	52 05	287	49 08	334
302	47 01	009	27 14	059	37 51	132	30 11	177	29 48	237	51 08	286	48 41	333
303	47 10	008	28 05	058	38 35	132	30 14	178	28 57	237	50 10	286	48 14	332
304	47 17	007	28 56	058	39 19	133	30 16	178	28 07	238	49 12	286	47 45	331
305	47 24	006	29 47	058	40 03	134	30 18	179	27 16	238	48 15	286	47 16	330
306	47 29	005	30 38	058	40 46	134	30 19	180	26 25	238	47 17	285	46 45	329
307	47 33	004	31 28	057	41 29	135	30 19	180	25 34	239	46 19	285	46 15	328
308	47 37	003	32 18	057	42 11	136	30 18	181	24 43	239	45 21	285	45 43	328
309	47 39	002	33 09	057	42 53	136	30 17	181	23 51	239	44 23	285	45 10	327
310	47 40	001	33 59	056	43 34	137	30 15	182	23 00	240	43 25	284	44 37	326
311	47 40	359	34 48	056	44 14	138	30 13	183	22 08	240	42 27	284	44 04	325
312	47 39	358	35 38	056	44 54	139	30 10	183	21 16	240	41 29	284	43 29	325
313	47 36	357	36 27	055	45 34	139	30 06	184	20 24	240	40 31	284	42 54	324
314	47 33	356	37 17	055	46 12	140	30 01	185	19 32	241	39 33	284	42 19	323
	◆Alpheratz		◆FOMALHAUT		Peacock		Nunki		◆Rasalhague		VEGA		DENEB	
315	38 06	054	46 51	141	29 56	185	48 08	224	38 35	284	41 42	323	47 29	355
316	38 54	054	47 28	142	29 50	186	47 27	225	37 37	284	41 06	322	47 23	354
317	39 43	054	48 04	143	29 44	186	46 44	225	36 38	283	40 28	321	47 17	353
318	40 31	053	48 40	144	29 37	187	46 01	226	35 40	283	39 51	321	47 09	352
319	41 19	053	49 15	145	29 29	188	45 18	227	34 42	283	39 13	320	47 01	351
320	42 06	052	49 49	146	29 21	188	44 34	228	33 43	283	38 34	320	46 51	350
321	42 54	052	50 22	147	29 12	189	43 49	228	32 45	283	37 55	319	46 40	349
322	43 41	051	50 55	148	29 02	190	43 04	229	31 47	283	37 15	318	46 29	348
323	44 27	051	51 26	149	28 52	190	42 19	230	30 48	283	36 35	318	46 16	347
324	45 14	050	51 56	150	28 41	191	41 33	230	29 50	283	35 55	317	46 02	346
325	45 59	050	52 25	151	28 29	191	40 47	231	28 51	283	35 14	317	45 48	345
326	46 45	049	52 54	153	28 17	192	40 00	231	27 53	283	34 33	317	45 32	344
327	47 30	048	53 21	154	28 05	192	39 13	232	26 54	283	33 52	316	45 15	344
328	48 14	048	53 46	155	27 52	193	38 25	233	25 56	283	33 10	316	44 58	343
329	48 58	047	54 11	156	27 38	194	37 38	233	24 57	282	32 28	315	44 40	342
	◆Alpheratz		Diphda		◆FOMALHAUT		Peacock		◆ALTAIR		VEGA		DENEB	
330	49 42	046	44 26	119	54 34	158	27 23	194	57 32	282	31 46	315	44 20	341
331	50 25	045	45 19	119	54 56	159	27 08	195	56 33	282	31 03	314	44 00	340
332	51 07	045	46 11	120	55 17	161	26 53	195	55 34	281	30 20	314	43 39	339
333	51 49	044	47 03	121	55 36	162	26 37	196	54 36	281	29 37	314	43 18	338
334	52 30	043	47 54	121	55 54	163	26 20	196	53 37	281	28 54	313	42 55	337
335	53 10	042	48 45	122	56 11	165	26 03	197	52 38	281	28 10	313	42 32	337
336	53 50	041	49 36	122	56 26	166	25 46	197	51 39	281	27 26	313	42 08	336
337	54 29	040	50 26	123	56 39	168	25 27	198	50 40	280	26 42	313	41 43	335
338	55 07	039	51 16	124	56 51	169	25 09	198	49 41	280	25 58	312	41 17	334
339	55 44	038	52 06	125	57 01	171	24 50	199	48 42	280	25 14	312	40 51	334
340	56 20	037	52 55	125	57 09	173	24 30	199	47 43	280	24 29	312	40 24	333
341	56 55	036	53 43	126	57 16	174	24 10	200	46 44	280	23 44	311	39 56	332
342	57 30	034	54 31	127	57 22	176	23 49	200	45 45	280	22 59	311	39 28	332
343	58 03	033	55 19	128	57 25	177	23 28	201	44 46	280	22 14	311	38 59	331
344	58 35	032	56 06	129	57 27	179	23 07	201	43 47	279	21 29	311	38 30	330
	Alpheratz		◆Hamal		Acamar		◆ACHERNAR		FOMALHAUT		◆ALTAIR		DENEB	
345	59 06	030	40 11	061	20 32	135	21 56	158	57 27	181	42 48	279	38 00	330
346	59 36	029	41 04	061	21 14	136	22 18	159	57 26	182	41 49	279	37 29	329
347	60 04	027	41 56	061	21 56	136	22 40	159	57 23	184	40 50	279	36 58	328
348	60 31	026	42 48	060	22 37	136	23 01	159	57 18	185	39 50	279	36 27	328
349	60 56	024	43 40	060	23 18	137	23 22	160	57 11	187	38 51	279	35 55	327
350	61 20	023	44 32	059	23 59	137	23 42	160	57 03	189	37 52	279	35 22	327
351	61 43	021	45 23	059	24 40	137	24 02	161	56 53	190	36 53	279	34 49	326
352	62 04	019	46 14	058	25 21	138	24 21	161	56 42	192	35 54	279	34 15	326
353	62 23	018	47 05	058	26 01	138	24 40	162	56 29	193	34 55	279	33 41	325
354	62 40	016	47 56	057	26 40	139	24 59	162	56 14	195	33 55	279	33 07	325
355	62 56	014	48 46	057	27 20	139	25 17	163	55 58	196	32 56	279	32 32	324
356	63 09	012	49 36	056	27 59	140	25 34	163	55 41	198	31 57	279	31 57	324
357	63 21	010	50 26	056	28 38	140	25 51	164	55 22	199	30 58	279	31 21	323
358	63 31	008	51 15	055	29 16	140	26 08	164	55 02	201	29 58	279	30 45	323
359	63 38	006	52 04	054	29 54	141	26 24	165	54 40	202	28 59	279	30 09	322

 LAT 2°N

LHA ♈	Hc	Zn	Hc	Zn	Hc	Zn	Hc	Zn	Hc	Zn	Hc	Zn	Hc	Zn
	Alpheratz		◆ Mirfak		ALDEBARAN		◆ ACHERNAR		FOMALHAUT		◆ ALTAIR		DENEB	
0	62 44	004	25 23	034	20 30	073	27 37	165	55 12	204	27 51	279	28 45	322
1	62 48	002	25 56	033	21 27	073	27 52	166	54 47	205	26 51	279	28 08	322
2	62 50	001	26 29	033	22 25	073	28 06	166	54 21	206	25 52	279	27 31	322
3	62 49	359	27 02	033	23 22	073	28 20	167	53 53	208	24 53	279	26 54	321
4	62 47	357	27 34	032	24 19	073	28 34	167	53 25	209	23 54	279	26 16	321
5	62 42	355	28 06	032	25 17	073	28 46	168	52 55	210	22 55	279	25 38	321
6	62 36	353	28 37	031	26 14	073	28 58	169	52 25	211	21 55	279	25 00	320
7	62 28	351	29 08	031	27 11	072	29 10	169	51 53	212	20 56	279	24 21	320
8	62 17	349	29 39	031	28 08	072	29 21	170	51 20	214	19 57	279	23 43	320
9	62 05	347	30 09	030	29 05	072	29 31	170	50 47	215	18 57	279	23 04	319
10	61 51	346	30 39	030	30 02	072	29 41	171	50 12	216	17 58	279	22 25	319
11	61 35	344	31 08	029	30 59	072	29 50	172	49 37	217	16 59	279	21 45	319
12	61 18	342	31 37	029	31 56	072	29 59	172	49 01	218	16 00	279	21 06	319
13	60 59	340	32 06	028	32 53	072	30 06	173	48 24	219	15 00	279	20 26	318
14	60 38	339	32 34	028	33 50	071	30 14	173	47 46	219	14 01	279	19 46	318
	CAPELLA		ALDEBARAN		◆ RIGEL		ACHERNAR		◆ FOMALHAUT		Enif		◆ Alpheratz	
15	18 56	041	34 47	071	25 34	100	30 20	174	47 08	220	40 54	281	60 15	337
16	19 36	041	35 43	071	26 33	100	30 26	175	46 28	221	39 56	281	59 51	336
17	20 15	041	36 40	071	27 32	100	30 31	175	45 49	222	38 57	281	59 26	334
18	20 54	041	37 37	071	28 31	100	30 36	176	45 08	223	37 58	281	58 59	333
19	21 33	041	38 33	070	29 30	101	30 40	176	44 27	223	36 59	281	58 31	331
20	22 12	040	39 30	070	30 29	101	30 43	177	43 46	224	36 00	281	58 02	330
21	22 51	040	40 26	070	31 28	101	30 46	178	43 04	225	35 01	281	57 31	329
22	23 29	040	41 22	070	32 27	101	30 48	178	42 21	226	34 02	281	56 59	327
23	24 07	039	42 18	069	33 25	101	30 50	179	41 38	226	33 03	281	56 26	326
24	24 45	039	43 14	069	34 24	101	30 50	180	40 54	227	32 04	280	55 52	325
25	25 23	039	44 10	069	35 23	102	30 50	180	40 10	228	31 06	280	55 17	324
26	26 00	038	45 06	068	36 22	102	30 50	181	39 26	228	30 07	280	54 41	323
27	26 37	038	46 02	068	37 20	102	30 48	182	38 41	229	29 08	280	54 04	322
28	27 14	038	46 57	068	38 19	102	30 46	182	37 56	229	28 09	280	53 27	321
29	27 51	037	47 53	067	39 18	102	30 44	183	37 10	230	27 10	280	52 48	320
	Mirfak		CAPELLA		◆ ALDEBARAN		RIGEL		◆ ACHERNAR		FOMALHAUT		◆ Alpheratz	
30	38 46	017	28 27	037	48 48	067	40 16	102	30 41	183	36 24	230	52 09	319
31	39 03	017	29 03	036	49 43	066	41 15	103	30 37	184	35 38	231	51 29	318
32	39 20	016	29 38	036	50 38	066	42 13	103	30 32	185	34 51	231	50 48	317
33	39 36	015	30 13	036	51 33	066	43 12	103	30 27	185	34 04	232	50 07	316
34	39 52	014	30 48	035	52 27	065	44 10	103	30 21	186	33 17	232	49 25	315
35	40 06	014	31 22	035	53 21	065	45 08	104	30 15	187	32 30	233	48 42	314
36	40 20	013	31 56	034	54 15	064	46 07	104	30 07	187	31 42	233	47 59	314
37	40 33	012	32 30	034	55 09	063	47 05	104	30 00	188	30 54	233	47 15	313
38	40 45	011	33 03	033	56 03	063	48 03	105	29 51	188	30 06	234	46 31	312
39	40 57	011	33 36	033	56 56	062	49 01	105	29 42	189	29 17	234	45 46	312
40	41 07	010	34 08	032	57 48	061	49 59	105	29 33	190	28 28	235	45 01	311
41	41 17	009	34 40	032	58 41	061	50 56	106	29 22	190	27 39	235	44 16	310
42	41 26	008	35 11	031	59 33	060	51 54	106	29 12	191	26 50	235	43 30	310
43	41 34	007	35 41	031	60 25	059	52 52	106	29 00	191	26 01	236	42 44	309
44	41 41	006	36 12	030	61 16	058	53 49	107	28 48	192	25 11	236	41 57	309
	CAPELLA		◆ PROCYON		SIRIUS		CANOPUS		◆ ACHERNAR		Diphda		◆ Alpheratz	
45	36 41	029	20 04	085	31 15	111	20 39	150	28 35	192	51 07	238	41 10	308
46	37 10	029	21 04	085	32 11	111	21 09	150	28 22	193	50 16	238	40 23	308
47	37 39	028	22 04	085	33 07	112	21 39	150	28 08	194	49 25	239	39 35	307
48	38 07	027	23 04	085	34 03	112	22 08	151	27 54	194	48 33	240	38 47	307
49	38 34	027	24 03	085	34 58	112	22 37	151	27 39	195	47 42	240	37 59	306
50	39 01	026	25 03	085	35 54	112	23 06	152	27 24	195	46 49	241	37 10	306
51	39 27	025	26 03	085	36 49	113	23 34	152	27 08	196	45 57	241	36 22	305
52	39 52	025	27 03	085	37 45	113	24 02	153	26 51	196	45 04	242	35 33	305
53	40 17	024	28 02	085	38 40	113	24 30	153	26 34	197	44 11	242	34 43	305
54	40 41	023	29 02	085	39 35	114	24 57	153	26 17	197	43 18	243	33 54	304
55	41 04	022	30 02	085	40 29	114	25 23	154	25 58	198	42 24	243	33 04	304
56	41 27	022	31 02	085	41 24	115	25 50	154	25 40	198	41 30	244	32 15	304
57	41 48	021	32 01	085	42 19	115	26 15	155	25 21	199	40 37	244	31 25	303
58	42 09	020	33 01	085	43 13	115	26 41	155	25 01	199	39 43	245	30 34	303
59	42 29	019	34 01	085	44 07	116	27 05	156	24 41	200	38 48	245	29 44	303
	◆ CAPELLA		PROCYON		◆ SIRIUS		CANOPUS		ACHERNAR		◆ Diphda		Alpheratz	
60	42 49	018	35 01	085	45 01	116	27 30	156	24 21	200	37 54	245	28 54	303
61	43 07	018	36 00	085	45 54	117	27 54	157	24 00	201	36 59	246	28 03	302
62	43 25	017	37 00	085	46 48	117	28 17	157	23 39	201	36 05	246	27 12	302
63	43 42	016	38 00	085	47 41	118	28 40	158	23 17	202	35 10	246	26 21	302
64	43 57	015	39 00	085	48 34	118	29 02	158	22 55	202	34 15	247	25 30	302
65	44 12	014	39 59	085	49 27	119	29 24	159	22 32	202	33 20	247	24 39	301
66	44 26	013	40 59	085	50 19	120	29 45	160	22 09	203	32 24	247	23 48	301
67	44 39	012	41 59	085	51 11	120	30 06	160	21 45	203	31 29	248	22 57	301
68	44 52	011	42 58	085	52 03	121	30 26	161	21 22	204	30 33	248	22 05	301
69	45 03	010	43 58	085	52 54	122	30 46	161	20 57	204	29 38	248	21 14	301
70	45 13	009	44 58	085	53 45	122	31 05	162	20 33	204	28 42	248	20 22	300
71	45 22	008	45 58	085	54 35	123	31 23	162	20 08	205	27 46	249	19 30	300
72	45 30	007	46 57	085	55 25	124	31 41	163	19 43	205	26 51	249	18 38	300
73	45 38	006	47 57	084	56 15	125	31 58	164	19 17	205	25 55	249	17 47	300
74	45 44	005	48 57	084	57 04	126	32 14	164	18 51	206	24 59	249	16 55	300
	CAPELLA		◆ POLLUX		PROCYON		SIRIUS		◆ CANOPUS		Acamar		◆ Hamal	
75	45 49	004	42 35	053	49 56	084	57 52	127	32 30	165	39 30	210	43 10	301
76	45 53	003	43 23	052	50 56	084	58 40	128	32 45	166	39 00	211	42 18	301
77	45 56	002	44 10	052	51 56	084	59 27	129	33 00	166	38 29	211	41 27	300
78	45 58	001	44 57	051	52 55	084	60 13	130	33 13	167	37 57	212	40 35	300
79	45 59	000	45 43	050	53 55	084	60 59	131	33 27	168	37 25	213	39 43	299
80	45 59	359	46 29	050	54 55	084	61 44	132	33 39	168	36 53	213	38 50	299
81	45 58	358	47 15	049	55 54	084	62 27	134	33 51	169	36 19	214	37 58	299
82	45 56	357	48 00	048	56 54	084	63 10	135	34 02	170	35 45	215	37 05	298
83	45 53	356	48 45	048	57 53	083	63 52	137	34 12	170	35 11	215	36 12	298
84	45 48	355	49 29	047	58 53	083	64 33	138	34 22	171	34 36	216	35 19	298
85	45 43	354	50 12	046	59 52	083	65 12	140	34 30	172	34 00	217	34 26	297
86	45 37	353	50 55	045	60 52	083	65 50	141	34 39	173	33 24	217	33 33	297
87	45 30	353	51 38	045	61 51	083	66 27	143	34 46	173	32 48	218	32 39	297
88	45 21	352	52 20	044	62 51	083	67 02	145	34 53	174	32 11	218	31 46	297
89	45 12	351	53 01	043	63 50	082	67 35	147	34 58	175	31 34	219	30 52	296

LHA ♈	Hc	Zn	Hc	Zn	Hc	Zn	Hc	Zn	Hc	Zn	Hc	Zn	Hc	Zn
	POLLUX		◆ REGULUS		Suhail		◆ CANOPUS		Acamar		◆ ALDEBARAN		CAPELLA	
90	53 41	042	27 31	078	27 59	143	35 03	176	30 56	219	64 54	307	45 02	350
91	54 21	041	28 29	078	28 35	143	35 08	176	30 18	220	64 05	305	44 50	349
92	54 59	040	29 28	077	29 10	144	35 11	177	29 40	220	63 16	304	44 38	348
93	55 37	039	30 26	077	29 45	144	35 14	178	29 01	221	62 26	303	44 25	347
94	56 14	038	31 25	077	30 20	145	35 16	178	28 21	221	61 36	302	44 11	346
95	56 50	036	32 23	077	30 54	145	35 17	179	27 42	222	60 45	301	43 56	345
96	57 25	035	33 22	077	31 28	146	35 18	180	27 02	222	59 53	300	43 40	344
97	57 59	034	34 20	077	32 01	147	35 17	181	26 22	222	59 01	300	43 23	343
98	58 32	033	35 18	077	32 34	147	35 16	181	25 41	223	58 09	299	43 05	342
99	59 04	031	36 17	077	33 07	148	35 14	182	25 00	223	57 16	298	42 47	342
100	59 34	030	37 15	077	33 38	148	35 12	183	24 19	224	56 23	298	42 27	341
101	60 04	028	38 13	076	34 10	149	35 08	184	23 38	224	55 30	297	42 07	340
102	60 31	027	39 12	076	34 40	149	35 04	184	22 56	224	54 36	296	41 46	339
103	60 58	025	40 10	076	35 10	150	34 59	185	22 14	225	53 43	296	41 24	338
104	61 22	024	41 08	076	35 40	151	34 53	186	21 32	225	52 48	295	41 02	338
	POLLUX		◆ REGULUS		Suhail		◆ CANOPUS		RIGEL		◆ ALDEBARAN		CAPELLA	
105	61 46	022	42 06	076	36 09	151	34 47	187	61 58	248	51 54	295	40 38	337
106	62 07	020	43 04	076	36 37	152	34 40	187	61 02	249	50 59	294	40 14	336
107	62 27	018	44 02	075	37 05	153	34 32	188	60 06	250	50 05	294	39 50	335
108	62 45	017	45 00	075	37 32	154	34 23	189	59 10	250	49 10	293	39 24	335
109	63 02	015	45 58	075	37 58	154	34 14	189	58 13	251	48 14	293	38 58	334
110	63 16	013	46 56	075	38 24	155	34 03	190	57 17	251	47 19	292	38 31	333
111	63 28	011	47 54	074	38 49	156	33 52	191	56 20	252	46 24	292	38 04	333
112	63 39	009	48 52	074	39 13	157	33 41	192	55 23	252	45 28	292	37 36	332
113	63 47	007	49 49	074	39 37	157	33 28	192	54 25	253	44 32	291	37 08	331
114	63 54	005	50 47	074	39 59	158	33 15	193	53 28	253	43 36	291	36 38	331
115	63 58	003	51 44	073	40 21	159	33 02	194	52 30	254	42 40	291	36 09	330
116	64 00	001	52 42	073	40 43	160	32 47	194	51 33	254	41 44	291	35 38	329
117	64 00	359	53 39	073	41 03	161	32 32	195	50 35	255	40 48	290	35 08	329
118	63 58	357	54 36	072	41 22	162	32 16	196	49 37	255	39 52	290	34 36	328
119	63 54	355	55 33	072	41 41	162	32 00	196	48 39	255	38 55	290	34 05	328
	Dubhe		◆ Denebola		Suhail		◆ CANOPUS		SIRIUS		BETELGEUSE		◆ CAPELLA	
120	21 03	022	31 57	074	41 58	163	31 43	197	63 48	224	58 39	281	33 32	327
121	21 25	021	32 55	074	42 15	164	31 25	197	63 06	225	57 40	281	33 00	327
122	21 46	021	33 53	074	42 31	165	31 07	198	62 23	226	56 41	280	32 26	326
123	22 08	021	34 50	074	42 46	166	30 48	199	61 39	228	55 42	280	31 53	326
124	22 28	020	35 48	074	43 00	167	30 29	199	60 55	229	54 43	280	31 19	325
125	22 49	020	36 45	073	43 13	168	30 09	200	60 09	230	53 44	280	30 45	325
126	23 09	019	37 43	073	43 25	169	29 48	200	59 22	231	52 45	280	30 10	324
127	23 29	019	38 40	073	43 36	170	29 27	201	58 35	232	51 46	279	29 35	324
128	23 48	019	39 37	073	43 46	171	29 05	202	57 47	233	50 46	279	28 59	323
129	24 07	018	40 35	073	43 55	172	28 43	202	56 59	234	49 47	279	28 23	323
130	24 26	018	41 32	072	44 03	173	28 20	203	56 10	235	48 48	279	27 47	323
131	24 44	018	42 29	072	44 10	174	27 57	203	55 20	236	47 49	279	27 11	322
132	25 02	017	43 26	072	44 16	175	27 33	204	54 30	237	46 49	279	26 34	322
133	25 19	017	44 23	072	44 21	176	27 09	204	53 40	238	45 50	279	25 57	322
134	25 36	016	45 20	071	44 25	177	26 44	205	52 49	238	44 51	278	25 19	321
	Dubhe		◆ SPICA		ACRUX		◆ CANOPUS		SIRIUS		BETELGEUSE		◆ CAPELLA	
135	25 53	016	22 35	103	14 19	159	26 19	205	51 58	239	43 52	278	24 42	321
136	26 09	015	23 34	103	14 41	159	25 53	206	51 06	240	42 52	278	24 04	321
137	26 25	015	24 32	103	15 02	159	25 27	206	50 14	240	41 53	278	23 25	320
138	26 40	015	25 30	103	15 24	159	25 01	207	49 22	241	40 54	278	22 47	320
139	26 55	014	26 29	104	15 45	160	24 34	207	48 29	242	39 54	278	22 08	320
140	27 09	014	27 27	104	16 05	160	24 06	207	47 36	242	38 55	278	21 30	319
141	27 23	013	28 25	104	16 26	160	23 38	208	46 43	243	37 55	278	20 50	319
142	27 37	013	29 23	104	16 46	161	23 10	208	45 49	243	36 56	278	20 11	319
143	27 49	012	30 22	104	17 06	161	22 42	209	44 56	244	35 57	278	19 32	319
144	28 02	012	31 20	104	17 25	161	22 13	209	44 02	244	34 57	278	18 52	318
145	28 14	011	32 18	105	17 44	162	21 43	209	43 08	245	33 58	278	18 12	318
146	28 25	011	33 16	105	18 03	162	21 14	210	42 13	245	32 58	278	17 32	318
147	28 36	010	34 14	105	18 21	162	20 44	210	41 19	246	31 59	277	16 52	318
148	28 46	010	35 11	105	18 40	163	20 13	211	40 24	246	30 59	277	16 12	318
149	28 56	009	36 09	105	18 57	163	19 43	211	39 29	246	30 00	277	15 31	318
	◆ Dubhe		ARCTURUS		◆ SPICA		ACRUX		◆ SIRIUS		PROCYON		POLLUX	
150	29 06	009	25 06	070	37 07	106	19 15	163	38 34	247	54 57	276	48 50	312
151	29 14	008	26 02	070	38 05	106	19 32	164	37 39	247	53 58	276	48 05	312
152	29 23	008	26 58	070	39 02	106	19 48	164	36 44	247	52 58	276	47 20	311
153	29 30	007	27 54	069	40 00	106	20 05	164	35 49	248	51 58	276	46 35	310
154	29 38	007	28 50	069	40 57	107	20 20	165	34 53	248	50 59	276	45 49	310
155	29 44	006	29 46	069	41 55	107	20 36	165	33 57	248	49 59	276	45 02	309
156	29 50	006	30 42	069	42 52	107	20 51	166	33 02	249	48 59	276	44 16	308
157	29 56	005	31 38	069	43 49	108	21 06	166	32 06	249	48 00	276	43 28	308
158	30 01	004	32 34	069	44 46	108	21 20	166	31 10	249	47 00	275	42 41	307
159	30 05	004	33 30	068	45 43	108	21 34	167	30 14	249	46 00	275	41 53	307
160	30 09	003	34 26	068	46 40	109	21 47	167	29 18	250	45 00	275	41 05	306
161	30 12	003	35 21	068	47 37	109	22 00	168	28 22	250	44 01	275	40 16	306
162	30 15	002	36 17	068	48 33	110	22 12	168	27 25	250	43 01	275	39 28	305
163	30 17	002	37 12	067	49 30	110	22 24	169	26 29	250	42 01	275	38 39	305
164	30 18	001	38 07	067	50 26	110	22 36	169	25 32	250	41 02	275	37 49	305
	Dubhe		◆ ARCTURUS		SPICA		◆ ACRUX		Suhail		PROCYON		◆ POLLUX	
165	30 19	001	39 03	067	51 22	111	22 47	170	38 06	206	40 02	275	37 00	304
166	30 20	000	39 58	067	52 18	111	22 58	170	37 39	206	39 02	275	36 10	304
167	30 20	000	40 53	066	53 14	112	23 08	170	37 13	207	38 02	275	35 20	303
168	30 19	359	41 47	066	54 09	112	23 18	171	36 45	208	37 03	275	34 30	303
169	30 17	358	42 42	066	55 05	113	23 27	171	36 17	208	36 03	275	33 40	303
170	30 16	358	43 37	065	56 00	114	23 36	172	35 48	209	35 03	275	32 49	302
171	30 13	357	44 31	065	56 55	114	23 44	172	35 19	210	34 03	275	31 59	302
172	30 10	357	45 25	064	57 49	115	23 52	173	34 49	210	33 04	275	31 08	302
173	30 06	356	46 19	064	58 43	116	23 59	173	34 18	211	32 04	275	30 17	302
174	30 02	356	47 13	064	59 37	116	24 06	174	33 47	212	31 04	275	29 26	301
175	29 57	355	48 07	063	60 31	117	24 13	174	33 15	212	30 04	275	28 34	301
176	29 52	355	49 00	063	61 24	118	24 19	175	32 43	213	29 05	275	27 43	301
177	29 46	354	49 53	062	62 16	119	24 24	175	32 10	213	28 05	275	26 51	301
178	29 40	354	50 46	062	63 09	120	24 29	176	31 37	214	27 05	275	26 00	300
179	29 33	353	51 39	061	64 00	121	24 33	176	31 04	214	26 05	275	25 08	300

 LAT 2°N

LHA ♈	Hc Zn	Hc Zn	Hc Zn	Hc Zn	Hc Zn	Hc Zn	Hc Zn
	◆ ARCTURUS	ANTARES	RIGIL KENT	◆ ACRUX	Suhail	◆ REGULUS	Dubhe
180	52 31 060	19 00 119	19 56 161	24 37 177	30 29 215	60 48 291	29 25 353
181	53 23 060	19 53 119	20 16 161	24 40 177	29 55 215	59 52 291	29 17 352
182	54 15 059	20 45 119	20 36 161	24 43 178	29 20 216	58 56 290	29 09 351
183	55 06 059	21 37 120	20 55 162	24 45 178	28 44 216	58 00 289	28 59 351
184	55 57 058	22 29 120	21 13 162	24 47 179	28 09 217	57 03 289	28 50 350
185	56 47 057	23 21 120	21 32 162	24 48 179	27 32 217	56 06 289	28 39 350
186	57 37 056	24 13 120	21 49 163	24 49 180	26 56 218	55 09 288	28 29 349
187	58 27 055	25 05 121	22 07 163	24 49 180	26 19 218	54 12 288	28 17 349
188	59 16 054	25 56 121	22 24 164	24 49 181	25 42 219	53 15 287	28 06 348
189	60 05 053	26 48 121	22 40 164	24 48 181	25 04 219	52 18 287	27 53 348
190	60 52 052	27 39 121	22 57 165	24 47 182	24 26 219	51 20 287	27 41 347
191	61 40 051	28 30 122	23 12 165	24 45 182	23 48 220	50 23 286	27 28 347
192	62 26 050	29 21 122	23 27 166	24 42 183	23 09 220	49 25 286	27 14 347
193	63 12 049	30 12 122	23 42 166	24 39 183	22 31 221	48 28 286	27 00 346
194	63 56 048	31 02 123	23 57 166	24 36 184	21 51 221	47 30 285	26 45 346
	◆ Alphecca	Rasalhague	ANTARES	◆ RIGIL KENT	ACRUX	◆ REGULUS	Dubhe
195	45 21 053	21 01 077	31 52 123	24 10 167	24 32 184	46 32 285	26 30 345
196	46 09 052	21 59 077	32 43 124	24 24 167	24 27 185	45 34 285	26 14 345
197	46 56 052	22 58 077	33 32 124	24 37 168	24 22 185	44 36 285	25 58 344
198	47 43 051	23 56 077	34 22 124	24 49 168	24 17 185	43 38 285	25 42 344
199	48 29 050	24 55 077	35 11 125	25 01 169	24 11 186	42 40 284	25 25 343
200	49 15 050	25 53 077	36 01 125	25 12 169	24 04 186	41 42 284	25 08 343
201	50 00 049	26 52 077	36 49 126	25 23 170	23 58 187	40 44 284	24 50 343
202	50 45 048	27 50 077	37 38 126	25 33 170	23 50 187	39 46 284	24 32 342
203	51 30 047	28 49 077	38 26 127	25 43 171	23 42 188	38 48 284	24 13 342
204	52 14 047	29 47 077	39 14 127	25 52 171	23 34 188	37 49 284	23 54 341
205	52 57 046	30 45 077	40 02 128	26 01 172	23 25 189	36 51 283	23 35 341
206	53 39 045	31 44 076	40 49 128	26 09 172	23 15 189	35 53 283	23 15 341
207	54 21 044	32 42 076	41 36 129	26 17 173	23 05 190	34 54 283	22 55 340
208	55 02 043	33 40 076	42 22 129	26 24 173	22 55 190	33 56 283	22 35 340
209	55 43 042	34 38 076	43 09 130	26 31 174	22 44 191	32 57 283	22 14 340
	◆ VEGA	Rasalhague	ANTARES	◆ RIGIL KENT	ACRUX	◆ REGULUS	Dubhe
210	17 14 050	35 37 076	43 54 131	26 37 174	22 33 191	31 59 283	21 53 339
211	18 00 050	36 35 076	44 39 131	26 42 175	22 21 192	31 00 283	21 32 339
212	18 46 049	37 33 076	45 24 132	26 47 176	22 09 192	30 02 283	21 10 339
213	19 31 049	38 31 076	46 08 133	26 52 176	21 56 192	29 03 283	20 48 338
214	20 17 049	39 29 075	46 52 134	26 55 177	21 43 193	28 05 282	20 26 338
215	21 02 049	40 27 075	47 35 134	26 59 177	21 30 193	27 06 282	20 03 338
216	21 47 049	41 25 075	48 18 135	27 01 178	21 16 194	26 08 282	19 40 337
217	22 32 048	42 23 075	49 00 136	27 03 178	21 02 194	25 09 282	19 17 337
218	23 17 048	43 21 075	49 41 137	27 05 179	20 47 194	24 10 282	18 53 337
219	24 01 048	44 18 074	50 22 138	27 06 179	20 32 195	23 12 282	18 30 336
220	24 46 048	45 16 074	51 02 139	27 06 180	20 16 195	22 13 282	18 06 336
221	25 30 047	46 14 074	51 41 140	27 06 180	20 00 196	21 15 282	17 41 336
222	26 14 047	47 11 074	52 19 141	27 05 181	19 44 196	20 16 282	17 17 336
223	26 57 047	48 09 073	52 57 142	27 04 182	19 27 196	19 17 282	16 52 335
224	27 41 046	49 06 073	53 33 143	27 02 182	19 10 197	18 19 282	16 27 335
	VEGA	◆ ALTAIR	Nunki	ANTARES	◆ RIGIL KENT	SPICA	◆ ARCTURUS
225	28 24 046	17 13 081	26 27 121	54 09 144	27 00 183	63 08 240	69 50 329
226	29 07 046	18 13 081	27 18 121	54 44 145	26 57 183	62 16 241	69 18 327
227	29 50 045	19 12 081	28 10 121	55 17 146	26 53 184	61 23 242	68 44 324
228	30 33 045	20 11 081	29 01 122	55 50 148	26 49 184	60 30 243	68 08 322
229	31 15 045	21 10 081	29 52 122	56 21 149	26 44 185	59 37 244	67 31 321
230	31 57 044	22 10 081	30 42 122	56 51 150	26 39 185	58 43 244	66 52 319
231	32 38 044	23 09 081	31 33 123	57 21 152	26 33 186	57 49 245	66 12 317
232	33 20 043	24 08 081	32 23 123	57 48 153	26 26 186	56 54 246	65 30 315
233	34 01 043	25 07 081	33 13 124	58 15 155	26 19 187	55 59 246	64 48 314
234	34 41 042	26 07 081	34 03 124	58 40 156	26 12 187	55 04 247	64 04 313
235	35 22 042	27 06 081	34 53 124	59 03 158	26 04 188	54 09 248	63 19 311
236	36 02 041	28 05 081	35 42 125	59 25 159	25 55 188	53 13 248	62 34 310
237	36 41 041	29 04 081	36 31 125	59 45 161	25 46 189	52 18 249	61 48 309
238	37 20 040	30 03 081	37 20 126	60 04 163	25 37 190	51 22 249	61 01 308
239	37 59 040	31 03 081	38 09 126	60 21 164	25 26 190	50 26 250	60 13 307
	VEGA	◆ ALTAIR	Nunki	◆ ANTARES	SPICA	◆ ARCTURUS	Alkaid
240	38 37 039	32 02 081	38 57 127	60 37 166	49 29 250	59 25 306	35 01 334
241	39 15 039	33 01 081	39 45 127	60 50 168	48 33 250	58 36 305	34 35 334
242	39 52 038	34 00 081	40 32 128	61 02 170	47 36 251	57 46 304	34 08 333
243	40 28 037	34 59 081	41 20 128	61 12 171	46 40 251	56 56 303	33 41 333
244	41 05 037	35 59 080	42 06 129	61 20 173	45 43 252	56 06 302	33 13 332
245	41 40 036	36 58 080	42 53 130	61 26 175	44 46 252	55 15 302	32 44 331
246	42 15 035	37 57 080	43 39 130	61 30 177	43 49 252	54 24 301	32 16 331
247	42 50 035	38 56 080	44 24 131	61 32 179	42 52 253	53 32 300	31 46 330
248	43 23 034	39 55 080	45 10 132	61 32 181	41 54 253	52 40 300	31 16 330
249	43 57 033	40 54 080	45 54 132	61 30 183	40 57 253	51 48 299	30 46 329
250	44 29 032	41 53 080	46 38 133	61 26 185	39 59 254	50 55 298	30 16 329
251	45 01 032	42 52 080	47 22 134	61 21 186	39 02 254	50 02 298	29 44 329
252	45 32 031	43 51 080	48 05 135	61 13 188	38 04 254	49 09 297	29 13 328
253	46 02 030	44 50 079	48 47 135	61 04 190	37 07 254	48 16 297	28 41 328
254	46 32 029	45 49 079	49 29 136	60 52 192	36 09 255	47 22 296	28 09 327
	◆ VEGA	ALTAIR	◆ Nunki	ANTARES	◆ SPICA	ARCTURUS	Alkaid
255	47 00 028	46 48 079	50 10 137	60 39 194	35 11 255	46 28 296	27 36 327
256	47 28 027	47 47 079	50 51 138	60 24 195	34 13 255	45 34 296	27 03 326
257	47 55 026	48 45 079	51 30 139	60 07 197	33 15 255	44 40 295	26 30 326
258	48 21 025	49 44 079	52 09 140	59 49 199	32 17 256	43 46 295	25 56 326
259	48 46 024	50 43 078	52 47 141	59 29 200	31 19 256	42 51 294	25 22 325
260	49 10 023	51 42 078	53 24 142	59 07 202	30 21 256	41 57 294	24 48 325
261	49 34 022	52 40 078	54 01 143	58 44 204	29 23 256	41 02 294	24 13 325
262	49 56 021	53 39 078	54 36 144	58 19 205	28 25 256	40 07 294	23 38 324
263	50 17 020	54 37 077	55 10 146	57 53 207	27 26 256	39 12 293	23 03 324
264	50 37 019	55 36 077	55 44 147	57 25 208	26 28 256	38 17 293	22 28 324
265	50 56 018	56 34 077	56 16 148	56 56 209	25 30 257	37 22 293	21 52 323
266	51 14 017	57 33 076	56 47 150	56 26 211	24 32 257	36 26 292	21 16 323
267	51 30 016	58 31 076	57 17 151	55 55 212	23 33 257	35 31 292	20 40 323
268	51 46 014	59 29 076	57 45 152	55 23 213	22 35 257	34 35 292	20 04 323
269	52 00 013	60 27 075	58 12 154	54 49 215	21 36 257	33 40 292	19 27 322

LHA ♈	Hc Zn	Hc Zn	Hc Zn	Hc Zn	Hc Zn	Hc Zn	Hc Zn
	VEGA	◆ DENEB	FOMALHAUT	◆ Peacock	Shaula	ANTARES	◆ ARCTURUS
270	52 13 012	34 00 033	12 19 121	24 16 159	50 27 188	54 15 216	32 44 292
271	52 25 011	34 33 033	13 11 121	24 37 159	50 18 189	53 39 217	31 48 291
272	52 36 009	35 05 032	14 02 121	24 58 160	50 08 190	53 03 218	30 52 291
273	52 45 008	35 37 032	14 53 121	25 18 160	49 56 192	52 25 219	29 56 291
274	52 53 007	36 08 031	15 45 121	25 38 161	49 43 193	51 47 220	29 00 291
275	52 59 006	36 39 031	16 36 122	25 58 161	49 30 194	51 08 221	28 04 291
276	53 04 004	37 09 030	17 27 122	26 17 162	49 15 195	50 28 222	27 08 290
277	53 08 003	37 39 029	18 17 122	26 35 162	48 58 196	49 48 223	26 12 290
278	53 11 002	38 08 029	19 08 122	26 53 163	48 41 197	49 07 224	25 15 290
279	53 12 000	38 36 028	19 59 123	27 11 163	48 22 199	48 25 225	24 19 290
280	53 12 359	39 04 027	20 49 123	27 28 164	48 03 200	47 42 225	23 23 290
281	53 10 358	39 31 027	21 40 123	27 44 164	47 42 201	46 59 226	22 26 290
282	53 07 357	39 58 026	22 30 123	28 00 165	47 20 202	46 16 227	21 30 290
283	53 03 355	40 24 025	23 20 124	28 15 165	46 58 203	45 32 228	20 34 290
284	52 57 354	40 49 024	24 10 124	28 30 166	46 34 204	44 47 228	19 37 290
	DENEB	Alpheratz	◆ FOMALHAUT	Peacock	◆ ANTARES	Rasalhague	◆ VEGA
285	41 13 024	12 04 061	25 00 124	28 44 167	44 02 229	66 36 298	52 51 353
286	41 37 023	12 56 060	25 49 124	28 58 167	43 16 230	65 43 297	52 42 351
287	42 00 022	13 48 060	26 39 125	29 11 168	42 30 230	64 49 296	52 33 350
288	42 22 021	14 40 060	27 28 125	29 23 168	41 44 231	63 55 295	52 22 349
289	42 44 021	15 32 060	28 17 125	29 35 169	40 57 232	63 00 294	52 10 348
290	43 04 020	16 24 060	29 06 126	29 46 170	40 10 232	62 05 293	51 56 347
291	43 24 019	17 16 060	29 54 126	29 57 170	39 22 233	61 10 293	51 42 345
292	43 43 018	18 08 060	30 42 126	30 07 171	38 34 233	60 15 292	51 26 344
293	44 01 017	19 00 060	31 31 127	30 16 171	37 46 234	59 19 292	51 09 343
294	44 18 016	19 52 060	32 18 127	30 25 172	36 57 234	58 23 291	50 51 342
295	44 35 015	20 43 059	33 06 128	30 33 173	36 09 235	57 27 290	50 32 341
296	44 50 014	21 35 059	33 53 128	30 41 173	35 20 235	56 31 290	50 11 340
297	45 04 013	22 27 059	34 40 129	30 47 174	34 30 236	55 34 289	49 50 339
298	45 18 012	23 18 059	35 27 129	30 53 174	33 41 236	54 38 289	49 27 337
299	45 30 012	24 09 059	36 13 130	30 59 175	32 51 236	53 41 289	49 04 336
	◆ DENEB	Alpheratz	◆ FOMALHAUT	Peacock	◆ ANTARES	Rasalhague	VEGA
300	45 42 011	25 01 059	36 59 130	31 04 176	32 01 237	52 44 288	48 39 335
301	45 52 010	25 52 058	37 45 131	31 08 176	31 10 237	51 47 288	48 14 334
302	46 02 009	26 43 058	38 30 131	31 11 177	30 20 238	50 50 288	47 48 333
303	46 10 008	27 33 058	39 15 132	31 14 178	29 29 238	49 53 287	47 20 333
304	46 17 007	28 24 058	40 00 132	31 16 178	28 38 238	48 56 287	46 52 332
305	46 24 006	29 15 057	40 44 133	31 18 179	27 47 239	47 58 287	46 23 331
306	46 29 005	30 05 057	41 28 134	31 19 180	26 56 239	47 01 286	45 54 330
307	46 33 004	30 55 057	42 11 134	31 19 180	26 05 239	46 03 286	45 23 329
308	46 37 003	31 45 056	42 54 135	31 18 181	25 13 239	45 05 286	44 52 328
309	46 39 002	32 35 056	43 36 136	31 17 181	24 22 240	44 08 286	44 20 327
310	46 40 000	33 25 056	44 18 136	31 15 182	23 30 240	43 10 285	43 47 327
311	46 40 359	34 15 056	44 59 137	31 13 183	22 38 240	42 12 285	43 14 326
312	46 39 358	35 04 055	45 39 138	31 09 183	21 46 240	41 14 285	42 40 325
313	46 37 357	35 53 055	46 19 139	31 06 184	20 54 241	40 16 285	42 06 324
314	46 33 356	36 42 054	46 58 140	31 01 185	20 01 241	39 18 285	41 30 324
	◆ Alpheratz	◆ FOMALHAUT	Peacock	Nunki	◆ Rasalhague	VEGA	DENEB
315	37 31 054	47 37 140	30 56 185	48 51 225	38 20 284	40 55 323	46 29 355
316	38 19 054	48 15 141	30 50 186	48 09 225	37 22 284	40 18 322	46 24 354
317	39 07 053	48 52 142	30 43 187	47 26 226	36 24 284	39 41 322	46 17 353
318	39 55 053	49 28 143	30 36 187	46 43 227	35 26 284	39 04 321	46 10 352
319	40 42 052	50 04 144	30 28 188	45 59 228	34 28 284	38 26 321	46 01 351
320	41 30 052	50 39 145	30 20 188	45 14 228	33 29 284	37 48 320	45 52 350
321	42 16 051	51 12 146	30 11 189	44 29 229	32 31 284	37 09 319	45 41 349
322	43 03 051	51 45 147	30 01 190	43 43 230	31 33 284	36 30 319	45 30 348
323	43 49 050	52 17 148	29 51 190	42 57 230	30 34 283	35 51 318	45 17 347
324	44 35 049	52 48 150	29 40 191	42 11 231	29 36 283	35 11 318	45 04 347
325	45 20 049	53 18 151	29 28 191	41 24 232	28 38 283	34 30 317	44 49 346
326	46 05 048	53 47 152	29 16 192	40 37 232	27 39 283	33 49 317	44 34 345
327	46 49 047	54 14 153	29 03 193	39 50 233	26 41 283	33 08 317	44 18 344
328	47 33 047	54 41 155	28 50 193	39 02 233	25 43 283	32 27 316	44 01 343
329	48 17 046	55 06 156	28 36 194	38 13 234	24 44 283	31 45 316	43 43 342
	◆ Alpheratz	Diphda	◆ FOMALHAUT	Peacock	◆ ALTAIR	VEGA	DENEB
330	49 00 045	44 55 118	55 30 157	28 22 194	57 19 283	31 03 315	43 24 341
331	49 42 045	45 48 118	55 52 159	28 06 195	56 20 283	30 21 315	43 04 340
332	50 24 044	46 40 119	56 14 160	27 51 195	55 22 283	29 38 315	42 43 339
333	51 05 043	47 33 120	56 33 161	27 35 196	54 23 283	28 55 314	42 22 339
334	51 45 042	48 25 120	56 52 163	27 18 196	53 25 282	28 12 314	41 59 338
335	52 25 041	49 16 121	57 09 164	27 01 197	52 26 282	27 29 314	41 36 337
336	53 04 040	50 08 121	57 24 166	26 43 198	51 27 282	26 45 313	41 13 336
337	53 42 039	50 59 122	57 38 168	26 25 198	50 29 282	26 02 313	40 48 336
338	54 20 038	51 49 123	57 50 169	26 06 199	49 30 281	25 18 313	40 23 335
339	54 56 037	52 39 124	58 00 171	25 46 199	48 31 281	24 33 312	39 57 334
340	55 32 036	53 29 124	58 09 172	25 27 200	47 32 281	23 49 312	39 31 333
341	56 06 035	54 18 125	58 16 174	25 06 200	46 33 281	23 04 312	39 03 333
342	56 40 033	55 07 126	58 21 176	24 46 200	45 35 281	22 19 312	38 35 332
343	57 12 032	55 55 127	58 25 177	24 25 201	44 36 281	21 35 311	38 07 331
344	57 44 031	56 43 128	58 27 179	24 03 201	43 37 280	20 49 311	37 38 331
	Alpheratz	◆ Hamal	Acamar	◆ ACHERNAR	FOMALHAUT	◆ ALTAIR	DENEB
345	58 14 030	39 42 061	21 14 135	22 51 158	58 27 181	42 38 280	37 08 330
346	58 43 028	40 34 060	21 57 135	23 14 158	58 26 182	41 39 280	36 38 329
347	59 10 027	41 26 060	22 39 136	23 36 159	58 23 184	40 40 280	36 07 329
348	59 37 025	42 18 059	23 20 136	23 57 159	58 18 186	39 41 280	35 36 328
349	60 02 024	43 09 059	24 02 136	24 18 160	58 11 187	38 41 280	35 04 328
350	60 25 022	44 01 059	24 43 137	24 39 160	58 02 189	37 42 280	34 32 327
351	60 47 020	44 52 058	25 24 137	24 59 161	57 52 190	36 43 280	33 59 327
352	61 07 019	45 42 058	26 05 137	25 18 161	57 41 192	35 44 280	33 26 326
353	61 25 017	46 33 057	26 45 138	25 37 162	57 27 194	34 45 279	32 52 326
354	61 42 015	47 23 056	27 25 138	25 56 162	57 12 195	33 46 279	32 18 325
355	61 57 014	48 13 056	28 05 139	26 14 163	56 56 197	32 47 279	31 43 325
356	62 10 012	49 02 055	28 44 139	26 32 163	56 38 198	31 48 279	31 08 324
357	62 22 010	49 51 055	29 23 140	26 49 164	56 18 200	30 48 279	30 33 324
358	62 31 008	50 40 054	30 02 140	27 05 164	55 58 201	29 49 279	29 57 323
359	62 39 006	51 29 053	30 40 141	27 22 165	55 35 202	28 50 279	29 21 323

 LAT 1°N

LHA ♈	Hc	Zn	Hc	Zn	Hc	Zn	Hc	Zn	Hc	Zn	Hc	Zn	Hc	Zn
	Alpheratz		◆ Mirfak		ALDEBARAN		◆ ACHERNAR		FOMALHAUT		◆ ALTAIR		DENEB	
0	61 45	004	24 33	034	20 12	073	28 35	165	56 07	204	27 41	280	27 57	323
1	61 48	002	25 06	033	21 10	073	28 50	166	55 41	206	26 42	279	27 21	322
2	61 50	001	25 39	033	22 07	073	29 05	166	55 14	207	25 43	279	26 44	322
3	61 49	359	26 11	032	23 04	072	29 19	167	54 46	208	24 43	279	26 07	322
4	61 47	357	26 43	032	24 01	072	29 32	167	54 17	210	23 44	279	25 29	321
5	61 43	355	27 15	032	24 58	072	29 45	168	53 47	211	22 45	279	24 52	321
6	61 36	353	27 46	031	25 55	072	29 57	169	53 16	212	21 46	279	24 14	321
7	61 28	351	28 17	031	26 53	072	30 09	169	52 43	213	20 47	279	23 35	320
8	61 18	350	28 47	030	27 50	072	30 20	170	52 10	214	19 47	279	22 57	320
9	61 07	348	29 17	030	28 46	072	30 30	170	51 36	215	18 48	279	22 18	320
10	60 53	346	29 47	029	29 43	071	30 40	171	51 01	216	17 49	279	21 39	319
11	60 38	344	30 16	029	30 40	071	30 49	171	50 25	217	16 50	279	21 00	319
12	60 21	343	30 45	028	31 37	071	30 58	172	49 48	218	15 50	279	20 21	319
13	60 02	341	31 13	028	32 34	071	31 06	173	49 10	219	14 51	279	19 41	319
14	59 42	339	31 41	027	33 30	071	31 13	173	48 32	220	13 52	279	19 01	318
	CAPELLA		ALDEBARAN		◆ RIGEL		ACHERNAR		◆ FOMALHAUT		Enif		◆ Alpheratz	
15	18 11	041	34 27	071	25 44	100	31 20	174	47 53	221	40 42	282	59 20	338
16	18 50	041	35 24	070	26 43	100	31 26	175	47 13	222	39 43	282	58 57	336
17	19 30	041	36 20	070	27 42	100	31 31	175	46 33	223	38 45	282	58 32	335
18	20 09	041	37 16	070	28 42	100	31 36	176	45 52	223	37 46	282	58 06	333
19	20 48	040	38 13	070	29 41	100	31 40	176	45 11	224	36 47	282	57 38	332
20	21 26	040	39 09	069	30 40	100	31 43	177	44 29	225	35 49	282	57 09	331
21	22 05	040	40 05	069	31 39	100	31 46	178	43 46	226	34 50	281	56 39	329
22	22 43	039	41 01	069	32 38	100	31 48	178	43 03	226	33 51	281	56 08	328
23	23 21	039	41 57	068	33 37	101	31 50	179	42 19	227	32 52	281	55 36	327
24	23 59	039	42 52	068	34 36	101	31 50	180	41 35	228	31 53	281	55 03	326
25	24 36	038	43 48	068	35 35	101	31 50	180	40 51	228	30 54	281	54 28	325
26	25 13	038	44 44	067	36 34	101	31 50	181	40 06	229	29 55	281	53 53	323
27	25 50	038	45 39	067	37 32	101	31 48	182	39 20	229	28 57	281	53 17	322
28	26 27	037	46 34	067	38 31	101	31 46	182	38 35	230	27 58	281	52 40	321
29	27 03	037	47 29	066	39 30	101	31 44	183	37 49	230	26 59	281	52 02	320
	Mirfak		CAPELLA		◆ ALDEBARAN		RIGEL		◆ ACHERNAR		FOMALHAUT		◆ Alpheratz	
30	37 48	017	27 39	037	48 24	066	40 29	102	31 40	183	37 02	231	51 23	319
31	38 06	017	28 14	036	49 19	065	41 28	102	31 37	184	36 16	231	50 44	318
32	38 23	016	28 50	036	50 13	065	42 26	102	31 32	185	35 29	232	50 04	318
33	38 39	015	29 24	035	51 07	064	43 25	102	31 27	185	34 41	232	49 23	317
34	38 54	014	29 59	035	52 01	064	44 24	102	31 21	186	33 54	233	48 42	316
35	39 08	014	30 33	034	52 55	063	45 22	103	31 14	187	33 06	233	48 00	315
36	39 22	013	31 07	034	53 48	063	46 21	103	31 07	187	32 18	234	47 17	314
37	39 35	012	31 40	033	54 42	062	47 19	103	30 59	188	31 29	234	46 34	314
38	39 47	011	32 13	033	55 34	061	48 17	104	30 51	188	30 41	234	45 50	313
39	39 58	010	32 45	032	56 27	061	49 16	104	30 42	189	29 52	235	45 06	312
40	40 08	010	33 17	032	57 19	060	50 14	104	30 32	190	29 03	235	44 22	312
41	40 18	009	33 48	031	58 11	059	51 12	104	30 21	190	28 14	235	43 37	311
42	40 26	008	34 19	031	59 02	058	52 10	105	30 10	191	27 24	236	42 51	310
43	40 34	007	34 50	030	59 53	057	53 08	105	29 59	191	26 35	236	42 05	310
44	40 41	006	35 20	030	60 43	057	54 06	105	29 47	192	25 45	236	41 19	309
	CAPELLA		◆ PROCYON		SIRIUS		CANOPUS		◆ ACHERNAR		Diphda		◆ Alpheratz	
45	35 49	029	19 59	085	31 37	110	21 31	150	29 34	193	51 39	239	40 33	309
46	36 18	028	20 59	085	32 33	111	22 01	150	29 21	193	50 47	239	39 46	308
47	36 46	028	21 59	085	33 29	111	22 31	150	29 07	194	49 55	240	38 58	308
48	37 14	027	22 58	085	34 25	111	23 01	151	28 52	194	49 03	241	38 11	307
49	37 41	026	23 58	085	35 21	111	23 30	151	28 37	195	48 11	241	37 23	307
50	38 07	026	24 58	085	36 16	112	23 59	151	28 22	195	47 18	242	36 35	306
51	38 33	025	25 58	085	37 12	112	24 27	152	28 05	196	46 25	242	35 46	306
52	38 58	024	26 57	085	38 08	112	24 55	152	27 49	196	45 32	243	34 58	306
53	39 22	024	27 57	085	39 03	113	25 23	153	27 31	197	44 38	243	34 09	305
54	39 46	023	28 57	085	39 58	113	25 50	153	27 14	197	43 45	244	33 20	305
55	40 09	022	29 57	085	40 54	113	26 17	154	26 56	198	42 51	244	32 31	305
56	40 31	021	30 56	085	41 49	114	26 44	154	26 37	198	41 57	245	31 41	304
57	40 52	021	31 56	085	42 43	114	27 10	155	26 18	199	41 02	245	30 51	304
58	41 13	020	32 56	084	43 38	114	27 35	155	25 58	199	40 08	245	30 01	304
59	41 33	019	33 55	084	44 33	115	28 00	156	25 38	200	39 13	246	29 11	303
	◆ CAPELLA		PROCYON		◆ SIRIUS		CANOPUS		ACHERNAR		◆ Diphda		Alpheratz	
60	41 52	018	34 55	084	45 27	115	28 25	156	25 17	200	38 19	246	28 21	303
61	42 10	017	35 55	084	46 21	116	28 49	157	24 56	201	37 24	246	27 31	303
62	42 27	016	36 55	084	47 15	116	29 12	157	24 34	201	36 29	247	26 40	302
63	42 44	016	37 54	084	48 09	117	29 35	158	24 13	202	35 33	247	25 50	302
64	42 59	015	38 54	084	49 02	117	29 58	158	23 50	202	34 38	247	24 59	302
65	43 14	014	39 54	084	49 55	118	30 20	159	23 27	203	33 43	248	24 08	302
66	43 28	013	40 53	084	50 48	118	30 41	159	23 04	203	32 47	248	23 17	302
67	43 41	012	41 53	084	51 41	119	31 02	160	22 41	203	31 52	248	22 26	301
68	43 53	011	42 53	084	52 33	120	31 23	160	22 17	204	30 56	248	21 34	301
69	44 04	010	43 52	084	53 25	120	31 42	161	21 52	204	30 00	249	20 43	301
70	44 14	009	44 52	084	54 16	121	32 02	162	21 28	205	29 04	249	19 51	301
71	44 23	008	45 51	084	55 07	122	32 20	162	21 02	205	28 08	249	19 00	301
72	44 31	007	46 51	083	55 58	123	32 38	163	20 37	205	27 12	249	18 08	300
73	44 38	006	47 51	083	56 48	124	32 55	164	20 11	206	26 16	249	17 16	300
74	44 44	005	48 50	083	57 38	124	33 12	164	19 45	206	25 20	250	16 25	300
	CAPELLA		◆ POLLUX		PROCYON		SIRIUS		◆ CANOPUS		Acamar		◆ Hamal	
75	44 49	004	41 59	052	49 50	083	58 27	125	33 28	165	40 22	210	42 39	302
76	44 53	003	42 46	051	50 49	083	59 16	126	33 43	166	39 51	211	41 48	301
77	44 56	002	43 33	051	51 49	083	60 04	127	33 58	166	39 20	212	40 56	301
78	44 58	001	44 19	050	52 48	083	60 51	129	34 12	167	38 48	213	40 05	300
79	44 59	000	45 05	050	53 48	083	61 38	130	34 25	168	38 16	213	39 13	300
80	44 59	359	45 50	049	54 47	082	62 23	131	34 38	168	37 42	214	38 21	300
81	44 58	358	46 35	048	55 47	082	63 08	132	34 50	169	37 09	215	37 29	299
82	44 56	357	47 20	048	56 46	082	63 52	134	35 01	170	36 34	215	36 36	299
83	44 53	357	48 04	047	57 46	082	64 35	135	35 11	170	36 00	216	35 44	299
84	44 49	356	48 48	046	58 45	082	65 17	137	35 21	171	35 24	216	34 51	298
85	44 44	355	49 31	045	59 44	081	65 58	138	35 30	172	34 49	217	33 58	298
86	44 37	354	50 13	045	60 44	081	66 37	140	35 38	173	34 12	218	33 05	298
87	44 30	353	50 55	044	61 43	081	67 15	142	35 46	173	33 35	218	32 12	297
88	44 22	352	51 36	043	62 42	081	67 51	144	35 52	174	32 58	219	31 19	297
89	44 13	351	52 16	042	63 41	080	68 26	146	35 58	175	32 21	219	30 25	297

LHA ♈	Hc	Zn	Hc	Zn	Hc	Zn	Hc	Zn	Hc	Zn	Hc	Zn	Hc	Zn
	POLLUX		◆ REGULUS		Suhail		◆ CANOPUS		Acamar		◆ ALDEBARAN		CAPELLA	
90	52 56	041	27 17	077	28 47	143	36 03	175	31 43	220	64 17	308	44 03	350
91	53 35	040	28 16	077	29 23	143	36 08	176	31 04	220	63 30	307	43 52	349
92	54 13	039	29 14	077	29 59	144	36 11	177	30 25	221	62 41	306	43 40	348
93	54 50	038	30 13	077	30 34	144	36 14	178	29 46	221	61 52	305	43 27	347
94	55 26	037	31 11	077	31 09	145	36 16	178	29 07	221	61 03	304	43 13	346
95	56 02	035	32 10	077	31 44	145	36 17	179	28 27	222	60 13	303	42 58	345
96	56 36	034	33 08	076	32 18	146	36 18	180	27 46	222	59 22	302	42 42	344
97	57 09	033	34 06	076	32 51	146	36 17	181	27 06	223	58 31	301	42 26	344
98	57 42	032	35 04	076	33 24	147	36 16	181	26 25	223	57 39	300	42 08	343
99	58 12	030	36 03	076	33 57	147	36 14	182	25 44	223	56 47	300	41 50	342
100	58 42	029	37 01	076	34 29	148	36 12	183	25 02	224	55 55	299	41 31	341
101	59 11	028	37 59	076	35 01	149	36 08	184	24 21	224	55 02	298	41 11	340
102	59 38	026	38 57	075	35 32	149	36 04	184	23 39	225	54 09	298	40 50	339
103	60 03	024	39 55	075	36 02	150	35 59	185	22 57	225	53 16	297	40 29	339
104	60 27	023	40 53	075	36 32	150	35 53	186	22 14	225	52 22	296	40 06	338
	POLLUX		◆ REGULUS		Suhail		◆ CANOPUS		RIGEL		◆ ALDEBARAN		CAPELLA	
105	60 50	021	41 51	075	37 02	151	35 47	187	62 20	250	51 28	296	39 43	337
106	61 11	020	42 49	075	37 30	152	35 39	187	61 23	251	50 34	295	39 20	336
107	61 30	018	43 47	074	37 58	152	35 31	188	60 26	251	49 40	295	38 55	336
108	61 48	016	44 44	074	38 26	153	35 22	189	59 29	252	48 45	294	38 30	335
109	62 03	014	45 42	074	38 52	154	35 13	190	58 32	252	47 51	294	38 04	334
110	62 17	013	46 40	074	39 18	155	35 02	190	57 35	253	46 56	293	37 38	334
111	62 30	011	47 37	073	39 44	155	34 51	191	56 38	253	46 01	293	37 11	333
112	62 40	009	48 35	073	40 08	156	34 40	192	55 40	254	45 05	293	36 43	332
113	62 48	007	49 32	073	40 32	157	34 27	192	54 42	254	44 10	292	36 15	332
114	62 54	005	50 29	072	40 55	158	34 14	193	53 45	255	43 14	292	35 46	331
115	62 58	003	51 26	072	41 17	159	34 00	194	52 47	255	42 19	292	35 17	330
116	63 00	001	52 23	072	41 39	160	33 45	194	51 49	255	41 23	291	34 47	330
117	63 00	359	53 20	071	41 59	160	33 30	195	50 51	256	40 27	291	34 16	329
118	62 59	357	54 17	071	42 19	161	33 14	196	49 52	256	39 31	291	33 45	329
119	62 55	355	55 14	070	42 38	162	32 58	196	48 54	256	38 35	291	33 14	328
	Dubhe		◆ Denebola		Suhail		◆ CANOPUS		SIRIUS		BETELGEUSE		◆ CAPELLA	
120	20 07	021	31 41	074	42 56	163	32 41	197	64 31	225	58 26	283	32 42	328
121	20 29	021	32 38	073	43 13	164	32 23	198	63 48	227	57 28	282	32 09	327
122	20 50	021	33 36	073	43 29	165	32 04	198	63 04	228	56 29	282	31 37	327
123	21 11	020	34 33	073	43 44	166	31 45	199	62 19	229	55 30	282	31 03	326
124	21 32	020	35 30	073	43 59	167	31 26	199	61 33	230	54 32	281	30 30	326
125	21 53	020	36 28	073	44 12	168	31 05	200	60 47	232	53 33	281	29 55	325
126	22 13	019	37 25	072	44 24	169	30 44	201	59 59	233	52 34	281	29 21	325
127	22 32	019	38 22	072	44 35	170	30 23	201	59 11	234	51 35	281	28 46	324
128	22 51	019	39 19	072	44 46	171	30 01	202	58 23	235	50 36	280	28 11	324
129	23 10	018	40 16	072	44 55	172	29 39	202	57 33	236	49 37	280	27 35	323
130	23 29	018	41 13	071	45 03	173	29 16	203	56 44	237	48 38	280	26 59	323
131	23 47	017	42 10	071	45 10	174	28 52	203	55 53	237	47 39	280	26 23	323
132	24 05	017	43 07	071	45 16	175	28 28	204	55 02	238	46 40	280	25 46	322
133	24 22	017	44 03	071	45 21	176	28 04	204	54 11	239	45 41	280	25 09	322
134	24 39	016	45 00	070	45 25	177	27 39	205	53 20	240	44 42	279	24 32	322
	Dubhe		◆ SPICA		ACRUX		◆ CANOPUS		SIRIUS		BETELGEUSE		◆ CAPELLA	
135	24 55	016	22 49	103	15 15	158	27 13	205	52 28	240	43 42	279	23 55	321
136	25 11	015	23 47	103	15 37	159	26 47	206	51 36	241	42 43	279	23 17	321
137	25 27	015	24 46	103	15 58	159	26 21	206	50 43	242	41 44	279	22 39	321
138	25 42	014	25 44	103	16 20	159	25 54	207	49 50	242	40 45	279	22 01	320
139	25 57	014	26 43	103	16 41	160	25 27	207	48 57	243	39 45	279	21 23	320
140	26 11	013	27 41	103	17 02	160	24 59	208	48 03	243	38 46	279	20 44	320
141	26 25	013	28 39	103	17 22	160	24 31	208	47 10	244	37 47	279	20 05	319
142	26 38	013	29 38	104	17 42	160	24 03	208	46 16	244	36 47	279	19 26	319
143	26 51	012	30 36	104	18 02	161	23 34	209	45 22	245	35 48	278	18 47	319
144	27 03	012	31 34	104	18 22	161	23 05	209	44 27	245	34 49	278	18 07	319
145	27 15	011	32 33	104	18 41	161	22 35	210	43 33	246	33 49	278	17 27	318
146	27 26	011	33 31	104	19 00	162	22 06	210	42 38	246	32 50	278	16 48	318
147	27 37	010	34 29	104	19 19	162	21 35	210	41 43	246	31 51	278	16 07	318
148	27 47	010	35 27	105	19 37	163	21 05	211	40 48	247	30 51	278	15 27	318
149	27 57	009	36 25	105	19 55	163	20 34	211	39 53	247	29 52	278	14 47	318
	◆ Dubhe		ARCTURUS		◆ SPICA		ACRUX		◆ SIRIUS		PROCYON		POLLUX	
150	28 06	009	24 45	069	37 23	105	20 12	163	38 58	247	54 50	278	48 09	313
151	28 15	008	25 41	069	38 21	105	20 29	164	38 02	248	53 50	277	47 25	312
152	28 23	008	26 37	069	39 19	105	20 46	164	37 07	248	52 51	277	46 41	312
153	28 31	007	27 33	069	40 17	106	21 02	164	36 11	248	51 51	277	45 56	311
154	28 38	007	28 29	069	41 14	106	21 18	165	35 15	249	50 52	277	45 10	310
155	28 45	006	29 25	069	42 12	106	21 34	165	34 19	249	49 52	277	44 24	310
156	28 51	005	30 21	068	43 09	106	21 49	166	33 23	249	48 53	277	43 38	309
157	28 56	005	31 16	068	44 07	107	22 04	166	32 27	249	47 53	277	42 51	309
158	29 01	004	32 12	068	45 04	107	22 18	166	31 31	250	46 54	277	42 04	308
159	29 05	004	33 07	068	46 02	107	22 32	167	30 35	250	45 54	276	41 17	308
160	29 09	003	34 03	067	46 59	108	22 45	167	29 39	250	44 54	276	40 29	307
161	29 12	003	34 58	067	47 56	108	22 59	168	28 42	250	43 55	276	39 41	307
162	29 15	002	35 53	067	48 53	108	23 11	168	27 46	250	42 55	276	38 53	306
163	29 17	002	36 49	067	49 50	109	23 23	169	26 49	251	41 55	276	38 04	306
164	29 18	001	37 44	066	50 46	109	23 35	169	25 52	251	40 56	276	37 15	305
	Dubhe		◆ ARCTURUS		SPICA		◆ ACRUX		Suhail		PROCYON		◆ POLLUX	
165	29 19	001	38 39	066	51 43	110	23 46	169	39 00	206	39 56	276	36 26	305
166	29 20	000	39 33	066	52 39	110	23 57	170	38 33	207	38 56	276	35 37	304
167	29 20	000	40 28	065	53 36	111	24 07	170	38 06	207	37 57	276	34 47	304
168	29 19	359	41 22	065	54 32	111	24 17	171	37 38	208	36 57	276	33 57	304
169	29 18	358	42 17	065	55 28	112	24 27	171	37 10	209	35 57	276	33 07	303
170	29 16	358	43 11	064	56 23	112	24 35	172	36 40	209	34 58	276	32 17	303
171	29 13	357	44 05	064	57 19	113	24 44	172	36 11	210	33 58	276	31 26	303
172	29 10	357	44 59	064	58 14	113	24 52	173	35 40	211	32 58	276	30 36	302
173	29 07	356	45 52	063	59 09	114	24 59	173	35 09	211	31 59	275	29 45	302
174	29 02	356	46 46	063	60 03	115	25 06	174	34 38	212	30 59	275	28 54	302
175	28 58	355	47 39	062	60 57	116	25 12	174	34 06	213	29 59	275	28 03	302
176	28 52	355	48 32	062	61 51	116	25 18	175	33 33	213	28 59	275	27 12	301
177	28 47	354	49 25	061	62 45	117	25 24	175	33 00	214	28 00	275	26 21	301
178	28 40	354	50 17	061	63 38	118	25 29	176	32 27	214	27 00	275	25 29	301
179	28 33	353	51 09	060	64 30	119	25 33	176	31 53	215	26 00	275	24 37	301

 LAT 1°N

LHA ♈	Hc	Zn	Hc	Zn	Hc	Zn	Hc	Zn	Hc	Zn	Hc	Zn	Hc	Zn
	◆ARCTURUS		ANTARES		RIGIL KENT		◆ACRUX		Suhail		◆REGULUS		Dubhe	
180	52 01	059	19 29	119	20 53	160	25 37	177	31 19	215	60 26	293	28 26	353
181	52 52	059	20 22	119	21 13	161	25 40	177	30 44	216	59 31	292	28 18	352
182	53 43	058	21 14	119	21 32	161	25 43	178	30 08	216	58 35	292	28 09	352
183	54 34	057	22 07	119	21 52	162	25 45	178	29 33	217	57 39	291	28 00	351
184	55 24	057	22 59	119	22 10	162	25 47	179	28 57	217	56 43	290	27 50	351
185	56 14	056	23 51	120	22 29	162	25 48	179	28 20	218	55 47	290	27 40	350
186	57 04	055	24 43	120	22 47	163	25 49	180	27 43	218	54 50	289	27 30	350
187	57 52	054	25 35	120	23 04	163	25 49	180	27 06	219	53 53	289	27 19	349
188	58 41	053	26 27	120	23 21	164	25 49	181	26 28	219	52 57	289	27 07	349
189	59 28	052	27 19	121	23 38	164	25 48	181	25 51	219	52 00	288	26 55	348
190	60 15	051	28 10	121	23 54	164	25 46	182	25 12	220	51 03	288	26 42	348
191	61 01	050	29 01	121	24 10	165	25 45	182	24 34	220	50 06	287	26 29	347
192	61 47	049	29 53	122	24 26	165	25 42	183	23 55	220	49 08	287	26 15	347
193	62 32	047	30 44	122	24 40	166	25 39	183	23 16	221	48 11	287	26 01	346
194	63 15	046	31 34	122	24 55	166	25 36	184	22 37	221	47 13	287	25 47	346
	◆Alphecca		Rasalhague		ANTARES		◆RIGIL KENT		ACRUX		◆REGULUS		Dubhe	
195	44 44	052	20 48	077	32 25	123	25 09	167	25 32	184	46 16	286	25 32	345
196	45 31	051	21 46	077	33 15	123	25 22	167	25 27	185	45 18	286	25 16	345
197	46 18	051	22 44	077	34 06	123	25 35	168	25 22	185	44 21	286	25 01	344
198	47 04	050	23 43	077	34 56	124	25 48	168	25 17	186	43 23	285	24 44	344
199	47 50	050	24 41	077	35 45	124	26 00	169	25 11	186	42 25	285	24 27	344
200	48 36	049	25 40	077	36 35	125	26 11	169	25 04	187	41 27	285	24 10	343
201	49 21	048	26 38	076	37 24	125	26 22	170	24 57	187	40 29	285	23 53	343
202	50 05	047	27 36	076	38 13	126	26 33	170	24 50	187	39 31	285	23 35	342
203	50 49	046	28 35	076	39 02	126	26 42	171	24 41	188	38 33	284	23 16	342
204	51 32	046	29 33	076	39 50	127	26 52	171	24 33	188	37 35	284	22 58	342
205	52 14	045	30 31	076	40 38	127	27 01	172	24 24	189	36 37	284	22 38	341
206	52 56	044	31 29	076	41 26	128	27 09	172	24 14	189	35 38	284	22 19	341
207	53 37	043	32 27	076	42 13	128	27 17	173	24 05	190	34 40	284	21 59	340
208	54 18	042	33 25	076	43 00	129	27 24	173	23 54	190	33 42	284	21 39	340
209	54 58	041	34 24	075	43 47	129	27 31	174	23 43	191	32 44	284	21 18	340
	◆VEGA		Rasalhague		ANTARES		◆RIGIL KENT		ACRUX		◆REGULUS		Dubhe	
210	16 36	050	35 22	075	44 33	130	27 37	174	23 32	191	31 45	283	20 57	339
211	17 21	049	36 20	075	45 19	131	27 42	175	23 20	192	30 47	283	20 36	339
212	18 07	049	37 18	075	46 04	131	27 47	176	23 08	192	29 49	283	20 14	339
213	18 52	049	38 15	075	46 49	132	27 51	176	22 55	192	28 50	283	19 52	338
214	19 37	049	39 13	075	47 33	133	27 55	177	22 42	193	27 52	283	19 30	338
215	20 22	049	40 11	074	48 17	134	27 59	177	22 28	193	26 53	283	19 08	338
216	21 07	048	41 09	074	49 00	134	28 01	178	22 14	194	25 55	283	18 45	337
217	21 52	048	42 07	074	49 43	135	28 03	178	22 00	194	24 56	283	18 22	337
218	22 36	048	43 04	074	50 25	136	28 05	179	21 45	195	23 58	283	17 58	337
219	23 21	048	44 02	073	51 06	137	28 06	179	21 30	195	22 59	283	17 35	337
220	24 05	047	44 59	073	51 46	138	28 06	180	21 14	195	22 00	282	17 11	336
221	24 49	047	45 57	073	52 26	139	28 06	180	20 58	196	21 02	282	16 46	336
222	25 33	047	46 54	073	53 05	140	28 05	181	20 41	196	20 03	282	16 22	336
223	26 16	046	47 51	072	53 43	141	28 04	182	20 25	196	19 05	282	15 57	336
224	26 59	046	48 48	072	54 21	142	28 02	182	20 07	197	18 06	282	15 32	335
	VEGA		◆ALTAIR		Nunki		ANTARES		◆RIGIL KENT		SPICA		◆ARCTURUS	
225	27 42	046	17 04	081	26 58	120	54 57	143	27 59	183	63 38	242	68 58	330
226	28 25	045	18 03	081	27 49	121	55 33	144	27 56	183	62 44	243	68 27	328
227	29 08	045	19 03	081	28 41	121	56 07	146	27 53	184	61 51	244	67 55	326
228	29 50	045	20 02	081	29 32	121	56 40	147	27 49	184	60 57	244	67 20	324
229	30 32	044	21 01	081	30 23	122	57 12	148	27 44	185	60 03	245	66 44	322
230	31 14	044	22 00	081	31 14	122	57 43	150	27 38	185	59 08	246	66 06	320
231	31 55	043	22 59	081	32 05	122	58 13	151	27 33	186	58 13	247	65 27	319
232	32 36	043	23 59	081	32 56	123	58 42	152	27 26	186	57 18	247	64 47	317
233	33 17	042	24 58	081	33 46	123	59 09	154	27 19	187	56 23	248	64 05	315
234	33 57	042	25 57	081	34 37	123	59 34	155	27 11	188	55 27	248	63 23	314
235	34 37	041	26 56	081	35 27	124	59 58	157	27 03	188	54 31	249	62 39	313
236	35 16	041	27 55	080	36 16	124	60 21	159	26 55	189	53 35	249	61 55	311
237	35 55	040	28 55	080	37 06	125	60 42	160	26 45	189	52 39	250	61 09	310
238	36 34	040	29 54	080	37 55	125	61 01	162	26 36	190	51 43	250	60 23	309
239	37 12	039	30 53	080	38 44	126	61 19	164	26 25	190	50 46	251	59 36	308
	VEGA		◆ALTAIR		Nunki		◆ANTARES		SPICA		◆ARCTURUS		Alkaid	
240	37 50	039	31 52	080	39 33	126	61 35	166	49 49	251	58 49	307	34 07	335
241	38 27	038	32 51	080	40 21	127	61 49	167	48 52	252	58 01	306	33 41	334
242	39 04	038	33 50	080	41 09	127	62 01	169	47 55	252	57 12	305	33 15	333
243	39 41	037	34 49	080	41 57	128	62 11	171	46 58	252	56 23	304	32 47	333
244	40 16	036	35 48	080	42 44	128	62 19	173	46 01	253	55 33	304	32 20	332
245	40 51	036	36 47	080	43 31	129	62 25	175	45 04	253	54 43	303	31 52	332
246	41 26	035	37 46	079	44 17	129	62 30	177	44 07	253	53 52	302	31 23	331
247	42 00	034	38 45	079	45 03	130	62 32	179	43 09	254	53 01	301	30 54	331
248	42 33	033	39 44	079	45 49	131	62 32	181	42 11	254	52 10	301	30 24	330
249	43 06	033	40 43	079	46 34	131	62 30	183	41 14	254	51 18	300	29 54	330
250	43 38	032	41 42	079	47 19	132	62 26	185	40 16	254	50 26	300	29 24	329
251	44 09	031	42 41	079	48 03	133	62 20	187	39 18	255	49 34	299	28 53	329
252	44 40	030	43 40	079	48 47	134	62 12	189	38 20	255	48 41	298	28 22	328
253	45 10	029	44 38	078	49 30	135	62 03	190	37 23	255	47 48	298	27 50	328
254	45 39	029	45 37	078	50 12	135	61 51	192	36 25	255	46 55	297	27 18	328
	◆VEGA		ALTAIR		◆Nunki		ANTARES		◆SPICA		ARCTURUS		Alkaid	
255	46 07	028	46 36	078	50 54	136	61 37	194	35 26	255	46 02	297	26 46	327
256	46 35	027	47 35	078	51 35	137	61 22	196	34 28	256	45 08	297	26 13	327
257	47 01	026	48 33	078	52 15	138	61 04	198	33 30	256	44 14	296	25 40	326
258	47 27	025	49 32	077	52 55	139	60 45	199	32 32	256	43 20	296	25 07	326
259	47 51	024	50 30	077	53 34	140	60 25	201	31 34	256	42 26	295	24 33	326
260	48 15	023	51 29	077	54 12	141	60 02	203	30 36	256	41 32	295	23 59	325
261	48 38	022	52 27	077	54 49	142	59 38	204	29 37	256	40 37	295	23 24	325
262	49 00	021	53 25	076	55 25	144	59 13	206	28 39	257	39 43	294	22 50	325
263	49 21	020	54 24	076	56 00	145	58 46	207	27 41	257	38 48	294	22 15	324
264	49 40	019	55 22	076	56 34	146	58 18	209	26 42	257	37 53	294	21 40	324
265	49 59	017	56 20	075	57 07	147	57 48	210	25 44	257	36 58	293	21 04	324
266	50 16	016	57 18	075	57 38	149	57 18	212	24 45	257	36 03	293	20 28	323
267	50 33	015	58 16	075	58 09	150	56 46	213	23 47	257	35 08	293	19 52	323
268	50 48	014	59 14	074	58 38	152	56 13	214	22 48	257	34 12	293	19 16	323
269	51 02	013	60 11	074	59 06	153	55 38	215	21 50	257	33 17	292	18 40	323

LHA ♈	Hc	Zn	Hc	Zn	Hc	Zn	Hc	Zn	Hc	Zn	Hc	Zn	Hc	Zn
	VEGA		◆DENEB		FOMALHAUT		◆Peacock		Shaula		ANTARES		◆ARCTURUS	
270	51 15	012	33 10	033	12 50	121	25 12	159	51 26	188	55 03	217	32 21	292
271	51 26	010	33 42	033	13 42	121	25 33	159	51 17	189	54 27	218	31 26	292
272	51 36	009	34 14	032	14 33	121	25 54	160	51 07	191	53 50	219	30 30	292
273	51 45	008	34 46	031	15 24	121	26 15	160	50 55	192	53 12	220	29 34	291
274	51 53	007	35 17	031	16 16	121	26 35	161	50 42	193	52 33	221	28 39	291
275	51 59	006	35 47	030	17 07	121	26 55	161	50 28	194	51 53	222	27 43	291
276	52 05	004	36 17	030	17 58	122	27 14	162	50 12	195	51 13	223	26 47	291
277	52 08	003	36 46	029	18 49	122	27 32	162	49 56	197	50 31	224	25 51	291
278	52 11	002	37 15	028	19 40	122	27 51	163	49 38	198	49 50	225	24 54	291
279	52 12	000	37 43	028	20 31	122	28 08	163	49 19	199	49 07	225	23 58	291
280	52 12	359	38 11	027	21 22	122	28 25	164	48 59	200	48 24	226	23 02	290
281	52 10	358	38 38	026	22 12	123	28 42	164	48 38	201	47 40	227	22 06	290
282	52 07	357	39 04	026	23 03	123	28 58	165	48 16	202	46 56	228	21 10	290
283	52 03	355	39 29	025	23 53	123	29 13	165	47 53	203	46 12	229	20 13	290
284	51 58	354	39 54	024	24 43	123	29 28	166	47 29	204	45 26	229	19 17	290
	DENEB		Alpheratz		◆FOMALHAUT		Peacock		◆ANTARES		Rasalhague		◆VEGA	
285	40 18	023	11 34	060	25 33	124	29 43	166	44 41	230	66 07	300	51 51	353
286	40 42	023	12 26	060	26 23	124	29 56	167	43 55	231	65 15	299	51 43	352
287	41 04	022	13 18	060	27 13	124	30 10	168	43 08	231	64 22	298	51 34	350
288	41 26	021	14 10	060	28 02	125	30 22	168	42 21	232	63 28	297	51 23	349
289	41 48	020	15 02	060	28 51	125	30 34	169	41 34	232	62 35	296	51 11	348
290	42 08	019	15 54	060	29 40	125	30 45	169	40 46	233	61 41	295	50 58	347
291	42 27	019	16 46	060	30 29	126	30 56	170	39 58	233	60 46	294	50 44	346
292	42 46	018	17 38	060	31 18	126	31 06	171	39 10	234	59 51	294	50 28	344
293	43 04	017	18 30	059	32 06	126	31 16	171	38 21	234	58 56	293	50 12	343
294	43 21	016	19 21	059	32 54	127	31 24	172	37 32	235	58 01	292	49 54	342
295	43 37	015	20 13	059	33 42	127	31 33	172	36 43	235	57 06	292	49 35	341
296	43 52	014	21 04	059	34 30	128	31 40	173	35 54	236	56 10	291	49 15	340
297	44 06	013	21 56	059	35 17	128	31 47	174	35 04	236	55 14	291	48 54	339
298	44 19	012	22 47	059	36 05	129	31 53	174	34 14	237	54 18	290	48 32	338
299	44 31	011	23 38	058	36 51	129	31 59	175	33 24	237	53 21	290	48 09	337
	◆DENEB		Alpheratz		◆FOMALHAUT		Peacock		◆ANTARES		Rasalhague		VEGA	
300	44 43	010	24 29	058	37 38	130	32 04	176	32 33	237	52 25	289	47 45	336
301	44 53	009	25 20	058	38 24	130	32 08	176	31 43	238	51 28	289	47 20	335
302	45 02	008	26 11	058	39 10	131	32 11	177	30 52	238	50 31	289	46 54	334
303	45 11	007	27 01	057	39 55	131	32 14	178	30 01	238	49 35	288	46 27	333
304	45 18	006	27 52	057	40 40	132	32 16	178	29 10	239	48 38	288	45 59	332
305	45 24	005	28 42	057	41 25	132	32 18	179	28 19	239	47 40	288	45 31	331
306	45 29	004	29 32	057	42 09	133	32 19	180	27 27	239	46 43	287	45 02	330
307	45 34	003	30 22	056	42 52	134	32 19	180	26 35	240	45 46	287	44 32	330
308	45 37	002	31 12	056	43 36	134	32 18	181	25 44	240	44 49	287	44 01	329
309	45 39	001	32 02	056	44 18	135	32 17	181	24 52	240	43 51	287	43 29	328
310	45 40	000	32 51	055	45 01	136	32 15	182	24 00	240	42 54	286	42 57	327
311	45 40	359	33 40	055	45 42	136	32 13	183	23 08	241	41 56	286	42 24	326
312	45 39	358	34 29	055	46 23	137	32 09	183	22 15	241	40 58	286	41 51	326
313	45 37	357	35 18	054	47 04	138	32 05	184	21 23	241	40 00	286	41 17	325
314	45 33	356	36 07	054	47 44	139	32 01	185	20 30	241	39 03	285	40 42	324
	◆Alpheratz		◆FOMALHAUT		Peacock		Nunki		◆Rasalhague		VEGA		DENEB	
315	36 55	053	48 23	140	31 56	185	49 34	225	38 05	285	40 06	324	45 29	355
316	37 43	053	49 01	141	31 50	186	48 51	226	37 07	285	39 31	323	45 24	354
317	38 31	052	49 39	141	31 43	187	48 07	227	36 09	285	38 54	322	45 18	353
318	39 18	052	50 16	142	31 36	187	47 23	228	35 11	285	38 17	322	45 10	353
319	40 05	051	50 52	143	31 28	188	46 39	228	34 13	285	37 40	321	45 02	352
320	40 52	051	51 28	144	31 19	189	45 54	229	33 15	284	37 02	321	44 53	351
321	41 38	050	52 02	145	31 10	189	45 08	230	32 17	284	36 24	320	44 42	350
322	42 25	050	52 36	147	31 00	190	44 22	230	31 18	284	35 45	319	44 31	349
323	43 10	049	53 08	148	30 50	190	43 35	231	30 20	284	35 05	319	44 19	348
324	43 55	049	53 40	149	30 39	191	42 48	232	29 22	284	34 26	318	44 06	347
325	44 40	048	54 10	150	30 27	192	42 01	232	28 24	284	33 46	318	43 51	346
326	45 25	047	54 40	151	30 15	192	41 14	233	27 26	284	33 05	317	43 36	345
327	46 09	047	55 08	153	30 02	193	40 26	233	26 27	284	32 25	317	43 20	344
328	46 52	046	55 35	154	29 48	193	39 37	234	25 29	283	31 44	317	43 03	343
329	47 35	045	56 01	155	29 34	194	38 49	234	24 31	283	31 02	316	42 45	342
	◆Alpheratz		Diphda		◆FOMALHAUT		Peacock		◆ALTAIR		VEGA		DENEB	
330	48 17	045	45 23	117	56 25	157	29 20	194	57 04	285	30 20	316	42 27	341
331	48 59	044	46 16	118	56 48	158	29 04	195	56 06	285	29 38	315	42 07	341
332	49 40	043	47 09	118	57 10	159	28 49	196	55 08	284	28 56	315	41 47	340
333	50 21	042	48 02	119	57 30	161	28 32	196	54 10	284	28 13	315	41 26	339
334	51 01	041	48 54	119	57 49	162	28 15	197	53 11	284	27 31	314	41 04	338
335	51 40	040	49 47	120	58 06	164	27 58	197	52 13	283	26 48	314	40 41	337
336	52 18	039	50 38	120	58 22	166	27 40	198	51 15	283	26 04	314	40 18	337
337	52 55	038	51 30	121	58 36	167	27 22	198	50 16	283	25 21	313	39 54	336
338	53 32	037	52 21	122	58 49	169	27 03	199	49 18	283	24 37	313	39 29	335
339	54 08	036	53 12	122	58 59	170	26 43	199	48 19	282	23 53	313	39 03	334
340	54 43	035	54 02	123	59 08	172	26 23	200	47 20	282	23 09	312	38 37	334
341	55 17	034	54 52	124	59 16	174	26 03	200	46 22	282	22 24	312	38 10	333
342	55 50	033	55 42	125	59 21	176	25 42	201	45 23	282	21 40	312	37 42	332
343	56 21	031	56 31	126	59 25	177	25 21	201	44 24	282	20 55	312	37 14	332
344	56 52	030	57 19	127	59 27	179	24 59	202	43 25	281	20 10	311	36 45	331
	Alpheratz		◆Hamal		Acamar		◆ACHERNAR		FOMALHAUT		◆ALTAIR		DENEB	
345	57 22	029	39 12	060	21 57	135	23 47	158	59 27	181	42 27	281	36 16	330
346	57 50	027	40 04	060	22 39	135	24 10	158	59 26	182	41 28	281	35 46	330
347	58 17	026	40 56	059	23 21	135	24 32	159	59 22	184	40 29	281	35 16	329
348	58 42	025	41 47	059	24 03	136	24 53	159	59 17	186	39 30	281	34 45	329
349	59 06	023	42 38	058	24 45	136	25 14	160	59 10	187	38 31	281	34 13	328
350	59 29	021	43 29	058	25 27	136	25 35	160	59 02	189	37 32	280	33 41	327
351	59 50	020	44 20	057	26 08	137	25 55	161	58 51	191	36 33	280	33 09	327
352	60 10	018	45 10	057	26 49	137	26 15	161	58 39	192	35 34	280	32 36	326
353	60 28	017	46 00	056	27 30	138	26 34	161	58 26	194	34 35	280	32 02	326
354	60 44	015	46 50	056	28 10	138	26 53	162	58 10	196	33 36	280	31 29	325
355	60 59	013	47 39	055	28 50	138	27 11	162	57 53	197	32 37	280	30 54	325
356	61 12	011	48 28	054	29 30	139	27 29	163	57 35	199	31 38	280	30 20	324
357	61 23	010	49 16	054	30 09	139	27 46	164	57 15	200	30 38	280	29 45	324
358	61 32	008	50 05	053	30 48	140	28 03	164	56 53	202	29 39	280	29 09	324
359	61 39	006	50 52	052	31 27	140	28 19	165	56 31	203	28 40	280	28 33	323

LAT 0°

LHA ♈	Hc	Zn	Hc	Zn	Hc	Zn	Hc	Zn	Hc	Zn	Hc	Zn	Hc	Zn
	Alpheratz		◆ Mirfak		ALDEBARAN		◆ ACHERNAR		FOMALHAUT		◆ ALTAIR		DENEB	
0	60 45	004	23 43	033	19 54	072	29 33	165	57 01	205	27 31	280	27 09	323
1	60 48	002	24 16	033	20 52	072	29 48	166	56 35	206	26 32	280	26 33	323
2	60 50	001	24 48	033	21 49	072	30 03	166	56 08	208	25 33	280	25 57	322
3	60 49	359	25 20	032	22 46	072	30 17	167	55 39	209	24 34	280	25 20	322
4	60 47	357	25 52	032	23 43	072	30 31	167	55 09	210	23 34	280	24 43	322
5	60 43	355	26 23	031	24 40	072	30 44	168	54 38	212	22 35	280	24 05	321
6	60 37	353	26 54	031	25 37	072	30 56	168	54 06	213	21 36	280	23 27	321
7	60 29	352	27 25	030	26 34	071	31 08	169	53 33	214	20 37	280	22 49	320
8	60 19	350	27 55	030	27 31	071	31 19	170	53 00	215	19 38	279	22 11	320
9	60 08	348	28 25	030	28 27	071	31 30	170	52 25	216	18 39	279	21 32	320
10	59 55	346	28 54	029	29 24	071	31 39	171	51 49	217	17 39	279	20 54	320
11	59 40	345	29 23	029	30 21	071	31 49	171	51 12	218	16 40	279	20 15	319
12	59 23	343	29 52	028	31 17	071	31 57	172	50 35	219	15 41	279	19 35	319
13	59 05	342	30 20	028	32 14	070	32 05	173	49 57	220	14 42	279	18 56	319
14	58 45	340	30 47	027	33 10	070	32 13	173	49 18	221	13 42	279	18 16	319
	CAPELLA		ALDEBARAN		◆ RIGEL		ACHERNAR		◆ FOMALHAUT		Enif		◆ Alpheratz	
15	17 26	041	34 07	070	25 54	099	32 20	174	48 38	222	40 29	283	58 24	338
16	18 05	041	35 03	070	26 53	099	32 26	175	47 58	223	39 30	283	58 01	337
17	18 44	041	35 59	069	27 52	099	32 31	175	47 17	223	38 32	283	57 37	336
18	19 23	040	36 55	069	28 52	099	32 36	176	46 35	224	37 33	283	57 12	334
19	20 02	040	37 51	069	29 51	099	32 40	176	45 53	225	36 35	283	56 45	333
20	20 40	040	38 47	069	30 50	100	32 43	177	45 11	226	35 36	282	56 17	331
21	21 19	039	39 43	068	31 49	100	32 46	178	44 28	226	34 37	282	55 48	330
22	21 57	039	40 39	068	32 48	100	32 48	178	43 44	227	33 39	282	55 17	329
23	22 34	039	41 34	068	33 47	100	32 50	179	43 00	228	32 40	282	54 46	328
24	23 12	038	42 30	067	34 46	100	32 50	180	42 15	228	31 41	282	54 13	326
25	23 49	038	43 25	067	35 46	100	32 50	180	41 30	229	30 43	282	53 39	325
26	24 26	038	44 20	067	36 45	100	32 50	181	40 45	229	29 44	281	53 05	324
27	25 02	037	45 15	066	37 44	100	32 48	182	39 59	230	28 45	281	52 29	323
28	25 39	037	46 10	066	38 43	101	32 46	182	39 13	230	27 46	281	51 53	322
29	26 15	037	47 04	065	39 42	101	32 44	183	38 27	231	26 47	281	51 16	321
	Mirfak		CAPELLA		◆ ALDEBARAN		RIGEL		◆ ACHERNAR		FOMALHAUT		◆ Alpheratz	
30	36 51	017	26 50	036	47 59	065	40 41	101	32 40	183	37 40	231	50 38	320
31	37 08	016	27 26	036	48 53	064	41 40	101	32 36	184	36 53	232	49 59	319
32	37 25	016	28 01	035	49 47	064	42 38	101	32 32	185	36 06	232	49 19	318
33	37 41	015	28 35	035	50 41	063	43 37	101	32 26	185	35 18	233	48 39	318
34	37 56	014	29 09	035	51 34	063	44 36	102	32 20	186	34 30	233	47 58	317
35	38 10	013	29 43	034	52 27	062	45 35	102	32 14	187	33 42	234	47 17	316
36	38 23	013	30 17	034	53 20	062	46 34	102	32 07	187	32 53	234	46 35	315
37	38 36	012	30 50	033	54 13	061	47 32	102	31 59	188	32 05	234	45 52	314
38	38 48	011	31 22	033	55 05	060	48 31	102	31 50	189	31 16	235	45 09	314
39	38 59	010	31 54	032	55 57	059	49 29	103	31 41	189	30 27	235	44 26	313
40	39 09	009	32 26	032	56 48	059	50 28	103	31 31	190	29 37	235	43 42	312
41	39 18	009	32 57	031	57 40	058	51 26	103	31 20	190	28 48	236	42 57	312
42	39 27	008	33 28	030	58 30	057	52 25	103	31 09	191	27 58	236	42 12	311
43	39 35	007	33 58	030	59 20	056	53 23	104	30 58	192	27 08	236	41 27	311
44	39 41	006	34 27	029	60 10	055	54 21	104	30 45	192	26 18	237	40 41	310
	CAPELLA		◆ PROCYON		SIRIUS		CANOPUS		◆ ACHERNAR		Diphda		◆ Hamal	
45	34 56	029	19 54	084	31 57	110	22 23	149	30 32	193	52 09	240	63 18	333
46	35 25	028	20 53	084	32 54	110	22 53	150	30 19	193	51 17	241	62 50	331
47	35 53	027	21 53	084	33 50	110	23 23	150	30 05	194	50 25	241	62 20	329
48	36 20	027	22 53	084	34 46	111	23 53	150	29 50	194	49 32	242	61 48	328
49	36 47	026	23 52	084	35 42	111	24 22	151	29 35	195	48 39	242	61 16	326
50	37 13	025	24 52	084	36 38	111	24 51	151	29 19	195	47 46	243	60 41	325
51	37 38	025	25 52	084	37 34	111	25 20	152	29 03	196	46 52	243	60 06	323
52	38 03	024	26 52	084	38 30	112	25 48	152	28 46	197	45 59	244	59 30	322
53	38 27	023	27 51	084	39 26	112	26 16	153	28 29	197	45 05	244	58 52	321
54	38 50	023	28 51	084	40 21	112	26 44	153	28 11	198	44 11	245	58 13	319
55	39 13	022	29 51	084	41 17	113	27 11	153	27 53	198	43 16	245	57 34	318
56	39 35	021	30 50	084	42 12	113	27 38	154	27 34	199	42 22	245	56 53	317
57	39 56	020	31 50	084	43 07	113	28 04	154	27 14	199	41 27	246	56 12	316
58	40 16	019	32 50	084	44 03	114	28 29	155	26 54	200	40 33	246	55 30	315
59	40 36	019	33 49	084	44 57	114	28 55	155	26 34	200	39 38	246	54 47	314
	CAPELLA		◆ PROCYON		SIRIUS		CANOPUS		◆ ACHERNAR		Diphda		◆ Hamal	
60	40 55	018	34 49	084	45 52	114	29 19	156	26 13	201	38 43	247	54 03	313
61	41 13	017	35 49	084	46 47	115	29 44	156	25 52	201	37 47	247	53 19	312
62	41 30	016	36 48	084	47 41	115	30 08	157	25 30	201	36 52	247	52 34	311
63	41 46	015	37 48	083	48 35	116	30 31	157	25 08	202	35 57	248	51 48	310
64	42 01	014	38 47	083	49 29	116	30 54	158	24 46	202	35 01	248	51 02	309
65	42 16	014	39 47	083	50 23	117	31 16	159	24 23	203	34 05	248	50 16	309
66	42 29	013	40 47	083	51 16	117	31 38	159	23 59	203	33 10	248	49 29	308
67	42 42	012	41 46	083	52 09	118	31 59	160	23 36	204	32 14	249	48 41	307
68	42 54	011	42 46	083	53 02	119	32 19	160	23 11	204	31 18	249	47 53	307
69	43 05	010	43 45	083	53 55	119	32 39	161	22 47	204	30 22	249	47 05	306
70	43 15	009	44 45	083	54 47	120	32 59	161	22 22	205	29 26	249	46 16	305
71	43 23	008	45 44	083	55 39	121	33 17	162	21 57	205	28 29	250	45 27	305
72	43 31	007	46 44	082	56 30	121	33 35	163	21 31	205	27 33	250	44 37	304
73	43 38	006	47 43	082	57 21	122	33 53	163	21 05	206	26 37	250	43 47	304
74	43 44	005	48 43	082	58 11	123	34 10	164	20 39	206	25 41	250	42 57	303
	CAPELLA		◆ POLLUX		PROCYON		SIRIUS		◆ CANOPUS		Acamar		◆ Hamal	
75	43 49	004	41 21	051	49 42	082	59 01	124	34 26	165	41 14	211	42 07	303
76	43 53	003	42 08	051	50 41	082	59 51	125	34 41	165	40 43	212	41 16	302
77	43 56	002	42 54	050	51 41	082	60 40	126	34 56	166	40 11	212	40 25	302
78	43 58	001	43 40	050	52 40	081	61 28	127	35 10	167	39 39	213	39 34	301
79	43 59	000	44 26	049	53 39	081	62 15	128	35 24	167	39 06	214	38 42	301
80	43 59	359	45 11	048	54 39	081	63 02	129	35 37	168	38 32	214	37 51	300
81	43 58	359	45 55	048	55 38	081	63 48	131	35 49	169	37 58	215	36 59	300
82	43 56	358	46 39	047	56 37	081	64 33	132	36 00	170	37 23	216	36 07	300
83	43 53	357	47 23	046	57 36	080	65 17	134	36 10	170	36 48	216	35 15	299
84	43 49	356	48 06	045	58 35	080	66 00	135	36 20	171	36 13	217	34 22	299
85	43 44	355	48 48	045	59 35	080	66 42	137	36 29	172	35 36	217	33 30	299
86	43 38	354	49 30	044	60 34	079	67 22	138	36 38	172	35 00	218	32 37	298
87	43 31	353	50 11	043	61 32	079	68 01	140	36 45	173	34 23	218	31 44	298
88	43 23	352	50 52	042	62 31	079	68 39	142	36 52	174	33 45	219	30 51	298
89	43 14	351	51 31	041	63 30	078	69 15	144	36 58	175	33 07	220	29 58	297

LHA ♈	Hc	Zn	Hc	Zn	Hc	Zn	Hc	Zn	Hc	Zn	Hc	Zn	Hc	Zn
	POLLUX		◆ REGULUS		Suhail		◆ CANOPUS		Acamar		◆ ALDEBARAN		CAPELLA	
90	52 10	040	27 04	077	29 34	142	37 03	175	32 29	220	63 39	310	43 04	350
91	52 49	039	28 02	076	30 11	143	37 08	176	31 50	220	62 53	309	42 53	349
92	53 26	038	29 00	076	30 47	143	37 11	177	31 11	221	62 06	307	42 41	348
93	54 02	037	29 59	076	31 23	144	37 14	178	30 31	221	61 18	306	42 28	347
94	54 38	036	30 57	076	31 58	144	37 16	178	29 51	222	60 29	305	42 14	346
95	55 13	035	31 55	076	32 33	145	37 17	179	29 11	222	59 40	304	42 00	345
96	55 46	033	32 53	076	33 07	145	37 18	180	28 31	223	58 50	303	41 44	345
97	56 19	032	33 52	076	33 41	146	37 17	181	27 50	223	57 59	302	41 28	344
98	56 50	031	34 50	075	34 15	146	37 16	181	27 09	223	57 09	302	41 11	343
99	57 20	030	35 48	075	34 47	147	37 14	182	26 27	224	56 17	301	40 53	342
100	57 49	028	36 46	075	35 20	148	37 12	183	25 46	224	55 26	300	40 34	341
101	58 17	027	37 44	075	35 52	148	37 08	184	25 04	225	54 33	299	40 14	340
102	58 44	025	38 42	075	36 23	149	37 04	184	24 22	225	53 41	299	39 54	340
103	59 08	024	39 39	074	36 54	149	36 59	185	23 39	225	52 48	298	39 33	339
104	59 32	022	40 37	074	37 24	150	36 53	186	22 56	225	51 55	297	39 11	338
	POLLUX		◆ REGULUS		Suhail		◆ CANOPUS		RIGEL		◆ ALDEBARAN		CAPELLA	
105	59 54	021	41 35	074	37 54	151	36 46	187	62 39	252	51 02	297	38 48	337
106	60 14	019	42 33	074	38 23	151	36 39	187	61 42	253	50 08	296	38 25	337
107	60 33	017	43 30	073	38 51	152	36 30	188	60 45	253	49 14	296	38 00	336
108	60 50	016	44 28	073	39 19	153	36 22	189	59 47	254	48 20	295	37 36	335
109	61 05	014	45 25	073	39 46	154	36 12	190	58 50	254	47 26	295	37 10	335
110	61 19	012	46 22	073	40 13	154	36 01	190	57 52	254	46 31	294	36 44	334
111	61 31	010	47 20	072	40 38	155	35 50	191	56 54	255	45 37	294	36 17	333
112	61 40	009	48 17	072	41 03	156	35 38	192	55 56	255	44 42	294	35 50	333
113	61 48	007	49 14	072	41 27	157	35 26	193	54 58	256	43 47	293	35 22	332
114	61 54	005	50 11	071	41 51	158	35 12	193	54 00	256	42 51	293	34 53	331
115	61 58	003	51 07	071	42 13	158	34 58	194	53 01	256	41 56	292	34 24	331
116	62 00	001	52 04	070	42 35	159	34 44	195	52 03	257	41 01	292	33 55	330
117	62 00	359	53 00	070	42 56	160	34 28	195	51 05	257	40 05	292	33 25	330
118	61 59	357	53 57	070	43 16	161	34 12	196	50 06	257	39 09	292	32 54	329
119	61 55	355	54 53	069	43 35	162	33 55	197	49 08	257	38 13	291	32 23	328
	Dubhe		◆ REGULUS		Suhail		◆ CANOPUS		SIRIUS		BETELGEUSE		◆ CAPELLA	
120	19 11	021	55 49	068	43 53	163	33 38	197	65 13	227	58 13	284	31 51	328
121	19 33	021	56 44	068	44 11	164	33 20	198	64 29	228	57 14	284	31 19	327
122	19 54	021	57 40	067	44 27	165	33 01	198	63 44	229	56 16	283	30 46	327
123	20 15	020	58 35	067	44 42	166	32 42	199	62 58	231	55 18	283	30 13	326
124	20 36	020	59 30	066	44 57	167	32 22	200	62 11	232	54 19	283	29 40	326
125	20 56	020	60 25	065	45 10	168	32 02	200	61 23	233	53 21	282	29 06	325
126	21 16	019	61 19	065	45 23	168	31 41	201	60 35	234	52 22	282	28 32	325
127	21 35	019	62 13	064	45 34	169	31 19	201	59 46	235	51 23	282	27 57	325
128	21 55	018	63 07	063	45 45	170	30 57	202	58 57	236	50 25	282	27 22	324
129	22 13	018	64 00	062	45 54	172	30 34	202	58 07	237	49 26	281	26 47	324
130	22 32	018	64 53	061	46 02	173	30 11	203	57 16	238	48 27	281	26 11	323
131	22 50	017	65 45	060	46 10	174	29 47	204	56 25	239	47 28	281	25 35	323
132	23 07	017	66 36	059	46 16	175	29 23	204	55 34	239	46 29	281	24 59	323
133	23 24	016	67 27	057	46 21	176	28 58	205	54 42	240	45 30	281	24 22	322
134	23 41	016	68 18	056	46 25	177	28 33	205	53 50	241	44 31	280	23 45	322
	Dubhe		◆ SPICA		ACRUX		◆ CANOPUS		SIRIUS		BETELGEUSE		◆ POLLUX	
135	23 58	016	23 02	102	16 11	158	28 07	206	52 57	241	43 32	280	56 54	329
136	24 13	015	24 00	102	16 33	159	27 41	206	52 04	242	42 33	280	56 23	328
137	24 29	015	24 59	102	16 54	159	27 15	207	51 11	243	41 34	280	55 50	327
138	24 44	014	25 57	103	17 16	159	26 48	207	50 18	243	40 35	280	55 17	325
139	24 59	014	26 56	103	17 37	159	26 20	207	49 24	244	39 36	280	54 42	324
140	25 13	013	27 55	103	17 58	160	25 52	208	48 30	244	38 37	279	54 07	323
141	25 26	013	28 53	103	18 19	160	25 24	208	47 36	245	37 37	279	53 30	322
142	25 39	012	29 52	103	18 39	160	24 56	209	46 41	245	36 38	279	52 53	321
143	25 52	012	30 50	103	18 59	161	24 27	209	45 47	246	35 39	279	52 15	320
144	26 04	011	31 48	103	19 19	161	23 57	209	44 52	246	34 40	279	51 36	319
145	26 16	011	32 47	103	19 38	161	23 28	210	43 57	246	33 40	279	50 56	318
146	26 27	011	33 45	104	19 57	162	22 57	210	43 02	247	32 41	279	50 16	317
147	26 38	010	34 43	104	20 16	162	22 27	211	42 07	247	31 42	279	49 35	316
148	26 48	010	35 42	104	20 34	162	21 56	211	41 12	247	30 43	279	48 53	316
149	26 58	009	36 40	104	20 52	163	21 25	211	40 16	248	29 43	279	48 11	315
	◆ Dubhe		ARCTURUS		◆ SPICA		ACRUX		◆ SIRIUS		PROCYON		POLLUX	
150	27 07	009	24 23	069	37 38	104	21 10	163	39 21	248	54 41	279	47 28	314
151	27 16	008	25 19	069	38 36	104	21 27	164	38 25	248	53 42	279	46 44	313
152	27 24	008	26 15	069	39 34	105	21 44	164	37 29	249	52 43	279	46 00	313
153	27 31	007	27 11	068	40 32	105	22 00	164	36 33	249	51 43	278	45 16	312
154	27 38	006	28 07	068	41 30	105	22 16	165	35 37	249	50 44	278	44 31	311
155	27 45	006	29 03	068	42 28	105	22 32	165	34 41	250	49 45	278	43 46	311
156	27 51	005	29 58	068	43 26	106	22 47	165	33 45	250	48 45	278	43 00	310
157	27 56	005	30 54	068	44 24	106	23 02	166	32 48	250	47 46	278	42 14	309
158	28 01	004	31 49	067	45 21	106	23 16	166	31 52	250	46 46	278	41 27	309
159	28 05	004	32 44	067	46 19	106	23 30	167	30 55	250	45 47	277	40 40	308
160	28 09	003	33 40	067	47 17	107	23 44	167	29 59	251	44 47	277	39 53	308
161	28 12	003	34 35	067	48 14	107	23 57	168	29 02	251	43 48	277	39 05	307
162	28 15	002	35 30	066	49 11	107	24 10	168	28 05	251	42 48	277	38 17	307
163	28 17	002	36 25	066	50 09	108	24 22	168	27 09	251	41 49	277	37 29	306
164	28 18	001	37 19	066	51 06	108	24 34	169	26 12	251	40 49	277	36 40	306
	Dubhe		◆ ARCTURUS		SPICA		◆ ACRUX		Suhail		PROCYON		◆ POLLUX	
165	28 19	001	38 14	065	52 03	108	24 45	169	39 54	206	39 49	277	35 52	305
166	28 20	000	39 08	065	52 59	109	24 56	170	39 27	207	38 50	277	35 02	305
167	28 20	000	40 03	065	53 56	109	25 06	170	38 59	208	37 50	277	34 13	305
168	28 19	359	40 57	064	54 53	110	25 16	171	38 31	208	36 51	276	33 24	304
169	28 18	358	41 51	064	55 49	110	25 26	171	38 02	209	35 51	276	32 34	304
170	28 16	358	42 45	064	56 45	111	25 35	172	37 33	210	34 51	276	31 44	303
171	28 13	357	43 38	063	57 41	111	25 43	172	37 02	210	33 52	276	30 54	303
172	28 10	357	44 32	063	58 37	112	25 51	173	36 32	211	32 52	276	30 04	303
173	28 07	356	45 25	062	59 32	113	25 59	173	36 01	212	31 53	276	29 13	303
174	28 03	356	46 18	062	60 28	113	26 06	174	35 29	212	30 53	276	28 22	302
175	27 58	355	47 11	061	61 23	114	26 12	174	34 56	213	29 53	276	27 32	302
176	27 53	355	48 03	061	62 17	115	26 18	175	34 24	213	28 53	276	26 41	302
177	27 47	354	48 55	060	63 12	116	26 23	175	33 50	214	27 54	276	25 49	301
178	27 41	354	49 47	060	64 06	116	26 28	176	33 16	215	26 54	276	24 58	301
179	27 34	353	50 39	059	64 59	117	26 33	176	32 42	215	25 54	276	24 07	301

 LAT 0°

LHA ♈	Hc	Zn	Hc	Zn	Hc	Zn	Hc	Zn	Hc	Zn	Hc	Zn	Hc	Zn
	◆ ARCTURUS		ANTARES		RIGIL KENT		◆ ACRUX		Suhail		◆ REGULUS		Dubhe	
180	51 30	058	19 58	118	21 49	160	26 37	177	32 07	216	60 02	294	27 26	353
181	52 21	058	20 50	118	22 09	161	26 40	177	31 32	216	59 07	294	27 18	352
182	53 11	057	21 43	119	22 29	161	26 43	178	30 57	217	58 12	293	27 10	352
183	54 01	056	22 36	119	22 48	161	26 45	178	30 21	217	57 17	292	27 01	351
184	54 51	055	23 28	119	23 07	162	26 47	179	29 44	218	56 21	292	26 51	351
185	55 40	055	24 21	119	23 26	162	26 48	179	29 07	218	55 25	291	26 41	350
186	56 29	054	25 13	120	23 44	163	26 49	180	28 30	218	54 29	291	26 31	350
187	57 17	053	26 05	120	24 02	163	26 49	180	27 53	219	53 33	290	26 20	349
188	58 04	052	26 57	120	24 19	163	26 49	181	27 15	219	52 37	290	26 08	349
189	58 51	051	27 49	120	24 36	164	26 48	181	26 37	220	51 40	289	25 56	348
190	59 37	050	28 41	121	24 52	164	26 46	182	25 58	220	50 44	289	25 44	348
191	60 22	049	29 32	121	25 08	165	26 45	182	25 20	220	49 47	289	25 31	347
192	61 07	047	30 24	121	25 24	165	26 42	183	24 41	221	48 50	288	25 17	347
193	61 51	046	31 15	121	25 39	166	26 39	183	24 01	221	47 53	288	25 03	346
194	62 33	045	32 06	122	25 53	166	26 36	184	23 22	221	46 56	288	24 49	346
	◆ Alphecca		Rasalhague		ANTARES		◆ RIGIL KENT		ACRUX		◆ REGULUS		Dubhe	
195	44 07	051	20 34	077	32 57	122	26 07	167	26 32	184	45 59	287	24 34	345
196	44 54	051	21 32	076	33 48	122	26 21	167	26 27	185	45 01	287	24 18	345
197	45 40	050	22 31	076	34 38	123	26 34	168	26 22	185	44 04	287	24 03	345
198	46 26	049	23 29	076	35 29	123	26 46	168	26 16	186	43 06	286	23 46	344
199	47 11	049	24 27	076	36 19	124	26 59	169	26 10	186	42 09	286	23 30	344
200	47 56	048	25 25	076	37 09	124	27 10	169	26 04	187	41 11	286	23 13	343
201	48 40	047	26 24	076	37 58	124	27 21	170	25 57	187	40 13	286	22 55	343
202	49 24	046	27 22	076	38 48	125	27 32	170	25 49	188	39 15	285	22 38	342
203	50 07	046	28 20	076	39 37	125	27 42	171	25 41	188	38 18	285	22 19	342
204	50 50	045	29 18	076	40 26	126	27 51	171	25 32	188	37 20	285	22 01	342
205	51 31	044	30 16	075	41 14	126	28 00	172	25 23	189	36 22	285	21 42	341
206	52 13	043	31 14	075	42 02	127	28 08	172	25 14	189	35 24	285	21 22	341
207	52 53	042	32 12	075	42 50	127	28 16	173	25 04	190	34 26	284	21 02	341
208	53 33	041	33 10	075	43 38	128	28 23	173	24 53	190	33 27	284	20 42	340
209	54 12	040	34 08	075	44 25	129	28 30	174	24 42	191	32 29	284	20 22	340
	◆ VEGA		Rasalhague		ANTARES		◆ RIGIL KENT		ACRUX		◆ REGULUS		Dubhe	
210	15 57	049	35 06	075	45 11	129	28 36	174	24 31	191	31 31	284	20 01	340
211	16 42	049	36 04	074	45 58	130	28 42	175	24 19	192	30 33	284	19 40	339
212	17 27	049	37 02	074	46 43	131	28 47	175	24 06	192	29 35	284	19 18	339
213	18 13	049	37 59	074	47 29	131	28 51	176	23 54	193	28 36	284	18 57	339
214	18 58	049	38 57	074	48 14	132	28 55	177	23 40	193	27 38	283	18 34	338
215	19 42	048	39 55	074	48 58	133	28 59	177	23 27	193	26 40	283	18 12	338
216	20 27	048	40 52	073	49 42	134	29 01	178	23 12	194	25 41	283	17 49	338
217	21 12	048	41 49	073	50 25	134	29 03	178	22 58	194	24 43	283	17 26	337
218	21 56	048	42 47	073	51 08	135	29 05	179	22 43	195	23 44	283	17 03	337
219	22 40	047	43 44	072	51 49	136	29 06	179	22 28	195	22 46	283	16 39	337
220	23 24	047	44 41	072	52 31	137	29 06	180	22 12	195	21 47	283	16 16	336
221	24 08	047	45 38	072	53 11	138	29 06	180	21 56	196	20 49	283	15 52	336
222	24 51	046	46 35	072	53 51	139	29 05	181	21 39	196	19 50	283	15 27	336
223	25 35	046	47 32	071	54 30	140	29 04	182	21 22	197	18 52	283	15 03	336
224	26 18	046	48 29	071	55 08	141	29 02	182	21 05	197	17 53	283	14 38	335
	VEGA		◆ ALTAIR		Nunki		ANTARES		◆ RIGIL KENT		SPICA		◆ ARCTURUS	
225	27 00	045	16 55	081	27 28	120	55 45	142	28 59	183	64 05	244	68 06	331
226	27 43	045	17 54	081	28 20	120	56 21	144	28 56	183	63 11	244	67 36	329
227	28 25	045	18 53	081	29 11	120	56 56	145	28 53	184	62 17	245	67 05	327
228	29 07	044	19 52	081	30 03	121	57 30	146	28 48	184	61 22	246	66 31	325
229	29 49	044	20 51	080	30 55	121	58 03	147	28 44	185	60 27	247	65 56	323
230	30 30	043	21 50	080	31 46	121	58 35	149	28 38	185	59 32	247	65 20	322
231	31 11	043	22 50	080	32 37	122	59 05	150	28 32	186	58 37	248	64 42	320
232	31 52	042	23 49	080	33 28	122	59 35	152	28 26	187	57 41	249	64 03	318
233	32 32	042	24 48	080	34 19	122	60 02	153	28 19	187	56 45	249	63 22	317
234	33 12	042	25 47	080	35 09	123	60 29	155	28 11	188	55 49	250	62 41	315
235	33 52	041	26 46	080	36 00	123	60 54	156	28 03	188	54 52	250	61 58	314
236	34 31	040	27 45	080	36 50	124	61 17	158	27 54	189	53 56	251	61 14	313
237	35 10	040	28 44	080	37 40	124	61 38	160	27 45	189	52 59	251	60 30	312
238	35 48	039	29 43	080	38 29	124	61 58	162	27 35	190	52 02	252	59 45	311
239	36 26	039	30 42	080	39 19	125	62 16	163	27 25	190	51 05	252	58 59	309
	VEGA		◆ ALTAIR		Nunki		◆ ANTARES		SPICA		◆ ARCTURUS		Alkaid	
240	37 03	038	31 41	080	40 08	125	62 33	165	50 08	252	58 12	308	33 13	335
241	37 40	038	32 40	079	40 56	126	62 47	167	49 11	253	57 25	307	32 47	334
242	38 17	037	33 39	079	41 45	126	63 00	169	48 14	253	56 37	306	32 21	334
243	38 52	036	34 38	079	42 33	127	63 10	171	47 16	253	55 48	306	31 54	333
244	39 28	036	35 37	079	43 21	128	63 19	173	46 19	254	54 59	305	31 27	333
245	40 03	035	36 36	079	44 08	128	63 25	175	45 21	254	54 10	304	30 59	332
246	40 37	034	37 35	079	44 55	129	63 30	177	44 23	254	53 20	303	30 30	332
247	41 10	034	38 34	079	45 42	129	63 32	179	43 26	254	52 29	303	30 02	331
248	41 43	033	39 32	078	46 28	130	63 32	181	42 28	255	51 39	302	29 32	331
249	42 15	032	40 31	078	47 14	131	63 30	183	41 30	255	50 47	301	29 03	330
250	42 47	031	41 30	078	47 59	131	63 26	185	40 32	255	49 56	301	28 32	330
251	43 18	031	42 29	078	48 44	132	63 20	187	39 34	255	49 04	300	28 02	329
252	43 48	030	43 27	078	49 28	133	63 12	189	38 36	256	48 12	299	27 31	329
253	44 17	029	44 26	077	50 12	134	63 02	191	37 38	256	47 20	299	26 59	328
254	44 46	028	45 24	077	50 55	135	62 49	193	36 39	256	46 27	298	26 28	328
	◆ VEGA		ALTAIR		◆ Nunki		ANTARES		◆ SPICA		ARCTURUS		Alkaid	
255	45 14	027	46 23	077	51 37	135	62 35	195	35 41	256	45 34	298	25 55	327
256	45 41	026	47 21	077	52 19	136	62 19	196	34 43	256	44 41	297	25 23	327
257	46 07	025	48 20	077	53 00	137	62 01	198	33 45	256	43 48	297	24 50	327
258	46 32	024	49 18	076	53 40	138	61 42	200	32 46	257	42 54	297	24 17	326
259	46 56	023	50 16	076	54 19	139	61 21	202	31 48	257	42 00	296	23 43	326
260	47 20	022	51 14	076	54 58	140	60 58	203	30 50	257	41 06	296	23 09	325
261	47 42	021	52 13	075	55 36	142	60 33	205	29 51	257	40 12	295	22 35	325
262	48 04	020	53 11	075	56 13	143	60 07	207	28 53	257	39 18	295	22 01	325
263	48 24	019	54 08	075	56 48	144	59 39	208	27 54	257	38 23	295	21 26	324
264	48 43	018	55 06	074	57 23	145	59 10	210	26 56	257	37 29	294	20 51	324
265	49 02	017	56 04	074	57 57	147	58 40	211	25 57	257	36 34	294	20 16	324
266	49 19	016	57 02	073	58 29	148	58 09	212	24 58	258	35 39	294	19 40	324
267	49 35	015	57 59	073	59 01	149	57 36	214	24 00	258	34 44	293	19 04	323
268	49 50	014	58 56	073	59 31	151	57 02	215	23 01	258	33 49	293	18 28	323
269	50 03	013	59 54	072	59 59	152	56 27	216	22 03	258	32 54	293	17 52	323

LHA ♈	Hc	Zn	Hc	Zn	Hc	Zn	Hc	Zn	Hc	Zn	Hc	Zn	Hc	Zn
	VEGA		◆ DENEB		FOMALHAUT		◆ Peacock		Shaula		ANTARES		◆ ARCTURUS	
270	50 16	011	32 19	033	13 20	120	26 07	159	52 26	188	55 51	217	31 59	293
271	50 27	010	32 51	032	14 12	121	26 29	159	52 16	190	55 14	219	31 03	292
272	50 37	009	33 23	032	15 04	121	26 50	159	52 06	191	54 36	220	30 08	292
273	50 46	008	33 54	031	15 55	121	27 11	160	51 54	192	53 57	221	29 12	292
274	50 53	007	34 25	030	16 47	121	27 32	160	51 40	193	53 18	222	28 16	292
275	51 00	005	34 55	030	17 38	121	27 51	161	51 26	195	52 37	223	27 21	292
276	51 05	004	35 25	029	18 30	121	28 11	161	51 10	196	51 56	224	26 25	291
277	51 08	003	35 54	029	19 21	122	28 30	162	50 53	197	51 14	225	25 29	291
278	51 11	002	36 22	028	20 12	122	28 48	162	50 35	198	50 32	225	24 33	291
279	51 12	000	36 50	027	21 03	122	29 06	163	50 16	199	49 49	226	23 37	291
280	51 12	359	37 17	027	21 54	122	29 23	164	49 56	200	49 05	227	22 41	291
281	51 10	358	37 44	026	22 44	122	29 40	164	49 34	202	48 21	228	21 45	291
282	51 08	357	38 10	025	23 35	123	29 56	165	49 12	203	47 36	229	20 49	290
283	51 03	355	38 35	025	24 26	123	30 11	165	48 48	204	46 51	229	19 52	290
284	50 58	354	38 59	024	25 16	123	30 27	166	48 24	205	46 05	230	18 56	290
	DENEB		Alpheratz		◆ FOMALHAUT		Peacock		◆ ANTARES		Rasalhague		◆ VEGA	
285	39 23	023	11 04	060	26 06	123	30 41	166	45 19	231	65 36	302	50 51	353
286	39 46	022	11 57	060	26 56	124	30 55	167	44 32	231	64 45	301	50 44	352
287	40 09	021	12 49	060	27 46	124	31 08	168	43 45	232	63 53	300	50 34	351
288	40 30	021	13 40	060	28 36	124	31 21	168	42 58	232	63 01	299	50 24	349
289	40 51	020	14 32	060	29 25	124	31 33	169	42 10	233	62 08	298	50 12	348
290	41 11	019	15 24	060	30 15	125	31 44	169	41 22	234	61 14	297	50 00	347
291	41 30	018	16 16	059	31 04	125	31 55	170	40 34	234	60 21	296	49 46	346
292	41 49	017	17 07	059	31 53	125	32 05	171	39 45	235	59 27	295	49 30	345
293	42 06	017	17 59	059	32 42	126	32 15	171	38 56	235	58 32	295	49 14	344
294	42 23	016	18 51	059	33 30	126	32 24	172	38 07	236	57 37	294	48 57	343
295	42 39	015	19 42	059	34 18	127	32 32	172	37 17	236	56 42	293	48 38	341
296	42 54	014	20 33	059	35 06	127	32 40	173	36 27	236	55 47	293	48 18	340
297	43 07	013	21 24	058	35 54	127	32 47	174	35 37	237	54 52	292	47 58	339
298	43 20	012	22 15	058	36 42	128	32 53	174	34 47	237	53 56	292	47 36	338
299	43 33	011	23 06	058	37 29	128	32 58	175	33 56	238	53 00	291	47 13	337
	◆ DENEB		Alpheratz		◆ FOMALHAUT		Peacock		◆ ANTARES		Rasalhague		VEGA	
300	43 44	010	23 57	058	38 16	129	33 03	176	33 06	238	52 04	291	46 50	336
301	43 54	009	24 48	058	39 02	129	33 08	176	32 15	238	51 08	290	46 25	335
302	44 03	008	25 38	057	39 48	130	33 11	177	31 24	239	50 12	290	46 00	334
303	44 11	007	26 29	057	40 34	130	33 14	178	30 32	239	49 15	289	45 34	333
304	44 18	006	27 19	057	41 20	131	33 16	178	29 41	239	48 18	289	45 06	333
305	44 24	005	28 09	056	42 05	132	33 18	179	28 49	239	47 22	289	44 38	332
306	44 30	004	28 59	056	42 49	132	33 19	180	27 58	240	46 25	288	44 09	331
307	44 34	003	29 49	056	43 34	133	33 19	180	27 06	240	45 28	288	43 40	330
308	44 37	002	30 38	055	44 17	134	33 18	181	26 14	240	44 31	288	43 09	329
309	44 39	001	31 28	055	45 01	134	33 17	182	25 22	240	43 34	287	42 38	328
310	44 40	000	32 17	055	45 43	135	33 15	182	24 29	241	42 36	287	42 07	328
311	44 40	359	33 06	054	46 26	136	33 13	183	23 37	241	41 39	287	41 34	327
312	44 39	359	33 54	054	47 07	136	33 09	183	22 44	241	40 41	287	41 01	326
313	44 37	358	34 43	054	47 48	137	33 05	184	21 52	241	39 44	286	40 27	325
314	44 34	357	35 31	053	48 29	138	33 01	185	20 59	241	38 46	286	39 53	325
	◆ Alpheratz		◆ FOMALHAUT		Peacock		Nunki		◆ Rasalhague		VEGA		DENEB	
315	36 19	053	49 08	139	32 55	185	50 16	226	37 49	286	39 18	324	44 29	356
316	37 07	052	49 47	140	32 49	186	49 32	227	36 51	286	38 43	323	44 24	355
317	37 54	052	50 26	141	32 43	187	48 48	228	35 53	286	38 07	323	44 18	354
318	38 41	051	51 03	142	32 35	187	48 03	229	34 55	285	37 30	322	44 11	353
319	39 28	051	51 40	143	32 27	188	47 18	229	33 57	285	36 53	322	44 03	352
320	40 14	050	52 16	144	32 19	189	46 32	230	33 00	285	36 15	321	43 54	351
321	41 00	050	52 51	145	32 09	189	45 46	231	32 02	285	35 37	320	43 43	350
322	41 46	049	53 25	146	31 59	190	45 00	231	31 04	285	34 59	320	43 32	349
323	42 31	049	53 59	147	31 49	190	44 13	232	30 05	285	34 20	319	43 20	348
324	43 16	048	54 31	148	31 38	191	43 25	232	29 07	284	33 41	319	43 07	347
325	44 00	047	55 02	149	31 26	192	42 38	233	28 09	284	33 01	318	42 53	346
326	44 44	047	55 32	151	31 13	192	41 50	234	27 11	284	32 21	318	42 38	345
327	45 27	046	56 01	152	31 00	193	41 01	234	26 13	284	31 41	317	42 22	344
328	46 10	045	56 29	153	30 47	193	40 12	235	25 15	284	31 00	317	42 06	343
329	46 52	045	56 55	155	30 33	194	39 23	235	24 16	284	30 19	317	41 48	343
	◆ Alpheratz		Diphda		◆ FOMALHAUT		Peacock		◆ ALTAIR		VEGA		DENEB	
330	47 34	044	45 50	116	57 20	156	30 18	195	56 48	286	29 37	316	41 30	342
331	48 15	043	46 43	117	57 44	157	30 02	195	55 50	286	28 56	316	41 11	341
332	48 56	042	47 37	117	58 06	159	29 46	196	54 52	286	28 14	315	40 51	340
333	49 36	041	48 30	118	58 27	160	29 30	196	53 54	285	27 31	315	40 30	339
334	50 15	040	49 23	118	58 46	162	29 13	197	52 57	285	26 49	315	40 08	338
335	50 54	039	50 16	119	59 04	164	28 55	197	51 58	285	26 06	314	39 46	338
336	51 31	038	51 08	119	59 20	165	28 37	198	51 00	284	25 23	314	39 23	337
337	52 08	037	52 00	120	59 35	167	28 19	198	50 02	284	24 39	314	38 59	336
338	52 44	036	52 52	121	59 47	169	27 59	199	49 04	284	23 56	313	38 34	335
339	53 19	035	53 44	121	59 59	170	27 40	199	48 06	283	23 12	313	38 09	335
340	53 53	034	54 35	122	60 08	172	27 20	200	47 07	283	22 28	313	37 43	334
341	54 27	033	55 25	123	60 15	174	26 59	200	46 09	283	21 44	312	37 16	333
342	54 59	032	56 16	124	60 21	175	26 38	201	45 10	283	20 59	312	36 49	333
343	55 30	031	57 05	124	60 25	177	26 16	201	44 12	282	20 15	312	36 21	332
344	56 00	029	57 55	125	60 27	179	25 55	202	43 13	282	19 30	312	35 53	331
	Alpheratz		◆ Hamal		Acamar		◆ ACHERNAR		FOMALHAUT		◆ ALTAIR		DENEB	
345	56 29	028	38 42	059	22 39	134	24 43	158	60 27	181	42 14	282	35 24	331
346	56 56	027	39 33	059	23 21	135	25 05	158	60 26	182	41 16	282	34 54	330
347	57 23	025	40 25	058	24 04	135	25 27	159	60 22	184	40 17	282	34 24	330
348	57 48	024	41 15	058	24 46	135	25 49	159	60 17	186	39 18	282	33 53	329
349	58 11	022	42 06	057	25 28	136	26 10	159	60 10	188	38 19	281	33 22	328
350	58 33	021	42 57	057	26 10	136	26 31	160	60 01	189	37 21	281	32 50	328
351	58 54	019	43 47	056	26 52	136	26 52	160	59 50	191	36 22	281	32 18	327
352	59 13	018	44 37	056	27 33	137	27 12	161	59 38	193	35 23	281	31 46	327
353	59 30	016	45 26	055	28 14	137	27 31	161	59 24	194	34 24	281	31 13	326
354	59 46	014	46 15	055	28 54	138	27 50	162	59 08	196	33 25	281	30 39	326
355	60 00	013	47 04	054	29 35	138	28 09	162	58 51	198	32 26	281	30 05	325
356	60 13	011	47 52	053	30 15	138	28 26	163	58 32	199	31 27	280	29 31	325
357	60 24	009	48 40	053	30 54	139	28 44	163	58 11	201	30 28	280	28 56	324
358	60 32	008	49 28	052	31 34	139	29 01	164	57 49	202	29 29	280	28 21	324
359	60 39	006	50 15	051	32 13	140	29 17	164	57 26	204	28 30	280	27 45	323

LHA ♈	Hc	Zn	Hc	Zn	Hc	Zn	Hc	Zn	Hc	Zn	Hc	Zn	Hc	Zn
	Alpheratz		◆ ALDEBARAN		RIGEL		ACHERNAR		◆ FOMALHAUT		ALTAIR		◆ DENEB	
0	59 45	004	19 36	072	11 13	098	30 31	165	57 55	206	27 20	281	26 21	323
1	59 48	002	20 33	072	12 12	098	30 46	165	57 28	207	26 21	280	25 45	323
2	59 50	001	21 30	072	13 12	098	31 01	166	57 00	209	25 22	280	25 09	323
3	59 49	359	22 27	072	14 11	098	31 16	167	56 31	210	24 23	280	24 32	322
4	59 47	357	23 24	071	15 10	098	31 29	167	56 01	211	23 24	280	23 55	322
5	59 43	355	24 21	071	16 10	098	31 42	168	55 29	212	22 25	280	23 18	321
6	59 37	354	25 18	071	17 09	098	31 55	168	54 57	214	21 26	280	22 41	321
7	59 30	352	26 14	071	18 08	098	32 07	169	54 23	215	20 27	280	22 03	321
8	59 20	350	27 11	071	19 08	098	32 18	169	53 48	216	19 28	280	21 25	320
9	59 09	349	28 08	071	20 07	098	32 29	170	53 13	217	18 29	280	20 46	320
10	58 56	347	29 04	070	21 06	098	32 39	171	52 37	218	17 29	280	20 08	320
11	58 42	345	30 01	070	22 06	098	32 48	171	51 59	219	16 30	280	19 29	320
12	58 26	344	30 57	070	23 05	098	32 57	172	51 21	220	15 31	280	18 50	319
13	58 08	342	31 53	070	24 05	099	33 05	173	50 42	221	14 32	279	18 11	319
14	57 49	341	32 50	070	25 04	099	33 12	173	50 03	222	13 33	279	17 31	319
	CAPELLA		ALDEBARAN		◆ RIGEL		ACHERNAR		◆ FOMALHAUT		Enif		◆ Alpheratz	
15	16 40	041	33 46	069	26 03	099	33 19	174	49 23	223	40 15	284	57 28	339
16	17 20	041	34 42	069	27 02	099	33 25	174	48 42	223	39 17	284	57 06	338
17	17 59	040	35 38	069	28 02	099	33 31	175	48 00	224	38 18	284	56 43	336
18	18 37	040	36 34	068	29 01	099	33 36	176	47 18	225	37 20	283	56 18	335
19	19 16	040	37 29	068	30 00	099	33 40	176	46 36	226	36 21	283	55 51	333
20	19 54	040	38 25	068	31 00	099	33 43	177	45 52	226	35 23	283	55 24	332
21	20 32	039	39 21	068	31 59	099	33 46	178	45 09	227	34 25	283	54 55	331
22	21 10	039	40 16	067	32 58	099	33 48	178	44 25	228	33 26	283	54 26	330
23	21 47	039	41 11	067	33 57	099	33 50	179	43 40	228	32 27	282	53 55	328
24	22 25	038	42 06	066	34 57	099	33 50	180	42 55	229	31 29	282	53 23	327
25	23 02	038	43 01	066	35 56	099	33 50	180	42 10	229	30 30	282	52 50	326
26	23 38	038	43 56	066	36 55	099	33 50	181	41 24	230	29 32	282	52 16	325
27	24 15	037	44 50	065	37 54	100	33 48	182	40 38	231	28 33	282	51 41	324
28	24 51	037	45 45	065	38 53	100	33 46	182	39 51	231	27 34	282	51 05	323
29	25 27	036	46 39	064	39 52	100	33 44	183	39 04	232	26 35	282	50 29	322
	CAPELLA		◆ BETELGEUSE		SIRIUS		CANOPUS		◆ ACHERNAR		FOMALHAUT		◆ Alpheratz	
30	26 02	036	30 34	081	18 02	107	15 03	145	33 40	184	38 17	232	49 51	321
31	26 37	036	31 33	081	18 59	107	15 37	145	33 36	184	37 30	233	49 13	320
32	27 12	035	32 32	081	19 57	107	16 11	145	33 32	185	36 42	233	48 34	319
33	27 46	035	33 31	080	20 54	108	16 45	146	33 26	185	35 54	233	47 55	318
34	28 20	034	34 30	080	21 51	108	17 19	146	33 20	186	35 06	234	47 14	317
35	28 53	034	35 30	080	22 48	108	17 52	146	33 13	187	34 17	234	46 34	317
36	29 27	033	36 29	080	23 45	108	18 26	146	33 06	187	33 28	235	45 52	316
37	29 59	033	37 28	080	24 42	108	18 59	147	32 58	188	32 39	235	45 10	315
38	30 32	032	38 27	080	25 39	108	19 32	147	32 49	189	31 50	235	44 27	314
39	31 03	032	39 26	080	26 36	108	20 04	147	32 40	189	31 01	236	43 44	314
40	31 35	031	40 25	079	27 33	108	20 37	148	32 30	190	30 11	236	43 01	313
41	32 05	031	41 24	079	28 30	109	21 09	148	32 19	190	29 21	236	42 17	312
42	32 36	030	42 23	079	29 27	109	21 41	148	32 08	191	28 31	237	41 32	312
43	33 06	030	43 21	079	30 24	109	22 12	148	31 56	192	27 41	237	40 47	311
44	33 35	029	44 20	079	31 21	109	22 43	149	31 44	192	26 51	237	40 02	311
	CAPELLA		◆ BETELGEUSE		SIRIUS		CANOPUS		◆ ACHERNAR		Diphda		◆ Hamal	
45	34 04	028	45 19	078	32 17	109	23 14	149	31 31	193	52 39	241	62 24	334
46	34 32	028	46 18	078	33 14	109	23 45	149	31 17	193	51 46	242	61 57	332
47	34 59	027	47 17	078	34 10	110	24 15	150	31 03	194	50 53	242	61 28	330
48	35 26	026	48 15	078	35 07	110	24 45	150	30 48	195	50 00	243	60 57	329
49	35 53	026	49 14	077	36 03	110	25 15	151	30 33	195	49 07	243	60 25	327
50	36 18	025	50 12	077	37 00	110	25 44	151	30 17	196	48 13	244	59 52	326
51	36 44	024	51 11	077	37 56	111	26 13	151	30 01	196	47 19	244	59 18	324
52	37 08	024	52 09	077	38 52	111	26 41	152	29 44	197	46 25	245	58 42	323
53	37 32	023	53 07	076	39 48	111	27 09	152	29 26	197	45 31	245	58 05	322
54	37 55	022	54 06	076	40 44	111	27 37	153	29 08	198	44 36	246	57 28	320
55	38 17	021	55 04	076	41 40	112	28 04	153	28 50	198	43 41	246	56 49	319
56	38 39	021	56 02	075	42 35	112	28 31	154	28 31	199	42 47	246	56 09	318
57	39 00	020	57 00	075	43 31	112	28 58	154	28 11	199	41 52	247	55 28	317
58	39 20	019	57 58	074	44 26	113	29 24	155	27 51	200	40 56	247	54 47	316
59	39 39	018	58 55	074	45 21	113	29 49	155	27 30	200	40 01	247	54 05	315
	◆ CAPELLA		POLLUX		◆ SIRIUS		CANOPUS		ACHERNAR		◆ Diphda		Hamal	
60	39 57	018	28 35	057	46 17	113	30 14	156	27 09	201	39 06	248	53 22	314
61	40 15	017	29 25	057	47 11	114	30 39	156	26 48	201	38 10	248	52 38	313
62	40 32	016	30 15	056	48 06	114	31 03	157	26 26	202	37 15	248	51 54	312
63	40 48	015	31 05	056	49 01	115	31 26	157	26 04	202	36 19	248	51 09	311
64	41 03	014	31 55	056	49 55	115	31 49	158	25 41	202	35 23	249	50 24	310
65	41 17	013	32 44	055	50 49	116	32 12	158	25 18	203	34 27	249	49 38	310
66	41 31	012	33 33	055	51 43	116	32 34	159	24 55	203	33 31	249	48 51	309
67	41 43	012	34 22	055	52 37	117	32 55	159	24 31	204	32 35	249	48 04	308
68	41 55	011	35 11	054	53 30	117	33 16	160	24 06	204	31 39	249	47 17	307
69	42 06	010	35 59	054	54 23	118	33 36	161	23 42	204	30 43	250	46 29	307
70	42 15	009	36 48	053	55 16	119	33 55	161	23 17	205	29 47	250	45 41	306
71	42 24	008	37 35	053	56 09	119	34 14	162	22 51	205	28 50	250	44 52	306
72	42 32	007	38 23	052	57 01	120	34 33	163	22 25	206	27 54	250	44 03	305
73	42 39	006	39 10	052	57 52	121	34 50	163	21 59	206	26 57	250	43 14	304
74	42 45	005	39 57	051	58 44	122	35 07	164	21 33	206	26 01	251	42 24	304
	CAPELLA		◆ POLLUX		REGULUS		Suhail		◆ CANOPUS		ACHERNAR		◆ Hamal	
75	42 49	004	40 44	051	12 13	078	20 33	137	35 24	164	21 06	207	41 34	303
76	42 53	003	41 30	050	13 12	078	21 13	137	35 39	165	20 39	207	40 44	303
77	42 56	002	42 16	049	14 10	077	21 55	137	35 54	166	20 12	207	39 53	302
78	42 58	001	43 01	049	15 09	077	22 35	138	36 09	167	19 44	208	39 02	302
79	42 59	000	43 46	048	16 07	077	23 16	138	36 22	167	19 16	208	38 11	301
80	42 59	359	44 30	048	17 06	077	23 56	138	36 35	168	18 48	208	37 20	301
81	42 58	359	45 14	047	18 04	077	24 36	139	36 47	169	18 20	208	36 29	301
82	42 56	358	45 58	046	19 03	077	25 15	139	36 59	169	17 51	209	35 37	300
83	42 53	357	46 41	045	20 01	077	25 55	139	37 10	170	17 22	209	34 45	300
84	42 49	356	47 23	045	21 00	077	26 34	140	37 19	171	16 53	209	33 53	300
85	42 44	355	48 05	044	21 58	077	27 12	140	37 29	172	16 24	209	33 01	299
86	42 38	354	48 46	043	22 56	077	27 51	140	37 37	172	15 54	210	32 08	299
87	42 31	353	49 27	042	23 55	077	28 29	141	37 45	173	15 24	210	31 16	299
88	42 23	352	50 07	041	24 53	076	29 07	141	37 52	174	14 54	210	30 23	298
89	42 14	351	50 46	040	25 51	076	29 44	142	37 58	175	14 24	210	29 30	298

LHA ♈	Hc	Zn	Hc	Zn	Hc	Zn	Hc	Zn	Hc	Zn	Hc	Zn	Hc	Zn
	POLLUX		◆ REGULUS		Suhail		◆ CANOPUS		Acamar		◆ ALDEBARAN		CAPELLA	
90	51 24	039	26 50	076	30 22	142	38 03	175	33 14	220	63 00	311	42 05	350
91	52 02	038	27 48	076	30 58	142	38 07	176	32 35	221	62 15	310	41 54	349
92	52 38	037	28 46	076	31 35	143	38 11	177	31 56	221	61 28	309	41 42	348
93	53 14	036	29 44	076	32 11	143	38 14	178	31 16	222	60 41	308	41 30	347
94	53 49	035	30 42	076	32 46	144	38 16	178	30 36	222	59 54	307	41 16	347
95	54 23	034	31 40	075	33 22	144	38 17	179	29 55	223	59 05	306	41 02	346
96	54 56	033	32 38	075	33 56	145	38 18	180	29 15	223	58 16	305	40 46	345
97	55 28	031	33 36	075	34 31	145	38 17	181	28 34	223	57 27	304	40 30	344
98	55 59	030	34 34	075	35 04	146	38 16	181	27 52	224	56 36	303	40 13	343
99	56 28	029	35 32	075	35 38	147	38 14	182	27 10	224	55 46	302	39 56	342
100	56 56	027	36 30	074	36 10	147	38 12	183	26 29	225	54 55	301	39 37	342
101	57 23	026	37 28	074	36 43	148	38 08	184	25 46	225	54 03	301	39 18	341
102	57 49	025	38 25	074	37 14	148	38 04	185	25 04	225	53 12	300	38 58	340
103	58 13	023	39 23	074	37 46	149	37 58	185	24 21	225	52 19	299	38 37	339
104	58 36	022	40 21	073	38 16	150	37 52	186	23 38	226	51 27	299	38 15	338
	POLLUX		◆ REGULUS		Suhail		◆ CANOPUS		RIGEL		◆ ALDEBARAN		CAPELLA	
105	58 58	020	41 18	073	38 46	150	37 46	187	62 57	254	50 34	298	37 53	338
106	59 17	018	42 15	073	39 16	151	37 38	188	61 59	254	49 41	297	37 29	337
107	59 36	017	43 13	073	39 44	152	37 30	188	61 01	255	48 48	297	37 06	336
108	59 52	015	44 10	072	40 12	152	37 21	189	60 03	255	47 54	296	36 41	336
109	60 07	013	45 07	072	40 40	153	37 11	190	59 05	256	47 00	296	36 16	335
110	60 20	012	46 04	072	41 07	154	37 00	191	58 07	256	46 06	295	35 50	334
111	60 31	010	47 01	071	41 33	155	36 49	191	57 09	256	45 12	295	35 24	334
112	60 41	008	47 58	071	41 58	156	36 37	192	56 10	257	44 17	295	34 57	333
113	60 49	006	48 54	071	42 22	156	36 24	193	55 12	257	43 23	294	34 29	332
114	60 54	005	49 51	070	42 46	157	36 11	193	54 14	257	42 28	294	34 01	332
115	60 58	003	50 47	070	43 09	158	35 56	194	53 15	258	41 33	293	33 32	331
116	61 00	001	51 43	069	43 31	159	35 42	195	52 16	258	40 38	293	33 03	330
117	61 00	359	52 39	069	43 52	160	35 26	195	51 18	258	39 42	293	32 33	330
118	60 59	357	53 35	068	44 12	161	35 10	196	50 19	258	38 47	292	32 02	329
119	60 55	356	54 31	068	44 32	162	34 53	197	49 20	259	37 51	292	31 32	329
	◆ REGULUS		Gienah		◆ ACRUX		CANOPUS		SIRIUS		◆ BETELGEUSE		POLLUX	
120	55 26	067	24 53	109	11 07	155	34 35	197	65 54	228	57 57	286	60 49	354
121	56 21	067	25 50	109	11 32	155	34 17	198	65 08	230	56 59	285	60 42	352
122	57 16	066	26 47	109	11 57	155	33 58	199	64 22	231	56 01	285	60 33	350
123	58 11	065	27 43	109	12 22	156	33 39	199	63 35	232	55 03	284	60 22	348
124	59 05	065	28 40	110	12 47	156	33 19	200	62 47	233	54 05	284	60 09	347
125	59 59	064	29 36	110	13 12	156	32 58	200	61 59	235	53 07	284	59 54	345
126	60 53	063	30 33	110	13 36	156	32 37	201	61 10	236	52 09	283	59 38	343
127	61 46	062	31 29	110	14 00	156	32 15	202	60 20	237	51 10	283	59 20	342
128	62 39	061	32 25	110	14 25	157	31 52	202	59 30	237	50 12	283	59 00	340
129	63 31	060	33 22	111	14 48	157	31 30	203	58 39	238	49 13	283	58 39	339
130	64 23	059	34 18	111	15 12	157	31 06	203	57 47	239	48 15	282	58 16	337
131	65 14	058	35 14	111	15 35	157	30 42	204	56 56	240	47 16	282	57 52	336
132	66 04	057	36 10	111	15 58	157	30 18	204	56 04	241	46 17	282	57 26	334
133	66 54	056	37 06	111	16 21	158	29 53	205	55 11	241	45 19	282	57 00	333
134	67 43	054	38 01	112	16 44	158	29 27	205	54 18	242	44 20	281	56 31	331
	Alioth		◆ SPICA		ACRUX		◆ CANOPUS		SIRIUS		BETELGEUSE		◆ POLLUX	
135	16 05	030	23 14	102	17 06	158	29 01	206	53 25	243	43 21	281	56 02	330
136	16 35	030	24 13	102	17 29	158	28 35	206	52 32	243	42 22	281	55 31	329
137	17 05	029	25 12	102	17 50	159	28 08	207	51 38	244	41 23	281	55 00	327
138	17 34	029	26 10	102	18 12	159	27 41	207	50 44	244	40 24	281	54 27	326
139	18 03	029	27 09	102	18 33	159	27 13	208	49 50	245	39 25	280	53 53	325
140	18 32	028	28 07	102	18 54	160	26 45	208	48 56	245	38 26	280	53 18	324
141	19 00	028	29 06	102	19 15	160	26 17	209	48 01	246	37 27	280	52 43	323
142	19 28	028	30 05	102	19 35	160	25 48	209	47 06	246	36 28	280	52 06	322
143	19 56	027	31 03	103	19 56	161	25 19	209	46 11	247	35 29	280	51 29	321
144	20 24	027	32 02	103	20 15	161	24 49	210	45 16	247	34 30	280	50 50	320
145	20 51	027	33 00	103	20 35	161	24 20	210	44 21	247	33 31	280	50 11	319
146	21 18	026	33 59	103	20 54	162	23 49	210	43 25	248	32 32	279	49 32	318
147	21 44	026	34 57	103	21 13	162	23 19	211	42 30	248	31 32	279	48 51	317
148	22 11	026	35 56	103	21 31	162	22 48	211	41 34	248	30 33	279	48 10	316
149	22 36	025	36 54	103	21 49	163	22 17	211	40 38	249	29 34	279	47 28	316
	Alioth		◆ ARCTURUS		SPICA		◆ ACRUX		CANOPUS		SIRIUS		◆ POLLUX	
150	23 02	025	24 02	069	37 52	103	22 07	163	21 45	212	39 43	249	46 46	315
151	23 27	024	24 57	068	38 51	104	22 24	163	21 13	212	38 46	249	46 03	314
152	23 52	024	25 53	068	39 49	104	22 41	164	20 41	212	37 50	249	45 20	313
153	24 16	024	26 49	068	40 47	104	22 58	164	20 09	213	36 54	250	44 36	313
154	24 40	023	27 44	068	41 45	104	23 14	165	19 36	213	35 58	250	43 51	312
155	25 03	023	28 40	068	42 44	104	23 30	165	19 04	213	35 01	250	43 06	311
156	25 26	022	29 35	067	43 42	105	23 45	165	18 31	214	34 05	250	42 21	311
157	25 49	022	30 30	067	44 40	105	24 00	166	17 57	214	33 08	251	41 35	310
158	26 11	021	31 26	067	45 38	105	24 15	166	17 24	214	32 12	251	40 49	309
159	26 32	021	32 21	067	46 35	105	24 29	167	16 50	214	31 15	251	40 03	309
160	26 54	020	33 16	066	47 33	106	24 42	167	16 16	215	30 18	251	39 16	308
161	27 14	020	34 11	066	48 31	106	24 56	167	15 42	215	29 22	251	38 28	308
162	27 34	019	35 05	066	49 29	106	25 08	168	15 08	215	28 25	251	37 41	307
163	27 54	019	36 00	065	50 26	107	25 21	168	14 33	215	27 28	252	36 53	307
164	28 13	018	36 54	065	51 24	107	25 33	169	13 59	215	26 31	252	36 05	306
	Alioth		◆ ARCTURUS		SPICA		◆ ACRUX		Suhail		SIRIUS		◆ POLLUX	
165	28 32	018	37 49	065	52 21	107	25 44	169	40 47	207	25 34	252	35 17	306
166	28 50	017	38 43	064	53 18	108	25 55	170	40 20	207	24 37	252	34 28	306
167	29 08	017	39 37	064	54 15	108	26 06	170	39 52	208	23 40	252	33 39	305
168	29 25	016	40 31	064	55 12	108	26 16	171	39 24	209	22 43	252	32 50	305
169	29 41	016	41 24	063	56 09	109	26 25	171	38 54	209	21 46	252	32 00	304
170	29 57	015	42 18	063	57 06	109	26 34	172	38 25	210	20 48	252	31 11	304
171	30 12	014	43 11	062	58 02	110	26 43	172	37 54	211	19 51	253	30 21	304
172	30 27	014	44 04	062	58 59	110	26 51	173	37 23	211	18 54	253	29 31	303
173	30 41	013	44 56	061	59 55	111	26 58	173	36 52	212	17 57	253	28 41	303
174	30 55	013	45 49	061	60 51	112	27 05	174	36 19	213	16 59	253	27 50	303
175	31 07	012	46 41	060	61 46	112	27 12	174	35 47	213	16 02	253	27 00	302
176	31 20	011	47 33	060	62 42	113	27 18	175	35 14	214	15 05	253	26 09	302
177	31 31	011	48 25	059	63 37	114	27 23	175	34 40	214	14 07	253	25 18	302
178	31 42	010	49 16	059	64 31	115	27 28	176	34 06	215	13 10	253	24 27	302
179	31 53	010	50 07	058	65 26	116	27 33	176	33 31	215	12 13	253	23 36	301

LHA ♈	Hc	Zn	Hc	Zn	Hc	Zn	Hc	Zn	Hc	Zn	Hc	Zn	Hc	Zn
	Alioth		◆ ARCTURUS		ANTARES		◆ ACRUX		Suhail		Alphard		◆ REGULUS	
180	32 02	009	50 58	057	20 26	118	27 37	177	32 56	216	51 28	257	59 37	296
181	32 12	008	51 48	057	21 19	118	27 40	177	32 21	217	50 30	257	58 42	295
182	32 20	008	52 38	056	22 12	118	27 43	178	31 45	217	49 31	258	57 48	294
183	32 28	007	53 27	055	23 05	118	27 45	178	31 08	217	48 32	258	56 53	294
184	32 35	006	54 16	054	23 57	119	27 47	179	30 32	218	47 34	258	55 58	293
185	32 41	006	55 05	053	24 50	119	27 48	179	29 55	218	46 35	258	55 03	293
186	32 47	005	55 52	052	25 42	119	27 49	180	29 17	219	45 36	259	54 08	292
187	32 52	004	56 40	052	26 35	119	27 49	180	28 39	219	44 37	259	53 12	292
188	32 56	004	57 26	051	27 27	120	27 49	181	28 01	220	43 39	259	52 16	291
189	33 00	003	58 12	049	28 19	120	27 48	181	27 23	220	42 40	259	51 20	291
190	33 03	002	58 58	048	29 11	120	27 46	182	26 44	220	41 41	259	50 24	290
191	33 05	002	59 42	047	30 03	120	27 44	182	26 05	221	40 42	259	49 27	290
192	33 06	001	60 26	046	30 55	121	27 42	183	25 26	221	39 43	259	48 31	289
193	33 07	000	61 08	045	31 46	121	27 39	183	24 46	221	38 44	260	47 34	289
194	33 07	000	61 50	043	32 38	121	27 35	184	24 07	222	37 45	260	46 37	289
	ARCTURUS		◆ Rasalhague		ANTARES		◆ ACRUX		Alphard		◆ REGULUS		Alioth	
195	62 31	042	20 20	076	33 29	122	27 31	184	36 46	260	45 40	288	33 07	359
196	63 10	041	21 18	076	34 20	122	27 27	185	35 47	260	44 43	288	33 05	358
197	63 49	039	22 16	076	35 11	122	27 22	185	34 48	260	43 46	288	33 03	358
198	64 26	037	23 14	076	36 01	123	27 16	186	33 49	260	42 49	287	33 01	357
199	65 02	036	24 13	076	36 52	123	27 10	186	32 50	260	41 52	287	32 57	356
200	65 36	034	25 11	076	37 42	123	27 03	187	31 50	260	40 54	287	32 53	356
201	66 08	032	26 09	075	38 32	124	26 56	187	30 51	260	39 57	286	32 49	355
202	66 39	030	27 07	075	39 22	124	26 49	188	29 52	261	38 59	286	32 43	354
203	67 08	028	28 05	075	40 11	125	26 40	188	28 53	261	38 01	286	32 37	354
204	67 35	026	29 03	075	41 00	125	26 32	189	27 54	261	37 04	286	32 30	353
205	68 00	023	30 01	075	41 49	126	26 23	189	26 54	261	36 06	286	32 23	353
206	68 23	021	30 59	075	42 38	126	26 13	189	25 55	261	35 08	285	32 14	352
207	68 43	019	31 57	075	43 26	127	26 03	190	24 56	261	34 10	285	32 06	351
208	69 02	016	32 54	074	44 14	127	25 52	190	23 57	261	33 12	285	31 56	351
209	69 17	014	33 52	074	45 02	128	25 41	191	22 58	261	32 14	285	31 46	350
	ARCTURUS		◆ VEGA		ANTARES		◆ RIGIL KENT		ACRUX		Gienah		◆ REGULUS	
210	69 30	011	15 17	049	45 49	128	29 36	174	25 29	191	59 38	235	31 16	285
211	69 40	008	16 03	049	46 36	129	29 42	175	25 17	192	58 48	236	30 18	284
212	69 47	006	16 48	049	47 22	130	29 47	175	25 05	192	57 58	237	29 20	284
213	69 52	003	17 33	048	48 08	130	29 51	176	24 52	193	57 08	238	28 22	284
214	69 54	000	18 18	048	48 53	131	29 55	177	24 39	193	56 17	239	27 24	284
215	69 53	357	19 02	048	49 38	132	29 58	177	24 25	194	55 25	239	26 25	284
216	69 48	355	19 47	048	50 23	133	30 01	178	24 11	194	54 33	240	25 27	284
217	69 42	352	20 31	047	51 07	133	30 03	178	23 56	194	53 41	241	24 29	284
218	69 32	349	21 15	047	51 50	134	30 05	179	23 41	195	52 49	241	23 31	283
219	69 19	347	21 59	047	52 32	135	30 06	179	23 25	195	51 56	242	22 32	283
220	69 04	344	22 43	047	53 14	136	30 06	180	23 10	196	51 03	243	21 34	283
221	68 47	342	23 27	046	53 55	137	30 06	180	22 53	196	50 09	243	20 35	283
222	68 27	339	24 10	046	54 36	138	30 05	181	22 37	196	49 16	244	19 37	283
223	68 04	337	24 53	046	55 15	139	30 04	182	22 20	197	48 22	244	18 39	283
224	67 40	335	25 36	045	55 54	140	30 02	182	22 02	197	47 28	245	17 40	283
	Alphecca		VEGA		◆ ALTAIR		ANTARES		◆ RIGIL KENT		SPICA		◆ ARCTURUS	
225	61 03	016	26 18	045	16 45	080	56 32	141	29 59	183	64 31	245	67 13	332
226	61 19	015	27 00	045	17 44	080	57 09	143	29 56	183	63 36	246	66 44	330
227	61 34	013	27 42	044	18 43	080	57 45	144	29 53	184	62 41	247	66 14	328
228	61 46	011	28 24	044	19 42	080	58 20	145	29 48	184	61 46	248	65 42	326
229	61 57	009	29 05	043	20 41	080	58 53	146	29 43	185	60 50	248	65 08	325
230	62 05	007	29 46	043	21 40	080	59 26	148	29 38	185	59 54	249	64 32	323
231	62 12	005	30 27	043	22 39	080	59 57	149	29 32	186	58 58	250	63 55	321
232	62 17	004	31 07	042	23 38	080	60 27	151	29 25	187	58 02	250	63 17	320
233	62 19	002	31 47	042	24 37	080	60 56	152	29 18	187	57 05	251	62 38	318
234	62 20	000	32 27	041	25 36	080	61 23	154	29 10	188	56 09	251	61 57	317
235	62 19	358	33 06	041	26 35	080	61 48	156	29 02	188	55 12	252	61 16	315
236	62 15	356	33 45	040	27 34	079	62 12	157	28 53	189	54 15	252	60 33	314
237	62 10	354	34 23	040	28 33	079	62 35	159	28 44	189	53 18	252	59 50	313
238	62 03	352	35 01	039	29 32	079	62 55	161	28 34	190	52 21	253	59 05	312
239	61 53	350	35 39	038	30 31	079	63 14	163	28 24	190	51 23	253	58 20	311
	VEGA		◆ ALTAIR		Nunki		◆ RIGIL KENT		SPICA		◆ ARCTURUS		Alphecca	
240	36 16	038	31 30	079	40 42	125	28 13	191	50 26	253	57 34	310	61 42	348
241	36 52	037	32 29	079	41 31	125	28 01	191	49 28	254	56 48	309	61 29	346
242	37 29	037	33 28	079	42 20	126	27 49	192	48 31	254	56 01	308	61 14	345
243	38 04	036	34 27	078	43 09	126	27 37	192	47 33	254	55 13	307	60 57	343
244	38 39	035	35 25	078	43 57	127	27 24	193	46 35	255	54 25	306	60 39	341
245	39 13	035	36 24	078	44 45	127	27 10	193	45 37	255	53 36	305	60 19	340
246	39 47	034	37 23	078	45 32	128	26 56	194	44 39	255	52 46	304	59 57	338
247	40 20	033	38 21	078	46 19	129	26 41	194	43 41	255	51 57	304	59 34	336
248	40 53	032	39 20	078	47 06	129	26 26	195	42 43	256	51 07	303	59 09	335
249	41 25	032	40 19	077	47 52	130	26 11	195	41 45	256	50 16	302	58 43	333
250	41 56	031	41 17	077	48 38	131	25 55	196	40 47	256	49 25	302	58 15	332
251	42 26	030	42 16	077	49 24	131	25 39	196	39 49	256	48 34	301	57 46	330
252	42 56	029	43 14	077	50 08	132	25 22	196	38 50	256	47 42	300	57 16	329
253	43 25	028	44 12	077	50 53	133	25 05	197	37 52	257	46 50	300	56 44	328
254	43 53	028	45 11	076	51 36	134	24 47	197	36 54	257	45 58	299	56 11	326
	◆ VEGA		ALTAIR		◆ Nunki		Shaula		ANTARES		◆ SPICA		ARCTURUS	
255	44 20	027	46 09	076	52 19	135	53 01	168	63 33	195	35 55	257	45 06	299
256	44 47	026	47 07	076	53 02	135	53 12	170	63 17	197	34 57	257	44 13	298
257	45 13	025	48 05	075	53 44	136	53 22	171	62 58	199	33 58	257	43 20	298
258	45 37	024	49 03	075	54 25	137	53 31	172	62 38	201	33 00	257	42 27	297
259	46 01	023	50 01	075	55 05	138	53 38	174	62 16	202	32 01	257	41 33	297
260	46 24	022	50 59	074	55 44	140	53 44	175	61 52	204	31 03	257	40 40	297
261	46 46	021	51 57	074	56 23	141	53 48	176	61 27	206	30 04	258	39 46	296
262	47 07	020	52 54	074	57 00	142	53 51	178	61 00	207	29 06	258	38 52	296
263	47 27	019	53 52	073	57 37	143	53 53	179	60 32	209	28 07	258	37 58	295
264	47 46	018	54 49	073	58 12	144	53 53	180	60 02	210	27 08	258	37 04	295
265	48 04	017	55 47	072	58 47	146	53 52	182	59 31	212	26 10	258	36 09	295
266	48 21	016	56 44	072	59 20	147	53 49	183	58 59	213	25 11	258	35 15	294
267	48 37	015	57 41	072	59 52	148	53 45	185	58 25	215	24 12	258	34 20	294
268	48 51	013	58 38	071	60 23	150	53 40	186	57 51	216	23 14	258	33 25	294
269	49 05	012	59 34	070	60 52	151	53 33	187	57 15	217	22 15	258	32 30	294

LAT 1°S

LHA ♈	Hc	Zn	Hc	Zn	Hc	Zn	Hc	Zn	Hc	Zn	Hc	Zn	Hc	Zn
	◆ VEGA		DENEB		Enif		◆ FOMALHAUT		Peacock		◆ ANTARES		ARCTURUS	
270	49 17	011	31 29	032	32 59	077	13 51	120	27 03	158	56 38	218	31 35	293
271	49 28	010	32 00	032	33 58	077	14 43	120	27 25	159	56 01	220	30 40	293
272	49 38	009	32 32	031	34 56	077	15 34	120	27 47	159	55 22	221	29 45	293
273	49 46	008	33 03	031	35 55	077	16 26	121	28 08	160	54 42	222	28 49	293
274	49 54	006	33 33	030	36 53	077	17 18	121	28 28	160	54 02	223	27 54	292
275	50 00	005	34 03	030	37 51	077	18 09	121	28 48	161	53 21	224	26 58	292
276	50 05	004	34 32	029	38 50	076	19 01	121	29 08	161	52 39	225	26 03	292
277	50 09	003	35 01	028	39 48	076	19 52	121	29 27	162	51 57	226	25 07	292
278	50 11	002	35 29	028	40 46	076	20 43	121	29 45	162	51 14	226	24 11	292
279	50 12	000	35 57	027	41 44	076	21 34	122	30 03	163	50 30	227	23 15	291
280	50 12	359	36 23	026	42 42	075	22 25	122	30 20	163	49 46	228	22 20	291
281	50 10	358	36 50	026	43 40	075	23 16	122	30 37	164	49 01	229	21 24	291
282	50 08	357	37 15	025	44 38	075	24 07	122	30 54	164	48 16	229	20 28	291
283	50 04	356	37 40	024	45 36	075	24 58	122	31 09	165	47 30	230	19 31	291
284	49 58	354	38 04	023	46 34	074	25 49	123	31 25	166	46 43	231	18 35	291
	DENEB		Enif		◆ FOMALHAUT		Peacock		◆ ANTARES		Rasalhague		◆ VEGA	
285	38 28	023	47 32	074	26 39	123	31 39	166	45 57	231	65 04	304	49 52	353
286	38 51	022	48 29	074	27 29	123	31 53	167	45 10	232	64 14	302	49 44	352
287	39 13	021	49 27	073	28 19	123	32 07	167	44 22	233	63 23	301	49 35	351
288	39 34	020	50 24	073	29 09	124	32 20	168	43 34	233	62 31	300	49 25	350
289	39 55	020	51 22	073	29 59	124	32 32	169	42 46	234	61 39	299	49 14	348
290	40 14	019	52 19	072	30 49	124	32 43	169	41 57	234	60 46	298	49 01	347
291	40 33	018	53 16	072	31 38	125	32 54	170	41 09	235	59 53	298	48 47	346
292	40 51	017	54 13	071	32 28	125	33 05	170	40 19	235	59 00	297	48 32	345
293	41 09	016	55 10	071	33 17	125	33 14	171	39 30	236	58 06	296	48 16	344
294	41 25	015	56 06	070	34 05	126	33 23	172	38 40	236	57 12	295	47 59	343
295	41 41	015	57 03	070	34 54	126	33 32	172	37 50	237	56 18	295	47 41	342
296	41 55	014	57 59	069	35 42	126	33 39	173	37 00	237	55 23	294	47 22	341
297	42 09	013	58 55	069	36 30	127	33 46	174	36 10	237	54 28	293	47 02	340
298	42 22	012	59 51	068	37 18	127	33 53	174	35 19	238	53 33	293	46 40	339
299	42 34	011	60 46	067	38 06	128	33 58	175	34 28	238	52 38	292	46 18	338
	◆ DENEB		Alpheratz		◆ FOMALHAUT		Peacock		◆ ANTARES		Rasalhague		VEGA	
300	42 45	010	23 25	057	38 53	128	34 03	176	33 37	238	51 42	292	45 55	337
301	42 55	009	24 15	057	39 40	129	34 08	176	32 46	239	50 47	291	45 31	336
302	43 04	008	25 06	057	40 27	129	34 11	177	31 55	239	49 51	291	45 06	335
303	43 12	007	25 56	057	41 13	130	34 14	178	31 03	239	48 55	291	44 40	334
304	43 19	006	26 46	056	41 59	130	34 16	178	30 11	240	47 58	290	44 13	333
305	43 25	005	27 36	056	42 44	131	34 18	179	29 20	240	47 02	290	43 45	332
306	43 30	004	28 25	056	43 29	132	34 19	180	28 28	240	46 05	289	43 17	331
307	43 34	003	29 15	055	44 14	132	34 19	180	27 36	240	45 09	289	42 48	330
308	43 37	002	30 04	055	44 58	133	34 18	181	26 43	241	44 12	289	42 18	330
309	43 39	001	30 53	055	45 42	133	34 17	182	25 51	241	43 15	288	41 47	329
310	43 40	000	31 42	054	46 25	134	34 15	182	24 58	241	42 18	288	41 16	328
311	43 40	000	32 31	054	47 08	135	34 12	183	24 06	241	41 21	288	40 44	327
312	43 39	359	33 19	053	47 50	136	34 09	184	23 13	241	40 24	287	40 11	327
313	43 37	358	34 07	053	48 32	136	34 05	184	22 21	242	39 27	287	39 38	326
314	43 34	357	34 55	053	49 13	137	34 00	185	21 28	242	38 29	287	39 04	325
	◆ Alpheratz		◆ FOMALHAUT		Peacock		Nunki		◆ Rasalhague		VEGA		DENEB	
315	35 42	052	49 53	138	33 55	185	50 57	227	37 32	287	38 29	325	43 30	356
316	36 30	052	50 33	139	33 49	186	50 13	228	36 34	286	37 54	324	43 25	355
317	37 17	051	51 12	140	33 42	187	49 28	229	35 37	286	37 19	323	43 18	354
318	38 03	051	51 50	141	33 35	187	48 43	229	34 39	286	36 42	323	43 11	353
319	38 49	050	52 28	142	33 27	188	47 57	230	33 41	286	36 06	322	43 03	352
320	39 35	050	53 04	143	33 18	189	47 11	231	32 44	286	35 29	321	42 54	351
321	40 21	049	53 40	144	33 09	189	46 24	231	31 46	285	34 51	321	42 44	350
322	41 06	049	54 15	145	32 59	190	45 37	232	30 48	285	34 13	320	42 33	349
323	41 51	048	54 49	146	32 48	191	44 49	233	29 50	285	33 34	320	42 21	348
324	42 35	047	55 22	147	32 37	191	44 02	233	28 52	285	32 55	319	42 09	347
325	43 19	047	55 53	149	32 25	192	43 13	234	27 54	285	32 16	319	41 55	346
326	44 02	046	56 24	150	32 12	192	42 25	234	26 56	285	31 36	318	41 40	345
327	44 45	045	56 54	151	31 59	193	41 36	235	25 58	284	30 56	318	41 25	345
328	45 28	045	57 22	153	31 45	194	40 47	235	25 00	284	30 16	317	41 08	344
329	46 09	044	57 49	154	31 31	194	39 57	236	24 02	284	29 35	317	40 51	343
	◆ Alpheratz		Hamal		Diphda		◆ FOMALHAUT		Nunki		◆ ALTAIR		DENEB	
330	46 51	043	25 03	063	46 16	115	58 15	155	39 08	236	56 30	288	40 33	342
331	47 31	042	25 56	063	47 10	116	58 39	157	38 18	237	55 33	287	40 14	341
332	48 11	041	26 50	063	48 04	116	59 02	158	37 28	237	54 35	287	39 54	340
333	48 50	040	27 43	063	48 57	117	59 23	160	36 37	237	53 38	287	39 34	340
334	49 29	040	28 36	062	49 51	117	59 43	161	35 46	238	52 40	286	39 12	339
335	50 07	039	29 29	062	50 44	118	60 01	163	34 56	238	51 43	286	38 50	338
336	50 44	038	30 22	062	51 37	118	60 18	165	34 05	238	50 45	285	38 27	337
337	51 20	037	31 15	061	52 30	119	60 33	166	33 13	239	49 47	285	38 04	337
338	51 56	036	32 08	061	53 22	119	60 46	168	32 22	239	48 49	285	37 40	336
339	52 30	035	33 00	061	54 14	120	60 58	170	31 30	239	47 51	284	37 15	335
340	53 04	033	33 52	060	55 06	121	61 07	172	30 39	240	46 53	284	36 49	334
341	53 36	032	34 44	060	55 57	122	61 15	173	29 47	240	45 55	284	36 23	334
342	54 08	031	35 36	060	56 48	122	61 21	175	28 55	240	44 57	284	35 56	333
343	54 38	030	36 28	059	57 39	123	61 25	177	28 03	241	43 58	283	35 28	332
344	55 07	029	37 20	059	58 29	124	61 27	179	27 10	241	43 00	283	35 00	332
	Alpheratz		◆ Hamal		◆ ACHERNAR		FOMALHAUT		Nunki		◆ ALTAIR		DENEB	
345	55 36	027	38 11	059	25 38	157	61 27	181	26 18	241	42 01	283	34 31	331
346	56 03	026	39 02	058	26 01	158	61 26	183	25 25	241	41 03	283	34 02	330
347	56 28	025	39 53	058	26 23	158	61 22	184	24 33	241	40 04	283	33 32	330
348	56 53	023	40 43	057	26 45	159	61 17	186	23 40	242	39 06	282	33 02	329
349	57 16	022	41 34	057	27 07	159	61 09	188	22 47	242	38 07	282	32 31	329
350	57 37	020	42 24	056	27 28	160	61 00	190	21 54	242	37 09	282	32 00	328
351	57 57	019	43 13	056	27 48	160	60 49	191	21 01	242	36 10	282	31 28	328
352	58 16	017	44 03	055	28 08	161	60 36	193	20 08	242	35 11	282	30 55	327
353	58 33	016	44 52	054	28 28	161	60 22	195	19 15	242	34 12	281	30 23	327
354	58 48	014	45 40	054	28 47	162	60 06	197	18 22	243	33 13	281	29 49	326
355	59 02	012	46 29	053	29 06	162	59 48	198	17 29	243	32 15	281	29 16	326
356	59 14	011	47 16	053	29 24	163	59 28	200	16 35	243	31 16	281	28 42	325
357	59 24	009	48 04	052	29 41	163	59 07	201	15 42	243	30 17	281	28 07	325
358	59 33	007	48 51	051	29 58	164	58 45	203	14 48	243	29 18	281	27 32	324
359	59 40	006	49 37	050	30 15	164	58 21	204	13 55	243	28 19	281	26 57	324

LHA ♈	Hc	Zn	Hc	Zn	Hc	Zn	Hc	Zn	Hc	Zn	Hc	Zn	Hc	Zn
	Alpheratz		◆ALDEBARAN		RIGEL		ACHERNAR		◆FOMALHAUT		ALTAIR		◆DENEB	
0	58 45	004	19 17	072	11 21	098	31 29	165	58 49	206	27 09	281	25 33	324
1	58 48	002	20 14	072	12 21	098	31 44	165	58 22	208	26 10	281	24 57	323
2	58 50	000	21 11	071	13 20	098	31 59	166	57 53	209	25 11	281	24 21	323
3	58 49	359	22 08	071	14 19	098	32 14	166	57 23	211	24 12	281	23 45	322
4	58 47	357	23 05	071	15 19	098	32 28	167	56 52	212	23 13	281	23 08	322
5	58 43	355	24 01	071	16 18	098	32 41	168	56 20	213	22 14	280	22 31	322
6	58 38	354	24 58	071	17 18	098	32 54	168	55 46	214	21 15	280	21 54	321
7	58 30	352	25 55	071	18 17	098	33 06	169	55 12	215	20 16	280	21 16	321
8	58 21	350	26 51	070	19 16	098	33 17	169	54 37	217	19 17	280	20 38	321
9	58 10	349	27 47	070	20 16	098	33 28	170	54 01	218	18 18	280	20 00	320
10	57 58	347	28 44	070	21 15	098	33 38	171	53 24	219	17 19	280	19 22	320
11	57 44	346	29 40	070	22 14	098	33 47	171	52 46	220	16 20	280	18 43	320
12	57 28	344	30 36	069	23 14	098	33 56	172	52 07	221	15 21	280	18 04	319
13	57 11	343	31 32	069	24 13	098	34 04	172	51 28	222	14 22	280	17 25	319
14	56 52	341	32 28	069	25 13	098	34 12	173	50 47	222	13 23	280	16 46	319
	CAPELLA		ALDEBARAN		◆RIGEL		ACHERNAR		◆FOMALHAUT		Enif		◆Alpheratz	
15	15 55	041	33 24	069	26 12	098	34 19	174	50 07	223	40 00	285	56 32	340
16	16 34	040	34 20	068	27 11	098	34 25	174	49 25	224	39 02	285	56 11	338
17	17 13	040	35 16	068	28 11	098	34 31	175	48 43	225	38 04	284	55 48	337
18	17 51	040	36 11	068	29 10	098	34 35	176	48 00	226	37 06	284	55 23	335
19	18 30	040	37 07	067	30 09	098	34 40	176	47 17	226	36 07	284	54 58	334
20	19 08	039	38 02	067	31 09	098	34 43	177	46 34	227	35 09	284	54 31	333
21	19 46	039	38 57	067	32 08	098	34 46	178	45 49	228	34 11	283	54 03	332
22	20 23	039	39 52	066	33 07	098	34 48	178	45 05	228	33 13	283	53 34	330
23	21 00	038	40 47	066	34 07	099	34 49	179	44 20	229	32 14	283	53 03	329
24	21 37	038	41 42	066	35 06	099	34 50	180	43 34	230	31 16	283	52 32	328
25	22 14	038	42 36	065	36 05	099	34 50	180	42 48	230	30 17	283	52 00	327
26	22 51	037	43 31	065	37 04	099	34 50	181	42 02	231	29 19	283	51 26	326
27	23 27	037	44 25	064	38 04	099	34 48	182	41 16	231	28 20	282	50 52	325
28	24 03	036	45 19	064	39 03	099	34 46	182	40 29	232	27 22	282	50 17	324
29	24 38	036	46 13	063	40 02	099	34 44	183	39 41	232	26 23	282	49 41	323
	CAPELLA		◆BETELGEUSE		SIRIUS		CANOPUS		◆ACHERNAR		FOMALHAUT		◆Alpheratz	
30	25 13	036	30 24	080	18 20	107	15 52	145	34 40	184	38 54	233	49 04	322
31	25 48	035	31 23	080	19 17	107	16 26	145	34 36	184	38 06	233	48 27	321
32	26 23	035	32 22	080	20 14	107	17 01	145	34 31	185	37 18	234	47 49	320
33	26 57	034	33 21	080	21 12	107	17 35	145	34 26	186	36 29	234	47 10	319
34	27 30	034	34 20	080	22 09	107	18 09	146	34 20	186	35 41	234	46 30	318
35	28 04	033	35 19	079	23 06	107	18 42	146	34 13	187	34 52	235	45 50	317
36	28 36	033	36 18	079	24 03	107	19 16	146	34 06	187	34 03	235	45 09	317
37	29 09	032	37 17	079	25 01	108	19 49	146	33 57	188	33 14	235	44 27	316
38	29 41	032	38 16	079	25 58	108	20 22	147	33 49	189	32 24	236	43 45	315
39	30 12	031	39 14	079	26 55	108	20 55	147	33 39	189	31 34	236	43 03	314
40	30 43	031	40 13	079	27 52	108	21 27	147	33 29	190	30 44	236	42 20	314
41	31 14	030	41 12	078	28 49	108	22 00	148	33 18	191	29 54	237	41 36	313
42	31 44	030	42 11	078	29 46	108	22 32	148	33 07	191	29 04	237	40 52	312
43	32 13	029	43 09	078	30 43	108	23 03	148	32 55	192	28 14	237	40 08	312
44	32 42	029	44 08	078	31 40	108	23 35	149	32 43	192	27 23	237	39 23	311
	CAPELLA		◆BETELGEUSE		SIRIUS		CANOPUS		◆ACHERNAR		Diphda		◆Hamal	
45	33 11	028	45 07	077	32 37	109	24 06	149	32 29	193	53 07	242	61 30	334
46	33 39	027	46 05	077	33 33	109	24 37	149	32 16	194	52 14	243	61 04	333
47	34 06	027	47 03	077	34 30	109	25 07	150	32 01	194	51 21	243	60 35	331
48	34 33	026	48 02	077	35 27	109	25 37	150	31 46	195	50 27	244	60 06	330
49	34 59	025	49 00	076	36 23	109	26 07	150	31 31	195	49 33	244	59 35	328
50	35 24	025	49 58	076	37 20	110	26 36	151	31 15	196	48 39	245	59 02	327
51	35 49	024	50 56	076	38 16	110	27 06	151	30 58	196	47 45	245	58 29	325
52	36 13	023	51 55	075	39 13	110	27 34	152	30 41	197	46 50	246	57 54	324
53	36 36	023	52 52	075	40 09	110	28 03	152	30 23	197	45 55	246	57 18	323
54	36 59	022	53 50	075	41 05	111	28 30	152	30 05	198	45 00	246	56 41	321
55	37 21	021	54 48	074	42 01	111	28 58	153	29 47	198	44 05	247	56 03	320
56	37 43	020	55 46	074	42 57	111	29 25	153	29 27	199	43 10	247	55 24	319
57	38 03	020	56 43	073	43 53	111	29 52	154	29 08	199	42 15	247	54 44	318
58	38 23	019	57 40	073	44 49	112	30 18	154	28 47	200	41 20	248	54 04	317
59	38 42	018	58 38	072	45 44	112	30 44	155	28 27	200	40 24	248	53 22	316
	◆CAPELLA		POLLUX		◆SIRIUS		CANOPUS		ACHERNAR		◆Diphda		Hamal	
60	39 00	017	28 02	057	46 40	113	31 09	155	28 06	201	39 28	248	52 40	315
61	39 18	016	28 52	056	47 35	113	31 34	156	27 44	201	38 33	249	51 57	314
62	39 34	016	29 42	056	48 30	113	31 58	156	27 22	202	37 37	249	51 14	313
63	39 50	015	30 31	056	49 25	114	32 22	157	26 59	202	36 41	249	50 29	312
64	40 05	014	31 21	055	50 20	114	32 45	158	26 37	203	35 45	249	49 45	311
65	40 19	013	32 10	055	51 15	115	33 07	158	26 13	203	34 49	249	48 59	310
66	40 32	012	32 58	054	52 09	115	33 30	159	25 50	203	33 52	250	48 13	310
67	40 45	011	33 47	054	53 03	116	33 51	159	25 25	204	32 56	250	47 27	309
68	40 56	011	34 35	054	53 57	116	34 12	160	25 01	204	32 00	250	46 40	308
69	41 06	010	35 24	053	54 51	117	34 32	160	24 36	205	31 03	250	45 53	308
70	41 16	009	36 11	053	55 44	117	34 52	161	24 11	205	30 07	250	45 05	307
71	41 25	008	36 59	052	56 37	118	35 11	162	23 45	205	29 10	251	44 17	306
72	41 32	007	37 46	052	57 30	119	35 30	162	23 19	206	28 14	251	43 28	306
73	41 39	006	38 33	051	58 23	120	35 48	163	22 53	206	27 17	251	42 40	305
74	41 45	005	39 19	051	59 14	120	36 05	164	22 27	206	26 21	251	41 50	305
	CAPELLA		◆POLLUX		REGULUS		Suhail		◆CANOPUS		ACHERNAR		◆Hamal	
75	41 50	004	40 05	050	12 00	077	21 17	137	36 21	164	22 00	207	41 01	304
76	41 53	003	40 51	049	12 59	077	21 58	137	36 37	165	21 33	207	40 11	304
77	41 56	002	41 36	049	13 57	077	22 39	137	36 53	166	21 05	207	39 21	303
78	41 58	001	42 21	048	14 56	077	23 19	137	37 07	166	20 37	208	38 30	303
79	41 59	000	43 06	047	15 54	077	24 00	138	37 21	167	20 09	208	37 40	302
80	41 59	359	43 50	047	16 52	077	24 40	138	37 34	168	19 41	208	36 49	302
81	41 58	359	44 33	046	17 51	077	25 20	138	37 46	169	19 12	209	35 58	301
82	41 56	358	45 16	045	18 49	077	26 00	139	37 58	169	18 44	209	35 06	301
83	41 53	357	45 58	045	19 48	077	26 40	139	38 09	170	18 15	209	34 15	300
84	41 49	356	46 40	044	20 46	076	27 19	139	38 19	171	17 45	209	33 23	300
85	41 44	355	47 22	043	21 44	076	27 58	140	38 28	171	17 16	210	32 31	300
86	41 38	354	48 02	042	22 42	076	28 37	140	38 36	172	16 46	210	31 39	299
87	41 32	353	48 42	041	23 41	076	29 15	140	38 44	173	16 16	210	30 47	299
88	41 24	352	49 21	040	24 39	076	29 53	141	38 51	174	15 46	210	29 54	299
89	41 15	351	50 00	039	25 37	076	30 31	141	38 57	174	15 16	210	29 01	298

LAT 2°S

LHA ♈	Hc	Zn	Hc	Zn	Hc	Zn	Hc	Zn	Hc	Zn	Hc	Zn	Hc	Zn
	POLLUX		◆REGULUS		Suhail		◆CANOPUS		Acamar		◆ALDEBARAN		CAPELLA	
90	50 37	038	26 35	076	31 09	142	39 03	175	34 00	221	62 20	313	41 05	350
91	51 14	037	27 33	075	31 46	142	39 07	176	33 21	221	61 35	312	40 55	349
92	51 50	036	28 31	075	32 22	142	39 11	177	32 41	222	60 50	310	40 43	349
93	52 26	035	29 29	075	32 59	143	39 14	178	32 01	222	60 04	309	40 31	348
94	53 00	034	30 27	075	33 35	143	39 16	178	31 20	223	59 17	308	40 18	347
95	53 33	033	31 25	075	34 10	144	39 17	179	30 39	223	58 30	307	40 04	346
96	54 05	032	32 23	075	34 45	144	39 18	180	29 58	223	57 41	306	39 49	345
97	54 36	031	33 21	074	35 20	145	39 17	181	29 17	224	56 53	305	39 33	344
98	55 06	029	34 18	074	35 54	146	39 16	182	28 35	224	56 03	304	39 16	343
99	55 35	028	35 16	074	36 28	146	39 14	182	27 53	225	55 13	303	38 58	343
100	56 03	027	36 13	074	37 01	147	39 11	183	27 11	225	54 23	303	38 40	342
101	56 29	025	37 11	073	37 33	147	39 08	184	26 29	225	53 32	302	38 21	341
102	56 54	024	38 08	073	38 05	148	39 03	185	25 46	225	52 41	301	38 01	340
103	57 18	023	39 06	073	38 37	149	38 58	185	25 03	226	51 50	300	37 40	339
104	57 40	021	40 03	073	39 08	149	38 52	186	24 20	226	50 58	300	37 19	339
	POLLUX		◆REGULUS		Suhail		◆CANOPUS		RIGEL		◆ALDEBARAN		CAPELLA	
105	58 01	020	41 00	072	39 38	150	38 45	187	63 13	256	50 05	299	36 57	338
106	58 20	018	41 57	072	40 08	151	38 38	188	62 14	256	49 13	298	36 34	337
107	58 38	016	42 54	072	40 37	151	38 29	188	61 16	257	48 20	298	36 11	337
108	58 54	015	43 51	071	41 06	152	38 20	189	60 18	257	47 27	297	35 46	336
109	59 09	013	44 48	071	41 33	153	38 10	190	59 19	257	46 33	297	35 22	335
110	59 21	011	45 45	071	42 00	154	37 59	191	58 21	258	45 40	296	34 56	334
111	59 32	010	46 41	070	42 27	154	37 48	191	57 22	258	44 46	296	34 30	334
112	59 42	008	47 37	070	42 52	155	37 36	192	56 24	258	43 52	295	34 03	333
113	59 49	006	48 34	069	43 17	156	37 23	193	55 25	258	42 58	295	33 36	333
114	59 55	005	49 30	069	43 41	157	37 09	194	54 26	259	42 03	295	33 08	332
115	59 58	003	50 26	069	44 04	158	36 55	194	53 27	259	41 09	294	32 39	331
116	60 00	001	51 21	068	44 27	159	36 40	195	52 28	259	40 14	294	32 10	331
117	60 00	359	52 17	068	44 48	159	36 24	196	51 29	259	39 19	293	31 41	330
118	59 59	357	53 12	067	45 09	160	36 07	196	50 30	260	38 24	293	31 11	330
119	59 55	356	54 07	066	45 29	161	35 50	197	49 31	260	37 28	293	30 40	329
	◆REGULUS		Gienah		◆ACRUX		CANOPUS		SIRIUS		◆BETELGEUSE		POLLUX	
120	55 02	066	25 13	109	12 01	155	35 32	198	66 33	230	57 40	287	59 50	354
121	55 57	065	26 09	109	12 27	155	35 14	198	65 46	231	56 43	287	59 43	352
122	56 51	064	27 06	109	12 52	155	34 55	199	64 59	233	55 45	286	59 33	350
123	57 45	064	28 03	109	13 17	155	34 35	199	64 11	234	54 48	286	59 23	349
124	58 38	063	29 00	109	13 42	156	34 15	200	63 22	235	53 50	285	59 10	347
125	59 32	062	29 56	109	14 07	156	33 54	201	62 33	236	52 52	285	58 56	345
126	60 25	061	30 53	109	14 31	156	33 33	201	61 43	237	51 54	285	58 40	344
127	61 17	060	31 49	110	14 55	156	33 11	202	60 52	238	50 56	284	58 23	342
128	62 09	060	32 46	110	15 20	156	32 48	202	60 01	239	49 58	284	58 03	341
129	63 00	058	33 42	110	15 43	157	32 25	203	59 10	240	49 00	284	57 43	339
130	63 51	057	34 39	110	16 07	157	32 01	204	58 18	241	48 01	283	57 21	338
131	64 41	056	35 35	110	16 31	157	31 37	204	57 25	241	47 03	283	56 57	336
132	65 31	055	36 31	111	16 54	157	31 12	205	56 32	242	46 05	283	56 32	335
133	66 19	054	37 27	111	17 17	158	30 47	205	55 39	243	45 06	283	56 06	333
134	67 07	052	38 23	111	17 40	158	30 22	206	54 46	243	44 08	282	55 39	332
	Alioth		◆SPICA		ACRUX		◆CANOPUS		SIRIUS		BETELGEUSE		◆POLLUX	
135	15 13	030	23 26	101	18 02	158	29 55	206	53 52	244	43 09	282	55 10	331
136	15 43	029	24 25	101	18 24	158	29 29	207	52 58	244	42 10	282	54 40	329
137	16 12	029	25 24	101	18 46	159	29 02	207	52 04	245	41 12	282	54 09	328
138	16 42	029	26 22	102	19 08	159	28 34	207	51 10	245	40 13	281	53 37	327
139	17 10	029	27 21	102	19 29	159	28 07	208	50 15	246	39 14	281	53 04	326
140	17 39	028	28 20	102	19 51	160	27 38	208	49 20	246	38 15	281	52 30	325
141	18 07	028	29 19	102	20 11	160	27 10	209	48 25	247	37 16	281	51 55	324
142	18 35	028	30 17	102	20 32	160	26 41	209	47 30	247	36 17	281	51 19	323
143	19 03	027	31 16	102	20 52	160	26 11	210	46 35	248	35 18	281	50 42	322
144	19 30	027	32 15	102	21 12	161	25 41	210	45 39	248	34 19	280	50 04	321
145	19 57	027	33 13	102	21 32	161	25 11	210	44 44	248	33 21	280	49 26	320
146	20 24	026	34 12	102	21 51	161	24 41	211	43 48	249	32 21	280	48 47	319
147	20 51	026	35 10	102	22 10	162	24 10	211	42 52	249	31 22	280	48 07	318
148	21 17	026	36 09	102	22 28	162	23 39	211	41 56	249	30 23	280	47 26	317
149	21 42	025	37 08	103	22 46	163	23 08	212	41 00	249	29 24	280	46 45	316
	Alioth		ARCTURUS		◆SPICA		ACRUX		◆CANOPUS		SIRIUS		◆POLLUX	
150	22 07	025	23 39	068	38 06	103	23 04	163	22 36	212	40 04	250	46 03	315
151	22 32	024	24 35	068	39 05	103	23 22	163	22 04	212	39 07	250	45 21	315
152	22 57	024	25 31	068	40 03	103	23 39	164	21 32	213	38 11	250	44 38	314
153	23 21	023	26 26	067	41 01	103	23 56	164	20 59	213	37 15	250	43 55	313
154	23 45	023	27 21	067	42 00	103	24 12	164	20 27	213	36 18	251	43 11	313
155	24 08	023	28 17	067	42 58	104	24 28	165	19 54	213	35 21	251	42 26	312
156	24 31	022	29 12	067	43 56	104	24 43	165	19 20	214	34 25	251	41 42	311
157	24 53	022	30 07	066	44 55	104	24 58	166	18 47	214	33 28	251	40 56	311
158	25 15	021	31 02	066	45 53	104	25 13	166	18 13	214	32 31	251	40 11	310
159	25 36	021	31 57	066	46 51	104	25 27	166	17 40	214	31 34	252	39 25	310
160	25 57	020	32 51	066	47 49	105	25 41	167	17 05	215	30 38	252	38 38	309
161	26 18	020	33 46	065	48 47	105	25 54	167	16 31	215	29 41	252	37 51	308
162	26 38	019	34 40	065	49 45	105	26 07	168	15 57	215	28 44	252	37 04	308
163	26 57	019	35 34	065	50 43	105	26 20	168	15 22	215	27 47	252	36 17	307
164	27 16	018	36 29	064	51 40	106	26 32	169	14 48	216	26 49	252	35 29	307
	Alioth		◆ARCTURUS		SPICA		◆ACRUX		Suhail		SIRIUS		◆POLLUX	
165	27 35	018	37 23	064	52 38	106	26 43	169	41 41	207	25 52	252	34 41	307
166	27 53	017	38 16	064	53 36	106	26 54	170	41 13	208	24 55	252	33 53	306
167	28 10	017	39 10	063	54 33	107	27 05	170	40 45	208	23 58	253	33 04	306
168	28 27	016	40 03	063	55 31	107	27 15	171	40 16	209	23 01	253	32 15	305
169	28 43	015	40 57	062	56 28	107	27 24	171	39 47	210	22 04	253	31 26	305
170	28 59	015	41 50	062	57 25	108	27 33	172	39 16	211	21 06	253	30 37	304
171	29 14	014	42 42	061	58 22	108	27 42	172	38 46	211	20 09	253	29 47	304
172	29 29	014	43 35	061	59 19	109	27 50	172	38 14	212	19 12	253	28 58	304
173	29 43	013	44 27	060	60 15	109	27 58	173	37 42	212	18 14	253	28 08	303
174	29 56	013	45 19	060	61 12	110	28 05	173	37 10	213	17 17	253	27 18	303
175	30 09	012	46 11	059	62 08	111	28 11	174	36 37	214	16 20	253	26 27	303
176	30 21	011	47 03	059	63 04	111	28 17	174	36 03	214	15 22	253	25 37	303
177	30 32	011	47 54	058	64 00	112	28 23	175	35 29	215	14 25	253	24 46	302
178	30 43	010	48 44	058	64 55	113	28 28	175	34 55	215	13 27	253	23 55	302
179	30 54	010	49 35	057	65 51	113	28 32	176	34 20	216	12 30	253	23 04	302

 LAT 2°S

LHA ♈	Alioth Hc	Zn	◆ARCTURUS Hc	Zn	ANTARES Hc	Zn	◆ACRUX Hc	Zn	Suhail Hc	Zn	Alphard Hc	Zn	◆REGULUS Hc	Zn
180	31 03	009	50 25	056	20 54	118	28 36	176	33 44	216	51 41	258	59 10	297
181	31 12	008	51 15	055	21 47	118	28 40	177	33 09	217	50 42	259	58 16	297
182	31 20	008	52 04	055	22 40	118	28 43	178	32 32	217	49 43	259	57 22	296
183	31 28	007	52 52	054	23 33	118	28 45	178	31 56	218	48 44	259	56 28	295
184	31 35	006	53 41	053	24 26	118	28 47	179	31 19	218	47 46	259	55 34	295
185	31 41	006	54 28	052	25 19	118	28 48	179	30 42	219	46 47	259	54 39	294
186	31 47	005	55 15	051	26 11	119	28 49	180	30 04	219	45 48	260	53 44	293
187	31 52	004	56 02	050	27 04	119	28 49	180	29 26	220	44 49	260	52 49	293
188	31 56	004	56 48	049	27 56	119	28 49	181	28 48	220	43 50	260	51 54	292
189	32 00	003	57 33	048	28 49	119	28 48	181	28 09	220	42 51	260	50 58	292
190	32 03	002	58 17	047	29 41	120	28 46	182	27 30	221	41 52	260	50 02	291
191	32 05	002	59 01	046	30 33	120	28 44	182	26 51	221	40 53	260	49 06	291
192	32 06	001	59 44	045	31 25	120	28 42	183	26 11	221	39 53	260	48 10	290
193	32 07	000	60 25	044	32 17	120	28 39	183	25 31	222	38 54	260	47 14	290
194	32 07	000	61 06	042	33 08	121	28 35	184	24 51	222	37 55	260	46 18	290

LHA ♈	ARCTURUS Hc	Zn	◆Rasalhague Hc	Zn	ANTARES Hc	Zn	◆ACRUX Hc	Zn	Alphard Hc	Zn	◆REGULUS Hc	Zn	Alioth Hc	Zn
195	61 46	041	20 05	076	34 00	121	28 31	184	36 56	261	45 21	289	32 07	359
196	62 24	039	21 03	076	34 51	121	28 27	185	35 57	261	44 24	289	32 05	358
197	63 02	038	22 02	076	35 42	122	28 22	185	34 58	261	43 28	288	32 03	358
198	63 38	036	23 00	075	36 33	122	28 16	186	33 59	261	42 31	288	32 01	357
199	64 12	034	23 58	075	37 24	122	28 10	186	32 59	261	41 34	288	31 57	356
200	64 46	033	24 56	075	38 15	123	28 03	187	32 00	261	40 36	288	31 53	356
201	65 17	031	25 54	075	39 05	123	27 56	187	31 01	261	39 39	287	31 49	355
202	65 47	029	26 51	075	39 55	124	27 48	188	30 02	261	38 42	287	31 43	355
203	66 15	027	27 49	075	40 45	124	27 40	188	29 02	261	37 45	287	31 37	354
204	66 41	025	28 47	074	41 35	124	27 31	189	28 03	261	36 47	286	31 31	353
205	67 05	023	29 45	074	42 24	125	27 22	189	27 04	261	35 50	286	31 23	353
206	67 27	020	30 43	074	43 13	125	27 12	190	26 05	261	34 52	286	31 15	352
207	67 47	018	31 40	074	44 02	126	27 02	190	25 05	261	33 54	286	31 06	351
208	68 04	016	32 38	074	44 50	126	26 51	191	24 06	261	32 57	285	30 57	351
209	68 19	013	33 35	073	45 38	127	26 40	191	23 07	261	31 59	285	30 47	350

LHA ♈	ARCTURUS Hc	Zn	◆VEGA Hc	Zn	ANTARES Hc	Zn	◆RIGIL KENT Hc	Zn	ACRUX Hc	Zn	Gienah Hc	Zn	◆REGULUS Hc	Zn
210	68 31	011	14 38	049	46 26	128	30 36	174	26 28	191	60 12	237	31 01	285
211	68 41	008	15 23	049	47 13	128	30 41	175	26 16	192	59 21	238	30 03	285
212	68 48	005	16 08	048	48 00	129	30 47	175	26 04	192	58 30	238	29 05	285
213	68 52	003	16 53	048	48 47	130	30 51	176	25 51	193	57 39	239	28 07	285
214	68 54	000	17 38	048	49 33	130	30 55	177	25 37	193	56 47	240	27 09	284
215	68 53	358	18 22	048	50 18	131	30 58	177	25 23	194	55 55	241	26 11	284
216	68 49	355	19 06	047	51 03	132	31 01	178	25 09	194	55 03	241	25 13	284
217	68 42	352	19 51	047	51 48	133	31 03	178	24 54	194	54 10	242	24 15	284
218	68 33	350	20 34	047	52 31	133	31 05	179	24 39	195	53 17	243	23 16	284
219	68 21	347	21 18	047	53 15	134	31 06	179	24 23	195	52 23	243	22 18	284
220	68 07	345	22 02	046	53 57	135	31 06	180	24 07	196	51 30	244	21 20	284
221	67 50	342	22 45	046	54 39	136	31 06	180	23 51	196	50 36	244	20 22	283
222	67 30	340	23 28	046	55 20	137	31 05	181	23 34	196	49 42	245	19 23	283
223	67 09	338	24 11	045	56 01	138	31 04	182	23 17	197	48 47	245	18 25	283
224	66 45	336	24 53	045	56 40	139	31 02	182	22 59	197	47 53	246	17 27	283

LHA ♈	Alphecca Hc	Zn	VEGA Hc	Zn	◆ALTAIR Hc	Zn	ANTARES Hc	Zn	◆RIGIL KENT Hc	Zn	SPICA Hc	Zn	◆ARCTURUS Hc	Zn
225	60 06	016	25 36	045	16 34	080	57 19	140	30 59	183	64 55	247	66 20	334
226	60 21	014	26 17	044	17 34	080	57 56	142	30 56	183	64 00	248	65 52	332
227	60 35	012	26 59	044	18 33	080	58 33	143	30 52	184	63 04	249	65 22	330
228	60 47	011	27 41	043	19 32	080	59 09	144	30 48	184	62 08	249	64 51	328
229	60 58	009	28 22	043	20 31	080	59 43	146	30 43	185	61 12	250	64 18	326
230	61 06	007	29 02	043	21 30	080	60 17	147	30 38	186	60 15	251	63 44	324
231	61 12	005	29 43	042	22 29	080	60 49	148	30 32	186	59 18	251	63 08	323
232	61 17	003	30 23	042	23 28	079	61 19	150	30 25	187	58 22	252	62 31	321
233	61 19	002	31 02	041	24 26	079	61 49	152	30 18	187	57 25	252	61 53	319
234	61 20	000	31 42	041	25 25	079	62 17	153	30 10	188	56 27	253	61 13	318
235	61 19	358	32 21	040	26 24	079	62 43	155	30 02	188	55 30	253	60 32	317
236	61 16	356	32 59	040	27 23	079	63 08	157	29 53	189	54 33	253	59 51	315
237	61 10	354	33 37	039	28 22	079	63 31	158	29 43	189	53 35	254	59 08	314
238	61 03	352	34 15	039	29 21	079	63 52	160	29 33	190	52 38	254	58 25	313
239	60 54	350	34 52	038	30 19	078	64 11	162	29 23	190	51 40	254	57 41	312

LHA ♈	VEGA Hc	Zn	◆ALTAIR Hc	Zn	Nunki Hc	Zn	◆RIGIL KENT Hc	Zn	SPICA Hc	Zn	◆ARCTURUS Hc	Zn	Alphecca Hc	Zn
240	35 28	037	31 18	078	41 16	124	29 12	191	50 42	255	56 56	311	60 43	349
241	36 05	037	32 17	078	42 05	124	29 00	191	49 44	255	56 10	310	60 31	347
242	36 40	036	33 16	078	42 55	125	28 48	192	48 47	255	55 23	309	60 16	345
243	37 15	035	34 14	078	43 44	125	28 35	192	47 49	255	54 36	308	60 00	343
244	37 50	035	35 13	078	44 33	126	28 22	193	46 50	256	53 49	307	59 42	342
245	38 24	034	36 11	077	45 21	127	28 08	193	45 52	256	53 01	306	59 23	340
246	38 57	033	37 10	077	46 09	127	27 54	194	44 54	256	52 12	305	59 01	339
247	39 30	033	38 08	077	46 57	128	27 40	194	43 56	256	51 23	305	58 39	337
248	40 02	032	39 07	077	47 44	128	27 24	195	42 58	256	50 33	304	58 14	335
249	40 33	031	40 05	077	48 31	129	27 09	195	41 59	257	49 44	303	57 49	334
250	41 04	030	41 03	076	49 17	130	26 53	196	41 01	257	48 53	303	57 22	333
251	41 34	030	42 02	076	50 03	130	26 36	196	40 03	257	48 02	302	56 54	331
252	42 03	029	43 00	076	50 48	131	26 19	197	39 04	257	47 11	301	56 24	330
253	42 32	028	43 58	076	51 33	132	26 02	197	38 06	257	46 20	301	55 53	328
254	43 00	027	44 56	075	52 17	133	25 44	197	37 07	257	45 28	300	55 21	327

LHA ♈	◆VEGA Hc	Zn	ALTAIR Hc	Zn	◆Nunki Hc	Zn	Shaula Hc	Zn	ANTARES Hc	Zn	◆SPICA Hc	Zn	ARCTURUS Hc	Zn
255	43 27	026	45 54	075	53 01	134	54 00	168	64 31	196	36 09	258	44 36	300
256	43 53	025	46 52	075	53 44	135	54 11	170	64 14	198	35 10	258	43 44	299
257	44 18	024	47 50	074	54 27	135	54 21	171	63 55	199	34 11	258	42 52	299
258	44 43	024	48 47	074	55 08	136	54 30	172	63 34	201	33 13	258	41 59	298
259	45 06	023	49 45	074	55 49	137	54 38	174	63 11	203	32 14	258	41 06	298
260	45 29	022	50 42	073	56 29	139	54 44	175	62 47	205	31 16	258	40 13	297
261	45 50	021	51 40	073	57 09	140	54 48	176	62 21	207	30 17	258	39 19	297
262	46 11	020	52 37	072	57 47	141	54 51	178	61 53	208	29 18	258	38 26	296
263	46 30	019	53 34	072	58 24	142	54 53	179	61 24	210	28 19	258	37 32	296
264	46 49	018	54 31	072	59 01	143	54 53	180	60 54	211	27 21	258	36 38	296
265	47 07	017	55 28	071	59 36	145	54 52	182	60 22	213	26 22	258	35 44	295
266	47 23	015	56 25	071	60 10	146	54 49	183	59 49	214	25 23	259	34 50	295
267	47 39	014	57 21	070	60 43	147	54 45	185	59 15	216	24 24	259	33 55	295
268	47 53	013	58 17	069	61 14	149	54 40	186	58 39	217	23 26	259	33 01	294
269	48 06	012	59 13	069	61 45	151	54 33	187	58 03	218	22 27	259	32 06	294

LHA ♈	◆VEGA Hc	Zn	DENEB Hc	Zn	Enif Hc	Zn	◆FOMALHAUT Hc	Zn	Peacock Hc	Zn	◆ANTARES Hc	Zn	ARCTURUS Hc	Zn
270	48 18	011	30 38	032	32 46	077	14 21	120	27 59	158	57 25	219	31 11	294
271	48 29	010	31 09	031	33 44	077	15 13	120	28 21	159	56 47	220	30 16	294
272	48 39	009	31 40	031	34 42	076	16 05	120	28 43	159	56 07	222	29 21	293
273	48 47	008	32 11	030	35 41	076	16 56	120	29 04	160	55 27	223	28 26	293
274	48 54	006	32 41	030	36 39	076	17 48	120	29 25	160	54 46	224	27 31	293
275	49 00	005	33 11	029	37 37	076	18 40	121	29 45	161	54 04	225	26 36	293
276	49 05	004	33 40	029	38 35	076	19 31	121	30 04	161	53 22	226	25 40	292
277	49 09	003	34 08	028	39 33	075	20 23	121	30 24	162	52 39	226	24 45	292
278	49 11	002	34 36	027	40 31	075	21 14	121	30 42	162	51 55	227	23 49	292
279	49 12	000	35 03	027	41 29	075	22 06	121	31 00	163	51 10	228	22 53	292
280	49 12	359	35 30	026	42 27	075	22 57	121	31 18	163	50 26	229	21 58	292
281	49 10	358	35 55	025	43 25	074	23 48	122	31 35	164	49 40	230	21 02	291
282	49 08	357	36 21	025	44 22	074	24 39	122	31 51	164	48 54	230	20 06	291
283	49 04	356	36 45	024	45 20	074	25 30	122	32 07	165	48 08	231	19 10	291
284	48 59	354	37 09	023	46 17	073	26 21	122	32 23	165	47 21	232	18 14	291

LHA ♈	DENEB Hc	Zn	Enif Hc	Zn	◆FOMALHAUT Hc	Zn	Peacock Hc	Zn	◆ANTARES Hc	Zn	Rasalhague Hc	Zn	◆VEGA Hc	Zn
285	37 33	022	47 15	073	27 11	122	32 38	166	46 34	232	64 30	305	48 52	353
286	37 55	022	48 12	073	28 02	123	32 52	167	45 46	233	63 41	304	48 45	352
287	38 17	021	49 09	072	28 52	123	33 05	167	44 58	233	62 51	303	48 36	351
288	38 38	020	50 06	072	29 43	123	33 18	168	44 10	234	62 00	302	48 26	350
289	38 58	019	51 03	071	30 33	124	33 31	168	43 21	235	61 09	301	48 15	349
290	39 18	019	52 00	071	31 22	124	33 42	169	42 32	235	60 17	300	48 02	348
291	39 36	018	52 57	071	32 12	124	33 53	170	41 43	236	59 25	299	47 49	346
292	39 54	017	53 53	070	33 02	124	34 04	170	40 53	236	58 32	298	47 34	345
293	40 11	016	54 49	070	33 51	125	34 13	171	40 03	236	57 39	297	47 19	344
294	40 27	015	55 45	069	34 40	125	34 23	172	39 13	237	56 46	297	47 02	343
295	40 43	014	56 41	068	35 29	126	34 31	172	38 23	237	55 52	296	46 44	342
296	40 57	013	57 37	068	36 18	126	34 39	173	37 33	238	54 58	295	46 25	341
297	41 10	013	58 32	067	37 06	126	34 46	174	36 42	238	54 04	295	46 05	340
298	41 23	012	59 27	066	37 54	127	34 52	174	35 51	238	53 09	294	45 44	339
299	41 35	011	60 22	066	38 42	127	34 58	175	35 00	239	52 15	294	45 22	338

LHA ♈	◆DENEB Hc	Zn	Alpheratz Hc	Zn	◆FOMALHAUT Hc	Zn	Peacock Hc	Zn	◆ANTARES Hc	Zn	Rasalhague Hc	Zn	VEGA Hc	Zn
300	41 45	010	22 53	057	39 30	128	35 03	176	34 08	239	51 19	293	45 00	337
301	41 55	009	23 43	057	40 17	128	35 07	176	33 17	239	50 24	293	44 36	336
302	42 04	008	24 33	056	41 04	129	35 11	177	32 25	240	49 29	292	44 11	335
303	42 12	007	25 23	056	41 51	129	35 14	178	31 33	240	48 33	292	43 46	334
304	42 19	006	26 12	056	42 37	130	35 16	178	30 42	240	47 37	291	43 19	333
305	42 25	005	27 02	056	43 23	130	35 18	179	29 49	240	46 41	291	42 52	333
306	42 30	004	27 51	055	44 09	131	35 19	180	28 57	241	45 45	290	42 24	332
307	42 34	003	28 41	055	44 54	131	35 19	180	28 05	241	44 49	290	41 55	331
308	42 37	002	29 30	055	45 39	132	35 18	181	27 13	241	43 52	290	41 26	330
309	42 39	001	30 18	054	46 23	133	35 17	182	26 20	241	42 56	289	40 56	329
310	42 40	000	31 07	054	47 07	133	35 15	182	25 27	241	41 59	289	40 25	329
311	42 40	000	31 55	053	47 50	134	35 12	183	24 35	242	41 02	289	39 53	328
312	42 39	359	32 43	053	48 33	135	35 09	184	23 42	242	40 05	288	39 21	327
313	42 37	358	33 31	053	49 15	136	35 05	184	22 49	242	39 08	288	38 48	326
314	42 34	357	34 18	052	49 57	136	35 00	185	21 56	242	38 11	288	38 14	326

LHA ♈	◆Alpheratz Hc	Zn	◆FOMALHAUT Hc	Zn	Peacock Hc	Zn	Nunki Hc	Zn	◆Rasalhague Hc	Zn	VEGA Hc	Zn	DENEB Hc	Zn
315	35 05	052	50 38	137	34 55	186	51 38	228	37 14	287	37 40	325	42 30	356
316	35 52	051	51 18	138	34 49	186	50 53	229	36 17	287	37 06	324	42 25	355
317	36 39	051	51 58	139	34 42	187	50 07	230	35 20	287	36 30	324	42 19	354
318	37 25	050	52 37	140	34 34	188	49 21	230	34 22	287	35 55	323	42 12	353
319	38 11	050	53 15	141	34 26	188	48 35	231	33 25	286	35 18	322	42 04	352
320	38 56	049	53 52	142	34 17	189	47 48	232	32 27	286	34 42	322	41 55	351
321	39 41	048	54 28	143	34 08	189	47 01	232	31 30	286	34 04	321	41 45	350
322	40 26	048	55 04	144	33 58	190	46 14	233	30 32	286	33 27	321	41 34	349
323	41 10	047	55 38	145	33 47	191	45 26	233	29 34	286	32 48	320	41 23	348
324	41 54	047	56 12	147	33 35	191	44 37	234	28 36	285	32 10	320	41 10	347
325	42 38	046	56 44	148	33 23	192	43 49	235	27 39	285	31 31	319	40 57	347
326	43 20	045	57 16	149	33 11	193	43 00	235	26 41	285	30 51	319	40 42	346
327	44 03	045	57 46	150	32 57	193	42 10	236	25 43	285	30 12	318	40 27	345
328	44 45	044	58 15	152	32 43	194	41 21	236	24 45	285	29 32	318	40 11	344
329	45 26	043	58 43	153	32 29	194	40 31	236	23 47	285	28 51	317	39 54	343

LHA ♈	◆Alpheratz Hc	Zn	Hamal Hc	Zn	Diphda Hc	Zn	◆FOMALHAUT Hc	Zn	Nunki Hc	Zn	◆ALTAIR Hc	Zn	DENEB Hc	Zn
330	46 06	042	24 36	063	46 41	114	59 09	155	39 41	237	56 11	289	39 36	342
331	46 47	041	25 29	063	47 35	115	59 34	156	38 50	237	55 14	289	39 17	341
332	47 26	041	26 22	062	48 30	115	59 58	158	38 00	238	54 17	288	38 58	341
333	48 05	040	27 15	062	49 24	116	60 20	159	37 09	238	53 20	288	38 37	340
334	48 43	039	28 08	062	50 18	116	60 40	161	36 18	238	52 23	287	38 16	339
335	49 20	038	29 01	062	51 12	117	60 59	163	35 27	239	51 26	287	37 54	338
336	49 56	037	29 54	061	52 05	117	61 16	164	34 36	239	50 28	287	37 32	338
337	50 32	036	30 46	061	52 58	118	61 31	166	33 44	239	49 31	286	37 09	337
338	51 07	035	31 38	061	53 51	118	61 45	168	32 52	240	48 33	286	36 45	336
339	51 40	034	32 30	060	54 44	119	61 57	170	32 01	240	47 36	286	36 20	335
340	52 13	033	33 22	060	55 36	120	62 07	171	31 09	240	46 38	285	35 55	335
341	52 45	032	34 14	060	56 28	120	62 15	173	30 16	240	45 40	285	35 29	334
342	53 16	030	35 06	059	57 20	121	62 21	175	29 24	241	44 42	285	35 02	333
343	53 46	029	35 57	059	58 11	122	62 25	177	28 32	241	43 44	284	34 35	333
344	54 15	028	36 48	058	59 02	123	62 27	179	27 39	241	42 46	284	34 07	332

LHA ♈	Alpheratz Hc	Zn	◆Hamal Hc	Zn	◆ACHERNAR Hc	Zn	FOMALHAUT Hc	Zn	Nunki Hc	Zn	◆ALTAIR Hc	Zn	DENEB Hc	Zn
345	54 42	027	37 39	058	26 33	157	62 27	181	26 47	241	41 48	284	33 39	331
346	55 09	025	38 30	057	26 56	158	62 26	183	25 54	242	40 49	284	33 10	331
347	55 34	024	39 20	057	27 19	158	62 22	184	25 01	242	39 51	283	32 40	330
348	55 57	023	40 10	056	27 41	159	62 16	186	24 08	242	38 53	283	32 10	330
349	56 20	021	41 00	056	28 03	159	62 09	188	23 15	242	37 54	283	31 40	329
350	56 41	020	41 50	055	28 24	160	61 59	190	22 22	242	36 56	283	31 09	328
351	57 00	018	42 39	055	28 45	160	61 48	192	21 29	242	35 57	283	30 37	328
352	57 18	017	43 28	054	29 05	160	61 35	194	20 36	243	34 59	282	30 05	327
353	57 35	015	44 16	054	29 25	161	61 20	195	19 43	243	34 00	282	29 32	327
354	57 50	014	45 05	053	29 44	161	61 03	197	18 49	243	33 01	282	28 59	326
355	58 03	012	45 52	052	30 03	162	60 45	199	17 56	243	32 03	282	28 26	326
356	58 15	010	46 40	052	30 21	163	60 25	200	17 03	243	31 04	282	27 52	325
357	58 25	009	47 26	051	30 39	163	60 03	202	16 09	243	30 05	281	27 18	325
358	58 33	007	48 13	050	30 56	164	59 40	203	15 16	243	29 06	281	26 43	325
359	58 40	006	48 59	050	31 13	164	59 15	205	14 22	243	28 08	281	26 08	324

LAT 3°S

LHA ♈	Hc	Zn	Hc	Zn	Hc	Zn	Hc	Zn	Hc	Zn	Hc	Zn	Hc	Zn
	Alpheratz		◆ALDEBARAN		RIGEL		ACHERNAR		◆FOMALHAUT		ALTAIR		◆DENEB	
0	57 45	004	18 58	071	11 29	098	32 27	165	59 43	207	26 57	282	24 45	324
1	57 48	002	19 55	071	12 29	098	32 42	165	59 15	209	25 58	281	24 09	324
2	57 50	000	20 52	071	13 28	098	32 58	166	58 45	210	25 00	281	23 33	323
3	57 49	359	21 48	071	14 28	098	33 12	166	58 15	211	24 01	281	22 57	323
4	57 47	357	22 45	071	15 27	098	33 26	167	57 43	213	23 02	281	22 21	322
5	57 43	356	23 42	070	16 26	098	33 39	167	57 10	214	22 03	281	21 44	322
6	57 38	354	24 38	070	17 26	098	33 52	168	56 36	215	21 04	281	21 07	322
7	57 31	352	25 34	070	18 25	098	34 04	169	56 01	216	20 05	281	20 30	321
8	57 22	351	26 31	070	19 24	098	34 16	169	55 25	217	19 07	281	19 52	321
9	57 11	349	27 27	070	20 24	098	34 27	170	54 48	219	18 08	280	19 14	321
10	56 59	348	28 23	069	21 23	098	34 37	170	54 10	220	17 09	280	18 36	320
11	56 46	346	29 19	069	22 23	098	34 47	171	53 32	221	16 10	280	17 57	320
12	56 30	345	30 15	069	23 22	098	34 56	172	52 52	222	15 11	280	17 19	320
13	56 14	343	31 11	069	24 21	098	35 04	172	52 12	222	14 12	280	16 40	319
14	55 55	342	32 06	068	25 21	098	35 12	173	51 31	223	13 13	280	16 01	319
	CAPELLA		ALDEBARAN		◆RIGEL		ACHERNAR		◆FOMALHAUT		Enif		◆Alpheratz	
15	15 09	040	33 02	068	26 20	098	35 19	174	50 50	224	39 44	286	55 36	340
16	15 48	040	33 58	068	27 20	098	35 25	174	50 08	225	38 46	285	55 15	339
17	16 27	040	34 53	067	28 19	098	35 30	175	49 25	226	37 49	285	54 52	337
18	17 05	040	35 48	067	29 18	098	35 35	176	48 42	226	36 51	285	54 29	336
19	17 43	039	36 43	067	30 18	098	35 40	176	47 58	227	35 53	285	54 04	335
20	18 21	039	37 38	066	31 17	098	35 43	177	47 14	228	34 55	284	53 37	333
21	18 59	039	38 33	066	32 16	098	35 46	178	46 29	229	33 57	284	53 10	332
22	19 36	038	39 28	066	33 16	098	35 48	178	45 44	229	32 59	284	52 41	331
23	20 13	038	40 22	065	34 15	098	35 49	179	44 59	230	32 00	284	52 12	330
24	20 50	038	41 17	065	35 14	098	35 50	180	44 13	230	31 02	283	51 41	329
25	21 27	037	42 11	064	36 14	098	35 50	180	43 27	231	30 04	283	51 09	327
26	22 03	037	43 05	064	37 13	098	35 50	181	42 40	231	29 05	283	50 37	326
27	22 39	037	43 58	063	38 12	098	35 48	182	41 53	232	28 07	283	50 03	325
28	23 14	036	44 52	063	39 12	098	35 46	182	41 05	232	27 09	283	49 29	324
29	23 50	036	45 45	062	40 11	098	35 43	183	40 18	233	26 10	283	48 53	323
	CAPELLA		◆BETELGEUSE		SIRIUS		CANOPUS		◆ACHERNAR		FOMALHAUT		◆Alpheratz	
30	24 24	035	30 13	080	18 37	107	16 41	145	35 40	184	39 30	233	48 17	322
31	24 59	035	31 12	079	19 35	107	17 15	145	35 36	184	38 42	234	47 40	321
32	25 33	035	32 11	079	20 32	107	17 50	145	35 31	185	37 53	234	47 02	321
33	26 07	034	33 10	079	21 29	107	18 24	145	35 26	186	37 04	235	46 24	320
34	26 40	034	34 09	079	22 27	107	18 58	146	35 19	186	36 15	235	45 45	319
35	27 13	033	35 08	079	23 24	107	19 32	146	35 13	187	35 26	235	45 05	318
36	27 46	033	36 06	079	24 21	107	20 06	146	35 05	188	34 37	236	44 25	317
37	28 18	032	37 05	078	25 19	107	20 39	146	34 57	188	33 47	236	43 44	317
38	28 50	032	38 04	078	26 16	107	21 12	147	34 48	189	32 58	236	43 02	316
39	29 21	031	39 02	078	27 13	107	21 45	147	34 38	189	32 08	237	42 20	315
40	29 52	031	40 01	078	28 10	107	22 18	147	34 28	190	31 17	237	41 38	314
41	30 22	030	40 59	077	29 07	108	22 50	147	34 17	191	30 27	237	40 55	314
42	30 52	029	41 58	077	30 04	108	23 22	148	34 06	191	29 37	237	40 11	313
43	31 21	029	42 56	077	31 02	108	23 54	148	33 54	192	28 46	238	39 27	312
44	31 50	028	43 55	077	31 59	108	24 26	148	33 41	193	27 55	238	38 43	312
	CAPELLA		◆BETELGEUSE		SIRIUS		CANOPUS		◆ACHERNAR		Diphda		◆Hamal	
45	32 18	028	44 53	076	32 56	108	24 57	149	33 28	193	53 35	243	60 36	335
46	32 45	027	45 51	076	33 53	108	25 28	149	33 14	194	52 41	244	60 10	334
47	33 12	026	46 49	076	34 49	108	25 59	149	33 00	194	51 47	244	59 43	332
48	33 39	026	47 47	076	35 46	109	26 29	150	32 44	195	50 53	245	59 14	330
49	34 04	025	48 45	075	36 43	109	26 59	150	32 29	195	49 59	245	58 44	329
50	34 30	024	49 43	075	37 40	109	27 29	151	32 13	196	49 04	246	58 12	327
51	34 54	024	50 41	074	38 36	109	27 58	151	31 56	197	48 09	246	57 39	326
52	35 18	023	51 39	074	39 33	109	28 27	151	31 39	197	47 14	247	57 05	325
53	35 41	022	52 36	074	40 30	110	28 55	152	31 21	198	46 19	247	56 30	323
54	36 03	022	53 34	073	41 26	110	29 24	152	31 02	198	45 24	247	55 54	322
55	36 25	021	54 31	073	42 22	110	29 51	153	30 43	199	44 29	248	55 17	321
56	36 46	020	55 28	072	43 19	110	30 19	153	30 24	199	43 33	248	54 39	320
57	37 07	019	56 25	072	44 15	111	30 45	154	30 04	200	42 38	248	54 00	319
58	37 26	019	57 22	071	45 11	111	31 12	154	29 44	200	41 42	249	53 20	318
59	37 45	018	58 19	071	46 07	111	31 38	155	29 23	201	40 46	249	52 39	317
	◆CAPELLA		POLLUX		◆SIRIUS		CANOPUS		ACHERNAR		◆Diphda		Hamal	
60	38 03	017	27 29	056	47 02	112	32 03	155	29 02	201	39 50	249	51 57	316
61	38 20	016	28 18	056	47 58	112	32 28	156	28 40	202	38 54	249	51 15	315
62	38 36	015	29 08	055	48 54	112	32 53	156	28 18	202	37 58	250	50 32	314
63	38 52	015	29 57	055	49 49	113	33 17	157	27 55	202	37 02	250	49 49	313
64	39 07	014	30 46	055	50 44	113	33 40	157	27 32	203	36 06	250	49 05	312
65	39 21	013	31 35	054	51 39	113	34 03	158	27 08	203	35 09	250	48 20	311
66	39 34	012	32 23	054	52 34	114	34 25	158	26 45	204	34 13	250	47 35	311
67	39 46	011	33 12	053	53 29	114	34 47	159	26 20	204	33 16	250	46 49	310
68	39 57	010	34 00	053	54 23	115	35 08	160	25 56	204	32 20	251	46 03	309
69	40 07	009	34 47	053	55 17	116	35 29	160	25 31	205	31 23	251	45 16	308
70	40 17	009	35 35	052	56 11	116	35 49	161	25 05	205	30 27	251	44 29	308
71	40 25	008	36 22	052	57 05	117	36 08	161	24 39	206	29 30	251	43 41	307
72	40 33	007	37 08	051	57 58	117	36 27	162	24 13	206	28 33	251	42 53	306
73	40 39	006	37 55	050	58 51	118	36 45	163	23 47	206	27 37	251	42 05	306
74	40 45	005	38 41	050	59 44	119	37 02	163	23 20	207	26 40	251	41 16	305
	CAPELLA		◆POLLUX		REGULUS		Suhail		◆CANOPUS		ACHERNAR		◆Hamal	
75	40 50	004	39 27	049	11 47	077	22 00	136	37 19	164	22 53	207	40 27	305
76	40 54	003	40 12	049	12 45	077	22 41	136	37 35	165	22 26	207	39 38	304
77	40 56	002	40 57	048	13 44	077	23 22	137	37 51	165	21 58	208	38 48	304
78	40 58	001	41 41	047	14 42	077	24 03	137	38 05	166	21 30	208	37 58	303
79	40 59	000	42 25	047	15 40	077	24 44	137	38 19	167	21 02	208	37 08	303
80	40 59	359	43 08	046	16 39	077	25 25	138	38 33	168	20 34	208	36 17	302
81	40 58	359	43 51	045	17 37	077	26 05	138	38 45	168	20 05	209	35 26	302
82	40 56	358	44 34	045	18 35	076	26 45	138	38 57	169	19 36	209	34 35	301
83	40 53	357	45 16	044	19 33	076	27 25	139	39 08	170	19 07	209	33 44	301
84	40 49	356	45 57	043	20 32	076	28 04	139	39 18	171	18 38	210	32 53	301
85	40 45	355	46 37	042	21 30	076	28 44	139	39 27	171	18 08	210	32 01	300
86	40 39	354	47 17	041	22 28	076	29 23	140	39 36	172	17 38	210	31 09	300
87	40 32	353	47 57	041	23 26	076	30 01	140	39 44	173	17 08	210	30 17	300
88	40 24	352	48 35	040	24 24	075	30 40	140	39 51	174	16 38	210	29 25	299
89	40 16	351	49 13	039	25 22	075	31 18	141	39 57	174	16 07	211	28 33	299

LHA ♈	Hc	Zn	Hc	Zn	Hc	Zn	Hc	Zn	Hc	Zn	Hc	Zn	Hc	Zn
	POLLUX		◆REGULUS		Suhail		◆CANOPUS		Acamar		◆ALDEBARAN		CAPELLA	
90	49 50	038	26 20	075	31 56	141	40 02	175	34 45	221	61 39	314	40 06	350
91	50 27	037	27 18	075	32 33	142	40 07	176	34 05	222	60 55	313	39 56	350
92	51 02	036	28 16	075	33 10	142	40 11	177	33 25	222	60 11	312	39 45	349
93	51 36	035	29 13	075	33 47	143	40 14	178	32 45	223	59 26	310	39 32	348
94	52 10	034	30 11	074	34 23	143	40 16	178	32 04	223	58 40	309	39 19	347
95	52 43	032	31 09	074	34 59	144	40 17	179	31 23	223	57 53	308	39 05	346
96	53 14	031	32 06	074	35 34	144	40 18	180	30 42	224	57 06	307	38 51	345
97	53 45	030	33 04	074	36 09	145	40 17	181	30 00	224	56 18	306	38 35	344
98	54 14	029	34 01	073	36 43	145	40 16	182	29 18	225	55 29	305	38 18	344
99	54 42	027	34 59	073	37 17	146	40 14	182	28 36	225	54 40	305	38 01	343
100	55 09	026	35 56	073	37 51	146	40 11	183	27 54	225	53 50	304	37 43	342
101	55 35	025	36 53	073	38 24	147	40 08	184	27 11	226	53 00	303	37 24	341
102	55 59	023	37 51	072	38 56	148	40 03	185	26 28	226	52 10	302	37 05	340
103	56 23	022	38 48	072	39 28	148	39 58	185	25 45	226	51 19	301	36 44	340
104	56 44	020	39 45	072	39 59	149	39 52	186	25 02	226	50 27	301	36 23	339
	POLLUX		◆REGULUS		Suhail		◆CANOPUS		RIGEL		◆ALDEBARAN		CAPELLA	
105	57 05	019	40 42	072	40 30	150	39 45	187	63 26	258	49 36	300	36 01	338
106	57 23	017	41 38	071	41 00	150	39 37	188	62 28	258	48 44	299	35 39	338
107	57 40	016	42 35	071	41 30	151	39 29	189	61 29	258	47 51	299	35 15	337
108	57 56	014	43 32	070	41 58	152	39 19	189	60 30	259	46 59	298	34 52	336
109	58 10	013	44 28	070	42 27	152	39 09	190	59 32	259	46 06	298	34 27	335
110	58 22	011	45 24	070	42 54	153	38 58	191	58 33	259	45 13	297	34 02	335
111	58 33	009	46 20	069	43 21	154	38 47	192	57 34	259	44 19	297	33 36	334
112	58 42	008	47 16	069	43 47	155	38 34	192	56 35	260	43 26	296	33 10	333
113	58 49	006	48 12	068	44 12	156	38 21	193	55 36	260	42 32	296	32 42	333
114	58 55	004	49 08	068	44 36	156	38 07	194	54 37	260	41 38	295	32 15	332
115	58 58	003	50 03	067	45 00	157	37 53	194	53 38	260	40 44	295	31 47	332
116	59 00	001	50 58	067	45 23	158	37 38	195	52 39	260	39 49	295	31 18	331
117	59 00	359	51 53	066	45 44	159	37 22	196	51 40	261	38 55	294	30 49	330
118	58 59	358	52 48	066	46 05	160	37 05	196	50 41	261	38 00	294	30 19	330
119	58 55	356	53 43	065	46 26	161	36 48	197	49 42	261	37 05	293	29 49	329
	◆REGULUS		Gienah		◆ACRUX		CANOPUS		SIRIUS		◆BETELGEUSE		POLLUX	
120	54 37	065	25 31	108	12 56	155	36 30	198	67 11	232	57 22	289	58 50	354
121	55 31	064	26 28	108	13 21	155	36 11	198	66 23	233	56 25	288	58 43	352
122	56 24	063	27 25	108	13 46	155	35 52	199	65 35	234	55 28	288	58 34	351
123	57 18	062	28 22	108	14 12	155	35 32	200	64 46	236	54 31	287	58 24	349
124	58 11	062	29 19	109	14 37	155	35 11	200	63 56	237	53 33	287	58 12	347
125	59 03	061	30 16	109	15 01	156	34 50	201	63 06	238	52 36	286	57 58	346
126	59 55	060	31 13	109	15 26	156	34 28	202	62 15	239	51 38	286	57 42	344
127	60 47	059	32 09	109	15 50	156	34 06	202	61 23	240	50 41	286	57 25	343
128	61 38	058	33 06	109	16 14	156	33 43	203	60 31	240	49 43	285	57 07	341
129	62 28	057	34 02	109	16 38	157	33 20	203	59 39	241	48 45	285	56 47	340
130	63 18	056	34 59	109	17 02	157	32 56	204	58 46	242	47 47	284	56 25	338
131	64 07	054	35 55	110	17 26	157	32 32	204	57 53	243	46 49	284	56 02	337
132	64 56	053	36 52	110	17 49	157	32 07	205	57 00	243	45 51	284	55 38	335
133	65 43	052	37 48	110	18 12	157	31 41	205	56 06	244	44 52	284	55 12	334
134	66 30	050	38 44	110	18 35	158	31 16	206	55 12	245	43 54	283	54 45	333
	Alioth		◆SPICA		ACRUX		◆CANOPUS		SIRIUS		BETELGEUSE		◆POLLUX	
135	14 21	030	23 38	101	18 58	158	30 49	206	54 10	245	42 56	283	54 17	331
136	14 51	029	24 37	101	19 20	158	30 22	207	53 24	246	41 57	283	53 48	330
137	15 20	029	25 35	101	19 42	159	29 55	207	52 29	246	40 59	283	53 18	329
138	15 49	029	26 34	101	20 04	159	29 28	208	51 34	247	40 00	282	52 46	328
139	16 18	028	27 33	101	20 26	159	29 00	208	50 39	247	39 02	282	52 14	327
140	16 46	028	28 32	101	20 47	159	28 31	209	49 44	247	38 03	282	51 40	325
141	17 14	028	29 31	101	21 08	160	28 02	209	48 48	248	37 05	282	51 06	324
142	17 42	028	30 29	101	21 28	160	27 33	209	47 53	248	36 06	281	50 31	323
143	18 10	027	31 28	101	21 49	160	27 03	210	46 57	249	35 07	281	49 55	322
144	18 37	027	32 27	101	22 09	161	26 33	210	46 01	249	34 08	281	49 18	321
145	19 04	026	33 26	101	22 28	161	26 03	211	45 05	249	33 10	281	48 40	320
146	19 30	026	34 24	102	22 48	161	25 32	211	44 09	249	32 11	281	48 01	320
147	19 56	026	35 23	102	23 07	162	25 02	211	43 13	250	31 12	281	47 22	319
148	20 22	025	36 22	102	23 25	162	24 30	212	42 17	250	30 13	280	46 42	318
149	20 48	025	37 20	102	23 44	162	23 59	212	41 21	250	29 14	280	46 02	317
	Alioth		ARCTURUS		◆SPICA		ACRUX		◆CANOPUS		SIRIUS		◆POLLUX	
150	21 13	025	23 17	068	38 19	102	24 02	163	23 27	212	40 24	250	45 20	316
151	21 38	024	24 12	067	39 18	102	24 19	163	22 55	213	39 28	251	44 39	315
152	22 02	024	25 08	067	40 16	102	24 36	164	22 22	213	38 31	251	43 56	315
153	22 26	023	26 03	067	41 15	102	24 53	164	21 50	213	37 34	251	43 13	314
154	22 49	023	26 58	067	42 13	102	25 10	164	21 17	213	36 38	251	42 30	313
155	23 12	022	27 53	067	43 12	103	25 26	165	20 44	214	35 41	251	41 46	313
156	23 35	022	28 48	066	44 10	103	25 41	165	20 10	214	34 44	252	41 02	312
157	23 57	022	29 43	066	45 09	103	25 56	166	19 37	214	33 47	252	40 17	311
158	24 19	021	30 37	066	46 07	103	26 11	166	19 03	214	32 50	252	39 32	311
159	24 40	021	31 32	065	47 05	103	26 25	166	18 29	215	31 53	252	38 46	310
160	25 01	020	32 26	065	48 04	104	26 39	167	17 55	215	30 56	252	38 00	310
161	25 21	020	33 20	065	49 02	104	26 53	167	17 20	215	29 59	252	37 14	309
162	25 41	019	34 15	064	50 00	104	27 06	168	16 46	215	29 02	252	36 27	309
163	26 00	019	35 09	064	50 58	104	27 18	168	16 11	215	28 05	253	35 40	308
164	26 19	018	36 02	064	51 56	104	27 30	169	15 36	216	27 08	253	34 53	308
	Alioth		◆ARCTURUS		SPICA		◆ACRUX		Suhail		SIRIUS		◆POLLUX	
165	26 38	018	36 56	063	52 54	105	27 42	169	42 34	207	26 10	253	34 05	307
166	26 55	017	37 49	063	53 52	105	27 53	170	42 06	208	25 13	253	33 17	307
167	27 13	016	38 43	062	54 50	105	28 04	170	41 38	209	24 16	253	32 29	306
168	27 29	016	39 36	062	55 48	106	28 14	170	41 08	209	23 18	253	31 40	306
169	27 45	015	40 28	062	56 45	106	28 24	171	40 38	210	22 21	253	30 52	305
170	28 01	015	41 21	061	57 43	106	28 33	171	40 08	211	21 24	253	30 03	305
171	28 16	014	42 13	061	58 40	107	28 41	172	39 37	212	20 26	253	29 14	305
172	28 30	014	43 06	060	59 37	107	28 50	172	39 05	212	19 29	253	28 24	304
173	28 44	013	43 57	060	60 35	108	28 57	173	38 33	213	18 32	253	27 34	304
174	28 57	012	44 49	059	61 32	108	29 04	173	38 00	214	17 34	253	26 45	304
175	29 10	012	45 40	058	62 28	109	29 11	174	37 27	214	16 37	253	25 55	303
176	29 22	011	46 31	058	63 25	109	29 17	174	36 53	215	15 39	253	25 04	303
177	29 33	011	47 22	057	64 21	110	29 23	175	36 18	215	14 42	253	24 14	303
178	29 44	010	48 12	057	65 18	111	29 28	175	35 44	216	13 45	253	23 23	302
179	29 54	009	49 02	056	66 14	111	29 32	176	35 08	216	12 47	254	22 33	302

LHA ♈	Hc	Zn	Hc	Zn	Hc	Zn	Hc	Zn	Hc	Zn	Hc	Zn	Hc	Zn
	Alioth		◆ ARCTURUS		ANTARES		◆ ACRUX		Suhail		Alphard		◆ REGULUS	
180	30 04	009	49 51	055	21 22	117	29 36	176	34 33	217	51 52	260	58 41	299
181	30 13	008	50 40	054	22 15	117	29 40	177	33 57	217	50 53	260	57 49	298
182	30 21	008	51 29	054	23 08	118	29 43	177	33 20	218	49 54	260	56 56	297
183	30 29	007	52 17	053	24 01	118	29 45	178	32 43	218	48 55	260	56 02	297
184	30 35	006	53 04	052	24 54	118	29 47	179	32 06	219	47 56	260	55 08	296
185	30 42	006	53 51	051	25 47	118	29 48	179	31 28	219	46 57	260	54 14	295
186	30 47	005	54 37	050	26 40	118	29 49	180	30 50	220	45 58	261	53 20	295
187	30 52	004	55 23	049	27 33	118	29 49	180	30 12	220	44 59	261	52 25	294
188	30 56	004	56 08	048	28 25	119	29 49	181	29 33	220	44 00	261	51 31	293
189	31 00	003	56 53	047	29 18	119	29 48	181	28 54	221	43 01	261	50 35	293
190	31 03	002	57 36	046	30 10	119	29 46	182	28 15	221	42 02	261	49 40	292
191	31 05	002	58 19	045	31 03	119	29 44	182	27 36	221	41 02	261	48 45	292
192	31 06	001	59 01	044	31 55	120	29 42	183	26 56	222	40 03	261	47 49	291
193	31 07	000	59 41	042	32 47	120	29 39	183	26 16	222	39 04	261	46 53	291
194	31 07	000	60 21	041	33 39	120	29 35	184	25 36	222	38 05	261	45 57	291
	ARCTURUS		◆ Rasalhague		ANTARES		◆ ACRUX		Alphard		◆ REGULUS		Alioth	
195	61 00	040	19 50	076	34 31	120	29 31	184	37 05	261	45 01	290	31 07	359
196	61 38	038	20 48	075	35 22	121	29 26	185	36 06	261	44 05	290	31 05	358
197	62 14	037	21 46	075	36 14	121	29 21	185	35 07	261	43 08	289	31 03	358
198	62 49	035	22 44	075	37 05	121	29 16	186	34 08	261	42 11	289	31 01	357
199	63 23	033	23 42	075	37 56	122	29 09	186	33 08	262	41 15	289	30 58	357
200	63 55	032	24 40	075	38 47	122	29 03	187	32 09	262	40 18	288	30 54	356
201	64 25	030	25 38	075	39 38	122	28 55	187	31 10	262	39 21	288	30 49	355
202	64 54	028	26 36	074	40 28	123	28 47	188	30 11	262	38 24	288	30 44	355
203	65 21	026	27 33	074	41 18	123	28 39	188	29 11	262	37 27	287	30 38	354
204	65 46	024	28 31	074	42 08	124	28 30	189	28 12	262	36 30	287	30 31	353
205	66 09	022	29 28	074	42 58	124	28 21	189	27 13	262	35 32	287	30 24	353
206	66 30	019	30 26	074	43 47	125	28 11	190	26 14	262	34 35	287	30 16	352
207	66 49	017	31 23	073	44 37	125	28 01	190	25 14	262	33 38	286	30 07	351
208	67 06	015	32 21	073	45 25	126	27 50	191	24 15	262	32 40	286	29 58	351
209	67 20	013	33 18	073	46 14	126	27 39	191	23 16	262	31 43	286	29 48	350
	ARCTURUS		◆ VEGA		ANTARES		◆ RIGIL KENT		ACRUX		Gienah		◆ REGULUS	
210	67 32	010	13 59	049	47 02	127	31 35	174	27 27	192	60 44	238	30 45	286
211	67 41	008	14 44	049	47 50	127	31 41	175	27 15	192	59 53	239	29 47	286
212	67 48	005	15 28	048	48 37	128	31 46	175	27 02	192	59 01	240	28 49	285
213	67 52	003	16 13	048	49 24	129	31 51	176	26 49	193	58 09	241	27 52	285
214	67 54	000	16 57	048	50 11	129	31 55	176	26 36	193	57 17	241	26 54	285
215	67 53	358	17 42	048	50 57	130	31 58	177	26 22	194	56 24	242	25 56	285
216	67 49	355	18 26	047	51 43	131	32 01	178	26 07	194	55 31	243	24 58	285
217	67 43	353	19 10	047	52 28	132	32 03	178	25 52	195	54 37	243	24 00	284
218	67 34	350	19 53	047	53 12	132	32 05	179	25 37	195	53 44	244	23 02	284
219	67 22	348	20 37	046	53 56	133	32 06	179	25 21	195	52 50	244	22 04	284
220	67 09	345	21 20	046	54 39	134	32 06	180	25 05	196	51 56	245	21 06	284
221	66 52	343	22 03	046	55 22	135	32 06	180	24 49	196	51 01	245	20 07	284
222	66 34	341	22 46	045	56 04	136	32 05	181	24 32	197	50 07	246	19 09	284
223	66 13	339	23 28	045	56 45	137	32 04	182	24 14	197	49 12	246	18 11	284
224	65 50	337	24 11	045	57 25	138	32 02	182	23 57	197	48 17	247	17 13	283
	Alphecca		VEGA		◆ ALTAIR		ANTARES		◆ RIGIL KENT		SPICA		◆ ARCTURUS	
225	59 08	016	24 53	044	16 24	080	58 05	139	31 59	183	65 17	249	65 26	335
226	59 23	014	25 34	044	17 23	080	58 43	141	31 56	183	64 21	250	64 59	333
227	59 37	012	26 16	043	18 22	080	59 21	142	31 52	184	63 25	251	64 30	331
228	59 48	010	26 57	043	19 21	079	59 57	143	31 48	184	62 28	251	64 00	329
229	59 58	009	27 38	043	20 20	079	60 32	145	31 43	185	61 31	252	63 28	327
230	60 06	007	28 18	042	21 19	079	61 07	146	31 37	186	60 34	252	62 55	325
231	60 13	005	28 58	042	22 17	079	61 39	147	31 31	186	59 37	253	62 20	324
232	60 17	003	29 38	041	23 16	079	62 11	149	31 24	187	58 40	253	61 44	322
233	60 19	001	30 17	041	24 15	079	62 41	151	31 17	187	57 42	254	61 07	321
234	60 20	000	30 56	040	25 14	079	63 10	152	31 09	188	56 45	254	60 28	319
235	60 19	358	31 35	040	26 13	079	63 37	154	31 01	188	55 47	254	59 48	318
236	60 16	356	32 13	039	27 11	078	64 02	156	30 52	189	54 49	255	59 08	317
237	60 11	354	32 50	039	28 10	078	64 26	158	30 42	189	53 52	255	58 26	315
238	60 04	353	33 28	038	29 09	078	64 48	160	30 32	190	52 54	255	57 43	314
239	59 55	351	34 04	038	30 07	078	65 08	161	30 22	190	51 56	256	57 00	313
	VEGA		◆ ALTAIR		Nunki		◆ RIGIL KENT		SPICA		◆ ARCTURUS		Alphecca	
240	34 41	037	31 06	078	41 49	123	30 10	191	50 58	256	56 16	312	59 45	349
241	35 16	036	32 04	078	42 39	124	29 59	192	49 59	256	55 31	311	59 32	347
242	35 52	036	33 03	077	43 29	124	29 46	192	49 01	256	54 45	310	59 18	346
243	36 26	035	34 01	077	44 18	125	29 34	193	48 03	256	53 59	309	59 02	344
244	37 00	034	35 00	077	45 07	125	29 20	193	47 05	257	53 12	308	58 45	342
245	37 34	034	35 58	077	45 56	126	29 07	194	46 06	257	52 25	307	58 26	341
246	38 07	033	36 56	077	46 45	126	28 52	194	45 08	257	51 37	306	58 05	339
247	38 39	032	37 54	076	47 33	127	28 38	194	44 10	257	50 49	306	57 43	338
248	39 11	032	38 53	076	48 21	127	28 22	195	43 11	257	50 00	305	57 20	336
249	39 42	031	39 51	076	49 08	128	28 07	195	42 13	258	49 10	304	56 55	335
250	40 12	030	40 49	076	49 55	129	27 51	196	41 14	258	48 20	304	56 28	333
251	40 42	029	41 47	075	50 41	129	27 34	196	40 16	258	47 30	303	56 01	332
252	41 11	028	42 45	075	51 27	130	27 17	197	39 17	258	46 40	302	55 32	331
253	41 39	028	43 43	075	52 13	131	26 59	197	38 18	258	45 49	302	55 02	329
254	42 06	027	44 40	074	52 58	132	26 41	198	37 20	258	44 58	301	54 31	328
	◆ VEGA		ALTAIR		◆ Nunki		Shaula		ANTARES		◆ SPICA		ARCTURUS	
255	42 33	026	45 38	074	53 42	133	54 58	168	65 29	196	36 21	258	44 06	300
256	42 59	025	46 35	074	54 26	134	55 10	169	65 11	198	35 23	258	43 14	300
257	43 23	024	47 33	073	55 09	134	55 21	171	64 52	200	34 24	258	42 22	299
258	43 47	023	48 30	073	55 51	135	55 30	172	64 30	202	33 25	259	41 30	299
259	44 11	022	49 27	073	56 33	136	55 37	173	64 06	204	32 26	259	40 38	298
260	44 33	021	50 25	072	57 14	138	55 43	175	63 41	206	31 28	259	39 45	298
261	44 54	020	51 22	072	57 54	139	55 48	176	63 14	207	30 29	259	38 52	298
262	45 14	019	52 18	071	58 33	140	55 51	178	62 46	209	29 30	259	37 59	297
263	45 34	018	53 15	071	59 11	141	55 53	179	62 16	211	28 31	259	37 05	297
264	45 52	017	54 11	070	59 48	142	55 53	180	61 45	212	27 33	259	36 12	296
265	46 09	016	55 08	070	60 25	144	55 52	182	61 12	214	26 34	259	35 18	296
266	46 25	015	56 04	069	60 59	145	55 49	183	60 38	215	25 35	259	34 24	296
267	46 40	014	57 00	069	61 33	147	55 45	185	60 03	217	24 36	259	33 30	295
268	46 54	013	57 55	068	62 06	148	55 39	186	59 27	218	23 37	259	32 36	295
269	47 07	012	58 51	067	62 37	150	55 32	188	58 49	219	22 39	259	31 41	295

LHA ♈	Hc	Zn	Hc	Zn	Hc	Zn	Hc	Zn	Hc	Zn	Hc	Zn	Hc	Zn
	◆ VEGA		DENEB		Enif		◆ FOMALHAUT		Peacock		◆ ANTARES		ARCTURUS	
270	47 19	011	29 47	032	32 32	076	14 51	120	28 55	158	58 11	220	30 47	294
271	47 30	010	30 18	031	33 30	076	15 43	120	29 17	158	57 32	222	29 52	294
272	47 39	009	30 49	031	34 28	076	16 35	120	29 39	159	56 52	223	28 57	294
273	47 47	007	31 19	030	35 26	076	17 27	120	30 00	159	56 11	224	28 02	294
274	47 55	006	31 49	029	36 24	075	18 18	120	30 21	160	55 29	225	27 07	293
275	48 00	005	32 18	029	37 22	075	19 10	120	30 41	160	54 46	226	26 12	293
276	48 05	004	32 47	028	38 20	075	20 02	120	31 01	161	54 03	227	25 17	293
277	48 09	003	33 15	028	39 18	075	20 54	121	31 20	161	53 20	227	24 22	293
278	48 11	002	33 42	027	40 15	074	21 45	121	31 39	162	52 35	228	23 26	292
279	48 12	000	34 09	026	41 13	074	22 37	121	31 58	162	51 50	229	22 31	292
280	48 12	359	34 36	026	42 10	074	23 28	121	32 15	163	51 05	230	21 35	292
281	48 10	358	35 01	025	43 08	073	24 19	121	32 33	164	50 19	231	20 40	292
282	48 08	357	35 26	024	44 05	073	25 10	121	32 49	164	49 32	231	19 44	292
283	48 04	356	35 50	024	45 03	073	26 02	122	33 05	165	48 45	232	18 48	291
284	47 59	355	36 14	023	46 00	072	26 53	122	33 21	165	47 58	233	17 53	291
	DENEB		Enif		◆ FOMALHAUT		Peacock		◆ ANTARES		Rasalhague		◆ VEGA	
285	36 37	022	46 57	072	27 43	122	33 36	166	47 10	233	63 54	307	47 53	353
286	36 59	021	47 54	072	28 34	122	33 50	166	46 22	234	63 06	306	47 45	352
287	37 21	021	48 50	071	29 25	122	34 04	167	45 33	234	62 17	305	47 37	351
288	37 41	020	49 47	071	30 15	123	34 17	168	44 45	235	61 28	303	47 27	350
289	38 01	019	50 44	070	31 05	123	34 29	168	43 56	235	60 37	302	47 16	349
290	38 21	018	51 40	070	31 56	123	34 41	169	43 06	236	59 46	301	47 04	348
291	38 39	017	52 36	069	32 46	124	34 52	170	42 16	236	58 55	301	46 51	347
292	38 57	017	53 32	069	33 35	124	35 03	170	41 27	237	58 03	300	46 36	346
293	39 13	016	54 28	068	34 25	124	35 13	171	40 36	237	57 11	299	46 21	345
294	39 29	015	55 23	068	35 15	125	35 22	171	39 46	238	56 18	298	46 04	344
295	39 44	014	56 19	067	36 04	125	35 30	172	38 55	238	55 25	297	45 47	342
296	39 59	013	57 14	066	36 53	125	35 38	173	38 04	238	54 32	297	45 28	341
297	40 12	012	58 08	066	37 42	126	35 45	173	37 13	239	53 38	296	45 09	340
298	40 24	012	59 03	065	38 30	126	35 52	174	36 22	239	52 44	295	44 48	339
299	40 36	011	59 57	064	39 18	127	35 58	175	35 31	239	51 50	295	44 27	338
	◆ DENEB		Alpheratz		◆ FOMALHAUT		Peacock		◆ ANTARES		Rasalhague		VEGA	
300	40 46	010	22 20	057	40 06	127	36 03	175	34 39	240	50 55	294	44 04	338
301	40 56	009	23 10	056	40 54	127	36 07	176	33 47	240	50 01	294	43 41	337
302	41 05	008	24 00	056	41 42	128	36 11	177	32 55	240	49 06	293	43 17	336
303	41 12	007	24 49	056	42 29	128	36 14	177	32 03	240	48 10	293	42 52	335
304	41 19	006	25 39	055	43 15	129	36 16	178	31 11	241	47 15	292	42 26	334
305	41 25	005	26 28	055	44 02	129	36 18	179	30 19	241	46 19	292	41 59	333
306	41 30	004	27 17	055	44 48	130	36 19	180	29 26	241	45 24	291	41 31	332
307	41 34	003	28 06	054	45 34	131	36 19	180	28 34	241	44 28	291	41 03	331
308	41 37	002	28 55	054	46 19	131	36 18	181	27 41	242	43 32	290	40 34	331
309	41 39	001	29 43	054	47 04	132	36 17	182	26 49	242	42 36	290	40 04	330
310	41 40	000	30 31	053	47 48	133	36 15	182	25 56	242	41 39	290	39 33	329
311	41 40	000	31 19	053	48 32	133	36 12	183	25 03	242	40 43	289	39 02	328
312	41 39	359	32 07	052	49 15	134	36 09	184	24 10	242	39 46	289	38 30	328
313	41 37	358	32 54	052	49 58	135	36 05	184	23 17	242	38 50	289	37 58	327
314	41 34	357	33 41	052	50 40	136	36 00	185	22 24	243	37 53	288	37 25	326
	◆ Alpheratz		◆ FOMALHAUT		Peacock		Nunki		◆ Rasalhague		VEGA		DENEB	
315	34 28	051	51 22	136	35 54	186	52 17	229	36 56	288	36 51	325	41 30	356
316	35 14	051	52 02	137	35 48	186	51 32	230	35 59	288	36 17	325	41 25	355
317	36 01	050	52 43	138	35 41	187	50 46	230	35 02	288	35 42	324	41 19	354
318	36 46	050	53 22	139	35 34	188	49 59	231	34 05	287	35 07	323	41 12	353
319	37 32	049	54 01	140	35 26	188	49 13	232	33 07	287	34 31	323	41 04	352
320	38 17	048	54 39	141	35 17	189	48 25	232	32 10	287	33 54	322	40 56	351
321	39 01	048	55 16	142	35 07	190	47 38	233	31 13	287	33 17	322	40 46	350
322	39 46	047	55 52	143	34 57	190	46 49	234	30 15	286	32 40	321	40 35	349
323	40 29	047	56 28	145	34 46	191	46 01	234	29 18	286	32 02	321	40 24	348
324	41 13	046	57 02	146	34 34	191	45 12	235	28 20	286	31 24	320	40 11	348
325	41 56	045	57 35	147	34 22	192	44 23	235	27 23	286	30 45	320	39 58	347
326	42 38	045	58 07	148	34 09	193	43 34	236	26 25	286	30 06	319	39 44	346
327	43 20	044	58 38	150	33 56	193	42 44	236	25 27	285	29 27	319	39 29	345
328	44 01	043	59 08	151	33 42	194	41 54	237	24 29	285	28 47	318	39 13	344
329	44 42	042	59 36	152	33 27	194	41 04	237	23 32	285	28 07	318	38 56	343
	◆ Alpheratz		Hamal		Diphda		◆ FOMALHAUT		Nunki		◆ ALTAIR		DENEB	
330	45 22	042	24 08	063	47 05	113	60 03	154	40 13	238	55 50	291	38 39	343
331	46 01	041	25 01	062	48 00	114	60 29	155	39 23	238	54 54	290	38 20	342
332	46 40	040	25 54	062	48 55	114	60 53	157	38 32	238	53 58	290	38 01	341
333	47 18	039	26 47	062	49 49	115	61 16	159	37 41	239	53 01	289	37 41	340
334	47 56	038	27 40	061	50 44	115	61 37	160	36 49	239	52 05	289	37 20	339
335	48 32	037	28 32	061	51 38	115	61 56	162	35 58	239	51 08	288	36 59	339
336	49 08	036	29 24	061	52 32	116	62 14	164	35 06	240	50 11	288	36 36	338
337	49 43	035	30 17	060	53 26	116	62 29	166	34 14	240	49 14	287	36 13	337
338	50 17	034	31 09	060	54 19	117	62 43	167	33 22	240	48 16	287	35 50	336
339	50 50	033	32 00	060	55 12	118	62 56	169	32 30	241	47 19	287	35 25	336
340	51 23	032	32 52	059	56 05	118	63 06	171	31 38	241	46 21	286	35 00	335
341	51 54	031	33 44	059	56 58	119	63 14	173	30 46	241	45 24	286	34 35	334
342	52 24	030	34 35	059	57 50	120	63 20	175	29 53	241	44 26	286	34 09	334
343	52 53	029	35 26	058	58 42	120	63 25	177	29 01	241	43 28	285	33 42	333
344	53 22	027	36 17	058	59 33	121	63 27	179	28 08	242	42 31	285	33 14	332
	Alpheratz		◆ Hamal		◆ ACHERNAR		FOMALHAUT		Nunki		◆ ALTAIR		DENEB	
345	53 48	026	37 07	057	27 29	157	63 27	181	27 15	242	41 33	285	32 46	332
346	54 14	025	37 57	057	27 52	158	63 26	183	26 22	242	40 35	284	32 17	331
347	54 39	023	38 47	056	28 15	158	63 22	185	25 29	242	39 37	284	31 48	331
348	55 02	022	39 37	056	28 37	158	63 16	187	24 36	242	38 39	284	31 18	330
349	55 24	021	40 26	055	28 59	159	63 08	188	23 43	243	37 40	284	30 48	329
350	55 44	019	41 15	055	29 20	159	62 58	190	22 50	243	36 42	283	30 17	329
351	56 03	018	42 04	054	29 41	160	62 47	192	21 57	243	35 44	283	29 46	328
352	56 21	016	42 53	054	30 01	160	62 33	194	21 03	243	34 45	283	29 14	328
353	56 37	015	43 41	053	30 21	161	62 17	196	20 10	243	33 47	283	28 42	327
354	56 52	013	44 28	052	30 41	161	62 00	198	19 17	243	32 49	283	28 09	327
355	57 05	012	45 15	052	31 00	162	61 41	199	18 23	243	31 50	282	27 36	326
356	57 16	010	46 02	051	31 18	162	61 21	201	17 30	243	30 52	282	27 03	326
357	57 26	009	46 48	050	31 36	163	60 58	203	16 36	243	29 53	282	26 29	325
358	57 34	007	47 34	049	31 54	163	60 35	204	15 42	244	28 54	282	25 54	325
359	57 40	005	48 19	049	32 10	164	60 09	206	14 49	244	27 56	282	25 20	324

 LAT 4°S

LHA ♈	Hc	Zn	Hc	Zn	Hc	Zn	Hc	Zn	Hc	Zn	Hc	Zn	Hc	Zn
	Alpheratz		◆ ALDEBARAN		RIGEL		ACHERNAR		◆ FOMALHAUT		ALTAIR		◆ DENEB	
0	56 45	004	18 39	071	11 37	098	33 24	164	60 36	208	26 45	282	23 56	324
1	56 48	002	19 36	071	12 37	098	33 40	165	60 07	210	25 46	282	23 21	324
2	56 50	000	20 32	071	13 36	097	33 56	165	59 37	211	24 48	282	22 45	323
3	56 49	359	21 29	070	14 35	097	34 10	166	59 05	212	23 49	282	22 09	323
4	56 47	357	22 25	070	15 35	097	34 25	167	58 33	214	22 50	281	21 33	323
5	56 44	356	23 21	070	16 34	097	34 38	167	57 59	215	21 52	281	20 57	322
6	56 38	354	24 17	070	17 33	097	34 51	168	57 25	216	20 53	281	20 20	322
7	56 31	353	25 14	070	18 33	097	35 03	168	56 49	217	19 54	281	19 43	321
8	56 23	351	26 10	069	19 32	097	35 15	169	56 12	218	18 55	281	19 05	321
9	56 12	349	27 06	069	20 32	097	35 26	170	55 35	219	17 57	281	18 28	321
10	56 01	348	28 02	069	21 31	097	35 36	170	54 56	220	16 58	281	17 50	320
11	55 47	346	28 57	069	22 30	097	35 46	171	54 17	221	15 59	280	17 11	320
12	55 33	345	29 53	068	23 30	097	35 55	172	53 37	222	15 00	280	16 33	320
13	55 16	343	30 49	068	24 29	097	36 03	172	52 56	223	14 01	280	15 54	320
14	54 58	342	31 44	068	25 28	097	36 11	173	52 15	224	13 02	280	15 15	319
	CAPELLA		ALDEBARAN		◆ RIGEL		ACHERNAR		◆ FOMALHAUT		Enif		◆ Alpheratz	
15	14 24	040	32 39	067	26 28	097	36 18	174	51 33	225	39 28	286	54 39	341
16	15 02	040	33 35	067	27 27	097	36 24	174	50 50	226	38 30	286	54 19	339
17	15 41	040	34 30	067	28 27	097	36 30	175	50 07	227	37 33	286	53 57	338
18	16 19	039	35 25	066	29 26	097	36 35	176	49 23	227	36 35	286	53 34	337
19	16 57	039	36 19	066	30 25	097	36 39	176	48 39	228	35 37	285	53 09	335
20	17 35	039	37 14	066	31 25	097	36 43	177	47 54	229	34 40	285	52 44	334
21	18 12	039	38 08	065	32 24	097	36 46	178	47 09	229	33 42	285	52 17	333
22	18 49	038	39 03	065	33 24	097	36 48	178	46 23	230	32 44	285	51 49	332
23	19 26	038	39 57	064	34 23	097	36 49	179	45 37	231	31 46	284	51 20	330
24	20 03	038	40 51	064	35 22	097	36 50	180	44 51	231	30 48	284	50 50	329
25	20 39	037	41 44	064	36 22	097	36 50	180	44 04	232	29 50	284	50 19	328
26	21 15	037	42 38	063	37 21	097	36 50	181	43 17	232	28 52	284	49 46	327
27	21 51	036	43 31	063	38 20	097	36 48	182	42 29	233	27 53	283	49 13	326
28	22 26	036	44 24	062	39 20	097	36 46	182	41 42	233	26 55	283	48 40	325
29	23 01	036	45 17	062	40 19	097	36 43	183	40 54	234	25 57	283	48 05	324
	CAPELLA		◆ BETELGEUSE		SIRIUS		CANOPUS		◆ ACHERNAR		FOMALHAUT		◆ Alpheratz	
30	23 36	035	30 02	079	18 54	106	17 30	144	36 40	184	40 05	234	47 29	323
31	24 10	035	31 01	079	19 52	106	18 05	145	36 36	184	39 17	234	46 53	322
32	24 44	034	32 00	079	20 49	106	18 39	145	36 31	185	38 28	235	46 16	321
33	25 17	034	32 58	078	21 46	106	19 13	145	36 25	186	37 39	235	45 38	320
34	25 50	033	33 57	078	22 44	106	19 48	145	36 19	186	36 50	236	45 00	320
35	26 23	033	34 56	078	23 41	107	20 21	146	36 12	187	36 00	236	44 20	319
36	26 55	032	35 54	078	24 39	107	20 55	146	36 04	188	35 10	236	43 41	318
37	27 27	032	36 53	078	25 36	107	21 29	146	35 56	188	34 21	237	43 00	317
38	27 59	031	37 51	077	26 33	107	22 02	146	35 47	189	33 31	237	42 19	316
39	28 29	031	38 49	077	27 31	107	22 35	147	35 38	190	32 40	237	41 38	316
40	29 00	030	39 48	077	28 28	107	23 08	147	35 27	190	31 50	237	40 56	315
41	29 30	030	40 46	077	29 25	107	23 41	147	35 16	191	30 59	238	40 13	314
42	29 59	029	41 44	076	30 22	107	24 13	147	35 05	191	30 09	238	39 30	314
43	30 28	029	42 42	076	31 20	107	24 45	148	34 53	192	29 18	238	38 47	313
44	30 57	028	43 40	076	32 17	107	25 17	148	34 40	193	28 27	238	38 03	312
	CAPELLA		◆ BETELGEUSE		SIRIUS		CANOPUS		◆ ACHERNAR		Diphda		◆ Hamal	
45	31 24	027	44 38	075	33 14	107	25 48	148	34 26	193	54 01	245	59 42	336
46	31 52	027	45 36	075	34 11	108	26 19	149	34 12	194	53 07	245	59 16	334
47	32 18	026	46 34	075	35 08	108	26 50	149	33 58	194	52 12	246	58 50	333
48	32 45	026	47 32	074	36 05	108	27 21	150	33 42	195	51 18	246	58 21	331
49	33 10	025	48 29	074	37 02	108	27 51	150	33 27	196	50 23	246	57 52	330
50	33 35	024	49 27	074	37 59	108	28 21	150	33 10	196	49 28	247	57 21	328
51	33 59	024	50 24	073	38 56	108	28 50	151	32 53	197	48 33	247	56 49	327
52	34 23	023	51 22	073	39 52	109	29 20	151	32 36	197	47 38	248	56 16	326
53	34 45	022	52 19	072	40 49	109	29 48	152	32 18	198	46 42	248	55 42	324
54	35 08	021	53 16	072	41 46	109	30 17	152	31 59	198	45 47	248	55 06	323
55	35 29	021	54 13	071	42 42	109	30 45	152	31 40	199	44 51	249	54 30	322
56	35 50	020	55 09	071	43 39	109	31 12	153	31 21	199	43 55	249	53 52	321
57	36 10	019	56 06	070	44 35	110	31 39	153	31 01	200	42 59	249	53 14	320
58	36 29	018	57 02	070	45 32	110	32 06	154	30 40	200	42 03	249	52 35	319
59	36 48	018	57 58	069	46 28	110	32 32	154	30 19	201	41 07	250	51 55	318
	◆ CAPELLA		POLLUX		◆ SIRIUS		CANOPUS		ACHERNAR		◆ Diphda		Hamal	
60	37 06	017	26 55	056	47 24	111	32 58	155	29 58	201	40 11	250	51 14	317
61	37 22	016	27 44	055	48 20	111	33 23	155	29 36	202	39 15	250	50 33	316
62	37 39	015	28 34	055	49 16	111	33 48	156	29 13	202	38 19	250	49 50	315
63	37 54	014	29 22	055	50 12	112	34 12	156	28 50	203	37 22	250	49 08	314
64	38 08	014	30 11	054	51 07	112	34 35	157	28 27	203	36 26	251	48 24	313
65	38 22	013	31 00	054	52 03	112	34 59	158	28 04	203	35 29	251	47 40	312
66	38 35	012	31 48	053	52 58	113	35 21	158	27 39	204	34 33	251	46 55	311
67	38 47	011	32 36	053	53 53	113	35 43	159	27 15	204	33 36	251	46 10	311
68	38 58	010	33 23	052	54 48	114	36 04	159	26 50	205	32 40	251	45 24	310
69	39 08	009	34 11	052	55 43	114	36 25	160	26 25	205	31 43	251	44 38	309
70	39 17	008	34 57	051	56 37	115	36 45	161	25 59	205	30 46	252	43 52	308
71	39 26	008	35 44	051	57 31	115	37 05	161	25 34	206	29 49	252	43 05	308
72	39 33	007	36 30	050	58 25	116	37 24	162	25 07	206	28 52	252	42 17	307
73	39 40	006	37 16	050	59 19	117	37 42	163	24 41	207	27 56	252	41 29	307
74	39 45	005	38 02	049	60 12	117	38 00	163	24 14	207	26 59	252	40 41	306
	CAPELLA		◆ POLLUX		REGULUS		Suhail		◆ CANOPUS		ACHERNAR		◆ Hamal	
75	39 50	004	38 47	049	11 33	077	22 43	136	38 17	164	23 47	207	39 52	305
76	39 54	003	39 32	048	12 32	077	23 25	136	38 33	165	23 19	207	39 04	305
77	39 56	002	40 16	047	13 30	077	24 06	136	38 48	165	22 51	208	38 14	304
78	39 58	001	41 00	047	14 28	077	24 47	137	39 04	166	22 23	208	37 25	304
79	39 59	000	41 44	046	15 26	076	25 28	137	39 18	167	21 55	208	36 35	303
80	39 59	000	42 27	045	16 25	076	26 09	137	39 31	167	21 26	209	35 45	303
81	39 58	359	43 09	045	17 23	076	26 49	138	39 44	168	20 58	209	34 54	302
82	39 56	358	43 51	044	18 21	076	27 30	138	39 56	169	20 29	209	34 04	302
83	39 53	357	44 32	043	19 19	076	28 10	138	40 07	170	19 59	209	33 13	302
84	39 50	356	45 13	042	20 17	076	28 50	139	40 17	170	19 30	210	32 22	301
85	39 45	355	45 53	042	21 15	076	29 29	139	40 27	171	19 00	210	31 31	301
86	39 39	354	46 32	041	22 13	075	30 08	139	40 35	172	18 30	210	30 39	300
87	39 32	353	47 11	040	23 11	075	30 47	140	40 43	173	18 00	210	29 47	300
88	39 25	352	47 49	039	24 09	075	31 26	140	40 50	174	17 29	211	28 55	300
89	39 16	351	48 26	038	25 07	075	32 04	140	40 57	174	16 59	211	28 03	299

LHA ♈	Hc	Zn	Hc	Zn	Hc	Zn	Hc	Zn	Hc	Zn	Hc	Zn	Hc	Zn
	POLLUX		◆ REGULUS		Suhail		◆ CANOPUS		Acamar		◆ ALDEBARAN		CAPELLA	
90	49 03	037	26 04	075	32 42	141	41 02	175	35 30	222	60 56	315	39 07	351
91	49 38	036	27 02	074	33 20	141	41 07	176	34 50	222	60 14	314	38 57	350
92	50 13	035	28 00	074	33 57	142	41 11	177	34 10	223	59 30	313	38 46	349
93	50 47	034	28 57	074	34 34	142	41 14	178	33 29	223	58 46	312	38 34	348
94	51 20	033	29 55	074	35 11	143	41 16	178	32 48	223	58 01	311	38 21	347
95	51 52	032	30 52	074	35 47	143	41 17	179	32 06	224	57 15	310	38 07	346
96	52 23	031	31 50	073	36 22	144	41 18	180	31 25	224	56 29	308	37 52	345
97	52 53	029	32 47	073	36 58	144	41 17	181	30 43	225	55 42	307	37 37	345
98	53 21	028	33 44	073	37 32	145	41 16	182	30 01	225	54 54	307	37 21	344
99	53 49	027	34 41	073	38 07	145	41 14	182	29 18	225	54 05	306	37 04	343
100	54 15	026	35 38	072	38 41	146	41 11	183	28 36	226	53 17	305	36 46	342
101	54 40	024	36 35	072	39 14	146	41 08	184	27 53	226	52 27	304	36 27	342
102	55 04	023	37 32	072	39 47	147	41 03	185	27 10	226	51 37	303	36 08	341
103	55 27	021	38 29	071	40 19	148	40 58	186	26 26	226	50 47	302	35 48	340
104	55 48	020	39 26	071	40 51	148	40 51	186	25 43	227	49 56	302	35 27	339
	POLLUX		◆ REGULUS		Suhail		◆ CANOPUS		RIGEL		◆ ALDEBARAN		CAPELLA	
105	56 08	019	40 22	071	41 22	149	40 44	187	63 38	260	49 05	301	35 05	339
106	56 26	017	41 19	070	41 52	150	40 37	188	62 39	260	48 14	300	34 43	338
107	56 43	015	42 15	070	42 22	150	40 28	189	61 40	260	47 22	300	34 20	337
108	56 58	014	43 11	070	42 51	151	40 18	189	60 41	260	46 30	299	33 57	336
109	57 12	012	44 07	069	43 20	152	40 08	190	59 42	261	45 38	299	33 32	336
110	57 24	011	45 03	069	43 47	153	39 57	191	58 43	261	44 45	298	33 07	335
111	57 34	009	45 59	068	44 15	154	39 45	192	57 44	261	43 52	298	32 42	334
112	57 43	008	46 54	068	44 41	154	39 33	192	56 45	261	42 59	297	32 16	334
113	57 50	006	47 49	067	45 06	155	39 20	193	55 46	261	42 05	297	31 49	333
114	57 55	004	48 45	067	45 31	156	39 06	194	54 47	261	41 12	296	31 22	333
115	57 59	003	49 40	066	45 55	157	38 51	195	53 48	262	40 18	296	30 54	332
116	58 00	001	50 34	066	46 18	158	38 35	195	52 48	262	39 24	295	30 25	331
117	58 01	359	51 29	065	46 40	159	38 19	196	51 49	262	38 30	295	29 56	331
118	57 59	358	52 23	065	47 02	160	38 02	197	50 50	262	37 35	294	29 27	330
119	57 55	356	53 17	064	47 22	161	37 45	197	49 51	262	36 41	294	28 57	330
	◆ REGULUS		Gienah		◆ ACRUX		CANOPUS		SIRIUS		◆ BETELGEUSE		POLLUX	
120	54 10	063	25 50	108	13 50	155	37 27	198	67 47	234	57 02	290	57 50	354
121	55 04	063	26 47	108	14 16	155	37 08	199	66 58	235	56 05	290	57 44	353
122	55 57	062	27 44	108	14 41	155	36 48	199	66 09	236	55 09	289	57 35	351
123	56 49	061	28 41	108	15 06	155	36 28	200	65 19	237	54 12	289	57 25	349
124	57 41	060	29 38	108	15 31	155	36 07	201	64 28	238	53 15	288	57 13	348
125	58 33	059	30 35	108	15 56	156	35 46	201	63 37	239	52 18	288	57 00	346
126	59 24	058	31 32	108	16 21	156	35 24	202	62 45	240	51 21	287	56 45	345
127	60 15	057	32 28	108	16 45	156	35 02	202	61 53	241	50 24	287	56 28	343
128	61 05	056	33 25	109	17 09	156	34 39	203	61 00	242	49 26	286	56 10	342
129	61 55	055	34 22	109	17 33	156	34 15	203	60 07	243	48 29	286	55 50	340
130	62 43	054	35 19	109	17 57	157	33 51	204	59 14	243	47 31	286	55 29	339
131	63 32	053	36 15	109	18 21	157	33 26	205	58 20	244	46 34	285	55 07	337
132	64 19	052	37 12	109	18 44	157	33 01	205	57 26	245	45 36	285	54 43	336
133	65 05	050	38 08	109	19 08	157	32 36	206	56 32	245	44 38	285	54 18	335
134	65 51	049	39 05	110	19 31	158	32 10	206	55 37	246	43 40	284	53 52	333
	Alioth		◆ SPICA		ACRUX		◆ CANOPUS		SIRIUS		BETELGEUSE		◆ POLLUX	
135	13 29	030	23 49	101	19 53	158	31 43	207	54 43	246	42 42	284	53 25	332
136	13 59	029	24 48	101	20 16	158	31 16	207	53 48	247	41 44	284	52 56	331
137	14 28	029	25 47	101	20 38	158	30 49	208	52 53	247	40 46	283	52 26	330
138	14 56	029	26 45	101	21 00	159	30 21	208	51 57	248	39 47	283	51 55	328
139	15 25	028	27 44	101	21 22	159	29 52	208	51 02	248	38 49	283	51 24	327
140	15 53	028	28 43	101	21 43	159	29 24	209	50 06	249	37 51	283	50 51	326
141	16 21	028	29 42	101	22 04	160	28 55	209	49 11	249	36 52	282	50 17	325
142	16 49	027	30 41	101	22 25	160	28 25	210	48 15	249	35 54	282	49 42	324
143	17 16	027	31 40	101	22 45	160	27 55	210	47 19	250	34 55	282	49 07	323
144	17 43	027	32 38	101	23 05	161	27 25	210	46 23	250	33 57	282	48 30	322
145	18 10	026	33 37	101	23 25	161	26 55	211	45 26	250	32 58	282	47 53	321
146	18 36	026	34 36	101	23 45	161	26 24	211	44 30	250	31 59	281	47 15	320
147	19 02	026	35 35	101	24 04	162	25 53	212	43 34	251	31 01	281	46 37	319
148	19 28	025	36 34	101	24 22	162	25 21	212	42 37	251	30 02	281	45 57	319
149	19 53	025	37 32	101	24 41	162	24 50	212	41 40	251	29 03	281	45 17	318
	Alioth		ARCTURUS		◆ SPICA		ACRUX		◆ CANOPUS		SIRIUS		◆ POLLUX	
150	20 18	024	22 54	067	38 31	101	24 59	163	24 18	213	40 44	251	44 37	317
151	20 43	024	23 49	067	39 30	101	25 17	163	23 45	213	39 47	251	43 56	316
152	21 07	024	24 44	067	40 28	101	25 34	163	23 13	213	38 50	252	43 14	315
153	21 31	023	25 39	067	41 27	101	25 51	164	22 40	213	37 53	252	42 31	315
154	21 54	023	26 34	066	42 26	102	26 07	164	22 07	214	36 57	252	41 49	314
155	22 17	022	27 29	066	43 24	102	26 23	165	21 34	214	36 00	252	41 05	313
156	22 39	022	28 23	066	44 23	102	26 39	165	21 00	214	35 03	252	40 21	313
157	23 01	021	29 18	065	45 21	102	26 54	165	20 26	214	34 06	252	39 37	312
158	23 23	021	30 12	065	46 20	102	27 09	166	19 52	215	33 08	253	38 52	311
159	23 44	020	31 07	065	47 19	102	27 24	166	19 18	215	32 11	253	38 07	311
160	24 05	020	32 01	064	48 17	102	27 38	167	18 44	215	31 14	253	37 22	310
161	24 25	019	32 55	064	49 15	103	27 51	167	18 09	215	30 17	253	36 36	310
162	24 44	019	33 48	064	50 14	103	28 04	168	17 35	215	29 20	253	35 50	309
163	25 04	018	34 42	063	51 12	103	28 17	168	17 00	216	28 22	253	35 03	309
164	25 22	018	35 35	063	52 10	103	28 29	168	16 25	216	27 25	253	34 16	308
	Alioth		◆ ARCTURUS		SPICA		◆ ACRUX		Suhail		SIRIUS		◆ POLLUX	
165	25 40	017	36 29	063	53 09	103	28 41	169	43 27	208	26 28	253	33 29	308
166	25 58	017	37 22	062	54 07	104	28 52	169	42 59	209	25 30	253	32 41	307
167	26 15	016	38 15	062	55 05	104	29 03	170	42 30	209	24 33	253	31 53	307
168	26 32	016	39 07	061	56 03	104	29 13	170	42 00	210	23 36	253	31 05	306
169	26 48	015	40 00	061	57 01	105	29 23	171	41 30	211	22 38	254	30 17	306
170	27 03	015	40 52	060	57 59	105	29 32	171	40 59	211	21 41	254	29 28	305
171	27 18	014	41 44	060	58 57	105	29 41	172	40 28	212	20 44	254	28 39	305
172	27 32	014	42 35	059	59 54	106	29 49	172	39 56	213	19 46	254	27 50	305
173	27 46	013	43 27	059	60 52	106	29 57	173	39 23	213	18 49	254	27 01	304
174	27 59	012	44 18	058	61 49	106	30 04	173	38 50	214	17 51	254	26 11	304
175	28 11	012	45 08	058	62 47	107	30 11	174	38 16	215	16 54	254	25 22	304
176	28 23	011	45 59	057	63 44	107	30 17	174	37 42	215	15 56	254	24 32	303
177	28 35	011	46 49	056	64 41	108	30 23	175	37 07	216	14 59	254	23 41	303
178	28 45	010	47 38	056	65 38	109	30 28	175	36 32	216	14 01	254	22 51	303
179	28 55	009	48 28	055	66 34	109	30 32	176	35 57	217	13 04	254	22 01	302

LAT 4°S

LHA ♈	Hc	Zn	Hc	Zn	Hc	Zn	Hc	Zn	Hc	Zn	Hc	Zn	Hc	Zn
	Alioth		◆ARCTURUS		ANTARES		◆ACRUX		Suhail		Alphard		◆REGULUS	
180	29 05	009	49 16	054	21 49	117	30 36	176	35 21	217	52 02	261	58 12	300
181	29 13	008	50 05	053	22 42	117	30 40	177	34 44	218	51 03	261	57 20	299
182	29 21	007	50 53	053	23 36	117	30 43	177	34 07	218	50 04	261	56 27	299
183	29 29	007	51 40	052	24 29	117	30 45	178	33 30	219	49 05	261	55 35	298
184	29 36	006	52 27	051	25 22	117	30 47	178	32 53	219	48 06	261	54 42	297
185	29 42	006	53 13	050	26 15	118	30 48	179	32 15	219	47 07	261	53 48	296
186	29 47	005	53 59	049	27 08	118	30 49	180	31 36	220	46 07	262	52 54	296
187	29 52	004	54 44	048	28 01	118	30 49	180	30 58	220	45 08	262	52 00	295
188	29 56	004	55 28	047	28 54	118	30 49	181	30 19	221	44 09	262	51 06	295
189	30 00	003	56 11	046	29 47	118	30 48	181	29 40	221	43 10	262	50 12	294
190	30 03	002	56 54	045	30 39	119	30 46	182	29 00	221	42 10	262	49 17	293
191	30 05	002	57 36	044	31 32	119	30 44	182	28 21	222	41 11	262	48 22	293
192	30 06	001	58 17	043	32 24	119	30 42	183	27 41	222	40 12	262	47 26	292
193	30 07	000	58 57	041	33 16	119	30 39	183	27 01	222	39 13	262	46 31	292
194	30 07	000	59 36	040	34 09	119	30 35	184	26 20	223	38 13	262	45 35	292
	ARCTURUS		◆Rasalhague		ANTARES		◆ACRUX		Alphard		◆REGULUS		Alioth	
195	60 13	038	19 35	075	35 01	120	30 31	184	37 14	262	44 40	291	30 07	359
196	60 50	037	20 33	075	35 52	120	30 26	185	36 15	262	43 44	291	30 05	358
197	61 25	035	21 31	075	36 44	120	30 21	185	35 16	262	42 48	290	30 04	358
198	62 00	034	22 29	075	37 36	121	30 15	186	34 16	262	41 51	290	30 01	357
199	62 32	032	23 26	074	38 27	121	30 09	186	33 17	262	40 55	290	29 58	357
200	63 03	030	24 24	074	39 18	121	30 02	187	32 18	262	39 59	289	29 54	356
201	63 33	029	25 22	074	40 09	122	29 55	187	31 18	262	39 02	289	29 49	355
202	64 01	027	26 19	074	41 00	122	29 47	188	30 19	262	38 05	288	29 44	355
203	64 27	025	27 17	074	41 51	122	29 39	188	29 20	262	37 09	288	29 38	354
204	64 51	023	28 14	073	42 41	123	29 30	189	28 20	262	36 12	288	29 31	353
205	65 13	021	29 11	073	43 31	123	29 20	189	27 21	262	35 15	288	29 24	353
206	65 34	019	30 09	073	44 21	124	29 10	190	26 22	262	34 18	287	29 16	352
207	65 52	017	31 06	073	45 11	124	29 00	190	25 23	262	33 20	287	29 08	351
208	66 08	014	32 03	072	46 00	125	28 49	191	24 23	262	32 23	287	28 58	351
209	66 22	012	33 00	072	46 49	125	28 38	191	23 24	262	31 26	287	28 49	350
	ARCTURUS		◆VEGA		ANTARES		◆RIGIL KENT		ACRUX		Gienah		◆REGULUS	
210	66 33	010	13 19	049	47 38	126	32 35	174	28 26	192	61 15	240	30 28	286
211	66 42	007	14 04	048	48 26	126	32 41	175	28 14	192	60 23	241	29 31	286
212	66 48	005	14 48	048	49 14	127	32 46	175	28 01	193	59 30	241	28 33	286
213	66 52	003	15 33	048	50 02	128	32 51	176	27 48	193	58 38	242	27 36	286
214	66 54	000	16 17	048	50 49	128	32 55	176	27 34	193	57 45	243	26 38	285
215	66 53	358	17 01	047	51 35	129	32 58	177	27 20	194	56 51	243	25 40	285
216	66 49	355	17 45	047	52 22	130	33 01	178	27 05	194	55 58	244	24 43	285
217	66 43	353	18 29	047	53 07	131	33 03	178	26 50	195	55 04	245	23 45	285
218	66 35	351	19 12	046	53 52	131	33 05	179	26 35	195	54 10	245	22 47	285
219	66 24	348	19 55	046	54 37	132	33 06	179	26 19	196	53 15	246	21 49	285
220	66 10	346	20 38	046	55 21	133	33 06	180	26 03	196	52 21	246	20 51	284
221	65 55	344	21 21	045	56 04	134	33 06	180	25 46	196	51 26	246	19 53	284
222	65 37	342	22 04	045	56 47	135	33 05	181	25 29	197	50 31	247	18 55	284
223	65 17	340	22 46	045	57 29	136	33 04	182	25 12	197	49 36	247	17 57	284
224	64 55	337	23 28	044	58 10	137	33 02	182	24 54	197	48 40	248	16 59	284
	Alphecca		VEGA		◆ALTAIR		ANTARES		◆RIGIL KENT		SPICA		◆ARCTURUS	
225	58 10	015	24 10	044	16 13	080	58 50	138	32 59	183	65 37	251	64 31	335
226	58 25	013	24 51	044	17 12	079	59 29	140	32 56	183	64 41	252	64 05	333
227	58 38	012	25 32	043	18 11	079	60 08	141	32 52	184	63 44	253	63 38	332
228	58 49	010	26 13	043	19 10	079	60 45	142	32 48	185	62 46	253	63 09	330
229	58 59	008	26 53	042	20 08	079	61 21	143	32 43	185	61 49	254	62 38	328
230	59 07	007	27 33	042	21 07	079	61 56	145	32 37	186	60 52	254	62 05	326
231	59 13	005	28 13	041	22 06	079	62 30	146	32 31	186	59 54	254	61 31	325
232	59 17	003	28 53	041	23 05	079	63 02	148	32 24	187	58 56	255	60 56	323
233	59 19	001	29 32	040	24 03	078	63 33	150	32 17	187	57 58	255	60 20	322
234	59 20	000	30 10	040	25 02	078	64 03	151	32 09	188	57 01	255	59 42	320
235	59 19	358	30 48	039	26 00	078	64 31	153	32 00	188	56 03	256	59 03	319
236	59 16	356	31 26	039	26 59	078	64 57	155	31 51	189	55 05	256	58 24	318
237	59 11	354	32 03	038	27 57	078	65 21	157	31 42	190	54 06	256	57 43	316
238	59 04	353	32 40	038	28 56	078	65 44	159	31 31	190	53 08	257	57 01	315
239	58 56	351	33 17	037	29 54	077	66 05	161	31 21	191	52 10	257	56 19	314
	VEGA		◆ALTAIR		Nunki		◆RIGIL KENT		SPICA		◆ARCTURUS		Alphecca	
240	33 53	037	30 53	077	42 22	122	31 09	191	51 12	257	55 35	313	58 46	349
241	34 28	036	31 51	077	43 12	123	30 58	192	50 13	257	54 51	312	58 34	348
242	35 03	035	32 49	077	44 02	123	30 45	192	49 15	257	54 06	311	58 20	346
243	35 37	035	33 48	076	44 52	124	30 32	193	48 17	258	53 21	310	58 05	344
244	36 11	034	34 46	076	45 42	124	30 19	193	47 18	258	52 35	309	57 48	343
245	36 44	033	35 44	076	46 31	125	30 05	194	46 20	258	51 48	308	57 29	341
246	37 16	033	36 42	076	47 20	125	29 51	194	45 21	258	51 01	307	57 09	340
247	37 48	032	37 40	076	48 08	126	29 36	195	44 22	258	50 13	307	56 48	338
248	38 20	031	38 38	075	48 57	127	29 20	195	43 24	258	49 25	306	56 25	337
249	38 50	030	39 36	075	49 45	127	29 05	196	42 25	258	48 36	305	56 00	335
250	39 20	030	40 33	075	50 32	128	28 48	196	41 27	259	47 47	304	55 35	334
251	39 49	029	41 31	074	51 19	129	28 32	196	40 28	259	46 57	304	55 08	333
252	40 18	028	42 29	074	52 06	129	28 14	197	39 29	259	46 07	303	54 39	331
253	40 46	027	43 26	074	52 52	130	27 57	197	38 31	259	45 17	302	54 10	330
254	41 13	026	44 24	073	53 37	131	27 39	198	37 32	259	44 26	302	53 40	329
	◆VEGA		ALTAIR		◆Nunki		Shaula		ANTARES		◆SPICA		ARCTURUS	
255	41 39	025	45 21	073	54 22	132	55 57	168	66 26	197	36 33	259	43 35	301
256	42 04	025	46 18	073	55 07	133	56 09	169	66 08	199	35 34	259	42 44	301
257	42 29	024	47 15	072	55 51	133	56 20	170	65 48	201	34 36	259	41 53	300
258	42 52	023	48 12	072	56 34	134	56 29	172	65 25	203	33 37	259	41 01	300
259	43 15	022	49 09	071	57 16	135	56 37	173	65 01	205	32 38	259	40 09	299
260	43 37	021	50 06	071	57 58	136	56 43	175	64 35	207	31 39	259	39 16	299
261	43 58	020	51 02	071	58 39	138	56 48	176	64 07	208	30 40	259	38 24	298
262	44 18	019	51 58	070	59 19	139	56 51	178	63 38	210	29 42	259	37 31	298
263	44 37	018	52 55	070	59 58	140	56 53	179	63 07	212	28 43	259	36 38	297
264	44 54	017	53 51	069	60 36	141	56 53	181	62 35	213	27 44	259	35 45	297
265	45 11	016	54 46	068	61 13	143	56 52	182	62 02	215	26 45	259	34 51	297
266	45 27	015	55 42	068	61 48	144	56 49	183	61 27	216	25 46	259	33 58	296
267	45 42	014	56 37	067	62 23	145	56 45	185	60 51	218	24 47	259	33 04	296
268	45 56	013	57 32	066	62 56	147	56 39	186	60 14	219	23 49	259	32 10	296
269	46 09	012	58 27	066	63 28	149	56 32	188	59 36	220	22 50	259	31 16	295

LHA ♈	Hc	Zn	Hc	Zn	Hc	Zn	Hc	Zn	Hc	Zn	Hc	Zn	Hc	Zn
	◆VEGA		DENEB		Enif		◆FOMALHAUT		Peacock		◆ANTARES		ARCTURUS	
270	46 20	011	28 56	031	32 17	076	15 21	120	29 50	158	58 56	221	30 22	295
271	46 31	009	29 27	031	33 15	075	16 13	120	30 13	158	58 16	223	29 27	295
272	46 40	008	29 57	030	34 13	075	17 05	120	30 35	159	57 35	224	28 33	294
273	46 48	007	30 27	030	35 11	075	17 57	120	30 56	159	56 54	225	27 38	294
274	46 55	006	30 57	029	36 08	075	18 48	120	31 17	160	56 11	226	26 44	294
275	47 01	005	31 26	029	37 06	074	19 40	120	31 38	160	55 28	227	25 49	293
276	47 05	004	31 54	028	38 04	074	20 32	120	31 58	161	54 44	228	24 54	293
277	47 09	003	32 22	027	39 01	074	21 24	120	32 17	161	54 00	228	23 59	293
278	47 11	002	32 49	027	39 59	073	22 16	120	32 36	162	53 15	229	23 03	293
279	47 12	000	33 15	026	40 56	073	23 07	121	32 55	162	52 29	230	22 08	292
280	47 12	359	33 41	025	41 53	073	23 59	121	33 13	163	51 43	231	21 13	292
281	47 10	358	34 07	025	42 50	072	24 50	121	33 30	163	50 56	231	20 17	292
282	47 08	357	34 31	024	43 47	072	25 42	121	33 47	164	50 09	232	19 22	292
283	47 04	356	34 55	023	44 44	072	26 33	121	34 03	165	49 22	233	18 26	292
284	46 59	355	35 19	023	45 41	071	27 24	121	34 19	165	48 34	233	17 31	291
	DENEB		Enif		◆FOMALHAUT		Peacock		◆ANTARES		Rasalhague		◆VEGA	
285	35 41	022	46 38	071	28 15	122	34 34	166	47 46	234	63 18	309	46 53	354
286	36 03	021	47 34	071	29 06	122	34 48	166	46 57	235	62 31	307	46 46	352
287	36 25	020	48 31	070	29 57	122	35 02	167	46 08	235	61 43	306	46 37	351
288	36 45	020	49 27	070	30 47	122	35 15	168	45 19	236	60 54	305	46 28	350
289	37 05	019	50 23	069	31 38	123	35 28	168	44 29	236	60 04	304	46 17	349
290	37 24	018	51 19	069	32 28	123	35 40	169	43 40	237	59 15	303	46 05	348
291	37 42	017	52 14	068	33 19	123	35 51	169	42 49	237	58 24	302	45 52	347
292	37 59	016	53 10	068	34 09	123	36 02	170	41 59	237	57 33	301	45 38	346
293	38 16	016	54 05	067	34 59	124	36 12	171	41 09	238	56 41	300	45 23	345
294	38 31	015	55 00	066	35 48	124	36 21	171	40 18	238	55 50	299	45 07	344
295	38 46	014	55 55	066	36 38	124	36 30	172	39 27	239	54 57	299	44 50	343
296	39 00	013	56 49	065	37 27	125	36 38	173	38 36	239	54 04	298	44 31	342
297	39 13	012	57 43	064	38 16	125	36 45	173	37 44	239	53 11	297	44 12	341
298	39 25	011	58 37	063	39 05	125	36 52	174	36 53	240	52 18	297	43 52	340
299	39 37	010	59 30	063	39 54	126	36 58	175	36 01	240	51 24	296	43 31	339
	◆DENEB		Alpheratz		◆FOMALHAUT		Peacock		◆ANTARES		Rasalhague		VEGA	
300	39 47	010	21 47	056	40 42	126	37 03	175	35 09	240	50 30	295	43 09	338
301	39 57	009	22 36	056	41 30	127	37 07	176	34 17	240	49 36	295	42 46	337
302	40 05	008	23 26	056	42 18	127	37 11	177	33 25	241	48 42	294	42 22	336
303	40 13	007	24 15	055	43 06	128	37 14	177	32 33	241	47 47	294	41 57	335
304	40 20	006	25 05	055	43 53	128	37 16	178	31 40	241	46 52	293	41 32	334
305	40 25	005	25 53	055	44 40	129	37 18	179	30 48	241	45 57	293	41 05	333
306	40 30	004	26 42	054	45 26	129	37 19	180	29 55	242	45 01	292	40 38	333
307	40 34	003	27 31	054	46 12	130	37 19	180	29 02	242	44 06	292	40 10	332
308	40 37	002	28 19	054	46 58	130	37 18	181	28 10	242	43 10	291	39 41	331
309	40 39	001	29 07	053	47 43	131	37 17	182	27 17	242	42 15	291	39 12	330
310	40 40	000	29 55	053	48 28	132	37 15	182	26 24	242	41 19	291	38 42	329
311	40 40	000	30 43	052	49 13	132	37 12	183	25 31	243	40 22	290	38 11	329
312	40 39	359	31 30	052	49 56	133	37 09	184	24 38	243	39 26	290	37 40	328
313	40 37	358	32 17	052	50 40	134	37 05	184	23 44	243	38 30	290	37 08	327
314	40 34	357	33 04	051	51 23	135	37 00	185	22 51	243	37 33	289	36 35	327
	◆Alpheratz		◆FOMALHAUT		Peacock		Nunki		◆Rasalhague		VEGA		DENEB	
315	33 50	051	52 05	136	36 54	186	52 56	230	36 37	289	36 02	326	40 30	356
316	34 36	050	52 46	136	36 48	186	52 10	231	35 40	289	35 28	325	40 25	355
317	35 22	050	53 27	137	36 41	187	51 24	231	34 43	288	34 53	325	40 19	354
318	36 07	049	54 07	138	36 33	188	50 37	232	33 46	288	34 18	324	40 13	353
319	36 52	048	54 47	139	36 25	188	49 49	233	32 49	288	33 43	323	40 05	352
320	37 37	048	55 25	140	36 16	189	49 01	233	31 52	287	33 07	323	39 56	351
321	38 21	047	56 03	141	36 06	190	48 13	234	30 55	287	32 30	322	39 47	350
322	39 05	047	56 40	142	35 56	190	47 25	235	29 58	287	31 53	322	39 36	350
323	39 48	046	57 16	144	35 45	191	46 36	235	29 01	287	31 16	321	39 25	349
324	40 31	045	57 51	145	35 33	192	45 46	236	28 03	287	30 38	320	39 13	348
325	41 13	045	58 25	146	35 21	192	44 57	236	27 06	286	30 00	320	39 00	347
326	41 55	044	58 58	147	35 08	193	44 07	237	26 09	286	29 21	319	38 46	346
327	42 36	043	59 29	149	34 54	193	43 17	237	25 11	286	28 42	319	38 31	345
328	43 17	043	60 00	150	34 40	194	42 27	237	24 13	286	28 02	318	38 15	344
329	43 57	042	60 29	152	34 25	195	41 36	238	23 16	285	27 22	318	37 59	344
	◆Alpheratz		Hamal		Diphda		◆FOMALHAUT		Nunki		◆ALTAIR		DENEB	
330	44 37	041	23 40	062	47 28	112	60 57	153	40 45	238	55 28	292	37 41	343
331	45 16	040	24 33	062	48 24	113	61 23	155	39 54	239	54 33	291	37 23	342
332	45 54	039	25 26	062	49 19	113	61 48	156	39 03	239	53 37	291	37 04	341
333	46 31	038	26 18	061	50 14	113	62 11	158	38 11	239	52 41	290	36 44	340
334	47 08	037	27 11	061	51 08	114	62 33	160	37 20	240	51 45	290	36 24	340
335	47 44	037	28 03	061	52 03	114	62 53	161	36 28	240	50 48	289	36 03	339
336	48 19	036	28 55	060	52 58	115	63 11	163	35 36	240	49 52	289	35 41	338
337	48 54	035	29 47	060	53 52	115	63 27	165	34 44	241	48 55	288	35 18	337
338	49 27	034	30 38	060	54 46	116	63 42	167	33 52	241	47 58	288	34 55	337
339	50 00	032	31 30	059	55 40	116	63 55	169	33 00	241	47 01	288	34 31	336
340	50 32	031	32 21	059	56 33	117	64 05	171	32 07	241	46 04	287	34 06	335
341	51 02	030	33 12	058	57 26	118	64 14	173	31 15	242	45 07	287	33 41	335
342	51 32	029	34 03	058	58 19	118	64 20	175	30 22	242	44 10	287	33 15	334
343	52 01	028	34 54	058	59 12	119	64 25	177	29 29	242	43 12	286	32 48	333
344	52 28	027	35 44	057	60 04	120	64 27	179	28 36	242	42 15	286	32 21	333
	Alpheratz		◆Hamal		◆ACHERNAR		FOMALHAUT		Nunki		◆ALTAIR		DENEB	
345	52 54	025	36 34	057	28 24	157	64 27	181	27 43	242	41 17	286	31 53	332
346	53 20	024	37 24	056	28 47	157	64 25	183	26 50	242	40 19	285	31 25	331
347	53 43	023	38 14	056	29 10	158	64 21	185	25 57	243	39 22	285	30 56	331
348	54 06	022	39 03	055	29 33	158	64 15	187	25 04	243	38 24	285	30 26	330
349	54 27	020	39 52	055	29 55	159	64 07	189	24 11	243	37 26	284	29 56	330
350	54 47	019	40 41	054	30 16	159	63 57	191	23 17	243	36 28	284	29 26	329
351	55 06	017	41 29	053	30 37	160	63 45	193	22 24	243	35 30	284	28 55	329
352	55 23	016	42 17	053	30 58	160	63 31	195	21 31	243	34 32	284	28 23	328
353	55 39	014	43 04	052	31 18	161	63 15	196	20 37	243	33 33	283	27 52	327
354	55 53	013	43 51	052	31 38	161	62 57	198	19 44	243	32 35	283	27 19	327
355	56 06	011	44 38	051	31 57	162	62 38	200	18 50	244	31 37	283	26 46	326
356	56 17	010	45 24	050	32 15	162	62 17	202	17 56	244	30 39	283	26 13	326
357	56 26	008	46 10	049	32 33	163	61 54	203	17 03	244	29 40	283	25 39	326
358	56 34	007	46 55	049	32 51	163	61 29	205	16 09	244	28 42	282	25 05	325
359	56 41	005	47 40	048	33 08	164	61 03	207	15 15	244	27 43	282	24 31	325

 LAT 5°S

LHA ♈	Hc	Zn	Hc	Zn	Hc	Zn	Hc	Zn	Hc	Zn	Hc	Zn	Hc	Zn
	Alpheratz		◆ ALDEBARAN		RIGEL		ACHERNAR		◆ FOMALHAUT		ALTAIR		◆ DENEB	
0	55 45	004	18 19	071	11 45	097	34 22	164	61 29	209	26 32	283	23 07	324
1	55 48	002	19 16	071	12 44	097	34 38	165	60 59	210	25 34	282	22 32	324
2	55 50	000	20 12	070	13 44	097	34 54	165	60 28	212	24 35	282	21 57	324
3	55 49	359	21 08	070	14 43	097	35 09	166	59 56	213	23 37	282	21 21	323
4	55 47	357	22 05	070	15 42	097	35 23	166	59 23	215	22 38	282	20 45	323
5	55 44	356	23 01	070	16 42	097	35 37	167	58 48	216	21 40	282	20 09	322
6	55 38	354	23 57	069	17 41	097	35 50	168	58 13	217	20 41	281	19 33	322
7	55 32	353	24 53	069	18 40	097	36 02	168	57 36	218	19 43	281	18 56	322
8	55 23	351	25 48	069	19 40	097	36 14	169	56 59	219	18 44	281	18 19	321
9	55 13	350	26 44	069	20 39	097	36 25	170	56 21	220	17 45	281	17 41	321
10	55 02	348	27 40	068	21 38	097	36 35	170	55 41	221	16 47	281	17 03	321
11	54 49	347	28 35	068	22 38	097	36 45	171	55 01	222	15 48	281	16 25	320
12	54 35	345	29 31	068	23 37	097	36 54	172	54 21	223	14 49	281	15 47	320
13	54 19	344	30 26	067	24 36	097	37 03	172	53 39	224	13 50	280	15 09	320
14	54 01	342	31 21	067	25 36	097	37 11	173	52 57	225	12 52	280	14 30	319
	CAPELLA		ALDEBARAN		◆ RIGEL		ACHERNAR		◆ FOMALHAUT		Enif		◆ Alpheratz	
15	13 38	040	32 16	067	26 35	097	37 18	173	52 15	226	39 10	287	53 43	341
16	14 16	040	33 11	067	27 34	097	37 24	174	51 32	227	38 13	287	53 23	340
17	14 55	040	34 06	066	28 34	097	37 30	175	50 48	227	37 16	287	53 01	338
18	15 33	039	35 00	066	29 33	097	37 35	176	50 03	228	36 19	286	52 39	337
19	16 10	039	35 55	065	30 33	097	37 39	176	49 19	229	35 21	286	52 15	336
20	16 48	039	36 49	065	31 32	097	37 43	177	48 33	230	34 24	286	51 50	335
21	17 25	038	37 43	065	32 31	097	37 46	178	47 48	230	33 26	285	51 23	333
22	18 02	038	38 37	064	33 31	097	37 48	178	47 02	231	32 28	285	50 56	332
23	18 39	038	39 31	064	34 30	097	37 49	179	46 15	231	31 31	285	50 27	331
24	19 15	037	40 24	063	35 30	096	37 50	180	45 28	232	30 33	285	49 58	330
25	19 51	037	41 17	063	36 29	096	37 50	180	44 41	232	29 35	284	49 27	329
26	20 27	037	42 10	062	37 28	096	37 50	181	43 53	233	28 37	284	48 56	328
27	21 02	036	43 03	062	38 28	096	37 48	182	43 06	233	27 39	284	48 24	327
28	21 37	036	43 56	061	39 27	096	37 46	182	42 17	234	26 41	284	47 50	326
29	22 12	035	44 48	061	40 26	097	37 43	183	41 29	234	25 43	284	47 16	325
	CAPELLA		◆ BETELGEUSE		SIRIUS		CANOPUS		◆ ACHERNAR		FOMALHAUT		◆ Alpheratz	
30	22 46	035	29 51	078	19 11	106	18 19	144	37 40	184	40 40	235	46 41	324
31	23 20	034	30 49	078	20 08	106	18 53	144	37 36	184	39 51	235	46 05	323
32	23 54	034	31 48	078	21 06	106	19 28	145	37 31	185	39 02	236	45 29	322
33	24 27	034	32 46	078	22 03	106	20 03	145	37 25	186	38 13	236	44 52	321
34	25 00	033	33 44	078	23 01	106	20 37	145	37 19	186	37 23	236	44 14	320
35	25 33	033	34 43	077	23 58	106	21 11	145	37 12	187	36 33	237	43 35	319
36	26 05	032	35 41	077	24 56	106	21 45	146	37 04	188	35 44	237	42 56	319
37	26 36	032	36 39	077	25 53	106	22 18	146	36 56	188	34 53	237	42 16	318
38	27 07	031	37 38	077	26 50	106	22 52	146	36 46	189	34 03	237	41 35	317
39	27 38	031	38 36	076	27 48	106	23 25	146	36 37	190	33 13	238	40 54	316
40	28 08	030	39 34	076	28 45	106	23 58	147	36 26	190	32 22	238	40 13	316
41	28 38	029	40 32	076	29 42	106	24 31	147	36 15	191	31 31	238	39 31	315
42	29 07	029	41 30	076	30 40	107	25 03	147	36 04	192	30 40	238	38 48	314
43	29 36	028	42 27	075	31 37	107	25 36	148	35 51	192	29 49	239	38 05	314
44	30 04	028	43 25	075	32 34	107	26 08	148	35 38	193	28 58	239	37 22	313
	CAPELLA		◆ BETELGEUSE		SIRIUS		CANOPUS		◆ ACHERNAR		Diphda		◆ Hamal	
45	30 31	027	44 23	075	33 32	107	26 39	148	35 25	193	54 26	246	58 47	337
46	30 58	027	45 20	074	34 29	107	27 11	149	35 11	194	53 32	246	58 22	335
47	31 24	026	46 18	074	35 26	107	27 42	149	34 56	195	52 37	247	57 56	333
48	31 50	025	47 15	073	36 23	107	28 12	149	34 40	195	51 42	247	57 29	332
49	32 15	025	48 12	073	37 20	107	28 43	150	34 24	196	50 46	248	57 00	331
50	32 40	024	49 10	073	38 17	107	29 13	150	34 08	196	49 51	248	56 30	329
51	33 04	023	50 07	072	39 14	108	29 43	150	33 51	197	48 56	248	55 59	328
52	33 27	023	51 03	072	40 11	108	30 12	151	33 33	197	48 00	249	55 26	326
53	33 50	022	52 00	071	41 08	108	30 41	151	33 15	198	47 04	249	54 53	325
54	34 12	021	52 57	071	42 05	108	31 10	152	32 56	199	46 08	249	54 18	324
55	34 33	020	53 53	070	43 02	108	31 38	152	32 37	199	45 12	250	53 42	323
56	34 53	020	54 49	070	43 58	108	32 05	153	32 17	200	44 16	250	53 06	322
57	35 13	019	55 45	069	44 55	109	32 33	153	31 57	200	43 20	250	52 28	321
58	35 32	018	56 41	068	45 52	109	33 00	154	31 36	201	42 24	250	51 50	319
59	35 51	017	57 36	068	46 48	109	33 26	154	31 15	201	41 28	250	51 10	318
	◆ CAPELLA		POLLUX		◆ SIRIUS		CANOPUS		ACHERNAR		◆ Diphda		Hamal	
60	36 08	017	26 21	055	47 45	109	33 52	155	30 53	201	40 31	251	50 30	317
61	36 25	016	27 10	055	48 41	110	34 17	155	30 31	202	39 35	251	49 49	316
62	36 41	015	27 59	055	49 37	110	34 42	156	30 09	202	38 39	251	49 08	316
63	36 56	014	28 48	054	50 33	110	35 07	156	29 46	203	37 42	251	48 26	315
64	37 10	013	29 36	054	51 29	111	35 31	157	29 22	203	36 45	251	47 43	314
65	37 24	013	30 24	053	52 25	111	35 54	157	28 58	204	35 49	251	46 59	313
66	37 36	012	31 12	053	53 21	112	36 17	158	28 34	204	34 52	252	46 15	312
67	37 48	011	31 59	052	54 16	112	36 39	158	28 10	205	33 55	252	45 31	311
68	37 59	010	32 46	052	55 11	112	37 01	159	27 45	205	32 58	252	44 46	311
69	38 09	009	33 33	051	56 07	113	37 22	160	27 19	205	32 02	252	44 00	310
70	38 18	008	34 20	051	57 02	113	37 42	160	26 54	206	31 05	252	43 14	309
71	38 26	007	35 06	050	57 56	114	38 02	161	26 28	206	30 08	252	42 28	309
72	38 34	007	35 52	050	58 51	114	38 21	162	26 01	206	29 11	252	41 41	308
73	38 40	006	36 38	049	59 45	115	38 40	162	25 34	207	28 14	252	40 53	307
74	38 45	005	37 23	049	60 39	116	38 57	163	25 07	207	27 17	252	40 05	307
	CAPELLA		◆ POLLUX		REGULUS		Suhail		◆ CANOPUS		ACHERNAR		◆ Hamal	
75	38 50	004	38 07	048	11 20	077	23 26	136	39 15	164	24 40	207	39 17	306
76	38 54	003	38 52	048	12 18	077	24 08	136	39 31	164	24 12	208	38 29	306
77	38 57	002	39 36	047	13 16	077	24 49	136	39 47	165	23 44	208	37 40	305
78	38 58	001	40 19	046	14 14	076	25 31	136	40 02	166	23 16	208	36 51	305
79	38 59	000	41 02	046	15 12	076	26 12	137	40 16	167	22 48	209	36 02	304
80	38 59	000	41 44	045	16 10	076	26 53	137	40 30	167	22 19	209	35 12	304
81	38 58	359	42 26	044	17 08	076	27 34	137	40 42	168	21 50	209	34 22	303
82	38 56	358	43 07	043	18 06	076	28 14	137	40 54	169	21 21	209	33 32	303
83	38 53	357	43 48	043	19 04	076	28 54	138	41 06	170	20 51	210	32 41	302
84	38 50	356	44 28	042	20 02	075	29 34	138	41 16	170	20 22	210	31 51	302
85	38 45	355	45 08	041	21 00	075	30 14	138	41 26	171	19 52	210	31 00	301
86	38 39	354	45 46	040	21 58	075	30 54	139	41 35	172	19 22	210	30 08	301
87	38 33	353	46 25	039	22 55	075	31 33	139	41 43	173	18 52	211	29 17	301
88	38 25	352	47 02	038	23 53	075	32 12	140	41 50	173	18 21	211	28 26	300
89	38 17	352	47 39	037	24 51	074	32 50	140	41 56	174	17 50	211	27 34	300

LHA ♈	Hc	Zn	Hc	Zn	Hc	Zn	Hc	Zn	Hc	Zn	Hc	Zn	Hc	Zn
	POLLUX		◆ REGULUS		Suhail		◆ CANOPUS		Acamar		◆ ALDEBARAN		CAPELLA	
90	48 14	036	25 48	074	33 29	140	42 02	175	36 15	222	60 13	317	38 08	351
91	48 49	035	26 46	074	34 07	141	42 07	176	35 34	223	59 32	315	37 58	350
92	49 24	034	27 43	074	34 44	141	42 11	177	34 54	223	58 49	314	37 47	349
93	49 57	033	28 40	074	35 21	142	42 14	177	34 13	224	58 06	313	37 35	348
94	50 29	032	29 38	073	35 58	142	42 16	178	33 31	224	57 22	312	37 22	347
95	51 01	031	30 35	073	36 35	143	42 17	179	32 50	224	56 37	311	37 09	346
96	51 31	030	31 32	073	37 11	143	42 18	180	32 08	225	55 51	310	36 54	346
97	52 00	029	32 29	072	37 46	144	42 17	181	31 25	225	55 05	309	36 39	345
98	52 28	027	33 26	072	38 21	144	42 16	182	30 43	225	54 18	308	36 23	344
99	52 55	026	34 23	072	38 56	145	42 14	182	30 00	226	53 30	307	36 06	343
100	53 21	025	35 20	072	39 30	145	42 11	183	29 18	226	52 42	306	35 49	343
101	53 46	024	36 16	071	40 04	146	42 07	184	28 34	226	51 53	305	35 30	342
102	54 09	022	37 13	071	40 37	147	42 03	185	27 51	227	51 04	304	35 11	341
103	54 31	021	38 09	071	41 10	147	41 57	186	27 08	227	50 14	303	34 51	340
104	54 52	019	39 06	070	41 42	148	41 51	186	26 24	227	49 24	303	34 31	340
	POLLUX		◆ REGULUS		Suhail		◆ CANOPUS		RIGEL		◆ ALDEBARAN		CAPELLA	
105	55 11	018	40 02	070	42 13	149	41 44	187	63 48	262	48 34	302	34 10	339
106	55 29	017	40 58	070	42 44	149	41 36	188	62 49	262	47 43	301	33 48	338
107	55 45	015	41 54	069	43 14	150	41 27	189	61 50	262	46 52	301	33 25	337
108	56 00	014	42 50	069	43 44	151	41 18	190	60 50	262	46 00	300	33 02	337
109	56 13	012	43 45	068	44 13	151	41 07	190	59 51	262	45 08	300	32 38	336
110	56 25	011	44 41	068	44 41	152	40 56	191	58 52	262	44 16	299	32 13	335
111	56 35	009	45 36	067	45 08	153	40 44	192	57 53	263	43 24	298	31 48	335
112	56 43	007	46 31	067	45 35	154	40 31	193	56 53	263	42 31	298	31 22	334
113	56 50	006	47 26	066	46 01	155	40 18	193	55 54	263	41 38	297	30 55	333
114	56 55	004	48 21	066	46 26	156	40 04	194	54 55	263	40 45	297	30 28	333
115	56 59	003	49 15	065	46 50	156	39 49	195	53 56	263	39 52	296	30 01	332
116	57 00	001	50 09	065	47 14	157	39 33	196	52 56	263	38 58	296	29 33	332
117	57 01	359	51 03	064	47 36	158	39 17	196	51 57	263	38 04	296	29 04	331
118	56 59	358	51 57	063	47 58	159	39 00	197	50 58	263	37 10	295	28 35	330
119	56 56	356	52 50	063	48 19	160	38 42	198	49 58	263	36 16	295	28 05	330
	◆ REGULUS		Gienah		◆ ACRUX		CANOPUS		SIRIUS		◆ BETELGEUSE		POLLUX	
120	53 43	062	26 08	107	14 44	155	38 24	198	68 22	236	56 40	292	56 51	354
121	54 35	061	27 05	107	15 10	155	38 05	199	67 32	237	55 44	291	56 44	353
122	55 28	061	28 02	107	15 35	155	37 45	200	66 42	238	54 49	290	56 36	351
123	56 20	060	28 59	107	16 00	155	37 25	200	65 50	239	53 52	290	56 26	350
124	57 11	059	29 56	107	16 26	155	37 04	201	64 59	240	52 56	289	56 14	348
125	58 02	058	30 53	108	16 51	155	36 42	201	64 07	241	52 00	289	56 01	347
126	58 52	057	31 50	108	17 15	156	36 20	202	63 14	242	51 03	288	55 47	345
127	59 42	056	32 47	108	17 40	156	35 57	203	62 21	243	50 06	288	55 30	344
128	60 31	055	33 44	108	18 04	156	35 34	203	61 28	244	49 09	287	55 13	342
129	61 20	054	34 41	108	18 28	156	35 10	204	60 34	244	48 12	287	54 54	341
130	62 08	053	35 38	108	18 52	156	34 46	204	59 40	245	47 15	287	54 33	339
131	62 55	051	36 34	108	19 16	157	34 21	205	58 46	246	46 17	286	54 12	338
132	63 41	050	37 31	108	19 40	157	33 56	205	57 51	246	45 20	286	53 48	337
133	64 26	049	38 28	109	20 03	157	33 30	206	56 56	247	44 22	285	53 24	335
134	65 10	047	39 24	109	20 26	157	33 03	206	56 01	247	43 25	285	52 58	334
	Alioth		◆ SPICA		ACRUX		◆ CANOPUS		SIRIUS		BETELGEUSE		◆ POLLUX	
135	12 37	029	24 00	100	20 49	158	32 37	207	55 06	248	42 27	285	52 31	333
136	13 06	029	24 59	100	21 11	158	32 09	207	54 11	248	41 29	284	52 03	331
137	13 35	029	25 57	100	21 34	158	31 42	208	53 15	249	40 31	284	51 34	330
138	14 04	029	26 56	100	21 56	159	31 14	208	52 20	249	39 33	284	51 04	329
139	14 32	028	27 55	100	22 17	159	30 45	209	51 24	249	38 35	284	50 33	328
140	15 00	028	28 54	100	22 39	159	30 16	209	50 28	250	37 37	283	50 01	327
141	15 28	028	29 53	100	23 00	159	29 47	210	49 32	250	36 39	283	49 28	326
142	15 56	027	30 52	100	23 21	160	29 17	210	48 35	250	35 41	283	48 53	325
143	16 23	027	31 50	100	23 42	160	28 47	210	47 39	251	34 42	283	48 19	324
144	16 50	027	32 49	100	24 02	160	28 17	211	46 43	251	33 44	282	47 43	323
145	17 16	026	33 48	100	24 22	161	27 46	211	45 46	251	32 46	282	47 06	322
146	17 42	026	34 47	100	24 41	161	27 15	211	44 50	251	31 47	282	46 29	321
147	18 08	025	35 46	100	25 01	161	26 44	212	43 53	252	30 49	282	45 51	320
148	18 34	025	36 45	100	25 19	162	26 12	212	42 56	252	29 50	282	45 12	319
149	18 59	025	37 43	100	25 38	162	25 40	212	41 59	252	28 51	281	44 33	318
	Alioth		ARCTURUS		◆ SPICA		ACRUX		◆ CANOPUS		SIRIUS		◆ POLLUX	
150	19 24	024	22 31	067	38 42	100	25 56	162	25 08	213	41 03	252	43 53	318
151	19 48	024	23 26	067	39 41	100	26 14	163	24 36	213	40 06	252	43 12	317
152	20 12	023	24 20	066	40 40	101	26 31	163	24 03	213	39 09	252	42 31	316
153	20 35	023	25 15	066	41 39	101	26 48	164	23 30	214	38 12	253	41 49	315
154	20 59	023	26 10	066	42 37	101	27 05	164	22 57	214	37 15	253	41 07	315
155	21 21	022	27 04	066	43 36	101	27 21	164	22 23	214	36 18	253	40 24	314
156	21 44	022	27 59	065	44 35	101	27 37	165	21 50	214	35 20	253	39 41	313
157	22 05	021	28 53	065	45 33	101	27 53	165	21 16	215	34 23	253	38 57	313
158	22 27	021	29 47	065	46 32	101	28 07	166	20 42	215	33 26	253	38 13	312
159	22 48	020	30 41	064	47 31	101	28 22	166	20 07	215	32 29	253	37 28	311
160	23 08	020	31 35	064	48 29	101	28 36	167	19 33	215	31 32	253	36 43	311
161	23 28	019	32 28	064	49 28	101	28 50	167	18 58	215	30 34	253	35 57	310
162	23 48	019	33 22	063	50 26	102	29 03	167	18 24	216	29 37	254	35 11	310
163	24 07	018	34 15	063	51 25	102	29 16	168	17 49	216	28 40	254	34 25	309
164	24 25	018	35 08	062	52 24	102	29 28	168	17 14	216	27 42	254	33 39	309
	Alioth		◆ ARCTURUS		SPICA		◆ ACRUX		Suhail		SIRIUS		◆ POLLUX	
165	24 43	017	36 01	062	53 22	102	29 40	169	44 20	208	26 45	254	32 52	308
166	25 00	017	36 53	062	54 20	102	29 51	169	43 52	209	25 47	254	32 05	308
167	25 17	016	37 46	061	55 19	103	30 02	170	43 22	210	24 50	254	31 17	307
168	25 34	016	38 38	061	56 17	103	30 12	170	42 52	211	23 53	254	30 29	307
169	25 50	015	39 30	060	57 15	103	30 22	171	42 22	211	22 55	254	29 41	306
170	26 05	015	40 22	060	58 14	103	30 31	171	41 50	212	21 58	254	28 53	306
171	26 20	014	41 13	059	59 12	104	30 40	172	41 18	213	21 00	254	28 05	305
172	26 34	013	42 04	059	60 10	104	30 49	172	40 46	213	20 03	254	27 16	305
173	26 47	013	42 55	058	61 08	104	30 56	173	40 13	214	19 05	254	26 27	305
174	27 00	012	43 46	057	62 06	105	31 04	173	39 39	214	18 08	254	25 38	304
175	27 13	012	44 36	057	63 03	105	31 10	174	39 05	215	17 10	254	24 48	304
176	27 24	011	45 26	056	64 01	105	31 17	174	38 31	216	16 13	254	23 58	304
177	27 36	010	46 15	055	64 59	106	31 22	175	37 56	216	15 16	254	23 09	303
178	27 46	010	47 04	055	65 56	106	31 27	175	37 20	217	14 18	254	22 19	303
179	27 56	009	47 53	054	66 53	107	31 32	176	36 44	217	13 21	254	21 28	303

LAT 5°S

LHA ♈	Hc Zn	Hc Zn	Hc Zn	Hc Zn	Hc Zn	Hc Zn	Hc Zn
	Alioth	◆ARCTURUS	ANTARES	◆ACRUX	Suhail	Alphard	◆REGULUS
180	28 05 009	48 41 053	22 16 117	31 36 176	36 08 218	52 11 262	57 41 302
181	28 14 008	49 29 053	23 09 117	31 40 177	35 31 218	51 12 262	56 50 301
182	28 22 007	50 16 052	24 03 117	31 43 177	34 54 219	50 13 262	55 58 300
183	28 29 007	51 03 051	24 56 117	31 45 178	34 17 219	49 13 262	55 06 299
184	28 36 006	51 49 050	25 49 117	31 47 178	33 39 219	48 14 262	54 14 298
185	28 42 006	52 34 049	26 43 117	31 48 179	33 01 220	47 15 263	53 21 298
186	28 48 005	53 19 048	27 36 117	31 49 180	32 22 220	46 16 263	52 28 297
187	28 52 004	54 03 047	28 29 117	31 49 180	31 44 221	45 16 263	51 34 296
188	28 57 004	54 47 046	29 22 118	31 49 181	31 04 221	44 17 263	50 41 296
189	29 00 003	55 29 045	30 15 118	31 48 181	30 25 221	43 18 263	49 47 295
190	29 03 002	56 11 044	31 08 118	31 46 182	29 45 222	42 19 263	48 52 295
191	29 05 002	56 52 043	32 00 118	31 44 182	29 05 222	41 19 263	47 58 294
192	29 06 001	57 32 041	32 53 118	31 42 183	28 25 222	40 20 263	47 03 293
193	29 07 000	58 11 040	33 45 119	31 39 183	27 45 223	39 21 263	46 08 293
194	29 07 000	58 49 039	34 38 119	31 35 184	27 04 223	38 21 263	45 13 292
	ARCTURUS	◆Rasalhague	ANTARES	◆ACRUX	Alphard	◆REGULUS	Alioth
195	59 26 037	19 20 075	35 30 119	31 31 184	37 22 263	44 18 292	29 07 359
196	60 02 036	20 17 075	36 22 119	31 26 185	36 23 263	43 22 292	29 05 359
197	60 36 034	21 15 074	37 14 120	31 21 185	35 23 263	42 27 291	29 04 358
198	61 09 033	22 13 074	38 06 120	31 15 186	34 24 263	41 31 291	29 01 357
199	61 41 031	23 10 074	38 58 120	31 09 186	33 25 263	40 35 290	28 58 357
200	62 11 030	24 08 074	39 49 121	31 02 187	32 26 263	39 39 290	28 54 356
201	62 40 028	25 05 074	40 41 121	30 54 187	31 26 263	38 42 290	28 49 355
202	63 07 026	26 02 073	41 32 121	30 46 188	30 27 263	37 46 289	28 44 355
203	63 32 024	26 59 073	42 23 122	30 38 188	29 28 263	36 49 289	28 38 354
204	63 56 022	27 57 073	43 13 122	30 29 189	28 28 263	35 53 289	28 32 353
205	64 17 020	28 54 073	44 04 123	30 19 189	27 29 263	34 56 288	28 25 353
206	64 37 018	29 51 072	44 54 123	30 09 190	26 30 263	33 59 288	28 17 352
207	64 54 016	30 48 072	45 44 123	29 59 190	25 30 263	33 02 288	28 08 352
208	65 10 014	31 45 072	46 34 124	29 48 191	24 31 263	32 05 287	27 59 351
209	65 23 012	32 41 072	47 23 124	29 37 191	23 32 263	31 08 287	27 50 350
	ARCTURUS	◆VEGA	ANTARES	◆RIGIL KENT	ACRUX	Gienah	◆REGULUS
210	65 34 009	12 39 048	48 13 125	33 35 174	29 25 192	61 44 241	30 11 287
211	65 42 007	13 24 048	49 01 126	33 41 175	29 12 192	60 52 242	29 14 287
212	65 48 005	14 08 048	49 50 126	33 46 175	28 59 193	59 59 243	28 17 286
213	65 52 003	14 52 048	50 38 127	33 51 176	28 46 193	59 05 244	27 19 286
214	65 54 000	15 36 047	51 26 127	33 55 176	28 32 194	58 12 244	26 22 286
215	65 53 358	16 20 047	52 13 128	33 58 177	28 18 194	57 18 245	25 24 286
216	65 49 356	17 04 047	53 00 129	34 01 178	28 03 194	56 23 245	24 27 285
217	65 44 353	17 47 046	53 46 130	34 03 178	27 48 195	55 29 246	23 29 285
218	65 35 351	18 31 046	54 32 130	34 05 179	27 33 195	54 34 246	22 31 285
219	65 25 349	19 14 046	55 17 131	34 06 179	27 17 196	53 39 247	21 34 285
220	65 12 347	19 56 046	56 02 132	34 06 180	27 00 196	52 44 247	20 36 285
221	64 57 344	20 39 045	56 46 133	34 06 180	26 44 196	51 49 248	19 38 285
222	64 40 342	21 21 045	57 29 134	34 05 181	26 27 197	50 54 248	18 40 284
223	64 21 340	22 03 044	58 12 135	34 04 182	26 09 197	49 58 248	17 42 284
224	64 00 338	22 45 044	58 53 136	34 02 182	25 51 198	49 03 249	16 44 284
	Alphecca	VEGA	◆ALTAIR	ANTARES	◆RIGIL KENT	SPICA	◆ARCTURUS
225	57 12 015	23 26 044	16 02 079	59 34 137	33 59 183	65 55 254	63 36 336
226	57 26 013	24 07 043	17 01 079	60 14 138	33 56 183	64 58 254	63 12 334
227	57 39 011	24 48 043	18 00 079	60 54 140	33 52 184	64 01 255	62 45 333
228	57 50 010	25 29 042	18 58 079	61 32 141	33 47 185	63 03 255	62 16 331
229	57 59 008	26 09 042	19 57 079	62 09 142	33 42 185	62 05 255	61 46 329
230	58 07 006	26 49 042	20 55 078	62 45 144	33 37 186	61 07 256	61 15 327
231	58 13 005	27 28 041	21 54 078	63 19 145	33 30 186	60 09 256	60 42 326
232	58 17 003	28 07 041	22 52 078	63 53 147	33 24 187	59 11 256	60 08 324
233	58 19 001	28 46 040	23 51 078	64 25 149	33 16 187	58 13 257	59 32 323
234	58 20 000	29 24 040	24 49 078	64 55 150	33 08 188	57 15 257	58 56 321
235	58 19 358	30 02 039	25 48 078	65 24 152	33 00 189	56 17 257	58 18 320
236	58 16 356	30 39 038	26 46 077	65 51 154	32 50 189	55 18 257	57 39 319
237	58 11 355	31 16 038	27 44 077	66 16 156	32 41 190	54 20 258	56 59 318
238	58 05 353	31 53 037	28 43 077	66 40 158	32 30 190	53 22 258	56 18 316
239	57 57 351	32 29 037	29 41 077	67 01 160	32 20 191	52 23 258	55 37 315
	VEGA	◆ALTAIR	Nunki	◆RIGIL KENT	SPICA	◆ARCTURUS	Alphecca
240	33 04 036	30 39 077	42 53 122	32 08 191	51 25 258	54 54 314	57 47 350
241	33 39 036	31 37 076	43 44 122	31 56 192	50 26 258	54 11 313	57 35 348
242	34 14 035	32 35 076	44 35 123	31 44 192	49 27 259	53 27 312	57 22 346
243	34 48 034	33 33 076	45 25 123	31 31 193	48 29 259	52 42 311	57 07 345
244	35 21 034	34 31 076	46 15 123	31 17 193	47 30 259	51 57 310	56 50 343
245	35 54 033	35 29 075	47 05 124	31 03 194	46 32 259	51 11 309	56 32 342
246	36 26 032	36 27 075	47 54 124	30 49 194	45 33 259	50 24 308	56 13 340
247	36 57 031	37 24 075	48 43 125	30 34 195	44 34 259	49 37 308	55 52 339
248	37 28 031	38 22 074	49 32 126	30 18 195	43 36 259	48 49 307	55 30 337
249	37 58 030	39 20 074	50 20 126	30 02 196	42 37 259	48 01 306	55 06 336
250	38 28 029	40 17 074	51 09 127	29 46 196	41 38 259	47 13 305	54 41 335
251	38 57 028	41 14 074	51 56 128	29 29 197	40 39 259	46 24 305	54 14 333
252	39 25 028	42 12 073	52 43 128	29 12 197	39 41 260	45 34 304	53 47 332
253	39 52 027	43 09 073	53 30 129	28 54 198	38 42 260	44 45 303	53 18 331
254	40 19 026	44 06 072	54 16 130	28 36 198	37 43 260	43 54 303	52 48 329
	◆VEGA	ALTAIR	◆Nunki	Shaula	ANTARES	◆SPICA	ARCTURUS
255	40 44 025	45 03 072	55 02 131	56 55 167	67 24 197	36 44 260	43 04 302
256	41 09 024	46 00 072	55 47 131	57 08 169	67 05 200	35 45 260	42 13 302
257	41 34 023	46 56 071	56 32 132	57 19 170	66 44 202	34 47 260	41 22 301
258	41 57 022	47 53 071	57 15 133	57 28 172	66 20 204	33 48 260	40 31 300
259	42 19 022	48 49 070	57 59 134	57 36 173	65 55 206	32 49 260	39 39 300
260	42 41 021	49 45 070	58 41 135	57 43 175	65 29 208	31 50 260	38 47 299
261	43 01 020	50 42 069	59 23 136	57 48 176	65 00 209	30 51 260	37 55 299
262	43 21 019	51 37 069	60 03 138	57 51 178	64 30 211	29 52 260	37 03 299
263	43 39 018	52 33 068	60 43 139	57 53 179	63 58 213	28 54 260	36 10 298
264	43 57 017	53 28 068	61 22 140	57 53 181	63 25 214	27 55 260	35 17 298
265	44 14 016	54 24 067	62 00 141	57 52 182	62 51 216	26 56 260	34 24 297
266	44 29 015	55 19 066	62 37 143	57 49 184	62 15 217	25 57 260	33 31 297
267	44 44 014	56 13 066	63 12 144	57 45 185	61 38 219	24 58 260	32 37 296
268	44 57 013	57 08 065	63 46 146	57 38 186	61 00 220	23 59 260	31 44 296
269	45 10 011	58 02 064	64 19 148	57 31 188	60 21 221	23 00 260	30 50 296

LHA ♈	Hc Zn	Hc Zn	Hc Zn	Hc Zn	Hc Zn	Hc Zn	Hc Zn
	◆VEGA	DENEB	Enif	◆FOMALHAUT	Peacock	◆ANTARES	ARCTURUS
270	45 21 010	28 05 031	32 02 075	15 50 119	30 46 158	59 41 223	29 56 295
271	45 31 009	28 35 031	33 00 075	16 42 119	31 08 158	59 00 224	29 02 295
272	45 40 008	29 05 030	33 57 074	17 34 119	31 31 158	58 18 225	28 08 295
273	45 48 007	29 35 029	34 55 074	18 26 120	31 52 159	57 36 226	27 14 294
274	45 55 006	30 04 029	35 52 074	19 18 120	32 13 159	56 53 227	26 19 294
275	46 01 005	30 33 028	36 50 074	20 10 120	32 34 160	56 09 228	25 25 294
276	46 05 004	31 01 028	37 47 073	21 02 120	32 54 160	55 24 229	24 30 294
277	46 09 003	31 28 027	38 44 073	21 54 120	33 14 161	54 39 229	23 35 293
278	46 11 002	31 55 026	39 41 073	22 46 120	33 33 162	53 53 230	22 40 293
279	46 12 000	32 21 026	40 38 072	23 37 120	33 52 162	53 07 231	21 45 293
280	46 12 359	32 47 025	41 35 072	24 29 120	34 10 163	52 21 232	20 50 293
281	46 11 358	33 12 024	42 32 072	25 21 120	34 28 163	51 33 232	19 55 292
282	46 08 357	33 37 024	43 28 071	26 12 121	34 45 164	50 46 233	18 59 292
283	46 04 356	34 00 023	44 25 071	27 04 121	35 01 164	49 58 234	18 04 292
284	45 59 355	34 23 022	45 21 070	27 55 121	35 17 165	49 09 234	17 09 292
	DENEB	Enif	◆FOMALHAUT	Peacock	◆ANTARES	Rasalhague	◆VEGA
285	34 46 022	46 18 070	28 46 121	35 32 166	48 21 235	62 40 310	45 53 354
286	35 07 021	47 14 070	29 37 121	35 47 166	47 32 235	61 54 309	45 46 353
287	35 28 020	48 10 069	30 28 122	36 01 167	46 42 236	61 07 308	45 38 351
288	35 48 019	49 05 069	31 19 122	36 14 167	45 52 236	60 19 306	45 29 350
289	36 08 019	50 01 068	32 10 122	36 27 168	45 02 237	59 30 305	45 18 349
290	36 27 018	50 56 067	33 01 122	36 39 169	44 12 237	58 41 304	45 06 348
291	36 44 017	51 51 067	33 51 122	36 50 169	43 22 238	57 52 303	44 54 347
292	37 02 016	52 46 066	34 41 123	37 01 170	42 31 238	57 01 302	44 40 346
293	37 18 015	53 41 066	35 32 123	37 11 171	41 40 239	56 11 301	44 25 345
294	37 33 015	54 35 065	36 22 123	37 21 171	40 49 239	55 20 301	44 09 344
295	37 48 014	55 29 064	37 11 124	37 29 172	39 58 239	54 28 300	43 52 343
296	38 02 013	56 23 064	38 01 124	37 37 173	39 06 240	53 36 299	43 34 342
297	38 15 012	57 16 063	38 50 124	37 45 173	38 15 240	52 43 298	43 15 341
298	38 27 011	58 09 062	39 40 125	37 51 174	37 23 240	51 51 298	42 56 340
299	38 38 010	59 02 061	40 29 125	37 57 175	36 31 241	50 58 297	42 35 339
	◆DENEB	Alpheratz	◆FOMALHAUT	Peacock	◆ANTARES	Rasalhague	VEGA
300	38 48 009	21 13 056	41 17 126	38 02 175	35 39 241	50 04 296	42 13 338
301	38 57 009	22 03 056	42 06 126	38 07 176	34 46 241	49 10 296	41 50 337
302	39 06 008	22 52 055	42 54 126	38 11 177	33 54 241	48 17 295	41 27 336
303	39 13 007	23 41 055	43 42 127	38 14 177	33 02 242	47 22 295	41 03 336
304	39 20 006	24 30 055	44 30 127	38 16 178	32 09 242	46 28 294	40 37 335
305	39 26 005	25 19 054	45 17 128	38 18 179	31 16 242	45 33 294	40 11 334
306	39 30 004	26 07 054	46 04 129	38 19 180	30 23 242	44 38 293	39 45 333
307	39 34 003	26 55 054	46 50 129	38 19 180	29 31 242	43 43 293	39 17 332
308	39 37 002	27 43 053	47 37 130	38 18 181	28 38 242	42 48 292	38 49 331
309	39 39 001	28 31 053	48 22 130	38 17 182	27 45 243	41 53 292	38 20 331
310	39 40 000	29 19 052	49 08 131	38 15 182	26 51 243	40 57 291	37 50 330
311	39 40 000	30 06 052	49 53 132	38 12 183	25 58 243	40 01 291	37 20 329
312	39 39 359	30 53 052	50 37 132	38 09 184	25 05 243	39 05 291	36 49 328
313	39 37 358	31 39 051	51 21 133	38 04 184	24 12 243	38 09 290	36 17 328
314	39 34 357	32 26 051	52 04 134	38 00 185	23 18 243	37 13 290	35 45 327
	◆Alpheratz	◆FOMALHAUT	Peacock	Nunki	◆Rasalhague	VEGA	DENEB
315	33 12 050	52 47 135	37 54 186	53 35 231	36 17 290	35 12 326	39 30 356
316	33 57 050	53 29 136	37 48 186	52 48 232	35 21 289	34 38 326	39 25 355
317	34 43 049	54 11 136	37 40 187	52 01 232	34 24 289	34 04 325	39 20 354
318	35 28 048	54 52 137	37 33 188	51 13 233	33 28 289	33 30 324	39 13 353
319	36 12 048	55 32 138	37 24 188	50 25 234	32 31 288	32 54 324	39 06 352
320	36 56 047	56 11 139	37 15 189	49 37 234	31 34 288	32 19 323	38 57 351
321	37 40 047	56 50 140	37 05 190	48 48 235	30 37 288	31 43 323	38 48 351
322	38 23 046	57 27 142	36 55 190	47 59 235	29 40 288	31 06 322	38 37 350
323	39 06 045	58 04 143	36 44 191	47 10 236	28 43 287	30 29 321	38 26 349
324	39 48 045	58 40 144	36 32 192	46 20 236	27 46 287	29 51 321	38 14 348
325	40 30 044	59 15 145	36 19 192	45 30 237	26 49 287	29 13 320	38 01 347
326	41 12 043	59 48 146	36 06 193	44 40 237	25 52 287	28 35 320	37 47 346
327	41 52 043	60 21 148	35 52 194	43 49 238	24 54 286	27 56 319	37 33 345
328	42 33 042	60 52 149	35 38 194	42 58 238	23 57 286	27 17 319	37 17 345
329	43 12 041	61 22 151	35 23 195	42 07 239	22 59 286	26 38 318	37 01 344
	◆Alpheratz	Hamal	Diphda	◆FOMALHAUT	Nunki	◆ALTAIR	DENEB
330	43 51 040	23 12 062	47 50 111	61 50 152	41 16 239	55 05 293	36 44 343
331	44 30 039	24 04 061	48 46 112	62 17 154	40 25 239	54 10 293	36 26 342
332	45 07 039	24 57 061	49 42 112	62 43 156	39 33 240	53 15 292	36 07 341
333	45 44 038	25 49 061	50 37 112	63 07 157	38 42 240	52 20 292	35 48 341
334	46 20 037	26 41 060	51 32 113	63 29 159	37 50 240	51 24 291	35 28 340
335	46 56 036	27 33 060	52 27 113	63 50 161	36 58 241	50 28 291	35 07 339
336	47 30 035	28 25 060	53 22 114	64 08 163	36 06 241	49 32 290	34 45 338
337	48 04 034	29 16 059	54 17 114	64 25 165	35 13 241	48 36 290	34 23 338
338	48 37 033	30 08 059	55 11 115	64 40 166	34 21 241	47 39 289	34 00 337
339	49 09 032	30 59 059	56 06 115	64 53 168	33 28 242	46 43 289	33 36 336
340	49 40 031	31 50 058	57 00 116	65 04 170	32 36 242	45 46 288	33 11 336
341	50 10 030	32 41 058	57 53 116	65 13 172	31 43 242	44 49 288	32 46 335
342	50 39 029	33 31 057	58 47 117	65 20 175	30 50 242	43 52 287	32 21 334
343	51 07 027	34 21 057	59 40 117	65 25 177	29 57 242	42 55 287	31 54 334
344	51 34 026	35 11 056	60 33 118	65 27 179	29 04 243	41 58 287	31 28 333
	Alpheratz	◆Hamal	◆ACHERNAR	FOMALHAUT	Nunki	◆ALTAIR	DENEB
345	52 00 025	36 01 056	29 19 157	65 27 181	28 11 243	41 01 286	31 00 332
346	52 25 024	36 50 056	29 43 157	65 25 183	27 18 243	40 03 286	30 32 332
347	52 48 022	37 40 055	30 06 158	65 21 185	26 25 243	39 06 286	30 03 331
348	53 10 021	38 28 054	30 28 158	65 15 187	25 31 243	38 08 285	29 34 331
349	53 31 020	39 17 054	30 50 158	65 07 189	24 38 243	37 10 285	29 05 330
350	53 51 018	40 05 053	31 12 159	64 56 191	23 44 243	36 13 285	28 34 329
351	54 09 017	40 53 053	31 33 159	64 44 193	22 51 244	35 15 285	28 04 329
352	54 25 016	41 40 052	31 54 160	64 29 195	21 57 244	34 17 284	27 32 328
353	54 41 014	42 27 051	32 15 160	64 13 197	21 04 244	33 19 284	27 01 328
354	54 55 013	43 14 051	32 34 161	63 54 199	20 10 244	32 21 284	26 29 327
355	55 07 011	44 00 050	32 54 161	63 34 201	19 17 244	31 23 284	25 56 327
356	55 18 010	44 45 049	33 12 162	63 12 202	18 23 244	30 25 283	25 23 326
357	55 27 008	45 30 049	33 31 162	62 49 204	17 29 244	29 27 283	24 50 326
358	55 35 007	46 15 048	33 48 163	62 23 206	16 35 244	28 29 283	24 16 325
359	55 41 005	46 59 047	34 06 164	61 57 207	15 42 244	27 30 283	23 42 325

LAT 6°S

LHA ♈	Hc	Zn	Hc	Zn	Hc	Zn	Hc	Zn	Hc	Zn	Hc	Zn	Hc	Zn
	◆ Alpheratz		ALDEBARAN		◆ RIGEL		ACHERNAR		◆ FOMALHAUT		ALTAIR		DENEB	
0	54 45	003	17 59	070	11 53	097	35 20	164	62 21	210	26 19	283	22 18	325
1	54 48	002	18 56	070	12 52	097	35 36	165	61 50	211	25 20	283	21 44	324
2	54 50	000	19 52	070	13 51	097	35 52	165	61 19	213	24 22	283	21 09	324
3	54 49	359	20 48	070	14 50	097	36 07	166	60 46	214	23 24	282	20 33	323
4	54 47	357	21 44	070	15 50	097	36 21	166	60 12	216	22 26	282	19 58	323
5	54 44	356	22 40	069	16 49	097	36 35	167	59 37	217	21 27	282	19 22	323
6	54 39	354	23 35	069	17 48	097	36 48	168	59 00	218	20 29	282	18 45	322
7	54 32	353	24 31	069	18 47	097	37 01	168	58 23	219	19 31	282	18 09	322
8	54 24	351	25 27	068	19 47	097	37 13	169	57 45	220	18 32	282	17 32	322
9	54 14	350	26 22	068	20 46	097	37 24	169	57 06	221	17 34	281	16 54	321
10	54 03	348	27 17	068	21 45	096	37 34	170	56 26	222	16 35	281	16 17	321
11	53 51	347	28 13	068	22 45	096	37 44	171	55 45	223	15 37	281	15 39	321
12	53 36	346	29 08	067	23 44	096	37 54	171	55 04	224	14 38	281	15 01	320
13	53 21	344	30 03	067	24 43	096	38 02	172	54 22	225	13 39	281	14 23	320
14	53 04	343	30 57	067	25 42	096	38 10	173	53 39	226	12 41	281	13 44	320
	Hamal		ALDEBARAN		◆ RIGEL		ACHERNAR		◆ FOMALHAUT		Enif		◆ Alpheratz	
15	56 07	029	31 52	066	26 42	096	38 17	173	52 56	227	38 52	288	52 46	341
16	56 35	027	32 47	066	27 41	096	38 24	174	52 12	228	37 55	288	52 26	340
17	57 02	026	33 41	066	28 40	096	38 30	175	51 28	228	36 59	287	52 05	339
18	57 27	024	34 35	065	29 40	096	38 35	175	50 43	229	36 02	287	51 43	338
19	57 51	023	35 29	065	30 39	096	38 39	176	49 58	230	35 04	287	51 20	336
20	58 14	021	36 23	064	31 38	096	38 43	177	49 12	230	34 07	286	50 55	335
21	58 34	020	37 17	064	32 38	096	38 46	178	48 26	231	33 10	286	50 30	334
22	58 54	018	38 10	063	33 37	096	38 48	178	47 39	232	32 12	286	50 03	333
23	59 11	016	39 04	063	34 37	096	38 49	179	46 52	232	31 15	285	49 35	332
24	59 27	015	39 57	063	35 36	096	38 50	180	46 05	233	30 17	285	49 06	330
25	59 41	013	40 50	062	36 35	096	38 50	180	45 17	233	29 20	285	48 36	329
26	59 53	011	41 42	062	37 35	096	38 50	181	44 29	234	28 22	285	48 05	328
27	60 04	009	42 35	061	38 34	096	38 48	182	43 41	234	27 24	284	47 33	327
28	60 13	007	43 27	060	39 33	096	38 46	182	42 52	235	26 27	284	47 01	326
29	60 19	006	44 18	060	40 33	096	38 43	183	42 04	235	25 29	284	46 27	325
	CAPELLA		◆ BETELGEUSE		SIRIUS		CANOPUS		◆ ACHERNAR		FOMALHAUT		◆ Alpheratz	
30	21 57	035	29 38	078	19 27	106	19 07	144	38 40	184	41 15	235	45 53	324
31	22 31	034	30 37	078	20 25	106	19 42	144	38 35	184	40 25	236	45 17	323
32	23 04	034	31 35	077	21 22	106	20 17	144	38 30	185	39 36	236	44 41	323
33	23 37	033	32 33	077	22 20	106	20 52	145	38 25	186	38 46	237	44 05	322
34	24 10	033	33 31	077	23 17	106	21 26	145	38 18	187	37 56	237	43 27	321
35	24 42	032	34 29	077	24 15	106	22 00	145	38 11	187	37 06	237	42 49	320
36	25 14	032	35 27	076	25 12	106	22 34	145	38 03	188	36 16	237	42 11	319
37	25 45	031	36 25	076	26 09	106	23 08	146	37 55	189	35 26	238	41 31	318
38	26 16	031	37 23	076	27 07	106	23 42	146	37 46	189	34 35	238	40 51	318
39	26 46	030	38 21	076	28 04	106	24 15	146	37 36	190	33 44	238	40 11	317
40	27 16	030	39 19	075	29 02	106	24 48	146	37 25	190	32 54	239	39 30	316
41	27 45	029	40 17	075	29 59	106	25 21	147	37 14	191	32 03	239	38 48	316
42	28 14	029	41 14	075	30 56	106	25 54	147	37 02	192	31 12	239	38 06	315
43	28 43	028	42 12	074	31 54	106	26 26	147	36 50	192	30 20	239	37 24	314
44	29 10	027	43 09	074	32 51	106	26 58	148	36 37	193	29 29	239	36 41	314
	CAPELLA		◆ BETELGEUSE		SIRIUS		CANOPUS		◆ ACHERNAR		FOMALHAUT		◆ Alpheratz	
45	29 38	027	44 06	074	33 49	106	27 30	148	36 23	194	28 38	240	35 57	313
46	30 04	026	45 04	073	34 46	106	28 02	148	36 09	194	27 46	240	35 13	312
47	30 30	026	46 01	073	35 43	106	28 33	149	35 54	195	26 55	240	34 29	312
48	30 56	025	46 58	072	36 40	106	29 04	149	35 38	195	26 03	240	33 44	311
49	31 21	024	47 54	072	37 38	107	29 35	149	35 22	196	25 12	240	32 59	311
50	31 45	024	48 51	071	38 35	107	30 05	150	35 05	197	24 20	240	32 14	310
51	32 09	023	49 48	071	39 32	107	30 35	150	34 48	197	23 28	240	31 28	310
52	32 32	022	50 44	071	40 29	107	31 04	151	34 30	198	22 36	240	30 42	309
53	32 54	022	51 40	070	41 26	107	31 33	151	34 12	198	21 44	241	29 56	309
54	33 16	021	52 36	069	42 23	107	32 02	151	33 53	199	20 52	241	29 09	308
55	33 37	020	53 32	069	43 20	107	32 31	152	33 34	199	20 00	241	28 22	308
56	33 57	019	54 27	068	44 17	108	32 59	152	33 14	200	19 08	241	27 35	307
57	34 16	019	55 23	068	45 14	108	33 26	153	32 53	200	18 16	241	26 47	307
58	34 35	018	56 18	067	46 11	108	33 53	153	32 32	201	17 24	241	26 00	307
59	34 53	017	57 13	066	47 07	108	34 20	154	32 11	201	16 32	241	25 12	306
	◆ CAPELLA		POLLUX		◆ SIRIUS		CANOPUS		ACHERNAR		◆ Diphda		Hamal	
60	35 11	016	25 47	055	48 04	108	34 46	154	31 49	202	40 51	251	49 46	318
61	35 27	016	26 36	055	49 01	109	35 12	155	31 27	202	39 54	252	49 06	317
62	35 43	015	27 24	054	49 57	109	35 37	155	31 04	203	38 58	252	48 25	316
63	35 58	014	28 12	054	50 53	109	36 01	156	30 41	203	38 01	252	47 43	315
64	36 12	013	29 00	053	51 50	110	36 26	156	30 17	204	37 04	252	47 01	315
65	36 25	012	29 48	053	52 46	110	36 49	157	29 53	204	36 07	252	46 18	314
66	36 37	012	30 35	052	53 42	110	37 12	158	29 29	204	35 11	252	45 35	313
67	36 49	011	31 22	052	54 38	111	37 35	158	29 04	205	34 14	252	44 51	312
68	37 00	010	32 09	051	55 34	111	37 57	159	28 39	205	33 17	252	44 06	311
69	37 10	009	32 56	051	56 29	111	38 18	159	28 13	206	32 20	253	43 21	311
70	37 19	008	33 42	050	57 25	112	38 38	160	27 48	206	31 23	253	42 36	310
71	37 27	007	34 28	050	58 20	112	38 59	161	27 21	206	30 26	253	41 50	309
72	37 34	007	35 13	049	59 15	113	39 18	161	26 55	207	29 29	253	41 03	309
73	37 40	006	35 58	049	60 10	114	39 37	162	26 28	207	28 32	253	40 17	308
74	37 46	005	36 43	048	61 04	114	39 55	163	26 01	207	27 35	253	39 29	307
	CAPELLA		POLLUX		◆ REGULUS		CANOPUS		◆ ACHERNAR		Diphda		◆ Hamal	
75	37 50	004	37 27	048	11 06	077	40 12	163	25 33	208	26 38	253	38 42	307
76	37 54	003	38 11	047	12 04	076	40 29	164	25 05	208	25 41	253	37 54	306
77	37 57	002	38 54	046	13 02	076	40 45	165	24 37	208	24 44	253	37 05	306
78	37 58	001	39 37	046	14 00	076	41 00	166	24 09	209	23 47	253	36 17	305
79	37 59	000	40 20	045	14 58	076	41 14	166	23 40	209	22 50	253	35 28	305
80	37 59	000	41 01	044	15 56	076	41 28	167	23 12	209	21 53	253	34 39	304
81	37 58	359	41 43	043	16 54	076	41 41	168	22 42	209	20 55	253	33 49	304
82	37 56	358	42 23	043	17 51	075	41 53	169	22 13	210	19 58	253	32 59	303
83	37 54	357	43 04	042	18 49	075	42 05	169	21 44	210	19 01	253	32 09	303
84	37 50	356	43 43	041	19 47	075	42 15	170	21 14	210	18 04	253	31 19	302
85	37 45	355	44 22	040	20 44	075	42 25	171	20 44	210	17 07	253	30 28	302
86	37 40	354	45 00	039	21 42	075	42 34	172	20 14	211	16 10	253	29 37	301
87	37 33	353	45 38	039	22 39	074	42 42	173	19 43	211	15 13	253	28 46	301
88	37 26	353	46 15	038	23 37	074	42 50	173	19 13	211	14 16	253	27 55	301
89	37 18	352	46 51	037	24 34	074	42 56	174	18 42	211	13 19	253	27 04	300

LHA ♈	Hc	Zn	Hc	Zn	Hc	Zn	Hc	Zn	Hc	Zn	Hc	Zn	Hc	Zn
	POLLUX		◆ REGULUS		Suhail		◆ CANOPUS		Acamar		◆ ALDEBARAN		CAPELLA	
90	47 26	036	25 32	074	34 15	140	43 02	175	36 59	223	59 29	318	37 09	351
91	48 00	035	26 29	074	34 53	140	43 07	176	36 18	223	58 48	317	36 59	350
92	48 34	034	27 26	073	35 31	141	43 11	177	35 37	224	58 07	315	36 48	349
93	49 07	033	28 23	073	36 08	141	43 14	177	34 56	224	57 24	314	36 36	348
94	49 38	032	29 20	073	36 45	142	43 16	178	34 14	224	56 41	313	36 24	347
95	50 09	030	30 17	072	37 22	142	43 17	179	33 32	225	55 57	312	36 10	347
96	50 39	029	31 14	072	37 58	143	43 18	180	32 50	225	55 12	311	35 56	346
97	51 07	028	32 11	072	38 34	143	43 17	181	32 08	225	54 27	310	35 41	345
98	51 35	027	33 07	072	39 10	144	43 16	182	31 25	226	53 40	309	35 25	344
99	52 01	026	34 04	071	39 45	144	43 14	182	30 42	226	52 54	308	35 09	343
100	52 26	024	35 00	071	40 19	145	43 11	183	29 59	226	52 06	307	34 51	343
101	52 50	023	35 57	071	40 53	146	43 07	184	29 16	227	51 18	306	34 33	342
102	53 13	022	36 53	070	41 27	146	43 03	185	28 32	227	50 30	305	34 15	341
103	53 35	020	37 49	070	42 00	147	42 57	186	27 48	227	49 41	304	33 55	340
104	53 55	019	38 45	070	42 32	147	42 51	187	27 05	227	48 51	304	33 35	340
	POLLUX		◆ REGULUS		Suhail		◆ CANOPUS		RIGEL		◆ ALDEBARAN		CAPELLA	
105	54 14	018	39 41	069	43 04	148	42 43	187	63 56	264	48 02	303	33 14	339
106	54 31	016	40 37	069	43 35	149	42 35	188	62 56	264	47 11	302	32 52	338
107	54 47	015	41 32	068	44 06	150	42 26	189	61 57	264	46 21	302	32 30	338
108	55 01	013	42 27	068	44 36	150	42 17	190	60 58	264	45 30	301	32 06	337
109	55 14	012	43 23	067	45 05	151	42 06	191	59 58	264	44 38	300	31 43	336
110	55 26	010	44 18	067	45 34	152	41 55	191	58 59	264	43 47	300	31 18	336
111	55 35	009	45 12	066	46 02	153	41 43	192	58 00	264	42 55	299	30 53	335
112	55 44	007	46 07	066	46 29	153	41 30	193	57 00	264	42 03	299	30 28	334
113	55 50	006	47 01	065	46 55	154	41 16	194	56 01	264	41 10	298	30 02	334
114	55 55	004	47 55	065	47 20	155	41 02	194	55 02	264	40 18	298	29 35	333
115	55 59	002	48 49	064	47 45	156	40 47	195	54 02	264	39 25	297	29 08	332
116	56 00	001	49 43	064	48 09	157	40 31	196	53 03	264	38 31	297	28 40	332
117	56 01	359	50 36	063	48 32	158	40 14	196	52 03	264	37 38	296	28 11	331
118	55 59	358	51 29	062	48 54	159	39 57	197	51 04	264	36 44	296	27 42	331
119	55 56	356	52 22	062	49 15	160	39 39	198	50 05	264	35 51	295	27 13	330
	◆ REGULUS		Gienah		◆ ACRUX		CANOPUS		RIGEL		◆ BETELGEUSE		CAPELLA	
120	53 14	061	26 25	107	15 38	154	39 21	199	49 05	264	56 17	293	26 43	330
121	54 06	060	27 23	107	16 04	155	39 01	199	48 06	264	55 22	292	26 13	329
122	54 58	059	28 20	107	16 30	155	38 41	200	47 07	264	54 27	292	25 42	329
123	55 49	058	29 17	107	16 55	155	38 21	200	46 07	264	53 31	291	25 11	328
124	56 39	058	30 14	107	17 20	155	38 00	201	45 08	264	52 36	291	24 39	328
125	57 29	057	31 11	107	17 45	155	37 38	202	44 08	264	51 40	290	24 07	327
126	58 19	056	32 08	107	18 10	155	37 15	202	43 09	264	50 43	289	23 34	327
127	59 08	055	33 05	107	18 35	156	36 53	203	42 10	264	49 47	289	23 01	326
128	59 56	053	34 02	107	18 59	156	36 29	203	41 10	264	48 51	288	22 28	326
129	60 44	052	34 59	107	19 23	156	36 05	204	40 11	264	47 54	288	21 54	325
130	61 31	051	35 56	107	19 47	156	35 40	205	39 11	264	46 57	288	21 20	325
131	62 17	050	36 53	108	20 11	157	35 15	205	38 12	264	46 00	287	20 45	324
132	63 02	048	37 50	108	20 35	157	34 50	206	37 13	264	45 03	287	20 10	324
133	63 46	047	38 47	108	20 58	157	34 24	206	36 13	264	44 06	286	19 35	324
134	64 29	045	39 43	108	21 21	157	33 57	207	35 14	264	43 09	286	18 59	323
	Dubhe		Denebola		◆ SPICA		ACRUX		◆ CANOPUS		SIRIUS		◆ POLLUX	
135	18 10	015	43 11	064	24 10	100	21 44	158	33 30	207	55 28	249	51 38	333
136	18 25	015	44 04	063	25 09	100	22 07	158	33 03	208	54 33	249	51 11	332
137	18 40	014	44 57	063	26 08	100	22 29	158	32 35	208	53 37	250	50 42	331
138	18 55	014	45 50	062	27 06	100	22 52	158	32 06	209	52 41	250	50 12	330
139	19 08	013	46 43	061	28 05	100	23 13	159	31 38	209	51 44	250	49 42	329
140	19 22	013	47 35	061	29 04	100	23 35	159	31 08	209	50 48	251	49 10	327
141	19 35	012	48 27	060	30 03	100	23 56	159	30 39	210	49 52	251	48 38	326
142	19 48	012	49 18	059	31 02	100	24 17	160	30 09	210	48 55	251	48 04	325
143	20 00	011	50 09	059	32 01	100	24 38	160	29 39	211	47 59	252	47 30	324
144	20 11	011	51 00	058	33 00	100	24 58	160	29 08	211	47 02	252	46 55	323
145	20 22	011	51 51	057	33 58	100	25 18	161	28 37	211	46 05	252	46 19	322
146	20 33	010	52 41	056	34 57	100	25 38	161	28 06	212	45 08	252	45 42	322
147	20 43	010	53 30	056	35 56	100	25 57	161	27 35	212	44 12	252	45 05	321
148	20 53	009	54 19	055	36 55	100	26 16	162	27 03	212	43 15	253	44 27	320
149	21 02	009	55 08	054	37 54	100	26 35	162	26 31	213	42 18	253	43 48	319
	Dubhe		ARCTURUS		◆ SPICA		ACRUX		◆ CANOPUS		SIRIUS		◆ POLLUX	
150	21 11	008	22 07	067	38 53	100	26 53	162	25 58	213	41 21	253	43 08	318
151	21 19	008	23 02	066	39 51	100	27 11	163	25 26	213	40 24	253	42 28	317
152	21 27	007	23 56	066	40 50	100	27 29	163	24 53	214	39 26	253	41 47	317
153	21 34	007	24 51	066	41 49	100	27 46	163	24 20	214	38 29	253	41 06	316
154	21 41	006	25 45	065	42 48	100	28 03	164	23 46	214	37 32	253	40 24	315
155	21 47	006	26 39	065	43 47	100	28 19	164	23 13	214	36 35	254	39 42	314
156	21 52	005	27 33	065	44 46	100	28 35	165	22 39	215	35 38	254	38 59	314
157	21 57	005	28 27	064	45 44	100	28 51	165	22 05	215	34 40	254	38 16	313
158	22 02	004	29 21	064	46 43	100	29 06	166	21 30	215	33 43	254	37 32	313
159	22 06	004	30 14	064	47 42	100	29 20	166	20 56	215	32 46	254	36 48	312
160	22 10	003	31 08	063	48 41	100	29 34	166	20 22	215	31 48	254	36 03	311
161	22 13	003	32 01	063	49 39	100	29 48	167	19 47	216	30 51	254	35 18	311
162	22 15	002	32 54	063	50 38	100	30 02	167	19 12	216	29 54	254	34 33	310
163	22 17	002	33 47	062	51 37	101	30 14	168	18 37	216	28 56	254	33 47	310
164	22 19	001	34 40	062	52 35	101	30 27	168	18 02	216	27 59	254	33 01	309
	Dubhe		◆ ARCTURUS		SPICA		◆ ACRUX		Suhail		SIRIUS		◆ POLLUX	
165	22 19	001	35 32	061	53 34	101	30 39	169	45 13	209	27 01	254	32 15	309
166	22 20	000	36 25	061	54 33	101	30 50	169	44 44	210	26 04	254	31 28	308
167	22 20	000	37 17	060	55 31	101	31 01	170	44 14	210	25 06	254	30 41	308
168	22 19	359	38 08	060	56 30	101	31 11	170	43 44	211	24 09	254	29 53	307
169	22 18	359	39 00	059	57 28	102	31 21	171	43 13	212	23 12	254	29 06	307
170	22 16	358	39 51	059	58 27	102	31 31	171	42 41	212	22 14	254	28 18	306
171	22 14	358	40 42	058	59 25	102	31 40	172	42 09	213	21 17	254	27 30	306
172	22 11	357	41 33	058	60 23	102	31 48	172	41 36	214	20 19	254	26 41	306
173	22 07	357	42 23	057	61 22	102	31 56	173	41 03	214	19 22	254	25 52	305
174	22 03	356	43 13	057	62 20	103	32 03	173	40 29	215	18 24	254	25 04	305
175	21 59	355	44 03	056	63 18	103	32 10	174	39 54	215	17 27	254	24 14	304
176	21 54	355	44 52	055	64 16	103	32 16	174	39 19	216	16 29	254	23 25	304
177	21 49	354	45 41	055	65 14	104	32 22	175	38 44	217	15 32	254	22 36	304
178	21 43	354	46 29	054	66 12	104	32 27	175	38 08	217	14 35	254	21 46	303
179	21 36	353	47 17	053	67 10	105	32 32	176	37 32	218	13 37	254	20 56	303

LAT 6°S

LHA ♈	Hc	Zn	Hc	Zn	Hc	Zn	Hc	Zn	Hc	Zn	Hc	Zn	Hc	Zn
	ARCTURUS		◆ANTARES		ACRUX		◆Suhail		Alphard		REGULUS		◆Dubhe	
180	48 05	052	22 43	116	32 36	176	36 56	218	52 19	263	57 09	303	21 29	353
181	48 52	052	23 36	116	32 39	177	36 18	219	51 19	264	56 18	302	21 22	353
182	49 38	051	24 30	116	32 42	177	35 41	219	50 20	264	55 28	301	21 13	352
183	50 24	050	25 23	116	32 45	178	35 03	219	49 21	264	54 36	300	21 05	352
184	51 10	049	26 17	117	32 47	178	34 25	220	48 21	264	53 45	300	20 56	351
185	51 54	048	27 10	117	32 48	179	33 47	220	47 22	264	52 53	299	20 46	351
186	52 39	047	28 03	117	32 49	180	33 08	221	46 23	264	52 00	298	20 36	350
187	53 22	046	28 56	117	32 49	180	32 29	221	45 24	264	51 07	297	20 26	350
188	54 05	045	29 49	117	32 49	181	31 49	221	44 24	264	50 14	297	20 15	349
189	54 46	044	30 43	117	32 48	181	31 10	222	43 25	264	49 21	296	20 03	349
190	55 27	043	31 36	117	32 46	182	30 30	222	42 26	264	48 27	296	19 51	348
191	56 08	042	32 28	118	32 44	182	29 50	222	41 26	264	47 33	295	19 39	348
192	56 47	040	33 21	118	32 42	183	29 09	223	40 27	264	46 39	294	19 26	347
193	57 25	039	34 14	118	32 39	183	28 29	223	39 28	264	45 44	294	19 13	347
194	58 02	038	35 07	118	32 35	184	27 48	223	38 28	264	44 50	293	18 59	346
	ARCTURUS		◆Rasalhague		ANTARES		◆ACRUX		Suhail		◆REGULUS		Dubhe	
195	58 38	036	19 04	074	35 59	119	32 31	184	27 07	224	43 55	293	18 45	346
196	59 13	035	20 01	074	36 51	119	32 26	185	26 25	224	43 00	292	18 30	346
197	59 46	033	20 59	074	37 44	119	32 20	185	25 44	224	42 04	292	18 15	345
198	60 19	032	21 56	074	38 36	119	32 15	186	25 02	224	41 09	292	18 00	345
199	60 50	030	22 53	074	39 28	120	32 08	186	24 21	225	40 13	291	17 44	344
200	61 19	029	23 51	073	40 19	120	32 01	187	23 39	225	39 18	291	17 27	344
201	61 47	027	24 48	073	41 11	120	31 54	187	22 56	225	38 22	290	17 11	344
202	62 13	025	25 45	073	42 03	121	31 46	188	22 14	225	37 26	290	16 54	343
203	62 37	023	26 42	073	42 54	121	31 37	188	21 32	225	36 30	290	16 36	343
204	63 00	021	27 39	072	43 45	121	31 28	189	20 49	226	35 33	289	16 18	342
205	63 21	019	28 36	072	44 36	122	31 19	189	20 07	226	34 37	289	16 00	342
206	63 40	017	29 32	072	45 26	122	31 09	190	19 24	226	33 41	289	15 41	342
207	63 57	015	30 29	072	46 17	123	30 58	190	18 41	226	32 44	288	15 22	341
208	64 11	013	31 26	071	47 07	123	30 47	191	17 58	226	31 47	288	15 03	341
209	64 24	011	32 22	071	47 57	124	30 35	191	17 15	226	30 50	288	14 43	341
	ARCTURUS		◆Rasalhague		ANTARES		◆RIGIL KENT		ACRUX		Gienah		◆REGULUS	
210	64 34	009	33 19	071	48 47	124	34 34	174	30 23	192	62 12	243	29 54	287
211	64 43	007	34 15	070	49 36	125	34 40	175	30 11	192	61 19	244	28 57	287
212	64 49	005	35 11	070	50 25	125	34 46	175	29 58	193	60 25	244	27 59	287
213	64 52	002	36 07	070	51 13	126	34 50	176	29 44	193	59 31	245	27 02	287
214	64 54	000	37 03	069	52 02	126	34 55	176	29 31	194	58 37	246	26 05	286
215	64 53	358	37 59	069	52 49	127	34 58	177	29 16	194	57 42	246	25 08	286
216	64 49	356	38 54	069	53 37	128	35 01	178	29 01	195	56 48	247	24 11	286
217	64 44	354	39 50	068	54 24	129	35 03	178	28 46	195	55 53	247	23 13	286
218	64 36	351	40 45	068	55 10	129	35 05	179	28 31	195	54 58	248	22 16	285
219	64 26	349	41 40	067	55 56	130	35 06	179	28 15	196	54 03	248	21 18	285
220	64 14	347	42 35	067	56 41	131	35 06	180	27 58	196	53 07	248	20 20	285
221	63 59	345	43 30	066	57 26	132	35 06	181	27 41	197	52 12	249	19 23	285
222	63 43	343	44 24	066	58 10	133	35 05	181	27 24	197	51 16	249	18 25	285
223	63 24	341	45 19	065	58 54	134	35 04	182	27 06	197	50 20	249	17 27	284
224	63 04	339	46 13	065	59 36	135	35 02	182	26 48	198	49 24	250	16 30	284
	Alphecca		◆VEGA		ALTAIR		◆Shaula		RIGIL KENT		◆SPICA		ARCTURUS	
225	56 14	014	22 43	043	15 51	079	43 02	137	34 59	183	66 11	256	62 41	337
226	56 28	013	23 24	043	16 49	079	43 42	138	34 56	183	65 14	256	62 17	335
227	56 40	011	24 04	043	17 48	079	44 22	138	34 52	184	64 16	257	61 51	333
228	56 51	010	24 44	042	18 46	078	45 02	139	34 47	185	63 18	257	61 24	332
229	57 00	008	25 24	042	19 45	078	45 41	140	34 42	185	62 19	257	60 55	330
230	57 07	006	26 04	041	20 43	078	46 19	140	34 36	186	61 21	258	60 24	328
231	57 13	005	26 43	041	21 42	078	46 57	141	34 30	186	60 23	258	59 52	327
232	57 17	003	27 21	040	22 40	078	47 34	142	34 23	187	59 25	258	59 19	325
233	57 20	001	28 00	040	23 38	078	48 11	142	34 16	188	58 26	258	58 44	324
234	57 20	000	28 38	039	24 36	077	48 47	143	34 08	188	57 28	258	58 08	322
235	57 19	358	29 15	039	25 35	077	49 23	144	33 59	189	56 29	259	57 31	321
236	57 16	356	29 52	038	26 33	077	49 57	145	33 50	189	55 31	259	56 53	320
237	57 11	355	30 29	038	27 31	077	50 31	146	33 40	190	54 32	259	56 14	319
238	57 05	353	31 05	037	28 29	076	51 04	147	33 29	190	53 33	259	55 34	317
239	56 57	352	31 40	036	29 27	076	51 37	148	33 19	191	52 35	259	54 54	316
	VEGA		◆ALTAIR		Shaula		◆RIGIL KENT		SPICA		◆ARCTURUS		Alphecca	
240	32 16	036	30 25	076	52 08	149	33 07	191	51 36	259	54 12	315	56 48	350
241	32 50	035	31 23	076	52 39	150	32 55	192	50 38	260	53 29	314	56 36	348
242	33 24	035	32 20	075	53 09	151	32 42	192	49 39	260	52 46	313	56 23	347
243	33 58	034	33 18	075	53 38	152	32 29	193	48 40	260	52 02	312	56 09	345
244	34 31	033	34 16	075	54 05	153	32 16	193	47 41	260	51 17	311	55 53	344
245	35 03	033	35 13	075	54 32	154	32 02	194	46 43	260	50 32	310	55 35	342
246	35 35	032	36 11	074	54 58	155	31 47	194	45 44	260	49 46	309	55 16	341
247	36 06	031	37 08	074	55 22	156	31 32	195	44 45	260	49 00	309	54 56	339
248	36 37	030	38 06	074	55 46	158	31 16	195	43 46	260	48 13	308	54 34	338
249	37 06	030	39 03	073	56 08	159	31 00	196	42 47	260	47 26	307	54 11	336
250	37 35	029	40 00	073	56 29	160	30 44	196	41 49	260	46 38	306	53 46	335
251	38 04	028	40 57	073	56 49	161	30 26	197	40 50	260	45 49	305	53 21	334
252	38 32	027	41 54	072	57 07	163	30 09	197	39 51	260	45 00	305	52 54	332
253	38 59	026	42 51	072	57 24	164	29 51	198	38 52	260	44 11	304	52 26	331
254	39 25	026	43 47	072	57 40	166	29 33	198	37 53	260	43 22	303	51 56	330
	VEGA		◆ALTAIR		Peacock		◆RIGIL KENT		SPICA		◆ARCTURUS		Alphecca	
255	39 50	025	44 44	071	25 12	152	29 14	199	36 55	260	42 32	303	51 26	329
256	40 15	024	45 40	071	25 41	152	28 55	199	35 56	260	41 41	302	50 55	328
257	40 38	023	46 37	070	26 09	152	28 35	199	34 57	260	40 51	302	50 22	327
258	41 01	022	47 33	070	26 36	153	28 15	200	33 58	260	40 00	301	49 49	325
259	41 23	021	48 28	069	27 04	153	27 55	200	32 59	260	39 09	301	49 14	324
260	41 44	020	49 24	069	27 31	153	27 34	201	32 00	260	38 17	300	48 39	323
261	42 05	019	50 20	068	27 57	154	27 13	201	31 01	260	37 26	300	48 03	322
262	42 24	018	51 15	068	28 24	154	26 51	201	30 03	260	36 34	299	47 26	321
263	42 42	017	52 10	067	28 50	154	26 29	202	29 04	260	35 41	299	46 49	320
264	43 00	016	53 05	066	29 15	155	26 07	202	28 05	260	34 49	298	46 10	320
265	43 16	015	54 00	066	29 41	155	25 45	202	27 06	260	33 56	298	45 31	319
266	43 31	014	54 54	065	30 06	156	25 22	203	26 07	260	33 03	297	44 52	318
267	43 46	013	55 48	064	30 30	156	24 58	203	25 08	260	32 10	297	44 11	317
268	43 59	012	56 42	064	30 54	156	24 35	203	24 10	260	31 17	297	43 30	316
269	44 11	011	57 35	063	31 18	157	24 11	204	23 11	260	30 24	296	42 49	315

LHA ♈	Hc	Zn	Hc	Zn	Hc	Zn	Hc	Zn	Hc	Zn	Hc	Zn	Hc	Zn
	◆VEGA		DENEB		Enif		◆FOMALHAUT		Peacock		◆ANTARES		ARCTURUS	
270	44 22	010	27 13	031	31 46	074	16 19	119	31 41	157	60 25	224	29 30	296
271	44 32	009	27 43	030	32 43	074	17 11	119	32 04	158	59 43	225	28 36	296
272	44 41	008	28 13	030	33 41	074	18 04	119	32 26	158	59 01	226	27 43	295
273	44 49	007	28 43	029	34 38	074	18 56	119	32 48	159	58 17	227	26 48	295
274	44 56	006	29 12	029	35 35	073	19 48	119	33 10	159	57 33	228	25 54	295
275	45 01	005	29 40	028	36 32	073	20 40	119	33 30	160	56 49	229	25 00	294
276	45 06	004	30 08	027	37 29	073	21 32	119	33 51	160	56 04	230	24 06	294
277	45 09	003	30 35	027	38 26	072	22 24	120	34 11	161	55 18	231	23 11	294
278	45 11	002	31 01	026	39 23	072	23 16	120	34 30	161	54 31	231	22 16	293
279	45 12	000	31 27	025	40 20	072	24 07	120	34 49	162	53 45	232	21 22	293
280	45 12	359	31 53	025	41 16	071	24 59	120	35 07	162	52 57	233	20 27	293
281	45 11	358	32 17	024	42 12	071	25 51	120	35 25	163	52 09	233	19 32	293
282	45 08	357	32 42	023	43 09	070	26 43	120	35 42	164	51 21	234	18 37	292
283	45 04	356	33 05	023	44 05	070	27 34	120	35 59	164	50 33	235	17 41	292
284	45 00	355	33 28	022	45 01	069	28 26	120	36 15	165	49 44	235	16 46	292
	DENEB		Enif		◆FOMALHAUT		Peacock		◆ANTARES		Rasalhague		◆VEGA	
285	33 50	021	45 57	069	29 17	121	36 30	165	48 55	236	62 00	312	44 54	354
286	34 11	021	46 52	069	30 08	121	36 45	166	48 05	236	61 15	310	44 47	353
287	34 32	020	47 48	068	30 59	121	36 59	167	47 15	237	60 29	309	44 39	352
288	34 52	019	48 43	067	31 51	121	37 13	167	46 25	237	59 43	308	44 29	351
289	35 11	018	49 38	067	32 42	121	37 25	168	45 35	238	58 55	307	44 19	349
290	35 29	018	50 33	066	33 32	122	37 38	169	44 44	238	58 07	306	44 08	348
291	35 47	017	51 27	066	34 23	122	37 49	169	43 53	239	57 18	305	43 55	347
292	36 04	016	52 21	065	35 14	122	38 00	170	43 02	239	56 29	304	43 42	346
293	36 20	015	53 15	064	36 04	122	38 10	170	42 11	239	55 39	303	43 27	345
294	36 35	014	54 09	064	36 54	123	38 20	171	41 20	240	54 48	302	43 11	344
295	36 50	014	55 03	063	37 44	123	38 29	172	40 28	240	53 57	301	42 55	343
296	37 03	013	55 56	062	38 34	123	38 37	172	39 36	240	53 06	300	42 37	342
297	37 16	012	56 48	061	39 24	124	38 44	173	38 44	241	52 14	300	42 19	341
298	37 28	011	57 40	061	40 14	124	38 51	174	37 52	241	51 22	299	41 59	340
299	37 39	010	58 32	060	41 03	124	38 57	175	37 00	241	50 30	298	41 39	339
	◆DENEB		Alpheratz		◆FOMALHAUT		Peacock		◆ANTARES		Rasalhague		VEGA	
300	37 49	009	20 40	056	41 52	125	39 02	175	36 08	241	49 37	297	41 17	339
301	37 58	008	21 29	055	42 41	125	39 07	176	35 15	242	48 44	297	40 55	338
302	38 06	008	22 18	055	43 29	126	39 11	177	34 23	242	47 50	296	40 32	337
303	38 14	007	23 07	055	44 18	126	39 14	177	33 30	242	46 57	296	40 08	336
304	38 20	006	23 55	054	45 06	127	39 16	178	32 37	242	46 03	295	39 43	335
305	38 26	005	24 44	054	45 53	127	39 18	179	31 44	242	45 09	295	39 18	334
306	38 31	004	25 32	054	46 41	128	39 19	179	30 51	243	44 14	294	38 51	333
307	38 34	003	26 20	053	47 28	128	39 19	180	29 58	243	43 20	294	38 24	333
308	38 37	002	27 07	053	48 15	129	39 18	181	29 05	243	42 25	293	37 56	332
309	38 39	001	27 55	052	49 01	129	39 17	182	28 12	243	41 30	293	37 27	331
310	38 40	000	28 42	052	49 47	130	39 15	182	27 19	243	40 35	292	36 58	330
311	38 40	000	29 29	052	50 32	131	39 12	183	26 25	243	39 39	292	36 28	329
312	38 39	359	30 15	051	51 17	131	39 09	184	25 32	243	38 44	291	35 58	329
313	38 37	358	31 01	051	52 02	132	39 04	184	24 39	244	37 48	291	35 26	328
314	38 34	357	31 47	050	52 46	133	38 59	185	23 45	244	36 53	291	34 54	327
	Alpheratz		◆Diphda		ACHERNAR		Peacock		◆Nunki		VEGA		◆DENEB	
315	32 33	050	34 04	108	16 02	148	38 54	186	54 12	232	34 22	327	38 30	356
316	33 18	049	35 01	108	16 33	148	38 47	187	53 25	233	33 49	326	38 26	355
317	34 03	049	35 58	108	17 04	148	38 40	187	52 37	233	33 15	325	38 20	354
318	34 48	048	36 55	108	17 36	149	38 32	188	51 49	234	32 41	325	38 14	353
319	35 32	047	37 51	108	18 07	149	38 24	189	51 00	235	32 06	324	38 06	352
320	36 15	047	38 48	108	18 38	149	38 14	189	50 11	235	31 31	323	37 58	352
321	36 59	046	39 45	108	19 08	149	38 04	190	49 22	236	30 55	323	37 49	351
322	37 41	046	40 41	108	19 39	149	37 54	191	48 33	236	30 19	322	37 38	350
323	38 24	045	41 38	109	20 09	149	37 42	191	47 43	237	29 42	322	37 27	349
324	39 06	044	42 34	109	20 40	150	37 31	192	46 53	237	29 05	321	37 16	348
325	39 47	044	43 31	109	21 10	150	37 18	193	46 02	238	28 27	321	37 03	347
326	40 28	043	44 27	109	21 39	150	37 05	193	45 12	238	27 49	320	36 49	346
327	41 08	042	45 23	109	22 09	150	36 51	194	44 21	239	27 11	320	36 35	346
328	41 48	041	46 20	110	22 38	151	36 36	194	43 30	239	26 32	319	36 19	345
329	42 27	041	47 16	110	23 08	151	36 21	195	42 38	239	25 53	319	36 03	344
	◆Alpheratz		Diphda		◆ACHERNAR		Peacock		Nunki		◆ALTAIR		DENEB	
330	43 05	040	48 12	110	23 37	151	36 05	196	41 47	240	54 41	295	35 47	343
331	43 43	039	49 08	111	24 05	151	35 49	196	40 55	240	53 46	294	35 29	342
332	44 20	038	50 04	111	24 34	152	35 32	197	40 03	240	52 52	293	35 10	342
333	44 57	037	50 59	111	25 02	152	35 15	197	39 11	241	51 57	293	34 51	341
334	45 32	036	51 55	112	25 29	152	34 57	198	38 19	241	51 02	292	34 31	340
335	46 07	035	52 50	112	25 57	153	34 38	198	37 27	241	50 06	292	34 11	339
336	46 41	034	53 46	112	26 24	153	34 19	199	36 35	242	49 11	291	33 49	339
337	47 14	033	54 41	113	26 51	153	33 59	200	35 42	242	48 15	291	33 27	338
338	47 47	032	55 36	113	27 18	154	33 39	200	34 49	242	47 19	290	33 04	337
339	48 18	031	56 30	114	27 44	154	33 18	201	33 57	242	46 23	290	32 41	337
340	48 49	030	57 25	114	28 10	154	32 57	201	33 04	242	45 27	289	32 17	336
341	49 18	029	58 19	115	28 36	155	32 35	202	32 11	243	44 30	289	31 52	335
342	49 47	028	59 13	115	29 01	155	32 13	202	31 18	243	43 34	288	31 27	334
343	50 14	027	60 07	116	29 26	156	31 51	203	30 25	243	42 37	288	31 01	334
344	50 40	026	61 01	117	29 50	156	31 28	203	29 32	243	41 40	288	30 34	333
	Alpheratz		◆Hamal		◆ACHERNAR		Peacock		Nunki		◆ALTAIR		DENEB	
345	51 06	024	35 27	055	30 14	156	31 04	203	28 38	243	40 43	287	30 07	333
346	51 30	023	36 16	055	30 38	157	30 40	204	27 45	243	39 46	287	29 39	332
347	51 53	022	37 05	054	31 01	157	30 16	204	26 52	244	38 49	287	29 11	331
348	52 14	021	37 53	054	31 24	158	29 51	205	25 58	244	37 52	286	28 42	331
349	52 35	019	38 41	053	31 46	158	29 26	205	25 05	244	36 54	286	28 13	330
350	52 54	018	39 29	053	32 08	159	29 00	206	24 11	244	35 57	286	27 43	330
351	53 11	017	40 16	052	32 30	159	28 35	206	23 17	244	34 59	285	27 12	329
352	53 28	015	41 03	051	32 51	160	28 08	206	22 24	244	34 02	285	26 41	329
353	53 43	014	41 49	051	33 11	160	27 41	207	21 30	244	33 04	285	26 10	328
354	53 56	012	42 35	050	33 31	161	27 15	207	20 37	244	32 06	284	25 38	328
355	54 08	011	43 21	049	33 51	161	26 48	207	19 43	244	31 09	284	25 06	327
356	54 19	009	44 06	049	34 09	162	26 20	208	18 49	244	30 11	284	24 33	327
357	54 28	008	44 50	048	34 28	162	25 52	208	17 55	244	29 13	284	24 00	326
358	54 35	006	45 34	047	34 46	163	25 24	208	17 02	244	28 15	283	23 27	326
359	54 41	005	46 18	046	35 03	163	24 55	209	16 08	244	27 17	283	22 53	325

LAT 7°S

LHA ♈	Hc Zn	Hc Zn	Hc Zn	Hc Zn	Hc Zn	Hc Zn	Hc Zn
	◆ Alpheratz	ALDEBARAN	◆ RIGEL	ACHERNAR	◆ FOMALHAUT	ALTAIR	DENEB
0	53 46 003	17 39 070	12 00 097	36 18 164	63 13 211	26 05 284	21 29 325
1	53 48 002	18 35 070	12 59 097	36 34 164	62 41 212	25 07 283	20 55 324
2	53 50 000	19 31 070	13 58 097	36 50 165	62 09 214	24 09 283	20 20 324
3	53 49 359	20 27 069	14 57 097	37 05 166	61 35 215	23 11 283	19 45 324
4	53 47 357	21 23 069	15 57 097	37 19 166	61 00 217	22 13 283	19 10 323
5	53 44 356	22 18 069	16 56 096	37 33 167	60 24 218	21 15 282	18 34 323
6	53 39 355	23 14 069	17 55 096	37 47 167	59 47 219	20 17 282	17 58 322
7	53 33 353	24 09 068	18 54 096	37 59 168	59 09 220	19 18 282	17 21 322
8	53 25 352	25 04 068	19 53 096	38 11 169	58 30 221	18 20 282	16 45 322
9	53 15 350	25 59 068	20 53 096	38 23 169	57 51 222	17 22 282	16 08 321
10	53 04 349	26 55 067	21 52 096	38 34 170	57 10 223	16 23 281	15 30 321
11	52 52 347	27 49 067	22 51 096	38 44 171	56 29 224	15 25 281	14 53 321
12	52 38 346	28 44 067	23 50 096	38 53 171	55 47 225	14 27 281	14 15 320
13	52 23 345	29 39 066	24 49 096	39 02 172	55 04 226	13 28 281	13 37 320
14	52 07 343	30 33 066	25 49 096	39 10 173	54 21 227	12 30 281	12 58 320
	Hamal	ALDEBARAN	◆ RIGEL	ACHERNAR	◆ FOMALHAUT	Enif	◆ Alpheratz
15	55 14 028	31 28 066	26 48 096	39 17 173	53 37 228	38 33 289	51 49 342
16	55 42 027	32 22 065	27 47 096	39 24 174	52 52 229	37 37 288	51 30 341
17	56 08 025	33 16 065	28 47 096	39 29 175	52 07 229	36 40 288	51 09 339
18	56 32 024	34 10 065	29 46 095	39 35 175	51 22 230	35 44 288	50 48 338
19	56 56 022	35 04 064	30 45 095	39 39 176	50 36 231	34 47 287	50 25 337
20	57 18 021	35 57 064	31 44 095	39 43 177	49 50 231	33 50 287	50 01 336
21	57 38 019	36 50 063	32 44 095	39 46 177	49 03 232	32 53 287	49 36 334
22	57 56 017	37 43 063	33 43 095	39 48 178	48 16 233	31 56 286	49 09 333
23	58 13 016	38 36 062	34 42 095	39 49 179	47 29 233	30 59 286	48 42 332
24	58 29 014	39 29 062	35 42 095	39 50 180	46 41 234	30 01 286	48 14 331
25	58 43 012	40 21 061	36 41 095	39 50 180	45 53 234	29 04 286	47 44 330
26	58 55 011	41 13 061	37 40 095	39 50 181	45 04 235	28 07 285	47 14 329
27	59 05 009	42 05 060	38 40 095	39 48 182	44 16 235	27 09 285	46 43 328
28	59 13 007	42 57 060	39 39 095	39 46 182	43 27 235	26 12 285	46 10 327
29	59 20 005	43 48 059	40 38 095	39 43 183	42 38 236	25 14 284	45 37 326
	CAPELLA	◆ BETELGEUSE	SIRIUS	CANOPUS	◆ ACHERNAR	FOMALHAUT	◆ Alpheratz
30	21 08 034	29 25 077	19 43 105	19 56 144	39 40 184	41 48 236	45 04 325
31	21 41 034	30 24 077	20 41 105	20 31 144	39 35 185	40 59 237	44 29 324
32	22 14 034	31 22 077	21 38 105	21 06 144	39 30 185	40 09 237	43 54 323
33	22 47 033	32 20 077	22 36 105	21 40 144	39 24 186	39 19 237	43 18 322
34	23 19 033	33 17 076	23 33 105	22 15 145	39 18 187	38 29 238	42 41 321
35	23 51 032	34 15 076	24 31 105	22 49 145	39 11 187	37 39 238	42 03 321
36	24 23 032	35 13 076	25 28 105	23 23 145	39 03 188	36 48 238	41 25 320
37	24 54 031	36 11 075	26 25 105	23 57 145	38 54 189	35 57 238	40 46 319
38	25 24 031	37 08 075	27 23 105	24 31 146	38 45 189	35 07 239	40 07 318
39	25 54 030	38 06 075	28 20 105	25 05 146	38 35 190	34 16 239	39 27 317
40	26 24 030	39 03 075	29 18 105	25 38 146	38 24 191	33 25 239	38 46 317
41	26 53 029	40 01 074	30 15 105	26 11 146	38 13 191	32 34 239	38 05 316
42	27 22 028	40 58 074	31 13 105	26 44 147	38 01 192	31 42 239	37 24 315
43	27 50 028	41 55 073	32 10 105	27 17 147	37 48 193	30 51 240	36 42 315
44	28 17 027	42 52 073	33 07 105	27 49 147	37 35 193	30 00 240	35 59 314
	CAPELLA	◆ BETELGEUSE	SIRIUS	CANOPUS	◆ ACHERNAR	FOMALHAUT	◆ Alpheratz
45	28 44 027	43 49 073	34 05 106	28 21 148	37 21 194	29 08 240	35 16 314
46	29 10 026	44 46 072	35 02 106	28 53 148	37 07 194	28 16 240	34 33 313
47	29 36 025	45 42 072	36 00 106	29 24 148	36 52 195	27 25 240	33 49 312
48	30 02 025	46 39 071	36 57 106	29 55 149	36 36 196	26 33 240	33 05 312
49	30 26 024	47 35 071	37 54 106	30 26 149	36 20 196	25 41 241	32 20 311
50	30 50 023	48 31 070	38 52 106	30 57 149	36 03 197	24 49 241	31 35 311
51	31 14 023	49 28 070	39 49 106	31 27 150	35 45 197	23 57 241	30 50 310
52	31 36 022	50 23 069	40 46 106	31 56 150	35 28 198	23 05 241	30 04 310
53	31 58 021	51 19 069	41 43 106	32 26 151	35 09 198	22 13 241	29 18 309
54	32 20 021	52 14 068	42 40 106	32 55 151	34 50 199	21 21 241	28 32 309
55	32 40 020	53 10 068	43 38 106	33 23 152	34 30 199	20 29 241	27 45 308
56	33 00 019	54 05 067	44 35 107	33 52 152	34 10 200	19 37 241	26 58 308
57	33 20 019	54 59 066	45 32 107	34 19 152	33 50 200	18 45 241	26 11 307
58	33 38 018	55 54 066	46 29 107	34 47 153	33 29 201	17 53 241	25 24 307
59	33 56 017	56 48 065	47 26 107	35 14 153	33 07 201	17 01 241	24 36 307
	◆ CAPELLA	POLLUX	◆ SIRIUS	CANOPUS	ACHERNAR	◆ Diphda	Hamal
60	34 13 016	25 12 055	48 22 107	35 40 154	32 45 202	41 10 252	49 01 319
61	34 29 015	26 01 054	49 19 108	36 06 154	32 22 202	40 13 252	48 21 318
62	34 45 015	26 49 054	50 16 108	36 31 155	31 59 203	39 16 253	47 41 317
63	34 59 014	27 37 053	51 13 108	36 56 156	31 36 203	38 19 253	47 00 316
64	35 13 013	28 24 053	52 09 108	37 21 156	31 12 204	37 22 253	46 19 315
65	35 26 012	29 11 052	53 06 109	37 44 157	30 48 204	36 25 253	45 37 314
66	35 39 011	29 58 052	54 02 109	38 08 157	30 24 205	35 29 253	44 54 314
67	35 50 011	30 45 051	54 58 109	38 30 158	29 59 205	34 32 253	44 10 313
68	36 01 010	31 32 051	55 54 110	38 52 159	29 33 205	33 35 253	43 26 312
69	36 10 009	32 18 050	56 50 110	39 14 159	29 08 206	32 38 253	42 42 311
70	36 19 008	33 03 050	57 46 110	39 35 160	28 42 206	31 41 253	41 57 311
71	36 27 007	33 49 049	58 42 111	39 55 160	28 15 206	30 44 253	41 12 310
72	36 34 006	34 34 049	59 38 111	40 15 161	27 48 207	29 46 253	40 26 309
73	36 41 006	35 18 048	60 33 112	40 34 162	27 21 207	28 49 253	39 39 309
74	36 46 005	36 03 048	61 28 112	40 52 162	26 54 208	27 52 253	38 53 308
	CAPELLA	POLLUX	◆ REGULUS	CANOPUS	◆ ACHERNAR	Diphda	◆ Hamal
75	36 50 004	36 46 047	10 52 076	41 10 163	26 26 208	26 55 253	38 06 307
76	36 54 003	37 30 046	11 50 076	41 26 164	25 58 208	25 58 253	37 18 307
77	36 57 002	38 13 046	12 48 076	41 43 165	25 30 208	25 01 253	36 30 306
78	36 58 001	38 55 045	13 45 076	41 58 165	25 02 209	24 04 253	35 42 306
79	36 59 000	39 37 044	14 43 076	42 13 166	24 33 209	23 07 253	34 53 305
80	36 59 000	40 18 044	15 41 076	42 27 167	24 04 209	22 10 253	34 05 305
81	36 58 359	40 59 043	16 39 075	42 40 168	23 35 210	21 13 253	33 16 304
82	36 56 358	41 39 042	17 36 075	42 52 168	23 05 210	20 16 253	32 26 304
83	36 54 357	42 19 041	18 34 075	43 04 169	22 36 210	19 19 253	31 36 303
84	36 50 356	42 58 040	19 31 075	43 14 170	22 06 210	18 21 253	30 46 303
85	36 45 355	43 36 040	20 29 074	43 24 171	21 35 210	17 24 253	29 56 302
86	36 40 354	44 14 039	21 26 074	43 34 172	21 05 211	16 27 253	29 06 302
87	36 34 353	44 51 038	22 23 074	43 42 172	20 35 211	15 30 253	28 15 302
88	36 26 353	45 27 037	23 20 074	43 49 173	20 04 211	14 33 253	27 24 301
89	36 18 352	46 02 036	24 18 074	43 56 174	19 33 211	13 36 253	26 33 301

LHA ♈	Hc Zn	Hc Zn	Hc Zn	Hc Zn	Hc Zn	Hc Zn	Hc Zn
	POLLUX	◆ REGULUS	Suhail	◆ CANOPUS	Acamar	◆ ALDEBARAN	CAPELLA
90	46 37 035	25 15 073	35 00 140	44 02 175	37 43 223	58 44 319	36 09 351
91	47 11 034	26 12 073	35 39 140	44 06 176	37 02 224	58 04 318	36 00 350
92	47 44 033	27 09 073	36 17 140	44 10 177	36 20 224	57 24 316	35 49 349
93	48 16 032	28 05 072	36 55 141	44 14 177	35 39 225	56 42 315	35 37 348
94	48 47 031	29 02 072	37 32 141	44 16 178	34 57 225	56 00 314	35 25 348
95	49 17 030	29 59 072	38 09 142	44 17 179	34 15 225	55 17 313	35 12 347
96	49 46 029	30 55 072	38 46 142	44 18 180	33 32 226	54 33 312	34 58 346
97	50 14 028	31 52 071	39 22 143	44 17 181	32 50 226	53 48 311	34 43 345
98	50 41 026	32 48 071	39 58 143	44 16 182	32 07 226	53 02 310	34 28 344
99	51 07 025	33 44 071	40 33 144	44 14 182	31 24 227	52 16 309	34 11 344
100	51 32 024	34 41 070	41 08 144	44 11 183	30 40 227	51 30 308	33 54 343
101	51 55 023	35 37 070	41 43 145	44 07 184	29 57 227	50 42 307	33 36 342
102	52 17 021	36 32 070	42 17 146	44 02 185	29 13 227	49 55 306	33 18 341
103	52 38 020	37 28 069	42 50 146	43 57 186	28 29 228	49 06 305	32 58 341
104	52 58 019	38 24 069	43 23 147	43 50 187	27 45 228	48 18 305	32 38 340
	POLLUX	◆ REGULUS	Suhail	◆ CANOPUS	RIGEL	◆ ALDEBARAN	CAPELLA
105	53 16 017	39 19 068	43 55 148	43 43 187	64 01 266	47 28 304	32 18 339
106	53 33 016	40 14 068	44 27 148	43 35 188	63 02 266	46 39 303	31 56 339
107	53 49 014	41 09 067	44 57 149	43 26 189	62 03 266	45 49 303	31 34 338
108	54 03 013	42 04 067	45 28 150	43 16 190	61 03 266	44 58 302	31 11 337
109	54 15 011	42 59 067	45 57 151	43 05 191	60 04 266	44 08 301	30 48 337
110	54 27 010	43 54 066	46 26 151	42 54 191	59 04 266	43 17 301	30 24 336
111	54 36 008	44 48 066	46 55 152	42 42 192	58 05 266	42 25 300	29 59 335
112	54 44 007	45 42 065	47 22 153	42 29 193	57 06 266	41 34 299	29 34 335
113	54 51 005	46 36 064	47 49 154	42 15 194	56 06 266	40 42 299	29 08 334
114	54 55 004	47 29 064	48 15 155	42 00 195	55 07 266	39 49 298	28 41 333
115	54 59 002	48 23 063	48 40 156	41 45 195	54 07 266	38 57 298	28 14 333
116	55 00 001	49 16 063	49 04 156	41 29 196	53 08 266	38 04 297	27 47 332
117	55 01 359	50 08 062	49 27 157	41 12 197	52 09 266	37 11 297	27 19 332
118	54 59 358	51 01 061	49 50 158	40 54 197	51 09 266	36 18 296	26 50 331
119	54 56 356	51 53 060	50 11 159	40 36 198	50 10 266	35 24 296	26 21 330
	◆ REGULUS	Gienah	◆ ACRUX	CANOPUS	RIGEL	◆ BETELGEUSE	CAPELLA
120	52 44 060	26 42 106	16 33 154	40 17 199	49 11 266	55 53 294	25 51 330
121	53 36 059	27 40 106	16 58 155	39 58 199	48 11 266	54 59 294	25 21 329
122	54 26 058	28 37 106	17 24 155	39 38 200	47 12 265	54 04 293	24 51 329
123	55 17 057	29 34 106	17 49 155	39 17 201	46 12 265	53 09 292	24 20 328
124	56 07 056	30 31 106	18 14 155	38 56 201	45 13 265	52 14 292	23 48 328
125	56 56 055	31 28 106	18 40 155	38 34 202	44 14 265	51 19 291	23 16 327
126	57 44 054	32 25 106	19 04 155	38 11 203	43 14 265	50 23 291	22 44 327
127	58 32 053	33 22 107	19 29 156	37 48 203	42 15 265	49 27 290	22 11 326
128	59 20 052	34 19 107	19 54 156	37 24 204	41 16 265	48 31 290	21 38 326
129	60 06 051	35 17 107	20 18 156	37 00 204	40 16 265	47 35 289	21 04 326
130	60 52 050	36 14 107	20 42 156	36 35 205	39 17 265	46 38 289	20 30 325
131	61 37 048	37 11 107	21 06 156	36 10 205	38 18 265	45 42 288	19 56 325
132	62 21 047	38 08 107	21 30 157	35 44 206	37 18 265	44 45 288	19 22 324
133	63 04 046	39 05 107	21 53 157	35 17 206	36 19 265	43 49 287	18 47 324
134	63 46 044	40 01 107	22 17 157	34 51 207	35 20 265	42 52 287	18 11 323
	Dubhe	Denebola	◆ SPICA	ACRUX	◆ CANOPUS	SIRIUS	◆ POLLUX
135	17 12 015	42 44 063	24 20 099	22 40 157	34 23 207	55 49 250	50 44 334
136	17 27 014	43 37 062	25 19 099	23 03 158	33 56 208	54 53 251	50 17 333
137	17 42 014	44 29 062	26 17 099	23 25 158	33 28 208	53 57 251	49 49 331
138	17 56 014	45 21 061	27 16 099	23 47 158	32 59 209	53 00 251	49 20 330
139	18 10 013	46 13 060	28 15 099	24 09 158	32 30 209	52 04 252	48 50 329
140	18 23 013	47 05 060	29 14 099	24 31 159	32 01 210	51 07 252	48 19 328
141	18 36 012	47 56 059	30 13 099	24 52 159	31 31 210	50 11 252	47 48 327
142	18 49 012	48 47 058	31 11 099	25 13 159	31 01 211	49 14 252	47 15 326
143	19 01 011	49 38 058	32 10 099	25 34 160	30 30 211	48 17 253	46 41 325
144	19 12 011	50 28 057	33 09 099	25 55 160	30 00 211	47 20 253	46 06 324
145	19 23 010	51 18 056	34 08 099	26 15 160	29 29 212	46 23 253	45 31 323
146	19 34 010	52 07 055	35 07 099	26 35 161	28 57 212	45 26 253	44 55 322
147	19 44 010	52 56 055	36 06 099	26 54 161	28 26 212	44 29 253	44 18 321
148	19 54 009	53 44 054	37 05 099	27 13 161	27 54 213	43 32 254	43 41 320
149	20 03 009	54 32 053	38 03 099	27 32 162	27 21 213	42 35 254	43 02 320
	Dubhe	ARCTURUS	◆ SPICA	ACRUX	◆ CANOPUS	SIRIUS	◆ POLLUX
150	20 11 008	21 43 066	39 02 099	27 51 162	26 49 213	41 38 254	42 23 319
151	20 20 008	22 37 066	40 01 099	28 09 163	26 16 214	40 41 254	41 44 318
152	20 27 007	23 32 066	41 00 099	28 26 163	25 43 214	39 43 254	41 04 317
153	20 34 007	24 26 065	41 59 099	28 43 163	25 10 214	38 46 254	40 23 316
154	20 41 006	25 20 065	42 58 099	29 00 164	24 36 214	37 49 254	39 42 316
155	20 47 006	26 14 065	43 56 099	29 17 164	24 02 215	36 51 254	39 00 315
156	20 53 005	27 07 064	44 55 099	29 33 165	23 28 215	35 54 254	38 18 314
157	20 58 005	28 01 064	45 54 099	29 49 165	22 54 215	34 57 254	37 35 314
158	21 02 004	28 54 064	46 53 099	30 04 165	22 20 215	33 59 255	36 51 313
159	21 06 004	29 48 063	47 52 099	30 18 166	21 45 216	33 02 255	36 08 312
160	21 10 003	30 41 063	48 51 099	30 33 166	21 11 216	32 05 255	35 24 312
161	21 13 003	31 34 062	49 49 099	30 47 167	20 36 216	31 07 255	34 39 311
162	21 15 002	32 26 062	50 48 099	31 00 167	20 01 216	30 10 255	33 54 311
163	21 17 002	33 19 062	51 47 099	31 13 168	19 26 216	29 12 255	33 09 310
164	21 19 001	34 11 061	52 46 099	31 25 168	18 50 216	28 15 255	32 23 310
	Dubhe	◆ ARCTURUS	SPICA	◆ ACRUX	Suhail	SIRIUS	◆ POLLUX
165	21 19 001	35 03 061	53 44 099	31 37 169	46 05 209	27 17 255	31 37 309
166	21 20 000	35 55 060	54 43 100	31 49 169	45 36 210	26 20 255	30 51 309
167	21 20 000	36 47 060	55 42 100	32 00 170	45 06 211	25 23 255	30 04 308
168	21 19 359	37 38 059	56 41 100	32 11 170	44 35 212	24 25 255	29 17 308
169	21 18 359	38 29 059	57 39 100	32 21 171	44 04 212	23 28 255	28 30 307
170	21 16 358	39 20 058	58 38 100	32 30 171	43 32 213	22 30 255	27 42 307
171	21 14 358	40 10 058	59 37 100	32 39 172	42 59 214	21 33 255	26 54 306
172	21 11 357	41 00 057	60 35 100	32 47 172	42 26 214	20 35 255	26 06 306
173	21 07 357	41 50 056	61 34 101	32 55 173	41 52 215	19 38 255	25 18 305
174	21 04 356	42 40 056	62 32 101	33 03 173	41 18 215	18 40 255	24 29 305
175	20 59 356	43 29 055	63 31 101	33 10 174	40 43 216	17 43 255	23 40 305
176	20 54 355	44 17 055	64 29 101	33 16 174	40 08 217	16 46 255	22 51 304
177	20 49 355	45 06 054	65 27 102	33 22 175	39 32 217	15 48 255	22 02 304
178	20 43 354	45 54 053	66 26 102	33 27 175	38 56 217	14 51 254	21 13 304
179	20 36 354	46 41 052	67 24 102	33 32 176	38 20 218	13 53 254	20 23 303

 LAT 7°S

LHA ♈	Hc	Zn	Hc	Zn	Hc	Zn	Hc	Zn	Hc	Zn	Hc	Zn	Hc	Zn
	ARCTURUS		◆ANTARES		ACRUX		◆Suhail		Alphard		REGULUS		◆Dubhe	
180	47 28	052	23 09	116	33 36	176	37 43	219	52 25	265	56 35	304	20 29	353
181	48 14	051	24 03	116	33 39	177	37 05	219	51 25	265	55 46	303	20 22	353
182	49 00	050	24 56	116	33 42	177	36 28	220	50 26	265	54 56	302	20 14	352
183	49 45	049	25 50	116	33 45	178	35 49	220	49 27	265	54 05	302	20 06	352
184	50 30	048	26 43	116	33 47	178	35 11	220	48 28	265	53 14	301	19 57	351
185	51 14	047	27 37	116	33 48	179	34 32	221	47 28	265	52 23	300	19 47	351
186	51 57	046	28 30	116	33 49	180	33 53	221	46 29	265	51 31	299	19 37	350
187	52 40	045	29 23	116	33 49	180	33 14	222	45 30	265	50 39	299	19 27	350
188	53 22	044	30 17	117	33 49	181	32 34	222	44 30	265	49 47	298	19 16	349
189	54 03	043	31 10	117	33 48	181	31 54	222	43 31	265	48 54	297	19 05	349
190	54 43	042	32 03	117	33 46	182	31 14	223	42 32	265	48 01	297	18 53	348
191	55 22	041	32 56	117	33 44	182	30 34	223	41 33	265	47 07	296	18 40	348
192	56 01	039	33 49	117	33 42	183	29 53	223	40 33	264	46 14	295	18 28	347
193	56 38	038	34 42	117	33 38	183	29 12	223	39 34	264	45 20	295	18 14	347
194	57 14	037	35 35	118	33 35	184	28 31	224	38 35	264	44 25	294	18 01	347
	ARCTURUS		◆Rasalhague		ANTARES		◆ACRUX		Suhail		◆REGULUS		Dubhe	
195	57 50	035	18 48	074	36 27	118	33 30	184	27 50	224	43 31	294	17 47	346
196	58 23	034	19 45	074	37 20	118	33 26	185	27 09	224	42 36	293	17 32	346
197	58 56	033	20 42	074	38 12	118	33 20	185	26 27	224	41 42	293	17 17	345
198	59 28	031	21 39	073	39 05	119	33 14	186	25 45	225	40 47	292	17 02	345
199	59 58	029	22 36	073	39 57	119	33 08	187	25 03	225	39 51	292	16 46	344
200	60 26	028	23 33	073	40 49	119	33 01	187	24 21	225	38 56	291	16 30	344
201	60 53	026	24 30	073	41 41	119	32 53	188	23 39	225	38 01	291	16 13	344
202	61 18	024	25 27	072	42 33	120	32 45	188	22 56	225	37 05	291	15 56	343
203	61 42	023	26 24	072	43 24	120	32 37	189	22 14	226	36 09	290	15 39	343
204	62 04	021	27 20	072	44 16	120	32 27	189	21 31	226	35 13	290	15 21	342
205	62 24	019	28 17	072	45 07	121	32 18	190	20 48	226	34 17	290	15 03	342
206	62 42	017	29 14	071	45 58	121	32 08	190	20 06	226	33 21	289	14 44	342
207	62 59	015	30 10	071	46 49	122	31 57	191	19 23	226	32 25	289	14 25	341
208	63 13	013	31 06	071	47 39	122	31 46	191	18 40	226	31 28	289	14 06	341
209	63 25	011	32 02	070	48 30	123	31 34	192	17 56	226	30 32	288	13 46	341
	ARCTURUS		◆Rasalhague		ANTARES		◆RIGIL KENT		ACRUX		Gienah		◆REGULUS	
210	63 35	009	32 58	070	49 20	123	35 34	174	31 22	192	62 39	245	29 35	288
211	63 43	007	33 54	070	50 09	124	35 40	175	31 09	192	61 45	245	28 39	288
212	63 49	004	34 50	069	50 59	124	35 46	175	30 56	193	60 50	246	27 42	287
213	63 52	002	35 46	069	51 48	125	35 50	176	30 43	193	59 56	247	26 45	287
214	63 54	000	36 41	069	52 37	125	35 54	176	30 29	194	59 01	247	25 48	287
215	63 53	358	37 37	068	53 25	126	35 58	177	30 14	194	58 06	248	24 51	287
216	63 50	356	38 32	068	54 13	127	36 01	178	30 00	195	57 11	248	23 54	286
217	63 44	354	39 27	067	55 01	127	36 03	178	29 44	195	56 15	249	22 57	286
218	63 37	352	40 22	067	55 48	128	36 05	179	29 28	196	55 20	249	21 59	286
219	63 27	350	41 17	066	56 34	129	36 06	179	29 12	196	54 24	249	21 02	286
220	63 15	348	42 11	066	57 20	130	36 06	180	28 56	196	53 28	250	20 05	285
221	63 01	345	43 05	066	58 06	131	36 06	181	28 39	197	52 33	250	19 07	285
222	62 45	343	43 59	065	58 51	132	36 05	181	28 21	197	51 37	250	18 10	285
223	62 27	342	44 53	064	59 35	133	36 04	182	28 04	198	50 40	251	17 12	285
224	62 08	340	45 47	064	60 18	134	36 02	182	27 45	198	49 44	251	16 15	285
	Alphecca		◆VEGA		ALTAIR		◆Shaula		RIGIL KENT		◆SPICA		ARCTURUS	
225	55 16	014	21 59	043	15 39	079	43 45	136	35 59	183	66 25	258	61 46	338
226	55 29	012	22 40	043	16 38	078	44 26	137	35 56	184	65 27	258	61 23	336
227	55 41	011	23 20	042	17 36	078	45 07	138	35 52	184	64 29	259	60 58	334
228	55 52	009	24 00	042	18 34	078	45 47	138	35 47	185	63 30	259	60 31	333
229	56 01	008	24 39	041	19 32	078	46 26	139	35 42	185	62 32	259	60 03	331
230	56 08	006	25 18	041	20 31	078	47 05	140	35 36	186	61 33	259	59 33	329
231	56 13	005	25 57	040	21 29	078	47 43	140	35 30	186	60 35	260	59 02	328
232	56 17	003	26 35	040	22 27	077	48 21	141	35 23	187	59 36	260	58 29	326
233	56 20	001	27 13	039	23 25	077	48 58	142	35 15	188	58 37	260	57 55	325
234	56 20	000	27 51	039	24 23	077	49 35	143	35 07	188	57 39	260	57 21	323
235	56 19	358	28 28	038	25 21	077	50 11	143	34 58	189	56 40	260	56 44	322
236	56 16	357	29 05	038	26 19	076	50 46	144	34 49	189	55 41	260	56 07	321
237	56 12	355	29 41	037	27 17	076	51 21	145	34 39	190	54 43	260	55 29	320
238	56 06	353	30 17	037	28 15	076	51 54	146	34 28	190	53 44	261	54 50	318
239	55 58	352	30 52	036	29 12	076	52 27	147	34 17	191	52 45	261	54 10	317
	VEGA		◆ALTAIR		Shaula		◆RIGIL KENT		SPICA		◆ARCTURUS		Alphecca	
240	31 27	035	30 10	075	52 59	148	34 06	191	51 47	261	53 29	316	55 48	350
241	32 01	035	31 08	075	53 31	149	33 54	192	50 48	261	52 47	315	55 37	349
242	32 35	034	32 05	075	54 01	150	33 41	193	49 49	261	52 05	314	55 25	347
243	33 08	033	33 03	075	54 30	151	33 28	193	48 50	261	51 22	313	55 11	346
244	33 40	033	34 00	074	54 59	152	33 14	194	47 51	261	50 38	312	54 55	344
245	34 12	032	34 57	074	55 26	153	33 00	194	46 53	261	49 53	311	54 38	343
246	34 44	031	35 54	074	55 52	154	32 45	195	45 54	261	49 08	310	54 20	341
247	35 15	031	36 51	073	56 17	156	32 30	195	44 55	261	48 22	309	54 00	340
248	35 45	030	37 48	073	56 41	157	32 14	196	43 56	261	47 36	309	53 38	338
249	36 14	029	38 45	073	57 04	158	31 58	196	42 57	261	46 49	308	53 16	337
250	36 43	028	39 42	072	57 25	160	31 41	197	41 58	261	46 02	307	52 52	336
251	37 11	028	40 39	072	57 45	161	31 24	197	41 00	261	45 14	306	52 27	334
252	37 38	027	41 35	071	58 04	162	31 06	197	40 01	261	44 26	306	52 00	333
253	38 05	026	42 32	071	58 22	164	30 48	198	39 02	261	43 37	305	51 33	332
254	38 31	025	43 28	071	58 38	165	30 30	198	38 03	261	42 48	304	51 04	331
	VEGA		◆ALTAIR		Peacock		◆RIGIL KENT		SPICA		◆ARCTURUS		Alphecca	
255	38 56	024	44 24	070	26 05	151	30 11	199	37 04	261	41 59	304	50 34	329
256	39 20	024	45 20	070	26 33	152	29 51	199	36 05	261	41 09	303	50 04	328
257	39 43	023	46 16	069	27 02	152	29 32	200	35 06	261	40 19	302	49 32	327
258	40 06	022	47 11	069	27 29	152	29 12	200	34 08	261	39 29	302	48 59	326
259	40 27	021	48 07	068	27 57	153	28 51	200	33 09	261	38 38	301	48 25	325
260	40 48	020	49 02	068	28 24	153	28 30	201	32 10	261	37 47	301	47 51	324
261	41 08	019	49 57	067	28 51	153	28 09	201	31 11	261	36 56	300	47 16	323
262	41 27	018	50 52	067	29 18	154	27 47	202	30 12	261	36 04	300	46 39	322
263	41 45	017	51 46	066	29 44	154	27 25	202	29 13	261	35 12	299	46 02	321
264	42 02	016	52 41	065	30 10	154	27 03	202	28 15	261	34 20	299	45 25	320
265	42 18	015	53 34	065	30 35	155	26 40	203	27 16	261	33 28	298	44 46	319
266	42 33	014	54 28	064	31 00	155	26 17	203	26 17	261	32 35	298	44 07	318
267	42 47	013	55 21	063	31 25	156	25 54	203	25 18	261	31 43	298	43 27	318
268	43 00	012	56 14	062	31 49	156	25 30	204	24 19	261	30 50	297	42 47	317
269	43 12	011	57 07	061	32 13	157	25 06	204	23 21	261	29 57	297	42 06	316

LHA ♈	Hc	Zn	Hc	Zn	Hc	Zn	Hc	Zn	Hc	Zn	Hc	Zn	Hc	Zn
	◆VEGA		DENEB		Enif		◆FOMALHAUT		Peacock		◆ANTARES		ARCTURUS	
270	43 23	010	26 22	031	31 29	074	16 48	119	32 36	157	61 08	225	29 04	296
271	43 33	009	26 52	030	32 27	073	17 40	119	32 59	158	60 25	226	28 10	296
272	43 42	008	27 21	030	33 24	073	18 33	119	33 22	158	59 42	227	27 17	296
273	43 49	007	27 50	029	34 21	073	19 25	119	33 44	159	58 58	228	26 23	295
274	43 56	006	28 19	028	35 18	073	20 17	119	34 06	159	58 13	229	25 29	295
275	44 01	005	28 47	028	36 14	072	21 09	119	34 27	160	57 28	230	24 35	295
276	44 06	004	29 14	027	37 11	072	22 01	119	34 47	160	56 42	231	23 41	294
277	44 09	003	29 41	027	38 07	071	22 53	119	35 07	161	55 55	232	22 47	294
278	44 11	001	30 07	026	39 04	071	23 45	119	35 27	161	55 08	232	21 52	294
279	44 12	000	30 33	025	40 00	071	24 37	119	35 46	162	54 21	233	20 58	294
280	44 12	359	30 58	025	40 56	070	25 29	119	36 04	162	53 33	234	20 03	293
281	44 11	358	31 23	024	41 52	070	26 21	120	36 22	163	52 45	235	19 08	293
282	44 08	357	31 46	023	42 48	069	27 12	120	36 40	163	51 56	235	18 14	293
283	44 05	356	32 10	023	43 44	069	28 04	120	36 56	164	51 07	236	17 19	293
284	44 00	355	32 32	022	44 39	069	28 56	120	37 13	165	50 18	236	16 24	292
	DENEB		Enif		◆FOMALHAUT		Peacock		◆ANTARES		Rasalhague		◆VEGA	
285	32 54	021	45 35	068	29 47	120	37 28	165	49 28	237	61 20	313	43 54	354
286	33 15	020	46 30	068	30 39	120	37 43	166	48 38	237	60 36	312	43 47	353
287	33 35	020	47 25	067	31 30	120	37 57	166	47 48	238	59 51	310	43 39	352
288	33 55	019	48 19	066	32 21	121	38 11	167	46 57	238	59 05	309	43 30	351
289	34 14	018	49 14	066	33 13	121	38 24	168	46 06	239	58 19	308	43 20	350
290	34 32	017	50 08	065	34 04	121	38 36	168	45 15	239	57 31	307	43 09	349
291	34 50	017	51 02	065	34 55	121	38 48	169	44 24	239	56 43	306	42 57	348
292	35 06	016	51 56	064	35 45	122	38 59	170	43 33	240	55 55	305	42 43	347
293	35 22	015	52 49	063	36 36	122	39 09	170	42 41	240	55 06	304	42 29	346
294	35 37	014	53 42	063	37 27	122	39 19	171	41 50	240	54 16	303	42 14	345
295	35 51	013	54 35	062	38 17	122	39 28	172	40 58	241	53 26	302	41 57	344
296	36 05	013	55 27	061	39 07	123	39 36	172	40 06	241	52 35	301	41 40	343
297	36 17	012	56 19	060	39 57	123	39 44	173	39 13	241	51 44	301	41 22	342
298	36 29	011	57 10	059	40 47	123	39 51	174	38 21	242	50 53	300	41 03	341
299	36 40	010	58 01	058	41 37	124	39 57	174	37 29	242	50 01	299	40 42	340
	◆DENEB		Alpheratz		◆FOMALHAUT		Peacock		◆ANTARES		Rasalhague		VEGA	
300	36 50	009	20 06	055	42 26	124	40 02	175	36 36	242	49 09	298	40 21	339
301	36 59	008	20 55	055	43 15	125	40 07	176	35 43	242	48 16	298	39 59	338
302	37 07	007	21 43	055	44 04	125	40 11	177	34 51	243	47 24	297	39 37	337
303	37 14	007	22 32	054	44 53	125	40 14	177	33 58	243	46 30	297	39 13	336
304	37 21	006	23 20	054	45 41	126	40 16	178	33 05	243	45 37	296	38 49	335
305	37 26	005	24 08	054	46 29	126	40 18	179	32 12	243	44 43	295	38 23	335
306	37 31	004	24 56	053	47 17	127	40 19	179	31 19	243	43 49	295	37 57	334
307	37 34	003	25 44	053	48 05	127	40 19	180	30 25	243	42 55	294	37 31	333
308	37 37	002	26 31	052	48 52	128	40 18	181	29 32	243	42 01	294	37 03	332
309	37 39	001	27 18	052	49 39	129	40 17	182	28 39	244	41 06	293	36 35	331
310	37 40	000	28 05	052	50 25	129	40 15	182	27 45	244	40 12	293	36 06	331
311	37 40	000	28 51	051	51 11	130	40 12	183	26 52	244	39 17	293	35 36	330
312	37 39	359	29 37	051	51 57	130	40 08	184	25 59	244	38 22	292	35 06	329
313	37 37	358	30 23	050	52 42	131	40 04	185	25 05	244	37 26	292	34 35	328
314	37 34	357	31 09	050	53 26	132	39 59	185	24 11	244	36 31	291	34 04	328
	Alpheratz		◆Diphda		ACHERNAR		Peacock		◆Nunki		VEGA		◆DENEB	
315	31 54	049	34 22	107	16 53	148	39 53	186	54 48	233	33 32	327	37 31	356
316	32 39	049	35 19	107	17 24	148	39 47	187	54 00	234	32 59	326	37 26	355
317	33 23	048	36 16	107	17 56	148	39 39	187	53 12	235	32 26	326	37 20	354
318	34 07	047	37 13	107	18 27	148	39 32	188	52 24	235	31 52	325	37 14	353
319	34 51	047	38 09	107	18 58	149	39 23	189	51 34	236	31 17	324	37 07	353
320	35 34	046	39 06	107	19 29	149	39 14	189	50 45	236	30 42	324	36 58	352
321	36 17	046	40 03	108	20 00	149	39 03	190	49 55	237	30 07	323	36 49	351
322	36 59	045	41 00	108	20 31	149	38 53	191	49 05	237	29 31	323	36 39	350
323	37 41	044	41 57	108	21 01	149	38 41	191	48 15	238	28 55	322	36 29	349
324	38 22	044	42 53	108	21 31	149	38 29	192	47 25	238	28 18	322	36 17	348
325	39 03	043	43 50	108	22 02	150	38 16	193	46 34	239	27 41	321	36 04	347
326	39 44	042	44 46	108	22 31	150	38 03	193	45 43	239	27 03	320	35 51	347
327	40 23	041	45 43	109	23 01	150	37 49	194	44 52	240	26 25	320	35 37	346
328	41 02	041	46 39	109	23 31	150	37 34	195	44 00	240	25 46	319	35 22	345
329	41 41	040	47 36	109	24 00	151	37 19	195	43 08	240	25 08	319	35 06	344
	◆Alpheratz		Diphda		◆ACHERNAR		Peacock		Nunki		◆ALTAIR		DENEB	
330	42 19	039	48 32	109	24 29	151	37 03	196	42 17	241	54 15	296	34 49	343
331	42 56	038	49 28	109	24 58	151	36 47	196	41 25	241	53 21	295	34 32	343
332	43 33	037	50 24	110	25 26	152	36 30	197	40 33	241	52 27	295	34 13	342
333	44 08	037	51 20	110	25 55	152	36 12	198	39 40	241	51 33	294	33 55	341
334	44 44	036	52 16	110	26 23	152	35 54	198	38 48	242	50 39	293	33 35	340
335	45 18	035	53 12	111	26 50	152	35 35	199	37 55	242	49 44	293	33 14	340
336	45 51	034	54 08	111	27 18	153	35 16	199	37 03	242	48 49	292	32 53	339
337	46 24	033	55 03	111	27 45	153	34 56	200	36 10	242	47 53	292	32 31	338
338	46 56	032	55 59	112	28 12	153	34 35	200	35 17	243	46 58	291	32 09	337
339	47 27	031	56 54	112	28 38	153	34 14	201	34 24	243	46 02	291	31 46	337
340	47 57	030	57 49	113	29 04	154	33 53	201	33 31	243	45 07	290	31 22	336
341	48 25	029	58 44	113	29 30	155	33 31	202	32 38	243	44 11	290	30 58	335
342	48 53	027	59 38	114	29 55	155	33 09	202	31 45	243	43 14	289	30 32	335
343	49 20	026	60 33	114	30 20	155	32 46	203	30 52	243	42 18	289	30 07	334
344	49 46	025	61 27	115	30 45	156	32 23	203	29 58	244	41 22	288	29 40	333
	Alpheratz		◆Hamal		◆ACHERNAR		Peacock		Nunki		◆ALTAIR		DENEB	
345	50 11	024	34 53	055	31 09	156	31 59	204	29 05	244	40 25	288	29 14	333
346	50 34	023	35 41	054	31 33	157	31 35	204	28 12	244	39 28	288	28 46	332
347	50 57	021	36 30	054	31 56	157	31 10	205	27 18	244	38 32	287	28 18	332
348	51 18	020	37 18	053	32 19	158	30 46	205	26 25	244	37 35	287	27 49	331
349	51 38	019	38 05	053	32 42	158	30 20	205	25 31	244	36 38	287	27 20	330
350	51 56	018	38 52	052	33 04	158	29 55	206	24 37	244	35 41	286	26 51	330
351	52 14	016	39 39	051	33 26	159	29 28	206	23 44	244	34 43	286	26 21	329
352	52 30	015	40 25	051	33 47	159	29 02	207	22 50	244	33 46	286	25 50	329
353	52 44	013	41 11	050	34 07	160	28 35	207	21 56	244	32 49	285	25 19	328
354	52 57	012	41 57	049	34 28	160	28 08	207	21 03	244	31 51	285	24 47	328
355	53 09	011	42 41	049	34 47	161	27 41	208	20 09	245	30 54	285	24 16	327
356	53 19	009	43 26	048	35 06	162	27 13	208	19 15	245	29 56	285	23 43	327
357	53 28	008	44 10	047	35 25	162	26 45	208	18 21	245	28 58	284	23 10	326
358	53 35	006	44 53	046	35 43	163	26 17	209	17 27	245	28 01	284	22 37	326
359	53 41	005	45 36	046	36 01	163	25 48	209	16 34	245	27 03	284	22 03	325

LAT 8°S

LHA ♈	Hc Zn	Hc Zn	Hc Zn	Hc Zn	Hc Zn	Hc Zn	Hc Zn
	◆ Alpheratz	ALDEBARAN	◆ RIGEL	ACHERNAR	◆ FOMALHAUT	ALTAIR	DENEB
0	52 46 003	17 19 070	12 07 097	37 15 164	64 04 212	25 51 284	20 40 325
1	52 48 002	18 14 070	13 06 097	37 32 164	63 32 213	24 53 284	20 06 325
2	52 50 000	19 10 069	14 05 096	37 48 165	62 59 215	23 55 283	19 32 324
3	52 49 359	20 06 069	15 04 096	38 03 165	62 24 216	22 57 283	18 57 324
4	52 47 358	21 01 069	16 03 096	38 18 166	61 48 218	22 00 283	18 21 323
5	52 44 356	21 56 068	17 02 096	38 32 167	61 11 219	21 02 283	17 46 323
6	52 39 355	22 52 068	18 01 096	38 45 167	60 33 220	20 04 283	17 10 323
7	52 33 353	23 47 068	19 01 096	38 58 168	59 55 221	19 06 282	16 34 322
8	52 25 352	24 42 068	20 00 096	39 10 168	59 15 222	18 08 282	15 57 322
9	52 16 350	25 37 067	20 59 096	39 22 169	58 34 224	17 09 282	15 21 322
10	52 06 349	26 31 067	21 58 096	39 33 170	57 53 225	16 11 282	14 43 321
11	51 53 348	27 26 067	22 57 096	39 43 170	57 11 226	15 13 282	14 06 321
12	51 40 346	28 20 066	23 56 095	39 52 171	56 28 226	14 15 281	13 29 321
13	51 25 345	29 15 066	24 55 095	40 01 172	55 45 227	13 17 281	12 51 320
14	51 09 344	30 09 066	25 54 095	40 09 173	55 01 228	12 18 281	12 13 320
	Hamal	ALDEBARAN	◆ RIGEL	ACHERNAR	◆ FOMALHAUT	Enif	◆ Alpheratz
15	54 21 027	31 03 065	26 54 095	40 17 173	54 17 229	38 14 289	50 52 342
16	54 48 026	31 57 065	27 53 095	40 23 174	53 32 230	37 18 289	50 33 341
17	55 13 025	32 50 064	28 52 095	40 29 175	52 46 230	36 22 289	50 13 340
18	55 37 023	33 44 064	29 51 095	40 34 175	52 00 231	35 25 288	49 52 338
19	56 00 022	34 37 063	30 50 095	40 39 176	51 14 232	34 29 288	49 29 337
20	56 21 020	35 30 063	31 50 095	40 43 177	50 27 232	33 32 288	49 06 336
21	56 41 019	36 23 063	32 49 095	40 46 177	49 40 233	32 35 287	48 41 335
22	56 59 017	37 16 062	33 48 095	40 48 178	48 52 233	31 39 287	48 16 334
23	57 16 015	38 08 062	34 47 094	40 49 179	48 04 234	30 42 287	47 49 333
24	57 31 014	39 00 061	35 47 094	40 50 180	47 16 234	29 45 286	47 21 332
25	57 44 012	39 52 061	36 46 094	40 50 180	46 28 235	28 48 286	46 52 330
26	57 56 010	40 44 060	37 45 094	40 50 181	45 39 235	27 51 286	46 22 329
27	58 05 009	41 35 059	38 44 094	40 48 182	44 50 236	26 53 285	45 52 328
28	58 14 007	42 26 059	39 44 094	40 46 182	44 01 236	25 56 285	45 20 327
29	58 20 005	43 16 058	40 43 094	40 43 183	43 11 237	24 59 285	44 48 326
	CAPELLA	◆ BETELGEUSE	SIRIUS	CANOPUS	◆ ACHERNAR	FOMALHAUT	◆ Alpheratz
30	20 18 034	29 12 077	19 59 105	20 44 144	40 39 184	42 21 237	44 14 325
31	20 51 034	30 10 077	20 56 105	21 19 144	40 35 185	41 32 237	43 40 325
32	21 24 033	31 08 076	21 54 105	21 54 144	40 30 185	40 41 238	43 05 324
33	21 57 033	32 05 076	22 51 105	22 29 144	40 24 186	39 51 238	42 30 323
34	22 29 032	33 03 076	23 49 105	23 04 144	40 17 187	39 01 238	41 54 322
35	23 00 032	34 01 075	24 46 105	23 38 145	40 10 187	38 10 238	41 17 321
36	23 32 031	34 58 075	25 44 105	24 13 145	40 02 188	37 19 239	40 39 320
37	24 02 031	35 55 075	26 41 105	24 47 145	39 54 189	36 29 239	40 01 320
38	24 33 030	36 53 074	27 38 105	25 21 145	39 44 189	35 38 239	39 22 319
39	25 02 030	37 50 074	28 36 105	25 54 146	39 34 190	34 47 239	38 42 318
40	25 32 029	38 47 074	29 33 105	26 28 146	39 23 191	33 55 240	38 02 317
41	26 00 029	39 44 073	30 31 105	27 01 146	39 12 191	33 04 240	37 22 317
42	26 29 028	40 41 073	31 28 105	27 34 146	39 00 192	32 13 240	36 41 316
43	26 56 028	41 38 073	32 26 105	28 07 147	38 47 193	31 21 240	35 59 315
44	27 24 027	42 34 072	33 23 105	28 39 147	38 34 193	30 30 240	35 17 315
	CAPELLA	◆ BETELGEUSE	SIRIUS	CANOPUS	◆ ACHERNAR	FOMALHAUT	◆ Alpheratz
45	27 50 026	43 31 072	34 21 105	29 12 147	38 20 194	29 38 240	34 35 314
46	28 17 026	44 27 071	35 18 105	29 43 148	38 05 195	28 46 241	33 52 313
47	28 42 025	45 23 071	36 15 105	30 15 148	37 50 195	27 54 241	33 08 313
48	29 07 025	46 19 070	37 13 105	30 46 148	37 34 196	27 02 241	32 25 312
49	29 31 024	47 15 070	38 10 105	31 17 149	37 17 196	26 11 241	31 40 312
50	29 55 023	48 11 069	39 08 105	31 48 149	37 00 197	25 19 241	30 56 311
51	30 18 023	49 06 069	40 05 105	32 18 149	36 43 198	24 27 241	30 11 311
52	30 41 022	50 02 068	41 02 105	32 48 150	36 25 198	23 35 241	29 26 310
53	31 02 021	50 57 068	42 00 105	33 18 150	36 06 199	22 42 241	28 40 310
54	31 23 020	51 52 067	42 57 105	33 47 151	35 47 199	21 50 241	27 54 309
55	31 44 020	52 46 066	43 54 106	34 16 151	35 27 200	20 58 241	27 08 309
56	32 04 019	53 40 066	44 51 106	34 45 152	35 07 200	20 06 241	26 21 308
57	32 23 018	54 34 065	45 49 106	35 13 152	34 46 201	19 14 241	25 35 308
58	32 41 018	55 28 064	46 46 106	35 40 153	34 24 201	18 22 241	24 47 307
59	32 59 017	56 22 063	47 43 106	36 07 153	34 03 202	17 30 241	24 00 307
	◆ CAPELLA	POLLUX	◆ SIRIUS	CANOPUS	ACHERNAR	◆ Diphda	Hamal
60	33 15 016	24 37 054	48 40 106	36 34 154	33 41 202	41 27 253	48 15 320
61	33 31 015	25 25 054	49 37 106	37 00 154	33 18 203	40 31 253	47 36 319
62	33 47 015	26 13 053	50 34 107	37 26 155	32 55 203	39 34 253	46 57 318
63	34 01 014	27 00 053	51 31 107	37 51 155	32 31 204	38 37 253	46 17 317
64	34 15 013	27 48 052	52 27 107	38 15 156	32 07 204	37 40 254	45 36 316
65	34 28 012	28 35 052	53 24 107	38 39 156	31 43 204	36 43 254	44 54 315
66	34 40 011	29 21 051	54 21 108	39 03 157	31 18 205	35 46 254	44 12 314
67	34 51 011	30 08 051	55 17 108	39 26 158	30 53 205	34 49 254	43 29 314
68	35 01 010	30 54 050	56 14 108	39 48 158	30 27 206	33 52 254	42 46 313
69	35 11 009	31 39 050	57 10 109	40 10 159	30 02 206	32 55 254	42 02 312
70	35 20 008	32 25 049	58 07 109	40 31 159	29 35 206	31 58 254	41 18 311
71	35 28 007	33 10 049	59 03 109	40 52 160	29 09 207	31 00 254	40 33 311
72	35 35 006	33 54 048	59 59 110	41 11 161	28 42 207	30 03 254	39 47 310
73	35 41 006	34 38 048	60 55 110	41 31 162	28 15 207	29 06 254	39 02 309
74	35 46 005	35 22 047	61 50 111	41 49 162	27 47 208	28 09 254	38 15 309
	CAPELLA	POLLUX	◆ REGULUS	CANOPUS	◆ ACHERNAR	Diphda	◆ Hamal
75	35 50 004	36 05 046	10 38 076	42 07 163	27 19 208	27 12 254	37 29 308
76	35 54 003	36 48 046	11 36 076	42 24 164	26 51 208	26 15 254	36 42 307
77	35 57 002	37 30 045	12 33 076	42 40 164	26 23 209	25 18 254	35 54 307
78	35 58 001	38 12 044	13 31 076	42 56 165	25 54 209	24 21 254	35 07 306
79	35 59 000	38 54 044	14 28 075	43 11 166	25 25 209	23 24 254	34 19 306
80	35 59 000	39 35 043	15 26 075	43 25 167	24 56 210	22 27 254	33 30 305
81	35 58 359	40 15 042	16 23 075	43 38 167	24 27 210	21 30 254	32 42 305
82	35 56 358	40 54 042	17 21 075	43 51 168	23 57 210	20 33 254	31 53 304
83	35 54 357	41 34 041	18 18 075	44 03 169	23 27 210	19 35 254	31 03 304
84	35 50 356	42 12 040	19 15 074	44 14 170	22 57 210	18 38 254	30 14 303
85	35 46 355	42 50 039	20 12 074	44 24 171	22 27 211	17 41 254	29 24 303
86	35 40 354	43 27 038	21 09 074	44 33 171	21 57 211	16 44 254	28 34 302
87	35 34 354	44 03 037	22 06 074	44 41 172	21 26 211	15 47 254	27 44 302
88	35 27 353	44 39 036	23 03 073	44 49 173	20 55 211	14 50 254	26 53 302
89	35 19 352	45 14 035	24 00 073	44 56 174	20 24 211	13 53 253	26 02 301

LHA ♈	Hc Zn	Hc Zn	Hc Zn	Hc Zn	Hc Zn	Hc Zn	Hc Zn
	POLLUX	◆ REGULUS	Suhail	◆ CANOPUS	Acamar	◆ ALDEBARAN	CAPELLA
90	45 48 034	24 57 073	35 46 139	45 01 175	38 26 224	57 58 320	35 10 351
91	46 21 033	25 54 073	36 25 139	45 06 176	37 45 224	57 20 319	35 00 350
92	46 53 032	26 51 072	37 03 140	45 10 177	37 03 225	56 40 317	34 50 349
93	47 25 031	27 47 072	37 41 140	45 14 177	36 21 225	55 59 316	34 39 349
94	47 55 030	28 44 072	38 19 141	45 16 178	35 39 225	55 18 315	34 26 348
95	48 25 029	29 40 071	38 56 141	45 17 179	34 57 226	54 35 314	34 14 347
96	48 53 028	30 36 071	39 33 142	45 18 180	34 14 226	53 52 313	34 00 346
97	49 21 027	31 32 071	40 10 142	45 17 181	33 31 226	53 08 312	33 45 345
98	49 47 026	32 28 070	40 46 143	45 16 182	32 48 227	52 24 311	33 30 345
99	50 13 025	33 24 070	41 22 143	45 14 183	32 05 227	51 38 310	33 14 344
100	50 37 023	34 20 070	41 57 144	45 11 183	31 21 227	50 52 309	32 57 343
101	51 00 022	35 16 069	42 32 145	45 07 184	30 37 228	50 06 308	32 39 342
102	51 21 021	36 11 069	43 06 145	45 02 185	29 53 228	49 19 307	32 21 342
103	51 42 020	37 06 068	43 40 146	44 56 186	29 09 228	48 31 306	32 02 341
104	52 01 018	38 02 068	44 13 146	44 50 187	28 25 228	47 43 306	31 42 340
	POLLUX	◆ REGULUS	Suhail	◆ CANOPUS	RIGEL	◆ ALDEBARAN	CAPELLA
105	52 19 017	38 57 068	44 45 147	44 42 188	64 05 268	46 55 305	31 21 339
106	52 36 015	39 51 067	45 17 148	44 34 188	63 05 268	46 06 304	31 00 339
107	52 51 014	40 46 067	45 49 148	44 25 189	62 06 268	45 16 303	30 38 338
108	53 04 013	41 41 066	46 20 149	44 15 190	61 07 268	44 26 303	30 16 337
109	53 17 011	42 35 066	46 50 150	44 04 191	60 07 267	43 36 302	29 53 337
110	53 27 010	43 29 065	47 19 151	43 53 192	59 08 267	42 46 301	29 29 336
111	53 37 008	44 23 065	47 48 152	43 40 192	58 09 267	41 55 301	29 05 335
112	53 45 007	45 16 064	48 15 152	43 27 193	57 09 267	41 04 300	28 40 335
113	53 51 005	46 10 063	48 43 153	43 13 194	56 10 267	40 12 300	28 14 334
114	53 56 004	47 03 063	49 09 154	42 58 195	55 11 267	39 20 299	27 48 334
115	53 59 002	47 55 062	49 34 155	42 43 196	54 11 267	38 28 299	27 21 333
116	54 00 001	48 48 062	49 59 156	42 26 196	53 12 267	37 36 298	26 54 332
117	54 01 359	49 40 061	50 23 157	42 09 197	52 13 267	36 44 298	26 26 332
118	53 59 358	50 31 060	50 45 158	41 52 198	51 13 267	35 51 297	25 58 331
119	53 56 356	51 23 059	51 07 159	41 33 198	50 14 267	34 58 297	25 29 331
	◆ REGULUS	SPICA	◆ ACRUX	CANOPUS	RIGEL	◆ BETELGEUSE	POLLUX
120	52 14 059	09 50 100	17 27 154	41 14 199	49 15 267	55 28 296	53 51 355
121	53 04 058	10 48 100	17 52 154	40 54 200	48 15 267	54 34 295	53 45 353
122	53 54 057	11 47 100	18 18 155	40 34 200	47 16 267	53 40 294	53 38 352
123	54 44 056	12 45 100	18 43 155	40 13 201	46 17 266	52 46 294	53 29 350
124	55 33 055	13 44 100	19 09 155	39 51 202	45 17 266	51 51 293	53 18 349
125	56 21 054	14 43 100	19 34 155	39 29 202	44 18 266	50 56 292	53 06 348
126	57 09 053	15 41 099	19 59 155	39 06 203	43 19 266	50 01 292	52 52 346
127	57 56 052	16 40 099	20 24 155	38 43 204	42 19 266	49 06 291	52 37 345
128	58 42 051	17 38 099	20 48 156	38 19 204	41 20 266	48 10 291	52 21 343
129	59 28 050	18 37 099	21 13 156	37 54 205	40 21 266	47 15 290	52 03 342
130	60 13 048	19 36 099	21 37 156	37 29 205	39 22 266	46 19 290	51 44 341
131	60 57 047	20 34 099	22 01 156	37 04 206	38 22 266	45 23 289	51 24 339
132	61 40 046	21 33 099	22 25 156	36 38 206	37 23 266	44 27 289	51 02 338
133	62 22 044	22 32 099	22 49 157	36 11 207	36 24 266	43 30 288	50 39 337
134	63 03 043	23 30 099	23 12 157	35 44 207	35 25 266	42 34 288	50 15 336
	Dubhe	Denebola	◆ SPICA	ACRUX	◆ CANOPUS	SIRIUS	◆ POLLUX
135	16 14 015	42 16 062	24 29 099	23 35 157	35 16 208	56 09 252	49 50 334
136	16 29 014	43 08 061	25 28 099	23 58 157	34 49 208	55 12 252	49 24 333
137	16 44 014	44 00 061	26 27 099	24 21 158	34 20 209	54 16 252	48 57 332
138	16 58 014	44 52 060	27 25 099	24 43 158	33 51 209	53 19 253	48 28 331
139	17 12 013	45 43 060	28 24 098	25 05 158	33 22 210	52 22 253	47 59 330
140	17 25 013	46 35 059	29 23 098	25 27 159	32 53 210	51 25 253	47 28 329
141	17 38 012	47 25 058	30 22 098	25 48 159	32 23 210	50 28 253	46 57 328
142	17 50 012	48 16 058	31 20 098	26 10 159	31 53 211	49 31 254	46 25 327
143	18 02 011	49 05 057	32 19 098	26 30 160	31 22 211	48 34 254	45 52 326
144	18 13 011	49 55 056	33 18 098	26 51 160	30 51 212	47 37 254	45 18 325
145	18 24 010	50 44 055	34 17 098	27 11 160	30 20 212	46 40 254	44 43 324
146	18 35 010	51 32 054	35 16 098	27 31 161	29 48 212	45 43 254	44 07 323
147	18 45 009	52 20 053	36 15 098	27 51 161	29 16 213	44 46 254	43 31 322
148	18 54 009	53 08 053	37 13 098	28 10 161	28 44 213	43 49 254	42 54 321
149	19 03 009	53 55 052	38 12 098	28 29 162	28 11 213	42 51 255	42 16 320
	Dubhe	ARCTURUS	◆ SPICA	ACRUX	◆ CANOPUS	SIRIUS	◆ POLLUX
150	19 12 008	21 18 066	39 11 098	28 48 162	27 39 214	41 54 255	41 38 319
151	19 20 008	22 13 066	40 10 098	29 06 162	27 06 214	40 57 255	40 59 319
152	19 28 007	23 07 065	41 09 098	29 24 163	26 33 214	39 59 255	40 19 318
153	19 35 007	24 00 065	42 08 098	29 41 163	25 59 214	39 02 255	39 39 317
154	19 41 006	24 54 065	43 06 098	29 58 164	25 25 215	38 05 255	38 58 316
155	19 47 006	25 48 064	44 05 098	30 15 164	24 52 215	37 07 255	38 17 316
156	19 53 005	26 41 064	45 04 098	30 31 164	24 17 215	36 10 255	37 35 315
157	19 58 005	27 34 063	46 03 098	30 46 165	23 43 215	35 13 255	36 53 314
158	20 02 004	28 28 063	47 02 098	31 02 165	23 09 216	34 15 255	36 10 314
159	20 06 004	29 20 063	48 01 098	31 17 166	22 34 216	33 18 255	35 27 313
160	20 10 003	30 13 062	48 59 098	31 31 166	21 59 216	32 20 255	34 43 312
161	20 13 003	31 06 062	49 58 098	31 45 167	21 24 216	31 23 255	33 59 312
162	20 15 002	31 58 061	50 57 098	31 59 167	20 49 216	30 25 255	33 15 311
163	20 17 002	32 50 061	51 56 098	32 12 168	20 14 216	29 28 255	32 30 311
164	20 19 001	33 42 061	52 55 098	32 24 168	19 39 217	28 30 255	31 45 310
	Dubhe	◆ ARCTURUS	SPICA	◆ ACRUX	Suhail	SIRIUS	◆ POLLUX
165	20 19 001	34 34 060	53 54 098	32 36 168	46 58 211	27 33 255	30 59 310
166	20 20 000	35 25 060	54 52 098	32 48 169	46 28 211	26 35 255	30 13 309
167	20 20 000	36 16 059	55 51 098	32 59 169	45 57 211	25 38 255	29 27 309
168	20 19 359	37 07 059	56 50 098	33 10 170	45 26 212	24 41 255	28 40 308
169	20 18 359	37 58 058	57 49 098	33 20 170	44 54 213	23 43 255	27 53 308
170	20 16 358	38 48 058	58 48 099	33 29 171	44 22 213	22 46 255	27 06 307
171	20 14 358	39 38 057	59 46 099	33 38 171	43 49 214	21 48 255	26 18 307
172	20 11 357	40 27 056	60 45 099	33 47 172	43 15 215	20 51 255	25 31 306
173	20 08 357	41 17 056	61 44 099	33 55 173	42 41 215	19 53 255	24 43 306
174	20 04 356	42 06 055	62 43 099	34 02 173	42 07 216	18 56 255	23 54 305
175	19 59 356	42 54 054	63 41 099	34 09 174	41 31 216	17 59 255	23 06 305
176	19 55 355	43 42 054	64 40 099	34 16 174	40 56 217	17 01 255	22 17 305
177	19 49 355	44 30 053	65 38 100	34 22 175	40 20 217	16 04 255	21 28 304
178	19 43 354	45 17 052	66 37 100	34 27 175	39 43 218	15 07 255	20 39 304
179	19 37 354	46 04 052	67 36 100	34 32 176	39 07 219	14 09 255	19 50 304

LHA ♈	Hc	Zn	Hc	Zn	Hc	Zn	Hc	Zn	Hc	Zn	Hc	Zn	Hc	Zn
	ARCTURUS		◆ ANTARES		ACRUX		◆ Suhail		Alphard		REGULUS		◆ Dubhe	
180	46 50	051	23 35	115	34 36	176	38 29	219	52 30	266	56 01	306	19 30	353
181	47 36	050	24 29	115	34 39	177	37 52	220	51 30	266	55 12	305	19 23	353
182	48 21	049	25 22	116	34 42	177	37 14	220	50 31	266	54 23	304	19 15	352
183	49 06	048	26 16	116	34 45	178	36 35	220	49 32	266	53 33	303	19 06	352
184	49 50	047	27 09	116	34 47	178	35 57	221	48 32	266	52 43	302	18 57	351
185	50 33	046	28 03	116	34 48	179	35 18	221	47 33	266	51 53	301	18 48	351
186	51 16	045	28 56	116	34 49	180	34 38	222	46 34	266	51 01	300	18 38	350
187	51 57	044	29 50	116	34 49	180	33 59	222	45 35	266	50 10	300	18 28	350
188	52 38	043	30 43	116	34 49	181	33 19	222	44 35	266	49 18	299	18 17	349
189	53 19	042	31 37	116	34 48	181	32 39	223	43 36	266	48 26	298	18 06	349
190	53 58	041	32 30	116	34 46	182	31 58	223	42 37	265	47 33	298	17 54	348
191	54 37	040	33 23	117	34 44	182	31 18	223	41 38	265	46 41	297	17 42	348
192	55 14	039	34 16	117	34 42	183	30 37	224	40 39	265	45 47	296	17 29	347
193	55 51	037	35 09	117	34 38	183	29 56	224	39 39	265	44 54	296	17 16	347
194	56 26	036	36 02	117	34 35	184	29 14	224	38 40	265	44 00	295	17 02	347
	ARCTURUS		◆ Rasalhague		ANTARES		◆ ACRUX		Suhail		◆ REGULUS		Dubhe	
195	57 00	035	18 31	074	36 55	117	34 30	184	28 33	224	43 06	295	16 48	346
196	57 34	033	19 28	074	37 48	117	34 25	185	27 51	225	42 12	294	16 34	346
197	58 05	032	20 25	073	38 41	118	34 20	186	27 10	225	41 18	294	16 19	345
198	58 36	030	21 22	073	39 33	118	34 14	186	26 28	225	40 23	293	16 04	345
199	59 05	029	22 19	073	40 26	118	34 07	187	25 45	225	39 29	293	15 48	344
200	59 33	027	23 16	073	41 18	118	34 00	187	25 03	225	38 34	292	15 32	344
201	59 59	025	24 12	072	42 10	119	33 53	188	24 21	226	37 39	292	15 16	344
202	60 24	024	25 09	072	43 02	119	33 45	188	23 38	226	36 43	291	14 59	343
203	60 47	022	26 05	072	43 54	119	33 36	189	22 56	226	35 48	291	14 41	343
204	61 08	020	27 02	071	44 46	120	33 27	189	22 13	226	34 52	291	14 24	343
205	61 27	018	27 58	071	45 37	120	33 17	190	21 30	226	33 57	290	14 06	342
206	61 45	016	28 54	071	46 29	120	33 07	190	20 47	226	33 01	290	13 47	342
207	62 01	014	29 50	071	47 20	121	32 56	191	20 04	226	32 05	289	13 28	341
208	62 14	012	30 46	070	48 11	121	32 45	191	19 21	227	31 09	289	13 09	341
209	62 26	010	31 42	070	49 02	122	32 33	192	18 38	227	30 13	289	12 50	341
	ARCTURUS		◆ Rasalhague		ANTARES		◆ RIGIL KENT		ACRUX		Gienah		◆ REGULUS	
210	62 36	008	32 38	069	49 52	122	36 34	174	32 21	192	63 03	247	29 16	289
211	62 43	006	33 33	069	50 42	123	36 40	174	32 08	193	62 09	247	28 20	288
212	62 49	004	34 29	069	51 32	123	36 45	175	31 55	193	61 14	248	27 24	288
213	62 52	002	35 24	068	52 22	124	36 50	176	31 41	194	60 19	248	26 27	288
214	62 54	000	36 19	068	53 11	124	36 54	176	31 27	194	59 24	249	25 30	287
215	62 53	358	37 14	068	54 00	125	36 58	177	31 13	194	58 28	249	24 34	287
216	62 50	356	38 09	067	54 48	126	37 01	177	30 58	195	57 32	250	23 37	287
217	62 45	354	39 04	067	55 37	126	37 03	178	30 42	195	56 37	250	22 40	287
218	62 37	352	39 58	066	56 24	127	37 05	179	30 26	196	55 41	250	21 43	286
219	62 28	350	40 52	066	57 11	128	37 06	179	30 10	196	54 45	251	20 46	286
220	62 17	348	41 46	065	57 58	129	37 06	180	29 53	197	53 49	251	19 49	286
221	62 03	346	42 40	065	58 44	129	37 06	181	29 36	197	52 52	251	18 51	286
222	61 48	344	43 34	064	59 30	130	37 05	181	29 19	197	51 56	252	17 54	285
223	61 30	342	44 27	064	60 15	131	37 04	182	29 01	198	51 00	252	16 57	285
224	61 11	340	45 20	063	60 59	132	37 02	182	28 43	198	50 03	252	15 59	285
	Alphecca		◆ VEGA		ALTAIR		◆ Shaula		RIGIL KENT		◆ SPICA		ARCTURUS	
225	54 18	014	21 15	043	15 27	078	44 29	136	36 59	183	66 37	260	60 50	338
226	54 31	012	21 55	042	16 25	078	45 10	136	36 55	184	65 38	260	60 28	337
227	54 42	011	22 35	042	17 24	078	45 51	137	36 51	184	64 39	261	60 03	335
228	54 53	009	23 15	041	18 22	078	46 31	138	36 47	185	63 41	261	59 37	333
229	55 01	008	23 54	041	19 20	078	47 11	138	36 42	185	62 42	261	59 10	332
230	55 08	006	24 33	041	20 18	077	47 50	139	36 36	186	61 43	261	58 41	330
231	55 14	004	25 11	040	21 16	077	48 29	140	36 29	187	60 45	261	58 11	329
232	55 17	003	25 49	040	22 14	077	49 08	140	36 22	187	59 46	261	57 39	327
233	55 20	001	26 27	039	23 11	077	49 45	141	36 15	188	58 47	261	57 06	326
234	55 20	000	27 04	039	24 09	076	50 22	142	36 06	188	57 48	262	56 32	324
235	55 19	358	27 41	038	25 07	076	50 59	143	35 58	189	56 50	262	55 57	323
236	55 16	357	28 17	037	26 05	076	51 35	143	35 48	189	55 51	262	55 21	322
237	55 12	355	28 53	037	27 02	076	52 10	144	35 38	190	54 52	262	54 43	320
238	55 06	353	29 29	036	28 00	075	52 44	145	35 27	191	53 53	262	54 05	319
239	54 58	352	30 03	036	28 57	075	53 17	146	35 16	191	52 54	262	53 26	318
	VEGA		◆ ALTAIR		Shaula		◆ RIGIL KENT		SPICA		◆ ARCTURUS		Alphecca	
240	30 38	035	29 55	075	53 50	147	35 05	192	51 56	262	52 46	317	54 49	350
241	31 12	034	30 52	075	54 22	148	34 52	192	50 57	262	52 05	316	54 39	349
242	31 45	034	31 49	074	54 53	149	34 40	193	49 58	262	51 23	315	54 26	347
243	32 18	033	32 46	074	55 23	150	34 26	193	48 59	262	50 40	314	54 13	346
244	32 50	032	33 43	074	55 51	151	34 12	194	48 00	262	49 57	313	53 58	344
245	33 22	032	34 40	073	56 19	153	33 58	194	47 01	262	49 13	312	53 41	343
246	33 53	031	35 37	073	56 46	154	33 43	195	46 03	262	48 29	311	53 23	342
247	34 23	030	36 34	073	57 12	155	33 28	195	45 04	262	47 44	310	53 03	340
248	34 53	030	37 31	072	57 36	156	33 12	196	44 05	262	46 58	309	52 43	339
249	35 22	029	38 27	072	57 59	158	32 55	196	43 06	262	46 12	309	52 20	337
250	35 50	028	39 23	071	58 21	159	32 39	197	42 07	262	45 25	308	51 57	336
251	36 18	027	40 20	071	58 42	160	32 21	197	41 08	262	44 38	307	51 32	335
252	36 45	027	41 16	071	59 01	162	32 03	198	40 09	262	43 51	306	51 07	334
253	37 11	026	42 12	070	59 19	163	31 45	198	39 11	262	43 03	306	50 40	332
254	37 36	025	43 08	070	59 36	165	31 27	199	38 12	262	42 14	305	50 12	331
	VEGA		◆ ALTAIR		Peacock		◆ RIGIL KENT		SPICA		◆ ARCTURUS		Alphecca	
255	38 01	024	44 03	069	26 58	151	31 08	199	37 13	262	41 25	304	49 43	330
256	38 25	023	44 59	069	27 26	151	30 48	199	36 14	262	40 36	304	49 12	329
257	38 48	022	45 54	068	27 54	152	30 28	200	35 15	262	39 46	303	48 41	328
258	39 10	021	46 49	068	28 22	152	30 08	200	34 16	262	38 57	303	48 09	327
259	39 31	021	47 44	067	28 50	152	29 47	201	33 18	262	38 06	302	47 36	326
260	39 52	020	48 39	067	29 18	153	29 26	201	32 19	262	37 16	301	47 02	325
261	40 11	019	49 33	066	29 45	153	29 05	201	31 20	262	36 25	301	46 27	324
262	40 30	018	50 27	065	30 11	153	28 43	202	30 21	262	35 34	300	45 52	323
263	40 48	017	51 21	065	30 38	154	28 21	202	29 22	262	34 43	300	45 15	322
264	41 04	016	52 15	064	31 04	154	27 58	202	28 24	262	33 51	299	44 38	321
265	41 20	015	53 08	063	31 29	155	27 35	203	27 25	261	32 59	299	44 00	320
266	41 35	014	54 01	063	31 55	155	27 12	203	26 26	261	32 07	299	43 22	319
267	41 49	013	54 54	062	32 20	155	26 49	203	25 27	261	31 15	298	42 43	318
268	42 01	012	55 46	061	32 44	156	26 25	204	24 29	261	30 22	298	42 03	317
269	42 13	011	56 38	060	33 08	156	26 01	204	23 30	261	29 30	297	41 22	317

LHA ♈	Hc	Zn	Hc	Zn	Hc	Zn	Hc	Zn	Hc	Zn	Hc	Zn	Hc	Zn
	◆ VEGA		DENEB		Enif		◆ FOMALHAUT		Peacock		◆ ANTARES		ARCTURUS	
270	42 24	010	25 30	030	31 12	073	17 17	119	33 32	157	61 50	226	28 37	297
271	42 34	009	26 00	030	32 09	073	18 09	119	33 55	157	61 06	227	27 44	297
272	42 42	008	26 29	029	33 06	073	19 01	119	34 18	158	60 22	228	26 50	296
273	42 50	007	26 58	029	34 03	072	19 54	119	34 40	158	59 37	229	25 57	296
274	42 56	006	27 26	028	34 59	072	20 46	119	35 02	159	58 52	230	25 03	296
275	43 02	005	27 54	027	35 56	072	21 38	119	35 23	159	58 06	231	24 10	295
276	43 06	004	28 21	027	36 52	071	22 30	119	35 44	160	57 19	232	23 16	295
277	43 09	003	28 47	026	37 48	071	23 22	119	36 04	160	56 32	233	22 22	295
278	43 11	001	29 13	026	38 44	070	24 14	119	36 24	161	55 44	234	21 28	294
279	43 12	000	29 39	025	39 40	070	25 06	119	36 43	161	54 56	234	20 34	294
280	43 12	359	30 04	024	40 36	070	25 58	119	37 02	162	54 08	235	19 39	294
281	43 11	358	30 28	024	41 31	069	26 50	119	37 20	163	53 19	236	18 45	293
282	43 08	357	30 51	023	42 27	069	27 42	119	37 37	163	52 30	236	17 50	293
283	43 05	356	31 14	022	43 22	068	28 34	119	37 54	164	51 40	237	16 55	293
284	43 00	355	31 36	022	44 17	068	29 26	119	38 10	164	50 50	237	16 01	293
	DENEB		Enif		◆ FOMALHAUT		Peacock		◆ ANTARES		Rasalhague		◆ VEGA	
285	31 58	021	45 12	067	30 17	120	38 26	165	50 00	238	60 39	314	42 55	354
286	32 19	020	46 06	067	31 09	120	38 41	166	49 10	238	59 56	313	42 48	353
287	32 39	019	47 01	066	32 00	120	38 56	166	48 19	239	59 12	312	42 40	352
288	32 58	019	47 55	065	32 52	120	39 09	167	47 28	239	58 27	310	42 31	351
289	33 17	018	48 49	065	33 43	120	39 23	168	46 37	240	57 41	309	42 21	350
290	33 35	017	49 42	064	34 34	121	39 35	168	45 46	240	56 55	308	42 10	349
291	33 52	016	50 36	064	35 25	121	39 47	169	44 54	240	56 08	307	41 58	348
292	34 08	016	51 29	063	36 17	121	39 58	170	44 03	241	55 20	306	41 45	347
293	34 24	015	52 22	062	37 07	121	40 09	170	43 11	241	54 32	305	41 31	346
294	34 39	014	53 14	061	37 58	121	40 18	171	42 19	241	53 43	304	41 16	345
295	34 53	013	54 06	061	38 49	122	40 27	172	41 27	242	52 54	303	41 00	344
296	35 06	012	54 57	060	39 39	122	40 36	172	40 34	242	52 04	302	40 43	343
297	35 18	012	55 48	059	40 29	122	40 43	173	39 42	242	51 13	302	40 25	342
298	35 30	011	56 39	058	41 20	123	40 50	174	38 49	242	50 23	301	40 06	341
299	35 41	010	57 29	057	42 10	123	40 56	174	37 57	243	49 31	300	39 46	340
	◆ DENEB		Alpheratz		◆ FOMALHAUT		Peacock		◆ ANTARES		Rasalhague		VEGA	
300	35 50	009	19 31	055	42 59	123	41 02	175	37 04	243	48 40	299	39 25	339
301	35 59	008	20 20	055	43 49	124	41 07	176	36 11	243	47 48	299	39 04	338
302	36 07	007	21 08	054	44 38	124	41 10	177	35 18	243	46 56	298	38 41	337
303	36 15	007	21 57	054	45 27	125	41 14	177	34 25	243	46 03	298	38 18	337
304	36 21	006	22 45	054	46 16	125	41 16	178	33 32	243	45 10	297	37 54	336
305	36 26	005	23 32	053	47 05	125	41 18	179	32 39	244	44 17	296	37 29	335
306	36 31	004	24 20	053	47 53	126	41 19	179	31 45	244	43 24	296	37 04	334
307	36 34	003	25 07	052	48 41	126	41 19	180	30 52	244	42 30	295	36 37	333
308	36 37	002	25 54	052	49 28	127	41 18	181	29 59	244	41 36	295	36 10	332
309	36 39	001	26 41	052	50 16	128	41 17	182	29 05	244	40 42	294	35 42	332
310	36 40	000	27 27	051	51 03	128	41 15	182	28 12	244	39 48	294	35 14	331
311	36 40	000	28 13	051	51 49	129	41 12	183	27 18	244	38 53	293	34 44	330
312	36 39	359	28 59	050	52 35	129	41 08	184	26 25	244	37 59	293	34 15	329
313	36 37	358	29 45	050	53 21	130	41 04	185	25 31	244	37 04	292	33 44	329
314	36 34	357	30 30	049	54 06	131	40 59	185	24 38	244	36 09	292	33 13	328
	Alpheratz		◆ Diphda		ACHERNAR		Peacock		◆ Nunki		VEGA		◆ DENEB	
315	31 14	049	34 39	106	17 43	148	40 53	186	55 24	234	32 41	327	36 31	356
316	31 59	048	35 36	106	18 15	148	40 46	187	54 35	235	32 09	327	36 26	355
317	32 43	048	36 33	106	18 46	148	40 39	187	53 47	236	31 36	326	36 21	354
318	33 26	047	37 30	106	19 18	148	40 31	188	52 57	236	31 02	325	36 14	353
319	34 10	046	38 27	107	19 49	148	40 22	189	52 08	237	30 28	325	36 07	353
320	34 52	046	39 24	107	20 20	149	40 13	190	51 18	237	29 54	324	35 59	352
321	35 35	045	40 21	107	20 51	149	40 03	190	50 28	238	29 19	324	35 50	351
322	36 17	044	41 18	107	21 22	149	39 52	191	49 37	238	28 43	323	35 40	350
323	36 58	044	42 15	107	21 53	149	39 40	192	48 47	239	28 07	322	35 30	349
324	37 39	043	43 11	107	22 23	149	39 28	192	47 56	239	27 31	322	35 18	348
325	38 19	042	44 08	107	22 53	150	39 15	193	47 04	240	26 54	321	35 06	348
326	38 59	042	45 05	107	23 23	150	39 01	194	46 13	240	26 17	321	34 52	347
327	39 38	041	46 02	108	23 53	150	38 47	194	45 22	240	25 39	320	34 38	346
328	40 17	040	46 58	108	24 23	150	38 32	195	44 30	241	25 01	320	34 24	345
329	40 55	039	47 55	108	24 52	150	38 17	195	43 38	241	24 22	319	34 08	344
	◆ Alpheratz		Diphda		◆ ACHERNAR		Peacock		Nunki		◆ ALTAIR		DENEB	
330	41 32	039	48 51	108	25 21	151	38 01	196	42 46	241	53 48	297	33 52	344
331	42 09	038	49 48	108	25 50	151	37 44	197	41 54	242	52 55	296	33 34	343
332	42 45	037	50 44	109	26 19	151	37 27	197	41 01	242	52 02	296	33 16	342
333	43 20	036	51 40	109	26 47	152	37 09	198	40 09	242	51 08	295	32 58	341
334	43 55	035	52 36	109	27 16	152	36 51	198	39 16	242	50 14	294	32 38	341
335	44 28	034	53 33	109	27 43	152	36 32	199	38 23	243	49 20	294	32 18	340
336	45 01	033	54 29	110	28 11	153	36 12	199	37 31	243	48 26	293	31 57	339
337	45 33	032	55 24	110	28 38	153	35 52	200	36 38	243	47 31	293	31 36	338
338	46 05	031	56 20	110	29 05	153	35 32	201	35 45	243	46 36	292	31 14	338
339	46 35	030	57 16	111	29 32	154	35 10	201	34 51	243	45 41	292	30 51	337
340	47 04	029	58 11	111	29 58	154	34 49	202	33 58	244	44 45	291	30 27	336
341	47 33	028	59 07	112	30 24	154	34 27	202	33 05	244	43 50	291	30 03	336
342	48 00	027	60 02	112	30 50	155	34 04	203	32 12	244	42 54	290	29 38	335
343	48 26	026	60 57	113	31 15	155	33 41	203	31 18	244	41 58	290	29 13	334
344	48 52	025	61 51	113	31 40	156	33 18	203	30 25	244	41 02	289	28 47	334
	Alpheratz		◆ Hamal		◆ ACHERNAR		Peacock		Nunki		◆ ALTAIR		DENEB	
345	49 16	023	34 18	054	32 04	156	32 54	204	29 31	244	40 06	289	28 20	333
346	49 39	022	35 06	054	32 28	156	32 30	204	28 38	244	39 10	288	27 53	332
347	50 01	021	35 54	053	32 52	157	32 05	205	27 44	244	38 14	288	27 25	332
348	50 22	020	36 41	053	33 15	157	31 40	205	26 51	245	37 17	288	26 57	331
349	50 41	018	37 28	052	33 37	158	31 14	206	25 57	245	36 20	287	26 28	331
350	50 59	017	38 15	051	34 00	158	30 49	206	25 03	245	35 23	287	25 59	330
351	51 16	016	39 01	051	34 22	159	30 22	206	24 09	245	34 26	287	25 29	330
352	51 32	015	39 47	050	34 43	159	29 56	207	23 16	245	33 29	286	24 59	329
353	51 46	013	40 32	049	35 04	160	29 29	207	22 22	245	32 32	286	24 28	329
354	51 59	012	41 17	049	35 24	160	29 01	207	21 28	245	31 35	286	23 57	328
355	52 10	010	42 02	048	35 44	161	28 34	208	20 34	245	30 38	285	23 25	328
356	52 20	009	42 45	047	36 03	161	28 06	208	19 41	245	29 41	285	22 53	327
357	52 29	008	43 29	046	36 22	162	27 38	208	18 47	245	28 43	285	22 20	327
358	52 36	006	44 12	046	36 40	162	27 09	209	17 53	245	27 46	285	21 47	326
359	52 42	005	44 54	045	36 58	163	26 41	209	16 59	245	26 48	284	21 14	326

LHA ♈	Hc	Zn	Hc	Zn	Hc	Zn	Hc	Zn	Hc	Zn	Hc	Zn	Hc	Zn
	◆ Alpheratz		ALDEBARAN		◆ RIGEL		ACHERNAR		◆ FOMALHAUT		ALTAIR		DENEB	
0	51 46	003	16 58	070	12 14	096	38 13	163	64 55	213	25 36	284	19 51	325
1	51 48	002	17 53	069	13 13	096	38 29	164	64 22	215	24 38	284	19 17	325
2	51 50	000	18 49	069	14 12	096	38 45	165	63 47	216	23 41	284	18 43	324
3	51 49	359	19 44	069	15 11	096	39 01	165	63 12	217	22 43	284	18 08	324
4	51 47	358	20 39	068	16 10	096	39 16	166	62 35	219	21 46	283	17 33	324
5	51 44	356	21 34	068	17 09	096	39 30	166	61 58	220	20 48	283	16 58	323
6	51 40	355	22 29	068	18 08	096	39 44	167	61 19	221	19 50	283	16 22	323
7	51 33	353	23 24	068	19 07	096	39 57	168	60 39	223	18 53	283	15 46	322
8	51 26	352	24 19	067	20 06	095	40 09	168	59 59	224	17 55	282	15 10	322
9	51 17	351	25 13	067	21 05	095	40 21	169	59 18	225	16 57	282	14 34	322
10	51 07	349	26 08	067	22 04	095	40 32	170	58 35	226	15 59	282	13 57	321
11	50 55	348	27 02	066	23 03	095	40 42	170	57 53	227	15 01	282	13 20	321
12	50 42	347	27 56	066	24 02	095	40 52	171	57 09	228	14 03	282	12 42	321
13	50 27	345	28 50	065	25 01	095	41 00	172	56 25	228	13 05	281	12 04	320
14	50 12	344	29 44	065	26 00	095	41 09	172	55 41	229	12 07	281	11 27	320
	Hamal		ALDEBARAN		◆ RIGEL		ACHERNAR		◆ FOMALHAUT		Enif		◆ Alpheratz	
15	53 28	027	30 37	065	26 59	095	41 16	173	54 56	230	37 54	290	49 55	343
16	53 54	025	31 31	064	27 58	095	41 23	174	54 10	231	36 58	290	49 36	341
17	54 19	024	32 24	064	28 57	094	41 29	175	53 24	231	36 02	289	49 17	340
18	54 42	023	33 17	063	29 56	094	41 34	175	52 37	232	35 06	289	48 56	339
19	55 04	021	34 10	063	30 55	094	41 39	176	51 50	233	34 10	289	48 34	338
20	55 25	020	35 03	062	31 54	094	41 43	177	51 03	233	33 14	288	48 11	337
21	55 44	018	35 55	062	32 53	094	41 46	177	50 15	234	32 17	288	47 47	335
22	56 02	017	36 47	061	33 52	094	41 48	178	49 27	234	31 21	288	47 22	334
23	56 18	015	37 39	061	34 52	094	41 49	179	48 39	235	30 24	287	46 55	333
24	56 32	013	38 31	060	35 51	094	41 50	180	47 51	235	29 28	287	46 28	332
25	56 45	012	39 22	060	36 50	094	41 50	180	47 02	236	28 31	287	46 00	331
26	56 56	010	40 13	059	37 49	093	41 50	181	46 13	236	27 34	286	45 31	330
27	57 06	008	41 04	059	38 48	093	41 48	182	45 23	237	26 37	286	45 00	329
28	57 14	007	41 54	058	39 47	093	41 46	182	44 34	237	25 40	286	44 29	328
29	57 20	005	42 45	057	40 47	093	41 43	183	43 44	237	24 43	285	43 57	327
	CAPELLA		◆ BETELGEUSE		SIRIUS		CANOPUS		◆ ACHERNAR		FOMALHAUT		◆ Alpheratz	
30	19 29	034	28 58	076	20 14	105	21 33	143	41 39	184	42 54	238	43 25	326
31	20 01	034	29 56	076	21 12	105	22 08	144	41 35	185	42 04	238	42 51	325
32	20 34	033	30 53	076	22 09	104	22 43	144	41 30	185	41 13	238	42 17	324
33	21 06	033	31 51	075	23 06	104	23 18	144	41 24	186	40 23	239	41 42	323
34	21 38	032	32 48	075	24 04	104	23 53	144	41 17	187	39 32	239	41 06	322
35	22 09	032	33 45	075	25 01	104	24 27	144	41 10	187	38 41	239	40 30	322
36	22 40	031	34 42	074	25 59	104	25 02	145	41 02	188	37 50	239	39 53	321
37	23 11	031	35 39	074	26 56	104	25 36	145	40 53	189	36 59	240	39 15	320
38	23 41	030	36 36	074	27 53	104	26 10	145	40 43	190	36 08	240	38 37	319
39	24 10	030	37 33	073	28 51	104	26 44	145	40 33	190	35 17	240	37 58	319
40	24 39	029	38 30	073	29 48	104	27 17	146	40 22	191	34 25	240	37 18	318
41	25 08	028	39 26	073	30 46	104	27 51	146	40 11	192	33 34	240	36 38	317
42	25 36	028	40 23	072	31 43	104	28 24	146	39 58	192	32 42	241	35 57	316
43	26 03	027	41 19	072	32 41	104	28 57	146	39 46	193	31 51	241	35 16	316
44	26 30	027	42 15	071	33 38	104	29 30	147	39 32	194	30 59	241	34 35	315
	CAPELLA		◆ BETELGEUSE		SIRIUS		CANOPUS		◆ ACHERNAR		FOMALHAUT		◆ Alpheratz	
45	26 57	026	43 11	071	34 36	104	30 02	147	39 18	194	30 07	241	33 53	314
46	27 22	026	44 07	070	35 33	104	30 34	147	39 03	195	29 15	241	33 10	314
47	27 48	025	45 03	070	36 31	104	31 06	148	38 48	195	28 23	241	32 27	313
48	28 12	024	45 59	069	37 28	104	31 37	148	38 32	196	27 32	241	31 44	313
49	28 36	024	46 54	069	38 25	104	32 09	148	38 15	197	26 40	241	31 00	312
50	29 00	023	47 49	068	39 23	104	32 40	149	37 58	197	25 47	241	30 16	312
51	29 23	022	48 44	068	40 20	104	33 10	149	37 40	198	24 55	242	29 32	311
52	29 45	022	49 39	067	41 18	104	33 40	150	37 22	198	24 03	242	28 47	311
53	30 06	021	50 33	067	42 15	104	34 10	150	37 03	199	23 11	242	28 02	310
54	30 27	020	51 28	066	43 12	105	34 40	150	36 43	199	22 19	242	27 16	310
55	30 47	020	52 22	065	44 10	105	35 09	151	36 23	200	21 27	242	26 30	309
56	31 07	019	53 15	065	45 07	105	35 37	151	36 03	200	20 35	242	25 44	309
57	31 26	018	54 09	064	46 04	105	36 05	152	35 42	201	19 42	242	24 58	308
58	31 44	017	55 02	063	47 02	105	36 33	152	35 20	201	18 50	242	24 11	308
59	32 01	017	55 54	062	47 59	105	37 01	153	34 58	202	17 58	242	23 24	307
	◆ CAPELLA		POLLUX		◆ SIRIUS		CANOPUS		ACHERNAR		◆ Diphda		Hamal	
60	32 18	016	24 02	054	48 56	105	37 27	153	34 36	202	41 44	254	47 29	320
61	32 33	015	24 50	053	49 53	105	37 54	154	34 13	203	40 47	254	46 51	319
62	32 49	014	25 37	053	50 50	106	38 20	154	33 50	203	39 50	254	46 12	319
63	33 03	014	26 24	052	51 47	106	38 45	155	33 26	204	38 53	254	45 33	318
64	33 16	013	27 11	052	52 45	106	39 10	155	33 02	204	37 56	254	44 52	317
65	33 29	012	27 58	052	53 41	106	39 34	156	32 37	205	36 59	254	44 11	316
66	33 41	011	28 44	051	54 38	106	39 58	157	32 12	205	36 02	254	43 30	315
67	33 52	010	29 30	051	55 35	107	40 21	157	31 47	205	35 05	254	42 48	314
68	34 02	010	30 15	050	56 32	107	40 44	158	31 21	206	34 08	254	42 05	313
69	34 12	009	31 00	049	57 29	107	41 06	159	30 55	206	33 11	254	41 22	313
70	34 20	008	31 45	049	58 25	107	41 27	159	30 29	207	32 14	254	40 38	312
71	34 28	007	32 30	048	59 22	108	41 48	160	30 02	207	31 17	254	39 53	311
72	34 35	006	33 14	048	60 18	108	42 08	161	29 35	207	30 20	254	39 09	311
73	34 41	005	33 58	047	61 14	109	42 27	161	29 08	208	29 23	254	38 23	310
74	34 46	005	34 41	047	62 11	109	42 46	162	28 40	208	28 26	254	37 38	309
	CAPELLA		POLLUX		◆ REGULUS		CANOPUS		◆ ACHERNAR		Diphda		◆ Hamal	
75	34 51	004	35 24	046	10 23	076	43 04	163	28 12	208	27 28	254	36 52	309
76	34 54	003	36 06	045	11 21	076	43 22	163	27 44	209	26 31	254	36 05	308
77	34 57	002	36 48	045	12 18	076	43 38	164	27 15	209	25 34	254	35 18	307
78	34 58	001	37 29	044	13 16	075	43 54	165	26 47	209	24 37	254	34 31	307
79	34 59	000	38 10	043	14 13	075	44 09	166	26 18	209	23 40	254	33 43	306
80	34 59	000	38 50	042	15 10	075	44 23	166	25 48	210	22 43	254	32 55	306
81	34 58	359	39 30	042	16 08	075	44 37	167	25 19	210	21 46	254	32 07	305
82	34 56	358	40 09	041	17 05	075	44 50	168	24 49	210	20 49	254	31 19	305
83	34 54	357	40 48	040	18 02	074	45 01	169	24 19	210	19 52	254	30 30	304
84	34 50	356	41 26	039	18 59	074	45 13	170	23 49	211	18 55	254	29 41	304
85	34 46	355	42 03	038	19 56	074	45 23	170	23 19	211	17 58	254	28 51	303
86	34 41	354	42 39	038	20 53	074	45 32	171	22 48	211	17 01	254	28 02	303
87	34 34	354	43 15	037	21 49	073	45 41	172	22 17	211	16 04	254	27 12	302
88	34 27	353	43 50	036	22 46	073	45 48	173	21 47	211	15 07	254	26 22	302
89	34 20	352	44 25	035	23 43	073	45 55	174	21 16	212	14 10	254	25 31	302

LAT 9°S

LHA ♈	Hc	Zn	Hc	Zn	Hc	Zn	Hc	Zn	Hc	Zn	Hc	Zn	Hc	Zn
	POLLUX		◆ REGULUS		Suhail		◆ CANOPUS		Acamar		◆ ALDEBARAN		CAPELLA	
90	44 58	034	24 39	072	36 31	139	46 01	175	39 09	224	57 12	321	34 11	351
91	45 31	033	25 36	072	37 10	139	46 06	176	38 28	225	56 34	320	34 01	350
92	46 03	032	26 32	072	37 49	139	46 10	176	37 46	225	55 55	318	33 51	350
93	46 33	031	27 28	071	38 27	140	46 13	177	37 04	226	55 16	317	33 40	349
94	47 03	030	28 24	071	39 05	140	46 16	178	36 21	226	54 35	316	33 28	348
95	47 32	029	29 20	071	39 43	141	46 17	179	35 38	226	53 53	315	33 15	347
96	48 00	028	30 16	070	40 20	141	46 18	180	34 56	227	53 11	314	33 01	346
97	48 27	026	31 12	070	40 57	142	46 17	181	34 12	227	52 28	313	32 47	346
98	48 53	025	32 08	070	41 34	142	46 16	182	33 29	227	51 44	312	32 32	345
99	49 18	024	33 03	069	42 10	143	46 14	183	32 45	227	51 00	311	32 16	344
100	49 42	023	33 59	069	42 45	143	46 11	183	32 02	228	50 14	310	31 59	343
101	50 04	022	34 54	069	43 20	144	46 07	184	31 18	228	49 29	309	31 42	343
102	50 25	020	35 49	068	43 55	145	46 02	185	30 34	228	48 42	308	31 24	342
103	50 45	019	36 44	068	44 29	145	45 56	186	29 49	228	47 55	307	31 05	341
104	51 04	018	37 39	067	45 03	146	45 49	187	29 05	229	47 08	306	30 45	340
	POLLUX		◆ REGULUS		Suhail		◆ CANOPUS		RIGEL		◆ ALDEBARAN		CAPELLA	
105	51 22	016	38 33	067	45 36	147	45 42	188	64 06	270	46 20	306	30 25	340
106	51 38	015	39 28	066	46 08	147	45 33	189	63 07	270	45 32	305	30 04	339
107	51 52	014	40 22	066	46 40	148	45 24	189	62 08	269	44 43	304	29 43	338
108	52 06	012	41 16	065	47 11	149	45 14	190	61 08	269	43 54	304	29 20	338
109	52 18	011	42 10	065	47 41	149	45 03	191	60 09	269	43 04	303	28 58	337
110	52 28	010	43 03	064	48 11	150	44 51	192	59 10	269	42 14	302	28 34	336
111	52 37	008	43 57	064	48 40	151	44 39	193	58 11	269	41 24	302	28 10	336
112	52 45	007	44 50	063	49 09	152	44 25	193	57 11	269	40 33	301	27 45	335
113	52 51	005	45 42	063	49 36	153	44 11	194	56 12	269	39 42	300	27 20	334
114	52 56	004	46 35	062	50 03	154	43 56	195	55 13	269	38 51	300	26 54	334
115	52 59	002	47 27	061	50 29	155	43 40	196	54 14	268	37 59	299	26 28	333
116	53 00	001	48 19	061	50 54	155	43 24	197	53 14	268	37 08	299	26 01	333
117	53 01	359	49 10	060	51 18	156	43 07	197	52 15	268	36 15	298	25 33	332
118	52 59	358	50 01	059	51 41	157	42 49	198	51 16	268	35 23	298	25 05	331
119	52 56	356	50 52	058	52 03	158	42 30	199	50 17	268	34 31	297	24 36	331
	◆ REGULUS		SPICA		◆ ACRUX		CANOPUS		RIGEL		◆ BETELGEUSE		POLLUX	
120	51 42	058	10 00	100	18 21	154	42 11	199	49 17	268	55 01	297	52 52	355
121	52 32	057	10 59	100	18 46	154	41 51	200	48 18	268	54 08	296	52 46	354
122	53 21	056	11 57	100	19 12	154	41 30	201	47 19	268	53 15	295	52 38	352
123	54 10	055	12 56	100	19 38	155	41 09	201	46 20	268	52 21	295	52 29	351
124	54 58	054	13 54	099	20 03	155	40 47	202	45 21	267	51 27	294	52 19	349
125	55 45	053	14 52	099	20 28	155	40 25	203	44 21	267	50 33	293	52 07	348
126	56 32	052	15 51	099	20 53	155	40 01	203	43 22	267	49 38	293	51 54	346
127	57 19	051	16 49	099	21 18	155	39 38	204	42 23	267	48 44	292	51 39	345
128	58 04	050	17 48	099	21 43	155	39 14	204	41 24	267	47 49	292	51 23	344
129	58 49	048	18 47	099	22 08	156	38 49	205	40 25	267	46 54	291	51 06	342
130	59 33	047	19 45	099	22 32	156	38 23	206	39 25	267	45 58	291	50 48	341
131	60 16	046	20 44	099	22 56	156	37 58	206	38 26	267	45 03	290	50 28	340
132	60 57	044	21 42	099	23 20	156	37 31	207	37 27	267	44 07	290	50 07	338
133	61 38	043	22 41	098	23 44	157	37 04	207	36 28	266	43 11	289	49 44	337
134	62 18	041	23 39	098	24 07	157	36 37	208	35 29	266	42 15	289	49 21	336
	Dubhe		Denebola		◆ SPICA		ACRUX		◆ CANOPUS		SIRIUS		◆ POLLUX	
135	15 16	015	41 47	061	24 38	098	24 30	157	36 09	208	56 27	253	48 56	335
136	15 31	014	42 39	061	25 37	098	24 53	157	35 41	209	55 30	253	48 30	334
137	15 46	014	43 31	060	26 35	098	25 16	158	35 13	209	54 33	254	48 04	333
138	16 00	013	44 22	059	27 34	098	25 39	158	34 44	210	53 36	254	47 36	331
139	16 13	013	45 13	059	28 33	098	26 01	158	34 14	210	52 39	254	47 07	330
140	16 26	013	46 03	058	29 31	098	26 23	158	33 45	210	51 42	254	46 37	329
141	16 39	012	46 53	057	30 30	098	26 44	159	33 14	211	50 45	255	46 06	328
142	16 51	012	47 43	057	31 29	098	27 06	159	32 44	211	49 48	255	45 35	327
143	17 03	011	48 32	056	32 28	098	27 27	159	32 13	212	48 51	255	45 02	326
144	17 14	011	49 21	055	33 26	098	27 47	160	31 42	212	47 53	255	44 29	325
145	17 25	010	50 09	054	34 25	098	28 08	160	31 10	212	46 56	255	43 54	324
146	17 36	010	50 57	053	35 24	097	28 28	160	30 39	213	45 59	255	43 19	323
147	17 46	009	51 44	052	36 23	097	28 48	161	30 07	213	45 02	255	42 44	322
148	17 55	009	52 31	051	37 21	097	29 07	161	29 34	213	44 04	255	42 07	322
149	18 04	008	53 17	051	38 20	097	29 26	161	29 02	214	43 07	255	41 30	321
	Dubhe		ARCTURUS		◆ SPICA		ACRUX		◆ CANOPUS		SIRIUS		◆ POLLUX	
150	18 13	008	20 54	065	39 19	097	29 45	162	28 29	214	42 10	256	40 52	320
151	18 21	008	21 48	065	40 18	097	30 03	162	27 56	214	41 12	256	40 14	319
152	18 28	007	22 41	065	41 17	097	30 21	163	27 22	214	40 15	256	39 35	318
153	18 35	007	23 35	064	42 15	097	30 38	163	26 49	215	39 17	256	38 55	318
154	18 42	006	24 28	064	43 14	097	30 55	163	26 15	215	38 20	256	38 15	317
155	18 48	006	25 21	064	44 13	097	31 12	164	25 41	215	37 22	256	37 34	316
156	18 53	005	26 15	063	45 12	097	31 28	164	25 06	215	36 25	256	36 53	315
157	18 58	005	27 07	063	46 11	097	31 44	165	24 32	216	35 28	256	36 11	315
158	19 03	004	28 00	063	47 10	097	32 00	165	23 57	216	34 30	256	35 29	314
159	19 07	004	28 53	062	48 08	097	32 15	166	23 23	216	33 33	256	34 46	313
160	19 10	003	29 45	062	49 07	097	32 29	166	22 48	216	32 35	256	34 03	313
161	19 13	003	30 37	061	50 06	097	32 43	166	22 13	216	31 38	256	33 19	312
162	19 15	002	31 29	061	51 05	097	32 57	167	21 38	217	30 40	256	32 35	312
163	19 17	002	32 21	060	52 04	097	33 10	167	21 02	217	29 43	256	31 51	311
164	19 19	001	33 12	060	53 03	097	33 23	168	20 27	217	28 45	256	31 06	311
	Dubhe		◆ ARCTURUS		SPICA		◆ ACRUX		Suhail		SIRIUS		◆ POLLUX	
165	19 19	001	34 03	060	54 01	097	33 35	168	47 50	210	27 48	256	30 21	310
166	19 20	000	34 54	059	55 00	097	33 47	169	47 19	211	26 51	256	29 35	310
167	19 20	000	35 45	059	55 59	097	33 58	169	46 48	212	25 53	256	28 49	309
168	19 19	359	36 35	058	56 58	097	34 09	170	46 17	213	24 56	256	28 03	309
169	19 18	359	37 26	057	57 57	097	34 19	170	45 45	213	23 58	256	27 16	308
170	19 16	358	38 15	057	58 56	097	34 29	171	45 12	214	23 01	256	26 30	308
171	19 14	358	39 05	056	59 54	097	34 38	171	44 38	215	22 04	255	25 42	307
172	19 11	357	39 54	056	60 53	097	34 46	172	44 04	215	21 06	255	24 55	307
173	19 08	357	40 43	055	61 52	097	34 54	172	43 30	216	20 09	255	24 07	306
174	19 04	356	41 31	054	62 51	097	35 02	173	42 55	216	19 11	255	23 19	306
175	19 00	356	42 19	054	63 50	097	35 09	173	42 20	217	18 14	255	22 31	305
176	18 55	355	43 06	053	64 49	097	35 15	174	41 44	218	17 17	255	21 43	305
177	18 49	355	43 54	052	65 47	097	35 21	175	41 07	218	16 20	255	20 54	305
178	18 44	354	44 40	051	66 46	098	35 27	175	40 30	219	15 22	255	20 05	304
179	18 37	354	45 26	051	67 45	098	35 31	176	39 53	219	14 25	255	19 16	304

LHA ♈	ARCTURUS Hc	Zn	◆ ANTARES Hc	Zn	ACRUX Hc	Zn	◆ Suhail Hc	Zn	Alphard Hc	Zn	REGULUS Hc	Zn	◆ Dubhe Hc	Zn
180	46 12	050	24 01	115	35 36	176	39 16	220	52 33	267	55 26	307	18 30	353
181	46 57	049	24 54	115	35 39	177	38 38	220	51 34	267	54 38	306	18 23	353
182	47 41	048	25 48	115	35 42	177	37 59	220	50 35	267	53 49	305	18 15	352
183	48 25	047	26 42	115	35 45	178	37 21	221	49 35	267	53 01	304	18 07	352
184	49 09	046	27 35	115	35 47	178	36 42	221	48 36	267	52 11	303	17 58	351
185	49 51	045	28 29	115	35 48	179	36 03	222	47 37	267	51 21	302	17 49	351
186	50 33	044	29 22	115	35 49	180	35 23	222	46 38	267	50 31	301	17 39	350
187	51 14	043	30 16	115	35 49	180	34 43	222	45 39	267	49 40	301	17 29	350
188	51 54	042	31 09	116	35 49	181	34 03	223	44 40	267	48 49	300	17 18	349
189	52 34	041	32 03	116	35 48	181	33 23	223	43 40	266	47 57	299	17 07	349
190	53 13	040	32 56	116	35 46	182	32 42	223	42 41	266	47 05	298	16 55	348
191	53 50	039	33 50	116	35 44	182	32 01	224	41 42	266	46 13	298	16 43	348
192	54 27	038	34 43	116	35 41	183	31 20	224	40 43	266	45 20	297	16 30	348
193	55 03	036	35 36	116	35 38	183	30 39	224	39 44	266	44 28	297	16 17	347
194	55 37	035	36 29	116	35 34	184	29 57	225	38 45	266	43 34	296	16 04	347

LHA ♈	ARCTURUS Hc	Zn	◆ Rasalhague Hc	Zn	ANTARES Hc	Zn	◆ ACRUX Hc	Zn	Suhail Hc	Zn	◆ REGULUS Hc	Zn	Dubhe Hc	Zn
195	56 11	034	18 14	074	37 22	117	35 30	184	29 16	225	42 41	295	15 50	346
196	56 43	032	19 11	073	38 15	117	35 25	185	28 34	225	41 47	295	15 36	346
197	57 14	031	20 08	073	39 08	117	35 20	186	27 52	225	40 54	294	15 21	345
198	57 44	029	21 04	073	40 01	117	35 14	186	27 10	225	39 59	294	15 06	345
199	58 12	028	22 01	072	40 54	117	35 07	187	26 28	226	39 05	293	14 50	345
200	58 39	026	22 57	072	41 46	118	35 00	187	25 45	226	38 11	293	14 34	344
201	59 05	025	23 54	072	42 39	118	34 52	188	25 03	226	37 16	293	14 18	344
202	59 28	023	24 50	072	43 31	118	34 44	188	24 20	226	36 21	292	14 01	343
203	59 51	021	25 46	071	44 23	118	34 35	189	23 37	226	35 26	292	13 44	343
204	60 11	019	26 42	071	45 15	119	34 26	189	22 54	226	34 31	291	13 27	343
205	60 30	018	27 38	071	46 07	119	34 16	190	22 11	227	33 36	291	13 09	342
206	60 47	016	28 34	070	46 59	119	34 06	190	21 28	227	32 40	290	12 50	342
207	61 02	014	29 30	070	47 50	120	33 55	191	20 45	227	31 45	290	12 32	341
208	61 16	012	30 25	070	48 41	120	33 44	191	20 02	227	30 49	290	12 13	341
209	61 27	010	31 21	069	49 33	121	33 32	192	19 19	227	29 53	289	11 53	341

LHA ♈	ARCTURUS Hc	Zn	◆ Rasalhague Hc	Zn	ANTARES Hc	Zn	◆ RIGIL KENT Hc	Zn	ACRUX Hc	Zn	Gienah Hc	Zn	◆ REGULUS Hc	Zn
210	61 36	008	32 16	069	50 23	121	37 33	174	33 19	192	63 26	248	28 57	289
211	61 44	006	33 12	068	51 14	122	37 40	174	33 07	193	62 31	249	28 01	289
212	61 49	004	34 07	068	52 04	122	37 45	175	32 53	193	61 36	249	27 05	288
213	61 52	002	35 01	068	52 55	123	37 50	176	32 40	194	60 40	250	26 09	288
214	61 54	000	35 56	067	53 44	123	37 54	176	32 25	194	59 45	250	25 12	288
215	61 53	358	36 51	067	54 34	124	37 58	177	32 11	195	58 49	251	24 16	287
216	61 50	356	37 45	066	55 23	124	38 01	177	31 56	195	57 53	251	23 19	287
217	61 45	354	38 39	066	56 12	125	38 03	178	31 40	195	56 57	251	22 23	287
218	61 38	352	39 33	065	57 00	126	38 05	179	31 24	196	56 00	252	21 26	287
219	61 29	350	40 27	065	57 48	127	38 06	179	31 08	196	55 04	252	20 29	286
220	61 18	348	41 21	064	58 35	127	38 06	180	30 51	197	54 08	252	19 32	286
221	61 05	346	42 14	064	59 22	128	38 06	181	30 34	197	53 11	253	18 35	286
222	60 50	345	43 07	063	60 08	129	38 05	181	30 16	197	52 15	253	17 38	286
223	60 33	343	44 00	063	60 54	130	38 04	182	29 58	198	51 18	253	16 41	285
224	60 15	341	44 52	062	61 39	131	38 02	182	29 40	198	50 21	253	15 44	285

LHA ♈	Alphecca Hc	Zn	◆ VEGA Hc	Zn	ALTAIR Hc	Zn	◆ Shaula Hc	Zn	RIGIL KENT Hc	Zn	◆ SPICA Hc	Zn	ARCTURUS Hc	Zn
225	53 19	013	20 31	043	15 15	078	45 11	135	37 59	183	66 46	262	59 54	339
226	53 32	012	21 11	042	16 13	078	45 53	136	37 55	184	65 47	263	59 32	337
227	53 43	010	21 51	042	17 11	078	46 34	136	37 51	184	64 48	263	59 09	336
228	53 53	009	22 30	041	18 09	077	47 15	137	37 47	185	63 49	263	58 44	334
229	54 02	007	23 09	041	19 07	077	47 56	137	37 41	185	62 51	263	58 17	332
230	54 09	006	23 47	040	20 04	077	48 35	138	37 35	186	61 52	263	57 49	331
231	54 14	004	24 25	040	21 02	077	49 15	139	37 29	187	60 53	263	57 19	329
232	54 17	003	25 03	039	22 00	077	49 53	139	37 22	187	59 54	263	56 48	328
233	54 20	001	25 40	039	22 57	076	50 32	140	37 14	188	58 55	263	56 16	327
234	54 20	000	26 17	038	23 55	076	51 09	141	37 06	188	57 56	263	55 43	325
235	54 19	358	26 54	038	24 52	076	51 46	142	36 57	189	56 58	263	55 09	324
236	54 16	357	27 30	037	25 50	075	52 23	143	36 47	190	55 59	263	54 33	323
237	54 12	355	28 05	037	26 47	075	52 58	144	36 37	190	55 00	263	53 57	321
238	54 06	354	28 40	036	27 44	075	53 33	144	36 26	191	54 01	263	53 19	320
239	53 59	352	29 15	035	28 42	075	54 07	145	36 15	191	53 02	263	52 41	319

LHA ♈	VEGA Hc	Zn	◆ ALTAIR Hc	Zn	Shaula Hc	Zn	◆ RIGIL KENT Hc	Zn	SPICA Hc	Zn	◆ ARCTURUS Hc	Zn	Alphecca Hc	Zn
240	29 49	035	29 39	074	54 40	146	36 03	192	52 03	263	52 01	318	53 50	351
241	30 22	034	30 36	074	55 13	147	35 51	192	51 04	263	51 21	317	53 40	349
242	30 55	033	31 33	074	55 44	148	35 38	193	50 06	263	50 40	316	53 28	348
243	31 27	033	32 29	073	56 14	150	35 25	193	49 07	263	49 58	315	53 14	346
244	31 59	032	33 26	073	56 44	151	35 11	194	48 08	263	49 16	314	53 00	345
245	32 30	031	34 23	073	57 12	152	34 56	194	47 09	263	48 33	313	52 43	343
246	33 01	031	35 19	072	57 40	153	34 41	195	46 10	263	47 49	312	52 26	342
247	33 31	030	36 16	072	58 06	154	34 26	195	45 11	263	47 05	311	52 07	341
248	34 00	029	37 12	072	58 31	156	34 10	196	44 13	263	46 20	310	51 47	339
249	34 29	029	38 08	071	58 55	157	33 53	196	43 14	263	45 34	309	51 25	338
250	34 57	028	39 04	071	59 17	158	33 36	197	42 15	263	44 48	309	51 02	337
251	35 24	027	40 00	070	59 38	160	33 19	197	41 16	263	44 02	308	50 38	335
252	35 51	026	40 56	070	59 58	161	33 01	198	40 17	263	43 15	307	50 13	334
253	36 17	025	41 51	069	60 17	163	32 42	198	39 19	263	42 27	306	49 46	333
254	36 42	025	42 46	069	60 33	164	32 23	199	38 20	263	41 39	306	49 19	332

LHA ♈	VEGA Hc	Zn	◆ ALTAIR Hc	Zn	Peacock Hc	Zn	◆ RIGIL KENT Hc	Zn	SPICA Hc	Zn	◆ ARCTURUS Hc	Zn	Alphecca Hc	Zn
255	37 06	024	43 42	068	27 50	151	32 04	199	37 21	263	40 51	305	48 50	331
256	37 29	023	44 37	068	28 19	151	31 45	200	36 22	263	40 02	304	48 21	330
257	37 52	022	45 31	067	28 47	151	31 25	200	35 23	263	39 13	304	47 50	328
258	38 14	021	46 25	067	29 15	152	31 04	200	34 25	262	38 24	303	47 19	327
259	38 35	020	47 20	066	29 43	152	30 43	201	33 26	262	37 34	303	46 46	326
260	38 55	019	48 15	066	30 11	152	30 22	201	32 27	262	36 44	302	46 13	325
261	39 14	018	49 08	065	30 38	153	30 00	202	31 28	262	35 54	302	45 39	324
262	39 33	018	50 02	064	31 05	153	29 39	202	30 30	262	35 03	301	45 04	323
263	39 50	017	50 55	064	31 32	154	29 16	202	29 31	262	34 12	301	44 28	322
264	40 07	016	51 48	063	31 58	154	28 54	203	28 32	262	33 21	300	43 52	321
265	40 22	015	52 41	062	32 24	154	28 31	203	27 34	262	32 30	300	43 14	321
266	40 37	014	53 33	061	32 49	155	28 07	203	26 35	262	31 38	299	42 36	320
267	40 50	013	54 25	061	33 14	155	27 44	204	25 36	262	30 46	299	41 58	319
268	41 03	012	55 16	060	33 39	156	27 20	204	24 38	262	29 54	298	41 18	318
269	41 14	011	56 07	059	34 03	156	26 56	204	23 39	262	29 02	298	40 38	317

LHA ♈	◆ VEGA Hc	Zn	DENEB Hc	Zn	Enif Hc	Zn	◆ FOMALHAUT Hc	Zn	Peacock Hc	Zn	◆ ANTARES Hc	Zn	ARCTURUS Hc	Zn
270	41 25	010	24 38	030	30 55	073	17 46	118	34 27	157	62 31	228	28 09	297
271	41 34	009	25 08	030	31 51	072	18 38	118	34 50	157	61 46	229	27 17	297
272	41 43	008	25 37	029	32 48	072	19 30	118	35 13	157	61 01	230	26 24	297
273	41 50	007	26 05	028	33 44	072	20 22	118	35 35	158	60 16	231	25 31	296
274	41 56	006	26 33	028	34 40	071	21 14	118	35 57	158	59 30	232	24 37	296
275	42 02	005	27 00	027	35 36	071	22 07	118	36 19	159	58 43	233	23 44	296
276	42 06	004	27 27	027	36 32	070	22 59	118	36 40	160	57 56	233	22 51	295
277	42 09	002	27 54	026	37 28	070	23 51	118	37 00	160	57 08	234	21 57	295
278	42 11	001	28 19	025	38 23	070	24 43	118	37 20	161	56 20	235	21 03	295
279	42 12	000	28 44	025	39 19	069	25 35	119	37 40	161	55 31	236	20 09	294
280	42 12	359	29 09	024	40 14	069	26 27	119	37 59	162	54 42	236	19 15	294
281	42 11	358	29 33	023	41 09	068	27 19	119	38 17	162	53 52	237	18 21	294
282	42 08	357	29 56	023	42 04	068	28 11	119	38 35	163	53 03	237	17 26	293
283	42 05	356	30 19	022	42 59	067	29 03	119	38 52	164	52 13	238	16 32	293
284	42 00	355	30 41	021	43 54	067	29 55	119	39 08	164	51 22	238	15 37	293

LHA ♈	DENEB Hc	Zn	Enif Hc	Zn	◆ FOMALHAUT Hc	Zn	Peacock Hc	Zn	◆ ANTARES Hc	Zn	Rasalhague Hc	Zn	◆ VEGA Hc	Zn
285	31 02	021	44 48	066	30 47	119	39 24	165	50 32	239	59 56	315	41 55	354
286	31 22	020	45 42	066	31 38	119	39 39	165	49 41	239	59 14	314	41 48	353
287	31 42	019	46 36	065	32 30	119	39 54	166	48 50	240	58 31	313	41 41	352
288	32 01	018	47 30	064	33 22	120	40 08	167	47 59	240	57 47	312	41 32	351
289	32 20	018	48 23	064	34 13	120	40 21	167	47 07	240	57 03	310	41 22	350
290	32 38	017	49 16	063	35 05	120	40 34	168	46 16	241	56 17	309	41 11	349
291	32 54	016	50 09	062	35 56	120	40 46	169	45 24	241	55 31	308	40 59	348
292	33 11	015	51 01	062	36 47	120	40 57	169	44 32	242	54 44	307	40 47	347
293	33 26	015	51 53	061	37 38	121	41 08	170	43 40	242	53 57	306	40 33	346
294	33 41	014	52 45	060	38 29	121	41 18	171	42 47	242	53 09	305	40 18	345
295	33 54	013	53 36	059	39 20	121	41 27	171	41 55	242	52 20	304	40 02	344
296	34 07	012	54 27	059	40 11	121	41 35	172	41 02	243	51 31	304	39 45	343
297	34 20	011	55 17	058	41 01	122	41 43	173	40 10	243	50 41	303	39 28	342
298	34 31	011	56 07	057	41 52	122	41 50	174	39 17	243	49 51	302	39 09	341
299	34 41	010	56 56	056	42 42	122	41 56	174	38 24	243	49 01	301	38 50	340

LHA ♈	◆ DENEB Hc	Zn	Alpheratz Hc	Zn	◆ FOMALHAUT Hc	Zn	Peacock Hc	Zn	◆ ANTARES Hc	Zn	Rasalhague Hc	Zn	VEGA Hc	Zn
300	34 51	009	18 57	055	43 32	123	42 02	175	37 31	243	48 10	300	38 29	339
301	35 00	008	19 45	054	44 22	123	42 06	176	36 38	244	47 19	300	38 08	339
302	35 08	007	20 33	054	45 11	123	42 10	177	35 45	244	46 27	299	37 46	338
303	35 15	006	21 21	054	46 01	124	42 14	177	34 52	244	45 35	298	37 23	337
304	35 21	006	22 09	053	46 50	124	42 16	178	33 58	244	44 43	298	36 59	336
305	35 26	005	22 56	053	47 39	125	42 18	179	33 05	244	43 50	297	36 35	335
306	35 31	004	23 44	053	48 28	125	42 19	179	32 12	244	42 57	297	36 10	334
307	35 34	003	24 30	052	49 16	126	42 19	180	31 18	244	42 04	296	35 44	334
308	35 37	002	25 17	052	50 04	126	42 18	181	30 25	245	41 11	296	35 17	333
309	35 39	001	26 03	051	50 52	127	42 17	182	29 31	245	40 17	295	34 49	332
310	35 40	000	26 49	051	51 39	127	42 15	182	28 38	245	39 23	295	34 21	331
311	35 40	000	27 35	050	52 26	128	42 12	183	27 44	245	38 29	294	33 52	331
312	35 39	359	28 20	050	53 13	128	42 08	184	26 50	245	37 35	294	33 23	330
313	35 37	358	29 06	049	53 59	129	42 04	185	25 57	245	36 41	293	32 53	329
314	35 34	357	29 50	049	54 45	130	41 59	185	25 03	245	35 46	293	32 22	328

LHA ♈	Alpheratz Hc	Zn	◆ Diphda Hc	Zn	ACHERNAR Hc	Zn	Peacock Hc	Zn	◆ Nunki Hc	Zn	VEGA Hc	Zn	◆ DENEB Hc	Zn
315	30 35	048	34 55	106	18 34	148	41 53	186	55 58	235	31 51	328	35 31	356
316	31 19	048	35 53	106	19 06	148	41 46	187	55 09	236	31 19	327	35 26	355
317	32 02	047	36 50	106	19 37	148	41 38	188	54 20	237	30 46	326	35 21	354
318	32 45	046	37 47	106	20 09	148	41 30	188	53 30	237	30 13	326	35 15	354
319	33 28	046	38 44	106	20 40	148	41 21	189	52 40	238	29 39	325	35 08	353
320	34 10	045	39 41	106	21 11	148	41 12	190	51 50	238	29 05	324	35 00	352
321	34 52	045	40 38	106	21 42	148	41 02	190	50 59	239	28 30	324	34 51	351
322	35 34	044	41 35	106	22 13	149	40 51	191	50 08	239	27 55	323	34 41	350
323	36 14	043	42 32	106	22 44	149	40 39	192	49 17	240	27 20	323	34 31	349
324	36 55	043	43 29	106	23 15	149	40 27	192	48 26	240	26 44	322	34 19	349
325	37 35	042	44 25	106	23 45	149	40 13	193	47 34	241	26 07	322	34 07	348
326	38 14	041	45 22	106	24 15	150	40 00	194	46 43	241	25 30	321	33 54	347
327	38 53	040	46 19	107	24 45	150	39 45	194	45 51	241	24 53	321	33 40	346
328	39 31	040	47 16	107	25 15	150	39 30	195	44 59	242	24 15	320	33 26	345
329	40 08	039	48 13	107	25 44	150	39 15	196	44 07	242	23 37	320	33 10	345

LHA ♈	◆ Alpheratz Hc	Zn	Diphda Hc	Zn	◆ ACHERNAR Hc	Zn	Peacock Hc	Zn	Nunki Hc	Zn	◆ ALTAIR Hc	Zn	DENEB Hc	Zn
330	40 45	038	49 09	107	26 14	150	38 58	196	43 14	242	53 20	298	32 54	344
331	41 21	037	50 06	107	26 43	151	38 42	197	42 22	242	52 28	298	32 37	343
332	41 57	036	51 03	107	27 12	151	38 24	197	41 29	243	51 35	297	32 19	342
333	42 31	035	51 59	108	27 40	151	38 06	198	40 36	243	50 42	296	32 01	341
334	43 05	035	52 56	108	28 08	152	37 48	199	39 43	243	49 49	296	31 42	341
335	43 39	034	53 52	108	28 36	152	37 28	199	38 51	243	48 55	295	31 22	340
336	44 11	033	54 48	108	29 04	152	37 09	200	37 58	244	48 01	294	31 01	339
337	44 42	032	55 44	109	29 32	153	36 48	200	37 04	244	47 07	294	30 40	339
338	45 13	031	56 40	109	29 59	153	36 28	201	36 11	244	46 13	293	30 18	338
339	45 43	030	57 36	109	30 25	153	36 06	201	35 18	244	45 18	293	29 55	337
340	46 12	029	58 32	110	30 52	154	35 45	202	34 25	244	44 23	292	29 32	337
341	46 40	028	59 28	110	31 18	154	35 22	202	33 31	244	43 28	291	29 08	336
342	47 06	026	60 24	111	31 44	154	35 00	203	32 38	244	42 33	291	28 44	335
343	47 32	025	61 19	111	32 09	155	34 36	203	31 44	245	41 38	291	28 19	335
344	47 57	024	62 14	112	32 34	155	34 13	204	30 51	245	40 42	290	27 53	334

LHA ♈	Alpheratz Hc	Zn	◆ Hamal Hc	Zn	◆ ACHERNAR Hc	Zn	Peacock Hc	Zn	Nunki Hc	Zn	◆ ALTAIR Hc	Zn	DENEB Hc	Zn
345	48 21	023	33 43	054	32 59	156	33 49	204	29 57	245	39 46	290	27 26	333
346	48 43	022	34 30	053	33 23	156	33 24	205	29 03	245	38 50	289	27 00	333
347	49 05	021	35 18	053	33 47	156	32 59	205	28 10	245	37 54	289	26 32	332
348	49 25	019	36 05	052	34 10	157	32 34	205	27 16	245	36 58	288	26 04	332
349	49 44	018	36 51	051	34 33	157	32 08	206	26 22	245	36 02	288	25 36	331
350	50 02	017	37 37	051	34 55	158	31 42	206	25 29	245	35 06	288	25 07	330
351	50 18	016	38 23	050	35 17	158	31 16	207	24 35	245	34 09	287	24 37	330
352	50 33	014	39 08	049	35 39	159	30 49	207	23 41	245	33 12	287	24 07	329
353	50 47	013	39 53	049	36 00	159	30 22	207	22 47	245	32 16	287	23 37	329
354	51 00	012	40 37	048	36 21	160	29 55	208	21 54	245	31 19	286	23 06	328
355	51 11	010	41 21	047	36 41	161	29 27	208	21 00	245	30 22	286	22 34	328
356	51 21	009	42 04	047	37 00	161	28 59	208	20 06	245	29 25	286	22 02	327
357	51 29	007	42 47	046	37 19	162	28 30	209	19 12	245	28 28	285	21 30	327
358	51 36	006	43 29	045	37 37	162	28 02	209	18 18	245	27 30	285	20 57	326
359	51 42	005	44 11	044	37 55	163	27 33	209	17 25	245	26 33	285	20 24	326

LHA ♈	Hc	Zn	Hc	Zn	Hc	Zn	Hc	Zn	Hc	Zn	Hc	Zn	Hc	Zn
	◆ Alpheratz		Hamal		ALDEBARAN		◆ RIGEL		ACHERNAR		◆ FOMALHAUT		Enif	
0	50 46	003	44 08	043	16 37	069	12 21	096	39 10	163	65 45	214	50 56	300
1	50 48	002	44 48	042	17 32	069	13 19	096	39 27	164	65 11	216	50 04	299
2	50 50	000	45 27	041	18 27	069	14 18	096	39 43	164	64 36	217	49 12	298
3	50 49	359	46 05	040	19 22	068	15 17	096	39 59	165	63 59	219	48 20	298
4	50 48	358	46 42	039	20 17	068	16 16	096	40 14	166	63 22	220	47 28	297
5	50 44	356	47 19	038	21 12	068	17 15	096	40 28	166	62 43	221	46 35	296
6	50 40	355	47 55	037	22 06	067	18 13	095	40 42	167	62 04	223	45 41	296
7	50 34	354	48 30	036	23 01	067	19 12	095	40 55	167	61 23	224	44 48	295
8	50 26	352	49 04	035	23 55	067	20 11	095	41 08	168	60 42	225	43 54	294
9	50 18	351	49 37	034	24 49	066	21 10	095	41 20	169	60 00	226	43 00	294
10	50 08	349	50 09	032	25 43	066	22 09	095	41 31	170	59 17	227	42 06	293
11	49 56	348	50 41	031	26 37	066	23 08	095	41 41	170	58 33	228	41 12	293
12	49 43	347	51 11	030	27 31	065	24 07	095	41 51	171	57 49	229	40 17	292
13	49 29	346	51 40	029	28 25	065	25 06	094	42 00	172	57 05	230	39 23	292
14	49 14	344	52 08	027	29 18	065	26 04	094	42 08	172	56 19	230	38 28	291
	Hamal		ALDEBARAN		◆ RIGEL		ACHERNAR		◆ FOMALHAUT		Enif		◆ Alpheratz	
15	52 34	026	30 11	064	27 03	094	42 16	173	55 34	231	37 33	291	48 57	343
16	53 00	025	31 04	064	28 02	094	42 23	174	54 48	232	36 37	290	48 39	342
17	53 24	023	31 57	063	29 01	094	42 29	174	54 01	232	35 42	290	48 20	341
18	53 47	022	32 50	063	30 00	094	42 34	175	53 14	233	34 46	290	48 00	339
19	54 08	021	33 42	062	30 59	094	42 39	176	52 26	234	33 50	289	47 38	338
20	54 28	019	34 35	062	31 58	093	42 42	177	51 39	234	32 55	289	47 16	337
21	54 47	018	35 26	061	32 57	093	42 45	177	50 50	235	31 59	288	46 52	336
22	55 04	016	36 18	061	33 56	093	42 48	178	50 02	235	31 03	288	46 27	335
23	55 20	015	37 10	060	34 55	093	42 49	179	49 13	236	30 06	288	46 02	334
24	55 34	013	38 01	060	35 54	093	42 50	180	48 24	236	29 10	287	45 35	333
25	55 46	011	38 52	059	36 53	093	42 50	180	47 35	237	28 14	287	45 07	331
26	55 57	010	39 42	059	37 52	093	42 50	181	46 46	237	27 17	287	44 38	330
27	56 07	008	40 32	058	38 51	092	42 48	182	45 56	237	26 20	286	44 09	329
28	56 14	007	41 22	057	39 50	092	42 46	183	45 06	238	25 24	286	43 38	328
29	56 20	005	42 12	057	40 49	092	42 43	183	44 16	238	24 27	286	43 07	327
	CAPELLA		◆ BETELGEUSE		SIRIUS		CANOPUS		◆ ACHERNAR		FOMALHAUT		◆ Alpheratz	
30	18 39	034	28 44	076	20 29	104	22 21	143	42 39	184	43 26	239	42 35	327
31	19 11	033	29 41	075	21 27	104	22 56	143	42 35	185	42 35	239	42 02	326
32	19 44	033	30 38	075	22 24	104	23 31	144	42 29	185	41 44	239	41 28	325
33	20 16	032	31 35	075	23 21	104	24 06	144	42 23	186	40 54	239	40 54	324
34	20 47	032	32 32	074	24 18	104	24 41	144	42 17	187	40 03	240	40 18	323
35	21 18	031	33 29	074	25 16	104	25 16	144	42 09	188	39 12	240	39 43	322
36	21 49	031	34 26	074	26 13	104	25 50	144	42 01	188	38 21	240	39 06	321
37	22 19	030	35 22	073	27 11	104	26 25	145	41 52	189	37 29	240	38 29	321
38	22 49	030	36 19	073	28 08	104	26 59	145	41 42	190	36 38	240	37 51	320
39	23 18	029	37 15	073	29 05	104	27 33	145	41 32	190	35 46	241	37 12	319
40	23 47	029	38 12	072	30 03	104	28 07	145	41 21	191	34 55	241	36 33	318
41	24 15	028	39 08	072	31 00	104	28 40	146	41 09	192	34 03	241	35 54	318
42	24 43	028	40 04	071	31 58	104	29 14	146	40 57	192	33 12	241	35 14	317
43	25 10	027	41 00	071	32 55	104	29 47	146	40 44	193	32 20	241	34 33	316
44	25 37	027	41 56	070	33 53	104	30 20	146	40 30	194	31 28	241	33 52	316
	CAPELLA		◆ BETELGEUSE		SIRIUS		CANOPUS		◆ ACHERNAR		FOMALHAUT		◆ Alpheratz	
45	26 03	026	42 51	070	34 50	104	30 52	147	40 16	194	30 36	241	33 11	315
46	26 28	025	43 47	069	35 47	103	31 25	147	40 01	195	29 44	242	32 29	314
47	26 53	025	44 42	069	36 45	103	31 57	147	39 45	196	28 52	242	31 46	314
48	27 18	024	45 37	068	37 42	103	32 28	148	39 29	196	28 00	242	31 03	313
49	27 41	023	46 32	068	38 40	103	33 00	148	39 12	197	27 08	242	30 20	313
50	28 05	023	47 27	067	39 37	104	33 31	148	38 55	197	26 16	242	29 36	312
51	28 27	022	48 21	067	40 35	104	34 02	149	38 37	198	25 24	242	28 52	311
52	28 49	021	49 15	066	41 32	104	34 32	149	38 18	199	24 32	242	28 08	311
53	29 10	021	50 09	065	42 30	104	35 02	150	37 59	199	23 40	242	27 23	310
54	29 31	020	51 03	065	43 27	104	35 32	150	37 40	200	22 47	242	26 38	310
55	29 51	019	51 56	064	44 24	104	36 01	151	37 20	200	21 55	242	25 52	309
56	30 10	019	52 49	063	45 22	104	36 30	151	36 59	201	21 03	242	25 06	309
57	30 29	018	53 41	063	46 19	104	36 58	151	36 38	201	20 11	242	24 20	309
58	30 46	017	54 34	062	47 17	104	37 26	152	36 16	202	19 19	242	23 34	308
59	31 04	016	55 26	061	48 14	104	37 54	152	35 54	202	18 26	242	22 47	308
	◆ CAPELLA		POLLUX		◆ SIRIUS		CANOPUS		ACHERNAR		◆ Diphda		Hamal	
60	31 20	016	23 26	053	49 11	104	38 21	153	35 31	203	42 01	255	46 43	321
61	31 36	015	24 14	053	50 09	104	38 48	153	35 08	203	41 03	255	46 05	320
62	31 50	014	25 01	053	51 06	104	39 14	154	34 45	204	40 06	255	45 27	319
63	32 04	013	25 47	052	52 03	104	39 39	155	34 21	204	39 09	255	44 48	318
64	32 18	013	26 34	052	53 00	105	40 05	155	33 57	205	38 12	255	44 08	317
65	32 30	012	27 20	051	53 57	105	40 29	156	33 32	205	37 15	255	43 28	317
66	32 42	011	28 06	051	54 55	105	40 53	156	33 07	205	36 18	255	42 47	316
67	32 53	010	28 51	050	55 52	105	41 17	157	32 41	206	35 21	255	42 06	315
68	33 03	009	29 37	050	56 49	105	41 39	158	32 15	206	34 24	255	41 23	314
69	33 12	009	30 21	049	57 46	106	42 02	158	31 49	207	33 27	255	40 41	313
70	33 21	008	31 06	048	58 42	106	42 23	159	31 23	207	32 30	255	39 57	313
71	33 29	007	31 50	048	59 39	106	42 44	160	30 56	207	31 33	255	39 14	312
72	33 35	006	32 33	047	60 36	106	43 05	160	30 28	208	30 36	255	38 29	311
73	33 41	005	33 17	047	61 33	107	43 24	161	30 01	208	29 38	255	37 45	310
74	33 46	005	33 59	046	62 29	107	43 43	162	29 33	208	28 41	255	37 00	310
	CAPELLA		POLLUX		◆ REGULUS		CANOPUS		◆ ACHERNAR		Diphda		◆ Hamal	
75	33 51	004	34 42	045	10 09	076	44 01	162	29 05	209	27 44	255	36 14	309
76	33 54	003	35 24	045	11 06	076	44 19	163	28 37	209	26 47	255	35 28	309
77	33 57	002	36 05	044	12 03	075	44 36	164	28 08	209	25 50	255	34 42	308
78	33 58	001	36 46	043	13 01	075	44 52	165	27 39	209	24 53	255	33 55	307
79	33 59	000	37 26	043	13 58	075	45 07	165	27 10	210	23 56	255	33 08	307
80	33 59	000	38 06	042	14 55	075	45 22	166	26 40	210	22 59	255	32 20	306
81	33 58	359	38 45	041	15 52	074	45 35	167	26 11	210	22 02	255	31 32	306
82	33 56	358	39 24	040	16 49	074	45 48	168	25 41	210	21 05	255	30 44	305
83	33 54	357	40 02	040	17 45	074	46 00	169	25 11	211	20 08	254	29 56	305
84	33 50	356	40 39	039	18 42	074	46 12	169	24 41	211	19 11	254	29 07	304
85	33 46	355	41 16	038	19 39	073	46 22	170	24 10	211	18 15	254	28 18	304
86	33 41	355	41 52	037	20 35	073	46 31	171	23 39	211	17 18	254	27 29	303
87	33 35	354	42 27	036	21 32	073	46 40	172	23 09	212	16 21	254	26 39	303
88	33 28	353	43 02	035	22 28	073	46 48	173	22 38	212	15 24	254	25 50	302
89	33 20	352	43 35	034	23 25	072	46 55	174	22 07	212	14 27	254	25 00	302

LHA ♈	Hc	Zn	Hc	Zn	Hc	Zn	Hc	Zn	Hc	Zn	Hc	Zn	Hc	Zn
	POLLUX		◆ REGULUS		Suhail		◆ CANOPUS		Acamar		◆ ALDEBARAN		CAPELLA	
90	44 08	033	24 21	072	37 16	138	47 01	175	39 52	225	56 25	322	33 12	351
91	44 40	032	25 17	072	37 55	138	47 06	175	39 10	225	55 48	321	33 02	350
92	45 11	031	26 13	071	38 34	139	47 10	176	38 28	226	55 10	319	32 52	350
93	45 42	030	27 09	071	39 13	139	47 13	177	37 45	226	54 31	318	32 41	349
94	46 11	029	28 05	071	39 51	140	47 16	178	37 03	226	53 51	317	32 29	348
95	46 40	028	29 00	070	40 29	140	47 17	179	36 20	227	53 11	316	32 17	347
96	47 07	027	29 56	070	41 07	141	47 18	180	35 37	227	52 29	315	32 03	347
97	47 33	026	30 51	070	41 44	141	47 17	181	34 53	227	51 47	314	31 49	346
98	47 59	025	31 47	069	42 21	142	47 16	182	34 10	228	51 04	313	31 34	345
99	48 23	024	32 42	069	42 57	142	47 14	183	33 26	228	50 20	312	31 18	344
100	48 46	022	33 37	068	43 33	143	47 11	184	32 42	228	49 36	311	31 02	343
101	49 08	021	34 32	068	44 09	143	47 07	184	31 58	228	48 50	310	30 45	343
102	49 29	020	35 26	068	44 44	144	47 02	185	31 13	229	48 05	309	30 27	342
103	49 49	019	36 21	067	45 18	145	46 56	186	30 29	229	47 19	308	30 08	341
104	50 07	017	37 15	067	45 52	145	46 49	187	29 44	229	46 32	307	29 49	341
	POLLUX		◆ REGULUS		Suhail		◆ CANOPUS		RIGEL		◆ ALDEBARAN		CAPELLA	
105	50 24	016	38 09	066	46 26	146	46 41	188	64 05	272	45 45	307	29 29	340
106	50 40	015	39 03	066	46 58	147	46 33	189	63 06	272	44 57	306	29 08	339
107	50 54	013	39 57	065	47 30	147	46 23	190	62 07	271	44 09	305	28 47	338
108	51 07	012	40 51	065	48 02	148	46 13	190	61 08	271	43 20	304	28 25	338
109	51 19	011	41 44	064	48 33	149	46 02	191	60 09	271	42 31	304	28 02	337
110	51 29	009	42 37	063	49 03	150	45 50	192	59 10	271	41 42	303	27 39	337
111	51 38	008	43 30	063	49 33	150	45 37	193	58 11	271	40 52	302	27 15	336
112	51 45	007	44 22	062	50 01	151	45 24	194	57 12	270	40 02	302	26 51	335
113	51 51	005	45 14	062	50 29	152	45 09	194	56 13	270	39 11	301	26 26	335
114	51 56	004	46 06	061	50 56	153	44 54	195	55 14	270	38 21	301	26 00	334
115	51 59	002	46 58	060	51 23	154	44 38	196	54 14	270	37 30	300	25 34	333
116	52 00	001	47 49	060	51 48	155	44 21	197	53 15	270	36 38	299	25 07	333
117	52 01	359	48 39	059	52 13	156	44 04	198	52 16	270	35 47	299	24 40	332
118	51 59	358	49 30	058	52 36	157	43 46	198	51 17	269	34 55	298	24 12	332
119	51 56	357	50 20	057	52 59	158	43 27	199	50 18	269	34 03	298	23 44	331
	◆ REGULUS		SPICA		◆ ACRUX		CANOPUS		RIGEL		◆ BETELGEUSE		POLLUX	
120	51 09	056	10 11	100	19 15	154	43 07	200	49 19	269	54 33	298	51 52	355
121	51 58	056	11 09	100	19 40	154	42 47	200	48 20	269	53 41	297	51 46	354
122	52 47	055	12 07	099	20 06	154	42 26	201	47 21	269	52 48	297	51 39	352
123	53 35	054	13 05	099	20 32	154	42 05	202	46 22	269	51 55	296	51 30	351
124	54 22	053	14 04	099	20 57	155	41 43	202	45 23	268	51 02	295	51 20	349
125	55 09	052	15 02	099	21 23	155	41 20	203	44 24	268	50 09	295	51 09	348
126	55 55	051	16 00	099	21 48	155	40 56	204	43 25	268	49 15	294	50 56	347
127	56 40	050	16 59	099	22 13	155	40 33	204	42 26	268	48 21	293	50 41	345
128	57 25	048	17 57	099	22 38	155	40 08	205	41 26	268	47 26	293	50 26	344
129	58 08	047	18 56	099	23 02	155	39 43	205	40 27	268	46 31	292	50 09	343
130	58 51	046	19 54	098	23 27	156	39 17	206	39 28	268	45 37	292	49 51	341
131	59 33	045	20 53	098	23 51	156	38 51	206	38 29	267	44 42	291	49 31	340
132	60 14	043	21 51	098	24 15	156	38 25	207	37 30	267	43 46	291	49 11	339
133	60 54	042	22 49	098	24 39	156	37 58	208	36 31	267	42 51	290	48 49	338
134	61 33	040	23 48	098	25 02	157	37 30	208	35 32	267	41 55	290	48 26	336
	Dubhe		Denebola		◆ SPICA		ACRUX		◆ CANOPUS		SIRIUS		◆ POLLUX	
135	14 18	015	41 18	060	24 47	098	25 26	157	37 02	208	56 43	255	48 02	335
136	14 33	014	42 09	060	25 45	098	25 49	157	36 34	209	55 46	255	47 36	334
137	14 47	014	43 00	059	26 44	098	26 12	157	36 05	209	54 49	255	47 10	333
138	15 01	013	43 51	059	27 42	098	26 34	158	35 36	210	53 52	255	46 43	332
139	15 15	013	44 41	058	28 41	097	26 56	158	35 06	210	52 55	255	46 15	331
140	15 28	013	45 31	057	29 39	097	27 18	158	34 36	211	51 58	256	45 45	330
141	15 40	012	46 20	056	30 38	097	27 40	159	34 06	211	51 00	256	45 15	329
142	15 53	012	47 09	056	31 37	097	28 02	159	33 35	212	50 03	256	44 44	328
143	16 04	011	47 58	055	32 35	097	28 23	159	33 04	212	49 06	256	44 12	327
144	16 16	011	48 46	054	33 34	097	28 44	160	32 33	212	48 08	256	43 39	326
145	16 26	010	49 34	053	34 33	097	29 04	160	32 01	213	47 11	256	43 05	325
146	16 37	010	50 21	052	35 31	097	29 24	160	31 29	213	46 14	256	42 31	324
147	16 46	009	51 07	051	36 30	097	29 44	161	30 57	213	45 16	256	41 56	323
148	16 56	009	51 53	050	37 29	097	30 04	161	30 24	214	44 19	256	41 20	322
149	17 05	008	52 38	049	38 27	096	30 23	161	29 51	214	43 22	256	40 43	321
	Dubhe		ARCTURUS		◆ SPICA		ACRUX		◆ CANOPUS		SIRIUS		◆ POLLUX	
150	17 13	008	20 29	065	39 26	096	30 42	162	29 18	214	42 24	256	40 06	320
151	17 21	007	21 22	065	40 25	096	31 00	162	28 45	214	41 27	256	39 28	320
152	17 29	007	22 16	064	41 24	096	31 18	162	28 12	215	40 29	256	38 50	319
153	17 35	007	23 09	064	42 22	096	31 36	163	27 38	215	39 32	256	38 11	318
154	17 42	006	24 02	064	43 21	096	31 53	163	27 04	215	38 34	257	37 31	317
155	17 48	006	24 55	063	44 20	096	32 10	164	26 30	215	37 37	257	36 51	317
156	17 53	005	25 47	063	45 19	096	32 26	164	25 55	216	36 39	257	36 10	316
157	17 58	005	26 40	063	46 17	096	32 42	165	25 21	216	35 42	257	35 28	315
158	18 03	004	27 32	062	47 16	096	32 58	165	24 46	216	34 45	256	34 47	315
159	18 07	004	28 25	062	48 15	096	33 13	165	24 11	216	33 47	256	34 04	314
160	18 10	003	29 16	061	49 14	096	33 28	166	23 36	216	32 50	256	33 22	313
161	18 13	003	30 08	061	50 13	096	33 42	166	23 01	217	31 52	256	32 38	313
162	18 15	002	31 00	060	51 11	096	33 55	167	22 26	217	30 55	256	31 55	312
163	18 17	002	31 51	060	52 10	095	34 09	167	21 50	217	29 57	256	31 11	312
164	18 19	001	32 42	059	53 09	095	34 22	168	21 15	217	29 00	256	30 27	311
	Dubhe		◆ ARCTURUS		SPICA		◆ ACRUX		Suhail		SIRIUS		◆ POLLUX	
165	18 19	001	33 33	059	54 08	095	34 34	168	48 41	211	28 02	256	29 42	310
166	18 20	000	34 23	058	55 07	095	34 46	169	48 11	212	27 05	256	28 57	310
167	18 20	000	35 13	058	56 05	095	34 57	169	47 39	212	26 08	256	28 11	309
168	18 19	359	36 03	057	57 04	095	35 08	170	47 07	213	25 10	256	27 25	309
169	18 18	359	36 53	057	58 03	095	35 18	170	46 35	214	24 13	256	26 39	308
170	18 16	358	37 42	056	59 02	095	35 28	171	46 01	215	23 16	256	25 53	308
171	18 14	358	38 31	056	60 01	095	35 37	171	45 28	215	22 18	256	25 06	308
172	18 11	357	39 20	055	61 00	095	35 46	172	44 53	216	21 21	256	24 19	307
173	18 08	357	40 08	054	61 59	095	35 54	172	44 18	216	20 24	256	23 32	307
174	18 04	356	40 56	054	62 57	095	36 01	173	43 43	217	19 27	256	22 44	306
175	18 00	356	41 43	053	63 56	095	36 09	173	43 07	218	18 29	256	21 56	306
176	17 55	355	42 30	052	64 55	095	36 15	174	42 31	218	17 32	255	21 08	305
177	17 50	355	43 17	052	65 54	095	36 21	174	41 54	219	16 35	255	20 20	305
178	17 44	354	44 03	051	66 53	095	36 26	175	41 17	219	15 38	255	19 32	305
179	17 38	354	44 48	050	67 52	095	36 31	176	40 40	220	14 41	255	18 43	304

LHA ♈	Hc	Zn	Hc	Zn	Hc	Zn	Hc	Zn	Hc	Zn	Hc	Zn	Hc	Zn
	ARCTURUS		◆ANTARES		ACRUX		◆Suhail		Alphard		REGULUS		◆Dubhe	
180	45 33	049	24 26	115	36 35	176	40 02	220	52 35	269	54 49	308	17 31	353
181	46 17	048	25 20	115	36 39	177	39 24	221	51 36	269	54 02	307	17 24	353
182	47 01	047	26 13	115	36 42	177	38 45	221	50 37	268	53 15	306	17 16	352
183	47 44	047	27 07	115	36 45	178	38 06	221	49 38	268	52 27	305	17 07	352
184	48 27	046	28 01	115	36 47	178	37 27	222	48 39	268	51 38	304	16 59	351
185	49 09	045	28 54	115	36 48	179	36 47	222	47 40	268	50 49	303	16 50	351
186	49 50	044	29 48	115	36 49	180	36 07	223	46 41	268	49 59	302	16 40	350
187	50 30	043	30 41	115	36 49	180	35 27	223	45 42	268	49 09	302	16 30	350
188	51 10	041	31 35	115	36 49	181	34 47	223	44 43	268	48 18	301	16 19	349
189	51 49	040	32 29	115	36 48	181	34 06	224	43 44	267	47 27	300	16 08	349
190	52 26	039	33 22	115	36 46	182	33 25	224	42 45	267	46 36	299	15 56	348
191	53 03	038	34 15	115	36 44	182	32 44	224	41 46	267	45 45	299	15 44	348
192	53 39	037	35 09	115	36 41	183	32 03	224	40 47	267	44 53	298	15 32	348
193	54 14	036	36 02	116	36 38	183	31 22	225	39 48	267	44 00	297	15 19	347
194	54 48	034	36 55	116	36 34	184	30 40	225	38 49	267	43 08	297	15 06	347
	ARCTURUS		◆Rasalhague		ANTARES		◆ACRUX		Suhail		◆REGULUS		Denebola	
195	55 21	033	17 57	073	37 49	116	36 30	185	29 58	225	42 15	296	59 58	324
196	55 52	032	18 54	073	38 42	116	36 25	185	29 16	225	41 22	296	59 23	323
197	56 22	030	19 50	073	39 35	116	36 19	186	28 34	226	40 28	295	58 46	321
198	56 51	029	20 46	072	40 28	116	36 13	186	27 52	226	39 35	295	58 09	320
199	57 19	027	21 43	072	41 21	117	36 07	187	27 09	226	38 41	294	57 30	319
200	57 45	026	22 39	072	42 14	117	35 59	187	26 27	226	37 47	294	56 51	317
201	58 10	024	23 35	071	43 06	117	35 52	188	25 44	226	36 53	293	56 10	316
202	58 33	022	24 31	071	43 59	117	35 43	188	25 01	226	35 58	293	55 29	315
203	58 55	021	25 27	071	44 51	118	35 34	189	24 19	227	35 04	292	54 46	314
204	59 15	019	26 23	071	45 44	118	35 25	189	23 36	227	34 09	292	54 03	313
205	59 33	017	27 18	070	46 36	118	35 15	190	22 53	227	33 14	291	53 19	311
206	59 49	015	28 14	070	47 28	118	35 05	190	22 09	227	32 19	291	52 35	310
207	60 04	014	29 09	069	48 20	119	34 54	191	21 26	227	31 24	291	51 49	309
208	60 17	012	30 04	069	49 11	119	34 42	191	20 43	227	30 28	290	51 03	308
209	60 28	010	30 59	069	50 03	120	34 30	192	20 00	227	29 33	290	50 17	308
	ARCTURUS		◆Rasalhague		ANTARES		◆RIGIL KENT		ACRUX		Gienah		◆REGULUS	
210	60 37	008	31 54	068	50 54	120	38 33	174	34 18	192	63 48	250	28 37	290
211	60 44	006	32 49	068	51 45	120	38 39	174	34 05	193	62 52	251	27 42	289
212	60 49	004	33 44	067	52 36	121	38 45	175	33 52	193	61 56	251	26 46	289
213	60 53	002	34 38	067	53 26	121	38 50	176	33 38	194	61 00	252	25 50	289
214	60 54	000	35 33	067	54 17	122	38 54	176	33 23	194	60 04	252	24 54	288
215	60 53	358	36 27	066	55 07	123	38 58	177	33 09	195	59 08	252	23 58	288
216	60 50	356	37 21	066	55 56	123	39 01	177	32 53	195	58 11	253	23 01	288
217	60 45	354	38 15	065	56 45	124	39 03	178	32 38	196	57 15	253	22 05	287
218	60 38	352	39 08	065	57 34	124	39 05	179	32 22	196	56 18	253	21 08	287
219	60 30	351	40 01	064	58 23	125	39 06	179	32 05	196	55 22	253	20 12	287
220	60 19	349	40 54	064	59 11	126	39 06	180	31 48	197	54 25	254	19 15	286
221	60 06	347	41 47	063	59 58	127	39 06	181	31 31	197	53 28	254	18 19	286
222	59 52	345	42 40	062	60 46	128	39 05	181	31 13	198	52 32	254	17 22	286
223	59 36	343	43 32	062	61 32	129	39 04	182	30 55	198	51 35	254	16 25	286
224	59 18	341	44 24	061	62 18	130	39 01	182	30 36	198	50 38	254	15 28	285
	Alphecca		◆VEGA		ALTAIR		◆Shaula		RIGIL KENT		◆SPICA		ARCTURUS	
225	52 21	013	19 47	042	15 03	078	45 54	134	38 59	183	66 52	265	58 58	340
226	52 33	012	20 26	042	16 00	078	46 36	135	38 55	184	65 53	265	58 37	338
227	52 44	010	21 06	041	16 58	077	47 17	135	38 51	184	64 55	265	58 14	336
228	52 54	009	21 45	041	17 56	077	47 59	136	38 46	185	63 56	265	57 50	335
229	53 02	007	22 23	040	18 53	077	48 39	137	38 41	185	62 57	265	57 24	333
230	53 09	006	23 01	040	19 51	077	49 20	137	38 35	186	61 58	265	56 56	332
231	53 14	004	23 39	039	20 48	076	50 00	138	38 29	187	60 59	265	56 27	330
232	53 18	003	24 16	039	21 46	076	50 39	139	38 21	187	60 00	265	55 57	329
233	53 20	001	24 53	038	22 43	076	51 18	139	38 14	188	59 02	265	55 26	327
234	53 20	000	25 30	038	23 40	076	51 56	140	38 05	189	58 03	265	54 54	326
235	53 19	358	26 06	037	24 37	075	52 33	141	37 56	189	57 04	265	54 20	325
236	53 16	357	26 42	037	25 34	075	53 10	142	37 46	190	56 05	265	53 45	323
237	53 12	355	27 17	036	26 32	075	53 46	143	37 36	190	55 06	265	53 10	322
238	53 07	354	27 51	036	27 28	074	54 21	144	37 25	191	54 07	265	52 33	321
239	53 00	352	28 26	035	28 25	074	54 56	145	37 14	191	53 09	265	51 55	320
	VEGA		◆ALTAIR		Shaula		◆RIGIL KENT		SPICA		◆ARCTURUS		Alphecca	
240	28 59	034	29 22	074	55 30	146	37 02	192	52 10	265	51 17	319	52 51	351
241	29 32	034	30 19	073	56 03	147	36 50	192	51 11	264	50 37	318	52 41	349
242	30 05	033	31 15	073	56 35	148	36 37	193	50 12	264	49 57	317	52 29	348
243	30 37	032	32 12	073	57 06	149	36 23	194	49 13	264	49 16	316	52 16	347
244	31 08	032	33 08	072	57 36	150	36 09	194	48 14	264	48 34	315	52 02	345
245	31 39	031	34 04	072	58 05	151	35 54	195	47 16	264	47 52	314	51 46	344
246	32 09	030	35 01	072	58 33	152	35 39	195	46 17	264	47 09	313	51 29	342
247	32 39	030	35 57	071	59 00	154	35 23	196	45 18	264	46 25	312	51 10	341
248	33 08	029	36 52	071	59 26	155	35 07	196	44 19	264	45 41	311	50 50	340
249	33 36	028	37 48	070	59 50	156	34 51	197	43 21	264	44 56	310	50 29	338
250	34 04	027	38 44	070	60 13	158	34 33	197	42 22	264	44 10	309	50 07	337
251	34 31	027	39 39	069	60 35	159	34 16	198	41 23	264	43 24	309	49 43	336
252	34 57	026	40 34	069	60 55	161	33 58	198	40 24	264	42 38	308	49 19	335
253	35 22	025	41 30	069	61 14	162	33 39	198	39 26	264	41 51	307	48 53	333
254	35 47	024	42 24	068	61 31	164	33 20	199	38 27	264	41 04	306	48 26	332
	VEGA		◆ALTAIR		Peacock		◆RIGIL KENT		SPICA		◆ARCTURUS		Alphecca	
255	36 11	023	43 19	068	28 42	151	33 01	199	37 28	263	40 16	306	47 58	331
256	36 34	023	44 14	067	29 11	151	32 41	200	36 30	263	39 28	305	47 29	330
257	36 56	022	45 08	066	29 40	151	32 21	200	35 31	263	38 40	305	46 59	329
258	37 18	021	46 02	066	30 08	152	32 00	201	34 32	263	37 51	304	46 28	328
259	37 39	020	46 56	065	30 36	152	31 39	201	33 33	263	37 02	303	45 56	327
260	37 58	019	47 49	065	31 04	152	31 18	201	32 35	263	36 12	303	45 24	326
261	38 17	018	48 42	064	31 31	153	30 56	202	31 36	263	35 22	302	44 50	325
262	38 35	017	49 35	063	31 58	153	30 34	202	30 38	263	34 32	302	44 16	324
263	38 53	016	50 28	063	32 25	153	30 12	202	29 39	263	33 42	301	43 40	323
264	39 09	015	51 20	062	32 52	154	29 49	203	28 40	263	32 51	301	43 04	322
265	39 24	014	52 12	061	33 18	154	29 26	203	27 42	262	32 00	300	42 28	321
266	39 38	014	53 04	060	33 43	154	29 02	204	26 43	262	31 09	300	41 50	320
267	39 52	013	53 55	059	34 08	155	28 39	204	25 45	262	30 17	299	41 12	319
268	40 04	012	54 45	059	34 33	155	28 15	204	24 46	262	29 25	299	40 34	319
269	40 15	011	55 36	058	34 58	156	27 50	204	23 48	262	28 34	298	39 54	318

LAT 10°S

LHA ♈	Hc	Zn	Hc	Zn	Hc	Zn	Hc	Zn	Hc	Zn	Hc	Zn	Hc	Zn
	◆VEGA		DENEB		Enif		◆FOMALHAUT		Peacock		◆ANTARES		ARCTURUS	
270	40 26	010	23 46	030	30 37	072	18 14	118	35 22	156	63 10	229	27 41	298
271	40 35	009	24 15	029	31 33	072	19 06	118	35 45	157	62 25	230	26 49	297
272	40 43	008	24 44	029	32 29	071	19 58	118	36 08	157	61 40	231	25 57	297
273	40 51	007	25 12	028	33 25	071	20 51	118	36 31	158	60 53	232	25 04	297
274	40 57	006	25 40	028	34 21	071	21 43	118	36 53	158	60 06	233	24 11	296
275	41 02	005	26 07	027	35 16	070	22 35	118	37 15	159	59 19	234	23 18	296
276	41 06	003	26 34	026	36 12	070	23 27	118	37 36	159	58 31	235	22 25	296
277	41 09	002	27 00	026	37 07	069	24 19	118	37 57	160	57 42	235	21 31	295
278	41 11	001	27 25	025	38 02	069	25 11	118	38 17	160	56 54	236	20 38	295
279	41 12	000	27 50	025	38 57	068	26 04	118	38 36	161	56 04	237	19 44	295
280	41 12	359	28 14	024	39 52	068	26 56	118	38 55	162	55 15	237	18 50	294
281	41 11	358	28 38	023	40 47	067	27 48	118	39 14	162	54 25	238	17 57	294
282	41 08	357	29 01	023	41 41	067	28 40	118	39 32	163	53 35	238	17 02	294
283	41 05	356	29 23	022	42 35	066	29 32	118	39 49	163	52 44	239	16 08	293
284	41 01	355	29 45	021	43 30	066	30 24	118	40 06	164	51 53	239	15 14	293
	DENEB		Enif		◆FOMALHAUT		Peacock		◆ANTARES		Rasalhague		◆VEGA	
285	30 06	020	44 23	065	31 16	119	40 22	165	51 02	240	59 13	317	40 55	354
286	30 26	020	45 17	065	32 07	119	40 37	165	50 11	240	58 32	315	40 49	353
287	30 46	019	46 10	064	32 59	119	40 52	166	49 20	241	57 50	314	40 41	352
288	31 04	018	47 03	063	33 51	119	41 06	166	48 28	241	57 07	313	40 33	351
289	31 23	018	47 56	063	34 43	119	41 20	167	47 36	241	56 23	312	40 23	350
290	31 40	017	48 48	062	35 34	119	41 33	168	46 44	242	55 39	310	40 12	349
291	31 57	016	49 40	061	36 26	119	41 45	169	45 52	242	54 54	309	40 01	348
292	32 13	015	50 32	061	37 17	120	41 56	169	45 00	242	54 07	308	39 48	347
293	32 28	014	51 23	060	38 08	120	42 07	170	44 07	243	53 21	307	39 34	346
294	32 42	014	52 14	059	39 00	120	42 17	171	43 15	243	52 34	306	39 20	345
295	32 56	013	53 05	058	39 51	120	42 26	171	42 22	243	51 46	305	39 04	344
296	33 09	012	53 55	057	40 42	121	42 35	172	41 29	243	50 57	305	38 48	343
297	33 21	011	54 44	056	41 32	121	42 42	173	40 37	244	50 08	304	38 31	342
298	33 32	011	55 33	055	42 23	121	42 50	173	39 44	244	49 19	303	38 12	342
299	33 42	010	56 22	054	43 14	121	42 56	174	38 51	244	48 29	302	37 53	341
	◆DENEB		Alpheratz		◆FOMALHAUT		Peacock		◆ANTARES		Rasalhague		VEGA	
300	33 52	009	18 22	055	44 04	122	43 01	175	37 57	244	47 39	301	37 33	340
301	34 01	008	19 10	054	44 54	122	43 06	176	37 04	244	46 48	301	37 12	339
302	34 08	007	19 58	054	45 44	122	43 10	176	36 11	244	45 57	300	36 50	338
303	34 15	006	20 46	053	46 34	123	43 14	177	35 18	245	45 06	299	36 28	337
304	34 21	006	21 33	053	47 23	123	43 16	178	34 24	245	44 14	299	36 04	336
305	34 27	005	22 20	053	48 13	124	43 18	179	33 31	245	43 22	298	35 40	335
306	34 31	004	23 07	052	49 02	124	43 19	179	32 37	245	42 30	297	35 15	335
307	34 35	003	23 53	052	49 50	125	43 19	180	31 44	245	41 37	297	34 50	334
308	34 37	002	24 40	051	50 39	125	43 18	181	30 50	245	40 45	296	34 23	333
309	34 39	001	25 26	051	51 27	126	43 17	182	29 57	245	39 52	296	33 56	332
310	34 40	000	26 11	050	52 15	126	43 15	182	29 03	245	38 58	295	33 28	332
311	34 40	000	26 57	050	53 03	127	43 12	183	28 09	245	38 05	295	33 00	331
312	34 39	359	27 42	049	53 50	127	43 08	184	27 16	245	37 11	294	32 31	330
313	34 37	358	28 26	049	54 36	128	43 03	185	26 22	245	36 17	294	32 01	329
314	34 34	357	29 10	048	55 23	129	42 58	185	25 28	245	35 23	293	31 31	329
	Alpheratz		◆Diphda		ACHERNAR		Peacock		◆Nunki		VEGA		◆DENEB	
315	29 54	048	35 11	105	19 25	147	42 52	186	56 32	237	31 00	328	34 31	356
316	30 38	047	36 08	105	19 56	148	42 45	187	55 42	237	30 28	327	34 27	355
317	31 21	047	37 05	105	20 28	148	42 38	188	54 52	238	29 56	327	34 21	354
318	32 04	046	38 03	105	21 00	148	42 30	188	54 02	239	29 23	326	34 15	354
319	32 46	045	39 00	105	21 31	148	42 21	189	53 12	239	28 50	325	34 08	353
320	33 28	045	39 57	105	22 02	148	42 11	190	52 21	240	28 16	325	34 00	352
321	34 09	044	40 54	105	22 33	148	42 01	191	51 30	240	27 42	324	33 52	351
322	34 50	043	41 51	105	23 04	148	41 49	191	50 38	240	27 07	324	33 42	350
323	35 31	043	42 48	105	23 35	149	41 38	192	49 47	241	26 32	323	33 32	349
324	36 10	042	43 45	105	24 06	149	41 25	193	48 55	241	25 56	322	33 20	349
325	36 50	041	44 42	105	24 36	149	41 12	193	48 03	242	25 20	322	33 08	348
326	37 29	041	45 39	105	25 07	149	40 58	194	47 11	242	24 43	321	32 56	347
327	38 07	040	46 36	106	25 37	149	40 43	195	46 19	242	24 06	321	32 42	346
328	38 44	039	47 33	106	26 07	150	40 28	195	45 27	243	23 29	320	32 28	345
329	39 21	038	48 30	106	26 36	150	40 13	196	44 34	243	22 51	320	32 12	345
	◆Alpheratz		Diphda		◆ACHERNAR		Peacock		Nunki		◆ALTAIR		DENEB	
330	39 58	037	49 26	106	27 06	150	39 56	196	43 42	243	52 51	300	31 56	344
331	40 33	037	50 23	106	27 35	151	39 39	197	42 49	243	52 00	299	31 40	343
332	41 08	036	51 20	106	28 04	151	39 21	198	41 56	244	51 08	298	31 22	342
333	41 42	035	52 17	106	28 33	151	39 03	198	41 03	244	50 15	297	31 04	342
334	42 16	034	53 13	107	29 01	151	38 44	199	40 10	244	49 23	297	30 45	341
335	42 48	033	54 10	107	29 29	152	38 25	199	39 17	244	48 30	296	30 25	340
336	43 20	032	55 06	107	29 57	152	38 05	200	38 24	244	47 36	295	30 05	340
337	43 51	031	56 03	107	30 25	152	37 45	201	37 31	244	46 43	295	29 44	339
338	44 21	030	56 59	108	30 52	153	37 24	201	36 37	245	45 49	294	29 22	338
339	44 51	029	57 56	108	31 19	153	37 02	202	35 44	245	44 55	293	29 00	337
340	45 19	028	58 52	108	31 46	153	36 40	202	34 50	245	44 00	293	28 37	337
341	45 46	027	59 48	109	32 12	154	36 18	203	33 57	245	43 06	292	28 13	336
342	46 13	026	60 44	109	32 38	154	35 55	203	33 03	245	42 11	292	27 49	335
343	46 38	025	61 40	109	33 03	155	35 32	204	32 10	245	41 16	291	27 24	335
344	47 02	024	62 35	110	33 29	155	35 08	204	31 16	245	40 21	291	26 59	334
	Alpheratz		◆Hamal		◆ACHERNAR		Peacock		Nunki		◆ALTAIR		DENEB	
345	47 25	023	33 07	053	33 53	155	34 43	204	30 22	245	39 26	290	26 33	334
346	47 48	021	33 54	053	34 18	156	34 19	205	29 29	245	38 30	290	26 06	333
347	48 09	020	34 41	052	34 42	156	33 54	205	28 35	245	37 35	290	25 39	332
348	48 28	019	35 27	051	35 05	157	33 28	206	27 41	245	36 39	289	25 11	332
349	48 47	018	36 13	051	35 28	157	33 02	206	26 47	246	35 43	289	24 43	331
350	49 04	016	36 59	050	35 51	158	32 36	207	25 54	246	34 47	288	24 14	331
351	49 20	015	37 44	050	36 13	158	32 10	207	25 00	246	33 51	288	23 45	330
352	49 35	014	38 29	049	36 35	159	31 43	207	24 06	246	32 55	288	23 15	330
353	49 49	013	39 13	048	36 56	159	31 15	208	23 12	246	31 58	287	22 45	329
354	50 01	011	39 57	047	37 17	160	30 48	208	22 19	246	31 02	287	22 15	328
355	50 12	010	40 40	047	37 37	160	30 20	208	21 25	246	30 05	286	21 44	328
356	50 22	009	41 23	046	37 57	161	29 52	209	20 31	246	29 08	286	21 12	327
357	50 30	007	42 05	045	38 16	161	29 23	209	19 37	246	28 12	286	20 40	327
358	50 37	006	42 47	044	38 35	162	28 54	209	18 43	245	27 15	286	20 08	326
359	50 42	005	43 28	043	38 53	163	28 25	210	17 50	245	26 18	285	19 35	326

 LAT 11°S

LHA ♈	Hc	Zn	Hc	Zn	Hc	Zn	Hc	Zn	Hc	Zn	Hc	Zn	Hc	Zn
	◆ Alpheratz		Hamal		ALDEBARAN		◆ RIGEL		ACHERNAR		◆ FOMALHAUT		Enif	
0	49 46	003	43 24	042	16 15	069	12 27	096	40 07	163	66 34	215	50 26	301
1	49 48	002	44 03	041	17 10	069	13 26	096	40 25	163	65 59	217	49 35	300
2	49 50	000	44 41	040	18 05	068	14 24	096	40 41	164	65 23	219	48 44	299
3	49 49	359	45 19	039	19 00	068	15 23	096	40 57	165	64 46	220	47 52	298
4	49 48	358	45 55	038	19 54	068	16 22	095	41 12	165	64 07	221	47 00	298
5	49 45	356	46 31	037	20 49	067	17 20	095	41 27	166	63 28	223	46 08	297
6	49 40	355	47 07	036	21 43	067	18 19	095	41 41	167	62 47	224	45 15	296
7	49 34	354	47 41	035	22 37	067	19 18	095	41 54	167	62 06	225	44 22	296
8	49 27	352	48 14	034	23 31	066	20 16	095	42 07	168	61 24	226	43 29	295
9	49 19	351	48 47	033	24 25	066	21 15	095	42 18	169	60 41	227	42 36	295
10	49 09	350	49 19	032	25 19	066	22 14	094	42 30	169	59 57	228	41 42	294
11	48 57	348	49 49	031	26 12	065	23 12	094	42 40	170	59 13	229	40 48	294
12	48 45	347	50 19	029	27 06	065	24 11	094	42 50	171	58 29	230	39 54	293
13	48 31	346	50 47	028	27 59	064	25 10	094	42 59	171	57 43	231	39 00	293
14	48 16	345	51 14	027	28 52	064	26 09	094	43 08	172	56 57	232	38 05	292
	Hamal		◆ ALDEBARAN		RIGEL		◆ ACHERNAR		FOMALHAUT		◆ Enif		Alpheratz	
15	51 40	026	29 45	064	27 07	094	43 15	173	56 11	232	37 11	292	48 00	343
16	52 05	024	30 38	063	28 06	093	43 22	174	55 24	233	36 16	291	47 42	342
17	52 29	023	31 30	063	29 05	093	43 28	174	54 37	234	35 21	291	47 24	341
18	52 51	022	32 22	062	30 04	093	43 34	175	53 49	234	34 26	290	47 04	340
19	53 12	020	33 14	062	31 03	093	43 38	176	53 01	235	33 30	290	46 43	339
20	53 32	019	34 06	061	32 01	093	43 42	177	52 13	235	32 35	289	46 21	337
21	53 50	017	34 57	061	33 00	093	43 45	177	51 25	236	31 39	289	45 57	336
22	54 06	016	35 49	060	33 59	093	43 48	178	50 36	236	30 44	289	45 33	335
23	54 22	014	36 40	060	34 58	092	43 49	179	49 47	237	29 48	288	45 08	334
24	54 35	013	37 30	059	35 57	092	43 50	180	48 57	237	28 52	288	44 42	333
25	54 48	011	38 21	058	36 56	092	43 50	180	48 08	238	27 56	288	44 14	332
26	54 58	010	39 11	058	37 55	092	43 50	181	47 18	238	26 59	287	43 46	331
27	55 07	008	40 00	057	38 53	092	43 48	182	46 28	238	26 03	287	43 17	330
28	55 15	006	40 50	057	39 52	092	43 46	183	45 37	239	25 07	287	42 47	329
29	55 21	005	41 39	056	40 51	091	43 43	183	44 47	239	24 10	286	42 16	328
	CAPELLA		◆ BETELGEUSE		SIRIUS		CANOPUS		◆ ACHERNAR		FOMALHAUT		◆ Alpheratz	
30	17 49	034	28 29	075	20 44	104	23 09	143	43 39	184	43 57	239	41 45	327
31	18 21	033	29 26	075	21 41	104	23 44	143	43 34	185	43 06	240	41 12	326
32	18 53	033	30 22	075	22 38	104	24 19	143	43 29	186	42 15	240	40 39	325
33	19 25	032	31 19	074	23 35	104	24 54	143	43 23	186	41 24	240	40 05	324
34	19 56	032	32 16	074	24 33	104	25 29	144	43 16	187	40 33	240	39 30	324
35	20 27	031	33 12	073	25 30	103	26 04	144	43 09	188	39 42	241	38 55	323
36	20 57	031	34 09	073	26 27	103	26 39	144	43 00	188	38 50	241	38 19	322
37	21 27	030	35 05	073	27 25	103	27 14	144	42 51	189	37 59	241	37 42	321
38	21 57	030	36 01	072	28 22	103	27 48	144	42 42	190	37 07	241	37 05	320
39	22 26	029	36 57	072	29 19	103	28 22	145	42 31	191	36 16	241	36 27	320
40	22 54	029	37 53	071	30 17	103	28 56	145	42 20	191	35 24	241	35 49	319
41	23 22	028	38 49	071	31 14	103	29 30	145	42 08	192	34 32	242	35 09	318
42	23 50	027	39 44	071	32 11	103	30 03	145	41 56	193	33 40	242	34 30	317
43	24 16	027	40 40	070	33 09	103	30 36	146	41 42	193	32 48	242	33 50	317
44	24 43	026	41 35	070	34 06	103	31 09	146	41 29	194	31 56	242	33 09	316
	◆ CAPELLA		BETELGEUSE		SIRIUS		◆ CANOPUS		ACHERNAR		◆ FOMALHAUT		Alpheratz	
45	25 09	026	42 30	069	35 04	103	31 42	146	41 14	195	31 04	242	32 28	315
46	25 34	025	43 25	069	36 01	103	32 15	147	40 59	195	30 12	242	31 46	315
47	25 59	024	44 20	068	36 59	103	32 47	147	40 43	196	29 20	242	31 04	314
48	26 23	024	45 15	068	37 56	103	33 19	147	40 27	196	28 28	242	30 22	314
49	26 46	023	46 09	067	38 53	103	33 51	148	40 10	197	27 36	242	29 39	313
50	27 09	023	47 03	066	39 51	103	34 22	148	39 52	198	26 44	242	28 56	312
51	27 31	022	47 57	066	40 48	103	34 53	148	39 34	198	25 52	242	28 12	312
52	27 53	021	48 50	065	41 46	103	35 23	149	39 15	199	25 00	242	27 28	311
53	28 14	021	49 44	064	42 43	103	35 54	149	38 56	199	24 07	242	26 44	311
54	28 35	020	50 36	064	43 41	103	36 24	150	38 36	200	23 15	242	25 59	310
55	28 54	019	51 29	063	44 38	103	36 53	150	38 16	200	22 23	242	25 14	310
56	29 13	018	52 21	062	45 36	103	37 22	151	37 55	201	21 31	242	24 29	309
57	29 31	018	53 13	061	46 33	103	37 51	151	37 34	202	20 39	242	23 43	309
58	29 49	017	54 05	061	47 30	103	38 19	152	37 12	202	19 47	242	22 57	308
59	30 06	016	54 56	060	48 28	103	38 47	152	36 49	203	18 54	242	22 11	308
	CAPELLA		POLLUX		◆ SIRIUS		CANOPUS		◆ ACHERNAR		Diphda		◆ Hamal	
60	30 22	016	22 50	053	49 25	103	39 14	153	36 27	203	42 16	256	45 56	322
61	30 38	015	23 37	053	50 23	103	39 41	153	36 03	203	41 19	256	45 19	321
62	30 52	014	24 24	052	51 20	103	40 08	154	35 40	204	40 22	256	44 41	320
63	31 06	013	25 10	052	52 17	103	40 34	154	35 16	204	39 24	256	44 03	319
64	31 19	013	25 56	051	53 15	103	40 59	155	34 51	205	38 27	256	43 24	318
65	31 32	012	26 42	051	54 12	103	41 24	155	34 26	205	37 30	256	42 44	317
66	31 43	011	27 28	050	55 09	104	41 48	156	34 01	206	36 33	256	42 04	316
67	31 54	010	28 13	050	56 07	104	42 12	157	33 35	206	35 36	256	41 23	316
68	32 04	009	28 57	049	57 04	104	42 35	157	33 09	206	34 39	256	40 41	315
69	32 13	009	29 42	049	58 01	104	42 57	158	32 43	207	33 42	256	39 59	314
70	32 22	008	30 26	048	58 58	104	43 19	159	32 16	207	32 45	256	39 17	313
71	32 29	007	31 09	047	59 55	104	43 40	159	31 49	208	31 48	256	38 33	312
72	32 36	006	31 53	047	60 52	105	44 01	160	31 22	208	30 51	256	37 50	312
73	32 42	005	32 35	046	61 49	105	44 21	161	30 54	208	29 54	256	37 06	311
74	32 47	004	33 18	046	62 46	105	44 40	161	30 26	209	28 57	255	36 21	310
	CAPELLA		POLLUX		◆ PROCYON		Suhail		CANOPUS		◆ ACHERNAR		◆ Hamal	
75	32 51	004	34 00	045	47 00	070	27 39	134	44 59	162	29 58	209	35 36	310
76	32 54	003	34 41	044	47 55	069	28 22	134	45 16	163	29 29	209	34 50	309
77	32 57	002	35 22	044	48 51	069	29 04	134	45 33	164	29 00	209	34 04	309
78	32 58	001	36 02	043	49 45	068	29 47	134	45 50	164	28 31	210	33 18	308
79	32 59	000	36 42	042	50 40	068	30 29	134	46 05	165	28 02	210	32 32	307
80	32 59	000	37 21	041	51 34	067	31 11	135	46 20	166	27 32	210	31 44	307
81	32 58	359	38 00	041	52 28	066	31 53	135	46 34	167	27 03	210	30 57	306
82	32 57	358	38 38	040	53 22	065	32 34	135	46 47	168	26 33	211	30 09	306
83	32 54	357	39 15	039	54 15	065	33 16	135	46 59	168	26 02	211	29 21	305
84	32 50	356	39 52	038	55 08	064	33 57	136	47 11	169	25 32	211	28 33	305
85	32 46	355	40 28	037	56 01	063	34 38	136	47 21	170	25 01	211	27 45	304
86	32 41	355	41 04	037	56 53	062	35 19	136	47 31	171	24 31	212	26 56	304
87	32 35	354	41 38	036	57 45	061	36 00	137	47 40	172	24 00	212	26 07	303
88	32 28	353	42 12	035	58 37	060	36 40	137	47 47	173	23 29	212	25 17	303
89	32 21	352	42 46	034	59 28	059	37 20	137	47 54	174	22 57	212	24 28	302

LHA ♈	Hc	Zn	Hc	Zn	Hc	Zn	Hc	Zn	Hc	Zn	Hc	Zn	Hc	Zn
	POLLUX		◆ REGULUS		Suhail		◆ CANOPUS		ACHERNAR		◆ ALDEBARAN		CAPELLA	
90	43 18	033	24 02	072	38 00	138	48 01	175	22 26	212	55 37	323	32 12	351
91	43 49	032	24 58	071	38 40	138	48 06	175	21 55	212	55 01	322	32 03	351
92	44 20	031	25 54	071	39 19	138	48 10	176	21 23	213	54 24	320	31 53	350
93	44 50	030	26 49	071	39 58	139	48 13	177	20 51	213	53 46	319	31 42	349
94	45 19	029	27 45	070	40 37	139	48 16	178	20 19	213	53 07	318	31 30	348
95	45 47	028	28 40	070	41 15	140	48 17	179	19 47	213	52 27	317	31 18	347
96	46 14	027	29 35	069	41 53	140	48 18	180	19 15	213	51 47	316	31 05	347
97	46 39	026	30 30	069	42 31	141	48 17	181	18 43	213	51 05	315	30 51	346
98	47 04	024	31 25	069	43 08	141	48 16	182	18 11	213	50 23	314	30 36	345
99	47 28	023	32 20	068	43 45	142	48 14	183	17 39	213	49 40	313	30 21	344
100	47 51	022	33 15	068	44 21	142	48 11	184	17 07	213	48 56	312	30 04	344
101	48 12	021	34 09	067	44 57	143	48 06	184	16 34	213	48 12	311	29 47	343
102	48 33	020	35 03	067	45 32	143	48 01	185	16 02	213	47 27	310	29 30	342
103	48 52	018	35 57	066	46 07	144	47 55	186	15 29	213	46 41	309	29 11	341
104	49 10	017	36 51	066	46 41	145	47 48	187	14 57	213	45 55	308	28 52	341
	POLLUX		◆ REGULUS		ACRUX		◆ CANOPUS		RIGEL		◆ ALDEBARAN		CAPELLA	
105	49 26	016	37 45	065	13 28	153	47 41	188	64 02	274	45 09	307	28 33	340
106	49 42	014	38 38	065	13 55	153	47 32	189	63 03	274	44 22	307	28 12	339
107	49 56	013	39 32	064	14 22	153	47 22	190	62 05	273	43 34	306	27 51	339
108	50 08	012	40 24	064	14 49	153	47 12	191	61 06	273	42 46	305	27 29	338
109	50 20	010	41 17	063	15 16	153	47 01	191	60 07	273	41 58	304	27 07	337
110	50 30	009	42 10	063	15 43	153	46 49	192	59 08	272	41 09	304	26 44	337
111	50 38	008	43 02	062	16 10	153	46 36	193	58 09	272	40 20	303	26 20	336
112	50 46	006	43 54	061	16 37	153	46 22	194	57 10	272	39 30	302	25 56	335
113	50 52	005	44 45	061	17 04	153	46 07	195	56 12	272	38 40	302	25 31	335
114	50 56	004	45 37	060	17 30	153	45 52	196	55 13	271	37 50	301	25 06	334
115	50 59	002	46 27	059	17 57	153	45 36	196	54 14	271	36 59	301	24 40	334
116	51 00	001	47 18	059	18 23	153	45 19	197	53 15	271	36 09	300	24 14	333
117	51 01	359	48 08	058	18 50	153	45 01	198	52 16	271	35 17	300	23 47	332
118	50 59	358	48 58	057	19 16	154	44 43	199	51 17	271	34 26	299	23 19	332
119	50 56	357	49 47	056	19 42	154	44 24	199	50 18	270	33 34	298	22 51	331
	◆ REGULUS		SPICA		◆ ACRUX		CANOPUS		◆ RIGEL		BETELGEUSE		POLLUX	
120	50 36	055	10 21	100	20 08	154	44 04	200	49 19	270	54 04	299	50 52	355
121	51 24	055	11 19	099	20 34	154	43 43	201	48 20	270	53 13	299	50 46	354
122	52 12	054	12 17	099	21 00	154	43 22	201	47 22	270	52 21	298	50 39	352
123	52 59	053	13 15	099	21 26	154	43 00	202	46 23	270	51 29	297	50 31	351
124	53 45	052	14 13	099	21 51	154	42 38	203	45 24	269	50 36	296	50 21	350
125	54 31	051	15 11	099	22 17	155	42 15	203	44 25	269	49 43	296	50 10	348
126	55 16	050	16 10	099	22 42	155	41 51	204	43 26	269	48 50	295	49 57	347
127	56 01	048	17 08	099	23 07	155	41 27	205	42 27	269	47 56	294	49 43	346
128	56 44	047	18 06	098	23 32	155	41 02	205	41 28	269	47 03	294	49 28	344
129	57 27	046	19 04	098	23 57	155	40 37	206	40 29	269	46 08	293	49 12	343
130	58 09	045	20 03	098	24 21	156	40 11	206	39 30	268	45 14	292	48 54	342
131	58 50	043	21 01	098	24 46	156	39 45	207	38 32	268	44 20	292	48 35	341
132	59 30	042	21 59	098	25 10	156	39 18	207	37 33	268	43 25	291	48 15	339
133	60 09	040	22 58	098	25 34	156	38 51	208	36 34	268	42 30	291	47 53	338
134	60 46	039	23 56	098	25 57	156	38 23	208	35 35	268	41 35	290	47 31	337
	REGULUS		◆ SPICA		ACRUX		◆ CANOPUS		SIRIUS		BETELGEUSE		◆ POLLUX	
135	61 23	037	24 54	097	26 21	157	37 55	209	56 58	256	40 40	290	47 07	336
136	61 58	036	25 53	097	26 44	157	37 26	209	56 01	256	39 44	289	46 42	335
137	62 32	034	26 51	097	27 07	157	36 57	210	55 04	256	38 48	289	46 17	333
138	63 04	032	27 50	097	27 30	157	36 28	210	54 07	256	37 53	289	45 50	332
139	63 34	030	28 48	097	27 52	158	35 58	211	53 09	257	36 57	288	45 22	331
140	64 03	028	29 47	097	28 14	158	35 28	211	52 12	257	36 01	288	44 53	330
141	64 30	026	30 45	097	28 36	158	34 57	211	51 15	257	35 05	287	44 24	329
142	64 56	024	31 44	097	28 58	159	34 26	212	50 17	257	34 08	287	43 53	328
143	65 19	022	32 42	096	29 19	159	33 55	212	49 20	257	33 12	287	43 22	327
144	65 40	020	33 41	096	29 40	159	33 23	213	48 22	257	32 15	286	42 49	326
145	65 59	018	34 39	096	30 00	160	32 52	213	47 25	257	31 19	286	42 16	325
146	66 16	015	35 38	096	30 21	160	32 19	213	46 28	257	30 22	285	41 42	324
147	66 31	013	36 37	096	30 41	160	31 47	214	45 30	257	29 25	285	41 08	324
148	66 43	011	37 35	096	31 00	161	31 14	214	44 33	257	28 28	285	40 32	323
149	66 52	008	38 34	096	31 20	161	30 41	214	43 35	257	27 31	284	39 56	322
	REGULUS		◆ ARCTURUS		SPICA		◆ ACRUX		CANOPUS		SIRIUS		◆ PROCYON	
150	67 00	006	20 03	065	39 32	096	31 39	161	30 08	214	42 38	257	51 36	293
151	67 04	003	20 56	064	40 31	095	31 57	162	29 34	215	41 40	257	50 42	293
152	67 06	001	21 50	064	41 30	095	32 15	162	29 01	215	40 43	257	49 48	292
153	67 06	358	22 42	064	42 28	095	32 33	163	28 27	215	39 45	257	48 53	291
154	67 03	356	23 35	063	43 27	095	32 50	163	27 53	216	38 48	257	47 58	291
155	66 57	353	24 28	063	44 26	095	33 07	163	27 18	216	37 50	257	47 03	290
156	66 49	351	25 20	063	45 24	095	33 24	164	26 44	216	36 53	257	46 07	290
157	66 38	348	26 12	062	46 23	095	33 40	164	26 09	216	35 56	257	45 12	289
158	66 25	346	27 04	062	47 22	095	33 56	165	25 34	216	34 58	257	44 16	289
159	66 09	344	27 56	061	48 20	095	34 11	165	24 59	217	34 01	257	43 20	288
160	65 52	341	28 47	061	49 19	095	34 26	166	24 24	217	33 03	257	42 24	288
161	65 32	339	29 39	060	50 18	094	34 40	166	23 49	217	32 06	257	41 28	287
162	65 10	337	30 30	060	51 16	094	34 54	167	23 14	217	31 09	257	40 31	287
163	64 45	335	31 21	059	52 15	094	35 07	167	22 38	217	30 11	257	39 35	286
164	64 19	333	32 11	059	53 14	094	35 20	168	22 03	217	29 14	257	38 38	286
	Denebola		◆ ARCTURUS		SPICA		◆ ACRUX		SIRIUS		◆ PROCYON		REGULUS	
165	61 41	026	33 02	058	54 13	094	35 33	168	28 16	257	37 42	285	63 51	331
166	62 06	024	33 52	058	55 11	094	35 44	169	27 19	257	36 45	285	63 22	329
167	62 29	022	34 41	057	56 10	094	35 56	169	26 22	257	35 48	285	62 51	327
168	62 51	020	35 31	057	57 09	094	36 07	170	25 25	257	34 51	284	62 18	325
169	63 10	018	36 20	056	58 08	094	36 17	170	24 27	256	33 54	284	61 43	324
170	63 28	016	37 09	056	59 07	094	36 27	171	23 30	256	32 57	284	61 08	322
171	63 43	014	37 57	055	60 05	093	36 36	171	22 33	256	31 59	283	60 31	320
172	63 57	012	38 45	054	61 04	093	36 45	172	21 36	256	31 02	283	59 53	319
173	64 08	010	39 33	054	62 03	093	36 53	172	20 38	256	30 04	283	59 13	317
174	64 17	008	40 20	053	63 02	093	37 01	173	19 41	256	29 07	282	58 33	316
175	64 24	006	41 07	052	64 01	093	37 08	173	18 44	256	28 09	282	57 52	315
176	64 28	003	41 53	052	64 59	093	37 15	174	17 47	256	27 12	282	57 09	313
177	64 30	001	42 39	051	65 58	093	37 21	174	16 50	256	26 14	281	56 26	312
178	64 30	359	43 24	050	66 57	093	37 26	175	15 53	256	25 16	281	55 42	311
179	64 28	357	44 09	049	67 56	093	37 31	176	14 56	255	24 18	281	54 58	310

 LAT 11°S

LHA ♈	Hc	Zn	Hc	Zn	Hc	Zn	Hc	Zn	Hc	Zn	Hc	Zn	Hc	Zn
	ARCTURUS		◆ ANTARES		ACRUX		◆ Suhail		Alphard		REGULUS		◆ Denebola	
180	44 53	048	24 51	114	37 35	176	40 47	221	52 36	270	54 12	309	64 23	354
181	45 37	048	25 44	114	37 39	177	40 09	221	51 37	270	53 26	308	64 16	352
182	46 20	047	26 38	114	37 42	177	39 30	222	50 38	270	52 39	307	64 07	350
183	47 03	046	27 32	114	37 45	178	38 51	222	49 39	269	51 52	306	63 56	348
184	47 45	045	28 25	114	37 47	178	38 11	222	48 40	269	51 04	305	63 42	346
185	48 26	044	29 19	114	37 48	179	37 31	223	47 41	269	50 15	304	63 26	343
186	49 06	043	30 13	114	37 49	180	36 51	223	46 42	269	49 26	303	63 09	341
187	49 46	042	31 06	114	37 49	180	36 11	223	45 43	269	48 37	303	62 49	339
188	50 25	041	32 00	114	37 49	181	35 30	224	44 45	269	47 47	302	62 27	337
189	51 03	040	32 54	115	37 48	181	34 50	224	43 46	268	46 57	301	62 04	336
190	51 40	038	33 47	115	37 46	182	34 09	224	42 47	268	46 06	300	61 38	334
191	52 16	037	34 41	115	37 44	182	33 27	225	41 48	268	45 15	300	61 12	332
192	52 51	036	35 34	115	37 41	183	32 46	225	40 49	268	44 24	299	60 43	330
193	53 25	035	36 28	115	37 38	183	32 04	225	39 50	268	43 32	298	60 13	329
194	53 58	033	37 21	115	37 34	184	31 22	225	38 51	268	42 40	298	59 42	327
	ARCTURUS		◆ Rasalhague		ANTARES		◆ ACRUX		Suhail		◆ REGULUS		Denebola	
195	54 30	032	17 40	073	38 15	115	37 30	185	30 40	226	41 48	297	59 09	325
196	55 01	031	18 36	073	39 08	115	37 25	185	29 58	226	40 55	297	58 35	324
197	55 30	029	19 32	072	40 01	115	37 19	186	29 16	226	40 03	296	57 59	322
198	55 58	028	20 28	072	40 54	116	37 13	186	28 34	226	39 09	295	57 23	321
199	56 25	026	21 24	072	41 47	116	37 06	187	27 51	226	38 16	295	56 45	320
200	56 51	025	22 20	071	42 40	116	36 59	187	27 08	227	37 23	294	56 06	318
201	57 15	023	23 16	071	43 33	116	36 51	188	26 26	227	36 29	294	55 27	317
202	57 37	022	24 11	071	44 26	116	36 43	188	25 43	227	35 35	293	54 46	316
203	57 58	020	25 07	070	45 19	117	36 34	189	25 00	227	34 41	293	54 04	315
204	58 18	018	26 02	070	46 11	117	36 24	190	24 17	227	33 46	292	53 22	314
205	58 35	017	26 58	070	47 04	117	36 14	190	23 33	227	32 52	292	52 39	312
206	58 51	015	27 53	069	47 56	118	36 04	191	22 50	227	31 57	292	51 55	311
207	59 06	013	28 48	069	48 48	118	35 53	191	22 07	227	31 02	291	51 11	310
208	59 18	011	29 43	069	49 40	118	35 41	192	21 24	227	30 07	291	50 26	309
209	59 29	009	30 37	068	50 32	119	35 29	192	20 40	227	29 12	290	49 40	309
	ARCTURUS		◆ Rasalhague		ANTARES		◆ RIGIL KENT		ACRUX		Gienah		◆ REGULUS	
210	59 38	008	31 32	068	51 24	119	39 33	174	35 17	193	64 07	252	28 17	290
211	59 45	006	32 26	067	52 15	119	39 39	174	35 04	193	63 11	253	27 22	290
212	59 49	004	33 21	067	53 06	120	39 45	175	34 50	194	62 15	253	26 26	289
213	59 53	002	34 15	066	53 57	120	39 50	175	34 36	194	61 18	253	25 30	289
214	59 54	000	35 09	066	54 48	121	39 54	176	34 22	194	60 22	254	24 35	289
215	59 53	358	36 02	065	55 38	121	39 58	177	34 07	195	59 25	254	23 39	288
216	59 50	356	36 56	065	56 28	122	40 01	177	33 51	195	58 29	254	22 43	288
217	59 46	355	37 49	064	57 18	123	40 03	178	33 36	196	57 32	254	21 47	288
218	59 39	353	38 42	064	58 08	123	40 05	179	33 19	196	56 35	255	20 51	287
219	59 30	351	39 35	063	58 57	124	40 06	179	33 03	197	55 38	255	19 54	287
220	59 20	349	40 27	063	59 46	125	40 06	180	32 46	197	54 41	255	18 58	287
221	59 08	347	41 20	062	60 34	125	40 06	181	32 28	197	53 44	255	18 02	287
222	58 54	345	42 12	062	61 22	126	40 05	181	32 10	198	52 48	255	17 05	286
223	58 38	344	43 03	061	62 09	127	40 04	182	31 52	198	51 51	255	16 09	286
224	58 21	342	43 55	060	62 55	128	40 01	182	31 33	199	50 54	256	15 12	286
	Alphecca		◆ VEGA		ALTAIR		◆ Shaula		RIGIL KENT		◆ SPICA		ARCTURUS	
225	51 22	013	19 02	042	14 50	078	46 35	134	39 59	183	66 57	267	58 02	340
226	51 34	011	19 42	042	15 47	077	47 18	134	39 55	184	65 58	267	57 41	339
227	51 45	010	20 21	041	16 45	077	48 00	135	39 51	184	64 59	267	57 19	337
228	51 55	008	20 59	041	17 42	077	48 41	135	39 46	185	64 00	267	56 55	335
229	52 03	007	21 37	040	18 39	077	49 23	136	39 41	186	63 01	267	56 30	334
230	52 09	006	22 15	040	19 37	076	50 04	136	39 35	186	62 02	267	56 03	332
231	52 14	004	22 53	039	20 34	076	50 44	137	39 28	187	61 04	267	55 35	331
232	52 18	003	23 30	039	21 31	076	51 24	138	39 21	187	60 05	267	55 06	329
233	52 20	001	24 06	038	22 28	075	52 03	139	39 13	188	59 06	266	54 35	328
234	52 20	000	24 42	038	23 25	075	52 41	139	39 04	189	58 07	266	54 04	327
235	52 19	358	25 18	037	24 22	075	53 20	140	38 55	189	57 09	266	53 31	325
236	52 17	357	25 53	036	25 19	075	53 57	141	38 46	190	56 10	266	52 57	324
237	52 13	355	26 28	036	26 15	074	54 34	142	38 35	190	55 11	266	52 22	323
238	52 07	354	27 03	035	27 12	074	55 10	143	38 24	191	54 12	266	51 46	322
239	52 00	352	27 36	035	28 09	074	55 45	144	38 13	192	53 14	266	51 09	321
	VEGA		◆ ALTAIR		Shaula		◆ RIGIL KENT		SPICA		◆ ARCTURUS		Alphecca	
240	28 10	034	29 05	073	56 19	145	38 01	192	52 15	266	50 31	319	51 52	351
241	28 42	033	30 01	073	56 53	146	37 48	193	51 16	266	49 53	318	51 42	350
242	29 15	033	30 58	073	57 25	147	37 35	193	50 17	266	49 13	317	51 30	348
243	29 46	032	31 54	072	57 57	148	37 21	194	49 19	265	48 33	316	51 18	347
244	30 17	031	32 50	072	58 28	149	37 07	194	48 20	265	47 52	315	51 04	345
245	30 48	031	33 46	071	58 57	150	36 52	195	47 21	265	47 10	314	50 48	344
246	31 18	030	34 41	071	59 26	152	36 37	195	46 22	265	46 28	314	50 31	343
247	31 47	029	35 37	071	59 53	153	36 21	196	45 24	265	45 45	313	50 13	341
248	32 15	029	36 32	070	60 20	154	36 05	196	44 25	265	45 01	312	49 54	340
249	32 43	028	37 28	070	60 45	156	35 48	197	43 26	265	44 17	311	49 33	339
250	33 11	027	38 23	069	61 08	157	35 31	197	42 28	265	43 32	310	49 11	338
251	33 37	026	39 18	069	61 31	159	35 13	198	41 29	265	42 47	309	48 48	336
252	34 03	026	40 13	068	61 51	160	34 55	198	40 31	265	42 01	309	48 24	335
253	34 28	025	41 07	068	62 11	162	34 36	199	39 32	264	41 15	308	47 59	334
254	34 52	024	42 02	067	62 29	163	34 17	199	38 33	264	40 28	307	47 33	333
	◆ VEGA		ALTAIR		◆ Peacock		RIGIL KENT		◆ SPICA		ARCTURUS		Alphecca	
255	35 16	023	42 56	067	29 34	150	33 57	200	37 35	264	39 41	306	47 05	332
256	35 39	022	43 50	066	30 04	151	33 38	200	36 36	264	38 53	306	46 37	331
257	36 01	022	44 43	066	30 32	151	33 17	200	35 37	264	38 05	305	46 07	330
258	36 22	021	45 37	065	31 01	151	32 56	201	34 39	264	37 17	305	45 37	328
259	36 42	020	46 30	064	31 29	152	32 35	201	33 40	264	36 28	304	45 06	327
260	37 02	019	47 23	064	31 57	152	32 14	202	32 42	264	35 39	303	44 34	326
261	37 20	018	48 16	063	32 25	152	31 52	202	31 43	263	34 50	303	44 01	325
262	37 38	017	49 08	062	32 52	153	31 30	202	30 45	263	34 00	302	43 27	324
263	37 55	016	50 00	062	33 19	153	31 07	203	29 46	263	33 10	302	42 52	324
264	38 11	015	50 51	061	33 45	153	30 44	203	28 48	263	32 20	301	42 17	323
265	38 26	014	51 43	060	34 11	154	30 21	203	27 49	263	31 29	301	41 41	322
266	38 40	013	52 33	059	34 37	154	29 57	204	26 51	263	30 39	300	41 04	321
267	38 53	012	53 24	058	35 03	155	29 34	204	25 52	263	29 48	300	40 26	320
268	39 05	011	54 14	057	35 28	155	29 09	204	24 54	263	28 56	299	39 48	319
269	39 16	010	55 03	056	35 52	156	28 45	205	23 56	262	28 05	299	39 09	318

LHA ♈	Hc	Zn	Hc	Zn	Hc	Zn	Hc	Zn	Hc	Zn	Hc	Zn	Hc	Zn
	◆ VEGA		ALTAIR		◆ FOMALHAUT		Peacock		RIGIL KENT		◆ ANTARES		ARCTURUS	
270	39 26	009	55 52	055	18 42	118	36 17	156	28 20	205	63 49	231	27 13	298
271	39 36	008	56 40	054	19 34	118	36 40	156	27 55	205	63 03	232	26 21	298
272	39 44	007	57 27	053	20 26	118	37 04	157	27 30	206	62 17	233	25 29	298
273	39 51	006	58 14	052	21 18	118	37 27	157	27 04	206	61 29	234	24 37	297
274	39 57	005	59 00	051	22 11	118	37 49	158	26 39	206	60 42	234	23 44	297
275	40 02	004	59 46	050	23 03	118	38 11	158	26 13	206	59 54	235	22 52	296
276	40 06	003	60 30	048	23 55	118	38 32	159	25 46	207	59 05	236	21 59	296
277	40 09	002	61 14	047	24 47	118	38 53	160	25 20	207	58 16	237	21 06	296
278	40 11	001	61 56	046	25 39	118	39 13	160	24 53	207	57 26	237	20 12	295
279	40 12	000	62 38	044	26 32	118	39 33	161	24 26	207	56 37	238	19 19	295
280	40 12	359	63 18	042	27 24	118	39 52	161	23 59	207	55 47	239	18 26	295
281	40 11	358	63 57	041	28 16	118	40 11	162	23 32	208	54 56	239	17 32	294
282	40 08	357	64 35	039	29 08	118	40 29	162	23 05	208	54 06	240	16 38	294
283	40 05	356	65 12	037	30 00	118	40 47	163	22 37	208	53 15	240	15 44	294
284	40 01	355	65 46	035	30 52	118	41 03	164	22 10	208	52 23	241	14 50	293
	◆ DENEB		◆ FOMALHAUT		Peacock		RIGIL KENT		◆ ANTARES		Rasalhague		VEGA	
285	29 09	020	31 44	118	41 20	164	21 42	208	51 32	241	58 29	318	39 55	354
286	29 29	020	32 36	118	41 35	165	21 14	208	50 40	241	57 49	316	39 49	353
287	29 49	019	33 28	118	41 50	166	20 46	209	49 49	242	57 08	315	39 42	352
288	30 07	018	34 20	118	42 05	166	20 18	209	48 57	242	56 26	314	39 33	351
289	30 25	017	35 12	119	42 18	167	19 49	209	48 05	242	55 43	313	39 24	350
290	30 43	017	36 03	119	42 31	168	19 21	209	47 12	243	54 59	312	39 13	349
291	30 59	016	36 55	119	42 43	168	18 52	209	46 20	243	54 15	310	39 02	348
292	31 15	015	37 46	119	42 55	169	18 24	209	45 27	243	53 30	309	38 49	347
293	31 30	014	38 38	119	43 06	170	17 55	209	44 35	244	52 44	308	38 36	346
294	31 44	014	39 29	119	43 16	170	17 26	209	43 42	244	51 58	307	38 22	345
295	31 57	013	40 21	120	43 25	171	16 57	209	42 49	244	51 10	306	38 07	345
296	32 10	012	41 12	120	43 34	172	16 28	209	41 56	244	50 23	306	37 50	344
297	32 22	011	42 03	120	43 42	173	15 59	210	41 03	244	49 35	305	37 33	343
298	32 33	010	42 54	120	43 49	173	15 30	210	40 10	245	48 46	304	37 15	342
299	32 43	010	43 44	121	43 56	174	15 01	210	39 17	245	47 57	303	36 56	341
	◆ DENEB		Alpheratz		◆ FOMALHAUT		Peacock		◆ ANTARES		Rasalhague		VEGA	
300	32 53	009	17 47	054	44 35	121	44 01	175	38 23	245	47 07	302	36 37	340
301	33 01	008	18 35	054	45 26	121	44 06	176	37 30	245	46 17	302	36 16	339
302	33 09	007	19 23	054	46 16	122	44 10	176	36 37	245	45 27	301	35 55	338
303	33 16	006	20 10	053	47 06	122	44 13	177	35 43	245	44 36	300	35 32	337
304	33 22	005	20 57	053	47 56	122	44 16	178	34 50	245	43 45	300	35 09	337
305	33 27	005	21 43	052	48 45	123	44 18	179	33 56	245	42 54	299	34 46	336
306	33 31	004	22 30	052	49 35	123	44 19	179	33 03	245	42 02	298	34 21	335
307	33 35	003	23 16	051	50 24	124	44 19	180	32 09	246	41 10	298	33 56	334
308	33 37	002	24 02	051	51 13	124	44 18	181	31 15	246	40 18	297	33 30	333
309	33 39	001	24 48	050	52 02	125	44 17	182	30 22	246	39 25	297	33 03	333
310	33 40	000	25 33	050	52 50	125	44 15	183	29 28	246	38 32	296	32 36	332
311	33 40	000	26 18	049	53 38	126	44 12	183	28 34	246	37 39	295	32 08	331
312	33 39	359	27 02	049	54 26	126	44 08	184	27 41	246	36 46	295	31 39	330
313	33 37	358	27 47	048	55 13	127	44 03	185	26 47	246	35 52	294	31 09	330
314	33 35	357	28 30	048	56 00	128	43 58	186	25 53	246	34 59	294	30 39	329
	Alpheratz		◆ Diphda		ACHERNAR		Peacock		◆ ANTARES		VEGA		◆ DENEB	
315	29 14	047	35 26	104	20 15	147	43 52	186	25 00	246	30 09	328	33 31	356
316	29 57	047	36 23	104	20 47	147	43 45	187	24 06	246	29 38	328	33 27	355
317	30 40	046	37 21	104	21 19	147	43 37	188	23 12	246	29 06	327	33 22	355
318	31 22	046	38 18	104	21 50	148	43 29	189	22 18	246	28 33	326	33 16	354
319	32 04	045	39 15	104	22 22	148	43 20	189	21 25	246	28 00	326	33 09	353
320	32 45	044	40 12	104	22 53	148	43 10	190	20 31	246	27 27	325	33 01	352
321	33 26	044	41 09	104	23 24	148	43 00	191	19 37	246	26 53	325	32 52	351
322	34 07	043	42 06	104	23 56	148	42 48	191	18 44	246	26 19	324	32 43	350
323	34 46	042	43 03	104	24 26	148	42 36	192	17 50	246	25 44	323	32 33	350
324	35 26	042	44 00	104	24 57	149	42 24	193	16 57	245	25 08	323	32 22	349
325	36 05	041	44 57	104	25 28	149	42 10	193	16 03	245	24 32	322	32 10	348
326	36 43	040	45 54	104	25 58	149	41 56	194	15 09	245	23 56	322	31 57	347
327	37 21	039	46 51	105	26 28	149	41 42	195	14 16	245	23 19	321	31 44	346
328	37 58	039	47 48	105	26 58	149	41 26	195	13 22	245	22 42	321	31 29	346
329	38 34	038	48 45	105	27 28	150	41 10	196	12 29	245	22 05	320	31 14	345
	◆ Alpheratz		Diphda		◆ ACHERNAR		Peacock		◆ Nunki		ALTAIR		DENEB	
330	39 10	037	49 42	105	27 58	150	40 54	197	44 09	244	52 21	301	30 59	344
331	39 45	036	50 39	105	28 27	150	40 36	197	43 16	244	51 30	300	30 42	343
332	40 19	035	51 36	105	28 56	151	40 19	198	42 23	244	50 39	299	30 25	343
333	40 53	034	52 33	105	29 25	151	40 00	199	41 29	245	49 47	298	30 07	342
334	41 26	034	53 30	105	29 54	151	39 41	199	40 36	245	48 55	298	29 48	341
335	41 58	033	54 27	105	30 22	151	39 22	200	39 43	245	48 03	297	29 29	340
336	42 29	032	55 23	106	30 50	152	39 01	200	38 50	245	47 10	296	29 09	340
337	43 00	031	56 20	106	31 18	152	38 41	201	37 56	245	46 17	296	28 48	339
338	43 29	030	57 17	106	31 45	152	38 20	201	37 03	245	45 24	295	28 27	338
339	43 58	029	58 13	106	32 12	153	37 58	202	36 09	245	44 30	294	28 05	338
340	44 26	028	59 10	107	32 39	153	37 36	202	35 16	245	43 37	294	27 42	337
341	44 53	027	60 06	107	33 06	154	37 13	203	34 22	246	42 43	293	27 18	336
342	45 19	026	61 02	107	33 32	154	36 50	203	33 28	246	41 48	293	26 55	336
343	45 43	024	61 59	108	33 57	154	36 26	204	32 35	246	40 54	292	26 30	335
344	46 07	023	62 55	108	34 23	155	36 02	204	31 41	246	39 59	292	26 05	334
	Alpheratz		◆ Hamal		◆ ACHERNAR		Peacock		Nunki		◆ ALTAIR		DENEB	
345	46 30	022	32 31	053	34 48	155	35 38	205	30 47	246	39 05	291	25 39	334
346	46 52	021	33 18	052	35 12	156	35 13	205	29 53	246	38 09	291	25 13	333
347	47 12	020	34 04	052	35 37	156	34 48	206	29 00	246	37 14	290	24 46	333
348	47 32	019	34 50	051	36 00	156	34 22	206	28 06	246	36 19	290	24 18	332
349	47 50	017	35 35	050	36 24	157	33 56	206	27 12	246	35 23	289	23 51	331
350	48 07	016	36 20	050	36 46	157	33 30	207	26 18	246	34 28	289	23 22	331
351	48 22	015	37 05	049	37 09	158	33 03	207	25 25	246	33 32	289	22 53	330
352	48 37	014	37 49	048	37 31	158	32 36	208	24 31	246	32 36	288	22 24	330
353	48 50	012	38 33	048	37 52	159	32 08	208	23 37	246	31 40	288	21 54	329
354	49 02	011	39 16	047	38 13	159	31 41	208	22 43	246	30 44	287	21 23	329
355	49 13	010	39 59	046	38 34	160	31 12	209	21 49	246	29 48	287	20 53	328
356	49 22	008	40 41	045	38 53	161	30 44	209	20 56	246	28 51	287	20 21	328
357	49 30	007	41 23	044	39 13	161	30 15	209	20 02	246	27 55	286	19 50	327
358	49 37	006	42 04	044	39 32	162	29 46	210	19 08	246	26 58	286	19 17	327
359	49 42	004	42 44	043	39 50	162	29 17	210	18 14	246	26 02	286	18 45	326

 LAT 12°S

LHA ♈	◆ Alpheratz Hc Zn	Hamal Hc Zn	ALDEBARAN Hc Zn	◆ RIGEL Hc Zn	ACHERNAR Hc Zn	◆ FOMALHAUT Hc Zn	Enif Hc Zn
0	48 46 003	42 39 041	15 54 069	12 33 096	41 05 163	67 22 217	49 54 302
1	48 48 002	43 17 040	16 48 068	13 32 095	41 22 163	66 46 218	49 04 301
2	48 50 000	43 55 040	17 43 068	14 30 095	41 39 164	66 09 220	48 14 300
3	48 49 359	44 32 039	18 37 068	15 29 095	41 55 164	65 31 221	47 23 299
4	48 48 358	45 08 038	19 31 067	16 27 095	42 10 165	64 52 223	46 32 299
5	48 45 356	45 44 037	20 26 067	17 26 095	42 25 166	64 11 224	45 40 298
6	48 40 355	46 18 036	21 20 067	18 24 095	42 39 166	63 30 225	44 48 297
7	48 35 354	46 52 035	22 13 066	19 23 095	42 52 167	62 48 226	43 56 297
8	48 28 352	47 25 033	23 07 066	20 21 094	43 05 168	62 05 228	43 03 296
9	48 19 351	47 56 032	24 01 066	21 20 094	43 17 168	61 21 229	42 10 296
10	48 10 350	48 27 031	24 54 065	22 18 094	43 29 169	60 37 229	41 17 295
11	47 59 349	48 57 030	25 47 065	23 17 094	43 39 170	59 52 230	40 24 294
12	47 46 347	49 26 029	26 40 064	24 15 094	43 49 171	59 07 231	39 30 294
13	47 33 346	49 54 028	27 33 064	25 14 093	43 58 171	58 21 232	38 37 293
14	47 18 345	50 21 026	28 26 064	26 12 093	44 07 172	57 34 233	37 43 293

LHA ♈	Hamal	◆ ALDEBARAN	RIGEL	◆ ACHERNAR	FOMALHAUT	◆ Enif	Alpheratz
15	50 46 025	29 18 063	27 11 093	44 15 173	56 47 233	36 48 292	47 02 344
16	51 10 024	30 10 063	28 10 093	44 22 174	56 00 234	35 54 292	46 45 342
17	51 33 022	31 02 062	29 08 093	44 28 174	55 12 235	34 59 291	46 27 341
18	51 55 021	31 54 062	30 07 093	44 34 175	54 24 235	34 05 291	46 07 340
19	52 16 020	32 45 061	31 05 092	44 38 176	53 36 236	33 10 290	45 47 339
20	52 35 018	33 37 061	32 04 092	44 42 177	52 47 236	32 15 290	45 25 338
21	52 52 017	34 28 060	33 03 092	44 45 177	51 58 237	31 19 290	45 02 337
22	53 09 015	35 18 060	34 01 092	44 48 178	51 09 237	30 24 289	44 39 336
23	53 23 014	36 09 059	35 00 092	44 49 179	50 19 238	29 29 289	44 14 334
24	53 37 012	36 59 058	35 59 091	44 50 180	49 29 238	28 33 288	43 48 333
25	53 49 011	37 49 058	36 57 091	44 50 180	48 39 239	27 37 288	43 21 332
26	53 59 009	38 38 057	37 56 091	44 50 181	47 49 239	26 41 288	42 54 331
27	54 08 008	39 27 057	38 55 091	44 48 182	46 59 239	25 45 287	42 25 330
28	54 15 006	40 16 056	39 53 091	44 46 183	46 08 240	24 49 287	41 56 329
29	54 21 005	41 05 055	40 52 090	44 43 183	45 18 240	23 53 287	41 25 328

LHA ♈	CAPELLA	◆ BETELGEUSE	SIRIUS	CANOPUS	◆ ACHERNAR	FOMALHAUT	◆ Alpheratz
30	16 59 033	28 13 075	20 58 104	23 56 143	44 39 184	44 27 240	40 54 328
31	17 31 033	29 10 074	21 55 103	24 32 143	44 34 185	43 36 240	40 22 327
32	18 03 033	30 06 074	22 52 103	25 07 143	44 29 186	42 45 241	39 50 326
33	18 34 032	31 02 074	23 49 103	25 43 143	44 23 186	41 53 241	39 16 325
34	19 05 032	31 59 073	24 47 103	26 18 143	44 16 187	41 02 241	38 42 324
35	19 36 031	32 55 073	25 44 103	26 53 144	44 08 188	40 11 241	38 07 323
36	20 06 031	33 51 072	26 41 103	27 27 144	44 00 189	39 19 241	37 32 322
37	20 35 030	34 47 072	27 38 103	28 02 144	43 51 189	38 28 242	36 55 322
38	21 05 030	35 43 072	28 35 103	28 37 144	43 41 190	37 36 242	36 19 321
39	21 33 029	36 38 071	29 33 103	29 11 144	43 30 191	36 44 242	35 41 320
40	22 01 028	37 34 071	30 30 103	29 45 145	43 19 191	35 52 242	35 03 319
41	22 29 028	38 29 070	31 27 102	30 19 145	43 07 192	35 00 242	34 25 319
42	22 56 027	39 24 070	32 25 102	30 53 145	42 54 193	34 08 242	33 46 318
43	23 23 027	40 19 069	33 22 102	31 26 145	42 41 193	33 16 242	33 06 317
44	23 49 026	41 14 069	34 19 102	31 59 146	42 27 194	32 24 242	32 26 317

LHA ♈	◆ CAPELLA	BETELGEUSE	SIRIUS	◆ CANOPUS	ACHERNAR	◆ FOMALHAUT	Alpheratz
45	24 15 026	42 09 068	35 17 102	32 32 146	42 12 195	31 32 243	31 45 316
46	24 40 025	43 03 068	36 14 102	33 05 146	41 57 195	30 40 243	31 04 315
47	25 04 024	43 57 067	37 11 102	33 37 147	41 41 196	29 48 243	30 22 315
48	25 28 024	44 51 067	38 09 102	34 09 147	41 24 197	28 56 243	29 40 314
49	25 51 023	45 45 066	39 06 102	34 41 147	41 07 197	28 04 243	28 58 313
50	26 14 022	46 38 065	40 04 102	35 13 148	40 49 198	27 12 243	28 15 313
51	26 36 022	47 32 065	41 01 102	35 44 148	40 31 199	26 20 243	27 32 312
52	26 57 021	48 24 064	41 59 102	36 15 148	40 12 199	25 27 243	26 48 312
53	27 18 020	49 17 063	42 56 102	36 45 149	39 53 200	24 35 243	26 04 311
54	27 38 020	50 09 063	43 53 102	37 15 149	39 33 200	23 43 243	25 20 311
55	27 57 019	51 01 062	44 51 102	37 45 150	39 12 201	22 51 243	24 35 310
56	28 16 018	51 53 061	45 48 102	38 14 150	38 51 201	21 59 243	23 50 310
57	28 34 018	52 44 060	46 46 102	38 43 151	38 29 202	21 06 243	23 05 309
58	28 52 017	53 35 059	47 43 102	39 12 151	38 07 202	20 14 243	22 19 309
59	29 08 016	54 25 058	48 41 102	39 40 152	37 45 203	19 22 243	21 34 308

LHA ♈	CAPELLA	POLLUX	◆ SIRIUS	CANOPUS	◆ ACHERNAR	Diphda	◆ Hamal
60	29 24 015	22 14 053	49 38 102	40 08 152	37 22 203	42 30 257	45 08 322
61	29 40 015	23 01 052	50 36 102	40 35 153	36 58 204	41 33 257	44 32 321
62	29 54 014	23 47 052	51 33 102	41 01 153	36 35 204	40 36 257	43 55 320
63	30 08 013	24 33 051	52 30 102	41 27 154	36 10 205	39 39 257	43 18 320
64	30 21 012	25 19 051	53 28 102	41 53 154	35 46 205	38 42 257	42 39 319
65	30 33 012	26 04 050	54 25 102	42 18 155	35 20 206	37 45 257	42 00 318
66	30 44 011	26 49 050	55 23 102	42 43 156	34 55 206	36 48 256	41 20 317
67	30 55 010	27 34 049	56 20 102	43 07 156	34 29 206	35 51 256	40 40 316
68	31 05 009	28 18 049	57 17 102	43 30 157	34 03 207	34 53 256	39 59 315
69	31 13 008	29 02 048	58 15 102	43 53 158	33 36 207	33 56 256	39 17 315
70	31 22 008	29 46 048	59 12 103	44 15 158	33 09 207	32 59 256	38 35 314
71	31 29 007	30 29 047	60 09 103	44 36 159	32 42 208	32 02 256	37 53 313
72	31 36 006	31 11 046	61 06 103	44 57 160	32 15 208	31 05 256	37 10 312
73	31 42 005	31 54 046	62 04 103	45 17 160	31 47 209	30 08 256	36 26 312
74	31 47 004	32 36 045	63 01 103	45 37 161	31 19 209	29 11 256	35 42 311

LHA ♈	CAPELLA	POLLUX	◆ PROCYON	Suhail	CANOPUS	◆ ACHERNAR	◆ Hamal
75	31 51 004	33 17 044	46 39 069	28 21 133	45 56 162	30 50 209	34 57 310
76	31 54 003	33 58 044	47 34 068	29 03 133	46 14 163	30 21 209	34 12 310
77	31 57 002	34 38 043	48 28 068	29 46 134	46 31 163	29 52 210	33 27 309
78	31 58 001	35 18 042	49 22 067	30 28 134	46 47 164	29 23 210	32 41 308
79	31 59 000	35 57 042	50 16 066	31 11 134	47 03 165	28 54 210	31 55 308
80	31 59 000	36 36 041	51 10 066	31 53 134	47 18 166	28 24 211	31 08 307
81	31 58 359	37 14 040	52 03 065	32 35 134	47 32 167	27 54 211	30 21 307
82	31 57 358	37 52 039	52 56 064	33 17 135	47 45 167	27 24 211	29 34 306
83	31 54 357	38 29 039	53 49 063	33 58 135	47 58 168	26 54 211	28 47 306
84	31 51 356	39 05 038	54 41 063	34 40 135	48 09 169	26 23 211	27 59 305
85	31 46 355	39 40 037	55 33 062	35 21 135	48 20 170	25 53 212	27 11 305
86	31 41 355	40 15 036	56 25 061	36 02 136	48 30 171	25 22 212	26 22 304
87	31 35 354	40 50 035	57 16 060	36 43 136	48 39 172	24 51 212	25 34 304
88	31 29 353	41 23 034	58 06 059	37 24 136	48 47 173	24 20 212	24 45 303
89	31 21 352	41 56 033	58 56 058	38 04 137	48 54 173	23 48 212	23 55 303

LHA ♈	POLLUX Hc Zn	◆ REGULUS Hc Zn	Suhail Hc Zn	◆ CANOPUS Hc Zn	ACHERNAR Hc Zn	◆ ALDEBARAN Hc Zn	CAPELLA Hc Zn
90	42 27 032	23 43 071	38 44 137	49 00 174	23 17 212	54 49 324	31 13 351
91	42 58 031	24 38 071	39 24 137	49 06 175	22 45 213	54 14 322	31 04 351
92	43 28 030	25 34 070	40 04 138	49 10 176	22 14 213	53 38 321	30 54 350
93	43 58 029	26 29 070	40 43 138	49 13 177	21 42 213	53 01 320	30 43 349
94	44 26 028	27 24 070	41 22 139	49 16 178	21 10 213	52 22 319	30 32 348
95	44 53 027	28 19 069	42 01 139	49 17 179	20 38 213	51 43 318	30 19 348
96	45 20 026	29 14 069	42 39 140	49 18 180	20 06 213	51 03 317	30 06 347
97	45 45 025	30 09 068	43 17 140	49 17 181	19 34 213	50 23 315	29 53 346
98	46 10 024	31 03 068	43 54 141	49 16 182	19 01 213	49 41 314	29 38 345
99	46 33 023	31 57 068	44 32 141	49 14 183	18 29 213	48 59 313	29 23 345
100	46 55 022	32 52 067	45 08 142	49 10 184	17 57 213	48 16 312	29 07 344
101	47 16 020	33 46 067	45 44 142	49 06 185	17 24 214	47 32 312	28 50 343
102	47 36 019	34 39 066	46 20 143	49 01 185	16 52 214	46 48 311	28 33 342
103	47 55 018	35 33 066	46 55 143	48 55 186	16 19 214	46 03 310	28 14 342
104	48 12 017	36 26 065	47 30 144	48 48 187	15 47 214	45 18 309	27 56 341

LHA ♈	POLLUX	◆ REGULUS	ACRUX	◆ CANOPUS	RIGEL	◆ ALDEBARAN	CAPELLA
105	48 28 015	37 20 065	14 22 153	48 40 188	63 57 276	44 32 308	27 36 340
106	48 43 014	38 12 064	14 49 153	48 31 189	62 59 276	43 45 307	27 16 340
107	48 57 013	39 05 064	15 16 153	48 22 190	62 00 275	42 59 307	26 55 339
108	49 10 012	39 58 063	15 43 153	48 11 191	61 02 275	42 11 306	26 34 338
109	49 21 010	40 50 062	16 10 153	48 00 192	60 03 274	41 23 305	26 12 338
110	49 31 009	41 42 062	16 37 153	47 47 193	59 05 274	40 35 304	25 49 337
111	49 39 008	42 33 061	17 03 153	47 34 193	58 06 274	39 47 304	25 25 336
112	49 46 006	43 25 061	17 30 153	47 20 194	57 08 273	38 58 303	25 02 336
113	49 52 005	44 16 060	17 57 153	47 05 195	56 09 273	38 08 302	24 37 335
114	49 56 004	45 06 059	18 24 153	46 50 196	55 10 273	37 19 302	24 12 334
115	49 59 002	45 56 058	18 50 153	46 33 197	54 12 273	36 29 301	23 46 334
116	50 00 001	46 46 058	19 17 153	46 16 197	53 13 272	35 38 301	23 20 333
117	50 01 359	47 36 057	19 43 153	45 58 198	52 15 272	34 48 300	22 54 333
118	49 59 358	48 25 056	20 10 153	45 40 199	51 16 272	33 57 300	22 26 332
119	49 56 357	49 13 055	20 36 153	45 20 200	50 17 272	33 06 299	21 59 332

LHA ♈	◆ REGULUS	SPICA	◆ ACRUX	CANOPUS	◆ RIGEL	BETELGEUSE	POLLUX
120	50 01 054	10 31 099	21 02 154	45 00 200	49 19 271	53 34 301	49 52 355
121	50 49 054	11 28 099	21 28 154	44 39 201	48 20 271	52 44 300	49 47 354
122	51 36 053	12 26 099	21 54 154	44 18 202	47 21 271	51 52 299	49 40 353
123	52 22 052	13 24 099	22 20 154	43 56 202	46 23 271	51 01 298	49 32 351
124	53 08 051	14 22 099	22 45 154	43 33 203	45 24 270	50 09 297	49 22 350
125	53 53 050	15 20 099	23 11 154	43 10 204	44 25 270	49 17 297	49 11 349
126	54 37 048	16 18 098	23 36 155	42 46 204	43 26 270	48 24 296	48 59 347
127	55 20 047	17 17 098	24 01 155	42 22 205	42 28 270	47 31 295	48 45 346
128	56 03 046	18 15 098	24 26 155	41 57 206	41 29 270	46 38 295	48 30 345
129	56 45 045	19 13 098	24 51 155	41 31 206	40 30 269	45 44 294	48 14 343
130	57 26 044	20 11 098	25 16 155	41 05 207	39 32 269	44 51 293	47 57 342
131	58 06 042	21 09 098	25 40 156	40 38 207	38 33 269	43 57 293	47 38 341
132	58 45 041	22 07 097	26 04 156	40 11 208	37 34 269	43 03 292	47 18 340
133	59 23 039	23 05 097	26 28 156	39 44 208	36 36 269	42 08 292	46 57 339
134	59 59 038	24 04 097	26 52 156	39 16 209	35 37 268	41 14 291	46 35 337

LHA ♈	REGULUS	◆ SPICA	ACRUX	◆ CANOPUS	SIRIUS	BETELGEUSE	◆ POLLUX
135	60 35 036	25 02 097	27 16 156	38 47 209	57 12 258	40 19 291	46 12 336
136	61 09 035	26 00 097	27 39 157	38 19 210	56 15 258	39 24 290	45 48 335
137	61 42 033	26 59 097	28 02 157	37 49 210	55 17 258	38 29 290	45 23 334
138	62 13 031	27 57 096	28 25 157	37 20 211	54 20 258	37 33 289	44 57 333
139	62 42 029	28 55 096	28 47 158	36 49 211	53 22 258	36 38 289	44 29 332
140	63 10 027	29 53 096	29 10 158	36 19 211	52 25 258	35 42 288	44 01 331
141	63 36 026	30 52 096	29 32 158	35 48 212	51 28 258	34 46 288	43 32 330
142	64 01 024	31 50 096	29 53 158	35 17 212	50 30 258	33 50 288	43 02 329
143	64 23 021	32 49 096	30 15 159	34 46 213	49 33 258	32 54 287	42 31 328
144	64 44 019	33 47 096	30 36 159	34 14 213	48 35 258	31 58 287	41 59 327
145	65 02 017	34 45 095	30 57 159	33 42 213	47 38 258	31 02 286	41 27 326
146	65 18 015	35 44 095	31 17 160	33 09 214	46 40 258	30 06 286	40 53 325
147	65 32 013	36 42 095	31 37 160	32 37 214	45 43 258	29 09 286	40 19 324
148	65 44 010	37 41 095	31 57 161	32 04 214	44 45 258	28 13 285	39 45 323
149	65 53 008	38 39 095	32 16 161	31 31 215	43 48 258	27 16 285	39 09 322

LHA ♈	REGULUS	◆ ARCTURUS	SPICA	◆ ACRUX	CANOPUS	SIRIUS	◆ PROCYON
150	66 00 006	19 38 064	39 38 095	32 35 161	30 57 215	42 50 258	51 12 294
151	66 04 003	20 30 064	40 36 095	32 54 162	30 24 215	41 53 258	50 19 294
152	66 06 001	21 23 064	41 35 094	33 12 162	29 50 215	40 56 258	49 25 293
153	66 06 358	22 16 063	42 33 094	33 30 162	29 16 216	39 58 258	48 31 292
154	66 03 356	23 08 063	43 32 094	33 48 163	28 42 216	39 01 258	47 36 292
155	65 57 353	24 00 063	44 30 094	34 05 163	28 07 216	38 03 258	46 42 291
156	65 49 351	24 52 062	45 29 094	34 21 164	27 32 216	37 06 258	45 47 291
157	65 39 349	25 44 062	46 27 094	34 38 164	26 58 216	36 09 258	44 52 290
158	65 27 346	26 36 061	47 26 094	34 54 165	26 23 217	35 11 258	43 56 289
159	65 12 344	27 27 061	48 25 093	35 09 165	25 48 217	34 14 258	43 01 289
160	64 55 342	28 18 060	49 23 093	35 24 166	25 12 217	33 16 258	42 05 288
161	64 35 340	29 09 060	50 22 093	35 38 166	24 37 217	32 19 258	41 10 288
162	64 14 338	30 00 059	51 20 093	35 52 166	24 02 217	31 22 258	40 14 288
163	63 51 336	30 50 059	52 19 093	36 06 167	23 26 217	30 24 257	39 18 287
164	63 26 334	31 40 058	53 18 093	36 19 167	22 50 218	29 27 257	38 22 287

LHA ♈	Denebola	◆ ARCTURUS	SPICA	◆ ACRUX	SIRIUS	◆ PROCYON	REGULUS
165	60 47 025	32 30 058	54 16 093	36 31 168	28 30 257	37 25 286	62 59 332
166	61 11 024	33 19 057	55 15 092	36 43 168	27 33 257	36 29 286	62 30 330
167	61 33 022	34 09 057	56 13 092	36 55 169	26 35 257	35 32 285	62 00 328
168	61 54 020	34 58 056	57 12 092	37 06 169	25 38 257	34 36 285	61 28 326
169	62 13 018	35 46 056	58 11 092	37 16 170	24 41 257	33 39 285	60 55 325
170	62 30 016	36 34 055	59 09 092	37 26 171	23 44 257	32 42 284	60 20 323
171	62 45 014	37 22 054	60 08 092	37 36 171	22 47 257	31 45 284	59 44 321
172	62 58 012	38 10 054	61 07 092	37 44 172	21 50 257	30 48 284	59 07 320
173	63 09 010	38 57 053	62 05 091	37 53 172	20 53 256	29 51 283	58 29 319
174	63 17 007	39 43 052	63 04 091	38 00 173	19 56 256	28 54 283	57 49 317
175	63 24 005	40 30 052	64 03 091	38 08 173	18 59 256	27 57 283	57 09 316
176	63 28 003	41 15 051	65 01 091	38 14 174	18 02 256	26 59 282	56 28 315
177	63 30 001	42 01 050	66 00 091	38 20 174	17 05 256	26 02 282	55 46 313
178	63 30 359	42 45 049	66 59 091	38 26 175	16 08 256	25 04 282	55 02 312
179	63 28 357	43 30 048	67 57 090	38 31 175	15 11 256	24 07 281	54 19 311

LHA ♈	ARCTURUS	◆ANTARES	ACRUX	◆Suhail	Alphard	REGULUS	◆Denebola
180	44 13 048	25 15 114	38 35 176	41 33 221	52 35 271	53 34 310	63 24 354
181	44 56 047	26 09 114	38 39 177	40 54 222	51 36 271	52 49 309	63 17 352
182	45 39 046	27 02 114	38 42 177	40 15 222	50 38 271	52 03 308	63 08 350
183	46 21 045	27 56 114	38 45 178	39 35 222	49 39 271	51 16 307	62 57 348
184	47 02 044	28 50 114	38 47 178	38 55 223	48 40 270	50 29 306	62 44 346
185	47 42 043	29 44 114	38 48 179	38 15 223	47 42 270	49 41 305	62 29 344
186	48 22 042	30 37 114	38 49 180	37 35 224	46 43 270	48 53 304	62 12 342
187	49 01 041	31 31 114	38 49 180	36 54 224	45 44 270	48 04 304	61 52 340
188	49 39 040	32 25 114	38 49 181	36 14 224	44 46 270	47 15 303	61 32 338
189	50 16 039	33 18 114	38 48 181	35 33 225	43 47 269	46 26 302	61 09 336
190	50 52 038	34 12 114	38 46 182	34 51 225	42 48 269	45 36 301	60 44 335
191	51 28 036	35 06 114	38 44 182	34 10 225	41 50 269	44 45 300	60 18 333
192	52 02 035	35 59 114	38 41 183	33 28 225	40 51 269	43 54 300	59 51 331
193	52 36 034	36 53 114	38 38 184	32 46 226	39 52 269	43 03 299	59 22 329
194	53 08 033	37 46 114	38 34 184	32 04 226	38 54 268	42 12 298	58 51 328

LHA ♈	ARCTURUS	◆Rasalhague	ANTARES	◆ACRUX	Suhail	◆REGULUS	Denebola
195	53 39 031	17 22 073	38 40 114	38 30 185	31 22 226	41 20 298	58 19 326
196	54 09 030	18 18 072	39 33 115	38 24 185	30 40 226	40 28 297	57 46 325
197	54 38 029	19 14 072	40 26 115	38 19 186	29 57 226	39 36 297	57 11 323
198	55 05 027	20 09 072	41 20 115	38 13 186	29 15 227	38 43 296	56 36 322
199	55 31 026	21 05 071	42 13 115	38 06 187	28 32 227	37 51 296	55 59 321
200	55 56 024	22 01 071	43 06 115	37 58 187	27 49 227	36 57 295	55 21 319
201	56 20 023	22 56 071	43 59 115	37 50 188	27 07 227	36 04 295	54 42 318
202	56 42 021	23 51 070	44 52 116	37 42 189	26 24 227	35 11 294	54 03 317
203	57 02 020	24 46 070	45 45 116	37 33 189	25 41 227	34 17 294	53 22 316
204	57 21 018	25 42 070	46 38 116	37 23 190	24 57 227	33 23 293	52 40 314
205	57 38 016	26 36 069	47 31 116	37 13 190	24 14 227	32 29 293	51 58 313
206	57 53 014	27 31 069	48 23 117	37 03 191	23 31 228	31 35 292	51 15 312
207	58 07 013	28 26 068	49 16 117	36 52 191	22 48 228	30 40 292	50 31 311
208	58 19 011	29 20 068	50 08 117	36 40 192	22 04 228	29 46 291	49 47 310
209	58 30 009	30 15 068	51 00 117	36 28 192	21 21 228	28 51 291	49 02 309

LHA ♈	ARCTURUS	◆Rasalhague	ANTARES	◆RIGIL KENT	ACRUX	Gienah	◆REGULUS
210	58 38 007	31 09 067	51 52 118	40 32 174	36 15 193	64 24 254	27 56 291
211	58 45 006	32 03 067	52 44 118	40 39 174	36 02 193	63 28 255	27 01 290
212	58 50 004	32 57 066	53 35 119	40 44 175	35 48 194	62 31 255	26 06 290
213	58 53 002	33 50 066	54 27 119	40 49 175	35 34 194	61 35 255	25 11 289
214	58 54 000	34 44 065	55 18 120	40 54 176	35 20 195	60 38 255	24 15 289
215	58 53 358	35 37 065	56 09 120	40 57 177	35 05 195	59 41 256	23 20 289
216	58 50 357	36 30 064	57 00 121	41 01 177	34 49 196	58 44 256	22 24 288
217	58 46 355	37 23 064	57 50 121	41 03 178	34 33 196	57 47 256	21 28 288
218	58 39 353	38 15 063	58 40 122	41 05 179	34 17 196	56 50 256	20 33 288
219	58 31 351	39 08 063	59 30 122	41 06 179	34 00 197	55 53 256	19 37 287
220	58 21 349	40 00 062	60 19 123	41 06 180	33 43 197	54 56 256	18 41 287
221	58 09 348	40 51 061	61 08 124	41 05 181	33 25 198	53 59 256	17 44 287
222	57 56 346	41 43 061	61 56 125	41 05 181	33 07 198	53 02 257	16 48 287
223	57 41 344	42 34 060	62 44 126	41 04 182	32 49 198	52 05 257	15 52 286
224	57 24 342	43 25 060	63 32 127	41 01 182	32 30 199	51 08 257	14 56 286

LHA ♈	Alphecca	◆VEGA	ALTAIR	◆Shaula	RIGIL KENT	◆SPICA	ARCTURUS
225	50 24 012	18 18 042	14 37 077	47 16 133	40 59 183	66 58 269	57 05 341
226	50 36 011	18 57 041	15 34 077	47 59 133	40 55 184	66 00 269	56 45 339
227	50 46 010	19 35 041	16 31 077	48 42 134	40 51 184	65 01 269	56 24 338
228	50 55 008	20 14 040	17 28 077	49 24 134	40 46 185	64 02 269	56 00 336
229	51 03 007	20 51 040	18 25 076	50 05 135	40 41 186	63 04 269	55 36 335
230	51 09 005	21 29 039	19 22 076	50 47 136	40 34 186	62 05 269	55 10 333
231	51 14 004	22 06 039	20 19 076	51 28 136	40 28 187	61 06 268	54 43 332
232	51 18 003	22 43 038	21 16 075	52 08 137	40 20 188	60 08 268	54 14 330
233	51 20 001	23 19 038	22 13 075	52 48 138	40 12 188	59 09 268	53 44 329
234	51 20 000	23 55 037	23 09 075	53 27 139	40 04 189	58 10 268	53 13 327
235	51 19 358	24 30 037	24 06 074	54 05 139	39 54 189	57 12 268	52 41 326
236	51 17 357	25 05 036	25 03 074	54 43 140	39 45 190	56 13 268	52 08 325
237	51 13 355	25 40 036	25 59 074	55 21 141	39 34 191	55 14 268	51 34 324
238	51 07 354	26 13 035	26 55 073	55 57 142	39 23 191	54 16 267	50 59 323
239	51 01 353	26 47 034	27 51 073	56 33 143	39 12 192	53 17 267	50 22 321

LHA ♈	VEGA	◆ALTAIR	Shaula	◆RIGIL KENT	SPICA	◆ARCTURUS	Alphecca
240	27 20 034	28 47 073	57 08 144	38 59 192	52 18 267	49 45 320	50 52 351
241	27 52 033	29 43 072	57 42 145	38 47 193	51 20 267	49 07 319	50 43 350
242	28 24 033	30 39 072	58 15 146	38 33 193	50 21 267	48 29 318	50 32 348
243	28 55 032	31 35 072	58 48 147	38 20 194	49 23 267	47 49 317	50 19 347
244	29 26 031	32 31 071	59 19 148	38 05 194	48 24 267	47 09 316	50 06 346
245	29 56 031	33 26 071	59 49 150	37 50 195	47 26 266	46 28 315	49 50 344
246	30 26 030	34 21 070	60 19 151	37 35 196	46 27 266	45 46 314	49 34 343
247	30 54 029	35 17 070	60 47 152	37 19 196	45 28 266	45 04 313	49 16 342
248	31 23 028	36 12 069	61 14 153	37 02 197	44 30 266	44 21 313	48 57 341
249	31 50 028	37 07 069	61 39 155	36 45 197	43 31 266	43 37 312	48 37 339
250	32 17 027	38 01 068	62 03 156	36 28 198	42 33 266	42 53 311	48 16 338
251	32 43 026	38 56 068	62 26 158	36 10 198	41 34 266	42 08 310	47 53 337
252	33 09 025	39 50 067	62 48 159	35 52 198	40 36 265	41 23 309	47 30 336
253	33 33 025	40 44 067	63 08 161	35 33 199	39 37 265	40 38 309	47 05 334
254	33 57 024	41 38 066	63 26 163	35 14 199	38 39 265	39 51 308	46 39 333

LHA ♈	◆VEGA	ALTAIR	◆Peacock	RIGIL KENT	◆SPICA	ARCTURUS	Alphecca
255	34 21 023	42 32 066	30 27 150	34 54 200	37 40 265	39 05 307	46 12 332
256	34 43 022	43 25 065	30 56 150	34 34 200	36 42 265	38 18 306	45 44 331
257	35 05 021	44 18 065	31 25 151	34 13 201	35 43 265	37 30 306	45 16 330
258	35 26 020	45 11 064	31 54 151	33 52 201	34 45 265	36 43 305	44 46 329
259	35 46 020	46 04 063	32 22 151	33 31 201	33 47 264	35 55 305	44 15 328
260	36 05 019	46 56 063	32 50 152	33 10 202	32 48 264	35 06 304	43 44 327
261	36 23 018	47 48 062	33 18 152	32 48 202	31 50 264	34 17 303	43 11 326
262	36 41 017	48 40 061	33 45 152	32 25 203	30 51 264	33 28 303	42 38 325
263	36 57 016	49 31 060	34 12 153	32 02 203	29 53 264	32 38 302	42 04 324
264	37 13 015	50 22 060	34 39 153	31 39 203	28 55 264	31 49 302	41 29 323
265	37 28 014	51 12 059	35 05 153	31 16 204	27 56 264	30 59 301	40 53 322
266	37 42 013	52 02 058	35 31 154	30 52 204	26 58 263	30 08 301	40 17 321
267	37 54 012	52 52 057	35 57 154	30 28 204	26 00 263	29 18 300	39 40 321
268	38 06 011	53 41 056	36 22 155	30 04 205	25 02 263	28 27 300	39 03 320
269	38 17 010	54 29 055	36 47 155	29 39 205	24 03 263	27 36 299	38 24 319

LHA ♈	◆VEGA	ALTAIR	◆FOMALHAUT	Peacock	RIGIL KENT	◆ANTARES	ARCTURUS
270	38 27 009	55 17 054	19 10 117	37 11 156	29 14 205	64 26 232	26 44 299
271	38 36 008	56 04 053	20 02 117	37 35 156	28 49 205	63 40 233	25 53 298
272	38 44 007	56 51 052	20 54 117	37 59 157	28 24 206	62 52 234	25 01 298
273	38 51 006	57 37 051	21 46 117	38 22 157	27 58 206	62 04 235	24 09 298
274	38 57 005	58 22 050	22 38 117	38 44 158	27 32 206	61 16 236	23 17 297
275	39 02 004	59 06 048	23 30 117	39 07 158	27 06 207	60 27 237	22 25 297
276	39 06 003	59 50 047	24 23 117	39 28 159	26 40 207	59 38 237	21 32 296
277	39 09 002	60 32 046	25 15 117	39 49 159	26 13 207	58 48 238	20 40 296
278	39 11 001	61 14 044	26 07 117	40 10 160	25 47 207	57 58 239	19 47 296
279	39 12 000	61 54 043	26 59 117	40 30 160	25 20 207	57 08 239	18 54 295
280	39 12 359	62 34 041	27 51 117	40 49 161	24 53 208	56 17 240	18 01 295
281	39 11 358	63 12 039	28 44 117	41 08 162	24 25 208	55 26 240	17 07 295
282	39 09 357	63 48 038	29 36 117	41 26 162	23 58 208	54 35 241	16 14 294
283	39 05 356	64 23 036	30 28 117	41 44 163	23 30 208	53 44 241	15 20 294
284	39 01 355	64 57 034	31 20 117	42 01 163	23 03 208	52 52 242	14 26 294

LHA ♈	◆DENEB	◆FOMALHAUT	Peacock	RIGIL KENT	◆ANTARES	Rasalhague	VEGA
285	28 13 020	32 12 118	42 17 164	22 35 208	52 01 242	57 44 319	38 56 354
286	28 33 019	33 04 118	42 33 165	22 07 209	51 09 242	57 05 317	38 49 353
287	28 52 019	33 56 118	42 48 165	21 38 209	50 17 243	56 25 316	38 42 352
288	29 10 018	34 48 118	43 03 166	21 10 209	49 24 243	55 44 315	38 34 351
289	29 28 017	35 40 118	43 17 167	20 42 209	48 32 243	55 02 314	38 25 350
290	29 45 016	36 32 118	43 30 167	20 13 209	47 39 244	54 19 313	38 14 349
291	30 01 016	37 24 118	43 42 168	19 45 209	46 47 244	53 36 311	38 03 348
292	30 17 015	38 15 118	43 54 169	19 16 209	45 54 244	52 51 310	37 51 348
293	30 32 014	39 07 118	44 05 170	18 47 209	45 01 244	52 06 309	37 38 347
294	30 46 013	39 58 119	44 15 170	18 18 209	44 08 245	51 21 308	37 24 346
295	30 59 013	40 50 119	44 25 171	17 49 210	43 15 245	50 34 307	37 09 345
296	31 11 012	41 41 119	44 33 172	17 20 210	42 22 245	49 48 307	36 53 344
297	31 23 011	42 32 119	44 41 173	16 51 210	41 29 245	49 00 306	36 36 343
298	31 34 010	43 24 120	44 49 173	16 22 210	40 35 245	48 12 305	36 18 342
299	31 44 009	44 15 120	44 55 174	15 53 210	39 42 245	47 24 304	36 00 341

LHA ♈	◆DENEB	Alpheratz	◆FOMALHAUT	Peacock	◆ANTARES	Rasalhague	VEGA
300	31 53 009	17 12 054	45 05 120	45 01 175	38 48 246	46 35 303	35 40 340
301	32 02 008	18 00 054	45 56 120	45 06 176	37 55 246	45 46 302	35 20 339
302	32 09 007	18 47 053	46 47 121	45 10 176	37 02 246	44 56 302	34 59 339
303	32 16 006	19 34 053	47 37 121	45 13 177	36 08 246	44 06 301	34 37 338
304	32 22 005	20 20 052	48 27 121	45 16 178	35 14 246	43 15 300	34 14 337
305	32 27 005	21 07 052	49 17 122	45 18 179	34 21 246	42 24 300	33 51 336
306	32 31 004	21 53 052	50 07 122	45 19 179	33 27 246	41 33 299	33 27 335
307	32 35 003	22 38 051	50 57 123	45 19 180	32 34 246	40 42 298	33 02 334
308	32 37 002	23 24 051	51 46 123	45 18 181	31 40 246	39 50 298	32 36 334
309	32 39 001	24 09 050	52 35 123	45 17 182	30 46 246	38 58 297	32 10 333
310	32 40 000	24 54 050	53 24 124	45 15 183	29 52 246	38 06 297	31 43 332
311	32 40 000	25 39 049	54 13 125	45 11 183	28 59 246	37 13 296	31 15 331
312	32 39 359	26 23 049	55 01 125	45 08 184	28 05 246	36 20 296	30 47 331
313	32 37 358	27 07 048	55 49 126	45 03 185	27 11 246	35 27 295	30 17 330
314	32 35 357	27 50 047	56 36 126	44 58 186	26 18 246	34 34 295	29 48 329

LHA ♈	Alpheratz	◆Diphda	ACHERNAR	Peacock	◆ANTARES	VEGA	◆DENEB
315	28 33 047	35 41 104	21 05 147	44 52 186	25 24 246	29 18 329	32 31 356
316	29 16 046	36 38 104	21 37 147	44 45 187	24 30 246	28 47 328	32 27 355
317	29 58 046	37 35 103	22 09 147	44 37 188	23 37 246	28 15 327	32 22 355
318	30 40 045	38 32 103	22 41 147	44 28 189	22 43 246	27 43 327	32 16 354
319	31 21 045	39 29 103	23 13 148	44 19 189	21 49 246	27 11 326	32 09 353
320	32 02 044	40 26 103	23 44 148	44 09 190	20 56 246	26 38 325	32 01 352
321	32 43 043	41 23 103	24 15 148	43 58 191	20 02 246	26 04 325	31 53 351
322	33 22 043	42 20 103	24 47 148	43 47 192	19 08 246	25 30 324	31 44 351
323	34 02 042	43 17 103	25 18 148	43 35 192	18 15 246	24 55 324	31 34 350
324	34 41 041	44 15 103	25 48 148	43 22 193	17 21 246	24 20 323	31 23 349
325	35 19 040	45 12 103	26 19 149	43 09 194	16 28 246	23 45 323	31 11 348
326	35 57 040	46 09 103	26 50 149	42 54 194	15 34 246	23 09 322	30 59 347
327	36 34 039	47 06 103	27 20 149	42 40 195	14 41 245	22 33 321	30 45 347
328	37 11 038	48 03 104	27 50 149	42 24 196	13 48 245	21 56 321	30 31 346
329	37 46 037	49 00 104	28 20 149	42 08 196	12 54 245	21 19 320	30 16 345

LHA ♈	◆Alpheratz	Diphda	◆ACHERNAR	Peacock	◆Nunki	ALTAIR	DENEB
330	38 22 037	49 57 104	28 50 150	41 51 197	44 35 245	51 50 302	30 01 344
331	38 56 036	50 54 104	29 19 150	41 34 198	43 41 245	51 00 301	29 45 344
332	39 30 035	51 51 104	29 48 150	41 16 198	42 48 245	50 09 300	29 28 343
333	40 03 034	52 48 104	30 17 151	40 57 199	41 55 245	49 18 299	29 10 342
334	40 36 033	53 45 104	30 46 151	40 38 199	41 01 245	48 27 299	28 51 341
335	41 07 032	54 42 104	31 15 151	40 18 200	40 08 246	47 35 298	28 32 341
336	41 38 031	55 39 104	31 43 151	39 58 201	39 15 246	46 43 297	28 12 340
337	42 08 030	56 36 104	32 11 152	39 37 201	38 21 246	45 51 297	27 52 339
338	42 37 029	57 32 105	32 38 152	39 15 202	37 27 246	44 58 296	27 31 339
339	43 05 028	58 29 105	33 06 152	38 54 202	36 34 246	44 05 295	27 09 338
340	43 33 027	59 26 105	33 33 153	38 31 203	35 40 246	43 12 295	26 47 337
341	43 59 026	60 23 105	33 59 153	38 08 203	34 47 246	42 19 294	26 23 337
342	44 24 025	61 19 105	34 26 154	37 45 204	33 53 246	41 25 293	26 00 336
343	44 49 024	62 16 106	34 51 154	37 21 204	32 59 246	40 31 293	25 36 335
344	45 12 023	63 12 106	35 17 154	36 57 205	32 05 246	39 37 292	25 11 335

LHA ♈	Alpheratz	◆Hamal	◆ACHERNAR	Peacock	Nunki	◆ALTAIR	DENEB
345	45 34 022	31 54 052	35 42 155	36 32 205	31 12 246	38 42 292	24 45 334
346	45 55 021	32 41 052	36 07 155	36 07 206	30 18 246	37 48 291	24 19 333
347	46 16 019	33 26 051	36 31 156	35 42 206	29 24 246	36 53 291	23 53 333
348	46 35 018	34 12 050	36 55 156	35 16 206	28 30 246	35 58 290	23 25 332
349	46 52 017	34 57 050	37 19 157	34 50 207	27 36 246	35 03 290	22 58 332
350	47 09 016	35 41 049	37 42 157	34 23 207	26 43 246	34 08 290	22 30 331
351	47 24 015	36 25 048	38 04 158	33 56 208	25 49 246	33 13 289	22 01 330
352	47 39 013	37 09 048	38 26 158	33 29 208	24 55 246	32 17 289	21 32 330
353	47 52 012	37 52 047	38 48 159	33 01 208	24 01 246	31 22 288	21 02 329
354	48 03 011	38 35 046	39 09 159	32 33 209	23 07 246	30 26 288	20 32 329
355	48 14 010	39 17 045	39 30 160	32 05 209	22 14 246	29 30 288	20 02 328
356	48 23 008	39 59 045	39 50 160	31 37 209	21 20 246	28 34 287	19 31 328
357	48 31 007	40 40 044	40 09 161	31 08 210	20 26 246	27 38 287	18 59 327
358	48 37 006	41 20 043	40 28 161	30 39 210	19 33 246	26 42 287	18 27 327
359	48 42 004	42 00 042	40 47 162	30 09 210	18 39 246	25 45 286	17 55 326

 LAT 13°S

LHA ♈	Hc	Zn	Hc	Zn	Hc	Zn	Hc	Zn	Hc	Zn	Hc	Zn	Hc	Zn
	◆ Alpheratz		Hamal		ALDEBARAN		◆ RIGEL		ACHERNAR		◆ FOMALHAUT		Enif	
0	47 46	003	41 54	041	15 32	068	12 39	096	42 02	162	68 10	218	49 22	303
1	47 49	002	42 31	040	16 26	068	13 38	095	42 19	163	67 33	220	48 33	302
2	47 50	000	43 08	039	17 20	068	14 36	095	42 36	164	66 55	222	47 43	301
3	47 49	359	43 45	038	18 14	067	15 34	095	42 52	164	66 15	223	46 53	300
4	47 48	358	44 20	037	19 08	067	16 32	095	43 08	165	65 35	224	46 02	300
5	47 45	356	44 55	036	20 02	067	17 31	095	43 23	166	64 54	226	45 11	299
6	47 40	355	45 29	035	20 56	066	18 29	094	43 37	166	64 12	227	44 20	298
7	47 35	354	46 02	034	21 49	066	19 27	094	43 51	167	63 29	228	43 28	298
8	47 28	353	46 34	033	22 42	066	20 25	094	44 04	168	62 45	229	42 36	297
9	47 20	351	47 06	032	23 36	065	21 24	094	44 16	168	62 00	230	41 44	296
10	47 10	350	47 36	031	24 29	065	22 22	094	44 28	169	61 15	231	40 52	296
11	47 00	349	48 05	029	25 21	064	23 20	093	44 38	170	60 30	232	39 59	295
12	46 48	348	48 33	028	26 14	064	24 19	093	44 48	170	59 44	233	39 06	295
13	46 35	346	49 01	027	27 06	063	25 17	093	44 58	171	58 57	233	38 12	294
14	46 20	345	49 27	026	27 59	063	26 16	093	45 06	172	58 10	234	37 19	294
	Hamal		◆ ALDEBARAN		RIGEL		◆ ACHERNAR		FOMALHAUT		◆ Enif		Alpheratz	
15	49 52	025	28 51	063	27 14	093	45 14	173	57 22	235	36 25	293	46 05	344
16	50 15	023	29 42	062	28 12	092	45 21	173	56 35	235	35 31	292	45 48	343
17	50 38	022	30 34	062	29 11	092	45 28	174	55 46	236	34 37	292	45 30	342
18	50 59	021	31 25	061	30 09	092	45 33	175	54 58	236	33 43	292	45 11	340
19	51 19	019	32 16	061	31 08	092	45 38	176	54 09	237	32 48	291	44 51	339
20	51 38	018	33 07	060	32 06	092	45 42	176	53 20	238	31 54	291	44 30	338
21	51 55	016	33 58	059	33 05	091	45 45	177	52 30	238	30 59	290	44 07	337
22	52 11	015	34 48	059	34 03	091	45 48	178	51 41	238	30 04	290	43 44	336
23	52 25	014	35 38	058	35 01	091	45 49	179	50 51	239	29 09	289	43 20	335
24	52 38	012	36 27	058	36 00	091	45 50	180	50 00	239	28 14	289	42 54	334
25	52 50	011	37 17	057	36 58	091	45 50	180	49 10	240	27 18	289	42 28	333
26	53 00	009	38 05	056	37 57	090	45 50	181	48 20	240	26 23	288	42 01	332
27	53 08	008	38 54	056	38 55	090	45 48	182	47 29	240	25 27	288	41 33	331
28	53 15	006	39 42	055	39 54	090	45 46	183	46 38	240	24 32	287	41 04	330
29	53 21	005	40 30	054	40 52	090	45 43	183	45 47	241	23 36	287	40 34	329
	CAPELLA		◆ BETELGEUSE		SIRIUS		CANOPUS		◆ ACHERNAR		FOMALHAUT		◆ Alpheratz	
30	16 09	033	27 57	074	21 12	103	24 44	142	45 39	184	44 56	241	40 03	328
31	16 41	033	28 53	074	22 09	103	25 20	143	45 34	185	44 05	241	39 32	327
32	17 12	032	29 49	073	23 06	103	25 55	143	45 29	186	43 14	241	39 00	326
33	17 43	032	30 45	073	24 03	103	26 31	143	45 22	186	42 22	242	38 27	325
34	18 14	031	31 41	073	25 00	103	27 06	143	45 15	187	41 31	242	37 53	324
35	18 44	031	32 37	072	25 57	102	27 41	143	45 08	188	40 39	242	37 19	324
36	19 14	030	33 32	072	26 54	102	28 16	143	44 59	189	39 47	242	36 44	323
37	19 43	030	34 28	071	27 51	102	28 51	144	44 50	189	38 56	242	36 08	322
38	20 12	029	35 23	071	28 48	102	29 25	144	44 40	190	38 04	242	35 32	321
39	20 41	029	36 18	070	29 45	102	30 00	144	44 29	191	37 12	243	34 55	320
40	21 09	028	37 14	070	30 43	102	30 34	144	44 18	192	36 20	243	34 18	320
41	21 36	028	38 08	070	31 40	102	31 08	145	44 05	192	35 28	243	33 39	319
42	22 03	027	39 03	069	32 37	102	31 42	145	43 53	193	34 36	243	33 01	318
43	22 29	027	39 58	069	33 34	102	32 15	145	43 39	194	33 44	243	32 22	318
44	22 55	026	40 52	068	34 32	102	32 49	145	43 25	194	32 52	243	31 42	317
	◆ CAPELLA		BETELGEUSE		SIRIUS		◆ CANOPUS		ACHERNAR		◆ FOMALHAUT		Alpheratz	
45	23 20	025	41 46	067	35 29	101	33 22	146	43 10	195	32 00	243	31 02	316
46	23 45	025	42 40	067	36 26	101	33 55	146	42 55	196	31 08	243	30 21	316
47	24 09	024	43 33	066	37 24	101	34 27	146	42 38	196	30 15	243	29 40	315
48	24 33	023	44 27	066	38 21	101	35 00	147	42 22	197	29 23	243	28 59	314
49	24 56	023	45 20	065	39 18	101	35 32	147	42 04	198	28 31	243	28 17	314
50	25 18	022	46 13	064	40 16	101	36 03	147	41 46	198	27 39	243	27 34	313
51	25 40	022	47 05	064	41 13	101	36 35	148	41 28	199	26 47	243	26 51	313
52	26 01	021	47 58	063	42 10	101	37 06	148	41 09	199	25 55	243	26 08	312
53	26 22	020	48 50	062	43 08	101	37 36	149	40 49	200	25 02	243	25 25	312
54	26 42	020	49 41	062	44 05	101	38 07	149	40 29	201	24 10	243	24 41	311
55	27 01	019	50 32	061	45 03	101	38 37	149	40 08	201	23 18	243	23 56	311
56	27 19	018	51 23	060	46 00	101	39 06	150	39 47	202	22 26	243	23 12	310
57	27 37	017	52 14	059	46 57	101	39 36	150	39 25	202	21 34	243	22 27	310
58	27 54	017	53 04	058	47 55	101	40 04	151	39 03	203	20 42	243	21 42	309
59	28 11	016	53 53	057	48 52	101	40 33	151	38 40	203	19 50	243	20 56	309
	CAPELLA		POLLUX		◆ SIRIUS		CANOPUS		◆ ACHERNAR		Diphda		◆ Hamal	
60	28 26	015	21 38	052	49 50	101	41 00	152	38 17	204	42 44	258	44 21	323
61	28 41	015	22 24	052	50 47	101	41 28	152	37 53	204	41 46	257	43 45	322
62	28 56	014	23 10	051	51 45	101	41 55	153	37 29	205	40 49	257	43 09	321
63	29 09	013	23 55	051	52 42	101	42 21	153	37 05	205	39 52	257	42 32	320
64	29 22	012	24 41	050	53 40	101	42 47	154	36 40	205	38 55	257	41 54	319
65	29 34	011	25 26	050	54 37	101	43 12	155	36 15	206	37 58	257	41 15	318
66	29 45	011	26 10	049	55 35	101	43 37	155	35 49	206	37 01	257	40 36	318
67	29 56	010	26 54	049	56 32	101	44 01	156	35 23	207	36 04	257	39 57	317
68	30 06	009	27 38	048	57 29	101	44 25	156	34 56	207	35 07	257	39 16	316
69	30 14	008	28 22	048	58 27	101	44 48	157	34 30	207	34 10	257	38 35	315
70	30 23	008	29 05	047	59 24	101	45 11	158	34 03	208	33 13	257	37 54	314
71	30 30	007	29 48	047	60 22	101	45 32	158	33 35	208	32 16	257	37 12	314
72	30 36	006	30 30	046	61 19	101	45 53	159	33 07	208	31 19	257	36 29	313
73	30 42	005	31 12	045	62 16	101	46 14	160	32 39	209	30 23	257	35 46	312
74	30 47	004	31 53	045	63 14	101	46 34	161	32 11	209	29 26	257	35 02	311
	CAPELLA		POLLUX		◆ PROCYON		Suhail		CANOPUS		◆ ACHERNAR		◆ Hamal	
75	30 51	004	32 34	044	46 17	068	29 01	133	46 53	161	31 42	209	34 18	311
76	30 54	003	33 14	043	47 11	067	29 44	133	47 11	162	31 14	210	33 34	310
77	30 57	002	33 54	043	48 05	067	30 27	133	47 28	163	30 44	210	32 49	310
78	30 58	001	34 34	042	48 59	066	31 10	133	47 45	164	30 15	210	32 04	309
79	30 59	000	35 12	041	49 52	065	31 52	133	48 01	165	29 46	211	31 18	308
80	30 59	000	35 51	040	50 45	065	32 34	134	48 16	165	29 16	211	30 32	308
81	30 58	359	36 28	040	51 37	064	33 17	134	48 30	166	28 46	211	29 45	307
82	30 57	358	37 05	039	52 30	063	33 59	134	48 44	167	28 15	211	28 59	307
83	30 54	357	37 42	038	53 22	062	34 41	134	48 57	168	27 45	211	28 12	306
84	30 51	356	38 17	037	54 13	061	35 22	135	49 08	169	27 14	212	27 24	306
85	30 47	356	38 52	036	55 04	060	36 04	135	49 19	170	26 44	212	26 36	305
86	30 42	355	39 27	036	55 55	060	36 45	135	49 29	171	26 13	212	25 48	305
87	30 36	354	40 00	035	56 45	059	37 26	135	49 38	172	25 42	212	25 00	304
88	30 29	353	40 33	034	57 35	058	38 07	136	49 46	172	25 10	212	24 12	304
89	30 22	352	41 05	033	58 24	056	38 48	136	49 54	173	24 39	213	23 23	303

LHA ♈	Hc	Zn	Hc	Zn	Hc	Zn	Hc	Zn	Hc	Zn	Hc	Zn	Hc	Zn
	POLLUX		◆ REGULUS		Suhail		◆ CANOPUS		ACHERNAR		◆ ALDEBARAN		CAPELLA	
90	41 37	032	23 23	071	39 28	136	50 00	174	24 07	213	54 01	325	30 14	352
91	42 07	031	24 18	070	40 08	137	50 05	175	23 36	213	53 26	323	30 05	351
92	42 37	030	25 13	070	40 48	137	50 10	176	23 04	213	52 51	322	29 55	350
93	43 05	029	26 08	070	41 28	138	50 13	177	22 32	213	52 14	321	29 44	349
94	43 33	028	27 03	069	42 07	138	50 16	178	22 00	213	51 37	320	29 33	348
95	44 00	027	27 58	069	42 46	138	50 17	179	21 28	213	50 59	318	29 21	348
96	44 26	026	28 52	068	43 24	139	50 18	180	20 56	213	50 19	317	29 08	347
97	44 51	025	29 46	068	44 03	139	50 17	181	20 24	213	49 39	316	28 54	346
98	45 15	024	30 40	067	44 41	140	50 16	182	19 51	214	48 59	315	28 40	345
99	45 37	022	31 34	067	45 18	140	50 14	183	19 19	214	48 17	314	28 25	345
100	45 59	021	32 28	067	45 55	141	50 10	184	18 47	214	47 35	313	28 09	344
101	46 20	020	33 22	066	46 32	142	50 06	185	18 14	214	46 52	312	27 53	343
102	46 39	019	34 15	066	47 08	142	50 01	186	17 42	214	46 09	311	27 35	343
103	46 58	018	35 08	065	47 43	143	49 55	187	17 09	214	45 24	311	27 17	342
104	47 15	016	36 01	065	48 18	143	49 48	187	16 37	214	44 40	310	26 59	341
	POLLUX		◆ REGULUS		ACRUX		◆ CANOPUS		RIGEL		◆ ALDEBARAN		CAPELLA	
105	47 31	015	36 54	064	15 15	152	49 39	188	63 50	278	43 55	309	26 40	340
106	47 45	014	37 46	063	15 42	152	49 31	189	62 52	277	43 09	308	26 20	340
107	47 59	013	38 38	063	16 09	152	49 21	190	61 54	277	42 22	307	25 59	339
108	48 11	011	39 30	062	16 36	152	49 10	191	60 56	277	41 36	307	25 38	338
109	48 22	010	40 22	062	17 03	153	48 58	192	59 58	276	40 49	306	25 16	338
110	48 31	009	41 13	061	17 30	153	48 46	193	59 00	276	40 01	305	24 54	337
111	48 40	007	42 04	060	17 57	153	48 32	194	58 01	275	39 13	304	24 31	336
112	48 46	006	42 55	060	18 24	153	48 18	194	57 03	275	38 25	304	24 07	336
113	48 52	005	43 45	059	18 50	153	48 03	195	56 05	275	37 36	303	23 43	335
114	48 56	003	44 35	058	19 17	153	47 47	196	55 07	274	36 47	303	23 18	335
115	48 59	002	45 25	058	19 44	153	47 31	197	54 08	274	35 57	302	22 53	334
116	49 00	001	46 14	057	20 10	153	47 13	198	53 10	274	35 07	301	22 27	333
117	49 01	359	47 03	056	20 37	153	46 55	198	52 12	273	34 17	301	22 00	333
118	48 59	358	47 51	055	21 03	153	46 36	199	51 13	273	33 27	300	21 33	332
119	48 57	357	48 39	054	21 30	153	46 17	200	50 15	273	32 36	300	21 06	332
	◆ REGULUS		SPICA		◆ ACRUX		CANOPUS		◆ RIGEL		BETELGEUSE		POLLUX	
120	49 26	053	10 40	099	21 56	153	45 56	201	49 17	273	53 03	302	48 53	355
121	50 13	053	11 38	099	22 22	154	45 35	201	48 18	272	52 13	301	48 47	354
122	50 59	052	12 36	099	22 48	154	45 14	202	47 20	272	51 23	300	48 40	353
123	51 44	051	13 34	099	23 14	154	44 51	203	46 21	272	50 32	299	48 32	351
124	52 29	050	14 31	098	23 39	154	44 28	203	45 23	271	49 41	298	48 23	350
125	53 13	049	15 29	098	24 05	154	44 05	204	44 24	271	48 49	298	48 12	349
126	53 57	047	16 27	098	24 30	154	43 41	205	43 26	271	47 57	297	48 00	347
127	54 39	046	17 25	098	24 56	155	43 16	205	42 27	271	47 05	296	47 47	346
128	55 21	045	18 23	098	25 21	155	42 51	206	41 29	271	46 12	296	47 32	345
129	56 02	044	19 21	098	25 46	155	42 25	206	40 31	270	45 20	295	47 17	344
130	56 42	043	20 19	097	26 10	155	41 59	207	39 32	270	44 26	294	47 00	342
131	57 21	041	21 17	097	26 35	155	41 32	208	38 34	270	43 33	294	46 41	341
132	57 59	040	22 15	097	26 59	156	41 04	208	37 35	270	42 39	293	46 22	340
133	58 36	038	23 13	097	27 23	156	40 37	209	36 37	269	41 46	293	46 02	339
134	59 12	037	24 11	097	27 47	156	40 08	209	35 38	269	40 51	292	45 40	338
	REGULUS		◆ SPICA		ACRUX		◆ CANOPUS		SIRIUS		BETELGEUSE		◆ POLLUX	
135	59 46	035	25 09	096	28 11	156	39 40	210	57 24	259	39 57	291	45 17	337
136	60 19	034	26 07	096	28 34	157	39 11	210	56 27	259	39 03	291	44 54	335
137	60 51	032	27 05	096	28 57	157	38 41	211	55 29	259	38 08	290	44 29	334
138	61 21	030	28 03	096	29 20	157	38 11	211	54 32	259	37 13	290	44 03	333
139	61 50	028	29 01	096	29 43	157	37 41	211	53 34	259	36 18	289	43 36	332
140	62 17	027	30 00	096	30 05	158	37 10	212	52 37	259	35 23	289	43 09	331
141	62 42	025	30 58	095	30 27	158	36 39	212	51 39	259	34 28	289	42 40	330
142	63 06	023	31 56	095	30 49	158	36 08	213	50 42	259	33 32	288	42 10	329
143	63 27	021	32 54	095	31 11	159	35 36	213	49 44	259	32 36	288	41 40	328
144	63 47	019	33 53	095	31 32	159	35 04	213	48 47	259	31 41	287	41 09	327
145	64 05	017	34 51	095	31 53	159	34 32	214	47 49	259	30 45	287	40 37	326
146	64 20	014	35 49	095	32 13	160	33 59	214	46 52	259	29 49	287	40 04	325
147	64 34	012	36 47	094	32 34	160	33 26	214	45 55	259	28 53	286	39 31	325
148	64 45	010	37 46	094	32 53	160	32 53	215	44 57	259	27 57	286	38 56	324
149	64 54	008	38 44	094	33 13	161	32 20	215	44 00	259	27 00	285	38 21	323
	REGULUS		◆ ARCTURUS		SPICA		◆ ACRUX		CANOPUS		SIRIUS		◆ PROCYON	
150	65 00	005	19 12	064	39 42	094	33 32	161	31 46	215	43 02	259	50 47	295
151	65 04	003	20 04	064	40 41	094	33 51	161	31 13	215	42 05	259	49 54	295
152	65 06	001	20 56	063	41 39	094	34 09	162	30 39	216	41 07	259	49 01	294
153	65 06	358	21 49	063	42 37	093	34 27	162	30 04	216	40 10	259	48 07	293
154	65 03	356	22 41	063	43 36	093	34 45	163	29 30	216	39 13	259	47 14	293
155	64 58	354	23 32	062	44 34	093	35 02	163	28 55	216	38 15	259	46 19	292
156	64 50	351	24 24	062	45 32	093	35 19	164	28 21	217	37 18	259	45 25	291
157	64 40	349	25 15	061	46 31	093	35 35	164	27 46	217	36 21	259	44 31	291
158	64 28	347	26 07	061	47 29	093	35 51	164	27 11	217	35 23	259	43 36	290
159	64 14	345	26 57	060	48 28	092	36 07	165	26 36	217	34 26	258	42 41	290
160	63 58	343	27 48	060	49 26	092	36 22	165	26 00	217	33 29	258	41 46	289
161	63 39	341	28 39	059	50 24	092	36 36	166	25 25	217	32 32	258	40 51	289
162	63 19	338	29 29	059	51 23	092	36 51	166	24 49	218	31 34	258	39 55	288
163	62 56	336	30 19	058	52 21	092	37 04	167	24 13	218	30 37	258	39 00	288
164	62 32	335	31 08	058	53 20	091	37 17	167	23 38	218	29 40	258	38 04	287
	Denebola		◆ ARCTURUS		SPICA		◆ ACRUX		SIRIUS		◆ PROCYON		REGULUS	
165	59 52	025	31 58	057	54 18	091	37 30	168	28 43	258	37 08	287	62 06	333
166	60 16	023	32 47	057	55 17	091	37 42	168	27 46	258	36 12	286	61 38	331
167	60 38	021	33 36	056	56 15	091	37 54	169	26 49	258	35 16	286	61 09	329
168	60 58	019	34 24	056	57 14	091	38 05	169	25 51	257	34 20	286	60 38	327
169	61 16	017	35 12	055	58 12	090	38 15	170	24 54	257	33 23	285	60 06	326
170	61 32	015	36 00	054	59 10	090	38 25	170	23 57	257	32 27	285	59 32	324
171	61 47	013	36 47	054	60 09	090	38 35	171	23 00	257	31 30	284	58 57	323
172	61 59	011	37 34	053	61 07	090	38 44	171	22 03	257	30 34	284	58 21	321
173	62 10	009	38 20	052	62 06	090	38 52	172	21 06	257	29 37	284	57 44	320
174	62 18	007	39 06	052	63 04	089	39 00	173	20 10	257	28 40	283	57 05	318
175	62 24	005	39 52	051	64 03	089	39 07	173	19 13	257	27 43	283	56 26	317
176	62 28	003	40 37	050	65 01	089	39 14	174	18 16	256	26 46	283	55 45	316
177	62 30	001	41 22	049	66 00	088	39 20	174	17 19	256	25 49	282	55 04	314
178	62 30	359	42 06	049	66 58	088	39 26	175	16 22	256	24 52	282	54 22	313
179	62 28	357	42 50	048	67 57	088	39 31	175	15 26	256	23 55	282	53 39	312

LAT 13°S

LHA ♈	Hc	Zn	Hc	Zn	Hc	Zn	Hc	Zn	Hc	Zn	Hc	Zn	Hc	Zn
	ARCTURUS		◆ ANTARES		ACRUX		◆ Suhail		Alphard		REGULUS		◆ Denebola	
180	43 33	047	25 39	113	39 35	176	42 18	222	52 33	273	52 55	311	62 24	355
181	44 15	046	26 33	113	39 39	177	41 39	222	51 35	272	52 11	310	62 17	353
182	44 57	045	27 26	113	39 42	177	40 59	223	50 36	272	51 25	309	62 09	351
183	45 38	044	28 20	113	39 45	178	40 19	223	49 38	272	50 40	308	61 58	349
184	46 18	043	29 14	113	39 47	178	39 39	223	48 39	272	49 53	307	61 45	347
185	46 58	042	30 08	113	39 48	179	38 59	224	47 41	271	49 06	306	61 31	345
186	47 37	041	31 01	113	39 49	179	38 18	224	46 42	271	48 19	305	61 14	343
187	48 15	040	31 55	113	39 49	180	37 37	224	45 44	271	47 31	304	60 56	341
188	48 53	039	32 49	113	39 49	181	36 56	225	44 46	271	46 42	304	60 36	339
189	49 29	038	33 42	113	39 48	181	36 15	225	43 47	270	45 53	303	60 14	337
190	50 05	037	34 36	113	39 46	182	35 34	225	42 49	270	45 04	302	59 50	335
191	50 39	036	35 30	113	39 44	182	34 52	226	41 50	270	44 14	301	59 25	334
192	51 13	035	36 23	113	39 41	183	34 10	226	40 52	270	43 24	301	58 58	332
193	51 46	033	37 17	114	39 38	184	33 28	226	39 53	269	42 34	300	58 30	330
194	52 17	032	38 11	114	39 34	184	32 46	226	38 55	269	41 43	299	58 00	329
	ARCTURUS		◆ Rasalhague		ANTARES		◆ ACRUX		Suhail		◆ REGULUS		Denebola	
195	52 48	031	17 04	072	39 04	114	39 29	185	32 04	226	40 52	299	57 29	327
196	53 17	029	17 59	072	39 58	114	39 24	185	31 21	227	40 00	298	56 57	326
197	53 45	028	18 55	072	40 51	114	39 18	186	30 39	227	39 09	297	56 23	324
198	54 12	027	19 50	071	41 45	114	39 12	186	29 56	227	38 17	297	55 48	323
199	54 37	025	20 46	071	42 38	114	39 05	187	29 13	227	37 24	296	55 12	321
200	55 01	024	21 41	071	43 31	114	38 58	188	28 30	227	36 32	296	54 35	320
201	55 24	022	22 36	070	44 24	114	38 50	188	27 47	227	35 39	295	53 57	319
202	55 45	021	23 31	070	45 18	115	38 41	189	27 04	228	34 46	295	53 19	318
203	56 05	019	24 26	070	46 11	115	38 32	189	26 21	228	33 53	294	52 39	317
204	56 24	017	25 20	069	47 04	115	38 23	190	25 38	228	32 59	294	51 58	315
205	56 40	016	26 15	069	47 57	115	38 12	190	24 55	228	32 06	293	51 17	314
206	56 55	014	27 09	068	48 50	116	38 02	191	24 11	228	31 12	293	50 34	313
207	57 09	012	28 04	068	49 42	116	37 50	191	23 28	228	30 18	292	49 51	312
208	57 20	011	28 58	068	50 35	116	37 39	192	22 44	228	29 24	292	49 08	311
209	57 30	009	29 52	067	51 27	116	37 26	192	22 01	228	28 29	291	48 24	310
	ARCTURUS		◆ Rasalhague		ANTARES		◆ RIGIL KENT		ACRUX		Gienah		◆ REGULUS	
210	57 39	007	30 45	067	52 20	117	41 32	173	37 14	193	64 40	256	27 35	291
211	57 45	005	31 39	066	53 12	117	41 38	174	37 00	193	63 43	256	26 40	291
212	57 50	004	32 32	066	54 04	117	41 44	175	36 47	194	62 46	257	25 45	290
213	57 53	002	33 26	065	54 55	118	41 49	175	36 32	194	61 49	257	24 51	290
214	57 54	000	34 18	065	55 47	118	41 54	176	36 18	195	60 52	257	23 56	290
215	57 53	358	35 11	064	56 38	119	41 57	177	36 03	195	59 55	257	23 00	289
216	57 50	357	36 04	064	57 30	119	42 00	177	35 47	196	58 58	257	22 05	289
217	57 46	355	36 56	063	58 20	120	42 03	178	35 31	196	58 01	257	21 10	288
218	57 40	353	37 48	063	59 11	120	42 05	179	35 14	197	57 04	258	20 14	288
219	57 32	351	38 40	062	60 01	121	42 06	179	34 58	197	56 07	258	19 19	288
220	57 22	350	39 31	061	60 51	122	42 06	180	34 40	197	55 10	258	18 23	287
221	57 11	348	40 22	061	61 41	122	42 06	181	34 22	198	54 13	258	17 27	287
222	56 58	346	41 13	060	62 30	123	42 05	181	34 04	198	53 15	258	16 31	287
223	56 43	345	42 04	059	63 19	124	42 04	182	33 46	199	52 18	258	15 35	286
224	56 27	343	42 54	059	64 07	125	42 01	183	33 27	199	51 21	258	14 39	286
	Alphecca		◆ VEGA		ALTAIR		◆ Shaula		RIGIL KENT		◆ SPICA		ARCTURUS	
225	49 25	012	17 33	042	14 24	077	47 57	132	41 58	183	66 58	272	56 09	341
226	49 37	011	18 12	041	15 20	077	48 40	132	41 55	184	65 59	272	55 49	340
227	49 47	009	18 50	041	16 17	077	49 23	133	41 51	184	65 01	271	55 28	338
228	49 56	008	19 28	040	17 14	076	50 05	134	41 46	185	64 02	271	55 05	337
229	50 03	007	20 05	040	18 11	076	50 48	134	41 40	186	63 04	271	54 42	335
230	50 10	005	20 43	039	19 08	076	51 29	135	41 34	186	62 05	270	54 16	334
231	50 14	004	21 19	039	20 04	075	52 11	135	41 27	187	61 07	270	53 50	332
232	50 18	003	21 56	038	21 01	075	52 51	136	41 20	188	60 08	270	53 22	331
233	50 20	001	22 32	038	21 57	075	53 32	137	41 12	188	59 10	270	52 53	330
234	50 20	000	23 07	037	22 53	074	54 11	138	41 03	189	58 12	270	52 23	328
235	50 19	358	23 42	037	23 50	074	54 50	138	40 54	189	57 13	269	51 51	327
236	50 17	357	24 17	036	24 46	074	55 29	139	40 44	190	56 15	269	51 19	326
237	50 13	356	24 51	035	25 42	073	56 07	140	40 33	191	55 16	269	50 45	324
238	50 08	354	25 24	035	26 38	073	56 44	141	40 22	191	54 18	269	50 11	323
239	50 01	353	25 57	034	27 34	073	57 20	142	40 10	192	53 19	269	49 35	322
	VEGA		◆ ALTAIR		Shaula		◆ RIGIL KENT		SPICA		◆ ARCTURUS		Alphecca	
240	26 30	034	28 29	072	57 56	143	39 58	192	52 21	268	48 59	321	49 53	351
241	27 02	033	29 25	072	58 31	144	39 45	193	51 22	268	48 22	320	49 44	350
242	27 33	032	30 20	071	59 05	145	39 32	194	50 24	268	47 44	319	49 33	349
243	28 04	032	31 16	071	59 38	146	39 18	194	49 26	268	47 05	318	49 21	347
244	28 35	031	32 11	071	60 10	147	39 03	195	48 27	268	46 25	317	49 07	346
245	29 04	030	33 06	070	60 41	149	38 48	195	47 29	267	45 45	316	48 53	345
246	29 33	030	34 01	070	61 11	150	38 33	196	46 30	267	45 04	315	48 37	343
247	30 02	029	34 56	069	61 40	151	38 16	196	45 32	267	44 22	314	48 19	342
248	30 30	028	35 50	069	62 07	153	38 00	197	44 34	267	43 40	313	48 01	341
249	30 57	027	36 45	068	62 33	154	37 43	197	43 35	267	42 57	312	47 41	340
250	31 23	027	37 39	068	62 58	156	37 25	198	42 37	267	42 14	312	47 20	338
251	31 49	026	38 33	067	63 22	157	37 07	198	41 38	266	41 30	311	46 58	337
252	32 14	025	39 27	067	63 44	159	36 49	199	40 40	266	40 45	310	46 35	336
253	32 39	024	40 20	066	64 04	160	36 30	199	39 42	266	40 00	309	46 11	335
254	33 02	023	41 14	066	64 23	162	36 10	200	38 43	266	39 14	308	45 45	334
	◆ VEGA		ALTAIR		◆ Peacock		RIGIL KENT		◆ SPICA		ARCTURUS		Alphecca	
255	33 25	023	42 07	065	31 18	150	35 50	200	37 45	266	38 28	308	45 19	333
256	33 48	022	42 59	064	31 48	150	35 30	200	36 47	266	37 42	307	44 52	332
257	34 09	021	43 52	064	32 17	150	35 09	201	35 49	265	36 55	306	44 24	331
258	34 29	020	44 44	063	32 46	151	34 48	201	34 50	265	36 08	306	43 54	329
259	34 49	019	45 36	062	33 14	151	34 27	202	33 52	265	35 20	305	43 24	328
260	35 08	018	46 28	062	33 42	151	34 05	202	32 54	265	34 32	305	42 53	327
261	35 26	018	47 19	061	34 10	152	33 43	202	31 56	265	33 44	304	42 21	326
262	35 43	017	48 10	060	34 38	152	33 20	203	30 57	265	32 55	303	41 49	326
263	36 00	016	49 01	059	35 05	152	32 58	203	29 59	264	32 06	303	41 15	325
264	36 15	015	49 51	059	35 32	153	32 34	204	29 01	264	31 17	302	40 41	324
265	36 29	014	50 41	058	35 59	153	32 11	204	28 03	264	30 27	302	40 06	323
266	36 43	013	51 30	057	36 25	154	31 47	204	27 05	264	29 37	301	39 30	322
267	36 56	012	52 19	056	36 51	154	31 23	205	26 07	264	28 47	301	38 54	321
268	37 07	011	53 07	055	37 16	154	30 58	205	25 09	264	27 57	300	38 17	320
269	37 18	010	53 54	054	37 41	155	30 34	205	24 10	263	27 06	300	37 39	319

LAT 13°S

LHA ♈	Hc	Zn	Hc	Zn	Hc	Zn	Hc	Zn	Hc	Zn	Hc	Zn	Hc	Zn
	◆ VEGA		ALTAIR		◆ FOMALHAUT		Peacock		RIGIL KENT		◆ ANTARES		ARCTURUS	
270	37 28	009	54 42	053	19 37	117	38 06	155	30 09	205	65 02	234	26 15	299
271	37 37	008	55 28	052	20 29	117	38 30	156	29 43	206	64 15	235	25 24	299
272	37 45	007	56 14	051	21 21	117	38 54	156	29 18	206	63 27	236	24 33	298
273	37 52	006	56 59	050	22 13	117	39 17	157	28 52	206	62 38	237	23 41	298
274	37 58	005	57 43	048	23 06	117	39 40	157	28 26	207	61 49	237	22 50	297
275	38 02	004	58 26	047	23 58	117	40 02	158	28 00	207	60 59	238	21 58	297
276	38 06	003	59 09	046	24 50	117	40 24	158	27 34	207	60 10	239	21 05	297
277	38 09	002	59 50	044	25 42	117	40 45	159	27 07	207	59 19	240	20 13	296
278	38 11	001	60 30	043	26 34	117	41 06	160	26 40	207	58 29	240	19 21	296
279	38 12	000	61 10	042	27 26	117	41 26	160	26 13	208	57 38	241	18 28	296
280	38 12	359	61 48	040	28 19	117	41 46	161	25 46	208	56 47	241	17 35	295
281	38 11	358	62 25	038	29 11	117	42 05	161	25 18	208	55 56	242	16 42	295
282	38 09	357	63 00	037	30 03	117	42 23	162	24 51	208	55 04	242	15 49	294
283	38 05	356	63 34	035	30 55	117	42 41	163	24 23	208	54 12	242	14 56	294
284	38 01	355	64 07	033	31 47	117	42 58	163	23 55	209	53 20	243	14 02	294
	◆ DENEB		◆ FOMALHAUT		Peacock		RIGIL KENT		◆ ANTARES		Rasalhague		VEGA	
285	27 17	020	32 40	117	43 15	164	23 27	209	52 28	243	56 59	320	37 56	354
286	27 36	019	33 32	117	43 31	164	22 59	209	51 36	244	56 21	319	37 50	353
287	27 55	018	34 24	117	43 46	165	22 31	209	50 43	244	55 41	317	37 43	352
288	28 13	018	35 16	117	44 01	166	22 03	209	49 51	244	55 01	316	37 35	352
289	28 31	017	36 08	117	44 15	167	21 34	209	48 58	244	54 20	315	37 25	351
290	28 48	016	37 00	117	44 28	167	21 06	209	48 05	245	53 38	314	37 15	350
291	29 04	016	37 52	117	44 41	168	20 37	209	47 13	245	52 56	312	37 04	349
292	29 19	015	38 43	118	44 53	169	20 08	209	46 20	245	52 12	311	36 52	348
293	29 33	014	39 35	118	45 04	169	19 39	210	45 26	245	51 28	310	36 39	347
294	29 47	013	40 27	118	45 14	170	19 10	210	44 33	246	50 43	309	36 26	346
295	30 00	013	41 18	118	45 24	171	18 42	210	43 40	246	49 57	308	36 11	345
296	30 13	012	42 10	118	45 33	172	18 13	210	42 47	246	49 11	307	35 55	344
297	30 24	011	43 01	118	45 41	172	17 43	210	41 53	246	48 25	307	35 39	343
298	30 35	010	43 53	119	45 48	173	17 14	210	41 00	246	47 38	306	35 21	342
299	30 45	009	44 44	119	45 55	174	16 45	210	40 06	246	46 50	305	35 03	341
	◆ DENEB		Alpheratz		◆ FOMALHAUT		Peacock		◆ ANTARES		Rasalhague		VEGA	
300	30 54	009	16 37	054	45 35	119	46 01	175	39 13	246	46 02	304	34 44	340
301	31 02	008	17 24	053	46 26	119	46 06	175	38 19	246	45 13	303	34 24	340
302	31 10	007	18 11	053	47 17	120	46 10	176	37 26	246	44 24	303	34 03	339
303	31 16	006	18 57	053	48 08	120	46 13	177	36 32	247	43 34	302	33 41	338
304	31 22	005	19 44	052	48 58	120	46 16	178	35 39	247	42 45	301	33 19	337
305	31 27	005	20 30	052	49 49	121	46 18	179	34 45	247	41 54	300	32 56	336
306	31 31	004	21 15	051	50 39	121	46 19	179	33 51	247	41 04	300	32 32	336
307	31 35	003	22 01	051	51 29	121	46 19	180	32 58	247	40 13	299	32 08	335
308	31 37	002	22 46	050	52 18	122	46 18	181	32 04	247	39 22	299	31 42	334
309	31 39	001	23 31	050	53 08	122	46 17	182	31 10	247	38 30	298	31 16	333
310	31 40	000	24 15	049	53 57	123	46 14	183	30 16	247	37 38	297	30 50	332
311	31 40	000	24 59	049	54 46	123	46 11	183	29 23	247	36 46	297	30 22	332
312	31 39	359	25 43	048	55 35	124	46 08	184	28 29	247	35 54	296	29 54	331
313	31 37	358	26 26	048	56 23	125	46 03	185	27 35	247	35 02	296	29 25	330
314	31 35	357	27 09	047	57 11	125	45 57	186	26 42	247	34 09	295	28 56	330
	Alpheratz		◆ Diphda		ACHERNAR		Peacock		◆ ANTARES		VEGA		◆ DENEB	
315	27 52	047	35 54	103	21 56	147	45 51	187	25 48	247	28 26	329	31 31	356
316	28 34	046	36 51	103	22 28	147	45 44	187	24 54	247	27 56	328	31 27	355
317	29 16	045	37 48	103	23 00	147	45 36	188	24 01	247	27 25	328	31 22	355
318	29 57	045	38 46	103	23 31	147	45 28	189	23 07	247	26 53	327	31 16	354
319	30 38	044	39 43	103	24 03	147	45 18	190	22 13	246	26 21	326	31 10	353
320	31 19	043	40 40	103	24 35	147	45 08	190	21 20	246	25 48	326	31 02	352
321	31 59	043	41 37	103	25 06	148	44 57	191	20 26	246	25 15	325	30 54	351
322	32 38	042	42 34	102	25 37	148	44 46	192	19 33	246	24 41	324	30 45	351
323	33 17	041	43 31	102	26 08	148	44 34	192	18 39	246	24 07	324	30 35	350
324	33 55	041	44 28	102	26 39	148	44 21	193	17 46	246	23 32	323	30 24	349
325	34 33	040	45 25	102	27 10	148	44 07	194	16 52	246	22 57	323	30 12	348
326	35 11	039	46 22	102	27 41	148	43 52	195	15 59	246	22 22	322	30 00	347
327	35 47	038	47 19	102	28 11	149	43 37	195	15 06	246	21 46	322	29 47	347
328	36 23	038	48 16	102	28 42	149	43 22	196	14 13	246	21 09	321	29 33	346
329	36 59	037	49 13	102	29 12	149	43 05	197	13 19	245	20 32	321	29 19	345
	◆ Alpheratz		Diphda		◆ ACHERNAR		Peacock		◆ Nunki		ALTAIR		DENEB	
330	37 33	036	50 10	102	29 41	149	42 48	197	45 00	246	51 18	303	29 03	344
331	38 07	035	51 08	102	30 11	150	42 31	198	44 06	246	50 29	302	28 47	344
332	38 41	034	52 05	103	30 40	150	42 13	198	43 13	246	49 39	301	28 30	343
333	39 13	033	53 02	103	31 10	150	41 54	199	42 20	246	48 49	300	28 13	342
334	39 45	033	53 59	103	31 39	151	41 34	200	41 26	246	47 58	300	27 55	341
335	40 16	032	54 56	103	32 07	151	41 14	200	40 32	246	47 07	299	27 36	341
336	40 47	031	55 53	103	32 36	151	40 54	201	39 39	246	46 15	298	27 16	340
337	41 16	030	56 50	103	33 04	151	40 33	201	38 45	247	45 24	297	26 56	339
338	41 45	029	57 47	103	33 31	152	40 11	202	37 52	247	44 32	297	26 35	339
339	42 12	028	58 44	103	33 59	152	39 49	202	36 58	247	43 39	296	26 13	338
340	42 39	027	59 41	103	34 26	153	39 27	203	36 04	247	42 47	295	25 51	337
341	43 05	026	60 37	103	34 53	153	39 03	203	35 10	247	41 54	295	25 28	337
342	43 30	025	61 34	104	35 19	153	38 40	204	34 17	247	41 01	294	25 05	336
343	43 54	024	62 31	104	35 45	154	38 16	204	33 23	247	40 07	294	24 41	335
344	44 17	023	63 28	104	36 11	154	37 52	205	32 29	247	39 14	293	24 16	335
	Alpheratz		◆ Hamal		◆ ACHERNAR		Peacock		Nunki		◆ ALTAIR		DENEB	
345	44 38	021	31 17	052	36 36	155	37 27	205	31 35	247	38 20	293	23 51	334
346	44 59	020	32 03	051	37 01	155	37 01	206	30 41	247	37 26	292	23 25	334
347	45 19	019	32 48	050	37 26	155	36 36	206	29 48	247	36 31	292	22 59	333
348	45 38	018	33 33	050	37 50	156	36 10	207	28 54	247	35 37	291	22 32	332
349	45 55	017	34 18	049	38 14	156	35 43	207	28 00	247	34 42	291	22 05	332
350	46 11	016	35 02	049	38 37	157	35 16	207	27 06	247	33 48	290	21 37	331
351	46 26	014	35 45	048	39 00	157	34 49	208	26 13	247	32 53	290	21 09	331
352	46 40	013	36 28	047	39 22	158	34 22	208	25 19	247	31 58	289	20 40	330
353	46 53	012	37 11	046	39 44	158	33 54	209	24 25	247	31 02	289	20 11	330
354	47 04	011	37 53	046	40 05	159	33 26	209	23 31	247	30 07	289	19 41	329
355	47 15	009	38 35	045	40 26	159	32 58	209	22 38	247	29 11	288	19 10	329
356	47 23	008	39 16	044	40 46	160	32 29	210	21 44	247	28 16	288	18 40	328
357	47 31	007	39 56	043	41 06	161	32 00	210	20 50	247	27 20	287	18 09	328
358	47 37	006	40 36	042	41 25	161	31 31	210	19 57	246	26 24	287	17 37	327
359	47 42	004	41 15	042	41 44	162	31 01	210	19 03	246	25 28	287	17 05	327

LAT 14°S

LHA ♈	Hc	Zn	Hc	Zn	Hc	Zn	Hc	Zn	Hc	Zn	Hc	Zn	Hc	Zn
	◆ Alpheratz		Hamal		ALDEBARAN		◆ RIGEL		ACHERNAR		◆ FOMALHAUT		Enif	
0	46 46	003	41 08	040	15 10	068	12 45	095	42 59	162	68 56	220	48 49	304
1	46 49	002	41 45	039	16 04	068	13 43	095	43 17	163	68 18	222	48 01	303
2	46 50	000	42 22	038	16 57	067	14 41	095	43 34	163	67 39	223	47 12	302
3	46 49	359	42 57	037	17 51	067	15 39	095	43 50	164	66 59	225	46 22	301
4	46 48	358	43 32	036	18 45	067	16 37	095	44 06	165	66 17	226	45 32	301
5	46 45	357	44 06	035	19 38	066	17 35	094	44 21	165	65 35	227	44 42	300
6	46 41	355	44 40	034	20 31	066	18 33	094	44 35	166	64 52	228	43 51	299
7	46 35	354	45 12	033	21 24	066	19 31	094	44 49	167	64 08	229	43 00	298
8	46 29	353	45 44	032	22 17	065	20 29	094	45 02	167	63 24	230	42 09	298
9	46 21	352	46 14	031	23 10	065	21 28	093	45 15	168	62 39	231	41 17	297
10	46 11	350	46 44	030	24 03	064	22 26	093	45 26	169	61 53	232	40 25	296
11	46 01	349	47 13	029	24 55	064	23 24	093	45 37	170	61 06	233	39 33	296
12	45 49	348	47 40	028	25 47	063	24 22	093	45 48	170	60 20	234	38 40	295
13	45 36	347	48 07	027	26 39	063	25 20	093	45 57	171	59 32	235	37 48	295
14	45 22	345	48 33	025	27 31	063	26 18	092	46 06	172	58 45	235	36 55	294
	Hamal		◆ ALDEBARAN		RIGEL		◆ ACHERNAR		FOMALHAUT		◆ Enif		Alpheratz	
15	48 57	024	28 23	062	27 16	092	46 14	173	57 57	236	36 01	294	45 07	344
16	49 20	023	29 14	062	28 15	092	46 21	173	57 08	237	35 08	293	44 51	343
17	49 42	022	30 05	061	29 13	092	46 27	174	56 19	237	34 14	293	44 33	342
18	50 03	020	30 56	061	30 11	091	46 33	175	55 30	238	33 21	292	44 14	341
19	50 22	019	31 47	060	31 09	091	46 38	176	54 41	238	32 27	292	43 55	340
20	50 40	018	32 37	059	32 07	091	46 42	176	53 51	239	31 32	291	43 34	338
21	50 57	016	33 27	059	33 06	091	46 45	177	53 02	239	30 38	291	43 12	337
22	51 13	015	34 17	058	34 04	090	46 48	178	52 11	239	29 44	290	42 49	336
23	51 27	013	35 06	058	35 02	090	46 49	179	51 21	240	28 49	290	42 25	335
24	51 40	012	35 55	057	36 00	090	46 50	180	50 31	240	27 54	289	42 00	334
25	51 51	010	36 44	056	36 59	090	46 50	180	49 40	241	26 59	289	41 35	333
26	52 01	009	37 32	056	37 57	090	46 50	181	48 49	241	26 04	289	41 08	332
27	52 09	007	38 20	055	38 55	089	46 48	182	47 58	241	25 09	288	40 40	331
28	52 16	006	39 08	054	39 53	089	46 46	183	47 07	241	24 13	288	40 12	330
29	52 21	005	39 55	054	40 51	089	46 42	184	46 16	242	23 18	288	39 43	329
	CAPELLA		◆ BETELGEUSE		SIRIUS		CANOPUS		◆ ACHERNAR		FOMALHAUT		◆ Alpheratz	
30	15 19	033	27 40	074	21 25	103	25 32	142	46 38	184	45 25	242	39 12	328
31	15 50	033	28 36	073	22 22	103	26 07	142	46 34	185	44 33	242	38 42	327
32	16 21	032	29 32	073	23 19	102	26 43	142	46 28	186	43 42	242	38 10	327
33	16 52	032	30 28	072	24 16	102	27 18	143	46 22	187	42 50	242	37 37	326
34	17 23	031	31 23	072	25 13	102	27 54	143	46 15	187	41 59	243	37 04	325
35	17 53	031	32 18	072	26 10	102	28 29	143	46 07	188	41 07	243	36 31	324
36	18 22	030	33 13	071	27 07	102	29 04	143	45 58	189	40 15	243	35 56	323
37	18 51	030	34 09	071	28 04	102	29 39	143	45 49	190	39 23	243	35 21	322
38	19 20	029	35 03	070	29 01	102	30 13	143	45 39	190	38 31	243	34 45	322
39	19 48	029	35 58	070	29 58	101	30 48	144	45 28	191	37 39	243	34 09	321
40	20 16	028	36 53	069	30 55	101	31 22	144	45 16	192	36 47	243	33 32	320
41	20 43	027	37 47	069	31 52	101	31 57	144	45 04	193	35 55	243	32 54	319
42	21 09	027	38 41	068	32 49	101	32 31	144	44 51	193	35 03	244	32 16	319
43	21 36	026	39 35	068	33 46	101	33 04	145	44 37	194	34 11	244	31 37	318
44	22 01	026	40 29	067	34 43	101	33 38	145	44 23	195	33 19	244	30 58	317
	◆ CAPELLA		BETELGEUSE		SIRIUS		◆ CANOPUS		ACHERNAR		◆ FOMALHAUT		Alpheratz	
45	22 26	025	41 23	067	35 40	101	34 11	145	44 08	195	32 27	244	30 18	317
46	22 51	025	42 16	066	36 38	101	34 44	146	43 52	196	31 35	244	29 38	316
47	23 14	024	43 09	065	37 35	101	35 17	146	43 36	197	30 42	244	28 58	315
48	23 38	023	44 02	065	38 32	100	35 49	146	43 19	197	29 50	244	28 16	315
49	24 01	023	44 54	064	39 29	100	36 22	147	43 01	198	28 58	244	27 35	314
50	24 23	022	45 47	063	40 27	100	36 54	147	42 43	198	28 06	244	26 53	314
51	24 44	021	46 38	063	41 24	100	37 25	147	42 25	199	27 14	244	26 11	313
52	25 05	021	47 30	062	42 21	100	37 57	148	42 05	200	26 21	244	25 28	312
53	25 25	020	48 21	061	43 19	100	38 27	148	41 45	200	25 29	244	24 45	312
54	25 45	019	49 12	061	44 16	100	38 58	149	41 25	201	24 37	244	24 01	311
55	26 04	019	50 03	060	45 13	100	39 28	149	41 04	201	23 45	244	23 17	311
56	26 22	018	50 53	059	46 11	100	39 58	149	40 43	202	22 53	243	22 33	310
57	26 40	017	51 42	058	47 08	100	40 28	150	40 21	202	22 01	243	21 49	310
58	26 57	017	52 31	057	48 05	100	40 57	150	39 58	203	21 09	243	21 04	309
59	27 13	016	53 20	056	49 03	100	41 25	151	39 35	203	20 17	243	20 19	309
	CAPELLA		POLLUX		◆ SIRIUS		CANOPUS		◆ ACHERNAR		Diphda		◆ Hamal	
60	27 29	015	21 01	052	50 00	099	41 53	151	39 12	204	42 56	258	43 33	324
61	27 43	014	21 47	052	50 58	099	42 21	152	38 48	204	41 59	258	42 58	323
62	27 57	014	22 32	051	51 55	099	42 48	152	38 24	205	41 02	258	42 22	322
63	28 11	013	23 18	051	52 53	099	43 15	153	37 59	205	40 05	258	41 45	321
64	28 23	012	24 02	050	53 50	099	43 41	154	37 34	206	39 08	258	41 08	320
65	28 35	011	24 47	050	54 48	099	44 07	154	37 08	206	38 11	258	40 30	319
66	28 46	011	25 31	049	55 45	099	44 32	155	36 43	207	37 14	258	39 52	318
67	28 57	010	26 15	049	56 42	099	44 56	155	36 16	207	36 17	258	39 13	317
68	29 06	009	26 58	048	57 40	099	45 20	156	35 50	207	35 20	258	38 33	316
69	29 15	008	27 41	047	58 37	099	45 43	157	35 23	208	34 23	258	37 52	316
70	29 23	008	28 24	047	59 35	099	46 06	157	34 56	208	33 27	258	37 11	315
71	29 30	007	29 06	046	60 32	099	46 28	158	34 28	208	32 30	257	36 30	314
72	29 37	006	29 48	046	61 30	099	46 49	159	34 00	209	31 33	257	35 48	313
73	29 42	005	30 29	045	62 27	099	47 10	160	33 32	209	30 36	257	35 05	313
74	29 47	004	31 10	044	63 25	099	47 30	160	33 03	209	29 39	257	34 22	312
	CAPELLA		POLLUX		◆ PROCYON		Suhail		CANOPUS		◆ ACHERNAR		◆ Hamal	
75	29 51	004	31 51	044	45 54	067	29 42	132	47 49	161	32 35	210	33 39	311
76	29 54	003	32 31	043	46 48	066	30 25	133	48 08	162	32 06	210	32 55	311
77	29 57	002	33 10	042	47 41	066	31 08	133	48 26	163	31 36	210	32 11	310
78	29 58	001	33 49	041	48 34	065	31 51	133	48 43	163	31 07	211	31 26	309
79	29 59	000	34 27	041	49 26	064	32 33	133	48 59	164	30 37	211	30 41	309
80	29 59	000	35 05	040	50 19	063	33 16	133	49 14	165	30 07	211	29 55	308
81	29 58	359	35 42	039	51 10	063	33 58	133	49 29	166	29 37	211	29 09	308
82	29 57	358	36 18	038	52 02	062	34 40	134	49 42	167	29 07	212	28 23	307
83	29 54	357	36 54	038	52 53	061	35 22	134	49 55	168	28 36	212	27 36	306
84	29 51	356	37 29	037	53 44	060	36 04	134	50 07	169	28 05	212	26 49	306
85	29 47	356	38 04	036	54 34	059	36 46	134	50 18	170	27 34	212	26 02	305
86	29 42	355	38 38	035	55 24	058	37 27	135	50 28	170	27 03	212	25 14	305
87	29 36	354	39 11	034	56 13	057	38 09	135	50 38	171	26 32	213	24 26	304
88	29 30	353	39 43	033	57 02	056	38 50	135	50 46	172	26 01	213	23 38	304
89	29 22	352	40 15	032	57 50	055	39 31	136	50 53	173	25 29	213	22 50	303

LHA ♈	Hc	Zn	Hc	Zn	Hc	Zn	Hc	Zn	Hc	Zn	Hc	Zn	Hc	Zn
	POLLUX		◆ REGULUS		Suhail		◆ CANOPUS		ACHERNAR		◆ ALDEBARAN		CAPELLA	
90	40 45	031	23 03	070	40 11	136	51 00	174	24 58	213	53 11	325	29 14	352
91	41 15	030	23 58	070	40 52	136	51 05	175	24 26	213	52 38	324	29 05	351
92	41 44	029	24 53	070	41 32	137	51 10	176	23 54	213	52 03	323	28 56	350
93	42 13	028	25 47	069	42 12	137	51 13	177	23 22	213	51 28	322	28 45	349
94	42 40	027	26 41	069	42 51	137	51 16	178	22 50	213	50 51	320	28 34	349
95	43 06	026	27 36	068	43 31	138	51 17	179	22 18	214	50 13	319	28 22	348
96	43 32	025	28 30	068	44 09	138	51 18	180	21 46	214	49 35	318	28 09	347
97	43 56	024	29 23	067	44 48	139	51 17	181	21 14	214	48 56	317	27 56	346
98	44 19	023	30 17	067	45 26	139	51 16	182	20 41	214	48 16	316	27 42	346
99	44 42	022	31 11	066	46 04	140	51 14	183	20 09	214	47 35	315	27 27	345
100	45 03	021	32 04	066	46 41	140	51 10	184	19 37	214	46 54	314	27 11	344
101	45 23	020	32 57	065	47 18	141	51 06	185	19 04	214	46 11	313	26 55	343
102	45 42	019	33 50	065	47 55	141	51 01	186	18 32	214	45 29	312	26 38	343
103	46 00	017	34 42	064	48 31	142	50 54	187	17 59	214	44 45	311	26 20	342
104	46 17	016	35 35	064	49 06	143	50 47	188	17 27	214	44 01	310	26 02	341
	POLLUX		◆ REGULUS		ACRUX		◆ CANOPUS		RIGEL		◆ ALDEBARAN		CAPELLA	
105	46 33	015	36 27	063	16 08	152	50 39	189	63 40	280	43 17	310	25 43	341
106	46 47	014	37 19	063	16 35	152	50 30	189	62 43	279	42 31	309	25 23	340
107	47 00	012	38 11	062	17 02	152	50 20	190	61 46	279	41 46	308	25 03	339
108	47 12	011	39 02	062	17 29	152	50 09	191	60 48	278	41 00	307	24 42	339
109	47 23	010	39 53	061	17 56	152	49 57	192	59 50	278	40 13	307	24 20	338
110	47 32	009	40 44	060	18 23	152	49 44	193	58 53	277	39 26	306	23 58	337
111	47 40	007	41 34	060	18 50	152	49 31	194	57 55	277	38 39	305	23 35	337
112	47 47	006	42 24	059	19 17	153	49 16	195	56 57	277	37 51	304	23 12	336
113	47 52	005	43 14	058	19 44	153	49 01	196	55 59	276	37 03	304	22 48	335
114	47 56	003	44 03	058	20 11	153	48 45	196	55 01	276	36 14	303	22 24	335
115	47 59	002	44 52	057	20 37	153	48 28	197	54 03	275	35 25	303	21 59	334
116	48 00	001	45 41	056	21 04	153	48 10	198	53 05	275	34 36	302	21 33	334
117	48 01	359	46 29	055	21 30	153	47 52	199	52 07	275	33 46	301	21 07	333
118	47 59	358	47 16	054	21 57	153	47 33	200	51 09	274	32 56	301	20 40	332
119	47 57	357	48 03	053	22 23	153	47 13	200	50 11	274	32 06	300	20 13	332
	◆ REGULUS		SPICA		◆ ACRUX		CANOPUS		◆ RIGEL		BETELGEUSE		POLLUX	
120	48 50	053	10 50	099	22 50	153	46 52	201	49 13	274	52 31	303	47 53	355
121	49 36	052	11 47	099	23 16	153	46 31	202	48 15	273	51 42	302	47 47	354
122	50 21	051	12 45	099	23 42	154	46 09	202	47 17	273	50 52	301	47 41	353
123	51 06	050	13 42	098	24 08	154	45 47	203	46 19	273	50 02	300	47 33	352
124	51 50	049	14 40	098	24 33	154	45 23	204	45 21	272	49 12	299	47 24	350
125	52 33	048	15 38	098	24 59	154	45 00	204	44 23	272	48 21	299	47 13	349
126	53 16	046	16 35	098	25 24	154	44 35	205	43 24	272	47 30	298	47 02	348
127	53 58	045	17 33	098	25 50	154	44 10	206	42 26	272	46 38	297	46 49	346
128	54 38	044	18 31	097	26 15	154	43 45	206	41 28	271	45 46	297	46 34	345
129	55 18	043	19 28	097	26 40	155	43 19	207	40 30	271	44 54	296	46 19	344
130	55 58	042	20 26	097	27 05	155	42 52	207	39 32	271	44 01	295	46 02	343
131	56 36	040	21 24	097	27 29	155	42 25	208	38 33	271	43 09	295	45 45	342
132	57 13	039	22 22	097	27 54	155	41 57	209	37 35	270	42 15	294	45 26	340
133	57 49	037	23 20	096	28 18	156	41 29	209	36 37	270	41 22	293	45 06	339
134	58 23	036	24 18	096	28 42	156	41 01	210	35 39	270	40 29	293	44 44	338
	REGULUS		◆ SPICA		ACRUX		◆ CANOPUS		SIRIUS		BETELGEUSE		◆ POLLUX	
135	58 57	034	25 15	096	29 06	156	40 32	210	57 34	261	39 35	292	44 22	337
136	59 29	033	26 13	096	29 29	156	40 02	211	56 37	261	38 41	292	43 59	336
137	60 00	031	27 11	096	29 52	157	39 33	211	55 39	261	37 47	291	43 35	335
138	60 29	029	28 09	095	30 15	157	39 02	211	54 42	261	36 52	291	43 09	334
139	60 57	028	29 07	095	30 38	157	38 32	212	53 45	261	35 58	290	42 43	333
140	61 23	026	30 05	095	31 01	157	38 01	212	52 47	261	35 03	290	42 16	332
141	61 47	024	31 03	095	31 23	158	37 30	213	51 50	261	34 08	289	41 48	331
142	62 10	022	32 01	095	31 45	158	36 58	213	50 52	261	33 13	289	41 19	330
143	62 31	020	32 59	094	32 07	158	36 26	213	49 55	261	32 18	288	40 49	329
144	62 50	018	33 57	094	32 28	159	35 54	214	48 57	260	31 23	288	40 18	328
145	63 07	016	34 55	094	32 49	159	35 22	214	48 00	260	30 27	288	39 47	327
146	63 22	014	35 53	094	33 10	159	34 49	214	47 03	260	29 31	287	39 15	326
147	63 35	012	36 52	094	33 30	160	34 16	215	46 05	260	28 36	287	38 42	325
148	63 46	010	37 50	093	33 50	160	33 43	215	45 08	260	27 40	286	38 08	324
149	63 54	007	38 48	093	34 10	160	33 09	215	44 10	260	26 44	286	37 33	323
	REGULUS		◆ ARCTURUS		SPICA		◆ ACRUX		CANOPUS		SIRIUS		◆ PROCYON	
150	64 00	005	18 45	064	39 46	093	34 29	161	32 35	216	43 13	260	50 21	297
151	64 04	003	19 37	063	40 44	093	34 48	161	32 01	216	42 16	260	49 28	296
152	64 06	001	20 29	063	41 42	093	35 06	162	31 27	216	41 18	260	48 36	295
153	64 06	358	21 21	063	42 40	092	35 25	162	30 53	216	40 21	260	47 43	294
154	64 03	356	22 13	062	43 39	092	35 42	162	30 18	216	39 24	260	46 50	294
155	63 58	354	23 04	062	44 37	092	36 00	163	29 44	217	38 27	260	45 56	293
156	63 51	352	23 55	061	45 35	092	36 17	163	29 09	217	37 29	259	45 03	292
157	63 41	350	24 46	061	46 33	092	36 33	164	28 34	217	36 32	259	44 09	292
158	63 30	347	25 37	060	47 31	091	36 49	164	27 59	217	35 35	259	43 15	291
159	63 16	345	26 28	060	48 29	091	37 05	165	27 23	217	34 38	259	42 20	291
160	63 00	343	27 18	059	49 28	091	37 20	165	26 48	218	33 41	259	41 26	290
161	62 42	341	28 08	059	50 26	091	37 35	166	26 12	218	32 43	259	40 31	290
162	62 23	339	28 58	058	51 24	091	37 49	166	25 37	218	31 46	259	39 36	289
163	62 01	337	29 47	058	52 22	090	38 03	167	25 01	218	30 49	259	38 41	289
164	61 37	335	30 36	057	53 21	090	38 16	167	24 25	218	29 52	259	37 46	288
	Denebola		◆ ARCTURUS		SPICA		◆ ACRUX		SIRIUS		◆ PROCYON		REGULUS	
165	58 58	024	31 25	057	54 19	090	38 29	168	28 55	258	36 50	288	61 12	333
166	59 20	022	32 14	056	55 17	090	38 41	168	27 58	258	35 55	287	60 45	332
167	59 41	020	33 02	056	56 15	089	38 52	169	27 01	258	34 59	287	60 17	330
168	60 01	019	33 50	055	57 13	089	39 04	169	26 04	258	34 03	286	59 47	328
169	60 18	017	34 37	054	58 12	089	39 14	170	25 07	258	33 07	286	59 16	327
170	60 34	015	35 24	054	59 10	089	39 24	170	24 10	258	32 11	285	58 43	325
171	60 48	013	36 11	053	60 08	088	39 34	171	23 14	258	31 15	285	58 09	324
172	61 00	011	36 58	052	61 06	088	39 43	171	22 17	257	30 19	285	57 34	322
173	61 10	009	37 43	052	62 04	088	39 52	172	21 20	257	29 22	284	56 57	321
174	61 18	007	38 29	051	63 03	087	39 59	172	20 23	257	28 26	284	56 20	319
175	61 25	005	39 14	050	64 01	087	40 07	173	19 26	257	27 29	284	55 41	318
176	61 29	003	39 59	050	64 59	087	40 14	174	18 30	257	26 33	283	55 02	317
177	61 30	001	40 43	049	65 57	086	40 20	174	17 33	257	25 36	283	54 22	315
178	61 30	359	41 26	048	66 55	086	40 25	175	16 37	256	24 39	283	53 40	314
179	61 28	357	42 09	047	67 53	085	40 30	175	15 40	256	23 42	282	52 58	313

LAT 14°S

LHA ♈	Hc	Zn	Hc	Zn	Hc	Zn	Hc	Zn	Hc	Zn	Hc	Zn	Hc	Zn
	ARCTURUS		◆ANTARES		ACRUX		◆Suhail		Alphard		REGULUS		◆Denebola	
180	42 51	046	26 03	113	40 35	176	43 02	222	52 30	274	52 15	312	61 24	355
181	43 33	045	26 56	113	40 39	177	42 23	223	51 32	274	51 32	311	61 18	353
182	44 14	044	27 50	113	40 42	177	41 43	223	50 33	273	50 47	310	61 10	351
183	44 55	044	28 44	113	40 45	178	41 03	224	49 35	273	50 02	309	60 59	349
184	45 34	043	29 37	113	40 47	178	40 23	224	48 37	273	49 17	308	60 47	347
185	46 13	042	30 31	113	40 48	179	39 42	224	47 39	272	48 31	307	60 33	345
186	46 52	041	31 25	113	40 49	179	39 01	225	46 41	272	47 44	306	60 17	343
187	47 29	040	32 18	113	40 49	180	38 20	225	45 43	272	46 57	305	59 59	341
188	48 06	038	33 12	113	40 49	181	37 39	225	44 44	272	46 09	304	59 40	339
189	48 42	037	34 06	113	40 48	181	36 57	226	43 46	271	45 21	304	59 18	338
190	49 16	036	35 00	113	40 46	182	36 16	226	42 48	271	44 32	303	58 55	336
191	49 50	035	35 53	113	40 44	182	35 34	226	41 50	271	43 43	302	58 31	334
192	50 23	034	36 47	113	40 41	183	34 52	226	40 52	271	42 53	301	58 05	333
193	50 55	033	37 41	113	40 38	184	34 10	227	39 53	270	42 03	301	57 37	331
194	51 26	031	38 34	113	40 34	184	33 27	227	38 55	270	41 13	300	57 09	329
	ARCTURUS		◆Rasalhague		ANTARES		◆ACRUX		Suhail		REGULUS		◆Denebola	
195	51 56	030	16 45	072	39 28	113	40 29	185	32 45	227	40 23	299	56 38	328
196	52 24	029	17 41	072	40 21	113	40 24	185	32 02	227	39 32	299	56 07	326
197	52 52	027	18 36	071	41 15	113	40 18	186	31 20	227	38 41	298	55 34	325
198	53 18	026	19 31	071	42 09	113	40 12	187	30 37	227	37 49	298	55 00	324
199	53 43	025	20 26	071	43 02	113	40 05	187	29 54	228	36 57	297	54 25	322
200	54 06	023	21 21	070	43 56	113	39 57	188	29 11	228	36 05	296	53 49	321
201	54 28	022	22 15	070	44 49	114	39 49	188	28 28	228	35 13	296	53 12	320
202	54 49	020	23 10	069	45 42	114	39 41	189	27 45	228	34 21	295	52 34	319
203	55 08	019	24 05	069	46 36	114	39 31	189	27 01	228	33 28	295	51 55	317
204	55 26	017	24 59	069	47 29	114	39 22	190	26 18	228	32 35	294	51 15	316
205	55 42	015	25 53	068	48 22	114	39 11	190	25 35	228	31 42	294	50 34	315
206	55 57	014	26 47	068	49 15	114	39 01	191	24 51	228	30 48	293	49 53	314
207	56 10	012	27 41	067	50 08	115	38 49	191	24 08	228	29 55	293	49 11	313
208	56 21	010	28 35	067	51 01	115	38 37	192	23 24	228	29 01	292	48 28	312
209	56 31	009	29 28	067	51 53	115	38 25	193	22 41	228	28 07	292	47 44	311
	ARCTURUS		◆Rasalhague		ANTARES		◆RIGIL KENT		ACRUX		Gienah		◆REGULUS	
210	56 39	007	30 21	066	52 46	116	42 32	173	38 12	193	64 53	258	27 13	292
211	56 45	005	31 14	066	53 38	116	42 38	174	37 59	194	63 56	258	26 19	291
212	56 50	004	32 07	065	54 31	116	42 44	175	37 45	194	62 59	259	25 24	291
213	56 53	002	33 00	065	55 23	117	42 49	175	37 31	195	62 02	259	24 30	290
214	56 54	000	33 53	064	56 15	117	42 53	176	37 16	195	61 05	259	23 35	290
215	56 53	358	34 45	064	57 07	117	42 57	177	37 00	195	60 08	259	22 40	290
216	56 50	357	35 37	063	57 58	118	43 00	177	36 45	196	59 10	259	21 46	289
217	56 46	355	36 29	062	58 50	118	43 03	178	36 29	196	58 13	259	20 51	289
218	56 40	353	37 20	062	59 41	119	43 05	179	36 12	197	57 16	259	19 55	288
219	56 33	352	38 11	061	60 32	119	43 06	179	35 55	197	56 19	259	19 00	288
220	56 23	350	39 02	061	61 22	120	43 06	180	35 37	198	55 22	259	18 05	288
221	56 12	348	39 53	060	62 12	121	43 06	181	35 20	198	54 25	259	17 09	287
222	55 59	347	40 43	059	63 02	122	43 05	181	35 01	198	53 27	259	16 14	287
223	55 45	345	41 33	059	63 51	122	43 04	182	34 43	199	52 30	259	15 18	287
224	55 29	343	42 22	058	64 40	123	43 01	183	34 24	199	51 33	259	14 22	286
	Alphecca		◆VEGA		ALTAIR		◆Shaula		RIGIL KENT		◆SPICA		ARCTURUS	
225	48 26	012	16 48	041	14 10	077	48 36	131	42 58	183	66 55	274	55 12	342
226	48 38	011	17 26	041	15 07	077	49 20	132	42 55	184	65 56	274	54 53	340
227	48 48	009	18 04	040	16 03	076	50 04	132	42 50	185	64 58	273	54 32	339
228	48 57	008	18 42	040	17 00	076	50 46	133	42 46	185	64 00	273	54 10	337
229	49 04	007	19 19	039	17 56	076	51 29	133	42 40	186	63 02	273	53 47	336
230	49 10	005	19 56	039	18 53	075	52 11	134	42 34	186	62 04	272	53 22	334
231	49 15	004	20 32	038	19 49	075	52 53	135	42 27	187	61 06	272	52 56	333
232	49 18	003	21 08	038	20 45	075	53 34	135	42 19	188	60 08	272	52 29	331
233	49 20	001	21 44	037	21 41	074	54 15	136	42 11	188	59 09	271	52 01	330
234	49 20	000	22 19	037	22 37	074	54 55	137	42 02	189	58 11	271	51 31	329
235	49 19	358	22 54	036	23 33	074	55 35	137	41 53	190	57 13	271	51 01	328
236	49 17	357	23 28	036	24 29	073	56 14	138	41 43	190	56 15	271	50 29	326
237	49 13	356	24 02	035	25 24	073	56 53	139	41 32	191	55 17	270	49 56	325
238	49 08	354	24 35	034	26 20	072	57 30	140	41 21	191	54 18	270	49 22	324
239	49 02	353	25 08	034	27 15	072	58 07	141	41 09	192	53 20	270	48 48	323
	VEGA		◆ALTAIR		Shaula		◆RIGIL KENT		SPICA		◆ARCTURUS		Alphecca	
240	25 40	033	28 11	072	58 44	142	40 57	193	52 22	270	48 12	322	48 54	352
241	26 11	033	29 06	071	59 19	143	40 44	193	51 24	269	47 36	321	48 45	350
242	26 43	032	30 01	071	59 54	144	40 30	194	50 25	269	46 58	320	48 34	349
243	27 13	031	30 56	070	60 27	145	40 16	194	49 27	269	46 20	319	48 22	348
244	27 43	031	31 51	070	61 00	146	40 01	195	48 29	269	45 41	318	48 09	346
245	28 12	030	32 45	070	61 32	148	39 46	195	47 31	269	45 02	317	47 55	345
246	28 41	029	33 40	069	62 02	149	39 30	196	46 33	268	44 21	316	47 39	344
247	29 09	029	34 34	069	62 32	150	39 14	196	45 34	268	43 40	315	47 22	343
248	29 37	028	35 28	068	63 00	152	38 57	197	44 36	268	42 59	314	47 04	341
249	30 04	027	36 22	068	63 27	153	38 40	197	43 38	268	42 16	313	46 45	340
250	30 30	026	37 16	067	63 53	155	38 22	198	42 40	268	41 33	312	46 24	339
251	30 55	026	38 09	066	64 17	156	38 04	198	41 42	267	40 50	311	46 03	338
252	31 20	025	39 03	066	64 39	158	37 45	199	40 44	267	40 06	311	45 40	336
253	31 44	024	39 56	065	65 01	160	37 26	199	39 45	267	39 22	310	45 16	335
254	32 07	023	40 48	065	65 20	161	37 07	200	38 47	267	38 37	309	44 52	334
	◆VEGA		ALTAIR		◆Peacock		RIGIL KENT		◆SPICA		ARCTURUS		Alphecca	
255	32 30	022	41 41	064	32 10	149	36 47	200	37 49	267	37 51	308	44 26	333
256	32 52	022	42 33	064	32 40	150	36 26	201	36 51	266	37 06	308	43 59	332
257	33 13	021	43 25	063	33 09	150	36 05	201	35 53	266	36 19	307	43 31	331
258	33 33	020	44 17	062	33 38	150	35 44	202	34 55	266	35 33	306	43 02	330
259	33 52	019	45 08	062	34 07	151	35 23	202	33 57	266	34 45	306	42 33	329
260	34 11	018	45 59	061	34 35	151	35 01	202	32 59	266	33 58	305	42 02	328
261	34 29	017	46 50	060	35 03	151	34 38	203	32 01	265	33 10	304	41 31	327
262	34 46	016	47 40	059	35 31	152	34 16	203	31 03	265	32 22	304	40 59	326
263	35 02	016	48 30	058	35 58	152	33 53	203	30 05	265	31 34	303	40 26	325
264	35 17	015	49 19	058	36 26	152	33 29	204	29 07	265	30 45	303	39 52	324
265	35 31	014	50 08	057	36 52	153	33 06	204	28 09	265	29 56	302	39 18	323
266	35 45	013	50 57	056	37 19	153	32 42	204	27 11	264	29 06	302	38 43	322
267	35 57	012	51 45	055	37 45	154	32 17	205	26 13	264	28 16	301	38 07	322
268	36 09	011	52 32	054	38 10	154	31 53	205	25 15	264	27 27	301	37 30	321
269	36 19	010	53 19	053	38 36	155	31 28	205	24 17	264	26 36	300	36 53	320

LHA ♈	Hc	Zn	Hc	Zn	Hc	Zn	Hc	Zn	Hc	Zn	Hc	Zn	Hc	Zn
	◆VEGA		ALTAIR		◆FOMALHAUT		Peacock		RIGIL KENT		◆ANTARES		ARCTURUS	
270	36 29	009	54 05	052	20 04	117	39 00	155	31 03	206	65 37	236	25 46	300
271	36 38	008	54 51	051	20 56	117	39 25	155	30 37	206	64 48	237	24 55	299
272	36 45	007	55 35	050	21 48	117	39 49	156	30 12	206	64 00	238	24 04	299
273	36 52	006	56 19	049	22 40	117	40 12	156	29 46	207	63 10	238	23 13	298
274	36 58	005	57 03	047	23 32	116	40 35	157	29 20	207	62 20	239	22 22	298
275	37 03	004	57 45	046	24 25	116	40 58	158	28 53	207	61 30	240	21 30	297
276	37 06	003	58 26	045	25 17	116	41 20	158	28 27	207	60 40	240	20 38	297
277	37 09	002	59 07	043	26 09	116	41 41	159	28 00	207	59 49	241	19 46	297
278	37 11	001	59 46	042	27 01	116	42 02	159	27 33	208	58 58	242	18 54	296
279	37 12	000	60 24	040	27 53	116	42 23	160	27 06	208	58 07	242	18 02	296
280	37 12	359	61 02	039	28 45	116	42 42	160	26 39	208	57 15	243	17 09	295
281	37 11	358	61 37	037	29 38	116	43 02	161	26 11	208	56 23	243	16 17	295
282	37 09	357	62 12	035	30 30	116	43 20	162	25 44	208	55 31	243	15 24	295
283	37 06	356	62 45	034	31 22	116	43 38	162	25 16	209	54 39	244	14 31	294
284	37 01	355	63 16	032	32 14	116	43 56	163	24 48	209	53 47	244	13 38	294
	◆DENEB		◆FOMALHAUT		Peacock		RIGIL KENT		◆ANTARES		Rasalhague		VEGA	
285	26 20	020	33 06	116	44 13	164	24 20	209	52 55	244	56 13	321	36 56	355
286	26 40	019	33 59	116	44 29	164	23 52	209	52 02	245	55 35	319	36 50	354
287	26 58	018	34 51	116	44 44	165	23 23	209	51 09	245	54 57	318	36 43	353
288	27 16	018	35 43	117	44 59	166	22 55	209	50 17	245	54 18	317	36 35	352
289	27 33	017	36 35	117	45 13	166	22 26	209	49 24	245	53 38	316	36 26	351
290	27 50	016	37 27	117	45 27	167	21 58	209	48 31	246	52 56	315	36 16	350
291	28 06	015	38 19	117	45 40	168	21 29	210	47 37	246	52 15	313	36 05	349
292	28 21	015	39 11	117	45 52	168	21 00	210	46 44	246	51 32	312	35 54	348
293	28 35	014	40 03	117	46 03	169	20 31	210	45 51	246	50 49	311	35 41	347
294	28 49	013	40 55	117	46 13	170	20 03	210	44 58	246	50 05	310	35 27	346
295	29 02	012	41 46	117	46 23	171	19 34	210	44 04	247	49 20	309	35 13	345
296	29 14	012	42 38	117	46 32	171	19 05	210	43 11	247	48 34	308	34 57	344
297	29 25	011	43 30	118	46 40	172	18 35	210	42 17	247	47 49	307	34 41	343
298	29 36	010	44 21	118	46 48	173	18 06	210	41 24	247	47 02	307	34 24	342
299	29 46	009	45 13	118	46 55	174	17 37	210	40 30	247	46 15	306	34 06	342
	◆DENEB		Alpheratz		◆FOMALHAUT		Peacock		◆ANTARES		Rasalhague		VEGA	
300	29 55	008	16 01	054	46 04	118	47 00	175	39 37	247	45 28	305	33 47	341
301	30 03	008	16 48	053	46 55	119	47 05	175	38 43	247	44 40	304	33 28	340
302	30 10	007	17 34	053	47 46	119	47 10	176	37 49	247	43 51	303	33 07	339
303	30 17	006	18 21	052	48 37	119	47 13	177	36 56	247	43 02	303	32 46	338
304	30 23	005	19 07	052	49 28	119	47 16	178	36 02	247	42 13	302	32 24	337
305	30 27	004	19 52	051	50 19	120	47 18	179	35 08	247	41 24	301	32 01	337
306	30 32	004	20 38	051	51 09	120	47 19	179	34 15	247	40 34	301	31 37	336
307	30 35	003	21 23	050	52 00	120	47 19	180	33 21	247	39 43	300	31 13	335
308	30 37	002	22 07	050	52 50	121	47 18	181	32 27	247	38 53	299	30 48	334
309	30 39	001	22 52	049	53 40	121	47 17	182	31 34	247	38 02	299	30 23	333
310	30 40	000	23 36	049	54 29	122	47 14	183	30 40	247	37 11	298	29 56	333
311	30 40	000	24 19	048	55 19	122	47 11	183	29 46	247	36 19	297	29 29	332
312	30 39	359	25 03	048	56 08	123	47 07	184	28 52	247	35 27	297	29 02	331
313	30 37	358	25 46	047	56 57	123	47 03	185	27 59	247	34 35	296	28 33	331
314	30 35	357	26 28	047	57 45	124	46 57	186	27 05	247	33 43	296	28 04	330
	Alpheratz		◆Diphda		ACHERNAR		Peacock		◆ANTARES		VEGA		◆DENEB	
315	27 11	046	36 07	102	22 46	147	46 51	187	26 11	247	27 35	329	30 31	356
316	27 52	046	37 04	102	23 18	147	46 44	187	25 18	247	27 05	329	30 27	356
317	28 34	045	38 01	102	23 50	147	46 36	188	24 24	247	26 34	328	30 22	355
318	29 15	044	38 58	102	24 22	147	46 27	189	23 31	247	26 03	327	30 17	354
319	29 55	044	39 55	102	24 53	147	46 17	190	22 37	247	25 31	327	30 10	353
320	30 35	043	40 52	102	25 25	147	46 07	190	21 44	247	24 59	326	30 03	352
321	31 14	042	41 49	102	25 57	147	45 56	191	20 50	247	24 26	325	29 54	351
322	31 53	042	42 46	102	26 28	147	45 45	192	19 57	247	23 52	325	29 45	351
323	32 32	041	43 43	102	26 59	148	45 32	193	19 03	246	23 19	324	29 36	350
324	33 10	040	44 40	101	27 30	148	45 19	193	18 10	246	22 44	324	29 25	349
325	33 47	040	45 37	101	28 01	148	45 05	194	17 17	246	22 09	323	29 14	348
326	34 24	039	46 35	101	28 32	148	44 51	195	16 24	246	21 34	322	29 01	348
327	35 00	038	47 32	101	29 03	148	44 35	196	15 30	246	20 58	322	28 49	347
328	35 36	037	48 29	101	29 33	149	44 19	196	14 37	246	20 22	321	28 35	346
329	36 10	036	49 26	101	30 03	149	44 03	197	13 44	246	19 46	321	28 20	345
	◆Alpheratz		Diphda		◆ACHERNAR		Peacock		◆Nunki		ALTAIR		DENEB	
330	36 45	036	50 23	101	30 33	149	43 46	198	45 24	247	50 45	304	28 05	345
331	37 18	035	51 20	101	31 03	149	43 28	198	44 30	247	49 56	303	27 49	344
332	37 51	034	52 17	101	31 32	150	43 09	199	43 37	247	49 07	302	27 33	343
333	38 23	033	53 14	101	32 02	150	42 50	199	42 43	247	48 18	301	27 16	342
334	38 55	032	54 11	101	32 31	150	42 31	200	41 50	247	47 28	301	26 58	342
335	39 25	031	55 08	101	32 59	151	42 11	201	40 56	247	46 38	300	26 39	341
336	39 55	030	56 05	101	33 28	151	41 50	201	40 02	247	45 47	299	26 20	340
337	40 24	029	57 02	101	33 56	151	41 29	202	39 09	247	44 56	298	26 00	340
338	40 52	028	58 00	101	34 24	151	41 07	202	38 15	247	44 04	298	25 39	339
339	41 19	027	58 57	102	34 52	152	40 45	203	37 21	247	43 13	297	25 18	338
340	41 45	026	59 54	102	35 19	152	40 22	203	36 27	247	42 20	296	24 56	338
341	42 11	025	60 51	102	35 46	153	39 58	204	35 34	248	41 28	296	24 33	337
342	42 35	024	61 48	102	36 13	153	39 35	204	34 40	248	40 36	295	24 10	336
343	42 59	023	62 45	102	36 39	153	39 11	205	33 46	248	39 43	294	23 46	336
344	43 21	022	63 41	102	37 05	154	38 46	205	32 52	248	38 50	294	23 22	335
	Alpheratz		◆Hamal		◆ACHERNAR		Peacock		Nunki		◆ALTAIR		DENEB	
345	43 43	021	30 40	051	37 30	154	38 21	206	31 58	248	37 56	293	22 57	334
346	44 03	020	31 25	051	37 56	155	37 55	206	31 05	248	37 03	293	22 32	334
347	44 22	019	32 10	050	38 20	155	37 29	207	30 11	247	36 09	292	22 06	333
348	44 40	018	32 54	049	38 45	156	37 03	207	29 17	247	35 15	292	21 39	333
349	44 58	016	33 38	049	39 09	156	36 37	207	28 23	247	34 21	291	21 12	332
350	45 13	015	34 22	048	39 32	156	36 10	208	27 30	247	33 27	291	20 44	331
351	45 28	014	35 05	047	39 55	157	35 42	208	26 36	247	32 32	290	20 16	331
352	45 42	013	35 47	047	40 18	157	35 15	209	25 42	247	31 37	290	19 48	330
353	45 54	012	36 29	046	40 40	158	34 47	209	24 48	247	30 43	289	19 19	330
354	46 05	010	37 11	045	41 01	159	34 18	209	23 55	247	29 48	289	18 49	329
355	46 15	009	37 52	044	41 22	159	33 50	210	23 01	247	28 53	289	18 19	329
356	46 24	008	38 32	044	41 43	160	33 21	210	22 08	247	27 57	288	17 49	328
357	46 32	007	39 12	043	42 03	160	32 52	210	21 14	247	27 02	288	17 18	328
358	46 38	005	39 51	042	42 22	161	32 22	210	20 21	247	26 07	287	16 47	327
359	46 43	004	40 30	041	42 41	161	31 53	211	19 27	247	25 11	287	16 15	327

 LAT 15°S

LHA ♈	Hc Zn	Hc Zn	Hc Zn	Hc Zn	Hc Zn	Hc Zn	Hc Zn
	◆ Alpheratz	Hamal	ALDEBARAN	◆ RIGEL	ACHERNAR	◆ FOMALHAUT	Enif
0	45 46 003	40 22 040	14 47 068	12 51 095	43 56 162	69 42 222	48 16 305
1	45 49 002	40 58 039	15 41 068	13 48 095	44 14 162	69 03 223	47 28 304
2	45 50 000	41 34 038	16 34 067	14 46 095	44 31 163	68 22 225	46 39 303
3	45 49 359	42 09 037	17 28 067	15 44 094	44 48 164	67 41 226	45 51 302
4	45 48 358	42 44 036	18 21 066	16 42 094	45 04 164	66 59 228	45 01 301
5	45 45 357	43 17 035	19 14 066	17 40 094	45 19 165	66 15 229	44 12 301
6	45 41 355	43 50 034	20 07 066	18 37 094	45 34 166	65 31 230	43 22 300
7	45 36 354	44 22 033	21 00 065	19 35 094	45 48 166	64 47 231	42 31 299
8	45 29 353	44 53 032	21 52 065	20 33 093	46 01 167	64 01 232	41 40 299
9	45 21 352	45 23 031	22 44 064	21 31 093	46 13 168	63 15 233	40 49 298
10	45 12 350	45 52 030	23 37 064	22 29 093	46 25 169	62 29 234	39 58 297
11	45 02 349	46 20 028	24 29 064	23 27 093	46 36 169	61 42 235	39 06 297
12	44 51 348	46 47 027	25 20 063	24 25 092	46 47 170	60 54 235	38 14 296
13	44 38 347	47 13 026	26 12 063	25 23 092	46 56 171	60 06 236	37 22 295
14	44 24 346	47 38 025	27 03 062	26 20 092	47 05 172	59 18 237	36 30 295
	Hamal	◆ ALDEBARAN	RIGEL	◆ ACHERNAR	FOMALHAUT	◆ Enif	Alpheratz
15	48 02 024	27 54 062	27 18 092	47 13 172	58 30 237	35 37 294	44 09 344
16	48 25 022	28 45 061	28 16 091	47 21 173	57 41 238	34 44 294	43 53 343
17	48 46 021	29 36 061	29 14 091	47 27 174	56 51 238	33 51 293	43 36 342
18	49 06 020	30 26 060	30 12 091	47 33 175	56 02 239	32 58 293	43 18 341
19	49 25 018	31 16 060	31 10 091	47 38 176	55 12 239	32 04 292	42 58 340
20	49 43 017	32 06 059	32 08 090	47 42 176	54 22 240	31 10 292	42 38 339
21	50 00 016	32 56 058	33 06 090	47 45 177	53 32 240	30 16 291	42 16 338
22	50 15 014	33 45 058	34 04 090	47 48 178	52 41 241	29 22 291	41 54 337
23	50 28 013	34 34 057	35 02 090	47 49 179	51 51 241	28 28 290	41 31 336
24	50 41 012	35 22 057	36 00 089	47 50 180	51 00 241	27 34 290	41 06 335
25	50 52 010	36 10 056	36 58 089	47 50 180	50 09 242	26 39 290	40 41 334
26	51 01 009	36 58 055	37 56 089	47 50 181	49 18 242	25 45 289	40 15 333
27	51 09 007	37 45 055	38 54 088	47 48 182	48 27 242	24 50 289	39 48 332
28	51 16 006	38 32 054	39 52 088	47 46 183	47 36 242	23 55 288	39 20 331
29	51 21 004	39 19 053	40 50 088	47 42 184	46 44 243	23 00 288	38 51 330
	CAPELLA	◆ BETELGEUSE	SIRIUS	CANOPUS	◆ ACHERNAR	FOMALHAUT	◆ Alpheratz
30	14 28 033	27 23 073	21 38 102	26 19 142	47 38 184	45 53 243	38 21 329
31	15 00 033	28 19 073	22 35 102	26 55 142	47 34 185	45 01 243	37 51 328
32	15 31 032	29 14 072	23 32 102	27 30 142	47 28 186	44 09 243	37 20 327
33	16 01 032	30 09 072	24 28 102	28 06 142	47 21 187	43 18 243	36 48 326
34	16 31 031	31 04 072	25 25 102	28 41 142	47 14 188	42 26 243	36 15 325
35	17 01 031	31 59 071	26 22 102	29 17 143	47 06 188	41 34 244	35 42 324
36	17 30 030	32 54 071	27 19 101	29 52 143	46 58 189	40 42 244	35 08 324
37	17 59 030	33 48 070	28 16 101	30 27 143	46 48 190	39 50 244	34 33 323
38	18 27 029	34 43 070	29 12 101	31 02 143	46 38 191	38 58 244	33 58 322
39	18 55 028	35 37 069	30 09 101	31 36 143	46 27 191	38 06 244	33 22 321
40	19 23 028	36 31 069	31 06 101	32 11 144	46 15 192	37 14 244	32 45 321
41	19 50 027	37 25 068	32 03 101	32 45 144	46 03 193	36 22 244	32 08 320
42	20 16 027	38 19 068	33 00 100	33 19 144	45 49 193	35 30 244	31 31 319
43	20 42 026	39 12 067	33 57 100	33 53 144	45 36 194	34 37 244	30 52 318
44	21 07 026	40 05 066	34 54 100	34 27 145	45 21 195	33 45 244	30 14 318
	◆ CAPELLA	BETELGEUSE	SIRIUS	◆ CANOPUS	ACHERNAR	◆ FOMALHAUT	Alpheratz
45	21 32 025	40 58 066	35 51 100	35 00 145	45 06 196	32 53 244	29 35 317
46	21 56 024	41 51 065	36 48 100	35 34 145	44 50 196	32 01 244	28 55 316
47	22 20 024	42 44 065	37 45 100	36 07 145	44 33 197	31 09 244	28 15 316
48	22 43 023	43 36 064	38 43 100	36 39 146	44 16 198	30 16 244	27 34 315
49	23 05 022	44 28 063	39 40 100	37 12 146	43 59 198	29 24 244	26 53 315
50	23 27 022	45 19 063	40 37 099	37 44 147	43 40 199	28 32 244	26 11 314
51	23 48 021	46 11 062	41 34 099	38 16 147	43 21 199	27 40 244	25 30 313
52	24 09 021	47 01 061	42 31 099	38 47 147	43 02 200	26 48 244	24 47 313
53	24 29 020	47 52 060	43 29 099	39 18 148	42 42 201	25 56 244	24 05 312
54	24 48 019	48 42 060	44 26 099	39 49 148	42 21 201	25 04 244	23 21 312
55	25 07 019	49 32 059	45 23 099	40 20 149	42 00 202	24 11 244	22 38 311
56	25 25 018	50 21 058	46 20 099	40 50 149	41 38 202	23 19 244	21 54 311
57	25 42 017	51 10 057	47 18 099	41 19 149	41 16 203	22 27 244	21 10 310
58	25 59 016	51 58 056	48 15 098	41 49 150	40 53 203	21 35 244	20 26 310
59	26 15 016	52 46 055	49 12 098	42 17 150	40 30 204	20 43 244	19 41 309
	CAPELLA	POLLUX	◆ SIRIUS	CANOPUS	◆ ACHERNAR	Diphda	◆ Hamal
60	26 31 015	20 24 052	50 10 098	42 46 151	40 07 204	43 08 259	42 44 324
61	26 45 014	21 09 051	51 07 098	43 14 151	39 43 205	42 11 259	42 10 323
62	26 59 014	21 55 051	52 04 098	43 41 152	39 18 205	41 14 259	41 35 322
63	27 12 013	22 39 050	53 02 098	44 08 153	38 53 206	40 17 259	40 59 321
64	27 25 012	23 24 050	53 59 098	44 35 153	38 28 206	39 20 259	40 22 320
65	27 36 011	24 08 049	54 56 098	45 00 154	38 02 207	38 23 259	39 45 320
66	27 47 011	24 52 049	55 54 098	45 26 154	37 36 207	37 26 259	39 07 319
67	27 58 010	25 35 048	56 51 098	45 51 155	37 10 207	36 29 259	38 28 318
68	28 07 009	26 18 048	57 49 098	46 15 156	36 43 208	35 33 258	37 49 317
69	28 16 008	27 01 047	58 46 098	46 38 156	36 16 208	34 36 258	37 09 316
70	28 24 007	27 43 046	59 44 098	47 01 157	35 48 208	33 39 258	36 29 315
71	28 31 007	28 25 046	60 41 098	47 24 158	35 21 209	32 42 258	35 48 315
72	28 37 006	29 06 045	61 39 098	47 45 158	34 53 209	31 46 258	35 06 314
73	28 43 005	29 47 045	62 36 098	48 06 159	34 24 209	30 49 258	34 24 313
74	28 47 004	30 27 044	63 33 098	48 27 160	33 56 210	29 52 258	33 42 312
	CAPELLA	POLLUX	◆ PROCYON	Suhail	◆ CANOPUS	ACHERNAR	◆ Hamal
75	28 51 004	31 07 043	45 30 066	30 22 132	48 46 161	33 27 210	32 59 312
76	28 55 003	31 46 042	46 23 065	31 05 132	49 05 161	32 57 210	32 16 311
77	28 57 002	32 25 042	47 16 065	31 48 132	49 23 162	32 28 211	31 32 310
78	28 58 001	33 04 041	48 08 064	32 31 132	49 40 163	31 58 211	30 47 310
79	28 59 000	33 41 040	49 00 063	33 14 133	49 57 164	31 29 211	30 03 309
80	28 59 000	34 19 040	49 51 062	33 57 133	50 12 165	30 58 211	29 18 309
81	28 58 359	34 55 039	50 42 062	34 39 133	50 27 166	30 28 212	28 32 308
82	28 57 358	35 31 038	51 33 061	35 21 133	50 41 167	29 58 212	27 46 307
83	28 54 357	36 07 037	52 24 060	36 04 133	50 54 167	29 27 212	27 00 307
84	28 51 356	36 41 036	53 13 059	36 46 134	51 06 168	28 56 212	26 14 306
85	28 47 356	37 15 035	54 03 058	37 28 134	51 17 169	28 25 212	25 27 306
86	28 42 355	37 49 035	54 52 057	38 09 134	51 28 170	27 54 213	24 40 305
87	28 36 354	38 21 034	55 40 056	38 51 134	51 37 171	27 23 213	23 52 305
88	28 30 353	38 53 033	56 28 055	39 32 135	51 45 172	26 51 213	23 05 304
89	28 23 352	39 24 032	57 15 054	40 13 135	51 53 173	26 20 213	22 17 304

LHA ♈	Hc Zn	Hc Zn	Hc Zn	Hc Zn	Hc Zn	Hc Zn	Hc Zn
	POLLUX	◆ REGULUS	Suhail	◆ CANOPUS	ACHERNAR	◆ ALDEBARAN	CAPELLA
90	39 54 031	22 43 070	40 54 135	51 59 174	25 48 213	52 22 326	28 15 352
91	40 24 030	23 37 070	41 35 136	52 05 175	25 16 213	51 49 325	28 06 351
92	40 52 029	24 31 069	42 15 136	52 09 176	24 44 213	51 15 324	27 57 350
93	41 20 028	25 25 069	42 55 136	52 13 177	24 12 214	50 40 322	27 46 349
94	41 47 027	26 19 068	43 35 137	52 16 178	23 40 214	50 04 321	27 35 349
95	42 12 026	27 13 068	44 15 137	52 17 179	23 08 214	49 28 320	27 24 348
96	42 37 025	28 07 067	44 54 138	52 18 180	22 36 214	48 50 319	27 11 347
97	43 01 024	29 00 067	45 33 138	52 17 181	22 04 214	48 12 318	26 58 346
98	43 24 023	29 53 066	46 11 139	52 16 182	21 31 214	47 32 317	26 44 346
99	43 46 022	30 46 066	46 50 139	52 13 183	20 59 214	46 52 316	26 29 345
100	44 07 021	31 39 065	47 27 140	52 10 184	20 26 214	46 11 315	26 14 344
101	44 27 019	32 32 065	48 05 140	52 06 185	19 54 214	45 30 314	25 58 344
102	44 45 018	33 24 064	48 42 141	52 00 186	19 21 214	44 48 313	25 41 343
103	45 03 017	34 16 064	49 18 141	51 54 187	18 49 214	44 05 312	25 23 342
104	45 19 016	35 08 063	49 54 142	51 46 188	18 16 214	43 22 311	25 05 341
	POLLUX	◆ REGULUS	ACRUX	◆ CANOPUS	RIGEL	◆ ALDEBARAN	CAPELLA
105	45 35 015	36 00 063	17 01 152	51 38 189	63 29 282	42 38 310	24 46 341
106	45 49 013	36 51 062	17 28 152	51 29 190	62 32 281	41 54 310	24 27 340
107	46 02 012	37 42 062	17 55 152	51 19 191	61 35 281	41 09 309	24 07 339
108	46 13 011	38 33 061	18 22 152	51 08 192	60 38 280	40 23 308	23 46 339
109	46 24 010	39 24 060	18 49 152	50 56 192	59 41 280	39 37 307	23 25 338
110	46 33 008	40 14 060	19 16 152	50 43 193	58 44 279	38 51 306	23 03 337
111	46 41 007	41 04 059	19 43 152	50 29 194	57 47 279	38 04 306	22 40 337
112	46 47 006	41 53 058	20 10 152	50 14 195	56 50 278	37 17 305	22 17 336
113	46 52 005	42 42 057	20 37 152	49 59 196	55 52 278	36 29 304	21 54 336
114	46 56 003	43 31 057	21 04 152	49 42 197	54 55 277	35 41 304	21 29 335
115	46 59 002	44 19 056	21 31 153	49 25 198	53 57 277	34 53 303	21 05 334
116	47 00 001	45 07 055	21 57 153	49 07 198	53 00 276	34 04 302	20 39 334
117	47 01 359	45 54 054	22 24 153	48 49 199	52 02 276	33 15 302	20 13 333
118	46 59 358	46 41 053	22 50 153	48 29 200	51 04 276	32 26 301	19 47 333
119	46 57 357	47 27 053	23 17 153	48 09 201	50 07 275	31 36 301	19 20 332
	◆ REGULUS	SPICA	◆ ACRUX	CANOPUS	◆ RIGEL	BETELGEUSE	POLLUX
120	48 13 052	10 59 099	23 43 153	47 48 201	49 09 275	51 58 304	46 53 356
121	48 58 051	11 56 099	24 09 153	47 27 202	48 11 274	51 10 303	46 48 354
122	49 43 050	12 54 098	24 35 153	47 05 203	47 13 274	50 21 302	46 41 353
123	50 27 049	13 51 098	25 01 153	46 42 204	46 15 274	49 32 301	46 34 352
124	51 10 048	14 48 098	25 27 154	46 18 204	45 18 274	48 42 300	46 25 350
125	51 52 047	15 46 098	25 53 154	45 54 205	44 20 273	47 52 300	46 14 349
126	52 34 045	16 43 097	26 18 154	45 29 206	43 22 273	47 01 299	46 03 348
127	53 15 044	17 41 097	26 44 154	45 04 206	42 24 273	46 10 298	45 50 347
128	53 55 043	18 38 097	27 09 154	44 38 207	41 26 272	45 19 297	45 36 345
129	54 34 042	19 36 097	27 34 154	44 12 207	40 28 272	44 27 297	45 21 344
130	55 12 041	20 33 097	27 59 155	43 45 208	39 30 272	43 35 296	45 05 343
131	55 50 039	21 31 096	28 24 155	43 18 208	38 32 271	42 43 295	44 48 342
132	56 26 038	22 29 096	28 48 155	42 50 209	37 34 271	41 51 295	44 29 341
133	57 01 036	23 26 096	29 12 155	42 21 210	36 36 271	40 58 294	44 09 340
134	57 34 035	24 24 096	29 37 156	41 53 210	35 38 271	40 05 294	43 49 338
	REGULUS	◆ SPICA	ACRUX	◆ CANOPUS	SIRIUS	BETELGEUSE	◆ POLLUX
135	58 07 033	25 21 096	30 00 156	41 23 210	57 43 262	39 12 293	43 27 337
136	58 38 032	26 19 095	30 24 156	40 54 211	56 46 262	38 18 292	43 04 336
137	59 08 030	27 17 095	30 47 156	40 24 211	55 48 262	37 25 292	42 40 335
138	59 37 029	28 15 095	31 11 157	39 53 212	54 51 262	36 31 291	42 15 334
139	60 03 027	29 12 095	31 33 157	39 23 212	53 54 262	35 37 291	41 50 333
140	60 29 025	30 10 094	31 56 157	38 52 213	52 56 262	34 42 290	41 23 332
141	60 52 023	31 08 094	32 18 157	38 20 213	51 59 262	33 48 290	40 55 331
142	61 14 021	32 06 094	32 40 158	37 48 213	51 01 262	32 53 289	40 27 330
143	61 35 019	33 04 094	33 02 158	37 16 214	50 04 262	31 59 289	39 58 329
144	61 53 017	34 01 094	33 24 158	36 44 214	49 07 262	31 04 288	39 27 328
145	62 09 015	34 59 093	33 45 159	36 11 214	48 09 262	30 09 288	38 57 327
146	62 24 013	35 57 093	34 06 159	35 38 215	47 12 261	29 14 288	38 25 326
147	62 36 011	36 55 093	34 26 159	35 05 215	46 15 261	28 18 287	37 52 325
148	62 46 009	37 53 093	34 46 160	34 32 215	45 18 261	27 23 287	37 19 325
149	62 55 007	38 51 092	35 06 160	33 58 216	44 20 261	26 27 286	36 45 324
	REGULUS	◆ ARCTURUS	SPICA	◆ ACRUX	CANOPUS	SIRIUS	◆ PROCYON
150	63 01 005	18 19 064	39 49 092	35 26 161	33 24 216	43 23 261	49 53 298
151	63 05 003	19 10 063	40 47 092	35 45 161	32 50 216	42 26 261	49 02 297
152	63 06 001	20 02 063	41 45 092	36 03 161	32 16 216	41 29 261	48 10 296
153	63 06 358	20 53 062	42 42 092	36 22 162	31 41 217	40 31 261	47 18 295
154	63 03 356	21 45 062	43 40 091	36 39 162	31 07 217	39 34 260	46 25 295
155	62 58 354	22 36 061	44 38 091	36 57 163	30 32 217	38 37 260	45 32 294
156	62 51 352	23 26 061	45 36 091	37 14 163	29 57 217	37 40 260	44 39 293
157	62 42 350	24 17 060	46 34 091	37 31 164	29 22 217	36 43 260	43 46 293
158	62 31 348	25 07 060	47 32 090	37 47 164	28 46 218	35 46 260	42 52 292
159	62 18 346	25 57 060	48 30 090	38 03 164	28 11 218	34 49 260	41 59 292
160	62 03 344	26 47 059	49 28 090	38 18 165	27 35 218	33 52 260	41 05 291
161	61 45 342	27 37 058	50 26 090	38 33 165	27 00 218	32 55 260	40 10 290
162	61 26 340	28 26 058	51 24 089	38 47 166	26 24 218	31 58 259	39 16 290
163	61 05 338	29 15 057	52 22 089	39 01 166	25 48 218	31 01 259	38 21 289
164	60 43 336	30 04 057	53 20 089	39 14 167	25 12 218	30 04 259	37 27 289
	Denebola	◆ ARCTURUS	SPICA	◆ ACRUX	SIRIUS	◆ PROCYON	REGULUS
165	58 03 023	30 52 056	54 18 088	39 27 167	29 07 259	36 32 288	60 18 334
166	58 25 022	31 40 056	55 16 088	39 39 168	28 10 259	35 37 288	59 52 332
167	58 45 020	32 28 055	56 14 088	39 51 168	27 13 259	34 41 287	59 25 331
168	59 04 018	33 15 054	57 12 088	40 03 169	26 16 258	33 46 287	58 56 329
169	59 21 016	34 02 054	58 09 087	40 13 170	25 20 258	32 51 287	58 25 328
170	59 36 014	34 49 053	59 07 087	40 24 170	24 23 258	31 55 286	57 54 326
171	59 50 013	35 35 053	60 05 086	40 33 171	23 26 258	30 59 286	57 21 324
172	60 01 011	36 21 052	61 03 086	40 42 171	22 30 258	30 03 285	56 46 323
173	60 11 009	37 06 051	62 01 086	40 51 172	21 33 258	29 07 285	56 11 322
174	60 19 007	37 51 050	62 59 085	40 59 172	20 36 257	28 11 284	55 34 320
175	60 25 005	38 35 050	63 56 085	41 06 173	19 40 257	27 15 284	54 57 319
176	60 29 003	39 19 049	64 54 084	41 13 174	18 43 257	26 19 284	54 18 318
177	60 31 001	40 03 048	65 52 084	41 19 174	17 47 257	25 23 283	53 38 316
178	60 30 359	40 46 047	66 49 084	41 25 175	16 50 257	24 26 283	52 58 315
179	60 28 357	41 28 046	67 47 083	41 30 175	15 54 256	23 30 283	52 17 314

LAT 15°S

LHA ♈	Hc	Zn	Hc	Zn	Hc	Zn	Hc	Zn	Hc	Zn	Hc	Zn	Hc	Zn
	ARCTURUS		◆ ANTARES		ACRUX		◆ Suhail		Alphard		REGULUS		◆ Denebola	
180	42 10	046	26 26	112	41 35	176	43 46	223	52 25	275	51 35	313	60 24	355
181	42 51	045	27 19	112	41 39	176	43 06	224	51 27	275	50 52	312	60 18	353
182	43 31	044	28 13	112	41 42	177	42 26	224	50 29	274	50 08	311	60 10	351
183	44 11	043	29 07	112	41 45	178	41 46	224	49 32	274	49 24	310	60 00	349
184	44 50	042	30 00	112	41 47	178	41 05	225	48 34	274	48 39	309	59 49	347
185	45 28	041	30 54	112	41 48	179	40 25	225	47 36	273	47 54	308	59 35	345
186	46 06	040	31 48	112	41 49	179	39 44	225	46 38	273	47 08	307	59 20	344
187	46 43	039	32 41	112	41 49	180	39 02	226	45 40	273	46 21	306	59 02	342
188	47 19	038	33 35	112	41 49	181	38 21	226	44 42	273	45 34	305	58 43	340
189	47 54	037	34 29	112	41 48	181	37 39	226	43 44	272	44 47	305	58 23	338
190	48 28	036	35 22	112	41 46	182	36 57	226	42 46	272	43 59	304	58 01	337
191	49 01	034	36 16	112	41 44	183	36 15	227	41 49	272	43 11	303	57 37	335
192	49 33	033	37 10	112	41 41	183	35 33	227	40 51	271	42 22	302	57 12	333
193	50 05	032	38 04	112	41 38	184	34 51	227	39 53	271	41 32	301	56 45	332
194	50 35	031	38 57	112	41 34	184	34 08	227	38 55	271	40 43	301	56 17	330
	ARCTURUS		◆ Rasalhague		ANTARES		◆ ACRUX		Suhail		◆ REGULUS		Denebola	
195	51 04	029	16 27	072	39 51	112	41 29	185	33 26	227	39 53	300	55 47	329
196	51 32	028	17 22	071	40 45	112	41 24	185	32 43	228	39 03	299	55 17	327
197	51 58	027	18 16	071	41 38	112	41 18	186	32 00	228	38 12	299	54 45	326
198	52 24	025	19 11	071	42 32	112	41 11	187	31 17	228	37 21	298	54 12	324
199	52 48	024	20 06	070	43 25	112	41 04	187	30 34	228	36 30	298	53 37	323
200	53 11	023	21 00	070	44 19	113	40 57	188	29 51	228	35 38	297	53 02	322
201	53 33	021	21 55	069	45 12	113	40 49	188	29 08	228	34 47	296	52 26	321
202	53 53	020	22 49	069	46 06	113	40 40	189	28 25	228	33 55	296	51 49	319
203	54 12	018	23 43	069	46 59	113	40 31	189	27 41	228	33 02	295	51 10	318
204	54 29	017	24 37	068	47 53	113	40 21	190	26 58	228	32 10	295	50 31	317
205	54 45	015	25 31	068	48 46	113	40 10	191	26 15	229	31 17	294	49 52	316
206	54 59	013	26 24	067	49 39	113	40 00	191	25 31	229	30 24	294	49 11	315
207	55 11	012	27 18	067	50 32	114	39 48	192	24 48	229	29 31	293	48 29	314
208	55 22	010	28 11	066	51 25	114	39 36	192	24 04	229	28 38	293	47 47	313
209	55 32	009	29 04	066	52 18	114	39 24	193	23 21	229	27 44	292	47 05	312
	ARCTURUS		◆ Rasalhague		ANTARES		◆ RIGIL KENT		ACRUX		Gienah		◆ REGULUS	
210	55 40	007	29 57	066	53 11	114	43 31	173	39 11	193	65 04	260	26 51	292
211	55 46	005	30 49	065	54 04	115	43 38	174	38 57	194	64 07	260	25 57	292
212	55 50	004	31 42	065	54 57	115	43 44	175	38 43	194	63 10	261	25 03	291
213	55 53	002	32 34	064	55 49	115	43 49	175	38 29	195	62 13	261	24 09	291
214	55 54	000	33 26	063	56 41	116	43 53	176	38 14	195	61 15	261	23 15	290
215	55 53	358	34 18	063	57 34	116	43 57	177	37 58	196	60 18	261	22 20	290
216	55 51	357	35 09	062	58 26	116	44 00	177	37 42	196	59 21	261	21 26	290
217	55 46	355	36 00	062	59 17	117	44 03	178	37 26	197	58 24	261	20 31	289
218	55 41	353	36 51	061	60 09	117	44 05	179	37 09	197	57 27	261	19 36	289
219	55 33	352	37 42	061	61 00	118	44 06	179	36 52	197	56 29	261	18 41	288
220	55 24	350	38 32	060	61 51	119	44 06	180	36 35	198	55 32	261	17 46	288
221	55 13	348	39 22	059	62 42	119	44 06	181	36 17	198	54 35	261	16 51	288
222	55 01	347	40 12	059	63 33	120	44 05	181	35 58	199	53 38	261	15 56	287
223	54 47	345	41 01	058	64 23	121	44 03	182	35 39	199	52 41	260	15 00	287
224	54 32	344	41 50	057	65 12	121	44 01	183	35 20	200	51 44	260	14 05	287
	Alphecca		◆ VEGA		ALTAIR		◆ Shaula		RIGIL KENT		◆ SPICA		ARCTURUS	
225	47 28	012	16 03	041	13 56	077	49 16	130	43 58	183	66 49	276	54 15	342
226	47 39	010	16 41	041	14 53	076	50 00	131	43 55	184	65 51	276	53 56	341
227	47 49	009	17 19	040	15 49	076	50 43	131	43 50	185	64 54	276	53 36	339
228	47 57	008	17 56	040	16 45	076	51 27	132	43 45	185	63 56	275	53 15	338
229	48 04	006	18 33	039	17 41	075	52 10	132	43 40	186	62 58	275	52 52	336
230	48 10	005	19 09	039	18 37	075	52 52	133	43 33	187	62 00	274	52 28	335
231	48 15	004	19 45	038	19 33	075	53 35	134	43 26	187	61 03	274	52 03	333
232	48 18	002	20 21	038	20 29	074	54 16	134	43 19	188	60 05	274	51 36	332
233	48 20	001	20 56	037	21 25	074	54 58	135	43 10	189	59 07	273	51 09	331
234	48 20	000	21 31	037	22 20	074	55 39	136	43 02	189	58 09	273	50 40	329
235	48 19	358	22 05	036	23 16	073	56 19	136	42 52	190	57 11	272	50 10	328
236	48 17	357	22 39	035	24 11	073	56 58	137	42 42	190	56 13	272	49 39	327
237	48 13	356	23 13	035	25 06	072	57 38	138	42 31	191	55 15	272	49 07	326
238	48 08	354	23 45	034	26 02	072	58 16	139	42 20	192	54 17	272	48 34	325
239	48 02	353	24 18	034	26 57	072	58 54	140	42 08	192	53 19	271	48 00	324
	VEGA		◆ ALTAIR		Shaula		◆ RIGIL KENT		SPICA		◆ ARCTURUS		Alphecca	
240	24 50	033	27 52	071	59 31	141	41 55	193	52 22	271	47 25	322	47 54	352
241	25 21	032	28 46	071	60 07	142	41 42	193	51 24	271	46 49	321	47 45	350
242	25 52	032	29 41	070	60 42	143	41 28	194	50 26	270	46 12	320	47 35	349
243	26 22	031	30 36	070	61 16	144	41 14	195	49 28	270	45 35	319	47 24	348
244	26 51	030	31 30	069	61 50	145	40 59	195	48 30	270	44 57	318	47 11	347
245	27 20	030	32 24	069	62 22	147	40 44	196	47 32	270	44 18	317	46 57	345
246	27 49	029	33 18	068	62 54	148	40 28	196	46 34	269	43 38	316	46 41	344
247	28 17	028	34 12	068	63 24	149	40 11	197	45 36	269	42 58	315	46 25	343
248	28 44	028	35 05	067	63 53	151	39 55	197	44 38	269	42 17	315	46 07	342
249	29 10	027	35 59	067	64 20	152	39 37	198	43 40	269	41 35	314	45 48	340
250	29 36	026	36 52	066	64 47	154	39 19	198	42 42	268	40 53	313	45 28	339
251	30 01	025	37 45	066	65 12	155	39 01	199	41 44	268	40 10	312	45 07	338
252	30 25	025	38 38	065	65 35	157	38 42	199	40 46	268	39 27	311	44 45	337
253	30 49	024	39 30	065	65 57	159	38 23	200	39 48	268	38 43	310	44 22	336
254	31 12	023	40 22	064	66 17	161	38 03	200	38 50	268	37 59	310	43 57	335
	◆ VEGA		ALTAIR		◆ Peacock		RIGIL KENT		◆ SPICA		ARCTURUS		Alphecca	
255	31 34	022	41 14	063	33 02	149	37 43	201	37 52	267	37 14	309	43 32	334
256	31 56	021	42 06	063	33 31	149	37 22	201	36 55	267	36 29	308	43 06	332
257	32 17	021	42 57	062	34 01	150	37 01	201	35 57	267	35 43	308	42 39	331
258	32 37	020	43 48	061	34 30	150	36 40	202	34 59	267	34 57	307	42 10	330
259	32 56	019	44 39	061	34 59	150	36 18	202	34 01	266	34 10	306	41 41	329
260	33 14	018	45 29	060	35 27	151	35 56	203	33 03	266	33 23	306	41 11	328
261	33 31	017	46 19	059	35 56	151	35 34	203	32 05	266	32 36	305	40 41	327
262	33 48	016	47 09	058	36 24	151	35 11	203	31 08	266	31 48	304	40 09	327
263	34 04	015	47 58	058	36 51	152	34 48	204	30 10	266	31 00	304	39 37	326
264	34 19	014	48 47	057	37 19	152	34 24	204	29 12	265	30 12	303	39 04	325
265	34 33	014	49 35	056	37 46	152	34 00	204	28 14	265	29 23	303	38 30	324
266	34 46	013	50 23	055	38 12	153	33 36	205	27 16	265	28 34	302	37 55	323
267	34 58	012	51 10	054	38 38	153	33 12	205	26 19	265	27 45	302	37 20	322
268	35 10	011	51 56	053	39 04	154	32 47	205	25 21	264	26 56	301	36 44	321
269	35 20	010	52 42	052	39 30	154	32 22	206	24 23	264	26 06	301	36 07	320

LHA ♈	Hc	Zn	Hc	Zn	Hc	Zn	Hc	Zn	Hc	Zn	Hc	Zn	Hc	Zn
	◆ VEGA		ALTAIR		◆ FOMALHAUT		Peacock		RIGIL KENT		◆ ANTARES		ARCTURUS	
270	35 30	009	53 28	051	20 31	116	39 55	155	31 57	206	66 10	238	25 16	300
271	35 38	008	54 12	050	21 23	116	40 19	155	31 31	206	65 21	239	24 26	300
272	35 46	007	54 56	049	22 15	116	40 43	156	31 06	207	64 31	239	23 35	299
273	35 52	006	55 39	047	23 07	116	41 07	156	30 40	207	63 41	240	22 44	299
274	35 58	005	56 21	046	23 59	116	41 30	157	30 13	207	62 51	241	21 53	298
275	36 03	004	57 03	045	24 51	116	41 53	157	29 47	207	62 00	241	21 02	298
276	36 07	003	57 43	044	25 43	116	42 15	158	29 20	207	61 09	242	20 11	297
277	36 09	002	58 23	042	26 35	116	42 37	158	28 53	208	60 17	243	19 19	297
278	36 11	001	59 01	041	27 27	116	42 58	159	28 26	208	59 26	243	18 28	297
279	36 12	000	59 38	039	28 20	116	43 19	159	27 59	208	58 34	243	17 36	296
280	36 12	359	60 14	038	29 12	116	43 39	160	27 32	208	57 42	244	16 44	296
281	36 11	358	60 49	036	30 04	116	43 58	161	27 04	208	56 50	244	15 51	295
282	36 09	357	61 23	034	30 56	116	44 17	161	26 36	209	55 58	245	14 59	295
283	36 06	356	61 55	033	31 48	116	44 35	162	26 09	209	55 05	245	14 06	295
284	36 02	356	62 25	031	32 41	116	44 53	163	25 41	209	54 13	245	13 13	294
	◆ DENEB		◆ FOMALHAUT		Peacock		RIGIL KENT		◆ ANTARES		Rasalhague		VEGA	
285	25 24	020	33 33	116	45 10	163	25 12	209	53 20	246	55 26	322	35 57	355
286	25 43	019	34 25	116	45 26	164	24 44	209	52 27	246	54 49	320	35 51	354
287	26 01	018	35 17	116	45 42	165	24 16	209	51 34	246	54 12	319	35 44	353
288	26 19	017	36 09	116	45 57	165	23 47	209	50 41	246	53 34	318	35 36	352
289	26 36	017	37 01	116	46 12	166	23 19	210	49 48	247	52 54	317	35 27	351
290	26 52	016	37 54	116	46 25	167	22 50	210	48 55	247	52 14	315	35 17	350
291	27 08	015	38 46	116	46 38	167	22 21	210	48 01	247	51 33	314	35 07	349
292	27 23	015	39 38	116	46 50	168	21 52	210	47 08	247	50 51	313	34 55	348
293	27 37	014	40 30	116	47 02	169	21 24	210	46 15	247	50 09	312	34 43	347
294	27 50	013	41 22	116	47 12	170	20 55	210	45 21	247	49 25	311	34 29	346
295	28 03	012	42 14	116	47 22	171	20 26	210	44 28	247	48 41	310	34 15	345
296	28 15	012	43 05	117	47 31	171	19 56	210	43 34	248	47 57	309	34 00	344
297	28 26	011	43 57	117	47 40	172	19 27	210	42 41	248	47 12	308	33 44	344
298	28 37	010	44 49	117	47 47	173	18 58	210	41 47	248	46 26	307	33 27	343
299	28 46	009	45 40	117	47 54	174	18 29	210	40 53	248	45 40	307	33 09	342
	◆ DENEB		Alpheratz		◆ FOMALHAUT		Peacock		◆ ANTARES		Rasalhague		VEGA	
300	28 55	008	15 26	053	46 32	117	48 00	174	40 00	248	44 53	306	32 50	341
301	29 03	008	16 12	053	47 23	118	48 05	175	39 06	248	44 06	305	32 31	340
302	29 11	007	16 58	052	48 15	118	48 10	176	38 12	248	43 18	304	32 11	339
303	29 17	006	17 44	052	49 06	118	48 13	177	37 19	248	42 30	303	31 50	338
304	29 23	005	18 29	052	49 57	118	48 16	178	36 25	248	41 41	303	31 28	338
305	29 28	004	19 15	051	50 48	119	48 18	179	35 31	248	40 52	302	31 06	337
306	29 32	004	20 00	051	51 39	119	48 19	179	34 38	248	40 03	301	30 43	336
307	29 35	003	20 44	050	52 29	119	48 19	180	33 44	248	39 13	301	30 19	335
308	29 37	002	21 29	050	53 20	120	48 18	181	32 50	248	38 23	300	29 54	334
309	29 39	001	22 12	049	54 10	120	48 17	182	31 56	248	37 33	299	29 29	334
310	29 40	000	22 56	049	55 00	120	48 14	183	31 03	248	36 42	299	29 03	333
311	29 40	000	23 39	048	55 50	121	48 11	184	30 09	248	35 51	298	28 36	332
312	29 39	359	24 22	048	56 40	121	48 07	184	29 15	248	35 00	298	28 09	332
313	29 37	358	25 05	047	57 29	122	48 02	185	28 22	248	34 08	297	27 41	331
314	29 35	357	25 47	046	58 18	123	47 57	186	27 28	248	33 16	296	27 12	330
	Alpheratz		◆ Diphda		ACHERNAR		Peacock		◆ ANTARES		VEGA		◆ DENEB	
315	26 29	046	36 20	101	23 36	146	47 50	187	26 35	248	26 43	329	29 32	356
316	27 10	045	37 17	101	24 08	146	47 43	188	25 41	247	26 13	329	29 28	356
317	27 51	045	38 13	101	24 40	147	47 35	188	24 48	247	25 43	328	29 23	355
318	28 31	044	39 10	101	25 12	147	47 26	189	23 54	247	25 12	327	29 17	354
319	29 11	043	40 07	101	25 44	147	47 17	190	23 01	247	24 41	327	29 10	353
320	29 51	043	41 04	101	26 15	147	47 06	191	22 07	247	24 09	326	29 03	352
321	30 30	042	42 01	101	26 47	147	46 55	191	21 14	247	23 36	326	28 55	352
322	31 08	041	42 58	101	27 18	147	46 43	192	20 21	247	23 03	325	28 46	351
323	31 46	041	43 55	101	27 50	147	46 31	193	19 27	247	22 30	324	28 36	350
324	32 24	040	44 52	101	28 21	148	46 17	194	18 34	247	21 56	324	28 26	349
325	33 01	039	45 49	100	28 52	148	46 03	194	17 41	246	21 21	323	28 15	348
326	33 37	038	46 46	100	29 23	148	45 48	195	16 48	246	20 47	323	28 03	348
327	34 13	038	47 43	100	29 54	148	45 33	196	15 55	246	20 11	322	27 50	347
328	34 48	037	48 40	100	30 24	148	45 17	196	15 02	246	19 35	322	27 37	346
329	35 22	036	49 37	100	30 54	149	45 00	197	14 09	246	18 59	321	27 22	345
	◆ Alpheratz		Diphda		◆ ACHERNAR		Peacock		◆ Nunki		ALTAIR		DENEB	
330	35 56	035	50 34	100	31 24	149	44 43	198	45 47	248	50 11	305	27 07	345
331	36 29	034	51 31	100	31 54	149	44 25	198	44 54	248	49 23	304	26 52	344
332	37 01	033	52 28	100	32 24	149	44 06	199	44 00	248	48 35	303	26 35	343
333	37 33	033	53 25	100	32 53	150	43 47	200	43 06	248	47 46	302	26 18	343
334	38 04	032	54 22	100	33 23	150	43 27	200	42 13	248	46 57	301	26 01	342
335	38 34	031	55 19	100	33 52	150	43 07	201	41 19	248	46 07	301	25 42	341
336	39 03	030	56 16	100	34 20	151	42 46	201	40 25	248	45 17	300	25 23	340
337	39 31	029	57 14	100	34 49	151	42 24	202	39 31	248	44 27	299	25 03	340
338	39 59	028	58 11	100	35 17	151	42 02	203	38 38	248	43 36	298	24 43	339
339	40 26	027	59 08	100	35 45	152	41 40	203	37 44	248	42 45	298	24 22	338
340	40 52	026	60 05	100	36 12	152	41 17	204	36 50	248	41 54	297	24 00	338
341	41 16	025	61 02	100	36 39	152	40 53	204	35 56	248	41 02	296	23 38	337
342	41 40	024	61 59	100	37 06	153	40 29	205	35 03	248	40 10	296	23 15	336
343	42 03	023	62 56	100	37 33	153	40 05	205	34 09	248	39 17	295	22 52	336
344	42 25	022	63 53	100	37 59	153	39 40	206	33 15	248	38 25	295	22 28	335
	Alpheratz		◆ Hamal		◆ ACHERNAR		Peacock		Nunki		◆ ALTAIR		DENEB	
345	42 46	021	30 02	051	38 24	154	39 15	206	32 21	248	37 32	294	22 03	335
346	43 06	020	30 47	050	38 50	154	38 49	207	31 27	248	36 39	294	21 38	334
347	43 25	018	31 31	050	39 15	155	38 23	207	30 34	248	35 46	293	21 12	333
348	43 43	017	32 15	049	39 39	155	37 57	207	29 40	248	34 52	292	20 46	333
349	44 00	016	32 59	048	40 03	156	37 30	208	28 46	248	33 59	292	20 19	332
350	44 16	015	33 42	048	40 27	156	37 03	208	27 52	248	33 05	291	19 52	332
351	44 30	014	34 24	047	40 50	157	36 35	209	26 59	248	32 11	291	19 24	331
352	44 43	013	35 06	046	41 13	157	36 07	209	26 05	248	31 17	291	18 56	330
353	44 55	011	35 48	045	41 35	158	35 39	209	25 12	248	30 22	290	18 27	330
354	45 06	010	36 28	045	41 57	158	35 11	210	24 18	248	29 28	290	17 58	329
355	45 16	009	37 09	044	42 18	159	34 42	210	23 24	247	28 33	289	17 28	329
356	45 25	008	37 49	043	42 39	159	34 13	210	22 31	247	27 38	289	16 58	328
357	45 32	007	38 28	042	42 59	160	33 44	211	21 37	247	26 43	288	16 27	328
358	45 38	005	39 07	041	43 19	161	33 14	211	20 44	247	25 48	288	15 56	327
359	45 43	004	39 45	041	43 38	161	32 44	211	19 51	247	24 53	288	15 25	327

LAT 16°S

LHA ♈	Hc	Zn	Hc	Zn	Hc	Zn	Hc	Zn	Hc	Zn	Hc	Zn	Hc	Zn
	◆ Alpheratz		Hamal		ALDEBARAN		◆ RIGEL		ACHERNAR		◆ Peacock		Enif	
0	44 46	003	39 35	039	14 24	068	12 56	095	44 53	161	33 05	212	47 41	306
1	44 49	002	40 11	038	15 18	067	13 53	095	45 11	162	32 35	212	46 54	305
2	44 50	000	40 47	037	16 11	067	14 51	094	45 29	163	32 04	212	46 06	304
3	44 49	359	41 21	036	17 04	067	15 48	094	45 45	163	31 33	212	45 18	303
4	44 48	358	41 55	035	17 57	066	16 46	094	46 01	164	31 02	213	44 30	302
5	44 45	357	42 28	034	18 49	066	17 44	094	46 17	165	30 31	213	43 41	301
6	44 41	355	43 00	033	19 42	065	18 41	093	46 32	165	30 00	213	42 51	301
7	44 36	354	43 31	032	20 34	065	19 39	093	46 46	166	29 28	213	42 02	300
8	44 29	353	44 02	031	21 26	064	20 36	093	46 59	167	28 57	213	41 11	299
9	44 22	352	44 31	030	22 18	064	21 34	093	47 12	168	28 25	214	40 21	299
10	44 13	351	45 00	029	23 10	064	22 32	092	47 24	168	27 53	214	39 30	298
11	44 03	349	45 27	028	24 02	063	23 29	092	47 35	169	27 21	214	38 39	297
12	43 52	348	45 54	027	24 53	063	24 27	092	47 46	170	26 49	214	37 48	297
13	43 39	347	46 19	026	25 44	062	25 24	092	47 56	171	26 16	214	36 56	296
14	43 26	346	46 44	024	26 35	062	26 22	091	48 05	171	25 44	214	36 04	296
	◆ Hamal		ALDEBARAN		RIGEL		◆ CANOPUS		ACHERNAR		◆ FOMALHAUT		Alpheratz	
15	47 07	023	27 26	061	27 20	091	18 02	141	48 13	172	59 01	239	43 11	345
16	47 29	022	28 16	061	28 17	091	18 39	141	48 20	173	58 12	239	42 56	344
17	47 50	021	29 06	060	29 15	091	19 15	141	48 27	174	57 22	240	42 39	342
18	48 10	019	29 56	060	30 13	090	19 51	141	48 33	175	56 32	240	42 21	341
19	48 28	018	30 46	059	31 10	090	20 28	141	48 38	175	55 42	241	42 02	340
20	48 46	017	31 35	058	32 08	090	21 04	141	48 42	176	54 52	241	41 42	339
21	49 02	015	32 24	058	33 06	089	21 40	141	48 45	177	54 01	241	41 21	338
22	49 17	014	33 13	057	34 03	089	22 17	141	48 48	178	53 10	242	40 59	337
23	49 30	013	34 01	057	35 01	089	22 53	141	48 49	179	52 19	242	40 36	336
24	49 42	011	34 49	056	35 59	089	23 29	141	48 50	180	51 28	242	40 12	335
25	49 53	010	35 36	055	36 56	088	24 06	141	48 50	180	50 37	243	39 47	334
26	50 02	009	36 24	055	37 54	088	24 42	141	48 49	181	49 46	243	39 21	333
27	50 10	007	37 10	054	38 52	088	25 18	141	48 48	182	48 54	243	38 55	332
28	50 16	006	37 57	053	39 49	087	25 54	141	48 45	183	48 03	243	38 27	331
29	50 21	004	38 43	052	40 47	087	26 30	141	48 42	184	47 11	244	37 59	330
	◆ Hamal		ALDEBARAN		◆ SIRIUS		CANOPUS		ACHERNAR		◆ FOMALHAUT		Alpheratz	
30	50 25	003	39 28	052	21 51	102	27 06	142	48 38	184	46 20	244	37 30	329
31	50 27	001	40 13	051	22 48	102	27 42	142	48 33	185	45 28	244	37 00	328
32	50 28	000	40 58	050	23 44	102	28 17	142	48 28	186	44 36	244	36 29	327
33	50 27	359	41 42	049	24 40	101	28 53	142	48 21	187	43 44	244	35 58	327
34	50 25	357	42 25	048	25 37	101	29 29	142	48 14	188	42 52	244	35 26	326
35	50 22	356	43 08	048	26 34	101	30 04	142	48 06	188	42 00	244	34 53	325
36	50 16	354	43 50	047	27 30	101	30 39	142	47 57	189	41 08	244	34 19	324
37	50 10	353	44 32	046	28 27	101	31 14	143	47 47	190	40 16	245	33 45	323
38	50 02	351	45 13	045	29 24	101	31 49	143	47 37	191	39 24	245	33 10	322
39	49 53	350	45 53	044	30 20	100	32 24	143	47 26	192	38 32	245	32 35	322
40	49 42	349	46 33	043	31 17	100	32 59	143	47 14	192	37 40	245	31 59	321
41	49 30	347	47 12	042	32 14	100	33 33	143	47 01	193	36 48	245	31 22	320
42	49 17	346	47 50	041	33 11	100	34 08	144	46 48	194	35 55	245	30 45	320
43	49 02	345	48 27	040	34 08	100	34 42	144	46 34	194	35 03	245	30 07	319
44	48 46	343	49 03	039	35 04	099	35 16	144	46 19	195	34 11	245	29 29	318
	◆ CAPELLA		BETELGEUSE		SIRIUS		◆ CANOPUS		ACHERNAR		◆ FOMALHAUT		Hamal	
45	20 37	025	40 33	065	36 01	099	35 49	144	46 04	196	33 19	245	48 29	342
46	21 01	024	41 26	064	36 58	099	36 23	145	45 48	197	32 27	245	48 10	341
47	21 25	024	42 17	064	37 55	099	36 56	145	45 31	197	31 34	245	47 50	339
48	21 47	023	43 09	063	38 52	099	37 29	145	45 13	198	30 42	245	47 29	338
49	22 10	022	44 00	062	39 49	099	38 01	146	44 56	198	29 50	245	47 07	337
50	22 31	022	44 51	062	40 46	099	38 34	146	44 37	199	28 58	245	46 44	336
51	22 52	021	45 42	061	41 43	098	39 06	146	44 18	200	28 06	245	46 20	334
52	23 13	020	46 32	060	42 40	098	39 37	147	43 58	200	27 14	245	45 54	333
53	23 32	020	47 22	059	43 37	098	40 09	147	43 38	201	26 22	245	45 28	332
54	23 52	019	48 11	059	44 35	098	40 40	148	43 17	201	25 30	244	45 00	331
55	24 10	018	49 00	058	45 32	098	41 11	148	42 56	202	24 38	244	44 32	330
56	24 28	018	49 49	057	46 29	098	41 41	149	42 34	203	23 46	244	44 02	329
57	24 45	017	50 37	056	47 26	098	42 11	149	42 11	203	22 54	244	43 32	328
58	25 02	016	51 24	055	48 23	097	42 40	149	41 48	204	22 02	244	43 01	327
59	25 17	016	52 11	054	49 20	097	43 09	150	41 25	204	21 10	244	42 28	326
	CAPELLA		BETELGEUSE		◆ SIRIUS		CANOPUS		◆ ACHERNAR		Diphda		◆ Hamal	
60	25 33	015	52 58	053	50 18	097	43 38	150	41 01	205	43 18	260	41 55	325
61	25 47	014	53 43	052	51 15	097	44 06	151	40 37	205	42 21	260	41 22	324
62	26 01	013	54 28	051	52 12	097	44 34	152	40 12	206	41 25	260	40 47	323
63	26 14	013	55 13	050	53 09	097	45 01	152	39 47	206	40 28	260	40 12	322
64	26 26	012	55 56	048	54 07	097	45 28	153	39 22	206	39 31	260	39 36	321
65	26 38	011	56 39	047	55 04	096	45 54	153	38 56	207	38 34	260	38 59	320
66	26 48	010	57 21	046	56 01	096	46 20	154	38 30	207	37 38	259	38 22	319
67	26 58	010	58 02	045	56 59	096	46 45	155	38 03	208	36 41	259	37 44	318
68	27 08	009	58 42	043	57 56	096	47 09	155	37 36	208	35 44	259	37 05	318
69	27 16	008	59 21	042	58 53	096	47 33	156	37 09	208	34 48	259	36 26	317
70	27 24	007	59 58	040	59 51	096	47 57	157	36 41	209	33 51	259	35 46	316
71	27 31	007	60 35	039	60 48	096	48 19	157	36 13	209	32 54	259	35 06	315
72	27 37	006	61 10	037	61 45	096	48 41	158	35 45	209	31 58	259	34 25	314
73	27 43	005	61 44	035	62 43	096	49 02	159	35 16	210	31 01	258	33 43	314
74	27 48	004	62 17	033	63 40	096	49 23	160	34 48	210	30 05	258	33 01	313
	CAPELLA		POLLUX		◆ PROCYON		Suhail		◆ CANOPUS		ACHERNAR		◆ Hamal	
75	27 51	003	30 23	043	45 05	065	31 02	132	49 43	160	34 18	210	32 19	312
76	27 55	003	31 02	042	45 58	064	31 45	132	50 02	161	33 49	211	31 36	312
77	27 57	002	31 40	041	46 49	064	32 29	132	50 20	162	33 20	211	30 53	311
78	27 58	001	32 18	041	47 41	063	33 12	132	50 37	163	32 50	211	30 09	310
79	27 59	000	32 56	040	48 32	062	33 54	132	50 54	164	32 20	211	29 25	310
80	27 59	000	33 32	039	49 23	061	34 37	132	51 10	164	31 50	212	28 40	309
81	27 58	359	34 08	038	50 13	061	35 20	132	51 25	165	31 19	212	27 55	308
82	27 57	358	34 44	038	51 03	060	36 02	133	51 39	166	30 49	212	27 10	308
83	27 54	357	35 19	037	51 53	059	36 45	133	51 52	167	30 18	212	26 24	307
84	27 51	356	35 53	036	52 42	058	37 27	133	52 05	168	29 47	213	25 38	307
85	27 47	356	36 26	035	53 31	057	38 09	133	52 16	169	29 16	213	24 52	306
86	27 42	355	36 59	034	54 19	056	38 51	134	52 27	170	28 44	213	24 05	306
87	27 37	354	37 31	033	55 06	055	39 33	134	52 36	171	28 13	213	23 18	305
88	27 30	353	38 02	032	55 53	054	40 14	134	52 45	172	27 42	213	22 31	305
89	27 23	353	38 33	031	56 39	053	40 56	134	52 52	173	27 10	213	21 43	304

LHA ♈	Hc	Zn	Hc	Zn	Hc	Zn	Hc	Zn	Hc	Zn	Hc	Zn	Hc	Zn
	POLLUX		◆ REGULUS		Suhail		◆ CANOPUS		ACHERNAR		◆ ALDEBARAN		CAPELLA	
90	39 03	031	22 22	070	41 37	135	52 59	174	26 38	213	51 32	327	27 16	352
91	39 32	030	23 16	069	42 18	135	53 05	175	26 06	214	51 00	326	27 07	351
92	40 00	029	24 10	069	42 58	135	53 09	176	25 34	214	50 27	324	26 57	350
93	40 27	028	25 03	068	43 39	136	53 13	177	25 02	214	49 53	323	26 47	349
94	40 53	027	25 57	068	44 19	136	53 16	178	24 30	214	49 17	322	26 36	349
95	41 18	026	26 50	067	44 59	137	53 17	179	23 58	214	48 41	321	26 25	348
96	41 43	025	27 43	067	45 38	137	53 18	180	23 26	214	48 04	320	26 12	347
97	42 06	023	28 36	066	46 17	137	53 17	181	22 53	214	47 27	319	25 59	347
98	42 29	022	29 29	066	46 56	138	53 16	182	22 21	214	46 48	318	25 46	346
99	42 50	021	30 22	065	47 35	138	53 13	183	21 48	214	46 09	317	25 31	345
100	43 11	020	31 14	065	48 13	139	53 10	184	21 16	214	45 29	316	25 16	344
101	43 30	019	32 06	064	48 51	139	53 05	185	20 43	214	44 48	315	25 00	344
102	43 48	018	32 58	064	49 28	140	53 00	186	20 11	214	44 07	314	24 43	343
103	44 06	017	33 50	063	50 05	141	52 53	187	19 38	214	43 25	313	24 26	342
104	44 22	016	34 41	063	50 41	141	52 46	188	19 06	214	42 42	312	24 08	342
	POLLUX		◆ REGULUS		◆ ACRUX		CANOPUS		◆ RIGEL		ALDEBARAN		CAPELLA	
105	44 37	014	35 32	062	17 54	152	52 37	189	63 16	284	41 59	311	23 50	341
106	44 50	013	36 23	061	18 21	152	52 28	190	62 20	283	41 15	310	23 31	340
107	45 03	012	37 13	061	18 48	152	52 18	191	61 23	282	40 31	309	23 11	340
108	45 14	011	38 04	060	19 15	152	52 06	192	60 27	282	39 46	309	22 50	339
109	45 24	010	38 53	060	19 42	152	51 54	193	59 30	281	39 01	308	22 29	338
110	45 33	008	39 43	059	20 09	152	51 41	194	58 34	281	38 15	307	22 07	338
111	45 41	007	40 32	058	20 36	152	51 27	195	57 37	280	37 29	306	21 45	337
112	45 47	006	41 21	057	21 03	152	51 12	195	56 40	280	36 42	306	21 22	336
113	45 53	005	42 09	057	21 30	152	50 56	196	55 43	279	35 55	305	20 59	336
114	45 56	003	42 57	056	21 57	152	50 40	197	54 46	279	35 07	304	20 35	335
115	45 59	002	43 45	055	22 24	152	50 22	198	53 49	278	34 20	304	20 10	335
116	46 00	001	44 32	054	22 50	152	50 04	199	52 52	278	33 31	303	19 45	334
117	46 01	359	45 19	054	23 17	153	49 45	200	51 55	277	32 43	302	19 20	333
118	45 59	358	46 05	053	23 44	153	49 26	200	50 58	277	31 54	302	18 54	333
119	45 57	357	46 50	052	24 10	153	49 05	201	50 00	276	31 05	301	18 27	332
	◆ REGULUS		SPICA		◆ ACRUX		CANOPUS		◆ RIGEL		BETELGEUSE		POLLUX	
120	47 35	051	11 08	099	24 36	153	48 44	202	49 03	276	51 24	305	45 53	356
121	48 20	050	12 05	098	25 03	153	48 22	203	48 06	276	50 36	304	45 48	354
122	49 04	049	13 02	098	25 29	153	48 00	203	47 08	275	49 48	303	45 42	353
123	49 47	048	13 59	098	25 55	153	47 37	204	46 11	275	49 00	302	45 34	352
124	50 29	047	14 57	098	26 21	153	47 13	205	45 13	275	48 11	301	45 25	351
125	51 11	046	15 54	097	26 47	154	46 48	205	44 16	274	47 21	301	45 15	349
126	51 52	045	16 51	097	27 12	154	46 23	206	43 18	274	46 32	300	45 04	348
127	52 32	043	17 48	097	27 38	154	45 58	207	42 21	273	45 41	299	44 52	347
128	53 11	042	18 45	097	28 03	154	45 32	207	41 23	273	44 51	298	44 38	346
129	53 49	041	19 43	096	28 28	154	45 05	208	40 26	273	44 00	298	44 23	345
130	54 26	040	20 40	096	28 53	154	44 38	208	39 28	273	43 09	297	44 07	343
131	55 03	038	21 37	096	29 18	155	44 10	209	38 30	272	42 17	296	43 50	342
132	55 38	037	22 35	096	29 43	155	43 42	209	37 33	272	41 25	296	43 32	341
133	56 12	036	23 32	096	30 07	155	43 14	210	36 35	272	40 33	295	43 13	340
134	56 45	034	24 30	095	30 31	155	42 45	210	35 37	271	39 41	294	42 53	339
	REGULUS		◆ SPICA		ACRUX		◆ CANOPUS		SIRIUS		BETELGEUSE		◆ POLLUX	
135	57 17	033	25 27	095	30 55	156	42 15	211	57 50	264	38 48	294	42 31	338
136	57 47	031	26 24	095	31 19	156	41 45	211	56 53	264	37 55	293	42 09	337
137	58 16	029	27 22	095	31 42	156	41 15	212	55 56	264	37 02	293	41 46	336
138	58 44	028	28 19	094	32 06	156	40 44	212	54 59	264	36 09	292	41 21	335
139	59 10	026	29 17	094	32 29	157	40 13	213	54 01	263	35 15	292	40 56	333
140	59 34	024	30 15	094	32 51	157	39 42	213	53 04	263	34 21	291	40 30	332
141	59 57	022	31 12	094	33 14	157	39 10	214	52 07	263	33 27	291	40 03	331
142	60 18	021	32 10	093	33 36	158	38 38	214	51 09	263	32 33	290	39 35	331
143	60 38	019	33 07	093	33 58	158	38 06	214	50 12	263	31 39	290	39 06	330
144	60 56	017	34 05	093	34 19	158	37 33	215	49 15	263	30 44	289	38 36	329
145	61 11	015	35 02	093	34 41	159	37 01	215	48 18	263	29 50	289	38 06	328
146	61 25	013	36 00	092	35 02	159	36 27	215	47 21	262	28 55	288	37 35	327
147	61 37	011	36 58	092	35 22	159	35 54	216	46 23	262	28 00	288	37 03	326
148	61 47	009	37 55	092	35 43	160	35 20	216	45 26	262	27 05	287	36 30	325
149	61 55	007	38 53	092	36 03	160	34 47	216	44 29	262	26 10	287	35 57	324
	REGULUS		◆ ARCTURUS		SPICA		◆ ACRUX		CANOPUS		SIRIUS		◆ PROCYON	
150	62 01	005	17 52	063	39 51	091	36 22	160	34 13	216	43 32	262	49 25	299
151	62 05	003	18 43	063	40 48	091	36 41	161	33 38	217	42 35	262	48 34	298
152	62 06	001	19 34	062	41 46	091	37 00	161	33 04	217	41 38	262	47 43	297
153	62 06	359	20 25	062	42 44	091	37 19	162	32 29	217	40 41	261	46 52	296
154	62 03	356	21 16	062	43 41	090	37 37	162	31 54	217	39 44	261	46 00	296
155	61 59	354	22 07	061	44 39	090	37 54	162	31 19	217	38 47	261	45 08	295
156	61 52	352	22 57	061	45 37	090	38 11	163	30 44	218	37 50	261	44 15	294
157	61 43	350	23 47	060	46 34	090	38 28	163	30 09	218	36 53	261	43 22	294
158	61 32	348	24 37	060	47 32	089	38 44	164	29 34	218	35 56	261	42 29	293
159	61 20	346	25 27	059	48 30	089	39 00	164	28 58	218	34 59	261	41 36	292
160	61 05	344	26 16	059	49 27	089	39 16	165	28 23	218	34 02	260	40 43	292
161	60 48	342	27 05	058	50 25	088	39 31	165	27 47	218	33 05	260	39 49	291
162	60 30	340	27 54	058	51 23	088	39 45	166	27 11	218	32 08	260	38 55	291
163	60 10	339	28 42	057	52 20	088	39 59	166	26 35	219	31 12	260	38 01	290
164	59 48	337	29 31	056	53 18	087	40 13	167	25 59	219	30 15	260	37 07	290
	Denebola		◆ ARCTURUS		SPICA		◆ ACRUX		SIRIUS		◆ PROCYON		REGULUS	
165	57 07	023	30 19	056	54 15	087	40 26	167	29 18	259	36 12	289	59 24	335
166	57 29	021	31 06	055	55 13	087	40 38	168	28 22	259	35 18	289	58 59	333
167	57 49	019	31 53	055	56 11	086	40 50	168	27 25	259	34 23	288	58 32	332
168	58 07	018	32 40	054	57 08	086	41 01	169	26 28	259	33 28	288	58 04	330
169	58 23	016	33 27	053	58 06	086	41 12	169	25 32	259	32 33	287	57 35	328
170	58 38	014	34 13	053	59 03	085	41 23	170	24 35	259	31 38	287	57 04	327
171	58 51	012	34 58	052	60 01	085	41 32	171	23 39	258	30 43	286	56 31	325
172	59 02	010	35 43	051	60 58	084	41 42	171	22 42	258	29 47	286	55 58	324
173	59 12	008	36 28	051	61 55	084	41 50	172	21 46	258	28 52	285	55 23	322
174	59 19	007	37 12	050	62 53	083	41 58	172	20 49	258	27 56	285	54 48	321
175	59 25	005	37 56	049	63 50	083	42 06	173	19 53	258	27 00	285	54 11	320
176	59 29	003	38 40	048	64 47	082	42 13	173	18 57	257	26 04	284	53 33	319
177	59 31	001	39 22	047	65 44	082	42 19	174	18 00	257	25 08	284	52 55	317
178	59 30	359	40 05	047	66 41	081	42 25	175	17 04	257	24 12	283	52 15	316
179	59 28	357	40 46	046	67 38	081	42 30	175	16 08	257	23 16	283	51 35	315

LHA ♈	Hc	Zn	Hc	Zn	Hc	Zn	Hc	Zn	Hc	Zn	Hc	Zn	Hc	Zn
	ARCTURUS		◆ANTARES		ACRUX		◆Suhail		Alphard		REGULUS		◆Denebola	
180	41 27	045	26 48	112	42 35	176	44 30	224	52 19	276	50 54	314	59 25	355
181	42 08	044	27 42	112	42 38	176	43 50	224	51 21	276	50 12	313	59 19	353
182	42 48	043	28 36	112	42 42	177	43 09	225	50 24	276	49 29	312	59 11	351
183	43 27	042	29 29	112	42 44	178	42 29	225	49 27	275	48 45	311	59 01	350
184	44 05	041	30 23	112	42 47	178	41 48	225	48 29	275	48 01	310	58 50	348
185	44 43	040	31 16	112	42 48	179	41 07	226	47 32	275	47 17	309	58 37	346
186	45 20	039	32 10	112	42 49	179	40 26	226	46 34	274	46 32	308	58 22	344
187	45 56	038	33 04	112	42 49	180	39 44	226	45 37	274	45 46	307	58 05	342
188	46 31	037	33 57	111	42 49	181	39 02	226	44 39	274	44 59	306	57 47	341
189	47 05	036	34 51	111	42 48	181	38 21	227	43 42	273	44 13	305	57 27	339
190	47 39	035	35 45	111	42 46	182	37 38	227	42 44	273	43 25	305	57 05	337
191	48 11	034	36 38	111	42 44	183	36 56	227	41 46	273	42 38	304	56 42	336
192	48 43	033	37 32	111	42 41	183	36 14	227	40 49	272	41 49	303	56 18	334
193	49 13	031	38 26	111	42 37	184	35 31	228	39 51	272	41 01	302	55 52	332
194	49 43	030	39 19	111	42 33	184	34 49	228	38 53	272	40 12	302	55 24	331
	ARCTURUS		◆Rasalhague		ANTARES		◆ACRUX		Suhail		◆REGULUS		Denebola	
195	50 11	029	16 08	071	40 13	111	42 29	185	34 06	228	39 22	301	54 56	329
196	50 39	028	17 02	071	41 07	111	42 23	186	33 23	228	38 33	300	54 26	328
197	51 05	026	17 57	071	42 01	111	42 17	186	32 40	228	37 43	300	53 55	327
198	51 30	025	18 51	070	42 54	111	42 11	187	31 57	228	36 52	299	53 22	325
199	51 53	023	19 45	070	43 48	112	42 04	187	31 14	228	36 02	298	52 49	324
200	52 16	022	20 39	070	44 41	112	41 56	188	30 31	229	35 11	298	52 15	323
201	52 37	021	21 33	069	45 35	112	41 48	189	29 48	229	34 20	297	51 39	321
202	52 56	019	22 27	069	46 29	112	41 39	189	29 04	229	33 28	297	51 03	320
203	53 14	018	23 21	068	47 22	112	41 30	190	28 21	229	32 36	296	50 25	319
204	53 31	016	24 14	068	48 16	112	41 20	190	27 38	229	31 44	295	49 47	318
205	53 47	015	25 08	067	49 09	112	41 09	191	26 54	229	30 52	295	49 08	317
206	54 00	013	26 01	067	50 03	112	40 58	191	26 11	229	30 00	294	48 28	316
207	54 13	011	26 54	066	50 56	112	40 47	192	25 27	229	29 07	294	47 48	315
208	54 23	010	27 47	066	51 49	113	40 35	192	24 44	229	28 14	293	47 06	314
209	54 32	008	28 39	066	52 42	113	40 22	193	24 00	229	27 21	293	46 24	313
	◆ARCTURUS		Rasalhague		◆ANTARES		RIGIL KENT		ACRUX		◆Suhail		REGULUS	
210	54 40	007	29 32	065	53 35	113	44 31	173	40 09	193	23 17	229	26 28	292
211	54 46	005	30 24	065	54 28	113	44 37	174	39 55	194	22 33	229	25 35	292
212	54 50	003	31 16	064	55 21	114	44 43	174	39 41	194	21 50	229	24 41	292
213	54 53	002	32 07	063	56 14	114	44 49	175	39 27	195	21 06	229	23 47	291
214	54 54	000	32 59	063	57 07	114	44 53	176	39 12	195	20 23	229	22 54	291
215	54 53	358	33 50	062	57 59	115	44 57	176	38 56	196	19 39	229	22 00	290
216	54 51	357	34 41	062	58 52	115	45 00	177	38 40	196	18 56	229	21 05	290
217	54 47	355	35 32	061	59 44	115	45 03	178	38 24	197	18 12	229	20 11	290
218	54 41	354	36 22	061	60 36	116	45 05	179	38 07	197	17 29	229	19 17	289
219	54 34	352	37 12	060	61 28	116	45 06	179	37 49	198	16 46	229	18 22	289
220	54 25	350	38 02	059	62 19	117	45 06	180	37 32	198	16 03	229	17 27	288
221	54 15	349	38 51	059	63 11	117	45 06	181	37 13	199	15 19	228	16 33	288
222	54 03	347	39 40	058	64 02	118	45 05	181	36 55	199	14 36	228	15 38	288
223	53 49	346	40 29	057	64 52	119	45 03	182	36 36	199	13 53	228	14 43	287
224	53 34	344	41 17	056	65 43	119	45 01	183	36 17	200	13 10	228	13 48	287
	Alphecca		◆VEGA		ALTAIR		◆Peacock		RIGIL KENT		◆SPICA		ARCTURUS	
225	46 29	011	15 18	041	13 42	076	17 51	145	44 58	183	66 41	279	53 17	343
226	46 40	010	15 55	041	14 38	076	18 24	145	44 54	184	65 44	278	52 59	341
227	46 49	009	16 33	040	15 34	076	18 57	145	44 50	185	64 47	278	52 40	340
228	46 58	008	17 10	040	16 30	075	19 30	145	44 45	185	63 50	277	52 19	338
229	47 05	006	17 46	039	17 26	075	20 03	145	44 39	186	62 52	277	51 57	337
230	47 10	005	18 22	039	18 21	075	20 36	145	44 33	187	61 55	276	51 34	335
231	47 15	004	18 58	038	19 17	074	21 09	145	44 26	187	60 58	276	51 09	334
232	47 18	002	19 33	037	20 12	074	21 41	145	44 18	188	60 00	275	50 43	333
233	47 20	001	20 08	037	21 08	074	22 14	145	44 10	189	59 03	275	50 16	331
234	47 20	000	20 43	036	22 03	073	22 47	145	44 01	189	58 05	274	49 48	330
235	47 19	358	21 17	036	22 58	073	23 20	145	43 51	190	57 08	274	49 19	329
236	47 17	357	21 50	035	23 53	072	23 53	145	43 41	191	56 10	274	48 48	328
237	47 13	356	22 23	035	24 48	072	24 25	146	43 30	191	55 13	273	48 17	326
238	47 09	355	22 56	034	25 43	072	24 58	146	43 18	192	54 15	273	47 45	325
239	47 02	353	23 28	033	26 38	071	25 30	146	43 06	192	53 17	273	47 11	324
	◆VEGA		ALTAIR		◆Peacock		RIGIL KENT		◆SPICA		ARCTURUS		Alphecca	
240	23 59	033	27 32	071	26 03	146	42 54	193	52 20	272	46 37	323	46 55	352
241	24 30	032	28 26	070	26 35	146	42 40	194	51 22	272	46 02	322	46 46	351
242	25 00	031	29 21	070	27 07	146	42 26	194	50 25	272	45 26	321	46 36	349
243	25 30	031	30 15	069	27 40	146	42 12	195	49 27	271	44 49	320	46 25	348
244	26 00	030	31 08	069	28 12	146	41 57	195	48 29	271	44 12	319	46 12	347
245	26 28	029	32 02	068	28 43	147	41 42	196	47 32	271	43 33	318	45 59	346
246	26 56	029	32 56	068	29 15	147	41 25	196	46 34	270	42 54	317	45 44	344
247	27 24	028	33 49	067	29 47	147	41 09	197	45 36	270	42 15	316	45 27	343
248	27 50	027	34 42	067	30 18	147	40 52	197	44 39	270	41 34	315	45 10	342
249	28 17	027	35 35	066	30 49	147	40 34	198	43 41	270	40 53	314	44 52	341
250	28 42	026	36 28	066	31 21	147	40 16	198	42 43	269	40 12	313	44 32	340
251	29 07	025	37 20	065	31 51	148	39 58	199	41 46	269	39 30	313	44 11	338
252	29 31	024	38 12	064	32 22	148	39 39	199	40 48	269	38 47	312	43 50	337
253	29 54	024	39 04	064	32 53	148	39 19	200	39 50	269	38 04	311	43 27	336
254	30 17	023	39 56	063	33 23	148	38 59	200	38 53	268	37 20	310	43 03	335
	◆VEGA		ALTAIR		◆Peacock		RIGIL KENT		◆SPICA		ARCTURUS		Alphecca	
255	30 39	022	40 47	063	33 53	149	38 39	201	37 55	268	36 36	310	42 38	334
256	31 00	021	41 38	062	34 23	149	38 18	201	36 57	268	35 51	309	42 12	333
257	31 20	020	42 29	061	34 52	149	37 57	202	36 00	268	35 06	308	41 46	332
258	31 40	019	43 19	061	35 22	150	37 36	202	35 02	267	34 20	307	41 18	331
259	31 59	019	44 09	060	35 51	150	37 14	203	34 04	267	33 35	307	40 50	330
260	32 17	018	44 59	059	36 20	150	36 51	203	33 07	267	32 48	306	40 20	329
261	32 34	017	45 48	058	36 48	151	36 29	203	32 09	267	32 01	306	39 50	328
262	32 51	016	46 37	057	37 16	151	36 06	204	31 12	266	31 14	305	39 19	327
263	33 06	015	47 25	057	37 44	151	35 43	204	30 14	266	30 27	304	38 47	326
264	33 21	014	48 13	056	38 12	152	35 19	204	29 17	266	29 39	304	38 14	325
265	33 35	013	49 01	055	38 39	152	34 55	205	28 19	266	28 51	303	37 41	324
266	33 48	013	49 48	054	39 06	153	34 31	205	27 22	265	28 02	303	37 07	323
267	34 00	012	50 34	053	39 32	153	34 06	205	26 24	265	27 14	302	36 32	323
268	34 11	011	51 20	052	39 58	153	33 41	206	25 27	265	26 25	302	35 57	322
269	34 21	010	52 05	051	40 24	154	33 16	206	24 29	265	25 35	301	35 21	321

LAT 16°S

LHA ♈	Hc	Zn	Hc	Zn	Hc	Zn	Hc	Zn	Hc	Zn	Hc	Zn	Hc	Zn
	◆VEGA		ALTAIR		◆FOMALHAUT		Peacock		RIGIL KENT		◆ANTARES		Alphecca	
270	34 30	009	52 49	050	20 58	116	40 49	154	32 51	206	66 41	240	34 44	320
271	34 39	008	53 33	049	21 49	116	41 14	155	32 25	207	65 51	240	34 07	319
272	34 46	007	54 16	048	22 41	116	41 38	155	31 59	207	65 01	241	33 29	319
273	34 53	006	54 58	046	23 33	116	42 02	156	31 33	207	64 10	242	32 50	318
274	34 58	005	55 40	045	24 25	116	42 25	156	31 07	207	63 19	242	32 11	317
275	35 03	004	56 20	044	25 17	116	42 48	157	30 40	208	62 28	243	31 32	316
276	35 07	003	56 59	043	26 09	116	43 11	157	30 13	208	61 36	244	30 52	316
277	35 09	002	57 38	041	27 01	115	43 33	158	29 46	208	60 44	244	30 11	315
278	35 11	001	58 15	040	27 53	115	43 54	159	29 19	208	59 52	245	29 30	314
279	35 12	000	58 52	038	28 46	115	44 15	159	28 52	208	59 00	245	28 49	314
280	35 12	359	59 27	037	29 38	115	44 35	160	28 24	209	58 08	245	28 07	313
281	35 11	358	60 00	035	30 30	115	44 55	160	27 57	209	57 15	246	27 24	312
282	35 09	357	60 33	033	31 22	115	45 14	161	27 29	209	56 23	246	26 42	312
283	35 06	357	61 04	032	32 14	115	45 32	162	27 01	209	55 30	246	25 58	311
284	35 02	356	61 33	030	33 06	115	45 50	162	26 33	209	54 37	247	25 15	311
	DENEB		◆FOMALHAUT		Peacock		RIGIL KENT		◆ANTARES		Rasalhague		◆VEGA	
285	24 27	019	33 59	115	46 08	163	26 05	209	53 44	247	54 38	323	34 57	355
286	24 46	019	34 51	115	46 24	164	25 36	209	52 51	247	54 03	321	34 51	354
287	25 04	018	35 43	115	46 40	164	25 08	210	51 58	247	53 26	320	34 44	353
288	25 22	017	36 35	115	46 55	165	24 39	210	51 05	247	52 49	319	34 36	352
289	25 38	017	37 27	115	47 10	166	24 11	210	50 11	248	52 10	318	34 28	351
290	25 55	016	38 20	115	47 24	167	23 42	210	49 18	248	51 31	316	34 18	350
291	26 10	015	39 12	115	47 37	167	23 13	210	48 25	248	50 51	315	34 08	349
292	26 25	014	40 04	115	47 49	168	22 44	210	47 31	248	50 10	314	33 56	348
293	26 39	014	40 56	115	48 01	169	22 15	210	46 37	248	49 28	313	33 44	347
294	26 52	013	41 48	116	48 11	170	21 46	210	45 44	248	48 46	312	33 31	346
295	27 05	012	42 40	116	48 22	170	21 17	210	44 50	248	48 02	311	33 17	345
296	27 16	011	43 32	116	48 31	171	20 48	210	43 57	248	47 19	310	33 02	345
297	27 27	011	44 24	116	48 39	172	20 19	210	43 03	248	46 34	309	32 46	344
298	27 38	010	45 16	116	48 47	173	19 50	210	42 09	249	45 49	308	32 29	343
299	27 47	009	46 07	116	48 54	174	19 21	210	41 16	249	45 04	307	32 12	342
	◆DENEB		Alpheratz		◆FOMALHAUT		Peacock		◆ANTARES		Rasalhague		VEGA	
300	27 56	008	14 50	053	46 59	116	49 00	174	40 22	249	44 18	307	31 54	341
301	28 04	008	15 36	053	47 51	117	49 05	175	39 28	249	43 31	306	31 35	340
302	28 11	007	16 21	052	48 42	117	49 09	176	38 35	249	42 44	305	31 15	339
303	28 17	006	17 07	052	49 34	117	49 13	177	37 41	249	41 56	304	30 54	339
304	28 23	005	17 52	051	50 25	117	49 16	178	36 47	249	41 08	303	30 33	338
305	28 28	004	18 37	051	51 16	118	49 18	179	35 53	249	40 20	303	30 11	337
306	28 32	004	19 21	050	52 07	118	49 19	179	35 00	249	39 31	302	29 48	336
307	28 35	003	20 06	050	52 58	118	49 19	180	34 06	249	38 42	301	29 24	335
308	28 37	002	20 50	049	53 49	118	49 18	181	33 12	249	37 53	301	29 00	335
309	28 39	001	21 33	049	54 40	119	49 17	182	32 19	248	37 03	300	28 35	334
310	28 40	000	22 16	048	55 30	119	49 14	183	31 25	248	36 13	299	28 09	333
311	28 40	000	22 59	048	56 20	120	49 11	184	30 31	248	35 22	299	27 43	332
312	28 39	359	23 42	047	57 10	120	49 07	184	29 38	248	34 32	298	27 16	332
313	28 37	358	24 24	047	58 00	121	49 02	185	28 44	248	33 41	298	26 49	331
314	28 35	357	25 06	046	58 50	121	48 56	186	27 51	248	32 49	297	26 20	330
	Alpheratz		◆Diphda		ACHERNAR		Peacock		◆ANTARES		VEGA		◆DENEB	
315	25 47	045	36 31	101	24 26	146	48 50	187	26 57	248	25 51	330	28 32	356
316	26 28	045	37 28	101	24 58	146	48 43	188	26 04	248	25 22	329	28 28	356
317	27 08	044	38 25	100	25 30	146	48 34	189	25 10	248	24 52	328	28 23	355
318	27 48	044	39 21	100	26 02	146	48 25	189	24 17	248	24 22	328	28 17	354
319	28 28	043	40 18	100	26 34	146	48 16	190	23 24	248	23 51	327	28 11	353
320	29 07	042	41 15	100	27 06	147	48 05	191	22 30	247	23 19	326	28 04	352
321	29 45	042	42 12	100	27 37	147	47 54	192	21 37	247	22 47	326	27 56	352
322	30 23	041	43 09	100	28 09	147	47 42	192	20 44	247	22 14	325	27 47	351
323	31 01	040	44 05	100	28 40	147	47 29	193	19 51	247	21 41	325	27 37	350
324	31 38	039	45 02	100	29 12	147	47 16	194	18 58	247	21 07	324	27 27	349
325	32 14	039	45 59	099	29 43	147	47 01	195	18 05	247	20 33	323	27 16	349
326	32 50	038	46 56	099	30 14	148	46 46	195	17 12	247	19 59	323	27 04	348
327	33 25	037	47 53	099	30 44	148	46 31	196	16 19	246	19 24	322	26 52	347
328	34 00	036	48 50	099	31 15	148	46 14	197	15 26	246	18 48	322	26 38	346
329	34 33	036	49 47	099	31 45	148	45 57	197	14 33	246	18 12	321	26 24	346
	◆Alpheratz		Diphda		◆ACHERNAR		Peacock		◆Nunki		ALTAIR		DENEB	
330	35 07	035	50 44	099	32 16	148	45 40	198	46 10	249	49 36	306	26 10	345
331	35 39	034	51 41	099	32 46	149	45 22	199	45 16	249	48 49	305	25 54	344
332	36 11	033	52 38	099	33 16	149	45 03	199	44 22	249	48 02	304	25 38	343
333	36 42	032	53 35	099	33 45	149	44 43	200	43 29	249	47 14	303	25 21	343
334	37 12	031	54 32	099	34 15	150	44 23	201	42 35	249	46 25	302	25 04	342
335	37 42	030	55 29	098	34 44	150	44 03	201	41 41	249	45 36	302	24 45	341
336	38 11	029	56 26	098	35 12	150	43 42	202	40 47	249	44 47	301	24 27	341
337	38 39	029	57 23	098	35 41	150	43 20	202	39 53	249	43 57	300	24 07	340
338	39 06	028	58 20	098	36 09	151	42 58	203	39 00	249	43 07	299	23 47	339
339	39 32	027	59 17	098	36 37	151	42 35	203	38 06	249	42 17	299	23 26	339
340	39 58	026	60 14	098	37 05	152	42 12	204	37 12	249	41 26	298	23 05	338
341	40 22	025	61 11	098	37 32	152	41 48	205	36 18	249	40 35	297	22 43	337
342	40 46	024	62 08	098	37 59	152	41 24	205	35 25	249	39 43	297	22 20	337
343	41 08	023	63 06	098	38 26	153	40 59	206	34 31	249	38 52	296	21 57	336
344	41 30	021	64 03	098	38 52	153	40 34	206	33 37	249	38 00	295	21 33	335
	Alpheratz		◆Hamal		◆ACHERNAR		Peacock		Nunki		◆ALTAIR		DENEB	
345	41 50	020	29 24	050	39 18	153	40 09	206	32 43	249	37 07	295	21 09	335
346	42 10	019	30 08	050	39 44	154	39 43	207	31 49	249	36 15	294	20 44	334
347	42 28	018	30 52	049	40 09	154	39 16	207	30 56	249	35 22	294	20 18	334
348	42 46	017	31 35	048	40 34	155	38 50	208	30 02	249	34 29	293	19 52	333
349	43 02	016	32 18	048	40 58	155	38 23	208	29 08	248	33 36	293	19 26	332
350	43 18	015	33 01	047	41 22	156	37 55	209	28 15	248	32 43	292	18 59	332
351	43 32	014	33 43	046	41 45	156	37 28	209	27 21	248	31 49	292	18 31	331
352	43 45	012	34 24	046	42 08	157	37 00	209	26 28	248	30 55	291	18 03	331
353	43 57	011	35 05	045	42 31	157	36 31	210	25 34	248	30 01	291	17 35	330
354	44 07	010	35 46	044	42 53	158	36 03	210	24 41	248	29 07	290	17 06	330
355	44 17	009	36 25	043	43 14	158	35 34	210	23 47	248	28 13	290	16 36	329
356	44 25	008	37 05	042	43 35	159	35 05	211	22 54	248	27 19	289	16 07	329
357	44 32	006	37 43	042	43 55	160	34 35	211	22 00	248	26 24	289	15 36	328
358	44 38	005	38 21	041	44 15	160	34 05	211	21 07	247	25 30	288	15 05	328
359	44 43	004	38 59	040	44 34	161	33 35	211	20 14	247	24 35	288	14 34	327

LHA ♈	Hc Zn	Hc Zn	Hc Zn	Hc Zn	Hc Zn	Hc Zn	Hc Zn
	◆ Alpheratz	Hamal	ALDEBARAN	◆ RIGEL	ACHERNAR	◆ Peacock	Enif
0	43 46 003	38 49 039	14 02 067	13 01 095	45 50 161	33 56 212	47 06 306
1	43 49 002	39 24 038	14 55 067	13 58 094	46 08 162	33 26 212	46 19 306
2	43 50 000	39 59 037	15 47 067	14 55 094	46 26 162	32 55 213	45 33 305
3	43 49 359	40 33 036	16 40 066	15 53 094	46 43 163	32 24 213	44 45 304
4	43 48 358	41 06 035	17 32 066	16 50 094	46 59 164	31 53 213	43 57 303
5	43 45 357	41 38 034	18 25 065	17 47 093	47 15 164	31 21 213	43 09 302
6	43 41 356	42 10 033	19 17 065	18 44 093	47 30 165	30 50 213	42 20 302
7	43 36 354	42 41 032	20 09 065	19 42 093	47 44 166	30 18 214	41 31 301
8	43 30 353	43 10 031	21 00 064	20 39 093	47 58 167	29 47 214	40 42 300
9	43 22 352	43 39 030	21 52 064	21 36 092	48 11 167	29 15 214	39 52 299
10	43 14 351	44 07 029	22 43 063	22 34 092	48 23 168	28 43 214	39 02 299
11	43 04 350	44 34 027	23 34 063	23 31 092	48 34 169	28 10 214	38 11 298
12	42 53 348	45 00 026	24 25 062	24 28 091	48 45 170	27 38 214	37 20 297
13	42 41 347	45 25 025	25 16 062	25 26 091	48 55 170	27 06 214	36 29 297
14	42 28 346	45 49 024	26 06 061	26 23 091	49 04 171	26 33 215	35 38 296
	◆ Hamal	ALDEBARAN	RIGEL	◆ CANOPUS	ACHERNAR	◆ FOMALHAUT	Alpheratz
15	46 12 023	26 57 061	27 21 091	18 49 141	49 12 172	59 32 240	42 13 345
16	46 33 022	27 46 060	28 18 090	19 25 141	49 20 173	58 42 241	41 58 344
17	46 54 020	28 36 060	29 15 090	20 02 141	49 26 174	57 52 241	41 41 343
18	47 13 019	29 25 059	30 13 090	20 38 141	49 32 175	57 01 242	41 24 342
19	47 31 018	30 14 058	31 10 089	21 14 141	49 37 175	56 11 242	41 05 341
20	47 48 016	31 03 058	32 07 089	21 51 141	49 42 176	55 20 242	40 46 339
21	48 04 015	31 52 057	33 05 089	22 27 141	49 45 177	54 29 243	40 25 338
22	48 18 014	32 40 057	34 02 088	23 03 141	49 48 178	53 38 243	40 04 337
23	48 31 013	33 28 056	35 00 088	23 40 141	49 49 179	52 47 243	39 41 336
24	48 43 011	34 15 055	35 57 088	24 16 141	49 50 180	51 56 244	39 17 335
25	48 54 010	35 02 055	36 54 088	24 52 141	49 50 180	51 04 244	38 53 334
26	49 03 008	35 49 054	37 52 087	25 28 141	49 49 181	50 13 244	38 28 333
27	49 10 007	36 35 053	38 49 087	26 05 141	49 48 182	49 21 244	38 02 332
28	49 17 006	37 21 053	39 46 087	26 41 141	49 45 183	48 29 244	37 35 331
29	49 22 004	38 06 052	40 43 086	27 17 141	49 42 184	47 38 245	37 07 331
	◆ Hamal	ALDEBARAN	◆ SIRIUS	CANOPUS	ACHERNAR	◆ FOMALHAUT	Alpheratz
30	49 25 003	38 51 051	22 03 102	27 53 141	49 38 185	46 46 245	36 38 330
31	49 27 001	39 35 050	23 00 101	28 29 141	49 33 185	45 54 245	36 09 329
32	49 28 000	40 19 049	23 56 101	29 05 141	49 27 186	45 02 245	35 39 328
33	49 27 359	41 02 049	24 52 101	29 40 142	49 21 187	44 10 245	35 08 327
34	49 25 357	41 45 048	25 48 101	30 16 142	49 13 188	43 18 245	34 36 326
35	49 22 356	42 27 047	26 45 101	30 51 142	49 05 189	42 26 245	34 04 325
36	49 17 354	43 09 046	27 41 100	31 27 142	48 56 189	41 34 245	33 31 324
37	49 10 353	43 50 045	28 38 100	32 02 142	48 46 190	40 42 245	32 57 324
38	49 03 352	44 30 044	29 34 100	32 37 142	48 36 191	39 49 245	32 23 323
39	48 54 350	45 10 043	30 31 100	33 12 143	48 24 192	38 57 245	31 48 322
40	48 43 349	45 49 042	31 27 100	33 47 143	48 12 193	38 05 245	31 12 321
41	48 32 348	46 27 041	32 24 099	34 21 143	48 00 193	37 13 245	30 36 321
42	48 18 346	47 04 040	33 21 099	34 56 143	47 46 194	36 21 245	29 59 320
43	48 04 345	47 41 039	34 17 099	35 30 143	47 32 195	35 28 245	29 22 319
44	47 48 344	48 16 038	35 14 099	36 04 144	47 17 195	34 36 245	28 44 319
	◆ CAPELLA	BETELGEUSE	SIRIUS	◆ CANOPUS	ACHERNAR	◆ FOMALHAUT	Hamal
45	19 43 025	40 08 064	36 11 099	36 38 144	47 01 196	33 44 245	47 32 342
46	20 07 024	40 59 064	37 07 098	37 12 144	46 45 197	32 52 245	47 13 341
47	20 30 023	41 51 063	38 04 098	37 45 145	46 28 197	32 00 245	46 54 340
48	20 52 023	42 41 062	39 01 098	38 18 145	46 11 198	31 08 245	46 34 338
49	21 14 022	43 32 062	39 58 098	38 51 145	45 52 199	30 15 245	46 12 337
50	21 35 022	44 22 061	40 55 098	39 23 146	45 34 199	29 23 245	45 49 336
51	21 56 021	45 12 060	41 52 097	39 56 146	45 14 200	28 31 245	45 25 335
52	22 16 020	46 02 059	42 48 097	40 28 146	44 54 201	27 39 245	45 00 334
53	22 36 020	46 51 058	43 45 097	40 59 147	44 34 201	26 47 245	44 34 333
54	22 55 019	47 40 058	44 42 097	41 30 147	44 13 202	25 55 245	44 07 331
55	23 13 018	48 28 057	45 39 097	42 01 148	43 51 202	25 03 245	43 40 330
56	23 31 018	49 16 056	46 36 097	42 32 148	43 29 203	24 11 245	43 11 329
57	23 48 017	50 03 055	47 33 096	43 02 149	43 06 203	23 20 245	42 41 328
58	24 04 016	50 49 054	48 30 096	43 32 149	42 43 204	22 28 244	42 10 327
59	24 20 015	51 35 053	49 27 096	44 01 149	42 20 205	21 36 244	41 39 326
	CAPELLA	BETELGEUSE	◆ SIRIUS	CANOPUS	◆ ACHERNAR	Diphda	◆ Hamal
60	24 35 015	52 21 052	50 24 096	44 30 150	41 56 205	43 28 261	41 06 325
61	24 49 014	53 06 051	51 21 096	44 59 151	41 31 205	42 31 261	40 33 324
62	25 02 013	53 50 050	52 19 096	45 27 151	41 06 206	41 35 261	39 59 323
63	25 15 013	54 33 049	53 16 095	45 54 152	40 41 206	40 38 261	39 25 322
64	25 27 012	55 16 047	54 13 095	46 21 152	40 15 207	39 41 261	38 49 321
65	25 39 011	55 58 046	55 10 095	46 48 153	39 49 207	38 45 260	38 13 321
66	25 49 010	56 39 045	56 07 095	47 14 153	39 23 208	37 48 260	37 36 320
67	25 59 010	57 19 043	57 04 095	47 39 154	38 56 208	36 52 260	36 59 319
68	26 08 009	57 57 042	58 02 095	48 04 155	38 29 208	35 55 260	36 21 318
69	26 17 008	58 35 041	58 59 094	48 28 155	38 01 209	34 59 260	35 42 317
70	26 25 007	59 12 039	59 56 094	48 51 156	37 33 209	34 02 260	35 03 316
71	26 32 007	59 48 038	60 53 094	49 14 157	37 05 210	33 06 259	34 23 316
72	26 38 006	60 22 036	61 50 094	49 37 158	36 37 210	32 09 259	33 42 315
73	26 43 005	60 55 034	62 48 094	49 58 158	36 08 210	31 13 259	33 02 314
74	26 48 004	61 26 032	63 45 093	50 19 159	35 39 210	30 17 259	32 20 313
	CAPELLA	POLLUX	◆ PROCYON	Suhail	◆ CANOPUS	ACHERNAR	◆ Hamal
75	26 52 003	29 39 042	44 40 064	31 42 131	50 39 160	35 10 211	31 38 313
76	26 55 003	30 17 042	45 31 063	32 25 131	50 58 161	34 41 211	30 56 312
77	26 57 002	30 55 041	46 22 063	33 08 131	51 17 162	34 11 211	30 13 311
78	26 58 001	31 33 040	47 13 062	33 51 131	51 35 162	33 41 212	29 30 311
79	26 59 000	32 09 039	48 04 061	34 34 132	51 52 163	33 11 212	28 46 310
80	26 59 000	32 46 039	48 54 060	35 17 132	52 08 164	32 41 212	28 02 309
81	26 58 359	33 21 038	49 43 060	36 00 132	52 23 165	32 10 212	27 18 309
82	26 57 358	33 56 037	50 33 059	36 43 132	52 37 166	31 39 212	26 33 308
83	26 54 357	34 30 036	51 21 058	37 25 132	52 51 167	31 08 213	25 48 308
84	26 51 356	35 04 035	52 10 057	38 08 132	53 03 168	30 37 213	25 02 307
85	26 47 356	35 37 035	52 57 056	38 50 133	53 15 169	30 06 213	24 16 307
86	26 43 355	36 09 034	53 45 055	39 32 133	53 26 170	29 35 213	23 30 306
87	26 37 354	36 41 033	54 31 054	40 14 133	53 35 171	29 03 213	22 43 305
88	26 31 353	37 12 032	55 17 053	40 56 133	53 44 172	28 32 214	21 56 305
89	26 24 353	37 42 031	56 02 051	41 37 134	53 52 173	28 00 214	21 09 304

LHA ♈	Hc Zn	Hc Zn	Hc Zn	Hc Zn	Hc Zn	Hc Zn	Hc Zn
	POLLUX	◆ REGULUS	Suhail	◆ CANOPUS	ACHERNAR	◆ ALDEBARAN	CAPELLA
90	38 11 030	22 01 069	42 19 134	53 59 174	27 28 214	50 41 327	26 16 352
91	38 39 029	22 54 069	43 00 134	54 04 175	26 56 214	50 10 326	26 08 351
92	39 07 028	23 48 068	43 41 135	54 09 176	26 24 214	49 38 325	25 58 350
93	39 34 027	24 41 068	44 21 135	54 13 177	25 52 214	49 04 324	25 48 350
94	39 59 026	25 34 067	45 02 135	54 16 178	25 20 214	48 30 323	25 38 349
95	40 24 025	26 27 067	45 42 136	54 17 179	24 48 214	47 55 321	25 26 348
96	40 48 024	27 20 066	46 22 136	54 18 180	24 15 214	47 19 320	25 14 347
97	41 11 023	28 12 066	47 01 137	54 17 181	23 43 214	46 42 319	25 01 347
98	41 33 022	29 04 065	47 40 137	54 16 182	23 10 214	46 04 318	24 47 346
99	41 54 021	29 56 065	48 19 138	54 13 183	22 38 214	45 25 317	24 33 345
100	42 14 020	30 48 064	48 58 138	54 10 184	22 05 215	44 46 316	24 18 344
101	42 33 019	31 40 064	49 36 139	54 05 185	21 33 215	44 06 315	24 02 344
102	42 51 018	32 31 063	50 14 139	54 00 186	21 00 215	43 25 314	23 46 343
103	43 08 016	33 22 063	50 51 140	53 53 187	20 28 215	42 44 313	23 29 342
104	43 24 015	34 13 062	51 27 140	53 45 188	19 55 215	42 02 313	23 11 342
	POLLUX	◆ REGULUS	◆ ACRUX	CANOPUS	◆ RIGEL	ALDEBARAN	CAPELLA
105	43 38 014	35 04 061	18 47 152	53 37 189	63 00 286	41 19 312	22 53 341
106	43 52 013	35 54 061	19 14 152	53 27 190	62 05 285	40 36 311	22 34 340
107	44 04 012	36 44 060	19 41 152	53 17 191	61 09 284	39 52 310	22 14 340
108	44 15 011	37 33 060	20 08 152	53 05 192	60 14 284	39 08 309	21 54 339
109	44 25 009	38 23 059	20 35 152	52 53 193	59 18 283	38 24 308	21 33 338
110	44 34 008	39 12 058	21 02 152	52 39 194	58 22 282	37 38 308	21 12 338
111	44 41 007	40 00 057	21 29 152	52 25 195	57 26 282	36 53 307	20 50 337
112	44 48 006	40 48 057	21 56 152	52 10 196	56 30 281	36 07 306	20 27 336
113	44 53 004	41 36 056	22 23 152	51 54 197	55 33 281	35 20 306	20 04 336
114	44 57 003	42 24 055	22 50 152	51 37 197	54 37 280	34 33 305	19 40 335
115	44 59 002	43 10 054	23 17 152	51 20 198	53 40 279	33 46 304	19 16 335
116	45 00 001	43 57 054	23 44 152	51 01 199	52 44 279	32 59 304	18 51 334
117	45 01 359	44 43 053	24 10 152	50 42 200	51 47 278	32 11 303	18 26 334
118	44 59 358	45 28 052	24 37 152	50 22 201	50 50 278	31 22 302	18 00 333
119	44 57 357	46 13 051	25 03 153	50 01 202	49 53 278	30 34 302	17 34 332
	◆ REGULUS	SPICA	◆ ACRUX	CANOPUS	◆ RIGEL	BETELGEUSE	POLLUX
120	46 57 050	11 17 098	25 30 153	49 40 202	48 56 277	50 49 306	44 53 356
121	47 41 049	12 14 098	25 56 153	49 18 203	47 59 277	50 02 305	44 48 354
122	48 24 048	13 11 098	26 22 153	48 55 204	47 02 276	49 15 304	44 42 353
123	49 06 047	14 08 098	26 48 153	48 31 204	46 05 276	48 27 303	44 35 352
124	49 48 046	15 04 097	27 14 153	48 07 205	45 08 276	47 39 302	44 26 351
125	50 29 045	16 01 097	27 40 153	47 43 206	44 11 275	46 51 302	44 16 350
126	51 09 044	16 58 097	28 06 153	47 17 206	43 14 275	46 01 301	44 05 348
127	51 48 043	17 55 097	28 32 154	46 51 207	42 17 274	45 12 300	43 53 347
128	52 26 041	18 52 096	28 57 154	46 25 208	41 19 274	44 22 299	43 40 346
129	53 04 040	19 49 096	29 22 154	45 58 208	40 22 274	43 32 298	43 26 345
130	53 40 039	20 46 096	29 47 154	45 31 209	39 25 273	42 41 298	43 10 344
131	54 15 037	21 43 096	30 12 154	45 03 209	38 28 273	41 50 297	42 53 343
132	54 50 036	22 41 095	30 37 155	44 34 210	37 30 273	40 59 296	42 35 341
133	55 23 035	23 38 095	31 01 155	44 05 210	36 33 272	40 07 296	42 17 340
134	55 55 033	24 35 095	31 26 155	43 36 211	35 36 272	39 16 295	41 57 339
	REGULUS	◆ SPICA	ACRUX	◆ CANOPUS	SIRIUS	BETELGEUSE	◆ POLLUX
135	56 26 032	25 32 095	31 50 155	43 06 211	57 56 265	38 23 294	41 36 338
136	56 55 030	26 29 094	32 14 156	42 36 212	56 59 265	37 31 294	41 14 337
137	57 24 029	27 26 094	32 37 156	42 06 212	56 02 265	36 38 293	40 51 336
138	57 50 027	28 24 094	33 01 156	41 35 213	55 05 265	35 46 293	40 27 335
139	58 16 025	29 21 094	33 24 156	41 04 213	54 07 265	34 53 292	40 02 334
140	58 39 024	30 18 093	33 46 157	40 32 214	53 10 265	33 59 292	39 37 333
141	59 02 022	31 16 093	34 09 157	40 00 214	52 13 264	33 06 291	39 10 332
142	59 22 020	32 13 093	34 31 157	39 28 214	51 16 264	32 12 291	38 42 331
143	59 41 018	33 10 093	34 53 158	38 55 215	50 19 264	31 19 290	38 14 330
144	59 58 016	34 08 092	35 15 158	38 23 215	49 22 264	30 25 290	37 45 329
145	60 13 014	35 05 092	35 37 158	37 50 215	48 25 264	29 30 289	37 15 328
146	60 27 013	36 02 092	35 58 159	37 16 216	47 28 264	28 36 289	36 44 327
147	60 38 011	37 00 091	36 18 159	36 43 216	46 31 263	27 42 288	36 13 326
148	60 48 009	37 57 091	36 39 159	36 09 216	45 34 263	26 47 288	35 41 325
149	60 55 007	38 54 091	36 59 160	35 35 216	44 37 263	25 52 287	35 08 325
	REGULUS	◆ ARCTURUS	SPICA	◆ ACRUX	CANOPUS	SIRIUS	◆ PROCYON
150	61 01 005	17 25 063	39 52 091	37 19 160	35 01 217	43 40 263	48 56 300
151	61 05 003	18 16 063	40 49 090	37 38 161	34 26 217	42 43 263	48 06 299
152	61 06 001	19 06 062	41 46 090	37 57 161	33 52 217	41 46 262	47 15 298
153	61 06 359	19 57 062	42 44 090	38 15 161	33 17 217	40 49 262	46 25 297
154	61 03 357	20 47 061	43 41 089	38 34 162	32 42 218	39 52 262	45 33 297
155	60 59 355	21 38 061	44 39 089	38 51 162	32 07 218	38 56 262	44 42 296
156	60 53 353	22 27 060	45 36 089	39 09 163	31 32 218	37 59 262	43 50 295
157	60 44 351	23 17 060	46 33 088	39 26 163	30 56 218	37 02 262	42 58 294
158	60 34 349	24 07 059	47 31 088	39 42 164	30 21 218	36 05 261	42 06 294
159	60 21 347	24 56 059	48 28 088	39 58 164	29 45 218	35 09 261	41 13 293
160	60 07 345	25 45 058	49 25 087	40 14 165	29 10 219	34 12 261	40 20 293
161	59 51 343	26 33 058	50 23 087	40 29 165	28 34 219	33 15 261	39 27 292
162	59 33 341	27 22 057	51 20 087	40 43 166	27 58 219	32 19 261	38 34 291
163	59 14 339	28 10 057	52 17 086	40 57 166	27 22 219	31 22 260	37 40 291
164	58 53 337	28 57 056	53 14 086	41 11 167	26 46 219	30 25 260	36 46 290
	Denebola	◆ ARCTURUS	SPICA	◆ ACRUX	SIRIUS	◆ PROCYON	REGULUS
165	56 12 022	29 45 055	54 12 086	41 24 167	29 29 260	35 53 290	58 30 336
166	56 33 020	30 32 055	55 09 085	41 37 168	28 32 260	34 58 289	58 05 334
167	56 52 019	31 18 054	56 06 085	41 49 168	27 36 260	34 04 289	57 39 332
168	57 09 017	32 05 053	57 03 084	42 00 169	26 40 259	33 10 288	57 12 331
169	57 25 015	32 50 053	58 00 084	42 11 169	25 43 259	32 15 288	56 43 329
170	57 40 014	33 36 052	58 57 084	42 22 170	24 47 259	31 20 287	56 13 328
171	57 52 012	34 21 051	59 54 083	42 32 170	23 50 259	30 26 287	55 42 326
172	58 03 010	35 06 051	60 51 083	42 41 171	22 54 259	29 31 286	55 09 325
173	58 12 008	35 50 050	61 48 082	42 50 172	21 58 258	28 36 286	54 36 323
174	58 20 006	36 34 049	62 45 081	42 58 172	21 02 258	27 40 285	54 01 322
175	58 25 005	37 17 048	63 42 081	43 05 173	20 06 258	26 45 285	53 25 321
176	58 29 003	37 59 048	64 38 080	43 12 173	19 10 258	25 49 285	52 48 319
177	58 31 001	38 42 047	65 35 080	43 19 174	18 14 258	24 54 284	52 10 318
178	58 30 359	39 23 046	66 31 079	43 25 175	17 18 257	23 58 284	51 32 317
179	58 28 357	40 04 045	67 27 078	43 30 175	16 22 257	23 02 283	50 52 316

LHA ♈	Hc Zn	Hc Zn	Hc Zn	Hc Zn	Hc Zn	Hc Zn	Hc Zn
	ARCTURUS	◆ ANTARES	ACRUX	◆ Suhail	Alphard	REGULUS	◆ Denebola
180	40 45 044	27 11 112	43 34 176	45 13 224	52 11 278	50 12 315	58 25 355
181	41 24 043	28 04 111	43 38 176	44 32 225	51 14 277	49 30 314	58 19 353
182	42 04 043	28 58 111	43 42 177	43 52 225	50 17 277	48 49 313	58 12 352
183	42 42 042	29 51 111	43 44 178	43 11 226	49 20 276	48 06 312	58 02 350
184	43 20 041	30 45 111	43 47 178	42 30 226	48 23 276	47 23 311	57 51 348
185	43 57 040	31 38 111	43 48 179	41 49 226	47 26 276	46 39 310	57 39 346
186	44 33 039	32 32 111	43 49 179	41 07 226	46 29 275	45 54 309	57 24 345
187	45 08 038	33 25 111	43 49 180	40 25 227	45 32 275	45 09 308	57 08 343
188	45 43 037	34 19 111	43 49 181	39 44 227	44 35 275	44 24 307	56 50 341
189	46 17 035	35 12 111	43 48 181	39 01 227	43 38 274	43 38 306	56 31 339
190	46 49 034	36 06 111	43 46 182	38 19 227	42 40 274	42 51 305	56 10 338
191	47 21 033	37 00 111	43 44 183	37 37 228	41 43 273	42 04 304	55 48 336
192	47 52 032	37 54 111	43 41 183	36 54 228	40 46 273	41 16 304	55 24 335
193	48 22 031	38 47 111	43 37 184	36 12 228	39 49 273	40 28 303	54 58 333
194	48 51 030	39 41 111	43 33 184	35 29 228	38 51 272	39 40 302	54 32 332
	ARCTURUS	◆ Rasalhague	ANTARES	◆ ACRUX	Suhail	◆ REGULUS	Denebola
195	49 19 028	15 48 071	40 35 111	43 28 185	34 46 228	38 51 302	54 04 330
196	49 45 027	16 43 071	41 28 111	43 23 186	34 03 229	38 02 301	53 35 329
197	50 11 026	17 37 070	42 22 111	43 17 186	33 20 229	37 13 300	53 04 327
198	50 35 024	18 31 070	43 16 111	43 11 187	32 37 229	36 23 300	52 33 326
199	50 58 023	19 25 070	44 09 111	43 03 187	31 54 229	35 33 299	52 00 325
200	51 20 022	20 18 069	45 03 111	42 56 188	31 11 229	34 43 298	51 27 323
201	51 40 020	21 12 069	45 57 111	42 47 189	30 27 229	33 52 298	50 52 322
202	51 59 019	22 05 068	46 50 111	42 38 189	29 44 229	33 01 297	50 16 321
203	52 17 017	22 59 068	47 44 111	42 29 190	29 00 229	32 10 297	49 40 320
204	52 34 016	23 52 067	48 38 111	42 19 190	28 17 229	31 18 296	49 02 319
205	52 48 014	24 44 067	49 31 111	42 08 191	27 34 229	30 27 295	48 24 318
206	53 02 013	25 37 067	50 25 111	41 57 191	26 50 229	29 35 295	47 45 317
207	53 14 011	26 30 066	51 18 111	41 46 192	26 06 229	28 43 294	47 05 315
208	53 24 010	27 22 066	52 12 111	41 33 193	25 23 229	27 50 294	46 24 314
209	53 33 008	28 14 065	53 05 112	41 21 193	24 39 229	26 58 293	45 43 313
	◆ ARCTURUS	Rasalhague	◆ ANTARES	RIGIL KENT	ACRUX	◆ Suhail	REGULUS
210	53 40 007	29 06 065	53 58 112	45 30 173	41 07 194	23 56 229	26 05 293
211	53 46 005	29 58 064	54 52 112	45 37 174	40 54 194	23 12 229	25 12 292
212	53 50 003	30 49 063	55 45 112	45 43 174	40 39 195	22 29 229	24 19 292
213	53 53 002	31 40 063	56 38 113	45 48 175	40 25 195	21 45 229	23 26 292
214	53 54 000	32 31 062	57 31 113	45 53 176	40 09 196	21 02 229	22 32 291
215	53 53 359	33 22 062	58 24 113	45 57 176	39 54 196	20 19 229	21 39 291
216	53 51 357	34 12 061	59 16 113	46 00 177	39 38 197	19 35 229	20 45 290
217	53 47 355	35 03 061	60 09 114	46 03 178	39 21 197	18 52 229	19 51 290
218	53 41 354	35 52 060	61 01 114	46 05 178	39 04 197	18 09 229	18 57 289
219	53 34 352	36 42 059	61 53 115	46 06 179	38 46 198	17 25 229	18 03 289
220	53 26 351	37 31 059	62 46 115	46 06 180	38 29 198	16 42 229	17 08 289
221	53 16 349	38 20 058	63 37 116	46 06 181	38 10 199	15 59 229	16 14 288
222	53 04 347	39 08 057	64 29 116	46 05 181	37 52 199	15 16 229	15 19 288
223	52 51 346	39 56 056	65 20 117	46 03 182	37 33 200	14 33 228	14 25 288
224	52 36 344	40 44 056	66 11 117	46 01 183	37 13 200	13 50 228	13 30 287
	Alphecca	◆ VEGA	ALTAIR	◆ Peacock	RIGIL KENT	◆ SPICA	ARCTURUS
225	45 30 011	14 32 041	13 28 076	18 40 145	45 58 183	66 31 281	52 20 343
226	45 41 010	15 10 040	14 24 076	19 13 145	45 54 184	65 34 280	52 03 342
227	45 50 009	15 47 040	15 19 075	19 46 145	45 50 185	64 38 280	51 44 340
228	45 58 008	16 23 039	16 15 075	20 19 145	45 45 185	63 41 279	51 23 339
229	46 05 006	17 00 039	17 10 075	20 52 145	45 39 186	62 44 279	51 02 337
230	46 11 005	17 35 038	18 05 074	21 25 145	45 32 187	61 48 278	50 39 336
231	46 15 004	18 11 038	19 01 074	21 58 145	45 25 187	60 51 277	50 15 335
232	46 18 002	18 46 037	19 56 074	22 31 145	45 18 188	59 54 277	49 50 333
233	46 20 001	19 20 037	20 51 073	23 04 145	45 09 189	58 57 276	49 23 332
234	46 20 000	19 54 036	21 45 073	23 36 145	45 00 189	58 00 276	48 56 331
235	46 19 358	20 28 036	22 40 072	24 09 145	44 50 190	57 03 276	48 27 329
236	46 17 357	21 01 035	23 35 072	24 42 145	44 40 191	56 06 275	47 57 328
237	46 14 356	21 34 034	24 29 072	25 15 145	44 29 191	55 08 275	47 27 327
238	46 09 355	22 06 034	25 24 071	25 47 145	44 17 192	54 11 274	46 55 326
239	46 03 353	22 38 033	26 18 071	26 20 145	44 05 193	53 14 274	46 22 325
	◆ VEGA	ALTAIR	◆ Peacock	RIGIL KENT	◆ SPICA	ARCTURUS	Alphecca
240	23 09 033	27 12 070	26 52 146	43 52 193	52 17 274	45 49 324	45 56 352
241	23 39 032	28 06 070	27 25 146	43 39 194	51 19 273	45 14 323	45 47 351
242	24 09 031	29 00 069	27 57 146	43 25 194	50 22 273	44 39 322	45 37 350
243	24 39 031	29 53 069	28 29 146	43 10 195	49 25 272	44 03 321	45 26 348
244	25 08 030	30 46 068	29 01 146	42 55 196	48 28 272	43 26 320	45 14 347
245	25 36 029	31 40 068	29 33 146	42 39 196	47 30 272	42 49 319	45 00 346
246	26 04 028	32 33 067	30 05 146	42 23 197	46 33 272	42 10 318	44 46 345
247	26 31 028	33 25 067	30 37 147	42 06 197	45 35 271	41 31 317	44 30 343
248	26 57 027	34 18 066	31 08 147	41 49 198	44 38 271	40 52 316	44 13 342
249	27 23 026	35 10 066	31 40 147	41 31 198	43 41 271	40 11 315	43 55 341
250	27 48 026	36 03 065	32 11 147	41 13 199	42 43 270	39 30 314	43 36 340
251	28 12 025	36 54 064	32 42 147	40 54 199	41 46 270	38 49 313	43 16 339
252	28 36 024	37 46 064	33 13 148	40 35 200	40 49 270	38 07 312	42 54 338
253	28 59 023	38 37 063	33 44 148	40 16 200	39 51 269	37 24 312	42 32 337
254	29 22 023	39 28 063	34 14 148	39 56 201	38 54 269	36 41 311	42 09 335
	◆ VEGA	ALTAIR	◆ Peacock	RIGIL KENT	◆ SPICA	ARCTURUS	Alphecca
255	29 43 022	40 19 062	34 44 148	39 35 201	37 56 269	35 57 310	41 44 334
256	30 04 021	41 10 061	35 14 149	39 14 202	36 59 269	35 13 309	41 19 333
257	30 24 020	42 00 060	35 44 149	38 53 202	36 02 268	34 29 309	40 53 332
258	30 43 019	42 49 060	36 13 149	38 31 202	35 04 268	33 44 308	40 26 331
259	31 02 018	43 39 059	36 43 150	38 09 203	34 07 268	32 58 307	39 58 330
260	31 20 018	44 28 058	37 12 150	37 47 203	33 10 267	32 13 307	39 29 329
261	31 37 017	45 16 057	37 40 150	37 24 204	32 12 267	31 26 306	38 59 328
262	31 53 016	46 04 057	38 09 151	37 01 204	31 15 267	30 40 305	38 28 327
263	32 08 015	46 52 056	38 37 151	36 37 204	30 18 267	29 53 305	37 57 326
264	32 23 014	47 39 055	39 04 151	36 13 205	29 21 266	29 05 304	37 25 326
265	32 36 013	48 26 054	39 32 152	35 49 205	28 23 266	28 18 304	36 52 325
266	32 49 012	49 12 053	39 59 152	35 25 205	27 26 266	27 30 303	36 19 324
267	33 01 011	49 57 052	40 25 153	35 00 206	26 29 266	26 42 302	35 45 323
268	33 12 011	50 42 051	40 52 153	34 35 206	25 32 265	25 53 302	35 10 322
269	33 22 010	51 27 050	41 17 153	34 10 206	24 34 265	25 04 301	34 34 321

LHA ♈	Hc Zn	Hc Zn	Hc Zn	Hc Zn	Hc Zn	Hc Zn	Hc Zn
	◆ VEGA	ALTAIR	◆ FOMALHAUT	Peacock	RIGIL KENT	◆ ANTARES	Alphecca
270	33 31 009	52 10 049	21 24 116	41 43 154	33 44 207	67 10 242	33 58 321
271	33 39 008	52 53 048	22 16 116	42 08 154	33 19 207	66 20 242	33 21 320
272	33 47 007	53 35 047	23 07 115	42 32 155	32 53 207	65 29 243	32 44 319
273	33 53 006	54 16 045	23 59 115	42 57 155	32 26 207	64 37 244	32 06 318
274	33 59 005	54 57 044	24 51 115	43 20 156	32 00 208	63 46 244	31 27 317
275	34 03 004	55 36 043	25 43 115	43 43 156	31 33 208	62 54 245	30 48 317
276	34 07 003	56 15 041	26 35 115	44 06 157	31 06 208	62 02 245	30 09 316
277	34 09 002	56 52 040	27 27 115	44 28 158	30 39 208	61 10 246	29 29 315
278	34 11 001	57 29 039	28 19 115	44 50 158	30 12 208	60 17 246	28 48 315
279	34 12 000	58 04 037	29 11 115	45 11 159	29 45 209	59 25 247	28 07 314
280	34 12 359	58 38 036	30 03 115	45 31 159	29 17 209	58 32 247	27 26 313
281	34 11 358	59 11 034	30 55 115	45 51 160	28 49 209	57 39 247	26 44 313
282	34 09 358	59 42 032	31 47 115	46 11 161	28 21 209	56 46 247	26 01 312
283	34 06 357	60 12 031	32 39 115	46 29 161	27 53 209	55 53 248	25 19 312
284	34 02 356	60 41 029	33 32 115	46 47 162	27 25 209	55 00 248	24 36 311
	DENEB	◆ FOMALHAUT	Peacock	RIGIL KENT	◆ ANTARES	Rasalhague	◆ VEGA
285	23 31 019	34 24 115	47 05 163	26 57 210	54 07 248	53 50 323	33 57 355
286	23 49 019	35 16 115	47 22 163	26 29 210	53 14 248	53 16 322	33 51 354
287	24 07 018	36 08 115	47 38 164	26 00 210	52 20 248	52 40 321	33 45 353
288	24 24 017	37 00 115	47 53 165	25 31 210	51 27 249	52 03 320	33 37 352
289	24 41 016	37 53 115	48 08 166	25 03 210	50 34 249	51 26 318	33 29 351
290	24 57 016	38 45 115	48 22 166	24 34 210	49 40 249	50 47 317	33 19 350
291	25 12 015	39 37 115	48 35 167	24 05 210	48 47 249	50 08 316	33 09 349
292	25 27 014	40 29 115	48 48 168	23 36 210	47 53 249	49 28 315	32 58 348
293	25 40 014	41 21 115	48 59 169	23 07 210	46 59 249	48 47 314	32 45 347
294	25 54 013	42 13 115	49 10 169	22 38 210	46 06 249	48 05 313	32 33 346
295	26 06 012	43 06 115	49 21 170	22 09 210	45 12 249	47 23 312	32 19 346
296	26 17 011	43 58 115	49 30 171	21 40 210	44 18 249	46 40 311	32 04 345
297	26 28 011	44 50 115	49 39 172	21 11 211	43 25 249	45 56 310	31 48 344
298	26 39 010	45 42 115	49 46 173	20 42 211	42 31 249	45 12 309	31 32 343
299	26 48 009	46 33 115	49 53 173	20 13 211	41 37 249	44 27 308	31 15 342
	◆ DENEB	Alpheratz	◆ FOMALHAUT	Peacock	◆ ANTARES	Rasalhague	VEGA
300	26 56 008	14 14 053	47 25 115	50 00 174	40 43 249	43 41 307	30 57 341
301	27 04 007	14 59 052	48 17 116	50 05 175	39 50 249	42 56 306	30 38 340
302	27 11 007	15 44 052	49 09 116	50 09 176	38 56 249	42 09 306	30 19 340
303	27 18 006	16 30 052	50 00 116	50 13 177	38 02 249	41 22 305	29 58 339
304	27 23 005	17 14 051	50 52 116	50 16 178	37 09 249	40 35 304	29 37 338
305	27 28 004	17 59 051	51 43 116	50 18 179	36 15 249	39 47 303	29 15 337
306	27 32 004	18 43 050	52 35 117	50 19 179	35 21 249	38 59 303	28 53 336
307	27 35 003	19 27 050	53 26 117	50 19 180	34 28 249	38 11 302	28 30 336
308	27 37 002	20 10 049	54 17 117	50 18 181	33 34 249	37 22 301	28 06 335
309	27 39 001	20 53 049	55 08 118	50 17 182	32 40 249	36 33 301	27 41 334
310	27 40 000	21 36 048	55 59 118	50 14 183	31 47 249	35 43 300	27 16 333
311	27 40 000	22 19 047	56 49 118	50 11 184	30 53 249	34 53 299	26 50 333
312	27 39 359	23 01 047	57 40 119	50 07 185	30 00 249	34 03 299	26 23 332
313	27 37 358	23 42 046	58 30 119	50 02 185	29 06 249	33 13 298	25 56 331
314	27 35 357	24 24 046	59 20 120	49 56 186	28 13 249	32 22 298	25 28 331
	Alpheratz	◆ Diphda	ACHERNAR	Peacock	◆ ANTARES	VEGA	◆ DENEB
315	25 05 045	36 42 100	25 15 146	49 49 187	27 20 248	25 00 330	27 32 356
316	25 45 044	37 39 100	25 48 146	49 42 188	26 26 248	24 31 329	27 28 356
317	26 25 044	38 35 100	26 20 146	49 34 189	25 33 248	24 01 329	27 23 355
318	27 05 043	39 32 099	26 52 146	49 25 190	24 40 248	23 31 328	27 18 354
319	27 44 043	40 28 099	27 24 146	49 15 190	23 46 248	23 00 327	27 11 353
320	28 22 042	41 25 099	27 56 146	49 04 191	22 53 248	22 29 327	27 04 353
321	29 00 041	42 22 099	28 27 146	48 53 192	22 00 248	21 57 326	26 56 352
322	29 38 041	43 18 099	28 59 147	48 40 193	21 07 248	21 25 325	26 48 351
323	30 14 040	44 15 099	29 31 147	48 27 193	20 14 247	20 52 325	26 38 350
324	30 51 039	45 12 099	30 02 147	48 14 194	19 21 247	20 19 324	26 28 349
325	31 27 038	46 08 098	30 33 147	47 59 195	18 28 247	19 45 324	26 17 349
326	32 02 038	47 05 098	31 04 147	47 44 196	17 35 247	19 11 323	26 06 348
327	32 37 037	48 02 098	31 35 148	47 28 196	16 43 247	18 36 323	25 53 347
328	33 11 036	48 59 098	32 06 148	47 12 197	15 50 247	18 01 322	25 40 346
329	33 44 035	49 56 098	32 36 148	46 55 198	14 57 246	17 26 322	25 26 346
	◆ Alpheratz	Diphda	◆ ACHERNAR	Peacock	◆ Nunki	ALTAIR	DENEB
330	34 17 034	50 53 098	33 07 148	46 37 198	46 31 249	49 01 307	25 12 345
331	34 49 034	51 49 098	33 37 148	46 18 199	45 37 250	48 15 306	24 56 344
332	35 21 033	52 46 097	34 07 149	45 59 200	44 44 250	47 28 305	24 41 344
333	35 51 032	53 43 097	34 37 149	45 40 200	43 50 250	46 41 304	24 24 343
334	36 21 031	54 40 097	35 06 149	45 19 201	42 56 250	45 53 303	24 07 342
335	36 50 030	55 37 097	35 35 149	44 59 202	42 02 250	45 05 302	23 49 341
336	37 18 029	56 34 097	36 04 150	44 37 202	41 09 250	44 16 302	23 30 341
337	37 46 028	57 31 097	36 33 150	44 15 203	40 15 250	43 27 301	23 11 340
338	38 13 027	58 28 097	37 02 150	43 53 203	39 21 250	42 37 300	22 51 339
339	38 38 026	59 25 097	37 30 151	43 30 204	38 27 250	41 48 299	22 30 339
340	39 03 025	60 22 096	37 58 151	43 06 204	37 33 250	40 57 299	22 09 338
341	39 27 024	61 19 096	38 25 152	42 42 205	36 40 250	40 07 298	21 47 337
342	39 50 023	62 16 096	38 52 152	42 18 205	35 46 249	39 16 297	21 25 337
343	40 13 022	63 13 096	39 19 152	41 53 206	34 52 249	38 25 297	21 02 336
344	40 34 021	64 10 096	39 46 153	41 28 206	33 58 249	37 34 296	20 39 335
	Alpheratz	◆ Hamal	◆ ACHERNAR	Peacock	Nunki	◆ ALTAIR	DENEB
345	40 54 020	28 46 050	40 12 153	41 02 207	33 05 249	36 42 295	20 15 335
346	41 13 019	29 29 049	40 38 154	40 36 207	32 11 249	35 50 295	19 50 334
347	41 31 018	30 13 049	41 03 154	40 10 208	31 17 249	34 58 294	19 25 334
348	41 48 017	30 55 048	41 28 154	39 43 208	30 24 249	34 05 294	18 59 333
349	42 05 016	31 38 047	41 52 155	39 16 209	29 30 249	33 13 293	18 33 333
350	42 20 015	32 20 047	42 16 155	38 48 209	28 37 249	32 20 293	18 06 332
351	42 33 013	33 01 046	42 40 156	38 20 209	27 43 249	31 27 292	17 39 331
352	42 46 012	33 42 045	43 03 156	37 52 210	26 50 249	30 34 292	17 11 331
353	42 58 011	34 22 044	43 26 157	37 23 210	25 56 249	29 40 291	16 43 330
354	43 08 010	35 02 044	43 48 158	36 55 210	25 03 248	28 46 291	16 14 330
355	43 18 009	35 42 043	44 10 158	36 26 211	24 10 248	27 53 290	15 45 329
356	43 26 008	36 20 042	44 31 159	35 56 211	23 16 248	26 59 290	15 15 329
357	43 33 006	36 58 041	44 52 159	35 26 211	22 23 248	26 05 289	14 45 328
358	43 38 005	37 36 040	45 12 160	34 57 212	21 30 248	25 10 289	14 15 328
359	43 43 004	38 13 039	45 31 160	34 26 212	20 37 248	24 16 288	13 44 327

 LAT 18°S

LHA ♈	Hc	Zn	Hc	Zn	Hc	Zn	Hc	Zn	Hc	Zn	Hc	Zn	Hc	Zn
	◆ Alpheratz		Hamal		ALDEBARAN		◆ RIGEL		ACHERNAR		◆ Peacock		Enif	
0	42 46	003	38 02	038	13 39	067	13 06	094	46 47	161	34 47	212	46 30	307
1	42 49	002	38 36	037	14 31	067	14 03	094	47 05	161	34 16	213	45 44	306
2	42 50	000	39 11	036	15 23	066	15 00	094	47 23	162	33 45	213	44 58	306
3	42 49	359	39 44	035	16 16	066	15 57	094	47 40	163	33 14	213	44 11	305
4	42 48	358	40 17	034	17 08	066	16 54	093	47 57	163	32 43	213	43 24	304
5	42 45	357	40 48	033	18 00	065	17 51	093	48 13	164	32 12	214	42 37	303
6	42 41	356	41 19	032	18 51	065	18 48	093	48 28	165	31 40	214	41 49	302
7	42 36	354	41 49	031	19 43	064	19 45	092	48 42	166	31 08	214	41 00	302
8	42 30	353	42 19	030	20 34	064	20 42	092	48 56	166	30 36	214	40 11	301
9	42 23	352	42 47	029	21 25	063	21 39	092	49 09	167	30 04	214	39 22	300
10	42 15	351	43 14	028	22 16	063	22 36	092	49 21	168	29 32	214	38 33	299
11	42 05	350	43 41	027	23 07	062	23 33	091	49 33	169	29 00	214	37 43	299
12	41 54	349	44 06	026	23 57	062	24 30	091	49 44	169	28 28	215	36 53	298
13	41 42	347	44 31	025	24 47	061	25 27	091	49 54	170	27 55	215	36 02	297
14	41 29	346	44 54	024	25 37	061	26 24	090	50 03	171	27 23	215	35 11	297
	◆ Hamal		ALDEBARAN		RIGEL		◆ CANOPUS		ACHERNAR		◆ FOMALHAUT		Alpheratz	
15	45 16	022	26 27	060	27 21	090	19 35	141	50 12	172	60 01	242	41 15	345
16	45 37	021	27 16	060	28 18	090	20 12	141	50 19	173	59 11	242	41 00	344
17	45 58	020	28 06	059	29 15	089	20 48	140	50 26	174	58 20	243	40 44	343
18	46 16	019	28 54	059	30 12	089	21 24	140	50 32	174	57 29	243	40 27	342
19	46 34	017	29 43	058	31 09	089	22 01	140	50 37	175	56 38	243	40 09	341
20	46 51	016	30 31	057	32 06	088	22 37	140	50 41	176	55 47	244	39 49	340
21	47 06	015	31 19	057	33 03	088	23 13	140	50 45	177	54 56	244	39 29	339
22	47 20	014	32 07	056	34 00	088	23 50	140	50 48	178	54 05	244	39 08	338
23	47 33	012	32 54	055	34 57	087	24 26	140	50 49	179	53 13	244	38 46	337
24	47 44	011	33 41	055	35 54	087	25 02	140	50 50	180	52 22	245	38 23	336
25	47 54	010	34 27	054	36 51	087	25 39	141	50 50	180	51 30	245	37 59	335
26	48 03	008	35 13	053	37 48	086	26 15	141	50 49	181	50 39	245	37 34	334
27	48 11	007	35 59	053	38 45	086	26 51	141	50 48	182	49 47	245	37 08	333
28	48 17	006	36 44	052	39 42	086	27 27	141	50 45	183	48 55	245	36 42	332
29	48 22	004	37 29	051	40 39	085	28 03	141	50 42	184	48 03	246	36 14	331
	◆ Hamal		ALDEBARAN		◆ SIRIUS		CANOPUS		ACHERNAR		◆ FOMALHAUT		Alpheratz	
30	48 25	003	38 13	050	22 15	101	28 39	141	50 38	185	47 11	246	35 46	330
31	48 27	001	38 57	050	23 11	101	29 15	141	50 33	185	46 19	246	35 17	329
32	48 28	000	39 40	049	24 07	101	29 51	141	50 27	186	45 27	246	34 48	328
33	48 27	359	40 23	048	25 03	101	30 27	141	50 20	187	44 35	246	34 17	327
34	48 25	357	41 05	047	25 59	100	31 03	141	50 13	188	43 43	246	33 46	326
35	48 22	356	41 46	046	26 56	100	31 38	141	50 04	189	42 51	246	33 14	326
36	48 17	354	42 27	045	27 52	100	32 14	142	49 55	190	41 58	246	32 42	325
37	48 11	353	43 07	044	28 48	100	32 49	142	49 45	190	41 06	246	32 09	324
38	48 03	352	43 47	043	29 44	099	33 24	142	49 35	191	40 14	246	31 35	323
39	47 55	350	44 26	042	30 41	099	34 00	142	49 23	192	39 22	246	31 00	322
40	47 44	349	45 04	041	31 37	099	34 34	142	49 11	193	38 30	246	30 25	322
41	47 33	348	45 41	040	32 33	099	35 09	143	48 58	194	37 37	246	29 50	321
42	47 20	346	46 18	039	33 30	099	35 44	143	48 44	194	36 45	246	29 13	320
43	47 06	345	46 54	038	34 26	098	36 18	143	48 30	195	35 53	246	28 37	320
44	46 51	344	47 29	037	35 23	098	36 52	143	48 15	196	35 01	246	27 59	319
	◆ CAPELLA		BETELGEUSE		SIRIUS		◆ CANOPUS		ACHERNAR		◆ FOMALHAUT		Hamal	
45	18 48	025	39 41	064	36 19	098	37 26	144	47 59	196	34 09	246	46 34	343
46	19 12	024	40 32	063	37 16	098	38 00	144	47 42	197	33 17	246	46 17	341
47	19 35	023	41 23	062	38 12	097	38 34	144	47 25	198	32 24	246	45 58	340
48	19 57	023	42 13	061	39 09	097	39 07	144	47 08	198	31 32	246	45 38	339
49	20 19	022	43 03	061	40 06	097	39 40	145	46 49	199	30 40	246	45 17	338
50	20 40	021	43 53	060	41 02	097	40 13	145	46 30	200	29 48	246	44 54	336
51	21 00	021	44 42	059	41 59	097	40 45	146	46 11	200	28 56	246	44 31	335
52	21 20	020	45 31	058	42 56	096	41 17	146	45 50	201	28 04	246	44 07	334
53	21 39	019	46 19	058	43 52	096	41 49	146	45 30	202	27 12	245	43 41	333
54	21 58	019	47 07	057	44 49	096	42 21	147	45 08	202	26 21	245	43 15	332
55	22 16	018	47 54	056	45 46	096	42 52	147	44 46	203	25 29	245	42 47	331
56	22 34	017	48 41	055	46 43	096	43 23	148	44 24	203	24 37	245	42 19	330
57	22 50	017	49 28	054	47 39	095	43 53	148	44 01	204	23 45	245	41 50	329
58	23 06	016	50 14	053	48 36	095	44 23	148	43 38	204	22 54	245	41 20	328
59	23 22	015	50 59	052	49 33	095	44 53	149	43 14	205	22 02	245	40 49	327
	CAPELLA		BETELGEUSE		◆ SIRIUS		CANOPUS		◆ ACHERNAR		Diphda		◆ Hamal	
60	23 37	015	51 44	051	50 30	095	45 22	149	42 50	205	43 37	262	40 17	326
61	23 51	014	52 27	050	51 27	094	45 51	150	42 25	206	42 40	262	39 44	325
62	24 04	013	53 11	049	52 24	094	46 19	151	42 00	206	41 44	262	39 11	324
63	24 17	012	53 53	048	53 21	094	46 47	151	41 35	207	40 47	262	38 37	323
64	24 29	012	54 35	046	54 18	094	47 14	152	41 09	207	39 51	261	38 02	322
65	24 40	011	55 16	045	55 15	094	47 41	152	40 42	208	38 54	261	37 26	321
66	24 50	010	55 56	044	56 11	093	48 07	153	40 16	208	37 58	261	36 50	320
67	25 00	010	56 35	042	57 08	093	48 33	154	39 49	208	37 02	261	36 13	319
68	25 09	009	57 13	041	58 05	093	48 58	154	39 21	209	36 05	261	35 36	318
69	25 18	008	57 49	040	59 02	093	49 22	155	38 54	209	35 09	260	34 58	318
70	25 25	007	58 25	038	59 59	092	49 46	156	38 26	210	34 13	260	34 19	317
71	25 32	006	59 00	036	60 56	092	50 09	156	37 58	210	33 17	260	33 40	316
72	25 38	006	59 33	035	61 53	092	50 32	157	37 29	210	32 20	260	33 00	315
73	25 43	005	60 05	033	62 51	092	50 54	158	37 00	211	31 24	260	32 20	315
74	25 48	004	60 36	032	63 48	091	51 15	159	36 31	211	30 28	259	31 39	314
	CAPELLA		POLLUX		◆ PROCYON		Suhail		◆ CANOPUS		ACHERNAR		◆ Hamal	
75	25 52	003	28 54	042	44 13	063	32 21	131	51 35	159	36 02	211	30 57	313
76	25 55	003	29 32	041	45 04	063	33 04	131	51 55	160	35 32	211	30 16	313
77	25 57	002	30 10	041	45 54	062	33 48	131	52 14	161	35 02	212	29 33	312
78	25 58	001	30 47	040	46 45	061	34 31	131	52 32	162	34 32	212	28 51	311
79	25 59	000	31 23	039	47 34	060	35 14	131	52 49	163	34 02	212	28 07	311
80	25 59	000	31 59	038	48 24	059	35 57	131	53 05	164	33 31	212	27 24	310
81	25 58	359	32 34	038	49 13	059	36 40	131	53 21	165	33 01	213	26 40	309
82	25 57	358	33 08	037	50 01	058	37 23	131	53 36	166	32 30	213	25 55	309
83	25 54	357	33 42	036	50 49	057	38 05	132	53 49	167	31 59	213	25 11	308
84	25 51	356	34 15	035	51 36	056	38 48	132	54 02	168	31 28	213	24 26	307
85	25 47	356	34 48	034	52 23	055	39 30	132	54 14	169	30 56	213	23 40	307
86	25 43	355	35 19	033	53 10	054	40 13	132	54 25	170	30 25	214	22 54	306
87	25 37	354	35 50	033	53 55	053	40 55	133	54 35	171	29 53	214	22 08	306
88	25 31	353	36 21	032	54 40	051	41 37	133	54 44	172	29 22	214	21 22	305
89	25 24	353	36 50	031	55 25	050	42 19	133	54 51	173	28 50	214	20 35	305

LHA ♈	Hc	Zn	Hc	Zn	Hc	Zn	Hc	Zn	Hc	Zn	Hc	Zn	Hc	Zn
	POLLUX		◆ REGULUS		Suhail		◆ CANOPUS		ACHERNAR		◆ ALDEBARAN		CAPELLA	
90	37 19	030	21 39	069	43 00	133	54 58	174	28 18	214	49 51	328	25 17	352
91	37 47	029	22 32	068	43 41	134	55 04	175	27 46	214	49 20	327	25 08	351
92	38 14	028	23 25	068	44 23	134	55 09	176	27 14	214	48 48	326	24 59	350
93	38 40	027	24 18	067	45 04	134	55 13	177	26 42	214	48 16	324	24 49	350
94	39 05	026	25 11	067	45 44	135	55 15	178	26 09	214	47 42	323	24 39	349
95	39 30	025	26 03	066	46 25	135	55 17	179	25 37	215	47 07	322	24 27	348
96	39 53	024	26 55	066	47 05	136	55 18	180	25 05	215	46 32	321	24 15	347
97	40 16	023	27 47	065	47 45	136	55 17	181	24 32	215	45 56	320	24 03	347
98	40 38	022	28 39	065	48 24	136	55 16	182	24 00	215	45 19	319	23 49	346
99	40 58	021	29 31	064	49 03	137	55 13	183	23 27	215	44 41	318	23 35	345
100	41 18	020	30 22	064	49 42	137	55 10	184	22 55	215	44 02	317	23 20	345
101	41 36	018	31 13	063	50 21	138	55 05	185	22 22	215	43 23	316	23 05	344
102	41 54	017	32 04	063	50 59	138	54 59	186	21 50	215	42 43	315	22 49	343
103	42 10	016	32 54	062	51 36	139	54 52	187	21 17	215	42 02	314	22 32	343
104	42 26	015	33 45	061	52 14	140	54 45	188	20 45	215	41 21	313	22 14	342
	POLLUX		◆ REGULUS		◆ ACRUX		CANOPUS		◆ RIGEL		ALDEBARAN		CAPELLA	
105	42 40	014	34 35	061	19 40	152	54 36	189	62 43	288	40 39	312	21 56	341
106	42 53	013	35 24	060	20 07	152	54 26	190	61 49	287	39 57	311	21 38	340
107	43 05	012	36 14	060	20 34	152	54 15	191	60 54	286	39 14	311	21 18	340
108	43 16	010	37 03	059	21 01	152	54 04	192	59 59	285	38 30	310	20 58	339
109	43 26	009	37 51	058	21 28	152	53 51	193	59 04	285	37 46	309	20 38	339
110	43 35	008	38 40	057	21 55	152	53 38	194	58 08	284	37 01	308	20 16	338
111	43 42	007	39 28	057	22 22	152	53 23	195	57 13	283	36 16	308	19 55	337
112	43 48	006	40 15	056	22 49	152	53 08	196	56 17	283	35 31	307	19 32	337
113	43 53	004	41 02	055	23 16	152	52 51	197	55 21	282	34 45	306	19 09	336
114	43 57	003	41 49	054	23 43	152	52 34	198	54 26	281	33 59	305	18 46	335
115	43 59	002	42 35	054	24 10	152	52 16	199	53 30	281	33 12	305	18 22	335
116	44 00	001	43 21	053	24 37	152	51 58	200	52 33	280	32 25	304	17 57	334
117	44 01	359	44 06	052	25 03	152	51 38	200	51 37	280	31 38	303	17 32	334
118	43 59	358	44 51	051	25 30	152	51 18	201	50 41	279	30 50	303	17 07	333
119	43 57	357	45 35	050	25 57	152	50 57	202	49 45	279	30 02	302	16 41	333
	◆ REGULUS		SPICA		◆ ACRUX		CANOPUS		◆ RIGEL		BETELGEUSE		POLLUX	
120	46 18	049	11 26	098	26 23	152	50 35	203	48 48	278	50 13	307	43 53	356
121	47 01	048	12 22	098	26 49	153	50 13	204	47 52	278	49 27	306	43 49	355
122	47 43	047	13 19	098	27 16	153	49 50	204	46 55	277	48 41	305	43 43	353
123	48 25	046	14 15	097	27 42	153	49 26	205	45 59	277	47 54	304	43 35	352
124	49 06	045	15 12	097	28 08	153	49 01	206	45 02	277	47 07	303	43 27	351
125	49 46	044	16 09	097	28 34	153	48 36	206	44 05	276	46 19	302	43 17	350
126	50 25	043	17 05	097	29 00	153	48 11	207	43 08	276	45 30	302	43 07	349
127	51 03	042	18 02	096	29 25	153	47 45	208	42 12	275	44 42	301	42 55	347
128	51 41	040	18 59	096	29 51	154	47 18	208	41 15	275	43 52	300	42 42	346
129	52 17	039	19 56	096	30 16	154	46 51	209	40 18	275	43 03	299	42 28	345
130	52 53	038	20 52	095	30 41	154	46 23	209	39 21	274	42 13	299	42 12	344
131	53 28	037	21 49	095	31 06	154	45 55	210	38 24	274	41 22	298	41 56	343
132	54 01	035	22 46	095	31 31	154	45 26	210	37 27	273	40 32	297	41 39	342
133	54 33	034	23 43	095	31 56	155	44 57	211	36 30	273	39 41	296	41 20	341
134	55 05	032	24 40	094	32 20	155	44 27	211	35 33	273	38 50	296	41 01	339
	REGULUS		◆ SPICA		ACRUX		◆ CANOPUS		SIRIUS		BETELGEUSE		◆ POLLUX	
135	55 35	031	25 37	094	32 44	155	43 57	212	58 00	267	37 58	295	40 40	338
136	56 03	029	26 34	094	33 08	155	43 27	212	57 03	267	37 06	295	40 19	337
137	56 31	028	27 30	094	33 32	156	42 56	213	56 06	267	36 14	294	39 56	336
138	56 57	026	28 27	093	33 55	156	42 25	213	55 09	266	35 22	293	39 33	335
139	57 21	025	29 24	093	34 19	156	41 54	214	54 12	266	34 30	293	39 08	334
140	57 44	023	30 21	093	34 42	156	41 22	214	53 15	266	33 37	292	38 43	333
141	58 06	021	31 18	092	35 04	157	40 50	214	52 18	266	32 44	292	38 17	332
142	58 26	020	32 15	092	35 27	157	40 17	215	51 21	265	31 51	291	37 50	331
143	58 44	018	33 12	092	35 49	157	39 45	215	50 25	265	30 58	291	37 22	330
144	59 00	016	34 10	092	36 11	158	39 12	215	49 28	265	30 04	290	36 53	329
145	59 15	014	35 07	091	36 32	158	38 38	216	48 31	265	29 11	290	36 24	328
146	59 28	012	36 04	091	36 53	158	38 05	216	47 34	265	28 17	289	35 54	328
147	59 39	010	37 01	091	37 14	159	37 31	216	46 37	264	27 23	289	35 23	327
148	59 48	008	37 58	090	37 35	159	36 57	217	45 40	264	26 29	288	34 51	326
149	59 56	006	38 55	090	37 55	159	36 23	217	44 44	264	25 34	288	34 19	325
	REGULUS		◆ ARCTURUS		SPICA		◆ ACRUX		CANOPUS		SIRIUS		◆ PROCYON	
150	60 01	004	16 57	063	39 52	090	38 15	160	35 49	217	43 47	264	48 26	301
151	60 05	003	17 48	062	40 49	089	38 34	160	35 14	217	42 50	264	47 36	300
152	60 06	001	18 38	062	41 46	089	38 54	161	34 39	218	41 54	263	46 47	299
153	60 06	359	19 28	061	42 43	089	39 12	161	34 05	218	40 57	263	45 57	298
154	60 04	357	20 18	061	43 40	088	39 31	162	33 29	218	40 00	263	45 06	297
155	59 59	355	21 08	060	44 37	088	39 48	162	32 54	218	39 04	263	44 15	297
156	59 53	353	21 58	060	45 34	088	40 06	162	32 19	218	38 07	263	43 24	296
157	59 45	351	22 47	059	46 31	087	40 23	163	31 43	219	37 10	262	42 33	295
158	59 35	349	23 36	059	47 28	087	40 40	163	31 08	219	36 14	262	41 41	295
159	59 23	347	24 24	058	48 25	087	40 56	164	30 32	219	35 17	262	40 49	294
160	59 09	345	25 13	058	49 22	086	41 11	164	29 56	219	34 21	262	39 57	293
161	58 54	343	26 01	057	50 19	086	41 27	165	29 21	219	33 24	261	39 04	293
162	58 37	342	26 49	057	51 16	086	41 41	165	28 45	219	32 28	261	38 12	292
163	58 18	340	27 36	056	52 13	085	41 56	166	28 09	219	31 32	261	37 19	292
164	57 57	338	28 23	055	53 10	085	42 09	166	27 32	219	30 35	261	36 25	291
	Denebola		◆ ARCTURUS		SPICA		◆ ACRUX		SIRIUS		◆ PROCYON		REGULUS	
165	55 16	022	29 10	055	54 06	084	42 23	167	29 39	261	35 32	290	57 35	336
166	55 36	020	29 57	054	55 03	084	42 35	167	28 43	260	34 38	290	57 11	335
167	55 55	018	30 43	054	56 00	083	42 47	168	27 46	260	33 45	289	56 46	333
168	56 12	017	31 29	053	56 57	083	42 59	168	26 50	260	32 51	289	56 20	331
169	56 28	015	32 14	052	57 53	082	43 10	169	25 54	260	31 57	288	55 52	330
170	56 41	013	32 59	052	58 50	082	43 21	170	24 58	259	31 02	288	55 22	328
171	56 54	011	33 43	051	59 46	081	43 31	170	24 02	259	30 08	287	54 52	327
172	57 04	010	34 27	050	60 43	081	43 40	171	23 06	259	29 13	287	54 20	326
173	57 13	008	35 11	049	61 39	080	43 49	171	22 10	259	28 19	286	53 47	324
174	57 20	006	35 54	049	62 35	080	43 57	172	21 14	259	27 24	286	53 13	323
175	57 25	004	36 37	048	63 31	079	44 05	173	20 18	258	26 29	286	52 38	322
176	57 29	003	37 19	047	64 27	078	44 12	173	19 22	258	25 34	285	52 02	320
177	57 31	001	38 00	046	65 23	077	44 18	174	18 26	258	24 39	285	51 25	319
178	57 30	359	38 41	045	66 18	077	44 24	174	17 31	258	23 44	284	50 47	318
179	57 29	357	39 22	045	67 14	076	44 30	175	16 35	257	22 48	284	50 09	317

LHA ♈	Hc	Zn	Hc	Zn	Hc	Zn	Hc	Zn	Hc	Zn	Hc	Zn	Hc	Zn
	ARCTURUS		◆ANTARES		ACRUX		◆Suhail		Alphard		REGULUS		◆Denebola	
180	40 02	044	27 33	111	44 34	176	45 55	225	52 03	279	49 29	316	57 25	355
181	40 41	043	28 26	111	44 38	176	45 15	226	51 06	279	48 49	314	57 19	354
182	41 19	042	29 19	111	44 42	177	44 34	226	50 10	278	48 08	313	57 12	352
183	41 57	041	30 12	111	44 44	178	43 53	226	49 13	278	47 26	312	57 03	350
184	42 34	040	31 06	111	44 46	178	43 11	227	48 17	277	46 43	311	56 53	348
185	43 10	039	31 59	110	44 48	179	42 30	227	47 20	277	46 00	310	56 40	347
186	43 46	038	32 53	110	44 49	179	41 48	227	46 23	276	45 17	309	56 26	345
187	44 21	037	33 46	110	44 49	180	41 06	227	45 26	276	44 32	309	56 11	343
188	44 55	036	34 40	110	44 49	181	40 24	228	44 30	275	43 47	308	55 53	342
189	45 28	035	35 33	110	44 48	181	39 42	228	43 33	275	43 02	307	55 35	340
190	46 00	034	36 27	110	44 46	182	39 00	228	42 36	275	42 16	306	55 14	338
191	46 31	033	37 21	110	44 44	183	38 17	228	41 39	274	41 30	305	54 52	337
192	47 01	031	38 14	110	44 41	183	37 34	228	40 42	274	40 43	304	54 29	335
193	47 30	030	39 08	110	44 37	184	36 52	229	39 45	274	39 55	304	54 05	334
194	47 59	029	40 02	110	44 33	185	36 09	229	38 48	273	39 08	303	53 39	332
	ARCTURUS		◆Rasalhague		ANTARES		◆ACRUX		Suhail		◆REGULUS		Denebola	
195	48 26	028	15 29	071	40 55	110	44 28	185	35 26	229	38 20	302	53 12	331
196	48 52	026	16 23	071	41 49	110	44 23	186	34 43	229	37 31	302	52 43	329
197	49 17	025	17 16	070	42 43	110	44 17	186	34 00	229	36 42	301	52 14	328
198	49 40	024	18 10	070	43 36	110	44 10	187	33 16	229	35 53	300	51 43	327
199	50 03	023	19 04	069	44 30	110	44 03	188	32 33	229	35 04	300	51 11	325
200	50 24	021	19 57	069	45 24	110	43 55	188	31 50	229	34 14	299	50 38	324
201	50 44	020	20 50	068	46 18	110	43 47	189	31 06	230	33 24	298	50 04	323
202	51 03	018	21 43	068	47 11	110	43 38	189	30 23	230	32 33	298	49 29	322
203	51 20	017	22 36	067	48 05	110	43 28	190	29 39	230	31 43	297	48 54	321
204	51 36	015	23 28	067	48 59	110	43 18	191	28 56	230	30 52	297	48 17	319
205	51 50	014	24 21	067	49 52	110	43 07	191	28 12	230	30 01	296	47 39	318
206	52 03	012	25 13	066	50 46	110	42 56	192	27 29	230	29 09	295	47 01	317
207	52 15	011	26 05	066	51 39	110	42 44	192	26 45	230	28 18	295	46 22	316
208	52 25	009	26 57	065	52 33	110	42 32	193	26 02	230	27 26	294	45 42	315
209	52 34	008	27 49	065	53 27	110	42 19	193	25 18	230	26 34	294	45 02	314
	◆ARCTURUS		Rasalhague		◆ANTARES		RIGIL KENT		ACRUX		◆Suhail		REGULUS	
210	52 41	006	28 40	064	54 20	111	46 30	173	42 06	194	24 35	230	25 41	293
211	52 46	005	29 31	063	55 13	111	46 37	174	41 52	194	23 51	230	24 49	293
212	52 50	003	30 22	063	56 07	111	46 43	174	41 37	195	23 08	230	23 56	292
213	52 53	002	31 13	062	57 00	111	46 48	175	41 22	195	22 24	230	23 03	292
214	52 54	000	32 03	062	57 53	111	46 53	176	41 07	196	21 41	229	22 10	291
215	52 53	359	32 53	061	58 46	112	46 57	176	40 51	196	20 58	229	21 17	291
216	52 51	357	33 43	061	59 39	112	47 00	177	40 35	197	20 14	229	20 24	291
217	52 47	355	34 33	060	60 32	112	47 03	178	40 18	197	19 31	229	19 30	290
218	52 42	354	35 22	059	61 25	113	47 05	178	40 01	198	18 48	229	18 37	290
219	52 35	352	36 11	059	62 18	113	47 06	179	39 44	198	18 05	229	17 43	289
220	52 27	351	36 59	058	63 10	113	47 06	180	39 25	199	17 22	229	16 49	289
221	52 17	349	37 48	057	64 02	114	47 06	181	39 07	199	16 39	229	15 55	289
222	52 05	348	38 35	057	64 55	114	47 05	181	38 48	199	15 56	229	15 01	288
223	51 53	346	39 23	056	65 46	115	47 03	182	38 29	200	15 13	229	14 07	288
224	51 38	345	40 10	055	66 38	115	47 01	183	38 09	200	14 30	228	13 12	287
	Alphecca		◆VEGA		ALTAIR		◆Peacock		RIGIL KENT		◆SPICA		ARCTURUS	
225	44 31	011	13 47	041	13 13	076	19 29	145	46 58	183	66 18	283	51 23	343
226	44 42	010	14 24	040	14 09	076	20 02	145	46 54	184	65 22	283	51 06	342
227	44 51	009	15 01	040	15 04	075	20 35	145	46 50	185	64 27	282	50 47	340
228	44 59	007	15 37	039	15 59	075	21 08	145	46 44	186	63 31	281	50 28	339
229	45 05	006	16 13	039	16 54	074	21 41	145	46 39	186	62 35	280	50 07	338
230	45 11	005	16 48	038	17 49	074	22 14	145	46 32	187	61 38	280	49 44	336
231	45 15	004	17 23	038	18 44	074	22 47	145	46 25	188	60 42	279	49 21	335
232	45 18	002	17 58	037	19 38	073	23 20	145	46 17	188	59 46	279	48 56	334
233	45 20	001	18 32	037	20 33	073	23 53	145	46 08	189	58 49	278	48 30	332
234	45 20	000	19 06	036	21 27	072	24 26	145	45 59	190	57 53	278	48 03	331
235	45 19	359	19 39	035	22 22	072	24 58	145	45 49	190	56 56	277	47 35	330
236	45 17	357	20 12	035	23 16	072	25 31	145	45 39	191	55 59	277	47 06	329
237	45 14	356	20 44	034	24 10	071	26 04	145	45 28	192	55 03	276	46 36	328
238	45 09	355	21 16	034	25 04	071	26 37	145	45 16	192	54 06	276	46 05	326
239	45 03	353	21 47	033	25 58	070	27 09	145	45 03	193	53 09	275	45 33	325
	◆VEGA		ALTAIR		◆Peacock		RIGIL KENT		◆SPICA		ARCTURUS		Alphecca	
240	22 18	032	26 51	070	27 42	145	44 50	193	52 12	275	45 00	324	44 56	352
241	22 48	032	27 45	069	28 14	145	44 37	194	51 15	274	44 27	323	44 48	351
242	23 18	031	28 38	069	28 47	145	44 23	195	50 19	274	43 52	322	44 38	350
243	23 47	030	29 31	068	29 19	146	44 08	195	49 22	274	43 17	321	44 27	348
244	24 15	030	30 24	068	29 51	146	43 53	196	48 25	273	42 40	320	44 15	347
245	24 43	029	31 17	067	30 23	146	43 37	196	47 28	273	42 03	319	44 02	346
246	25 11	028	32 09	067	30 55	146	43 20	197	46 31	273	41 26	318	43 48	345
247	25 37	028	33 01	066	31 27	146	43 04	197	45 34	272	40 47	317	43 32	344
248	26 04	027	33 53	066	31 59	146	42 46	198	44 37	272	40 08	316	43 16	343
249	26 29	026	34 45	065	32 30	147	42 28	199	43 40	272	39 29	316	42 58	341
250	26 54	025	35 37	064	33 01	147	42 10	199	42 43	271	38 48	315	42 39	340
251	27 18	025	36 28	064	33 33	147	41 51	200	41 46	271	38 08	314	42 20	339
252	27 41	024	37 19	063	34 03	147	41 32	200	40 48	271	37 26	313	41 59	338
253	28 04	023	38 10	062	34 34	147	41 12	201	39 51	270	36 44	312	41 37	337
254	28 26	022	39 00	062	35 05	148	40 52	201	38 54	270	36 02	311	41 14	336
	◆VEGA		ALTAIR		◆Peacock		RIGIL KENT		◆SPICA		ARCTURUS		Alphecca	
255	28 47	022	39 50	061	35 35	148	40 31	201	37 57	270	35 19	311	40 50	335
256	29 08	021	40 40	060	36 05	148	40 10	202	37 00	269	34 35	310	40 25	334
257	29 28	020	41 30	060	36 35	149	39 48	202	36 03	269	33 51	309	40 00	333
258	29 47	019	42 19	059	37 05	149	39 27	203	35 06	269	33 07	309	39 33	332
259	30 05	018	43 07	058	37 34	149	39 04	203	34 09	268	32 22	308	39 05	331
260	30 23	017	43 56	057	38 03	149	38 42	204	33 12	268	31 36	307	38 37	330
261	30 39	017	44 44	057	38 32	150	38 19	204	32 15	268	30 51	307	38 08	329
262	30 55	016	45 31	056	39 01	150	37 55	204	31 18	268	30 05	306	37 38	328
263	31 10	015	46 18	055	39 29	151	37 32	205	30 21	267	29 18	305	37 07	327
264	31 24	014	47 04	054	39 57	151	37 08	205	29 24	267	28 32	305	36 35	326
265	31 38	013	47 50	053	40 24	151	36 44	205	28 27	267	27 44	304	36 03	325
266	31 50	012	48 35	052	40 52	152	36 19	206	27 30	266	26 57	303	35 30	324
267	32 02	011	49 20	051	41 18	152	35 54	206	26 33	266	26 09	303	34 57	323
268	32 13	010	50 04	050	41 45	153	35 29	206	25 36	266	25 21	302	34 22	323
269	32 23	010	50 48	049	42 11	153	35 04	207	24 39	266	24 33	302	33 47	322

LHA ♈	Hc	Zn	Hc	Zn	Hc	Zn	Hc	Zn	Hc	Zn	Hc	Zn	Hc	Zn
	◆VEGA		ALTAIR		◆FOMALHAUT		Peacock		RIGIL KENT		◆ANTARES		Alphecca	
270	32 32	009	51 30	048	21 50	115	42 37	154	34 38	207	67 38	244	33 11	321
271	32 40	008	52 12	047	22 41	115	43 02	154	34 12	207	66 47	244	32 35	320
272	32 47	007	52 54	046	23 33	115	43 27	154	33 46	207	65 55	245	31 58	319
273	32 53	006	53 34	044	24 25	115	43 51	155	33 20	208	65 03	246	31 21	319
274	32 59	005	54 13	043	25 16	115	44 15	156	32 53	208	64 11	246	30 43	318
275	33 03	004	54 52	042	26 08	115	44 38	156	32 26	208	63 19	247	30 04	317
276	33 07	003	55 30	041	27 00	115	45 01	157	31 59	208	62 26	247	29 25	316
277	33 10	002	56 06	039	27 52	114	45 24	157	31 32	209	61 34	247	28 46	316
278	33 11	001	56 42	038	28 44	114	45 45	158	31 05	209	60 41	248	28 06	315
279	33 12	000	57 16	036	29 36	114	46 07	158	30 37	209	59 48	248	27 25	314
280	33 12	359	57 49	035	30 28	114	46 27	159	30 10	209	58 55	248	26 44	314
281	33 11	358	58 21	033	31 20	114	46 48	160	29 42	209	58 02	249	26 03	313
282	33 09	358	58 51	032	32 12	114	47 07	160	29 14	209	57 09	249	25 21	313
283	33 06	357	59 21	030	33 04	114	47 26	161	28 46	210	56 16	249	24 39	312
284	33 02	356	59 48	028	33 56	114	47 44	162	28 17	210	55 22	249	23 56	311
	DENEB		◆FOMALHAUT		Peacock		RIGIL KENT		◆ANTARES		Rasalhague		◆VEGA	
285	22 34	019	34 48	114	48 02	162	27 49	210	54 29	249	53 02	324	32 57	355
286	22 52	018	35 41	114	48 19	163	27 21	210	53 35	250	52 28	323	32 52	354
287	23 10	018	36 33	114	48 35	164	26 52	210	52 42	250	51 53	322	32 45	353
288	23 27	017	37 25	114	48 51	164	26 23	210	51 48	250	51 17	320	32 38	352
289	23 43	016	38 17	114	49 06	165	25 55	210	50 55	250	50 41	319	32 29	351
290	23 59	016	39 09	114	49 20	166	25 26	210	50 01	250	50 03	318	32 20	350
291	24 14	015	40 02	114	49 34	167	24 57	210	49 07	250	49 24	317	32 10	349
292	24 28	014	40 54	114	49 46	168	24 28	211	48 14	250	48 45	316	31 59	348
293	24 42	013	41 46	114	49 58	168	23 59	211	47 20	250	48 05	315	31 47	348
294	24 55	013	42 38	114	50 09	169	23 30	211	46 26	250	47 24	314	31 34	347
295	25 07	012	43 30	114	50 20	170	23 01	211	45 33	250	46 42	313	31 21	346
296	25 19	011	44 22	114	50 29	171	22 32	211	44 39	250	46 00	312	31 06	345
297	25 29	010	45 15	114	50 38	172	22 03	211	43 45	250	45 17	311	30 51	344
298	25 39	010	46 07	114	50 46	172	21 33	211	42 52	250	44 34	310	30 35	343
299	25 49	009	46 59	114	50 53	173	21 04	211	41 58	250	43 49	309	30 18	342
	◆DENEB		Alpheratz		◆FOMALHAUT		Peacock		◆ANTARES		Rasalhague		VEGA	
300	25 57	008	13 37	053	47 51	114	50 59	174	41 04	250	43 05	308	30 00	342
301	26 05	007	14 22	052	48 43	115	51 05	175	40 11	250	42 20	307	29 42	341
302	26 12	007	15 07	052	49 34	115	51 09	176	39 17	250	41 34	306	29 22	340
303	26 18	006	15 52	051	50 26	115	51 13	177	38 23	250	40 48	306	29 02	339
304	26 23	005	16 37	051	51 18	115	51 16	178	37 30	250	40 01	305	28 42	338
305	26 28	004	17 21	050	52 10	115	51 18	179	36 36	250	39 14	304	28 20	337
306	26 32	004	18 04	050	53 01	115	51 19	179	35 42	250	38 27	303	27 58	337
307	26 35	003	18 48	049	53 53	116	51 19	180	34 49	250	37 39	303	27 35	336
308	26 38	002	19 31	049	54 44	116	51 18	181	33 55	250	36 50	302	27 11	335
309	26 39	001	20 14	048	55 35	116	51 17	182	33 02	250	36 02	301	26 47	334
310	26 40	000	20 56	048	56 26	117	51 14	183	32 08	250	35 13	301	26 22	334
311	26 40	000	21 38	047	57 17	117	51 11	184	31 15	249	34 24	300	25 56	333
312	26 39	359	22 20	047	58 08	117	51 07	185	30 21	249	33 34	299	25 30	332
313	26 37	358	23 01	046	58 59	118	51 02	185	29 28	249	32 44	299	25 03	332
314	26 35	357	23 42	046	59 49	118	50 56	186	28 35	249	31 54	298	24 36	331
	Alpheratz		◆Diphda		ACHERNAR		Peacock		◆ANTARES		VEGA		◆DENEB	
315	24 22	045	36 52	099	26 05	146	50 49	187	27 41	249	24 08	330	26 32	356
316	25 02	044	37 48	099	26 37	146	50 41	188	26 48	249	23 39	329	26 28	356
317	25 42	044	38 45	099	27 09	146	50 33	189	25 55	249	23 10	329	26 23	355
318	26 21	043	39 41	099	27 42	146	50 24	190	25 02	249	22 40	328	26 18	354
319	26 59	042	40 38	098	28 14	146	50 14	191	24 09	248	22 10	328	26 12	353
320	27 37	042	41 34	098	28 46	146	50 03	191	23 16	248	21 39	327	26 05	353
321	28 15	041	42 30	098	29 17	146	49 51	192	22 23	248	21 07	326	25 57	352
322	28 52	040	43 27	098	29 49	146	49 39	193	21 30	248	20 35	326	25 48	351
323	29 29	039	44 23	098	30 21	146	49 26	194	20 37	248	20 03	325	25 39	350
324	30 05	039	45 20	098	30 52	147	49 12	194	19 44	248	19 30	324	25 29	350
325	30 40	038	46 17	097	31 23	147	48 57	195	18 51	247	18 57	324	25 18	349
326	31 15	037	47 13	097	31 55	147	48 42	196	17 59	247	18 23	323	25 07	348
327	31 49	036	48 10	097	32 26	147	48 26	197	17 06	247	17 48	323	24 55	347
328	32 22	036	49 07	097	32 56	147	48 09	197	16 14	247	17 14	322	24 42	347
329	32 55	035	50 03	097	33 27	148	47 52	198	15 21	247	16 39	322	24 28	346
	◆Alpheratz		Diphda		◆ACHERNAR		Peacock		◆Nunki		ALTAIR		DENEB	
330	33 28	034	51 00	096	33 58	148	47 34	199	46 52	250	48 25	308	24 14	345
331	33 59	033	51 57	096	34 28	148	47 15	199	45 58	251	47 39	307	23 59	344
332	34 30	032	52 53	096	34 58	148	46 56	200	45 04	251	46 53	306	23 43	344
333	35 00	031	53 50	096	35 28	149	46 36	201	44 10	251	46 07	305	23 27	343
334	35 30	031	54 47	096	35 58	149	46 15	201	43 17	251	45 20	304	23 09	342
335	35 58	030	55 44	096	36 27	149	45 54	202	42 23	251	44 32	303	22 52	342
336	36 26	029	56 40	095	36 56	149	45 33	203	41 29	250	43 44	302	22 33	341
337	36 53	028	57 37	095	37 25	150	45 10	203	40 35	250	42 56	302	22 14	340
338	37 19	027	58 34	095	37 54	150	44 48	204	39 41	250	42 07	301	21 55	340
339	37 45	026	59 31	095	38 22	150	44 25	204	38 48	250	41 18	300	21 34	339
340	38 09	025	60 28	095	38 50	151	44 01	205	37 54	250	40 28	299	21 13	338
341	38 33	024	61 25	095	39 18	151	43 37	205	37 00	250	39 38	299	20 52	338
342	38 55	023	62 22	094	39 45	152	43 12	206	36 07	250	38 48	298	20 30	337
343	39 17	022	63 18	094	40 12	152	42 47	206	35 13	250	37 58	297	20 07	336
344	39 38	021	64 15	094	40 39	152	42 22	207	34 19	250	37 07	297	19 44	336
	Alpheratz		◆Hamal		◆ACHERNAR		Peacock		Nunki		◆ALTAIR		DENEB	
345	39 58	020	28 07	049	41 05	153	41 56	207	33 26	250	36 16	296	19 20	335
346	40 16	019	28 50	049	41 31	153	41 29	208	32 32	250	35 24	296	18 56	334
347	40 34	018	29 33	048	41 57	154	41 03	208	31 38	250	34 33	295	18 31	334
348	40 51	017	30 15	048	42 22	154	40 36	209	30 45	250	33 41	294	18 05	333
349	41 07	015	30 57	047	42 47	155	40 08	209	29 52	249	32 49	294	17 39	333
350	41 21	014	31 38	046	43 11	155	39 40	209	28 58	249	31 56	293	17 13	332
351	41 35	013	32 19	045	43 35	156	39 12	210	28 05	249	31 04	293	16 46	332
352	41 48	012	33 00	045	43 58	156	38 44	210	27 11	249	30 11	292	16 19	331
353	41 59	011	33 39	044	44 21	157	38 15	210	26 18	249	29 18	292	15 51	330
354	42 09	010	34 19	043	44 43	157	37 46	211	25 25	249	28 25	291	15 22	330
355	42 18	009	34 57	042	45 05	158	37 17	211	24 32	249	27 32	291	14 53	329
356	42 26	007	35 35	042	45 27	158	36 47	211	23 39	249	26 38	290	14 24	329
357	42 33	006	36 13	041	45 48	159	36 18	212	22 45	248	25 45	290	13 54	328
358	42 39	005	36 50	040	46 08	160	35 48	212	21 52	248	24 51	289	13 24	328
359	42 43	004	37 26	039	46 27	160	35 17	212	20 59	248	23 57	289	12 53	327

LAT 19°S

LHA ♈	Hc	Zn	Hc	Zn	Hc	Zn	Hc	Zn	Hc	Zn	Hc	Zn	Hc	Zn
	◆ Alpheratz		Hamal		ALDEBARAN		◆ RIGEL		ACHERNAR		◆ Peacock		Enif	
0	41 47	003	37 14	038	13 15	067	13 10	094	47 43	160	35 37	213	45 53	308
1	41 49	002	37 49	037	14 07	067	14 07	094	48 02	161	35 07	213	45 08	307
2	41 50	000	38 22	036	14 59	066	15 04	094	48 20	162	34 36	213	44 23	306
3	41 49	359	38 55	035	15 51	066	16 00	093	48 37	162	34 04	213	43 37	305
4	41 48	358	39 27	034	16 43	065	16 57	093	48 54	163	33 33	214	42 50	305
5	41 45	357	39 58	033	17 34	065	17 54	093	49 10	164	33 01	214	42 04	304
6	41 42	356	40 29	032	18 25	064	18 50	092	49 26	165	32 30	214	41 16	303
7	41 37	354	40 58	031	19 17	064	19 47	092	49 40	165	31 58	214	40 28	302
8	41 31	353	41 27	030	20 07	063	20 44	092	49 54	166	31 26	214	39 40	302
9	41 24	352	41 55	029	20 58	063	21 40	091	50 08	167	30 54	215	38 52	301
10	41 15	351	42 21	028	21 48	062	22 37	091	50 20	168	30 22	215	38 03	300
11	41 06	350	42 47	027	22 39	062	23 34	091	50 32	168	29 49	215	37 14	299
12	40 55	349	43 12	025	23 29	061	24 30	090	50 43	169	29 17	215	36 24	299
13	40 44	348	43 36	024	24 18	061	25 27	090	50 53	170	28 44	215	35 34	298
14	40 31	347	43 59	023	25 08	060	26 24	090	51 02	171	28 12	215	34 44	297
	◆ Hamal		ALDEBARAN		RIGEL		◆ CANOPUS		ACHERNAR		◆ FOMALHAUT		Alpheratz	
15	44 21	022	25 57	060	27 21	090	20 22	140	51 11	172	60 29	243	40 17	345
16	44 41	021	26 46	059	28 17	089	20 58	140	51 19	173	59 38	244	40 03	344
17	45 01	020	27 35	059	29 14	089	21 34	140	51 26	173	58 47	244	39 47	343
18	45 20	018	28 23	058	30 11	089	22 10	140	51 32	174	57 56	244	39 30	342
19	45 37	017	29 11	058	31 08	088	22 47	140	51 37	175	57 05	245	39 12	341
20	45 53	016	29 59	057	32 04	088	23 23	140	51 41	176	56 13	245	38 53	340
21	46 08	015	30 46	056	33 01	087	23 59	140	51 45	177	55 22	245	38 33	339
22	46 22	013	31 33	056	33 58	087	24 36	140	51 47	178	54 30	245	38 12	338
23	46 34	012	32 20	055	34 54	087	25 12	140	51 49	179	53 39	246	37 51	337
24	46 45	011	33 06	054	35 51	086	25 48	140	51 50	180	52 47	246	37 28	336
25	46 55	009	33 52	054	36 47	086	26 25	140	51 50	180	51 55	246	37 05	335
26	47 04	008	34 37	053	37 44	086	27 01	140	51 49	181	51 03	246	36 40	334
27	47 11	007	35 22	052	38 41	085	27 37	140	51 48	182	50 11	246	36 15	333
28	47 17	005	36 07	051	39 37	085	28 14	140	51 45	183	49 19	246	35 49	332
29	47 22	004	36 51	051	40 34	084	28 50	140	51 42	184	48 27	247	35 22	331
	◆ Hamal		ALDEBARAN		◆ SIRIUS		CANOPUS		ACHERNAR		◆ FOMALHAUT		Alpheratz	
30	47 25	003	37 34	050	22 27	101	29 26	141	51 38	185	47 35	247	34 54	330
31	47 27	001	38 18	049	23 22	101	30 02	141	51 32	186	46 43	247	34 26	329
32	47 28	000	39 00	048	24 18	100	30 38	141	51 26	186	45 51	247	33 57	329
33	47 27	359	39 42	047	25 14	100	31 14	141	51 20	187	44 59	247	33 27	328
34	47 25	357	40 24	047	26 10	100	31 50	141	51 12	188	44 07	247	32 56	327
35	47 22	356	41 04	046	27 06	100	32 25	141	51 04	189	43 15	247	32 25	326
36	47 17	355	41 45	045	28 02	099	33 01	141	50 54	190	42 22	247	31 53	325
37	47 11	353	42 24	044	28 58	099	33 36	141	50 44	191	41 30	247	31 20	324
38	47 04	352	43 03	043	29 54	099	34 12	142	50 33	191	40 38	247	30 47	324
39	46 55	351	43 41	042	30 50	099	34 47	142	50 22	192	39 46	247	30 13	323
40	46 45	349	44 19	041	31 46	098	35 22	142	50 09	193	38 54	247	29 38	322
41	46 34	348	44 55	040	32 42	098	35 57	142	49 56	194	38 01	247	29 03	321
42	46 22	347	45 31	039	33 38	098	36 31	142	49 42	195	37 09	247	28 27	321
43	46 08	345	46 06	038	34 35	098	37 06	143	49 28	195	36 17	247	27 51	320
44	45 53	344	46 41	036	35 31	097	37 40	143	49 12	196	35 25	247	27 14	319
	◆ CAPELLA		BETELGEUSE		SIRIUS		◆ CANOPUS		ACHERNAR		◆ FOMALHAUT		Hamal	
45	17 54	024	39 14	063	36 27	097	38 15	143	48 56	197	34 33	247	45 37	343
46	18 17	024	40 05	062	37 23	097	38 48	143	48 40	197	33 41	247	45 20	342
47	18 39	023	40 55	061	38 20	097	39 22	144	48 22	198	32 49	247	45 01	340
48	19 01	023	41 44	061	39 16	096	39 56	144	48 04	199	31 57	246	44 42	339
49	19 23	022	42 33	060	40 12	096	40 29	144	47 46	199	31 05	246	44 21	338
50	19 44	021	43 22	059	41 09	096	41 02	145	47 27	200	30 13	246	43 59	337
51	20 04	021	44 11	058	42 05	096	41 35	145	47 07	201	29 21	246	43 36	336
52	20 24	020	44 59	058	43 02	095	42 07	145	46 46	201	28 29	246	43 12	335
53	20 43	019	45 47	057	43 58	095	42 39	146	46 25	202	27 37	246	42 48	333
54	21 01	019	46 34	056	44 55	095	43 11	146	46 04	203	26 45	246	42 22	332
55	21 19	018	47 20	055	45 51	095	43 42	147	45 42	203	25 54	246	41 55	331
56	21 36	017	48 07	054	46 48	094	44 13	147	45 19	204	25 02	245	41 27	330
57	21 53	017	48 52	053	47 44	094	44 44	147	44 56	204	24 10	245	40 58	329
58	22 09	016	49 37	052	48 41	094	45 14	148	44 33	205	23 19	245	40 29	328
59	22 24	015	50 22	051	49 38	094	45 44	148	44 09	205	22 27	245	39 58	327
	CAPELLA		BETELGEUSE		◆ SIRIUS		CANOPUS		◆ ACHERNAR		Diphda		◆ Hamal	
60	22 38	015	51 05	050	50 34	093	46 14	149	43 44	206	43 44	263	39 27	326
61	22 52	014	51 48	049	51 31	093	46 43	149	43 19	206	42 48	263	38 55	325
62	23 06	013	52 31	048	52 28	093	47 11	150	42 54	207	41 52	263	38 22	324
63	23 18	012	53 12	047	53 24	093	47 39	151	42 28	207	40 56	262	37 49	323
64	23 30	012	53 53	045	54 21	092	48 07	151	42 02	208	39 59	262	37 15	322
65	23 41	011	54 33	044	55 18	092	48 34	152	41 36	208	39 03	262	36 40	322
66	23 51	010	55 12	043	56 14	092	49 00	152	41 09	208	38 07	262	36 04	321
67	24 01	009	55 50	041	57 11	092	49 26	153	40 41	209	37 11	262	35 28	320
68	24 10	009	56 27	040	58 08	091	49 52	154	40 14	209	36 15	261	34 51	319
69	24 18	008	57 03	039	59 04	091	50 17	154	39 46	210	35 19	261	34 13	318
70	24 26	007	57 38	037	60 01	091	50 41	155	39 18	210	34 23	261	33 35	317
71	24 32	006	58 11	036	60 58	090	51 04	156	38 49	210	33 27	261	32 56	317
72	24 38	006	58 44	034	61 55	090	51 27	157	38 21	211	32 31	260	32 17	316
73	24 44	005	59 15	032	62 51	090	51 49	157	37 52	211	31 35	260	31 37	315
74	24 48	004	59 44	031	63 48	089	52 11	158	37 22	211	30 39	260	30 57	314
	CAPELLA		POLLUX		◆ PROCYON		Suhail		◆ CANOPUS		ACHERNAR		◆ Hamal	
75	24 52	003	28 10	042	43 46	062	33 00	130	52 31	159	36 53	212	30 16	314
76	24 55	003	28 47	041	44 36	062	33 43	130	52 51	160	36 23	212	29 35	313
77	24 57	002	29 24	040	45 26	061	34 27	130	53 10	161	35 53	212	28 53	312
78	24 59	001	30 00	039	46 15	060	35 10	130	53 29	162	35 23	212	28 11	312
79	24 59	000	30 36	039	47 04	059	35 53	130	53 46	162	34 52	213	27 28	311
80	24 59	000	31 11	038	47 53	058	36 36	131	54 03	163	34 22	213	26 45	310
81	24 58	359	31 46	037	48 41	058	37 19	131	54 19	164	33 51	213	26 02	310
82	24 57	358	32 20	036	49 28	057	38 02	131	54 34	165	33 20	213	25 18	309
83	24 55	357	32 53	036	50 16	056	38 45	131	54 48	166	32 49	213	24 34	308
84	24 51	357	33 26	035	51 02	055	39 28	131	55 01	167	32 18	214	23 49	308
85	24 48	356	33 58	034	51 48	054	40 10	131	55 13	168	31 46	214	23 04	307
86	24 43	355	34 29	033	52 34	053	40 53	132	55 24	169	31 15	214	22 19	307
87	24 38	354	35 00	032	53 18	052	41 35	132	55 34	170	30 43	214	21 33	306
88	24 32	353	35 29	031	54 02	050	42 17	132	55 43	171	30 11	214	20 47	306
89	24 25	353	35 58	030	54 46	049	42 59	132	55 51	172	29 39	214	20 01	305

LHA ♈	Hc	Zn	Hc	Zn	Hc	Zn	Hc	Zn	Hc	Zn	Hc	Zn	Hc	Zn
	POLLUX		◆ REGULUS		Suhail		◆ CANOPUS		ACHERNAR		◆ ALDEBARAN		CAPELLA	
90	36 27	029	21 17	068	43 41	133	55 58	173	29 08	214	49 00	329	24 17	352
91	36 54	028	22 10	068	44 23	133	56 04	174	28 35	214	48 30	328	24 09	351
92	37 21	027	23 03	067	45 04	133	56 09	176	28 03	215	47 59	326	24 00	350
93	37 46	027	23 55	067	45 45	134	56 13	177	27 31	215	47 27	325	23 50	350
94	38 11	026	24 47	066	46 26	134	56 15	178	26 59	215	46 54	324	23 40	349
95	38 35	025	25 39	066	47 07	134	56 17	179	26 26	215	46 20	323	23 29	348
96	38 58	024	26 31	065	47 47	135	56 18	180	25 54	215	45 45	322	23 17	348
97	39 21	022	27 22	065	48 28	135	56 17	181	25 22	215	45 10	321	23 04	347
98	39 42	021	28 13	064	49 07	136	56 16	182	24 49	215	44 33	320	22 51	346
99	40 02	020	29 04	064	49 47	136	56 13	183	24 17	215	43 56	319	22 37	345
100	40 21	019	29 55	063	50 26	137	56 09	184	23 44	215	43 18	318	22 22	345
101	40 40	018	30 46	063	51 05	137	56 05	185	23 12	215	42 40	317	22 07	344
102	40 57	017	31 36	062	51 43	138	55 59	186	22 39	215	42 00	316	21 51	343
103	41 13	016	32 26	062	52 21	138	55 52	187	22 06	215	41 20	315	21 35	343
104	41 28	015	33 16	061	52 59	139	55 44	189	21 34	215	40 40	314	21 17	342
	POLLUX		◆ REGULUS		◆ ACRUX		CANOPUS		◆ RIGEL		ALDEBARAN		CAPELLA	
105	41 42	014	34 05	060	20 33	152	55 35	190	62 24	289	39 58	313	20 59	341
106	41 55	013	34 54	060	21 00	152	55 25	191	61 30	289	39 17	312	20 41	341
107	42 07	011	35 43	059	21 27	152	55 14	192	60 36	288	38 34	311	20 22	340
108	42 17	010	36 31	058	21 54	152	55 02	193	59 42	287	37 51	310	20 02	339
109	42 27	009	37 20	058	22 21	152	54 49	194	58 48	286	37 08	310	19 42	339
110	42 35	008	38 07	057	22 48	152	54 36	195	57 53	285	36 24	309	19 21	338
111	42 42	007	38 54	056	23 15	152	54 21	196	56 58	285	35 40	308	18 59	337
112	42 48	005	39 41	055	23 42	152	54 05	196	56 03	284	34 55	307	18 37	337
113	42 53	004	40 28	055	24 09	152	53 49	197	55 08	283	34 10	307	18 15	336
114	42 57	003	41 14	054	24 36	152	53 31	198	54 13	283	33 24	306	17 51	336
115	42 59	002	41 59	053	25 03	152	53 13	199	53 18	282	32 38	305	17 28	335
116	43 00	001	42 44	052	25 30	152	52 54	200	52 22	282	31 51	305	17 03	334
117	43 01	359	43 29	051	25 56	152	52 34	201	51 27	281	31 04	304	16 38	334
118	42 59	358	44 13	050	26 23	152	52 14	202	50 31	280	30 17	303	16 13	333
119	42 57	357	44 56	049	26 50	152	51 52	202	49 35	280	29 30	303	15 47	333
	◆ REGULUS		SPICA		◆ ACRUX		CANOPUS		◆ RIGEL		BETELGEUSE		POLLUX	
120	45 39	048	11 34	098	27 16	152	51 30	203	48 39	279	49 37	308	42 54	356
121	46 21	047	12 30	098	27 43	152	51 08	204	47 43	279	48 52	307	42 49	355
122	47 02	046	13 27	097	28 09	152	50 44	205	46 47	278	48 06	306	42 43	353
123	47 43	045	14 23	097	28 35	153	50 20	205	45 51	278	47 20	305	42 36	352
124	48 23	044	15 19	097	29 01	153	49 55	206	44 55	278	46 33	304	42 28	351
125	49 02	043	16 16	097	29 27	153	49 30	207	43 58	277	45 46	303	42 18	350
126	49 41	042	17 12	096	29 53	153	49 04	207	43 02	277	44 59	302	42 08	349
127	50 18	041	18 08	096	30 19	153	48 38	208	42 06	276	44 10	302	41 56	348
128	50 55	040	19 05	096	30 44	153	48 11	209	41 09	276	43 22	301	41 43	346
129	51 31	038	20 01	095	31 10	153	47 43	209	40 13	275	42 33	300	41 30	345
130	52 05	037	20 58	095	31 35	154	47 15	210	39 16	275	41 44	299	41 15	344
131	52 39	036	21 54	095	32 00	154	46 47	210	38 20	275	40 54	299	40 59	343
132	53 12	035	22 51	095	32 25	154	46 18	211	37 23	274	40 04	298	40 42	342
133	53 43	033	23 47	094	32 50	154	45 48	211	36 26	274	39 14	297	40 23	341
134	54 14	032	24 44	094	33 14	155	45 18	212	35 30	273	38 23	297	40 04	340
	REGULUS		◆ SPICA		ACRUX		◆ CANOPUS		SIRIUS		BETELGEUSE		◆ POLLUX	
135	54 43	030	25 41	094	33 38	155	44 48	212	58 02	269	37 32	296	39 44	339
136	55 11	029	26 37	093	34 03	155	44 18	213	57 06	268	36 41	295	39 23	338
137	55 38	027	27 34	093	34 26	155	43 47	213	56 09	268	35 50	295	39 01	337
138	56 03	026	28 31	093	34 50	156	43 15	214	55 12	268	34 58	294	38 38	336
139	56 27	024	29 27	092	35 13	156	42 44	214	54 15	268	34 06	293	38 14	335
140	56 49	022	30 24	092	35 36	156	42 11	215	53 19	267	33 14	293	37 49	334
141	57 10	021	31 21	092	35 59	156	41 39	215	52 22	267	32 22	292	37 24	333
142	57 29	019	32 17	092	36 22	157	41 07	215	51 25	267	31 29	292	36 57	332
143	57 47	017	33 14	091	36 44	157	40 34	216	50 29	266	30 36	291	36 30	331
144	58 03	015	34 11	091	37 06	157	40 00	216	49 32	266	29 43	291	36 02	330
145	58 17	014	35 08	091	37 28	158	39 27	216	48 36	266	28 50	290	35 33	329
146	58 29	012	36 04	090	37 49	158	38 53	217	47 39	266	27 57	290	35 03	328
147	58 40	010	37 01	090	38 10	158	38 19	217	46 42	265	27 03	289	34 33	327
148	58 49	008	37 58	090	38 31	159	37 45	217	45 46	265	26 10	289	34 01	326
149	58 56	006	38 54	089	38 51	159	37 11	217	44 49	265	25 16	288	33 30	325
	REGULUS		◆ ARCTURUS		SPICA		◆ ACRUX		CANOPUS		SIRIUS		◆ PROCYON	
150	59 01	004	16 30	062	39 51	089	39 11	160	36 36	218	43 53	265	47 55	302
151	59 05	002	17 20	062	40 48	089	39 31	160	36 02	218	42 56	265	47 06	301
152	59 06	001	18 10	061	41 45	088	39 50	160	35 27	218	42 00	264	46 17	300
153	59 06	359	18 59	061	42 41	088	40 09	161	34 52	218	41 04	264	45 28	299
154	59 04	357	19 49	061	43 38	088	40 27	161	34 17	218	40 07	264	44 38	298
155	58 59	355	20 38	060	44 35	087	40 45	162	33 41	219	39 11	264	43 48	298
156	58 53	353	21 27	060	45 31	087	41 03	162	33 06	219	38 14	263	42 58	297
157	58 46	351	22 16	059	46 28	086	41 20	163	32 30	219	37 18	263	42 07	296
158	58 36	349	23 04	058	47 25	086	41 37	163	31 55	219	36 22	263	41 16	295
159	58 24	347	23 53	058	48 21	086	41 53	164	31 19	219	35 25	263	40 24	295
160	58 11	346	24 41	057	49 18	085	42 09	164	30 43	219	34 29	262	39 33	294
161	57 56	344	25 28	057	50 14	085	42 24	165	30 07	219	33 33	262	38 41	293
162	57 40	342	26 16	056	51 11	084	42 39	165	29 31	219	32 37	262	37 49	293
163	57 21	340	27 03	056	52 07	084	42 54	166	28 55	220	31 41	262	36 56	292
164	57 01	339	27 49	055	53 03	083	43 08	166	28 19	220	30 45	261	36 04	292
	Denebola		◆ ARCTURUS		SPICA		◆ ACRUX		SIRIUS		◆ PROCYON		REGULUS	
165	54 20	021	28 36	054	54 00	083	43 21	167	29 49	261	35 11	291	56 40	337
166	54 40	019	29 21	054	54 56	082	43 34	167	28 52	261	34 18	291	56 17	335
167	54 58	018	30 07	053	55 52	082	43 46	168	27 56	261	33 24	290	55 52	334
168	55 14	016	30 52	052	56 48	081	43 58	168	27 01	260	32 31	289	55 27	332
169	55 30	015	31 37	052	57 44	081	44 09	169	26 05	260	31 37	289	54 59	331
170	55 43	013	32 21	051	58 40	080	44 20	169	25 09	260	30 44	288	54 31	329
171	55 55	011	33 05	050	59 36	080	44 30	170	24 13	260	29 50	288	54 01	328
172	56 05	009	33 49	050	60 32	079	44 39	171	23 17	259	28 56	287	53 30	326
173	56 14	008	34 32	049	61 28	078	44 48	171	22 21	259	28 02	287	52 58	325
174	56 20	006	35 14	048	62 23	078	44 57	172	21 26	259	27 07	286	52 25	324
175	56 25	004	35 56	047	63 18	077	45 04	172	20 30	259	26 13	286	51 51	322
176	56 29	003	36 38	047	64 14	076	45 12	173	19 34	258	25 18	286	51 16	321
177	56 31	001	37 19	046	65 09	075	45 18	174	18 38	258	24 23	285	50 40	320
178	56 30	359	37 59	045	66 03	074	45 24	174	17 43	258	23 29	285	50 03	319
179	56 29	357	38 39	044	66 58	074	45 29	175	16 48	258	22 34	284	49 25	317

LHA ♈	Hc	Zn	Hc	Zn	Hc	Zn	Hc	Zn	Hc	Zn	Hc	Zn	Hc	Zn
	ARCTURUS		◆ANTARES		ACRUX		◆Suhail		Alphard		REGULUS		◆Denebola	
180	39 18	043	27 54	111	45 34	176	46 37	226	51 52	280	48 46	316	56 25	356
181	39 57	042	28 47	110	45 38	176	45 57	226	50 57	280	48 06	315	56 20	354
182	40 34	041	29 40	110	45 42	177	45 15	227	50 01	279	47 26	314	56 13	352
183	41 11	040	30 33	110	45 44	178	44 34	227	49 05	279	46 45	313	56 04	350
184	41 48	039	31 27	110	45 46	178	43 52	227	48 08	278	46 03	312	55 54	349
185	42 24	038	32 20	110	45 48	179	43 11	228	47 12	278	45 21	311	55 42	347
186	42 58	037	33 13	110	45 49	179	42 29	228	46 16	277	44 38	310	55 28	345
187	43 33	036	34 07	110	45 49	180	41 47	228	45 20	277	43 54	309	55 13	344
188	44 06	035	35 00	110	45 49	181	41 04	228	44 23	276	43 10	308	54 56	342
189	44 38	034	35 54	109	45 48	181	40 22	228	43 27	276	42 26	308	54 38	340
190	45 10	033	36 47	109	45 46	182	39 39	229	42 31	276	41 40	307	54 18	339
191	45 40	032	37 41	109	45 44	183	38 57	229	41 34	275	40 55	306	53 57	337
192	46 10	031	38 34	109	45 41	183	38 14	229	40 38	275	40 09	305	53 35	336
193	46 38	030	39 28	109	45 37	184	37 31	229	39 41	274	39 22	304	53 11	334
194	47 06	028	40 22	109	45 33	185	36 48	229	38 44	274	38 35	304	52 46	333
	ARCTURUS		◆Rasalhague		ANTARES		◆ACRUX		Suhail		◆REGULUS		Denebola	
195	47 32	027	15 09	071	41 15	109	45 28	185	36 05	229	37 47	303	52 19	331
196	47 58	026	16 03	070	42 09	109	45 22	186	35 22	230	37 00	302	51 51	330
197	48 22	025	16 56	070	43 03	109	45 16	186	34 39	230	36 11	301	51 23	329
198	48 45	023	17 49	069	43 56	109	45 10	187	33 55	230	35 23	301	50 53	327
199	49 07	022	18 42	069	44 50	109	45 02	188	33 12	230	34 34	300	50 21	326
200	49 28	021	19 35	069	45 44	109	44 54	188	32 29	230	33 45	299	49 49	325
201	49 47	019	20 28	068	46 37	109	44 46	189	31 45	230	32 55	299	49 16	324
202	50 06	018	21 20	068	47 31	109	44 37	190	31 02	230	32 05	298	48 42	322
203	50 22	017	22 13	067	48 25	109	44 27	190	30 18	230	31 15	298	48 07	321
204	50 38	015	23 05	067	49 19	109	44 17	191	29 35	230	30 25	297	47 31	320
205	50 52	014	23 57	066	50 12	109	44 06	191	28 51	230	29 34	296	46 54	319
206	51 05	012	24 49	066	51 06	109	43 55	192	28 08	230	28 43	296	46 17	318
207	51 16	011	25 40	065	52 00	109	43 43	192	27 24	230	27 52	295	45 38	317
208	51 26	009	26 31	065	52 53	109	43 30	193	26 41	230	27 01	295	44 59	316
209	51 34	008	27 23	064	53 47	109	43 17	194	25 57	230	26 09	294	44 20	315
	◆ARCTURUS		Rasalhague		◆ANTARES		RIGIL KENT		ACRUX		◆Suhail		REGULUS	
210	51 41	006	28 14	064	54 40	109	47 29	173	43 04	194	25 14	230	25 17	294
211	51 46	005	29 04	063	55 34	109	47 36	173	42 50	195	24 30	230	24 25	293
212	51 50	003	29 55	062	56 27	109	47 42	174	42 35	195	23 47	230	23 33	293
213	51 53	002	30 45	062	57 21	110	47 48	175	42 20	196	23 03	230	22 41	292
214	51 54	000	31 35	061	58 14	110	47 53	176	42 05	196	22 20	230	21 48	292
215	51 53	359	32 24	061	59 08	110	47 57	176	41 49	197	21 37	230	20 55	291
216	51 51	357	33 13	060	60 01	110	48 00	177	41 32	197	20 53	230	20 03	291
217	51 47	356	34 02	059	60 54	111	48 03	178	41 16	198	20 10	230	19 10	291
218	51 42	354	34 51	059	61 47	111	48 05	178	40 58	198	19 27	229	18 16	290
219	51 35	353	35 39	058	62 40	111	48 06	179	40 40	198	18 44	229	17 23	290
220	51 27	351	36 27	057	63 33	111	48 06	180	40 22	199	18 01	229	16 29	289
221	51 18	350	37 15	057	64 26	112	48 06	181	40 04	199	17 18	229	15 36	289
222	51 07	348	38 02	056	65 18	112	48 05	181	39 45	200	16 35	229	14 42	288
223	50 54	347	38 49	055	66 11	113	48 03	182	39 26	200	15 53	229	13 48	288
224	50 40	345	39 35	054	67 03	113	48 01	183	39 06	201	15 10	229	12 54	288
	Alphecca		◆VEGA		ALTAIR		◆Peacock		RIGIL KENT		◆SPICA		ARCTURUS	
225	43 32	011	13 01	041	12 59	076	20 18	145	47 58	184	66 03	286	50 25	344
226	43 42	010	13 38	040	13 54	075	20 51	145	47 54	184	65 08	285	50 09	342
227	43 51	008	14 14	040	14 48	075	21 24	145	47 49	185	64 13	284	49 51	341
228	43 59	007	14 50	039	15 43	075	21 57	145	47 44	186	63 18	283	49 31	340
229	44 06	006	15 26	039	16 38	074	22 30	144	47 38	186	62 23	282	49 11	338
230	44 11	005	16 01	038	17 32	074	23 03	144	47 32	187	61 27	282	48 49	337
231	44 15	004	16 36	037	18 27	073	23 36	144	47 24	188	60 32	281	48 26	336
232	44 18	002	17 10	037	19 21	073	24 09	145	47 16	188	59 36	280	48 02	334
233	44 20	001	17 44	036	20 15	072	24 42	145	47 08	189	58 40	280	47 37	333
234	44 20	000	18 17	036	21 09	072	25 15	145	46 58	190	57 44	279	47 11	332
235	44 19	359	18 50	035	22 03	072	25 47	145	46 48	190	56 48	279	46 43	331
236	44 17	357	19 23	035	22 57	071	26 20	145	46 38	191	55 52	278	46 15	329
237	44 14	356	19 54	034	23 50	071	26 53	145	46 26	192	54 56	278	45 45	328
238	44 09	355	20 26	033	24 44	070	27 26	145	46 14	192	53 59	277	45 15	327
239	44 04	354	20 57	033	25 37	070	27 58	145	46 02	193	53 03	277	44 44	326
	◆VEGA		ALTAIR		◆Peacock		RIGIL KENT		◆SPICA		ARCTURUS		Alphecca	
240	21 27	032	26 30	069	28 31	145	45 49	194	52 07	276	44 11	325	43 57	352
241	21 57	031	27 23	069	29 04	145	45 35	194	51 10	276	43 38	324	43 48	351
242	22 26	031	28 16	068	29 36	145	45 21	195	50 14	275	43 04	323	43 39	350
243	22 55	030	29 09	068	30 08	145	45 06	196	49 17	275	42 30	322	43 29	349
244	23 23	029	30 01	067	30 41	145	44 50	196	48 21	274	41 54	321	43 17	347
245	23 51	029	30 53	067	31 13	146	44 34	197	47 24	274	41 18	320	43 04	346
246	24 18	028	31 45	066	31 45	146	44 18	197	46 27	274	40 41	319	42 50	345
247	24 44	027	32 37	065	32 17	146	44 01	198	45 31	273	40 03	318	42 35	344
248	25 10	027	33 28	065	32 48	146	43 43	198	44 34	273	39 25	317	42 19	343
249	25 35	026	34 20	064	33 20	146	43 25	199	43 38	272	38 46	316	42 01	342
250	25 59	025	35 11	064	33 51	146	43 07	199	42 41	272	38 06	315	41 43	341
251	26 23	024	36 01	063	34 23	147	42 47	200	41 44	272	37 26	314	41 23	339
252	26 46	024	36 52	062	34 54	147	42 28	200	40 47	271	36 45	314	41 03	338
253	27 09	023	37 42	062	35 25	147	42 08	201	39 51	271	36 04	313	40 42	337
254	27 31	022	38 32	061	35 55	147	41 48	201	38 54	271	35 22	312	40 19	336
	◆VEGA		ALTAIR		◆Peacock		RIGIL KENT		◆SPICA		ARCTURUS		Alphecca	
255	27 51	021	39 21	060	36 26	148	41 27	202	37 57	270	34 39	311	39 56	335
256	28 12	021	40 10	060	36 56	148	41 06	202	37 01	270	33 56	310	39 31	334
257	28 31	020	40 59	059	37 26	148	40 44	203	36 04	270	33 13	310	39 06	333
258	28 50	019	41 47	058	37 56	148	40 22	203	35 07	269	32 29	309	38 40	332
259	29 08	018	42 35	057	38 26	149	39 59	203	34 10	269	31 45	308	38 13	331
260	29 25	017	43 23	057	38 55	149	39 37	204	33 14	269	31 00	308	37 45	330
261	29 42	016	44 10	056	39 24	149	39 14	204	32 17	268	30 15	307	37 16	329
262	29 57	016	44 57	055	39 53	150	38 50	205	31 20	268	29 29	306	36 47	328
263	30 12	015	45 43	054	40 21	150	38 26	205	30 24	268	28 44	306	36 17	327
264	30 26	014	46 29	053	40 49	151	38 02	205	29 27	268	27 57	305	35 46	326
265	30 39	013	47 14	052	41 17	151	37 38	206	28 30	267	27 11	304	35 14	326
266	30 52	012	47 58	051	41 44	151	37 13	206	27 33	267	26 24	304	34 41	325
267	31 03	011	48 42	050	42 11	152	36 48	206	26 37	267	25 36	303	34 08	324
268	31 14	010	49 25	049	42 38	152	36 23	207	25 40	266	24 49	303	33 34	323
269	31 23	009	50 08	048	43 04	153	35 57	207	24 44	266	24 01	302	33 00	322

LHA ♈	Hc	Zn	Hc	Zn	Hc	Zn	Hc	Zn	Hc	Zn	Hc	Zn	Hc	Zn
	◆VEGA		ALTAIR		◆FOMALHAUT		Peacock		RIGIL KENT		◆ANTARES		Alphecca	
270	31 32	009	50 50	047	22 15	115	43 30	153	35 31	207	68 03	246	32 25	321
271	31 40	008	51 31	046	23 07	115	43 56	154	35 05	207	67 12	247	31 49	321
272	31 47	007	52 11	045	23 58	115	44 21	154	34 39	208	66 19	247	31 13	320
273	31 54	006	52 51	043	24 50	115	44 45	155	34 13	208	65 27	248	30 36	319
274	31 59	005	53 29	042	25 41	114	45 09	155	33 46	208	64 34	248	29 58	318
275	32 03	004	54 07	041	26 33	114	45 33	156	33 19	208	63 42	248	29 20	318
276	32 07	003	54 44	040	27 25	114	45 56	156	32 52	209	62 49	249	28 42	317
277	32 10	002	55 19	038	28 17	114	46 19	157	32 25	209	61 56	249	28 03	316
278	32 11	001	55 54	037	29 08	114	46 41	157	31 57	209	61 03	249	27 23	315
279	32 12	000	56 27	035	30 00	114	47 02	158	31 30	209	60 10	250	26 43	315
280	32 12	359	56 59	034	30 52	114	47 23	159	31 02	209	59 16	250	26 03	314
281	32 11	358	57 30	032	31 44	114	47 44	159	30 34	210	58 23	250	25 22	314
282	32 09	358	58 00	031	32 36	114	48 04	160	30 06	210	57 30	250	24 40	313
283	32 06	357	58 28	029	33 28	113	48 23	161	29 38	210	56 36	250	23 59	312
284	32 02	356	58 55	027	34 20	113	48 41	161	29 09	210	55 43	251	23 16	312
	DENEB		◆FOMALHAUT		Peacock		RIGIL KENT		◆ANTARES		Rasalhague		◆VEGA	
285	21 37	019	35 12	113	48 59	162	28 41	210	54 49	251	52 13	325	31 58	355
286	21 55	018	36 05	113	49 16	163	28 13	210	53 56	251	51 40	324	31 52	354
287	22 13	018	36 57	113	49 33	163	27 44	210	53 02	251	51 06	322	31 46	353
288	22 30	017	37 49	113	49 49	164	27 15	210	52 08	251	50 31	321	31 38	352
289	22 46	016	38 41	113	50 04	165	26 46	211	51 15	251	49 55	320	31 30	351
290	23 01	016	39 33	113	50 18	166	26 18	211	50 21	251	49 18	319	31 21	350
291	23 16	015	40 25	113	50 32	166	25 49	211	49 27	251	48 40	318	31 11	349
292	23 30	014	41 18	113	50 45	167	25 20	211	48 34	251	48 02	317	31 00	349
293	23 44	013	42 10	113	50 57	168	24 51	211	47 40	251	47 22	316	30 48	348
294	23 56	013	43 02	113	51 08	169	24 22	211	46 46	251	46 42	314	30 36	347
295	24 08	012	43 54	113	51 19	170	23 52	211	45 53	251	46 01	313	30 22	346
296	24 20	011	44 46	113	51 28	171	23 23	211	44 59	251	45 20	312	30 08	345
297	24 30	010	45 39	113	51 37	171	22 54	211	44 05	251	44 38	312	29 53	344
298	24 40	010	46 31	113	51 45	172	22 25	211	43 11	251	43 55	311	29 37	343
299	24 49	009	47 23	113	51 53	173	21 56	211	42 18	251	43 11	310	29 21	343
	◆DENEB		Alpheratz		◆FOMALHAUT		Peacock		◆ANTARES		Rasalhague		VEGA	
300	24 58	008	13 01	053	48 15	113	51 59	174	41 24	251	42 27	309	29 03	342
301	25 05	007	13 46	052	49 07	114	52 04	175	40 30	251	41 43	308	28 45	341
302	25 12	007	14 30	052	49 59	114	52 09	176	39 37	251	40 58	307	28 26	340
303	25 18	006	15 15	051	50 51	114	52 13	177	38 43	251	40 13	306	28 06	339
304	25 24	005	15 59	051	51 43	114	52 16	178	37 50	251	39 27	306	27 46	338
305	25 28	004	16 42	050	52 35	114	52 18	178	36 56	251	38 40	305	27 25	338
306	25 32	003	17 26	050	53 26	114	52 19	179	36 03	251	37 53	304	27 03	337
307	25 35	003	18 09	049	54 18	114	52 19	180	35 09	250	37 06	303	26 40	336
308	25 38	002	18 51	049	55 10	115	52 18	181	34 16	250	36 18	303	26 17	335
309	25 39	001	19 34	048	56 01	115	52 17	182	33 22	250	35 30	302	25 53	335
310	25 40	000	20 16	047	56 52	115	52 14	183	32 29	250	34 42	301	25 28	334
311	25 40	000	20 57	047	57 44	116	52 11	184	31 35	250	33 53	301	25 03	333
312	25 39	359	21 38	046	58 35	116	52 06	185	30 42	250	33 04	300	24 37	332
313	25 37	358	22 19	046	59 26	116	52 01	186	29 49	250	32 15	299	24 10	332
314	25 35	357	22 59	045	60 17	117	51 55	186	28 56	250	31 25	299	23 43	331
	Alpheratz		◆Diphda		ACHERNAR		Peacock		◆ANTARES		VEGA		◆DENEB	
315	23 39	044	37 01	098	26 54	145	51 48	187	28 03	249	23 16	330	25 32	356
316	24 19	044	37 57	098	27 27	145	51 41	188	27 09	249	22 47	330	25 28	356
317	24 58	043	38 54	098	27 59	145	51 32	189	26 16	249	22 18	329	25 24	355
318	25 37	043	39 50	098	28 31	146	51 23	190	25 23	249	21 49	328	25 18	354
319	26 15	042	40 46	098	29 03	146	51 13	191	24 30	249	21 19	328	25 12	353
320	26 52	041	41 42	097	29 35	146	51 02	192	23 38	249	20 48	327	25 05	353
321	27 29	041	42 38	097	30 07	146	50 50	192	22 45	248	20 17	326	24 57	352
322	28 06	040	43 35	097	30 39	146	50 37	193	21 52	248	19 46	326	24 49	351
323	28 42	039	44 31	097	31 11	146	50 24	194	20 59	248	19 14	325	24 40	350
324	29 18	038	45 27	097	31 42	146	50 10	195	20 07	248	18 41	325	24 30	350
325	29 52	038	46 24	096	32 14	146	49 55	196	19 14	248	18 08	324	24 19	349
326	30 27	037	47 20	096	32 45	147	49 40	196	18 22	248	17 35	324	24 08	348
327	31 00	036	48 17	096	33 16	147	49 23	197	17 29	247	17 01	323	23 56	347
328	31 34	035	49 13	096	33 47	147	49 06	198	16 37	247	16 26	322	23 43	347
329	32 06	034	50 10	095	34 18	147	48 49	198	15 45	247	15 51	322	23 30	346
	◆Alpheratz		Diphda		◆ACHERNAR		Peacock		◆Nunki		ALTAIR		DENEB	
330	32 38	034	51 06	095	34 48	147	48 30	199	47 11	252	47 47	309	23 16	345
331	33 09	033	52 02	095	35 19	148	48 12	200	46 17	251	47 03	308	23 01	344
332	33 39	032	52 59	095	35 49	148	47 52	200	45 24	251	46 18	307	22 45	344
333	34 09	031	53 56	095	36 19	148	47 32	201	44 30	251	45 32	306	22 29	343
334	34 38	030	54 52	094	36 49	148	47 11	202	43 36	251	44 46	305	22 12	342
335	35 06	029	55 49	094	37 18	149	46 50	202	42 42	251	43 59	304	21 55	342
336	35 33	028	56 45	094	37 48	149	46 28	203	41 49	251	43 12	303	21 37	341
337	36 00	027	57 42	094	38 17	149	46 06	204	40 55	251	42 24	302	21 18	340
338	36 26	027	58 39	093	38 46	150	45 43	204	40 01	251	41 36	302	20 58	340
339	36 50	026	59 35	093	39 14	150	45 19	205	39 07	251	40 47	301	20 38	339
340	37 15	025	60 32	093	39 42	150	44 55	205	38 14	251	39 58	300	20 18	338
341	37 38	024	61 28	093	40 10	151	44 31	206	37 20	251	39 09	299	19 56	338
342	38 00	023	62 25	092	40 38	151	44 06	206	36 27	251	38 20	299	19 35	337
343	38 21	022	63 22	092	41 05	151	43 41	207	35 33	251	37 30	298	19 12	336
344	38 42	021	64 19	092	41 32	152	43 15	207	34 39	251	36 40	297	18 49	336
	Alpheratz		◆Hamal		◆ACHERNAR		Peacock		Nunki		◆ALTAIR		DENEB	
345	39 01	020	27 28	049	41 58	152	42 49	208	33 46	251	35 49	297	18 26	335
346	39 20	018	28 10	048	42 25	153	42 22	208	32 52	250	34 58	296	18 02	335
347	39 37	017	28 53	048	42 50	153	41 56	209	31 59	250	34 07	296	17 37	334
348	39 53	016	29 34	047	43 16	154	41 28	209	31 06	250	33 16	295	17 12	333
349	40 09	015	30 16	046	43 41	154	41 01	209	30 12	250	32 24	294	16 46	333
350	40 23	014	30 57	046	44 05	155	40 33	210	29 19	250	31 33	294	16 20	332
351	40 37	013	31 37	045	44 29	155	40 04	210	28 26	250	30 40	293	15 53	332
352	40 49	012	32 17	044	44 53	156	39 36	210	27 33	250	29 48	293	15 26	331
353	41 00	011	32 56	043	45 16	156	39 07	211	26 39	249	28 56	292	14 58	331
354	41 10	010	33 35	043	45 39	157	38 38	211	25 46	249	28 03	292	14 30	330
355	41 19	008	34 13	042	46 01	157	38 08	211	24 53	249	27 10	291	14 02	329
356	41 27	007	34 50	041	46 22	158	37 39	212	24 00	249	26 17	291	13 33	329
357	41 33	006	35 27	040	46 43	159	37 09	212	23 07	249	25 24	290	13 03	328
358	41 39	005	36 04	039	47 04	159	36 38	212	22 14	249	24 31	290	12 33	328
359	41 43	004	36 39	039	47 24	160	36 08	213	21 22	248	23 37	289	12 03	327

LAT 20°S

LHA ♈	Hc Zn	Hc Zn	Hc Zn	Hc Zn	Hc Zn	Hc Zn	Hc Zn
	◆ Alpheratz	Hamal	ALDEBARAN	◆ RIGEL	ACHERNAR	◆ Peacock	Enif
0	40 47 003	36 27 037	12 52 067	13 15 094	48 40 160	36 28 213	45 16 309
1	40 49 001	37 00 036	13 43 066	14 11 094	48 59 161	35 57 213	44 32 308
2	40 50 000	37 33 035	14 35 066	15 07 093	49 17 161	35 26 214	43 47 307
3	40 49 359	38 05 034	15 26 065	16 04 093	49 35 162	34 54 214	43 02 306
4	40 48 358	38 37 033	16 18 065	17 00 093	49 52 163	34 23 214	42 16 305
5	40 45 357	39 08 032	17 09 065	17 56 092	50 08 164	33 51 214	41 30 305
6	40 42 356	39 37 031	17 59 064	18 53 092	50 23 164	33 19 214	40 43 304
7	40 37 355	40 06 030	18 50 064	19 49 092	50 38 165	32 47 215	39 56 303
8	40 31 353	40 35 029	19 40 063	20 45 091	50 53 166	32 15 215	39 09 302
9	40 24 352	41 02 028	20 31 063	21 42 091	51 06 167	31 43 215	38 21 301
10	40 16 351	41 28 027	21 21 062	22 38 091	51 19 167	31 11 215	37 32 301
11	40 07 350	41 54 026	22 10 062	23 34 090	51 31 168	30 39 215	36 44 300
12	39 57 349	42 18 025	23 00 061	24 31 090	51 42 169	30 06 215	35 55 299
13	39 45 348	42 41 024	23 49 061	25 27 090	51 52 170	29 34 215	35 06 299
14	39 33 347	43 04 023	24 38 060	26 23 089	52 02 171	29 01 215	34 16 298
	◆ Hamal	ALDEBARAN	RIGEL	◆ CANOPUS	ACHERNAR	◆ FOMALHAUT	Alpheratz
15	43 25 022	25 27 059	27 20 089	21 08 140	52 10 172	60 55 245	39 19 346
16	43 45 020	26 15 059	28 16 089	21 44 140	52 18 172	60 04 245	39 05 345
17	44 05 019	27 03 058	29 13 088	22 20 140	52 25 173	59 13 246	38 49 343
18	44 23 018	27 51 058	30 09 088	22 56 140	52 31 174	58 21 246	38 33 342
19	44 40 017	28 38 057	31 05 088	23 33 140	52 37 175	57 30 246	38 15 341
20	44 55 016	29 26 056	32 02 087	24 09 140	52 41 176	56 38 246	37 57 340
21	45 10 014	30 12 056	32 58 087	24 45 140	52 45 177	55 46 247	37 37 339
22	45 23 013	30 59 055	33 54 086	25 22 140	52 47 178	54 55 247	37 17 338
23	45 35 012	31 45 054	34 50 086	25 58 140	52 49 179	54 03 247	36 55 337
24	45 46 011	32 31 054	35 47 086	26 34 140	52 50 179	53 11 247	36 33 336
25	45 56 009	33 16 053	36 43 085	27 11 140	52 50 180	52 19 247	36 10 335
26	46 05 008	34 01 052	37 39 085	27 47 140	52 49 181	51 27 247	35 46 334
27	46 12 007	34 45 052	38 35 084	28 23 140	52 48 182	50 35 247	35 21 333
28	46 18 005	35 29 051	39 31 084	29 00 140	52 45 183	49 43 248	34 56 332
29	46 22 004	36 13 050	40 27 084	29 36 140	52 42 184	48 51 248	34 29 332
	◆ Hamal	ALDEBARAN	◆ SIRIUS	CANOPUS	ACHERNAR	◆ FOMALHAUT	Alpheratz
30	46 25 003	36 55 049	22 38 100	30 12 140	52 37 185	47 59 248	34 02 331
31	46 27 001	37 38 048	23 33 100	30 48 140	52 32 186	47 06 248	33 34 330
32	46 28 000	38 20 048	24 29 100	31 24 140	52 26 187	46 14 248	33 05 329
33	46 27 359	39 01 047	25 24 100	32 00 140	52 19 187	45 22 248	32 36 328
34	46 25 357	39 42 046	26 20 099	32 36 141	52 11 188	44 30 248	32 06 327
35	46 22 356	40 22 045	27 16 099	33 12 141	52 03 189	43 38 248	31 35 326
36	46 18 355	41 02 044	28 11 099	33 47 141	51 53 190	42 45 248	31 03 326
37	46 12 353	41 41 043	29 07 099	34 23 141	51 43 191	41 53 248	30 31 325
38	46 05 352	42 19 042	30 03 098	34 58 141	51 32 192	41 01 248	29 58 324
39	45 56 351	42 56 041	30 59 098	35 34 141	51 20 192	40 09 248	29 25 323
40	45 47 349	43 33 040	31 54 098	36 09 141	51 08 193	39 17 248	28 51 322
41	45 36 348	44 09 039	32 50 097	36 44 142	50 54 194	38 25 248	28 16 322
42	45 23 347	44 44 038	33 46 097	37 19 142	50 40 195	37 32 248	27 41 321
43	45 10 346	45 19 037	34 42 097	37 54 142	50 26 196	36 40 247	27 05 320
44	44 55 344	45 52 036	35 38 097	38 28 142	50 10 196	35 48 247	26 29 320
	◆ CAPELLA	BETELGEUSE	SIRIUS	◆ CANOPUS	ACHERNAR	◆ FOMALHAUT	Hamal
45	16 59 024	38 46 062	36 34 096	39 02 143	49 54 197	34 56 247	44 40 343
46	17 22 024	39 36 061	37 30 096	39 36 143	49 37 198	34 04 247	44 23 342
47	17 44 023	40 25 061	38 26 096	40 10 143	49 19 199	33 12 247	44 05 341
48	18 06 022	41 14 060	39 22 096	40 44 143	49 01 199	32 20 247	43 46 340
49	18 27 022	42 03 059	40 19 095	41 17 144	48 42 200	31 28 247	43 25 338
50	18 48 021	42 51 058	41 15 095	41 51 144	48 23 201	30 37 247	43 04 337
51	19 08 020	43 39 058	42 11 095	42 24 144	48 03 201	29 45 247	42 42 336
52	19 27 020	44 26 057	43 07 095	42 56 145	47 42 202	28 53 247	42 18 335
53	19 46 019	45 13 056	44 03 094	43 28 145	47 21 202	28 01 246	41 54 334
54	20 04 019	46 00 055	44 59 094	44 00 146	46 59 203	27 10 246	41 28 333
55	20 22 018	46 45 054	45 56 094	44 32 146	46 37 204	26 18 246	41 02 332
56	20 39 017	47 31 053	46 52 093	45 03 146	46 14 204	25 27 246	40 35 331
57	20 55 016	48 16 052	47 48 093	45 34 147	45 51 205	24 35 246	40 07 330
58	21 11 016	49 00 051	48 45 093	46 05 147	45 27 205	23 44 246	39 38 329
59	21 26 015	49 43 050	49 41 093	46 35 148	45 03 206	22 53 245	39 08 328
	CAPELLA	BETELGEUSE	◆ SIRIUS	CANOPUS	◆ ACHERNAR	Diphda	◆ Hamal
60	21 40 014	50 26 049	50 37 092	47 05 148	44 38 206	43 51 264	38 37 327
61	21 54 014	51 09 048	51 34 092	47 34 149	44 13 207	42 55 264	38 06 326
62	22 07 013	51 50 047	52 30 092	48 03 149	43 47 207	41 59 264	37 34 325
63	22 19 012	52 31 046	53 26 091	48 31 150	43 21 208	41 03 263	37 01 324
64	22 31 012	53 10 044	54 23 091	48 59 151	42 55 208	40 07 263	36 27 323
65	22 42 011	53 49 043	55 19 091	49 27 151	42 28 208	39 11 263	35 53 322
66	22 52 010	54 27 042	56 15 090	49 54 152	42 01 209	38 15 263	35 17 321
67	23 02 009	55 05 040	57 12 090	50 20 153	41 34 209	37 19 262	34 42 320
68	23 11 009	55 41 039	58 08 090	50 46 153	41 06 210	36 23 262	34 05 319
69	23 19 008	56 16 038	59 05 089	51 11 154	40 38 210	35 28 262	33 28 319
70	23 26 007	56 49 036	60 01 089	51 35 155	40 10 210	34 32 262	32 51 318
71	23 33 006	57 22 035	60 57 089	51 59 155	39 41 211	33 36 261	32 13 317
72	23 39 006	57 54 033	61 54 088	52 22 156	39 12 211	32 40 261	31 34 316
73	23 44 005	58 24 031	62 50 088	52 45 157	38 43 211	31 45 261	30 55 315
74	23 48 004	58 52 030	63 46 087	53 06 158	38 14 212	30 49 261	30 15 315
	CAPELLA	POLLUX	◆ PROCYON	Suhail	◆ CANOPUS	ACHERNAR	◆ Hamal
75	23 52 003	27 25 041	43 18 062	33 39 130	53 27 159	37 44 212	29 35 314
76	23 55 003	28 02 041	44 07 061	34 22 130	53 48 159	37 14 212	28 54 313
77	23 57 002	28 38 040	44 56 060	35 05 130	54 07 160	36 44 212	28 13 313
78	23 59 001	29 14 039	45 45 059	35 49 130	54 26 161	36 13 213	27 31 312
79	23 59 000	29 49 038	46 33 058	36 32 130	54 43 162	35 43 213	26 49 311
80	23 59 000	30 24 038	47 21 058	37 15 130	55 00 163	35 12 213	26 06 311
81	23 58 359	30 58 037	48 08 057	37 58 130	55 16 164	34 41 213	25 23 310
82	23 57 358	31 31 036	48 55 056	38 41 130	55 32 165	34 10 214	24 40 309
83	23 55 357	32 04 035	49 41 055	39 24 130	55 46 166	33 39 214	23 56 309
84	23 52 357	32 36 034	50 27 054	40 07 131	55 59 167	33 08 214	23 12 308
85	23 48 356	33 08 033	51 12 053	40 50 131	56 11 168	32 36 214	22 27 308
86	23 43 355	33 39 033	51 57 052	41 32 131	56 23 169	32 05 214	21 43 307
87	23 38 354	34 09 032	52 41 051	42 15 131	56 33 170	31 33 214	20 57 306
88	23 32 354	34 38 031	53 24 049	42 57 131	56 42 171	31 01 214	20 12 306
89	23 25 353	35 07 030	54 06 048	43 39 132	56 50 172	30 29 215	19 26 305

LHA ♈	Hc Zn	Hc Zn	Hc Zn	Hc Zn	Hc Zn	Hc Zn	Hc Zn
	POLLUX	◆ REGULUS	Suhail	◆ CANOPUS	ACHERNAR	◆ ALDEBARAN	CAPELLA
90	35 34 029	20 55 068	44 21 132	56 58 173	29 57 215	48 08 329	23 18 352
91	36 01 028	21 47 068	45 03 132	57 04 174	29 25 215	47 39 328	23 10 351
92	36 27 027	22 39 067	45 45 133	57 09 175	28 53 215	47 09 327	23 01 351
93	36 53 026	23 31 067	46 26 133	57 13 177	28 20 215	46 37 326	22 51 350
94	37 17 025	24 23 066	47 08 133	57 15 178	27 48 215	46 05 325	22 41 349
95	37 41 024	25 14 066	47 49 134	57 17 179	27 16 215	45 32 323	22 30 348
96	38 03 023	26 05 065	48 29 134	57 18 180	26 43 215	44 58 322	22 18 348
97	38 25 022	26 56 064	49 10 134	57 17 181	26 11 215	44 23 321	22 06 347
98	38 46 021	27 47 064	49 50 135	57 16 182	25 38 215	43 47 320	21 53 346
99	39 06 020	28 38 063	50 30 135	57 13 183	25 06 215	43 11 319	21 39 346
100	39 25 019	29 28 063	51 09 136	57 09 184	24 33 215	42 34 318	21 25 345
101	39 42 018	30 18 062	51 49 136	57 04 185	24 01 215	41 56 317	21 09 344
102	39 59 017	31 08 062	52 27 137	56 58 187	23 28 215	41 17 316	20 54 343
103	40 15 016	31 57 061	53 06 137	56 51 188	22 56 215	40 38 315	20 37 343
104	40 30 015	32 46 060	53 44 138	56 43 189	22 23 215	39 58 314	20 20 342
	POLLUX	◆ REGULUS	◆ ACRUX	CANOPUS	◆ RIGEL	ALDEBARAN	CAPELLA
105	40 44 014	33 35 060	21 25 151	56 34 190	62 03 291	39 17 314	20 03 341
106	40 56 012	34 24 059	21 52 151	56 24 191	61 10 290	38 36 313	19 44 341
107	41 08 011	35 12 058	22 20 151	56 13 192	60 17 289	37 54 312	19 25 340
108	41 18 010	36 00 058	22 47 151	56 01 193	59 24 289	37 12 311	19 06 339
109	41 27 009	36 47 057	23 14 151	55 48 194	58 30 288	36 29 310	18 46 339
110	41 36 008	37 34 056	23 41 151	55 34 195	57 37 287	35 46 309	18 25 338
111	41 43 007	38 21 055	24 08 151	55 19 196	56 42 286	35 02 309	18 04 338
112	41 49 005	39 07 055	24 35 151	55 03 197	55 48 285	34 18 308	17 42 337
113	41 53 004	39 53 054	25 02 151	54 46 198	54 54 285	33 33 307	17 20 336
114	41 57 003	40 38 053	25 29 151	54 28 199	53 59 284	32 48 307	16 57 336
115	41 59 002	41 23 052	25 56 152	54 10 200	53 04 283	32 03 306	16 33 335
116	42 00 001	42 07 051	26 22 152	53 50 200	52 10 283	31 17 305	16 09 334
117	42 01 359	42 51 050	26 49 152	53 30 201	51 14 282	30 31 304	15 45 334
118	41 59 358	43 34 050	27 16 152	53 09 202	50 19 282	29 44 304	15 20 333
119	41 57 357	44 17 049	27 43 152	52 48 203	49 24 281	28 57 303	14 54 333
	◆ REGULUS	SPICA	◆ ACRUX	CANOPUS	◆ RIGEL	BETELGEUSE	POLLUX
120	44 59 048	11 43 098	28 09 152	52 25 204	48 29 281	49 00 309	41 54 356
121	45 40 047	12 38 098	28 36 152	52 02 205	47 33 280	48 15 308	41 49 355
122	46 21 046	13 34 097	29 02 152	51 39 205	46 38 279	47 31 307	41 43 354
123	47 01 045	14 30 097	29 28 152	51 14 206	45 42 279	46 45 306	41 37 352
124	47 40 044	15 26 097	29 54 152	50 49 207	44 46 278	45 59 305	41 28 351
125	48 18 042	16 22 096	30 21 153	50 24 207	43 50 278	45 13 304	41 19 350
126	48 56 041	17 18 096	30 46 153	49 57 208	42 55 278	44 26 303	41 09 349
127	49 33 040	18 14 096	31 12 153	49 31 209	41 59 277	43 39 302	40 58 348
128	50 08 039	19 11 095	31 38 153	49 03 209	41 03 277	42 51 302	40 45 347
129	50 43 038	20 07 095	32 03 153	48 35 210	40 07 276	42 03 301	40 32 346
130	51 17 036	21 03 095	32 29 153	48 07 210	39 11 276	41 14 300	40 17 344
131	51 50 035	21 59 094	32 54 154	47 38 211	38 14 275	40 25 299	40 01 343
132	52 22 034	22 55 094	33 19 154	47 09 212	37 18 275	39 36 299	39 44 342
133	52 53 032	23 52 094	33 44 154	46 39 212	36 22 275	38 46 298	39 27 341
134	53 23 031	24 48 093	34 08 154	46 09 213	35 26 274	37 56 297	39 08 340
	REGULUS	◆ SPICA	ACRUX	◆ CANOPUS	SIRIUS	BETELGEUSE	◆ POLLUX
135	53 51 030	25 44 093	34 33 154	45 39 213	58 03 270	37 06 297	38 48 339
136	54 18 028	26 40 093	34 57 155	45 08 213	57 06 270	36 15 296	38 28 338
137	54 44 027	27 37 093	35 21 155	44 37 214	56 10 270	35 24 295	38 06 337
138	55 09 025	28 33 092	35 45 155	44 05 214	55 14 269	34 33 295	37 43 336
139	55 32 023	29 29 092	36 08 156	43 33 215	54 17 269	33 42 294	37 20 335
140	55 53 022	30 26 092	36 31 156	43 01 215	53 21 269	32 50 293	36 56 334
141	56 14 020	31 22 091	36 54 156	42 28 215	52 25 268	31 59 293	36 30 333
142	56 32 018	32 19 091	37 17 156	41 55 216	51 28 268	31 06 292	36 04 332
143	56 49 017	33 15 091	37 39 157	41 22 216	50 32 268	30 14 292	35 37 331
144	57 05 015	34 11 090	38 01 157	40 49 216	49 36 267	29 22 291	35 10 330
145	57 19 013	35 08 090	38 23 157	40 15 217	48 39 267	28 29 291	34 41 329
146	57 31 012	36 04 090	38 45 158	39 41 217	47 43 267	27 36 290	34 12 328
147	57 41 010	37 00 089	39 06 158	39 07 217	46 47 267	26 43 290	33 42 327
148	57 50 008	37 57 089	39 27 158	38 33 218	45 50 266	25 50 289	33 11 327
149	57 57 006	38 53 088	39 47 159	37 58 218	44 54 266	24 57 289	32 40 326
	REGULUS	◆ ARCTURUS	SPICA	◆ ACRUX	CANOPUS	SIRIUS	◆ PROCYON
150	58 02 004	16 02 062	39 50 088	40 07 159	37 24 218	43 58 266	47 23 303
151	58 05 002	16 51 062	40 46 088	40 27 160	36 49 218	43 02 265	46 35 302
152	58 06 001	17 41 061	41 42 087	40 47 160	36 14 218	42 05 265	45 47 301
153	58 06 359	18 30 061	42 39 087	41 06 161	35 39 219	41 09 265	44 58 300
154	58 04 357	19 19 060	43 35 087	41 24 161	35 04 219	40 13 265	44 09 299
155	58 00 355	20 08 060	44 31 086	41 42 161	34 28 219	39 17 264	43 20 298
156	57 54 353	20 57 059	45 27 086	42 00 162	33 53 219	38 21 264	42 30 298
157	57 46 351	21 45 059	46 24 085	42 17 162	33 17 219	37 25 264	41 40 297
158	57 37 350	22 33 058	47 20 085	42 34 163	32 41 219	36 29 264	40 50 296
159	57 26 348	23 21 058	48 16 084	42 51 163	32 05 220	35 33 263	39 59 296
160	57 13 346	24 08 057	49 12 084	43 07 164	31 29 220	34 37 263	39 08 295
161	56 59 344	24 55 056	50 08 084	43 22 164	30 53 220	33 41 263	38 16 294
162	56 42 343	25 42 056	51 04 083	43 37 165	30 17 220	32 45 263	37 25 294
163	56 25 341	26 29 055	52 00 083	43 52 165	29 41 220	31 49 262	36 33 293
164	56 05 339	27 15 055	52 56 082	44 06 166	29 05 220	30 53 262	35 41 292
	Denebola	◆ ARCTURUS	SPICA	◆ ACRUX	SIRIUS	◆ PROCYON	REGULUS
165	53 24 021	28 00 054	53 52 082	44 19 166	29 57 262	34 49 292	55 45 338
166	53 43 019	28 46 053	54 47 081	44 32 167	29 02 261	33 56 291	55 22 336
167	54 01 017	29 31 053	55 43 080	44 45 168	28 06 261	33 04 291	54 59 334
168	54 17 016	30 16 052	56 39 080	44 57 168	27 10 261	32 11 290	54 33 333
169	54 31 014	31 00 051	57 34 079	45 08 169	26 15 261	31 18 290	54 07 331
170	54 44 013	31 44 051	58 29 079	45 19 169	25 19 260	30 24 289	53 39 330
171	54 56 011	32 27 050	59 25 078	45 29 170	24 23 260	29 31 288	53 10 328
172	55 06 009	33 10 049	60 20 077	45 39 170	23 28 260	28 38 288	52 40 327
173	55 14 008	33 52 048	61 15 077	45 48 171	22 32 260	27 44 287	52 09 326
174	55 21 006	34 34 048	62 09 076	45 56 172	21 37 259	26 50 287	51 37 324
175	55 26 004	35 16 047	63 04 075	46 04 172	20 42 259	25 56 286	51 03 323
176	55 29 002	35 56 046	63 58 074	46 11 173	19 46 259	25 02 286	50 29 322
177	55 31 001	36 37 045	64 52 073	46 18 174	18 51 258	24 08 286	49 54 321
178	55 30 359	37 16 044	65 46 072	46 24 174	17 56 258	23 13 285	49 17 319
179	55 29 357	37 56 044	66 40 071	46 29 175	17 01 258	22 19 285	48 40 318

LAT 20°S

LHA ♈	Hc	Zn	Hc	Zn	Hc	Zn	Hc	Zn	Hc	Zn	Hc	Zn	Hc	Zn
	ARCTURUS		◆ ANTARES		ACRUX		◆ Suhail		Alphard		REGULUS		◆ Denebola	
180	38 34	043	28 15	110	46 34	176	47 19	227	51 41	282	48 02	317	55 25	356
181	39 12	042	29 08	110	46 38	176	46 38	227	50 46	281	47 24	316	55 20	354
182	39 49	041	30 01	110	46 41	177	45 56	227	49 50	280	46 44	315	55 13	352
183	40 26	040	30 54	110	46 44	177	45 15	228	48 55	280	46 04	314	55 05	351
184	41 01	039	31 47	109	46 46	178	44 33	228	47 59	279	45 23	313	54 55	349
185	41 36	038	32 40	109	46 48	179	43 51	228	47 04	279	44 41	312	54 43	347
186	42 11	037	33 33	109	46 49	179	43 09	228	46 08	278	43 59	311	54 30	346
187	42 44	036	34 27	109	46 49	180	42 27	229	45 12	278	43 16	310	54 15	344
188	43 17	035	35 20	109	46 49	181	41 44	229	44 16	277	42 33	309	53 59	342
189	43 48	034	36 13	109	46 48	181	41 01	229	43 20	277	41 49	308	53 41	341
190	44 19	033	37 07	109	46 46	182	40 19	229	42 24	277	41 04	307	53 22	339
191	44 49	031	38 00	109	46 44	183	39 36	229	41 28	276	40 19	307	53 02	338
192	45 18	030	38 54	108	46 41	183	38 53	230	40 32	276	39 34	306	52 40	336
193	45 46	029	39 47	108	46 37	184	38 10	230	39 36	275	38 48	305	52 17	335
194	46 13	028	40 41	108	46 33	185	37 27	230	38 40	275	38 01	304	51 52	333
	ARCTURUS		◆ Rasalhague		ANTARES		◆ ACRUX		Suhail		◆ REGULUS		Denebola	
195	46 39	027	14 49	070	41 34	108	46 28	185	36 44	230	37 15	304	51 26	332
196	47 04	026	15 42	070	42 28	108	46 22	186	36 01	230	36 27	303	50 59	331
197	47 28	024	16 35	070	43 22	108	46 16	187	35 17	230	35 40	302	50 31	329
198	47 50	023	17 28	069	44 15	108	46 09	187	34 34	230	34 52	301	50 02	328
199	48 12	022	18 20	069	45 09	108	46 02	188	33 50	230	34 04	301	49 31	327
200	48 32	020	19 13	068	46 03	108	45 54	188	33 07	230	33 15	300	49 00	326
201	48 51	019	20 05	068	46 56	108	45 45	189	32 24	230	32 26	299	48 28	324
202	49 08	018	20 57	067	47 50	108	45 36	190	31 40	231	31 37	299	47 54	323
203	49 25	016	21 49	067	48 44	108	45 26	190	30 57	231	30 47	298	47 20	322
204	49 40	015	22 41	066	49 37	108	45 16	191	30 13	231	29 57	298	46 45	321
205	49 54	013	23 32	066	50 31	108	45 05	191	29 29	231	29 07	297	46 09	320
206	50 06	012	24 24	065	51 25	108	44 53	192	28 46	231	28 17	296	45 32	319
207	50 17	011	25 15	065	52 18	108	44 41	193	28 02	231	27 26	296	44 54	318
208	50 27	009	26 06	064	53 12	108	44 29	193	27 19	230	26 35	295	44 16	317
209	50 35	008	26 56	064	54 06	108	44 16	194	26 35	230	25 44	295	43 37	316
	◆ ARCTURUS		Rasalhague		◆ ANTARES		RIGIL KENT		ACRUX		◆ Suhail		REGULUS	
210	50 41	006	27 47	063	55 00	108	48 29	173	44 02	194	25 52	230	24 53	294
211	50 47	005	28 37	062	55 53	108	48 36	173	43 48	195	25 09	230	24 01	294
212	50 51	003	29 27	062	56 47	108	48 42	174	43 33	195	24 25	230	23 10	293
213	50 53	002	30 16	061	57 40	108	48 48	175	43 18	196	23 42	230	22 18	293
214	50 54	000	31 05	061	58 34	108	48 52	175	43 02	196	22 59	230	21 26	292
215	50 53	359	31 54	060	59 27	108	48 57	176	42 46	197	22 15	230	20 33	292
216	50 51	357	32 43	059	60 21	109	49 00	177	42 30	197	21 32	230	19 41	291
217	50 47	356	33 32	059	61 14	109	49 03	178	42 13	198	20 49	230	18 48	291
218	50 42	354	34 20	058	62 08	109	49 05	178	41 55	198	20 06	230	17 56	290
219	50 36	353	35 07	057	63 01	109	49 06	179	41 37	199	19 23	230	17 03	290
220	50 28	351	35 55	057	63 54	110	49 06	180	41 19	199	18 40	229	16 10	289
221	50 19	350	36 42	056	64 47	110	49 06	181	41 00	200	17 57	229	15 16	289
222	50 08	348	37 28	055	65 40	110	49 05	181	40 41	200	17 15	229	14 23	289
223	49 56	347	38 14	054	66 33	111	49 03	182	40 22	200	16 32	229	13 30	288
224	49 42	345	39 00	054	67 26	111	49 01	183	40 02	201	15 50	229	12 36	288
	Alphecca		◆ VEGA		ALTAIR		◆ Peacock		RIGIL KENT		◆ SPICA		ARCTURUS	
225	42 33	011	12 16	040	12 44	075	21 07	144	48 58	184	65 46	288	49 28	344
226	42 43	010	12 52	040	13 38	075	21 40	144	48 54	184	64 52	287	49 11	343
227	42 52	008	13 28	039	14 33	075	22 13	144	48 49	185	63 58	286	48 54	341
228	43 00	007	14 04	039	15 27	074	22 46	144	48 44	186	63 04	285	48 35	340
229	43 06	006	14 39	038	16 21	074	23 19	144	48 38	186	62 09	284	48 15	339
230	43 11	005	15 14	038	17 15	073	23 52	144	48 31	187	61 14	283	47 54	337
231	43 15	003	15 48	037	18 09	073	24 25	144	48 24	188	60 19	283	47 32	336
232	43 18	002	16 22	037	19 03	073	24 57	144	48 16	189	59 24	282	47 08	335
233	43 20	001	16 55	036	19 57	072	25 30	144	48 07	189	58 29	281	46 43	333
234	43 20	000	17 28	036	20 50	072	26 03	144	47 57	190	57 34	281	46 18	332
235	43 19	359	18 01	035	21 44	071	26 36	144	47 47	191	56 38	280	45 51	331
236	43 17	357	18 33	034	22 37	071	27 09	144	47 36	191	55 43	280	45 23	330
237	43 14	356	19 05	034	23 30	070	27 42	144	47 25	192	54 47	279	44 54	329
238	43 10	355	19 36	033	24 23	070	28 15	144	47 13	193	53 51	278	44 25	328
239	43 04	354	20 06	033	25 16	069	28 47	145	47 00	193	52 55	278	43 54	326
	◆ VEGA		ALTAIR		◆ Peacock		RIGIL KENT		◆ SPICA		ARCTURUS		Alphecca	
240	20 36	032	26 09	069	29 20	145	46 47	194	52 00	277	43 22	325	42 57	352
241	21 06	031	27 01	068	29 53	145	46 33	195	51 04	277	42 50	324	42 49	351
242	21 35	031	27 53	068	30 25	145	46 19	195	50 08	276	42 16	323	42 40	350
243	22 03	030	28 46	067	30 58	145	46 04	196	49 12	276	41 42	322	42 30	349
244	22 31	029	29 37	067	31 30	145	45 48	196	48 15	276	41 07	321	42 18	348
245	22 58	029	30 29	066	32 02	145	45 32	197	47 19	275	40 32	320	42 06	347
246	23 25	028	31 20	066	32 34	145	45 15	198	46 23	275	39 55	319	41 52	345
247	23 51	027	32 12	065	33 06	146	44 58	198	45 27	274	39 18	318	41 37	344
248	24 16	026	33 03	064	33 38	146	44 40	199	44 31	274	38 41	318	41 21	343
249	24 41	026	33 53	064	34 10	146	44 22	199	43 34	273	38 02	317	41 04	342
250	25 05	025	34 44	063	34 41	146	44 03	200	42 38	273	37 23	316	40 46	341
251	25 29	024	35 34	062	35 13	146	43 44	200	41 42	273	36 44	315	40 27	340
252	25 51	023	36 24	062	35 44	146	43 24	201	40 46	272	36 03	314	40 07	339
253	26 13	023	37 13	061	36 15	147	43 04	201	39 49	272	35 23	313	39 46	338
254	26 35	022	38 02	060	36 46	147	42 43	202	38 53	272	34 41	312	39 24	336
	◆ VEGA		ALTAIR		◆ Peacock		RIGIL KENT		◆ SPICA		ARCTURUS		Alphecca	
255	26 56	021	38 51	060	37 17	147	42 22	202	37 56	271	33 59	312	39 01	335
256	27 16	020	39 40	059	37 47	147	42 01	203	37 00	271	33 17	311	38 37	334
257	27 35	020	40 28	058	38 17	148	41 39	203	36 04	270	32 34	310	38 13	333
258	27 53	019	41 16	057	38 47	148	41 17	203	35 07	270	31 51	310	37 47	332
259	28 11	018	42 03	057	39 17	148	40 54	204	34 11	270	31 07	309	37 20	331
260	28 28	017	42 50	056	39 46	149	40 32	204	33 15	269	30 23	308	36 53	330
261	28 44	016	43 36	055	40 15	149	40 08	205	32 18	269	29 39	307	36 25	330
262	29 00	015	44 22	054	40 44	149	39 45	205	31 22	269	28 54	307	35 56	329
263	29 14	015	45 07	053	41 13	150	39 21	205	30 25	268	28 08	306	35 26	328
264	29 28	014	45 52	052	41 41	150	38 56	206	29 29	268	27 23	306	34 56	327
265	29 41	013	46 37	051	42 09	150	38 32	206	28 33	268	26 37	305	34 24	326
266	29 53	012	47 20	050	42 37	151	38 07	206	27 36	267	25 50	304	33 52	325
267	30 04	011	48 03	049	43 04	151	37 42	207	26 40	267	25 03	304	33 20	324
268	30 15	010	48 46	048	43 31	152	37 16	207	25 44	267	24 16	303	32 46	323
269	30 24	009	49 28	047	43 58	152	36 51	207	24 47	267	23 29	303	32 12	323

LHA ♈	Hc	Zn	Hc	Zn	Hc	Zn	Hc	Zn	Hc	Zn	Hc	Zn	Hc	Zn
	◆ VEGA		ALTAIR		◆ FOMALHAUT		Peacock		RIGIL KENT		◆ ANTARES		Alphecca	
270	30 33	008	50 09	046	22 40	115	44 24	153	36 25	208	68 27	248	31 38	322
271	30 41	008	50 49	045	23 32	114	44 49	153	35 59	208	67 34	249	31 03	321
272	30 48	007	51 28	044	24 23	114	45 15	154	35 32	208	66 42	249	30 27	320
273	30 54	006	52 07	043	25 14	114	45 39	154	35 06	208	65 49	250	29 50	319
274	30 59	005	52 45	041	26 06	114	46 04	155	34 39	209	64 56	250	29 13	319
275	31 04	004	53 21	040	26 58	114	46 28	155	34 12	209	64 03	250	28 36	318
276	31 07	003	53 57	039	27 49	114	46 51	156	33 45	209	63 10	251	27 58	317
277	31 10	002	54 32	037	28 41	114	47 14	156	33 17	209	62 16	251	27 19	317
278	31 11	001	55 06	036	29 33	113	47 36	157	32 50	209	61 23	251	26 40	316
279	31 12	000	55 38	034	30 24	113	47 58	158	32 22	210	60 30	251	26 01	315
280	31 12	359	56 09	033	31 16	113	48 19	158	31 54	210	59 36	252	25 21	314
281	31 11	359	56 39	031	32 08	113	48 40	159	31 26	210	58 43	252	24 40	314
282	31 09	358	57 08	030	33 00	113	49 00	160	30 58	210	57 49	252	23 59	313
283	31 06	357	57 36	028	33 52	113	49 19	160	30 30	210	56 56	252	23 18	313
284	31 02	356	58 02	027	34 44	113	49 38	161	30 01	210	56 02	252	22 36	312
	DENEB		◆ FOMALHAUT		Peacock		RIGIL KENT		◆ ANTARES		Rasalhague		◆ VEGA	
285	20 40	019	35 36	113	49 56	162	29 33	210	55 08	252	51 24	326	30 58	355
286	20 58	018	36 28	113	50 14	162	29 04	211	54 15	252	50 51	324	30 52	354
287	21 16	017	37 20	112	50 30	163	28 36	211	53 21	252	50 18	323	30 46	353
288	21 32	017	38 12	112	50 46	164	28 07	211	52 27	252	49 44	322	30 39	352
289	21 48	016	39 04	112	51 02	165	27 38	211	51 34	252	49 09	321	30 31	351
290	22 03	015	39 56	112	51 16	165	27 09	211	50 40	252	48 33	320	30 22	350
291	22 18	015	40 49	112	51 30	166	26 40	211	49 46	252	47 56	318	30 12	350
292	22 32	014	41 41	112	51 43	167	26 11	211	48 52	252	47 18	317	30 01	349
293	22 45	013	42 33	112	51 56	168	25 42	211	47 59	252	46 39	316	29 50	348
294	22 58	013	43 25	112	52 07	169	25 13	211	47 05	252	46 00	315	29 37	347
295	23 10	012	44 17	112	52 18	170	24 44	211	46 11	252	45 20	314	29 24	346
296	23 21	011	45 10	112	52 28	170	24 15	211	45 18	252	44 39	313	29 10	345
297	23 31	010	46 02	112	52 37	171	23 46	211	44 24	252	43 58	312	28 55	344
298	23 41	010	46 54	112	52 45	172	23 16	211	43 30	252	43 15	311	28 40	344
299	23 50	009	47 46	112	52 52	173	22 47	211	42 37	252	42 33	310	28 23	343
	◆ DENEB		Alpheratz		◆ FOMALHAUT		Peacock		◆ ANTARES		Rasalhague		VEGA	
300	23 58	008	12 24	052	48 38	112	52 59	174	41 43	252	41 50	309	28 06	342
301	24 06	007	13 09	052	49 30	112	53 04	175	40 50	252	41 06	309	27 48	341
302	24 13	007	13 53	051	50 22	113	53 09	176	39 56	252	40 22	308	27 30	340
303	24 19	006	14 37	051	51 15	113	53 13	177	39 03	252	39 37	307	27 10	339
304	24 24	005	15 20	050	52 07	113	53 16	178	38 09	252	38 51	306	26 50	339
305	24 28	004	16 04	050	52 59	113	53 18	178	37 16	251	38 06	305	26 29	338
306	24 32	003	16 47	049	53 50	113	53 19	179	36 22	251	37 19	305	26 07	337
307	24 35	003	17 29	049	54 42	113	53 19	180	35 29	251	36 33	304	25 45	336
308	24 38	002	18 11	048	55 34	113	53 18	181	34 35	251	35 46	303	25 22	336
309	24 39	001	18 53	048	56 26	114	53 16	182	33 42	251	34 59	302	24 59	335
310	24 40	000	19 35	047	57 17	114	53 14	183	32 49	251	34 11	302	24 34	334
311	24 40	000	20 16	047	58 09	114	53 11	184	31 56	251	33 23	301	24 09	333
312	24 39	359	20 57	046	59 00	114	53 06	185	31 03	250	32 34	300	23 44	333
313	24 38	358	21 37	045	59 52	115	53 01	186	30 09	250	31 45	300	23 18	332
314	24 35	357	22 17	045	60 43	115	52 55	187	29 16	250	30 56	299	22 51	331
	Alpheratz		◆ Diphda		ACHERNAR		Peacock		◆ ANTARES		VEGA		◆ DENEB	
315	22 57	044	37 10	098	27 44	145	52 48	188	28 23	250	22 23	331	24 32	357
316	23 36	044	38 06	097	28 16	145	52 40	188	27 30	250	21 55	330	24 28	356
317	24 14	043	39 01	097	28 48	145	52 31	189	26 38	250	21 27	329	24 24	355
318	24 52	042	39 57	097	29 20	145	52 22	190	25 45	249	20 58	329	24 19	354
319	25 30	042	40 53	097	29 53	145	52 12	191	24 52	249	20 28	328	24 12	353
320	26 07	041	41 49	097	30 25	145	52 00	192	23 59	249	19 58	327	24 06	353
321	26 44	040	42 45	096	30 57	146	51 49	193	23 07	249	19 27	327	23 58	352
322	27 20	039	43 42	096	31 29	146	51 36	193	22 14	249	18 56	326	23 50	351
323	27 55	039	44 38	096	32 00	146	51 22	194	21 22	248	18 24	325	23 41	350
324	28 30	038	45 34	096	32 32	146	51 08	195	20 29	248	17 52	325	23 31	350
325	29 05	037	46 30	095	33 03	146	50 53	196	19 37	248	17 19	324	23 21	349
326	29 39	036	47 26	095	33 35	146	50 37	197	18 45	248	16 46	324	23 09	348
327	30 12	036	48 22	095	34 06	146	50 21	197	17 52	248	16 13	323	22 58	347
328	30 44	035	49 18	095	34 37	147	50 03	198	17 00	247	15 39	323	22 45	347
329	31 16	034	50 15	094	35 08	147	49 46	199	16 08	247	15 04	322	22 32	346
	◆ Alpheratz		Diphda		◆ ACHERNAR		Peacock		◆ Nunki		ALTAIR		DENEB	
330	31 48	033	51 11	094	35 39	147	49 27	200	47 30	253	47 10	309	22 18	345
331	32 18	032	52 07	094	36 09	147	49 08	200	46 36	252	46 26	308	22 03	345
332	32 48	032	53 03	093	36 40	148	48 48	201	45 42	252	45 41	308	21 48	344
333	33 17	031	54 00	093	37 10	148	48 28	202	44 49	252	44 56	307	21 32	343
334	33 46	030	54 56	093	37 40	148	48 07	202	43 55	252	44 11	306	21 15	342
335	34 13	029	55 52	093	38 10	148	47 45	203	43 01	252	43 25	305	20 58	342
336	34 40	028	56 49	092	38 39	149	47 23	203	42 07	252	42 38	304	20 40	341
337	35 07	027	57 45	092	39 08	149	47 00	204	41 14	252	41 51	303	20 21	340
338	35 32	026	58 41	092	39 37	149	46 37	205	40 20	252	41 04	302	20 02	340
339	35 56	025	59 38	091	40 06	150	46 14	205	39 26	252	40 16	302	19 42	339
340	36 20	024	60 34	091	40 34	150	45 49	206	38 33	252	39 28	301	19 22	338
341	36 43	023	61 30	091	41 02	150	45 25	206	37 39	252	38 39	300	19 01	338
342	37 04	022	62 27	091	41 30	151	45 00	207	36 46	252	37 50	299	18 39	337
343	37 25	021	63 23	090	41 58	151	44 34	207	35 52	251	37 01	299	18 17	337
344	37 45	020	64 19	090	42 25	151	44 08	208	34 59	251	36 12	298	17 55	336
	Alpheratz		◆ Hamal		◆ ACHERNAR		Peacock		Nunki		◆ ALTAIR		DENEB	
345	38 04	019	26 48	049	42 51	152	43 42	208	34 06	251	35 22	297	17 31	335
346	38 23	018	27 30	048	43 18	152	43 15	209	33 12	251	34 31	297	17 07	335
347	38 40	017	28 12	047	43 44	153	42 48	209	32 19	251	33 41	296	16 43	334
348	38 56	016	28 53	047	44 09	153	42 21	209	31 26	251	32 50	296	16 18	334
349	39 11	015	29 34	046	44 35	154	41 53	210	30 32	251	31 59	295	15 53	333
350	39 25	014	30 14	045	44 59	154	41 25	210	29 39	250	31 08	294	15 27	332
351	39 38	013	30 54	045	45 24	155	40 56	211	28 46	250	30 17	294	15 00	332
352	39 50	012	31 33	044	45 48	155	40 27	211	27 53	250	29 25	293	14 34	331
353	40 01	011	32 12	043	46 11	156	39 58	211	27 00	250	28 33	293	14 06	331
354	40 11	009	32 50	042	46 34	156	39 29	212	26 07	250	27 41	292	13 38	330
355	40 20	008	33 28	041	46 56	157	38 59	212	25 14	250	26 48	292	13 10	330
356	40 27	007	34 05	041	47 18	158	38 30	212	24 22	249	25 56	291	12 41	329
357	40 34	006	34 41	040	47 39	158	37 59	212	23 29	249	25 03	291	12 12	329
358	40 39	005	35 17	039	48 00	159	37 29	213	22 36	249	24 10	290	11 42	328
359	40 43	004	35 52	038	48 20	159	36 59	213	21 44	249	23 17	290	11 12	328

LAT 21°S

LHA ♈	Hc	Zn	Hc	Zn	Hc	Zn	Hc	Zn	Hc	Zn	Hc	Zn	Hc	Zn
	◆ Alpheratz		Hamal		◆ RIGEL		CANOPUS		ACHERNAR		◆ Peacock		Enif	
0	39 47	003	35 39	037	13 19	094	13 01	142	49 36	160	37 18	214	44 38	310
1	39 49	001	36 12	036	14 15	093	13 36	142	49 55	160	36 47	214	43 54	309
2	39 50	000	36 44	035	15 11	093	14 11	141	50 14	161	36 15	214	43 10	308
3	39 49	359	37 16	034	16 07	093	14 46	141	50 32	162	35 44	214	42 26	307
4	39 48	358	37 47	033	17 03	092	15 21	141	50 49	162	35 12	214	41 41	306
5	39 46	357	38 17	032	17 58	092	15 56	141	51 05	163	34 41	215	40 55	305
6	39 42	356	38 46	031	18 54	092	16 31	141	51 21	164	34 09	215	40 10	304
7	39 37	355	39 15	030	19 50	091	17 07	141	51 36	165	33 37	215	39 23	304
8	39 32	354	39 42	029	20 46	091	17 42	141	51 51	166	33 05	215	38 36	303
9	39 25	352	40 09	028	21 42	091	18 18	140	52 04	166	32 32	215	37 49	302
10	39 17	351	40 35	027	22 38	090	18 54	140	52 17	167	32 00	215	37 01	301
11	39 08	350	41 00	026	23 35	090	19 30	140	52 29	168	31 28	215	36 13	301
12	38 58	349	41 23	025	24 31	090	20 05	140	52 41	169	30 55	216	35 25	300
13	38 47	348	41 46	024	25 27	089	20 41	140	52 51	170	30 22	216	34 36	299
14	38 34	347	42 08	022	26 23	089	21 18	140	53 01	170	29 50	216	33 47	299
	◆ Hamal		ALDEBARAN		RIGEL		◆ CANOPUS		ACHERNAR		◆ FOMALHAUT		Alpheratz	
15	42 29	021	24 56	059	27 19	088	21 54	140	53 10	171	61 20	246	38 21	346
16	42 49	020	25 44	058	28 15	088	22 30	140	53 18	172	60 28	247	38 07	345
17	43 08	019	26 31	058	29 11	088	23 06	140	53 25	173	59 37	247	37 52	344
18	43 26	018	27 19	057	30 06	087	23 42	140	53 31	174	58 45	247	37 35	343
19	43 42	017	28 06	057	31 02	087	24 19	140	53 36	175	57 53	248	37 18	342
20	43 57	015	28 52	056	31 58	087	24 55	140	53 41	176	57 02	248	37 00	341
21	44 12	014	29 38	055	32 54	086	25 31	140	53 45	177	56 10	248	36 41	340
22	44 25	013	30 24	055	33 50	086	26 08	140	53 47	178	55 18	248	36 21	339
23	44 37	012	31 10	054	34 46	085	26 44	140	53 49	179	54 26	248	36 00	338
24	44 47	010	31 55	053	35 42	085	27 20	140	53 50	179	53 34	248	35 38	337
25	44 57	009	32 40	053	36 38	085	27 57	140	53 50	180	52 42	248	35 16	336
26	45 05	008	33 24	052	37 33	084	28 33	140	53 49	181	51 49	249	34 52	335
27	45 12	007	34 08	051	38 29	084	29 09	140	53 48	182	50 57	249	34 28	334
28	45 18	005	34 51	050	39 25	083	29 46	140	53 45	183	50 05	249	34 02	333
29	45 22	004	35 34	050	40 20	083	30 22	140	53 42	184	49 13	249	33 36	332
	◆ Hamal		ALDEBARAN		◆ SIRIUS		CANOPUS		ACHERNAR		◆ FOMALHAUT		Alpheratz	
30	45 25	003	36 16	049	22 48	100	30 58	140	53 37	185	48 21	249	33 10	331
31	45 27	001	36 58	048	23 43	100	31 34	140	53 32	186	47 29	249	32 42	330
32	45 28	000	37 39	047	24 39	099	32 10	140	53 26	187	46 36	249	32 14	329
33	45 27	359	38 20	046	25 34	099	32 46	140	53 19	188	45 44	249	31 45	328
34	45 25	357	39 00	045	26 29	099	33 22	140	53 11	189	44 52	249	31 15	328
35	45 22	356	39 40	044	27 25	099	33 58	140	53 02	189	44 00	249	30 45	327
36	45 18	355	40 18	043	28 20	098	34 34	140	52 52	190	43 08	249	30 14	326
37	45 12	353	40 57	043	29 16	098	35 09	141	52 42	191	42 16	249	29 42	325
38	45 05	352	41 34	042	30 11	098	35 45	141	52 31	192	41 23	249	29 09	324
39	44 57	351	42 11	041	31 07	097	36 20	141	52 19	193	40 31	248	28 36	324
40	44 48	350	42 47	040	32 02	097	36 56	141	52 06	194	39 39	248	28 03	323
41	44 37	348	43 22	039	32 58	097	37 31	141	51 53	194	38 47	248	27 29	322
42	44 25	347	43 57	037	33 53	097	38 06	141	51 38	195	37 55	248	26 54	321
43	44 12	346	44 31	036	34 49	096	38 41	142	51 23	196	37 03	248	26 19	321
44	43 58	345	45 03	035	35 45	096	39 15	142	51 08	197	36 11	248	25 43	320
	◆ CAPELLA		BETELGEUSE		SIRIUS		◆ CANOPUS		ACHERNAR		◆ FOMALHAUT		Hamal	
45	16 04	024	38 18	061	36 40	096	39 50	142	50 51	197	35 19	248	43 42	343
46	16 27	024	39 07	061	37 36	095	40 24	142	50 34	198	34 27	248	43 26	342
47	16 49	023	39 56	060	38 32	095	40 58	143	50 16	199	33 35	248	43 08	341
48	17 11	022	40 44	059	39 28	095	41 32	143	49 58	200	32 44	248	42 49	340
49	17 31	022	41 32	058	40 24	094	42 06	143	49 39	200	31 52	247	42 29	339
50	17 52	021	42 19	058	41 20	094	42 39	144	49 19	201	31 00	247	42 09	338
51	18 12	020	43 06	057	42 15	094	43 12	144	48 59	202	30 08	247	41 47	336
52	18 31	020	43 53	056	43 11	093	43 45	144	48 38	202	29 17	247	41 24	335
53	18 49	019	44 39	055	44 07	093	44 18	145	48 16	203	28 25	247	41 00	334
54	19 07	018	45 25	054	45 03	093	44 50	145	47 54	203	27 34	247	40 35	333
55	19 25	018	46 10	053	45 59	093	45 22	145	47 32	204	26 42	247	40 09	332
56	19 42	017	46 54	052	46 55	092	45 53	146	47 09	205	25 51	246	39 43	331
57	19 58	016	47 38	051	47 51	092	46 24	146	46 45	205	25 00	246	39 15	330
58	20 13	016	48 22	050	48 47	092	46 55	147	46 21	206	24 09	246	38 46	329
59	20 28	015	49 05	049	49 43	091	47 26	147	45 57	206	23 17	246	38 17	328
	CAPELLA		BETELGEUSE		◆ SIRIUS		CANOPUS		◆ ACHERNAR		Diphda		◆ Hamal	
60	20 42	014	49 47	048	50 39	091	47 56	148	45 32	207	43 57	265	37 47	327
61	20 56	014	50 28	047	51 35	091	48 25	148	45 06	207	43 01	265	37 16	326
62	21 09	013	51 09	046	52 31	090	48 55	149	44 41	208	42 05	264	36 45	325
63	21 21	012	51 48	045	53 27	090	49 23	149	44 14	208	41 10	264	36 12	324
64	21 32	011	52 27	043	54 23	090	49 51	150	43 48	209	40 14	264	35 39	323
65	21 43	011	53 05	042	55 19	089	50 19	151	43 21	209	39 18	264	35 05	322
66	21 53	010	53 42	041	56 15	089	50 46	151	42 54	209	38 22	263	34 31	322
67	22 03	009	54 19	040	57 11	089	51 13	152	42 26	210	37 27	263	33 55	321
68	22 11	009	54 54	038	58 07	088	51 39	153	41 58	210	36 31	263	33 20	320
69	22 19	008	55 28	037	59 03	088	52 04	153	41 30	210	35 36	263	32 43	319
70	22 27	007	56 01	035	59 59	087	52 29	154	41 01	211	34 40	262	32 06	318
71	22 33	006	56 32	034	60 55	087	52 53	155	40 33	211	33 45	262	31 29	317
72	22 39	006	57 03	032	61 51	086	53 17	156	40 03	211	32 49	262	30 50	317
73	22 44	005	57 32	031	62 47	086	53 40	156	39 34	212	31 54	261	30 12	316
74	22 48	004	58 00	029	63 43	085	54 02	157	39 05	212	30 58	261	29 32	315
	◆ CAPELLA		POLLUX		PROCYON		◆ Suhail		CANOPUS		◆ ACHERNAR		Hamal	
75	22 52	003	26 40	041	42 49	061	34 17	129	54 23	158	38 35	212	28 53	314
76	22 55	003	27 16	040	43 38	060	35 00	129	54 44	159	38 05	213	28 13	314
77	22 57	002	27 52	040	44 26	059	35 43	129	55 03	160	37 34	213	27 32	313
78	22 59	001	28 27	039	45 14	058	36 27	129	55 22	161	37 04	213	26 51	312
79	22 59	000	29 02	038	46 01	058	37 10	129	55 40	162	36 33	213	26 09	312
80	22 59	000	29 36	037	46 48	057	37 53	129	55 58	163	36 02	214	25 27	311
81	22 58	359	30 10	036	47 35	056	38 37	130	56 14	164	35 31	214	24 44	310
82	22 57	358	30 43	036	48 21	055	39 20	130	56 29	165	35 00	214	24 02	310
83	22 55	357	31 15	035	49 06	054	40 03	130	56 44	166	34 29	214	23 18	309
84	22 52	357	31 47	034	49 51	053	40 46	130	56 57	167	33 57	214	22 35	309
85	22 48	356	32 18	033	50 35	052	41 29	130	57 10	168	33 26	214	21 51	308
86	22 44	355	32 48	032	51 19	051	42 11	130	57 21	169	32 54	215	21 06	307
87	22 38	354	33 18	031	52 02	050	42 54	131	57 32	170	32 22	215	20 22	307
88	22 32	354	33 46	031	52 44	048	43 37	131	57 41	171	31 50	215	19 37	306
89	22 26	353	34 14	030	53 26	047	44 19	131	57 50	172	31 18	215	18 51	306

LHA ♈	Hc	Zn	Hc	Zn	Hc	Zn	Hc	Zn	Hc	Zn	Hc	Zn	Hc	Zn
	POLLUX		◆ REGULUS		ACRUX		CANOPUS		◆ ACHERNAR		◆ ALDEBARAN		CAPELLA	
90	34 42	029	20 33	068	15 38	152	57 57	173	30 46	215	47 16	330	22 18	352
91	35 08	028	21 24	067	16 04	152	58 03	174	30 14	215	46 48	329	22 10	351
92	35 34	027	22 16	067	16 30	152	58 08	175	29 42	215	46 18	327	22 02	351
93	35 59	026	23 07	066	16 57	152	58 12	176	29 09	215	45 48	326	21 52	350
94	36 23	025	23 58	066	17 23	152	58 15	178	28 37	215	45 16	325	21 42	349
95	36 46	024	24 49	065	17 50	152	58 17	179	28 05	215	44 44	324	21 31	348
96	37 08	023	25 40	065	18 16	152	58 18	180	27 32	215	44 10	323	21 20	348
97	37 29	022	26 30	064	18 43	152	58 17	181	27 00	215	43 36	322	21 07	347
98	37 50	021	27 21	063	19 10	151	58 16	182	26 27	215	43 01	321	20 54	346
99	38 09	020	28 11	063	19 36	151	58 13	183	25 55	216	42 25	320	20 41	346
100	38 28	019	29 00	062	20 03	151	58 09	185	25 22	216	41 49	319	20 27	345
101	38 45	018	29 50	062	20 30	151	58 04	186	24 50	216	41 11	318	20 12	344
102	39 02	017	30 39	061	20 57	151	57 58	187	24 17	215	40 34	317	19 56	344
103	39 17	016	31 28	060	21 24	151	57 51	188	23 45	215	39 55	316	19 40	343
104	39 32	014	32 16	060	21 51	151	57 43	189	23 12	215	39 16	315	19 23	342
	POLLUX		◆ REGULUS		Gienah		◆ ACRUX		CANOPUS		◆ RIGEL		BETELGEUSE	
105	39 45	013	33 05	059	16 02	103	22 18	151	57 33	190	61 40	293	57 32	329
106	39 58	012	33 52	058	16 56	103	22 45	151	57 23	191	60 49	292	57 03	328
107	40 09	011	34 40	058	17 51	103	23 12	151	57 12	192	59 57	291	56 32	326
108	40 19	010	35 27	057	18 45	102	23 39	151	56 59	193	59 04	290	56 00	325
109	40 28	009	36 14	056	19 40	102	24 06	151	56 46	194	58 11	289	55 28	323
110	40 36	008	37 00	056	20 35	102	24 33	151	56 32	195	57 18	288	54 53	322
111	40 43	006	37 46	055	21 30	101	25 00	151	56 16	196	56 25	288	54 18	320
112	40 49	005	38 32	054	22 25	101	25 27	151	56 00	197	55 32	287	53 42	319
113	40 53	004	39 17	053	23 20	101	25 54	151	55 43	198	54 38	286	53 05	318
114	40 57	003	40 02	052	24 15	101	26 21	151	55 25	199	53 44	285	52 27	317
115	40 59	002	40 46	052	25 10	100	26 48	151	55 06	200	52 50	285	51 48	315
116	41 00	001	41 29	051	26 05	100	27 15	151	54 47	201	51 56	284	51 08	314
117	41 01	359	42 12	050	27 00	100	27 42	151	54 26	202	51 01	283	50 28	313
118	40 59	358	42 55	049	27 56	099	28 09	151	54 05	203	50 07	283	49 46	312
119	40 57	357	43 37	048	28 51	099	28 35	152	53 43	204	49 12	282	49 04	311
	◆ REGULUS		SPICA		◆ ACRUX		CANOPUS		◆ RIGEL		BETELGEUSE		POLLUX	
120	44 18	047	11 51	098	29 02	152	53 20	204	48 17	282	48 21	310	40 54	356
121	44 58	046	12 46	097	29 29	152	52 57	205	47 22	281	47 38	309	40 49	355
122	45 38	045	13 42	097	29 55	152	52 33	206	46 27	281	46 54	308	40 44	354
123	46 18	044	14 37	097	30 21	152	52 08	207	45 32	280	46 10	307	40 37	353
124	46 56	043	15 33	096	30 48	152	51 43	207	44 37	279	45 24	306	40 29	351
125	47 34	042	16 29	096	31 14	152	51 17	208	43 42	279	44 39	305	40 20	350
126	48 10	041	17 24	096	31 40	152	50 50	209	42 46	278	43 53	304	40 10	349
127	48 46	039	18 20	095	32 06	153	50 23	209	41 51	278	43 06	303	39 59	348
128	49 21	038	19 16	095	32 31	153	49 55	210	40 55	278	42 19	302	39 47	347
129	49 56	037	20 12	095	32 57	153	49 27	210	40 00	277	41 31	302	39 33	346
130	50 29	036	21 08	094	33 22	153	48 59	211	39 04	277	40 44	301	39 19	345
131	51 01	034	22 04	094	33 48	153	48 30	212	38 08	276	39 55	300	39 04	344
132	51 32	033	22 59	094	34 13	154	48 00	212	37 13	276	39 07	299	38 47	342
133	52 02	032	23 55	093	34 38	154	47 30	213	36 17	275	38 18	299	38 30	341
134	52 31	030	24 51	093	35 02	154	47 00	213	35 21	275	37 28	298	38 12	340
	REGULUS		◆ SPICA		ACRUX		◆ CANOPUS		SIRIUS		BETELGEUSE		◆ POLLUX	
135	52 59	029	25 47	093	35 27	154	46 29	214	58 02	272	36 39	297	37 52	339
136	53 25	027	26 43	092	35 51	154	45 58	214	57 06	271	35 49	297	37 32	338
137	53 50	026	27 39	092	36 15	155	45 26	214	56 10	271	34 58	296	37 11	337
138	54 14	024	28 35	092	36 39	155	44 54	215	55 14	271	34 08	295	36 49	336
139	54 36	023	29 31	091	37 03	155	44 22	215	54 18	270	33 17	295	36 26	335
140	54 58	021	30 27	091	37 26	156	43 50	216	53 22	270	32 26	294	36 02	334
141	55 17	020	31 23	091	37 49	156	43 17	216	52 26	270	31 35	293	35 37	333
142	55 35	018	32 19	090	38 12	156	42 44	216	51 30	269	30 43	293	35 11	332
143	55 52	016	33 15	090	38 34	156	42 11	217	50 34	269	29 52	292	34 45	331
144	56 07	015	34 11	090	38 57	157	41 37	217	49 38	269	29 00	292	34 18	330
145	56 20	013	35 07	089	39 19	157	41 03	217	48 42	268	28 08	291	33 50	330
146	56 32	011	36 03	089	39 40	157	40 29	218	47 46	268	27 15	291	33 21	329
147	56 42	009	36 59	088	40 02	158	39 55	218	46 50	268	26 23	290	32 51	328
148	56 50	008	37 55	088	40 23	158	39 20	218	45 54	267	25 30	290	32 21	327
149	56 57	006	38 51	088	40 43	159	38 46	218	44 58	267	24 37	289	31 50	326
	REGULUS		◆ ARCTURUS		SPICA		◆ ACRUX		CANOPUS		SIRIUS		◆ PROCYON	
150	57 02	004	15 34	062	39 47	087	41 03	159	38 11	219	44 02	267	46 50	303
151	57 05	002	16 23	061	40 43	087	41 23	159	37 36	219	43 06	266	46 03	303
152	57 06	001	17 12	061	41 39	086	41 43	160	37 01	219	42 10	266	45 16	302
153	57 06	359	18 01	060	42 35	086	42 02	160	36 26	219	41 14	266	44 28	301
154	57 04	357	18 49	060	43 31	086	42 21	161	35 50	219	40 18	265	43 40	300
155	57 00	355	19 38	059	44 27	085	42 39	161	35 15	219	39 23	265	42 51	299
156	56 54	353	20 26	059	45 22	085	42 57	162	34 39	220	38 27	265	42 02	298
157	56 47	352	21 14	058	46 18	084	43 15	162	34 03	220	37 31	265	41 12	298
158	56 38	350	22 01	058	47 14	084	43 32	163	33 27	220	36 35	264	40 23	297
159	56 27	348	22 48	057	48 10	083	43 48	163	32 51	220	35 39	264	39 33	296
160	56 15	346	23 35	057	49 05	083	44 04	164	32 15	220	34 44	264	38 42	296
161	56 01	345	24 22	056	50 01	082	44 20	164	31 39	220	33 48	263	37 52	295
162	55 45	343	25 08	055	50 56	082	44 35	165	31 03	220	32 52	263	37 01	294
163	55 28	341	25 54	055	51 52	081	44 50	165	30 27	220	31 57	263	36 09	294
164	55 09	340	26 40	054	52 47	081	45 04	166	29 51	220	31 01	263	35 18	293
	◆ ARCTURUS		ANTARES		◆ ACRUX		CANOPUS		SIRIUS		◆ PROCYON		REGULUS	
165	27 25	054	15 31	113	45 18	166	29 14	220	30 06	262	34 26	292	54 49	338
166	28 10	053	16 23	113	45 31	167	28 38	220	29 10	262	33 34	292	54 27	336
167	28 54	052	17 15	112	45 43	167	28 02	220	28 15	262	32 42	291	54 04	335
168	29 38	052	18 07	112	45 55	168	27 25	220	27 19	261	31 50	291	53 40	333
169	30 22	051	18 58	112	46 07	168	26 49	220	26 24	261	30 57	290	53 14	332
170	31 05	050	19 50	112	46 18	169	26 13	220	25 29	261	30 05	290	52 47	331
171	31 48	049	20 43	111	46 28	170	25 36	220	24 33	261	29 12	289	52 19	329
172	32 30	049	21 35	111	46 38	170	25 00	220	23 38	260	28 19	288	51 50	328
173	33 12	048	22 27	111	46 47	171	24 24	220	22 43	260	27 26	288	51 19	326
174	33 53	047	23 19	111	46 55	172	23 47	220	21 48	260	26 32	287	50 48	325
175	34 34	046	24 12	111	47 03	172	23 11	220	20 53	259	25 39	287	50 15	324
176	35 15	046	25 04	110	47 11	173	22 35	220	19 58	259	24 45	286	49 42	323
177	35 54	045	25 57	110	47 17	173	21 59	220	19 03	259	23 51	286	49 07	321
178	36 33	044	26 49	110	47 23	174	21 23	220	18 08	259	22 57	286	48 32	320
179	37 12	043	27 42	110	47 29	175	20 47	220	17 13	258	22 03	285	47 55	319

LHA ♈	Hc Zn	Hc Zn	Hc Zn	Hc Zn	Hc Zn	Hc Zn	Hc Zn
	ARCTURUS	◆ANTARES	ACRUX	◆Suhail	Alphard	REGULUS	◆Denebola
180	37 50 042	28 35 110	47 34 175	48 00 228	51 28 283	47 18 318	54 25 356
181	38 27 041	29 28 109	47 38 176	47 18 228	50 34 282	46 40 317	54 20 354
182	39 04 040	30 21 109	47 41 177	46 37 228	49 39 282	46 01 316	54 14 352
183	39 39 039	31 14 109	47 44 177	45 55 228	48 44 281	45 22 315	54 06 351
184	40 15 038	32 07 109	47 46 178	45 13 229	47 49 280	44 42 314	53 56 349
185	40 49 037	33 00 109	47 48 179	44 31 229	46 54 280	44 01 313	53 45 348
186	41 22 036	33 53 108	47 49 179	43 48 229	45 59 279	43 19 312	53 32 346
187	41 55 035	34 46 108	47 49 180	43 06 229	45 03 279	42 37 311	53 18 344
188	42 27 034	35 39 108	47 49 181	42 23 230	44 08 278	41 55 310	53 02 343
189	42 58 033	36 32 108	47 48 181	41 40 230	43 12 278	41 11 309	52 45 341
190	43 29 032	37 26 108	47 46 182	40 58 230	42 17 277	40 27 308	52 26 340
191	43 58 031	38 19 108	47 43 183	40 15 230	41 21 277	39 43 307	52 06 338
192	44 26 030	39 12 108	47 40 183	39 32 230	40 26 277	38 58 306	51 45 337
193	44 54 029	40 06 108	47 37 184	38 49 230	39 30 276	38 13 306	51 22 335
194	45 20 027	40 59 107	47 32 185	38 05 231	38 34 276	37 27 305	50 58 334
	ARCTURUS	◆Rasalhague	ANTARES	◆ACRUX	Suhail	◆REGULUS	Denebola
195	45 45 026	14 29 070	41 53 107	47 27 185	37 22 231	36 41 304	50 33 333
196	46 10 025	15 22 070	42 46 107	47 22 186	36 39 231	35 55 303	50 07 331
197	46 33 024	16 14 069	43 40 107	47 16 187	35 55 231	35 08 303	49 39 330
198	46 55 023	17 06 069	44 33 107	47 09 187	35 12 231	34 20 302	49 11 329
199	47 16 021	17 58 068	45 27 107	47 01 188	34 28 231	33 33 301	48 41 327
200	47 35 020	18 50 068	46 20 107	46 53 189	33 45 231	32 45 301	48 10 326
201	47 54 019	19 42 067	47 14 107	46 44 189	33 02 231	31 56 300	47 39 325
202	48 11 017	20 34 067	48 08 107	46 35 190	32 18 231	31 08 299	47 06 324
203	48 27 016	21 25 066	49 01 107	46 25 190	31 34 231	30 19 299	46 33 323
204	48 42 015	22 16 066	49 55 107	46 15 191	30 51 231	29 29 298	45 58 322
205	48 55 013	23 07 065	50 49 107	46 04 192	30 07 231	28 40 297	45 23 320
206	49 07 012	23 58 065	51 42 107	45 52 192	29 24 231	27 50 297	44 47 319
207	49 18 010	24 49 064	52 36 106	45 40 193	28 40 231	27 00 296	44 10 318
208	49 27 009	25 39 064	53 30 106	45 27 193	27 57 231	26 09 296	43 32 317
209	49 35 007	26 29 063	54 24 106	45 14 194	27 13 231	25 19 295	42 54 316
	ARCTURUS	◆Rasalhague	ANTARES	◆RIGIL KENT	ACRUX	Gienah	◆Denebola
210	49 42 006	27 19 063	55 17 107	49 28 172	45 00 195	65 24 273	42 15 315
211	49 47 005	28 09 062	56 11 107	49 35 173	44 46 195	64 28 273	41 35 314
212	49 51 003	28 58 061	57 05 107	49 42 174	44 31 196	63 32 272	40 55 313
213	49 53 002	29 47 061	57 58 107	49 47 175	44 16 196	62 36 272	40 14 313
214	49 54 000	30 36 060	58 52 107	49 52 175	44 00 197	61 40 272	39 32 312
215	49 53 359	31 24 060	59 46 107	49 56 176	43 44 197	60 44 271	38 50 311
216	49 51 357	32 12 059	60 39 107	50 00 177	43 27 198	59 48 271	38 07 310
217	49 48 356	33 00 058	61 33 107	50 03 178	43 10 198	58 52 270	37 24 309
218	49 43 354	33 48 058	62 26 107	50 05 178	42 52 199	57 56 270	36 40 308
219	49 36 353	34 35 057	63 20 107	50 06 179	42 34 199	57 00 270	35 56 308
220	49 29 351	35 21 056	64 13 108	50 06 180	42 16 199	56 04 269	35 11 307
221	49 20 350	36 08 055	65 07 108	50 06 181	41 57 200	55 08 269	34 26 306
222	49 09 349	36 54 055	66 00 108	50 05 181	41 38 200	54 12 269	33 41 305
223	48 57 347	37 39 054	66 53 108	50 03 182	41 18 201	53 16 268	32 55 305
224	48 44 346	38 24 053	67 46 109	50 01 183	40 58 201	52 20 268	32 09 304
	Alphecca	Rasalhague	◆ALTAIR	Peacock	◆RIGIL KENT	◆SPICA	ARCTURUS
225	41 34 011	39 09 052	12 29 075	21 56 144	49 58 184	65 27 290	48 30 344
226	41 44 009	39 53 051	13 23 075	22 29 144	49 54 184	64 34 289	48 14 343
227	41 53 008	40 36 051	14 17 074	23 01 144	49 49 185	63 41 288	47 57 342
228	42 00 007	41 19 050	15 11 074	23 34 144	49 44 186	62 47 287	47 39 340
229	42 06 006	42 01 049	16 04 074	24 07 144	49 37 187	61 53 286	47 19 339
230	42 11 005	42 43 048	16 58 073	24 40 144	49 31 187	60 59 285	46 59 338
231	42 15 003	43 24 047	17 52 073	25 13 144	49 23 188	60 05 284	46 37 336
232	42 18 002	44 05 046	18 45 072	25 46 144	49 15 189	59 11 284	46 14 335
233	42 20 001	44 45 045	19 38 072	26 19 144	49 06 190	58 16 283	45 50 334
234	42 20 000	45 24 044	20 31 071	26 52 144	48 56 190	57 22 282	45 24 333
235	42 19 359	46 03 043	21 24 071	27 25 144	48 46 191	56 27 282	44 58 332
236	42 17 357	46 40 042	22 17 070	27 58 144	48 35 192	55 32 281	44 31 330
237	42 14 356	47 17 041	23 10 070	28 31 144	48 24 192	54 37 280	44 03 329
238	42 10 355	47 53 039	24 02 069	29 03 144	48 11 193	53 42 280	43 34 328
239	42 04 354	48 28 038	24 55 069	29 36 144	47 59 194	52 47 279	43 04 327
	VEGA	◆ALTAIR	Peacock	◆RIGIL KENT	SPICA	◆ARCTURUS	Alphecca
240	19 45 032	25 47 068	30 09 144	47 45 194	51 51 279	42 33 326	41 58 353
241	20 14 031	26 39 068	30 42 144	47 31 195	50 56 278	42 01 325	41 50 351
242	20 43 030	27 30 067	31 14 144	47 16 195	50 00 278	41 28 324	41 41 350
243	21 11 030	28 22 067	31 47 145	47 01 196	49 05 277	40 55 323	41 31 349
244	21 39 029	29 13 066	32 19 145	46 45 197	48 09 277	40 21 322	41 20 348
245	22 05 028	30 04 066	32 51 145	46 29 197	47 13 276	39 45 321	41 07 347
246	22 32 028	30 55 065	33 24 145	46 12 198	46 18 276	39 10 320	40 54 346
247	22 57 027	31 46 064	33 56 145	45 55 198	45 22 275	38 33 319	40 39 344
248	23 22 026	32 36 064	34 28 145	45 37 199	44 26 275	37 56 318	40 24 343
249	23 47 025	33 26 063	34 59 145	45 18 199	43 30 274	37 18 317	40 07 342
250	24 11 025	34 16 062	35 31 146	44 59 200	42 34 274	36 40 316	39 50 341
251	24 34 024	35 06 062	36 03 146	44 40 201	41 39 274	36 01 315	39 31 340
252	24 56 023	35 55 061	36 34 146	44 20 201	40 43 273	35 21 315	39 11 339
253	25 18 023	36 44 060	37 05 146	44 00 202	39 47 273	34 41 314	38 51 338
254	25 39 022	37 32 060	37 36 147	43 39 202	38 51 272	34 01 313	38 29 337
	◆VEGA	ALTAIR	◆Peacock	RIGIL KENT	◆SPICA	ARCTURUS	Alphecca
255	26 00 021	38 21 059	38 07 147	43 18 202	37 55 272	33 19 312	38 07 336
256	26 19 020	39 08 058	38 37 147	42 56 203	36 59 271	32 38 311	37 43 335
257	26 38 019	39 56 057	39 08 147	42 34 203	36 03 271	31 55 311	37 19 334
258	26 56 019	40 43 057	39 38 148	42 12 204	35 07 271	31 13 310	36 54 333
259	27 14 018	41 29 056	40 08 148	41 49 204	34 11 270	30 30 309	36 28 332
260	27 31 017	42 16 055	40 37 148	41 26 205	33 15 270	29 46 309	36 01 331
261	27 46 016	43 01 054	41 07 149	41 03 205	32 19 270	29 02 308	35 33 330
262	28 02 015	43 46 053	41 36 149	40 39 205	31 23 269	28 18 307	35 05 329
263	28 16 014	44 31 052	42 05 149	40 15 206	30 27 269	27 33 307	34 35 328
264	28 30 014	45 15 051	42 33 150	39 50 206	29 31 269	26 48 306	34 05 327
265	28 42 013	45 59 051	43 01 150	39 26 206	28 35 268	26 02 305	33 35 326
266	28 54 012	46 42 050	43 29 150	39 01 207	27 39 268	25 16 305	33 03 325
267	29 05 011	47 24 049	43 57 151	38 35 207	26 43 268	24 30 304	32 31 325
268	29 16 010	48 06 047	44 24 151	38 10 207	25 47 267	23 43 303	31 58 324
269	29 25 009	48 46 046	44 50 152	37 44 208	24 51 267	22 56 303	31 25 323

LAT 21°S

LHA ♈	Hc Zn	Hc Zn	Hc Zn	Hc Zn	Hc Zn	Hc Zn	Hc Zn
	◆VEGA	ALTAIR	◆FOMALHAUT	Peacock	RIGIL KENT	◆ANTARES	Alphecca
270	29 34 008	49 27 045	23 05 114	45 17 152	37 18 208	68 48 251	30 51 322
271	29 41 007	50 06 044	23 56 114	45 43 153	36 52 208	67 55 251	30 16 321
272	29 48 007	50 45 043	24 48 114	46 08 153	36 25 208	67 02 251	29 41 321
273	29 54 006	51 22 042	25 39 114	46 33 154	35 58 209	66 09 252	29 05 320
274	29 59 005	51 59 040	26 30 114	46 58 154	35 31 209	65 15 252	28 28 319
275	30 04 004	52 35 039	27 22 113	47 22 155	35 04 209	64 22 252	27 51 318
276	30 07 003	53 10 038	28 13 113	47 46 155	34 37 209	63 29 253	27 14 318
277	30 10 002	53 44 037	29 05 113	48 09 156	34 10 209	62 35 253	26 36 317
278	30 11 001	54 17 035	29 56 113	48 31 157	33 42 210	61 42 253	25 57 316
279	30 12 000	54 48 034	30 48 113	48 53 157	33 14 210	60 48 253	25 18 315
280	30 12 359	55 19 032	31 39 113	49 15 158	32 46 210	59 54 253	24 39 315
281	30 11 359	55 48 031	32 31 112	49 36 158	32 18 210	59 01 253	23 59 314
282	30 09 358	56 16 029	33 23 112	49 56 159	31 50 210	58 07 253	23 18 314
283	30 06 357	56 43 028	34 15 112	50 16 160	31 22 210	57 13 253	22 37 313
284	30 03 356	57 08 026	35 07 112	50 35 160	30 53 211	56 20 253	21 56 312
	◆DENEB	FOMALHAUT	◆ACHERNAR	RIGIL KENT	◆ANTARES	Rasalhague	VEGA
285	19 44 019	35 59 112	12 32 147	30 25 211	55 26 253	50 34 326	29 58 355
286	20 01 018	36 51 112	13 03 147	29 56 211	54 32 254	50 02 325	29 53 354
287	20 18 017	37 43 112	13 33 146	29 27 211	53 39 254	49 30 324	29 46 353
288	20 35 017	38 35 112	14 05 146	28 58 211	52 45 254	48 56 323	29 39 352
289	20 51 016	39 27 112	14 36 146	28 29 211	51 51 253	48 22 321	29 31 351
290	21 06 015	40 19 112	15 07 146	28 01 211	50 58 253	47 47 320	29 23 350
291	21 20 015	41 11 111	15 38 146	27 32 211	50 04 253	47 10 319	29 13 350
292	21 34 014	42 03 111	16 10 146	27 02 211	49 10 253	46 33 318	29 02 349
293	21 47 013	42 55 111	16 42 146	26 33 211	48 16 253	45 56 317	28 51 348
294	21 59 012	43 47 111	17 13 145	26 04 211	47 23 253	45 17 316	28 39 347
295	22 11 012	44 40 111	17 45 145	25 35 211	46 29 253	44 38 315	28 26 346
296	22 22 011	45 32 111	18 17 145	25 06 211	45 36 253	43 58 314	28 12 345
297	22 32 010	46 24 111	18 49 145	24 37 211	44 42 253	43 17 313	27 58 344
298	22 42 009	47 16 111	19 21 145	24 08 211	43 48 253	42 36 312	27 42 344
299	22 51 009	48 08 111	19 53 145	23 38 211	42 55 253	41 54 311	27 26 343
	DENEB	Enif	◆FOMALHAUT	ACHERNAR	◆RIGIL KENT	ANTARES	◆VEGA
300	22 59 008	49 44 042	49 01 111	20 26 145	23 09 211	42 01 253	27 09 342
301	23 06 007	50 21 041	49 53 111	20 58 145	22 40 211	41 08 253	26 51 341
302	23 13 006	50 57 040	50 45 111	21 30 145	22 11 211	40 14 253	26 33 340
303	23 19 006	51 33 039	51 37 111	22 03 145	21 42 211	39 21 252	26 14 340
304	23 24 005	52 07 037	52 29 112	22 35 145	21 13 211	38 28 252	25 54 339
305	23 29 004	52 41 036	53 21 112	23 08 145	20 44 211	37 34 252	25 33 338
306	23 32 003	53 13 035	54 13 112	23 40 145	20 15 211	36 41 252	25 12 337
307	23 35 003	53 44 033	55 05 112	24 13 145	19 46 211	35 48 252	24 50 337
308	23 38 002	54 15 032	55 57 112	24 45 144	19 17 211	34 55 252	24 28 336
309	23 39 001	54 44 030	56 49 112	25 18 144	18 48 211	34 01 252	24 04 335
310	23 40 000	55 11 029	57 41 112	25 50 144	18 19 211	33 08 251	23 40 334
311	23 40 000	55 38 027	58 33 113	26 23 145	17 51 211	32 15 251	23 16 334
312	23 39 359	56 03 026	59 24 113	26 55 145	17 22 211	31 22 251	22 50 333
313	23 38 358	56 26 024	60 16 113	27 28 145	16 54 211	30 29 251	22 25 332
314	23 35 357	56 48 022	61 07 113	28 00 145	16 25 210	29 36 251	21 58 331
	Alpheratz	◆Diphda	ACHERNAR	◆Peacock	ANTARES	◆ALTAIR	DENEB
315	22 13 044	37 17 097	28 33 145	53 47 188	28 44 250	55 41 329	23 32 357
316	22 52 043	38 13 097	29 05 145	53 40 189	27 51 250	55 12 327	23 29 356
317	23 30 043	39 09 096	29 37 145	53 31 189	26 58 250	54 41 326	23 24 355
318	24 08 042	40 04 096	30 10 145	53 21 190	26 06 250	54 09 325	23 19 354
319	24 45 041	41 00 096	30 42 145	53 11 191	25 13 250	53 36 323	23 13 353
320	25 22 041	41 56 096	31 14 145	52 59 192	24 20 249	53 02 322	23 06 353
321	25 58 040	42 52 095	31 46 145	52 47 193	23 28 249	52 27 320	22 59 352
322	26 33 039	43 47 095	32 18 145	52 34 194	22 36 249	51 50 319	22 51 351
323	27 08 038	44 43 095	32 50 145	52 20 195	21 43 249	51 13 318	22 42 350
324	27 43 038	45 39 094	33 22 146	52 06 195	20 51 249	50 35 317	22 32 350
325	28 17 037	46 35 094	33 53 146	51 51 196	19 59 248	49 57 316	22 22 349
326	28 50 036	47 31 094	34 25 146	51 35 197	19 07 248	49 17 314	22 11 348
327	29 23 035	48 27 094	34 56 146	51 18 198	18 15 248	48 37 313	21 59 348
328	29 55 035	49 22 093	35 27 146	51 00 198	17 23 248	47 56 312	21 47 347
329	30 27 034	50 18 093	35 58 146	50 42 199	16 31 247	47 14 311	21 33 346
	◆Alpheratz	Diphda	◆ACHERNAR	Peacock	◆Nunki	ALTAIR	DENEB
330	30 57 033	51 14 093	36 29 147	50 24 200	47 47 254	46 31 310	21 20 345
331	31 28 032	52 10 092	37 00 147	50 04 201	46 54 254	45 48 309	21 05 345
332	31 57 031	53 06 092	37 30 147	49 44 201	46 00 253	45 05 308	20 50 344
333	32 26 030	54 02 092	38 01 147	49 24 202	45 06 253	44 20 307	20 34 343
334	32 54 030	54 58 091	38 31 148	49 02 203	44 13 253	43 36 306	20 18 343
335	33 21 029	55 54 091	39 01 148	48 40 203	43 19 253	42 50 306	20 01 342
336	33 47 028	56 50 091	39 30 148	48 18 204	42 25 253	42 04 305	19 43 341
337	34 13 027	57 46 090	40 00 149	47 55 204	41 32 253	41 18 304	19 25 341
338	34 38 026	58 42 090	40 29 149	47 32 205	40 38 253	40 32 303	19 06 340
339	35 02 025	59 38 090	40 58 149	47 08 206	39 45 253	39 44 302	18 46 339
340	35 25 024	60 34 089	41 26 149	46 43 206	38 51 253	38 57 302	18 26 339
341	35 47 023	61 30 089	41 54 150	46 19 207	37 58 252	38 09 301	18 05 338
342	36 09 022	62 26 089	42 22 150	45 53 207	37 04 252	37 21 300	17 44 337
343	36 29 021	63 22 088	42 50 151	45 27 208	36 11 252	36 32 299	17 22 337
344	36 49 020	64 18 088	43 17 151	45 01 208	35 18 252	35 43 299	17 00 336
	Alpheratz	◆Hamal	◆ACHERNAR	Peacock	Nunki	◆ALTAIR	Enif
345	37 08 019	26 09 048	43 44 151	44 35 209	34 25 252	34 54 298	53 59 327
346	37 26 018	26 50 048	44 11 152	44 08 209	33 31 252	34 04 297	53 28 326
347	37 42 017	27 31 047	44 37 152	43 41 209	32 38 252	33 14 297	52 56 325
348	37 58 016	28 12 046	45 03 153	43 13 210	31 45 251	32 24 296	52 23 323
349	38 13 015	28 52 046	45 28 153	42 45 210	30 52 251	31 34 295	51 49 322
350	38 27 014	29 32 045	45 53 154	42 16 211	29 59 251	30 43 295	51 14 321
351	38 40 013	30 11 044	46 18 154	41 48 211	29 06 251	29 52 294	50 38 319
352	38 51 012	30 50 043	46 42 155	41 19 211	28 13 251	29 01 294	50 01 318
353	39 02 010	31 28 043	47 06 155	40 50 212	27 21 250	28 10 293	49 23 317
354	39 12 009	32 06 042	47 29 156	40 20 212	26 28 250	27 18 293	48 45 316
355	39 20 008	32 43 041	47 51 156	39 50 212	25 35 250	26 26 292	48 05 315
356	39 28 007	33 19 040	48 13 157	39 20 213	24 43 250	25 34 292	47 25 314
357	39 34 006	33 55 039	48 35 158	38 50 213	23 50 250	24 42 291	46 44 313
358	39 39 005	34 30 038	48 56 158	38 19 213	22 58 249	23 50 291	46 03 312
359	39 44 004	35 05 038	49 16 159	37 49 213	22 05 249	22 57 290	45 21 311

LHA ♈	Hc	Zn	Hc	Zn	Hc	Zn	Hc	Zn	Hc	Zn	Hc	Zn	Hc	Zn
	◆ Alpheratz		Hamal		◆ RIGEL		CANOPUS		ACHERNAR		◆ Peacock		Enif	
0	38 47	003	34 50	036	13 23	094	13 48	142	50 32	159	38 08	214	43 59	310
1	38 49	001	35 23	035	14 18	093	14 23	141	50 52	160	37 36	214	43 17	310
2	38 50	000	35 55	034	15 14	093	14 58	141	51 10	161	37 05	214	42 33	309
3	38 49	359	36 26	034	16 09	092	15 32	141	51 28	161	36 34	215	41 50	308
4	38 48	358	36 56	033	17 05	092	16 07	141	51 46	162	36 02	215	41 05	307
5	38 46	357	37 26	032	18 00	092	16 43	141	52 03	163	35 30	215	40 21	306
6	38 42	356	37 55	031	18 56	091	17 18	141	52 19	164	34 58	215	39 35	305
7	38 38	355	38 23	030	19 52	091	17 53	140	52 34	164	34 26	215	38 50	304
8	38 32	354	38 50	029	20 47	091	18 29	140	52 49	165	33 54	215	38 03	304
9	38 25	353	39 16	028	21 43	090	19 04	140	53 03	166	33 21	216	37 17	303
10	38 17	351	39 41	027	22 39	090	19 40	140	53 16	167	32 49	216	36 30	302
11	38 09	350	40 05	025	23 34	089	20 16	140	53 28	168	32 16	216	35 43	301
12	37 59	349	40 29	024	24 30	089	20 51	140	53 39	169	31 44	216	34 55	301
13	37 48	348	40 51	023	25 25	089	21 27	140	53 50	169	31 11	216	34 07	300
14	37 36	347	41 13	022	26 21	088	22 03	140	54 00	170	30 38	216	33 18	299
	◆ Hamal		ALDEBARAN		RIGEL		◆ CANOPUS		ACHERNAR		◆ FOMALHAUT		Alpheratz	
15	41 33	021	24 25	059	27 17	088	22 39	140	54 09	171	61 43	248	37 23	346
16	41 53	020	25 12	058	28 12	088	23 15	139	54 17	172	60 51	248	37 09	345
17	42 11	019	25 59	057	29 08	087	23 52	139	54 24	173	59 59	249	36 54	344
18	42 28	018	26 46	057	30 03	087	24 28	139	54 31	174	59 07	249	36 38	343
19	42 45	016	27 32	056	30 59	086	25 04	139	54 36	175	58 16	249	36 21	342
20	43 00	015	28 18	056	31 54	086	25 40	139	54 41	176	57 24	249	36 03	341
21	43 14	014	29 04	055	32 50	086	26 17	139	54 45	177	56 32	249	35 45	340
22	43 26	013	29 49	054	33 45	085	26 53	139	54 47	178	55 39	249	35 25	339
23	43 38	011	30 34	053	34 41	085	27 29	139	54 49	179	54 47	250	35 05	338
24	43 48	010	31 19	053	35 36	084	28 06	139	54 50	179	53 55	250	34 43	337
25	43 58	009	32 03	052	36 31	084	28 42	139	54 50	180	53 03	250	34 21	336
26	44 06	008	32 46	051	37 27	083	29 18	139	54 49	181	52 11	250	33 58	335
27	44 12	006	33 30	051	38 22	083	29 55	139	54 48	182	51 19	250	33 34	334
28	44 18	005	34 12	050	39 17	082	30 31	139	54 45	183	50 26	250	33 09	333
29	44 22	004	34 55	049	40 12	082	31 07	139	54 41	184	49 34	250	32 43	332
	Hamal		◆ ALDEBARAN		SIRIUS		◆ CANOPUS		ACHERNAR		◆ FOMALHAUT		Alpheratz	
30	44 26	003	35 36	048	22 58	100	31 44	139	54 37	185	48 42	250	32 17	331
31	44 27	001	36 18	047	23 53	099	32 20	139	54 32	186	47 50	250	31 50	330
32	44 28	000	36 58	046	24 48	099	32 56	140	54 25	187	46 58	250	31 22	330
33	44 27	359	37 38	046	25 43	099	33 32	140	54 18	188	46 06	250	30 54	329
34	44 26	357	38 18	045	26 38	098	34 08	140	54 10	189	45 13	250	30 24	328
35	44 22	356	38 57	044	27 33	098	34 44	140	54 01	190	44 21	250	29 54	327
36	44 18	355	39 35	043	28 28	098	35 20	140	53 52	191	43 29	250	29 24	326
37	44 13	354	40 12	042	29 24	097	35 56	140	53 41	191	42 37	249	28 53	325
38	44 06	352	40 49	041	30 19	097	36 31	140	53 30	192	41 45	249	28 21	325
39	43 58	351	41 25	040	31 14	097	37 07	140	53 17	193	40 53	249	27 48	324
40	43 48	350	42 01	039	32 09	096	37 42	141	53 04	194	40 01	249	27 15	323
41	43 38	349	42 35	038	33 05	096	38 18	141	52 51	195	39 09	249	26 41	322
42	43 26	347	43 09	037	34 00	096	38 53	141	52 36	196	38 17	249	26 07	322
43	43 14	346	43 42	036	34 55	096	39 28	141	52 21	196	37 25	249	25 32	321
44	43 00	345	44 14	035	35 51	095	40 02	141	52 05	197	36 33	249	24 57	320
	◆ CAPELLA		BETELGEUSE		SIRIUS		◆ CANOPUS		ACHERNAR		◆ FOMALHAUT		Hamal	
45	15 09	024	37 49	061	36 46	095	40 37	142	51 48	198	35 41	249	42 45	344
46	15 32	023	38 37	060	37 41	095	41 12	142	51 31	199	34 50	248	42 29	343
47	15 54	023	39 25	059	38 37	094	41 46	142	51 13	199	33 58	248	42 11	341
48	16 15	022	40 13	058	39 32	094	42 20	142	50 54	200	33 06	248	41 53	340
49	16 36	022	41 00	058	40 28	094	42 54	143	50 35	201	32 14	248	41 33	339
50	16 56	021	41 47	057	41 23	093	43 27	143	50 15	201	31 23	248	41 13	338
51	17 15	020	42 33	056	42 19	093	44 01	143	49 54	202	30 31	248	40 52	337
52	17 34	020	43 19	055	43 15	093	44 34	144	49 33	203	29 40	248	40 29	336
53	17 53	019	44 04	054	44 10	092	45 06	144	49 11	203	28 49	247	40 06	335
54	18 11	018	44 49	053	45 06	092	45 39	144	48 49	204	27 57	247	39 41	333
55	18 28	018	45 34	052	46 01	092	46 11	145	48 26	204	27 06	247	39 16	332
56	18 44	017	46 17	051	46 57	091	46 43	145	48 03	205	26 15	247	38 50	331
57	19 00	016	47 01	050	47 53	091	47 14	146	47 39	206	25 24	247	38 23	330
58	19 15	016	47 43	049	48 48	091	47 45	146	47 15	206	24 33	246	37 55	329
59	19 30	015	48 25	048	49 44	090	48 16	147	46 50	207	23 42	246	37 26	328
	CAPELLA		BETELGEUSE		◆ SIRIUS		CANOPUS		◆ ACHERNAR		Diphda		◆ Hamal	
60	19 44	014	49 06	047	50 39	090	48 46	147	46 25	207	44 02	266	36 57	327
61	19 57	014	49 47	046	51 35	089	49 16	148	46 00	208	43 06	266	36 26	326
62	20 10	013	50 26	045	52 31	089	49 46	148	45 34	208	42 11	265	35 55	326
63	20 22	012	51 05	044	53 26	089	50 15	149	45 07	209	41 15	265	35 23	325
64	20 33	011	51 43	043	54 22	088	50 43	149	44 41	209	40 20	265	34 51	324
65	20 44	011	52 21	041	55 18	088	51 11	150	44 13	209	39 24	264	34 17	323
66	20 54	010	52 57	040	56 13	087	51 39	151	43 46	210	38 29	264	33 44	322
67	21 03	009	53 32	039	57 09	087	52 06	151	43 18	210	37 34	264	33 09	321
68	21 12	009	54 06	037	58 04	086	52 32	152	42 50	211	36 38	264	32 34	320
69	21 20	008	54 39	036	59 00	086	52 58	153	42 22	211	35 43	263	31 58	319
70	21 27	007	55 12	034	59 55	086	53 23	153	41 53	211	34 48	263	31 21	319
71	21 33	006	55 42	033	60 51	085	53 48	154	41 24	212	33 53	263	30 44	318
72	21 39	006	56 12	031	61 46	084	54 11	155	40 55	212	32 58	262	30 07	317
73	21 44	005	56 40	030	62 41	084	54 35	156	40 25	212	32 02	262	29 28	316
74	21 49	004	57 07	028	63 37	083	54 57	157	39 55	212	31 07	262	28 50	316
	◆ CAPELLA		POLLUX		PROCYON		◆ Suhail		CANOPUS		◆ ACHERNAR		Hamal	
75	21 52	003	25 54	041	42 19	060	34 54	129	55 19	157	39 25	213	28 11	315
76	21 55	003	26 30	040	43 07	059	35 38	129	55 40	158	38 55	213	27 31	314
77	21 57	002	27 06	039	43 55	058	36 21	129	56 00	159	38 25	213	26 51	313
78	21 59	001	27 40	038	44 42	058	37 05	129	56 19	160	37 54	214	26 10	313
79	21 59	000	28 15	038	45 29	057	37 48	129	56 37	161	37 23	214	25 29	312
80	21 59	000	28 48	037	46 15	056	38 31	129	56 55	162	36 52	214	24 47	311
81	21 58	359	29 21	036	47 01	055	39 15	129	57 12	163	36 21	214	24 05	311
82	21 57	358	29 54	035	47 46	054	39 58	129	57 27	164	35 50	214	23 23	310
83	21 55	357	30 26	034	48 30	053	40 41	129	57 42	165	35 18	214	22 40	309
84	21 52	357	30 57	034	49 14	052	41 24	129	57 56	166	34 47	215	21 57	309
85	21 48	356	31 27	033	49 58	051	42 07	129	58 09	167	34 15	215	21 14	308
86	21 44	355	31 57	032	50 41	050	42 50	130	58 20	168	33 43	215	20 30	308
87	21 39	354	32 26	031	51 23	049	43 33	130	58 31	169	33 11	215	19 46	307
88	21 33	354	32 55	030	52 04	047	44 16	130	58 41	171	32 39	215	19 01	306
89	21 26	353	33 22	029	52 45	046	44 58	130	58 49	172	32 07	215	18 16	306

LHA ♈	Hc	Zn	Hc	Zn	Hc	Zn	Hc	Zn	Hc	Zn	Hc	Zn	Hc	Zn
	POLLUX		◆ REGULUS		ACRUX		CANOPUS		◆ ACHERNAR		◆ ALDEBARAN		CAPELLA	
90	33 49	028	20 10	067	16 31	152	58 57	173	31 35	215	46 24	330	21 19	352
91	34 15	027	21 01	067	16 57	152	59 03	174	31 03	215	45 56	329	21 11	351
92	34 40	027	21 52	066	17 23	152	59 08	175	30 31	216	45 27	328	21 02	351
93	35 05	026	22 43	066	17 50	152	59 12	176	29 58	216	44 57	327	20 53	350
94	35 28	025	23 33	065	18 16	152	59 15	178	29 26	216	44 27	326	20 43	349
95	35 51	024	24 24	065	18 42	152	59 17	179	28 53	216	43 55	325	20 32	349
96	36 13	023	25 14	064	19 09	151	59 18	180	28 21	216	43 22	324	20 21	348
97	36 34	022	26 04	064	19 36	151	59 17	181	27 48	216	42 49	322	20 09	347
98	36 54	021	26 54	063	20 02	151	59 16	182	27 16	216	42 14	321	19 56	346
99	37 13	020	27 43	062	20 29	151	59 13	183	26 43	216	41 39	320	19 43	346
100	37 31	018	28 32	062	20 56	151	59 09	185	26 11	216	41 03	319	19 29	345
101	37 48	017	29 21	061	21 23	151	59 04	186	25 38	216	40 27	318	19 14	344
102	38 04	016	30 10	061	21 50	151	58 58	187	25 06	216	39 50	317	18 59	344
103	38 20	015	30 58	060	22 16	151	58 50	188	24 33	216	39 12	317	18 43	343
104	38 34	014	31 46	059	22 43	151	58 42	189	24 01	216	38 33	316	18 26	342
	POLLUX		◆ REGULUS		Gienah		◆ ACRUX		CANOPUS		◆ RIGEL		BETELGEUSE	
105	38 47	013	32 34	059	16 15	103	23 10	151	58 32	190	61 16	295	56 40	330
106	38 59	012	33 21	058	17 09	103	23 38	151	58 22	191	60 25	294	56 12	329
107	39 10	011	34 08	057	18 04	102	24 05	151	58 10	193	59 34	293	55 42	327
108	39 20	010	34 54	056	18 58	102	24 32	151	57 58	194	58 43	292	55 11	326
109	39 29	009	35 40	056	19 53	102	24 59	151	57 44	195	57 51	291	54 39	324
110	39 37	008	36 26	055	20 47	101	25 26	151	57 29	196	56 59	290	54 06	323
111	39 43	006	37 12	054	21 42	101	25 53	151	57 14	197	56 06	289	53 32	321
112	39 49	005	37 56	053	22 36	101	26 20	151	56 57	198	55 13	288	52 57	320
113	39 54	004	38 41	053	23 31	100	26 47	151	56 40	199	54 21	287	52 20	319
114	39 57	003	39 25	052	24 26	100	27 14	151	56 22	200	53 27	287	51 43	317
115	39 59	002	40 08	051	25 20	100	27 41	151	56 02	201	52 34	286	51 05	316
116	40 00	001	40 51	050	26 15	099	28 08	151	55 42	202	51 40	285	50 26	315
117	40 01	359	41 33	049	27 10	099	28 35	151	55 22	202	50 47	285	49 46	314
118	40 00	358	42 15	048	28 05	099	29 01	151	55 00	203	49 53	284	49 06	313
119	39 57	357	42 56	047	29 00	099	29 28	151	54 38	204	48 59	283	48 25	312
	◆ REGULUS		SPICA		◆ ACRUX		CANOPUS		◆ RIGEL		BETELGEUSE		POLLUX	
120	43 37	046	11 59	097	29 55	151	54 15	205	48 04	283	47 43	311	39 54	356
121	44 16	045	12 54	097	30 21	152	53 51	206	47 10	282	47 00	310	39 50	355
122	44 56	044	13 49	097	30 48	152	53 27	206	46 16	282	46 17	309	39 44	354
123	45 34	043	14 44	096	31 14	152	53 01	207	45 21	281	45 33	308	39 38	353
124	46 12	042	15 40	096	31 41	152	52 36	208	44 26	280	44 49	307	39 30	351
125	46 49	041	16 35	096	32 07	152	52 10	209	43 32	280	44 04	306	39 21	350
126	47 25	040	17 30	095	32 33	152	51 43	209	42 37	279	43 19	305	39 11	349
127	48 00	039	18 26	095	32 59	152	51 15	210	41 42	279	42 33	304	39 00	348
128	48 34	037	19 21	095	33 25	152	50 47	210	40 47	278	41 46	303	38 48	347
129	49 07	036	20 17	094	33 50	153	50 19	211	39 52	278	41 00	302	38 35	346
130	49 40	035	21 12	094	34 16	153	49 50	212	38 57	277	40 12	302	38 21	345
131	50 11	034	22 08	094	34 41	153	49 21	212	38 02	277	39 25	301	38 06	344
132	50 42	032	23 03	093	35 06	153	48 51	213	37 06	276	38 37	300	37 50	343
133	51 11	031	23 59	093	35 31	153	48 20	213	36 11	276	37 49	299	37 33	342
134	51 39	030	24 54	093	35 56	154	47 50	214	35 16	276	37 00	299	37 15	341
	REGULUS		◆ SPICA		ACRUX		◆ CANOPUS		SIRIUS		BETELGEUSE		◆ POLLUX	
135	52 06	028	25 50	092	36 21	154	47 19	214	57 59	273	36 11	298	36 56	340
136	52 32	027	26 45	092	36 45	154	46 47	215	57 03	273	35 22	297	36 36	339
137	52 56	025	27 41	091	37 09	154	46 16	215	56 08	273	34 32	297	36 15	338
138	53 19	024	28 37	091	37 33	155	45 43	215	55 12	272	33 42	296	35 54	337
139	53 41	022	29 32	091	37 57	155	45 11	216	54 17	272	32 52	295	35 31	336
140	54 02	021	30 28	090	38 20	155	44 38	216	53 21	271	32 01	295	35 07	335
141	54 21	019	31 23	090	38 44	155	44 05	217	52 25	271	31 11	294	34 43	334
142	54 38	018	32 19	090	39 07	156	43 32	217	51 30	271	30 20	293	34 18	333
143	54 54	016	33 15	089	39 29	156	42 58	217	50 34	270	29 29	293	33 52	332
144	55 09	014	34 10	089	39 52	156	42 25	218	49 39	270	28 37	292	33 25	331
145	55 22	013	35 06	088	40 14	157	41 51	218	48 43	269	27 46	292	32 58	330
146	55 33	011	36 02	088	40 36	157	41 16	218	47 47	269	26 54	291	32 30	329
147	55 43	009	36 57	088	40 57	157	40 42	218	46 52	269	26 02	291	32 01	328
148	55 51	007	37 53	087	41 18	158	40 07	219	45 56	268	25 10	290	31 31	327
149	55 57	006	38 48	087	41 39	158	39 33	219	45 00	268	24 17	290	31 00	326
	REGULUS		◆ ARCTURUS		SPICA		◆ ACRUX		CANOPUS		SIRIUS		◆ PROCYON	
150	56 02	004	15 05	062	39 44	086	41 59	159	38 58	219	44 05	268	46 17	304
151	56 05	002	15 54	061	40 39	086	42 19	159	38 23	219	43 09	267	45 31	303
152	56 06	001	16 43	061	41 35	086	42 39	159	37 47	219	42 14	267	44 44	303
153	56 06	359	17 31	060	42 30	085	42 58	160	37 12	220	41 18	267	43 57	302
154	56 04	357	18 19	060	43 26	085	43 17	160	36 36	220	40 23	266	43 09	301
155	56 00	355	19 07	059	44 21	084	43 36	161	36 01	220	39 27	266	42 21	300
156	55 55	354	19 55	059	45 16	084	43 54	161	35 25	220	38 32	266	41 33	299
157	55 48	352	20 42	058	46 12	083	44 12	162	34 49	220	37 36	265	40 44	298
158	55 39	350	21 29	057	47 07	083	44 29	162	34 13	220	36 41	265	39 55	298
159	55 28	348	22 16	057	48 02	082	44 46	163	33 37	220	35 45	265	39 06	297
160	55 16	347	23 02	056	48 57	082	45 02	163	33 01	220	34 50	264	38 16	296
161	55 03	345	23 48	056	49 52	081	45 18	164	32 25	221	33 55	264	37 26	296
162	54 48	343	24 34	055	50 47	081	45 33	164	31 49	221	32 59	264	36 36	295
163	54 31	342	25 19	054	51 42	080	45 48	165	31 13	221	32 04	263	35 45	294
164	54 13	340	26 04	054	52 37	079	46 02	165	30 36	221	31 09	263	34 54	294
	◆ ARCTURUS		ANTARES		◆ ACRUX		CANOPUS		SIRIUS		◆ PROCYON		REGULUS	
165	26 49	053	15 54	113	46 16	166	30 00	221	30 14	263	34 03	293	53 53	339
166	27 33	052	16 46	112	46 29	167	29 24	221	29 18	263	33 12	292	53 32	337
167	28 17	052	17 37	112	46 42	167	28 47	221	28 23	262	32 20	292	53 10	336
168	29 01	051	18 29	112	46 54	168	28 11	221	27 28	262	31 29	291	52 46	334
169	29 44	050	19 21	112	47 06	168	27 35	221	26 33	262	30 37	291	52 21	333
170	30 27	050	20 12	111	47 17	169	26 58	221	25 38	261	29 44	290	51 55	331
171	31 09	049	21 04	111	47 27	169	26 22	221	24 43	261	28 52	290	51 27	330
172	31 51	048	21 56	111	47 37	170	25 46	221	23 48	261	28 00	289	50 59	328
173	32 32	047	22 48	111	47 46	171	25 09	221	22 53	260	27 07	288	50 29	327
174	33 13	047	23 40	110	47 55	171	24 33	221	21 58	260	26 14	288	49 58	326
175	33 53	046	24 33	110	48 03	172	23 57	221	21 04	260	25 21	287	49 27	324
176	34 32	045	25 25	110	48 10	173	23 21	221	20 09	259	24 28	287	48 54	323
177	35 11	044	26 17	110	48 17	173	22 45	220	19 14	259	23 35	286	48 20	322
178	35 50	043	27 10	109	48 23	174	22 08	220	18 20	259	22 41	286	47 45	321
179	36 28	042	28 02	109	48 29	175	21 32	220	17 25	259	21 48	285	47 10	320

LHA ♈	Hc	Zn	Hc	Zn	Hc	Zn	Hc	Zn	Hc	Zn	Hc	Zn	Hc	Zn
	ARCTURUS		◆ANTARES		ACRUX		◆Suhail		Alphard		REGULUS		◆Denebola	
180	37 05	042	28 55	109	48 33	175	48 40	228	51 15	284	46 33	319	53 26	356
181	37 42	041	29 47	109	48 38	176	47 58	229	50 20	283	45 56	317	53 21	354
182	38 18	040	30 40	109	48 41	177	47 16	229	49 26	283	45 18	316	53 14	353
183	38 53	039	31 33	108	48 44	177	46 34	229	48 32	282	44 39	315	53 07	351
184	39 27	038	32 26	108	48 46	178	45 52	229	47 37	282	44 00	314	52 57	349
185	40 01	037	33 18	108	48 48	179	45 10	230	46 43	281	43 20	313	52 46	348
186	40 34	036	34 11	108	48 49	179	44 27	230	45 48	280	42 39	312	52 34	346
187	41 06	035	35 04	108	48 49	180	43 45	230	44 54	280	41 58	311	52 20	345
188	41 38	034	35 57	107	48 49	181	43 02	230	43 59	279	41 16	311	52 05	343
189	42 08	033	36 51	107	48 48	181	42 19	231	43 04	279	40 33	310	51 48	342
190	42 38	032	37 44	107	48 46	182	41 36	231	42 09	278	39 50	309	51 30	340
191	43 06	030	38 37	107	48 43	183	40 53	231	41 14	278	39 07	308	51 10	339
192	43 34	029	39 30	107	48 40	184	40 10	231	40 18	277	38 22	307	50 49	337
193	44 01	028	40 23	107	48 37	184	39 27	231	39 23	277	37 38	306	50 27	336
194	44 27	027	41 17	107	48 32	185	38 43	231	38 28	276	36 53	306	50 04	335
	ARCTURUS		◆Rasalhague		ANTARES		◆ACRUX		Suhail		◆REGULUS		Denebola	
195	44 51	026	14 08	070	42 10	106	48 27	186	38 00	231	36 07	305	49 40	333
196	45 15	025	15 01	069	43 03	106	48 21	186	37 16	231	35 21	304	49 14	332
197	45 38	023	15 53	069	43 57	106	48 15	187	36 33	231	34 35	303	48 47	331
198	45 59	022	16 44	069	44 50	106	48 08	188	35 50	231	33 48	303	48 19	329
199	46 20	021	17 36	068	45 44	106	48 01	188	35 06	231	33 01	302	47 50	328
200	46 39	020	18 28	068	46 37	106	47 52	189	34 23	231	32 14	301	47 20	327
201	46 57	018	19 19	067	47 31	106	47 44	189	33 39	231	31 26	300	46 49	326
202	47 14	017	20 10	067	48 24	106	47 34	190	32 56	231	30 38	300	46 17	324
203	47 29	016	21 01	066	49 18	106	47 24	191	32 12	231	29 50	299	45 45	323
204	47 44	014	21 52	066	50 12	105	47 14	191	31 29	231	29 01	299	45 11	322
205	47 57	013	22 42	065	51 05	105	47 02	192	30 45	231	28 12	298	44 36	321
206	48 08	011	23 33	064	51 59	105	46 51	192	30 02	231	27 23	297	44 01	320
207	48 19	010	24 23	064	52 52	105	46 38	193	29 18	231	26 33	297	43 25	319
208	48 28	009	25 12	063	53 46	105	46 25	194	28 35	231	25 43	296	42 48	318
209	48 36	007	26 02	063	54 40	105	46 12	194	27 51	231	24 53	296	42 10	317
	ARCTURUS		◆Rasalhague		ANTARES		◆RIGIL KENT		ACRUX		Gienah		◆Denebola	
210	48 42	006	26 51	062	55 34	105	50 28	172	45 58	195	65 19	276	41 32	316
211	48 47	004	27 40	062	56 27	105	50 35	173	45 44	195	64 24	275	40 53	315
212	48 51	003	28 29	061	57 21	105	50 41	174	45 29	196	63 28	274	40 13	314
213	48 53	002	29 18	060	58 15	105	50 47	174	45 13	196	62 33	274	39 33	313
214	48 54	000	30 06	060	59 08	105	50 52	175	44 57	197	61 37	273	38 52	312
215	48 53	359	30 54	059	60 02	105	50 56	176	44 41	197	60 42	273	38 10	311
216	48 51	357	31 41	058	60 56	105	51 00	177	44 24	198	59 46	273	37 28	311
217	48 48	356	32 28	058	61 49	105	51 03	178	44 07	198	58 50	272	36 46	310
218	48 43	354	33 15	057	62 43	105	51 04	178	43 49	199	57 55	272	36 03	309
219	48 37	353	34 02	056	63 37	105	51 06	179	43 31	199	56 59	271	35 19	308
220	48 29	352	34 48	056	64 30	106	51 06	180	43 12	200	56 04	271	34 35	307
221	48 21	350	35 33	055	65 24	106	51 06	181	42 53	200	55 08	270	33 51	307
222	48 10	349	36 19	054	66 17	106	51 05	181	42 34	201	54 12	270	33 06	306
223	47 59	347	37 03	053	67 11	106	51 03	182	42 14	201	53 17	270	32 21	305
224	47 46	346	37 48	052	68 04	106	51 01	183	41 54	201	52 21	269	31 35	304
	Alphecca		Rasalhague		◆ALTAIR		Peacock		◆RIGIL KENT		◆SPICA		ARCTURUS	
225	40 35	010	38 32	052	12 13	075	22 44	144	50 57	184	65 05	292	47 32	345
226	40 45	009	39 15	051	13 07	075	23 17	144	50 53	185	64 14	291	47 17	343
227	40 53	008	39 58	050	14 00	074	23 50	144	50 49	185	63 21	290	47 00	342
228	41 01	007	40 40	049	14 54	074	24 23	144	50 43	186	62 29	289	46 42	341
229	41 07	006	41 22	048	15 47	073	24 56	144	50 37	187	61 36	288	46 23	339
230	41 12	005	42 03	047	16 40	073	25 29	144	50 30	188	60 43	287	46 03	338
231	41 15	003	42 43	046	17 34	072	26 02	144	50 23	188	59 49	286	45 42	337
232	41 18	002	43 23	045	18 26	072	26 34	144	50 14	189	58 56	285	45 19	336
233	41 20	001	44 02	044	19 19	071	27 07	144	50 05	190	58 02	285	44 56	334
234	41 20	000	44 41	043	20 12	071	27 40	144	49 55	190	57 08	284	44 31	333
235	41 19	359	45 18	042	21 04	070	28 13	144	49 45	191	56 14	283	44 05	332
236	41 17	357	45 55	041	21 57	070	28 46	144	49 34	192	55 20	282	43 39	331
237	41 14	356	46 31	040	22 49	069	29 19	144	49 22	192	54 25	282	43 11	330
238	41 10	355	47 07	039	23 41	069	29 52	144	49 10	193	53 31	281	42 43	329
239	41 05	354	47 41	038	24 33	068	30 25	144	48 57	194	52 36	281	42 13	327
	VEGA		◆ALTAIR		Peacock		◆RIGIL KENT		SPICA		◆ARCTURUS		Alphecca	
240	18 54	031	25 24	068	30 58	144	48 43	194	51 41	280	41 43	326	40 58	353
241	19 23	031	26 16	067	31 30	144	48 29	195	50 47	279	41 12	325	40 51	352
242	19 51	030	27 07	067	32 03	144	48 14	196	49 52	279	40 40	324	40 42	350
243	20 19	030	27 58	066	32 35	144	47 59	196	48 57	278	40 07	323	40 32	349
244	20 46	029	28 49	066	33 08	144	47 43	197	48 02	278	39 33	322	40 21	348
245	21 13	028	29 39	065	33 40	144	47 26	198	47 06	277	38 59	321	40 09	347
246	21 39	027	30 30	064	34 13	145	47 09	198	46 11	277	38 24	320	39 56	346
247	22 04	027	31 20	064	34 45	145	46 52	199	45 16	276	37 48	319	39 42	345
248	22 29	026	32 10	063	35 17	145	46 34	199	44 21	276	37 11	319	39 26	344
249	22 53	025	32 59	063	35 49	145	46 15	200	43 25	275	36 34	318	39 10	342
250	23 16	025	33 48	062	36 20	145	45 56	200	42 30	275	35 56	317	38 53	341
251	23 39	024	34 37	061	36 52	145	45 36	201	41 34	274	35 18	316	38 34	340
252	24 01	023	35 26	061	37 24	146	45 16	201	40 39	274	34 39	315	38 15	339
253	24 23	022	36 14	060	37 55	146	44 56	202	39 43	274	34 00	314	37 55	338
254	24 43	022	37 02	059	38 26	146	44 35	202	38 48	273	33 19	313	37 34	337
	◆VEGA		ALTAIR		◆Peacock		RIGIL KENT		◆SPICA		ARCTURUS		Alphecca	
255	25 04	021	37 49	058	38 57	146	44 13	203	37 52	273	32 39	313	37 12	336
256	25 23	020	38 37	058	39 28	147	43 52	203	36 57	272	31 58	312	36 49	335
257	25 42	019	39 23	057	39 58	147	43 29	204	36 01	272	31 16	311	36 25	334
258	26 00	018	40 10	056	40 28	147	43 07	204	35 06	272	30 34	310	36 00	333
259	26 17	018	40 55	055	40 59	147	42 44	205	34 10	271	29 51	310	35 35	332
260	26 33	017	41 41	054	41 28	148	42 21	205	33 14	271	29 08	309	35 08	331
261	26 49	016	42 26	053	41 58	148	41 57	205	32 19	270	28 25	308	34 41	330
262	27 04	015	43 10	053	42 27	148	41 33	206	31 23	270	27 41	308	34 13	329
263	27 18	014	43 54	052	42 56	149	41 09	206	30 27	270	26 57	307	33 44	328
264	27 31	013	44 38	051	43 25	149	40 44	206	29 32	269	26 12	306	33 15	328
265	27 44	013	45 20	050	43 53	150	40 19	207	28 36	269	25 27	306	32 44	327
266	27 56	012	46 02	049	44 21	150	39 54	207	27 41	269	24 42	305	32 14	326
267	28 06	011	46 44	048	44 49	150	39 29	207	26 45	268	23 56	304	31 42	325
268	28 17	010	47 25	047	45 16	151	39 03	208	25 49	268	23 10	304	31 10	324
269	28 26	009	48 05	046	45 43	151	38 37	208	24 54	267	22 24	303	30 37	323

LAT 22°S

LHA ♈	Hc	Zn	Hc	Zn	Hc	Zn	Hc	Zn	Hc	Zn	Hc	Zn	Hc	Zn
	◆VEGA		ALTAIR		◆FOMALHAUT		Peacock		RIGIL KENT		◆ANTARES		Alphecca	
270	28 34	008	48 44	044	23 30	114	46 10	152	38 11	208	69 06	253	30 03	322
271	28 42	007	49 23	043	24 21	114	46 36	152	37 44	208	68 13	253	29 29	322
272	28 49	007	50 00	042	25 12	113	47 02	153	37 18	209	67 20	254	28 54	321
273	28 55	006	50 37	041	26 03	113	47 27	153	36 51	209	66 26	254	28 19	320
274	29 00	005	51 13	040	26 54	113	47 52	154	36 24	209	65 33	254	27 43	319
275	29 04	004	51 48	038	27 45	113	48 16	154	35 57	209	64 39	254	27 06	319
276	29 07	003	52 22	037	28 36	113	48 40	155	35 29	210	63 46	254	26 29	318
277	29 10	002	52 55	036	29 28	112	49 03	155	35 02	210	62 52	255	25 52	317
278	29 11	001	53 27	034	30 19	112	49 26	156	34 34	210	61 58	255	25 14	317
279	29 12	000	53 58	033	31 11	112	49 49	157	34 06	210	61 05	255	24 35	316
280	29 12	359	54 28	031	32 02	112	50 10	157	33 38	210	60 11	255	23 56	315
281	29 11	359	54 56	030	32 54	112	50 31	158	33 10	210	59 17	255	23 17	314
282	29 09	358	55 23	028	33 45	112	50 52	159	32 42	211	58 24	255	22 37	314
283	29 06	357	55 49	027	34 37	112	51 12	159	32 13	211	57 30	255	21 56	313
284	29 03	356	56 14	025	35 29	111	51 31	160	31 45	211	56 36	255	21 16	313
	◆DENEB		FOMALHAUT		◆ACHERNAR		RIGIL KENT		◆ANTARES		Rasalhague		VEGA	
285	18 47	019	36 21	111	13 22	147	31 16	211	55 42	255	49 44	327	28 58	355
286	19 04	018	37 13	111	13 53	146	30 47	211	54 49	255	49 13	326	28 53	354
287	19 21	017	38 05	111	14 23	146	30 19	211	53 55	255	48 41	325	28 47	353
288	19 37	017	38 56	111	14 54	146	29 50	211	53 01	255	48 08	323	28 40	352
289	19 53	016	39 48	111	15 25	146	29 21	211	52 08	255	47 35	322	28 32	351
290	20 08	015	40 40	111	15 57	146	28 52	211	51 14	255	47 00	321	28 23	351
291	20 22	014	41 33	111	16 28	146	28 23	211	50 20	255	46 25	320	28 14	350
292	20 36	014	42 25	111	16 59	145	27 54	212	49 27	255	45 48	319	28 04	349
293	20 48	013	43 17	110	17 31	145	27 25	212	48 33	254	45 11	318	27 52	348
294	21 01	012	44 09	110	18 03	145	26 55	212	47 40	254	44 34	317	27 40	347
295	21 12	012	45 01	110	18 34	145	26 26	212	46 46	254	43 55	316	27 28	346
296	21 23	011	45 53	110	19 06	145	25 57	212	45 53	254	43 16	315	27 14	345
297	21 33	010	46 45	110	19 38	145	25 28	212	44 59	254	42 36	314	27 00	345
298	21 43	009	47 37	110	20 10	145	24 59	212	44 06	254	41 55	313	26 45	344
299	21 51	009	48 30	110	20 42	145	24 30	212	43 12	254	41 14	312	26 29	343
	DENEB		Enif		◆FOMALHAUT		ACHERNAR		◆RIGIL KENT		ANTARES		◆VEGA	
300	21 59	008	48 59	042	49 22	110	21 15	145	24 00	212	42 19	254	26 12	342
301	22 07	007	49 35	040	50 14	110	21 47	145	23 31	212	41 25	253	25 55	341
302	22 13	006	50 11	039	51 06	110	22 19	144	23 02	212	40 32	253	25 36	341
303	22 19	006	50 46	038	51 58	110	22 52	144	22 33	212	39 39	253	25 18	340
304	22 24	005	51 19	037	52 51	110	23 24	144	22 04	211	38 46	253	24 58	339
305	22 29	004	51 52	035	53 43	110	23 56	144	21 35	211	37 52	253	24 38	338
306	22 32	003	52 24	034	54 35	110	24 29	144	21 06	211	36 59	253	24 17	337
307	22 35	003	52 54	033	55 27	111	25 01	144	20 37	211	36 06	253	23 55	337
308	22 38	002	53 23	031	56 19	111	25 34	144	20 08	211	35 13	252	23 33	336
309	22 39	001	53 52	030	57 11	111	26 06	144	19 40	211	34 20	252	23 10	335
310	22 40	000	54 18	028	58 03	111	26 39	144	19 11	211	33 27	252	22 46	334
311	22 40	000	54 44	027	58 55	111	27 12	144	18 42	211	32 34	252	22 22	334
312	22 39	359	55 08	025	59 47	111	27 44	144	18 14	211	31 42	252	21 57	333
313	22 38	358	55 31	023	60 39	111	28 17	144	17 45	211	30 49	251	21 31	332
314	22 35	357	55 53	022	61 30	112	28 49	144	17 17	211	29 56	251	21 05	332
	Alpheratz		◆Diphda		ACHERNAR		◆Peacock		ANTARES		◆ALTAIR		DENEB	
315	21 30	044	37 24	096	29 21	144	54 47	188	29 03	251	54 49	330	22 32	357
316	22 08	043	38 20	096	29 54	144	54 39	189	28 11	251	54 21	328	22 29	356
317	22 46	042	39 15	096	30 26	144	54 30	190	27 18	251	53 51	327	22 24	355
318	23 23	042	40 10	095	30 59	145	54 20	191	26 26	250	53 20	325	22 19	354
319	24 00	041	41 06	095	31 31	145	54 09	192	25 34	250	52 48	324	22 13	354
320	24 36	040	42 01	095	32 03	145	53 58	192	24 41	250	52 14	323	22 07	353
321	25 12	040	42 57	094	32 35	145	53 45	193	23 49	250	51 40	321	21 59	352
322	25 47	039	43 52	094	33 07	145	53 32	194	22 57	249	51 05	320	21 51	351
323	26 21	038	44 48	094	33 39	145	53 18	195	22 05	249	50 28	319	21 42	351
324	26 55	037	45 43	093	34 11	145	53 04	196	21 13	249	49 51	318	21 33	350
325	27 29	037	46 39	093	34 43	145	52 48	197	20 21	249	49 13	316	21 23	349
326	28 02	036	47 34	093	35 14	145	52 32	197	19 29	248	48 35	315	21 12	348
327	28 34	035	48 30	093	35 46	146	52 15	198	18 38	248	47 55	314	21 00	348
328	29 06	034	49 25	092	36 17	146	51 57	199	17 46	248	47 15	313	20 48	347
329	29 37	033	50 21	092	36 48	146	51 39	200	16 54	248	46 34	312	20 35	346
	◆Alpheratz		Diphda		◆ACHERNAR		Peacock		◆Nunki		ALTAIR		DENEB	
330	30 07	033	51 17	091	37 19	146	51 20	200	48 04	255	45 52	311	20 22	345
331	30 37	032	52 12	091	37 50	146	51 00	201	47 10	255	45 10	310	20 07	345
332	31 06	031	53 08	091	38 21	147	50 40	202	46 16	254	44 27	309	19 52	344
333	31 34	030	54 03	090	38 51	147	50 19	202	45 23	254	43 44	308	19 37	343
334	32 01	029	54 59	090	39 21	147	49 58	203	44 29	254	43 00	307	19 21	343
335	32 28	028	55 55	090	39 51	147	49 36	204	43 36	254	42 15	306	19 04	342
336	32 54	027	56 50	089	40 21	148	49 13	204	42 42	254	41 30	305	18 46	341
337	33 19	027	57 46	089	40 51	148	48 50	205	41 49	254	40 44	305	18 28	341
338	33 44	026	58 42	088	41 20	148	48 26	206	40 56	254	39 58	304	18 09	340
339	34 07	025	59 37	088	41 49	149	48 02	206	40 02	253	39 12	303	17 50	339
340	34 30	024	60 33	088	42 18	149	47 37	207	39 09	253	38 25	302	17 30	339
341	34 52	023	61 28	087	42 46	149	47 12	207	38 16	253	37 38	301	17 10	338
342	35 13	022	62 24	087	43 14	150	46 47	208	37 22	253	36 50	301	16 49	337
343	35 33	021	63 19	086	43 42	150	46 21	208	36 29	253	36 02	300	16 27	337
344	35 53	020	64 15	086	44 10	151	45 54	209	35 36	253	35 14	299	16 05	336
	Alpheratz		◆Hamal		◆ACHERNAR		Peacock		Nunki		◆ALTAIR		Enif	
345	36 11	019	25 28	048	44 37	151	45 27	209	34 43	252	34 25	299	53 08	328
346	36 28	018	26 10	047	45 04	151	45 00	209	33 50	252	33 36	298	52 38	327
347	36 45	017	26 50	047	45 30	152	44 33	210	32 57	252	32 47	297	52 07	325
348	37 00	016	27 30	046	45 56	152	44 05	210	32 04	252	31 57	297	51 35	324
349	37 15	015	28 10	045	46 22	153	43 37	211	31 11	252	31 08	296	51 01	323
350	37 28	014	28 49	044	46 47	153	43 08	211	30 18	252	30 18	295	50 27	321
351	37 41	012	29 28	044	47 12	154	42 39	211	29 26	251	29 27	295	49 52	320
352	37 53	011	30 06	043	47 36	154	42 10	212	28 33	251	28 37	294	49 16	319
353	38 03	010	30 44	042	48 00	155	41 41	212	27 40	251	27 46	294	48 39	318
354	38 12	009	31 21	041	48 23	155	41 11	212	26 48	251	26 55	293	48 01	317
355	38 21	008	31 57	041	48 46	156	40 41	213	25 55	250	26 03	293	47 23	316
356	38 28	007	32 33	040	49 08	157	40 11	213	25 03	250	25 12	292	46 43	314
357	38 34	006	33 09	039	49 30	157	39 40	213	24 11	250	24 20	291	46 03	313
358	38 40	005	33 43	038	49 51	158	39 10	214	23 18	250	23 28	291	45 23	312
359	38 44	004	34 17	037	50 12	159	38 39	214	22 26	250	22 36	290	44 41	311

LHA ♈	Hc	Zn	Hc	Zn	Hc	Zn	Hc	Zn	Hc	Zn	Hc	Zn	Hc	Zn
	◆ Alpheratz		Hamal		◆ RIGEL		CANOPUS		ACHERNAR		◆ Peacock		Enif	
0	37 47	003	34 02	036	13 26	093	14 35	141	51 28	159	38 57	214	43 20	311
1	37 49	001	34 34	035	14 21	093	15 10	141	51 48	159	38 26	215	42 38	310
2	37 50	000	35 05	034	15 17	093	15 44	141	52 07	160	37 54	215	41 56	309
3	37 49	359	35 36	033	16 12	092	16 19	141	52 25	161	37 23	215	41 13	308
4	37 48	358	36 06	032	17 07	092	16 54	141	52 43	162	36 51	215	40 29	308
5	37 46	357	36 35	031	18 02	091	17 29	141	53 00	162	36 19	215	39 45	307
6	37 42	356	37 03	030	18 57	091	18 04	140	53 16	163	35 47	216	39 00	306
7	37 38	355	37 30	029	19 53	091	18 39	140	53 32	164	35 15	216	38 15	305
8	37 32	354	37 57	028	20 48	090	19 15	140	53 47	165	34 42	216	37 30	304
9	37 26	353	38 23	027	21 43	090	19 50	140	54 01	166	34 10	216	36 44	303
10	37 18	352	38 47	026	22 38	089	20 26	140	54 14	167	33 37	216	35 58	303
11	37 09	350	39 11	025	23 33	089	21 01	140	54 27	167	33 05	216	35 11	302
12	37 00	349	39 34	024	24 29	089	21 37	140	54 38	168	32 32	216	34 24	301
13	36 49	348	39 56	023	25 24	088	22 13	139	54 49	169	31 59	216	33 37	300
14	36 37	347	40 17	022	26 19	088	22 49	139	54 59	170	31 27	216	32 49	300
	◆ Hamal		ALDEBARAN		RIGEL		◆ CANOPUS		ACHERNAR		◆ FOMALHAUT		Alpheratz	
15	40 37	021	23 54	058	27 14	087	23 25	139	55 08	171	62 04	250	36 25	346
16	40 56	020	24 40	058	28 09	087	24 01	139	55 16	172	61 12	250	36 11	345
17	41 14	018	25 27	057	29 05	087	24 37	139	55 24	173	60 20	250	35 56	344
18	41 31	017	26 13	056	30 00	086	25 13	139	55 30	174	59 28	250	35 41	343
19	41 47	016	26 59	056	30 55	086	25 50	139	55 36	175	58 36	251	35 24	342
20	42 02	015	27 44	055	31 50	085	26 26	139	55 41	176	57 44	251	35 07	341
21	42 15	014	28 29	054	32 45	085	27 02	139	55 44	177	56 52	251	34 48	340
22	42 28	012	29 14	054	33 40	084	27 38	139	55 47	178	56 00	251	34 29	339
23	42 39	011	29 58	053	34 35	084	28 15	139	55 49	178	55 08	251	34 09	338
24	42 49	010	30 42	052	35 30	084	28 51	139	55 50	179	54 15	251	33 48	337
25	42 58	009	31 26	052	36 25	083	29 27	139	55 50	180	53 23	251	33 26	336
26	43 06	008	32 09	051	37 19	083	30 04	139	55 49	181	52 31	251	33 03	335
27	43 13	006	32 51	050	38 14	082	30 40	139	55 48	182	51 39	251	32 40	334
28	43 18	005	33 33	049	39 09	082	31 16	139	55 45	183	50 47	251	32 15	333
29	43 23	004	34 15	048	40 03	081	31 53	139	55 41	184	49 55	251	31 50	332
	Hamal		◆ ALDEBARAN		SIRIUS		◆ CANOPUS		ACHERNAR		◆ FOMALHAUT		Alpheratz	
30	43 26	003	34 56	048	23 08	099	32 29	139	55 37	185	49 02	251	31 24	332
31	43 27	001	35 37	047	24 03	099	33 05	139	55 31	186	48 10	251	30 58	331
32	43 28	000	36 17	046	24 57	098	33 41	139	55 25	187	47 18	251	30 30	330
33	43 27	359	36 56	045	25 52	098	34 18	139	55 18	188	46 26	251	30 02	329
34	43 26	357	37 35	044	26 47	098	34 54	139	55 09	189	45 34	251	29 33	328
35	43 23	356	38 13	043	27 41	098	35 30	139	55 00	190	44 42	251	29 04	327
36	43 18	355	38 51	042	28 36	097	36 06	139	54 50	191	43 50	250	28 34	327
37	43 13	354	39 27	041	29 31	097	36 41	140	54 40	192	42 58	250	28 03	326
38	43 06	352	40 04	040	30 26	097	37 17	140	54 28	193	42 06	250	27 32	325
39	42 58	351	40 39	039	31 21	096	37 53	140	54 16	193	41 14	250	27 00	324
40	42 49	350	41 14	038	32 16	096	38 28	140	54 03	194	40 22	250	26 27	323
41	42 39	349	41 48	037	33 11	096	39 04	140	53 49	195	39 30	250	25 54	323
42	42 28	348	42 21	036	34 06	095	39 39	140	53 34	196	38 38	250	25 20	322
43	42 15	346	42 53	035	35 01	095	40 14	141	53 18	197	37 46	250	24 46	321
44	42 02	345	43 25	034	35 56	095	40 49	141	53 02	197	36 55	249	24 11	320
	◆ CAPELLA		BETELGEUSE		SIRIUS		◆ CANOPUS		ACHERNAR		◆ FOMALHAUT		Hamal	
45	14 15	024	37 19	060	36 51	094	41 24	141	52 45	198	36 03	249	41 47	344
46	14 37	023	38 07	059	37 46	094	41 59	141	52 28	199	35 11	249	41 31	343
47	14 58	023	38 54	058	38 41	093	42 33	142	52 09	200	34 20	249	41 14	342
48	15 19	022	39 41	058	39 36	093	43 07	142	51 50	200	33 28	249	40 56	340
49	15 40	021	40 28	057	40 31	093	43 41	142	51 31	201	32 37	249	40 37	339
50	16 00	021	41 14	056	41 26	092	44 15	142	51 11	202	31 45	248	40 17	338
51	16 19	020	41 59	055	42 22	092	44 49	143	50 50	202	30 54	248	39 56	337
52	16 38	020	42 44	054	43 17	092	45 22	143	50 28	203	30 03	248	39 34	336
53	16 56	019	43 29	053	44 12	091	45 55	144	50 06	204	29 11	248	39 11	335
54	17 14	018	44 13	053	45 07	091	46 27	144	49 44	204	28 20	248	38 48	334
55	17 31	018	44 57	052	46 03	091	47 00	144	49 21	205	27 29	247	38 23	333
56	17 47	017	45 40	051	46 58	090	47 32	145	48 57	206	26 38	247	37 57	332
57	18 03	016	46 22	050	47 53	090	48 04	145	48 33	206	25 47	247	37 31	331
58	18 18	016	47 04	049	48 48	089	48 35	146	48 09	207	24 57	247	37 03	330
59	18 32	015	47 45	048	49 43	089	49 06	146	47 44	207	24 06	247	36 35	329
	CAPELLA		BETELGEUSE		◆ SIRIUS		CANOPUS		◆ ACHERNAR		Diphda		◆ Hamal	
60	18 46	014	48 25	046	50 39	089	49 37	147	47 19	208	44 05	267	36 06	328
61	18 59	013	49 05	045	51 34	088	50 07	147	46 53	208	43 10	267	35 36	327
62	19 12	013	49 44	044	52 29	088	50 37	148	46 26	209	42 15	266	35 06	326
63	19 23	012	50 22	043	53 24	087	51 06	148	46 00	209	41 20	266	34 34	325
64	19 35	011	50 59	042	54 19	087	51 35	149	45 33	209	40 25	266	34 02	324
65	19 45	011	51 35	040	55 15	086	52 03	149	45 06	210	39 30	265	33 30	323
66	19 55	010	52 11	039	56 10	086	52 31	150	44 38	210	38 35	265	32 56	322
67	20 04	009	52 45	038	57 05	085	52 58	151	44 10	211	37 40	265	32 22	321
68	20 13	008	53 18	036	58 00	085	53 25	151	43 42	211	36 45	264	31 47	321
69	20 20	008	53 51	035	58 55	084	53 51	152	43 13	211	35 50	264	31 12	320
70	20 27	007	54 22	034	59 50	084	54 17	153	42 44	212	34 55	264	30 36	319
71	20 34	006	54 52	032	60 45	083	54 41	154	42 15	212	34 00	263	30 00	318
72	20 39	006	55 21	031	61 39	083	55 06	154	41 45	212	33 05	263	29 23	317
73	20 44	005	55 48	029	62 34	082	55 29	155	41 16	213	32 10	263	28 45	317
74	20 49	004	56 14	027	63 29	081	55 52	156	40 46	213	31 16	262	28 07	316
	◆ CAPELLA		POLLUX		PROCYON		◆ Suhail		CANOPUS		◆ ACHERNAR		Hamal	
75	20 52	003	25 09	040	41 49	059	35 31	128	56 14	157	40 16	213	27 28	315
76	20 55	003	25 44	040	42 36	058	36 15	128	56 35	158	39 45	213	26 49	314
77	20 57	002	26 19	039	43 23	058	36 58	128	56 56	159	39 15	214	26 09	314
78	20 59	001	26 53	038	44 09	057	37 42	128	57 15	160	38 44	214	25 29	313
79	20 59	000	27 27	037	44 55	056	38 25	128	57 34	161	38 13	214	24 49	312
80	20 59	000	28 00	037	45 41	055	39 09	128	57 52	162	37 42	214	24 08	312
81	20 58	359	28 33	036	46 26	054	39 52	128	58 09	163	37 11	215	23 26	311
82	20 57	358	29 05	035	47 10	053	40 35	128	58 25	164	36 39	215	22 44	310
83	20 55	357	29 36	034	47 54	052	41 19	128	58 40	165	36 08	215	22 02	310
84	20 52	357	30 07	033	48 37	051	42 02	129	58 54	166	35 36	215	21 19	309
85	20 48	356	30 37	032	49 20	050	42 45	129	59 07	167	35 04	215	20 36	309
86	20 44	355	31 06	032	50 01	049	43 28	129	59 19	168	34 32	215	19 53	308
87	20 39	354	31 35	031	50 43	048	44 11	129	59 30	169	34 00	215	19 09	307
88	20 33	354	32 03	030	51 23	046	44 54	129	59 40	170	33 28	216	18 25	307
89	20 27	353	32 30	029	52 03	045	45 36	129	59 49	171	32 56	216	17 41	306

LHA ♈	Hc	Zn	Hc	Zn	Hc	Zn	Hc	Zn	Hc	Zn	Hc	Zn	Hc	Zn
	POLLUX		◆ REGULUS		ACRUX		CANOPUS		◆ ACHERNAR		◆ ALDEBARAN		CAPELLA	
90	32 56	028	19 46	067	17 24	152	59 56	173	32 24	216	45 32	331	20 20	352
91	33 22	027	20 37	066	17 50	152	60 03	174	31 52	216	45 05	330	20 12	351
92	33 47	026	21 28	066	18 16	152	60 08	175	31 19	216	44 36	329	20 03	351
93	34 11	025	22 18	065	18 42	152	60 12	176	30 47	216	44 07	327	19 54	350
94	34 34	024	23 08	065	19 09	152	60 15	177	30 15	216	43 37	326	19 44	349
95	34 56	023	23 58	064	19 35	151	60 17	179	29 42	216	43 06	325	19 34	349
96	35 17	022	24 48	064	20 02	151	60 18	180	29 10	216	42 34	324	19 22	348
97	35 38	021	25 37	063	20 28	151	60 17	181	28 37	216	42 01	323	19 10	347
98	35 58	020	26 26	063	20 55	151	60 16	182	28 05	216	41 27	322	18 58	346
99	36 16	019	27 15	062	21 22	151	60 13	184	27 32	216	40 53	321	18 45	346
100	36 34	018	28 04	061	21 48	151	60 09	185	26 59	216	40 18	320	18 31	345
101	36 51	017	28 52	061	22 15	151	60 03	186	26 27	216	39 42	319	18 16	344
102	37 07	016	29 40	060	22 42	151	59 57	187	25 54	216	39 05	318	18 01	344
103	37 22	015	30 28	059	23 09	151	59 50	188	25 22	216	38 28	317	17 45	343
104	37 35	014	31 15	059	23 36	151	59 41	190	24 49	216	37 50	316	17 29	342
	POLLUX		◆ REGULUS		Gienah		◆ ACRUX		CANOPUS		◆ RIGEL		BETELGEUSE	
105	37 48	013	32 02	058	16 28	103	24 03	151	59 31	191	60 50	296	55 48	331
106	38 00	012	32 49	057	17 22	102	24 30	151	59 21	192	60 01	295	55 20	329
107	38 11	011	33 35	057	18 16	102	24 57	151	59 09	193	59 10	294	54 52	328
108	38 21	010	34 21	056	19 10	102	25 24	151	58 56	194	58 20	293	54 22	326
109	38 30	009	35 06	055	20 04	101	25 51	151	58 42	195	57 29	292	53 50	325
110	38 37	007	35 51	054	20 59	101	26 18	151	58 27	196	56 38	291	53 18	324
111	38 44	006	36 36	054	21 53	101	26 45	151	58 11	197	55 46	290	52 45	322
112	38 49	005	37 20	053	22 47	100	27 12	151	57 54	198	54 54	290	52 10	321
113	38 54	004	38 04	052	23 42	100	27 39	151	57 37	199	54 02	289	51 35	320
114	38 57	003	38 47	051	24 36	100	28 06	151	57 18	200	53 09	288	50 59	318
115	38 59	002	39 30	050	25 30	099	28 33	151	56 58	201	52 17	287	50 21	317
116	39 01	001	40 12	049	26 25	099	29 00	151	56 38	202	51 24	286	49 43	316
117	39 01	359	40 54	048	27 20	099	29 27	151	56 17	203	50 31	286	49 04	315
118	39 00	358	41 35	047	28 14	098	29 54	151	55 55	204	49 38	285	48 25	314
119	38 57	357	42 15	047	29 09	098	30 21	151	55 32	205	48 44	284	47 44	312
	◆ REGULUS		SPICA		◆ ACRUX		CANOPUS		◆ RIGEL		BETELGEUSE		POLLUX	
120	42 55	046	12 06	097	30 47	151	55 09	205	47 51	284	47 03	311	38 54	356
121	43 34	045	13 01	097	31 14	151	54 45	206	46 57	283	46 22	310	38 50	355
122	44 12	044	13 56	096	31 41	151	54 20	207	46 03	283	45 39	309	38 44	354
123	44 50	042	14 51	096	32 07	151	53 55	208	45 09	282	44 56	308	38 38	353
124	45 27	041	15 46	096	32 33	152	53 29	208	44 15	281	44 13	307	38 30	352
125	46 03	040	16 41	095	33 00	152	53 02	209	43 21	281	43 29	307	38 22	350
126	46 38	039	17 36	095	33 26	152	52 35	210	42 27	280	42 44	306	38 12	349
127	47 13	038	18 31	095	33 52	152	52 07	210	41 32	280	41 59	305	38 02	348
128	47 46	037	19 26	094	34 18	152	51 39	211	40 38	279	41 13	304	37 50	347
129	48 19	036	20 21	094	34 43	152	51 10	212	39 43	279	40 27	303	37 37	346
130	48 51	034	21 16	094	35 09	152	50 41	212	38 49	278	39 41	302	37 23	345
131	49 21	033	22 11	093	35 34	153	50 11	213	37 54	278	38 54	301	37 08	344
132	49 51	032	23 06	093	36 00	153	49 41	213	36 59	277	38 07	301	36 53	343
133	50 19	030	24 01	092	36 25	153	49 10	214	36 04	277	37 19	300	36 36	342
134	50 47	029	24 57	092	36 50	153	48 39	214	35 09	276	36 31	299	36 18	341
	REGULUS		◆ SPICA		ACRUX		◆ CANOPUS		SIRIUS		BETELGEUSE		◆ POLLUX	
135	51 13	028	25 52	092	37 14	154	48 08	215	57 54	275	35 43	299	36 00	340
136	51 38	026	26 47	091	37 39	154	47 36	215	56 59	275	34 54	298	35 40	339
137	52 02	025	27 42	091	38 03	154	47 04	216	56 04	274	34 05	297	35 20	338
138	52 24	023	28 37	091	38 27	154	46 32	216	55 09	274	33 16	296	34 58	337
139	52 45	022	29 33	090	38 51	155	45 59	216	54 14	273	32 26	296	34 36	336
140	53 05	020	30 28	090	39 15	155	45 26	217	53 19	273	31 36	295	34 13	335
141	53 24	019	31 23	089	39 38	155	44 53	217	52 24	272	30 46	295	33 49	334
142	53 41	017	32 18	089	40 01	155	44 20	217	51 29	272	29 56	294	33 25	333
143	53 56	016	33 14	089	40 24	156	43 46	218	50 33	271	29 05	293	32 59	332
144	54 10	014	34 09	088	40 47	156	43 12	218	49 38	271	28 14	293	32 33	331
145	54 23	012	35 04	088	41 09	156	42 38	218	48 43	271	27 23	292	32 06	330
146	54 34	011	35 59	087	41 31	157	42 03	219	47 48	270	26 32	292	31 38	329
147	54 43	009	36 54	087	41 52	157	41 29	219	46 52	270	25 41	291	31 10	328
148	54 51	007	37 49	086	42 14	158	40 54	219	45 57	269	24 49	291	30 40	328
149	54 57	006	38 45	086	42 35	158	40 19	219	45 02	269	23 57	290	30 10	327
	REGULUS		◆ ARCTURUS		SPICA		◆ ACRUX		CANOPUS		SIRIUS		◆ PROCYON	
150	55 02	004	14 37	061	39 40	086	42 55	158	39 44	220	44 07	269	45 43	305
151	55 05	002	15 25	061	40 35	085	43 15	159	39 09	220	43 12	268	44 57	304
152	55 06	001	16 13	060	41 30	085	43 35	159	38 33	220	42 16	268	44 11	303
153	55 06	359	17 01	060	42 25	084	43 55	160	37 58	220	41 21	268	43 25	302
154	55 04	357	17 49	059	43 20	084	44 14	160	37 22	220	40 26	267	42 38	302
155	55 00	355	18 36	059	44 14	083	44 32	160	36 47	220	39 31	267	41 51	301
156	54 55	354	19 23	058	45 09	083	44 51	161	36 11	221	38 36	266	41 03	300
157	54 48	352	20 10	058	46 04	082	45 09	161	35 35	221	37 41	266	40 15	299
158	54 40	350	20 56	057	46 59	082	45 26	162	34 59	221	36 46	266	39 27	298
159	54 30	349	21 43	057	47 53	081	45 43	162	34 23	221	35 50	265	38 38	298
160	54 18	347	22 29	056	48 48	081	45 59	163	33 47	221	34 55	265	37 49	297
161	54 05	345	23 14	055	49 42	080	46 15	163	33 10	221	34 00	265	37 00	296
162	53 50	344	23 59	055	50 37	079	46 31	164	32 34	221	33 05	264	36 10	296
163	53 34	342	24 44	054	51 31	079	46 46	165	31 58	221	32 10	264	35 20	295
164	53 16	341	25 29	053	52 25	078	47 00	165	31 22	221	31 16	264	34 30	294
	◆ ARCTURUS		ANTARES		◆ ACRUX		CANOPUS		SIRIUS		◆ PROCYON		REGULUS	
165	26 13	053	16 17	112	47 14	166	30 45	221	30 21	263	33 39	294	52 57	339
166	26 57	052	17 09	112	47 27	166	30 09	221	29 26	263	32 49	293	52 37	338
167	27 40	051	18 00	112	47 40	167	29 33	221	28 31	263	31 58	292	52 15	336
168	28 23	051	18 51	112	47 53	167	28 56	221	27 36	262	31 07	292	51 52	335
169	29 06	050	19 43	111	48 04	168	28 20	221	26 41	262	30 15	291	51 28	333
170	29 48	049	20 34	111	48 15	169	27 44	221	25 47	262	29 24	291	51 02	332
171	30 29	049	21 26	111	48 26	169	27 07	221	24 52	261	28 32	290	50 35	330
172	31 10	048	22 17	110	48 36	170	26 31	221	23 58	261	27 40	289	50 08	329
173	31 51	047	23 09	110	48 45	171	25 55	221	23 03	261	26 48	289	49 39	328
174	32 31	046	24 01	110	48 54	171	25 18	221	22 09	260	25 55	288	49 09	326
175	33 11	045	24 53	110	49 02	172	24 42	221	21 14	260	25 03	288	48 37	325
176	33 50	045	25 45	109	49 10	173	24 06	221	20 20	260	24 10	287	48 05	324
177	34 28	044	26 37	109	49 17	173	23 30	221	19 25	260	23 17	287	47 32	323
178	35 06	043	27 29	109	49 23	174	22 54	221	18 31	259	22 24	286	46 59	322
179	35 43	042	28 22	109	49 28	175	22 18	221	17 37	259	21 31	286	46 24	320

LAT 23°S

LHA ♈	ARCTURUS Hc	Zn	◆ ANTARES Hc	Zn	ACRUX Hc	Zn	◆ Suhail Hc	Zn	Alphard Hc	Zn	REGULUS Hc	Zn	◆ Denebola Hc	Zn
180	36 20	041	29 14	108	49 33	175	49 19	229	50 59	285	45 48	319	52 26	356
181	36 56	040	30 06	108	49 38	176	48 38	230	50 06	285	45 12	318	52 21	354
182	37 31	039	30 59	108	49 41	177	47 55	230	49 12	284	44 34	317	52 15	353
183	38 06	038	31 51	108	49 44	177	47 13	230	48 19	283	43 56	316	52 07	351
184	38 40	037	32 44	108	49 46	178	46 31	230	47 25	283	43 18	315	51 58	350
185	39 13	036	33 37	107	49 48	179	45 48	231	46 31	282	42 38	314	51 47	348
186	39 45	035	34 29	107	49 49	179	45 06	231	45 37	281	41 58	313	51 35	347
187	40 17	034	35 22	107	49 49	180	44 23	231	44 43	281	41 18	312	51 22	345
188	40 48	033	36 15	107	49 49	181	43 40	231	43 48	280	40 36	311	51 07	344
189	41 17	032	37 08	107	49 48	181	42 57	231	42 54	280	39 55	310	50 51	342
190	41 46	031	38 01	106	49 46	182	42 14	231	42 00	279	39 12	309	50 33	341
191	42 15	030	38 54	106	49 43	183	41 31	231	41 05	279	38 29	309	50 14	339
192	42 42	029	39 47	106	49 40	184	40 47	232	40 10	278	37 46	308	49 54	338
193	43 08	028	40 40	106	49 36	184	40 04	232	39 16	278	37 02	307	49 33	336
194	43 33	027	41 33	106	49 32	185	39 21	232	38 21	277	36 18	306	49 10	335

LHA ♈	ARCTURUS Hc	Zn	◆ Rasalhague Hc	Zn	ANTARES Hc	Zn	◆ ACRUX Hc	Zn	Suhail Hc	Zn	◆ REGULUS Hc	Zn	Denebola Hc	Zn
195	43 57	025	13 48	070	42 26	106	49 27	186	38 37	232	35 33	305	48 46	334
196	44 21	024	14 39	069	43 20	105	49 21	186	37 54	232	34 48	305	48 21	332
197	44 43	023	15 31	069	44 13	105	49 15	187	37 10	232	34 02	304	47 55	331
198	45 04	022	16 22	068	45 06	105	49 08	188	36 27	232	33 16	303	47 28	330
199	45 24	021	17 14	068	46 00	105	49 00	188	35 43	232	32 29	302	46 59	329
200	45 42	019	18 05	067	46 53	105	48 52	189	35 00	232	31 43	302	46 30	327
201	46 00	018	18 55	067	47 46	105	48 43	190	34 16	232	30 55	301	46 00	326
202	46 16	017	19 46	066	48 40	105	48 33	190	33 33	232	30 08	300	45 29	325
203	46 32	015	20 36	066	49 33	104	48 23	191	32 49	232	29 20	300	44 56	324
204	46 46	014	21 27	065	50 27	104	48 12	192	32 06	232	28 32	299	44 23	323
205	46 58	013	22 17	065	51 20	104	48 01	192	31 22	232	27 43	298	43 50	322
206	47 10	011	23 06	064	52 14	104	47 49	193	30 39	232	26 55	298	43 15	321
207	47 20	010	23 56	063	53 08	104	47 37	193	29 55	232	26 06	297	42 39	320
208	47 29	009	24 45	063	54 01	104	47 24	194	29 12	232	25 17	297	42 03	318
209	47 36	007	25 34	062	54 55	104	47 10	194	28 29	232	24 27	296	41 26	317

LHA ♈	ARCTURUS Hc	Zn	◆ Rasalhague Hc	Zn	ANTARES Hc	Zn	◆ RIGIL KENT Hc	Zn	ACRUX Hc	Zn	Gienah Hc	Zn	◆ Denebola Hc	Zn
210	47 42	006	26 23	062	55 49	104	51 27	172	46 56	195	65 12	278	40 49	317
211	47 47	004	27 12	061	56 42	104	51 34	173	46 42	196	64 17	277	40 10	316
212	47 51	003	28 00	060	57 36	104	51 41	174	46 26	196	63 22	276	39 31	315
213	47 53	002	28 48	060	58 30	104	51 47	174	46 11	197	62 28	276	38 52	314
214	47 54	000	29 35	059	59 23	103	51 52	175	45 55	197	61 33	275	38 11	313
215	47 53	359	30 23	059	60 17	103	51 56	176	45 38	198	60 38	275	37 31	312
216	47 51	357	31 09	058	61 11	103	52 00	177	45 21	198	59 43	274	36 49	311
217	47 48	356	31 56	057	62 04	103	52 02	178	45 04	199	58 47	274	36 07	310
218	47 43	354	32 42	056	62 58	103	52 04	178	44 46	199	57 52	273	35 25	309
219	47 37	353	33 28	056	63 52	104	52 06	179	44 27	200	56 57	273	34 42	309
220	47 30	352	34 13	055	64 45	104	52 06	180	44 09	200	56 02	272	33 59	308
221	47 21	350	34 58	054	65 39	104	52 06	181	43 49	201	55 07	272	33 15	307
222	47 12	349	35 43	053	66 33	104	52 05	181	43 30	201	54 12	271	32 31	306
223	47 00	348	36 27	053	67 26	104	52 03	182	43 10	201	53 16	271	31 46	306
224	46 48	346	37 11	052	68 20	104	52 01	183	42 50	202	52 21	271	31 01	305

LHA ♈	Alphecca Hc	Zn	Rasalhague Hc	Zn	◆ ALTAIR Hc	Zn	Peacock Hc	Zn	◆ RIGIL KENT Hc	Zn	◆ SPICA Hc	Zn	ARCTURUS Hc	Zn
225	39 36	010	37 54	051	11 58	075	23 33	144	51 57	184	64 42	294	46 34	345
226	39 46	009	38 37	050	12 51	074	24 05	144	51 53	185	63 51	293	46 19	344
227	39 54	008	39 19	049	13 44	074	24 38	144	51 48	185	63 00	292	46 03	342
228	40 01	007	40 00	048	14 37	073	25 11	143	51 43	186	62 09	290	45 45	341
229	40 07	006	40 41	047	15 30	073	25 44	143	51 37	187	61 17	290	45 27	340
230	40 12	004	41 22	047	16 23	073	26 17	143	51 30	188	60 25	289	45 07	338
231	40 16	003	42 01	046	17 15	072	26 50	143	51 22	188	59 32	288	44 46	337
232	40 18	002	42 41	045	18 08	072	27 23	143	51 13	189	58 39	287	44 24	336
233	40 20	001	43 19	044	19 00	071	27 56	143	51 04	190	57 46	286	44 01	335
234	40 20	000	43 57	043	19 52	071	28 29	143	50 54	191	56 53	285	43 37	334
235	40 19	359	44 34	041	20 44	070	29 02	143	50 44	191	56 00	285	43 12	332
236	40 17	357	45 10	040	21 36	070	29 35	143	50 33	192	55 06	284	42 46	331
237	40 14	356	45 45	039	22 28	069	30 07	143	50 21	193	54 12	283	42 19	330
238	40 10	355	46 20	038	23 19	069	30 40	143	50 08	193	53 19	282	41 51	329
239	40 05	354	46 53	037	24 10	068	31 13	144	49 55	194	52 25	282	41 22	328

LHA ♈	VEGA Hc	Zn	◆ ALTAIR Hc	Zn	Peacock Hc	Zn	◆ RIGIL KENT Hc	Zn	SPICA Hc	Zn	◆ ARCTURUS Hc	Zn	Alphecca Hc	Zn
240	18 03	031	25 02	067	31 46	144	49 41	195	51 30	281	40 53	327	39 59	353
241	18 31	031	25 52	067	32 19	144	49 27	195	50 36	281	40 22	326	39 51	352
242	18 59	030	26 43	066	32 51	144	49 12	196	49 42	280	39 51	325	39 43	350
243	19 27	029	27 34	066	33 24	144	48 56	197	48 47	279	39 19	324	39 33	349
244	19 53	029	28 24	065	33 57	144	48 40	197	47 53	279	38 46	323	39 22	348
245	20 20	028	29 14	065	34 29	144	48 24	198	46 58	278	38 12	322	39 10	347
246	20 45	027	30 04	064	35 01	144	48 06	199	46 04	278	37 37	321	38 58	346
247	21 10	027	30 53	063	35 34	144	47 48	199	45 09	277	37 02	320	38 44	345
248	21 35	026	31 42	063	36 06	144	47 30	200	44 14	277	36 26	319	38 29	344
249	21 58	025	32 31	062	36 38	145	47 11	200	43 19	276	35 50	318	38 13	343
250	22 22	024	33 20	061	37 10	145	46 52	201	42 24	276	35 13	317	37 56	342
251	22 44	024	34 08	061	37 41	145	46 32	201	41 29	275	34 35	316	37 38	341
252	23 06	023	34 56	060	38 13	145	46 12	202	40 34	275	33 56	316	37 19	339
253	23 27	022	35 43	059	38 44	145	45 51	202	39 39	274	33 18	315	36 59	338
254	23 48	021	36 31	058	39 16	146	45 30	203	38 44	274	32 38	314	36 39	337

LHA ♈	◆ VEGA Hc	Zn	ALTAIR Hc	Zn	◆ Peacock Hc	Zn	RIGIL KENT Hc	Zn	◆ SPICA Hc	Zn	ARCTURUS Hc	Zn	Alphecca Hc	Zn
255	24 07	021	37 18	058	39 47	146	45 09	203	37 49	274	31 58	313	36 17	336
256	24 26	020	38 04	057	40 18	146	44 47	204	36 54	273	31 17	312	35 54	335
257	24 45	019	38 50	056	40 48	146	44 24	204	35 59	273	30 36	312	35 31	334
258	25 03	018	39 36	055	41 19	147	44 02	205	35 04	272	29 55	311	35 07	333
259	25 19	017	40 21	054	41 49	147	43 38	205	34 08	272	29 13	310	34 41	332
260	25 36	017	41 06	054	42 19	147	43 15	205	33 13	271	28 30	309	34 16	332
261	25 51	016	41 50	053	42 49	148	42 51	206	32 18	271	27 48	309	33 49	331
262	26 06	015	42 33	052	43 18	148	42 27	206	31 23	271	27 04	308	33 21	330
263	26 20	014	43 17	051	43 47	148	42 03	206	30 27	270	26 21	307	32 53	329
264	26 33	013	43 59	050	44 16	149	41 38	207	29 32	270	25 37	307	32 24	328
265	26 45	013	44 41	049	44 45	149	41 13	207	28 37	269	24 52	306	31 54	327
266	26 57	012	45 23	048	45 13	149	40 47	207	27 42	269	24 07	305	31 24	326
267	27 08	011	46 03	047	45 41	150	40 22	208	26 47	269	23 22	305	30 53	325
268	27 17	010	46 43	046	46 08	150	39 56	208	25 51	268	22 37	304	30 21	324
269	27 27	009	47 22	045	46 36	151	39 30	208	24 56	268	21 51	304	29 48	324

LHA ♈	◆ VEGA Hc	Zn	ALTAIR Hc	Zn	◆ FOMALHAUT Hc	Zn	Peacock Hc	Zn	RIGIL KENT Hc	Zn	◆ ANTARES Hc	Zn	Alphecca Hc	Zn
270	27 35	008	48 01	044	23 54	113	47 02	151	39 04	209	69 22	256	29 15	323
271	27 42	007	48 39	043	24 44	113	47 29	152	38 37	209	68 29	256	28 42	322
272	27 49	006	49 16	041	25 35	113	47 55	152	38 10	209	67 35	256	28 07	321
273	27 55	006	49 52	040	26 26	113	48 20	153	37 43	209	66 42	256	27 33	320
274	28 00	005	50 27	039	27 17	113	48 45	153	37 16	210	65 48	256	26 57	320
275	28 04	004	51 01	038	28 08	112	49 10	154	36 49	210	64 54	256	26 21	319
276	28 07	003	51 34	036	28 59	112	49 34	154	36 21	210	64 01	256	25 45	318
277	28 10	002	52 07	035	29 50	112	49 58	155	35 54	210	63 07	257	25 08	318
278	28 11	001	52 38	034	30 42	112	50 21	156	35 26	210	62 13	257	24 30	317
279	28 12	000	53 08	032	31 33	112	50 44	156	34 58	211	61 20	257	23 52	316
280	28 12	359	53 36	031	32 24	111	51 06	157	34 30	211	60 26	257	23 13	315
281	28 11	359	54 04	029	33 16	111	51 27	158	34 01	211	59 32	257	22 34	315
282	28 09	358	54 30	028	34 07	111	51 48	158	33 33	211	58 38	256	21 55	314
283	28 06	357	54 55	026	34 59	111	52 08	159	33 05	211	57 45	256	21 15	313
284	28 03	356	55 19	025	35 51	111	52 27	160	32 36	211	56 51	256	20 35	313

LHA ♈	◆ DENEB Hc	Zn	FOMALHAUT Hc	Zn	◆ ACHERNAR Hc	Zn	RIGIL KENT Hc	Zn	◆ ANTARES Hc	Zn	Rasalhague Hc	Zn	VEGA Hc	Zn
285	17 50	019	36 42	111	14 12	147	32 07	211	55 57	256	48 53	328	27 59	355
286	18 07	018	37 34	110	14 43	146	31 39	211	55 04	256	48 23	326	27 53	354
287	18 24	017	38 26	110	15 13	146	31 10	212	54 10	256	47 52	325	27 47	353
288	18 40	016	39 18	110	15 44	146	30 41	212	53 16	256	47 20	324	27 40	352
289	18 55	016	40 09	110	16 15	146	30 12	212	52 23	256	46 47	323	27 33	352
290	19 10	015	41 01	110	16 46	146	29 43	212	51 29	256	46 13	322	27 24	351
291	19 24	014	41 53	110	17 17	145	29 14	212	50 36	256	45 39	321	27 15	350
292	19 37	014	42 45	110	17 49	145	28 45	212	49 42	256	45 03	319	27 05	349
293	19 50	013	43 37	110	18 20	145	28 16	212	48 49	256	44 27	318	26 54	348
294	20 02	012	44 29	110	18 52	145	27 46	212	47 55	255	43 50	317	26 42	347
295	20 13	012	45 21	109	19 24	145	27 17	212	47 02	255	43 12	316	26 29	346
296	20 24	011	46 13	109	19 55	145	26 48	212	46 08	255	42 33	315	26 16	346
297	20 34	010	47 06	109	20 27	145	26 19	212	45 15	255	41 54	314	26 02	345
298	20 44	009	47 58	109	20 59	145	25 50	212	44 22	255	41 14	313	25 47	344
299	20 52	009	48 50	109	21 31	144	25 21	212	43 28	255	40 34	312	25 31	343

LHA ♈	DENEB Hc	Zn	Enif Hc	Zn	◆ FOMALHAUT Hc	Zn	ACHERNAR Hc	Zn	◆ RIGIL KENT Hc	Zn	ANTARES Hc	Zn	◆ VEGA Hc	Zn
300	21 00	008	48 14	041	49 42	109	22 03	144	24 51	212	42 35	254	25 15	342
301	21 07	007	48 49	040	50 34	109	22 36	144	24 22	212	41 42	254	24 58	342
302	21 14	006	49 24	038	51 26	109	23 08	144	23 53	212	40 49	254	24 40	341
303	21 20	006	49 58	037	52 19	109	23 40	144	23 24	212	39 56	254	24 21	340
304	21 25	005	50 31	036	53 11	109	24 13	144	22 55	212	39 03	254	24 02	339
305	21 29	004	51 03	035	54 03	109	24 45	144	22 26	212	38 10	254	23 42	338
306	21 33	003	51 34	033	54 55	109	25 18	144	21 57	212	37 17	253	23 21	338
307	21 36	003	52 03	032	55 47	109	25 50	144	21 28	211	36 24	253	23 00	337
308	21 38	002	52 32	030	56 40	109	26 23	144	21 00	211	35 31	253	22 38	336
309	21 39	001	52 59	029	57 32	109	26 55	144	20 31	211	34 38	253	22 15	335
310	21 40	000	53 25	028	58 24	109	27 28	144	20 02	211	33 45	253	21 52	335
311	21 40	000	53 50	026	59 16	110	28 00	144	19 34	211	32 53	253	21 28	334
312	21 39	359	54 14	024	60 08	110	28 33	144	19 05	211	32 00	252	21 03	333
313	21 38	358	54 36	023	61 00	110	29 05	144	18 37	211	31 08	252	20 38	333
314	21 35	357	54 57	021	61 52	110	29 38	144	18 09	211	30 15	252	20 12	332

LHA ♈	Alpheratz Hc	Zn	◆ Diphda Hc	Zn	ACHERNAR Hc	Zn	◆ Peacock Hc	Zn	ANTARES Hc	Zn	◆ ALTAIR Hc	Zn	DENEB Hc	Zn
315	20 46	043	37 30	095	30 10	144	55 46	188	29 23	252	53 57	330	21 33	357
316	21 24	043	38 25	095	30 43	144	55 38	189	28 30	251	53 30	329	21 29	356
317	22 01	042	39 20	095	31 15	144	55 29	190	27 38	251	53 00	327	21 24	355
318	22 38	041	40 15	094	31 47	144	55 19	191	26 46	251	52 30	326	21 19	354
319	23 14	041	41 11	094	32 20	144	55 08	192	25 54	251	51 59	325	21 14	354
320	23 50	040	42 06	094	32 52	144	54 56	193	25 02	250	51 26	323	21 07	353
321	24 25	039	43 01	093	33 24	144	54 44	194	24 10	250	50 53	322	21 00	352
322	25 00	039	43 56	093	33 56	145	54 30	194	23 18	250	50 18	321	20 52	351
323	25 34	038	44 51	093	34 28	145	54 16	195	22 26	250	49 43	320	20 43	351
324	26 08	037	45 46	092	35 00	145	54 01	196	21 34	249	49 07	318	20 34	350
325	26 41	036	46 41	092	35 32	145	53 46	197	20 43	249	48 30	317	20 24	349
326	27 13	036	47 37	092	36 03	145	53 29	198	19 51	249	47 52	316	20 13	348
327	27 45	035	48 32	091	36 35	145	53 12	199	19 00	249	47 13	315	20 02	348
328	28 16	034	49 27	091	37 06	145	52 54	199	18 08	248	46 34	314	19 50	347
329	28 47	033	50 22	091	37 38	146	52 35	200	17 17	248	45 53	313	19 37	346

LHA ♈	◆ Alpheratz Hc	Zn	Diphda Hc	Zn	◆ ACHERNAR Hc	Zn	Peacock Hc	Zn	◆ Nunki Hc	Zn	ALTAIR Hc	Zn	DENEB Hc	Zn
330	29 16	032	51 17	090	38 09	146	52 16	201	48 19	256	45 13	312	19 23	346
331	29 46	031	52 13	090	38 40	146	51 56	201	47 26	256	44 31	311	19 09	345
332	30 14	031	53 08	089	39 11	146	51 36	202	46 32	255	43 49	310	18 55	344
333	30 42	030	54 03	089	39 41	146	51 14	203	45 39	255	43 06	309	18 39	343
334	31 09	029	54 58	089	40 12	147	50 53	204	44 45	255	42 23	308	18 23	343
335	31 35	028	55 54	088	40 42	147	50 30	204	43 52	255	41 39	307	18 07	342
336	32 01	027	56 49	088	41 12	147	50 07	205	42 59	255	40 55	306	17 49	341
337	32 26	027	57 44	087	41 41	148	49 44	205	42 05	255	40 10	305	17 32	341
338	32 50	025	58 39	087	42 11	148	49 20	206	41 12	254	39 25	305	17 13	340
339	33 13	024	59 34	086	42 40	148	48 56	207	40 19	254	38 39	304	16 54	339
340	33 35	023	60 29	086	43 09	149	48 31	207	39 26	254	37 53	303	16 34	339
341	33 57	022	61 24	085	43 38	149	48 05	208	38 33	254	37 06	302	16 14	338
342	34 17	022	62 19	085	44 06	149	47 40	208	37 40	254	36 19	301	15 53	338
343	34 37	021	63 14	084	44 34	150	47 13	209	36 47	254	35 32	301	15 32	337
344	34 56	020	64 09	084	45 02	150	46 47	209	35 54	253	34 44	300	15 10	336

LHA ♈	Alpheratz Hc	Zn	◆ Hamal Hc	Zn	◆ ACHERNAR Hc	Zn	Peacock Hc	Zn	Nunki Hc	Zn	◆ ALTAIR Hc	Zn	Enif Hc	Zn
345	35 14	019	24 48	048	45 29	150	46 20	210	35 01	253	33 56	299	52 17	329
346	35 31	018	25 29	047	45 56	151	45 52	210	34 08	253	33 08	299	51 47	327
347	35 47	016	26 09	046	46 23	151	45 25	210	33 15	253	32 19	298	51 17	326
348	36 03	015	26 49	046	46 49	152	44 56	211	32 22	253	31 30	297	50 46	325
349	36 17	014	27 28	045	47 15	152	44 28	211	31 30	252	30 41	297	50 13	323
350	36 30	013	28 06	044	47 41	153	43 59	212	30 37	252	29 51	296	49 40	322
351	36 42	012	28 45	043	48 06	153	43 30	212	29 45	252	29 02	295	49 06	321
352	36 54	011	29 22	043	48 30	154	43 01	212	28 52	252	28 12	295	48 30	320
353	37 04	010	29 59	042	48 54	154	42 31	213	28 00	251	27 21	294	47 54	319
354	37 13	009	30 36	041	49 18	155	42 01	213	27 08	251	26 31	294	47 17	317
355	37 21	008	31 12	040	49 41	156	41 31	213	26 15	251	25 40	293	46 40	316
356	37 29	007	31 47	039	50 03	156	41 01	213	25 23	251	24 49	292	46 01	315
357	37 35	006	32 22	039	50 25	157	40 30	214	24 31	250	23 58	292	45 22	314
358	37 40	005	32 56	038	50 47	157	39 59	214	23 39	250	23 07	291	44 42	313
359	37 44	004	33 29	037	51 08	158	39 28	214	22 47	250	22 15	291	44 01	312

LHA ♈	Hc	Zn	Hc	Zn	Hc	Zn	Hc	Zn	Hc	Zn	Hc	Zn	Hc	Zn
	◆ Alpheratz		Hamal		◆ RIGEL		CANOPUS		ACHERNAR		◆ Peacock		Enif	
0	36 47	002	33 13	036	13 30	093	15 22	141	52 24	158	39 47	215	42 40	312
1	36 49	001	33 45	035	14 24	093	15 56	141	52 44	159	39 15	215	41 59	311
2	36 50	000	34 15	034	15 19	092	16 31	141	53 03	160	38 43	215	41 17	310
3	36 49	359	34 45	033	16 14	092	17 06	141	53 22	160	38 12	216	40 35	309
4	36 48	358	35 15	032	17 09	091	17 40	141	53 40	161	37 40	216	39 52	308
5	36 46	357	35 43	031	18 03	091	18 15	140	53 57	162	37 08	216	39 09	307
6	36 42	356	36 11	030	18 58	091	18 50	140	54 14	163	36 36	216	38 25	306
7	36 38	355	36 38	029	19 53	090	19 25	140	54 30	164	36 03	216	37 41	306
8	36 33	354	37 04	028	20 48	090	20 01	140	54 45	164	35 31	216	36 56	305
9	36 26	353	37 29	027	21 43	089	20 36	140	54 59	165	34 58	216	36 11	304
10	36 19	352	37 53	026	22 37	089	21 12	140	55 12	166	34 26	217	35 25	303
11	36 10	351	38 17	025	23 32	089	21 47	139	55 25	167	33 53	217	34 39	303
12	36 01	350	38 39	024	24 27	088	22 23	139	55 37	168	33 20	217	33 53	302
13	35 50	348	39 01	023	25 22	088	22 59	139	55 48	169	32 48	217	33 06	301
14	35 39	347	39 21	022	26 17	087	23 34	139	55 58	170	32 15	217	32 19	300
	◆ Hamal		ALDEBARAN		RIGEL		◆ CANOPUS		ACHERNAR		◆ FOMALHAUT		Alpheratz	
15	39 41	020	23 22	058	27 11	087	24 10	139	56 07	171	62 24	252	35 26	346
16	40 00	019	24 08	057	28 06	086	24 46	139	56 16	172	61 32	252	35 13	345
17	40 17	018	24 54	057	29 01	086	25 22	139	56 23	173	60 40	252	34 59	344
18	40 34	017	25 40	056	29 55	086	25 59	139	56 30	174	59 48	252	34 43	343
19	40 49	016	26 25	055	30 50	085	26 35	139	56 36	175	58 55	252	34 27	342
20	41 04	015	27 10	055	31 45	085	27 11	139	56 40	175	58 03	252	34 10	341
21	41 17	013	27 54	054	32 39	084	27 47	139	56 44	176	57 11	252	33 52	340
22	41 29	012	28 38	053	33 34	084	28 23	139	56 47	177	56 19	252	33 33	339
23	41 40	011	29 22	053	34 28	083	29 00	138	56 49	178	55 27	252	33 13	338
24	41 50	010	30 05	052	35 23	083	29 36	138	56 50	179	54 34	252	32 53	337
25	41 59	009	30 48	051	36 17	082	30 12	138	56 50	180	53 42	252	32 31	336
26	42 07	007	31 31	050	37 11	082	30 49	138	56 49	181	52 50	252	32 09	336
27	42 13	006	32 13	050	38 05	081	31 25	138	56 48	182	51 58	252	31 46	335
28	42 19	005	32 54	049	39 00	081	32 01	138	56 45	183	51 06	252	31 22	334
29	42 23	004	33 35	048	39 54	080	32 38	138	56 41	184	50 14	252	30 57	333
	Hamal		◆ ALDEBARAN		SIRIUS		◆ CANOPUS		ACHERNAR		◆ FOMALHAUT		Alpheratz	
30	42 26	002	34 15	047	23 18	099	33 14	139	56 36	185	49 21	252	30 32	332
31	42 27	001	34 55	046	24 12	098	33 50	139	56 31	186	48 29	252	30 05	331
32	42 28	000	35 35	045	25 06	098	34 27	139	56 24	187	47 37	252	29 38	330
33	42 27	359	36 13	045	26 00	098	35 03	139	56 17	188	46 45	252	29 11	329
34	42 26	358	36 52	044	26 55	097	35 39	139	56 09	189	45 53	252	28 42	328
35	42 23	356	37 29	043	27 49	097	36 15	139	55 59	190	45 01	251	28 13	328
36	42 19	355	38 06	042	28 43	097	36 51	139	55 49	191	44 09	251	27 44	327
37	42 13	354	38 42	041	29 38	096	37 27	139	55 38	192	43 17	251	27 13	326
38	42 07	353	39 18	040	30 32	096	38 03	139	55 27	193	42 26	251	26 42	325
39	41 59	351	39 53	039	31 27	096	38 39	139	55 14	194	41 34	251	26 11	324
40	41 50	350	40 27	038	32 22	095	39 14	140	55 01	195	40 42	251	25 39	324
41	41 40	349	41 00	037	33 16	095	39 50	140	54 47	196	39 50	251	25 06	323
42	41 29	348	41 32	036	34 11	095	40 25	140	54 32	196	38 58	250	24 33	322
43	41 17	347	42 04	035	35 05	094	41 00	140	54 16	197	38 07	250	23 59	321
44	41 04	345	42 35	034	36 00	094	41 36	140	53 59	198	37 15	250	23 24	321
	◆ CAPELLA		BETELGEUSE		SIRIUS		◆ CANOPUS		ACHERNAR		◆ FOMALHAUT		Hamal	
45	13 20	024	36 49	059	36 55	093	42 10	141	53 42	199	36 24	250	40 49	344
46	13 42	023	37 36	059	37 49	093	42 45	141	53 24	199	35 32	250	40 34	343
47	14 03	023	38 23	058	38 44	093	43 20	141	53 06	200	34 41	250	40 17	342
48	14 24	022	39 09	057	39 39	092	43 54	141	52 47	201	33 49	249	40 00	341
49	14 44	021	39 55	056	40 34	092	44 28	142	52 27	202	32 58	249	39 41	340
50	15 04	021	40 40	055	41 29	092	45 02	142	52 06	202	32 07	249	39 22	339
51	15 23	020	41 25	054	42 23	091	45 36	142	51 45	203	31 16	249	39 01	337
52	15 41	019	42 09	054	43 18	091	46 10	143	51 24	204	30 25	249	38 40	336
53	15 59	019	42 53	053	44 13	090	46 43	143	51 01	204	29 34	248	38 17	335
54	16 17	018	43 36	052	45 08	090	47 16	143	50 39	205	28 43	248	37 54	334
55	16 33	017	44 19	051	46 03	090	47 48	144	50 15	205	27 52	248	37 29	333
56	16 49	017	45 01	050	46 57	089	48 21	144	49 51	206	27 01	248	37 04	332
57	17 05	016	45 43	049	47 52	089	48 53	144	49 27	207	26 11	248	36 38	331
58	17 20	015	46 24	048	48 47	088	49 24	145	49 02	207	25 20	247	36 11	330
59	17 34	015	47 04	047	49 42	088	49 56	145	48 37	208	24 29	247	35 44	329
	CAPELLA		BETELGEUSE		◆ SIRIUS		CANOPUS		◆ ACHERNAR		Diphda		◆ Hamal	
60	17 48	014	47 43	046	50 37	087	50 27	146	48 12	208	44 08	268	35 15	328
61	18 01	013	48 22	044	51 31	087	50 57	146	47 46	209	43 13	268	34 46	327
62	18 13	013	49 00	043	52 26	086	51 27	147	47 19	209	42 19	267	34 16	326
63	18 25	012	49 37	042	53 21	086	51 57	148	46 52	210	41 24	267	33 45	325
64	18 36	011	50 14	041	54 15	085	52 26	148	46 25	210	40 29	266	33 14	324
65	18 46	011	50 49	040	55 10	085	52 55	149	45 57	210	39 34	266	32 41	324
66	18 56	010	51 24	038	56 05	084	53 23	149	45 30	211	38 40	266	32 09	323
67	19 05	009	51 57	037	56 59	084	53 50	150	45 01	211	37 45	265	31 35	322
68	19 13	008	52 30	036	57 54	083	54 17	151	44 33	212	36 50	265	31 01	321
69	19 21	008	53 01	034	58 48	083	54 44	151	44 04	212	35 56	265	30 26	320
70	19 28	007	53 32	033	59 42	082	55 10	152	43 35	212	35 01	264	29 51	319
71	19 34	006	54 01	031	60 37	081	55 35	153	43 06	213	34 07	264	29 15	319
72	19 40	005	54 29	030	61 31	081	56 00	154	42 36	213	33 12	264	28 38	318
73	19 45	005	54 55	028	62 25	080	56 23	155	42 06	213	32 18	263	28 01	317
74	19 49	004	55 21	027	63 19	079	56 47	155	41 36	213	31 23	263	27 24	316
	◆ CAPELLA		POLLUX		PROCYON		◆ Suhail		CANOPUS		◆ ACHERNAR		Hamal	
75	19 52	003	24 23	040	41 18	058	36 08	127	57 09	156	41 06	214	26 45	316
76	19 55	003	24 58	039	42 04	058	36 52	127	57 31	157	40 35	214	26 07	315
77	19 57	002	25 32	039	42 50	057	37 35	127	57 51	158	40 04	214	25 28	314
78	19 59	001	26 06	038	43 36	056	38 19	127	58 11	159	39 34	214	24 48	313
79	19 59	000	26 39	037	44 21	055	39 02	128	58 31	160	39 03	215	24 08	313
80	19 59	000	27 12	036	45 06	054	39 46	128	58 49	161	38 31	215	23 28	312
81	19 58	359	27 44	035	45 50	053	40 29	128	59 06	162	38 00	215	22 47	311
82	19 57	358	28 16	035	46 34	052	41 12	128	59 22	163	37 28	215	22 05	311
83	19 55	357	28 46	034	47 16	051	41 56	128	59 38	164	36 57	215	21 24	310
84	19 52	357	29 17	033	47 59	050	42 39	128	59 52	165	36 25	215	20 41	309
85	19 48	356	29 46	032	48 41	049	43 22	128	60 05	167	35 53	216	19 59	309
86	19 44	355	30 15	031	49 22	048	44 05	128	60 18	168	35 21	216	19 16	308
87	19 39	354	30 43	030	50 02	047	44 48	128	60 29	169	34 49	216	18 33	308
88	19 34	354	31 11	030	50 41	046	45 31	128	60 39	170	34 17	216	17 49	307
89	19 27	353	31 37	029	51 20	044	46 14	129	60 48	171	33 45	216	17 05	306

LAT 24°S

LHA ♈	Hc	Zn	Hc	Zn	Hc	Zn	Hc	Zn	Hc	Zn	Hc	Zn	Hc	Zn
	POLLUX		◆ REGULUS		ACRUX		CANOPUS		◆ ACHERNAR		◆ ALDEBARAN		CAPELLA	
90	32 03	028	19 23	067	18 17	152	60 56	172	33 13	216	44 39	331	19 20	352
91	32 28	027	20 13	066	18 43	152	61 02	174	32 40	216	44 13	330	19 12	352
92	32 53	026	21 03	066	19 09	152	61 08	175	32 08	216	43 45	329	19 04	351
93	33 16	025	21 53	065	19 35	151	61 12	176	31 35	216	43 16	328	18 55	350
94	33 39	024	22 42	064	20 01	151	61 15	177	31 03	216	42 47	327	18 45	349
95	34 01	023	23 32	064	20 28	151	61 17	179	30 30	216	42 16	326	18 35	349
96	34 22	022	24 21	063	20 54	151	61 18	180	29 58	216	41 45	325	18 24	348
97	34 42	021	25 10	063	21 21	151	61 17	181	29 25	216	41 13	324	18 12	347
98	35 01	020	25 58	062	21 47	151	61 15	182	28 53	216	40 40	322	17 59	347
99	35 20	019	26 47	061	22 14	151	61 13	184	28 20	216	40 06	321	17 46	346
100	35 37	018	27 35	061	22 41	151	61 08	185	27 48	216	39 32	320	17 33	345
101	35 54	017	28 22	060	23 07	151	61 03	186	27 15	216	38 56	319	17 18	345
102	36 09	016	29 10	060	23 34	151	60 57	187	26 43	216	38 20	319	17 03	344
103	36 24	015	29 57	059	24 01	151	60 49	189	26 10	216	37 44	318	16 48	343
104	36 37	014	30 44	058	24 28	151	60 40	190	25 38	216	37 06	317	16 32	342
	POLLUX		◆ REGULUS		Gienah		◆ ACRUX		CANOPUS		◆ RIGEL		BETELGEUSE	
105	36 50	013	31 30	057	16 41	102	24 55	150	60 30	191	60 23	298	54 55	332
106	37 01	012	32 16	057	17 35	102	25 22	150	60 19	192	59 34	297	54 29	330
107	37 12	011	33 02	056	18 28	102	25 49	150	60 07	193	58 45	296	54 01	329
108	37 22	010	33 47	055	19 22	101	26 16	150	59 54	194	57 56	295	53 31	327
109	37 30	008	34 32	055	20 16	101	26 43	150	59 40	196	57 05	294	53 01	326
110	37 38	007	35 16	054	21 10	101	27 10	150	59 25	197	56 15	293	52 30	324
111	37 44	006	36 00	053	22 04	100	27 37	150	59 08	198	55 24	292	51 57	323
112	37 50	005	36 44	052	22 58	100	28 04	150	58 51	199	54 33	291	51 24	322
113	37 54	004	37 27	051	23 52	100	28 32	150	58 33	200	53 42	290	50 49	320
114	37 57	003	38 09	050	24 46	099	28 59	150	58 14	201	52 50	289	50 14	319
115	37 59	002	38 51	050	25 40	099	29 26	151	57 54	202	51 58	288	49 37	318
116	38 01	001	39 33	049	26 34	099	29 53	151	57 34	203	51 06	288	49 00	317
117	38 01	000	40 14	048	27 28	098	30 19	151	57 12	204	50 14	287	48 22	316
118	38 00	358	40 54	047	28 23	098	30 46	151	56 50	204	49 21	286	47 43	314
119	37 57	357	41 34	046	29 17	097	31 13	151	56 27	205	48 29	286	47 04	313
	◆ REGULUS		SPICA		◆ ACRUX		CANOPUS		◆ RIGEL		BETELGEUSE		POLLUX	
120	42 13	045	12 14	097	31 40	151	56 03	206	47 36	285	46 23	312	37 54	356
121	42 51	044	13 08	097	32 07	151	55 39	207	46 43	284	45 42	311	37 50	355
122	43 29	043	14 02	096	32 33	151	55 13	208	45 50	284	45 01	310	37 45	354
123	44 05	042	14 57	096	33 00	151	54 48	208	44 56	283	44 19	309	37 39	353
124	44 42	041	15 52	095	33 26	151	54 21	209	44 03	282	43 36	308	37 31	352
125	45 17	040	16 46	095	33 52	151	53 54	210	43 09	282	42 53	307	37 23	351
126	45 52	038	17 41	095	34 19	152	53 27	211	42 15	281	42 09	306	37 13	350
127	46 25	037	18 35	094	34 45	152	52 59	211	41 22	281	41 24	306	37 03	348
128	46 58	036	19 30	094	35 11	152	52 30	212	40 28	280	40 39	305	36 51	347
129	47 30	035	20 25	094	35 36	152	52 01	212	39 34	280	39 54	304	36 39	346
130	48 01	034	21 19	093	36 02	152	51 31	213	38 40	279	39 08	303	36 25	345
131	48 31	032	22 14	093	36 28	152	51 01	213	37 45	278	38 22	302	36 11	344
132	49 00	031	23 09	092	36 53	153	50 31	214	36 51	278	37 36	301	35 55	343
133	49 27	030	24 04	092	37 18	153	50 00	214	35 57	277	36 49	301	35 39	342
134	49 54	028	24 59	092	37 43	153	49 29	215	35 02	277	36 01	300	35 22	341
	REGULUS		◆ SPICA		ACRUX		◆ CANOPUS		SIRIUS		BETELGEUSE		◆ POLLUX	
135	50 20	027	25 53	091	38 08	153	48 57	215	57 48	277	35 14	299	35 03	340
136	50 44	026	26 48	091	38 33	153	48 25	216	56 54	276	34 26	298	34 44	339
137	51 07	024	27 43	090	38 57	154	47 53	216	55 59	276	33 37	298	34 24	338
138	51 29	023	28 38	090	39 21	154	47 20	217	55 05	275	32 49	297	34 03	337
139	51 50	021	29 33	090	39 45	154	46 48	217	54 10	274	32 00	296	33 41	336
140	52 09	020	30 27	089	40 09	154	46 14	217	53 16	274	31 10	296	33 19	335
141	52 27	018	31 22	089	40 33	155	45 41	218	52 21	273	30 21	295	32 55	334
142	52 43	017	32 17	088	40 56	155	45 07	218	51 26	273	29 31	294	32 31	333
143	52 59	015	33 12	088	41 19	155	44 33	218	50 31	273	28 41	294	32 06	332
144	53 12	014	34 06	087	41 41	156	43 59	219	49 37	272	27 51	293	31 40	331
145	53 24	012	35 01	087	42 04	156	43 25	219	48 42	272	27 00	293	31 14	331
146	53 35	010	35 56	087	42 26	156	42 50	219	47 47	271	26 10	292	30 46	330
147	53 44	009	36 51	086	42 48	157	42 15	219	46 52	271	25 19	292	30 18	329
148	53 52	007	37 45	086	43 09	157	41 40	220	45 57	270	24 28	291	29 50	328
149	53 58	005	38 40	085	43 30	158	41 05	220	45 03	270	23 36	290	29 20	327
	REGULUS		◆ ARCTURUS		SPICA		◆ ACRUX		CANOPUS		SIRIUS		◆ PROCYON	
150	54 02	004	14 08	061	39 35	085	43 51	158	40 30	220	44 08	270	45 08	306
151	54 05	002	14 56	061	40 29	084	44 11	158	39 55	220	43 13	269	44 23	305
152	54 06	000	15 43	060	41 24	084	44 31	159	39 19	220	42 18	269	43 38	304
153	54 06	359	16 31	060	42 18	083	44 51	159	38 44	221	41 23	268	42 52	303
154	54 04	357	17 18	059	43 13	083	45 10	160	38 08	221	40 29	268	42 06	302
155	54 01	355	18 05	059	44 07	082	45 29	160	37 32	221	39 34	268	41 20	302
156	53 55	354	18 51	058	45 01	082	45 47	161	36 56	221	38 39	267	40 33	301
157	53 49	352	19 38	057	45 55	081	46 05	161	36 20	221	37 44	267	39 46	300
158	53 41	351	20 24	057	46 50	081	46 23	162	35 44	221	36 50	267	38 58	299
159	53 31	349	21 09	056	47 44	080	46 40	162	35 08	221	35 55	266	38 10	298
160	53 19	347	21 55	056	48 37	079	46 57	163	34 32	221	35 00	266	37 22	298
161	53 07	346	22 40	055	49 31	079	47 13	163	33 56	221	34 06	265	36 33	297
162	52 52	344	23 25	054	50 25	078	47 28	164	33 19	221	33 11	265	35 44	296
163	52 37	343	24 09	054	51 19	078	47 43	164	32 43	221	32 16	265	34 55	296
164	52 20	341	24 53	053	52 12	077	47 58	165	32 07	222	31 22	264	34 05	295
	◆ ARCTURUS		ANTARES		◆ ACRUX		CANOPUS		SIRIUS		◆ PROCYON		REGULUS	
165	25 37	052	16 40	112	48 12	165	31 30	222	30 27	264	33 15	294	52 01	340
166	26 20	052	17 31	112	48 26	166	30 54	222	29 33	264	32 25	294	51 41	338
167	27 03	051	18 22	111	48 39	167	30 18	222	28 38	263	31 35	293	51 20	337
168	27 45	050	19 13	111	48 51	167	29 41	222	27 44	263	30 44	292	50 58	335
169	28 27	050	20 04	111	49 03	168	29 05	222	26 49	263	29 53	292	50 34	334
170	29 08	049	20 55	111	49 14	168	28 29	221	25 55	262	29 02	291	50 09	332
171	29 49	048	21 47	110	49 25	169	27 52	221	25 01	262	28 11	291	49 43	331
172	30 30	047	22 38	110	49 35	170	27 16	221	24 07	262	27 20	290	49 16	330
173	31 10	047	23 30	110	49 44	170	26 40	221	23 12	261	26 28	289	48 48	328
174	31 49	046	24 21	110	49 52	171	26 04	221	22 18	261	25 36	289	48 18	327
175	32 28	045	25 13	109	50 02	172	25 28	221	21 24	261	24 44	288	47 48	326
176	33 07	044	26 05	109	50 09	172	24 51	221	20 30	260	23 52	288	47 17	325
177	33 45	043	26 57	109	50 16	173	24 15	221	19 36	260	23 00	287	46 45	323
178	34 22	042	27 49	108	50 22	174	23 40	221	18 42	260	22 07	287	46 11	322
179	34 59	042	28 41	108	50 28	174	23 04	221	17 48	259	21 15	286	45 37	321

LHA ♈	Hc	Zn	Hc	Zn	Hc	Zn	Hc	Zn	Hc	Zn	Hc	Zn	Hc	Zn
	ARCTURUS		◆ANTARES		ACRUX		◆Suhail		Alphard		REGULUS		◆Denebola	
180	35 35	041	29 33	108	50 33	175	49 58	230	50 43	286	45 02	320	51 26	356
181	36 10	040	30 25	108	50 37	176	49 16	230	49 50	286	44 27	319	51 21	355
182	36 45	039	31 17	107	50 41	177	48 34	231	48 58	285	43 50	318	51 15	353
183	37 19	038	32 10	107	50 44	177	47 51	231	48 04	284	43 13	317	51 08	351
184	37 52	037	33 02	107	50 46	178	47 09	231	47 11	284	42 35	316	50 59	350
185	38 24	036	33 54	107	50 48	179	46 26	231	46 18	283	41 56	315	50 49	348
186	38 56	035	34 47	107	50 49	179	45 43	231	45 24	282	41 17	314	50 37	347
187	39 27	034	35 39	106	50 49	180	45 00	232	44 31	282	40 37	313	50 24	345
188	39 57	033	36 32	106	50 49	181	44 17	232	43 37	281	39 57	312	50 09	344
189	40 27	032	37 25	106	50 48	182	43 34	232	42 43	281	39 16	311	49 54	342
190	40 55	031	38 18	106	50 46	182	42 51	232	41 49	280	38 34	310	49 36	341
191	41 22	030	39 10	105	50 43	183	42 08	232	40 55	280	37 52	309	49 18	340
192	41 49	028	40 03	105	50 40	184	41 24	232	40 01	279	37 09	308	48 58	338
193	42 15	027	40 56	105	50 36	184	40 41	232	39 07	279	36 26	308	48 37	337
194	42 39	026	41 49	105	50 32	185	39 57	232	38 13	278	35 42	307	48 15	336
	ARCTURUS		◆Rasalhague		ANTARES		◆ACRUX		Suhail		◆REGULUS		Denebola	
195	43 03	025	13 27	069	42 42	105	50 27	186	39 14	232	34 58	306	47 52	334
196	43 26	024	14 18	069	43 35	104	50 21	186	38 31	233	34 13	305	47 28	333
197	43 47	023	15 09	068	44 28	104	50 14	187	37 47	233	33 28	304	47 02	332
198	44 08	021	16 00	068	45 21	104	50 07	188	37 04	233	32 43	304	46 36	330
199	44 27	020	16 51	067	46 15	104	49 59	188	36 20	233	31 57	303	46 08	329
200	44 46	019	17 41	067	47 08	104	49 51	189	35 36	233	31 11	302	45 39	328
201	45 03	018	18 32	066	48 01	104	49 42	190	34 53	233	30 24	302	45 10	327
202	45 19	016	19 22	066	48 54	103	49 32	190	34 09	233	29 37	301	44 39	326
203	45 34	015	20 12	065	49 48	103	49 22	191	33 26	232	28 50	300	44 08	324
204	45 47	014	21 01	065	50 41	103	49 11	192	32 42	232	28 03	300	43 35	323
205	46 00	012	21 51	064	51 34	103	49 00	192	31 59	232	27 15	299	43 02	322
206	46 11	011	22 40	064	52 28	103	48 48	193	31 16	232	26 27	298	42 28	321
207	46 21	010	23 29	063	53 21	103	48 35	194	30 32	232	25 38	298	41 54	320
208	46 29	008	24 18	062	54 15	103	48 22	194	29 49	232	24 49	297	41 18	319
209	46 37	007	25 06	062	55 08	102	48 08	195	29 06	232	24 00	296	40 42	318
	ARCTURUS		◆Rasalhague		ANTARES		◆RIGIL KENT		ACRUX		Gienah		◆Denebola	
210	46 43	006	25 54	061	56 02	102	52 27	172	47 54	195	65 03	280	40 05	317
211	46 47	004	26 42	061	56 56	102	52 34	173	47 39	196	64 09	279	39 27	316
212	46 51	003	27 30	060	57 49	102	52 41	173	47 24	196	63 15	278	38 49	315
213	46 53	002	28 17	059	58 43	102	52 46	174	47 08	197	62 20	278	38 10	314
214	46 54	000	29 04	059	59 36	102	52 52	175	46 52	198	61 26	277	37 30	313
215	46 53	359	29 51	058	60 30	102	52 56	176	46 35	198	60 32	277	36 50	313
216	46 51	357	30 37	057	61 24	102	53 00	177	46 18	199	59 37	276	36 10	312
217	46 48	356	31 23	057	62 17	102	53 02	177	46 00	199	58 43	275	35 28	311
218	46 44	355	32 09	056	63 11	102	53 04	178	45 42	200	57 48	275	34 47	310
219	46 38	353	32 54	055	64 05	102	53 06	179	45 24	200	56 53	274	34 04	309
220	46 31	352	33 39	054	64 59	102	53 06	180	45 05	200	55 59	274	33 22	308
221	46 22	351	34 23	054	65 52	101	53 06	181	44 46	201	55 04	273	32 38	308
222	46 13	349	35 07	053	66 46	102	53 05	181	44 26	201	54 09	273	31 55	307
223	46 02	348	35 50	052	67 40	102	53 03	182	44 06	202	53 15	272	31 11	306
224	45 50	346	36 33	051	68 33	102	53 01	183	43 45	202	52 20	272	30 26	305
	Alphecca		Rasalhague		◆ALTAIR		Peacock		◆RIGIL KENT		◆SPICA		ARCTURUS	
225	38 37	010	37 16	050	11 42	075	24 21	143	52 57	184	64 17	296	45 36	345
226	38 46	009	37 58	050	12 35	074	24 54	143	52 53	185	63 27	294	45 21	344
227	38 54	008	38 39	049	13 27	074	25 26	143	52 48	185	62 37	293	45 06	343
228	39 01	007	39 20	048	14 20	073	25 59	143	52 43	186	61 47	292	44 49	341
229	39 07	006	40 00	047	15 12	073	26 32	143	52 36	187	60 56	291	44 31	340
230	39 12	004	40 40	046	16 04	072	27 05	143	52 29	188	60 05	290	44 11	339
231	39 16	003	41 19	045	16 57	072	27 38	143	52 21	189	59 13	289	43 51	338
232	39 18	002	41 58	044	17 49	071	28 11	143	52 13	189	58 21	288	43 30	336
233	39 20	001	42 35	043	18 40	071	28 44	143	52 03	190	57 29	288	43 07	335
234	39 20	000	43 12	042	19 32	070	29 17	143	51 53	191	56 37	287	42 44	334
235	39 19	359	43 48	041	20 24	070	29 50	143	51 43	192	55 44	286	42 19	333
236	39 18	357	44 24	040	21 15	069	30 23	143	51 31	192	54 51	285	41 54	332
237	39 15	356	44 58	039	22 06	069	30 56	143	51 19	193	53 58	284	41 27	331
238	39 11	355	45 32	038	22 57	068	31 28	143	51 07	194	53 05	284	41 00	330
239	39 05	354	46 05	036	23 48	068	32 01	143	50 53	194	52 12	283	40 31	328
	VEGA		◆ALTAIR		Peacock		◆RIGIL KENT		SPICA		◆ARCTURUS		Alphecca	
240	17 12	031	24 38	067	32 34	143	50 39	195	51 18	282	40 02	327	38 59	353
241	17 40	031	25 29	066	33 07	143	50 25	196	50 25	282	39 32	326	38 52	352
242	18 07	030	26 19	066	33 40	143	50 10	196	49 31	281	39 02	325	38 43	351
243	18 34	029	27 09	065	34 12	143	49 54	197	48 37	281	38 30	324	38 34	350
244	19 01	028	27 58	065	34 45	144	49 37	198	47 43	280	37 58	323	38 23	348
245	19 27	028	28 48	064	35 17	144	49 21	198	46 49	279	37 24	322	38 12	347
246	19 52	027	29 37	063	35 50	144	49 03	199	45 55	279	36 51	321	37 59	346
247	20 17	026	30 26	063	36 22	144	48 45	199	45 01	278	36 16	320	37 46	345
248	20 41	026	31 14	062	36 54	144	48 27	200	44 06	278	35 41	320	37 31	344
249	21 04	025	32 03	061	37 27	144	48 08	201	43 12	277	35 05	319	37 15	343
250	21 27	024	32 51	061	37 59	144	47 48	201	42 18	277	34 28	318	36 59	342
251	21 49	024	33 38	060	38 30	145	47 28	202	41 23	276	33 51	317	36 41	341
252	22 11	023	34 26	059	39 02	145	47 08	202	40 29	276	33 13	316	36 23	340
253	22 31	022	35 12	059	39 34	145	46 47	203	39 34	275	32 35	315	36 03	339
254	22 52	021	35 59	058	40 05	145	46 25	203	38 40	275	31 56	314	35 43	338
	◆VEGA		ALTAIR		◆Peacock		RIGIL KENT		◆SPICA		ARCTURUS		Alphecca	
255	23 11	020	36 45	057	40 36	145	46 04	204	37 45	274	31 17	314	35 22	337
256	23 30	020	37 31	056	41 07	146	45 41	204	36 50	274	30 37	313	35 00	336
257	23 48	019	38 16	055	41 38	146	45 19	205	35 56	273	29 56	312	34 37	335
258	24 06	018	39 01	055	42 09	146	44 56	205	35 01	273	29 15	311	34 13	334
259	24 22	017	39 46	054	42 39	146	44 33	205	34 06	273	28 34	311	33 48	333
260	24 38	017	40 30	053	43 09	147	44 09	206	33 11	272	27 52	310	33 23	332
261	24 53	016	41 13	052	43 39	147	43 45	206	32 17	272	27 10	309	32 56	331
262	25 08	015	41 56	051	44 09	147	43 21	206	31 22	271	26 27	308	32 29	330
263	25 22	014	42 38	050	44 38	148	42 56	207	30 27	271	25 44	308	32 02	329
264	25 34	013	43 20	049	45 07	148	42 31	207	29 32	270	25 00	307	31 33	328
265	25 47	012	44 01	048	45 36	149	42 06	208	28 37	270	24 17	306	31 04	327
266	25 58	012	44 42	047	46 05	149	41 41	208	27 43	270	23 32	306	30 34	326
267	26 09	011	45 22	046	46 33	149	41 15	208	26 48	269	22 48	305	30 03	325
268	26 18	010	46 01	045	47 00	150	40 49	208	25 53	269	22 03	305	29 32	325
269	26 27	009	46 40	044	47 28	150	40 23	209	24 58	268	21 17	304	29 00	324

LHA ♈	Hc	Zn	Hc	Zn	Hc	Zn	Hc	Zn	Hc	Zn	Hc	Zn	Hc	Zn
	◆VEGA		ALTAIR		◆FOMALHAUT		Peacock		RIGIL KENT		◆ANTARES		Alphecca	
270	26 36	008	47 17	043	24 17	113	47 55	151	39 56	209	69 36	258	28 27	323
271	26 43	007	47 54	042	25 08	113	48 22	151	39 30	209	68 42	258	27 54	322
272	26 49	006	48 30	041	25 58	113	48 48	152	39 03	210	67 49	258	27 21	322
273	26 55	006	49 06	039	26 49	112	49 14	152	38 36	210	66 55	258	26 46	321
274	27 00	005	49 40	038	27 40	112	49 39	153	38 08	210	66 01	259	26 11	320
275	27 04	004	50 13	037	28 31	112	50 04	153	37 41	210	65 07	258	25 36	319
276	27 07	003	50 46	036	29 22	112	50 28	154	37 13	210	64 14	258	25 00	319
277	27 10	002	51 17	034	30 13	111	50 52	154	36 45	211	63 20	258	24 23	318
278	27 11	001	51 47	033	31 04	111	51 16	155	36 17	211	62 26	258	23 46	317
279	27 12	000	52 17	031	31 55	111	51 38	156	35 49	211	61 33	258	23 09	316
280	27 12	359	52 45	030	32 46	111	52 01	156	35 21	211	60 39	258	22 31	316
281	27 11	359	53 12	029	33 37	111	52 22	157	34 53	211	59 45	258	21 52	315
282	27 09	358	53 37	027	34 29	110	52 43	158	34 24	211	58 52	258	21 13	314
283	27 07	357	54 02	026	35 20	110	53 04	158	33 56	211	57 58	258	20 34	314
284	27 03	356	54 25	024	36 11	110	53 24	159	33 27	212	57 04	258	19 54	313
	◆DENEB		FOMALHAUT		◆ACHERNAR		RIGIL KENT		◆ANTARES		Rasalhague		VEGA	
285	16 53	018	37 03	110	15 02	146	32 59	212	56 11	258	48 02	328	26 59	355
286	17 10	018	37 55	110	15 32	146	32 30	212	55 17	258	47 33	327	26 54	354
287	17 26	017	38 46	110	16 03	146	32 01	212	54 24	258	47 03	326	26 48	353
288	17 42	016	39 38	109	16 34	146	31 32	212	53 30	257	46 31	325	26 41	352
289	17 57	016	40 30	109	17 05	146	31 03	212	52 37	257	45 59	323	26 33	352
290	18 12	015	41 21	109	17 36	145	30 34	212	51 43	257	45 26	322	26 25	351
291	18 26	014	42 13	109	18 07	145	30 05	212	50 50	257	44 52	321	26 16	350
292	18 39	014	43 05	109	18 38	145	29 36	212	49 57	257	44 17	320	26 06	349
293	18 52	013	43 57	109	19 10	145	29 07	212	49 03	257	43 42	319	25 55	348
294	19 03	012	44 49	109	19 41	145	28 37	212	48 10	256	43 05	318	25 43	347
295	19 15	011	45 41	108	20 13	145	28 08	212	47 17	256	42 28	317	25 31	347
296	19 25	011	46 33	108	20 44	145	27 39	212	46 23	256	41 51	316	25 18	346
297	19 35	010	47 25	108	21 16	144	27 10	212	45 30	256	41 12	315	25 04	345
298	19 44	009	48 17	108	21 48	144	26 41	212	44 37	256	40 33	314	24 49	344
299	19 53	009	49 09	108	22 20	144	26 11	212	43 44	256	39 53	313	24 34	343
	DENEB		Enif		◆FOMALHAUT		ACHERNAR		◆RIGIL KENT		ANTARES		◆VEGA	
300	20 01	008	47 28	040	50 01	108	22 52	144	25 42	212	42 51	255	24 18	342
301	20 08	007	48 03	039	50 53	108	23 24	144	25 13	212	41 58	255	24 01	342
302	20 14	006	48 37	038	51 45	108	23 57	144	24 44	212	41 05	255	23 43	341
303	20 20	006	49 10	036	52 38	108	24 29	144	24 15	212	40 12	255	23 25	340
304	20 25	005	49 42	035	53 30	108	25 01	144	23 46	212	39 19	255	23 06	339
305	20 29	004	50 13	034	54 22	108	25 34	144	23 17	212	38 26	254	22 46	339
306	20 33	003	50 43	033	55 14	108	26 06	144	22 48	212	37 33	254	22 26	338
307	20 36	003	51 12	031	56 06	108	26 38	144	22 20	212	36 41	254	22 05	337
308	20 38	002	51 40	030	56 59	108	27 11	144	21 51	212	35 48	254	21 43	336
309	20 39	001	52 07	028	57 51	108	27 43	144	21 22	211	34 56	253	21 21	336
310	20 40	000	52 32	027	58 43	108	28 16	144	20 54	211	34 03	253	20 58	335
311	20 40	000	52 56	025	59 35	108	28 48	144	20 25	211	33 11	253	20 34	334
312	20 39	359	53 19	024	60 27	108	29 21	144	19 57	211	32 18	253	20 10	333
313	20 38	358	53 41	022	61 19	108	29 54	144	19 28	211	31 26	253	19 45	333
314	20 35	357	54 01	021	62 11	108	30 26	144	19 00	211	30 34	252	19 20	332
	Alpheratz		◆Diphda		ACHERNAR		◆Peacock		ANTARES		◆ALTAIR		DENEB	
315	20 03	043	37 36	095	30 59	144	56 46	188	29 41	252	53 05	331	20 33	357
316	20 40	042	38 30	094	31 31	144	56 37	189	28 49	252	52 38	330	20 29	356
317	21 17	042	39 25	094	32 03	144	56 28	190	27 57	252	52 10	328	20 25	355
318	21 53	041	40 20	094	32 36	144	56 18	191	27 05	251	51 40	327	20 20	354
319	22 29	040	41 14	093	33 08	144	56 07	192	26 13	251	51 10	325	20 14	354
320	23 04	040	42 09	093	33 41	144	55 55	193	25 22	251	50 38	324	20 08	353
321	23 39	039	43 04	093	34 13	144	55 42	194	24 30	251	50 05	323	20 00	352
322	24 13	038	43 59	092	34 45	144	55 28	195	23 38	250	49 32	322	19 53	351
323	24 47	038	44 53	092	35 17	144	55 14	196	22 47	250	48 57	320	19 44	351
324	25 20	037	45 48	091	35 49	144	54 59	197	21 55	250	48 22	319	19 35	350
325	25 52	036	46 43	091	36 21	145	54 43	197	21 04	249	47 45	318	19 25	349
326	26 24	035	47 38	091	36 53	145	54 26	198	20 13	249	47 08	317	19 14	349
327	26 55	034	48 33	090	37 24	145	54 09	199	19 21	249	46 30	316	19 03	348
328	27 26	034	49 27	090	37 56	145	53 51	200	18 30	249	45 52	315	18 51	347
329	27 56	033	50 22	089	38 27	145	53 32	201	17 39	248	45 12	314	18 39	346
	◆Alpheratz		Diphda		◆ACHERNAR		Peacock		◆Nunki		ALTAIR		DENEB	
330	28 26	032	51 17	089	38 58	145	53 12	201	48 33	257	44 32	313	18 25	346
331	28 54	031	52 12	089	39 29	146	52 52	202	47 40	257	43 52	312	18 11	345
332	29 22	030	53 07	088	40 00	146	52 31	203	46 47	256	43 10	311	17 57	344
333	29 50	030	54 01	088	40 31	146	52 10	203	45 53	256	42 28	310	17 42	344
334	30 16	029	54 56	087	41 02	146	51 48	204	45 00	256	41 46	309	17 26	343
335	30 42	028	55 51	087	41 32	147	51 25	205	44 07	256	41 03	308	17 10	342
336	31 07	027	56 46	086	42 02	147	51 02	205	43 14	256	40 19	307	16 53	342
337	31 32	026	57 40	086	42 32	147	50 38	206	42 21	256	39 35	306	16 35	341
338	31 55	025	58 35	085	43 02	147	50 14	206	41 28	255	38 50	305	16 17	340
339	32 18	024	59 30	085	43 31	148	49 49	207	40 35	255	38 05	304	15 58	340
340	32 40	023	60 24	084	44 00	148	49 24	208	39 42	255	37 20	304	15 38	339
341	33 01	022	61 19	084	44 29	148	48 58	208	38 49	255	36 34	303	15 18	338
342	33 22	021	62 13	083	44 57	149	48 32	209	37 56	254	35 48	302	14 58	338
343	33 41	020	63 07	082	45 26	149	48 06	209	37 03	254	35 01	301	14 37	337
344	34 00	019	64 02	082	45 54	150	47 39	210	36 10	254	34 14	301	14 15	336
	Alpheratz		◆Hamal		◆ACHERNAR		Peacock		Nunki		◆ALTAIR		Enif	
345	34 17	018	24 08	047	46 21	150	47 12	210	35 18	254	33 27	300	51 25	329
346	34 34	017	24 48	047	46 49	150	46 44	210	34 25	254	32 39	299	50 57	328
347	34 50	016	25 27	046	47 15	151	46 16	211	33 33	253	31 51	298	50 27	327
348	35 05	015	26 06	045	47 42	151	45 48	211	32 40	253	31 03	298	49 57	325
349	35 19	014	26 45	044	48 08	152	45 19	212	31 48	253	30 14	297	49 25	324
350	35 32	013	27 23	044	48 34	152	44 50	212	30 55	253	29 25	296	48 52	323
351	35 44	012	28 01	043	48 59	153	44 21	212	30 03	252	28 36	296	48 19	322
352	35 55	011	28 38	042	49 24	153	43 51	213	29 11	252	27 46	295	47 44	320
353	36 05	010	29 14	041	49 48	154	43 22	213	28 19	252	26 57	294	47 09	319
354	36 14	009	29 50	041	50 12	154	42 52	213	27 27	252	26 07	294	46 33	318
355	36 22	008	30 26	040	50 35	155	42 21	214	26 35	251	25 16	293	45 56	317
356	36 29	007	31 00	039	50 58	156	41 51	214	25 43	251	24 26	293	45 18	316
357	36 35	006	31 35	038	51 21	156	41 20	214	24 51	251	23 35	292	44 40	315
358	36 40	005	32 08	037	51 42	157	40 49	214	23 59	251	22 45	292	44 01	314
359	36 44	004	32 41	036	52 03	158	40 18	215	23 08	250	21 54	291	43 21	313

LHA ♈	Hc	Zn	Hc	Zn	Hc	Zn	Hc	Zn	Hc	Zn	Hc	Zn	Hc	Zn
	◆ Alpheratz		Hamal		◆ RIGEL		CANOPUS		ACHERNAR		◆ Peacock		Enif	
0	35 47	002	32 24	035	13 33	093	16 09	141	53 20	158	40 36	215	42 00	313
1	35 49	001	32 55	034	14 27	092	16 43	141	53 40	159	40 04	216	41 19	312
2	35 50	000	33 25	033	15 21	092	17 17	141	53 59	159	39 32	216	40 39	311
3	35 49	359	33 55	032	16 16	092	17 52	141	54 18	160	39 00	216	39 57	310
4	35 48	358	34 24	031	17 10	091	18 27	140	54 37	161	38 28	216	39 15	309
5	35 46	357	34 52	030	18 04	091	19 01	140	54 54	162	37 56	216	38 32	308
6	35 43	356	35 19	030	18 59	090	19 36	140	55 11	162	37 24	216	37 49	307
7	35 38	355	35 45	029	19 53	090	20 11	140	55 27	163	36 52	217	37 06	306
8	35 33	354	36 11	028	20 47	089	20 46	140	55 42	164	36 19	217	36 21	305
9	35 27	353	36 35	027	21 42	089	21 22	139	55 57	165	35 46	217	35 37	305
10	35 19	352	36 59	025	22 36	089	21 57	139	56 11	166	35 14	217	34 52	304
11	35 11	351	37 22	024	23 31	088	22 33	139	56 24	167	34 41	217	34 07	303
12	35 02	350	37 44	023	24 25	088	23 08	139	56 36	168	34 08	217	33 21	302
13	34 52	349	38 05	022	25 19	087	23 44	139	56 47	169	33 36	217	32 35	302
14	34 40	348	38 26	021	26 14	087	24 20	139	56 57	169	33 03	217	31 48	301
	◆ Hamal		ALDEBARAN		RIGEL		◆ CANOPUS		ACHERNAR		◆ FOMALHAUT		Alpheratz	
15	38 45	020	22 50	058	27 08	086	24 56	139	57 07	170	62 42	254	34 28	347
16	39 03	019	23 35	057	28 02	086	25 31	139	57 15	171	61 50	254	34 15	346
17	39 20	018	24 21	056	28 56	086	26 07	138	57 23	172	60 57	254	34 01	344
18	39 36	017	25 06	056	29 51	085	26 44	138	57 30	173	60 05	254	33 46	343
19	39 51	016	25 50	055	30 45	085	27 20	138	57 35	174	59 13	254	33 30	342
20	40 06	014	26 35	054	31 39	084	27 56	138	57 40	175	58 21	254	33 13	341
21	40 19	013	27 19	054	32 33	084	28 32	138	57 44	176	57 29	254	32 55	341
22	40 30	012	28 02	053	33 27	083	29 08	138	57 47	177	56 36	254	32 37	340
23	40 41	011	28 45	052	34 21	083	29 45	138	57 49	178	55 44	254	32 17	339
24	40 51	010	29 28	051	35 15	082	30 21	138	57 50	179	54 52	254	31 57	338
25	41 00	009	30 10	051	36 09	082	30 57	138	57 50	180	54 00	254	31 36	337
26	41 07	007	30 52	050	37 02	081	31 34	138	57 49	181	53 08	253	31 14	336
27	41 14	006	31 33	049	37 56	081	32 10	138	57 47	182	52 16	253	30 51	335
28	41 19	005	32 14	048	38 50	080	32 46	138	57 45	183	51 24	253	30 28	334
29	41 23	004	32 55	047	39 43	079	33 23	138	57 41	184	50 32	253	30 04	333
	Hamal		◆ ALDEBARAN		SIRIUS		◆ CANOPUS		ACHERNAR		◆ FOMALHAUT		Alpheratz	
30	41 26	002	33 34	047	23 26	098	33 59	138	57 36	185	49 40	253	29 39	332
31	41 27	001	34 14	046	24 20	098	34 35	138	57 30	186	48 48	253	29 13	331
32	41 28	000	34 52	045	25 14	098	35 12	138	57 24	187	47 56	253	28 46	330
33	41 27	359	35 31	044	26 08	097	35 48	138	57 16	188	47 04	253	28 19	330
34	41 26	358	36 08	043	27 02	097	36 24	138	57 08	189	46 12	253	27 51	329
35	41 23	356	36 45	042	27 56	096	37 00	138	56 58	190	45 20	252	27 23	328
36	41 19	355	37 21	041	28 50	096	37 36	138	56 48	191	44 28	252	26 53	327
37	41 14	354	37 57	040	29 44	096	38 12	139	56 37	192	43 36	252	26 24	326
38	41 07	353	38 32	039	30 38	095	38 48	139	56 25	193	42 45	252	25 53	325
39	41 00	351	39 06	038	31 32	095	39 24	139	56 12	194	41 53	252	25 22	325
40	40 51	350	39 39	037	32 27	095	40 00	139	55 59	195	41 01	252	24 50	324
41	40 41	349	40 12	036	33 21	094	40 35	139	55 44	196	40 10	251	24 18	323
42	40 31	348	40 44	035	34 15	094	41 11	139	55 29	197	39 18	251	23 45	322
43	40 19	347	41 15	034	35 09	093	41 46	140	55 13	197	38 27	251	23 12	322
44	40 06	346	41 45	033	36 04	093	42 21	140	54 56	198	37 35	251	22 38	321
	◆ CAPELLA		BETELGEUSE		SIRIUS		◆ CANOPUS		ACHERNAR		◆ FOMALHAUT		Hamal	
45	12 25	024	36 18	059	36 58	093	42 57	140	54 39	199	36 44	251	39 52	344
46	12 46	023	37 04	058	37 52	092	43 31	140	54 21	200	35 53	250	39 36	343
47	13 08	022	37 50	057	38 47	092	44 06	140	54 02	201	35 01	250	39 20	342
48	13 28	022	38 36	056	39 41	091	44 41	141	53 43	201	34 10	250	39 03	341
49	13 48	021	39 21	056	40 35	091	45 15	141	53 22	202	33 19	250	38 45	340
50	14 08	021	40 05	055	41 30	091	45 49	141	53 02	203	32 28	250	38 26	339
51	14 26	020	40 50	054	42 24	090	46 23	142	52 40	203	31 37	249	38 06	338
52	14 45	019	41 33	053	43 18	090	46 57	142	52 18	204	30 46	249	37 45	337
53	15 02	019	42 16	052	44 13	089	47 30	142	51 56	205	29 56	249	37 23	336
54	15 20	018	42 59	051	45 07	089	48 04	143	51 33	205	29 05	249	37 00	335
55	15 36	017	43 41	050	46 02	089	48 36	143	51 09	206	28 14	248	36 36	334
56	15 52	017	44 22	049	46 56	088	49 09	143	50 45	207	27 24	248	36 11	332
57	16 07	016	45 03	048	47 50	088	49 41	144	50 21	207	26 33	248	35 46	331
58	16 22	015	45 43	047	48 45	087	50 13	144	49 56	208	25 43	248	35 19	330
59	16 36	015	46 22	046	49 39	087	50 45	145	49 30	208	24 53	247	34 52	330
	CAPELLA		BETELGEUSE		◆ SIRIUS		CANOPUS		◆ ACHERNAR		Diphda		◆ Hamal	
60	16 50	014	47 01	045	50 33	086	51 16	145	49 04	209	44 10	269	34 24	329
61	17 02	013	47 39	044	51 27	086	51 47	146	48 38	209	43 15	268	33 55	328
62	17 15	013	48 16	043	52 22	085	52 17	146	48 11	210	42 21	268	33 26	327
63	17 26	012	48 53	041	53 16	085	52 47	147	47 44	210	41 27	268	32 56	326
64	17 37	011	49 28	040	54 10	084	53 17	147	47 17	211	40 32	267	32 25	325
65	17 47	010	50 03	039	55 04	084	53 46	148	46 49	211	39 38	267	31 53	324
66	17 57	010	50 36	038	55 58	083	54 14	149	46 21	211	38 44	267	31 21	323
67	18 06	009	51 09	036	56 52	082	54 42	149	45 53	212	37 49	266	30 48	322
68	18 14	008	51 41	035	57 46	082	55 10	150	45 24	212	36 55	266	30 14	321
69	18 21	008	52 12	034	58 40	081	55 36	151	44 55	212	36 01	265	29 40	321
70	18 28	007	52 41	032	59 33	080	56 03	152	44 25	213	35 07	265	29 05	320
71	18 34	006	53 09	031	60 27	080	56 28	152	43 56	213	34 13	265	28 30	319
72	18 40	005	53 37	029	61 20	079	56 53	153	43 26	213	33 19	264	27 54	318
73	18 45	005	54 03	028	62 14	078	57 18	154	42 56	214	32 24	264	27 17	317
74	18 49	004	54 27	026	63 07	077	57 41	155	42 26	214	31 30	264	26 40	317
	◆ CAPELLA		POLLUX		PROCYON		◆ Suhail		CANOPUS		◆ ACHERNAR		Hamal	
75	18 52	003	23 37	040	40 46	058	36 44	127	58 04	156	41 55	214	26 02	316
76	18 55	003	24 11	039	41 32	057	37 28	127	58 26	157	41 25	214	25 24	315
77	18 57	002	24 45	038	42 17	056	38 11	127	58 47	158	40 54	215	24 46	314
78	18 59	001	25 18	038	43 02	055	38 55	127	59 07	159	40 23	215	24 07	314
79	18 59	000	25 51	037	43 46	054	39 38	127	59 27	160	39 52	215	23 27	313
80	18 59	000	26 24	036	44 30	053	40 22	127	59 45	161	39 20	215	22 47	312
81	18 58	359	26 55	035	45 14	052	41 05	127	60 03	162	38 49	215	22 07	312
82	18 57	358	27 26	034	45 56	051	41 49	127	60 20	163	38 17	216	21 26	311
83	18 55	357	27 57	034	46 38	050	42 32	127	60 35	164	37 46	216	20 45	310
84	18 52	357	28 26	033	47 20	049	43 16	127	60 50	165	37 14	216	20 03	310
85	18 49	356	28 55	032	48 01	048	43 59	127	61 04	166	36 42	216	19 21	309
86	18 44	355	29 24	031	48 41	047	44 42	127	61 16	167	36 10	216	18 39	308
87	18 39	354	29 51	030	49 20	046	45 25	128	61 28	168	35 38	216	17 56	308
88	18 34	354	30 18	029	49 59	045	46 08	128	61 38	170	35 06	216	17 13	307
89	18 28	353	30 45	028	50 37	044	46 51	128	61 47	171	34 33	216	16 30	307

LAT 25°S

LHA ♈	Hc	Zn	Hc	Zn	Hc	Zn	Hc	Zn	Hc	Zn	Hc	Zn	Hc	Zn
	POLLUX		◆ REGULUS		ACRUX		CANOPUS		◆ ACHERNAR		◆ ALDEBARAN		CAPELLA	
90	31 10	027	18 59	066	19 10	152	61 55	172	34 01	217	43 47	332	18 21	352
91	31 35	027	19 49	066	19 36	152	62 02	173	33 29	217	43 21	331	18 13	352
92	31 59	026	20 38	065	20 02	151	62 08	175	32 56	217	42 53	330	18 05	351
93	32 22	025	21 27	065	20 28	151	62 12	176	32 24	217	42 25	328	17 56	350
94	32 44	024	22 16	064	20 54	151	62 15	177	31 51	217	41 56	327	17 46	349
95	33 06	023	23 05	064	21 20	151	62 17	179	31 19	217	41 27	326	17 36	349
96	33 26	022	23 54	063	21 47	151	62 18	180	30 46	217	40 56	325	17 25	348
97	33 46	021	24 42	062	22 13	151	62 17	181	30 14	217	40 24	324	17 13	347
98	34 05	020	25 30	062	22 40	151	62 15	183	29 41	217	39 52	323	17 01	347
99	34 23	019	26 18	061	23 06	151	62 12	184	29 09	217	39 19	322	16 48	346
100	34 40	018	27 05	060	23 33	151	62 08	185	28 36	217	38 45	321	16 35	345
101	34 56	017	27 52	060	24 00	150	62 03	186	28 04	217	38 10	320	16 21	345
102	35 11	016	28 39	059	24 27	150	61 56	188	27 31	217	37 35	319	16 06	344
103	35 26	015	29 26	058	24 53	150	61 48	189	26 59	217	36 59	318	15 50	343
104	35 39	014	30 12	058	25 20	150	61 39	190	26 26	217	36 23	317	15 34	343
	POLLUX		◆ REGULUS		Gienah		◆ ACRUX		CANOPUS		◆ RIGEL		BETELGEUSE	
105	35 51	013	30 58	057	16 54	102	25 47	150	61 29	191	59 54	299	54 02	332
106	36 03	012	31 43	056	17 47	102	26 14	150	61 18	193	59 07	298	53 36	331
107	36 13	010	32 28	056	18 40	101	26 41	150	61 06	194	58 18	297	53 09	329
108	36 22	009	33 13	055	19 34	101	27 08	150	60 52	195	57 30	296	52 41	328
109	36 31	008	33 57	054	20 27	101	27 35	150	60 38	196	56 41	295	52 11	326
110	36 38	007	34 41	053	21 21	100	28 02	150	60 22	197	55 51	294	51 41	325
111	36 45	006	35 24	052	22 14	100	28 30	150	60 05	198	55 01	293	51 09	324
112	36 50	005	36 07	052	23 08	099	28 57	150	59 48	199	54 11	292	50 36	322
113	36 54	004	36 49	051	24 01	099	29 24	150	59 30	200	53 21	291	50 03	321
114	36 57	003	37 31	050	24 55	099	29 51	150	59 10	201	52 30	290	49 28	320
115	36 59	002	38 12	049	25 49	098	30 18	150	58 50	202	51 39	290	48 52	319
116	37 01	001	38 53	048	26 43	098	30 45	150	58 29	203	50 48	289	48 16	317
117	37 01	000	39 33	047	27 37	098	31 12	150	58 07	204	49 56	288	47 39	316
118	37 00	358	40 13	046	28 31	097	31 39	150	57 44	205	49 04	287	47 01	315
119	36 58	357	40 52	045	29 24	097	32 05	150	57 21	206	48 12	287	46 22	314
	◆ REGULUS		SPICA		◆ ACRUX		CANOPUS		◆ RIGEL		BETELGEUSE		POLLUX	
120	41 30	044	12 21	097	32 32	151	56 57	207	47 20	286	45 43	313	36 54	356
121	42 07	043	13 15	096	32 59	151	56 32	208	46 28	285	45 03	312	36 50	355
122	42 44	042	14 09	096	33 26	151	56 06	208	45 35	285	44 22	311	36 45	354
123	43 21	041	15 03	096	33 52	151	55 40	209	44 42	284	43 40	310	36 39	353
124	43 56	040	15 57	095	34 19	151	55 14	210	43 49	283	42 58	309	36 32	352
125	44 31	039	16 51	095	34 45	151	54 46	211	42 56	283	42 16	308	36 23	351
126	45 04	038	17 45	094	35 11	151	54 18	211	42 03	282	41 33	307	36 14	350
127	45 37	037	18 40	094	35 37	151	53 50	212	41 10	281	40 49	306	36 04	349
128	46 09	036	19 34	094	36 03	151	53 21	212	40 17	281	40 05	305	35 53	348
129	46 41	034	20 28	093	36 29	152	52 51	213	39 23	280	39 20	304	35 40	346
130	47 11	033	21 23	093	36 55	152	52 22	214	38 30	280	38 35	304	35 27	345
131	47 40	032	22 17	092	37 21	152	51 51	214	37 36	279	37 50	303	35 13	344
132	48 08	031	23 11	092	37 46	152	51 20	215	36 42	279	37 04	302	34 58	343
133	48 35	029	24 06	092	38 12	152	50 49	215	35 49	278	36 18	301	34 42	342
134	49 01	028	25 00	091	38 37	153	50 18	216	34 55	278	35 31	301	34 25	341
	REGULUS		◆ SPICA		ACRUX		◆ CANOPUS		SIRIUS		BETELGEUSE		◆ POLLUX	
135	49 26	027	25 54	091	39 02	153	49 46	216	57 41	278	34 44	300	34 07	340
136	49 50	025	26 49	090	39 26	153	49 14	217	56 47	278	33 57	299	33 48	339
137	50 12	024	27 43	090	39 51	153	48 41	217	55 53	277	33 09	298	33 28	338
138	50 34	022	28 37	089	40 15	154	48 08	217	54 59	276	32 21	298	33 08	337
139	50 54	021	29 32	089	40 39	154	47 35	218	54 05	276	31 33	297	32 47	336
140	51 12	019	30 26	089	41 03	154	47 02	218	53 11	275	30 44	296	32 24	335
141	51 30	018	31 21	088	41 27	154	46 28	218	52 16	275	29 55	296	32 01	334
142	51 46	016	32 15	088	41 50	155	45 54	219	51 22	274	29 06	295	31 37	334
143	52 01	015	33 09	087	42 13	155	45 20	219	50 28	274	28 17	294	31 13	333
144	52 14	013	34 04	087	42 36	155	44 46	219	49 34	273	27 27	294	30 48	332
145	52 26	012	34 58	086	42 59	156	44 11	220	48 39	273	26 37	293	30 21	331
146	52 36	010	35 52	086	43 21	156	43 36	220	47 45	272	25 47	293	29 55	330
147	52 45	009	36 46	085	43 43	156	43 02	220	46 51	272	24 57	292	29 27	329
148	52 52	007	37 40	085	44 04	157	42 26	220	45 56	271	24 06	291	28 59	328
149	52 58	005	38 35	084	44 26	157	41 51	220	45 02	271	23 15	291	28 30	327
	REGULUS		◆ ARCTURUS		SPICA		◆ ACRUX		CANOPUS		SIRIUS		◆ PROCYON	
150	53 02	004	13 39	061	39 29	084	44 46	158	41 16	221	44 08	271	44 32	307
151	53 05	002	14 26	060	40 23	083	45 07	158	40 40	221	43 13	270	43 48	306
152	53 06	000	15 13	060	41 17	083	45 27	158	40 05	221	42 19	270	43 04	305
153	53 06	359	16 00	059	42 11	082	45 47	159	39 29	221	41 25	269	42 19	304
154	53 04	357	16 47	059	43 05	082	46 06	159	38 53	221	40 30	269	41 34	303
155	53 01	356	17 33	058	43 58	081	46 25	160	38 17	221	39 36	268	40 48	302
156	52 56	354	18 19	058	44 52	081	46 44	160	37 41	222	38 41	268	40 02	301
157	52 49	352	19 05	057	45 46	080	47 02	161	37 05	222	37 47	268	39 15	301
158	52 41	351	19 51	056	46 39	080	47 20	161	36 29	222	36 53	267	38 28	300
159	52 32	349	20 36	056	47 33	079	47 37	162	35 53	222	35 58	267	37 41	299
160	52 21	348	21 21	055	48 26	078	47 54	162	35 17	222	35 04	267	36 53	298
161	52 09	346	22 05	055	49 19	078	48 10	163	34 40	222	34 10	266	36 05	298
162	51 55	344	22 49	054	50 12	077	48 26	163	34 04	222	33 16	266	35 17	297
163	51 39	343	23 33	053	51 05	076	48 41	164	33 28	222	32 21	265	34 28	296
164	51 23	341	24 17	053	51 58	076	48 56	165	32 51	222	31 27	265	33 39	295
	◆ ARCTURUS		ANTARES		◆ ACRUX		CANOPUS		SIRIUS		◆ PROCYON		REGULUS	
165	25 00	052	17 03	112	49 10	165	32 15	222	30 33	265	32 50	295	51 05	340
166	25 42	051	17 53	111	49 24	166	31 39	222	29 39	264	32 01	294	50 46	338
167	26 25	051	18 44	111	49 37	166	31 02	222	28 45	264	31 11	294	50 25	337
168	27 06	050	19 35	111	49 50	167	30 26	222	27 51	264	30 21	293	50 03	336
169	27 48	049	20 25	111	50 02	168	29 50	222	26 57	263	29 31	292	49 40	334
170	28 29	048	21 16	110	50 13	168	29 13	222	26 03	263	28 40	292	49 16	333
171	29 09	048	22 07	110	50 24	169	28 37	222	25 09	262	27 50	291	48 51	332
172	29 49	047	22 59	110	50 34	170	28 01	222	24 15	262	26 59	290	48 24	330
173	30 28	046	23 50	109	50 44	170	27 25	222	23 21	262	26 08	290	47 56	329
174	31 07	045	24 41	109	50 53	171	26 49	222	22 27	261	25 17	289	47 28	328
175	31 46	044	25 33	109	51 01	172	26 13	222	21 34	261	24 25	289	46 58	326
176	32 24	044	26 24	109	51 09	172	25 37	221	20 40	261	23 34	288	46 28	325
177	33 01	043	27 16	108	51 16	173	25 01	221	19 46	260	22 42	288	45 56	324
178	33 37	042	28 07	108	51 22	174	24 25	221	18 53	260	21 50	287	45 24	323
179	34 14	041	28 59	108	51 28	174	23 49	221	17 59	259	20 58	287	44 50	322

LHA ♈	ARCTURUS Hc	Zn	◆ANTARES Hc	Zn	ACRUX Hc	Zn	◆Suhail Hc	Zn	Alphard Hc	Zn	REGULUS Hc	Zn	◆Denebola Hc	Zn
180	34 49	040	29 51	107	51 33	175	50 36	231	50 26	288	44 16	321	50 26	356
181	35 24	039	30 43	107	51 37	176	49 54	231	49 34	287	43 41	319	50 22	355
182	35 58	038	31 35	107	51 41	176	49 11	232	48 41	286	43 06	318	50 16	353
183	36 31	037	32 27	107	51 44	177	48 29	232	47 49	285	42 29	317	50 09	352
184	37 04	036	33 19	106	51 46	178	47 46	232	46 57	285	41 52	316	50 00	350
185	37 36	035	34 11	106	51 48	179	47 03	232	46 04	284	41 14	315	49 50	349
186	38 07	034	35 04	106	51 49	179	46 20	232	45 11	283	40 35	314	49 39	347
187	38 37	033	35 56	106	51 49	180	45 37	232	44 18	283	39 56	313	49 26	346
188	39 07	032	36 48	105	51 49	181	44 54	233	43 25	282	39 16	312	49 12	344
189	39 35	031	37 41	105	51 47	182	44 11	233	42 32	282	38 36	312	48 56	343
190	40 03	030	38 33	105	51 46	182	43 27	233	41 38	281	37 55	311	48 40	341
191	40 30	029	39 26	105	51 43	183	42 44	233	40 45	280	37 14	310	48 22	340
192	40 56	028	40 19	104	51 40	184	42 01	233	39 52	280	36 31	309	48 03	339
193	41 21	027	41 11	104	51 36	184	41 17	233	38 58	279	35 49	308	47 42	337
194	41 45	026	42 04	104	51 31	185	40 34	233	38 04	279	35 06	307	47 21	336

LHA ♈	ARCTURUS Hc	Zn	◆Rasalhague Hc	Zn	ANTARES Hc	Zn	◆ACRUX Hc	Zn	Suhail Hc	Zn	◆REGULUS Hc	Zn	Denebola Hc	Zn
195	42 09	025	13 06	069	42 57	104	51 26	186	39 50	233	34 22	306	46 58	335
196	42 31	023	13 56	069	43 50	104	51 20	187	39 07	233	33 38	306	46 34	333
197	42 52	022	14 47	068	44 43	103	51 14	187	38 23	233	32 54	305	46 09	332
198	43 12	021	15 37	068	45 35	103	51 07	188	37 40	233	32 09	304	45 43	331
199	43 31	020	16 28	067	46 28	103	50 59	189	36 56	233	31 24	303	45 16	330
200	43 49	019	17 18	067	47 22	103	50 50	189	36 13	233	30 39	303	44 48	328
201	44 06	017	18 07	066	48 15	102	50 41	190	35 29	233	29 53	302	44 19	327
202	44 21	016	18 57	066	49 08	102	50 31	191	34 46	233	29 06	301	43 50	326
203	44 36	015	19 46	065	50 01	102	50 21	191	34 02	233	28 20	301	43 19	325
204	44 49	013	20 36	064	50 54	102	50 10	192	33 19	233	27 33	300	42 47	324
205	45 01	012	21 25	064	51 47	102	49 58	193	32 35	233	26 46	299	42 15	323
206	45 12	011	22 13	063	52 41	102	49 46	193	31 52	233	25 58	299	41 41	322
207	45 22	010	23 02	063	53 34	101	49 33	194	31 09	233	25 10	298	41 07	321
208	45 30	008	23 50	062	54 27	101	49 20	194	30 26	233	24 22	297	40 32	320
209	45 37	007	24 38	061	55 21	101	49 06	195	29 42	233	23 34	297	39 57	319

LHA ♈	ARCTURUS Hc	Zn	◆Rasalhague Hc	Zn	ANTARES Hc	Zn	◆RIGIL KENT Hc	Zn	ACRUX Hc	Zn	Gienah Hc	Zn	◆Denebola Hc	Zn
210	45 43	006	25 25	061	56 14	101	53 26	172	48 52	196	64 52	282	39 21	318
211	45 48	004	26 13	060	57 07	101	53 34	173	48 37	196	63 58	281	38 44	317
212	45 51	003	27 00	060	58 01	100	53 40	173	48 22	197	63 05	280	38 06	316
213	45 53	001	27 47	059	58 54	100	53 46	174	48 06	197	62 11	280	37 28	315
214	45 54	000	28 33	058	59 48	100	53 51	175	47 49	198	61 18	279	36 49	314
215	45 53	359	29 19	058	60 41	100	53 56	176	47 32	198	60 24	278	36 09	313
216	45 51	357	30 05	057	61 35	100	53 59	177	47 15	199	59 30	278	35 29	312
217	45 48	356	30 50	056	62 29	100	54 02	177	46 57	199	58 36	277	34 49	311
218	45 44	355	31 35	055	63 22	100	54 04	178	46 39	200	57 42	276	34 08	311
219	45 38	353	32 19	055	64 16	099	54 06	179	46 20	200	56 48	276	33 26	310
220	45 31	352	33 04	054	65 09	099	54 06	180	46 01	201	55 54	275	32 44	309
221	45 23	351	33 47	053	66 03	099	54 06	181	45 42	201	55 00	275	32 02	308
222	45 14	349	34 31	052	66 57	099	54 05	182	45 22	202	54 06	274	31 19	307
223	45 03	348	35 13	051	67 50	099	54 03	182	45 01	202	53 11	274	30 35	307
224	44 51	347	35 56	051	68 44	099	54 00	183	44 41	203	52 17	273	29 51	306

LHA ♈	Alphecca Hc	Zn	Rasalhague Hc	Zn	◆ALTAIR Hc	Zn	Peacock Hc	Zn	◆RIGIL KENT Hc	Zn	◆SPICA Hc	Zn	ARCTURUS Hc	Zn
225	37 38	010	36 37	050	11 26	074	25 09	143	53 57	184	63 50	297	44 38	345
226	37 47	009	37 19	049	12 18	074	25 42	143	53 53	185	63 02	296	44 24	344
227	37 55	008	37 59	048	13 10	073	26 14	143	53 48	186	62 13	295	44 08	343
228	38 02	007	38 40	047	14 02	073	26 47	143	53 42	186	61 23	294	43 52	342
229	38 08	005	39 19	046	14 54	072	27 20	143	53 36	187	60 33	293	43 34	340
230	38 12	004	39 58	045	15 46	072	27 53	143	53 29	188	59 43	292	43 15	339
231	38 16	003	40 36	044	16 38	071	28 26	143	53 21	189	58 52	291	42 55	338
232	38 18	002	41 14	043	17 29	071	28 59	143	53 12	190	58 01	290	42 34	337
233	38 20	001	41 51	042	18 20	070	29 32	143	53 02	190	57 10	289	42 13	336
234	38 20	000	42 27	041	19 12	070	30 05	143	52 52	191	56 19	288	41 50	334
235	38 19	359	43 03	040	20 03	069	30 37	143	52 41	192	55 27	287	41 26	333
236	38 18	358	43 38	039	20 53	069	31 10	143	52 30	193	54 35	287	41 01	332
237	38 15	356	44 11	038	21 44	068	31 43	143	52 18	193	53 43	286	40 35	331
238	38 11	355	44 44	037	22 34	068	32 16	143	52 05	194	52 50	285	40 08	330
239	38 06	354	45 17	036	23 25	067	32 49	143	51 51	195	51 58	284	39 40	329

LHA ♈	VEGA Hc	Zn	◆ALTAIR Hc	Zn	Peacock Hc	Zn	◆RIGIL KENT Hc	Zn	SPICA Hc	Zn	◆ARCTURUS Hc	Zn	Alphecca Hc	Zn
240	16 20	031	24 15	067	33 22	143	51 37	195	51 05	284	39 12	328	38 00	353
241	16 48	030	25 04	066	33 55	143	51 22	196	50 12	283	38 42	327	37 52	352
242	17 15	030	25 54	065	34 28	143	51 07	197	49 19	282	38 12	326	37 44	351
243	17 42	029	26 43	065	35 00	143	50 51	197	48 26	282	37 41	325	37 35	350
244	18 08	028	27 32	064	35 33	143	50 35	198	47 32	281	37 09	324	37 25	349
245	18 33	028	28 21	064	36 06	143	50 17	199	46 39	280	36 37	323	37 13	347
246	18 58	027	29 10	063	36 38	143	50 00	199	45 45	280	36 04	322	37 01	346
247	19 23	026	29 58	062	37 11	143	49 42	200	44 52	279	35 30	321	36 48	345
248	19 47	026	30 46	062	37 43	144	49 23	200	43 58	279	34 55	320	36 33	344
249	20 10	025	31 34	061	38 15	144	49 04	201	43 04	278	34 20	319	36 18	343
250	20 32	024	32 21	060	38 47	144	48 44	202	42 10	278	33 44	318	36 02	342
251	20 54	023	33 08	059	39 19	144	48 24	202	41 16	277	33 07	317	35 45	341
252	21 15	023	33 55	059	39 51	144	48 03	203	40 22	277	32 30	316	35 27	340
253	21 36	022	34 41	058	40 23	144	47 42	203	39 28	276	31 52	316	35 08	339
254	21 56	021	35 27	057	40 54	145	47 20	204	38 34	276	31 14	315	34 47	338

LHA ♈	◆VEGA Hc	Zn	ALTAIR Hc	Zn	◆Peacock Hc	Zn	RIGIL KENT Hc	Zn	◆SPICA Hc	Zn	ARCTURUS Hc	Zn	Alphecca Hc	Zn
255	22 15	020	36 12	056	41 25	145	46 59	204	37 40	275	30 35	314	34 27	337
256	22 34	020	36 57	056	41 57	145	46 36	204	36 46	275	29 56	313	34 05	336
257	22 51	019	37 42	055	42 28	145	46 13	205	35 52	274	29 16	312	33 42	335
258	23 08	018	38 26	054	42 58	146	45 50	205	34 57	274	28 36	312	33 19	334
259	23 25	017	39 10	053	43 29	146	45 27	206	34 03	273	27 55	311	32 55	333
260	23 41	016	39 53	052	43 59	146	45 03	206	33 09	273	27 14	310	32 30	332
261	23 56	016	40 36	051	44 29	147	44 39	207	32 14	272	26 32	310	32 04	331
262	24 10	015	41 18	050	44 59	147	44 14	207	31 20	272	25 50	309	31 37	330
263	24 23	014	42 00	049	45 29	147	43 50	207	30 26	271	25 07	308	31 10	329
264	24 36	013	42 41	049	45 58	148	43 25	208	29 31	271	24 24	307	30 42	329
265	24 48	012	43 21	048	46 27	148	42 59	208	28 37	271	23 41	307	30 13	328
266	24 59	011	44 01	047	46 56	148	42 34	208	27 43	270	22 57	306	29 44	327
267	25 10	011	44 40	045	47 24	149	42 08	209	26 48	270	22 13	305	29 14	326
268	25 19	010	45 19	044	47 52	149	41 42	209	25 54	269	21 29	305	28 43	325
269	25 28	009	45 56	043	48 20	150	41 15	209	25 00	269	20 44	304	28 11	324

LHA ♈	VEGA Hc	Zn	◆ALTAIR Hc	Zn	FOMALHAUT Hc	Zn	◆Peacock Hc	Zn	RIGIL KENT Hc	Zn	◆ANTARES Hc	Zn	Alphecca Hc	Zn
270	25 36	008	46 33	042	24 41	113	48 47	150	40 49	209	69 47	261	27 39	323
271	25 43	007	47 09	041	25 31	112	49 14	151	40 22	210	68 53	261	27 07	323
272	25 50	006	47 45	040	26 21	112	49 40	151	39 55	210	67 59	261	26 33	322
273	25 55	006	48 19	039	27 12	112	50 07	152	39 28	210	67 06	261	26 00	321
274	26 00	005	48 53	037	28 02	112	50 32	152	39 00	210	66 12	261	25 25	320
275	26 04	004	49 25	036	28 53	111	50 57	153	38 33	211	65 18	261	24 50	320
276	26 07	003	49 57	035	29 43	111	51 22	153	38 05	211	64 25	261	24 15	319
277	26 10	002	50 27	034	30 34	111	51 46	154	37 37	211	63 31	260	23 39	318
278	26 11	001	50 57	032	31 25	111	52 10	155	37 09	211	62 37	260	23 02	317
279	26 12	000	51 25	031	32 16	110	52 33	155	36 41	211	61 44	260	22 25	317
280	26 12	359	51 53	029	33 07	110	52 55	156	36 13	211	60 50	260	21 48	316
281	26 11	359	52 19	028	33 58	110	53 17	157	35 44	212	59 57	260	21 10	315
282	26 09	358	52 44	027	34 49	110	53 39	157	35 16	212	59 03	260	20 31	315
283	26 07	357	53 07	025	35 40	110	54 00	158	34 47	212	58 10	260	19 52	314
284	26 03	356	53 30	023	36 32	109	54 20	159	34 18	212	57 16	259	19 13	313

LHA ♈	◆DENEB Hc	Zn	FOMALHAUT Hc	Zn	◆ACHERNAR Hc	Zn	RIGIL KENT Hc	Zn	◆ANTARES Hc	Zn	Rasalhague Hc	Zn	VEGA Hc	Zn
285	15 56	018	37 23	109	15 52	146	33 50	212	56 23	259	47 11	329	25 59	355
286	16 13	018	38 14	109	16 22	146	33 21	212	55 29	259	46 42	328	25 54	354
287	16 29	017	39 06	109	16 53	146	32 52	212	54 36	259	46 13	326	25 48	353
288	16 45	016	39 57	109	17 23	146	32 23	212	53 43	259	45 42	325	25 41	353
289	17 00	016	40 49	108	17 54	145	31 54	212	52 49	259	45 11	324	25 34	352
290	17 14	015	41 41	108	18 25	145	31 25	212	51 56	258	44 38	323	25 26	351
291	17 28	014	42 32	108	18 56	145	30 56	212	51 03	258	44 05	322	25 17	350
292	17 41	014	43 24	108	19 27	145	30 26	212	50 10	258	43 31	321	25 07	349
293	17 53	013	44 16	108	19 59	145	29 57	212	49 16	258	42 56	320	24 56	348
294	18 05	012	45 08	108	20 30	145	29 28	212	48 23	258	42 21	319	24 45	347
295	18 16	011	45 59	107	21 02	144	28 59	212	47 30	257	41 44	318	24 33	347
296	18 26	011	46 51	107	21 33	144	28 30	212	46 37	257	41 07	316	24 20	346
297	18 36	010	47 43	107	22 05	144	28 01	212	45 44	257	40 29	316	24 06	345
298	18 45	009	48 35	107	22 37	144	27 31	212	44 51	257	39 51	315	23 52	344
299	18 53	009	49 27	107	23 09	144	27 02	212	43 58	257	39 12	314	23 36	343

LHA ♈	DENEB Hc	Zn	Enif Hc	Zn	◆FOMALHAUT Hc	Zn	ACHERNAR Hc	Zn	◆RIGIL KENT Hc	Zn	ANTARES Hc	Zn	◆VEGA Hc	Zn
300	19 01	008	46 42	039	50 19	107	23 41	144	26 33	212	43 06	256	23 20	343
301	19 08	007	47 16	038	51 11	107	24 13	144	26 04	212	42 13	256	23 04	342
302	19 15	006	47 49	037	52 03	107	24 45	144	25 35	212	41 20	256	22 46	341
303	19 20	006	48 22	036	52 55	107	25 17	144	25 06	212	40 27	256	22 28	340
304	19 25	005	48 53	035	53 48	107	25 50	144	24 37	212	39 35	255	22 10	339
305	19 29	004	49 23	033	54 40	106	26 22	143	24 08	212	38 42	255	21 50	339
306	19 33	003	49 52	032	55 32	106	26 54	143	23 39	212	37 50	255	21 30	338
307	19 36	003	50 21	031	56 24	106	27 27	143	23 11	212	36 57	255	21 09	337
308	19 38	002	50 48	029	57 16	106	27 59	143	22 42	212	36 05	254	20 48	336
309	19 39	001	51 14	028	58 08	106	28 32	143	22 13	212	35 12	254	20 26	336
310	19 40	000	51 38	026	59 01	106	29 04	143	21 45	212	34 20	254	20 03	335
311	19 40	000	52 02	025	59 53	106	29 37	143	21 16	211	33 28	254	19 40	334
312	19 39	359	52 24	023	60 45	106	30 09	143	20 48	211	32 36	253	19 16	334
313	19 38	358	52 45	022	61 37	106	30 42	143	20 20	211	31 44	253	18 52	333
314	19 36	357	53 05	020	62 29	106	31 14	143	19 52	211	30 52	253	18 26	332

LHA ♈	Alpheratz Hc	Zn	◆Diphda Hc	Zn	ACHERNAR Hc	Zn	◆Peacock Hc	Zn	ANTARES Hc	Zn	◆ALTAIR Hc	Zn	DENEB Hc	Zn
315	19 19	043	37 40	094	31 47	143	57 45	189	30 00	253	52 13	332	19 33	357
316	19 56	042	38 34	094	32 19	143	57 37	190	29 08	252	51 46	330	19 29	356
317	20 32	042	39 29	093	32 52	143	57 27	191	28 16	252	51 19	329	19 25	355
318	21 08	041	40 23	093	33 24	143	57 17	191	27 24	252	50 50	327	19 20	354
319	21 43	040	41 17	092	33 57	143	57 05	192	26 33	252	50 20	326	19 14	354
320	22 18	039	42 12	092	34 29	144	56 53	193	25 41	251	49 49	325	19 08	353
321	22 52	039	43 06	092	35 01	144	56 40	194	24 50	251	49 17	324	19 01	352
322	23 26	038	44 00	091	35 33	144	56 26	195	23 58	251	48 45	322	18 53	351
323	23 59	037	44 55	091	36 06	144	56 12	196	23 07	250	48 11	321	18 45	351
324	24 32	036	45 49	090	36 38	144	55 56	197	22 16	250	47 36	320	18 36	350
325	25 04	036	46 44	090	37 10	144	55 40	198	21 25	250	47 01	319	18 26	349
326	25 35	035	47 38	090	37 41	144	55 23	199	20 34	249	46 24	318	18 16	349
327	26 06	034	48 32	089	38 13	144	55 05	199	19 43	249	45 47	316	18 04	348
328	26 36	033	49 27	089	38 45	145	54 47	200	18 52	249	45 09	315	17 53	347
329	27 06	033	50 21	088	39 16	145	54 28	201	18 01	249	44 31	314	17 40	346

LHA ♈	◆Alpheratz Hc	Zn	Diphda Hc	Zn	◆ACHERNAR Hc	Zn	Peacock Hc	Zn	◆Nunki Hc	Zn	ALTAIR Hc	Zn	DENEB Hc	Zn
330	27 35	032	51 15	088	39 48	145	54 08	202	48 46	258	43 51	313	17 27	346
331	28 03	031	52 10	087	40 19	145	53 47	202	47 53	258	43 12	312	17 14	345
332	28 31	030	53 04	087	40 50	145	53 26	203	47 00	258	42 31	311	16 59	344
333	28 57	029	53 58	086	41 21	146	53 05	204	46 07	257	41 50	310	16 44	344
334	29 24	028	54 53	086	41 51	146	52 42	205	45 14	257	41 08	309	16 29	343
335	29 49	027	55 47	085	42 22	146	52 19	205	44 21	257	40 26	308	16 12	342
336	30 14	027	56 41	085	42 52	146	51 56	206	43 28	257	39 43	308	15 56	342
337	30 38	026	57 35	084	43 22	147	51 32	206	42 35	256	38 59	307	15 38	341
338	31 01	025	58 29	084	43 52	147	51 08	207	41 42	256	38 16	306	15 20	340
339	31 23	024	59 23	083	44 22	147	50 43	208	40 50	256	37 31	305	15 02	340
340	31 45	023	60 17	082	44 51	148	50 17	208	39 57	256	36 47	304	14 42	339
341	32 06	022	61 11	082	45 20	148	49 51	209	39 04	255	36 01	303	14 23	338
342	32 26	021	62 05	081	45 49	148	49 25	209	38 12	255	35 16	303	14 02	338
343	32 45	020	62 58	080	46 17	149	48 58	210	37 19	255	34 30	302	13 41	337
344	33 03	019	63 52	080	46 45	149	48 31	210	36 27	255	33 43	301	13 20	336

LHA ♈	Alpheratz Hc	Zn	◆Hamal Hc	Zn	◆ACHERNAR Hc	Zn	Peacock Hc	Zn	Nunki Hc	Zn	◆ALTAIR Hc	Zn	Enif Hc	Zn
345	33 20	018	23 27	047	47 13	149	48 04	211	35 34	255	32 57	300	50 33	330
346	33 37	017	24 06	046	47 41	150	47 36	211	34 42	254	32 10	300	50 06	329
347	33 52	016	24 45	046	48 08	150	47 08	211	33 49	254	31 22	299	49 37	327
348	34 07	015	25 24	045	48 34	151	46 39	212	32 57	254	30 34	298	49 07	326
349	34 21	014	26 02	044	49 01	151	46 10	212	32 05	253	29 46	298	48 36	325
350	34 33	013	26 40	043	49 27	152	45 41	213	31 13	253	28 58	297	48 04	324
351	34 45	012	27 17	043	49 52	152	45 11	213	30 21	253	28 09	296	47 32	322
352	34 56	011	27 53	042	50 17	153	44 42	213	29 29	253	27 21	296	46 58	321
353	35 06	010	28 29	041	50 42	153	44 12	214	28 37	252	26 31	295	46 23	320
354	35 15	009	29 05	040	51 06	154	43 42	214	27 45	252	25 42	294	45 48	319
355	35 23	008	29 39	039	51 30	155	43 11	214	26 54	252	24 52	294	45 12	318
356	35 29	007	30 14	039	51 53	155	42 40	214	26 02	252	24 03	293	44 35	317
357	35 35	006	30 47	038	52 15	156	42 09	215	25 10	251	23 13	293	43 57	316
358	35 40	005	31 20	037	52 37	156	41 38	215	24 19	251	22 22	292	43 19	315
359	35 44	004	31 53	036	52 59	157	41 07	215	23 28	251	21 32	292	42 40	314

LHA ♈	Hc	Zn	Hc	Zn	Hc	Zn	Hc	Zn	Hc	Zn	Hc	Zn	Hc	Zn
	◆ Alpheratz		Hamal		◆ RIGEL		CANOPUS		ACHERNAR		◆ Peacock		Enif	
0	34 47	002	31 35	035	13 35	093	16 56	141	54 15	157	41 24	216	41 19	313
1	34 49	001	32 05	034	14 29	092	17 30	141	54 36	158	40 53	216	40 39	312
2	34 50	000	32 35	033	15 23	092	18 04	141	54 55	159	40 21	216	39 59	311
3	34 49	359	33 04	032	16 17	091	18 38	140	55 15	160	39 49	216	39 18	310
4	34 48	358	33 32	031	17 11	091	19 13	140	55 33	160	39 17	217	38 37	309
5	34 46	357	34 00	030	18 05	090	19 47	140	55 51	161	38 44	217	37 55	309
6	34 43	356	34 27	029	18 59	090	20 22	140	56 08	162	38 12	217	37 13	308
7	34 39	355	34 52	028	19 53	090	20 57	140	56 24	163	37 40	217	36 30	307
8	34 33	354	35 17	027	20 47	089	21 32	139	56 40	164	37 07	217	35 46	306
9	34 27	353	35 42	026	21 41	089	22 07	139	56 55	165	36 34	217	35 03	305
10	34 20	352	36 05	025	22 35	088	22 43	139	57 09	165	36 02	217	34 18	304
11	34 12	351	36 28	024	23 28	088	23 18	139	57 22	166	35 29	217	33 34	304
12	34 03	350	36 49	023	24 22	087	23 53	139	57 34	167	34 56	217	32 48	303
13	33 53	349	37 10	022	25 16	087	24 29	139	57 46	168	34 23	218	32 03	302
14	33 42	348	37 30	021	26 10	086	25 05	139	57 56	169	33 50	218	31 17	301
	◆ Hamal		ALDEBARAN		RIGEL		◆ CANOPUS		ACHERNAR		◆ FOMALHAUT		Alpheratz	
15	37 48	020	22 17	057	27 04	086	25 40	138	58 06	170	62 58	255	33 30	347
16	38 06	019	23 02	057	27 58	085	26 16	138	58 15	171	62 06	255	33 17	346
17	38 23	018	23 47	056	28 51	085	26 52	138	58 22	172	61 13	255	33 03	345
18	38 39	017	24 32	055	29 45	084	27 28	138	58 29	173	60 21	255	32 48	344
19	38 54	015	25 16	055	30 39	084	28 04	138	58 35	174	59 29	255	32 33	343
20	39 07	014	26 00	054	31 32	083	28 40	138	58 40	175	58 37	255	32 16	342
21	39 20	013	26 43	053	32 26	083	29 17	138	58 44	176	57 45	255	31 59	341
22	39 32	012	27 26	052	33 19	082	29 53	138	58 47	177	56 53	255	31 41	340
23	39 42	011	28 08	052	34 13	082	30 29	138	58 49	178	56 00	255	31 22	339
24	39 52	010	28 50	051	35 06	081	31 05	138	58 50	179	55 08	255	31 02	338
25	40 00	008	29 32	050	35 59	081	31 42	138	58 50	180	54 16	255	30 41	337
26	40 08	007	30 13	049	36 53	080	32 18	138	58 49	182	53 24	255	30 19	336
27	40 14	006	30 54	049	37 46	080	32 54	138	58 47	183	52 32	255	29 57	335
28	40 19	005	31 34	048	38 39	079	33 31	138	58 45	184	51 40	254	29 34	334
29	40 23	004	32 14	047	39 32	079	34 07	138	58 41	185	50 48	254	29 10	333
	Hamal		ALDEBARAN		◆ SIRIUS		CANOPUS		◆ ACHERNAR		FOMALHAUT		◆ Alpheratz	
30	40 26	002	32 53	046	23 35	098	34 43	138	58 36	186	49 56	254	28 45	332
31	40 27	001	33 32	045	24 28	097	35 20	138	58 30	187	49 05	254	28 20	332
32	40 28	000	34 10	044	25 22	097	35 56	138	58 23	188	48 13	254	27 54	331
33	40 27	359	34 47	044	26 15	097	36 32	138	58 16	189	47 21	254	27 27	330
34	40 26	358	35 24	043	27 09	096	37 09	138	58 07	190	46 29	254	27 00	329
35	40 23	356	36 00	042	28 02	096	37 45	138	57 57	191	45 37	253	26 32	328
36	40 19	355	36 36	041	28 56	096	38 21	138	57 47	192	44 46	253	26 03	327
37	40 14	354	37 11	040	29 50	095	38 57	138	57 36	193	43 54	253	25 34	327
38	40 08	353	37 45	039	30 44	095	39 33	138	57 24	194	43 03	253	25 04	326
39	40 00	352	38 19	038	31 37	094	40 09	138	57 11	194	42 11	253	24 33	325
40	39 52	350	38 51	037	32 31	094	40 45	138	56 57	195	41 20	252	24 02	324
41	39 43	349	39 23	036	33 25	094	41 21	139	56 42	196	40 28	252	23 30	323
42	39 32	348	39 55	035	34 19	093	41 56	139	56 27	197	39 37	252	22 57	323
43	39 20	347	40 25	034	35 13	093	42 32	139	56 10	198	38 46	252	22 25	322
44	39 08	346	40 54	033	36 06	092	43 07	139	55 53	199	37 55	252	21 51	321
	◆ ALDEBARAN		BETELGEUSE		SIRIUS		◆ CANOPUS		ACHERNAR		◆ FOMALHAUT		Hamal	
45	41 23	032	35 47	058	37 00	092	43 42	139	55 36	200	37 03	251	38 54	345
46	41 51	030	36 32	057	37 54	092	44 17	140	55 17	200	36 12	251	38 39	344
47	42 18	029	37 17	057	38 48	091	44 52	140	54 58	201	35 21	251	38 23	342
48	42 44	028	38 02	056	39 42	091	45 27	140	54 38	202	34 30	251	38 06	341
49	43 09	027	38 47	055	40 36	090	46 02	140	54 18	203	33 40	250	37 49	340
50	43 33	026	39 30	054	41 30	090	46 36	141	53 57	203	32 49	250	37 30	339
51	43 56	025	40 14	053	42 24	089	47 10	141	53 35	204	31 58	250	37 10	338
52	44 18	023	40 57	052	43 18	089	47 44	141	53 13	205	31 07	250	36 49	337
53	44 38	022	41 39	051	44 12	088	48 18	142	52 50	205	30 17	249	36 28	336
54	44 58	021	42 21	050	45 06	088	48 51	142	52 27	206	29 26	249	36 05	335
55	45 17	020	43 02	049	46 00	087	49 24	142	52 03	207	28 36	249	35 42	334
56	45 34	018	43 43	048	46 53	087	49 57	143	51 39	207	27 46	249	35 18	333
57	45 50	017	44 23	047	47 47	087	50 30	143	51 14	208	26 56	248	34 53	332
58	46 05	016	45 02	046	48 41	086	51 02	144	50 49	208	26 05	248	34 27	331
59	46 19	014	45 40	045	49 35	085	51 34	144	50 23	209	25 15	248	34 00	330
	ALDEBARAN		BETELGEUSE		◆ SIRIUS		CANOPUS		◆ ACHERNAR		FOMALHAUT		◆ Hamal	
60	46 32	013	46 18	044	50 29	085	52 05	145	49 57	209	24 26	248	33 33	329
61	46 43	011	46 56	043	51 22	084	52 36	145	49 30	210	23 36	247	33 04	328
62	46 53	010	47 32	042	52 16	084	53 07	146	49 03	210	22 46	247	32 36	327
63	47 02	009	48 07	041	53 09	083	53 37	146	48 36	211	21 56	247	32 06	326
64	47 10	007	48 42	039	54 03	083	54 07	147	48 08	211	21 07	246	31 35	325
65	47 16	006	49 16	038	54 56	082	54 36	147	47 40	211	20 18	246	31 04	324
66	47 21	005	49 49	037	55 50	081	55 05	148	47 12	212	19 28	246	30 33	323
67	47 24	003	50 21	036	56 43	081	55 34	149	46 43	212	18 39	246	30 00	323
68	47 27	002	50 51	034	57 36	080	56 01	149	46 14	213	17 50	245	29 27	322
69	47 28	000	51 21	033	58 29	079	56 29	150	45 45	213	17 01	245	28 53	321
70	47 27	359	51 50	031	59 22	079	56 55	151	45 16	213	16 12	245	28 19	320
71	47 26	357	52 18	030	60 15	078	57 21	152	44 46	214	15 24	244	27 44	319
72	47 22	356	52 44	029	61 08	077	57 47	152	44 16	214	14 35	244	27 09	319
73	47 18	355	53 09	027	62 00	076	58 11	153	43 46	214	13 47	244	26 33	318
74	47 12	353	53 33	026	62 53	076	58 35	154	43 16	214	12 59	243	25 56	317
	BETELGEUSE		PROCYON		◆ Suhail		CANOPUS		◆ ACHERNAR		Hamal		◆ ALDEBARAN	
75	53 56	024	40 14	057	37 20	126	58 58	155	42 45	215	25 19	316	47 05	352
76	54 17	022	40 59	056	38 04	126	59 21	156	42 14	215	24 42	315	46 57	350
77	54 37	021	41 43	055	38 47	126	59 42	157	41 43	215	24 04	315	46 47	349
78	54 55	019	42 27	054	39 31	126	60 03	158	41 12	215	23 25	314	46 36	348
79	55 13	018	43 11	053	40 14	126	60 23	159	40 41	216	22 46	313	46 24	346
80	55 28	016	43 54	052	40 58	126	60 42	160	40 09	216	22 07	313	46 11	345
81	55 42	014	44 37	052	41 41	126	61 00	161	39 38	216	21 27	312	45 56	344
82	55 54	012	45 19	051	42 25	126	61 17	162	39 06	216	20 47	311	45 41	342
83	56 05	011	46 00	049	43 08	126	61 33	163	38 34	216	20 06	311	45 24	341
84	56 14	009	46 40	048	43 51	126	61 48	164	38 02	216	19 25	310	45 05	340
85	56 22	007	47 20	047	44 35	126	62 02	166	37 30	216	18 43	309	44 46	338
86	56 28	005	48 00	046	45 18	127	62 15	167	36 58	217	18 01	309	44 26	337
87	56 32	004	48 38	045	46 01	127	62 26	168	36 26	217	17 19	308	44 04	336
88	56 35	002	49 16	044	46 45	127	62 37	169	35 54	217	16 37	308	43 42	335
89	56 35	000	49 53	043	47 28	127	62 46	171	35 21	217	15 54	307	43 18	333

LHA ♈	Hc	Zn	Hc	Zn	Hc	Zn	Hc	Zn	Hc	Zn	Hc	Zn	Hc	Zn
	POLLUX		◆ REGULUS		ACRUX		◆ CANOPUS		ACHERNAR		◆ RIGEL		BETELGEUSE	
90	30 17	027	18 35	066	20 03	152	62 55	172	34 49	217	69 15	327	56 35	358
91	30 41	026	19 24	065	20 29	151	63 02	173	34 17	217	68 45	325	56 32	356
92	31 04	025	20 13	065	20 54	151	63 07	175	33 44	217	68 13	323	56 28	355
93	31 27	024	21 02	064	21 20	151	63 12	176	33 12	217	67 39	320	56 22	353
94	31 49	023	21 50	064	21 47	151	63 15	177	32 39	217	67 04	318	56 14	351
95	32 10	023	22 38	063	22 13	151	63 17	179	32 07	217	66 28	316	56 05	349
96	32 30	022	23 26	063	22 39	151	63 18	180	31 34	217	65 50	314	55 54	348
97	32 50	021	24 14	062	23 05	151	63 17	181	31 02	217	65 11	313	55 42	346
98	33 08	020	25 01	061	23 32	151	63 15	183	30 29	217	64 30	311	55 28	344
99	33 26	019	25 48	061	23 59	150	63 12	184	29 57	217	63 49	309	55 12	342
100	33 43	018	26 35	060	24 25	150	63 08	185	29 24	217	63 07	308	54 55	341
101	33 59	017	27 22	059	24 52	150	63 02	187	28 52	217	62 24	306	54 37	339
102	34 14	016	28 08	059	25 19	150	62 56	188	28 19	217	61 40	305	54 17	338
103	34 28	015	28 54	058	25 46	150	62 48	189	27 47	217	60 55	303	53 56	336
104	34 41	014	29 39	057	26 12	150	62 38	190	27 14	217	60 10	302	53 33	334
	POLLUX		◆ REGULUS		Gienah		◆ ACRUX		CANOPUS		◆ RIGEL		BETELGEUSE	
105	34 53	012	30 25	056	17 06	102	26 39	150	62 28	192	59 24	301	53 09	333
106	35 04	011	31 09	056	17 59	101	27 06	150	62 16	193	58 37	300	52 44	331
107	35 14	010	31 54	055	18 52	101	27 33	150	62 04	194	57 50	299	52 17	330
108	35 23	009	32 38	054	19 45	101	28 00	150	61 50	195	57 03	297	51 50	328
109	35 31	008	33 21	053	20 38	100	28 27	150	61 35	197	56 15	296	51 21	327
110	35 39	007	34 04	053	21 31	100	28 54	150	61 19	198	55 26	295	50 51	326
111	35 45	006	34 47	052	22 24	099	29 22	150	61 02	199	54 37	294	50 20	324
112	35 50	005	35 29	051	23 17	099	29 49	150	60 45	200	53 48	293	49 48	323
113	35 54	004	36 11	050	24 11	099	30 16	150	60 26	201	52 58	293	49 16	322
114	35 57	003	36 52	049	25 04	098	30 43	150	60 06	202	52 08	292	48 42	321
115	35 59	002	37 33	048	25 57	098	31 10	150	59 45	203	51 18	291	48 07	319
116	36 01	001	38 13	047	26 51	098	31 37	150	59 24	204	50 28	290	47 32	318
117	36 01	000	38 52	047	27 44	097	32 04	150	59 02	205	49 37	289	46 55	317
118	36 00	358	39 31	046	28 38	097	32 31	150	58 39	206	48 46	288	46 18	316
119	35 58	357	40 09	045	29 31	096	32 58	150	58 15	207	47 54	288	45 40	315
	◆ REGULUS		SPICA		◆ ACRUX		CANOPUS		◆ RIGEL		BETELGEUSE		POLLUX	
120	40 47	044	12 28	097	33 24	150	57 50	207	47 03	287	45 02	314	35 55	356
121	41 24	043	13 21	096	33 51	150	57 25	208	46 11	286	44 22	313	35 51	355
122	42 00	042	14 15	096	34 18	150	56 59	209	45 19	286	43 42	312	35 45	354
123	42 35	041	15 09	095	34 44	150	56 32	210	44 27	285	43 02	311	35 39	353
124	43 10	039	16 02	095	35 11	151	56 05	211	43 35	284	42 20	310	35 32	352
125	43 44	038	16 56	094	35 37	151	55 38	211	42 43	284	41 39	309	35 24	351
126	44 17	037	17 50	094	36 04	151	55 09	212	41 50	283	40 56	308	35 15	350
127	44 49	036	18 44	094	36 30	151	54 41	213	40 58	282	40 13	307	35 05	349
128	45 20	035	19 38	093	36 56	151	54 11	213	40 05	282	39 30	306	34 54	348
129	45 51	034	20 31	093	37 22	151	53 42	214	39 12	281	38 46	305	34 42	347
130	46 20	033	21 25	092	37 48	151	53 11	214	38 19	281	38 02	304	34 29	346
131	46 49	031	22 19	092	38 14	152	52 41	215	37 26	280	37 17	303	34 15	345
132	47 16	030	23 13	092	38 39	152	52 10	215	36 33	279	36 32	303	34 00	344
133	47 43	029	24 07	091	39 05	152	51 38	216	35 40	279	35 46	302	33 45	343
134	48 08	027	25 01	091	39 30	152	51 06	216	34 46	278	35 00	301	33 28	342
	REGULUS		◆ SPICA		ACRUX		◆ CANOPUS		RIGEL		BETELGEUSE		◆ POLLUX	
135	48 32	026	25 55	090	39 55	152	50 34	217	33 53	278	34 14	300	33 10	341
136	48 55	025	26 49	090	40 20	153	50 02	217	33 00	277	33 27	300	32 52	340
137	49 17	023	27 43	089	40 44	153	49 29	218	32 06	277	32 40	299	32 33	339
138	49 38	022	28 37	089	41 09	153	48 56	218	31 12	276	31 53	298	32 13	338
139	49 58	020	29 30	088	41 33	153	48 22	218	30 19	276	31 05	297	31 52	337
140	50 16	019	30 24	088	41 57	154	47 49	219	29 25	275	30 17	297	31 30	336
141	50 33	018	31 18	088	42 21	154	47 15	219	28 31	275	29 29	296	31 07	335
142	50 48	016	32 12	087	42 44	154	46 41	219	27 38	274	28 40	295	30 44	334
143	51 03	015	33 06	087	43 07	155	46 06	220	26 44	274	27 52	295	30 20	333
144	51 15	013	34 00	086	43 30	155	45 32	220	25 50	273	27 03	294	29 55	332
145	51 27	011	34 54	086	43 53	155	44 57	220	24 56	273	26 13	294	29 29	331
146	51 37	010	35 47	085	44 16	156	44 22	220	24 02	273	25 24	293	29 02	330
147	51 45	008	36 41	085	44 38	156	43 47	221	23 09	272	24 34	292	28 35	329
148	51 53	007	37 35	084	44 59	156	43 12	221	22 15	272	23 44	292	28 08	329
149	51 58	005	38 28	084	45 21	157	42 37	221	21 21	271	22 54	291	27 39	328
	REGULUS		◆ Denebola		SPICA		◆ ACRUX		CANOPUS		◆ SIRIUS		PROCYON	
150	52 02	004	41 30	037	39 22	083	45 42	157	42 01	221	44 07	272	43 56	308
151	52 05	002	42 01	035	40 15	083	46 03	158	41 26	221	43 13	271	43 13	307
152	52 06	000	42 32	034	41 09	082	46 23	158	40 50	222	42 19	271	42 29	306
153	52 06	359	43 02	033	42 02	082	46 43	158	40 14	222	41 25	270	41 45	305
154	52 04	357	43 31	032	42 56	081	47 02	159	39 38	222	40 31	270	41 01	304
155	52 01	356	44 00	031	43 49	080	47 22	159	39 02	222	39 37	269	40 16	303
156	51 56	354	44 27	030	44 42	080	47 40	160	38 26	222	38 43	269	39 30	302
157	51 50	353	44 53	029	45 35	079	47 59	160	37 50	222	37 49	268	38 44	301
158	51 42	351	45 18	027	46 28	079	48 17	161	37 14	222	36 55	268	37 58	301
159	51 33	349	45 42	026	47 21	078	48 34	161	36 38	222	36 01	268	37 12	300
160	51 22	348	46 06	025	48 13	077	48 51	162	36 01	222	35 07	267	36 25	299
161	51 10	346	46 28	023	49 06	077	49 07	163	35 25	222	34 14	267	35 37	298
162	50 57	345	46 49	022	49 58	076	49 23	163	34 49	222	33 20	266	34 50	298
163	50 42	343	47 08	021	50 50	075	49 39	164	34 12	222	32 26	266	34 02	297
164	50 26	342	47 27	019	51 42	074	49 54	164	33 36	222	31 32	266	33 13	296
	ARCTURUS		◆ ANTARES		ACRUX		◆ CANOPUS		SIRIUS		PROCYON		◆ REGULUS	
165	24 23	052	17 25	112	50 08	165	33 00	222	30 38	265	32 25	295	50 08	340
166	25 05	051	18 15	111	50 22	165	32 23	222	29 45	265	31 36	295	49 50	339
167	25 46	050	19 05	111	50 35	166	31 47	222	28 51	264	30 47	294	49 30	338
168	26 28	049	19 56	111	50 48	167	31 11	222	27 57	264	29 57	293	49 08	336
169	27 08	049	20 46	110	51 00	167	30 34	222	27 04	264	29 08	293	48 46	335
170	27 49	048	21 37	110	51 12	168	29 58	222	26 10	263	28 18	292	48 22	333
171	28 29	047	22 28	110	51 23	169	29 22	222	25 17	263	27 28	292	47 58	332
172	29 08	046	23 19	109	51 33	169	28 46	222	24 23	262	26 38	291	47 32	331
173	29 47	046	24 10	109	51 43	170	28 09	222	23 30	262	25 47	290	47 05	329
174	30 25	045	25 01	109	51 52	171	27 33	222	22 36	262	24 56	290	46 37	328
175	31 03	044	25 52	108	52 00	171	26 57	222	21 43	261	24 06	289	46 08	327
176	31 40	043	26 43	108	52 08	172	26 21	222	20 50	261	23 15	289	45 38	326
177	32 17	042	27 34	108	52 15	173	25 46	222	19 56	261	22 23	288	45 07	325
178	32 53	042	28 26	107	52 22	173	25 10	222	19 03	260	21 32	287	44 36	323
179	33 28	041	29 17	107	52 27	174	24 34	221	18 10	260	20 41	287	44 03	322

 LAT 26°S

LHA ♈	Hc Zn	Hc Zn	Hc Zn	Hc Zn	Hc Zn	Hc Zn	Hc Zn
	◆ARCTURUS	ANTARES	◆RIGIL KENT	ACRUX	CANOPUS	◆Alphard	REGULUS
180	34 03 040	30 09 107	45 49 153	52 33 175	23 58 221	50 07 289	43 30 321
181	34 37 039	31 00 107	46 13 154	52 37 176	23 23 221	49 16 288	42 56 320
182	35 11 038	31 52 106	46 37 154	52 41 176	22 48 221	48 24 287	42 21 319
183	35 43 037	32 44 106	47 00 154	52 44 177	22 12 221	47 33 286	41 45 318
184	36 15 036	33 36 106	47 23 155	52 46 178	21 37 221	46 41 286	41 08 317
185	36 47 035	34 28 105	47 46 155	52 48 179	21 02 220	45 49 285	40 31 316
186	37 17 034	35 20 105	48 08 156	52 49 179	20 27 220	44 57 284	39 53 315
187	37 47 033	36 12 105	48 30 156	52 49 180	19 52 220	44 04 284	39 15 314
188	38 16 032	37 04 105	48 52 157	52 49 181	19 18 220	43 12 283	38 36 313
189	38 44 031	37 56 104	49 13 157	52 47 182	18 43 220	42 19 282	37 56 312
190	39 11 030	38 48 104	49 33 158	52 46 182	18 09 220	41 27 282	37 16 311
191	39 38 029	39 41 104	49 53 158	52 43 183	17 34 219	40 34 281	36 35 310
192	40 03 028	40 33 104	50 13 159	52 40 184	17 00 219	39 41 281	35 54 309
193	40 28 027	41 26 103	50 32 160	52 36 185	16 26 219	38 48 280	35 12 309
194	40 51 025	42 18 103	50 51 160	52 31 185	15 53 219	37 55 280	34 29 308
	ARCTURUS	◆Rasalhague	ANTARES	RIGIL KENT	◆ACRUX	Suhail	◆REGULUS
195	41 14 024	12 44 069	43 11 103	51 09 161	52 26 186	40 26 234	33 46 307
196	41 36 023	13 34 069	44 03 103	51 26 161	52 20 187	39 42 234	33 03 306
197	41 56 022	14 25 068	44 56 102	51 43 162	52 13 187	38 59 234	32 19 305
198	42 16 021	15 14 067	45 49 102	51 59 163	52 06 188	38 15 234	31 35 305
199	42 34 020	16 04 067	46 41 102	52 15 163	51 58 189	37 32 234	30 51 304
200	42 52 018	16 54 066	47 34 102	52 30 164	51 49 190	36 48 234	30 06 303
201	43 08 017	17 43 066	48 27 101	52 45 165	51 40 190	36 05 234	29 21 302
202	43 24 016	18 32 065	49 20 101	52 59 165	51 30 191	35 22 234	28 35 302
203	43 38 015	19 21 065	50 13 101	53 12 166	51 20 192	34 38 234	27 49 301
204	43 51 013	20 10 064	51 06 101	53 25 167	51 09 192	33 55 233	27 03 300
205	44 02 012	20 58 064	51 59 100	53 37 168	50 57 193	33 11 233	26 16 300
206	44 13 011	21 46 063	52 52 100	53 48 168	50 45 194	32 28 233	25 29 299
207	44 22 009	22 34 062	53 45 100	53 58 169	50 32 194	31 45 233	24 42 298
208	44 31 008	23 22 062	54 38 100	54 08 170	50 18 195	31 02 233	23 54 298
209	44 38 007	24 09 061	55 31 100	54 17 171	50 04 195	30 19 233	23 06 297
	◆ARCTURUS	Rasalhague	◆Nunki	RIGIL KENT	ACRUX	◆Suhail	Denebola
210	44 43 005	24 56 060	24 33 109	54 25 172	49 50 196	29 36 233	38 36 318
211	44 48 004	25 43 060	25 24 108	54 33 172	49 35 197	28 53 233	38 00 317
212	44 51 003	26 29 059	26 16 108	54 40 173	49 19 197	28 10 233	37 23 316
213	44 53 001	27 15 058	27 07 108	54 46 174	49 03 198	27 27 232	36 45 315
214	44 54 000	28 01 058	27 58 107	54 51 175	48 46 198	26 44 232	36 07 314
215	44 53 359	28 47 057	28 50 107	54 56 176	48 29 199	26 02 232	35 28 314
216	44 51 357	29 32 056	29 42 107	54 59 176	48 12 199	25 19 232	34 49 313
217	44 48 356	30 16 056	30 33 107	55 02 177	47 54 200	24 37 232	34 09 312
218	44 44 355	31 01 055	31 25 106	55 04 178	47 35 200	23 54 232	33 29 311
219	44 39 353	31 45 054	32 17 106	55 06 179	47 16 201	23 12 231	32 48 310
220	44 32 352	32 28 053	33 09 106	55 06 180	46 57 201	22 30 231	32 06 309
221	44 24 351	33 11 053	34 01 105	55 06 181	46 37 202	21 48 231	31 24 309
222	44 15 350	33 54 052	34 53 105	55 05 182	46 17 202	21 06 231	30 42 308
223	44 04 348	34 36 051	35 45 105	55 03 182	45 57 202	20 25 231	29 59 307
224	43 53 347	35 17 050	36 37 105	55 00 183	45 36 203	19 43 230	29 16 306
	Alphecca	Rasalhague	◆Nunki	Peacock	◆RIGIL KENT	SPICA	◆ARCTURUS
225	36 39 010	35 59 049	37 29 104	25 57 143	54 57 184	63 22 299	43 40 346
226	36 48 009	36 39 048	38 21 104	26 29 143	54 53 185	62 34 298	43 26 344
227	36 56 008	37 19 047	39 14 104	27 02 143	54 48 186	61 46 297	43 11 343
228	37 02 007	37 59 047	40 06 103	27 35 143	54 42 187	60 58 296	42 55 342
229	37 08 005	38 37 046	40 59 103	28 08 143	54 35 187	60 09 294	42 38 341
230	37 12 004	39 16 045	41 51 103	28 41 142	54 28 188	59 20 293	42 19 339
231	37 16 003	39 53 044	42 44 103	29 13 142	54 20 189	58 30 292	42 00 338
232	37 18 002	40 30 043	43 36 102	29 46 142	54 11 190	57 40 291	41 39 337
233	37 20 001	41 06 042	44 29 102	30 19 142	54 01 190	56 50 290	41 18 336
234	37 20 000	41 42 041	45 22 102	30 52 142	53 51 191	55 59 290	40 55 335
235	37 19 359	42 17 040	46 15 102	31 25 142	53 40 192	55 08 289	40 32 334
236	37 18 358	42 51 039	47 07 101	31 58 142	53 28 193	54 17 288	40 07 333
237	37 15 356	43 24 037	48 00 101	32 31 142	53 16 194	53 26 287	39 42 331
238	37 11 355	43 56 036	48 53 101	33 04 142	53 03 194	52 34 286	39 16 330
239	37 06 354	44 28 035	49 46 101	33 37 142	52 49 195	51 42 286	38 49 329
	◆VEGA	ALTAIR	◆Peacock	RIGIL KENT	◆SPICA	ARCTURUS	Alphecca
240	15 29 031	23 51 066	34 10 142	52 35 196	50 50 285	38 21 328	37 00 353
241	15 56 030	24 40 066	34 43 142	52 20 196	49 58 284	37 52 327	36 53 352
242	16 23 030	25 29 065	35 15 143	52 04 197	49 05 283	37 22 326	36 45 351
243	16 49 029	26 18 064	35 48 143	51 48 198	48 13 283	36 52 325	36 36 350
244	17 15 028	27 06 064	36 21 143	51 32 198	47 20 282	36 21 324	36 26 349
245	17 40 027	27 54 063	36 54 143	51 14 199	46 27 281	35 49 323	36 15 348
246	18 05 027	28 42 062	37 26 143	50 56 200	45 35 281	35 16 322	36 03 347
247	18 29 026	29 30 062	37 59 143	50 38 200	44 42 280	34 43 321	35 50 345
248	18 52 025	30 17 061	38 31 143	50 19 201	43 48 280	34 09 320	35 36 344
249	19 15 025	31 04 060	39 03 143	50 00 201	42 55 279	33 34 320	35 21 343
250	19 37 024	31 51 060	39 35 143	49 40 202	42 02 278	32 59 319	35 05 342
251	19 59 023	32 37 059	40 08 144	49 19 202	41 08 278	32 23 318	34 48 341
252	20 20 022	33 23 058	40 39 144	48 58 203	40 15 277	31 46 317	34 30 340
253	20 40 022	34 09 057	41 11 144	48 37 204	39 22 277	31 09 316	34 11 339
254	21 00 021	34 54 057	41 43 144	48 15 204	38 28 276	30 32 315	33 52 338
	◆VEGA	ALTAIR	FOMALHAUT	◆Peacock	RIGIL KENT	◆SPICA	ARCTURUS
255	21 19 020	35 39 056	12 47 117	42 14 144	47 53 204	37 34 276	29 53 314
256	21 37 019	36 23 055	13 35 117	42 46 145	47 31 205	36 41 275	29 15 314
257	21 55 019	37 07 054	14 24 116	43 17 145	47 08 205	35 47 275	28 35 313
258	22 11 018	37 51 053	15 12 116	43 48 145	46 44 206	34 53 274	27 56 312
259	22 28 017	38 34 052	16 01 116	44 19 145	46 21 206	33 59 274	27 15 311
260	22 43 016	39 16 052	16 50 115	44 49 146	45 57 207	33 06 273	26 35 311
261	22 58 015	39 58 051	17 38 115	45 19 146	45 32 207	32 12 273	25 54 310
262	23 12 015	40 40 050	18 27 115	45 49 146	45 08 207	31 18 272	25 12 309
263	23 25 014	41 21 049	19 17 114	46 19 147	44 43 208	30 24 272	24 30 308
264	23 38 013	42 01 048	20 06 114	46 49 147	44 18 208	29 30 272	23 48 308
265	23 49 012	42 40 047	20 55 114	47 18 147	43 52 208	28 36 271	23 05 307
266	24 00 011	43 19 046	21 45 113	47 47 148	43 26 209	27 42 271	22 22 306
267	24 11 011	43 58 045	22 34 113	48 15 148	43 00 209	26 48 270	21 38 306
268	24 20 010	44 35 044	23 24 113	48 44 149	42 34 209	25 54 270	20 54 305
269	24 29 009	45 12 043	24 14 112	49 11 149	42 07 210	25 00 269	20 10 305

LHA ♈	Hc Zn	Hc Zn	Hc Zn	Hc Zn	Hc Zn	Hc Zn	Hc Zn
	VEGA	◆ALTAIR	FOMALHAUT	◆Peacock	RIGIL KENT	◆ANTARES	Alphecca
270	24 37 008	45 48 042	25 04 112	49 39 150	41 41 210	69 55 264	26 51 324
271	24 44 007	46 24 040	25 54 112	50 06 150	41 14 210	69 01 264	26 19 323
272	24 50 006	46 58 039	26 44 112	50 33 151	40 47 210	68 08 263	25 46 322
273	24 56 005	47 32 038	27 34 111	50 59 151	40 19 211	67 14 263	25 13 321
274	25 00 005	48 05 037	28 24 111	51 25 152	39 52 211	66 20 263	24 39 321
275	25 04 004	48 37 036	29 14 111	51 50 152	39 24 211	65 27 263	24 04 320
276	25 08 003	49 07 034	30 05 111	52 15 153	38 56 211	64 33 263	23 29 319
277	25 10 002	49 37 033	30 55 110	52 40 153	38 28 211	63 40 262	22 54 318
278	25 11 001	50 06 032	31 46 110	53 04 154	38 00 212	62 47 262	22 18 318
279	25 12 000	50 34 030	32 37 110	53 27 155	37 32 212	61 53 262	21 41 317
280	25 12 359	51 00 029	33 27 110	53 50 155	37 04 212	61 00 262	21 04 316
281	25 11 359	51 26 027	34 18 109	54 12 156	36 35 212	60 06 262	20 27 316
282	25 09 358	51 50 026	35 09 109	54 34 157	36 07 212	59 13 261	19 49 315
283	25 07 357	52 13 024	36 00 109	54 55 157	35 38 212	58 20 261	19 10 314
284	25 03 356	52 34 023	36 51 109	55 15 158	35 09 212	57 26 261	18 32 314
	◆DENEB	FOMALHAUT	◆ACHERNAR	RIGIL KENT	◆ANTARES	Rasalhague	VEGA
285	14 59 018	37 42 108	16 42 146	34 40 212	56 33 261	46 20 329	24 59 355
286	15 16 018	38 34 108	17 12 146	34 11 212	55 40 261	45 52 328	24 54 354
287	15 32 017	39 25 108	17 42 146	33 42 213	54 47 260	45 23 327	24 49 353
288	15 47 016	40 16 108	18 13 145	33 13 213	53 54 260	44 53 326	24 42 353
289	16 02 016	41 07 108	18 44 145	32 44 213	53 01 260	44 22 325	24 35 352
290	16 16 015	41 59 107	19 14 145	32 15 213	52 08 260	43 50 323	24 26 351
291	16 29 014	42 50 107	19 45 145	31 46 213	51 15 259	43 18 322	24 18 350
292	16 42 013	43 42 107	20 16 145	31 17 213	50 22 259	42 45 321	24 08 349
293	16 55 013	44 34 107	20 48 145	30 48 213	49 29 259	42 10 320	23 57 348
294	17 06 012	45 25 107	21 19 144	30 19 213	48 36 259	41 36 319	23 46 348
295	17 17 011	46 17 106	21 50 144	29 49 213	47 43 258	41 00 318	23 34 347
296	17 27 011	47 09 106	22 22 144	29 20 213	46 50 258	40 23 317	23 21 346
297	17 37 010	48 00 106	22 54 144	28 51 213	45 57 258	39 46 316	23 08 345
298	17 46 009	48 52 106	23 25 144	28 22 213	45 05 258	39 09 315	22 54 344
299	17 54 008	49 44 106	23 57 144	27 53 213	44 12 257	38 30 314	22 39 344
	DENEB	Enif	◆FOMALHAUT	ACHERNAR	◆RIGIL KENT	ANTARES	◆VEGA
300	18 02 008	45 55 039	50 36 106	24 29 144	27 24 213	43 19 257	22 23 343
301	18 09 007	46 29 038	51 28 106	25 01 144	26 55 213	42 27 257	22 07 342
302	18 15 006	47 01 036	52 20 105	25 33 143	26 26 213	41 34 257	21 50 341
303	18 20 006	47 33 035	53 12 105	26 05 143	25 57 212	40 42 256	21 32 340
304	18 25 005	48 03 034	54 04 105	26 38 143	25 28 212	39 49 256	21 14 340
305	18 29 004	48 33 033	54 56 105	27 10 143	24 59 212	38 57 256	20 54 339
306	18 33 003	49 01 031	55 48 105	27 42 143	24 30 212	38 05 256	20 35 338
307	18 36 003	49 29 030	56 40 105	28 15 143	24 01 212	37 13 255	20 14 337
308	18 38 002	49 55 029	57 32 105	28 47 143	23 33 212	36 20 255	19 53 337
309	18 39 001	50 20 027	58 24 105	29 20 143	23 04 212	35 28 255	19 31 336
310	18 40 000	50 45 026	59 17 105	29 52 143	22 36 212	34 36 255	19 09 335
311	18 40 000	51 07 024	60 09 105	30 25 143	22 07 212	33 44 254	18 46 334
312	18 39 359	51 29 023	61 01 105	30 57 143	21 39 212	32 52 254	18 22 334
313	18 38 358	51 49 021	61 53 105	31 30 143	21 11 211	32 01 254	17 58 333
314	18 36 357	52 08 020	62 45 105	32 02 143	20 43 211	31 09 253	17 33 332
	Alpheratz	◆Diphda	ACHERNAR	◆RIGIL KENT	ANTARES	◆ALTAIR	DENEB
315	18 35 043	37 44 093	32 35 143	20 15 211	30 17 253	51 20 332	18 33 357
316	19 11 042	38 38 093	33 07 143	19 47 211	29 26 253	50 54 331	18 29 356
317	19 47 041	39 32 092	33 40 143	19 20 211	28 34 253	50 27 329	18 25 355
318	20 22 041	40 26 092	34 12 143	18 52 211	27 43 252	49 59 328	18 20 354
319	20 57 040	41 19 092	34 45 143	18 25 210	26 51 252	49 30 327	18 15 354
320	21 31 039	42 13 091	35 17 143	17 57 210	26 00 252	49 00 325	18 08 353
321	22 05 038	43 07 091	35 49 143	17 30 210	25 09 251	48 29 324	18 02 352
322	22 38 038	44 01 090	36 22 143	17 03 210	24 18 251	47 57 323	17 54 352
323	23 11 037	44 55 090	36 54 143	16 37 210	23 27 251	47 24 322	17 46 351
324	23 43 036	45 49 089	37 26 144	16 10 209	22 36 250	46 50 321	17 37 350
325	24 15 035	46 43 089	37 58 144	15 44 209	21 45 250	46 15 319	17 27 349
326	24 46 035	47 37 088	38 30 144	15 17 209	20 55 250	45 40 318	17 17 349
327	25 16 034	48 31 088	39 02 144	14 51 209	20 04 250	45 03 317	17 06 348
328	25 46 033	49 25 088	39 33 144	14 25 209	19 14 249	44 26 316	16 54 347
329	26 15 032	50 19 087	40 05 144	14 00 208	18 23 249	43 49 315	16 42 347
	◆Alpheratz	Diphda	◆ACHERNAR	Peacock	◆Nunki	ALTAIR	Enif
330	26 44 031	51 12 087	40 36 144	55 04 202	48 58 259	43 10 314	53 52 354
331	27 11 031	52 06 086	41 08 145	54 43 203	48 05 259	42 31 313	53 45 352
332	27 39 030	53 00 085	41 39 145	54 21 204	47 13 259	41 51 312	53 37 350
333	28 05 029	53 54 085	42 10 145	53 59 204	46 20 258	41 11 311	53 27 349
334	28 31 028	54 47 084	42 41 145	53 37 205	45 27 258	40 30 310	53 16 347
335	28 56 027	55 41 084	43 11 146	53 14 206	44 34 258	39 48 309	53 03 346
336	29 20 026	56 35 083	43 42 146	52 50 206	43 42 258	39 06 308	52 49 344
337	29 44 025	57 28 083	44 12 146	52 26 207	42 49 257	38 23 307	52 34 342
338	30 06 025	58 22 082	44 42 146	52 01 208	41 56 257	37 40 306	52 17 341
339	30 28 024	59 15 081	45 12 147	51 36 208	41 04 257	36 57 306	51 58 339
340	30 50 023	60 08 081	45 41 147	51 10 209	40 11 257	36 13 305	51 39 338
341	31 10 022	61 01 080	46 11 147	50 44 209	39 19 256	35 28 304	51 17 336
342	31 30 021	61 54 079	46 40 148	50 17 210	38 27 256	34 43 303	50 55 335
343	31 48 020	62 47 078	47 08 148	49 50 210	37 34 256	33 58 302	50 32 333
344	32 06 019	63 40 078	47 37 148	49 23 211	36 42 255	33 12 302	50 07 332
	Alpheratz	◆Hamal	◆ACHERNAR	Peacock	Nunki	◆ALTAIR	Enif
345	32 23 018	22 46 047	48 05 149	48 55 211	35 50 255	32 26 301	49 41 331
346	32 39 017	23 25 046	48 32 149	48 27 212	34 58 255	31 40 300	49 14 329
347	32 55 016	24 03 045	49 00 150	47 59 212	34 06 255	30 53 300	48 46 328
348	33 09 015	24 41 045	49 27 150	47 30 212	33 14 254	30 06 299	48 17 327
349	33 22 014	25 19 044	49 53 151	47 01 213	32 22 254	29 18 298	47 47 325
350	33 35 013	25 56 043	50 19 151	46 31 213	31 30 254	28 31 297	47 16 324
351	33 46 012	26 32 042	50 45 152	46 02 214	30 38 254	27 43 297	46 44 323
352	33 57 011	27 08 041	51 11 152	45 32 214	29 47 253	26 54 296	46 11 322
353	34 07 010	27 44 041	51 35 153	45 02 214	28 55 253	26 06 296	45 37 321
354	34 15 009	28 19 040	52 00 153	44 31 214	28 03 253	25 17 295	45 03 319
355	34 23 008	28 53 039	52 24 154	44 00 215	27 12 252	24 28 294	44 27 318
356	34 30 007	29 27 038	52 47 155	43 30 215	26 21 252	23 39 294	43 51 317
357	34 36 006	30 00 037	53 10 155	42 59 215	25 29 252	22 49 293	43 14 316
358	34 40 005	30 32 037	53 32 156	42 27 216	24 38 251	21 59 293	42 36 315
359	34 44 003	31 04 036	53 54 157	41 56 216	23 47 251	21 10 292	41 58 314

LHA ♈	Hc	Zn	Hc	Zn	Hc	Zn	Hc	Zn	Hc	Zn	Hc	Zn	Hc	Zn
	◆ Alpheratz		Hamal		◆ RIGEL		CANOPUS		ACHERNAR		◆ Peacock		Enif	
0	33 47	002	30 46	034	13 38	092	17 42	141	55 10	157	42 13	216	40 38	314
1	33 49	001	31 16	034	14 31	092	18 16	141	55 31	157	41 41	217	39 59	313
2	33 50	000	31 45	033	15 25	091	18 50	140	55 51	158	41 09	217	39 19	312
3	33 49	359	32 13	032	16 18	091	19 24	140	56 11	159	40 37	217	38 39	311
4	33 48	358	32 41	031	17 12	091	19 59	140	56 30	160	40 05	217	37 59	310
5	33 46	357	33 08	030	18 05	090	20 33	140	56 48	161	39 32	217	37 17	309
6	33 43	356	33 34	029	18 59	090	21 08	139	57 05	161	39 00	217	36 36	308
7	33 39	355	33 59	028	19 52	089	21 43	139	57 22	162	38 27	218	35 54	307
8	33 34	354	34 24	027	20 46	089	22 18	139	57 37	163	37 55	218	35 11	307
9	33 28	353	34 48	026	21 39	088	22 53	139	57 53	164	37 22	218	34 28	306
10	33 21	352	35 11	025	22 32	088	23 28	139	58 07	165	36 49	218	33 44	305
11	33 13	351	35 33	024	23 26	087	24 03	139	58 20	166	36 16	218	33 00	304
12	33 04	350	35 54	023	24 19	087	24 38	138	58 33	167	35 44	218	32 16	303
13	32 54	349	36 14	022	25 13	086	25 14	138	58 44	168	35 11	218	31 31	303
14	32 43	348	36 33	021	26 06	086	25 50	138	58 55	169	34 38	218	30 46	302
	◆ Hamal		ALDEBARAN		RIGEL		◆ CANOPUS		ACHERNAR		◆ FOMALHAUT		Alpheratz	
15	36 52	020	21 45	057	26 59	085	26 25	138	59 05	170	63 12	257	32 31	347
16	37 09	018	22 29	056	27 53	085	27 01	138	59 14	171	62 20	257	32 19	346
17	37 26	017	23 13	056	28 46	084	27 37	138	59 22	172	61 28	257	32 05	345
18	37 41	016	23 57	055	29 39	084	28 13	138	59 29	173	60 35	257	31 51	344
19	37 56	015	24 41	054	30 32	083	28 49	138	59 35	174	59 43	257	31 35	343
20	38 09	014	25 24	053	31 25	083	29 25	138	59 40	175	58 51	257	31 19	342
21	38 22	013	26 07	053	32 18	082	30 01	137	59 44	176	57 59	257	31 02	341
22	38 33	012	26 49	052	33 11	082	30 37	137	59 47	177	57 07	257	30 44	340
23	38 43	011	27 31	051	34 04	081	31 13	137	59 49	178	56 15	256	30 26	339
24	38 53	009	28 12	051	34 57	081	31 50	137	59 50	179	55 23	256	30 06	338
25	39 01	008	28 54	050	35 50	080	32 26	137	59 50	180	54 31	256	29 46	337
26	39 08	007	29 34	049	36 42	080	33 02	137	59 49	182	53 39	256	29 24	336
27	39 14	006	30 14	048	37 35	079	33 39	137	59 47	183	52 48	256	29 03	335
28	39 19	005	30 54	047	38 27	078	34 15	137	59 44	184	51 56	256	28 40	334
29	39 23	004	31 33	047	39 19	078	34 51	137	59 40	185	51 04	256	28 16	334
	Hamal		ALDEBARAN		◆ SIRIUS		CANOPUS		◆ ACHERNAR		FOMALHAUT		◆ Alpheratz	
30	39 26	002	32 11	046	23 43	097	35 28	137	59 36	186	50 12	255	27 52	333
31	39 27	001	32 49	045	24 36	097	36 04	137	59 30	187	49 20	255	27 27	332
32	39 28	000	33 27	044	25 29	097	36 40	137	59 23	188	48 29	255	27 02	331
33	39 27	359	34 04	043	26 22	096	37 17	137	59 15	189	47 37	255	26 35	330
34	39 26	358	34 40	042	27 15	096	37 53	137	59 06	190	46 46	255	26 08	329
35	39 23	356	35 15	041	28 08	095	38 29	137	58 56	191	45 54	254	25 41	328
36	39 19	355	35 50	040	29 02	095	39 05	137	58 46	192	45 03	254	25 12	328
37	39 14	354	36 25	039	29 55	095	39 41	138	58 34	193	44 11	254	24 43	327
38	39 08	353	36 58	038	30 48	094	40 18	138	58 22	194	43 20	254	24 14	326
39	39 01	352	37 31	037	31 42	094	40 54	138	58 09	195	42 29	254	23 44	325
40	38 53	351	38 03	036	32 35	093	41 29	138	57 54	196	41 37	253	23 13	324
41	38 44	349	38 35	035	33 28	093	42 05	138	57 40	197	40 46	253	22 42	324
42	38 33	348	39 05	034	34 22	092	42 41	138	57 24	198	39 55	253	22 10	323
43	38 22	347	39 35	033	35 15	092	43 17	138	57 07	198	39 04	253	21 37	322
44	38 09	346	40 04	032	36 09	092	43 52	138	56 50	199	38 13	252	21 04	321
	◆ ALDEBARAN		BETELGEUSE		SIRIUS		◆ CANOPUS		ACHERNAR		◆ FOMALHAUT		Hamal	
45	40 32	031	35 15	058	37 02	091	44 28	139	56 32	200	37 22	252	37 56	345
46	40 59	030	36 00	057	37 55	091	45 03	139	56 13	201	36 31	252	37 41	344
47	41 25	029	36 44	056	38 49	090	45 38	139	55 54	202	35 41	252	37 26	343
48	41 51	028	37 28	055	39 42	090	46 13	139	55 34	202	34 50	251	37 09	342
49	42 15	027	38 12	054	40 36	089	46 47	140	55 13	203	33 59	251	36 52	340
50	42 39	025	38 55	053	41 29	089	47 22	140	54 52	204	33 09	251	36 34	339
51	43 01	024	39 37	052	42 23	088	47 56	140	54 30	205	32 18	251	36 14	338
52	43 22	023	40 20	052	43 16	088	48 31	140	54 07	205	31 28	250	35 54	337
53	43 43	022	41 01	051	44 10	087	49 04	141	53 44	206	30 38	250	35 33	336
54	44 02	020	41 42	050	45 03	087	49 38	141	53 21	207	29 47	250	35 11	335
55	44 20	019	42 23	049	45 56	086	50 11	142	52 57	207	28 57	249	34 48	334
56	44 37	018	43 02	048	46 50	086	50 45	142	52 32	208	28 07	249	34 24	333
57	44 53	017	43 42	047	47 43	085	51 17	142	52 07	208	27 17	249	34 00	332
58	45 08	015	44 20	046	48 36	085	51 50	143	51 41	209	26 28	249	33 34	331
59	45 21	014	44 58	044	49 29	084	52 22	143	51 15	209	25 38	248	33 08	330
	ALDEBARAN		BETELGEUSE		◆ SIRIUS		CANOPUS		◆ ACHERNAR		FOMALHAUT		◆ Hamal	
60	45 33	013	45 35	043	50 23	084	52 54	144	50 49	210	24 48	248	32 41	329
61	45 44	011	46 11	042	51 16	083	53 25	144	50 22	210	23 59	248	32 14	328
62	45 54	010	46 47	041	52 09	083	53 56	145	49 55	211	23 09	247	31 45	327
63	46 03	009	47 22	040	53 02	082	54 27	145	49 28	211	22 20	247	31 16	326
64	46 10	007	47 56	039	53 55	081	54 57	146	49 00	212	21 31	247	30 46	326
65	46 16	006	48 28	037	54 48	081	55 27	147	48 31	212	20 42	246	30 15	325
66	46 21	004	49 01	036	55 40	080	55 56	147	48 03	212	19 53	246	29 44	324
67	46 25	003	49 32	035	56 33	079	56 25	148	47 34	213	19 04	246	29 12	323
68	46 27	002	50 02	034	57 25	079	56 53	149	47 05	213	18 15	246	28 40	322
69	46 28	000	50 31	032	58 18	078	57 20	149	46 35	214	17 27	245	28 07	321
70	46 27	359	50 59	031	59 10	077	57 47	150	46 06	214	16 38	245	27 33	320
71	46 26	357	51 26	029	60 02	076	58 14	151	45 36	214	15 50	244	26 59	320
72	46 23	356	51 51	028	60 54	075	58 40	152	45 06	214	15 02	244	26 24	319
73	46 18	355	52 16	027	61 45	075	59 05	152	44 35	215	14 14	244	25 48	318
74	46 13	353	52 39	025	62 37	074	59 29	153	44 05	215	13 26	243	25 12	317
	BETELGEUSE		PROCYON		◆ Suhail		CANOPUS		◆ ACHERNAR		Hamal		◆ ALDEBARAN	
75	53 01	023	39 41	056	37 55	126	59 53	154	43 34	215	24 36	317	46 06	352
76	53 22	022	40 25	055	38 39	126	60 15	155	43 03	215	23 59	316	45 58	351
77	53 41	020	41 09	055	39 22	126	60 37	156	42 32	216	23 21	315	45 48	349
78	53 59	019	41 52	054	40 06	126	60 59	157	42 01	216	22 43	314	45 38	348
79	54 15	017	42 35	053	40 49	125	61 19	158	41 29	216	22 05	314	45 26	347
80	54 30	015	43 17	052	41 33	125	61 38	159	40 58	216	21 26	313	45 13	345
81	54 44	014	43 59	051	42 16	126	61 57	160	40 26	216	20 47	312	44 59	344
82	54 56	012	44 40	050	43 00	126	62 14	162	39 54	217	20 07	312	44 43	343
83	55 06	010	45 21	049	43 43	126	62 30	163	39 22	217	19 27	311	44 27	341
84	55 15	009	46 00	048	44 27	126	62 46	164	38 50	217	18 46	310	44 09	340
85	55 22	007	46 40	047	45 10	126	63 00	165	38 18	217	18 05	310	43 50	339
86	55 28	005	47 18	045	45 54	126	63 13	166	37 46	217	17 24	309	43 30	338
87	55 32	003	47 56	044	46 37	126	63 25	168	37 14	217	16 42	308	43 09	336
88	55 35	002	48 33	043	47 20	126	63 36	169	36 42	217	16 00	308	42 47	335
89	55 35	000	49 09	042	48 04	126	63 46	170	36 09	217	15 17	307	42 24	334

LAT 27°S

LHA ♈	Hc	Zn	Hc	Zn	Hc	Zn	Hc	Zn	Hc	Zn	Hc	Zn	Hc	Zn
	POLLUX		◆ REGULUS		ACRUX		◆ CANOPUS		ACHERNAR		◆ RIGEL		BETELGEUSE	
90	29 23	027	18 10	066	20 55	151	63 54	172	35 37	217	68 24	329	55 35	358
91	29 47	026	18 59	065	21 21	151	64 01	173	35 04	217	67 56	326	55 32	356
92	30 10	025	19 47	065	21 47	151	64 07	174	34 32	217	67 25	324	55 28	355
93	30 32	024	20 35	064	22 13	151	64 12	176	33 59	217	66 53	322	55 22	353
94	30 54	023	21 23	063	22 39	151	64 15	177	33 27	217	66 19	320	55 15	351
95	31 15	022	22 11	063	23 05	151	64 17	179	32 54	217	65 44	318	55 06	350
96	31 35	021	22 58	062	23 31	151	64 18	180	32 22	217	65 07	316	54 56	348
97	31 54	020	23 45	062	23 58	150	64 17	181	31 49	217	64 29	314	54 44	346
98	32 12	019	24 32	061	24 24	150	64 15	183	31 17	217	63 51	312	54 30	344
99	32 29	018	25 19	060	24 51	150	64 12	184	30 44	217	63 11	311	54 15	343
100	32 46	017	26 05	060	25 17	150	64 08	185	30 12	217	62 30	309	53 59	341
101	33 01	016	26 51	059	25 44	150	64 02	187	29 39	217	61 48	308	53 41	340
102	33 16	015	27 37	058	26 11	150	63 55	188	29 07	217	61 05	306	53 21	338
103	33 29	014	28 22	057	26 37	150	63 47	190	28 35	217	60 22	305	53 01	336
104	33 42	013	29 07	057	27 04	150	63 37	191	28 02	217	59 37	304	52 39	335
	POLLUX		◆ REGULUS		Gienah		◆ ACRUX		CANOPUS		◆ RIGEL		BETELGEUSE	
105	33 54	012	29 51	056	17 18	101	27 31	150	63 27	192	58 53	302	52 16	333
106	34 05	011	30 35	055	18 10	101	27 58	150	63 15	193	58 07	301	51 51	332
107	34 15	010	31 19	054	19 03	101	28 25	150	63 02	195	57 21	300	51 25	331
108	34 24	009	32 02	054	19 56	100	28 52	150	62 48	196	56 34	299	50 58	329
109	34 32	008	32 45	053	20 48	100	29 19	150	62 33	197	55 47	298	50 31	328
110	34 39	007	33 28	052	21 41	099	29 46	150	62 16	198	55 00	297	50 01	326
111	34 45	006	34 10	051	22 34	099	30 13	150	61 59	199	54 12	296	49 31	325
112	34 50	005	34 51	050	23 27	099	30 40	150	61 41	201	53 23	295	49 00	324
113	34 54	004	35 32	050	24 19	098	31 07	150	61 22	202	52 35	294	48 28	323
114	34 57	003	36 13	049	25 12	098	31 35	150	61 01	203	51 46	293	47 55	321
115	34 59	002	36 52	048	26 05	097	32 02	150	60 40	204	50 56	292	47 21	320
116	35 01	001	37 32	047	26 58	097	32 29	150	60 19	205	50 07	291	46 47	319
117	35 01	000	38 11	046	27 51	097	32 56	150	59 56	206	49 16	290	46 11	318
118	35 00	358	38 49	045	28 45	096	33 23	150	59 32	207	48 26	289	45 35	317
119	34 58	357	39 26	044	29 38	096	33 49	150	59 08	207	47 36	289	44 58	316
	◆ REGULUS		SPICA		◆ ACRUX		CANOPUS		◆ RIGEL		BETELGEUSE		POLLUX	
120	40 03	043	12 34	096	34 16	150	58 43	208	46 45	288	44 20	314	34 55	356
121	40 39	042	13 28	096	34 43	150	58 18	209	45 54	287	43 41	313	34 51	355
122	41 15	041	14 21	095	35 10	150	57 51	210	45 03	287	43 02	312	34 46	354
123	41 49	040	15 14	095	35 37	150	57 24	211	44 12	286	42 22	311	34 40	353
124	42 23	039	16 07	095	36 03	150	56 57	211	43 20	285	41 42	310	34 33	352
125	42 57	038	17 01	094	36 30	150	56 29	212	42 28	284	41 01	309	34 25	351
126	43 29	037	17 54	094	36 56	150	56 00	213	41 36	284	40 19	308	34 16	350
127	44 00	036	18 47	093	37 22	151	55 31	213	40 44	283	39 37	308	34 06	349
128	44 31	034	19 41	093	37 49	151	55 01	214	39 52	283	38 55	307	33 55	348
129	45 01	033	20 34	092	38 15	151	54 31	215	39 00	282	38 11	306	33 44	347
130	45 30	032	21 28	092	38 41	151	54 01	215	38 08	281	37 28	305	33 31	346
131	45 57	031	22 21	092	39 06	151	53 30	216	37 15	281	36 44	304	33 17	345
132	46 24	029	23 14	091	39 32	151	52 58	216	36 23	280	35 59	303	33 03	344
133	46 50	028	24 08	091	39 57	152	52 27	217	35 30	280	35 14	302	32 47	343
134	47 15	027	25 01	090	40 23	152	51 54	217	34 37	279	34 29	302	32 31	342
	REGULUS		◆ SPICA		ACRUX		◆ CANOPUS		RIGEL		BETELGEUSE		◆ POLLUX	
135	47 38	026	25 55	090	40 48	152	51 22	218	33 44	279	33 43	301	32 14	341
136	48 01	024	26 48	089	41 13	152	50 49	218	32 52	278	32 57	300	31 56	340
137	48 22	023	27 42	089	41 38	153	50 16	218	31 59	277	32 11	299	31 37	339
138	48 42	021	28 35	088	42 02	153	49 43	219	31 06	277	31 24	299	31 17	338
139	49 01	020	29 29	088	42 27	153	49 09	219	30 12	276	30 37	298	30 56	337
140	49 19	019	30 22	087	42 51	153	48 35	219	29 19	276	29 50	297	30 35	336
141	49 35	017	31 15	087	43 15	154	48 01	220	28 26	275	29 02	297	30 13	335
142	49 51	016	32 09	086	43 38	154	47 27	220	27 33	275	28 14	296	29 50	334
143	50 04	014	33 02	086	44 02	154	46 52	220	26 40	274	27 26	295	29 26	333
144	50 17	013	33 55	085	44 25	155	46 18	221	25 46	274	26 38	295	29 02	332
145	50 28	011	34 49	085	44 48	155	45 43	221	24 53	273	25 49	294	28 36	331
146	50 38	010	35 42	084	45 10	155	45 08	221	24 00	273	25 00	293	28 10	331
147	50 46	008	36 35	084	45 32	156	44 33	221	23 06	273	24 11	293	27 44	330
148	50 53	007	37 28	083	45 54	156	43 57	221	22 13	272	23 21	292	27 16	329
149	50 59	005	38 21	083	46 16	156	43 22	222	21 19	272	22 32	292	26 48	328
	REGULUS		◆ Denebola		SPICA		◆ ACRUX		CANOPUS		◆ SIRIUS		PROCYON	
150	51 03	004	40 41	036	39 14	082	46 37	157	42 46	222	44 04	272	43 19	308
151	51 05	002	41 12	035	40 07	082	46 58	157	42 10	222	43 11	272	42 37	307
152	51 06	000	41 43	034	41 00	081	47 18	158	41 35	222	42 18	272	41 54	306
153	51 06	359	42 12	033	41 53	081	47 39	158	40 59	222	41 24	271	41 11	305
154	51 04	357	42 40	032	42 46	080	47 58	159	40 23	222	40 31	271	40 27	305
155	51 01	356	43 08	030	43 38	079	48 18	159	39 47	222	39 37	270	39 43	304
156	50 56	354	43 35	029	44 31	079	48 37	160	39 10	223	38 44	270	38 58	303
157	50 50	353	44 00	028	45 23	078	48 55	160	38 34	223	37 50	269	38 13	302
158	50 43	351	44 25	027	46 15	078	49 13	161	37 58	223	36 57	269	37 27	301
159	50 34	350	44 48	026	47 08	077	49 31	161	37 22	223	36 03	268	36 42	300
160	50 24	348	45 11	024	48 00	076	49 48	162	36 45	223	35 10	268	35 55	300
161	50 12	347	45 32	023	48 51	075	50 04	162	36 09	223	34 17	267	35 09	299
162	49 59	345	45 53	022	49 43	075	50 21	163	35 33	223	33 23	267	34 22	298
163	49 44	344	46 12	020	50 34	074	50 36	163	34 56	223	32 30	267	33 34	297
164	49 29	342	46 30	019	51 26	073	50 51	164	34 20	223	31 36	266	32 47	297
	ARCTURUS		◆ ANTARES		ACRUX		◆ CANOPUS		SIRIUS		PROCYON		◆ REGULUS	
165	23 45	051	17 47	111	51 06	164	33 44	223	30 43	266	31 59	296	49 12	341
166	24 27	051	18 36	111	51 20	165	33 07	223	29 50	265	31 11	295	48 54	339
167	25 08	050	19 26	111	51 33	166	32 31	223	28 57	265	30 22	295	48 34	338
168	25 48	049	20 17	110	51 46	166	31 55	223	28 03	265	29 33	294	48 13	337
169	26 29	048	21 07	110	51 59	167	31 19	223	27 10	264	28 44	293	47 52	335
170	27 08	048	21 57	110	52 10	168	30 42	223	26 17	264	27 55	293	47 29	334
171	27 48	047	22 48	109	52 21	168	30 06	223	25 24	263	27 06	292	47 05	333
172	28 26	046	23 38	109	52 32	169	29 30	222	24 31	263	26 16	291	46 39	331
173	29 05	045	24 29	109	52 42	170	28 54	222	23 38	263	25 26	291	46 13	330
174	29 42	044	25 20	108	52 51	170	28 18	222	22 45	262	24 36	290	45 46	329
175	30 20	044	26 10	108	53 00	171	27 42	222	21 52	262	23 46	290	45 18	328
176	30 56	043	27 01	108	53 07	172	27 06	222	20 59	261	22 55	289	44 48	326
177	31 32	042	27 52	107	53 15	173	26 30	222	20 06	261	22 05	288	44 18	325
178	32 08	041	28 43	107	53 21	173	25 55	222	19 13	261	21 14	288	43 47	324
179	32 42	040	29 35	107	53 27	174	25 19	222	18 21	260	20 23	287	43 16	323

LAT 27°S

LHA ♈	Hc	Zn	Hc	Zn	Hc	Zn	Hc	Zn	Hc	Zn	Hc	Zn	Hc	Zn
	◆ ARCTURUS		ANTARES		◆ RIGIL KENT		ACRUX		CANOPUS		◆ Alphard		REGULUS	
180	33 17	039	30 26	106	46 43	153	53 32	175	24 43	222	49 47	290	42 43	322
181	33 50	038	31 17	106	47 07	153	53 37	176	24 08	221	48 57	289	42 09	321
182	34 23	037	32 09	106	47 31	154	53 41	176	23 33	221	48 06	288	41 35	320
183	34 55	037	33 00	105	47 54	154	53 44	177	22 58	221	47 15	287	41 00	319
184	35 27	036	33 52	105	48 18	154	53 46	178	22 23	221	46 24	287	40 24	318
185	35 57	035	34 43	105	48 41	155	53 48	179	21 48	221	45 33	286	39 48	317
186	36 27	034	35 35	105	49 03	155	53 49	179	21 13	221	44 41	285	39 11	316
187	36 56	033	36 27	104	49 25	156	53 49	180	20 38	220	43 50	285	38 33	315
188	37 25	032	37 19	104	49 47	156	53 49	181	20 04	220	42 58	284	37 55	314
189	37 52	030	38 11	104	50 08	157	53 47	182	19 29	220	42 06	283	37 16	313
190	38 19	029	39 03	103	50 29	157	53 46	182	18 55	220	41 14	283	36 36	312
191	38 45	028	39 55	103	50 49	158	53 43	183	18 21	219	40 22	282	35 56	311
192	39 10	027	40 47	103	51 09	159	53 40	184	17 47	219	39 29	281	35 15	310
193	39 34	026	41 39	102	51 28	159	53 36	185	17 13	219	38 37	281	34 34	309
194	39 57	025	42 31	102	51 47	160	53 31	185	16 40	219	37 44	280	33 52	308
	ARCTURUS		◆ Rasalhague		ANTARES		RIGIL KENT		◆ ACRUX		Suhail		◆ REGULUS	
195	40 19	024	12 23	069	43 23	102	52 05	160	53 26	186	41 01	235	33 10	308
196	40 40	023	13 12	068	44 16	102	52 23	161	53 20	187	40 18	234	32 28	307
197	41 01	022	14 02	068	45 08	101	52 40	162	53 13	188	39 34	234	31 44	306
198	41 20	020	14 51	067	46 01	101	52 57	162	53 05	188	38 51	234	31 01	305
199	41 38	019	15 40	067	46 53	101	53 13	163	52 57	189	38 07	234	30 17	304
200	41 55	018	16 29	066	47 46	101	53 28	164	52 49	190	37 24	234	29 33	304
201	42 11	017	17 18	066	48 38	100	53 43	164	52 39	190	36 40	234	28 48	303
202	42 26	016	18 07	065	49 31	100	53 57	165	52 29	191	35 57	234	28 03	302
203	42 40	014	18 55	064	50 24	100	54 10	166	52 18	192	35 14	234	27 18	302
204	42 52	013	19 43	064	51 16	099	54 23	167	52 07	193	34 30	234	26 32	301
205	43 04	012	20 31	063	52 09	099	54 35	167	51 55	193	33 47	234	25 46	300
206	43 14	011	21 19	063	53 02	099	54 46	168	51 43	194	33 04	234	25 00	300
207	43 23	009	22 06	062	53 55	099	54 57	169	51 30	194	32 21	234	24 13	299
208	43 31	008	22 53	061	54 48	098	55 07	170	51 16	195	31 38	234	23 26	298
209	43 38	007	23 40	061	55 40	098	55 16	170	51 02	196	30 55	233	22 39	298
	◆ ARCTURUS		Rasalhague		◆ Nunki		RIGIL KENT		ACRUX		◆ Suhail		Denebola	
210	43 44	005	24 26	060	24 52	108	55 25	171	50 47	196	30 12	233	37 51	319
211	43 48	004	25 12	059	25 43	108	55 32	172	50 32	197	29 29	233	37 16	318
212	43 51	003	25 58	059	26 34	108	55 39	173	50 16	197	28 46	233	36 39	317
213	43 53	001	26 44	058	27 25	107	55 46	174	50 00	198	28 03	233	36 02	316
214	43 54	000	27 29	057	28 16	107	55 51	175	49 43	199	27 21	233	35 25	315
215	43 53	359	28 14	057	29 07	107	55 55	176	49 26	199	26 38	233	34 47	314
216	43 51	357	28 58	056	29 59	106	55 59	176	49 08	200	25 56	232	34 08	313
217	43 49	356	29 42	055	30 50	106	56 02	177	48 50	200	25 14	232	33 29	312
218	43 44	355	30 26	054	31 41	106	56 04	178	48 31	201	24 32	232	32 49	312
219	43 39	354	31 09	054	32 33	105	56 06	179	48 12	201	23 50	232	32 09	311
220	43 32	352	31 52	053	33 25	105	56 06	180	47 53	202	23 08	232	31 28	310
221	43 25	351	32 34	052	34 16	105	56 06	181	47 33	202	22 26	231	30 47	309
222	43 16	350	33 16	051	35 08	104	56 05	182	47 13	202	21 44	231	30 05	308
223	43 06	348	33 58	050	36 00	104	56 03	182	46 52	203	21 03	231	29 23	308
224	42 54	347	34 39	050	36 52	104	56 00	183	46 31	203	20 21	231	28 40	307
	Alphecca		Rasalhague		◆ Nunki		Peacock		◆ RIGIL KENT		SPICA		◆ ARCTURUS	
225	35 40	010	35 19	049	37 44	104	26 45	143	55 57	184	62 52	301	42 42	346
226	35 49	009	35 59	048	38 36	103	27 17	142	55 52	185	62 05	300	42 28	345
227	35 56	008	36 38	047	39 28	103	27 50	142	55 47	186	61 19	298	42 14	343
228	36 03	006	37 17	046	40 20	103	28 22	142	55 41	187	60 31	297	41 58	342
229	36 08	005	37 55	045	41 12	102	28 55	142	55 35	188	59 44	296	41 41	341
230	36 13	004	38 33	044	42 04	102	29 28	142	55 27	188	58 55	295	41 23	340
231	36 16	003	39 10	043	42 57	102	30 01	142	55 19	189	58 07	294	41 04	339
232	36 18	002	39 46	042	43 49	102	30 34	142	55 10	190	57 18	293	40 44	337
233	36 20	001	40 21	041	44 41	101	31 07	142	55 00	191	56 28	292	40 23	336
234	36 20	000	40 56	040	45 34	101	31 40	142	54 50	192	55 38	291	40 01	335
235	36 19	359	41 30	039	46 26	101	32 12	142	54 39	192	54 48	290	39 38	334
236	36 18	358	42 04	038	47 19	100	32 45	142	54 27	193	53 58	289	39 14	333
237	36 15	356	42 36	037	48 11	100	33 18	142	54 14	194	53 07	288	38 49	332
238	36 11	355	43 08	036	49 04	100	33 51	142	54 01	195	52 17	288	38 24	331
239	36 06	354	43 39	035	49 57	100	34 24	142	53 47	195	51 25	287	37 57	330
	◆ VEGA		ALTAIR		◆ Peacock		RIGIL KENT		◆ SPICA		ARCTURUS		Alphecca	
240	14 37	031	23 26	066	34 57	142	53 33	196	50 34	286	37 30	329	36 00	353
241	15 04	030	24 15	065	35 30	142	53 18	197	49 43	285	37 01	328	35 54	352
242	15 31	029	25 03	065	36 03	142	53 02	198	48 51	285	36 32	327	35 46	351
243	15 57	029	25 51	064	36 36	142	52 45	198	47 59	284	36 03	326	35 37	350
244	16 22	028	26 39	063	37 08	142	52 28	199	47 07	283	35 32	325	35 27	349
245	16 47	027	27 27	063	37 41	142	52 11	199	46 15	282	35 01	324	35 16	348
246	17 11	027	28 14	062	38 14	142	51 53	200	45 23	282	34 29	323	35 04	347
247	17 35	026	29 01	061	38 46	143	51 34	201	44 30	281	33 56	322	34 52	346
248	17 58	025	29 48	061	39 19	143	51 15	201	43 38	281	33 22	321	34 38	345
249	18 21	025	30 34	060	39 51	143	50 55	202	42 45	280	32 48	320	34 23	344
250	18 42	024	31 20	059	40 24	143	50 35	202	41 53	279	32 14	319	34 08	343
251	19 04	023	32 06	058	40 56	143	50 15	203	41 00	279	31 38	318	33 51	341
252	19 24	022	32 51	058	41 28	143	49 54	203	40 07	278	31 02	317	33 34	340
253	19 44	022	33 36	057	42 00	143	49 32	204	39 14	278	30 26	316	33 15	339
254	20 04	021	34 21	056	42 31	144	49 10	204	38 21	277	29 49	316	32 56	338
	◆ VEGA		ALTAIR		FOMALHAUT		◆ Peacock		RIGIL KENT		◆ SPICA		ARCTURUS	
255	20 22	020	35 05	055	13 14	117	43 03	144	48 48	205	37 28	277	29 11	315
256	20 40	019	35 49	054	14 02	116	43 34	144	48 25	205	36 35	276	28 33	314
257	20 58	019	36 32	054	14 50	116	44 06	144	48 02	206	35 42	276	27 54	313
258	21 14	018	37 15	053	15 38	116	44 37	145	47 38	206	34 48	275	27 15	313
259	21 30	017	37 57	052	16 27	115	45 08	145	47 15	207	33 55	275	26 36	312
260	21 45	016	38 39	051	17 15	115	45 38	145	46 50	207	33 02	274	25 55	311
261	22 00	015	39 20	050	18 04	115	46 09	145	46 26	207	32 08	274	25 15	310
262	22 14	015	40 01	049	18 52	114	46 39	146	46 01	208	31 15	273	24 34	310
263	22 27	014	40 41	048	19 41	114	47 09	146	45 36	208	30 22	273	23 52	309
264	22 39	013	41 20	047	20 30	114	47 39	146	45 10	209	29 28	272	23 11	308
265	22 51	012	41 59	046	21 19	113	48 08	147	44 45	209	28 35	272	22 28	307
266	23 02	011	42 37	045	22 08	113	48 37	147	44 19	209	27 41	271	21 46	307
267	23 12	010	43 15	044	22 57	113	49 06	148	43 53	209	26 48	271	21 03	306
268	23 21	010	43 52	043	23 47	112	49 35	148	43 26	210	25 54	270	20 19	305
269	23 30	009	44 28	042	24 36	112	50 03	148	43 00	210	25 01	270	19 36	305

LHA ♈	Hc	Zn	Hc	Zn	Hc	Zn	Hc	Zn	Hc	Zn	Hc	Zn	Hc	Zn
	VEGA		◆ ALTAIR		FOMALHAUT		◆ Peacock		RIGIL KENT		◆ ANTARES		Alphecca	
270	23 37	008	45 03	041	25 26	112	50 31	149	42 33	210	70 00	266	26 03	324
271	23 44	007	45 38	040	26 16	111	50 58	149	42 06	211	69 07	266	25 31	323
272	23 51	006	46 12	039	27 05	111	51 25	150	41 38	211	68 13	266	24 59	322
273	23 56	005	46 44	037	27 55	111	51 52	150	41 11	211	67 20	266	24 26	322
274	24 01	005	47 16	036	28 45	111	52 18	151	40 43	211	66 27	265	23 52	321
275	24 05	004	47 47	035	29 35	110	52 43	152	40 15	211	65 33	265	23 18	320
276	24 08	003	48 18	034	30 26	110	53 09	152	39 48	212	64 40	265	22 44	319
277	24 10	002	48 47	032	31 16	110	53 33	153	39 19	212	63 47	264	22 09	319
278	24 11	001	49 15	031	32 06	109	53 58	153	38 51	212	62 54	264	21 33	318
279	24 12	000	49 42	030	32 57	109	54 21	154	38 23	212	62 00	264	20 57	317
280	24 12	359	50 07	028	33 47	109	54 44	155	37 54	212	61 07	264	20 21	317
281	24 11	359	50 32	027	34 38	109	55 07	155	37 26	212	60 14	263	19 44	316
282	24 09	358	50 56	025	35 29	108	55 29	156	36 57	212	59 21	263	19 06	315
283	24 07	357	51 18	024	36 19	108	55 50	157	36 29	213	58 28	263	18 28	315
284	24 04	356	51 39	022	37 10	108	56 11	158	36 00	213	57 35	262	17 50	314
	◆ DENEB		FOMALHAUT		◆ ACHERNAR		RIGIL KENT		◆ ANTARES		Rasalhague		VEGA	
285	14 02	018	38 01	108	17 32	146	35 31	213	56 42	262	45 28	330	23 59	355
286	14 18	017	38 52	107	18 02	146	35 02	213	55 49	262	45 01	329	23 55	354
287	14 34	017	39 43	107	18 32	145	34 33	213	54 56	262	44 32	328	23 49	353
288	14 49	016	40 34	107	19 02	145	34 04	213	54 03	261	44 03	326	23 42	353
289	15 04	015	41 25	107	19 33	145	33 35	213	53 11	261	43 33	325	23 35	352
290	15 18	015	42 16	107	20 03	145	33 06	213	52 18	261	43 02	324	23 27	351
291	15 31	014	43 08	106	20 34	145	32 37	213	51 25	261	42 30	323	23 18	350
292	15 44	013	43 59	106	21 05	145	32 07	213	50 32	260	41 58	322	23 09	349
293	15 56	013	44 50	106	21 36	144	31 38	213	49 40	260	41 24	321	22 59	348
294	16 07	012	45 42	106	22 08	144	31 09	213	48 47	260	40 50	320	22 48	348
295	16 18	011	46 33	105	22 39	144	30 40	213	47 54	260	40 15	319	22 36	347
296	16 28	011	47 25	105	23 10	144	30 11	213	47 02	259	39 39	318	22 23	346
297	16 38	010	48 17	105	23 42	144	29 41	213	46 09	259	39 03	317	22 10	345
298	16 47	009	49 08	105	24 14	144	29 12	213	45 17	259	38 26	316	21 56	344
299	16 55	008	50 00	105	24 45	143	28 43	213	44 24	258	37 48	315	21 41	344
	DENEB		Enif		◆ FOMALHAUT		ACHERNAR		◆ RIGIL KENT		ANTARES		◆ VEGA	
300	17 02	008	45 08	038	50 52	105	25 17	143	28 14	213	43 32	258	21 26	343
301	17 09	007	45 41	037	51 43	104	25 49	143	27 45	213	42 40	258	21 10	342
302	17 15	006	46 13	036	52 35	104	26 21	143	27 16	213	41 48	258	20 53	341
303	17 21	006	46 43	035	53 27	104	26 53	143	26 47	213	40 55	257	20 35	340
304	17 25	005	47 13	033	54 19	104	27 26	143	26 18	213	40 03	257	20 17	340
305	17 30	004	47 42	032	55 11	104	27 58	143	25 50	213	39 11	257	19 58	339
306	17 33	003	48 10	031	56 03	104	28 30	143	25 21	212	38 19	256	19 39	338
307	17 36	003	48 37	029	56 55	103	29 03	143	24 52	212	37 27	256	19 19	337
308	17 38	002	49 02	028	57 47	103	29 35	143	24 24	212	36 35	256	18 58	337
309	17 39	001	49 27	027	58 39	103	30 07	143	23 55	212	35 44	256	18 36	336
310	17 40	000	49 50	025	59 31	103	30 40	143	23 27	212	34 52	255	18 14	335
311	17 40	000	50 13	024	60 23	103	31 12	143	22 58	212	34 00	255	17 52	335
312	17 39	359	50 34	022	61 15	103	31 45	143	22 30	212	33 09	255	17 29	334
313	17 38	358	50 53	021	62 07	103	32 17	143	22 02	212	32 17	254	17 05	333
314	17 36	357	51 12	019	62 59	103	32 50	143	21 34	211	31 26	254	16 40	332
	Alpheratz		◆ Diphda		ACHERNAR		◆ RIGIL KENT		ANTARES		◆ ALTAIR		DENEB	
315	17 50	042	37 47	092	33 23	143	21 06	211	30 34	254	50 26	333	17 33	357
316	18 26	042	38 40	092	33 55	143	20 39	211	29 43	253	50 01	331	17 29	356
317	19 02	041	39 34	092	34 28	143	20 11	211	28 52	253	49 35	330	17 25	355
318	19 36	040	40 27	091	35 00	143	19 44	211	28 01	253	49 08	329	17 21	354
319	20 11	040	41 21	091	35 32	143	19 16	211	27 10	252	48 40	327	17 15	354
320	20 45	039	42 14	090	36 05	143	18 49	210	26 19	252	48 10	326	17 09	353
321	21 18	038	43 08	090	36 37	143	18 22	210	25 28	252	47 40	325	17 02	352
322	21 51	037	44 01	089	37 10	143	17 55	210	24 37	252	47 09	324	16 55	352
323	22 23	037	44 54	089	37 42	143	17 29	210	23 46	251	46 37	322	16 46	351
324	22 55	036	45 48	088	38 14	143	17 02	210	22 56	251	46 03	321	16 38	350
325	23 26	035	46 41	088	38 46	143	16 36	209	22 05	251	45 30	320	16 28	349
326	23 56	034	47 35	087	39 18	143	16 10	209	21 15	250	44 55	319	16 18	349
327	24 26	034	48 28	087	39 50	143	15 44	209	20 25	250	44 19	318	16 07	348
328	24 56	033	49 21	086	40 22	144	15 18	209	19 35	250	43 43	317	15 56	347
329	25 24	032	50 15	086	40 54	144	14 52	208	18 45	249	43 06	316	15 44	347
	◆ Alpheratz		Diphda		◆ ACHERNAR		Peacock		◆ Nunki		ALTAIR		Enif	
330	25 52	031	51 08	085	41 25	144	55 59	203	49 09	260	42 28	315	52 53	354
331	26 20	030	52 01	085	41 57	144	55 38	204	48 17	260	41 50	314	52 46	352
332	26 46	030	52 55	084	42 28	144	55 16	204	47 24	260	41 11	313	52 38	351
333	27 12	029	53 48	084	42 59	145	54 54	205	46 31	259	40 31	312	52 29	349
334	27 38	028	54 41	083	43 30	145	54 31	206	45 39	259	39 51	311	52 18	347
335	28 02	027	55 34	082	44 01	145	54 07	206	44 46	259	39 10	310	52 05	346
336	28 26	026	56 27	082	44 31	145	53 43	207	43 54	259	38 29	309	51 52	344
337	28 49	025	57 20	081	45 02	146	53 19	208	43 02	258	37 47	308	51 36	343
338	29 12	024	58 12	080	45 32	146	52 54	208	42 09	258	37 04	307	51 20	341
339	29 33	023	59 05	080	46 02	146	52 28	209	41 17	258	36 21	306	51 02	340
340	29 54	022	59 58	079	46 31	146	52 02	209	40 25	257	35 38	305	50 43	338
341	30 14	022	60 50	078	47 01	147	51 36	210	39 33	257	34 54	305	50 22	337
342	30 33	021	61 42	077	47 30	147	51 09	210	38 41	257	34 10	304	50 01	335
343	30 52	020	62 34	077	47 59	147	50 42	211	37 49	256	33 25	303	49 38	334
344	31 09	019	63 26	076	48 28	148	50 14	211	36 57	256	32 40	302	49 14	333
	Alpheratz		◆ Hamal		◆ ACHERNAR		Peacock		Nunki		◆ ALTAIR		Enif	
345	31 26	018	22 04	046	48 56	148	49 46	212	36 05	256	31 55	301	48 49	331
346	31 42	017	22 43	046	49 24	149	49 18	212	35 13	256	31 09	301	48 22	330
347	31 57	016	23 21	045	49 51	149	48 49	213	34 21	255	30 23	300	47 55	329
348	32 11	015	23 58	044	50 19	150	48 20	213	33 30	255	29 37	299	47 27	327
349	32 24	014	24 35	043	50 45	150	47 51	213	32 38	255	28 50	299	46 57	326
350	32 36	013	25 12	043	51 12	151	47 21	214	31 46	254	28 03	298	46 27	325
351	32 48	012	25 48	042	51 38	151	46 51	214	30 55	254	27 15	297	45 56	324
352	32 58	011	26 23	041	52 04	152	46 21	214	30 04	254	26 28	297	45 24	322
353	33 08	010	26 58	040	52 29	152	45 51	215	29 12	253	25 40	296	44 51	321
354	33 16	009	27 33	040	52 53	153	45 20	215	28 21	253	24 52	295	44 17	320
355	33 24	008	28 06	039	53 18	153	44 50	215	27 30	253	24 03	295	43 42	319
356	33 30	007	28 39	038	53 41	154	44 19	216	26 39	253	23 14	294	43 07	318
357	33 36	006	29 12	037	54 04	155	43 47	216	25 48	252	22 25	293	42 30	317
358	33 41	005	29 44	036	54 27	155	43 16	216	24 57	252	21 36	293	41 54	316
359	33 44	003	30 15	035	54 49	156	42 44	216	24 06	252	20 47	292	41 16	315

LAT 28°S

LHA ♈	Hc	Zn	Hc	Zn	Hc	Zn	Hc	Zn	Hc	Zn	Hc	Zn	Hc	Zn
	◆ Alpheratz		Hamal		◆ RIGEL		CANOPUS		ACHERNAR		◆ Peacock		Enif	
0	32 47	002	29 56	034	13 40	092	18 28	141	56 05	156	43 01	217	39 56	314
1	32 49	001	30 25	033	14 33	092	19 02	140	56 26	157	42 29	217	39 18	313
2	32 50	000	30 54	032	15 26	091	19 36	140	56 47	158	41 57	217	38 39	313
3	32 49	359	31 22	031	16 19	091	20 10	140	57 07	158	41 25	218	38 00	312
4	32 48	358	31 49	030	17 12	090	20 44	140	57 26	159	40 52	218	37 20	311
5	32 46	357	32 16	029	18 05	090	21 19	139	57 44	160	40 20	218	36 39	310
6	32 43	356	32 41	029	18 58	089	21 53	139	58 02	161	39 47	218	35 58	309
7	32 39	355	33 06	028	19 51	089	22 28	139	58 19	162	39 15	218	35 17	308
8	32 34	354	33 30	027	20 44	088	23 03	139	58 35	163	38 42	218	34 35	307
9	32 28	353	33 54	026	21 37	088	23 38	139	58 50	164	38 09	218	33 52	306
10	32 21	352	34 16	025	22 30	087	24 13	138	59 05	165	37 37	218	33 09	306
11	32 13	351	34 38	024	23 23	087	24 48	138	59 18	166	37 04	218	32 26	305
12	32 05	350	34 59	023	24 16	086	25 23	138	59 31	167	36 31	218	31 42	304
13	31 55	349	35 18	021	25 09	086	25 59	138	59 43	168	35 58	218	30 58	303
14	31 44	348	35 37	020	26 01	085	26 34	138	59 54	169	35 25	218	30 14	302
	◆ Hamal		ALDEBARAN		RIGEL		◆ CANOPUS		ACHERNAR		◆ FOMALHAUT		Alpheratz	
15	35 55	019	21 12	056	26 54	085	27 10	138	60 04	170	63 24	259	31 33	347
16	36 12	018	21 56	056	27 47	084	27 45	138	60 13	171	62 32	259	31 20	346
17	36 28	017	22 39	055	28 40	084	28 21	137	60 21	172	61 40	259	31 07	345
18	36 44	016	23 23	054	29 32	083	28 57	137	60 28	173	60 48	259	30 53	344
19	36 58	015	24 06	054	30 25	083	29 33	137	60 34	174	59 56	259	30 38	343
20	37 11	014	24 48	053	31 17	082	30 09	137	60 40	175	59 04	259	30 22	342
21	37 23	013	25 30	052	32 10	082	30 45	137	60 44	176	58 12	258	30 05	341
22	37 34	012	26 12	052	33 02	081	31 21	137	60 47	177	57 20	258	29 48	340
23	37 44	010	26 53	051	33 55	081	31 57	137	60 49	178	56 28	258	29 29	339
24	37 54	009	27 34	050	34 47	080	32 34	137	60 50	179	55 37	258	29 10	338
25	38 02	008	28 15	049	35 39	079	33 10	137	60 50	180	54 45	258	28 50	337
26	38 09	007	28 55	049	36 31	079	33 46	137	60 49	182	53 53	257	28 30	336
27	38 15	006	29 34	048	37 23	078	34 22	137	60 47	183	53 02	257	28 08	336
28	38 19	005	30 13	047	38 15	078	34 59	137	60 44	184	52 10	257	27 46	335
29	38 23	004	30 51	046	39 06	077	35 35	137	60 40	185	51 18	257	27 23	334
	Hamal		ALDEBARAN		◆ SIRIUS		CANOPUS		◆ ACHERNAR		FOMALHAUT		◆ Alpheratz	
30	38 26	002	31 29	045	23 50	097	36 11	137	60 35	186	50 27	257	26 59	333
31	38 27	001	32 07	044	24 43	097	36 48	137	60 29	187	49 35	256	26 34	332
32	38 28	000	32 43	044	25 36	096	37 24	137	60 22	188	48 44	256	26 09	331
33	38 28	359	33 20	043	26 28	096	38 00	137	60 14	189	47 52	256	25 43	330
34	38 26	358	33 55	042	27 21	095	38 37	137	60 05	190	47 01	256	25 17	330
35	38 23	356	34 30	041	28 14	095	39 13	137	59 55	191	46 10	255	24 50	329
36	38 19	355	35 05	040	29 07	094	39 49	137	59 44	192	45 19	255	24 22	328
37	38 15	354	35 38	039	29 59	094	40 25	137	59 33	193	44 27	255	23 53	327
38	38 09	353	36 11	038	30 52	094	41 02	137	59 20	194	43 36	255	23 24	326
39	38 02	352	36 43	037	31 45	093	41 38	137	59 07	195	42 45	254	22 54	325
40	37 54	351	37 15	036	32 38	093	42 14	137	58 52	196	41 54	254	22 24	325
41	37 45	350	37 46	035	33 31	092	42 50	137	58 37	197	41 03	254	21 53	324
42	37 34	348	38 16	034	34 24	092	43 25	138	58 21	198	40 12	254	21 22	323
43	37 23	347	38 45	033	35 17	091	44 01	138	58 04	199	39 22	253	20 50	322
44	37 11	346	39 13	032	36 10	091	44 37	138	57 47	200	38 31	253	20 17	322
	◆ ALDEBARAN		BETELGEUSE		SIRIUS		◆ CANOPUS		ACHERNAR		◆ FOMALHAUT		Hamal	
45	39 40	031	34 42	057	37 03	090	45 12	138	57 28	201	37 40	253	36 58	345
46	40 07	030	35 26	056	37 56	090	45 48	138	57 09	201	36 50	253	36 44	344
47	40 33	028	36 10	055	38 49	089	46 23	138	56 50	202	35 59	252	36 29	343
48	40 58	027	36 54	054	39 42	089	46 58	139	56 29	203	35 09	252	36 13	342
49	41 21	026	37 36	054	40 35	089	47 33	139	56 08	204	34 18	252	35 55	341
50	41 44	025	38 19	053	41 28	088	48 08	139	55 47	204	33 28	251	35 37	340
51	42 06	024	39 01	052	42 21	088	48 42	139	55 24	205	32 38	251	35 19	339
52	42 27	023	39 42	051	43 14	087	49 17	140	55 02	206	31 48	251	34 59	338
53	42 47	021	40 23	050	44 06	086	49 51	140	54 38	206	30 58	251	34 38	336
54	43 06	020	41 03	049	44 59	086	50 25	140	54 14	207	30 08	250	34 16	335
55	43 23	019	41 43	048	45 52	085	50 58	141	53 50	208	29 18	250	33 54	334
56	43 40	018	42 22	047	46 45	085	51 32	141	53 25	208	28 28	250	33 31	333
57	43 55	016	43 00	046	47 38	084	52 05	142	53 00	209	27 39	249	33 07	332
58	44 10	015	43 38	045	48 30	084	52 37	142	52 34	209	26 49	249	32 42	331
59	44 23	014	44 15	044	49 23	083	53 10	142	52 08	210	26 00	249	32 16	331
	ALDEBARAN		BETELGEUSE		◆ SIRIUS		CANOPUS		◆ ACHERNAR		FOMALHAUT		◆ Hamal	
60	44 35	012	44 51	043	50 16	083	53 42	143	51 41	210	25 10	248	31 50	330
61	44 46	011	45 27	042	51 08	082	54 14	143	51 14	211	24 21	248	31 22	329
62	44 55	010	46 01	040	52 00	081	54 45	144	50 46	211	23 32	248	30 54	328
63	45 04	008	46 35	039	52 53	081	55 16	145	50 19	212	22 43	247	30 26	327
64	45 11	007	47 08	038	53 45	080	55 46	145	49 51	212	21 54	247	29 56	326
65	45 17	006	47 41	037	54 37	079	56 17	146	49 22	213	21 05	247	29 26	325
66	45 21	004	48 12	036	55 29	079	56 46	146	48 53	213	20 17	246	28 56	324
67	45 25	003	48 42	034	56 21	078	57 15	147	48 24	213	19 28	246	28 24	323
68	45 27	002	49 12	033	57 13	077	57 44	148	47 55	214	18 40	246	27 52	322
69	45 28	000	49 40	032	58 04	076	58 12	148	47 25	214	17 52	245	27 20	322
70	45 27	359	50 07	030	58 56	075	58 39	149	46 55	214	17 03	245	26 47	321
71	45 26	358	50 33	029	59 47	075	59 06	150	46 25	215	16 16	245	26 13	320
72	45 23	356	50 58	027	60 38	074	59 32	151	45 55	215	15 28	244	25 38	319
73	45 19	355	51 22	026	61 29	073	59 58	152	45 25	215	14 40	244	25 04	318
74	45 13	353	51 44	024	62 19	072	60 22	153	44 54	216	13 52	244	24 28	318
	BETELGEUSE		PROCYON		◆ Suhail		CANOPUS		◆ ACHERNAR		Hamal		◆ ALDEBARAN	
75	52 06	023	39 07	056	38 30	125	60 46	154	44 23	216	23 52	317	45 06	352
76	52 26	021	39 51	055	39 13	125	61 10	154	43 52	216	23 16	316	44 59	351
77	52 45	020	40 34	054	39 57	125	61 32	155	43 21	216	22 39	315	44 49	349
78	53 02	018	41 16	053	40 40	125	61 54	156	42 49	216	22 01	315	44 39	348
79	53 18	017	41 58	052	41 24	125	62 14	158	42 18	217	21 23	314	44 28	347
80	53 32	015	42 40	051	42 07	125	62 34	159	41 46	217	20 45	313	44 15	345
81	53 45	013	43 21	050	42 51	125	62 53	160	41 14	217	20 06	313	44 01	344
82	53 57	012	44 01	049	43 34	125	63 11	161	40 42	217	19 27	312	43 46	343
83	54 07	010	44 41	048	44 18	125	63 28	162	40 10	217	18 47	311	43 30	342
84	54 16	009	45 20	047	45 01	125	63 43	163	39 38	217	18 07	311	43 13	340
85	54 23	007	45 58	046	45 45	125	63 58	165	39 06	217	17 27	310	42 54	339
86	54 28	005	46 36	045	46 28	125	64 11	166	38 34	218	16 46	309	42 35	338
87	54 32	003	47 12	044	47 12	125	64 24	167	38 02	218	16 05	309	42 14	337
88	54 35	002	47 49	042	47 55	125	64 35	169	37 29	218	15 23	308	41 53	335
89	54 35	000	48 24	041	48 38	125	64 45	170	36 57	218	14 41	307	41 30	334

LHA ♈	Hc	Zn	Hc	Zn	Hc	Zn	Hc	Zn	Hc	Zn	Hc	Zn	Hc	Zn
	POLLUX		◆ REGULUS		ACRUX		◆ CANOPUS		ACHERNAR		◆ RIGEL		BETELGEUSE	
90	28 30	027	17 45	065	21 48	151	64 53	171	36 24	218	67 33	330	54 35	358
91	28 53	026	18 33	065	22 14	151	65 01	173	35 52	218	67 05	328	54 32	357
92	29 16	025	19 21	064	22 39	151	65 07	174	35 19	218	66 36	325	54 28	355
93	29 38	024	20 09	064	23 05	151	65 11	176	34 47	218	66 05	323	54 23	353
94	29 59	023	20 56	063	23 31	151	65 15	177	34 14	218	65 33	321	54 16	351
95	30 19	022	21 43	062	23 57	150	65 17	178	33 42	218	64 59	319	54 07	350
96	30 39	021	22 30	062	24 24	150	65 18	180	33 09	218	64 24	317	53 57	348
97	30 57	020	23 17	061	24 50	150	65 17	181	32 37	218	63 47	316	53 45	346
98	31 15	019	24 03	060	25 16	150	65 15	183	32 04	218	63 09	314	53 32	345
99	31 32	018	24 49	060	25 43	150	65 12	184	31 32	218	62 31	312	53 18	343
100	31 48	017	25 35	059	26 09	150	65 07	186	30 59	218	61 51	311	53 02	342
101	32 04	016	26 20	058	26 36	150	65 02	187	30 27	218	61 10	309	52 44	340
102	32 18	015	27 05	058	27 03	150	64 54	188	29 55	218	60 29	308	52 26	339
103	32 31	014	27 49	057	27 29	150	64 46	190	29 22	218	59 47	306	52 06	337
104	32 44	013	28 34	056	27 56	150	64 36	191	28 50	217	59 04	305	51 44	336
	POLLUX		◆ REGULUS		Gienah		◆ ACRUX		CANOPUS		◆ RIGEL		BETELGEUSE	
105	32 56	012	29 18	056	17 30	101	28 23	149	64 25	193	58 20	304	51 22	334
106	33 06	011	30 01	055	18 22	101	28 50	149	64 13	194	57 36	302	50 58	333
107	33 16	010	30 44	054	19 14	100	29 17	149	64 00	195	56 51	301	50 33	331
108	33 25	009	31 27	053	20 06	100	29 44	149	63 45	196	56 05	300	50 07	330
109	33 33	008	32 09	052	20 58	099	30 11	149	63 30	198	55 19	299	49 40	328
110	33 40	007	32 51	052	21 51	099	30 38	149	63 13	199	54 32	298	49 11	327
111	33 45	006	33 32	051	22 43	099	31 05	149	62 56	200	53 45	297	48 42	326
112	33 50	005	34 13	050	23 35	098	31 32	149	62 37	201	52 58	296	48 12	324
113	33 54	004	34 53	049	24 28	098	31 59	149	62 17	202	52 10	295	47 40	323
114	33 57	003	35 33	048	25 20	097	32 26	149	61 57	203	51 22	294	47 08	322
115	33 59	002	36 12	047	26 13	097	32 53	149	61 35	204	50 33	293	46 35	321
116	34 01	001	36 51	046	27 05	097	33 20	149	61 13	205	49 44	292	46 01	320
117	34 01	000	37 29	045	27 58	096	33 47	149	60 50	206	48 55	291	45 26	318
118	34 00	358	38 06	044	28 51	096	34 14	149	60 26	207	48 06	291	44 51	317
119	33 58	357	38 43	044	29 44	095	34 41	149	60 01	208	47 16	290	44 15	316
	◆ REGULUS		SPICA		◆ ACRUX		CANOPUS		◆ RIGEL		BETELGEUSE		POLLUX	
120	39 19	043	12 41	096	35 08	150	59 36	209	46 26	289	43 38	315	33 55	356
121	39 54	041	13 34	096	35 35	150	59 10	210	45 36	288	43 00	314	33 51	355
122	40 29	040	14 26	095	36 02	150	58 43	211	44 45	287	42 21	313	33 46	354
123	41 03	039	15 19	095	36 28	150	58 16	211	43 55	287	41 42	312	33 40	353
124	41 36	038	16 12	094	36 55	150	57 48	212	43 04	286	41 03	311	33 34	352
125	42 09	037	17 05	094	37 22	150	57 19	213	42 13	285	40 22	310	33 26	351
126	42 41	036	17 58	093	37 48	150	56 50	214	41 22	285	39 42	309	33 17	350
127	43 11	035	18 51	093	38 15	150	56 21	214	40 30	284	39 00	308	33 07	349
128	43 41	034	19 44	093	38 41	150	55 51	215	39 39	283	38 18	307	32 57	348
129	44 10	033	20 36	092	39 07	151	55 20	215	38 47	283	37 36	306	32 45	347
130	44 38	031	21 29	092	39 33	151	54 49	216	37 56	282	36 53	306	32 33	346
131	45 06	030	22 22	091	39 59	151	54 18	216	37 04	282	36 10	305	32 19	345
132	45 32	029	23 15	091	40 25	151	53 46	217	36 12	281	35 26	304	32 05	344
133	45 57	028	24 08	090	40 50	151	53 14	217	35 20	280	34 42	303	31 50	343
134	46 21	026	25 01	090	41 16	151	52 42	218	34 27	280	33 57	302	31 34	342
	REGULUS		◆ SPICA		ACRUX		◆ CANOPUS		RIGEL		BETELGEUSE		◆ POLLUX	
135	46 44	025	25 54	089	41 41	152	52 09	218	33 35	279	33 12	302	31 17	341
136	47 06	024	26 47	089	42 06	152	51 36	219	32 43	279	32 27	301	30 59	340
137	47 27	022	27 40	088	42 31	152	51 03	219	31 50	278	31 41	300	30 41	339
138	47 46	021	28 33	088	42 56	152	50 29	220	30 58	278	30 55	299	30 21	338
139	48 05	020	29 26	087	43 20	153	49 56	220	30 05	277	30 09	299	30 01	337
140	48 22	018	30 19	087	43 44	153	49 21	220	29 13	276	29 22	298	29 40	336
141	48 38	017	31 12	086	44 08	153	48 47	221	28 20	276	28 35	297	29 18	335
142	48 53	015	32 05	086	44 32	153	48 13	221	27 27	275	27 48	296	28 56	334
143	49 06	014	32 58	085	44 56	154	47 38	221	26 35	275	27 00	296	28 32	333
144	49 18	013	33 50	085	45 19	154	47 03	221	25 42	274	26 12	295	28 08	333
145	49 29	011	34 43	084	45 42	154	46 28	222	24 49	274	25 24	294	27 44	332
146	49 39	010	35 36	084	46 04	155	45 53	222	23 56	273	24 36	294	27 18	331
147	49 47	008	36 28	083	46 27	155	45 17	222	23 03	273	23 47	293	26 52	330
148	49 53	007	37 21	083	46 49	156	44 42	222	22 10	272	22 59	293	26 25	329
149	49 59	005	38 13	082	47 11	156	44 06	222	21 17	272	22 10	292	25 57	328
	REGULUS		◆ Denebola		SPICA		◆ ACRUX		CANOPUS		◆ SIRIUS		PROCYON	
150	50 03	003	39 53	036	39 06	082	47 32	156	43 31	222	44 01	273	42 42	309
151	50 05	002	40 23	034	39 58	081	47 53	157	42 55	223	43 08	273	42 00	308
152	50 06	000	40 53	033	40 51	080	48 14	157	42 19	223	42 16	272	41 18	307
153	50 06	359	41 21	032	41 43	080	48 34	158	41 43	223	41 23	272	40 36	306
154	50 04	357	41 49	031	42 35	079	48 54	158	41 07	223	40 30	271	39 53	305
155	50 01	356	42 16	030	43 27	078	49 14	159	40 31	223	39 37	271	39 09	304
156	49 57	354	42 42	029	44 19	078	49 33	159	39 54	223	38 44	270	38 25	304
157	49 51	353	43 07	028	45 10	077	49 51	160	39 18	223	37 51	270	37 41	303
158	49 44	351	43 31	026	46 02	076	50 10	160	38 42	223	36 58	270	36 56	302
159	49 35	350	43 54	025	46 53	076	50 27	161	38 06	223	36 05	269	36 11	301
160	49 25	348	44 16	024	47 45	075	50 45	161	37 29	223	35 12	269	35 25	300
161	49 14	347	44 37	023	48 36	074	51 02	162	36 53	223	34 19	268	34 39	299
162	49 01	345	44 57	021	49 27	074	51 18	162	36 17	223	33 26	268	33 53	299
163	48 47	344	45 16	020	50 17	073	51 34	163	35 40	223	32 33	267	33 06	298
164	48 32	343	45 33	019	51 08	072	51 49	163	35 04	223	31 40	267	32 19	297
	ARCTURUS		◆ ANTARES		ACRUX		◆ CANOPUS		SIRIUS		PROCYON		◆ REGULUS	
165	23 08	051	18 08	111	52 04	164	34 28	223	30 47	266	31 32	297	48 15	341
166	23 48	050	18 58	111	52 18	165	33 51	223	29 54	266	30 45	296	47 57	340
167	24 29	050	19 47	110	52 32	165	33 15	223	29 02	266	29 57	295	47 38	338
168	25 09	049	20 37	110	52 45	166	32 39	223	28 09	265	29 09	294	47 18	337
169	25 49	048	21 27	109	52 57	167	32 02	223	27 16	265	28 20	294	46 57	336
170	26 28	047	22 17	109	53 09	167	31 26	223	26 23	264	27 32	293	46 35	334
171	27 06	046	23 07	109	53 20	168	30 50	223	25 31	264	26 43	292	46 11	333
172	27 45	046	23 57	108	53 31	169	30 14	223	24 38	263	25 54	292	45 47	332
173	28 22	045	24 48	108	53 41	169	29 38	223	23 45	263	25 05	291	45 21	331
174	28 59	044	25 38	108	53 50	170	29 02	223	22 53	263	24 15	291	44 54	329
175	29 36	043	26 29	107	53 59	171	28 26	223	22 00	262	23 25	290	44 27	328
176	30 12	042	27 19	107	54 07	172	27 51	222	21 08	262	22 36	289	43 58	327
177	30 47	042	28 10	107	54 14	172	27 15	222	20 15	261	21 45	289	43 29	326
178	31 22	041	29 01	106	54 21	173	26 39	222	19 23	261	20 55	288	42 59	325
179	31 56	040	29 51	106	54 27	174	26 04	222	18 31	260	20 05	288	42 28	323

LAT 28°S

LHA ♈	Hc	Zn	Hc	Zn	Hc	Zn	Hc	Zn	Hc	Zn	Hc	Zn	Hc	Zn
	◆ ARCTURUS		ANTARES		◆ RIGIL KENT		ACRUX		CANOPUS		◆ Alphard		REGULUS	
180	32 30	039	30 42	106	47 36	152	54 32	175	25 28	222	49 26	291	41 56	322
181	33 03	038	31 33	105	48 00	153	54 37	175	24 53	222	48 37	290	41 23	321
182	33 35	037	32 25	105	48 24	153	54 41	176	24 18	222	47 47	289	40 49	320
183	34 07	036	33 16	105	48 48	154	54 44	177	23 43	221	46 57	289	40 15	319
184	34 38	035	34 07	104	49 12	154	54 46	178	23 08	221	46 06	288	39 40	318
185	35 08	034	34 58	104	49 35	154	54 48	179	22 33	221	45 16	287	39 04	317
186	35 37	033	35 50	104	49 57	155	54 49	179	21 58	221	44 25	286	38 28	316
187	36 06	032	36 41	103	50 20	155	54 49	180	21 24	221	43 34	286	37 51	315
188	36 34	031	37 33	103	50 42	156	54 49	181	20 49	220	42 43	285	37 13	314
189	37 01	030	38 24	103	51 03	156	54 47	182	20 15	220	41 52	284	36 35	313
190	37 27	029	39 16	103	51 24	157	54 46	182	19 41	220	41 00	284	35 56	312
191	37 52	028	40 08	102	51 45	157	54 43	183	19 07	220	40 09	283	35 16	311
192	38 16	027	41 00	102	52 05	158	54 40	184	18 33	219	39 17	282	34 36	311
193	38 40	026	41 51	102	52 24	159	54 35	185	18 00	219	38 25	282	33 56	310
194	39 03	025	42 43	101	52 43	159	54 31	186	17 26	219	37 33	281	33 15	309
	ARCTURUS		◆ Rasalhague		ANTARES		RIGIL KENT		◆ ACRUX		Suhail		◆ REGULUS	
195	39 24	024	12 01	069	43 35	101	53 02	160	54 25	186	41 36	235	32 33	308
196	39 45	022	12 50	068	44 27	101	53 20	161	54 19	187	40 52	235	31 51	307
197	40 05	021	13 39	068	45 20	100	53 37	161	54 12	188	40 09	235	31 09	306
198	40 23	020	14 28	067	46 12	100	53 54	162	54 05	189	39 25	235	30 26	306
199	40 41	019	15 17	066	47 04	100	54 10	163	53 56	189	38 42	235	29 43	305
200	40 58	018	16 05	066	47 56	099	54 25	163	53 48	190	37 58	235	28 59	304
201	41 13	017	16 53	065	48 48	099	54 40	164	53 38	191	37 15	235	28 15	303
202	41 28	015	17 41	065	49 41	099	54 55	165	53 28	191	36 32	235	27 31	303
203	41 41	014	18 29	064	50 33	099	55 08	165	53 17	192	35 48	235	26 46	302
204	41 54	013	19 17	063	51 25	098	55 21	166	53 06	193	35 05	235	26 01	301
205	42 05	012	20 04	063	52 18	098	55 34	167	52 54	193	34 22	234	25 16	301
206	42 15	010	20 51	062	53 10	098	55 45	168	52 41	194	33 39	234	24 30	300
207	42 24	009	21 38	062	54 03	097	55 56	169	52 28	195	32 56	234	23 44	299
208	42 32	008	22 24	061	54 56	097	56 06	169	52 14	195	32 13	234	22 57	299
209	42 38	007	23 10	060	55 48	097	56 15	170	52 00	196	31 30	234	22 11	298
	◆ ARCTURUS		Rasalhague		◆ Nunki		RIGIL KENT		ACRUX		◆ Suhail		Denebola	
210	42 44	005	23 56	060	25 11	108	56 24	171	51 45	197	30 47	234	37 06	319
211	42 48	004	24 42	059	26 01	107	56 32	172	51 29	197	30 05	234	36 31	318
212	42 51	003	25 27	058	26 52	107	56 39	173	51 13	198	29 22	233	35 55	317
213	42 53	001	26 12	058	27 42	107	56 45	174	50 57	198	28 39	233	35 19	316
214	42 54	000	26 56	057	28 33	106	56 51	175	50 40	199	27 57	233	34 42	315
215	42 53	359	27 41	056	29 24	106	56 55	175	50 23	199	27 15	233	34 05	315
216	42 52	358	28 24	055	30 15	106	56 59	176	50 05	200	26 33	233	33 27	314
217	42 49	356	29 08	055	31 06	105	57 02	177	49 46	201	25 50	233	32 48	313
218	42 45	355	29 51	054	31 57	105	57 04	178	49 27	201	25 08	232	32 09	312
219	42 39	354	30 33	053	32 48	105	57 06	179	49 08	202	24 27	232	31 29	311
220	42 33	352	31 16	052	33 40	104	57 06	180	48 49	202	23 45	232	30 49	310
221	42 25	351	31 57	052	34 31	104	57 06	181	48 29	202	23 03	232	30 09	310
222	42 17	350	32 39	051	35 23	104	57 05	182	48 08	203	22 22	231	29 28	309
223	42 07	349	33 19	050	36 14	103	57 03	183	47 47	203	21 40	231	28 46	308
224	41 56	347	34 00	049	37 06	103	57 00	183	47 26	204	20 59	231	28 04	307
	Alphecca		Rasalhague		◆ Nunki		Peacock		◆ RIGIL KENT		SPICA		◆ ARCTURUS	
225	34 41	010	34 39	048	37 57	103	27 32	142	56 57	184	62 20	303	41 44	346
226	34 49	009	35 19	047	38 49	102	28 05	142	56 52	185	61 35	301	41 30	345
227	34 57	007	35 57	046	39 41	102	28 37	142	56 47	186	60 49	300	41 16	344
228	35 03	006	36 35	045	40 32	102	29 10	142	56 41	187	60 03	299	41 01	342
229	35 08	005	37 13	045	41 24	102	29 42	142	56 34	188	59 17	298	40 44	341
230	35 13	004	37 50	044	42 16	101	30 15	142	56 27	189	58 29	296	40 27	340
231	35 16	003	38 26	043	43 08	101	30 48	142	56 18	189	57 42	295	40 08	339
232	35 18	002	39 01	042	44 00	101	31 21	142	56 09	190	56 54	294	39 48	338
233	35 20	001	39 36	041	44 52	100	31 54	142	55 59	191	56 05	293	39 28	337
234	35 20	000	40 10	040	45 45	100	32 27	142	55 49	192	55 16	292	39 06	335
235	35 19	359	40 44	039	46 37	100	33 00	142	55 37	193	54 27	291	38 44	334
236	35 18	358	41 16	037	47 29	099	33 33	142	55 25	194	53 38	290	38 21	333
237	35 15	357	41 48	036	48 21	099	34 05	142	55 13	194	52 48	290	37 56	332
238	35 11	355	42 19	035	49 14	099	34 38	142	54 59	195	51 58	289	37 31	331
239	35 07	354	42 49	034	50 06	098	35 11	142	54 45	196	51 08	288	37 05	330
	◆ VEGA		ALTAIR		◆ Peacock		RIGIL KENT		◆ SPICA		ARCTURUS		Alphecca	
240	13 46	031	23 01	065	35 44	142	54 30	197	50 17	287	36 38	329	35 01	353
241	14 12	030	23 49	065	36 17	142	54 15	197	49 26	286	36 11	328	34 54	352
242	14 39	029	24 37	064	36 50	142	53 59	198	48 35	286	35 42	327	34 46	351
243	15 04	029	25 25	063	37 23	142	53 42	199	47 44	285	35 13	326	34 38	350
244	15 29	028	26 12	063	37 56	142	53 25	199	46 53	284	34 43	325	34 28	349
245	15 54	027	26 59	062	38 29	142	53 07	200	46 02	283	34 12	324	34 18	348
246	16 18	027	27 46	061	39 01	142	52 49	201	45 10	283	33 41	323	34 06	347
247	16 41	026	28 32	061	39 34	142	52 30	201	44 18	282	33 09	322	33 53	346
248	17 04	025	29 18	060	40 06	142	52 11	202	43 26	282	32 36	321	33 40	345
249	17 26	024	30 04	059	40 39	142	51 51	202	42 34	281	32 02	320	33 26	344
250	17 48	024	30 49	059	41 11	142	51 31	203	41 42	280	31 28	319	33 10	343
251	18 09	023	31 34	058	41 44	143	51 10	203	40 50	280	30 53	319	32 54	342
252	18 29	022	32 19	057	42 16	143	50 48	204	39 58	279	30 18	318	32 37	341
253	18 49	021	33 03	056	42 48	143	50 27	204	39 06	278	29 42	317	32 19	340
254	19 08	021	33 47	055	43 20	143	50 05	205	38 13	278	29 06	316	32 00	339
	◆ VEGA		ALTAIR		FOMALHAUT		◆ Peacock		RIGIL KENT		◆ SPICA		ARCTURUS	
255	19 26	020	34 30	055	13 41	116	43 51	143	49 42	205	37 21	277	28 29	315
256	19 44	019	35 13	054	14 29	116	44 23	144	49 19	206	36 28	277	27 51	314
257	20 01	018	35 56	053	15 16	116	44 54	144	48 56	206	35 35	276	27 13	314
258	20 17	018	36 38	052	16 04	115	45 26	144	48 32	207	34 43	276	26 35	313
259	20 33	017	37 20	051	16 52	115	45 57	144	48 08	207	33 50	275	25 55	312
260	20 48	016	38 01	050	17 40	115	46 27	145	47 44	208	32 57	275	25 16	311
261	21 02	015	38 41	049	18 28	114	46 58	145	47 19	208	32 04	274	24 36	311
262	21 16	014	39 21	048	19 17	114	47 29	145	46 54	208	31 11	274	23 56	310
263	21 29	014	40 00	048	20 05	114	47 59	145	46 29	209	30 19	273	23 15	309
264	21 41	013	40 39	047	20 54	113	48 29	146	46 03	209	29 26	273	22 33	308
265	21 52	012	41 17	046	21 43	113	48 58	146	45 37	209	28 33	272	21 52	308
266	22 03	011	41 55	045	22 31	113	49 28	147	45 11	210	27 40	272	21 10	307
267	22 13	010	42 32	043	23 20	112	49 57	147	44 45	210	26 47	271	20 27	306
268	22 23	010	43 08	042	24 09	112	50 25	147	44 18	210	25 54	271	19 44	306
269	22 30	009	43 43	041	24 59	112	50 54	148	43 51	211	25 01	270	19 01	305

LHA ♈	Hc	Zn	Hc	Zn	Hc	Zn	Hc	Zn	Hc	Zn	Hc	Zn	Hc	Zn
	VEGA		◆ ALTAIR		FOMALHAUT		◆ Peacock		RIGIL KENT		◆ ANTARES		Alphecca	
270	22 38	008	44 18	040	25 48	111	51 22	148	43 24	211	70 02	269	25 14	324
271	22 45	007	44 51	039	26 37	111	51 49	149	42 57	211	69 09	269	24 43	324
272	22 51	006	45 24	038	27 27	111	52 17	149	42 30	211	68 16	268	24 11	323
273	22 56	005	45 57	037	28 17	110	52 44	150	42 02	211	67 23	268	23 39	322
274	23 01	005	46 28	035	29 06	110	53 10	150	41 34	212	66 30	268	23 06	321
275	23 05	004	46 58	034	29 56	110	53 36	151	41 07	212	65 37	267	22 32	320
276	23 08	003	47 27	033	30 46	109	54 02	151	40 39	212	64 45	267	21 58	320
277	23 10	002	47 56	032	31 36	109	54 27	152	40 10	212	63 52	266	21 24	319
278	23 11	001	48 23	030	32 26	109	54 51	153	39 42	212	62 59	266	20 49	318
279	23 12	000	48 49	029	33 16	109	55 15	153	39 14	213	62 06	266	20 13	318
280	23 12	359	49 14	028	34 06	108	55 39	154	38 45	213	61 13	265	19 37	317
281	23 11	359	49 39	026	34 57	108	56 01	155	38 17	213	60 20	265	19 01	316
282	23 09	358	50 01	025	35 47	108	56 24	155	37 48	213	59 28	265	18 24	315
283	23 07	357	50 23	023	36 38	107	56 45	156	37 19	213	58 35	264	17 46	315
284	23 04	356	50 44	022	37 28	107	57 06	157	36 50	213	57 42	264	17 08	314
	◆ DENEB		FOMALHAUT		◆ ACHERNAR		RIGIL KENT		◆ ANTARES		Rasalhague		VEGA	
285	13 05	018	38 19	107	18 21	146	36 21	213	56 49	264	44 36	330	23 00	355
286	13 21	017	39 10	107	18 51	145	35 52	213	55 57	263	44 09	329	22 55	354
287	13 37	017	40 00	106	19 21	145	35 23	213	55 04	263	43 42	328	22 49	354
288	13 52	016	40 51	106	19 51	145	34 54	213	54 12	263	43 13	327	22 43	353
289	14 06	015	41 42	106	20 22	145	34 25	213	53 19	262	42 44	326	22 36	352
290	14 20	015	42 33	106	20 52	145	33 56	213	52 27	262	42 13	325	22 28	351
291	14 33	014	43 24	105	21 23	144	33 27	213	51 34	262	41 42	323	22 19	350
292	14 46	013	44 15	105	21 54	144	32 58	213	50 42	262	41 10	322	22 10	349
293	14 57	013	45 06	105	22 25	144	32 28	213	49 49	261	40 37	321	22 00	349
294	15 09	012	45 58	105	22 56	144	31 59	213	48 57	261	40 04	320	21 49	348
295	15 19	011	46 49	104	23 27	144	31 30	213	48 05	261	39 30	319	21 37	347
296	15 29	011	47 40	104	23 59	144	31 01	213	47 12	260	38 55	318	21 25	346
297	15 39	010	48 32	104	24 30	143	30 32	213	46 20	260	38 19	317	21 12	345
298	15 47	009	49 23	104	25 02	143	30 03	213	45 28	260	37 43	316	20 58	345
299	15 55	008	50 15	104	25 34	143	29 33	213	44 36	259	37 06	315	20 44	344
	DENEB		Enif		◆ FOMALHAUT		ACHERNAR		◆ RIGIL KENT		ANTARES		◆ VEGA	
300	16 03	008	44 21	038	51 06	103	26 05	143	29 04	213	43 44	259	20 29	343
301	16 10	007	44 53	036	51 58	103	26 37	143	28 35	213	42 52	259	20 13	342
302	16 16	006	45 24	035	52 49	103	27 09	143	28 07	213	42 00	258	19 56	341
303	16 21	005	45 54	034	53 41	103	27 41	143	27 38	213	41 08	258	19 39	341
304	16 26	005	46 23	033	54 33	102	28 13	143	27 09	213	40 16	258	19 21	340
305	16 30	004	46 51	031	55 24	102	28 46	143	26 40	213	39 25	258	19 02	339
306	16 33	003	47 18	030	56 16	102	29 18	142	26 11	213	38 33	257	18 43	338
307	16 36	003	47 44	029	57 08	102	29 50	142	25 43	213	37 41	257	18 23	338
308	16 38	002	48 09	028	58 00	102	30 23	142	25 14	213	36 50	257	18 03	337
309	16 39	001	48 33	026	58 52	102	30 55	142	24 46	212	35 58	256	17 42	336
310	16 40	000	48 56	025	59 44	101	31 27	142	24 18	212	35 07	256	17 20	335
311	16 40	000	49 18	023	60 36	101	32 00	142	23 49	212	34 15	256	16 58	335
312	16 39	359	49 38	022	61 28	101	32 32	142	23 21	212	33 24	255	16 35	334
313	16 38	358	49 57	021	62 20	101	33 05	142	22 53	212	32 33	255	16 11	333
314	16 36	357	50 15	019	63 12	101	33 37	142	22 25	212	31 42	255	15 47	333
	Alpheratz		◆ Diphda		ACHERNAR		◆ RIGIL KENT		ANTARES		◆ ALTAIR		DENEB	
315	17 06	042	37 49	092	34 10	142	21 58	212	30 51	254	49 33	333	16 33	357
316	17 41	041	38 42	091	34 43	142	21 30	211	30 00	254	49 08	332	16 30	356
317	18 16	041	39 35	091	35 15	142	21 02	211	29 09	254	48 43	331	16 26	355
318	18 51	040	40 28	090	35 48	142	20 35	211	28 18	253	48 17	329	16 21	355
319	19 25	039	41 21	090	36 20	142	20 08	211	27 27	253	47 49	328	16 15	354
320	19 58	039	42 14	089	36 52	142	19 41	211	26 37	253	47 20	327	16 09	353
321	20 31	038	43 07	089	37 25	142	19 14	210	25 46	252	46 51	325	16 03	352
322	21 03	037	44 00	088	37 57	142	18 47	210	24 56	252	46 20	324	15 55	352
323	21 35	036	44 53	088	38 30	142	18 21	210	24 06	252	45 49	323	15 47	351
324	22 06	036	45 46	087	39 02	143	17 54	210	23 15	251	45 17	322	15 38	350
325	22 37	035	46 38	087	39 34	143	17 28	210	22 25	251	44 43	321	15 29	349
326	23 07	034	47 31	086	40 06	143	17 02	209	21 35	251	44 09	320	15 19	349
327	23 36	033	48 24	086	40 38	143	16 36	209	20 45	250	43 35	318	15 08	348
328	24 05	033	49 17	085	41 10	143	16 11	209	19 56	250	42 59	317	14 57	347
329	24 33	032	50 10	085	41 42	143	15 45	209	19 06	250	42 23	316	14 45	347
	◆ Alpheratz		Diphda		◆ ACHERNAR		Peacock		◆ Nunki		ALTAIR		Enif	
330	25 01	031	51 03	084	42 13	143	56 54	203	49 19	261	41 46	315	51 53	354
331	25 28	030	51 55	083	42 45	144	56 33	204	48 26	261	41 08	314	51 47	352
332	25 54	029	52 48	083	43 16	144	56 11	205	47 34	261	40 30	313	51 39	351
333	26 20	028	53 40	082	43 48	144	55 48	206	46 42	260	39 51	312	51 30	349
334	26 45	028	54 33	082	44 19	144	55 25	206	45 50	260	39 11	311	51 19	348
335	27 09	027	55 25	081	44 50	144	55 01	207	44 58	260	38 31	310	51 07	346
336	27 32	026	56 17	080	45 20	145	54 37	208	44 05	259	37 51	309	50 54	345
337	27 55	025	57 10	080	45 51	145	54 12	208	43 13	259	37 10	309	50 39	343
338	28 17	024	58 02	079	46 21	145	53 47	209	42 21	259	36 28	308	50 23	342
339	28 38	023	58 53	078	46 51	146	53 21	209	41 29	259	35 46	307	50 06	340
340	28 59	022	59 45	077	47 21	146	52 54	210	40 38	258	35 03	306	49 47	339
341	29 18	021	60 37	076	47 51	146	52 28	211	39 46	258	34 20	305	49 27	337
342	29 37	020	61 28	076	48 20	147	52 01	211	38 54	258	33 36	304	49 06	336
343	29 55	019	62 19	075	48 49	147	51 33	212	38 02	257	32 52	304	48 44	334
344	30 13	018	63 10	074	49 18	147	51 05	212	37 11	257	32 08	303	48 20	333
	Alpheratz		◆ Hamal		◆ ACHERNAR		Peacock		Nunki		◆ ALTAIR		Enif	
345	30 29	018	21 23	046	49 47	148	50 37	212	36 19	257	31 23	302	47 56	332
346	30 44	017	22 01	045	50 15	148	50 08	213	35 28	256	30 38	301	47 30	330
347	30 59	016	22 38	045	50 43	149	49 40	213	34 36	256	29 53	301	47 04	329
348	31 13	015	23 15	044	51 10	149	49 10	214	33 45	256	29 07	300	46 36	328
349	31 26	014	23 52	043	51 37	149	48 41	214	32 53	255	28 21	299	46 07	327
350	31 38	013	24 28	042	52 04	150	48 11	214	32 02	255	27 34	298	45 38	325
351	31 49	012	25 03	042	52 30	150	47 41	215	31 11	255	26 48	298	45 07	324
352	31 59	011	25 38	041	52 56	151	47 11	215	30 20	254	26 01	297	44 36	323
353	32 08	010	26 12	040	53 22	152	46 40	215	29 29	254	25 13	296	44 04	322
354	32 17	009	26 46	039	53 47	152	46 09	216	28 38	254	24 26	296	43 30	321
355	32 24	008	27 19	038	54 11	153	45 38	216	27 47	253	23 38	295	42 57	320
356	32 31	007	27 52	038	54 35	153	45 07	216	26 57	253	22 50	294	42 22	319
357	32 36	005	28 24	037	54 58	154	44 36	216	26 06	253	22 01	294	41 46	317
358	32 41	004	28 55	036	55 21	155	44 04	217	25 16	252	21 13	293	41 10	316
359	32 44	003	29 26	035	55 44	155	43 33	217	24 25	252	20 24	293	40 33	315

LHA ♈	Hc	Zn	Hc	Zn	Hc	Zn	Hc	Zn	Hc	Zn	Hc	Zn	Hc	Zn
	◆ Alpheratz		Hamal		◆ RIGEL		CANOPUS		ACHERNAR		◆ Peacock		Enif	
0	31 47	002	29 06	034	13 42	092	19 15	140	57 00	156	43 49	218	39 14	315
1	31 49	001	29 35	033	14 35	091	19 48	140	57 22	156	43 16	218	38 36	314
2	31 50	000	30 03	032	15 27	091	20 22	140	57 42	157	42 44	218	37 58	313
3	31 49	359	30 31	031	16 20	090	20 56	140	58 02	158	42 12	218	37 20	312
4	31 48	358	30 57	030	17 12	090	21 30	139	58 22	159	41 40	218	36 40	311
5	31 46	357	31 23	029	18 05	089	22 04	139	58 41	160	41 07	218	36 01	310
6	31 43	356	31 49	028	18 57	089	22 39	139	58 58	160	40 34	218	35 20	309
7	31 39	355	32 13	027	19 50	088	23 13	139	59 16	161	40 02	219	34 40	309
8	31 34	354	32 37	026	20 42	088	23 48	139	59 32	162	39 29	219	33 58	308
9	31 28	353	33 00	025	21 35	087	24 23	138	59 48	163	38 56	219	33 17	307
10	31 22	352	33 22	024	22 27	087	24 58	138	60 02	164	38 23	219	32 34	306
11	31 14	351	33 43	023	23 19	086	25 33	138	60 16	165	37 51	219	31 52	305
12	31 06	350	34 03	022	24 12	086	26 08	138	60 29	166	37 18	219	31 09	304
13	30 56	349	34 22	021	25 04	085	26 43	138	60 41	167	36 45	219	30 25	304
14	30 46	348	34 41	020	25 56	085	27 18	138	60 53	168	36 12	219	29 41	303
	◆ Hamal		ALDEBARAN		RIGEL		◆ CANOPUS		ACHERNAR		◆ FOMALHAUT		Alpheratz	
15	34 59	019	20 38	056	26 49	084	27 54	137	61 03	169	63 34	261	30 34	347
16	35 15	018	21 22	056	27 41	084	28 30	137	61 12	170	62 42	261	30 22	346
17	35 31	017	22 05	055	28 33	083	29 05	137	61 20	171	61 50	261	30 09	345
18	35 46	016	22 48	054	29 25	083	29 41	137	61 28	173	60 59	261	29 55	344
19	36 00	015	23 30	053	30 17	082	30 17	137	61 34	174	60 07	260	29 41	343
20	36 13	014	24 12	053	31 09	082	30 53	137	61 39	175	59 15	260	29 25	342
21	36 25	013	24 53	052	32 01	081	31 29	137	61 44	176	58 23	260	29 09	341
22	36 36	011	25 35	051	32 53	081	32 05	137	61 47	177	57 32	260	28 51	340
23	36 45	010	26 15	050	33 44	080	32 41	136	61 49	178	56 40	259	28 33	339
24	36 54	009	26 56	050	34 36	079	33 17	136	61 50	179	55 49	259	28 15	338
25	37 02	008	27 35	049	35 28	079	33 53	136	61 50	180	54 57	259	27 55	338
26	37 09	007	28 15	048	36 19	078	34 30	136	61 49	182	54 06	259	27 34	337
27	37 15	006	28 53	047	37 10	078	35 06	136	61 47	183	53 14	258	27 13	336
28	37 20	005	29 32	047	38 01	077	35 42	136	61 44	184	52 23	258	26 51	335
29	37 23	003	30 10	046	38 53	076	36 19	136	61 40	185	51 31	258	26 29	334
	Hamal		ALDEBARAN		◆ SIRIUS		CANOPUS		◆ ACHERNAR		FOMALHAUT		◆ Alpheratz	
30	37 26	002	30 47	045	23 57	097	36 55	136	61 35	186	50 40	258	26 05	333
31	37 28	001	31 24	044	24 50	096	37 31	136	61 29	187	49 49	257	25 41	332
32	37 28	000	32 00	043	25 42	096	38 08	136	61 22	188	48 58	257	25 17	331
33	37 28	359	32 35	042	26 34	095	38 44	136	61 13	190	48 07	257	24 51	331
34	37 26	358	33 10	041	27 26	095	39 20	136	61 04	191	47 15	257	24 25	330
35	37 23	357	33 45	040	28 19	094	39 57	136	60 54	192	46 24	256	23 58	329
36	37 20	355	34 18	039	29 11	094	40 33	136	60 43	193	45 33	256	23 31	328
37	37 15	354	34 51	038	30 03	093	41 09	136	60 31	194	44 43	256	23 03	327
38	37 09	353	35 24	038	30 56	093	41 45	136	60 18	195	43 52	256	22 34	327
39	37 02	352	35 55	037	31 48	093	42 21	137	60 04	196	43 01	255	22 05	326
40	36 54	351	36 26	036	32 41	092	42 58	137	59 50	197	42 10	255	21 35	325
41	36 46	350	36 56	035	33 33	092	43 34	137	59 34	198	41 20	255	21 05	324
42	36 36	349	37 26	033	34 25	091	44 09	137	59 18	199	40 29	254	20 34	323
43	36 25	347	37 54	032	35 18	091	44 45	137	59 01	199	39 38	254	20 02	323
44	36 13	346	38 22	031	36 10	090	45 21	137	58 43	200	38 48	254	19 30	322
	◆ ALDEBARAN		BETELGEUSE		SIRIUS		◆ CANOPUS		ACHERNAR		◆ FOMALHAUT		Hamal	
45	38 49	030	34 09	056	37 03	090	45 57	137	58 24	201	37 58	254	36 00	345
46	39 15	029	34 53	056	37 55	089	46 32	138	58 05	202	37 07	253	35 46	344
47	39 40	028	35 36	055	38 48	089	47 08	138	57 45	203	36 17	253	35 31	343
48	40 04	027	36 18	054	39 40	088	47 43	138	57 24	204	35 27	253	35 16	342
49	40 27	026	37 00	053	40 33	088	48 18	138	57 03	204	34 37	252	34 59	341
50	40 50	025	37 42	052	41 25	087	48 53	138	56 41	205	33 47	252	34 41	340
51	41 11	023	38 23	051	42 18	087	49 28	139	56 19	206	32 57	252	34 23	339
52	41 32	022	39 04	050	43 10	086	50 02	139	55 55	206	32 07	251	34 03	338
53	41 51	021	39 44	049	44 02	086	50 36	139	55 32	207	31 17	251	33 43	337
54	42 09	020	40 23	048	44 55	085	51 11	140	55 08	208	30 28	251	33 22	336
55	42 26	019	41 02	047	45 47	084	51 44	140	54 43	208	29 38	251	33 00	335
56	42 43	017	41 41	046	46 39	084	52 18	140	54 18	209	28 49	250	32 37	334
57	42 58	016	42 18	045	47 31	083	52 51	141	53 52	210	28 00	250	32 13	333
58	43 12	015	42 55	044	48 23	083	53 24	141	53 26	210	27 10	250	31 49	332
59	43 24	014	43 31	043	49 15	082	53 57	142	52 59	211	26 21	249	31 24	331
	ALDEBARAN		BETELGEUSE		◆ SIRIUS		CANOPUS		◆ ACHERNAR		FOMALHAUT		◆ Hamal	
60	43 36	012	44 07	042	50 07	081	54 30	142	52 32	211	25 32	249	30 58	330
61	43 47	011	44 42	041	50 59	081	55 02	143	52 05	212	24 43	249	30 31	329
62	43 56	010	45 16	040	51 51	080	55 33	143	51 37	212	23 55	248	30 04	328
63	44 04	008	45 49	039	52 42	079	56 05	144	51 09	213	23 06	248	29 35	327
64	44 11	007	46 21	037	53 34	079	56 35	144	50 41	213	22 17	248	29 07	326
65	44 17	006	46 52	036	54 25	078	57 06	145	50 12	213	21 29	247	28 37	325
66	44 21	004	47 23	035	55 17	077	57 36	145	49 43	214	20 41	247	28 07	324
67	44 25	003	47 52	034	56 08	076	58 05	146	49 14	214	19 52	246	27 36	324
68	44 27	002	48 21	032	56 59	076	58 34	147	48 45	214	19 04	246	27 05	323
69	44 28	000	48 49	031	57 49	075	59 03	148	48 15	215	18 16	246	26 33	322
70	44 27	359	49 15	030	58 40	074	59 31	148	47 45	215	17 29	245	26 00	321
71	44 26	358	49 40	028	59 30	073	59 58	149	47 14	215	16 41	245	25 27	320
72	44 23	356	50 05	027	60 20	072	60 24	150	46 44	216	15 53	245	24 53	319
73	44 19	355	50 28	025	61 10	071	60 50	151	46 13	216	15 06	244	24 19	319
74	44 14	354	50 50	024	61 59	070	61 15	152	45 42	216	14 19	244	23 44	318
	BETELGEUSE		PROCYON		◆ Suhail		CANOPUS		◆ ACHERNAR		Hamal		◆ ALDEBARAN	
75	51 10	022	38 33	055	39 04	124	61 40	153	45 11	216	23 08	317	44 07	352
76	51 30	021	39 16	054	39 47	124	62 04	154	44 40	217	22 32	316	43 59	351
77	51 48	019	39 58	053	40 31	124	62 27	155	44 09	217	21 56	316	43 50	350
78	52 05	018	40 40	052	41 14	124	62 49	156	43 37	217	21 19	315	43 40	348
79	52 20	016	41 21	051	41 58	124	63 10	157	43 06	217	20 42	314	43 29	347
80	52 34	015	42 02	050	42 41	124	63 30	158	42 34	217	20 04	314	43 17	346
81	52 47	013	42 42	049	43 25	124	63 49	159	42 02	217	19 25	313	43 03	344
82	52 58	012	43 21	048	44 08	124	64 07	160	41 30	218	18 47	312	42 49	343
83	53 08	010	44 00	047	44 52	124	64 25	162	40 58	218	18 08	311	42 33	342
84	53 16	008	44 38	046	45 35	124	64 41	163	40 26	218	17 28	311	42 16	341
85	53 23	007	45 16	045	46 19	124	64 56	164	39 54	218	16 48	310	41 58	339
86	53 29	005	45 53	044	47 02	124	65 09	165	39 21	218	16 08	309	41 39	338
87	53 32	003	46 29	043	47 46	124	65 22	167	38 49	218	15 27	309	41 19	337
88	53 35	002	47 04	042	48 29	124	65 33	168	38 17	218	14 46	308	40 58	336
89	53 35	000	47 38	040	49 13	124	65 44	170	37 44	218	14 05	308	40 36	335

LAT 29°S

LHA ♈	Hc	Zn	Hc	Zn	Hc	Zn	Hc	Zn	Hc	Zn	Hc	Zn	Hc	Zn
	POLLUX		◆ REGULUS		ACRUX		◆ CANOPUS		ACHERNAR		◆ RIGEL		BETELGEUSE	
90	27 36	026	17 20	065	22 41	151	65 53	171	37 12	218	66 41	331	53 35	358
91	27 59	026	18 08	065	23 06	151	66 00	172	36 39	218	66 14	329	53 32	357
92	28 21	025	18 55	064	23 32	151	66 06	174	36 07	218	65 46	327	53 29	355
93	28 43	024	19 42	063	23 58	150	66 11	175	35 34	218	65 17	325	53 23	353
94	29 04	023	20 29	063	24 23	150	66 15	177	35 02	218	64 45	323	53 16	352
95	29 23	022	21 15	062	24 49	150	66 17	178	34 29	218	64 13	321	53 08	350
96	29 43	021	22 02	061	25 16	150	66 18	180	33 57	218	63 39	319	52 58	348
97	30 01	020	22 48	061	25 42	150	66 17	181	33 24	218	63 04	317	52 47	347
98	30 18	019	23 33	060	26 08	150	66 15	183	32 52	218	62 27	315	52 34	345
99	30 35	018	24 19	059	26 35	150	66 12	184	32 19	218	61 50	314	52 20	344
100	30 51	017	25 04	059	27 01	150	66 07	186	31 47	218	61 11	312	52 05	342
101	31 06	016	25 48	058	27 28	150	66 01	187	31 14	218	60 32	311	51 48	341
102	31 20	015	26 33	057	27 54	149	65 54	189	30 42	218	59 52	309	51 30	339
103	31 33	014	27 17	057	28 21	149	65 45	190	30 10	218	59 11	308	51 10	337
104	31 45	013	28 00	056	28 48	149	65 35	192	29 37	218	58 29	306	50 50	336
	POLLUX		◆ REGULUS		Gienah		◆ ACRUX		CANOPUS		◆ RIGEL		BETELGEUSE	
105	31 57	012	28 43	055	17 41	101	29 15	149	65 24	193	57 46	305	50 28	335
106	32 07	011	29 26	054	18 33	100	29 42	149	65 11	194	57 03	304	50 05	333
107	32 17	010	30 09	054	19 24	100	30 08	149	64 58	196	56 19	303	49 40	332
108	32 26	009	30 51	053	20 16	099	30 35	149	64 43	197	55 34	301	49 15	330
109	32 33	008	31 32	052	21 08	099	31 02	149	64 27	198	54 49	300	48 48	329
110	32 40	007	32 13	051	22 00	099	31 29	149	64 10	200	54 04	299	48 21	328
111	32 46	006	32 54	050	22 52	098	31 56	149	63 52	201	53 18	298	47 52	326
112	32 51	005	33 34	049	23 44	098	32 24	149	63 33	202	52 31	297	47 23	325
113	32 55	004	34 14	049	24 36	097	32 51	149	63 13	203	51 44	296	46 52	324
114	32 58	003	34 53	048	25 28	097	33 18	149	62 52	204	50 57	295	46 21	323
115	33 00	002	35 31	047	26 20	096	33 45	149	62 30	205	50 09	294	45 48	321
116	33 01	001	36 09	046	27 12	096	34 12	149	62 07	206	49 21	293	45 15	320
117	33 01	000	36 46	045	28 04	096	34 39	149	61 43	207	48 33	292	44 41	319
118	33 00	358	37 23	044	28 56	095	35 06	149	61 19	208	47 44	292	44 07	318
119	32 58	357	37 59	043	29 49	095	35 33	149	60 54	209	46 55	291	43 31	317
	◆ REGULUS		SPICA		◆ ACRUX		CANOPUS		◆ RIGEL		BETELGEUSE		POLLUX	
120	38 35	042	12 47	096	36 00	149	60 28	210	46 06	290	42 55	316	32 55	356
121	39 09	041	13 40	095	36 27	149	60 02	211	45 17	289	42 18	315	32 51	355
122	39 43	040	14 32	095	36 53	149	59 34	212	44 27	288	41 40	314	32 46	354
123	40 17	039	15 24	094	37 20	149	59 07	212	43 37	288	41 02	313	32 41	353
124	40 49	038	16 16	094	37 47	149	58 38	213	42 47	287	40 23	312	32 34	352
125	41 21	037	17 09	094	38 14	150	58 09	214	41 57	286	39 44	311	32 26	351
126	41 52	036	18 01	093	38 40	150	57 40	214	41 06	286	39 04	310	32 18	350
127	42 22	034	18 54	093	39 06	150	57 10	215	40 15	285	38 23	309	32 08	349
128	42 51	033	19 46	092	39 33	150	56 40	216	39 25	284	37 42	308	31 58	348
129	43 20	032	20 38	092	39 59	150	56 09	216	38 34	284	37 00	307	31 47	347
130	43 47	031	21 31	091	40 25	150	55 38	217	37 43	283	36 18	306	31 35	346
131	44 14	030	22 23	091	40 51	150	55 06	217	36 51	282	35 35	305	31 22	345
132	44 39	028	23 16	090	41 17	151	54 34	218	36 00	282	34 52	304	31 08	344
133	45 04	027	24 08	090	41 43	151	54 02	218	35 09	281	34 09	304	30 53	343
134	45 27	026	25 01	089	42 08	151	53 29	219	34 17	280	33 25	303	30 37	342
	REGULUS		◆ SPICA		ACRUX		◆ CANOPUS		RIGEL		BETELGEUSE		◆ POLLUX	
135	45 50	025	25 53	089	42 34	151	52 56	219	33 25	280	32 41	302	30 20	341
136	46 11	023	26 46	088	42 59	151	52 23	220	32 34	279	31 56	301	30 03	340
137	46 31	022	27 38	088	43 24	152	51 49	220	31 42	279	31 11	301	29 45	339
138	46 50	021	28 31	087	43 49	152	51 15	220	30 50	278	30 26	300	29 26	338
139	47 08	019	29 23	087	44 13	152	50 41	221	29 58	278	29 40	299	29 06	337
140	47 25	018	30 15	086	44 38	152	50 07	221	29 06	277	28 54	298	28 45	336
141	47 41	017	31 08	086	45 02	153	49 32	221	28 14	276	28 08	298	28 24	335
142	47 55	015	32 00	085	45 26	153	48 58	222	27 22	276	27 21	297	28 02	335
143	48 08	014	32 52	085	45 49	153	48 23	222	26 29	275	26 34	296	27 39	334
144	48 20	012	33 45	084	46 13	154	47 48	222	25 37	275	25 47	296	27 15	333
145	48 30	011	34 37	084	46 36	154	47 13	222	24 45	274	24 59	295	26 51	332
146	48 39	009	35 29	083	46 59	154	46 37	222	23 52	274	24 12	294	26 26	331
147	48 47	008	36 21	082	47 21	155	46 02	223	23 00	273	23 24	294	26 00	330
148	48 54	006	37 13	082	47 43	155	45 26	223	22 08	273	22 35	293	25 33	329
149	48 59	005	38 05	081	48 05	156	44 50	223	21 15	272	21 47	292	25 06	328
	REGULUS		◆ Denebola		SPICA		◆ ACRUX		CANOPUS		◆ SIRIUS		PROCYON	
150	49 03	003	39 04	035	38 57	081	48 27	156	44 15	223	43 57	274	42 03	310
151	49 05	002	39 33	034	39 48	080	48 48	156	43 39	223	43 05	274	41 23	309
152	49 06	000	40 02	033	40 40	079	49 09	157	43 03	223	42 13	273	40 42	308
153	49 06	359	40 30	032	41 32	079	49 30	157	42 27	223	41 20	273	40 00	307
154	49 04	357	40 58	031	42 23	078	49 50	158	41 50	224	40 28	272	39 18	306
155	49 01	356	41 24	030	43 14	078	50 09	158	41 14	224	39 35	272	38 35	305
156	48 57	354	41 49	028	44 05	077	50 29	159	40 38	224	38 43	271	37 52	304
157	48 51	353	42 14	027	44 57	076	50 48	159	40 02	224	37 50	271	37 08	303
158	48 44	352	42 37	026	45 47	076	51 06	160	39 25	224	36 58	270	36 24	302
159	48 36	350	43 00	025	46 38	075	51 24	160	38 49	224	36 05	270	35 40	302
160	48 26	349	43 21	024	47 29	074	51 41	161	38 13	224	35 13	269	34 55	301
161	48 15	347	43 42	022	48 19	073	51 58	161	37 36	224	34 20	269	34 10	300
162	48 03	346	44 01	021	49 09	073	52 15	162	37 00	224	33 28	268	33 24	299
163	47 49	344	44 19	020	49 59	072	52 31	163	36 24	224	32 36	268	32 38	299
164	47 34	343	44 37	018	50 49	071	52 46	163	35 47	224	31 43	267	31 52	298
	ARCTURUS		◆ ANTARES		ACRUX		◆ CANOPUS		SIRIUS		PROCYON		◆ REGULUS	
165	22 30	051	18 29	111	53 01	164	35 11	224	30 51	267	31 05	297	47 18	341
166	23 10	050	19 19	110	53 16	164	34 35	224	29 58	267	30 18	296	47 01	340
167	23 50	049	20 08	110	53 30	165	33 59	224	29 06	266	29 31	296	46 43	339
168	24 29	048	20 57	109	53 43	166	33 22	224	28 14	266	28 44	295	46 23	337
169	25 08	048	21 47	109	53 55	166	32 46	224	27 21	265	27 56	294	46 02	336
170	25 47	047	22 36	109	54 07	167	32 10	223	26 29	265	27 08	294	45 40	335
171	26 25	046	23 26	108	54 19	168	31 34	223	25 37	264	26 20	293	45 18	334
172	27 03	045	24 16	108	54 30	169	30 58	223	24 45	264	25 31	292	44 54	332
173	27 40	045	25 06	108	54 40	169	30 22	223	23 52	263	24 43	292	44 29	331
174	28 16	044	25 56	107	54 49	170	29 46	223	23 00	263	23 54	291	44 03	330
175	28 52	043	26 46	107	54 58	171	29 10	223	22 08	263	23 05	290	43 36	329
176	29 28	042	27 36	107	55 06	171	28 35	223	21 16	262	22 15	290	43 08	327
177	30 02	041	28 27	106	55 14	172	27 59	223	20 24	262	21 26	289	42 39	326
178	30 37	040	29 17	106	55 20	173	27 24	223	19 32	261	20 36	289	42 10	325
179	31 10	039	30 08	106	55 26	174	26 48	222	18 41	261	19 46	288	41 39	324

LAT 29°S

LHA ♈	Hc	Zn	Hc	Zn	Hc	Zn	Hc	Zn	Hc	Zn	Hc	Zn	Hc	Zn
	◆ARCTURUS		ANTARES		◆RIGIL KENT		ACRUX		CANOPUS		◆Alphard		REGULUS	
180	31 43	039	30 58	105	48 29	152	55 32	175	26 13	222	49 04	292	41 08	323
181	32 16	038	31 49	105	48 53	152	55 36	175	25 38	222	48 15	291	40 36	322
182	32 47	037	32 40	104	49 18	153	55 40	176	25 03	222	47 26	290	40 03	321
183	33 18	036	33 31	104	49 42	153	55 44	177	24 28	222	46 37	290	39 29	320
184	33 49	035	34 22	104	50 05	153	55 46	178	23 53	221	45 47	289	38 55	319
185	34 18	034	35 13	103	50 29	154	55 48	179	23 18	221	44 58	288	38 20	318
186	34 47	033	36 04	103	50 52	154	55 49	179	22 44	221	44 08	287	37 44	317
187	35 15	032	36 55	103	51 14	155	55 49	180	22 09	221	43 17	286	37 08	316
188	35 42	031	37 46	102	51 36	155	55 49	181	21 35	221	42 27	286	36 31	315
189	36 09	030	38 37	102	51 58	156	55 47	182	21 01	220	41 36	285	35 53	314
190	36 34	029	39 29	102	52 19	156	55 45	183	20 27	220	40 46	284	35 15	313
191	36 59	028	40 20	101	52 40	157	55 43	183	19 53	220	39 55	284	34 36	312
192	37 23	027	41 12	101	53 00	158	55 39	184	19 20	220	39 04	283	33 57	311
193	37 46	025	42 03	101	53 20	158	55 35	185	18 46	219	38 13	282	33 17	310
194	38 08	024	42 55	100	53 39	159	55 30	186	18 13	219	37 21	282	32 37	309
	ARCTURUS		◆Rasalhague		ANTARES		RIGIL KENT		◆ACRUX		Suhail		◆REGULUS	
195	38 29	023	11 39	068	43 46	100	53 58	159	55 25	186	42 10	236	31 56	309
196	38 49	022	12 28	068	44 38	100	54 16	160	55 19	187	41 26	236	31 15	308
197	39 09	021	13 16	067	45 30	099	54 34	161	55 12	188	40 43	236	30 33	307
198	39 27	020	14 04	067	46 22	099	54 51	161	55 04	189	39 59	236	29 51	306
199	39 44	019	14 52	066	47 13	099	55 07	162	54 56	190	39 16	236	29 08	305
200	40 01	017	15 40	066	48 05	098	55 23	163	54 47	190	38 33	236	28 25	305
201	40 16	016	16 28	065	48 57	098	55 38	164	54 37	191	37 49	236	27 42	304
202	40 30	015	17 15	064	49 49	098	55 53	164	54 27	192	37 06	235	26 58	303
203	40 43	014	18 03	064	50 41	097	56 06	165	54 16	192	36 23	235	26 14	302
204	40 55	013	18 50	063	51 33	097	56 20	166	54 04	193	35 40	235	25 30	302
205	41 06	011	19 36	063	52 25	097	56 32	167	53 52	194	34 57	235	24 45	301
206	41 16	010	20 23	062	53 18	096	56 44	167	53 39	194	34 14	235	24 00	300
207	41 25	009	21 09	061	54 10	096	56 55	168	53 26	195	33 31	235	23 14	300
208	41 32	008	21 55	061	55 02	096	57 05	169	53 12	196	32 48	235	22 29	299
209	41 39	006	22 40	060	55 54	095	57 15	170	52 57	196	32 05	234	21 42	298
	◆ARCTURUS		Rasalhague		◆Nunki		RIGIL KENT		ACRUX		◆Suhail		Denebola	
210	41 44	005	23 26	059	25 29	107	57 23	171	52 42	197	31 23	234	36 20	320
211	41 48	004	24 11	059	26 19	107	57 31	172	52 27	198	30 40	234	35 46	319
212	41 51	003	24 55	058	27 09	107	57 38	173	52 10	198	29 57	234	35 11	318
213	41 53	001	25 39	057	27 59	106	57 45	173	51 54	199	29 15	234	34 36	317
214	41 54	000	26 23	056	28 50	106	57 50	174	51 37	199	28 33	234	33 59	316
215	41 53	359	27 07	056	29 40	105	57 55	175	51 19	200	27 51	233	33 23	315
216	41 52	358	27 50	055	30 31	105	57 59	176	51 01	200	27 09	233	32 45	314
217	41 49	356	28 33	054	31 22	105	58 02	177	50 42	201	26 27	233	32 07	313
218	41 45	355	29 15	053	32 13	104	58 04	178	50 23	201	25 45	233	31 29	312
219	41 40	354	29 57	053	33 03	104	58 06	179	50 04	202	25 03	232	30 50	312
220	41 33	353	30 39	052	33 54	104	58 06	180	49 44	202	24 22	232	30 10	311
221	41 26	351	31 20	051	34 45	103	58 06	181	49 24	203	23 40	232	29 30	310
222	41 18	350	32 00	050	35 36	103	58 05	182	49 03	203	22 59	232	28 50	309
223	41 08	349	32 40	049	36 28	103	58 03	183	48 42	204	22 18	231	28 09	308
224	40 57	348	33 20	049	37 19	102	58 00	184	48 21	204	21 37	231	27 28	308
	Alphecca		Rasalhague		◆Nunki		Peacock		◆RIGIL KENT		SPICA		◆ARCTURUS	
225	33 42	009	33 59	048	38 10	102	28 19	142	57 56	184	61 47	304	40 45	346
226	33 50	008	34 38	047	39 01	102	28 52	142	57 52	185	61 03	303	40 32	345
227	33 57	007	35 16	046	39 53	101	29 24	142	57 47	186	60 19	301	40 18	344
228	34 03	006	35 53	045	40 44	101	29 57	142	57 41	187	59 34	300	40 03	343
229	34 09	005	36 30	044	41 36	101	30 30	141	57 34	188	58 48	299	39 47	342
230	34 13	004	37 06	043	42 28	100	31 02	141	57 26	189	58 02	298	39 30	340
231	34 16	003	37 41	042	43 19	100	31 35	141	57 17	190	57 15	297	39 12	339
232	34 18	002	38 16	041	44 11	100	32 08	141	57 08	191	56 28	296	38 53	338
233	34 20	001	38 50	040	45 03	099	32 41	141	56 58	191	55 41	295	38 33	337
234	34 20	000	39 24	039	45 54	099	33 14	141	56 47	192	54 53	294	38 12	336
235	34 19	359	39 56	038	46 46	099	33 46	141	56 36	193	54 05	293	37 50	335
236	34 18	358	40 28	037	47 38	098	34 19	141	56 24	194	53 16	292	37 27	334
237	34 15	357	40 59	036	48 30	098	34 52	141	56 11	195	52 27	291	37 03	333
238	34 11	355	41 30	035	49 22	098	35 25	141	55 57	195	51 38	290	36 39	331
239	34 07	354	41 59	034	50 14	097	35 58	141	55 43	196	50 48	289	36 13	330
	◆VEGA		ALTAIR		◆Peacock		RIGIL KENT		◆SPICA		ARCTURUS		Alphecca	
240	12 54	030	22 36	065	36 31	141	55 28	197	49 59	288	35 47	329	34 01	353
241	13 20	030	23 24	064	37 04	141	55 12	198	49 09	287	35 20	328	33 55	352
242	13 46	029	24 11	064	37 37	141	54 56	198	48 19	287	34 52	327	33 47	351
243	14 11	028	24 58	063	38 10	141	54 39	199	47 28	286	34 23	326	33 39	350
244	14 36	028	25 44	062	38 43	141	54 22	200	46 38	285	33 54	325	33 29	349
245	15 00	027	26 31	062	39 16	141	54 04	200	45 47	284	33 24	324	33 19	348
246	15 24	026	27 17	061	39 48	141	53 45	201	44 56	284	32 53	324	33 08	347
247	15 47	026	28 03	060	40 21	142	53 26	202	44 05	283	32 21	323	32 55	346
248	16 09	025	28 48	060	40 54	142	53 06	202	43 14	282	31 49	322	32 42	345
249	16 31	024	29 33	059	41 26	142	52 46	203	42 23	282	31 16	321	32 28	344
250	16 53	024	30 18	058	41 59	142	52 26	203	41 31	281	30 42	320	32 13	343
251	17 13	023	31 02	057	42 31	142	52 05	204	40 40	281	30 08	319	31 57	342
252	17 33	022	31 46	057	43 03	142	51 43	204	39 48	280	29 34	318	31 40	341
253	17 53	021	32 30	056	43 35	142	51 21	205	38 56	279	28 58	317	31 23	340
254	18 11	021	33 13	055	44 07	143	50 59	205	38 04	279	28 22	316	31 04	339
	◆VEGA		ALTAIR		FOMALHAUT		◆Peacock		RIGIL KENT		◆SPICA		ARCTURUS	
255	18 30	020	33 55	054	14 08	116	44 39	143	50 36	206	37 12	278	27 46	316
256	18 47	019	34 38	053	14 55	116	45 11	143	50 13	206	36 21	278	27 09	315
257	19 04	018	35 20	052	15 42	115	45 43	143	49 49	207	35 28	277	26 32	314
258	19 20	018	36 01	052	16 30	115	46 14	143	49 25	207	34 36	276	25 54	313
259	19 35	017	36 42	051	17 17	115	46 45	144	49 01	208	33 44	276	25 15	312
260	19 50	016	37 22	050	18 05	114	47 16	144	48 37	208	32 52	275	24 36	312
261	20 04	015	38 02	049	18 53	114	47 47	144	48 12	209	32 00	275	23 57	311
262	20 18	014	38 41	048	19 41	114	48 18	144	47 47	209	31 07	274	23 17	310
263	20 30	014	39 20	047	20 29	113	48 48	145	47 21	209	30 15	274	22 37	310
264	20 42	013	39 58	046	21 17	113	49 18	145	46 55	210	29 23	273	21 56	309
265	20 53	012	40 35	045	22 06	113	49 48	146	46 29	210	28 30	273	21 15	308
266	21 04	011	41 12	044	22 54	112	50 17	146	46 03	210	27 38	272	20 33	307
267	21 14	010	41 48	043	23 43	112	50 47	146	45 37	210	26 45	272	19 51	307
268	21 23	009	42 23	042	24 32	112	51 16	147	45 10	211	25 53	271	19 09	306
269	21 31	009	42 58	041	25 21	111	51 44	147	44 43	211	25 00	271	18 27	305

LHA ♈	Hc	Zn	Hc	Zn	Hc	Zn	Hc	Zn	Hc	Zn	Hc	Zn	Hc	Zn
	VEGA		◆ALTAIR		FOMALHAUT		◆Peacock		RIGIL KENT		◆ANTARES		Alphecca	
270	21 38	008	43 32	040	26 10	111	52 13	148	44 16	211	70 02	272	24 25	325
271	21 45	007	44 05	038	26 59	111	52 41	148	43 48	212	69 09	271	23 54	324
272	21 51	006	44 37	037	27 48	110	53 08	149	43 21	212	68 17	271	23 23	323
273	21 57	005	45 08	036	28 37	110	53 35	149	42 53	212	67 24	270	22 51	322
274	22 01	005	45 39	035	29 27	110	54 02	150	42 25	212	66 32	270	22 19	321
275	22 05	004	46 08	034	30 16	109	54 28	150	41 57	212	65 39	269	21 46	321
276	22 08	003	46 37	032	31 06	109	54 54	151	41 29	212	64 47	269	21 12	320
277	22 10	002	47 05	031	31 55	109	55 19	151	41 01	213	63 54	268	20 38	319
278	22 11	001	47 31	030	32 45	108	55 44	152	40 33	213	63 02	268	20 04	318
279	22 12	000	47 57	029	33 35	108	56 09	153	40 04	213	62 09	268	19 29	318
280	22 12	359	48 21	027	34 25	108	56 32	153	39 36	213	61 17	267	18 53	317
281	22 11	359	48 45	026	35 15	107	56 56	154	39 07	213	60 25	267	18 17	316
282	22 09	358	49 07	024	36 05	107	57 18	155	38 38	213	59 32	266	17 41	316
283	22 07	357	49 28	023	36 55	107	57 40	156	38 09	213	58 40	266	17 04	315
284	22 04	356	49 48	022	37 46	106	58 01	156	37 40	213	57 47	266	16 27	314
	◆DENEB		FOMALHAUT		◆ACHERNAR		RIGIL KENT		◆ANTARES		Rasalhague		VEGA	
285	12 08	018	38 36	106	19 11	146	37 11	214	56 55	265	43 43	331	22 00	355
286	12 24	017	39 26	106	19 40	145	36 42	214	56 03	265	43 17	330	21 55	354
287	12 39	017	40 17	106	20 10	145	36 13	214	55 11	265	42 50	329	21 50	354
288	12 54	016	41 07	105	20 41	145	35 44	214	54 18	264	42 23	327	21 43	353
289	13 08	015	41 58	105	21 11	145	35 15	214	53 26	264	41 54	326	21 36	352
290	13 22	015	42 49	105	21 41	144	34 46	214	52 34	263	41 24	325	21 29	351
291	13 35	014	43 40	104	22 12	144	34 17	214	51 42	263	40 54	324	21 20	350
292	13 47	013	44 30	104	22 43	144	33 48	214	50 50	263	40 23	323	21 11	349
293	13 59	013	45 21	104	23 14	144	33 18	214	49 58	262	39 51	322	21 01	349
294	14 10	012	46 12	104	23 45	144	32 49	214	49 06	262	39 18	321	20 50	348
295	14 20	011	47 03	103	24 16	144	32 20	214	48 14	262	38 44	320	20 39	347
296	14 30	010	47 54	103	24 47	143	31 51	214	47 22	261	38 10	319	20 27	346
297	14 40	010	48 46	103	25 18	143	31 22	214	46 30	261	37 35	318	20 14	345
298	14 48	009	49 37	103	25 50	143	30 53	214	45 38	261	36 59	317	20 00	345
299	14 56	008	50 28	102	26 22	143	30 24	214	44 47	260	36 23	316	19 46	344
	DENEB		Enif		◆FOMALHAUT		ACHERNAR		◆RIGIL KENT		ANTARES		◆VEGA	
300	15 03	008	43 33	037	51 19	102	26 53	143	29 55	214	43 55	260	19 31	343
301	15 10	007	44 04	036	52 11	102	27 25	143	29 26	213	43 03	260	19 16	342
302	15 16	006	44 35	035	53 02	102	27 57	143	28 57	213	42 12	259	18 59	342
303	15 21	005	45 04	033	53 53	101	28 29	142	28 28	213	41 20	259	18 42	341
304	15 26	005	45 32	032	54 45	101	29 01	142	27 59	213	40 29	259	18 25	340
305	15 30	004	46 00	031	55 36	101	29 33	142	27 30	213	39 37	258	18 06	339
306	15 33	003	46 26	030	56 28	101	30 05	142	27 02	213	38 46	258	17 47	338
307	15 36	003	46 52	028	57 20	100	30 38	142	26 33	213	37 55	258	17 28	338
308	15 38	002	47 16	027	58 11	100	31 10	142	26 05	213	37 03	257	17 08	337
309	15 39	001	47 39	026	59 03	100	31 42	142	25 36	213	36 12	257	16 47	336
310	15 40	000	48 01	024	59 55	100	32 15	142	25 08	212	35 21	257	16 25	336
311	15 40	000	48 22	023	60 46	099	32 47	142	24 40	212	34 30	256	16 03	335
312	15 39	359	48 42	022	61 38	099	33 20	142	24 12	212	33 39	256	15 41	334
313	15 38	358	49 01	020	62 30	099	33 52	142	23 44	212	32 48	256	15 17	333
314	15 36	357	49 18	019	63 22	099	34 25	142	23 16	212	31 57	255	14 54	333
	Alpheratz		◆Diphda		ACHERNAR		◆RIGIL KENT		ANTARES		◆ALTAIR		DENEB	
315	16 22	042	37 50	091	34 57	142	22 49	212	31 07	255	48 39	334	15 33	357
316	16 56	041	38 43	090	35 30	142	22 21	212	30 16	255	48 15	333	15 30	356
317	17 31	041	39 35	090	36 02	142	21 54	211	29 26	254	47 51	331	15 26	355
318	18 05	040	40 28	089	36 35	142	21 27	211	28 35	254	47 25	330	15 21	355
319	18 38	039	41 20	089	37 07	142	20 59	211	27 45	253	46 58	329	15 16	354
320	19 11	038	42 13	088	37 40	142	20 32	211	26 55	253	46 30	327	15 10	353
321	19 43	038	43 05	088	38 12	142	20 06	211	26 04	253	46 01	326	15 03	352
322	20 15	037	43 57	087	38 45	142	19 39	210	25 14	252	45 31	325	14 56	352
323	20 47	036	44 50	087	39 17	142	19 13	210	24 24	252	45 01	324	14 48	351
324	21 17	035	45 42	086	39 49	142	18 46	210	23 34	252	44 29	322	14 39	350
325	21 47	035	46 35	086	40 22	142	18 20	210	22 45	251	43 57	321	14 30	350
326	22 17	034	47 27	085	40 54	142	17 54	209	21 55	251	43 24	320	14 20	349
327	22 46	033	48 19	085	41 26	142	17 29	209	21 05	251	42 50	319	14 10	348
328	23 15	032	49 11	084	41 58	143	17 03	209	20 16	250	42 15	318	13 59	347
329	23 42	032	50 04	083	42 30	143	16 38	209	19 27	250	41 39	317	13 47	347
	◆Alpheratz		Diphda		◆ACHERNAR		Peacock		◆Nunki		ALTAIR		Enif	
330	24 09	031	50 56	083	43 01	143	57 49	204	49 27	262	41 03	316	50 53	354
331	24 36	030	51 48	082	43 33	143	57 27	205	48 35	262	40 26	315	50 47	353
332	25 02	029	52 40	082	44 05	143	57 05	206	47 43	262	39 49	314	50 40	351
333	25 27	028	53 31	081	44 36	143	56 42	206	46 51	261	39 10	313	50 31	349
334	25 51	027	54 23	080	45 07	144	56 18	207	46 00	261	38 32	312	50 20	348
335	26 15	027	55 15	079	45 38	144	55 54	208	45 08	261	37 52	311	50 09	346
336	26 38	026	56 06	079	46 09	144	55 30	208	44 16	260	37 12	310	49 56	345
337	27 01	025	56 58	078	46 40	144	55 05	209	43 24	260	36 32	309	49 42	343
338	27 22	024	57 49	077	47 10	145	54 39	210	42 33	260	35 51	308	49 26	342
339	27 43	023	58 40	076	47 41	145	54 13	210	41 41	259	35 10	307	49 09	341
340	28 03	022	59 31	076	48 11	145	53 46	211	40 49	259	34 28	307	48 51	339
341	28 22	021	60 22	075	48 41	146	53 19	211	39 58	259	33 45	306	48 32	338
342	28 41	020	61 12	074	49 10	146	52 52	212	39 06	258	33 02	305	48 11	336
343	28 59	019	62 03	073	49 39	146	52 24	212	38 15	258	32 19	304	47 50	335
344	29 16	018	62 53	072	50 08	147	51 56	213	37 24	258	31 35	303	47 27	334
	Alpheratz		◆Hamal		◆ACHERNAR		Peacock		Nunki		◆ALTAIR		Enif	
345	29 32	017	20 41	046	50 37	147	51 28	213	36 33	257	30 51	303	47 03	332
346	29 47	016	21 19	045	51 06	147	50 59	214	35 41	257	30 07	302	46 38	331
347	30 01	015	21 55	044	51 34	148	50 30	214	34 50	257	29 22	301	46 12	330
348	30 15	014	22 32	044	52 01	148	50 00	214	33 59	256	28 37	300	45 45	328
349	30 27	013	23 08	043	52 29	149	49 30	215	33 08	256	27 51	300	45 17	327
350	30 39	012	23 43	042	52 56	149	49 00	215	32 17	256	27 06	299	44 48	326
351	30 50	011	24 18	041	53 22	150	48 30	215	31 27	255	26 20	298	44 18	325
352	31 00	010	24 53	041	53 49	150	48 00	216	30 36	255	25 33	297	43 48	324
353	31 09	009	25 26	040	54 14	151	47 29	216	29 45	255	24 46	297	43 16	322
354	31 17	008	26 00	039	54 39	152	46 58	216	28 55	254	23 59	296	42 44	321
355	31 25	007	26 32	038	55 04	152	46 27	217	28 04	254	23 12	295	42 11	320
356	31 31	006	27 04	037	55 29	153	45 55	217	27 14	254	22 25	295	41 37	319
357	31 36	005	27 36	036	55 52	153	45 24	217	26 24	253	21 37	294	41 02	318
358	31 41	004	28 07	036	56 15	154	44 52	217	25 34	253	20 49	294	40 27	317
359	31 45	003	28 37	035	56 38	155	44 21	217	24 43	252	20 01	293	39 50	316

LAT 30°S

LHA ♈	Hc	Zn	Hc	Zn	Hc	Zn	Hc	Zn	Hc	Zn	Hc	Zn	Hc	Zn
	◆ Alpheratz		Hamal		◆ RIGEL		CANOPUS		ACHERNAR		◆ Peacock		Enif	
0	30 47	002	28 16	033	13 44	092	20 01	140	57 55	155	44 36	218	38 31	316
1	30 49	001	28 45	033	14 36	091	20 34	140	58 16	156	44 04	218	37 54	315
2	30 50	000	29 12	032	15 28	091	21 08	140	58 37	156	43 31	219	37 17	314
3	30 49	359	29 39	031	16 20	090	21 42	139	58 58	157	42 59	219	36 39	313
4	30 48	358	30 06	030	17 12	090	22 16	139	59 18	158	42 27	219	36 01	312
5	30 46	357	30 31	029	18 04	089	22 50	139	59 37	159	41 54	219	35 22	311
6	30 43	356	30 56	028	18 56	089	23 24	139	59 55	160	41 21	219	34 42	310
7	30 39	355	31 20	027	19 48	088	23 58	138	60 12	161	40 49	219	34 02	309
8	30 35	354	31 43	026	20 40	088	24 33	138	60 29	162	40 16	219	33 21	308
9	30 29	353	32 05	025	21 32	087	25 07	138	60 45	163	39 43	219	32 40	307
10	30 22	352	32 27	024	22 24	087	25 42	138	61 00	164	39 10	219	31 59	307
11	30 15	351	32 48	023	23 15	086	26 17	138	61 14	165	38 37	219	31 17	306
12	30 06	350	33 07	022	24 07	086	26 52	137	61 28	166	38 04	219	30 35	305
13	29 57	349	33 26	021	24 59	085	27 27	137	61 40	167	37 31	219	29 52	304
14	29 47	348	33 45	020	25 51	084	28 03	137	61 51	168	36 58	219	29 09	303
	◆ Hamal		ALDEBARAN		RIGEL		◆ CANOPUS		ACHERNAR		◆ FOMALHAUT		Alpheratz	
15	34 02	019	20 05	056	26 42	084	28 38	137	62 02	169	63 42	263	29 36	347
16	34 18	018	20 48	055	27 34	083	29 13	137	62 11	170	62 51	263	29 24	346
17	34 34	017	21 30	054	28 26	083	29 49	137	62 20	171	61 59	263	29 11	345
18	34 48	016	22 12	054	29 17	082	30 25	137	62 27	172	61 07	262	28 58	344
19	35 02	015	22 54	053	30 09	082	31 01	136	62 34	173	60 16	262	28 43	343
20	35 14	014	23 35	052	31 00	081	31 36	136	62 39	175	59 25	262	28 28	342
21	35 26	012	24 16	052	31 51	080	32 12	136	62 44	176	58 33	262	28 12	341
22	35 37	011	24 57	051	32 43	080	32 48	136	62 47	177	57 42	261	27 55	341
23	35 46	010	25 37	050	33 34	079	33 24	136	62 49	178	56 50	261	27 37	340
24	35 55	009	26 17	049	34 25	079	34 00	136	62 50	179	55 59	261	27 19	339
25	36 03	008	26 56	049	35 16	078	34 37	136	62 50	181	55 08	260	26 59	338
26	36 09	007	27 34	048	36 06	077	35 13	136	62 49	182	54 17	260	26 39	337
27	36 15	006	28 13	047	36 57	077	35 49	136	62 47	183	53 26	260	26 19	336
28	36 20	005	28 50	046	37 48	076	36 25	136	62 44	184	52 34	259	25 57	335
29	36 23	003	29 28	045	38 38	075	37 02	136	62 40	185	51 43	259	25 35	334
	Hamal		ALDEBARAN		◆ SIRIUS		CANOPUS		◆ ACHERNAR		FOMALHAUT		◆ Alpheratz	
30	36 26	002	30 04	044	24 04	096	37 38	136	62 35	186	50 52	259	25 12	333
31	36 28	001	30 40	044	24 56	096	38 14	136	62 28	188	50 01	259	24 48	332
32	36 28	000	31 16	043	25 47	095	38 51	136	62 21	189	49 10	258	24 24	332
33	36 28	359	31 51	042	26 39	095	39 27	136	62 13	190	48 20	258	23 59	331
34	36 26	358	32 25	041	27 31	094	40 03	136	62 03	191	47 29	258	23 33	330
35	36 23	357	32 59	040	28 23	094	40 40	136	61 53	192	46 38	257	23 07	329
36	36 20	355	33 32	039	29 15	093	41 16	136	61 42	193	45 47	257	22 40	328
37	36 15	354	34 04	038	30 07	093	41 52	136	61 29	194	44 57	257	22 12	328
38	36 10	353	34 36	037	30 58	092	42 29	136	61 16	195	44 06	257	21 44	327
39	36 03	352	35 07	036	31 50	092	43 05	136	61 02	196	43 16	256	21 15	326
40	35 55	351	35 37	035	32 42	091	43 41	136	60 47	197	42 25	256	20 46	325
41	35 46	350	36 07	034	33 34	091	44 17	136	60 31	198	41 35	256	20 16	324
42	35 37	349	36 35	033	34 26	090	44 53	136	60 15	199	40 45	255	19 45	324
43	35 26	348	37 03	032	35 18	090	45 29	136	59 57	200	39 54	255	19 14	323
44	35 15	347	37 31	031	36 10	089	46 05	136	59 39	201	39 04	255	18 43	322
	◆ ALDEBARAN		BETELGEUSE		SIRIUS		◆ CANOPUS		ACHERNAR		◆ FOMALHAUT		Hamal	
45	37 57	030	33 36	056	37 02	089	46 41	137	59 20	202	38 14	254	35 02	345
46	38 22	029	34 19	055	37 54	088	47 16	137	59 01	203	37 24	254	34 48	344
47	38 47	028	35 01	054	38 46	088	47 52	137	58 40	203	36 34	254	34 34	343
48	39 11	027	35 43	053	39 38	087	48 27	137	58 19	204	35 44	253	34 18	342
49	39 33	025	36 24	052	40 30	087	49 02	137	57 58	205	34 55	253	34 02	341
50	39 55	024	37 05	051	41 22	086	49 37	138	57 35	206	34 05	253	33 45	340
51	40 16	023	37 45	051	42 14	086	50 12	138	57 12	206	33 15	252	33 27	339
52	40 36	022	38 25	050	43 05	085	50 47	138	56 49	207	32 26	252	33 08	338
53	40 55	021	39 05	049	43 57	085	51 22	138	56 25	208	31 37	252	32 48	337
54	41 13	020	39 43	048	44 49	084	51 56	139	56 00	208	30 47	251	32 27	336
55	41 30	018	40 21	047	45 40	083	52 30	139	55 35	209	29 58	251	32 05	335
56	41 45	017	40 59	046	46 32	083	53 04	140	55 10	210	29 09	251	31 43	334
57	42 00	016	41 36	045	47 24	082	53 38	140	54 44	210	28 20	250	31 20	333
58	42 14	015	42 12	044	48 15	082	54 11	140	54 18	211	27 31	250	30 56	332
59	42 26	013	42 47	042	49 06	081	54 44	141	53 51	211	26 42	250	30 31	331
	ALDEBARAN		BETELGEUSE		◆ SIRIUS		CANOPUS		◆ ACHERNAR		FOMALHAUT		◆ Hamal	
60	42 38	012	43 22	041	49 58	080	55 17	141	53 24	212	25 54	249	30 06	330
61	42 48	011	43 56	040	50 49	080	55 49	142	52 56	212	25 05	249	29 40	329
62	42 57	009	44 29	039	51 40	079	56 21	142	52 28	213	24 17	249	29 13	328
63	43 05	008	45 02	038	52 31	078	56 53	143	52 00	213	23 28	248	28 45	327
64	43 12	007	45 33	037	53 21	077	57 24	143	51 31	214	22 40	248	28 17	327
65	43 17	006	46 04	036	54 12	077	57 55	144	51 02	214	21 52	248	27 48	326
66	43 22	004	46 34	034	55 03	076	58 25	145	50 33	214	21 04	247	27 18	325
67	43 25	003	47 02	033	55 53	075	58 55	145	50 04	215	20 16	247	26 48	324
68	43 27	002	47 30	032	56 43	074	59 24	146	49 34	215	19 28	246	26 17	323
69	43 28	000	47 57	030	57 33	073	59 53	147	49 04	215	18 41	246	25 45	322
70	43 27	359	48 23	029	58 22	072	60 21	147	48 34	216	17 53	246	25 13	321
71	43 26	358	48 47	028	59 12	071	60 49	148	48 03	216	17 06	245	24 40	321
72	43 23	356	49 11	026	60 01	070	61 16	149	47 33	216	16 19	245	24 07	320
73	43 19	355	49 34	025	60 50	069	61 42	150	47 02	217	15 32	245	23 33	319
74	43 14	354	49 55	023	61 38	068	62 08	151	46 31	217	14 45	244	22 59	318
	BETELGEUSE		PROCYON		◆ Suhail		CANOPUS		◆ ACHERNAR		Hamal		◆ ALDEBARAN	
75	50 15	022	37 58	054	39 37	124	62 33	152	46 00	217	22 24	317	43 08	352
76	50 34	021	38 40	053	40 21	124	62 57	153	45 28	217	21 49	317	43 00	351
77	50 51	019	39 22	053	41 04	123	63 21	154	44 57	217	21 13	316	42 51	350
78	51 08	018	40 03	052	41 48	123	63 43	155	44 25	218	20 37	315	42 42	348
79	51 23	016	40 43	051	42 31	123	64 05	156	43 53	218	20 00	314	42 31	347
80	51 36	014	41 23	050	43 14	123	64 25	157	43 21	218	19 22	314	42 19	346
81	51 49	013	42 02	049	43 58	123	64 45	158	42 50	218	18 45	313	42 05	345
82	52 00	011	42 41	048	44 41	123	65 04	160	42 17	218	18 06	312	41 51	343
83	52 09	010	43 19	047	45 25	123	65 21	161	41 45	218	17 28	312	41 36	342
84	52 17	008	43 57	045	46 08	123	65 38	162	41 13	218	16 49	311	41 19	341
85	52 24	007	44 33	044	46 52	123	65 53	163	40 41	218	16 09	310	41 02	340
86	52 29	005	45 09	043	47 35	123	66 07	165	40 08	219	15 30	310	40 43	339
87	52 33	003	45 44	042	48 19	123	66 20	166	39 36	219	14 49	309	40 24	337
88	52 35	002	46 19	041	49 02	123	66 32	168	39 04	219	14 09	308	40 03	336
89	52 35	000	46 52	040	49 46	123	66 43	169	38 31	219	13 28	308	39 42	335

LHA ♈	Hc	Zn	Hc	Zn	Hc	Zn	Hc	Zn	Hc	Zn	Hc	Zn	Hc	Zn
	POLLUX		◆ REGULUS		ACRUX		◆ CANOPUS		ACHERNAR		◆ RIGEL		BETELGEUSE	
90	26 42	026	16 55	065	23 33	151	66 52	171	37 59	219	65 48	332	52 35	358
91	27 05	025	17 42	064	23 58	151	67 00	172	37 26	219	65 23	330	52 33	357
92	27 27	024	18 29	064	24 24	150	67 06	174	36 54	219	64 56	328	52 29	355
93	27 48	024	19 15	063	24 50	150	67 11	175	36 21	219	64 27	326	52 24	353
94	28 08	023	20 01	062	25 16	150	67 15	177	35 49	219	63 57	324	52 17	352
95	28 28	022	20 47	062	25 42	150	67 17	178	35 16	219	63 26	322	52 09	350
96	28 47	021	21 33	061	26 08	150	67 18	180	34 44	219	62 53	320	51 59	349
97	29 05	020	22 18	060	26 34	150	67 17	181	34 11	219	62 19	318	51 49	347
98	29 22	019	23 03	060	27 00	150	67 15	183	33 39	219	61 44	317	51 36	346
99	29 38	018	23 48	059	27 26	149	67 12	185	33 06	219	61 08	315	51 23	344
100	29 54	017	24 32	058	27 53	149	67 07	186	32 34	219	60 31	313	51 08	342
101	30 08	016	25 16	058	28 19	149	67 01	188	32 01	218	59 52	312	50 51	341
102	30 22	015	26 00	057	28 46	149	66 53	189	31 29	218	59 13	310	50 34	339
103	30 35	014	26 43	056	29 13	149	66 44	191	30 57	218	58 33	309	50 15	338
104	30 47	013	27 26	055	29 39	149	66 34	192	30 25	218	57 53	308	49 55	337
	POLLUX		◆ REGULUS		Gienah		◆ ACRUX		CANOPUS		◆ RIGEL		BETELGEUSE	
105	30 58	012	28 09	055	17 52	100	30 06	149	66 22	194	57 11	306	49 33	335
106	31 08	011	28 51	054	18 43	100	30 33	149	66 09	195	56 29	305	49 11	334
107	31 18	010	29 33	053	19 34	100	31 00	149	65 55	196	55 46	304	48 47	332
108	31 26	009	30 14	052	20 26	099	31 27	149	65 40	198	55 02	303	48 23	331
109	31 34	008	30 55	051	21 17	099	31 54	149	65 24	199	54 18	301	47 57	330
110	31 40	007	31 35	051	22 08	098	32 21	149	65 06	200	53 34	300	47 30	328
111	31 46	006	32 15	050	23 00	098	32 48	149	64 48	202	52 49	299	47 02	327
112	31 51	005	32 55	049	23 51	097	33 15	149	64 28	203	52 03	298	46 33	326
113	31 55	004	33 34	048	24 43	097	33 42	149	64 08	204	51 17	297	46 04	324
114	31 58	003	34 12	047	25 35	096	34 09	149	63 46	205	50 31	296	45 33	323
115	32 00	002	34 50	046	26 26	096	34 36	149	63 24	206	49 44	295	45 01	322
116	32 01	001	35 27	045	27 18	095	35 03	149	63 01	207	48 57	294	44 29	321
117	32 01	000	36 04	044	28 10	095	35 30	149	62 37	208	48 09	293	43 56	320
118	32 00	358	36 40	043	29 02	095	35 57	149	62 12	209	47 22	293	43 22	319
119	31 58	357	37 15	042	29 53	094	36 24	149	61 46	210	46 33	292	42 47	317
	◆ REGULUS		SPICA		◆ ACRUX		CANOPUS		◆ RIGEL		BETELGEUSE		POLLUX	
120	37 50	041	12 53	096	36 51	149	61 20	211	45 45	291	42 12	316	31 55	356
121	38 24	040	13 45	095	37 18	149	60 53	212	44 56	290	41 35	315	31 51	355
122	38 57	039	14 37	095	37 45	149	60 25	212	44 07	289	40 59	314	31 47	354
123	39 30	038	15 29	094	38 12	149	59 57	213	43 18	289	40 21	313	31 41	353
124	40 02	037	16 20	094	38 38	149	59 28	214	42 29	288	39 43	312	31 35	352
125	40 33	036	17 12	093	39 05	149	58 59	215	41 39	287	39 04	311	31 27	351
126	41 03	035	18 04	093	39 32	149	58 29	215	40 50	286	38 25	310	31 19	350
127	41 32	034	18 56	092	39 58	149	57 59	216	40 00	286	37 45	309	31 10	349
128	42 01	033	19 48	092	40 25	150	57 28	217	39 10	285	37 05	309	30 59	348
129	42 29	032	20 40	091	40 51	150	56 57	217	38 19	284	36 24	308	30 48	347
130	42 56	030	21 32	091	41 17	150	56 25	218	37 29	284	35 42	307	30 36	346
131	43 21	029	22 24	090	41 43	150	55 54	218	36 38	283	35 01	306	30 24	345
132	43 46	028	23 16	090	42 09	150	55 21	219	35 48	282	34 18	305	30 10	344
133	44 10	027	24 08	089	42 35	150	54 49	219	34 57	282	33 35	304	29 55	343
134	44 33	026	25 00	089	43 01	151	54 16	220	34 06	281	32 52	303	29 40	342
	REGULUS		◆ SPICA		ACRUX		◆ CANOPUS		RIGEL		BETELGEUSE		◆ POLLUX	
135	44 55	024	25 52	088	43 26	151	53 42	220	33 15	280	32 09	303	29 24	341
136	45 16	023	26 44	088	43 51	151	53 09	220	32 24	280	31 25	302	29 07	340
137	45 36	022	27 36	087	44 16	151	52 35	221	31 32	279	30 40	301	28 49	339
138	45 54	020	28 27	087	44 41	151	52 01	221	30 41	279	29 56	300	28 30	338
139	46 12	019	29 19	086	45 06	152	51 27	221	29 50	278	29 11	300	28 11	338
140	46 28	018	30 11	086	45 31	152	50 52	222	28 58	278	28 25	299	27 50	337
141	46 43	016	31 03	085	45 55	152	50 17	222	28 07	277	27 40	298	27 29	336
142	46 57	015	31 55	085	46 19	153	49 42	222	27 15	276	26 54	297	27 07	335
143	47 10	013	32 46	084	46 43	153	49 07	223	26 23	276	26 07	297	26 45	334
144	47 21	012	33 38	083	47 06	153	48 32	223	25 32	275	25 21	296	26 22	333
145	47 31	011	34 30	083	47 30	154	47 57	223	24 40	275	24 34	295	25 58	332
146	47 40	009	35 21	082	47 53	154	47 21	223	23 48	274	23 47	295	25 33	331
147	47 48	008	36 13	082	48 15	154	46 46	223	22 56	274	22 59	294	25 08	330
148	47 54	006	37 04	081	48 38	155	46 10	224	22 04	273	22 12	293	24 42	330
149	47 59	005	37 55	081	49 00	155	45 34	224	21 13	273	21 24	293	24 15	329
	REGULUS		◆ Denebola		SPICA		◆ ACRUX		CANOPUS		◆ SIRIUS		PROCYON	
150	48 03	003	38 14	035	38 47	080	49 22	155	44 58	224	43 52	275	41 25	310
151	48 05	002	38 44	034	39 38	079	49 43	156	44 22	224	43 00	275	40 45	309
152	48 06	000	39 12	032	40 29	079	50 04	156	43 46	224	42 09	274	40 05	308
153	48 06	359	39 39	031	41 20	078	50 25	157	43 10	224	41 17	274	39 24	308
154	48 04	357	40 06	030	42 10	077	50 45	157	42 34	224	40 25	273	38 42	307
155	48 02	356	40 32	029	43 01	077	51 05	158	41 57	224	39 33	273	38 00	306
156	47 57	355	40 56	028	43 51	076	51 25	158	41 21	224	38 41	272	37 18	305
157	47 52	353	41 20	027	44 42	075	51 44	159	40 45	224	37 49	272	36 35	304
158	47 45	352	41 43	026	45 32	075	52 02	159	40 09	224	36 57	271	35 52	303
159	47 37	350	42 05	024	46 22	074	52 20	160	39 32	224	36 05	271	35 08	302
160	47 27	349	42 26	023	47 12	073	52 38	160	38 56	224	35 13	270	34 24	301
161	47 17	347	42 46	022	48 01	072	52 55	161	38 19	224	34 21	270	33 39	301
162	47 05	346	43 05	021	48 51	071	53 12	162	37 43	224	33 29	269	32 54	300
163	46 51	345	43 23	019	49 40	071	53 28	162	37 07	224	32 37	269	32 09	299
164	46 37	343	43 40	018	50 29	070	53 44	163	36 30	224	31 45	268	31 24	298
	ARCTURUS		◆ ANTARES		ACRUX		◆ CANOPUS		SIRIUS		PROCYON		◆ REGULUS	
165	21 51	050	18 50	110	53 59	163	35 54	224	30 54	268	30 38	298	46 21	342
166	22 31	050	19 39	110	54 14	164	35 18	224	30 02	267	29 51	297	46 05	340
167	23 11	049	20 28	109	54 28	165	34 42	224	29 10	267	29 05	296	45 47	339
168	23 49	048	21 17	109	54 41	165	34 06	224	28 18	266	28 18	295	45 28	338
169	24 28	047	22 06	109	54 54	166	33 29	224	27 26	266	27 31	295	45 07	337
170	25 06	047	22 56	108	55 06	167	32 53	224	26 34	265	26 44	294	44 46	335
171	25 43	046	23 45	108	55 17	167	32 17	224	25 42	265	25 56	293	44 24	334
172	26 20	045	24 34	108	55 28	168	31 41	224	24 51	264	25 08	293	44 00	333
173	26 57	044	25 24	107	55 39	169	31 06	224	23 59	264	24 20	292	43 36	331
174	27 33	043	26 14	107	55 48	170	30 30	223	23 07	263	23 32	291	43 11	330
175	28 08	042	27 03	106	55 57	170	29 54	223	22 16	263	22 44	291	42 45	329
176	28 43	042	27 53	106	56 06	171	29 19	223	21 24	262	21 55	290	42 17	328
177	29 17	041	28 43	106	56 13	172	28 43	223	20 33	262	21 06	290	41 49	327
178	29 51	040	29 33	105	56 20	173	28 08	223	19 41	262	20 17	289	41 20	326
179	30 24	039	30 24	105	56 26	174	27 32	223	18 50	261	19 28	288	40 51	324

LHA ♈	Hc	Zn	Hc	Zn	Hc	Zn	Hc	Zn	Hc	Zn	Hc	Zn	Hc	Zn
	◆ ARCTURUS		ANTARES		◆ RIGIL KENT		ACRUX		CANOPUS		◆ Alphard		REGULUS	
180	30 56	038	31 14	105	49 22	151	56 32	174	26 57	223	48 41	293	40 20	323
181	31 28	037	32 04	104	49 46	152	56 36	175	26 22	222	47 53	292	39 49	322
182	31 59	036	32 55	104	50 11	152	56 40	176	25 47	222	47 05	291	39 16	321
183	32 29	035	33 45	103	50 35	152	56 44	177	25 12	222	46 17	291	38 43	320
184	32 59	034	34 36	103	50 59	153	56 46	178	24 38	222	45 28	290	38 10	319
185	33 28	033	35 26	103	51 23	153	56 48	178	24 03	222	44 39	289	37 35	318
186	33 56	032	36 17	102	51 46	154	56 49	179	23 29	221	43 49	288	37 00	317
187	34 24	031	37 08	102	52 08	154	56 49	180	22 54	221	43 00	287	36 25	316
188	34 51	030	37 59	102	52 31	155	56 49	181	22 20	221	42 10	287	35 49	315
189	35 16	029	38 50	101	52 53	155	56 47	182	21 46	221	41 20	286	35 12	314
190	35 42	028	39 41	101	53 14	156	56 45	183	21 13	220	40 30	285	34 34	313
191	36 06	027	40 32	101	53 35	156	56 43	183	20 39	220	39 40	285	33 56	312
192	36 29	026	41 23	100	53 56	157	56 39	184	20 06	220	38 50	284	33 17	312
193	36 52	025	42 14	100	54 16	158	56 35	185	19 32	220	37 59	283	32 38	311
194	37 13	024	43 05	099	54 35	158	56 30	186	18 59	219	37 09	283	31 59	310
	ARCTURUS		◆ Rasalhague		ANTARES		RIGIL KENT		◆ ACRUX		Suhail		◆ REGULUS	
195	37 34	023	11 17	068	43 56	099	54 54	159	56 24	187	42 43	237	31 19	309
196	37 54	022	12 05	068	44 48	099	55 12	160	56 18	187	41 59	237	30 38	308
197	38 13	021	12 53	067	45 39	098	55 30	160	56 11	188	41 16	237	29 57	307
198	38 31	020	13 41	067	46 30	098	55 47	161	56 03	189	40 33	236	29 15	307
199	38 47	018	14 28	066	47 22	098	56 04	162	55 55	190	39 49	236	28 34	306
200	39 03	017	15 15	065	48 13	097	56 20	162	55 46	191	39 06	236	27 51	305
201	39 18	016	16 03	065	49 05	097	56 36	163	55 36	191	38 23	236	27 08	304
202	39 32	015	16 49	064	49 57	096	56 50	164	55 25	192	37 40	236	26 25	304
203	39 45	014	17 36	063	50 48	096	57 04	165	55 14	193	36 57	236	25 42	303
204	39 57	012	18 22	063	51 40	096	57 18	165	55 03	193	36 14	236	24 58	302
205	40 07	011	19 08	062	52 32	095	57 30	166	54 50	194	35 31	236	24 14	301
206	40 17	010	19 54	062	53 23	095	57 42	167	54 37	195	34 48	235	23 29	301
207	40 25	009	20 40	061	54 15	095	57 53	168	54 24	195	34 05	235	22 44	300
208	40 33	008	21 25	060	55 07	094	58 04	169	54 10	196	33 22	235	21 59	299
209	40 39	006	22 10	060	55 59	094	58 14	170	53 55	197	32 40	235	21 14	299
	◆ ARCTURUS		Rasalhague		◆ Nunki		RIGIL KENT		ACRUX		◆ Suhail		Denebola	
210	40 44	005	22 55	059	25 46	107	58 23	171	53 40	197	31 57	235	35 34	320
211	40 48	004	23 39	058	26 36	106	58 31	171	53 24	198	31 15	235	35 01	319
212	40 51	003	24 23	058	27 26	106	58 38	172	53 07	199	30 33	234	34 26	318
213	40 53	001	25 07	057	28 16	106	58 44	173	52 51	199	29 50	234	33 52	317
214	40 54	000	25 50	056	29 06	105	58 50	174	52 33	200	29 08	234	33 16	316
215	40 53	359	26 33	055	29 56	105	58 55	175	52 15	200	28 26	234	32 40	316
216	40 52	358	27 15	055	30 46	105	58 59	176	51 57	201	27 45	234	32 03	315
217	40 49	356	27 58	054	31 37	104	59 02	177	51 38	201	27 03	233	31 26	314
218	40 45	355	28 39	053	32 27	104	59 04	178	51 19	202	26 21	233	30 48	313
219	40 40	354	29 21	052	33 18	103	59 06	179	51 00	202	25 40	233	30 10	312
220	40 34	353	30 02	051	34 08	103	59 06	180	50 40	203	24 58	233	29 31	311
221	40 27	351	30 42	051	34 59	103	59 06	181	50 19	203	24 17	232	28 52	310
222	40 18	350	31 22	050	35 50	102	59 05	182	49 58	204	23 36	232	28 12	310
223	40 09	349	32 01	049	36 40	102	59 03	183	49 37	204	22 55	232	27 32	309
224	39 59	348	32 40	048	37 31	102	59 00	184	49 16	205	22 15	231	26 51	308
	Alphecca		Rasalhague		◆ Nunki		Peacock		◆ RIGIL KENT		SPICA		◆ ARCTURUS	
225	32 42	009	33 19	047	38 22	101	29 06	142	58 56	185	61 13	306	39 47	347
226	32 50	008	33 56	046	39 13	101	29 39	141	58 52	185	60 30	304	39 34	345
227	32 58	007	34 34	045	40 04	101	30 11	141	58 46	186	59 47	303	39 21	344
228	33 04	006	35 10	044	40 55	100	30 44	141	58 40	187	59 03	302	39 06	343
229	33 09	005	35 46	044	41 47	100	31 16	141	58 33	188	58 18	300	38 50	342
230	33 13	004	36 22	043	42 38	099	31 49	141	58 25	189	57 33	299	38 34	341
231	33 16	003	36 57	042	43 29	099	32 22	141	58 17	190	56 48	298	38 16	340
232	33 18	002	37 31	041	44 20	099	32 54	141	58 07	191	56 02	297	37 57	338
233	33 20	001	38 04	040	45 12	098	33 27	141	57 57	192	55 15	296	37 38	337
234	33 20	000	38 37	039	46 03	098	34 00	141	57 46	193	54 28	295	37 17	336
235	33 19	359	39 09	037	46 55	098	34 33	141	57 34	193	53 41	294	36 55	335
236	33 18	358	39 40	036	47 46	097	35 06	141	57 22	194	52 53	293	36 33	334
237	33 15	357	40 11	035	48 38	097	35 39	141	57 09	195	52 05	292	36 10	333
238	33 12	356	40 40	034	49 29	096	36 12	141	56 55	196	51 17	291	35 46	332
239	33 07	354	41 09	033	50 21	096	36 45	141	56 40	197	50 28	290	35 21	331
	◆ VEGA		ALTAIR		◆ Peacock		RIGIL KENT		◆ SPICA		ARCTURUS		Alphecca	
240	12 02	030	22 11	065	37 18	141	56 25	197	49 39	289	34 55	330	33 02	353
241	12 28	030	22 58	064	37 51	141	56 09	198	48 50	289	34 28	329	32 55	352
242	12 54	029	23 44	063	38 24	141	55 53	199	48 01	288	34 01	328	32 48	351
243	13 19	028	24 30	063	38 57	141	55 36	200	47 11	287	33 33	327	32 40	350
244	13 43	028	25 16	062	39 29	141	55 18	200	46 22	286	33 04	326	32 30	349
245	14 07	027	26 02	061	40 02	141	55 00	201	45 32	285	32 35	325	32 20	348
246	14 30	026	26 47	061	40 35	141	54 41	202	44 41	285	32 04	324	32 09	347
247	14 53	026	27 33	060	41 08	141	54 22	202	43 51	284	31 33	323	31 57	346
248	15 15	025	28 17	059	41 40	141	54 02	203	43 01	283	31 02	322	31 44	345
249	15 37	024	29 02	058	42 13	141	53 42	203	42 10	283	30 29	321	31 30	344
250	15 58	023	29 46	058	42 46	141	53 21	204	41 19	282	29 56	320	31 16	343
251	16 18	023	30 29	057	43 18	141	52 59	204	40 28	281	29 23	319	31 00	342
252	16 38	022	31 13	056	43 50	142	52 38	205	39 37	281	28 49	318	30 44	341
253	16 57	021	31 56	055	44 23	142	52 16	206	38 46	280	28 14	318	30 26	340
254	17 15	020	32 38	054	44 55	142	51 53	206	37 55	279	27 39	317	30 08	339
	◆ VEGA		ALTAIR		FOMALHAUT		◆ Peacock		RIGIL KENT		◆ SPICA		ARCTURUS	
255	17 33	020	33 20	054	14 34	116	45 27	142	51 30	207	37 04	279	27 03	316
256	17 50	019	34 02	053	15 21	116	45 59	142	51 07	207	36 12	278	26 27	315
257	18 07	018	34 43	052	16 08	115	46 30	143	50 43	207	35 21	278	25 50	314
258	18 23	017	35 23	051	16 55	115	47 02	143	50 19	208	34 29	277	25 12	314
259	18 38	017	36 04	050	17 42	114	47 33	143	49 54	208	33 38	277	24 34	313
260	18 52	016	36 43	049	18 30	114	48 04	143	49 29	209	32 46	276	23 56	312
261	19 06	015	37 22	048	19 17	114	48 35	144	49 04	209	31 54	275	23 17	311
262	19 19	014	38 01	047	20 05	113	49 06	144	48 39	209	31 03	275	22 38	311
263	19 32	013	38 39	046	20 53	113	49 37	144	48 13	210	30 11	274	21 58	310
264	19 44	013	39 16	045	21 41	113	50 07	144	47 47	210	29 19	274	21 18	309
265	19 55	012	39 52	044	22 29	112	50 37	145	47 21	210	28 27	273	20 38	308
266	20 05	011	40 28	043	23 17	112	51 07	145	46 55	211	27 35	273	19 57	308
267	20 15	010	41 04	042	24 05	111	51 36	146	46 28	211	26 43	272	19 15	307
268	20 23	009	41 38	041	24 53	111	52 06	146	46 01	211	25 51	272	18 34	306
269	20 32	009	42 12	040	25 42	111	52 34	146	45 34	212	24 59	271	17 52	306

LAT 30°S

LHA ♈	Hc	Zn	Hc	Zn	Hc	Zn	Hc	Zn	Hc	Zn	Hc	Zn	Hc	Zn
	VEGA		◆ ALTAIR		FOMALHAUT		◆ Peacock		RIGIL KENT		◆ ANTARES		Alphecca	
270	20 39	008	42 45	039	26 31	110	53 03	147	45 07	212	69 58	275	23 36	325
271	20 46	007	43 18	038	27 19	110	53 31	147	44 39	212	69 06	274	23 06	324
272	20 52	006	43 49	037	28 08	110	53 59	148	44 12	212	68 14	273	22 35	323
273	20 57	005	44 20	036	28 57	109	54 26	148	43 44	212	67 23	273	22 04	322
274	21 01	004	44 49	034	29 46	109	54 54	149	43 16	213	66 31	272	21 32	322
275	21 05	004	45 18	033	30 36	109	55 20	150	42 48	213	65 39	272	20 59	321
276	21 08	003	45 46	032	31 25	108	55 46	150	42 20	213	64 47	271	20 26	320
277	21 10	002	46 13	031	32 14	108	56 12	151	41 51	213	63 55	271	19 53	319
278	21 11	001	46 39	029	33 04	108	56 37	151	41 23	213	63 03	270	19 19	319
279	21 12	000	47 04	028	33 53	107	57 02	152	40 54	213	62 11	270	18 44	318
280	21 12	359	47 28	027	34 43	107	57 26	153	40 26	214	61 19	269	18 09	317
281	21 11	359	47 50	025	35 33	107	57 49	153	39 57	214	60 27	269	17 34	317
282	21 09	358	48 12	024	36 22	106	58 12	154	39 28	214	59 35	268	16 58	316
283	21 07	357	48 33	023	37 12	106	58 35	155	38 59	214	58 43	268	16 21	315
284	21 04	356	48 52	021	38 02	106	58 56	156	38 30	214	57 51	267	15 45	315
	◆ DENEB		FOMALHAUT		◆ ACHERNAR		RIGIL KENT		◆ ANTARES		Rasalhague		VEGA	
285	11 11	018	38 52	105	20 00	145	38 01	214	56 59	267	42 51	331	21 00	355
286	11 27	017	39 42	105	20 30	145	37 32	214	56 07	266	42 25	330	20 55	354
287	11 42	017	40 33	105	21 00	145	37 03	214	55 16	266	41 59	329	20 50	354
288	11 56	016	41 23	104	21 30	145	36 34	214	54 24	266	41 32	328	20 44	353
289	12 10	015	42 13	104	22 00	144	36 05	214	53 32	265	41 04	327	20 37	352
290	12 24	015	43 04	104	22 30	144	35 36	214	52 40	265	40 35	326	20 29	351
291	12 37	014	43 54	104	23 01	144	35 06	214	51 49	264	40 05	324	20 21	350
292	12 49	013	44 45	103	23 31	144	34 37	214	50 57	264	39 35	323	20 12	350
293	13 00	013	45 35	103	24 02	144	34 08	214	50 05	264	39 03	322	20 02	349
294	13 11	012	46 26	103	24 33	143	33 39	214	49 14	263	38 31	321	19 52	348
295	13 22	011	47 17	102	25 04	143	33 10	214	48 22	263	37 58	320	19 40	347
296	13 31	010	48 07	102	25 35	143	32 41	214	47 30	262	37 25	319	19 28	346
297	13 40	010	48 58	102	26 06	143	32 12	214	46 39	262	36 50	318	19 16	346
298	13 49	009	49 49	101	26 38	143	31 42	214	45 48	262	36 15	317	19 02	345
299	13 57	008	50 40	101	27 09	143	31 13	214	44 56	261	35 40	316	18 48	344
	DENEB		Enif		◆ FOMALHAUT		ACHERNAR		◆ RIGIL KENT		ANTARES		◆ VEGA	
300	14 04	008	42 45	036	51 31	101	27 41	142	30 44	214	44 05	261	18 34	343
301	14 10	007	43 16	035	52 22	101	28 13	142	30 16	214	43 14	261	18 18	342
302	14 16	006	43 45	034	53 13	100	28 44	142	29 47	214	42 22	260	18 02	342
303	14 22	005	44 14	033	54 04	100	29 16	142	29 18	214	41 31	260	17 46	341
304	14 26	005	44 41	032	54 56	100	29 48	142	28 49	214	40 40	259	17 28	340
305	14 30	004	45 08	030	55 47	099	30 20	142	28 21	213	39 49	259	17 10	339
306	14 33	003	45 34	029	56 38	099	30 53	142	27 52	213	38 58	259	16 52	339
307	14 36	003	45 59	028	57 30	099	31 25	142	27 24	213	38 07	258	16 32	338
308	14 38	002	46 22	027	58 21	099	31 57	142	26 55	213	37 16	258	16 12	337
309	14 39	001	46 45	025	59 12	098	32 29	141	26 27	213	36 25	258	15 52	336
310	14 40	000	47 07	024	60 04	098	33 02	141	25 59	213	35 35	257	15 31	336
311	14 40	000	47 27	022	60 55	098	33 34	141	25 31	213	34 44	257	15 09	335
312	14 39	359	47 46	021	61 47	097	34 07	141	25 03	212	33 53	257	14 47	334
313	14 38	358	48 05	020	62 38	097	34 39	141	24 35	212	33 03	256	14 24	334
314	14 36	357	48 21	018	63 30	097	35 12	141	24 07	212	32 12	256	14 00	333
	Alpheratz		◆ Diphda		ACHERNAR		◆ RIGIL KENT		ANTARES		◆ ALTAIR		DENEB	
315	15 37	042	37 51	090	35 44	141	23 40	212	31 22	255	47 45	334	14 33	357
316	16 11	041	38 43	090	36 17	141	23 12	212	30 32	255	47 22	333	14 30	356
317	16 45	040	39 35	089	36 49	141	22 45	212	29 42	255	46 58	332	14 26	355
318	17 19	040	40 27	089	37 22	141	22 18	211	28 52	254	46 33	330	14 21	355
319	17 52	039	41 18	088	37 54	141	21 51	211	28 02	254	46 07	329	14 16	354
320	18 24	038	42 10	087	38 27	141	21 24	211	27 12	254	45 39	328	14 10	353
321	18 56	038	43 02	087	38 59	141	20 57	211	26 22	253	45 11	327	14 04	352
322	19 27	037	43 54	086	39 32	141	20 31	211	25 32	253	44 42	325	13 56	352
323	19 58	036	44 46	086	40 04	141	20 04	210	24 43	252	44 12	324	13 49	351
324	20 28	035	45 38	085	40 36	142	19 38	210	23 53	252	43 41	323	13 40	350
325	20 58	035	46 30	085	41 09	142	19 12	210	23 04	252	43 10	322	13 31	350
326	21 27	034	47 21	084	41 41	142	18 47	210	22 14	251	42 37	321	13 21	349
327	21 56	033	48 13	083	42 13	142	18 21	209	21 25	251	42 04	320	13 11	348
328	22 24	032	49 05	083	42 45	142	17 56	209	20 36	251	41 30	319	13 00	347
329	22 51	031	49 56	082	43 17	142	17 30	209	19 47	250	40 55	317	12 48	347
	◆ Alpheratz		Diphda		◆ ACHERNAR		Peacock		◆ Nunki		ALTAIR		Enif	
330	23 18	031	50 48	082	43 49	142	58 44	205	49 34	264	40 20	316	49 53	354
331	23 44	030	51 39	081	44 21	142	58 22	206	48 43	263	39 44	315	49 48	353
332	24 09	029	52 30	080	44 52	143	57 59	206	47 51	263	39 07	314	49 40	351
333	24 34	028	53 21	080	45 24	143	57 36	207	47 00	263	38 29	313	49 32	350
334	24 58	027	54 12	079	45 55	143	57 12	208	46 08	262	37 51	312	49 22	348
335	25 21	026	55 03	078	46 27	143	56 47	208	45 17	262	37 13	312	49 10	347
336	25 44	025	55 54	077	46 58	143	56 22	209	44 25	261	36 34	311	48 58	345
337	26 06	025	56 45	077	47 28	144	55 57	210	43 34	261	35 54	310	48 44	344
338	26 27	024	57 35	076	47 59	144	55 31	210	42 43	261	35 14	309	48 29	342
339	26 48	023	58 25	075	48 30	144	55 05	211	41 52	260	34 33	308	48 12	341
340	27 07	022	59 15	074	49 00	145	54 38	211	41 00	260	33 52	307	47 55	340
341	27 26	021	60 05	073	49 30	145	54 10	212	40 09	260	33 10	306	47 36	338
342	27 45	020	60 55	072	50 00	145	53 43	212	39 18	259	32 28	305	47 16	337
343	28 02	019	61 44	071	50 29	146	53 15	213	38 27	259	31 45	305	46 55	335
344	28 19	018	62 33	070	50 58	146	52 46	213	37 36	258	31 02	304	46 33	334
	Alpheratz		◆ Hamal		◆ ACHERNAR		Peacock		Nunki		◆ ALTAIR		Enif	
345	28 34	017	19 59	046	51 27	146	52 18	214	36 45	258	30 19	303	46 10	333
346	28 49	016	20 36	045	51 56	147	51 48	214	35 55	258	29 35	302	45 45	331
347	29 03	015	21 12	044	52 24	147	51 19	215	35 04	257	28 51	301	45 20	330
348	29 17	014	21 48	043	52 52	148	50 49	215	34 13	257	28 06	301	44 54	329
349	29 29	013	22 24	043	53 20	148	50 19	215	33 23	257	27 22	300	44 27	328
350	29 41	012	22 59	042	53 47	149	49 49	216	32 32	256	26 36	299	43 58	327
351	29 51	011	23 33	041	54 14	149	49 19	216	31 42	256	25 51	299	43 29	325
352	30 01	010	24 07	040	54 40	150	48 48	216	30 51	255	25 05	298	42 59	324
353	30 10	009	24 40	039	55 06	150	48 17	217	30 01	255	24 19	297	42 28	323
354	30 18	008	25 13	039	55 32	151	47 46	217	29 11	255	23 33	297	41 57	322
355	30 25	007	25 45	038	55 57	151	47 15	217	28 21	254	22 46	296	41 24	321
356	30 31	006	26 16	037	56 22	152	46 43	217	27 31	254	21 59	295	40 51	320
357	30 37	005	26 47	036	56 46	153	46 12	218	26 41	254	21 12	295	40 17	319
358	30 41	004	27 18	035	57 09	153	45 40	218	25 51	253	20 25	294	39 42	318
359	30 45	003	27 47	034	57 32	154	45 08	218	25 01	253	19 37	293	39 07	317

LHA ♈	Hc	Zn	Hc	Zn	Hc	Zn	Hc	Zn	Hc	Zn	Hc	Zn	Hc	Zn
	◆ Alpheratz		Hamal		◆ RIGEL		CANOPUS		ACHERNAR		◆ Peacock		Enif	
0	29 47	002	27 26	033	13 46	091	20 47	140	58 49	154	45 23	219	37 48	316
1	29 49	001	27 54	032	14 37	091	21 20	140	59 11	155	44 51	219	37 12	315
2	29 50	000	28 21	031	15 29	090	21 53	139	59 32	156	44 18	219	36 35	314
3	29 49	359	28 48	030	16 20	090	22 27	139	59 53	157	43 46	219	35 58	313
4	29 48	358	29 13	030	17 11	089	23 01	139	60 13	157	43 13	219	35 21	312
5	29 46	357	29 38	029	18 03	089	23 35	139	60 33	158	42 40	219	34 42	311
6	29 43	356	30 03	028	18 54	088	24 09	138	60 51	159	42 08	220	34 03	310
7	29 40	355	30 26	027	19 46	088	24 43	138	61 09	160	41 35	220	33 24	310
8	29 35	354	30 49	026	20 37	087	25 17	138	61 26	161	41 02	220	32 44	309
9	29 29	353	31 11	025	21 28	087	25 52	138	61 42	162	40 29	220	32 04	308
10	29 23	352	31 32	024	22 20	086	26 27	138	61 58	163	39 56	220	31 23	307
11	29 16	351	31 52	023	23 11	086	27 01	137	62 12	164	39 23	220	30 42	306
12	29 07	350	32 12	022	24 02	085	27 36	137	62 26	165	38 51	220	30 00	305
13	28 58	349	32 30	021	24 54	085	28 11	137	62 38	166	38 18	220	29 18	305
14	28 48	348	32 48	020	25 45	084	28 46	137	62 50	167	37 45	220	28 35	304
	◆ Hamal		ALDEBARAN		RIGEL		◆ CANOPUS		ACHERNAR		◆ FOMALHAUT		Alpheratz	
15	33 05	019	19 31	056	26 36	083	29 22	137	63 01	169	63 48	265	28 37	347
16	33 21	018	20 13	055	27 27	083	29 57	136	63 10	170	62 57	265	28 26	346
17	33 36	017	20 55	054	28 18	082	30 33	136	63 19	171	62 06	265	28 13	345
18	33 50	015	21 37	053	29 09	082	31 08	136	63 27	172	61 14	264	28 00	344
19	34 04	014	22 18	053	30 00	081	31 44	136	63 33	173	60 23	264	27 46	344
20	34 16	013	22 59	052	30 50	080	32 20	136	63 39	174	59 32	264	27 31	343
21	34 27	012	23 39	051	31 41	080	32 55	136	63 43	176	58 41	263	27 15	342
22	34 38	011	24 19	051	32 32	079	33 31	136	63 47	177	57 50	263	26 58	341
23	34 47	010	24 58	050	33 22	079	34 07	136	63 49	178	56 59	262	26 41	340
24	34 56	009	25 37	049	34 13	078	34 43	135	63 50	179	56 08	262	26 23	339
25	35 03	008	26 16	048	35 03	077	35 19	135	63 50	181	55 17	262	26 04	338
26	35 10	007	26 54	047	35 53	077	35 56	135	63 49	182	54 26	261	25 44	337
27	35 15	006	27 32	047	36 43	076	36 32	135	63 47	183	53 35	261	25 24	336
28	35 20	005	28 09	046	37 33	075	37 08	135	63 44	184	52 45	261	25 03	335
29	35 23	003	28 45	045	38 22	075	37 44	135	63 40	185	51 54	260	24 41	334
	Hamal		ALDEBARAN		◆ SIRIUS		CANOPUS		◆ ACHERNAR		FOMALHAUT		◆ Alpheratz	
30	35 26	002	29 21	044	24 10	096	38 21	135	63 34	187	51 03	260	24 18	334
31	35 28	001	29 57	043	25 01	095	38 57	135	63 28	188	50 13	260	23 55	333
32	35 28	000	30 32	042	25 53	095	39 33	135	63 20	189	49 22	259	23 31	332
33	35 28	359	31 06	041	26 44	094	40 10	135	63 12	190	48 31	259	23 06	331
34	35 26	358	31 40	040	27 35	094	40 46	135	63 02	191	47 41	259	22 41	330
35	35 24	357	32 13	040	28 27	093	41 22	135	62 51	192	46 51	258	22 15	329
36	35 20	356	32 45	039	29 18	093	41 59	135	62 40	194	46 00	258	21 49	329
37	35 15	354	33 17	038	30 09	092	42 35	135	62 27	195	45 10	258	21 22	328
38	35 10	353	33 48	037	31 01	092	43 11	135	62 14	196	44 20	257	20 54	327
39	35 03	352	34 18	036	31 52	091	43 48	135	62 00	197	43 30	257	20 25	326
40	34 56	351	34 48	035	32 43	091	44 24	135	61 44	198	42 39	257	19 56	325
41	34 47	350	35 17	034	33 35	090	45 00	135	61 28	199	41 49	256	19 27	325
42	34 38	349	35 45	033	34 26	090	45 36	135	61 11	200	40 59	256	18 57	324
43	34 28	348	36 12	032	35 18	089	46 12	136	60 54	201	40 10	256	18 26	323
44	34 16	347	36 39	031	36 09	089	46 48	136	60 35	202	39 20	255	17 55	322
	◆ ALDEBARAN		BETELGEUSE		SIRIUS		◆ CANOPUS		ACHERNAR		◆ FOMALHAUT		Hamal	
45	37 05	030	33 02	055	37 01	088	47 24	136	60 16	202	38 30	255	34 04	346
46	37 30	028	33 44	054	37 52	088	48 00	136	59 56	203	37 40	255	33 51	345
47	37 54	027	34 25	054	38 43	087	48 35	136	59 35	204	36 51	254	33 36	343
48	38 17	026	35 07	053	39 35	087	49 11	136	59 14	205	36 01	254	33 21	342
49	38 39	025	35 47	052	40 26	086	49 46	137	58 52	206	35 12	254	33 05	341
50	39 00	024	36 27	051	41 17	085	50 22	137	58 29	206	34 23	253	32 48	340
51	39 21	023	37 07	050	42 09	085	50 57	137	58 06	207	33 33	253	32 31	339
52	39 40	022	37 46	049	43 00	084	51 32	137	57 42	208	32 44	253	32 12	338
53	39 59	020	38 25	048	43 51	084	52 06	138	57 18	209	31 55	252	31 53	337
54	40 16	019	39 03	047	44 42	083	52 41	138	56 53	209	31 06	252	31 32	336
55	40 33	018	39 40	046	45 33	082	53 15	138	56 28	210	30 17	252	31 11	335
56	40 48	017	40 17	045	46 24	082	53 49	139	56 02	210	29 28	251	30 49	334
57	41 02	016	40 53	044	47 15	081	54 23	139	55 36	211	28 40	251	30 26	333
58	41 16	014	41 28	043	48 06	080	54 57	139	55 09	212	27 51	251	30 03	332
59	41 28	013	42 03	042	48 56	080	55 30	140	54 42	212	27 03	250	29 39	331
	ALDEBARAN		◆ BETELGEUSE		SIRIUS		◆ CANOPUS		ACHERNAR		◆ FOMALHAUT		Hamal	
60	41 39	012	42 37	041	49 47	079	56 03	140	54 14	213	26 15	250	29 14	330
61	41 49	011	43 10	040	50 37	078	56 36	141	53 47	213	25 26	249	28 48	330
62	41 58	009	43 42	039	51 27	078	57 08	141	53 18	213	24 38	249	28 22	329
63	42 05	008	44 14	037	52 18	077	57 40	142	52 50	214	23 50	249	27 54	328
64	42 12	007	44 45	036	53 08	076	58 12	142	52 21	214	23 02	248	27 27	327
65	42 17	005	45 15	035	53 57	075	58 43	143	51 52	215	22 15	248	26 58	326
66	42 22	004	45 44	034	54 47	074	59 14	144	51 22	215	21 27	248	26 29	325
67	42 25	003	46 12	032	55 37	074	59 44	144	50 53	215	20 40	247	25 59	324
68	42 27	002	46 39	031	56 26	073	60 14	145	50 23	216	19 52	247	25 29	323
69	42 28	000	47 05	030	57 15	072	60 43	146	49 53	216	19 05	246	24 58	323
70	42 27	359	47 30	029	58 03	071	61 12	146	49 22	216	18 18	246	24 26	322
71	42 26	358	47 54	027	58 52	070	61 40	147	48 52	217	17 31	246	23 54	321
72	42 23	356	48 17	026	59 40	069	62 07	148	48 21	217	16 44	245	23 21	320
73	42 19	355	48 39	024	60 28	068	62 34	149	47 50	217	15 58	245	22 48	319
74	42 14	354	49 00	023	61 15	067	63 00	150	47 19	217	15 11	244	22 14	318
	BETELGEUSE		◆ PROCYON		Suhail		◆ ACRUX		ACHERNAR		◆ Diphda		ALDEBARAN	
75	49 19	022	37 23	054	40 10	123	18 24	154	46 47	218	31 08	267	42 08	352
76	49 38	020	38 04	053	40 54	123	18 47	154	46 16	218	30 17	266	42 01	351
77	49 55	019	38 45	052	41 37	123	19 10	153	45 44	218	29 25	266	41 52	350
78	50 10	017	39 25	051	42 20	123	19 33	153	45 12	218	28 34	265	41 43	349
79	50 25	016	40 05	050	43 04	123	19 56	153	44 41	218	27 43	265	41 32	347
80	50 38	014	40 44	049	43 47	122	20 20	153	44 09	218	26 51	264	41 20	346
81	50 50	013	41 23	048	44 30	122	20 44	152	43 37	219	26 00	264	41 08	345
82	51 01	011	42 00	047	45 14	122	21 08	152	43 04	219	25 09	263	40 54	344
83	51 10	010	42 38	046	45 57	122	21 32	152	42 32	219	24 18	263	40 39	342
84	51 18	008	43 14	045	46 41	122	21 56	152	42 00	219	23 27	263	40 23	341
85	51 24	006	43 50	044	47 24	122	22 21	151	41 28	219	22 36	262	40 06	340
86	51 29	005	44 25	043	48 08	122	22 45	151	40 55	219	21 45	262	39 48	339
87	51 33	003	45 00	041	48 51	122	23 10	151	40 23	219	20 54	261	39 29	338
88	51 35	002	45 33	040	49 35	122	23 35	151	39 50	219	20 04	261	39 08	337
89	51 35	000	46 06	039	50 18	122	24 00	151	39 18	219	19 13	260	38 48	335

LAT 31°S

LHA ♈	Hc	Zn	Hc	Zn	Hc	Zn	Hc	Zn	Hc	Zn	Hc	Zn	Hc	Zn
	PROCYON		REGULUS		◆ Suhail		ACRUX		◆ ACHERNAR		RIGEL		◆ BETELGEUSE	
90	46 38	038	16 29	065	51 02	122	24 25	151	38 45	219	64 55	333	51 35	358
91	47 09	037	17 16	064	51 45	122	24 51	150	38 13	219	64 31	331	51 33	357
92	47 39	035	18 02	063	52 29	122	25 16	150	37 40	219	64 05	329	51 29	355
93	48 09	034	18 48	063	53 12	122	25 42	150	37 08	219	63 37	327	51 24	354
94	48 37	033	19 33	062	53 56	123	26 08	150	36 35	219	63 09	325	51 18	352
95	49 04	031	20 19	061	54 39	123	26 33	150	36 03	219	62 38	323	51 10	350
96	49 30	030	21 04	061	55 22	123	26 59	150	35 30	219	62 07	321	51 01	349
97	49 56	029	21 48	060	56 05	123	27 25	149	34 58	219	61 34	320	50 50	347
98	50 20	027	22 33	059	56 48	123	27 52	149	34 25	219	61 00	318	50 38	346
99	50 43	026	23 17	059	57 31	123	28 18	149	33 53	219	60 25	316	50 25	344
100	51 04	024	24 01	058	58 14	124	28 44	149	33 21	219	59 49	315	50 10	343
101	51 25	023	24 44	057	58 57	124	29 11	149	32 48	219	59 12	313	49 54	341
102	51 44	021	25 27	056	59 39	124	29 37	149	32 16	219	58 34	312	49 37	340
103	52 02	020	26 10	056	60 22	125	30 04	149	31 44	219	57 55	310	49 19	338
104	52 19	018	26 52	055	61 04	125	30 31	149	31 12	219	57 15	309	49 00	337
	PROCYON		REGULUS		◆ Gienah		ACRUX		◆ ACHERNAR		RIGEL		◆ BETELGEUSE	
105	52 34	017	27 34	054	18 03	100	30 57	149	30 40	218	56 35	308	48 39	336
106	52 48	015	28 15	053	18 53	100	31 24	149	30 08	218	55 54	306	48 17	334
107	53 01	013	28 57	053	19 44	099	31 51	148	29 36	218	55 12	305	47 54	333
108	53 12	012	29 37	052	20 35	099	32 18	148	29 04	218	54 30	304	47 30	331
109	53 22	010	30 17	051	21 26	098	32 45	148	28 33	218	53 47	303	47 05	330
110	53 30	008	30 57	050	22 17	098	33 12	148	28 01	218	53 03	302	46 39	329
111	53 37	007	31 36	049	23 08	097	33 39	148	27 30	218	52 19	300	46 12	328
112	53 42	005	32 15	048	23 59	097	34 06	148	26 58	217	51 34	299	45 44	326
113	53 46	003	32 53	048	24 50	096	34 33	148	26 27	217	50 49	298	45 15	325
114	53 48	002	33 31	047	25 41	096	35 00	148	25 56	217	50 04	297	44 45	324
115	53 49	000	34 08	046	26 32	095	35 27	148	25 25	217	49 18	296	44 14	323
116	53 48	358	34 45	045	27 23	095	35 54	148	24 54	217	48 32	295	43 42	321
117	53 46	357	35 21	044	28 15	094	36 21	148	24 24	217	47 45	294	43 10	320
118	53 42	355	35 56	043	29 06	094	36 48	148	23 53	216	46 58	294	42 37	319
119	53 37	353	36 31	042	29 57	094	37 15	148	23 23	216	46 11	293	42 03	318
	REGULUS		◆ SPICA		ACRUX		◆ CANOPUS		RIGEL		BETELGEUSE		◆ PROCYON	
120	37 05	041	12 59	095	37 42	148	62 11	212	45 23	292	41 28	317	53 30	352
121	37 38	040	13 50	095	38 09	148	61 44	213	44 35	291	40 52	316	53 22	350
122	38 11	039	14 42	094	38 36	148	61 16	213	43 47	290	40 16	315	53 12	348
123	38 43	038	15 33	094	39 03	149	60 47	214	42 59	289	39 40	314	53 01	347
124	39 14	037	16 24	093	39 30	149	60 18	215	42 10	289	39 02	313	52 49	345
125	39 44	036	17 16	093	39 57	149	59 48	216	41 21	288	38 24	312	52 35	344
126	40 14	035	18 07	092	40 23	149	59 18	216	40 32	287	37 46	311	52 19	342
127	40 43	033	18 58	092	40 50	149	58 47	217	39 43	286	37 07	310	52 03	340
128	41 10	032	19 50	091	41 16	149	58 16	218	38 54	286	36 27	309	51 45	339
129	41 38	031	20 41	091	41 43	149	57 45	218	38 04	285	35 47	308	51 26	337
130	42 04	030	21 33	090	42 09	149	57 13	219	37 14	284	35 06	307	51 05	336
131	42 29	029	22 24	090	42 35	150	56 40	219	36 24	284	34 25	306	50 44	334
132	42 53	028	23 15	089	43 01	150	56 08	220	35 34	283	33 43	306	50 21	333
133	43 17	026	24 07	089	43 27	150	55 35	220	34 44	282	33 01	305	49 57	331
134	43 39	025	24 58	088	43 53	150	55 01	221	33 54	282	32 19	304	49 32	330
	◆ REGULUS		SPICA		◆ ACRUX		CANOPUS		◆ RIGEL		BETELGEUSE		PROCYON	
135	44 00	024	25 50	088	44 18	150	54 28	221	33 03	281	31 36	303	49 05	329
136	44 21	023	26 41	087	44 44	150	53 54	221	32 13	281	30 53	302	48 38	327
137	44 40	021	27 32	087	45 09	151	53 20	222	31 22	280	30 09	302	48 10	326
138	44 58	020	28 24	086	45 34	151	52 46	222	30 32	279	29 25	301	47 41	325
139	45 15	019	29 15	086	45 59	151	52 11	222	29 41	279	28 41	300	47 11	323
140	45 31	017	30 06	085	46 23	151	51 36	223	28 50	278	27 56	299	46 39	322
141	45 45	016	30 58	085	46 48	152	51 02	223	27 59	278	27 11	299	46 08	321
142	45 59	015	31 49	084	47 12	152	50 27	223	27 08	277	26 26	298	45 35	320
143	46 11	013	32 40	083	47 36	152	49 51	223	26 17	276	25 40	297	45 01	319
144	46 22	012	33 31	083	48 00	153	49 16	224	25 26	276	24 54	296	44 27	317
145	46 32	010	34 22	082	48 23	153	48 40	224	24 35	275	24 08	296	43 52	316
146	46 41	009	35 13	082	48 46	153	48 05	224	23 43	275	23 22	295	43 16	315
147	46 48	008	36 04	081	49 09	154	47 29	224	22 52	274	22 35	294	42 39	314
148	46 55	006	36 54	080	49 32	154	46 53	224	22 01	274	21 48	294	42 02	313
149	46 59	005	37 45	080	49 54	155	46 17	224	21 09	273	21 01	293	41 24	312
	REGULUS		◆ Denebola		SPICA		◆ ACRUX		CANOPUS		◆ SIRIUS		PROCYON	
150	47 03	003	37 25	034	38 36	079	50 16	155	45 41	225	43 46	276	40 46	311
151	47 05	002	37 53	033	39 26	078	50 38	155	45 05	225	42 55	276	40 07	310
152	47 06	000	38 21	032	40 16	078	50 59	156	44 29	225	42 04	275	39 27	309
153	47 06	359	38 48	031	41 07	077	51 20	156	43 53	225	41 12	275	38 47	308
154	47 05	358	39 14	030	41 57	076	51 40	157	43 17	225	40 21	274	38 06	307
155	47 02	356	39 39	029	42 47	076	52 00	157	42 40	225	39 30	273	37 25	306
156	46 58	355	40 03	028	43 36	075	52 20	158	42 04	225	38 38	273	36 43	305
157	46 52	353	40 27	026	44 26	074	52 39	158	41 28	225	37 47	272	36 01	305
158	46 45	352	40 49	025	45 15	074	52 58	159	40 51	225	36 56	272	35 19	304
159	46 38	350	41 11	024	46 05	073	53 17	159	40 15	225	36 04	271	34 36	303
160	46 28	349	41 31	023	46 54	072	53 34	160	39 39	225	35 13	271	33 52	302
161	46 18	348	41 50	022	47 42	071	53 52	161	39 02	225	34 21	270	33 08	301
162	46 06	346	42 09	020	48 31	070	54 09	161	38 26	225	33 30	270	32 24	300
163	45 53	345	42 26	019	49 19	069	54 25	162	37 50	225	32 39	269	31 40	300
164	45 39	343	42 43	018	50 07	069	54 41	162	37 13	225	31 47	269	30 55	299
	ARCTURUS		◆ ANTARES		ACRUX		◆ CANOPUS		SIRIUS		PROCYON		◆ REGULUS	
165	21 13	050	19 11	110	54 56	163	36 37	225	30 56	268	30 10	298	45 24	342
166	21 52	049	19 59	110	55 11	164	36 01	225	30 04	268	29 24	297	45 08	341
167	22 31	049	20 48	109	55 25	164	35 25	225	29 13	267	28 38	297	44 50	339
168	23 09	048	21 37	109	55 39	165	34 49	225	28 22	267	27 52	296	44 32	338
169	23 47	047	22 25	108	55 52	166	34 12	224	27 30	266	27 06	295	44 13	337
170	24 24	046	23 14	108	56 04	166	33 36	224	26 39	266	26 19	295	43 52	336
171	25 01	045	24 03	108	56 16	167	33 01	224	25 48	265	25 32	294	43 30	334
172	25 38	045	24 52	107	56 27	168	32 25	224	24 56	265	24 45	293	43 07	333
173	26 14	044	25 41	107	56 38	169	31 49	224	24 05	264	23 58	292	42 43	332
174	26 49	043	26 31	106	56 47	169	31 13	224	23 14	264	23 10	292	42 19	331
175	27 24	042	27 20	106	56 56	170	30 38	224	22 23	263	22 22	291	41 53	330
176	27 58	041	28 10	106	57 05	171	30 02	224	21 32	263	21 34	291	41 26	328
177	28 32	040	28 59	105	57 12	172	29 27	223	20 41	262	20 46	290	40 59	327
178	29 05	040	29 49	105	57 19	173	28 52	223	19 50	262	19 57	289	40 31	326
179	29 37	039	30 39	104	57 26	173	28 16	223	18 59	261	19 09	289	40 02	325

LAT 31°S

LHA ♈	Hc	Zn	Hc	Zn	Hc	Zn	Hc	Zn	Hc	Zn	Hc	Zn	Hc	Zn
	◆ ARCTURUS		ANTARES		◆ RIGIL KENT		ACRUX		CANOPUS		◆ Alphard		REGULUS	
180	30 09	038	31 29	104	50 14	151	57 31	174	27 41	223	48 17	294	39 32	324
181	30 40	037	32 19	104	50 39	151	57 36	175	27 06	223	47 30	293	39 01	323
182	31 11	036	33 09	103	51 04	151	57 40	176	26 32	222	46 43	292	38 29	322
183	31 40	035	33 59	103	51 28	152	57 43	177	25 57	222	45 55	291	37 57	321
184	32 09	034	34 49	102	51 52	152	57 46	178	25 22	222	45 07	291	37 24	320
185	32 38	033	35 39	102	52 16	153	57 48	178	24 48	222	44 19	290	36 51	319
186	33 06	032	36 29	102	52 39	153	57 49	179	24 14	222	43 30	289	36 16	318
187	33 33	031	37 20	101	53 02	154	57 49	180	23 40	221	42 42	288	35 41	317
188	33 59	030	38 10	101	53 25	154	57 49	181	23 06	221	41 53	288	35 06	316
189	34 24	029	39 01	101	53 47	155	57 47	182	22 32	221	41 03	287	34 30	315
190	34 49	028	39 51	100	54 09	155	57 45	183	21 58	221	40 14	286	33 53	314
191	35 12	027	40 42	100	54 30	156	57 43	183	21 25	220	39 25	285	33 15	313
192	35 35	026	41 33	099	54 51	157	57 39	184	20 52	220	38 35	285	32 37	312
193	35 57	025	42 24	099	55 11	157	57 35	185	20 18	220	37 45	284	31 59	311
194	36 18	024	43 14	099	55 31	158	57 30	186	19 46	220	36 55	283	31 20	310
	ARCTURUS		◆ ANTARES		RIGIL KENT		◆ ACRUX		Suhail		REGULUS		◆ Denebola	
195	36 39	023	44 05	098	55 50	158	57 24	187	43 15	238	30 41	309	41 29	337
196	36 58	022	44 56	098	56 08	159	57 18	188	42 32	237	30 01	309	41 09	336
197	37 16	020	45 47	097	56 27	160	57 10	188	41 49	237	29 20	308	40 47	335
198	37 34	019	46 38	097	56 44	160	57 03	189	41 05	237	28 39	307	40 25	333
199	37 50	018	47 29	097	57 01	161	56 54	190	40 22	237	27 58	306	40 01	332
200	38 06	017	48 20	096	57 17	162	56 45	191	39 39	237	27 17	305	39 37	331
201	38 21	016	49 12	096	57 33	163	56 35	192	38 56	237	26 34	305	39 12	330
202	38 34	015	50 03	095	57 48	163	56 24	192	38 13	237	25 52	304	38 46	329
203	38 47	013	50 54	095	58 02	164	56 13	193	37 30	237	25 09	303	38 19	328
204	38 58	012	51 45	094	58 16	165	56 01	194	36 47	236	24 26	302	37 51	327
205	39 08	011	52 37	094	58 29	166	55 48	194	36 04	236	23 42	302	37 22	326
206	39 18	010	53 28	094	58 41	167	55 35	195	35 22	236	22 58	301	36 53	325
207	39 26	009	54 19	093	58 52	168	55 21	196	34 39	236	22 14	300	36 23	324
208	39 33	007	55 11	093	59 03	169	55 07	197	33 56	236	21 30	300	35 52	323
209	39 39	006	56 02	092	59 13	169	54 52	197	33 14	236	20 45	299	35 20	322
	◆ ARCTURUS		Rasalhague		◆ Nunki		RIGIL KENT		ACRUX		◆ Suhail		SPICA	
210	39 44	005	22 24	059	26 03	106	59 22	170	54 37	198	32 32	235	68 44	336
211	39 48	004	23 07	058	26 53	106	59 30	171	54 21	198	31 49	235	68 22	334
212	39 51	003	23 51	057	27 42	106	59 37	172	54 04	199	31 07	235	67 59	332
213	39 53	001	24 34	056	28 32	105	59 44	173	53 47	200	30 25	235	67 33	329
214	39 54	000	25 16	056	29 22	105	59 50	174	53 30	200	29 43	234	67 06	327
215	39 53	359	25 59	055	30 11	104	59 55	175	53 12	201	29 02	234	66 37	325
216	39 52	358	26 41	054	31 01	104	59 59	176	52 53	201	28 20	234	66 07	323
217	39 49	356	27 22	053	31 51	104	60 02	177	52 34	202	27 38	234	65 35	321
218	39 45	355	28 03	053	32 41	103	60 04	178	52 15	202	26 57	233	65 01	319
219	39 40	354	28 44	052	33 31	103	60 06	179	51 55	203	26 16	233	64 27	317
220	39 34	353	29 24	051	34 21	102	60 06	180	51 35	203	25 35	233	63 51	315
221	39 27	352	30 04	050	35 12	102	60 06	181	51 14	204	24 54	233	63 14	313
222	39 19	350	30 43	049	36 02	102	60 05	182	50 53	204	24 13	232	62 36	312
223	39 10	349	31 22	048	36 52	101	60 03	183	50 32	205	23 32	232	61 57	310
224	39 00	348	32 00	048	37 43	101	60 00	184	50 10	205	22 52	232	61 18	309
	Alphecca		Rasalhague		◆ Nunki		Peacock		◆ RIGIL KENT		SPICA		◆ ARCTURUS	
225	31 43	009	32 38	047	38 33	100	29 53	141	59 56	185	60 37	307	38 49	347
226	31 51	008	33 15	046	39 24	100	30 26	141	59 51	186	59 56	306	38 36	346
227	31 58	007	33 51	045	40 15	100	30 58	141	59 46	187	59 14	304	38 23	344
228	32 04	006	34 27	044	41 05	099	31 30	141	59 40	188	58 31	303	38 09	343
229	32 09	005	35 03	043	41 56	099	32 03	141	59 32	188	57 47	302	37 53	342
230	32 13	004	35 38	042	42 47	098	32 36	141	59 24	189	57 03	301	37 37	341
231	32 16	003	36 12	041	43 38	098	33 08	141	59 16	190	56 19	299	37 20	340
232	32 19	002	36 45	040	44 29	098	33 41	140	59 06	191	55 34	298	37 01	339
233	32 20	001	37 18	039	45 20	097	34 14	140	58 56	192	54 48	297	36 42	338
234	32 20	000	37 50	038	46 11	097	34 46	140	58 44	193	54 02	296	36 22	336
235	32 19	359	38 21	037	47 02	096	35 19	140	58 33	194	53 16	295	36 01	335
236	32 18	358	38 52	036	47 53	096	35 52	140	58 20	195	52 29	294	35 39	334
237	32 15	357	39 22	035	48 44	096	36 25	140	58 07	195	51 42	293	35 16	333
238	32 12	356	39 51	034	49 36	095	36 58	140	57 52	196	50 55	292	34 53	332
239	32 07	355	40 19	033	50 27	095	37 31	140	57 38	197	50 07	291	34 28	331
	Rasalhague		ALTAIR		◆ Nunki		Peacock		◆ RIGIL KENT		SPICA		◆ ARCTURUS	
240	40 46	031	21 45	064	51 18	094	38 04	140	57 22	198	49 19	290	34 03	330
241	41 12	030	22 31	064	52 09	094	38 37	140	57 06	199	48 31	290	33 37	329
242	41 38	029	23 17	063	53 01	093	39 10	140	56 50	199	47 42	289	33 10	328
243	42 03	028	24 03	062	53 52	093	39 43	140	56 32	200	46 53	288	32 43	327
244	42 26	027	24 48	062	54 43	093	40 16	140	56 14	201	46 04	287	32 14	326
245	42 49	026	25 33	061	55 35	092	40 49	140	55 56	201	45 15	286	31 45	325
246	43 11	024	26 18	060	56 26	092	41 21	140	55 37	202	44 26	286	31 16	324
247	43 31	023	27 02	059	57 18	091	41 54	140	55 17	203	43 36	285	30 45	323
248	43 51	022	27 46	059	58 09	091	42 27	141	54 57	203	42 46	284	30 14	322
249	44 09	020	28 30	058	59 00	090	43 00	141	54 37	204	41 56	284	29 43	321
250	44 27	019	29 13	057	59 52	090	43 32	141	54 15	204	41 06	283	29 10	321
251	44 43	018	29 56	056	60 43	089	44 05	141	53 54	205	40 16	282	28 37	320
252	44 58	017	30 39	056	61 35	089	44 37	141	53 32	206	39 26	282	28 04	319
253	45 12	015	31 21	055	62 26	088	45 10	141	53 10	206	38 35	281	27 30	318
254	45 25	014	32 03	054	63 17	087	45 42	141	52 47	207	37 45	280	26 55	317
	VEGA		◆ ALTAIR		FOMALHAUT		◆ Peacock		RIGIL KENT		◆ SPICA		ARCTURUS	
255	16 37	020	32 44	053	15 00	116	46 14	141	52 23	207	36 54	280	26 20	316
256	16 53	019	33 25	052	15 47	115	46 46	142	52 00	208	36 03	279	25 44	316
257	17 10	018	34 06	051	16 33	115	47 18	142	51 36	208	35 12	278	25 08	315
258	17 25	017	34 45	050	17 20	115	47 49	142	51 12	208	34 22	278	24 31	314
259	17 40	017	35 25	050	18 07	114	48 21	142	50 47	209	33 31	277	23 54	313
260	17 55	016	36 04	049	18 54	114	48 52	143	50 22	209	32 39	277	23 16	312
261	18 08	015	36 42	048	19 41	113	49 23	143	49 57	210	31 48	276	22 38	312
262	18 21	014	37 20	047	20 28	113	49 54	143	49 31	210	30 57	275	21 59	311
263	18 34	013	37 57	046	21 16	113	50 25	143	49 05	210	30 06	275	21 20	310
264	18 45	013	38 33	045	22 03	112	50 56	144	48 39	211	29 15	274	20 40	309
265	18 56	012	39 09	044	22 51	112	51 26	144	48 13	211	28 23	274	20 00	309
266	19 06	011	39 45	043	23 39	111	51 56	144	47 46	211	27 32	273	19 20	308
267	19 16	010	40 19	042	24 27	111	52 26	145	47 19	212	26 41	273	18 39	307
268	19 24	009	40 53	041	25 15	111	52 55	145	46 52	212	25 49	272	17 58	307
269	19 32	009	41 26	040	26 03	110	53 24	146	46 25	212	24 58	272	17 17	306

LHA ♈	Hc	Zn	Hc	Zn	Hc	Zn	Hc	Zn	Hc	Zn	Hc	Zn	Hc	Zn
	VEGA		ALTAIR		◆ FOMALHAUT		ACHERNAR		◆ RIGIL KENT		ANTARES		◆ Rasalhague	
270	19 40	008	41 58	038	26 51	110	13 51	149	45 58	212	69 52	277	46 03	351
271	19 46	007	42 30	037	27 40	110	14 18	149	45 30	213	69 01	277	45 55	350
272	19 52	006	43 01	036	28 28	109	14 44	149	45 02	213	68 10	276	45 46	349
273	19 57	005	43 31	035	29 17	109	15 11	148	44 34	213	67 18	275	45 35	347
274	20 01	004	44 00	034	30 06	108	15 38	148	44 06	213	66 27	274	45 23	346
275	20 05	004	44 28	033	30 54	108	16 05	148	43 38	213	65 36	274	45 10	345
276	20 08	003	44 55	031	31 43	108	16 33	148	43 10	213	64 45	273	44 56	343
277	20 10	002	45 21	030	32 32	107	17 00	147	42 41	214	63 53	273	44 40	342
278	20 11	001	45 47	029	33 22	107	17 28	147	42 13	214	63 02	272	44 24	341
279	20 12	000	46 11	027	34 11	107	17 56	147	41 44	214	62 10	271	44 06	339
280	20 12	359	46 34	026	35 00	106	18 25	146	41 16	214	61 19	271	43 47	338
281	20 11	359	46 56	025	35 49	106	18 53	146	40 47	214	60 28	270	43 27	337
282	20 10	358	47 17	023	36 39	106	19 22	146	40 18	214	59 36	270	43 07	335
283	20 07	357	47 37	022	37 29	105	19 51	146	39 49	214	58 45	269	42 45	334
284	20 04	356	47 56	021	38 18	105	20 20	145	39 20	214	57 53	269	42 22	333
	ALTAIR		Enif		◆ FOMALHAUT		ACHERNAR		◆ RIGIL KENT		ANTARES		◆ Rasalhague	
285	48 13	019	33 06	051	39 08	105	20 49	145	38 51	214	57 02	268	41 58	332
286	48 30	018	33 45	050	39 58	104	21 19	145	38 22	214	56 10	268	41 33	331
287	48 45	016	34 24	049	40 48	104	21 49	145	37 53	215	55 19	267	41 08	329
288	48 59	015	35 03	048	41 37	104	22 18	144	37 24	215	54 28	267	40 41	328
289	49 12	013	35 41	047	42 28	103	22 48	144	36 54	215	53 36	266	40 14	327
290	49 23	012	36 18	046	43 18	103	23 19	144	36 25	215	52 45	266	39 45	326
291	49 33	011	36 55	045	44 08	103	23 49	144	35 56	215	51 54	266	39 16	325
292	49 42	009	37 31	044	44 58	102	24 19	144	35 27	215	51 03	265	38 46	324
293	49 49	007	38 07	043	45 48	102	24 50	143	34 58	215	50 11	265	38 16	323
294	49 55	006	38 42	042	46 39	102	25 21	143	34 28	215	49 20	264	37 44	322
295	50 00	004	39 16	041	47 29	101	25 52	143	33 59	214	48 29	264	37 12	321
296	50 03	003	39 50	040	48 19	101	26 23	143	33 30	214	47 38	264	36 39	320
297	50 05	002	40 23	039	49 10	101	26 54	143	33 01	214	46 47	263	36 05	319
298	50 05	000	40 55	038	50 01	100	27 25	142	32 32	214	45 56	263	35 31	318
299	50 05	358	41 26	037	50 51	100	27 57	142	32 03	214	45 05	262	34 56	317
	Enif		◆ FOMALHAUT		ACHERNAR		◆ RIGIL KENT		ANTARES		Rasalhague		◆ ALTAIR	
300	41 57	036	51 42	100	28 28	142	31 34	214	44 14	262	34 21	316	50 02	357
301	42 26	035	52 33	099	29 00	142	31 05	214	43 23	262	33 45	315	49 59	355
302	42 55	034	53 23	099	29 32	142	30 37	214	42 32	261	33 08	314	49 54	354
303	43 23	032	54 14	099	30 04	142	30 08	214	41 41	261	32 31	313	49 47	352
304	43 50	031	55 05	098	30 35	142	29 39	214	40 50	260	31 53	312	49 40	351
305	44 16	030	55 56	098	31 07	141	29 11	214	40 00	260	31 15	311	49 31	349
306	44 41	029	56 47	098	31 40	141	28 42	214	39 09	260	30 36	311	49 20	348
307	45 05	027	57 38	097	32 12	141	28 14	213	38 19	259	29 56	310	49 09	346
308	45 29	026	58 29	097	32 44	141	27 45	213	37 28	259	29 17	309	48 56	345
309	45 51	025	59 20	097	33 16	141	27 17	213	36 38	258	28 36	308	48 41	343
310	46 12	023	60 11	096	33 49	141	26 49	213	35 47	258	27 56	307	48 26	342
311	46 32	022	61 02	096	34 21	141	26 21	213	34 57	258	27 14	306	48 09	340
312	46 50	021	61 53	096	34 53	141	25 53	213	34 07	257	26 33	306	47 51	339
313	47 08	019	62 45	095	35 26	141	25 26	213	33 17	257	25 51	305	47 32	338
314	47 24	018	63 36	095	35 58	141	24 58	212	32 27	256	25 09	304	47 12	336
	Alpheratz		◆ Diphda		ACHERNAR		◆ RIGIL KENT		ANTARES		Rasalhague		◆ ALTAIR	
315	14 52	042	37 50	089	36 31	141	24 30	212	31 37	256	24 26	303	46 51	335
316	15 26	041	38 42	089	37 03	141	24 03	212	30 47	256	23 43	303	46 28	334
317	15 59	040	39 33	088	37 36	141	23 36	212	29 57	255	22 59	302	46 05	332
318	16 32	039	40 25	088	38 08	141	23 09	212	29 07	255	22 16	301	45 40	331
319	17 05	039	41 16	087	38 41	141	22 42	211	28 18	255	21 31	301	45 15	330
320	17 37	038	42 07	087	39 13	141	22 15	211	27 28	254	20 47	300	44 48	328
321	18 08	037	42 59	086	39 46	141	21 49	211	26 39	254	20 02	299	44 21	327
322	18 39	037	43 50	085	40 18	141	21 22	211	25 50	253	19 17	299	43 53	326
323	19 10	036	44 41	085	40 51	141	20 56	211	25 00	253	18 32	298	43 23	325
324	19 39	035	45 32	084	41 23	141	20 30	210	24 11	253	17 46	297	42 53	324
325	20 09	034	46 23	084	41 56	141	20 04	210	23 22	252	17 01	297	42 22	322
326	20 37	034	47 15	083	42 28	141	19 39	210	22 33	252	16 15	296	41 51	321
327	21 05	033	48 06	082	43 00	141	19 13	210	21 45	251	15 28	295	41 18	320
328	21 33	032	48 56	082	43 32	141	18 48	209	20 56	251	14 42	295	40 45	319
329	22 00	031	49 47	081	44 04	141	18 23	209	20 07	251	13 55	294	40 11	318
	◆ Alpheratz		Diphda		◆ ACHERNAR		Peacock		◆ Nunki		ALTAIR		Enif	
330	22 26	030	50 38	080	44 36	142	59 38	205	49 41	265	39 36	317	48 54	354
331	22 52	029	51 29	080	45 08	142	59 16	206	48 49	264	39 01	316	48 48	353
332	23 17	029	52 19	079	45 40	142	58 53	207	47 58	264	38 25	315	48 41	351
333	23 41	028	53 10	078	46 12	142	58 29	208	47 07	264	37 48	314	48 33	350
334	24 05	027	54 00	077	46 43	142	58 05	208	46 16	263	37 11	313	48 23	348
335	24 28	026	54 50	077	47 14	143	57 40	209	45 25	263	36 33	312	48 12	347
336	24 50	025	55 40	076	47 46	143	57 15	210	44 34	262	35 54	311	48 00	346
337	25 11	024	56 30	075	48 17	143	56 49	210	43 43	262	35 15	310	47 46	344
338	25 32	023	57 19	074	48 47	143	56 23	211	42 52	262	34 36	309	47 32	343
339	25 52	023	58 09	073	49 18	144	55 56	212	42 01	261	33 56	308	47 16	341
340	26 12	022	58 58	072	49 48	144	55 29	212	41 10	261	33 15	308	46 59	340
341	26 30	021	59 47	071	50 19	144	55 01	213	40 20	260	32 34	307	46 40	339
342	26 48	020	60 35	070	50 49	145	54 33	213	39 29	260	31 53	306	46 21	337
343	27 05	019	61 24	069	51 18	145	54 05	214	38 38	260	31 11	305	46 01	336
344	27 22	018	62 12	068	51 48	145	53 36	214	37 48	259	30 29	304	45 39	335
	Alpheratz		◆ Hamal		◆ ACHERNAR		Peacock		◆ Nunki		ALTAIR		Enif	
345	27 37	017	19 17	045	52 17	146	53 07	215	36 57	259	29 46	303	45 16	333
346	27 52	016	19 53	045	52 46	146	52 38	215	36 07	258	29 03	303	44 53	332
347	28 05	015	20 29	044	53 15	146	52 08	215	35 17	258	28 19	302	44 28	331
348	28 18	014	21 05	043	53 43	147	51 38	216	34 26	258	27 36	301	44 02	329
349	28 31	013	21 39	042	54 11	147	51 08	216	33 36	257	26 51	300	43 36	328
350	28 42	012	22 14	042	54 38	148	50 38	216	32 46	257	26 07	300	43 08	327
351	28 52	011	22 48	041	55 05	148	50 07	217	31 56	256	25 22	299	42 40	326
352	29 02	010	23 21	040	55 32	149	49 36	217	31 06	256	24 37	298	42 10	325
353	29 11	009	23 54	039	55 58	150	49 05	217	30 16	256	23 52	298	41 40	324
354	29 19	008	24 26	038	56 24	150	48 34	218	29 26	255	23 06	297	41 09	322
355	29 26	007	24 57	037	56 50	151	48 02	218	28 37	255	22 20	296	40 38	321
356	29 32	006	25 28	037	57 15	151	47 31	218	27 47	255	21 34	296	40 05	320
357	29 37	005	25 59	036	57 39	152	46 59	218	26 58	254	20 47	295	39 32	319
358	29 41	004	26 29	035	58 03	153	46 27	218	26 08	254	20 00	294	38 58	318
359	29 45	003	26 58	034	58 26	153	45 55	219	25 19	253	19 13	294	38 23	317

LHA ♈	Hc	Zn	Hc	Zn	Hc	Zn	Hc	Zn	Hc	Zn	Hc	Zn	Hc	Zn
	◆ Alpheratz		Hamal		◆ RIGEL		CANOPUS		ACHERNAR		◆ Peacock		Enif	
0	28 47	002	26 36	033	13 47	091	21 33	140	59 43	153	46 09	219	37 05	317
1	28 49	001	27 03	032	14 38	091	22 06	139	60 05	154	45 37	220	36 29	316
2	28 50	000	27 30	031	15 29	090	22 39	139	60 27	155	45 05	220	35 53	315
3	28 49	359	27 56	030	16 20	090	23 12	139	60 48	156	44 32	220	35 17	314
4	28 48	358	28 21	029	17 11	089	23 46	139	61 08	157	43 59	220	34 40	313
5	28 46	357	28 46	028	18 01	088	24 20	138	61 28	158	43 27	220	34 02	312
6	28 44	356	29 09	027	18 52	088	24 54	138	61 47	159	42 54	220	33 24	311
7	28 40	355	29 32	026	19 43	087	25 28	138	62 05	160	42 21	220	32 46	310
8	28 35	354	29 55	025	20 34	087	26 02	138	62 23	161	41 48	220	32 06	309
9	28 30	353	30 16	025	21 25	086	26 36	137	62 39	162	41 15	220	31 27	308
10	28 23	352	30 37	024	22 16	086	27 11	137	62 55	163	40 42	220	30 47	308
11	28 16	351	30 57	023	23 06	085	27 45	137	63 10	164	40 09	220	30 06	307
12	28 08	350	31 16	022	23 57	085	28 20	137	63 24	165	39 36	220	29 25	306
13	27 59	349	31 34	021	24 48	084	28 55	137	63 36	166	39 03	220	28 44	305
14	27 49	348	31 52	019	25 38	083	29 30	136	63 48	167	38 31	220	28 02	304
	◆ Hamal		ALDEBARAN		RIGEL		◆ CANOPUS		ACHERNAR		◆ FOMALHAUT		Alpheratz	
15	32 08	018	18 57	055	26 29	083	30 05	136	63 59	168	63 52	267	27 39	347
16	32 24	017	19 39	055	27 19	082	30 40	136	64 09	169	63 01	267	27 27	347
17	32 39	016	20 20	054	28 10	082	31 16	136	64 18	171	62 10	266	27 15	346
18	32 53	015	21 01	053	29 00	081	31 51	136	64 26	172	61 20	266	27 02	345
19	33 06	014	21 41	052	29 50	081	32 27	136	64 33	173	60 29	266	26 48	344
20	33 18	013	22 22	052	30 40	080	33 03	135	64 39	174	59 38	265	26 33	343
21	33 29	012	23 01	051	31 30	079	33 38	135	64 43	175	58 47	265	26 18	342
22	33 39	011	23 41	050	32 20	079	34 14	135	64 47	177	57 57	264	26 02	341
23	33 48	010	24 19	049	33 10	078	34 50	135	64 49	178	57 06	264	25 45	340
24	33 57	009	24 58	049	34 00	077	35 26	135	64 50	179	56 16	264	25 27	339
25	34 04	008	25 36	048	34 49	077	36 02	135	64 50	181	55 25	263	25 08	338
26	34 10	007	26 13	047	35 39	076	36 38	135	64 49	182	54 35	263	24 49	337
27	34 16	006	26 50	046	36 28	075	37 14	135	64 47	183	53 44	262	24 29	336
28	34 20	004	27 27	045	37 17	075	37 50	135	64 44	184	52 54	262	24 08	335
29	34 24	003	28 03	045	38 06	074	38 27	135	64 39	186	52 03	262	23 47	335
	Hamal		ALDEBARAN		◆ SIRIUS		CANOPUS		◆ ACHERNAR		FOMALHAUT		◆ Alpheratz	
30	34 26	002	28 38	044	24 16	095	39 03	135	64 34	187	51 13	261	23 24	334
31	34 28	001	29 13	043	25 07	095	39 39	134	64 27	188	50 23	261	23 02	333
32	34 28	000	29 47	042	25 57	094	40 16	134	64 19	189	49 32	261	22 38	332
33	34 28	359	30 21	041	26 48	094	40 52	134	64 11	191	48 42	260	22 14	331
34	34 26	358	30 54	040	27 39	093	41 28	134	64 01	192	47 52	260	21 49	330
35	34 24	357	31 26	039	28 30	093	42 05	134	63 50	193	47 02	260	21 24	330
36	34 20	356	31 58	038	29 20	092	42 41	134	63 38	194	46 12	259	20 57	329
37	34 16	354	32 29	037	30 11	092	43 17	134	63 25	195	45 22	259	20 31	328
38	34 10	353	33 00	036	31 02	091	43 54	134	63 12	196	44 32	258	20 03	327
39	34 04	352	33 29	035	31 53	091	44 30	135	62 57	197	43 42	258	19 36	326
40	33 57	351	33 59	034	32 44	090	45 06	135	62 41	198	42 53	258	19 07	326
41	33 48	350	34 27	033	33 35	090	45 42	135	62 25	199	42 03	257	18 38	325
42	33 39	349	34 54	032	34 26	089	46 19	135	62 08	200	41 13	257	18 08	324
43	33 29	348	35 21	031	35 17	089	46 55	135	61 50	201	40 24	257	17 38	323
44	33 18	347	35 47	030	36 07	088	47 31	135	61 31	202	39 34	256	17 08	323
	◆ ALDEBARAN		BETELGEUSE		SIRIUS		◆ CANOPUS		ACHERNAR		◆ FOMALHAUT		Hamal	
45	36 12	029	32 27	055	36 58	087	48 07	135	61 11	203	38 45	256	33 06	346
46	36 37	028	33 09	054	37 49	087	48 43	135	60 51	204	37 56	256	32 53	345
47	37 00	027	33 50	053	38 40	086	49 18	135	60 30	205	37 06	255	32 39	344
48	37 23	026	34 30	052	39 31	086	49 54	136	60 08	206	36 17	255	32 24	343
49	37 45	025	35 10	051	40 21	085	50 30	136	59 46	206	35 28	254	32 08	342
50	38 05	024	35 49	050	41 12	085	51 05	136	59 23	207	34 39	254	31 52	341
51	38 25	022	36 28	049	42 03	084	51 40	136	58 59	208	33 50	254	31 34	339
52	38 44	021	37 07	048	42 53	083	52 15	136	58 35	209	33 02	253	31 16	338
53	39 02	020	37 44	047	43 44	083	52 50	137	58 10	209	32 13	253	30 57	337
54	39 19	019	38 22	046	44 34	082	53 25	137	57 45	210	31 24	253	30 37	336
55	39 35	018	38 58	045	45 24	081	54 00	137	57 20	211	30 36	252	30 17	335
56	39 50	017	39 34	044	46 15	081	54 34	138	56 53	211	29 47	252	29 55	335
57	40 04	015	40 09	043	47 05	080	55 08	138	56 27	212	28 59	251	29 33	334
58	40 17	014	40 44	042	47 55	079	55 42	138	56 00	212	28 11	251	29 10	333
59	40 29	013	41 18	041	48 45	079	56 16	139	55 33	213	27 23	251	28 46	332
	ALDEBARAN		◆ BETELGEUSE		SIRIUS		◆ CANOPUS		ACHERNAR		◆ FOMALHAUT		Hamal	
60	40 40	012	41 51	040	49 35	078	56 49	139	55 05	213	26 35	250	28 21	331
61	40 50	010	42 24	039	50 24	077	57 22	140	54 37	214	25 47	250	27 56	330
62	40 58	009	42 55	038	51 14	076	57 55	140	54 08	214	24 59	249	27 30	329
63	41 06	008	43 26	037	52 03	076	58 27	141	53 39	215	24 12	249	27 04	328
64	41 12	007	43 56	036	52 52	075	58 59	141	53 10	215	23 24	249	26 36	327
65	41 18	005	44 25	034	53 41	074	59 30	142	52 41	215	22 37	248	26 08	326
66	41 22	004	44 54	033	54 30	073	60 02	143	52 11	216	21 50	248	25 40	325
67	41 25	003	45 21	032	55 19	072	60 32	143	51 41	216	21 03	248	25 10	324
68	41 27	002	45 47	031	56 07	071	61 02	144	51 11	216	20 16	247	24 41	324
69	41 28	000	46 13	029	56 55	070	61 32	145	50 41	217	19 29	247	24 10	323
70	41 27	359	46 37	028	57 43	069	62 01	145	50 10	217	18 42	246	23 39	322
71	41 26	358	47 01	027	58 30	068	62 30	146	49 39	217	17 56	246	23 07	321
72	41 23	356	47 23	025	59 17	067	62 58	147	49 08	218	17 09	245	22 35	320
73	41 19	355	47 44	024	60 04	066	63 25	148	48 37	218	16 23	245	22 02	320
74	41 15	354	48 04	023	60 51	065	63 52	149	48 06	218	15 37	245	21 29	319
	BETELGEUSE		◆ PROCYON		Suhail		◆ ACRUX		ACHERNAR		◆ Diphda		ALDEBARAN	
75	48 23	021	36 47	053	40 43	122	19 18	154	47 35	218	31 11	267	41 09	353
76	48 41	020	37 28	052	41 26	122	19 40	153	47 03	218	30 20	267	41 02	351
77	48 58	018	38 08	051	42 09	122	20 03	153	46 31	219	29 29	266	40 53	350
78	49 13	017	38 47	050	42 52	122	20 26	153	45 59	219	28 39	266	40 44	349
79	49 27	015	39 26	049	43 35	122	20 50	153	45 27	219	27 48	265	40 34	348
80	49 40	014	40 04	048	44 19	122	21 13	152	44 55	219	26 57	265	40 22	346
81	49 52	012	40 42	047	45 02	122	21 37	152	44 23	219	26 06	264	40 10	345
82	50 02	011	41 19	046	45 45	122	22 01	152	43 51	219	25 16	264	39 56	344
83	50 11	009	41 56	045	46 29	121	22 25	152	43 19	219	24 25	263	39 41	343
84	50 18	008	42 31	044	47 12	121	22 49	151	42 46	220	23 35	263	39 26	342
85	50 24	006	43 06	043	47 56	121	23 13	151	42 14	220	22 44	262	39 09	340
86	50 29	005	43 41	042	48 39	121	23 38	151	41 42	220	21 54	262	38 52	339
87	50 33	003	44 14	041	49 23	121	24 02	151	41 09	220	21 03	261	38 33	338
88	50 35	002	44 47	040	50 06	121	24 27	151	40 37	220	20 13	261	38 13	337
89	50 35	000	45 19	038	50 50	121	24 52	150	40 04	220	19 23	261	37 53	336

LAT 32°S

LHA ♈	Hc	Zn	Hc	Zn	Hc	Zn	Hc	Zn	Hc	Zn	Hc	Zn	Hc	Zn
	PROCYON		REGULUS		◆ Suhail		ACRUX		◆ ACHERNAR		RIGEL		◆ BETELGEUSE	
90	45 51	037	16 04	064	51 33	121	25 17	150	39 32	220	64 01	334	50 35	358
91	46 21	036	16 49	064	52 17	121	25 43	150	38 59	220	63 38	332	50 33	357
92	46 50	035	17 35	063	53 00	121	26 08	150	38 27	220	63 13	330	50 29	355
93	47 19	033	18 20	062	53 44	121	26 34	150	37 54	220	62 47	328	50 24	354
94	47 46	032	19 05	062	54 27	121	26 59	150	37 22	220	62 19	326	50 18	352
95	48 13	031	19 50	061	55 11	122	27 25	149	36 49	220	61 50	324	50 11	351
96	48 38	029	20 34	060	55 54	122	27 51	149	36 17	220	61 20	322	50 02	349
97	49 03	028	21 18	060	56 37	122	28 17	149	35 44	220	60 48	321	49 51	348
98	49 26	027	22 02	059	57 21	122	28 43	149	35 12	219	60 15	319	49 40	346
99	49 48	025	22 45	058	58 04	122	29 09	149	34 39	219	59 41	317	49 27	345
100	50 10	024	23 28	058	58 47	122	29 36	149	34 07	219	59 06	316	49 13	343
101	50 29	022	24 11	057	59 30	123	30 02	149	33 35	219	58 30	314	48 58	342
102	50 48	021	24 54	056	60 13	123	30 29	149	33 03	219	57 54	313	48 41	340
103	51 06	019	25 36	055	60 55	123	30 55	148	32 31	219	57 16	311	48 23	339
104	51 22	018	26 17	055	61 38	123	31 22	148	31 59	219	56 37	310	48 04	337
	PROCYON		REGULUS		◆ Gienah		ACRUX		◆ ACHERNAR		RIGEL		◆ BETELGEUSE	
105	51 37	016	26 59	054	18 13	100	31 49	148	31 27	219	55 58	309	47 44	336
106	51 50	015	27 39	053	19 03	099	32 15	148	30 55	219	55 18	307	47 23	335
107	52 02	013	28 20	052	19 54	099	32 42	148	30 23	219	54 37	306	47 01	333
108	52 13	011	29 00	051	20 44	098	33 09	148	29 51	218	53 56	305	46 37	332
109	52 22	010	29 39	051	21 34	098	33 36	148	29 20	218	53 14	304	46 13	331
110	52 30	008	30 18	050	22 25	097	34 03	148	28 48	218	52 31	303	45 47	329
111	52 37	007	30 57	049	23 15	097	34 30	148	28 17	218	51 48	302	45 21	328
112	52 42	005	31 35	048	24 06	096	34 57	148	27 46	218	51 04	300	44 53	327
113	52 46	003	32 13	047	24 56	096	35 24	148	27 15	218	50 20	299	44 25	326
114	52 48	002	32 50	046	25 47	095	35 51	148	26 44	217	49 36	298	43 56	324
115	52 49	000	33 26	045	26 38	095	36 18	148	26 13	217	48 51	297	43 26	323
116	52 48	358	34 02	044	27 28	094	36 45	148	25 42	217	48 05	296	42 55	322
117	52 46	357	34 37	043	28 19	094	37 12	148	25 12	217	47 20	295	42 23	321
118	52 42	355	35 12	042	29 10	093	37 39	148	24 41	217	46 34	295	41 51	320
119	52 37	353	35 46	041	30 01	093	38 06	148	24 11	216	45 47	294	41 18	319
	REGULUS		◆ SPICA		ACRUX		◆ CANOPUS		RIGEL		BETELGEUSE		◆ PROCYON	
120	36 19	040	13 05	095	38 33	148	63 02	213	45 00	293	40 44	318	52 31	352
121	36 52	039	13 55	095	39 00	148	62 34	214	44 13	292	40 09	317	52 23	350
122	37 24	038	14 46	094	39 27	148	62 05	214	43 26	291	39 34	316	52 14	349
123	37 55	037	15 37	094	39 54	148	61 36	215	42 38	290	38 58	315	52 03	347
124	38 26	036	16 28	093	40 21	148	61 07	216	41 51	290	38 21	313	51 51	345
125	38 55	035	17 18	093	40 48	148	60 37	217	41 02	289	37 44	313	51 37	344
126	39 24	034	18 09	092	41 14	148	60 06	217	40 14	288	37 06	312	51 22	342
127	39 52	033	19 00	092	41 41	149	59 35	218	39 26	287	36 28	311	51 06	341
128	40 20	032	19 51	091	42 08	149	59 03	219	38 37	287	35 49	310	50 49	339
129	40 46	031	20 42	091	42 34	149	58 31	219	37 48	286	35 10	309	50 30	338
130	41 12	030	21 33	090	43 00	149	57 59	220	36 59	285	34 30	308	50 10	336
131	41 36	028	22 24	089	43 27	149	57 27	220	36 10	284	33 49	307	49 49	335
132	42 00	027	23 15	089	43 53	149	56 54	221	35 20	284	33 08	306	49 27	333
133	42 23	026	24 05	088	44 19	149	56 20	221	34 31	283	32 27	305	49 04	332
134	42 45	025	24 56	088	44 45	150	55 47	221	33 41	282	31 45	304	48 39	331
	◆ REGULUS		SPICA		◆ ACRUX		CANOPUS		◆ RIGEL		BETELGEUSE		PROCYON	
135	43 05	023	25 47	087	45 10	150	55 13	222	32 52	282	31 03	304	48 14	329
136	43 25	022	26 38	087	45 36	150	54 39	222	32 02	281	30 21	303	47 47	328
137	43 44	021	27 29	086	46 01	150	54 05	223	31 12	280	29 38	302	47 20	327
138	44 01	020	28 20	086	46 26	150	53 30	223	30 22	280	28 54	301	46 52	325
139	44 18	018	29 10	085	46 51	151	52 55	223	29 31	279	28 11	300	46 22	324
140	44 33	017	30 01	085	47 16	151	52 20	223	28 41	279	27 27	300	45 52	323
141	44 48	016	30 52	084	47 41	151	51 45	224	27 51	278	26 42	299	45 21	322
142	45 01	014	31 42	083	48 05	152	51 10	224	27 00	277	25 58	298	44 49	320
143	45 13	013	32 33	083	48 29	152	50 35	224	26 10	277	25 13	298	44 16	319
144	45 24	012	33 23	082	48 53	152	49 59	224	25 19	276	24 27	297	43 42	318
145	45 33	010	34 13	082	49 17	153	49 23	225	24 29	276	23 42	296	43 08	317
146	45 42	009	35 04	081	49 40	153	48 48	225	23 38	275	22 56	295	42 33	316
147	45 49	007	35 54	080	50 03	153	48 12	225	22 47	275	22 10	295	41 57	315
148	45 55	006	36 44	080	50 26	154	47 36	225	21 57	274	21 24	294	41 21	314
149	46 00	005	37 34	079	50 48	154	47 00	225	21 06	274	20 37	293	40 44	313
	REGULUS		◆ Denebola		SPICA		◆ ACRUX		CANOPUS		◆ SIRIUS		PROCYON	
150	46 03	003	36 35	034	38 24	078	51 10	154	46 24	225	43 39	277	40 06	312
151	46 05	002	37 03	033	39 14	078	51 32	155	45 48	225	42 48	277	39 28	311
152	46 06	000	37 30	032	40 03	077	51 54	155	45 11	225	41 58	276	38 49	310
153	46 06	359	37 56	031	40 53	076	52 15	156	44 35	225	41 07	275	38 10	309
154	46 05	358	38 22	029	41 42	076	52 35	156	43 59	226	40 17	275	37 30	308
155	46 02	356	38 46	028	42 31	075	52 56	157	43 22	226	39 26	274	36 49	307
156	45 58	355	39 10	027	43 20	074	53 16	157	42 46	226	38 35	274	36 08	306
157	45 53	353	39 33	026	44 09	073	53 35	158	42 10	226	37 44	273	35 27	305
158	45 46	352	39 55	025	44 58	073	53 54	158	41 33	226	36 53	273	34 45	304
159	45 38	351	40 16	024	45 46	072	54 13	159	40 57	226	36 03	272	34 03	303
160	45 29	349	40 36	022	46 35	071	54 31	159	40 21	226	35 12	271	33 20	303
161	45 19	348	40 55	021	47 23	070	54 48	160	39 44	226	34 21	271	32 37	302
162	45 08	346	41 13	020	48 10	069	55 05	161	39 08	225	33 30	270	31 54	301
163	44 56	345	41 29	019	48 58	068	55 22	161	38 32	225	32 39	270	31 10	300
164	44 42	344	41 45	018	49 45	068	55 38	162	37 56	225	31 48	269	30 26	299
	ARCTURUS		◆ ANTARES		ACRUX		◆ CANOPUS		SIRIUS		PROCYON		◆ REGULUS	
165	20 34	050	19 31	110	55 54	163	37 19	225	30 57	269	29 41	299	44 27	342
166	21 13	049	20 19	109	56 09	163	36 43	225	30 06	268	28 56	298	44 11	341
167	21 51	048	21 07	109	56 23	164	36 07	225	29 16	268	28 11	297	43 54	340
168	22 29	047	21 56	108	56 37	165	35 31	225	28 25	267	27 26	296	43 36	339
169	23 06	047	22 44	108	56 50	165	34 55	225	27 34	267	26 40	296	43 17	337
170	23 43	046	23 32	108	57 03	166	34 19	225	26 43	266	25 54	295	42 57	336
171	24 19	045	24 21	107	57 14	167	33 43	225	25 52	266	25 08	294	42 36	335
172	24 55	044	25 10	107	57 26	168	33 08	225	25 02	265	24 21	294	42 13	334
173	25 30	043	25 59	106	57 36	168	32 32	224	24 11	265	23 34	293	41 50	332
174	26 05	043	26 47	106	57 46	169	31 56	224	23 20	264	22 47	292	41 26	331
175	26 39	042	27 36	105	57 56	170	31 21	224	22 30	264	22 00	292	41 01	330
176	27 13	041	28 26	105	58 04	171	30 46	224	21 39	263	21 13	291	40 35	329
177	27 46	040	29 15	105	58 12	172	30 10	224	20 49	263	20 25	290	40 08	328
178	28 18	039	30 04	105	58 19	172	29 35	224	19 58	262	19 37	290	39 41	327
179	28 50	038	30 53	104	58 25	173	29 00	223	19 08	262	18 49	289	39 12	325

LHA ♈	◆ ARCTURUS Hc	Zn	ANTARES Hc	Zn	◆ RIGIL KENT Hc	Zn	ACRUX Hc	Zn	CANOPUS Hc	Zn	◆ Alphard Hc	Zn	REGULUS Hc	Zn
180	29 21	037	31 43	103	51 06	150	58 31	174	28 25	223	47 52	295	38 43	324
181	29 52	037	32 32	103	51 31	150	58 36	175	27 50	223	47 06	294	38 13	323
182	30 22	036	33 22	103	51 56	151	58 40	176	27 16	223	46 19	293	37 42	322
183	30 51	035	34 12	102	52 21	151	58 43	177	26 41	223	45 33	292	37 11	321
184	31 20	034	35 01	102	52 45	152	58 46	178	26 07	222	44 45	292	36 38	320
185	31 48	033	35 51	101	53 09	152	58 48	178	25 33	222	43 58	291	36 05	319
186	32 15	032	36 41	101	53 33	153	58 49	179	24 58	222	43 10	290	35 32	318
187	32 41	031	37 31	101	53 56	153	58 49	180	24 24	222	42 22	289	34 57	317
188	33 07	030	38 21	100	54 19	154	58 49	181	23 51	221	41 34	288	34 23	316
189	33 32	029	39 11	100	54 41	154	58 47	182	23 17	221	40 46	288	33 47	315
190	33 56	028	40 02	099	55 03	155	58 45	183	22 44	221	39 57	287	33 11	314
191	34 19	027	40 52	099	55 25	155	58 42	184	22 10	221	39 08	286	32 34	313
192	34 41	026	41 42	098	55 46	156	58 39	184	21 37	220	38 19	285	31 57	313
193	35 03	025	42 32	098	56 06	157	58 35	185	21 04	220	37 30	285	31 19	312
194	35 23	023	43 23	098	56 26	157	58 29	186	20 32	220	36 41	284	30 41	311

LHA ♈	ARCTURUS Hc	Zn	◆ ANTARES Hc	Zn	RIGIL KENT Hc	Zn	◆ ACRUX Hc	Zn	Suhail Hc	Zn	REGULUS Hc	Zn	◆ Denebola Hc	Zn
195	35 43	022	44 13	097	56 46	158	58 24	187	43 47	238	30 02	310	40 34	337
196	36 02	021	45 04	097	57 04	159	58 17	188	43 04	238	29 23	309	40 14	336
197	36 20	020	45 54	096	57 23	159	58 10	189	42 21	238	28 43	308	39 53	335
198	36 37	019	46 45	096	57 41	160	58 02	189	41 38	238	28 03	307	39 31	334
199	36 53	018	47 36	095	57 58	161	57 53	190	40 55	238	27 23	307	39 08	333
200	37 09	017	48 26	095	58 14	161	57 44	191	40 11	238	26 42	306	38 44	332
201	37 23	016	49 17	095	58 30	162	57 33	192	39 29	238	26 00	305	38 20	330
202	37 36	014	50 08	094	58 45	163	57 23	193	38 46	237	25 18	304	37 54	329
203	37 48	013	50 59	094	59 00	164	57 11	193	38 03	237	24 36	304	37 28	328
204	37 59	012	51 49	093	59 14	165	56 59	194	37 20	237	23 54	303	37 01	327
205	38 10	011	52 40	093	59 27	166	56 46	195	36 37	237	23 11	302	36 33	326
206	38 19	010	53 31	092	59 39	166	56 33	196	35 55	237	22 27	301	36 04	325
207	38 27	009	54 22	092	59 51	167	56 19	196	35 12	236	21 44	301	35 34	324
208	38 34	007	55 13	091	60 02	168	56 05	197	34 30	236	21 00	300	35 04	323
209	38 40	006	56 04	091	60 12	169	55 49	198	33 48	236	20 16	299	34 33	322

LHA ♈	◆ ARCTURUS Hc	Zn	Rasalhague Hc	Zn	◆ Nunki Hc	Zn	RIGIL KENT Hc	Zn	ACRUX Hc	Zn	◆ Suhail Hc	Zn	SPICA Hc	Zn
210	38 45	005	21 52	058	26 20	106	60 21	170	55 34	198	33 06	236	67 48	337
211	38 49	004	22 35	057	27 09	105	60 29	171	55 18	199	32 24	236	67 28	335
212	38 51	003	23 18	057	27 58	105	60 37	172	55 01	200	31 42	235	67 06	333
213	38 53	001	24 00	056	28 47	105	60 44	173	54 44	200	31 00	235	66 41	330
214	38 54	000	24 42	055	29 37	104	60 49	174	54 26	201	30 18	235	66 15	328
215	38 53	359	25 24	055	30 26	104	60 54	175	54 08	201	29 37	235	65 48	326
216	38 52	358	26 05	054	31 15	103	60 59	176	53 49	202	28 55	234	65 18	324
217	38 49	356	26 46	053	32 05	103	61 02	177	53 30	202	28 14	234	64 48	322
218	38 45	355	27 26	052	32 55	103	61 04	178	53 10	203	27 33	234	64 16	320
219	38 41	354	28 06	051	33 44	102	61 06	179	52 50	203	26 52	234	63 43	318
220	38 35	353	28 46	051	34 34	102	61 06	180	52 30	204	26 11	233	63 08	316
221	38 28	352	29 25	050	35 24	101	61 06	181	52 09	204	25 30	233	62 32	315
222	38 20	350	30 04	049	36 14	101	61 05	182	51 48	205	24 49	233	61 56	313
223	38 11	349	30 42	048	37 04	101	61 03	183	51 26	205	24 09	232	61 18	312
224	38 01	348	31 19	047	37 54	100	61 00	184	51 04	206	23 29	232	60 40	310

LHA ♈	Alphecca Hc	Zn	Rasalhague Hc	Zn	◆ Nunki Hc	Zn	Peacock Hc	Zn	◆ RIGIL KENT Hc	Zn	SPICA Hc	Zn	◆ ARCTURUS Hc	Zn
225	30 44	009	31 56	046	38 44	100	30 40	141	60 56	185	60 00	309	37 50	347
226	30 52	008	32 33	045	39 34	099	31 12	141	60 51	186	59 20	307	37 38	346
227	30 58	007	33 09	044	40 24	099	31 44	141	60 45	187	58 39	306	37 25	345
228	31 04	006	33 44	044	41 15	098	32 17	140	60 39	188	57 57	304	37 11	343
229	31 09	005	34 19	043	42 05	098	32 49	140	60 32	189	57 15	303	36 56	342
230	31 13	004	34 53	042	42 55	098	33 22	140	60 24	190	56 32	302	36 40	341
231	31 16	003	35 26	041	43 46	097	33 54	140	60 15	191	55 49	301	36 23	340
232	31 19	002	35 59	040	44 36	097	34 27	140	60 05	192	55 05	300	36 05	339
233	31 20	001	36 31	039	45 27	096	35 00	140	59 54	192	54 20	298	35 47	338
234	31 20	000	37 03	038	46 18	096	35 33	140	59 43	193	53 35	297	35 27	337
235	31 19	359	37 33	037	47 08	095	36 05	140	59 31	194	52 50	296	35 06	336
236	31 18	358	38 03	035	47 59	095	36 38	140	59 18	195	52 04	295	34 45	335
237	31 15	357	38 32	034	48 50	095	37 11	140	59 04	196	51 18	294	34 23	334
238	31 12	356	39 01	033	49 40	094	37 44	140	58 50	197	50 31	293	34 00	332
239	31 08	355	39 28	032	50 31	094	38 17	140	58 35	198	49 45	292	33 36	331

LHA ♈	Rasalhague Hc	Zn	ALTAIR Hc	Zn	◆ Nunki Hc	Zn	Peacock Hc	Zn	◆ RIGIL KENT Hc	Zn	SPICA Hc	Zn	◆ ARCTURUS Hc	Zn
240	39 55	031	21 19	064	51 22	093	38 50	140	58 19	198	48 57	292	33 11	330
241	40 21	030	22 04	063	52 13	093	39 23	140	58 03	199	48 10	291	32 46	329
242	40 45	029	22 49	063	53 04	092	39 56	140	57 46	200	47 22	290	32 19	328
243	41 09	028	23 34	062	53 54	092	40 29	140	57 28	201	46 34	289	31 52	327
244	41 33	026	24 19	061	54 45	091	41 02	140	57 10	201	45 46	288	31 25	326
245	41 55	025	25 04	060	55 36	091	41 35	140	56 52	202	44 58	287	30 56	326
246	42 16	024	25 48	060	56 27	090	42 07	140	56 32	203	44 09	287	30 27	325
247	42 36	023	26 31	059	57 18	090	42 40	140	56 12	203	43 20	286	29 57	324
248	42 55	021	27 15	058	58 09	089	43 13	140	55 52	204	42 31	285	29 27	323
249	43 13	020	27 58	057	59 00	088	43 46	140	55 31	204	41 42	284	28 56	322
250	43 30	019	28 41	057	59 51	088	44 18	140	55 10	205	40 52	284	28 24	321
251	43 46	018	29 23	056	60 41	087	44 51	140	54 48	206	40 03	283	27 51	320
252	44 01	016	30 05	055	61 32	087	45 24	140	54 26	206	39 13	282	27 18	319
253	44 14	015	30 46	054	62 23	086	45 56	140	54 03	207	38 24	282	26 45	318
254	44 27	014	31 27	053	63 14	085	46 28	141	53 40	207	37 34	281	26 11	317

LHA ♈	VEGA Hc	Zn	◆ ALTAIR Hc	Zn	FOMALHAUT Hc	Zn	◆ Peacock Hc	Zn	RIGIL KENT Hc	Zn	◆ SPICA Hc	Zn	ARCTURUS Hc	Zn
255	15 40	020	32 08	053	15 26	116	47 01	141	53 17	208	36 44	280	25 36	317
256	15 57	019	32 48	052	16 12	115	47 33	141	52 53	208	35 54	280	25 01	316
257	16 13	018	33 28	051	16 58	115	48 05	141	52 29	209	35 03	279	24 25	315
258	16 28	017	34 07	050	17 45	114	48 37	141	52 04	209	34 13	278	23 49	314
259	16 43	016	34 46	049	18 31	114	49 08	142	51 39	209	33 23	278	23 12	313
260	16 57	016	35 24	048	19 18	113	49 40	142	51 14	210	32 32	277	22 35	313
261	17 10	015	36 01	047	20 05	113	50 11	142	50 49	210	31 42	277	21 58	312
262	17 23	014	36 38	046	20 52	113	50 42	142	50 23	211	30 51	276	21 19	311
263	17 35	013	37 15	045	21 39	112	51 13	143	49 57	211	30 01	275	20 41	310
264	17 46	013	37 51	044	22 26	112	51 44	143	49 31	211	29 10	275	20 02	310
265	17 57	012	38 26	043	23 13	111	52 14	143	49 04	212	28 19	274	19 23	309
266	18 07	011	39 00	042	24 01	111	52 45	144	48 37	212	27 28	274	18 43	308
267	18 16	010	39 34	041	24 48	111	53 15	144	48 10	212	26 38	273	18 03	308
268	18 25	009	40 07	040	25 36	110	53 44	145	47 43	212	25 47	273	17 22	307
269	18 33	009	40 40	039	26 24	110	54 14	145	47 16	213	24 56	272	16 41	306

LHA ♈	VEGA Hc	Zn	ALTAIR Hc	Zn	◆ FOMALHAUT Hc	Zn	ACHERNAR Hc	Zn	◆ RIGIL KENT Hc	Zn	ANTARES Hc	Zn	◆ Rasalhague Hc	Zn
270	18 40	008	41 11	038	27 12	109	14 43	149	46 48	213	69 43	280	45 04	352
271	18 47	007	41 42	037	28 00	109	15 09	149	46 21	213	68 53	279	44 56	350
272	18 52	006	42 12	036	28 48	109	15 35	149	45 53	213	68 02	278	44 47	349
273	18 57	005	42 41	034	29 36	108	16 02	148	45 25	214	67 12	277	44 36	347
274	19 02	004	43 10	033	30 24	108	16 29	148	44 57	214	66 21	277	44 25	346
275	19 05	004	43 37	032	31 13	108	16 56	148	44 28	214	65 31	276	44 12	345
276	19 08	003	44 04	031	32 01	107	17 23	147	44 00	214	64 40	275	43 58	343
277	19 10	002	44 29	030	32 50	107	17 51	147	43 31	214	63 49	275	43 43	342
278	19 11	001	44 54	028	33 39	106	18 18	147	43 03	214	62 59	274	43 27	341
279	19 12	000	45 17	027	34 28	106	18 46	147	42 34	214	62 08	273	43 10	340
280	19 12	359	45 40	026	35 17	106	19 15	146	42 05	215	61 17	273	42 52	338
281	19 11	359	46 02	024	36 06	105	19 43	146	41 36	215	60 26	272	42 32	337
282	19 10	358	46 22	023	36 55	105	20 12	146	41 07	215	59 35	272	42 12	336
283	19 07	357	46 41	022	37 44	105	20 40	145	40 38	215	58 45	271	41 51	335
284	19 04	356	47 00	020	38 33	104	21 09	145	40 09	215	57 54	270	41 28	333

LHA ♈	ALTAIR Hc	Zn	Enif Hc	Zn	◆ FOMALHAUT Hc	Zn	ACHERNAR Hc	Zn	◆ RIGIL KENT Hc	Zn	ANTARES Hc	Zn	◆ Rasalhague Hc	Zn
285	47 17	019	32 28	050	39 23	104	21 38	145	39 40	215	57 03	270	41 05	332
286	47 33	018	33 06	049	40 12	103	22 08	145	39 11	215	56 12	269	40 41	331
287	47 47	016	33 45	049	41 02	103	22 37	144	38 42	215	55 21	269	40 16	330
288	48 01	015	34 23	048	41 51	103	23 07	144	38 13	215	54 30	268	39 50	329
289	48 13	013	35 00	047	42 41	102	23 37	144	37 44	215	53 39	268	39 23	328
290	48 24	012	35 37	046	43 31	102	24 07	144	37 14	215	52 49	267	38 55	327
291	48 34	010	36 13	045	44 20	102	24 37	143	36 45	215	51 58	267	38 27	325
292	48 42	009	36 48	044	45 10	101	25 08	143	36 16	215	51 07	266	37 58	324
293	48 50	007	37 23	043	46 00	101	25 38	143	35 47	215	50 16	266	37 28	323
294	48 55	006	37 57	042	46 50	101	26 09	143	35 18	215	49 25	266	36 57	322
295	49 00	004	38 31	041	47 40	100	26 40	143	34 49	215	48 35	265	36 25	321
296	49 03	003	39 04	040	48 30	100	27 11	142	34 20	215	47 44	265	35 53	320
297	49 05	001	39 36	039	49 20	099	27 42	142	33 51	215	46 53	264	35 20	319
298	49 05	000	40 07	038	50 11	099	28 13	142	33 22	215	46 03	264	34 47	318
299	49 05	358	40 38	036	51 01	099	28 44	142	32 53	215	45 12	263	34 12	317

LHA ♈	Enif Hc	Zn	◆ FOMALHAUT Hc	Zn	ACHERNAR Hc	Zn	◆ RIGIL KENT Hc	Zn	ANTARES Hc	Zn	Rasalhague Hc	Zn	◆ ALTAIR Hc	Zn
300	41 08	035	51 51	098	29 16	142	32 24	215	44 22	263	33 38	316	49 02	357
301	41 37	034	52 42	098	29 47	142	31 55	214	43 31	262	33 02	315	48 59	355
302	42 05	033	53 32	098	30 19	141	31 26	214	42 41	262	32 26	314	48 54	354
303	42 32	032	54 22	097	30 51	141	30 57	214	41 50	262	31 49	314	48 48	352
304	42 59	031	55 13	097	31 22	141	30 29	214	41 00	261	31 12	313	48 40	351
305	43 24	029	56 04	096	31 54	141	30 00	214	40 10	261	30 35	312	48 32	349
306	43 49	028	56 54	096	32 26	141	29 32	214	39 20	260	29 57	311	48 22	348
307	44 12	027	57 45	096	32 58	141	29 04	214	38 30	260	29 18	310	48 10	346
308	44 35	026	58 35	095	33 31	141	28 35	214	37 39	260	28 39	309	47 58	345
309	44 56	024	59 26	095	34 03	141	28 07	213	36 49	259	27 59	308	47 44	344
310	45 17	023	60 17	094	34 35	141	27 39	213	36 00	259	27 19	308	47 29	342
311	45 36	022	61 07	094	35 07	141	27 11	213	35 10	258	26 39	307	47 13	341
312	45 54	020	61 58	094	35 40	140	26 44	213	34 20	258	25 58	306	46 55	339
313	46 11	019	62 49	093	36 12	140	26 16	213	33 30	257	25 16	305	46 37	338
314	46 27	018	63 40	093	36 45	140	25 49	213	32 41	257	24 35	305	46 17	337

LHA ♈	Alpheratz Hc	Zn	◆ Diphda Hc	Zn	ACHERNAR Hc	Zn	◆ RIGIL KENT Hc	Zn	ANTARES Hc	Zn	Rasalhague Hc	Zn	◆ ALTAIR Hc	Zn
315	14 07	041	37 49	089	37 17	140	25 21	212	31 51	257	23 53	304	45 56	335
316	14 41	041	38 40	088	37 50	140	24 54	212	31 01	256	23 10	303	45 35	334
317	15 14	040	39 31	087	38 22	140	24 27	212	30 12	256	22 27	302	45 12	333
318	15 46	039	40 22	087	38 55	140	24 00	212	29 23	255	21 44	302	44 48	331
319	16 18	039	41 12	086	39 27	140	23 33	212	28 34	255	21 01	301	44 23	330
320	16 49	038	42 03	086	40 00	140	23 07	211	27 44	255	20 17	300	43 57	329
321	17 20	037	42 54	085	40 32	140	22 40	211	26 55	254	19 33	300	43 30	328
322	17 51	036	43 45	084	41 05	140	22 14	211	26 07	254	18 48	299	43 03	326
323	18 21	036	44 35	084	41 37	140	21 48	211	25 18	253	18 04	298	42 34	325
324	18 50	035	45 26	083	42 10	140	21 22	210	24 29	253	17 19	298	42 05	324
325	19 19	034	46 16	083	42 42	140	20 56	210	23 40	253	16 34	297	41 35	323
326	19 47	033	47 07	082	43 14	141	20 31	210	22 52	252	15 48	296	41 04	322
327	20 15	033	47 57	081	43 47	141	20 05	210	22 04	252	15 02	296	40 32	321
328	20 42	032	48 47	081	44 19	141	19 40	209	21 15	251	14 16	295	39 59	320
329	21 08	031	49 37	080	44 51	141	19 15	209	20 27	251	13 30	294	39 26	319

LHA ♈	◆ Alpheratz Hc	Zn	Diphda Hc	Zn	◆ ACHERNAR Hc	Zn	Peacock Hc	Zn	◆ Nunki Hc	Zn	ALTAIR Hc	Zn	Enif Hc	Zn
330	21 34	030	50 27	079	45 23	141	60 32	206	49 45	266	38 52	318	47 54	354
331	21 59	029	51 17	078	45 55	141	60 09	207	48 55	266	38 17	317	47 48	353
332	22 24	028	52 07	078	46 27	141	59 46	208	48 04	265	37 42	316	47 42	352
333	22 48	028	52 57	077	46 59	141	59 22	209	47 13	265	37 06	315	47 34	350
334	23 11	027	53 46	076	47 30	142	58 57	209	46 23	264	36 29	314	47 24	349
335	23 34	026	54 36	075	48 02	142	58 32	210	45 32	264	35 52	313	47 14	347
336	23 56	025	55 25	074	48 33	142	58 07	211	44 41	263	35 15	312	47 02	346
337	24 17	024	56 14	074	49 04	142	57 40	211	43 51	263	34 36	311	46 49	344
338	24 37	023	57 02	073	49 35	143	57 14	212	43 00	262	33 58	310	46 34	343
339	24 57	022	57 51	072	50 06	143	56 47	212	42 10	262	33 18	309	46 19	342
340	25 16	021	58 39	071	50 37	143	56 19	213	41 20	262	32 38	308	46 02	340
341	25 34	021	59 27	070	51 07	143	55 51	213	40 29	261	31 58	307	45 44	339
342	25 52	020	60 15	069	51 37	144	55 23	214	39 39	261	31 17	306	45 26	338
343	26 08	019	61 02	068	52 07	144	54 55	214	38 49	260	30 36	306	45 06	336
344	26 24	018	61 49	067	52 37	144	54 26	215	37 59	260	29 55	305	44 45	335

LHA ♈	Alpheratz Hc	Zn	◆ Hamal Hc	Zn	◆ ACHERNAR Hc	Zn	Peacock Hc	Zn	◆ Nunki Hc	Zn	ALTAIR Hc	Zn	Enif Hc	Zn
345	26 40	017	18 35	045	53 06	145	53 56	215	37 09	260	29 13	304	44 23	334
346	26 54	016	19 11	044	53 35	145	53 27	216	36 19	259	28 30	303	44 00	332
347	27 08	015	19 46	044	54 04	146	52 57	216	35 29	259	27 47	302	43 35	331
348	27 20	014	20 21	043	54 33	146	52 27	216	34 39	258	27 04	302	43 10	330
349	27 32	013	20 55	042	55 01	147	51 56	217	33 49	258	26 21	301	42 45	329
350	27 43	012	21 29	041	55 29	147	51 26	217	32 59	257	25 37	300	42 18	328
351	27 54	011	22 02	040	55 56	148	50 55	217	32 10	257	24 53	299	41 50	326
352	28 03	010	22 35	040	56 23	148	50 24	218	31 20	257	24 08	299	41 21	325
353	28 12	009	23 07	039	56 50	149	49 53	218	30 31	256	23 23	298	40 52	324
354	28 19	008	23 39	038	57 16	149	49 21	218	29 41	256	22 38	297	40 22	323
355	28 26	007	24 10	037	57 42	150	48 50	219	28 52	255	21 53	297	39 51	322
356	28 32	006	24 40	036	58 07	151	48 18	219	28 03	255	21 08	296	39 19	321
357	28 37	005	25 10	036	58 32	151	47 46	219	27 14	255	20 22	295	38 46	320
358	28 41	004	25 39	035	58 56	152	47 14	219	26 25	254	19 35	295	38 13	319
359	28 45	003	26 08	034	59 20	153	46 42	219	25 36	254	18 49	294	37 39	318

LAT 33°S

LHA ♈	Hc	Zn	Hc	Zn	Hc	Zn	Hc	Zn	Hc	Zn	Hc	Zn	Hc	Zn
	◆ Alpheratz		Hamal		◆ RIGEL		CANOPUS		ACHERNAR		◆ Peacock		Enif	
0	27 47	002	25 46	033	13 48	091	22 18	139	60 36	153	46 55	220	36 21	317
1	27 49	001	26 12	032	14 38	090	22 51	139	60 59	153	46 23	220	35 46	316
2	27 50	000	26 38	031	15 29	090	23 24	139	61 21	154	45 50	220	35 11	315
3	27 49	359	27 04	030	16 19	089	23 57	139	61 43	155	45 18	221	34 35	314
4	27 48	358	27 29	029	17 09	089	24 31	138	62 03	156	44 45	221	33 59	313
5	27 46	357	27 53	028	18 00	088	25 04	138	62 23	157	44 12	221	33 22	312
6	27 44	356	28 16	027	18 50	088	25 38	138	62 43	158	43 39	221	32 45	311
7	27 40	355	28 39	026	19 40	087	26 12	138	63 01	159	43 07	221	32 07	311
8	27 36	354	29 01	025	20 30	086	26 46	137	63 19	160	42 34	221	31 28	310
9	27 30	353	29 22	024	21 21	086	27 20	137	63 36	161	42 01	221	30 49	309
10	27 24	352	29 42	023	22 11	085	27 55	137	63 52	162	41 28	221	30 10	308
11	27 17	351	30 01	022	23 01	085	28 29	137	64 07	163	40 55	221	29 30	307
12	27 09	350	30 20	021	23 51	084	29 04	136	64 21	164	40 22	221	28 50	306
13	27 00	350	30 38	020	24 41	084	29 39	136	64 35	165	39 49	221	28 09	306
14	26 51	349	30 55	019	25 31	083	30 13	136	64 47	167	39 16	221	27 28	305
	◆ Hamal		ALDEBARAN		RIGEL		◆ CANOPUS		ACHERNAR		◆ FOMALHAUT		Alpheratz	
15	31 11	018	18 23	055	26 21	082	30 48	136	64 58	168	63 54	269	26 40	348
16	31 27	017	19 04	054	27 11	082	31 24	136	65 08	169	63 03	269	26 29	347
17	31 41	016	19 44	054	28 01	081	31 59	135	65 17	170	62 13	268	26 17	346
18	31 55	015	20 25	053	28 50	081	32 34	135	65 25	171	61 23	268	26 04	345
19	32 07	014	21 05	052	29 40	080	33 10	135	65 32	173	60 33	267	25 50	344
20	32 19	013	21 44	051	30 29	079	33 45	135	65 38	174	59 42	267	25 36	343
21	32 30	012	22 23	051	31 19	079	34 21	135	65 43	175	58 52	266	25 21	342
22	32 40	011	23 02	050	32 08	078	34 56	135	65 47	177	58 02	266	25 05	341
23	32 49	010	23 40	049	32 57	077	35 32	135	65 49	178	57 12	266	24 48	340
24	32 57	009	24 18	048	33 46	077	36 08	134	65 50	179	56 21	265	24 31	339
25	33 04	008	24 55	047	34 35	076	36 44	134	65 50	181	55 31	265	24 12	338
26	33 11	007	25 32	047	35 24	075	37 20	134	65 49	182	54 41	264	23 53	337
27	33 16	005	26 09	046	36 13	075	37 56	134	65 47	183	53 51	264	23 34	337
28	33 20	004	26 44	045	37 01	074	38 32	134	65 44	185	53 01	263	23 13	336
29	33 24	003	27 20	044	37 49	073	39 09	134	65 39	186	52 11	263	22 52	335
	Hamal		ALDEBARAN		◆ SIRIUS		CANOPUS		◆ ACHERNAR		FOMALHAUT		◆ Alpheratz	
30	33 26	002	27 54	043	24 21	095	39 45	134	65 33	187	51 21	263	22 31	334
31	33 28	001	28 29	042	25 11	094	40 21	134	65 26	188	50 31	262	22 08	333
32	33 28	000	29 02	042	26 01	094	40 57	134	65 19	190	49 42	262	21 45	332
33	33 28	359	29 35	041	26 52	093	41 34	134	65 10	191	48 52	261	21 21	331
34	33 26	358	30 08	040	27 42	093	42 10	134	65 00	192	48 02	261	20 57	331
35	33 24	357	30 40	039	28 32	092	42 46	134	64 48	193	47 12	261	20 32	330
36	33 20	356	31 11	038	29 22	092	43 23	134	64 36	195	46 23	260	20 06	329
37	33 16	355	31 41	037	30 13	091	43 59	134	64 23	196	45 33	260	19 40	328
38	33 11	353	32 11	036	31 03	091	44 35	134	64 09	197	44 44	259	19 13	327
39	33 05	352	32 40	035	31 53	090	45 12	134	63 54	198	43 54	259	18 46	327
40	32 57	351	33 09	034	32 44	089	45 48	134	63 38	199	43 05	259	18 17	326
41	32 49	350	33 37	033	33 34	089	46 24	134	63 21	200	42 16	258	17 49	325
42	32 40	349	34 04	032	34 24	088	47 01	134	63 04	201	41 26	258	17 20	324
43	32 30	348	34 30	031	35 15	088	47 37	134	62 45	202	40 37	257	16 50	323
44	32 19	347	34 55	030	36 05	087	48 13	134	62 26	203	39 48	257	16 20	323
	◆ ALDEBARAN		BETELGEUSE		SIRIUS		◆ CANOPUS		ACHERNAR		◆ FOMALHAUT		Hamal	
45	35 20	029	31 52	054	36 55	087	48 49	134	62 06	204	38 59	257	32 08	346
46	35 44	028	32 33	053	37 45	086	49 25	134	61 45	205	38 10	256	31 55	345
47	36 07	027	33 13	052	38 35	085	50 01	135	61 24	206	37 21	256	31 41	344
48	36 29	026	33 53	052	39 26	085	50 37	135	61 02	206	36 33	255	31 27	343
49	36 50	024	34 32	051	40 16	084	51 12	135	60 39	207	35 44	255	31 11	342
50	37 10	023	35 11	050	41 06	084	51 48	135	60 16	208	34 55	255	30 55	341
51	37 30	022	35 49	049	41 56	083	52 23	135	59 52	209	34 07	254	30 38	340
52	37 48	021	36 27	048	42 46	082	52 59	136	59 28	209	33 19	254	30 20	339
53	38 06	020	37 04	047	43 36	082	53 34	136	59 03	210	32 30	254	30 02	338
54	38 23	019	37 40	046	44 25	081	54 09	136	58 37	211	31 42	253	29 42	337
55	38 38	018	38 16	045	45 15	080	54 43	136	58 11	211	30 54	253	29 22	336
56	38 53	016	38 51	044	46 05	080	55 18	137	57 45	212	30 06	252	29 01	335
57	39 07	015	39 26	043	46 54	079	55 52	137	57 18	213	29 18	252	28 39	334
58	39 19	014	40 00	042	47 43	078	56 27	137	56 50	213	28 30	252	28 16	333
59	39 31	013	40 33	041	48 33	077	57 00	138	56 23	214	27 43	251	27 53	332
	ALDEBARAN		◆ BETELGEUSE		SIRIUS		◆ CANOPUS		ACHERNAR		◆ FOMALHAUT		Hamal	
60	39 41	011	41 05	040	49 22	077	57 34	138	55 55	214	26 55	251	27 29	331
61	39 51	010	41 37	039	50 10	076	58 07	139	55 26	215	26 08	250	27 04	330
62	39 59	009	42 08	037	50 59	075	58 40	139	54 58	215	25 20	250	26 39	329
63	40 07	008	42 38	036	51 48	074	59 13	140	54 29	215	24 33	250	26 13	328
64	40 13	007	43 07	035	52 36	073	59 45	140	53 59	216	23 46	249	25 46	327
65	40 18	005	43 36	034	53 24	073	60 17	141	53 30	216	22 59	249	25 18	326
66	40 22	004	44 03	033	54 12	072	60 49	141	53 00	217	22 12	248	24 50	326
67	40 25	003	44 30	031	55 00	071	61 20	142	52 30	217	21 26	248	24 22	325
68	40 27	002	44 56	030	55 47	070	61 51	143	51 59	217	20 39	247	23 52	324
69	40 28	000	45 20	029	56 34	069	62 21	144	51 29	218	19 53	247	23 22	323
70	40 27	359	45 44	028	57 21	068	62 50	144	50 58	218	19 06	247	22 52	322
71	40 26	358	46 07	026	58 07	067	63 19	145	50 27	218	18 20	246	22 21	321
72	40 23	356	46 29	025	58 54	066	63 48	146	49 56	218	17 34	246	21 49	321
73	40 20	355	46 49	024	59 39	065	64 16	147	49 24	219	16 48	245	21 17	320
74	40 15	354	47 09	022	60 24	063	64 43	148	48 53	219	16 03	245	20 44	319
	BETELGEUSE		◆ PROCYON		Suhail		◆ ACRUX		ACHERNAR		◆ Diphda		ALDEBARAN	
75	47 27	021	36 11	053	41 14	121	20 12	154	48 21	219	31 13	268	40 09	353
76	47 45	019	36 51	052	41 57	121	20 34	153	47 50	219	30 23	267	40 02	351
77	48 01	018	37 30	051	42 40	121	20 57	153	47 18	219	29 33	267	39 54	350
78	48 16	017	38 09	050	43 23	121	21 20	153	46 46	219	28 43	266	39 45	349
79	48 29	015	38 47	049	44 07	121	21 43	152	46 14	220	27 52	266	39 35	348
80	48 42	014	39 24	048	44 50	121	22 06	152	45 42	220	27 02	265	39 24	347
81	48 53	012	40 01	047	45 33	121	22 30	152	45 10	220	26 12	265	39 12	345
82	49 03	011	40 37	046	46 16	121	22 54	152	44 37	220	25 22	264	38 58	344
83	49 11	009	41 13	045	47 00	120	23 17	152	44 05	220	24 32	264	38 44	343
84	49 19	008	41 48	044	47 43	120	23 42	151	43 33	220	23 42	263	38 29	342
85	49 25	006	42 22	042	48 27	120	24 06	151	43 00	220	22 52	263	38 13	341
86	49 29	005	42 56	041	49 10	120	24 30	151	42 28	220	22 02	262	37 55	339
87	49 33	003	43 29	040	49 53	120	24 55	151	41 55	220	21 12	262	37 37	338
88	49 35	002	44 01	039	50 37	120	25 20	150	41 23	220	20 22	261	37 18	337
89	49 35	000	44 32	038	51 21	120	25 44	150	40 50	220	19 33	261	36 58	336

LHA ♈	Hc	Zn	Hc	Zn	Hc	Zn	Hc	Zn	Hc	Zn	Hc	Zn	Hc	Zn
	PROCYON		REGULUS		◆ Suhail		ACRUX		◆ ACHERNAR		RIGEL		◆ BETELGEUSE	
90	45 03	037	15 37	064	52 04	120	26 10	150	40 18	220	63 07	335	49 35	358
91	45 32	035	16 23	063	52 48	120	26 35	150	39 45	220	62 45	333	49 33	357
92	46 01	034	17 07	063	53 31	120	27 00	150	39 13	220	62 21	331	49 29	355
93	46 29	033	17 52	062	54 15	120	27 25	150	38 40	220	61 56	329	49 25	354
94	46 55	032	18 36	061	54 58	120	27 51	149	38 08	220	61 29	327	49 19	352
95	47 21	030	19 21	061	55 42	120	28 17	149	37 35	220	61 01	325	49 11	351
96	47 46	029	20 04	060	56 25	120	28 43	149	37 03	220	60 32	324	49 03	349
97	48 10	028	20 48	059	57 08	120	29 09	149	36 30	220	60 01	322	48 53	348
98	48 32	026	21 31	059	57 52	121	29 35	149	35 58	220	59 30	320	48 42	346
99	48 54	025	22 14	058	58 35	121	30 01	149	35 26	220	58 57	319	48 29	345
100	49 15	023	22 56	057	59 18	121	30 27	148	34 53	220	58 23	317	48 15	343
101	49 34	022	23 38	056	60 01	121	30 53	148	34 21	220	57 48	315	48 01	342
102	49 52	020	24 20	056	60 44	121	31 20	148	33 49	220	57 12	314	47 44	341
103	50 09	019	25 01	055	61 27	122	31 46	148	33 17	219	56 36	313	47 27	339
104	50 25	017	25 42	054	62 10	122	32 13	148	32 45	219	55 58	311	47 09	338
	PROCYON		REGULUS		◆ Gienah		ACRUX		◆ ACHERNAR		RIGEL		◆ BETELGEUSE	
105	50 39	016	26 23	053	18 23	099	32 39	148	32 13	219	55 20	310	46 49	336
106	50 52	014	27 03	053	19 13	099	33 06	148	31 42	219	54 41	309	46 29	335
107	51 04	013	27 43	052	20 03	098	33 33	148	31 10	219	54 01	307	46 07	334
108	51 14	011	28 22	051	20 52	098	34 00	148	30 38	219	53 21	306	45 44	332
109	51 23	010	29 01	050	21 42	097	34 27	148	30 07	219	52 40	305	45 20	331
110	51 31	008	29 39	049	22 32	097	34 54	148	29 36	218	51 58	304	44 55	330
111	51 37	006	30 17	048	23 22	096	35 21	148	29 04	218	51 16	303	44 30	329
112	51 42	005	30 55	048	24 12	096	35 48	148	28 33	218	50 34	301	44 03	327
113	51 46	003	31 32	047	25 02	095	36 15	147	28 02	218	49 50	300	43 36	326
114	51 48	002	32 08	046	25 52	095	36 42	147	27 31	218	49 07	299	43 07	325
115	51 49	000	32 44	045	26 43	094	37 09	147	27 01	217	48 23	298	42 38	324
116	51 48	358	33 19	044	27 33	094	37 36	147	26 30	217	47 38	297	42 08	323
117	51 46	357	33 53	043	28 23	093	38 03	147	26 00	217	46 53	296	41 37	321
118	51 43	355	34 27	042	29 13	093	38 30	147	25 29	217	46 08	296	41 05	320
119	51 38	354	35 01	041	30 03	092	38 57	147	24 59	217	45 23	295	40 32	319
	REGULUS		◆ SPICA		ACRUX		◆ CANOPUS		RIGEL		BETELGEUSE		◆ PROCYON	
120	35 33	040	13 10	095	39 24	148	63 52	214	44 37	294	39 59	318	51 31	352
121	36 05	039	14 00	094	39 51	148	63 24	215	43 50	293	39 25	317	51 24	350
122	36 37	038	14 50	094	40 18	148	62 55	216	43 04	292	38 51	316	51 15	349
123	37 07	037	15 41	093	40 45	148	62 25	216	42 17	291	38 16	315	51 04	347
124	37 37	036	16 31	093	41 12	148	61 55	217	41 30	290	37 40	314	50 53	346
125	38 06	035	17 21	092	41 39	148	61 24	218	40 43	290	37 03	313	50 39	344
126	38 34	034	18 11	092	42 05	148	60 53	218	39 55	289	36 26	312	50 25	343
127	39 02	033	19 02	091	42 32	148	60 22	219	39 07	288	35 49	311	50 10	341
128	39 29	031	19 52	091	42 59	148	59 50	220	38 20	287	35 10	310	49 53	340
129	39 54	030	20 42	090	43 25	148	59 18	220	37 31	287	34 32	309	49 35	338
130	40 19	029	21 33	090	43 52	148	58 45	221	36 43	286	33 53	308	49 15	337
131	40 43	028	22 23	089	44 18	149	58 12	221	35 55	285	33 13	308	48 55	335
132	41 07	027	23 13	089	44 44	149	57 39	222	35 06	284	32 33	307	48 33	334
133	41 29	026	24 04	088	45 10	149	57 05	222	34 17	284	31 52	306	48 11	333
134	41 50	024	24 54	087	45 36	149	56 31	222	33 28	283	31 11	305	47 47	331
	◆ REGULUS		SPICA		◆ ACRUX		CANOPUS		◆ RIGEL		BETELGEUSE		PROCYON	
135	42 10	023	25 44	087	46 02	149	55 57	223	32 39	282	30 30	304	47 22	330
136	42 29	022	26 34	086	46 28	149	55 23	223	31 50	282	29 48	303	46 56	329
137	42 48	021	27 25	086	46 53	150	54 48	224	31 01	281	29 06	302	46 30	327
138	43 05	019	28 15	085	47 18	150	54 14	224	30 11	280	28 23	302	46 02	326
139	43 21	018	29 05	085	47 43	150	53 39	224	29 22	280	27 40	301	45 33	325
140	43 36	017	29 55	084	48 08	150	53 04	224	28 32	279	26 57	300	45 04	323
141	43 50	015	30 45	083	48 33	151	52 28	225	27 42	279	26 13	299	44 33	322
142	44 03	014	31 35	083	48 58	151	51 53	225	26 52	278	25 29	299	44 02	321
143	44 14	013	32 25	082	49 22	151	51 17	225	26 03	277	24 45	298	43 30	320
144	44 25	011	33 15	082	49 46	152	50 42	225	25 13	277	24 00	297	42 57	319
145	44 34	010	34 04	081	50 10	152	50 06	225	24 23	276	23 15	297	42 24	318
146	44 42	009	34 54	080	50 33	152	49 30	226	23 33	276	22 30	296	41 50	317
147	44 49	007	35 43	080	50 56	153	48 54	226	22 42	275	21 45	295	41 15	315
148	44 55	006	36 33	079	51 19	153	48 18	226	21 52	274	20 59	294	40 39	314
149	45 00	005	37 22	078	51 42	153	47 42	226	21 02	274	20 13	294	40 03	313
	REGULUS		◆ Denebola		SPICA		◆ ACRUX		CANOPUS		◆ SIRIUS		PROCYON	
150	45 03	003	35 45	033	38 11	078	52 04	154	47 06	226	43 31	278	39 26	312
151	45 05	002	36 12	032	39 00	077	52 26	154	46 29	226	42 41	278	38 48	311
152	45 06	000	36 39	031	39 49	076	52 48	155	45 53	226	41 51	277	38 10	310
153	45 06	359	37 05	030	40 38	075	53 09	155	45 17	226	41 01	276	37 32	309
154	45 05	358	37 29	029	41 27	075	53 30	156	44 41	226	40 11	276	36 53	308
155	45 02	356	37 54	028	42 15	074	53 51	156	44 04	226	39 21	275	36 13	308
156	44 58	355	38 17	027	43 04	073	54 11	157	43 28	226	38 31	274	35 33	307
157	44 53	353	38 39	026	43 52	072	54 30	157	42 52	226	37 41	274	34 52	306
158	44 47	352	39 00	025	44 39	072	54 50	158	42 15	226	36 50	273	34 11	305
159	44 39	351	39 21	023	45 27	071	55 09	158	41 39	226	36 00	273	33 29	304
160	44 30	349	39 40	022	46 15	070	55 27	159	41 03	226	35 10	272	32 48	303
161	44 21	348	39 59	021	47 02	069	55 45	160	40 26	226	34 20	272	32 05	302
162	44 10	347	40 16	020	47 49	068	56 02	160	39 50	226	33 29	271	31 22	301
163	43 57	345	40 33	019	48 35	067	56 19	161	39 14	226	32 39	270	30 39	301
164	43 44	344	40 48	017	49 21	066	56 35	161	38 38	226	31 49	270	29 56	300
	ARCTURUS		◆ ANTARES		ACRUX		◆ CANOPUS		SIRIUS		PROCYON		◆ REGULUS	
165	19 55	049	19 51	109	56 51	162	38 01	226	30 58	269	29 12	299	43 30	343
166	20 33	049	20 39	109	57 06	163	37 25	226	30 08	269	28 28	298	43 14	341
167	21 11	048	21 27	108	57 21	163	36 49	226	29 18	268	27 44	298	42 58	340
168	21 48	047	22 14	108	57 35	164	36 13	226	28 27	268	26 59	297	42 40	339
169	22 25	046	23 02	108	57 48	165	35 37	225	27 37	267	26 14	296	42 22	338
170	23 01	046	23 50	107	58 01	166	35 02	225	26 47	267	25 28	295	42 02	336
171	23 37	045	24 38	107	58 13	166	34 26	225	25 57	266	24 43	295	41 41	335
172	24 12	044	25 27	106	58 24	167	33 50	225	25 06	266	23 57	294	41 20	334
173	24 46	043	26 15	106	58 35	168	33 15	225	24 16	265	23 11	293	40 57	333
174	25 21	042	27 04	105	58 45	169	32 39	225	23 26	265	22 25	293	40 34	332
175	25 54	041	27 52	105	58 55	170	32 04	225	22 36	264	21 38	292	40 09	330
176	26 27	041	28 41	105	59 03	170	31 29	224	21 46	264	20 51	291	39 44	329
177	27 00	040	29 30	104	59 11	171	30 53	224	20 56	263	20 04	291	39 18	328
178	27 32	039	30 18	104	59 18	172	30 18	224	20 06	263	19 17	290	38 51	327
179	28 03	038	31 07	103	59 25	173	29 43	224	19 16	262	18 30	289	38 23	326

LHA ♈	◆ ARCTURUS Hc	Zn	ANTARES Hc	Zn	◆ RIGIL KENT Hc	Zn	ACRUX Hc	Zn	CANOPUS Hc	Zn	◆ Alphard Hc	Zn	REGULUS Hc	Zn
180	28 34	037	31 56	103	51 58	149	59 31	174	29 09	224	47 26	296	37 54	325
181	29 04	036	32 46	102	52 23	150	59 36	175	28 34	223	46 41	295	37 25	324
182	29 33	035	33 35	102	52 49	150	59 40	176	28 00	223	45 55	294	36 55	323
183	30 02	034	34 24	101	53 13	151	59 43	177	27 25	223	45 09	293	36 24	322
184	30 30	033	35 13	101	53 38	151	59 46	177	26 51	223	44 23	292	35 52	321
185	30 57	032	36 03	101	54 02	152	59 48	178	26 17	223	43 36	292	35 20	320
186	31 24	031	36 52	100	54 26	152	59 49	179	25 43	222	42 49	291	34 47	319
187	31 49	030	37 42	100	54 49	152	59 49	180	25 09	222	42 02	290	34 13	318
188	32 14	029	38 31	099	55 12	153	59 49	181	24 36	222	41 15	289	33 39	317
189	32 39	028	39 21	099	55 35	154	59 47	182	24 02	221	40 27	288	33 04	316
190	33 02	027	40 11	098	55 57	154	59 45	183	23 29	221	39 39	288	32 29	315
191	33 25	026	41 01	098	56 19	155	59 42	184	22 56	221	38 51	287	31 53	314
192	33 47	025	41 50	098	56 40	155	59 39	185	22 23	221	38 03	286	31 16	313
193	34 08	024	42 40	097	57 01	156	59 34	185	21 50	220	37 15	285	30 39	312
194	34 28	023	43 30	097	57 21	157	59 29	186	21 18	220	36 26	285	30 02	311

LHA ♈	ARCTURUS Hc	Zn	◆ ANTARES Hc	Zn	RIGIL KENT Hc	Zn	◆ ACRUX Hc	Zn	Suhail Hc	Zn	REGULUS Hc	Zn	◆ Denebola Hc	Zn
195	34 48	022	44 20	096	57 41	157	59 23	187	44 18	239	29 24	310	39 38	338
196	35 06	021	45 10	096	58 00	158	59 16	188	43 35	239	28 45	310	39 19	337
197	35 24	020	46 00	095	58 19	159	59 09	189	42 52	239	28 06	309	38 58	335
198	35 41	019	46 51	095	58 37	159	59 01	190	42 09	239	27 26	308	38 37	334
199	35 56	018	47 41	094	58 54	160	58 52	191	41 26	239	26 47	307	38 15	333
200	36 11	017	48 31	094	59 11	161	58 42	191	40 43	238	26 06	306	37 51	332
201	36 25	015	49 21	093	59 27	162	58 32	192	40 00	238	25 25	306	37 27	331
202	36 38	014	50 11	093	59 43	163	58 21	193	39 18	238	24 44	305	37 02	330
203	36 50	013	51 02	092	59 57	163	58 10	194	38 35	238	24 03	304	36 37	329
204	37 01	012	51 52	092	60 11	164	57 57	195	37 52	238	23 21	303	36 10	328
205	37 11	011	52 42	091	60 25	165	57 44	195	37 10	237	22 39	302	35 43	327
206	37 20	010	53 33	091	60 37	166	57 31	196	36 28	237	21 56	302	35 15	325
207	37 27	008	54 23	090	60 49	167	57 17	197	35 45	237	21 13	301	34 46	324
208	37 34	007	55 13	090	61 00	168	57 02	197	35 03	237	20 30	300	34 16	323
209	37 40	006	56 04	089	61 10	169	56 47	198	34 21	237	19 46	300	33 46	322

LHA ♈	◆ ARCTURUS Hc	Zn	Rasalhague Hc	Zn	◆ Nunki Hc	Zn	RIGIL KENT Hc	Zn	ACRUX Hc	Zn	◆ Suhail Hc	Zn	SPICA Hc	Zn
210	37 45	005	21 20	058	26 36	105	61 20	170	56 31	199	33 39	236	66 53	338
211	37 49	004	22 03	057	27 25	105	61 28	171	56 14	199	32 57	236	66 33	336
212	37 51	002	22 45	056	28 13	105	61 36	172	55 57	200	32 15	236	66 12	334
213	37 53	001	23 27	056	29 02	104	61 43	173	55 40	201	31 34	236	65 49	331
214	37 54	000	24 08	055	29 51	104	61 49	174	55 22	201	30 52	235	65 24	329
215	37 53	359	24 49	054	30 40	103	61 54	175	55 03	202	30 11	235	64 57	327
216	37 52	358	25 30	053	31 29	103	61 58	176	54 44	202	29 30	235	64 30	325
217	37 49	357	26 10	053	32 18	102	62 02	177	54 25	203	28 49	235	64 00	323
218	37 46	355	26 50	052	33 07	102	62 04	178	54 05	203	28 08	234	63 29	321
219	37 41	354	27 29	051	33 57	101	62 06	179	53 45	204	27 27	234	62 57	320
220	37 35	353	28 08	050	34 46	101	62 06	180	53 24	204	26 46	234	62 24	318
221	37 29	352	28 46	049	35 35	101	62 06	181	53 03	205	26 06	233	61 50	316
222	37 21	351	29 24	048	36 25	100	62 05	182	52 42	205	25 26	233	61 14	314
223	37 12	349	30 01	048	37 14	100	62 03	183	52 20	206	24 45	233	60 38	313
224	37 02	348	30 38	047	38 04	099	62 00	184	51 58	206	24 05	233	60 01	311

LHA ♈	Alphecca Hc	Zn	Rasalhague Hc	Zn	◆ Nunki Hc	Zn	Peacock Hc	Zn	◆ RIGIL KENT Hc	Zn	SPICA Hc	Zn	◆ ARCTURUS Hc	Zn
225	29 45	009	31 15	046	38 54	099	31 26	140	61 56	185	59 22	310	36 52	347
226	29 52	008	31 50	045	39 43	098	31 58	140	61 51	186	58 43	308	36 40	346
227	29 59	007	32 26	044	40 33	098	32 31	140	61 45	187	58 03	307	36 27	345
228	30 05	006	33 00	043	41 23	098	33 03	140	61 38	188	57 23	306	36 14	344
229	30 10	005	33 34	042	42 13	097	33 35	140	61 31	189	56 42	304	35 59	343
230	30 13	004	34 08	041	43 03	097	34 08	140	61 23	190	56 00	303	35 43	341
231	30 16	003	34 41	040	43 53	096	34 40	140	61 14	191	55 18	302	35 27	340
232	30 19	002	35 13	039	44 43	096	35 13	140	61 04	192	54 35	301	35 09	339
233	30 20	001	35 44	038	45 33	095	35 46	139	60 53	193	53 51	300	34 51	338
234	30 20	000	36 15	037	46 23	095	36 18	139	60 41	194	53 07	299	34 32	337
235	30 19	359	36 45	036	47 13	094	36 51	139	60 29	195	52 23	298	34 12	336
236	30 18	358	37 14	035	48 04	094	37 24	139	60 16	196	51 38	296	33 51	335
237	30 16	357	37 43	034	48 54	093	37 57	139	60 02	196	50 53	295	33 29	334
238	30 12	356	38 10	033	49 44	093	38 30	139	59 47	197	50 07	295	33 06	333
239	30 08	355	38 37	032	50 34	092	39 02	139	59 32	198	49 21	294	32 43	332

LHA ♈	Rasalhague Hc	Zn	ALTAIR Hc	Zn	◆ Nunki Hc	Zn	Peacock Hc	Zn	◆ RIGIL KENT Hc	Zn	SPICA Hc	Zn	◆ ARCTURUS Hc	Zn
240	39 03	031	20 52	064	51 25	092	39 35	139	59 16	199	48 35	293	32 19	331
241	39 28	029	21 37	063	52 15	091	40 08	139	59 00	200	47 48	292	31 54	330
242	39 53	028	22 22	062	53 05	091	40 41	139	58 42	200	47 01	291	31 28	329
243	40 16	027	23 06	061	53 55	090	41 14	139	58 25	201	46 14	290	31 02	328
244	40 39	026	23 50	061	54 46	090	41 47	139	58 06	202	45 27	289	30 34	327
245	41 00	025	24 34	060	55 36	089	42 20	139	57 47	203	44 39	288	30 07	326
246	41 21	024	25 17	059	56 26	089	42 53	139	57 28	203	43 51	288	29 38	325
247	41 40	022	26 00	059	57 17	088	43 26	139	57 07	204	43 03	287	29 09	324
248	41 59	021	26 43	058	58 07	087	43 59	139	56 47	204	42 15	286	28 39	323
249	42 17	020	27 25	057	58 57	087	44 32	139	56 26	205	41 26	285	28 08	322
250	42 33	019	28 07	056	59 47	086	45 04	139	56 04	206	40 38	285	27 37	321
251	42 49	017	28 49	055	60 38	086	45 37	140	55 42	206	39 49	284	27 05	320
252	43 03	016	29 30	055	61 28	085	46 10	140	55 20	207	39 00	283	26 33	320
253	43 16	015	30 11	054	62 18	084	46 42	140	54 57	207	38 11	282	26 00	319
254	43 29	013	30 51	053	63 08	083	47 15	140	54 33	208	37 22	282	25 26	318

LHA ♈	VEGA Hc	Zn	◆ ALTAIR Hc	Zn	FOMALHAUT Hc	Zn	◆ Peacock Hc	Zn	RIGIL KENT Hc	Zn	◆ SPICA Hc	Zn	ARCTURUS Hc	Zn
255	14 43	019	31 31	052	15 52	115	47 47	140	54 10	208	36 32	281	24 52	317
256	15 00	019	32 11	051	16 38	115	48 19	140	53 46	209	35 43	280	24 18	316
257	15 16	018	32 50	050	17 23	114	48 51	140	53 21	209	34 54	280	23 43	315
258	15 31	017	33 28	049	18 09	114	49 23	141	52 56	210	34 04	279	23 07	315
259	15 45	016	34 06	048	18 55	114	49 55	141	52 31	210	33 14	278	22 31	314
260	15 59	016	34 44	048	19 42	113	50 27	141	52 06	210	32 24	278	21 54	313
261	16 12	015	35 20	047	20 28	113	50 58	141	51 40	211	31 34	277	21 17	312
262	16 25	014	35 57	046	21 14	112	51 29	142	51 14	211	30 44	277	20 40	311
263	16 37	013	36 32	045	22 01	112	52 01	142	50 48	212	29 54	276	20 02	311
264	16 48	012	37 07	044	22 48	111	52 32	142	50 22	212	29 04	275	19 24	310
265	16 58	012	37 42	043	23 35	111	53 02	143	49 55	212	28 14	275	18 45	309
266	17 08	011	38 16	042	24 22	111	53 33	143	49 28	212	27 24	274	18 06	309
267	17 17	010	38 49	041	25 09	110	54 03	143	49 01	213	26 34	274	17 26	308
268	17 26	009	39 21	040	25 56	110	54 33	144	48 34	213	25 44	273	16 46	307
269	17 34	008	39 53	038	26 44	109	55 02	144	48 06	213	24 53	273	16 06	306

LAT 33°S

LHA ♈	VEGA Hc	Zn	ALTAIR Hc	Zn	◆ FOMALHAUT Hc	Zn	ACHERNAR Hc	Zn	◆ RIGIL KENT Hc	Zn	ANTARES Hc	Zn	◆ Rasalhague Hc	Zn
270	17 41	008	40 24	037	27 31	109	15 35	149	47 39	213	69 31	283	44 05	352
271	17 47	007	40 54	036	28 19	109	16 00	149	47 11	214	68 42	282	43 57	350
272	17 53	006	41 23	035	29 07	108	16 27	149	46 43	214	67 52	281	43 48	349
273	17 58	005	41 52	034	29 55	108	16 53	148	46 15	214	67 03	280	43 38	348
274	18 02	004	42 19	033	30 43	107	17 20	148	45 46	214	66 13	279	43 27	346
275	18 05	004	42 46	032	31 31	107	17 47	148	45 18	214	65 23	278	43 14	345
276	18 08	003	43 12	030	32 19	107	18 14	147	44 49	215	64 34	277	43 01	344
277	18 10	002	43 37	029	33 07	106	18 41	147	44 21	215	63 44	277	42 46	342
278	18 11	001	44 01	028	33 55	106	19 09	147	43 52	215	62 54	276	42 30	341
279	18 12	000	44 24	027	34 44	105	19 36	146	43 23	215	62 04	275	42 14	340
280	18 12	359	44 46	025	35 32	105	20 04	146	42 54	215	61 13	275	41 56	339
281	18 11	359	45 07	024	36 21	105	20 33	146	42 26	215	60 23	274	41 37	337
282	18 10	358	45 27	023	37 10	104	21 01	145	41 57	215	59 33	273	41 17	336
283	18 07	357	45 46	021	37 59	104	21 30	145	41 27	215	58 43	273	40 56	335
284	18 04	356	46 03	020	38 48	103	21 58	145	40 58	215	57 52	272	40 35	334

LHA ♈	ALTAIR Hc	Zn	Enif Hc	Zn	◆ FOMALHAUT Hc	Zn	ACHERNAR Hc	Zn	◆ RIGIL KENT Hc	Zn	ANTARES Hc	Zn	◆ Rasalhague Hc	Zn
285	46 20	019	31 49	050	39 37	103	22 28	145	40 29	215	57 02	271	40 12	333
286	46 35	017	32 27	049	40 26	103	22 57	144	40 00	215	56 12	271	39 48	331
287	46 50	016	33 05	048	41 15	102	23 26	144	39 31	215	55 22	270	39 24	330
288	47 03	014	33 42	047	42 04	102	23 56	144	39 02	215	54 31	270	38 58	329
289	47 15	013	34 19	046	42 53	101	24 25	144	38 33	215	53 41	269	38 32	328
290	47 25	012	34 55	045	43 43	101	24 55	143	38 03	215	52 51	269	38 05	327
291	47 35	010	35 30	044	44 32	101	25 25	143	37 34	215	52 00	268	37 37	326
292	47 43	009	36 05	043	45 21	100	25 56	143	37 05	215	51 10	268	37 09	325
293	47 50	007	36 39	042	46 11	100	26 26	143	36 36	215	50 20	267	36 39	324
294	47 56	006	37 13	041	47 01	100	26 57	143	36 07	215	49 29	267	36 09	323
295	48 00	004	37 45	040	47 50	099	27 27	142	35 38	215	48 39	266	35 38	322
296	48 03	003	38 18	039	48 40	099	27 58	142	35 09	215	47 49	266	35 07	321
297	48 05	001	38 49	038	49 30	098	28 29	142	34 40	215	46 59	265	34 35	320
298	48 05	000	39 20	037	50 20	098	29 00	142	34 11	215	46 09	265	34 02	319
299	48 05	358	39 50	036	51 09	098	29 31	142	33 42	215	45 19	264	33 28	318

LHA ♈	Enif Hc	Zn	◆ FOMALHAUT Hc	Zn	ACHERNAR Hc	Zn	◆ RIGIL KENT Hc	Zn	ANTARES Hc	Zn	Rasalhague Hc	Zn	◆ ALTAIR Hc	Zn
300	40 19	035	51 59	097	30 03	141	33 13	215	44 29	264	32 54	317	48 03	357
301	40 47	034	52 49	097	30 34	141	32 44	215	43 39	263	32 19	316	47 59	355
302	41 15	033	53 39	096	31 06	141	32 16	215	42 49	263	31 44	315	47 54	354
303	41 41	031	54 29	096	31 37	141	31 47	215	41 59	263	31 08	314	47 48	352
304	42 07	030	55 19	095	32 09	141	31 18	214	41 09	262	30 31	313	47 41	351
305	42 32	029	56 10	095	32 41	141	30 50	214	40 19	262	29 55	312	47 33	350
306	42 56	028	57 00	095	33 13	141	30 22	214	39 29	261	29 17	311	47 23	348
307	43 18	026	57 50	094	33 45	140	29 53	214	38 40	261	28 39	311	47 12	347
308	43 40	025	58 40	094	34 17	140	29 25	214	37 50	260	28 01	310	47 00	345
309	44 01	024	59 30	093	34 49	140	28 57	214	37 00	260	27 22	309	46 46	344
310	44 21	023	60 21	093	35 21	140	28 29	214	36 11	259	26 42	308	46 32	342
311	44 40	021	61 11	092	35 54	140	28 02	213	35 21	259	26 02	307	46 16	341
312	44 58	020	62 01	092	36 26	140	27 34	213	34 32	259	25 22	306	45 59	340
313	45 15	019	62 51	091	36 58	140	27 06	213	33 43	258	24 41	306	45 41	338
314	45 30	017	63 42	091	37 31	140	26 39	213	32 54	258	24 00	305	45 22	337

LHA ♈	Alpheratz Hc	Zn	◆ Diphda Hc	Zn	ACHERNAR Hc	Zn	◆ RIGIL KENT Hc	Zn	ANTARES Hc	Zn	Rasalhague Hc	Zn	◆ ALTAIR Hc	Zn
315	13 22	041	37 47	088	38 03	140	26 12	213	32 04	257	23 19	304	45 02	336
316	13 55	041	38 37	087	38 36	140	25 45	212	31 15	257	22 37	303	44 41	334
317	14 28	040	39 28	087	39 08	140	25 18	212	30 26	256	21 55	303	44 18	333
318	15 00	039	40 18	086	39 41	140	24 51	212	29 38	256	21 13	302	43 55	332
319	15 31	038	41 08	085	40 13	140	24 24	212	28 49	256	20 30	301	43 31	331
320	16 02	038	41 58	085	40 46	140	23 58	212	28 00	255	19 47	301	43 06	329
321	16 33	037	42 48	084	41 18	140	23 31	211	27 12	255	19 03	300	42 40	328
322	17 03	036	43 38	084	41 51	140	23 05	211	26 23	254	18 19	299	42 13	327
323	17 32	035	44 28	083	42 23	140	22 39	211	25 35	254	17 35	299	41 45	326
324	18 01	035	45 18	082	42 56	140	22 14	211	24 46	253	16 51	298	41 16	325
325	18 29	034	46 08	082	43 28	140	21 48	210	23 58	253	16 06	297	40 47	324
326	18 57	033	46 58	081	44 01	140	21 23	210	23 10	253	15 21	297	40 16	322
327	19 24	032	47 47	080	44 33	140	20 57	210	22 22	252	14 36	296	39 45	321
328	19 51	032	48 37	079	45 05	140	20 33	210	21 34	252	13 51	295	39 13	320
329	20 17	031	49 26	079	45 37	140	20 08	209	20 47	251	13 05	295	38 41	319

LHA ♈	◆ Alpheratz Hc	Zn	Diphda Hc	Zn	◆ ACHERNAR Hc	Zn	Peacock Hc	Zn	◆ Nunki Hc	Zn	ALTAIR Hc	Zn	Enif Hc	Zn
330	20 42	030	50 16	078	46 10	140	61 26	207	49 49	267	38 07	318	46 54	355
331	21 07	029	51 05	077	46 42	140	61 03	208	48 59	267	37 34	317	46 49	353
332	21 31	028	51 54	076	47 14	141	60 39	209	48 08	266	36 59	316	46 42	352
333	21 55	027	52 43	076	47 45	141	60 14	209	47 18	266	36 24	315	46 34	350
334	22 18	027	53 31	075	48 17	141	59 49	210	46 28	265	35 48	314	46 25	349
335	22 40	026	54 20	074	48 49	141	59 24	211	45 38	265	35 11	313	46 15	347
336	23 01	025	55 08	073	49 20	141	58 58	211	44 48	264	34 34	312	46 03	346
337	23 22	024	55 56	072	49 52	142	58 31	212	43 58	264	33 57	311	45 51	345
338	23 42	023	56 44	071	50 23	142	58 05	213	43 08	263	33 19	310	45 37	343
339	24 01	022	57 31	070	50 54	142	57 37	213	42 18	263	32 40	309	45 22	342
340	24 20	021	58 19	069	51 24	142	57 09	214	41 28	262	32 01	309	45 06	341
341	24 38	020	59 05	068	51 55	143	56 41	214	40 38	262	31 22	308	44 48	339
342	24 55	020	59 52	067	52 25	143	56 13	215	39 48	262	30 42	307	44 30	338
343	25 12	019	60 38	066	52 56	143	55 44	215	38 58	261	30 01	306	44 11	337
344	25 27	018	61 24	065	53 26	144	55 15	216	38 09	261	29 20	305	43 50	335

LHA ♈	Alpheratz Hc	Zn	◆ Hamal Hc	Zn	◆ ACHERNAR Hc	Zn	Peacock Hc	Zn	◆ Nunki Hc	Zn	ALTAIR Hc	Zn	Enif Hc	Zn
345	25 42	017	17 52	045	53 55	144	54 45	216	37 19	260	28 39	304	43 29	334
346	25 56	016	18 28	044	54 25	144	54 15	217	36 30	260	27 57	304	43 06	333
347	26 10	015	19 02	043	54 54	145	53 45	217	35 40	259	27 15	303	42 43	332
348	26 22	014	19 37	043	55 22	145	53 15	217	34 51	259	26 33	302	42 18	330
349	26 34	013	20 10	042	55 51	146	52 44	218	34 01	259	25 50	301	41 53	329
350	26 45	012	20 44	041	56 19	146	52 13	218	33 12	258	25 07	301	41 27	328
351	26 55	011	21 16	040	56 47	147	51 42	218	32 23	258	24 23	300	41 00	327
352	27 04	010	21 49	039	57 14	147	51 11	219	31 34	257	23 39	299	40 32	326
353	27 12	009	22 20	039	57 41	148	50 40	219	30 45	257	22 55	298	40 03	325
354	27 20	008	22 51	038	58 07	149	50 08	219	29 56	256	22 11	298	39 34	323
355	27 27	007	23 22	037	58 34	149	49 36	219	29 07	256	21 26	297	39 03	322
356	27 32	006	23 52	036	58 59	150	49 04	219	28 18	256	20 41	296	38 32	321
357	27 37	005	24 21	035	59 24	150	48 32	220	27 29	255	19 56	296	38 00	320
358	27 42	004	24 50	034	59 49	151	48 00	220	26 41	255	19 10	295	37 28	319
359	27 45	003	25 18	034	60 13	152	47 28	220	25 52	254	18 25	294	36 55	318

LAT 34°S

LHA ♈	Hc	Zn	Hc	Zn	Hc	Zn	Hc	Zn	Hc	Zn	Hc	Zn	Hc	Zn
	◆ Alpheratz		Hamal		◆ RIGEL		CANOPUS		ACHERNAR		◆ Peacock		Enif	
0	26 47	002	24 55	032	13 49	091	23 04	139	61 29	152	47 41	221	35 37	318
1	26 49	001	25 21	032	14 39	090	23 36	139	61 52	153	47 09	221	35 03	317
2	26 50	000	25 47	031	15 28	090	24 09	139	62 15	153	46 36	221	34 28	316
3	26 49	359	26 12	030	16 18	089	24 42	138	62 37	154	46 03	221	33 53	315
4	26 48	358	26 36	029	17 08	088	25 15	138	62 58	155	45 30	221	33 18	314
5	26 46	357	27 00	028	17 58	088	25 49	138	63 19	156	44 58	221	32 41	313
6	26 44	356	27 23	027	18 47	087	26 22	137	63 38	157	44 25	221	32 05	312
7	26 40	355	27 45	026	19 37	087	26 56	137	63 57	158	43 52	221	31 27	311
8	26 36	354	28 06	025	20 27	086	27 30	137	64 15	159	43 19	221	30 50	310
9	26 31	353	28 27	024	21 16	086	28 04	137	64 33	160	42 46	221	30 11	309
10	26 24	352	28 47	023	22 06	085	28 38	136	64 49	161	42 13	221	29 33	308
11	26 18	352	29 06	022	22 55	084	29 13	136	65 04	162	41 40	221	28 54	308
12	26 10	351	29 24	021	23 45	084	29 47	136	65 19	164	41 07	221	28 14	307
13	26 01	350	29 42	020	24 34	083	30 22	136	65 33	165	40 34	221	27 34	306
14	25 52	349	29 58	019	25 24	083	30 56	136	65 45	166	40 01	221	26 53	305
	◆ Hamal		ALDEBARAN		RIGEL		◆ CANOPUS		ACHERNAR		◆ FOMALHAUT		Alpheratz	
15	30 14	018	17 48	055	26 13	082	31 31	135	65 57	167	63 53	271	25 42	348
16	30 29	017	18 29	054	27 02	081	32 06	135	66 07	168	63 04	271	25 31	347
17	30 43	016	19 09	053	27 51	081	32 41	135	66 17	170	62 14	270	25 19	346
18	30 57	015	19 48	053	28 40	080	33 17	135	66 25	171	61 24	270	25 06	345
19	31 09	014	20 28	052	29 29	079	33 52	135	66 32	172	60 34	269	24 53	344
20	31 21	013	21 07	051	30 18	079	34 27	135	66 38	174	59 45	269	24 39	343
21	31 31	012	21 45	050	31 07	078	35 03	134	66 43	175	58 55	268	24 24	342
22	31 41	011	22 23	050	31 55	077	35 38	134	66 46	176	58 05	268	24 08	341
23	31 50	010	23 01	049	32 44	077	36 14	134	66 49	178	57 15	267	23 52	340
24	31 58	009	23 38	048	33 32	076	36 50	134	66 50	179	56 26	267	23 35	339
25	32 05	008	24 15	047	34 20	075	37 26	134	66 50	181	55 36	266	23 17	338
26	32 11	007	24 51	046	35 08	075	38 02	134	66 49	182	54 47	266	22 58	338
27	32 16	005	25 27	045	35 56	074	38 38	134	66 47	183	53 57	265	22 39	337
28	32 20	004	26 02	045	36 44	073	39 14	133	66 43	185	53 07	265	22 19	336
29	32 24	003	26 36	044	37 32	072	39 50	133	66 39	186	52 18	264	21 58	335
	Hamal		ALDEBARAN		◆ SIRIUS		CANOPUS		◆ ACHERNAR		FOMALHAUT		◆ Alpheratz	
30	32 26	002	27 11	043	24 26	094	40 26	133	66 33	187	51 28	264	21 37	334
31	32 28	001	27 44	042	25 15	094	41 02	133	66 26	189	50 39	263	21 15	333
32	32 28	000	28 17	041	26 05	093	41 39	133	66 18	190	49 50	263	20 52	332
33	32 28	359	28 50	040	26 55	093	42 15	133	66 08	191	49 00	262	20 28	332
34	32 26	358	29 22	039	27 44	092	42 51	133	65 58	193	48 11	262	20 04	331
35	32 24	357	29 53	038	28 34	092	43 28	133	65 47	194	47 22	262	19 40	330
36	32 21	356	30 23	037	29 24	091	44 04	133	65 34	195	46 33	261	19 15	329
37	32 16	355	30 53	037	30 14	091	44 40	133	65 21	196	45 43	261	18 49	328
38	32 11	354	31 23	036	31 03	090	45 17	133	65 07	197	44 54	260	18 22	328
39	32 05	352	31 51	035	31 53	089	45 53	133	64 51	199	44 05	260	17 55	327
40	31 58	351	32 19	034	32 43	089	46 29	133	64 35	200	43 16	260	17 28	326
41	31 50	350	32 46	033	33 33	088	47 06	133	64 18	201	42 28	259	17 00	325
42	31 41	349	33 13	032	34 22	088	47 42	133	64 00	202	41 39	259	16 31	324
43	31 31	348	33 38	031	35 12	087	48 18	133	63 41	203	40 50	258	16 02	324
44	31 21	347	34 03	030	36 02	087	48 54	133	63 21	204	40 01	258	15 32	323
	◆ ALDEBARAN		BETELGEUSE		SIRIUS		◆ CANOPUS		ACHERNAR		◆ FOMALHAUT		Hamal	
45	34 27	028	31 17	054	36 51	086	49 30	133	63 01	205	39 13	257	31 09	346
46	34 51	027	31 57	053	37 41	085	50 07	134	62 40	206	38 24	257	30 57	345
47	35 13	026	32 36	052	38 30	085	50 43	134	62 18	206	37 36	257	30 44	344
48	35 35	025	33 15	051	39 20	084	51 18	134	61 55	207	36 47	256	30 29	343
49	35 55	024	33 54	050	40 09	083	51 54	134	61 32	208	35 59	256	30 14	342
50	36 15	023	34 32	049	40 59	083	52 30	134	61 09	209	35 11	255	29 59	341
51	36 34	022	35 09	048	41 48	082	53 06	134	60 44	210	34 23	255	29 42	340
52	36 52	021	35 46	047	42 37	081	53 41	135	60 20	210	33 35	255	29 24	339
53	37 10	020	36 22	046	43 26	081	54 16	135	59 54	211	32 47	254	29 06	338
54	37 26	018	36 58	045	44 15	080	54 52	135	59 28	212	31 59	254	28 47	337
55	37 41	017	37 33	044	45 04	079	55 27	135	59 02	212	31 11	253	28 27	336
56	37 55	016	38 08	043	45 53	079	56 01	136	58 35	213	30 24	253	28 06	335
57	38 09	015	38 41	042	46 42	078	56 36	136	58 08	213	29 36	252	27 45	334
58	38 21	014	39 15	041	47 31	077	57 10	136	57 40	214	28 49	252	27 23	333
59	38 32	013	39 47	040	48 19	076	57 45	137	57 12	214	28 02	252	27 00	332
	ALDEBARAN		◆ BETELGEUSE		SIRIUS		◆ CANOPUS		ACHERNAR		◆ FOMALHAUT		Hamal	
60	38 42	011	40 19	039	49 07	076	58 18	137	56 44	215	27 15	251	26 36	331
61	38 52	010	40 50	038	49 55	075	58 52	138	56 15	215	26 28	251	26 12	330
62	39 00	009	41 20	037	50 43	074	59 25	138	55 46	216	25 41	250	25 47	329
63	39 07	008	41 49	036	51 31	073	59 58	139	55 17	216	24 54	250	25 22	329
64	39 13	006	42 18	035	52 18	072	60 31	139	54 48	217	24 07	250	24 55	328
65	39 18	005	42 46	033	53 06	071	61 04	140	54 18	217	23 21	249	24 28	327
66	39 22	004	43 13	032	53 53	070	61 35	140	53 48	217	22 34	249	24 01	326
67	39 25	003	43 39	031	54 39	069	62 07	141	53 17	218	21 48	248	23 32	325
68	39 27	001	44 04	030	55 26	068	62 38	142	52 47	218	21 02	248	23 04	324
69	39 28	000	44 28	028	56 12	067	63 09	142	52 16	218	20 16	247	22 34	323
70	39 27	359	44 51	027	56 58	066	63 39	143	51 45	219	19 30	247	22 04	322
71	39 26	358	45 13	026	57 43	065	64 08	144	51 14	219	18 44	246	21 34	322
72	39 23	357	45 34	024	58 28	064	64 37	145	50 43	219	17 59	246	21 02	321
73	39 20	355	45 54	023	59 13	063	65 06	146	50 11	219	17 13	246	20 31	320
74	39 15	354	46 13	022	59 57	062	65 33	147	49 40	220	16 28	245	19 59	319
	BETELGEUSE		◆ PROCYON		Suhail		◆ ACRUX		ACHERNAR		◆ Diphda		ALDEBARAN	
75	46 31	020	35 34	052	41 45	121	21 05	153	49 08	220	31 15	269	39 10	353
76	46 48	019	36 13	051	42 28	121	21 28	153	48 36	220	30 25	268	39 03	352
77	47 04	018	36 52	050	43 11	120	21 50	153	48 04	220	29 36	268	38 55	350
78	47 18	016	37 30	049	43 54	120	22 13	153	47 32	220	28 46	267	38 46	349
79	47 31	015	38 07	048	44 37	120	22 36	152	47 00	220	27 56	266	38 36	348
80	47 43	013	38 44	047	45 20	120	22 59	152	46 28	220	27 07	266	38 25	347
81	47 54	012	39 20	046	46 03	120	23 23	152	45 55	221	26 17	265	38 14	346
82	48 04	010	39 55	045	46 46	120	23 46	152	45 23	221	25 28	265	38 01	344
83	48 12	009	40 30	044	47 30	120	24 10	151	44 51	221	24 38	264	37 47	343
84	48 19	007	41 04	043	48 13	119	24 34	151	44 18	221	23 49	264	37 32	342
85	48 25	006	41 38	042	48 56	119	24 58	151	43 46	221	22 59	263	37 16	341
86	48 30	004	42 11	041	49 40	119	25 23	151	43 13	221	22 10	263	36 59	340
87	48 33	003	42 43	040	50 23	119	25 47	150	42 41	221	21 20	262	36 41	339
88	48 35	001	43 14	038	51 07	119	26 12	150	42 08	221	20 31	262	36 23	337
89	48 35	000	43 44	037	51 50	119	26 37	150	41 36	221	19 42	261	36 03	336

LHA ♈	Hc	Zn	Hc	Zn	Hc	Zn	Hc	Zn	Hc	Zn	Hc	Zn	Hc	Zn
	PROCYON		REGULUS		◆ Suhail		ACRUX		◆ ACHERNAR		RIGEL		◆ BETELGEUSE	
90	44 14	036	15 11	064	52 34	119	27 01	150	41 03	221	62 12	336	48 35	358
91	44 43	035	15 56	063	53 17	119	27 27	150	40 31	221	61 51	334	48 33	357
92	45 11	034	16 40	063	54 01	119	27 52	149	39 58	221	61 28	332	48 30	356
93	45 38	032	17 24	062	54 44	119	28 17	149	39 26	221	61 04	330	48 25	354
94	46 04	031	18 08	061	55 28	119	28 43	149	38 53	221	60 38	328	48 19	353
95	46 29	030	18 51	060	56 11	119	29 08	149	38 21	221	60 11	326	48 12	351
96	46 53	028	19 34	060	56 55	119	29 34	149	37 48	221	59 43	325	48 04	350
97	47 16	027	20 17	059	57 38	119	30 00	149	37 16	221	59 14	323	47 54	348
98	47 38	026	21 00	058	58 22	119	30 26	148	36 44	220	58 43	321	47 43	347
99	47 59	024	21 42	058	59 05	119	30 52	148	36 11	220	58 11	320	47 31	345
100	48 19	023	22 24	057	59 48	119	31 18	148	35 39	220	57 39	318	47 18	344
101	48 38	021	23 05	056	60 32	120	31 44	148	35 07	220	57 05	317	47 03	342
102	48 56	020	23 46	055	61 15	120	32 11	148	34 35	220	56 30	315	46 48	341
103	49 12	019	24 27	055	61 58	120	32 37	148	34 03	220	55 55	314	46 31	340
104	49 27	017	25 07	054	62 41	120	33 04	148	33 31	220	55 18	312	46 13	338
	PROCYON		REGULUS		◆ Gienah		ACRUX		◆ ACHERNAR		RIGEL		◆ BETELGEUSE	
105	49 41	016	25 47	053	18 33	099	33 30	148	33 00	220	54 41	311	45 54	337
106	49 54	014	26 27	052	19 22	099	33 57	148	32 28	219	54 03	310	45 34	336
107	50 05	013	27 06	051	20 11	098	34 24	147	31 56	219	53 25	308	45 13	334
108	50 15	011	27 44	051	21 01	098	34 50	147	31 25	219	52 45	307	44 51	333
109	50 24	009	28 22	050	21 50	097	35 17	147	30 54	219	52 05	306	44 28	332
110	50 32	008	29 00	049	22 39	097	35 44	147	30 22	219	51 25	305	44 03	330
111	50 38	006	29 37	048	23 29	096	36 11	147	29 51	219	50 43	304	43 38	329
112	50 43	005	30 14	047	24 18	096	36 38	147	29 20	218	50 02	303	43 12	328
113	50 46	003	30 50	046	25 08	095	37 05	147	28 49	218	49 20	301	42 46	327
114	50 48	002	31 26	045	25 57	094	37 32	147	28 19	218	48 37	300	42 18	325
115	50 49	000	32 01	044	26 47	094	37 59	147	27 48	218	47 54	299	41 49	324
116	50 48	358	32 35	043	27 37	093	38 26	147	27 18	218	47 10	298	41 20	323
117	50 46	357	33 09	042	28 26	093	38 53	147	26 48	217	46 26	297	40 50	322
118	50 43	355	33 43	042	29 16	092	39 20	147	26 17	217	45 42	296	40 19	321
119	50 38	354	34 15	041	30 06	092	39 48	147	25 47	217	44 57	296	39 47	320
	REGULUS		◆ SPICA		ACRUX		◆ CANOPUS		RIGEL		BETELGEUSE		◆ PROCYON	
120	34 47	040	13 15	095	40 15	147	64 41	215	44 12	295	39 14	319	50 32	352
121	35 19	039	14 05	094	40 42	147	64 13	216	43 27	294	38 41	318	50 25	351
122	35 49	037	14 54	094	41 09	147	63 43	217	42 41	293	38 07	317	50 16	349
123	36 19	036	15 44	093	41 36	147	63 13	218	41 55	292	37 33	316	50 06	348
124	36 48	035	16 34	093	42 02	147	62 42	218	41 09	291	36 58	315	49 54	346
125	37 17	034	17 23	092	42 29	147	62 11	219	40 22	290	36 22	314	49 42	345
126	37 44	033	18 13	091	42 56	147	61 40	220	39 36	290	35 46	313	49 28	343
127	38 11	032	19 03	091	43 23	148	61 08	220	38 49	289	35 09	312	49 13	342
128	38 37	031	19 53	090	43 50	148	60 36	221	38 01	288	34 31	311	48 56	340
129	39 02	030	20 42	090	44 16	148	60 03	221	37 14	287	33 54	310	48 39	339
130	39 27	029	21 32	089	44 43	148	59 30	222	36 26	287	33 15	309	48 20	337
131	39 50	028	22 22	089	45 09	148	58 57	222	35 39	286	32 36	308	48 00	336
132	40 13	026	23 11	088	45 35	148	58 23	223	34 51	285	31 57	307	47 39	334
133	40 34	025	24 01	088	46 01	148	57 49	223	34 03	284	31 17	306	47 17	333
134	40 55	024	24 51	087	46 27	149	57 15	224	33 14	284	30 37	305	46 54	332
	◆ REGULUS		SPICA		◆ ACRUX		CANOPUS		◆ RIGEL		BETELGEUSE		PROCYON	
135	41 15	023	25 41	086	46 53	149	56 41	224	32 26	283	29 56	305	46 30	330
136	41 34	022	26 30	086	47 19	149	56 06	224	31 37	282	29 15	304	46 05	329
137	41 51	020	27 20	085	47 45	149	55 32	225	30 49	282	28 33	303	45 39	328
138	42 08	019	28 09	085	48 10	149	54 57	225	30 00	281	27 51	302	45 12	327
139	42 24	018	28 59	084	48 35	150	54 21	225	29 11	280	27 09	301	44 44	325
140	42 38	016	29 48	083	49 00	150	53 46	225	28 22	280	26 26	301	44 15	324
141	42 52	015	30 38	083	49 25	150	53 11	226	27 33	279	25 43	300	43 46	323
142	43 04	014	31 27	082	49 50	150	52 35	226	26 44	278	25 00	299	43 15	322
143	43 16	013	32 16	081	50 14	151	51 59	226	25 55	278	24 16	298	42 44	320
144	43 26	011	33 05	081	50 39	151	51 24	226	25 05	277	23 32	298	42 12	319
145	43 35	010	33 54	080	51 03	151	50 48	226	24 16	277	22 48	297	41 39	318
146	43 43	009	34 43	080	51 26	152	50 12	226	23 26	276	22 04	296	41 06	317
147	43 50	007	35 32	079	51 50	152	49 36	227	22 37	275	21 19	295	40 32	316
148	43 56	006	36 21	078	52 13	152	48 59	227	21 47	275	20 34	295	39 57	315
149	44 00	004	37 10	078	52 36	153	48 23	227	20 58	274	19 49	294	39 21	314
	REGULUS		◆ Denebola		SPICA		◆ ACRUX		CANOPUS		◆ SIRIUS		PROCYON	
150	44 03	003	34 55	033	37 58	077	52 58	153	47 47	227	43 22	279	38 45	313
151	44 05	002	35 22	032	38 46	076	53 20	154	47 11	227	42 33	278	38 08	312
152	44 06	000	35 48	031	39 35	075	53 42	154	46 34	227	41 43	278	37 31	311
153	44 06	359	36 13	030	40 23	075	54 04	155	45 58	227	40 54	277	36 53	310
154	44 05	358	36 37	029	41 11	074	54 25	155	45 22	227	40 05	277	36 15	309
155	44 02	356	37 00	028	41 58	073	54 45	156	44 45	227	39 15	276	35 36	308
156	43 58	355	37 23	026	42 46	072	55 06	156	44 09	227	38 26	275	34 57	307
157	43 53	354	37 45	025	43 33	072	55 26	157	43 33	227	37 36	275	34 17	306
158	43 47	352	38 06	024	44 20	071	55 45	157	42 56	227	36 47	274	33 36	305
159	43 40	351	38 26	023	45 07	070	56 04	158	42 20	227	35 57	273	32 56	305
160	43 31	350	38 44	022	45 54	069	56 23	158	41 44	227	35 07	273	32 15	304
161	43 22	348	39 03	021	46 40	068	56 41	159	41 08	227	34 18	272	31 33	303
162	43 11	347	39 20	019	47 26	067	56 58	160	40 31	227	33 28	272	30 51	302
163	42 59	346	39 36	018	48 12	066	57 15	160	39 55	227	32 38	271	30 09	301
164	42 46	344	39 51	017	48 57	065	57 32	161	39 19	227	31 48	271	29 26	300
	ARCTURUS		◆ ANTARES		ACRUX		◆ CANOPUS		SIRIUS		PROCYON		◆ REGULUS	
165	19 16	049	20 11	109	57 48	162	38 43	226	30 59	270	28 43	300	42 32	343
166	19 54	048	20 58	108	58 03	162	38 07	226	30 09	269	27 59	299	42 17	342
167	20 31	048	21 45	108	58 18	163	37 31	226	29 19	269	27 16	298	42 01	340
168	21 07	047	22 33	108	58 32	164	36 55	226	28 29	268	26 32	297	41 44	339
169	21 43	046	23 20	107	58 46	165	36 19	226	27 40	268	25 47	297	41 26	338
170	22 19	045	24 08	107	58 59	165	35 44	226	26 50	267	25 03	296	41 07	337
171	22 54	044	24 55	106	59 11	166	35 08	226	26 00	267	24 18	295	40 47	336
172	23 28	044	25 43	106	59 23	167	34 32	226	25 11	266	23 32	294	40 26	334
173	24 03	043	26 31	105	59 34	168	33 57	225	24 21	266	22 47	294	40 04	333
174	24 36	042	27 19	105	59 44	169	33 22	225	23 31	265	22 01	293	39 41	332
175	25 09	041	28 07	104	59 54	169	32 46	225	22 42	265	21 15	292	39 17	331
176	25 42	040	28 56	104	60 02	170	32 11	225	21 52	264	20 29	292	38 52	330
177	26 13	039	29 44	104	60 10	171	31 36	225	21 03	264	19 43	291	38 27	329
178	26 45	039	30 32	103	60 18	172	31 01	224	20 14	263	18 56	290	38 00	327
179	27 15	038	31 21	103	60 24	173	30 27	224	19 24	262	18 10	290	37 33	326

 LAT 34°S

LHA ♈	Hc	Zn	Hc	Zn	Hc	Zn	Hc	Zn	Hc	Zn	Hc	Zn	Hc	Zn
	◆ ARCTURUS		ANTARES		◆ RIGIL KENT		ACRUX		CANOPUS		◆ Alphard		REGULUS	
180	27 46	037	32 09	102	52 49	149	60 30	174	29 52	224	47 00	297	37 05	325
181	28 15	036	32 58	102	53 15	149	60 35	175	29 17	224	46 15	296	36 36	324
182	28 44	035	33 47	101	53 40	150	60 40	176	28 43	224	45 30	295	36 07	323
183	29 12	034	34 36	101	54 06	150	60 43	176	28 09	223	44 45	294	35 37	322
184	29 39	033	35 24	100	54 30	150	60 46	177	27 35	223	44 00	293	35 06	321
185	30 06	032	36 13	100	54 55	151	60 48	178	27 01	223	43 14	293	34 34	320
186	30 32	031	37 02	099	55 19	151	60 49	179	26 27	223	42 28	292	34 02	319
187	30 58	030	37 52	099	55 42	152	60 49	180	25 54	222	41 41	291	33 29	318
188	31 22	029	38 41	099	56 06	152	60 49	181	25 20	222	40 55	290	32 55	317
189	31 46	028	39 30	098	56 29	153	60 47	182	24 47	222	40 08	289	32 21	316
190	32 09	027	40 19	098	56 51	153	60 45	183	24 14	222	39 21	288	31 46	315
191	32 31	026	41 09	097	57 13	154	60 42	184	23 41	221	38 33	288	31 11	314
192	32 53	025	41 58	097	57 35	155	60 38	185	23 08	221	37 46	287	30 35	313
193	33 13	024	42 47	096	57 56	155	60 34	186	22 36	221	36 58	286	29 59	313
194	33 33	023	43 37	096	58 16	156	60 29	187	22 04	220	36 10	285	29 22	312
	ARCTURUS		◆ ANTARES		RIGIL KENT		◆ ACRUX		Suhail		REGULUS		◆ Denebola	
195	33 52	022	44 26	095	58 36	157	60 23	187	44 49	240	28 45	311	38 43	338
196	34 10	021	45 16	095	58 56	157	60 16	188	44 06	240	28 07	310	38 24	337
197	34 27	020	46 05	094	59 15	158	60 08	189	43 23	240	27 28	309	38 04	336
198	34 44	019	46 55	094	59 33	159	60 00	190	42 40	240	26 49	308	37 43	335
199	34 59	017	47 45	093	59 51	160	59 51	191	41 57	239	26 10	307	37 21	333
200	35 14	016	48 34	093	60 08	160	59 41	192	41 14	239	25 31	307	36 58	332
201	35 27	015	49 24	092	60 24	161	59 31	193	40 32	239	24 50	306	36 35	331
202	35 40	014	50 14	092	60 40	162	59 20	193	39 49	239	24 10	305	36 10	330
203	35 51	013	51 04	091	60 55	163	59 08	194	39 07	239	23 29	304	35 45	329
204	36 02	012	51 53	091	61 09	164	58 55	195	38 24	238	22 48	304	35 19	328
205	36 12	011	52 43	090	61 23	165	58 42	196	37 42	238	22 06	303	34 53	327
206	36 20	009	53 33	090	61 36	166	58 28	196	37 00	238	21 24	302	34 25	326
207	36 28	008	54 23	089	61 48	166	58 14	197	36 18	238	20 42	301	33 57	325
208	36 35	007	55 12	088	61 59	167	57 59	198	35 36	237	19 59	301	33 28	324
209	36 40	006	56 02	088	62 09	168	57 44	199	34 54	237	19 16	300	32 58	323
	◆ ARCTURUS		Rasalhague		◆ Nunki		RIGIL KENT		ACRUX		◆ Suhail		SPICA	
210	36 45	005	20 48	058	26 52	105	62 19	169	57 27	199	34 12	237	65 57	339
211	36 49	004	21 30	057	27 40	104	62 28	170	57 11	200	33 30	237	65 38	337
212	36 51	002	22 12	056	28 28	104	62 36	171	56 54	201	32 49	236	65 18	335
213	36 53	001	22 53	055	29 16	104	62 43	172	56 36	201	32 08	236	64 56	333
214	36 54	000	23 33	055	30 05	103	62 49	173	56 18	202	31 26	236	64 32	330
215	36 53	359	24 14	054	30 53	103	62 54	174	55 59	202	30 45	236	64 07	328
216	36 52	358	24 54	053	31 42	102	62 58	176	55 40	203	30 04	235	63 40	326
217	36 49	357	25 33	052	32 31	102	63 02	177	55 20	203	29 23	235	63 12	324
218	36 46	355	26 12	051	33 19	101	63 04	178	55 00	204	28 43	235	62 42	323
219	36 41	354	26 51	051	34 08	101	63 06	179	54 40	205	28 02	234	62 11	321
220	36 36	353	27 29	050	34 57	100	63 06	180	54 19	205	27 22	234	61 39	319
221	36 29	352	28 07	049	35 46	100	63 06	181	53 58	205	26 41	234	61 06	317
222	36 22	351	28 44	048	36 35	099	63 05	182	53 36	206	26 01	234	60 32	316
223	36 13	350	29 21	047	37 24	099	63 02	183	53 14	206	25 21	233	59 57	314
224	36 04	348	29 57	046	38 13	099	62 59	184	52 52	207	24 42	233	59 20	313
	Alphecca		Rasalhague		◆ Nunki		Peacock		◆ RIGIL KENT		SPICA		◆ ARCTURUS	
225	28 46	009	30 33	045	39 02	098	32 12	140	62 55	185	58 43	311	35 53	347
226	28 53	008	31 08	044	39 52	098	32 44	140	62 50	186	58 05	310	35 42	346
227	28 59	007	31 42	044	40 41	097	33 17	140	62 45	187	57 27	308	35 29	345
228	29 05	006	32 16	043	41 30	097	33 49	140	62 38	188	56 47	307	35 16	344
229	29 10	005	32 50	042	42 20	096	34 21	139	62 30	189	56 07	306	35 02	343
230	29 14	004	33 22	041	43 09	096	34 53	139	62 22	190	55 27	304	34 46	342
231	29 17	003	33 55	040	43 59	095	35 26	139	62 12	191	54 45	303	34 30	341
232	29 19	002	34 26	039	44 48	095	35 58	139	62 02	192	54 03	302	34 13	339
233	29 20	001	34 57	038	45 38	094	36 31	139	61 51	193	53 21	301	33 55	338
234	29 20	000	35 27	037	46 28	094	37 04	139	61 39	194	52 38	300	33 36	337
235	29 19	359	35 56	036	47 17	093	37 36	139	61 27	195	51 55	299	33 17	336
236	29 18	358	36 25	035	48 07	093	38 09	139	61 13	196	51 11	298	32 56	335
237	29 16	357	36 53	034	48 57	092	38 42	139	60 59	197	50 26	297	32 35	334
238	29 12	356	37 20	032	49 46	092	39 15	139	60 45	198	49 42	296	32 13	333
239	29 08	355	37 46	031	50 36	091	39 48	139	60 29	199	48 57	295	31 50	332
	Rasalhague		ALTAIR		◆ Nunki		Peacock		◆ RIGIL KENT		SPICA		◆ ARCTURUS	
240	38 11	030	20 25	063	51 26	091	40 21	139	60 13	199	48 11	294	31 26	331
241	38 36	029	21 09	063	52 16	090	40 54	139	59 56	200	47 26	293	31 02	330
242	39 00	028	21 53	062	53 05	089	41 26	139	59 39	201	46 39	292	30 37	329
243	39 23	027	22 37	061	53 55	089	41 59	139	59 20	202	45 53	291	30 11	328
244	39 45	026	23 21	060	54 45	088	42 32	139	59 02	202	45 07	290	29 44	327
245	40 06	024	24 04	060	55 35	088	43 05	139	58 42	203	44 20	289	29 17	326
246	40 26	023	24 46	059	56 24	087	43 38	139	58 23	204	43 33	288	28 49	325
247	40 45	022	25 29	058	57 14	086	44 11	139	58 02	205	42 45	288	28 20	324
248	41 03	021	26 11	057	58 03	086	44 44	139	57 41	205	41 58	287	27 51	323
249	41 20	020	26 52	057	58 53	085	45 17	139	57 20	206	41 10	286	27 21	322
250	41 36	018	27 34	056	59 43	084	45 50	139	56 58	206	40 22	285	26 50	322
251	41 51	017	28 15	055	60 32	084	46 22	139	56 36	207	39 34	285	26 19	321
252	42 05	016	28 55	054	61 22	083	46 55	139	56 13	207	38 46	284	25 47	320
253	42 18	014	29 35	053	62 11	082	47 28	139	55 50	208	37 58	283	25 15	319
254	42 30	013	30 15	052	63 00	082	48 00	139	55 26	209	37 09	282	24 42	318
	VEGA		◆ ALTAIR		FOMALHAUT		◆ Peacock		RIGIL KENT		◆ SPICA		ARCTURUS	
255	13 47	019	30 54	052	16 17	115	48 33	139	55 02	209	36 21	282	24 08	317
256	14 03	019	31 33	051	17 03	115	49 05	140	54 38	209	35 32	281	23 34	317
257	14 19	018	32 11	050	17 48	114	49 37	140	54 13	210	34 43	280	23 00	316
258	14 33	017	32 49	049	18 33	114	50 09	140	53 48	210	33 54	280	22 25	315
259	14 48	016	33 26	048	19 19	113	50 41	140	53 23	211	33 05	279	21 49	314
260	15 01	016	34 03	047	20 05	113	51 13	140	52 58	211	32 16	278	21 13	313
261	15 14	015	34 39	046	20 51	112	51 45	141	52 32	212	31 27	278	20 37	312
262	15 27	014	35 15	045	21 37	112	52 16	141	52 06	212	30 37	277	20 00	312
263	15 38	013	35 49	044	22 23	111	52 48	141	51 39	212	29 48	277	19 23	311
264	15 49	012	36 24	043	23 10	111	53 19	141	51 13	213	28 58	276	18 45	310
265	16 00	012	36 58	042	23 56	111	53 50	142	50 46	213	28 09	275	18 07	309
266	16 09	011	37 31	041	24 43	110	54 20	142	50 19	213	27 19	275	17 28	309
267	16 18	010	38 03	040	25 29	110	54 51	142	49 51	213	26 30	274	16 49	308
268	16 27	009	38 35	039	26 16	109	55 21	143	49 24	214	25 40	274	16 10	307
269	16 34	008	39 06	038	27 03	109	55 51	143	48 56	214	24 51	273	15 30	307

LHA ♈	Hc	Zn	Hc	Zn	Hc	Zn	Hc	Zn	Hc	Zn	Hc	Zn	Hc	Zn
	VEGA		ALTAIR		◆ FOMALHAUT		ACHERNAR		◆ RIGIL KENT		ANTARES		◆ Rasalhague	
270	16 41	008	39 36	037	27 50	108	16 26	149	48 28	214	69 16	285	43 05	352
271	16 47	007	40 05	036	28 38	108	16 52	149	48 00	214	68 28	284	42 58	351
272	16 53	006	40 34	035	29 25	108	17 18	148	47 32	215	67 40	283	42 49	349
273	16 58	005	41 02	033	30 13	107	17 44	148	47 04	215	66 51	282	42 39	348
274	17 02	004	41 29	032	31 00	107	18 10	148	46 36	215	66 03	281	42 28	347
275	17 05	004	41 55	031	31 48	106	18 37	147	46 07	215	65 14	280	42 16	345
276	17 08	003	42 20	030	32 36	106	19 04	147	45 39	215	64 25	279	42 03	344
277	17 10	002	42 44	029	33 23	106	19 31	147	45 10	215	63 36	279	41 49	343
278	17 11	001	43 08	027	34 11	105	19 59	146	44 41	215	62 46	278	41 33	341
279	17 12	000	43 30	026	34 59	105	20 26	146	44 12	215	61 57	277	41 17	340
280	17 12	359	43 52	025	35 48	104	20 54	146	43 43	216	61 08	276	41 00	339
281	17 11	359	44 12	024	36 36	104	21 22	146	43 14	216	60 18	276	40 41	338
282	17 10	358	44 31	022	37 24	103	21 50	145	42 45	216	59 29	275	40 22	337
283	17 07	357	44 50	021	38 13	103	22 19	145	42 16	216	58 39	274	40 02	335
284	17 04	356	45 07	020	39 01	103	22 48	145	41 47	216	57 50	274	39 41	334
	ALTAIR		Enif		◆ FOMALHAUT		ACHERNAR		◆ RIGIL KENT		ANTARES		◆ Rasalhague	
285	45 23	018	31 10	049	39 50	102	23 16	144	41 18	216	57 00	273	39 19	333
286	45 38	017	31 48	048	40 38	102	23 45	144	40 49	216	56 10	272	38 56	332
287	45 52	016	32 25	048	41 27	101	24 15	144	40 20	216	55 20	272	38 32	331
288	46 05	014	33 01	047	42 16	101	24 44	144	39 51	216	54 31	271	38 07	330
289	46 16	013	33 37	046	43 05	101	25 14	143	39 21	216	53 41	271	37 41	328
290	46 27	011	34 12	045	43 54	100	25 43	143	38 52	216	52 51	270	37 15	327
291	46 36	010	34 47	044	44 43	100	26 13	143	38 23	216	52 02	269	36 48	326
292	46 44	008	35 21	043	45 32	099	26 43	143	37 54	216	51 12	269	36 20	325
293	46 51	007	35 54	042	46 21	099	27 14	142	37 25	216	50 22	268	35 51	324
294	46 56	006	36 27	041	47 10	098	27 44	142	36 56	216	49 32	268	35 21	323
295	47 00	004	36 59	040	47 59	098	28 15	142	36 27	216	48 43	267	34 51	322
296	47 03	003	37 31	039	48 49	098	28 45	142	35 58	216	47 53	267	34 20	321
297	47 05	001	38 02	038	49 38	097	29 16	142	35 29	216	47 03	266	33 49	320
298	47 05	000	38 32	037	50 27	097	29 47	141	35 00	215	46 14	266	33 16	319
299	47 05	358	39 01	035	51 17	096	30 18	141	34 31	215	45 24	265	32 44	318
	Enif		◆ FOMALHAUT		ACHERNAR		◆ RIGIL KENT		ANTARES		Rasalhague		◆ ALTAIR	
300	39 29	034	52 06	096	30 49	141	34 02	215	44 35	265	32 10	317	47 03	357
301	39 57	033	52 56	095	31 21	141	33 33	215	43 45	264	31 36	316	46 59	355
302	40 24	032	53 45	095	31 52	141	33 05	215	42 56	264	31 01	315	46 55	354
303	40 50	031	54 35	094	32 24	141	32 36	215	42 06	263	30 26	314	46 49	353
304	41 15	030	55 24	094	32 55	140	32 08	215	41 17	263	29 50	314	46 42	351
305	41 39	029	56 14	094	33 27	140	31 39	215	40 27	262	29 14	313	46 34	350
306	42 02	027	57 04	093	33 59	140	31 11	215	39 38	262	28 37	312	46 24	348
307	42 25	026	57 53	093	34 31	140	30 43	214	38 49	262	28 00	311	46 14	347
308	42 46	025	58 43	092	35 03	140	30 15	214	38 00	261	27 22	310	46 02	346
309	43 06	024	59 33	092	35 35	140	29 47	214	37 11	261	26 44	309	45 49	344
310	43 26	022	60 22	091	36 07	140	29 19	214	36 22	260	26 05	308	45 35	343
311	43 44	021	61 12	090	36 39	140	28 52	214	35 33	260	25 26	308	45 19	341
312	44 01	020	62 02	090	37 12	139	28 24	214	34 44	259	24 46	307	45 03	340
313	44 18	018	62 52	089	37 44	139	27 57	213	33 55	259	24 06	306	44 45	339
314	44 33	017	63 41	089	38 16	139	27 29	213	33 06	258	23 26	305	44 27	337
	Alpheratz		◆ Diphda		ACHERNAR		◆ RIGIL KENT		ANTARES		Rasalhague		◆ ALTAIR	
315	12 37	041	37 44	087	38 49	139	27 02	213	32 17	258	22 45	305	44 07	336
316	13 09	040	38 34	086	39 21	139	26 35	213	31 29	257	22 04	304	43 46	335
317	13 41	040	39 24	086	39 54	139	26 08	213	30 40	257	21 22	303	43 25	334
318	14 13	039	40 13	085	40 26	139	25 42	212	29 52	257	20 41	302	43 02	332
319	14 44	038	41 03	085	40 59	139	25 15	212	29 04	256	19 58	302	42 39	331
320	15 15	038	41 52	084	41 31	139	24 49	212	28 15	256	19 16	301	42 14	330
321	15 45	037	42 42	083	42 04	139	24 23	212	27 27	255	18 33	300	41 49	329
322	16 14	036	43 31	083	42 36	139	23 57	211	26 39	255	17 50	299	41 22	327
323	16 43	035	44 20	082	43 09	139	23 31	211	25 51	254	17 06	299	40 55	326
324	17 11	034	45 10	081	43 41	139	23 05	211	25 03	254	16 23	298	40 27	325
325	17 39	034	45 59	081	44 14	139	22 40	211	24 16	253	15 39	297	39 58	324
326	18 07	033	46 48	080	44 46	139	22 14	210	23 28	253	14 54	297	39 29	323
327	18 33	032	47 37	079	45 19	139	21 49	210	22 40	252	14 10	296	38 58	322
328	19 00	031	48 25	078	45 51	139	21 25	210	21 53	252	13 25	295	38 27	321
329	19 25	031	49 14	078	46 23	140	21 00	210	21 06	252	12 40	295	37 55	320
	◆ Alpheratz		Diphda		◆ ACHERNAR		Peacock		◆ Nunki		ALTAIR		Enif	
330	19 50	030	50 03	077	46 56	140	62 19	208	49 51	268	37 23	319	45 55	355
331	20 15	029	50 51	076	47 28	140	61 55	209	49 02	268	36 49	318	45 49	353
332	20 38	028	51 39	075	48 00	140	61 31	209	48 12	267	36 16	317	45 43	352
333	21 01	027	52 27	074	48 32	140	61 06	210	47 22	267	35 41	316	45 35	350
334	21 24	026	53 15	074	49 04	140	60 41	211	46 32	266	35 06	315	45 26	349
335	21 46	026	54 03	073	49 35	140	60 15	212	45 43	266	34 30	314	45 16	348
336	22 07	025	54 50	072	50 07	141	59 49	212	44 53	265	33 54	313	45 05	346
337	22 27	024	55 37	071	50 38	141	59 22	213	44 04	265	33 17	312	44 53	345
338	22 47	023	56 24	070	51 10	141	58 55	214	43 14	264	32 40	311	44 39	344
339	23 06	022	57 10	069	51 41	141	58 27	214	42 25	264	32 02	310	44 25	342
340	23 24	021	57 57	068	52 12	142	57 59	215	41 35	263	31 24	309	44 09	341
341	23 42	020	58 42	067	52 43	142	57 31	215	40 46	263	30 45	308	43 52	340
342	23 59	019	59 28	066	53 13	142	57 02	216	39 57	262	30 05	307	43 34	338
343	24 15	018	60 13	064	53 44	143	56 33	216	39 07	262	29 26	307	43 15	337
344	24 30	018	60 58	063	54 14	143	56 03	217	38 18	262	28 45	306	42 56	336
	Alpheratz		◆ Hamal		◆ ACHERNAR		Peacock		◆ Nunki		ALTAIR		Enif	
345	24 45	017	17 10	045	54 44	143	55 33	217	37 29	261	28 05	305	42 35	335
346	24 59	016	17 44	044	55 13	144	55 03	217	36 40	261	27 24	304	42 13	333
347	25 12	015	18 19	043	55 42	144	54 33	218	35 51	260	26 42	303	41 50	332
348	25 24	014	18 52	042	56 12	145	54 02	218	35 02	260	26 01	302	41 26	331
349	25 35	013	19 25	042	56 40	145	53 31	218	34 13	259	25 18	302	41 01	330
350	25 46	012	19 58	041	57 09	145	53 00	219	33 24	259	24 36	301	40 36	328
351	25 56	011	20 30	040	57 37	146	52 29	219	32 35	258	23 53	300	40 09	327
352	26 05	010	21 02	039	58 04	146	51 58	219	31 47	258	23 10	299	39 42	326
353	26 13	009	21 33	038	58 32	147	51 26	220	30 58	257	22 27	299	39 14	325
354	26 21	008	22 04	038	58 58	148	50 54	220	30 10	257	21 43	298	38 45	324
355	26 27	007	22 34	037	59 25	148	50 23	220	29 21	257	20 59	297	38 16	323
356	26 33	006	23 03	036	59 51	149	49 50	220	28 33	256	20 14	297	37 45	322
357	26 38	005	23 32	035	60 16	150	49 18	220	27 45	256	19 30	296	37 14	321
358	26 42	004	24 00	034	60 41	150	48 46	221	26 56	255	18 45	295	36 42	320
359	26 45	003	24 28	033	61 05	151	48 14	221	26 08	255	18 00	295	36 10	319

 LAT 35°S

LHA ♈	Hc	Zn	Hc	Zn	Hc	Zn	Hc	Zn	Hc	Zn	Hc	Zn	Hc	Zn
	◆ Alpheratz		Hamal		◆ RIGEL		CANOPUS		ACHERNAR		◆ Peacock		Enif	
0	25 47	002	24 04	032	13 49	090	23 49	139	62 22	151	48 26	222	34 52	318
1	25 49	001	24 30	031	14 39	090	24 21	139	62 45	152	47 54	222	34 19	317
2	25 50	000	24 55	030	15 28	089	24 54	138	63 08	153	47 21	222	33 45	316
3	25 49	359	25 20	029	16 17	089	25 27	138	63 31	153	46 48	222	33 11	315
4	25 48	358	25 44	029	17 06	088	26 00	138	63 52	154	46 15	222	32 36	314
5	25 47	357	26 07	028	17 55	087	26 33	137	64 13	155	45 42	222	32 00	313
6	25 44	356	26 29	027	18 44	087	27 06	137	64 33	156	45 10	222	31 24	312
7	25 40	355	26 51	026	19 33	086	27 40	137	64 53	157	44 37	222	30 48	312
8	25 36	354	27 12	025	20 22	086	28 14	137	65 11	158	44 04	222	30 11	311
9	25 31	354	27 32	024	21 11	085	28 48	136	65 29	159	43 31	222	29 33	310
10	25 25	353	27 52	023	22 00	085	29 22	136	65 46	161	42 58	222	28 55	309
11	25 18	352	28 10	022	22 49	084	29 56	136	66 02	162	42 25	222	28 17	308
12	25 11	351	28 28	021	23 38	083	30 30	136	66 16	163	41 52	222	27 38	307
13	25 02	350	28 45	020	24 27	083	31 05	135	66 30	164	41 19	222	26 58	306
14	24 53	349	29 02	019	25 15	082	31 39	135	66 43	165	40 46	222	26 19	306
	◆ Hamal		ALDEBARAN		RIGEL		◆ CANOPUS		ACHERNAR		◆ FOMALHAUT		Alpheratz	
15	29 17	018	17 13	054	26 04	081	32 14	135	66 55	167	63 51	273	24 43	348
16	29 32	017	17 53	054	26 53	081	32 49	135	67 06	168	63 02	273	24 32	347
17	29 46	016	18 33	053	27 41	080	33 24	135	67 16	169	62 13	272	24 21	346
18	29 59	015	19 12	052	28 30	079	33 59	134	67 24	171	61 23	272	24 08	345
19	30 11	014	19 51	052	29 18	079	34 34	134	67 31	172	60 34	271	23 55	344
20	30 22	013	20 29	051	30 06	078	35 09	134	67 38	173	59 45	270	23 41	343
21	30 33	012	21 07	050	30 54	077	35 45	134	67 43	175	58 56	270	23 27	342
22	30 42	011	21 44	049	31 42	077	36 20	134	67 46	176	58 07	269	23 11	341
23	30 51	010	22 21	048	32 30	076	36 56	134	67 49	178	57 18	269	22 55	340
24	30 59	009	22 58	048	33 17	075	37 31	133	67 50	179	56 29	268	22 38	340
25	31 05	008	23 34	047	34 05	075	38 07	133	67 50	181	55 39	268	22 21	339
26	31 11	006	24 09	046	34 52	074	38 43	133	67 49	182	54 50	267	22 03	338
27	31 17	005	24 44	045	35 39	073	39 19	133	67 47	183	54 01	267	21 44	337
28	31 21	004	25 19	044	36 26	072	39 55	133	67 43	185	53 12	266	21 24	336
29	31 24	003	25 53	043	37 13	072	40 31	133	67 38	186	52 23	266	21 04	335
	Hamal		ALDEBARAN		◆ SIRIUS		CANOPUS		◆ ACHERNAR		FOMALHAUT		◆ Alpheratz	
30	31 26	002	26 27	043	24 30	094	41 07	133	67 32	188	51 34	265	20 43	334
31	31 28	001	27 00	042	25 19	093	41 43	133	67 25	189	50 45	265	20 21	333
32	31 28	000	27 32	041	26 08	093	42 19	133	67 17	190	49 56	264	19 59	333
33	31 28	359	28 04	040	26 57	092	42 56	132	67 07	192	49 08	264	19 36	332
34	31 26	358	28 35	039	27 46	092	43 32	132	66 57	193	48 19	263	19 12	331
35	31 24	357	29 06	038	28 36	091	44 08	132	66 45	194	47 30	263	18 48	330
36	31 21	356	29 36	037	29 25	091	44 45	132	66 32	196	46 41	262	18 23	329
37	31 17	355	30 05	036	30 14	090	45 21	132	66 18	197	45 53	262	17 58	328
38	31 12	354	30 34	035	31 03	089	45 57	132	66 04	198	45 04	261	17 32	328
39	31 06	353	31 02	034	31 52	089	46 34	132	65 48	199	44 15	261	17 05	327
40	30 59	351	31 29	033	32 41	088	47 10	132	65 31	200	43 27	260	16 38	326
41	30 51	350	31 56	032	33 30	088	47 46	132	65 14	201	42 38	260	16 10	325
42	30 42	349	32 21	031	34 19	087	48 23	132	64 55	203	41 50	260	15 42	325
43	30 33	348	32 46	030	35 09	086	48 59	132	64 36	204	41 02	259	15 13	324
44	30 22	347	33 11	029	35 58	086	49 35	133	64 16	205	40 13	259	14 44	323
	◆ ALDEBARAN		BETELGEUSE		SIRIUS		◆ CANOPUS		ACHERNAR		◆ FOMALHAUT		Hamal	
45	33 34	028	30 41	053	36 47	085	50 11	133	63 55	206	39 25	258	30 11	346
46	33 57	027	31 21	052	37 36	085	50 48	133	63 34	206	38 37	258	29 59	345
47	34 19	026	31 59	051	38 24	084	51 24	133	63 11	207	37 49	257	29 46	344
48	34 40	025	32 37	051	39 13	083	52 00	133	62 49	208	37 01	257	29 32	343
49	35 01	024	33 15	050	40 02	083	52 36	133	62 25	209	36 13	257	29 17	342
50	35 20	023	33 52	049	40 51	082	53 11	133	62 01	210	35 26	256	29 02	341
51	35 39	022	34 29	048	41 39	081	53 47	133	61 36	211	34 38	256	28 46	340
52	35 56	020	35 05	047	42 28	081	54 23	134	61 11	211	33 51	255	28 28	339
53	36 13	019	35 41	046	43 16	080	54 58	134	60 45	212	33 03	255	28 10	338
54	36 29	018	36 16	045	44 05	079	55 34	134	60 19	213	32 16	254	27 52	337
55	36 44	017	36 50	044	44 53	078	56 09	134	59 52	213	31 28	254	27 32	336
56	36 58	016	37 24	043	45 41	078	56 44	135	59 25	214	30 41	253	27 12	335
57	37 11	015	37 57	042	46 29	077	57 19	135	58 58	214	29 54	253	26 51	334
58	37 23	014	38 29	041	47 17	076	57 53	135	58 30	215	29 07	253	26 29	333
59	37 34	012	39 01	040	48 04	075	58 28	136	58 02	215	28 20	252	26 07	332
	ALDEBARAN		◆ BETELGEUSE		SIRIUS		◆ CANOPUS		ACHERNAR		◆ FOMALHAUT		Hamal	
60	37 44	011	39 32	039	48 52	075	59 02	136	57 33	216	27 34	252	25 44	331
61	37 53	010	40 02	037	49 39	074	59 36	137	57 04	216	26 47	251	25 20	331
62	38 01	009	40 32	036	50 26	073	60 10	137	56 35	217	26 01	251	24 55	330
63	38 08	008	41 00	035	51 13	072	60 43	137	56 05	217	25 14	250	24 30	329
64	38 14	006	41 28	034	52 00	071	61 16	138	55 35	218	24 28	250	24 04	328
65	38 18	005	41 55	033	52 46	070	61 49	139	55 05	218	23 42	250	23 38	327
66	38 22	004	42 22	032	53 32	069	62 21	139	54 35	218	22 56	249	23 11	326
67	38 25	003	42 47	030	54 18	068	62 53	140	54 04	219	22 10	249	22 43	325
68	38 27	001	43 11	029	55 03	067	63 25	140	53 34	219	21 24	248	22 15	324
69	38 28	000	43 35	028	55 48	066	63 56	141	53 03	219	20 39	248	21 46	324
70	38 27	359	43 57	027	56 33	065	64 26	142	52 32	219	19 53	247	21 17	323
71	38 26	358	44 19	025	57 17	064	64 56	143	52 00	220	19 08	247	20 46	322
72	38 24	357	44 39	024	58 01	063	65 26	144	51 29	220	18 23	246	20 16	321
73	38 20	355	44 59	023	58 45	062	65 55	144	50 57	220	17 38	246	19 45	320
74	38 16	354	45 17	021	59 28	060	66 23	145	50 26	220	16 53	245	19 13	319
	BETELGEUSE		◆ PROCYON		Suhail		◆ ACRUX		ACHERNAR		◆ Diphda		ALDEBARAN	
75	45 35	020	34 57	051	42 16	120	21 59	153	49 54	220	31 16	269	38 10	353
76	45 51	019	35 35	050	42 58	120	22 21	153	49 22	221	30 27	269	38 03	352
77	46 06	017	36 13	049	43 41	120	22 44	153	48 50	221	29 38	268	37 56	351
78	46 20	016	36 50	049	44 24	119	23 06	152	48 18	221	28 49	268	37 47	349
79	46 33	014	37 27	048	45 07	119	23 29	152	47 45	221	28 00	267	37 38	348
80	46 45	013	38 03	047	45 50	119	23 52	152	47 13	221	27 11	266	37 27	347
81	46 55	012	38 38	046	46 33	119	24 16	152	46 41	221	26 22	266	37 15	346
82	47 05	010	39 13	044	47 16	119	24 39	151	46 08	221	25 33	265	37 03	345
83	47 13	009	39 47	043	47 59	119	25 03	151	45 36	221	24 44	265	36 49	343
84	47 20	007	40 20	042	48 42	118	25 27	151	45 03	221	23 55	264	36 35	342
85	47 25	006	40 53	041	49 25	118	25 51	151	44 31	221	23 06	264	36 19	341
86	47 30	004	41 25	040	50 09	118	26 15	150	43 58	221	22 17	263	36 03	340
87	47 33	003	41 56	039	50 52	118	26 39	150	43 26	221	21 28	263	35 46	339
88	47 35	001	42 27	038	51 35	118	27 04	150	42 53	221	20 40	262	35 27	338
89	47 35	000	42 57	037	52 19	118	27 28	150	42 21	221	19 51	262	35 08	337

LHA ♈	Hc	Zn	Hc	Zn	Hc	Zn	Hc	Zn	Hc	Zn	Hc	Zn	Hc	Zn
	PROCYON		REGULUS		◆ Suhail		ACRUX		◆ ACHERNAR		RIGEL		◆ BETELGEUSE	
90	43 25	035	14 45	064	53 02	118	27 53	150	41 48	221	61 17	336	47 35	359
91	43 54	034	15 28	063	53 46	118	28 18	149	41 16	221	60 57	335	47 33	357
92	44 21	033	16 12	062	54 29	118	28 43	149	40 43	221	60 35	333	47 30	356
93	44 47	032	16 55	062	55 13	118	29 09	149	40 11	221	60 12	331	47 25	354
94	45 12	030	17 39	061	55 56	118	29 34	149	39 38	221	59 47	329	47 20	353
95	45 37	029	18 21	060	56 40	118	30 00	149	39 06	221	59 21	327	47 13	351
96	46 00	028	19 04	059	57 23	118	30 25	148	38 34	221	58 54	326	47 05	350
97	46 23	027	19 46	059	58 07	118	30 51	148	38 01	221	58 26	324	46 55	348
98	46 44	025	20 28	058	58 50	118	31 17	148	37 29	221	57 56	322	46 45	347
99	47 05	024	21 09	057	59 34	118	31 43	148	36 57	221	57 25	321	46 33	345
100	47 24	022	21 51	057	60 17	118	32 09	148	36 25	221	56 54	319	46 20	344
101	47 42	021	22 31	056	61 01	118	32 35	148	35 53	221	56 21	318	46 06	342
102	47 59	020	23 12	055	61 44	118	33 01	148	35 21	220	55 47	316	45 51	341
103	48 15	018	23 52	054	62 27	118	33 28	147	34 49	220	55 13	315	45 35	340
104	48 30	017	24 32	053	63 10	119	33 54	147	34 17	220	54 38	313	45 17	339
	PROCYON		REGULUS		◆ Gienah		ACRUX		◆ ACHERNAR		RIGEL		◆ BETELGEUSE	
105	48 43	015	25 11	053	18 42	099	34 21	147	33 46	220	54 01	312	44 59	337
106	48 56	014	25 50	052	19 31	098	34 47	147	33 14	220	53 25	311	44 39	336
107	49 07	012	26 28	051	20 20	098	35 14	147	32 43	220	52 47	309	44 19	335
108	49 16	011	27 06	050	21 08	097	35 41	147	32 11	220	52 09	308	43 57	333
109	49 25	009	27 43	049	21 57	097	36 08	147	31 40	219	51 30	307	43 35	332
110	49 32	008	28 20	048	22 46	096	36 35	147	31 09	219	50 50	306	43 11	331
111	49 38	006	28 57	048	23 35	096	37 01	147	30 38	219	50 10	305	42 47	330
112	49 43	005	29 33	047	24 24	095	37 28	147	30 07	219	49 29	303	42 21	328
113	49 46	003	30 09	046	25 13	095	37 55	147	29 37	219	48 48	302	41 55	327
114	49 48	002	30 43	045	26 02	094	38 22	147	29 06	218	48 06	301	41 28	326
115	49 49	000	31 18	044	26 51	093	38 49	147	28 36	218	47 24	300	41 00	325
116	49 48	358	31 52	043	27 40	093	39 17	147	28 05	218	46 41	299	40 32	324
117	49 46	357	32 25	042	28 29	092	39 44	147	27 35	218	45 58	298	40 02	323
118	49 43	355	32 57	041	29 18	092	40 11	147	27 05	217	45 15	297	39 32	321
119	49 38	354	33 29	040	30 07	091	40 38	147	26 35	217	44 31	296	39 01	320
	REGULUS		◆ SPICA		ACRUX		◆ CANOPUS		RIGEL		BETELGEUSE		◆ PROCYON	
120	34 01	039	13 20	095	41 05	147	65 30	216	43 47	295	38 29	319	49 33	352
121	34 31	038	14 09	094	41 32	147	65 01	217	43 02	295	37 57	318	49 25	351
122	35 01	037	14 58	093	41 59	147	64 31	218	42 17	294	37 24	317	49 17	349
123	35 31	036	15 47	093	42 26	147	64 00	219	41 32	293	36 50	316	49 07	348
124	35 59	035	16 36	092	42 53	147	63 29	219	40 47	292	36 15	315	48 56	346
125	36 27	034	17 25	092	43 20	147	62 58	220	40 01	291	35 40	314	48 44	345
126	36 54	033	18 14	091	43 47	147	62 26	221	39 15	290	35 05	313	48 30	343
127	37 20	032	19 04	091	44 13	147	61 54	221	38 29	290	34 29	312	48 16	342
128	37 46	031	19 53	090	44 40	147	61 21	222	37 42	289	33 52	311	48 00	340
129	38 10	029	20 42	089	45 07	147	60 48	222	36 56	288	33 15	310	47 43	339
130	38 34	028	21 31	089	45 33	147	60 15	223	36 09	287	32 37	309	47 25	338
131	38 57	027	22 20	088	46 00	147	59 41	223	35 22	286	31 59	309	47 05	336
132	39 19	026	23 09	088	46 26	148	59 07	224	34 35	286	31 20	308	46 45	335
133	39 40	025	23 58	087	46 52	148	58 33	224	33 47	285	30 41	307	46 24	334
134	40 00	024	24 47	086	47 18	148	57 58	225	33 00	284	30 02	306	46 01	332
	◆ REGULUS		SPICA		◆ ACRUX		CANOPUS		◆ RIGEL		BETELGEUSE		PROCYON	
135	40 20	022	25 36	086	47 44	148	57 24	225	32 12	284	29 22	305	45 38	331
136	40 38	021	26 25	085	48 10	148	56 49	225	31 24	283	28 41	304	45 14	330
137	40 55	020	27 14	085	48 36	149	56 14	226	30 36	282	28 00	303	44 48	328
138	41 11	019	28 03	084	49 02	149	55 39	226	29 48	282	27 19	303	44 22	327
139	41 27	017	28 52	083	49 27	149	55 03	226	29 00	281	26 37	302	43 55	326
140	41 41	016	29 41	083	49 52	149	54 28	226	28 12	280	25 56	301	43 27	325
141	41 54	015	30 30	082	50 17	150	53 52	227	27 23	280	25 13	300	42 58	323
142	42 06	014	31 18	082	50 42	150	53 17	227	26 35	279	24 31	299	42 28	322
143	42 17	012	32 07	081	51 07	150	52 41	227	25 46	278	23 48	299	41 58	321
144	42 27	011	32 55	080	51 31	150	52 05	227	24 57	278	23 04	298	41 26	320
145	42 36	010	33 44	080	51 55	151	51 29	227	24 09	277	22 21	297	40 54	319
146	42 44	008	34 32	079	52 19	151	50 53	227	23 20	276	21 37	297	40 22	318
147	42 50	007	35 20	078	52 42	151	50 17	227	22 31	276	20 53	296	39 48	317
148	42 56	006	36 08	077	53 06	152	49 40	227	21 42	275	20 09	295	39 14	316
149	43 00	004	36 56	077	53 29	152	49 04	228	20 53	275	19 24	294	38 39	315
	REGULUS		◆ Denebola		SPICA		◆ ACRUX		CANOPUS		◆ SIRIUS		PROCYON	
150	43 03	003	34 04	033	37 44	076	53 52	153	48 28	228	43 12	280	38 04	314
151	43 05	002	34 31	032	38 32	075	54 14	153	47 52	228	42 23	279	37 28	313
152	43 06	000	34 56	031	39 19	075	54 36	154	47 15	228	41 35	279	36 52	312
153	43 06	359	35 20	029	40 06	074	54 58	154	46 39	228	40 46	278	36 15	311
154	43 05	358	35 44	028	40 53	073	55 19	155	46 02	228	39 57	277	35 37	310
155	43 02	356	36 07	027	41 40	072	55 40	155	45 26	228	39 09	277	34 59	309
156	42 59	355	36 29	026	42 27	071	56 01	156	44 50	228	38 20	276	34 20	308
157	42 54	354	36 50	025	43 14	071	56 21	156	44 13	228	37 31	275	33 41	307
158	42 48	352	37 11	024	44 00	070	56 40	157	43 37	228	36 42	275	33 02	306
159	42 41	351	37 30	023	44 46	069	57 00	157	43 01	228	35 53	274	32 21	305
160	42 32	350	37 49	022	45 32	068	57 18	158	42 25	227	35 04	274	31 41	304
161	42 23	348	38 06	020	46 17	067	57 37	158	41 48	227	34 15	273	31 00	303
162	42 13	347	38 23	019	47 02	066	57 55	159	41 12	227	33 26	272	30 19	302
163	42 01	346	38 39	018	47 47	065	58 12	160	40 36	227	32 37	272	29 37	302
164	41 49	345	38 53	017	48 31	064	58 29	160	40 00	227	31 47	271	28 55	301
	ARCTURUS		◆ ANTARES		ACRUX		◆ CANOPUS		SIRIUS		PROCYON		◆ REGULUS	
165	18 37	049	20 30	109	58 45	161	39 24	227	30 58	271	28 13	300	41 35	343
166	19 14	048	21 17	108	59 00	162	38 48	227	30 09	270	27 30	299	41 20	342
167	19 50	047	22 04	108	59 15	163	38 12	227	29 20	269	26 47	298	41 05	341
168	20 26	047	22 51	107	59 30	163	37 36	227	28 31	269	26 04	298	40 48	340
169	21 01	046	23 38	107	59 44	164	37 01	227	27 42	268	25 20	297	40 30	338
170	21 36	045	24 25	106	59 57	165	36 25	226	26 53	268	24 36	296	40 12	337
171	22 11	044	25 12	106	60 09	166	35 50	226	26 04	267	23 52	295	39 52	336
172	22 45	043	25 59	105	60 21	166	35 14	226	25 14	267	23 07	295	39 31	335
173	23 18	043	26 47	105	60 32	167	34 39	226	24 25	266	22 23	294	39 10	333
174	23 51	042	27 34	104	60 43	168	34 04	226	23 36	266	21 38	293	38 48	332
175	24 24	041	28 22	104	60 52	169	33 29	225	22 47	265	20 52	293	38 24	331
176	24 56	040	29 10	103	61 01	170	32 54	225	21 58	264	20 07	292	38 00	330
177	25 27	039	29 58	103	61 10	171	32 19	225	21 10	264	19 21	291	37 35	329
178	25 58	038	30 46	102	61 17	172	31 44	225	20 21	263	18 35	291	37 09	328
179	26 28	037	31 34	102	61 24	173	31 09	225	19 32	263	17 49	290	36 43	327

 LAT 35°S

LHA ♈	Hc	Zn	Hc	Zn	Hc	Zn	Hc	Zn	Hc	Zn	Hc	Zn	Hc	Zn
	◆ ARCTURUS		ANTARES		◆ RIGIL KENT		ACRUX		CANOPUS		◆ Alphard		REGULUS	
180	26 57	036	32 22	102	53 40	148	61 30	174	30 35	224	46 32	298	36 16	326
181	27 26	036	33 10	101	54 06	148	61 35	174	30 01	224	45 48	297	35 47	325
182	27 55	035	33 58	101	54 32	149	61 39	175	29 26	224	45 04	296	35 19	324
183	28 22	034	34 46	100	54 57	149	61 43	176	28 52	224	44 20	295	34 49	323
184	28 49	033	35 35	100	55 22	150	61 46	177	28 19	223	43 35	294	34 19	321
185	29 15	032	36 23	099	55 47	150	61 48	178	27 45	223	42 50	293	33 48	320
186	29 41	031	37 12	099	56 11	151	61 49	179	27 11	223	42 05	293	33 16	319
187	30 06	030	38 01	098	56 35	151	61 49	180	26 38	223	41 20	292	32 44	319
188	30 30	029	38 49	098	56 59	152	61 49	181	26 05	222	40 34	291	32 11	318
189	30 53	028	39 38	097	57 22	152	61 47	182	25 32	222	39 48	290	31 38	317
190	31 16	027	40 27	097	57 45	153	61 45	183	24 59	222	39 01	289	31 04	316
191	31 37	026	41 16	096	58 07	153	61 42	184	24 26	222	38 15	288	30 29	315
192	31 58	025	42 04	096	58 29	154	61 38	185	23 54	221	37 28	288	29 54	314
193	32 18	024	42 53	095	58 50	155	61 34	186	23 21	221	36 41	287	29 18	313
194	32 38	023	43 42	095	59 11	155	61 28	187	22 49	221	35 54	286	28 42	312
	ARCTURUS		◆ ANTARES		RIGIL KENT		◆ ACRUX		Suhail		REGULUS		◆ Denebola	
195	32 56	022	44 31	094	59 31	156	61 22	188	45 18	241	28 05	311	37 47	338
196	33 14	021	45 20	094	59 51	157	61 15	189	44 36	241	27 28	310	37 29	337
197	33 31	019	46 09	093	60 10	157	61 08	189	43 53	241	26 50	310	37 09	336
198	33 47	018	46 58	093	60 29	158	60 59	190	43 10	240	26 12	309	36 49	335
199	34 02	017	47 48	092	60 47	159	60 50	191	42 27	240	25 34	308	36 27	334
200	34 16	016	48 37	092	61 04	160	60 40	192	41 45	240	24 55	307	36 05	333
201	34 29	015	49 26	091	61 21	161	60 29	193	41 02	240	24 15	306	35 42	332
202	34 41	014	50 15	091	61 37	161	60 18	194	40 20	239	23 35	305	35 18	330
203	34 53	013	51 04	090	61 52	162	60 06	195	39 38	239	22 55	305	34 54	329
204	35 03	012	51 53	089	62 07	163	59 53	195	38 55	239	22 14	304	34 28	328
205	35 13	011	52 42	089	62 20	164	59 40	196	38 13	239	21 33	303	34 02	327
206	35 21	009	53 32	088	62 34	165	59 26	197	37 31	239	20 52	302	33 35	326
207	35 29	008	54 21	088	62 46	166	59 11	198	36 49	238	20 11	302	33 08	325
208	35 35	007	55 10	087	62 57	167	58 56	198	36 08	238	19 29	301	32 39	324
209	35 41	006	55 59	086	63 08	168	58 40	199	35 26	238	18 46	300	32 10	323
	◆ ARCTURUS		Rasalhague		◆ Nunki		RIGIL KENT		ACRUX		◆ Suhail		SPICA	
210	35 45	005	20 16	057	27 07	104	63 18	169	58 24	200	34 45	238	65 01	340
211	35 49	004	20 57	056	27 55	104	63 27	170	58 07	200	34 03	237	64 43	338
212	35 52	002	21 38	056	28 42	103	63 35	171	57 50	201	33 22	237	64 24	336
213	35 53	001	22 18	055	29 30	103	63 42	172	57 32	202	32 41	237	64 02	333
214	35 54	000	22 58	054	30 18	103	63 48	173	57 13	202	32 00	236	63 40	331
215	35 53	359	23 38	053	31 06	102	63 54	174	56 54	203	31 19	236	63 15	329
216	35 52	358	24 17	053	31 54	102	63 58	175	56 35	204	30 38	236	62 50	327
217	35 49	357	24 56	052	32 42	101	64 01	176	56 15	204	29 57	236	62 22	326
218	35 46	355	25 35	051	33 31	101	64 04	178	55 55	205	29 17	235	61 54	324
219	35 42	354	26 13	050	34 19	100	64 06	179	55 34	205	28 37	235	61 24	322
220	35 36	353	26 50	049	35 07	100	64 06	180	55 13	206	27 57	235	60 53	320
221	35 30	352	27 27	048	35 56	099	64 06	181	54 52	206	27 17	234	60 21	319
222	35 23	351	28 04	048	36 44	099	64 05	182	54 30	207	26 37	234	59 48	317
223	35 14	350	28 40	047	37 33	098	64 02	183	54 08	207	25 57	234	59 14	315
224	35 05	349	29 15	046	38 22	098	63 59	184	53 45	207	25 18	233	58 39	314
	Alphecca		Rasalhague		◆ Nunki		Peacock		◆ RIGIL KENT		SPICA		◆ ARCTURUS	
225	27 46	009	29 50	045	39 10	097	32 58	140	63 55	185	58 03	312	34 55	347
226	27 53	008	30 25	044	39 59	097	33 30	139	63 50	186	57 27	311	34 43	346
227	28 00	007	30 59	043	40 48	096	34 02	139	63 44	188	56 49	309	34 31	345
228	28 05	006	31 32	042	41 37	096	34 34	139	63 37	189	56 11	308	34 18	344
229	28 10	005	32 05	041	42 26	095	35 06	139	63 29	190	55 32	307	34 04	343
230	28 14	004	32 37	040	43 15	095	35 39	139	63 21	191	54 52	306	33 49	342
231	28 17	003	33 08	039	44 04	094	36 11	139	63 11	192	54 12	304	33 34	341
232	28 19	002	33 39	038	44 53	094	36 44	139	63 01	193	53 31	303	33 17	340
233	28 20	001	34 09	037	45 42	093	37 16	139	62 50	194	52 50	302	32 59	339
234	28 20	000	34 39	036	46 31	093	37 49	138	62 38	195	52 08	301	32 41	338
235	28 20	359	35 07	035	47 20	092	38 21	138	62 25	196	51 25	300	32 22	336
236	28 18	358	35 35	034	48 09	092	38 54	138	62 11	197	50 42	299	32 02	335
237	28 16	357	36 03	033	48 58	091	39 27	138	61 57	197	49 59	298	31 41	334
238	28 13	356	36 29	032	49 48	091	40 00	138	61 42	198	49 15	297	31 19	333
239	28 08	355	36 55	031	50 37	090	40 32	138	61 26	199	48 31	296	30 57	332
	Rasalhague		ALTAIR		◆ Nunki		Peacock		◆ RIGIL KENT		SPICA		◆ ARCTURUS	
240	37 20	030	19 58	063	51 26	089	41 05	138	61 09	200	47 47	295	30 34	331
241	37 44	029	20 42	062	52 15	089	41 38	138	60 52	201	47 02	294	30 10	330
242	38 07	028	21 25	061	53 04	088	42 11	138	60 34	202	46 17	293	29 45	329
243	38 29	026	22 08	061	53 53	088	42 44	138	60 16	202	45 31	292	29 20	328
244	38 50	025	22 51	060	54 42	087	43 17	138	59 57	203	44 45	291	28 54	327
245	39 11	024	23 33	059	55 31	086	43 50	138	59 37	204	44 00	290	28 27	326
246	39 31	023	24 15	058	56 20	086	44 23	138	59 17	205	43 13	289	27 59	326
247	39 49	022	24 57	058	57 09	085	44 56	138	58 57	205	42 27	289	27 31	325
248	40 07	020	25 38	057	57 58	084	45 29	138	58 35	206	41 40	288	27 02	324
249	40 24	019	26 19	056	58 47	084	46 02	138	58 14	206	40 53	287	26 33	323
250	40 39	018	27 00	055	59 36	083	46 35	138	57 52	207	40 06	286	26 03	322
251	40 54	017	27 40	055	60 25	082	47 07	138	57 29	208	39 19	285	25 32	321
252	41 08	016	28 20	054	61 13	081	47 40	138	57 06	208	38 31	285	25 01	320
253	41 20	014	28 59	053	62 02	080	48 13	138	56 43	209	37 44	284	24 29	319
254	41 32	013	29 38	052	62 50	080	48 45	138	56 19	209	36 56	283	23 57	318
	VEGA		◆ ALTAIR		FOMALHAUT		◆ Peacock		RIGIL KENT		◆ SPICA		ARCTURUS	
255	12 50	019	30 17	051	16 43	115	49 18	139	55 55	210	36 08	283	23 24	318
256	13 06	018	30 55	050	17 27	114	49 50	139	55 30	210	35 20	282	22 51	317
257	13 21	018	31 32	049	18 12	114	50 23	139	55 05	211	34 32	281	22 17	316
258	13 36	017	32 09	048	18 57	113	50 55	139	54 40	211	33 43	280	21 42	315
259	13 50	016	32 46	048	19 43	113	51 27	139	54 15	211	32 55	280	21 08	314
260	14 04	015	33 22	047	20 28	112	51 59	140	53 49	212	32 07	279	20 32	314
261	14 16	015	33 57	046	21 13	112	52 31	140	53 23	212	31 18	278	19 56	313
262	14 28	014	34 32	045	21 59	111	53 03	140	52 56	213	30 29	278	19 20	312
263	14 40	013	35 06	044	22 45	111	53 34	140	52 30	213	29 41	277	18 43	311
264	14 51	012	35 40	043	23 31	111	54 05	141	52 03	213	28 52	277	18 06	310
265	15 01	012	36 13	042	24 17	110	54 36	141	51 36	214	28 03	276	17 29	310
266	15 10	011	36 45	041	25 03	110	55 07	141	51 09	214	27 14	275	16 51	309
267	15 19	010	37 17	040	25 49	109	55 38	142	50 41	214	26 25	275	16 12	308
268	15 27	009	37 48	039	26 36	109	56 08	142	50 14	214	25 36	274	15 33	308
269	15 35	008	38 18	037	27 22	108	56 39	142	49 46	215	24 47	274	14 54	307

LHA ♈	Hc	Zn	Hc	Zn	Hc	Zn	Hc	Zn	Hc	Zn	Hc	Zn	Hc	Zn
	VEGA		ALTAIR		◆ FOMALHAUT		ACHERNAR		◆ RIGIL KENT		ANTARES		◆ Rasalhague	
270	15 42	008	38 48	036	28 09	108	17 17	149	49 18	215	68 59	288	42 06	352
271	15 48	007	39 16	035	28 56	107	17 43	149	48 50	215	68 12	287	41 59	351
272	15 53	006	39 44	034	29 43	107	18 09	148	48 22	215	67 25	285	41 50	349
273	15 58	005	40 11	033	30 30	107	18 35	148	47 53	215	66 38	284	41 40	348
274	16 02	004	40 38	032	31 17	106	19 01	148	47 25	215	65 50	283	41 30	347
275	16 05	004	41 03	031	32 04	106	19 28	147	46 56	216	65 02	282	41 18	346
276	16 08	003	41 28	029	32 52	105	19 54	147	46 27	216	64 14	281	41 05	344
277	16 10	002	41 52	028	33 39	105	20 21	147	45 59	216	63 26	281	40 51	343
278	16 11	001	42 14	027	34 27	104	20 49	146	45 30	216	62 37	280	40 36	342
279	16 12	000	42 36	026	35 14	104	21 16	146	45 01	216	61 49	279	40 21	341
280	16 12	359	42 57	024	36 02	104	21 44	146	44 32	216	61 00	278	40 04	339
281	16 11	359	43 17	023	36 50	103	22 12	145	44 03	216	60 11	277	39 46	338
282	16 10	358	43 36	022	37 38	103	22 40	145	43 34	216	59 23	277	39 27	337
283	16 07	357	43 54	021	38 26	102	23 08	145	43 05	216	58 34	276	39 07	336
284	16 05	356	44 10	019	39 14	102	23 36	144	42 36	216	57 45	275	38 47	335
	ALTAIR		Enif		◆ FOMALHAUT		ACHERNAR		◆ RIGIL KENT		ANTARES		◆ Rasalhague	
285	44 26	018	30 31	049	40 02	101	24 05	144	42 07	216	56 56	274	38 25	333
286	44 41	017	31 08	048	40 50	101	24 34	144	41 37	216	56 07	274	38 03	332
287	44 54	015	31 44	047	41 39	101	25 03	144	41 08	216	55 18	273	37 39	331
288	45 07	014	32 20	046	42 27	100	25 32	143	40 39	216	54 29	273	37 15	330
289	45 18	013	32 55	045	43 15	100	26 02	143	40 10	216	53 40	272	36 50	329
290	45 28	011	33 29	044	44 04	099	26 31	143	39 41	216	52 51	271	36 24	328
291	45 37	010	34 03	043	44 52	099	27 01	143	39 11	216	52 01	271	35 58	327
292	45 44	008	34 37	042	45 41	098	27 31	142	38 42	216	51 12	270	35 30	326
293	45 51	007	35 10	041	46 30	098	28 01	142	38 13	216	50 23	270	35 02	325
294	45 56	006	35 42	040	47 18	097	28 31	142	37 44	216	49 34	269	34 33	324
295	46 00	004	36 13	039	48 07	097	29 02	142	37 15	216	48 45	268	34 04	323
296	46 03	003	36 44	038	48 56	096	29 32	141	36 46	216	47 56	268	33 33	322
297	46 05	001	37 14	037	49 45	096	30 03	141	36 17	216	47 07	267	33 02	321
298	46 05	000	37 43	036	50 34	096	30 34	141	35 48	216	46 18	267	32 31	320
299	46 05	358	38 12	035	51 23	095	31 05	141	35 20	216	45 28	266	31 59	319
	Enif		◆ FOMALHAUT		ACHERNAR		◆ RIGIL KENT		ANTARES		Rasalhague		◆ ALTAIR	
300	38 40	034	52 12	095	31 36	141	34 51	216	44 39	266	31 26	318	46 03	357
301	39 07	033	53 01	094	32 07	140	34 22	216	43 50	265	30 52	317	46 00	356
302	39 33	032	53 50	094	32 38	140	33 54	215	43 01	265	30 18	316	45 55	354
303	39 58	030	54 39	093	33 10	140	33 25	215	42 13	264	29 44	315	45 49	353
304	40 23	029	55 28	093	33 41	140	32 57	215	41 24	264	29 09	314	45 43	351
305	40 46	028	56 17	092	34 13	140	32 29	215	40 35	263	28 33	313	45 35	350
306	41 09	027	57 06	091	34 45	140	32 01	215	39 46	263	27 57	312	45 25	349
307	41 31	026	57 55	091	35 17	140	31 32	215	38 57	262	27 20	311	45 15	347
308	41 52	024	58 44	090	35 49	139	31 05	215	38 09	262	26 43	311	45 04	346
309	42 11	023	59 33	090	36 21	139	30 37	214	37 20	261	26 06	310	44 51	344
310	42 30	022	60 23	089	36 53	139	30 09	214	36 31	261	25 28	309	44 37	343
311	42 48	021	61 12	089	37 25	139	29 41	214	35 43	260	24 49	308	44 22	342
312	43 05	019	62 01	088	37 57	139	29 14	214	34 54	260	24 10	307	44 06	340
313	43 21	018	62 50	087	38 29	139	28 47	214	34 06	259	23 31	306	43 49	339
314	43 35	017	63 39	087	39 02	139	28 19	213	33 18	259	22 51	306	43 31	338
	Alpheratz		◆ Diphda		ACHERNAR		◆ RIGIL KENT		ANTARES		Rasalhague		◆ ALTAIR	
315	11 52	041	37 41	086	39 34	139	27 52	213	32 30	259	22 11	305	43 12	336
316	12 24	040	38 30	086	40 06	139	27 26	213	31 42	258	21 30	304	42 52	335
317	12 55	040	39 19	085	40 39	139	26 59	213	30 53	258	20 50	303	42 31	334
318	13 26	039	40 08	084	41 11	139	26 32	213	30 06	257	20 08	303	42 09	333
319	13 57	038	40 57	084	41 44	139	26 06	212	29 18	257	19 27	302	41 46	331
320	14 27	037	41 45	083	42 16	139	25 40	212	28 30	256	18 45	301	41 22	330
321	14 56	037	42 34	082	42 49	139	25 14	212	27 42	256	18 03	300	40 57	329
322	15 25	036	43 23	082	43 22	139	24 48	212	26 55	255	17 20	300	40 32	328
323	15 54	035	44 11	081	43 54	139	24 22	211	26 07	255	16 37	299	40 05	327
324	16 22	034	45 00	080	44 27	139	23 57	211	25 20	254	15 54	298	39 38	326
325	16 49	034	45 48	080	44 59	139	23 31	211	24 33	254	15 11	298	39 09	324
326	17 16	033	46 37	079	45 32	139	23 06	211	23 45	253	14 27	297	38 41	323
327	17 43	032	47 25	078	46 04	139	22 41	210	22 58	253	13 43	296	38 11	322
328	18 08	031	48 13	077	46 36	139	22 17	210	22 11	252	12 59	296	37 40	321
329	18 34	030	49 01	076	47 09	139	21 52	210	21 25	252	12 15	295	37 09	320
	◆ Alpheratz		Diphda		◆ ACHERNAR		Peacock		◆ Nunki		ALTAIR		Enif	
330	18 58	030	49 48	076	47 41	139	63 12	209	49 52	270	36 37	319	44 55	355
331	19 22	029	50 36	075	48 13	139	62 48	210	49 03	269	36 05	318	44 50	353
332	19 45	028	51 23	074	48 45	139	62 23	210	48 14	268	35 32	317	44 44	352
333	20 08	027	52 10	073	49 17	139	61 58	211	47 25	268	34 58	316	44 36	351
334	20 30	026	52 57	072	49 49	140	61 32	212	46 36	267	34 24	315	44 27	349
335	20 51	025	53 44	071	50 21	140	61 06	213	45 47	267	33 49	314	44 18	348
336	21 12	025	54 30	070	50 53	140	60 39	213	44 58	266	33 13	313	44 07	347
337	21 32	024	55 17	069	51 25	140	60 12	214	44 09	266	32 37	312	43 55	345
338	21 52	023	56 02	068	51 56	140	59 45	214	43 20	265	32 00	311	43 42	344
339	22 10	022	56 48	067	52 27	141	59 17	215	42 31	265	31 23	310	43 28	343
340	22 28	021	57 33	066	52 59	141	58 48	216	41 42	264	30 46	310	43 12	341
341	22 45	020	58 18	065	53 30	141	58 19	216	40 53	264	30 07	309	42 56	340
342	23 02	019	59 02	064	54 00	141	57 50	217	40 04	263	29 29	308	42 39	339
343	23 18	018	59 46	063	54 31	142	57 21	217	39 15	263	28 50	307	42 20	337
344	23 33	017	60 30	062	55 01	142	56 51	217	38 27	262	28 10	306	42 01	336
	Alpheratz		◆ Hamal		◆ ACHERNAR		Peacock		◆ Nunki		ALTAIR		Enif	
345	23 47	016	16 27	044	55 31	142	56 21	218	37 38	262	27 30	305	41 40	335
346	24 01	016	17 01	044	56 01	143	55 51	218	36 49	261	26 50	304	41 19	334
347	24 14	015	17 35	043	56 31	143	55 20	219	36 01	261	26 09	304	40 57	332
348	24 26	014	18 08	042	57 00	144	54 49	219	35 12	260	25 28	303	40 34	331
349	24 37	013	18 41	041	57 29	144	54 18	219	34 24	260	24 47	302	40 10	330
350	24 47	012	19 13	041	57 58	145	53 47	220	33 35	259	24 05	301	39 45	329
351	24 57	011	19 44	040	58 26	145	53 16	220	32 47	259	23 23	301	39 19	328
352	25 06	010	20 16	039	58 54	146	52 44	220	31 59	258	22 40	300	38 52	327
353	25 14	009	20 46	038	59 22	146	52 12	220	31 11	258	21 58	299	38 25	326
354	25 21	008	21 16	037	59 49	147	51 40	221	30 23	258	21 14	298	37 57	324
355	25 28	007	21 46	036	60 16	147	51 08	221	29 35	257	20 31	298	37 28	323
356	25 33	006	22 15	036	60 42	148	50 36	221	28 47	257	19 47	297	36 58	322
357	25 38	005	22 43	035	61 08	149	50 04	221	27 59	256	19 03	296	36 27	321
358	25 42	004	23 11	034	61 33	149	49 31	221	27 12	256	18 19	296	35 56	320
359	25 45	003	23 38	033	61 58	150	48 59	221	26 24	255	17 35	295	35 24	319

 LAT 36°S

LHA ♈	Hc Zn	Hc Zn	Hc Zn	Hc Zn	Hc Zn	Hc Zn	Hc Zn
	Alpheratz	◆Hamal	RIGEL	◆CANOPUS	Peacock	◆Nunki	Enif
0	24 47 002	23 13 032	13 50 090	24 34 139	49 11 222	25 52 255	34 07 319
1	24 49 001	23 39 031	14 38 090	25 06 138	48 38 222	25 05 255	33 35 318
2	24 50 000	24 03 030	15 27 089	25 39 138	48 05 223	24 18 254	33 02 317
3	24 49 359	24 27 029	16 15 088	26 11 138	47 33 223	23 32 254	32 28 316
4	24 48 358	24 51 028	17 04 088	26 44 137	47 00 223	22 45 253	31 54 315
5	24 47 357	25 13 027	17 52 087	27 17 137	46 27 223	21 59 253	31 19 314
6	24 44 356	25 35 026	18 41 087	27 50 137	45 54 223	21 13 252	30 44 313
7	24 41 355	25 57 026	19 29 086	28 24 136	45 21 223	20 26 252	30 08 312
8	24 36 355	26 17 025	20 18 085	28 57 136	44 48 223	19 40 251	29 32 311
9	24 31 354	26 37 024	21 06 085	29 31 136	44 15 223	18 55 251	28 55 310
10	24 25 353	26 56 023	21 54 084	30 05 136	43 42 223	18 09 250	28 17 309
11	24 19 352	27 15 022	22 43 083	30 39 135	43 09 223	17 23 250	27 40 308
12	24 11 351	27 32 021	23 31 083	31 13 135	42 36 223	16 38 249	27 01 308
13	24 03 350	27 49 020	24 19 082	31 47 135	42 03 223	15 52 249	26 23 307
14	23 54 349	28 05 019	25 07 082	32 22 135	41 30 223	15 07 248	25 44 306
	◆Hamal	ALDEBARAN	RIGEL	◆CANOPUS	Peacock	◆FOMALHAUT	Alpheratz
15	28 20 018	16 39 054	25 55 081	32 56 135	40 58 223	63 46 275	23 44 348
16	28 34 017	17 18 054	26 43 080	33 31 134	40 25 222	62 58 275	23 34 347
17	28 48 016	17 57 053	27 31 080	34 06 134	39 52 222	62 09 274	23 22 346
18	29 01 015	18 35 052	28 18 079	34 40 134	39 19 222	61 21 273	23 10 345
19	29 13 014	19 13 051	29 06 078	35 16 134	38 47 222	60 32 273	22 57 344
20	29 24 013	19 51 050	29 53 078	35 51 133	38 14 222	59 44 272	22 44 343
21	29 34 012	20 28 050	30 41 077	36 26 133	37 42 222	58 55 271	22 30 342
22	29 43 011	21 05 049	31 28 076	37 01 133	37 09 222	58 07 271	22 14 341
23	29 52 010	21 41 048	32 15 076	37 37 133	36 37 222	57 18 270	21 59 341
24	29 59 008	22 17 047	33 02 075	38 12 133	36 05 222	56 30 270	21 42 340
25	30 06 007	22 52 046	33 49 074	38 48 133	35 33 221	55 41 269	21 25 339
26	30 12 006	23 27 046	34 35 073	39 24 133	35 01 221	54 53 268	21 07 338
27	30 17 005	24 02 045	35 22 073	40 00 132	34 29 221	54 04 268	20 48 337
28	30 21 004	24 36 044	36 08 072	40 35 132	33 57 221	53 16 267	20 29 336
29	30 24 003	25 09 043	36 54 071	41 11 132	33 25 221	52 27 267	20 09 335
	Hamal	◆ALDEBARAN	RIGEL	SIRIUS	◆CANOPUS	Peacock	◆FOMALHAUT
30	30 26 002	25 42 042	37 40 070	24 34 093	41 47 132	32 54 221	51 39 266
31	30 28 001	26 15 041	38 25 069	25 22 093	42 24 132	32 22 220	50 50 266
32	30 28 000	26 46 040	39 11 069	26 11 092	43 00 132	31 51 220	50 02 265
33	30 28 359	27 18 040	39 56 068	26 59 092	43 36 132	31 20 220	49 14 265
34	30 26 358	27 48 039	40 40 067	27 48 091	44 12 132	30 49 220	48 25 264
35	30 24 357	28 18 038	41 25 066	28 36 091	44 48 132	30 18 219	47 37 264
36	30 21 356	28 48 037	42 09 065	29 25 090	45 25 132	29 47 219	46 49 263
37	30 17 355	29 16 036	42 53 064	30 13 089	46 01 132	29 16 219	46 01 263
38	30 12 354	29 44 035	43 37 063	31 02 089	46 37 132	28 46 219	45 12 262
39	30 06 353	30 12 034	44 20 062	31 51 088	47 14 132	28 15 219	44 24 262
40	29 59 352	30 39 033	45 03 061	32 39 088	47 50 131	27 45 218	43 36 261
41	29 52 350	31 05 032	45 45 060	33 28 087	48 26 132	27 15 218	42 48 261
42	29 43 349	31 30 031	46 27 059	34 16 086	49 03 132	26 45 218	42 00 260
43	29 34 348	31 55 030	47 09 058	35 04 086	49 39 132	26 16 217	41 13 260
44	29 24 347	32 18 029	47 50 057	35 53 085	50 15 132	25 46 217	40 25 260
	◆ALDEBARAN	RIGEL	SIRIUS	◆CANOPUS	ACHERNAR	◆FOMALHAUT	Hamal
45	32 41 028	48 30 056	36 41 084	50 52 132	64 49 206	39 37 259	29 13 346
46	33 04 027	49 10 055	37 29 084	51 28 132	64 27 207	38 50 259	29 01 345
47	33 25 026	49 50 054	38 18 083	52 04 132	64 05 208	38 02 258	28 48 344
48	33 46 025	50 29 053	39 06 082	52 40 132	63 41 209	37 14 258	28 35 343
49	34 06 024	51 07 052	39 54 082	53 16 132	63 17 210	36 27 257	28 20 342
50	34 25 022	51 45 050	40 42 081	53 52 132	62 53 211	35 40 257	28 05 341
51	34 43 021	52 22 049	41 30 080	54 28 132	62 28 211	34 53 256	27 49 340
52	35 00 020	52 58 048	42 18 080	55 04 133	62 02 212	34 05 256	27 32 339
53	35 16 019	53 34 047	43 05 079	55 40 133	61 36 213	33 18 255	27 15 338
54	35 32 018	54 09 045	43 53 078	56 15 133	61 09 214	32 32 255	26 56 337
55	35 46 017	54 43 044	44 40 077	56 50 133	60 42 214	31 45 255	26 37 336
56	36 00 016	55 16 042	45 28 077	57 26 134	60 15 215	30 58 254	26 18 335
57	36 13 015	55 48 041	46 15 076	58 01 134	59 47 215	30 11 254	25 57 334
58	36 24 013	56 20 039	47 02 075	58 36 134	59 19 216	29 25 253	25 36 334
59	36 35 012	56 50 038	47 49 074	59 10 135	58 50 216	28 38 253	25 14 333
	ALDEBARAN	◆BETELGEUSE	SIRIUS	◆ACRUX	ACHERNAR	◆FOMALHAUT	Hamal
60	36 45 011	38 45 038	48 35 073	17 48 158	58 21 217	27 52 252	24 51 332
61	36 54 010	39 14 037	49 22 073	18 06 157	57 52 217	27 06 252	24 28 331
62	37 01 009	39 43 036	50 08 072	18 25 157	57 23 218	26 20 251	24 04 330
63	37 08 007	40 11 035	50 54 071	18 44 157	56 53 218	25 34 251	23 39 329
64	37 14 006	40 39 034	51 39 070	19 03 156	56 23 218	24 48 250	23 14 328
65	37 19 005	41 05 032	52 25 069	19 23 156	55 52 219	24 03 250	22 48 327
66	37 22 004	41 30 031	53 10 068	19 43 156	55 22 219	23 17 249	22 21 326
67	37 25 003	41 55 030	53 55 067	20 03 155	54 51 219	22 32 249	21 54 325
68	37 27 001	42 19 029	54 39 066	20 23 155	54 20 220	21 46 249	21 26 325
69	37 28 000	42 42 027	55 23 065	20 44 155	53 49 220	21 01 248	20 58 324
70	37 27 359	43 04 026	56 07 064	21 05 154	53 18 220	20 16 248	20 29 323
71	37 26 358	43 25 025	56 50 063	21 26 154	52 46 220	19 32 247	19 59 322
72	37 24 357	43 45 024	57 33 061	21 47 154	52 15 221	18 47 247	19 29 321
73	37 20 355	44 04 022	58 16 060	22 09 154	51 43 221	18 02 246	18 58 321
74	37 16 354	44 22 021	58 57 059	22 30 153	51 11 221	17 18 246	18 27 320
	BETELGEUSE	◆SIRIUS	Suhail	◆ACRUX	ACHERNAR	◆Diphda	ALDEBARAN
75	44 38 020	59 39 058	42 45 119	22 52 153	50 39 221	31 17 270	37 11 353
76	44 54 018	60 19 056	43 28 119	23 14 153	50 07 221	30 28 269	37 04 352
77	45 09 017	60 59 055	44 10 119	23 37 152	49 35 222	29 40 269	36 57 351
78	45 23 016	61 39 053	44 53 118	23 59 152	49 03 222	28 51 268	36 48 349
79	45 35 014	62 17 052	45 36 118	24 22 152	48 30 222	28 03 268	36 39 348
80	45 46 013	62 55 050	46 18 118	24 45 152	47 58 222	27 14 267	36 29 347
81	45 57 011	63 32 049	47 01 118	25 08 151	47 26 222	26 26 266	36 17 346
82	46 06 010	64 08 047	47 44 118	25 32 151	46 53 222	25 37 266	36 05 345
83	46 14 009	64 43 045	48 27 118	25 55 151	46 21 222	24 49 265	35 52 344
84	46 20 007	65 17 043	49 10 117	26 19 151	45 48 222	24 01 265	35 38 342
85	46 26 006	65 49 041	49 53 117	26 43 150	45 16 222	23 12 264	35 22 341
86	46 30 004	66 21 039	50 36 117	27 07 150	44 43 222	22 24 264	35 06 340
87	46 33 003	66 51 037	51 20 117	27 31 150	44 11 222	21 36 263	34 50 339
88	46 35 001	67 20 035	52 03 117	27 56 150	43 38 222	20 48 262	34 32 338
89	46 35 000	67 47 033	52 46 117	28 20 149	43 06 222	20 00 262	34 13 337

LHA ♈	Hc Zn	Hc Zn	Hc Zn	Hc Zn	Hc Zn	Hc Zn	Hc Zn
	PROCYON	REGULUS	◆Suhail	ACRUX	◆ACHERNAR	RIGEL	◆BETELGEUSE
90	42 36 035	14 18 063	53 30 117	28 45 149	42 33 222	60 22 337	46 35 359
91	43 04 034	15 01 063	54 13 117	29 10 149	42 01 222	60 03 335	46 33 357
92	43 30 032	15 44 062	54 56 116	29 35 149	41 28 222	59 42 333	46 30 356
93	43 56 031	16 27 061	55 40 116	30 00 149	40 56 222	59 19 332	46 26 354
94	44 21 030	17 09 061	56 23 116	30 25 148	40 23 222	58 56 330	46 20 353
95	44 44 029	17 51 060	57 07 116	30 51 148	39 51 222	58 31 328	46 14 351
96	45 07 027	18 33 059	57 50 116	31 16 148	39 19 222	58 04 326	46 06 350
97	45 29 026	19 15 058	58 34 116	31 42 148	38 47 222	57 37 325	45 57 349
98	45 50 025	19 56 058	59 18 116	32 08 148	38 14 221	57 08 323	45 46 347
99	46 10 023	20 37 057	60 01 116	32 34 148	37 42 221	56 39 322	45 35 346
100	46 28 022	21 17 056	60 45 116	33 00 148	37 10 221	56 08 320	45 23 344
101	46 46 021	21 57 055	61 28 116	33 26 147	36 38 221	55 36 319	45 09 343
102	47 03 019	22 37 055	62 11 116	33 52 147	36 07 221	55 04 317	44 54 342
103	47 18 018	23 17 054	62 55 117	34 18 147	35 35 221	54 30 316	44 38 340
104	47 32 016	23 56 053	63 38 117	34 45 147	35 03 221	53 56 314	44 21 339
	PROCYON	REGULUS	◆Gienah	ACRUX	◆ACHERNAR	RIGEL	◆BETELGEUSE
105	47 45 015	24 34 052	18 51 098	35 11 147	34 32 220	53 21 313	44 03 338
106	47 57 013	25 12 051	19 39 098	35 38 147	34 00 220	52 45 312	43 44 336
107	48 08 012	25 50 051	20 27 097	36 04 147	33 29 220	52 08 310	43 24 335
108	48 17 011	26 27 050	21 16 097	36 31 147	32 58 220	51 31 309	43 04 334
109	48 26 009	27 04 049	22 04 096	36 58 146	32 26 220	50 53 308	42 42 333
110	48 33 008	27 41 048	22 52 096	37 25 146	31 55 220	50 14 307	42 19 331
111	48 39 006	28 16 047	23 40 095	37 52 146	31 25 219	49 35 306	41 55 330
112	48 43 005	28 52 046	24 29 095	38 18 146	30 54 219	48 56 304	41 30 329
113	48 46 003	29 27 045	25 17 094	38 45 146	30 23 219	48 15 303	41 05 328
114	48 48 002	30 01 044	26 06 093	39 12 146	29 53 219	47 34 302	40 38 326
115	48 49 000	30 34 044	26 54 093	39 39 146	29 23 218	46 53 301	40 11 325
116	48 48 359	31 08 043	27 43 092	40 06 146	28 52 218	46 11 300	39 43 324
117	48 46 357	31 40 042	28 31 092	40 34 146	28 22 218	45 29 299	39 14 323
118	48 43 356	32 12 041	29 20 091	41 01 146	27 53 218	44 47 298	38 45 322
119	48 39 354	32 43 040	30 08 091	41 28 146	27 23 218	44 04 297	38 14 321
	REGULUS	◆SPICA	ACRUX	◆CANOPUS	RIGEL	BETELGEUSE	◆PROCYON
120	33 14 039	13 25 094	41 55 146	66 18 218	43 20 296	37 43 320	48 33 352
121	33 44 038	14 13 094	42 22 146	65 48 219	42 37 295	37 12 319	48 26 351
122	34 13 037	15 01 093	42 49 146	65 18 219	41 53 295	36 39 318	48 18 350
123	34 42 036	15 50 093	43 16 146	64 47 220	41 08 294	36 06 317	48 08 348
124	35 10 035	16 38 092	43 43 146	64 15 221	40 24 293	35 33 316	47 58 347
125	35 37 034	17 27 091	44 10 146	63 43 221	39 39 292	34 59 315	47 46 345
126	36 04 032	18 15 091	44 37 146	63 11 222	38 54 291	34 24 314	47 33 344
127	36 29 031	19 04 090	45 03 146	62 38 223	38 08 290	33 48 313	47 19 342
128	36 54 030	19 53 090	45 30 147	62 05 223	37 23 289	33 12 312	47 03 341
129	37 18 029	20 41 089	45 57 147	61 32 224	36 37 289	32 36 311	46 47 339
130	37 41 028	21 30 088	46 24 147	60 58 224	35 51 288	31 59 310	46 29 338
131	38 04 027	22 18 088	46 50 147	60 24 225	35 05 287	31 21 309	46 10 337
132	38 25 026	23 07 087	47 17 147	59 50 225	34 18 286	30 43 308	45 51 335
133	38 46 024	23 55 087	47 43 147	59 15 225	33 31 286	30 05 307	45 30 334
134	39 05 023	24 44 086	48 09 147	58 41 226	32 45 285	29 26 306	45 08 333
	◆REGULUS	SPICA	◆ACRUX	CANOPUS	◆RIGEL	BETELGEUSE	PROCYON
135	39 24 022	25 32 085	48 35 148	58 06 226	31 58 284	28 47 306	44 45 331
136	39 42 021	26 20 085	49 01 148	57 31 226	31 10 284	28 07 305	44 22 330
137	39 59 020	27 09 084	49 27 148	56 56 227	30 23 283	27 27 304	43 57 329
138	40 14 018	27 57 084	49 53 148	56 20 227	29 36 282	26 47 303	43 31 328
139	40 29 017	28 45 083	50 18 148	55 45 227	28 48 281	26 06 302	43 05 326
140	40 43 016	29 33 082	50 44 149	55 09 227	28 01 281	25 24 301	42 38 325
141	40 56 015	30 21 082	51 09 149	54 33 228	27 13 280	24 43 301	42 09 324
142	41 08 013	31 09 081	51 34 149	53 57 228	26 25 279	24 01 300	41 40 323
143	41 19 012	31 57 080	51 58 150	53 21 228	25 37 279	23 19 299	41 11 322
144	41 28 011	32 45 080	52 23 150	52 45 228	24 49 278	22 36 298	40 40 320
145	41 37 010	33 33 079	52 47 150	52 09 228	24 01 278	21 53 298	40 09 319
146	41 44 008	34 20 078	53 11 150	51 33 228	23 13 277	21 10 297	39 37 318
147	41 51 007	35 08 077	53 35 151	50 57 228	22 25 276	20 27 296	39 04 317
148	41 56 006	35 55 077	53 59 151	50 21 228	21 36 276	19 43 295	38 31 316
149	42 00 004	36 42 076	54 22 152	49 44 228	20 48 275	18 59 295	37 57 315
	REGULUS	◆SPICA	ACRUX	◆Miaplacidus	CANOPUS	SIRIUS	◆PROCYON
150	42 03 003	37 29 075	54 45 152	55 38 187	49 08 228	43 01 281	37 23 314
151	42 05 002	38 16 075	55 07 152	55 32 188	48 32 228	42 13 280	36 47 313
152	42 06 000	39 03 074	55 30 153	55 25 188	47 55 228	41 25 280	36 12 312
153	42 06 359	39 49 073	55 51 153	55 18 189	47 19 228	40 37 279	35 35 311
154	42 05 358	40 36 072	56 13 154	55 10 189	46 43 228	39 49 278	34 58 310
155	42 02 356	41 22 071	56 34 154	55 02 190	46 06 228	39 01 278	34 21 309
156	41 59 355	42 08 071	56 55 155	54 53 191	45 30 228	38 13 277	33 43 308
157	41 54 354	42 53 070	57 15 155	54 44 191	44 54 228	37 25 276	33 05 307
158	41 48 352	43 39 069	57 35 156	54 35 192	44 17 228	36 37 276	32 26 306
159	41 41 351	44 24 068	57 55 157	54 25 192	43 41 228	35 48 275	31 47 306
160	41 33 350	45 09 067	58 14 157	54 14 193	43 05 228	35 00 274	31 07 305
161	41 24 349	45 53 066	58 32 158	54 03 193	42 29 228	34 11 274	30 27 304
162	41 14 347	46 38 065	58 50 158	53 52 194	41 53 228	33 23 273	29 46 303
163	41 03 346	47 21 064	59 08 159	53 41 194	41 17 228	32 34 272	29 06 302
164	40 51 345	48 05 063	59 25 160	53 29 195	40 41 228	31 46 272	28 24 301
	ARCTURUS	◆ANTARES	ACRUX	◆CANOPUS	SIRIUS	PROCYON	◆REGULUS
165	17 57 049	20 49 108	59 41 161	40 05 228	30 57 271	27 43 301	40 38 344
166	18 34 048	21 35 108	59 57 161	39 29 228	30 09 271	27 01 300	40 23 342
167	19 09 047	22 22 107	60 13 162	38 53 227	29 20 270	26 18 299	40 08 341
168	19 45 046	23 08 107	60 27 163	38 17 227	28 32 269	25 36 298	39 52 340
169	20 20 046	23 55 106	60 41 164	37 42 227	27 43 269	24 53 297	39 35 339
170	20 54 045	24 41 106	60 55 164	37 06 227	26 55 268	24 09 297	39 16 337
171	21 28 044	25 28 105	61 07 165	36 31 227	26 06 268	23 26 296	38 57 336
172	22 01 043	26 15 105	61 19 166	35 56 227	25 18 267	22 42 295	38 37 335
173	22 34 042	27 02 104	61 31 167	35 21 226	24 29 267	21 58 294	38 16 334
174	23 07 041	27 49 104	61 41 168	34 45 226	23 41 266	21 14 294	37 54 333
175	23 38 041	28 36 103	61 51 169	34 11 226	22 52 265	20 29 293	37 32 332
176	24 10 040	29 23 103	62 01 170	33 36 226	22 04 265	19 44 292	37 08 330
177	24 40 039	30 11 102	62 09 170	33 01 226	21 16 264	18 59 292	36 44 329
178	25 11 038	30 58 102	62 17 171	32 26 225	20 27 264	18 14 291	36 19 328
179	25 40 037	31 46 101	62 23 172	31 52 225	19 39 263	17 29 290	35 53 327

LAT 36°S

LHA ♈	Hc	Zn	Hc	Zn	Hc	Zn	Hc	Zn	Hc	Zn	Hc	Zn	Hc	Zn
	ARCTURUS		◆ANTARES		RIGIL KENT		ACRUX		◆CANOPUS		Alphard		◆REGULUS	
180	26 09	036	32 33	101	54 31	147	62 30	173	31 18	225	46 03	299	35 26	326
181	26 37	035	33 21	100	54 57	148	62 35	174	30 44	225	45 21	298	34 58	325
182	27 05	034	34 09	100	55 23	148	62 39	175	30 10	224	44 37	297	34 30	324
183	27 32	033	34 57	099	55 49	148	62 43	176	29 36	224	43 54	296	34 01	323
184	27 58	032	35 45	099	56 14	149	62 46	177	29 02	224	43 10	295	33 32	322
185	28 24	031	36 33	098	56 39	149	62 48	178	28 28	224	42 26	294	33 01	321
186	28 49	031	37 21	098	57 03	150	62 49	179	27 55	223	41 42	293	32 30	320
187	29 13	030	38 09	097	57 27	150	62 49	180	27 22	223	40 57	292	31 59	319
188	29 37	029	38 57	097	57 51	151	62 49	181	26 49	223	40 12	292	31 27	318
189	30 00	028	39 45	096	58 15	151	62 47	182	26 16	222	39 27	291	30 54	317
190	30 22	027	40 33	096	58 38	152	62 45	183	25 43	222	38 41	290	30 21	316
191	30 43	026	41 22	095	59 00	153	62 42	184	25 11	222	37 56	289	29 47	315
192	31 04	025	42 10	095	59 22	153	62 38	185	24 39	222	37 10	288	29 12	314
193	31 24	023	42 58	094	59 44	154	62 33	186	24 06	221	36 23	288	28 37	313
194	31 42	022	43 47	094	60 05	155	62 28	187	23 35	221	35 37	287	28 02	312
	ARCTURUS		◆ANTARES		RIGIL KENT		◆ACRUX		Suhail		◆REGULUS		Denebola	
195	32 01	021	44 35	093	60 26	155	62 22	188	45 47	242	27 25	312	36 51	339
196	32 18	020	45 24	093	60 46	156	62 15	189	45 05	242	26 49	311	36 33	337
197	32 34	019	46 12	092	61 05	157	62 07	190	44 22	241	26 12	310	36 14	336
198	32 50	018	47 01	092	61 24	157	61 58	191	43 39	241	25 34	309	35 54	335
199	33 04	017	47 49	091	61 43	158	61 49	192	42 57	241	24 57	308	35 33	334
200	33 18	016	48 38	090	62 00	159	61 39	192	42 14	241	24 18	307	35 12	333
201	33 31	015	49 26	090	62 17	160	61 28	193	41 32	240	23 39	307	34 49	332
202	33 43	014	50 15	089	62 33	161	61 16	194	40 50	240	23 00	306	34 26	331
203	33 54	013	51 03	089	62 49	162	61 04	195	40 08	240	22 21	305	34 02	330
204	34 04	012	51 52	088	63 04	163	60 51	196	39 26	240	21 41	304	33 37	329
205	34 14	010	52 40	087	63 18	164	60 37	197	38 44	239	21 01	303	33 12	328
206	34 22	009	53 29	087	63 31	165	60 23	197	38 02	239	20 20	303	32 45	327
207	34 29	008	54 17	086	63 44	166	60 08	198	37 21	239	19 39	302	32 18	326
208	34 36	007	55 06	085	63 56	167	59 53	199	36 39	239	18 58	301	31 50	325
209	34 41	006	55 54	085	64 07	168	59 37	200	35 58	238	18 16	301	31 22	324
	ARCTURUS		◆ANTARES		Peacock		RIGIL KENT		◆ACRUX		Suhail		◆SPICA	
210	34 46	005	56 42	084	26 04	143	64 17	169	59 20	200	35 16	238	64 04	341
211	34 49	004	57 31	083	26 33	142	64 26	170	59 03	201	34 35	238	63 47	338
212	34 52	002	58 19	083	27 03	142	64 34	171	58 46	202	33 54	238	63 29	336
213	34 53	001	59 07	082	27 33	142	64 41	172	58 27	202	33 13	237	63 08	334
214	34 54	000	59 55	081	28 03	142	64 48	173	58 09	203	32 33	237	62 47	332
215	34 53	359	60 43	080	28 33	141	64 53	174	57 49	204	31 52	237	62 23	330
216	34 52	358	61 31	079	29 04	141	64 58	175	57 30	204	31 12	236	61 59	328
217	34 50	357	62 18	079	29 34	141	65 01	176	57 10	205	30 31	236	61 33	327
218	34 46	355	63 06	078	30 05	141	65 04	178	56 49	205	29 51	236	61 05	325
219	34 42	354	63 53	077	30 36	140	65 06	179	56 28	206	29 11	235	60 37	323
220	34 37	353	64 40	076	31 07	140	65 06	180	56 07	206	28 31	235	60 07	321
221	34 30	352	65 27	075	31 38	140	65 06	181	55 45	207	27 52	235	59 36	320
222	34 23	351	66 14	074	32 09	140	65 05	182	55 23	207	27 12	234	59 04	318
223	34 15	350	67 00	072	32 41	140	65 02	183	55 01	208	26 33	234	58 31	316
224	34 06	349	67 46	071	33 12	139	64 59	184	54 38	208	25 54	234	57 57	315
	Alphecca		Rasalhague		◆Nunki		Peacock		◆RIGIL KENT		◆SPICA		ARCTURUS	
225	26 47	009	29 08	045	39 18	096	33 44	139	64 55	186	57 23	313	33 56	348
226	26 54	008	29 42	044	40 06	096	34 16	139	64 50	187	56 47	312	33 45	346
227	27 00	007	30 15	043	40 54	095	34 48	139	64 44	188	56 11	311	33 33	345
228	27 06	006	30 47	042	41 43	095	35 19	139	64 36	189	55 33	309	33 21	344
229	27 10	005	31 19	041	42 31	094	35 52	139	64 29	190	54 55	308	33 07	343
230	27 14	004	31 51	040	43 19	094	36 24	138	64 20	191	54 17	307	32 52	342
231	27 17	003	32 22	039	44 08	093	36 56	138	64 10	192	53 38	305	32 37	341
232	27 19	002	32 52	038	44 56	093	37 28	138	63 59	193	52 58	304	32 21	340
233	27 20	001	33 21	037	45 45	092	38 01	138	63 48	194	52 17	303	32 04	339
234	27 20	000	33 50	036	46 33	092	38 33	138	63 36	195	51 36	302	31 46	338
235	27 20	359	34 18	035	47 22	091	39 06	138	63 22	196	50 55	301	31 27	337
236	27 18	358	34 46	034	48 10	091	39 39	138	63 09	197	50 13	300	31 07	336
237	27 16	357	35 12	033	48 59	090	40 11	138	62 54	198	49 31	299	30 47	335
238	27 13	356	35 38	032	49 47	089	40 44	138	62 39	199	48 48	298	30 26	334
239	27 09	355	36 03	031	50 36	089	41 17	137	62 22	200	48 05	297	30 04	333
	Rasalhague		ALTAIR		◆Nunki		Peacock		◆RIGIL KENT		SPICA		◆ARCTURUS	
240	36 27	029	19 31	063	51 25	088	41 50	137	62 06	201	47 21	296	29 41	332
241	36 51	028	20 13	062	52 13	087	42 23	137	61 48	201	46 37	295	29 18	331
242	37 13	027	20 56	061	53 01	087	42 56	137	61 30	202	45 53	294	28 53	330
243	37 35	026	21 38	060	53 50	086	43 28	137	61 11	203	45 08	293	28 29	329
244	37 56	025	22 21	060	54 38	086	44 01	137	60 52	204	44 23	292	28 03	328
245	38 16	024	23 02	059	55 27	085	44 34	137	60 32	205	43 38	291	27 37	327
246	38 35	023	23 44	058	56 15	084	45 07	137	60 12	205	42 53	290	27 10	326
247	38 53	021	24 25	057	57 03	083	45 40	137	59 51	206	42 07	289	26 42	325
248	39 11	020	25 05	057	57 51	083	46 13	137	59 29	207	41 21	289	26 14	324
249	39 27	019	25 46	056	58 40	082	46 46	137	59 07	207	40 35	288	25 45	323
250	39 42	018	26 26	055	59 28	081	47 19	137	58 45	208	39 49	287	25 16	322
251	39 57	017	27 05	054	60 15	080	47 52	137	58 22	208	39 02	286	24 46	321
252	40 10	015	27 44	053	61 03	079	48 25	138	57 59	209	38 16	285	24 15	320
253	40 22	014	28 23	052	61 51	079	48 57	138	57 35	209	37 29	285	23 44	320
254	40 33	013	29 01	052	62 38	078	49 30	138	57 11	210	36 42	284	23 12	319
	Rasalhague		◆ALTAIR		FOMALHAUT		◆ACHERNAR		RIGIL KENT		◆SPICA		ARCTURUS	
255	40 44	012	29 39	051	17 08	114	12 23	155	56 47	210	35 55	283	22 40	318
256	40 53	010	30 16	050	17 52	114	12 44	154	56 22	211	35 07	283	22 07	317
257	41 01	009	30 53	049	18 36	113	13 05	154	55 57	211	34 20	282	21 34	316
258	41 08	008	31 29	048	19 21	113	13 27	153	55 31	212	33 32	281	21 00	315
259	41 14	006	32 05	047	20 06	113	13 48	153	55 05	212	32 45	280	20 26	315
260	41 19	005	32 40	046	20 51	112	14 11	153	54 39	213	31 57	280	19 51	314
261	41 22	004	33 15	045	21 36	112	14 33	152	54 13	213	31 09	279	19 15	313
262	41 25	002	33 49	044	22 21	111	14 56	152	53 47	213	30 21	278	18 40	312
263	41 27	001	34 23	043	23 06	111	15 19	151	53 20	214	29 33	278	18 04	311
264	41 27	000	34 56	042	23 52	110	15 43	151	52 53	214	28 45	277	17 27	311
265	41 26	359	35 28	041	24 37	110	16 06	151	52 26	214	27 57	276	16 50	310
266	41 25	357	36 00	040	25 23	109	16 30	150	51 58	215	27 08	276	16 13	309
267	41 22	356	36 31	039	26 09	109	16 54	150	51 31	215	26 20	275	15 35	309
268	41 18	355	37 01	038	26 55	108	17 19	149	51 03	215	25 32	275	14 57	308
269	41 13	353	37 30	037	27 41	108	17 44	149	50 35	215	24 43	274	14 18	307

LHA ♈	Hc	Zn	Hc	Zn	Hc	Zn	Hc	Zn	Hc	Zn	Hc	Zn	Hc	Zn
	ALTAIR		Enif		◆FOMALHAUT		ACHERNAR		◆RIGIL KENT		ANTARES		◆Rasalhague	
270	37 59	036	19 58	061	28 27	107	18 09	149	50 07	215	68 40	290	41 07	352
271	38 27	035	20 40	060	29 14	107	18 34	148	49 39	216	67 54	289	40 59	351
272	38 55	034	21 22	059	30 00	107	19 00	148	49 10	216	67 08	288	40 51	350
273	39 21	033	22 03	058	30 47	106	19 26	148	48 42	216	66 22	287	40 42	348
274	39 47	031	22 44	058	31 34	106	19 52	147	48 13	216	65 35	286	40 31	347
275	40 12	030	23 25	057	32 20	105	20 18	147	47 45	216	64 48	284	40 20	346
276	40 36	029	24 06	056	33 07	105	20 45	147	47 16	216	64 01	283	40 07	344
277	40 59	028	24 46	055	33 54	104	21 11	146	46 47	216	63 14	283	39 54	343
278	41 21	027	25 25	054	34 41	104	21 38	146	46 18	217	62 26	282	39 39	342
279	41 42	025	26 05	054	35 29	103	22 06	146	45 49	217	61 39	281	39 24	341
280	42 02	024	26 44	053	36 16	103	22 33	145	45 20	217	60 51	280	39 08	340
281	42 22	023	27 22	052	37 03	102	23 01	145	44 51	217	60 03	279	38 50	338
282	42 40	022	28 00	051	37 51	102	23 29	145	44 22	217	59 15	278	38 32	337
283	42 57	020	28 38	050	38 38	102	23 57	144	43 53	217	58 27	277	38 13	336
284	43 14	019	29 15	049	39 26	101	24 25	144	43 24	217	57 39	277	37 52	335
	ALTAIR		Enif		◆FOMALHAUT		ACHERNAR		◆RIGIL KENT		ANTARES		◆Rasalhague	
285	43 29	018	29 51	048	40 13	101	24 54	144	42 55	217	56 50	276	37 31	334
286	43 43	016	30 27	048	41 01	100	25 22	144	42 25	217	56 02	275	37 09	333
287	43 56	015	31 03	047	41 49	100	25 51	143	41 56	217	55 14	275	36 47	331
288	44 08	014	31 38	046	42 37	099	26 20	143	41 27	217	54 25	274	36 23	330
289	44 19	012	32 12	045	43 25	099	26 50	143	40 58	217	53 37	273	35 59	329
290	44 29	011	32 46	044	44 13	098	27 19	143	40 29	217	52 48	273	35 33	328
291	44 38	010	33 20	043	45 01	098	27 49	142	40 00	217	52 00	272	35 07	327
292	44 45	008	33 52	042	45 49	097	28 18	142	39 31	217	51 11	271	34 41	326
293	44 51	007	34 24	041	46 37	097	28 48	142	39 02	217	50 23	271	34 13	325
294	44 57	005	34 56	040	47 25	096	29 18	142	38 32	217	49 34	270	33 45	324
295	45 01	004	35 27	039	48 14	096	29 49	141	38 04	217	48 46	270	33 16	323
296	45 03	003	35 57	038	49 02	095	30 19	141	37 35	217	47 57	269	32 46	322
297	45 05	001	36 26	037	49 50	095	30 50	141	37 06	216	47 09	268	32 16	321
298	45 05	000	36 55	036	50 39	094	31 20	141	36 37	216	46 20	268	31 45	320
299	45 05	358	37 23	035	51 27	094	31 51	140	36 08	216	45 32	267	31 14	319
	Enif		◆FOMALHAUT		ACHERNAR		◆RIGIL KENT		ANTARES		◆Rasalhague		ALTAIR	
300	37 50	033	52 16	093	32 22	140	35 40	216	44 43	267	30 41	318	45 03	357
301	38 16	032	53 04	093	32 53	140	35 11	216	43 55	266	30 09	317	45 00	356
302	38 42	031	53 53	092	33 25	140	34 43	216	43 06	266	29 35	316	44 55	354
303	39 06	030	54 41	092	33 56	140	34 14	216	42 18	265	29 01	315	44 50	353
304	39 30	029	55 30	091	34 27	140	33 46	216	41 30	265	28 27	314	44 43	351
305	39 53	028	56 18	091	34 59	139	33 18	215	40 41	264	27 52	313	44 36	350
306	40 15	027	57 07	090	35 30	139	32 50	215	39 53	264	27 17	313	44 27	349
307	40 37	025	57 55	089	36 02	139	32 22	215	39 05	263	26 41	312	44 17	347
308	40 57	024	58 44	089	36 34	139	31 54	215	38 17	263	26 04	311	44 05	346
309	41 16	023	59 32	088	37 06	139	31 26	215	37 29	262	25 27	310	43 53	345
310	41 34	022	60 21	087	37 38	139	30 58	215	36 41	262	24 50	309	43 40	343
311	41 52	020	61 09	087	38 10	139	30 31	214	35 53	261	24 12	308	43 25	342
312	42 08	019	61 58	086	38 42	138	30 04	214	35 05	261	23 34	308	43 10	341
313	42 24	018	62 46	085	39 14	138	29 36	214	34 17	260	22 55	307	42 53	339
314	42 38	016	63 35	085	39 47	138	29 09	214	33 29	260	22 16	306	42 36	338
	Enif		◆Diphda		ACHERNAR		◆RIGIL KENT		ANTARES		Nunki		◆ALTAIR	
315	42 51	015	37 36	085	40 19	138	28 43	214	32 41	259	61 56	282	42 17	337
316	43 03	014	38 25	085	40 51	138	28 16	213	31 54	259	61 08	281	41 57	336
317	43 14	013	39 13	084	41 24	138	27 49	213	31 06	258	60 20	280	41 37	334
318	43 24	011	40 01	083	41 56	138	27 23	213	30 19	258	59 32	279	41 15	333
319	43 33	010	40 50	083	42 29	138	26 57	213	29 31	257	58 44	278	40 53	332
320	43 41	009	41 38	082	43 01	138	26 30	212	28 44	257	57 56	277	40 30	331
321	43 48	007	42 26	081	43 34	138	26 05	212	27 57	256	57 08	277	40 06	330
322	43 53	006	43 14	081	44 06	138	25 39	212	27 10	256	56 20	276	39 41	328
323	43 57	004	44 01	080	44 39	138	25 13	212	26 23	255	55 31	275	39 15	327
324	44 00	003	44 49	079	45 11	138	24 48	211	25 36	255	54 43	275	38 48	326
325	44 02	002	45 37	079	45 44	138	24 23	211	24 49	254	53 55	274	38 20	325
326	44 03	000	46 24	078	46 16	138	23 58	211	24 02	254	53 06	273	37 52	324
327	44 03	359	47 12	077	46 49	138	23 33	211	23 16	253	52 18	273	37 23	323
328	44 02	358	47 59	076	47 21	138	23 09	210	22 29	253	51 29	272	36 53	322
329	43 59	356	48 46	075	47 54	138	22 44	210	21 43	252	50 41	271	36 23	321
	◆Alpheratz		Diphda		◆ACHERNAR		RIGIL KENT		◆Nunki		ALTAIR		Enif	
330	18 06	029	49 33	075	48 26	138	22 20	210	49 52	271	35 52	320	43 55	355
331	18 29	029	50 20	074	48 58	138	21 56	209	49 04	270	35 20	319	43 50	353
332	18 52	028	51 06	073	49 31	138	21 32	209	48 15	270	34 48	318	43 44	352
333	19 15	027	51 52	072	50 03	139	21 09	209	47 27	269	34 15	317	43 37	351
334	19 36	026	52 38	071	50 35	139	20 46	208	46 38	268	33 41	316	43 29	349
335	19 57	025	53 24	070	51 07	139	20 23	208	45 50	268	33 07	315	43 19	348
336	20 18	024	54 10	069	51 39	139	20 00	208	45 01	267	32 32	314	43 08	347
337	20 37	023	54 55	068	52 10	139	19 38	207	44 13	267	31 56	313	42 57	345
338	20 56	023	55 40	067	52 42	139	19 15	207	43 24	266	31 21	312	42 44	344
339	21 15	022	56 24	066	53 13	140	18 53	207	42 36	266	30 44	311	42 30	343
340	21 32	021	57 08	065	53 45	140	18 32	206	41 47	265	30 07	310	42 15	342
341	21 49	020	57 52	064	54 16	140	18 10	206	40 59	265	29 30	309	42 00	340
342	22 05	019	58 35	063	54 47	140	17 49	206	40 11	264	28 52	308	41 43	339
343	22 21	018	59 18	061	55 18	141	17 28	205	39 22	264	28 14	307	41 25	338
344	22 36	017	60 01	060	55 48	141	17 07	205	38 34	263	27 35	307	41 06	336
	◆Alpheratz		Diphda		◆CANOPUS		RIGIL KENT		◆Nunki		ALTAIR		Enif	
345	22 50	016	60 42	059	16 56	144	16 47	205	37 46	263	26 56	306	40 46	335
346	23 03	015	61 24	057	17 25	143	16 27	204	36 58	262	26 16	305	40 25	334
347	23 15	015	62 04	056	17 54	143	16 07	204	36 10	262	25 36	304	40 04	333
348	23 27	014	62 44	055	18 24	143	15 48	204	35 22	261	24 55	303	39 41	332
349	23 38	013	63 23	053	18 53	142	15 28	203	34 34	261	24 15	302	39 17	330
350	23 49	012	64 02	051	19 23	142	15 09	203	33 46	260	23 34	302	38 53	329
351	23 58	011	64 39	050	19 53	142	14 51	202	32 58	260	22 52	301	38 28	328
352	24 07	010	65 16	048	20 23	141	14 32	202	32 11	259	22 10	300	38 02	327
353	24 15	009	65 51	046	20 54	141	14 14	202	31 23	259	21 28	299	37 35	326
354	24 22	008	66 26	044	21 25	140	13 57	201	30 35	258	20 46	299	37 08	325
355	24 28	007	66 59	042	21 56	140	13 39	201	29 48	258	20 03	298	36 39	324
356	24 34	006	67 31	040	22 27	140	13 22	200	29 01	257	19 20	297	36 10	323
357	24 38	005	68 02	038	22 58	139	13 06	200	28 13	257	18 37	297	35 40	322
358	24 42	004	68 31	036	23 30	139	12 49	200	27 26	256	17 53	296	35 10	321
359	24 45	003	68 59	034	24 02	139	12 33	199	26 39	256	17 09	295	34 39	320

LAT 37°S

LHA ♈	Hc	Zn	Hc	Zn	Hc	Zn	Hc	Zn	Hc	Zn	Hc	Zn	Hc	Zn
	Alpheratz		◆ Hamal		RIGEL		◆ CANOPUS		Peacock		◆ Nunki		Enif	
0	23 48	002	22 22	032	13 50	090	25 19	138	49 55	223	26 07	256	33 22	319
1	23 49	001	22 47	031	14 38	089	25 51	138	49 22	223	25 21	255	32 50	318
2	23 50	000	23 11	030	15 26	089	26 23	138	48 49	223	24 35	255	32 18	317
3	23 49	359	23 35	029	16 13	088	26 56	137	48 16	223	23 48	254	31 45	316
4	23 48	358	23 58	028	17 01	087	27 28	137	47 44	223	23 02	254	31 11	315
5	23 47	357	24 20	027	17 49	087	28 01	137	47 11	223	22 17	253	30 37	314
6	23 44	356	24 42	026	18 37	086	28 34	136	46 38	223	21 31	253	30 03	313
7	23 41	356	25 03	025	19 25	086	29 07	136	46 05	223	20 45	252	29 28	312
8	23 37	355	25 23	024	20 13	085	29 40	136	45 32	223	20 00	252	28 52	311
9	23 32	354	25 42	023	21 00	084	30 14	136	44 59	223	19 14	251	28 16	311
10	23 26	353	26 01	022	21 48	084	30 47	135	44 26	223	18 29	251	27 39	310
11	23 19	352	26 19	022	22 36	083	31 21	135	43 53	223	17 44	250	27 02	309
12	23 12	351	26 36	021	23 23	082	31 55	135	43 20	223	16 59	250	26 25	308
13	23 04	350	26 52	020	24 11	082	32 29	135	42 47	223	16 14	249	25 47	307
14	22 55	349	27 08	019	24 58	081	33 04	134	42 14	223	15 29	249	25 08	306
	◆ Hamal		ALDEBARAN		RIGEL		◆ CANOPUS		Peacock		◆ FOMALHAUT		Alpheratz	
15	27 23	018	16 03	054	25 45	080	33 38	134	41 42	223	63 39	277	22 46	348
16	27 37	017	16 42	053	26 32	080	34 12	134	41 09	223	62 52	277	22 35	347
17	27 50	016	17 20	053	27 20	079	34 47	134	40 36	223	62 04	276	22 24	346
18	28 03	015	17 58	052	28 07	078	35 22	133	40 04	223	61 16	275	22 12	345
19	28 14	014	18 35	051	28 53	078	35 57	133	39 31	223	60 29	274	22 00	344
20	28 25	013	19 12	050	29 40	077	36 32	133	38 59	223	59 41	274	21 46	343
21	28 35	011	19 49	049	30 27	076	37 07	133	38 26	222	58 53	273	21 32	342
22	28 44	010	20 25	049	31 13	076	37 42	133	37 54	222	58 05	272	21 18	342
23	28 53	009	21 01	048	32 00	075	38 17	132	37 22	222	57 17	272	21 02	341
24	29 00	008	21 36	047	32 46	074	38 53	132	36 50	222	56 29	271	20 46	340
25	29 06	007	22 11	046	33 32	073	39 28	132	36 18	222	55 41	271	20 29	339
26	29 12	006	22 45	045	34 18	073	40 04	132	35 46	222	54 54	270	20 11	338
27	29 17	005	23 19	045	35 03	072	40 40	132	35 14	222	54 06	269	19 53	337
28	29 21	004	23 53	044	35 49	071	41 16	132	34 42	221	53 18	269	19 34	336
29	29 24	003	24 25	043	36 34	070	41 51	131	34 11	221	52 30	268	19 15	335
	Hamal		◆ ALDEBARAN		RIGEL		SIRIUS		◆ CANOPUS		Peacock		◆ FOMALHAUT	
30	29 26	002	24 58	042	37 19	069	24 37	093	42 27	131	33 39	221	51 42	268
31	29 28	001	25 29	041	38 04	069	25 25	092	43 03	131	33 08	221	50 54	267
32	29 28	000	26 01	040	38 48	068	26 13	092	43 39	131	32 37	221	50 06	266
33	29 28	359	26 31	039	39 33	067	27 01	091	44 16	131	32 05	220	49 18	266
34	29 26	358	27 01	038	40 16	066	27 49	091	44 52	131	31 35	220	48 31	265
35	29 24	357	27 31	037	41 00	065	28 37	090	45 28	131	31 04	220	47 43	265
36	29 21	356	28 00	036	41 44	064	29 25	089	46 04	131	30 33	220	46 55	264
37	29 17	355	28 28	036	42 27	063	30 12	089	46 41	131	30 03	219	46 07	264
38	29 12	354	28 55	035	43 09	062	31 00	088	47 17	131	29 32	219	45 20	263
39	29 07	353	29 22	034	43 52	062	31 48	088	47 53	131	29 02	219	44 32	263
40	29 00	352	29 48	033	44 33	061	32 36	087	48 29	131	28 32	219	43 45	262
41	28 53	351	30 14	032	45 15	060	33 24	086	49 06	131	28 02	218	42 57	262
42	28 44	350	30 38	031	45 56	059	34 12	086	49 42	131	27 33	218	42 10	261
43	28 35	349	31 02	030	46 37	057	35 00	085	50 19	131	27 03	218	41 23	261
44	28 25	347	31 26	029	47 17	056	35 47	084	50 55	131	26 34	218	40 35	260
	◆ ALDEBARAN		RIGEL		SIRIUS		◆ CANOPUS		ACHERNAR		◆ FOMALHAUT		Hamal	
45	31 48	028	47 56	055	36 35	084	51 31	131	65 43	207	39 48	260	28 14	346
46	32 10	026	48 36	054	37 22	083	52 07	131	65 20	208	39 01	259	28 03	345
47	32 31	025	49 14	053	38 10	082	52 44	131	64 57	209	38 14	259	27 50	344
48	32 51	024	49 52	052	38 57	082	53 20	131	64 33	210	37 27	258	27 37	343
49	33 11	023	50 30	051	39 45	081	53 56	131	64 09	211	36 40	258	27 23	342
50	33 29	022	51 06	049	40 32	080	54 32	131	63 44	212	35 53	257	27 08	341
51	33 47	021	51 42	048	41 19	079	55 08	131	63 19	213	35 06	257	26 53	340
52	34 04	020	52 18	047	42 06	079	55 44	132	62 53	213	34 20	257	26 36	339
53	34 20	019	52 52	046	42 53	078	56 20	132	62 26	214	33 33	256	26 19	339
54	34 35	018	53 26	044	43 40	077	56 56	132	61 59	215	32 47	256	26 01	338
55	34 49	017	53 59	043	44 27	076	57 31	132	61 32	215	32 00	255	25 42	337
56	35 02	016	54 31	041	45 13	076	58 07	132	61 04	216	31 14	255	25 23	336
57	35 14	014	55 03	040	46 00	075	58 42	133	60 36	216	30 28	254	25 03	335
58	35 26	013	55 33	038	46 46	074	59 17	133	60 07	217	29 42	254	24 42	334
59	35 36	012	56 02	037	47 32	073	59 52	133	59 38	217	28 56	253	24 20	333
	ALDEBARAN		◆ BETELGEUSE		SIRIUS		◆ ACRUX		ACHERNAR		◆ FOMALHAUT		Hamal	
60	35 46	011	37 58	038	48 17	072	18 43	158	59 09	218	28 10	253	23 58	332
61	35 54	010	38 26	036	49 03	071	19 02	157	58 40	218	27 25	252	23 35	331
62	36 02	009	38 54	035	49 48	071	19 20	157	58 10	219	26 39	252	23 12	330
63	36 09	007	39 22	034	50 33	070	19 39	157	57 40	219	25 54	251	22 47	329
64	36 14	006	39 48	033	51 18	069	19 58	156	57 09	219	25 08	251	22 23	328
65	36 19	005	40 14	032	52 03	068	20 18	156	56 39	220	24 23	250	21 57	327
66	36 23	004	40 39	031	52 47	067	20 38	156	56 08	220	23 38	250	21 31	327
67	36 25	003	41 03	030	53 31	066	20 57	155	55 37	220	22 53	249	21 04	326
68	36 27	001	41 26	028	54 14	065	21 18	155	55 06	221	22 08	249	20 37	325
69	36 28	000	41 48	027	54 57	063	21 38	155	54 35	221	21 24	248	20 09	324
70	36 27	359	42 10	026	55 40	062	21 59	154	54 03	221	20 39	248	19 41	323
71	36 26	358	42 30	025	56 22	061	22 20	154	53 32	221	19 55	247	19 12	322
72	36 24	357	42 50	023	57 04	060	22 41	154	53 00	222	19 11	247	18 42	322
73	36 20	355	43 08	022	57 45	059	23 02	153	52 28	222	18 27	246	18 12	321
74	36 16	354	43 25	021	58 26	057	23 24	153	51 56	222	17 43	246	17 42	320
	BETELGEUSE		◆ SIRIUS		Suhail		◆ ACRUX		ACHERNAR		◆ Diphda		ALDEBARAN	
75	43 42	019	59 06	056	43 14	118	23 46	153	51 24	222	31 17	270	36 11	353
76	43 57	018	59 45	055	43 56	118	24 08	152	50 52	222	30 29	270	36 05	352
77	44 12	017	60 24	053	44 39	118	24 30	152	50 20	222	29 41	269	35 57	351
78	44 25	015	61 02	052	45 21	118	24 52	152	49 47	222	28 53	269	35 49	350
79	44 37	014	61 40	050	46 04	117	25 15	152	49 15	223	28 05	268	35 40	348
80	44 48	013	62 16	049	46 46	117	25 38	151	48 43	223	27 17	267	35 30	347
81	44 58	011	62 52	047	47 29	117	26 01	151	48 10	223	26 29	267	35 19	346
82	45 07	010	63 26	045	48 12	117	26 24	151	47 38	223	25 41	266	35 07	345
83	45 14	008	64 00	044	48 54	117	26 48	151	47 05	223	24 54	266	34 54	344
84	45 21	007	64 33	042	49 37	116	27 11	150	46 33	223	24 06	265	34 40	343
85	45 26	006	65 04	040	50 20	116	27 35	150	46 00	223	23 18	265	34 26	342
86	45 30	004	65 34	038	51 03	116	27 59	150	45 28	223	22 30	264	34 10	340
87	45 33	003	66 03	036	51 46	116	28 23	150	44 55	223	21 43	263	33 53	339
88	45 35	001	66 31	034	52 30	116	28 47	149	44 22	223	20 55	263	33 36	338
89	45 35	000	66 57	032	53 13	116	29 12	149	43 50	223	20 08	262	33 18	337

LHA ♈	Hc	Zn	Hc	Zn	Hc	Zn	Hc	Zn	Hc	Zn	Hc	Zn	Hc	Zn
	PROCYON		REGULUS		◆ Suhail		ACRUX		◆ ACHERNAR		RIGEL		◆ BETELGEUSE	
90	41 47	034	13 51	063	53 56	115	29 36	149	43 17	223	59 27	338	45 35	359
91	42 14	033	14 33	062	54 39	115	30 01	149	42 45	223	59 08	336	45 33	357
92	42 40	032	15 16	062	55 23	115	30 26	149	42 13	223	58 48	334	45 30	356
93	43 04	031	15 58	061	56 06	115	30 51	148	41 40	222	58 26	332	45 26	354
94	43 29	029	16 40	060	56 49	115	31 16	148	41 08	222	58 03	331	45 21	353
95	43 52	028	17 21	060	57 33	115	31 42	148	40 36	222	57 39	329	45 14	352
96	44 14	027	18 02	059	58 16	115	32 07	148	40 03	222	57 14	327	45 07	350
97	44 35	026	18 43	058	59 00	115	32 33	148	39 31	222	56 48	326	44 58	349
98	44 55	024	19 24	057	59 43	115	32 58	147	38 59	222	56 20	324	44 48	347
99	45 14	023	20 04	057	60 27	115	33 24	147	38 27	222	55 51	323	44 37	346
100	45 33	022	20 44	056	61 10	115	33 50	147	37 55	222	55 22	321	44 25	345
101	45 50	020	21 23	055	61 54	115	34 16	147	37 23	222	54 51	320	44 11	343
102	46 06	019	22 02	054	62 37	115	34 42	147	36 52	221	54 20	318	43 57	342
103	46 21	017	22 41	054	63 21	115	35 09	147	36 20	221	53 47	317	43 42	341
104	46 35	016	23 19	053	64 04	115	35 35	147	35 48	221	53 14	315	43 25	339
	PROCYON		REGULUS		◆ Gienah		ACRUX		◆ ACHERNAR		RIGEL		◆ BETELGEUSE	
105	46 47	015	23 57	052	19 00	098	36 01	146	35 17	221	52 40	314	43 08	338
106	46 59	013	24 35	051	19 47	098	36 28	146	34 46	221	52 05	313	42 49	337
107	47 09	012	25 12	050	20 35	097	36 54	146	34 14	221	51 29	311	42 30	335
108	47 18	010	25 48	049	21 23	096	37 21	146	33 43	220	50 53	310	42 10	334
109	47 26	009	26 25	049	22 10	096	37 48	146	33 12	220	50 16	309	41 48	333
110	47 33	007	27 00	048	22 58	095	38 15	146	32 42	220	49 38	308	41 26	332
111	47 39	006	27 35	047	23 46	095	38 41	146	32 11	220	49 00	307	41 03	330
112	47 43	004	28 10	046	24 33	094	39 08	146	31 40	220	48 21	305	40 39	329
113	47 46	003	28 44	045	25 21	094	39 35	146	31 10	219	47 42	304	40 14	328
114	47 48	002	29 18	044	26 09	093	40 02	146	30 40	219	47 02	303	39 48	327
115	47 49	000	29 51	043	26 57	092	40 29	146	30 09	219	46 22	302	39 22	326
116	47 48	359	30 23	042	27 45	092	40 56	146	29 39	219	45 41	301	38 54	325
117	47 46	357	30 55	041	28 33	091	41 23	146	29 10	218	45 00	300	38 26	324
118	47 43	356	31 26	040	29 21	091	41 50	146	28 40	218	44 18	299	37 57	322
119	47 39	354	31 57	039	30 09	090	42 17	146	28 11	218	43 36	298	37 28	321
	REGULUS		◆ SPICA		ACRUX		◆ CANOPUS		RIGEL		BETELGEUSE		◆ PROCYON	
120	32 27	038	13 29	094	42 44	146	67 05	219	42 53	297	36 57	320	47 34	353
121	32 56	037	14 17	093	43 11	146	66 35	220	42 11	296	36 26	319	47 27	351
122	33 25	036	15 05	093	43 39	146	66 04	221	41 27	295	35 55	318	47 19	350
123	33 53	035	15 52	092	44 06	146	65 32	221	40 44	294	35 23	317	47 10	348
124	34 20	034	16 40	092	44 33	146	65 00	222	40 00	294	34 50	316	46 59	347
125	34 47	033	17 28	091	45 00	146	64 28	223	39 16	293	34 16	315	46 48	345
126	35 13	032	18 16	090	45 26	146	63 55	223	38 32	292	33 42	314	46 35	344
127	35 38	031	19 04	090	45 53	146	63 22	224	37 47	291	33 07	313	46 21	343
128	36 02	030	19 52	089	46 20	146	62 48	225	37 02	290	32 32	312	46 07	341
129	36 26	029	20 40	089	46 47	146	62 15	225	36 17	289	31 56	311	45 51	340
130	36 48	028	21 28	088	47 14	146	61 41	225	35 32	289	31 20	310	45 33	338
131	37 10	026	22 16	087	47 40	146	61 06	226	34 46	288	30 43	309	45 15	337
132	37 31	025	23 04	087	48 07	146	60 32	226	34 01	287	30 06	309	44 56	336
133	37 51	024	23 51	086	48 33	147	59 57	227	33 15	286	29 29	308	44 36	334
134	38 10	023	24 39	086	49 00	147	59 22	227	32 29	286	28 50	307	44 15	333
	◆ REGULUS		SPICA		◆ ACRUX		CANOPUS		◆ RIGEL		BETELGEUSE		PROCYON	
135	38 28	022	25 27	085	49 26	147	58 47	227	31 43	285	28 12	306	43 53	332
136	38 46	021	26 15	084	49 52	147	58 12	228	30 56	284	27 33	305	43 30	331
137	39 02	019	27 02	084	50 18	147	57 36	228	30 10	283	26 53	304	43 06	329
138	39 18	018	27 50	083	50 44	148	57 01	228	29 23	283	26 14	303	42 41	328
139	39 32	017	28 37	082	51 09	148	56 25	228	28 36	282	25 33	303	42 15	327
140	39 45	016	29 25	082	51 35	148	55 49	228	27 49	281	24 53	302	41 48	326
141	39 58	014	30 12	081	52 00	148	55 13	229	27 02	281	24 12	301	41 21	324
142	40 09	013	30 59	080	52 25	149	54 37	229	26 15	280	23 31	300	40 53	323
143	40 20	012	31 47	080	52 50	149	54 01	229	25 28	279	22 49	299	40 24	322
144	40 29	011	32 34	079	53 15	149	53 25	229	24 40	279	22 07	299	39 54	321
145	40 38	009	33 21	078	53 39	149	52 49	229	23 53	278	21 25	298	39 23	320
146	40 45	008	34 08	078	54 03	150	52 13	229	23 06	277	20 43	297	38 52	319
147	40 51	007	34 54	077	54 27	150	51 36	229	22 18	277	20 00	296	38 20	318
148	40 56	006	35 41	076	54 51	151	51 00	229	21 30	276	19 17	296	37 48	317
149	41 01	004	36 27	075	55 14	151	50 24	229	20 43	275	18 34	295	37 14	316
	REGULUS		◆ SPICA		ACRUX		◆ Miaplacidus		CANOPUS		SIRIUS		◆ PROCYON	
150	41 04	003	37 14	075	55 38	151	56 37	187	49 47	229	42 49	282	36 41	315
151	41 05	002	38 00	074	56 00	152	56 31	188	49 11	229	42 02	281	36 06	314
152	41 06	000	38 46	073	56 23	152	56 24	188	48 35	229	41 15	280	35 31	313
153	41 06	359	39 31	072	56 45	153	56 17	189	47 58	229	40 28	280	34 56	312
154	41 05	358	40 17	071	57 07	153	56 09	190	47 22	229	39 40	279	34 20	311
155	41 02	356	41 02	071	57 28	154	56 01	190	46 46	229	38 53	278	33 43	310
156	40 59	355	41 47	070	57 49	154	55 52	191	46 09	229	38 05	278	33 06	309
157	40 54	354	42 32	069	58 10	155	55 43	191	45 33	229	37 18	277	32 28	308
158	40 49	353	43 17	068	58 30	155	55 33	192	44 57	229	36 30	276	31 50	307
159	40 42	351	44 01	067	58 50	156	55 23	192	44 21	229	35 43	276	31 12	306
160	40 34	350	44 45	066	59 09	157	55 13	193	43 45	229	34 55	275	30 33	305
161	40 26	349	45 29	065	59 28	157	55 02	193	43 09	229	34 07	274	29 53	304
162	40 16	348	46 12	064	59 46	158	54 50	194	42 33	229	33 19	274	29 14	303
163	40 05	346	46 55	063	60 04	159	54 39	194	41 57	229	32 32	273	28 33	303
164	39 53	345	47 38	062	60 21	159	54 27	195	41 21	228	31 44	272	27 53	302
	ARCTURUS		◆ ANTARES		ACRUX		◆ CANOPUS		SIRIUS		PROCYON		◆ REGULUS	
165	17 18	048	21 08	108	60 38	160	40 45	228	30 56	272	27 12	301	39 40	344
166	17 53	048	21 53	107	60 54	161	40 09	228	30 08	271	26 31	300	39 26	343
167	18 28	047	22 39	107	61 10	161	39 34	228	29 20	271	25 49	299	39 11	341
168	19 03	046	23 25	106	61 24	162	38 58	228	28 32	270	25 07	299	38 55	340
169	19 37	045	24 11	106	61 39	163	38 23	228	27 44	269	24 25	298	38 39	339
170	20 11	044	24 57	105	61 52	164	37 47	227	26 56	269	23 42	297	38 21	338
171	20 45	044	25 44	105	62 05	165	37 12	227	26 08	268	23 00	296	38 02	337
172	21 17	043	26 30	104	62 18	166	36 37	227	25 20	268	22 16	296	37 43	335
173	21 50	042	27 16	104	62 29	166	36 02	227	24 33	267	21 33	295	37 22	334
174	22 21	041	28 03	103	62 40	167	35 27	227	23 45	266	20 49	294	37 01	333
175	22 53	040	28 50	103	62 50	168	34 52	226	22 57	266	20 06	293	36 39	332
176	23 23	039	29 37	102	62 59	169	34 17	226	22 09	265	19 21	293	36 16	331
177	23 54	039	30 23	102	63 08	170	33 43	226	21 21	265	18 37	292	35 52	330
178	24 23	038	31 10	101	63 16	171	33 08	226	20 34	264	17 53	291	35 27	329
179	24 52	037	31 57	101	63 23	172	32 34	226	19 46	264	17 08	291	35 02	328

LHA ♈	ARCTURUS Hc	Zn	◆ANTARES Hc	Zn	RIGIL KENT Hc	Zn	ACRUX Hc	Zn	◆CANOPUS Hc	Zn	Alphard Hc	Zn	◆REGULUS Hc	Zn
180	25 21	036	32 44	100	55 21	147	63 29	173	32 00	225	45 34	300	34 36	326
181	25 48	035	33 32	100	55 48	147	63 34	174	31 26	225	44 52	299	34 09	325
182	26 15	034	34 19	099	56 14	147	63 39	175	30 52	225	44 10	298	33 42	324
183	26 42	033	35 06	099	56 40	148	63 43	176	30 19	224	43 27	297	33 13	323
184	27 08	032	35 54	098	57 05	148	63 46	177	29 45	224	42 44	296	32 44	322
185	27 33	031	36 41	098	57 30	149	63 48	178	29 12	224	42 01	295	32 15	321
186	27 57	030	37 29	097	57 55	149	63 49	179	28 39	224	41 18	294	31 44	320
187	28 21	029	38 16	097	58 19	150	63 49	180	28 06	223	40 34	293	31 14	319
188	28 44	028	39 04	096	58 44	150	63 49	181	27 33	223	39 50	292	30 42	318
189	29 07	027	39 51	096	59 07	151	63 47	182	27 00	223	39 05	292	30 10	317
190	29 28	026	40 39	095	59 30	151	63 45	183	26 28	222	38 20	291	29 37	316
191	29 49	025	41 27	095	59 53	152	63 42	184	25 55	222	37 35	290	29 04	316
192	30 09	024	42 15	094	60 16	152	63 38	185	25 23	222	36 50	289	28 30	315
193	30 28	023	43 02	093	60 38	153	63 33	186	24 52	222	36 05	288	27 56	314
194	30 47	022	43 50	093	60 59	154	63 27	187	24 20	221	35 19	288	27 21	313

LHA ♈	ARCTURUS Hc	Zn	◆ANTARES Hc	Zn	RIGIL KENT Hc	Zn	◆ACRUX Hc	Zn	Suhail Hc	Zn	◆REGULUS Hc	Zn	Denebola Hc	Zn
195	31 05	021	44 38	092	61 20	154	63 21	188	46 15	243	26 46	312	35 55	339
196	31 21	020	45 26	092	61 40	155	63 14	189	45 33	242	26 10	311	35 38	338
197	31 38	019	46 14	091	62 00	156	63 06	190	44 50	242	25 33	310	35 19	337
198	31 53	018	47 02	091	62 19	157	62 57	191	44 08	242	24 57	309	35 00	335
199	32 07	017	47 50	090	62 38	158	62 47	192	43 26	242	24 19	309	34 39	334
200	32 21	016	48 38	089	62 56	158	62 37	193	42 43	241	23 42	308	34 18	333
201	32 33	015	49 26	089	63 13	159	62 26	194	42 01	241	23 04	307	33 56	332
202	32 45	014	50 14	088	63 30	160	62 14	195	41 19	241	22 25	306	33 34	331
203	32 56	013	51 01	087	63 46	161	62 02	196	40 38	241	21 46	305	33 10	330
204	33 06	011	51 49	087	64 01	162	61 49	196	39 56	240	21 07	305	32 46	329
205	33 15	010	52 37	086	64 16	163	61 35	197	39 14	240	20 27	304	32 21	328
206	33 23	009	53 25	085	64 29	164	61 20	198	38 33	240	19 47	303	31 55	327
207	33 30	008	54 13	085	64 42	165	61 05	199	37 51	240	19 07	302	31 29	326
208	33 36	007	55 00	084	64 54	166	60 50	199	37 10	239	18 26	302	31 01	325
209	33 41	006	55 48	083	65 05	167	60 33	200	36 29	239	17 45	301	30 34	324

LHA ♈	ARCTURUS Hc	Zn	◆ANTARES Hc	Zn	Peacock Hc	Zn	RIGIL KENT Hc	Zn	◆ACRUX Hc	Zn	Suhail Hc	Zn	◆SPICA Hc	Zn
210	33 46	005	56 36	083	26 51	142	65 15	168	60 16	201	35 48	239	63 08	341
211	33 49	004	57 23	082	27 21	142	65 25	169	59 59	202	35 07	238	62 51	339
212	33 52	002	58 10	081	27 50	142	65 33	170	59 41	202	34 26	238	62 34	337
213	33 53	001	58 58	080	28 20	141	65 41	172	59 23	203	33 46	238	62 14	335
214	33 54	000	59 45	079	28 50	141	65 47	173	59 04	204	33 05	237	61 53	333
215	33 53	359	60 32	079	29 20	141	65 53	174	58 44	204	32 25	237	61 31	331
216	33 52	358	61 19	078	29 50	141	65 58	175	58 24	205	31 45	237	61 07	329
217	33 50	357	62 05	077	30 21	140	66 01	176	58 04	205	31 05	236	60 42	328
218	33 46	356	62 52	076	30 51	140	66 04	177	57 43	206	30 25	236	60 16	326
219	33 42	354	63 38	075	31 22	140	66 06	179	57 22	206	29 45	236	59 48	324
220	33 37	353	64 24	074	31 53	140	66 06	180	57 01	207	29 05	235	59 20	322
221	33 31	352	65 10	073	32 24	140	66 06	181	56 39	207	28 26	235	58 50	321
222	33 24	351	65 56	071	32 55	139	66 05	182	56 17	208	27 47	235	58 19	319
223	33 16	350	66 41	070	33 26	139	66 02	183	55 54	208	27 08	234	57 47	318
224	33 07	349	67 26	069	33 58	139	65 59	185	55 31	209	26 29	234	57 15	316

LHA ♈	Alphecca Hc	Zn	Rasalhague Hc	Zn	◆Nunki Hc	Zn	Peacock Hc	Zn	◆RIGIL KENT Hc	Zn	◆SPICA Hc	Zn	ARCTURUS Hc	Zn
225	25 48	009	28 25	044	39 24	096	34 29	139	65 55	186	56 41	315	32 57	348
226	25 55	008	28 58	043	40 12	095	35 01	139	65 49	187	56 06	313	32 47	347
227	26 01	007	29 31	042	40 59	095	35 33	138	65 43	188	55 31	312	32 35	345
228	26 06	006	30 03	041	41 47	094	36 04	138	65 36	189	54 55	310	32 23	344
229	26 10	005	30 34	040	42 35	093	36 36	138	65 28	190	54 18	309	32 09	343
230	26 14	004	31 05	039	43 23	093	37 08	138	65 18	191	53 40	308	31 55	342
231	26 17	003	31 35	038	44 11	092	37 41	138	65 09	193	53 02	307	31 40	341
232	26 19	002	32 04	038	44 59	092	38 13	138	64 58	194	52 24	305	31 24	340
233	26 20	001	32 33	037	45 47	091	38 45	137	64 46	195	51 44	304	31 08	339
234	26 20	000	33 01	035	46 34	091	39 18	137	64 33	196	51 04	303	30 50	338
235	26 20	359	33 29	034	47 22	090	39 50	137	64 20	197	50 24	302	30 32	337
236	26 18	358	33 56	033	48 10	089	40 23	137	64 06	198	49 43	301	30 13	336
237	26 16	357	34 22	032	48 58	089	40 55	137	63 51	199	49 01	300	29 53	335
238	26 13	356	34 47	031	49 46	088	41 28	137	63 35	200	48 20	299	29 32	334
239	26 09	355	35 11	030	50 34	088	42 01	137	63 19	200	47 37	298	29 10	333

LHA ♈	Rasalhague Hc	Zn	ALTAIR Hc	Zn	◆Nunki Hc	Zn	Peacock Hc	Zn	◆RIGIL KENT Hc	Zn	SPICA Hc	Zn	◆ARCTURUS Hc	Zn
240	35 35	029	19 03	062	51 22	087	42 34	137	63 02	201	46 55	297	28 48	332
241	35 58	028	19 45	062	52 10	086	43 06	137	62 44	202	46 12	296	28 25	331
242	36 20	027	20 27	061	52 57	086	43 39	137	62 25	203	45 28	295	28 02	330
243	36 41	026	21 09	060	53 45	085	44 12	137	62 06	204	44 45	294	27 37	329
244	37 02	025	21 50	059	54 33	084	44 45	137	61 47	205	44 01	293	27 12	328
245	37 21	023	22 31	059	55 21	083	45 18	137	61 27	205	43 16	292	26 46	327
246	37 40	022	23 12	058	56 08	083	45 51	137	61 06	206	42 32	291	26 20	326
247	37 57	021	23 52	057	56 56	082	46 24	137	60 45	207	41 47	290	25 53	325
248	38 14	020	24 32	056	57 43	081	46 57	137	60 23	207	41 02	289	25 25	324
249	38 30	019	25 12	055	58 30	080	47 30	137	60 01	208	40 17	289	24 57	323
250	38 45	018	25 51	055	59 17	079	48 03	137	59 38	209	39 31	288	24 28	322
251	38 59	016	26 30	054	60 04	079	48 36	137	59 15	209	38 45	287	23 59	322
252	39 12	015	27 08	053	60 51	078	49 09	137	58 51	210	37 59	286	23 29	321
253	39 24	014	27 46	052	61 38	077	49 41	137	58 27	210	37 13	285	22 58	320
254	39 35	013	28 24	051	62 25	076	50 14	137	58 03	211	36 27	285	22 27	319

LHA ♈	Rasalhague Hc	Zn	◆ALTAIR Hc	Zn	FOMALHAUT Hc	Zn	◆ACHERNAR Hc	Zn	RIGIL KENT Hc	Zn	◆SPICA Hc	Zn	ARCTURUS Hc	Zn
255	39 45	011	29 01	050	17 32	114	13 17	155	57 38	211	35 41	284	21 55	318
256	39 54	010	29 37	049	18 16	114	13 38	154	57 13	212	34 54	283	21 23	317
257	40 02	009	30 13	048	19 00	113	13 59	154	56 48	212	34 07	282	20 50	316
258	40 08	008	30 49	048	19 44	113	14 20	153	56 22	213	33 20	282	20 17	316
259	40 14	006	31 24	047	20 29	112	14 42	153	55 56	213	32 33	281	19 43	315
260	40 19	005	31 59	046	21 13	112	15 04	152	55 30	213	31 46	280	19 09	314
261	40 22	004	32 33	045	21 58	111	15 26	152	55 03	214	30 59	280	18 34	313
262	40 25	002	33 06	044	22 42	111	15 49	152	54 37	214	30 12	279	17 59	312
263	40 27	001	33 39	043	23 27	110	16 12	151	54 10	214	29 24	278	17 24	312
264	40 27	000	34 11	042	24 12	110	16 35	151	53 42	215	28 37	278	16 48	311
265	40 26	359	34 43	041	24 57	109	16 58	150	53 15	215	27 49	277	16 11	310
266	40 25	357	35 14	040	25 43	109	17 22	150	52 48	215	27 02	276	15 35	309
267	40 22	356	35 44	039	26 28	108	17 46	150	52 20	215	26 14	276	14 57	309
268	40 18	355	36 13	038	27 14	108	18 11	149	51 52	216	25 27	275	14 20	308
269	40 13	353	36 42	037	27 59	107	18 35	149	51 24	216	24 39	274	13 42	307

LHA ♈	ALTAIR Hc	Zn	Enif Hc	Zn	◆FOMALHAUT Hc	Zn	ACHERNAR Hc	Zn	◆RIGIL KENT Hc	Zn	ANTARES Hc	Zn	◆Rasalhague Hc	Zn
270	37 10	035	19 28	060	28 45	107	19 00	149	50 56	216	68 18	293	40 07	352
271	37 38	034	20 10	060	29 31	106	19 25	148	50 27	216	67 33	291	40 00	351
272	38 04	033	20 51	059	30 17	106	19 51	148	49 59	216	66 49	290	39 52	350
273	38 30	032	21 32	058	31 03	105	20 16	147	49 30	217	66 03	289	39 43	348
274	38 55	031	22 12	057	31 49	105	20 42	147	49 02	217	65 18	288	39 33	347
275	39 20	030	22 52	056	32 36	105	21 08	147	48 33	217	64 32	287	39 22	346
276	39 43	029	23 32	056	33 22	104	21 35	146	48 04	217	63 46	285	39 10	345
277	40 05	027	24 11	055	34 09	104	22 01	146	47 35	217	63 00	284	38 56	343
278	40 27	026	24 50	054	34 55	103	22 28	146	47 06	217	62 13	283	38 42	342
279	40 48	025	25 29	053	35 42	103	22 55	145	46 37	217	61 26	283	38 27	341
280	41 07	024	26 07	052	36 29	102	23 22	145	46 08	217	60 40	282	38 11	340
281	41 26	022	26 45	052	37 16	102	23 50	145	45 39	217	59 53	281	37 54	339
282	41 44	021	27 22	051	38 03	101	24 18	144	45 10	217	59 05	280	37 36	338
283	42 01	020	27 59	050	38 50	101	24 46	144	44 41	217	58 18	279	37 18	336
284	42 17	019	28 35	049	39 37	100	25 14	144	44 12	218	57 31	278	36 58	335

LHA ♈	ALTAIR Hc	Zn	Enif Hc	Zn	◆FOMALHAUT Hc	Zn	ACHERNAR Hc	Zn	◆RIGIL KENT Hc	Zn	ANTARES Hc	Zn	◆Rasalhague Hc	Zn
285	42 32	017	29 11	048	40 24	100	25 42	144	43 42	218	56 43	278	36 37	334
286	42 45	016	29 47	047	41 11	099	26 11	143	43 13	218	55 56	277	36 16	333
287	42 58	015	30 21	046	41 59	099	26 39	143	42 44	218	55 08	276	35 54	332
288	43 10	013	30 56	045	42 46	098	27 08	143	42 15	217	54 21	275	35 31	331
289	43 20	012	31 30	044	43 33	098	27 37	142	41 46	217	53 33	275	35 07	330
290	43 30	011	32 03	043	44 21	097	28 07	142	41 17	217	52 45	274	34 42	329
291	43 38	009	32 35	042	45 09	097	28 36	142	40 48	217	51 57	273	34 17	327
292	43 46	008	33 07	041	45 56	096	29 06	142	40 18	217	51 09	273	33 51	326
293	43 52	007	33 39	040	46 44	096	29 35	141	39 49	217	50 21	272	33 24	325
294	43 57	005	34 10	039	47 31	095	30 05	141	39 20	217	49 34	271	32 56	324
295	44 01	004	34 40	038	48 19	095	30 35	141	38 52	217	48 46	271	32 28	323
296	44 03	003	35 09	037	49 07	094	31 06	141	38 23	217	47 58	270	31 59	322
297	44 05	001	35 38	036	49 55	094	31 36	140	37 54	217	47 10	270	31 29	321
298	44 05	000	36 06	035	50 43	093	32 07	140	37 25	217	46 22	269	30 59	320
299	44 05	358	36 33	034	51 31	093	32 37	140	36 57	217	45 34	268	30 28	319

LHA ♈	Enif Hc	Zn	◆FOMALHAUT Hc	Zn	ACHERNAR Hc	Zn	◆RIGIL KENT Hc	Zn	ANTARES Hc	Zn	◆Rasalhague Hc	Zn	ALTAIR Hc	Zn
300	37 00	033	52 18	092	33 08	140	36 28	217	44 46	268	29 57	318	44 03	357
301	37 25	032	53 06	091	33 39	140	35 59	216	43 58	267	29 25	317	44 00	356
302	37 50	031	53 54	091	34 10	139	35 31	216	43 10	267	28 52	317	43 56	354
303	38 14	030	54 42	090	34 41	139	35 03	216	42 23	266	28 19	316	43 50	353
304	38 38	028	55 30	090	35 13	139	34 35	216	41 35	266	27 45	315	43 44	352
305	39 00	027	56 18	089	35 44	139	34 06	216	40 47	265	27 11	314	43 36	350
306	39 22	026	57 06	088	36 16	139	33 39	216	39 59	264	26 36	313	43 28	349
307	39 42	025	57 54	088	36 47	139	33 11	215	39 12	264	26 01	312	43 18	348
308	40 02	024	58 42	087	37 19	138	32 43	215	38 24	263	25 25	311	43 07	346
309	40 21	023	59 29	086	37 51	138	32 15	215	37 36	263	24 48	310	42 55	345
310	40 39	021	60 17	086	38 23	138	31 48	215	36 49	262	24 12	310	42 42	344
311	40 56	020	61 05	085	38 55	138	31 20	215	36 01	262	23 35	309	42 28	342
312	41 11	019	61 53	084	39 27	138	30 53	215	35 14	261	22 57	308	42 13	341
313	41 26	018	62 40	083	39 59	138	30 26	214	34 27	261	22 19	307	41 57	340
314	41 40	016	63 28	083	40 31	138	29 59	214	33 39	260	21 41	306	41 40	338

LHA ♈	Enif Hc	Zn	◆Diphda Hc	Zn	ACHERNAR Hc	Zn	◆RIGIL KENT Hc	Zn	ANTARES Hc	Zn	Nunki Hc	Zn	◆ALTAIR Hc	Zn
315	41 53	015	37 31	085	41 04	138	29 32	214	32 52	260	61 43	283	41 22	337
316	42 05	014	38 19	084	41 36	138	29 06	214	32 05	259	60 56	282	41 03	336
317	42 16	012	39 07	083	42 08	137	28 39	213	31 18	259	60 09	282	40 43	335
318	42 25	011	39 54	083	42 41	137	28 13	213	30 31	258	59 22	281	40 22	334
319	42 34	010	40 42	082	43 13	137	27 47	213	29 44	258	58 35	280	40 00	332
320	42 42	008	41 29	081	43 46	137	27 21	213	28 57	257	57 48	279	39 37	331
321	42 48	007	42 16	081	44 18	137	26 55	212	28 11	257	57 00	278	39 14	330
322	42 53	006	43 03	080	44 51	137	26 30	212	27 24	256	56 13	277	38 49	329
323	42 57	004	43 51	079	45 23	137	26 04	212	26 38	256	55 25	277	38 24	328
324	43 01	003	44 38	078	45 56	137	25 39	212	25 51	255	54 38	276	37 58	327
325	43 02	002	45 24	078	46 28	137	25 14	211	25 05	255	53 50	275	37 31	325
326	43 03	000	46 11	077	47 01	137	24 49	211	24 19	254	53 02	275	37 04	324
327	43 03	359	46 58	076	47 33	137	24 25	211	23 33	254	52 14	274	36 35	323
328	43 02	358	47 44	075	48 06	137	24 00	210	22 47	253	51 27	273	36 06	322
329	42 59	356	48 30	074	48 38	137	23 36	210	22 01	253	50 39	273	35 37	321

LHA ♈	◆Alpheratz Hc	Zn	Diphda Hc	Zn	◆ACHERNAR Hc	Zn	RIGIL KENT Hc	Zn	◆Nunki Hc	Zn	ALTAIR Hc	Zn	Enif Hc	Zn
330	17 14	029	49 16	073	49 11	137	23 12	210	49 51	272	35 06	320	42 55	355
331	17 37	028	50 02	073	49 43	138	22 48	210	49 03	271	34 35	319	42 51	354
332	17 59	028	50 48	072	50 15	138	22 25	209	48 15	271	34 03	318	42 45	352
333	18 21	027	51 33	071	50 47	138	22 02	209	47 27	270	33 31	317	42 38	351
334	18 42	026	52 18	070	51 20	138	21 39	209	46 39	269	32 58	316	42 30	350
335	19 03	025	53 03	069	51 52	138	21 16	208	45 51	269	32 24	315	42 20	348
336	19 23	024	53 48	068	52 24	138	20 53	208	45 03	268	31 50	314	42 10	347
337	19 42	023	54 32	067	52 56	138	20 31	208	44 15	268	31 16	313	41 59	346
338	20 01	022	55 16	066	53 27	139	20 09	207	43 28	267	30 40	312	41 46	344
339	20 19	022	55 59	065	53 59	139	19 47	207	42 40	267	30 05	311	41 33	343
340	20 36	021	56 42	064	54 30	139	19 25	207	41 52	266	29 28	310	41 18	342
341	20 53	020	57 25	062	55 02	139	19 04	206	41 04	265	28 52	310	41 03	341
342	21 09	019	58 07	061	55 33	140	18 43	206	40 16	265	28 15	309	40 47	339
343	21 24	018	58 49	060	56 04	140	18 22	206	39 29	264	27 37	308	40 29	338
344	21 38	017	59 30	059	56 35	140	18 02	205	38 41	264	26 59	307	40 11	337

LHA ♈	◆Alpheratz Hc	Zn	Diphda Hc	Zn	◆CANOPUS Hc	Zn	RIGIL KENT Hc	Zn	◆Nunki Hc	Zn	ALTAIR Hc	Zn	Enif Hc	Zn
345	21 52	016	60 11	057	17 45	144	17 42	205	37 53	263	26 20	306	39 51	336
346	22 05	015	60 51	056	18 13	143	17 22	204	37 06	263	25 41	305	39 31	334
347	22 17	014	61 30	054	18 42	143	17 02	204	36 18	262	25 02	304	39 10	333
348	22 29	013	62 09	053	19 11	142	16 43	204	35 31	262	24 22	304	38 48	332
349	22 40	013	62 46	051	19 41	142	16 23	203	34 43	261	23 42	303	38 25	331
350	22 50	012	63 24	050	20 10	142	16 05	203	33 56	261	23 02	302	38 01	330
351	22 59	011	64 00	048	20 40	141	15 46	202	33 09	260	22 21	301	37 37	329
352	23 08	010	64 35	046	21 10	141	15 28	202	32 22	260	21 40	301	37 11	327
353	23 15	009	65 09	045	21 40	141	15 10	202	31 35	259	20 59	300	36 45	326
354	23 22	008	65 42	043	22 11	140	14 53	201	30 48	259	20 17	299	36 18	325
355	23 28	007	66 14	041	22 42	140	14 35	201	30 01	258	19 35	298	35 51	324
356	23 34	006	66 45	039	23 13	140	14 19	200	29 14	258	18 52	298	35 22	323
357	23 38	005	67 14	037	23 44	139	14 02	200	28 27	257	18 10	297	34 53	322
358	23 42	004	67 42	035	24 15	139	13 46	200	27 40	257	17 27	296	34 24	321
359	23 45	003	68 09	032	24 47	139	13 30	199	26 54	256	16 44	295	33 53	320

LHA ♈	Hc	Zn	Hc	Zn	Hc	Zn	Hc	Zn	Hc	Zn	Hc	Zn	Hc	Zn
	Alpheratz		◆ Hamal		RIGEL		◆ CANOPUS		Peacock		◆ Nunki		Enif	
0	22 48	002	21 31	031	13 49	090	26 03	138	50 38	224	26 22	256	32 37	319
1	22 49	001	21 56	031	14 37	089	26 35	138	50 06	224	25 36	256	32 05	318
2	22 50	000	22 19	030	15 24	088	27 07	137	49 33	224	24 50	255	31 34	317
3	22 49	359	22 42	029	16 11	088	27 39	137	49 00	224	24 05	255	31 02	317
4	22 48	358	23 05	028	16 59	087	28 12	137	48 27	224	23 19	254	30 29	316
5	22 47	357	23 27	027	17 46	087	28 44	136	47 54	224	22 34	254	29 55	315
6	22 44	356	23 48	026	18 33	086	29 17	136	47 21	224	21 48	253	29 21	314
7	22 41	356	24 08	025	19 20	085	29 50	136	46 48	224	21 03	252	28 47	313
8	22 37	355	24 28	024	20 07	085	30 23	135	46 15	224	20 18	252	28 12	312
9	22 32	354	24 47	023	20 54	084	30 57	135	45 42	224	19 33	251	27 37	311
10	22 26	353	25 05	022	21 41	083	31 30	135	45 09	224	18 49	251	27 01	310
11	22 20	352	25 23	021	22 28	083	32 04	135	44 36	224	18 04	250	26 24	309
12	22 13	351	25 40	020	23 15	082	32 37	134	44 03	224	17 20	250	25 47	308
13	22 05	350	25 56	019	24 02	081	33 11	134	43 31	224	16 35	249	25 10	308
14	21 56	349	26 11	018	24 48	081	33 45	134	42 58	224	15 51	249	24 33	307
	◆ Hamal		ALDEBARAN		RIGEL		◆ CANOPUS		Peacock		◆ FOMALHAUT		Alpheratz	
15	26 26	017	15 28	054	25 35	080	34 19	134	42 25	224	63 30	279	21 47	348
16	26 39	016	16 06	053	26 22	079	34 54	133	41 53	224	62 44	279	21 37	347
17	26 52	015	16 44	052	27 08	079	35 28	133	41 20	224	61 57	278	21 26	346
18	27 05	014	17 21	052	27 54	078	36 03	133	40 47	223	61 10	277	21 14	345
19	27 16	013	17 58	051	28 40	077	36 38	133	40 15	223	60 23	276	21 02	344
20	27 27	012	18 34	050	29 26	076	37 12	132	39 43	223	59 36	275	20 49	343
21	27 36	011	19 10	049	30 12	076	37 47	132	39 10	223	58 49	275	20 35	343
22	27 45	010	19 45	048	30 58	075	38 23	132	38 38	223	58 02	274	20 21	342
23	27 53	009	20 21	048	31 44	074	38 58	132	38 06	223	57 15	273	20 05	341
24	28 01	008	20 55	047	32 29	074	39 33	132	37 34	223	56 27	273	19 50	340
25	28 07	007	21 29	046	33 14	073	40 08	131	37 02	222	55 40	272	19 33	339
26	28 13	006	22 03	045	33 59	072	40 44	131	36 30	222	54 53	271	19 16	338
27	28 17	005	22 36	044	34 44	071	41 19	131	35 59	222	54 06	271	18 58	337
28	28 21	004	23 09	043	35 29	070	41 55	131	35 27	222	53 18	270	18 39	336
29	28 24	003	23 41	043	36 13	070	42 31	131	34 56	222	52 31	269	18 20	336
	Hamal		◆ ALDEBARAN		RIGEL		SIRIUS		◆ CANOPUS		Peacock		◆ FOMALHAUT	
30	28 26	002	24 13	042	36 58	069	24 40	092	43 07	131	34 24	221	51 44	269
31	28 28	001	24 44	041	37 42	068	25 27	092	43 43	131	33 53	221	50 57	268
32	28 28	000	25 15	040	38 25	067	26 15	091	44 19	130	33 22	221	50 09	268
33	28 28	359	25 45	039	39 09	066	27 02	091	44 55	130	32 51	221	49 22	267
34	28 26	358	26 14	038	39 52	065	27 49	090	45 31	130	32 20	220	48 35	267
35	28 24	357	26 43	037	40 35	064	28 36	089	46 07	130	31 50	220	47 48	266
36	28 21	356	27 11	036	41 17	064	29 24	089	46 43	130	31 19	220	47 00	265
37	28 17	355	27 39	035	41 59	063	30 11	088	47 19	130	30 49	220	46 13	265
38	28 13	354	28 06	034	42 41	062	30 58	088	47 56	130	30 19	219	45 26	264
39	28 07	353	28 32	033	43 23	061	31 45	087	48 32	130	29 49	219	44 39	264
40	28 01	352	28 58	032	44 04	060	32 33	086	49 08	130	29 19	219	43 52	263
41	27 53	351	29 22	031	44 44	059	33 20	086	49 45	130	28 49	219	43 05	263
42	27 45	350	29 47	030	45 24	058	34 07	085	50 21	130	28 20	218	42 18	262
43	27 36	349	30 10	029	46 04	057	34 54	084	50 57	130	27 51	218	41 32	262
44	27 27	348	30 33	028	46 43	056	35 41	084	51 34	130	27 21	218	40 45	261
	◆ ALDEBARAN		RIGEL		SIRIUS		◆ CANOPUS		ACHERNAR		◆ FOMALHAUT		Hamal	
45	30 55	027	47 22	054	36 28	083	52 10	130	66 36	208	39 58	261	27 16	347
46	31 16	026	48 00	053	37 15	082	52 46	130	66 13	209	39 12	260	27 05	346
47	31 37	025	48 38	052	38 02	082	53 23	130	65 49	210	38 25	260	26 53	345
48	31 56	024	49 15	051	38 48	081	53 59	130	65 25	211	37 39	259	26 40	344
49	32 15	023	49 51	050	39 35	080	54 35	130	65 00	212	36 52	259	26 26	343
50	32 34	022	50 27	049	40 21	079	55 11	130	64 35	213	36 06	258	26 11	342
51	32 51	021	51 02	047	41 08	079	55 47	130	64 09	214	35 20	258	25 56	341
52	33 07	020	51 36	046	41 54	078	56 23	130	63 42	214	34 33	257	25 40	340
53	33 23	019	52 10	045	42 40	077	56 59	131	63 16	215	33 47	257	25 23	339
54	33 37	018	52 43	043	43 26	076	57 35	131	62 48	216	33 01	256	25 06	338
55	33 51	016	53 15	042	44 12	076	58 11	131	62 20	216	32 16	256	24 47	337
56	34 04	015	53 46	040	44 58	075	58 47	131	61 52	217	31 30	255	24 28	336
57	34 16	014	54 16	039	45 43	074	59 22	131	61 24	217	30 44	255	24 09	335
58	34 27	013	54 46	038	46 29	073	59 58	132	60 55	218	29 59	254	23 48	334
59	34 38	012	55 14	036	47 14	072	60 33	132	60 26	218	29 13	254	23 27	333
	ALDEBARAN		◆ BETELGEUSE		SIRIUS		◆ ACRUX		ACHERNAR		◆ FOMALHAUT		Hamal	
60	34 47	011	37 10	037	47 59	071	19 39	157	59 56	219	28 28	253	23 05	332
61	34 55	010	37 38	036	48 43	070	19 57	157	59 26	219	27 43	253	22 43	331
62	35 03	008	38 05	035	49 28	069	20 15	157	58 56	220	26 57	252	22 20	330
63	35 09	007	38 32	034	50 12	068	20 34	156	58 26	220	26 13	252	21 56	329
64	35 15	006	38 58	033	50 56	068	20 53	156	57 55	220	25 28	251	21 32	329
65	35 19	005	39 23	031	51 39	067	21 13	156	57 25	221	24 43	251	21 07	328
66	35 23	004	39 47	030	52 22	065	21 32	155	56 54	221	23 58	250	20 41	327
67	35 25	003	40 11	029	53 05	064	21 52	155	56 22	221	23 14	250	20 15	326
68	35 27	001	40 33	028	53 48	063	22 12	155	55 51	222	22 30	249	19 48	325
69	35 28	000	40 55	027	54 30	062	22 32	154	55 20	222	21 45	249	19 21	324
70	35 27	359	41 16	025	55 11	061	22 53	154	54 48	222	21 01	248	18 53	323
71	35 26	358	41 35	024	55 53	060	23 14	154	54 16	222	20 18	248	18 24	323
72	35 24	357	41 54	023	56 33	059	23 35	153	53 44	222	19 34	247	17 55	322
73	35 21	356	42 12	022	57 13	057	23 56	153	53 12	223	18 50	247	17 26	321
74	35 17	354	42 29	020	57 53	056	24 17	153	52 40	223	18 07	246	16 56	320
	BETELGEUSE		◆ SIRIUS		Suhail		◆ ACRUX		ACHERNAR		◆ Diphda		ALDEBARAN	
75	42 45	019	58 32	055	43 42	117	24 39	153	52 08	223	31 16	271	35 11	353
76	43 00	018	59 10	053	44 24	117	25 01	152	51 36	223	30 29	270	35 05	352
77	43 14	016	59 48	052	45 06	117	25 23	152	51 04	223	29 41	270	34 58	351
78	43 27	015	60 25	051	45 48	117	25 45	152	50 31	223	28 54	269	34 50	350
79	43 39	014	61 01	049	46 31	116	26 08	151	49 59	223	28 07	269	34 41	349
80	43 49	012	61 36	047	47 13	116	26 30	151	49 26	223	27 20	268	34 32	347
81	43 59	011	62 10	046	47 56	116	26 53	151	48 54	223	26 32	267	34 21	346
82	44 08	010	62 44	044	48 38	116	27 16	151	48 21	223	25 45	267	34 09	345
83	44 15	008	63 16	042	49 21	116	27 40	150	47 49	223	24 58	266	33 56	344
84	44 21	007	63 47	041	50 03	115	28 03	150	47 16	223	24 11	266	33 43	343
85	44 26	006	64 18	039	50 46	115	28 27	150	46 44	223	23 24	265	33 29	342
86	44 30	004	64 47	037	51 29	115	28 51	150	46 11	223	22 36	264	33 13	341
87	44 33	003	65 14	035	52 12	115	29 15	149	45 39	223	21 49	264	32 57	340
88	44 35	001	65 41	033	52 55	115	29 39	149	45 06	223	21 02	263	32 40	338
89	44 35	000	66 05	031	53 38	114	30 03	149	44 34	223	20 16	263	32 23	337

LHA ♈	Hc	Zn	Hc	Zn	Hc	Zn	Hc	Zn	Hc	Zn	Hc	Zn	Hc	Zn
	PROCYON		REGULUS		◆ Suhail		ACRUX		◆ ACHERNAR		RIGEL		◆ BETELGEUSE	
90	40 57	034	13 24	063	54 21	114	30 28	149	44 01	223	58 31	338	44 35	359
91	41 23	033	14 06	062	55 04	114	30 52	148	43 29	223	58 13	337	44 33	357
92	41 48	032	14 47	062	55 48	114	31 17	148	42 57	223	57 54	335	44 30	356
93	42 13	030	15 29	061	56 31	114	31 42	148	42 24	223	57 33	333	44 26	354
94	42 36	029	16 10	060	57 14	114	32 07	148	41 52	223	57 11	331	44 21	353
95	42 59	028	16 51	059	57 57	113	32 32	148	41 20	223	56 48	330	44 15	352
96	43 20	027	17 31	059	58 41	113	32 58	147	40 48	223	56 23	328	44 07	350
97	43 41	025	18 11	058	59 24	113	33 23	147	40 16	223	55 58	327	43 59	349
98	44 01	024	18 51	057	60 08	113	33 49	147	39 44	223	55 31	325	43 49	348
99	44 19	023	19 31	056	60 51	113	34 15	147	39 12	222	55 03	323	43 39	346
100	44 37	021	20 10	056	61 35	113	34 40	147	38 40	222	54 35	322	43 27	345
101	44 53	020	20 49	055	62 18	113	35 06	147	38 08	222	54 05	320	43 14	344
102	45 09	019	21 27	054	63 02	113	35 32	146	37 36	222	53 35	319	43 00	342
103	45 24	017	22 05	053	63 45	113	35 59	146	37 05	222	53 03	318	42 45	341
104	45 37	016	22 43	052	64 29	113	36 25	146	36 34	222	52 31	316	42 29	340
	PROCYON		REGULUS		◆ Gienah		ACRUX		◆ ACHERNAR		RIGEL		◆ BETELGEUSE	
105	45 49	014	23 20	052	19 08	098	36 51	146	36 02	221	51 58	315	42 12	338
106	46 00	013	23 57	051	19 55	097	37 18	146	35 31	221	51 24	314	41 54	337
107	46 11	012	24 33	050	20 42	097	37 44	146	35 00	221	50 49	312	41 35	336
108	46 19	010	25 09	049	21 29	096	38 11	146	34 29	221	50 14	311	41 15	335
109	46 27	009	25 45	048	22 16	095	38 37	146	33 58	221	49 38	310	40 55	333
110	46 34	007	26 20	047	23 03	095	39 04	146	33 27	220	49 01	309	40 33	332
111	46 39	006	26 54	046	23 50	094	39 31	145	32 57	220	48 24	307	40 10	331
112	46 43	004	27 28	045	24 38	094	39 58	145	32 26	220	47 46	306	39 47	330
113	46 46	003	28 02	045	25 25	093	40 25	145	31 56	220	47 08	305	39 23	329
114	46 48	001	28 35	044	26 12	093	40 52	145	31 26	219	46 29	304	38 58	327
115	46 49	000	29 07	043	26 59	092	41 19	145	30 56	219	45 49	303	38 32	326
116	46 48	359	29 39	042	27 46	091	41 46	145	30 26	219	45 09	302	38 05	325
117	46 47	357	30 10	041	28 34	091	42 13	145	29 57	219	44 29	301	37 38	324
118	46 44	356	30 41	040	29 21	090	42 40	145	29 27	218	43 48	300	37 10	323
119	46 39	354	31 11	039	30 08	089	43 07	145	28 58	218	43 07	299	36 41	322
	REGULUS		◆ SPICA		ACRUX		◆ CANOPUS		RIGEL		BETELGEUSE		◆ PROCYON	
120	31 40	038	13 33	094	43 34	145	67 51	221	42 26	298	36 11	321	46 34	353
121	32 09	037	14 20	093	44 01	145	67 20	222	41 44	297	35 41	320	46 28	351
122	32 37	036	15 07	093	44 28	145	66 48	222	41 01	296	35 10	319	46 20	350
123	33 04	035	15 55	092	44 55	145	66 16	223	40 19	295	34 38	318	46 11	348
124	33 31	034	16 42	091	45 22	145	65 44	224	39 36	294	34 06	317	46 01	347
125	33 57	033	17 29	091	45 49	145	65 11	224	38 53	293	33 33	316	45 50	346
126	34 22	032	18 16	090	46 16	145	64 38	225	38 09	293	33 00	315	45 38	344
127	34 46	031	19 04	090	46 43	145	64 04	225	37 25	292	32 26	314	45 24	343
128	35 10	030	19 51	089	47 10	145	63 31	226	36 41	291	31 52	313	45 10	342
129	35 33	028	20 38	088	47 37	145	62 56	226	35 57	290	31 17	312	44 54	340
130	35 55	027	21 26	088	48 03	146	62 22	227	35 13	289	30 41	311	44 38	339
131	36 16	026	22 13	087	48 30	146	61 48	227	34 28	288	30 05	310	44 20	337
132	36 37	025	23 00	086	48 57	146	61 13	228	33 43	288	29 29	309	44 01	336
133	36 56	024	23 47	086	49 23	146	60 38	228	32 58	287	28 52	308	43 42	335
134	37 15	023	24 34	085	49 50	146	60 03	228	32 12	286	28 14	307	43 21	334
	◆ REGULUS		SPICA		◆ ACRUX		CANOPUS		◆ RIGEL		BETELGEUSE		PROCYON	
135	37 33	022	25 21	084	50 16	146	59 27	229	31 27	285	27 36	306	43 00	332
136	37 49	020	26 08	084	50 42	146	58 52	229	30 41	285	26 58	306	42 37	331
137	38 05	019	26 55	083	51 08	147	58 16	229	29 55	284	26 19	305	42 14	330
138	38 20	018	27 42	082	51 34	147	57 40	229	29 09	283	25 40	304	41 50	329
139	38 35	017	28 29	082	52 00	147	57 04	229	28 23	283	25 01	303	41 24	327
140	38 48	016	29 16	081	52 25	147	56 29	230	27 37	282	24 21	302	40 59	326
141	39 00	014	30 03	080	52 51	148	55 53	230	26 51	281	23 41	301	40 32	325
142	39 11	013	30 49	080	53 16	148	55 16	230	26 04	280	23 00	301	40 04	324
143	39 21	012	31 36	079	53 41	148	54 40	230	25 18	280	22 20	300	39 36	323
144	39 30	011	32 22	078	54 06	148	54 04	230	24 31	279	21 38	299	39 07	322
145	39 38	009	33 08	078	54 31	149	53 28	230	23 44	278	20 57	298	38 37	320
146	39 46	008	33 54	077	54 55	149	52 51	230	22 58	278	20 15	298	38 07	319
147	39 52	007	34 40	076	55 19	149	52 15	230	22 11	277	19 33	297	37 36	318
148	39 57	005	35 26	075	55 43	150	51 39	230	21 24	276	18 51	296	37 04	317
149	40 01	004	36 12	075	56 07	150	51 02	230	20 37	276	18 08	295	36 31	316
	REGULUS		◆ SPICA		ACRUX		◆ Miaplacidus		CANOPUS		SIRIUS		◆ PROCYON	
150	40 04	003	36 57	074	56 30	151	57 37	187	50 26	230	42 36	283	35 58	315
151	40 06	002	37 43	073	56 53	151	57 30	188	49 50	230	41 50	282	35 25	314
152	40 06	000	38 28	072	57 16	152	57 24	189	49 13	230	41 03	281	34 50	313
153	40 06	359	39 13	071	57 38	152	57 16	189	48 37	230	40 17	281	34 16	312
154	40 05	358	39 57	071	58 00	152	57 08	190	48 01	230	39 31	280	33 40	311
155	40 03	357	40 42	070	58 22	153	57 00	190	47 25	230	38 44	279	33 04	310
156	39 59	355	41 26	069	58 43	154	56 51	191	46 48	230	37 57	278	32 28	309
157	39 55	354	42 10	068	59 04	154	56 42	192	46 12	230	37 10	278	31 51	308
158	39 49	353	42 54	067	59 24	155	56 32	192	45 36	230	36 23	277	31 14	307
159	39 43	351	43 37	066	59 44	155	56 22	193	45 00	230	35 36	276	30 36	307
160	39 35	350	44 20	065	60 04	156	56 11	193	44 24	230	34 49	276	29 58	306
161	39 27	349	45 03	064	60 23	157	56 00	194	43 48	229	34 02	275	29 19	305
162	39 17	348	45 46	063	60 42	157	55 49	194	43 12	229	33 15	274	28 40	304
163	39 06	346	46 28	062	61 00	158	55 37	195	42 36	229	32 28	274	28 01	303
164	38 55	345	47 09	061	61 17	159	55 25	195	42 00	229	31 41	273	27 21	302
	ARCTURUS		◆ ANTARES		ACRUX		◆ CANOPUS		SIRIUS		PROCYON		◆ REGULUS	
165	16 38	048	21 26	108	61 34	159	41 25	229	30 54	272	26 41	301	38 42	344
166	17 13	047	22 11	107	61 51	160	40 49	229	30 06	272	26 00	301	38 29	343
167	17 47	047	22 56	106	62 06	161	40 13	229	29 19	271	25 19	300	38 14	342
168	18 21	046	23 42	106	62 22	162	39 38	228	28 32	271	24 38	299	37 59	340
169	18 55	045	24 27	105	62 36	163	39 03	228	27 45	270	23 57	298	37 43	339
170	19 28	044	25 13	105	62 50	163	38 28	228	26 57	269	23 15	297	37 25	338
171	20 01	043	25 59	104	63 03	164	37 52	228	26 10	269	22 33	297	37 07	337
172	20 33	043	26 45	104	63 16	165	37 17	228	25 23	268	21 50	296	36 48	336
173	21 05	042	27 31	103	63 27	166	36 43	227	24 36	267	21 08	295	36 28	335
174	21 36	041	28 17	103	63 39	167	36 08	227	23 48	267	20 25	294	36 07	333
175	22 07	040	29 03	102	63 49	168	35 33	227	23 01	266	19 42	294	35 46	332
176	22 37	039	29 49	102	63 58	169	34 59	227	22 14	266	18 58	293	35 23	331
177	23 07	038	30 35	101	64 07	170	34 24	226	21 27	265	18 15	292	35 00	330
178	23 36	037	31 22	101	64 15	171	33 50	226	20 40	264	17 31	292	34 36	329
179	24 04	037	32 08	100	64 22	172	33 16	226	19 53	264	16 47	291	34 11	328

LAT 38°S

LHA ♈	Hc Zn	Hc Zn	Hc Zn	Hc Zn	Hc Zn	Hc Zn	Hc Zn
	ARCTURUS	◆ANTARES	RIGIL KENT	ACRUX	◆CANOPUS	Alphard	◆REGULUS
180	24 32 036	32 55 100	56 11 146	64 29 173	32 42 226	45 04 301	33 46 327
181	24 59 035	33 41 099	56 38 146	64 34 174	32 08 225	44 23 300	33 20 326
182	25 26 034	34 28 099	57 04 146	64 39 175	31 35 225	43 41 299	32 53 325
183	25 52 033	35 15 098	57 30 147	64 43 176	31 01 225	43 00 298	32 25 324
184	26 17 032	36 02 098	57 56 147	64 45 177	30 28 225	42 18 297	31 57 323
185	26 42 031	36 49 097	58 21 148	64 48 178	29 55 224	41 35 296	31 28 322
186	27 06 030	37 36 096	58 46 148	64 49 179	29 22 224	40 53 295	30 58 321
187	27 29 029	38 23 096	59 11 149	64 49 180	28 49 224	40 10 294	30 28 320
188	27 51 028	39 10 095	59 35 149	64 49 181	28 16 223	39 26 293	29 57 319
189	28 13 027	39 57 095	59 59 150	64 47 182	27 44 223	38 43 292	29 26 318
190	28 34 026	40 44 094	60 23 150	64 45 183	27 12 223	37 59 291	28 54 317
191	28 55 025	41 31 094	60 46 151	64 42 184	26 40 222	37 15 291	28 21 316
192	29 14 024	42 18 093	61 09 152	64 38 185	26 08 222	36 30 290	27 48 315
193	29 33 023	43 06 092	61 31 152	64 33 186	25 36 222	35 46 289	27 14 314
194	29 51 022	43 53 092	61 53 153	64 27 187	25 05 221	35 01 288	26 40 313
	ARCTURUS	◆ANTARES	RIGIL KENT	◆ACRUX	Suhail	◆REGULUS	Denebola
195	30 09 021	44 40 091	62 14 154	64 20 188	46 42 244	26 05 312	34 59 339
196	30 25 020	45 27 091	62 35 154	64 13 189	46 00 243	25 30 311	34 42 338
197	30 41 019	46 15 090	62 55 155	64 05 190	45 18 243	24 54 311	34 24 337
198	30 56 018	47 02 089	63 14 156	63 56 191	44 36 243	24 18 310	34 05 336
199	31 10 017	47 49 089	63 33 157	63 46 192	43 54 243	23 42 309	33 45 335
200	31 23 016	48 36 088	63 52 158	63 36 193	43 12 242	23 05 308	33 25 334
201	31 35 015	49 24 088	64 09 159	63 24 194	42 30 242	22 27 307	33 03 333
202	31 47 013	50 11 087	64 26 159	63 12 195	41 48 242	21 50 306	32 41 331
203	31 57 012	50 58 086	64 43 160	63 00 196	41 07 241	21 11 306	32 18 330
204	32 07 011	51 45 086	64 58 161	62 46 197	40 25 241	20 33 305	31 54 329
205	32 16 010	52 32 085	65 13 162	62 32 198	39 44 241	19 54 304	31 30 328
206	32 23 009	53 19 084	65 27 163	62 17 199	39 03 241	19 14 303	31 05 327
207	32 30 008	54 06 083	65 40 164	62 02 199	38 21 240	18 35 303	30 39 326
208	32 37 007	54 53 083	65 52 165	61 46 200	37 40 240	17 55 302	30 12 325
209	32 42 006	55 40 082	66 04 167	61 30 201	36 59 240	17 14 301	29 45 324
	ARCTURUS	◆ANTARES	Peacock	RIGIL KENT	◆ACRUX	Suhail	◆SPICA
210	32 46 005	56 27 081	27 39 142	66 14 168	61 12 202	36 19 239	62 11 342
211	32 49 003	57 14 080	28 08 142	66 24 169	60 55 202	35 38 239	61 55 340
212	32 52 002	58 00 079	28 37 141	66 32 170	60 37 203	34 58 239	61 38 338
213	32 53 001	58 47 079	29 07 141	66 40 171	60 18 204	34 17 238	61 20 336
214	32 54 000	59 33 078	29 36 141	66 47 172	59 59 204	33 37 238	61 00 334
215	32 53 359	60 19 077	30 06 141	66 53 174	59 39 205	32 57 238	60 38 332
216	32 52 358	61 05 076	30 36 140	66 57 175	59 19 205	32 17 237	60 15 330
217	32 50 357	61 51 075	31 07 140	67 01 176	58 58 206	31 38 237	59 51 329
218	32 47 356	62 36 074	31 37 140	67 04 177	58 37 207	30 58 237	59 26 327
219	32 43 354	63 21 073	32 08 140	67 06 179	58 16 207	30 19 236	59 00 325
220	32 38 353	64 07 072	32 38 139	67 06 180	57 54 208	29 39 236	58 32 323
221	32 32 352	64 51 071	33 09 139	67 06 181	57 32 208	29 00 236	58 03 322
222	32 25 351	65 36 069	33 40 139	67 05 182	57 09 209	28 21 235	57 33 320
223	32 17 350	66 20 068	34 11 139	67 02 184	56 47 209	27 43 235	57 03 319
224	32 08 349	67 03 067	34 43 138	66 59 185	56 24 209	27 04 234	56 31 317
	Alphecca	Rasalhague	◆Nunki	Peacock	◆RIGIL KENT	◆SPICA	ARCTURUS
225	24 48 009	27 42 044	39 29 095	35 14 138	66 54 186	55 58 316	31 59 348
226	24 55 008	28 14 043	40 17 094	35 46 138	66 49 187	55 25 314	31 48 347
227	25 01 007	28 46 042	41 04 094	36 17 138	66 42 188	54 51 313	31 37 346
228	25 06 006	29 17 041	41 51 093	36 49 138	66 35 190	54 16 311	31 25 345
229	25 11 005	29 48 040	42 38 093	37 21 138	66 27 191	53 40 310	31 12 343
230	25 14 004	30 18 039	43 25 092	37 53 137	66 17 192	53 03 309	30 58 342
231	25 17 003	30 48 038	44 13 091	38 25 137	66 07 193	52 26 308	30 43 341
232	25 19 002	31 17 037	45 00 091	38 57 137	65 56 194	51 48 306	30 28 340
233	25 20 001	31 45 036	45 47 090	39 29 137	65 44 195	51 10 305	30 12 339
234	25 20 000	32 12 035	46 35 090	40 02 137	65 31 196	50 31 304	29 54 338
235	25 20 359	32 39 034	47 22 089	40 34 137	65 17 197	49 52 303	29 36 337
236	25 18 358	33 05 033	48 09 088	41 07 137	65 03 198	49 12 302	29 18 336
237	25 16 357	33 31 032	48 56 088	41 39 136	64 48 199	48 31 301	28 58 335
238	25 13 356	33 55 031	49 44 087	42 12 136	64 32 200	47 50 300	28 38 334
239	25 09 355	34 19 030	50 31 086	42 44 136	64 15 201	47 09 299	28 17 333
	Rasalhague	ALTAIR	◆Nunki	Peacock	◆RIGIL KENT	SPICA	◆ARCTURUS
240	34 43 029	18 35 062	51 18 086	43 17 136	63 57 202	46 27 298	27 55 332
241	35 05 028	19 16 061	52 05 085	43 50 136	63 39 203	45 45 297	27 33 331
242	35 26 027	19 58 060	52 52 084	44 23 136	63 21 204	45 03 296	27 10 330
243	35 47 025	20 39 060	53 39 083	44 56 136	63 01 205	44 20 295	26 46 329
244	36 07 024	21 19 059	54 26 083	45 29 136	62 41 205	43 37 294	26 21 328
245	36 26 023	22 00 058	55 13 082	46 01 136	62 21 206	42 53 293	25 56 327
246	36 44 022	22 40 057	56 00 081	46 34 136	62 00 207	42 10 292	25 30 326
247	37 01 021	23 19 057	56 46 080	47 07 136	61 38 208	41 26 291	25 04 325
248	37 18 020	23 58 056	57 33 080	47 40 136	61 16 208	40 41 290	24 37 325
249	37 33 018	24 37 055	58 19 079	48 13 136	60 53 209	39 57 289	24 09 324
250	37 48 017	25 16 054	59 06 078	48 46 136	60 30 209	39 12 289	23 41 323
251	38 01 016	25 54 053	59 52 077	49 19 136	60 07 210	38 27 288	23 12 322
252	38 14 015	26 32 052	60 38 076	49 52 136	59 43 211	37 42 287	22 42 321
253	38 26 014	27 09 052	61 23 075	50 25 136	59 19 211	36 57 286	22 12 320
254	38 36 012	27 46 051	62 09 074	50 58 136	58 54 212	36 11 285	21 42 319
	Rasalhague	◆ALTAIR	FOMALHAUT	◆ACHERNAR	RIGIL KENT	◆SPICA	ARCTURUS
255	38 46 011	28 22 050	17 57 114	14 11 154	58 29 212	35 26 285	21 10 318
256	38 55 010	28 58 049	18 40 113	14 32 154	58 04 213	34 40 284	20 39 318
257	39 02 009	29 33 048	19 24 113	14 53 154	57 38 213	33 54 283	20 07 317
258	39 09 007	30 08 047	20 07 112	15 14 153	57 12 213	33 08 282	19 34 316
259	39 14 006	30 43 046	20 51 112	15 35 153	56 46 214	32 22 282	19 01 315
260	39 19 005	31 16 045	21 35 111	15 57 152	56 20 214	31 35 281	18 27 314
261	39 23 004	31 50 044	22 19 111	16 19 152	55 53 215	30 49 280	17 53 314
262	39 25 002	32 22 043	23 03 110	16 42 152	55 26 215	30 02 280	17 19 313
263	39 27 001	32 55 042	23 48 110	17 04 151	54 59 215	29 15 279	16 44 312
264	39 27 000	33 26 041	24 32 109	17 27 151	54 32 215	28 29 278	16 08 311
265	39 26 359	33 57 040	25 17 109	17 51 150	54 04 216	27 42 278	15 33 310
266	39 25 357	34 27 039	26 02 108	18 14 150	53 36 216	26 55 277	14 56 310
267	39 22 356	34 57 038	26 47 108	18 38 150	53 08 216	26 08 276	14 20 309
268	39 18 355	35 26 037	27 32 107	19 02 149	52 40 216	25 21 276	13 43 308
269	39 13 354	35 54 036	28 17 107	19 27 149	52 12 217	24 34 275	13 05 307

LHA ♈	Hc Zn	Hc Zn	Hc Zn	Hc Zn	Hc Zn	Hc Zn	Hc Zn
	ALTAIR	Enif	◆FOMALHAUT	ACHERNAR	◆RIGIL KENT	ANTARES	◆Rasalhague
270	36 21 035	18 58 060	29 02 106	19 51 148	51 44 217	67 54 295	39 08 352
271	36 48 034	19 39 059	29 48 106	20 16 148	51 15 217	67 11 293	39 01 351
272	37 14 033	20 20 058	30 33 105	20 41 148	50 47 217	66 27 292	38 53 350
273	37 39 032	21 00 058	31 19 105	21 07 147	50 18 217	65 43 291	38 44 349
274	38 04 031	21 40 057	32 05 104	21 32 147	49 49 217	64 59 290	38 34 347
275	38 27 029	22 19 056	32 50 104	21 58 147	49 21 218	64 14 289	38 23 346
276	38 50 028	22 58 055	33 36 103	22 25 146	48 52 218	63 29 287	38 12 345
277	39 12 027	23 37 055	34 22 103	22 51 146	48 23 218	62 44 286	37 59 344
278	39 33 026	24 15 054	35 09 102	23 18 146	47 54 218	61 58 285	37 45 343
279	39 53 025	24 53 053	35 55 102	23 44 145	47 25 218	61 12 284	37 30 341
280	40 12 023	25 30 052	36 41 101	24 12 145	46 56 218	60 27 283	37 15 340
281	40 31 022	26 07 051	37 27 101	24 39 145	46 27 218	59 41 282	36 58 339
282	40 48 021	26 44 050	38 14 100	25 06 144	45 57 218	58 54 282	36 41 338
283	41 05 020	27 20 049	39 00 100	25 34 144	45 28 218	58 08 281	36 23 337
284	41 20 018	27 56 049	39 47 099	26 02 144	44 59 218	57 21 280	36 03 335
	ALTAIR	Enif	◆FOMALHAUT	ACHERNAR	◆RIGIL KENT	ANTARES	◆Rasalhague
285	41 34 017	28 31 048	40 34 099	26 30 143	44 30 218	56 35 279	35 43 334
286	41 48 016	29 06 047	41 21 098	26 59 143	44 01 218	55 48 278	35 23 333
287	42 00 015	29 40 046	42 07 098	27 27 143	43 31 218	55 01 277	35 01 332
288	42 12 013	30 13 045	42 54 097	27 56 142	43 02 218	54 14 277	34 38 331
289	42 22 012	30 47 044	43 41 097	28 25 142	42 33 218	53 27 276	34 15 330
290	42 31 011	31 19 043	44 28 096	28 54 142	42 04 218	52 40 275	33 51 329
291	42 39 009	31 51 042	45 15 096	29 23 142	41 35 218	51 53 275	33 26 328
292	42 46 008	32 22 041	46 02 095	29 53 141	41 06 218	51 06 274	33 01 327
293	42 52 007	32 53 040	46 49 095	30 22 141	40 37 218	50 19 273	32 34 326
294	42 57 005	33 23 039	47 36 094	30 52 141	40 08 218	49 31 273	32 07 325
295	43 01 004	33 52 038	48 24 094	31 22 141	39 39 218	48 44 272	31 40 324
296	43 03 003	34 21 037	49 11 093	31 52 140	39 10 217	47 57 271	31 11 323
297	43 05 001	34 49 036	49 58 092	32 22 140	38 42 217	47 10 271	30 42 322
298	43 05 000	35 17 035	50 45 092	32 53 140	38 13 217	46 22 270	30 13 321
299	43 05 358	35 43 034	51 33 091	33 23 140	37 44 217	45 35 269	29 43 320
	Enif	◆FOMALHAUT	ACHERNAR	◆RIGIL KENT	ANTARES	◆Rasalhague	ALTAIR
300	36 09 033	52 20 091	33 54 139	37 16 217	44 48 269	29 12 319	43 03 357
301	36 34 032	53 07 090	34 25 139	36 48 217	44 01 268	28 40 318	43 00 356
302	36 59 030	53 54 089	34 56 139	36 19 217	43 13 268	28 08 317	42 56 354
303	37 22 029	54 42 089	35 27 139	35 51 217	42 26 267	27 36 316	42 51 353
304	37 45 028	55 29 088	35 58 139	35 23 216	41 39 266	27 03 315	42 45 352
305	38 07 027	56 16 088	36 29 138	34 55 216	40 52 266	26 29 314	42 37 350
306	38 28 026	57 03 087	37 01 138	34 27 216	40 05 265	25 55 313	42 29 349
307	38 48 025	57 51 086	37 32 138	33 59 216	39 18 265	25 20 312	42 19 348
308	39 07 023	58 38 085	38 04 138	33 32 216	38 30 264	24 45 312	42 09 346
309	39 25 022	59 25 085	38 36 138	33 04 215	37 43 264	24 09 311	41 57 345
310	39 43 021	60 12 084	39 07 138	32 37 215	36 56 263	23 33 310	41 45 344
311	39 59 020	60 59 083	39 39 138	32 10 215	36 10 263	22 57 309	41 31 343
312	40 15 018	61 46 082	40 11 137	31 43 215	35 23 262	22 20 308	41 16 341
313	40 29 017	62 33 082	40 43 137	31 16 215	34 36 261	21 43 307	41 01 340
314	40 43 016	63 19 081	41 15 137	30 49 214	33 49 261	21 05 307	40 44 339
	Enif	◆Diphda	ACHERNAR	◆RIGIL KENT	ANTARES	Nunki	◆ALTAIR
315	40 55 015	37 25 084	41 48 137	30 22 214	33 03 260	61 28 285	40 26 338
316	41 07 013	38 12 083	42 20 137	29 56 214	32 16 260	60 42 284	40 08 336
317	41 17 012	38 59 083	42 52 137	29 29 214	31 29 259	59 56 283	39 48 335
318	41 27 011	39 46 082	43 25 137	29 03 213	30 43 259	59 10 282	39 28 334
319	41 35 010	40 33 081	43 57 137	28 37 213	29 57 258	58 24 281	39 07 333
320	41 42 008	41 19 080	44 29 137	28 11 213	29 10 258	57 37 281	38 45 332
321	41 48 007	42 06 080	45 02 137	27 46 213	28 24 257	56 51 280	38 22 330
322	41 54 006	42 52 079	45 34 137	27 20 212	27 38 257	56 04 279	37 58 329
323	41 58 004	43 39 078	46 07 137	26 55 212	26 52 256	55 17 278	37 33 328
324	42 01 003	44 25 077	46 39 137	26 30 212	26 06 256	54 31 277	37 08 327
325	42 03 002	45 11 077	47 12 137	26 05 212	25 21 255	53 44 277	36 42 326
326	42 03 000	45 57 076	47 45 137	25 41 211	24 35 255	52 57 276	36 15 325
327	42 03 359	46 43 075	48 17 137	25 16 211	23 49 254	52 10 275	35 47 324
328	42 02 358	47 28 074	48 50 137	24 52 211	23 04 254	51 22 274	35 19 323
329	41 59 356	48 14 073	49 22 137	24 28 210	22 19 253	50 35 274	34 50 322
	◆Alpheratz	Diphda	◆ACHERNAR	RIGIL KENT	◆Nunki	ALTAIR	Enif
330	16 21 029	48 59 072	49 54 137	24 04 210	49 48 273	34 20 320	41 56 355
331	16 44 028	49 44 071	50 27 137	23 41 210	49 01 272	33 50 319	41 51 354
332	17 06 027	50 28 070	50 59 137	23 17 209	48 14 272	33 18 318	41 45 352
333	17 27 027	51 13 070	51 32 137	22 54 209	47 26 271	32 47 317	41 38 351
334	17 48 026	51 57 069	52 04 137	22 31 209	46 39 271	32 15 316	41 30 350
335	18 08 025	52 41 068	52 36 137	22 09 208	45 52 270	31 42 316	41 22 348
336	18 28 024	53 24 067	53 08 137	21 46 208	45 05 269	31 08 315	41 12 347
337	18 47 023	54 08 066	53 40 138	21 24 208	44 17 269	30 34 314	41 01 346
338	19 05 022	54 50 064	54 12 138	21 02 207	43 30 268	30 00 313	40 49 345
339	19 23 021	55 33 063	54 44 138	20 40 207	42 43 268	29 25 312	40 35 343
340	19 40 021	56 15 062	55 15 138	20 19 207	41 56 267	28 49 311	40 21 342
341	19 56 020	56 56 061	55 47 138	19 58 206	41 08 266	28 13 310	40 06 341
342	20 12 019	57 38 060	56 18 139	19 37 206	40 21 266	27 37 309	39 50 340
343	20 27 018	58 18 058	56 49 139	19 16 206	39 34 265	27 00 308	39 33 338
344	20 41 017	58 58 057	57 20 139	18 56 205	38 47 265	26 23 307	39 16 337
	◆Alpheratz	Diphda	◆CANOPUS	RIGIL KENT	◆Nunki	ALTAIR	Enif
345	20 54 016	59 38 056	18 33 143	18 36 205	38 00 264	25 45 307	38 57 336
346	21 07 015	60 16 054	19 01 143	18 16 205	37 13 264	25 07 306	38 37 335
347	21 19 014	60 54 053	19 30 143	17 57 204	36 26 263	24 28 305	38 16 334
348	21 31 013	61 32 052	19 59 142	17 38 204	35 39 262	23 49 304	37 55 332
349	21 41 012	62 08 050	20 28 142	17 19 203	34 52 262	23 10 303	37 33 331
350	21 51 012	62 44 048	20 57 141	17 00 203	34 05 261	22 30 302	37 09 330
351	22 00 011	63 19 047	21 27 141	16 42 203	33 19 261	21 50 302	36 46 329
352	22 08 010	63 53 045	21 57 141	16 24 202	32 32 260	21 09 301	36 21 328
353	22 16 009	64 26 043	22 27 140	16 06 202	31 45 260	20 29 300	35 55 327
354	22 23 008	64 58 041	22 57 140	15 49 201	30 59 259	19 48 299	35 29 326
355	22 29 007	65 28 039	23 27 140	15 31 201	30 13 259	19 06 299	35 02 325
356	22 34 006	65 58 037	23 58 139	15 15 201	29 26 258	18 25 298	34 34 324
357	22 39 005	66 26 035	24 29 139	14 58 200	28 40 258	17 43 297	34 06 323
358	22 42 004	66 53 033	25 00 139	14 42 200	27 54 257	17 00 296	33 37 321
359	22 45 003	67 18 031	25 32 138	14 26 199	27 08 257	16 18 296	33 07 320

LAT 39°S

LHA ♈	Hc	Zn	Hc	Zn	Hc	Zn	Hc	Zn	Hc	Zn	Hc	Zn	Hc	Zn
	Alpheratz		◆Hamal		RIGEL		◆CANOPUS		Peacock		◆Nunki		Enif	
0	21 48	002	20 40	031	13 49	089	26 48	138	51 21	225	26 36	257	31 51	320
1	21 49	001	21 04	030	14 36	089	27 19	137	50 48	225	25 51	256	31 20	319
2	21 50	000	21 27	030	15 22	088	27 51	137	50 15	225	25 05	256	30 49	318
3	21 49	359	21 50	029	16 09	087	28 23	137	49 43	225	24 20	255	30 18	317
4	21 48	358	22 12	028	16 55	087	28 55	136	49 10	225	23 35	254	29 46	316
5	21 47	357	22 33	027	17 42	086	29 28	136	48 37	225	22 51	254	29 13	315
6	21 44	357	22 54	026	18 28	086	30 00	136	48 04	225	22 06	253	28 40	314
7	21 41	356	23 14	025	19 15	085	30 33	135	47 31	225	21 21	253	28 06	313
8	21 37	355	23 33	024	20 01	084	31 06	135	46 58	225	20 37	252	27 32	312
9	21 32	354	23 52	023	20 48	084	31 39	135	46 25	225	19 52	252	26 57	311
10	21 27	353	24 10	022	21 34	083	32 12	134	45 52	225	19 08	251	26 22	310
11	21 21	352	24 27	021	22 20	082	32 45	134	45 19	225	18 24	251	25 46	310
12	21 14	351	24 43	020	23 06	082	33 19	134	44 46	225	17 40	250	25 10	309
13	21 06	350	24 59	019	23 52	081	33 53	134	44 14	225	16 56	250	24 34	308
14	20 57	349	25 14	018	24 38	080	34 27	133	43 41	224	16 13	249	23 57	307
	◆Hamal		ALDEBARAN		RIGEL		◆CANOPUS		Peacock		◆FOMALHAUT		Alpheratz	
15	25 28	017	14 52	054	25 24	080	35 01	133	43 08	224	63 19	281	20 48	348
16	25 42	016	15 30	053	26 10	079	35 35	133	42 36	224	62 34	281	20 38	347
17	25 55	015	16 07	052	26 56	078	36 09	133	42 03	224	61 48	280	20 28	346
18	26 06	014	16 43	051	27 41	077	36 43	132	41 31	224	61 02	279	20 16	345
19	26 18	013	17 19	050	28 27	077	37 18	132	40 58	224	60 16	278	20 04	344
20	26 28	012	17 55	050	29 12	076	37 53	132	40 26	224	59 29	277	19 51	344
21	26 37	011	18 31	049	29 57	075	38 28	132	39 54	224	58 43	276	19 38	343
22	26 46	010	19 06	048	30 42	074	39 02	131	39 22	223	57 57	276	19 24	342
23	26 54	009	19 40	047	31 27	074	39 37	131	38 50	223	57 10	275	19 09	341
24	27 01	008	20 14	046	32 12	073	40 13	131	38 18	223	56 24	274	18 53	340
25	27 07	007	20 48	046	32 56	072	40 48	131	37 46	223	55 37	273	18 37	339
26	27 13	006	21 21	045	33 41	071	41 23	131	37 15	223	54 51	273	18 20	338
27	27 18	005	21 53	044	34 25	071	41 59	130	36 43	222	54 04	272	18 02	337
28	27 21	004	22 25	043	35 09	070	42 34	130	36 12	222	53 18	271	17 44	337
29	27 24	003	22 57	042	35 52	069	43 10	130	35 40	222	52 31	271	17 25	336
	Hamal		◆ALDEBARAN		RIGEL		SIRIUS		◆CANOPUS		Peacock		◆FOMALHAUT	
30	27 26	002	23 28	041	36 36	068	24 42	092	43 46	130	35 09	222	51 44	270
31	27 28	001	23 59	040	37 19	067	25 29	091	44 21	130	34 38	222	50 58	270
32	27 28	000	24 29	040	38 02	066	26 16	091	44 57	130	34 07	221	50 11	269
33	27 28	359	24 58	039	38 44	065	27 02	090	45 33	130	33 36	221	49 24	268
34	27 26	358	25 27	038	39 26	065	27 49	090	46 09	129	33 06	221	48 38	268
35	27 24	357	25 55	037	40 08	064	28 35	089	46 45	129	32 35	221	47 51	267
36	27 21	356	26 23	036	40 50	063	29 22	088	47 21	129	32 05	220	47 05	267
37	27 18	355	26 50	035	41 31	062	30 09	088	47 58	129	31 35	220	46 18	266
38	27 13	354	27 16	034	42 12	061	30 55	087	48 34	129	31 05	220	45 32	265
39	27 08	353	27 42	033	42 53	060	31 42	086	49 10	129	30 35	220	44 45	265
40	27 01	352	28 07	032	43 33	059	32 28	086	49 46	129	30 05	219	43 59	264
41	26 54	351	28 31	031	44 13	058	33 15	085	50 23	129	29 36	219	43 12	264
42	26 46	350	28 55	030	44 52	057	34 01	084	50 59	129	29 07	219	42 26	263
43	26 38	349	29 18	029	45 31	056	34 48	084	51 35	129	28 38	218	41 40	263
44	26 28	348	29 40	028	46 09	055	35 34	083	52 12	129	28 09	218	40 54	262
	◆ALDEBARAN		RIGEL		SIRIUS		◆CANOPUS		ACHERNAR		◆FOMALHAUT		Hamal	
45	30 02	027	46 47	054	36 20	082	52 48	129	67 28	210	40 07	262	26 18	347
46	30 22	026	47 24	052	37 06	081	53 24	129	67 05	211	39 21	261	26 07	346
47	30 42	025	48 01	051	37 52	081	54 01	129	66 41	212	38 35	260	25 55	345
48	31 02	024	48 37	050	38 38	080	54 37	129	66 16	212	37 49	260	25 42	344
49	31 20	023	49 12	049	39 24	079	55 13	129	65 51	213	37 04	259	25 29	343
50	31 38	022	49 47	048	40 10	079	55 50	129	65 25	214	36 18	259	25 14	342
51	31 55	021	50 21	046	40 56	078	56 26	129	64 59	215	35 32	258	24 59	341
52	32 11	020	50 54	045	41 41	077	57 02	129	64 32	216	34 46	258	24 44	340
53	32 26	018	51 27	044	42 26	076	57 38	129	64 04	216	34 01	257	24 27	339
54	32 40	017	51 59	042	43 12	075	58 14	130	63 37	217	33 15	257	24 10	338
55	32 54	016	52 30	041	43 57	075	58 50	130	63 08	217	32 30	256	23 52	337
56	33 06	015	53 00	040	44 42	074	59 26	130	62 40	218	31 45	256	23 33	336
57	33 18	014	53 29	038	45 26	073	60 01	130	62 11	219	31 00	255	23 14	335
58	33 29	013	53 58	037	46 11	072	60 37	130	61 42	219	30 15	255	22 54	334
59	33 39	012	54 25	035	46 55	071	61 12	131	61 12	220	29 30	254	22 33	333
	ALDEBARAN		◆BETELGEUSE		SIRIUS		◆ACRUX		ACHERNAR		◆FOMALHAUT		Hamal	
60	33 48	011	36 22	037	47 39	070	20 34	157	60 42	220	28 45	254	22 12	332
61	33 56	009	36 49	036	48 23	069	20 52	157	60 12	220	28 00	253	21 50	331
62	34 03	008	37 16	034	49 06	068	21 11	157	59 42	221	27 16	253	21 27	330
63	34 10	007	37 42	033	49 49	067	21 29	156	59 11	221	26 31	252	21 04	330
64	34 15	006	38 07	032	50 32	066	21 48	156	58 41	221	25 47	252	20 40	329
65	34 19	005	38 32	031	51 15	065	22 07	156	58 10	222	25 02	251	20 16	328
66	34 23	004	38 55	030	51 57	064	22 27	155	57 38	222	24 18	251	19 51	327
67	34 25	003	39 18	029	52 39	063	22 46	155	57 07	222	23 34	250	19 25	326
68	34 27	001	39 40	027	53 20	062	23 06	155	56 36	223	22 51	250	18 59	325
69	34 28	000	40 01	026	54 01	061	23 26	154	56 04	223	22 07	249	18 32	324
70	34 27	359	40 21	025	54 42	060	23 47	154	55 32	223	21 24	249	18 04	324
71	34 26	358	40 41	024	55 22	059	24 07	154	55 00	223	20 40	248	17 36	323
72	34 24	357	40 59	023	56 01	057	24 28	153	54 28	223	19 57	248	17 08	322
73	34 21	356	41 16	021	56 40	056	24 49	153	53 56	224	19 14	247	16 39	321
74	34 17	354	41 33	020	57 19	055	25 11	153	53 24	224	18 31	247	16 09	320
	BETELGEUSE		◆SIRIUS		Suhail		◆ACRUX		ACHERNAR		◆Diphda		ALDEBARAN	
75	41 48	019	57 57	053	44 09	117	25 32	152	52 52	224	31 14	272	34 12	353
76	42 03	017	58 34	052	44 51	116	25 54	152	52 19	224	30 28	271	34 06	352
77	42 16	016	59 10	051	45 33	116	26 16	152	51 47	224	29 41	270	33 59	351
78	42 29	015	59 45	049	46 15	116	26 38	151	51 15	224	28 55	270	33 51	350
79	42 40	014	60 21	048	46 57	116	27 00	151	50 42	224	28 08	269	33 43	349
80	42 51	012	60 55	046	47 39	115	27 23	151	50 10	224	27 21	268	33 33	348
81	43 00	011	61 28	044	48 21	115	27 46	151	49 37	224	26 35	268	33 22	346
82	43 08	010	62 00	043	49 04	115	28 09	150	49 05	224	25 48	267	33 11	345
83	43 16	008	62 31	041	49 46	114	28 32	150	48 32	224	25 02	267	32 59	344
84	43 22	007	63 01	039	50 29	114	28 55	150	48 00	224	24 15	266	32 46	343
85	43 27	005	63 30	037	51 11	114	29 19	150	47 27	224	23 29	265	32 32	342
86	43 30	004	63 58	036	51 54	114	29 42	149	46 55	224	22 42	265	32 17	341
87	43 33	003	64 25	034	52 36	114	30 06	149	46 22	224	21 56	264	32 01	340
88	43 35	001	64 50	032	53 19	113	30 30	149	45 50	224	21 09	264	31 45	339
89	43 35	000	65 13	030	54 02	113	30 55	149	45 17	224	20 23	263	31 27	338

LHA ♈	Hc	Zn	Hc	Zn	Hc	Zn	Hc	Zn	Hc	Zn	Hc	Zn	Hc	Zn
	PROCYON		REGULUS		◆Suhail		ACRUX		◆ACHERNAR		RIGEL		◆BETELGEUSE	
90	40 07	033	12 56	063	54 45	113	31 19	148	44 45	224	57 35	339	43 35	359
91	40 33	032	13 38	062	55 28	113	31 43	148	44 12	224	57 18	337	43 33	357
92	40 57	031	14 19	061	56 11	112	32 08	148	43 40	224	56 59	336	43 30	356
93	41 21	030	14 59	061	56 54	112	32 33	148	43 08	224	56 39	334	43 27	355
94	41 44	029	15 40	060	57 37	112	32 58	148	42 36	224	56 18	332	43 22	353
95	42 05	027	16 20	059	58 21	112	33 23	147	42 04	223	55 56	330	43 15	352
96	42 26	026	17 00	058	59 04	112	33 48	147	41 32	223	55 32	329	43 08	350
97	42 46	025	17 39	058	59 47	112	34 14	147	41 00	223	55 08	327	43 00	349
98	43 06	024	18 19	057	60 31	112	34 39	147	40 28	223	54 42	326	42 51	348
99	43 24	022	18 57	056	61 14	111	35 05	147	39 56	223	54 15	324	42 40	346
100	43 41	021	19 36	055	61 57	111	35 31	146	39 24	223	53 47	323	42 29	345
101	43 57	020	20 14	054	62 41	111	35 56	146	38 52	223	53 19	321	42 16	344
102	44 12	018	20 52	054	63 24	111	36 22	146	38 21	222	52 49	320	42 03	343
103	44 26	017	21 29	053	64 08	111	36 48	146	37 50	222	52 18	318	41 48	341
104	44 39	016	22 06	052	64 51	111	37 15	146	37 18	222	51 47	317	41 33	340
	PROCYON		REGULUS		◆Gienah		ACRUX		◆ACHERNAR		RIGEL		◆BETELGEUSE	
105	44 51	014	22 43	051	19 16	097	37 41	146	36 47	222	51 15	316	41 16	339
106	45 02	013	23 19	050	20 03	097	38 07	146	36 16	222	50 42	314	40 59	337
107	45 12	011	23 55	050	20 49	096	38 34	145	35 45	221	50 08	313	40 41	336
108	45 20	010	24 30	049	21 35	096	39 00	145	35 14	221	49 34	312	40 21	335
109	45 28	009	25 05	048	22 22	095	39 27	145	34 44	221	48 59	311	40 01	334
110	45 34	007	25 39	047	23 08	094	39 53	145	34 13	221	48 23	309	39 40	333
111	45 39	006	26 13	046	23 55	094	40 20	145	33 43	221	47 47	308	39 18	331
112	45 44	004	26 46	045	24 41	093	40 47	145	33 12	220	47 10	307	38 55	330
113	45 46	003	27 19	044	25 28	093	41 14	145	32 42	220	46 33	306	38 32	329
114	45 48	001	27 51	043	26 14	092	41 41	145	32 12	220	45 55	305	38 07	328
115	45 49	000	28 23	042	27 01	091	42 08	145	31 42	220	45 16	304	37 42	327
116	45 48	359	28 54	041	27 48	091	42 35	145	31 13	219	44 37	303	37 16	326
117	45 47	357	29 24	040	28 34	090	43 02	145	30 43	219	43 58	302	36 49	324
118	45 44	356	29 54	039	29 21	090	43 29	145	30 14	219	43 18	301	36 22	323
119	45 40	354	30 24	039	30 07	089	43 56	145	29 45	219	42 38	300	35 53	322
	REGULUS		◆SPICA		ACRUX		◆CANOPUS		RIGEL		BETELGEUSE		◆PROCYON	
120	30 52	038	13 37	094	44 23	145	68 36	222	41 57	299	35 25	321	45 34	353
121	31 20	037	14 23	093	44 50	145	68 04	223	41 16	298	34 55	320	45 28	351
122	31 48	036	15 10	092	45 17	145	67 32	224	40 35	297	34 25	319	45 21	350
123	32 15	034	15 57	092	45 44	145	67 00	225	39 53	296	33 54	318	45 12	349
124	32 41	033	16 43	091	46 11	145	66 27	225	39 11	295	33 22	317	45 02	347
125	33 06	032	17 30	090	46 38	145	65 53	226	38 28	294	32 50	316	44 52	346
126	33 31	031	18 16	090	47 05	145	65 20	226	37 46	293	32 18	315	44 40	345
127	33 55	030	19 03	089	47 32	145	64 46	227	37 03	292	31 45	314	44 27	343
128	34 18	029	19 50	089	47 59	145	64 12	227	36 20	292	31 11	313	44 13	342
129	34 40	028	20 36	088	48 26	145	63 37	228	35 36	291	30 37	312	43 58	340
130	35 01	027	21 23	087	48 53	145	63 03	228	34 52	290	30 02	311	43 42	339
131	35 22	026	22 09	087	49 19	145	62 28	229	34 08	289	29 26	310	43 24	338
132	35 42	025	22 56	086	49 46	145	61 53	229	33 24	288	28 51	309	43 06	337
133	36 01	024	23 42	085	50 13	145	61 17	229	32 40	288	28 14	309	42 47	335
134	36 19	022	24 29	085	50 39	145	60 42	230	31 55	287	27 38	308	42 27	334
	◆REGULUS		SPICA		◆ACRUX		CANOPUS		◆RIGEL		BETELGEUSE		PROCYON	
135	36 37	021	25 15	084	51 06	146	60 06	230	31 11	286	27 01	307	42 06	333
136	36 53	020	26 02	083	51 32	146	59 31	230	30 26	285	26 23	306	41 45	331
137	37 09	019	26 48	083	51 58	146	58 55	230	29 41	285	25 45	305	41 22	330
138	37 23	018	27 34	082	52 24	146	58 19	230	28 55	284	25 07	304	40 58	329
139	37 37	017	28 20	081	52 50	146	57 43	231	28 10	283	24 28	303	40 34	328
140	37 50	015	29 06	081	53 16	147	57 07	231	27 25	282	23 49	303	40 09	327
141	38 02	014	29 52	080	53 41	147	56 31	231	26 39	282	23 10	302	39 43	325
142	38 13	013	30 38	079	54 07	147	55 55	231	25 53	281	22 30	301	39 16	324
143	38 22	012	31 24	078	54 32	147	55 18	231	25 07	280	21 50	300	38 48	323
144	38 31	010	32 09	078	54 57	148	54 42	231	24 21	280	21 09	299	38 20	322
145	38 39	009	32 55	077	55 22	148	54 06	231	23 35	279	20 28	299	37 51	321
146	38 46	008	33 40	076	55 46	148	53 29	231	22 49	278	19 47	298	37 21	320
147	38 52	007	34 26	075	56 11	149	52 53	231	22 03	277	19 06	297	36 51	319
148	38 57	005	35 11	075	56 35	149	52 17	231	21 17	277	18 24	296	36 20	318
149	39 01	004	35 55	074	56 59	149	51 40	231	20 31	276	17 42	296	35 48	317
	REGULUS		◆SPICA		ACRUX		◆Miaplacidus		CANOPUS		SIRIUS		◆PROCYON	
150	39 04	003	36 40	073	57 22	150	58 36	188	51 04	231	42 22	284	35 16	316
151	39 06	002	37 25	072	57 45	150	58 30	188	50 28	231	41 37	283	34 43	315
152	39 06	000	38 09	072	58 08	151	58 23	189	49 51	231	40 51	282	34 09	314
153	39 06	359	38 53	071	58 31	151	58 15	190	49 15	231	40 06	281	33 35	313
154	39 05	358	39 37	070	58 53	152	58 07	190	48 39	231	39 20	281	33 01	312
155	39 03	357	40 21	069	59 15	152	57 59	191	48 03	231	38 34	280	32 26	311
156	38 59	355	41 04	068	59 37	153	57 50	191	47 27	231	37 48	279	31 50	310
157	38 55	354	41 47	067	59 58	153	57 40	192	46 50	231	37 02	278	31 14	309
158	38 50	353	42 30	066	60 18	154	57 31	193	46 14	231	36 16	278	30 37	308
159	38 43	352	43 13	065	60 39	155	57 20	193	45 38	231	35 30	277	30 00	307
160	38 36	350	43 55	064	60 59	155	57 10	194	45 02	230	34 43	276	29 23	306
161	38 28	349	44 37	063	61 18	156	56 58	194	44 26	230	33 57	276	28 45	305
162	38 18	348	45 18	062	61 37	156	56 47	195	43 51	230	33 10	275	28 07	304
163	38 08	347	45 59	061	61 55	157	56 35	195	43 15	230	32 24	274	27 28	304
164	37 57	345	46 40	060	62 13	158	56 22	196	42 39	230	31 37	274	26 49	303
	ARCTURUS		◆ANTARES		ACRUX		◆CANOPUS		SIRIUS		PROCYON		◆REGULUS	
165	15 58	048	21 44	107	62 30	159	42 04	230	30 51	273	26 09	302	37 45	344
166	16 32	047	22 29	107	62 47	159	41 28	229	30 04	272	25 30	301	37 31	343
167	17 06	046	23 13	106	63 03	160	40 53	229	29 18	272	24 50	300	37 17	342
168	17 40	046	23 58	106	63 18	161	40 18	229	28 31	271	24 09	299	37 02	341
169	18 13	045	24 43	105	63 33	162	39 42	229	27 44	270	23 28	299	36 46	339
170	18 45	044	25 28	104	63 47	163	39 07	229	26 58	270	22 47	298	36 30	338
171	19 17	043	26 13	104	64 01	164	38 32	228	26 11	269	22 06	297	36 12	337
172	19 49	042	26 59	103	64 14	165	37 58	228	25 25	269	21 24	296	35 53	336
173	20 20	041	27 44	103	64 26	165	37 23	228	24 38	268	20 42	295	35 34	335
174	20 51	041	28 30	102	64 37	166	36 48	228	23 51	267	20 00	295	35 14	334
175	21 21	040	29 15	102	64 47	167	36 14	227	23 05	267	19 17	294	34 53	333
176	21 50	039	30 01	101	64 57	168	35 40	227	22 18	266	18 35	293	34 31	331
177	22 19	038	30 47	101	65 06	169	35 05	227	21 32	265	17 52	293	34 08	330
178	22 48	037	31 33	100	65 14	170	34 31	227	20 45	265	17 09	292	33 45	329
179	23 16	036	32 19	100	65 22	171	33 58	226	19 59	264	16 25	291	33 21	328

 LAT 39°S

LHA ♈	ARCTURUS Hc	Zn	◆ ANTARES Hc	Zn	RIGIL KENT Hc	Zn	ACRUX Hc	Zn	◆ CANOPUS Hc	Zn	Alphard Hc	Zn	◆ REGULUS Hc	Zn
180	23 43	035	33 05	099	57 01	145	65 28	173	33 24	226	44 33	302	32 56	327
181	24 10	034	33 51	098	57 27	145	65 34	174	32 50	226	43 53	301	32 30	326
182	24 36	034	34 37	098	57 54	146	65 39	175	32 17	226	43 12	300	32 04	325
183	25 01	033	35 23	097	58 20	146	65 42	176	31 44	225	42 31	299	31 37	324
184	25 26	032	36 09	097	58 46	146	65 45	177	31 11	225	41 50	298	31 09	323
185	25 50	031	36 56	096	59 12	147	65 48	178	30 38	225	41 09	297	30 41	322
186	26 13	030	37 42	096	59 37	147	65 49	179	30 05	224	40 27	296	30 12	321
187	26 36	029	38 28	095	60 02	148	65 49	180	29 32	224	39 45	295	29 42	320
188	26 58	028	39 15	095	60 27	148	65 48	181	29 00	224	39 02	294	29 12	319
189	27 20	027	40 01	094	60 51	149	65 47	182	28 28	223	38 20	293	28 41	318
190	27 40	026	40 48	093	61 15	149	65 45	183	27 56	223	37 36	292	28 10	317
191	28 00	025	41 35	093	61 38	150	65 41	185	27 24	223	36 53	291	27 38	316
192	28 20	024	42 21	092	62 01	151	65 37	186	26 52	223	36 10	290	27 05	315
193	28 38	023	43 08	092	62 24	151	65 32	187	26 21	222	35 26	290	26 32	314
194	28 56	022	43 54	091	62 46	152	65 26	188	25 50	222	34 42	289	25 59	314

LHA ♈	ARCTURUS Hc	Zn	◆ ANTARES Hc	Zn	RIGIL KENT Hc	Zn	◆ ACRUX Hc	Zn	Suhail Hc	Zn	◆ REGULUS Hc	Zn	Denebola Hc	Zn
195	29 13	021	44 41	090	63 08	153	65 20	189	47 09	245	25 25	313	34 03	339
196	29 29	020	45 28	090	63 29	154	65 12	190	46 26	244	24 50	312	33 46	338
197	29 44	019	46 14	089	63 49	154	65 04	191	45 45	244	24 15	311	33 29	337
198	29 58	018	47 01	088	64 09	155	64 55	192	45 03	244	23 40	310	33 10	336
199	30 12	017	47 47	088	64 28	156	64 45	193	44 21	243	23 04	309	32 51	335
200	30 25	015	48 34	087	64 47	157	64 34	194	43 39	243	22 28	308	32 31	334
201	30 37	014	49 21	086	65 05	158	64 22	195	42 58	243	21 51	308	32 10	333
202	30 48	013	50 07	086	65 22	159	64 10	196	42 16	243	21 14	307	31 48	332
203	30 58	012	50 54	085	65 39	160	63 57	197	41 35	242	20 36	306	31 26	331
204	31 08	011	51 40	084	65 55	161	63 43	197	40 54	242	19 58	305	31 03	330
205	31 17	010	52 26	084	66 10	162	63 29	198	40 13	242	19 20	304	30 39	329
206	31 24	009	53 13	083	66 24	163	63 14	199	39 32	241	18 41	304	30 14	328
207	31 31	008	53 59	082	66 38	164	62 59	200	38 51	241	18 02	303	29 49	327
208	31 37	007	54 45	081	66 50	165	62 42	201	38 10	241	17 23	302	29 23	326
209	31 42	006	55 31	080	67 02	166	62 25	202	37 29	240	16 43	301	28 56	325

LHA ♈	ARCTURUS Hc	Zn	◆ ANTARES Hc	Zn	Peacock Hc	Zn	RIGIL KENT Hc	Zn	◆ ACRUX Hc	Zn	Suhail Hc	Zn	◆ SPICA Hc	Zn
210	31 46	005	56 17	080	28 26	142	67 13	167	62 08	202	36 49	240	61 14	342
211	31 49	003	57 03	079	28 55	141	67 23	168	61 50	203	36 09	240	60 59	340
212	31 52	002	57 48	078	29 24	141	67 31	170	61 32	204	35 29	239	60 42	339
213	31 53	001	58 34	077	29 53	141	67 39	171	61 13	204	34 49	239	60 25	337
214	31 54	000	59 19	076	30 23	141	67 46	172	60 53	205	34 09	239	60 05	335
215	31 53	359	60 04	075	30 53	140	67 52	173	60 33	206	33 29	238	59 45	333
216	31 52	358	60 49	074	31 23	140	67 57	175	60 13	206	32 49	238	59 23	331
217	31 50	357	61 34	073	31 53	140	68 01	176	59 52	207	32 10	238	59 00	329
218	31 47	356	62 19	072	32 23	139	68 04	177	59 31	207	31 31	237	58 36	328
219	31 43	355	63 03	071	32 53	139	68 06	178	59 09	208	30 52	237	58 10	326
220	31 38	353	63 47	070	33 24	139	68 06	180	58 47	208	30 13	236	57 43	324
221	31 32	352	64 30	069	33 54	139	68 06	181	58 25	209	29 34	236	57 16	323
222	31 25	351	65 13	067	34 25	138	68 04	182	58 02	209	28 55	236	56 47	321
223	31 18	350	65 56	066	34 56	138	68 02	184	57 39	210	28 17	235	56 17	320
224	31 09	349	66 39	065	35 27	138	67 58	185	57 16	210	27 39	235	55 47	318

LHA ♈	Alphecca Hc	Zn	Rasalhague Hc	Zn	◆ Nunki Hc	Zn	Peacock Hc	Zn	◆ RIGIL KENT Hc	Zn	◆ SPICA Hc	Zn	ARCTURUS Hc	Zn
225	23 49	009	26 58	043	39 34	094	35 59	138	67 54	186	55 15	317	31 00	348
226	23 56	008	27 30	043	40 21	093	36 30	138	67 48	188	54 43	315	30 50	347
227	24 02	007	28 01	042	41 07	093	37 02	137	67 42	189	54 09	314	30 39	346
228	24 07	006	28 32	041	41 54	092	37 33	137	67 34	190	53 35	312	30 27	345
229	24 11	005	29 02	040	42 40	092	38 05	137	67 25	191	53 01	311	30 14	344
230	24 14	004	29 32	039	43 27	091	38 37	137	67 16	192	52 25	310	30 01	343
231	24 17	003	30 00	038	44 14	090	39 09	137	67 05	194	51 49	309	29 47	342
232	24 19	002	30 29	037	45 00	090	39 41	136	66 54	195	51 12	307	29 31	340
233	24 20	001	30 56	036	45 47	089	40 13	136	66 42	196	50 35	306	29 15	339
234	24 20	000	31 23	035	46 33	088	40 45	136	66 29	197	49 57	305	28 59	338
235	24 20	359	31 49	034	47 20	088	41 17	136	66 14	198	49 19	304	28 41	337
236	24 18	358	32 15	033	48 07	087	41 50	136	66 00	199	48 40	303	28 23	336
237	24 16	357	32 40	032	48 53	086	42 22	136	65 44	200	48 00	302	28 04	335
238	24 13	356	33 04	031	49 40	086	42 55	136	65 28	201	47 20	301	27 44	334
239	24 09	355	33 27	030	50 26	085	43 27	136	65 11	202	46 40	300	27 23	333

LHA ♈	Rasalhague Hc	Zn	ALTAIR Hc	Zn	◆ Nunki Hc	Zn	Peacock Hc	Zn	◆ RIGIL KENT Hc	Zn	SPICA Hc	Zn	◆ ARCTURUS Hc	Zn
240	33 50	028	18 06	062	51 13	084	44 00	135	64 53	203	45 59	299	27 02	332
241	34 12	027	18 47	061	51 59	084	44 33	135	64 34	204	45 18	297	26 40	331
242	34 33	026	19 28	060	52 45	083	45 06	135	64 15	205	44 36	297	26 17	330
243	34 53	025	20 08	059	53 32	082	45 38	135	63 56	205	43 55	296	25 54	329
244	35 12	024	20 48	059	54 18	081	46 11	135	63 35	206	43 12	295	25 30	329
245	35 31	023	21 28	058	55 04	081	46 44	135	63 14	207	42 30	294	25 05	328
246	35 49	022	22 07	057	55 50	080	47 17	135	62 53	208	41 47	293	24 40	327
247	36 05	021	22 46	056	56 36	079	47 50	135	62 31	208	41 04	292	24 14	326
248	36 21	019	23 25	055	57 21	078	48 23	135	62 09	209	40 20	291	23 48	325
249	36 36	018	24 03	055	58 07	077	48 56	135	61 46	210	39 37	290	23 20	324
250	36 50	017	24 41	054	58 52	076	49 29	135	61 22	210	38 53	289	22 53	323
251	37 04	016	25 18	053	59 37	075	50 02	135	60 59	211	38 09	288	22 24	322
252	37 16	015	25 55	052	60 22	074	50 35	135	60 34	211	37 24	288	21 55	321
253	37 27	013	26 31	051	61 07	073	51 08	135	60 10	212	36 40	287	21 26	320
254	37 38	012	27 08	050	61 52	072	51 41	135	59 45	213	35 55	286	20 56	320

LHA ♈	Rasalhague Hc	Zn	◆ ALTAIR Hc	Zn	FOMALHAUT Hc	Zn	◆ ACHERNAR Hc	Zn	RIGIL KENT Hc	Zn	◆ SPICA Hc	Zn	ARCTURUS Hc	Zn
255	37 47	011	27 43	049	18 21	114	15 05	154	59 20	213	35 10	285	20 25	319
256	37 55	010	28 18	049	19 04	113	15 26	154	58 54	213	34 25	285	19 54	318
257	38 03	009	28 53	048	19 47	113	15 46	153	58 28	214	33 40	284	19 23	317
258	38 09	007	29 27	047	20 30	112	16 07	153	58 02	214	32 55	283	18 51	316
259	38 15	006	30 01	046	21 13	111	16 29	153	57 36	215	32 09	282	18 18	315
260	38 19	005	30 34	045	21 57	111	16 50	152	57 09	215	31 24	282	17 45	315
261	38 23	004	31 07	044	22 40	110	17 12	152	56 42	215	30 38	281	17 12	314
262	38 25	002	31 39	043	23 24	110	17 34	151	56 15	216	29 52	280	16 38	313
263	38 27	001	32 10	042	24 08	109	17 57	151	55 48	216	29 06	279	16 04	312
264	38 27	000	32 41	041	24 52	109	18 20	151	55 20	216	28 20	279	15 29	311
265	38 26	359	33 11	040	25 36	108	18 43	150	54 52	217	27 34	278	14 54	311
266	38 25	357	33 41	039	26 20	108	19 06	150	54 25	217	26 48	277	14 18	310
267	38 22	356	34 10	038	27 05	107	19 30	149	53 57	217	26 01	277	13 42	309
268	38 19	355	34 38	037	27 49	107	19 54	149	53 28	217	25 15	276	13 06	308
269	38 14	354	35 05	036	28 34	106	20 18	149	53 00	217	24 29	275	12 29	308

LHA ♈	ALTAIR Hc	Zn	Enif Hc	Zn	◆ FOMALHAUT Hc	Zn	ACHERNAR Hc	Zn	◆ RIGIL KENT Hc	Zn	ANTARES Hc	Zn	◆ Rasalhague Hc	Zn
270	35 32	035	18 28	060	29 19	106	20 42	148	52 32	218	67 27	297	38 08	352
271	35 58	033	19 08	059	30 04	105	21 07	148	52 03	218	66 46	296	38 02	351
272	36 24	032	19 48	058	30 49	105	21 32	147	51 34	218	66 03	294	37 54	350
273	36 48	031	20 28	057	31 34	104	21 57	147	51 06	218	65 21	293	37 45	349
274	37 12	030	21 07	057	32 19	104	22 23	147	50 37	218	64 37	292	37 36	348
275	37 35	029	21 45	056	33 05	103	22 48	146	50 08	218	63 54	290	37 25	346
276	37 57	028	22 24	055	33 50	103	23 14	146	49 39	218	63 10	289	37 14	345
277	38 19	027	23 02	054	34 36	102	23 41	146	49 10	219	62 26	288	37 01	344
278	38 39	025	23 39	053	35 21	102	24 07	145	48 41	219	61 41	287	36 48	343
279	38 59	024	24 16	052	36 07	101	24 34	145	48 12	219	60 57	286	36 34	342
280	39 17	023	24 53	052	36 53	101	25 01	145	47 43	219	60 12	285	36 18	340
281	39 35	022	25 30	051	37 38	100	25 28	144	47 14	219	59 27	284	36 02	339
282	39 52	021	26 06	050	38 24	100	25 55	144	46 44	219	58 41	283	35 45	338
283	40 08	019	26 41	049	39 10	099	26 23	144	46 15	219	57 56	282	35 27	337
284	40 23	018	27 16	048	39 56	099	26 50	143	45 46	219	57 10	281	35 09	336

LHA ♈	ALTAIR Hc	Zn	Enif Hc	Zn	◆ FOMALHAUT Hc	Zn	ACHERNAR Hc	Zn	◆ RIGIL KENT Hc	Zn	ANTARES Hc	Zn	◆ Rasalhague Hc	Zn
285	40 37	017	27 50	047	40 43	098	27 18	143	45 17	219	56 25	281	34 49	335
286	40 50	016	28 24	046	41 29	098	27 46	143	44 48	219	55 39	280	34 29	334
287	41 02	014	28 58	045	42 15	097	28 15	142	44 19	219	54 53	279	34 08	332
288	41 13	013	29 31	044	43 01	096	28 43	142	43 49	219	54 06	278	33 46	331
289	41 23	012	30 03	044	43 48	096	29 12	142	43 20	219	53 20	277	33 23	330
290	41 32	010	30 35	043	44 34	095	29 41	142	42 51	219	52 34	277	33 00	329
291	41 40	009	31 06	042	45 21	095	30 10	141	42 22	218	51 48	276	32 35	328
292	41 47	008	31 37	041	46 07	094	30 39	141	41 53	218	51 01	275	32 10	327
293	41 53	006	32 07	040	46 54	094	31 09	141	41 24	218	50 15	274	31 45	326
294	41 57	005	32 36	039	47 40	093	31 38	140	40 55	218	49 28	274	31 18	325
295	42 01	004	33 05	038	48 27	092	32 08	140	40 27	218	48 42	273	30 51	324
296	42 04	003	33 33	037	49 13	092	32 38	140	39 58	218	47 55	272	30 24	323
297	42 05	001	34 01	035	50 00	091	33 08	140	39 29	218	47 08	272	29 55	322
298	42 05	000	34 27	034	50 47	091	33 38	139	39 01	218	46 22	271	29 26	321
299	42 05	359	34 53	033	51 33	090	34 09	139	38 32	218	45 35	270	28 57	320

LHA ♈	Enif Hc	Zn	◆ FOMALHAUT Hc	Zn	ACHERNAR Hc	Zn	◆ RIGIL KENT Hc	Zn	ANTARES Hc	Zn	◆ Rasalhague Hc	Zn	ALTAIR Hc	Zn
300	35 18	032	52 20	089	34 39	139	38 04	217	44 49	270	28 26	319	42 03	357
301	35 43	031	53 06	089	35 10	139	37 35	217	44 02	269	27 56	318	42 00	356
302	36 07	030	53 53	088	35 41	139	37 07	217	43 15	269	27 24	317	41 56	355
303	36 30	029	54 40	087	36 12	138	36 39	217	42 29	268	26 52	316	41 51	353
304	36 52	028	55 26	087	36 43	138	36 11	217	41 42	267	26 20	315	41 45	352
305	37 13	027	56 13	086	37 14	138	35 43	217	40 56	267	25 47	315	41 38	351
306	37 33	025	56 59	085	37 45	138	35 16	216	40 09	266	25 13	314	41 30	349
307	37 53	024	57 46	085	38 17	138	34 48	216	39 23	266	24 40	313	41 21	348
308	38 12	023	58 32	084	38 48	137	34 20	216	38 36	265	24 05	312	41 11	347
309	38 30	022	59 18	083	39 20	137	33 53	216	37 50	264	23 30	311	40 59	345
310	38 47	021	60 05	082	39 52	137	33 26	216	37 03	264	22 55	310	40 47	344
311	39 03	019	60 51	081	40 23	137	32 59	215	36 17	263	22 19	309	40 34	343
312	39 18	018	61 37	081	40 55	137	32 32	215	35 31	263	21 43	309	40 19	342
313	39 32	017	62 23	080	41 27	137	32 05	215	34 44	262	21 06	308	40 04	340
314	39 45	016	63 09	079	41 59	137	31 38	215	33 58	262	20 29	307	39 48	339

LHA ♈	Enif Hc	Zn	◆ Diphda Hc	Zn	ACHERNAR Hc	Zn	◆ RIGIL KENT Hc	Zn	ANTARES Hc	Zn	Nunki Hc	Zn	◆ ALTAIR Hc	Zn
315	39 57	014	37 18	083	42 31	136	31 12	215	33 12	261	61 11	287	39 31	338
316	40 08	013	38 05	082	43 04	136	30 45	214	32 26	261	60 27	286	39 13	337
317	40 18	012	38 51	082	43 36	136	30 19	214	31 40	260	59 42	285	38 54	335
318	40 28	011	39 37	081	44 08	136	29 53	214	30 54	259	58 57	284	38 34	334
319	40 36	009	40 23	080	44 40	136	29 27	214	30 09	259	58 11	283	38 13	333
320	40 43	008	41 09	079	45 13	136	29 02	213	29 23	258	57 26	282	37 52	332
321	40 49	007	41 55	079	45 45	136	28 36	213	28 37	258	56 40	281	37 29	331
322	40 54	006	42 40	078	46 18	136	28 11	213	27 52	257	55 54	280	37 06	330
323	40 58	004	43 26	077	46 50	136	27 46	212	27 06	257	55 08	280	36 42	328
324	41 01	003	44 11	076	47 23	136	27 21	212	26 21	256	54 22	279	36 17	327
325	41 03	002	44 56	076	47 55	136	26 56	212	25 36	256	53 36	278	35 52	326
326	41 03	000	45 42	075	48 28	136	26 32	212	24 51	255	52 50	277	35 26	325
327	41 03	359	46 26	074	49 00	136	26 08	211	24 06	255	52 04	276	34 59	324
328	41 02	358	47 11	073	49 33	136	25 43	211	23 21	254	51 17	276	34 31	323
329	40 59	356	47 56	072	50 05	136	25 20	211	22 36	253	50 31	275	34 03	322

LHA ♈	◆ Alpheratz Hc	Zn	Diphda Hc	Zn	◆ ACHERNAR Hc	Zn	RIGIL KENT Hc	Zn	◆ Nunki Hc	Zn	ALTAIR Hc	Zn	Enif Hc	Zn
330	15 29	029	48 40	071	50 38	136	24 56	210	49 44	274	33 33	321	40 56	355
331	15 51	028	49 24	070	51 10	136	24 33	210	48 58	274	33 04	320	40 51	354
332	16 13	027	50 08	069	51 43	136	24 09	210	48 11	273	32 33	319	40 46	352
333	16 34	026	50 51	068	52 15	136	23 46	209	47 25	272	32 02	318	40 39	351
334	16 54	026	51 34	067	52 47	136	23 24	209	46 38	272	31 31	317	40 31	350
335	17 14	025	52 17	066	53 20	136	23 01	209	45 51	271	30 59	316	40 23	349
336	17 33	024	53 00	065	53 52	136	22 39	208	45 05	270	30 26	315	40 13	347
337	17 52	023	53 42	064	54 24	137	22 17	208	44 18	270	29 53	314	40 02	346
338	18 10	022	54 24	063	54 56	137	21 55	208	43 32	269	29 19	313	39 51	345
339	18 27	021	55 05	062	55 28	137	21 34	207	42 45	268	28 45	312	39 38	344
340	18 44	020	55 46	061	56 00	137	21 13	207	41 58	268	28 10	311	39 24	342
341	19 00	020	56 27	060	56 31	137	20 52	207	41 12	267	27 35	310	39 10	341
342	19 15	019	57 07	058	57 03	138	20 31	206	40 25	267	26 59	309	38 54	340
343	19 30	018	57 46	057	57 34	138	20 10	206	39 39	266	26 23	309	38 38	339
344	19 44	017	58 25	056	58 05	138	19 50	205	38 52	265	25 46	308	38 20	337

LHA ♈	◆ Alpheratz Hc	Zn	Diphda Hc	Zn	◆ CANOPUS Hc	Zn	RIGIL KENT Hc	Zn	◆ Nunki Hc	Zn	ALTAIR Hc	Zn	Enif Hc	Zn
345	19 57	016	59 03	054	19 21	143	19 30	205	38 06	265	25 09	307	38 02	336
346	20 09	015	59 41	053	19 49	143	19 11	205	37 19	264	24 31	306	37 43	335
347	20 21	014	60 18	052	20 17	142	18 51	204	36 33	264	23 54	305	37 23	334
348	20 32	013	60 54	050	20 46	142	18 32	204	35 47	263	23 15	304	37 02	333
349	20 43	012	61 29	049	21 15	142	18 14	204	35 00	263	22 37	304	36 40	332
350	20 52	011	62 04	047	21 44	141	17 55	203	34 14	262	21 58	303	36 17	330
351	21 01	011	62 37	045	22 13	141	17 37	203	33 28	262	21 18	302	35 54	329
352	21 09	010	63 10	044	22 43	140	17 19	202	32 42	261	20 38	301	35 30	328
353	21 17	009	63 42	042	23 13	140	17 02	202	31 56	260	19 58	300	35 05	327
354	21 23	008	64 12	040	23 43	140	16 44	201	31 10	260	19 18	300	34 39	326
355	21 29	007	64 42	038	24 13	139	16 27	201	30 24	259	18 37	299	34 13	325
356	21 34	006	65 10	036	24 44	139	16 11	201	29 38	259	17 56	298	33 46	324
357	21 39	005	65 37	034	25 14	139	15 55	200	28 53	258	17 15	297	33 18	323
358	21 43	004	66 02	032	25 45	138	15 39	200	28 07	258	16 34	297	32 50	322
359	21 45	003	66 26	030	26 16	138	15 23	199	27 21	257	15 52	296	32 21	321

LHA ♈	Hc	Zn	Hc	Zn	Hc	Zn	Hc	Zn	Hc	Zn	Hc	Zn	Hc	Zn
	Alpheratz		◆ Hamal		RIGEL		◆ CANOPUS		Peacock		◆ Nunki		Enif	
0	20 48	002	19 49	031	13 48	089	27 32	137	52 04	226	26 50	257	31 05	320
1	20 49	001	20 12	030	14 34	089	28 03	137	51 31	226	26 05	257	30 35	319
2	20 50	000	20 35	029	15 20	088	28 35	137	50 58	226	25 20	256	30 05	318
3	20 49	359	20 57	028	16 06	087	29 07	136	50 25	226	24 36	255	29 34	317
4	20 49	358	21 19	028	16 52	087	29 38	136	49 52	226	23 51	255	29 02	316
5	20 47	357	21 40	027	17 38	086	30 11	136	49 19	226	23 07	254	28 31	315
6	20 44	357	22 00	026	18 24	085	30 43	135	48 46	226	22 23	254	27 58	314
7	20 41	356	22 19	025	19 09	085	31 15	135	48 13	226	21 39	253	27 25	314
8	20 37	355	22 38	024	19 55	084	31 48	135	47 40	226	20 55	253	26 51	313
9	20 33	354	22 57	023	20 41	083	32 21	134	47 07	226	20 11	252	26 17	312
10	20 27	353	23 14	022	21 26	083	32 54	134	46 34	226	19 27	252	25 43	311
11	20 21	352	23 31	021	22 12	082	33 27	134	46 02	225	18 44	251	25 08	310
12	20 14	351	23 47	020	22 57	081	34 00	133	45 29	225	18 00	250	24 32	309
13	20 07	350	24 02	019	23 43	080	34 34	133	44 56	225	17 17	250	23 56	308
14	19 59	349	24 17	018	24 28	080	35 08	133	44 24	225	16 34	249	23 20	307
	◆ Hamal		ALDEBARAN		RIGEL		◆ CANOPUS		Peacock		◆ FOMALHAUT		Alpheratz	
15	24 31	017	14 17	053	25 13	079	35 41	133	43 51	225	63 07	283	19 50	348
16	24 44	016	14 53	053	25 58	078	36 15	132	43 18	225	62 22	282	19 40	347
17	24 57	015	15 30	052	26 43	078	36 49	132	42 46	225	61 37	281	19 29	346
18	25 08	014	16 06	051	27 28	077	37 24	132	42 14	225	60 52	281	19 18	345
19	25 19	013	16 41	050	28 13	076	37 58	131	41 41	224	60 06	280	19 06	345
20	25 29	012	17 16	049	28 57	075	38 32	131	41 09	224	59 21	279	18 54	344
21	25 39	011	17 51	049	29 42	075	39 07	131	40 37	224	58 36	278	18 41	343
22	25 47	010	18 25	048	30 26	074	39 42	131	40 05	224	57 50	277	18 27	342
23	25 55	009	18 59	047	31 10	073	40 17	131	39 33	224	57 04	276	18 12	341
24	26 02	008	19 33	046	31 54	072	40 52	130	39 02	224	56 19	276	17 57	340
25	26 08	007	20 06	045	32 38	072	41 27	130	38 30	223	55 33	275	17 41	339
26	26 13	006	20 38	045	33 21	071	42 02	130	37 59	223	54 47	274	17 24	338
27	26 18	005	21 10	044	34 04	070	42 37	130	37 27	223	54 01	273	17 07	338
28	26 21	004	21 41	043	34 48	069	43 13	130	36 56	223	53 15	273	16 49	337
29	26 24	003	22 12	042	35 30	068	43 48	129	36 25	223	52 29	272	16 31	336
	Hamal		◆ ALDEBARAN		RIGEL		SIRIUS		◆ CANOPUS		Peacock		◆ FOMALHAUT	
30	26 26	002	22 43	041	36 13	067	24 44	092	44 24	129	35 54	222	51 44	271
31	26 28	001	23 13	040	36 55	067	25 30	091	44 59	129	35 23	222	50 58	271
32	26 28	000	23 42	039	37 37	066	26 16	090	45 35	129	34 52	222	50 12	270
33	26 28	359	24 11	038	38 19	065	27 02	090	46 11	129	34 21	222	49 26	269
34	26 26	358	24 39	037	39 00	064	27 48	089	46 47	129	33 51	221	48 40	269
35	26 24	357	25 07	037	39 41	063	28 34	088	47 23	128	33 21	221	47 54	268
36	26 21	356	25 34	036	40 22	062	29 20	088	47 59	128	32 51	221	47 08	268
37	26 18	355	26 00	035	41 03	061	30 06	087	48 35	128	32 21	221	46 22	267
38	26 13	354	26 26	034	41 43	060	30 52	086	49 11	128	31 51	220	45 36	266
39	26 08	353	26 51	033	42 22	059	31 38	086	49 47	128	31 21	220	44 50	266
40	26 02	352	27 16	032	43 02	058	32 23	085	50 24	128	30 52	220	44 04	265
41	25 55	351	27 40	031	43 40	057	33 09	084	51 00	128	30 23	219	43 19	265
42	25 47	350	28 03	030	44 19	056	33 55	084	51 36	128	29 53	219	42 33	264
43	25 39	349	28 25	029	44 56	055	34 41	083	52 12	128	29 25	219	41 47	263
44	25 29	348	28 47	028	45 34	054	35 26	082	52 49	128	28 56	218	41 01	263
	◆ ALDEBARAN		RIGEL		SIRIUS		◆ CANOPUS		ACHERNAR		◆ FOMALHAUT		Hamal	
45	29 08	027	46 11	053	36 12	081	53 25	128	68 20	211	40 16	262	25 19	347
46	29 28	026	46 47	052	36 57	081	54 01	128	67 56	212	39 30	262	25 08	346
47	29 48	025	47 23	050	37 42	080	54 38	128	67 31	213	38 45	261	24 57	345
48	30 07	024	47 58	049	38 28	079	55 14	128	67 06	214	37 59	261	24 44	344
49	30 25	023	48 32	048	39 13	078	55 51	128	66 41	215	37 14	260	24 31	343
50	30 42	022	49 06	047	39 58	078	56 27	128	66 14	215	36 29	260	24 17	342
51	30 58	020	49 39	046	40 42	077	57 03	128	65 47	216	35 44	259	24 03	341
52	31 14	019	50 12	044	41 27	076	57 39	128	65 20	217	34 59	259	23 47	340
53	31 29	018	50 43	043	42 12	075	58 15	128	64 52	217	34 14	258	23 31	339
54	31 43	017	51 14	042	42 56	075	58 52	128	64 24	218	33 29	257	23 14	338
55	31 56	016	51 44	040	43 40	074	59 28	128	63 56	219	32 44	257	22 57	337
56	32 08	015	52 14	039	44 24	073	60 04	129	63 27	219	31 59	256	22 39	336
57	32 20	014	52 42	037	45 08	072	60 39	129	62 58	220	31 15	256	22 20	335
58	32 30	013	53 09	036	45 52	071	61 15	129	62 28	220	30 30	255	22 00	334
59	32 40	012	53 36	034	46 35	070	61 51	129	61 58	221	29 46	255	21 40	333
	ALDEBARAN		◆ BETELGEUSE		SIRIUS		◆ ACRUX		ACHERNAR		◆ FOMALHAUT		Hamal	
60	32 49	011	35 34	036	47 18	069	21 29	157	61 28	221	29 01	254	21 19	332
61	32 57	009	36 00	035	48 01	068	21 47	157	60 58	222	28 17	254	20 57	332
62	33 04	008	36 26	034	48 44	067	22 06	156	60 27	222	27 33	253	20 35	331
63	33 10	007	36 52	033	49 26	066	22 24	156	59 56	222	26 49	253	20 12	330
64	33 15	006	37 16	032	50 08	065	22 43	156	59 25	223	26 05	252	19 49	329
65	33 20	005	37 40	031	50 49	064	23 02	155	58 54	223	25 22	252	19 25	328
66	33 23	004	38 03	029	51 30	063	23 21	155	58 23	223	24 38	251	19 00	327
67	33 25	003	38 25	028	52 11	062	23 41	155	57 51	223	23 55	251	18 35	326
68	33 27	001	38 47	027	52 52	061	24 00	154	57 19	224	23 11	250	18 09	325
69	33 28	000	39 07	026	53 32	060	24 20	154	56 48	224	22 28	250	17 43	325
70	33 27	359	39 27	025	54 11	059	24 41	154	56 16	224	21 45	249	17 16	324
71	33 26	358	39 46	023	54 50	057	25 01	153	55 44	224	21 02	248	16 49	323
72	33 24	357	40 04	022	55 29	056	25 22	153	55 12	224	20 20	248	16 21	322
73	33 21	356	40 21	021	56 07	055	25 43	153	54 39	225	19 37	247	15 52	321
74	33 17	354	40 37	020	56 44	054	26 04	152	54 07	225	18 55	247	15 23	320
	BETELGEUSE		◆ SIRIUS		Suhail		◆ ACRUX		ACHERNAR		◆ Diphda		ALDEBARAN	
75	40 52	018	57 20	052	44 36	116	26 25	152	53 35	225	31 12	272	33 12	353
76	41 06	017	57 56	051	45 17	115	26 47	152	53 02	225	30 27	272	33 06	352
77	41 19	016	58 32	049	45 59	115	27 09	152	52 30	225	29 41	271	33 00	351
78	41 31	015	59 06	048	46 41	115	27 31	151	51 57	225	28 55	270	32 52	350
79	41 42	013	59 40	046	47 22	115	27 53	151	51 25	225	28 09	270	32 44	349
80	41 52	012	60 13	045	48 04	114	28 15	151	50 52	225	27 23	269	32 34	348
81	42 01	011	60 45	043	48 46	114	28 38	150	50 20	225	26 37	268	32 24	347
82	42 09	009	61 16	042	49 28	114	29 01	150	49 47	225	25 51	268	32 13	345
83	42 16	008	61 46	040	50 10	113	29 24	150	49 15	225	25 05	267	32 01	344
84	42 22	007	62 15	038	50 53	113	29 47	150	48 42	225	24 19	266	31 48	343
85	42 27	005	62 42	036	51 35	113	30 10	149	48 10	225	23 33	266	31 35	342
86	42 31	004	63 09	034	52 17	113	30 34	149	47 37	225	22 47	265	31 20	341
87	42 33	003	63 34	032	53 00	112	30 58	149	47 05	225	22 02	265	31 05	340
88	42 35	001	63 58	031	53 42	112	31 22	149	46 32	225	21 16	264	30 49	339
89	42 35	000	64 21	028	54 25	112	31 46	148	46 00	225	20 30	263	30 32	338

LAT 40°S

LHA ♈	Hc	Zn	Hc	Zn	Hc	Zn	Hc	Zn	Hc	Zn	Hc	Zn	Hc	Zn
	PROCYON		REGULUS		◆ Suhail		ACRUX		◆ ACHERNAR		RIGEL		◆ BETELGEUSE	
90	39 17	033	12 29	063	55 08	112	32 10	148	45 28	225	56 39	340	42 35	359
91	39 42	032	13 09	062	55 51	111	32 34	148	44 55	225	56 22	338	42 33	357
92	40 06	031	13 50	061	56 33	111	32 59	148	44 23	224	56 05	336	42 31	356
93	40 29	029	14 30	060	57 16	111	33 24	147	43 51	224	55 45	334	42 27	355
94	40 51	028	15 10	060	57 59	111	33 48	147	43 19	224	55 25	333	42 22	353
95	41 12	027	15 49	059	58 42	110	34 13	147	42 47	224	55 03	331	42 16	352
96	41 32	026	16 28	058	59 25	110	34 39	147	42 15	224	54 41	330	42 09	351
97	41 52	024	17 07	057	60 09	110	35 04	147	41 43	224	54 17	328	42 01	349
98	42 10	023	17 46	057	60 52	110	35 29	146	41 11	224	53 52	327	41 52	348
99	42 28	022	18 24	056	61 35	110	35 55	146	40 40	224	53 26	325	41 42	347
100	42 45	021	19 02	055	62 18	110	36 20	146	40 08	223	52 59	324	41 31	345
101	43 00	019	19 39	054	63 02	109	36 46	146	39 36	223	52 32	322	41 19	344
102	43 15	018	20 16	053	63 45	109	37 12	146	39 05	223	52 03	321	41 06	343
103	43 29	017	20 53	053	64 28	109	37 38	145	38 34	223	51 33	319	40 51	342
104	43 41	015	21 29	052	65 12	109	38 04	145	38 03	223	51 03	318	40 36	340
	PROCYON		REGULUS		◆ Gienah		ACRUX		◆ ACHERNAR		RIGEL		◆ BETELGEUSE	
105	43 53	014	22 05	051	19 24	097	38 30	145	37 32	222	50 32	317	40 20	339
106	44 03	013	22 40	050	20 09	096	38 57	145	37 01	222	50 00	315	40 03	338
107	44 13	011	23 15	049	20 55	096	39 23	145	36 30	222	49 27	314	39 46	337
108	44 21	010	23 50	048	21 41	095	39 49	145	35 59	222	48 54	313	39 27	335
109	44 29	008	24 24	047	22 27	095	40 16	145	35 29	222	48 20	312	39 07	334
110	44 35	007	24 58	047	23 13	094	40 43	145	34 58	221	47 45	310	38 47	333
111	44 40	006	25 31	046	23 58	093	41 09	144	34 28	221	47 10	309	38 25	332
112	44 44	004	26 04	045	24 44	093	41 36	144	33 58	221	46 34	308	38 03	331
113	44 47	003	26 36	044	25 30	092	42 03	144	33 28	221	45 57	307	37 40	329
114	44 48	001	27 07	043	26 16	092	42 30	144	32 58	220	45 20	306	37 16	328
115	44 49	000	27 38	042	27 02	091	42 56	144	32 29	220	44 43	305	36 52	327
116	44 48	359	28 09	041	27 48	090	43 23	144	31 59	220	44 04	304	36 26	326
117	44 47	357	28 39	040	28 34	090	43 50	144	31 30	219	43 26	303	36 00	325
118	44 44	356	29 08	039	29 20	089	44 17	144	31 01	219	42 47	302	35 33	324
119	44 40	354	29 37	038	30 06	088	44 44	144	30 32	219	42 08	301	35 06	323
	REGULUS		◆ SPICA		ACRUX		◆ CANOPUS		RIGEL		BETELGEUSE		◆ PROCYON	
120	30 05	037	13 40	093	45 11	144	69 20	224	41 28	300	34 38	322	44 35	353
121	30 32	036	14 26	093	45 39	144	68 48	225	40 48	299	34 09	321	44 29	352
122	30 59	035	15 12	092	46 06	144	68 15	226	40 07	298	33 39	320	44 22	350
123	31 25	034	15 58	091	46 33	144	67 42	226	39 26	297	33 09	319	44 13	349
124	31 51	033	16 44	091	47 00	144	67 08	227	38 45	296	32 38	318	44 04	348
125	32 15	032	17 30	090	47 27	144	66 35	228	38 04	295	32 07	317	43 53	346
126	32 39	031	18 16	089	47 54	144	66 01	228	37 22	294	31 35	316	43 42	345
127	33 03	030	19 02	089	48 21	144	65 26	229	36 40	293	31 03	315	43 29	343
128	33 25	029	19 48	088	48 48	144	64 52	229	35 57	292	30 30	314	43 16	342
129	33 47	028	20 34	088	49 15	144	64 17	229	35 14	291	29 56	313	43 01	341
130	34 08	027	21 20	087	49 42	144	63 42	230	34 32	291	29 22	312	42 45	339
131	34 28	026	22 06	086	50 08	144	63 07	230	33 48	290	28 47	311	42 29	338
132	34 48	024	22 52	086	50 35	144	62 31	230	33 05	289	28 12	310	42 11	337
133	35 06	023	23 37	085	51 02	145	61 56	231	32 22	288	27 37	309	41 53	336
134	35 24	022	24 23	084	51 28	145	61 20	231	31 38	287	27 01	308	41 33	334
	◆ REGULUS		SPICA		◆ ACRUX		CANOPUS		◆ RIGEL		BETELGEUSE		PROCYON	
135	35 41	021	25 09	084	51 55	145	60 45	231	30 54	287	26 25	307	41 13	333
136	35 57	020	25 54	083	52 21	145	60 09	231	30 10	286	25 48	306	40 52	332
137	36 12	019	26 40	082	52 48	145	59 33	232	29 25	285	25 10	305	40 30	331
138	36 26	017	27 25	081	53 14	145	58 57	232	28 41	284	24 33	305	40 07	329
139	36 40	016	28 11	081	53 40	146	58 21	232	27 56	284	23 55	304	39 43	328
140	36 52	015	28 56	080	54 06	146	57 44	232	27 12	283	23 16	303	39 18	327
141	37 03	014	29 41	079	54 31	146	57 08	232	26 27	282	22 38	302	38 53	326
142	37 14	013	30 27	079	54 57	146	56 32	232	25 42	281	21 59	301	38 27	325
143	37 24	011	31 12	078	55 22	147	55 56	232	24 57	281	21 19	301	38 00	324
144	37 32	010	31 56	077	55 47	147	55 19	232	24 11	280	20 39	300	37 32	323
145	37 40	009	32 41	076	56 12	147	54 43	232	23 26	279	19 59	299	37 04	321
146	37 47	008	33 26	076	56 37	148	54 07	232	22 41	279	19 19	298	36 35	320
147	37 52	007	34 10	075	57 02	148	53 30	232	21 55	278	18 38	297	36 05	319
148	37 57	005	34 54	074	57 26	148	52 54	232	21 10	277	17 57	297	35 35	318
149	38 01	004	35 39	073	57 50	149	52 18	232	20 24	277	17 16	296	35 04	317
	REGULUS		◆ SPICA		ACRUX		◆ Miaplacidus		CANOPUS		SIRIUS		◆ PROCYON	
150	38 04	003	36 22	072	58 14	149	59 36	188	51 41	232	42 08	285	34 33	316
151	38 06	002	37 06	072	58 37	149	59 29	189	51 05	232	41 23	284	34 00	315
152	38 06	000	37 50	071	59 00	150	59 22	189	50 29	232	40 38	283	33 28	314
153	38 06	359	38 33	070	59 23	150	59 14	190	49 52	232	39 53	282	32 54	313
154	38 05	358	39 16	069	59 46	151	59 06	190	49 16	232	39 08	281	32 21	312
155	38 03	357	39 59	068	60 08	151	58 58	191	48 40	232	38 23	281	31 46	311
156	38 00	355	40 41	067	60 30	152	58 49	192	48 04	232	37 38	280	31 11	310
157	37 55	354	41 24	066	60 51	153	58 39	192	47 28	232	36 53	279	30 36	309
158	37 50	353	42 06	065	61 12	153	58 29	193	46 52	231	36 07	278	30 00	308
159	37 44	352	42 47	065	61 33	154	58 19	193	46 16	231	35 22	278	29 24	307
160	37 37	350	43 29	064	61 53	154	58 08	194	45 40	231	34 36	277	28 47	307
161	37 29	349	44 10	063	62 12	155	57 56	195	45 05	231	33 51	276	28 10	306
162	37 20	348	44 50	062	62 32	156	57 45	195	44 29	231	33 05	276	27 33	305
163	37 10	347	45 30	061	62 50	156	57 33	196	43 53	231	32 19	275	26 55	304
164	36 59	346	46 10	060	63 08	157	57 20	196	43 18	230	31 33	274	26 16	303
	ARCTURUS		◆ ANTARES		ACRUX		◆ CANOPUS		SIRIUS		PROCYON		◆ REGULUS	
165	15 17	048	22 01	107	63 26	158	42 42	230	30 47	274	25 38	302	36 47	344
166	15 51	047	22 45	106	63 43	159	42 07	230	30 02	273	24 59	301	36 34	343
167	16 25	046	23 30	106	63 59	160	41 32	230	29 16	272	24 19	301	36 20	342
168	16 57	045	24 14	105	64 15	160	40 57	230	28 30	272	23 39	300	36 06	341
169	17 30	045	24 58	105	64 30	161	40 22	229	27 44	271	22 59	299	35 50	340
170	18 02	044	25 43	104	64 45	162	39 47	229	26 58	270	22 19	298	35 34	339
171	18 33	043	26 28	103	64 58	163	39 12	229	26 12	270	21 38	297	35 17	337
172	19 05	042	27 12	103	65 11	164	38 37	229	25 26	269	20 57	297	34 59	336
173	19 35	041	27 57	102	65 24	165	38 03	229	24 40	268	20 16	296	34 40	335
174	20 05	040	28 42	102	65 35	166	37 29	228	23 54	268	19 35	295	34 20	334
175	20 35	040	29 27	101	65 46	167	36 54	228	23 08	267	18 53	294	33 59	333
176	21 04	039	30 12	101	65 56	168	36 20	228	22 22	266	18 11	294	33 38	332
177	21 32	038	30 58	100	66 05	169	35 46	228	21 36	266	17 29	293	33 16	331
178	22 00	037	31 43	100	66 13	170	35 12	227	20 50	265	16 46	292	32 53	330
179	22 27	036	32 28	099	66 21	171	34 39	227	20 05	265	16 03	291	32 29	329

LAT 40°S

LHA ♈	Hc	Zn	Hc	Zn	Hc	Zn	Hc	Zn	Hc	Zn	Hc	Zn	Hc	Zn
	ARCTURUS		◆ANTARES		RIGIL KENT		ACRUX		◆CANOPUS		Alphard		◆REGULUS	
180	22 54	035	33 14	098	57 49	144	66 28	172	34 05	227	44 01	302	32 05	328
181	23 20	034	33 59	098	58 16	144	66 33	173	33 32	226	43 22	301	31 40	326
182	23 46	033	34 45	097	58 43	145	66 38	174	32 59	226	42 42	300	31 14	325
183	24 10	032	35 30	097	59 09	145	66 42	176	32 26	226	42 02	299	30 48	324
184	24 35	031	36 16	096	59 36	145	66 45	177	31 53	225	41 22	298	30 21	323
185	24 58	030	37 02	095	60 02	146	66 47	178	31 20	225	40 42	297	29 53	322
186	25 21	029	37 48	095	60 27	146	66 49	179	30 48	225	40 01	296	29 25	321
187	25 44	029	38 33	094	60 52	147	66 49	180	30 15	225	39 19	296	28 56	320
188	26 05	028	39 19	094	61 17	147	66 48	181	29 43	224	38 38	295	28 26	319
189	26 26	027	40 05	093	61 42	148	66 47	182	29 11	224	37 56	294	27 56	319
190	26 46	026	40 51	092	62 06	149	66 45	184	28 39	224	37 14	293	27 25	318
191	27 06	025	41 37	092	62 30	149	66 41	185	28 08	223	36 31	292	26 54	317
192	27 25	024	42 23	091	62 53	150	66 37	186	27 36	223	35 48	291	26 22	316
193	27 43	023	43 09	091	63 16	150	66 32	187	27 05	223	35 05	290	25 50	315
194	28 00	022	43 55	090	63 39	151	66 26	188	26 34	222	34 22	290	25 17	314
	ARCTURUS		◆ANTARES		RIGIL KENT		◆ACRUX		Suhail		◆REGULUS		Denebola	
195	28 16	021	44 41	089	64 01	152	66 19	189	47 34	246	24 44	313	33 07	340
196	28 32	020	45 27	089	64 22	153	66 11	190	46 52	245	24 10	312	32 51	338
197	28 47	018	46 13	088	64 43	153	66 03	191	46 10	245	23 36	311	32 33	337
198	29 01	017	46 59	087	65 03	154	65 53	192	45 29	245	23 01	310	32 15	336
199	29 15	016	47 44	087	65 23	155	65 43	193	44 47	244	22 26	310	31 56	335
200	29 27	015	48 30	086	65 42	156	65 32	194	44 06	244	21 50	309	31 37	334
201	29 39	014	49 16	085	66 00	157	65 20	195	43 25	244	21 14	308	31 16	333
202	29 50	013	50 02	085	66 18	158	65 08	196	42 43	243	20 38	307	30 55	332
203	30 00	012	50 48	084	66 35	159	64 55	197	42 02	243	20 01	306	30 33	331
204	30 09	011	51 33	083	66 51	160	64 41	198	41 22	243	19 24	305	30 11	330
205	30 17	010	52 19	082	67 07	161	64 26	199	40 41	242	18 46	305	29 47	329
206	30 25	009	53 04	081	67 21	162	64 11	200	40 00	242	18 08	304	29 23	328
207	30 32	008	53 50	081	67 35	163	63 55	201	39 20	242	17 30	303	28 59	327
208	30 37	007	54 35	080	67 48	164	63 38	201	38 39	241	16 51	302	28 33	326
209	30 42	006	55 20	079	68 00	165	63 21	202	37 59	241	16 12	302	28 07	325
	ARCTURUS		◆ANTARES		Peacock		RIGIL KENT		◆ACRUX		Suhail		◆SPICA	
210	30 46	004	56 05	078	29 13	141	68 11	167	63 03	203	37 19	241	60 16	343
211	30 50	003	56 50	077	29 41	141	68 21	168	62 45	204	36 39	240	60 02	341
212	30 52	002	57 35	076	30 10	141	68 30	169	62 26	204	35 59	240	59 46	339
213	30 53	001	58 20	075	30 40	140	68 39	170	62 07	205	35 19	240	59 29	337
214	30 54	000	59 04	074	31 09	140	68 46	172	61 47	206	34 40	239	59 11	336
215	30 53	359	59 48	073	31 39	140	68 52	173	61 27	206	34 00	239	58 51	334
216	30 52	358	60 32	072	32 08	140	68 57	174	61 06	207	33 21	238	58 30	332
217	30 50	357	61 16	071	32 38	139	69 01	176	60 45	208	32 42	238	58 08	330
218	30 47	356	61 59	070	33 08	139	69 04	177	60 24	208	32 03	238	57 45	329
219	30 43	355	62 42	069	33 39	139	69 06	178	60 02	209	31 24	237	57 20	327
220	30 38	354	63 25	068	34 09	139	69 06	180	59 40	209	30 46	237	56 54	325
221	30 33	352	64 07	067	34 39	138	69 06	181	59 17	210	30 07	237	56 28	324
222	30 26	351	64 49	065	35 10	138	69 04	183	58 54	210	29 29	236	56 00	322
223	30 19	350	65 31	064	35 41	138	69 02	184	58 31	211	28 51	236	55 31	321
224	30 11	349	66 12	063	36 12	138	68 58	185	58 07	211	28 13	235	55 02	319
	Alphecca		Rasalhague		◆Nunki		Peacock		◆RIGIL KENT		◆SPICA		ARCTURUS	
225	22 50	009	26 15	043	39 38	093	36 43	137	68 53	187	54 31	318	30 01	348
226	22 56	008	26 46	042	40 24	093	37 14	137	68 48	188	54 00	316	29 52	347
227	23 02	007	27 16	041	41 10	092	37 46	137	68 41	189	53 27	315	29 41	346
228	23 07	006	27 46	040	41 56	091	38 17	137	68 33	190	52 55	313	29 29	345
229	23 11	005	28 16	039	42 42	091	38 49	136	68 24	192	52 21	312	29 17	344
230	23 14	004	28 45	038	43 28	090	39 20	136	68 14	193	51 46	311	29 04	343
231	23 17	003	29 13	037	44 14	089	39 52	136	68 04	194	51 11	310	28 50	342
232	23 19	002	29 41	036	44 59	089	40 24	136	67 52	195	50 36	308	28 35	341
233	23 20	001	30 07	035	45 45	088	40 56	136	67 39	197	49 59	307	28 19	340
234	23 20	000	30 34	034	46 31	087	41 28	136	67 26	198	49 22	306	28 03	339
235	23 20	359	30 59	033	47 17	087	42 00	135	67 11	199	48 45	305	27 46	338
236	23 18	358	31 24	032	48 03	086	42 33	135	66 56	200	48 07	304	27 28	337
237	23 16	357	31 49	031	48 49	085	43 05	135	66 40	201	47 28	303	27 09	336
238	23 13	356	32 12	030	49 35	085	43 38	135	66 24	202	46 49	301	26 50	335
239	23 10	355	32 35	029	50 20	084	44 10	135	66 06	203	46 10	300	26 30	334
	Rasalhague		ALTAIR		◆Nunki		Peacock		◆RIGIL KENT		SPICA		◆ARCTURUS	
240	32 57	028	17 38	061	51 06	083	44 43	135	65 48	204	45 30	299	26 09	333
241	33 18	027	18 18	061	51 52	082	45 15	135	65 29	205	44 50	298	25 47	332
242	33 39	026	18 58	060	52 37	082	45 48	135	65 10	206	44 09	297	25 25	331
243	33 59	025	19 37	059	53 23	081	46 21	134	64 49	206	43 28	296	25 02	330
244	34 17	024	20 17	058	54 08	080	46 54	134	64 29	207	42 47	295	24 39	329
245	34 35	023	20 56	057	54 53	079	47 26	134	64 08	208	42 05	295	24 15	328
246	34 53	021	21 34	057	55 38	078	47 59	134	63 46	209	41 23	294	23 50	327
247	35 09	020	22 12	056	56 23	077	48 32	134	63 23	209	40 41	293	23 25	326
248	35 25	019	22 50	055	57 08	076	49 05	134	63 01	210	39 58	292	22 58	325
249	35 39	018	23 28	054	57 53	076	49 38	134	62 37	211	39 16	291	22 32	324
250	35 53	017	24 05	053	58 37	075	50 11	134	62 14	211	38 33	290	22 05	323
251	36 06	016	24 42	053	59 21	074	50 44	134	61 50	212	37 49	289	21 37	322
252	36 18	014	25 18	052	60 05	073	51 17	134	61 25	212	37 06	288	21 09	321
253	36 29	013	25 54	051	60 49	072	51 50	134	61 00	213	36 22	288	20 40	321
254	36 39	012	26 29	050	61 32	070	52 23	134	60 35	213	35 38	287	20 10	320
	Rasalhague		◆ALTAIR		FOMALHAUT		◆ACHERNAR		RIGIL KENT		◆SPICA		ARCTURUS	
255	36 48	011	27 04	049	18 45	113	15 59	154	60 10	214	34 54	286	19 40	319
256	36 56	010	27 39	048	19 27	113	16 19	154	59 44	214	34 10	285	19 10	318
257	37 04	008	28 12	047	20 10	112	16 40	153	59 18	215	33 25	284	18 39	317
258	37 10	007	28 46	046	20 52	112	17 01	153	58 51	215	32 41	284	18 07	316
259	37 15	006	29 19	045	21 35	111	17 22	152	58 25	216	31 56	283	17 35	316
260	37 19	005	29 51	044	22 18	111	17 43	152	57 58	216	31 11	282	17 03	315
261	37 23	004	30 23	043	23 01	110	18 05	152	57 31	216	30 26	281	16 30	314
262	37 25	002	30 54	042	23 44	110	18 27	151	57 03	217	29 41	281	15 57	313
263	37 27	001	31 25	041	24 28	109	18 49	151	56 36	217	28 56	280	15 23	312
264	37 27	000	31 55	040	25 11	108	19 12	150	56 08	217	28 11	279	14 49	312
265	37 26	359	32 25	039	25 55	108	19 35	150	55 40	217	27 25	279	14 14	311
266	37 25	357	32 54	038	26 39	107	19 58	150	55 12	218	26 40	278	13 39	310
267	37 22	356	33 22	037	27 23	107	20 21	149	54 44	218	25 54	277	13 04	309
268	37 19	355	33 50	036	28 07	106	20 45	149	54 16	218	25 08	276	12 28	309
269	37 14	354	34 16	035	28 51	106	21 09	148	53 47	218	24 23	276	11 52	308

LHA ♈	Hc	Zn	Hc	Zn	Hc	Zn	Hc	Zn	Hc	Zn	Hc	Zn	Hc	Zn
	ALTAIR		Enif		◆FOMALHAUT		ACHERNAR		◆RIGIL KENT		ANTARES		◆Rasalhague	
270	34 43	034	17 58	059	29 35	105	21 33	148	53 19	218	66 59	299	37 09	353
271	35 08	033	18 37	059	30 19	105	21 58	148	52 50	219	66 19	298	37 02	351
272	35 33	032	19 16	058	31 04	104	22 22	147	52 21	219	65 38	296	36 55	350
273	35 57	031	19 55	057	31 49	104	22 47	147	51 53	219	64 56	295	36 46	349
274	36 20	030	20 33	056	32 33	103	23 13	146	51 24	219	64 14	294	36 37	348
275	36 42	029	21 11	055	33 18	103	23 38	146	50 55	219	63 32	292	36 27	346
276	37 04	027	21 49	055	34 03	102	24 04	146	50 26	219	62 49	291	36 16	345
277	37 25	026	22 26	054	34 48	102	24 30	145	49 57	219	62 06	290	36 04	344
278	37 45	025	23 03	053	35 33	101	24 56	145	49 28	219	61 23	289	35 51	343
279	38 04	024	23 40	052	36 18	101	25 23	145	48 58	219	60 39	288	35 37	342
280	38 22	023	24 16	051	37 03	100	25 49	144	48 29	219	59 55	287	35 22	341
281	38 39	022	24 52	050	37 49	099	26 16	144	48 00	219	59 11	286	35 06	339
282	38 56	020	25 27	050	38 34	099	26 43	144	47 31	219	58 27	285	34 50	338
283	39 11	019	26 01	049	39 20	098	27 11	143	47 02	219	57 42	284	34 32	337
284	39 26	018	26 36	048	40 05	098	27 38	143	46 33	219	56 58	283	34 14	336
	ALTAIR		Enif		◆FOMALHAUT		ACHERNAR		◆RIGIL KENT		ANTARES		◆Rasalhague	
285	39 40	017	27 10	047	40 51	097	28 06	143	46 03	219	56 13	282	33 55	335
286	39 52	015	27 43	046	41 36	097	28 34	142	45 34	219	55 28	281	33 35	334
287	40 04	014	28 16	045	42 22	096	29 02	142	45 05	219	54 43	280	33 14	333
288	40 15	013	28 48	044	43 08	096	29 31	142	44 36	219	53 57	279	32 53	332
289	40 24	012	29 19	043	43 53	095	29 59	141	44 07	219	53 12	279	32 31	331
290	40 33	010	29 51	042	44 39	094	30 28	141	43 38	219	52 26	278	32 08	330
291	40 41	009	30 21	041	45 25	094	30 57	141	43 09	219	51 41	277	31 44	328
292	40 47	008	30 51	040	46 11	093	31 26	141	42 40	219	50 55	276	31 20	327
293	40 53	006	31 21	039	46 57	093	31 55	140	42 11	219	50 10	276	30 55	326
294	40 58	005	31 49	038	47 43	092	32 25	140	41 42	219	49 24	275	30 29	325
295	41 01	004	32 17	037	48 29	091	32 54	140	41 14	219	48 38	274	30 03	324
296	41 04	002	32 45	036	49 15	091	33 24	140	40 45	219	47 52	273	29 35	323
297	41 05	001	33 12	035	50 01	090	33 54	139	40 16	218	47 06	273	29 08	322
298	41 05	000	33 38	034	50 47	089	34 24	139	39 48	218	46 20	272	28 39	321
299	41 05	359	34 03	033	51 33	089	34 54	139	39 20	218	45 34	271	28 10	320
	Enif		◆FOMALHAUT		ACHERNAR		◆RIGIL KENT		ANTARES		◆Rasalhague		ALTAIR	
300	34 28	032	52 19	088	35 24	139	38 51	218	44 48	271	27 41	320	41 03	357
301	34 51	031	53 04	087	35 55	138	38 23	218	44 02	270	27 11	319	41 00	356
302	35 15	030	53 50	087	36 26	138	37 55	218	43 16	269	26 40	318	40 57	355
303	35 37	029	54 36	086	36 56	138	37 27	217	42 30	269	26 09	317	40 52	353
304	35 59	027	55 22	085	37 27	138	36 59	217	41 45	268	25 37	316	40 46	352
305	36 19	026	56 08	085	37 58	137	36 31	217	40 59	268	25 05	315	40 39	351
306	36 39	025	56 54	084	38 30	137	36 04	217	40 13	267	24 32	314	40 31	349
307	36 58	024	57 39	083	39 01	137	35 36	217	39 27	266	23 59	313	40 22	348
308	37 17	023	58 25	082	39 32	137	35 09	216	38 41	266	23 25	312	40 12	347
309	37 34	022	59 10	081	40 04	137	34 42	216	37 55	265	22 51	311	40 01	346
310	37 50	020	59 56	081	40 35	137	34 14	216	37 09	265	22 16	311	39 49	344
311	38 06	019	60 41	080	41 07	136	33 47	216	36 24	264	21 41	310	39 36	343
312	38 21	018	61 26	079	41 39	136	33 21	216	35 38	263	21 05	309	39 22	342
313	38 34	017	62 11	078	42 11	136	32 54	215	34 52	263	20 29	308	39 08	341
314	38 47	016	62 56	077	42 43	136	32 27	215	34 07	262	19 53	307	38 52	339
	Enif		◆Diphda		ACHERNAR		◆RIGIL KENT		ANTARES		Nunki		◆ALTAIR	
315	38 59	014	37 11	082	43 15	136	32 01	215	33 21	262	60 53	289	38 35	338
316	39 10	013	37 56	082	43 47	136	31 35	215	32 36	261	60 09	288	38 18	337
317	39 20	012	38 42	081	44 19	136	31 09	214	31 50	261	59 25	287	37 59	336
318	39 29	011	39 27	080	44 51	135	30 43	214	31 05	260	58 41	286	37 40	335
319	39 36	009	40 12	079	45 23	135	30 17	214	30 20	259	57 57	285	37 20	333
320	39 43	008	40 57	079	45 56	135	29 52	214	29 35	259	57 12	284	36 59	332
321	39 49	007	41 42	078	46 28	135	29 27	213	28 50	258	56 28	283	36 37	331
322	39 54	005	42 27	077	47 00	135	29 01	213	28 05	258	55 43	282	36 14	330
323	39 58	004	43 12	076	47 33	135	28 36	213	27 20	257	54 58	281	35 51	329
324	40 01	003	43 57	075	48 05	135	28 12	212	26 35	257	54 12	280	35 27	328
325	40 03	002	44 41	075	48 38	135	27 47	212	25 50	256	53 27	279	35 02	327
326	40 03	000	45 25	074	49 10	135	27 23	212	25 06	256	52 42	278	34 36	326
327	40 03	359	46 09	073	49 43	135	26 59	211	24 21	255	51 56	278	34 10	324
328	40 02	358	46 53	072	50 16	135	26 35	211	23 37	254	51 11	277	33 43	323
329	39 59	356	47 37	071	50 48	135	26 11	211	22 53	254	50 25	276	33 15	322
	◆Alpheratz		Diphda		◆ACHERNAR		RIGIL KENT		◆Nunki		ALTAIR		Enif	
330	14 36	029	48 20	070	51 21	135	25 48	211	49 39	275	32 47	321	39 56	355
331	14 58	028	49 03	069	51 53	135	25 24	210	48 53	275	32 18	320	39 52	354
332	15 19	027	49 46	068	52 26	135	25 01	210	48 08	274	31 48	319	39 46	353
333	15 40	026	50 29	067	52 58	135	24 39	210	47 22	273	31 18	318	39 40	351
334	16 00	026	51 11	066	53 30	135	24 16	209	46 36	273	30 47	317	39 32	350
335	16 20	025	51 53	065	54 03	135	23 54	209	45 50	272	30 16	316	39 24	349
336	16 38	024	52 34	064	54 35	135	23 32	209	45 04	271	29 43	315	39 14	348
337	16 57	023	53 15	063	55 07	136	23 10	208	44 18	271	29 11	314	39 04	346
338	17 14	022	53 56	062	55 39	136	22 48	208	43 32	270	28 38	314	38 53	345
339	17 31	021	54 37	061	56 11	136	22 27	207	42 46	269	28 04	313	38 40	344
340	17 47	020	55 16	060	56 43	136	22 06	207	42 00	269	27 30	312	38 27	343
341	18 03	019	55 56	058	57 15	136	21 45	207	41 14	268	26 56	311	38 13	341
342	18 18	019	56 35	057	57 47	137	21 25	206	40 28	267	26 21	310	37 58	340
343	18 32	018	57 13	056	58 18	137	21 04	206	39 42	267	25 45	309	37 42	339
344	18 46	017	57 51	054	58 50	137	20 44	206	38 56	266	25 09	308	37 25	338
	◆Alpheratz		Diphda		◆CANOPUS		RIGIL KENT		◆Nunki		ALTAIR		Enif	
345	18 59	016	58 28	053	20 09	143	20 25	205	38 11	266	24 33	307	37 07	337
346	19 11	015	59 04	052	20 37	143	20 05	205	37 25	265	23 56	306	36 48	335
347	19 23	014	59 40	050	21 05	142	19 46	204	36 39	264	23 19	306	36 29	334
348	19 34	013	60 15	049	21 33	142	19 27	204	35 53	264	22 41	305	36 08	333
349	19 44	012	60 49	047	22 02	141	19 09	204	35 08	263	22 03	304	35 47	332
350	19 53	011	61 22	046	22 31	141	18 50	203	34 22	263	21 25	303	35 25	331
351	20 02	010	61 55	044	23 00	141	18 32	203	33 36	262	20 46	302	35 02	330
352	20 10	010	62 26	042	23 29	140	18 15	202	32 51	262	20 07	302	34 39	329
353	20 17	009	62 57	040	23 59	140	17 57	202	32 05	261	19 28	301	34 14	328
354	20 24	008	63 26	039	24 28	139	17 40	202	31 20	260	18 48	300	33 49	326
355	20 30	007	63 54	037	24 58	139	17 23	201	30 35	260	18 08	299	33 24	325
356	20 35	006	64 21	035	25 29	139	17 07	201	29 50	259	17 28	298	32 57	324
357	20 39	005	64 47	033	25 59	138	16 51	200	29 04	259	16 47	298	32 30	323
358	20 43	004	65 11	031	26 30	138	16 35	200	28 19	258	16 07	297	32 02	322
359	20 46	003	65 34	029	27 01	138	16 20	199	27 35	258	15 25	296	31 34	321

LHA ♈	Hc	Zn	Hc	Zn	Hc	Zn	Hc	Zn	Hc	Zn	Hc	Zn	Hc	Zn
	Alpheratz		Hamal		◆ RIGEL		CANOPUS		◆ RIGIL KENT		Peacock		◆ Enif	
0	19 48	002	18 57	031	13 47	089	28 16	137	17 01	199	52 45	227	30 19	321
1	19 49	001	19 20	030	14 32	088	28 47	136	16 46	199	52 12	227	29 49	320
2	19 50	000	19 43	029	15 18	088	29 18	136	16 32	198	51 39	227	29 20	319
3	19 49	359	20 04	028	16 03	087	29 50	136	16 18	198	51 06	227	28 50	318
4	19 49	358	20 25	027	16 48	086	30 21	135	16 04	197	50 33	227	28 19	317
5	19 47	357	20 46	026	17 33	086	30 53	135	15 51	197	50 00	227	27 48	316
6	19 45	357	21 06	026	18 18	085	31 25	135	15 38	196	49 27	227	27 16	315
7	19 41	356	21 25	025	19 04	084	31 58	134	15 25	196	48 55	227	26 43	314
8	19 38	355	21 43	024	19 49	084	32 30	134	15 13	196	48 22	226	26 11	313
9	19 33	354	22 01	023	20 34	083	33 03	134	15 01	195	47 49	226	25 37	312
10	19 28	353	22 18	022	21 18	082	33 35	133	14 49	195	47 16	226	25 03	311
11	19 22	352	22 35	021	22 03	081	34 08	133	14 38	194	46 43	226	24 29	310
12	19 15	351	22 51	020	22 48	081	34 41	133	14 27	194	46 11	226	23 54	309
13	19 08	350	23 06	019	23 33	080	35 15	133	14 17	193	45 38	226	23 19	309
14	19 00	349	23 20	018	24 17	079	35 48	132	14 06	193	45 06	226	22 44	308
	◆ Hamal		RIGEL		◆ CANOPUS		RIGIL KENT		◆ Peacock		FOMALHAUT		Alpheratz	
15	23 34	017	25 02	079	36 22	132	13 57	192	44 33	226	62 52	285	18 51	348
16	23 47	016	25 46	078	36 55	132	13 47	192	44 01	226	62 08	284	18 41	347
17	23 59	015	26 30	077	37 29	131	13 38	191	43 28	225	61 24	283	18 31	346
18	24 10	014	27 14	076	38 03	131	13 29	191	42 56	225	60 40	282	18 20	346
19	24 21	013	27 58	076	38 38	131	13 21	190	42 24	225	59 55	281	18 08	345
20	24 31	012	28 42	075	39 12	131	13 13	190	41 52	225	59 11	280	17 56	344
21	24 40	011	29 26	074	39 46	130	13 05	189	41 20	225	58 26	280	17 43	343
22	24 48	010	30 09	073	40 21	130	12 58	189	40 48	225	57 42	279	17 30	342
23	24 56	009	30 52	073	40 55	130	12 51	188	40 17	224	56 57	278	17 15	341
24	25 02	008	31 35	072	41 30	130	12 45	188	39 45	224	56 12	277	17 00	340
25	25 08	007	32 18	071	42 05	129	12 39	187	39 13	224	55 27	276	16 45	339
26	25 14	006	33 01	070	42 40	129	12 33	187	38 42	224	54 42	276	16 28	339
27	25 18	005	33 44	069	43 15	129	12 28	187	38 11	224	53 57	275	16 11	338
28	25 22	004	34 26	068	43 51	129	12 23	186	37 40	223	53 12	274	15 54	337
29	25 24	003	35 08	068	44 26	129	12 18	186	37 09	223	52 27	273	15 36	336
	◆ Hamal		RIGEL		SIRIUS		◆ CANOPUS		RIGIL KENT		◆ Peacock		FOMALHAUT	
30	25 26	002	35 50	067	24 46	091	45 01	128	12 14	185	36 38	223	51 41	273
31	25 28	001	36 31	066	25 31	090	45 37	128	12 10	185	36 07	223	50 56	272
32	25 28	000	37 12	065	26 16	090	46 13	128	12 07	184	35 37	222	50 11	271
33	25 28	359	37 53	064	27 02	089	46 48	128	12 04	184	35 06	222	49 26	271
34	25 26	358	38 34	063	27 47	088	47 24	128	12 01	183	34 36	222	48 40	270
35	25 24	357	39 14	062	28 32	088	48 00	128	11 59	183	34 06	222	47 55	269
36	25 22	356	39 54	061	29 17	087	48 36	127	11 57	182	33 36	221	47 10	269
37	25 18	355	40 33	060	30 02	086	49 12	127	11 56	182	33 06	221	46 24	268
38	25 14	354	41 12	059	30 48	086	49 48	127	11 55	181	32 36	221	45 39	267
39	25 08	353	41 51	058	31 33	085	50 24	127	11 54	181	32 07	220	44 54	267
40	25 02	352	42 29	057	32 18	084	51 00	127	11 54	180	31 38	220	44 09	266
41	24 56	351	43 07	056	33 03	084	51 36	127	11 54	180	31 09	220	43 24	266
42	24 48	350	43 45	055	33 48	083	52 12	127	11 54	179	30 40	219	42 39	265
43	24 40	349	44 22	054	34 33	082	52 49	127	11 55	179	30 11	219	41 53	264
44	24 31	348	44 58	053	35 18	081	53 25	127	11 57	178	29 43	219	41 08	264
	◆ RIGEL		SIRIUS		CANOPUS		◆ RIGIL KENT		Peacock		◆ FOMALHAUT		Hamal	
45	45 34	052	36 02	081	54 01	127	11 58	178	29 14	219	40 23	263	24 21	347
46	46 09	051	36 47	080	54 38	127	12 00	177	28 46	218	39 38	263	24 10	346
47	46 44	050	37 32	079	55 14	127	12 03	177	28 18	218	38 54	262	23 59	345
48	47 18	048	38 16	078	55 50	127	12 06	176	27 51	218	38 09	261	23 47	344
49	47 52	047	39 00	078	56 27	127	12 09	176	27 23	217	37 24	261	23 34	343
50	48 25	046	39 44	077	57 03	127	12 13	175	26 56	217	36 39	260	23 20	342
51	48 57	045	40 29	076	57 39	127	12 17	175	26 29	216	35 55	260	23 06	341
52	49 28	043	41 12	075	58 16	127	12 21	174	26 02	216	35 10	259	22 51	340
53	49 59	042	41 56	074	58 52	127	12 26	174	25 35	216	34 26	259	22 35	339
54	50 29	041	42 40	074	59 28	127	12 31	173	25 09	215	33 41	258	22 19	338
55	50 58	039	43 23	073	60 04	127	12 37	173	24 43	215	32 57	258	22 02	337
56	51 27	038	44 06	072	60 40	127	12 43	172	24 17	215	32 13	257	21 44	336
57	51 54	037	44 49	071	61 17	127	12 49	172	23 52	214	31 29	256	21 25	335
58	52 21	035	45 32	070	61 52	128	12 56	171	23 26	214	30 45	256	21 06	334
59	52 46	034	46 14	069	62 28	128	13 03	171	23 01	214	30 01	255	20 46	334
	ALDEBARAN		◆ SIRIUS		Suhail		◆ RIGIL KENT		ACHERNAR		◆ Diphda		Hamal	
60	31 50	010	46 56	068	34 59	120	13 10	170	62 13	222	42 21	284	20 26	333
61	31 58	009	47 38	067	35 39	120	13 18	170	61 42	223	41 37	283	20 05	332
62	32 05	008	48 20	066	36 18	120	13 27	169	61 11	223	40 53	282	19 43	331
63	32 11	007	49 01	065	36 57	119	13 35	169	60 40	223	40 08	282	19 20	330
64	32 16	006	49 42	064	37 37	119	13 44	168	60 09	224	39 24	281	18 58	329
65	32 20	005	50 23	063	38 17	118	13 54	168	59 38	224	38 40	280	18 34	328
66	32 23	004	51 03	062	38 57	118	14 03	167	59 06	224	37 55	279	18 10	327
67	32 26	002	51 43	061	39 37	118	14 13	167	58 34	225	37 10	279	17 45	326
68	32 27	001	52 22	060	40 17	117	14 24	166	58 02	225	36 25	278	17 20	326
69	32 28	000	53 01	059	40 57	117	14 35	166	57 30	225	35 40	277	16 54	325
70	32 27	359	53 39	057	41 38	117	14 46	166	56 58	225	34 55	276	16 28	324
71	32 26	358	54 17	056	42 18	116	14 57	165	56 26	225	34 10	276	16 01	323
72	32 24	357	54 55	055	42 59	116	15 09	165	55 54	225	33 25	275	15 33	322
73	32 21	356	55 32	054	43 40	116	15 21	164	55 22	226	32 40	274	15 05	321
74	32 17	355	56 08	052	44 21	115	15 34	164	54 49	226	31 55	274	14 37	321
	BETELGEUSE		◆ SIRIUS		Suhail		◆ RIGIL KENT		ACHERNAR		◆ Diphda		ALDEBARAN	
75	39 55	018	56 43	051	45 02	115	15 47	163	54 17	226	31 10	273	32 13	353
76	40 08	017	57 18	050	45 43	115	16 00	163	53 45	226	30 25	272	32 07	352
77	40 21	016	57 52	048	46 24	114	16 14	162	53 12	226	29 39	272	32 00	351
78	40 33	014	58 26	047	47 05	114	16 28	162	52 40	226	28 54	271	31 53	350
79	40 44	013	58 58	045	47 47	114	16 42	161	52 07	226	28 09	270	31 45	349
80	40 53	012	59 30	044	48 28	113	16 56	161	51 35	226	27 23	270	31 36	348
81	41 02	011	60 01	042	49 10	113	17 11	161	51 02	226	26 38	269	31 26	347
82	41 10	009	60 30	040	49 52	113	17 27	160	50 29	226	25 53	268	31 15	346
83	41 17	008	60 59	039	50 34	112	17 42	160	49 57	226	25 08	268	31 03	345
84	41 22	007	61 27	037	51 16	112	17 58	159	49 24	226	24 22	267	30 51	343
85	41 27	005	61 54	035	51 58	112	18 14	159	48 52	226	23 37	266	30 37	342
86	41 31	004	62 19	033	52 40	111	18 31	158	48 19	226	22 52	266	30 23	341
87	41 33	003	62 43	031	53 22	111	18 47	158	47 47	226	22 07	265	30 08	340
88	41 35	001	63 06	030	54 04	111	19 05	158	47 15	226	21 22	264	29 53	339
89	41 35	000	63 28	028	54 47	110	19 22	157	46 42	226	20 37	264	29 36	338

LAT 41°S

LHA ♈	Hc	Zn	Hc	Zn	Hc	Zn	Hc	Zn	Hc	Zn	Hc	Zn	Hc	Zn
	PROCYON		Alphard		◆ Suhail		RIGIL KENT		◆ ACHERNAR		RIGEL		◆ BETELGEUSE	
90	38 27	033	33 55	070	55 29	110	19 40	157	46 10	225	55 43	340	41 35	359
91	38 51	031	34 37	069	56 12	110	19 58	156	45 38	225	55 27	338	41 33	357
92	39 14	030	35 19	068	56 54	110	20 16	156	45 06	225	55 10	337	41 31	356
93	39 36	029	36 01	067	57 37	109	20 35	156	44 34	225	54 51	335	41 27	355
94	39 58	028	36 43	067	58 20	109	20 54	155	44 02	225	54 31	333	41 22	353
95	40 19	027	37 25	066	59 03	109	21 13	155	43 30	225	54 11	332	41 17	352
96	40 38	025	38 06	065	59 45	109	21 32	154	42 58	225	53 49	330	41 10	351
97	40 57	024	38 46	064	60 28	108	21 52	154	42 26	224	53 26	329	41 02	349
98	41 15	023	39 27	063	61 11	108	22 12	154	41 54	224	53 02	327	40 53	348
99	41 32	022	40 07	062	61 54	108	22 32	153	41 23	224	52 37	326	40 44	347
100	41 49	020	40 47	061	62 37	108	22 53	153	40 51	224	52 11	324	40 33	346
101	42 04	019	41 26	060	63 21	108	23 14	152	40 20	224	51 44	323	40 21	344
102	42 18	018	42 05	059	64 04	107	23 35	152	39 49	224	51 16	321	40 08	343
103	42 31	016	42 44	058	64 47	107	23 56	152	39 18	223	50 48	320	39 55	342
104	42 43	015	43 22	057	65 30	107	24 18	151	38 47	223	50 18	319	39 40	341
	PROCYON		REGULUS		◆ Gienah		RIGIL KENT		◆ ACHERNAR		RIGEL		◆ BETELGEUSE	
105	42 55	014	21 27	051	19 31	097	24 39	151	38 16	223	49 48	317	39 24	339
106	43 05	012	22 02	050	20 16	096	25 01	151	37 45	223	49 17	316	39 08	338
107	43 14	011	22 36	049	21 01	095	25 24	150	37 14	222	48 45	315	38 50	337
108	43 22	010	23 10	048	21 46	095	25 46	150	36 44	222	48 13	314	38 32	336
109	43 29	008	23 43	047	22 31	094	26 09	150	36 13	222	47 39	312	38 13	334
110	43 35	007	24 16	046	23 17	094	26 32	149	35 43	222	47 06	311	37 53	333
111	43 40	006	24 49	045	24 02	093	26 55	149	35 13	221	46 31	310	37 32	332
112	43 44	004	25 21	044	24 47	092	27 19	149	34 43	221	45 56	309	37 11	331
113	43 47	003	25 52	044	25 32	092	27 42	148	34 13	221	45 21	308	36 48	330
114	43 48	001	26 23	043	26 18	091	28 06	148	33 44	221	44 45	307	36 25	329
115	43 49	000	26 54	042	27 03	090	28 30	148	33 14	220	44 08	305	36 01	327
116	43 48	359	27 23	041	27 48	090	28 55	147	32 45	220	43 31	304	35 36	326
117	43 47	357	27 53	040	28 33	089	29 19	147	32 16	220	42 53	303	35 11	325
118	43 44	356	28 21	039	29 19	088	29 44	147	31 47	220	42 15	302	34 45	324
119	43 40	355	28 49	038	30 04	088	30 09	147	31 18	219	41 37	301	34 18	323
	REGULUS		◆ SPICA		RIGIL KENT		◆ ACHERNAR		RIGEL		BETELGEUSE		◆ PROCYON	
120	29 17	037	13 44	093	30 34	146	30 50	219	40 58	300	33 50	322	43 35	353
121	29 44	036	14 29	092	30 59	146	30 21	219	40 19	299	33 22	321	43 29	352
122	30 10	035	15 14	092	31 24	146	29 53	218	39 39	298	32 53	320	43 22	350
123	30 35	034	15 59	091	31 50	145	29 25	218	38 59	297	32 24	319	43 14	349
124	31 00	033	16 45	090	32 16	145	28 57	218	38 19	297	31 54	318	43 05	348
125	31 24	032	17 30	090	32 42	145	28 30	217	37 38	296	31 23	317	42 55	346
126	31 48	031	18 15	089	33 08	145	28 02	217	36 57	295	30 52	316	42 44	345
127	32 10	030	19 01	088	33 34	144	27 35	217	36 16	294	30 20	315	42 32	344
128	32 32	029	19 46	088	34 01	144	27 08	216	35 34	293	29 48	314	42 19	342
129	32 54	027	20 31	087	34 27	144	26 42	216	34 52	292	29 15	313	42 04	341
130	33 14	026	21 16	086	34 54	144	26 15	216	34 10	291	28 42	312	41 49	340
131	33 34	025	22 01	086	35 21	143	25 49	215	33 28	290	28 08	311	41 33	339
132	33 53	024	22 47	085	35 48	143	25 23	215	32 45	290	27 34	310	41 16	337
133	34 11	023	23 32	084	36 15	143	24 57	215	32 03	289	26 59	309	40 58	336
134	34 28	022	24 17	084	36 43	143	24 31	214	31 20	288	26 24	308	40 39	335
	REGULUS		◆ SPICA		RIGIL KENT		◆ ACHERNAR		CANOPUS		SIRIUS		◆ PROCYON	
135	34 45	021	25 02	083	37 10	143	24 06	214	61 22	233	52 18	300	40 19	333
136	35 00	020	25 47	082	37 38	142	23 41	213	60 46	233	51 39	299	39 59	332
137	35 15	018	26 32	082	38 06	142	23 16	213	60 10	233	50 59	298	39 37	331
138	35 29	017	27 16	081	38 33	142	22 52	213	59 33	233	50 19	297	39 15	330
139	35 42	016	28 01	080	39 01	142	22 27	212	58 57	233	49 38	296	38 52	329
140	35 54	015	28 46	079	39 30	142	22 03	212	58 21	233	48 57	295	38 28	328
141	36 05	014	29 30	079	39 58	141	21 39	211	57 45	233	48 16	294	38 03	326
142	36 15	013	30 14	078	40 26	141	21 16	211	57 08	233	47 34	293	37 38	325
143	36 25	011	30 59	077	40 54	141	20 53	211	56 32	233	46 52	292	37 11	324
144	36 33	010	31 43	076	41 23	141	20 30	210	55 56	233	46 10	291	36 45	323
145	36 41	009	32 27	076	41 51	141	20 07	210	55 19	233	45 28	290	36 17	322
146	36 47	008	33 10	075	42 20	141	19 45	209	54 43	233	44 45	289	35 49	321
147	36 53	006	33 54	074	42 49	141	19 22	209	54 07	233	44 02	288	35 20	320
148	36 57	005	34 38	073	43 17	140	19 01	209	53 30	233	43 19	287	34 50	319
149	37 01	004	35 21	073	43 46	140	18 39	208	52 54	233	42 35	286	34 20	318
	REGULUS		◆ SPICA		RIGIL KENT		◆ ACHERNAR		CANOPUS		SIRIUS		◆ PROCYON	
150	37 04	003	36 04	072	44 15	140	18 18	208	52 18	233	41 52	285	33 49	317
151	37 06	002	36 47	071	44 44	140	17 57	207	51 41	233	41 08	285	33 18	316
152	37 06	000	37 30	070	45 13	140	17 36	207	51 05	233	40 24	284	32 46	315
153	37 06	359	38 12	069	45 42	140	17 16	206	50 29	233	39 40	283	32 13	314
154	37 05	358	38 54	068	46 11	140	16 56	206	49 53	233	38 56	282	31 40	313
155	37 03	357	39 36	067	46 40	140	16 36	206	49 17	233	38 12	281	31 07	312
156	37 00	355	40 18	067	47 09	140	16 17	205	48 41	233	37 27	281	30 32	311
157	36 56	354	40 59	066	47 39	140	15 58	205	48 05	232	36 43	280	29 58	310
158	36 51	353	41 40	065	48 08	140	15 39	204	47 29	232	35 58	279	29 23	309
159	36 45	352	42 21	064	48 37	140	15 21	204	46 53	232	35 13	278	28 47	308
160	36 38	351	43 01	063	49 06	140	15 03	203	46 18	232	34 29	278	28 11	307
161	36 30	349	43 42	062	49 35	140	14 45	203	45 42	232	33 44	277	27 35	306
162	36 21	348	44 21	061	50 05	140	14 28	202	45 06	232	32 59	276	26 58	305
163	36 11	347	45 01	060	50 34	140	14 11	202	44 31	231	32 14	276	26 21	304
164	36 01	346	45 39	059	51 03	140	13 54	201	43 56	231	31 29	275	25 43	303
	SPICA		◆ ANTARES		RIGIL KENT		ACHERNAR		◆ CANOPUS		SIRIUS		◆ REGULUS	
165	46 18	058	22 18	106	51 32	140	13 38	201	43 20	231	30 43	274	35 49	345
166	46 56	057	23 02	106	52 01	140	13 22	200	42 45	231	29 58	273	35 37	343
167	47 33	055	23 46	105	52 30	140	13 07	200	42 10	231	29 13	273	35 23	342
168	48 10	054	24 29	105	52 59	140	12 51	199	41 35	230	28 28	272	35 09	341
169	48 47	053	25 13	104	53 28	140	12 37	199	41 00	230	27 42	271	34 54	340
170	49 23	052	25 57	104	53 56	141	12 22	198	40 26	230	26 57	271	34 38	339
171	49 58	051	26 41	103	54 25	141	12 08	198	39 51	230	26 12	270	34 21	338
172	50 33	049	27 25	102	54 54	141	11 54	197	39 17	229	25 27	269	34 04	337
173	51 07	048	28 10	102	55 22	141	11 41	197	38 42	229	24 41	269	33 45	335
174	51 40	047	28 54	101	55 51	141	11 28	196	38 08	229	23 56	268	33 26	334
175	52 13	046	29 39	101	56 19	142	11 16	196	37 34	229	23 11	268	33 06	333
176	52 45	044	30 23	100	56 47	142	11 03	195	37 00	228	22 26	267	32 45	332
177	53 16	043	31 08	099	57 15	142	10 52	195	36 27	228	21 40	266	32 23	331
178	53 47	041	31 52	099	57 43	142	10 40	194	35 53	228	20 55	266	32 01	330
179	54 16	040	32 37	098	58 10	143	10 29	194	35 19	227	20 10	265	31 38	329

LAT 41°S

LHA ♈	◆ ARCTURUS Hc	Zn	ANTARES Hc	Zn	◆ RIGIL KENT Hc	Zn	ACHERNAR Hc	Zn	CANOPUS Hc	Zn	◆ Suhail Hc	Zn	REGULUS Hc	Zn
180	22 05	035	33 22	098	58 37	143	10 19	193	34 46	227	58 31	251	31 14	328
181	22 30	034	34 07	097	59 05	143	10 09	193	34 13	227	57 49	251	30 50	327
182	22 55	033	34 52	097	59 32	144	09 59	192	33 40	227	57 06	250	30 25	326
183	23 20	032	35 37	096	59 58	144	09 49	192	33 07	226	56 23	250	29 59	325
184	23 43	031	36 22	095	60 25	144	09 40	191	32 35	226	55 41	250	29 33	324
185	24 07	030	37 07	095	60 51	145	09 32	191	32 02	226	54 58	250	29 05	323
186	24 29	029	37 52	094	61 17	145	09 24	190	31 30	225	54 16	249	28 38	322
187	24 51	028	38 37	094	61 42	146	09 16	190	30 58	225	53 34	249	28 09	321
188	25 12	027	39 23	093	62 08	146	09 09	189	30 26	225	52 51	249	27 41	320
189	25 32	026	40 08	092	62 33	147	09 02	188	29 54	224	52 09	248	27 11	319
190	25 52	025	40 53	092	62 57	147	08 55	188	29 23	224	51 27	248	26 41	318
191	26 11	024	41 38	091	63 21	148	08 49	187	28 51	224	50 45	248	26 10	317
192	26 30	023	42 24	090	63 45	149	08 44	187	28 20	223	50 03	248	25 39	316
193	26 47	022	43 09	090	64 08	149	08 39	186	27 49	223	49 21	247	25 08	315
194	27 04	021	43 54	089	64 31	150	08 34	186	27 19	222	48 40	247	24 35	314

LHA ♈	◆ ARCTURUS Hc	Zn	ANTARES Hc	Zn	◆ Peacock Hc	Zn	ACHERNAR Hc	Zn	CANOPUS Hc	Zn	◆ Suhail Hc	Zn	REGULUS Hc	Zn
195	27 20	020	44 40	088	23 16	146	08 29	185	26 48	222	47 58	247	24 03	313
196	27 36	019	45 25	088	23 41	146	08 26	185	26 18	222	47 17	246	23 30	313
197	27 50	018	46 10	087	24 07	145	08 22	184	25 48	221	46 35	246	22 56	312
198	28 04	017	46 55	086	24 32	145	08 19	184	25 18	221	45 54	246	22 22	311
199	28 17	016	47 40	086	24 58	145	08 16	183	24 49	221	45 13	245	21 47	310
200	28 29	015	48 26	085	25 25	144	08 14	183	24 19	220	44 32	245	21 12	309
201	28 41	014	49 11	084	25 51	144	08 12	182	23 50	220	43 51	245	20 37	308
202	28 51	013	49 56	083	26 18	144	08 11	181	23 21	219	43 10	244	20 01	307
203	29 01	012	50 41	083	26 45	143	08 10	181	22 53	219	42 29	244	19 25	307
204	29 10	011	51 25	082	27 12	143	08 10	180	22 24	219	41 49	244	18 49	306
205	29 18	010	52 10	081	27 39	143	08 10	180	21 56	218	41 08	243	18 12	305
206	29 26	009	52 55	080	28 07	142	08 10	179	21 28	218	40 28	243	17 34	304
207	29 32	008	53 39	079	28 35	142	08 11	179	21 01	217	39 48	242	16 57	303
208	29 38	007	54 24	078	29 03	142	08 12	178	20 33	217	39 08	242	16 19	303
209	29 43	006	55 08	078	29 31	141	08 14	178	20 06	216	38 28	242	15 40	302

LHA ♈	◆ ARCTURUS Hc	Zn	ANTARES Hc	Zn	◆ Peacock Hc	Zn	ACHERNAR Hc	Zn	CANOPUS Hc	Zn	◆ Suhail Hc	Zn	SPICA Hc	Zn
210	29 47	004	55 52	077	29 59	141	08 16	177	19 40	216	37 48	241	59 19	343
211	29 50	003	56 36	076	30 28	141	08 19	176	19 13	216	37 08	241	59 05	342
212	29 52	002	57 20	075	30 57	140	08 22	176	18 47	215	36 29	241	58 50	340
213	29 53	001	58 04	074	31 26	140	08 25	175	18 21	215	35 49	240	58 34	338
214	29 54	000	58 47	073	31 55	140	08 29	175	17 55	214	35 10	240	58 16	336
215	29 53	359	59 30	072	32 24	139	08 33	174	17 30	214	34 31	239	57 57	334
216	29 52	358	60 13	071	32 54	139	08 38	174	17 05	213	33 52	239	57 37	333
217	29 50	357	60 56	070	33 24	139	08 43	173	16 40	213	33 13	239	57 16	331
218	29 47	356	61 38	068	33 53	139	08 49	173	16 16	212	32 35	238	56 53	329
219	29 43	355	62 20	067	34 23	138	08 55	172	15 52	212	31 56	238	56 30	328
220	29 39	354	63 01	066	34 54	138	09 01	172	15 28	211	31 18	237	56 05	326
221	29 33	352	63 43	065	35 24	138	09 08	171	15 04	211	30 40	237	55 39	325
222	29 27	351	64 23	063	35 55	138	09 15	171	14 41	210	30 02	237	55 12	323
223	29 20	350	65 04	062	36 25	137	09 23	170	14 19	210	29 25	236	54 45	321
224	29 12	349	65 43	061	36 56	137	09 31	169	13 56	210	28 47	236	54 16	320

LHA ♈	Rasalhague Hc	Zn	◆ Nunki Hc	Zn	Peacock Hc	Zn	ACHERNAR Hc	Zn	◆ ACRUX Hc	Zn	SPICA Hc	Zn	◆ ARCTURUS Hc	Zn
225	25 31	043	39 41	092	37 27	137	09 39	169	58 34	212	53 46	319	29 03	348
226	26 01	042	40 26	092	37 58	137	09 48	168	58 10	213	53 16	317	28 53	347
227	26 31	041	41 11	091	38 29	136	09 57	168	57 45	213	52 45	316	28 43	346
228	27 01	040	41 57	090	39 00	136	10 07	167	57 21	213	52 13	314	28 31	345
229	27 29	039	42 42	090	39 32	136	10 17	167	56 56	214	51 40	313	28 19	344
230	27 58	038	43 27	089	40 03	136	10 28	166	56 30	214	51 07	312	28 06	343
231	28 25	037	44 12	088	40 35	136	10 39	166	56 05	214	50 33	311	27 53	342
232	28 52	036	44 58	088	41 07	135	10 50	165	55 39	215	49 58	309	27 38	341
233	29 18	035	45 43	087	41 39	135	11 02	165	55 14	215	49 23	308	27 23	340
234	29 44	034	46 28	086	42 11	135	11 14	164	54 48	215	48 47	307	27 07	339
235	30 09	033	47 13	086	42 43	135	11 26	164	54 22	215	48 10	306	26 50	338
236	30 34	032	47 58	085	43 15	135	11 39	163	53 56	215	47 33	305	26 33	337
237	30 57	031	48 43	084	43 47	134	11 53	163	53 29	216	46 56	303	26 14	336
238	31 20	030	49 28	083	44 20	134	12 06	162	53 03	216	46 18	302	25 56	335
239	31 43	029	50 13	083	44 52	134	12 20	162	52 36	216	45 39	301	25 36	334

LHA ♈	Rasalhague Hc	Zn	◆ ALTAIR Hc	Zn	Peacock Hc	Zn	◆ ACHERNAR Hc	Zn	ACRUX Hc	Zn	◆ SPICA Hc	Zn	ARCTURUS Hc	Zn
240	32 04	028	17 09	061	45 25	134	12 35	161	52 10	216	45 00	300	25 16	333
241	32 25	027	17 48	060	45 57	134	12 49	161	51 43	216	44 21	299	24 55	332
242	32 45	026	18 28	060	46 30	134	13 05	160	51 16	216	43 41	298	24 33	331
243	33 04	025	19 06	059	47 03	134	13 20	160	50 49	216	43 01	297	24 10	330
244	33 22	023	19 45	058	47 35	134	13 36	159	50 23	216	42 21	296	23 47	329
245	33 40	022	20 23	057	48 08	134	13 52	159	49 56	217	41 40	295	23 24	328
246	33 57	021	21 01	056	48 41	133	14 09	158	49 29	217	40 59	294	23 00	327
247	34 13	020	21 39	056	49 14	133	14 26	158	49 02	217	40 17	293	22 35	326
248	34 28	019	22 16	055	49 47	133	14 43	157	48 35	217	39 36	293	22 09	325
249	34 42	018	22 53	054	50 20	133	15 01	157	48 08	217	38 54	292	21 43	324
250	34 56	017	23 29	053	50 53	133	15 19	156	47 41	217	38 12	291	21 17	324
251	35 08	015	24 05	052	51 26	133	15 37	156	47 13	217	37 29	290	20 49	323
252	35 20	014	24 41	051	51 58	133	15 55	155	46 46	217	36 47	289	20 22	322
253	35 30	013	25 16	050	52 31	133	16 14	155	46 19	217	36 04	288	19 53	321
254	35 40	012	25 50	050	53 04	133	16 34	155	45 52	217	35 21	287	19 24	320

LHA ♈	Rasalhague Hc	Zn	◆ ALTAIR Hc	Zn	FOMALHAUT Hc	Zn	◆ ACHERNAR Hc	Zn	RIGIL KENT Hc	Zn	◆ SPICA Hc	Zn	Alphecca Hc	Zn
255	35 49	011	26 25	049	19 08	113	16 53	154	60 59	215	34 37	287	19 33	340
256	35 57	010	26 58	048	19 50	112	17 13	154	60 33	215	33 54	286	19 17	339
257	36 04	008	27 32	047	20 32	112	17 34	153	60 07	216	33 10	285	19 00	338
258	36 10	007	28 04	046	21 14	111	17 54	153	59 40	216	32 26	284	18 43	337
259	36 15	006	28 37	045	21 56	111	18 15	152	59 13	217	31 42	284	18 25	336
260	36 20	005	29 08	044	22 39	110	18 36	152	58 46	217	30 58	283	18 07	336
261	36 23	004	29 39	043	23 21	110	18 58	151	58 19	217	30 14	282	17 48	335
262	36 25	002	30 10	042	24 04	109	19 19	151	57 51	218	29 30	281	17 28	334
263	36 27	001	30 40	041	24 47	109	19 42	151	57 24	218	28 45	281	17 08	333
264	36 27	000	31 10	040	25 30	108	20 04	150	56 56	218	28 01	280	16 47	332
265	36 26	359	31 38	039	26 13	107	20 27	150	56 28	218	27 16	279	16 25	331
266	36 25	357	32 07	038	26 56	107	20 49	149	55 59	219	26 31	278	16 03	330
267	36 22	356	32 34	037	27 40	106	21 13	149	55 31	219	25 46	278	15 40	329
268	36 19	355	33 01	036	28 23	106	21 36	149	55 03	219	25 01	277	15 17	329
269	36 15	354	33 27	035	29 07	105	22 00	148	54 34	219	24 16	276	14 53	328

LHA ♈	ALTAIR Hc	Zn	Enif Hc	Zn	◆ FOMALHAUT Hc	Zn	ACHERNAR Hc	Zn	◆ RIGIL KENT Hc	Zn	ANTARES Hc	Zn	◆ Rasalhague Hc	Zn
270	33 53	034	17 27	059	29 51	105	22 24	148	54 06	219	66 29	301	36 09	353
271	34 18	033	18 06	058	30 34	104	22 48	147	53 37	219	65 50	300	36 03	351
272	34 42	032	18 44	058	31 18	104	23 13	147	53 08	220	65 10	298	35 56	350
273	35 05	031	19 22	057	32 02	103	23 38	147	52 39	220	64 30	297	35 48	349
274	35 28	029	20 00	056	32 47	103	24 03	146	52 10	220	63 49	295	35 39	348
275	35 50	028	20 37	055	33 31	102	24 28	146	51 41	220	63 08	294	35 29	347
276	36 11	027	21 14	054	34 15	101	24 53	145	51 12	220	62 27	293	35 18	345
277	36 31	026	21 51	053	35 00	101	25 19	145	50 43	220	61 45	292	35 06	344
278	36 50	025	22 27	053	35 44	100	25 45	145	50 14	220	61 03	291	34 53	343
279	37 09	024	23 03	052	36 29	100	26 12	144	49 45	220	60 20	289	34 40	342
280	37 27	022	23 38	051	37 13	099	26 38	144	49 15	220	59 37	288	34 25	341
281	37 44	021	24 13	050	37 58	099	27 05	144	48 46	220	58 54	287	34 10	340
282	38 00	020	24 48	049	38 43	098	27 32	143	48 17	220	58 11	286	33 54	339
283	38 15	019	25 22	048	39 28	098	27 59	143	47 48	220	57 27	285	33 37	337
284	38 29	018	25 55	047	40 13	097	28 26	143	47 19	220	56 44	284	33 19	336

LHA ♈	ALTAIR Hc	Zn	Enif Hc	Zn	◆ FOMALHAUT Hc	Zn	ACHERNAR Hc	Zn	◆ RIGIL KENT Hc	Zn	ANTARES Hc	Zn	◆ Rasalhague Hc	Zn
285	38 42	016	26 28	046	40 58	096	28 54	142	46 50	220	56 00	283	33 01	335
286	38 54	015	27 01	046	41 43	096	29 21	142	46 20	220	55 15	283	32 41	334
287	39 06	014	27 33	045	42 28	095	29 49	142	45 51	220	54 31	282	32 21	333
288	39 16	013	28 05	044	43 13	095	30 18	141	45 22	220	53 47	281	32 00	332
289	39 26	011	28 36	043	43 58	094	30 46	141	44 53	220	53 02	280	31 38	331
290	39 34	010	29 06	042	44 43	093	31 14	141	44 24	220	52 18	279	31 16	330
291	39 41	009	29 36	041	45 28	093	31 43	140	43 55	220	51 33	278	30 53	329
292	39 48	008	30 05	040	46 14	092	32 12	140	43 27	220	50 48	278	30 29	328
293	39 53	006	30 34	039	46 59	091	32 41	140	42 58	219	50 03	277	30 05	327
294	39 58	005	31 02	038	47 44	091	33 10	140	42 29	219	49 18	276	29 40	326
295	40 01	004	31 29	037	48 30	090	33 40	139	42 00	219	48 33	275	29 14	325
296	40 04	002	31 56	036	49 15	090	34 09	139	41 32	219	47 48	275	28 47	324
297	40 05	001	32 22	035	50 00	089	34 39	139	41 03	219	47 03	274	28 20	323
298	40 05	000	32 48	034	50 45	088	35 09	139	40 35	219	46 17	273	27 52	322
299	40 05	359	33 13	033	51 31	088	35 39	138	40 07	219	45 32	272	27 24	321

LHA ♈	◆ Enif Hc	Zn	FOMALHAUT Hc	Zn	◆ ACHERNAR Hc	Zn	RIGIL KENT Hc	Zn	◆ ANTARES Hc	Zn	Rasalhague Hc	Zn	ALTAIR Hc	Zn
300	33 37	032	52 16	087	36 09	138	39 38	218	44 47	272	26 55	320	40 03	357
301	34 00	030	53 01	086	36 40	138	39 10	218	44 02	271	26 26	319	40 01	356
302	34 22	029	53 46	085	37 10	138	38 42	218	43 16	270	25 56	318	39 57	355
303	34 44	028	54 31	085	37 41	137	38 14	218	42 31	270	25 25	317	39 52	353
304	35 05	027	55 16	084	38 11	137	37 47	218	41 46	269	24 54	316	39 46	352
305	35 25	026	56 01	083	38 42	137	37 19	218	41 01	268	24 22	315	39 40	351
306	35 45	025	56 46	082	39 13	137	36 52	217	40 15	268	23 50	314	39 32	350
307	36 03	024	57 31	081	39 45	136	36 24	217	39 30	267	23 17	313	39 23	348
308	36 21	022	58 16	081	40 16	136	35 57	217	38 45	267	22 44	313	39 14	347
309	36 38	021	59 00	080	40 47	136	35 30	217	38 00	266	22 11	312	39 03	346
310	36 54	020	59 45	079	41 19	136	35 03	216	37 15	265	21 37	311	38 51	345
311	37 09	019	60 29	078	41 50	136	34 36	216	36 29	265	21 02	310	38 39	343
312	37 24	018	61 13	077	42 22	136	34 09	216	35 44	264	20 27	309	38 25	342
313	37 37	017	61 57	076	42 54	135	33 43	216	34 59	264	19 52	308	38 11	341
314	37 49	015	62 41	075	43 25	135	33 16	215	34 14	263	19 16	308	37 56	340

LHA ♈	Enif Hc	Zn	◆ Diphda Hc	Zn	ACHERNAR Hc	Zn	Miaplacidus Hc	Zn	◆ RIGIL KENT Hc	Zn	ANTARES Hc	Zn	◆ ALTAIR Hc	Zn
315	38 01	014	37 02	082	43 57	135	20 48	181	32 50	215	33 29	262	37 40	338
316	38 11	013	37 47	081	44 29	135	20 48	181	32 24	215	32 45	262	37 22	337
317	38 21	012	38 32	080	45 01	135	20 47	180	31 58	215	32 00	261	37 05	336
318	38 30	010	39 16	079	45 34	135	20 47	180	31 33	214	31 15	261	36 46	335
319	38 37	009	40 01	079	46 06	135	20 47	180	31 07	214	30 31	260	36 26	334
320	38 44	008	40 45	078	46 38	135	20 47	179	30 42	214	29 46	259	36 06	333
321	38 50	007	41 29	077	47 10	134	20 48	179	30 17	214	29 01	259	35 44	331
322	38 54	005	42 13	076	47 43	134	20 49	179	29 52	213	28 17	258	35 22	330
323	38 58	004	42 57	075	48 15	134	20 50	178	29 27	213	27 33	258	35 00	329
324	39 01	003	43 41	075	48 48	134	20 51	178	29 02	213	26 49	257	34 36	328
325	39 03	002	44 25	074	49 20	134	20 53	178	28 38	212	26 04	257	34 12	327
326	39 03	000	45 08	073	49 53	134	20 55	177	28 14	212	25 20	256	33 47	326
327	39 03	359	45 51	072	50 25	134	20 58	177	27 50	212	24 37	255	33 21	325
328	39 02	358	46 34	071	50 58	134	21 00	176	27 26	211	23 53	255	32 55	324
329	38 59	356	47 17	070	51 30	134	21 03	176	27 03	211	23 09	254	32 28	323

LHA ♈	◆ Diphda Hc	Zn	ACHERNAR Hc	Zn	◆ Miaplacidus Hc	Zn	RIGIL KENT Hc	Zn	Nunki Hc	Zn	◆ ALTAIR Hc	Zn	Enif Hc	Zn
330	47 59	069	52 03	134	21 07	176	26 39	211	49 33	277	32 00	322	38 56	355
331	48 41	068	52 35	134	21 10	175	26 16	210	48 48	276	31 31	321	38 52	354
332	49 23	067	53 08	134	21 14	175	25 53	210	48 03	275	31 02	320	38 47	353
333	50 05	066	53 40	134	21 18	175	25 31	210	47 18	274	30 33	319	38 40	351
334	50 46	065	54 13	134	21 22	174	25 08	209	46 32	274	30 03	318	38 33	350
335	51 27	064	54 45	134	21 27	174	24 46	209	45 47	273	29 32	317	38 25	349
336	52 08	063	55 17	134	21 32	174	24 24	209	45 02	272	29 01	316	38 16	348
337	52 48	062	55 50	135	21 37	173	24 03	208	44 17	272	28 29	315	38 06	346
338	53 27	061	56 22	135	21 43	173	23 41	208	43 32	271	27 56	314	37 55	345
339	54 07	060	56 54	135	21 49	172	23 20	208	42 46	270	27 24	313	37 43	344
340	54 45	058	57 26	135	21 55	172	22 59	207	42 01	270	26 50	312	37 30	343
341	55 24	057	57 58	135	22 01	172	22 39	207	41 16	269	26 16	311	37 16	342
342	56 02	056	58 30	135	22 08	171	22 18	207	40 30	268	25 42	310	37 01	340
343	56 39	055	59 02	136	22 15	171	21 58	206	39 45	268	25 07	309	36 46	339
344	57 15	053	59 33	136	22 22	171	21 38	206	39 00	267	24 32	308	36 29	338

LHA ♈	◆ Alpheratz Hc	Zn	Diphda Hc	Zn	◆ CANOPUS Hc	Zn	RIGIL KENT Hc	Zn	◆ Nunki Hc	Zn	ALTAIR Hc	Zn	Enif Hc	Zn
345	18 01	016	57 51	052	20 57	143	21 19	205	38 15	266	23 56	308	36 12	337
346	18 13	015	58 27	050	21 24	142	21 00	205	37 30	266	23 20	307	35 54	336
347	18 25	014	59 01	049	21 52	142	20 41	205	36 44	265	22 44	306	35 34	335
348	18 35	013	59 35	047	22 20	141	20 22	204	35 59	265	22 07	305	35 15	333
349	18 45	012	60 08	046	22 49	141	20 04	204	35 14	264	21 30	304	34 54	332
350	18 55	011	60 40	044	23 17	141	19 45	203	34 29	263	20 52	303	34 33	331
351	19 03	010	61 11	043	23 46	140	19 28	203	33 44	263	20 14	303	34 10	330
352	19 11	010	61 41	041	24 15	140	19 10	203	32 59	262	19 36	302	33 47	329
353	19 18	009	62 10	039	24 44	139	18 53	202	32 15	262	18 57	301	33 24	328
354	19 24	008	62 39	037	25 14	139	18 36	202	31 30	261	18 18	300	32 59	327
355	19 30	007	63 06	036	25 44	139	18 19	201	30 45	260	17 39	299	32 34	326
356	19 35	006	63 31	034	26 14	138	18 03	201	30 00	260	16 59	298	32 08	325
357	19 39	005	63 56	032	26 44	138	17 47	200	29 16	259	16 19	298	31 42	324
358	19 43	004	64 19	030	27 14	138	17 31	200	28 31	259	15 39	297	31 15	323
359	19 46	003	64 41	028	27 45	137	17 16	200	27 47	258	14 59	296	30 47	322

LHA ♈	Alpheratz Hc Zn	Hamal Hc Zn	◆RIGEL Hc Zn	CANOPUS Hc Zn	◆RIGIL KENT Hc Zn	Peacock Hc Zn	◆Enif Hc Zn
0	18 48 002	18 06 031	13 46 089	28 59 136	17 58 199	53 26 228	29 32 321
1	18 49 001	18 28 030	14 31 088	29 30 136	17 43 199	52 53 228	29 04 320
2	18 50 000	18 50 029	15 15 087	30 01 136	17 29 198	52 20 228	28 35 319
3	18 49 359	19 11 028	16 00 087	30 33 135	17 15 198	51 47 228	28 05 318
4	18 49 358	19 32 027	16 44 086	31 04 135	17 02 197	51 14 228	27 35 317
5	18 47 358	19 52 026	17 29 085	31 36 135	16 48 197	50 41 228	27 04 316
6	18 45 357	20 12 025	18 13 085	32 07 134	16 35 197	50 08 227	26 33 315
7	18 42 356	20 30 024	18 57 084	32 39 134	16 23 196	49 35 227	26 02 314
8	18 38 355	20 48 024	19 42 083	33 12 134	16 11 196	49 03 227	25 30 313
9	18 33 354	21 06 023	20 26 082	33 44 133	15 59 195	48 30 227	24 57 312
10	18 28 353	21 23 022	21 10 082	34 16 133	15 47 195	47 57 227	24 24 312
11	18 22 352	21 39 021	21 54 081	34 49 133	15 36 194	47 25 227	23 50 311
12	18 16 351	21 54 020	22 38 080	35 22 132	15 25 194	46 52 227	23 16 310
13	18 09 350	22 09 019	23 22 080	35 55 132	15 15 193	46 20 227	22 42 309
14	18 01 349	22 23 018	24 06 079	36 28 132	15 05 193	45 47 227	22 07 308

LHA ♈	◆Hamal	RIGEL	◆CANOPUS	RIGIL KENT	◆Peacock	FOMALHAUT	Alpheratz
15	22 36 017	24 50 078	37 02 131	14 55 192	45 15 226	62 35 287	17 52 348
16	22 49 016	25 33 077	37 35 131	14 46 192	44 42 226	61 52 286	17 43 347
17	23 01 015	26 17 077	38 09 131	14 37 191	44 10 226	61 09 285	17 33 347
18	23 12 014	27 00 076	38 43 131	14 28 191	43 38 226	60 26 284	17 22 346
19	23 22 013	27 43 075	39 17 130	14 20 190	43 06 226	59 43 283	17 11 345
20	23 32 012	28 26 074	39 51 130	14 12 190	42 34 226	58 59 282	16 59 344
21	23 41 011	29 09 074	40 25 130	14 05 189	42 02 225	58 16 281	16 46 343
22	23 49 010	29 52 073	40 59 129	13 57 189	41 31 225	57 32 280	16 32 342
23	23 56 009	30 34 072	41 34 129	13 51 188	40 59 225	56 48 279	16 18 341
24	24 03 008	31 16 071	42 08 129	13 44 188	40 28 225	56 04 279	16 04 340
25	24 09 007	31 58 070	42 43 129	13 38 188	39 56 225	55 20 278	15 48 339
26	24 14 006	32 40 070	43 18 128	13 33 187	39 25 224	54 35 277	15 33 339
27	24 18 005	33 22 069	43 53 128	13 27 187	38 54 224	53 51 276	15 16 338
28	24 22 004	34 03 068	44 28 128	13 22 186	38 23 224	53 07 275	14 59 337
29	24 24 003	34 45 067	45 03 128	13 18 186	37 52 224	52 22 275	14 41 336

LHA ♈	◆Hamal	RIGEL	SIRIUS	◆CANOPUS	RIGIL KENT	◆Peacock	FOMALHAUT
30	24 26 002	35 26 066	24 47 091	45 38 128	13 14 185	37 22 223	51 38 274
31	24 28 001	36 06 065	25 31 090	46 14 127	13 10 185	36 51 223	50 53 273
32	24 28 000	36 46 064	26 16 089	46 49 127	13 07 184	36 21 223	50 09 272
33	24 28 359	37 26 063	27 00 089	47 25 127	13 04 184	35 51 223	49 24 272
34	24 26 358	38 06 062	27 45 088	48 00 127	13 01 183	35 20 222	48 40 271
35	24 25 357	38 46 061	28 29 087	48 36 127	12 59 183	34 51 222	47 55 270
36	24 22 356	39 25 061	29 14 087	49 12 127	12 57 182	34 21 222	47 11 270
37	24 18 355	40 03 060	29 58 086	49 48 126	12 56 182	33 51 221	46 26 269
38	24 14 354	40 41 059	30 43 085	50 24 126	12 55 181	33 22 221	45 41 268
39	24 09 353	41 19 058	31 27 084	51 00 126	12 54 181	32 53 221	44 57 268
40	24 03 352	41 57 057	32 12 084	51 36 126	12 54 180	32 24 220	44 12 267
41	23 56 351	42 34 055	32 56 083	52 12 126	12 54 180	31 55 220	43 28 267
42	23 49 350	43 10 054	33 40 082	52 48 126	12 54 179	31 26 220	42 43 266
43	23 41 349	43 46 053	34 24 082	53 24 126	12 55 179	30 58 220	41 59 265
44	23 32 348	44 22 052	35 08 081	54 00 126	12 57 178	30 29 219	41 14 265

LHA ♈	◆RIGEL	SIRIUS	CANOPUS	◆RIGIL KENT	Peacock	◆FOMALHAUT	Hamal
45	44 57 051	35 52 080	54 37 126	12 58 178	30 01 219	40 30 264	23 22 347
46	45 31 050	36 36 079	55 13 125	13 00 177	29 33 219	39 46 263	23 12 346
47	46 05 049	37 20 079	55 49 125	13 03 177	29 06 218	39 01 263	23 01 345
48	46 38 048	38 04 078	56 26 125	13 06 176	28 38 218	38 17 262	22 49 344
49	47 11 046	38 47 077	57 02 125	13 09 176	28 11 218	37 33 262	22 36 343
50	47 43 045	39 30 076	57 38 125	13 13 175	27 44 217	36 49 261	22 23 342
51	48 14 044	40 14 075	58 15 125	13 17 175	27 17 217	36 05 261	22 09 341
52	48 45 043	40 57 074	58 51 125	13 21 174	26 50 216	35 21 260	21 54 340
53	49 14 041	41 40 074	59 27 125	13 26 174	26 24 216	34 37 259	21 39 339
54	49 43 040	42 22 073	60 04 126	13 31 173	25 58 216	33 53 259	21 23 338
55	50 12 039	43 05 072	60 40 126	13 36 173	25 32 215	33 10 258	21 06 337
56	50 39 037	43 47 071	61 16 126	13 42 172	25 06 215	32 26 258	20 49 336
57	51 06 036	44 29 070	61 52 126	13 49 172	24 41 215	31 43 257	20 31 336
58	51 31 034	45 11 069	62 28 126	13 55 171	24 16 214	30 59 257	20 12 335
59	51 56 033	45 52 068	63 04 126	14 02 171	23 51 214	30 16 256	19 52 334

LHA ♈	ALDEBARAN	◆SIRIUS	Suhail	◆RIGIL KENT	ACHERNAR	◆Diphda	Hamal
60	30 51 010	46 34 067	35 29 120	14 10 170	62 57 224	42 06 285	19 32 333
61	30 58 009	47 15 066	36 08 119	14 17 170	62 26 224	41 23 284	19 12 332
62	31 05 008	47 55 065	36 47 119	14 26 169	61 55 224	40 40 283	18 50 331
63	31 11 007	48 36 064	37 26 118	14 34 169	61 23 225	39 56 282	18 28 330
64	31 16 006	49 16 063	38 06 118	14 43 168	60 52 225	39 12 282	18 06 329
65	31 20 005	49 55 062	38 45 118	14 52 168	60 20 225	38 29 281	17 43 328
66	31 23 004	50 34 061	39 25 117	15 02 167	59 48 226	37 45 280	17 19 328
67	31 26 002	51 13 060	40 04 117	15 12 167	59 17 226	37 01 279	16 55 327
68	31 27 001	51 51 059	40 44 117	15 22 166	58 45 226	36 17 278	16 30 326
69	31 28 000	52 29 058	41 24 116	15 33 166	58 13 226	35 33 278	16 05 325
70	31 27 359	53 07 056	42 04 116	15 44 165	57 40 226	34 48 277	15 39 324
71	31 26 358	53 44 055	42 44 115	15 55 165	57 08 226	34 04 276	15 13 323
72	31 24 357	54 20 054	43 25 115	16 07 165	56 36 227	33 20 276	14 46 322
73	31 21 356	54 56 053	44 05 115	16 19 164	56 03 227	32 35 275	14 18 322
74	31 18 355	55 31 051	44 46 114	16 31 164	55 31 227	31 51 274	13 50 321

LHA ♈	BETELGEUSE	◆SIRIUS	Suhail	◆RIGIL KENT	ACHERNAR	◆Diphda	ALDEBARAN
75	38 58 018	56 05 050	45 26 114	16 44 163	54 59 227	31 06 273	31 13 353
76	39 11 017	56 39 048	46 07 114	16 57 163	54 26 227	30 22 273	31 08 352
77	39 23 015	57 12 047	46 48 113	17 11 162	53 54 227	29 37 272	31 01 351
78	39 35 014	57 44 046	47 29 113	17 25 162	53 21 227	28 53 271	30 54 350
79	39 45 013	58 15 044	48 10 113	17 39 161	52 48 227	28 08 271	30 46 349
80	39 55 012	58 46 042	48 52 112	17 53 161	52 16 227	27 24 270	30 37 348
81	40 03 010	59 16 041	49 33 112	18 08 160	51 43 227	26 39 269	30 27 347
82	40 11 009	59 44 039	50 14 111	18 23 160	51 11 227	25 55 269	30 17 346
83	40 17 008	60 12 038	50 56 111	18 38 160	50 38 227	25 10 268	30 05 345
84	40 23 007	60 39 036	51 37 111	18 54 159	50 06 227	24 25 267	29 53 344
85	40 27 005	61 04 034	52 19 110	19 10 159	49 33 227	23 41 267	29 40 343
86	40 31 004	61 29 032	53 01 110	19 26 158	49 01 227	22 56 266	29 26 341
87	40 33 003	61 52 030	53 43 110	19 43 158	48 29 226	22 12 265	29 12 340
88	40 35 001	62 14 029	54 25 109	20 00 157	47 56 226	21 27 265	28 56 339
89	40 35 000	62 35 027	55 07 109	20 17 157	47 24 226	20 43 264	28 40 338

LAT 42°S

LHA ♈	PROCYON Hc Zn	Alphard Hc Zn	◆Suhail Hc Zn	RIGIL KENT Hc Zn	◆ACHERNAR Hc Zn	RIGEL Hc Zn	◆BETELGEUSE Hc Zn
90	37 36 032	33 34 069	55 49 109	20 35 157	46 52 226	54 46 341	40 35 359
91	37 59 031	34 16 069	56 31 109	20 53 156	46 20 226	54 31 339	40 33 357
92	38 22 030	34 57 068	57 14 108	21 11 156	45 48 226	54 14 337	40 31 356
93	38 44 029	35 38 067	57 56 108	21 29 155	45 16 226	53 56 336	40 27 355
94	39 05 027	36 19 066	58 39 108	21 48 155	44 44 226	53 38 334	40 23 353
95	39 25 026	36 59 065	59 21 107	22 07 155	44 12 225	53 17 333	40 17 352
96	39 44 025	37 40 064	60 04 107	22 26 154	43 40 225	52 56 331	40 11 351
97	40 02 024	38 20 063	60 46 107	22 46 154	43 09 225	52 34 329	40 03 350
98	40 20 022	38 59 062	61 29 106	23 06 153	42 37 225	52 11 328	39 55 348
99	40 36 021	39 39 061	62 12 106	23 26 153	42 06 225	51 47 326	39 45 347
100	40 52 020	40 17 060	62 55 106	23 46 153	41 34 225	51 22 325	39 35 346
101	41 07 019	40 56 059	63 38 106	24 07 152	41 03 224	50 56 324	39 23 345
102	41 21 017	41 34 058	64 21 105	24 28 152	40 32 224	50 29 322	39 11 343
103	41 34 016	42 12 057	65 04 105	24 49 152	40 01 224	50 01 321	38 58 342
104	41 45 015	42 49 056	65 47 105	25 10 151	39 30 224	49 33 320	38 43 341

LHA ♈	PROCYON	REGULUS	◆Gienah	RIGIL KENT	◆ACHERNAR	RIGEL	◆BETELGEUSE
105	41 56 013	20 49 050	19 38 096	25 32 151	38 59 223	49 03 318	38 28 340
106	42 06 012	21 23 049	20 22 096	25 54 150	38 29 223	48 33 317	38 12 338
107	42 15 011	21 57 049	21 07 095	26 16 150	37 58 223	48 02 316	37 55 337
108	42 23 009	22 30 048	21 51 094	26 38 150	37 28 223	47 31 314	37 38 336
109	42 30 008	23 02 047	22 36 094	27 01 149	36 58 222	46 59 313	37 19 335
110	42 36 007	23 35 046	23 20 093	27 24 149	36 28 222	46 26 312	36 59 334
111	42 40 005	24 07 045	24 05 093	27 47 149	35 58 222	45 52 311	36 39 332
112	42 44 004	24 38 044	24 49 092	28 10 148	35 28 222	45 18 310	36 18 331
113	42 47 003	25 09 043	25 34 091	28 33 148	34 59 221	44 44 308	35 56 330
114	42 48 001	25 39 042	26 18 091	28 57 148	34 29 221	44 09 307	35 34 329
115	42 49 000	26 09 041	27 03 090	29 21 147	34 00 221	43 33 306	35 10 328
116	42 48 359	26 38 040	27 48 089	29 45 147	33 31 221	42 57 305	34 46 327
117	42 47 357	27 06 039	28 32 089	30 09 147	33 02 220	42 20 304	34 22 326
118	42 44 356	27 34 038	29 17 088	30 34 146	32 33 220	41 43 303	33 56 325
119	42 41 355	28 02 037	30 01 087	30 59 146	32 05 220	41 05 302	33 30 324

LHA ♈	REGULUS	◆SPICA	RIGIL KENT	◆ACHERNAR	RIGEL	BETELGEUSE	◆PROCYON
120	28 29 036	13 47 093	31 24 146	31 36 219	40 27 301	33 03 322	42 36 353
121	28 55 035	14 31 092	31 49 146	31 08 219	39 49 300	32 36 321	42 30 352
122	29 20 034	15 16 091	32 14 145	30 40 219	39 10 299	32 07 320	42 23 351
123	29 45 033	16 01 091	32 39 145	30 12 218	38 31 298	31 39 319	42 15 349
124	30 10 032	16 45 090	33 05 145	29 45 218	37 52 297	31 09 318	42 07 348
125	30 33 031	17 30 089	33 31 144	29 17 218	37 12 296	30 39 317	41 57 347
126	30 56 030	18 14 089	33 57 144	28 50 217	36 32 295	30 09 316	41 46 345
127	31 18 029	18 59 088	34 23 144	28 23 217	35 51 294	29 38 315	41 34 344
128	31 40 028	19 43 087	34 49 144	27 57 217	35 10 294	29 06 314	41 21 343
129	32 00 027	20 28 087	35 16 143	27 30 216	34 29 293	28 34 313	41 08 341
130	32 20 026	21 12 086	35 42 143	27 04 216	33 48 292	28 02 313	40 53 340
131	32 40 025	21 57 085	36 09 143	26 38 216	33 07 291	27 28 312	40 37 339
132	32 58 024	22 41 085	36 36 143	26 12 215	32 25 290	26 55 311	40 21 338
133	33 16 023	23 26 084	37 03 143	25 46 215	31 43 289	26 21 310	40 03 336
134	33 32 022	24 10 083	37 30 142	25 21 214	31 01 289	25 46 309	39 45 335

LHA ♈	REGULUS	◆SPICA	RIGIL KENT	◆ACHERNAR	CANOPUS	SIRIUS	◆PROCYON
135	33 49 020	24 54 083	37 58 142	24 56 214	61 57 234	51 48 301	39 26 334
136	34 04 019	25 38 082	38 25 142	24 31 214	61 21 234	51 09 300	39 06 333
137	34 18 018	26 23 081	38 53 142	24 06 213	60 45 234	50 31 299	38 45 331
138	34 32 017	27 07 080	39 21 141	23 42 213	60 09 234	49 51 298	38 23 330
139	34 44 016	27 50 080	39 48 141	23 18 213	59 33 235	49 12 297	38 00 329
140	34 56 015	28 34 079	40 16 141	22 54 212	58 56 235	48 32 296	37 37 328
141	35 07 014	29 18 078	40 44 141	22 30 212	58 20 235	47 51 295	37 13 327
142	35 17 012	30 02 077	41 13 141	22 07 211	57 44 235	47 11 294	36 48 326
143	35 26 011	30 45 077	41 41 141	21 44 211	57 07 235	46 30 293	36 23 325
144	35 34 010	31 28 076	42 09 140	21 21 210	56 31 235	45 48 292	35 57 323
145	35 41 009	32 12 075	42 38 140	20 59 210	55 55 235	45 07 291	35 30 322
146	35 48 008	32 55 074	43 06 140	20 37 210	55 18 235	44 25 290	35 02 321
147	35 53 006	33 37 074	43 35 140	20 15 209	54 42 234	43 43 289	34 34 320
148	35 58 005	34 20 073	44 04 140	19 53 209	54 06 234	43 01 288	34 05 319
149	36 01 004	35 03 072	44 32 140	19 32 208	53 29 234	42 18 287	33 35 318

LHA ♈	REGULUS	◆SPICA	RIGIL KENT	◆ACHERNAR	CANOPUS	SIRIUS	◆PROCYON
150	36 04 003	35 45 071	45 01 140	19 11 208	52 53 234	41 36 286	33 05 317
151	36 06 002	36 27 070	45 30 140	18 50 207	52 17 234	40 53 285	32 35 316
152	36 06 000	37 09 069	45 59 139	18 30 207	51 41 234	40 10 285	32 03 315
153	36 06 359	37 50 068	46 28 139	18 10 207	51 05 234	39 26 284	31 32 314
154	36 05 358	38 32 068	46 57 139	17 50 206	50 29 234	38 43 283	30 59 313
155	36 03 357	39 13 067	47 26 139	17 30 206	49 53 234	37 59 282	30 26 312
156	36 00 356	39 54 066	47 55 139	17 11 205	49 17 233	37 16 281	29 53 311
157	35 56 354	40 34 065	48 24 139	16 53 205	48 41 233	36 32 281	29 19 310
158	35 51 353	41 14 064	48 53 139	16 34 204	48 05 233	35 48 280	28 45 309
159	35 45 352	41 54 063	49 23 139	16 16 204	47 30 233	35 04 279	28 10 308
160	35 39 351	42 34 062	49 52 139	15 58 203	46 54 233	34 20 278	27 35 307
161	35 31 350	43 13 061	50 21 139	15 41 203	46 19 233	33 36 278	26 59 307
162	35 22 348	43 52 060	50 50 139	15 23 202	45 43 232	32 52 277	26 23 306
163	35 13 347	44 30 059	51 19 139	15 07 202	45 08 232	32 07 276	25 47 305
164	35 02 346	45 08 058	51 48 139	14 50 201	44 33 232	31 23 275	25 10 304

LHA ♈	SPICA	◆ANTARES	RIGIL KENT	ACHERNAR	◆CANOPUS	SIRIUS	◆REGULUS
165	45 45 057	22 35 106	52 18 139	14 34 201	43 58 232	30 39 275	34 51 345
166	46 22 056	23 18 105	52 47 139	14 18 200	43 23 232	29 54 274	34 39 344
167	46 59 055	24 01 105	53 16 139	14 03 200	42 48 231	29 10 273	34 26 342
168	47 35 053	24 44 104	53 45 139	13 48 199	42 13 231	28 25 273	34 12 341
169	48 10 052	25 28 104	54 14 140	13 33 199	41 39 231	27 41 272	33 58 340
170	48 45 051	26 11 103	54 43 140	13 19 198	41 04 231	26 56 271	33 42 339
171	49 20 050	26 54 102	55 11 140	13 05 198	40 30 230	26 12 271	33 26 338
172	49 54 049	27 38 102	55 40 140	12 52 197	39 56 230	25 27 270	33 08 337
173	50 27 047	28 22 101	56 09 140	12 38 197	39 21 230	24 42 269	32 50 336
174	50 59 046	29 06 101	56 37 140	12 26 196	38 47 229	23 58 269	32 32 335
175	51 31 045	29 49 100	57 05 141	12 13 196	38 14 229	23 13 268	32 12 333
176	52 02 043	30 33 099	57 34 141	12 01 195	37 40 229	22 29 267	31 52 332
177	52 32 042	31 17 099	58 02 141	11 50 195	37 06 229	21 44 267	31 31 331
178	53 01 041	32 01 098	58 30 141	11 38 194	36 33 228	21 00 266	31 09 330
179	53 30 039	32 46 098	58 57 142	11 28 194	36 00 228	20 15 265	30 47 329

 LAT 42°S

LHA ♈	Hc	Zn	Hc	Zn	Hc	Zn	Hc	Zn	Hc	Zn	Hc	Zn	Hc	Zn
	◆ARCTURUS		ANTARES		◆RIGIL KENT		ACHERNAR		CANOPUS		◆Suhail		REGULUS	
180	21 15	035	33 30	097	59 25	142	11 17	193	35 27	228	58 50	252	30 23	328
181	21 41	034	34 14	096	59 52	142	11 07	193	34 54	227	58 08	252	30 00	327
182	22 05	033	34 58	096	60 20	143	10 57	192	34 21	227	57 25	252	29 35	326
183	22 29	032	35 43	095	60 47	143	10 48	192	33 49	227	56 43	252	29 10	325
184	22 52	031	36 27	095	61 13	143	10 39	191	33 16	226	56 01	251	28 44	324
185	23 15	030	37 12	094	61 40	144	10 31	191	32 44	226	55 19	251	28 18	323
186	23 37	029	37 56	093	62 06	144	10 23	190	32 12	226	54 36	251	27 51	322
187	23 58	028	38 41	093	62 32	145	10 15	190	31 40	225	53 54	250	27 23	321
188	24 19	027	39 25	092	62 57	145	10 08	189	31 08	225	53 13	250	26 55	320
189	24 39	026	40 10	091	63 23	146	10 01	188	30 37	225	52 31	250	26 26	319
190	24 58	025	40 54	091	63 47	146	09 55	188	30 06	224	51 49	249	25 56	318
191	25 17	024	41 39	090	64 12	147	09 49	187	29 35	224	51 07	249	25 26	317
192	25 34	023	42 24	089	64 36	148	09 43	187	29 04	224	50 26	249	24 56	316
193	25 52	022	43 08	089	65 00	148	09 38	186	28 33	223	49 44	248	24 25	316
194	26 08	021	43 53	088	65 23	149	09 33	186	28 03	223	49 03	248	23 53	315
	◆ARCTURUS		ANTARES		◆Peacock		ACHERNAR		CANOPUS		◆Suhail		REGULUS	
195	26 24	020	44 37	087	24 06	146	09 29	185	27 33	222	48 22	248	23 21	314
196	26 39	019	45 22	087	24 31	146	09 25	185	27 03	222	47 40	247	22 49	313
197	26 53	018	46 06	086	24 56	145	09 22	184	26 33	222	46 59	247	22 16	312
198	27 07	017	46 51	085	25 21	145	09 19	184	26 03	221	46 18	247	21 43	311
199	27 19	016	47 35	084	25 47	144	09 16	183	25 34	221	45 38	246	21 09	310
200	27 31	015	48 20	084	26 13	144	09 14	183	25 05	220	44 57	246	20 35	309
201	27 43	014	49 04	083	26 40	144	09 12	182	24 36	220	44 16	245	20 00	309
202	27 53	013	49 48	082	27 06	143	09 11	181	24 07	220	43 36	245	19 25	308
203	28 02	012	50 32	081	27 33	143	09 10	181	23 39	219	42 55	245	18 49	307
204	28 11	011	51 16	081	28 00	143	09 10	180	23 11	219	42 15	244	18 13	306
205	28 19	010	52 00	080	28 27	142	09 10	180	22 43	218	41 35	244	17 37	305
206	28 26	009	52 44	079	28 54	142	09 10	179	22 16	218	40 55	244	17 01	304
207	28 33	008	53 28	078	29 22	142	09 11	179	21 48	218	40 15	243	16 24	304
208	28 38	007	54 11	077	29 50	141	09 12	178	21 21	217	39 35	243	15 46	303
209	28 43	005	54 55	076	30 18	141	09 14	178	20 55	217	38 56	242	15 09	302
	◆ARCTURUS		ANTARES		◆Peacock		ACHERNAR		CANOPUS		◆Suhail		SPICA	
210	28 47	004	55 38	075	30 46	141	09 16	177	20 28	216	38 16	242	58 21	344
211	28 50	003	56 21	074	31 14	140	09 18	176	20 02	216	37 37	242	58 08	342
212	28 52	002	57 04	073	31 43	140	09 21	176	19 36	215	36 58	241	57 54	340
213	28 53	001	57 46	072	32 12	140	09 25	175	19 10	215	36 19	241	57 38	339
214	28 54	000	58 29	071	32 41	139	09 29	175	18 45	214	35 40	240	57 21	337
215	28 53	359	59 11	070	33 10	139	09 33	174	18 20	214	35 01	240	57 03	335
216	28 52	358	59 52	069	33 39	139	09 38	174	17 55	213	34 23	240	56 44	333
217	28 50	357	60 34	068	34 09	138	09 43	173	17 31	213	33 44	239	56 23	332
218	28 47	356	61 15	067	34 38	138	09 48	173	17 06	213	33 06	239	56 01	330
219	28 44	355	61 56	066	35 08	138	09 54	172	16 43	212	32 28	238	55 39	328
220	28 39	354	62 36	064	35 38	138	10 00	172	16 19	212	31 50	238	55 15	327
221	28 34	353	63 16	063	36 08	137	10 07	171	15 56	211	31 13	237	54 50	325
222	28 28	351	63 56	062	36 39	137	10 14	170	15 33	211	30 35	237	54 24	324
223	28 20	350	64 35	060	37 09	137	10 22	170	15 10	210	29 58	237	53 57	322
224	28 13	349	65 13	059	37 40	137	10 30	169	14 48	210	29 21	236	53 30	321
	Rasalhague		◆Nunki		Peacock		ACHERNAR		◆ACRUX		SPICA		◆ARCTURUS	
225	24 47	042	39 43	092	38 10	136	10 38	169	59 25	213	53 01	319	28 04	348
226	25 16	042	40 27	091	38 41	136	10 47	168	59 00	214	52 32	318	27 55	347
227	25 46	041	41 12	090	39 12	136	10 56	168	58 36	214	52 02	317	27 44	346
228	26 14	040	41 57	090	39 44	136	11 06	167	58 11	214	51 31	315	27 33	345
229	26 43	039	42 41	089	40 15	135	11 16	167	57 45	215	50 59	314	27 22	344
230	27 10	038	43 26	088	40 46	135	11 26	166	57 20	215	50 26	313	27 09	343
231	27 37	037	44 10	087	41 18	135	11 37	166	56 54	215	49 53	311	26 56	342
232	28 04	036	44 55	087	41 49	135	11 48	165	56 29	215	49 20	310	26 41	341
233	28 29	035	45 39	086	42 21	134	12 00	165	56 03	216	48 45	309	26 27	340
234	28 54	034	46 24	085	42 53	134	12 12	164	55 37	216	48 10	308	26 11	339
235	29 19	033	47 08	085	43 25	134	12 24	164	55 11	216	47 35	307	25 55	338
236	29 43	032	47 53	084	43 57	134	12 37	163	54 44	216	46 59	305	25 37	337
237	30 06	031	48 37	083	44 29	134	12 50	163	54 18	216	46 22	304	25 20	336
238	30 28	030	49 21	082	45 01	134	13 03	162	53 51	217	45 45	303	25 01	335
239	30 50	029	50 05	081	45 34	133	13 17	162	53 25	217	45 08	302	24 42	334
	Rasalhague		◆ALTAIR		Peacock		◆ACHERNAR		ACRUX		◆SPICA		ARCTURUS	
240	31 11	028	16 40	061	46 06	133	13 31	161	52 58	217	44 30	301	24 22	333
241	31 31	026	17 19	060	46 39	133	13 46	161	52 31	217	43 51	300	24 02	332
242	31 51	025	17 57	059	47 11	133	14 01	160	52 04	217	43 12	299	23 40	331
243	32 09	024	18 35	058	47 44	133	14 16	160	51 38	217	42 33	298	23 18	330
244	32 27	023	19 13	058	48 16	133	14 32	159	51 11	217	41 54	297	22 56	329
245	32 44	022	19 51	057	48 49	133	14 48	159	50 44	217	41 14	296	22 33	328
246	33 01	021	20 28	056	49 22	133	15 04	158	50 17	217	40 34	295	22 09	327
247	33 16	020	21 05	055	49 55	133	15 21	158	49 50	217	39 53	294	21 45	326
248	33 31	019	21 41	054	50 28	133	15 38	157	49 23	217	39 12	293	21 20	326
249	33 45	018	22 17	054	51 00	132	15 56	157	48 55	217	38 31	292	20 54	325
250	33 58	016	22 53	053	51 33	132	16 13	156	48 28	217	37 50	292	20 28	324
251	34 10	015	23 28	052	52 06	132	16 32	156	48 01	217	37 08	291	20 02	323
252	34 22	014	24 03	051	52 39	132	16 50	155	47 34	217	36 27	290	19 34	322
253	34 32	013	24 37	050	53 12	132	17 09	155	47 07	217	35 44	289	19 07	321
254	34 42	012	25 11	049	53 45	132	17 28	154	46 40	217	35 02	288	18 38	320
	Rasalhague		◆ALTAIR		FOMALHAUT		◆ACHERNAR		RIGIL KENT		◆SPICA		Alphecca	
255	34 50	011	25 45	048	19 32	113	17 47	154	61 48	216	34 20	287	18 36	340
256	34 58	009	26 18	047	20 13	112	18 07	154	61 22	216	33 37	286	18 21	339
257	35 05	008	26 50	046	20 54	111	18 27	153	60 55	217	32 54	286	18 04	338
258	35 11	007	27 22	046	21 36	111	18 47	153	60 28	217	32 11	285	17 48	337
259	35 16	006	27 54	045	22 17	110	19 08	152	60 01	218	31 28	284	17 30	337
260	35 20	005	28 25	044	22 59	110	19 29	152	59 34	218	30 45	283	17 12	336
261	35 23	003	28 55	043	23 41	109	19 50	151	59 06	218	30 01	283	16 53	335
262	35 25	002	29 25	042	24 24	109	20 12	151	58 39	219	29 18	282	16 34	334
263	35 27	001	29 55	041	25 06	108	20 34	150	58 11	219	28 34	281	16 14	333
264	35 27	000	30 23	040	25 48	108	20 56	150	57 43	219	27 50	280	15 54	332
265	35 26	359	30 52	039	26 31	107	21 18	150	57 14	219	27 06	280	15 33	331
266	35 25	357	31 19	038	27 14	106	21 41	149	56 46	220	26 22	279	15 11	330
267	35 23	356	31 46	037	27 56	106	22 04	149	56 18	220	25 38	278	14 49	330
268	35 19	355	32 12	036	28 39	105	22 27	148	55 49	220	24 54	277	14 26	329
269	35 15	354	32 38	035	29 22	105	22 51	148	55 20	220	24 10	277	14 02	328

LHA ♈	Hc	Zn	Hc	Zn	Hc	Zn	Hc	Zn	Hc	Zn	Hc	Zn	Hc	Zn
	ALTAIR		Enif		◆FOMALHAUT		ACHERNAR		◆RIGIL KENT		ANTARES		◆Rasalhague	
270	33 03	033	16 56	059	30 06	104	23 15	148	54 52	220	65 57	303	35 10	353
271	33 27	032	17 34	058	30 49	104	23 39	147	54 23	220	65 19	302	35 04	352
272	33 51	031	18 12	057	31 32	103	24 03	147	53 54	221	64 41	300	34 57	350
273	34 13	030	18 49	056	32 16	102	24 28	146	53 25	221	64 02	299	34 49	349
274	34 35	029	19 26	056	32 59	102	24 52	146	52 56	221	63 23	297	34 40	348
275	34 57	028	20 03	055	33 43	101	25 18	146	52 27	221	62 43	296	34 30	347
276	35 17	027	20 39	054	34 27	101	25 43	145	51 58	221	62 03	295	34 20	346
277	35 37	026	21 15	053	35 11	100	26 08	145	51 29	221	61 22	293	34 08	345
278	35 56	025	21 50	052	35 55	100	26 34	144	50 59	221	60 41	292	33 56	343
279	36 14	023	22 26	051	36 39	099	27 00	144	50 30	221	59 59	291	33 43	342
280	36 31	022	23 00	051	37 23	098	27 26	144	50 01	221	59 18	290	33 28	341
281	36 48	021	23 34	050	38 07	098	27 53	143	49 32	221	58 36	289	33 14	340
282	37 03	020	24 08	049	38 51	097	28 20	143	49 03	221	57 53	288	32 58	339
283	37 18	019	24 42	048	39 35	097	28 47	143	48 34	221	57 11	287	32 41	338
284	37 32	017	25 15	047	40 20	096	29 14	142	48 04	221	56 28	286	32 24	337
	ALTAIR		Enif		◆FOMALHAUT		ACHERNAR		◆RIGIL KENT		ANTARES		◆Rasalhague	
285	37 44	016	25 47	046	41 04	095	29 41	142	47 35	221	55 45	285	32 06	336
286	37 56	015	26 19	045	41 48	095	30 09	142	47 06	221	55 02	284	31 47	334
287	38 07	014	26 50	044	42 33	094	30 36	141	46 37	221	54 18	283	31 27	333
288	38 18	012	27 21	043	43 17	094	31 04	141	46 08	221	53 35	282	31 07	332
289	38 27	011	27 51	042	44 02	093	31 32	141	45 39	220	52 51	281	30 46	331
290	38 35	010	28 21	041	44 46	092	32 01	140	45 10	220	52 07	280	30 24	330
291	38 42	009	28 50	040	45 31	092	32 29	140	44 41	220	51 23	280	30 02	329
292	38 48	007	29 19	039	46 15	091	32 58	140	44 13	220	50 39	279	29 38	328
293	38 54	006	29 47	038	47 00	090	33 27	139	43 44	220	49 55	278	29 14	327
294	38 58	005	30 14	037	47 45	090	33 56	139	43 15	220	49 11	277	28 50	326
295	39 01	004	30 41	036	48 29	089	34 25	139	42 47	220	48 27	276	28 25	325
296	39 04	002	31 07	035	49 14	088	34 55	139	42 18	220	47 43	276	27 59	324
297	39 05	001	31 33	034	49 58	088	35 24	138	41 50	219	46 58	275	27 32	323
298	39 05	000	31 58	033	50 43	087	35 54	138	41 22	219	46 14	274	27 05	322
299	39 05	359	32 22	032	51 27	086	36 24	138	40 53	219	45 29	273	26 37	321
	◆Enif		FOMALHAUT		◆ACHERNAR		RIGIL KENT		◆ANTARES		Rasalhague		ALTAIR	
300	32 45	031	52 12	086	36 54	138	40 25	219	44 45	273	26 09	320	39 03	357
301	33 08	030	52 56	085	37 24	137	39 57	219	44 00	272	25 40	319	39 01	356
302	33 30	029	53 41	084	37 54	137	39 29	219	43 16	271	25 11	318	38 57	355
303	33 51	028	54 25	083	38 25	137	39 02	218	42 31	271	24 41	317	38 53	353
304	34 12	027	55 09	082	38 55	137	38 34	218	41 46	270	24 11	316	38 47	352
305	34 31	026	55 53	082	39 26	136	38 06	218	41 02	269	23 40	316	38 40	351
306	34 50	025	56 37	081	39 57	136	37 39	218	40 17	269	23 08	315	38 33	350
307	35 08	023	57 21	080	40 28	136	37 12	218	39 33	268	22 36	314	38 25	348
308	35 26	022	58 05	079	40 59	136	36 45	217	38 48	267	22 04	313	38 15	347
309	35 42	021	58 49	078	41 30	135	36 18	217	38 04	267	21 31	312	38 05	346
310	35 58	020	59 32	077	42 01	135	35 51	217	37 19	266	20 57	311	37 54	345
311	36 12	019	60 16	076	42 33	135	35 24	217	36 35	265	20 24	310	37 41	344
312	36 26	018	60 59	075	43 04	135	34 58	216	35 50	265	19 49	309	37 28	342
313	36 39	016	61 42	074	43 36	135	34 31	216	35 06	264	19 15	309	37 14	341
314	36 51	015	62 25	073	44 08	135	34 05	216	34 21	264	18 40	308	36 59	340
	Enif		◆Diphda		ACHERNAR		Miaplacidus		◆RIGIL KENT		ANTARES		◆ALTAIR	
315	37 03	014	36 53	081	44 40	134	21 48	181	33 39	216	33 37	263	36 44	339
316	37 13	013	37 37	080	45 11	134	21 48	181	33 13	215	32 53	262	36 27	338
317	37 22	011	38 21	079	45 43	134	21 47	180	32 48	215	32 09	262	36 10	336
318	37 31	010	39 05	079	46 15	134	21 47	180	32 22	215	31 25	261	35 51	335
319	37 38	009	39 49	078	46 48	134	21 47	180	31 57	214	30 41	261	35 32	334
320	37 45	008	40 32	077	47 20	134	21 47	179	31 31	214	29 57	260	35 12	333
321	37 50	007	41 15	076	47 52	134	21 48	179	31 06	214	29 13	259	34 52	332
322	37 55	005	41 59	075	48 24	134	21 49	179	30 42	214	28 29	259	34 30	331
323	37 58	004	42 42	074	48 57	133	21 50	178	30 17	213	27 45	258	34 08	330
324	38 01	003	43 25	074	49 29	133	21 51	178	29 53	213	27 02	258	33 45	328
325	38 03	002	44 07	073	50 02	133	21 53	178	29 29	213	26 18	257	33 21	327
326	38 03	000	44 50	072	50 34	133	21 55	177	29 05	212	25 35	256	32 57	326
327	38 03	359	45 32	071	51 06	133	21 58	177	28 41	212	24 51	256	32 32	325
328	38 02	358	46 14	070	51 39	133	22 00	176	28 17	212	24 08	255	32 06	324
329	38 00	357	46 56	069	52 12	133	22 03	176	27 54	211	23 25	255	31 40	323
	◆Diphda		ACHERNAR		◆Miaplacidus		RIGIL KENT		Nunki		◆ALTAIR		Enif	
330	47 37	068	52 44	133	22 06	176	27 31	211	49 25	278	31 13	322	37 56	355
331	48 19	067	53 17	133	22 10	175	27 08	211	48 41	277	30 45	321	37 52	354
332	48 59	066	53 49	133	22 14	175	26 45	210	47 57	276	30 17	320	37 47	353
333	49 40	065	54 22	133	22 18	175	26 23	210	47 12	275	29 48	319	37 41	352
334	50 20	064	54 54	133	22 22	174	26 01	210	46 28	275	29 18	318	37 34	350
335	51 00	063	55 27	133	22 27	174	25 39	209	45 44	274	28 48	317	37 26	349
336	51 40	062	55 59	133	22 32	173	25 17	209	44 59	273	28 17	316	37 17	348
337	52 19	061	56 31	133	22 37	173	24 56	209	44 15	273	27 46	315	37 07	347
338	52 58	060	57 04	134	22 42	173	24 34	208	43 30	272	27 15	314	36 57	345
339	53 36	058	57 36	134	22 48	172	24 13	208	42 45	271	26 42	313	36 45	344
340	54 13	057	58 08	134	22 54	172	23 53	207	42 01	271	26 10	312	36 32	343
341	54 51	056	58 40	134	23 00	172	23 32	207	41 16	270	25 37	312	36 19	342
342	55 27	055	59 12	134	23 07	171	23 12	207	40 32	269	25 03	311	36 05	341
343	56 03	053	59 44	134	23 14	171	22 52	206	39 47	269	24 29	310	35 49	339
344	56 39	052	60 16	135	23 21	171	22 32	206	39 03	268	23 54	309	35 33	338
	◆Alpheratz		Diphda		◆CANOPUS		RIGIL KENT		◆Nunki		ALTAIR		Enif	
345	17 04	016	57 14	051	21 44	143	22 13	206	38 18	267	23 20	308	35 16	337
346	17 15	015	57 48	049	22 12	142	21 54	205	37 33	267	22 44	307	34 59	336
347	17 27	014	58 21	048	22 39	142	21 35	205	36 49	266	22 08	306	34 40	335
348	17 37	013	58 54	046	23 07	141	21 17	204	36 05	265	21 32	305	34 21	334
349	17 47	012	59 26	045	23 35	141	20 58	204	35 20	265	20 56	305	34 01	333
350	17 56	011	59 57	043	24 03	140	20 40	204	34 36	264	20 19	304	33 40	332
351	18 04	010	60 27	041	24 32	140	20 23	203	33 51	263	19 42	303	33 18	330
352	18 12	009	60 56	040	25 01	140	20 05	203	33 07	263	19 04	302	32 56	329
353	18 19	009	61 24	038	25 30	139	19 48	202	32 23	262	18 26	301	32 33	328
354	18 25	008	61 51	036	25 59	139	19 32	202	31 39	262	17 48	301	32 09	327
355	18 31	007	62 16	035	26 29	138	19 15	201	30 55	261	17 09	300	31 44	326
356	18 35	006	62 41	033	26 58	138	18 59	201	30 11	260	16 30	299	31 19	325
357	18 40	005	63 05	031	27 28	138	18 43	201	29 27	260	15 51	298	30 53	324
358	18 43	004	63 27	029	27 58	137	18 28	200	28 43	259	15 12	297	30 27	323
359	18 46	003	63 47	027	28 29	137	18 13	200	27 59	259	14 32	297	30 00	322

LAT 43°S

LHA ♈	Hc	Zn	Hc	Zn	Hc	Zn	Hc	Zn	Hc	Zn	Hc	Zn	Hc	Zn
	Alpheratz		Hamal		◆ RIGEL		CANOPUS		◆ RIGIL KENT		Peacock		◆ Enif	
0	17 48	002	17 14	031	13 44	088	29 43	136	18 54	199	54 06	229	28 45	321
1	17 49	001	17 36	030	14 28	088	30 13	136	18 40	199	53 33	229	28 18	320
2	17 50	000	17 58	029	15 12	087	30 44	135	18 26	198	53 00	229	27 49	319
3	17 49	359	18 18	028	15 56	086	31 15	135	18 12	198	52 27	229	27 20	318
4	17 49	358	18 39	027	16 40	086	31 46	135	17 59	198	51 54	229	26 51	317
5	17 47	358	18 58	026	17 23	085	32 18	134	17 46	197	51 21	228	26 21	317
6	17 45	357	19 17	025	18 07	084	32 49	134	17 33	197	50 49	228	25 51	316
7	17 42	356	19 36	024	18 51	084	33 21	134	17 21	196	50 16	228	25 20	315
8	17 38	355	19 53	023	19 34	083	33 53	133	17 08	196	49 43	228	24 48	314
9	17 34	354	20 11	022	20 18	082	34 25	133	16 57	195	49 10	228	24 16	313
10	17 29	353	20 27	022	21 01	081	34 57	132	16 45	195	48 38	228	23 44	312
11	17 23	352	20 43	021	21 45	081	35 30	132	16 34	194	48 05	228	23 11	311
12	17 17	351	20 58	020	22 28	080	36 02	132	16 24	194	47 33	228	22 38	310
13	17 10	350	21 12	019	23 11	079	36 35	131	16 13	193	47 00	228	22 04	309
14	17 02	349	21 26	018	23 54	078	37 08	131	16 03	193	46 28	227	21 30	308
	◆ Hamal		RIGEL		◆ CANOPUS		RIGIL KENT		◆ Peacock		FOMALHAUT		Alpheratz	
15	21 39	017	24 37	078	37 41	131	15 54	192	45 56	227	62 16	289	16 53	348
16	21 51	016	25 20	077	38 14	131	15 45	192	45 24	227	61 35	288	16 44	348
17	22 03	015	26 02	076	38 48	130	15 36	191	44 52	227	60 53	287	16 34	347
18	22 14	014	26 45	075	39 21	130	15 27	191	44 20	227	60 11	286	16 24	346
19	22 24	013	27 27	075	39 55	130	15 19	190	43 48	226	59 28	285	16 13	345
20	22 33	012	28 10	074	40 29	129	15 11	190	43 16	226	58 46	284	16 01	344
21	22 42	011	28 52	073	41 03	129	15 04	190	42 44	226	58 03	283	15 48	343
22	22 50	010	29 34	072	41 37	129	14 57	189	42 13	226	57 20	282	15 35	342
23	22 57	009	30 15	071	42 11	129	14 50	189	41 41	226	56 37	281	15 22	341
24	23 04	008	30 57	071	42 46	128	14 44	188	41 10	225	55 54	280	15 07	340
25	23 09	007	31 38	070	43 20	128	14 38	188	40 39	225	55 11	279	14 52	340
26	23 14	006	32 19	069	43 55	128	14 32	187	40 08	225	54 27	278	14 37	339
27	23 18	005	33 00	068	44 30	127	14 27	187	39 37	225	53 44	278	14 20	338
28	23 22	004	33 41	067	45 05	127	14 22	186	39 06	224	53 00	277	14 04	337
29	23 25	003	34 21	066	45 40	127	14 18	186	38 36	224	52 17	276	13 46	336
	◆ Hamal		RIGEL		SIRIUS		◆ CANOPUS		RIGIL KENT		◆ Peacock		FOMALHAUT	
30	23 26	002	35 01	065	24 47	090	46 15	127	14 14	185	38 05	224	51 33	275
31	23 28	001	35 41	065	25 31	089	46 50	127	14 10	185	37 35	224	50 49	274
32	23 28	000	36 20	064	26 15	089	47 25	126	14 07	184	37 05	223	50 06	274
33	23 28	359	36 59	063	26 59	088	48 00	126	14 04	184	36 35	223	49 22	273
34	23 27	358	37 38	062	27 42	087	48 36	126	14 01	183	36 05	223	48 38	272
35	23 25	357	38 17	061	28 26	087	49 12	126	13 59	183	35 35	222	47 54	272
36	23 22	356	38 55	060	29 10	086	49 47	126	13 57	182	35 05	222	47 10	271
37	23 19	355	39 32	059	29 54	085	50 23	125	13 56	182	34 36	222	46 26	270
38	23 14	354	40 10	058	30 38	085	50 59	125	13 55	181	34 07	222	45 43	269
39	23 09	353	40 47	057	31 21	084	51 35	125	13 54	181	33 38	221	44 59	269
40	23 04	352	41 23	056	32 05	083	52 11	125	13 54	180	33 09	221	44 15	268
41	22 57	351	41 59	055	32 48	082	52 47	125	13 54	180	32 40	221	43 31	267
42	22 50	350	42 35	054	33 32	082	53 23	125	13 54	179	32 12	220	42 47	267
43	22 42	349	43 10	053	34 15	081	53 59	125	13 55	179	31 44	220	42 03	266
44	22 33	348	43 45	051	34 58	080	54 35	124	13 57	178	31 16	220	41 20	266
	◆ RIGEL		SIRIUS		CANOPUS		◆ RIGIL KENT		Peacock		◆ FOMALHAUT		Hamal	
45	44 19	050	35 42	079	55 11	124	13 58	178	30 48	219	40 36	265	22 24	347
46	44 52	049	36 25	079	55 47	124	14 00	177	30 20	219	39 52	264	22 14	346
47	45 25	048	37 08	078	56 24	124	14 03	177	29 53	219	39 09	264	22 03	345
48	45 57	047	37 50	077	57 00	124	14 06	176	29 25	218	38 25	263	21 51	344
49	46 29	046	38 33	076	57 36	124	14 09	176	28 58	218	37 41	262	21 39	343
50	47 00	044	39 16	075	58 13	124	14 12	175	28 32	217	36 58	262	21 26	342
51	47 30	043	39 58	074	58 49	124	14 16	175	28 05	217	36 15	261	21 12	341
52	48 00	042	40 40	074	59 25	124	14 21	174	27 39	217	35 31	261	20 58	340
53	48 29	041	41 22	073	60 02	124	14 25	174	27 13	216	34 48	260	20 43	339
54	48 57	039	42 04	072	60 38	124	14 30	173	26 47	216	34 05	259	20 27	339
55	49 25	038	42 46	071	61 14	124	14 36	173	26 21	216	33 22	259	20 11	338
56	49 51	037	43 27	070	61 51	124	14 42	172	25 56	215	32 39	258	19 54	337
57	50 17	035	44 08	069	62 27	124	14 48	172	25 30	215	31 56	258	19 36	336
58	50 42	034	44 49	068	63 03	124	14 54	171	25 05	214	31 13	257	19 18	335
59	51 05	032	45 30	067	63 39	125	15 01	171	24 41	214	30 30	257	18 59	334
	ALDEBARAN		◆ SIRIUS		Suhail		◆ RIGIL KENT		ACHERNAR		◆ Diphda		Hamal	
60	29 52	010	46 10	066	35 59	119	15 09	170	63 39	225	41 50	286	18 39	333
61	29 59	009	46 50	065	36 37	119	15 16	170	63 08	225	41 08	285	18 19	332
62	30 06	008	47 30	064	37 16	118	15 24	169	62 37	226	40 25	284	17 58	331
63	30 11	007	48 09	063	37 55	118	15 33	169	62 05	226	39 43	283	17 36	330
64	30 16	006	48 48	062	38 33	117	15 42	168	61 34	226	39 00	282	17 14	329
65	30 20	005	49 27	061	39 13	117	15 51	168	61 02	227	38 17	282	16 52	329
66	30 23	004	50 05	060	39 52	117	16 00	167	60 30	227	37 34	281	16 29	328
67	30 26	002	50 42	059	40 31	116	16 10	167	59 58	227	36 51	280	16 05	327
68	30 27	001	51 20	058	41 10	116	16 20	166	59 26	227	36 08	279	15 41	326
69	30 28	000	51 57	056	41 50	115	16 31	166	58 54	227	35 24	278	15 16	325
70	30 27	359	52 33	055	42 30	115	16 42	165	58 21	227	34 41	278	14 50	324
71	30 26	358	53 09	054	43 10	115	16 53	165	57 49	228	33 57	277	14 25	323
72	30 24	357	53 44	053	43 50	114	17 05	164	57 17	228	33 14	276	13 58	323
73	30 22	356	54 19	051	44 30	114	17 17	164	56 44	228	32 30	275	13 31	322
74	30 18	355	54 53	050	45 10	113	17 29	164	56 12	228	31 46	275	13 04	321
	BETELGEUSE		◆ SIRIUS		Suhail		◆ RIGIL KENT		ACHERNAR		◆ Diphda		ALDEBARAN	
75	38 00	018	55 26	049	45 50	113	17 42	163	55 39	228	31 03	274	30 13	354
76	38 13	016	55 59	047	46 31	113	17 55	163	55 07	228	30 19	273	30 08	352
77	38 25	015	56 30	046	47 11	112	18 08	162	54 34	228	29 35	273	30 02	351
78	38 36	014	57 02	044	47 52	112	18 22	162	54 02	228	28 51	272	29 55	350
79	38 47	013	57 32	043	48 33	111	18 35	161	53 29	228	28 07	271	29 47	349
80	38 56	011	58 01	041	49 14	111	18 50	161	52 57	228	27 23	271	29 38	348
81	39 04	010	58 30	040	49 55	111	19 04	160	52 24	228	26 39	270	29 29	347
82	39 11	009	58 58	038	50 36	110	19 19	160	51 52	228	25 56	269	29 19	346
83	39 18	008	59 24	037	51 17	110	19 35	159	51 19	228	25 12	269	29 07	345
84	39 23	006	59 50	035	51 58	110	19 50	159	50 47	228	24 28	268	28 56	344
85	39 28	005	60 14	033	52 40	109	20 06	159	50 14	228	23 44	267	28 43	343
86	39 31	004	60 38	031	53 21	109	20 22	158	49 42	227	23 00	267	28 29	342
87	39 34	003	61 00	030	54 03	108	20 39	158	49 10	227	22 16	266	28 15	341
88	39 35	001	61 21	028	54 44	108	20 55	157	48 37	227	21 33	265	28 00	340
89	39 35	000	61 41	026	55 26	108	21 13	157	48 05	227	20 49	265	27 45	338

LHA ♈	Hc	Zn	Hc	Zn	Hc	Zn	Hc	Zn	Hc	Zn	Hc	Zn	Hc	Zn
	PROCYON		Alphard		◆ Suhail		RIGIL KENT		◆ ACHERNAR		RIGEL		◆ BETELGEUSE	
90	36 45	032	33 13	069	56 08	107	21 30	156	47 33	227	53 50	341	39 35	359
91	37 08	031	33 53	068	56 50	107	21 48	156	47 01	227	53 35	339	39 33	357
92	37 30	029	34 34	067	57 32	107	22 06	156	46 29	227	53 19	338	39 31	356
93	37 51	028	35 14	066	58 14	106	22 24	155	45 57	227	53 02	336	39 28	355
94	38 11	027	35 54	065	58 56	106	22 42	155	45 26	226	52 43	335	39 23	354
95	38 31	026	36 34	064	59 38	106	23 01	154	44 54	226	52 24	333	39 18	352
96	38 50	025	37 13	063	60 20	105	23 20	154	44 22	226	52 04	332	39 11	351
97	39 07	023	37 52	062	61 03	105	23 40	154	43 51	226	51 42	330	39 04	350
98	39 24	022	38 31	062	61 45	105	23 59	153	43 19	226	51 20	329	38 56	348
99	39 40	021	39 09	061	62 28	104	24 19	153	42 48	225	50 57	327	38 47	347
100	39 56	020	39 47	060	63 10	104	24 39	152	42 17	225	50 32	326	38 36	346
101	40 10	018	40 25	059	63 53	104	25 00	152	41 46	225	50 07	324	38 25	345
102	40 23	017	41 02	058	64 36	103	25 20	152	41 15	225	49 41	323	38 13	343
103	40 36	016	41 39	057	65 18	103	25 41	151	40 44	225	49 14	322	38 00	342
104	40 47	015	42 15	055	66 01	103	26 03	151	40 13	224	48 47	320	37 47	341
	PROCYON		REGULUS		◆ Gienah		RIGIL KENT		◆ ACHERNAR		RIGEL		◆ BETELGEUSE	
105	40 58	013	20 10	050	19 44	096	26 24	151	39 43	224	48 18	319	37 32	340
106	41 08	012	20 44	049	20 28	095	26 46	150	39 12	224	47 49	318	37 16	339
107	41 16	011	21 17	048	21 12	095	27 08	150	38 42	224	47 19	316	37 00	337
108	41 24	009	21 49	047	21 56	094	27 30	149	38 12	223	46 49	315	36 43	336
109	41 30	008	22 21	047	22 39	093	27 52	149	37 42	223	46 17	314	36 25	335
110	41 36	007	22 53	046	23 23	093	28 15	149	37 12	223	45 45	313	36 06	334
111	41 41	005	23 24	045	24 07	092	28 38	148	36 42	222	45 13	312	35 46	333
112	41 44	004	23 55	044	24 51	091	29 01	148	36 13	222	44 40	310	35 25	332
113	41 47	003	24 25	043	25 35	091	29 24	148	35 43	222	44 06	309	35 04	330
114	41 48	001	24 54	042	26 19	090	29 48	147	35 14	222	43 32	308	34 42	329
115	41 49	000	25 23	041	27 03	089	30 11	147	34 45	221	42 57	307	34 19	328
116	41 48	359	25 52	040	27 46	089	30 35	147	34 16	221	42 22	306	33 56	327
117	41 47	357	26 20	039	28 30	088	30 59	146	33 48	221	41 46	305	33 32	326
118	41 44	356	26 47	038	29 14	087	31 24	146	33 19	220	41 10	304	33 07	325
119	41 41	355	27 14	037	29 58	087	31 48	146	32 51	220	40 33	303	32 41	324
	REGULUS		◆ SPICA		RIGIL KENT		◆ ACHERNAR		RIGEL		BETELGEUSE		◆ PROCYON	
120	27 40	036	13 50	093	32 13	146	32 23	220	39 56	302	32 15	323	41 36	353
121	28 06	035	14 33	092	32 38	145	31 55	219	39 19	301	31 48	322	41 31	352
122	28 31	034	15 17	091	33 03	145	31 27	219	38 41	300	31 21	321	41 24	351
123	28 55	033	16 01	091	33 28	145	30 59	219	38 02	299	30 53	320	41 16	349
124	29 19	032	16 45	090	33 54	144	30 32	218	37 24	298	30 24	319	41 08	348
125	29 42	031	17 29	089	34 20	144	30 05	218	36 45	297	29 55	318	40 58	347
126	30 04	030	18 13	088	34 45	144	29 38	218	36 06	296	29 25	317	40 48	345
127	30 26	029	18 57	088	35 11	144	29 11	217	35 26	295	28 55	316	40 36	344
128	30 47	028	19 41	087	35 38	143	28 45	217	34 46	294	28 24	315	40 24	343
129	31 07	027	20 24	086	36 04	143	28 18	217	34 06	293	27 53	314	40 11	342
130	31 26	026	21 08	086	36 30	143	27 52	216	33 26	292	27 21	313	39 56	340
131	31 45	025	21 52	085	36 57	143	27 26	216	32 45	292	26 48	312	39 41	339
132	32 03	024	22 36	084	37 24	142	27 01	216	32 04	291	26 16	311	39 25	338
133	32 20	022	23 19	084	37 51	142	26 35	215	31 23	290	25 42	310	39 08	337
134	32 37	021	24 03	083	38 18	142	26 10	215	30 41	289	25 08	309	38 50	335
	REGULUS		◆ SPICA		RIGIL KENT		◆ ACHERNAR		CANOPUS		SIRIUS		◆ PROCYON	
135	32 52	020	24 46	082	38 45	142	25 45	214	62 32	236	51 16	302	38 32	334
136	33 07	019	25 30	081	39 12	141	25 21	214	61 56	236	50 39	301	38 12	333
137	33 21	018	26 13	081	39 40	141	24 56	214	61 19	236	50 01	300	37 52	332
138	33 34	017	26 56	080	40 07	141	24 32	213	60 43	236	49 23	299	37 31	331
139	33 46	016	27 39	079	40 35	141	24 08	213	60 07	236	48 44	298	37 09	329
140	33 58	015	28 23	078	41 03	141	23 45	212	59 30	236	48 05	297	36 46	328
141	34 09	013	29 05	078	41 31	140	23 21	212	58 54	236	47 26	296	36 23	327
142	34 18	012	29 48	077	41 59	140	22 58	212	58 18	236	46 46	295	35 59	326
143	34 27	011	30 31	076	42 27	140	22 36	211	57 41	236	46 06	294	35 34	325
144	34 35	010	31 13	075	42 55	140	22 13	211	57 05	236	45 26	293	35 08	324
145	34 42	009	31 56	075	43 24	140	21 51	210	56 29	236	44 45	292	34 42	323
146	34 48	008	32 38	074	43 52	140	21 29	210	55 52	236	44 04	291	34 15	322
147	34 54	006	33 20	073	44 21	139	21 07	209	55 16	236	43 23	290	33 48	321
148	34 58	005	34 02	072	44 49	139	20 46	209	54 40	236	42 42	289	33 19	320
149	35 01	004	34 44	071	45 18	139	20 25	209	54 04	235	42 00	288	32 51	319
	REGULUS		◆ SPICA		RIGIL KENT		◆ ACHERNAR		CANOPUS		SIRIUS		◆ PROCYON	
150	35 04	003	35 25	070	45 47	139	20 04	208	53 28	235	41 18	287	32 21	317
151	35 06	002	36 06	069	46 15	139	19 43	208	52 52	235	40 36	286	31 51	316
152	35 06	000	36 47	069	46 44	139	19 23	207	52 16	235	39 54	285	31 21	315
153	35 06	359	37 28	068	47 13	139	19 03	207	51 40	235	39 12	285	30 50	314
154	35 05	358	38 08	067	47 42	139	18 44	206	51 04	235	38 29	284	30 18	313
155	35 03	357	38 49	066	48 11	139	18 25	206	50 28	235	37 46	283	29 46	313
156	35 00	356	39 28	065	48 40	138	18 06	205	49 52	234	37 04	282	29 14	312
157	34 56	354	40 08	064	49 09	138	17 47	205	49 17	234	36 21	281	28 40	311
158	34 52	353	40 47	063	49 39	138	17 29	204	48 41	234	35 38	281	28 07	310
159	34 46	352	41 26	062	50 08	138	17 11	204	48 06	234	34 54	280	27 33	309
160	34 39	351	42 05	061	50 37	138	16 53	203	47 30	234	34 11	279	26 58	308
161	34 32	350	42 43	060	51 06	138	16 36	203	46 55	233	33 28	278	26 24	307
162	34 24	348	43 21	059	51 35	138	16 19	202	46 20	233	32 44	278	25 48	306
163	34 14	347	43 58	058	52 04	138	16 02	202	45 45	233	32 01	277	25 13	305
164	34 04	346	44 35	057	52 34	138	15 46	201	45 10	233	31 17	276	24 37	304
	SPICA		◆ ANTARES		RIGIL KENT		ACHERNAR		◆ CANOPUS		SIRIUS		◆ REGULUS	
165	45 12	056	22 51	106	53 03	138	15 30	201	44 35	233	30 33	275	33 53	345
166	45 48	055	23 34	105	53 32	138	15 15	201	44 00	232	29 50	275	33 41	344
167	46 24	054	24 16	104	54 01	139	14 59	200	43 25	232	29 06	274	33 29	343
168	46 59	053	24 59	104	54 30	139	14 45	200	42 51	232	28 22	273	33 15	342
169	47 33	051	25 42	103	54 59	139	14 30	199	42 16	232	27 38	273	33 01	340
170	48 07	050	26 24	103	55 28	139	14 16	199	41 42	231	26 54	272	32 46	339
171	48 41	049	27 07	102	55 57	139	14 02	198	41 08	231	26 11	271	32 30	338
172	49 13	048	27 50	101	56 26	139	13 49	197	40 34	231	25 27	270	32 13	337
173	49 46	046	28 33	101	56 54	139	13 36	197	40 00	230	24 43	270	31 56	336
174	50 17	045	29 16	100	57 23	139	13 23	196	39 26	230	23 59	269	31 37	335
175	50 48	044	30 00	100	57 51	140	13 11	196	38 53	230	23 15	268	31 18	334
176	51 18	042	30 43	099	58 20	140	12 59	195	38 19	229	22 31	268	30 59	333
177	51 47	041	31 26	098	58 48	140	12 48	195	37 46	229	21 47	267	30 38	332
178	52 15	040	32 10	098	59 16	140	12 37	194	37 13	229	21 04	266	30 17	331
179	52 43	038	32 53	097	59 44	141	12 26	194	36 40	229	20 20	266	29 55	330

LAT 43°S

LHA ♈	Hc Zn	Hc Zn	Hc Zn	Hc Zn	Hc Zn	Hc Zn	Hc Zn
	◆ARCTURUS	ANTARES	◆RIGIL KENT	ACHERNAR	CANOPUS	◆Suhail	REGULUS
180	20 26 034	33 37 096	60 12 141	12 15 193	36 07 228	59 08 254	29 32 328
181	20 51 034	34 21 096	60 40 141	12 06 193	35 34 228	58 25 254	29 09 327
182	21 14 033	35 04 095	61 07 142	11 56 192	35 02 228	57 43 253	28 45 326
183	21 38 032	35 48 095	61 34 142	11 47 192	34 29 227	57 01 253	28 21 325
184	22 01 031	36 32 094	62 01 142	11 38 191	33 57 227	56 19 253	27 55 324
185	22 23 030	37 15 093	62 28 143	11 30 191	33 25 227	55 37 252	27 30 323
186	22 44 029	37 59 093	62 54 143	11 22 190	32 54 226	54 56 252	27 03 322
187	23 05 028	38 43 092	63 20 144	11 14 190	32 22 226	54 14 252	26 36 321
188	23 25 027	39 27 091	63 46 144	11 07 189	31 51 225	53 32 251	26 08 320
189	23 45 026	40 11 091	64 12 145	11 01 189	31 20 225	52 51 251	25 40 320
190	24 04 025	40 55 090	64 37 145	10 54 188	30 49 225	52 10 251	25 11 319
191	24 22 024	41 39 089	65 02 146	10 48 187	30 18 224	51 28 250	24 42 318
192	24 39 023	42 23 089	65 26 146	10 43 187	29 47 224	50 47 250	24 12 317
193	24 56 022	43 06 088	65 50 147	10 38 186	29 17 224	50 06 249	23 42 316
194	25 12 021	43 50 087	66 14 148	10 33 186	28 47 223	49 25 249	23 11 315
	◆ARCTURUS	ANTARES	◆Peacock	ACHERNAR	CANOPUS	◆Suhail	REGULUS
195	25 28 020	44 34 086	24 55 146	10 29 185	28 17 223	48 44 249	22 40 314
196	25 42 019	45 18 086	25 20 145	10 25 185	27 47 222	48 03 248	22 08 313
197	25 56 018	46 02 085	25 45 145	10 22 184	27 18 222	47 22 248	21 36 312
198	26 09 017	46 45 084	26 10 145	10 19 184	26 48 222	46 42 247	21 03 311
199	26 22 016	47 29 083	26 36 144	10 16 183	26 19 221	46 01 247	20 30 311
200	26 33 015	48 12 083	27 02 144	10 14 183	25 50 221	45 21 247	19 56 310
201	26 44 014	48 56 082	27 28 143	10 12 182	25 22 220	44 41 246	19 22 309
202	26 54 013	49 39 081	27 54 143	10 11 181	24 54 220	44 01 246	18 48 308
203	27 04 012	50 23 080	28 21 143	10 10 181	24 26 220	43 21 246	18 13 307
204	27 12 011	51 06 079	28 47 142	10 10 180	23 58 219	42 41 245	17 38 306
205	27 20 010	51 49 078	29 14 142	10 10 180	23 30 219	42 01 245	17 02 305
206	27 27 009	52 32 078	29 41 142	10 10 179	23 03 218	41 21 244	16 27 305
207	27 33 008	53 14 077	30 09 141	10 11 179	22 36 218	40 42 244	15 50 304
208	27 39 006	53 57 076	30 36 141	10 12 178	22 09 217	40 02 244	15 14 303
209	27 43 005	54 40 075	31 04 141	10 14 178	21 43 217	39 23 243	14 37 302
	◆ARCTURUS	ANTARES	◆Peacock	ACHERNAR	CANOPUS	◆Suhail	SPICA
210	27 47 004	55 22 074	31 32 140	10 16 177	21 16 216	38 44 243	57 23 344
211	27 50 003	56 04 073	32 00 140	10 18 176	20 50 216	38 05 242	57 11 343
212	27 52 002	56 46 072	32 29 140	10 21 176	20 25 216	37 26 242	56 57 341
213	27 53 001	57 27 071	32 57 139	10 25 175	19 59 215	36 48 241	56 42 339
214	27 54 000	58 09 070	33 26 139	10 28 175	19 34 215	36 09 241	56 26 337
215	27 53 359	58 50 069	33 55 139	10 33 174	19 10 214	35 31 241	56 09 336
216	27 52 358	59 30 068	34 24 138	10 37 174	18 45 214	34 53 240	55 50 334
217	27 50 357	60 11 066	34 53 138	10 42 173	18 21 213	34 15 240	55 30 332
218	27 47 356	60 51 065	35 23 138	10 48 173	17 57 213	33 37 239	55 09 331
219	27 44 355	61 30 064	35 52 137	10 53 172	17 33 212	32 59 239	54 47 329
220	27 39 354	62 09 063	36 22 137	11 00 172	17 10 212	32 22 238	54 24 328
221	27 34 353	62 48 061	36 52 137	11 06 171	16 47 211	31 45 238	54 00 326
222	27 28 352	63 26 060	37 22 137	11 13 170	16 25 211	31 08 238	53 36 325
223	27 21 351	64 04 058	37 53 136	11 21 170	16 02 210	30 31 237	53 10 323
224	27 14 349	64 41 057	38 23 136	11 29 169	15 40 210	29 54 237	52 43 322
	Rasalhague	◆Nunki	Peacock	ACHERNAR	◆ACRUX	SPICA	◆ARCTURUS
225	24 02 042	39 44 091	38 54 136	11 37 169	60 15 214	52 15 320	27 05 348
226	24 31 041	40 28 090	39 24 135	11 46 168	59 50 215	51 47 319	26 56 347
227	25 00 040	41 12 089	39 55 135	11 55 168	59 25 215	51 18 318	26 46 346
228	25 28 039	41 56 089	40 26 135	12 04 167	59 00 215	50 48 316	26 35 345
229	25 56 038	42 39 088	40 57 135	12 14 167	58 34 215	50 17 315	26 24 344
230	26 23 037	43 23 087	41 28 134	12 24 166	58 09 216	49 45 314	26 11 343
231	26 49 036	44 07 086	42 00 134	12 35 166	57 43 216	49 13 312	25 58 342
232	27 15 035	44 51 086	42 31 134	12 46 165	57 17 216	48 40 311	25 45 341
233	27 40 034	45 35 085	43 03 134	12 58 165	56 51 217	48 07 310	25 30 340
234	28 04 033	46 18 084	43 35 134	13 09 164	56 25 217	47 33 309	25 15 339
235	28 28 032	47 02 084	44 06 133	13 22 164	55 59 217	46 59 307	24 59 338
236	28 52 031	47 45 083	44 38 133	13 34 163	55 32 217	46 23 306	24 42 337
237	29 14 030	48 29 082	45 10 133	13 47 163	55 06 217	45 48 305	24 25 336
238	29 36 029	49 12 081	45 43 133	14 00 162	54 39 217	45 12 304	24 07 335
239	29 57 028	49 56 080	46 15 133	14 14 162	54 13 218	44 35 303	23 48 334
	Rasalhague	◆ALTAIR	Peacock	◆ACHERNAR	ACRUX	◆SPICA	ARCTURUS
240	30 18 027	16 10 061	46 47 133	14 28 161	53 46 218	43 58 302	23 29 333
241	30 37 026	16 49 060	47 19 132	14 43 161	53 19 218	43 21 301	23 08 332
242	30 56 025	17 26 059	47 52 132	14 57 160	52 52 218	42 43 300	22 48 331
243	31 15 024	18 04 058	48 24 132	15 13 160	52 25 218	42 05 299	22 26 330
244	31 32 023	18 41 057	48 57 132	15 28 159	51 58 218	41 26 298	22 04 329
245	31 49 022	19 18 057	49 30 132	15 44 159	51 31 218	40 47 297	21 42 329
246	32 05 021	19 54 056	50 02 132	16 00 158	51 04 218	40 08 296	21 19 328
247	32 20 020	20 30 055	50 35 132	16 17 158	50 37 218	39 28 295	20 55 327
248	32 34 019	21 06 054	51 08 132	16 34 157	50 10 218	38 48 294	20 30 326
249	32 48 017	21 41 053	51 41 132	16 51 157	49 43 218	38 08 293	20 05 325
250	33 00 016	22 16 052	52 13 131	17 08 156	49 16 218	37 28 292	19 40 324
251	33 12 015	22 51 051	52 46 131	17 26 156	48 49 218	36 47 291	19 14 323
252	33 23 014	23 25 051	53 19 131	17 45 155	48 22 218	36 06 290	18 47 322
253	33 34 013	23 59 050	53 52 131	18 03 155	47 55 218	35 25 290	18 20 321
254	33 43 012	24 32 049	54 25 131	18 22 154	47 28 218	34 43 289	17 52 320
	Rasalhague	◆ALTAIR	FOMALHAUT	◆ACHERNAR	RIGIL KENT	◆SPICA	Alphecca
255	33 51 010	25 05 048	19 54 112	18 41 154	62 36 217	34 02 288	17 40 340
256	33 59 009	25 37 047	20 35 112	19 01 153	62 10 218	33 20 287	17 25 339
257	34 05 008	26 09 046	21 16 111	19 21 153	61 43 218	32 38 286	17 09 338
258	34 11 007	26 40 045	21 57 111	19 41 152	61 16 218	31 55 285	16 52 338
259	34 16 006	27 11 044	22 38 110	20 01 152	60 48 219	31 13 285	16 35 337
260	34 20 005	27 41 043	23 19 109	20 22 152	60 21 219	30 31 284	16 17 336
261	34 23 003	28 11 042	24 01 109	20 43 151	59 53 219	29 48 283	15 59 335
262	34 25 002	28 40 041	24 43 108	21 04 151	59 25 220	29 05 282	15 40 334
263	34 27 001	29 09 040	25 24 108	21 26 150	58 57 220	28 22 282	15 21 333
264	34 27 000	29 37 039	26 06 107	21 48 150	58 29 220	27 39 281	15 01 332
265	34 26 359	30 05 038	26 48 107	22 10 149	58 00 220	26 56 280	14 40 331
266	34 25 358	30 32 037	27 30 106	22 33 149	57 32 221	26 13 279	14 19 331
267	34 23 356	30 58 036	28 13 105	22 55 149	57 03 221	25 29 279	13 57 330
268	34 19 355	31 23 035	28 55 105	23 18 148	56 35 221	24 46 278	13 34 329
269	34 15 354	31 48 034	29 37 104	23 42 148	56 06 221	24 02 277	13 11 328

LHA ♈	Hc Zn	Hc Zn	Hc Zn	Hc Zn	Hc Zn	Hc Zn	Hc Zn
	ALTAIR	Enif	◆FOMALHAUT	ACHERNAR	◆RIGIL KENT	ANTARES	◆Rasalhague
270	32 13 033	16 25 059	30 20 104	24 05 147	55 37 221	65 23 305	34 10 353
271	32 36 032	17 02 058	31 03 103	24 29 147	55 08 221	64 47 303	34 04 352
272	32 59 031	17 39 057	31 46 102	24 53 146	54 39 221	64 10 302	33 57 350
273	33 21 030	18 16 056	32 28 102	25 17 146	54 10 221	63 33 300	33 50 349
274	33 43 029	18 52 055	33 11 101	25 42 146	53 41 222	62 54 299	33 41 348
275	34 04 028	19 28 055	33 54 101	26 07 145	53 12 222	62 16 298	33 32 347
276	34 24 026	20 04 054	34 38 100	26 32 145	52 43 222	61 37 296	33 21 346
277	34 43 025	20 39 053	35 21 100	26 57 145	52 14 222	60 57 295	33 10 345
278	35 01 024	21 14 052	36 04 099	27 23 144	51 45 222	60 17 294	32 58 344
279	35 19 023	21 48 051	36 48 098	27 49 144	51 15 222	59 37 293	32 45 342
280	35 36 022	22 22 050	37 31 098	28 15 143	50 46 222	58 56 292	32 32 341
281	35 52 021	22 56 049	38 15 097	28 41 143	50 17 222	58 15 290	32 17 340
282	36 07 020	23 29 049	38 58 096	29 07 143	49 48 222	57 34 289	32 02 339
283	36 21 018	24 01 048	39 42 096	29 34 142	49 19 222	56 53 288	31 46 338
284	36 34 017	24 33 047	40 25 095	30 01 142	48 50 222	56 11 287	31 29 337
	ALTAIR	Enif	◆FOMALHAUT	ACHERNAR	◆RIGIL KENT	ANTARES	◆Rasalhague
285	36 47 016	25 05 046	41 09 095	30 28 142	48 20 221	55 29 286	31 11 336
286	36 58 015	25 36 045	41 53 094	30 56 141	47 51 221	54 47 285	30 53 335
287	37 09 014	26 07 044	42 37 093	31 23 141	47 22 221	54 04 284	30 34 334
288	37 19 012	26 37 043	43 21 093	31 51 141	46 53 221	53 22 283	30 14 333
289	37 28 011	27 07 042	44 04 092	32 19 140	46 25 221	52 39 283	29 53 331
290	37 36 010	27 36 041	44 48 091	32 47 140	45 56 221	51 56 282	29 32 330
291	37 43 009	28 05 040	45 32 091	33 15 140	45 27 221	51 13 281	29 10 329
292	37 49 007	28 33 039	46 16 090	33 44 139	44 58 221	50 30 280	28 47 328
293	37 54 006	29 00 038	47 00 089	34 12 139	44 30 221	49 46 279	28 24 327
294	37 58 005	29 27 037	47 44 089	34 41 139	44 01 221	49 03 278	28 00 326
295	38 01 004	29 53 036	48 28 088	35 10 138	43 33 220	48 20 278	27 35 325
296	38 04 002	30 18 035	49 11 087	35 39 138	43 04 220	47 36 277	27 10 324
297	38 05 001	30 43 034	49 55 086	36 09 138	42 36 220	46 52 276	26 44 323
298	38 05 000	31 07 033	50 39 086	36 38 138	42 08 220	46 09 275	26 18 322
299	38 05 359	31 31 032	51 23 085	37 08 137	41 40 220	45 25 274	25 51 321
	◆Enif	FOMALHAUT	◆ACHERNAR	RIGIL KENT	◆ANTARES	Rasalhague	ALTAIR
300	31 54 031	52 06 084	37 38 137	41 12 220	44 41 274	25 23 320	38 03 357
301	32 16 030	52 50 083	38 08 137	40 44 219	43 57 273	24 55 320	38 01 356
302	32 37 029	53 34 083	38 38 136	40 16 219	43 14 272	24 26 319	37 57 355
303	32 58 028	54 17 082	39 08 136	39 48 219	42 30 272	23 57 318	37 53 354
304	33 18 026	55 01 081	39 39 136	39 21 219	41 46 271	23 27 317	37 48 352
305	33 37 025	55 44 080	40 09 136	38 54 218	41 02 270	22 57 316	37 41 351
306	33 56 024	56 27 079	40 40 136	38 26 218	40 18 270	22 26 315	37 34 350
307	34 13 023	57 10 078	41 11 135	37 59 218	39 34 269	21 54 314	37 26 349
308	34 30 022	57 53 077	41 42 135	37 32 218	38 50 268	21 23 313	37 17 347
309	34 46 021	58 36 076	42 13 135	37 05 218	38 07 268	20 50 312	37 07 346
310	35 01 020	59 18 076	42 44 135	36 39 217	37 23 267	20 18 311	36 56 345
311	35 16 018	60 01 075	43 15 134	36 12 217	36 39 266	19 45 311	36 44 344
312	35 29 017	60 43 073	43 46 134	35 46 217	35 55 266	19 11 310	36 31 343
313	35 42 016	61 25 072	44 18 134	35 20 217	35 11 265	18 37 309	36 18 341
314	35 53 015	62 06 071	44 50 134	34 54 216	34 28 264	18 03 308	36 03 340
	Enif	◆Diphda	ACHERNAR	Miaplacidus	◆RIGIL KENT	ANTARES	◆ALTAIR
315	36 04 014	36 43 080	45 21 134	22 48 181	34 28 216	33 44 264	35 48 339
316	36 14 013	37 27 079	45 53 134	22 48 181	34 02 216	33 00 263	35 32 338
317	36 23 011	38 10 079	46 25 133	22 47 181	33 36 215	32 17 262	35 15 337
318	36 31 010	38 53 078	46 57 133	22 47 180	33 11 215	31 33 262	34 57 336
319	36 39 009	39 35 077	47 29 133	22 47 180	32 46 215	30 50 261	34 38 334
320	36 45 008	40 18 076	48 01 133	22 47 179	32 21 215	30 07 261	34 19 333
321	36 50 006	41 01 075	48 33 133	22 48 179	31 56 214	29 23 260	33 59 332
322	36 55 005	41 43 074	49 05 133	22 49 179	31 32 214	28 40 259	33 38 331
323	36 58 004	42 25 074	49 38 133	22 50 178	31 07 214	27 57 259	33 16 330
324	37 01 003	43 07 073	50 10 132	22 51 178	30 43 213	27 14 258	32 54 329
325	37 03 002	43 49 072	50 42 132	22 53 178	30 19 213	26 31 258	32 31 328
326	37 03 000	44 31 071	51 15 132	22 55 177	29 55 213	25 49 257	32 07 327
327	37 03 359	45 12 070	51 47 132	22 58 177	29 32 212	25 06 256	31 42 326
328	37 02 358	45 53 069	52 20 132	23 00 176	29 08 212	24 23 256	31 17 325
329	37 00 357	46 34 068	52 52 132	23 03 176	28 45 212	23 41 255	30 52 324
	◆Diphda	ACHERNAR	◆Miaplacidus	RIGIL KENT	Nunki	◆ALTAIR	Enif
330	47 14 067	53 25 132	23 06 176	28 22 211	49 17 279	30 25 322	36 57 355
331	47 55 066	53 57 132	23 10 175	27 59 211	48 33 278	29 58 321	36 53 354
332	48 35 065	54 30 132	23 13 175	27 37 211	47 50 277	29 30 320	36 48 353
333	49 14 064	55 02 132	23 17 175	27 15 210	47 06 277	29 02 319	36 42 352
334	49 54 063	55 35 132	23 22 174	26 53 210	46 23 276	28 33 318	36 35 350
335	50 32 062	56 07 132	23 26 174	26 31 210	45 39 275	28 04 317	36 27 349
336	51 11 061	56 40 132	23 31 173	26 09 209	44 55 274	27 34 317	36 19 348
337	51 49 060	57 12 132	23 36 173	25 48 209	44 11 274	27 04 316	36 09 347
338	52 27 058	57 45 132	23 42 173	25 27 208	43 28 273	26 33 315	35 59 346
339	53 04 057	58 17 133	23 48 172	25 06 208	42 44 272	26 01 314	35 47 344
340	53 40 056	58 49 133	23 54 172	24 46 208	42 00 271	25 29 313	35 35 343
341	54 17 055	59 22 133	24 00 172	24 26 207	41 16 271	24 57 312	35 22 342
342	54 52 053	59 54 133	24 06 171	24 06 207	40 32 270	24 24 311	35 08 341
343	55 27 052	60 26 133	24 13 171	23 46 207	39 48 269	23 50 310	34 53 340
344	56 01 051	60 58 133	24 20 171	23 26 206	39 04 269	23 17 309	34 38 339
	◆Alpheratz	Diphda	◆CANOPUS	RIGIL KENT	◆Nunki	ALTAIR	Enif
345	16 06 016	56 35 049	22 32 142	23 07 206	38 20 268	22 42 308	34 21 337
346	16 17 015	57 08 048	22 59 142	22 48 205	37 37 267	22 08 307	34 04 336
347	16 28 014	57 40 047	23 26 141	22 30 205	36 53 267	21 33 307	33 46 335
348	16 38 013	58 12 045	23 54 141	22 11 205	36 09 266	20 57 306	33 27 334
349	16 48 012	58 43 044	24 22 141	21 53 204	35 25 265	20 22 305	33 07 333
350	16 57 011	59 12 042	24 50 140	21 35 204	34 42 265	19 45 304	32 47 332
351	17 05 010	59 41 040	25 18 140	21 18 203	33 58 264	19 09 303	32 26 331
352	17 13 009	60 09 039	25 46 139	21 01 203	33 14 264	18 32 302	32 04 330
353	17 19 008	60 36 037	26 15 139	20 44 202	32 31 263	17 55 302	31 42 329
354	17 26 008	61 02 035	26 44 138	20 27 202	31 47 262	17 17 301	31 18 328
355	17 31 007	61 27 033	27 13 138	20 11 202	31 04 262	16 39 300	30 55 326
356	17 36 006	61 50 032	27 43 138	19 55 201	30 20 261	16 01 299	30 30 325
357	17 40 005	62 13 030	28 12 137	19 39 201	29 37 260	15 23 298	30 05 324
358	17 43 004	62 34 028	28 42 137	19 24 200	28 54 260	14 44 298	29 39 323
359	17 46 003	62 54 026	29 13 136	19 09 200	28 11 259	14 05 297	29 12 322

LHA ♈	Hc Zn	Hc Zn	Hc Zn	Hc Zn	Hc Zn	Hc Zn	Hc Zn
	Alpheratz	Hamal	◆RIGEL	CANOPUS	◆RIGIL KENT	Peacock	◆Enif
0	16 48 002	16 22 030	13 43 088	30 26 136	19 51 199	54 45 230	27 58 322
1	16 49 001	16 44 030	14 26 087	30 56 135	19 37 199	54 12 230	27 31 321
2	16 50 000	17 05 029	15 09 087	31 27 135	19 23 199	53 39 230	27 04 320
3	16 49 359	17 25 028	15 52 086	31 57 135	19 09 198	53 06 230	26 35 319
4	16 49 358	17 45 027	16 35 085	32 28 134	18 56 198	52 34 229	26 07 318
5	16 47 358	18 04 026	17 18 085	32 59 134	18 43 197	52 01 229	25 37 317
6	16 45 357	18 23 025	18 01 084	33 31 133	18 30 197	51 28 229	25 08 316
7	16 42 356	18 41 024	18 44 083	34 02 133	18 18 196	50 55 229	24 37 315
8	16 38 355	18 58 023	19 27 082	34 34 133	18 06 196	50 23 229	24 07 314
9	16 34 354	19 15 022	20 09 082	35 05 132	17 55 195	49 50 229	23 35 313
10	16 29 353	19 31 021	20 52 081	35 38 132	17 43 195	49 18 229	23 04 312
11	16 24 352	19 47 020	21 35 080	36 10 132	17 33 194	48 45 229	22 31 311
12	16 17 351	20 01 020	22 17 080	36 42 131	17 22 194	48 13 228	21 59 310
13	16 10 350	20 15 019	23 00 079	37 15 131	17 12 193	47 41 228	21 26 310
14	16 03 349	20 29 018	23 42 078	37 47 131	17 02 193	47 08 228	20 52 309
	◆Hamal	RIGEL	◆CANOPUS	RIGIL KENT	◆Peacock	FOMALHAUT	Alpheratz
15	20 41 017	24 24 077	38 20 130	16 52 192	46 36 228	61 56 291	15 54 348
16	20 53 016	25 06 076	38 53 130	16 43 192	46 04 228	61 15 290	15 46 348
17	21 05 015	25 48 076	39 26 130	16 34 192	45 32 228	60 35 288	15 36 347
18	21 15 014	26 30 075	40 00 129	16 26 191	45 01 227	59 54 287	15 26 346
19	21 25 013	27 11 074	40 33 129	16 18 191	44 29 227	59 12 286	15 15 345
20	21 35 012	27 53 073	41 07 129	16 10 190	43 57 227	58 31 285	15 03 344
21	21 43 011	28 34 073	41 40 128	16 03 190	43 26 227	57 49 284	14 51 343
22	21 51 010	29 15 072	42 14 128	15 56 189	42 54 226	57 07 283	14 38 342
23	21 58 009	29 56 071	42 48 128	15 49 189	42 23 226	56 25 282	14 25 341
24	22 04 008	30 37 070	43 23 128	15 43 188	41 52 226	55 43 282	14 11 341
25	22 10 007	31 17 069	43 57 127	15 37 188	41 21 226	55 00 281	13 56 340
26	22 15 006	31 57 068	44 31 127	15 32 187	40 50 226	54 18 280	13 41 339
27	22 19 005	32 37 067	45 06 127	15 26 187	40 19 225	53 35 279	13 25 338
28	22 22 004	33 17 067	45 41 126	15 22 186	39 49 225	52 53 278	13 08 337
29	22 25 003	33 56 066	46 15 126	15 17 186	39 18 225	52 10 277	12 51 336
	◆Hamal	RIGEL	SIRIUS	◆CANOPUS	RIGIL KENT	◆Peacock	FOMALHAUT
30	22 27 002	34 36 065	24 47 090	46 50 126	15 13 185	38 48 224	51 27 276
31	22 28 001	35 15 064	25 30 089	47 25 126	15 10 185	38 18 224	50 44 276
32	22 28 000	35 53 063	26 13 088	48 00 125	15 06 184	37 48 224	50 01 275
33	22 28 359	36 31 062	26 56 088	48 35 125	15 03 184	37 18 224	49 18 274
34	22 27 358	37 09 061	27 40 087	49 11 125	15 01 183	36 49 223	48 35 273
35	22 25 357	37 47 060	28 23 086	49 46 125	14 59 183	36 19 223	47 52 273
36	22 22 356	38 24 059	29 06 085	50 22 125	14 57 182	35 50 223	47 09 272
37	22 19 355	39 01 058	29 49 085	50 57 124	14 56 182	35 21 222	46 26 271
38	22 15 354	39 38 057	30 32 084	51 33 124	14 55 181	34 52 222	45 43 270
39	22 10 353	40 14 056	31 14 083	52 09 124	14 54 181	34 23 222	44 59 270
40	22 04 352	40 49 055	31 57 083	52 44 124	14 54 180	33 54 221	44 16 269
41	21 58 351	41 24 054	32 40 082	53 20 124	14 54 180	33 26 221	43 33 268
42	21 51 350	41 59 053	33 23 081	53 56 124	14 54 179	32 58 221	42 50 268
43	21 43 349	42 33 052	34 05 080	54 32 123	14 55 179	32 30 220	42 07 267
44	21 35 348	43 07 051	34 48 079	55 08 123	14 57 178	32 02 220	41 24 266
	◆RIGEL	SIRIUS	CANOPUS	◆RIGIL KENT	Peacock	◆FOMALHAUT	Hamal
45	43 40 050	35 30 079	55 44 123	14 58 178	31 34 220	40 41 266	21 25 347
46	44 13 048	36 12 078	56 21 123	15 00 177	31 07 219	39 58 265	21 16 346
47	44 45 047	36 55 077	56 57 123	15 03 177	30 39 219	39 15 264	21 05 345
48	45 16 046	37 37 076	57 33 123	15 05 176	30 12 219	38 32 264	20 54 344
49	45 47 045	38 18 075	58 09 123	15 09 176	29 46 218	37 49 263	20 42 343
50	46 17 044	39 00 075	58 46 123	15 12 175	29 19 218	37 06 263	20 29 342
51	46 46 042	39 42 074	59 22 123	15 16 175	28 53 217	36 23 262	20 15 341
52	47 15 041	40 23 073	59 58 123	15 20 174	28 27 217	35 41 261	20 01 341
53	47 43 040	41 04 072	60 35 123	15 25 174	28 01 217	34 58 261	19 47 340
54	48 10 039	41 45 071	61 11 123	15 30 173	27 35 216	34 15 260	19 31 339
55	48 37 037	42 26 070	61 47 123	15 35 173	27 10 216	33 33 260	19 15 338
56	49 03 036	43 06 069	62 24 123	15 41 172	26 44 215	32 51 259	18 59 337
57	49 27 034	43 46 068	63 00 123	15 47 172	26 20 215	32 08 258	18 41 336
58	49 51 033	44 26 067	63 36 123	15 54 171	25 55 215	31 26 258	18 23 335
59	50 15 032	45 06 066	64 13 123	16 01 171	25 30 214	30 44 257	18 05 334
	ALDEBARAN	◆SIRIUS	Suhail	◆RIGIL KENT	ACHERNAR	◆Diphda	Hamal
60	28 53 010	45 45 065	36 28 118	16 08 170	64 21 227	41 34 287	17 45 333
61	29 00 009	46 24 064	37 06 118	16 15 170	63 50 227	40 52 286	17 26 332
62	29 06 008	47 03 063	37 44 118	16 23 169	63 18 227	40 10 285	17 05 331
63	29 12 007	47 41 062	38 22 117	16 32 169	62 47 227	39 29 284	16 44 330
64	29 17 006	48 19 061	39 01 117	16 40 168	62 15 228	38 47 283	16 23 330
65	29 20 005	48 57 060	39 39 116	16 49 168	61 43 228	38 05 282	16 01 329
66	29 23 004	49 34 059	40 18 116	16 59 167	61 11 228	37 22 282	15 38 328
67	29 26 002	50 11 058	40 57 115	17 09 167	60 38 228	36 40 281	15 15 327
68	29 27 001	50 47 057	41 36 115	17 19 166	60 06 228	35 58 280	14 51 326
69	29 28 000	51 23 055	42 15 115	17 29 166	59 34 229	35 15 279	14 26 325
70	29 27 359	51 58 054	42 55 114	17 40 165	59 02 229	34 32 278	14 02 324
71	29 26 358	52 33 053	43 34 114	17 51 165	58 29 229	33 50 278	13 36 324
72	29 24 357	53 07 052	44 14 113	18 03 164	57 57 229	33 07 277	13 10 323
73	29 22 356	53 41 050	44 53 113	18 14 164	57 24 229	32 24 276	12 44 322
74	29 18 355	54 14 049	45 33 112	18 27 163	56 52 229	31 41 275	12 17 321
	BETELGEUSE	◆SIRIUS	Suhail	◆RIGIL KENT	ACHERNAR	◆Diphda	ALDEBARAN
75	37 03 017	54 46 048	46 13 112	18 39 163	56 19 229	30 58 275	29 14 354
76	37 16 016	55 17 046	46 53 112	18 52 162	55 47 229	30 15 274	29 09 353
77	37 27 015	55 48 045	47 33 111	19 05 162	55 14 229	29 32 273	29 03 351
78	37 38 014	56 18 043	48 14 111	19 18 162	54 41 229	28 49 272	28 56 350
79	37 48 013	56 48 042	48 54 110	19 32 161	54 09 229	28 06 272	28 48 349
80	37 57 011	57 16 040	49 35 110	19 46 161	53 36 229	27 23 271	28 40 348
81	38 05 010	57 43 039	50 15 110	20 01 160	53 04 229	26 39 270	28 30 347
82	38 12 009	58 10 037	50 56 109	20 16 160	52 32 229	25 56 270	28 20 346
83	38 18 008	58 36 036	51 37 109	20 31 159	51 59 229	25 13 269	28 10 345
84	38 24 006	59 00 034	52 18 108	20 46 159	51 27 229	24 30 268	27 58 344
85	38 28 005	59 24 032	52 59 108	21 02 158	50 54 228	23 47 268	27 46 343
86	38 31 004	59 46 030	53 40 108	21 18 158	50 22 228	23 04 267	27 33 342
87	38 34 003	60 08 029	54 21 107	21 34 158	49 50 228	22 21 266	27 19 341
88	38 35 001	60 28 027	55 02 107	21 51 157	49 18 228	21 38 266	27 04 340
89	38 35 000	60 47 025	55 44 106	22 08 157	48 46 228	20 55 265	26 49 339

LAT 44°S

LHA ♈	Hc Zn	Hc Zn	Hc Zn	Hc Zn	Hc Zn	Hc Zn	Hc Zn
	PROCYON	Alphard	◆Suhail	RIGIL KENT	◆ACHERNAR	RIGEL	◆BETELGEUSE
90	35 54 031	32 50 068	56 25 106	22 25 156	48 14 228	52 53 341	38 35 359
91	36 16 030	33 30 067	57 07 106	22 42 156	47 42 228	52 39 340	38 34 357
92	36 37 029	34 10 066	57 48 105	23 00 155	47 10 227	52 23 338	38 31 356
93	36 58 028	34 50 065	58 30 105	23 18 155	46 38 227	52 07 337	38 28 355
94	37 18 027	35 29 065	59 12 104	23 37 155	46 07 227	51 49 335	38 24 354
95	37 37 025	36 07 064	59 54 104	23 55 154	45 35 227	51 30 334	38 18 352
96	37 55 024	36 46 063	60 35 104	24 14 154	45 04 227	51 11 332	38 12 351
97	38 12 023	37 24 062	61 17 103	24 33 153	44 32 226	50 50 331	38 05 350
98	38 29 022	38 02 061	61 59 103	24 53 153	44 01 226	50 29 329	37 57 349
99	38 44 021	38 40 060	62 42 102	25 13 153	43 30 226	50 06 328	37 48 347
100	38 59 019	39 17 059	63 24 102	25 32 152	42 59 226	49 43 326	37 38 346
101	39 13 018	39 53 058	64 06 102	25 53 152	42 28 226	49 18 325	37 27 345
102	39 26 017	40 30 057	64 48 101	26 13 151	41 57 225	48 53 324	37 16 344
103	39 38 016	41 06 056	65 31 101	26 34 151	41 27 225	48 27 322	37 03 343
104	39 49 014	41 41 055	66 13 100	26 55 151	40 56 225	48 00 321	36 50 341
	PROCYON	REGULUS	◆Gienah	RIGIL KENT	◆ACHERNAR	RIGEL	◆BETELGEUSE
105	40 00 013	19 32 050	19 51 096	27 16 150	40 26 225	47 33 320	36 36 340
106	40 09 012	20 04 049	20 34 095	27 38 150	39 55 224	47 05 318	36 20 339
107	40 17 010	20 37 048	21 17 094	28 00 150	39 25 224	46 36 317	36 04 338
108	40 25 009	21 09 047	22 00 094	28 21 149	38 55 224	46 06 316	35 48 337
109	40 31 008	21 40 046	22 43 093	28 44 149	38 26 224	45 35 315	35 30 335
110	40 36 007	22 11 045	23 26 092	29 06 148	37 56 223	45 04 313	35 12 334
111	40 41 005	22 41 044	24 09 092	29 29 148	37 26 223	44 33 312	34 53 333
112	40 44 004	23 11 044	24 52 091	29 52 148	36 57 223	44 01 311	34 33 332
113	40 47 003	23 41 043	25 35 090	30 15 147	36 28 222	43 28 310	34 12 331
114	40 48 001	24 10 042	26 18 090	30 38 147	35 59 222	42 54 309	33 51 330
115	40 49 000	24 38 041	27 02 089	31 02 147	35 30 222	42 21 308	33 28 329
116	40 48 359	25 06 040	27 45 088	31 25 146	35 01 221	41 46 307	33 06 327
117	40 47 357	25 33 039	28 28 087	31 49 146	34 33 221	41 11 306	32 42 326
118	40 44 356	26 00 038	29 11 087	32 14 146	34 05 221	40 36 305	32 18 325
119	40 41 355	26 26 037	29 54 086	32 38 145	33 36 220	40 00 304	31 53 324
	REGULUS	◆SPICA	RIGIL KENT	◆ACHERNAR	RIGEL	BETELGEUSE	◆PROCYON
120	26 52 036	13 52 092	33 02 145	33 09 220	39 24 302	31 27 323	40 37 353
121	27 17 035	14 35 092	33 27 145	32 41 220	38 47 301	31 01 322	40 31 352
122	27 41 034	15 18 091	33 52 145	32 13 219	38 10 300	30 34 321	40 25 351
123	28 05 033	16 02 090	34 17 144	31 46 219	37 33 300	30 07 320	40 17 350
124	28 28 032	16 45 090	34 43 144	31 19 219	36 55 299	29 39 319	40 09 348
125	28 50 031	17 28 089	35 08 144	30 52 218	36 17 298	29 11 318	40 00 347
126	29 12 030	18 11 088	35 34 143	30 25 218	35 39 297	28 41 317	39 50 346
127	29 33 029	18 54 087	36 00 143	29 59 218	35 00 296	28 12 316	39 39 344
128	29 54 028	19 37 087	36 25 143	29 32 217	34 21 295	27 42 315	39 27 343
129	30 13 027	20 20 086	36 52 143	29 06 217	33 42 294	27 11 314	39 14 342
130	30 32 026	21 03 085	37 18 142	28 41 217	33 02 293	26 40 313	39 00 341
131	30 51 024	21 46 085	37 44 142	28 15 216	32 22 292	26 08 312	38 45 339
132	31 08 023	22 29 084	38 11 142	27 50 216	31 42 291	25 36 311	38 29 338
133	31 25 022	23 12 083	38 38 142	27 24 215	31 02 290	25 03 310	38 13 337
134	31 41 021	23 55 082	39 05 141	27 00 215	30 22 290	24 30 310	37 56 336
	REGULUS	◆SPICA	RIGIL KENT	◆ACHERNAR	CANOPUS	SIRIUS	◆PROCYON
135	31 56 020	24 38 082	39 32 141	26 35 215	63 05 237	50 44 303	37 38 335
136	32 10 019	25 21 081	39 59 141	26 10 214	62 29 237	50 07 302	37 19 333
137	32 24 018	26 03 080	40 26 141	25 46 214	61 53 237	49 31 301	36 59 332
138	32 37 017	26 46 079	40 54 140	25 22 213	61 16 237	48 53 300	36 38 331
139	32 49 016	27 28 079	41 21 140	24 59 213	60 40 237	48 16 299	36 17 330
140	33 00 014	28 10 078	41 49 140	24 35 213	60 03 237	47 38 298	35 55 329
141	33 10 013	28 52 077	42 17 140	24 12 212	59 27 237	46 59 297	35 32 328
142	33 20 012	29 34 076	42 45 140	23 49 212	58 51 237	46 21 296	35 09 326
143	33 28 011	30 16 076	43 13 139	23 27 211	58 14 237	45 42 295	34 45 325
144	33 36 010	30 58 075	43 41 139	23 05 211	57 38 237	45 02 294	34 20 324
145	33 43 009	31 39 074	44 09 139	22 43 210	57 02 237	44 22 293	33 54 323
146	33 49 007	32 21 073	44 37 139	22 21 210	56 26 237	43 42 292	33 28 322
147	33 54 006	33 02 072	45 06 139	21 59 210	55 50 237	43 02 291	33 01 321
148	33 58 005	33 43 071	45 34 139	21 38 209	55 13 237	42 22 290	32 34 320
149	34 02 004	34 24 071	46 03 138	21 17 209	54 37 237	41 41 289	32 06 319
	REGULUS	◆SPICA	RIGIL KENT	◆ACHERNAR	CANOPUS	SIRIUS	◆PROCYON
150	34 04 003	35 04 070	46 32 138	20 57 208	54 01 236	41 00 288	31 37 318
151	34 06 002	35 45 069	47 00 138	20 37 208	53 25 236	40 19 287	31 08 317
152	34 06 000	36 25 068	47 29 138	20 17 207	52 50 236	39 38 286	30 38 316
153	34 06 359	37 05 067	47 58 138	19 57 207	52 14 236	38 56 285	30 08 315
154	34 05 358	37 44 066	48 27 138	19 38 206	51 38 236	38 14 285	29 37 314
155	34 03 357	38 24 065	48 56 138	19 19 206	51 02 236	37 33 284	29 05 313
156	34 00 356	39 03 064	49 25 138	19 00 205	50 27 235	36 51 283	28 34 312
157	33 57 354	39 41 063	49 54 138	18 41 205	49 51 235	36 08 282	28 01 311
158	33 52 353	40 20 062	50 23 138	18 23 205	49 16 235	35 26 281	27 28 310
159	33 46 352	40 58 061	50 52 138	18 06 204	48 41 235	34 44 281	26 55 309
160	33 40 351	41 36 060	51 21 137	17 48 204	48 05 235	34 01 280	26 21 308
161	33 33 350	42 13 059	51 51 137	17 31 203	47 30 234	33 19 279	25 47 307
162	33 25 349	42 50 058	52 20 137	17 14 203	46 55 234	32 36 278	25 13 306
163	33 16 347	43 26 057	52 49 137	16 58 202	46 20 234	31 53 277	24 38 306
164	33 06 346	44 02 056	53 18 137	16 42 202	45 45 234	31 10 277	24 03 305
	SPICA	◆ANTARES	RIGIL KENT	ACHERNAR	◆CANOPUS	SIRIUS	◆REGULUS
165	44 38 055	23 07 105	53 47 137	16 26 201	45 11 233	30 28 276	32 55 345
166	45 13 054	23 49 105	54 16 138	16 11 201	44 36 233	29 45 275	32 44 344
167	45 48 053	24 31 104	54 46 138	15 56 200	44 02 233	29 02 274	32 32 343
168	46 22 052	25 13 103	55 15 138	15 41 200	43 27 233	28 18 274	32 18 342
169	46 56 050	25 55 103	55 44 138	15 27 199	42 53 232	27 35 273	32 04 341
170	47 29 049	26 37 102	56 13 138	15 13 199	42 19 232	26 52 272	31 50 339
171	48 01 048	27 19 101	56 42 138	14 59 198	41 45 232	26 09 272	31 34 338
172	48 33 047	28 02 101	57 11 138	14 46 198	41 12 231	25 26 271	31 18 337
173	49 04 046	28 44 100	57 39 138	14 33 197	40 38 231	24 43 270	31 01 336
174	49 34 044	29 27 100	58 08 138	14 21 197	40 04 231	24 00 270	30 43 335
175	50 04 043	30 09 099	58 37 139	14 09 196	39 31 230	23 17 269	30 25 334
176	50 33 042	30 52 098	59 05 139	13 57 195	38 58 230	22 33 268	30 05 333
177	51 02 040	31 35 098	59 34 139	13 46 195	38 25 230	21 50 267	29 45 332
178	51 29 039	32 17 097	60 02 139	13 35 194	37 52 229	21 07 267	29 25 331
179	51 56 037	33 00 096	60 30 139	13 24 194	37 19 229	20 24 266	29 03 330

LHA ♈	Hc	Zn	Hc	Zn	Hc	Zn	Hc	Zn	Hc	Zn	Hc	Zn	Hc	Zn
	◆ARCTURUS		ANTARES		◆RIGIL KENT		ACHERNAR		CANOPUS		◆Suhail		REGULUS	
180	19 36	034	33 43	096	60 58	140	13 14	193	36 47	229	59 23	256	28 41	329
181	20 00	033	34 26	095	61 26	140	13 04	193	36 14	228	58 41	255	28 18	328
182	20 24	032	35 09	094	61 54	140	12 55	192	35 42	228	58 00	255	27 55	327
183	20 47	031	35 52	094	62 21	141	12 46	192	35 10	228	57 18	255	27 31	326
184	21 09	031	36 35	093	62 48	141	12 37	191	34 38	227	56 36	254	27 06	325
185	21 31	030	37 18	092	63 15	142	12 29	191	34 07	227	55 55	254	26 41	324
186	21 52	029	38 02	092	63 42	142	12 21	190	33 35	227	55 14	253	26 15	323
187	22 12	028	38 45	091	64 08	142	12 14	190	33 04	226	54 32	253	25 49	322
188	22 32	027	39 28	090	64 35	143	12 06	189	32 33	226	53 51	253	25 22	321
189	22 51	026	40 11	090	65 00	143	12 00	189	32 02	226	53 10	252	24 54	320
190	23 09	025	40 54	089	65 26	144	11 54	188	31 31	225	52 29	252	24 26	319
191	23 27	024	41 37	088	65 51	145	11 48	187	31 01	225	51 48	251	23 58	318
192	23 44	023	42 20	088	66 16	145	11 42	187	30 30	224	51 07	251	23 29	317
193	24 00	022	43 04	087	66 40	146	11 37	186	30 00	224	50 26	251	22 59	316
194	24 16	021	43 47	086	67 04	147	11 33	186	29 30	224	49 46	250	22 29	315
	◆ARCTURUS		ANTARES		◆Peacock		ACHERNAR		CANOPUS		◆Suhail		REGULUS	
195	24 31	020	44 30	085	25 45	145	11 29	185	29 01	223	49 05	250	21 58	314
196	24 45	019	45 13	085	26 09	145	11 25	185	28 31	223	48 25	249	21 27	313
197	24 59	018	45 56	084	26 34	145	11 22	184	28 02	222	47 44	249	20 55	313
198	25 12	017	46 39	083	26 59	144	11 19	184	27 33	222	47 04	248	20 23	312
199	25 24	016	47 21	082	27 25	144	11 16	183	27 04	222	46 24	248	19 51	311
200	25 35	015	48 04	081	27 50	143	11 14	183	26 36	221	45 44	248	19 18	310
201	25 46	014	48 47	081	28 16	143	11 12	182	26 07	221	45 04	247	18 45	309
202	25 56	013	49 29	080	28 42	143	11 11	181	25 39	220	44 25	247	18 11	308
203	26 05	012	50 12	079	29 08	142	11 10	181	25 12	220	43 45	246	17 37	307
204	26 13	011	50 54	078	29 35	142	11 10	180	24 44	219	43 05	246	17 02	307
205	26 21	010	51 36	077	30 01	142	11 10	180	24 17	219	42 26	246	16 27	306
206	26 28	009	52 18	076	30 28	141	11 10	179	23 50	219	41 47	245	15 52	305
207	26 34	007	53 00	075	30 55	141	11 11	179	23 23	218	41 08	245	15 17	304
208	26 39	006	53 42	074	31 23	141	11 12	178	22 57	218	40 29	244	14 41	303
209	26 43	005	54 23	073	31 50	140	11 14	178	22 30	217	39 50	244	14 05	303
	◆ARCTURUS		ANTARES		◆Peacock		ACHERNAR		CANOPUS		◆Suhail		SPICA	
210	26 47	004	55 04	072	32 18	140	11 16	177	22 05	217	39 11	243	56 26	345
211	26 50	003	55 45	071	32 46	139	11 18	176	21 39	216	38 33	243	56 14	343
212	26 52	002	56 26	070	33 14	139	11 21	176	21 13	216	37 54	243	56 00	341
213	26 53	001	57 07	069	33 43	139	11 24	175	20 48	215	37 16	242	55 46	340
214	26 54	000	57 47	068	34 11	138	11 28	175	20 24	215	36 38	242	55 30	338
215	26 53	359	58 27	067	34 40	138	11 32	174	19 59	214	36 00	241	55 14	336
216	26 52	358	59 07	066	35 09	138	11 37	174	19 35	214	35 22	241	54 56	335
217	26 50	357	59 46	065	35 38	137	11 42	173	19 11	213	34 45	240	54 37	333
218	26 48	356	60 25	064	36 07	137	11 47	173	18 47	213	34 07	240	54 17	331
219	26 44	355	61 03	062	36 36	137	11 53	172	18 24	212	33 30	239	53 56	330
220	26 40	354	61 41	061	37 06	137	11 59	172	18 01	212	32 53	239	53 34	328
221	26 35	353	62 18	060	37 36	136	12 06	171	17 38	211	32 16	239	53 10	327
222	26 29	352	62 55	058	38 06	136	12 13	170	17 16	211	31 39	238	52 46	325
223	26 22	351	63 32	057	38 36	136	12 20	170	16 54	210	31 03	238	52 21	324
224	26 15	350	64 07	055	39 06	135	12 28	169	16 32	210	30 27	237	51 56	323
	Rasalhague		◆Nunki		Peacock		ACHERNAR		◆ACRUX		SPICA		◆ARCTURUS	
225	23 18	042	39 44	090	39 36	135	12 36	169	61 04	215	51 29	321	26 06	349
226	23 46	041	40 27	089	40 07	135	12 44	168	60 39	216	51 01	320	25 58	347
227	24 14	040	41 11	088	40 37	135	12 53	168	60 14	216	50 33	318	25 48	346
228	24 42	039	41 54	088	41 08	134	13 03	167	59 49	216	50 04	317	25 37	345
229	25 09	038	42 37	087	41 39	134	13 13	167	59 23	216	49 34	316	25 26	344
230	25 35	037	43 20	086	42 10	134	13 23	166	58 57	217	49 04	314	25 14	343
231	26 01	036	44 03	086	42 41	134	13 33	166	58 31	217	48 33	313	25 01	342
232	26 26	035	44 46	085	43 13	133	13 44	165	58 05	217	48 01	312	24 48	341
233	26 50	034	45 29	084	43 44	133	13 55	165	57 39	217	47 28	311	24 34	340
234	27 14	033	46 12	083	44 16	133	14 07	164	57 13	218	46 55	309	24 19	339
235	27 38	032	46 55	082	44 47	133	14 19	164	56 46	218	46 22	308	24 03	338
236	28 00	031	47 37	082	45 19	133	14 32	163	56 20	218	45 48	307	23 47	337
237	28 22	030	48 20	081	45 51	132	14 44	162	55 53	218	45 13	306	23 30	336
238	28 44	029	49 03	080	46 23	132	14 57	162	55 27	218	44 38	305	23 12	335
239	29 04	028	49 45	079	46 55	132	15 11	161	55 00	218	44 02	304	22 54	334
	Rasalhague		◆ALTAIR		Peacock		◆ACHERNAR		ACRUX		◆SPICA		ARCTURUS	
240	29 24	027	15 41	060	47 27	132	15 25	161	54 33	218	43 26	303	22 35	333
241	29 43	026	16 18	060	48 00	132	15 39	160	54 06	219	42 50	302	22 15	332
242	30 02	025	16 55	059	48 32	131	15 54	160	53 39	219	42 13	301	21 55	332
243	30 20	024	17 32	058	49 04	131	16 09	159	53 12	219	41 35	300	21 34	331
244	30 37	023	18 08	057	49 37	131	16 24	159	52 45	219	40 58	299	21 13	330
245	30 53	022	18 45	056	50 09	131	16 40	158	52 18	219	40 20	298	20 51	329
246	31 09	021	19 20	055	50 42	131	16 56	158	51 51	219	39 41	297	20 28	328
247	31 23	019	19 56	055	51 15	131	17 12	157	51 24	219	39 02	296	20 05	327
248	31 37	018	20 31	054	51 47	131	17 29	157	50 57	219	38 23	295	19 41	326
249	31 50	017	21 05	053	52 20	131	17 46	157	50 30	219	37 44	294	19 16	325
250	32 03	016	21 39	052	52 53	130	18 03	156	50 03	219	37 05	293	18 51	324
251	32 14	015	22 13	051	53 26	130	18 21	156	49 36	219	36 25	292	18 26	323
252	32 25	014	22 47	050	53 59	130	18 39	155	49 09	219	35 45	291	18 00	322
253	32 35	013	23 20	049	54 31	130	18 57	155	48 42	219	35 04	290	17 33	321
254	32 44	012	23 52	048	55 04	130	19 16	154	48 15	219	34 24	289	17 06	321
	Rasalhague		◆ALTAIR		FOMALHAUT		◆ACHERNAR		RIGIL KENT		◆SPICA		Alphecca	
255	32 52	010	24 24	048	20 17	112	19 35	154	63 24	218	33 43	289	16 43	340
256	33 00	009	24 56	047	20 57	111	19 54	153	62 57	219	33 02	288	16 28	339
257	33 06	008	25 27	046	21 37	111	20 14	153	62 30	219	32 21	287	16 13	339
258	33 12	007	25 58	045	22 18	110	20 34	152	62 02	220	31 39	286	15 57	338
259	33 16	006	26 28	044	22 58	110	20 54	152	61 35	220	30 58	285	15 40	337
260	33 20	005	26 58	043	23 39	109	21 15	151	61 07	220	30 16	284	15 23	336
261	33 23	003	27 27	042	24 20	108	21 35	151	60 39	220	29 34	284	15 05	335
262	33 25	002	27 55	041	25 01	108	21 57	150	60 11	221	28 52	283	14 46	334
263	33 27	001	28 23	040	25 42	107	22 18	150	59 43	221	28 10	282	14 27	333
264	33 27	000	28 51	039	26 24	107	22 40	150	59 14	221	27 28	281	14 07	332
265	33 26	359	29 17	038	27 05	106	23 02	149	58 46	221	26 45	281	13 47	332
266	33 25	358	29 44	037	27 47	105	23 24	149	58 17	222	26 03	280	13 26	331
267	33 23	356	30 09	036	28 28	105	23 46	148	57 49	222	25 20	279	13 05	330
268	33 20	355	30 34	035	29 10	104	24 09	148	57 20	222	24 38	278	12 43	329
269	33 16	354	30 59	034	29 52	104	24 32	147	56 51	222	23 55	278	12 21	328

LHA ♈	Hc	Zn	Hc	Zn	Hc	Zn	Hc	Zn	Hc	Zn	Hc	Zn	Hc	Zn
	ALTAIR		Enif		◆FOMALHAUT		ACHERNAR		◆RIGIL KENT		ANTARES		◆Rasalhague	
270	31 22	033	15 54	058	30 34	103	24 56	147	56 22	222	64 48	307	33 11	353
271	31 45	032	16 30	058	31 16	102	25 19	147	55 53	222	64 13	305	33 05	352
272	32 08	031	17 07	057	31 58	102	25 43	146	55 24	222	63 38	304	32 58	351
273	32 29	030	17 42	056	32 40	101	26 07	146	54 55	222	63 01	302	32 51	349
274	32 50	028	18 18	055	33 23	101	26 32	145	54 26	222	62 25	301	32 42	348
275	33 10	027	18 53	054	34 05	100	26 56	145	53 57	223	61 47	299	32 33	347
276	33 30	026	19 28	053	34 48	099	27 21	145	53 27	223	61 09	298	32 23	346
277	33 49	025	20 03	053	35 30	099	27 46	144	52 58	223	60 31	297	32 12	345
278	34 06	024	20 37	052	36 13	098	28 11	144	52 29	223	59 52	295	32 01	344
279	34 24	023	21 10	051	36 56	098	28 37	143	52 00	223	59 13	294	31 48	343
280	34 40	022	21 44	050	37 39	097	29 03	143	51 31	223	58 34	293	31 35	341
281	34 55	020	22 16	049	38 22	096	29 29	143	51 02	222	57 54	292	31 21	340
282	35 10	019	22 49	048	39 04	096	29 55	142	50 32	222	57 13	291	31 06	339
283	35 24	018	23 21	047	39 47	095	30 22	142	50 03	222	56 33	290	30 50	338
284	35 37	017	23 52	046	40 30	094	30 48	142	49 34	222	55 52	289	30 34	337
	ALTAIR		Enif		◆FOMALHAUT		ACHERNAR		◆RIGIL KENT		ANTARES		◆Rasalhague	
285	35 49	016	24 23	045	41 14	094	31 15	141	49 05	222	55 11	288	30 17	336
286	36 00	015	24 54	045	41 57	093	31 42	141	48 36	222	54 30	287	29 59	335
287	36 11	013	25 24	044	42 40	092	32 10	141	48 07	222	53 49	286	29 40	334
288	36 20	012	25 53	043	43 23	092	32 37	140	47 38	222	53 07	285	29 21	333
289	36 29	011	26 22	042	44 06	091	33 05	140	47 10	222	52 25	284	29 01	332
290	36 37	010	26 51	041	44 49	090	33 33	140	46 41	222	51 43	283	28 40	331
291	36 43	008	27 19	040	45 32	090	34 01	139	46 12	222	51 01	282	28 18	330
292	36 49	007	27 46	039	46 15	089	34 29	139	45 43	221	50 19	281	27 56	329
293	36 54	006	28 13	038	46 59	088	34 57	139	45 15	221	49 36	280	27 33	328
294	36 58	005	28 39	037	47 42	088	35 26	138	44 46	221	48 54	279	27 10	327
295	37 02	004	29 04	036	48 25	087	35 55	138	44 18	221	48 11	279	26 46	326
296	37 04	002	29 29	035	49 08	086	36 24	138	43 50	221	47 28	278	26 21	325
297	37 05	001	29 53	034	49 51	085	36 53	137	43 22	221	46 46	277	25 56	324
298	37 05	000	30 17	033	50 34	085	37 22	137	42 54	220	46 03	276	25 30	323
299	37 05	359	30 40	032	51 17	084	37 52	137	42 26	220	45 20	275	25 04	322
	◆Enif		FOMALHAUT		◆ACHERNAR		RIGIL KENT		◆ANTARES		Rasalhague		ALTAIR	
300	31 02	031	52 00	083	38 22	136	41 58	220	44 37	275	24 37	321	37 03	357
301	31 24	029	52 43	082	38 51	136	41 30	220	43 54	274	24 09	320	37 01	356
302	31 45	028	53 25	081	39 21	136	41 02	220	43 11	273	23 41	319	36 58	355
303	32 05	027	54 08	080	39 51	136	40 35	219	42 28	273	23 12	318	36 53	354
304	32 24	026	54 50	080	40 22	135	40 08	219	41 44	272	22 43	317	36 48	352
305	32 43	025	55 33	079	40 52	135	39 40	219	41 01	271	22 13	316	36 42	351
306	33 01	024	56 15	078	41 22	135	39 13	219	40 18	270	21 43	315	36 35	350
307	33 18	023	56 57	077	41 53	135	38 46	219	39 35	270	21 13	314	36 27	349
308	33 34	022	57 39	076	42 24	134	38 20	218	38 52	269	20 42	313	36 18	348
309	33 50	021	58 21	075	42 55	134	37 53	218	38 09	268	20 10	313	36 08	346
310	34 05	019	59 02	074	43 26	134	37 26	218	37 26	268	19 38	312	35 58	345
311	34 19	018	59 44	073	43 57	134	37 00	218	36 42	267	19 06	311	35 46	344
312	34 32	017	60 25	072	44 28	134	36 34	217	35 59	266	18 33	310	35 34	343
313	34 44	016	61 06	071	44 59	133	36 08	217	35 16	266	17 59	309	35 21	342
314	34 55	015	61 46	070	45 31	133	35 42	217	34 33	265	17 26	308	35 07	340
	Enif		◆Diphda		ACHERNAR		Miaplacidus		◆RIGIL KENT		ANTARES		◆ALTAIR	
315	35 06	014	36 33	079	46 02	133	23 48	181	35 16	216	33 50	264	34 52	339
316	35 16	012	37 15	079	46 34	133	23 48	181	34 51	216	33 07	264	34 36	338
317	35 24	011	37 57	078	47 06	133	23 47	181	34 25	216	32 25	263	34 19	337
318	35 32	010	38 40	077	47 38	132	23 47	180	34 00	216	31 42	262	34 02	336
319	35 39	009	39 22	076	48 10	132	23 47	180	33 35	215	30 59	262	33 44	335
320	35 46	008	40 03	075	48 42	132	23 47	179	33 10	215	30 16	261	33 25	334
321	35 51	006	40 45	074	49 14	132	23 48	179	32 46	215	29 34	261	33 06	332
322	35 55	005	41 27	074	49 46	132	23 49	179	32 21	214	28 51	260	32 45	331
323	35 59	004	42 08	073	50 18	132	23 50	178	31 57	214	28 09	259	32 24	330
324	36 01	003	42 49	072	50 50	132	23 51	178	31 33	214	27 26	259	32 02	329
325	36 03	001	43 30	071	51 22	131	23 53	177	31 09	213	26 44	258	31 40	328
326	36 03	000	44 11	070	51 55	131	23 55	177	30 46	213	26 02	257	31 17	327
327	36 03	359	44 51	069	52 27	131	23 57	177	30 22	213	25 20	257	30 53	326
328	36 02	358	45 31	068	53 00	131	24 00	176	29 59	212	24 38	256	30 28	325
329	36 00	357	46 11	067	53 32	131	24 03	176	29 36	212	23 56	256	30 03	324
	◆Diphda		ACHERNAR		◆Miaplacidus		RIGIL KENT		Nunki		◆ALTAIR		Enif	
330	46 51	066	54 05	131	24 06	176	29 13	212	49 07	280	29 37	323	35 57	355
331	47 30	065	54 37	131	24 09	175	28 51	211	48 24	279	29 11	322	35 53	354
332	48 09	064	55 10	131	24 13	175	28 29	211	47 41	278	28 44	321	35 48	353
333	48 48	063	55 42	131	24 17	174	28 06	211	46 59	278	28 16	320	35 42	352
334	49 26	062	56 15	131	24 21	174	27 45	210	46 16	277	27 48	319	35 36	351
335	50 04	061	56 47	131	24 26	174	27 23	210	45 33	276	27 20	318	35 28	349
336	50 41	060	57 20	131	24 31	173	27 02	209	44 50	275	26 50	317	35 20	348
337	51 18	059	57 52	131	24 36	173	26 41	209	44 07	275	26 21	316	35 11	347
338	51 55	057	58 25	131	24 41	173	26 20	209	43 24	274	25 50	315	35 00	346
339	52 31	056	58 57	131	24 47	172	25 59	208	42 41	273	25 20	314	34 49	345
340	53 06	055	59 29	131	24 53	172	25 39	208	41 58	272	24 48	313	34 38	343
341	53 42	054	60 02	132	24 59	172	25 19	208	41 15	272	24 17	312	34 25	342
342	54 16	052	60 34	132	25 06	171	24 59	207	40 32	271	23 44	311	34 11	341
343	54 50	051	61 06	132	25 12	171	24 39	207	39 48	270	23 12	310	33 57	340
344	55 23	050	61 38	132	25 19	170	24 20	206	39 05	270	22 39	310	33 42	339
	◆Alpheratz		Diphda		◆CANOPUS		RIGIL KENT		◆Nunki		ALTAIR		Enif	
345	15 08	016	55 56	048	23 19	142	24 01	206	38 22	269	22 05	309	33 26	338
346	15 19	015	56 28	047	23 46	142	23 42	206	37 39	268	21 31	308	33 09	337
347	15 30	014	56 59	045	24 13	141	23 24	205	36 56	267	20 57	307	32 51	335
348	15 40	013	57 29	044	24 40	141	23 06	205	36 13	267	20 22	306	32 33	334
349	15 49	012	57 59	042	25 08	140	22 48	204	35 30	266	19 47	305	32 14	333
350	15 58	011	58 27	041	25 35	140	22 30	204	34 47	265	19 12	304	31 54	332
351	16 06	010	58 55	039	26 03	139	22 13	203	34 04	265	18 36	304	31 34	331
352	16 13	009	59 22	038	26 32	139	21 56	203	33 21	264	18 00	303	31 12	330
353	16 20	008	59 48	036	27 00	139	21 39	203	32 38	264	17 23	302	30 50	329
354	16 26	008	60 13	034	27 29	138	21 23	202	31 55	263	16 46	301	30 28	328
355	16 31	007	60 36	032	27 58	138	21 07	202	31 12	262	16 09	300	30 04	327
356	16 36	006	60 59	031	28 27	137	20 51	201	30 29	262	15 32	299	29 40	326
357	16 40	005	61 20	029	28 56	137	20 36	201	29 47	261	14 54	299	29 16	325
358	16 43	004	61 41	027	29 26	136	20 20	200	29 04	260	14 16	298	28 51	324
359	16 46	003	62 00	025	29 56	136	20 05	200	28 22	260	13 38	297	28 25	323

LHA ♈	Hc	Zn	Hc	Zn	Hc	Zn	Hc	Zn	Hc	Zn	Hc	Zn	Hc	Zn
	Alpheratz		Hamal		◆RIGEL		CANOPUS		◆RIGIL KENT		Peacock		◆Enif	
0	15 48	002	15 31	030	13 41	088	31 09	135	20 47	200	55 23	231	27 11	322
1	15 49	001	15 52	029	14 23	087	31 39	135	20 33	199	54 51	231	26 45	321
2	15 50	000	16 12	029	15 05	086	32 09	134	20 20	199	54 18	231	26 18	320
3	15 49	359	16 32	028	15 48	086	32 39	134	20 06	198	53 45	231	25 50	319
4	15 49	358	16 52	027	16 30	085	33 10	134	19 53	198	53 12	230	25 22	318
5	15 47	358	17 10	026	17 12	084	33 41	133	19 40	197	52 39	230	24 54	317
6	15 45	357	17 29	025	17 54	084	34 12	133	19 28	197	52 07	230	24 24	316
7	15 42	356	17 46	024	18 37	083	34 43	133	19 16	196	51 34	230	23 55	315
8	15 39	355	18 03	023	19 19	082	35 14	132	19 04	196	51 02	230	23 25	314
9	15 35	354	18 20	022	20 01	081	35 46	132	18 53	195	50 29	230	22 54	313
10	15 30	353	18 35	021	20 42	081	36 17	131	18 41	195	49 57	230	22 23	313
11	15 24	352	18 50	020	21 24	080	36 49	131	18 31	194	49 24	230	21 52	312
12	15 18	351	19 05	019	22 06	079	37 21	131	18 20	194	48 52	229	21 20	311
13	15 11	350	19 18	018	22 48	078	37 54	130	18 10	194	48 20	229	20 47	310
14	15 04	349	19 32	017	23 29	078	38 26	130	18 00	193	47 48	229	20 15	309
	◆Hamal		RIGEL		◆CANOPUS		RIGIL KENT		◆Peacock		FOMALHAUT		Alpheratz	
15	19 44	017	24 10	077	38 59	130	17 51	193	47 16	229	61 34	292	14 56	349
16	19 56	016	24 52	076	39 31	129	17 42	192	46 44	229	60 55	291	14 47	348
17	20 07	015	25 33	075	40 04	129	17 33	192	46 13	228	60 15	290	14 38	347
18	20 17	014	26 14	074	40 37	129	17 25	191	45 41	228	59 35	289	14 27	346
19	20 27	013	26 55	074	41 11	128	17 17	191	45 09	228	58 55	288	14 17	345
20	20 36	012	27 35	073	41 44	128	17 09	190	44 38	228	58 14	287	14 06	344
21	20 44	011	28 16	072	42 17	128	17 02	190	44 07	227	57 33	286	13 54	343
22	20 52	010	28 56	071	42 51	127	16 55	189	43 35	227	56 53	285	13 41	342
23	20 59	009	29 36	070	43 25	127	16 49	189	43 04	227	56 11	284	13 28	341
24	21 05	008	30 16	069	43 59	127	16 42	188	42 33	227	55 30	283	13 14	341
25	21 10	007	30 55	069	44 33	126	16 37	188	42 03	226	54 49	282	13 00	340
26	21 15	006	31 35	068	45 07	126	16 31	187	41 32	226	54 07	281	12 45	339
27	21 19	005	32 14	067	45 41	126	16 26	187	41 01	226	53 25	280	12 29	338
28	21 22	004	32 53	066	46 16	126	16 21	186	40 31	226	52 44	279	12 13	337
29	21 25	003	33 31	065	46 50	125	16 17	186	40 01	225	52 02	279	11 56	336
	◆Hamal		RIGEL		SIRIUS		◆CANOPUS		RIGIL KENT		◆Peacock		FOMALHAUT	
30	21 27	002	34 10	064	24 46	089	47 25	125	16 13	185	39 31	225	51 20	278
31	21 28	001	34 48	063	25 29	089	48 00	125	16 09	185	39 01	225	50 38	277
32	21 28	000	35 26	062	26 11	088	48 35	125	16 06	184	38 31	224	49 55	276
33	21 28	359	36 03	061	26 54	087	49 10	124	16 03	184	38 02	224	49 13	275
34	21 27	358	36 40	060	27 36	086	49 45	124	16 01	183	37 32	224	48 31	274
35	21 25	357	37 17	059	28 18	086	50 20	124	15 59	183	37 03	223	47 49	274
36	21 22	356	37 53	058	29 01	085	50 55	124	15 57	182	36 34	223	47 06	273
37	21 19	355	38 29	057	29 43	084	51 31	123	15 56	182	36 05	223	46 24	272
38	21 15	354	39 05	056	30 25	083	52 06	123	15 55	181	35 36	222	45 42	272
39	21 10	353	39 40	055	31 07	083	52 42	123	15 54	181	35 08	222	44 59	271
40	21 05	352	40 15	054	31 49	082	53 17	123	15 54	180	34 39	222	44 17	270
41	20 59	351	40 49	053	32 31	081	53 53	123	15 54	180	34 11	221	43 34	269
42	20 52	350	41 23	052	33 13	080	54 29	122	15 54	179	33 43	221	42 52	269
43	20 44	349	41 56	051	33 55	080	55 05	122	15 55	179	33 15	221	42 09	268
44	20 36	348	42 29	050	34 36	079	55 41	122	15 57	178	32 48	220	41 27	267
	◆RIGEL		SIRIUS		CANOPUS		◆RIGIL KENT		Peacock		◆FOMALHAUT		Hamal	
45	43 01	049	35 18	078	56 17	122	15 58	178	32 20	220	40 45	267	20 27	347
46	43 33	048	35 59	077	56 53	122	16 00	177	31 53	220	40 02	266	20 17	346
47	44 04	047	36 41	076	57 29	122	16 03	177	31 26	219	39 20	265	20 07	345
48	44 34	045	37 22	075	58 05	121	16 05	176	30 59	219	38 38	265	19 56	344
49	45 04	044	38 03	075	58 41	121	16 08	176	30 33	219	37 56	264	19 44	343
50	45 33	043	38 44	074	59 17	121	16 12	175	30 06	218	37 13	263	19 32	343
51	46 02	042	39 24	073	59 54	121	16 16	175	29 40	218	36 31	263	19 19	342
52	46 30	040	40 05	072	60 30	121	16 20	174	29 14	217	35 49	262	19 05	341
53	46 57	039	40 45	071	61 06	121	16 25	174	28 49	217	35 07	261	18 50	340
54	47 23	038	41 25	070	61 43	121	16 30	173	28 23	217	34 25	261	18 35	339
55	47 49	037	42 05	069	62 19	121	16 35	173	27 58	216	33 43	260	18 20	338
56	48 14	035	42 44	068	62 55	121	16 41	172	27 33	216	33 02	260	18 03	337
57	48 38	034	43 24	067	63 32	121	16 47	172	27 09	215	32 20	259	17 46	336
58	49 01	032	44 03	066	64 08	121	16 53	171	26 44	215	31 38	258	17 29	335
59	49 23	031	44 41	065	64 44	121	17 00	171	26 20	215	30 57	258	17 11	334
	ALDEBARAN		◆SIRIUS		Suhail		◆RIGIL KENT		ACHERNAR		◆Diphda		Hamal	
60	27 54	010	45 20	064	36 56	118	17 07	170	65 02	228	41 16	287	16 52	333
61	28 01	009	45 58	063	37 34	117	17 14	170	64 30	228	40 35	287	16 33	332
62	28 07	008	46 36	062	38 11	117	17 22	169	63 58	229	39 55	286	16 13	331
63	28 12	007	47 13	061	38 49	116	17 31	169	63 27	229	39 14	285	15 52	331
64	28 17	006	47 50	060	39 27	116	17 39	168	62 54	229	38 33	284	15 31	330
65	28 21	005	48 27	059	40 06	115	17 48	168	62 22	229	37 51	283	15 09	329
66	28 24	003	49 03	058	40 44	115	17 57	167	61 50	229	37 10	282	14 47	328
67	28 26	002	49 39	057	41 22	115	18 07	167	61 18	230	36 29	281	14 24	327
68	28 27	001	50 14	056	42 01	114	18 17	166	60 45	230	35 47	281	14 01	326
69	28 28	000	50 49	054	42 40	114	18 27	166	60 13	230	35 05	280	13 37	325
70	28 27	359	51 23	053	43 19	113	18 38	165	59 41	230	34 23	279	13 13	325
71	28 26	358	51 56	052	43 58	113	18 49	165	59 08	230	33 41	278	12 48	324
72	28 25	357	52 30	051	44 37	112	19 00	164	58 36	230	32 59	278	12 23	323
73	28 22	356	53 02	049	45 16	112	19 12	164	58 03	230	32 17	277	11 57	322
74	28 18	355	53 34	048	45 56	111	19 24	163	57 31	230	31 35	276	11 30	321
	BETELGEUSE		◆SIRIUS		Suhail		◆RIGIL KENT		ACHERNAR		◆Diphda		ALDEBARAN	
75	36 06	017	54 05	047	46 35	111	19 36	163	56 58	230	30 53	275	28 14	354
76	36 18	016	54 36	045	47 15	111	19 49	162	56 26	230	30 11	275	28 09	353
77	36 30	015	55 05	044	47 55	110	20 02	162	55 53	230	29 28	274	28 03	352
78	36 40	014	55 34	042	48 35	110	20 15	161	55 21	230	28 46	273	27 57	350
79	36 50	012	56 03	041	49 15	109	20 29	161	54 48	230	28 04	272	27 49	349
80	36 58	011	56 30	039	49 55	109	20 43	161	54 16	230	27 21	272	27 41	348
81	37 06	010	56 56	038	50 35	108	20 57	160	53 43	230	26 39	271	27 32	347
82	37 13	009	57 22	036	51 15	108	21 12	160	53 11	230	25 56	270	27 22	346
83	37 19	007	57 47	035	51 56	108	21 27	159	52 38	230	25 14	269	27 12	345
84	37 24	006	58 10	033	52 36	107	21 42	159	52 06	229	24 31	269	27 00	344
85	37 28	005	58 33	031	53 17	107	21 58	158	51 34	229	23 49	268	26 48	343
86	37 31	004	58 54	030	53 57	106	22 13	158	51 02	229	23 07	267	26 35	342
87	37 34	002	59 15	028	54 38	106	22 30	157	50 30	229	22 24	267	26 22	341
88	37 35	001	59 34	026	55 19	105	22 46	157	49 58	229	21 42	266	26 08	340
89	37 35	000	59 52	024	56 00	105	23 03	157	49 26	229	21 00	265	25 53	339

LAT 45°S

LHA ♈	Hc	Zn	Hc	Zn	Hc	Zn	Hc	Zn	Hc	Zn	Hc	Zn	Hc	Zn
	PROCYON		Alphard		◆Suhail		RIGIL KENT		◆ACHERNAR		RIGEL		◆BETELGEUSE	
90	35 03	031	32 28	068	56 41	105	23 20	156	48 54	229	51 56	342	37 35	359
91	35 24	030	33 07	067	57 22	104	23 37	156	48 22	228	51 42	340	37 34	357
92	35 45	029	33 46	066	58 03	104	23 55	155	47 50	228	51 27	339	37 31	356
93	36 05	028	34 24	065	58 44	103	24 13	155	47 19	228	51 11	337	37 28	355
94	36 24	026	35 03	064	59 26	103	24 31	154	46 47	228	50 55	336	37 24	354
95	36 43	025	35 41	063	60 07	102	24 49	154	46 16	228	50 37	334	37 19	353
96	37 00	024	36 18	062	60 49	102	25 08	154	45 45	227	50 18	333	37 13	351
97	37 17	023	36 55	061	61 30	101	25 27	153	45 13	227	49 58	331	37 06	350
98	37 33	022	37 32	060	62 12	101	25 46	153	44 42	227	49 37	330	36 58	349
99	37 48	020	38 09	059	62 54	101	26 06	152	44 11	227	49 15	328	36 49	348
100	38 03	019	38 45	058	63 35	100	26 26	152	43 40	227	48 53	327	36 40	346
101	38 16	018	39 21	057	64 17	100	26 46	152	43 10	226	48 29	326	36 29	345
102	38 29	017	39 57	056	64 59	099	27 06	151	42 39	226	48 05	324	36 18	344
103	38 40	015	40 32	055	65 41	099	27 26	151	42 09	226	47 40	323	36 06	343
104	38 51	014	41 06	054	66 23	098	27 47	150	41 38	226	47 14	322	35 53	342
	PROCYON		REGULUS		◆Gienah		RIGIL KENT		◆ACHERNAR		RIGEL		◆BETELGEUSE	
105	39 01	013	18 53	049	19 56	095	28 08	150	41 08	225	46 47	320	35 39	340
106	39 10	012	19 25	049	20 39	095	28 30	150	40 38	225	46 19	319	35 24	339
107	39 18	010	19 56	048	21 21	094	28 51	149	40 08	225	45 51	318	35 09	338
108	39 25	009	20 28	047	22 03	093	29 13	149	39 38	224	45 23	317	34 53	337
109	39 32	008	20 58	046	22 46	093	29 35	149	39 09	224	44 53	315	34 35	336
110	39 37	006	21 29	045	23 28	092	29 57	148	38 39	224	44 23	314	34 18	335
111	39 41	005	21 58	044	24 10	091	30 20	148	38 10	224	43 52	313	33 59	333
112	39 44	004	22 28	043	24 53	090	30 42	147	37 41	223	43 21	312	33 40	332
113	39 47	003	22 56	042	25 35	090	31 05	147	37 12	223	42 49	311	33 19	331
114	39 48	001	23 25	041	26 18	089	31 28	147	36 43	223	42 17	310	32 59	330
115	39 49	000	23 52	040	27 00	088	31 52	146	36 15	222	41 44	308	32 37	329
116	39 48	359	24 20	039	27 43	088	32 15	146	35 46	222	41 10	307	32 15	328
117	39 47	357	24 46	039	28 25	087	32 39	146	35 18	222	40 36	306	31 52	327
118	39 45	356	25 13	038	29 07	086	33 03	145	34 50	221	40 02	305	31 28	326
119	39 41	355	25 38	037	29 50	085	33 27	145	34 22	221	39 27	304	31 04	325
	REGULUS		◆SPICA		RIGIL KENT		◆ACHERNAR		RIGEL		BETELGEUSE		◆PROCYON	
120	26 03	036	13 55	092	33 52	145	33 54	221	38 52	303	30 39	324	39 37	354
121	26 27	035	14 37	091	34 16	144	33 27	220	38 16	302	30 14	323	39 32	352
122	26 51	034	15 19	091	34 41	144	32 59	220	37 40	301	29 48	322	39 26	351
123	27 14	033	16 02	090	35 06	144	32 32	220	37 03	300	29 21	320	39 18	350
124	27 37	032	16 44	089	35 31	144	32 05	219	36 26	299	28 54	319	39 10	348
125	27 59	031	17 27	089	35 56	143	31 39	219	35 49	298	28 26	318	39 01	347
126	28 20	030	18 09	088	36 22	143	31 12	218	35 12	297	27 57	317	38 52	346
127	28 41	028	18 51	087	36 47	143	30 46	218	34 34	296	27 28	317	38 41	345
128	29 00	027	19 34	086	37 13	142	30 20	218	33 56	295	26 59	316	38 29	343
129	29 20	026	20 16	086	37 39	142	29 54	217	33 17	295	26 29	315	38 17	342
130	29 38	025	20 58	085	38 05	142	29 29	217	32 38	294	25 59	314	38 03	341
131	29 56	024	21 41	084	38 32	142	29 03	217	31 59	293	25 28	313	37 49	340
132	30 13	023	22 23	083	38 58	141	28 38	216	31 20	292	24 56	312	37 34	338
133	30 29	022	23 05	083	39 25	141	28 13	216	30 41	291	24 24	311	37 18	337
134	30 45	021	23 47	082	39 51	141	27 49	215	30 01	290	23 52	310	37 01	336
	REGULUS		◆SPICA		RIGIL KENT		◆ACHERNAR		CANOPUS		SIRIUS		◆PROCYON	
135	31 00	020	24 29	081	40 18	141	27 24	215	63 37	239	50 10	304	36 43	335
136	31 14	019	25 11	080	40 45	140	27 00	215	63 01	239	49 35	303	36 25	334
137	31 27	018	25 53	080	41 12	140	26 36	214	62 24	239	48 59	302	36 06	333
138	31 39	016	26 34	079	41 40	140	26 12	214	61 48	239	48 23	301	35 46	331
139	31 51	015	27 16	078	42 07	140	25 49	213	61 11	239	47 47	300	35 25	330
140	32 02	014	27 57	077	42 35	139	25 26	213	60 35	239	47 09	299	35 04	329
141	32 12	013	28 39	077	43 02	139	25 03	212	59 59	239	46 32	298	34 41	328
142	32 21	012	29 20	076	43 30	139	24 40	212	59 23	239	45 54	297	34 19	327
143	32 29	011	30 01	075	43 58	139	24 18	212	58 46	239	45 16	296	33 55	326
144	32 37	010	30 42	074	44 26	139	23 56	211	58 10	239	44 38	295	33 31	325
145	32 43	008	31 23	073	44 54	138	23 34	211	57 34	238	43 59	294	33 06	324
146	32 49	007	32 03	072	45 22	138	23 13	210	56 58	238	43 20	293	32 40	322
147	32 54	006	32 43	072	45 51	138	22 52	210	56 22	238	42 41	292	32 14	321
148	32 58	005	33 24	071	46 19	138	22 31	209	55 46	238	42 01	291	31 48	320
149	33 02	004	34 04	070	46 48	138	22 10	209	55 10	238	41 21	290	31 20	319
	REGULUS		◆SPICA		RIGIL KENT		◆ACHERNAR		CANOPUS		SIRIUS		◆PROCYON	
150	33 04	003	34 43	069	47 16	138	21 50	208	54 34	238	40 41	289	30 52	318
151	33 06	002	35 23	068	47 45	137	21 30	208	53 58	237	40 01	288	30 24	317
152	33 06	000	36 02	067	48 14	137	21 10	208	53 22	237	39 20	287	29 55	316
153	33 06	359	36 41	066	48 42	137	20 50	207	52 47	237	38 40	286	29 25	315
154	33 05	358	37 20	065	49 11	137	20 31	207	52 11	237	37 59	285	28 55	314
155	33 03	357	37 58	064	49 40	137	20 12	206	51 36	237	37 18	284	28 24	313
156	33 00	356	38 36	064	50 09	137	19 54	206	51 00	236	36 37	284	27 53	312
157	32 57	355	39 14	063	50 38	137	19 36	205	50 25	236	35 55	283	27 22	311
158	32 52	353	39 52	062	51 07	137	19 18	205	49 50	236	35 14	282	26 50	310
159	32 47	352	40 29	061	51 36	137	19 00	204	49 15	236	34 32	281	26 17	310
160	32 41	351	41 06	060	52 05	137	18 43	204	48 40	235	33 51	280	25 44	309
161	32 34	350	41 42	059	52 34	137	18 26	203	48 05	235	33 09	280	25 11	308
162	32 26	349	42 18	058	53 04	137	18 10	203	47 30	235	32 27	279	24 37	307
163	32 17	348	42 54	056	53 33	137	17 54	202	46 55	235	31 45	278	24 03	306
164	32 08	346	43 29	055	54 02	137	17 38	202	46 21	234	31 03	277	23 28	305
	SPICA		◆ANTARES		RIGIL KENT		ACHERNAR		◆CANOPUS		SIRIUS		◆REGULUS	
165	44 03	054	23 23	105	54 31	137	17 22	201	45 46	234	30 21	277	31 57	345
166	44 38	053	24 04	104	55 00	137	17 07	201	45 12	234	29 39	276	31 46	344
167	45 11	052	24 45	103	55 30	137	16 52	200	44 38	234	28 57	275	31 34	343
168	45 44	051	25 26	103	55 59	137	16 38	200	44 04	233	28 14	274	31 21	342
169	46 17	050	26 08	102	56 28	137	16 23	199	43 30	233	27 32	274	31 08	341
170	46 49	048	26 49	102	56 57	137	16 10	199	42 56	233	26 50	273	30 53	340
171	47 21	047	27 31	101	57 26	137	15 56	198	42 22	232	26 07	272	30 38	339
172	47 51	046	28 13	100	57 55	137	15 43	198	41 49	232	25 25	271	30 23	338
173	48 22	045	28 54	100	58 24	137	15 31	197	41 15	232	24 42	271	30 06	336
174	48 51	043	29 36	099	58 53	137	15 18	197	40 42	231	24 00	270	29 49	335
175	49 20	042	30 18	098	59 21	137	15 06	196	40 09	231	23 18	269	29 31	334
176	49 48	041	31 00	098	59 50	138	14 55	196	39 36	231	22 35	269	29 12	333
177	50 16	040	31 42	097	60 19	138	14 44	195	39 03	230	21 53	268	28 52	332
178	50 42	038	32 24	096	60 47	138	14 33	195	38 31	230	21 10	267	28 32	331
179	51 08	037	33 07	096	61 15	138	14 22	194	37 58	230	20 28	266	28 11	330

LHA ♈	Hc	Zn	Hc	Zn	Hc	Zn	Hc	Zn	Hc	Zn	Hc	Zn	Hc	Zn
	◆ ARCTURUS		ANTARES		◆ RIGIL KENT		ACHERNAR		CANOPUS		◆ Suhail		REGULUS	
180	18 47	034	33 49	095	61 43	139	14 12	193	37 26	229	59 37	257	27 50	329
181	19 10	033	34 31	094	62 12	139	14 03	193	36 54	229	58 56	257	27 28	328
182	19 33	032	35 14	094	62 39	139	13 53	192	36 22	229	58 15	256	27 05	327
183	19 55	031	35 56	093	63 07	139	13 44	192	35 50	228	57 33	256	26 41	326
184	20 17	030	36 38	092	63 34	140	13 36	191	35 19	228	56 52	256	26 17	325
185	20 38	029	37 21	092	64 02	140	13 28	191	34 47	228	56 11	255	25 53	324
186	20 59	028	38 03	091	64 29	141	13 20	190	34 16	227	55 30	255	25 28	323
187	21 19	028	38 45	090	64 56	141	13 13	190	33 45	227	54 49	254	25 02	322
188	21 38	027	39 28	090	65 22	142	13 06	189	33 14	226	54 08	254	24 35	321
189	21 57	026	40 10	089	65 48	142	12 59	189	32 44	226	53 28	253	24 08	320
190	22 15	025	40 53	088	66 14	143	12 53	188	32 13	226	52 47	253	23 41	319
191	22 32	024	41 35	087	66 40	143	12 47	187	31 43	225	52 07	253	23 13	318
192	22 49	023	42 17	087	67 05	144	12 42	187	31 13	225	51 26	252	22 45	317
193	23 05	022	43 00	086	67 30	145	12 37	186	30 43	224	50 46	252	22 16	316
194	23 20	021	43 42	085	67 54	145	12 33	186	30 14	224	50 06	251	21 46	315
	◆ ARCTURUS		ANTARES		◆ Peacock		ACHERNAR		CANOPUS		◆ Suhail		REGULUS	
195	23 35	020	44 24	084	26 34	145	12 28	185	29 44	224	49 26	251	21 16	315
196	23 49	019	45 07	084	26 58	145	12 25	185	29 15	223	48 45	250	20 46	314
197	24 02	018	45 49	083	27 23	144	12 21	184	28 46	223	48 06	250	20 15	313
198	24 14	017	46 31	082	27 48	144	12 19	184	28 17	222	47 26	249	19 43	312
199	24 26	016	47 13	081	28 13	144	12 16	183	27 49	222	46 46	249	19 12	311
200	24 37	015	47 55	080	28 38	143	12 14	183	27 21	221	46 07	249	18 39	310
201	24 48	014	48 36	080	29 04	143	12 12	182	26 53	221	45 27	248	18 07	309
202	24 57	013	49 18	079	29 30	142	12 11	181	26 25	221	44 48	248	17 34	308
203	25 06	012	50 00	078	29 56	142	12 10	181	25 58	220	44 09	247	17 00	308
204	25 14	011	50 41	077	30 22	142	12 10	180	25 30	220	43 29	247	16 27	307
205	25 22	010	51 22	076	30 48	141	12 10	180	25 03	219	42 51	246	15 52	306
206	25 28	008	52 03	075	31 15	141	12 10	179	24 37	219	42 12	246	15 18	305
207	25 34	007	52 44	074	31 42	140	12 11	179	24 10	218	41 33	246	14 43	304
208	25 39	006	53 25	073	32 09	140	12 12	178	23 44	218	40 55	245	14 08	304
209	25 44	005	54 05	072	32 36	140	12 14	178	23 18	217	40 16	245	13 32	303
	◆ ARCTURUS		ANTARES		◆ Peacock		ACHERNAR		CANOPUS		◆ Suhail		SPICA	
210	25 47	004	54 46	071	33 04	139	12 16	177	22 53	217	39 38	244	55 28	345
211	25 50	003	55 26	070	33 31	139	12 18	176	22 27	216	39 00	244	55 16	343
212	25 52	002	56 05	069	33 59	139	12 21	176	22 02	216	38 22	243	55 04	342
213	25 53	001	56 45	068	34 27	138	12 24	175	21 37	216	37 44	243	54 50	340
214	25 54	000	57 24	067	34 56	138	12 28	175	21 13	215	37 06	242	54 35	339
215	25 53	359	58 03	066	35 24	138	12 32	174	20 49	215	36 29	242	54 19	337
216	25 52	358	58 41	064	35 53	137	12 36	174	20 25	214	35 51	241	54 01	335
217	25 50	357	59 19	063	36 22	137	12 41	173	20 01	214	35 14	241	53 43	334
218	25 48	356	59 57	062	36 51	137	12 47	173	19 38	213	34 37	241	53 24	332
219	25 44	355	60 34	061	37 20	136	12 52	172	19 15	213	34 00	240	53 04	331
220	25 40	354	61 11	059	37 49	136	12 58	171	18 52	212	33 24	240	52 42	329
221	25 35	353	61 47	058	38 19	136	13 05	171	18 30	212	32 47	239	52 20	328
222	25 29	352	62 23	057	38 49	135	13 12	170	18 08	211	32 11	239	51 57	326
223	25 23	351	62 58	055	39 18	135	13 19	170	17 46	211	31 35	238	51 33	325
224	25 16	350	63 33	053	39 48	135	13 27	169	17 24	210	30 59	238	51 08	323
	Rasalhague		◆ Nunki		Peacock		ACHERNAR		◆ ACRUX		SPICA		◆ ARCTURUS	
225	22 33	042	39 44	089	40 19	135	13 35	169	61 53	216	50 42	322	25 08	349
226	23 01	041	40 26	088	40 49	134	13 43	168	61 28	217	50 15	320	24 59	348
227	23 28	040	41 08	088	41 19	134	13 52	168	61 02	217	49 48	319	24 49	347
228	23 55	039	41 51	087	41 50	134	14 01	167	60 37	217	49 20	318	24 39	346
229	24 21	038	42 33	086	42 21	133	14 11	167	60 11	217	48 51	317	24 28	345
230	24 47	037	43 15	085	42 52	133	14 21	166	59 45	218	48 21	315	24 17	343
231	25 12	036	43 58	085	43 23	133	14 31	166	59 19	218	47 51	314	24 04	342
232	25 37	035	44 40	084	43 54	133	14 42	165	58 53	218	47 20	313	23 51	341
233	26 01	034	45 22	083	44 25	132	14 53	165	58 26	218	46 49	312	23 37	340
234	26 24	033	46 04	082	44 56	132	15 05	164	58 00	219	46 17	310	23 23	339
235	26 47	032	46 46	081	45 28	132	15 17	163	57 34	219	45 44	309	23 07	338
236	27 09	031	47 28	081	45 59	132	15 29	163	57 07	219	45 11	308	22 51	337
237	27 30	030	48 10	080	46 31	132	15 42	162	56 40	219	44 37	307	22 35	337
238	27 51	029	48 52	079	47 03	131	15 55	162	56 13	219	44 03	306	22 18	336
239	28 11	028	49 33	078	47 35	131	16 08	161	55 47	219	43 28	305	22 00	335
	Rasalhague		◆ ALTAIR		Peacock		◆ ACHERNAR		ACRUX		◆ SPICA		ARCTURUS	
240	28 31	027	15 11	060	48 07	131	16 22	161	55 20	219	42 53	304	21 41	334
241	28 49	026	15 48	059	48 39	131	16 36	160	54 53	219	42 18	302	21 22	333
242	29 08	025	16 24	058	49 11	131	16 50	160	54 26	220	41 42	301	21 02	332
243	29 25	024	17 00	058	49 43	130	17 05	159	53 59	220	41 05	300	20 42	331
244	29 41	022	17 36	057	50 16	130	17 20	159	53 32	220	40 29	299	20 21	330
245	29 57	021	18 11	056	50 48	130	17 36	158	53 05	220	39 51	298	19 59	329
246	30 12	020	18 46	055	51 21	130	17 51	158	52 38	220	39 14	297	19 37	328
247	30 27	019	19 21	054	51 53	130	18 08	157	52 11	220	38 36	296	19 14	327
248	30 40	018	19 55	053	52 26	130	18 24	157	51 43	220	37 58	296	18 51	326
249	30 53	017	20 29	053	52 59	130	18 41	156	51 16	220	37 20	295	18 27	325
250	31 05	016	21 02	052	53 31	129	18 58	156	50 49	220	36 41	294	18 03	324
251	31 16	015	21 36	051	54 04	129	19 16	155	50 22	220	36 02	293	17 38	323
252	31 27	014	22 08	050	54 37	129	19 33	155	49 55	219	35 23	292	17 12	323
253	31 36	013	22 41	049	55 10	129	19 51	154	49 28	219	34 43	291	16 46	322
254	31 45	011	23 12	048	55 43	129	20 10	154	49 01	219	34 03	290	16 19	321
	Rasalhague		◆ ALTAIR		FOMALHAUT		◆ ACHERNAR		RIGIL KENT		◆ SPICA		Alphecca	
255	31 53	010	23 44	047	20 39	112	20 29	153	64 10	220	33 23	289	15 47	340
256	32 00	009	24 15	046	21 19	111	20 48	153	63 43	220	32 43	288	15 32	340
257	32 07	008	24 45	045	21 59	110	21 07	153	63 16	220	32 03	288	15 17	339
258	32 12	007	25 15	044	22 38	110	21 27	152	62 48	221	31 22	287	15 01	338
259	32 17	006	25 45	044	23 18	109	21 47	152	62 20	221	30 42	286	14 45	337
260	32 20	005	26 13	043	23 59	109	22 07	151	61 52	221	30 01	285	14 28	336
261	32 23	003	26 42	042	24 39	108	22 28	151	61 24	222	29 20	284	14 10	335
262	32 25	002	27 10	041	25 19	107	22 49	150	60 56	222	28 38	283	13 52	334
263	32 27	001	27 37	040	26 00	107	23 10	150	60 28	222	27 57	283	13 34	333
264	32 27	000	28 04	039	26 40	106	23 31	149	59 59	222	27 16	282	13 14	333
265	32 26	359	28 30	038	27 21	106	23 53	149	59 30	223	26 34	281	12 54	332
266	32 25	358	28 56	037	28 02	105	24 15	149	59 02	223	25 52	280	12 34	331
267	32 23	357	29 21	036	28 43	104	24 37	148	58 33	223	25 11	280	12 13	330
268	32 20	355	29 45	035	29 24	104	25 00	148	58 04	223	24 29	279	11 52	329
269	32 16	354	30 09	033	30 06	103	25 23	147	57 35	223	23 47	278	11 29	328

LHA ♈	Hc	Zn	Hc	Zn	Hc	Zn	Hc	Zn	Hc	Zn	Hc	Zn	Hc	Zn
	ALTAIR		Enif		◆ FOMALHAUT		ACHERNAR		◆ RIGIL KENT		ANTARES		◆ Rasalhague	
270	30 32	032	15 22	058	30 47	102	25 46	147	57 06	223	64 12	308	32 11	353
271	30 54	031	15 58	057	31 29	102	26 09	146	56 37	223	63 38	307	32 06	352
272	31 16	030	16 34	056	32 10	101	26 33	146	56 08	223	63 04	305	31 59	351
273	31 37	029	17 09	056	32 52	101	26 57	146	55 39	223	62 29	304	31 52	350
274	31 57	028	17 44	055	33 34	100	27 21	145	55 10	223	61 53	302	31 44	348
275	32 17	027	18 18	054	34 15	099	27 45	145	54 40	223	61 17	301	31 35	347
276	32 36	026	18 52	053	34 57	099	28 10	144	54 11	223	60 40	300	31 25	346
277	32 54	025	19 26	052	35 39	098	28 35	144	53 42	223	60 03	298	31 14	345
278	33 12	024	19 59	051	36 21	097	29 00	144	53 13	223	59 26	297	31 03	344
279	33 28	023	20 32	051	37 03	097	29 25	143	52 44	223	58 48	296	30 51	343
280	33 44	021	21 05	050	37 46	096	29 51	143	52 15	223	58 09	295	30 38	342
281	33 59	020	21 37	049	38 28	096	30 17	142	51 45	223	57 31	293	30 24	341
282	34 13	019	22 09	048	39 10	095	30 43	142	51 16	223	56 51	292	30 10	339
283	34 27	018	22 40	047	39 52	094	31 09	142	50 47	223	56 12	291	29 54	338
284	34 39	017	23 11	046	40 35	094	31 35	141	50 18	223	55 32	290	29 38	337
	ALTAIR		Enif		◆ FOMALHAUT		ACHERNAR		◆ RIGIL KENT		ANTARES		◆ Rasalhague	
285	34 51	016	23 41	045	41 17	093	32 02	141	49 49	223	54 52	289	29 22	336
286	35 02	014	24 11	044	41 59	092	32 29	141	49 20	223	54 12	288	29 04	335
287	35 12	013	24 40	043	42 42	091	32 56	140	48 52	223	53 32	287	28 46	334
288	35 22	012	25 09	042	43 24	091	33 23	140	48 23	223	52 51	286	28 27	333
289	35 30	011	25 37	041	44 07	090	33 51	139	47 54	223	52 10	285	28 08	332
290	35 37	010	26 05	040	44 49	089	34 18	139	47 25	222	51 29	284	27 47	331
291	35 44	008	26 32	039	45 31	089	34 46	139	46 57	222	50 48	283	27 26	330
292	35 50	007	26 59	038	46 14	088	35 14	138	46 28	222	50 06	282	27 05	329
293	35 55	006	27 25	037	46 56	087	35 42	138	46 00	222	49 25	281	26 43	328
294	35 59	005	27 51	036	47 39	086	36 11	138	45 31	222	48 43	281	26 20	327
295	36 02	004	28 15	035	48 21	086	36 39	137	45 03	222	48 02	280	25 56	326
296	36 04	002	28 40	034	49 03	085	37 08	137	44 35	221	47 20	279	25 32	325
297	36 05	001	29 03	033	49 45	084	37 37	137	44 07	221	46 38	278	25 08	324
298	36 05	000	29 26	032	50 28	083	38 06	137	43 39	221	45 56	277	24 42	323
299	36 05	359	29 49	031	51 10	083	38 35	136	43 11	221	45 14	276	24 16	322
	◆ Enif		FOMALHAUT		◆ ACHERNAR		RIGIL KENT		◆ ANTARES		Rasalhague		ALTAIR	
300	30 11	030	51 52	082	39 05	136	42 44	221	44 31	276	23 50	321	36 03	357
301	30 32	029	52 34	081	39 34	136	42 16	220	43 49	275	23 23	320	36 01	356
302	30 52	028	53 16	080	40 04	135	41 48	220	43 07	274	22 56	319	35 58	355
303	31 12	027	53 57	079	40 34	135	41 21	220	42 24	273	22 28	318	35 54	354
304	31 30	026	54 39	078	41 04	135	40 54	220	41 42	273	21 59	317	35 49	353
305	31 49	025	55 20	077	41 34	135	40 27	220	41 00	272	21 30	316	35 43	351
306	32 06	024	56 02	076	42 05	134	40 00	219	40 17	271	21 01	316	35 36	350
307	32 23	023	56 43	075	42 35	134	39 33	219	39 35	271	20 31	315	35 28	349
308	32 39	021	57 24	074	43 06	134	39 06	219	38 52	270	20 00	314	35 19	348
309	32 54	020	58 04	073	43 36	134	38 40	219	38 10	269	19 29	313	35 10	347
310	33 08	019	58 45	072	44 07	133	38 14	218	37 28	268	18 58	312	35 00	345
311	33 22	018	59 25	071	44 38	133	37 47	218	36 45	268	18 26	311	34 48	344
312	33 34	017	60 05	070	45 09	133	37 21	218	36 03	267	17 54	310	34 36	343
313	33 46	016	60 45	069	45 40	133	36 56	217	35 20	266	17 21	309	34 24	342
314	33 57	015	61 25	068	46 12	132	36 30	217	34 38	266	16 48	309	34 10	341
	Enif		◆ Diphda		ACHERNAR		Miaplacidus		◆ RIGIL KENT		ANTARES		◆ ALTAIR	
315	34 08	013	36 21	079	46 43	132	24 48	181	36 04	217	33 56	265	33 56	339
316	34 17	012	37 03	078	47 14	132	24 48	181	35 39	217	33 14	264	33 40	338
317	34 26	011	37 44	077	47 46	132	24 47	181	35 14	216	32 31	264	33 24	337
318	34 33	010	38 26	076	48 18	132	24 47	180	34 49	216	31 49	263	33 07	336
319	34 40	009	39 07	075	48 50	131	24 47	180	34 24	216	31 07	262	32 50	335
320	34 46	007	39 48	075	49 21	131	24 47	179	33 59	215	30 25	262	32 31	334
321	34 51	006	40 29	074	49 53	131	24 48	179	33 35	215	29 43	261	32 12	333
322	34 55	005	41 09	073	50 25	131	24 49	179	33 11	215	29 01	260	31 53	332
323	34 59	004	41 50	072	50 57	131	24 50	178	32 47	214	28 20	260	31 32	331
324	35 01	003	42 30	071	51 30	131	24 51	178	32 23	214	27 38	259	31 11	329
325	35 03	001	43 10	070	52 02	131	24 53	177	31 59	214	26 56	259	30 49	328
326	35 03	000	43 50	069	52 34	130	24 55	177	31 36	213	26 15	258	30 26	327
327	35 03	359	44 29	068	53 06	130	24 57	177	31 13	213	25 33	257	30 03	326
328	35 02	358	45 08	067	53 39	130	25 00	176	30 50	213	24 52	257	29 39	325
329	35 00	357	45 47	066	54 11	130	25 03	176	30 27	212	24 11	256	29 15	324
	◆ Diphda		ACHERNAR		◆ Miaplacidus		RIGIL KENT		Nunki		◆ ALTAIR		Enif	
330	46 26	065	54 44	130	25 06	176	30 04	212	48 56	281	28 50	323	34 57	355
331	47 04	064	55 16	130	25 09	175	29 42	212	48 14	280	28 24	322	34 53	354
332	47 42	063	55 49	130	25 13	175	29 20	211	47 32	280	27 57	321	34 49	353
333	48 20	062	56 21	130	25 17	174	28 58	211	46 50	279	27 31	320	34 43	352
334	48 57	061	56 54	130	25 21	174	28 36	210	46 08	278	27 03	319	34 37	351
335	49 34	060	57 26	130	25 26	174	28 15	210	45 26	277	26 35	318	34 29	350
336	50 10	059	57 59	130	25 30	173	27 54	210	44 44	276	26 06	317	34 21	348
337	50 46	057	58 31	130	25 36	173	27 33	209	44 02	276	25 37	316	34 12	347
338	51 22	056	59 04	130	25 41	173	27 12	209	43 20	275	25 08	315	34 02	346
339	51 57	055	59 36	130	25 47	172	26 52	209	42 37	274	24 38	314	33 52	345
340	52 32	054	60 09	130	25 52	172	26 32	208	41 55	273	24 07	313	33 40	344
341	53 06	053	60 41	130	25 59	171	26 12	208	41 13	272	23 36	313	33 28	342
342	53 39	051	61 13	130	26 05	171	25 52	207	40 30	272	23 05	312	33 14	341
343	54 12	050	61 46	130	26 12	171	25 33	207	39 48	271	22 33	311	33 00	340
344	54 44	049	62 18	131	26 19	170	25 14	207	39 05	270	22 00	310	32 46	339
	◆ Alpheratz		Diphda		◆ CANOPUS		RIGIL KENT		◆ Nunki		ALTAIR		Enif	
345	14 10	016	55 15	047	24 07	142	24 55	206	38 23	270	21 28	309	32 30	338
346	14 21	015	55 46	046	24 33	141	24 37	206	37 40	269	20 54	308	32 14	337
347	14 32	014	56 16	044	25 00	141	24 18	205	36 58	268	20 21	307	31 57	336
348	14 42	013	56 46	043	25 27	140	24 00	205	36 16	268	19 47	306	31 39	335
349	14 51	012	57 14	041	25 54	140	23 43	204	35 33	267	19 12	305	31 20	333
350	14 59	011	57 42	040	26 21	139	23 25	204	34 51	266	18 38	305	31 01	332
351	15 07	010	58 08	038	26 49	139	23 08	204	34 09	266	18 03	304	30 41	331
352	15 14	009	58 34	037	27 17	138	22 51	203	33 26	265	17 27	303	30 20	330
353	15 21	008	58 59	035	27 45	138	22 35	203	32 44	264	16 51	302	29 59	329
354	15 27	008	59 23	033	28 13	138	22 19	202	32 02	264	16 15	301	29 37	328
355	15 32	007	59 45	032	28 42	137	22 03	202	31 20	263	15 39	301	29 14	327
356	15 36	006	60 07	030	29 11	137	21 47	201	30 38	262	15 02	300	28 51	326
357	15 40	005	60 28	028	29 40	136	21 32	201	29 56	262	14 25	299	28 27	325
358	15 43	004	60 47	026	30 09	136	21 17	201	29 14	261	13 48	298	28 02	324
359	15 46	003	61 05	024	30 39	136	21 02	200	28 32	260	13 10	297	27 37	323

LAT 46°S

LHA ♈	Hc	Zn	Hc	Zn	Hc	Zn	Hc	Zn	Hc	Zn	Hc	Zn	Hc	Zn
	Alpheratz		Hamal		◆ RIGEL		CANOPUS		◆ RIGIL KENT		Peacock		◆ FOMALHAUT	
0	14 48	002	14 39	030	13 38	088	31 51	135	21 44	200	56 01	232	69 37	319
1	14 49	001	14 59	029	14 20	087	32 21	134	21 30	199	55 28	232	69 09	316
2	14 50	000	15 20	028	15 02	086	32 51	134	21 16	199	54 55	232	68 40	314
3	14 49	359	15 39	027	15 43	085	33 21	134	21 03	198	54 23	232	68 09	312
4	14 49	358	15 58	027	16 25	085	33 51	133	20 50	198	53 50	232	67 38	311
5	14 47	358	16 16	026	17 06	084	34 22	133	20 38	197	53 17	231	67 06	309
6	14 45	357	16 34	025	17 48	083	34 52	132	20 25	197	52 45	231	66 33	307
7	14 42	356	16 51	024	18 29	083	35 23	132	20 13	196	52 12	231	66 00	305
8	14 39	355	17 08	023	19 10	082	35 54	132	20 02	196	51 40	231	65 25	304
9	14 35	354	17 24	022	19 51	081	36 25	131	19 50	196	51 08	231	64 50	302
10	14 30	353	17 39	021	20 33	080	36 57	131	19 39	195	50 35	231	64 15	301
11	14 25	352	17 54	020	21 14	079	37 28	130	19 29	195	50 03	230	63 39	299
12	14 19	351	18 08	019	21 54	079	38 00	130	19 18	194	49 31	230	63 02	298
13	14 12	350	18 21	018	22 35	078	38 32	130	19 08	194	48 59	230	62 25	297
14	14 05	349	18 34	017	23 16	077	39 04	129	18 59	193	48 27	230	61 48	295
	Hamal		◆ RIGEL		SIRIUS		CANOPUS		◆ RIGIL KENT		Peacock		◆ FOMALHAUT	
15	18 46	016	23 57	076	14 23	099	39 37	129	18 50	193	47 55	230	61 10	294
16	18 58	016	24 37	076	15 04	099	40 09	129	18 41	192	47 24	229	60 32	293
17	19 09	015	25 17	075	15 45	098	40 42	128	18 32	192	46 52	229	59 53	292
18	19 19	014	25 57	074	16 26	097	41 15	128	18 24	191	46 21	229	59 14	291
19	19 28	013	26 37	073	17 08	097	41 47	128	18 16	191	45 49	229	58 35	290
20	19 37	012	27 17	072	17 49	096	42 21	127	18 08	190	45 18	228	57 56	288
21	19 45	011	27 57	071	18 31	095	42 54	127	18 01	190	44 47	228	57 16	287
22	19 53	010	28 36	071	19 12	094	43 27	127	17 54	189	44 16	228	56 36	286
23	19 59	009	29 15	070	19 54	094	44 01	126	17 48	189	43 45	228	55 56	285
24	20 05	008	29 55	069	20 35	093	44 34	126	17 42	188	43 14	227	55 16	284
25	20 11	007	30 33	068	21 17	092	45 08	126	17 36	188	42 44	227	54 36	283
26	20 15	006	31 12	067	21 59	092	45 42	125	17 31	187	42 13	227	53 55	282
27	20 19	005	31 50	066	22 40	091	46 16	125	17 26	187	41 43	226	53 14	282
28	20 22	004	32 28	065	23 22	090	46 50	125	17 21	186	41 13	226	52 33	281
29	20 25	003	33 06	065	24 04	090	47 25	124	17 17	186	40 43	226	51 52	280
	Hamal		◆ RIGEL		SIRIUS		CANOPUS		◆ RIGIL KENT		Peacock		◆ FOMALHAUT	
30	20 27	002	33 43	064	24 45	089	47 59	124	17 13	185	40 13	226	51 11	279
31	20 28	001	34 21	063	25 27	088	48 34	124	17 09	185	39 43	225	50 30	278
32	20 28	000	34 57	062	26 09	087	49 08	124	17 06	184	39 14	225	49 49	277
33	20 28	359	35 34	061	26 50	087	49 43	123	17 03	184	38 44	225	49 07	276
34	20 27	358	36 10	060	27 32	086	50 18	123	17 01	183	38 15	224	48 26	276
35	20 25	357	36 46	059	28 13	085	50 53	123	16 59	183	37 46	224	47 44	275
36	20 22	356	37 21	058	28 55	084	51 28	123	16 57	182	37 17	224	47 03	274
37	20 19	355	37 57	057	29 36	084	52 03	122	16 56	182	36 49	223	46 21	273
38	20 15	354	38 31	056	30 18	083	52 38	122	16 55	181	36 20	223	45 39	273
39	20 11	353	39 05	055	30 59	082	53 14	122	16 54	181	35 52	223	44 58	272
40	20 05	352	39 39	054	31 40	081	53 49	122	16 54	180	35 24	222	44 16	271
41	19 59	351	40 13	053	32 22	080	54 25	121	16 54	180	34 56	222	43 34	270
42	19 53	350	40 46	052	33 03	080	55 00	121	16 54	179	34 28	222	42 53	270
43	19 45	349	41 18	050	33 44	079	55 36	121	16 55	179	34 00	221	42 11	269
44	19 37	348	41 50	049	34 24	078	56 12	121	16 56	178	33 33	221	41 29	268
	RIGEL		SIRIUS		◆ CANOPUS		RIGIL KENT		◆ Peacock		FOMALHAUT		◆ Hamal	
45	42 21	048	35 05	077	56 48	121	16 58	178	33 06	220	40 48	267	19 28	347
46	42 52	047	35 46	076	57 24	120	17 00	177	32 39	220	40 06	267	19 19	346
47	43 22	046	36 26	076	58 00	120	17 02	177	32 12	220	39 25	266	19 09	345
48	43 52	045	37 06	075	58 36	120	17 05	176	31 46	219	38 43	265	18 58	345
49	44 21	043	37 47	074	59 12	120	17 08	176	31 20	219	38 01	265	18 47	344
50	44 49	042	38 26	073	59 48	120	17 12	175	30 53	219	37 20	264	18 34	343
51	45 17	041	39 06	072	60 24	120	17 15	175	30 28	218	36 39	263	18 22	342
52	45 44	040	39 46	071	61 00	120	17 20	174	30 02	218	35 57	263	18 08	341
53	46 10	038	40 25	070	61 37	120	17 24	173	29 37	217	35 16	262	17 54	340
54	46 36	037	41 04	069	62 13	119	17 29	173	29 11	217	34 35	261	17 39	339
55	47 01	036	41 43	068	62 49	119	17 34	172	28 47	217	33 53	261	17 24	338
56	47 25	035	42 22	067	63 26	119	17 40	172	28 22	216	33 12	260	17 08	337
57	47 48	033	43 00	066	64 02	119	17 46	171	27 57	216	32 31	260	16 52	336
58	48 10	032	43 38	066	64 38	119	17 52	171	27 33	215	31 50	259	16 34	335
59	48 32	030	44 16	065	65 15	119	17 59	170	27 09	215	31 09	258	16 17	334
	◆ ALDEBARAN		BETELGEUSE		SIRIUS		◆ Suhail		RIGIL KENT		◆ ACHERNAR		Diphda	
60	26 55	010	30 39	034	44 53	063	37 24	117	18 06	170	65 41	230	40 58	288
61	27 01	009	31 02	033	45 31	062	38 01	117	18 13	170	65 09	230	40 18	287
62	27 07	008	31 24	032	46 07	061	38 38	116	18 21	169	64 37	230	39 38	286
63	27 13	007	31 46	031	46 44	060	39 16	116	18 29	169	64 05	230	38 58	286
64	27 17	006	32 07	030	47 20	059	39 53	115	18 38	168	63 33	231	38 18	285
65	27 21	005	32 27	029	47 55	058	40 31	115	18 47	168	63 01	231	37 37	284
66	27 24	003	32 47	027	48 31	057	41 09	114	18 56	167	62 29	231	36 57	283
67	27 26	002	33 05	026	49 05	056	41 47	114	19 05	167	61 56	231	36 16	282
68	27 27	001	33 24	025	49 39	055	42 25	113	19 15	166	61 24	231	35 35	281
69	27 28	000	33 41	024	50 13	053	43 04	113	19 25	166	60 51	231	34 55	281
70	27 27	359	33 57	023	50 46	052	43 42	112	19 36	165	60 19	231	34 13	280
71	27 26	358	34 13	022	51 19	051	44 21	112	19 47	165	59 46	231	33 32	279
72	27 25	357	34 28	021	51 51	050	44 59	111	19 58	164	59 14	231	32 51	278
73	27 22	356	34 43	019	52 23	048	45 38	111	20 10	164	58 41	231	32 10	277
74	27 19	355	34 56	018	52 53	047	46 17	111	20 21	163	58 09	231	31 28	277
	BETELGEUSE		SIRIUS		◆ Suhail		RIGIL KENT		◆ ACHERNAR		Diphda		◆ ALDEBARAN	
75	35 09	017	53 24	046	46 56	110	20 34	163	57 36	231	30 47	276	27 14	354
76	35 21	016	53 53	044	47 36	110	20 46	162	57 04	231	30 06	275	27 10	353
77	35 32	015	54 22	043	48 15	109	20 59	162	56 31	231	29 24	274	27 04	352
78	35 42	013	54 50	041	48 54	109	21 12	161	55 59	231	28 42	274	26 57	351
79	35 51	012	55 17	040	49 34	108	21 26	161	55 26	231	28 01	273	26 50	349
80	35 59	011	55 43	038	50 13	108	21 40	160	54 54	231	27 19	272	26 42	348
81	36 07	010	56 09	037	50 53	107	21 54	160	54 21	231	26 38	271	26 33	347
82	36 14	009	56 33	035	51 33	107	22 08	159	53 49	231	25 56	271	26 24	346
83	36 19	007	56 57	034	52 13	106	22 23	159	53 17	231	25 14	270	26 14	345
84	36 24	006	57 20	032	52 53	106	22 38	159	52 45	230	24 32	269	26 03	344
85	36 28	005	57 41	030	53 33	105	22 53	158	52 13	230	23 51	269	25 51	343
86	36 31	004	58 02	029	54 13	105	23 09	158	51 41	230	23 09	268	25 38	342
87	36 34	002	58 21	027	54 54	104	23 25	157	51 09	230	22 28	267	25 25	341
88	36 35	001	58 40	025	55 34	104	23 41	157	50 37	230	21 46	266	25 11	340
89	36 35	000	58 57	024	56 15	104	23 58	156	50 05	230	21 04	266	24 57	339

LHA ♈	Hc	Zn	Hc	Zn	Hc	Zn	Hc	Zn	Hc	Zn	Hc	Zn	Hc	Zn
	PROCYON		Alphard		◆ Suhail		RIGIL KENT		◆ ACHERNAR		◆ RIGEL		BETELGEUSE	
90	34 11	031	32 05	067	56 55	103	24 15	156	49 33	229	50 59	342	36 35	359
91	34 32	029	32 43	066	57 36	103	24 32	156	49 02	229	50 46	341	36 34	358
92	34 52	028	33 21	065	58 17	102	24 49	155	48 30	229	50 31	339	36 31	356
93	35 12	027	33 59	064	58 57	102	25 07	155	47 59	229	50 16	338	36 28	355
94	35 30	026	34 36	063	59 38	101	25 25	154	47 27	229	50 00	336	36 24	354
95	35 48	025	35 13	062	60 19	101	25 43	154	46 56	228	49 42	335	36 19	353
96	36 05	024	35 50	061	61 00	100	26 02	153	46 25	228	49 24	333	36 14	351
97	36 22	022	36 26	060	61 41	100	26 20	153	45 54	228	49 05	332	36 07	350
98	36 37	021	37 02	059	62 22	099	26 40	153	45 23	228	48 45	330	35 59	349
99	36 52	020	37 38	058	63 04	099	26 59	152	44 52	227	48 24	329	35 51	348
100	37 06	019	38 13	057	63 45	098	27 18	152	44 21	227	48 02	328	35 42	347
101	37 19	018	38 48	056	64 26	098	27 38	151	43 51	227	47 39	326	35 31	345
102	37 31	016	39 23	055	65 07	097	27 58	151	43 21	227	47 16	325	35 20	344
103	37 42	015	39 57	054	65 49	096	28 19	151	42 50	226	46 51	324	35 09	343
104	37 53	014	40 31	053	66 30	096	28 39	150	42 20	226	46 26	322	34 56	342
	PROCYON		REGULUS		◆ Gienah		RIGIL KENT		◆ ACHERNAR		RIGEL		◆ BETELGEUSE	
105	38 03	013	18 14	049	20 02	095	29 00	150	41 50	226	46 00	321	34 43	341
106	38 11	011	18 45	048	20 43	094	29 21	149	41 20	226	45 34	320	34 28	339
107	38 19	010	19 16	047	21 25	094	29 43	149	40 51	225	45 07	319	34 13	338
108	38 26	009	19 46	047	22 06	093	30 04	149	40 21	225	44 39	317	33 57	337
109	38 32	008	20 16	046	22 48	092	30 26	148	39 52	225	44 10	316	33 41	336
110	38 37	006	20 46	045	23 30	091	30 48	148	39 22	224	43 41	315	33 23	335
111	38 41	005	21 15	044	24 11	091	31 10	148	38 53	224	43 11	314	33 05	334
112	38 45	004	21 44	043	24 53	090	31 33	147	38 25	224	42 41	313	32 46	333
113	38 47	003	22 12	042	25 35	089	31 56	147	37 56	223	42 10	311	32 27	331
114	38 48	001	22 40	041	26 16	089	32 19	146	37 27	223	41 38	310	32 07	330
115	38 49	000	23 07	040	26 58	088	32 42	146	36 59	223	41 06	309	31 46	329
116	38 48	359	23 33	039	27 40	087	33 05	146	36 31	222	40 33	308	31 24	328
117	38 47	357	23 59	038	28 21	086	33 29	145	36 03	222	40 00	307	31 02	327
118	38 45	356	24 25	037	29 03	086	33 52	145	35 35	222	39 27	306	30 39	326
119	38 42	355	24 50	036	29 44	085	34 16	145	35 07	221	38 53	305	30 15	325
	REGULUS		◆ SPICA		RIGIL KENT		◆ ACHERNAR		RIGEL		BETELGEUSE		◆ PROCYON	
120	25 14	035	13 57	092	34 40	144	34 40	221	38 18	304	29 51	324	38 37	354
121	25 38	034	14 38	091	35 05	144	34 12	221	37 44	303	29 26	323	38 32	352
122	26 01	033	15 20	090	35 29	144	33 45	220	37 08	302	29 01	322	38 26	351
123	26 24	032	16 02	090	35 54	143	33 19	220	36 33	301	28 34	321	38 19	350
124	26 46	031	16 43	089	36 19	143	32 52	220	35 57	300	28 08	320	38 12	349
125	27 07	030	17 25	088	36 44	143	32 25	219	35 20	299	27 41	319	38 03	347
126	27 28	029	18 07	088	37 09	143	31 59	219	34 44	298	27 13	318	37 53	346
127	27 48	028	18 48	087	37 35	142	31 33	218	34 07	297	26 45	317	37 43	345
128	28 07	027	19 30	086	38 01	142	31 07	218	33 30	296	26 16	316	37 32	344
129	28 26	026	20 11	085	38 26	142	30 42	218	32 52	295	25 47	315	37 19	342
130	28 44	025	20 53	085	38 52	141	30 16	217	32 14	294	25 17	314	37 06	341
131	29 01	024	21 34	084	39 18	141	29 51	217	31 36	293	24 47	313	36 53	340
132	29 18	023	22 16	083	39 45	141	29 26	216	30 58	292	24 16	312	36 38	339
133	29 34	022	22 57	082	40 11	141	29 02	216	30 19	292	23 45	311	36 22	338
134	29 49	021	23 38	082	40 38	140	28 37	216	29 40	291	23 13	310	36 06	336
	◆ REGULUS		SPICA		◆ RIGIL KENT		ACHERNAR		◆ CANOPUS		SIRIUS		PROCYON	
135	30 03	020	24 20	081	41 04	140	28 13	215	64 07	241	49 36	305	35 49	335
136	30 17	019	25 01	080	41 31	140	27 49	215	63 31	241	49 02	304	35 31	334
137	30 30	017	25 42	079	41 58	139	27 26	214	62 54	241	48 27	303	35 12	333
138	30 42	016	26 23	078	42 25	139	27 02	214	62 18	241	47 52	302	34 53	332
139	30 53	015	27 03	078	42 53	139	26 39	214	61 42	241	47 16	301	34 33	331
140	31 04	014	27 44	077	43 20	139	26 16	213	61 05	240	46 40	300	34 12	329
141	31 13	013	28 24	076	43 48	139	25 54	213	60 29	240	46 04	299	33 50	328
142	31 22	012	29 05	075	44 15	138	25 31	212	59 53	240	45 27	297	33 28	327
143	31 30	011	29 45	074	44 43	138	25 09	212	59 17	240	44 50	296	33 05	326
144	31 38	010	30 25	074	45 11	138	24 47	211	58 41	240	44 12	295	32 42	325
145	31 44	008	31 05	073	45 39	138	24 26	211	58 05	240	43 35	294	32 18	324
146	31 50	007	31 45	072	46 07	138	24 05	210	57 29	240	42 56	293	31 53	323
147	31 55	006	32 24	071	46 35	137	23 44	210	56 53	239	42 18	292	31 27	322
148	31 59	005	33 04	070	47 03	137	23 23	210	56 17	239	41 39	291	31 01	321
149	32 02	004	33 43	069	47 32	137	23 02	209	55 41	239	41 01	291	30 35	320
	◆ REGULUS		SPICA		◆ RIGIL KENT		ACHERNAR		◆ CANOPUS		SIRIUS		PROCYON	
150	32 04	003	34 22	068	48 00	137	22 42	209	55 06	239	40 21	290	30 07	319
151	32 06	001	35 00	068	48 29	137	22 23	208	54 30	239	39 42	289	29 40	318
152	32 06	000	35 39	067	48 57	137	22 03	208	53 54	238	39 02	288	29 11	317
153	32 06	359	36 17	066	49 26	136	21 44	207	53 19	238	38 23	287	28 42	316
154	32 05	358	36 55	065	49 55	136	21 25	207	52 44	238	37 43	286	28 13	315
155	32 03	357	37 32	064	50 24	136	21 06	206	52 08	238	37 03	285	27 43	314
156	32 01	356	38 09	063	50 53	136	20 48	206	51 33	237	36 22	284	27 13	313
157	31 57	355	38 46	062	51 22	136	20 30	205	50 58	237	35 42	284	26 42	312
158	31 53	353	39 23	061	51 51	136	20 12	205	50 23	237	35 01	283	26 11	311
159	31 48	352	39 59	060	52 20	136	19 55	204	49 48	237	34 20	282	25 39	310
160	31 42	351	40 35	059	52 49	136	19 38	204	49 13	236	33 40	281	25 07	309
161	31 35	350	41 10	058	53 18	136	19 21	203	48 39	236	32 59	280	24 34	308
162	31 27	349	41 45	057	53 47	136	19 05	203	48 04	236	32 18	279	24 01	307
163	31 19	348	42 20	056	54 16	136	18 49	202	47 30	236	31 36	279	23 28	306
164	31 09	347	42 54	055	54 45	136	18 33	202	46 55	235	30 55	278	22 54	305
	SPICA		◆ ANTARES		RIGIL KENT		ACHERNAR		◆ CANOPUS		SIRIUS		◆ REGULUS	
165	43 28	053	23 38	104	55 14	136	18 18	201	46 21	235	30 14	277	30 59	345
166	44 01	052	24 18	104	55 44	136	18 03	201	45 47	235	29 32	276	30 48	344
167	44 34	051	24 59	103	56 13	136	17 48	200	45 13	234	28 51	276	30 37	343
168	45 06	050	25 40	102	56 42	136	17 34	200	44 39	234	28 10	275	30 24	342
169	45 38	049	26 20	102	57 11	136	17 20	199	44 06	234	27 28	274	30 11	341
170	46 09	048	27 01	101	57 40	136	17 07	199	43 32	233	26 46	273	29 57	340
171	46 40	046	27 42	100	58 09	136	16 53	198	42 59	233	26 05	273	29 42	339
172	47 09	045	28 23	100	58 38	136	16 40	198	42 25	233	25 23	272	29 27	338
173	47 39	044	29 04	099	59 07	136	16 28	197	41 52	232	24 41	271	29 11	337
174	48 07	043	29 45	098	59 36	136	16 16	197	41 19	232	24 00	270	28 54	336
175	48 35	041	30 27	098	60 05	136	16 04	196	40 46	232	23 18	270	28 36	335
176	49 02	040	31 08	097	60 34	136	15 53	196	40 14	231	22 36	269	28 18	333
177	49 29	039	31 49	096	61 03	137	15 41	195	39 41	231	21 55	268	27 59	332
178	49 55	037	32 31	096	61 31	137	15 31	195	39 09	231	21 13	268	27 40	331
179	50 20	036	33 12	095	62 00	137	15 21	194	38 37	230	20 31	267	27 19	330

 LAT 46°S

LHA ♈	Hc	Zn	Hc	Zn	Hc	Zn	Hc	Zn	Hc	Zn	Hc	Zn	Hc	Zn
	◆ ARCTURUS		ANTARES		◆ Peacock		ACHERNAR		CANOPUS		◆ Suhail		REGULUS	
180	17 57	034	33 54	094	21 54	152	15 11	194	38 05	230	59 49	259	26 58	329
181	18 20	033	34 35	094	22 14	151	15 01	193	37 33	230	59 09	259	26 37	328
182	18 42	032	35 17	093	22 35	151	14 52	192	37 01	229	58 28	258	26 14	327
183	19 04	031	35 59	092	22 55	150	14 43	192	36 30	229	57 47	258	25 52	326
184	19 25	030	36 40	092	23 16	150	14 35	191	35 59	228	57 06	257	25 28	325
185	19 46	029	37 22	091	23 37	149	14 27	191	35 28	228	56 26	257	25 04	324
186	20 06	028	38 04	090	23 58	149	14 19	190	34 57	228	55 45	256	24 40	323
187	20 25	027	38 45	090	24 20	148	14 12	190	34 26	227	55 05	256	24 14	322
188	20 44	026	39 27	089	24 42	148	14 05	189	33 55	227	54 24	255	23 49	321
189	21 02	025	40 09	088	25 04	148	13 59	189	33 25	226	53 44	255	23 22	320
190	21 20	024	40 50	087	25 27	147	13 52	188	32 55	226	53 04	254	22 56	319
191	21 37	023	41 32	087	25 50	147	13 47	188	32 25	226	52 24	254	22 28	319
192	21 53	023	42 14	086	26 13	146	13 42	187	31 55	225	51 44	253	22 00	318
193	22 09	022	42 55	085	26 36	146	13 37	186	31 26	225	51 04	253	21 32	317
194	22 24	021	43 37	084	26 59	145	13 32	186	30 57	224	50 24	252	21 03	316
	ARCTURUS		◆ ANTARES		Peacock		◆ ACHERNAR		CANOPUS		Suhail		◆ REGULUS	
195	22 38	020	44 18	083	27 23	145	13 28	185	30 28	224	49 45	252	20 34	315
196	22 52	019	44 59	083	27 47	144	13 25	185	29 59	224	49 05	251	20 04	314
197	23 05	018	45 41	082	28 12	144	13 21	184	29 30	223	48 26	251	19 34	313
198	23 17	017	46 22	081	28 36	144	13 18	184	29 02	223	47 46	251	19 03	312
199	23 28	016	47 03	080	29 01	143	13 16	183	28 34	222	47 07	250	18 32	311
200	23 39	015	47 44	079	29 26	143	13 14	183	28 06	222	46 28	250	18 01	310
201	23 49	014	48 25	078	29 51	142	13 12	182	27 38	221	45 49	249	17 29	310
202	23 59	013	49 06	078	30 17	142	13 11	181	27 11	221	45 10	249	16 56	309
203	24 07	011	49 46	077	30 43	142	13 10	181	26 43	220	44 31	248	16 24	308
204	24 15	010	50 27	076	31 09	141	13 10	180	26 16	220	43 53	248	15 50	307
205	24 23	009	51 07	075	31 35	141	13 10	180	25 50	220	43 14	247	15 17	306
206	24 29	008	51 47	074	32 01	140	13 10	179	25 23	219	42 36	247	14 43	305
207	24 35	007	52 27	073	32 28	140	13 11	179	24 57	219	41 58	246	14 09	305
208	24 40	006	53 07	072	32 55	140	13 12	178	24 31	218	41 19	246	13 35	304
209	24 44	005	53 46	071	33 22	139	13 14	178	24 06	218	40 41	245	13 00	303
	◆ ARCTURUS		ANTARES		◆ Peacock		ACHERNAR		CANOPUS		◆ Suhail		SPICA	
210	24 47	004	54 26	070	33 49	139	13 16	177	23 40	217	40 04	245	54 30	346
211	24 50	003	55 05	069	34 17	139	13 18	176	23 15	217	39 26	244	54 19	344
212	24 52	002	55 43	068	34 44	138	13 21	176	22 51	216	38 48	244	54 06	342
213	24 53	001	56 22	067	35 12	138	13 24	175	22 26	216	38 11	244	53 53	341
214	24 54	000	57 00	065	35 40	138	13 28	175	22 02	215	37 34	243	53 39	339
215	24 53	359	57 37	064	36 08	137	13 32	174	21 38	215	36 57	243	53 23	337
216	24 52	358	58 15	063	36 37	137	13 36	174	21 14	214	36 20	242	53 07	336
217	24 50	357	58 52	062	37 05	136	13 41	173	20 51	214	35 43	242	52 49	334
218	24 48	356	59 28	060	37 34	136	13 46	173	20 28	213	35 07	241	52 31	333
219	24 45	355	60 04	059	38 03	136	13 52	172	20 05	213	34 30	241	52 11	331
220	24 40	354	60 40	058	38 32	135	13 58	171	19 43	212	33 54	240	51 51	330
221	24 36	353	61 15	056	39 02	135	14 04	171	19 21	212	33 18	240	51 29	328
222	24 30	352	61 49	055	39 31	135	14 11	170	18 59	211	32 42	239	51 07	327
223	24 24	351	62 23	053	40 01	135	14 18	170	18 37	211	32 06	239	50 43	325
224	24 17	350	62 56	052	40 31	134	14 26	169	18 16	210	31 31	238	50 19	324
	ANTARES		◆ Nunki		Peacock		ACHERNAR		◆ CANOPUS		◆ SPICA		ARCTURUS	
225	63 29	050	39 42	088	41 00	134	14 34	169	17 55	210	49 54	323	24 09	349
226	64 00	049	40 24	087	41 31	134	14 42	168	17 35	209	49 29	321	24 00	348
227	64 31	047	41 05	087	42 01	133	14 51	168	17 15	209	49 02	320	23 51	347
228	65 01	045	41 47	086	42 31	133	15 00	167	16 55	208	48 35	319	23 41	346
229	65 30	043	42 29	085	43 02	133	15 09	167	16 36	208	48 07	317	23 30	345
230	65 59	042	43 10	084	43 32	132	15 19	166	16 16	207	47 39	316	23 19	344
231	66 26	040	43 52	084	44 03	132	15 29	165	15 58	206	47 09	315	23 07	343
232	66 52	038	44 33	083	44 34	132	15 40	165	15 39	206	46 39	314	22 54	342
233	67 17	036	45 14	082	45 05	132	15 51	164	15 21	205	46 09	312	22 41	341
234	67 40	034	45 55	081	45 36	131	16 02	164	15 03	205	45 38	311	22 26	340
235	68 03	031	46 37	080	46 08	131	16 14	163	14 46	204	45 06	310	22 12	339
236	68 24	029	47 18	079	46 39	131	16 26	163	14 29	204	44 34	309	21 56	338
237	68 44	027	47 59	079	47 11	131	16 39	162	14 13	203	44 01	308	21 40	337
238	69 02	025	48 39	078	47 42	130	16 52	162	13 56	203	43 28	306	21 23	336
239	69 18	022	49 20	077	48 14	130	17 05	161	13 40	202	42 54	305	21 06	335
	Rasalhague		◆ ALTAIR		FOMALHAUT		◆ ACHERNAR		ACRUX		◆ SPICA		ARCTURUS	
240	27 37	027	14 41	060	11 40	121	17 18	161	56 06	220	42 20	304	20 47	334
241	27 55	025	15 17	059	12 16	120	17 32	160	55 39	220	41 45	303	20 29	333
242	28 13	024	15 53	058	12 52	119	17 46	160	55 12	220	41 10	302	20 09	332
243	28 30	023	16 28	057	13 28	119	18 01	159	54 45	220	40 35	301	19 49	331
244	28 46	022	17 03	057	14 05	118	18 16	159	54 18	220	39 59	300	19 29	330
245	29 01	021	17 37	056	14 42	118	18 31	158	53 51	221	39 23	299	19 08	329
246	29 16	020	18 12	055	15 19	117	18 47	158	53 24	220	38 46	298	18 46	328
247	29 30	019	18 46	054	15 56	116	19 03	157	52 56	220	38 09	297	18 24	327
248	29 43	018	19 19	053	16 34	116	19 19	157	52 29	220	37 32	296	18 01	326
249	29 56	017	19 52	052	17 11	115	19 36	156	52 02	220	36 54	295	17 38	325
250	30 07	016	20 25	051	17 49	114	19 53	156	51 35	220	36 16	294	17 14	325
251	30 18	015	20 58	051	18 27	114	20 10	155	51 08	220	35 38	293	16 49	324
252	30 28	014	21 30	050	19 05	113	20 28	155	50 41	220	35 00	292	16 24	323
253	30 38	012	22 01	049	19 44	112	20 46	154	50 15	220	34 21	292	15 59	322
254	30 46	011	22 32	048	20 22	112	21 04	154	49 48	220	33 42	291	15 33	321
	Rasalhague		◆ ALTAIR		FOMALHAUT		◆ ACHERNAR		ACRUX		◆ SPICA		ANTARES	
255	30 54	010	23 03	047	21 01	111	21 22	153	49 21	220	33 03	290	69 35	341
256	31 01	009	23 33	046	21 40	111	21 41	153	48 54	220	32 24	289	69 21	338
257	31 07	008	24 03	045	22 19	110	22 00	152	48 27	220	31 44	288	69 05	336
258	31 12	007	24 32	044	22 58	109	22 20	152	48 01	220	31 05	287	68 47	333
259	31 17	006	25 01	043	23 38	109	22 40	151	47 34	220	30 25	286	68 27	331
260	31 21	004	25 29	042	24 17	108	23 00	151	47 08	219	29 45	286	68 06	329
261	31 23	003	25 57	041	24 57	108	23 20	151	46 41	219	29 05	285	67 44	327
262	31 25	002	26 24	040	25 37	107	23 41	150	46 15	219	28 24	284	67 21	325
263	31 27	001	26 51	039	26 17	106	24 02	150	45 49	219	27 44	283	66 56	323
264	31 27	000	27 17	038	26 57	106	24 23	149	45 23	219	27 03	282	66 30	321
265	31 26	359	27 42	037	27 37	105	24 44	149	44 57	219	26 22	282	66 03	319
266	31 25	358	28 07	036	28 17	104	25 06	148	44 31	218	25 41	281	65 35	317
267	31 23	356	28 32	035	28 58	104	25 28	148	44 05	218	25 00	280	65 06	315
268	31 20	355	28 55	034	29 38	103	25 51	147	43 39	218	24 19	279	64 36	313
269	31 16	354	29 19	033	30 19	103	26 13	147	43 13	218	23 38	278	64 05	312

LHA ♈	Hc	Zn	Hc	Zn	Hc	Zn	Hc	Zn	Hc	Zn	Hc	Zn	Hc	Zn
	◆ ALTAIR		FOMALHAUT		◆ ACHERNAR		RIGIL KENT		◆ SPICA		ANTARES		Rasalhague	
270	29 41	032	31 00	102	26 36	147	57 49	224	22 57	278	63 34	310	31 12	353
271	30 03	031	31 41	101	26 59	146	57 20	224	22 15	277	63 02	308	31 06	352
272	30 24	030	32 22	101	27 23	146	56 51	224	21 34	276	62 29	307	31 00	351
273	30 45	029	33 03	100	27 46	145	56 22	224	20 53	275	61 55	305	30 53	350
274	31 04	028	33 44	099	28 10	145	55 53	224	20 11	275	61 20	304	30 45	349
275	31 24	027	34 25	099	28 34	144	55 24	224	19 30	274	60 46	302	30 36	347
276	31 42	026	35 06	098	28 59	144	54 54	224	18 48	273	60 10	301	30 27	346
277	32 00	025	35 47	097	29 23	144	54 25	224	18 06	272	59 34	300	30 16	345
278	32 17	023	36 29	097	29 48	143	53 56	224	17 25	272	58 58	298	30 05	344
279	32 33	022	37 10	096	30 13	143	53 27	224	16 43	271	58 21	297	29 54	343
280	32 48	021	37 52	095	30 38	142	52 58	224	16 01	270	57 44	296	29 41	342
281	33 03	020	38 33	095	31 04	142	52 29	224	15 20	270	57 06	295	29 28	341
282	33 17	019	39 15	094	31 30	142	52 00	224	14 38	269	56 28	294	29 13	340
283	33 30	018	39 56	093	31 56	141	51 31	224	13 56	268	55 50	293	28 59	339
284	33 42	017	40 38	093	32 22	141	51 02	224	13 15	267	55 11	291	28 43	338
	ALTAIR		Enif		◆ FOMALHAUT		ACHERNAR		◆ RIGIL KENT		ANTARES		◆ Rasalhague	
285	33 53	015	22 59	045	41 19	092	32 48	140	50 33	224	54 32	290	28 27	336
286	34 04	014	23 28	044	42 01	091	33 15	140	50 04	224	53 53	289	28 10	335
287	34 14	013	23 56	043	42 43	091	33 42	140	49 35	224	53 13	288	27 52	334
288	34 23	012	24 25	042	43 25	090	34 09	139	49 07	223	52 34	287	27 34	333
289	34 31	011	24 52	041	44 06	089	34 36	139	48 38	223	51 54	286	27 15	332
290	34 38	009	25 19	040	44 48	088	35 03	139	48 09	223	51 14	285	26 55	331
291	34 45	008	25 46	039	45 30	088	35 31	138	47 41	223	50 33	284	26 34	330
292	34 50	007	26 12	038	46 11	087	35 59	138	47 12	223	49 53	283	26 13	329
293	34 55	006	26 37	037	46 53	086	36 27	138	46 44	223	49 12	283	25 52	328
294	34 59	005	27 02	036	47 34	085	36 55	137	46 16	223	48 32	282	25 29	327
295	35 02	003	27 26	035	48 16	085	37 23	137	45 48	222	47 51	281	25 07	326
296	35 04	002	27 50	034	48 57	084	37 52	137	45 20	222	47 10	280	24 43	325
297	35 05	001	28 13	033	49 39	083	38 21	136	44 52	222	46 29	279	24 19	324
298	35 05	000	28 36	032	50 20	082	38 49	136	44 24	222	45 48	278	23 54	323
299	35 05	359	28 57	031	51 01	081	39 19	136	43 56	222	45 06	277	23 29	322
	◆ Enif		FOMALHAUT		◆ ACHERNAR		RIGIL KENT		◆ ANTARES		Rasalhague		ALTAIR	
300	29 19	030	51 42	080	39 48	135	43 29	221	44 25	277	23 03	321	35 03	357
301	29 39	029	52 23	080	40 17	135	43 01	221	43 43	276	22 37	320	35 01	356
302	29 59	028	53 04	079	40 47	135	42 34	221	43 02	275	22 10	319	34 58	355
303	30 18	027	53 45	078	41 16	134	42 07	221	42 20	274	21 43	319	34 54	354
304	30 36	026	54 26	077	41 46	134	41 40	220	41 39	274	21 15	318	34 49	353
305	30 54	025	55 06	076	42 16	134	41 13	220	40 57	273	20 47	317	34 43	351
306	31 11	023	55 47	075	42 46	134	40 46	220	40 16	272	20 18	316	34 37	350
307	31 27	022	56 27	074	43 16	133	40 20	220	39 34	271	19 48	315	34 29	349
308	31 43	021	57 07	073	43 47	133	39 53	219	38 52	271	19 19	314	34 21	348
309	31 57	020	57 47	072	44 17	133	39 27	219	38 11	270	18 48	313	34 12	347
310	32 11	019	58 26	071	44 48	133	39 01	219	37 29	269	18 18	312	34 02	346
311	32 25	018	59 05	070	45 19	132	38 35	218	36 47	268	17 47	311	33 51	344
312	32 37	017	59 44	069	45 50	132	38 09	218	36 06	268	17 15	310	33 39	343
313	32 49	016	60 23	067	46 21	132	37 43	218	35 24	267	16 43	310	33 27	342
314	32 59	014	61 01	066	46 52	132	37 18	218	34 42	266	16 11	309	33 13	341
	◆ Enif		Diphda		◆ ACHERNAR		Miaplacidus		RIGIL KENT		◆ ANTARES		ALTAIR	
315	33 09	013	36 09	078	47 23	131	25 48	181	36 52	217	34 01	266	32 59	340
316	33 18	012	36 50	077	47 54	131	25 48	181	36 27	217	33 19	265	32 44	339
317	33 27	011	37 31	076	48 26	131	25 47	181	36 02	217	32 38	264	32 29	337
318	33 34	010	38 11	075	48 57	131	25 47	180	35 37	216	31 56	264	32 12	336
319	33 41	009	38 51	075	49 29	131	25 47	180	35 13	216	31 15	263	31 55	335
320	33 47	007	39 31	074	50 01	130	25 47	179	34 48	216	30 34	262	31 38	334
321	33 52	006	40 11	073	50 32	130	25 48	179	34 24	215	29 52	262	31 19	333
322	33 56	005	40 51	072	51 04	130	25 49	179	34 00	215	29 11	261	31 00	332
323	33 59	004	41 30	071	51 36	130	25 50	178	33 36	215	28 30	260	30 40	331
324	34 01	003	42 10	070	52 08	130	25 51	178	33 12	214	27 49	260	30 19	330
325	34 03	001	42 49	069	52 40	130	25 53	177	32 49	214	27 08	259	29 58	329
326	34 03	000	43 28	068	53 13	129	25 55	177	32 26	214	26 27	258	29 36	328
327	34 03	359	44 06	067	53 45	129	25 57	177	32 03	213	25 46	258	29 13	327
328	34 02	358	44 45	066	54 17	129	26 00	176	31 40	213	25 06	257	28 50	326
329	34 00	357	45 22	065	54 49	129	26 03	176	31 18	213	24 25	256	28 26	325
	◆ Diphda		ACHERNAR		◆ Miaplacidus		RIGIL KENT		ANTARES		◆ ALTAIR		Enif	
330	46 00	064	55 22	129	26 06	176	30 55	212	23 45	256	28 01	323	33 57	356
331	46 38	063	55 54	129	26 09	175	30 33	212	23 04	255	27 36	322	33 54	354
332	47 15	062	56 27	129	26 13	175	30 11	211	22 24	255	27 11	321	33 49	353
333	47 51	061	56 59	129	26 17	174	29 50	211	21 44	254	26 44	320	33 44	352
334	48 27	060	57 32	129	26 21	174	29 28	211	21 04	253	26 18	319	33 37	351
335	49 03	059	58 04	129	26 25	174	29 07	210	20 24	253	25 50	319	33 30	350
336	49 39	058	58 37	129	26 30	173	28 46	210	19 44	252	25 22	318	33 22	348
337	50 14	056	59 09	129	26 35	173	28 25	210	19 05	251	24 54	317	33 14	347
338	50 48	055	59 42	129	26 40	173	28 05	209	18 25	251	24 25	316	33 04	346
339	51 22	054	60 14	129	26 46	172	27 45	209	17 46	250	23 56	315	32 54	345
340	51 56	053	60 47	129	26 52	172	27 25	208	17 07	249	23 26	314	32 42	344
341	52 29	052	61 19	129	26 58	171	27 05	208	16 28	249	22 55	313	32 30	343
342	53 01	050	61 52	129	27 04	171	26 46	208	15 49	248	22 25	312	32 18	342
343	53 33	049	62 24	129	27 11	171	26 26	207	15 11	247	21 53	311	32 04	340
344	54 04	048	62 56	129	27 18	170	26 08	207	14 32	247	21 22	310	31 50	339
	◆ Diphda		Acamar		◆ CANOPUS		Miaplacidus		RIGIL KENT		◆ Nunki		Enif	
345	54 34	046	47 04	105	24 54	141	27 25	170	25 49	206	38 23	270	31 34	338
346	55 04	045	47 45	104	25 20	141	27 32	170	25 31	206	37 41	270	31 19	337
347	55 33	043	48 25	104	25 46	141	27 40	169	25 13	205	37 00	269	31 02	336
348	56 01	042	49 06	103	26 13	140	27 48	169	24 55	205	36 18	268	30 45	335
349	56 29	040	49 46	102	26 40	140	27 56	168	24 37	205	35 36	268	30 27	334
350	56 55	039	50 27	102	27 07	139	28 05	168	24 20	204	34 55	267	30 08	333
351	57 21	037	51 08	101	27 34	139	28 13	168	24 03	204	34 13	266	29 48	332
352	57 46	036	51 49	101	28 02	138	28 22	167	23 46	203	33 31	266	29 28	331
353	58 09	034	52 30	100	28 30	138	28 31	167	23 30	203	32 50	265	29 07	329
354	58 32	032	53 11	100	28 58	137	28 41	167	23 14	202	32 08	264	28 46	328
355	58 54	031	53 52	099	29 26	137	28 51	166	22 58	202	31 27	263	28 24	327
356	59 15	029	54 33	099	29 55	137	29 00	166	22 43	202	30 46	263	28 01	326
357	59 34	027	55 14	098	30 23	136	29 11	166	22 28	201	30 04	262	27 37	325
358	59 53	025	55 56	097	30 52	136	29 21	165	22 13	201	29 23	261	27 13	324
359	60 10	024	56 37	097	31 22	135	29 32	165	21 58	200	28 42	261	26 49	323

LAT 47°S

LHA ♈	Hc	Zn	Hc	Zn	Hc	Zn	Hc	Zn	Hc	Zn	Hc	Zn	Hc	Zn
	Alpheratz		Hamal		◆ RIGEL		CANOPUS		◆ RIGIL KENT		Peacock		◆ FOMALHAUT	
0	13 48	002	13 47	030	13 36	087	32 33	134	22 40	200	56 37	233	68 51	320
1	13 49	001	14 07	029	14 17	087	33 03	134	22 27	199	56 05	233	68 25	318
2	13 50	000	14 27	028	14 57	086	33 32	134	22 13	199	55 32	233	67 57	316
3	13 49	359	14 46	027	15 38	085	34 02	133	22 00	198	54 59	233	67 28	314
4	13 49	358	15 04	026	16 19	084	34 32	133	21 47	198	54 27	233	66 58	312
5	13 47	358	15 22	026	17 00	084	35 02	132	21 35	198	53 54	232	66 28	311
6	13 45	357	15 40	025	17 40	083	35 32	132	21 23	197	53 22	232	65 56	309
7	13 42	356	15 57	024	18 21	082	36 03	131	21 11	197	52 49	232	65 24	307
8	13 39	355	16 13	023	19 01	081	36 34	131	20 59	196	52 17	232	64 51	306
9	13 35	354	16 28	022	19 42	081	37 05	131	20 48	196	51 45	232	64 18	304
10	13 31	353	16 43	021	20 22	080	37 36	130	20 37	195	51 13	232	63 43	303
11	13 25	352	16 58	020	21 02	079	38 07	130	20 27	195	50 41	231	63 09	301
12	13 19	351	17 11	019	21 43	078	38 39	129	20 17	194	50 09	231	62 33	300
13	13 13	350	17 25	018	22 23	078	39 10	129	20 07	194	49 37	231	61 58	298
14	13 06	350	17 37	017	23 02	077	39 42	129	19 57	193	49 06	231	61 21	297
	Hamal		◆ RIGEL		SIRIUS		CANOPUS		◆ RIGIL KENT		Peacock		◆ FOMALHAUT	
15	17 49	016	23 42	076	14 32	099	40 14	128	19 48	193	48 34	230	60 45	296
16	18 00	015	24 22	075	15 13	098	40 46	128	19 39	192	48 02	230	60 08	295
17	18 11	014	25 01	074	15 53	098	41 19	128	19 31	192	47 31	230	59 30	293
18	18 20	014	25 41	074	16 34	097	41 51	127	19 23	191	47 00	230	58 53	292
19	18 30	013	26 20	073	17 15	096	42 24	127	19 15	191	46 29	229	58 15	291
20	18 38	012	26 59	072	17 55	096	42 57	127	19 07	190	45 58	229	57 36	290
21	18 46	011	27 38	071	18 36	095	43 30	126	19 00	190	45 27	229	56 58	289
22	18 53	010	28 16	070	19 17	094	44 03	126	18 54	189	44 56	229	56 19	288
23	19 00	009	28 55	069	19 58	093	44 36	126	18 47	189	44 25	228	55 40	287
24	19 06	008	29 33	068	20 38	093	45 09	125	18 41	188	43 55	228	55 00	286
25	19 11	007	30 11	068	21 19	092	45 43	125	18 36	188	43 24	228	54 21	285
26	19 16	006	30 48	067	22 00	091	46 16	124	18 30	187	42 54	227	53 41	284
27	19 19	005	31 26	066	22 41	091	46 50	124	18 25	187	42 24	227	53 01	283
28	19 22	004	32 03	065	23 22	090	47 24	124	18 21	186	41 54	227	52 21	282
29	19 25	003	32 40	064	24 03	089	47 58	124	18 16	186	41 24	227	51 41	281
	Hamal		◆ RIGEL		SIRIUS		CANOPUS		◆ RIGIL KENT		Peacock		◆ FOMALHAUT	
30	19 27	002	33 16	063	24 44	088	48 32	123	18 13	185	40 55	226	51 01	280
31	19 28	001	33 53	062	25 25	088	49 07	123	18 09	185	40 25	226	50 21	279
32	19 28	000	34 29	061	26 06	087	49 41	123	18 06	184	39 56	226	49 40	278
33	19 28	359	35 04	060	26 47	086	50 16	122	18 03	184	39 27	225	49 00	278
34	19 27	358	35 40	059	27 27	085	50 50	122	18 01	183	38 58	225	48 19	277
35	19 25	357	36 15	058	28 08	085	51 25	122	17 59	183	38 29	225	47 39	276
36	19 23	356	36 49	057	28 49	084	52 00	121	17 57	182	38 01	224	46 58	275
37	19 19	355	37 23	056	29 29	083	52 35	121	17 56	182	37 32	224	46 17	274
38	19 16	354	37 57	055	30 10	082	53 10	121	17 55	181	37 04	223	45 36	274
39	19 11	353	38 31	054	30 51	081	53 45	121	17 54	181	36 36	223	44 55	273
40	19 06	352	39 03	053	31 31	081	54 20	120	17 54	180	36 08	223	44 15	272
41	19 00	351	39 36	052	32 11	080	54 56	120	17 54	180	35 40	222	43 34	271
42	18 54	350	40 08	051	32 52	079	55 31	120	17 54	179	35 13	222	42 53	271
43	18 46	349	40 39	050	33 32	078	56 06	120	17 55	179	34 45	222	42 12	270
44	18 38	348	41 10	049	34 12	077	56 42	119	17 56	178	34 18	221	41 31	269
	RIGEL		SIRIUS		◆ CANOPUS		RIGIL KENT		◆ Peacock		FOMALHAUT		◆ Hamal	
45	41 41	048	34 51	077	57 18	119	17 58	178	33 51	221	40 50	268	18 30	347
46	42 11	046	35 31	076	57 53	119	18 00	177	33 25	220	40 09	268	18 21	346
47	42 40	045	36 11	075	58 29	119	18 02	177	32 58	220	39 28	267	18 11	346
48	43 09	044	36 50	074	59 05	119	18 05	176	32 32	220	38 47	266	18 00	345
49	43 37	043	37 29	073	59 41	118	18 08	175	32 06	219	38 07	266	17 49	344
50	44 04	042	38 09	072	60 17	118	18 11	175	31 40	219	37 26	265	17 37	343
51	44 31	040	38 47	071	60 53	118	18 15	174	31 15	219	36 45	264	17 25	342
52	44 57	039	39 26	070	61 29	118	18 19	174	30 49	218	36 04	263	17 12	341
53	45 23	038	40 04	069	62 05	118	18 24	173	30 24	218	35 24	263	16 58	340
54	45 48	037	40 43	069	62 42	118	18 29	173	29 59	217	34 43	262	16 43	339
55	46 12	035	41 21	068	63 18	118	18 34	172	29 35	217	34 03	261	16 28	338
56	46 35	034	41 58	067	63 54	118	18 39	172	29 10	216	33 22	261	16 13	337
57	46 57	033	42 36	066	64 30	117	18 45	171	28 46	216	32 42	260	15 57	336
58	47 19	031	43 13	065	65 07	117	18 52	171	28 22	216	32 02	260	15 40	335
59	47 40	030	43 50	064	65 43	117	18 58	170	27 58	215	31 21	259	15 23	334
	◆ ALDEBARAN		BETELGEUSE		SIRIUS		◆ Suhail		RIGIL KENT		◆ ACHERNAR		Diphda	
60	25 56	010	29 49	034	44 26	063	37 51	116	19 05	170	66 19	232	40 39	289
61	26 02	009	30 11	033	45 02	062	38 27	116	19 12	169	65 47	232	40 00	288
62	26 08	008	30 33	032	45 38	060	39 04	115	19 20	169	65 15	232	39 21	287
63	26 13	007	30 54	030	46 14	059	39 41	115	19 28	168	64 43	232	38 42	286
64	26 17	006	31 15	029	46 49	058	40 18	114	19 37	168	64 11	232	38 02	285
65	26 21	004	31 34	028	47 23	057	40 56	114	19 45	167	63 38	232	37 23	285
66	26 24	003	31 53	027	47 57	056	41 33	113	19 54	167	63 06	232	36 43	284
67	26 26	002	32 12	026	48 31	055	42 11	113	20 04	166	62 33	233	36 03	283
68	26 27	001	32 29	025	49 04	054	42 49	112	20 13	166	62 01	233	35 23	282
69	26 28	000	32 46	024	49 37	052	43 26	112	20 23	166	61 28	233	34 43	281
70	26 27	359	33 02	023	50 09	051	44 04	111	20 34	165	60 56	233	34 03	280
71	26 26	358	33 18	022	50 41	050	44 43	111	20 45	165	60 23	233	33 23	280
72	26 25	357	33 32	020	51 12	049	45 21	111	20 56	164	59 51	233	32 42	279
73	26 22	356	33 46	019	51 42	047	45 59	110	21 07	164	59 18	233	32 02	278
74	26 19	355	33 59	018	52 12	046	46 38	110	21 19	163	58 46	233	31 21	277
	BETELGEUSE		SIRIUS		◆ Suhail		RIGIL KENT		◆ ACHERNAR		Diphda		◆ ALDEBARAN	
75	34 11	017	52 41	045	47 16	109	21 31	163	58 13	233	30 41	276	26 15	354
76	34 23	016	53 10	043	47 55	109	21 43	162	57 41	232	30 00	276	26 10	353
77	34 33	014	53 37	042	48 34	108	21 56	162	57 08	232	29 19	275	26 04	352
78	34 43	013	54 04	041	49 13	108	22 09	161	56 36	232	28 38	274	25 58	351
79	34 52	012	54 31	039	49 52	107	22 22	161	56 03	232	27 58	273	25 51	350
80	35 00	011	54 56	038	50 31	107	22 36	160	55 31	232	27 17	273	25 43	348
81	35 08	010	55 20	036	51 10	106	22 50	160	54 59	232	26 36	272	25 35	347
82	35 14	009	55 44	035	51 50	106	23 04	159	54 27	232	25 55	271	25 26	346
83	35 20	007	56 07	033	52 29	105	23 19	159	53 55	232	25 14	270	25 16	345
84	35 25	006	56 29	031	53 09	105	23 34	158	53 23	232	24 33	270	25 05	344
85	35 29	005	56 49	030	53 48	104	23 49	158	52 51	231	23 52	269	24 53	343
86	35 32	004	57 09	028	54 28	104	24 04	158	52 19	231	23 11	268	24 41	342
87	35 34	002	57 28	026	55 08	103	24 20	157	51 47	231	22 30	267	24 28	341
88	35 35	001	57 46	025	55 48	103	24 36	157	51 15	231	21 49	267	24 15	340
89	35 35	000	58 02	023	56 28	102	24 53	156	50 43	231	21 09	266	24 01	339

LHA ♈	Hc	Zn	Hc	Zn	Hc	Zn	Hc	Zn	Hc	Zn	Hc	Zn	Hc	Zn
	PROCYON		Alphard		◆ Suhail		RIGIL KENT		◆ ACHERNAR		◆ RIGEL		BETELGEUSE	
90	33 19	030	31 41	066	57 08	102	25 09	156	50 12	230	50 02	343	35 35	359
91	33 40	029	32 18	065	57 48	101	25 26	155	49 40	230	49 49	341	35 34	358
92	33 59	028	32 55	065	58 28	100	25 44	155	49 09	230	49 35	340	35 32	356
93	34 18	027	33 32	064	59 09	100	26 01	154	48 38	230	49 20	338	35 29	355
94	34 36	026	34 09	063	59 49	099	26 19	154	48 07	229	49 05	337	35 25	354
95	34 54	025	34 45	062	60 29	099	26 37	154	47 35	229	48 48	335	35 20	353
96	35 10	023	35 21	061	61 10	098	26 55	153	47 04	229	48 30	334	35 14	351
97	35 26	022	35 56	060	61 50	098	27 14	153	46 34	229	48 12	332	35 08	350
98	35 41	021	36 32	059	62 31	097	27 33	152	46 03	228	47 53	331	35 00	349
99	35 55	020	37 06	058	63 11	097	27 52	152	45 32	228	47 32	330	34 52	348
100	36 09	019	37 41	057	63 52	096	28 11	152	45 02	228	47 11	328	34 43	347
101	36 22	017	38 15	056	64 33	095	28 31	151	44 32	228	46 49	327	34 33	345
102	36 34	016	38 48	055	65 14	095	28 51	151	44 01	227	46 26	326	34 23	344
103	36 45	015	39 22	054	65 54	094	29 11	150	43 31	227	46 03	324	34 11	343
104	36 55	014	39 54	053	66 35	094	29 31	150	43 01	227	45 39	323	33 59	342
	PROCYON		REGULUS		◆ Gienah		RIGIL KENT		◆ ACHERNAR		RIGEL		◆ BETELGEUSE	
105	37 04	013	17 34	049	20 07	095	29 52	149	42 32	227	45 14	322	33 46	341
106	37 12	011	18 05	048	20 48	094	30 13	149	42 02	226	44 48	320	33 32	340
107	37 20	010	18 35	047	21 28	093	30 34	149	41 33	226	44 21	319	33 17	338
108	37 27	009	19 05	046	22 09	092	30 55	148	41 03	226	43 54	318	33 02	337
109	37 33	008	19 34	045	22 50	092	31 17	148	40 34	225	43 27	317	32 46	336
110	37 38	006	20 03	045	23 31	091	31 39	148	40 05	225	42 58	316	32 29	335
111	37 42	005	20 32	044	24 12	090	32 01	147	39 36	225	42 29	314	32 11	334
112	37 45	004	21 00	043	24 53	090	32 23	147	39 08	224	42 00	313	31 53	333
113	37 47	003	21 27	042	25 34	089	32 46	146	38 39	224	41 30	312	31 34	332
114	37 48	001	21 54	041	26 15	088	33 08	146	38 11	224	40 59	311	31 14	331
115	37 49	000	22 21	040	26 56	087	33 31	146	37 43	223	40 28	310	30 54	330
116	37 48	359	22 47	039	27 36	087	33 55	145	37 15	223	39 56	309	30 33	328
117	37 47	358	23 12	038	28 17	086	34 18	145	36 47	223	39 24	308	30 11	327
118	37 45	356	23 37	037	28 58	085	34 41	145	36 19	222	38 51	307	29 49	326
119	37 42	355	24 01	036	29 39	084	35 05	144	35 52	222	38 18	306	29 26	325
	REGULUS		◆ SPICA		RIGIL KENT		◆ ACHERNAR		RIGEL		BETELGEUSE		◆ PROCYON	
120	24 25	035	13 58	092	35 29	144	35 25	221	37 45	304	29 02	324	37 38	354
121	24 48	034	14 39	091	35 53	144	34 58	221	37 11	303	28 38	323	37 33	352
122	25 11	033	15 20	090	36 18	143	34 31	221	36 36	302	28 13	322	37 27	351
123	25 33	032	16 01	089	36 42	143	34 04	220	36 02	301	27 48	321	37 20	350
124	25 54	031	16 42	089	37 07	143	33 38	220	35 27	300	27 22	320	37 13	349
125	26 15	030	17 23	088	37 32	142	33 12	220	34 51	299	26 55	319	37 04	348
126	26 35	029	18 04	087	37 57	142	32 46	219	34 15	299	26 28	318	36 55	346
127	26 55	028	18 45	086	38 22	142	32 20	219	33 39	298	26 01	317	36 45	345
128	27 14	027	19 25	086	38 48	141	31 55	218	33 03	297	25 33	316	36 34	344
129	27 32	026	20 06	085	39 13	141	31 29	218	32 26	296	25 04	315	36 22	343
130	27 49	025	20 47	084	39 39	141	31 04	218	31 49	295	24 35	314	36 10	341
131	28 06	024	21 28	083	40 05	141	30 39	217	31 12	294	24 06	313	35 56	340
132	28 22	023	22 08	083	40 31	140	30 15	217	30 34	293	23 36	312	35 42	339
133	28 38	022	22 49	082	40 57	140	29 50	216	29 57	292	23 05	312	35 27	338
134	28 53	021	23 29	081	41 24	140	29 26	216	29 19	291	22 34	311	35 11	337
	◆ REGULUS		SPICA		◆ RIGIL KENT		ACHERNAR		◆ CANOPUS		SIRIUS		PROCYON	
135	29 07	019	24 10	080	41 50	139	29 02	216	64 36	243	49 01	306	34 54	335
136	29 20	018	24 50	080	42 17	139	28 39	215	63 59	242	48 28	305	34 37	334
137	29 32	017	25 30	079	42 44	139	28 15	215	63 23	242	47 54	304	34 19	333
138	29 44	016	26 10	078	43 11	139	27 52	214	62 47	242	47 20	303	34 00	332
139	29 55	015	26 50	077	43 38	138	27 29	214	62 11	242	46 45	302	33 41	331
140	30 05	014	27 30	076	44 05	138	27 06	213	61 34	242	46 10	300	33 20	330
141	30 15	013	28 10	076	44 32	138	26 44	213	60 58	242	45 35	299	32 59	329
142	30 23	012	28 49	075	45 00	138	26 22	212	60 22	242	44 59	298	32 38	328
143	30 31	011	29 29	074	45 27	137	26 00	212	59 46	242	44 23	297	32 15	326
144	30 38	009	30 08	073	45 55	137	25 39	212	59 10	241	43 46	296	31 53	325
145	30 45	008	30 47	072	46 23	137	25 17	211	58 34	241	43 09	295	31 29	324
146	30 50	007	31 26	071	46 51	137	24 56	211	57 59	241	42 32	294	31 05	323
147	30 55	006	32 04	070	47 19	137	24 35	210	57 23	241	41 55	293	30 40	322
148	30 59	005	32 43	070	47 47	136	24 15	210	56 47	241	41 17	292	30 15	321
149	31 02	004	33 21	069	48 15	136	23 55	209	56 12	240	40 39	291	29 49	320
	◆ REGULUS		SPICA		◆ RIGIL KENT		ACHERNAR		◆ CANOPUS		SIRIUS		PROCYON	
150	31 04	003	33 59	068	48 44	136	23 35	209	55 36	240	40 01	290	29 22	319
151	31 06	001	34 37	067	49 12	136	23 15	208	55 01	240	39 22	289	28 55	318
152	31 06	000	35 14	066	49 41	136	22 56	208	54 25	240	38 44	289	28 27	317
153	31 06	359	35 52	065	50 09	136	22 37	207	53 50	239	38 05	288	27 59	316
154	31 05	358	36 29	064	50 38	135	22 18	207	53 15	239	37 26	287	27 31	315
155	31 03	357	37 05	063	51 07	135	22 00	206	52 40	239	36 46	286	27 01	314
156	31 01	356	37 42	062	51 35	135	21 42	206	52 05	239	36 07	285	26 32	313
157	30 57	355	38 18	061	52 04	135	21 24	205	51 30	238	35 27	284	26 02	312
158	30 53	353	38 53	060	52 33	135	21 07	205	50 55	238	34 48	283	25 31	311
159	30 48	352	39 29	059	53 02	135	20 50	204	50 21	238	34 08	283	25 00	310
160	30 42	351	40 03	058	53 31	135	20 33	204	49 46	237	33 28	282	24 29	309
161	30 36	350	40 38	057	54 00	135	20 16	203	49 12	237	32 48	281	23 57	308
162	30 28	349	41 12	056	54 29	135	20 00	203	48 37	237	32 07	280	23 25	307
163	30 20	348	41 46	055	54 59	135	19 45	202	48 03	237	31 27	279	22 52	307
164	30 11	347	42 19	054	55 28	135	19 29	202	47 29	236	30 47	278	22 19	306
	SPICA		◆ ANTARES		RIGIL KENT		ACHERNAR		◆ CANOPUS		SIRIUS		◆ REGULUS	
165	42 52	053	23 52	104	55 57	135	19 14	201	46 55	236	30 06	278	30 01	346
166	43 24	052	24 32	103	56 26	135	18 59	201	46 21	236	29 26	277	29 51	344
167	43 56	050	25 12	103	56 55	135	18 45	200	45 48	235	28 45	276	29 39	343
168	44 27	049	25 52	102	57 24	135	18 31	200	45 14	235	28 04	275	29 28	342
169	44 58	048	26 32	101	57 54	135	18 17	199	44 41	235	27 23	275	29 14	341
170	45 28	047	27 12	101	58 23	135	18 03	199	44 07	234	26 43	274	29 01	340
171	45 58	046	27 53	100	58 52	135	17 50	198	43 34	234	26 02	273	28 47	339
172	46 27	044	28 33	099	59 21	135	17 38	198	43 01	234	25 21	272	28 31	338
173	46 55	043	29 13	099	59 50	135	17 25	197	42 28	233	24 40	272	28 16	337
174	47 23	042	29 54	098	60 19	135	17 13	197	41 56	233	23 59	271	27 59	336
175	47 50	041	30 35	097	60 48	135	17 02	196	41 23	232	23 18	270	27 42	335
176	48 16	039	31 15	097	61 17	135	16 50	196	40 51	232	22 37	269	27 24	334
177	48 42	038	31 56	096	61 46	135	16 39	195	40 19	232	21 56	269	27 06	333
178	49 07	037	32 37	095	62 14	135	16 29	195	39 47	231	21 15	268	26 47	332
179	49 31	035	33 17	094	62 43	136	16 19	194	39 15	231	20 35	267	26 27	331

 LAT 47°S

LHA ♈	Hc	Zn	Hc	Zn	Hc	Zn	Hc	Zn	Hc	Zn	Hc	Zn	Hc	Zn
	◆ ARCTURUS		ANTARES		◆ Peacock		ACHERNAR		CANOPUS		◆ Suhail		REGULUS	
180	17 07	034	33 58	094	22 47	151	16 09	194	38 43	231	60 00	261	26 07	330
181	17 30	033	34 39	093	23 07	151	15 59	193	38 12	230	59 20	260	25 46	329
182	17 51	032	35 20	092	23 27	151	15 50	192	37 40	230	58 39	260	25 24	328
183	18 13	031	36 01	092	23 47	150	15 42	192	37 09	229	57 59	259	25 02	327
184	18 33	030	36 42	091	24 08	150	15 34	191	36 38	229	57 19	259	24 39	326
185	18 54	029	37 23	090	24 29	149	15 26	191	36 07	229	56 39	258	24 15	325
186	19 13	028	38 04	089	24 50	149	15 18	190	35 37	228	55 59	258	23 51	324
187	19 32	027	38 44	089	25 11	148	15 11	190	35 06	228	55 19	257	23 27	323
188	19 50	026	39 25	088	25 33	148	15 04	189	34 36	227	54 39	257	23 02	322
189	20 08	025	40 06	087	25 55	147	14 58	189	34 06	227	53 59	256	22 36	321
190	20 25	024	40 47	086	26 17	147	14 52	188	33 36	227	53 20	256	22 10	320
191	20 42	023	41 28	086	26 40	146	14 46	188	33 07	226	52 40	255	21 43	319
192	20 58	022	42 09	085	27 02	146	14 41	187	32 37	226	52 01	255	21 16	318
193	21 13	021	42 49	084	27 25	145	14 36	186	32 08	225	51 21	254	20 48	317
194	21 28	020	43 30	083	27 49	145	14 32	186	31 39	225	50 42	254	20 20	316
	ARCTURUS		◆ ANTARES		Peacock		◆ ACHERNAR		CANOPUS		Suhail		◆ REGULUS	
195	21 42	019	44 11	082	28 12	145	14 28	185	31 11	224	50 03	253	19 51	315
196	21 55	018	44 51	082	28 36	144	14 24	185	30 42	224	49 24	253	19 22	314
197	22 07	017	45 32	081	29 00	144	14 21	184	30 14	224	48 45	252	18 53	313
198	22 19	016	46 12	080	29 25	143	14 18	184	29 46	223	48 06	252	18 23	312
199	22 31	015	46 52	079	29 49	143	14 16	183	29 18	223	47 27	251	17 52	312
200	22 41	014	47 32	078	30 14	142	14 14	183	28 50	222	46 48	251	17 22	311
201	22 51	013	48 12	077	30 39	142	14 12	182	28 23	222	46 10	250	16 50	310
202	23 00	012	48 52	076	31 04	142	14 11	181	27 56	221	45 31	250	16 19	309
203	23 09	011	49 32	076	31 30	141	14 10	181	27 29	221	44 53	249	15 47	308
204	23 16	010	50 11	075	31 55	141	14 10	180	27 02	220	44 15	249	15 14	307
205	23 23	009	50 51	074	32 21	140	14 10	180	26 36	220	43 37	248	14 41	306
206	23 30	008	51 30	073	32 47	140	14 10	179	26 10	219	42 59	248	14 08	306
207	23 35	007	52 09	072	33 14	140	14 11	179	25 44	219	42 21	247	13 35	305
208	23 40	006	52 48	071	33 40	139	14 12	178	25 18	218	41 44	247	13 01	304
209	23 44	005	53 26	070	34 07	139	14 14	178	24 53	218	41 06	246	12 27	303
	◆ ARCTURUS		ANTARES		◆ Peacock		ACHERNAR		CANOPUS		◆ Suhail		SPICA	
210	23 48	004	54 04	069	34 34	139	14 16	177	24 28	217	40 29	246	53 31	346
211	23 50	003	54 42	067	35 01	138	14 18	176	24 03	217	39 51	245	53 21	344
212	23 52	002	55 20	066	35 29	138	14 21	176	23 39	217	39 14	245	53 09	343
213	23 53	001	55 57	065	35 56	137	14 24	175	23 15	216	38 37	244	52 57	341
214	23 54	000	56 34	064	36 24	137	14 27	175	22 51	216	38 01	244	52 43	339
215	23 53	359	57 11	063	36 52	137	14 31	174	22 27	215	37 24	243	52 28	338
216	23 52	358	57 47	062	37 20	136	14 36	174	22 04	215	36 48	243	52 12	336
217	23 51	357	58 23	060	37 49	136	14 40	173	21 41	214	36 11	242	51 55	335
218	23 48	356	58 58	059	38 17	136	14 46	173	21 18	214	35 35	242	51 37	333
219	23 45	355	59 33	058	38 46	135	14 51	172	20 56	213	34 59	241	51 18	332
220	23 41	354	60 07	056	39 15	135	14 57	171	20 33	212	34 23	241	50 59	330
221	23 36	353	60 41	055	39 44	135	15 03	171	20 12	212	33 48	240	50 38	329
222	23 31	352	61 14	053	40 13	134	15 10	170	19 50	211	33 12	240	50 16	327
223	23 25	351	61 47	052	40 43	134	15 17	170	19 29	211	32 37	239	49 54	326
224	23 18	350	62 19	050	41 12	134	15 25	169	19 08	210	32 02	239	49 31	325
	ANTARES		◆ Nunki		Peacock		ACHERNAR		◆ CANOPUS		◆ SPICA		ARCTURUS	
225	62 50	049	39 40	087	41 42	133	15 32	169	18 48	210	49 07	323	23 10	349
226	63 20	047	40 21	087	42 12	133	15 41	168	18 27	209	48 42	322	23 02	348
227	63 50	046	41 02	086	42 42	133	15 49	168	18 07	209	48 16	321	22 53	347
228	64 18	044	41 42	085	43 12	132	15 58	167	17 48	208	47 50	319	22 43	346
229	64 46	042	42 23	084	43 42	132	16 08	166	17 29	208	47 23	318	22 33	345
230	65 13	040	43 04	083	44 13	132	16 17	166	17 10	207	46 55	317	22 21	344
231	65 39	038	43 44	083	44 43	131	16 27	165	16 51	207	46 27	315	22 10	343
232	66 04	036	44 25	082	45 14	131	16 38	165	16 33	206	45 58	314	21 57	342
233	66 28	034	45 05	081	45 45	131	16 49	164	16 15	206	45 28	313	21 44	341
234	66 50	032	45 46	080	46 16	131	17 00	164	15 58	205	44 58	312	21 30	340
235	67 11	030	46 26	079	46 47	130	17 12	163	15 41	204	44 27	311	21 16	339
236	67 31	028	47 06	078	47 18	130	17 24	163	15 24	204	43 56	310	21 00	338
237	67 50	026	47 46	078	47 49	130	17 36	162	15 08	203	43 24	308	20 45	337
238	68 07	024	48 26	077	48 21	130	17 49	162	14 52	203	42 52	307	20 28	336
239	68 23	021	49 06	076	48 52	129	18 02	161	14 36	202	42 19	306	20 11	335
	Rasalhague		◆ ALTAIR		FOMALHAUT		◆ ACHERNAR		ACRUX		◆ SPICA		ARCTURUS	
240	26 43	026	14 11	060	12 10	121	18 15	161	56 51	221	41 46	305	19 54	334
241	27 01	025	14 46	059	12 46	120	18 29	160	56 24	221	41 12	304	19 35	333
242	27 18	024	15 21	058	13 21	119	18 43	160	55 57	221	40 38	303	19 16	332
243	27 35	023	15 55	057	13 57	119	18 57	159	55 30	221	40 03	302	18 57	331
244	27 50	022	16 30	056	14 33	118	19 12	159	55 03	221	39 28	301	18 37	330
245	28 05	021	17 04	055	15 09	117	19 27	158	54 36	221	38 53	300	18 16	329
246	28 20	020	17 37	055	15 46	117	19 42	158	54 09	221	38 17	299	17 55	328
247	28 33	019	18 10	054	16 23	116	19 58	157	53 42	221	37 41	298	17 33	327
248	28 46	018	18 43	053	16 59	115	20 14	157	53 15	221	37 05	297	17 11	327
249	28 58	017	19 16	052	17 37	115	20 31	156	52 48	221	36 28	296	16 48	326
250	29 10	016	19 48	051	18 14	114	20 47	156	52 21	221	35 51	295	16 25	325
251	29 20	014	20 19	050	18 51	113	21 04	155	51 54	221	35 14	294	16 01	324
252	29 30	013	20 51	049	19 29	113	21 22	155	51 27	221	34 37	293	15 36	323
253	29 39	012	21 21	048	20 07	112	21 40	154	51 00	221	33 59	292	15 12	322
254	29 48	011	21 52	048	20 45	112	21 58	154	50 33	221	33 21	291	14 46	321
	Rasalhague		◆ ALTAIR		FOMALHAUT		◆ ACHERNAR		ACRUX		◆ SPICA		ANTARES	
255	29 55	010	22 22	047	21 23	111	22 16	153	50 07	221	32 43	290	68 39	341
256	30 02	009	22 51	046	22 01	110	22 35	153	49 40	221	32 04	290	68 25	339
257	30 08	008	23 20	045	22 40	110	22 54	152	49 13	221	31 26	289	68 10	337
258	30 13	007	23 49	044	23 18	109	23 13	152	48 47	220	30 47	288	67 53	335
259	30 17	006	24 17	043	23 57	108	23 32	151	48 20	220	30 08	287	67 34	332
260	30 21	004	24 45	042	24 36	108	23 52	151	47 54	220	29 28	286	67 15	330
261	30 24	003	25 12	041	25 15	107	24 12	150	47 28	220	28 49	285	66 54	328
262	30 26	002	25 38	040	25 54	106	24 33	150	47 01	220	28 09	284	66 31	326
263	30 27	001	26 04	039	26 33	106	24 53	149	46 35	220	27 30	284	66 08	324
264	30 27	000	26 30	038	27 13	105	25 14	149	46 09	219	26 50	283	65 43	322
265	30 27	359	26 55	037	27 52	105	25 36	148	45 43	219	26 10	282	65 18	320
266	30 25	358	27 19	036	28 32	104	25 57	148	45 17	219	25 30	281	64 51	318
267	30 23	357	27 43	035	29 12	103	26 19	148	44 52	219	24 50	280	64 23	316
268	30 20	355	28 06	034	29 52	103	26 41	147	44 26	219	24 09	280	63 55	315
269	30 17	354	28 28	033	30 32	102	27 03	147	44 01	218	23 29	279	63 25	313

LHA ♈	Hc	Zn	Hc	Zn	Hc	Zn	Hc	Zn	Hc	Zn	Hc	Zn	Hc	Zn
	◆ ALTAIR		FOMALHAUT		◆ ACHERNAR		RIGIL KENT		◆ SPICA		ANTARES		Rasalhague	
270	28 50	032	31 12	101	27 26	146	58 32	225	22 49	278	62 55	311	30 12	353
271	29 11	031	31 52	101	27 49	146	58 03	225	22 08	277	62 24	310	30 07	352
272	29 32	030	32 32	100	28 12	145	57 34	225	21 27	277	61 52	308	30 01	351
273	29 52	029	33 13	099	28 35	145	57 04	225	20 47	276	61 19	307	29 54	350
274	30 11	028	33 53	099	28 59	145	56 35	225	20 06	275	60 46	305	29 46	349
275	30 30	026	34 33	098	29 23	144	56 06	225	19 25	274	60 13	304	29 38	348
276	30 48	025	35 14	097	29 47	144	55 37	225	18 44	274	59 39	303	29 28	346
277	31 05	024	35 55	097	30 11	143	55 08	225	18 04	273	59 04	301	29 18	345
278	31 21	023	36 35	096	30 36	143	54 39	225	17 23	272	58 29	300	29 08	344
279	31 37	022	37 16	095	31 01	142	54 10	225	16 42	271	57 53	299	28 56	343
280	31 52	021	37 57	095	31 26	142	53 40	225	16 01	271	57 17	297	28 44	342
281	32 06	020	38 38	094	31 51	142	53 11	225	15 20	270	56 40	296	28 31	341
282	32 20	019	39 18	093	32 17	141	52 42	225	14 39	269	56 03	295	28 17	340
283	32 33	018	39 59	093	32 42	141	52 14	225	13 58	268	55 26	294	28 03	339
284	32 44	016	40 40	092	33 08	140	51 45	225	13 17	268	54 48	293	27 48	338
	ALTAIR		Enif		◆ FOMALHAUT		ACHERNAR		◆ RIGIL KENT		ANTARES		◆ Rasalhague	
285	32 56	015	22 16	045	41 21	091	33 34	140	51 16	225	54 11	292	27 32	337
286	33 06	014	22 44	044	42 02	090	34 01	140	50 47	225	53 32	291	27 15	336
287	33 15	013	23 12	043	42 43	090	34 27	139	50 18	224	52 54	290	26 58	335
288	33 24	012	23 40	042	43 24	089	34 54	139	49 50	224	52 15	289	26 40	334
289	33 32	011	24 07	041	44 05	088	35 21	139	49 21	224	51 36	288	26 21	332
290	33 39	009	24 33	040	44 46	087	35 48	138	48 53	224	50 57	287	26 02	331
291	33 45	008	24 59	039	45 27	087	36 16	138	48 24	224	50 18	286	25 42	330
292	33 51	007	25 25	038	46 07	086	36 43	137	47 56	224	49 38	285	25 22	329
293	33 55	006	25 49	037	46 48	085	37 11	137	47 28	223	48 59	284	25 01	328
294	33 59	005	26 14	036	47 29	084	37 39	137	47 00	223	48 19	283	24 39	327
295	34 02	003	26 37	035	48 10	083	38 07	136	46 32	223	47 39	282	24 17	326
296	34 04	002	27 00	034	48 50	083	38 35	136	46 04	223	46 59	281	23 54	325
297	34 05	001	27 23	033	49 31	082	39 04	136	45 36	223	46 19	280	23 30	324
298	34 05	000	27 45	032	50 11	081	39 32	135	45 09	222	45 38	279	23 06	323
299	34 05	359	28 06	031	50 52	080	40 01	135	44 41	222	44 58	278	22 42	323
	◆ Enif		FOMALHAUT		◆ ACHERNAR		RIGIL KENT		◆ ANTARES		Rasalhague		ALTAIR	
300	28 27	030	51 32	079	40 30	135	44 14	222	44 17	278	22 16	322	34 04	357
301	28 46	029	52 12	078	40 59	134	43 46	222	43 37	277	21 51	321	34 01	356
302	29 06	028	52 52	077	41 29	134	43 19	221	42 56	276	21 24	320	33 58	355
303	29 24	026	53 32	076	41 58	134	42 52	221	42 15	275	20 58	319	33 54	354
304	29 42	025	54 11	075	42 28	134	42 25	221	41 35	274	20 31	318	33 50	353
305	29 59	024	54 51	075	42 57	133	41 59	221	40 54	274	20 03	317	33 44	352
306	30 16	023	55 30	073	43 27	133	41 32	220	40 13	273	19 35	316	33 37	350
307	30 32	022	56 09	072	43 57	133	41 06	220	39 32	272	19 06	315	33 30	349
308	30 47	021	56 48	071	44 28	132	40 39	220	38 51	271	18 37	314	33 22	348
309	31 01	020	57 27	070	44 58	132	40 13	220	38 10	271	18 07	313	33 13	347
310	31 15	019	58 05	069	45 28	132	39 47	219	37 29	270	17 37	312	33 03	346
311	31 27	018	58 44	068	45 59	132	39 21	219	36 48	269	17 07	312	32 53	345
312	31 39	017	59 21	067	46 30	131	38 56	219	36 08	268	16 36	311	32 42	343
313	31 51	015	59 59	066	47 00	131	38 30	218	35 27	268	16 05	310	32 30	342
314	32 01	014	60 36	065	47 31	131	38 05	218	34 46	267	15 33	309	32 17	341
	◆ Enif		Diphda		◆ ACHERNAR		Miaplacidus		RIGIL KENT		◆ ANTARES		ALTAIR	
315	32 11	013	35 56	077	48 02	131	26 48	181	37 40	218	34 05	266	32 03	340
316	32 20	012	36 36	076	48 33	130	26 48	181	37 15	217	33 24	266	31 49	339
317	32 28	011	37 16	076	49 05	130	26 47	181	36 50	217	32 43	265	31 33	338
318	32 35	010	37 55	075	49 36	130	26 47	180	36 25	217	32 03	264	31 17	337
319	32 41	008	38 35	074	50 08	130	26 47	180	36 01	216	31 22	264	31 01	335
320	32 47	007	39 14	073	50 39	129	26 47	179	35 37	216	30 41	263	30 43	334
321	32 52	006	39 53	072	51 11	129	26 48	179	35 13	216	30 01	262	30 25	333
322	32 56	005	40 32	071	51 42	129	26 49	179	34 49	215	29 20	262	30 07	332
323	32 59	004	41 11	070	52 14	129	26 50	178	34 25	215	28 40	261	29 47	331
324	33 01	003	41 49	069	52 46	129	26 51	178	34 02	215	27 59	260	29 27	330
325	33 03	001	42 27	068	53 18	129	26 53	177	33 39	214	27 19	260	29 06	329
326	33 03	000	43 05	067	53 50	128	26 55	177	33 16	214	26 39	259	28 45	328
327	33 03	359	43 43	066	54 22	128	26 57	177	32 53	214	25 59	258	28 23	327
328	33 02	358	44 20	065	54 55	128	27 00	176	32 30	213	25 19	258	28 00	326
329	33 00	357	44 57	064	55 27	128	27 02	176	32 08	213	24 39	257	27 37	325
	◆ Diphda		ACHERNAR		◆ Miaplacidus		RIGIL KENT		ANTARES		◆ ALTAIR		Enif	
330	45 34	063	55 59	128	27 06	175	31 46	213	23 59	256	27 13	324	32 57	356
331	46 10	062	56 31	128	27 09	175	31 24	212	23 19	256	26 49	323	32 54	354
332	46 46	061	57 04	128	27 12	175	31 02	212	22 40	255	26 24	322	32 49	353
333	47 22	060	57 36	128	27 16	174	30 41	211	22 00	254	25 58	321	32 44	352
334	47 57	059	58 09	127	27 21	174	30 20	211	21 21	254	25 32	320	32 38	351
335	48 32	058	58 41	127	27 25	174	29 59	211	20 42	253	25 05	319	32 31	350
336	49 06	057	59 14	127	27 30	173	29 38	210	20 03	252	24 38	318	32 24	349
337	49 40	055	59 46	127	27 35	173	29 17	210	19 24	252	24 10	317	32 15	347
338	50 14	054	60 19	127	27 40	172	28 57	209	18 45	251	23 42	316	32 06	346
339	50 47	053	60 51	127	27 45	172	28 37	209	18 06	250	23 13	315	31 56	345
340	51 19	052	61 24	127	27 51	172	28 17	209	17 28	250	22 44	314	31 45	344
341	51 51	051	61 56	127	27 57	171	27 58	208	16 50	249	22 15	313	31 33	343
342	52 22	049	62 29	127	28 03	171	27 39	208	16 12	248	21 44	312	31 21	342
343	52 53	048	63 01	128	28 10	171	27 20	207	15 34	248	21 14	311	31 07	341
344	53 23	047	63 34	128	28 17	170	27 01	207	14 56	247	20 43	310	30 53	339
	◆ Diphda		Acamar		◆ CANOPUS		Miaplacidus		RIGIL KENT		◆ Nunki		Enif	
345	53 52	045	47 19	104	25 40	141	28 24	170	26 43	207	38 22	271	30 39	338
346	54 21	044	47 59	103	26 06	141	28 31	169	26 25	206	37 41	270	30 23	337
347	54 49	042	48 39	102	26 32	140	28 39	169	26 07	206	37 00	270	30 07	336
348	55 16	041	49 19	102	26 59	140	28 47	169	25 49	205	36 19	269	29 50	335
349	55 43	039	49 59	101	27 25	139	28 55	168	25 32	205	35 38	268	29 33	334
350	56 08	038	50 39	101	27 52	139	29 03	168	25 15	204	34 57	268	29 14	333
351	56 33	036	51 19	100	28 19	138	29 12	168	24 58	204	34 17	267	28 55	332
352	56 57	035	51 59	100	28 46	138	29 21	167	24 41	204	33 36	266	28 36	331
353	57 20	033	52 40	099	29 14	137	29 30	167	24 25	203	32 55	265	28 16	330
354	57 41	032	53 20	098	29 42	137	29 39	167	24 09	203	32 14	265	27 55	329
355	58 02	030	54 01	098	30 10	137	29 49	166	23 54	202	31 33	264	27 33	328
356	58 22	028	54 41	097	30 38	136	29 59	166	23 39	202	30 53	263	27 11	327
357	58 41	026	55 22	097	31 06	136	30 09	166	23 24	201	30 12	263	26 48	326
358	58 59	025	56 03	096	31 35	135	30 19	165	23 09	201	29 32	262	26 25	325
359	59 15	023	56 43	095	32 04	135	30 30	165	22 55	200	28 51	261	26 01	324

LHA ♈	Hc Zn	Hc Zn	Hc Zn	Hc Zn	Hc Zn	Hc Zn	Hc Zn
	Alpheratz	**Hamal**	**◆RIGEL**	**CANOPUS**	**◆RIGIL KENT**	**Peacock**	**◆FOMALHAUT**
0	12 48 002	12 55 030	13 33 087	33 15 134	23 37 200	57 13 234	68 05 322
1	12 49 001	13 15 029	14 13 086	33 44 133	23 23 200	56 40 234	67 39 320
2	12 50 000	13 34 028	14 53 086	34 13 133	23 10 199	56 08 234	67 13 318
3	12 49 359	13 53 027	15 33 085	34 43 133	22 57 199	55 35 234	66 46 316
4	12 49 358	14 11 026	16 13 084	35 12 132	22 44 198	55 03 234	66 17 314
5	12 47 358	14 28 025	16 53 083	35 42 132	22 32 198	54 30 234	65 48 312
6	12 45 357	14 45 025	17 33 083	36 12 131	22 20 197	53 58 233	65 18 311
7	12 43 356	15 02 024	18 13 082	36 43 131	22 08 197	53 26 233	64 47 309
8	12 39 355	15 17 023	18 52 081	37 13 130	21 57 196	52 54 233	64 15 307
9	12 36 354	15 33 022	19 32 080	37 44 130	21 46 196	52 22 233	63 43 306
10	12 31 353	15 47 021	20 11 080	38 14 130	21 35 195	51 50 233	63 10 304
11	12 26 352	16 01 020	20 51 079	38 45 129	21 25 195	51 18 232	62 37 303
12	12 20 351	16 15 019	21 30 078	39 17 129	21 15 194	50 46 232	62 03 301
13	12 14 350	16 28 018	22 09 077	39 48 128	21 05 194	50 15 232	61 28 300
14	12 07 350	16 40 017	22 48 076	40 19 128	20 56 193	49 43 232	60 53 299
	Hamal	**◆RIGEL**	**SIRIUS**	**CANOPUS**	**◆RIGIL KENT**	**Peacock**	**◆FOMALHAUT**
15	16 51 016	23 27 076	14 42 099	40 51 128	20 47 193	49 12 231	60 18 297
16	17 02 015	24 06 075	15 21 098	41 23 127	20 38 192	48 40 231	59 42 296
17	17 12 014	24 45 074	16 01 097	41 55 127	20 30 192	48 09 231	59 06 295
18	17 22 013	25 23 073	16 41 097	42 27 127	20 21 191	47 38 231	58 29 294
19	17 31 012	26 02 072	17 21 096	43 00 126	20 14 191	47 07 230	57 52 293
20	17 40 012	26 40 071	18 01 095	43 32 126	20 06 190	46 36 230	57 15 291
21	17 47 011	27 18 071	18 41 095	44 05 125	19 59 190	46 06 230	56 38 290
22	17 54 010	27 56 070	19 21 094	44 37 125	19 53 189	45 35 229	56 00 289
23	18 01 009	28 33 069	20 01 093	45 10 125	19 47 189	45 05 229	55 22 288
24	18 06 008	29 10 068	20 41 092	45 43 124	19 41 188	44 35 229	54 43 287
25	18 11 007	29 47 067	21 21 092	46 17 124	19 35 188	44 04 228	54 05 286
26	18 16 006	30 24 066	22 01 091	46 50 124	19 30 187	43 34 228	53 26 285
27	18 20 005	31 01 065	22 42 090	47 24 123	19 25 187	43 05 228	52 47 284
28	18 23 004	31 37 064	23 22 089	47 57 123	19 20 186	42 35 228	52 08 283
29	18 25 003	32 13 063	24 02 089	48 31 123	19 16 186	42 05 227	51 29 282
	Hamal	**◆RIGEL**	**SIRIUS**	**CANOPUS**	**◆RIGIL KENT**	**Peacock**	**◆FOMALHAUT**
30	18 27 002	32 49 062	24 42 088	49 05 122	19 12 185	41 36 227	50 50 281
31	18 28 001	33 24 061	25 22 087	49 39 122	19 09 185	41 07 227	50 11 280
32	18 28 000	33 59 061	26 02 086	50 13 122	19 06 184	40 38 226	49 31 280
33	18 28 359	34 34 060	26 42 086	50 47 121	19 03 184	40 09 226	48 51 279
34	18 27 358	35 09 059	27 22 085	51 22 121	19 01 183	39 40 225	48 12 278
35	18 25 357	35 43 058	28 02 084	51 56 121	18 59 183	39 12 225	47 32 277
36	18 23 356	36 16 057	28 42 083	52 31 120	18 57 182	38 43 225	46 52 276
37	18 20 355	36 50 056	29 22 082	53 05 120	18 56 182	38 15 224	46 12 275
38	18 16 354	37 23 055	30 02 082	53 40 120	18 55 181	37 47 224	45 32 275
39	18 12 353	37 55 053	30 41 081	54 15 119	18 54 181	37 19 224	44 52 274
40	18 06 352	38 27 052	31 21 080	54 50 119	18 54 180	36 52 223	44 12 273
41	18 01 351	38 59 051	32 00 079	55 25 119	18 54 180	36 24 223	43 32 272
42	17 54 350	39 30 050	32 40 078	56 00 119	18 54 179	35 57 222	42 52 271
43	17 47 349	40 00 049	33 19 078	56 36 118	18 55 179	35 30 222	42 12 271
44	17 40 348	40 31 048	33 58 077	57 11 118	18 56 178	35 03 222	41 31 270
	RIGEL	**SIRIUS**	**◆CANOPUS**	**RIGIL KENT**	**◆Peacock**	**FOMALHAUT**	**◆Hamal**
45	41 00 047	34 37 076	57 46 118	18 58 178	34 37 221	40 51 269	17 31 348
46	41 29 046	35 16 075	58 22 118	19 00 177	34 10 221	40 11 268	17 22 347
47	41 58 045	35 55 074	58 58 117	19 02 176	33 44 221	39 31 268	17 13 346
48	42 25 043	36 33 073	59 33 117	19 05 176	33 18 220	38 51 267	17 02 345
49	42 53 042	37 12 072	60 09 117	19 08 175	32 52 220	38 11 266	16 51 344
50	43 19 041	37 50 071	60 45 117	19 11 175	32 27 219	37 31 266	16 40 343
51	43 45 040	38 28 071	61 21 117	19 15 174	32 02 219	36 51 265	16 28 342
52	44 11 039	39 06 070	61 57 116	19 19 174	31 36 218	36 11 264	16 15 341
53	44 35 037	39 43 069	62 33 116	19 23 173	31 12 218	35 31 264	16 01 340
54	44 59 036	40 20 068	63 09 116	19 28 173	30 47 218	34 51 263	15 47 339
55	45 23 035	40 57 067	63 45 116	19 33 172	30 23 217	34 11 262	15 33 338
56	45 45 033	41 34 066	64 21 116	19 39 172	29 58 217	33 31 261	15 18 337
57	46 07 032	42 11 065	64 57 116	19 45 171	29 34 216	32 52 261	15 02 336
58	46 28 031	42 47 064	65 33 115	19 51 171	29 11 216	32 12 260	14 45 335
59	46 48 029	43 23 063	66 10 115	19 57 170	28 47 215	31 33 259	14 28 335
	◆ALDEBARAN	**BETELGEUSE**	**SIRIUS**	**◆Suhail**	**RIGIL KENT**	**◆ACHERNAR**	**Diphda**
60	24 56 010	28 59 033	43 58 062	38 17 116	20 04 170	66 56 233	40 19 290
61	25 03 009	29 21 032	44 33 061	38 53 115	20 11 169	66 24 234	39 41 289
62	25 08 008	29 42 031	45 08 060	39 30 115	20 19 169	65 51 234	39 03 288
63	25 13 007	30 02 030	45 43 059	40 06 114	20 27 168	65 19 234	38 24 287
64	25 18 006	30 22 029	46 17 057	40 43 114	20 35 168	64 47 234	37 46 286
65	25 21 004	30 41 028	46 50 056	41 20 113	20 44 167	64 14 234	37 07 285
66	25 24 003	31 00 027	47 23 055	41 57 113	20 53 167	63 42 234	36 28 284
67	25 26 002	31 18 026	47 56 054	42 34 112	21 02 166	63 09 234	35 49 284
68	25 27 001	31 35 025	48 28 053	43 11 112	21 12 166	62 37 234	35 10 283
69	25 28 000	31 51 024	49 00 052	43 49 111	21 22 165	62 04 234	34 31 282
70	25 27 359	32 07 022	49 31 050	44 26 111	21 32 165	61 31 234	33 52 281
71	25 26 358	32 22 021	50 02 049	45 04 110	21 42 164	60 59 234	33 12 280
72	25 25 357	32 36 020	50 32 048	45 41 110	21 53 164	60 26 234	32 33 279
73	25 22 356	32 49 019	51 01 046	46 19 109	22 05 163	59 54 234	31 53 279
74	25 19 355	33 02 018	51 30 045	46 57 109	22 16 163	59 21 234	31 13 278
	BETELGEUSE	**SIRIUS**	**◆Suhail**	**RIGIL KENT**	**◆ACHERNAR**	**Diphda**	**◆ALDEBARAN**
75	33 14 017	51 58 044	47 35 108	22 28 162	58 49 234	30 34 277	25 15 354
76	33 25 015	52 26 042	48 14 107	22 40 162	58 17 234	29 54 276	25 11 353
77	33 35 014	52 53 041	48 52 107	22 53 162	57 44 234	29 14 275	25 05 352
78	33 45 013	53 19 040	49 31 106	23 06 161	57 12 234	28 34 275	24 59 351
79	33 54 012	53 44 038	50 09 106	23 19 161	56 40 233	27 54 274	24 52 350
80	34 02 011	54 08 037	50 48 105	23 32 160	56 08 233	27 14 273	24 45 349
81	34 09 010	54 32 035	51 26 105	23 46 160	55 35 233	26 34 272	24 36 348
82	34 15 008	54 54 034	52 05 104	24 00 159	55 03 233	25 53 272	24 27 347
83	34 20 007	55 16 032	52 44 104	24 15 159	54 31 233	25 13 271	24 17 345
84	34 25 006	55 37 031	53 23 103	24 30 158	53 59 233	24 33 270	24 07 344
85	34 29 005	55 57 029	54 02 103	24 45 158	53 28 232	23 53 269	23 56 343
86	34 32 004	56 16 027	54 42 102	25 00 157	52 56 232	23 13 269	23 44 342
87	34 34 002	56 34 026	55 21 102	25 15 157	52 24 232	22 33 268	23 32 341
88	34 35 001	56 51 024	56 00 101	25 31 156	51 53 232	21 53 267	23 18 340
89	34 35 000	57 07 022	56 40 101	25 48 156	51 21 232	21 13 266	23 05 339

LHA ♈	Hc Zn	Hc Zn	Hc Zn	Hc Zn	Hc Zn	Hc Zn	Hc Zn
	PROCYON	**Alphard**	**◆Suhail**	**RIGIL KENT**	**◆ACHERNAR**	**◆RIGEL**	**BETELGEUSE**
90	32 27 030	31 17 066	57 19 100	26 04 156	50 50 231	49 04 343	34 35 359
91	32 47 029	31 53 065	57 59 099	26 21 155	50 18 231	48 52 341	34 34 358
92	33 06 028	32 29 064	58 38 099	26 38 155	49 47 231	48 39 340	34 32 356
93	33 25 027	33 05 063	59 18 098	26 55 154	49 16 231	48 25 339	34 29 355
94	33 42 025	33 41 062	59 58 098	27 13 154	48 45 230	48 10 337	34 25 354
95	33 59 024	34 16 061	60 38 097	27 31 153	48 14 230	47 53 336	34 20 353
96	34 15 023	34 51 060	61 17 097	27 49 153	47 44 230	47 36 334	34 15 352
97	34 31 022	35 26 059	61 57 096	28 07 153	47 13 230	47 19 333	34 09 350
98	34 45 021	36 00 058	62 37 095	28 26 152	46 42 229	47 00 332	34 01 349
99	34 59 020	36 34 057	63 17 095	28 45 152	46 12 229	46 40 330	33 54 348
100	35 12 018	37 08 056	63 57 094	29 04 151	45 42 229	46 20 329	33 45 347
101	35 24 017	37 41 055	64 37 093	29 23 151	45 12 228	45 59 327	33 35 346
102	35 36 016	38 14 054	65 18 093	29 43 150	44 42 228	45 37 326	33 25 344
103	35 47 015	38 46 053	65 58 092	30 03 150	44 12 228	45 14 325	33 14 343
104	35 56 014	39 18 052	66 38 091	30 23 150	43 42 228	44 51 324	33 02 342
	PROCYON	**REGULUS**	**◆Gienah**	**RIGIL KENT**	**◆ACHERNAR**	**RIGEL**	**◆BETELGEUSE**
105	36 05 012	16 55 049	20 11 094	30 44 149	43 13 227	44 26 322	32 49 341
106	36 14 011	17 25 048	20 51 094	31 04 149	42 43 227	44 01 321	32 36 340
107	36 21 010	17 54 047	21 31 093	31 25 148	42 14 227	43 36 320	32 22 339
108	36 27 009	18 24 046	22 12 092	31 46 148	41 45 226	43 10 319	32 07 338
109	36 33 007	18 52 045	22 52 091	32 08 148	41 16 226	42 43 317	31 51 336
110	36 38 006	19 20 044	23 32 091	32 29 147	40 47 226	42 15 316	31 35 335
111	36 42 005	19 48 043	24 12 090	32 51 147	40 19 225	41 47 315	31 17 334
112	36 45 004	20 16 042	24 52 089	33 13 146	39 50 225	41 18 314	31 00 333
113	36 47 003	20 42 041	25 32 088	33 36 146	39 22 225	40 49 313	30 41 332
114	36 48 001	21 09 041	26 12 088	33 58 146	38 54 224	40 19 312	30 22 331
115	36 49 000	21 35 040	26 53 087	34 21 145	38 26 224	39 49 310	30 02 330
116	36 48 359	22 00 039	27 33 086	34 44 145	37 59 223	39 18 309	29 42 329
117	36 47 358	22 25 038	28 13 085	35 07 145	37 31 223	38 47 308	29 21 328
118	36 45 356	22 49 037	28 53 085	35 30 144	37 04 223	38 15 307	28 59 327
119	36 42 355	23 13 036	29 33 084	35 54 144	36 37 222	37 43 306	28 36 326
	REGULUS	**◆SPICA**	**RIGIL KENT**	**◆ACHERNAR**	**RIGEL**	**BETELGEUSE**	**◆PROCYON**
120	23 36 035	14 00 091	36 18 144	36 10 222	37 11 305	28 13 325	36 38 354
121	23 59 034	14 40 091	36 42 143	35 43 222	36 37 304	27 50 324	36 33 353
122	24 21 033	15 20 090	37 06 143	35 16 221	36 04 303	27 26 323	36 28 351
123	24 42 032	16 00 089	37 30 143	34 50 221	35 30 302	27 01 322	36 21 350
124	25 03 031	16 40 088	37 54 142	34 24 220	34 56 301	26 36 320	36 14 349
125	25 23 030	17 21 088	38 19 142	33 58 220	34 21 300	26 10 319	36 06 348
126	25 43 029	18 01 087	38 44 142	33 32 220	33 47 299	25 44 319	35 57 346
127	26 02 028	18 41 086	39 09 141	33 07 219	33 11 298	25 17 318	35 47 345
128	26 20 027	19 21 085	39 34 141	32 41 219	32 36 297	24 49 317	35 36 344
129	26 38 026	20 01 085	40 00 141	32 16 218	32 00 296	24 22 316	35 25 343
130	26 55 025	20 41 084	40 25 140	31 52 218	31 24 295	23 53 315	35 13 342
131	27 11 024	21 21 083	40 51 140	31 27 218	30 47 294	23 24 314	35 00 340
132	27 27 022	22 00 082	41 17 140	31 03 217	30 11 294	22 55 313	34 46 339
133	27 42 021	22 40 081	41 43 139	30 38 217	29 34 293	22 25 312	34 31 338
134	27 56 020	23 20 081	42 09 139	30 15 216	28 57 292	21 55 311	34 16 337
	◆REGULUS	**SPICA**	**◆RIGIL KENT**	**ACHERNAR**	**◆CANOPUS**	**SIRIUS**	**PROCYON**
135	28 10 019	23 59 080	42 36 139	29 51 216	65 02 244	48 25 307	34 00 336
136	28 23 018	24 39 079	43 02 139	29 28 215	64 26 244	47 53 306	33 43 335
137	28 35 017	25 18 078	43 29 138	29 04 215	63 50 244	47 20 305	33 25 333
138	28 46 016	25 58 077	43 56 138	28 41 215	63 14 244	46 47 304	33 07 332
139	28 57 015	26 37 077	44 22 138	28 19 214	62 38 244	46 13 302	32 48 331
140	29 07 014	27 16 076	44 49 137	27 56 214	62 02 244	45 39 301	32 28 330
141	29 16 013	27 54 075	45 17 137	27 34 213	61 26 243	45 05 300	32 08 329
142	29 25 012	28 33 074	45 44 137	27 12 213	60 50 243	44 30 299	31 47 328
143	29 32 010	29 12 073	46 11 137	26 51 212	60 14 243	43 55 298	31 25 327
144	29 39 009	29 50 072	46 39 137	26 30 212	59 38 243	43 19 297	31 03 326
145	29 45 008	30 28 072	47 07 136	26 09 211	59 03 243	42 43 296	30 40 325
146	29 51 007	31 06 071	47 34 136	25 48 211	58 27 242	42 07 295	30 17 324
147	29 55 006	31 44 070	48 02 136	25 27 210	57 51 242	41 31 294	29 52 323
148	29 59 005	32 22 069	48 30 136	25 07 210	57 16 242	40 54 293	29 28 321
149	30 02 004	32 59 068	48 58 135	24 47 210	56 41 242	40 17 292	29 02 320
	◆REGULUS	**SPICA**	**◆RIGIL KENT**	**ACHERNAR**	**◆CANOPUS**	**SIRIUS**	**PROCYON**
150	30 04 003	33 36 067	49 27 135	24 27 209	56 05 241	39 40 291	28 37 319
151	30 06 001	34 13 066	49 55 135	24 08 209	55 30 241	39 02 290	28 10 318
152	30 06 000	34 50 065	50 23 135	23 49 208	54 55 241	38 24 289	27 43 317
153	30 06 359	35 26 064	50 52 135	23 30 208	54 20 241	37 46 288	27 16 316
154	30 05 358	36 02 063	51 20 135	23 12 207	53 45 240	37 08 288	26 48 315
155	30 03 357	36 38 062	51 49 134	22 54 207	53 10 240	36 30 287	26 20 314
156	30 01 356	37 13 061	52 18 134	22 36 206	52 36 240	35 51 286	25 51 313
157	29 58 355	37 48 060	52 47 134	22 18 206	52 01 239	35 12 285	25 21 313
158	29 54 354	38 23 059	53 15 134	22 01 205	51 27 239	34 34 284	24 51 312
159	29 49 352	38 57 058	53 44 134	21 44 205	50 52 239	33 54 283	24 21 311
160	29 43 351	39 31 057	54 13 134	21 28 204	50 18 238	33 15 282	23 51 310
161	29 36 350	40 05 056	54 42 134	21 11 204	49 44 238	32 36 282	23 19 309
162	29 29 349	40 38 055	55 11 134	20 56 203	49 10 238	31 57 281	22 48 308
163	29 21 348	41 11 054	55 40 134	20 40 203	48 36 237	31 17 280	22 16 307
164	29 13 347	41 43 053	56 09 133	20 25 202	48 02 237	30 38 279	21 44 306
	SPICA	**◆ANTARES**	**RIGIL KENT**	**ACHERNAR**	**◆CANOPUS**	**SIRIUS**	**◆REGULUS**
165	42 15 052	24 07 103	56 39 133	20 10 202	47 28 237	29 58 278	29 03 346
166	42 47 051	24 46 103	57 08 133	19 55 201	46 55 236	29 18 277	28 53 345
167	43 18 050	25 25 102	57 37 133	19 41 201	46 21 236	28 38 277	28 42 344
168	43 48 049	26 04 101	58 06 133	19 27 200	45 48 236	27 58 276	28 30 342
169	44 18 047	26 44 101	58 35 133	19 13 200	45 15 235	27 18 275	28 18 341
170	44 47 046	27 23 100	59 04 133	19 00 199	44 42 235	26 38 274	28 04 340
171	45 16 045	28 03 099	59 34 133	18 47 198	44 09 235	25 58 274	27 50 339
172	45 44 044	28 42 099	60 03 133	18 35 198	43 37 234	25 18 273	27 36 338
173	46 11 043	29 22 098	60 32 134	18 22 197	43 04 234	24 38 272	27 21 337
174	46 38 041	30 02 097	61 01 134	18 11 197	42 32 234	23 58 271	27 05 336
175	47 04 040	30 42 097	61 30 134	17 59 196	42 00 233	23 18 271	26 48 335
176	47 30 039	31 22 096	61 59 134	17 48 196	41 28 233	22 38 270	26 31 334
177	47 54 037	32 02 095	62 28 134	17 37 195	40 56 233	21 58 269	26 13 333
178	48 18 036	32 42 095	62 57 134	17 27 195	40 24 232	21 17 268	25 54 332
179	48 42 035	33 22 094	63 26 134	17 17 194	39 52 232	20 37 268	25 35 331

 LAT 48°S

LHA ♈	Hc Zn	Hc Zn	Hc Zn	Hc Zn	Hc Zn	Hc Zn	Hc Zn
	◆ ARCTURUS	ANTARES	◆ Peacock	ACHERNAR	CANOPUS	◆ Suhail	REGULUS
180	16 17 033	34 02 093	23 40 151	17 07 194	39 21 231	60 09 262	25 15 330
181	16 39 033	34 42 092	23 59 151	16 58 193	38 50 231	59 29 262	24 54 329
182	17 00 032	35 22 092	24 19 150	16 49 193	38 19 230	58 49 261	24 33 328
183	17 21 031	36 02 091	24 39 150	16 40 192	37 48 230	58 10 261	24 12 327
184	17 41 030	36 42 090	24 59 149	16 32 191	37 17 230	57 30 260	23 49 326
185	18 01 029	37 22 089	25 20 149	16 25 191	36 47 229	56 50 260	23 26 325
186	18 20 028	38 03 089	25 41 148	16 17 190	36 17 229	56 11 259	23 03 324
187	18 39 027	38 43 088	26 02 148	16 10 190	35 47 228	55 32 258	22 39 323
188	18 57 026	39 23 087	26 23 147	16 03 189	35 17 228	54 52 258	22 15 322
189	19 14 025	40 03 086	26 45 147	15 57 189	34 47 227	54 13 257	21 49 321
190	19 31 024	40 43 086	27 07 147	15 51 188	34 18 227	53 34 257	21 24 320
191	19 47 023	41 23 085	27 29 146	15 46 188	33 48 227	52 55 256	20 58 319
192	20 02 022	42 03 084	27 52 146	15 41 187	33 19 226	52 16 256	20 31 318
193	20 17 021	42 43 083	28 15 145	15 36 186	32 50 226	51 37 255	20 04 317
194	20 31 020	43 23 082	28 38 145	15 32 186	32 22 225	50 58 255	19 37 316
	ARCTURUS	◆ ANTARES	Peacock	◆ ACHERNAR	CANOPUS	Suhail	◆ REGULUS
195	20 45 019	44 02 082	29 01 144	15 28 185	31 53 225	50 20 254	19 09 315
196	20 58 018	44 42 081	29 25 144	15 24 185	31 25 224	49 41 254	18 40 314
197	21 10 017	45 22 080	29 49 143	15 21 184	30 57 224	49 03 253	18 11 314
198	21 22 016	46 01 079	30 13 143	15 18 184	30 29 223	48 24 253	17 42 313
199	21 33 015	46 40 078	30 37 143	15 16 183	30 02 223	47 46 252	17 12 312
200	21 43 014	47 20 077	31 01 142	15 14 183	29 35 223	47 08 252	16 42 311
201	21 53 013	47 59 076	31 26 142	15 12 182	29 08 222	46 30 251	16 12 310
202	22 02 012	48 38 075	31 51 141	15 11 181	28 41 222	45 52 251	15 41 309
203	22 10 011	49 16 074	32 16 141	15 10 181	28 14 221	45 14 250	15 10 308
204	22 17 010	49 55 073	32 42 140	15 10 180	27 48 221	44 36 250	14 38 307
205	22 24 009	50 33 072	33 07 140	15 10 180	27 22 220	43 59 249	14 06 307
206	22 30 008	51 11 071	33 33 140	15 10 179	26 56 220	43 21 249	13 33 306
207	22 36 007	51 49 070	33 59 139	15 11 179	26 31 219	42 44 248	13 01 305
208	22 40 006	52 27 069	34 26 139	15 12 178	26 05 219	42 07 248	12 28 304
209	22 44 005	53 05 068	34 52 138	15 14 178	25 40 218	41 30 247	11 54 303
	◆ ARCTURUS	ANTARES	◆ Peacock	ACHERNAR	CANOPUS	◆ Suhail	SPICA
210	22 48 004	53 42 067	35 19 138	15 15 177	25 16 218	40 53 246	52 33 346
211	22 50 003	54 19 066	35 46 138	15 18 176	24 51 217	40 16 246	52 23 345
212	22 52 002	54 55 065	36 13 137	15 21 176	24 27 217	39 40 245	52 12 343
213	22 53 001	55 31 064	36 40 137	15 24 175	24 03 216	39 03 245	52 00 341
214	22 54 000	56 07 063	37 08 137	15 27 175	23 40 216	38 27 244	51 46 340
215	22 53 359	56 43 061	37 36 136	15 31 174	23 16 215	37 51 244	51 32 338
216	22 52 358	57 18 060	38 04 136	15 35 174	22 53 215	37 15 243	51 17 337
217	22 51 357	57 52 059	38 32 135	15 40 173	22 30 214	36 39 243	51 01 335
218	22 48 356	58 26 058	39 00 135	15 45 172	22 08 214	36 03 242	50 43 334
219	22 45 355	59 00 056	39 28 135	15 51 172	21 46 213	35 28 242	50 25 332
220	22 41 354	59 33 055	39 57 134	15 56 171	21 24 213	34 53 241	50 06 331
221	22 37 353	60 06 053	40 26 134	16 03 171	21 02 212	34 17 241	49 46 330
222	22 31 352	60 38 052	40 55 134	16 09 170	20 41 212	33 42 240	49 26 328
223	22 25 351	61 09 051	41 24 133	16 16 170	20 20 211	33 08 240	49 04 327
224	22 19 350	61 40 049	41 53 133	16 23 169	20 00 211	32 33 239	48 41 325
	ANTARES	◆ Nunki	Peacock	ACHERNAR	◆ CANOPUS	◆ SPICA	ARCTURUS
225	62 10 047	39 37 087	42 23 133	16 31 169	19 40 210	48 18 324	22 11 349
226	62 39 046	40 17 086	42 52 132	16 39 168	19 20 209	47 54 323	22 03 348
227	63 07 044	40 57 085	43 22 132	16 48 168	19 00 209	47 30 321	21 54 347
228	63 35 042	41 37 084	43 52 132	16 57 167	18 41 208	47 04 320	21 45 346
229	64 01 041	42 17 083	44 22 131	17 06 166	18 22 208	46 38 319	21 35 345
230	64 27 039	42 56 083	44 52 131	17 16 166	18 03 207	46 11 317	21 24 344
231	64 52 037	43 36 082	45 23 131	17 26 165	17 45 207	45 44 316	21 12 343
232	65 15 035	44 16 081	45 53 130	17 36 165	17 27 206	45 16 315	21 00 342
233	65 38 033	44 56 080	46 24 130	17 47 164	17 09 206	44 47 314	20 47 341
234	65 59 031	45 35 079	46 55 130	17 58 164	16 52 205	44 18 313	20 34 340
235	66 19 029	46 14 078	47 25 130	18 09 163	16 35 205	43 48 311	20 20 339
236	66 38 027	46 54 077	47 56 129	18 21 163	16 19 204	43 17 310	20 05 338
237	66 56 025	47 33 076	48 28 129	18 33 162	16 03 203	42 46 309	19 50 337
238	67 12 023	48 12 076	48 59 129	18 45 162	15 47 203	42 15 308	19 34 336
239	67 26 020	48 50 075	49 30 129	18 58 161	15 32 202	41 43 307	19 17 335
	Rasalhague	◆ ALTAIR	FOMALHAUT	◆ ACHERNAR	ACRUX	◆ SPICA	ARCTURUS
240	25 49 026	13 40 059	12 41 120	19 12 161	57 36 222	41 11 306	19 00 334
241	26 07 025	14 15 059	13 16 120	19 25 160	57 09 222	40 38 305	18 42 333
242	26 23 024	14 49 058	13 51 119	19 39 160	56 42 222	40 05 304	18 23 332
243	26 39 023	15 23 057	14 26 118	19 53 159	56 15 222	39 31 303	18 04 331
244	26 55 022	15 56 056	15 01 118	20 08 158	55 48 222	38 57 302	17 45 330
245	27 09 021	16 29 055	15 37 117	20 23 158	55 21 222	38 23 301	17 25 329
246	27 23 020	17 02 054	16 13 116	20 38 157	54 54 222	37 48 300	17 04 328
247	27 37 019	17 35 054	16 49 116	20 53 157	54 27 222	37 13 299	16 43 328
248	27 49 018	18 07 053	17 25 115	21 09 156	54 00 222	36 38 298	16 21 327
249	28 01 017	18 39 052	18 01 114	21 25 156	53 33 222	36 02 297	15 59 326
250	28 12 015	19 10 051	18 38 114	21 42 155	53 06 222	35 26 296	15 36 325
251	28 22 014	19 41 050	19 15 113	21 59 155	52 39 222	34 49 295	15 12 324
252	28 32 013	20 11 049	19 52 112	22 16 154	52 12 222	34 13 294	14 49 323
253	28 41 012	20 42 048	20 29 112	22 34 154	51 45 222	33 36 293	14 24 322
254	28 49 011	21 11 047	21 06 111	22 51 153	51 18 222	32 59 292	13 59 321
	Rasalhague	◆ ALTAIR	FOMALHAUT	◆ ACHERNAR	ACRUX	◆ SPICA	ANTARES
255	28 56 010	21 40 046	21 44 111	23 09 153	50 52 222	32 21 291	67 42 342
256	29 03 009	22 09 045	22 22 110	23 28 152	50 25 221	31 44 290	67 29 340
257	29 08 008	22 38 044	23 00 109	23 47 152	49 59 221	31 06 289	67 14 338
258	29 13 007	23 06 044	23 38 109	24 06 152	49 32 221	30 28 288	66 58 336
259	29 18 005	23 33 043	24 16 108	24 25 151	49 06 221	29 50 288	66 41 333
260	29 21 004	24 00 042	24 54 107	24 44 151	48 39 221	29 11 287	66 22 331
261	29 24 003	24 26 041	25 32 107	25 04 150	48 13 221	28 33 286	66 02 329
262	29 26 002	24 52 040	26 11 106	25 24 150	47 47 220	27 54 285	65 41 327
263	29 27 001	25 17 039	26 50 105	25 45 149	47 21 220	27 15 284	65 19 325
264	29 27 000	25 42 038	27 28 105	26 06 149	46 55 220	26 36 283	64 56 323
265	29 27 359	26 07 037	28 07 104	26 27 148	46 29 220	25 57 283	64 31 321
266	29 25 358	26 30 036	28 46 103	26 48 148	46 04 220	25 18 282	64 06 320
267	29 23 357	26 53 035	29 25 103	27 10 147	45 38 219	24 39 281	63 39 318
268	29 20 355	27 16 034	30 05 102	27 31 147	45 13 219	23 59 280	63 12 316
269	29 17 354	27 38 033	30 44 101	27 53 146	44 47 219	23 20 279	62 44 314

LHA ♈	Hc Zn	Hc Zn	Hc Zn	Hc Zn	Hc Zn	Hc Zn	Hc Zn
	◆ ALTAIR	FOMALHAUT	◆ ACHERNAR	RIGIL KENT	◆ SPICA	ANTARES	Rasalhague
270	27 59 032	31 23 101	28 16 146	59 14 227	22 40 279	62 14 313	29 12 353
271	28 20 030	32 03 100	28 38 146	58 44 227	22 00 278	61 45 311	29 07 352
272	28 40 029	32 42 099	29 01 145	58 15 227	21 20 277	61 14 310	29 01 351
273	28 59 028	33 22 099	29 24 145	57 46 227	20 40 276	60 43 308	28 55 350
274	29 18 027	34 02 098	29 48 144	57 17 227	20 00 275	60 11 307	28 47 349
275	29 36 026	34 41 097	30 11 144	56 48 227	19 21 275	59 39 305	28 39 348
276	29 53 025	35 21 097	30 35 143	56 19 227	18 40 274	59 06 304	28 30 347
277	30 10 024	36 01 096	30 59 143	55 50 226	18 00 273	58 32 303	28 20 345
278	30 26 023	36 41 095	31 24 142	55 20 226	17 20 272	57 58 301	28 10 344
279	30 41 022	37 21 095	31 48 142	54 51 226	16 40 272	57 23 300	27 59 343
280	30 56 021	38 01 094	32 13 142	54 22 226	16 00 271	56 48 299	27 47 342
281	31 10 020	38 41 093	32 38 141	53 53 226	15 20 270	56 13 298	27 34 341
282	31 23 018	39 21 092	33 03 141	53 25 226	14 40 269	55 37 296	27 21 340
283	31 35 017	40 02 092	33 29 140	52 56 226	14 00 269	55 01 295	27 07 339
284	31 47 016	40 42 091	33 54 140	52 27 226	13 19 268	54 25 294	26 52 338
	ALTAIR	Enif	◆ FOMALHAUT	ACHERNAR	◆ RIGIL KENT	ANTARES	◆ Rasalhague
285	31 58 015	21 33 044	41 22 090	34 20 140	51 58 226	53 48 293	26 37 337
286	32 08 014	22 01 043	42 02 089	34 46 139	51 29 225	53 11 292	26 20 336
287	32 17 013	22 28 042	42 42 089	35 13 139	51 01 225	52 34 291	26 04 335
288	32 25 012	22 55 041	43 22 088	35 39 138	50 32 225	51 56 290	25 46 334
289	32 33 010	23 21 040	44 02 087	36 06 138	50 04 225	51 18 289	25 28 333
290	32 40 009	23 47 040	44 42 086	36 33 138	49 36 225	50 40 288	25 09 332
291	32 46 008	24 12 039	45 22 086	37 00 137	49 07 225	50 01 287	24 50 331
292	32 51 007	24 37 038	46 02 085	37 27 137	48 39 224	49 23 286	24 30 330
293	32 56 006	25 01 037	46 42 084	37 55 137	48 11 224	48 44 285	24 10 329
294	32 59 005	25 25 036	47 22 083	38 22 136	47 43 224	48 05 284	23 48 328
295	33 02 003	25 48 035	48 02 082	38 50 136	47 15 224	47 26 283	23 27 327
296	33 04 002	26 10 034	48 42 082	39 18 136	46 48 224	46 47 282	23 04 326
297	33 05 001	26 32 033	49 22 081	39 47 135	46 20 223	46 08 281	22 41 325
298	33 05 000	26 54 031	50 01 080	40 15 135	45 53 223	45 28 280	22 18 324
299	33 05 359	27 14 030	50 41 079	40 44 134	45 25 223	44 49 279	21 54 323
	◆ Enif	FOMALHAUT	◆ ACHERNAR	RIGIL KENT	◆ ANTARES	Rasalhague	ALTAIR
300	27 34 029	51 20 078	41 12 134	44 58 223	44 09 279	21 29 322	33 04 357
301	27 54 028	51 59 077	41 41 134	44 31 222	43 29 278	21 04 321	33 01 356
302	28 12 027	52 38 076	42 10 133	44 04 222	42 49 277	20 39 320	32 58 355
303	28 31 026	53 17 075	42 39 133	43 37 222	42 09 276	20 13 319	32 55 354
304	28 48 025	53 56 074	43 09 133	43 11 222	41 29 275	19 46 318	32 50 353
305	29 05 024	54 34 073	43 38 133	42 44 221	40 49 275	19 19 317	32 45 352
306	29 21 023	55 13 072	44 08 132	42 18 221	40 09 274	18 51 316	32 38 350
307	29 36 022	55 51 071	44 38 132	41 51 221	39 29 273	18 23 315	32 31 349
308	29 51 021	56 29 070	45 08 132	41 25 220	38 49 272	17 55 314	32 23 348
309	30 05 020	57 06 069	45 38 131	40 59 220	38 09 271	17 26 314	32 15 347
310	30 18 019	57 43 068	46 08 131	40 33 220	37 29 271	16 57 313	32 05 346
311	30 30 017	58 20 067	46 38 131	40 08 220	36 49 270	16 27 312	31 55 345
312	30 42 016	58 57 065	47 09 130	39 42 219	36 09 269	15 57 311	31 44 344
313	30 53 015	59 33 064	47 39 130	39 17 219	35 29 268	15 26 310	31 32 342
314	31 03 014	60 09 063	48 10 130	38 52 219	34 48 268	14 55 309	31 20 341
	◆ Enif	Diphda	◆ ACHERNAR	Miaplacidus	RIGIL KENT	◆ ANTARES	ALTAIR
315	31 12 013	35 43 077	48 41 130	27 48 181	38 27 218	34 08 267	31 07 340
316	31 21 012	36 22 076	49 12 129	27 47 181	38 02 218	33 28 266	30 53 339
317	31 29 011	37 01 075	49 43 129	27 47 181	37 38 218	32 48 266	30 38 338
318	31 36 010	37 39 074	50 14 129	27 47 180	37 13 217	32 08 265	30 22 337
319	31 42 008	38 18 073	50 45 129	27 47 180	36 49 217	31 28 264	30 06 336
320	31 48 007	38 56 072	51 17 128	27 47 179	36 25 217	30 48 264	29 49 335
321	31 52 006	39 34 071	51 48 128	27 48 179	36 01 216	30 08 263	29 32 334
322	31 56 005	40 12 070	52 20 128	27 49 179	35 38 216	29 29 262	29 14 332
323	31 59 004	40 50 069	52 52 128	27 50 178	35 14 215	28 49 261	28 55 331
324	32 01 003	41 27 068	53 23 128	27 51 178	34 51 215	28 09 261	28 35 330
325	32 03 001	42 04 067	53 55 127	27 53 177	34 28 215	27 30 260	28 15 329
326	32 03 000	42 41 066	54 27 127	27 55 177	34 05 214	26 50 259	27 54 328
327	32 03 359	43 18 065	54 59 127	27 57 177	33 43 214	26 11 259	27 33 327
328	32 02 358	43 54 064	55 31 127	28 00 176	33 20 214	25 31 258	27 10 326
329	32 00 357	44 30 063	56 03 127	28 02 176	32 58 213	24 52 257	26 48 325
	◆ Diphda	ACHERNAR	◆ Miaplacidus	RIGIL KENT	ANTARES	◆ ALTAIR	Enif
330	45 06 062	56 35 127	28 05 175	32 36 213	24 13 257	26 25 324	31 58 356
331	45 42 061	57 08 127	28 09 175	32 15 213	23 34 256	26 01 323	31 54 354
332	46 17 060	57 40 126	28 12 175	31 53 212	22 55 255	25 36 322	31 50 353
333	46 51 059	58 12 126	28 16 174	31 32 212	22 16 255	25 11 321	31 45 352
334	47 26 058	58 45 126	28 20 174	31 11 211	21 38 254	24 46 320	31 39 351
335	47 59 057	59 17 126	28 25 174	30 50 211	20 59 253	24 20 319	31 32 350
336	48 33 056	59 50 126	28 29 173	30 30 211	20 21 253	23 53 318	31 25 349
337	49 06 055	60 22 126	28 34 173	30 09 210	19 43 252	23 26 317	31 16 348
338	49 38 053	60 55 126	28 39 172	29 49 210	19 05 251	22 59 316	31 07 346
339	50 10 052	61 27 126	28 45 172	29 30 209	18 27 251	22 31 315	30 58 345
340	50 42 051	62 00 126	28 51 172	29 10 209	17 49 250	22 02 314	30 47 344
341	51 12 050	62 32 126	28 56 171	28 51 208	17 11 249	21 33 313	30 36 343
342	51 43 048	63 05 126	29 03 171	28 32 208	16 34 249	21 04 313	30 24 342
343	52 12 047	63 37 126	29 09 170	28 13 208	15 56 248	20 34 312	30 11 341
344	52 41 046	64 10 126	29 16 170	27 55 207	15 19 247	20 04 311	29 57 340
	◆ Diphda	Acamar	◆ CANOPUS	Miaplacidus	RIGIL KENT	◆ Nunki	Enif
345	53 10 044	47 32 103	26 27 141	29 23 170	27 36 207	38 20 272	29 43 339
346	53 37 043	48 12 102	26 52 140	29 30 169	27 18 206	37 40 271	29 28 338
347	54 04 041	48 51 101	27 18 140	29 38 169	27 01 206	37 00 270	29 12 336
348	54 31 040	49 30 101	27 44 139	29 46 169	26 43 205	36 20 270	28 56 335
349	54 56 039	50 10 100	28 10 139	29 54 168	26 26 205	35 40 269	28 39 334
350	55 21 037	50 49 100	28 37 138	30 02 168	26 09 205	35 00 268	28 21 333
351	55 44 035	51 29 099	29 04 138	30 10 168	25 53 204	34 20 268	28 02 332
352	56 07 034	52 09 098	29 31 138	30 19 167	25 36 204	33 39 267	27 43 331
353	56 29 032	52 48 098	29 58 137	30 28 167	25 20 203	32 59 266	27 24 330
354	56 50 031	53 28 097	30 25 137	30 38 166	25 05 203	32 19 265	27 03 329
355	57 10 029	54 08 096	30 53 136	30 47 166	24 49 202	31 39 265	26 42 328
356	57 29 027	54 48 096	31 21 136	30 57 166	24 34 202	30 59 264	26 21 327
357	57 47 026	55 28 095	31 49 135	31 07 165	24 19 201	30 19 263	25 58 326
358	58 04 024	56 08 094	32 18 135	31 17 165	24 05 201	29 40 263	25 36 325
359	58 20 022	56 48 094	32 46 134	31 28 165	23 51 200	29 00 262	25 12 324

 LAT 49°S

LHA ♈	Hc	Zn	Hc	Zn	Hc	Zn	Hc	Zn	Hc	Zn	Hc	Zn	Hc	Zn
	Alpheratz		Hamal		◆ RIGEL		CANOPUS		◆ RIGIL KENT		Peacock		◆ FOMALHAUT	
0	11 48	002	12 03	030	13 30	087	33 56	133	24 33	200	57 47	236	67 17	323
1	11 49	001	12 22	029	14 09	086	34 25	133	24 20	200	57 15	236	66 53	321
2	11 50	000	12 41	028	14 48	085	34 54	133	24 07	199	56 42	235	66 28	319
3	11 49	359	12 59	027	15 28	085	35 23	132	23 54	199	56 10	235	66 02	318
4	11 49	358	13 17	026	16 07	084	35 52	132	23 41	198	55 38	235	65 35	316
5	11 47	358	13 34	025	16 46	083	36 22	131	23 29	198	55 05	235	65 07	314
6	11 45	357	13 51	024	17 25	082	36 52	131	23 17	197	54 33	235	64 38	312
7	11 43	356	14 07	024	18 04	082	37 22	130	23 06	197	54 01	234	64 09	311
8	11 40	355	14 22	023	18 43	081	37 52	130	22 55	196	53 29	234	63 38	309
9	11 36	354	14 37	022	19 22	080	38 22	129	22 44	196	52 58	234	63 07	307
10	11 31	353	14 51	021	20 00	079	38 52	129	22 33	195	52 26	234	62 36	306
11	11 26	352	15 05	020	20 39	078	39 23	129	22 23	195	51 54	233	62 04	304
12	11 21	351	15 18	019	21 17	078	39 54	128	22 13	194	51 23	233	61 31	303
13	11 15	350	15 30	018	21 56	077	40 25	128	22 03	194	50 51	233	60 58	302
14	11 08	350	15 42	017	22 34	076	40 56	127	21 54	193	50 20	233	60 24	300
	Hamal		◆ RIGEL		SIRIUS		CANOPUS		◆ RIGIL KENT		Peacock		◆ FOMALHAUT	
15	15 54	016	23 12	075	14 51	099	41 28	127	21 45	193	49 49	232	59 50	299
16	16 04	015	23 50	074	15 30	098	41 59	127	21 36	192	49 18	232	59 15	298
17	16 14	014	24 28	073	16 09	097	42 31	126	21 28	192	48 47	232	58 40	296
18	16 24	013	25 06	073	16 48	096	43 03	126	21 20	191	48 16	231	58 04	295
19	16 33	012	25 43	072	17 27	096	43 35	125	21 13	191	47 45	231	57 29	294
20	16 41	011	26 20	071	18 06	095	44 07	125	21 05	190	47 15	231	56 52	293
21	16 48	011	26 58	070	18 45	094	44 39	125	20 59	190	46 44	230	56 16	292
22	16 55	010	27 34	069	19 25	093	45 12	124	20 52	189	46 14	230	55 39	291
23	17 01	009	28 11	068	20 04	093	45 44	124	20 46	189	45 44	230	55 02	289
24	17 07	008	28 48	067	20 43	092	46 17	123	20 40	188	45 14	230	54 25	288
25	17 12	007	29 24	066	21 23	091	46 50	123	20 34	188	44 44	229	53 48	287
26	17 16	006	30 00	066	22 02	090	47 23	123	20 29	187	44 14	229	53 10	286
27	17 20	005	30 35	065	22 41	090	47 56	122	20 24	187	43 45	229	52 32	285
28	17 23	004	31 11	064	23 21	089	48 29	122	20 20	186	43 15	228	51 54	284
29	17 25	003	31 46	063	24 00	088	49 03	122	20 16	186	42 46	228	51 16	283
	Hamal		◆ RIGEL		SIRIUS		CANOPUS		◆ RIGIL KENT		Peacock		◆ FOMALHAUT	
30	17 27	002	32 21	062	24 39	087	49 36	121	20 12	185	42 17	227	50 38	283
31	17 28	001	32 55	061	25 19	087	50 10	121	20 09	185	41 48	227	49 59	282
32	17 28	000	33 30	060	25 58	086	50 44	121	20 06	184	41 19	227	49 20	281
33	17 28	359	34 04	059	26 37	085	51 18	120	20 03	184	40 51	226	48 42	280
34	17 27	358	34 37	058	27 16	084	51 52	120	20 00	183	40 22	226	48 03	279
35	17 25	357	35 10	057	27 56	084	52 26	120	19 58	183	39 54	226	47 24	278
36	17 23	356	35 43	056	28 35	083	53 00	119	19 57	182	39 26	225	46 45	277
37	17 20	355	36 16	055	29 14	082	53 35	119	19 56	182	38 58	225	46 06	276
38	17 16	354	36 48	054	29 53	081	54 09	119	19 55	181	38 30	225	45 27	276
39	17 12	353	37 19	053	30 31	080	54 44	118	19 54	181	38 03	224	44 48	275
40	17 07	352	37 50	052	31 10	079	55 19	118	19 54	180	37 35	224	44 08	274
41	17 01	351	38 21	051	31 49	079	55 54	118	19 54	180	37 08	223	43 29	273
42	16 55	350	38 51	050	32 27	078	56 29	117	19 54	179	36 41	223	42 50	272
43	16 48	349	39 21	049	33 06	077	57 04	117	19 55	179	36 14	223	42 10	272
44	16 41	349	39 50	047	33 44	076	57 39	117	19 56	178	35 48	222	41 31	271
	RIGEL		SIRIUS		◆ CANOPUS		RIGIL KENT		◆ Peacock		FOMALHAUT		◆ Hamal	
45	40 19	046	34 22	075	58 14	116	19 58	177	35 22	222	40 52	270	16 33	348
46	40 47	045	35 00	074	58 49	116	20 00	177	34 55	221	40 12	269	16 24	347
47	41 15	044	35 38	073	59 24	116	20 02	176	34 30	221	39 33	269	16 14	346
48	41 42	043	36 16	073	60 00	116	20 05	176	34 04	221	38 54	268	16 04	345
49	42 08	042	36 53	072	60 35	115	20 08	175	33 38	220	38 14	267	15 54	344
50	42 34	040	37 30	071	61 11	115	20 11	175	33 13	220	37 35	266	15 42	343
51	42 59	039	38 07	070	61 47	115	20 15	174	32 48	219	36 56	266	15 31	342
52	43 24	038	38 44	069	62 22	115	20 19	174	32 23	219	36 16	265	15 18	341
53	43 47	037	39 21	068	62 58	114	20 23	173	31 59	218	35 37	264	15 05	340
54	44 11	035	39 57	067	63 34	114	20 28	173	31 34	218	34 58	264	14 51	339
55	44 33	034	40 33	066	64 10	114	20 33	172	31 10	218	34 19	263	14 37	338
56	44 55	033	41 09	065	64 46	114	20 38	172	30 46	217	33 40	262	14 22	337
57	45 16	032	41 45	064	65 22	114	20 44	171	30 23	217	33 01	261	14 07	336
58	45 36	030	42 20	063	65 58	113	20 50	171	29 59	216	32 22	261	13 51	336
59	45 55	029	42 55	062	66 34	113	20 56	170	29 36	216	31 43	260	13 34	335
	◆ ALDEBARAN		BETELGEUSE		SIRIUS		◆ Suhail		RIGIL KENT		◆ ACHERNAR		Diphda	
60	23 57	010	28 09	033	43 29	061	38 43	115	21 03	170	67 31	235	39 58	291
61	24 03	009	28 30	032	44 04	060	39 18	114	21 10	169	66 59	235	39 21	290
62	24 09	008	28 50	031	44 38	059	39 54	114	21 18	169	66 26	236	38 44	289
63	24 14	007	29 10	030	45 11	058	40 30	113	21 26	168	65 54	236	38 06	288
64	24 18	005	29 30	029	45 44	057	41 07	113	21 34	168	65 21	236	37 29	287
65	24 21	004	29 48	028	46 17	055	41 43	112	21 42	167	64 49	236	36 51	286
66	24 24	003	30 06	027	46 49	054	42 19	112	21 51	167	64 16	236	36 13	285
67	24 26	002	30 24	026	47 21	053	42 56	111	22 00	166	63 44	236	35 35	284
68	24 27	001	30 40	024	47 52	052	43 33	111	22 10	166	63 11	236	34 57	283
69	24 28	000	30 56	023	48 22	051	44 10	110	22 20	165	62 39	236	34 18	283
70	24 27	359	31 11	022	48 53	049	44 47	110	22 30	165	62 06	236	33 40	282
71	24 27	358	31 26	021	49 22	048	45 24	109	22 40	164	61 34	236	33 01	281
72	24 25	357	31 39	020	49 51	047	46 01	109	22 51	164	61 01	236	32 23	280
73	24 22	356	31 53	019	50 20	046	46 38	108	23 02	163	60 29	235	31 44	279
74	24 19	355	32 05	018	50 48	044	47 16	108	23 14	163	59 56	235	31 05	278
	BETELGEUSE		SIRIUS		◆ Suhail		RIGIL KENT		◆ ACHERNAR		Diphda		◆ ALDEBARAN	
75	32 16	016	51 15	043	47 54	107	23 25	162	59 24	235	30 26	278	24 16	354
76	32 27	015	51 41	042	48 31	106	23 37	162	58 52	235	29 47	277	24 11	353
77	32 37	014	52 07	040	49 09	106	23 50	161	58 19	235	29 08	276	24 06	352
78	32 46	013	52 32	039	49 47	105	24 03	161	57 47	235	28 29	275	24 00	351
79	32 55	012	52 56	037	50 25	105	24 16	160	57 15	235	27 49	274	23 53	350
80	33 03	011	53 20	036	51 03	104	24 29	160	56 43	234	27 10	274	23 46	349
81	33 09	009	53 42	034	51 41	104	24 43	160	56 11	234	26 31	273	23 38	348
82	33 16	008	54 04	033	52 20	103	24 56	159	55 39	234	25 52	272	23 29	347
83	33 21	007	54 25	031	52 58	103	25 11	159	55 07	234	25 12	271	23 19	346
84	33 25	006	54 45	030	53 36	102	25 25	158	54 35	234	24 33	271	23 09	345
85	33 29	005	55 04	028	54 15	101	25 40	158	54 04	233	23 53	270	22 58	344
86	33 32	004	55 23	027	54 54	101	25 55	157	53 32	233	23 14	269	22 47	343
87	33 34	002	55 40	025	55 32	100	26 11	157	53 01	233	22 35	268	22 35	341
88	33 35	001	55 56	023	56 11	100	26 26	156	52 29	233	21 55	268	22 22	340
89	33 35	000	56 11	022	56 50	099	26 42	156	51 58	233	21 16	267	22 08	339

LHA ♈	Hc	Zn	Hc	Zn	Hc	Zn	Hc	Zn	Hc	Zn	Hc	Zn	Hc	Zn
	PROCYON		Alphard		◆ Suhail		RIGIL KENT		◆ ACHERNAR		◆ RIGEL		BETELGEUSE	
90	31 35	030	30 52	065	57 29	098	26 59	155	51 27	232	48 07	343	33 35	359
91	31 55	029	31 27	064	58 08	098	27 15	155	50 56	232	47 55	342	33 34	358
92	32 13	027	32 03	063	58 47	097	27 32	154	50 25	232	47 42	340	33 32	356
93	32 31	026	32 38	062	59 26	097	27 49	154	49 54	232	47 29	339	33 29	355
94	32 48	025	33 13	062	60 05	096	28 06	154	49 23	231	47 14	338	33 25	354
95	33 04	024	33 47	061	60 44	095	28 24	153	48 52	231	46 59	336	33 21	353
96	33 20	023	34 21	060	61 23	095	28 42	153	48 22	231	46 42	335	33 15	352
97	33 35	022	34 55	059	62 03	094	29 00	152	47 51	230	46 25	333	33 09	351
98	33 49	021	35 28	058	62 42	093	29 19	152	47 21	230	46 07	332	33 02	349
99	34 02	019	36 01	057	63 21	093	29 37	151	46 51	230	45 48	331	32 55	348
100	34 15	018	36 34	056	64 01	092	29 56	151	46 21	229	45 28	329	32 46	347
101	34 27	017	37 06	055	64 40	091	30 16	151	45 51	229	45 08	328	32 37	346
102	34 38	016	37 38	053	65 19	091	30 35	150	45 22	229	44 47	327	32 27	345
103	34 49	015	38 10	052	65 59	090	30 55	150	44 52	229	44 25	325	32 16	344
104	34 58	013	38 41	051	66 38	089	31 15	149	44 22	228	44 02	324	32 05	342
	PROCYON		REGULUS		◆ Gienah		RIGIL KENT		◆ ACHERNAR		RIGEL		◆ BETELGEUSE	
105	35 07	012	16 15	049	20 16	094	31 35	149	43 53	228	43 39	323	31 52	341
106	35 15	011	16 44	048	20 55	093	31 56	148	43 24	228	43 15	322	31 39	340
107	35 22	010	17 13	047	21 34	092	32 16	148	42 55	227	42 50	320	31 26	339
108	35 28	009	17 42	046	22 14	092	32 37	148	42 26	227	42 24	319	31 11	338
109	35 34	007	18 10	045	22 53	091	32 58	147	41 58	227	41 58	318	30 56	337
110	35 38	006	18 37	044	23 32	090	33 20	147	41 29	226	41 32	317	30 40	336
111	35 42	005	19 05	043	24 12	089	33 41	146	41 01	226	41 04	316	30 23	334
112	35 45	004	19 31	042	24 51	089	34 03	146	40 33	225	40 37	314	30 06	333
113	35 47	002	19 57	041	25 30	088	34 25	146	40 05	225	40 08	313	29 48	332
114	35 48	001	20 23	040	26 10	087	34 48	145	39 37	225	39 39	312	29 29	331
115	35 49	000	20 48	039	26 49	086	35 10	145	39 09	224	39 10	311	29 10	330
116	35 48	359	21 13	038	27 28	086	35 33	145	38 42	224	38 40	310	28 50	329
117	35 47	358	21 37	037	28 07	085	35 56	144	38 15	224	38 10	309	28 30	328
118	35 45	356	22 01	036	28 47	084	36 19	144	37 48	223	37 39	308	28 09	327
119	35 42	355	22 24	036	29 26	083	36 42	143	37 21	223	37 07	307	27 47	326
	REGULUS		◆ SPICA		RIGIL KENT		◆ ACHERNAR		RIGEL		BETELGEUSE		◆ PROCYON	
120	22 47	035	14 01	091	37 06	143	36 54	222	36 36	306	27 24	325	35 38	354
121	23 09	034	14 41	090	37 29	143	36 28	222	36 04	305	27 02	324	35 34	353
122	23 30	033	15 20	090	37 53	142	36 01	222	35 31	304	26 38	323	35 28	351
123	23 51	032	15 59	089	38 17	142	35 35	221	34 58	303	26 14	322	35 22	350
124	24 11	031	16 39	088	38 42	142	35 09	221	34 25	302	25 49	321	35 15	349
125	24 31	030	17 18	087	39 06	141	34 44	220	33 51	301	25 24	320	35 07	348
126	24 50	029	17 57	087	39 31	141	34 18	220	33 17	300	24 59	319	34 58	347
127	25 09	028	18 37	086	39 56	141	33 53	220	32 43	299	24 32	318	34 49	345
128	25 27	026	19 16	085	40 21	140	33 28	219	32 08	298	24 06	317	34 39	344
129	25 44	025	19 55	084	40 46	140	33 03	219	31 33	297	23 39	316	34 28	343
130	26 00	024	20 34	083	41 11	140	32 39	218	30 58	296	23 11	315	34 16	342
131	26 16	023	21 13	083	41 37	139	32 14	218	30 22	295	22 43	314	34 03	341
132	26 32	022	21 52	082	42 03	139	31 50	218	29 46	294	22 14	313	33 50	340
133	26 46	021	22 31	081	42 28	139	31 26	217	29 10	293	21 45	312	33 35	338
134	27 00	020	23 10	080	42 54	139	31 03	217	28 34	292	21 16	311	33 21	337
	◆ REGULUS		SPICA		◆ RIGIL KENT		ACHERNAR		◆ CANOPUS		SIRIUS		PROCYON	
135	27 13	019	23 49	079	43 21	138	30 39	216	65 27	246	47 49	308	33 05	336
136	27 26	018	24 27	079	43 47	138	30 16	216	64 51	246	47 18	307	32 49	335
137	27 38	017	25 06	078	44 13	138	29 53	215	64 15	246	46 46	306	32 32	334
138	27 49	016	25 44	077	44 40	137	29 31	215	63 39	246	46 14	304	32 14	333
139	27 59	015	26 23	076	45 07	137	29 08	214	63 03	246	45 41	303	31 55	332
140	28 09	014	27 01	075	45 33	137	28 46	214	62 28	245	45 08	302	31 36	330
141	28 18	013	27 39	075	46 00	137	28 24	214	61 52	245	44 34	301	31 16	329
142	28 26	011	28 17	074	46 28	136	28 03	213	61 16	245	44 00	300	30 56	328
143	28 33	010	28 54	073	46 55	136	27 42	213	60 41	245	43 26	299	30 35	327
144	28 40	009	29 32	072	47 22	136	27 20	212	60 05	244	42 52	298	30 13	326
145	28 46	008	30 09	071	47 50	136	27 00	212	59 30	244	42 17	297	29 51	325
146	28 51	007	30 46	070	48 17	135	26 39	211	58 54	244	41 41	296	29 28	324
147	28 56	006	31 23	069	48 45	135	26 19	211	58 19	244	41 06	295	29 05	323
148	28 59	005	32 00	068	49 13	135	25 59	210	57 44	243	40 30	294	28 41	322
149	29 02	004	32 36	067	49 41	135	25 39	210	57 09	243	39 54	293	28 16	321
	◆ REGULUS		SPICA		◆ RIGIL KENT		ACHERNAR		◆ CANOPUS		SIRIUS		PROCYON	
150	29 04	003	33 13	067	50 09	134	25 20	209	56 33	243	39 17	292	27 51	320
151	29 06	001	33 49	066	50 37	134	25 01	209	55 59	242	38 41	291	27 25	319
152	29 06	000	34 24	065	51 05	134	24 42	208	55 24	242	38 04	290	26 59	318
153	29 06	359	35 00	064	51 34	134	24 23	208	54 49	242	37 27	289	26 32	317
154	29 05	358	35 35	063	52 02	134	24 05	207	54 14	241	36 50	288	26 05	316
155	29 04	357	36 10	062	52 31	134	23 47	207	53 40	241	36 12	287	25 37	315
156	29 01	356	36 44	061	52 59	133	23 30	206	53 05	241	35 34	286	25 09	314
157	28 58	355	37 18	060	53 28	133	23 12	206	52 31	240	34 57	286	24 41	313
158	28 54	354	37 52	059	53 57	133	22 55	205	51 57	240	34 19	285	24 12	312
159	28 49	353	38 26	058	54 25	133	22 39	205	51 23	240	33 40	284	23 42	311
160	28 44	351	38 59	057	54 54	133	22 22	204	50 49	239	33 02	283	23 12	310
161	28 37	350	39 32	056	55 23	133	22 06	204	50 15	239	32 24	282	22 42	309
162	28 30	349	40 04	055	55 52	133	21 51	203	49 41	239	31 45	281	22 11	308
163	28 23	348	40 36	054	56 21	132	21 35	203	49 08	238	31 07	280	21 40	307
164	28 14	347	41 07	052	56 50	132	21 20	202	48 34	238	30 28	280	21 08	306
	SPICA		◆ ANTARES		RIGIL KENT		ACHERNAR		◆ CANOPUS		SIRIUS		◆ REGULUS	
165	41 38	051	24 20	103	57 19	132	21 05	202	48 01	238	29 49	279	28 05	346
166	42 09	050	24 59	102	57 48	132	20 51	201	47 28	237	29 10	278	27 55	345
167	42 39	049	25 37	102	58 18	132	20 37	201	46 55	237	28 31	277	27 44	344
168	43 08	048	26 16	101	58 47	132	20 23	200	46 22	237	27 52	276	27 33	343
169	43 37	047	26 55	100	59 16	132	20 10	200	45 49	236	27 13	276	27 21	342
170	44 05	046	27 33	100	59 45	132	19 57	199	45 16	236	26 34	275	27 08	340
171	44 33	044	28 12	099	60 14	132	19 44	199	44 44	235	25 54	274	26 54	339
172	45 00	043	28 51	098	60 44	132	19 32	198	44 11	235	25 15	273	26 40	338
173	45 27	042	29 30	097	61 13	132	19 20	198	43 39	235	24 36	273	26 25	337
174	45 53	041	30 09	097	61 42	132	19 08	197	43 07	234	23 56	272	26 10	336
175	46 18	039	30 48	096	62 11	132	18 57	196	42 35	234	23 17	271	25 54	335
176	46 43	038	31 28	095	62 40	132	18 46	196	42 04	233	22 38	270	25 37	334
177	47 07	037	32 07	095	63 09	133	18 35	195	41 32	233	21 58	269	25 19	333
178	47 30	035	32 46	094	63 38	133	18 25	195	41 01	233	21 19	269	25 01	332
179	47 52	034	33 25	093	64 07	133	18 15	194	40 29	232	20 40	268	24 42	331

LAT 49°S

LHA ♈	Hc Zn	Hc Zn	Hc Zn	Hc Zn	Hc Zn	Hc Zn	Hc Zn
	◆ ARCTURUS	ANTARES	◆ Peacock	ACHERNAR	CANOPUS	◆ Suhail	REGULUS
180	15 27 033	34 05 092	24 32 151	18 06 194	39 58 232	60 16 264	24 23 330
181	15 48 032	34 44 092	24 52 151	17 56 193	39 28 231	59 37 264	24 03 329
182	16 09 032	35 23 091	25 11 150	17 48 193	38 57 231	58 57 263	23 42 328
183	16 30 031	36 03 090	25 31 150	17 39 192	38 26 231	58 18 262	23 21 327
184	16 49 030	36 42 089	25 51 149	17 31 192	37 56 230	57 39 262	23 00 326
185	17 08 029	37 21 089	26 11 149	17 23 191	37 26 230	57 01 261	22 37 325
186	17 27 028	38 01 088	26 32 148	17 16 190	36 56 229	56 22 261	22 14 324
187	17 45 027	38 40 087	26 53 148	17 09 190	36 26 229	55 43 260	21 51 323
188	18 03 026	39 19 086	27 14 147	17 03 189	35 57 228	55 04 259	21 27 322
189	18 20 025	39 59 086	27 35 147	16 56 189	35 27 228	54 26 259	21 03 321
190	18 36 024	40 38 085	27 57 146	16 51 188	34 58 228	53 47 258	20 38 320
191	18 52 023	41 17 084	28 19 146	16 45 188	34 29 227	53 08 258	20 12 319
192	19 07 022	41 56 083	28 41 145	16 40 187	34 01 227	52 30 257	19 47 318
193	19 21 021	42 35 082	29 04 145	16 36 187	33 32 226	51 52 256	19 20 317
194	19 35 020	43 14 081	29 27 144	16 31 186	33 04 226	51 14 256	18 53 317
	ARCTURUS	◆ ANTARES	Peacock	◆ ACHERNAR	CANOPUS	Suhail	◆ REGULUS
195	19 48 019	43 53 081	29 50 144	16 27 185	32 36 225	50 35 255	18 26 316
196	20 01 018	44 32 080	30 13 144	16 24 185	32 08 225	49 57 255	17 58 315
197	20 13 017	45 10 079	30 37 143	16 21 184	31 40 224	49 19 254	17 30 314
198	20 24 016	45 49 078	31 00 143	16 18 184	31 13 224	48 42 254	17 01 313
199	20 35 015	46 27 077	31 24 142	16 16 183	30 46 223	48 04 253	16 32 312
200	20 45 014	47 06 076	31 49 142	16 14 183	30 19 223	47 26 253	16 03 311
201	20 54 013	47 44 075	32 13 141	16 12 182	29 52 222	46 49 252	15 33 310
202	21 03 012	48 22 074	32 38 141	16 11 181	29 26 222	46 11 252	15 03 309
203	21 11 011	49 00 073	33 03 140	16 10 181	28 59 222	45 34 251	14 32 309
204	21 18 010	49 37 072	33 28 140	16 10 180	28 33 221	44 57 250	14 01 308
205	21 25 009	50 15 071	33 53 140	16 10 180	28 08 221	44 20 250	13 30 307
206	21 31 008	50 52 070	34 19 139	16 10 179	27 42 220	43 43 249	12 58 306
207	21 36 007	51 29 069	34 45 139	16 11 179	27 17 220	43 06 249	12 26 305
208	21 41 006	52 05 068	35 11 138	16 12 178	26 52 219	42 29 248	11 54 304
209	21 45 005	52 42 067	35 37 138	16 13 177	26 27 219	41 53 248	11 21 303
	◆ ARCTURUS	ANTARES	◆ Peacock	ACHERNAR	CANOPUS	◆ Suhail	SPICA
210	21 48 004	53 18 066	36 04 138	16 15 177	26 03 218	41 17 247	51 35 347
211	21 50 003	53 54 065	36 30 137	16 18 176	25 39 218	40 40 247	51 25 345
212	21 52 002	54 29 064	36 57 137	16 20 176	25 15 217	40 04 246	51 14 343
213	21 53 001	55 04 063	37 24 136	16 23 175	24 51 217	39 28 246	51 03 342
214	21 54 000	55 39 061	37 51 136	16 27 175	24 28 216	38 52 245	50 50 340
215	21 53 359	56 13 060	38 19 136	16 31 174	24 05 216	38 17 245	50 36 339
216	21 52 358	56 47 059	38 46 135	16 35 174	23 42 215	37 41 244	50 22 337
217	21 51 357	57 21 058	39 14 135	16 40 173	23 20 214	37 06 244	50 06 336
218	21 48 356	57 54 056	39 42 134	16 45 172	22 58 214	36 31 243	49 49 334
219	21 45 355	58 26 055	40 10 134	16 50 172	22 36 213	35 56 242	49 32 333
220	21 41 354	58 58 054	40 39 134	16 56 171	22 14 213	35 21 242	49 14 332
221	21 37 353	59 30 052	41 07 133	17 02 171	21 53 212	34 46 241	48 54 330
222	21 32 352	60 00 051	41 36 133	17 08 170	21 32 212	34 12 241	48 34 329
223	21 26 351	60 30 049	42 05 133	17 15 170	21 12 211	33 38 240	48 14 327
224	21 19 350	61 00 048	42 34 132	17 22 169	20 51 211	33 04 240	47 52 326
	ANTARES	◆ Nunki	Peacock	ACHERNAR	◆ CANOPUS	◆ SPICA	ARCTURUS
225	61 29 046	39 33 086	43 03 132	17 30 169	20 31 210	47 30 325	21 12 349
226	61 56 044	40 12 085	43 32 132	17 38 168	20 12 210	47 06 323	21 04 348
227	62 24 043	40 51 084	44 02 131	17 46 167	19 52 209	46 42 322	20 56 347
228	62 50 041	41 30 083	44 32 131	17 55 167	19 33 209	46 18 321	20 47 346
229	63 15 039	42 09 082	45 01 131	18 04 166	19 15 208	45 53 319	20 37 345
230	63 40 038	42 48 082	45 31 130	18 14 166	18 56 207	45 27 318	20 26 344
231	64 03 036	43 27 081	46 02 130	18 24 165	18 38 207	45 00 317	20 15 343
232	64 26 034	44 06 080	46 32 130	18 34 165	18 21 206	44 33 316	20 03 342
233	64 47 032	44 45 079	47 02 129	18 44 164	18 04 206	44 05 314	19 51 341
234	65 07 030	45 23 078	47 33 129	18 55 164	17 47 205	43 37 313	19 37 340
235	65 26 028	46 02 077	48 03 129	19 06 163	17 30 205	43 08 312	19 24 339
236	65 44 026	46 40 076	48 34 128	19 18 163	17 14 204	42 38 311	19 09 338
237	66 01 024	47 18 075	49 05 128	19 30 162	16 58 204	42 08 310	18 54 337
238	66 16 022	47 56 074	49 36 128	19 42 161	16 42 203	41 38 309	18 39 336
239	66 30 020	48 34 074	50 07 128	19 55 161	16 27 202	41 07 308	18 22 335
	Rasalhague	◆ ALTAIR	FOMALHAUT	◆ ACHERNAR	ACRUX	◆ SPICA	ARCTURUS
240	24 56 026	13 10 059	13 11 120	20 08 160	58 20 223	40 35 306	18 06 334
241	25 12 025	13 44 058	13 45 119	20 21 160	57 53 223	40 04 305	17 48 333
242	25 29 024	14 17 058	14 20 119	20 35 159	57 26 223	39 31 304	17 30 332
243	25 44 023	14 50 057	14 54 118	20 49 159	56 59 223	38 59 303	17 12 331
244	25 59 022	15 23 056	15 29 117	21 03 158	56 32 223	38 26 302	16 53 330
245	26 13 021	15 55 055	16 04 117	21 18 158	56 05 223	37 52 301	16 33 330
246	26 27 020	16 27 054	16 39 116	21 33 157	55 38 223	37 18 300	16 13 329
247	26 40 019	16 59 053	17 15 115	21 49 157	55 11 223	36 44 299	15 52 328
248	26 52 017	17 30 052	17 50 115	22 04 156	54 44 223	36 09 298	15 31 327
249	27 03 016	18 01 052	18 26 114	22 20 156	54 17 223	35 35 297	15 09 326
250	27 14 015	18 32 051	19 02 113	22 37 155	53 50 223	34 59 296	14 47 325
251	27 24 014	19 02 050	19 38 113	22 53 155	53 23 223	34 24 295	14 24 324
252	27 33 013	19 32 049	20 15 112	23 10 154	52 56 223	33 48 294	14 01 323
253	27 42 012	20 01 048	20 51 111	23 27 154	52 30 223	33 12 293	13 37 322
254	27 50 011	20 30 047	21 28 111	23 45 153	52 03 223	32 36 293	13 12 321
	Rasalhague	◆ ALTAIR	FOMALHAUT	◆ ACHERNAR	ACRUX	◆ SPICA	ANTARES
255	27 57 010	20 59 046	22 05 110	24 03 153	51 36 222	32 00 292	66 44 343
256	28 03 009	21 27 045	22 42 109	24 21 152	51 10 222	31 23 291	66 32 341
257	28 09 008	21 55 044	23 19 109	24 39 152	50 43 222	30 46 290	66 19 339
258	28 14 007	22 22 043	23 56 108	24 58 151	50 17 222	30 09 289	66 03 336
259	28 18 005	22 49 042	24 34 107	25 17 151	49 51 222	29 31 288	65 47 334
260	28 21 004	23 15 041	25 11 107	25 37 150	49 25 222	28 54 287	65 29 332
261	28 24 003	23 41 040	25 49 106	25 56 150	48 59 221	28 16 286	65 11 330
262	28 26 002	24 06 039	26 27 105	26 16 149	48 33 221	27 38 285	64 51 328
263	28 27 001	24 31 038	27 05 105	26 36 149	48 07 221	27 00 285	64 29 326
264	28 27 000	24 55 037	27 43 104	26 57 148	47 41 221	26 22 284	64 07 325
265	28 27 359	25 18 036	28 21 103	27 18 148	47 15 221	25 44 283	63 44 323
266	28 25 358	25 41 035	29 00 103	27 39 147	46 50 220	25 06 282	63 19 321
267	28 23 357	26 04 034	29 38 102	28 00 147	46 24 220	24 27 281	62 54 319
268	28 21 355	26 26 033	30 17 101	28 22 147	45 59 220	23 48 281	62 28 317
269	28 17 354	26 47 032	30 55 101	28 43 146	45 34 220	23 10 280	62 01 316

LHA ♈	Hc Zn	Hc Zn	Hc Zn	Hc Zn	Hc Zn	Hc Zn	Hc Zn
	◆ ALTAIR	FOMALHAUT	◆ ACHERNAR	RIGIL KENT	◆ SPICA	ANTARES	Rasalhague
270	27 08 031	31 34 100	29 05 146	59 54 228	22 31 279	61 33 314	28 13 353
271	27 28 030	32 13 099	29 28 145	59 25 228	21 52 278	61 05 313	28 08 352
272	27 48 029	32 52 099	29 50 145	58 56 228	21 13 277	60 35 311	28 02 351
273	28 06 028	33 31 098	30 13 144	58 27 228	20 34 277	60 05 310	27 56 350
274	28 25 027	34 10 097	30 36 144	57 58 228	19 55 276	59 35 308	27 48 349
275	28 42 026	34 49 097	31 00 143	57 29 228	19 15 275	59 03 307	27 40 348
276	28 59 025	35 28 096	31 23 143	57 00 228	18 36 274	58 32 305	27 32 347
277	29 15 024	36 07 095	31 47 143	56 30 228	17 57 273	57 59 304	27 22 346
278	29 31 023	36 46 095	32 11 142	56 01 227	17 18 273	57 26 303	27 12 345
279	29 46 022	37 26 094	32 35 142	55 32 227	16 38 272	56 53 301	27 01 343
280	30 00 021	38 05 093	33 00 141	55 03 227	15 59 271	56 19 300	26 50 342
281	30 13 019	38 44 092	33 25 141	54 35 227	15 20 270	55 45 299	26 37 341
282	30 26 018	39 24 092	33 50 140	54 06 227	14 40 270	55 10 298	26 24 340
283	30 38 017	40 03 091	34 15 140	53 37 227	14 01 269	54 35 296	26 11 339
284	30 49 016	40 42 090	34 40 140	53 08 227	13 22 268	54 00 295	25 56 338
	ALTAIR	Enif	◆ FOMALHAUT	ACHERNAR	◆ RIGIL KENT	ANTARES	◆ Rasalhague
285	31 00 015	20 50 044	41 22 089	35 06 139	52 40 227	53 24 294	25 41 337
286	31 09 014	21 17 043	42 01 089	35 32 139	52 11 226	52 48 293	25 26 336
287	31 18 013	21 44 042	42 40 088	35 58 138	51 43 226	52 11 292	25 09 335
288	31 27 011	22 10 041	43 20 087	36 24 138	51 14 226	51 35 291	24 52 334
289	31 34 010	22 36 040	43 59 086	36 50 138	50 46 226	50 58 290	24 35 333
290	31 41 009	23 01 039	44 38 085	37 17 137	50 18 226	50 21 289	24 17 332
291	31 47 008	23 25 038	45 17 085	37 44 137	49 50 225	49 43 288	23 58 331
292	31 52 007	23 49 037	45 57 084	38 11 136	49 22 225	49 06 287	23 38 330
293	31 56 006	24 13 036	46 36 083	38 38 136	48 54 225	48 28 286	23 18 329
294	31 59 005	24 36 035	47 15 082	39 06 136	48 26 225	47 50 285	22 58 328
295	32 02 003	24 59 034	47 54 081	39 33 135	47 59 225	47 12 284	22 36 327
296	32 04 002	25 20 033	48 32 080	40 01 135	47 31 224	46 34 283	22 15 326
297	32 05 001	25 42 032	49 11 080	40 29 135	47 04 224	45 55 282	21 52 325
298	32 05 000	26 02 031	49 50 079	40 57 134	46 36 224	45 17 281	21 29 324
299	32 05 359	26 23 030	50 28 078	41 25 134	46 09 224	44 38 280	21 06 323
	◆ Enif	FOMALHAUT	◆ ACHERNAR	RIGIL KENT	◆ ANTARES	Rasalhague	ALTAIR
300	26 42 029	51 07 077	41 54 134	45 42 223	43 59 280	20 42 322	32 04 358
301	27 01 028	51 45 076	42 22 133	45 15 223	43 21 279	20 18 321	32 02 356
302	27 19 027	52 23 075	42 51 133	44 48 223	42 42 278	19 53 320	31 59 355
303	27 37 026	53 01 074	43 20 132	44 22 222	42 03 277	19 27 319	31 55 354
304	27 54 025	53 39 073	43 49 132	43 55 222	41 23 276	19 01 318	31 50 353
305	28 10 024	54 16 072	44 19 132	43 29 222	40 44 275	18 35 317	31 45 352
306	28 25 023	54 54 071	44 48 131	43 03 222	40 05 275	18 08 316	31 39 351
307	28 40 022	55 31 070	45 17 131	42 37 221	39 26 274	17 41 316	31 32 349
308	28 55 021	56 07 069	45 47 131	42 11 221	38 47 273	17 13 315	31 25 348
309	29 08 020	56 44 067	46 17 131	41 45 221	38 07 272	16 45 314	31 16 347
310	29 21 018	57 20 066	46 47 130	41 19 220	37 28 271	16 16 313	31 07 346
311	29 33 017	57 56 065	47 17 130	40 54 220	36 49 271	15 47 312	30 57 345
312	29 44 016	58 31 064	47 47 130	40 29 220	36 09 270	15 18 311	30 47 344
313	29 55 015	59 07 063	48 18 129	40 04 219	35 30 269	14 48 310	30 35 343
314	30 05 014	59 41 061	48 48 129	39 39 219	34 50 268	14 17 309	30 23 341
	◆ Enif	Diphda	◆ ACHERNAR	Miaplacidus	RIGIL KENT	◆ ANTARES	ALTAIR
315	30 14 013	35 28 076	49 19 129	28 48 181	39 14 219	34 11 268	30 10 340
316	30 22 012	36 07 075	49 50 129	28 47 181	38 49 218	33 32 267	29 57 339
317	30 30 011	36 45 074	50 20 128	28 47 181	38 25 218	32 52 266	29 42 338
318	30 37 009	37 22 073	50 51 128	28 47 180	38 01 218	32 13 266	29 27 337
319	30 43 008	38 00 072	51 23 128	28 47 180	37 37 217	31 34 265	29 11 336
320	30 48 007	38 37 071	51 54 127	28 47 179	37 13 217	30 55 264	28 55 335
321	30 53 006	39 14 070	52 25 127	28 48 179	36 50 217	30 16 263	28 38 334
322	30 56 005	39 51 070	52 56 127	28 49 179	36 26 216	29 37 263	28 20 333
323	30 59 004	40 28 069	53 28 127	28 50 178	36 03 216	28 58 262	28 02 332
324	31 01 003	41 05 068	53 59 127	28 51 178	35 40 216	28 19 261	27 43 331
325	31 03 001	41 41 067	54 31 126	28 53 177	35 17 215	27 40 261	27 23 330
326	31 03 000	42 17 066	55 03 126	28 55 177	34 55 215	27 01 260	27 03 328
327	31 03 359	42 53 065	55 35 126	28 57 177	34 32 214	26 22 259	26 42 327
328	31 02 358	43 28 064	56 07 126	28 59 176	34 10 214	25 44 258	26 21 326
329	31 00 357	44 03 063	56 39 126	29 02 176	33 48 214	25 05 258	25 59 325
	◆ Diphda	ACHERNAR	◆ Miaplacidus	RIGIL KENT	ANTARES	◆ ALTAIR	Enif
330	44 38 061	57 11 125	29 05 175	33 27 213	24 27 257	25 36 324	30 58 356
331	45 12 060	57 43 125	29 08 175	33 05 213	23 48 256	25 13 323	30 54 355
332	45 46 059	58 15 125	29 12 175	32 44 212	23 10 256	24 49 322	30 50 353
333	46 20 058	58 47 125	29 16 174	32 23 212	22 32 255	24 25 321	30 45 352
334	46 53 057	59 20 125	29 20 174	32 02 212	21 54 254	24 00 320	30 40 351
335	47 26 056	59 52 125	29 24 173	31 42 211	21 16 254	23 34 319	30 33 350
336	47 59 055	60 24 125	29 29 173	31 21 211	20 39 253	23 09 318	30 26 349
337	48 31 054	60 57 125	29 34 173	31 01 210	20 01 252	22 42 317	30 18 348
338	49 02 052	61 29 124	29 39 172	30 41 210	19 24 252	22 15 317	30 09 347
339	49 33 051	62 02 124	29 44 172	30 22 210	18 46 251	21 48 316	30 00 345
340	50 03 050	62 34 124	29 50 172	30 03 209	18 09 250	21 20 315	29 49 344
341	50 33 049	63 07 124	29 56 171	29 43 209	17 32 250	20 52 314	29 38 343
342	51 02 047	63 39 124	30 02 171	29 25 208	16 55 249	20 23 313	29 27 342
343	51 31 046	64 12 124	30 08 170	29 06 208	16 19 248	19 54 312	29 14 341
344	51 59 045	64 44 124	30 15 170	28 48 207	15 42 248	19 25 311	29 01 340
	◆ Diphda	Acamar	◆ CANOPUS	Miaplacidus	RIGIL KENT	◆ Nunki	Enif
345	52 26 043	47 45 101	27 13 141	30 22 170	28 30 207	38 18 273	28 47 339
346	52 53 042	48 23 101	27 39 140	30 29 169	28 12 207	37 39 272	28 32 338
347	53 19 041	49 02 100	28 04 140	30 37 169	27 55 206	36 59 271	28 17 337
348	53 44 039	49 41 100	28 30 139	30 44 169	27 37 206	36 20 270	28 01 336
349	54 09 038	50 20 099	28 56 139	30 52 168	27 20 205	35 40 270	27 45 334
350	54 32 036	50 59 098	29 22 138	31 01 168	27 04 205	35 01 269	27 27 333
351	54 55 035	51 38 098	29 48 138	31 09 167	26 47 204	34 22 268	27 09 332
352	55 17 033	52 17 097	30 15 137	31 18 167	26 31 204	33 42 267	26 51 331
353	55 38 032	52 56 096	30 42 137	31 27 167	26 16 203	33 03 267	26 32 330
354	55 58 030	53 35 096	31 09 136	31 36 166	26 00 203	32 24 266	26 12 329
355	56 17 028	54 14 095	31 36 136	31 45 166	25 45 203	31 45 265	25 51 328
356	56 36 027	54 53 094	32 04 135	31 55 166	25 30 202	31 05 265	25 30 327
357	56 54 025	55 33 094	32 32 135	32 05 165	25 15 202	30 26 264	25 09 326
358	57 09 023	56 12 093	33 00 134	32 15 165	25 01 201	29 47 263	24 46 325
359	57 24 022	56 51 092	33 28 134	32 25 165	24 47 201	29 08 262	24 24 324

LAT 50°S

LHA ♈	Hc	Zn	Hc	Zn	Hc	Zn	Hc	Zn	Hc	Zn	Hc	Zn	Hc	Zn
	Alpheratz		Hamal		◆RIGEL		CANOPUS		◆RIGIL KENT		Peacock		◆FOMALHAUT	
0	10 48	002	11 11	030	13 27	087	34 38	133	25 29	200	58 20	237	66 29	325
1	10 49	001	11 30	029	14 05	086	35 06	132	25 16	200	57 48	237	66 06	323
2	10 50	000	11 48	028	14 44	085	35 34	132	25 03	199	57 16	237	65 42	321
3	10 49	359	12 06	027	15 22	084	36 03	132	24 51	199	56 44	236	65 17	319
4	10 49	358	12 23	026	16 00	084	36 32	131	24 38	198	56 12	236	64 51	317
5	10 47	358	12 40	025	16 39	083	37 01	131	24 26	198	55 40	236	64 25	315
6	10 45	357	12 56	024	17 17	082	37 31	130	24 15	197	55 08	236	63 57	314
7	10 43	356	13 12	023	17 55	081	38 00	130	24 03	197	54 36	235	63 29	312
8	10 40	355	13 27	023	18 33	080	38 30	129	23 52	196	54 04	235	63 00	310
9	10 36	354	13 41	022	19 11	080	39 00	129	23 41	196	53 33	235	62 30	309
10	10 32	353	13 55	021	19 49	079	39 30	128	23 31	195	53 01	235	62 00	307
11	10 27	352	14 08	020	20 27	078	40 00	128	23 21	195	52 30	234	61 29	306
12	10 21	351	14 21	019	21 04	077	40 31	128	23 11	194	51 58	234	60 58	304
13	10 15	351	14 33	018	21 42	076	41 01	127	23 02	194	51 27	234	60 26	303
14	10 09	350	14 45	017	22 19	076	41 32	127	22 52	193	50 56	234	59 53	302
	Hamal		◆RIGEL		SIRIUS		CANOPUS		◆RIGIL KENT		Peacock		◆FOMALHAUT	
15	14 56	016	22 57	075	15 00	098	42 03	126	22 44	193	50 25	233	59 20	300
16	15 06	015	23 34	074	15 38	098	42 35	126	22 35	192	49 54	233	58 46	299
17	15 16	014	24 11	073	16 16	097	43 06	125	22 27	192	49 24	233	58 13	298
18	15 25	013	24 47	072	16 54	096	43 37	125	22 19	191	48 53	232	57 38	297
19	15 34	012	25 24	071	17 33	095	44 09	125	22 12	191	48 23	232	57 04	295
20	15 42	011	26 01	070	18 11	095	44 41	124	22 05	190	47 52	232	56 29	294
21	15 49	010	26 37	070	18 50	094	45 13	124	21 58	190	47 22	231	55 53	293
22	15 56	010	27 13	069	19 28	093	45 45	123	21 51	189	46 52	231	55 18	292
23	16 02	009	27 49	068	20 07	092	46 17	123	21 45	189	46 22	231	54 42	291
24	16 07	008	28 24	067	20 45	092	46 50	123	21 39	188	45 52	230	54 06	290
25	16 12	007	29 00	066	21 24	091	47 22	122	21 34	188	45 23	230	53 29	289
26	16 16	006	29 35	065	22 02	090	47 55	122	21 29	187	44 53	230	52 52	288
27	16 20	005	30 10	064	22 41	089	48 28	121	21 24	187	44 24	229	52 16	287
28	16 23	004	30 44	063	23 19	089	49 01	121	21 20	186	43 55	229	51 39	286
29	16 25	003	31 18	062	23 58	088	49 34	121	21 16	186	43 26	229	51 01	285
	Hamal		◆RIGEL		SIRIUS		CANOPUS		◆RIGIL KENT		Peacock		◆FOMALHAUT	
30	16 27	002	31 52	061	24 37	087	50 07	120	21 12	185	42 57	228	50 24	284
31	16 28	001	32 26	060	25 15	086	50 41	120	21 08	185	42 28	228	49 46	283
32	16 28	000	32 59	059	25 53	085	51 14	120	21 05	184	42 00	227	49 09	282
33	16 28	359	33 32	058	26 32	085	51 48	119	21 03	184	41 32	227	48 31	281
34	16 27	358	34 05	057	27 10	084	52 21	119	21 00	183	41 04	227	47 53	280
35	16 25	357	34 37	056	27 49	083	52 55	118	20 58	183	40 36	226	47 15	279
36	16 23	356	35 09	055	28 27	082	53 29	118	20 57	182	40 08	226	46 37	278
37	16 20	355	35 41	054	29 05	081	54 03	118	20 55	182	39 40	226	45 59	277
38	16 16	354	36 12	053	29 43	081	54 38	117	20 55	181	39 13	225	45 20	277
39	16 12	353	36 43	052	30 21	080	55 12	117	20 54	181	38 45	225	44 42	276
40	16 08	352	37 13	051	30 59	079	55 46	117	20 54	180	38 18	224	44 04	275
41	16 02	351	37 43	050	31 37	078	56 21	116	20 54	180	37 52	224	43 25	274
42	15 56	350	38 12	049	32 14	077	56 55	116	20 54	179	37 25	224	42 47	273
43	15 49	350	38 41	048	32 52	076	57 30	116	20 55	179	36 58	223	42 08	273
44	15 42	349	39 09	047	33 29	075	58 05	115	20 56	178	36 32	223	41 30	272
	RIGEL		SIRIUS		◆CANOPUS		RIGIL KENT		◆Peacock		FOMALHAUT		◆Hamal	
45	39 37	046	34 07	075	58 40	115	20 58	177	36 06	222	40 51	271	15 34	348
46	40 04	045	34 44	074	59 15	115	21 00	177	35 40	222	40 13	270	15 25	347
47	40 31	043	35 21	073	59 50	114	21 02	176	35 15	221	39 34	269	15 16	346
48	40 57	042	35 57	072	60 25	114	21 05	176	34 49	221	38 55	269	15 07	345
49	41 23	041	36 34	071	61 00	114	21 07	175	34 24	221	38 17	268	14 56	344
50	41 48	040	37 10	070	61 36	113	21 11	175	33 59	220	37 38	267	14 45	343
51	42 12	039	37 46	069	62 11	113	21 14	174	33 34	220	37 00	266	14 34	342
52	42 36	037	38 22	068	62 47	113	21 18	174	33 10	219	36 21	266	14 21	341
53	42 59	036	38 58	067	63 22	113	21 23	173	32 46	219	35 43	265	14 09	340
54	43 22	035	39 33	066	63 58	112	21 27	173	32 22	218	35 04	264	13 55	339
55	43 43	034	40 09	065	64 34	112	21 32	172	31 58	218	34 26	264	13 41	338
56	44 04	032	40 43	064	65 09	112	21 38	172	31 34	217	33 48	263	13 27	337
57	44 24	031	41 18	063	65 45	112	21 43	171	31 11	217	33 10	262	13 12	337
58	44 44	030	41 52	062	66 21	111	21 49	171	30 48	217	32 31	261	12 56	336
59	45 03	028	42 26	061	66 57	111	21 56	170	30 25	216	31 53	261	12 40	335
	◆ALDEBARAN		BETELGEUSE		SIRIUS		◆Suhail		RIGIL KENT		◆ACHERNAR		Diphda	
60	22 58	010	27 18	033	43 00	060	39 08	114	22 02	170	68 04	237	39 36	291
61	23 04	009	27 39	032	43 33	059	39 43	114	22 09	169	67 32	237	39 00	290
62	23 10	008	27 59	031	44 06	058	40 18	113	22 17	169	66 59	237	38 24	290
63	23 14	006	28 18	030	44 38	057	40 54	113	22 24	168	66 27	238	37 48	289
64	23 18	005	28 37	029	45 11	056	41 30	112	22 32	168	65 54	238	37 11	288
65	23 22	004	28 55	027	45 42	055	42 05	111	22 41	167	65 22	238	36 34	287
66	23 24	003	29 13	026	46 13	053	42 41	111	22 50	167	64 49	237	35 57	286
67	23 26	002	29 29	025	46 44	052	43 17	110	22 59	166	64 17	237	35 20	285
68	23 27	001	29 45	024	47 14	051	43 54	110	23 08	166	63 44	237	34 43	284
69	23 28	000	30 01	023	47 44	050	44 30	109	23 18	165	63 12	237	34 05	283
70	23 27	359	30 16	022	48 13	049	45 06	109	23 28	165	62 39	237	33 27	282
71	23 27	358	30 30	021	48 42	047	45 43	108	23 38	164	62 07	237	32 50	282
72	23 25	357	30 43	020	49 10	046	46 20	108	23 49	164	61 34	237	32 12	281
73	23 23	356	30 56	019	49 37	045	46 57	107	24 00	163	61 02	237	31 34	280
74	23 20	355	31 08	017	50 04	043	47 33	106	24 11	163	60 30	237	30 56	279
	BETELGEUSE		SIRIUS		◆Suhail		RIGIL KENT		◆ACHERNAR		Diphda		◆ALDEBARAN	
75	31 19	016	50 31	042	48 10	106	24 23	162	59 58	237	30 18	278	23 16	354
76	31 29	015	50 56	041	48 48	105	24 35	162	59 25	236	29 40	277	23 11	353
77	31 39	014	51 21	039	49 25	105	24 47	161	58 53	236	29 01	277	23 06	352
78	31 48	013	51 45	038	50 02	104	24 59	161	58 21	236	28 23	276	23 01	351
79	31 56	012	52 08	037	50 40	104	25 12	160	57 49	236	27 44	275	22 54	350
80	32 04	011	52 31	035	51 17	103	25 25	160	57 17	236	27 06	274	22 47	349
81	32 10	009	52 53	034	51 55	102	25 39	159	56 45	236	26 28	273	22 39	348
82	32 16	008	53 14	032	52 33	102	25 52	159	56 14	235	25 49	273	22 30	347
83	32 21	007	53 34	031	53 10	101	26 07	158	55 42	235	25 11	272	22 21	346
84	32 26	006	53 53	029	53 48	101	26 21	158	55 10	235	24 32	271	22 11	345
85	32 29	005	54 11	028	54 26	100	26 36	157	54 39	235	23 53	270	22 01	344
86	32 32	004	54 29	026	55 04	099	26 50	157	54 08	234	23 15	270	21 50	343
87	32 34	002	54 45	024	55 42	099	27 06	157	53 36	234	22 36	269	21 38	342
88	32 35	001	55 01	023	56 20	098	27 21	156	53 05	234	21 58	268	21 25	341
89	32 35	000	55 15	021	56 59	098	27 37	156	52 34	234	21 19	267	21 12	340

LHA ♈	Hc	Zn	Hc	Zn	Hc	Zn	Hc	Zn	Hc	Zn	Hc	Zn	Hc	Zn
	PROCYON		Alphard		◆Suhail		RIGIL KENT		◆ACHERNAR		◆RIGEL		BETELGEUSE	
90	30 43	029	30 26	065	57 37	097	27 53	155	52 03	233	47 09	344	32 35	359
91	31 02	028	31 01	064	58 15	096	28 09	155	51 32	233	46 58	342	32 34	358
92	31 20	027	31 36	063	58 53	096	28 26	154	51 01	233	46 46	341	32 32	356
93	31 37	026	32 10	062	59 32	095	28 43	154	50 31	232	46 33	339	32 29	355
94	31 54	025	32 44	061	60 10	094	29 00	153	50 00	232	46 19	338	32 26	354
95	32 09	024	33 17	060	60 49	094	29 18	153	49 30	232	46 04	337	32 21	353
96	32 25	023	33 50	059	61 27	093	29 35	152	49 00	232	45 48	335	32 16	352
97	32 39	021	34 23	058	62 06	092	29 53	152	48 29	231	45 31	334	32 10	351
98	32 53	020	34 56	057	62 44	091	30 12	152	47 59	231	45 14	332	32 04	349
99	33 06	019	35 28	056	63 23	091	30 30	151	47 29	231	44 56	331	31 56	348
100	33 18	018	36 00	055	64 02	090	30 49	151	47 00	230	44 37	330	31 48	347
101	33 30	017	36 31	054	64 40	089	31 08	150	46 30	230	44 17	329	31 39	346
102	33 40	016	37 02	053	65 19	088	31 27	150	46 01	230	43 56	327	31 29	345
103	33 50	014	37 33	052	65 57	088	31 47	149	45 31	229	43 35	326	31 19	344
104	34 00	013	38 03	051	66 36	087	32 06	149	45 02	229	43 13	325	31 08	343
	PROCYON		REGULUS		◆Gienah		RIGIL KENT		◆ACHERNAR		RIGEL		◆BETELGEUSE	
105	34 08	012	15 35	048	20 19	093	32 26	149	44 33	229	42 51	323	30 56	341
106	34 16	011	16 04	047	20 58	093	32 47	148	44 04	228	42 27	322	30 43	340
107	34 23	010	16 32	047	21 36	092	33 07	148	43 36	228	42 03	321	30 30	339
108	34 29	008	17 00	046	22 15	091	33 28	147	43 07	228	41 39	320	30 16	338
109	34 34	007	17 27	045	22 54	090	33 49	147	42 39	227	41 14	319	30 01	337
110	34 39	006	17 54	044	23 32	090	34 10	147	42 10	227	40 48	317	29 45	336
111	34 42	005	18 21	043	24 11	089	34 31	146	41 42	226	40 21	316	29 29	335
112	34 45	004	18 47	042	24 49	088	34 53	146	41 15	226	39 54	315	29 12	334
113	34 47	002	19 12	041	25 28	087	35 15	145	40 47	226	39 27	314	28 55	333
114	34 48	001	19 37	040	26 06	087	35 37	145	40 19	225	38 59	313	28 37	331
115	34 49	000	20 02	039	26 45	086	35 59	145	39 52	225	38 30	312	28 18	330
116	34 48	359	20 26	038	27 23	085	36 22	144	39 25	225	38 01	311	27 59	329
117	34 47	358	20 50	037	28 02	084	36 44	144	38 58	224	37 32	310	27 39	328
118	34 45	356	21 13	036	28 40	083	37 07	143	38 31	224	37 02	308	27 18	327
119	34 42	355	21 35	035	29 18	083	37 30	143	38 04	223	36 31	307	26 57	326
	REGULUS		◆SPICA		RIGIL KENT		◆ACHERNAR		RIGEL		BETELGEUSE		◆PROCYON	
120	21 57	034	14 02	091	37 54	143	37 38	223	36 00	306	26 35	325	34 39	354
121	22 19	033	14 41	090	38 17	142	37 12	223	35 29	305	26 13	324	34 34	353
122	22 39	032	15 19	089	38 41	142	36 46	222	34 57	304	25 50	323	34 29	352
123	23 00	031	15 58	089	39 05	142	36 20	222	34 25	303	25 27	322	34 23	350
124	23 20	030	16 36	088	39 29	141	35 55	221	33 53	302	25 03	321	34 16	349
125	23 39	029	17 15	087	39 53	141	35 29	221	33 20	301	24 38	320	34 08	348
126	23 57	028	17 53	086	40 17	141	35 04	220	32 47	300	24 13	319	34 00	347
127	24 15	027	18 32	085	40 42	140	34 39	220	32 14	299	23 48	318	33 51	346
128	24 33	026	19 10	085	41 07	140	34 14	220	31 40	298	23 22	317	33 41	344
129	24 50	025	19 49	084	41 32	139	33 50	219	31 06	297	22 55	316	33 30	343
130	25 06	024	20 27	083	41 57	139	33 26	219	30 31	296	22 28	315	33 19	342
131	25 21	023	21 05	082	42 22	139	33 02	218	29 57	296	22 01	314	33 06	341
132	25 36	022	21 43	081	42 48	139	32 38	218	29 22	295	21 33	313	32 53	340
133	25 50	021	22 22	081	43 13	138	32 14	217	28 47	294	21 05	312	32 40	339
134	26 04	020	23 00	080	43 39	138	31 51	217	28 11	293	20 36	311	32 25	337
	◆REGULUS		SPICA		◆RIGIL KENT		ACHERNAR		◆CANOPUS		SIRIUS		PROCYON	
135	26 17	019	23 37	079	44 05	138	31 28	217	65 50	248	47 12	309	32 10	336
136	26 29	018	24 15	078	44 31	137	31 05	216	65 14	248	46 41	308	31 54	335
137	26 40	017	24 53	077	44 57	137	30 42	216	64 39	248	46 10	306	31 38	334
138	26 51	016	25 31	077	45 24	137	30 20	215	64 03	248	45 39	305	31 20	333
139	27 01	015	26 08	076	45 50	136	29 58	215	63 27	247	45 08	304	31 03	332
140	27 10	014	26 45	075	46 17	136	29 36	214	62 52	247	44 35	303	30 44	331
141	27 19	012	27 22	074	46 44	136	29 14	214	62 16	247	44 03	302	30 25	330
142	27 27	011	27 59	073	47 11	136	28 53	213	61 41	247	43 30	301	30 05	329
143	27 34	010	28 36	072	47 38	135	28 32	213	61 05	246	42 57	300	29 45	327
144	27 41	009	29 13	071	48 05	135	28 11	212	60 30	246	42 23	299	29 23	326
145	27 47	008	29 49	071	48 32	135	27 51	212	59 55	246	41 49	298	29 02	325
146	27 52	007	30 26	070	49 00	135	27 30	211	59 20	245	41 15	297	28 40	324
147	27 56	006	31 02	069	49 27	134	27 10	211	58 45	245	40 40	296	28 17	323
148	28 00	005	31 37	068	49 55	134	26 51	210	58 10	245	40 05	295	27 53	322
149	28 02	004	32 13	067	50 23	134	26 31	210	57 35	244	39 30	294	27 29	321
	◆REGULUS		SPICA		◆RIGIL KENT		ACHERNAR		◆CANOPUS		SIRIUS		PROCYON	
150	28 04	003	32 48	066	50 51	134	26 12	210	57 00	244	38 55	293	27 05	320
151	28 06	001	33 24	065	51 19	133	25 53	209	56 26	244	38 19	292	26 40	319
152	28 06	000	33 58	064	51 47	133	25 35	209	55 51	243	37 43	291	26 15	318
153	28 06	359	34 33	063	52 15	133	25 16	208	55 17	243	37 07	290	25 49	317
154	28 05	358	35 07	062	52 43	133	24 59	208	54 42	243	36 30	289	25 22	316
155	28 04	357	35 41	061	53 12	133	24 41	207	54 08	242	35 54	288	24 55	315
156	28 01	356	36 15	060	53 40	132	24 23	207	53 34	242	35 17	287	24 28	314
157	27 58	355	36 48	059	54 09	132	24 06	206	53 00	242	34 40	286	24 00	313
158	27 54	354	37 21	058	54 37	132	23 50	205	52 26	241	34 03	285	23 31	312
159	27 50	353	37 53	057	55 06	132	23 33	205	51 52	241	33 26	284	23 03	311
160	27 44	351	38 26	056	55 35	132	23 17	204	51 19	241	32 48	284	22 33	310
161	27 38	350	38 57	055	56 03	132	23 01	204	50 45	240	32 11	283	22 04	309
162	27 31	349	39 29	054	56 32	131	22 46	203	50 12	240	31 33	282	21 34	308
163	27 24	348	40 00	053	57 01	131	22 31	203	49 39	239	30 55	281	21 03	308
164	27 16	347	40 30	052	57 30	131	22 16	202	49 05	239	30 17	280	20 33	307
	SPICA		◆ANTARES		RIGIL KENT		ACHERNAR		◆CANOPUS		SIRIUS		◆REGULUS	
165	41 00	051	24 34	103	57 59	131	22 01	202	48 32	239	29 39	279	27 07	346
166	41 30	049	25 11	102	58 28	131	21 47	201	48 00	238	29 01	279	26 57	345
167	41 59	048	25 49	101	58 57	131	21 33	201	47 27	238	28 23	278	26 47	344
168	42 28	047	26 27	100	59 27	131	21 20	200	46 54	237	27 45	277	26 35	343
169	42 56	046	27 05	100	59 56	131	21 06	200	46 22	237	27 07	276	26 24	342
170	43 23	045	27 43	099	60 25	131	20 53	199	45 50	237	26 28	275	26 11	341
171	43 50	044	28 21	098	60 54	131	20 41	199	45 17	236	25 50	275	25 58	340
172	44 16	042	28 59	098	61 23	131	20 29	198	44 45	236	25 11	274	25 44	339
173	44 42	041	29 38	097	61 52	131	20 17	198	44 14	235	24 33	273	25 30	337
174	45 07	040	30 16	096	62 22	131	20 05	197	43 42	235	23 54	272	25 15	336
175	45 31	039	30 54	095	62 51	131	19 54	197	43 10	235	23 16	271	24 59	335
176	45 55	037	31 33	095	63 20	131	19 43	196	42 39	234	22 37	271	24 43	334
177	46 18	036	32 11	094	63 49	131	19 33	195	42 08	234	21 59	270	24 26	333
178	46 41	035	32 50	093	64 18	131	19 23	195	41 37	233	21 20	269	24 08	332
179	47 02	033	33 28	092	64 47	131	19 13	194	41 06	233	20 42	268	23 50	331

LHA ♈	Hc	Zn	Hc	Zn	Hc	Zn	Hc	Zn	Hc	Zn	Hc	Zn	Hc	Zn
	◆ARCTURUS		ANTARES		◆Peacock		ACHERNAR		CANOPUS		◆Suhail		REGULUS	
180	14 37	033	34 07	092	25 25	151	19 04	194	40 35	233	60 21	266	23 31	330
181	14 58	032	34 45	091	25 44	150	18 55	193	40 05	232	59 42	265	23 11	329
182	15 18	031	35 24	090	26 03	150	18 46	193	39 34	232	59 04	265	22 51	328
183	15 38	030	36 02	089	26 23	149	18 38	192	39 04	231	58 26	264	22 31	327
184	15 57	030	36 41	089	26 42	149	18 30	192	38 34	231	57 47	263	22 10	326
185	16 16	029	37 20	088	27 02	148	18 22	191	38 04	230	57 09	263	21 48	325
186	16 34	028	37 58	087	27 23	148	18 15	190	37 35	230	56 31	262	21 26	324
187	16 52	027	38 37	086	27 43	147	18 08	190	37 05	229	55 53	261	21 03	323
188	17 09	026	39 15	086	28 04	147	18 02	189	36 36	229	55 15	261	20 40	322
189	17 25	025	39 53	085	28 26	146	17 56	189	36 07	229	54 37	260	20 16	321
190	17 41	024	40 32	084	28 47	146	17 50	188	35 39	228	53 59	260	19 52	320
191	17 56	023	41 10	083	29 09	145	17 45	188	35 10	228	53 21	259	19 27	320
192	18 11	022	41 48	082	29 31	145	17 40	187	34 42	227	52 43	258	19 02	319
193	18 25	021	42 27	081	29 53	145	17 35	187	34 13	227	52 05	258	18 36	318
194	18 39	020	43 05	080	30 15	144	17 31	186	33 45	226	51 27	257	18 10	317
	ARCTURUS		◆ANTARES		Peacock		◆ACHERNAR		CANOPUS		Suhail		◆REGULUS	
195	18 52	019	43 43	080	30 38	144	17 27	185	33 18	226	50 50	257	17 43	316
196	19 04	018	44 21	079	31 01	143	17 24	185	32 50	225	50 12	256	17 16	315
197	19 16	017	44 58	078	31 24	143	17 21	184	32 23	225	49 35	255	16 48	314
198	19 27	016	45 36	077	31 48	142	17 18	184	31 56	224	48 58	255	16 20	313
199	19 37	015	46 13	076	32 12	142	17 16	183	31 29	224	48 21	254	15 52	312
200	19 47	014	46 51	075	32 36	141	17 14	183	31 02	223	47 44	254	15 23	311
201	19 56	013	47 28	074	33 00	141	17 12	182	30 36	223	47 07	253	14 54	310
202	20 04	012	48 05	073	33 24	140	17 11	181	30 10	222	46 30	253	14 25	310
203	20 12	011	48 42	072	33 49	140	17 10	181	29 44	222	45 53	252	13 55	309
204	20 19	010	49 18	071	34 14	140	17 10	180	29 18	221	45 16	251	13 25	308
205	20 26	009	49 55	070	34 39	139	17 10	180	28 53	221	44 40	251	12 54	307
206	20 32	008	50 31	069	35 04	139	17 10	179	28 28	220	44 04	250	12 23	306
207	20 37	007	51 07	068	35 30	138	17 11	179	28 03	220	43 27	250	11 52	305
208	20 41	006	51 43	067	35 55	138	17 12	178	27 39	219	42 51	249	11 20	304
209	20 45	005	52 18	066	36 21	137	17 13	177	27 14	219	42 15	249	10 48	304
	◆ARCTURUS		ANTARES		◆Peacock		ACHERNAR		CANOPUS		◆Suhail		SPICA	
210	20 48	004	52 53	065	36 48	137	17 15	177	26 50	218	41 39	248	50 37	347
211	20 50	003	53 28	064	37 14	137	17 18	176	26 26	218	41 04	248	50 27	345
212	20 52	002	54 02	062	37 41	136	17 20	176	26 03	217	40 28	247	50 17	344
213	20 53	001	54 36	061	38 07	136	17 23	175	25 40	217	39 53	246	50 06	342
214	20 54	000	55 10	060	38 34	135	17 27	175	25 17	216	39 17	246	49 53	341
215	20 53	359	55 43	059	39 01	135	17 30	174	24 54	216	38 42	245	49 40	339
216	20 52	358	56 16	058	39 29	135	17 35	174	24 31	215	38 07	245	49 26	338
217	20 51	357	56 48	056	39 56	134	17 39	173	24 09	215	37 32	244	49 11	336
218	20 48	356	57 20	055	40 24	134	17 44	172	23 48	214	36 58	244	48 55	335
219	20 45	355	57 51	054	40 52	133	17 49	172	23 26	214	36 23	243	48 38	333
220	20 42	354	58 22	052	41 20	133	17 55	171	23 05	213	35 49	243	48 21	332
221	20 37	353	58 52	051	41 48	133	18 01	171	22 44	213	35 15	242	48 02	331
222	20 32	352	59 22	049	42 17	132	18 07	170	22 23	212	34 41	241	47 43	329
223	20 27	351	59 51	048	42 45	132	18 14	170	22 03	212	34 07	241	47 23	328
224	20 20	350	60 19	046	43 14	132	18 21	169	21 43	211	33 33	240	47 02	327
	ANTARES		◆Nunki		Peacock		ACHERNAR		◆CANOPUS		◆SPICA		ARCTURUS	
225	60 46	045	39 28	085	43 43	131	18 29	168	21 23	210	46 40	325	20 13	349
226	61 13	043	40 06	084	44 12	131	18 37	168	21 04	210	46 18	324	20 06	348
227	61 39	042	40 44	083	44 41	131	18 45	167	20 45	209	45 55	323	19 57	347
228	62 04	040	41 23	082	45 11	130	18 54	167	20 26	209	45 31	321	19 48	346
229	62 29	038	42 01	082	45 40	130	19 03	166	20 08	208	45 07	320	19 39	345
230	62 52	036	42 39	081	46 10	129	19 12	166	19 50	208	44 42	319	19 28	344
231	63 14	035	43 17	080	46 40	129	19 22	165	19 32	207	44 16	318	19 18	343
232	63 36	033	43 55	079	47 10	129	19 32	165	19 15	207	43 50	316	19 06	342
233	63 56	031	44 33	078	47 40	128	19 42	164	18 58	206	43 23	315	18 54	341
234	64 15	029	45 10	077	48 10	128	19 53	164	18 41	205	42 55	314	18 41	340
235	64 33	027	45 48	076	48 40	128	20 04	163	18 24	205	42 27	313	18 28	339
236	64 50	025	46 25	075	49 11	128	20 15	162	18 08	204	41 59	312	18 14	338
237	65 06	023	47 03	074	49 42	127	20 27	162	17 53	204	41 30	310	17 59	337
238	65 20	021	47 40	073	50 12	127	20 39	161	17 37	203	41 00	309	17 44	336
239	65 33	019	48 16	072	50 43	127	20 52	161	17 23	203	40 30	308	17 28	335
	Rasalhague		◆ALTAIR		FOMALHAUT		◆ACHERNAR		ACRUX		◆SPICA		ARCTURUS	
240	24 02	026	12 39	059	13 41	120	21 05	160	59 03	225	40 00	307	17 12	334
241	24 18	025	13 12	058	14 15	119	21 18	160	58 36	225	39 29	306	16 55	333
242	24 34	024	13 45	057	14 48	119	21 31	159	58 09	225	38 57	305	16 37	333
243	24 49	023	14 17	056	15 22	118	21 45	159	57 42	225	38 25	304	16 19	332
244	25 03	022	14 49	056	15 57	117	21 59	158	57 15	224	37 53	303	16 00	331
245	25 17	020	15 21	055	16 31	117	22 14	158	56 48	224	37 21	302	15 41	330
246	25 30	019	15 52	054	17 06	116	22 29	157	56 21	224	36 48	301	15 21	329
247	25 43	018	16 23	053	17 40	115	22 44	157	55 54	224	36 14	300	15 01	328
248	25 55	017	16 54	052	18 15	114	22 59	156	55 27	224	35 41	299	14 40	327
249	26 06	016	17 24	051	18 51	114	23 15	156	55 00	224	35 07	298	14 19	326
250	26 16	015	17 54	050	19 26	113	23 31	155	54 33	224	34 33	297	13 57	325
251	26 26	014	18 23	049	20 01	112	23 47	155	54 07	224	33 58	296	13 35	324
252	26 35	013	18 52	049	20 37	112	24 04	154	53 40	224	33 23	295	13 12	323
253	26 43	012	19 21	048	21 13	111	24 21	154	53 13	224	32 48	294	12 49	323
254	26 51	011	19 49	047	21 49	110	24 38	153	52 47	223	32 13	293	12 25	322
	Rasalhague		◆ALTAIR		FOMALHAUT		◆ACHERNAR		ACRUX		◆SPICA		ANTARES	
255	26 58	010	20 17	046	22 25	110	24 56	153	52 20	223	31 37	292	65 47	344
256	27 04	009	20 45	045	23 02	109	25 14	152	51 54	223	31 01	291	65 35	342
257	27 09	008	21 12	044	23 38	108	25 32	152	51 28	223	30 25	290	65 22	339
258	27 14	006	21 38	043	24 15	108	25 51	151	51 01	223	29 49	289	65 08	337
259	27 18	005	22 04	042	24 52	107	26 10	151	50 35	223	29 13	289	64 53	335
260	27 21	004	22 30	041	25 29	106	26 29	150	50 09	222	28 36	288	64 36	333
261	27 24	003	22 55	040	26 06	106	26 48	150	49 43	222	27 59	287	64 18	331
262	27 26	002	23 19	039	26 43	105	27 08	149	49 17	222	27 22	286	63 59	329
263	27 27	001	23 43	038	27 20	104	27 28	149	48 52	222	26 45	285	63 39	328
264	27 27	000	24 07	037	27 58	104	27 48	148	48 26	222	26 08	284	63 18	326
265	27 27	359	24 30	036	28 35	103	28 08	148	48 01	221	25 30	283	62 56	324
266	27 25	358	24 52	035	29 13	102	28 29	147	47 35	221	24 53	283	62 32	322
267	27 23	357	25 14	034	29 51	102	28 50	147	47 10	221	24 15	282	62 08	320
268	27 21	356	25 36	033	30 28	101	29 11	146	46 45	221	23 37	281	61 43	319
269	27 17	354	25 56	032	31 06	100	29 33	146	46 20	220	22 59	280	61 17	317

LAT 50°S

LHA ♈	Hc	Zn	Hc	Zn	Hc	Zn	Hc	Zn	Hc	Zn	Hc	Zn	Hc	Zn
	◆ALTAIR		FOMALHAUT		◆ACHERNAR		RIGIL KENT		◆SPICA		ANTARES		Rasalhague	
270	26 17	031	31 44	099	29 55	145	60 34	229	22 21	279	60 51	316	27 13	353
271	26 36	030	32 22	099	30 17	145	60 05	229	21 43	279	60 23	314	27 08	352
272	26 55	029	33 01	098	30 39	144	59 36	229	21 05	278	59 55	312	27 03	351
273	27 13	028	33 39	097	31 02	144	59 07	229	20 27	277	59 26	311	26 57	350
274	27 31	027	34 17	097	31 25	143	58 38	229	19 48	276	58 57	309	26 49	349
275	27 48	026	34 55	096	31 48	143	58 09	229	19 10	275	58 27	308	26 42	348
276	28 05	025	35 34	095	32 11	143	57 39	229	18 32	275	57 56	307	26 33	347
277	28 20	024	36 12	094	32 35	142	57 10	229	17 53	274	57 25	305	26 24	346
278	28 35	022	36 51	094	32 58	142	56 42	229	17 15	273	56 53	304	26 14	345
279	28 50	021	37 29	093	33 22	141	56 13	228	16 36	272	56 21	303	26 04	344
280	29 04	020	38 08	092	33 47	141	55 44	228	15 58	271	55 48	301	25 52	343
281	29 17	019	38 46	092	34 11	140	55 15	228	15 19	271	55 15	300	25 40	341
282	29 29	018	39 25	091	34 36	140	54 46	228	14 40	270	54 42	299	25 28	340
283	29 41	017	40 03	090	35 01	140	54 18	228	14 02	269	54 08	298	25 15	339
284	29 52	016	40 42	089	35 26	139	53 49	228	13 23	268	53 33	297	25 01	338
	ALTAIR		Enif		◆FOMALHAUT		ACHERNAR		◆RIGIL KENT		ANTARES		◆Rasalhague	
285	30 02	015	20 07	044	41 20	088	35 51	139	53 21	228	52 59	295	24 46	337
286	30 11	014	20 33	043	41 59	088	36 17	138	52 52	227	52 24	294	24 31	336
287	30 20	012	20 59	042	42 38	087	36 42	138	52 24	227	51 48	293	24 15	335
288	30 28	011	21 25	041	43 16	086	37 08	137	51 56	227	51 13	292	23 58	334
289	30 35	010	21 50	040	43 54	085	37 35	137	51 28	227	50 37	291	23 41	333
290	30 41	009	22 14	039	44 33	084	38 01	137	51 00	227	50 01	290	23 24	332
291	30 47	008	22 38	038	45 11	084	38 27	136	50 32	226	49 24	289	23 05	331
292	30 52	007	23 02	037	45 50	083	38 54	136	50 04	226	48 48	288	22 46	330
293	30 56	006	23 25	036	46 28	082	39 21	135	49 36	226	48 11	287	22 27	329
294	31 00	004	23 47	035	47 06	081	39 48	135	49 09	226	47 34	286	22 07	328
295	31 02	003	24 09	034	47 44	080	40 16	135	48 41	225	46 57	285	21 46	327
296	31 04	002	24 30	033	48 22	079	40 43	134	48 14	225	46 20	284	21 25	326
297	31 05	001	24 51	032	49 00	078	41 11	134	47 46	225	45 42	283	21 03	325
298	31 05	000	25 11	031	49 37	077	41 39	134	47 19	225	45 05	282	20 41	324
299	31 05	359	25 31	030	50 15	077	42 07	133	46 52	224	44 27	281	20 18	323
	◆Enif		FOMALHAUT		◆ACHERNAR		RIGIL KENT		◆ANTARES		Rasalhague		ALTAIR	
300	25 50	029	50 52	076	42 35	133	46 25	224	43 49	281	19 55	322	31 04	358
301	26 08	028	51 30	075	43 03	132	45 59	224	43 11	280	19 31	321	31 02	356
302	26 26	027	52 07	074	43 32	132	45 32	223	42 33	279	19 06	320	30 59	355
303	26 43	026	52 44	073	44 00	132	45 06	223	41 55	278	18 42	319	30 55	354
304	26 59	025	53 20	072	44 29	131	44 39	223	41 16	277	18 16	319	30 51	353
305	27 15	024	53 57	071	44 58	131	44 13	223	40 38	276	17 51	318	30 46	352
306	27 30	023	54 33	069	45 27	131	43 47	222	40 00	275	17 24	317	30 40	351
307	27 45	022	55 09	068	45 57	130	43 21	222	39 21	275	16 58	316	30 33	350
308	27 58	020	55 45	067	46 26	130	42 56	222	38 43	274	16 31	315	30 26	348
309	28 12	019	56 20	066	46 56	130	42 30	221	38 04	273	16 03	314	30 18	347
310	28 24	018	56 55	065	47 25	129	42 05	221	37 26	272	15 35	313	30 09	346
311	28 36	017	57 30	064	47 55	129	41 40	221	36 47	271	15 07	312	29 59	345
312	28 47	016	58 04	062	48 25	129	41 15	220	36 09	271	14 38	311	29 49	344
313	28 57	015	58 38	061	48 55	128	40 50	220	35 30	270	14 09	310	29 38	343
314	29 07	014	59 12	060	49 26	128	40 25	220	34 52	269	13 39	310	29 26	342
	◆Enif		Diphda		◆ACHERNAR		Miaplacidus		RIGIL KENT		◆ANTARES		ALTAIR	
315	29 15	013	35 13	075	49 56	128	29 48	181	40 01	219	34 13	268	29 14	341
316	29 23	012	35 51	074	50 27	128	29 47	181	39 36	219	33 35	268	29 00	339
317	29 31	010	36 28	073	50 57	127	29 47	181	39 12	219	32 56	267	28 46	338
318	29 37	009	37 05	072	51 28	127	29 47	180	38 48	218	32 18	266	28 32	337
319	29 43	008	37 41	072	51 59	127	29 47	180	38 25	218	31 39	265	28 17	336
320	29 49	007	38 18	071	52 30	126	29 47	179	38 01	217	31 01	265	28 01	335
321	29 53	006	38 54	070	53 01	126	29 48	179	37 38	217	30 22	264	27 44	334
322	29 56	005	39 30	069	53 32	126	29 49	179	37 14	217	29 44	263	27 27	333
323	29 59	004	40 06	068	54 03	126	29 50	178	36 51	216	29 06	263	27 09	332
324	30 01	003	40 41	067	54 35	125	29 51	178	36 29	216	28 27	262	26 51	331
325	30 03	001	41 17	066	55 06	125	29 53	177	36 06	216	27 49	261	26 31	330
326	30 03	000	41 52	065	55 38	125	29 55	177	35 44	215	27 11	260	26 12	329
327	30 03	359	42 27	064	56 09	125	29 57	177	35 22	215	26 33	260	25 51	328
328	30 02	358	43 01	063	56 41	125	29 59	176	35 00	214	25 55	259	25 31	327
329	30 00	357	43 35	062	57 13	124	30 02	176	34 38	214	25 18	258	25 09	326
	◆Diphda		ACHERNAR		◆Miaplacidus		RIGIL KENT		ANTARES		◆ALTAIR		Enif	
330	44 09	061	57 45	124	30 05	175	34 17	214	24 40	258	24 47	325	29 58	356
331	44 42	060	58 17	124	30 08	175	33 55	213	24 02	257	24 24	324	29 55	355
332	45 15	058	58 49	124	30 12	175	33 34	213	23 25	256	24 01	323	29 51	353
333	45 48	057	59 21	124	30 15	174	33 14	212	22 47	255	23 38	322	29 46	352
334	46 20	056	59 53	123	30 20	174	32 53	212	22 10	255	23 13	321	29 40	351
335	46 52	055	60 25	123	30 24	173	32 33	212	21 33	254	22 49	320	29 34	350
336	47 24	054	60 58	123	30 28	173	32 13	211	20 56	253	22 24	319	29 27	349
337	47 55	053	61 30	123	30 33	173	31 53	211	20 19	253	21 58	318	29 19	348
338	48 25	052	62 02	123	30 38	172	31 33	210	19 42	252	21 32	317	29 11	347
339	48 55	050	62 35	123	30 44	172	31 14	210	19 06	251	21 05	316	29 01	346
340	49 24	049	63 07	123	30 49	171	30 55	209	18 29	251	20 38	315	28 52	344
341	49 53	048	63 40	123	30 55	171	30 36	209	17 53	250	20 10	314	28 41	343
342	50 21	046	64 12	123	31 01	171	30 17	209	17 17	249	19 43	313	28 29	342
343	50 49	045	64 45	123	31 08	170	29 59	208	16 41	248	19 14	312	28 17	341
344	51 16	044	65 17	122	31 14	170	29 41	208	16 05	248	18 45	311	28 05	340
	◆Diphda		Acamar		◆CANOPUS		Miaplacidus		RIGIL KENT		◆Nunki		Enif	
345	51 42	042	47 56	100	28 00	140	31 21	170	29 23	207	38 15	274	27 51	339
346	52 08	041	48 34	100	28 24	140	31 28	169	29 06	207	37 36	273	27 37	338
347	52 33	040	49 12	099	28 50	139	31 36	169	28 48	206	36 58	272	27 22	337
348	52 57	038	49 50	098	29 15	139	31 43	168	28 31	206	36 19	271	27 07	336
349	53 21	037	50 28	098	29 40	138	31 51	168	28 15	205	35 40	270	26 50	335
350	53 44	035	51 07	097	30 06	138	31 59	168	27 58	205	35 02	270	26 34	334
351	54 06	034	51 45	096	30 32	137	32 08	167	27 42	205	34 23	269	26 16	333
352	54 27	032	52 23	096	30 59	137	32 16	167	27 26	204	33 45	268	25 58	332
353	54 47	031	53 02	095	31 25	136	32 25	167	27 11	204	33 06	267	25 39	331
354	55 06	029	53 40	094	31 52	136	32 34	166	26 55	203	32 28	267	25 20	329
355	55 24	028	54 19	094	32 19	135	32 43	166	26 40	203	31 49	266	25 00	328
356	55 42	026	54 57	093	32 46	135	32 53	165	26 25	202	31 11	265	24 40	327
357	55 58	024	55 36	092	33 14	134	33 03	165	26 11	202	30 32	264	24 19	326
358	56 14	023	56 14	091	33 41	134	33 13	165	25 57	201	29 54	264	23 57	325
359	56 28	021	56 53	091	34 09	133	33 23	164	25 43	201	29 16	263	23 35	324

LAT 51°S

LHA ♈	Hc	Zn	Hc	Zn	Hc	Zn	Hc	Zn	Hc	Zn	Hc	Zn	Hc	Zn
	Diphda		◆ RIGEL		CANOPUS		Miaplacidus		◆ RIGIL KENT		Peacock		◆ FOMALHAUT	
0	55 45	019	13 23	086	35 18	132	34 31	164	26 26	201	58 52	238	65 39	326
1	55 57	017	14 01	086	35 46	132	34 42	163	26 13	200	58 20	238	65 18	324
2	56 07	016	14 38	085	36 14	131	34 53	163	26 00	200	57 48	238	64 55	322
3	56 17	014	15 16	084	36 43	131	35 04	163	25 47	199	57 16	238	64 31	320
4	56 26	012	15 53	083	37 11	131	35 15	162	25 35	199	56 44	237	64 07	319
5	56 33	011	16 31	083	37 40	130	35 27	162	25 23	198	56 13	237	63 41	317
6	56 39	009	17 08	082	38 09	130	35 39	162	25 12	198	55 41	237	63 15	315
7	56 45	007	17 46	081	38 38	129	35 51	161	25 01	197	55 09	237	62 48	314
8	56 49	005	18 23	080	39 08	129	36 03	161	24 50	197	54 38	236	62 21	312
9	56 52	004	19 00	079	39 37	128	36 15	161	24 39	196	54 07	236	61 52	310
10	56 54	002	19 37	078	40 07	128	36 28	160	24 29	196	53 35	236	61 23	309
11	56 54	000	20 14	078	40 37	127	36 41	160	24 19	195	53 04	235	60 53	307
12	56 54	358	20 51	077	41 07	127	36 54	160	24 09	195	52 33	235	60 23	306
13	56 52	357	21 28	076	41 37	126	37 07	159	24 00	194	52 02	235	59 52	305
14	56 49	355	22 04	075	42 08	126	37 20	159	23 51	194	51 31	235	59 21	303
	◆ RIGEL		SIRIUS		CANOPUS		◆ RIGIL KENT		Peacock		◆ FOMALHAUT		Diphda	
15	22 41	074	15 08	098	42 39	126	23 42	193	51 01	234	58 49	302	56 45	353
16	23 17	073	15 46	097	43 09	125	23 34	193	50 30	234	58 17	301	56 40	351
17	23 53	073	16 23	097	43 40	125	23 26	192	50 00	234	57 44	299	56 34	350
18	24 29	072	17 01	096	44 11	124	23 18	192	49 29	233	57 11	298	56 27	348
19	25 05	071	17 38	095	44 43	124	23 11	191	48 59	233	56 37	297	56 19	346
20	25 40	070	18 16	094	45 14	123	23 04	190	48 29	233	56 03	296	56 09	345
21	26 16	069	18 53	094	45 46	123	22 57	190	47 59	232	55 29	294	55 59	343
22	26 51	068	19 31	093	46 18	123	22 50	189	47 30	232	54 55	293	55 47	341
23	27 26	067	20 09	092	46 50	122	22 44	189	47 00	231	54 20	292	55 34	340
24	28 00	066	20 47	091	47 22	122	22 39	188	46 30	231	53 45	291	55 21	338
25	28 35	065	21 24	090	47 54	121	22 33	188	46 01	231	53 09	290	55 06	336
26	29 09	065	22 02	090	48 26	121	22 28	187	45 32	230	52 34	289	54 51	335
27	29 43	064	22 40	089	48 59	120	22 24	187	45 03	230	51 58	288	54 34	333
28	30 17	063	23 18	088	49 31	120	22 19	186	44 34	230	51 22	287	54 17	332
29	30 50	062	23 55	087	50 04	120	22 15	186	44 05	229	50 46	286	53 58	330
	◆ RIGEL		SIRIUS		CANOPUS		◆ RIGIL KENT		Peacock		◆ FOMALHAUT		Diphda	
30	31 23	061	24 33	087	50 37	119	22 12	185	43 37	229	50 09	285	53 39	329
31	31 56	060	25 11	086	51 10	119	22 08	185	43 09	229	49 33	284	53 19	327
32	32 29	059	25 48	085	51 43	118	22 05	184	42 40	228	48 56	283	52 58	326
33	33 01	058	26 26	084	52 16	118	22 03	184	42 12	228	48 19	282	52 36	324
34	33 32	057	27 04	083	52 50	118	22 00	183	41 44	227	47 42	281	52 14	323
35	34 04	056	27 41	082	53 23	117	21 58	183	41 17	227	47 05	280	51 51	321
36	34 35	055	28 18	082	53 57	117	21 57	182	40 49	227	46 28	279	51 27	320
37	35 06	054	28 56	081	54 31	116	21 55	182	40 22	226	45 50	278	51 02	319
38	35 36	053	29 33	080	55 05	116	21 55	181	39 55	226	45 13	278	50 37	317
39	36 06	052	30 10	079	55 38	116	21 54	181	39 28	225	44 35	277	50 11	316
40	36 35	051	30 47	078	56 13	115	21 54	180	39 01	225	43 58	276	49 44	315
41	37 04	050	31 24	077	56 47	115	21 54	180	38 35	224	43 20	275	49 17	313
42	37 32	048	32 01	077	57 21	115	21 54	179	38 08	224	42 43	274	48 49	312
43	38 00	047	32 37	076	57 55	114	21 55	179	37 42	224	42 05	273	48 21	311
44	38 28	046	33 14	075	58 30	114	21 56	178	37 16	223	41 27	273	47 52	310
	RIGEL		◆ SIRIUS		CANOPUS		◆ RIGIL KENT		Peacock		FOMALHAUT		◆ Diphda	
45	38 55	045	33 50	074	59 04	113	21 58	177	36 50	223	40 50	272	47 23	308
46	39 21	044	34 27	073	59 39	113	22 00	177	36 25	222	40 12	271	46 53	307
47	39 47	043	35 03	072	60 14	113	22 02	176	36 00	222	39 34	270	46 23	306
48	40 13	042	35 38	071	60 49	112	22 04	176	35 34	221	38 56	269	45 52	305
49	40 37	040	36 14	070	61 24	112	22 07	175	35 10	221	38 19	269	45 21	304
50	41 02	039	36 49	069	61 59	112	22 10	175	34 45	221	37 41	268	44 49	303
51	41 25	038	37 25	068	62 34	111	22 14	174	34 20	220	37 03	267	44 17	301
52	41 48	037	38 00	067	63 09	111	22 18	174	33 56	220	36 25	266	43 45	300
53	42 10	036	38 34	066	63 44	111	22 22	173	33 32	219	35 48	266	43 12	299
54	42 32	034	39 09	065	64 20	110	22 27	173	33 08	219	35 10	265	42 39	298
55	42 53	033	39 43	064	64 55	110	22 32	172	32 45	218	34 33	264	42 05	297
56	43 13	032	40 17	063	65 31	110	22 37	172	32 22	218	33 55	263	41 32	296
57	43 33	030	40 51	062	66 06	109	22 43	171	31 59	217	33 18	263	40 58	295
58	43 52	029	41 24	061	66 42	109	22 48	171	31 36	217	32 40	262	40 23	294
59	44 10	028	41 57	060	67 18	109	22 55	170	31 13	216	32 03	261	39 49	293
	RIGEL		◆ SIRIUS		Suhail		◆ RIGIL KENT		Peacock		FOMALHAUT		◆ Diphda	
60	44 27	027	42 30	059	39 32	114	23 01	170	30 51	216	31 25	261	39 14	292
61	44 43	025	43 02	058	40 07	113	23 08	169	30 29	216	30 48	260	38 39	291
62	44 59	024	43 34	057	40 42	112	23 16	169	30 07	215	30 11	259	38 04	290
63	45 14	023	44 05	056	41 17	112	23 23	168	29 45	215	29 34	258	37 28	289
64	45 28	021	44 36	055	41 52	111	23 31	168	29 24	214	28 57	258	36 52	288
65	45 41	020	45 07	054	42 27	111	23 39	167	29 03	214	28 20	257	36 16	287
66	45 54	018	45 37	053	43 02	110	23 48	167	28 42	213	27 44	256	35 40	287
67	46 05	017	46 07	051	43 38	109	23 57	166	28 22	213	27 07	256	35 04	286
68	46 16	016	46 36	050	44 14	109	24 06	166	28 02	212	26 30	255	34 28	285
69	46 25	014	47 05	049	44 49	108	24 16	165	27 42	212	25 54	254	33 51	284
70	46 34	013	47 33	048	45 25	108	24 26	165	27 22	211	25 18	254	33 14	283
71	46 42	011	48 01	047	46 01	107	24 36	164	27 03	211	24 42	253	32 37	282
72	46 49	010	48 28	045	46 37	107	24 46	164	26 44	210	24 06	252	32 00	281
73	46 55	008	48 55	044	47 14	106	24 57	163	26 25	210	23 30	251	31 23	280
74	47 00	007	49 20	043	47 50	105	25 08	163	26 06	209	22 54	251	30 46	280
	RIGEL		◆ SIRIUS		Suhail		◆ RIGIL KENT		Peacock		ACHERNAR		◆ Diphda	
75	47 04	006	49 46	041	48 26	105	25 20	162	25 48	209	60 30	238	30 09	279
76	47 07	004	50 10	040	49 03	104	25 31	162	25 30	208	59 58	238	29 32	278
77	47 10	003	50 34	039	49 40	104	25 43	161	25 12	208	59 26	238	28 54	277
78	47 11	001	50 57	037	50 16	103	25 56	161	24 55	207	58 54	237	28 17	276
79	47 11	000	51 20	036	50 53	102	26 09	160	24 38	207	58 22	237	27 39	275
80	47 10	358	51 42	034	51 30	102	26 22	160	24 21	206	57 51	237	27 01	275
81	47 09	357	52 03	033	52 07	101	26 35	159	24 05	206	57 19	237	26 24	274
82	47 06	355	52 23	031	52 44	101	26 48	159	23 49	205	56 47	237	25 46	273
83	47 03	354	52 42	030	53 21	100	27 02	158	23 33	204	56 16	236	25 08	272
84	46 58	352	53 01	029	53 59	099	27 16	158	23 18	204	55 45	236	24 31	271
85	46 53	351	53 18	027	54 36	099	27 31	157	23 02	203	55 13	236	23 53	271
86	46 46	350	53 35	025	55 13	098	27 46	157	22 48	203	54 42	236	23 15	270
87	46 39	348	53 51	024	55 51	097	28 01	156	22 33	202	54 11	235	22 37	269
88	46 31	347	54 05	022	56 28	097	28 16	156	22 19	202	53 40	235	22 00	268
89	46 22	345	54 19	021	57 06	096	28 32	155	22 05	201	53 09	235	21 22	268

LHA ♈	Hc	Zn	Hc	Zn	Hc	Zn	Hc	Zn	Hc	Zn	Hc	Zn	Hc	Zn
	PROCYON		◆ Suhail		RIGIL KENT		◆ Peacock		ACHERNAR		◆ RIGEL		BETELGEUSE	
90	29 51	029	57 43	095	28 47	155	21 52	201	52 38	234	46 12	344	31 35	359
91	30 09	028	58 21	095	29 04	154	21 38	200	52 08	234	46 01	342	31 34	358
92	30 26	027	58 58	094	29 20	154	21 26	200	51 37	234	45 49	341	31 32	357
93	30 43	026	59 36	093	29 37	154	21 13	199	51 07	233	45 36	340	31 29	355
94	30 59	025	60 14	093	29 54	153	21 01	199	50 37	233	45 23	338	31 26	354
95	31 14	024	60 52	092	30 11	153	20 49	198	50 06	233	45 09	337	31 22	353
96	31 29	022	61 29	091	30 28	152	20 38	197	49 36	232	44 53	336	31 17	352
97	31 43	021	62 07	090	30 46	152	20 26	197	49 07	232	44 37	334	31 11	351
98	31 56	020	62 45	089	31 04	151	20 16	196	48 37	232	44 21	333	31 05	350
99	32 09	019	63 23	089	31 23	151	20 05	196	48 07	231	44 03	332	30 57	348
100	32 21	018	64 00	088	31 41	150	19 55	195	47 38	231	43 45	330	30 49	347
101	32 32	017	64 38	087	32 00	150	19 45	195	47 08	231	43 26	329	30 41	346
102	32 43	015	65 16	086	32 19	150	19 36	194	46 39	230	43 06	328	30 31	345
103	32 52	014	65 53	085	32 38	149	19 27	194	46 10	230	42 45	326	30 21	344
104	33 01	013	66 31	084	32 58	149	19 18	193	45 41	230	42 24	325	30 10	343
	PROCYON		REGULUS		◆ Gienah		RIGIL KENT		◆ ACHERNAR		RIGEL		◆ SIRIUS	
105	33 09	012	14 55	048	20 23	093	33 17	148	45 13	229	42 02	324	55 37	354
106	33 17	011	15 23	047	21 01	092	33 37	148	44 44	229	41 40	323	55 33	352
107	33 24	010	15 51	046	21 38	092	33 58	147	44 16	229	41 17	322	55 27	351
108	33 29	008	16 18	045	22 16	091	34 18	147	43 47	228	40 53	320	55 20	349
109	33 35	007	16 45	044	22 54	090	34 39	147	43 19	228	40 28	319	55 13	347
110	33 39	006	17 11	044	23 32	089	35 00	146	42 51	228	40 03	318	55 04	346
111	33 42	005	17 37	043	24 09	088	35 21	146	42 23	227	39 38	317	54 54	344
112	33 45	004	18 02	042	24 47	088	35 42	145	41 56	227	39 12	316	54 43	342
113	33 47	002	18 27	041	25 25	087	36 04	145	41 28	226	38 45	315	54 31	341
114	33 48	001	18 51	040	26 02	086	36 26	145	41 01	226	38 18	313	54 18	339
115	33 49	000	19 15	039	26 40	085	36 48	144	40 34	226	37 50	312	54 04	338
116	33 48	359	19 39	038	27 18	085	37 10	144	40 07	225	37 22	311	53 49	336
117	33 47	358	20 02	037	27 55	084	37 32	143	39 41	225	36 53	310	53 33	334
118	33 45	356	20 24	036	28 33	083	37 55	143	39 14	224	36 24	309	53 16	333
119	33 43	355	20 46	035	29 10	082	38 18	143	38 48	224	35 55	308	52 59	331
	REGULUS		◆ SPICA		RIGIL KENT		Peacock		◆ ACHERNAR		RIGEL		◆ SIRIUS	
120	21 07	034	14 03	091	38 41	142	17 50	184	38 22	224	35 25	307	52 40	330
121	21 28	033	14 41	090	39 04	142	17 47	183	37 56	223	34 54	306	52 21	328
122	21 49	032	15 18	089	39 28	141	17 45	183	37 30	223	34 23	305	52 01	327
123	22 09	031	15 56	088	39 51	141	17 44	182	37 05	222	33 52	304	51 40	325
124	22 28	030	16 34	087	40 15	141	17 43	182	36 39	222	33 21	303	51 18	324
125	22 46	029	17 12	087	40 39	140	17 42	181	36 14	221	32 49	302	50 55	323
126	23 05	028	17 49	086	41 03	140	17 41	180	35 50	221	32 17	301	50 32	321
127	23 22	027	18 27	085	41 28	140	17 41	180	35 25	221	31 44	300	50 08	320
128	23 39	026	19 05	084	41 52	139	17 41	179	35 00	220	31 11	299	49 43	319
129	23 55	025	19 42	083	42 17	139	17 42	179	34 36	220	30 38	298	49 18	317
130	24 11	024	20 20	083	42 42	139	17 43	178	34 12	219	30 04	297	48 52	316
131	24 26	023	20 57	082	43 07	138	17 45	178	33 49	219	29 31	296	48 26	315
132	24 40	022	21 34	081	43 32	138	17 46	177	33 25	218	28 56	295	47 58	313
133	24 54	021	22 12	080	43 58	138	17 49	176	33 02	218	28 22	294	47 31	312
134	25 07	020	22 49	079	44 23	137	17 51	176	32 39	217	27 48	293	47 02	311
	◆ REGULUS		SPICA		◆ RIGIL KENT		Peacock		ACHERNAR		◆ CANOPUS		SIRIUS	
135	25 20	019	23 26	079	44 49	137	17 54	175	32 16	217	66 11	251	46 34	310
136	25 32	018	24 03	078	45 15	137	17 58	175	31 53	216	65 36	250	46 04	308
137	25 43	017	24 40	077	45 41	136	18 01	174	31 31	216	65 00	250	45 34	307
138	25 53	016	25 16	076	46 07	136	18 05	174	31 09	216	64 25	250	45 04	306
139	26 03	015	25 53	075	46 33	136	18 10	173	30 47	215	63 49	249	44 33	305
140	26 12	013	26 29	074	47 00	135	18 15	172	30 25	215	63 14	249	44 02	304
141	26 21	012	27 06	074	47 27	135	18 20	172	30 04	214	62 39	249	43 31	303
142	26 28	011	27 42	073	47 53	135	18 25	171	29 43	214	62 04	248	42 59	302
143	26 35	010	28 18	072	48 20	134	18 31	171	29 22	213	61 29	248	42 27	301
144	26 42	009	28 53	071	48 47	134	18 38	170	29 02	213	60 54	248	41 54	300
145	26 47	008	29 29	070	49 14	134	18 44	170	28 42	212	60 19	247	41 21	298
146	26 52	007	30 04	069	49 42	134	18 51	169	28 22	212	59 44	247	40 47	297
147	26 56	006	30 40	068	50 09	133	18 59	168	28 02	211	59 09	247	40 14	296
148	27 00	005	31 15	067	50 36	133	19 07	168	27 42	211	58 35	246	39 40	295
149	27 02	004	31 49	066	51 04	133	19 15	167	27 23	210	58 00	246	39 06	294
	◆ REGULUS		SPICA		◆ RIGIL KENT		Peacock		ACHERNAR		◆ CANOPUS		SIRIUS	
150	27 04	003	32 24	065	51 32	133	19 23	167	27 04	210	57 26	245	38 31	293
151	27 06	001	32 58	064	52 00	132	19 32	166	26 46	209	56 52	245	37 56	292
152	27 06	000	33 32	063	52 27	132	19 41	166	26 27	209	56 17	245	37 21	292
153	27 06	359	34 05	062	52 55	132	19 51	165	26 09	208	55 43	244	36 46	291
154	27 05	358	34 39	062	53 24	132	20 01	164	25 52	208	55 09	244	36 11	290
155	27 04	357	35 12	061	53 52	132	20 11	164	25 34	207	54 35	244	35 35	289
156	27 01	356	35 45	060	54 20	131	20 22	163	25 17	207	54 02	243	34 59	288
157	26 58	355	36 17	059	54 49	131	20 33	163	25 00	206	53 28	243	34 23	287
158	26 55	354	36 49	057	55 17	131	20 44	162	24 44	206	52 55	242	33 47	286
159	26 50	353	37 21	056	55 46	131	20 56	162	24 28	205	52 21	242	33 10	285
160	26 45	352	37 52	055	56 14	131	21 08	161	24 12	205	51 48	242	32 34	284
161	26 39	350	38 23	054	56 43	130	21 20	161	23 56	204	51 15	241	31 57	283
162	26 32	349	38 53	053	57 12	130	21 33	160	23 41	204	50 42	241	31 20	282
163	26 25	348	39 23	052	57 40	130	21 46	160	23 26	203	50 09	240	30 44	282
164	26 17	347	39 53	051	58 09	130	21 59	159	23 11	203	49 36	240	30 07	281
	◆ SPICA		ANTARES		◆ Peacock		ACHERNAR		CANOPUS		◆ SIRIUS		REGULUS	
165	40 22	050	24 47	102	22 13	158	22 57	202	49 03	240	29 29	280	26 08	346
166	40 51	049	25 23	101	22 27	158	22 43	202	48 31	239	28 52	279	25 59	345
167	41 19	048	26 01	101	22 42	157	22 29	201	47 58	239	28 15	278	25 49	344
168	41 47	047	26 38	100	22 56	157	22 16	200	47 26	238	27 37	277	25 38	343
169	42 14	045	27 15	099	23 11	156	22 03	200	46 54	238	27 00	277	25 27	342
170	42 40	044	27 52	099	23 27	156	21 50	199	46 22	238	26 22	276	25 15	341
171	43 06	043	28 30	098	23 42	155	21 38	199	45 50	237	25 45	275	25 02	340
172	43 32	042	29 07	097	23 58	155	21 26	198	45 19	237	25 07	274	24 48	339
173	43 57	041	29 45	096	24 15	154	21 14	198	44 47	236	24 30	273	24 34	338
174	44 21	039	30 22	096	24 31	154	21 03	197	44 16	236	23 52	273	24 20	337
175	44 44	038	31 00	095	24 48	153	20 52	197	43 45	235	23 14	272	24 04	336
176	45 07	037	31 37	094	25 05	153	20 41	196	43 14	235	22 36	271	23 49	335
177	45 30	035	32 15	093	25 23	152	20 31	196	42 43	235	21 59	270	23 32	334
178	45 51	034	32 53	093	25 41	152	20 21	195	42 12	234	21 21	270	23 15	332
179	46 12	033	33 30	092	25 59	151	20 11	194	41 42	234	20 43	269	22 57	331

LAT 51°S

LHA ♈	Hc	Zn	Hc	Zn	Hc	Zn	Hc	Zn	Hc	Zn	Hc	Zn	Hc	Zn
	◆ SPICA		ANTARES		◆ Peacock		ACHERNAR		CANOPUS		◆ Suhail		REGULUS	
180	46 32	031	34 08	091	26 17	151	20 02	194	41 11	233	60 24	268	22 39	330
181	46 51	030	34 46	090	26 36	150	19 53	193	40 41	233	59 47	267	22 20	329
182	47 10	029	35 24	089	26 55	150	19 45	193	40 11	232	59 09	266	22 00	328
183	47 28	027	36 01	089	27 14	149	19 36	192	39 42	232	58 31	266	21 40	327
184	47 45	026	36 39	088	27 34	149	19 29	192	39 12	231	57 54	265	21 20	326
185	48 01	025	37 17	087	27 53	148	19 21	191	38 43	231	57 16	264	20 59	326
186	48 16	023	37 55	086	28 14	148	19 14	191	38 13	230	56 38	263	20 37	325
187	48 31	022	38 32	086	28 34	147	19 07	190	37 44	230	56 01	263	20 15	324
188	48 44	020	39 10	085	28 55	147	19 01	189	37 15	230	55 23	262	19 52	323
189	48 57	019	39 47	084	29 15	146	18 55	189	36 47	229	54 46	262	19 29	322
190	49 09	017	40 25	083	29 37	146	18 49	188	36 18	229	54 09	261	19 05	321
191	49 19	016	41 02	082	29 58	145	18 44	188	35 50	228	53 32	260	18 41	320
192	49 29	014	41 40	081	30 20	145	18 39	187	35 22	228	52 54	260	18 17	319
193	49 38	013	42 17	080	30 42	144	18 35	187	34 54	227	52 17	259	17 51	318
194	49 46	011	42 54	080	31 04	144	18 31	186	34 27	227	51 40	258	17 26	317
	◆ ARCTURUS		ANTARES		◆ Peacock		ACHERNAR		CANOPUS		◆ Suhail		Denebola	
195	17 55	019	43 31	079	31 26	143	18 27	185	33 59	226	51 03	258	22 44	342
196	18 07	018	44 08	078	31 49	143	18 23	185	33 32	226	50 26	257	22 32	341
197	18 18	017	44 45	077	32 12	142	18 20	184	33 05	225	49 50	257	22 19	340
198	18 29	016	45 22	076	32 35	142	18 18	184	32 39	225	49 13	256	22 06	338
199	18 39	015	45 58	075	32 59	141	18 15	183	32 12	224	48 36	255	21 51	337
200	18 49	014	46 35	074	33 22	141	18 14	183	31 46	224	48 00	255	21 37	336
201	18 57	013	47 11	073	33 46	141	18 12	182	31 20	223	47 24	254	21 21	335
202	19 06	012	47 47	072	34 10	140	18 11	181	30 54	223	46 47	254	21 05	334
203	19 13	011	48 23	071	34 35	140	18 10	181	30 29	222	46 11	253	20 49	333
204	19 20	010	48 59	070	34 59	139	18 10	180	30 03	222	45 35	252	20 32	332
205	19 26	009	49 34	069	35 24	139	18 10	180	29 38	221	44 59	252	20 14	331
206	19 32	008	50 09	068	35 49	138	18 10	179	29 14	221	44 23	251	19 56	331
207	19 37	007	50 44	067	36 14	138	18 11	179	28 49	220	43 48	251	19 37	330
208	19 41	006	51 19	066	36 40	137	18 12	178	28 25	220	43 12	250	19 17	329
209	19 45	005	51 53	065	37 05	137	18 13	177	28 01	219	42 37	250	18 57	328
	◆ ARCTURUS		ANTARES		◆ Peacock		ACHERNAR		CANOPUS		◆ Suhail		SPICA	
210	19 48	004	52 27	064	37 31	137	18 15	177	27 37	219	42 01	249	49 38	347
211	19 51	003	53 00	062	37 57	136	18 17	176	27 14	218	41 26	248	49 29	346
212	19 52	002	53 34	061	38 24	136	18 20	176	26 50	218	40 51	248	49 19	344
213	19 53	001	54 07	060	38 50	135	18 23	175	26 27	217	40 16	247	49 08	343
214	19 54	000	54 39	059	39 17	135	18 26	175	26 05	217	39 41	247	48 57	341
215	19 53	359	55 11	058	39 44	134	18 30	174	25 42	216	39 07	246	48 44	340
216	19 52	358	55 43	056	40 11	134	18 34	173	25 20	216	38 32	246	48 30	338
217	19 51	357	56 14	055	40 38	134	18 39	173	24 59	215	37 58	245	48 16	337
218	19 49	356	56 45	054	41 05	133	18 43	172	24 37	214	37 24	244	48 01	335
219	19 46	355	57 15	052	41 33	133	18 49	172	24 16	214	36 50	244	47 45	334
220	19 42	354	57 45	051	42 01	132	18 54	171	23 55	213	36 16	243	47 28	333
221	19 38	353	58 14	050	42 29	132	19 00	171	23 34	213	35 43	243	47 10	331
222	19 33	352	58 42	048	42 57	132	19 07	170	23 14	212	35 09	242	46 51	330
223	19 27	351	59 10	047	43 25	131	19 13	170	22 54	212	34 36	242	46 32	328
224	19 21	350	59 37	045	43 54	131	19 20	169	22 34	211	34 03	241	46 12	327
	ANTARES		◆ Nunki		Peacock		ACHERNAR		◆ CANOPUS		Suhail		◆ SPICA	
225	60 03	044	39 22	084	44 22	131	19 28	168	22 15	211	33 30	240	45 51	326
226	60 29	042	39 59	083	44 51	130	19 35	168	21 56	210	32 57	240	45 29	325
227	60 54	040	40 37	082	45 20	130	19 44	167	21 37	210	32 25	239	45 07	323
228	61 18	039	41 14	082	45 49	129	19 52	167	21 19	209	31 52	239	44 44	322
229	61 41	037	41 52	081	46 18	129	20 01	166	21 01	208	31 20	238	44 21	321
230	62 03	035	42 29	080	46 48	129	20 10	166	20 43	208	30 48	238	43 56	319
231	62 24	033	43 06	079	47 17	128	20 20	165	20 25	207	30 16	237	43 32	318
232	62 45	032	43 43	078	47 47	128	20 29	165	20 08	207	29 45	236	43 06	317
233	63 04	030	44 20	077	48 17	128	20 40	164	19 51	206	29 14	236	42 40	316
234	63 22	028	44 57	076	48 47	127	20 50	163	19 35	206	28 42	235	42 13	315
235	63 40	026	45 33	075	49 17	127	21 01	163	19 19	205	28 12	235	41 46	313
236	63 56	024	46 10	074	49 47	127	21 13	162	19 03	204	27 41	234	41 19	312
237	64 10	022	46 46	073	50 18	126	21 24	162	18 48	204	27 10	233	40 50	311
238	64 24	020	47 22	072	50 48	126	21 36	161	18 33	203	26 40	233	40 22	310
239	64 36	018	47 58	071	51 19	126	21 48	161	18 18	203	26 10	232	39 53	309
	◆ ANTARES		Nunki		◆ FOMALHAUT		ACHERNAR		CANOPUS		◆ ACRUX		SPICA	
240	64 48	016	48 34	070	14 11	120	22 01	160	18 04	202	59 45	226	39 23	308
241	64 57	014	49 09	069	14 44	119	22 14	160	17 50	201	59 18	226	38 53	307
242	65 06	012	49 44	068	15 17	118	22 27	159	17 36	201	58 51	226	38 22	306
243	65 13	010	50 19	067	15 50	118	22 41	159	17 23	200	58 24	226	37 52	305
244	65 19	008	50 54	066	16 24	117	22 55	158	17 10	200	57 57	226	37 20	304
245	65 23	006	51 28	065	16 58	116	23 09	158	16 57	199	57 30	225	36 49	303
246	65 26	003	52 02	064	17 32	116	23 24	157	16 45	198	57 03	225	36 17	301
247	65 28	001	52 36	063	18 06	115	23 39	156	16 33	198	56 36	225	35 44	300
248	65 28	359	53 09	062	18 40	114	23 54	156	16 22	197	56 10	225	35 12	299
249	65 26	357	53 42	060	19 15	114	24 10	155	16 11	197	55 43	225	34 39	298
250	65 24	355	54 15	059	19 49	113	24 25	155	16 00	196	55 16	225	34 05	297
251	65 20	353	54 47	058	20 24	112	24 42	154	15 50	195	54 50	225	33 32	297
252	65 14	351	55 19	057	20 59	111	24 58	154	15 40	195	54 23	225	32 58	296
253	65 07	348	55 51	055	21 34	111	25 15	153	15 31	194	53 56	225	32 23	295
254	64 59	346	56 21	054	22 10	110	25 32	153	15 22	194	53 30	224	31 49	294
	ALTAIR		◆ FOMALHAUT		ACHERNAR		CANOPUS		◆ ACRUX		SPICA		◆ ANTARES	
255	19 35	046	22 45	109	25 49	152	15 13	193	53 04	224	31 14	293	64 49	344
256	20 02	045	23 21	109	26 07	152	15 04	192	52 37	224	30 39	292	64 38	342
257	20 28	044	23 57	108	26 25	151	14 57	192	52 11	224	30 04	291	64 26	340
258	20 54	043	24 33	107	26 43	151	14 49	191	51 45	224	29 29	290	64 13	338
259	21 19	042	25 09	107	27 02	150	14 42	191	51 19	223	28 53	289	63 58	336
260	21 44	041	25 45	106	27 21	150	14 35	190	50 53	223	28 17	288	63 42	334
261	22 09	040	26 22	105	27 40	149	14 29	189	50 27	223	27 42	287	63 25	332
262	22 33	039	26 58	105	27 59	149	14 23	189	50 02	223	27 05	286	63 07	330
263	22 56	038	27 35	104	28 19	148	14 17	188	49 36	223	26 29	286	62 48	329
264	23 19	037	28 12	103	28 39	148	14 12	188	49 11	222	25 53	285	62 28	327
265	23 41	036	28 48	102	28 59	147	14 07	187	48 45	222	25 16	284	62 07	325
266	24 03	035	29 25	102	29 19	147	14 03	186	48 20	222	24 39	283	61 45	323
267	24 25	034	30 02	101	29 40	146	13 59	186	47 55	222	24 03	282	61 22	322
268	24 45	033	30 39	100	30 01	146	13 56	185	47 30	221	23 26	281	60 58	320
269	25 05	032	31 17	100	30 23	145	13 53	184	47 05	221	22 48	281	60 33	318

LHA ♈	Hc	Zn	Hc	Zn	Hc	Zn	Hc	Zn	Hc	Zn	Hc	Zn	Hc	Zn
	◆ ALTAIR		FOMALHAUT		◆ ACHERNAR		CANOPUS		RIGIL KENT		◆ SPICA		ANTARES	
270	25 25	031	31 54	099	30 44	145	13 50	184	61 13	231	22 11	280	60 08	317
271	25 44	030	32 31	098	31 06	145	13 48	183	60 44	230	21 34	279	59 41	315
272	26 03	029	33 09	097	31 28	144	13 46	183	60 15	230	20 57	278	59 14	314
273	26 20	028	33 46	097	31 50	144	13 44	182	59 46	230	20 19	277	58 47	312
274	26 38	027	34 24	096	32 13	143	13 43	181	59 16	230	19 42	276	58 18	311
275	26 54	026	35 01	095	32 36	143	13 42	181	58 47	230	19 04	276	57 49	309
276	27 10	024	35 39	095	32 59	142	13 42	180	58 19	230	18 27	275	57 20	308
277	27 25	023	36 16	094	33 22	142	13 42	179	57 50	230	17 49	274	56 50	307
278	27 40	022	36 54	093	33 45	141	13 43	179	57 21	230	17 11	273	56 19	305
279	27 54	021	37 32	092	34 09	141	13 44	178	56 52	230	16 34	273	55 48	304
280	28 07	020	38 10	091	34 33	140	13 45	178	56 23	229	15 56	272	55 17	303
281	28 20	019	38 47	091	34 57	140	13 47	177	55 55	229	15 18	271	54 45	301
282	28 32	018	39 25	090	35 22	140	13 49	176	55 26	229	14 40	270	54 12	300
283	28 43	017	40 03	089	35 46	139	13 52	176	54 58	229	14 03	269	53 39	299
284	28 54	016	40 41	088	36 11	139	13 55	175	54 29	229	13 25	269	53 06	298
	◆ ALTAIR		FOMALHAUT		◆ ACHERNAR		CANOPUS		◆ RIGIL KENT		ANTARES		Rasalhague	
285	29 04	015	41 18	088	36 36	138	13 59	174	54 01	229	52 32	297	23 51	337
286	29 13	013	41 56	087	37 01	138	14 02	174	53 33	228	51 58	295	23 36	336
287	29 21	012	42 34	086	37 27	137	14 07	173	53 04	228	51 24	294	23 20	335
288	29 29	011	43 11	085	37 52	137	14 11	173	52 36	228	50 50	293	23 04	334
289	29 36	010	43 49	084	38 18	137	14 17	172	52 08	228	50 15	292	22 48	333
290	29 42	009	44 27	083	38 44	136	14 22	171	51 41	227	49 40	291	22 30	332
291	29 48	008	45 04	083	39 11	136	14 28	171	51 13	227	49 04	290	22 13	331
292	29 52	007	45 41	082	39 37	135	14 34	170	50 45	227	48 29	289	21 54	330
293	29 57	006	46 19	081	40 04	135	14 41	169	50 18	227	47 53	288	21 35	329
294	30 00	004	46 56	080	40 31	135	14 48	169	49 50	226	47 17	287	21 16	328
295	30 02	003	47 33	079	40 58	134	14 55	168	49 23	226	46 41	286	20 56	327
296	30 04	002	48 10	078	41 25	134	15 03	168	48 56	226	46 04	285	20 35	326
297	30 05	001	48 47	077	41 52	133	15 12	167	48 29	226	45 28	284	20 14	325
298	30 05	000	49 24	076	42 20	133	15 20	166	48 02	225	44 51	283	19 52	324
299	30 05	359	50 00	075	42 47	133	15 29	166	47 35	225	44 14	282	19 30	323
	FOMALHAUT		◆ ACHERNAR		CANOPUS		◆ RIGIL KENT		ANTARES		Nunki		◆ ALTAIR	
300	50 37	074	43 15	132	15 39	165	47 08	225	43 37	281	62 27	328	30 04	358
301	51 13	073	43 43	132	15 49	165	46 42	224	43 00	281	62 06	326	30 02	356
302	51 49	072	44 12	131	15 59	164	46 15	224	42 23	280	61 45	324	29 59	355
303	52 25	071	44 40	131	16 09	163	45 49	224	41 46	279	61 22	323	29 56	354
304	53 01	070	45 09	131	16 20	163	45 23	224	41 09	278	60 59	321	29 51	353
305	53 36	069	45 37	130	16 32	162	44 57	223	40 31	277	60 35	319	29 46	352
306	54 11	068	46 06	130	16 43	162	44 31	223	39 54	276	60 10	318	29 41	351
307	54 46	067	46 35	130	16 56	161	44 06	223	39 16	275	59 44	316	29 34	350
308	55 21	066	47 04	129	17 08	160	43 40	222	38 39	275	59 17	315	29 27	348
309	55 55	065	47 34	129	17 21	160	43 15	222	38 01	274	58 50	313	29 19	347
310	56 29	064	48 03	129	17 34	159	42 50	222	37 23	273	58 22	312	29 11	346
311	57 03	062	48 33	128	17 48	159	42 25	221	36 45	272	57 54	310	29 01	345
312	57 36	061	49 03	128	18 02	158	42 00	221	36 08	271	57 24	309	28 51	344
313	58 09	060	49 32	128	18 16	157	41 36	221	35 30	271	56 55	307	28 41	343
314	58 41	058	50 02	127	18 31	157	41 11	220	34 52	270	56 24	306	28 29	342
	◆ FOMALHAUT		ACHERNAR		◆ CANOPUS		RIGIL KENT		◆ ANTARES		Nunki		ALTAIR	
315	59 13	057	50 33	127	18 46	156	40 47	220	34 14	269	55 54	305	28 17	341
316	59 45	056	51 03	127	19 01	156	40 23	219	33 37	268	55 22	303	28 04	340
317	60 16	054	51 33	126	19 17	155	39 59	219	32 59	268	54 50	302	27 51	339
318	60 46	053	52 04	126	19 33	155	39 35	219	32 21	267	54 18	301	27 37	337
319	61 16	051	52 34	126	19 49	154	39 12	218	31 44	266	53 46	300	27 22	336
320	61 45	050	53 05	125	20 06	153	38 48	218	31 06	265	53 13	298	27 06	335
321	62 14	048	53 36	125	20 23	153	38 25	218	30 28	265	52 39	297	26 50	334
322	62 42	047	54 07	125	20 40	152	38 02	217	29 51	264	52 06	296	26 33	333
323	63 09	045	54 38	125	20 58	152	37 40	217	29 13	263	51 32	295	26 16	332
324	63 35	044	55 09	124	21 16	151	37 17	216	28 36	262	50 57	294	25 58	331
325	64 01	042	55 40	124	21 34	151	36 55	216	27 58	262	50 23	293	25 40	330
326	64 26	040	56 12	124	21 53	150	36 33	216	27 21	261	49 48	292	25 20	329
327	64 49	038	56 43	123	22 12	149	36 11	215	26 44	260	49 12	291	25 01	328
328	65 12	036	57 15	123	22 32	149	35 49	215	26 07	259	48 37	290	24 40	327
329	65 34	034	57 46	123	22 51	148	35 28	214	25 30	259	48 01	289	24 19	326
	◆ FOMALHAUT		ACHERNAR		◆ CANOPUS		RIGIL KENT		◆ ANTARES		Nunki		ALTAIR	
330	65 55	033	58 18	123	23 11	148	35 07	214	24 53	258	47 25	288	23 58	325
331	66 15	031	58 50	123	23 31	147	34 45	214	24 16	257	46 49	287	23 36	324
332	66 33	029	59 22	122	23 52	147	34 25	213	23 39	257	46 13	286	23 14	323
333	66 51	026	59 54	122	24 13	146	34 04	213	23 02	256	45 37	285	22 50	322
334	67 07	024	60 26	122	24 34	146	33 44	212	22 26	255	45 00	284	22 27	321
335	67 22	022	60 58	122	24 56	145	33 24	212	21 49	254	44 23	283	22 03	320
336	67 36	020	61 30	122	25 17	145	33 04	211	21 13	254	43 47	282	21 38	319
337	67 48	018	62 02	121	25 39	144	32 44	211	20 37	253	43 10	281	21 13	318
338	67 59	016	62 34	121	26 02	143	32 25	211	20 01	252	42 32	280	20 48	317
339	68 08	013	63 07	121	26 24	143	32 06	210	19 25	252	41 55	279	20 22	316
340	68 16	011	63 39	121	26 47	142	31 47	210	18 49	251	41 18	279	19 56	315
341	68 22	009	64 11	121	27 10	142	31 28	209	18 13	250	40 41	278	19 29	314
342	68 27	006	64 44	121	27 34	141	31 10	209	17 38	249	40 03	277	19 01	313
343	68 30	004	65 16	121	27 57	141	30 52	208	17 03	249	39 26	276	18 34	312
344	68 32	001	65 49	121	28 21	140	30 34	208	16 28	248	38 48	275	18 06	311
	◆ Diphda		Acamar		◆ CANOPUS		Miaplacidus		RIGIL KENT		◆ Nunki		FOMALHAUT	
345	50 58	042	48 06	099	28 46	140	32 20	169	30 16	208	38 10	274	68 32	359
346	51 23	040	48 44	099	29 10	139	32 27	169	29 59	207	37 33	274	68 31	357
347	51 47	039	49 21	098	29 35	139	32 34	169	29 42	207	36 55	273	68 28	354
348	52 10	037	49 58	097	30 00	138	32 42	168	29 25	206	36 17	272	68 24	352
349	52 33	036	50 36	097	30 25	138	32 50	168	29 09	206	35 40	271	68 18	350
350	52 54	035	51 13	096	30 51	137	32 58	168	28 53	205	35 02	270	68 10	347
351	53 16	033	51 51	095	31 16	137	33 06	167	28 37	205	34 24	270	68 01	345
352	53 36	032	52 29	094	31 42	136	33 15	167	28 21	204	33 46	269	67 51	343
353	53 55	030	53 06	094	32 08	136	33 23	166	28 05	204	33 09	268	67 39	341
354	54 14	029	53 44	093	32 35	135	33 32	166	27 50	203	32 31	267	67 25	338
355	54 31	027	54 22	092	33 02	135	33 42	166	27 36	203	31 53	267	67 11	336
356	54 48	025	54 59	092	33 28	134	33 51	165	27 21	202	31 15	266	66 55	334
357	55 04	024	55 37	091	33 56	134	34 01	165	27 07	202	30 38	265	66 38	332
358	55 18	022	56 15	090	34 23	133	34 11	165	26 53	201	30 00	264	66 19	330
359	55 32	021	56 53	089	34 50	133	34 21	164	26 39	201	29 23	264	66 00	328

 LAT 52°S

LHA ♈	Hc	Zn	Hc	Zn	Hc	Zn	Hc	Zn	Hc	Zn	Hc	Zn	Hc	Zn
	Diphda		◆ RIGEL		CANOPUS		Miaplacidus		◆ RIGIL KENT		Peacock		◆ FOMALHAUT	
0	54 48	019	13 19	086	35 58	132	35 29	164	27 22	201	59 23	240	64 49	327
1	54 59	017	13 56	085	36 26	131	35 40	163	27 09	200	58 51	240	64 29	325
2	55 10	015	14 33	085	36 54	131	35 50	163	26 56	200	58 20	239	64 07	323
3	55 19	014	15 10	084	37 22	130	36 01	163	26 44	199	57 48	239	63 45	322
4	55 27	012	15 46	083	37 50	130	36 12	162	26 32	199	57 16	239	63 21	320
5	55 34	010	16 23	082	38 19	129	36 24	162	26 20	198	56 45	238	62 57	318
6	55 40	009	17 00	081	38 47	129	36 36	161	26 09	198	56 13	238	62 32	317
7	55 45	007	17 36	081	39 16	129	36 47	161	25 58	197	55 42	238	62 06	315
8	55 49	005	18 12	080	39 45	128	36 59	161	25 47	197	55 11	238	61 40	313
9	55 52	004	18 49	079	40 14	128	37 12	160	25 37	196	54 40	237	61 13	312
10	55 54	002	19 25	078	40 44	127	37 24	160	25 27	196	54 09	237	60 45	310
11	55 54	000	20 01	077	41 13	127	37 37	160	25 17	195	53 38	237	60 16	309
12	55 54	358	20 37	076	41 43	126	37 50	159	25 07	195	53 07	236	59 47	307
13	55 52	357	21 13	076	42 13	126	38 03	159	24 58	194	52 36	236	59 18	306
14	55 50	355	21 49	075	42 43	125	38 16	159	24 49	194	52 06	236	58 47	305
	◆ RIGEL		SIRIUS		CANOPUS		◆ RIGIL KENT		Peacock		◆ FOMALHAUT		Diphda	
15	22 24	074	15 16	098	43 13	125	24 40	193	51 35	235	58 17	303	55 46	353
16	23 00	073	15 53	097	43 44	124	24 32	193	51 05	235	57 46	302	55 41	352
17	23 35	072	16 30	096	44 14	124	24 24	192	50 35	235	57 14	301	55 35	350
18	24 10	071	17 06	095	44 45	123	24 17	192	50 05	234	56 42	299	55 28	348
19	24 45	070	17 43	095	45 16	123	24 09	191	49 35	234	56 10	298	55 20	347
20	25 19	070	18 20	094	45 47	123	24 03	191	49 05	233	55 37	297	55 11	345
21	25 54	069	18 57	093	46 18	122	23 56	190	48 36	233	55 04	296	55 01	343
22	26 28	068	19 34	092	46 49	122	23 50	190	48 06	233	54 30	295	54 50	342
23	27 02	067	20 11	092	47 21	121	23 44	189	47 37	232	53 56	293	54 38	340
24	27 36	066	20 48	091	47 53	121	23 38	188	47 08	232	53 22	292	54 25	339
25	28 10	065	21 25	090	48 24	120	23 33	188	46 39	232	52 48	291	54 11	337
26	28 43	064	22 02	089	48 56	120	23 28	187	46 10	231	52 14	290	53 56	335
27	29 16	063	22 39	088	49 29	119	23 23	187	45 41	231	51 39	289	53 40	334
28	29 49	062	23 15	088	50 01	119	23 19	186	45 13	230	51 04	288	53 24	332
29	30 22	061	23 52	087	50 33	119	23 15	186	44 44	230	50 29	287	53 06	331
	◆ RIGEL		SIRIUS		CANOPUS		◆ RIGIL KENT		Peacock		◆ FOMALHAUT		Diphda	
30	30 54	060	24 29	086	51 06	118	23 11	185	44 16	230	49 53	286	52 48	329
31	31 26	059	25 06	085	51 38	118	23 08	185	43 48	229	49 18	285	52 28	328
32	31 57	058	25 43	084	52 11	117	23 05	184	43 20	229	48 42	284	52 08	326
33	32 28	057	26 20	084	52 44	117	23 02	184	42 52	228	48 06	283	51 48	325
34	32 59	056	26 56	083	53 17	116	23 00	183	42 25	228	47 30	282	51 26	324
35	33 30	055	27 33	082	53 50	116	22 58	183	41 57	228	46 54	281	51 04	322
36	34 00	054	28 09	081	54 23	116	22 57	182	41 30	227	46 17	280	50 41	321
37	34 30	053	28 46	080	54 57	115	22 55	182	41 03	227	45 41	279	50 17	319
38	34 59	052	29 22	079	55 30	115	22 55	181	40 36	226	45 05	279	49 53	318
39	35 28	051	29 58	079	56 04	114	22 54	181	40 10	226	44 28	278	49 28	317
40	35 57	050	30 35	078	56 38	114	22 54	180	39 43	225	43 51	277	49 02	315
41	36 25	049	31 11	077	57 11	114	22 54	180	39 17	225	43 15	276	48 36	314
42	36 52	048	31 47	076	57 45	113	22 54	179	38 51	225	42 38	275	48 09	313
43	37 20	047	32 22	075	58 19	113	22 55	178	38 25	224	42 01	274	47 42	312
44	37 46	046	32 58	074	58 53	112	22 56	178	38 00	224	41 24	273	47 14	310
	RIGEL		◆ SIRIUS		CANOPUS		◆ RIGIL KENT		Peacock		FOMALHAUT		◆ Diphda	
45	38 12	045	33 33	073	59 28	112	22 58	177	37 34	223	40 47	273	46 45	309
46	38 38	043	34 09	072	60 02	112	23 00	177	37 09	223	40 10	272	46 16	308
47	39 03	042	34 44	071	60 36	111	23 02	176	36 44	222	39 33	271	45 47	307
48	39 28	041	35 19	071	61 11	111	23 04	176	36 19	222	38 57	270	45 17	306
49	39 52	040	35 53	070	61 45	110	23 07	175	35 55	221	38 20	269	44 47	305
50	40 15	039	36 28	069	62 20	110	23 10	175	35 30	221	37 43	269	44 16	303
51	40 38	037	37 02	068	62 55	110	23 14	174	35 06	221	37 06	268	43 45	302
52	41 00	036	37 36	067	63 30	109	23 18	174	34 42	220	36 29	267	43 14	301
53	41 22	035	38 10	066	64 05	109	23 22	173	34 19	220	35 52	266	42 42	300
54	41 42	034	38 44	065	64 40	108	23 26	173	33 55	219	35 15	266	42 10	299
55	42 03	033	39 17	064	65 15	108	23 31	172	33 32	219	34 38	265	41 38	298
56	42 22	031	39 50	063	65 50	108	23 36	172	33 09	218	34 01	264	41 05	297
57	42 41	030	40 23	062	66 25	107	23 42	171	32 46	218	33 25	263	40 32	296
58	42 59	029	40 55	061	67 00	107	23 48	171	32 24	217	32 48	263	39 58	295
59	43 17	027	41 27	060	67 36	107	23 54	170	32 01	217	32 12	262	39 25	294
	RIGEL		◆ SIRIUS		Suhail		◆ RIGIL KENT		Peacock		FOMALHAUT		◆ Diphda	
60	43 33	026	41 59	059	39 56	113	24 00	170	31 39	216	31 35	261	38 51	293
61	43 49	025	42 30	057	40 30	112	24 07	169	31 18	216	30 58	260	38 17	292
62	44 04	023	43 01	056	41 04	112	24 14	169	30 56	215	30 22	260	37 42	291
63	44 18	022	43 31	055	41 38	111	24 22	168	30 35	215	29 46	259	37 08	290
64	44 32	021	44 02	054	42 13	110	24 30	168	30 14	214	29 10	258	36 33	289
65	44 45	019	44 31	053	42 48	110	24 38	167	29 53	214	28 33	258	35 58	288
66	44 57	018	45 00	052	43 22	109	24 46	166	29 33	213	27 57	257	35 23	287
67	45 08	017	45 29	051	43 57	109	24 55	166	29 12	213	27 22	256	34 47	286
68	45 18	015	45 58	049	44 32	108	25 04	165	28 52	212	26 46	255	34 12	285
69	45 27	014	46 25	048	45 08	107	25 14	165	28 33	212	26 10	255	33 36	285
70	45 36	013	46 53	047	45 43	107	25 23	164	28 13	211	25 34	254	33 00	284
71	45 43	011	47 19	046	46 18	106	25 33	164	27 54	211	24 59	253	32 24	283
72	45 50	010	47 46	044	46 54	106	25 44	163	27 35	210	24 24	253	31 48	282
73	45 56	008	48 11	043	47 30	105	25 54	163	27 17	210	23 48	252	31 12	281
74	46 00	007	48 36	042	48 05	104	26 05	162	26 59	209	23 13	251	30 36	280
	RIGEL		◆ SIRIUS		Suhail		◆ RIGIL KENT		Peacock		ACHERNAR		◆ Diphda	
75	46 04	005	49 00	041	48 41	104	26 17	162	26 41	209	61 01	240	29 59	279
76	46 07	004	49 24	039	49 17	103	26 28	161	26 23	208	60 29	239	29 23	278
77	46 10	003	49 47	038	49 53	102	26 40	161	26 06	208	59 57	239	28 46	278
78	46 11	001	50 09	037	50 29	102	26 52	160	25 49	207	59 26	239	28 10	277
79	46 11	000	50 31	035	51 05	101	27 05	160	25 32	207	58 54	239	27 33	276
80	46 10	358	50 52	034	51 42	101	27 18	159	25 15	206	58 23	238	26 56	275
81	46 09	357	51 12	032	52 18	100	27 31	159	24 59	206	57 51	238	26 19	274
82	46 06	355	51 31	031	52 54	099	27 44	158	24 43	205	57 20	238	25 43	274
83	46 03	354	51 50	029	53 31	099	27 58	158	24 28	205	56 49	238	25 06	273
84	45 59	353	52 08	028	54 08	098	28 12	158	24 12	204	56 17	237	24 29	272
85	45 54	351	52 24	026	54 44	097	28 26	157	23 58	204	55 46	237	23 52	271
86	45 47	350	52 40	025	55 21	097	28 41	157	23 43	203	55 16	237	23 15	270
87	45 40	348	52 56	023	55 58	096	28 56	156	23 29	202	54 45	236	22 38	270
88	45 33	347	53 10	022	56 34	095	29 11	156	23 15	202	54 14	236	22 01	269
89	45 24	346	53 23	020	57 11	094	29 26	155	23 01	201	53 43	236	21 24	268

LHA ♈	Hc	Zn	Hc	Zn	Hc	Zn	Hc	Zn	Hc	Zn	Hc	Zn	Hc	Zn
	PROCYON		◆ Suhail		RIGIL KENT		◆ Peacock		ACHERNAR		◆ RIGEL		BETELGEUSE	
90	28 58	029	57 48	094	29 42	155	22 48	201	53 13	235	45 14	344	30 35	359
91	29 16	028	58 25	093	29 58	154	22 35	200	52 43	235	45 04	343	30 34	358
92	29 33	027	59 02	092	30 14	154	22 22	200	52 12	235	44 52	341	30 32	357
93	29 49	025	59 39	092	30 30	153	22 10	199	51 42	234	44 40	340	30 30	355
94	30 04	024	60 16	091	30 47	153	21 58	199	51 12	234	44 27	339	30 26	354
95	30 19	023	60 53	090	31 04	152	21 46	198	50 42	234	44 13	337	30 22	353
96	30 34	022	61 29	089	31 21	152	21 35	198	50 13	233	43 59	336	30 17	352
97	30 47	021	62 06	088	31 39	151	21 24	197	49 43	233	43 43	335	30 12	351
98	31 00	020	62 43	088	31 57	151	21 13	196	49 14	233	43 27	333	30 06	350
99	31 12	019	63 20	087	32 15	151	21 03	196	48 44	232	43 10	332	29 59	349
100	31 24	018	63 57	086	32 33	150	20 53	195	48 15	232	42 52	331	29 51	347
101	31 35	016	64 34	085	32 52	150	20 43	195	47 46	232	42 34	330	29 42	346
102	31 45	015	65 11	084	33 10	149	20 34	194	47 17	231	42 15	328	29 33	345
103	31 54	014	65 47	083	33 30	149	20 25	194	46 48	231	41 55	327	29 23	344
104	32 03	013	66 24	082	33 49	148	20 17	193	46 20	231	41 35	326	29 13	343
	PROCYON		REGULUS		◆ Gienah		RIGIL KENT		◆ ACHERNAR		RIGEL		◆ SIRIUS	
105	32 11	012	14 15	048	20 26	093	34 08	148	45 51	230	41 14	324	54 38	354
106	32 18	011	14 42	047	21 03	092	34 28	147	45 23	230	40 52	323	54 33	352
107	32 24	009	15 09	046	21 40	091	34 48	147	44 55	229	40 29	322	54 28	351
108	32 30	008	15 36	045	22 17	090	35 08	147	44 27	229	40 06	321	54 21	349
109	32 35	007	16 02	044	22 54	090	35 29	146	43 59	229	39 43	320	54 14	348
110	32 39	006	16 27	043	23 31	089	35 50	146	43 32	228	39 19	319	54 06	346
111	32 43	005	16 52	042	24 08	088	36 10	145	43 04	228	38 54	317	53 56	344
112	32 45	004	17 17	042	24 44	087	36 32	145	42 37	227	38 29	316	53 46	343
113	32 47	002	17 41	041	25 21	086	36 53	144	42 10	227	38 03	315	53 34	341
114	32 48	001	18 05	040	25 58	086	37 14	144	41 43	227	37 36	314	53 22	340
115	32 49	000	18 28	039	26 35	085	37 36	144	41 16	226	37 10	313	53 08	338
116	32 49	359	18 51	038	27 12	084	37 58	143	40 49	226	36 42	312	52 54	336
117	32 47	358	19 14	037	27 48	083	38 20	143	40 23	225	36 14	311	52 39	335
118	32 45	356	19 36	036	28 25	082	38 43	142	39 57	225	35 46	310	52 23	333
119	32 43	355	19 57	035	29 02	081	39 05	142	39 31	224	35 18	309	52 06	332
	REGULUS		◆ SPICA		RIGIL KENT		Peacock		◆ ACHERNAR		RIGEL		◆ SIRIUS	
120	20 18	034	14 03	090	39 28	142	18 50	184	39 05	224	34 48	307	51 48	330
121	20 38	033	14 40	090	39 51	141	18 47	183	38 40	224	34 19	306	51 30	329
122	20 58	032	15 17	089	40 15	141	18 45	183	38 14	223	33 49	305	51 10	328
123	21 17	031	15 54	088	40 38	141	18 44	182	37 49	223	33 19	304	50 50	326
124	21 36	030	16 31	087	41 01	140	18 43	182	37 24	222	32 48	303	50 29	325
125	21 54	029	17 08	086	41 25	140	18 42	181	36 59	222	32 17	302	50 07	323
126	22 12	028	17 45	086	41 49	139	18 41	180	36 35	221	31 46	301	49 45	322
127	22 29	027	18 22	085	42 13	139	18 41	180	36 10	221	31 14	300	49 22	321
128	22 45	026	18 58	084	42 38	139	18 41	179	35 46	221	30 42	299	48 58	319
129	23 01	025	19 35	083	43 02	138	18 42	179	35 22	220	30 09	298	48 34	318
130	23 16	024	20 12	082	43 27	138	18 43	178	34 59	220	29 37	297	48 09	317
131	23 31	023	20 48	082	43 52	138	18 45	178	34 35	219	29 04	297	47 43	315
132	23 45	022	21 25	081	44 17	137	18 46	177	34 12	219	28 31	296	47 17	314
133	23 58	021	22 01	080	44 42	137	18 49	176	33 49	218	27 57	295	46 50	313
134	24 11	020	22 38	079	45 07	137	18 51	176	33 26	218	27 24	294	46 23	312
	◆ REGULUS		SPICA		◆ RIGIL KENT		Peacock		ACHERNAR		◆ CANOPUS		SIRIUS	
135	24 23	019	23 14	078	45 33	136	18 54	175	33 04	217	66 30	253	45 55	310
136	24 34	018	23 50	077	45 58	136	18 57	175	32 41	217	65 55	252	45 27	309
137	24 45	017	24 26	076	46 24	136	19 01	174	32 19	216	65 20	252	44 58	308
138	24 55	015	25 02	076	46 50	135	19 05	173	31 58	216	64 45	252	44 28	307
139	25 05	014	25 37	075	47 16	135	19 09	173	31 36	215	64 10	251	43 59	306
140	25 14	013	26 13	074	47 42	135	19 14	172	31 15	215	63 35	251	43 29	305
141	25 22	012	26 48	073	48 09	134	19 19	172	30 54	214	63 00	250	42 58	304
142	25 29	011	27 24	072	48 35	134	19 25	171	30 33	214	62 25	250	42 27	302
143	25 36	010	27 59	071	49 02	134	19 31	171	30 12	213	61 50	250	41 56	301
144	25 42	009	28 34	070	49 29	133	19 37	170	29 52	213	61 16	249	41 24	300
145	25 48	008	29 08	069	49 56	133	19 43	169	29 32	213	60 41	249	40 52	299
146	25 53	007	29 43	069	50 23	133	19 50	169	29 12	212	60 07	249	40 19	298
147	25 57	006	30 17	068	50 50	133	19 58	168	28 53	212	59 33	248	39 47	297
148	26 00	005	30 51	067	51 17	132	20 05	168	28 34	211	58 58	248	39 14	296
149	26 03	004	31 25	066	51 44	132	20 13	167	28 15	211	58 24	247	38 40	295
	◆ REGULUS		SPICA		◆ RIGIL KENT		Peacock		ACHERNAR		◆ CANOPUS		SIRIUS	
150	26 05	002	31 58	065	52 12	132	20 22	167	27 56	210	57 50	247	38 07	294
151	26 06	001	32 32	064	52 40	131	20 30	166	27 38	210	57 16	247	37 33	293
152	26 06	000	33 05	063	53 07	131	20 39	165	27 20	209	56 42	246	36 59	292
153	26 06	359	33 37	062	53 35	131	20 49	165	27 02	208	56 09	246	36 25	291
154	26 05	358	34 10	061	54 03	131	20 59	164	26 45	208	55 35	245	35 50	290
155	26 04	357	34 42	060	54 31	130	21 09	164	26 28	207	55 02	245	35 15	289
156	26 02	356	35 14	059	54 59	130	21 19	163	26 11	207	54 28	244	34 40	288
157	25 59	355	35 45	058	55 28	130	21 30	163	25 54	206	53 55	244	34 05	288
158	25 55	354	36 16	057	55 56	130	21 41	162	25 38	206	53 22	244	33 30	287
159	25 51	353	36 47	056	56 24	130	21 53	162	25 22	205	52 49	243	32 55	286
160	25 46	352	37 18	055	56 53	129	22 05	161	25 06	205	52 16	243	32 19	285
161	25 40	351	37 47	054	57 21	129	22 17	160	24 51	204	51 43	242	31 43	284
162	25 33	349	38 17	053	57 50	129	22 29	160	24 36	204	51 10	242	31 07	283
163	25 26	348	38 46	052	58 19	129	22 42	159	24 21	203	50 38	242	30 31	282
164	25 19	347	39 15	050	58 47	129	22 55	159	24 07	203	50 05	241	29 55	281
	◆ SPICA		ANTARES		◆ Peacock		ACHERNAR		CANOPUS		◆ SIRIUS		REGULUS	
165	39 43	049	24 59	102	23 09	158	23 52	202	49 33	241	29 19	280	25 10	346
166	40 11	048	25 35	101	23 23	158	23 39	202	49 01	240	28 42	280	25 01	345
167	40 38	047	26 11	100	23 37	157	23 25	201	48 29	240	28 06	279	24 51	344
168	41 05	046	26 48	099	23 51	157	23 12	201	47 57	239	27 29	278	24 41	343
169	41 31	045	27 24	099	24 06	156	22 59	200	47 25	239	26 53	277	24 30	342
170	41 57	044	28 01	098	24 21	156	22 47	199	46 54	238	26 16	276	24 18	341
171	42 22	042	28 37	097	24 37	155	22 35	199	46 23	238	25 39	275	24 06	340
172	42 47	041	29 14	096	24 53	155	22 23	198	45 51	238	25 03	275	23 53	339
173	43 11	040	29 51	096	25 09	154	22 11	198	45 20	237	24 26	274	23 39	338
174	43 34	039	30 28	095	25 25	153	22 00	197	44 49	237	23 49	273	23 25	337
175	43 57	037	31 04	094	25 42	153	21 49	197	44 18	236	23 12	272	23 10	336
176	44 19	036	31 41	093	25 59	152	21 39	196	43 48	236	22 35	271	22 54	335
177	44 41	035	32 18	093	26 16	152	21 29	196	43 17	235	21 58	271	22 38	334
178	45 01	034	32 55	092	26 33	151	21 19	195	42 47	235	21 21	270	22 22	333
179	45 21	032	33 32	091	26 51	151	21 09	195	42 17	234	20 44	269	22 04	332

 LAT 52°S

LHA ♈	Hc	Zn	Hc	Zn	Hc	Zn	Hc	Zn	Hc	Zn	Hc	Zn	Hc	Zn
	◆ SPICA		ANTARES		◆ Peacock		ACHERNAR		CANOPUS		◆ Suhail		REGULUS	
180	45 41	031	34 09	090	27 09	150	21 00	194	41 47	234	60 26	269	21 46	331
181	45 59	030	34 46	090	27 28	150	20 52	193	41 17	233	59 49	269	21 28	330
182	46 17	028	35 23	089	27 46	149	20 43	193	40 48	233	59 12	268	21 09	329
183	46 34	027	36 00	088	28 05	149	20 35	192	40 18	233	58 35	267	20 50	328
184	46 51	026	36 37	087	28 25	148	20 27	192	39 49	232	57 58	266	20 30	327
185	47 06	024	37 14	086	28 44	148	20 20	191	39 20	232	57 21	266	20 09	326
186	47 21	023	37 50	086	29 04	147	20 13	191	38 51	231	56 44	265	19 48	325
187	47 35	021	38 27	085	29 24	147	20 06	190	38 23	231	56 08	264	19 27	324
188	47 48	020	39 04	084	29 45	146	20 00	189	37 54	230	55 31	264	19 04	323
189	48 00	018	39 41	083	30 05	146	19 54	189	37 26	230	54 54	263	18 42	322
190	48 11	017	40 17	082	30 26	145	19 49	188	36 58	229	54 18	262	18 19	321
191	48 22	016	40 54	081	30 47	145	19 44	188	36 30	229	53 41	262	17 55	320
192	48 31	014	41 30	080	31 09	144	19 39	187	36 02	228	53 04	261	17 31	319
193	48 40	013	42 07	080	31 30	144	19 34	187	35 35	228	52 28	260	17 07	318
194	48 47	011	42 43	079	31 52	143	19 30	186	35 08	227	51 52	260	16 42	317
	◆ ARCTURUS		ANTARES		◆ Peacock		ACHERNAR		CANOPUS		◆ Suhail		Denebola	
195	16 58	019	43 19	078	32 14	143	19 27	185	34 41	227	51 15	259	21 47	342
196	17 10	018	43 55	077	32 37	142	19 23	185	34 14	226	50 39	258	21 36	341
197	17 21	017	44 31	076	32 59	142	19 20	184	33 47	226	50 03	258	21 23	340
198	17 31	016	45 07	075	33 22	141	19 18	184	33 21	225	49 27	257	21 10	339
199	17 41	015	45 42	074	33 45	141	19 15	183	32 55	225	48 51	256	20 56	338
200	17 50	014	46 18	073	34 09	141	19 14	183	32 29	224	48 15	256	20 42	337
201	17 59	013	46 53	072	34 32	140	19 12	182	32 03	224	47 39	255	20 27	336
202	18 07	012	47 28	071	34 56	140	19 11	181	31 38	223	47 04	255	20 11	335
203	18 14	011	48 03	070	35 20	139	19 10	181	31 13	223	46 28	254	19 55	334
204	18 21	010	48 38	069	35 45	139	19 10	180	30 48	222	45 53	253	19 38	333
205	18 27	009	49 12	068	36 09	138	19 10	180	30 23	222	45 17	253	19 21	332
206	18 33	008	49 46	067	36 34	138	19 10	179	29 59	221	44 42	252	19 03	331
207	18 38	007	50 20	066	36 59	137	19 11	179	29 35	221	44 07	252	18 45	330
208	18 42	006	50 53	065	37 24	137	19 12	178	29 11	220	43 32	251	18 26	329
209	18 45	005	51 27	064	37 49	136	19 13	177	28 47	220	42 57	250	18 07	328
	◆ ARCTURUS		ANTARES		◆ Peacock		ACHERNAR		CANOPUS		◆ Suhail		SPICA	
210	18 48	004	52 00	062	38 15	136	19 15	177	28 24	219	42 22	250	48 40	347
211	18 51	003	52 32	061	38 40	136	19 17	176	28 01	218	41 48	249	48 31	346
212	18 52	002	53 04	060	39 06	135	19 20	176	27 38	218	41 13	249	48 22	344
213	18 53	001	53 36	059	39 33	135	19 23	175	27 15	217	40 39	248	48 11	343
214	18 54	000	54 08	058	39 59	134	19 26	175	26 53	217	40 05	247	48 00	341
215	18 53	359	54 39	056	40 25	134	19 30	174	26 31	216	39 31	247	47 48	340
216	18 53	358	55 09	055	40 52	133	19 34	173	26 09	216	38 57	246	47 35	339
217	18 51	357	55 39	054	41 19	133	19 38	173	25 48	215	38 23	246	47 21	337
218	18 49	356	56 09	052	41 46	133	19 43	172	25 26	215	37 50	245	47 06	336
219	18 46	355	56 38	051	42 14	132	19 48	172	25 06	214	37 16	244	46 51	334
220	18 42	354	57 06	050	42 41	132	19 54	171	24 45	214	36 43	244	46 34	333
221	18 38	353	57 34	048	43 09	131	19 59	171	24 25	213	36 10	243	46 17	332
222	18 34	352	58 02	047	43 36	131	20 06	170	24 05	213	35 37	243	45 59	330
223	18 28	351	58 28	045	44 04	131	20 12	169	23 45	212	35 04	242	45 41	329
224	18 22	350	58 54	044	44 33	130	20 19	169	23 26	211	34 32	242	45 21	328
	ANTARES		◆ Nunki		Peacock		ACHERNAR		◆ CANOPUS		Suhail		◆ SPICA	
225	59 19	042	39 15	083	45 01	130	20 26	168	23 07	211	33 59	241	45 01	326
226	59 44	041	39 52	082	45 29	129	20 34	168	22 48	210	33 27	240	44 40	325
227	60 08	039	40 29	082	45 58	129	20 42	167	22 29	210	32 55	240	44 19	324
228	60 31	038	41 05	081	46 27	129	20 50	167	22 11	209	32 23	239	43 57	323
229	60 53	036	41 41	080	46 56	128	20 59	166	21 53	209	31 52	239	43 34	321
230	61 14	034	42 18	079	47 25	128	21 08	166	21 36	208	31 20	238	43 11	320
231	61 34	032	42 54	078	47 54	127	21 18	165	21 19	207	30 49	237	42 47	319
232	61 53	031	43 30	077	48 24	127	21 27	164	21 02	207	30 18	237	42 22	318
233	62 12	029	44 06	076	48 53	127	21 37	164	20 45	206	29 47	236	41 57	316
234	62 29	027	44 42	075	49 23	126	21 48	163	20 29	206	29 16	236	41 31	315
235	62 45	025	45 17	074	49 53	126	21 59	163	20 13	205	28 46	235	41 05	314
236	63 01	023	45 53	073	50 23	126	22 10	162	19 58	205	28 16	234	40 38	313
237	63 15	021	46 28	072	50 53	125	22 21	162	19 43	204	27 46	234	40 11	312
238	63 28	019	47 03	071	51 23	125	22 33	161	19 28	203	27 16	233	39 43	311
239	63 39	018	47 38	070	51 53	125	22 45	161	19 13	203	26 47	233	39 15	310
	◆ ANTARES		Nunki		◆ FOMALHAUT		ACHERNAR		CANOPUS		◆ ACRUX		SPICA	
240	63 50	016	48 13	069	14 41	120	22 57	160	18 59	202	60 27	227	38 46	308
241	63 59	014	48 47	068	15 13	119	23 10	159	18 45	202	60 00	227	38 17	307
242	64 07	012	49 21	067	15 45	118	23 23	159	18 32	201	59 33	227	37 47	306
243	64 14	009	49 55	066	16 18	117	23 37	158	18 19	200	59 06	227	37 17	305
244	64 19	007	50 29	065	16 51	117	23 51	158	18 06	200	58 39	227	36 47	304
245	64 23	005	51 02	064	17 24	116	24 05	157	17 54	199	58 12	227	36 16	303
246	64 26	003	51 35	063	17 57	115	24 19	157	17 42	199	57 45	227	35 45	302
247	64 28	001	52 08	062	18 31	115	24 34	156	17 30	198	57 18	226	35 14	301
248	64 28	359	52 40	060	19 04	114	24 49	156	17 19	197	56 52	226	34 42	300
249	64 27	357	53 12	059	19 38	113	25 04	155	17 08	197	56 25	226	34 10	299
250	64 24	355	53 44	058	20 12	112	25 20	155	16 58	196	55 58	226	33 37	298
251	64 20	353	54 15	057	20 47	112	25 36	154	16 48	196	55 32	226	33 04	297
252	64 15	351	54 46	056	21 21	111	25 52	154	16 38	195	55 05	226	32 31	296
253	64 08	349	55 16	054	21 56	110	26 08	153	16 29	194	54 39	225	31 58	295
254	64 01	347	55 46	053	22 30	110	26 25	153	16 20	194	54 13	225	31 25	294
	ALTAIR		◆ FOMALHAUT		ACHERNAR		CANOPUS		◆ ACRUX		SPICA		◆ ANTARES	
255	18 53	045	23 05	109	26 42	152	16 11	193	53 46	225	30 51	293	63 51	345
256	19 19	044	23 40	108	27 00	152	16 03	192	53 20	225	30 17	292	63 41	343
257	19 45	043	24 15	108	27 18	151	15 55	192	52 54	225	29 42	291	63 30	341
258	20 10	042	24 51	107	27 36	151	15 48	191	52 28	224	29 08	291	63 17	339
259	20 35	041	25 26	106	27 54	150	15 41	191	52 02	224	28 33	290	63 03	337
260	20 59	041	26 02	105	28 12	150	15 34	190	51 37	224	27 58	289	62 48	335
261	21 23	040	26 37	105	28 31	149	15 28	189	51 11	224	27 23	288	62 32	333
262	21 46	039	27 13	104	28 50	149	15 22	189	50 46	224	26 48	287	62 15	331
263	22 09	038	27 49	103	29 10	148	15 17	188	50 20	223	26 13	286	61 57	330
264	22 31	037	28 25	103	29 30	148	15 12	188	49 55	223	25 37	285	61 38	328
265	22 53	036	29 01	102	29 49	147	15 07	187	49 30	223	25 01	284	61 17	326
266	23 14	035	29 37	101	30 10	147	15 03	186	49 05	223	24 26	284	60 56	324
267	23 35	034	30 13	100	30 30	146	14 59	186	48 40	222	23 50	283	60 34	323
268	23 55	033	30 50	100	30 51	146	14 55	185	48 15	222	23 13	282	60 11	321
269	24 14	032	31 26	099	31 12	145	14 52	184	47 50	222	22 37	281	59 48	319

LHA ♈	Hc	Zn	Hc	Zn	Hc	Zn	Hc	Zn	Hc	Zn	Hc	Zn	Hc	Zn
	◆ ALTAIR		FOMALHAUT		◆ ACHERNAR		CANOPUS		RIGIL KENT		◆ SPICA		ANTARES	
270	24 33	031	32 03	098	31 33	145	14 50	184	61 50	232	22 01	280	59 23	318
271	24 52	029	32 39	098	31 55	144	14 47	183	61 21	232	21 25	279	58 58	316
272	25 10	028	33 16	097	32 16	144	14 46	183	60 52	232	20 48	278	58 32	315
273	25 27	027	33 53	096	32 38	143	14 44	182	60 23	232	20 11	278	58 06	313
274	25 44	026	34 30	095	33 01	143	14 43	181	59 54	232	19 35	277	57 39	312
275	26 00	025	35 06	095	33 23	142	14 42	181	59 25	231	18 58	276	57 11	310
276	26 15	024	35 43	094	33 46	142	14 42	180	58 57	231	18 21	275	56 43	309
277	26 30	023	36 20	093	34 09	141	14 42	179	58 28	231	17 45	274	56 14	308
278	26 44	022	36 57	092	34 32	141	14 43	179	57 59	231	17 08	274	55 44	306
279	26 58	021	37 34	091	34 55	140	14 44	178	57 30	231	16 31	273	55 14	305
280	27 11	020	38 11	091	35 19	140	14 45	178	57 02	231	15 54	272	54 44	304
281	27 23	019	38 48	090	35 43	140	14 47	177	56 33	230	15 17	271	54 13	303
282	27 35	018	39 25	089	36 07	139	14 49	176	56 05	230	14 40	270	53 41	301
283	27 46	017	40 02	088	36 31	139	14 52	176	55 37	230	14 03	270	53 10	300
284	27 56	016	40 38	088	36 56	138	14 55	175	55 08	230	13 26	269	52 38	299
	◆ ALTAIR		FOMALHAUT		◆ ACHERNAR		CANOPUS		◆ RIGIL KENT		ANTARES		Rasalhague	
285	28 06	014	41 15	087	37 21	138	14 58	174	54 40	230	52 05	298	22 55	338
286	28 14	013	41 52	086	37 46	137	15 02	174	54 12	229	51 32	297	22 41	337
287	28 23	012	42 29	085	38 11	137	15 06	173	53 44	229	50 59	295	22 26	336
288	28 30	011	43 06	084	38 36	136	15 11	173	53 16	229	50 25	294	22 10	335
289	28 37	010	43 43	083	39 02	136	15 16	172	52 48	229	49 52	293	21 54	334
290	28 43	009	44 19	083	39 27	136	15 21	171	52 21	228	49 18	292	21 37	332
291	28 48	008	44 56	082	39 53	135	15 27	171	51 53	228	48 43	291	21 20	331
292	28 53	007	45 32	081	40 20	135	15 33	170	51 26	228	48 09	290	21 02	330
293	28 57	006	46 09	080	40 46	134	15 40	169	50 58	228	47 34	289	20 44	330
294	29 00	004	46 45	079	41 12	134	15 47	169	50 31	227	46 59	288	20 25	329
295	29 02	003	47 21	078	41 39	133	15 54	168	50 04	227	46 24	287	20 05	328
296	29 04	002	47 57	077	42 06	133	16 02	168	49 37	227	45 48	286	19 45	327
297	29 05	001	48 33	076	42 33	133	16 10	167	49 10	226	45 13	285	19 24	326
298	29 05	000	49 09	075	43 00	132	16 19	166	48 44	226	44 37	284	19 03	325
299	29 05	359	49 45	074	43 28	132	16 27	166	48 17	226	44 01	283	18 42	324
	FOMALHAUT		◆ ACHERNAR		CANOPUS		◆ RIGIL KENT		ANTARES		Nunki		◆ ALTAIR	
300	50 20	073	43 55	131	16 37	165	47 51	226	43 25	282	61 36	329	29 04	358
301	50 55	072	44 23	131	16 46	165	47 24	225	42 49	281	61 16	327	29 02	356
302	51 30	071	44 51	131	16 56	164	46 58	225	42 13	281	60 56	325	28 59	355
303	52 05	070	45 19	130	17 07	163	46 32	225	41 36	280	60 34	324	28 56	354
304	52 40	069	45 47	130	17 18	163	46 06	224	41 00	279	60 12	322	28 52	353
305	53 14	068	46 16	130	17 29	162	45 41	224	40 23	278	59 49	320	28 47	352
306	53 48	067	46 44	129	17 40	162	45 15	224	39 47	277	59 25	319	28 42	351
307	54 22	066	47 13	129	17 52	161	44 50	223	39 10	276	59 00	317	28 35	350
308	54 56	065	47 42	128	18 05	160	44 25	223	38 33	275	58 35	316	28 28	349
309	55 29	063	48 11	128	18 17	160	44 00	223	37 56	275	58 09	314	28 21	347
310	56 02	062	48 40	128	18 30	159	43 35	222	37 20	274	57 42	313	28 12	346
311	56 34	061	49 10	127	18 44	159	43 10	222	36 43	273	57 14	311	28 03	345
312	57 06	060	49 39	127	18 57	158	42 45	221	36 06	272	56 46	310	27 54	344
313	57 38	058	50 09	127	19 11	157	42 21	221	35 29	271	56 18	309	27 43	343
314	58 09	057	50 38	126	19 26	157	41 57	221	34 52	271	55 49	307	27 32	342
	◆ FOMALHAUT		ACHERNAR		◆ CANOPUS		RIGIL KENT		◆ ANTARES		Nunki		ALTAIR	
315	58 40	056	51 08	126	19 40	156	41 33	220	34 15	270	55 19	306	27 20	341
316	59 10	054	51 38	126	19 56	156	41 09	220	33 38	269	54 49	305	27 08	340
317	59 40	053	52 08	125	20 11	155	40 45	220	33 01	268	54 18	303	26 55	339
318	60 09	052	52 38	125	20 27	154	40 22	219	32 24	267	53 47	302	26 41	338
319	60 38	050	53 09	125	20 43	154	39 59	219	31 47	267	53 15	301	26 27	337
320	61 06	049	53 39	124	20 59	153	39 36	218	31 11	266	52 44	300	26 12	336
321	61 33	047	54 10	124	21 16	153	39 13	218	30 34	265	52 11	298	25 56	334
322	62 00	045	54 41	124	21 33	152	38 50	218	29 57	264	51 39	297	25 40	333
323	62 26	044	55 11	123	21 51	152	38 28	217	29 20	264	51 06	296	25 23	332
324	62 51	042	55 42	123	22 09	151	38 05	217	28 43	263	50 32	295	25 06	331
325	63 16	040	56 13	123	22 27	150	37 43	216	28 07	262	49 59	294	24 48	330
326	63 39	039	56 44	122	22 45	150	37 21	216	27 30	261	49 25	293	24 29	329
327	64 02	037	57 16	122	23 04	149	37 00	216	26 54	261	48 51	292	24 10	328
328	64 24	035	57 47	122	23 23	149	36 38	215	26 17	260	48 16	291	23 50	327
329	64 44	033	58 18	122	23 42	148	36 17	215	25 41	259	47 42	290	23 30	326
	◆ FOMALHAUT		ACHERNAR		◆ CANOPUS		RIGIL KENT		◆ ANTARES		Nunki		ALTAIR	
330	65 04	031	58 50	121	24 02	148	35 56	214	25 05	258	47 07	289	23 09	325
331	65 23	029	59 21	121	24 22	147	35 35	214	24 29	258	46 32	288	22 47	324
332	65 41	027	59 53	121	24 42	146	35 15	214	23 53	257	45 56	287	22 26	323
333	65 57	025	60 25	121	25 03	146	34 55	213	23 17	256	45 21	286	22 03	322
334	66 12	023	60 57	120	25 23	145	34 34	213	22 41	256	44 45	285	21 40	321
335	66 26	021	61 29	120	25 45	145	34 15	212	22 05	255	44 09	284	21 17	320
336	66 39	019	62 00	120	26 06	144	33 55	212	21 30	254	43 34	283	20 53	319
337	66 51	017	62 33	120	26 28	144	33 36	211	20 54	253	42 57	282	20 29	318
338	67 01	015	63 05	120	26 50	143	33 17	211	20 19	253	42 21	281	20 04	317
339	67 10	013	63 37	119	27 12	143	32 58	211	19 44	252	41 45	280	19 39	316
340	67 17	010	64 09	119	27 35	142	32 39	210	19 09	251	41 09	279	19 13	315
341	67 23	008	64 41	119	27 57	142	32 21	210	18 34	251	40 32	279	18 47	314
342	67 28	006	65 14	119	28 20	141	32 02	209	17 59	250	39 56	278	18 20	314
343	67 31	004	65 46	119	28 44	141	31 45	209	17 24	249	39 19	277	17 53	313
344	67 32	001	66 18	119	29 07	140	31 27	208	16 50	248	38 42	276	17 26	312
	◆ Diphda		Acamar		◆ CANOPUS		Miaplacidus		RIGIL KENT		◆ Nunki		FOMALHAUT	
345	50 13	041	48 15	098	29 31	139	33 19	169	31 10	208	38 05	275	67 32	359
346	50 37	039	48 52	097	29 55	139	33 26	169	30 53	207	37 29	274	67 31	357
347	51 00	038	49 29	097	30 20	138	33 33	169	30 36	207	36 52	273	67 28	355
348	51 22	037	50 05	096	30 44	138	33 41	168	30 19	206	36 15	273	67 24	352
349	51 44	035	50 42	095	31 09	137	33 48	168	30 03	206	35 38	272	67 19	350
350	52 05	034	51 19	095	31 34	137	33 56	167	29 47	205	35 01	271	67 11	348
351	52 25	032	51 56	094	32 00	136	34 05	167	29 31	205	34 24	270	67 03	346
352	52 44	031	52 33	093	32 25	136	34 13	167	29 16	205	33 47	269	66 53	343
353	53 03	029	53 10	092	32 51	135	34 22	166	29 00	204	33 10	269	66 42	341
354	53 21	028	53 46	092	33 17	135	34 31	166	28 45	204	32 33	268	66 29	339
355	53 38	026	54 23	091	33 44	134	34 40	165	28 31	203	31 56	267	66 16	337
356	53 54	025	55 00	090	34 10	134	34 49	165	28 16	203	31 20	266	66 01	335
357	54 09	023	55 37	089	34 37	133	34 59	165	28 02	202	30 43	266	65 45	333
358	54 23	022	56 14	088	35 04	133	35 09	164	27 49	202	30 06	265	65 27	331
359	54 36	020	56 51	088	35 31	132	35 19	164	27 35	201	29 29	264	65 09	329

LAT 53°S

LHA ♈	Diphda Hc	Zn	◆ RIGEL Hc	Zn	CANOPUS Hc	Zn	Miaplacidus Hc	Zn	◆ RIGIL KENT Hc	Zn	Peacock Hc	Zn	◆ FOMALHAUT Hc	Zn
0	53 51	018	13 15	086	36 38	131	36 27	163	28 18	201	59 53	241	63 59	328
1	54 02	016	13 51	085	37 06	131	36 37	163	28 05	200	59 21	241	63 39	326
2	54 12	015	14 27	084	37 33	130	36 48	163	27 53	200	58 50	241	63 19	325
3	54 20	013	15 03	084	38 01	130	36 58	162	27 41	199	58 18	240	62 57	323
4	54 28	012	15 39	083	38 28	129	37 10	162	27 29	199	57 47	240	62 35	321
5	54 35	010	16 15	082	38 56	129	37 21	162	27 17	198	57 15	240	62 12	319
6	54 41	008	16 50	081	39 25	128	37 32	161	27 06	198	56 44	239	61 48	318
7	54 46	007	17 26	080	39 53	128	37 44	161	26 55	197	56 13	239	61 24	316
8	54 49	005	18 02	079	40 22	127	37 56	160	26 45	197	55 42	239	60 58	315
9	54 52	003	18 37	079	40 50	127	38 08	160	26 34	196	55 12	238	60 32	313
10	54 54	002	19 12	078	41 19	126	38 21	160	26 24	196	54 41	238	60 05	312
11	54 54	000	19 48	077	41 49	126	38 33	159	26 15	195	54 10	238	59 38	310
12	54 54	358	20 23	076	42 18	125	38 46	159	26 05	195	53 40	237	59 10	309
13	54 52	357	20 58	075	42 47	125	38 59	159	25 56	194	53 09	237	58 42	307
14	54 50	355	21 33	074	43 17	124	39 12	158	25 47	194	52 39	237	58 13	306

LHA ♈	◆ RIGEL Hc	Zn	SIRIUS Hc	Zn	CANOPUS Hc	Zn	◆ RIGIL KENT Hc	Zn	Peacock Hc	Zn	◆ FOMALHAUT Hc	Zn	Diphda Hc	Zn
15	22 07	073	15 24	098	43 47	124	25 39	193	52 09	236	57 43	305	54 46	354
16	22 42	073	16 00	097	44 17	124	25 31	193	51 39	236	57 13	303	54 42	352
17	23 16	072	16 36	096	44 47	123	25 23	192	51 09	236	56 43	302	54 36	350
18	23 50	071	17 12	095	45 18	123	25 15	192	50 40	235	56 12	301	54 29	349
19	24 24	070	17 48	094	45 48	122	25 08	191	50 10	235	55 41	299	54 22	347
20	24 58	069	18 24	094	46 19	122	25 01	191	49 41	234	55 09	298	54 13	345
21	25 32	068	19 00	093	46 50	121	24 55	190	49 11	234	54 37	297	54 04	344
22	26 05	067	19 36	092	47 20	121	24 49	190	48 42	234	54 05	296	53 53	342
23	26 38	066	20 12	091	47 52	120	24 43	189	48 13	233	53 32	295	53 42	341
24	27 11	065	20 48	090	48 23	120	24 37	189	47 44	233	52 59	294	53 29	339
25	27 44	065	21 24	090	48 54	119	24 32	188	47 16	232	52 26	292	53 16	338
26	28 17	064	22 01	089	49 26	119	24 27	188	46 47	232	51 52	291	53 02	336
27	28 49	063	22 37	088	49 58	118	24 23	187	46 19	232	51 19	290	52 46	334
28	29 21	062	23 13	087	50 29	118	24 19	187	45 51	231	50 45	289	52 30	333
29	29 52	061	23 49	086	51 01	117	24 15	186	45 22	231	50 10	288	52 14	331

LHA ♈	◆ RIGEL Hc	Zn	SIRIUS Hc	Zn	CANOPUS Hc	Zn	◆ RIGIL KENT Hc	Zn	Peacock Hc	Zn	◆ FOMALHAUT Hc	Zn	Diphda Hc	Zn
30	30 24	060	24 25	086	51 33	117	24 11	185	44 55	230	49 36	287	51 56	330
31	30 55	059	25 01	085	52 06	117	24 08	185	44 27	230	49 01	286	51 37	329
32	31 25	058	25 37	084	52 38	116	24 05	184	43 59	230	48 27	285	51 18	327
33	31 56	057	26 13	083	53 11	116	24 02	184	43 32	229	47 52	284	50 58	326
34	32 26	056	26 48	082	53 43	115	24 00	183	43 05	229	47 17	283	50 37	324
35	32 55	055	27 24	081	54 16	115	23 58	183	42 38	228	46 41	282	50 16	323
36	33 25	054	28 00	081	54 49	114	23 57	182	42 11	228	46 06	281	49 54	322
37	33 54	053	28 35	080	55 22	114	23 55	182	41 44	227	45 31	280	49 31	320
38	34 22	052	29 11	079	55 55	113	23 55	181	41 18	227	44 55	280	49 08	319
39	34 50	051	29 46	078	56 28	113	23 54	181	40 51	227	44 19	279	48 44	318
40	35 18	049	30 22	077	57 01	113	23 54	180	40 25	226	43 44	278	48 19	316
41	35 45	048	30 57	076	57 35	112	23 54	180	39 59	226	43 08	277	47 54	315
42	36 12	047	31 32	075	58 08	112	23 54	179	39 34	225	42 32	276	47 28	314
43	36 38	046	32 07	074	58 42	111	23 55	178	39 08	225	41 56	275	47 01	312
44	37 04	045	32 41	074	59 15	111	23 56	178	38 43	224	41 20	274	46 34	311

LHA ♈	RIGEL Hc	Zn	◆ SIRIUS Hc	Zn	CANOPUS Hc	Zn	◆ RIGIL KENT Hc	Zn	Peacock Hc	Zn	FOMALHAUT Hc	Zn	◆ Diphda Hc	Zn
45	37 29	044	33 16	073	59 49	110	23 58	177	38 18	224	40 44	274	46 07	310
46	37 54	043	33 50	072	60 23	110	23 59	177	37 53	223	40 08	273	45 39	309
47	38 18	042	34 24	071	60 57	109	24 02	176	37 28	223	39 32	272	45 11	308
48	38 42	041	34 58	070	61 31	109	24 04	176	37 04	222	38 56	271	44 42	306
49	39 05	039	35 32	069	62 05	109	24 07	175	36 39	222	38 20	270	44 13	305
50	39 28	038	36 06	068	62 40	108	24 10	175	36 15	222	37 44	269	43 43	304
51	39 50	037	36 39	067	63 14	108	24 13	174	35 52	221	37 07	269	43 13	303
52	40 11	036	37 12	066	63 49	107	24 17	174	35 28	221	36 31	268	42 43	302
53	40 32	035	37 45	065	64 23	107	24 21	173	35 05	220	35 55	267	42 12	301
54	40 52	033	38 18	064	64 58	106	24 26	173	34 41	220	35 19	266	41 41	300
55	41 12	032	38 50	063	65 32	106	24 31	172	34 18	219	34 43	266	41 09	299
56	41 31	031	39 22	062	66 07	106	24 36	172	33 56	219	34 07	265	40 37	298
57	41 49	030	39 54	061	66 42	105	24 41	171	33 33	218	33 31	264	40 05	297
58	42 06	028	40 25	060	67 17	105	24 47	171	33 11	218	32 55	263	39 33	296
59	42 23	027	40 56	059	67 52	104	24 53	170	32 49	217	32 20	263	39 00	295

LHA ♈	RIGEL Hc	Zn	◆ SIRIUS Hc	Zn	Suhail Hc	Zn	◆ RIGIL KENT Hc	Zn	Peacock Hc	Zn	FOMALHAUT Hc	Zn	◆ Diphda Hc	Zn
60	42 39	026	41 27	058	40 18	112	24 59	170	32 28	217	31 44	262	38 27	294
61	42 54	024	41 57	057	40 52	111	25 06	169	32 06	216	31 08	261	37 54	293
62	43 09	023	42 27	056	41 26	111	25 13	168	31 45	216	30 33	260	37 21	292
63	43 23	022	42 57	054	41 59	110	25 21	168	31 24	215	29 57	260	36 47	291
64	43 36	020	43 26	053	42 33	110	25 28	167	31 03	215	29 21	259	36 13	290
65	43 48	019	43 55	052	43 08	109	25 36	167	30 43	214	28 46	258	35 39	289
66	43 59	018	44 23	051	43 42	108	25 45	166	30 23	214	28 11	257	35 05	288
67	44 10	016	44 51	050	44 16	108	25 53	166	30 03	213	27 36	257	34 30	287
68	44 20	015	45 18	049	44 51	107	26 02	165	29 43	213	27 01	256	33 56	286
69	44 29	014	45 45	047	45 25	106	26 12	165	29 24	212	26 26	255	33 21	285
70	44 37	012	46 11	046	46 00	106	26 21	164	29 05	212	25 51	254	32 46	284
71	44 44	011	46 37	045	46 35	105	26 31	164	28 46	211	25 16	254	32 11	283
72	44 51	010	47 02	044	47 10	105	26 41	163	28 27	211	24 41	253	31 36	283
73	44 56	008	47 27	042	47 45	104	26 52	163	28 09	210	24 07	252	31 00	282
74	45 01	007	47 51	041	48 20	103	27 03	162	27 51	210	23 33	252	30 25	281

LHA ♈	RIGEL Hc	Zn	◆ SIRIUS Hc	Zn	Suhail Hc	Zn	◆ RIGIL KENT Hc	Zn	Peacock Hc	Zn	ACHERNAR Hc	Zn	◆ Diphda Hc	Zn
75	45 05	005	48 15	040	48 55	103	27 14	162	27 33	209	61 31	241	29 49	280
76	45 08	004	48 37	039	49 30	102	27 25	161	27 16	209	60 59	241	29 14	279
77	45 10	003	49 00	037	50 05	101	27 37	161	26 59	208	60 27	241	28 38	278
78	45 11	001	49 21	036	50 41	101	27 49	160	26 42	208	59 56	240	28 02	277
79	45 11	000	49 42	034	51 16	100	28 01	160	26 25	207	59 25	240	27 26	277
80	45 10	358	50 02	033	51 52	099	28 14	159	26 09	206	58 53	240	26 51	276
81	45 09	357	50 21	032	52 28	099	28 27	159	25 53	206	58 22	239	26 15	275
82	45 07	356	50 40	030	53 03	098	28 40	158	25 37	205	57 51	239	25 39	274
83	45 03	354	50 57	029	53 39	097	28 54	158	25 22	205	57 20	239	25 03	273
84	44 59	353	51 14	027	54 15	097	29 07	157	25 07	204	56 49	239	24 27	272
85	44 54	351	51 31	026	54 51	096	29 21	157	24 52	204	56 19	238	23 50	272
86	44 48	350	51 46	024	55 27	095	29 36	156	24 38	203	55 48	238	23 14	271
87	44 42	349	52 00	023	56 03	094	29 50	156	24 24	203	55 17	238	22 38	270
88	44 34	347	52 14	021	56 39	094	30 05	155	24 10	202	54 47	237	22 02	269
89	44 26	346	52 27	020	57 15	093	30 20	155	23 57	202	54 17	237	21 26	268

LHA ♈	PROCYON Hc	Zn	◆ Suhail Hc	Zn	RIGIL KENT Hc	Zn	◆ Peacock Hc	Zn	ACHERNAR Hc	Zn	◆ RIGEL Hc	Zn	BETELGEUSE Hc	Zn
90	28 06	029	57 51	092	30 36	154	23 44	201	53 46	237	44 16	344	29 35	359
91	28 23	027	58 27	091	30 52	154	23 31	200	53 16	236	44 06	343	29 34	358
92	28 39	026	59 03	091	31 08	153	23 18	200	52 46	236	43 55	342	29 32	357
93	28 55	025	59 39	090	31 24	153	23 06	199	52 17	236	43 44	340	29 30	355
94	29 10	024	60 15	089	31 40	153	22 55	199	51 47	235	43 31	339	29 26	354
95	29 24	023	60 52	088	31 57	152	22 43	198	51 17	235	43 18	338	29 23	353
96	29 38	022	61 28	087	32 14	152	22 32	198	50 48	234	43 04	336	29 18	352
97	29 51	021	62 04	086	32 32	151	22 21	197	50 19	234	42 49	335	29 13	351
98	30 04	020	62 40	086	32 49	151	22 11	197	49 49	234	42 33	334	29 06	350
99	30 15	019	63 16	085	33 07	150	22 01	196	49 20	233	42 17	333	29 00	349
100	30 27	017	63 52	084	33 25	150	21 51	195	48 52	233	42 00	331	28 52	348
101	30 37	016	64 27	083	33 43	149	21 41	195	48 23	233	41 42	330	28 44	346
102	30 47	015	65 03	082	34 02	149	21 32	194	47 54	232	41 24	329	28 35	345
103	30 56	014	65 39	081	34 21	148	21 24	194	47 26	232	41 05	327	28 26	344
104	31 04	013	66 15	080	34 40	148	21 15	193	46 58	231	40 45	326	28 16	343

LHA ♈	PROCYON Hc	Zn	REGULUS Hc	Zn	◆ Gienah Hc	Zn	RIGIL KENT Hc	Zn	◆ ACHERNAR Hc	Zn	RIGEL Hc	Zn	◆ SIRIUS Hc	Zn
105	31 12	012	13 35	048	20 29	092	34 59	147	46 29	231	40 25	325	53 38	354
106	31 19	011	14 01	047	21 05	092	35 19	147	46 01	231	40 04	324	53 34	353
107	31 25	009	14 28	046	21 41	091	35 38	147	45 34	230	39 42	323	53 29	351
108	31 31	008	14 53	045	22 17	090	35 58	146	45 06	230	39 20	321	53 23	349
109	31 36	007	15 19	044	22 53	089	36 19	146	44 39	229	38 57	320	53 15	348
110	31 40	006	15 44	043	23 29	088	36 39	145	44 11	229	38 34	319	53 07	346
111	31 43	005	16 08	042	24 05	088	37 00	145	43 44	229	38 10	318	52 58	345
112	31 46	004	16 32	041	24 41	087	37 21	144	43 17	228	37 45	317	52 48	343
113	31 47	002	16 56	040	25 17	086	37 42	144	42 50	228	37 20	316	52 37	342
114	31 48	001	17 19	039	25 53	085	38 03	144	42 24	227	36 55	314	52 25	340
115	31 49	000	17 42	038	26 29	084	38 24	143	41 57	227	36 29	313	52 13	339
116	31 49	359	18 04	038	27 05	083	38 46	143	41 31	226	36 02	312	51 59	337
117	31 47	358	18 26	037	27 41	083	39 08	142	41 05	226	35 35	311	51 45	336
118	31 46	357	18 47	036	28 17	082	39 30	142	40 39	226	35 08	310	51 29	334
119	31 43	355	19 08	035	28 53	081	39 53	142	40 13	225	34 40	309	51 13	333

LHA ♈	REGULUS Hc	Zn	◆ SPICA Hc	Zn	RIGIL KENT Hc	Zn	Peacock Hc	Zn	◆ ACHERNAR Hc	Zn	RIGEL Hc	Zn	◆ SIRIUS Hc	Zn
120	19 28	034	14 04	090	40 15	141	19 49	184	39 48	225	34 12	308	50 56	331
121	19 48	033	14 40	089	40 38	141	19 47	183	39 23	224	33 43	307	50 38	330
122	20 07	032	15 16	088	41 01	140	19 45	183	38 58	224	33 14	306	50 19	328
123	20 26	031	15 52	088	41 24	140	19 44	182	38 33	223	32 45	305	50 00	327
124	20 44	030	16 28	087	41 47	140	19 42	182	38 08	223	32 15	304	49 40	325
125	21 01	029	17 04	086	42 11	139	19 42	181	37 44	222	31 45	303	49 19	324
126	21 18	028	17 40	085	42 35	139	19 41	180	37 19	222	31 14	302	48 57	323
127	21 35	027	18 16	084	42 58	138	19 41	180	36 55	221	30 43	301	48 35	321
128	21 51	026	18 52	084	43 23	138	19 41	179	36 32	221	30 12	300	48 12	320
129	22 06	025	19 28	083	43 47	138	19 42	179	36 08	221	29 41	299	47 49	319
130	22 21	024	20 04	082	44 11	137	19 43	178	35 45	220	29 09	298	47 25	317
131	22 35	023	20 39	081	44 36	137	19 45	177	35 22	220	28 37	297	47 00	316
132	22 49	022	21 15	080	45 00	137	19 46	177	34 59	219	28 05	296	46 35	315
133	23 02	021	21 50	079	45 25	136	19 48	176	34 36	219	27 32	295	46 09	314
134	23 14	020	22 26	079	45 50	136	19 51	176	34 13	218	26 59	294	45 43	312

LHA ♈	◆ REGULUS Hc	Zn	SPICA Hc	Zn	◆ RIGIL KENT Hc	Zn	Peacock Hc	Zn	ACHERNAR Hc	Zn	◆ CANOPUS Hc	Zn	SIRIUS Hc	Zn
135	23 26	018	23 01	078	46 16	135	19 54	175	33 51	218	66 47	255	45 16	311
136	23 37	017	23 36	077	46 41	135	19 57	175	33 29	217	66 12	255	44 48	310
137	23 48	016	24 12	076	47 07	135	20 01	174	33 08	217	65 37	254	44 20	309
138	23 58	015	24 47	075	47 32	134	20 05	173	32 46	216	65 03	254	43 52	308
139	24 07	014	25 21	074	47 58	134	20 09	173	32 25	216	64 28	253	43 23	307
140	24 15	013	25 56	073	48 24	134	20 14	172	32 04	215	63 53	253	42 54	305
141	24 23	012	26 31	073	48 50	133	20 19	172	31 43	215	63 19	252	42 24	304
142	24 31	011	27 05	072	49 17	133	20 24	171	31 23	214	62 45	252	41 54	303
143	24 37	010	27 39	071	49 43	133	20 30	171	31 02	214	62 10	251	41 24	302
144	24 43	009	28 13	070	50 10	133	20 36	170	30 42	213	61 36	251	40 53	301
145	24 48	008	28 47	069	50 36	132	20 42	169	30 23	213	61 02	251	40 22	300
146	24 53	007	29 21	068	51 03	132	20 49	169	30 03	212	60 28	250	39 51	299
147	24 57	006	29 54	067	51 30	132	20 56	168	29 44	212	59 54	250	39 19	298
148	25 00	005	30 27	066	51 57	131	21 04	168	29 25	211	59 20	249	38 47	297
149	25 03	004	31 00	065	52 24	131	21 12	167	29 07	211	58 47	249	38 15	296

LHA ♈	◆ REGULUS Hc	Zn	SPICA Hc	Zn	◆ RIGIL KENT Hc	Zn	Peacock Hc	Zn	ACHERNAR Hc	Zn	◆ CANOPUS Hc	Zn	SIRIUS Hc	Zn
150	25 05	002	31 33	064	52 52	131	21 20	167	28 48	210	58 13	248	37 42	295
151	25 06	001	32 05	063	53 19	130	21 29	166	28 30	210	57 39	248	37 09	294
152	25 06	000	32 37	062	53 46	130	21 38	165	28 12	209	57 06	248	36 36	293
153	25 06	359	33 09	061	54 14	130	21 47	165	27 55	209	56 33	247	36 03	292
154	25 05	358	33 40	060	54 42	130	21 56	164	27 38	208	55 59	247	35 29	291
155	25 04	357	34 12	059	55 10	129	22 06	164	27 21	208	55 26	246	34 55	290
156	25 02	356	34 43	058	55 38	129	22 17	163	27 04	207	54 53	246	34 21	289
157	24 59	355	35 13	057	56 06	129	22 27	163	26 48	207	54 21	245	33 47	288
158	24 55	354	35 43	056	56 34	129	22 38	162	26 32	206	53 48	245	33 13	287
159	24 51	353	36 13	055	57 02	128	22 50	161	26 16	206	53 15	244	32 38	286
160	24 46	352	36 43	054	57 30	128	23 01	161	26 01	205	52 43	244	32 03	285
161	24 41	351	37 12	053	57 59	128	23 13	160	25 45	205	52 10	243	31 28	285
162	24 34	350	37 40	052	58 27	128	23 26	160	25 31	204	51 38	243	30 53	284
163	24 28	348	38 09	051	58 56	128	23 38	159	25 16	203	51 06	243	30 18	283
164	24 20	347	38 36	050	59 24	127	23 51	159	25 02	203	50 34	242	29 43	282

LHA ♈	◆ SPICA Hc	Zn	ANTARES Hc	Zn	◆ Peacock Hc	Zn	ACHERNAR Hc	Zn	CANOPUS Hc	Zn	◆ SIRIUS Hc	Zn	REGULUS Hc	Zn
165	39 04	049	25 11	101	24 05	158	24 48	202	50 02	242	29 08	281	24 12	346
166	39 31	048	25 46	100	24 18	158	24 34	202	49 30	241	28 32	280	24 03	345
167	39 57	046	26 22	100	24 32	157	24 21	201	48 59	241	27 56	279	23 53	344
168	40 23	045	26 57	099	24 46	156	24 08	201	48 27	240	27 21	278	23 43	343
169	40 48	044	27 33	098	25 01	156	23 56	200	47 56	240	26 45	278	23 33	342
170	41 13	043	28 09	097	25 16	155	23 43	200	47 25	239	26 09	277	23 21	341
171	41 38	042	28 45	097	25 31	155	23 31	199	46 54	239	25 33	276	23 09	340
172	42 01	041	29 21	096	25 47	154	23 20	199	46 23	238	24 57	275	22 57	339
173	42 25	039	29 57	095	26 02	154	23 08	198	45 52	238	24 21	274	22 43	338
174	42 47	038	30 33	094	26 19	153	22 57	197	45 22	237	23 45	274	22 29	337
175	43 09	037	31 09	094	26 35	153	22 47	197	44 51	237	23 09	273	22 15	336
176	43 30	036	31 45	093	26 52	152	22 36	196	44 21	237	22 33	272	22 00	335
177	43 51	034	32 21	092	27 09	152	22 26	196	43 51	236	21 57	271	21 44	334
178	44 11	033	32 57	091	27 26	151	22 17	195	43 21	236	21 21	270	21 28	333
179	44 31	032	33 33	090	27 44	151	22 07	195	42 52	235	20 45	269	21 11	332

 LAT 53°S

LHA ♈	Hc	Zn	Hc	Zn	Hc	Zn	Hc	Zn	Hc	Zn	Hc	Zn	Hc	Zn
	◆ SPICA		ANTARES		◆ Peacock		ACHERNAR		CANOPUS		◆ Suhail		REGULUS	
180	44 49	030	34 09	090	28 01	150	21 59	194	42 22	235	60 25	271	20 54	331
181	45 07	029	34 45	089	28 20	150	21 50	194	41 53	234	59 49	270	20 36	330
182	45 24	028	35 21	088	28 38	149	21 42	193	41 24	234	59 13	270	20 18	329
183	45 41	026	35 57	087	28 57	149	21 34	192	40 55	233	58 37	269	19 59	328
184	45 56	025	36 33	086	29 16	148	21 26	192	40 26	233	58 01	268	19 39	327
185	46 11	024	37 09	086	29 35	147	21 19	191	39 57	232	57 25	267	19 20	326
186	46 26	022	37 45	085	29 54	147	21 12	191	39 29	232	56 49	267	18 59	325
187	46 39	021	38 21	084	30 14	146	21 06	190	39 00	231	56 13	266	18 38	324
188	46 51	020	38 57	083	30 34	146	20 59	190	38 32	231	55 37	265	18 17	323
189	47 03	018	39 33	082	30 55	145	20 54	189	38 05	230	55 01	264	17 55	322
190	47 14	017	40 09	081	31 15	145	20 48	188	37 37	230	54 25	264	17 32	321
191	47 24	015	40 44	080	31 36	144	20 43	188	37 09	229	53 49	263	17 09	320
192	47 33	014	41 20	080	31 57	144	20 38	187	36 42	229	53 13	262	16 46	319
193	47 41	012	41 55	079	32 19	143	20 34	187	36 15	228	52 38	262	16 22	318
194	47 48	011	42 31	078	32 40	143	20 30	186	35 48	228	52 02	261	15 58	317
	◆ ARCTURUS		ANTARES		◆ Peacock		ACHERNAR		CANOPUS		◆ Suhail		Denebola	
195	16 01	019	43 06	077	33 02	143	20 26	186	35 22	227	51 26	260	20 50	342
196	16 13	018	43 41	076	33 24	142	20 23	185	34 55	227	50 51	260	20 39	341
197	16 23	017	44 16	075	33 47	142	20 20	184	34 29	226	50 15	259	20 27	340
198	16 34	016	44 51	074	34 09	141	20 18	184	34 03	226	49 40	258	20 14	339
199	16 43	015	45 25	073	34 32	141	20 15	183	33 37	225	49 04	258	20 01	338
200	16 52	014	46 00	072	34 55	140	20 13	183	33 12	225	48 29	257	19 47	337
201	17 00	013	46 34	071	35 18	140	20 12	182	32 47	224	47 54	256	19 32	336
202	17 08	012	47 08	070	35 42	139	20 11	181	32 22	224	47 19	256	19 17	335
203	17 15	011	47 42	069	36 05	139	20 10	181	31 57	223	46 44	255	19 01	334
204	17 22	010	48 16	068	36 29	138	20 10	180	31 32	223	46 09	254	18 45	333
205	17 28	009	48 49	067	36 54	138	20 10	180	31 08	222	45 35	254	18 28	332
206	17 33	008	49 22	066	37 18	137	20 10	179	30 44	222	45 00	253	18 11	331
207	17 38	007	49 55	065	37 43	137	20 11	179	30 20	221	44 26	252	17 53	330
208	17 42	006	50 27	064	38 07	136	20 12	178	29 57	220	43 51	252	17 35	329
209	17 46	005	50 59	062	38 32	136	20 13	177	29 33	220	43 17	251	17 16	328
	◆ ARCTURUS		ANTARES		◆ Peacock		ACHERNAR		CANOPUS		◆ Suhail		SPICA	
210	17 48	004	51 31	061	38 58	135	20 15	177	29 10	219	42 43	251	47 41	348
211	17 51	003	52 03	060	39 23	135	20 17	176	28 48	219	42 09	250	47 33	346
212	17 52	002	52 34	059	39 49	135	20 20	176	28 25	218	41 35	249	47 24	345
213	17 53	001	53 05	058	40 15	134	20 23	175	28 03	218	41 01	249	47 14	343
214	17 54	000	53 35	057	40 41	134	20 26	175	27 41	217	40 28	248	47 03	342
215	17 53	359	54 05	055	41 07	133	20 29	174	27 19	217	39 54	248	46 51	340
216	17 53	358	54 34	054	41 33	133	20 33	173	26 58	216	39 21	247	46 39	339
217	17 51	357	55 03	053	42 00	132	20 38	173	26 37	216	38 48	246	46 25	338
218	17 49	356	55 32	051	42 27	132	20 42	172	26 16	215	38 15	246	46 11	336
219	17 46	355	56 00	050	42 54	131	20 47	172	25 55	214	37 42	245	45 56	335
220	17 43	354	56 27	049	43 21	131	20 53	171	25 35	214	37 09	245	45 41	334
221	17 39	353	56 54	047	43 48	131	20 59	171	25 15	213	36 37	244	45 24	332
222	17 34	352	57 20	046	44 15	130	21 05	170	24 55	213	36 04	243	45 07	331
223	17 29	351	57 46	044	44 43	130	21 11	169	24 36	212	35 32	243	44 49	330
224	17 23	350	58 10	043	45 11	129	21 18	169	24 17	212	35 00	242	44 30	328
	ANTARES		◆ Nunki		Peacock		ACHERNAR		◆ CANOPUS		Suhail		◆ SPICA	
225	58 35	041	39 08	082	45 39	129	21 25	168	23 58	211	34 28	242	44 11	327
226	58 58	040	39 44	082	46 07	129	21 33	168	23 39	210	33 56	241	43 51	326
227	59 21	038	40 19	081	46 35	128	21 41	167	23 21	210	33 25	240	43 30	324
228	59 43	037	40 55	080	47 04	128	21 49	167	23 03	209	32 54	240	43 09	323
229	60 04	035	41 30	079	47 33	127	21 57	166	22 46	209	32 23	239	42 47	322
230	60 24	033	42 06	078	48 01	127	22 06	165	22 29	208	31 52	239	42 24	321
231	60 43	031	42 41	077	48 30	127	22 15	165	22 12	208	31 21	238	42 01	319
232	61 02	030	43 16	076	48 59	126	22 25	164	21 55	207	30 51	237	41 37	318
233	61 19	028	43 51	075	49 29	126	22 35	164	21 39	206	30 20	237	41 13	317
234	61 36	026	44 26	074	49 58	125	22 45	163	21 23	206	29 50	236	40 48	316
235	61 51	024	45 01	073	50 27	125	22 56	163	21 08	205	29 20	236	40 23	315
236	62 05	023	45 35	072	50 57	125	23 07	162	20 52	205	28 51	235	39 57	314
237	62 19	021	46 09	071	51 27	124	23 18	162	20 37	204	28 21	234	39 30	312
238	62 31	019	46 44	070	51 57	124	23 30	161	20 23	203	27 52	234	39 04	311
239	62 42	017	47 17	069	52 27	124	23 42	160	20 09	203	27 23	233	38 36	310
	◆ ANTARES		Nunki		◆ FOMALHAUT		ACHERNAR		CANOPUS		◆ ACRUX		SPICA	
240	62 52	015	47 51	068	15 10	119	23 54	160	19 55	202	61 07	228	38 08	309
241	63 01	013	48 25	067	15 42	119	24 06	159	19 41	202	60 40	228	37 40	308
242	63 08	011	48 58	066	16 13	118	24 19	159	19 28	201	60 13	228	37 11	307
243	63 15	009	49 31	065	16 45	117	24 33	158	19 15	201	59 46	228	36 42	306
244	63 20	007	50 03	064	17 18	116	24 46	158	19 03	200	59 19	228	36 13	305
245	63 24	005	50 36	063	17 50	116	25 00	157	18 51	199	58 53	228	35 43	304
246	63 26	003	51 07	062	18 23	115	25 14	157	18 39	199	58 26	228	35 13	303
247	63 28	001	51 39	061	18 56	114	25 29	156	18 27	198	57 59	228	34 42	302
248	63 28	359	52 10	059	19 29	114	25 43	156	18 16	197	57 33	227	34 11	301
249	63 27	357	52 41	058	20 02	113	25 58	155	18 06	197	57 06	227	33 40	300
250	63 24	355	53 12	057	20 35	112	26 14	154	17 56	196	56 40	227	33 09	299
251	63 20	353	53 42	056	21 09	111	26 30	154	17 46	196	56 13	227	32 37	298
252	63 16	351	54 11	054	21 42	111	26 46	153	17 36	195	55 47	227	32 05	297
253	63 09	349	54 40	053	22 16	110	27 02	153	17 27	194	55 21	227	31 32	296
254	63 02	347	55 09	052	22 50	109	27 18	152	17 18	194	54 54	226	31 00	295
	ALTAIR		◆ FOMALHAUT		ACHERNAR		CANOPUS		◆ ACRUX		SPICA		◆ ANTARES	
255	18 11	045	23 24	109	27 35	152	17 10	193	54 28	226	30 27	294	62 53	345
256	18 36	044	23 59	108	27 53	151	17 02	193	54 02	226	29 54	293	62 44	343
257	19 01	043	24 33	107	28 10	151	16 54	192	53 37	226	29 20	292	62 33	341
258	19 26	042	25 08	106	28 28	150	16 47	191	53 11	225	28 47	291	62 21	340
259	19 50	041	25 42	106	28 46	150	16 40	191	52 45	225	28 13	290	62 08	338
260	20 13	040	26 17	105	29 04	149	16 33	190	52 20	225	27 39	289	61 53	336
261	20 36	039	26 52	104	29 23	149	16 27	189	51 54	225	27 05	288	61 38	334
262	20 59	038	27 27	104	29 42	148	16 21	189	51 29	224	26 30	287	61 22	332
263	21 21	037	28 02	103	30 01	148	16 16	188	51 04	224	25 56	287	61 05	331
264	21 43	036	28 38	102	30 20	147	16 11	188	50 38	224	25 21	286	60 46	329
265	22 04	035	29 13	101	30 40	147	16 07	187	50 13	224	24 46	285	60 27	327
266	22 24	034	29 48	101	31 00	146	16 02	186	49 49	223	24 11	284	60 07	325
267	22 45	033	30 24	100	31 20	146	15 59	186	49 24	223	23 36	283	59 46	324
268	23 04	032	31 00	099	31 40	145	15 55	185	48 59	223	23 01	282	59 24	322
269	23 23	031	31 35	098	32 01	145	15 52	184	48 35	222	22 26	281	59 02	321

LHA ♈	Hc	Zn	Hc	Zn	Hc	Zn	Hc	Zn	Hc	Zn	Hc	Zn	Hc	Zn
	◆ ALTAIR		FOMALHAUT		◆ ACHERNAR		CANOPUS		RIGIL KENT		◆ SPICA		ANTARES	
270	23 42	030	32 11	098	32 22	144	15 50	184	62 27	233	21 50	281	58 39	319
271	24 00	029	32 47	097	32 43	144	15 47	183	61 58	233	21 15	280	58 15	317
272	24 17	028	33 23	096	33 05	143	15 46	183	61 29	233	20 39	279	57 50	316
273	24 34	027	33 59	095	33 26	143	15 44	182	61 00	233	20 03	278	57 24	314
274	24 50	026	34 35	095	33 48	142	15 43	181	60 31	233	19 27	277	56 58	313
275	25 06	025	35 11	094	34 10	142	15 42	181	60 02	233	18 52	276	56 32	312
276	25 21	024	35 47	093	34 33	141	15 42	180	59 34	233	18 16	276	56 04	310
277	25 35	023	36 23	092	34 56	141	15 42	179	59 05	232	17 40	275	55 36	309
278	25 49	022	36 59	092	35 18	140	15 43	179	58 36	232	17 04	274	55 08	308
279	26 02	021	37 35	091	35 42	140	15 44	178	58 08	232	16 28	273	54 39	306
280	26 15	020	38 11	090	36 05	140	15 45	178	57 39	232	15 52	272	54 10	305
281	26 26	019	38 47	089	36 28	139	15 47	177	57 11	232	15 16	272	53 40	304
282	26 38	018	39 23	088	36 52	139	15 49	176	56 43	231	14 39	271	53 10	302
283	26 48	017	39 59	087	37 16	138	15 52	176	56 15	231	14 03	270	52 39	301
284	26 58	015	40 35	087	37 40	138	15 55	175	55 47	231	13 27	269	52 08	300
	◆ ALTAIR		FOMALHAUT		◆ ACHERNAR		CANOPUS		◆ RIGIL KENT		ANTARES		Rasalhague	
285	27 07	014	41 11	086	38 05	137	15 58	174	55 19	231	51 37	299	22 00	338
286	27 16	013	41 47	085	38 29	137	16 02	174	54 51	230	51 05	298	21 46	337
287	27 24	012	42 23	084	38 54	136	16 06	173	54 23	230	50 33	297	21 31	336
288	27 31	011	42 59	083	39 19	136	16 10	173	53 55	230	50 00	295	21 16	335
289	27 38	010	43 35	082	39 45	135	16 15	172	53 28	230	49 27	294	21 00	334
290	27 44	009	44 11	082	40 10	135	16 21	171	53 00	229	48 54	293	20 44	333
291	27 49	008	44 47	081	40 36	135	16 26	171	52 33	229	48 21	292	20 27	332
292	27 53	007	45 22	080	41 02	134	16 32	170	52 06	229	47 48	291	20 10	331
293	27 57	005	45 58	079	41 28	134	16 39	169	51 39	228	47 14	290	19 52	330
294	28 00	004	46 33	078	41 54	133	16 46	169	51 12	228	46 40	289	19 33	329
295	28 03	003	47 08	077	42 20	133	16 53	168	50 45	228	46 05	288	19 14	328
296	28 04	002	47 43	076	42 47	132	17 00	168	50 18	228	45 31	287	18 55	327
297	28 05	001	48 18	075	43 13	132	17 08	167	49 51	227	44 56	286	18 35	326
298	28 05	000	48 53	074	43 40	132	17 17	166	49 25	227	44 22	285	18 14	325
299	28 05	359	49 28	073	44 08	131	17 26	166	48 59	227	43 47	284	17 53	324
	FOMALHAUT		◆ ACHERNAR		CANOPUS		◆ RIGIL KENT		ANTARES		Nunki		◆ ALTAIR	
300	50 02	072	44 35	131	17 35	165	48 32	226	43 12	283	60 44	330	28 04	358
301	50 36	071	45 02	130	17 44	164	48 06	226	42 37	282	60 26	328	28 02	357
302	51 10	070	45 30	130	17 54	164	47 41	226	42 01	281	60 06	326	27 59	355
303	51 44	069	45 58	129	18 04	163	47 15	225	41 26	281	59 46	325	27 56	354
304	52 18	068	46 26	129	18 15	163	46 49	225	40 50	280	59 24	323	27 52	353
305	52 51	067	46 54	129	18 26	162	46 24	225	40 15	279	59 02	321	27 48	352
306	53 24	066	47 22	128	18 37	161	45 58	224	39 39	278	58 39	320	27 42	351
307	53 57	064	47 50	128	18 49	161	45 33	224	39 03	277	58 16	318	27 36	350
308	54 29	063	48 19	128	19 01	160	45 08	224	38 27	276	57 51	317	27 30	349
309	55 01	062	48 48	127	19 13	160	44 44	223	37 51	275	57 26	315	27 22	348
310	55 33	061	49 17	127	19 26	159	44 19	223	37 15	275	57 01	314	27 14	347
311	56 05	060	49 46	126	19 39	158	43 54	222	36 39	274	56 34	312	27 05	345
312	56 36	058	50 15	126	19 53	158	43 30	222	36 03	273	56 07	311	26 56	344
313	57 06	057	50 44	126	20 07	157	43 06	222	35 27	272	55 40	310	26 46	343
314	57 36	056	51 13	125	20 21	157	42 42	221	34 51	271	55 12	308	26 35	342
	◆ FOMALHAUT		ACHERNAR		◆ CANOPUS		RIGIL KENT		◆ ANTARES		Nunki		ALTAIR	
315	58 06	054	51 43	125	20 35	156	42 18	221	34 15	270	54 43	307	26 24	341
316	58 35	053	52 13	125	20 50	155	41 55	221	33 39	270	54 14	306	26 12	340
317	59 04	052	52 42	124	21 05	155	41 31	220	33 03	269	53 45	304	25 59	339
318	59 32	050	53 12	124	21 21	154	41 08	220	32 27	268	53 15	303	25 46	338
319	59 59	049	53 42	123	21 37	154	40 45	219	31 51	267	52 44	302	25 32	337
320	60 26	047	54 13	123	21 53	153	40 22	219	31 14	266	52 13	301	25 17	336
321	60 52	046	54 43	123	22 09	152	40 00	219	30 38	266	51 42	300	25 02	335
322	61 18	044	55 13	122	22 26	152	39 37	218	30 02	265	51 11	298	24 46	334
323	61 42	043	55 44	122	22 43	151	39 15	218	29 27	264	50 39	297	24 30	333
324	62 06	041	56 14	122	23 01	151	38 53	217	28 51	263	50 06	296	24 13	332
325	62 30	039	56 45	121	23 19	150	38 31	217	28 15	263	49 34	295	23 55	330
326	62 52	038	57 16	121	23 37	150	38 10	217	27 39	262	49 01	294	23 37	329
327	63 14	036	57 47	121	23 55	149	37 48	216	27 03	261	48 28	293	23 19	328
328	63 34	034	58 18	121	24 14	148	37 27	216	26 28	260	47 54	292	22 59	327
329	63 54	032	58 49	120	24 33	148	37 06	215	25 52	260	47 21	291	22 40	326
	◆ FOMALHAUT		ACHERNAR		◆ CANOPUS		RIGIL KENT		◆ ANTARES		Nunki		ALTAIR	
330	64 13	030	59 20	120	24 52	147	36 46	215	25 17	259	46 47	290	22 20	325
331	64 30	028	59 52	120	25 12	147	36 25	214	24 41	258	46 13	289	21 59	324
332	64 47	026	60 23	119	25 32	146	36 05	214	24 06	257	45 39	288	21 37	323
333	65 03	025	60 55	119	25 52	146	35 45	214	23 31	257	45 04	287	21 16	322
334	65 17	023	61 26	119	26 13	145	35 25	213	22 56	256	44 29	286	20 53	321
335	65 30	021	61 58	119	26 34	145	35 05	213	22 21	255	43 55	285	20 31	320
336	65 42	018	62 30	118	26 55	144	34 46	212	21 46	254	43 20	284	20 07	319
337	65 53	016	63 02	118	27 16	143	34 27	212	21 11	254	42 44	283	19 44	318
338	66 03	014	63 33	118	27 38	143	34 08	211	20 36	253	42 09	282	19 20	318
339	66 11	012	64 05	118	28 00	142	33 49	211	20 02	252	41 34	281	18 55	317
340	66 18	010	64 37	117	28 22	142	33 31	210	19 28	252	40 58	280	18 30	316
341	66 24	008	65 10	117	28 44	141	33 13	210	18 54	251	40 23	279	18 05	315
342	66 28	006	65 42	117	29 07	141	32 55	209	18 19	250	39 47	278	17 39	314
343	66 31	004	66 14	117	29 30	140	32 37	209	17 46	249	39 11	278	17 12	313
344	66 32	001	66 46	117	29 53	140	32 20	209	17 12	249	38 36	277	16 46	312
	◆ Diphda		Acamar		◆ CANOPUS		Miaplacidus		RIGIL KENT		◆ Nunki		FOMALHAUT	
345	49 27	040	48 23	097	30 17	139	34 18	169	32 03	208	38 00	276	66 32	359
346	49 50	039	48 59	096	30 41	139	34 25	169	31 46	208	37 24	275	66 31	357
347	50 12	037	49 35	096	31 05	138	34 32	168	31 29	207	36 48	274	66 29	355
348	50 34	036	50 11	095	31 29	138	34 39	168	31 13	207	36 12	273	66 25	353
349	50 55	035	50 47	094	31 53	137	34 47	168	30 57	206	35 36	273	66 19	350
350	51 15	033	51 23	093	32 18	136	34 55	167	30 41	206	35 00	272	66 13	348
351	51 34	032	51 59	093	32 43	136	35 03	167	30 25	205	34 23	271	66 05	346
352	51 53	030	52 35	092	33 08	135	35 11	166	30 10	205	33 47	270	65 56	344
353	52 11	029	53 11	091	33 34	135	35 20	166	29 55	204	33 11	269	65 45	342
354	52 28	027	53 47	090	33 59	134	35 29	165	29 40	204	32 35	269	65 33	340
355	52 44	026	54 24	089	34 25	134	35 38	165	29 26	203	31 59	268	65 20	338
356	52 59	024	55 00	089	34 52	133	35 47	165	29 12	203	31 23	267	65 06	336
357	53 13	023	55 36	088	35 18	133	35 57	165	28 58	202	30 47	266	64 51	334
358	53 27	021	56 12	087	35 44	132	36 06	164	28 44	202	30 11	265	64 34	332
359	53 40	020	56 48	086	36 11	132	36 16	164	28 31	201	29 35	265	64 17	330

 LAT 54°S

LHA ♈	Hc	Zn	Hc	Zn	Hc	Zn	Hc	Zn	Hc	Zn	Hc	Zn	Hc	Zn
	Diphda		◆ RIGEL		CANOPUS		Miaplacidus		◆ RIGIL KENT		Peacock		◆ FOMALHAUT	
0	52 54	018	13 11	086	37 18	131	37 24	163	29 14	201	60 21	243	63 07	329
1	53 04	016	13 46	085	37 45	130	37 34	163	29 01	201	59 49	243	62 49	328
2	53 14	015	14 21	084	38 12	130	37 45	162	28 49	200	59 18	242	62 29	326
3	53 22	013	14 56	083	38 39	129	37 56	162	28 37	200	58 47	242	62 09	324
4	53 29	011	15 31	082	39 06	129	38 07	162	28 26	199	58 16	241	61 48	322
5	53 36	010	16 06	082	39 34	128	38 18	161	28 14	199	57 45	241	61 26	321
6	53 41	008	16 41	081	40 02	128	38 29	161	28 03	198	57 14	241	61 03	319
7	53 46	007	17 16	080	40 30	127	38 41	161	27 52	198	56 44	240	60 40	317
8	53 50	005	17 50	079	40 58	127	38 53	160	27 42	197	56 13	240	60 16	316
9	53 52	003	18 25	078	41 26	126	39 05	160	27 32	196	55 42	240	59 51	314
10	53 54	002	19 00	077	41 55	126	39 17	159	27 22	196	55 12	239	59 25	313
11	53 54	000	19 34	077	42 23	125	39 29	159	27 12	195	54 42	239	58 59	311
12	53 54	359	20 08	076	42 52	125	39 42	159	27 03	195	54 12	239	58 32	310
13	53 52	357	20 42	075	43 21	124	39 55	158	26 54	194	53 42	238	58 05	309
14	53 50	355	21 16	074	43 51	124	40 08	158	26 46	194	53 12	238	57 37	307
	◆ RIGEL		SIRIUS		CANOPUS		◆ RIGIL KENT		Peacock		◆ FOMALHAUT		Diphda	
15	21 50	073	15 32	097	44 20	123	26 37	193	52 42	237	57 09	306	53 47	354
16	22 24	072	16 07	096	44 50	123	26 29	193	52 12	237	56 40	304	53 42	352
17	22 57	071	16 42	096	45 20	122	26 22	192	51 43	237	56 11	303	53 37	350
18	23 31	070	17 17	095	45 49	122	26 14	192	51 13	236	55 41	302	53 31	349
19	24 04	070	17 52	094	46 20	121	26 07	191	50 44	236	55 11	301	53 23	347
20	24 37	069	18 28	093	46 50	121	26 00	191	50 15	235	54 40	299	53 15	346
21	25 09	068	19 03	092	47 20	120	25 54	190	49 46	235	54 09	298	53 06	344
22	25 42	067	19 38	092	47 51	120	25 48	190	49 17	235	53 38	297	52 56	343
23	26 14	066	20 13	091	48 21	119	25 42	189	48 49	234	53 06	296	52 45	341
24	26 46	065	20 49	090	48 52	119	25 37	189	48 20	234	52 35	295	52 33	340
25	27 18	064	21 24	089	49 23	118	25 32	188	47 52	233	52 02	294	52 20	338
26	27 50	063	21 59	088	49 54	118	25 27	188	47 24	233	51 30	293	52 07	336
27	28 21	062	22 34	088	50 26	117	25 22	187	46 56	232	50 57	291	51 52	335
28	28 52	061	23 10	087	50 57	117	25 18	187	46 28	232	50 24	290	51 37	334
29	29 23	060	23 45	086	51 29	116	25 14	186	46 00	232	49 51	289	51 21	332
	◆ RIGEL		SIRIUS		CANOPUS		◆ RIGIL KENT		Peacock		FOMALHAUT		◆ Diphda	
30	29 53	059	24 20	085	52 00	116	25 11	185	45 33	231	49 18	288	51 04	331
31	30 23	058	24 55	084	52 32	115	25 08	185	45 05	231	48 44	287	50 46	329
32	30 53	057	25 30	083	53 04	115	25 05	184	44 38	230	48 10	286	50 28	328
33	31 23	056	26 05	083	53 36	114	25 02	184	44 11	230	47 36	285	50 08	326
34	31 52	055	26 40	082	54 08	114	25 00	183	43 44	229	47 02	284	49 49	325
35	32 21	054	27 15	081	54 40	113	24 58	183	43 17	229	46 28	283	49 28	324
36	32 49	053	27 50	080	55 13	113	24 57	182	42 51	229	45 54	282	49 07	322
37	33 17	052	28 24	079	55 45	113	24 55	182	42 25	228	45 19	281	48 45	321
38	33 45	051	28 59	078	56 18	112	24 55	181	41 58	228	44 45	281	48 22	320
39	34 12	050	29 34	077	56 51	112	24 54	181	41 32	227	44 10	280	47 59	318
40	34 39	049	30 08	077	57 24	111	24 54	180	41 07	227	43 35	279	47 35	317
41	35 05	048	30 42	076	57 56	111	24 54	180	40 41	226	43 00	278	47 11	316
42	35 31	047	31 16	075	58 30	110	24 54	179	40 16	226	42 25	277	46 46	314
43	35 57	046	31 50	074	59 03	110	24 55	178	39 51	225	41 50	276	46 21	313
44	36 22	045	32 24	073	59 36	109	24 56	178	39 26	225	41 15	275	45 55	312
	RIGEL		◆ SIRIUS		CANOPUS		◆ RIGIL KENT		Peacock		FOMALHAUT		◆ Diphda	
45	36 46	043	32 58	072	60 09	109	24 58	177	39 01	224	40 40	274	45 28	311
46	37 10	042	33 31	071	60 43	108	24 59	177	38 36	224	40 05	274	45 01	310
47	37 34	041	34 04	070	61 16	108	25 01	176	38 12	223	39 30	273	44 34	308
48	37 56	040	34 37	069	61 50	107	25 04	176	37 48	223	38 54	272	44 06	307
49	38 19	039	35 10	068	62 24	107	25 07	175	37 24	222	38 19	271	43 38	306
50	38 41	038	35 43	067	62 58	106	25 10	175	37 00	222	37 44	270	43 09	305
51	39 02	036	36 15	066	63 31	106	25 13	174	36 37	222	37 08	269	42 40	304
52	39 23	035	36 48	065	64 05	105	25 17	174	36 13	221	36 33	269	42 10	303
53	39 43	034	37 19	064	64 39	105	25 21	173	35 50	221	35 58	268	41 41	302
54	40 02	033	37 51	063	65 14	104	25 25	173	35 27	220	35 23	267	41 10	301
55	40 21	032	38 22	062	65 48	104	25 30	172	35 05	220	34 48	266	40 40	300
56	40 39	030	38 54	061	66 22	103	25 35	172	34 43	219	34 12	265	40 09	298
57	40 57	029	39 24	060	66 56	103	25 40	171	34 20	219	33 37	265	39 38	297
58	41 13	028	39 55	059	67 31	102	25 46	170	33 59	218	33 02	264	39 06	296
59	41 30	027	40 25	058	68 05	102	25 52	170	33 37	218	32 27	263	38 35	295
	RIGEL		◆ SIRIUS		Suhail		◆ RIGIL KENT		Peacock		FOMALHAUT		◆ Diphda	
60	41 45	025	40 55	057	40 40	111	25 58	169	33 15	217	31 52	262	38 03	294
61	42 00	024	41 24	056	41 13	111	26 05	169	32 54	217	31 17	262	37 31	293
62	42 14	023	41 53	055	41 46	110	26 12	168	32 33	216	30 42	261	36 58	292
63	42 27	021	42 22	054	42 20	109	26 19	168	32 13	216	30 08	260	36 25	291
64	42 40	020	42 50	053	42 53	109	26 27	167	31 52	215	29 33	259	35 52	290
65	42 51	019	43 18	051	43 27	108	26 35	167	31 32	215	28 58	259	35 19	290
66	43 02	017	43 45	050	44 00	107	26 43	166	31 12	214	28 24	258	34 46	289
67	43 13	016	44 12	049	44 34	107	26 51	166	30 53	214	27 49	257	34 12	288
68	43 22	015	44 38	048	45 08	106	27 00	165	30 33	213	27 15	256	33 39	287
69	43 31	013	45 04	047	45 42	105	27 09	165	30 14	213	26 41	256	33 05	286
70	43 38	012	45 30	045	46 16	105	27 19	164	29 55	212	26 07	255	32 31	285
71	43 45	011	45 54	044	46 50	104	27 29	164	29 37	211	25 33	254	31 57	284
72	43 51	009	46 19	043	47 24	103	27 39	163	29 19	211	24 59	253	31 22	283
73	43 57	008	46 43	042	47 58	103	27 49	163	29 01	210	24 25	253	30 48	282
74	44 01	007	47 06	040	48 33	102	28 00	162	28 43	210	23 51	252	30 13	281
	RIGEL		◆ SIRIUS		Suhail		◆ RIGIL KENT		Peacock		ACHERNAR		◆ Diphda	
75	44 05	005	47 28	039	49 07	101	28 11	162	28 26	209	61 59	243	29 39	280
76	44 08	004	47 50	038	49 42	101	28 22	161	28 08	209	61 27	243	29 04	280
77	44 10	003	48 12	036	50 17	100	28 34	161	27 52	208	60 56	242	28 29	279
78	44 11	001	48 32	035	50 51	099	28 45	160	27 35	208	60 25	242	27 54	278
79	44 11	000	48 52	034	51 26	099	28 58	160	27 19	207	59 54	242	27 19	277
80	44 11	358	49 11	032	52 01	098	29 10	159	27 03	207	59 23	241	26 44	276
81	44 09	357	49 30	031	52 36	097	29 23	159	26 47	206	58 52	241	26 09	275
82	44 07	356	49 48	030	53 11	097	29 36	158	26 32	206	58 21	241	25 34	275
83	44 04	354	50 05	028	53 46	096	29 49	158	26 17	205	57 51	240	24 59	274
84	44 00	353	50 21	027	54 21	095	30 03	157	26 02	204	57 20	240	24 24	273
85	43 55	351	50 36	025	54 56	094	30 16	157	25 47	204	56 50	240	23 49	272
86	43 49	350	50 51	024	55 32	094	30 31	156	25 33	203	56 19	239	23 13	271
87	43 43	349	51 05	022	56 07	093	30 45	156	25 19	203	55 49	239	22 38	270
88	43 36	347	51 18	021	56 42	092	31 00	155	25 06	202	55 19	238	22 03	270
89	43 27	346	51 30	019	57 17	091	31 15	155	24 53	202	54 49	238	21 27	269

LHA ♈	Hc	Zn	Hc	Zn	Hc	Zn	Hc	Zn	Hc	Zn	Hc	Zn	Hc	Zn
	PROCYON		◆ Suhail		RIGIL KENT		◆ Peacock		ACHERNAR		◆ RIGEL		BETELGEUSE	
90	27 13	028	57 52	091	31 30	154	24 40	201	54 19	238	43 19	345	28 35	359
91	27 29	027	58 28	090	31 45	154	24 27	201	53 49	237	43 09	343	28 34	358
92	27 45	026	59 03	089	32 01	153	24 15	200	53 20	237	42 58	342	28 32	357
93	28 00	025	59 38	088	32 17	153	24 03	199	52 50	237	42 47	341	28 30	355
94	28 15	024	60 14	087	32 34	152	23 51	199	52 21	236	42 35	339	28 27	354
95	28 29	023	60 49	086	32 50	152	23 40	198	51 52	236	42 22	338	28 23	353
96	28 42	022	61 24	086	33 07	151	23 29	198	51 22	235	42 09	337	28 18	352
97	28 55	021	61 59	085	33 24	151	23 18	197	50 53	235	41 54	335	28 13	351
98	29 07	019	62 34	084	33 41	150	23 08	197	50 25	235	41 39	334	28 07	350
99	29 19	018	63 09	083	33 59	150	22 58	196	49 56	234	41 24	333	28 01	349
100	29 29	017	63 44	082	34 17	149	22 49	196	49 27	234	41 07	332	27 54	348
101	29 39	016	64 19	081	34 35	149	22 39	195	48 59	233	40 50	330	27 46	347
102	29 49	015	64 54	080	34 53	148	22 30	194	48 31	233	40 32	329	27 37	345
103	29 58	014	65 28	079	35 12	148	22 22	194	48 03	233	40 14	328	27 28	344
104	30 06	013	66 03	078	35 31	148	22 14	193	47 35	232	39 55	327	27 18	343
	PROCYON		REGULUS		◆ Gienah		RIGIL KENT		◆ ACHERNAR		RIGEL		◆ SIRIUS	
105	30 13	012	12 54	048	20 31	092	35 50	147	47 07	232	39 35	325	52 38	354
106	30 20	010	13 20	047	21 06	091	36 09	147	46 39	231	39 15	324	52 34	353
107	30 26	009	13 46	046	21 41	090	36 28	146	46 12	231	38 54	323	52 29	351
108	30 31	008	14 11	045	22 17	090	36 48	146	45 44	231	38 33	322	52 23	350
109	30 36	007	14 35	044	22 52	089	37 08	145	45 17	230	38 11	321	52 17	348
110	30 40	006	15 00	043	23 27	088	37 28	145	44 50	230	37 48	320	52 09	347
111	30 43	005	15 24	042	24 02	087	37 49	144	44 24	229	37 25	318	52 00	345
112	30 46	004	15 47	041	24 38	086	38 09	144	43 57	229	37 01	317	51 51	344
113	30 47	002	16 10	040	25 13	085	38 30	144	43 30	228	36 37	316	51 40	342
114	30 48	001	16 32	039	25 48	085	38 51	143	43 04	228	36 12	315	51 29	340
115	30 49	000	16 55	038	26 23	084	39 12	143	42 38	227	35 47	314	51 17	339
116	30 49	359	17 16	037	26 58	083	39 34	142	42 12	227	35 22	313	51 04	337
117	30 47	358	17 37	036	27 33	082	39 55	142	41 46	227	34 55	312	50 50	336
118	30 46	357	17 58	035	28 08	081	40 17	141	41 21	226	34 29	311	50 35	335
119	30 43	355	18 18	034	28 43	080	40 39	141	40 56	226	34 02	310	50 20	333
	REGULUS		◆ SPICA		RIGIL KENT		Peacock		◆ ACHERNAR		RIGEL		◆ SIRIUS	
120	18 38	033	14 04	090	41 02	141	20 49	184	40 30	225	33 35	309	50 03	332
121	18 57	033	14 39	089	41 24	140	20 47	183	40 06	225	33 07	307	49 46	330
122	19 16	032	15 14	088	41 47	140	20 45	183	39 41	224	32 39	306	49 28	329
123	19 34	031	15 49	087	42 10	139	20 44	182	39 16	224	32 10	305	49 10	327
124	19 52	030	16 25	087	42 33	139	20 42	182	38 52	223	31 41	304	48 50	326
125	20 09	029	17 00	086	42 56	139	20 42	181	38 28	223	31 12	303	48 30	325
126	20 25	028	17 35	085	43 19	138	20 41	180	38 04	222	30 42	302	48 10	323
127	20 41	027	18 10	084	43 43	138	20 41	180	37 40	222	30 12	301	47 48	322
128	20 57	026	18 45	083	44 07	137	20 41	179	37 17	222	29 42	300	47 26	321
129	21 12	025	19 20	082	44 31	137	20 42	179	36 53	221	29 11	299	47 04	319
130	21 26	024	19 55	082	44 55	137	20 43	178	36 30	221	28 41	298	46 40	318
131	21 40	022	20 30	081	45 19	136	20 44	177	36 08	220	28 09	298	46 17	317
132	21 53	021	21 05	080	45 44	136	20 46	177	35 45	220	27 38	297	45 52	316
133	22 06	020	21 39	079	46 08	135	20 48	176	35 23	219	27 06	296	45 27	314
134	22 18	019	22 14	078	46 33	135	20 51	176	35 00	219	26 34	295	45 02	313
	◆ REGULUS		SPICA		◆ RIGIL KENT		Peacock		ACHERNAR		◆ CANOPUS		SIRIUS	
135	22 29	018	22 48	077	46 58	135	20 54	175	34 39	218	67 01	257	44 36	312
136	22 40	017	23 23	076	47 23	134	20 57	175	34 17	218	66 27	257	44 09	311
137	22 50	016	23 57	076	47 49	134	21 00	174	33 55	217	65 53	256	43 42	310
138	23 00	015	24 31	075	48 14	134	21 04	173	33 34	217	65 18	256	43 15	308
139	23 09	014	25 05	074	48 40	133	21 08	173	33 13	216	64 44	255	42 47	307
140	23 17	013	25 39	073	49 05	133	21 13	172	32 53	216	64 10	255	42 19	306
141	23 25	012	26 12	072	49 31	133	21 18	172	32 32	215	63 36	254	41 50	305
142	23 32	011	26 46	071	49 57	132	21 23	171	32 12	215	63 02	254	41 21	304
143	23 38	010	27 19	070	50 23	132	21 29	170	31 52	214	62 29	253	40 52	303
144	23 44	009	27 52	069	50 50	132	21 35	170	31 32	214	61 55	253	40 22	302
145	23 49	008	28 25	068	51 16	131	21 41	169	31 13	213	61 21	252	39 52	301
146	23 53	007	28 58	067	51 43	131	21 48	169	30 54	213	60 48	252	39 21	300
147	23 57	006	29 30	067	52 09	131	21 55	168	30 35	212	60 14	251	38 51	299
148	24 00	005	30 03	066	52 36	130	22 02	168	30 16	212	59 41	251	38 19	298
149	24 03	004	30 35	065	53 03	130	22 10	167	29 58	211	59 07	250	37 48	297
	◆ REGULUS		SPICA		◆ RIGIL KENT		Peacock		ACHERNAR		◆ CANOPUS		SIRIUS	
150	24 05	002	31 06	064	53 30	130	22 18	166	29 40	211	58 34	250	37 16	296
151	24 06	001	31 38	063	53 57	129	22 27	166	29 22	210	58 01	249	36 44	295
152	24 06	000	32 09	062	54 25	129	22 36	165	29 05	210	57 28	249	36 12	294
153	24 06	359	32 40	061	54 52	129	22 45	165	28 47	209	56 55	248	35 40	293
154	24 05	358	33 10	060	55 20	129	22 54	164	28 30	208	56 23	248	35 07	292
155	24 04	357	33 41	059	55 47	128	23 04	164	28 14	208	55 50	248	34 34	291
156	24 02	356	34 11	058	56 15	128	23 14	163	27 57	207	55 17	247	34 01	290
157	23 59	355	34 40	057	56 43	128	23 25	162	27 41	207	54 45	247	33 28	289
158	23 56	354	35 10	056	57 11	127	23 35	162	27 26	206	54 13	246	32 54	288
159	23 52	353	35 39	055	57 39	127	23 47	161	27 10	206	53 41	246	32 21	287
160	23 47	352	36 07	054	58 07	127	23 58	161	26 55	205	53 08	245	31 47	286
161	23 41	351	36 35	052	58 35	127	24 10	160	26 40	205	52 37	245	31 13	285
162	23 35	350	37 03	051	59 04	127	24 22	160	26 25	204	52 05	244	30 39	284
163	23 29	349	37 31	050	59 32	126	24 34	159	26 11	204	51 33	244	30 05	283
164	23 21	348	37 57	049	60 00	126	24 47	158	25 57	203	51 01	243	29 30	282
	◆ SPICA		ANTARES		◆ Peacock		ACHERNAR		CANOPUS		◆ SIRIUS		REGULUS	
165	38 24	048	25 22	101	25 00	158	25 43	203	50 30	243	28 56	282	23 14	346
166	38 50	047	25 57	100	25 14	157	25 30	202	49 59	242	28 21	281	23 05	345
167	39 16	046	26 32	099	25 27	157	25 17	201	49 28	242	27 46	280	22 56	344
168	39 41	045	27 07	098	25 41	156	25 04	201	48 57	241	27 12	279	22 46	343
169	40 05	044	27 41	098	25 56	156	24 52	200	48 26	241	26 37	278	22 35	342
170	40 29	042	28 16	097	26 10	155	24 40	200	47 55	240	26 02	277	22 24	341
171	40 53	041	28 51	096	26 25	155	24 28	199	47 25	240	25 27	276	22 13	340
172	41 16	040	29 27	095	26 41	154	24 16	199	46 54	239	24 52	276	22 01	339
173	41 38	039	30 02	095	26 56	154	24 05	198	46 24	239	24 17	275	21 48	338
174	42 00	038	30 37	094	27 12	153	23 55	198	45 54	238	23 41	274	21 34	337
175	42 21	036	31 12	093	27 28	152	23 44	197	45 24	238	23 06	273	21 20	336
176	42 41	035	31 47	092	27 45	152	23 34	196	44 54	237	22 31	272	21 06	335
177	43 01	034	32 23	091	28 01	151	23 24	196	44 24	237	21 56	271	20 50	334
178	43 21	033	32 58	091	28 18	151	23 15	195	43 55	236	21 21	271	20 35	333
179	43 39	031	33 33	090	28 36	150	23 05	195	43 26	236	20 45	270	20 19	332

LHA ♈	Hc Zn	Hc Zn	Hc Zn	Hc Zn	Hc Zn	Hc Zn	Hc Zn
	◆ SPICA	ANTARES	◆ Peacock	ACHERNAR	CANOPUS	◆ Suhail	REGULUS
180	43 57 030	34 08 089	28 53 150	22 57 194	42 57 235	60 23 273	20 02 331
181	44 15 029	34 44 088	29 11 149	22 48 194	42 28 235	59 48 272	19 44 330
182	44 31 027	35 19 087	29 29 149	22 40 193	41 59 234	59 13 271	19 26 329
183	44 47 026	35 54 087	29 48 148	22 32 192	41 30 234	58 37 270	19 08 328
184	45 02 025	36 29 086	30 06 148	22 25 192	41 02 233	58 02 270	18 49 327
185	45 16 023	37 04 085	30 25 147	22 18 191	40 34 233	57 27 269	18 30 326
186	45 30 022	37 39 084	30 45 147	22 11 191	40 06 232	56 52 268	18 10 325
187	45 43 021	38 14 083	31 04 146	22 05 190	39 38 232	56 16 267	17 49 324
188	45 55 019	38 49 082	31 24 146	21 59 190	39 10 231	55 41 267	17 29 323
189	46 06 018	39 24 081	31 44 145	21 53 189	38 43 231	55 06 266	17 07 322
190	46 16 016	39 59 081	32 04 145	21 48 188	38 15 230	54 31 265	16 45 321
191	46 26 015	40 34 080	32 25 144	21 43 188	37 48 230	53 56 264	16 23 320
192	46 35 014	41 09 079	32 46 144	21 38 187	37 22 229	53 21 264	16 00 319
193	46 42 012	41 43 078	33 07 143	21 34 187	36 55 229	52 46 263	15 37 318
194	46 50 011	42 18 077	33 28 143	21 30 186	36 28 228	52 11 262	15 14 318
	◆ ARCTURUS	ANTARES	◆ Peacock	ACHERNAR	CANOPUS	◆ Suhail	Denebola
195	15 05 019	42 52 076	33 50 142	21 26 186	36 02 228	51 36 261	19 53 342
196	15 16 018	43 26 075	34 11 142	21 23 185	35 36 227	51 01 261	19 42 341
197	15 26 017	44 00 074	34 33 141	21 20 184	35 10 227	50 26 260	19 30 340
198	15 36 016	44 34 073	34 56 141	21 17 184	34 45 226	49 51 259	19 18 339
199	15 45 015	45 07 072	35 18 140	21 15 183	34 20 226	49 17 259	19 05 338
200	15 54 014	45 41 071	35 41 140	21 13 183	33 54 225	48 42 258	18 51 337
201	16 02 013	46 14 070	36 04 139	21 12 182	33 30 225	48 08 257	18 37 336
202	16 10 012	46 47 069	36 27 139	21 11 181	33 05 224	47 33 257	18 23 335
203	16 17 011	47 20 068	36 50 138	21 10 181	32 41 224	46 59 256	18 07 334
204	16 23 010	47 53 067	37 14 138	21 10 180	32 16 223	46 25 255	17 52 333
205	16 29 009	48 25 066	37 38 137	21 10 180	31 52 222	45 51 255	17 35 332
206	16 34 008	48 57 065	38 02 137	21 10 179	31 29 222	45 17 254	17 19 331
207	16 38 007	49 29 064	38 26 136	21 11 179	31 05 221	44 43 253	17 01 330
208	16 42 006	50 00 063	38 51 136	21 12 178	30 42 221	44 09 253	16 43 329
209	16 46 005	50 31 061	39 15 135	21 13 177	30 19 220	43 36 252	16 25 328
	◆ ARCTURUS	ANTARES	◆ Peacock	ACHERNAR	CANOPUS	◆ Suhail	SPICA
210	16 49 004	51 02 060	39 40 135	21 15 177	29 57 220	43 02 252	46 42 348
211	16 51 003	51 33 059	40 05 134	21 17 176	29 34 219	42 29 251	46 35 346
212	16 52 002	52 03 058	40 31 134	21 20 176	29 12 219	41 56 250	46 26 345
213	16 53 001	52 32 057	40 56 133	21 22 175	28 50 218	41 22 250	46 16 344
214	16 54 000	53 01 055	41 22 133	21 26 175	28 28 218	40 49 249	46 06 342
215	16 53 359	53 30 054	41 48 133	21 29 174	28 07 217	40 17 248	45 55 341
216	16 53 358	53 59 053	42 14 132	21 33 173	27 46 216	39 44 248	45 43 339
217	16 51 357	54 27 052	42 40 132	21 37 173	27 25 216	39 11 247	45 30 338
218	16 49 356	54 54 050	43 06 131	21 42 172	27 05 215	38 39 247	45 16 337
219	16 46 355	55 21 049	43 33 131	21 47 172	26 45 215	38 07 246	45 02 335
220	16 43 354	55 47 047	44 00 130	21 52 171	26 25 214	37 35 245	44 47 334
221	16 39 353	56 13 046	44 27 130	21 58 170	26 05 214	37 03 245	44 31 333
222	16 35 352	56 38 045	44 54 129	22 04 170	25 46 213	36 31 244	44 14 331
223	16 30 351	57 02 043	45 21 129	22 10 169	25 27 212	35 59 243	43 57 330
224	16 24 350	57 26 042	45 49 129	22 17 169	25 08 212	35 28 243	43 39 329
	ANTARES	◆ Nunki	Peacock	ACHERNAR	◆ CANOPUS	Suhail	◆ SPICA
225	57 49 040	39 00 082	46 16 128	22 24 168	24 49 211	34 56 242	43 21 327
226	58 12 039	39 34 081	46 44 128	22 31 168	24 31 211	34 25 242	43 01 326
227	58 33 037	40 09 080	47 12 127	22 39 167	24 13 210	33 54 241	42 41 325
228	58 54 036	40 44 079	47 40 127	22 47 166	23 56 210	33 24 240	42 21 324
229	59 14 034	41 18 078	48 09 126	22 56 166	23 38 209	32 53 240	42 00 322
230	59 33 032	41 53 077	48 37 126	23 04 165	23 22 208	32 23 239	41 38 321
231	59 52 031	42 27 076	49 06 126	23 13 165	23 05 208	31 53 238	41 15 320
232	60 09 029	43 01 075	49 34 125	23 23 164	22 49 207	31 23 238	40 52 319
233	60 26 027	43 35 074	50 03 125	23 33 164	22 33 207	30 53 237	40 29 318
234	60 42 025	44 09 073	50 32 124	23 43 163	22 17 206	30 23 237	40 05 316
235	60 56 024	44 43 072	51 01 124	23 53 163	22 02 205	29 54 236	39 40 315
236	61 10 022	45 16 071	51 31 124	24 04 162	21 47 205	29 25 235	39 15 314
237	61 22 020	45 50 070	52 00 123	24 15 161	21 32 204	28 56 235	38 50 313
238	61 34 018	46 23 069	52 30 123	24 26 161	21 18 204	28 27 234	38 24 312
239	61 45 016	46 56 068	52 59 122	24 38 160	21 04 203	27 59 234	37 57 311
	◆ ANTARES	Nunki	◆ FOMALHAUT	ACHERNAR	CANOPUS	◆ ACRUX	SPICA
240	61 54 015	47 28 067	15 39 119	24 50 160	20 50 202	61 46 230	37 30 310
241	62 02 013	48 01 066	16 10 118	25 03 159	20 37 202	61 19 230	37 03 309
242	62 09 011	48 33 065	16 41 118	25 15 159	20 24 201	60 53 230	36 35 307
243	62 15 009	49 05 064	17 13 117	25 28 158	20 11 201	60 26 229	36 07 306
244	62 20 007	49 36 063	17 44 116	25 42 158	19 59 200	59 59 229	35 38 305
245	62 24 005	50 08 062	18 16 115	25 55 157	19 47 199	59 32 229	35 10 304
246	62 26 003	50 39 061	18 48 115	26 09 156	19 36 199	59 06 229	34 40 303
247	62 28 001	51 09 059	19 20 114	26 23 156	19 25 198	58 39 229	34 11 302
248	62 28 359	51 39 058	19 52 113	26 38 155	19 14 198	58 13 229	33 41 301
249	62 27 357	52 09 057	20 25 113	26 53 155	19 03 197	57 46 228	33 10 300
250	62 24 355	52 38 056	20 58 112	27 08 154	18 53 196	57 20 228	32 40 299
251	62 21 353	53 07 055	21 30 111	27 23 154	18 43 196	56 54 228	32 09 298
252	62 16 351	53 36 053	22 03 110	27 39 153	18 34 195	56 28 228	31 38 297
253	62 10 350	54 04 052	22 37 110	27 55 153	18 25 194	56 01 228	31 06 296
254	62 03 348	54 32 051	23 10 109	28 12 152	18 16 194	55 35 227	30 34 295
	ALTAIR	◆ FOMALHAUT	ACHERNAR	CANOPUS	◆ ACRUX	SPICA	◆ ANTARES
255	17 28 045	23 43 108	28 28 152	18 08 193	55 10 227	30 02 294	61 55 346
256	17 53 044	24 17 107	28 45 151	18 00 193	54 44 227	29 30 293	61 46 344
257	18 17 043	24 51 107	29 02 151	17 53 192	54 18 227	28 58 293	61 36 342
258	18 41 042	25 24 106	29 20 150	17 45 191	53 53 226	28 25 292	61 24 340
259	19 04 041	25 58 105	29 38 150	17 39 191	53 27 226	27 52 291	61 12 338
260	19 27 040	26 33 104	29 56 149	17 32 190	53 02 226	27 19 290	60 59 337
261	19 50 039	27 07 104	30 14 148	17 26 190	52 36 226	26 46 289	60 44 335
262	20 12 038	27 41 103	30 32 148	17 21 189	52 11 225	26 12 288	60 29 333
263	20 33 037	28 15 102	30 51 147	17 15 188	51 46 225	25 38 287	60 12 331
264	20 54 036	28 50 102	31 10 147	17 11 188	51 21 225	25 05 286	59 55 330
265	21 15 035	29 25 101	31 30 146	17 06 187	50 57 224	24 31 285	59 37 328
266	21 35 034	29 59 100	31 49 146	17 02 186	50 32 224	23 57 284	59 17 326
267	21 54 033	30 34 099	32 09 145	16 58 186	50 07 224	23 22 284	58 57 325
268	22 13 032	31 09 099	32 29 145	16 55 185	49 43 224	22 48 283	58 37 323
269	22 32 031	31 44 098	32 50 144	16 52 184	49 19 223	22 14 282	58 15 322

LAT 54°S

LHA ♈	Hc Zn	Hc Zn	Hc Zn	Hc Zn	Hc Zn	Hc Zn	Hc Zn
	◆ ALTAIR	FOMALHAUT	◆ ACHERNAR	CANOPUS	RIGIL KENT	◆ SPICA	ANTARES
270	22 50 030	32 19 097	33 11 144	16 49 184	63 02 235	21 39 281	57 53 320
271	23 07 029	32 54 096	33 31 143	16 47 183	62 33 235	21 04 280	57 30 319
272	23 24 028	33 29 095	33 53 143	16 45 183	62 04 235	20 30 279	57 06 317
273	23 40 027	34 04 095	34 14 142	16 44 182	61 35 235	19 55 278	56 42 316
274	23 56 026	34 39 094	34 36 142	16 43 181	61 07 234	19 20 278	56 17 314
275	24 11 025	35 14 093	34 57 141	16 42 181	60 38 234	18 45 277	55 51 313
276	24 26 024	35 50 092	35 20 141	16 42 180	60 09 234	18 10 276	55 25 311
277	24 40 023	36 25 092	35 42 140	16 42 179	59 41 234	17 35 275	54 58 310
278	24 53 022	37 00 091	36 05 140	16 43 179	59 13 234	16 59 274	54 31 309
279	25 06 021	37 35 090	36 27 139	16 44 178	58 44 233	16 24 273	54 03 307
280	25 18 020	38 11 089	36 50 139	16 45 178	58 16 233	15 49 273	53 35 306
281	25 30 019	38 46 088	37 14 139	16 47 177	57 48 233	15 14 272	53 06 305
282	25 40 017	39 21 087	37 37 138	16 49 176	57 20 233	14 39 271	52 37 304
283	25 51 016	39 56 087	38 01 138	16 52 176	56 52 232	14 03 270	52 07 302
284	26 00 015	40 32 086	38 25 137	16 54 175	56 24 232	13 28 269	51 37 301
	◆ ALTAIR	FOMALHAUT	◆ ACHERNAR	CANOPUS	◆ RIGIL KENT	ANTARES	Rasalhague
285	26 09 014	41 07 085	38 49 137	16 58 174	55 56 232	51 07 300	21 04 338
286	26 18 013	41 42 084	39 13 136	17 01 174	55 28 232	50 36 299	20 51 337
287	26 25 012	42 17 083	39 37 136	17 05 173	55 01 231	50 05 298	20 36 336
288	26 32 011	42 52 082	40 02 135	17 10 172	54 33 231	49 34 297	20 22 335
289	26 39 010	43 27 081	40 27 135	17 15 172	54 06 231	49 02 295	20 07 334
290	26 44 009	44 02 081	40 52 134	17 20 171	53 39 230	48 30 294	19 51 333
291	26 49 008	44 36 080	41 18 134	17 25 171	53 12 230	47 58 293	19 34 332
292	26 54 007	45 11 079	41 43 133	17 31 170	52 45 230	47 25 292	19 17 331
293	26 57 005	45 45 078	42 09 133	17 38 169	52 18 229	46 53 291	19 00 330
294	27 00 004	46 20 077	42 35 133	17 45 169	51 51 229	46 20 290	18 42 329
295	27 03 003	46 54 076	43 01 132	17 52 168	51 25 229	45 46 289	18 24 328
296	27 04 002	47 28 075	43 27 132	17 59 167	50 58 228	45 13 288	18 05 327
297	27 05 001	48 02 074	43 53 131	18 07 167	50 32 228	44 39 287	17 45 326
298	27 05 000	48 36 073	44 20 131	18 15 166	50 06 228	44 06 286	17 25 325
299	27 05 359	49 10 072	44 47 130	18 24 166	49 39 227	43 32 285	17 05 324
	FOMALHAUT	◆ ACHERNAR	CANOPUS	◆ RIGIL KENT	ANTARES	Nunki	◆ ALTAIR
300	49 43 071	45 14 130	18 33 165	49 14 227	42 57 284	59 52 331	27 04 358
301	50 16 070	45 41 130	18 42 164	48 48 227	42 23 283	59 35 329	27 02 357
302	50 49 069	46 08 129	18 52 164	48 22 226	41 49 282	59 16 327	27 00 355
303	51 22 068	46 36 129	19 02 163	47 57 226	41 14 281	58 56 326	26 57 354
304	51 55 067	47 03 128	19 12 163	47 31 226	40 40 281	58 36 324	26 53 353
305	52 27 066	47 31 128	19 23 162	47 06 225	40 05 280	58 15 322	26 48 352
306	52 59 064	47 59 127	19 34 161	46 41 225	39 30 279	57 53 321	26 43 351
307	53 31 063	48 27 127	19 46 161	46 16 225	38 55 278	57 31 319	26 37 350
308	54 02 062	48 55 127	19 57 160	45 52 224	38 20 277	57 07 318	26 31 349
309	54 33 061	49 23 126	20 10 159	45 27 224	37 45 276	56 43 316	26 23 348
310	55 03 060	49 52 126	20 22 159	45 03 224	37 10 275	56 19 315	26 16 347
311	55 34 058	50 21 125	20 35 158	44 38 223	36 35 274	55 53 314	26 07 346
312	56 04 057	50 50 125	20 48 158	44 14 223	36 00 274	55 28 312	25 58 344
313	56 33 056	51 18 125	21 02 157	43 51 222	35 25 273	55 01 311	25 48 343
314	57 02 055	51 48 124	21 16 156	43 27 222	34 49 272	54 34 309	25 38 342
	◆ FOMALHAUT	ACHERNAR	◆ CANOPUS	RIGIL KENT	◆ ANTARES	Nunki	ALTAIR
315	57 30 053	52 17 124	21 30 156	43 03 222	34 14 271	54 07 308	25 27 341
316	57 58 052	52 46 123	21 45 155	42 40 221	33 39 270	53 39 307	25 15 340
317	58 26 050	53 16 123	22 00 155	42 17 221	33 04 269	53 10 306	25 03 339
318	58 53 049	53 45 123	22 15 154	41 54 220	32 28 269	52 41 304	24 50 338
319	59 19 047	54 15 122	22 30 153	41 31 220	31 53 268	52 12 303	24 36 337
320	59 45 046	54 45 122	22 46 153	41 09 220	31 18 267	51 42 302	24 22 336
321	60 10 044	55 15 122	23 03 152	40 47 219	30 43 266	51 12 301	24 08 335
322	60 34 043	55 45 121	23 19 152	40 24 219	30 07 266	50 42 299	23 52 334
323	60 58 041	56 15 121	23 36 151	40 02 218	29 32 265	50 11 298	23 36 333
324	61 21 040	56 45 121	23 53 151	39 41 218	28 57 264	49 39 297	23 20 332
325	61 43 038	57 16 120	24 11 150	39 19 217	28 22 263	49 08 296	23 03 331
326	62 04 036	57 46 120	24 29 149	38 58 217	27 47 262	48 36 295	22 46 330
327	62 25 035	58 17 119	24 47 149	38 37 217	27 12 262	48 04 294	22 27 329
328	62 44 033	58 48 119	25 05 148	38 16 216	26 37 261	47 32 293	22 09 328
329	63 03 031	59 19 119	25 24 148	37 55 216	26 03 260	46 59 292	21 50 327
	◆ FOMALHAUT	ACHERNAR	◆ CANOPUS	RIGIL KENT	◆ ANTARES	Nunki	ALTAIR
330	63 21 029	59 50 118	25 43 147	37 35 215	25 28 259	46 26 291	21 30 326
331	63 37 027	60 21 118	26 02 147	37 14 215	24 53 259	45 53 290	21 10 325
332	63 53 026	60 52 118	26 22 146	36 54 214	24 19 258	45 20 289	20 49 324
333	64 08 024	61 23 118	26 42 145	36 35 214	23 44 257	44 46 288	20 28 323
334	64 21 022	61 54 117	27 02 145	36 15 213	23 10 256	44 13 287	20 06 322
335	64 34 020	62 26 117	27 22 144	35 56 213	22 36 256	43 39 286	19 44 321
336	64 45 018	62 57 117	27 43 144	35 37 213	22 02 255	43 05 285	19 22 320
337	64 55 016	63 29 116	28 04 143	35 18 212	21 28 254	42 31 284	18 59 319
338	65 04 014	64 01 116	28 25 143	34 59 212	20 54 253	41 56 283	18 35 318
339	65 12 012	64 32 116	28 47 142	34 41 211	20 20 253	41 22 282	18 11 317
340	65 19 010	65 04 115	29 09 141	34 22 211	19 47 252	40 47 281	17 47 316
341	65 24 008	65 36 115	29 31 141	34 05 210	19 13 251	40 13 280	17 22 315
342	65 28 005	66 08 115	29 53 140	33 47 210	18 40 250	39 38 279	16 57 314
343	65 31 003	66 40 115	30 16 140	33 30 209	18 07 250	39 03 278	16 32 313
344	65 32 001	67 12 114	30 39 139	33 12 209	17 34 249	38 28 278	16 06 312
	◆ Diphda	Acamar	◆ CANOPUS	Miaplacidus	RIGIL KENT	◆ Nunki	FOMALHAUT
345	48 41 039	48 30 096	31 02 139	35 17 169	32 55 208	37 53 277	65 32 359
346	49 03 038	49 05 095	31 25 138	35 24 169	32 39 208	37 18 276	65 31 357
347	49 24 037	49 40 094	31 49 138	35 31 168	32 22 207	36 43 275	65 29 355
348	49 45 035	50 15 094	32 13 137	35 38 168	32 06 207	36 08 274	65 25 353
349	50 05 034	50 51 093	32 37 137	35 46 167	31 50 206	35 33 273	65 20 351
350	50 24 032	51 26 092	33 01 136	35 53 167	31 35 206	34 57 272	65 14 349
351	50 43 031	52 01 091	33 26 135	36 01 167	31 20 206	34 22 272	65 06 347
352	51 01 030	52 36 091	33 51 135	36 10 166	31 04 205	33 47 271	64 58 345
353	51 18 028	53 12 090	34 16 134	36 18 166	30 50 205	33 12 270	64 48 343
354	51 34 027	53 47 089	34 41 134	36 27 165	30 35 204	32 36 269	64 37 341
355	51 50 025	54 22 088	35 07 133	36 36 165	30 21 204	32 01 268	64 25 339
356	52 04 024	54 58 087	35 33 133	36 45 165	30 07 203	31 26 268	64 11 337
357	52 18 022	55 33 086	35 59 132	36 54 164	29 53 203	30 51 267	63 57 335
358	52 31 021	56 08 086	36 25 132	37 04 164	29 40 202	30 15 266	63 41 333
359	52 43 019	56 43 085	36 51 131	37 14 164	29 27 202	29 40 265	63 25 331

LHA ♈	Hc	Zn	Hc	Zn	Hc	Zn	Hc	Zn	Hc	Zn	Hc	Zn	Hc	Zn
	Diphda		◆RIGEL		CANOPUS		Miaplacidus		◆RIGIL KENT		Peacock		◆FOMALHAUT	
0	51 57	017	13 06	086	37 57	130	38 21	163	30 10	201	60 47	244	62 15	330
1	52 07	016	13 41	085	38 23	130	38 32	163	29 58	201	60 16	244	61 58	329
2	52 16	014	14 15	084	38 50	129	38 42	162	29 46	200	59 45	244	61 39	327
3	52 24	013	14 49	083	39 16	129	38 53	162	29 34	200	59 15	243	61 20	325
4	52 31	011	15 23	082	39 43	128	39 03	161	29 22	199	58 44	243	61 00	323
5	52 37	010	15 57	081	40 11	128	39 15	161	29 11	199	58 13	243	60 39	322
6	52 42	008	16 31	081	40 38	127	39 26	161	29 00	198	57 43	242	60 18	320
7	52 46	006	17 05	080	41 06	126	39 37	160	28 50	198	57 13	242	59 55	319
8	52 50	005	17 39	079	41 33	126	39 49	160	28 39	197	56 42	241	59 32	317
9	52 52	003	18 13	078	42 01	125	40 01	160	28 29	197	56 12	241	59 08	316
10	52 54	002	18 46	077	42 29	125	40 13	159	28 20	196	55 42	241	58 44	314
11	52 54	000	19 20	076	42 58	124	40 25	159	28 10	196	55 12	240	58 19	313
12	52 54	359	19 53	075	43 26	124	40 38	158	28 01	195	54 42	240	57 53	311
13	52 53	357	20 26	074	43 55	123	40 51	158	27 52	195	54 13	239	57 27	310
14	52 50	355	20 59	074	44 24	123	41 04	158	27 44	194	53 43	239	57 00	308
	◆RIGEL		SIRIUS		CANOPUS		◆RIGIL KENT		Peacock		◆FOMALHAUT		Diphda	
15	21 32	073	15 39	097	44 53	122	27 36	193	53 14	238	56 33	307	52 47	354
16	22 05	072	16 14	096	45 22	122	27 28	193	52 45	238	56 05	306	52 43	352
17	22 38	071	16 48	095	45 51	121	27 20	192	52 15	238	55 37	304	52 38	351
18	23 10	070	17 22	095	46 21	121	27 13	192	51 46	237	55 09	303	52 32	349
19	23 42	069	17 57	094	46 50	120	27 06	191	51 18	237	54 40	302	52 25	348
20	24 15	068	18 31	093	47 20	120	26 59	191	50 49	236	54 10	301	52 17	346
21	24 46	067	19 05	092	47 50	119	26 53	190	50 20	236	53 40	299	52 08	345
22	25 18	066	19 40	091	48 20	119	26 47	190	49 52	236	53 10	298	51 59	343
23	25 49	065	20 14	090	48 50	118	26 41	189	49 24	235	52 40	297	51 48	341
24	26 21	065	20 48	090	49 21	118	26 36	189	48 55	235	52 09	296	51 37	340
25	26 52	064	21 23	089	49 51	117	26 31	188	48 27	234	51 38	295	51 25	338
26	27 22	063	21 57	088	50 22	117	26 26	188	48 00	234	51 06	294	51 11	337
27	27 53	062	22 32	087	50 53	116	26 22	187	47 32	233	50 35	293	50 58	336
28	28 23	061	23 06	086	51 24	116	26 18	187	47 04	233	50 03	291	50 43	334
29	28 53	060	23 40	086	51 55	115	26 14	186	46 37	232	49 31	290	50 28	333
	◆RIGEL		SIRIUS		CANOPUS		◆RIGIL KENT		Peacock		◆FOMALHAUT		Diphda	
30	29 22	059	24 15	085	52 26	115	26 10	185	46 10	232	48 58	289	50 11	331
31	29 52	058	24 49	084	52 57	114	26 07	185	45 43	232	48 26	288	49 54	330
32	30 21	057	25 23	083	53 29	114	26 05	184	45 16	231	47 53	287	49 37	328
33	30 49	056	25 57	082	54 00	113	26 02	184	44 49	231	47 20	286	49 18	327
34	31 17	055	26 31	081	54 32	113	26 00	183	44 23	230	46 47	285	48 59	326
35	31 45	054	27 05	080	55 04	112	25 58	183	43 56	230	46 14	284	48 39	324
36	32 13	053	27 39	080	55 36	112	25 57	182	43 30	229	45 40	283	48 19	323
37	32 40	052	28 13	079	56 08	111	25 55	182	43 04	229	45 07	282	47 58	322
38	33 07	051	28 47	078	56 40	111	25 55	181	42 39	228	44 33	282	47 36	320
39	33 33	050	29 20	077	57 12	110	25 54	181	42 13	228	43 59	281	47 14	319
40	33 59	048	29 54	076	57 44	110	25 54	180	41 48	227	43 25	280	46 51	318
41	34 25	047	30 27	075	58 17	109	25 54	180	41 22	227	42 51	279	46 28	316
42	34 50	046	31 00	074	58 49	109	25 54	179	40 57	226	42 17	278	46 04	315
43	35 14	045	31 33	073	59 22	108	25 55	178	40 33	226	41 43	277	45 39	314
44	35 39	044	32 06	072	59 55	108	25 56	178	40 08	225	41 09	276	45 14	313
	RIGEL		◆SIRIUS		CANOPUS		◆RIGIL KENT		Peacock		FOMALHAUT		◆Diphda	
45	36 02	043	32 39	071	60 28	107	25 58	177	39 43	225	40 35	275	44 49	312
46	36 25	042	33 11	070	61 01	107	25 59	177	39 19	224	40 01	274	44 23	310
47	36 48	041	33 44	070	61 34	106	26 01	176	38 55	224	39 26	274	43 56	309
48	37 10	040	34 16	069	62 07	105	26 04	176	38 31	224	38 52	273	43 29	308
49	37 32	038	34 48	068	62 40	105	26 06	175	38 08	223	38 17	272	43 02	307
50	37 53	037	35 19	067	63 13	104	26 09	175	37 45	223	37 43	271	42 34	306
51	38 14	036	35 51	066	63 47	104	26 13	174	37 21	222	37 09	270	42 06	305
52	38 34	035	36 22	065	64 20	103	26 16	174	36 58	222	36 34	269	41 38	304
53	38 53	034	36 53	064	64 54	103	26 20	173	36 36	221	36 00	269	41 09	302
54	39 12	032	37 24	063	65 27	102	26 25	173	36 13	221	35 25	268	40 40	301
55	39 30	031	37 54	062	66 01	102	26 29	172	35 51	220	34 51	267	40 10	300
56	39 47	030	38 24	061	66 35	101	26 34	171	35 29	220	34 17	266	39 40	299
57	40 04	029	38 54	060	67 09	101	26 40	171	35 07	219	33 42	265	39 10	298
58	40 20	027	39 24	058	67 42	100	26 45	170	34 46	219	33 08	265	38 39	297
59	40 36	026	39 53	057	68 16	099	26 51	170	34 24	218	32 34	264	38 09	296
	RIGEL		◆SIRIUS		Suhail		◆RIGIL KENT		Peacock		FOMALHAUT		◆Diphda	
60	40 51	025	40 22	056	41 02	110	26 57	169	34 03	218	32 00	263	37 38	295
61	41 05	024	40 50	055	41 34	110	27 04	169	33 42	217	31 26	262	37 06	294
62	41 18	022	41 18	054	42 06	109	27 11	168	33 22	216	30 51	261	36 35	293
63	41 31	021	41 46	053	42 39	108	27 18	168	33 01	216	30 17	261	36 03	292
64	41 43	020	42 13	052	43 12	108	27 25	167	32 41	215	29 44	260	35 31	291
65	41 54	019	42 40	051	43 45	107	27 33	167	32 22	215	29 10	259	34 59	290
66	42 05	017	43 06	050	44 18	106	27 41	166	32 02	214	28 36	258	34 26	289
67	42 15	016	43 32	048	44 51	106	27 50	166	31 43	214	28 02	258	33 54	288
68	42 24	015	43 58	047	45 24	105	27 58	165	31 24	213	27 29	257	33 21	287
69	42 32	013	44 23	046	45 57	104	28 07	165	31 05	213	26 55	256	32 48	286
70	42 40	012	44 47	045	46 30	104	28 17	164	30 46	212	26 22	255	32 15	286
71	42 46	011	45 11	044	47 04	103	28 26	164	30 28	212	25 49	255	31 42	285
72	42 52	009	45 35	042	47 38	102	28 36	163	30 10	211	25 16	254	31 08	284
73	42 57	008	45 58	041	48 11	102	28 46	162	29 52	211	24 42	253	30 35	283
74	43 02	007	46 20	040	48 45	101	28 57	162	29 35	210	24 10	252	30 01	282
	RIGEL		◆SIRIUS		Suhail		◆RIGIL KENT		Peacock		ACHERNAR		◆Diphda	
75	43 05	005	46 42	038	49 19	100	29 08	161	29 18	210	62 25	245	29 28	281
76	43 08	004	47 03	037	49 53	100	29 19	161	29 01	209	61 54	244	28 54	280
77	43 10	002	47 23	036	50 27	099	29 30	160	28 44	209	61 23	244	28 20	279
78	43 11	001	47 43	035	51 01	098	29 42	160	28 28	208	60 52	243	27 46	278
79	43 11	000	48 02	033	51 35	097	29 54	159	28 12	207	60 22	243	27 12	278
80	43 11	358	48 21	032	52 09	097	30 06	159	27 56	207	59 51	243	26 38	277
81	43 09	357	48 38	030	52 43	096	30 19	158	27 41	206	59 21	242	26 03	276
82	43 07	356	48 55	029	53 17	095	30 31	158	27 26	206	58 50	242	25 29	275
83	43 04	354	49 12	028	53 52	095	30 44	157	27 11	205	58 20	242	24 55	274
84	43 00	353	49 27	026	54 26	094	30 58	157	26 56	205	57 50	241	24 21	273
85	42 56	352	49 42	025	55 00	093	31 12	156	26 42	204	57 19	241	23 46	272
86	42 50	350	49 56	023	55 35	092	31 25	156	26 28	204	56 49	240	23 12	272
87	42 44	349	50 09	022	56 09	091	31 40	155	26 15	203	56 20	240	22 37	271
88	42 37	348	50 22	020	56 43	091	31 54	155	26 01	202	55 50	240	22 03	270
89	42 29	346	50 33	019	57 18	090	32 09	154	25 48	202	55 20	239	21 29	269

LAT 55°S

LHA ♈	Hc	Zn	Hc	Zn	Hc	Zn	Hc	Zn	Hc	Zn	Hc	Zn	Hc	Zn
	PROCYON		◆Suhail		RIGIL KENT		◆Peacock		ACHERNAR		◆RIGEL		BETELGEUSE	
90	26 20	028	57 52	089	32 24	154	25 36	201	54 51	239	42 21	345	27 35	359
91	26 36	027	58 27	088	32 39	153	25 23	201	54 21	239	42 11	344	27 34	358
92	26 51	026	59 01	087	32 55	153	25 11	200	53 52	238	42 01	342	27 32	357
93	27 06	025	59 35	086	33 11	152	24 59	200	53 23	238	41 50	341	27 30	356
94	27 20	024	60 10	086	33 27	152	24 48	199	52 54	237	41 39	340	27 27	354
95	27 34	023	60 44	085	33 43	151	24 37	199	52 25	237	41 27	338	27 23	353
96	27 47	022	61 18	084	34 00	151	24 26	198	51 56	236	41 13	337	27 19	352
97	27 59	020	61 52	083	34 16	150	24 16	197	51 27	236	41 00	336	27 14	351
98	28 11	019	62 27	082	34 33	150	24 06	197	50 59	236	40 45	335	27 08	350
99	28 22	018	63 01	081	34 51	150	23 56	196	50 31	235	40 30	333	27 02	349
100	28 32	017	63 34	080	35 08	149	23 46	196	50 02	235	40 14	332	26 55	348
101	28 42	016	64 08	079	35 26	149	23 37	195	49 34	234	39 58	331	26 47	347
102	28 51	015	64 42	078	35 44	148	23 29	194	49 06	234	39 41	330	26 39	346
103	28 59	014	65 16	077	36 03	148	23 20	194	48 39	234	39 23	328	26 30	344
104	29 07	013	65 49	075	36 21	147	23 12	193	48 11	233	39 05	327	26 21	343
	PROCYON		REGULUS		◆Gienah		RIGIL KENT		◆ACHERNAR		RIGEL		◆SIRIUS	
105	29 14	011	12 14	047	20 33	092	36 40	147	47 44	233	38 46	326	51 38	355
106	29 21	010	12 39	046	21 07	091	36 59	146	47 16	232	38 26	325	51 35	353
107	29 27	009	13 04	046	21 42	090	37 18	146	46 49	232	38 06	324	51 30	351
108	29 32	008	13 28	045	22 16	089	37 38	145	46 22	231	37 45	322	51 24	350
109	29 36	007	13 52	044	22 50	088	37 57	145	45 55	231	37 24	321	51 18	348
110	29 40	006	14 16	043	23 25	088	38 17	144	45 29	230	37 02	320	51 11	347
111	29 43	005	14 39	042	23 59	087	38 37	144	45 02	230	36 40	319	51 02	345
112	29 46	003	15 02	041	24 34	086	38 58	144	44 36	230	36 17	318	50 53	344
113	29 47	002	15 24	040	25 08	085	39 18	143	44 10	229	35 54	317	50 43	342
114	29 49	001	15 46	039	25 42	084	39 39	143	43 44	229	35 30	316	50 32	341
115	29 49	000	16 07	038	26 16	083	40 00	142	43 18	228	35 05	314	50 21	339
116	29 49	359	16 28	037	26 50	082	40 21	142	42 53	228	34 41	313	50 08	338
117	29 48	358	16 49	036	27 25	082	40 43	141	42 27	227	34 15	312	49 55	337
118	29 46	357	17 09	035	27 59	081	41 04	141	42 02	227	33 50	311	49 41	335
119	29 43	355	17 29	034	28 33	080	41 26	140	41 37	226	33 23	310	49 26	334
	REGULUS		◆SPICA		RIGIL KENT		Peacock		◆ACHERNAR		RIGEL		◆SIRIUS	
120	17 48	033	14 03	090	41 48	140	21 49	184	41 13	226	32 57	309	49 10	332
121	18 06	032	14 38	089	42 10	140	21 47	183	40 48	225	32 30	308	48 54	331
122	18 25	031	15 12	088	42 33	139	21 45	183	40 24	225	32 03	307	48 37	329
123	18 42	030	15 46	087	42 55	139	21 44	182	39 59	224	31 35	306	48 19	328
124	18 59	029	16 21	086	43 18	138	21 42	182	39 35	224	31 07	305	48 00	327
125	19 16	028	16 55	085	43 41	138	21 42	181	39 12	223	30 39	304	47 41	325
126	19 32	027	17 29	085	44 04	138	21 41	180	38 48	223	30 10	303	47 21	324
127	19 48	026	18 04	084	44 27	137	21 41	180	38 25	223	29 41	302	47 01	323
128	20 03	025	18 38	083	44 51	137	21 41	179	38 01	222	29 11	301	46 39	321
129	20 17	024	19 12	082	45 14	136	21 42	179	37 39	222	28 42	300	46 18	320
130	20 31	023	19 46	081	45 38	136	21 43	178	37 16	221	28 12	299	45 55	319
131	20 44	022	20 20	080	46 02	136	21 44	177	36 53	221	27 41	298	45 32	318
132	20 57	021	20 54	080	46 27	135	21 46	177	36 31	220	27 11	297	45 09	316
133	21 09	020	21 28	079	46 51	135	21 48	176	36 09	220	26 40	296	44 45	315
134	21 21	019	22 01	078	47 15	134	21 51	176	35 47	219	26 09	295	44 20	314
	◆REGULUS		SPICA		◆RIGIL KENT		Peacock		ACHERNAR		◆CANOPUS		SIRIUS	
135	21 32	018	22 35	077	47 40	134	21 53	175	35 26	219	67 13	260	43 55	313
136	21 43	017	23 08	076	48 05	134	21 56	175	35 04	218	66 40	259	43 30	312
137	21 52	016	23 42	075	48 30	133	22 00	174	34 43	218	66 06	258	43 04	310
138	22 02	015	24 15	074	48 55	133	22 04	173	34 22	217	65 32	258	42 37	309
139	22 10	014	24 48	073	49 20	132	22 08	173	34 02	217	64 59	257	42 11	308
140	22 18	013	25 21	073	49 46	132	22 12	172	33 41	216	64 25	257	41 43	307
141	22 26	012	25 54	072	50 12	132	22 17	172	33 21	216	63 52	256	41 15	306
142	22 33	011	26 26	071	50 37	131	22 23	171	33 01	215	63 18	256	40 47	305
143	22 39	010	26 59	070	51 03	131	22 28	170	32 42	215	62 45	255	40 19	304
144	22 44	009	27 31	069	51 29	131	22 34	170	32 22	214	62 12	255	39 50	303
145	22 49	008	28 03	068	51 55	130	22 40	169	32 03	213	61 38	254	39 21	301
146	22 54	007	28 35	067	52 22	130	22 47	169	31 44	213	61 05	254	38 51	300
147	22 57	006	29 06	066	52 48	130	22 54	168	31 26	212	60 32	253	38 21	299
148	23 01	005	29 37	065	53 15	129	23 01	167	31 07	212	60 00	253	37 51	298
149	23 03	004	30 09	064	53 41	129	23 09	167	30 49	211	59 27	252	37 21	297
	◆REGULUS		SPICA		◆RIGIL KENT		Peacock		ACHERNAR		◆CANOPUS		SIRIUS	
150	23 05	002	30 39	063	54 08	129	23 17	166	30 32	211	58 54	251	36 50	296
151	23 06	001	31 10	062	54 35	128	23 25	166	30 14	210	58 22	251	36 19	295
152	23 06	000	31 40	061	55 02	128	23 34	165	29 57	210	57 49	250	35 48	294
153	23 06	359	32 10	060	55 29	128	23 43	165	29 40	209	57 17	250	35 16	293
154	23 05	358	32 40	059	55 57	127	23 52	164	29 23	209	56 44	249	34 45	292
155	23 04	357	33 09	058	56 24	127	24 02	163	29 07	208	56 12	249	34 13	291
156	23 02	356	33 39	057	56 52	127	24 12	163	28 51	208	55 40	248	33 41	290
157	22 59	355	34 07	056	57 19	127	24 22	162	28 35	207	55 08	248	33 08	289
158	22 56	354	34 36	055	57 47	126	24 32	162	28 19	207	54 36	247	32 36	288
159	22 52	353	35 04	054	58 15	126	24 43	161	28 04	206	54 05	247	32 03	288
160	22 47	352	35 31	053	58 43	126	24 55	161	27 49	205	53 33	246	31 30	287
161	22 42	351	35 59	052	59 11	125	25 06	160	27 34	205	53 02	246	30 57	286
162	22 36	350	36 26	051	59 39	125	25 18	159	27 20	204	52 30	245	30 24	285
163	22 30	349	36 52	050	60 07	125	25 30	159	27 06	204	51 59	245	29 50	284
164	22 23	348	37 18	049	60 35	125	25 43	158	26 52	203	51 28	244	29 17	283
	◆SPICA		ANTARES		◆Peacock		ACHERNAR		CANOPUS		◆SIRIUS		REGULUS	
165	37 44	048	25 33	100	25 56	158	26 39	203	50 57	244	28 43	282	22 15	347
166	38 09	046	26 07	100	26 09	157	26 26	202	50 26	243	28 10	281	22 07	346
167	38 34	045	26 41	099	26 23	157	26 13	202	49 56	243	27 36	280	21 58	344
168	38 58	044	27 15	098	26 36	156	26 00	201	49 25	242	27 02	280	21 48	343
169	39 21	043	27 49	097	26 50	156	25 48	201	48 55	242	26 28	279	21 38	342
170	39 45	042	28 23	096	27 05	155	25 36	200	48 24	241	25 54	278	21 28	341
171	40 07	041	28 58	096	27 20	154	25 25	199	47 54	241	25 20	277	21 16	340
172	40 29	039	29 32	095	27 35	154	25 13	199	47 24	240	24 46	276	21 04	339
173	40 51	038	30 06	094	27 50	153	25 02	198	46 54	240	24 11	275	20 52	338
174	41 12	037	30 41	093	28 05	153	24 52	198	46 25	239	23 37	274	20 39	337
175	41 32	036	31 15	092	28 21	152	24 41	197	45 55	239	23 03	274	20 25	336
176	41 52	035	31 49	092	28 38	152	24 31	197	45 26	238	22 28	273	20 11	335
177	42 11	033	32 24	091	28 54	151	24 22	196	44 57	238	21 54	272	19 56	334
178	42 30	032	32 58	090	29 11	151	24 12	195	44 28	237	21 20	271	19 41	333
179	42 48	031	33 33	089	29 28	150	24 04	195	43 59	237	20 45	270	19 25	332

 LAT 55°S

LHA ♈	Hc	Zn	Hc	Zn	Hc	Zn	Hc	Zn	Hc	Zn	Hc	Zn	Hc	Zn
	◆SPICA		ANTARES		◆Peacock		ACHERNAR		CANOPUS		◆Suhail		REGULUS	
180	43 05	029	34 07	088	29 45	150	23 55	194	43 30	236	60 19	275	19 09	331
181	43 22	028	34 41	088	30 03	149	23 47	194	43 02	236	59 45	274	18 52	330
182	43 38	027	35 16	087	30 21	148	23 39	193	42 33	235	59 10	273	18 35	329
183	43 53	026	35 50	086	30 39	148	23 31	193	42 05	235	58 36	272	18 17	328
184	44 07	024	36 24	085	30 57	147	23 24	192	41 37	234	58 02	271	17 59	327
185	44 21	023	36 59	084	31 16	147	23 17	191	41 10	234	57 27	270	17 40	326
186	44 34	022	37 33	083	31 35	146	23 10	191	40 42	233	56 53	270	17 21	325
187	44 46	020	38 07	082	31 54	146	23 04	190	40 15	233	56 18	269	17 01	324
188	44 58	019	38 41	081	32 13	145	22 58	190	39 47	232	55 44	268	16 40	323
189	45 09	018	39 15	081	32 33	145	22 52	189	39 20	231	55 10	267	16 20	322
190	45 19	016	39 49	080	32 53	144	22 47	189	38 53	231	54 35	266	15 59	321
191	45 28	015	40 23	079	33 13	144	22 42	188	38 27	230	54 01	266	15 37	321
192	45 36	013	40 56	078	33 34	143	22 37	187	38 00	230	53 27	265	15 15	320
193	45 44	012	41 30	077	33 55	143	22 33	187	37 34	229	52 52	264	14 52	319
194	45 51	011	42 03	076	34 16	142	22 29	186	37 08	229	52 18	263	14 29	318
	◆ARCTURUS		ANTARES		◆Peacock		ACHERNAR		CANOPUS		◆Suhail		Denebola	
195	14 08	019	42 37	075	34 37	142	22 26	186	36 42	228	51 44	263	18 56	342
196	14 18	018	43 10	074	34 58	141	22 23	185	36 17	228	51 10	262	18 45	341
197	14 28	017	43 43	073	35 20	141	22 20	184	35 51	227	50 36	261	18 34	340
198	14 38	016	44 16	072	35 42	140	22 17	184	35 26	227	50 02	261	18 22	339
199	14 47	015	44 48	071	36 04	140	22 15	183	35 01	226	49 28	260	18 09	338
200	14 56	014	45 21	070	36 26	139	22 13	183	34 37	226	48 54	259	17 56	337
201	15 03	013	45 53	069	36 49	139	22 12	182	34 12	225	48 20	258	17 42	336
202	15 11	012	46 25	068	37 12	138	22 11	182	33 48	225	47 47	258	17 28	335
203	15 18	011	46 57	067	37 35	138	22 10	181	33 24	224	47 13	257	17 13	334
204	15 24	010	47 29	066	37 58	137	22 10	180	33 00	223	46 40	256	16 58	333
205	15 29	009	48 00	065	38 22	137	22 10	180	32 37	223	46 06	256	16 42	332
206	15 34	008	48 31	064	38 45	136	22 10	179	32 13	222	45 33	255	16 26	331
207	15 39	007	49 02	063	39 09	136	22 11	179	31 50	222	45 00	254	16 09	330
208	15 43	006	49 32	062	39 33	135	22 12	178	31 27	221	44 27	254	15 52	329
209	15 46	005	50 02	060	39 58	135	22 13	177	31 05	221	43 54	253	15 34	328
	◆ARCTURUS		ANTARES		◆Peacock		ACHERNAR		CANOPUS		◆Suhail		SPICA	
210	15 49	004	50 32	059	40 22	134	22 15	177	30 43	220	43 21	252	45 44	348
211	15 51	003	51 01	058	40 47	134	22 17	176	30 21	220	42 48	252	45 36	347
212	15 52	002	51 30	057	41 12	133	22 19	176	29 59	219	42 15	251	45 28	345
213	15 53	001	51 59	056	41 37	133	22 22	175	29 37	218	41 43	250	45 19	344
214	15 54	000	52 27	054	42 02	132	22 25	174	29 16	218	41 11	250	45 09	342
215	15 53	359	52 55	053	42 28	132	22 29	174	28 55	217	40 38	249	44 58	341
216	15 53	358	53 22	052	42 54	131	22 33	173	28 34	217	40 06	249	44 46	340
217	15 51	357	53 49	050	43 20	131	22 37	173	28 14	216	39 34	248	44 34	338
218	15 49	356	54 15	049	43 46	131	22 41	172	27 54	216	39 02	247	44 21	337
219	15 47	355	54 41	048	44 12	130	22 46	172	27 34	215	38 31	247	44 07	336
220	15 43	354	55 06	046	44 38	130	22 51	171	27 14	214	37 59	246	43 53	334
221	15 40	353	55 31	045	45 05	129	22 57	170	26 55	214	37 28	245	43 38	333
222	15 35	352	55 55	044	45 32	129	23 03	170	26 36	213	36 57	245	43 22	332
223	15 30	351	56 18	042	45 59	128	23 09	169	26 17	213	36 26	244	43 05	331
224	15 25	350	56 41	041	46 26	128	23 16	169	25 59	212	35 55	243	42 48	329
	ANTARES		◆Nunki		Peacock		ACHERNAR		◆CANOPUS		Suhail		◆SPICA	
225	57 03	039	38 50	081	46 53	127	23 23	168	25 41	212	35 24	243	42 30	328
226	57 24	038	39 24	080	47 21	127	23 30	168	25 23	211	34 54	242	42 11	327
227	57 45	036	39 58	079	47 48	126	23 37	167	25 05	210	34 23	242	41 52	325
228	58 05	035	40 32	078	48 16	126	23 45	166	24 48	210	33 53	241	41 32	324
229	58 24	033	41 06	077	48 44	126	23 54	166	24 31	209	33 23	240	41 12	323
230	58 42	031	41 39	076	49 12	125	24 02	165	24 14	209	32 53	240	40 51	322
231	59 00	030	42 12	075	49 40	125	24 11	165	23 58	208	32 24	239	40 29	321
232	59 17	028	42 46	074	50 09	124	24 21	164	23 42	207	31 54	238	40 07	319
233	59 32	026	43 19	073	50 37	124	24 30	164	23 26	207	31 25	238	39 44	318
234	59 47	025	43 52	072	51 06	123	24 40	163	23 11	206	30 56	237	39 21	317
235	60 01	023	44 24	071	51 35	123	24 50	162	22 56	206	30 27	236	38 58	316
236	60 14	021	44 57	070	52 03	123	25 01	162	22 41	205	29 59	236	38 33	315
237	60 26	019	45 29	069	52 33	122	25 12	161	22 27	204	29 30	235	38 09	314
238	60 37	018	46 01	068	53 02	122	25 23	161	22 13	204	29 02	235	37 43	312
239	60 47	016	46 33	067	53 31	121	25 35	160	21 59	203	28 34	234	37 18	311
	◆ANTARES		Nunki		◆FOMALHAUT		ACHERNAR		CANOPUS		◆ACRUX		SPICA	
240	60 56	014	47 05	066	16 08	119	25 46	160	21 46	203	62 25	231	36 52	310
241	61 04	012	47 36	065	16 39	118	25 59	159	21 33	202	61 58	231	36 25	309
242	61 10	010	48 07	064	17 09	117	26 11	158	21 20	201	61 31	231	35 58	308
243	61 16	009	48 38	063	17 40	117	26 24	158	21 08	201	61 04	231	35 31	307
244	61 21	007	49 09	062	18 11	116	26 37	157	20 55	200	60 38	231	35 03	306
245	61 24	005	49 39	061	18 42	115	26 50	157	20 44	200	60 11	230	34 35	305
246	61 26	003	50 09	060	19 13	114	27 04	156	20 32	199	59 45	230	34 07	304
247	61 28	001	50 38	058	19 44	114	27 18	156	20 22	198	59 18	230	33 38	303
248	61 28	359	51 07	057	20 16	113	27 32	155	20 11	198	58 52	230	33 09	302
249	61 27	357	51 36	056	20 48	112	27 47	155	20 01	197	58 26	230	32 40	301
250	61 25	355	52 04	055	21 20	111	28 02	154	19 51	196	58 00	229	32 10	300
251	61 21	354	52 32	054	21 52	111	28 17	154	19 41	196	57 33	229	31 40	299
252	61 17	352	53 00	052	22 24	110	28 33	153	19 32	195	57 07	229	31 10	298
253	61 11	350	53 27	051	22 57	109	28 48	152	19 23	195	56 42	229	30 39	297
254	61 05	348	53 53	050	23 29	108	29 05	152	19 15	194	56 16	228	30 08	296
	ALTAIR		◆FOMALHAUT		ACHERNAR		CANOPUS		◆ACRUX		SPICA		◆ANTARES	
255	16 46	045	24 02	108	29 21	151	19 06	193	55 50	228	29 37	295	60 57	346
256	17 10	044	24 35	107	29 38	151	18 59	193	55 24	228	29 06	294	60 48	344
257	17 33	043	25 08	106	29 54	150	18 51	192	54 59	228	28 34	293	60 39	343
258	17 56	042	25 41	105	30 12	150	18 44	191	54 33	227	28 03	292	60 28	341
259	18 19	041	26 14	105	30 29	149	18 38	191	54 08	227	27 31	291	60 16	339
260	18 41	040	26 47	104	30 47	149	18 31	190	53 43	227	26 58	290	60 03	337
261	19 03	039	27 21	103	31 05	148	18 25	190	53 18	227	26 26	289	59 50	336
262	19 24	038	27 54	102	31 23	148	18 20	189	52 53	226	25 53	288	59 35	334
263	19 45	037	28 28	102	31 42	147	18 15	188	52 28	226	25 21	287	59 19	332
264	20 06	036	29 02	101	32 01	147	18 10	188	52 04	226	24 48	287	59 03	331
265	20 26	035	29 35	100	32 20	146	18 06	187	51 39	225	24 15	286	58 45	329
266	20 45	034	30 09	099	32 39	146	18 02	186	51 15	225	23 42	285	58 27	327
267	21 04	033	30 43	099	32 59	145	17 58	186	50 50	225	23 08	284	58 08	326
268	21 23	032	31 17	098	33 18	145	17 55	185	50 26	224	22 35	283	57 48	324
269	21 40	031	31 52	097	33 39	144	17 52	184	50 02	224	22 01	282	57 28	323

LHA ♈	Hc	Zn	Hc	Zn	Hc	Zn	Hc	Zn	Hc	Zn	Hc	Zn	Hc	Zn
	◆ALTAIR		FOMALHAUT		◆ACHERNAR		CANOPUS		RIGIL KENT		◆SPICA		ANTARES	
270	21 58	030	32 26	096	33 59	144	17 49	184	63 35	237	21 27	281	57 07	321
271	22 15	029	33 00	096	34 19	143	17 47	183	63 07	237	20 54	280	56 45	320
272	22 31	028	33 34	095	34 40	142	17 45	183	62 38	236	20 20	280	56 22	318
273	22 47	027	34 09	094	35 01	142	17 44	182	62 09	236	19 46	279	55 59	317
274	23 02	026	34 43	093	35 23	141	17 43	181	61 41	236	19 12	278	55 35	315
275	23 17	025	35 17	092	35 44	141	17 42	181	61 12	236	18 38	277	55 10	314
276	23 31	024	35 52	092	36 06	140	17 42	180	60 44	235	18 03	276	54 45	312
277	23 44	023	36 26	091	36 28	140	17 42	179	60 16	235	17 29	275	54 19	311
278	23 57	022	37 00	090	36 50	140	17 43	179	59 48	235	16 55	275	53 53	310
279	24 10	021	37 35	089	37 13	139	17 44	178	59 19	235	16 21	274	53 26	308
280	24 21	019	38 09	088	37 35	139	17 45	178	58 51	234	15 46	273	52 59	307
281	24 33	018	38 44	088	37 58	138	17 47	177	58 24	234	15 12	272	52 32	306
282	24 43	017	39 18	087	38 21	138	17 49	176	57 56	234	14 37	271	52 03	305
283	24 53	016	39 52	086	38 45	137	17 51	176	57 28	234	14 03	270	51 35	303
284	25 02	015	40 27	085	39 08	137	17 54	175	57 00	233	13 29	270	51 06	302
	◆ALTAIR		FOMALHAUT		◆ACHERNAR		CANOPUS		◆RIGIL KENT		ANTARES		Rasalhague	
285	25 11	014	41 01	084	39 32	136	17 57	174	56 33	233	50 37	301	20 09	338
286	25 19	013	41 35	083	39 56	136	18 01	174	56 05	233	50 07	300	19 55	337
287	25 27	012	42 09	082	40 20	135	18 05	173	55 38	232	49 37	299	19 42	336
288	25 33	011	42 43	081	40 45	135	18 09	172	55 11	232	49 07	298	19 27	335
289	25 40	010	43 17	081	41 09	134	18 14	172	54 44	232	48 36	296	19 13	334
290	25 45	009	43 51	080	41 34	134	18 19	171	54 17	231	48 05	295	18 57	333
291	25 50	008	44 25	079	41 59	133	18 25	171	53 50	231	47 34	294	18 41	332
292	25 54	006	44 59	078	42 24	133	18 31	170	53 23	231	47 02	293	18 25	331
293	25 58	005	45 32	077	42 49	132	18 37	169	52 57	230	46 30	292	18 08	330
294	26 01	004	46 06	076	43 15	132	18 43	169	52 30	230	45 58	291	17 51	329
295	26 03	003	46 39	075	43 41	131	18 50	168	52 04	230	45 26	290	17 33	328
296	26 04	002	47 12	074	44 07	131	18 58	167	51 38	229	44 54	289	17 14	327
297	26 05	001	47 45	073	44 33	131	19 05	167	51 11	229	44 21	288	16 55	326
298	26 05	000	48 18	072	44 59	130	19 13	166	50 45	229	43 48	287	16 36	325
299	26 05	359	48 51	071	45 25	130	19 22	166	50 20	228	43 15	286	16 16	324
	FOMALHAUT		◆ACHERNAR		CANOPUS		◆RIGIL KENT		ANTARES		Nunki		◆ALTAIR	
300	49 23	070	45 52	129	19 31	165	49 54	228	42 42	285	59 00	331	26 04	358
301	49 55	069	46 19	129	19 40	164	49 29	228	42 09	284	58 43	330	26 02	357
302	50 27	068	46 46	128	19 49	164	49 03	227	41 36	283	58 25	328	26 00	355
303	50 59	067	47 13	128	19 59	163	48 38	227	41 02	282	58 07	327	25 57	354
304	51 30	065	47 40	127	20 09	162	48 13	227	40 28	281	57 47	325	25 53	353
305	52 02	064	48 07	127	20 20	162	47 48	226	39 54	280	57 27	323	25 49	352
306	52 32	063	48 35	127	20 31	161	47 23	226	39 21	280	57 06	322	25 44	351
307	53 03	062	49 03	126	20 42	161	46 59	225	38 47	279	56 45	320	25 38	350
308	53 33	061	49 31	126	20 54	160	46 34	225	38 13	278	56 22	319	25 32	349
309	54 03	060	49 59	125	21 06	159	46 10	225	37 38	277	55 59	317	25 25	348
310	54 33	058	50 27	125	21 18	159	45 46	224	37 04	276	55 36	316	25 17	347
311	55 02	057	50 55	124	21 31	158	45 22	224	36 30	275	55 12	315	25 09	346
312	55 30	056	51 24	124	21 44	157	44 58	223	35 56	274	54 47	313	25 00	345
313	55 59	055	51 52	124	21 57	157	44 35	223	35 21	273	54 22	312	24 51	344
314	56 27	053	52 21	123	22 11	156	44 11	223	34 47	273	53 56	311	24 41	342
	◆FOMALHAUT		ACHERNAR		◆CANOPUS		RIGIL KENT		◆ANTARES		Nunki		ALTAIR	
315	56 54	052	52 50	123	22 25	156	43 48	222	34 13	272	53 29	309	24 30	341
316	57 21	051	53 19	122	22 39	155	43 25	222	33 38	271	53 02	308	24 19	340
317	57 47	049	53 48	122	22 54	154	43 02	221	33 04	270	52 35	307	24 07	339
318	58 13	048	54 17	122	23 09	154	42 40	221	32 29	269	52 07	305	23 54	338
319	58 38	046	54 47	121	23 24	153	42 17	221	31 55	269	51 39	304	23 41	337
320	59 03	045	55 16	121	23 40	153	41 55	220	31 21	268	51 10	303	23 28	336
321	59 26	043	55 46	120	23 56	152	41 33	220	30 46	267	50 41	302	23 13	335
322	59 50	042	56 15	120	24 12	151	41 11	219	30 12	266	50 12	301	22 58	334
323	60 12	040	56 45	120	24 29	151	40 49	219	29 38	265	49 42	299	22 43	333
324	60 34	039	57 15	119	24 45	150	40 28	218	29 03	265	49 12	298	22 27	332
325	60 55	037	57 45	119	25 03	150	40 07	218	28 29	264	48 41	297	22 11	331
326	61 15	035	58 16	118	25 20	149	39 46	217	27 55	263	48 10	296	21 54	330
327	61 35	034	58 46	118	25 38	149	39 25	217	27 21	262	47 39	295	21 36	329
328	61 54	032	59 16	118	25 56	148	39 04	217	26 47	261	47 08	294	21 18	328
329	62 11	030	59 47	117	26 14	147	38 44	216	26 13	261	46 36	293	21 00	327
	◆FOMALHAUT		ACHERNAR		◆CANOPUS		RIGIL KENT		◆ANTARES		Nunki		ALTAIR	
330	62 28	028	60 18	117	26 33	147	38 23	216	25 39	260	46 04	292	20 40	326
331	62 44	027	60 48	117	26 52	146	38 04	215	25 05	259	45 32	291	20 21	325
332	62 59	025	61 19	116	27 11	146	37 44	215	24 31	258	45 00	290	20 01	324
333	63 13	023	61 50	116	27 31	145	37 24	214	23 57	258	44 27	289	19 40	323
334	63 26	021	62 21	115	27 51	144	37 05	214	23 24	257	43 55	288	19 19	322
335	63 37	019	62 52	115	28 11	144	36 46	213	22 50	256	43 22	287	18 58	321
336	63 48	017	63 23	115	28 31	143	36 27	213	22 17	255	42 49	286	18 36	320
337	63 58	015	63 55	114	28 52	143	36 08	213	21 44	255	42 16	285	18 14	319
338	64 06	013	64 26	114	29 13	142	35 50	212	21 11	254	41 42	284	17 51	318
339	64 13	011	64 57	114	29 34	142	35 32	212	20 38	253	41 09	283	17 28	317
340	64 20	009	65 29	113	29 56	141	35 14	211	20 05	252	40 35	282	17 04	316
341	64 25	007	66 01	113	30 17	141	34 56	211	19 32	251	40 02	281	16 40	315
342	64 28	005	66 32	113	30 39	140	34 39	210	19 00	251	39 28	280	16 15	314
343	64 31	003	67 04	113	31 02	139	34 22	210	18 27	250	38 54	279	15 51	313
344	64 32	001	67 36	112	31 24	139	34 05	209	17 55	249	38 20	278	15 25	312
	◆Diphda		Acamar		◆CANOPUS		Miaplacidus		RIGIL KENT		◆Nunki		FOMALHAUT	
345	47 54	039	48 36	095	31 47	138	36 16	169	33 48	209	37 46	277	64 32	359
346	48 15	037	49 10	094	32 10	138	36 23	169	33 32	208	37 12	277	64 31	357
347	48 36	036	49 44	093	32 33	137	36 29	168	33 16	208	36 37	276	64 29	355
348	48 56	035	50 19	092	32 57	137	36 37	168	33 00	207	36 03	275	64 26	353
349	49 15	033	50 53	092	33 20	136	36 44	167	32 44	207	35 29	274	64 21	351
350	49 34	032	51 28	091	33 44	136	36 52	167	32 29	206	34 54	273	64 15	349
351	49 51	030	52 02	090	34 09	135	37 00	166	32 14	206	34 20	272	64 08	347
352	50 08	029	52 36	089	34 33	134	37 08	166	31 59	205	33 46	272	64 00	345
353	50 25	028	53 11	088	34 58	134	37 16	166	31 44	205	33 11	271	63 50	343
354	50 40	026	53 45	088	35 23	133	37 25	165	31 30	204	32 37	270	63 40	341
355	50 55	025	54 20	087	35 48	133	37 34	165	31 16	204	32 02	269	63 28	339
356	51 09	023	54 54	086	36 13	132	37 43	165	31 02	203	31 28	268	63 16	338
357	51 22	022	55 28	085	36 39	132	37 52	164	30 49	203	30 54	267	63 02	336
358	51 35	020	56 02	084	37 04	131	38 02	164	30 35	202	30 19	267	62 48	334
359	51 46	019	56 37	083	37 30	131	38 11	163	30 23	202	29 45	266	62 32	332

LAT 56°S

LHA ♈	Hc Zn	Hc Zn	Hc Zn	Hc Zn	Hc Zn	Hc Zn	Hc Zn
	Diphda	◆ RIGEL	CANOPUS	Miaplacidus	◆ RIGIL KENT	Peacock	◆ FOMALHAUT
0	51 00 017	13 02 085	38 35 130	39 19 163	31 06 201	61 12 246	61 23 331
1	51 09 015	13 35 084	39 01 129	39 29 162	30 54 201	60 42 246	61 06 329
2	51 17 014	14 08 084	39 27 128	39 39 162	30 42 200	60 11 245	60 49 328
3	51 25 012	14 42 083	39 54 128	39 50 162	30 30 200	59 41 245	60 31 326
4	51 32 011	15 15 082	40 20 127	40 00 161	30 19 199	59 11 244	60 12 324
5	51 38 009	15 48 081	40 47 127	40 11 161	30 08 199	58 40 244	59 52 323
6	51 43 008	16 21 080	41 14 126	40 22 160	29 57 198	58 10 244	59 31 321
7	51 47 006	16 54 079	41 41 126	40 34 160	29 47 198	57 40 243	59 10 320
8	51 50 005	17 27 079	42 08 125	40 45 160	29 37 197	57 10 243	58 48 318
9	51 52 003	18 00 078	42 36 125	40 57 159	29 27 197	56 41 242	58 25 317
10	51 54 002	18 33 077	43 03 124	41 09 159	29 17 196	56 11 242	58 02 315
11	51 54 000	19 05 076	43 31 124	41 21 159	29 08 196	55 42 241	57 38 314
12	51 54 359	19 38 075	43 59 123	41 34 158	28 59 195	55 12 241	57 13 312
13	51 53 357	20 10 074	44 27 123	41 46 158	28 50 195	54 43 241	56 48 311
14	51 50 356	20 42 073	44 56 122	41 59 157	28 42 194	54 14 240	56 23 310
	◆ RIGEL	SIRIUS	CANOPUS	◆ RIGIL KENT	Peacock	◆ FOMALHAUT	Diphda
15	21 14 072	15 47 097	45 24 122	28 34 194	53 45 240	55 56 308	51 47 354
16	21 46 071	16 20 096	45 53 121	28 26 193	53 16 239	55 30 307	51 43 352
17	22 18 071	16 53 095	46 22 120	28 19 193	52 47 239	55 03 306	51 39 351
18	22 50 070	17 27 094	46 51 120	28 12 192	52 18 238	54 35 304	51 33 349
19	23 21 069	18 00 093	47 20 119	28 05 191	51 50 238	54 07 303	51 26 348
20	23 52 068	18 34 093	47 49 119	27 58 191	51 22 237	53 39 302	51 19 346
21	24 23 067	19 07 092	48 19 118	27 52 190	50 53 237	53 10 301	51 10 345
22	24 54 066	19 41 091	48 48 118	27 46 190	50 25 236	52 41 299	51 01 343
23	25 24 065	20 14 090	49 18 117	27 41 189	49 57 236	52 12 298	50 51 342
24	25 55 064	20 48 089	49 48 117	27 35 189	49 30 236	51 42 297	50 40 340
25	26 25 063	21 21 088	50 18 116	27 30 188	49 02 235	51 12 296	50 29 339
26	26 54 062	21 55 088	50 48 116	27 26 188	48 35 235	50 42 295	50 16 337
27	27 24 061	22 29 087	51 19 115	27 21 187	48 07 234	50 11 294	50 03 336
28	27 53 060	23 02 086	51 49 115	27 17 187	47 40 234	49 40 293	49 49 335
29	28 22 059	23 35 085	52 20 114	27 14 186	47 13 233	49 09 292	49 34 333
	◆ RIGEL	SIRIUS	CANOPUS	◆ RIGIL KENT	Peacock	◆ FOMALHAUT	Diphda
30	28 51 058	24 09 084	52 50 114	27 10 186	46 46 233	48 38 290	49 19 332
31	29 19 057	24 42 083	53 21 113	27 07 185	46 20 232	48 06 289	49 02 330
32	29 47 056	25 16 083	53 52 112	27 04 184	45 53 232	47 35 288	48 45 329
33	30 15 055	25 49 082	54 23 112	27 02 184	45 27 231	47 03 287	48 28 328
34	30 43 054	26 22 081	54 54 111	27 00 183	45 01 231	46 31 286	48 10 326
35	31 10 053	26 55 080	55 26 111	26 58 183	44 35 230	45 58 285	47 51 325
36	31 36 052	27 28 079	55 57 110	26 57 182	44 09 230	45 26 284	47 31 324
37	32 03 051	28 01 078	56 29 110	26 55 182	43 44 229	44 53 283	47 11 322
38	32 29 050	28 34 077	57 00 109	26 54 181	43 18 229	44 21 282	46 50 321
39	32 54 049	29 06 076	57 32 109	26 54 181	42 53 229	43 48 282	46 28 320
40	33 19 048	29 39 075	58 04 108	26 54 180	42 28 228	43 15 281	46 06 318
41	33 44 047	30 11 075	58 36 108	26 54 180	42 03 228	42 42 280	45 44 317
42	34 08 046	30 44 074	59 08 107	26 54 179	41 38 227	42 09 279	45 21 316
43	34 32 045	31 16 073	59 40 106	26 55 178	41 14 227	41 36 278	44 57 315
44	34 55 044	31 48 072	60 12 106	26 56 178	40 50 226	41 02 277	44 33 313
	RIGEL	◆ SIRIUS	CANOPUS	◆ RIGIL KENT	Peacock	FOMALHAUT	◆ Diphda
45	35 18 042	32 19 071	60 44 105	26 57 177	40 26 226	40 29 276	44 09 312
46	35 41 041	32 51 070	61 17 105	26 59 177	40 02 225	39 56 275	43 44 311
47	36 02 040	33 22 069	61 49 104	27 01 176	39 38 225	39 22 274	43 18 310
48	36 24 039	33 54 068	62 22 104	27 04 176	39 15 224	38 49 273	42 52 309
49	36 45 038	34 25 067	62 55 103	27 06 175	38 52 224	38 15 273	42 26 308
50	37 05 037	34 55 066	63 27 102	27 09 175	38 29 223	37 42 272	41 59 306
51	37 25 036	35 26 065	64 00 102	27 12 174	38 06 223	37 08 271	41 32 305
52	37 44 034	35 56 064	64 33 101	27 16 174	37 43 222	36 35 270	41 04 304
53	38 03 033	36 26 063	65 06 101	27 20 173	37 21 222	36 01 269	40 36 303
54	38 21 032	36 56 062	65 39 100	27 24 172	36 59 221	35 27 268	40 08 302
55	38 38 031	37 25 061	66 12 099	27 29 172	36 37 221	34 54 268	39 39 301
56	38 55 030	37 55 060	66 45 099	27 34 171	36 15 220	34 20 267	39 11 300
57	39 11 028	38 23 059	67 18 098	27 39 171	35 54 219	33 47 266	38 41 299
58	39 27 027	38 52 058	67 52 098	27 44 170	35 32 219	33 13 265	38 12 298
59	39 42 026	39 20 057	68 25 097	27 50 170	35 11 218	32 40 264	37 42 297
	RIGEL	◆ SIRIUS	Suhail	◆ RIGIL KENT	Peacock	FOMALHAUT	◆ Diphda
60	39 56 025	39 48 056	41 22 110	27 56 169	34 51 218	32 07 264	37 12 296
61	40 10 023	40 16 055	41 54 109	28 03 169	34 30 217	31 33 263	36 42 295
62	40 23 022	40 43 053	42 26 108	28 09 168	34 10 217	31 00 262	36 11 294
63	40 35 021	41 09 052	42 58 108	28 16 168	33 50 216	30 27 261	35 40 293
64	40 47 020	41 36 051	43 30 107	28 24 167	33 30 216	29 54 261	35 09 292
65	40 58 018	42 02 050	44 02 106	28 31 167	33 11 215	29 21 260	34 38 291
66	41 08 017	42 27 049	44 34 106	28 39 166	32 51 215	28 48 259	34 06 290
67	41 17 016	42 52 048	45 06 105	28 48 165	32 32 214	28 15 258	33 35 289
68	41 26 014	43 17 046	45 39 104	28 56 165	32 14 214	27 42 257	33 03 288
69	41 34 013	43 41 045	46 12 103	29 05 164	31 55 213	27 09 257	32 31 287
70	41 41 012	44 04 044	46 44 103	29 14 164	31 37 213	26 37 256	31 59 286
71	41 47 010	44 27 043	47 17 102	29 24 163	31 19 212	26 04 255	31 26 285
72	41 53 009	44 50 042	47 50 101	29 33 163	31 01 212	25 32 254	30 54 284
73	41 58 008	45 12 040	48 23 101	29 44 162	30 44 211	25 00 254	30 21 283
74	42 02 006	45 33 039	48 56 100	29 54 162	30 27 210	24 27 253	29 49 282
	RIGEL	◆ SIRIUS	Suhail	◆ RIGIL KENT	Peacock	ACHERNAR	◆ Diphda
75	42 05 005	45 54 038	49 29 099	30 04 161	30 10 210	62 50 246	29 16 282
76	42 08 004	46 15 037	50 02 098	30 15 161	29 53 209	62 20 246	28 43 281
77	42 10 002	46 34 035	50 35 098	30 27 160	29 37 209	61 49 246	28 10 280
78	42 11 001	46 53 034	51 09 097	30 38 160	29 21 208	61 19 245	27 37 279
79	42 11 000	47 12 033	51 42 096	30 50 159	29 05 208	60 48 245	27 04 278
80	42 11 358	47 29 031	52 15 095	31 02 159	28 50 207	60 18 244	26 30 277
81	42 09 357	47 46 030	52 49 095	31 14 158	28 35 207	59 48 244	25 57 276
82	42 07 356	48 03 028	53 22 094	31 27 158	28 20 206	59 18 244	25 24 275
83	42 04 354	48 18 027	53 56 093	31 40 157	28 05 205	58 48 243	24 50 275
84	42 01 353	48 33 026	54 29 092	31 53 157	27 51 205	58 18 243	24 17 274
85	41 56 352	48 48 024	55 03 092	32 06 156	27 37 204	57 48 242	23 43 273
86	41 51 350	49 01 023	55 36 091	32 20 156	27 23 204	57 18 242	23 10 272
87	41 45 349	49 14 021	56 10 090	32 34 155	27 10 203	56 49 241	22 36 271
88	41 38 348	49 26 020	56 43 089	32 48 155	26 57 203	56 19 241	22 03 270
89	41 31 346	49 37 019	57 17 088	33 03 154	26 44 202	55 50 241	21 29 270

LHA ♈	Hc Zn	Hc Zn	Hc Zn	Hc Zn	Hc Zn	Hc Zn	Hc Zn
	SIRIUS	Alphard	◆ Suhail	RIGIL KENT	◆ Peacock	ACHERNAR	◆ RIGEL
90	49 47 017	27 44 062	57 50 087	33 18 154	26 31 202	55 21 240	41 23 345
91	49 56 016	28 14 061	58 24 087	33 33 153	26 19 201	54 52 240	41 14 344
92	50 05 014	28 43 060	58 57 086	33 48 153	26 07 200	54 23 239	41 04 343
93	50 13 013	29 12 059	59 31 085	34 04 152	25 56 200	53 54 239	40 54 341
94	50 20 011	29 40 058	60 04 084	34 19 152	25 45 199	53 26 238	40 42 340
95	50 26 010	30 08 057	60 37 083	34 36 151	25 34 199	52 57 238	40 31 339
96	50 31 008	30 36 056	61 11 082	34 52 151	25 23 198	52 29 238	40 18 337
97	50 35 007	31 04 055	61 44 081	35 08 150	25 13 198	52 00 237	40 05 336
98	50 39 005	31 31 054	62 17 080	35 25 150	25 03 197	51 32 237	39 51 335
99	50 42 004	31 58 053	62 50 079	35 42 149	24 53 196	51 04 236	39 37 334
100	50 43 002	32 25 052	63 23 078	36 00 149	24 44 196	50 37 236	39 21 332
101	50 44 001	32 51 051	63 56 077	36 17 148	24 35 195	50 09 235	39 05 331
102	50 44 359	33 16 050	64 28 076	36 35 148	24 27 195	49 41 235	38 49 330
103	50 43 358	33 42 049	65 01 074	36 53 147	24 18 194	49 14 234	38 32 329
104	50 41 356	34 07 047	65 33 073	37 11 147	24 10 193	48 47 234	38 14 328
	Alphard	◆ Gienah	RIGIL KENT	◆ Peacock	ACHERNAR	◆ RIGEL	SIRIUS
105	34 31 046	20 34 091	37 30 146	24 03 193	48 20 234	37 56 326	50 39 355
106	34 55 045	21 08 090	37 49 146	23 55 192	47 53 233	37 37 325	50 35 353
107	35 19 044	21 41 090	38 08 145	23 48 192	47 26 233	37 18 324	50 31 352
108	35 42 043	22 15 089	38 27 145	23 42 191	46 59 232	36 58 323	50 25 350
109	36 05 042	22 49 088	38 46 144	23 36 191	46 33 232	36 37 322	50 19 349
110	36 27 041	23 22 087	39 06 144	23 30 190	46 07 231	36 16 321	50 12 347
111	36 48 040	23 56 086	39 26 144	23 24 189	45 41 231	35 54 319	50 04 346
112	37 10 038	24 29 085	39 46 143	23 19 189	45 15 230	35 32 318	49 56 344
113	37 30 037	25 02 085	40 06 143	23 14 188	44 49 230	35 10 317	49 46 343
114	37 50 036	25 36 084	40 26 142	23 09 188	44 23 229	34 47 316	49 36 341
115	38 10 035	26 09 083	40 47 142	23 05 187	43 58 229	34 23 315	49 24 340
116	38 29 034	26 42 082	41 08 141	23 01 186	43 33 228	33 59 314	49 12 338
117	38 47 033	27 16 081	41 29 141	22 58 186	43 08 228	33 35 313	49 00 337
118	39 05 031	27 49 080	41 50 140	22 54 185	42 43 227	33 10 312	48 46 336
119	39 22 030	28 22 079	42 12 140	22 51 185	42 19 227	32 45 311	48 32 334
	REGULUS	◆ SPICA	RIGIL KENT	Peacock	◆ ACHERNAR	RIGEL	◆ SIRIUS
120	16 58 033	14 03 089	42 34 139	22 49 184	41 54 226	32 19 310	48 17 333
121	17 16 032	14 36 089	42 56 139	22 47 183	41 30 226	31 53 308	48 01 331
122	17 33 031	15 10 088	43 18 139	22 45 183	41 06 226	31 26 307	47 45 330
123	17 50 030	15 43 087	43 40 138	22 44 182	40 42 225	31 00 306	47 28 329
124	18 07 029	16 17 086	44 02 138	22 42 182	40 18 225	30 32 305	47 10 327
125	18 23 028	16 50 085	44 25 137	22 42 181	39 55 224	30 05 304	46 51 326
126	18 39 027	17 24 084	44 48 137	22 41 180	39 32 224	29 37 303	46 32 325
127	18 54 026	17 57 083	45 11 136	22 41 180	39 09 223	29 09 302	46 13 323
128	19 08 025	18 30 083	45 34 136	22 41 179	38 46 223	28 40 301	45 52 322
129	19 22 024	19 04 082	45 58 136	22 42 179	38 23 222	28 12 300	45 31 321
130	19 36 023	19 37 081	46 21 135	22 43 178	38 01 222	27 42 299	45 10 320
131	19 49 022	20 10 080	46 45 135	22 44 177	37 39 221	27 13 298	44 48 318
132	20 01 021	20 43 079	47 09 134	22 46 177	37 17 221	26 43 297	44 25 317
133	20 13 020	21 16 078	47 33 134	22 48 176	36 55 220	26 14 297	44 02 316
134	20 24 019	21 49 077	47 57 134	22 50 176	36 34 220	25 43 296	43 39 315
	REGULUS	◆ SPICA	RIGIL KENT	◆ Peacock	ACHERNAR	CANOPUS	◆ SIRIUS
135	20 35 018	22 21 077	48 22 133	22 53 175	36 12 219	67 23 262	43 14 313
136	20 45 017	22 54 076	48 46 133	22 56 174	35 51 219	66 50 261	42 50 312
137	20 55 016	23 26 075	49 11 132	23 00 174	35 31 218	66 17 261	42 25 311
138	21 04 015	23 59 074	49 36 132	23 03 173	35 10 217	65 44 260	41 59 310
139	21 12 014	24 31 073	50 01 132	23 07 173	34 50 217	65 11 259	41 33 309
140	21 20 013	25 03 072	50 26 131	23 12 172	34 30 216	64 38 259	41 07 308
141	21 27 012	25 35 071	50 51 131	23 17 172	34 10 216	64 05 258	40 40 306
142	21 34 011	26 06 070	51 17 130	23 22 171	33 50 215	63 32 258	40 13 305
143	21 40 010	26 38 069	51 42 130	23 27 170	33 31 215	62 59 257	39 45 304
144	21 45 009	27 09 068	52 08 130	23 33 170	33 12 214	62 27 256	39 17 303
145	21 50 008	27 40 067	52 34 129	23 39 169	32 53 214	61 54 256	38 49 302
146	21 54 007	28 11 066	53 00 129	23 46 169	32 35 213	61 21 255	38 21 301
147	21 58 006	28 42 066	53 26 129	23 52 168	32 16 213	60 49 255	37 52 300
148	22 01 005	29 12 065	53 52 128	24 00 167	31 58 212	60 17 254	37 23 299
149	22 03 003	29 42 064	54 19 128	24 07 167	31 40 212	59 45 254	36 53 298
	REGULUS	◆ SPICA	RIGIL KENT	◆ Peacock	ACHERNAR	CANOPUS	◆ SIRIUS
150	22 05 002	30 12 063	54 45 128	24 15 166	31 23 211	59 12 253	36 23 297
151	22 06 001	30 42 062	55 12 127	24 23 166	31 06 211	58 40 253	35 53 296
152	22 06 000	31 11 061	55 39 127	24 32 165	30 49 210	58 08 252	35 23 295
153	22 06 359	31 40 060	56 06 127	24 40 164	30 32 210	57 37 251	34 52 294
154	22 05 358	32 09 059	56 33 126	24 50 164	30 16 209	57 05 251	34 22 293
155	22 04 357	32 38 058	57 00 126	24 59 163	30 00 208	56 33 250	33 51 292
156	22 02 356	33 06 057	57 27 126	25 09 163	29 44 208	56 02 250	33 19 291
157	22 00 355	33 34 056	57 54 125	25 19 162	29 28 207	55 30 249	32 48 290
158	21 56 354	34 01 055	58 22 125	25 29 162	29 13 207	54 59 249	32 16 289
159	21 53 353	34 28 053	58 49 125	25 40 161	28 58 206	54 28 248	31 45 288
160	21 48 352	34 55 052	59 17 124	25 51 160	28 43 206	53 57 248	31 13 287
161	21 43 351	35 21 051	59 45 124	26 03 160	28 29 205	53 26 247	30 40 286
162	21 37 350	35 47 050	60 13 124	26 14 159	28 15 205	52 55 247	30 08 285
163	21 31 349	36 13 049	60 41 123	26 26 159	28 01 204	52 24 246	29 36 284
164	21 24 348	36 38 048	61 09 123	26 39 158	27 47 203	51 53 245	29 03 284
	◆ SPICA	ANTARES	◆ Peacock	ACHERNAR	CANOPUS	◆ SIRIUS	REGULUS
165	37 03 047	25 44 100	26 51 158	27 34 203	51 23 245	28 31 283	21 17 347
166	37 27 046	26 17 099	27 04 157	27 21 202	50 53 244	27 58 282	21 09 346
167	37 51 045	26 50 098	27 18 156	27 09 202	50 22 244	27 25 281	21 00 345
168	38 14 044	27 23 097	27 31 156	26 56 201	49 52 243	26 52 280	20 51 344
169	38 37 042	27 56 097	27 45 156	26 44 201	49 22 243	26 19 279	20 41 343
170	39 00 041	28 30 096	27 59 155	26 33 200	48 53 242	25 46 278	20 31 341
171	39 22 040	29 03 095	28 14 154	26 21 200	48 23 242	25 12 277	20 20 340
172	39 43 039	29 37 094	28 28 154	26 10 199	47 54 241	24 39 277	20 08 339
173	40 04 038	30 10 093	28 43 153	25 59 198	47 24 241	24 06 276	19 56 338
174	40 24 036	30 44 093	28 59 153	25 49 198	46 55 240	23 32 275	19 44 337
175	40 44 035	31 17 092	29 14 152	25 39 197	46 26 240	22 59 274	19 30 336
176	41 03 034	31 51 091	29 30 151	25 29 197	45 57 239	22 25 273	19 17 335
177	41 21 033	32 24 090	29 46 151	25 19 196	45 28 239	21 52 272	19 02 334
178	41 39 032	32 58 089	30 03 150	25 10 196	45 00 238	21 18 271	18 48 333
179	41 56 030	33 31 089	30 20 150	25 01 195	44 32 238	20 45 271	18 32 332

LHA ♈	Hc	Zn	Hc	Zn	Hc	Zn	Hc	Zn	Hc	Zn	Hc	Zn	Hc	Zn
	◆SPICA		ANTARES		◆Peacock		ACHERNAR		CANOPUS		◆SIRIUS		Alphard	
180	42 13	029	34 05	088	30 37	149	24 53	194	44 03	237	20 11	270	34 11	313
181	42 29	028	34 38	087	30 54	149	24 45	194	43 35	236	19 38	269	33 46	312
182	42 44	026	35 12	086	31 12	148	24 37	193	43 07	236	19 04	268	33 21	311
183	42 59	025	35 45	085	31 29	148	24 29	193	42 40	235	18 31	267	32 55	310
184	43 13	024	36 19	084	31 48	147	24 22	192	42 12	235	17 57	267	32 29	308
185	43 26	023	36 52	083	32 06	147	24 15	191	41 45	234	17 24	266	32 02	307
186	43 38	021	37 25	082	32 25	146	24 09	191	41 18	234	16 50	265	31 36	306
187	43 50	020	37 59	082	32 43	145	24 03	190	40 51	233	16 17	264	31 08	305
188	44 01	019	38 32	081	33 03	145	23 57	190	40 24	233	15 43	263	30 41	304
189	44 11	017	39 05	080	33 22	144	23 51	189	39 57	232	15 10	262	30 13	303
190	44 21	016	39 38	079	33 42	144	23 46	189	39 31	232	14 37	262	29 45	302
191	44 30	015	40 11	078	34 02	143	23 41	188	39 05	231	14 04	261	29 16	301
192	44 38	013	40 43	077	34 22	143	23 37	187	38 39	231	13 31	260	28 48	300
193	44 45	012	41 16	076	34 42	142	23 33	187	38 13	230	12 58	259	28 18	299
194	44 52	010	41 48	075	35 03	142	23 29	186	37 47	229	12 25	258	27 49	298
	SPICA		◆ANTARES		Peacock		◆ACHERNAR		CANOPUS		Suhail		◆Alphard	
195	44 57	009	42 21	074	35 24	141	23 25	186	37 22	229	51 51	264	27 19	297
196	45 02	008	42 53	073	35 45	141	23 22	185	36 57	228	51 18	263	26 49	296
197	45 06	006	43 25	072	36 06	140	23 20	184	36 32	228	50 44	262	26 19	296
198	45 09	005	43 57	071	36 28	140	23 17	184	36 07	227	50 11	262	25 49	295
199	45 12	003	44 29	070	36 50	139	23 15	183	35 43	227	49 38	261	25 18	294
200	45 13	002	45 00	069	37 12	139	23 13	183	35 18	226	49 05	260	24 47	293
201	45 14	001	45 31	068	37 34	138	23 12	182	34 54	226	48 32	260	24 16	292
202	45 14	359	46 02	067	37 56	138	23 11	182	34 31	225	47 59	259	23 45	291
203	45 13	358	46 33	066	38 19	137	23 10	181	34 07	224	47 26	258	23 14	290
204	45 12	357	47 04	065	38 42	137	23 10	180	33 44	224	46 53	257	22 42	289
205	45 09	355	47 34	064	39 05	136	23 10	180	33 20	223	46 21	257	22 10	288
206	45 06	354	48 04	063	39 29	136	23 10	179	32 57	223	45 48	256	21 38	287
207	45 02	352	48 34	062	39 52	135	23 11	179	32 35	222	45 15	255	21 06	286
208	44 57	351	49 03	060	40 16	135	23 12	178	32 12	222	44 43	255	20 34	285
209	44 51	350	49 32	059	40 40	134	23 13	177	31 50	221	44 11	254	20 02	285
	ANTARES		◆Nunki		Peacock		ACHERNAR		◆CANOPUS		Suhail		◆SPICA	
210	50 01	058	30 19	093	41 04	134	23 15	177	31 28	220	43 38	253	44 45	348
211	50 29	057	30 53	092	41 28	133	23 17	176	31 07	220	43 06	253	44 38	347
212	50 57	056	31 26	091	41 53	133	23 19	176	30 45	219	42 34	252	44 30	345
213	51 24	055	32 00	090	42 18	132	23 22	175	30 24	219	42 03	251	44 21	344
214	51 52	053	32 33	090	42 43	132	23 25	174	30 03	218	41 31	251	44 11	343
215	52 18	052	33 07	089	43 08	131	23 28	174	29 43	218	40 59	250	44 01	341
216	52 44	051	33 40	088	43 33	131	23 32	173	29 22	217	40 28	249	43 50	340
217	53 10	049	34 14	087	43 59	130	23 36	173	29 02	216	39 56	249	43 38	339
218	53 35	048	34 47	086	44 24	130	23 41	172	28 42	216	39 25	248	43 26	337
219	54 00	047	35 21	085	44 50	129	23 46	172	28 23	215	38 54	247	43 13	336
220	54 24	045	35 54	084	45 16	129	23 51	171	28 04	215	38 23	247	42 59	335
221	54 48	044	36 28	084	45 43	128	23 56	170	27 45	214	37 53	246	42 44	334
222	55 11	043	37 01	083	46 09	128	24 02	170	27 26	214	37 22	245	42 29	332
223	55 33	041	37 34	082	46 35	127	24 08	169	27 08	213	36 52	245	42 13	331
224	55 55	040	38 07	081	47 02	127	24 15	169	26 49	212	36 21	244	41 56	330
	ANTARES		◆Nunki		Peacock		ACHERNAR		◆CANOPUS		Suhail		◆SPICA	
225	56 16	038	38 40	080	47 29	126	24 21	168	26 32	212	35 51	243	41 39	328
226	56 37	037	39 13	079	47 56	126	24 28	167	26 14	211	35 21	243	41 21	327
227	56 56	035	39 46	078	48 23	126	24 36	167	25 57	211	34 52	242	41 03	326
228	57 15	034	40 19	077	48 51	125	24 44	166	25 40	210	34 22	242	40 43	325
229	57 34	032	40 52	076	49 18	125	24 52	166	25 23	209	33 53	241	40 24	324
230	57 51	031	41 24	075	49 46	124	25 00	165	25 07	209	33 23	240	40 04	322
231	58 08	029	41 57	074	50 14	124	25 09	165	24 51	208	32 54	240	39 43	321
232	58 23	027	42 29	073	50 42	123	25 18	164	24 35	208	32 26	239	39 21	320
233	58 38	026	43 01	073	51 10	123	25 28	163	24 20	207	31 57	238	39 00	319
234	58 53	024	43 33	072	51 38	122	25 37	163	24 05	206	31 29	238	38 37	318
235	59 06	022	44 05	071	52 07	122	25 47	162	23 50	206	31 00	237	38 14	316
236	59 18	021	44 36	069	52 35	121	25 58	162	23 36	205	30 32	236	37 51	315
237	59 29	019	45 08	068	53 04	121	26 09	161	23 21	205	30 04	236	37 27	314
238	59 40	017	45 39	067	53 33	121	26 20	161	23 08	204	29 37	235	37 03	313
239	59 49	015	46 10	066	54 02	120	26 31	160	22 54	203	29 09	234	36 38	312
	◆ANTARES		Nunki		◆FOMALHAUT		ACHERNAR		CANOPUS		◆ACRUX		SPICA	
240	59 58	014	46 40	065	16 37	119	26 43	159	22 41	203	63 02	233	36 13	311
241	60 05	012	47 11	064	17 07	118	26 55	159	22 28	202	62 35	233	35 47	310
242	60 11	010	47 41	063	17 36	117	27 07	158	22 16	202	62 08	232	35 21	309
243	60 17	008	48 10	062	18 06	116	27 19	158	22 04	201	61 42	232	34 55	308
244	60 21	006	48 40	061	18 37	116	27 32	157	21 52	200	61 15	232	34 28	307
245	60 24	005	49 09	060	19 07	115	27 45	157	21 40	200	60 49	232	34 01	305
246	60 27	003	49 38	059	19 38	114	27 59	156	21 29	199	60 23	232	33 33	304
247	60 28	001	50 06	057	20 08	113	28 13	155	21 18	198	59 56	231	33 06	303
248	60 28	359	50 34	056	20 39	113	28 27	155	21 08	198	59 30	231	32 37	302
249	60 27	357	51 02	055	21 10	112	28 41	154	20 58	197	59 04	231	32 09	301
250	60 25	356	51 29	054	21 41	111	28 56	154	20 48	197	58 38	231	31 40	300
251	60 22	354	51 56	052	22 13	110	29 11	153	20 39	196	58 12	230	31 11	299
252	60 18	352	52 22	051	22 44	110	29 26	153	20 30	195	57 46	230	30 42	298
253	60 12	350	52 48	050	23 16	109	29 42	152	20 21	195	57 21	230	30 12	297
254	60 06	348	53 14	049	23 48	108	29 57	152	20 13	194	56 55	230	29 42	296
	ALTAIR		◆FOMALHAUT		ACHERNAR		CANOPUS		◆ACRUX		SPICA		◆ANTARES	
255	16 03	044	24 20	107	30 13	151	20 05	193	56 30	229	29 12	295	59 59	347
256	16 26	043	24 52	107	30 30	151	19 57	193	56 04	229	28 41	294	59 51	345
257	16 49	042	25 24	106	30 47	150	19 50	192	55 39	229	28 11	294	59 41	343
258	17 11	042	25 57	105	31 03	149	19 43	192	55 14	228	27 40	293	59 31	341
259	17 34	041	26 29	104	31 21	149	19 37	191	54 49	228	27 09	292	59 20	340
260	17 55	040	27 02	104	31 38	148	19 30	190	54 24	228	26 37	291	59 08	338
261	18 16	039	27 34	103	31 56	148	19 25	190	53 59	228	26 06	290	58 55	336
262	18 37	038	28 07	102	32 14	147	19 19	189	53 34	227	25 34	289	58 41	335
263	18 57	037	28 40	101	32 32	147	19 14	188	53 10	227	25 02	288	58 26	333
264	19 17	036	29 13	100	32 51	146	19 09	188	52 45	227	24 30	287	58 10	331
265	19 36	035	29 46	100	33 09	146	19 05	187	52 21	226	23 58	286	57 54	330
266	19 55	034	30 19	099	33 28	145	19 01	186	51 57	226	23 26	285	57 37	328
267	20 14	033	30 52	098	33 48	145	18 58	186	51 33	226	22 54	284	57 18	327
268	20 32	032	31 25	097	34 07	144	18 54	185	51 09	225	22 21	283	57 00	325
269	20 49	031	31 59	097	34 27	144	18 52	185	50 45	225	21 48	283	56 40	323

LAT 56°S

LHA ♈	Hc	Zn	Hc	Zn	Hc	Zn	Hc	Zn	Hc	Zn	Hc	Zn	Hc	Zn
	◆ALTAIR		FOMALHAUT		◆ACHERNAR		CANOPUS		RIGIL KENT		◆SPICA		ANTARES	
270	21 06	030	32 32	096	34 47	143	18 49	184	64 08	238	21 15	282	56 20	322
271	21 22	029	33 05	095	35 07	143	18 47	183	63 39	238	20 43	281	55 59	321
272	21 38	028	33 39	094	35 28	142	18 45	183	63 11	238	20 10	280	55 37	319
273	21 53	027	34 12	093	35 49	142	18 44	182	62 42	238	19 36	279	55 15	318
274	22 08	026	34 46	093	36 10	141	18 43	181	62 14	237	19 03	278	54 52	316
275	22 22	025	35 19	092	36 31	141	18 42	181	61 46	237	18 30	277	54 28	315
276	22 36	024	35 53	091	36 52	140	18 42	180	61 18	237	17 57	277	54 04	313
277	22 49	022	36 27	090	37 14	140	18 42	179	60 49	237	17 23	276	53 40	312
278	23 02	021	37 00	089	37 36	139	18 43	179	60 21	236	16 50	275	53 14	311
279	23 13	020	37 34	088	37 58	139	18 44	178	59 54	236	16 17	274	52 49	309
280	23 25	019	38 07	088	38 20	138	18 45	177	59 26	236	15 43	273	52 23	308
281	23 36	018	38 41	087	38 43	138	18 47	177	58 58	235	15 10	272	51 56	307
282	23 46	017	39 14	086	39 06	137	18 49	176	58 31	235	14 36	271	51 29	306
283	23 55	016	39 48	085	39 29	137	18 51	176	58 03	235	14 02	271	51 01	304
284	24 04	015	40 21	084	39 52	136	18 54	175	57 36	235	13 29	270	50 34	303
	◆ALTAIR		FOMALHAUT		◆ACHERNAR		CANOPUS		◆RIGIL KENT		ANTARES		Nunki	
285	24 13	014	40 54	083	40 15	136	18 57	174	57 08	234	50 05	302	60 16	358
286	24 21	013	41 28	082	40 39	135	19 01	174	56 41	234	49 37	301	60 15	356
287	24 28	012	42 01	081	41 03	135	19 05	173	56 14	234	49 08	300	60 12	355
288	24 34	011	42 34	081	41 27	134	19 09	172	55 47	233	48 39	299	60 08	353
289	24 40	010	43 07	080	41 51	134	19 13	172	55 20	233	48 09	297	60 04	351
290	24 46	009	43 40	079	42 15	133	19 18	171	54 54	233	47 39	296	59 58	349
291	24 50	007	44 13	078	42 40	133	19 24	170	54 27	232	47 09	295	59 51	348
292	24 54	006	44 46	077	43 05	132	19 30	170	54 01	232	46 38	294	59 43	346
293	24 58	005	45 18	076	43 30	132	19 36	169	53 34	232	46 07	293	59 35	344
294	25 01	004	45 51	075	43 55	131	19 42	169	53 08	231	45 36	292	59 25	342
295	25 03	003	46 23	074	44 20	131	19 49	168	52 42	231	45 05	291	59 14	341
296	25 04	002	46 55	073	44 46	130	19 56	167	52 16	230	44 34	290	59 03	339
297	25 05	001	47 27	072	45 11	130	20 04	167	51 50	230	44 02	289	58 50	337
298	25 05	000	47 59	071	45 37	129	20 12	166	51 25	230	43 30	288	58 37	335
299	25 05	359	48 30	070	46 03	129	20 20	165	50 59	229	42 58	287	58 22	334
	FOMALHAUT		◆ACHERNAR		CANOPUS		◆RIGIL KENT		ANTARES		Nunki		◆ALTAIR	
300	49 02	069	46 29	128	20 29	165	50 34	229	42 26	286	58 07	332	25 04	358
301	49 33	068	46 56	128	20 38	164	50 09	229	41 54	285	57 51	331	25 02	357
302	50 04	067	47 22	127	20 47	164	49 44	228	41 21	284	57 34	329	25 00	356
303	50 35	065	47 49	127	20 57	163	49 19	228	40 49	283	57 16	327	24 57	354
304	51 05	064	48 16	127	21 07	162	48 54	227	40 16	282	56 58	326	24 54	353
305	51 35	063	48 43	126	21 17	162	48 29	227	39 43	281	56 39	324	24 49	352
306	52 05	062	49 10	126	21 28	161	48 05	227	39 10	280	56 19	323	24 44	351
307	52 34	061	49 38	125	21 39	160	47 41	226	38 37	279	55 58	321	24 39	350
308	53 03	060	50 05	125	21 50	160	47 16	226	38 04	278	55 37	320	24 33	349
309	53 32	058	50 33	124	22 02	159	46 52	225	37 31	278	55 15	318	24 26	348
310	54 01	057	51 01	124	22 14	159	46 29	225	36 58	277	54 52	317	24 19	347
311	54 29	056	51 28	123	22 26	158	46 05	225	36 24	276	54 29	316	24 11	346
312	54 56	055	51 57	123	22 39	157	45 42	224	35 51	275	54 05	314	24 02	345
313	55 23	053	52 25	122	22 52	157	45 18	224	35 17	274	53 41	313	23 53	344
314	55 50	052	52 53	122	23 06	156	44 55	223	34 44	273	53 16	312	23 43	343
	◆FOMALHAUT		ACHERNAR		◆CANOPUS		RIGIL KENT		◆ANTARES		Nunki		ALTAIR	
315	56 16	051	53 22	122	23 19	156	44 32	223	34 10	272	52 51	310	23 33	342
316	56 42	049	53 50	121	23 34	155	44 10	222	33 37	272	52 25	309	23 22	340
317	57 07	048	54 19	121	23 48	154	43 47	222	33 03	271	51 59	308	23 11	339
318	57 32	047	54 48	120	24 03	154	43 25	222	32 30	270	51 32	306	22 59	338
319	57 56	045	55 17	120	24 18	153	43 03	221	31 56	269	51 05	305	22 46	337
320	58 20	044	55 46	119	24 33	152	42 41	221	31 23	268	50 37	304	22 33	336
321	58 42	042	56 15	119	24 49	152	42 19	220	30 49	268	50 09	303	22 19	335
322	59 05	041	56 45	119	25 05	151	41 57	220	30 16	267	49 41	302	22 05	334
323	59 26	039	57 14	118	25 21	151	41 36	219	29 42	266	49 12	300	21 50	333
324	59 47	037	57 44	118	25 38	150	41 15	219	29 09	265	48 43	299	21 34	332
325	60 07	036	58 14	117	25 54	149	40 54	218	28 35	264	48 13	298	21 18	331
326	60 26	034	58 44	117	26 12	149	40 33	218	28 02	263	47 44	297	21 02	330
327	60 45	033	59 14	117	26 29	148	40 12	218	27 29	263	47 13	296	20 45	329
328	61 02	031	59 44	116	26 47	148	39 52	217	26 55	262	46 43	295	20 27	328
329	61 19	029	60 14	116	27 05	147	39 32	217	26 22	261	46 13	294	20 09	327
	◆FOMALHAUT		ACHERNAR		◆CANOPUS		RIGIL KENT		◆ANTARES		Nunki		ALTAIR	
330	61 35	027	60 44	115	27 23	147	39 12	216	25 49	260	45 42	293	19 51	326
331	61 50	026	61 14	115	27 42	146	38 52	216	25 16	260	45 11	292	19 32	325
332	62 04	024	61 45	115	28 01	145	38 33	215	24 43	259	44 39	291	19 12	324
333	62 17	022	62 15	114	28 20	145	38 14	215	24 10	258	44 08	290	18 52	323
334	62 29	020	62 46	114	28 40	144	37 55	214	23 37	257	43 36	289	18 32	322
335	62 41	018	63 17	113	28 59	144	37 36	214	23 05	256	43 04	288	18 11	321
336	62 51	017	63 48	113	29 19	143	37 17	213	22 32	256	42 32	287	17 50	320
337	63 00	015	64 19	113	29 40	142	36 59	213	22 00	255	42 00	286	17 28	319
338	63 08	013	64 50	112	30 00	142	36 41	212	21 27	254	41 28	285	17 06	318
339	63 15	011	65 21	112	30 21	141	36 23	212	20 55	253	40 55	284	16 44	317
340	63 20	009	65 52	111	30 42	141	36 05	211	20 23	253	40 22	283	16 21	316
341	63 25	007	66 23	111	31 04	140	35 48	211	19 51	252	39 50	282	15 57	315
342	63 29	005	66 55	111	31 25	140	35 31	211	19 19	251	39 17	281	15 33	314
343	63 31	003	67 26	110	31 47	139	35 14	210	18 48	250	38 44	280	15 09	314
344	63 32	001	67 57	110	32 09	138	34 57	210	18 16	250	38 11	279	14 45	313
	◆Diphda		Acamar		CANOPUS		◆Miaplacidus		RIGIL KENT		◆Nunki		FOMALHAUT	
345	47 07	038	48 40	094	32 32	138	37 15	169	34 41	209	37 37	278	63 32	359
346	47 28	037	49 14	093	32 54	137	37 21	168	34 25	209	37 04	277	63 31	357
347	47 47	035	49 47	092	33 17	137	37 28	168	34 09	208	36 31	276	63 29	355
348	48 06	034	50 21	091	33 40	136	37 35	168	33 53	208	35 58	276	63 26	353
349	48 25	033	50 54	090	34 04	136	37 43	167	33 38	207	35 24	275	63 22	351
350	48 42	031	51 28	090	34 27	135	37 50	167	33 22	207	34 51	274	63 16	350
351	49 00	030	52 01	089	34 51	135	37 58	166	33 08	206	34 17	273	63 09	348
352	49 16	028	52 35	088	35 15	134	38 06	166	32 53	206	33 44	272	63 02	346
353	49 32	027	53 08	087	35 39	133	38 14	166	32 39	205	33 10	271	62 53	344
354	49 46	026	53 42	086	36 04	133	38 23	165	32 25	205	32 37	270	62 43	342
355	50 01	024	54 15	085	36 28	132	38 32	165	32 11	204	32 03	270	62 32	340
356	50 14	023	54 49	084	36 53	132	38 41	164	31 57	204	31 29	269	62 20	338
357	50 27	021	55 22	083	37 18	131	38 50	164	31 44	203	30 56	268	62 07	336
358	50 38	020	55 55	083	37 44	131	38 59	164	31 31	203	30 22	267	61 53	335
359	50 49	018	56 29	082	38 09	130	39 09	163	31 18	202	29 49	266	61 39	333

LAT 57°S

LHA ♈	Hc	Zn	Hc	Zn	Hc	Zn	Hc	Zn	Hc	Zn	Hc	Zn	Hc	Zn
	Diphda		◆ RIGEL		CANOPUS		Miaplacidus		◆ RIGIL KENT		Peacock		◆ FOMALHAUT	
0	50 02	017	12 57	085	39 13	129	40 16	162	32 02	202	61 36	248	60 30	332
1	50 11	015	13 29	084	39 39	128	40 26	162	31 50	201	61 06	247	60 14	330
2	50 19	014	14 02	083	40 04	128	40 36	162	31 38	201	60 36	247	59 58	329
3	50 26	012	14 34	083	40 30	127	40 46	161	31 27	200	60 06	246	59 41	327
4	50 33	011	15 06	082	40 56	127	40 57	161	31 15	200	59 36	246	59 22	325
5	50 38	009	15 39	081	41 23	126	41 08	161	31 05	199	59 06	245	59 03	324
6	50 43	008	16 11	080	41 49	126	41 19	160	30 54	199	58 36	245	58 44	322
7	50 47	006	16 43	079	42 16	125	41 30	160	30 44	198	58 07	245	58 24	321
8	50 50	005	17 15	078	42 43	124	41 42	159	30 34	197	57 37	244	58 03	319
9	50 52	003	17 47	077	43 10	124	41 53	159	30 24	197	57 08	244	57 41	318
10	50 54	002	18 19	076	43 37	123	42 05	159	30 15	196	56 39	243	57 19	316
11	50 54	000	18 51	076	44 04	123	42 17	158	30 06	196	56 10	243	56 56	315
12	50 54	359	19 22	075	44 32	122	42 29	158	29 57	195	55 41	242	56 32	313
13	50 53	357	19 54	074	44 59	122	42 42	157	29 48	195	55 12	242	56 08	312
14	50 51	356	20 25	073	45 27	121	42 54	157	29 40	194	54 43	241	55 44	311
	◆ RIGEL		SIRIUS		CANOPUS		◆ RIGIL KENT		Peacock		◆ FOMALHAUT		Diphda	
15	20 56	072	15 53	096	45 55	121	29 32	194	54 14	241	55 19	309	50 48	354
16	21 27	071	16 26	096	46 24	120	29 25	193	53 46	240	54 53	308	50 44	353
17	21 58	070	16 58	095	46 52	120	29 17	193	53 18	240	54 27	307	50 39	351
18	22 29	069	17 31	094	47 20	119	29 10	192	52 49	239	54 01	305	50 34	350
19	22 59	068	18 04	093	47 49	118	29 04	192	52 21	239	53 34	304	50 27	348
20	23 29	067	18 36	092	48 18	118	28 57	191	51 53	238	53 07	303	50 20	347
21	23 59	066	19 09	091	48 47	117	28 51	191	51 26	238	52 39	302	50 12	345
22	24 29	066	19 42	091	49 16	117	28 45	190	50 58	238	52 11	301	50 04	344
23	24 59	065	20 14	090	49 45	116	28 40	189	50 31	237	51 43	299	49 54	342
24	25 28	064	20 47	089	50 15	116	28 35	189	50 03	237	51 14	298	49 44	341
25	25 57	063	21 20	088	50 44	115	28 30	188	49 36	236	50 45	297	49 33	339
26	26 26	062	21 52	087	51 14	115	28 25	188	49 09	236	50 16	296	49 21	338
27	26 55	061	22 25	086	51 44	114	28 21	187	48 42	235	49 47	295	49 08	336
28	27 23	060	22 58	086	52 14	113	28 17	187	48 15	235	49 17	294	48 55	335
29	27 51	059	23 30	085	52 44	113	28 13	186	47 49	234	48 47	293	48 40	334
	◆ RIGEL		SIRIUS		CANOPUS		◆ RIGIL KENT		Peacock		◆ FOMALHAUT		Diphda	
30	28 19	058	24 03	084	53 14	112	28 10	186	47 22	234	48 16	292	48 26	332
31	28 47	057	24 35	083	53 44	112	28 07	185	46 56	233	47 46	290	48 10	331
32	29 14	056	25 07	082	54 14	111	28 04	184	46 30	233	47 15	289	47 54	330
33	29 41	055	25 40	081	54 45	111	28 02	184	46 04	232	46 44	288	47 37	328
34	30 07	054	26 12	080	55 16	110	28 00	183	45 38	232	46 13	287	47 19	327
35	30 33	053	26 44	079	55 46	109	27 58	183	45 13	231	45 42	286	47 01	326
36	30 59	052	27 16	079	56 17	109	27 56	182	44 48	231	45 10	285	46 42	324
37	31 25	051	27 48	078	56 48	108	27 55	182	44 22	230	44 39	284	46 23	323
38	31 50	050	28 20	077	57 19	108	27 54	181	43 57	230	44 07	283	46 03	322
39	32 14	049	28 52	076	57 50	107	27 54	181	43 33	229	43 35	282	45 43	320
40	32 39	047	29 24	075	58 22	107	27 54	180	43 08	229	43 03	282	45 21	319
41	33 03	046	29 55	074	58 53	106	27 54	180	42 43	228	42 31	281	45 00	318
42	33 26	045	30 26	073	59 25	105	27 54	179	42 19	228	41 59	280	44 38	317
43	33 49	044	30 58	072	59 56	105	27 55	178	41 55	227	41 27	279	44 15	315
44	34 12	043	31 29	071	60 28	104	27 56	178	41 31	227	40 55	278	43 52	314
	RIGEL		◆ SIRIUS		CANOPUS		◆ RIGIL KENT		Peacock		FOMALHAUT		◆ Diphda	
45	34 34	042	31 59	070	60 59	104	27 57	177	41 07	226	40 22	277	43 28	313
46	34 55	041	32 30	069	61 31	103	27 59	177	40 44	226	39 50	276	43 04	312
47	35 16	040	33 00	068	62 03	102	28 01	176	40 21	225	39 17	275	42 39	311
48	35 37	039	33 31	067	62 35	102	28 03	176	39 58	225	38 45	274	42 14	309
49	35 57	037	34 01	066	63 07	101	28 06	175	39 35	224	38 12	273	41 49	308
50	36 17	036	34 31	065	63 39	100	28 09	175	39 12	224	37 39	273	41 23	307
51	36 36	035	35 00	064	64 11	100	28 12	174	38 50	223	37 07	272	40 57	306
52	36 54	034	35 30	063	64 44	099	28 16	173	38 28	223	36 34	271	40 30	305
53	37 12	033	35 59	062	65 16	099	28 20	173	38 06	222	36 01	270	40 03	304
54	37 30	032	36 27	061	65 48	098	28 24	172	37 44	222	35 29	269	39 36	303
55	37 47	030	36 56	060	66 21	097	28 28	172	37 22	221	34 56	268	39 08	302
56	38 03	029	37 24	059	66 53	096	28 33	171	37 01	220	34 23	268	38 40	301
57	38 18	028	37 52	058	67 26	096	28 38	171	36 40	220	33 51	267	38 12	300
58	38 34	027	38 20	057	67 58	095	28 43	170	36 19	219	33 18	266	37 43	299
59	38 48	026	38 47	056	68 31	094	28 49	170	35 58	219	32 45	265	37 15	297
	RIGEL		◆ SIRIUS		Suhail		◆ RIGIL KENT		Peacock		FOMALHAUT		◆ Diphda	
60	39 02	024	39 14	055	41 42	109	28 55	169	35 38	218	32 13	264	36 45	296
61	39 15	023	39 40	054	42 13	108	29 02	169	35 18	218	31 40	263	36 16	295
62	39 27	022	40 07	053	42 44	107	29 08	168	34 58	217	31 08	263	35 46	294
63	39 39	021	40 32	052	43 15	107	29 15	168	34 38	217	30 36	262	35 17	293
64	39 50	019	40 58	050	43 47	106	29 22	167	34 19	216	30 03	261	34 46	292
65	40 01	018	41 23	049	44 18	105	29 30	166	33 59	216	29 31	260	34 16	291
66	40 10	017	41 47	048	44 50	105	29 38	166	33 41	215	28 59	260	33 46	291
67	40 19	015	42 11	047	45 21	104	29 46	165	33 22	215	28 27	259	33 15	290
68	40 28	014	42 35	046	45 53	103	29 54	165	33 03	214	27 55	258	32 44	289
69	40 35	013	42 58	045	46 25	102	30 03	164	32 45	214	27 23	257	32 13	288
70	40 42	012	43 21	043	46 57	102	30 12	164	32 27	213	26 51	256	31 42	287
71	40 48	010	43 43	042	47 29	101	30 21	163	32 10	212	26 19	256	31 10	286
72	40 54	009	44 05	041	48 01	100	30 31	163	31 52	212	25 48	255	30 39	285
73	40 58	008	44 26	040	48 33	100	30 41	162	31 35	211	25 16	254	30 07	284
74	41 02	006	44 47	038	49 06	099	30 51	162	31 18	211	24 45	253	29 35	283
	RIGEL		◆ SIRIUS		Suhail		◆ RIGIL KENT		Peacock		ACHERNAR		◆ Diphda	
75	41 06	005	45 07	037	49 38	098	31 01	161	31 02	210	63 13	248	29 04	282
76	41 08	004	45 26	036	50 10	097	31 12	161	30 45	210	62 43	248	28 32	281
77	41 10	002	45 45	035	50 43	097	31 23	160	30 29	209	62 13	247	27 59	280
78	41 11	001	46 03	033	51 15	096	31 34	159	30 14	209	61 43	247	27 27	279
79	41 11	000	46 21	032	51 48	095	31 46	159	29 58	208	61 13	246	26 55	279
80	41 11	358	46 38	031	52 20	094	31 58	158	29 43	207	60 43	246	26 23	278
81	41 09	357	46 54	029	52 53	093	32 10	158	29 28	207	60 13	245	25 50	277
82	41 07	356	47 10	028	53 26	093	32 22	157	29 14	206	59 44	245	25 18	276
83	41 05	355	47 25	027	53 58	092	32 35	157	28 59	206	59 14	245	24 45	275
84	41 01	353	47 39	025	54 31	091	32 48	156	28 45	205	58 45	244	24 13	274
85	40 57	352	47 53	024	55 04	090	33 01	156	28 31	205	58 15	244	23 40	273
86	40 52	351	48 06	022	55 36	089	33 15	155	28 18	204	57 46	243	23 07	273
87	40 46	349	48 18	021	56 09	088	33 28	155	28 05	203	57 17	243	22 35	272
88	40 40	348	48 29	020	56 42	088	33 43	154	27 52	203	56 48	242	22 02	271
89	40 33	347	48 40	018	57 14	087	33 57	154	27 39	202	56 19	242	21 29	270

LHA ♈	Hc	Zn	Hc	Zn	Hc	Zn	Hc	Zn	Hc	Zn	Hc	Zn	Hc	Zn
	SIRIUS		Alphard		◆ Suhail		RIGIL KENT		◆ Peacock		ACHERNAR		◆ RIGEL	
90	48 50	017	27 16	061	57 47	086	34 11	153	27 27	202	55 50	241	40 25	345
91	48 59	015	27 44	060	58 19	085	34 26	153	27 15	201	55 22	241	40 16	344
92	49 07	014	28 12	059	58 52	084	34 41	152	27 04	201	54 53	241	40 07	343
93	49 14	012	28 40	058	59 24	083	34 57	152	26 52	200	54 25	240	39 57	342
94	49 21	011	29 08	057	59 57	082	35 12	151	26 41	199	53 56	240	39 46	340
95	49 27	010	29 35	056	60 29	081	35 28	151	26 31	199	53 28	239	39 35	339
96	49 32	008	30 02	055	61 01	080	35 44	150	26 20	198	53 00	239	39 23	338
97	49 36	007	30 29	054	61 33	079	36 00	150	26 10	198	52 32	238	39 10	337
98	49 39	005	30 56	053	62 05	078	36 17	149	26 00	197	52 05	238	38 57	335
99	49 42	004	31 22	052	62 37	077	36 34	149	25 51	196	51 37	237	38 43	334
100	49 43	002	31 47	051	63 09	076	36 51	148	25 42	196	51 10	237	38 28	333
101	49 44	001	32 12	050	63 41	075	37 08	148	25 33	195	50 43	236	38 13	332
102	49 44	359	32 37	049	64 12	074	37 26	147	25 25	195	50 15	236	37 57	330
103	49 43	358	33 02	048	64 43	072	37 43	147	25 16	194	49 48	235	37 40	329
104	49 42	356	33 26	047	65 15	071	38 01	146	25 09	194	49 22	235	37 23	328
	Alphard		◆ Gienah		RIGIL KENT		◆ Peacock		ACHERNAR		◆ RIGEL		SIRIUS	
105	33 50	046	20 35	091	38 20	146	25 01	193	48 55	234	37 06	327	49 39	355
106	34 13	045	21 08	090	38 38	145	24 54	192	48 28	234	36 48	326	49 36	353
107	34 36	044	21 41	089	38 57	145	24 47	192	48 02	234	36 29	324	49 31	352
108	34 58	043	22 13	088	39 16	144	24 41	191	47 36	233	36 10	323	49 26	350
109	35 20	041	22 46	088	39 35	144	24 35	191	47 10	233	35 50	322	49 20	349
110	35 41	040	23 19	087	39 54	143	24 29	190	46 44	232	35 30	321	49 14	347
111	36 02	039	23 51	086	40 14	143	24 23	189	46 18	232	35 09	320	49 06	346
112	36 22	038	24 24	085	40 33	143	24 18	189	45 53	231	34 47	319	48 58	345
113	36 42	037	24 56	084	40 53	142	24 13	188	45 27	231	34 26	318	48 49	343
114	37 02	036	25 29	083	41 14	142	24 09	188	45 02	230	34 03	316	48 39	342
115	37 20	034	26 01	082	41 34	141	24 05	187	44 37	230	33 41	315	48 28	340
116	37 39	033	26 34	081	41 55	141	24 01	186	44 12	229	33 17	314	48 17	339
117	37 56	032	27 06	081	42 15	140	23 57	186	43 48	229	32 54	313	48 04	337
118	38 13	031	27 38	080	42 36	140	23 54	185	43 23	228	32 30	312	47 52	336
119	38 30	030	28 10	079	42 58	139	23 51	185	42 59	228	32 05	311	47 38	335
	REGULUS		◆ SPICA		RIGIL KENT		Peacock		◆ ACHERNAR		RIGEL		◆ SIRIUS	
120	16 07	033	14 02	089	43 19	139	23 49	184	42 35	227	31 41	310	47 24	333
121	16 25	032	14 35	088	43 41	138	23 47	183	42 11	227	31 15	309	47 08	332
122	16 42	031	15 07	087	44 03	138	23 45	183	41 48	226	30 50	308	46 53	331
123	16 59	030	15 40	087	44 24	138	23 43	182	41 24	226	30 24	307	46 36	329
124	17 15	029	16 12	086	44 47	137	23 42	182	41 01	225	29 57	306	46 19	328
125	17 30	028	16 45	085	45 09	137	23 42	181	40 38	225	29 31	305	46 02	327
126	17 45	027	17 18	084	45 32	136	23 41	180	40 15	224	29 04	304	45 43	325
127	18 00	026	17 50	083	45 54	136	23 41	180	39 52	224	28 37	303	45 24	324
128	18 14	025	18 22	082	46 17	135	23 41	179	39 30	223	28 09	302	45 05	323
129	18 28	024	18 55	081	46 40	135	23 42	179	39 08	223	27 41	301	44 45	321
130	18 41	023	19 27	081	47 03	134	23 43	178	38 46	222	27 13	300	44 24	320
131	18 53	022	19 59	080	47 27	134	23 44	177	38 24	222	26 44	299	44 03	319
132	19 05	021	20 31	079	47 50	134	23 46	177	38 02	221	26 16	298	43 41	318
133	19 17	020	21 03	078	48 14	133	23 48	176	37 41	221	25 47	297	43 19	316
134	19 28	019	21 35	077	48 38	133	23 50	176	37 20	220	25 17	296	42 56	315
	REGULUS		◆ SPICA		RIGIL KENT		◆ Peacock		ACHERNAR		CANOPUS		◆ SIRIUS	
135	19 38	018	22 07	076	49 02	132	23 53	175	36 59	220	67 30	264	42 33	314
136	19 48	017	22 39	075	49 26	132	23 56	174	36 38	219	66 58	264	42 09	313
137	19 57	016	23 10	074	49 51	132	23 59	174	36 18	218	66 25	263	41 45	312
138	20 06	015	23 42	073	50 15	131	24 03	173	35 58	218	65 53	262	41 20	311
139	20 14	014	24 13	073	50 40	131	24 07	173	35 38	217	65 21	262	40 55	309
140	20 21	013	24 44	072	51 05	130	24 11	172	35 18	217	64 48	261	40 30	308
141	20 28	012	25 15	071	51 30	130	24 16	171	34 58	216	64 16	260	40 04	307
142	20 35	011	25 46	070	51 55	129	24 21	171	34 39	216	63 44	260	39 38	306
143	20 41	010	26 16	069	52 20	129	24 26	170	34 20	215	63 12	259	39 11	305
144	20 46	009	26 47	068	52 46	129	24 32	170	34 01	215	62 40	258	38 44	304
145	20 51	008	27 17	067	53 11	128	24 38	169	33 43	214	62 08	258	38 17	303
146	20 55	007	27 47	066	53 37	128	24 44	168	33 25	214	61 36	257	37 49	302
147	20 58	006	28 16	065	54 03	128	24 51	168	33 07	213	61 04	256	37 21	301
148	21 01	004	28 46	064	54 29	127	24 58	167	32 49	213	60 32	256	36 53	300
149	21 03	003	29 15	063	54 55	127	25 06	167	32 31	212	60 01	255	36 25	299
	REGULUS		◆ SPICA		RIGIL KENT		◆ Peacock		ACHERNAR		CANOPUS		◆ SIRIUS	
150	21 05	002	29 44	062	55 21	126	25 13	166	32 14	211	59 29	255	35 56	298
151	21 06	001	30 13	061	55 48	126	25 21	166	31 57	211	58 58	254	35 27	297
152	21 06	000	30 42	060	56 14	126	25 30	165	31 41	210	58 26	254	34 57	296
153	21 06	359	31 10	059	56 41	125	25 38	164	31 24	210	57 55	253	34 28	295
154	21 06	358	31 38	058	57 07	125	25 47	164	31 08	209	57 24	252	33 58	294
155	21 04	357	32 05	057	57 34	125	25 57	163	30 52	209	56 53	252	33 28	293
156	21 02	356	32 32	056	58 01	124	26 06	163	30 37	208	56 22	251	32 58	292
157	21 00	355	32 59	055	58 28	124	26 16	162	30 21	208	55 51	251	32 27	291
158	20 57	354	33 26	054	58 56	124	26 26	161	30 06	207	55 20	250	31 56	290
159	20 53	353	33 52	053	59 23	123	26 37	161	29 52	207	54 49	249	31 26	289
160	20 49	352	34 18	052	59 50	123	26 48	160	29 37	206	54 19	249	30 55	288
161	20 44	351	34 44	051	60 18	123	26 59	160	29 23	205	53 48	248	30 23	287
162	20 38	350	35 09	050	60 45	122	27 10	159	29 09	205	53 18	248	29 52	286
163	20 32	349	35 34	049	61 13	122	27 22	159	28 56	204	52 48	247	29 21	285
164	20 26	348	35 58	048	61 41	122	27 34	158	28 42	204	52 18	247	28 49	284
	◆ SPICA		ANTARES		◆ Peacock		ACHERNAR		CANOPUS		◆ SIRIUS		REGULUS	
165	36 22	046	25 54	099	27 47	157	28 29	203	51 48	246	28 17	283	20 18	347
166	36 45	045	26 26	099	28 00	157	28 17	203	51 18	246	27 45	282	20 11	346
167	37 08	044	26 58	098	28 13	156	28 04	202	50 48	245	27 13	281	20 02	345
168	37 31	043	27 31	097	28 26	156	27 52	201	50 19	244	26 41	280	19 53	344
169	37 53	042	28 03	096	28 39	155	27 40	201	49 49	244	26 09	280	19 44	343
170	38 14	041	28 36	095	28 53	155	27 29	200	49 20	243	25 37	279	19 34	342
171	38 35	040	29 08	094	29 08	154	27 18	200	48 51	243	25 04	278	19 23	341
172	38 56	038	29 41	094	29 22	153	27 07	199	48 22	242	24 32	277	19 12	340
173	39 16	037	30 13	093	29 37	153	26 56	199	47 53	242	24 00	276	19 00	339
174	39 36	036	30 46	092	29 52	152	26 46	198	47 24	241	23 27	275	18 48	338
175	39 54	035	31 19	091	30 07	152	26 36	197	46 56	241	22 54	274	18 35	337
176	40 13	034	31 51	090	30 23	151	26 26	197	46 28	240	22 22	274	18 22	336
177	40 31	032	32 24	090	30 39	151	26 17	196	45 59	239	21 49	273	18 08	335
178	40 48	031	32 57	089	30 55	150	26 08	196	45 31	239	21 17	272	17 54	334
179	41 04	030	33 29	088	31 11	149	25 59	195	45 03	238	20 44	271	17 39	333

LHA ♈	Hc	Zn	Hc	Zn	Hc	Zn	Hc	Zn	Hc	Zn	Hc	Zn	Hc	Zn
	◆ SPICA		ANTARES		◆ Peacock		ACHERNAR		CANOPUS		◆ SIRIUS		Alphard	
180	41 20	029	34 02	087	31 28	149	25 51	195	44 36	238	20 11	270	33 30	313
181	41 36	027	34 35	086	31 45	148	25 43	194	44 08	237	19 39	269	33 06	312
182	41 50	026	35 07	085	32 02	148	25 35	193	43 41	237	19 06	268	32 41	311
183	42 04	025	35 40	084	32 20	147	25 28	193	43 13	236	18 33	268	32 17	310
184	42 18	023	36 12	084	32 38	147	25 21	192	42 46	236	18 01	267	31 51	309
185	42 30	022	36 45	083	32 56	146	25 14	192	42 20	235	17 28	266	31 26	308
186	42 42	021	37 17	082	33 14	146	25 08	191	41 53	234	16 55	265	31 00	307
187	42 54	020	37 49	081	33 33	145	25 02	190	41 26	234	16 23	264	30 33	306
188	43 04	018	38 22	080	33 52	145	24 56	190	41 00	233	15 50	264	30 07	305
189	43 14	017	38 54	079	34 11	144	24 51	189	40 34	233	15 18	263	29 40	304
190	43 23	016	39 26	078	34 30	143	24 46	189	40 08	232	14 46	262	29 13	303
191	43 32	014	39 58	077	34 50	143	24 41	188	39 42	232	14 13	261	28 45	302
192	43 39	013	40 29	076	35 09	142	24 36	187	39 17	231	13 41	260	28 17	301
193	43 46	012	41 01	075	35 30	142	24 32	187	38 51	231	13 09	259	27 49	300
194	43 53	010	41 33	074	35 50	141	24 29	186	38 26	230	12 37	259	27 20	299
	SPICA		◆ ANTARES		Peacock		◆ ACHERNAR		CANOPUS		Suhail		◆ Alphard	
195	43 58	009	42 04	073	36 10	141	24 25	186	38 01	229	51 57	265	26 52	298
196	44 03	008	42 35	072	36 31	140	24 22	185	37 37	229	51 24	264	26 23	297
197	44 06	006	43 06	071	36 52	140	24 19	184	37 12	228	50 52	264	25 53	296
198	44 10	005	43 37	070	37 13	139	24 17	184	36 48	228	50 19	263	25 24	295
199	44 12	003	44 08	069	37 35	139	24 15	183	36 24	227	49 47	262	24 54	294
200	44 13	002	44 38	068	37 57	138	24 13	183	36 00	227	49 14	261	24 24	293
201	44 14	001	45 09	067	38 18	138	24 12	182	35 36	226	48 42	261	23 54	292
202	44 14	359	45 39	066	38 41	137	24 11	182	35 13	225	48 10	260	23 24	291
203	44 13	358	46 08	065	39 03	137	24 10	181	34 50	225	47 38	259	22 53	290
204	44 12	357	46 38	064	39 25	136	24 10	180	34 27	224	47 06	258	22 22	289
205	44 10	355	47 07	063	39 48	136	24 10	180	34 04	224	46 34	258	21 51	289
206	44 06	354	47 36	062	40 11	135	24 10	179	33 41	223	46 02	257	21 20	288
207	44 03	352	48 05	061	40 34	135	24 11	179	33 19	223	45 30	256	20 49	287
208	43 58	351	48 33	060	40 58	134	24 12	178	32 57	222	44 58	256	20 18	286
209	43 52	350	49 01	058	41 21	134	24 13	177	32 35	221	44 27	255	19 46	285
	ANTARES		◆ Nunki		Peacock		ACHERNAR		◆ CANOPUS		Suhail		◆ SPICA	
210	49 29	057	30 22	092	41 45	133	24 15	177	32 14	221	43 55	254	43 46	348
211	49 56	056	30 55	091	42 09	133	24 17	176	31 53	220	43 24	254	43 39	347
212	50 23	055	31 27	091	42 33	132	24 19	176	31 32	220	42 53	253	43 32	346
213	50 49	054	32 00	090	42 58	132	24 22	175	31 11	219	42 21	252	43 23	344
214	51 15	052	32 33	089	43 22	131	24 25	174	30 50	219	41 50	251	43 14	343
215	51 41	051	33 05	088	43 47	130	24 28	174	30 30	218	41 19	251	43 04	342
216	52 06	050	33 38	087	44 12	130	24 32	173	30 10	217	40 49	250	42 54	340
217	52 31	048	34 10	086	44 37	130	24 36	173	29 50	217	40 18	249	42 42	339
218	52 55	047	34 43	086	45 02	129	24 40	172	29 31	216	39 47	249	42 30	338
219	53 19	046	35 16	085	45 28	129	24 45	171	29 12	216	39 17	248	42 18	336
220	53 42	044	35 48	084	45 54	128	24 50	171	28 53	215	38 47	247	42 04	335
221	54 04	043	36 21	083	46 19	128	24 55	170	28 34	214	38 17	247	41 50	334
222	54 26	042	36 53	082	46 45	127	25 01	170	28 16	214	37 47	246	41 35	333
223	54 48	040	37 25	081	47 12	127	25 07	169	27 58	213	37 17	245	41 20	331
224	55 09	039	37 58	080	47 38	126	25 13	168	27 40	213	36 47	245	41 04	330
	ANTARES		◆ Nunki		Peacock		ACHERNAR		◆ CANOPUS		Suhail		◆ SPICA	
225	55 29	037	38 30	079	48 04	126	25 20	168	27 23	212	36 18	244	40 48	329
226	55 48	036	39 02	078	48 31	125	25 27	167	27 05	211	35 49	243	40 30	328
227	56 07	034	39 34	077	48 58	125	25 34	167	26 48	211	35 19	243	40 13	326
228	56 25	033	40 06	076	49 25	124	25 42	166	26 32	210	34 50	242	39 54	325
229	56 43	031	40 37	076	49 52	124	25 50	166	26 15	210	34 22	241	39 35	324
230	56 59	030	41 09	075	50 19	123	25 58	165	25 59	209	33 53	241	39 16	323
231	57 15	028	41 40	074	50 47	123	26 07	164	25 44	208	33 25	240	38 56	322
232	57 30	027	42 12	073	51 14	122	26 16	164	25 28	208	32 56	239	38 35	320
233	57 44	025	42 43	072	51 42	122	26 25	163	25 13	207	32 28	239	38 14	319
234	57 58	023	43 14	071	52 10	121	26 35	163	24 58	207	32 00	238	37 53	318
235	58 10	022	43 44	070	52 38	121	26 45	162	24 44	206	31 33	237	37 31	317
236	58 22	020	44 15	069	53 06	120	26 55	162	24 30	205	31 05	237	37 08	316
237	58 32	018	44 45	068	53 34	120	27 05	161	24 16	205	30 38	236	36 45	315
238	58 42	017	45 15	066	54 03	119	27 16	160	24 02	204	30 11	236	36 22	314
239	58 51	015	45 45	065	54 31	119	27 27	160	23 49	204	29 44	235	35 58	312
	◆ ANTARES		Nunki		◆ FOMALHAUT		ACHERNAR		CANOPUS		◆ ACRUX		SPICA	
240	58 59	013	46 15	064	17 06	118	27 39	159	23 36	203	63 37	234	35 33	311
241	59 06	012	46 44	063	17 34	118	27 50	159	23 24	202	63 11	234	35 09	310
242	59 12	010	47 13	062	18 04	117	28 03	158	23 12	202	62 44	234	34 44	309
243	59 17	008	47 42	061	18 33	116	28 15	158	23 00	201	62 18	234	34 18	308
244	59 21	006	48 10	060	19 02	115	28 28	157	22 48	200	61 52	233	33 52	307
245	59 24	005	48 38	059	19 32	114	28 40	156	22 37	200	61 25	233	33 26	306
246	59 27	003	49 06	058	20 02	114	28 54	156	22 26	199	60 59	233	32 59	305
247	59 28	001	49 33	056	20 32	113	29 07	155	22 15	199	60 33	233	32 32	304
248	59 28	359	50 00	055	21 02	112	29 21	155	22 05	198	60 07	232	32 05	303
249	59 27	358	50 27	054	21 32	111	29 35	154	21 55	197	59 41	232	31 37	302
250	59 25	356	50 53	053	22 03	111	29 50	154	21 46	197	59 16	232	31 09	301
251	59 22	354	51 19	051	22 33	110	30 04	153	21 37	196	58 50	232	30 41	300
252	59 18	352	51 44	050	23 04	109	30 19	152	21 28	195	58 24	231	30 13	299
253	59 13	350	52 09	049	23 35	108	30 35	152	21 19	195	57 59	231	29 44	298
254	59 07	349	52 34	048	24 06	108	30 50	151	21 11	194	57 33	231	29 15	297
	ALTAIR		◆ FOMALHAUT		ACHERNAR		CANOPUS		◆ ACRUX		SPICA		◆ ANTARES	
255	15 20	044	24 37	107	31 06	151	21 03	193	57 08	230	28 46	296	59 00	347
256	15 43	043	25 09	106	31 22	150	20 56	193	56 43	230	28 16	295	58 53	345
257	16 05	042	25 40	105	31 38	150	20 49	192	56 18	230	27 47	294	58 44	344
258	16 26	041	26 12	105	31 55	149	20 42	192	55 53	230	27 17	293	58 34	342
259	16 48	040	26 44	104	32 12	149	20 36	191	55 28	229	26 46	292	58 24	340
260	17 09	039	27 15	103	32 29	148	20 29	190	55 04	229	26 16	291	58 12	339
261	17 29	038	27 47	102	32 47	147	20 24	190	54 39	229	25 45	290	58 00	337
262	17 49	037	28 19	101	33 04	147	20 18	189	54 15	228	25 15	289	57 46	335
263	18 09	036	28 51	101	33 22	146	20 14	188	53 50	228	24 44	288	57 32	334
264	18 28	035	29 23	100	33 40	146	20 09	188	53 26	228	24 13	287	57 17	332
265	18 47	035	29 56	099	33 59	145	20 05	187	53 02	227	23 41	287	57 02	331
266	19 05	034	30 28	098	34 18	145	20 01	186	52 38	227	23 10	286	56 45	329
267	19 23	033	31 00	098	34 36	144	19 57	186	52 14	227	22 38	285	56 28	327
268	19 40	032	31 33	097	34 56	144	19 54	185	51 51	226	22 07	284	56 10	326
269	19 57	031	32 05	096	35 15	143	19 51	185	51 27	226	21 35	283	55 51	324

LHA ♈	Hc	Zn	Hc	Zn	Hc	Zn	Hc	Zn	Hc	Zn	Hc	Zn	Hc	Zn
	◆ ALTAIR		FOMALHAUT		◆ ACHERNAR		CANOPUS		RIGIL KENT		◆ SPICA		ANTARES	
270	20 14	029	32 38	095	35 35	143	19 49	184	64 38	240	21 03	282	55 32	323
271	20 29	028	33 10	094	35 55	142	19 47	183	64 10	240	20 31	281	55 12	321
272	20 45	027	33 43	093	36 15	142	19 45	183	63 42	240	19 59	280	54 51	320
273	21 00	026	34 16	093	36 35	141	19 44	182	63 14	239	19 27	279	54 30	319
274	21 14	025	34 48	092	36 56	141	19 43	181	62 45	239	18 55	279	54 08	317
275	21 28	024	35 21	091	37 17	140	19 42	181	62 17	239	18 22	278	53 46	316
276	21 41	023	35 54	090	37 38	140	19 42	180	61 50	238	17 50	277	53 23	314
277	21 54	022	36 26	089	37 59	139	19 42	179	61 22	238	17 17	276	52 59	313
278	22 06	021	36 59	088	38 21	138	19 43	179	60 54	238	16 45	275	52 35	312
279	22 17	020	37 32	088	38 43	138	19 44	178	60 26	238	16 12	274	52 10	310
280	22 28	019	38 04	087	39 05	137	19 45	177	59 59	237	15 40	273	51 45	309
281	22 39	018	38 37	086	39 27	137	19 47	177	59 31	237	15 07	273	51 20	308
282	22 49	017	39 09	085	39 49	136	19 49	176	59 04	237	14 34	272	50 54	307
283	22 58	016	39 42	084	40 12	136	19 51	176	58 37	236	14 02	271	50 27	305
284	23 07	015	40 14	083	40 35	135	19 54	175	58 10	236	13 29	270	50 00	304
	◆ ALTAIR		FOMALHAUT		◆ ACHERNAR		CANOPUS		◆ RIGIL KENT		ANTARES		Nunki	
285	23 15	014	40 47	082	40 58	135	19 57	174	57 43	236	49 33	303	59 16	358
286	23 22	013	41 19	081	41 21	134	20 00	174	57 16	235	49 05	302	59 15	357
287	23 29	012	41 51	081	41 44	134	20 04	173	56 49	235	48 38	301	59 12	355
288	23 35	011	42 24	080	42 08	133	20 08	172	56 23	234	48 09	300	59 09	353
289	23 41	010	42 56	079	42 32	133	20 13	172	55 56	234	47 41	298	59 04	351
290	23 46	009	43 28	078	42 56	132	20 18	171	55 30	234	47 12	297	58 59	350
291	23 51	007	44 00	077	43 20	132	20 23	170	55 03	233	46 43	296	58 53	348
292	23 55	006	44 31	076	43 45	131	20 29	170	54 37	233	46 13	295	58 45	346
293	23 58	005	45 03	075	44 09	131	20 35	169	54 11	233	45 43	294	58 37	344
294	24 01	004	45 34	074	44 34	130	20 41	168	53 45	232	45 13	293	58 28	343
295	24 03	003	46 06	073	44 59	130	20 48	168	53 20	232	44 43	292	58 18	341
296	24 04	002	46 37	072	45 24	129	20 55	167	52 54	231	44 13	291	58 07	339
297	24 05	001	47 08	071	45 49	129	21 02	167	52 28	231	43 42	290	57 55	338
298	24 05	000	47 39	070	46 15	128	21 10	166	52 03	231	43 11	289	57 42	336
299	24 05	359	48 09	069	46 41	128	21 18	165	51 38	230	42 40	288	57 28	335
	FOMALHAUT		◆ ACHERNAR		CANOPUS		◆ RIGIL KENT		ANTARES		Nunki		◆ ALTAIR	
300	48 40	068	47 06	128	21 26	165	51 13	230	42 09	287	57 14	333	24 04	358
301	49 10	067	47 32	127	21 35	164	50 48	229	41 38	286	56 58	331	24 02	357
302	49 40	066	47 59	127	21 44	163	50 23	229	41 06	285	56 42	330	24 00	356
303	50 09	064	48 25	126	21 54	163	49 59	229	40 35	284	56 26	328	23 57	354
304	50 38	063	48 51	126	22 04	162	49 34	228	40 03	283	56 08	327	23 54	353
305	51 07	062	49 18	125	22 14	162	49 10	228	39 31	282	55 50	325	23 50	352
306	51 36	061	49 45	125	22 24	161	48 46	227	38 59	281	55 31	324	23 45	351
307	52 05	060	50 12	124	22 35	160	48 22	227	38 27	280	55 11	322	23 40	350
308	52 33	059	50 39	124	22 46	160	47 58	227	37 55	279	54 51	321	23 34	349
309	53 00	057	51 06	123	22 58	159	47 34	226	37 22	278	54 30	319	23 28	348
310	53 28	056	51 33	123	23 10	158	47 11	226	36 50	278	54 08	318	23 20	347
311	53 55	055	52 01	122	23 22	158	46 48	225	36 18	277	53 46	317	23 13	346
312	54 21	054	52 29	122	23 35	157	46 24	225	35 45	276	53 23	315	23 04	345
313	54 47	052	52 57	121	23 47	157	46 02	224	35 13	275	53 00	314	22 56	344
314	55 13	051	53 25	121	24 01	156	45 39	224	34 40	274	52 36	313	22 46	343
	◆ FOMALHAUT		ACHERNAR		◆ CANOPUS		RIGIL KENT		◆ ANTARES		Nunki		ALTAIR	
315	55 38	050	53 53	120	24 14	155	45 16	224	34 07	273	52 12	311	22 36	342
316	56 03	048	54 21	120	24 28	155	44 54	223	33 35	272	51 47	310	22 26	341
317	56 27	047	54 49	120	24 42	154	44 32	223	33 02	271	51 22	309	22 14	340
318	56 50	045	55 18	119	24 56	153	44 09	222	32 29	271	50 56	307	22 03	338
319	57 13	044	55 46	119	25 11	153	43 48	222	31 57	270	50 30	306	21 50	337
320	57 36	043	56 15	118	25 26	152	43 26	221	31 24	269	50 03	305	21 38	336
321	57 57	041	56 44	118	25 42	152	43 04	221	30 51	268	49 36	304	21 24	335
322	58 19	040	57 13	117	25 57	151	42 43	220	30 19	267	49 09	303	21 10	334
323	58 39	038	57 42	117	26 13	150	42 22	220	29 46	266	48 41	301	20 56	333
324	58 59	036	58 11	116	26 29	150	42 01	219	29 14	266	48 13	300	20 41	332
325	59 18	035	58 41	116	26 46	149	41 41	219	28 41	265	47 45	299	20 26	331
326	59 36	033	59 10	115	27 03	149	41 20	219	28 08	264	47 16	298	20 10	330
327	59 54	032	59 40	115	27 20	148	41 00	218	27 36	263	46 47	297	19 53	329
328	60 11	030	60 09	115	27 37	147	40 40	218	27 04	262	46 18	296	19 36	328
329	60 27	028	60 39	114	27 55	147	40 20	217	26 31	262	45 48	295	19 19	327
	◆ FOMALHAUT		ACHERNAR		◆ CANOPUS		RIGIL KENT		◆ ANTARES		Nunki		ALTAIR	
330	60 42	027	61 09	114	28 13	146	40 00	217	25 59	261	45 18	294	19 01	326
331	60 56	025	61 39	113	28 32	146	39 41	216	25 27	260	44 48	293	18 43	325
332	61 09	023	62 09	113	28 50	145	39 22	216	24 55	259	44 18	292	18 24	324
333	61 22	021	62 39	112	29 09	144	39 03	215	24 22	258	43 47	290	18 04	323
334	61 33	020	63 09	112	29 28	144	38 44	215	23 50	258	43 17	289	17 45	322
335	61 44	018	63 40	112	29 48	143	38 25	214	23 19	257	42 46	288	17 24	321
336	61 53	016	64 10	111	30 07	143	38 07	214	22 47	256	42 15	287	17 04	320
337	62 02	014	64 41	111	30 27	142	37 49	213	22 15	255	41 43	286	16 43	319
338	62 09	012	65 11	110	30 47	142	37 31	213	21 44	255	41 12	286	16 21	318
339	62 16	011	65 42	110	31 08	141	37 14	212	21 12	254	40 40	285	15 59	317
340	62 21	009	66 13	109	31 29	140	36 56	212	20 41	253	40 09	284	15 37	317
341	62 26	007	66 44	109	31 50	140	36 39	211	20 10	252	39 37	283	15 14	316
342	62 29	005	67 15	108	32 11	139	36 22	211	19 39	251	39 05	282	14 51	315
343	62 31	003	67 46	108	32 32	139	36 06	210	19 08	251	38 33	281	14 28	314
344	62 32	001	68 17	108	32 54	138	35 49	210	18 37	250	38 01	280	14 04	313
	◆ Diphda		Acamar		CANOPUS		◆ Miaplacidus		RIGIL KENT		◆ Nunki		FOMALHAUT	
345	46 20	037	48 43	093	33 16	137	38 13	169	35 33	209	37 28	279	62 32	359
346	46 39	036	49 16	092	33 38	137	38 20	168	35 17	209	36 56	278	62 32	357
347	46 58	035	49 49	091	34 01	136	38 27	168	35 02	208	36 24	277	62 29	356
348	47 16	033	50 21	090	34 23	136	38 34	167	34 46	208	35 51	276	62 26	354
349	47 34	032	50 54	089	34 46	135	38 41	167	34 31	207	35 19	275	62 22	352
350	47 51	031	51 27	088	35 09	135	38 49	167	34 16	207	34 46	275	62 17	350
351	48 07	029	51 59	087	35 33	134	38 56	166	34 01	206	34 14	274	62 11	348
352	48 23	028	52 32	087	35 56	133	39 04	166	33 47	206	33 41	273	62 04	346
353	48 38	027	53 05	086	36 20	133	39 12	165	33 33	205	33 08	272	61 55	344
354	48 52	025	53 37	085	36 44	132	39 21	165	33 19	205	32 36	271	61 46	343
355	49 06	024	54 10	084	37 09	132	39 30	164	33 05	204	32 03	270	61 36	341
356	49 19	022	54 42	083	37 33	131	39 38	164	32 52	204	31 30	269	61 24	339
357	49 31	021	55 15	082	37 58	131	39 47	164	32 39	203	30 58	269	61 12	337
358	49 42	019	55 47	081	38 23	130	39 57	163	32 26	203	30 25	268	60 59	335
359	49 52	018	56 19	080	38 48	130	40 06	163	32 14	202	29 52	267	60 45	334

LAT 58°S

LHA ♈	Hc Zn	Hc Zn	Hc Zn	Hc Zn	Hc Zn	Hc Zn	Hc Zn
	Diphda	◆ RIGEL	CANOPUS	Miaplacidus	◆ RIGIL KENT	Peacock	◆ FOMALHAUT
0	49 04 016	12 51 085	39 51 128	41 13 162	32 57 202	61 58 250	59 37 333
1	49 13 015	13 23 084	40 16 128	41 23 162	32 46 201	61 28 249	59 22 331
2	49 21 013	13 55 083	40 41 127	41 33 161	32 34 201	60 58 249	59 06 330
3	49 28 012	14 26 082	41 06 127	41 43 161	32 23 200	60 29 248	58 50 328
4	49 34 010	14 58 081	41 32 126	41 54 161	32 12 200	59 59 248	58 33 326
5	49 39 009	15 29 081	41 58 125	42 04 160	32 01 199	59 30 247	58 15 325
6	49 44 007	16 00 080	42 24 125	42 15 160	31 51 199	59 01 247	57 56 323
7	49 47 006	16 32 079	42 50 124	42 26 159	31 41 198	58 32 246	57 37 322
8	49 50 005	17 03 078	43 16 124	42 38 159	31 31 198	58 03 246	57 17 320
9	49 52 003	17 34 077	43 43 123	42 49 159	31 22 197	57 34 245	56 56 319
10	49 54 002	18 05 076	44 09 123	43 01 158	31 12 197	57 05 245	56 35 317
11	49 54 000	18 35 075	44 36 122	43 13 158	31 03 196	56 37 244	56 13 316
12	49 54 359	19 06 074	45 03 121	43 25 157	30 55 196	56 08 244	55 51 315
13	49 53 357	19 37 073	45 31 121	43 37 157	30 46 195	55 40 243	55 28 313
14	49 51 356	20 07 073	45 58 120	43 50 157	30 38 194	55 11 243	55 04 312
	◆ RIGEL	SIRIUS	CANOPUS	◆ RIGIL KENT	Peacock	◆ FOMALHAUT	Diphda
15	20 37 072	16 00 096	46 26 120	30 31 194	54 43 242	54 40 310	49 48 354
16	21 07 071	16 32 095	46 53 119	30 23 193	54 15 242	54 16 309	49 44 353
17	21 37 070	17 03 094	47 21 119	30 16 193	53 47 241	53 51 308	49 40 351
18	22 07 069	17 35 094	47 49 118	30 09 192	53 19 241	53 26 307	49 35 350
19	22 37 068	18 07 093	48 17 117	30 02 192	52 52 240	53 00 305	49 29 348
20	23 06 067	18 39 092	48 45 117	29 56 191	52 24 240	52 34 304	49 22 347
21	23 35 066	19 10 091	49 14 116	29 50 191	51 57 239	52 07 303	49 14 345
22	24 04 065	19 42 090	49 42 116	29 44 190	51 30 239	51 40 302	49 06 344
23	24 33 064	20 14 089	50 11 115	29 39 190	51 03 238	51 13 300	48 57 343
24	25 01 063	20 46 089	50 40 115	29 34 189	50 36 238	50 46 299	48 47 341
25	25 30 062	21 17 088	51 09 114	29 29 188	50 09 237	50 18 298	48 36 340
26	25 58 061	21 49 087	51 38 113	29 25 188	49 42 237	49 49 297	48 25 338
27	26 25 060	22 21 086	52 07 113	29 20 187	49 16 236	49 21 296	48 13 337
28	26 53 059	22 53 085	52 37 112	29 16 187	48 50 236	48 52 295	48 00 336
29	27 20 058	23 24 084	53 06 112	29 13 186	48 24 235	48 23 294	47 47 334
	◆ RIGEL	SIRIUS	CANOPUS	◆ RIGIL KENT	Peacock	◆ FOMALHAUT	Diphda
30	27 47 057	23 56 083	53 36 111	29 10 186	47 58 235	47 54 293	47 32 333
31	28 14 056	24 27 082	54 06 110	29 07 185	47 32 234	47 24 291	47 18 331
32	28 40 055	24 59 082	54 35 110	29 04 185	47 06 234	46 55 290	47 02 330
33	29 06 054	25 30 081	55 05 109	29 02 184	46 41 233	46 25 289	46 46 329
34	29 32 053	26 02 080	55 35 109	29 00 183	46 15 233	45 55 288	46 29 327
35	29 57 052	26 33 079	56 06 108	28 58 183	45 50 232	45 25 287	46 12 326
36	30 22 051	27 04 078	56 36 107	28 56 182	45 25 231	44 54 286	45 54 325
37	30 47 050	27 35 077	57 06 107	28 55 182	45 00 231	44 24 285	45 35 324
38	31 11 049	28 06 076	57 37 106	28 54 181	44 36 230	43 53 284	45 16 322
39	31 35 048	28 37 075	58 07 106	28 54 181	44 11 230	43 22 283	44 56 321
40	31 58 047	29 08 074	58 38 105	28 54 180	43 47 229	42 51 282	44 36 320
41	32 21 046	29 38 073	59 09 104	28 54 180	43 23 229	42 20 281	44 15 319
42	32 44 045	30 09 072	59 40 104	28 54 179	42 59 228	41 49 281	43 54 317
43	33 06 044	30 39 072	60 11 103	28 55 178	42 36 228	41 17 280	43 32 316
44	33 28 043	31 09 071	60 42 102	28 56 178	42 12 227	40 46 279	43 10 315
	RIGEL	◆ SIRIUS	CANOPUS	◆ RIGIL KENT	Peacock	FOMALHAUT	◆ Diphda
45	33 49 042	31 39 070	61 13 102	28 57 177	41 49 227	40 14 278	42 47 314
46	34 10 040	32 08 069	61 44 101	28 59 177	41 26 226	39 43 277	42 24 312
47	34 30 039	32 38 068	62 15 101	29 01 176	41 03 226	39 11 276	42 00 311
48	34 50 038	33 07 067	62 46 100	29 03 176	40 40 225	38 40 275	41 36 310
49	35 09 037	33 36 066	63 18 099	29 06 175	40 18 225	38 08 274	41 11 309
50	35 28 036	34 05 065	63 49 098	29 09 175	39 55 224	37 36 273	40 46 308
51	35 47 035	34 34 064	64 21 098	29 12 174	39 33 224	37 04 272	40 21 307
52	36 05 034	35 02 063	64 52 097	29 15 173	39 12 223	36 33 272	39 55 306
53	36 22 032	35 30 062	65 24 096	29 19 173	38 50 223	36 01 271	39 29 305
54	36 39 031	35 58 061	65 55 096	29 23 172	38 28 222	35 29 270	39 03 303
55	36 55 030	36 26 060	66 27 095	29 28 172	38 07 222	34 57 269	38 36 302
56	37 10 029	36 53 059	66 59 094	29 32 171	37 46 221	34 26 268	38 09 301
57	37 25 028	37 20 058	67 30 093	29 37 171	37 26 220	33 54 267	37 42 300
58	37 40 026	37 47 056	68 02 093	29 43 170	37 05 220	33 22 267	37 14 299
59	37 54 025	38 13 055	68 34 092	29 48 170	36 45 219	32 50 266	36 47 298
	RIGEL	◆ SIRIUS	Suhail	◆ RIGIL KENT	Peacock	FOMALHAUT	◆ Diphda
60	38 07 024	38 39 054	42 01 108	29 54 169	36 25 219	32 19 265	36 18 297
61	38 19 023	39 05 053	42 31 107	30 00 168	36 05 218	31 47 264	35 50 296
62	38 31 021	39 30 052	43 01 106	30 07 168	35 45 218	31 15 263	35 21 295
63	38 43 020	39 55 051	43 32 106	30 14 167	35 26 217	30 44 262	34 52 294
64	38 53 019	40 19 050	44 03 105	30 21 167	35 07 217	30 12 262	34 23 293
65	39 03 018	40 43 049	44 33 104	30 28 166	34 48 216	29 41 261	33 54 292
66	39 13 016	41 07 048	45 04 104	30 36 166	34 29 216	29 10 260	33 24 291
67	39 21 015	41 30 046	45 35 103	30 44 165	34 11 215	28 38 259	32 55 290
68	39 29 014	41 53 045	46 06 102	30 52 165	33 53 214	28 07 258	32 25 289
69	39 37 013	42 15 044	46 37 101	31 01 164	33 35 214	27 36 258	31 55 288
70	39 43 011	42 37 043	47 09 101	31 09 164	33 18 213	27 05 257	31 24 287
71	39 49 010	42 59 042	47 40 100	31 19 163	33 00 213	26 34 256	30 54 286
72	39 54 009	43 19 040	48 11 099	31 28 162	32 43 212	26 03 255	30 23 285
73	39 59 008	43 40 039	48 43 098	31 38 162	32 26 212	25 33 255	29 53 284
74	40 03 006	44 00 038	49 14 098	31 48 161	32 10 211	25 02 254	29 22 284
	RIGEL	◆ SIRIUS	Suhail	◆ RIGIL KENT	Peacock	ACHERNAR	◆ Diphda
75	40 06 005	44 19 037	49 46 097	31 58 161	31 54 211	63 35 250	28 51 283
76	40 08 004	44 37 035	50 17 096	32 09 160	31 38 210	63 05 249	28 20 282
77	40 10 002	44 56 034	50 49 095	32 19 160	31 22 209	62 35 249	27 48 281
78	40 11 001	45 13 033	51 21 095	32 30 159	31 06 209	62 06 249	27 17 280
79	40 11 000	45 30 031	51 52 094	32 42 159	30 51 208	61 36 248	26 46 279
80	40 11 358	45 46 030	52 24 093	32 54 158	30 36 208	61 07 248	26 14 278
81	40 09 357	46 02 029	52 56 092	33 05 158	30 22 207	60 37 247	25 43 277
82	40 07 356	46 17 027	53 28 091	33 18 157	30 07 207	60 08 247	25 11 276
83	40 05 355	46 31 026	53 59 090	33 30 157	29 53 206	59 39 246	24 40 276
84	40 01 353	46 45 025	54 31 090	33 43 156	29 39 205	59 10 246	24 08 275
85	39 57 352	46 58 023	55 03 089	33 56 156	29 26 205	58 41 245	23 36 274
86	39 53 351	47 10 022	55 35 088	34 09 155	29 13 204	58 12 245	23 05 273
87	39 47 349	47 22 021	56 06 087	34 23 155	29 00 204	57 44 244	22 33 272
88	39 41 348	47 33 019	56 38 086	34 37 154	28 47 203	57 15 244	22 01 271
89	39 34 347	47 43 018	57 10 085	34 51 153	28 35 202	56 47 243	21 29 270

LHA ♈	Hc Zn	Hc Zn	Hc Zn	Hc Zn	Hc Zn	Hc Zn	Hc Zn
	SIRIUS	Alphard	◆ Suhail	RIGIL KENT	◆ Peacock	ACHERNAR	◆ RIGEL
90	47 52 016	26 47 061	57 42 084	35 05 153	28 23 202	56 18 243	39 27 346
91	48 01 015	27 14 060	58 13 083	35 19 152	28 11 201	55 50 242	39 18 344
92	48 09 014	27 42 059	58 45 082	35 34 152	28 00 201	55 22 242	39 09 343
93	48 16 012	28 09 058	59 16 081	35 49 151	27 49 200	54 54 241	39 00 342
94	48 22 011	28 35 057	59 48 080	36 05 151	27 38 200	54 26 241	38 50 341
95	48 28 009	29 02 056	60 19 079	36 20 150	27 27 199	53 59 240	38 39 339
96	48 32 008	29 28 055	60 50 078	36 36 150	27 17 198	53 31 240	38 27 338
97	48 36 006	29 54 054	61 21 077	36 52 149	27 07 198	53 04 239	38 15 337
98	48 39 005	30 19 053	61 52 076	37 08 149	26 58 197	52 36 239	38 02 336
99	48 42 004	30 45 052	62 23 075	37 25 148	26 49 197	52 09 238	37 49 334
100	48 43 002	31 09 051	62 54 074	37 42 148	26 40 196	51 42 238	37 35 333
101	48 44 001	31 34 050	63 24 073	37 59 147	26 31 195	51 15 237	37 20 332
102	48 44 359	31 58 049	63 54 072	38 16 147	26 23 195	50 49 237	37 05 331
103	48 43 358	32 22 048	64 24 070	38 34 146	26 15 194	50 22 236	36 49 330
104	48 42 356	32 45 046	64 54 069	38 51 146	26 07 194	49 56 236	36 32 328
	Alphard	◆ Gienah	RIGIL KENT	◆ Peacock	ACHERNAR	◆ RIGEL	SIRIUS
105	33 08 045	20 36 091	39 09 145	26 00 193	49 29 235	36 16 327	48 39 355
106	33 30 044	21 08 090	39 27 145	25 53 192	49 03 235	35 58 326	48 36 353
107	33 52 043	21 40 089	39 46 144	25 46 192	48 37 234	35 40 325	48 32 352
108	34 14 042	22 12 088	40 04 144	25 40 191	48 12 234	35 21 324	48 27 351
109	34 35 041	22 43 087	40 23 143	25 33 191	47 46 233	35 02 323	48 21 349
110	34 55 040	23 15 086	40 42 143	25 28 190	47 21 233	34 43 321	48 15 348
111	35 15 039	23 47 085	41 01 142	25 22 189	46 55 232	34 23 320	48 08 346
112	35 35 038	24 18 084	41 21 142	25 17 189	46 30 232	34 02 319	48 00 345
113	35 54 036	24 50 084	41 41 142	25 13 188	46 05 231	33 41 318	47 51 343
114	36 13 035	25 22 083	42 01 141	25 08 188	45 40 231	33 20 317	47 42 342
115	36 31 034	25 53 082	42 21 141	25 04 187	45 16 230	32 58 316	47 32 341
116	36 48 033	26 25 081	42 41 140	25 00 186	44 51 230	32 35 315	47 21 339
117	37 05 032	26 56 080	43 01 140	24 57 186	44 27 229	32 13 314	47 09 338
118	37 22 030	27 27 079	43 22 139	24 54 185	44 03 229	31 49 313	46 57 336
119	37 37 029	27 58 078	43 43 139	24 51 185	43 39 228	31 26 312	46 44 335
	REGULUS	◆ SPICA	RIGIL KENT	Peacock	◆ ACHERNAR	RIGEL	◆ SIRIUS
120	15 17 033	14 01 089	44 04 138	24 49 184	43 16 228	31 02 310	46 30 334
121	15 34 032	14 33 088	44 25 138	24 47 183	42 52 227	30 37 309	46 15 332
122	15 50 031	15 04 087	44 47 137	24 45 183	42 29 227	30 13 308	46 00 331
123	16 07 030	15 36 086	45 08 137	24 43 182	42 06 226	29 48 307	45 45 330
124	16 22 029	16 08 085	45 30 136	24 42 182	41 43 226	29 22 306	45 28 328
125	16 37 028	16 39 085	45 52 136	24 42 181	41 20 225	28 56 305	45 11 327
126	16 52 027	17 11 084	46 15 135	24 41 180	40 58 225	28 30 304	44 54 326
127	17 06 026	17 43 083	46 37 135	24 41 180	40 35 224	28 04 303	44 36 325
128	17 20 025	18 14 082	47 00 135	24 41 179	40 13 224	27 37 302	44 17 323
129	17 33 024	18 46 081	47 22 134	24 42 179	39 52 223	27 10 301	43 58 322
130	17 46 023	19 17 080	47 45 134	24 43 178	39 30 223	26 43 300	43 38 321
131	17 58 022	19 48 079	48 08 133	24 44 177	39 08 222	26 15 299	43 17 320
132	18 09 021	20 19 078	48 32 133	24 46 177	38 47 222	25 47 298	42 57 318
133	18 20 020	20 51 078	48 55 132	24 48 176	38 26 221	25 19 297	42 35 317
134	18 31 019	21 22 077	49 19 132	24 50 176	38 06 221	24 51 296	42 13 316
	REGULUS	◆ SPICA	RIGIL KENT	◆ Peacock	ACHERNAR	CANOPUS	◆ SIRIUS
135	18 41 018	21 52 076	49 42 131	24 53 175	37 45 220	67 35 267	41 51 315
136	18 50 017	22 23 075	50 06 131	24 56 174	37 25 219	67 03 266	41 28 314
137	18 59 016	22 54 074	50 30 131	24 59 174	37 05 219	66 31 265	41 05 312
138	19 08 015	23 24 073	50 54 130	25 02 173	36 45 218	66 00 264	40 41 311
139	19 16 014	23 55 072	51 19 130	25 06 173	36 25 218	65 28 264	40 17 310
140	19 23 013	24 25 071	51 43 129	25 11 172	36 06 217	64 57 263	39 53 309
141	19 30 012	24 55 070	52 08 129	25 15 171	35 47 217	64 25 262	39 28 308
142	19 36 011	25 25 069	52 33 128	25 20 171	35 28 216	63 54 262	39 02 307
143	19 42 010	25 54 068	52 58 128	25 26 170	35 09 216	63 22 261	38 37 306
144	19 47 009	26 24 067	53 23 128	25 31 170	34 51 215	62 51 260	38 11 305
145	19 51 008	26 53 066	53 48 127	25 37 169	34 32 215	62 19 260	37 44 303
146	19 55 007	27 22 066	54 14 127	25 43 168	34 14 214	61 48 259	37 18 302
147	19 58 006	27 51 065	54 39 126	25 50 168	33 57 213	61 17 258	36 51 301
148	20 01 004	28 20 064	55 05 126	25 57 167	33 39 213	60 46 258	36 23 300
149	20 03 003	28 48 063	55 31 126	26 04 167	33 22 212	60 15 257	35 56 299
	REGULUS	◆ SPICA	RIGIL KENT	◆ Peacock	ACHERNAR	CANOPUS	◆ SIRIUS
150	20 05 002	29 16 062	55 56 125	26 11 166	33 05 212	59 44 256	35 28 298
151	20 06 001	29 44 061	56 22 125	26 19 165	32 49 211	59 13 256	35 00 297
152	20 06 000	30 11 060	56 49 124	26 27 165	32 32 211	58 42 255	34 31 296
153	20 06 359	30 39 059	57 15 124	26 36 164	32 16 210	58 12 254	34 03 295
154	20 06 358	31 06 058	57 41 124	26 45 164	32 00 210	57 41 254	33 34 294
155	20 04 357	31 32 057	58 08 123	26 54 163	31 45 209	57 11 253	33 05 293
156	20 02 356	31 59 056	58 34 123	27 03 162	31 29 208	56 40 253	32 35 292
157	20 00 355	32 25 055	59 01 123	27 13 162	31 14 208	56 10 252	32 06 291
158	19 57 354	32 51 053	59 28 122	27 23 161	31 00 207	55 40 251	31 36 290
159	19 53 353	33 16 052	59 55 122	27 34 161	30 45 207	55 10 251	31 06 289
160	19 49 352	33 41 051	60 22 121	27 44 160	30 31 206	54 40 250	30 36 288
161	19 45 351	34 06 050	60 49 121	27 55 159	30 17 206	54 10 250	30 06 287
162	19 39 350	34 30 049	61 17 121	28 06 159	30 04 205	53 40 249	29 35 286
163	19 33 349	34 54 048	61 44 120	28 18 158	29 50 205	53 10 248	29 05 286
164	19 27 348	35 17 047	62 11 120	28 30 158	29 37 204	52 41 248	28 34 285
	◆ SPICA	ANTARES	◆ Peacock	ACHERNAR	CANOPUS	◆ SIRIUS	REGULUS
165	35 40 046	26 03 099	28 42 157	29 24 203	52 12 247	28 03 284	19 20 347
166	36 03 045	26 34 098	28 55 157	29 12 203	51 42 247	27 32 283	19 12 346
167	36 25 044	27 06 097	29 07 156	29 00 202	51 13 246	27 01 282	19 04 345
168	36 47 043	27 38 096	29 20 155	28 48 202	50 44 246	26 30 281	18 56 344
169	37 08 041	28 09 096	29 34 155	28 36 201	50 15 245	25 59 280	18 47 343
170	37 29 040	28 41 095	29 48 154	28 25 200	49 47 244	25 27 279	18 37 342
171	37 49 039	29 13 094	30 01 154	28 14 200	49 18 244	24 56 278	18 27 341
172	38 09 038	29 44 093	30 16 153	28 03 199	48 50 243	24 24 277	18 16 340
173	38 28 037	30 16 092	30 30 153	27 53 199	48 21 243	23 53 277	18 05 339
174	38 47 036	30 48 091	30 45 152	27 43 198	47 53 242	23 21 276	17 53 338
175	39 05 034	31 20 091	31 00 151	27 33 198	47 25 241	22 50 275	17 40 337
176	39 23 033	31 51 090	31 15 151	27 24 197	46 57 241	22 18 274	17 27 336
177	39 40 032	32 23 089	31 31 150	27 15 196	46 29 240	21 46 273	17 14 335
178	39 56 031	32 55 088	31 47 150	27 06 196	46 02 240	21 14 272	17 00 334
179	40 12 029	33 27 087	32 03 149	26 57 195	45 34 239	20 43 271	16 46 333

 LAT 58°S

LHA ♈	Hc	Zn	Hc	Zn	Hc	Zn	Hc	Zn	Hc	Zn	Hc	Zn	Hc	Zn
	◆ SPICA		ANTARES		◆ Peacock		ACHERNAR		CANOPUS		◆ SIRIUS		Alphard	
180	40 27	028	33 59	086	32 20	149	26 49	195	45 07	239	20 11	271	32 49	314
181	40 42	027	34 30	085	32 36	148	26 41	194	44 40	238	19 39	270	32 25	313
182	40 56	026	35 02	085	32 53	147	26 34	193	44 13	237	19 07	269	32 02	312
183	41 10	024	35 34	084	33 10	147	26 26	193	43 47	237	18 35	268	31 38	311
184	41 23	023	36 05	083	33 28	146	26 20	192	43 20	236	18 04	267	31 13	309
185	41 35	022	36 37	082	33 46	146	26 13	192	42 54	236	17 32	266	30 49	308
186	41 46	021	37 08	081	34 04	145	26 07	191	42 27	235	17 00	265	30 24	307
187	41 57	019	37 39	080	34 22	145	26 01	190	42 01	235	16 29	265	29 58	306
188	42 07	018	38 11	079	34 40	144	25 55	190	41 36	234	15 57	264	29 32	305
189	42 17	017	38 42	078	34 59	144	25 50	189	41 10	233	15 25	263	29 06	304
190	42 25	015	39 13	077	35 18	143	25 45	189	40 44	233	14 54	262	28 40	303
191	42 34	014	39 44	076	35 37	142	25 40	188	40 19	232	14 22	261	28 13	302
192	42 41	013	40 15	075	35 57	142	25 36	188	39 54	232	13 51	260	27 46	301
193	42 48	011	40 45	074	36 17	141	25 32	187	39 29	231	13 20	260	27 19	300
194	42 53	010	41 16	073	36 37	141	25 28	186	39 05	231	12 48	259	26 51	299
	SPICA		◆ ANTARES		Peacock		◆ ACHERNAR		CANOPUS		Suhail		◆ Alphard	
195	42 59	009	41 46	072	36 57	140	25 25	186	38 40	230	52 01	267	26 23	298
196	43 03	007	42 17	071	37 17	140	25 22	185	38 16	229	51 29	266	25 55	297
197	43 07	006	42 47	070	37 38	139	25 19	185	37 52	229	50 58	265	25 27	296
198	43 10	005	43 16	069	37 59	139	25 17	184	37 28	228	50 26	264	24 58	295
199	43 12	003	43 46	068	38 20	138	25 15	183	37 04	228	49 54	263	24 29	294
200	43 14	002	44 16	067	38 41	138	25 13	183	36 41	227	49 23	263	24 00	294
201	43 14	001	44 45	066	39 03	137	25 12	182	36 18	227	48 51	262	23 31	293
202	43 14	359	45 14	065	39 24	137	25 11	182	35 55	226	48 20	261	23 02	292
203	43 14	358	45 43	064	39 46	136	25 10	181	35 32	225	47 48	260	22 32	291
204	43 12	357	46 11	063	40 08	136	25 10	180	35 09	225	47 17	260	22 02	290
205	43 10	355	46 39	062	40 31	135	25 10	180	34 47	224	46 46	259	21 32	289
206	43 07	354	47 07	061	40 53	134	25 10	179	34 25	224	46 15	258	21 02	288
207	43 03	353	47 35	060	41 16	134	25 11	179	34 03	223	45 44	257	20 32	287
208	42 59	351	48 02	059	41 39	133	25 12	178	33 42	222	45 13	257	20 01	286
209	42 53	350	48 29	057	42 02	133	25 13	177	33 20	222	44 42	256	19 31	285
	ANTARES		◆ Nunki		Peacock		ACHERNAR		◆ CANOPUS		Suhail		◆ SPICA	
210	48 56	056	30 24	092	42 26	132	25 15	177	32 59	221	44 11	255	42 47	349
211	49 22	055	30 56	091	42 49	132	25 17	176	32 38	221	43 40	254	42 41	347
212	49 48	054	31 28	090	43 13	131	25 19	176	32 18	220	43 10	254	42 33	346
213	50 13	053	31 59	089	43 37	131	25 21	175	31 57	220	42 39	253	42 25	345
214	50 38	051	32 31	088	44 01	130	25 24	174	31 37	219	42 09	252	42 17	343
215	51 03	050	33 03	087	44 26	130	25 28	174	31 17	218	41 39	252	42 07	342
216	51 27	049	33 35	087	44 50	129	25 31	173	30 58	218	41 09	251	41 57	341
217	51 51	047	34 06	086	45 15	129	25 35	173	30 38	217	40 39	250	41 46	339
218	52 14	046	34 38	085	45 40	128	25 40	172	30 19	217	40 09	250	41 35	338
219	52 36	045	35 10	084	46 05	128	25 44	171	30 00	216	39 39	249	41 22	337
220	52 59	044	35 41	083	46 30	127	25 49	171	29 42	215	39 09	248	41 10	336
221	53 20	042	36 13	082	46 56	127	25 54	170	29 24	215	38 40	247	40 56	334
222	53 41	041	36 44	081	47 21	126	26 00	170	29 06	214	38 11	247	40 42	333
223	54 02	039	37 16	080	47 47	126	26 06	169	28 48	214	37 42	246	40 27	332
224	54 22	038	37 47	079	48 13	125	26 12	168	28 30	213	37 13	245	40 12	331
	ANTARES		◆ Nunki		Peacock		ACHERNAR		◆ CANOPUS		Suhail		◆ SPICA	
225	54 41	036	38 18	078	48 39	125	26 19	168	28 13	212	36 44	245	39 56	329
226	54 59	035	38 49	078	49 05	124	26 26	167	27 56	212	36 15	244	39 40	328
227	55 17	034	39 20	077	49 32	124	26 33	167	27 40	211	35 47	243	39 23	327
228	55 35	032	39 51	076	49 58	123	26 40	166	27 24	211	35 18	243	39 05	326
229	55 51	031	40 22	075	50 25	123	26 48	165	27 08	210	34 50	242	38 47	324
230	56 07	029	40 52	074	50 52	122	26 56	165	26 52	209	34 22	241	38 28	323
231	56 22	027	41 23	073	51 19	122	27 05	164	26 36	209	33 54	241	38 09	322
232	56 36	026	41 53	072	51 46	121	27 13	164	26 21	208	33 27	240	37 49	321
233	56 50	024	42 23	071	52 13	121	27 23	163	26 07	207	32 59	239	37 29	320
234	57 02	023	42 53	070	52 40	120	27 32	163	25 52	207	32 32	239	37 08	319
235	57 14	021	43 23	069	53 08	120	27 42	162	25 38	206	32 05	238	36 47	317
236	57 25	019	43 52	068	53 36	119	27 52	161	25 24	206	31 38	237	36 25	316
237	57 35	018	44 22	067	54 04	119	28 02	161	25 10	205	31 11	237	36 03	315
238	57 45	016	44 51	066	54 32	118	28 13	160	24 57	204	30 45	236	35 40	314
239	57 53	015	45 20	065	55 00	118	28 24	160	24 44	204	30 19	235	35 17	313
	◆ ANTARES		Nunki		◆ FOMALHAUT		ACHERNAR		CANOPUS		◆ ACRUX		SPICA	
240	58 01	013	45 48	063	17 34	118	28 35	159	24 32	203	64 11	236	34 54	312
241	58 07	011	46 17	062	18 02	117	28 46	158	24 19	202	63 45	236	34 30	311
242	58 13	010	46 45	061	18 30	116	28 58	158	24 07	202	63 19	236	34 05	310
243	58 18	008	47 12	060	18 59	116	29 10	157	23 56	201	62 53	235	33 41	309
244	58 22	006	47 40	059	19 28	115	29 23	157	23 44	201	62 27	235	33 16	308
245	58 25	004	48 07	058	19 57	114	29 35	156	23 33	200	62 01	235	32 50	307
246	58 27	003	48 33	057	20 26	113	29 48	156	23 23	199	61 35	234	32 25	305
247	58 28	001	49 00	055	20 55	113	30 02	155	23 12	199	61 09	234	31 59	304
248	58 28	359	49 26	054	21 24	112	30 15	154	23 02	198	60 43	234	31 32	303
249	58 27	358	49 51	053	21 54	111	30 29	154	22 53	197	60 18	234	31 05	302
250	58 25	356	50 17	052	22 24	110	30 43	153	22 43	197	59 52	233	30 38	301
251	58 22	354	50 41	051	22 54	110	30 58	153	22 34	196	59 27	233	30 11	300
252	58 19	352	51 06	049	23 24	109	31 12	152	22 25	196	59 01	233	29 44	299
253	58 14	351	51 30	048	23 54	108	31 27	152	22 17	195	58 36	232	29 16	298
254	58 08	349	51 53	047	24 24	107	31 43	151	22 09	194	58 11	232	28 48	297
	ALTAIR		◆ FOMALHAUT		ACHERNAR		CANOPUS		◆ ACRUX		SPICA		◆ ANTARES	
255	14 37	044	24 55	106	31 58	150	22 02	194	57 46	232	28 19	296	58 02	347
256	14 59	043	25 25	106	32 14	150	21 54	193	57 21	231	27 51	295	57 55	346
257	15 20	042	25 56	105	32 30	149	21 47	192	56 56	231	27 22	294	57 46	344
258	15 41	041	26 27	104	32 46	149	21 41	192	56 31	231	26 53	294	57 37	342
259	16 02	040	26 58	103	33 03	148	21 34	191	56 07	230	26 24	293	57 27	341
260	16 22	039	27 29	103	33 20	148	21 28	190	55 43	230	25 54	292	57 16	339
261	16 42	038	28 00	102	33 37	147	21 23	190	55 18	230	25 24	291	57 04	338
262	17 02	037	28 31	101	33 54	147	21 18	189	54 54	229	24 55	290	56 52	336
263	17 21	036	29 02	100	34 12	146	21 13	188	54 30	229	24 25	289	56 38	334
264	17 39	035	29 33	099	34 30	145	21 08	188	54 06	229	23 54	288	56 24	333
265	17 58	034	30 05	099	34 48	145	21 04	187	53 42	228	23 24	287	56 09	331
266	18 15	033	30 36	098	35 06	144	21 00	187	53 19	228	22 54	286	55 54	330
267	18 32	032	31 08	097	35 25	144	20 57	186	52 55	227	22 23	285	55 37	328
268	18 49	031	31 39	096	35 44	143	20 54	185	52 32	227	21 52	284	55 20	327
269	19 06	030	32 11	095	36 03	143	20 51	185	52 09	227	21 21	283	55 02	325

LHA ♈	Hc	Zn	Hc	Zn	Hc	Zn	Hc	Zn	Hc	Zn	Hc	Zn	Hc	Zn
	◆ ALTAIR		FOMALHAUT		◆ ACHERNAR		CANOPUS		RIGIL KENT		◆ SPICA		ANTARES	
270	19 21	029	32 43	094	36 22	142	20 49	184	65 07	242	20 50	282	54 44	324
271	19 37	028	33 14	094	36 42	142	20 47	183	64 39	242	20 19	282	54 25	322
272	19 51	027	33 46	093	37 02	141	20 45	183	64 11	241	19 48	281	54 05	321
273	20 06	026	34 18	092	37 22	141	20 44	182	63 43	241	19 17	280	53 45	319
274	20 20	025	34 50	091	37 42	140	20 43	181	63 16	241	18 45	279	53 24	318
275	20 33	024	35 22	090	38 03	140	20 42	181	62 48	240	18 14	278	53 02	317
276	20 46	023	35 53	089	38 23	139	20 42	180	62 20	240	17 42	277	52 40	315
277	20 58	022	36 25	089	38 44	138	20 42	179	61 53	240	17 11	276	52 18	314
278	21 10	021	36 57	088	39 06	138	20 43	179	61 25	239	16 39	275	51 54	313
279	21 21	020	37 29	087	39 27	137	20 44	178	60 58	239	16 08	275	51 31	311
280	21 32	019	38 00	086	39 49	137	20 45	177	60 31	239	15 36	274	51 07	310
281	21 42	018	38 32	085	40 10	136	20 47	177	60 04	238	15 04	273	50 42	309
282	21 51	017	39 04	084	40 32	136	20 49	176	59 37	238	14 32	272	50 17	308
283	22 00	016	39 35	083	40 55	135	20 51	176	59 10	238	14 01	271	49 52	306
284	22 09	015	40 07	082	41 17	135	20 54	175	58 43	237	13 29	270	49 26	305
	◆ ALTAIR		FOMALHAUT		◆ ACHERNAR		CANOPUS		◆ RIGIL KENT		ANTARES		Nunki	
285	22 16	014	40 38	082	41 40	134	20 57	174	58 16	237	49 00	304	58 16	358
286	22 24	013	41 10	081	42 03	134	21 00	174	57 50	236	48 33	303	58 15	357
287	22 30	012	41 41	080	42 26	133	21 04	173	57 23	236	48 06	302	58 12	355
288	22 37	011	42 12	079	42 49	133	21 08	172	56 57	236	47 39	300	58 09	353
289	22 42	010	42 44	078	43 12	132	21 12	172	56 31	235	47 12	299	58 05	352
290	22 47	008	43 15	077	43 36	132	21 17	171	56 05	235	46 44	298	58 00	350
291	22 51	007	43 45	076	44 00	131	21 22	170	55 39	235	46 16	297	57 54	348
292	22 55	006	44 16	075	44 24	131	21 28	170	55 13	234	45 47	296	57 47	347
293	22 58	005	44 47	074	44 48	130	21 34	169	54 47	234	45 19	295	57 39	345
294	23 01	004	45 17	073	45 13	130	21 40	168	54 22	233	44 50	294	57 30	343
295	23 03	003	45 48	072	45 37	129	21 46	168	53 56	233	44 20	293	57 21	342
296	23 04	002	46 18	071	46 02	129	21 53	167	53 31	232	43 51	292	57 10	340
297	23 05	001	46 48	070	46 27	128	22 00	166	53 06	232	43 21	291	56 59	338
298	23 05	000	47 17	069	46 52	128	22 08	166	52 41	232	42 52	290	56 47	337
299	23 05	359	47 47	068	47 17	127	22 16	165	52 16	231	42 22	289	56 34	335
	FOMALHAUT		◆ ACHERNAR		CANOPUS		◆ RIGIL KENT		ANTARES		Nunki		◆ ALTAIR	
300	48 16	067	47 43	127	22 24	165	51 51	231	41 51	288	56 20	334	23 04	358
301	48 45	066	48 08	126	22 33	164	51 27	230	41 21	287	56 06	332	23 03	357
302	49 14	064	48 34	126	22 42	163	51 02	230	40 50	286	55 50	331	23 00	356
303	49 43	063	49 00	125	22 51	163	50 38	230	40 20	285	55 34	329	22 58	355
304	50 11	062	49 26	125	23 01	162	50 14	229	39 49	284	55 18	327	22 54	353
305	50 39	061	49 52	124	23 11	161	49 50	229	39 18	283	55 00	326	22 50	352
306	51 07	060	50 18	124	23 21	161	49 26	228	38 47	282	54 42	325	22 46	351
307	51 34	059	50 45	123	23 32	160	49 02	228	38 16	281	54 23	323	22 41	350
308	52 01	057	51 12	123	23 43	160	48 39	227	37 45	280	54 04	322	22 35	349
309	52 28	056	51 39	122	23 54	159	48 16	227	37 13	279	53 44	320	22 29	348
310	52 54	055	52 06	122	24 06	158	47 53	226	36 42	278	53 23	319	22 22	347
311	53 20	054	52 33	121	24 18	158	47 30	226	36 10	277	53 02	317	22 15	346
312	53 45	052	53 00	121	24 30	157	47 07	226	35 39	276	52 40	316	22 07	345
313	54 10	051	53 27	120	24 42	156	46 44	225	35 07	276	52 18	315	21 58	344
314	54 35	050	53 55	120	24 55	156	46 22	225	34 35	275	51 55	313	21 49	343
	◆ FOMALHAUT		ACHERNAR		◆ CANOPUS		RIGIL KENT		◆ ANTARES		Nunki		ALTAIR	
315	54 59	049	54 23	119	25 08	155	45 59	224	34 04	274	51 32	312	21 39	342
316	55 22	047	54 50	119	25 22	155	45 37	224	33 32	273	51 08	311	21 29	341
317	55 45	046	55 18	118	25 36	154	45 15	223	33 00	272	50 44	310	21 18	340
318	56 08	044	55 46	118	25 50	153	44 54	223	32 28	271	50 19	308	21 07	339
319	56 30	043	56 14	117	26 04	153	44 32	222	31 57	270	49 54	307	20 55	338
320	56 51	042	56 43	117	26 19	152	44 11	222	31 25	270	49 28	306	20 43	337
321	57 12	040	57 11	116	26 34	151	43 50	221	30 53	269	49 02	305	20 30	336
322	57 32	039	57 40	116	26 50	151	43 29	221	30 21	268	48 36	304	20 16	335
323	57 52	037	58 08	115	27 05	150	43 08	221	29 50	267	48 09	302	20 02	333
324	58 10	036	58 37	115	27 21	150	42 47	220	29 18	266	47 42	301	19 48	332
325	58 28	034	59 06	114	27 37	149	42 27	220	28 46	265	47 15	300	19 33	331
326	58 46	032	59 35	114	27 54	148	42 07	219	28 14	265	46 47	299	19 18	330
327	59 03	031	60 04	113	28 11	148	41 47	219	27 43	264	46 19	298	19 02	329
328	59 18	029	60 33	113	28 28	147	41 27	218	27 11	263	45 51	297	18 45	328
329	59 34	028	61 03	112	28 45	147	41 08	218	26 40	262	45 22	296	18 28	327
	◆ FOMALHAUT		ACHERNAR		◆ CANOPUS		RIGIL KENT		◆ ANTARES		Nunki		ALTAIR	
330	59 48	026	61 32	112	29 03	146	40 48	217	26 08	261	44 54	295	18 11	326
331	60 01	024	62 02	112	29 21	145	40 29	217	25 37	260	44 25	293	17 53	325
332	60 14	023	62 31	111	29 39	145	40 10	216	25 06	260	43 55	292	17 35	324
333	60 26	021	63 01	111	29 58	144	39 52	216	24 34	259	43 26	291	17 16	323
334	60 36	019	63 31	110	30 16	144	39 33	215	24 03	258	42 56	290	16 57	322
335	60 46	017	64 01	110	30 36	143	39 15	215	23 32	257	42 26	289	16 38	322
336	60 55	016	64 31	109	30 55	142	38 57	214	23 01	256	41 56	288	16 18	321
337	61 03	014	65 01	109	31 14	142	38 39	214	22 30	256	41 26	287	15 57	320
338	61 11	012	65 31	108	31 34	141	38 22	213	21 59	255	40 55	286	15 36	319
339	61 17	010	66 01	108	31 54	141	38 04	213	21 29	254	40 25	285	15 15	318
340	61 22	008	66 32	107	32 15	140	37 47	212	20 58	253	39 54	284	14 53	317
341	61 26	007	67 02	107	32 35	139	37 30	212	20 28	253	39 23	283	14 31	316
342	61 29	005	67 33	106	32 56	139	37 14	211	19 58	252	38 52	283	14 09	315
343	61 31	003	68 03	106	33 17	138	36 57	211	19 28	251	38 21	282	13 46	314
344	61 32	001	68 34	105	33 38	138	36 41	210	18 58	250	37 50	281	13 23	313
	◆ Diphda		Acamar		CANOPUS		◆ Miaplacidus		RIGIL KENT		◆ Nunki		FOMALHAUT	
345	45 32	037	48 45	091	34 00	137	39 12	168	36 25	210	37 19	280	61 32	359
346	45 50	035	49 17	091	34 22	136	39 19	168	36 10	209	36 47	279	61 32	357
347	46 09	034	49 49	090	34 44	136	39 25	168	35 54	209	36 16	278	61 30	356
348	46 26	033	50 21	089	35 06	135	39 32	167	35 39	208	35 44	277	61 27	354
349	46 43	031	50 53	088	35 29	135	39 40	167	35 24	208	35 13	276	61 23	352
350	46 59	030	51 24	087	35 51	134	39 47	166	35 10	207	34 41	275	61 18	350
351	47 15	029	51 56	086	36 14	133	39 55	166	34 55	207	34 09	274	61 12	348
352	47 30	027	52 28	085	36 37	133	40 02	166	34 41	206	33 38	274	61 05	347
353	47 44	026	52 59	084	37 01	132	40 10	165	34 27	206	33 06	273	60 57	345
354	47 58	025	53 31	083	37 24	132	40 19	165	34 13	205	32 34	272	60 49	343
355	48 11	023	54 03	083	37 48	131	40 27	164	34 00	205	32 02	271	60 39	341
356	48 23	022	54 34	082	38 12	131	40 36	164	33 47	204	31 31	270	60 28	340
357	48 34	020	55 06	081	38 37	130	40 45	163	33 34	204	30 59	269	60 17	338
358	48 45	019	55 37	080	39 01	129	40 54	163	33 22	203	30 27	268	60 04	336
359	48 55	018	56 08	079	39 26	129	41 04	163	33 09	202	29 55	268	59 51	335

LHA ♈	Hc	Zn	Hc	Zn	Hc	Zn	Hc	Zn	Hc	Zn	Hc	Zn	Hc	Zn
	Diphda		◆RIGEL		CANOPUS		Miaplacidus		◆RIGIL KENT		Peacock		◆FOMALHAUT	
0	48 07	016	12 46	085	40 27	128	42 10	162	33 53	202	62 18	251	58 43	334
1	48 15	014	13 17	084	40 52	127	42 20	162	33 41	202	61 49	251	58 29	332
2	48 22	013	13 47	083	41 17	126	42 30	161	33 30	201	61 20	250	58 14	330
3	48 29	012	14 18	082	41 42	126	42 40	161	33 19	201	60 51	250	57 59	329
4	48 35	010	14 48	081	42 07	125	42 50	160	33 08	200	60 22	249	57 42	327
5	48 40	009	15 19	080	42 32	125	43 01	160	32 58	200	59 53	249	57 25	326
6	48 44	007	15 49	079	42 58	124	43 11	159	32 48	199	59 24	248	57 08	324
7	48 48	006	16 20	078	43 23	124	43 22	159	32 38	198	58 55	248	56 49	323
8	48 51	004	16 50	078	43 49	123	43 34	159	32 28	198	58 27	247	56 30	321
9	48 53	003	17 20	077	44 15	122	43 45	158	32 19	197	57 59	246	56 11	320
10	48 54	002	17 50	076	44 41	122	43 56	158	32 10	197	57 30	246	55 50	318
11	48 54	000	18 20	075	45 08	121	44 08	157	32 01	196	57 02	245	55 30	317
12	48 54	359	18 50	074	45 34	121	44 20	157	31 53	196	56 34	245	55 08	316
13	48 53	357	19 19	073	46 01	120	44 32	157	31 44	195	56 06	244	54 46	314
14	48 51	356	19 49	072	46 28	119	44 45	156	31 36	195	55 38	244	54 24	313
	◆RIGEL		SIRIUS		CANOPUS		◆RIGIL KENT		Peacock		◆FOMALHAUT		Diphda	
15	20 18	071	16 06	096	46 55	119	31 29	194	55 11	243	54 01	312	48 48	354
16	20 47	070	16 37	095	47 22	118	31 21	193	54 43	243	53 38	310	48 45	353
17	21 16	069	17 08	094	47 49	118	31 14	193	54 16	242	53 14	309	48 41	351
18	21 45	069	17 39	093	48 17	117	31 08	192	53 48	242	52 50	308	48 36	350
19	22 14	068	18 09	092	48 44	116	31 01	192	53 21	241	52 25	306	48 30	349
20	22 42	067	18 40	092	49 12	116	30 55	191	52 54	241	52 00	305	48 23	347
21	23 11	066	19 11	091	49 40	115	30 49	191	52 27	240	51 34	304	48 16	346
22	23 39	065	19 42	090	50 08	115	30 43	190	52 01	240	51 08	303	48 08	344
23	24 07	064	20 13	089	50 36	114	30 38	190	51 34	239	50 42	301	48 00	343
24	24 34	063	20 44	088	51 04	113	30 33	189	51 08	239	50 16	300	47 50	342
25	25 02	062	21 15	087	51 33	113	30 28	188	50 41	238	49 49	299	47 40	340
26	25 29	061	21 46	086	52 01	112	30 24	188	50 15	238	49 22	298	47 29	339
27	25 56	060	22 17	086	52 30	112	30 20	187	49 49	237	48 54	297	47 18	337
28	26 22	059	22 47	085	52 59	111	30 16	187	49 23	237	48 27	296	47 05	336
29	26 48	058	23 18	084	53 28	110	30 13	186	48 58	236	47 59	295	46 52	335
	◆RIGEL		SIRIUS		CANOPUS		◆RIGIL KENT		Peacock		◆FOMALHAUT		Diphda	
30	27 14	057	23 49	083	53 57	110	30 09	186	48 32	235	47 30	294	46 39	333
31	27 40	056	24 19	082	54 26	109	30 06	185	48 07	235	47 02	292	46 25	332
32	28 06	055	24 50	081	54 55	109	30 04	185	47 41	234	46 33	291	46 10	331
33	28 31	054	25 20	080	55 25	108	30 01	184	47 16	234	46 04	290	45 54	329
34	28 56	053	25 51	079	55 54	107	29 59	183	46 52	233	45 35	289	45 38	328
35	29 20	052	26 21	078	56 24	107	29 58	183	46 27	233	45 06	288	45 22	327
36	29 44	051	26 51	078	56 53	106	29 56	182	46 02	232	44 37	287	45 04	325
37	30 08	050	27 22	077	57 23	105	29 55	182	45 38	232	44 07	286	44 47	324
38	30 31	049	27 52	076	57 53	105	29 54	181	45 14	231	43 37	285	44 28	323
39	30 54	048	28 21	075	58 23	104	29 54	181	44 50	231	43 08	284	44 09	322
40	31 17	047	28 51	074	58 53	103	29 54	180	44 26	230	42 38	283	43 50	320
41	31 39	045	29 21	073	59 23	103	29 54	180	44 02	230	42 07	282	43 30	319
42	32 01	044	29 50	072	59 53	102	29 54	179	43 39	229	41 37	281	43 09	318
43	32 22	043	30 20	071	60 23	101	29 55	178	43 16	229	41 07	280	42 48	317
44	32 43	042	30 49	070	60 54	101	29 56	178	42 52	228	40 36	280	42 27	316
	RIGEL		◆SIRIUS		CANOPUS		◆RIGIL KENT		Peacock		FOMALHAUT		◆Diphda	
45	33 04	041	31 18	069	61 24	100	29 57	177	42 30	227	40 06	279	42 05	314
46	33 24	040	31 46	068	61 54	099	29 59	177	42 07	227	39 35	278	41 43	313
47	33 44	039	32 15	067	62 25	099	30 01	176	41 44	226	39 05	277	41 20	312
48	34 03	038	32 43	066	62 56	098	30 03	176	41 22	226	38 34	276	40 57	311
49	34 21	037	33 11	065	63 26	097	30 06	175	41 00	225	38 03	275	40 33	310
50	34 40	035	33 39	064	63 57	096	30 08	174	40 38	225	37 32	274	40 09	309
51	34 57	034	34 07	063	64 28	096	30 12	174	40 17	224	37 02	273	39 45	307
52	35 14	033	34 35	062	64 58	095	30 15	173	39 55	224	36 31	272	39 20	306
53	35 31	032	35 02	061	65 29	094	30 19	173	39 34	223	36 00	271	38 55	305
54	35 47	031	35 29	060	66 00	093	30 23	172	39 13	223	35 29	271	38 30	304
55	36 03	030	35 55	059	66 31	093	30 27	172	38 52	222	34 58	270	38 04	303
56	36 18	028	36 22	058	67 02	092	30 32	171	38 31	221	34 27	269	37 38	302
57	36 32	027	36 48	057	67 33	091	30 37	171	38 11	221	33 56	268	37 12	301
58	36 46	026	37 13	056	68 04	090	30 42	170	37 51	220	33 25	267	36 45	300
59	36 59	025	37 39	055	68 34	089	30 47	169	37 31	220	32 54	266	36 18	299
	RIGEL		◆SIRIUS		Suhail		◆RIGIL KENT		Peacock		FOMALHAUT		◆Diphda	
60	37 12	024	38 04	054	42 19	107	30 53	169	37 11	219	32 24	266	35 51	298
61	37 24	022	38 28	053	42 48	106	30 59	168	36 52	219	31 53	265	35 23	297
62	37 36	021	38 53	051	43 18	106	31 05	168	36 33	218	31 22	264	34 56	296
63	37 46	020	39 17	050	43 48	105	31 12	167	36 14	218	30 51	263	34 28	295
64	37 57	019	39 40	049	44 18	104	31 19	167	35 55	217	30 21	262	33 59	294
65	38 06	017	40 04	048	44 48	103	31 26	166	35 36	217	29 50	261	33 31	293
66	38 15	016	40 26	047	45 18	103	31 34	166	35 18	216	29 20	261	33 02	292
67	38 23	015	40 49	046	45 48	102	31 42	165	35 00	215	28 49	260	32 34	291
68	38 31	014	41 11	045	46 18	101	31 50	164	34 42	215	28 19	259	32 05	290
69	38 38	012	41 32	043	46 49	100	31 58	164	34 25	214	27 49	258	31 35	289
70	38 44	011	41 53	042	47 19	100	32 07	163	34 08	214	27 18	257	31 06	288
71	38 50	010	42 13	041	47 50	099	32 16	163	33 51	213	26 48	257	30 37	287
72	38 55	009	42 33	040	48 20	098	32 25	162	33 34	213	26 18	256	30 07	286
73	39 00	007	42 53	039	48 51	097	32 35	162	33 17	212	25 48	255	29 37	285
74	39 03	006	43 12	037	49 21	096	32 45	161	33 01	211	25 18	254	29 07	284
	RIGEL		◆SIRIUS		Suhail		◆RIGIL KENT		Peacock		ACHERNAR		◆Diphda	
75	39 06	005	43 30	036	49 52	096	32 55	161	32 45	211	63 55	252	28 37	283
76	39 08	004	43 48	035	50 23	095	33 05	160	32 29	210	63 25	251	28 07	282
77	39 10	002	44 06	033	50 54	094	33 16	160	32 14	210	62 56	251	27 37	281
78	39 11	001	44 22	032	51 25	093	33 27	159	31 59	209	62 27	250	27 06	281
79	39 11	000	44 39	031	51 55	092	33 38	159	31 44	209	61 58	250	26 36	280
80	39 11	358	44 54	030	52 26	092	33 49	158	31 29	208	61 29	249	26 06	279
81	39 09	357	45 09	028	52 57	091	34 01	157	31 15	207	61 00	249	25 35	278
82	39 08	356	45 23	027	53 28	090	34 13	157	31 01	207	60 31	248	25 04	277
83	39 05	355	45 37	026	53 59	089	34 25	156	30 47	206	60 03	248	24 34	276
84	39 02	353	45 50	024	54 30	088	34 38	156	30 34	206	59 34	247	24 03	275
85	38 58	352	46 03	023	55 01	087	34 50	155	30 20	205	59 06	247	23 32	274
86	38 53	351	46 14	022	55 32	086	35 04	155	30 07	204	58 37	246	23 01	273
87	38 48	350	46 25	020	56 03	085	35 17	154	29 55	204	58 09	246	22 30	272
88	38 42	348	46 36	019	56 33	085	35 30	154	29 42	203	57 41	245	22 00	272
89	38 36	347	46 46	018	57 04	084	35 44	153	29 30	203	57 13	245	21 29	271

LAT 59°S

LHA ♈	Hc	Zn	Hc	Zn	Hc	Zn	Hc	Zn	Hc	Zn	Hc	Zn	Hc	Zn
	SIRIUS		Alphard		◆Suhail		RIGIL KENT		◆Peacock		ACHERNAR		◆RIGEL	
90	46 54	016	26 17	060	57 35	083	35 58	153	29 19	202	56 45	244	38 28	346
91	47 03	015	26 44	059	58 05	082	36 13	152	29 07	202	56 17	244	38 20	345
92	47 10	013	27 10	058	58 36	081	36 27	152	28 56	201	55 50	243	38 12	343
93	47 17	012	27 37	057	59 06	080	36 42	151	28 45	200	55 22	243	38 03	342
94	47 23	011	28 03	056	59 37	079	36 57	151	28 34	200	54 55	242	37 53	341
95	47 28	009	28 28	055	60 07	078	37 12	150	28 24	199	54 28	242	37 42	340
96	47 33	008	28 53	054	60 37	077	37 28	150	28 14	199	54 01	241	37 31	338
97	47 37	006	29 18	053	61 07	076	37 44	149	28 04	198	53 34	241	37 20	337
98	47 40	005	29 43	052	61 37	074	38 00	148	27 55	197	53 07	240	37 07	336
99	47 42	003	30 07	051	62 07	073	38 16	148	27 46	197	52 40	239	36 54	335
100	47 43	002	30 31	050	62 36	072	38 32	147	27 37	196	52 14	239	36 41	334
101	47 44	001	30 55	049	63 05	071	38 49	147	27 29	196	51 47	238	36 27	332
102	47 44	359	31 18	048	63 34	070	39 06	146	27 21	195	51 21	238	36 12	331
103	47 43	358	31 41	047	64 03	069	39 23	146	27 13	194	50 55	237	35 57	330
104	47 42	356	32 03	046	64 32	067	39 41	145	27 05	194	50 29	237	35 41	329
	Alphard		◆Gienah		RIGIL KENT		◆Peacock		ACHERNAR		◆RIGEL		SIRIUS	
105	32 25	045	20 37	090	39 58	145	26 58	193	50 03	236	35 25	328	47 39	355
106	32 47	044	21 07	089	40 16	144	26 51	193	49 37	236	35 08	326	47 36	354
107	33 08	043	21 38	088	40 34	144	26 45	192	49 12	235	34 51	325	47 32	352
108	33 29	042	22 09	088	40 53	143	26 38	191	48 47	235	34 33	324	47 28	351
109	33 49	040	22 40	087	41 11	143	26 32	191	48 21	234	34 15	323	47 22	349
110	34 09	039	23 11	086	41 30	142	26 27	190	47 56	234	33 56	322	47 16	348
111	34 28	038	23 42	085	41 49	142	26 22	190	47 31	233	33 36	321	47 10	346
112	34 47	037	24 12	084	42 08	141	26 17	189	47 07	233	33 17	320	47 02	345
113	35 06	036	24 43	083	42 27	141	26 12	188	46 42	232	32 56	318	46 54	344
114	35 24	035	25 14	082	42 47	140	26 08	188	46 18	232	32 36	317	46 45	342
115	35 41	034	25 44	081	43 07	140	26 04	187	45 54	231	32 15	316	46 35	341
116	35 58	032	26 15	080	43 27	139	26 00	187	45 30	231	31 53	315	46 24	340
117	36 14	031	26 45	080	43 47	139	25 57	186	45 06	230	31 31	314	46 13	338
118	36 30	030	27 16	079	44 07	139	25 54	185	44 42	230	31 09	313	46 02	337
119	36 45	029	27 46	078	44 28	138	25 51	185	44 19	229	30 46	312	45 49	336
	REGULUS		◆SPICA		RIGIL KENT		Peacock		◆ACHERNAR		RIGEL		◆SIRIUS	
120	14 26	033	13 59	089	44 49	138	25 49	184	43 56	229	30 23	311	45 36	334
121	14 43	032	14 30	088	45 10	137	25 46	183	43 33	228	29 59	310	45 22	333
122	14 59	031	15 01	087	45 31	137	25 45	183	43 10	227	29 35	309	45 08	332
123	15 14	030	15 32	086	45 52	136	25 43	182	42 47	227	29 11	308	44 53	330
124	15 30	029	16 03	085	46 14	136	25 42	182	42 25	226	28 46	307	44 37	329
125	15 44	028	16 34	084	46 35	135	25 42	181	42 02	226	28 21	306	44 21	328
126	15 58	027	17 04	083	46 57	135	25 41	180	41 40	225	27 56	305	44 04	326
127	16 12	026	17 35	083	47 19	134	25 41	180	41 18	225	27 31	304	43 47	325
128	16 25	025	18 06	082	47 41	134	25 41	179	40 57	224	27 05	303	43 29	324
129	16 38	024	18 36	081	48 04	133	25 42	179	40 35	224	26 39	302	43 10	323
130	16 50	023	19 07	080	48 26	133	25 43	178	40 14	223	26 12	301	42 51	321
131	17 02	022	19 37	079	48 49	132	25 44	177	39 53	223	25 46	300	42 32	320
132	17 13	021	20 07	078	49 12	132	25 46	177	39 32	222	25 19	299	42 12	319
133	17 24	020	20 37	077	49 35	131	25 48	176	39 11	222	24 51	298	41 51	318
134	17 34	019	21 08	076	49 58	131	25 50	176	38 51	221	24 24	297	41 30	317
	REGULUS		◆SPICA		RIGIL KENT		◆Peacock		ACHERNAR		CANOPUS		◆SIRIUS	
135	17 44	018	21 37	075	50 22	131	25 52	175	38 31	220	67 37	269	41 08	315
136	17 53	017	22 07	074	50 45	130	25 55	174	38 11	220	67 06	268	40 47	314
137	18 02	016	22 37	074	51 09	130	25 59	174	37 51	219	66 35	268	40 24	313
138	18 10	015	23 07	073	51 33	129	26 02	173	37 32	219	66 04	267	40 01	312
139	18 17	014	23 36	072	51 57	129	26 06	173	37 12	218	65 34	266	39 38	311
140	18 24	013	24 05	071	52 21	128	26 10	172	36 53	218	65 03	265	39 15	310
141	18 31	012	24 34	070	52 45	128	26 15	171	36 34	217	64 32	264	38 51	308
142	18 37	011	25 03	069	53 10	127	26 19	171	36 16	217	64 01	264	38 26	307
143	18 42	010	25 32	068	53 34	127	26 25	170	35 58	216	63 31	263	38 01	306
144	18 47	009	26 01	067	53 59	127	26 30	169	35 39	216	63 00	262	37 36	305
145	18 52	008	26 29	066	54 24	126	26 36	169	35 22	215	62 29	261	37 11	304
146	18 55	007	26 57	065	54 49	126	26 42	168	35 04	214	61 59	261	36 45	303
147	18 59	005	27 25	064	55 14	125	26 48	168	34 47	214	61 28	260	36 19	302
148	19 01	004	27 53	063	55 40	125	26 55	167	34 30	213	60 58	259	35 53	301
149	19 03	003	28 20	062	56 05	124	27 02	166	34 13	213	60 28	259	35 26	300
	REGULUS		◆SPICA		RIGIL KENT		◆Peacock		ACHERNAR		CANOPUS		◆SIRIUS	
150	19 05	002	28 47	061	56 31	124	27 10	166	33 56	212	59 57	258	34 59	299
151	19 06	001	29 14	060	56 56	124	27 17	165	33 40	212	59 27	257	34 32	298
152	19 06	000	29 41	059	57 22	123	27 25	165	33 24	211	58 57	257	34 04	297
153	19 06	359	30 07	058	57 48	123	27 34	164	33 08	210	58 27	256	33 37	296
154	19 06	358	30 33	057	58 14	122	27 42	163	32 52	210	57 57	255	33 09	295
155	19 04	357	30 59	056	58 40	122	27 51	163	32 37	209	57 27	255	32 41	294
156	19 03	356	31 25	055	59 06	122	28 01	162	32 22	209	56 57	254	32 12	293
157	19 00	355	31 50	054	59 33	121	28 10	162	32 07	208	56 28	253	31 44	292
158	18 57	354	32 15	053	59 59	121	28 20	161	31 53	208	55 58	253	31 15	291
159	18 54	353	32 39	052	60 26	120	28 30	160	31 39	207	55 29	252	30 46	290
160	18 50	352	33 03	051	60 53	120	28 41	160	31 25	206	54 59	252	30 17	289
161	18 45	351	33 27	050	61 20	119	28 51	159	31 11	206	54 30	251	29 47	288
162	18 40	350	33 50	049	61 47	119	29 02	159	30 58	205	54 01	250	29 18	287
163	18 35	349	34 13	048	62 14	119	29 14	159	30 45	205	53 32	250	28 48	286
164	18 28	348	34 36	046	62 41	118	29 25	158	30 32	204	53 03	249	28 19	285
	◆SPICA		ANTARES		◆Peacock		ACHERNAR		CANOPUS		◆SIRIUS		REGULUS	
165	34 58	045	26 12	098	29 37	157	30 19	204	52 34	248	27 49	284	18 22	347
166	35 20	044	26 43	098	29 50	156	30 07	203	52 05	248	27 19	283	18 14	346
167	35 41	043	27 13	097	30 02	156	29 55	202	51 37	247	26 49	282	18 06	345
168	36 02	042	27 44	096	30 15	155	29 44	202	51 08	247	26 18	281	17 58	344
169	36 23	041	28 15	095	30 28	155	29 32	201	50 40	246	25 48	281	17 49	343
170	36 43	040	28 46	094	30 42	154	29 21	201	50 12	245	25 18	280	17 40	342
171	37 02	039	29 16	093	30 55	153	29 10	200	49 44	245	24 47	279	17 30	341
172	37 21	037	29 47	093	31 09	153	29 00	199	49 16	244	24 16	278	17 20	340
173	37 40	036	30 18	092	31 23	152	28 50	199	48 48	244	23 46	277	17 09	339
174	37 58	035	30 49	091	31 38	152	28 40	198	48 21	243	23 15	276	16 57	338
175	38 15	034	31 20	090	31 53	151	28 30	198	47 53	242	22 44	275	16 45	337
176	38 32	033	31 51	089	32 08	151	28 21	197	47 26	242	22 14	274	16 33	336
177	38 49	031	32 22	088	32 23	150	28 12	197	46 59	241	21 43	273	16 20	335
178	39 05	030	32 53	087	32 39	149	28 04	196	46 32	241	21 12	273	16 06	334
179	39 20	029	33 23	087	32 55	149	27 55	195	46 05	240	20 41	272	15 53	333

 LAT 59°S

LHA ♈	Hc Zn	Hc Zn	Hc Zn	Hc Zn	Hc Zn	Hc Zn	Hc Zn
	◆ SPICA	ANTARES	◆ Peacock	ACHERNAR	CANOPUS	◆ SIRIUS	Alphard
180	39 35 028	33 54 086	33 11 148	27 47 195	45 38 240	20 10 271	32 07 314
181	39 49 027	34 25 085	33 27 148	27 39 194	45 12 239	19 39 270	31 45 313
182	40 02 025	34 56 084	33 44 147	27 32 194	44 45 238	19 08 269	31 22 312
183	40 15 024	35 27 083	34 01 147	27 25 193	44 19 238	18 37 268	30 59 311
184	40 27 023	35 57 082	34 18 146	27 18 192	43 53 237	18 07 267	30 35 310
185	40 39 022	36 28 081	34 35 145	27 12 192	43 27 237	17 36 267	30 11 309
186	40 50 020	36 58 080	34 53 145	27 06 191	43 01 236	17 05 266	29 47 308
187	41 00 019	37 29 079	35 11 144	27 00 191	42 36 235	16 34 265	29 22 307
188	41 10 018	37 59 078	35 29 144	26 54 190	42 10 235	16 03 264	28 57 306
189	41 19 016	38 29 077	35 47 143	26 49 189	41 45 234	15 33 263	28 32 305
190	41 28 015	38 59 076	36 06 143	26 44 189	41 20 234	15 02 262	28 07 304
191	41 35 014	39 29 076	36 25 142	26 40 188	40 56 233	14 31 262	27 41 303
192	41 42 013	39 59 075	36 44 141	26 35 188	40 31 232	14 01 261	27 15 302
193	41 49 011	40 29 074	37 03 141	26 31 187	40 07 232	13 30 260	26 48 301
194	41 54 010	40 58 073	37 23 140	26 28 186	39 42 231	13 00 259	26 22 300
	SPICA	◆ ANTARES	Peacock	◆ ACHERNAR	CANOPUS	Suhail	◆ Alphard
195	41 59 009	41 28 072	37 43 140	26 25 186	39 18 231	52 04 268	25 55 299
196	42 04 007	41 57 071	38 03 139	26 22 185	38 55 230	51 33 267	25 27 298
197	42 07 006	42 26 070	38 23 139	26 19 185	38 31 229	51 02 266	25 00 297
198	42 10 005	42 55 069	38 44 138	26 17 184	38 08 229	50 31 265	24 32 296
199	42 12 003	43 24 067	39 04 138	26 15 183	37 44 228	50 01 265	24 04 295
200	42 14 002	43 52 066	39 25 137	26 13 183	37 21 228	49 30 264	23 36 294
201	42 14 001	44 20 065	39 46 137	26 12 182	36 59 227	48 59 263	23 08 293
202	42 14 359	44 48 064	40 08 136	26 11 182	36 36 227	48 29 262	22 39 292
203	42 14 358	45 16 063	40 29 135	26 10 181	36 14 226	47 58 261	22 11 291
204	42 12 357	45 43 062	40 51 135	26 10 180	35 52 225	47 27 261	21 42 290
205	42 10 355	46 11 061	41 13 134	26 10 180	35 30 225	46 57 260	21 13 289
206	42 07 354	46 37 060	41 35 134	26 10 179	35 08 224	46 27 259	20 43 288
207	42 04 353	47 04 059	41 58 133	26 11 179	34 47 224	45 56 258	20 14 287
208	41 59 351	47 30 058	42 20 133	26 12 178	34 26 223	45 26 258	19 44 287
209	41 54 350	47 56 056	42 43 132	26 13 177	34 05 222	44 56 257	19 15 286
	ANTARES	◆ Nunki	Peacock	ACHERNAR	◆ CANOPUS	Suhail	◆ SPICA
210	48 22 055	30 25 091	43 06 132	26 14 177	33 44 222	44 26 256	41 49 349
211	48 47 054	30 56 090	43 29 131	26 16 176	33 23 221	43 56 255	41 42 347
212	49 12 053	31 27 089	43 53 131	26 19 176	33 03 221	43 26 255	41 35 346
213	49 36 052	31 58 089	44 16 130	26 21 175	32 43 220	42 56 254	41 28 345
214	50 00 050	32 29 088	44 40 130	26 24 174	32 24 219	42 27 253	41 19 344
215	50 24 049	33 00 087	45 04 129	26 27 174	32 04 219	41 57 252	41 10 342
216	50 47 048	33 31 086	45 28 128	26 31 173	31 45 218	41 28 252	41 00 341
217	51 10 047	34 02 085	45 52 128	26 35 172	31 26 218	40 58 251	40 50 340
218	51 32 045	34 32 084	46 17 127	26 39 172	31 07 217	40 29 250	40 39 338
219	51 54 044	35 03 083	46 41 127	26 43 171	30 49 216	40 00 250	40 27 337
220	52 15 043	35 34 082	47 06 126	26 48 171	30 31 216	39 31 249	40 15 336
221	52 35 041	36 04 081	47 31 126	26 53 170	30 13 215	39 03 248	40 02 335
222	52 56 040	36 35 081	47 56 125	26 59 169	29 55 214	38 34 248	39 49 333
223	53 15 038	37 05 080	48 22 125	27 05 169	29 38 214	38 06 247	39 34 332
224	53 34 037	37 36 079	48 47 124	27 11 168	29 21 213	37 37 246	39 20 331
	ANTARES	◆ Nunki	Peacock	ACHERNAR	◆ CANOPUS	Suhail	◆ SPICA
225	53 52 036	38 06 078	49 13 124	27 17 168	29 04 213	37 09 245	39 04 330
226	54 10 034	38 36 077	49 38 123	27 24 167	28 47 212	36 41 245	38 49 329
227	54 27 033	39 06 076	50 04 123	27 31 167	28 31 211	36 13 244	38 32 327
228	54 43 031	39 36 075	50 30 122	27 38 166	28 15 211	35 45 243	38 15 326
229	54 59 030	40 06 074	50 57 122	27 46 165	27 59 210	35 18 243	37 58 325
230	55 14 028	40 35 073	51 23 121	27 54 165	27 44 210	34 50 242	37 40 324
231	55 28 027	41 05 072	51 50 121	28 02 164	27 29 209	34 23 241	37 21 323
232	55 42 025	41 34 071	52 16 120	28 11 164	27 14 208	33 56 241	37 02 321
233	55 55 024	42 03 070	52 43 120	28 20 163	27 00 208	33 29 240	36 43 320
234	56 07 022	42 32 069	53 10 119	28 29 162	26 46 207	33 03 239	36 23 319
235	56 18 021	43 01 068	53 37 118	28 39 162	26 32 206	32 36 239	36 02 318
236	56 29 019	43 29 067	54 04 118	28 48 161	26 18 206	32 10 238	35 41 317
237	56 38 017	43 58 066	54 32 117	28 59 161	26 05 205	31 44 237	35 20 316
238	56 47 016	44 26 065	54 59 117	29 09 160	25 52 205	31 18 236	34 58 315
239	56 55 014	44 53 064	55 27 116	29 20 159	25 39 204	30 52 236	34 36 313
	◆ ANTARES	Nunki	◆ FOMALHAUT	ACHERNAR	CANOPUS	◆ ACRUX	SPICA
240	57 02 013	45 21 063	18 02 118	29 31 159	25 27 203	64 44 238	34 13 312
241	57 09 011	45 48 061	18 29 117	29 42 158	25 15 203	64 18 237	33 50 311
242	57 14 009	46 15 060	18 57 116	29 54 158	25 03 202	63 52 237	33 27 310
243	57 18 008	46 42 059	19 25 115	30 06 157	24 51 201	63 26 237	33 03 309
244	57 22 006	47 08 058	19 53 115	30 18 156	24 40 201	63 00 237	32 39 308
245	57 25 004	47 34 057	20 21 114	30 30 156	24 30 200	62 35 236	32 14 307
246	57 27 003	48 00 056	20 49 113	30 43 155	24 19 199	62 09 236	31 50 306
247	57 28 001	48 25 054	21 18 112	30 56 155	24 09 199	61 43 236	31 24 305
248	57 28 359	48 50 053	21 47 111	31 09 154	23 59 198	61 18 235	30 59 304
249	57 27 358	49 15 052	22 15 111	31 23 154	23 50 198	60 53 235	30 33 303
250	57 25 356	49 39 051	22 44 110	31 37 153	23 41 197	60 27 235	30 07 302
251	57 23 354	50 03 050	23 14 109	31 51 152	23 32 196	60 02 234	29 41 301
252	57 19 353	50 26 048	23 43 108	32 05 152	23 23 196	59 37 234	29 14 300
253	57 15 351	50 49 047	24 12 108	32 20 151	23 15 195	59 12 234	28 47 299
254	57 09 349	51 11 046	24 42 107	32 35 151	23 07 194	58 47 233	28 20 298
	ALTAIR	◆ FOMALHAUT	ACHERNAR	CANOPUS	◆ ACRUX	SPICA	◆ ANTARES
255	13 54 044	25 11 106	32 50 150	23 00 194	58 23 233	27 52 297	57 03 348
256	14 15 043	25 41 105	33 06 150	22 53 193	57 58 233	27 25 296	56 56 346
257	14 36 042	26 11 104	33 22 149	22 46 192	57 33 232	26 57 295	56 48 344
258	14 56 041	26 41 104	33 38 148	22 39 192	57 09 232	26 29 294	56 40 343
259	15 16 040	27 11 103	33 54 148	22 33 191	56 45 232	26 00 293	56 30 341
260	15 36 039	27 41 102	34 11 147	22 28 190	56 21 231	25 32 292	56 20 340
261	15 55 038	28 12 101	34 27 147	22 22 190	55 57 231	25 03 291	56 09 338
262	16 14 037	28 42 100	34 44 146	22 17 189	55 33 230	24 34 290	55 57 337
263	16 32 036	29 12 100	35 02 146	22 12 189	55 09 230	24 05 289	55 44 335
264	16 50 035	29 43 099	35 19 145	22 08 188	54 45 230	23 36 288	55 31 333
265	17 08 034	30 13 098	35 37 145	22 04 187	54 22 229	23 06 287	55 17 332
266	17 25 033	30 44 097	35 55 144	22 00 187	53 59 229	22 37 286	55 02 330
267	17 42 032	31 15 096	36 13 143	21 57 186	53 35 228	22 07 286	54 46 329
268	17 58 031	31 46 095	36 32 143	21 54 185	53 12 228	21 37 285	54 30 327
269	18 14 030	32 16 095	36 51 142	21 51 185	52 49 228	21 07 284	54 13 326

LHA ♈	Hc Zn	Hc Zn	Hc Zn	Hc Zn	Hc Zn	Hc Zn	Hc Zn
	◆ ALTAIR	FOMALHAUT	◆ ACHERNAR	CANOPUS	RIGIL KENT	◆ SPICA	ANTARES
270	18 29 029	32 47 094	37 10 142	21 49 184	65 34 244	20 37 283	53 55 325
271	18 44 028	33 18 093	37 29 141	21 47 183	65 07 244	20 07 282	53 37 323
272	18 58 027	33 49 092	37 48 141	21 45 183	64 39 243	19 37 281	53 18 322
273	19 12 026	34 20 091	38 08 140	21 44 182	64 11 243	19 06 280	52 59 320
274	19 25 025	34 51 090	38 28 140	21 43 181	63 44 243	18 36 279	52 39 319
275	19 38 024	35 22 090	38 48 139	21 42 181	63 17 242	18 05 278	52 18 318
276	19 51 023	35 52 089	39 09 138	21 42 180	62 49 242	17 35 277	51 57 316
277	20 02 022	36 23 088	39 29 138	21 42 179	62 22 241	17 04 277	51 36 315
278	20 14 021	36 54 087	39 50 137	21 43 179	61 55 241	16 33 276	51 13 314
279	20 25 020	37 25 086	40 11 137	21 44 178	61 28 241	16 03 275	50 51 312
280	20 35 019	37 56 085	40 32 136	21 45 177	61 01 240	15 32 274	50 28 311
281	20 45 018	38 27 084	40 54 136	21 47 177	60 34 240	15 01 273	50 04 310
282	20 54 017	38 57 083	41 15 135	21 48 176	60 08 239	14 30 272	49 40 309
283	21 02 016	39 28 083	41 37 135	21 51 175	59 41 239	13 59 271	49 16 307
284	21 11 015	39 59 082	41 59 134	21 53 175	59 15 239	13 28 271	48 51 306
	◆ ALTAIR	FOMALHAUT	◆ ACHERNAR	CANOPUS	◆ RIGIL KENT	ANTARES	Nunki
285	21 18 014	40 29 081	42 22 134	21 56 174	58 48 238	48 26 305	57 16 358
286	21 25 013	41 00 080	42 44 133	22 00 174	58 22 238	48 00 304	57 15 357
287	21 32 012	41 30 079	43 07 133	22 03 173	57 56 237	47 35 303	57 13 355
288	21 38 011	42 00 078	43 29 132	22 07 172	57 30 237	47 08 301	57 10 353
289	21 43 009	42 30 077	43 53 132	22 12 172	57 04 237	46 42 300	57 06 352
290	21 48 008	43 00 076	44 16 131	22 16 171	56 39 236	46 15 299	57 01 350
291	21 52 007	43 30 075	44 39 130	22 21 170	56 13 236	45 48 298	56 55 349
292	21 56 006	44 00 074	45 03 130	22 27 170	55 48 235	45 20 297	56 49 347
293	21 59 005	44 30 073	45 27 129	22 32 169	55 22 235	44 53 296	56 41 345
294	22 01 004	44 59 072	45 51 129	22 39 168	54 57 234	44 25 295	56 33 344
295	22 03 003	45 28 071	46 15 128	22 45 168	54 32 234	43 57 294	56 24 342
296	22 04 002	45 58 070	46 39 128	22 52 167	54 07 234	43 28 293	56 14 340
297	22 05 001	46 26 069	47 03 127	22 59 166	53 42 233	43 00 292	56 03 339
298	22 05 000	46 55 068	47 28 127	23 06 166	53 18 233	42 31 291	55 52 337
299	22 05 359	47 24 067	47 53 126	23 14 165	52 53 232	42 02 290	55 39 336
	FOMALHAUT	◆ ACHERNAR	CANOPUS	◆ RIGIL KENT	ANTARES	Nunki	◆ ALTAIR
300	47 52 066	48 18 126	23 22 164	52 29 232	41 33 289	55 26 334	22 04 358
301	48 20 065	48 43 125	23 31 164	52 04 231	41 03 288	55 12 333	22 03 357
302	48 48 063	49 08 125	23 39 163	51 40 231	40 34 287	54 58 331	22 01 356
303	49 15 062	49 34 124	23 48 163	51 16 230	40 04 286	54 43 330	21 58 355
304	49 42 061	50 00 124	23 58 162	50 53 230	39 34 285	54 27 328	21 55 353
305	50 09 060	50 25 123	24 08 161	50 29 230	39 04 284	54 10 327	21 51 352
306	50 36 059	50 51 123	24 18 161	50 06 229	38 34 283	53 53 325	21 47 351
307	51 02 058	51 17 122	24 28 160	49 42 229	38 04 282	53 35 324	21 42 350
308	51 28 056	51 44 122	24 39 159	49 19 228	37 34 281	53 17 323	21 36 349
309	51 54 055	52 10 121	24 50 159	48 56 228	37 03 280	52 57 321	21 30 348
310	52 19 054	52 37 121	25 01 158	48 34 227	36 33 279	52 38 320	21 23 347
311	52 44 053	53 03 120	25 13 157	48 11 227	36 02 278	52 18 318	21 16 346
312	53 08 051	53 30 120	25 25 157	47 48 226	35 32 277	51 57 317	21 09 345
313	53 32 050	53 57 119	25 37 156	47 26 226	35 01 276	51 35 316	21 00 344
314	53 55 049	54 24 119	25 50 156	47 04 225	34 30 275	51 14 314	20 52 343
	◆ FOMALHAUT	ACHERNAR	◆ CANOPUS	RIGIL KENT	◆ ANTARES	Nunki	ALTAIR
315	54 19 047	54 51 118	26 03 155	46 42 225	33 59 275	50 51 313	20 42 342
316	54 41 046	55 19 118	26 16 154	46 20 224	33 29 274	50 28 312	20 32 341
317	55 03 045	55 46 117	26 30 154	45 59 224	32 58 273	50 05 311	20 22 340
318	55 25 043	56 14 116	26 44 153	45 37 224	32 27 272	49 41 309	20 11 339
319	55 45 042	56 41 116	26 58 152	45 16 223	31 56 271	49 17 308	20 00 338
320	56 06 041	57 09 115	27 12 152	44 55 223	31 25 270	48 53 307	19 48 337
321	56 26 039	57 37 115	27 27 151	44 34 222	30 54 269	48 28 306	19 35 336
322	56 45 038	58 05 114	27 42 151	44 14 222	30 23 268	48 03 304	19 22 335
323	57 03 036	58 33 114	27 57 150	43 53 221	29 52 268	47 37 303	19 09 334
324	57 21 035	59 02 113	28 13 149	43 33 221	29 21 267	47 11 302	18 55 333
325	57 38 033	59 30 113	28 29 149	43 13 220	28 51 266	46 44 301	18 40 332
326	57 55 032	59 59 112	28 45 148	42 53 220	28 20 265	46 18 300	18 25 331
327	58 11 030	60 27 112	29 02 147	42 34 219	27 49 264	45 51 299	18 10 330
328	58 26 028	60 56 111	29 18 147	42 14 219	27 18 263	45 24 298	17 54 329
329	58 40 027	61 25 111	29 35 146	41 55 218	26 48 263	44 56 297	17 38 328
	◆ FOMALHAUT	ACHERNAR	◆ CANOPUS	RIGIL KENT	◆ ANTARES	Nunki	ALTAIR
330	58 54 025	61 54 110	29 53 146	41 36 218	26 17 262	44 28 295	17 21 327
331	59 06 024	62 23 110	30 10 145	41 17 217	25 47 261	44 00 294	17 04 326
332	59 18 022	62 52 109	30 28 144	40 59 217	25 16 260	43 32 293	16 46 325
333	59 29 020	63 21 109	30 46 144	40 40 216	24 46 259	43 04 292	16 28 324
334	59 40 019	63 51 108	31 05 143	40 22 216	24 15 259	42 35 291	16 09 323
335	59 49 017	64 20 108	31 23 143	40 04 215	23 45 258	42 06 290	15 50 322
336	59 57 015	64 49 107	31 42 142	39 46 215	23 15 257	41 37 289	15 31 321
337	60 05 013	65 19 107	32 01 141	39 29 214	22 45 256	41 08 288	15 11 320
338	60 12 012	65 49 106	32 21 141	39 12 214	22 15 255	40 38 287	14 51 319
339	60 18 010	66 18 105	32 40 140	38 55 213	21 45 254	40 09 286	14 31 318
340	60 22 008	66 48 105	33 00 140	38 38 213	21 15 254	39 39 285	14 10 317
341	60 26 006	67 18 104	33 21 139	38 21 212	20 46 253	39 09 284	13 48 316
342	60 29 005	67 48 104	33 41 138	38 05 212	20 16 252	38 39 283	13 27 315
343	60 31 003	68 18 103	34 02 138	37 49 211	19 47 251	38 09 282	13 05 314
344	60 32 001	68 48 103	34 23 137	37 33 211	19 18 250	37 39 281	12 42 313
	◆ Diphda	Acamar	CANOPUS	◆ Miaplacidus	RIGIL KENT	◆ Nunki	FOMALHAUT
345	44 43 036	48 46 090	34 44 137	40 11 168	37 17 210	37 08 280	60 32 359
346	45 01 035	49 17 089	35 05 136	40 17 168	37 02 210	36 38 280	60 32 358
347	45 19 034	49 48 089	35 27 135	40 24 167	36 47 209	36 07 279	60 30 356
348	45 35 032	50 19 088	35 49 135	40 31 167	36 32 209	35 37 278	60 27 354
349	45 52 031	50 50 087	36 11 134	40 38 167	36 17 208	35 06 277	60 23 352
350	46 07 030	51 21 086	36 33 134	40 45 166	36 03 208	34 35 276	60 19 351
351	46 22 028	51 51 085	36 55 133	40 53 166	35 49 207	34 05 275	60 13 349
352	46 37 027	52 22 084	37 18 132	41 00 165	35 35 206	33 34 274	60 07 347
353	46 50 026	52 53 083	37 41 132	41 08 165	35 21 206	33 03 273	59 59 345
354	47 03 024	53 24 082	38 04 131	41 17 164	35 08 205	32 32 272	59 51 344
355	47 16 023	53 54 081	38 28 131	41 25 164	34 55 205	32 01 272	59 42 342
356	47 27 021	54 25 080	38 51 130	41 34 164	34 42 204	31 30 271	59 32 340
357	47 38 020	54 55 079	39 15 129	41 42 163	34 29 204	30 59 270	59 21 339
358	47 48 019	55 25 078	39 39 129	41 52 163	34 17 203	30 28 269	59 09 337
359	47 58 017	55 56 077	40 03 128	42 01 162	34 05 203	29 58 268	58 57 335

LAT 60°S

LHA ♈	Hc Zn	Hc Zn	Hc Zn	Hc Zn	Hc Zn	Hc Zn	Hc Zn
	Diphda	◆RIGEL	CANOPUS	Miaplacidus	◆RIGIL KENT	Peacock	◆FOMALHAUT
0	47 09 016	12 40 084	41 04 127	43 07 162	34 48 202	62 36 253	57 49 334
1	47 17 014	13 10 084	41 28 126	43 17 161	34 37 202	62 08 253	57 36 333
2	47 24 013	13 40 083	41 52 126	43 27 161	34 26 201	61 39 252	57 22 331
3	47 30 011	14 09 082	42 17 125	43 37 160	34 15 201	61 11 251	57 07 330
4	47 36 010	14 39 081	42 41 125	43 47 160	34 05 200	60 42 251	56 52 328
5	47 41 009	15 09 080	43 06 124	43 57 160	33 54 200	60 14 250	56 36 327
6	47 45 007	15 38 079	43 31 123	44 08 159	33 44 199	59 46 250	56 19 325
7	47 48 006	16 08 078	43 56 123	44 18 159	33 35 199	59 18 249	56 01 324
8	47 51 004	16 37 077	44 21 122	44 29 158	33 25 198	58 50 249	55 43 322
9	47 53 003	17 06 076	44 47 122	44 41 158	33 16 198	58 22 248	55 24 321
10	47 54 002	17 35 076	45 13 121	44 52 158	33 07 197	57 54 247	55 05 319
11	47 54 000	18 04 075	45 38 120	45 04 157	32 59 196	57 26 247	54 45 318
12	47 54 359	18 33 074	46 04 120	45 15 157	32 50 196	56 59 246	54 25 317
13	47 53 357	19 02 073	46 31 119	45 27 156	32 42 195	56 31 246	54 04 315
14	47 51 356	19 30 072	46 57 118	45 39 156	32 34 195	56 04 245	53 43 314
	◆RIGEL	SIRIUS	CANOPUS	◆RIGIL KENT	Peacock	◆FOMALHAUT	Diphda
15	19 59 071	16 12 096	47 23 118	32 27 194	55 37 245	53 21 313	47 49 354
16	20 27 070	16 42 095	47 50 117	32 20 194	55 10 244	52 59 311	47 45 353
17	20 55 069	17 12 094	48 17 117	32 13 193	54 43 244	52 36 310	47 41 352
18	21 23 068	17 42 093	48 44 116	32 06 193	54 16 243	52 13 309	47 37 350
19	21 51 067	18 12 092	49 11 115	32 00 192	53 50 242	51 49 307	47 31 349
20	22 18 066	18 42 091	49 38 115	31 54 191	53 23 242	51 25 306	47 25 347
21	22 46 065	19 12 090	50 05 114	31 48 191	52 57 241	51 00 305	47 18 346
22	23 13 064	19 42 090	50 32 114	31 42 190	52 30 241	50 36 304	47 10 345
23	23 40 063	20 12 089	51 00 113	31 37 190	52 04 240	50 10 302	47 02 343
24	24 07 062	20 42 088	51 28 112	31 32 189	51 38 240	49 45 301	46 53 342
25	24 33 061	21 12 087	51 56 112	31 28 189	51 13 239	49 19 300	46 43 340
26	24 59 060	21 42 086	52 24 111	31 23 188	50 47 239	48 53 299	46 33 339
27	25 25 059	22 12 085	52 52 110	31 19 187	50 21 238	48 27 298	46 22 338
28	25 51 058	22 42 084	53 20 110	31 16 187	49 56 238	48 00 297	46 10 336
29	26 16 057	23 11 083	53 48 109	31 12 186	49 31 237	47 33 296	45 58 335
	◆RIGEL	SIRIUS	CANOPUS	◆RIGIL KENT	Peacock	◆FOMALHAUT	Diphda
30	26 42 056	23 41 082	54 16 108	31 09 186	49 06 236	47 06 295	45 45 334
31	27 06 055	24 11 082	54 45 108	31 06 185	48 41 236	46 39 293	45 32 332
32	27 31 054	24 40 081	55 14 107	31 04 185	48 16 235	46 11 292	45 17 331
33	27 55 053	25 10 080	55 42 107	31 01 184	47 51 235	45 43 291	45 03 330
34	28 19 052	25 40 079	56 11 106	30 59 183	47 27 234	45 15 290	44 47 329
35	28 43 051	26 09 078	56 40 105	30 58 183	47 03 234	44 47 289	44 31 327
36	29 06 050	26 38 077	57 09 105	30 56 182	46 39 233	44 18 288	44 15 326
37	29 29 049	27 07 076	57 38 104	30 55 182	46 15 233	43 50 287	43 58 325
38	29 52 048	27 36 075	58 07 103	30 54 181	45 51 232	43 21 286	43 40 323
39	30 14 047	28 05 074	58 37 102	30 54 181	45 27 231	42 52 285	43 22 322
40	30 36 046	28 34 073	59 06 102	30 54 180	45 04 231	42 23 284	43 03 321
41	30 57 045	29 03 072	59 35 101	30 54 180	44 41 230	41 54 283	42 44 320
42	31 18 044	29 31 071	60 05 100	30 54 179	44 18 230	41 25 282	42 25 319
43	31 39 043	30 00 070	60 34 100	30 55 178	43 55 229	40 55 281	42 05 317
44	31 59 042	30 28 069	61 04 099	30 56 178	43 32 229	40 26 280	41 44 316
	RIGEL	◆SIRIUS	CANOPUS	◆RIGIL KENT	Peacock	FOMALHAUT	◆Diphda
45	32 19 041	30 56 069	61 34 098	30 57 177	43 10 228	39 56 279	41 23 315
46	32 38 040	31 24 068	62 03 097	30 59 177	42 48 228	39 27 279	41 02 314
47	32 57 038	31 51 067	62 33 097	31 01 176	42 26 227	38 57 278	40 40 313
48	33 15 037	32 19 066	63 03 096	31 03 176	42 04 227	38 27 277	40 17 311
49	33 33 036	32 46 065	63 33 095	31 05 175	41 42 226	37 58 276	39 55 310
50	33 51 035	33 13 064	64 03 094	31 08 174	41 21 225	37 28 275	39 32 309
51	34 08 034	33 40 063	64 33 094	31 11 174	40 59 225	36 58 274	39 08 308
52	34 24 033	34 06 061	65 02 093	31 15 173	40 38 224	36 28 273	38 44 307
53	34 40 032	34 32 060	65 32 092	31 18 173	40 17 224	35 58 272	38 20 306
54	34 56 030	34 58 059	66 02 091	31 22 172	39 57 223	35 28 271	37 56 305
55	35 10 029	35 24 058	66 32 090	31 26 172	39 36 223	34 58 270	37 31 304
56	35 25 028	35 49 057	67 02 089	31 31 171	39 16 222	34 28 270	37 06 303
57	35 39 027	36 15 056	67 32 089	31 36 170	38 56 221	33 58 269	36 40 302
58	35 52 026	36 39 055	68 02 088	31 41 170	38 36 221	33 28 268	36 15 300
59	36 05 025	37 04 054	68 32 087	31 46 169	38 17 220	32 58 267	35 49 299
	RIGEL	◆SIRIUS	Suhail	◆RIGIL KENT	Peacock	FOMALHAUT	◆Diphda
60	36 17 023	37 28 053	42 36 106	31 52 169	37 58 220	32 28 266	35 22 298
61	36 29 022	37 52 052	43 05 105	31 58 168	37 39 219	31 58 265	34 56 297
62	36 40 021	38 15 051	43 34 105	32 04 168	37 20 219	31 28 264	34 29 296
63	36 50 020	38 38 050	44 03 104	32 11 167	37 01 218	30 58 264	34 02 295
64	37 00 018	39 01 049	44 32 103	32 18 167	36 43 218	30 29 263	33 35 294
65	37 09 017	39 23 047	45 01 102	32 25 166	36 25 217	29 59 262	33 08 293
66	37 18 016	39 45 046	45 30 102	32 32 165	36 07 216	29 29 261	32 40 292
67	37 25 015	40 07 045	46 00 101	32 40 165	35 49 216	29 00 260	32 12 291
68	37 33 014	40 28 044	46 29 100	32 48 164	35 32 215	28 30 260	31 44 290
69	37 40 012	40 48 043	46 59 099	32 56 164	35 14 215	28 01 259	31 16 289
70	37 46 011	41 08 042	47 29 099	33 04 163	34 57 214	27 31 258	30 47 288
71	37 51 010	41 28 040	47 58 098	33 13 163	34 41 213	27 02 257	30 19 287
72	37 56 009	41 47 039	48 28 097	33 22 162	34 24 213	26 33 256	29 50 287
73	38 00 007	42 06 038	48 58 096	33 32 162	34 08 212	26 04 255	29 21 286
74	38 03 006	42 24 037	49 28 095	33 41 161	33 52 212	25 35 255	28 52 285
	RIGEL	◆SIRIUS	Suhail	◆RIGIL KENT	Peacock	ACHERNAR	◆Diphda
75	38 06 005	42 42 035	49 58 095	33 51 160	33 37 211	64 12 254	28 23 284
76	38 09 004	42 59 034	50 27 094	34 01 160	33 21 211	63 43 253	27 54 283
77	38 10 002	43 15 033	50 57 093	34 12 159	33 06 210	63 15 253	27 25 282
78	38 11 001	43 31 032	51 27 092	34 23 159	32 51 209	62 46 252	26 55 281
79	38 11 000	43 47 030	51 57 091	34 34 158	32 37 209	62 18 252	26 26 280
80	38 11 359	44 02 029	52 27 090	34 45 158	32 22 208	61 49 251	25 56 279
81	38 10 357	44 16 028	52 57 089	34 56 157	32 08 208	61 21 250	25 27 278
82	38 08 356	44 30 027	53 27 089	35 08 157	31 54 207	60 53 250	24 57 277
83	38 05 355	44 43 025	53 57 088	35 20 156	31 41 206	60 25 249	24 27 276
84	38 02 353	44 56 024	54 27 087	35 32 156	31 28 206	59 57 249	23 57 276
85	37 59 352	45 07 023	54 57 086	35 45 155	31 15 205	59 29 248	23 27 275
86	37 54 351	45 19 021	55 27 085	35 58 154	31 02 205	59 01 248	22 58 274
87	37 49 350	45 29 020	55 57 084	36 11 154	30 50 204	58 33 247	22 28 273
88	37 43 348	45 39 019	56 27 083	36 24 153	30 37 204	58 06 247	21 58 272
89	37 37 347	45 48 017	56 57 082	36 38 153	30 26 203	57 38 246	21 28 271

LHA ♈	Hc Zn	Hc Zn	Hc Zn	Hc Zn	Hc Zn	Hc Zn	Hc Zn
	SIRIUS	Alphard	◆Suhail	RIGIL KENT	◆Peacock	ACHERNAR	◆RIGEL
90	45 57 016	25 47 060	57 26 081	36 51 152	30 14 202	57 11 245	37 30 346
91	46 05 015	26 13 059	57 56 080	37 06 152	30 03 202	56 43 245	37 23 345
92	46 12 013	26 39 058	58 25 079	37 20 151	29 52 201	56 16 244	37 14 344
93	46 18 012	27 04 057	58 55 078	37 34 151	29 41 201	55 49 244	37 06 342
94	46 24 010	27 29 056	59 24 077	37 49 150	29 31 200	55 22 243	36 56 341
95	46 29 009	27 54 055	59 53 076	38 04 150	29 21 199	54 56 243	36 46 340
96	46 33 008	28 18 054	60 22 075	38 20 149	29 11 199	54 29 242	36 36 339
97	46 37 006	28 42 053	60 51 074	38 35 149	29 01 198	54 03 242	36 24 337
98	46 40 005	29 06 052	61 20 073	38 51 148	28 52 198	53 36 241	36 12 336
99	46 42 003	29 30 051	61 48 071	39 07 148	28 43 197	53 10 241	36 00 335
100	46 43 002	29 53 050	62 17 070	39 23 147	28 35 196	52 44 240	35 47 334
101	46 44 001	30 15 049	62 45 069	39 39 147	28 27 196	52 18 240	35 34 333
102	46 44 359	30 38 048	63 13 068	39 56 146	28 19 195	51 52 239	35 20 331
103	46 43 358	31 00 047	63 40 067	40 13 145	28 11 195	51 27 238	35 05 330
104	46 42 356	31 21 046	64 08 065	40 30 145	28 04 194	51 01 238	34 50 329
	Alphard	◆Gienah	RIGIL KENT	◆Peacock	ACHERNAR	◆RIGEL	SIRIUS
105	31 43 044	20 36 090	40 47 144	27 56 193	50 36 237	34 34 328	46 40 355
106	32 03 043	21 06 089	41 05 144	27 50 193	50 11 237	34 18 327	46 37 354
107	32 24 042	21 36 088	41 23 143	27 43 192	49 46 236	34 01 326	46 33 352
108	32 44 041	22 06 087	41 41 143	27 37 191	49 21 236	33 44 325	46 29 351
109	33 03 040	22 36 086	41 59 142	27 31 191	48 56 235	33 27 323	46 24 349
110	33 22 039	23 06 085	42 17 142	27 26 190	48 31 235	33 08 322	46 18 348
111	33 41 038	23 36 084	42 36 141	27 21 190	48 07 234	32 50 321	46 11 347
112	33 59 037	24 06 084	42 55 141	27 16 189	47 43 234	32 31 320	46 04 345
113	34 17 036	24 36 083	43 14 140	27 11 188	47 19 233	32 11 319	45 56 344
114	34 34 034	25 06 082	43 33 140	27 07 188	46 55 233	31 51 318	45 47 343
115	34 51 033	25 35 081	43 52 139	27 03 187	46 31 232	31 31 317	45 38 341
116	35 07 032	26 05 080	44 12 139	27 00 187	46 08 231	31 10 316	45 28 340
117	35 23 031	26 34 079	44 32 138	26 56 186	45 44 231	30 49 315	45 18 339
118	35 38 030	27 04 078	44 52 138	26 53 185	45 21 230	30 27 313	45 06 337
119	35 52 029	27 33 077	45 12 137	26 51 185	44 58 230	30 06 312	44 54 336
	REGULUS	◆SPICA	RIGIL KENT	Peacock	◆ACHERNAR	RIGEL	◆SIRIUS
120	13 36 033	13 58 088	45 33 137	26 48 184	44 35 229	29 43 311	44 42 335
121	13 52 032	14 28 087	45 53 136	26 46 184	44 12 229	29 20 310	44 29 333
122	14 07 031	14 58 087	46 14 136	26 45 183	43 50 228	28 57 309	44 15 332
123	14 22 030	15 28 086	46 35 135	26 43 182	43 28 228	28 34 308	44 00 331
124	14 37 029	15 58 085	46 56 135	26 42 182	43 06 227	28 10 307	43 46 329
125	14 51 028	16 27 084	47 17 134	26 42 181	42 44 227	27 46 306	43 30 328
126	15 05 027	16 57 083	47 39 134	26 41 180	42 22 226	27 22 305	43 14 327
127	15 18 026	17 27 082	48 01 133	26 41 180	42 01 225	26 57 304	42 57 326
128	15 31 025	17 57 081	48 23 133	26 41 179	41 39 225	26 32 303	42 40 324
129	15 43 024	18 26 080	48 45 132	26 42 179	41 18 224	26 07 302	42 22 323
130	15 55 023	18 56 080	49 07 132	26 43 178	40 57 224	25 41 301	42 04 322
131	16 06 022	19 25 079	49 29 132	26 44 177	40 37 223	25 16 300	41 45 321
132	16 17 021	19 55 078	49 52 131	26 46 177	40 16 223	24 50 299	41 26 320
133	16 27 020	20 24 077	50 14 131	26 48 176	39 56 222	24 23 298	41 06 318
134	16 37 019	20 53 076	50 37 130	26 50 176	39 36 222	23 57 297	40 46 317
	REGULUS	◆SPICA	RIGIL KENT	◆Peacock	ACHERNAR	CANOPUS	◆SIRIUS
135	16 47 018	21 22 075	51 00 130	26 52 175	39 16 221	67 37 272	40 26 316
136	16 56 017	21 51 074	51 24 129	26 55 174	38 57 220	67 07 271	40 04 315
137	17 04 016	22 20 073	51 47 129	26 58 174	38 37 220	66 37 270	39 43 314
138	17 12 015	22 48 072	52 10 128	27 02 173	38 18 219	66 07 269	39 21 312
139	17 19 014	23 17 071	52 34 128	27 05 172	37 59 219	65 37 268	38 59 311
140	17 26 013	23 45 070	52 58 127	27 10 172	37 41 218	65 07 267	38 36 310
141	17 32 012	24 13 069	53 22 127	27 14 171	37 22 218	64 37 266	38 13 309
142	17 38 011	24 41 068	53 46 126	27 19 171	37 04 217	64 07 266	37 49 308
143	17 43 010	25 09 067	54 10 126	27 24 170	36 46 217	63 37 265	37 26 307
144	17 48 009	25 37 067	54 34 125	27 29 169	36 28 216	63 07 264	37 01 306
145	17 52 007	26 04 066	54 59 125	27 35 169	36 11 215	62 37 263	36 37 305
146	17 56 006	26 32 065	55 24 125	27 41 168	35 53 215	62 08 263	36 12 304
147	17 59 005	26 59 064	55 48 124	27 47 168	35 36 214	61 38 262	35 47 303
148	18 01 004	27 25 063	56 13 124	27 54 167	35 20 214	61 08 261	35 22 302
149	18 03 003	27 52 062	56 38 123	28 01 166	35 03 213	60 38 260	34 56 300
	REGULUS	◆SPICA	RIGIL KENT	◆Peacock	ACHERNAR	CANOPUS	◆SIRIUS
150	18 05 002	28 18 061	57 03 123	28 08 166	34 47 213	60 09 260	34 30 299
151	18 06 001	28 44 060	57 29 122	28 15 165	34 31 212	59 39 259	34 04 298
152	18 06 000	29 10 059	57 54 122	28 23 165	34 15 211	59 10 258	33 37 297
153	18 06 359	29 35 058	58 20 121	28 31 164	34 00 211	58 41 258	33 10 296
154	18 06 358	30 01 057	58 45 121	28 40 163	33 44 210	58 11 257	32 43 295
155	18 04 357	30 25 056	59 11 120	28 49 163	33 29 210	57 42 256	32 16 294
156	18 03 356	30 50 055	59 37 120	28 58 162	33 15 209	57 13 256	31 49 293
157	18 00 355	31 14 054	60 03 120	29 07 162	33 00 209	56 44 255	31 21 292
158	17 58 354	31 38 052	60 29 119	29 17 161	32 46 208	56 15 254	30 53 291
159	17 54 353	32 02 051	60 56 119	29 27 160	32 32 207	55 46 254	30 25 290
160	17 50 352	32 25 050	61 22 118	29 37 160	32 18 207	55 18 253	29 57 289
161	17 46 351	32 48 049	61 48 118	29 47 159	32 05 206	54 49 252	29 29 289
162	17 41 350	33 11 048	62 15 117	29 58 159	31 52 206	54 21 252	29 00 288
163	17 36 349	33 33 047	62 42 117	30 09 158	31 39 205	53 52 251	28 31 287
164	17 30 348	33 55 046	63 08 117	30 21 157	31 27 204	53 24 250	28 03 286
	◆SPICA	ANTARES	◆Peacock	ACHERNAR	CANOPUS	◆SIRIUS	REGULUS
165	34 16 045	26 20 098	30 33 157	31 14 204	52 56 250	27 34 285	17 23 347
166	34 37 044	26 50 097	30 45 156	31 02 203	52 28 249	27 05 284	17 16 346
167	34 57 043	27 20 096	30 57 156	30 51 203	52 00 248	26 35 283	17 09 345
168	35 18 042	27 50 095	31 09 155	30 39 202	51 32 248	26 06 282	17 01 344
169	35 37 040	28 20 095	31 22 154	30 28 201	51 04 247	25 37 281	16 52 343
170	35 56 039	28 50 094	31 35 154	30 17 201	50 36 247	25 07 280	16 43 342
171	36 15 038	29 20 093	31 49 153	30 07 200	50 09 246	24 38 279	16 33 341
172	36 33 037	29 50 092	32 02 153	29 57 200	49 42 245	24 08 278	16 23 340
173	36 51 036	30 20 091	32 16 152	29 47 199	49 14 245	23 38 277	16 13 339
174	37 09 035	30 50 090	32 31 151	29 37 198	48 47 244	23 09 277	16 02 338
175	37 25 033	31 20 089	32 45 151	29 28 198	48 20 243	22 39 276	15 50 337
176	37 42 032	31 50 089	33 00 150	29 18 197	47 54 243	22 09 275	15 38 336
177	37 57 031	32 20 088	33 15 150	29 10 197	47 27 242	21 39 274	15 26 335
178	38 13 030	32 50 087	33 30 149	29 01 196	47 01 242	21 09 273	15 13 334
179	38 27 029	33 19 086	33 46 148	28 53 196	46 34 241	20 39 272	14 59 333

LAT 60°S

LHA ♈	Hc	Zn	Hc	Zn	Hc	Zn	Hc	Zn	Hc	Zn	Hc	Zn	Hc	Zn
	◆ SPICA		ANTARES		◆ Peacock		ACHERNAR		CANOPUS		◆ SIRIUS		Alphard	
180	38 41	027	33 49	085	34 02	148	28 45	195	46 08	240	20 09	271	31 25	315
181	38 55	026	34 19	084	34 18	147	28 38	194	45 42	240	19 39	270	31 03	314
182	39 08	025	34 49	083	34 34	147	28 30	194	45 16	239	19 09	270	30 41	312
183	39 20	024	35 19	082	34 51	146	28 23	193	44 51	239	18 39	269	30 19	311
184	39 32	022	35 49	081	35 07	146	28 17	192	44 25	238	18 09	268	29 56	310
185	39 43	021	36 18	080	35 24	145	28 10	192	44 00	237	17 39	267	29 33	309
186	39 54	020	36 48	079	35 42	144	28 04	191	43 35	237	17 09	266	29 10	308
187	40 04	019	37 17	079	35 59	144	27 59	191	43 10	236	16 39	265	28 46	307
188	40 13	017	37 46	078	36 17	143	27 53	190	42 45	236	16 09	264	28 22	306
189	40 22	016	38 16	077	36 35	143	27 48	189	42 20	235	15 39	264	27 58	305
190	40 30	015	38 45	076	36 53	142	27 43	189	41 56	234	15 10	263	27 33	304
191	40 37	014	39 14	075	37 12	142	27 39	188	41 31	234	14 40	262	27 08	303
192	40 44	012	39 43	074	37 31	141	27 35	188	41 07	233	14 10	261	26 43	302
193	40 50	011	40 11	073	37 50	140	27 31	187	40 43	233	13 41	260	26 17	301
194	40 55	010	40 40	072	38 09	140	27 27	186	40 20	232	13 11	259	25 52	300
	SPICA		◆ ANTARES		Peacock		◆ ACHERNAR		CANOPUS		Suhail		◆ Alphard	
195	41 00	008	41 08	071	38 28	139	27 24	186	39 56	231	52 06	269	25 26	299
196	41 04	007	41 37	070	38 48	139	27 21	185	39 33	231	51 36	268	24 59	298
197	41 07	006	42 05	069	39 08	138	27 19	185	39 10	230	51 06	267	24 33	297
198	41 10	005	42 33	068	39 28	138	27 17	184	38 47	230	50 36	267	24 06	296
199	41 12	003	43 00	067	39 48	137	27 15	183	38 24	229	50 06	266	23 39	295
200	41 14	002	43 28	066	40 09	137	27 13	183	38 02	228	49 36	265	23 12	294
201	41 14	001	43 55	065	40 30	136	27 12	182	37 39	228	49 06	264	22 44	293
202	41 14	359	44 22	063	40 51	135	27 11	182	37 17	227	48 36	263	22 17	292
203	41 14	358	44 48	062	41 12	135	27 10	181	36 55	226	48 06	262	21 49	291
204	41 12	357	45 15	061	41 33	134	27 10	180	36 34	226	47 37	262	21 21	291
205	41 10	355	45 41	060	41 55	134	27 10	180	36 12	225	47 07	261	20 53	290
206	41 07	354	46 07	059	42 17	133	27 10	179	35 51	225	46 37	260	20 24	289
207	41 04	353	46 33	058	42 39	133	27 11	179	35 30	224	46 08	259	19 56	288
208	41 00	352	46 58	057	43 01	132	27 12	178	35 09	223	45 38	259	19 27	287
209	40 55	350	47 23	056	43 23	132	27 13	177	34 49	223	45 09	258	18 58	286
	ANTARES		◆ Nunki		Peacock		ACHERNAR		◆ CANOPUS		Suhail		◆ SPICA	
210	47 47	054	30 26	091	43 46	131	27 14	177	34 29	222	44 40	257	40 50	349
211	48 11	053	30 56	090	44 08	130	27 16	176	34 09	222	44 11	256	40 44	348
212	48 35	052	31 26	089	44 31	130	27 18	175	33 49	221	43 42	256	40 37	346
213	48 59	051	31 56	088	44 54	129	27 21	175	33 29	220	43 13	255	40 30	345
214	49 22	049	32 26	087	45 18	129	27 24	174	33 10	220	42 44	254	40 22	344
215	49 44	048	32 56	086	45 41	128	27 27	174	32 51	219	42 15	253	40 13	343
216	50 06	047	33 26	085	46 05	128	27 30	173	32 32	219	41 46	253	40 04	341
217	50 28	046	33 56	084	46 29	127	27 34	172	32 13	218	41 18	252	39 54	340
218	50 49	044	34 26	083	46 53	127	27 38	172	31 55	217	40 49	251	39 43	339
219	51 10	043	34 56	083	47 17	126	27 43	171	31 37	217	40 21	250	39 32	338
220	51 30	042	35 25	082	47 41	125	27 48	171	31 19	216	39 53	250	39 20	336
221	51 50	040	35 55	081	48 06	125	27 53	170	31 02	215	39 24	249	39 08	335
222	52 09	039	36 25	080	48 30	124	27 58	169	30 44	215	38 57	248	38 55	334
223	52 28	038	36 54	079	48 55	124	28 04	169	30 28	214	38 29	248	38 41	333
224	52 46	036	37 23	078	49 20	123	28 10	168	30 11	214	38 01	247	38 27	331
	ANTARES		◆ Nunki		Peacock		ACHERNAR		◆ CANOPUS		Suhail		◆ SPICA	
225	53 03	035	37 53	077	49 45	123	28 16	168	29 54	213	37 34	246	38 12	330
226	53 20	033	38 22	076	50 11	122	28 23	167	29 38	212	37 06	245	37 57	329
227	53 36	032	38 51	075	50 36	122	28 29	166	29 22	212	36 39	245	37 42	328
228	53 52	031	39 20	074	51 02	121	28 37	166	29 07	211	36 12	244	37 25	327
229	54 07	029	39 49	073	51 28	121	28 44	165	28 51	210	35 45	243	37 08	325
230	54 21	028	40 17	072	51 54	120	28 52	165	28 36	210	35 18	243	36 51	324
231	54 35	026	40 46	071	52 20	119	29 00	164	28 21	209	34 52	242	36 33	323
232	54 48	025	41 14	070	52 46	119	29 09	163	28 07	209	34 25	241	36 15	322
233	55 00	023	41 42	069	53 12	118	29 17	163	27 53	208	33 59	240	35 56	321
234	55 11	022	42 10	068	53 39	118	29 26	162	27 39	207	33 33	240	35 37	320
235	55 22	020	42 38	067	54 05	117	29 36	162	27 25	207	33 07	239	35 17	318
236	55 32	019	43 05	066	54 32	117	29 45	161	27 12	206	32 42	238	34 57	317
237	55 41	017	43 32	065	54 59	116	29 55	160	26 59	205	32 16	238	34 37	316
238	55 49	015	44 00	064	55 26	116	30 05	160	26 46	205	31 51	237	34 16	315
239	55 57	014	44 26	063	55 53	115	30 16	159	26 34	204	31 26	236	33 54	314
	◆ ANTARES		Nunki		◆ FOMALHAUT		ACHERNAR		CANOPUS		◆ ACRUX		SPICA	
240	56 04	012	44 53	062	18 30	117	30 27	159	26 22	203	65 15	240	33 33	313
241	56 10	011	45 19	061	18 56	117	30 38	158	26 10	203	64 50	239	33 10	312
242	56 15	009	45 45	059	19 23	116	30 49	157	25 59	202	64 24	239	32 48	311
243	56 19	007	46 11	058	19 50	115	31 01	157	25 47	202	63 58	239	32 25	310
244	56 22	006	46 36	057	20 18	114	31 13	156	25 36	201	63 33	238	32 02	309
245	56 25	004	47 01	056	20 45	113	31 25	156	25 26	200	63 07	238	31 38	308
246	56 27	003	47 26	055	21 13	113	31 37	155	25 16	200	62 42	238	31 14	306
247	56 28	001	47 50	054	21 40	112	31 50	154	25 06	199	62 17	237	30 50	305
248	56 28	359	48 14	052	22 08	111	32 03	154	24 56	198	61 51	237	30 25	304
249	56 27	358	48 38	051	22 36	110	32 17	153	24 47	198	61 26	237	30 00	303
250	56 25	356	49 01	050	23 05	110	32 30	153	24 38	197	61 01	236	29 35	302
251	56 23	354	49 24	049	23 33	109	32 44	152	24 29	196	60 36	236	29 10	301
252	56 20	353	49 46	047	24 01	108	32 58	152	24 21	196	60 12	235	28 44	300
253	56 15	351	50 08	046	24 30	107	33 13	151	24 13	195	59 47	235	28 18	299
254	56 10	350	50 29	045	24 59	106	33 27	150	24 05	194	59 22	235	27 52	298
	ALTAIR		◆ FOMALHAUT		ACHERNAR		CANOPUS		◆ ACRUX		SPICA		◆ ANTARES	
255	13 10	044	25 28	106	33 42	150	23 58	194	58 58	234	27 25	297	56 05	348
256	13 31	043	25 57	105	33 58	149	23 51	193	58 34	234	26 58	296	55 58	346
257	13 51	042	26 26	104	34 13	149	23 44	192	58 10	234	26 31	295	55 51	345
258	14 11	041	26 55	103	34 29	148	23 38	192	57 46	233	26 04	294	55 43	344
259	14 30	040	27 24	102	34 45	148	23 32	191	57 22	233	25 37	293	55 33	342
260	14 49	039	27 54	101	35 01	147	23 27	191	56 58	232	25 09	292	55 24	340
261	15 08	038	28 23	101	35 17	146	23 21	190	56 34	232	24 41	292	55 13	339
262	15 26	037	28 52	100	35 34	146	23 16	189	56 10	232	24 13	291	55 02	337
263	15 44	036	29 22	099	35 51	145	23 12	189	55 47	231	23 45	290	54 50	336
264	16 01	035	29 52	098	36 08	145	23 07	188	55 24	231	23 17	289	54 37	334
265	16 18	034	30 21	097	36 26	144	23 03	187	55 01	230	22 48	288	54 24	333
266	16 35	033	30 51	097	36 43	144	23 00	187	54 38	230	22 20	287	54 09	331
267	16 51	032	31 21	096	37 01	143	22 56	186	54 15	230	21 51	286	53 55	330
268	17 07	031	31 51	095	37 20	142	22 53	185	53 52	229	21 22	285	53 39	328
269	17 22	030	32 21	094	37 38	142	22 51	185	53 29	229	20 53	284	53 23	327

LHA ♈	Hc	Zn	Hc	Zn	Hc	Zn	Hc	Zn	Hc	Zn	Hc	Zn	Hc	Zn
	◆ ALTAIR		FOMALHAUT		◆ ACHERNAR		CANOPUS		RIGIL KENT		◆ SPICA		ANTARES	
270	17 37	029	32 51	093	37 57	141	22 49	184	66 00	246	20 24	283	53 06	325
271	17 51	028	33 21	092	38 16	141	22 47	183	65 32	246	19 54	282	52 49	324
272	18 05	027	33 51	091	38 35	140	22 45	183	65 05	245	19 25	281	52 31	323
273	18 18	026	34 21	091	38 54	140	22 44	182	64 38	245	18 56	280	52 12	321
274	18 31	025	34 51	090	39 14	139	22 43	181	64 11	244	18 26	280	51 53	320
275	18 43	024	35 21	089	39 33	138	22 42	181	63 44	244	17 56	279	51 34	318
276	18 55	023	35 51	088	39 53	138	22 42	180	63 17	244	17 27	278	51 13	317
277	19 07	022	36 21	087	40 14	137	22 42	179	62 50	243	16 57	277	50 53	316
278	19 18	021	36 51	086	40 34	137	22 43	179	62 23	243	16 27	276	50 32	315
279	19 28	020	37 21	085	40 55	136	22 44	178	61 57	242	15 57	275	50 10	313
280	19 38	019	37 50	084	41 15	136	22 45	177	61 30	242	15 27	274	49 48	312
281	19 47	018	38 20	084	41 36	135	22 46	177	61 04	241	14 58	273	49 25	311
282	19 56	017	38 50	083	41 58	135	22 48	176	60 38	241	14 28	273	49 02	309
283	20 05	016	39 20	082	42 19	134	22 51	175	60 11	241	13 58	272	48 39	308
284	20 12	015	39 49	081	42 41	134	22 53	175	59 45	240	13 28	271	48 15	307
	◆ ALTAIR		FOMALHAUT		◆ ACHERNAR		CANOPUS		◆ RIGIL KENT		ANTARES		Nunki	
285	20 20	014	40 19	080	43 03	133	22 56	174	59 19	240	47 51	306	56 16	358
286	20 27	013	40 48	079	43 25	132	22 59	173	58 54	239	47 27	305	56 15	357
287	20 33	011	41 18	078	43 47	132	23 03	173	58 28	239	47 02	303	56 13	355
288	20 39	010	41 47	077	44 09	131	23 07	172	58 02	238	46 37	302	56 10	354
289	20 44	009	42 16	076	44 32	131	23 11	172	57 37	238	46 11	301	56 06	352
290	20 48	008	42 45	075	44 55	130	23 16	171	57 12	237	45 45	300	56 02	350
291	20 52	007	43 14	074	45 18	130	23 20	170	56 46	237	45 19	299	55 56	349
292	20 56	006	43 43	073	45 41	129	23 26	170	56 21	237	44 53	298	55 50	347
293	20 59	005	44 12	072	46 04	129	23 31	169	55 56	236	44 26	297	55 43	346
294	21 01	004	44 40	071	46 28	128	23 37	168	55 31	236	43 59	296	55 35	344
295	21 03	003	45 08	070	46 52	128	23 44	168	55 07	235	43 32	295	55 27	343
296	21 04	002	45 36	069	47 15	127	23 50	167	54 42	235	43 05	294	55 17	341
297	21 05	001	46 04	068	47 39	126	23 57	166	54 18	234	42 37	292	55 07	339
298	21 05	000	46 32	067	48 04	126	24 04	166	53 53	234	42 09	291	54 56	338
299	21 05	359	47 00	066	48 28	125	24 12	165	53 29	233	41 41	290	54 44	336
	FOMALHAUT		◆ ACHERNAR		CANOPUS		◆ RIGIL KENT		ANTARES		Nunki		◆ ALTAIR	
300	47 27	065	48 53	125	24 20	164	53 05	233	41 13	289	54 32	335	21 04	358
301	47 54	064	49 17	124	24 28	164	52 42	232	40 45	288	54 19	333	21 03	357
302	48 20	062	49 42	124	24 37	163	52 18	232	40 16	287	54 05	332	21 01	356
303	48 47	061	50 07	123	24 46	162	51 54	231	39 47	286	53 51	330	20 58	355
304	49 13	060	50 32	123	24 55	162	51 31	231	39 19	285	53 36	329	20 55	354
305	49 39	059	50 58	122	25 04	161	51 08	231	38 50	284	53 20	328	20 51	352
306	50 04	058	51 23	122	25 14	160	50 45	230	38 21	284	53 03	326	20 47	351
307	50 30	057	51 49	121	25 24	160	50 22	230	37 51	283	52 46	325	20 42	350
308	50 55	055	52 15	121	25 35	159	49 59	229	37 22	282	52 29	323	20 37	349
309	51 19	054	52 41	120	25 46	159	49 36	229	36 53	281	52 10	322	20 31	348
310	51 43	053	53 07	119	25 57	158	49 14	228	36 23	280	51 52	321	20 25	347
311	52 07	052	53 33	119	26 08	157	48 52	228	35 53	279	51 32	319	20 18	346
312	52 30	050	53 59	118	26 20	157	48 30	227	35 24	278	51 13	318	20 11	345
313	52 53	049	54 26	118	26 32	156	48 08	227	34 54	277	50 52	317	20 03	344
314	53 16	048	54 52	117	26 45	155	47 46	226	34 24	276	50 31	315	19 54	343
	◆ FOMALHAUT		ACHERNAR		◆ CANOPUS		RIGIL KENT		◆ ANTARES		Nunki		ALTAIR	
315	53 38	046	55 19	117	26 57	155	47 24	226	33 54	275	50 10	314	19 45	342
316	53 59	045	55 46	116	27 10	154	47 03	225	33 24	274	49 48	313	19 36	341
317	54 20	044	56 13	116	27 23	153	46 42	225	32 54	273	49 26	311	19 26	340
318	54 41	042	56 40	115	27 37	153	46 21	224	32 25	273	49 03	310	19 15	339
319	55 01	041	57 07	115	27 51	152	46 00	224	31 55	272	48 40	309	19 04	338
320	55 20	040	57 34	114	28 05	152	45 39	223	31 25	271	48 16	308	18 52	337
321	55 39	038	58 02	113	28 19	151	45 19	223	30 55	270	47 52	307	18 40	336
322	55 57	037	58 29	113	28 34	150	44 58	222	30 25	269	47 28	305	18 28	335
323	56 15	035	58 57	112	28 49	150	44 38	222	29 55	268	47 04	304	18 15	334
324	56 32	034	59 25	112	29 04	149	44 18	221	29 25	267	46 39	303	18 01	333
325	56 48	032	59 53	111	29 20	148	43 59	221	28 55	266	46 13	302	17 47	332
326	57 04	031	60 21	111	29 36	148	43 39	220	28 25	266	45 48	301	17 33	331
327	57 19	029	60 49	110	29 52	147	43 20	220	27 55	265	45 22	300	17 18	330
328	57 33	028	61 17	110	30 08	147	43 01	219	27 25	264	44 55	298	17 03	329
329	57 46	026	61 45	109	30 25	146	42 42	219	26 55	263	44 29	297	16 47	328
	◆ FOMALHAUT		ACHERNAR		◆ CANOPUS		RIGIL KENT		◆ ANTARES		Nunki		ALTAIR	
330	57 59	024	62 14	108	30 42	145	42 23	218	26 25	262	44 02	296	16 31	327
331	58 11	023	62 42	108	30 59	145	42 05	218	25 56	261	43 35	295	16 14	326
332	58 22	021	63 11	107	31 17	144	41 46	217	25 26	261	43 08	294	15 57	325
333	58 33	020	63 40	107	31 35	143	41 28	217	24 56	260	42 40	293	15 40	324
334	58 43	018	64 08	106	31 53	143	41 11	216	24 27	259	42 13	292	15 22	323
335	58 51	016	64 37	106	32 11	142	40 53	216	23 58	258	41 45	291	15 03	322
336	58 59	015	65 06	105	32 29	142	40 36	215	23 28	257	41 17	290	14 45	321
337	59 07	013	65 35	104	32 48	141	40 18	215	22 59	256	40 48	289	14 25	320
338	59 13	011	66 04	104	33 07	140	40 01	214	22 30	256	40 20	288	14 06	319
339	59 18	010	66 33	103	33 26	140	39 45	214	22 01	255	39 51	287	13 46	318
340	59 23	008	67 03	103	33 46	139	39 28	213	21 32	254	39 23	286	13 26	317
341	59 27	006	67 32	102	34 06	138	39 12	213	21 03	253	38 54	285	13 05	316
342	59 29	004	68 01	101	34 26	138	38 56	212	20 35	252	38 25	284	12 44	315
343	59 31	003	68 31	101	34 46	137	38 40	212	20 06	252	37 56	283	12 23	314
344	59 31	001	69 00	100	35 06	137	38 24	211	19 38	251	37 26	282	12 01	313
	◆ Diphda		Acamar		CANOPUS		◆ Miaplacidus		RIGIL KENT		◆ Nunki		FOMALHAUT	
345	43 55	036	48 46	089	35 27	136	41 10	168	38 09	211	36 57	281	59 32	359
346	44 12	034	49 16	088	35 48	135	41 16	168	37 54	210	36 27	280	59 32	358
347	44 29	033	49 46	087	36 09	135	41 23	167	37 39	209	35 58	279	59 30	356
348	44 45	032	50 16	086	36 31	134	41 29	167	37 24	209	35 28	278	59 27	354
349	45 00	030	50 46	086	36 52	134	41 36	166	37 10	208	34 58	278	59 24	352
350	45 15	029	51 16	085	37 14	133	41 43	166	36 56	208	34 29	277	59 20	351
351	45 29	028	51 45	084	37 36	132	41 51	165	36 42	207	33 59	276	59 14	349
352	45 43	026	52 15	083	37 58	132	41 58	165	36 28	207	33 29	275	59 08	347
353	45 56	025	52 45	082	38 21	131	42 06	165	36 15	206	32 59	274	59 01	346
354	46 08	024	53 15	081	38 43	131	42 14	164	36 02	206	32 29	273	58 53	344
355	46 20	022	53 44	080	39 06	130	42 23	164	35 49	205	31 59	272	58 45	342
356	46 31	021	54 14	079	39 29	129	42 31	163	35 36	205	31 29	271	58 35	341
357	46 42	020	54 43	078	39 53	129	42 40	163	35 24	204	30 59	270	58 25	339
358	46 52	018	55 12	077	40 16	128	42 49	162	35 12	204	30 29	270	58 14	338
359	47 01	017	55 41	076	40 40	128	42 58	162	35 00	203	29 59	269	58 02	336

LHA ♈	Hc	Zn	Hc	Zn	Hc	Zn	Hc	Zn	Hc	Zn	Hc	Zn	Hc	Zn
	Diphda		◆ RIGEL		CANOPUS		Miaplacidus		◆ RIGIL KENT		Peacock		◆ FOMALHAUT	
0	46 11	015	12 34	084	41 40	126	44 04	161	35 44	203	62 53	255	56 55	335
1	46 19	014	13 03	083	42 03	126	44 14	161	35 33	202	62 25	254	56 43	333
2	46 25	013	13 32	082	42 27	125	44 23	160	35 22	202	61 57	254	56 29	332
3	46 31	011	14 01	082	42 51	124	44 33	160	35 11	201	61 29	253	56 15	330
4	46 37	010	14 29	081	43 15	124	44 43	160	35 01	201	61 01	253	56 01	329
5	46 41	008	14 58	080	43 39	123	44 53	159	34 51	200	60 33	252	55 45	327
6	46 45	007	15 27	079	44 04	123	45 04	159	34 41	199	60 06	251	55 29	326
7	46 48	006	15 55	078	44 28	122	45 14	158	34 32	199	59 38	251	55 13	325
8	46 51	004	16 24	077	44 53	121	45 25	158	34 22	198	59 11	250	54 55	323
9	46 53	003	16 52	076	45 18	121	45 36	158	34 13	198	58 44	250	54 38	322
10	46 54	002	17 20	075	45 43	120	45 47	157	34 05	197	58 16	249	54 19	320
11	46 54	000	17 48	074	46 08	119	45 59	157	33 56	197	57 49	248	54 01	319
12	46 54	359	18 16	073	46 34	119	46 10	156	33 48	196	57 22	248	53 41	317
13	46 53	357	18 44	072	46 59	118	46 22	156	33 40	195	56 55	247	53 21	316
14	46 51	356	19 12	072	47 25	118	46 34	155	33 32	195	56 29	247	53 01	315
	◆ RIGEL		SIRIUS		CANOPUS		◆ RIGIL KENT		Peacock		◆ FOMALHAUT		Diphda	
15	19 39	071	16 18	095	47 51	117	33 25	194	56 02	246	52 40	313	46 49	355
16	20 06	070	16 47	094	48 17	116	33 18	194	55 36	245	52 19	312	46 46	353
17	20 34	069	17 16	094	48 43	116	33 11	193	55 09	245	51 57	311	46 42	352
18	21 01	068	17 45	093	49 09	115	33 05	193	54 43	244	51 35	310	46 37	350
19	21 27	067	18 14	092	49 36	114	32 59	192	54 17	244	51 12	308	46 32	349
20	21 54	066	18 43	091	50 02	114	32 53	192	53 51	243	50 49	307	46 26	348
21	22 21	065	19 12	090	50 29	113	32 47	191	53 25	243	50 26	306	46 20	346
22	22 47	064	19 41	089	50 56	112	32 42	190	52 59	242	50 02	305	46 13	345
23	23 13	063	20 10	088	51 23	112	32 36	190	52 34	241	49 38	303	46 05	344
24	23 39	062	20 39	087	51 50	111	32 32	189	52 08	241	49 13	302	45 56	342
25	24 04	061	21 08	087	52 17	110	32 27	189	51 43	240	48 49	301	45 47	341
26	24 29	060	21 37	086	52 44	110	32 23	188	51 18	240	48 24	300	45 37	340
27	24 55	059	22 06	085	53 12	109	32 19	188	50 53	239	47 58	299	45 26	338
28	25 19	058	22 35	084	53 39	108	32 15	187	50 28	239	47 33	298	45 15	337
29	25 44	057	23 04	083	54 07	108	32 12	186	50 03	238	47 07	297	45 04	336
	◆ RIGEL		SIRIUS		CANOPUS		◆ RIGIL KENT		Peacock		◆ FOMALHAUT		Diphda	
30	26 08	056	23 33	082	54 35	107	32 09	186	49 38	237	46 41	296	44 51	334
31	26 32	055	24 02	081	55 03	106	32 06	185	49 14	237	46 14	294	44 38	333
32	26 56	054	24 31	080	55 31	106	32 03	185	48 50	236	45 48	293	44 25	332
33	27 19	053	24 59	079	55 59	105	32 01	184	48 26	236	45 21	292	44 11	330
34	27 42	052	25 28	078	56 27	104	31 59	184	48 02	235	44 54	291	43 56	329
35	28 05	051	25 56	077	56 55	104	31 58	183	47 38	235	44 27	290	43 41	328
36	28 28	050	26 24	077	57 23	103	31 56	182	47 14	234	43 59	289	43 25	327
37	28 50	049	26 53	076	57 52	102	31 55	182	46 51	233	43 32	288	43 09	325
38	29 11	048	27 21	075	58 20	102	31 54	181	46 28	233	43 04	287	42 52	324
39	29 33	047	27 49	074	58 49	101	31 54	181	46 04	232	42 36	286	42 34	323
40	29 54	046	28 17	073	59 17	100	31 54	180	45 42	232	42 08	285	42 17	322
41	30 14	045	28 44	072	59 46	099	31 54	180	45 19	231	41 40	284	41 58	320
42	30 35	044	29 12	071	60 15	099	31 54	179	44 56	231	41 12	283	41 39	319
43	30 54	042	29 39	070	60 43	098	31 55	178	44 34	230	40 43	282	41 20	318
44	31 14	041	30 07	069	61 12	097	31 56	178	44 12	229	40 15	281	41 00	317
	RIGEL		◆ SIRIUS		CANOPUS		◆ RIGIL KENT		Peacock		FOMALHAUT		◆ Diphda	
45	31 33	040	30 34	068	61 41	096	31 57	177	43 50	229	39 46	280	40 40	316
46	31 51	039	31 01	067	62 10	096	31 59	177	43 28	228	39 18	279	40 20	314
47	32 10	038	31 27	066	62 39	095	32 01	176	43 06	228	38 49	278	39 59	313
48	32 27	037	31 54	065	63 08	094	32 03	176	42 45	227	38 20	277	39 37	312
49	32 45	036	32 20	064	63 37	093	32 05	175	42 24	227	37 51	277	39 16	311
50	33 01	035	32 46	063	64 06	092	32 08	174	42 02	226	37 22	276	38 53	310
51	33 18	034	33 12	062	64 35	092	32 11	174	41 42	225	36 53	275	38 31	309
52	33 34	032	33 37	061	65 04	091	32 14	173	41 21	225	36 24	274	38 08	308
53	33 49	031	34 03	060	65 33	090	32 18	173	41 01	224	35 55	273	37 45	306
54	34 04	030	34 28	059	66 02	089	32 22	172	40 40	224	35 26	272	37 21	305
55	34 18	029	34 52	058	66 32	088	32 26	172	40 20	223	34 57	271	36 57	304
56	34 32	028	35 17	057	67 01	087	32 30	171	40 01	223	34 28	270	36 33	303
57	34 45	027	35 41	056	67 30	086	32 35	170	39 41	222	33 59	269	36 09	302
58	34 58	025	36 05	055	67 59	085	32 40	170	39 22	221	33 30	269	35 44	301
59	35 10	024	36 28	053	68 28	084	32 45	169	39 02	221	33 01	268	35 19	300
	RIGEL		◆ SIRIUS		Suhail		◆ RIGIL KENT		Peacock		FOMALHAUT		◆ Diphda	
60	35 22	023	36 52	052	42 52	105	32 51	169	38 44	220	32 32	267	34 54	299
61	35 33	022	37 14	051	43 20	104	32 57	168	38 25	220	32 03	266	34 28	298
62	35 43	021	37 37	050	43 48	104	33 03	168	38 06	219	31 34	265	34 02	297
63	35 53	019	37 59	049	44 17	103	33 09	167	37 48	219	31 05	264	33 36	296
64	36 03	018	38 21	048	44 45	102	33 16	166	37 30	218	30 36	263	33 10	295
65	36 12	017	38 42	047	45 13	101	33 23	166	37 12	217	30 07	263	32 43	294
66	36 20	016	39 03	046	45 42	101	33 30	165	36 55	217	29 38	262	32 17	293
67	36 27	015	39 24	045	46 11	100	33 38	165	36 38	216	29 09	261	31 50	292
68	36 34	013	39 44	043	46 39	099	33 45	164	36 20	216	28 41	260	31 23	291
69	36 41	012	40 04	042	47 08	098	33 54	164	36 04	215	28 12	259	30 56	290
70	36 47	011	40 23	041	47 37	097	34 02	163	35 47	214	27 43	258	30 28	289
71	36 52	010	40 42	040	48 06	097	34 11	162	35 31	214	27 15	258	30 01	288
72	36 57	008	41 00	039	48 35	096	34 19	162	35 15	213	26 47	257	29 33	287
73	37 00	007	41 18	037	49 04	095	34 29	161	34 59	213	26 18	256	29 05	286
74	37 04	006	41 36	036	49 33	094	34 38	161	34 43	212	25 50	255	28 37	285
	RIGEL		◆ SIRIUS		Suhail		◆ RIGIL KENT		Peacock		ACHERNAR		◆ Diphda	
75	37 07	005	41 53	035	50 02	093	34 48	160	34 28	212	64 28	256	28 09	284
76	37 09	003	42 09	034	50 31	092	34 58	160	34 13	211	64 00	255	27 41	283
77	37 10	002	42 25	032	51 00	092	35 08	159	33 58	210	63 32	255	27 12	282
78	37 11	001	42 40	031	51 29	091	35 18	159	33 43	210	63 04	254	26 44	281
79	37 11	000	42 55	030	51 58	090	35 29	158	33 29	209	62 36	253	26 15	281
80	37 11	359	43 09	029	52 27	089	35 40	157	33 15	209	62 08	253	25 47	280
81	37 10	357	43 23	027	52 56	088	35 52	157	33 01	208	61 40	252	25 18	279
82	37 08	356	43 36	026	53 25	087	36 03	156	32 48	207	61 12	252	24 49	278
83	37 06	355	43 49	025	53 54	086	36 15	156	32 35	207	60 45	251	24 20	277
84	37 03	354	44 01	024	54 23	085	36 27	155	32 22	206	60 17	250	23 51	276
85	36 59	352	44 12	022	54 52	084	36 39	155	32 09	206	59 50	250	23 22	275
86	36 55	351	44 23	021	55 21	083	36 52	154	31 56	205	59 23	249	22 53	274
87	36 50	350	44 33	020	55 50	083	37 05	154	31 44	204	58 56	249	22 24	273
88	36 45	349	44 42	018	56 19	082	37 18	153	31 32	204	58 29	248	21 55	272
89	36 39	347	44 51	017	56 48	081	37 31	153	31 21	203	58 02	247	21 26	272

LAT 61°S

LHA ♈	Hc	Zn	Hc	Zn	Hc	Zn	Hc	Zn	Hc	Zn	Hc	Zn	Hc	Zn
	◆ SIRIUS		Suhail		◆ RIGIL KENT		Peacock		◆ ACHERNAR		Acamar		RIGEL	
90	44 59	016	57 16	080	37 45	152	31 10	203	57 35	247	55 38	286	36 32	346
91	45 07	014	57 45	079	37 58	151	30 59	202	57 08	246	55 10	285	36 25	345
92	45 13	013	58 13	078	38 12	151	30 48	201	56 42	246	54 41	284	36 17	344
93	45 20	012	58 42	076	38 27	150	30 37	201	56 15	245	54 13	283	36 08	343
94	45 25	010	59 10	075	38 41	150	30 27	200	55 49	245	53 45	282	35 59	341
95	45 30	009	59 38	074	38 56	149	30 17	200	55 23	244	53 16	281	35 50	340
96	45 34	007	60 06	073	39 11	149	30 08	199	54 57	243	52 48	280	35 40	339
97	45 37	006	60 34	072	39 26	148	29 58	198	54 31	243	52 19	279	35 29	338
98	45 40	005	61 01	071	39 42	148	29 49	198	54 05	242	51 50	278	35 18	337
99	45 42	003	61 28	070	39 57	147	29 41	197	53 39	242	51 21	277	35 06	335
100	45 44	002	61 56	069	40 13	147	29 32	196	53 13	241	50 52	276	34 53	334
101	45 44	001	62 23	067	40 29	146	29 24	196	52 48	241	50 23	275	34 40	333
102	45 44	359	62 49	066	40 46	146	29 16	195	52 23	240	49 54	274	34 27	332
103	45 43	358	63 16	065	41 02	145	29 09	195	51 58	240	49 25	273	34 13	331
104	45 42	357	63 42	064	41 19	144	29 02	194	51 33	239	48 56	272	33 58	329
	Alphard		◆ Gienah		RIGIL KENT		◆ Peacock		ACHERNAR		◆ RIGEL		SIRIUS	
105	31 00	044	20 36	089	41 36	144	28 55	193	51 08	238	33 43	328	45 40	355
106	31 20	043	21 05	088	41 53	143	28 48	193	50 43	238	33 28	327	45 37	354
107	31 39	042	21 34	088	42 11	143	28 42	192	50 18	237	33 12	326	45 34	352
108	31 59	041	22 03	087	42 28	142	28 36	192	49 54	237	32 55	325	45 29	351
109	32 17	040	22 32	086	42 46	142	28 30	191	49 30	236	32 38	324	45 25	350
110	32 36	039	23 01	085	43 04	141	28 25	190	49 06	236	32 21	323	45 19	348
111	32 54	037	23 30	084	43 23	141	28 20	190	48 42	235	32 03	322	45 13	347
112	33 11	036	23 59	083	43 41	140	28 15	189	48 18	235	31 45	320	45 06	346
113	33 28	035	24 28	082	44 00	140	28 11	188	47 54	234	31 26	319	44 58	344
114	33 45	034	24 57	081	44 19	139	28 07	188	47 31	233	31 07	318	44 50	343
115	34 01	033	25 25	080	44 38	139	28 03	187	47 08	233	30 47	317	44 41	342
116	34 16	032	25 54	080	44 57	138	27 59	187	46 45	232	30 27	316	44 32	340
117	34 31	031	26 23	079	45 17	138	27 56	186	46 22	232	30 07	315	44 22	339
118	34 46	029	26 51	078	45 36	137	27 53	185	45 59	231	29 46	314	44 11	338
119	35 00	028	27 19	077	45 56	137	27 50	185	45 36	231	29 25	313	43 59	336
	Alphard		◆ SPICA		RIGIL KENT		◆ Peacock		ACHERNAR		◆ RIGEL		SIRIUS	
120	35 13	027	13 56	088	46 16	136	27 48	184	45 14	230	29 03	312	43 47	335
121	35 26	026	14 25	087	46 36	136	27 46	184	44 52	229	28 42	311	43 35	334
122	35 39	025	14 54	086	46 57	135	27 45	183	44 30	229	28 19	310	43 22	332
123	35 50	023	15 23	085	47 17	135	27 43	182	44 08	228	27 57	309	43 08	331
124	36 02	022	15 52	085	47 38	134	27 42	182	43 46	228	27 34	308	42 54	330
125	36 13	021	16 21	084	47 59	134	27 42	181	43 25	227	27 11	307	42 39	329
126	36 23	020	16 50	083	48 20	133	27 41	180	43 04	227	26 47	306	42 23	327
127	36 32	019	17 19	082	48 42	133	27 41	180	42 42	226	26 23	305	42 08	326
128	36 41	017	17 47	081	49 03	132	27 41	179	42 22	226	25 59	304	41 51	325
129	36 50	016	18 16	080	49 25	132	27 42	179	42 01	225	25 35	303	41 34	324
130	36 58	015	18 45	079	49 47	131	27 43	178	41 40	224	25 10	302	41 17	322
131	37 05	014	19 13	078	50 09	131	27 44	177	41 20	224	24 45	301	40 59	321
132	37 11	013	19 42	077	50 31	130	27 46	177	41 00	223	24 20	300	40 40	320
133	37 17	011	20 10	076	50 53	130	27 47	176	40 40	223	23 55	299	40 21	319
134	37 23	010	20 38	076	51 16	129	27 50	175	40 21	222	23 29	298	40 02	318
	REGULUS		◆ SPICA		RIGIL KENT		◆ Peacock		ACHERNAR		CANOPUS		◆ SIRIUS	
135	15 50	018	21 06	075	51 38	129	27 52	175	40 01	222	67 34	274	39 42	317
136	15 58	017	21 34	074	52 01	128	27 55	174	39 42	221	67 05	273	39 22	315
137	16 06	016	22 02	073	52 24	128	27 58	174	39 23	220	66 36	272	39 01	314
138	16 14	015	22 30	072	52 47	127	28 01	173	39 04	220	66 07	271	38 40	313
139	16 21	014	22 58	071	53 10	127	28 05	172	38 46	219	65 38	270	38 19	312
140	16 27	013	23 25	070	53 34	126	28 09	172	38 28	219	65 08	269	37 57	311
141	16 33	012	23 52	069	53 57	126	28 13	171	38 09	218	64 39	269	37 35	310
142	16 39	011	24 19	068	54 21	125	28 18	171	37 52	218	64 10	268	37 12	309
143	16 44	009	24 46	067	54 45	125	28 23	170	37 34	217	63 41	267	36 49	307
144	16 49	008	25 13	066	55 09	124	28 28	169	37 17	216	63 12	266	36 26	306
145	16 53	007	25 39	065	55 33	124	28 34	169	36 59	216	62 43	265	36 03	305
146	16 56	006	26 06	064	55 57	123	28 39	168	36 43	215	62 14	265	35 39	304
147	16 59	005	26 32	063	56 21	123	28 46	167	36 26	215	61 45	264	35 14	303
148	17 02	004	26 57	062	56 46	122	28 52	167	36 09	214	61 16	263	34 50	302
149	17 04	003	27 23	061	57 11	122	28 59	166	35 53	214	60 48	262	34 25	301
	REGULUS		◆ SPICA		RIGIL KENT		◆ Peacock		ACHERNAR		CANOPUS		◆ SIRIUS	
150	17 05	002	27 48	060	57 35	121	29 06	166	35 37	213	60 19	261	34 00	300
151	17 06	001	28 14	059	58 00	121	29 13	165	35 22	212	59 50	261	33 35	299
152	17 06	000	28 38	058	58 25	120	29 21	164	35 06	212	59 21	260	33 09	298
153	17 06	359	29 03	057	58 50	120	29 29	164	34 51	211	58 53	259	32 43	297
154	17 06	358	29 27	056	59 16	119	29 37	163	34 36	211	58 24	259	32 17	296
155	17 04	357	29 51	055	59 41	119	29 46	163	34 21	210	57 56	258	31 51	295
156	17 03	356	30 15	054	60 07	119	29 55	162	34 07	209	57 27	257	31 25	294
157	17 01	355	30 38	053	60 32	118	30 04	161	33 53	209	56 59	256	30 58	293
158	16 58	354	31 02	052	60 58	118	30 13	161	33 39	208	56 31	256	30 31	292
159	16 55	353	31 24	051	61 24	117	30 23	160	33 25	208	56 03	255	30 04	291
160	16 51	352	31 47	050	61 50	117	30 33	160	33 12	207	55 35	254	29 37	290
161	16 47	351	32 09	049	62 16	116	30 43	159	32 59	206	55 07	254	29 09	289
162	16 42	350	32 30	048	62 42	116	30 54	158	32 46	206	54 39	253	28 42	288
163	16 37	349	32 52	047	63 08	115	31 05	158	32 33	205	54 11	252	28 14	287
164	16 31	348	33 13	046	63 34	115	31 16	157	32 21	205	53 43	252	27 46	286
	◆ SPICA		ANTARES		◆ Peacock		ACHERNAR		CANOPUS		◆ SIRIUS		Alphard	
165	33 33	044	26 28	097	31 28	156	32 09	204	53 16	251	27 18	285	35 02	332
166	33 53	043	26 57	097	31 39	156	31 57	203	52 48	250	26 50	284	34 48	331
167	34 13	042	27 26	096	31 51	155	31 46	203	52 21	250	26 22	283	34 34	330
168	34 33	041	27 55	095	32 04	155	31 35	202	51 54	249	25 53	282	34 19	328
169	34 51	040	28 24	094	32 16	154	31 24	202	51 27	248	25 25	282	34 03	327
170	35 10	039	28 53	093	32 29	153	31 13	201	51 00	248	24 56	281	33 47	326
171	35 28	038	29 22	092	32 42	153	31 03	200	50 33	247	24 28	280	33 31	325
172	35 45	037	29 51	091	32 56	152	30 53	200	50 06	246	23 59	279	33 14	324
173	36 02	035	30 20	091	33 09	152	30 43	199	49 40	246	23 30	278	32 56	323
174	36 19	034	30 50	090	33 23	151	30 34	199	49 13	245	23 01	277	32 39	322
175	36 35	033	31 19	089	33 37	150	30 25	198	48 47	244	22 33	276	32 20	321
176	36 51	032	31 48	088	33 52	150	30 16	197	48 21	244	22 04	275	32 02	319
177	37 06	031	32 17	087	34 07	149	30 07	197	47 55	243	21 35	274	31 42	318
178	37 20	029	32 46	086	34 22	149	29 59	196	47 29	243	21 06	273	31 23	317
179	37 34	028	33 15	085	34 37	148	29 51	196	47 03	242	20 37	273	31 03	316

LAT 61°S

LHA ♈	Hc	Zn	Hc	Zn	Hc	Zn	Hc	Zn	Hc	Zn	Hc	Zn	Hc	Zn
	SPICA		◆ANTARES		Peacock		◆ACHERNAR		CANOPUS		Suhail		◆Alphard	
180	37 48	027	33 44	084	34 52	148	29 43	195	46 37	241	59 17	285	30 43	315
181	38 01	026	34 13	083	35 08	147	29 36	194	46 12	241	58 49	284	30 22	314
182	38 13	025	34 42	082	35 24	146	29 29	194	45 47	240	58 21	283	30 01	313
183	38 25	023	35 10	082	35 40	146	29 22	193	45 22	239	57 53	282	29 39	312
184	38 36	022	35 39	081	35 57	145	29 15	193	44 57	239	57 24	281	29 17	311
185	38 47	021	36 08	080	36 13	145	29 09	192	44 32	238	56 55	280	28 55	310
186	38 57	020	36 36	079	36 30	144	29 03	191	44 07	238	56 27	279	28 33	309
187	39 07	018	37 05	078	36 48	143	28 58	191	43 43	237	55 58	278	28 10	308
188	39 16	017	37 33	077	37 05	143	28 52	190	43 18	236	55 29	277	27 47	307
189	39 24	016	38 01	076	37 23	142	28 47	190	42 54	236	55 00	276	27 23	306
190	39 32	015	38 30	075	37 41	142	28 43	189	42 30	235	54 31	275	26 59	305
191	39 39	013	38 58	074	37 59	141	28 38	188	42 07	234	54 02	274	26 35	304
192	39 45	012	39 26	073	38 17	141	28 34	188	41 43	234	53 33	273	26 11	303
193	39 51	011	39 53	072	38 36	140	28 31	187	41 20	233	53 04	272	25 46	302
194	39 56	010	40 21	071	38 55	139	28 27	186	40 56	233	52 35	271	25 21	301
	SPICA		◆ANTARES		Peacock		◆ACHERNAR		CANOPUS		Suhail		◆Alphard	
195	40 01	008	40 48	070	39 14	139	28 24	186	40 33	232	52 06	270	24 56	300
196	40 05	007	41 15	069	39 33	138	28 21	185	40 11	231	51 37	269	24 31	299
197	40 08	006	41 43	068	39 52	138	28 19	185	39 48	231	51 08	269	24 05	298
198	40 10	004	42 09	067	40 12	137	28 16	184	39 25	230	50 39	268	23 39	297
199	40 12	003	42 36	066	40 32	136	28 14	183	39 03	230	50 10	267	23 13	296
200	40 14	002	43 02	065	40 52	136	28 13	183	38 41	229	49 41	266	22 47	295
201	40 14	001	43 29	064	41 13	135	28 12	182	38 19	228	49 12	265	22 20	294
202	40 14	359	43 55	063	41 33	135	28 11	182	37 58	228	48 43	264	21 53	293
203	40 14	358	44 20	061	41 54	134	28 10	181	37 36	227	48 14	264	21 27	292
204	40 12	357	44 46	060	42 15	134	28 10	180	37 15	226	47 45	263	20 59	291
205	40 10	356	45 11	059	42 36	133	28 10	180	36 54	226	47 16	262	20 32	290
206	40 08	354	45 36	058	42 57	132	28 10	179	36 34	225	46 47	261	20 05	289
207	40 04	353	46 00	057	43 19	132	28 11	179	36 13	225	46 18	260	19 37	288
208	40 01	352	46 24	056	43 41	131	28 11	178	35 53	224	45 50	260	19 10	287
209	39 56	350	46 48	055	44 03	131	28 13	177	35 33	223	45 21	259	18 42	286
	ANTARES		◆Nunki		Peacock		ACHERNAR		◆CANOPUS		Suhail		◆SPICA	
210	47 12	053	30 27	090	44 25	130	28 14	177	35 13	223	44 53	258	39 51	349
211	47 35	052	30 56	089	44 47	130	28 16	176	34 53	222	44 24	257	39 45	348
212	47 58	051	31 25	088	45 09	129	28 18	175	34 34	221	43 56	257	39 39	347
213	48 20	050	31 54	087	45 32	129	28 21	175	34 15	221	43 28	256	39 32	345
214	48 42	049	32 23	086	45 55	128	28 24	174	33 56	220	43 00	255	39 24	344
215	49 04	047	32 52	086	46 18	127	28 27	174	33 37	220	42 32	254	39 16	343
216	49 25	046	33 21	085	46 41	127	28 30	173	33 19	219	42 04	253	39 07	342
217	49 46	045	33 50	084	47 05	126	28 34	172	33 01	218	41 36	253	38 57	340
218	50 06	044	34 19	083	47 28	126	28 38	172	32 43	218	41 08	252	38 47	339
219	50 26	042	34 47	082	47 52	125	28 42	171	32 25	217	40 40	251	38 36	338
220	50 45	041	35 16	081	48 16	125	28 47	171	32 08	216	40 13	251	38 25	337
221	51 04	040	35 45	080	48 40	124	28 52	170	31 51	216	39 46	250	38 13	335
222	51 22	038	36 14	079	49 04	123	28 57	169	31 34	215	39 18	249	38 01	334
223	51 40	037	36 42	078	49 28	123	29 02	169	31 17	215	38 51	248	37 48	333
224	51 57	036	37 10	077	49 53	122	29 08	168	31 01	214	38 24	248	37 34	332
	ANTARES		◆Nunki		FOMALHAUT		ACHERNAR		◆CANOPUS		Suhail		◆SPICA	
225	52 14	034	37 39	076	12 52	129	29 14	167	30 45	213	37 58	247	37 20	331
226	52 30	033	38 07	075	13 15	128	29 21	167	30 29	213	37 31	246	37 06	329
227	52 45	031	38 35	074	13 38	128	29 28	166	30 13	212	37 04	245	36 51	328
228	53 00	030	39 03	073	14 01	127	29 35	166	29 58	211	36 38	245	36 35	327
229	53 14	028	39 31	072	14 25	126	29 42	165	29 43	211	36 12	244	36 19	326
230	53 28	027	39 58	071	14 48	125	29 50	164	29 28	210	35 46	243	36 02	325
231	53 41	026	40 26	070	15 12	124	29 58	164	29 14	209	35 20	243	35 45	323
232	53 53	024	40 53	069	15 36	124	30 06	163	29 00	209	34 54	242	35 28	322
233	54 05	023	41 20	068	16 01	123	30 15	163	28 46	208	34 29	241	35 10	321
234	54 15	021	41 47	067	16 25	122	30 23	162	28 32	208	34 03	240	34 51	320
235	54 25	020	42 14	066	16 50	121	30 33	161	28 19	207	33 38	240	34 32	319
236	54 35	018	42 40	065	17 15	120	30 42	161	28 06	206	33 13	239	34 13	318
237	54 43	017	43 07	064	17 40	120	30 52	160	27 53	206	32 48	238	33 53	317
238	54 51	015	43 33	063	18 06	119	31 02	160	27 41	205	32 23	238	33 33	316
239	54 59	013	43 58	062	18 31	118	31 12	159	27 29	204	31 59	237	33 13	314
	◆ANTARES		Nunki		◆FOMALHAUT		ACHERNAR		CANOPUS		◆ACRUX		SPICA	
240	55 05	012	44 24	061	18 57	117	31 23	158	27 17	204	65 45	242	32 52	313
241	55 11	010	44 49	060	19 23	116	31 33	158	27 05	203	65 19	241	32 30	312
242	55 15	009	45 14	059	19 49	116	31 44	157	26 54	202	64 54	241	32 09	311
243	55 19	007	45 39	057	20 16	115	31 56	157	26 43	202	64 29	240	31 47	310
244	55 23	006	46 03	056	20 42	114	32 08	156	26 32	201	64 03	240	31 24	309
245	55 25	004	46 27	055	21 09	113	32 20	155	26 22	200	63 38	240	31 01	308
246	55 27	002	46 51	054	21 36	112	32 32	155	26 12	200	63 13	239	30 38	307
247	55 28	001	47 14	053	22 03	112	32 44	154	26 03	199	62 48	239	30 15	306
248	55 28	359	47 37	052	22 30	111	32 57	154	25 53	198	62 23	238	29 51	305
249	55 27	358	48 00	050	22 57	110	33 10	153	25 44	198	61 59	238	29 27	304
250	55 26	356	48 22	049	23 24	109	33 24	152	25 35	197	61 34	238	29 03	303
251	55 23	355	48 44	048	23 52	108	33 37	152	25 27	197	61 10	237	28 38	302
252	55 20	353	49 05	047	24 20	107	33 51	151	25 19	196	60 45	237	28 13	301
253	55 16	351	49 26	045	24 48	107	34 05	151	25 11	195	60 21	237	27 48	300
254	55 11	350	49 46	044	25 15	106	34 19	150	25 04	195	59 57	236	27 23	299
	Nunki		◆FOMALHAUT		ACHERNAR		CANOPUS		◆ACRUX		SPICA		◆ANTARES	
255	50 06	043	25 43	105	34 34	149	24 56	194	59 32	236	26 57	298	55 06	348
256	50 26	041	26 12	104	34 49	149	24 50	193	59 09	235	26 31	297	55 00	347
257	50 45	040	26 40	103	35 04	148	24 43	193	58 45	235	26 05	296	54 53	345
258	51 03	039	27 08	103	35 20	148	24 37	192	58 21	234	25 39	295	54 45	344
259	51 21	037	27 37	102	35 35	147	24 31	191	57 57	234	25 13	294	54 36	342
260	51 39	036	28 05	101	35 51	147	24 25	191	57 34	234	24 46	293	54 27	341
261	51 56	035	28 34	100	36 07	146	24 20	190	57 11	233	24 19	292	54 17	339
262	52 12	033	29 02	099	36 24	145	24 15	189	56 47	233	23 52	291	54 06	338
263	52 27	032	29 31	098	36 40	145	24 11	189	56 24	232	23 25	290	53 55	336
264	52 43	030	30 00	098	36 57	144	24 07	188	56 01	232	22 57	289	53 43	335
265	52 57	029	30 29	097	37 14	144	24 03	187	55 38	231	22 30	288	53 30	333
266	53 11	028	30 58	096	37 32	143	23 59	187	55 16	231	22 02	287	53 17	332
267	53 24	026	31 27	095	37 49	143	23 56	186	54 53	231	21 34	286	53 03	330
268	53 36	025	31 56	094	38 07	142	23 53	185	54 31	230	21 06	285	52 48	329
269	53 48	023	32 25	093	38 25	141	23 51	185	54 09	230	20 38	284	52 33	327

LHA ♈	Hc	Zn	Hc	Zn	Hc	Zn	Hc	Zn	Hc	Zn	Hc	Zn	Hc	Zn
	◆ALTAIR		FOMALHAUT		◆ACHERNAR		CANOPUS		◆RIGIL KENT		SPICA		ANTARES	
270	16 44	029	32 54	093	38 43	141	23 48	184	66 23	248	20 10	284	52 17	326
271	16 58	028	33 23	092	39 02	140	23 47	183	65 56	248	19 42	283	52 00	325
272	17 11	027	33 52	091	39 21	140	23 45	183	65 29	247	19 13	282	51 43	323
273	17 24	026	34 21	090	39 40	139	23 44	182	65 03	247	18 45	281	51 25	322
274	17 37	025	34 50	089	39 59	139	23 43	181	64 36	246	18 16	280	51 07	321
275	17 49	024	35 19	088	40 18	138	23 42	181	64 09	246	17 47	279	50 48	319
276	18 00	023	35 48	087	40 38	137	23 42	180	63 43	245	17 18	278	50 29	318
277	18 11	022	36 17	086	40 57	137	23 42	179	63 16	245	16 50	277	50 09	317
278	18 22	021	36 46	085	41 17	136	23 43	179	62 50	244	16 21	276	49 49	315
279	18 32	020	37 15	085	41 38	136	23 44	178	62 24	244	15 52	275	49 29	314
280	18 41	019	37 44	084	41 58	135	23 45	177	61 58	243	15 23	275	49 07	313
281	18 50	018	38 13	083	42 19	135	23 46	177	61 32	243	14 54	274	48 46	312
282	18 59	017	38 42	082	42 40	134	23 48	176	61 06	243	14 25	273	48 24	310
283	19 07	016	39 11	081	43 01	133	23 50	175	60 40	242	13 56	272	48 02	309
284	19 14	015	39 39	080	43 22	133	23 53	175	60 15	242	13 27	271	47 39	308
	◆ALTAIR		FOMALHAUT		◆ACHERNAR		CANOPUS		◆RIGIL KENT		ANTARES		Nunki	
285	19 21	013	40 08	079	43 43	132	23 56	174	59 49	241	47 16	307	55 16	359
286	19 28	012	40 36	078	44 05	132	23 59	173	59 24	241	46 52	306	55 15	357
287	19 34	011	41 05	077	44 27	131	24 02	173	58 58	240	46 28	304	55 13	355
288	19 40	010	41 33	076	44 49	131	24 06	172	58 33	240	46 04	303	55 10	354
289	19 44	009	42 01	075	45 11	130	24 10	171	58 08	239	45 40	302	55 07	352
290	19 49	008	42 29	074	45 33	129	24 15	171	57 43	239	45 15	301	55 03	351
291	19 53	007	42 57	073	45 56	129	24 20	170	57 18	238	44 50	300	54 57	349
292	19 56	006	43 25	072	46 19	128	24 25	169	56 54	238	44 24	299	54 52	348
293	19 59	005	43 53	071	46 41	128	24 30	169	56 29	237	43 59	298	54 45	346
294	20 01	004	44 20	070	47 05	127	24 36	168	56 05	237	43 33	297	54 37	344
295	20 03	003	44 47	069	47 28	127	24 42	168	55 40	236	43 07	295	54 29	343
296	20 05	002	45 14	068	47 51	126	24 49	167	55 16	236	42 40	294	54 20	341
297	20 05	001	45 41	067	48 15	126	24 55	166	54 52	235	42 14	293	54 11	340
298	20 05	000	46 08	066	48 39	125	25 02	166	54 28	235	41 47	292	54 00	338
299	20 05	359	46 34	065	49 02	124	25 10	165	54 05	234	41 20	291	53 49	337
	FOMALHAUT		◆ACHERNAR		CANOPUS		◆RIGIL KENT		ANTARES		Nunki		◆ALTAIR	
300	47 01	064	49 26	124	25 18	164	53 41	234	40 53	290	53 38	335	20 04	358
301	47 27	063	49 51	123	25 26	164	53 18	233	40 25	289	53 25	334	20 03	357
302	47 52	061	50 15	123	25 34	163	52 54	233	39 58	288	53 12	333	20 01	356
303	48 18	060	50 40	122	25 43	162	52 31	232	39 30	287	52 58	331	19 58	355
304	48 43	059	51 04	122	25 52	162	52 08	232	39 02	286	52 44	330	19 55	354
305	49 08	058	51 29	121	26 01	161	51 45	231	38 34	285	52 29	328	19 52	353
306	49 32	057	51 54	121	26 11	160	51 23	231	38 06	284	52 13	327	19 48	351
307	49 56	056	52 19	120	26 21	160	51 00	231	37 38	283	51 57	325	19 43	350
308	50 20	054	52 45	119	26 31	159	50 38	230	37 10	282	51 40	324	19 38	349
309	50 43	053	53 10	119	26 42	158	50 16	230	36 41	281	51 23	323	19 33	348
310	51 07	052	53 36	118	26 52	158	49 54	229	36 12	280	51 05	321	19 26	347
311	51 29	051	54 01	118	27 04	157	49 32	229	35 44	280	50 47	320	19 20	346
312	51 52	049	54 27	117	27 15	156	49 10	228	35 15	279	50 28	319	19 13	345
313	52 13	048	54 53	117	27 27	156	48 48	228	34 46	278	50 08	317	19 05	344
314	52 35	047	55 19	116	27 39	155	48 27	227	34 17	277	49 48	316	18 57	343
	◆FOMALHAUT		ACHERNAR		◆CANOPUS		RIGIL KENT		◆ANTARES		Nunki		ALTAIR	
315	52 56	046	55 45	115	27 51	154	48 06	227	33 49	276	49 28	315	18 48	342
316	53 16	044	56 12	115	28 04	154	47 45	226	33 20	275	49 07	314	18 39	341
317	53 36	043	56 38	114	28 17	153	47 24	226	32 51	274	48 46	312	18 29	340
318	53 56	041	57 05	114	28 30	153	47 03	225	32 22	273	48 24	311	18 19	339
319	54 15	040	57 31	113	28 44	152	46 43	225	31 52	272	48 02	310	18 08	338
320	54 33	039	57 58	113	28 58	151	46 23	224	31 23	271	47 39	309	17 57	337
321	54 51	037	58 25	112	29 12	151	46 02	223	30 54	270	47 16	307	17 46	336
322	55 09	036	58 52	111	29 26	150	45 43	223	30 25	270	46 53	306	17 34	335
323	55 25	034	59 19	111	29 41	149	45 23	222	29 56	269	46 29	305	17 21	334
324	55 41	033	59 46	110	29 56	149	45 03	222	29 27	268	46 05	304	17 08	333
325	55 57	031	60 14	110	30 11	148	44 44	221	28 58	267	45 41	303	16 55	332
326	56 12	030	60 41	109	30 27	147	44 25	221	28 29	266	45 17	302	16 41	331
327	56 26	028	61 09	108	30 42	147	44 06	220	28 00	265	44 52	300	16 26	330
328	56 40	027	61 36	108	30 58	146	43 47	220	27 31	264	44 26	299	16 11	329
329	56 52	025	62 04	107	31 15	146	43 28	219	27 02	264	44 01	298	15 56	328
	◆FOMALHAUT		Diphda		ACHERNAR		◆CANOPUS		RIGIL KENT		◆ANTARES		Nunki	
330	57 04	024	38 04	053	62 32	107	31 31	145	43 10	219	26 33	263	43 35	297
331	57 16	022	38 27	051	63 00	106	31 48	144	42 52	218	26 04	262	43 09	296
332	57 26	021	38 50	050	63 28	105	32 05	144	42 34	218	25 36	261	42 43	295
333	57 36	019	39 12	049	63 56	105	32 23	143	42 16	217	25 07	260	42 16	294
334	57 45	017	39 34	048	64 24	104	32 40	142	41 59	217	24 38	259	41 50	293
335	57 54	016	39 55	047	64 52	104	32 58	142	41 41	216	24 10	259	41 23	292
336	58 01	014	40 16	046	65 21	103	33 16	141	41 24	216	23 41	258	40 56	291
337	58 08	013	40 37	045	65 49	102	33 35	141	41 08	215	23 13	257	40 28	290
338	58 14	011	40 57	043	66 17	102	33 53	140	40 51	215	22 45	256	40 01	289
339	58 19	009	41 17	042	66 46	101	34 12	139	40 34	214	22 16	255	39 33	288
340	58 24	008	41 36	041	67 15	100	34 31	139	40 18	214	21 48	254	39 06	287
341	58 27	006	41 55	040	67 43	100	34 50	138	40 02	213	21 20	254	38 38	286
342	58 30	004	42 13	039	68 12	099	35 10	137	39 47	213	20 53	253	38 10	285
343	58 31	003	42 31	037	68 41	098	35 30	137	39 31	212	20 25	252	37 41	284
344	58 32	001	42 49	036	69 09	098	35 50	136	39 16	211	19 57	251	37 13	283
	◆Diphda		Acamar		◆CANOPUS		RIGIL KENT		◆ANTARES		Nunki		FOMALHAUT	
345	43 06	035	48 44	088	36 10	136	39 01	211	19 30	250	36 45	282	58 32	359
346	43 22	034	49 13	087	36 31	135	38 46	210	19 02	250	36 16	281	58 32	358
347	43 38	032	49 42	086	36 51	134	38 31	210	18 35	249	35 48	280	58 30	356
348	43 53	031	50 11	085	37 12	134	38 17	209	18 08	248	35 19	279	58 28	354
349	44 08	030	50 40	084	37 33	133	38 03	209	17 41	247	34 50	278	58 24	353
350	44 22	029	51 09	083	37 55	132	37 49	208	17 15	246	34 21	277	58 20	351
351	44 36	027	51 38	082	38 16	132	37 35	208	16 48	245	33 53	276	58 15	349
352	44 49	026	52 07	081	38 38	131	37 22	207	16 22	245	33 24	275	58 10	348
353	45 02	025	52 36	080	39 00	131	37 09	207	15 56	244	32 55	275	58 03	346
354	45 13	023	53 04	079	39 22	130	36 56	206	15 29	243	32 26	274	57 56	345
355	45 25	022	53 33	078	39 45	129	36 43	205	15 04	242	31 57	273	57 48	343
356	45 35	021	54 01	077	40 07	129	36 31	205	14 38	241	31 28	272	57 39	341
357	45 45	019	54 30	076	40 30	128	36 19	204	14 13	241	30 58	271	57 29	340
358	45 55	018	54 58	075	40 53	127	36 07	204	13 47	240	30 29	270	57 18	338
359	46 03	017	55 26	074	41 16	127	35 55	203	13 22	239	30 00	269	57 07	337

 LAT 62°S

LHA ♈	Hc	Zn	Hc	Zn	Hc	Zn	Hc	Zn	Hc	Zn	Hc	Zn	Hc	Zn
	Diphda		◆ RIGEL		CANOPUS		Miaplacidus		◆ RIGIL KENT		Peacock		◆ FOMALHAUT	
0	45 13	015	12 28	084	42 15	126	45 01	161	36 39	203	63 07	257	56 01	336
1	45 20	014	12 56	083	42 38	125	45 10	161	36 28	202	62 40	256	55 49	334
2	45 27	012	13 24	082	43 01	124	45 20	160	36 18	202	62 13	256	55 36	333
3	45 32	011	13 52	081	43 24	124	45 29	160	36 07	201	61 45	255	55 23	331
4	45 37	010	14 20	080	43 48	123	45 39	159	35 57	201	61 18	254	55 09	330
5	45 42	008	14 47	079	44 12	122	45 49	159	35 47	200	60 51	254	54 54	328
6	45 46	007	15 15	079	44 35	122	45 59	158	35 38	200	60 24	253	54 39	327
7	45 49	006	15 42	078	45 00	121	46 10	158	35 28	199	59 57	252	54 24	325
8	45 51	004	16 10	077	45 24	120	46 21	158	35 19	198	59 30	252	54 07	324
9	45 53	003	16 37	076	45 48	120	46 31	157	35 10	198	59 04	251	53 50	323
10	45 54	001	17 05	075	46 13	119	46 42	157	35 02	197	58 37	250	53 33	321
11	45 54	000	17 32	074	46 37	118	46 54	156	34 54	197	58 11	250	53 15	320
12	45 54	359	17 59	073	47 02	118	47 05	156	34 46	196	57 44	249	52 57	318
13	45 53	357	18 26	072	47 27	117	47 17	155	34 38	196	57 18	249	52 38	317
14	45 51	356	18 52	071	47 52	117	47 29	155	34 30	195	56 52	248	52 18	316
	◆ RIGEL		SIRIUS		CANOPUS		◆ RIGIL KENT		Peacock		◆ FOMALHAUT		Diphda	
15	19 19	070	16 23	095	48 18	116	34 23	195	56 26	247	51 58	314	45 49	355
16	19 45	069	16 51	094	48 43	115	34 16	194	56 00	247	51 38	313	45 46	353
17	20 12	068	17 19	093	49 09	115	34 10	193	55 34	246	51 17	312	45 43	352
18	20 38	067	17 47	092	49 34	114	34 03	193	55 08	246	50 56	311	45 38	351
19	21 04	066	18 16	091	50 00	113	33 57	192	54 43	245	50 34	309	45 33	349
20	21 29	066	18 44	091	50 26	113	33 51	192	54 17	244	50 12	308	45 28	348
21	21 55	065	19 12	090	50 52	112	33 46	191	53 52	244	49 50	307	45 21	347
22	22 20	064	19 40	089	51 18	111	33 41	190	53 27	243	49 27	306	45 15	345
23	22 45	063	20 08	088	51 45	111	33 36	190	53 02	243	49 04	304	45 07	344
24	23 10	062	20 36	087	52 11	110	33 31	189	52 37	242	48 41	303	44 59	343
25	23 35	061	21 05	086	52 38	109	33 26	189	52 12	241	48 17	302	44 50	341
26	23 59	060	21 33	085	53 04	109	33 22	188	51 47	241	47 53	301	44 41	340
27	24 24	059	22 01	084	53 31	108	33 18	188	51 23	240	47 29	300	44 31	339
28	24 47	058	22 29	083	53 58	107	33 15	187	50 59	240	47 04	299	44 20	337
29	25 11	057	22 57	083	54 25	106	33 11	186	50 34	239	46 39	298	44 09	336
	◆ RIGEL		SIRIUS		CANOPUS		◆ RIGIL KENT		Peacock		◆ FOMALHAUT		Diphda	
30	25 35	056	23 25	082	54 52	106	33 08	186	50 10	238	46 14	296	43 57	335
31	25 58	055	23 52	081	55 19	105	33 06	185	49 46	238	45 49	295	43 45	333
32	26 21	054	24 20	080	55 46	104	33 03	185	49 23	237	45 23	294	43 32	332
33	26 43	053	24 48	079	56 14	104	33 01	184	48 59	237	44 58	293	43 18	331
34	27 05	052	25 15	078	56 41	103	32 59	184	48 36	236	44 32	292	43 04	330
35	27 27	051	25 43	077	57 08	102	32 58	183	48 12	235	44 05	291	42 50	328
36	27 49	050	26 10	076	57 36	101	32 56	182	47 49	235	43 39	290	42 35	327
37	28 10	048	26 38	075	58 04	101	32 55	182	47 26	234	43 13	289	42 19	326
38	28 31	047	27 05	074	58 31	100	32 54	181	47 03	234	42 46	288	42 03	325
39	28 51	046	27 32	073	58 59	099	32 54	181	46 41	233	42 19	287	41 46	323
40	29 12	045	27 59	072	59 27	098	32 54	180	46 18	233	41 52	286	41 29	322
41	29 32	044	28 25	071	59 55	098	32 54	180	45 56	232	41 25	285	41 12	321
42	29 51	043	28 52	070	60 23	097	32 54	179	45 34	231	40 58	284	40 54	320
43	30 10	042	29 18	069	60 51	096	32 55	178	45 12	231	40 30	283	40 35	319
44	30 29	041	29 45	068	61 19	095	32 56	178	44 50	230	40 03	282	40 17	317
	RIGEL		◆ SIRIUS		CANOPUS		◆ RIGIL KENT		Peacock		FOMALHAUT		◆ Diphda	
45	30 47	040	30 11	067	61 47	095	32 57	177	44 29	230	39 35	281	39 57	316
46	31 05	039	30 37	066	62 15	094	32 59	177	44 07	229	39 07	280	39 38	315
47	31 22	038	31 02	065	62 43	093	33 00	176	43 46	228	38 40	279	39 17	314
48	31 39	037	31 28	064	63 11	092	33 02	175	43 25	228	38 12	278	38 57	313
49	31 56	035	31 53	063	63 39	091	33 05	175	43 04	227	37 44	277	38 36	312
50	32 12	034	32 18	062	64 08	090	33 08	174	42 44	227	37 16	276	38 15	310
51	32 28	033	32 43	061	64 36	089	33 10	174	42 23	226	36 48	275	37 53	309
52	32 43	032	33 08	060	65 04	089	33 14	173	42 03	226	36 20	275	37 31	308
53	32 57	031	33 32	059	65 32	088	33 17	173	41 43	225	35 52	274	37 09	307
54	33 12	030	33 56	058	66 00	087	33 21	172	41 23	224	35 24	273	36 46	306
55	33 25	029	34 20	057	66 28	086	33 25	171	41 04	224	34 55	272	36 23	305
56	33 39	027	34 44	056	66 56	085	33 29	171	40 45	223	34 27	271	36 00	304
57	33 51	026	35 07	055	67 24	084	33 34	170	40 25	223	33 59	270	35 37	303
58	34 04	025	35 30	054	67 52	083	33 39	170	40 06	222	33 31	269	35 13	302
59	34 15	024	35 52	053	68 20	082	33 44	169	39 48	221	33 03	268	34 49	301
	RIGEL		◆ SIRIUS		Suhail		◆ RIGIL KENT		Peacock		FOMALHAUT		◆ Diphda	
60	34 27	023	36 15	052	43 07	104	33 50	169	39 29	221	32 35	267	34 24	300
61	34 37	022	36 37	051	43 35	104	33 55	168	39 11	220	32 07	267	34 00	299
62	34 47	020	36 58	050	44 02	103	34 01	167	38 53	220	31 38	266	33 35	298
63	34 57	019	37 20	048	44 29	102	34 08	167	38 35	219	31 10	265	33 10	297
64	35 06	018	37 41	047	44 57	101	34 14	166	38 17	218	30 42	264	32 44	296
65	35 14	017	38 01	046	45 25	100	34 21	166	38 00	218	30 14	263	32 19	295
66	35 22	016	38 21	045	45 52	100	34 28	165	37 43	217	29 46	262	31 53	294
67	35 29	014	38 41	044	46 20	099	34 35	165	37 26	217	29 18	261	31 27	293
68	35 36	013	39 00	043	46 48	098	34 43	164	37 09	216	28 51	261	31 01	292
69	35 42	012	39 19	042	47 16	097	34 51	163	36 53	215	28 23	260	30 35	291
70	35 48	011	39 38	040	47 44	096	34 59	163	36 36	215	27 55	259	30 08	290
71	35 53	010	39 56	039	48 12	096	35 08	162	36 20	214	27 28	258	29 42	289
72	35 57	008	40 13	038	48 40	095	35 16	162	36 05	214	27 00	257	29 15	288
73	36 01	007	40 30	037	49 08	094	35 25	161	35 49	213	26 33	256	28 48	287
74	36 04	006	40 47	036	49 36	093	35 35	161	35 34	212	26 05	256	28 21	286
	RIGEL		◆ SIRIUS		Suhail		◆ RIGIL KENT		Peacock		ACHERNAR		◆ Diphda	
75	36 07	005	41 03	034	50 04	092	35 44	160	35 19	212	64 41	258	27 54	285
76	36 09	003	41 19	033	50 33	091	35 54	159	35 04	211	64 14	257	27 27	284
77	36 10	002	41 34	032	51 01	090	36 04	159	34 50	211	63 47	257	26 59	283
78	36 11	001	41 49	031	51 29	089	36 14	158	34 35	210	63 19	256	26 32	282
79	36 11	000	42 03	030	51 57	089	36 25	158	34 21	209	62 52	255	26 04	281
80	36 11	359	42 17	028	52 25	088	36 36	157	34 08	209	62 25	255	25 36	280
81	36 10	357	42 30	027	52 53	087	36 47	157	33 54	208	61 58	254	25 09	279
82	36 08	356	42 42	026	53 22	086	36 58	156	33 41	208	61 31	253	24 41	278
83	36 06	355	42 54	024	53 50	085	37 10	155	33 28	207	61 04	253	24 13	277
84	36 03	354	43 05	023	54 18	084	37 21	155	33 15	206	60 37	252	23 45	276
85	36 00	352	43 16	022	54 46	083	37 33	154	33 03	206	60 10	251	23 17	276
86	35 56	351	43 26	021	55 14	082	37 46	154	32 51	205	59 43	251	22 49	275
87	35 51	350	43 36	019	55 41	081	37 58	153	32 39	205	59 17	250	22 21	274
88	35 46	349	43 45	018	56 09	080	38 11	153	32 27	204	58 50	250	21 53	273
89	35 40	348	43 53	017	56 37	079	38 24	152	32 16	203	58 24	249	21 24	272

LHA ♈	Hc	Zn	Hc	Zn	Hc	Zn	Hc	Zn	Hc	Zn	Hc	Zn	Hc	Zn
	◆ SIRIUS		Suhail		◆ RIGIL KENT		Peacock		◆ ACHERNAR		Acamar		RIGEL	
90	44 01	015	57 05	078	38 37	152	32 05	203	57 58	248	55 20	287	35 34	346
91	44 08	014	57 32	077	38 51	151	31 54	202	57 32	248	54 53	286	35 27	345
92	44 15	013	57 59	076	39 05	150	31 44	202	57 06	247	54 26	285	35 19	344
93	44 21	011	58 27	075	39 19	150	31 33	201	56 40	247	53 59	284	35 11	343
94	44 26	010	58 54	074	39 33	149	31 24	200	56 14	246	53 32	283	35 03	342
95	44 31	009	59 21	073	39 47	149	31 14	200	55 48	245	53 04	282	34 53	340
96	44 34	007	59 48	072	40 02	148	31 04	199	55 23	245	52 37	281	34 44	339
97	44 38	006	60 14	070	40 17	148	30 55	198	54 57	244	52 09	280	34 33	338
98	44 40	005	60 41	069	40 32	147	30 47	198	54 32	244	51 41	279	34 22	337
99	44 42	003	61 07	068	40 48	147	30 38	197	54 07	243	51 13	278	34 11	336
100	44 44	002	61 33	067	41 03	146	30 30	197	53 42	242	50 45	277	33 59	334
101	44 44	001	61 59	066	41 19	146	30 22	196	53 17	242	50 17	276	33 47	333
102	44 44	359	62 24	064	41 35	145	30 14	195	52 52	241	49 49	275	33 34	332
103	44 43	358	62 49	063	41 51	144	30 07	195	52 27	241	49 21	274	33 20	331
104	44 42	357	63 14	062	42 08	144	30 00	194	52 03	240	48 53	274	33 07	330
	Alphard		◆ Gienah		RIGIL KENT		◆ Peacock		ACHERNAR		◆ RIGEL		SIRIUS	
105	30 16	044	20 35	089	42 24	143	29 53	194	51 39	240	32 52	329	44 40	355
106	30 36	043	21 03	088	42 41	143	29 47	193	51 14	239	32 37	328	44 37	354
107	30 55	041	21 31	087	42 58	142	29 41	192	50 50	238	32 22	326	44 34	353
108	31 13	040	22 00	086	43 16	142	29 35	192	50 26	238	32 06	325	44 30	351
109	31 31	039	22 28	085	43 33	141	29 29	191	50 03	237	31 50	324	44 25	350
110	31 49	038	22 56	085	43 51	141	29 24	190	49 39	237	31 33	323	44 20	349
111	32 06	037	23 24	084	44 09	140	29 19	190	49 16	236	31 16	322	44 14	347
112	32 23	036	23 52	083	44 27	140	29 14	189	48 52	235	30 58	321	44 08	346
113	32 39	035	24 20	082	44 45	139	29 10	189	48 29	235	30 40	320	44 00	345
114	32 55	034	24 47	081	45 04	139	29 06	188	48 06	234	30 22	319	43 53	343
115	33 10	033	25 15	080	45 23	138	29 02	187	47 44	234	30 03	318	43 44	342
116	33 25	031	25 43	079	45 42	138	28 59	187	47 21	233	29 44	316	43 35	341
117	33 39	030	26 11	078	46 01	137	28 56	186	46 58	233	29 24	315	43 26	339
118	33 53	029	26 38	077	46 20	136	28 53	185	46 36	232	29 04	314	43 15	338
119	34 07	028	27 05	076	46 39	136	28 50	185	46 14	231	28 44	313	43 04	337
	Alphard		◆ SPICA		RIGIL KENT		◆ Peacock		ACHERNAR		◆ RIGEL		SIRIUS	
120	34 20	027	13 54	088	46 59	135	28 48	184	45 52	231	28 23	312	42 53	335
121	34 32	026	14 22	087	47 19	135	28 46	184	45 30	230	28 02	311	42 41	334
122	34 44	024	14 50	086	47 39	134	28 45	183	45 09	230	27 41	310	42 28	333
123	34 55	023	15 18	085	47 59	134	28 43	182	44 47	229	27 19	309	42 15	332
124	35 06	022	15 46	084	48 20	133	28 42	182	44 26	229	26 57	308	42 02	330
125	35 16	021	16 14	083	48 40	133	28 42	181	44 05	228	26 35	307	41 48	329
126	35 26	020	16 42	082	49 01	132	28 41	180	43 44	227	26 12	306	41 33	328
127	35 35	018	17 10	082	49 22	132	28 41	180	43 24	227	25 49	305	41 18	327
128	35 44	017	17 38	081	49 43	131	28 41	179	43 03	226	25 26	304	41 02	325
129	35 52	016	18 06	080	50 04	131	28 42	179	42 43	226	25 02	303	40 46	324
130	36 00	015	18 33	079	50 26	130	28 43	178	42 23	225	24 39	302	40 29	323
131	36 06	014	19 01	078	50 47	130	28 44	177	42 03	224	24 15	301	40 12	322
132	36 13	012	19 28	077	51 09	129	28 45	177	41 44	224	23 50	300	39 54	321
133	36 19	011	19 56	076	51 31	129	28 47	176	41 24	223	23 26	299	39 36	319
134	36 24	010	20 23	075	51 53	128	28 49	175	41 05	223	23 01	298	39 17	318
	REGULUS		◆ SPICA		RIGIL KENT		◆ Peacock		ACHERNAR		CANOPUS		◆ SIRIUS	
135	14 52	018	20 50	074	52 15	128	28 52	175	40 46	222	67 28	276	38 58	317
136	15 01	017	21 17	073	52 38	127	28 54	174	40 27	222	67 00	275	38 39	316
137	15 08	016	21 44	072	53 00	127	28 57	174	40 09	221	66 32	274	38 19	315
138	15 16	015	22 11	071	53 23	126	29 01	173	39 50	220	66 04	273	37 59	314
139	15 22	013	22 38	070	53 46	126	29 04	172	39 32	220	65 36	273	37 39	313
140	15 29	012	23 04	070	54 09	125	29 08	172	39 14	219	65 08	272	37 18	311
141	15 35	011	23 30	069	54 32	125	29 13	171	38 56	219	64 40	271	36 56	310
142	15 40	010	23 57	068	54 55	124	29 17	170	38 39	218	64 12	270	36 35	309
143	15 45	009	24 23	067	55 18	124	29 22	170	38 22	217	63 43	269	36 13	308
144	15 49	008	24 48	066	55 42	123	29 27	169	38 05	217	63 15	268	35 50	307
145	15 53	007	25 14	065	56 06	123	29 32	169	37 48	216	62 47	267	35 28	306
146	15 56	006	25 39	064	56 29	122	29 38	168	37 31	216	62 19	266	35 05	305
147	15 59	005	26 04	063	56 53	122	29 44	167	37 15	215	61 51	266	34 41	304
148	16 02	004	26 29	062	57 17	121	29 51	167	36 59	215	61 23	265	34 18	303
149	16 04	003	26 54	061	57 42	121	29 57	166	36 43	214	60 55	264	33 54	302
	REGULUS		◆ SPICA		RIGIL KENT		◆ Peacock		ACHERNAR		CANOPUS		◆ SIRIUS	
150	16 05	002	27 18	060	58 06	120	30 04	165	36 28	213	60 27	263	33 30	301
151	16 06	001	27 43	059	58 30	120	30 11	165	36 12	213	59 59	262	33 05	300
152	16 06	000	28 07	058	58 55	119	30 19	164	35 57	212	59 31	262	32 41	299
153	16 06	359	28 30	057	59 20	119	30 27	164	35 42	212	59 03	261	32 16	298
154	16 06	358	28 54	056	59 45	118	30 35	163	35 28	211	58 35	260	31 51	296
155	16 05	357	29 17	055	60 09	117	30 43	162	35 13	210	58 08	259	31 26	295
156	16 03	356	29 40	054	60 34	117	30 52	162	34 59	210	57 40	259	31 00	294
157	16 01	355	30 02	053	61 00	116	31 01	161	34 45	209	57 12	258	30 34	293
158	15 58	354	30 24	052	61 25	116	31 10	161	34 32	209	56 45	257	30 08	292
159	15 55	353	30 46	050	61 50	115	31 19	160	34 18	208	56 17	256	29 42	292
160	15 52	352	31 08	049	62 16	115	31 29	159	34 05	207	55 50	256	29 16	291
161	15 47	351	31 29	048	62 41	114	31 39	159	33 53	207	55 23	255	28 50	290
162	15 43	350	31 50	047	63 07	114	31 50	158	33 40	206	54 56	254	28 23	289
163	15 38	349	32 10	046	63 33	113	32 00	157	33 28	206	54 29	254	27 56	288
164	15 32	348	32 31	045	63 59	113	32 11	157	33 16	205	54 02	253	27 29	287
	◆ SPICA		ANTARES		◆ Peacock		ACHERNAR		CANOPUS		◆ SIRIUS		Alphard	
165	32 50	044	26 36	097	32 23	156	33 04	204	53 35	252	27 02	286	34 09	332
166	33 10	043	27 04	096	32 34	156	32 52	204	53 08	252	26 35	285	33 56	331
167	33 29	042	27 32	095	32 46	155	32 41	203	52 41	251	26 08	284	33 42	330
168	33 47	041	28 00	094	32 58	154	32 30	203	52 15	250	25 40	283	33 27	329
169	34 05	040	28 28	093	33 10	154	32 20	202	51 48	250	25 13	282	33 13	328
170	34 23	038	28 56	093	33 23	153	32 09	201	51 22	249	24 45	281	32 57	327
171	34 40	037	29 24	092	33 36	153	31 59	201	50 56	248	24 17	280	32 41	325
172	34 57	036	29 53	091	33 49	152	31 49	200	50 30	248	23 50	279	32 25	324
173	35 13	035	30 21	090	34 02	151	31 40	199	50 04	247	23 22	278	32 09	323
174	35 29	034	30 49	089	34 16	151	31 31	199	49 38	246	22 54	277	31 51	322
175	35 45	033	31 17	088	34 30	150	31 22	198	49 12	246	22 26	276	31 34	321
176	36 00	031	31 45	087	34 44	150	31 13	198	48 47	245	21 58	276	31 16	320
177	36 14	030	32 13	086	34 58	149	31 05	197	48 21	244	21 30	275	30 58	319
178	36 28	029	32 41	085	35 13	148	30 56	196	47 56	244	21 02	274	30 39	318
179	36 42	028	33 09	085	35 28	148	30 49	196	47 31	243	20 34	273	30 20	317

 LAT 62°S

LHA ♈	Hc	Zn	Hc	Zn	Hc	Zn	Hc	Zn	Hc	Zn	Hc	Zn	Hc	Zn
	SPICA		◆ANTARES		Peacock		◆ACHERNAR		CANOPUS		Suhail		◆Alphard	
180	36 54	027	33 37	084	35 43	147	30 41	195	47 06	242	59 01	287	30 00	315
181	37 07	026	34 05	083	35 58	147	30 34	195	46 41	242	58 34	285	29 40	314
182	37 19	024	34 33	082	36 14	146	30 27	194	46 16	241	58 07	284	29 20	313
183	37 30	023	35 01	081	36 30	145	30 20	193	45 52	240	57 40	283	28 59	312
184	37 41	022	35 29	080	36 46	145	30 14	193	45 27	240	57 12	282	28 38	311
185	37 51	021	35 57	079	37 02	144	30 08	192	45 03	239	56 45	281	28 17	310
186	38 01	019	36 24	078	37 19	144	30 02	192	44 39	238	56 17	280	27 55	309
187	38 10	018	36 52	077	37 36	143	29 57	191	44 15	238	55 49	279	27 33	308
188	38 18	017	37 19	076	37 53	142	29 51	190	43 51	237	55 21	278	27 11	307
189	38 26	016	37 46	075	38 10	142	29 47	190	43 28	236	54 53	277	26 48	306
190	38 34	014	38 14	074	38 28	141	29 42	189	43 04	236	54 25	276	26 25	305
191	38 40	013	38 41	073	38 45	141	29 38	188	42 41	235	53 57	275	26 02	304
192	38 46	012	39 08	072	39 03	140	29 34	188	42 18	235	53 29	274	25 38	303
193	38 52	011	39 34	071	39 22	139	29 30	187	41 55	234	53 01	273	25 15	302
194	38 57	009	40 01	070	39 40	139	29 27	187	41 32	233	52 33	273	24 51	301
	SPICA		◆ANTARES		Peacock		◆ACHERNAR		CANOPUS		Suhail		◆Alphard	
195	39 01	008	40 27	069	39 59	138	29 24	186	41 10	233	52 05	272	24 26	300
196	39 05	007	40 53	068	40 18	138	29 21	185	40 48	232	51 37	271	24 02	299
197	39 08	006	41 20	067	40 37	137	29 18	185	40 26	231	51 09	270	23 37	298
198	39 11	004	41 45	066	40 56	136	29 16	184	40 04	231	50 40	269	23 12	297
199	39 12	003	42 11	065	41 15	136	29 14	183	39 42	230	50 12	268	22 47	296
200	39 14	002	42 36	064	41 35	135	29 13	183	39 20	230	49 44	267	22 21	295
201	39 14	001	43 02	063	41 55	135	29 12	182	38 59	229	49 16	266	21 56	294
202	39 14	359	43 27	062	42 15	134	29 11	182	38 38	228	48 48	266	21 30	293
203	39 14	358	43 51	061	42 35	134	29 10	181	38 17	228	48 20	265	21 04	292
204	39 12	357	44 16	060	42 56	133	29 10	180	37 56	227	47 52	264	20 38	291
205	39 11	356	44 40	058	43 17	132	29 10	180	37 36	226	47 24	263	20 12	290
206	39 08	354	45 04	057	43 38	132	29 10	179	37 16	226	46 56	262	19 45	289
207	39 05	353	45 27	056	43 59	131	29 11	178	36 56	225	46 28	261	19 18	288
208	39 01	352	45 50	055	44 20	131	29 11	178	36 36	224	46 00	261	18 52	288
209	38 57	351	46 13	054	44 41	130	29 13	177	36 16	224	45 32	260	18 25	287
	ANTARES		◆Nunki		Peacock		ACHERNAR		◆CANOPUS		Suhail		◆SPICA	
210	46 36	053	30 26	089	45 03	129	29 14	177	35 57	223	45 05	259	38 52	349
211	46 58	051	30 54	088	45 25	129	29 16	176	35 38	223	44 37	258	38 46	348
212	47 20	050	31 22	088	45 47	128	29 18	175	35 19	222	44 10	257	38 40	347
213	47 41	049	31 51	087	46 09	128	29 21	175	35 00	221	43 42	257	38 33	346
214	48 02	048	32 19	086	46 32	127	29 23	174	34 42	221	43 15	256	38 26	344
215	48 23	047	32 47	085	46 54	127	29 26	174	34 23	220	42 47	255	38 18	343
216	48 43	045	33 15	084	47 17	126	29 30	173	34 05	219	42 20	254	38 10	342
217	49 03	044	33 43	083	47 40	125	29 33	172	33 48	219	41 53	254	38 01	341
218	49 22	043	34 11	082	48 03	125	29 37	172	33 30	218	41 26	253	37 51	339
219	49 41	041	34 39	081	48 26	124	29 41	171	33 13	217	40 59	252	37 41	338
220	50 00	040	35 06	080	48 49	124	29 46	170	32 56	217	40 33	251	37 30	337
221	50 18	039	35 34	079	49 13	123	29 51	170	32 39	216	40 06	251	37 19	336
222	50 35	038	36 02	078	49 37	122	29 56	169	32 23	216	39 39	250	37 07	334
223	50 52	036	36 29	077	50 00	122	30 01	169	32 06	215	39 13	249	36 54	333
224	51 08	035	36 57	076	50 24	121	30 07	168	31 50	214	38 47	248	36 41	332
	ANTARES		◆Nunki		FOMALHAUT		ACHERNAR		◆CANOPUS		Suhail		◆SPICA	
225	51 24	033	37 24	075	13 30	129	30 13	167	31 35	214	38 21	248	36 28	331
226	51 39	032	37 51	074	13 52	128	30 19	167	31 19	213	37 55	247	36 14	330
227	51 54	031	38 18	074	14 14	127	30 26	166	31 04	212	37 29	246	36 00	329
228	52 08	029	38 45	073	14 37	127	30 33	166	30 49	212	37 03	245	35 45	327
229	52 21	028	39 12	072	15 00	126	30 40	165	30 34	211	36 38	245	35 29	326
230	52 34	026	39 39	071	15 23	125	30 48	164	30 20	210	36 12	244	35 13	325
231	52 47	025	40 05	069	15 46	124	30 55	164	30 06	210	35 47	243	34 57	324
232	52 58	024	40 31	068	16 09	123	31 03	163	29 52	209	35 22	242	34 40	323
233	53 09	022	40 58	067	16 33	122	31 12	162	29 39	208	34 57	242	34 23	322
234	53 19	021	41 23	066	16 57	122	31 20	162	29 25	208	34 33	241	34 05	320
235	53 29	019	41 49	065	17 21	121	31 29	161	29 12	207	34 08	240	33 47	319
236	53 38	018	42 15	064	17 45	120	31 39	161	29 00	206	33 44	240	33 28	318
237	53 46	016	42 40	063	18 10	119	31 48	160	28 47	206	33 19	239	33 09	317
238	53 53	015	43 05	062	18 34	118	31 58	159	28 35	205	32 55	238	32 50	316
239	54 00	013	43 30	061	18 59	118	32 08	159	28 23	205	32 32	237	32 30	315
	◆ANTARES		Nunki		◆FOMALHAUT		ACHERNAR		CANOPUS		◆ACRUX		SPICA	
240	54 06	012	43 54	060	19 24	117	32 18	158	28 12	204	66 13	243	32 10	314
241	54 12	010	44 18	059	19 50	116	32 29	158	28 00	203	65 48	243	31 50	313
242	54 16	009	44 42	058	20 15	115	32 40	157	27 49	203	65 22	243	31 29	312
243	54 20	007	45 06	057	20 41	114	32 51	156	27 39	202	64 57	242	31 08	311
244	54 23	006	45 29	055	21 06	114	33 02	156	27 28	201	64 33	242	30 46	310
245	54 25	004	45 52	054	21 32	113	33 14	155	27 18	201	64 08	241	30 24	308
246	54 27	002	46 15	053	21 58	112	33 26	155	27 09	200	63 43	241	30 02	307
247	54 28	001	46 37	052	22 24	111	33 38	154	26 59	199	63 19	241	29 39	306
248	54 28	359	46 59	051	22 51	110	33 51	153	26 50	199	62 54	240	29 17	305
249	54 27	358	47 21	049	23 17	110	34 04	153	26 41	198	62 30	240	28 54	304
250	54 26	356	47 42	048	23 44	109	34 17	152	26 33	197	62 05	239	28 30	303
251	54 23	355	48 03	047	24 11	108	34 30	152	26 24	197	61 41	239	28 06	302
252	54 20	353	48 23	046	24 38	107	34 43	151	26 16	196	61 17	238	27 42	301
253	54 17	352	48 43	045	25 05	106	34 57	150	26 09	195	60 53	238	27 18	300
254	54 12	350	49 03	043	25 32	105	35 11	150	26 02	195	60 29	238	26 54	299
	Nunki		◆FOMALHAUT		ACHERNAR		CANOPUS		◆ACRUX		SPICA		◆ANTARES	
255	49 22	042	25 59	105	35 26	149	25 55	194	60 06	237	26 29	298	54 07	349
256	49 41	041	26 26	104	35 40	149	25 48	193	59 42	237	26 04	297	54 01	347
257	49 59	039	26 54	103	35 55	148	25 42	193	59 19	236	25 39	296	53 55	346
258	50 16	038	27 21	102	36 10	147	25 36	192	58 55	236	25 14	295	53 47	344
259	50 33	037	27 49	101	36 25	147	25 30	191	58 32	235	24 48	294	53 39	343
260	50 50	035	28 16	100	36 41	146	25 24	191	58 09	235	24 22	293	53 30	341
261	51 06	034	28 44	100	36 57	146	25 19	190	57 46	234	23 56	292	53 21	340
262	51 21	033	29 12	099	37 13	145	25 15	189	57 23	234	23 30	291	53 11	338
263	51 36	031	29 40	098	37 29	144	25 10	189	57 00	234	23 04	290	53 00	337
264	51 51	030	30 08	097	37 46	144	25 06	188	56 38	233	22 37	290	52 48	335
265	52 04	028	30 36	096	38 02	143	25 02	187	56 15	233	22 11	289	52 36	334
266	52 17	027	31 04	095	38 19	143	24 59	187	55 53	232	21 44	288	52 24	332
267	52 30	026	31 32	094	38 37	142	24 56	186	55 31	232	21 17	287	52 10	331
268	52 42	024	32 00	094	38 54	141	24 53	185	55 09	231	20 50	286	51 56	330
269	52 53	023	32 28	093	39 12	141	24 50	185	54 47	231	20 23	285	51 42	328

LHA ♈	Hc	Zn	Hc	Zn	Hc	Zn	Hc	Zn	Hc	Zn	Hc	Zn	Hc	Zn
	◆ALTAIR		FOMALHAUT		◆ACHERNAR		CANOPUS		◆RIGIL KENT		SPICA		ANTARES	
270	15 51	029	32 56	092	39 30	140	24 48	184	66 44	250	19 56	284	51 27	327
271	16 05	028	33 24	091	39 48	140	24 46	183	66 18	250	19 28	283	51 11	325
272	16 18	027	33 52	090	40 06	139	24 45	183	65 52	249	19 01	282	50 55	324
273	16 30	026	34 21	089	40 25	139	24 44	182	65 25	249	18 33	281	50 38	323
274	16 42	025	34 49	088	40 43	138	24 43	181	64 59	248	18 05	280	50 21	321
275	16 54	024	35 17	087	41 02	137	24 42	181	64 33	248	17 38	279	50 03	320
276	17 05	023	35 45	087	41 22	137	24 42	180	64 07	247	17 10	278	49 44	319
277	17 15	022	36 13	086	41 41	136	24 42	179	63 41	247	16 42	278	49 26	317
278	17 25	021	36 41	085	42 01	136	24 43	179	63 15	246	16 14	277	49 06	316
279	17 35	020	37 09	084	42 20	135	24 44	178	62 49	246	15 46	276	48 47	315
280	17 44	019	37 37	083	42 40	134	24 45	177	62 24	245	15 18	275	48 26	314
281	17 53	018	38 05	082	43 01	134	24 46	177	61 58	245	14 50	274	48 06	312
282	18 01	017	38 33	081	43 21	133	24 48	176	61 33	244	14 22	273	47 45	311
283	18 09	015	39 01	080	43 42	133	24 50	175	61 08	244	13 54	272	47 23	310
284	18 16	014	39 28	079	44 02	132	24 53	175	60 42	243	13 25	271	47 02	309
	◆ALTAIR		FOMALHAUT		◆ACHERNAR		CANOPUS		◆RIGIL KENT		ANTARES		Nunki	
285	18 23	013	39 56	078	44 23	132	24 55	174	60 17	243	46 39	308	54 16	359
286	18 29	012	40 24	077	44 45	131	24 58	173	59 52	242	46 17	306	54 15	357
287	18 35	011	40 51	076	45 06	130	25 02	173	59 28	242	45 54	305	54 13	355
288	18 40	010	41 18	075	45 27	130	25 06	172	59 03	241	45 31	304	54 11	354
289	18 45	009	41 46	074	45 49	129	25 10	171	58 38	241	45 07	303	54 07	352
290	18 50	008	42 13	073	46 11	129	25 14	171	58 14	240	44 44	302	54 03	351
291	18 53	007	42 39	072	46 33	128	25 19	170	57 49	240	44 20	301	53 58	349
292	18 57	006	43 06	071	46 55	128	25 24	169	57 25	239	43 55	300	53 53	348
293	18 59	005	43 33	070	47 18	127	25 29	169	57 01	239	43 31	298	53 47	346
294	19 02	004	43 59	069	47 40	126	25 35	168	56 37	238	43 06	297	53 40	345
295	19 03	003	44 25	068	48 03	126	25 41	167	56 13	238	42 41	296	53 32	343
296	19 05	002	44 51	067	48 26	125	25 47	167	55 49	237	42 15	295	53 23	342
297	19 05	001	45 17	066	48 49	125	25 54	166	55 26	237	41 50	294	53 14	340
298	19 05	000	45 43	065	49 13	124	26 01	165	55 02	236	41 24	293	53 05	339
299	19 05	359	46 08	064	49 36	123	26 08	165	54 39	236	40 58	292	52 54	337
	FOMALHAUT		◆ACHERNAR		CANOPUS		◆RIGIL KENT		ANTARES		Nunki		◆ALTAIR	
300	46 33	063	50 00	123	26 15	164	54 16	235	40 32	291	52 43	336	19 04	358
301	46 58	062	50 23	122	26 23	163	53 53	235	40 05	290	52 31	335	19 03	357
302	47 23	060	50 47	122	26 31	163	53 30	234	39 39	289	52 19	333	19 01	356
303	47 47	059	51 11	121	26 40	162	53 07	234	39 12	288	52 06	332	18 59	355
304	48 11	058	51 35	121	26 49	161	52 45	233	38 45	287	51 52	330	18 56	354
305	48 35	057	52 00	120	26 58	161	52 22	233	38 18	286	51 38	329	18 52	353
306	48 59	056	52 24	119	27 07	160	52 00	232	37 51	285	51 23	328	18 49	352
307	49 22	055	52 49	119	27 17	159	51 38	231	37 24	284	51 08	326	18 44	350
308	49 45	053	53 13	118	27 27	159	51 16	231	36 56	283	50 52	325	18 39	349
309	50 07	052	53 38	118	27 37	158	50 54	230	36 29	282	50 35	323	18 34	348
310	50 29	051	54 03	117	27 48	158	50 33	230	36 01	281	50 18	322	18 28	347
311	50 51	050	54 29	116	27 59	157	50 11	229	35 34	280	50 00	321	18 22	346
312	51 12	048	54 54	116	28 10	156	49 50	229	35 06	279	49 42	319	18 15	345
313	51 33	047	55 19	115	28 22	156	49 29	228	34 38	278	49 24	318	18 07	344
314	51 53	046	55 45	115	28 33	155	49 08	228	34 10	277	49 05	317	17 59	343
	◆FOMALHAUT		ACHERNAR		◆CANOPUS		RIGIL KENT		◆ANTARES		Nunki		ALTAIR	
315	52 13	045	56 10	114	28 45	154	48 47	227	33 42	277	48 45	316	17 51	342
316	52 33	043	56 36	114	28 58	154	48 26	227	33 14	276	48 25	314	17 42	341
317	52 52	042	57 02	113	29 11	153	48 06	226	32 46	275	48 05	313	17 33	340
318	53 11	041	57 28	112	29 23	152	47 45	226	32 18	274	47 44	312	17 23	339
319	53 29	039	57 54	112	29 37	152	47 25	225	31 50	273	47 23	311	17 13	338
320	53 46	038	58 20	111	29 50	151	47 05	225	31 22	272	47 02	309	17 02	337
321	54 03	036	58 47	110	30 04	150	46 46	224	30 54	271	46 40	308	16 51	336
322	54 20	035	59 13	110	30 18	150	46 26	224	30 25	270	46 17	307	16 39	335
323	54 36	034	59 40	109	30 32	149	46 07	223	29 57	269	45 55	306	16 27	334
324	54 51	032	60 06	109	30 47	148	45 48	223	29 29	268	45 32	305	16 15	333
325	55 06	031	60 33	108	31 02	148	45 29	222	29 01	268	45 08	304	16 02	332
326	55 20	029	61 00	107	31 17	147	45 10	222	28 33	267	44 45	302	15 48	331
327	55 33	028	61 27	107	31 32	146	44 51	221	28 05	266	44 21	301	15 34	330
328	55 46	026	61 54	106	31 48	146	44 33	221	27 37	265	43 57	300	15 20	329
329	55 58	025	62 21	105	32 04	145	44 15	220	27 09	264	43 32	299	15 05	328
	◆FOMALHAUT		Diphda		ACHERNAR		◆CANOPUS		RIGIL KENT		◆ANTARES		Nunki	
330	56 09	023	37 27	052	62 48	105	32 20	145	43 57	219	26 41	263	43 07	298
331	56 20	022	37 49	051	63 15	104	32 37	144	43 39	219	26 13	262	42 42	297
332	56 30	020	38 11	050	63 43	104	32 53	143	43 21	218	25 45	262	42 17	296
333	56 40	019	38 32	049	64 10	103	33 10	143	43 04	218	25 17	261	41 52	295
334	56 48	017	38 53	047	64 38	102	33 28	142	42 47	217	24 49	260	41 26	294
335	56 56	015	39 14	046	65 05	101	33 45	141	42 30	217	24 21	259	41 00	293
336	57 03	014	39 34	045	65 33	101	34 03	141	42 13	216	23 54	258	40 34	292
337	57 10	012	39 54	044	66 01	100	34 21	140	41 56	216	23 26	257	40 08	291
338	57 15	011	40 13	043	66 28	099	34 39	139	41 40	215	22 59	256	39 41	290
339	57 20	009	40 32	042	66 56	099	34 57	139	41 24	215	22 31	256	39 15	289
340	57 24	007	40 51	041	67 24	098	35 16	138	41 08	214	22 04	255	38 48	288
341	57 27	006	41 09	039	67 52	097	35 35	138	40 52	214	21 37	254	38 21	287
342	57 30	004	41 26	038	68 20	097	35 54	137	40 37	213	21 10	253	37 54	286
343	57 32	003	41 44	037	68 48	096	36 13	136	40 22	212	20 43	252	37 27	285
344	57 32	001	42 00	036	69 16	095	36 33	136	40 07	212	20 16	252	36 59	284
	◆Diphda		Acamar		◆CANOPUS		RIGIL KENT		◆ANTARES		Nunki		FOMALHAUT	
345	42 16	034	48 42	087	36 53	135	39 52	211	19 50	251	36 32	283	57 32	359
346	42 32	033	49 10	086	37 13	134	39 37	211	19 23	250	36 04	282	57 32	358
347	42 47	032	49 38	085	37 33	134	39 23	210	18 57	249	35 37	281	57 30	356
348	43 02	031	50 06	084	37 53	133	39 09	210	18 31	248	35 09	280	57 28	355
349	43 16	029	50 34	083	38 14	132	38 55	209	18 05	247	34 41	279	57 25	353
350	43 30	028	51 02	082	38 35	132	38 42	209	17 39	247	34 13	278	57 21	351
351	43 43	027	51 30	081	38 56	131	38 28	208	17 13	246	33 46	277	57 16	350
352	43 55	026	51 57	080	39 17	131	38 15	207	16 47	245	33 18	276	57 11	348
353	44 07	024	52 25	079	39 39	130	38 02	207	16 22	244	32 50	275	57 05	347
354	44 18	023	52 53	078	40 01	129	37 50	206	15 57	243	32 21	274	56 58	345
355	44 29	022	53 20	077	40 22	129	37 37	206	15 32	242	31 53	273	56 50	343
356	44 39	020	53 48	076	40 45	128	37 25	205	15 07	242	31 25	273	56 42	342
357	44 49	019	54 15	075	41 07	127	37 13	205	14 42	241	30 57	272	56 33	340
358	44 57	018	54 42	074	41 29	127	37 02	204	14 17	240	30 29	271	56 23	339
359	45 06	016	55 09	073	41 52	126	36 50	204	13 53	239	30 01	270	56 12	337

LAT 63°S

LHA ♈	Hc	Zn	Hc	Zn	Hc	Zn	Hc	Zn	Hc	Zn	Hc	Zn	Hc	Zn
	Diphda		◆ RIGEL		CANOPUS		Miaplacidus		◆ RIGIL KENT		Peacock		◆ FOMALHAUT	
0	44 15	015	12 22	084	42 49	125	45 58	161	37 34	203	63 20	259	55 06	336
1	44 22	013	12 49	083	43 12	124	46 07	160	37 24	203	62 53	258	54 55	335
2	44 28	012	13 16	082	43 34	123	46 16	160	37 13	202	62 27	257	54 43	333
3	44 33	011	13 42	081	43 57	123	46 26	159	37 03	202	62 00	257	54 30	332
4	44 38	009	14 09	080	44 20	122	46 35	159	36 53	201	61 34	256	54 17	330
5	44 42	008	14 36	079	44 43	122	46 45	158	36 43	200	61 07	255	54 03	329
6	44 46	007	15 03	078	45 07	121	46 55	158	36 34	200	60 41	255	53 49	328
7	44 49	005	15 30	077	45 30	120	47 05	158	36 25	199	60 15	254	53 34	326
8	44 51	004	15 56	076	45 54	120	47 16	157	36 16	199	59 49	253	53 19	325
9	44 53	003	16 22	076	46 18	119	47 27	157	36 07	198	59 22	253	53 02	323
10	44 54	001	16 49	075	46 41	118	47 38	156	35 59	198	58 57	252	52 46	322
11	44 54	000	17 15	074	47 06	118	47 49	156	35 51	197	58 31	251	52 29	321
12	44 54	359	17 41	073	47 30	117	48 00	155	35 43	196	58 05	251	52 11	319
13	44 53	357	18 07	072	47 54	116	48 11	155	35 36	196	57 39	250	51 53	318
14	44 52	356	18 33	071	48 19	116	48 23	155	35 28	195	57 14	249	51 35	317
	◆ RIGEL		SIRIUS		CANOPUS		◆ RIGIL KENT		Peacock		◆ FOMALHAUT		Diphda	
15	18 58	070	16 28	095	48 43	115	35 21	195	56 48	249	51 16	315	44 49	355
16	19 24	069	16 55	094	49 08	114	35 14	194	56 23	248	50 57	314	44 47	353
17	19 49	068	17 23	093	49 33	114	35 08	194	55 58	247	50 37	313	44 43	352
18	20 15	067	17 50	092	49 58	113	35 02	193	55 33	247	50 17	311	44 39	351
19	20 40	066	18 17	091	50 23	112	34 56	192	55 08	246	49 56	310	44 34	349
20	21 04	065	18 44	090	50 48	111	34 50	192	54 43	246	49 35	309	44 29	348
21	21 29	064	19 11	089	51 14	111	34 45	191	54 18	245	49 14	308	44 23	347
22	21 53	063	19 39	088	51 39	110	34 40	191	53 53	244	48 52	307	44 17	345
23	22 18	062	20 06	088	52 05	109	34 35	190	53 29	244	48 30	305	44 09	344
24	22 42	061	20 33	087	52 31	109	34 30	189	53 05	243	48 08	304	44 02	343
25	23 05	060	21 00	086	52 57	108	34 26	189	52 40	242	47 45	303	43 53	341
26	23 29	059	21 27	085	53 23	107	34 22	188	52 16	242	47 22	302	43 44	340
27	23 52	058	21 55	084	53 49	107	34 18	188	51 52	241	46 59	301	43 35	339
28	24 15	057	22 22	083	54 15	106	34 14	187	51 28	241	46 35	300	43 25	338
29	24 38	056	22 49	082	54 41	105	34 11	187	51 05	240	46 11	298	43 14	336
	◆ RIGEL		SIRIUS		CANOPUS		◆ RIGIL KENT		Peacock		◆ FOMALHAUT		Diphda	
30	25 01	055	23 16	081	55 07	104	34 08	186	50 41	239	45 47	297	43 03	335
31	25 23	054	23 42	080	55 34	104	34 05	185	50 18	239	45 23	296	42 51	334
32	25 45	053	24 09	079	56 00	103	34 03	185	49 55	238	44 58	295	42 39	332
33	26 06	052	24 36	078	56 27	102	34 01	184	49 32	238	44 34	294	42 26	331
34	26 28	051	25 03	077	56 54	101	33 59	184	49 09	237	44 09	293	42 13	330
35	26 49	050	25 29	077	57 20	101	33 57	183	48 46	236	43 43	292	41 59	329
36	27 10	049	25 56	076	57 47	100	33 56	182	48 23	236	43 18	291	41 44	328
37	27 30	048	26 22	075	58 14	099	33 55	182	48 01	235	42 53	290	41 29	326
38	27 50	047	26 48	074	58 41	098	33 54	181	47 39	235	42 27	289	41 14	325
39	28 10	046	27 14	073	59 08	098	33 54	181	47 16	234	42 01	288	40 58	324
40	28 29	045	27 40	072	59 35	097	33 54	180	46 55	233	41 35	287	40 42	323
41	28 48	044	28 06	071	60 02	096	33 54	180	46 33	233	41 09	286	40 25	321
42	29 07	043	28 32	070	60 29	095	33 54	179	46 11	232	40 43	285	40 08	320
43	29 25	042	28 57	069	60 56	094	33 55	178	45 50	232	40 16	284	39 50	319
44	29 43	041	29 22	068	61 23	094	33 56	178	45 28	231	39 50	283	39 32	318
	RIGEL		◆ SIRIUS		CANOPUS		◆ RIGIL KENT		Peacock		FOMALHAUT		◆ Diphda	
45	30 01	040	29 48	067	61 51	093	33 57	177	45 07	230	39 23	282	39 14	317
46	30 18	038	30 13	066	62 18	092	33 59	177	44 46	230	38 56	281	38 55	316
47	30 35	037	30 37	065	62 45	091	34 00	176	44 26	229	38 30	280	38 36	314
48	30 51	036	31 02	064	63 12	090	34 02	175	44 05	229	38 03	279	38 16	313
49	31 07	035	31 26	063	63 40	089	34 05	175	43 45	228	37 36	278	37 56	312
50	31 22	034	31 50	062	64 07	088	34 07	174	43 25	227	37 09	277	37 36	311
51	31 37	033	32 14	061	64 34	087	34 10	174	43 05	227	36 42	276	37 15	310
52	31 52	032	32 38	060	65 01	086	34 13	173	42 45	226	36 15	275	36 54	309
53	32 06	031	33 01	059	65 28	085	34 17	172	42 26	226	35 48	274	36 32	308
54	32 20	029	33 24	058	65 55	084	34 20	172	42 06	225	35 20	273	36 11	307
55	32 33	028	33 47	057	66 23	083	34 24	171	41 47	224	34 53	273	35 49	306
56	32 45	027	34 10	056	66 50	082	34 29	171	41 28	224	34 26	272	35 26	304
57	32 58	026	34 32	055	67 17	081	34 33	170	41 09	223	33 59	271	35 04	303
58	33 09	025	34 54	053	67 43	080	34 38	170	40 51	223	33 31	270	34 41	302
59	33 20	024	35 16	052	68 10	079	34 43	169	40 32	222	33 04	269	34 18	301
	RIGEL		◆ SIRIUS		Suhail		◆ RIGIL KENT		Peacock		FOMALHAUT		◆ Diphda	
60	33 31	023	35 37	051	43 22	103	34 48	168	40 14	221	32 37	268	33 54	300
61	33 41	021	35 58	050	43 48	103	34 54	168	39 56	221	32 10	267	33 31	299
62	33 51	020	36 19	049	44 15	102	35 00	167	39 39	220	31 43	266	33 07	298
63	34 00	019	36 40	048	44 41	101	35 06	167	39 21	220	31 15	265	32 43	297
64	34 09	018	37 00	047	45 08	100	35 12	166	39 04	219	30 48	265	32 18	296
65	34 17	017	37 19	046	45 35	099	35 19	165	38 47	218	30 21	264	31 54	295
66	34 24	015	37 39	045	46 02	099	35 26	165	38 30	218	29 54	263	31 29	294
67	34 31	014	37 58	043	46 29	098	35 33	164	38 14	217	29 27	262	31 04	293
68	34 38	013	38 16	042	46 56	097	35 41	164	37 57	217	29 00	261	30 39	292
69	34 44	012	38 34	041	47 23	096	35 48	163	37 41	216	28 33	260	30 13	291
70	34 49	011	38 52	040	47 50	095	35 57	163	37 25	215	28 06	259	29 48	290
71	34 54	009	39 09	039	48 17	094	36 05	162	37 10	215	27 40	259	29 22	289
72	34 58	008	39 26	038	48 44	094	36 13	161	36 54	214	27 13	258	28 57	288
73	35 01	007	39 42	036	49 12	093	36 22	161	36 39	213	26 46	257	28 31	287
74	35 04	006	39 58	035	49 39	092	36 31	160	36 24	213	26 20	256	28 04	286
	RIGEL		◆ SIRIUS		Suhail		◆ RIGIL KENT		Peacock		ACHERNAR		◆ Diphda	
75	35 07	005	40 14	034	50 06	091	36 40	160	36 10	212	64 53	260	27 38	285
76	35 09	003	40 29	033	50 33	090	36 50	159	35 55	212	64 26	259	27 12	284
77	35 10	002	40 43	032	51 01	089	37 00	159	35 41	211	63 59	259	26 45	283
78	35 11	001	40 57	030	51 28	088	37 10	158	35 27	210	63 33	258	26 19	282
79	35 11	000	41 11	029	51 55	087	37 20	157	35 14	210	63 06	257	25 52	281
80	35 11	359	41 24	028	52 22	086	37 31	157	35 00	209	62 40	256	25 26	281
81	35 10	357	41 36	027	52 49	085	37 42	156	34 47	209	62 13	256	24 59	280
82	35 08	356	41 48	025	53 17	085	37 53	156	34 34	208	61 47	255	24 32	279
83	35 06	355	41 59	024	53 44	084	38 04	155	34 21	207	61 21	254	24 05	278
84	35 03	354	42 10	023	54 11	083	38 16	155	34 09	207	60 54	254	23 38	277
85	35 00	353	42 21	022	54 38	082	38 27	154	33 57	206	60 28	253	23 11	276
86	34 56	351	42 30	020	55 05	081	38 39	153	33 45	206	60 02	252	22 44	275
87	34 52	350	42 39	019	55 31	080	38 52	153	33 33	205	59 36	252	22 17	274
88	34 47	349	42 48	018	55 58	079	39 04	152	33 22	204	59 10	251	21 49	273
89	34 41	348	42 56	016	56 25	078	39 17	152	33 11	204	58 45	251	21 22	272

LHA ♈	Hc	Zn	Hc	Zn	Hc	Zn	Hc	Zn	Hc	Zn	Hc	Zn	Hc	Zn
	◆ SIRIUS		Suhail		◆ RIGIL KENT		Peacock		◆ ACHERNAR		Acamar		RIGEL	
90	43 03	015	56 51	077	39 30	151	33 00	203	58 19	250	55 02	289	34 35	347
91	43 10	014	57 18	075	39 43	151	32 50	202	57 54	249	54 36	288	34 29	345
92	43 16	012	57 44	074	39 57	150	32 39	202	57 28	249	54 10	287	34 22	344
93	43 22	011	58 10	073	40 10	150	32 29	201	57 03	248	53 44	286	34 14	343
94	43 27	010	58 36	072	40 24	149	32 20	201	56 38	247	53 17	285	34 06	342
95	43 31	009	59 02	071	40 39	148	32 10	200	56 13	247	52 51	284	33 57	341
96	43 35	007	59 28	070	40 53	148	32 01	199	55 48	246	52 24	282	33 47	339
97	43 38	006	59 53	069	41 08	147	31 52	199	55 23	246	51 58	281	33 38	338
98	43 41	005	60 19	068	41 22	147	31 44	198	54 58	245	51 31	280	33 27	337
99	43 42	003	60 44	066	41 37	146	31 35	197	54 33	244	51 04	279	33 16	336
100	43 44	002	61 08	065	41 53	146	31 27	197	54 09	244	50 37	279	33 05	335
101	43 44	001	61 33	064	42 08	145	31 20	196	53 45	243	50 10	278	32 53	334
102	43 44	359	61 57	063	42 24	144	31 12	196	53 20	242	49 43	277	32 41	332
103	43 44	358	62 21	061	42 40	144	31 05	195	52 56	242	49 16	276	32 28	331
104	43 42	357	62 45	060	42 56	143	30 58	194	52 32	241	48 49	275	32 15	330
	Alphard		◆ Gienah		RIGIL KENT		◆ Peacock		ACHERNAR		◆ RIGEL		SIRIUS	
105	29 33	043	20 34	089	43 12	143	30 52	194	52 09	241	32 01	329	43 40	355
106	29 51	042	21 01	088	43 29	142	30 45	193	51 45	240	31 46	328	43 38	354
107	30 09	041	21 28	087	43 46	142	30 39	192	51 21	239	31 32	327	43 35	353
108	30 27	040	21 56	086	44 03	141	30 33	192	50 58	239	31 17	326	43 31	351
109	30 44	039	22 23	085	44 20	141	30 28	191	50 35	238	31 01	324	43 26	350
110	31 01	038	22 50	084	44 37	140	30 23	191	50 12	238	30 45	323	43 21	349
111	31 18	037	23 17	083	44 55	140	30 18	190	49 49	237	30 29	322	43 16	347
112	31 34	036	23 44	082	45 13	139	30 14	189	49 26	236	30 12	321	43 09	346
113	31 49	034	24 11	081	45 31	138	30 09	189	49 03	236	29 54	320	43 03	345
114	32 05	033	24 38	080	45 49	138	30 05	188	48 41	235	29 37	319	42 55	343
115	32 19	032	25 05	080	46 07	137	30 02	187	48 19	235	29 19	318	42 47	342
116	32 34	031	25 31	079	46 26	137	29 58	187	47 57	234	29 00	317	42 39	341
117	32 47	030	25 58	078	46 44	136	29 55	186	47 35	233	28 41	316	42 29	340
118	33 01	029	26 25	077	47 03	136	29 53	186	47 13	233	28 22	315	42 20	338
119	33 14	028	26 51	076	47 22	135	29 50	185	46 51	232	28 03	314	42 09	337
	Alphard		◆ SPICA		RIGIL KENT		◆ Peacock		ACHERNAR		◆ RIGEL		SIRIUS	
120	33 26	026	13 51	088	47 42	135	29 48	184	46 30	232	27 43	313	41 58	336
121	33 38	025	14 19	087	48 01	134	29 46	184	46 08	231	27 23	312	41 47	335
122	33 49	024	14 46	086	48 21	134	29 44	183	45 47	230	27 02	310	41 35	333
123	34 00	023	15 13	085	48 41	133	29 43	182	45 26	230	26 41	309	41 22	332
124	34 11	022	15 40	084	49 01	133	29 42	182	45 06	229	26 20	308	41 09	331
125	34 20	021	16 07	083	49 21	132	29 42	181	44 45	229	25 58	307	40 56	330
126	34 30	019	16 34	082	49 41	131	29 41	180	44 25	228	25 37	306	40 42	328
127	34 38	018	17 01	081	50 02	131	29 41	180	44 05	227	25 15	305	40 27	327
128	34 47	017	17 28	080	50 22	130	29 41	179	43 45	227	24 52	304	40 12	326
129	34 54	016	17 55	079	50 43	130	29 42	179	43 25	226	24 30	303	39 57	325
130	35 02	015	18 22	079	51 04	129	29 43	178	43 05	226	24 07	302	39 41	324
131	35 08	013	18 48	078	51 25	129	29 44	177	42 46	225	23 44	301	39 24	322
132	35 14	012	19 15	077	51 47	128	29 45	177	42 27	225	23 20	300	39 08	321
133	35 20	011	19 41	076	52 08	128	29 47	176	42 08	224	22 57	299	38 50	320
134	35 25	010	20 08	075	52 30	127	29 49	175	41 49	223	22 33	298	38 32	319
	REGULUS		◆ SPICA		RIGIL KENT		◆ Peacock		ACHERNAR		CANOPUS		◆ SIRIUS	
135	13 55	017	20 34	074	52 51	127	29 51	175	41 30	223	67 20	279	38 14	318
136	14 03	016	21 00	073	53 13	126	29 54	174	41 12	222	66 53	278	37 56	316
137	14 11	015	21 26	072	53 36	126	29 57	173	40 54	222	66 26	277	37 37	315
138	14 18	014	21 52	071	53 58	125	30 00	173	40 36	221	65 59	276	37 17	314
139	14 24	013	22 17	070	54 20	124	30 04	172	40 18	220	65 32	275	36 58	313
140	14 30	012	22 43	069	54 43	124	30 08	172	40 00	220	65 05	274	36 38	312
141	14 36	011	23 08	068	55 05	123	30 12	171	39 43	219	64 38	273	36 17	311
142	14 41	010	23 34	067	55 28	123	30 16	170	39 26	219	64 11	272	35 56	310
143	14 46	009	23 59	066	55 51	122	30 21	170	39 09	218	63 43	271	35 35	309
144	14 50	008	24 23	065	56 14	122	30 26	169	38 53	217	63 16	270	35 14	308
145	14 54	007	24 48	064	56 37	121	30 31	168	38 36	217	62 49	269	34 52	306
146	14 57	006	25 12	063	57 01	121	30 37	168	38 20	216	62 22	268	34 30	305
147	15 00	005	25 37	062	57 24	120	30 43	167	38 04	216	61 55	267	34 08	304
148	15 02	004	26 01	061	57 48	120	30 49	167	37 48	215	61 27	267	33 45	303
149	15 04	003	26 24	060	58 12	119	30 55	166	37 33	214	61 00	266	33 22	302
	REGULUS		◆ SPICA		RIGIL KENT		◆ Peacock		ACHERNAR		CANOPUS		◆ SIRIUS	
150	15 05	002	26 48	059	58 35	119	31 02	165	37 18	214	60 33	265	32 59	301
151	15 06	001	27 11	058	58 59	118	31 09	165	37 03	213	60 06	264	32 36	300
152	15 06	000	27 34	057	59 23	118	31 17	164	36 48	213	59 39	263	32 12	299
153	15 06	359	27 57	056	59 48	117	31 24	163	36 33	212	59 12	263	31 48	298
154	15 06	358	28 20	055	60 12	116	31 32	163	36 19	211	58 45	262	31 24	297
155	15 05	357	28 42	054	60 36	116	31 40	162	36 05	211	58 18	261	31 00	296
156	15 03	356	29 04	053	61 01	115	31 49	162	35 51	210	57 51	260	30 35	295
157	15 01	355	29 25	052	61 26	115	31 57	161	35 38	209	57 24	259	30 10	294
158	14 59	354	29 47	051	61 50	114	32 06	160	35 24	209	56 57	259	29 45	293
159	14 56	353	30 08	050	62 15	114	32 16	160	35 11	208	56 31	258	29 20	292
160	14 52	352	30 29	049	62 40	113	32 25	159	34 59	208	56 04	257	28 55	291
161	14 48	351	30 49	048	63 05	113	32 35	158	34 46	207	55 38	256	28 29	290
162	14 44	350	31 09	047	63 31	112	32 45	158	34 34	206	55 11	256	28 04	289
163	14 39	349	31 29	046	63 56	112	32 56	157	34 22	206	54 45	255	27 38	288
164	14 34	348	31 48	045	64 21	111	33 06	157	34 10	205	54 19	254	27 12	287
	◆ SPICA		ANTARES		◆ Peacock		ACHERNAR		CANOPUS		◆ SIRIUS		Alphard	
165	32 07	044	26 43	096	33 17	156	33 59	205	53 52	254	26 46	286	33 16	333
166	32 25	042	27 10	096	33 29	155	33 47	204	53 26	253	26 19	285	33 03	331
167	32 44	041	27 37	095	33 40	155	33 36	203	53 00	252	25 53	284	32 50	330
168	33 01	040	28 04	094	33 52	154	33 26	203	52 34	251	25 27	283	32 36	329
169	33 19	039	28 31	093	34 04	154	33 15	202	52 09	251	25 00	282	32 22	328
170	33 36	038	28 59	092	34 16	153	33 05	202	51 43	250	24 33	281	32 07	327
171	33 52	037	29 26	091	34 29	152	32 55	201	51 18	249	24 07	281	31 52	326
172	34 08	036	29 53	090	34 42	152	32 46	200	50 52	249	23 40	280	31 36	325
173	34 24	035	30 20	089	34 55	151	32 36	200	50 27	248	23 13	279	31 20	324
174	34 39	033	30 48	088	35 08	150	32 27	199	50 02	247	22 46	278	31 04	322
175	34 54	032	31 15	088	35 22	150	32 19	198	49 37	247	22 19	277	30 47	321
176	35 08	031	31 42	087	35 35	149	32 10	198	49 12	246	21 52	276	30 30	320
177	35 22	030	32 09	086	35 49	149	32 02	197	48 47	245	21 25	275	30 12	319
178	35 36	029	32 36	085	36 04	148	31 54	197	48 22	245	20 58	274	29 54	318
179	35 48	028	33 03	084	36 18	147	31 46	196	47 58	244	20 31	273	29 36	317

 LAT 63°S

LHA ♈	Hc	Zn	Hc	Zn	Hc	Zn	Hc	Zn	Hc	Zn	Hc	Zn	Hc	Zn
	SPICA		◆ANTARES		Peacock		◆ACHERNAR		CANOPUS		Suhail		◆Alphard	
180	36 01	026	33 30	083	36 33	147	31 39	195	47 33	243	58 43	288	29 17	316
181	36 13	025	33 57	082	36 48	146	31 32	195	47 09	243	58 17	287	28 58	315
182	36 24	024	34 24	081	37 03	146	31 25	194	46 45	242	57 51	286	28 38	314
183	36 35	023	34 51	080	37 19	145	31 19	193	46 21	241	57 25	285	28 19	313
184	36 45	022	35 18	079	37 35	144	31 12	193	45 57	241	56 59	284	27 58	312
185	36 55	020	35 45	078	37 51	144	31 06	192	45 33	240	56 32	283	27 38	311
186	37 04	019	36 11	077	38 07	143	31 01	192	45 10	239	56 05	282	27 17	310
187	37 13	018	36 38	076	38 23	143	30 55	191	44 47	239	55 39	281	26 56	308
188	37 21	017	37 04	075	38 40	142	30 50	190	44 23	238	55 12	280	26 34	307
189	37 28	016	37 31	074	38 57	141	30 46	190	44 00	237	54 45	279	26 13	306
190	37 35	014	37 57	073	39 14	141	30 41	189	43 38	237	54 18	278	25 50	305
191	37 42	013	38 23	072	39 32	140	30 37	189	43 15	236	53 51	277	25 28	304
192	37 48	012	38 49	071	39 49	139	30 33	188	42 52	235	53 24	276	25 06	303
193	37 53	011	39 15	070	40 07	139	30 30	187	42 30	235	52 57	275	24 43	302
194	37 58	009	39 40	069	40 25	138	30 26	187	42 08	234	52 30	274	24 20	301
	SPICA		◆ANTARES		Peacock		◆ACHERNAR		CANOPUS		Suhail		◆Alphard	
195	38 02	008	40 06	068	40 43	138	30 23	186	41 46	233	52 02	273	23 56	300
196	38 05	007	40 31	067	41 02	137	30 21	185	41 24	233	51 35	272	23 33	299
197	38 08	006	40 56	066	41 20	136	30 18	185	41 03	232	51 08	271	23 09	298
198	38 11	004	41 21	065	41 39	136	30 16	184	40 41	231	50 41	270	22 45	297
199	38 13	003	41 45	064	41 58	135	30 14	183	40 20	231	50 14	269	22 20	296
200	38 14	002	42 10	063	42 18	135	30 13	183	39 59	230	49 46	268	21 56	295
201	38 14	001	42 34	062	42 37	134	30 12	182	39 38	229	49 19	268	21 31	295
202	38 14	359	42 58	061	42 57	133	30 11	182	39 18	229	48 52	267	21 06	294
203	38 14	358	43 21	060	43 17	133	30 10	181	38 57	228	48 25	266	20 41	293
204	38 12	357	43 45	059	43 37	132	30 10	180	38 37	228	47 58	265	20 16	292
205	38 11	356	44 08	058	43 57	132	30 10	180	38 17	227	47 30	264	19 51	291
206	38 08	354	44 31	056	44 17	131	30 10	179	37 57	226	47 03	263	19 25	290
207	38 05	353	44 53	055	44 38	130	30 11	178	37 38	226	46 36	262	18 59	289
208	38 02	352	45 16	054	44 59	130	30 11	178	37 18	225	46 09	262	18 33	288
209	37 58	351	45 37	053	45 20	129	30 13	177	36 59	224	45 42	261	18 07	287
	ANTARES		◆Nunki		Peacock		ACHERNAR		◆CANOPUS		Suhail		◆SPICA	
210	45 59	052	30 25	089	45 41	129	30 14	177	36 40	224	45 16	260	37 53	349
211	46 20	051	30 52	088	46 02	128	30 16	176	36 22	223	44 49	259	37 48	348
212	46 41	049	31 20	087	46 24	127	30 18	175	36 03	222	44 22	258	37 42	347
213	47 02	048	31 47	086	46 45	127	30 20	175	35 45	222	43 55	258	37 35	346
214	47 22	047	32 14	085	47 07	126	30 23	174	35 27	221	43 29	257	37 28	344
215	47 41	046	32 41	084	47 29	126	30 26	173	35 09	220	43 02	256	37 21	343
216	48 01	044	33 08	083	47 52	125	30 29	173	34 52	220	42 36	255	37 13	342
217	48 20	043	33 35	082	48 14	124	30 33	172	34 34	219	42 10	254	37 04	341
218	48 38	042	34 02	081	48 37	124	30 36	172	34 17	218	41 44	254	36 55	340
219	48 56	041	34 29	081	48 59	123	30 41	171	34 00	218	41 17	253	36 45	338
220	49 14	039	34 56	080	49 22	123	30 45	170	33 44	217	40 51	252	36 35	337
221	49 31	038	35 23	079	49 45	122	30 50	170	33 27	217	40 26	251	36 24	336
222	49 47	037	35 49	078	50 08	121	30 55	169	33 11	216	40 00	251	36 13	335
223	50 03	035	36 16	077	50 32	121	31 00	168	32 55	215	39 34	250	36 01	334
224	50 19	034	36 42	076	50 55	120	31 06	168	32 40	215	39 09	249	35 48	332
	ANTARES		◆Nunki		FOMALHAUT		ACHERNAR		◆CANOPUS		Suhail		◆SPICA	
225	50 34	033	37 09	075	14 08	129	31 12	167	32 25	214	38 43	248	35 35	331
226	50 48	031	37 35	074	14 29	128	31 18	167	32 09	213	38 18	248	35 22	330
227	51 02	030	38 01	073	14 51	127	31 24	166	31 55	213	37 53	247	35 08	329
228	51 16	029	38 27	072	15 13	126	31 31	165	31 40	212	37 28	246	34 54	328
229	51 28	027	38 53	071	15 35	125	31 38	165	31 26	211	37 03	245	34 39	327
230	51 40	026	39 18	070	15 57	125	31 45	164	31 12	211	36 38	245	34 24	325
231	51 52	024	39 44	069	16 19	124	31 53	163	30 58	210	36 14	244	34 08	324
232	52 03	023	40 09	068	16 42	123	32 01	163	30 45	209	35 50	243	33 52	323
233	52 13	022	40 34	067	17 05	122	32 09	162	30 31	209	35 25	242	33 36	322
234	52 23	020	40 59	066	17 28	121	32 17	162	30 18	208	35 01	242	33 19	321
235	52 32	019	41 24	065	17 52	121	32 26	161	30 06	207	34 37	241	33 01	320
236	52 40	017	41 48	063	18 15	120	32 35	160	29 53	207	34 14	240	32 44	319
237	52 48	016	42 13	062	18 39	119	32 44	160	29 41	206	33 50	239	32 25	318
238	52 55	014	42 37	061	19 03	118	32 54	159	29 29	205	33 27	239	32 07	316
239	53 02	013	43 00	060	19 27	117	33 04	159	29 18	205	33 04	238	31 48	315
	◆ANTARES		Nunki		◆FOMALHAUT		ACHERNAR		CANOPUS		◆ACRUX		SPICA	
240	53 07	011	43 24	059	19 51	116	33 14	158	29 07	204	66 39	246	31 29	314
241	53 12	010	43 47	058	20 16	116	33 24	157	28 56	203	66 14	245	31 09	313
242	53 17	008	44 10	057	20 40	115	33 35	157	28 45	203	65 49	245	30 49	312
243	53 20	007	44 33	056	21 05	114	33 46	156	28 34	202	65 25	244	30 28	311
244	53 23	005	44 55	055	21 30	113	33 57	155	28 24	201	65 00	244	30 08	310
245	53 25	004	45 17	053	21 55	112	34 08	155	28 15	201	64 36	243	29 47	309
246	53 27	002	45 39	052	22 21	112	34 20	154	28 05	200	64 11	243	29 25	308
247	53 28	001	46 00	051	22 46	111	34 32	154	27 56	199	63 47	242	29 04	307
248	53 28	359	46 21	050	23 11	110	34 44	153	27 47	199	63 23	242	28 42	306
249	53 27	358	46 42	049	23 37	109	34 57	152	27 38	198	62 59	241	28 19	305
250	53 26	356	47 02	047	24 03	108	35 10	152	27 30	197	62 35	241	27 57	304
251	53 24	355	47 22	046	24 29	107	35 23	151	27 22	197	62 12	240	27 34	303
252	53 21	353	47 41	045	24 55	107	35 36	151	27 14	196	61 48	240	27 11	302
253	53 17	352	48 00	044	25 21	106	35 49	150	27 07	195	61 24	240	26 48	301
254	53 13	350	48 19	042	25 47	105	36 03	149	27 00	195	61 01	239	26 24	300
	Nunki		◆FOMALHAUT		ACHERNAR		CANOPUS		◆ACRUX		SPICA		◆ANTARES	
255	48 37	041	26 14	104	36 17	149	26 53	194	60 38	239	26 01	299	53 08	349
256	48 55	040	26 40	103	36 31	148	26 46	193	60 14	238	25 36	298	53 03	347
257	49 12	039	27 07	102	36 46	148	26 40	193	59 51	238	25 12	297	52 56	346
258	49 29	037	27 33	102	37 01	147	26 34	192	59 28	237	24 48	296	52 49	344
259	49 45	036	28 00	101	37 16	146	26 29	191	59 06	237	24 23	295	52 42	343
260	50 01	035	28 27	100	37 31	146	26 23	191	58 43	236	23 58	294	52 34	342
261	50 16	033	28 54	099	37 46	145	26 18	190	58 20	236	23 33	293	52 25	340
262	50 31	032	29 21	098	38 02	145	26 14	189	57 58	235	23 08	292	52 15	339
263	50 45	031	29 48	097	38 18	144	26 10	189	57 35	235	22 43	291	52 05	337
264	50 58	029	30 15	096	38 34	143	26 06	188	57 13	234	22 17	290	51 54	336
265	51 11	028	30 42	096	38 50	143	26 02	187	56 51	234	21 52	289	51 42	334
266	51 24	026	31 09	095	39 07	142	25 58	187	56 29	233	21 26	288	51 30	333
267	51 36	025	31 36	094	39 24	142	25 55	186	56 07	233	21 00	287	51 18	332
268	51 47	024	32 03	093	39 41	141	25 53	185	55 46	232	20 34	286	51 04	330
269	51 58	022	32 31	092	39 58	140	25 50	185	55 24	232	20 07	285	50 51	329

LHA ♈	Hc	Zn	Hc	Zn	Hc	Zn	Hc	Zn	Hc	Zn	Hc	Zn	Hc	Zn
	◆ALTAIR		FOMALHAUT		◆ACHERNAR		CANOPUS		◆RIGIL KENT		SPICA		ANTARES	
270	14 59	029	32 58	091	40 16	140	25 48	184	67 04	253	19 41	284	50 36	327
271	15 12	028	33 25	090	40 33	139	25 46	183	66 38	252	19 15	283	50 21	326
272	15 24	027	33 52	089	40 51	139	25 45	183	66 12	251	18 48	282	50 06	325
273	15 36	026	34 19	089	41 09	138	25 44	182	65 46	251	18 21	281	49 50	323
274	15 47	025	34 47	088	41 28	137	25 43	181	65 20	250	17 55	281	49 33	322
275	15 59	024	35 14	087	41 46	137	25 42	181	64 55	250	17 28	280	49 16	321
276	16 09	023	35 41	086	42 05	136	25 42	180	64 29	249	17 01	279	48 59	320
277	16 19	022	36 08	085	42 24	136	25 42	179	64 04	249	16 34	278	48 41	318
278	16 29	021	36 35	084	42 43	135	25 43	179	63 39	248	16 07	277	48 23	317
279	16 39	019	37 02	083	43 03	134	25 44	178	63 13	247	15 40	276	48 04	316
280	16 47	018	37 29	082	43 22	134	25 45	177	62 48	247	15 13	275	47 45	314
281	16 56	017	37 56	081	43 42	133	25 46	177	62 23	246	14 46	274	47 25	313
282	17 04	016	38 23	080	44 02	133	25 48	176	61 58	246	14 18	273	47 05	312
283	17 11	015	38 50	079	44 22	132	25 50	175	61 33	245	13 51	272	46 45	311
284	17 18	014	39 17	078	44 42	131	25 52	175	61 09	245	13 24	272	46 24	310
	◆ALTAIR		FOMALHAUT		◆ACHERNAR		CANOPUS		◆RIGIL KENT		ANTARES		Nunki	
285	17 25	013	39 43	077	45 03	131	25 55	174	60 44	244	46 03	308	53 16	359
286	17 31	012	40 10	076	45 24	130	25 58	173	60 20	244	45 41	307	53 15	357
287	17 36	011	40 36	075	45 44	130	26 01	173	59 55	243	45 19	306	53 14	356
288	17 41	010	41 03	074	46 06	129	26 05	172	59 31	243	44 57	305	53 11	354
289	17 46	009	41 29	073	46 27	128	26 09	171	59 07	242	44 34	304	53 08	353
290	17 50	008	41 55	072	46 48	128	26 13	171	58 43	242	44 12	303	53 04	351
291	17 54	007	42 21	071	47 10	127	26 18	170	58 19	241	43 49	302	52 59	350
292	17 57	006	42 46	070	47 32	127	26 23	169	57 55	240	43 25	300	52 54	348
293	18 00	005	43 12	069	47 54	126	26 28	169	57 32	240	43 02	299	52 48	347
294	18 02	004	43 37	068	48 16	125	26 33	168	57 08	239	42 38	298	52 42	345
295	18 03	003	44 03	067	48 38	125	26 39	167	56 45	239	42 14	297	52 34	344
296	18 05	002	44 28	066	49 00	124	26 45	167	56 22	238	41 49	296	52 26	342
297	18 05	001	44 52	065	49 23	124	26 52	166	55 58	238	41 25	295	52 18	341
298	18 05	000	45 17	064	49 46	123	26 59	165	55 35	237	41 00	294	52 08	339
299	18 05	359	45 41	063	50 09	122	27 06	165	55 13	237	40 35	293	51 59	338
	FOMALHAUT		◆ACHERNAR		CANOPUS		◆RIGIL KENT		ANTARES		Nunki		◆ALTAIR	
300	46 06	062	50 32	122	27 13	164	54 50	236	40 10	292	51 48	337	18 04	358
301	46 29	061	50 55	121	27 21	163	54 27	236	39 44	291	51 37	335	18 03	357
302	46 53	060	51 18	121	27 29	163	54 05	235	39 19	290	51 25	334	18 01	356
303	47 16	058	51 42	120	27 37	162	53 43	235	38 53	289	51 13	332	17 59	355
304	47 39	057	52 05	119	27 46	161	53 20	234	38 27	288	51 00	331	17 56	354
305	48 02	056	52 29	119	27 54	161	52 58	234	38 01	287	50 46	330	17 53	353
306	48 25	055	52 53	118	28 04	160	52 37	233	37 35	286	50 32	328	17 49	352
307	48 47	054	53 17	118	28 13	159	52 15	232	37 09	285	50 18	327	17 45	351
308	49 09	052	53 41	117	28 23	159	51 53	232	36 42	284	50 02	325	17 40	350
309	49 30	051	54 06	116	28 33	158	51 32	231	36 16	283	49 47	324	17 35	348
310	49 51	050	54 30	116	28 43	157	51 11	231	35 49	282	49 30	323	17 29	347
311	50 12	049	54 55	115	28 54	157	50 50	230	35 23	281	49 14	322	17 23	346
312	50 32	048	55 19	115	29 05	156	50 29	230	34 56	280	48 57	320	17 17	345
313	50 52	046	55 44	114	29 16	155	50 08	229	34 29	279	48 39	319	17 09	344
314	51 11	045	56 09	113	29 28	155	49 48	229	34 02	278	48 21	318	17 02	343
	◆FOMALHAUT		ACHERNAR		◆CANOPUS		RIGIL KENT		◆ANTARES		Nunki		ALTAIR	
315	51 30	044	56 34	113	29 39	154	49 27	228	33 35	277	48 02	316	16 54	342
316	51 49	042	56 59	112	29 52	153	49 07	228	33 08	276	47 43	315	16 45	341
317	52 07	041	57 25	111	30 04	153	48 47	227	32 41	275	47 24	314	16 36	340
318	52 25	040	57 50	111	30 17	152	48 27	227	32 14	274	47 04	313	16 27	339
319	52 42	038	58 16	110	30 29	151	48 07	226	31 46	273	46 44	311	16 17	338
320	52 59	037	58 41	110	30 43	151	47 48	226	31 19	273	46 23	310	16 07	337
321	53 15	036	59 07	109	30 56	150	47 28	225	30 52	272	46 02	309	15 56	336
322	53 30	034	59 33	108	31 10	149	47 09	224	30 25	271	45 41	308	15 45	335
323	53 45	033	59 59	108	31 24	149	46 50	224	29 58	270	45 19	307	15 33	334
324	54 00	031	60 25	107	31 38	148	46 32	223	29 30	269	44 57	306	15 21	333
325	54 14	030	60 51	106	31 53	147	46 13	223	29 03	268	44 35	304	15 09	332
326	54 27	029	61 17	106	32 07	147	45 54	222	28 36	267	44 12	303	14 56	331
327	54 40	027	61 43	105	32 22	146	45 36	222	28 09	266	43 49	302	14 42	330
328	54 52	026	62 10	104	32 38	146	45 18	221	27 42	265	43 26	301	14 29	329
329	55 03	024	62 36	104	32 53	145	45 00	221	27 14	265	43 03	300	14 14	328
	◆FOMALHAUT		Diphda		ACHERNAR		◆CANOPUS		RIGIL KENT		◆ANTARES		Nunki	
330	55 14	023	36 50	051	63 03	103	33 09	144	44 43	220	26 47	264	42 39	299
331	55 24	021	37 11	050	63 29	102	33 25	144	44 25	220	26 20	263	42 15	298
332	55 34	020	37 32	049	63 56	102	33 41	143	44 08	219	25 53	262	41 51	297
333	55 43	018	37 53	048	64 23	101	33 58	142	43 51	218	25 26	261	41 26	296
334	55 51	017	38 13	047	64 49	100	34 15	142	43 34	218	24 59	260	41 01	295
335	55 58	015	38 32	046	65 16	099	34 32	141	43 18	217	24 33	259	40 37	293
336	56 05	014	38 52	045	65 43	099	34 49	140	43 01	217	24 06	259	40 12	292
337	56 11	012	39 11	043	66 10	098	35 07	140	42 45	216	23 39	258	39 46	291
338	56 16	010	39 29	042	66 37	097	35 24	139	42 29	216	23 13	257	39 21	290
339	56 21	009	39 47	041	67 04	096	35 42	138	42 13	215	22 46	256	38 55	289
340	56 25	007	40 05	040	67 31	096	36 01	138	41 58	215	22 20	255	38 29	288
341	56 28	006	40 22	039	67 58	095	36 19	137	41 42	214	21 53	254	38 03	287
342	56 30	004	40 39	038	68 25	094	36 38	136	41 27	213	21 27	254	37 37	286
343	56 32	003	40 55	036	68 53	093	36 57	136	41 12	213	21 01	253	37 11	285
344	56 32	001	41 11	035	69 20	092	37 16	135	40 58	212	20 35	252	36 45	284
	◆Diphda		Acamar		◆CANOPUS		RIGIL KENT		◆ANTARES		Nunki		FOMALHAUT	
345	41 27	034	48 38	086	37 35	134	40 43	212	20 09	251	36 18	283	56 32	359
346	41 42	033	49 05	085	37 55	134	40 29	211	19 44	250	35 52	282	56 32	358
347	41 56	031	49 32	084	38 14	133	40 15	211	19 18	249	35 25	281	56 30	356
348	42 10	030	49 59	083	38 34	133	40 01	210	18 53	249	34 58	281	56 28	355
349	42 24	029	50 26	082	38 54	132	39 48	210	18 27	248	34 32	280	56 25	353
350	42 37	028	50 53	081	39 15	131	39 34	209	18 02	247	34 05	279	56 22	352
351	42 49	026	51 20	080	39 35	131	39 21	208	17 37	246	33 38	278	56 17	350
352	43 01	025	51 47	079	39 56	130	39 08	208	17 13	245	33 11	277	56 12	348
353	43 12	024	52 13	078	40 17	129	38 56	207	16 48	244	32 44	276	56 06	347
354	43 23	023	52 40	077	40 38	129	38 43	207	16 23	244	32 17	275	56 00	345
355	43 33	021	53 06	076	41 00	128	38 31	206	15 59	243	31 49	274	55 53	344
356	43 43	020	53 33	075	41 21	127	38 19	206	15 35	242	31 22	273	55 45	342
357	43 52	019	53 59	074	41 43	127	38 08	205	15 11	241	30 55	272	55 36	341
358	44 00	017	54 25	073	42 05	126	37 56	204	14 47	240	30 28	271	55 27	339
359	44 08	016	54 51	072	42 27	125	37 45	204	14 24	239	30 01	270	55 17	338

LAT 64°S

LHA ♈	Hc	Zn	Hc	Zn	Hc	Zn	Hc	Zn	Hc	Zn	Hc	Zn	Hc	Zn
	Diphda		◆RIGEL		CANOPUS		Miaplacidus		◆RIGIL KENT		Peacock		◆FOMALHAUT	
0	43 17	015	12 15	084	43 23	124	46 54	160	38 29	204	63 31	261	54 11	337
1	43 24	013	12 41	083	43 45	123	47 03	160	38 19	203	63 05	260	54 00	335
2	43 29	012	13 07	082	44 07	123	47 12	159	38 09	202	62 39	259	53 49	334
3	43 35	011	13 33	081	44 29	122	47 22	159	37 59	202	62 13	259	53 37	332
4	43 39	009	13 59	080	44 52	121	47 31	159	37 49	201	61 47	258	53 25	331
5	43 43	008	14 25	079	45 14	121	47 41	158	37 40	201	61 21	257	53 12	330
6	43 46	007	14 51	078	45 37	120	47 51	158	37 30	200	60 56	256	52 58	328
7	43 49	005	15 16	077	46 00	119	48 01	157	37 22	200	60 30	256	52 44	327
8	43 51	004	15 42	076	46 23	119	48 11	157	37 13	199	60 05	255	52 29	325
9	43 53	003	16 07	075	46 46	118	48 22	156	37 04	198	59 40	254	52 14	324
10	43 54	001	16 33	074	47 09	117	48 32	156	36 56	198	59 14	254	51 58	323
11	43 54	000	16 58	073	47 33	117	48 43	155	36 48	197	58 49	253	51 42	321
12	43 54	359	17 23	072	47 56	116	48 54	155	36 41	197	58 24	252	51 26	320
13	43 53	357	17 48	072	48 20	115	49 05	154	36 33	196	57 59	252	51 09	319
14	43 52	356	18 13	071	48 44	115	49 17	154	36 26	195	57 34	251	50 51	317
	◆RIGEL		SIRIUS		CANOPUS		◆RIGIL KENT		Peacock		◆FOMALHAUT		Diphda	
15	18 38	070	16 33	094	49 08	114	36 19	195	57 09	250	50 33	316	43 50	355
16	19 02	069	16 59	093	49 32	113	36 13	194	56 45	250	50 15	315	43 47	354
17	19 27	068	17 25	093	49 56	112	36 06	194	56 20	249	49 56	314	43 44	352
18	19 51	067	17 52	092	50 21	112	36 00	193	55 56	248	49 36	312	43 40	351
19	20 15	066	18 18	091	50 45	111	35 54	193	55 31	248	49 17	311	43 35	350
20	20 39	065	18 44	090	51 10	110	35 49	192	55 07	247	48 57	310	43 30	348
21	21 03	064	19 11	089	51 35	110	35 44	191	54 43	246	48 37	309	43 25	347
22	21 26	063	19 37	088	51 59	109	35 38	191	54 19	246	48 16	307	43 18	346
23	21 49	062	20 03	087	52 24	108	35 34	190	53 55	245	47 55	306	43 12	344
24	22 13	061	20 29	086	52 49	107	35 29	190	53 31	244	47 33	305	43 04	343
25	22 35	060	20 56	085	53 15	107	35 25	189	53 07	244	47 12	304	42 56	342
26	22 58	059	21 22	084	53 40	106	35 21	188	52 44	243	46 50	303	42 48	341
27	23 20	058	21 48	084	54 05	105	35 17	188	52 21	242	46 28	302	42 39	339
28	23 43	057	22 14	083	54 31	104	35 14	187	51 57	242	46 05	301	42 29	338
29	24 05	056	22 40	082	54 56	104	35 11	187	51 34	241	45 42	299	42 19	337
	◆RIGEL		SIRIUS		CANOPUS		◆RIGIL KENT		Peacock		◆FOMALHAUT		Diphda	
30	24 26	055	23 06	081	55 22	103	35 08	186	51 11	240	45 19	298	42 08	335
31	24 48	054	23 32	080	55 47	102	35 05	185	50 48	240	44 56	297	41 57	334
32	25 09	053	23 58	079	56 13	101	35 03	185	50 26	239	44 32	296	41 45	333
33	25 30	052	24 24	078	56 39	101	35 01	184	50 03	239	44 09	295	41 33	332
34	25 50	051	24 49	077	57 05	100	34 59	184	49 41	238	43 45	294	41 20	330
35	26 10	050	25 15	076	57 31	099	34 57	183	49 19	237	43 21	293	41 07	329
36	26 30	049	25 40	075	57 57	098	34 56	182	48 57	237	42 56	292	40 54	328
37	26 50	048	26 06	074	58 23	098	34 55	182	48 35	236	42 32	291	40 39	327
38	27 09	047	26 31	073	58 49	097	34 54	181	48 13	235	42 07	290	40 25	326
39	27 28	046	26 56	072	59 15	096	34 54	181	47 51	235	41 42	289	40 10	324
40	27 47	045	27 21	071	59 41	095	34 54	180	47 30	234	41 17	288	39 54	323
41	28 05	043	27 46	070	60 07	094	34 54	180	47 09	234	40 52	287	39 38	322
42	28 23	042	28 11	069	60 34	093	34 54	179	46 48	233	40 27	286	39 22	321
43	28 40	041	28 35	068	61 00	093	34 55	178	46 27	232	40 01	285	39 05	320
44	28 58	040	29 00	067	61 26	092	34 56	178	46 06	232	39 36	284	38 48	318
	RIGEL		◆SIRIUS		CANOPUS		◆RIGIL KENT		Peacock		FOMALHAUT		◆Diphda	
45	29 14	039	29 24	066	61 52	091	34 57	177	45 45	231	39 10	283	38 30	317
46	29 31	038	29 48	065	62 19	090	34 58	177	45 25	231	38 45	282	38 12	316
47	29 47	037	30 12	064	62 45	089	35 00	176	45 05	230	38 19	281	37 53	315
48	30 02	036	30 35	063	63 11	088	35 02	175	44 45	229	37 53	280	37 35	314
49	30 18	035	30 59	062	63 38	087	35 04	175	44 25	229	37 27	279	37 16	313
50	30 32	034	31 22	061	64 04	086	35 07	174	44 05	228	37 01	278	36 56	312
51	30 47	033	31 45	060	64 30	085	35 10	174	43 46	227	36 35	277	36 36	310
52	31 01	031	32 07	059	64 56	084	35 13	173	43 26	227	36 09	276	36 16	309
53	31 14	030	32 30	058	65 22	083	35 16	172	43 07	226	35 43	275	35 56	308
54	31 27	029	32 52	057	65 49	082	35 20	172	42 48	226	35 16	274	35 35	307
55	31 40	028	33 14	056	66 15	081	35 24	171	42 30	225	34 50	273	35 14	306
56	31 52	027	33 36	055	66 40	080	35 28	171	42 11	224	34 24	272	34 52	305
57	32 04	026	33 57	054	67 06	079	35 32	170	41 53	224	33 58	271	34 31	304
58	32 15	025	34 18	053	67 32	078	35 37	169	41 35	223	33 31	271	34 09	303
59	32 25	023	34 39	052	67 58	077	35 42	169	41 17	223	33 05	270	33 46	302
	RIGEL		◆SIRIUS		Suhail		◆RIGIL KENT		Peacock		FOMALHAUT		◆Diphda	
60	32 36	022	35 00	051	43 35	102	35 47	168	40 59	222	32 39	269	33 24	301
61	32 45	021	35 20	050	44 01	102	35 53	168	40 42	221	32 12	268	33 01	300
62	32 55	020	35 40	049	44 27	101	35 58	167	40 24	221	31 46	267	32 38	299
63	33 03	019	35 59	047	44 52	100	36 04	166	40 07	220	31 20	266	32 15	298
64	33 12	018	36 18	046	45 18	099	36 11	166	39 51	219	30 54	265	31 52	297
65	33 19	016	36 37	045	45 44	098	36 17	165	39 34	219	30 27	264	31 28	296
66	33 26	015	36 56	044	46 10	098	36 24	165	39 18	218	30 01	263	31 04	295
67	33 33	014	37 14	043	46 36	097	36 31	164	39 01	218	29 35	263	30 40	294
68	33 39	013	37 31	042	47 03	096	36 38	164	38 45	217	29 09	262	30 16	293
69	33 45	012	37 49	041	47 29	095	36 46	163	38 30	216	28 43	261	29 52	292
70	33 50	011	38 06	039	47 55	094	36 54	162	38 14	216	28 17	260	29 27	291
71	33 54	009	38 22	038	48 21	093	37 02	162	37 59	215	27 51	259	29 02	290
72	33 58	008	38 38	037	48 48	092	37 10	161	37 44	215	27 26	258	28 38	289
73	34 02	007	38 54	036	49 14	092	37 19	161	37 29	214	27 00	257	28 13	288
74	34 05	006	39 09	035	49 40	091	37 28	160	37 15	213	26 34	257	27 47	287
	RIGEL		◆SIRIUS		Suhail		◆RIGIL KENT		Peacock		ACHERNAR		◆Diphda	
75	34 07	005	39 24	034	50 06	090	37 37	159	37 00	213	65 02	262	27 22	286
76	34 09	003	39 38	032	50 33	089	37 46	159	36 46	212	64 36	261	26 57	285
77	34 10	002	39 52	031	50 59	088	37 56	158	36 32	211	64 10	261	26 31	284
78	34 11	001	40 05	030	51 25	087	38 06	158	36 19	211	63 44	260	26 06	283
79	34 11	000	40 18	029	51 52	086	38 16	157	36 05	210	63 19	259	25 40	282
80	34 11	359	40 31	027	52 18	085	38 26	157	35 52	210	62 53	258	25 14	281
81	34 10	357	40 42	026	52 44	084	38 37	156	35 40	209	62 27	258	24 48	280
82	34 08	356	40 54	025	53 10	083	38 47	155	35 27	208	62 01	257	24 23	279
83	34 06	355	41 05	024	53 36	082	38 58	155	35 15	208	61 36	256	23 57	278
84	34 04	354	41 15	022	54 02	081	39 10	154	35 02	207	61 10	256	23 30	277
85	34 01	353	41 25	021	54 28	080	39 21	154	34 51	206	60 45	255	23 04	276
86	33 57	351	41 34	020	54 54	079	39 33	153	34 39	206	60 19	254	22 38	275
87	33 53	350	41 43	019	55 20	078	39 45	153	34 28	205	59 54	253	22 12	275
88	33 48	349	41 51	017	55 46	077	39 57	152	34 17	205	59 29	253	21 46	274
89	33 43	348	41 58	016	56 11	076	40 10	151	34 06	204	59 04	252	21 19	273

LHA ♈	Hc	Zn	Hc	Zn	Hc	Zn	Hc	Zn	Hc	Zn	Hc	Zn	Hc	Zn
	◆SIRIUS		Suhail		◆RIGIL KENT		Peacock		◆ACHERNAR		Acamar		RIGEL	
90	42 05	015	56 37	075	40 23	151	33 55	203	58 39	251	54 42	290	33 37	347
91	42 12	014	57 02	074	40 36	150	33 45	203	58 14	251	54 17	289	33 31	345
92	42 18	012	57 27	073	40 49	150	33 35	202	57 49	250	53 52	288	33 24	344
93	42 23	011	57 52	072	41 02	149	33 25	201	57 25	249	53 27	287	33 16	343
94	42 28	010	58 17	071	41 16	149	33 16	201	57 00	249	53 02	286	33 09	342
95	42 32	008	58 42	070	41 30	148	33 07	200	56 36	248	52 36	285	33 00	341
96	42 35	007	59 06	068	41 44	147	32 58	200	56 11	247	52 11	284	32 51	340
97	42 38	006	59 31	067	41 58	147	32 49	199	55 47	247	51 45	283	32 42	338
98	42 41	004	59 55	066	42 12	146	32 41	198	55 23	246	51 19	282	32 32	337
99	42 42	003	60 19	065	42 27	146	32 33	198	54 59	246	50 54	281	32 22	336
100	42 44	002	60 42	064	42 42	145	32 25	197	54 35	245	50 28	280	32 11	335
101	42 44	001	61 06	062	42 57	145	32 17	196	54 11	244	50 02	279	31 59	334
102	42 44	359	61 29	061	43 13	144	32 10	196	53 48	244	49 36	278	31 47	333
103	42 44	358	61 52	060	43 28	143	32 03	195	53 24	243	49 10	277	31 35	332
104	42 42	357	62 14	058	43 44	143	31 56	194	53 01	242	48 43	276	31 22	330
	Alphard		◆Gienah		RIGIL KENT		◆Peacock		ACHERNAR		◆RIGEL		SIRIUS	
105	28 49	043	20 32	088	44 00	142	31 50	194	52 37	242	31 09	329	42 40	355
106	29 07	042	20 59	087	44 16	142	31 44	193	52 14	241	30 56	328	42 38	354
107	29 24	041	21 25	086	44 33	141	31 38	193	51 51	241	30 42	327	42 35	353
108	29 41	040	21 51	086	44 49	141	31 32	192	51 29	240	30 27	326	42 31	351
109	29 58	039	22 17	085	45 06	140	31 27	191	51 06	239	30 12	325	42 27	350
110	30 14	037	22 43	084	45 23	139	31 22	191	50 43	239	29 57	324	42 22	349
111	30 30	036	23 10	083	45 40	139	31 17	190	50 21	238	29 41	323	42 17	348
112	30 45	035	23 36	082	45 58	138	31 13	189	49 59	237	29 25	322	42 11	346
113	31 00	034	24 02	081	46 15	138	31 09	189	49 37	237	29 08	320	42 05	345
114	31 14	033	24 28	080	46 33	137	31 05	188	49 15	236	28 51	319	41 58	344
115	31 28	032	24 53	079	46 51	137	31 01	187	48 53	236	28 34	318	41 50	342
116	31 42	031	25 19	078	47 09	136	30 58	187	48 31	235	28 16	317	41 42	341
117	31 55	030	25 45	077	47 27	136	30 55	186	48 10	234	27 58	316	41 33	340
118	32 08	028	26 10	076	47 46	135	30 52	186	47 49	234	27 40	315	41 24	339
119	32 20	027	26 36	075	48 05	134	30 50	185	47 28	233	27 21	314	41 14	337
	Alphard		◆SPICA		RIGIL KENT		◆Peacock		ACHERNAR		◆RIGEL		SIRIUS	
120	32 32	026	13 49	087	48 24	134	30 48	184	47 07	232	27 02	313	41 04	336
121	32 44	025	14 15	086	48 43	133	30 46	184	46 46	232	26 43	312	40 53	335
122	32 54	024	14 41	086	49 02	133	30 44	183	46 25	231	26 23	311	40 41	334
123	33 05	023	15 08	085	49 21	132	30 43	182	46 05	231	26 03	310	40 29	332
124	33 15	022	15 34	084	49 41	132	30 42	182	45 45	230	25 43	309	40 17	331
125	33 24	020	16 00	083	50 00	131	30 42	181	45 24	229	25 22	308	40 04	330
126	33 33	019	16 26	082	50 20	131	30 41	180	45 05	229	25 01	307	39 51	329
127	33 41	018	16 52	081	50 40	130	30 41	180	44 45	228	24 40	306	39 37	328
128	33 49	017	17 18	080	51 01	129	30 41	179	44 25	228	24 18	305	39 22	326
129	33 57	016	17 44	079	51 21	129	30 42	179	44 06	227	23 56	304	39 08	325
130	34 03	014	18 09	078	51 42	128	30 43	178	43 47	226	23 34	303	38 52	324
131	34 10	013	18 35	077	52 02	128	30 44	177	43 28	226	23 12	302	38 37	323
132	34 16	012	19 01	076	52 23	127	30 45	177	43 09	225	22 50	301	38 21	322
133	34 21	011	19 26	075	52 44	127	30 47	176	42 51	225	22 27	300	38 04	320
134	34 25	010	19 52	074	53 05	126	30 49	175	42 32	224	22 04	299	37 47	319
	REGULUS		◆SPICA		RIGIL KENT		◆Peacock		ACHERNAR		CANOPUS		◆SIRIUS	
135	12 58	017	20 17	074	53 27	126	30 51	175	42 14	223	67 10	281	37 30	318
136	13 05	016	20 42	073	53 48	125	30 54	174	41 56	223	66 44	280	37 12	317
137	13 13	015	21 07	072	54 10	124	30 57	173	41 38	222	66 18	279	36 54	316
138	13 19	014	21 32	071	54 32	124	31 00	173	41 21	222	65 52	278	36 35	315
139	13 26	013	21 57	070	54 54	123	31 03	172	41 04	221	65 26	277	36 17	314
140	13 32	012	22 21	069	55 16	123	31 07	172	40 46	220	65 00	276	35 57	313
141	13 37	011	22 46	068	55 38	122	31 11	171	40 30	220	64 34	275	35 38	311
142	13 42	010	23 10	067	56 00	122	31 15	170	40 13	219	64 08	274	35 18	310
143	13 46	009	23 34	066	56 23	121	31 20	170	39 56	218	63 41	273	34 58	309
144	13 51	008	23 58	065	56 45	121	31 25	169	39 40	218	63 15	272	34 37	308
145	13 54	007	24 22	064	57 08	120	31 30	168	39 24	217	62 49	271	34 16	307
146	13 57	006	24 45	063	57 31	119	31 35	168	39 08	217	62 22	270	33 55	306
147	14 00	005	25 09	062	57 54	119	31 41	167	38 53	216	61 56	269	33 34	305
148	14 02	004	25 32	061	58 17	118	31 47	166	38 37	215	61 30	268	33 12	304
149	14 04	003	25 55	060	58 40	118	31 54	166	38 22	215	61 04	268	32 50	303
	REGULUS		◆SPICA		RIGIL KENT		◆Peacock		ACHERNAR		CANOPUS		◆SIRIUS	
150	14 05	002	26 17	059	59 03	117	32 00	165	38 07	214	60 37	267	32 28	302
151	14 06	001	26 40	058	59 27	117	32 07	165	37 53	214	60 11	266	32 05	301
152	14 06	000	27 02	057	59 50	116	32 14	164	37 38	213	59 45	265	31 43	300
153	14 06	359	27 24	056	60 14	115	32 22	163	37 24	212	59 19	264	31 20	299
154	14 06	358	27 45	055	60 38	115	32 29	163	37 10	212	58 53	263	30 56	298
155	14 05	357	28 07	054	61 02	114	32 37	162	36 56	211	58 26	263	30 33	297
156	14 03	356	28 28	053	61 26	114	32 46	161	36 43	210	58 00	262	30 09	296
157	14 01	355	28 48	052	61 50	113	32 54	161	36 30	210	57 34	261	29 45	295
158	13 59	354	29 09	051	62 14	113	33 03	160	36 17	209	57 08	260	29 21	294
159	13 56	353	29 29	050	62 39	112	33 12	159	36 04	209	56 43	259	28 57	293
160	13 53	352	29 49	049	63 03	111	33 21	159	35 52	208	56 17	259	28 33	292
161	13 49	351	30 09	047	63 28	111	33 31	158	35 39	207	55 51	258	28 08	291
162	13 45	350	30 28	046	63 52	110	33 41	158	35 27	207	55 25	257	27 44	290
163	13 40	349	30 47	045	64 17	110	33 51	157	35 16	206	55 00	256	27 19	289
164	13 35	348	31 05	044	64 42	109	34 02	156	35 04	206	54 34	256	26 54	288
	◆SPICA		ANTARES		◆Peacock		ACHERNAR		CANOPUS		◆SIRIUS		Alphard	
165	31 23	043	26 49	096	34 12	156	34 53	205	54 09	255	26 29	287	32 22	333
166	31 41	042	27 15	095	34 23	155	34 42	204	53 43	254	26 03	286	32 10	332
167	31 58	041	27 42	094	34 34	154	34 31	204	53 18	253	25 38	285	31 57	331
168	32 15	040	28 08	093	34 46	154	34 21	203	52 53	253	25 13	284	31 44	329
169	32 32	039	28 34	092	34 58	153	34 11	202	52 28	252	24 47	283	31 31	328
170	32 48	038	29 00	091	35 10	153	34 01	202	52 03	251	24 21	282	31 17	327
171	33 04	036	29 27	091	35 22	152	33 51	201	51 38	251	23 55	281	31 02	326
172	33 20	035	29 53	090	35 34	151	33 42	201	51 13	250	23 30	280	30 47	325
173	33 35	034	30 19	089	35 47	151	33 33	200	50 49	249	23 04	279	30 32	324
174	33 49	033	30 46	088	36 00	150	33 24	199	50 24	248	22 38	278	30 16	323
175	34 03	032	31 12	087	36 13	149	33 15	199	50 00	248	22 12	277	30 00	322
176	34 17	031	31 38	086	36 27	149	33 07	198	49 36	247	21 46	276	29 44	321
177	34 30	030	32 04	085	36 41	148	32 59	197	49 11	246	21 19	275	29 27	319
178	34 43	028	32 31	084	36 55	148	32 51	197	48 47	246	20 53	275	29 10	318
179	34 55	027	32 57	083	37 09	147	32 44	196	48 24	245	20 27	274	28 52	317

LAT 64°S

LHA ♈	Hc	Zn	Hc	Zn	Hc	Zn	Hc	Zn	Hc	Zn	Hc	Zn	Hc	Zn
	SPICA		◆ ANTARES		Peacock		◆ ACHERNAR		CANOPUS		Suhail		◆ Alphard	
180	35 07	026	33 23	082	37 23	146	32 37	196	48 00	244	58 24	290	28 34	316
181	35 18	025	33 49	081	37 38	146	32 30	195	47 36	244	57 59	289	28 16	315
182	35 29	024	34 15	080	37 53	145	32 23	194	47 13	243	57 34	287	27 57	314
183	35 39	023	34 41	079	38 08	144	32 17	194	46 49	242	57 09	286	27 38	313
184	35 49	021	35 07	079	38 23	144	32 11	193	46 26	241	56 44	285	27 18	312
185	35 59	020	35 32	078	38 39	143	32 05	192	46 03	241	56 18	284	26 59	311
186	36 07	019	35 58	077	38 55	143	32 00	192	45 40	240	55 53	283	26 39	310
187	36 16	018	36 23	076	39 11	142	31 54	191	45 18	239	55 27	282	26 18	309
188	36 23	017	36 49	075	39 27	141	31 49	190	44 55	239	55 01	281	25 58	308
189	36 31	015	37 14	074	39 44	141	31 45	190	44 33	238	54 35	280	25 37	307
190	36 37	014	37 39	073	40 00	140	31 40	189	44 10	237	54 09	279	25 16	306
191	36 43	013	38 04	072	40 17	140	31 36	189	43 48	237	53 43	278	24 54	305
192	36 49	012	38 29	071	40 35	139	31 33	188	43 26	236	53 17	277	24 32	304
193	36 54	010	38 54	070	40 52	138	31 29	187	43 05	235	52 51	276	24 10	303
194	36 59	009	39 19	069	41 10	138	31 26	187	42 43	235	52 25	275	23 48	302
	SPICA		◆ ANTARES		Peacock		◆ ACHERNAR		CANOPUS		Suhail		◆ Alphard	
195	37 02	008	39 43	068	41 27	137	31 23	186	42 22	234	51 59	274	23 26	301
196	37 06	007	40 07	067	41 45	136	31 20	185	42 00	233	51 32	273	23 03	300
197	37 09	006	40 31	065	42 04	136	31 18	185	41 39	233	51 06	272	22 40	299
198	37 11	004	40 55	064	42 22	135	31 16	184	41 18	232	50 40	271	22 17	298
199	37 13	003	41 19	063	42 41	135	31 14	184	40 58	231	50 14	271	21 53	297
200	37 14	002	41 42	062	42 59	134	31 13	183	40 37	231	49 47	270	21 30	296
201	37 14	001	42 05	061	43 18	133	31 12	182	40 17	230	49 21	269	21 06	295
202	37 14	359	42 28	060	43 38	133	31 11	182	39 57	229	48 55	268	20 42	294
203	37 14	358	42 51	059	43 57	132	31 10	181	39 37	229	48 28	267	20 18	293
204	37 13	357	43 13	058	44 17	132	31 10	180	39 17	228	48 02	266	19 54	292
205	37 11	356	43 35	057	44 36	131	31 10	180	38 58	227	47 36	265	19 29	291
206	37 09	354	43 57	056	44 56	130	31 10	179	38 39	227	47 10	264	19 05	290
207	37 06	353	44 19	054	45 17	130	31 11	178	38 20	226	46 44	264	18 40	289
208	37 02	352	44 40	053	45 37	129	31 11	178	38 01	226	46 18	263	18 15	288
209	36 58	351	45 01	052	45 57	128	31 13	177	37 42	225	45 51	262	17 50	287
	ANTARES		◆ Nunki		Peacock		ACHERNAR		◆ CANOPUS		Suhail		◆ SPICA	
210	45 22	051	30 24	088	46 18	128	31 14	177	37 24	224	45 25	261	36 54	350
211	45 42	050	30 50	087	46 39	127	31 16	176	37 05	224	45 00	260	36 49	348
212	46 02	049	31 16	086	47 00	127	31 18	175	36 47	223	44 34	259	36 43	347
213	46 21	047	31 42	085	47 21	126	31 20	175	36 30	222	44 08	259	36 37	346
214	46 40	046	32 09	085	47 42	125	31 23	174	36 12	222	43 42	258	36 31	345
215	46 59	045	32 35	084	48 04	125	31 25	173	35 55	221	43 16	257	36 23	343
216	47 18	044	33 01	083	48 26	124	31 29	173	35 38	220	42 51	256	36 16	342
217	47 36	042	33 27	082	48 48	124	31 32	172	35 21	220	42 25	255	36 07	341
218	47 53	041	33 53	081	49 10	123	31 36	171	35 04	219	42 00	255	35 58	340
219	48 10	040	34 19	080	49 32	122	31 40	171	34 48	218	41 35	254	35 49	339
220	48 27	039	34 45	079	49 54	122	31 44	170	34 31	218	41 09	253	35 39	337
221	48 43	037	35 10	078	50 17	121	31 49	170	34 15	217	40 44	252	35 29	336
222	48 59	036	35 36	077	50 39	120	31 54	169	34 00	216	40 19	251	35 18	335
223	49 14	035	36 02	076	51 02	120	31 59	168	33 44	216	39 54	251	35 07	334
224	49 29	033	36 27	075	51 25	119	32 04	168	33 29	215	39 30	250	34 55	333
	ANTARES		◆ Nunki		FOMALHAUT		ACHERNAR		◆ CANOPUS		Suhail		◆ SPICA	
225	49 43	032	36 52	074	14 45	129	32 10	167	33 14	214	39 05	249	34 43	332
226	49 57	031	37 18	073	15 06	128	32 16	166	33 00	214	38 41	248	34 30	330
227	50 10	029	37 43	072	15 27	127	32 22	166	32 45	213	38 16	248	34 17	329
228	50 23	028	38 08	071	15 48	126	32 29	165	32 31	212	37 52	247	34 03	328
229	50 35	027	38 33	070	16 09	125	32 36	165	32 17	212	37 28	246	33 49	327
230	50 46	025	38 57	069	16 31	124	32 43	164	32 03	211	37 04	245	33 34	326
231	50 57	024	39 22	068	16 53	124	32 50	163	31 50	210	36 40	244	33 20	325
232	51 08	023	39 46	067	17 15	123	32 58	163	31 37	210	36 16	244	33 04	324
233	51 17	021	40 10	066	17 37	122	33 06	162	31 24	209	35 53	243	32 48	322
234	51 27	020	40 34	065	17 59	121	33 14	161	31 11	208	35 30	242	32 32	321
235	51 35	018	40 58	064	18 22	120	33 23	161	30 59	208	35 06	241	32 15	320
236	51 43	017	41 21	063	18 45	119	33 32	160	30 47	207	34 43	241	31 58	319
237	51 50	015	41 44	062	19 08	119	33 41	160	30 35	206	34 21	240	31 41	318
238	51 57	014	42 07	060	19 31	118	33 50	159	30 23	206	33 58	239	31 23	317
239	52 03	013	42 30	059	19 54	117	34 00	158	30 12	205	33 35	238	31 05	316
	◆ ANTARES		Nunki		◆ FOMALHAUT		ACHERNAR		CANOPUS		◆ ACRUX		SPICA	
240	52 09	011	42 53	058	20 18	116	34 09	158	30 01	204	67 02	248	30 46	315
241	52 13	010	43 15	057	20 42	115	34 20	157	29 51	204	66 38	247	30 28	314
242	52 17	008	43 37	056	21 05	115	34 30	156	29 40	203	66 14	247	30 08	313
243	52 21	007	43 58	055	21 29	114	34 41	156	29 30	202	65 50	246	29 49	311
244	52 24	005	44 20	054	21 54	113	34 52	155	29 20	202	65 26	246	29 29	310
245	52 26	004	44 41	053	22 18	112	35 03	155	29 11	201	65 02	245	29 09	309
246	52 27	002	45 02	051	22 42	111	35 14	154	29 01	200	64 38	245	28 48	308
247	52 28	001	45 22	050	23 07	110	35 26	153	28 52	200	64 14	244	28 28	307
248	52 28	359	45 42	049	23 32	110	35 38	153	28 44	199	63 51	244	28 06	306
249	52 27	358	46 02	048	23 57	109	35 50	152	28 35	198	63 27	243	27 45	305
250	52 26	356	46 21	047	24 22	108	36 02	151	28 27	198	63 04	243	27 23	304
251	52 24	355	46 40	045	24 47	107	36 15	151	28 19	197	62 40	242	27 02	303
252	52 21	354	46 59	044	25 12	106	36 28	150	28 12	196	62 17	242	26 39	302
253	52 18	352	47 17	043	25 37	105	36 41	150	28 05	196	61 54	241	26 17	301
254	52 14	351	47 34	042	26 03	104	36 55	149	27 58	195	61 31	241	25 54	300
	Nunki		◆ FOMALHAUT		ACHERNAR		CANOPUS		◆ ACRUX		SPICA		◆ ANTARES	
255	47 52	040	26 28	104	37 08	148	27 51	194	61 08	240	25 32	299	52 09	349
256	48 09	039	26 54	103	37 22	148	27 45	194	60 45	240	25 08	298	52 04	348
257	48 25	038	27 19	102	37 36	147	27 39	193	60 23	239	24 45	297	51 58	346
258	48 41	037	27 45	101	37 51	147	27 33	192	60 00	239	24 22	296	51 52	345
259	48 56	035	28 11	100	38 05	146	27 27	192	59 38	238	23 58	295	51 44	343
260	49 11	034	28 37	099	38 20	145	27 22	191	59 16	238	23 34	294	51 37	342
261	49 26	033	29 03	099	38 35	145	27 18	190	58 53	237	23 10	293	51 28	341
262	49 40	031	29 29	098	38 51	144	27 13	190	58 31	237	22 46	292	51 19	339
263	49 53	030	29 55	097	39 06	143	27 09	189	58 09	236	22 21	291	51 09	338
264	50 06	029	30 21	096	39 22	143	27 05	188	57 48	236	21 57	290	50 59	336
265	50 18	027	30 47	095	39 38	142	27 01	188	57 26	235	21 32	289	50 48	335
266	50 30	026	31 14	094	39 54	142	26 58	187	57 05	235	21 07	288	50 37	334
267	50 41	025	31 40	093	40 11	141	26 55	186	56 43	234	20 42	287	50 25	332
268	50 52	023	32 06	092	40 27	140	26 52	185	56 22	234	20 17	286	50 12	331
269	51 02	022	32 32	091	40 44	140	26 50	185	56 01	233	19 51	286	49 59	329

LHA ♈	Hc	Zn	Hc	Zn	Hc	Zn	Hc	Zn	Hc	Zn	Hc	Zn	Hc	Zn
	◆ ALTAIR		FOMALHAUT		◆ ACHERNAR		CANOPUS		◆ RIGIL KENT		SPICA		ANTARES	
270	14 06	028	32 59	091	41 01	139	26 48	184	67 20	255	19 26	285	49 45	328
271	14 18	027	33 25	090	41 19	139	26 46	183	66 55	254	19 01	284	49 31	327
272	14 30	026	33 51	089	41 36	138	26 45	183	66 30	254	18 35	283	49 17	325
273	14 42	025	34 18	088	41 54	137	26 44	182	66 05	253	18 09	282	49 01	324
274	14 53	024	34 44	087	42 12	137	26 43	181	65 40	252	17 43	281	48 46	323
275	15 04	023	35 10	086	42 30	136	26 42	181	65 15	252	17 18	280	48 30	322
276	15 14	022	35 36	085	42 48	136	26 42	180	64 50	251	16 52	279	48 13	320
277	15 24	021	36 03	084	43 07	135	26 42	179	64 25	251	16 26	278	47 56	319
278	15 33	020	36 29	083	43 25	134	26 43	179	64 00	250	16 00	277	47 39	318
279	15 42	019	36 55	082	43 44	134	26 44	178	63 35	249	15 33	276	47 21	316
280	15 50	018	37 21	081	44 03	133	26 45	177	63 11	249	15 07	275	47 02	315
281	15 59	017	37 47	080	44 23	132	26 46	177	62 46	248	14 41	274	46 44	314
282	16 06	016	38 13	079	44 42	132	26 48	176	62 22	248	14 15	274	46 24	313
283	16 13	015	38 39	079	45 02	131	26 50	175	61 58	247	13 49	273	46 05	312
284	16 20	014	39 04	078	45 22	131	26 52	175	61 34	246	13 22	272	45 45	310
	◆ ALTAIR		FOMALHAUT		◆ ACHERNAR		CANOPUS		◆ RIGIL KENT		ANTARES		Nunki	
285	16 26	013	39 30	077	45 42	130	26 55	174	61 10	246	45 25	309	52 16	359
286	16 32	012	39 55	076	46 02	129	26 58	173	60 46	245	45 04	308	52 15	357
287	16 38	011	40 21	075	46 22	129	27 01	173	60 22	245	44 44	307	52 14	356
288	16 42	010	40 46	074	46 43	128	27 04	172	59 58	244	44 22	306	52 11	354
289	16 47	009	41 11	073	47 04	128	27 08	171	59 34	244	44 01	305	52 08	353
290	16 51	008	41 36	072	47 25	127	27 12	171	59 11	243	43 39	303	52 05	351
291	16 54	007	42 01	071	47 46	126	27 17	170	58 47	242	43 17	302	52 00	350
292	16 57	006	42 26	069	48 07	126	27 22	169	58 24	242	42 55	301	51 55	348
293	17 00	005	42 50	068	48 28	125	27 27	169	58 01	241	42 32	300	51 50	347
294	17 02	004	43 15	067	48 50	125	27 32	168	57 38	241	42 09	299	51 44	346
295	17 04	003	43 39	066	49 12	124	27 38	167	57 15	240	41 46	298	51 37	344
296	17 05	002	44 03	065	49 34	123	27 44	167	56 52	240	41 23	297	51 29	343
297	17 05	001	44 27	064	49 56	123	27 50	166	56 30	239	40 59	296	51 21	341
298	17 05	000	44 50	063	50 18	122	27 57	165	56 07	239	40 35	295	51 12	340
299	17 05	359	45 14	062	50 40	121	28 04	164	55 45	238	40 11	294	51 03	338
	FOMALHAUT		◆ ACHERNAR		CANOPUS		◆ RIGIL KENT		ANTARES		Nunki		◆ ALTAIR	
300	45 37	061	51 03	121	28 11	164	55 23	237	39 47	293	50 53	337	17 04	358
301	46 00	060	51 26	120	28 18	163	55 01	237	39 23	292	50 42	336	17 03	357
302	46 22	059	51 48	120	28 26	162	54 39	236	38 58	291	50 31	334	17 01	356
303	46 45	057	52 11	119	28 34	162	54 17	236	38 33	290	50 19	333	16 59	355
304	47 07	056	52 34	118	28 42	161	53 55	235	38 08	289	50 07	331	16 57	354
305	47 28	055	52 58	118	28 51	160	53 34	235	37 43	288	49 54	330	16 53	353
306	47 50	054	53 21	117	29 00	160	53 12	234	37 18	287	49 41	329	16 50	352
307	48 11	053	53 44	116	29 09	159	52 51	234	36 53	286	49 27	327	16 46	351
308	48 32	052	54 08	116	29 19	158	52 30	233	36 28	285	49 13	326	16 41	350
309	48 52	050	54 32	115	29 29	158	52 09	232	36 02	284	48 58	325	16 36	349
310	49 12	049	54 56	115	29 39	157	51 48	232	35 37	283	48 42	324	16 31	348
311	49 32	048	55 20	114	29 49	156	51 28	231	35 11	282	48 27	322	16 25	346
312	49 51	047	55 44	113	30 00	156	51 07	231	34 45	281	48 10	321	16 18	345
313	50 10	045	56 08	113	30 11	155	50 47	230	34 19	280	47 53	320	16 12	344
314	50 29	044	56 32	112	30 22	154	50 27	230	33 53	279	47 36	318	16 04	343
	◆ FOMALHAUT		ACHERNAR		◆ CANOPUS		RIGIL KENT		◆ ANTARES		Nunki		ALTAIR	
315	50 47	043	56 57	111	30 33	154	50 07	229	33 27	278	47 18	317	15 57	342
316	51 04	042	57 21	111	30 45	153	49 47	229	33 01	277	47 00	316	15 48	341
317	51 22	040	57 46	110	30 57	152	49 27	228	32 35	276	46 42	315	15 40	340
318	51 38	039	58 11	109	31 09	152	49 08	227	32 09	275	46 23	313	15 31	339
319	51 55	038	58 36	109	31 22	151	48 49	227	31 42	274	46 04	312	15 21	338
320	52 10	036	59 01	108	31 35	150	48 30	226	31 16	273	45 44	311	15 11	337
321	52 26	035	59 26	107	31 48	150	48 11	226	30 50	272	45 24	310	15 01	336
322	52 41	033	59 51	107	32 01	149	47 52	225	30 24	271	45 04	309	14 50	335
323	52 55	032	60 16	106	32 15	148	47 33	225	29 57	270	44 43	308	14 39	334
324	53 08	031	60 41	105	32 29	148	47 15	224	29 31	270	44 22	306	14 27	333
325	53 22	029	61 07	105	32 43	147	46 57	224	29 05	269	44 01	305	14 15	332
326	53 34	028	61 32	104	32 57	146	46 39	223	28 38	268	43 39	304	14 03	331
327	53 46	026	61 58	103	33 12	146	46 21	222	28 12	267	43 17	303	13 50	330
328	53 58	025	62 24	102	33 27	145	46 03	222	27 46	266	42 55	302	13 37	329
329	54 08	024	62 49	102	33 42	144	45 46	221	27 20	265	42 32	301	13 23	328
	◆ FOMALHAUT		Diphda		ACHERNAR		◆ CANOPUS		RIGIL KENT		◆ ANTARES		Nunki	
330	54 19	022	36 13	051	63 15	101	33 58	144	45 28	221	26 54	264	42 10	300
331	54 28	021	36 33	050	63 41	100	34 13	143	45 11	220	26 27	263	41 47	299
332	54 37	019	36 53	049	64 07	100	34 29	142	44 55	220	26 01	263	41 23	297
333	54 46	018	37 12	047	64 33	099	34 45	142	44 38	219	25 35	262	41 00	296
334	54 53	016	37 31	046	64 59	098	35 02	141	44 21	218	25 09	261	40 36	295
335	55 00	015	37 50	045	65 25	097	35 18	141	44 05	218	24 43	260	40 12	294
336	55 07	013	38 09	044	65 51	096	35 35	140	43 49	217	24 17	259	39 48	293
337	55 12	012	38 27	043	66 17	096	35 52	139	43 33	217	23 52	258	39 24	292
338	55 17	010	38 45	042	66 43	095	36 09	139	43 18	216	23 26	257	39 00	291
339	55 21	009	39 02	041	67 10	094	36 27	138	43 02	216	23 00	256	38 35	290
340	55 25	007	39 19	039	67 36	093	36 45	137	42 47	215	22 35	256	38 10	289
341	55 28	006	39 35	038	68 02	092	37 03	137	42 32	215	22 09	255	37 45	288
342	55 30	004	39 51	037	68 28	091	37 21	136	42 17	214	21 44	254	37 20	287
343	55 32	002	40 07	036	68 55	091	37 39	135	42 03	213	21 19	253	36 55	286
344	55 32	001	40 22	035	69 21	090	37 58	135	41 48	213	20 54	252	36 30	285
	◆ Diphda		Acamar		◆ CANOPUS		RIGIL KENT		◆ ANTARES		Nunki		FOMALHAUT	
345	40 37	033	48 33	085	38 17	134	41 34	212	20 29	251	36 04	284	55 32	359
346	40 51	032	48 59	084	38 36	133	41 20	212	20 04	251	35 39	283	55 32	358
347	41 05	031	49 25	083	38 55	133	41 06	211	19 39	250	35 13	282	55 31	356
348	41 18	030	49 51	082	39 15	132	40 53	211	19 15	249	34 47	281	55 29	355
349	41 31	029	50 17	081	39 34	131	40 40	210	18 50	248	34 21	280	55 26	353
350	41 43	027	50 43	080	39 54	131	40 27	209	18 26	247	33 55	279	55 22	352
351	41 55	026	51 09	079	40 14	130	40 14	209	18 02	246	33 29	278	55 18	350
352	42 06	025	51 34	078	40 34	129	40 01	208	17 38	245	33 03	277	55 13	349
353	42 17	024	52 00	077	40 55	129	39 49	208	17 14	245	32 37	277	55 08	347
354	42 27	022	52 26	076	41 15	128	39 37	207	16 50	244	32 11	276	55 02	346
355	42 37	021	52 51	075	41 36	127	39 25	207	16 27	243	31 45	275	54 55	344
356	42 46	020	53 16	074	41 57	127	39 13	206	16 03	242	31 19	274	54 47	343
357	42 55	018	53 41	072	42 19	126	39 02	205	15 40	241	30 52	273	54 39	341
358	43 03	017	54 06	071	42 40	125	38 51	205	15 17	240	30 26	272	54 30	340
359	43 10	016	54 31	070	43 01	125	38 40	204	14 54	240	30 00	271	54 21	338

LAT 65°S

LHA ♈	Hc	Zn	Hc	Zn	Hc	Zn	Hc	Zn	Hc	Zn	Hc	Zn	Hc	Zn
	Diphda		◆ RIGEL		CANOPUS		Miaplacidus		◆ RIGIL KENT		Peacock		◆ FOMALHAUT	
0	42 19	014	12 08	083	43 56	123	47 51	160	39 24	204	63 39	263	53 16	337
1	42 25	013	12 33	082	44 18	123	47 59	160	39 14	203	63 14	262	53 06	336
2	42 31	012	12 58	081	44 39	122	48 08	159	39 04	203	62 49	261	52 55	334
3	42 36	010	13 23	081	45 01	121	48 18	159	38 54	202	62 24	260	52 44	333
4	42 40	009	13 48	080	45 23	120	48 27	158	38 45	202	61 59	260	52 32	332
5	42 44	008	14 13	079	45 44	120	48 36	158	38 36	201	61 34	259	52 20	330
6	42 47	007	14 38	078	46 07	119	48 46	157	38 27	200	61 09	258	52 07	329
7	42 49	005	15 03	077	46 29	118	48 56	157	38 18	200	60 44	257	51 54	328
8	42 52	004	15 27	076	46 51	118	49 06	156	38 10	199	60 20	257	51 40	326
9	42 53	003	15 52	075	47 14	117	49 17	156	38 01	199	59 55	256	51 25	325
10	42 54	001	16 16	074	47 36	116	49 27	155	37 53	198	59 30	255	51 10	324
11	42 54	000	16 41	073	47 59	116	49 38	155	37 46	197	59 06	254	50 55	322
12	42 54	359	17 05	072	48 22	115	49 49	154	37 38	197	58 42	254	50 39	321
13	42 53	358	17 29	071	48 45	114	50 00	154	37 31	196	58 17	253	50 23	320
14	42 52	356	17 53	070	49 08	113	50 11	154	37 24	196	57 53	252	50 06	318
	◆ RIGEL		SIRIUS		CANOPUS		◆ RIGIL KENT		Peacock		◆ FOMALHAUT		Diphda	
15	18 17	069	16 37	094	49 32	113	37 17	195	57 29	252	49 49	317	42 50	355
16	18 40	068	17 03	093	49 55	112	37 11	194	57 05	251	49 32	316	42 47	354
17	19 04	067	17 28	092	50 19	111	37 05	194	56 41	250	49 14	314	42 44	352
18	19 27	066	17 53	091	50 42	111	36 59	193	56 17	250	48 56	313	42 41	351
19	19 50	065	18 19	090	51 06	110	36 53	193	55 53	249	48 37	312	42 36	350
20	20 13	064	18 44	090	51 30	109	36 47	192	55 30	248	48 18	311	42 32	348
21	20 36	064	19 09	089	51 54	108	36 42	191	55 06	248	47 59	310	42 26	347
22	20 59	063	19 35	088	52 18	108	36 37	191	54 43	247	47 39	308	42 20	346
23	21 21	062	20 00	087	52 42	107	36 33	190	54 20	246	47 19	307	42 14	345
24	21 43	061	20 25	086	53 07	106	36 28	190	53 57	246	46 59	306	42 07	343
25	22 05	060	20 51	085	53 31	105	36 24	189	53 34	245	46 38	305	41 59	342
26	22 27	059	21 16	084	53 56	105	36 20	188	53 11	244	46 17	304	41 51	341
27	22 48	058	21 41	083	54 20	104	36 17	188	52 48	244	45 56	303	41 43	340
28	23 10	057	22 06	082	54 45	103	36 13	187	52 25	243	45 34	301	41 33	338
29	23 31	056	22 31	081	55 10	102	36 10	187	52 03	242	45 12	300	41 24	337
	◆ RIGEL		SIRIUS		CANOPUS		◆ RIGIL KENT		Peacock		◆ FOMALHAUT		Diphda	
30	23 52	055	22 56	080	55 34	102	36 07	186	51 40	242	44 50	299	41 14	336
31	24 12	054	23 21	079	55 59	101	36 05	185	51 18	241	44 28	298	41 03	335
32	24 32	053	23 46	078	56 24	100	36 03	185	50 56	240	44 06	297	40 52	333
33	24 52	051	24 11	078	56 49	099	36 01	184	50 34	240	43 43	296	40 40	332
34	25 12	050	24 36	077	57 14	098	35 59	184	50 12	239	43 20	295	40 28	331
35	25 31	049	25 00	076	57 39	098	35 57	183	49 51	238	42 57	294	40 16	330
36	25 51	048	25 25	075	58 05	097	35 56	182	49 29	238	42 34	293	40 03	328
37	26 09	047	25 49	074	58 30	096	35 55	182	49 08	237	42 10	292	39 49	327
38	26 28	046	26 13	073	58 55	095	35 54	181	48 47	236	41 46	291	39 35	326
39	26 46	045	26 38	072	59 20	094	35 54	181	48 25	236	41 23	290	39 21	325
40	27 04	044	27 02	071	59 46	093	35 54	180	48 05	235	40 59	289	39 06	324
41	27 21	043	27 26	070	60 11	093	35 54	179	47 44	235	40 34	287	38 51	322
42	27 38	042	27 49	069	60 36	092	35 54	179	47 23	234	40 10	286	38 35	321
43	27 55	041	28 13	068	61 02	091	35 55	178	47 03	233	39 46	285	38 19	320
44	28 12	040	28 36	067	61 27	090	35 56	178	46 43	233	39 21	284	38 02	319
	RIGEL		◆ SIRIUS		CANOPUS		◆ RIGIL KENT		Peacock		FOMALHAUT		◆ Diphda	
45	28 28	039	28 59	066	61 52	089	35 57	177	46 23	232	38 57	283	37 46	318
46	28 43	038	29 22	065	62 18	088	35 58	176	46 03	231	38 32	282	37 28	317
47	28 59	037	29 45	064	62 43	087	36 00	176	45 43	231	38 07	282	37 11	316
48	29 14	036	30 08	063	63 08	086	36 02	175	45 23	230	37 42	281	36 53	314
49	29 28	034	30 30	062	63 34	085	36 04	175	45 04	229	37 17	280	36 35	313
50	29 42	033	30 53	061	63 59	084	36 07	174	44 45	229	36 52	279	36 16	312
51	29 56	032	31 15	060	64 24	083	36 09	173	44 26	228	36 27	278	35 57	311
52	30 09	031	31 36	059	64 49	082	36 12	173	44 07	228	36 02	277	35 38	310
53	30 22	030	31 58	058	65 14	081	36 16	172	43 49	227	35 37	276	35 18	309
54	30 35	029	32 19	057	65 39	080	36 19	172	43 30	226	35 12	275	34 58	308
55	30 47	028	32 40	056	66 04	079	36 23	171	43 12	226	34 46	274	34 38	307
56	30 58	027	33 01	054	66 29	078	36 27	170	42 54	225	34 21	273	34 18	306
57	31 09	025	33 22	053	66 54	077	36 31	170	42 36	224	33 56	272	33 57	305
58	31 20	024	33 42	052	67 18	076	36 36	169	42 18	224	33 30	271	33 36	303
59	31 30	023	34 02	051	67 43	074	36 41	169	42 01	223	33 05	270	33 14	302
	RIGEL		◆ SIRIUS		Suhail		◆ RIGIL KENT		Peacock		FOMALHAUT		◆ Diphda	
60	31 40	022	34 21	050	43 48	102	36 46	168	41 44	223	32 40	269	32 53	301
61	31 49	021	34 41	049	44 12	101	36 51	168	41 27	222	32 14	268	32 31	300
62	31 58	020	35 00	048	44 37	100	36 57	167	41 10	221	31 49	268	32 09	299
63	32 06	019	35 18	047	45 02	099	37 03	166	40 53	221	31 24	267	31 47	298
64	32 14	017	35 37	046	45 27	098	37 09	166	40 37	220	30 58	266	31 24	297
65	32 22	016	35 55	045	45 53	097	37 15	165	40 21	219	30 33	265	31 02	296
66	32 28	015	36 12	044	46 18	097	37 22	165	40 05	219	30 08	264	30 39	295
67	32 35	014	36 30	042	46 43	096	37 29	164	39 49	218	29 43	263	30 16	294
68	32 41	013	36 47	041	47 08	095	37 36	163	39 33	217	29 17	262	29 53	293
69	32 46	012	37 03	040	47 33	094	37 43	163	39 18	217	28 52	261	29 29	292
70	32 51	010	37 19	039	47 59	093	37 51	162	39 03	216	28 27	261	29 06	291
71	32 55	009	37 35	038	48 24	092	37 59	162	38 48	216	28 02	260	28 42	290
72	32 59	008	37 50	037	48 49	091	38 07	161	38 33	215	27 37	259	28 18	289
73	33 02	007	38 05	035	49 15	090	38 15	160	38 19	214	27 13	258	27 54	288
74	33 05	006	38 20	034	49 40	089	38 24	160	38 05	214	26 48	257	27 30	287
	RIGEL		◆ SIRIUS		Suhail		◆ RIGIL KENT		Peacock		ACHERNAR		◆ Diphda	
75	33 07	005	38 34	033	50 06	089	38 33	159	37 51	213	65 09	264	27 06	286
76	33 09	003	38 47	032	50 31	088	38 42	159	37 37	212	64 44	263	26 41	285
77	33 10	002	39 00	031	50 56	087	38 51	158	37 24	212	64 19	263	26 17	284
78	33 11	001	39 13	029	51 21	086	39 01	157	37 10	211	63 54	262	25 52	283
79	33 11	000	39 25	028	51 47	085	39 11	157	36 57	211	63 29	261	25 27	282
80	33 11	359	39 37	027	52 12	084	39 21	156	36 44	210	63 04	260	25 03	281
81	33 10	357	39 48	026	52 37	083	39 31	156	36 32	209	62 39	260	24 38	281
82	33 08	356	39 59	025	53 02	082	39 42	155	36 20	209	62 14	259	24 13	280
83	33 07	355	40 10	023	53 27	081	39 53	154	36 08	208	61 49	258	23 48	279
84	33 04	354	40 19	022	53 52	080	40 04	154	35 56	207	61 24	257	23 23	278
85	33 01	353	40 29	021	54 17	079	40 15	153	35 44	207	61 00	257	22 57	277
86	32 58	352	40 37	020	54 42	078	40 26	153	35 33	206	60 35	256	22 32	276
87	32 54	350	40 46	018	55 07	077	40 38	152	35 22	205	60 10	255	22 07	275
88	32 49	349	40 53	017	55 32	076	40 50	152	35 11	205	59 46	254	21 42	274
89	32 44	348	41 01	016	55 56	075	41 02	151	35 01	204	59 22	254	21 16	273

LHA ♈	Hc	Zn	Hc	Zn	Hc	Zn	Hc	Zn	Hc	Zn	Hc	Zn	Hc	Zn
	◆ SIRIUS		Suhail		◆ RIGIL KENT		Peacock		◆ ACHERNAR		Acamar		RIGEL	
90	41 07	015	56 20	074	41 15	150	34 50	204	58 57	253	54 20	291	32 39	347
91	41 13	013	56 45	073	41 27	150	34 40	203	58 33	252	53 57	290	32 33	346
92	41 19	012	57 09	071	41 40	149	34 31	202	58 09	252	53 33	289	32 26	344
93	41 24	011	57 33	070	41 53	149	34 21	202	57 45	251	53 09	288	32 19	343
94	41 29	010	57 57	069	42 07	148	34 12	201	57 21	250	52 44	287	32 11	342
95	41 32	008	58 20	068	42 20	147	34 03	200	56 57	250	52 20	286	32 03	341
96	41 36	007	58 44	067	42 34	147	33 54	200	56 34	249	51 56	285	31 55	340
97	41 39	006	59 07	066	42 48	146	33 46	199	56 10	248	51 31	284	31 46	339
98	41 41	004	59 30	064	43 02	146	33 38	198	55 46	248	51 07	283	31 37	338
99	41 43	003	59 52	063	43 17	145	33 30	198	55 23	247	50 42	282	31 27	336
100	41 44	002	60 15	062	43 31	145	33 22	197	55 00	246	50 17	281	31 16	335
101	41 44	001	60 37	061	43 46	144	33 15	197	54 37	246	49 52	280	31 05	334
102	41 44	359	60 59	059	44 01	143	33 08	196	54 14	245	49 27	279	30 54	333
103	41 44	358	61 21	058	44 16	143	33 01	195	53 51	244	49 02	278	30 42	332
104	41 42	357	61 42	057	44 32	142	32 54	195	53 28	244	48 37	277	30 30	331
	Alphard		◆ Gienah		RIGIL KENT		◆ Peacock		ACHERNAR		◆ RIGEL		SIRIUS	
105	28 05	042	20 30	088	44 47	142	32 48	194	53 05	243	30 18	330	41 41	355
106	28 22	041	20 56	087	45 03	141	32 42	193	52 43	242	30 05	328	41 38	354
107	28 38	040	21 21	086	45 19	141	32 36	193	52 20	242	29 51	327	41 36	353
108	28 55	039	21 46	085	45 35	140	32 31	192	51 58	241	29 37	326	41 32	352
109	29 11	038	22 11	084	45 52	139	32 26	191	51 36	240	29 23	325	41 28	350
110	29 26	037	22 37	083	46 08	139	32 21	191	51 14	240	29 08	324	41 24	349
111	29 41	036	23 02	082	46 25	138	32 16	190	50 52	239	28 53	323	41 19	348
112	29 56	035	23 27	081	46 42	138	32 12	189	50 31	238	28 38	322	41 13	347
113	30 10	034	23 52	080	46 59	137	32 08	189	50 09	238	28 22	321	41 07	345
114	30 24	033	24 17	080	47 17	136	32 04	188	49 48	237	28 06	320	41 00	344
115	30 37	032	24 42	079	47 34	136	32 01	188	49 27	237	27 49	319	40 53	343
116	30 50	030	25 07	078	47 52	135	31 57	187	49 05	236	27 32	318	40 45	341
117	31 03	029	25 31	077	48 10	135	31 55	186	48 45	235	27 15	317	40 37	340
118	31 15	028	25 56	076	48 28	134	31 52	186	48 24	235	26 57	315	40 28	339
119	31 27	027	26 20	075	48 46	134	31 50	185	48 03	234	26 39	314	40 18	338
	Alphard		◆ SPICA		RIGIL KENT		◆ Peacock		ACHERNAR		◆ RIGEL		SIRIUS	
120	31 38	026	13 46	087	49 05	133	31 48	184	47 43	233	26 21	313	40 09	337
121	31 49	025	14 11	086	49 23	132	31 46	184	47 23	233	26 02	312	39 58	335
122	32 00	024	14 36	085	49 42	132	31 44	183	47 02	232	25 43	311	39 47	334
123	32 09	022	15 02	084	50 01	131	31 43	182	46 42	231	25 24	310	39 36	333
124	32 19	021	15 27	083	50 20	131	31 42	182	46 23	231	25 05	309	39 24	332
125	32 28	020	15 52	083	50 40	130	31 42	181	46 03	230	24 45	308	39 12	330
126	32 36	019	16 17	082	50 59	130	31 41	180	45 44	230	24 25	307	38 59	329
127	32 44	018	16 42	081	51 19	129	31 41	180	45 25	229	24 05	306	38 46	328
128	32 52	017	17 07	080	51 38	128	31 41	179	45 06	228	23 44	305	38 32	327
129	32 59	015	17 32	079	51 58	128	31 42	179	44 47	228	23 23	304	38 18	326
130	33 05	014	17 57	078	52 18	127	31 43	178	44 28	227	23 02	303	38 04	324
131	33 11	013	18 22	077	52 39	127	31 44	177	44 10	226	22 41	302	37 49	323
132	33 17	012	18 46	076	52 59	126	31 45	177	43 51	226	22 19	301	37 33	322
133	33 22	011	19 11	075	53 20	126	31 47	176	43 33	225	21 57	300	37 18	321
134	33 26	010	19 35	074	53 40	125	31 49	175	43 15	225	21 35	299	37 01	320
	REGULUS		◆ SPICA		RIGIL KENT		◆ Peacock		ACHERNAR		CANOPUS		◆ SIRIUS	
135	12 01	017	20 00	073	54 01	124	31 51	175	42 58	224	66 57	283	36 45	319
136	12 08	016	20 24	072	54 22	124	31 53	174	42 40	223	66 33	282	36 28	318
137	12 15	015	20 48	071	54 43	123	31 56	173	42 23	223	66 08	281	36 11	316
138	12 21	014	21 12	070	55 05	123	31 59	173	42 06	222	65 43	280	35 53	315
139	12 27	013	21 36	069	55 26	122	32 03	172	41 49	221	65 18	279	35 35	314
140	12 33	012	21 59	068	55 48	122	32 06	171	41 32	221	64 53	278	35 17	313
141	12 38	011	22 23	067	56 09	121	32 10	171	41 16	220	64 28	277	34 58	312
142	12 43	010	22 46	066	56 31	120	32 14	170	40 59	220	64 02	276	34 39	311
143	12 47	009	23 09	065	56 53	120	32 19	169	40 43	219	63 37	275	34 20	310
144	12 51	008	23 32	064	57 15	119	32 24	169	40 27	218	63 12	274	34 00	309
145	12 55	007	23 55	063	57 37	119	32 29	168	40 12	218	62 47	273	33 40	308
146	12 58	006	24 18	062	58 00	118	32 34	168	39 56	217	62 21	272	33 20	306
147	13 00	005	24 40	061	58 22	117	32 40	167	39 41	216	61 56	271	32 59	305
148	13 02	004	25 02	060	58 45	117	32 46	166	39 26	216	61 31	270	32 38	304
149	13 04	003	25 24	059	59 07	116	32 52	166	39 11	215	61 05	269	32 17	303
	REGULUS		◆ SPICA		RIGIL KENT		◆ Peacock		ACHERNAR		CANOPUS		◆ SIRIUS	
150	13 05	002	25 46	058	59 30	116	32 58	165	38 57	215	60 40	268	31 56	302
151	13 06	001	26 07	057	59 53	115	33 05	164	38 43	214	60 14	268	31 34	301
152	13 06	000	26 29	056	60 16	114	33 12	164	38 29	213	59 49	267	31 13	300
153	13 06	359	26 50	055	60 39	114	33 19	163	38 15	213	59 24	266	30 51	299
154	13 06	358	27 10	054	61 02	113	33 27	162	38 01	212	58 59	265	30 28	298
155	13 05	357	27 31	053	61 26	113	33 34	162	37 48	211	58 33	264	30 06	297
156	13 03	356	27 51	052	61 49	112	33 42	161	37 35	211	58 08	263	29 43	296
157	13 01	355	28 11	051	62 13	111	33 51	161	37 22	210	57 43	263	29 20	295
158	12 59	354	28 31	050	62 36	111	33 59	160	37 09	210	57 18	262	28 57	294
159	12 56	353	28 50	049	63 00	110	34 08	159	36 57	209	56 53	261	28 34	293
160	12 53	352	29 09	048	63 24	110	34 17	159	36 44	208	56 28	260	28 11	292
161	12 50	351	29 28	047	63 48	109	34 27	158	36 33	208	56 03	259	27 47	291
162	12 46	350	29 46	046	64 12	108	34 36	157	36 21	207	55 38	259	27 23	290
163	12 41	349	30 04	045	64 36	108	34 46	157	36 09	206	55 13	258	26 59	289
164	12 36	348	30 22	044	65 00	107	34 56	156	35 58	206	54 48	257	26 35	288
	◆ SPICA		ANTARES		◆ Peacock		ACHERNAR		CANOPUS		◆ SIRIUS		Alphard	
165	30 39	043	26 55	095	35 07	155	35 47	205	54 24	256	26 11	287	31 29	333
166	30 56	042	27 20	094	35 17	155	35 37	205	53 59	255	25 47	286	31 17	332
167	31 13	041	27 46	094	35 28	154	35 26	204	53 35	255	25 22	285	31 05	331
168	31 29	039	28 11	093	35 40	154	35 16	203	53 10	254	24 58	284	30 53	330
169	31 45	038	28 36	092	35 51	153	35 06	203	52 45	253	24 33	283	30 40	329
170	32 01	037	29 02	091	36 03	152	34 57	202	52 22	252	24 09	282	30 26	328
171	32 16	036	29 27	090	36 15	152	34 47	201	51 58	252	23 44	281	30 12	326
172	32 31	035	29 52	089	36 27	151	34 38	201	51 34	251	23 19	280	29 58	325
173	32 45	034	30 18	088	36 39	150	34 29	200	51 10	250	22 54	280	29 43	324
174	32 59	033	30 43	087	36 52	150	34 21	200	50 46	250	22 29	279	29 28	323
175	33 12	032	31 08	086	37 05	149	34 12	199	50 22	249	22 04	278	29 13	322
176	33 25	030	31 34	085	37 18	148	34 04	198	49 59	248	21 39	277	28 57	321
177	33 38	029	31 59	084	37 31	148	33 56	198	49 35	247	21 13	276	28 41	320
178	33 50	028	32 24	084	37 45	147	33 49	197	49 12	247	20 48	275	28 25	319
179	34 02	027	32 49	083	37 59	147	33 42	196	48 48	246	20 23	274	28 08	318

LAT 65°S

LHA ♈	Hc	Zn	Hc	Zn	Hc	Zn	Hc	Zn	Hc	Zn	Hc	Zn	Hc	Zn
	SPICA		◆ANTARES		Peacock		◆ACHERNAR		CANOPUS		Suhail		◆Alphard	
180	34 13	026	33 14	082	38 13	146	33 35	196	48 25	245	58 03	291	27 50	317
181	34 24	025	33 40	081	38 27	145	33 28	195	48 02	245	57 39	290	27 33	316
182	34 34	023	34 05	080	38 42	145	33 21	194	47 40	244	57 15	289	27 15	314
183	34 44	022	34 29	079	38 57	144	33 15	194	47 17	243	56 51	288	26 57	313
184	34 53	021	34 54	078	39 12	143	33 09	193	46 54	242	56 27	287	26 38	312
185	35 02	020	35 19	077	39 27	143	33 04	193	46 32	242	56 03	286	26 19	311
186	35 11	019	35 44	076	39 42	142	32 58	192	46 10	241	55 38	285	26 00	310
187	35 18	018	36 08	075	39 58	142	32 53	191	45 48	240	55 14	283	25 40	309
188	35 26	016	36 33	074	40 14	141	32 48	191	45 26	240	54 49	282	25 21	308
189	35 33	015	36 57	073	40 30	140	32 44	190	45 04	239	54 24	281	25 01	307
190	35 39	014	37 21	072	40 46	140	32 40	189	44 42	238	53 59	280	24 40	306
191	35 45	013	37 45	071	41 03	139	32 36	189	44 21	238	53 34	279	24 20	305
192	35 50	012	38 09	070	41 20	138	32 32	188	43 59	237	53 09	278	23 59	304
193	35 55	010	38 33	069	41 37	138	32 29	187	43 38	236	52 44	277	23 38	303
194	35 59	009	38 56	068	41 54	137	32 25	187	43 17	236	52 19	276	23 16	302
	SPICA		◆ANTARES		Peacock		◆ACHERNAR		CANOPUS		Suhail		◆Alphard	
195	36 03	008	39 20	067	42 11	136	32 23	186	42 56	235	51 54	275	22 55	301
196	36 06	007	39 43	066	42 29	136	32 20	185	42 36	234	51 28	275	22 33	300
197	36 09	005	40 06	065	42 46	135	32 18	185	42 15	233	51 03	274	22 11	299
198	36 11	004	40 29	064	43 04	135	32 16	184	41 55	233	50 38	273	21 49	298
199	36 13	003	40 51	063	43 23	134	32 14	184	41 35	232	50 12	272	21 26	297
200	36 14	002	41 14	061	43 41	133	32 13	183	41 15	231	49 47	271	21 04	296
201	36 14	001	41 36	060	43 59	133	32 11	182	40 55	231	49 22	270	20 41	295
202	36 14	359	41 58	059	44 18	132	32 11	182	40 36	230	48 56	269	20 18	294
203	36 14	358	42 20	058	44 37	131	32 10	181	40 16	229	48 31	268	19 54	293
204	36 13	357	42 41	057	44 56	131	32 10	180	39 57	229	48 06	267	19 31	292
205	36 11	356	43 02	056	45 15	130	32 10	180	39 38	228	47 40	266	19 08	291
206	36 09	355	43 23	055	45 35	130	32 10	179	39 19	227	47 15	265	18 44	290
207	36 06	353	43 44	054	45 55	129	32 10	178	39 01	227	46 50	265	18 20	289
208	36 03	352	44 04	053	46 14	128	32 11	178	38 42	226	46 25	264	17 56	288
209	35 59	351	44 24	051	46 34	128	32 12	177	38 24	225	45 59	263	17 32	288
	ANTARES		◆Nunki		Peacock		ACHERNAR		◆CANOPUS		Suhail		◆SPICA	
210	44 44	050	30 21	088	46 55	127	32 14	177	38 06	225	45 34	262	35 55	350
211	45 03	049	30 47	087	47 15	126	32 16	176	37 49	224	45 09	261	35 50	348
212	45 22	048	31 12	086	47 35	126	32 17	175	37 31	223	44 44	260	35 45	347
213	45 40	047	31 37	085	47 56	125	32 20	175	37 14	223	44 19	260	35 39	346
214	45 59	045	32 02	084	48 17	124	32 22	174	36 57	222	43 54	259	35 33	345
215	46 17	044	32 28	083	48 38	124	32 25	173	36 40	221	43 30	258	35 26	344
216	46 34	043	32 53	082	48 59	123	32 28	173	36 23	221	43 05	257	35 18	342
217	46 51	042	33 18	081	49 20	123	32 32	172	36 07	220	42 40	256	35 10	341
218	47 08	041	33 43	080	49 42	122	32 35	171	35 51	219	42 15	255	35 02	340
219	47 24	039	34 08	079	50 03	121	32 39	171	35 35	219	41 51	255	34 53	339
220	47 40	038	34 33	078	50 25	121	32 43	170	35 19	218	41 27	254	34 44	338
221	47 55	037	34 58	077	50 47	120	32 48	169	35 03	217	41 02	253	34 34	337
222	48 10	035	35 22	076	51 09	119	32 53	169	34 48	217	40 38	252	34 24	335
223	48 25	034	35 47	075	51 31	119	32 58	168	34 33	216	40 14	251	34 13	334
224	48 39	033	36 11	074	51 53	118	33 03	168	34 18	215	39 50	251	34 02	333
	ANTARES		◆Nunki		FOMALHAUT		ACHERNAR		◆CANOPUS		Suhail		◆SPICA	
225	48 52	032	36 36	073	15 23	128	33 09	167	34 04	215	39 26	250	33 50	332
226	49 05	030	37 00	072	15 43	128	33 14	166	33 49	214	39 02	249	33 38	331
227	49 18	029	37 24	071	16 03	127	33 21	166	33 35	213	38 39	248	33 25	330
228	49 30	028	37 48	070	16 23	126	33 27	165	33 22	213	38 15	247	33 12	328
229	49 41	026	38 12	069	16 44	125	33 34	164	33 08	212	37 52	247	32 59	327
230	49 52	025	38 35	068	17 05	124	33 41	164	32 55	211	37 29	246	32 45	326
231	50 02	023	38 59	067	17 26	123	33 48	163	32 42	211	37 06	245	32 30	325
232	50 12	022	39 22	066	17 47	123	33 55	162	32 29	210	36 43	244	32 16	324
233	50 21	021	39 45	065	18 09	122	34 03	162	32 16	209	36 20	244	32 01	323
234	50 30	019	40 08	064	18 30	121	34 11	161	32 04	209	35 57	243	31 45	322
235	50 38	018	40 31	063	18 52	120	34 19	161	31 52	208	35 35	242	31 29	321
236	50 46	017	40 53	062	19 14	119	34 28	160	31 40	207	35 13	241	31 13	319
237	50 53	015	41 15	061	19 36	118	34 37	159	31 29	207	34 50	241	30 56	318
238	50 59	014	41 37	060	19 59	117	34 46	159	31 17	206	34 28	240	30 39	317
239	51 05	012	41 59	059	20 21	117	34 55	158	31 07	205	34 07	239	30 22	316
	◆ANTARES		Nunki		◆FOMALHAUT		ACHERNAR		CANOPUS		◆ACRUX		SPICA	
240	51 10	011	42 21	058	20 44	116	35 05	157	30 56	205	67 24	250	30 04	315
241	51 14	009	42 42	056	21 07	115	35 15	157	30 45	204	67 00	249	29 46	314
242	51 18	008	43 03	055	21 30	114	35 25	156	30 35	203	66 37	249	29 28	313
243	51 21	007	43 24	054	21 53	113	35 35	156	30 25	203	66 13	248	29 09	312
244	51 24	005	43 44	053	22 17	112	35 46	155	30 16	202	65 49	248	28 50	311
245	51 26	004	44 04	052	22 40	112	35 57	154	30 07	201	65 26	247	28 31	310
246	51 27	002	44 24	051	23 04	111	36 08	154	29 58	201	65 03	247	28 11	309
247	51 28	001	44 43	049	23 28	110	36 19	153	29 49	200	64 39	246	27 51	308
248	51 28	359	45 02	048	23 52	109	36 31	152	29 40	199	64 16	246	27 31	307
249	51 27	358	45 21	047	24 16	108	36 43	152	29 32	198	63 53	245	27 10	306
250	51 26	357	45 40	046	24 40	107	36 55	151	29 24	198	63 30	244	26 50	305
251	51 24	355	45 58	045	25 04	107	37 07	150	29 17	197	63 08	244	26 29	304
252	51 22	354	46 15	043	25 28	106	37 20	150	29 09	196	62 45	243	26 07	303
253	51 19	352	46 33	042	25 53	105	37 33	149	29 02	196	62 22	243	25 46	302
254	51 15	351	46 49	041	26 17	104	37 46	149	28 56	195	62 00	242	25 24	301
	Nunki		◆FOMALHAUT		ACHERNAR		CANOPUS		◆ACRUX		SPICA		◆ANTARES	
255	47 06	040	26 42	103	37 59	148	28 49	194	61 37	242	25 02	300	51 10	349
256	47 22	038	27 07	102	38 13	147	28 43	194	61 15	241	24 40	299	51 05	348
257	47 37	037	27 32	101	38 27	147	28 37	193	60 53	241	24 18	298	51 00	347
258	47 53	036	27 56	101	38 41	146	28 31	192	60 31	240	23 55	297	50 54	345
259	48 07	035	28 21	100	38 55	145	28 26	192	60 09	240	23 32	296	50 47	344
260	48 21	033	28 46	099	39 09	145	28 21	191	59 47	239	23 09	295	50 39	342
261	48 35	032	29 12	098	39 24	144	28 17	190	59 25	239	22 46	294	50 31	341
262	48 48	031	29 37	097	39 39	144	28 12	190	59 04	238	22 23	293	50 23	340
263	49 01	029	30 02	096	39 54	143	28 08	189	58 42	237	21 59	292	50 14	338
264	49 13	028	30 27	095	40 10	142	28 04	188	58 21	237	21 36	291	50 04	337
265	49 25	027	30 52	094	40 25	142	28 01	188	58 00	236	21 12	290	49 54	335
266	49 36	025	31 18	094	40 41	141	27 58	187	57 39	236	20 48	289	49 43	334
267	49 47	024	31 43	093	40 57	140	27 55	186	57 18	235	20 24	288	49 32	333
268	49 57	023	32 08	092	41 13	140	27 52	186	56 57	235	20 00	287	49 20	331
269	50 06	021	32 34	091	41 30	139	27 50	185	56 36	234	19 35	286	49 07	330

LHA ♈	Hc	Zn	Hc	Zn	Hc	Zn	Hc	Zn	Hc	Zn	Hc	Zn	Hc	Zn
	◆ALTAIR		FOMALHAUT		◆ACHERNAR		CANOPUS		◆RIGIL KENT		SPICA		ANTARES	
270	13 13	028	32 59	090	41 46	139	27 48	184	67 35	257	19 11	285	48 54	329
271	13 25	027	33 24	089	42 03	138	27 46	183	67 10	256	18 46	284	48 41	327
272	13 37	026	33 50	088	42 20	137	27 45	183	66 46	256	18 22	283	48 27	326
273	13 48	025	34 15	087	42 38	137	27 44	182	66 21	255	17 57	282	48 13	325
274	13 58	024	34 40	086	42 55	136	27 43	181	65 57	254	17 32	281	47 58	324
275	14 08	023	35 06	085	43 13	135	27 42	181	65 32	254	17 07	280	47 42	322
276	14 18	022	35 31	084	43 31	135	27 42	180	65 08	253	16 42	279	47 27	321
277	14 28	021	35 56	083	43 49	134	27 42	179	64 44	253	16 17	278	47 11	320
278	14 37	020	36 21	083	44 07	134	27 43	179	64 20	252	15 52	277	46 54	318
279	14 45	019	36 46	082	44 25	133	27 44	178	63 56	251	15 27	277	46 37	317
280	14 54	018	37 11	081	44 44	132	27 45	177	63 32	251	15 02	276	46 19	316
281	15 01	017	37 36	080	45 03	132	27 46	177	63 08	250	14 36	275	46 02	315
282	15 09	016	38 01	079	45 22	131	27 48	176	62 44	249	14 11	274	45 43	314
283	15 15	015	38 26	078	45 41	130	27 50	175	62 20	249	13 46	273	45 25	312
284	15 22	014	38 51	077	46 01	130	27 52	175	61 57	248	13 20	272	45 06	311
	◆ALTAIR		FOMALHAUT		◆ACHERNAR		CANOPUS		◆RIGIL KENT		ANTARES		Nunki	
285	15 28	013	39 16	076	46 20	129	27 54	174	61 33	248	44 47	310	51 16	359
286	15 34	012	39 40	075	46 40	129	27 57	173	61 10	247	44 27	309	51 15	357
287	15 39	011	40 04	074	47 00	128	28 00	173	60 47	246	44 07	308	51 14	356
288	15 43	010	40 29	073	47 20	127	28 04	172	60 23	246	43 47	306	51 12	354
289	15 48	009	40 53	072	47 40	127	28 08	171	60 00	245	43 26	305	51 09	353
290	15 51	008	41 17	071	48 00	126	28 12	170	59 37	245	43 06	304	51 05	351
291	15 55	007	41 41	070	48 21	125	28 16	170	59 15	244	42 44	303	51 01	350
292	15 58	006	42 04	069	48 42	125	28 21	169	58 52	243	42 23	302	50 57	349
293	16 00	005	42 28	068	49 03	124	28 25	168	58 29	243	42 01	301	50 51	347
294	16 02	004	42 51	067	49 24	124	28 31	168	58 07	242	41 40	300	50 45	346
295	16 04	003	43 14	065	49 45	123	28 36	167	57 44	242	41 17	299	50 39	344
296	16 05	002	43 37	064	50 06	122	28 42	166	57 22	241	40 55	298	50 32	343
297	16 05	001	44 00	063	50 28	122	28 48	166	57 00	240	40 33	297	50 24	342
298	16 05	000	44 23	062	50 49	121	28 55	165	56 38	240	40 10	295	50 16	340
299	16 05	359	44 45	061	51 11	120	29 01	164	56 16	239	39 47	294	50 07	339
	FOMALHAUT		◆ACHERNAR		CANOPUS		◆RIGIL KENT		ANTARES		Nunki		◆ALTAIR	
300	45 07	060	51 33	120	29 08	164	55 54	239	39 24	293	49 58	337	16 04	358
301	45 29	059	51 55	119	29 16	163	55 33	238	39 00	292	49 48	336	16 03	357
302	45 51	058	52 17	118	29 23	162	55 11	238	38 37	291	49 37	335	16 02	356
303	46 12	057	52 40	118	29 31	162	54 50	237	38 13	290	49 26	333	16 00	355
304	46 33	055	53 02	117	29 39	161	54 29	236	37 49	289	49 14	332	15 57	354
305	46 54	054	53 25	117	29 48	160	54 08	236	37 25	288	49 02	331	15 54	353
306	47 14	053	53 48	116	29 56	160	53 47	235	37 01	287	48 50	329	15 50	352
307	47 34	052	54 11	115	30 05	159	53 26	235	36 37	286	48 36	328	15 47	351
308	47 54	051	54 34	115	30 15	158	53 06	234	36 12	285	48 23	327	15 42	350
309	48 13	050	54 57	114	30 24	158	52 45	233	35 48	284	48 09	325	15 37	349
310	48 33	048	55 20	113	30 34	157	52 25	233	35 23	283	47 54	324	15 32	348
311	48 51	047	55 43	113	30 44	156	52 05	232	34 58	282	47 39	323	15 27	347
312	49 10	046	56 07	112	30 54	156	51 45	232	34 34	281	47 23	322	15 20	346
313	49 28	045	56 30	111	31 05	155	51 25	231	34 09	280	47 07	320	15 14	345
314	49 45	043	56 54	111	31 16	154	51 05	231	33 44	279	46 51	319	15 07	343
	◆FOMALHAUT		ACHERNAR		◆CANOPUS		RIGIL KENT		◆ANTARES		Nunki		ALTAIR	
315	50 02	042	57 18	110	31 27	153	50 46	230	33 19	278	46 34	318	14 59	342
316	50 19	041	57 42	109	31 39	153	50 26	229	32 53	278	46 17	317	14 52	341
317	50 36	039	58 06	108	31 50	152	50 07	229	32 28	277	45 59	315	14 43	340
318	50 51	038	58 30	108	32 02	151	49 48	228	32 03	276	45 41	314	14 35	339
319	51 07	037	58 54	107	32 14	151	49 29	228	31 38	275	45 23	313	14 26	338
320	51 22	035	59 18	106	32 27	150	49 11	227	31 13	274	45 04	312	14 16	337
321	51 36	034	59 43	106	32 40	149	48 52	227	30 47	273	44 45	311	14 06	336
322	51 50	033	60 07	105	32 53	149	48 34	226	30 22	272	44 26	309	13 56	335
323	52 04	031	60 32	104	33 06	148	48 16	225	29 57	271	44 06	308	13 45	334
324	52 17	030	60 56	104	33 20	147	47 58	225	29 31	270	43 46	307	13 34	333
325	52 29	029	61 21	103	33 33	147	47 40	224	29 06	269	43 26	306	13 22	332
326	52 41	027	61 46	102	33 47	146	47 22	224	28 41	268	43 05	305	13 10	331
327	52 52	026	62 11	101	34 02	145	47 05	223	28 15	267	42 44	304	12 58	330
328	53 03	024	62 35	101	34 16	145	46 48	223	27 50	267	42 23	303	12 45	329
329	53 13	023	63 00	100	34 31	144	46 31	222	27 25	266	42 01	301	12 32	328
	◆FOMALHAUT		Diphda		ACHERNAR		◆CANOPUS		RIGIL KENT		◆ANTARES		Nunki	
330	53 23	022	35 34	050	63 25	099	34 46	143	46 14	221	26 59	265	41 40	300
331	53 32	020	35 54	049	63 51	098	35 01	143	45 57	221	26 34	264	41 18	299
332	53 40	019	36 13	048	64 16	097	35 17	142	45 41	220	26 09	263	40 55	298
333	53 48	017	36 31	047	64 41	097	35 32	141	45 24	220	25 44	262	40 33	297
334	53 56	016	36 50	046	65 06	096	35 48	141	45 08	219	25 19	261	40 10	296
335	54 02	014	37 08	045	65 31	095	36 04	140	44 52	219	24 54	260	39 47	295
336	54 08	013	37 25	044	65 57	094	36 21	139	44 37	218	24 29	259	39 24	294
337	54 13	011	37 43	042	66 22	093	36 37	139	44 21	217	24 04	259	39 01	293
338	54 18	010	38 00	041	66 47	093	36 54	138	44 06	217	23 39	258	38 38	292
339	54 22	008	38 16	040	67 12	092	37 11	137	43 51	216	23 14	257	38 14	291
340	54 25	007	38 32	039	67 38	091	37 29	137	43 36	216	22 50	256	37 50	290
341	54 28	005	38 48	038	68 03	090	37 46	136	43 21	215	22 25	255	37 26	289
342	54 30	004	39 03	037	68 29	089	38 04	135	43 07	214	22 01	254	37 02	288
343	54 32	002	39 18	035	68 54	088	38 22	135	42 52	214	21 36	253	36 38	287
344	54 32	001	39 33	034	69 19	087	38 40	134	42 38	213	21 12	253	36 14	286
	◆Diphda		Acamar		◆CANOPUS		RIGIL KENT		◆ANTARES		Nunki		FOMALHAUT	
345	39 47	033	48 26	083	38 58	133	42 25	213	20 48	252	35 49	285	54 32	359
346	40 00	032	48 51	082	39 17	133	42 11	212	20 24	251	35 25	284	54 32	358
347	40 13	031	49 17	081	39 36	132	41 58	212	20 00	250	35 00	283	54 31	356
348	40 26	029	49 42	080	39 54	131	41 44	211	19 36	249	34 35	282	54 29	355
349	40 38	028	50 07	080	40 14	131	41 32	210	19 12	248	34 10	281	54 26	353
350	40 50	027	50 31	079	40 33	130	41 19	210	18 49	247	33 45	280	54 23	352
351	41 01	026	50 56	077	40 52	129	41 06	209	18 26	247	33 20	279	54 19	350
352	41 12	024	51 21	076	41 12	129	40 54	209	18 02	246	32 55	278	54 15	349
353	41 22	023	51 46	075	41 32	128	40 42	208	17 39	245	32 30	277	54 09	347
354	41 32	022	52 10	074	41 52	127	40 30	207	17 16	244	32 05	276	54 04	346
355	41 41	021	52 34	073	42 12	127	40 19	207	16 54	243	31 40	275	53 57	345
356	41 50	019	52 59	072	42 33	126	40 07	206	16 31	242	31 14	274	53 50	343
357	41 58	018	53 23	071	42 53	125	39 56	206	16 09	242	30 49	273	53 42	342
358	42 06	017	53 47	070	43 14	125	39 45	205	15 47	241	30 24	272	53 34	340
359	42 13	016	54 10	069	43 35	124	39 35	205	15 25	240	29 58	272	53 25	339

LAT 66°S

LHA ♈	Hc	Zn	Hc	Zn	Hc	Zn	Hc	Zn	Hc	Zn	Hc	Zn	Hc	Zn
	Diphda		◆RIGEL		CANOPUS		Miaplacidus		◆RIGIL KENT		Peacock		◆FOMALHAUT	
0	41 21	014	12 01	083	44 29	122	48 47	160	40 19	204	63 46	265	52 20	338
1	41 27	013	12 25	082	44 50	122	48 56	159	40 09	204	63 21	264	52 11	336
2	41 32	012	12 49	081	45 10	121	49 04	159	39 59	203	62 57	263	52 01	335
3	41 37	010	13 13	080	45 31	120	49 13	158	39 50	202	62 33	262	51 50	334
4	41 41	009	13 37	079	45 53	120	49 22	158	39 41	202	62 09	262	51 39	332
5	41 44	008	14 01	078	46 14	119	49 32	157	39 32	201	61 45	261	51 27	331
6	41 47	006	14 25	078	46 35	118	49 41	157	39 23	201	61 21	260	51 15	330
7	41 50	005	14 49	077	46 57	117	49 51	156	39 14	200	60 57	259	51 03	328
8	41 52	004	15 13	076	47 19	117	50 01	156	39 06	199	60 33	258	50 50	327
9	41 53	003	15 36	075	47 40	116	50 11	155	38 58	199	60 09	258	50 36	326
10	41 54	001	16 00	074	48 02	115	50 21	155	38 50	198	59 45	257	50 22	324
11	41 54	000	16 23	073	48 25	115	50 32	154	38 43	198	59 21	256	50 08	323
12	41 54	359	16 46	072	48 47	114	50 43	154	38 36	197	58 58	255	49 53	322
13	41 53	358	17 09	071	49 09	113	50 53	153	38 29	196	58 34	255	49 37	320
14	41 52	356	17 32	070	49 32	112	51 04	153	38 22	196	58 10	254	49 21	319
	◆RIGEL		CANOPUS		Miaplacidus		◆RIGIL KENT		Peacock		◆FOMALHAUT		Diphda	
15	17 55	069	49 54	112	51 15	153	38 15	195	57 47	253	49 05	318	41 50	355
16	18 18	068	50 17	111	51 27	152	38 09	195	57 24	252	48 49	317	41 48	354
17	18 41	067	50 40	110	51 38	152	38 03	194	57 01	252	48 32	315	41 45	352
18	19 03	066	51 03	109	51 50	151	37 57	193	56 37	251	48 14	314	41 41	351
19	19 25	065	51 26	109	52 02	151	37 51	193	56 14	250	47 57	313	41 37	350
20	19 47	064	51 49	108	52 14	150	37 46	192	55 51	250	47 39	312	41 33	349
21	20 09	063	52 12	107	52 26	150	37 41	192	55 29	249	47 20	310	41 28	347
22	20 31	062	52 36	106	52 39	149	37 36	191	55 06	248	47 01	309	41 22	346
23	20 52	061	52 59	106	52 51	149	37 32	190	54 43	248	46 42	308	41 16	345
24	21 14	060	53 23	105	53 04	148	37 27	190	54 21	247	46 23	307	41 09	344
25	21 35	059	53 46	104	53 17	148	37 23	189	53 58	246	46 03	306	41 02	342
26	21 55	058	54 10	103	53 30	147	37 20	189	53 36	245	45 43	305	40 55	341
27	22 16	057	54 34	103	53 43	147	37 16	188	53 14	245	45 23	303	40 46	340
28	22 37	056	54 58	102	53 56	147	37 13	187	52 52	244	45 03	302	40 38	339
29	22 57	055	55 22	101	54 10	146	37 10	187	52 30	243	44 42	301	40 29	337
	◆RIGEL		CANOPUS		Miaplacidus		◆RIGIL KENT		Peacock		◆FOMALHAUT		Diphda	
30	23 17	054	55 46	100	54 23	146	37 07	186	52 08	243	44 21	300	40 19	336
31	23 36	053	56 10	099	54 37	145	37 05	186	51 47	242	43 59	299	40 09	335
32	23 56	052	56 34	099	54 51	145	37 02	185	51 25	241	43 38	298	39 58	334
33	24 15	051	56 58	098	55 05	144	37 00	184	51 04	241	43 16	297	39 47	332
34	24 34	050	57 22	097	55 20	144	36 59	184	50 43	240	42 54	296	39 36	331
35	24 52	049	57 46	096	55 34	144	36 57	183	50 22	239	42 32	295	39 24	330
36	25 11	048	58 11	095	55 49	143	36 56	183	50 01	239	42 10	293	39 11	329
37	25 29	047	58 35	094	56 03	143	36 55	182	49 40	238	41 48	292	38 58	328
38	25 46	046	58 59	093	56 18	142	36 54	181	49 19	237	41 25	291	38 45	326
39	26 04	045	59 24	093	56 33	142	36 54	181	48 59	237	41 02	290	38 32	325
40	26 21	044	59 48	092	56 49	141	36 54	180	48 38	236	40 39	289	38 17	324
41	26 37	043	60 13	091	57 04	141	36 54	179	48 18	235	40 16	288	38 03	323
42	26 54	042	60 37	090	57 19	140	36 54	179	47 58	235	39 53	287	37 48	322
43	27 10	041	61 01	089	57 35	140	36 55	178	47 38	234	39 29	286	37 33	321
44	27 26	040	61 26	088	57 51	140	36 56	178	47 19	233	39 06	285	37 17	319
	RIGEL		◆SIRIUS		Suhail		◆RIGIL KENT		Peacock		◆FOMALHAUT		Diphda	
45	27 41	038	28 35	065	38 09	113	36 57	177	46 59	233	38 42	284	37 01	318
46	27 56	037	28 57	064	38 32	112	36 58	176	46 40	232	38 19	283	36 45	317
47	28 11	036	29 19	063	38 54	111	37 00	176	46 21	232	37 55	282	36 28	316
48	28 25	035	29 40	062	39 17	110	37 02	175	46 02	231	37 31	281	36 11	315
49	28 39	034	30 02	061	39 40	110	37 04	175	45 43	230	37 07	280	35 53	314
50	28 52	033	30 23	060	40 03	109	37 06	174	45 24	230	36 43	279	35 35	313
51	29 05	032	30 44	059	40 26	108	37 09	173	45 06	229	36 19	278	35 17	312
52	29 18	031	31 05	058	40 50	107	37 12	173	44 47	228	35 55	277	34 59	310
53	29 30	030	31 26	057	41 13	106	37 15	172	44 29	228	35 30	277	34 40	309
54	29 42	029	31 46	056	41 36	106	37 19	172	44 11	227	35 06	276	34 21	308
55	29 54	027	32 06	055	42 00	105	37 22	171	43 54	226	34 42	275	34 02	307
56	30 05	026	32 26	054	42 24	104	37 26	170	43 36	226	34 18	274	33 42	306
57	30 15	025	32 46	053	42 47	103	37 30	170	43 19	225	33 53	273	33 23	305
58	30 25	024	33 05	052	43 11	102	37 35	169	43 01	224	33 29	272	33 02	304
59	30 35	023	33 24	051	43 35	101	37 40	169	42 44	224	33 04	271	32 42	303
	RIGEL		◆SIRIUS		Suhail		◆RIGIL KENT		Peacock		◆FOMALHAUT		Diphda	
60	30 44	022	33 43	050	43 59	101	37 45	168	42 28	223	32 40	270	32 21	302
61	30 53	021	34 01	049	44 23	100	37 50	167	42 11	222	32 16	269	32 01	301
62	31 02	020	34 19	047	44 47	099	37 55	167	41 55	222	31 51	268	31 40	300
63	31 10	018	34 37	046	45 11	098	38 01	166	41 38	221	31 27	267	31 18	299
64	31 17	017	34 55	045	45 35	097	38 07	166	41 23	221	31 02	266	30 57	298
65	31 24	016	35 12	044	46 00	096	38 13	165	41 07	220	30 38	265	30 35	297
66	31 31	015	35 29	043	46 24	095	38 20	164	40 51	219	30 14	265	30 13	296
67	31 37	014	35 45	042	46 48	095	38 26	164	40 36	219	29 50	264	29 51	295
68	31 42	013	36 01	041	47 13	094	38 33	163	40 21	218	29 25	263	29 29	294
69	31 47	011	36 17	040	47 37	093	38 40	163	40 06	217	29 01	262	29 06	293
70	31 52	010	36 32	038	48 01	092	38 48	162	39 51	217	28 37	261	28 44	292
71	31 56	009	36 47	037	48 26	091	38 56	161	39 37	216	28 13	260	28 21	291
72	32 00	008	37 02	036	48 50	090	39 04	161	39 22	215	27 49	259	27 58	290
73	32 03	007	37 16	035	49 15	089	39 12	160	39 08	215	27 25	258	27 35	289
74	32 05	006	37 30	034	49 39	088	39 20	159	38 54	214	27 01	258	27 12	288
	RIGEL		◆SIRIUS		Suhail		◆RIGIL KENT		Peacock		◆FOMALHAUT		Diphda	
75	32 07	004	37 43	033	50 03	087	39 29	159	38 41	214	26 37	257	26 49	287
76	32 09	003	37 56	031	50 28	086	39 38	158	38 28	213	26 14	256	26 25	286
77	32 10	002	38 09	030	50 52	085	39 47	158	38 14	212	25 50	255	26 02	285
78	32 11	001	38 21	029	51 16	084	39 56	157	38 01	212	25 26	254	25 38	284
79	32 11	000	38 32	028	51 41	084	40 06	156	37 49	211	25 03	253	25 14	283
80	32 11	359	38 44	027	52 05	083	40 16	156	37 36	210	24 40	252	24 50	282
81	32 10	357	38 54	025	52 29	082	40 26	155	37 24	210	24 16	252	24 27	281
82	32 09	356	39 05	024	52 53	081	40 36	155	37 12	209	23 53	251	24 03	280
83	32 07	355	39 14	023	53 17	080	40 47	154	37 01	208	23 30	250	23 38	279
84	32 04	354	39 24	022	53 41	079	40 57	154	36 49	208	23 08	249	23 14	278
85	32 02	353	39 33	021	54 05	078	41 08	153	36 38	207	22 45	248	22 50	277
86	31 58	352	39 41	019	54 29	076	41 20	152	36 27	206	22 22	247	22 26	276
87	31 54	350	39 49	018	54 52	075	41 31	152	36 16	206	22 00	246	22 02	275
88	31 50	349	39 56	017	55 16	074	41 43	151	36 06	205	21 38	246	21 37	274
89	31 45	348	40 03	016	55 39	073	41 55	151	35 55	205	21 15	245	21 13	274

LHA ♈	Hc	Zn	Hc	Zn	Hc	Zn	Hc	Zn	Hc	Zn	Hc	Zn	Hc	Zn
	◆SIRIUS		Suhail		◆RIGIL KENT		Peacock		◆ACHERNAR		Acamar		RIGEL	
90	40 09	014	56 03	072	42 07	150	35 45	204	59 14	255	53 58	293	31 40	347
91	40 15	013	56 26	071	42 19	149	35 36	203	58 51	254	53 35	292	31 34	346
92	40 20	012	56 49	070	42 32	149	35 26	203	58 27	253	53 12	291	31 28	345
93	40 25	011	57 12	069	42 45	148	35 17	202	58 04	252	52 49	289	31 21	343
94	40 29	009	57 34	068	42 58	148	35 08	201	57 41	252	52 26	288	31 14	342
95	40 33	008	57 57	067	43 11	147	34 59	201	57 17	251	52 03	287	31 07	341
96	40 36	007	58 19	065	43 24	146	34 51	200	56 54	250	51 40	286	30 59	340
97	40 39	006	58 41	064	43 38	146	34 42	199	56 32	250	51 16	285	30 50	339
98	40 41	004	59 03	063	43 52	145	34 35	199	56 09	249	50 53	284	30 41	338
99	40 43	003	59 25	062	44 06	145	34 27	198	55 46	248	50 29	283	30 32	337
100	40 44	002	59 46	060	44 20	144	34 19	197	55 23	248	50 05	282	30 22	336
101	40 44	001	60 07	059	44 34	143	34 12	197	55 01	247	49 41	281	30 11	334
102	40 44	359	60 28	058	44 49	143	34 05	196	54 39	246	49 17	280	30 01	333
103	40 44	358	60 49	057	45 04	142	33 59	195	54 16	245	48 53	279	29 49	332
104	40 43	357	61 09	055	45 19	142	33 52	195	53 54	245	48 29	278	29 38	331
	Alphard		◆Gienah		RIGIL KENT		◆Peacock		ACHERNAR		◆RIGEL		SIRIUS	
105	27 21	042	20 28	088	45 34	141	33 46	194	53 32	244	29 26	330	40 41	356
106	27 37	041	20 52	087	45 50	140	33 40	193	53 10	243	29 13	329	40 39	354
107	27 53	040	21 17	086	46 05	140	33 35	193	52 48	243	29 00	328	40 36	353
108	28 08	039	21 41	085	46 21	139	33 30	192	52 27	242	28 47	327	40 33	352
109	28 23	038	22 05	084	46 37	139	33 25	192	52 05	241	28 34	325	40 29	350
110	28 38	037	22 29	083	46 53	138	33 20	191	51 44	241	28 20	324	40 25	349
111	28 52	036	22 54	082	47 10	137	33 15	190	51 23	240	28 05	323	40 20	348
112	29 06	035	23 18	081	47 26	137	33 11	190	51 02	239	27 50	322	40 15	347
113	29 20	033	23 42	080	47 43	136	33 07	189	50 41	239	27 35	321	40 09	345
114	29 33	032	24 06	079	48 00	136	33 04	188	50 20	238	27 20	320	40 02	344
115	29 46	031	24 30	078	48 17	135	33 00	188	49 59	237	27 04	319	39 55	343
116	29 59	030	24 54	077	48 34	135	32 57	187	49 39	237	26 48	318	39 48	342
117	30 11	029	25 17	076	48 52	134	32 54	186	49 18	236	26 31	317	39 40	341
118	30 22	028	25 41	075	49 10	133	32 52	186	48 58	236	26 14	316	39 32	339
119	30 33	027	26 04	074	49 27	133	32 49	185	48 38	235	25 57	315	39 23	338
	Alphard		◆SPICA		RIGIL KENT		◆Peacock		ACHERNAR		◆RIGEL		SIRIUS	
120	30 44	026	13 43	087	49 45	132	32 47	184	48 18	234	25 40	314	39 13	337
121	30 55	024	14 07	086	50 04	132	32 46	184	47 58	234	25 22	313	39 04	336
122	31 04	023	14 31	085	50 22	131	32 44	183	47 39	233	25 04	312	38 53	334
123	31 14	022	14 56	084	50 40	130	32 43	182	47 20	232	24 45	311	38 43	333
124	31 23	021	15 20	083	50 59	130	32 42	182	47 00	232	24 27	310	38 31	332
125	31 31	020	15 44	082	51 18	129	32 42	181	46 41	231	24 08	308	38 20	331
126	31 40	019	16 08	081	51 37	129	32 41	180	46 22	230	23 49	307	38 08	330
127	31 47	018	16 32	080	51 56	128	32 41	180	46 04	230	23 29	306	37 55	328
128	31 54	016	16 56	079	52 15	127	32 41	179	45 45	229	23 09	305	37 42	327
129	32 01	015	17 20	079	52 35	127	32 42	179	45 27	228	22 49	304	37 29	326
130	32 07	014	17 44	078	52 54	126	32 43	178	45 09	228	22 29	303	37 15	325
131	32 13	013	18 08	077	53 14	126	32 44	177	44 51	227	22 09	302	37 01	324
132	32 18	012	18 32	076	53 34	125	32 45	177	44 33	227	21 48	301	36 46	323
133	32 23	011	18 55	075	53 54	124	32 47	176	44 15	226	21 27	300	36 31	321
134	32 27	009	19 19	074	54 14	124	32 49	175	43 58	225	21 06	299	36 15	320
	Alphard		◆SPICA		RIGIL KENT		◆Peacock		ACHERNAR		◆CANOPUS		SIRIUS	
135	32 31	008	19 42	073	54 35	123	32 51	175	43 40	225	66 42	286	36 00	319
136	32 34	007	20 05	072	54 55	123	32 53	174	43 23	224	66 19	285	35 44	318
137	32 37	006	20 29	071	55 16	122	32 56	173	43 07	223	65 55	283	35 27	317
138	32 39	005	20 52	070	55 36	121	32 59	173	42 50	223	65 31	282	35 10	316
139	32 41	004	21 14	069	55 57	121	33 02	172	42 33	222	65 07	281	34 53	315
140	32 42	002	21 37	068	56 18	120	33 06	171	42 17	221	64 43	280	34 35	314
141	32 43	001	22 00	067	56 40	120	33 09	171	42 01	221	64 19	279	34 18	312
142	32 43	000	22 22	066	57 01	119	33 14	170	41 45	220	63 55	278	33 59	311
143	32 43	359	22 44	065	57 22	118	33 18	169	41 30	220	63 31	277	33 41	310
144	32 43	358	23 06	064	57 44	118	33 23	169	41 14	219	63 07	276	33 22	309
145	32 41	357	23 28	063	58 05	117	33 27	168	40 59	218	62 42	275	33 03	308
146	32 40	355	23 50	062	58 27	117	33 33	167	40 44	218	62 18	274	32 44	307
147	32 37	354	24 11	061	58 49	116	33 38	167	40 29	217	61 54	273	32 24	306
148	32 35	353	24 33	060	59 11	115	33 44	166	40 15	216	61 29	272	32 04	305
149	32 32	352	24 54	059	59 33	115	33 50	165	40 00	216	61 05	271	31 44	304
	◆SPICA		RIGIL KENT		◆Peacock		ACHERNAR		◆CANOPUS		SIRIUS		Alphard	
150	25 14	058	59 55	114	33 56	165	39 46	215	60 40	270	31 24	303	32 28	351
151	25 35	057	60 18	113	34 03	164	39 32	214	60 16	269	31 03	302	32 24	350
152	25 55	056	60 40	113	34 09	164	39 18	214	59 52	268	30 42	301	32 19	348
153	26 15	055	61 03	112	34 16	163	39 05	213	59 27	268	30 21	300	32 14	347
154	26 35	054	61 25	112	34 24	162	38 52	213	59 03	267	30 00	299	32 08	346
155	26 55	053	61 48	111	34 31	162	38 39	212	58 39	266	29 38	298	32 02	345
156	27 14	052	62 11	110	34 39	161	38 26	211	58 14	265	29 17	297	31 55	344
157	27 33	051	62 34	110	34 47	160	38 13	211	57 50	264	28 55	296	31 48	343
158	27 52	050	62 57	109	34 56	160	38 01	210	57 26	263	28 33	295	31 41	341
159	28 11	049	63 20	108	35 04	159	37 49	209	57 01	262	28 10	294	31 33	340
160	28 29	048	63 43	108	35 13	158	37 37	209	56 37	262	27 48	293	31 24	339
161	28 47	047	64 07	107	35 22	158	37 26	208	56 13	261	27 25	292	31 15	338
162	29 04	046	64 30	106	35 32	157	37 14	207	55 49	260	27 02	291	31 06	337
163	29 22	044	64 53	106	35 41	156	37 03	207	55 25	259	26 39	290	30 56	336
164	29 38	043	65 17	105	35 51	156	36 52	206	55 01	258	26 16	289	30 46	335
	◆SPICA		ANTARES		◆Peacock		ACHERNAR		◆CANOPUS		SIRIUS		Alphard	
165	29 55	042	27 00	095	36 01	155	36 42	206	54 37	258	25 53	288	30 35	333
166	30 11	041	27 25	094	36 12	154	36 31	205	54 14	257	25 30	287	30 24	332
167	30 27	040	27 49	093	36 22	154	36 21	204	53 50	256	25 06	286	30 13	331
168	30 43	039	28 14	092	36 33	153	36 11	204	53 26	255	24 43	285	30 01	330
169	30 58	038	28 38	091	36 44	153	36 02	203	53 03	254	24 19	284	29 48	329
170	31 13	037	29 02	090	36 56	152	35 52	202	52 39	254	23 56	283	29 35	328
171	31 27	036	29 27	089	37 07	151	35 43	202	52 16	253	23 32	282	29 22	327
172	31 41	035	29 51	089	37 19	151	35 34	201	51 52	252	23 08	281	29 09	326
173	31 55	033	30 16	088	37 31	150	35 25	200	51 29	251	22 44	280	28 55	325
174	32 08	032	30 40	087	37 44	149	35 17	200	51 06	251	22 20	279	28 40	323
175	32 21	031	31 04	086	37 56	149	35 09	199	50 43	250	21 56	278	28 26	322
176	32 33	030	31 29	085	38 09	148	35 01	198	50 20	249	21 31	277	28 11	321
177	32 45	029	31 53	084	38 22	147	34 54	198	49 58	248	21 07	276	27 55	320
178	32 57	028	32 17	083	38 35	147	34 46	197	49 35	248	20 43	275	27 39	319
179	33 08	027	32 41	082	38 49	146	34 39	197	49 12	247	20 19	274	27 23	318

 LAT 66°S

LHA ♈	Hc	Zn	Hc	Zn	Hc	Zn	Hc	Zn	Hc	Zn	Hc	Zn	Hc	Zn
	◆SPICA		ANTARES		◆Peacock		ACHERNAR		◆CANOPUS		SIRIUS		Alphard	
180	33 19	025	33 05	081	39 03	145	34 32	196	48 50	246	19 54	273	27 07	317
181	33 29	024	33 30	080	39 17	145	34 26	195	48 28	246	19 30	273	26 50	316
182	33 39	023	33 54	079	39 31	144	34 19	195	48 06	245	19 05	272	26 33	315
183	33 48	022	34 17	078	39 45	144	34 13	194	47 44	244	18 41	271	26 15	314
184	33 57	021	34 41	077	40 00	143	34 08	193	47 22	243	18 17	270	25 57	313
185	34 06	020	35 05	076	40 15	142	34 02	193	47 00	243	17 52	269	25 39	312
186	34 14	018	35 29	075	40 30	142	33 57	192	46 38	242	17 28	268	25 21	311
187	34 21	017	35 52	074	40 45	141	33 52	191	46 17	241	17 03	267	25 02	310
188	34 28	016	36 16	073	41 00	140	33 47	191	45 56	241	16 39	266	24 43	309
189	34 35	015	36 39	072	41 16	140	33 43	190	45 34	240	16 15	265	24 24	308
190	34 41	014	37 02	071	41 32	139	33 39	189	45 13	239	15 50	264	24 05	307
191	34 46	013	37 25	070	41 48	138	33 35	189	44 53	238	15 26	263	23 45	306
192	34 51	011	37 48	069	42 04	138	33 31	188	44 32	238	15 02	263	23 25	304
193	34 56	010	38 11	068	42 21	137	33 28	187	44 11	237	14 38	262	23 05	303
194	35 00	009	38 33	067	42 37	136	33 25	187	43 51	236	14 14	261	22 44	302
	◆SPICA		ANTARES		◆Peacock		ACHERNAR		◆CANOPUS		Suhail		Alphard	
195	35 04	008	38 56	066	42 54	136	33 22	186	43 31	236	51 47	277	22 24	301
196	35 07	007	39 18	065	43 11	135	33 20	186	43 11	235	51 23	276	22 03	300
197	35 09	005	39 40	064	43 29	135	33 18	185	42 51	234	50 59	275	21 42	299
198	35 11	004	40 02	063	43 46	134	33 16	184	42 31	234	50 34	274	21 20	298
199	35 13	003	40 23	062	44 04	133	33 14	184	42 11	233	50 10	273	20 59	298
200	35 14	002	40 45	061	44 22	133	33 13	183	41 52	232	49 46	272	20 37	297
201	35 14	001	41 06	060	44 40	132	33 11	182	41 33	231	49 21	271	20 15	296
202	35 14	359	41 27	059	44 58	131	33 11	182	41 14	231	48 57	270	19 53	295
203	35 14	358	41 48	057	45 16	131	33 10	181	40 55	230	48 32	269	19 31	294
204	35 13	357	42 08	056	45 35	130	33 10	180	40 36	229	48 08	268	19 08	293
205	35 11	356	42 28	055	45 54	129	33 10	180	40 18	229	47 44	267	18 46	292
206	35 09	355	42 48	054	46 13	129	33 10	179	40 00	228	47 19	267	18 23	291
207	35 07	353	43 08	053	46 32	128	33 10	178	39 42	227	46 55	266	18 00	290
208	35 04	352	43 27	052	46 51	127	33 11	178	39 24	227	46 31	265	17 37	289
209	35 00	351	43 46	051	47 11	127	33 12	177	39 06	226	46 06	264	17 14	288
	◆ANTARES		Nunki		◆FOMALHAUT		ACHERNAR		CANOPUS		◆Suhail		SPICA	
210	44 05	049	30 19	087	11 39	141	33 14	176	38 49	225	45 42	263	34 56	350
211	44 23	048	30 43	086	11 54	140	33 15	176	38 32	225	45 18	262	34 51	349
212	44 41	047	31 07	085	12 10	139	33 17	175	38 15	224	44 54	261	34 46	347
213	44 59	046	31 32	084	12 26	138	33 19	175	37 58	223	44 30	260	34 41	346
214	45 16	045	31 56	083	12 43	137	33 22	174	37 41	223	44 06	260	34 35	345
215	45 33	044	32 20	082	12 59	137	33 25	173	37 25	222	43 42	259	34 28	344
216	45 50	042	32 44	081	13 16	136	33 28	173	37 08	221	43 18	258	34 21	343
217	46 06	041	33 08	080	13 34	135	33 31	172	36 53	221	42 54	257	34 14	342
218	46 22	040	33 32	079	13 51	134	33 34	171	36 37	220	42 30	256	34 06	340
219	46 37	039	33 56	078	14 09	133	33 38	171	36 21	219	42 07	255	33 57	339
220	46 52	037	34 20	078	14 27	132	33 42	170	36 06	218	41 43	255	33 48	338
221	47 07	036	34 44	077	14 45	131	33 47	169	35 51	218	41 19	254	33 39	337
222	47 21	035	35 08	076	15 03	131	33 51	169	35 36	217	40 56	253	33 29	336
223	47 35	034	35 31	075	15 22	130	33 56	168	35 21	216	40 33	252	33 19	335
224	47 48	032	35 55	074	15 41	129	34 02	167	35 07	216	40 10	251	33 08	333
	◆ANTARES		Nunki		◆FOMALHAUT		ACHERNAR		CANOPUS		◆Suhail		SPICA	
225	48 01	031	36 18	073	16 00	128	34 07	167	34 53	215	39 46	251	32 57	332
226	48 13	030	36 41	072	16 19	127	34 13	166	34 39	214	39 24	250	32 45	331
227	48 25	028	37 04	071	16 39	126	34 19	165	34 25	214	39 01	249	32 33	330
228	48 36	027	37 27	070	16 58	126	34 25	165	34 12	213	38 38	248	32 21	329
229	48 47	026	37 50	069	17 18	125	34 31	164	33 59	212	38 15	247	32 08	328
230	48 57	024	38 13	067	17 38	124	34 38	164	33 46	212	37 53	247	31 55	327
231	49 07	023	38 35	066	17 59	123	34 45	163	33 33	211	37 31	246	31 41	325
232	49 16	022	38 57	065	18 19	122	34 53	162	33 21	210	37 08	245	31 27	324
233	49 25	020	39 19	064	18 40	121	35 00	162	33 08	210	36 46	244	31 13	323
234	49 33	019	39 41	063	19 01	121	35 08	161	32 57	209	36 24	243	30 58	322
235	49 41	018	40 03	062	19 22	120	35 16	160	32 45	208	36 03	243	30 43	321
236	49 48	016	40 25	061	19 43	119	35 24	160	32 33	208	35 41	242	30 27	320
237	49 55	015	40 46	060	20 05	118	35 33	159	32 22	207	35 20	241	30 11	319
238	50 01	013	41 07	059	20 26	117	35 42	158	32 11	206	34 58	240	29 55	318
239	50 06	012	41 28	058	20 48	116	35 51	158	32 01	206	34 37	240	29 38	317
	◆ANTARES		Nunki		◆FOMALHAUT		ACHERNAR		CANOPUS		◆ACRUX		SPICA	
240	50 11	011	41 48	057	21 10	115	36 00	157	31 50	205	67 43	252	29 21	316
241	50 15	009	42 08	056	21 32	115	36 10	156	31 40	204	67 20	252	29 04	314
242	50 19	008	42 28	055	21 55	114	36 20	156	31 30	203	66 57	251	28 47	313
243	50 22	006	42 48	053	22 17	113	36 30	155	31 21	203	66 34	250	28 29	312
244	50 24	005	43 08	052	22 39	112	36 40	155	31 11	202	66 11	250	28 10	311
245	50 26	004	43 27	051	23 02	111	36 51	154	31 02	201	65 48	249	27 52	310
246	50 27	002	43 46	050	23 25	110	37 02	153	30 54	201	65 26	249	27 33	309
247	50 28	001	44 04	049	23 48	110	37 13	153	30 45	200	65 03	248	27 14	308
248	50 28	359	44 22	048	24 11	109	37 24	152	30 37	199	64 40	247	26 55	307
249	50 27	358	44 40	046	24 34	108	37 36	151	30 29	199	64 18	247	26 35	306
250	50 26	357	44 58	045	24 57	107	37 47	151	30 21	198	63 55	246	26 15	305
251	50 24	355	45 15	044	25 21	106	37 59	150	30 14	197	63 33	246	25 55	304
252	50 22	354	45 32	043	25 44	105	38 12	149	30 07	197	63 11	245	25 35	303
253	50 19	352	45 48	042	26 08	104	38 24	149	30 00	196	62 49	245	25 14	302
254	50 16	351	46 04	040	26 32	104	38 37	148	29 53	195	62 27	244	24 53	301
	◆Nunki		FOMALHAUT		◆ACHERNAR		CANOPUS		◆ACRUX		SPICA		ANTARES	
255	46 19	039	26 55	103	38 50	148	29 47	195	62 05	243	24 32	300	50 11	350
256	46 35	038	27 19	102	39 03	147	29 41	194	61 43	243	24 11	299	50 07	348
257	46 49	037	27 43	101	39 17	146	29 36	193	61 21	242	23 50	298	50 01	347
258	47 04	035	28 07	100	39 30	146	29 30	192	61 00	242	23 29	297	49 56	345
259	47 18	034	28 31	099	39 44	145	29 25	192	60 39	241	23 06	296	49 49	344
260	47 31	033	28 55	098	39 58	144	29 20	191	60 17	241	22 44	295	49 42	343
261	47 44	031	29 20	097	40 13	144	29 16	190	59 56	240	22 22	294	49 35	341
262	47 57	030	29 44	097	40 27	143	29 11	190	59 35	239	22 00	293	49 27	340
263	48 09	029	30 08	096	40 42	142	29 07	189	59 14	239	21 37	292	49 18	339
264	48 20	028	30 32	095	40 57	142	29 04	188	58 53	238	21 14	291	49 09	337
265	48 31	026	30 57	094	41 12	141	29 00	188	58 32	238	20 51	290	48 59	336
266	48 42	025	31 21	093	41 28	141	28 57	187	58 12	237	20 28	289	48 49	335
267	48 52	024	31 45	092	41 43	140	28 54	186	57 51	237	20 05	288	48 38	333
268	49 01	022	32 10	091	41 59	139	28 52	186	57 31	236	19 42	287	48 27	332
269	49 10	021	32 34	090	42 15	139	28 50	185	57 11	236	19 19	286	48 15	331

LHA ♈	Hc	Zn	Hc	Zn	Hc	Zn	Hc	Zn	Hc	Zn	Hc	Zn	Hc	Zn
	◆Nunki		FOMALHAUT		◆ACHERNAR		CANOPUS		◆ACRUX		SPICA		ANTARES	
270	49 19	020	32 59	089	42 31	138	28 48	184	56 51	235	18 55	285	48 03	329
271	49 26	018	33 23	088	42 48	137	28 46	184	56 31	234	18 32	284	47 50	328
272	49 34	017	33 47	087	43 04	137	28 45	183	56 11	234	18 08	283	47 37	327
273	49 40	015	34 12	087	43 21	136	28 44	182	55 51	233	17 44	282	47 23	325
274	49 47	014	34 36	086	43 38	135	28 43	181	55 32	233	17 20	281	47 09	324
275	49 52	013	35 00	085	43 55	135	28 42	181	55 13	232	16 56	281	46 55	323
276	49 57	011	35 25	084	44 13	134	28 42	180	54 53	232	16 32	280	46 40	322
277	50 02	010	35 49	083	44 30	134	28 42	179	54 34	231	16 08	279	46 25	320
278	50 06	008	36 13	082	44 48	133	28 43	179	54 15	231	15 44	278	46 09	319
279	50 09	007	36 37	081	45 06	132	28 44	178	53 57	230	15 20	277	45 53	318
280	50 12	006	37 01	080	45 24	132	28 45	177	53 38	229	14 56	276	45 36	317
281	50 14	004	37 25	079	45 43	131	28 46	177	53 20	229	14 31	275	45 19	315
282	50 15	003	37 49	078	46 01	130	28 47	176	53 01	228	14 07	274	45 02	314
283	50 16	001	38 13	077	46 20	130	28 49	175	52 43	228	13 43	273	44 44	313
284	50 17	000	38 37	076	46 39	129	28 52	175	52 25	227	13 18	272	44 26	312
	◆ALTAIR		FOMALHAUT		◆ACHERNAR		CANOPUS		◆RIGIL KENT		ANTARES		Nunki	
285	14 30	013	39 00	075	46 58	128	28 54	174	61 55	249	44 08	311	50 16	359
286	14 35	012	39 24	074	47 17	128	28 57	173	61 33	249	43 49	310	50 15	357
287	14 40	011	39 47	073	47 36	127	29 00	172	61 10	248	43 30	308	50 14	356
288	14 44	010	40 11	072	47 56	126	29 03	172	60 47	247	43 11	307	50 12	354
289	14 48	009	40 34	071	48 16	126	29 07	171	60 25	247	42 51	306	50 09	353
290	14 52	008	40 57	070	48 35	125	29 11	170	60 02	246	42 32	305	50 06	352
291	14 55	007	41 20	069	48 55	125	29 15	170	59 40	245	42 11	304	50 02	350
292	14 58	006	41 42	068	49 16	124	29 19	169	59 18	245	41 51	303	49 58	349
293	15 00	005	42 05	067	49 36	123	29 24	168	58 56	244	41 30	302	49 53	347
294	15 02	004	42 27	066	49 56	123	29 29	168	58 34	244	41 09	301	49 47	346
295	15 04	003	42 49	065	50 17	122	29 35	167	58 12	243	40 48	299	49 41	345
296	15 05	002	43 11	064	50 38	121	29 40	166	57 51	242	40 27	298	49 34	343
297	15 05	001	43 33	062	50 59	121	29 46	166	57 29	242	40 05	297	49 27	342
298	15 05	000	43 54	061	51 20	120	29 53	165	57 08	241	39 44	296	49 19	341
299	15 05	359	44 16	060	51 41	119	29 59	164	56 46	241	39 22	295	49 11	339
	◆FOMALHAUT		ACHERNAR		◆CANOPUS		RIGIL KENT		◆ANTARES		Nunki		ALTAIR	
300	44 37	059	52 02	119	30 06	163	56 25	240	38 59	294	49 02	338	15 04	358
301	44 58	058	52 24	118	30 13	163	56 04	239	38 37	293	48 53	337	15 03	357
302	45 18	057	52 45	117	30 20	162	55 43	239	38 14	292	48 43	335	15 02	356
303	45 38	056	53 07	117	30 28	161	55 22	238	37 52	291	48 32	334	15 00	355
304	45 59	055	53 29	116	30 36	161	55 02	238	37 29	290	48 21	333	14 57	354
305	46 18	053	53 51	115	30 44	160	54 41	237	37 06	289	48 10	331	14 54	353
306	46 38	052	54 13	115	30 52	159	54 21	236	36 43	288	47 58	330	14 51	352
307	46 57	051	54 35	114	31 01	159	54 00	236	36 19	287	47 45	329	14 47	351
308	47 16	050	54 58	113	31 10	158	53 40	235	35 56	286	47 32	327	14 43	350
309	47 34	049	55 20	113	31 19	157	53 20	235	35 33	285	47 19	326	14 39	349
310	47 52	047	55 43	112	31 29	157	53 01	234	35 09	284	47 05	325	14 34	348
311	48 10	046	56 06	111	31 39	156	52 41	233	34 45	283	46 51	324	14 28	347
312	48 28	045	56 28	110	31 49	155	52 21	233	34 21	282	46 36	322	14 22	346
313	48 45	044	56 51	110	31 59	155	52 02	232	33 57	281	46 21	321	14 16	345
314	49 01	043	57 14	109	32 10	154	51 43	232	33 33	280	46 05	320	14 09	344
	◆FOMALHAUT		ACHERNAR		◆CANOPUS		Miaplacidus		RIGIL KENT		◆ANTARES		Nunki	
315	49 18	041	57 37	108	32 21	153	45 48	182	51 24	231	33 09	279	45 49	319
316	49 33	040	58 01	108	32 32	153	45 47	181	51 05	230	32 45	278	45 33	317
317	49 49	039	58 24	107	32 43	152	45 47	181	50 46	230	32 21	277	45 16	316
318	50 04	037	58 47	106	32 55	151	45 47	180	50 28	229	31 57	276	44 59	315
319	50 19	036	59 11	105	33 07	150	45 47	180	50 09	229	31 33	275	44 42	314
320	50 33	035	59 34	105	33 19	150	45 47	179	49 51	228	31 08	274	44 24	313
321	50 46	033	59 58	104	33 31	149	45 47	179	49 33	227	30 44	273	44 06	311
322	51 00	032	60 22	103	33 44	148	45 48	178	49 15	227	30 20	273	43 47	310
323	51 12	031	60 46	103	33 57	148	45 49	178	48 57	226	29 55	272	43 29	309
324	51 25	029	61 09	102	34 10	147	45 50	177	48 40	226	29 31	271	43 09	308
325	51 36	028	61 33	101	34 23	146	45 51	177	48 23	225	29 06	270	42 50	307
326	51 48	027	61 57	100	34 37	146	45 53	176	48 05	224	28 42	269	42 30	306
327	51 58	025	62 21	099	34 51	145	45 55	176	47 48	224	28 18	268	42 10	304
328	52 08	024	62 45	099	35 05	144	45 57	175	47 32	223	27 53	267	41 50	303
329	52 18	023	63 10	098	35 19	144	45 59	175	47 15	223	27 29	266	41 30	302
	◆FOMALHAUT		ACHERNAR		◆CANOPUS		Miaplacidus		RIGIL KENT		◆ANTARES		Nunki	
330	52 27	021	63 34	097	35 34	143	46 01	174	46 58	222	27 04	265	41 09	301
331	52 36	020	63 58	096	35 49	142	46 04	174	46 42	222	26 40	264	40 48	300
332	52 44	018	64 22	095	36 04	142	46 06	173	46 26	221	26 16	263	40 27	299
333	52 51	017	64 47	095	36 19	141	46 09	173	46 10	220	25 52	263	40 05	298
334	52 58	015	65 11	094	36 35	140	46 13	172	45 55	220	25 28	262	39 43	297
335	53 04	014	65 35	093	36 50	140	46 16	172	45 39	219	25 03	261	39 22	296
336	53 10	013	66 00	092	37 06	139	46 20	171	45 24	219	24 39	260	39 00	295
337	53 15	011	66 24	091	37 22	138	46 23	171	45 09	218	24 15	259	38 37	294
338	53 19	010	66 49	090	37 39	138	46 27	170	44 54	217	23 51	258	38 15	293
339	53 23	008	67 13	089	37 55	137	46 32	170	44 39	217	23 28	257	37 52	292
340	53 26	007	67 37	088	38 12	136	46 36	169	44 24	216	23 04	256	37 29	291
341	53 28	005	68 02	087	38 29	135	46 41	169	44 10	216	22 40	256	37 07	290
342	53 30	004	68 26	086	38 46	135	46 46	168	43 56	215	22 17	255	36 43	289
343	53 32	002	68 50	085	39 04	134	46 51	168	43 42	214	21 53	254	36 20	288
344	53 32	001	69 15	084	39 21	133	46 56	167	43 28	214	21 30	253	35 57	287
	Diphda		◆CANOPUS		Miaplacidus		RIGIL KENT		◆ANTARES		Nunki		◆FOMALHAUT	
345	38 56	033	39 39	133	47 01	167	43 15	213	21 06	252	35 33	286	53 33	359
346	39 09	031	39 57	132	47 07	166	43 02	213	20 43	251	35 10	285	53 32	358
347	39 22	030	40 15	131	47 13	166	42 49	212	20 20	250	34 46	284	53 31	357
348	39 34	029	40 34	131	47 19	165	42 36	211	19 57	250	34 22	283	53 29	355
349	39 45	028	40 52	130	47 25	165	42 23	211	19 34	249	33 59	282	53 27	354
350	39 56	027	41 11	129	47 32	164	42 11	210	19 12	248	33 35	281	53 24	352
351	40 07	025	41 30	129	47 38	164	41 59	210	18 49	247	33 11	280	53 20	351
352	40 17	024	41 49	128	47 45	163	41 47	209	18 27	246	32 47	279	53 16	349
353	40 27	023	42 09	127	47 52	163	41 35	208	18 05	245	32 22	278	53 11	348
354	40 36	022	42 28	127	47 59	162	41 23	208	17 43	244	31 58	277	53 05	346
355	40 45	020	42 48	126	48 07	162	41 12	207	17 21	243	31 34	276	52 59	345
356	40 53	019	43 08	125	48 14	162	41 01	207	16 59	243	31 10	275	52 53	343
357	41 01	018	43 28	124	48 22	161	40 50	206	16 37	242	30 45	274	52 45	342
358	41 08	017	43 48	124	48 30	161	40 39	205	16 16	241	30 21	273	52 38	341
359	41 15	015	44 08	123	48 39	160	40 29	205	15 55	240	29 57	272	52 29	339

 LAT 67°S

LHA ♈	Hc	Zn	Hc	Zn	Hc	Zn	Hc	Zn	Hc	Zn	Hc	Zn	Hc	Zn
	Diphda		◆ RIGEL		CANOPUS		Miaplacidus		◆ RIGIL KENT		Peacock		◆ FOMALHAUT	
0	40 23	014	11 54	083	45 01	122	49 43	159	41 14	205	63 50	267	51 25	338
1	40 28	013	12 17	082	45 21	121	49 52	159	41 04	204	63 27	266	51 16	337
2	40 33	011	12 40	081	45 41	120	50 00	158	40 54	203	63 03	265	51 06	336
3	40 37	010	13 03	080	46 01	119	50 09	158	40 45	203	62 40	264	50 56	334
4	40 41	009	13 26	079	46 22	119	50 18	157	40 36	202	62 17	263	50 46	333
5	40 45	008	13 49	078	46 42	118	50 27	157	40 28	202	61 53	263	50 35	332
6	40 48	006	14 12	077	47 03	117	50 36	156	40 19	201	61 30	262	50 23	330
7	40 50	005	14 35	076	47 24	116	50 46	156	40 11	200	61 07	261	50 12	329
8	40 52	004	14 58	075	47 45	116	50 56	155	40 03	200	60 44	260	49 59	328
9	40 53	003	15 20	074	48 06	115	51 06	155	39 55	199	60 21	259	49 46	326
10	40 54	001	15 43	073	48 28	114	51 16	154	39 47	199	59 58	259	49 33	325
11	40 54	000	16 05	073	48 49	114	51 26	154	39 40	198	59 35	258	49 19	324
12	40 54	359	16 28	072	49 11	113	51 36	153	39 33	197	59 12	257	49 05	322
13	40 53	358	16 50	071	49 32	112	51 47	153	39 26	197	58 49	256	48 51	321
14	40 52	356	17 12	070	49 54	111	51 58	152	39 19	196	58 26	255	48 36	320
	◆ RIGEL		CANOPUS		Miaplacidus		◆ RIGIL KENT		Peacock		◆ FOMALHAUT		Diphda	
15	17 34	069	50 16	111	52 09	152	39 13	195	58 04	255	48 21	319	40 50	355
16	17 55	068	50 38	110	52 20	151	39 07	195	57 41	254	48 05	317	40 48	354
17	18 17	067	51 00	109	52 31	151	39 01	194	57 19	253	47 49	316	40 45	353
18	18 39	066	51 22	108	52 42	151	38 55	194	56 56	252	47 32	315	40 42	351
19	19 00	065	51 45	107	52 54	150	38 50	193	56 34	252	47 15	314	40 38	350
20	19 21	064	52 07	107	53 06	150	38 45	192	56 12	251	46 58	312	40 34	349
21	19 42	063	52 30	106	53 18	149	38 40	192	55 50	250	46 41	311	40 29	348
22	20 03	062	52 52	105	53 30	149	38 35	191	55 28	250	46 23	310	40 24	346
23	20 23	061	53 15	104	53 42	148	38 31	191	55 06	249	46 05	309	40 18	345
24	20 44	060	53 38	104	53 55	148	38 27	190	54 44	248	45 47	308	40 12	344
25	21 04	059	54 00	103	54 07	147	38 23	189	54 22	247	45 28	307	40 05	343
26	21 24	058	54 23	102	54 20	147	38 19	189	54 01	247	45 09	305	39 58	341
27	21 43	057	54 46	101	54 33	146	38 16	188	53 39	246	44 50	304	39 50	340
28	22 03	056	55 09	100	54 46	146	38 12	187	53 18	245	44 30	303	39 42	339
29	22 22	055	55 32	100	54 59	145	38 09	187	52 56	245	44 10	302	39 33	338
	◆ RIGEL		CANOPUS		Miaplacidus		◆ RIGIL KENT		Peacock		◆ FOMALHAUT		Diphda	
30	22 41	054	55 56	099	55 13	145	38 07	186	52 35	244	43 50	301	39 24	336
31	23 00	053	56 19	098	55 26	144	38 04	186	52 14	243	43 30	300	39 14	335
32	23 19	052	56 42	097	55 40	144	38 02	185	51 54	242	43 10	299	39 04	334
33	23 37	051	57 05	096	55 54	144	38 00	184	51 33	242	42 49	298	38 54	333
34	23 55	050	57 29	095	56 08	143	37 59	184	51 12	241	42 28	296	38 43	332
35	24 13	049	57 52	094	56 22	143	37 57	183	50 52	240	42 07	295	38 32	330
36	24 30	048	58 15	094	56 36	142	37 56	183	50 31	240	41 46	294	38 20	329
37	24 47	047	58 39	093	56 51	142	37 55	182	50 11	239	41 24	293	38 08	328
38	25 04	046	59 02	092	57 05	141	37 54	181	49 51	238	41 03	292	37 55	327
39	25 21	045	59 26	091	57 20	141	37 54	181	49 31	238	40 41	291	37 42	326
40	25 37	043	59 49	090	57 35	140	37 54	180	49 12	237	40 19	290	37 29	325
41	25 53	042	60 12	089	57 50	140	37 54	179	48 52	236	39 57	289	37 15	323
42	26 09	041	60 36	088	58 05	139	37 54	179	48 33	236	39 35	288	37 01	322
43	26 24	040	60 59	087	58 21	139	37 55	178	48 13	235	39 12	287	36 46	321
44	26 39	039	61 23	086	58 36	139	37 56	178	47 54	234	38 50	286	36 31	320
	RIGEL		◆ SIRIUS		Suhail		◆ RIGIL KENT		Peacock		◆ FOMALHAUT		Diphda	
45	26 54	038	28 09	065	38 32	112	37 57	177	47 35	234	38 27	285	36 16	319
46	27 08	037	28 31	064	38 54	111	37 58	176	47 16	233	38 05	284	36 00	318
47	27 22	036	28 51	063	39 16	110	38 00	176	46 58	232	37 42	283	35 44	317
48	27 36	035	29 12	062	39 38	110	38 01	175	46 39	232	37 19	282	35 28	315
49	27 49	034	29 33	061	40 00	109	38 04	175	46 21	231	36 56	281	35 12	314
50	28 02	033	29 53	060	40 22	108	38 06	174	46 03	230	36 33	280	34 55	313
51	28 14	032	30 13	059	40 45	107	38 09	173	45 45	230	36 10	279	34 37	312
52	28 26	031	30 33	058	41 07	106	38 11	173	45 27	229	35 47	278	34 20	311
53	28 38	029	30 53	057	41 30	106	38 15	172	45 09	228	35 23	277	34 02	310
54	28 49	028	31 12	056	41 52	105	38 18	171	44 52	228	35 00	276	33 44	309
55	29 00	027	31 32	055	42 15	104	38 21	171	44 35	227	34 37	275	33 25	308
56	29 11	026	31 51	053	42 38	103	38 25	170	44 18	226	34 13	274	33 07	307
57	29 21	025	32 09	052	43 01	102	38 29	170	44 01	226	33 50	273	32 48	306
58	29 31	024	32 28	051	43 23	101	38 34	169	43 45	225	33 27	272	32 29	305
59	29 40	023	32 46	050	43 47	101	38 38	168	43 28	224	33 03	272	32 09	303
	RIGEL		◆ SIRIUS		Suhail		◆ RIGIL KENT		Peacock		◆ FOMALHAUT		Diphda	
60	29 49	022	33 04	049	44 10	100	38 43	168	43 11	224	32 40	271	31 50	302
61	29 57	020	33 21	048	44 33	099	38 48	167	42 55	223	32 16	270	31 30	301
62	30 05	019	33 39	047	44 56	098	38 54	167	42 39	222	31 53	269	31 10	300
63	30 13	018	33 56	046	45 19	097	38 59	166	42 23	222	31 29	268	30 49	299
64	30 20	017	34 12	045	45 42	096	39 05	165	42 08	221	31 06	267	30 29	298
65	30 26	016	34 29	044	46 06	095	39 11	165	41 53	221	30 43	266	30 08	297
66	30 33	015	34 45	043	46 29	094	39 17	164	41 37	220	30 19	265	29 47	296
67	30 38	014	35 00	041	46 53	094	39 24	163	41 23	219	29 56	264	29 26	295
68	30 44	012	35 16	040	47 16	093	39 31	163	41 08	219	29 32	263	29 05	294
69	30 48	011	35 31	039	47 39	092	39 38	162	40 53	218	29 09	262	28 43	293
70	30 53	010	35 45	038	48 03	091	39 45	162	40 39	217	28 46	262	28 21	292
71	30 57	009	35 59	037	48 26	090	39 52	161	40 25	217	28 23	261	28 00	291
72	31 00	008	36 13	036	48 50	089	40 00	160	40 11	216	28 00	260	27 38	290
73	31 03	007	36 27	035	49 13	088	40 08	160	39 57	215	27 37	259	27 16	289
74	31 06	006	36 40	033	49 37	087	40 16	159	39 44	215	27 14	258	26 53	288
	RIGEL		◆ SIRIUS		Suhail		◆ RIGIL KENT		Peacock		◆ FOMALHAUT		Diphda	
75	31 08	004	36 53	032	50 00	086	40 25	159	39 31	214	26 51	257	26 31	287
76	31 09	003	37 05	031	50 23	085	40 33	158	39 18	213	26 28	256	26 09	286
77	31 10	002	37 17	030	50 47	084	40 42	157	39 05	213	26 05	255	25 46	285
78	31 11	001	37 28	029	51 10	083	40 52	157	38 52	212	25 43	255	25 23	284
79	31 11	000	37 39	028	51 33	082	41 01	156	38 40	211	25 20	254	25 01	283
80	31 11	359	37 50	026	51 56	081	41 10	156	38 28	211	24 58	253	24 38	282
81	31 10	357	38 00	025	52 20	080	41 20	155	38 16	210	24 35	252	24 15	281
82	31 09	356	38 10	024	52 43	079	41 30	154	38 05	209	24 13	251	23 52	280
83	31 07	355	38 19	023	53 06	078	41 41	154	37 53	209	23 51	250	23 29	280
84	31 05	354	38 28	022	53 29	077	41 51	153	37 42	208	23 29	249	23 06	279
85	31 02	353	38 36	020	53 51	076	42 02	153	37 31	207	23 07	249	22 42	278
86	30 59	352	38 44	019	54 14	075	42 13	152	37 20	207	22 45	248	22 19	277
87	30 55	351	38 52	018	54 37	074	42 24	151	37 10	206	22 24	247	21 56	276
88	30 51	349	38 59	017	54 59	073	42 35	151	37 00	205	22 02	246	21 32	275
89	30 47	348	39 05	015	55 22	072	42 47	150	36 50	205	21 41	245	21 09	274

LHA ♈	Hc	Zn	Hc	Zn	Hc	Zn	Hc	Zn	Hc	Zn	Hc	Zn	Hc	Zn
	◆ SIRIUS		Suhail		◆ RIGIL KENT		Peacock		◆ ACHERNAR		Acamar		RIGEL	
90	39 11	014	55 44	071	42 59	149	36 40	204	59 29	256	53 34	294	30 42	347
91	39 17	013	56 06	070	43 11	149	36 31	204	59 06	255	53 12	293	30 36	346
92	39 22	012	56 28	069	43 23	148	36 21	203	58 44	255	52 51	292	30 30	345
93	39 26	011	56 49	067	43 35	148	36 12	202	58 21	254	52 29	291	30 24	344
94	39 30	009	57 11	066	43 48	147	36 04	202	57 59	253	52 07	290	30 17	343
95	39 34	008	57 32	065	44 01	146	35 55	201	57 36	252	51 45	288	30 10	341
96	39 37	007	57 53	064	44 14	146	35 47	200	57 14	252	51 22	287	30 02	340
97	39 39	006	58 14	063	44 27	145	35 39	200	56 52	251	51 00	286	29 54	339
98	39 41	004	58 35	061	44 41	145	35 31	199	56 30	250	50 37	285	29 45	338
99	39 43	003	58 56	060	44 54	144	35 24	198	56 08	250	50 15	284	29 36	337
100	39 44	002	59 16	059	45 08	143	35 17	198	55 46	249	49 52	283	29 27	336
101	39 44	001	59 36	058	45 22	143	35 10	197	55 24	248	49 29	282	29 17	335
102	39 44	359	59 55	056	45 37	142	35 03	196	55 02	247	49 06	281	29 07	334
103	39 44	358	60 15	055	45 51	142	34 57	196	54 41	247	48 43	280	28 56	332
104	39 43	357	60 34	054	46 06	141	34 50	195	54 19	246	48 20	279	28 45	331
	Alphard		◆ Gienah		RIGIL KENT		◆ Peacock		ACHERNAR		◆ RIGEL		SIRIUS	
105	26 36	042	20 25	087	46 21	140	34 44	194	53 58	245	28 34	330	39 41	356
106	26 51	041	20 48	086	46 36	140	34 39	194	53 36	245	28 22	329	39 39	354
107	27 06	040	21 12	085	46 51	139	34 33	193	53 15	244	28 10	328	39 36	353
108	27 21	039	21 35	084	47 06	139	34 28	192	52 54	243	27 57	327	39 33	352
109	27 36	038	21 58	083	47 22	138	34 23	192	52 33	243	27 44	326	39 30	351
110	27 50	036	22 22	082	47 38	137	34 19	191	52 13	242	27 31	325	39 26	349
111	28 04	035	22 45	082	47 54	137	34 14	190	51 52	241	27 17	324	39 21	348
112	28 17	034	23 08	081	48 10	136	34 10	190	51 32	241	27 03	323	39 16	347
113	28 30	033	23 31	080	48 26	136	34 06	189	51 11	240	26 48	321	39 11	346
114	28 43	032	23 54	079	48 43	135	34 03	188	50 51	239	26 34	320	39 04	344
115	28 55	031	24 17	078	48 59	134	34 00	188	50 31	239	26 19	319	38 58	343
116	29 07	030	24 40	077	49 16	134	33 57	187	50 11	238	26 03	318	38 51	342
117	29 18	029	25 03	076	49 33	133	33 54	186	49 51	237	25 47	317	38 43	341
118	29 29	028	25 25	075	49 50	132	33 51	186	49 32	237	25 31	316	38 36	340
119	29 40	026	25 48	074	50 08	132	33 49	185	49 12	236	25 15	315	38 27	338
	Alphard		◆ SPICA		RIGIL KENT		◆ Peacock		ACHERNAR		◆ RIGEL		SIRIUS	
120	29 50	025	13 39	087	50 25	131	33 47	184	48 53	235	24 58	314	38 18	337
121	30 00	024	14 03	086	50 43	131	33 46	184	48 34	235	24 41	313	38 09	336
122	30 09	023	14 26	085	51 01	130	33 44	183	48 15	234	24 24	312	37 59	335
123	30 18	022	14 49	084	51 19	129	33 43	182	47 56	233	24 06	311	37 49	334
124	30 27	021	15 13	083	51 37	129	33 42	182	47 37	233	23 48	310	37 38	332
125	30 35	020	15 36	082	51 55	128	33 42	181	47 19	232	23 30	309	37 27	331
126	30 43	019	15 59	081	52 14	128	33 41	180	47 00	231	23 12	308	37 16	330
127	30 50	017	16 22	080	52 33	127	33 41	180	46 42	231	22 53	307	37 04	329
128	30 57	016	16 45	079	52 51	126	33 41	179	46 24	230	22 34	306	36 51	328
129	31 03	015	17 08	078	53 10	126	33 42	178	46 06	229	22 15	305	36 39	326
130	31 09	014	17 31	077	53 29	125	33 43	178	45 49	229	21 56	304	36 26	325
131	31 14	013	17 54	076	53 49	125	33 44	177	45 31	228	21 36	303	36 12	324
132	31 19	012	18 17	075	54 08	124	33 45	177	45 14	227	21 16	302	35 58	323
133	31 24	011	18 39	074	54 28	123	33 46	176	44 57	227	20 56	301	35 44	322
134	31 28	009	19 02	073	54 47	123	33 48	175	44 40	226	20 36	300	35 29	321
	Alphard		◆ SPICA		RIGIL KENT		◆ Peacock		ACHERNAR		◆ CANOPUS		SIRIUS	
135	31 32	008	19 24	072	55 07	122	33 50	175	44 23	225	66 25	288	35 14	320
136	31 35	007	19 47	072	55 27	121	33 53	174	44 06	225	66 02	287	34 59	318
137	31 37	006	20 09	071	55 47	121	33 55	173	43 50	224	65 40	286	34 43	317
138	31 39	005	20 31	070	56 07	120	33 58	173	43 34	223	65 17	284	34 27	316
139	31 41	004	20 53	069	56 28	120	34 02	172	43 18	223	64 55	283	34 11	315
140	31 42	002	21 14	068	56 48	119	34 05	171	43 02	222	64 32	282	33 54	314
141	31 43	001	21 36	067	57 09	118	34 09	171	42 46	221	64 09	281	33 37	313
142	31 43	000	21 58	066	57 29	118	34 13	170	42 31	221	63 46	280	33 20	312
143	31 43	359	22 19	065	57 50	117	34 17	169	42 16	220	63 23	279	33 02	311
144	31 43	358	22 40	064	58 11	116	34 21	169	42 01	219	62 59	278	32 44	310
145	31 41	357	23 01	063	58 32	116	34 26	168	41 46	219	62 36	277	32 26	309
146	31 40	355	23 22	062	58 53	115	34 31	167	41 31	218	62 13	276	32 07	308
147	31 38	354	23 42	061	59 15	114	34 36	167	41 17	218	61 49	275	31 49	306
148	31 35	353	24 02	060	59 36	114	34 42	166	41 03	217	61 26	274	31 30	305
149	31 32	352	24 23	059	59 57	113	34 48	165	40 49	216	61 03	273	31 11	304
	◆ SPICA		RIGIL KENT		◆ Peacock		ACHERNAR		◆ CANOPUS		SIRIUS		Alphard	
150	24 43	058	60 19	112	34 54	165	40 35	216	60 39	272	30 51	303	31 29	351
151	25 02	057	60 41	112	35 00	164	40 22	215	60 16	271	30 31	302	31 25	350
152	25 22	056	61 03	111	35 07	163	40 08	214	59 52	270	30 11	301	31 20	349
153	25 41	055	61 25	110	35 14	163	39 55	214	59 29	269	29 51	300	31 15	347
154	26 00	054	61 47	110	35 21	162	39 42	213	59 05	268	29 31	299	31 10	346
155	26 19	053	62 09	109	35 28	161	39 30	212	58 42	267	29 10	298	31 04	345
156	26 37	051	62 31	108	35 36	161	39 17	212	58 18	267	28 49	297	30 58	344
157	26 55	050	62 53	108	35 44	160	39 05	211	57 55	266	28 29	296	30 51	343
158	27 13	049	63 15	107	35 52	159	38 53	210	57 32	265	28 07	295	30 44	342
159	27 31	048	63 38	106	36 00	159	38 41	210	57 09	264	27 46	294	30 36	340
160	27 48	047	64 00	106	36 09	158	38 30	209	56 45	263	27 25	293	30 28	339
161	28 05	046	64 23	105	36 18	157	38 18	208	56 22	262	27 03	292	30 20	338
162	28 22	045	64 46	104	36 27	157	38 07	208	55 59	261	26 41	291	30 11	337
163	28 39	044	65 08	104	36 36	156	37 57	207	55 36	261	26 19	290	30 01	336
164	28 55	043	65 31	103	36 46	155	37 46	206	55 13	260	25 57	289	29 52	335
	◆ SPICA		ANTARES		◆ Peacock		ACHERNAR		◆ CANOPUS		SIRIUS		Alphard	
165	29 11	042	27 05	094	36 56	155	37 36	206	54 50	259	25 35	288	29 42	334
166	29 26	041	27 29	093	37 06	154	37 26	205	54 27	258	25 12	287	29 31	333
167	29 41	040	27 52	093	37 16	153	37 16	205	54 04	257	24 50	286	29 20	331
168	29 56	039	28 16	092	37 27	153	37 06	204	53 41	257	24 27	285	29 09	330
169	30 11	038	28 39	091	37 38	152	36 57	203	53 18	256	24 05	284	28 57	329
170	30 25	036	29 02	090	37 49	152	36 48	203	52 55	255	23 42	283	28 45	328
171	30 38	035	29 26	089	38 00	151	36 39	202	52 33	254	23 19	282	28 32	327
172	30 52	034	29 49	088	38 11	150	36 30	201	52 10	253	22 56	281	28 19	326
173	31 05	033	30 13	087	38 23	150	36 22	201	51 48	253	22 33	280	28 06	325
174	31 17	032	30 36	086	38 35	149	36 14	200	51 25	252	22 10	279	27 52	324
175	31 30	031	31 00	085	38 47	148	36 06	199	51 03	251	21 47	278	27 38	323
176	31 41	030	31 23	084	39 00	148	35 58	199	50 41	250	21 24	278	27 24	322
177	31 53	029	31 46	083	39 12	147	35 51	198	50 19	250	21 00	277	27 09	321
178	32 04	027	32 09	082	39 25	146	35 43	197	49 57	249	20 37	276	26 54	319
179	32 14	026	32 33	081	39 39	146	35 37	197	49 35	248	20 14	275	26 38	318

LHA ♈	Hc	Zn	Hc	Zn	Hc	Zn	Hc	Zn	Hc	Zn	Hc	Zn	Hc	Zn
	◆ SPICA		ANTARES		◆ Peacock		ACHERNAR		◆ CANOPUS		SIRIUS		Alphard	
180	32 25	025	32 56	080	39 52	145	35 30	196	49 14	247	19 50	274	26 23	317
181	32 34	024	33 19	079	40 05	144	35 24	195	48 52	247	19 27	273	26 07	316
182	32 44	023	33 42	078	40 19	144	35 18	195	48 31	246	19 04	272	25 50	315
183	32 53	022	34 05	077	40 33	143	35 12	194	48 09	245	18 40	271	25 34	314
184	33 01	021	34 28	076	40 47	142	35 06	193	47 48	244	18 17	270	25 17	313
185	33 09	019	34 50	076	41 02	142	35 01	193	47 27	244	17 53	269	24 59	312
186	33 17	018	35 13	075	41 16	141	34 56	192	47 06	243	17 30	268	24 42	311
187	33 24	017	35 36	074	41 31	140	34 51	192	46 45	242	17 06	267	24 24	310
188	33 31	016	35 58	073	41 46	140	34 46	191	46 25	241	16 43	266	24 06	309
189	33 37	015	36 20	072	42 02	139	34 42	190	46 04	241	16 20	266	23 48	308
190	33 42	014	36 42	070	42 17	138	34 38	190	45 44	240	15 56	265	23 29	307
191	33 48	012	37 04	069	42 33	138	34 34	189	45 24	239	15 33	264	23 10	306
192	33 53	011	37 26	068	42 48	137	34 31	188	45 03	239	15 10	263	22 51	305
193	33 57	010	37 48	067	43 05	136	34 28	188	44 44	238	14 46	262	22 32	304
194	34 01	009	38 10	066	43 21	136	34 25	187	44 24	237	14 23	261	22 12	303
	◆ SPICA		ANTARES		◆ Peacock		ACHERNAR		◆ CANOPUS		Suhail		Alphard	
195	34 04	008	38 31	065	43 37	135	34 22	186	44 04	236	51 40	278	21 52	302
196	34 07	007	38 52	064	43 54	135	34 19	186	43 45	236	51 16	277	21 32	301
197	34 09	005	39 13	063	44 11	134	34 17	185	43 25	235	50 53	276	21 12	300
198	34 11	004	39 34	062	44 28	133	34 15	184	43 06	234	50 30	275	20 51	299
199	34 13	003	39 55	061	44 45	133	34 14	184	42 47	234	50 06	274	20 31	298
200	34 14	002	40 15	060	45 02	132	34 12	183	42 29	233	49 43	273	20 10	297
201	34 14	001	40 35	059	45 20	131	34 11	182	42 10	232	49 20	272	19 49	296
202	34 14	359	40 55	058	45 37	131	34 11	182	41 52	231	48 56	271	19 28	295
203	34 14	358	41 15	057	45 55	130	34 10	181	41 33	231	48 33	270	19 06	294
204	34 13	357	41 34	056	46 13	129	34 10	180	41 15	230	48 09	269	18 45	293
205	34 11	356	41 54	054	46 32	129	34 10	180	40 57	229	47 46	269	18 23	292
206	34 09	355	42 13	053	46 50	128	34 10	179	40 40	229	47 22	268	18 01	291
207	34 07	353	42 31	052	47 09	127	34 10	178	40 22	228	46 59	267	17 39	290
208	34 04	352	42 50	051	47 27	127	34 11	178	40 05	227	46 36	266	17 17	289
209	34 01	351	43 08	050	47 46	126	34 12	177	39 48	227	46 12	265	16 55	288
	◆ ANTARES		Nunki		◆ FOMALHAUT		ACHERNAR		CANOPUS		◆ Suhail		SPICA	
210	43 26	049	30 15	086	12 25	141	34 14	176	39 31	226	45 49	264	33 57	350
211	43 43	048	30 38	085	12 40	140	34 15	176	39 14	225	45 26	263	33 53	349
212	44 00	046	31 02	085	12 56	139	34 17	175	38 58	224	45 02	262	33 48	348
213	44 17	045	31 25	084	13 11	138	34 19	174	38 41	224	44 39	261	33 42	346
214	44 33	044	31 48	083	13 27	137	34 22	174	38 25	223	44 16	261	33 37	345
215	44 50	043	32 12	082	13 43	136	34 24	173	38 09	222	43 53	260	33 30	344
216	45 05	042	32 35	081	13 59	136	34 27	173	37 53	222	43 30	259	33 24	343
217	45 21	040	32 58	080	14 16	135	34 30	172	37 38	221	43 07	258	33 17	342
218	45 36	039	33 21	079	14 33	134	34 34	171	37 23	220	42 44	257	33 09	341
219	45 50	038	33 44	078	14 50	133	34 38	171	37 08	220	42 21	256	33 01	339
220	46 04	037	34 07	077	15 07	132	34 41	170	36 53	219	41 58	256	32 53	338
221	46 18	035	34 30	076	15 24	131	34 46	169	36 38	218	41 36	255	32 44	337
222	46 32	034	34 52	075	15 42	130	34 50	169	36 24	218	41 13	254	32 34	336
223	46 45	033	35 15	074	16 00	130	34 55	168	36 10	217	40 51	253	32 25	335
224	46 57	032	35 37	073	16 18	129	35 00	167	35 56	216	40 28	252	32 14	334
	◆ ANTARES		Nunki		◆ FOMALHAUT		ACHERNAR		CANOPUS		◆ Suhail		SPICA	
225	47 09	030	36 00	072	16 37	128	35 05	167	35 42	215	40 06	251	32 04	333
226	47 21	029	36 22	071	16 55	127	35 11	166	35 28	215	39 44	251	31 53	331
227	47 32	028	36 44	070	17 14	126	35 17	165	35 15	214	39 22	250	31 41	330
228	47 43	026	37 06	069	17 33	125	35 23	165	35 02	213	39 00	249	31 29	329
229	47 53	025	37 28	068	17 52	124	35 29	164	34 49	213	38 38	248	31 17	328
230	48 03	024	37 49	067	18 12	124	35 36	163	34 37	212	38 16	247	31 05	327
231	48 12	023	38 11	066	18 31	123	35 43	163	34 24	211	37 55	247	30 52	326
232	48 21	021	38 32	065	18 51	122	35 50	162	34 12	211	37 33	246	30 38	325
233	48 29	020	38 53	064	19 11	121	35 57	161	34 01	210	37 12	245	30 25	323
234	48 37	019	39 14	063	19 31	120	36 05	161	33 49	209	36 51	244	30 10	322
235	48 44	017	39 35	061	19 52	119	36 12	160	33 38	209	36 30	243	29 56	321
236	48 50	016	39 55	060	20 12	119	36 21	159	33 27	208	36 09	243	29 41	320
237	48 57	014	40 16	059	20 33	118	36 29	159	33 16	207	35 48	242	29 26	319
238	49 02	013	40 36	058	20 54	117	36 38	158	33 05	206	35 28	241	29 10	318
239	49 07	012	40 55	057	21 15	116	36 46	157	32 55	206	35 07	240	28 55	317
	◆ ANTARES		Nunki		◆ FOMALHAUT		ACHERNAR		CANOPUS		◆ ACRUX		SPICA	
240	49 12	010	41 15	056	21 36	115	36 55	157	32 45	205	68 01	255	28 38	316
241	49 16	009	41 34	055	21 57	114	37 05	156	32 35	204	67 38	254	28 22	315
242	49 19	008	41 53	054	22 19	113	37 14	156	32 25	204	67 16	253	28 05	314
243	49 22	006	42 12	053	22 40	113	37 24	155	32 16	203	66 53	253	27 48	313
244	49 24	005	42 31	052	23 02	112	37 34	154	32 07	202	66 31	252	27 31	312
245	49 26	004	42 49	050	23 24	111	37 45	154	31 58	202	66 09	251	27 13	311
246	49 27	002	43 07	049	23 46	110	37 55	153	31 50	201	65 46	251	26 55	310
247	49 28	001	43 24	048	24 08	109	38 06	152	31 42	200	65 24	250	26 37	309
248	49 28	359	43 42	047	24 30	108	38 17	152	31 34	200	65 02	249	26 18	307
249	49 27	358	43 58	046	24 52	107	38 28	151	31 26	199	64 40	249	26 00	306
250	49 26	357	44 15	044	25 15	107	38 40	150	31 18	198	64 19	248	25 41	305
251	49 25	355	44 31	043	25 37	106	38 51	150	31 11	197	63 57	248	25 22	304
252	49 22	354	44 47	042	26 00	105	39 03	149	31 04	197	63 35	247	25 02	303
253	49 20	353	45 03	041	26 23	104	39 16	148	30 58	196	63 14	246	24 42	302
254	49 16	351	45 18	040	26 45	103	39 28	148	30 51	195	62 52	246	24 22	301
	◆ Nunki		FOMALHAUT		◆ ACHERNAR		CANOPUS		◆ ACRUX		SPICA		ANTARES	
255	45 33	038	27 08	102	39 41	147	30 45	195	62 31	245	24 02	300	49 12	350
256	45 47	037	27 31	101	39 53	146	30 39	194	62 10	245	23 42	299	49 08	348
257	46 01	036	27 54	100	40 06	146	30 34	193	61 49	244	23 21	298	49 03	347
258	46 15	035	28 17	100	40 20	145	30 29	193	61 28	243	23 01	297	48 58	346
259	46 28	033	28 40	099	40 33	145	30 24	192	61 07	243	22 40	296	48 51	344
260	46 40	032	29 04	098	40 47	144	30 19	191	60 46	242	22 19	295	48 45	343
261	46 53	031	29 27	097	41 01	143	30 15	191	60 25	242	21 57	294	48 38	342
262	47 05	030	29 50	096	41 15	143	30 10	190	60 05	241	21 36	293	48 30	340
263	47 16	028	30 14	095	41 29	142	30 07	189	59 44	240	21 14	292	48 22	339
264	47 27	027	30 37	094	41 44	141	30 03	188	59 24	240	20 53	291	48 13	338
265	47 37	026	31 00	093	41 59	141	30 00	188	59 04	239	20 31	290	48 04	336
266	47 47	024	31 24	092	42 14	140	29 57	187	58 44	239	20 09	289	47 55	335
267	47 57	023	31 47	091	42 29	139	29 54	186	58 24	238	19 46	288	47 44	334
268	48 06	022	32 11	090	42 44	139	29 52	186	58 04	237	19 24	288	47 34	332
269	48 14	020	32 34	090	43 00	138	29 49	185	57 44	237	19 02	287	47 23	331

LHA ♈	Hc	Zn	Hc	Zn	Hc	Zn	Hc	Zn	Hc	Zn	Hc	Zn	Hc	Zn
	◆ Nunki		FOMALHAUT		◆ ACHERNAR		CANOPUS		◆ ACRUX		SPICA		ANTARES	
270	48 22	019	32 58	089	43 16	137	29 48	184	57 25	236	18 39	286	47 11	330
271	48 29	018	33 21	088	43 32	137	29 46	184	57 05	236	18 17	285	46 59	329
272	48 36	016	33 44	087	43 48	136	29 45	183	56 46	235	17 54	284	46 47	327
273	48 43	015	34 08	086	44 04	135	29 44	182	56 27	235	17 31	283	46 34	326
274	48 48	014	34 31	085	44 21	135	29 43	181	56 08	234	17 08	282	46 21	325
275	48 54	012	34 54	084	44 37	134	29 42	181	55 49	233	16 45	281	46 07	324
276	48 58	011	35 18	083	44 54	133	29 42	180	55 30	233	16 22	280	45 53	322
277	49 03	010	35 41	082	45 11	133	29 42	179	55 12	232	15 59	279	45 38	321
278	49 06	008	36 04	081	45 29	132	29 43	179	54 53	232	15 36	278	45 23	320
279	49 09	007	36 27	080	45 46	132	29 43	178	54 35	231	15 13	277	45 08	319
280	49 12	006	36 50	079	46 04	131	29 44	177	54 17	230	14 49	276	44 52	317
281	49 14	004	37 13	078	46 22	130	29 46	177	53 59	230	14 26	275	44 36	316
282	49 15	003	37 36	077	46 40	130	29 47	176	53 41	229	14 03	274	44 20	315
283	49 16	001	37 59	076	46 58	129	29 49	175	53 23	229	13 39	273	44 03	314
284	49 17	000	38 22	075	47 16	128	29 51	174	53 05	228	13 16	272	43 46	313
	◆ ALTAIR		FOMALHAUT		◆ ACHERNAR		CANOPUS		◆ RIGIL KENT		ANTARES		Nunki	
285	13 31	013	38 44	074	47 35	128	29 54	174	62 16	251	43 28	311	49 16	359
286	13 36	012	39 07	073	47 53	127	29 56	173	61 54	250	43 11	310	49 16	357
287	13 41	011	39 29	072	48 12	126	29 59	172	61 31	250	42 53	309	49 14	356
288	13 45	010	39 52	071	48 31	126	30 03	172	61 10	249	42 34	308	49 12	355
289	13 49	009	40 14	070	48 50	125	30 06	171	60 48	248	42 16	307	49 10	353
290	13 53	008	40 36	069	49 10	124	30 10	170	60 26	248	41 57	306	49 07	352
291	13 56	007	40 57	068	49 29	124	30 14	170	60 04	247	41 38	305	49 03	350
292	13 58	006	41 19	067	49 49	123	30 18	169	59 43	246	41 18	303	48 59	349
293	14 01	005	41 41	066	50 08	122	30 23	168	59 21	246	40 59	302	48 54	348
294	14 02	004	42 02	065	50 28	122	30 28	168	59 00	245	40 39	301	48 49	346
295	14 04	003	42 23	064	50 48	121	30 33	167	58 39	244	40 18	300	48 43	345
296	14 05	002	42 44	063	51 09	120	30 39	166	58 18	244	39 58	299	48 37	344
297	14 05	001	43 05	062	51 29	120	30 44	165	57 57	243	39 38	298	48 30	342
298	14 05	000	43 25	061	51 49	119	30 50	165	57 36	243	39 17	297	48 23	341
299	14 05	359	43 46	059	52 10	118	30 57	164	57 15	242	38 56	296	48 15	340
	◆ FOMALHAUT		ACHERNAR		◆ CANOPUS		RIGIL KENT		◆ ANTARES		Nunki		ALTAIR	
300	44 06	058	52 31	118	31 03	163	56 55	241	38 35	295	48 06	338	14 05	358
301	44 25	057	52 51	117	31 10	163	56 34	241	38 13	294	47 57	337	14 03	357
302	44 45	056	53 12	116	31 17	162	56 14	240	37 52	293	47 48	336	14 02	356
303	45 04	055	53 34	115	31 25	161	55 53	239	37 30	292	47 38	334	14 00	355
304	45 23	054	53 55	115	31 32	161	55 33	239	37 08	291	47 28	333	13 58	354
305	45 42	053	54 16	114	31 40	160	55 13	238	36 46	290	47 17	332	13 55	353
306	46 01	051	54 38	113	31 49	159	54 53	238	36 24	289	47 06	331	13 52	352
307	46 19	050	54 59	113	31 57	158	54 34	237	36 02	288	46 54	329	13 48	351
308	46 37	049	55 21	112	32 06	158	54 14	236	35 39	287	46 42	328	13 44	350
309	46 54	048	55 43	111	32 15	157	53 55	236	35 17	286	46 29	327	13 40	349
310	47 11	047	56 05	111	32 24	156	53 35	235	34 54	285	46 16	325	13 35	348
311	47 28	045	56 27	110	32 34	156	53 16	234	34 31	284	46 02	324	13 30	347
312	47 45	044	56 49	109	32 43	155	52 57	234	34 09	283	45 48	323	13 24	346
313	48 01	043	57 11	108	32 53	154	52 39	233	33 46	282	45 34	322	13 18	345
314	48 17	042	57 33	108	33 04	154	52 20	233	33 23	281	45 19	320	13 12	344
	◆ FOMALHAUT		ACHERNAR		◆ CANOPUS		Miaplacidus		RIGIL KENT		◆ ANTARES		Nunki	
315	48 32	040	57 56	107	33 14	153	46 48	182	52 01	232	33 00	280	45 04	319
316	48 47	039	58 18	106	33 25	152	46 47	181	51 43	231	32 36	279	44 49	318
317	49 02	038	58 41	105	33 36	152	46 47	181	51 25	231	32 13	278	44 33	317
318	49 16	037	59 03	105	33 47	151	46 47	180	51 07	230	31 50	277	44 17	316
319	49 30	035	59 26	104	33 59	150	46 47	180	50 49	230	31 27	276	44 00	314
320	49 43	034	59 49	103	34 11	150	46 47	179	50 31	229	31 03	275	43 43	313
321	49 56	033	60 12	102	34 23	149	46 47	179	50 13	228	30 40	274	43 26	312
322	50 09	031	60 35	102	34 35	148	46 48	178	49 56	228	30 17	273	43 08	311
323	50 21	030	60 58	101	34 48	147	46 49	178	49 39	227	29 53	272	42 51	310
324	50 32	029	61 21	100	35 00	147	46 50	177	49 22	226	29 30	271	42 32	309
325	50 43	027	61 44	099	35 13	146	46 51	177	49 05	226	29 06	270	42 14	307
326	50 54	026	62 07	098	35 26	145	46 53	176	48 48	225	28 43	269	41 55	306
327	51 04	025	62 30	098	35 40	145	46 54	176	48 31	225	28 19	269	41 36	305
328	51 13	023	62 53	097	35 54	144	46 56	175	48 15	224	27 56	268	41 17	304
329	51 23	022	63 17	096	36 08	143	46 58	175	47 59	223	27 33	267	40 57	303
	◆ FOMALHAUT		ACHERNAR		◆ CANOPUS		Miaplacidus		RIGIL KENT		◆ ANTARES		Nunki	
330	51 31	021	63 40	095	36 22	143	47 01	174	47 43	223	27 09	266	40 38	302
331	51 39	019	64 03	094	36 36	142	47 03	174	47 27	222	26 46	265	40 17	301
332	51 47	018	64 27	093	36 51	141	47 06	173	47 11	222	26 22	264	39 57	300
333	51 53	016	64 50	092	37 05	140	47 09	173	46 56	221	25 59	263	39 37	299
334	52 00	015	65 14	092	37 21	140	47 12	172	46 40	220	25 36	262	39 16	298
335	52 06	014	65 37	091	37 36	139	47 15	172	46 25	220	25 13	261	38 55	296
336	52 11	012	66 01	090	37 51	138	47 19	171	46 10	219	24 50	260	38 34	295
337	52 16	011	66 24	089	38 07	138	47 23	171	45 56	219	24 26	260	38 13	294
338	52 20	009	66 47	088	38 23	137	47 27	170	45 41	218	24 03	259	37 51	293
339	52 23	008	67 11	087	38 39	136	47 31	170	45 27	217	23 41	258	37 30	292
340	52 26	007	67 34	086	38 55	136	47 35	169	45 13	217	23 18	257	37 08	291
341	52 29	005	67 58	085	39 12	135	47 40	169	44 59	216	22 55	256	36 46	290
342	52 31	004	68 21	084	39 28	134	47 44	168	44 45	216	22 32	255	36 24	289
343	52 32	002	68 44	083	39 45	134	47 49	168	44 31	215	22 10	254	36 02	288
344	52 32	001	69 08	082	40 02	133	47 54	167	44 18	214	21 47	253	35 40	287
	Diphda		◆ CANOPUS		Miaplacidus		RIGIL KENT		◆ ANTARES		Nunki		◆ FOMALHAUT	
345	38 06	032	40 20	132	48 00	167	44 05	214	21 25	252	35 17	286	52 33	359
346	38 18	031	40 37	131	48 05	166	43 52	213	21 02	252	34 54	285	52 32	358
347	38 30	030	40 55	131	48 11	166	43 39	213	20 40	251	34 32	284	52 31	357
348	38 41	029	41 13	130	48 17	165	43 27	212	20 18	250	34 09	283	52 29	355
349	38 52	027	41 31	129	48 23	165	43 15	211	19 56	249	33 46	282	52 27	354
350	39 03	026	41 49	129	48 29	164	43 02	211	19 34	248	33 23	281	52 24	352
351	39 13	025	42 07	128	48 36	164	42 51	210	19 13	247	33 00	280	52 21	351
352	39 22	024	42 26	127	48 43	163	42 39	210	18 51	246	32 37	279	52 17	349
353	39 32	023	42 45	127	48 49	163	42 27	209	18 30	246	32 14	278	52 12	348
354	39 40	021	43 04	126	48 57	162	42 16	208	18 08	245	31 51	277	52 07	347
355	39 49	020	43 23	125	49 04	162	42 05	208	17 47	244	31 27	276	52 01	345
356	39 56	019	43 42	124	49 11	161	41 54	207	17 26	243	31 04	276	51 55	344
357	40 04	018	44 01	124	49 19	161	41 44	206	17 06	242	30 41	275	51 48	342
358	40 11	016	44 21	123	49 27	160	41 34	206	16 45	241	30 17	274	51 41	341
359	40 17	015	44 41	122	49 35	160	41 23	205	16 25	240	29 54	273	51 33	340

LHA ♈	Hc	Zn	Hc	Zn	Hc	Zn	Hc	Zn	Hc	Zn	Hc	Zn	Hc	Zn
	Diphda		◆RIGEL		CANOPUS		Miaplacidus		◆RIGIL KENT		Peacock		◆FOMALHAUT	
0	39 25	014	11 46	083	45 32	121	50 39	159	42 08	205	63 52	269	50 29	339
1	39 30	012	12 08	082	45 51	120	50 47	158	41 59	204	63 30	268	50 20	337
2	39 34	011	12 31	081	46 11	119	50 56	158	41 49	204	63 07	267	50 11	336
3	39 38	010	12 53	080	46 30	118	51 04	157	41 40	203	62 45	266	50 02	335
4	39 42	009	13 15	079	46 50	118	51 13	157	41 32	203	62 22	265	49 52	333
5	39 45	008	13 37	078	47 10	117	51 22	156	41 23	202	62 00	264	49 42	332
6	39 48	006	13 59	077	47 30	116	51 31	156	41 15	201	61 38	264	49 31	331
7	39 50	005	14 21	076	47 50	115	51 41	155	41 07	201	61 15	263	49 20	329
8	39 52	004	14 42	075	48 11	115	51 50	155	40 59	200	60 53	262	49 08	328
9	39 53	003	15 04	074	48 31	114	52 00	154	40 52	199	60 31	261	48 56	327
10	39 54	001	15 26	073	48 52	113	52 10	154	40 44	199	60 09	260	48 44	326
11	39 54	000	15 47	072	49 13	112	52 20	153	40 37	198	59 47	259	48 31	324
12	39 54	359	16 08	071	49 33	112	52 30	153	40 30	198	59 24	259	48 18	323
13	39 53	358	16 30	070	49 54	111	52 40	152	40 23	197	59 02	258	48 04	322
14	39 52	356	16 51	069	50 15	110	52 51	152	40 17	196	58 41	257	47 50	321
	◆RIGEL		CANOPUS		Miaplacidus		◆RIGIL KENT		Peacock		◆FOMALHAUT		Diphda	
15	17 12	068	50 36	109	53 01	151	40 11	196	58 19	256	47 35	319	39 51	355
16	17 33	067	50 58	109	53 12	151	40 05	195	57 57	255	47 20	318	39 48	354
17	17 53	066	51 19	108	53 23	150	39 59	194	57 35	255	47 05	317	39 46	353
18	18 14	065	51 41	107	53 35	150	39 54	194	57 14	254	46 50	316	39 43	351
19	18 34	064	52 02	106	53 46	149	39 48	193	56 52	253	46 34	314	39 39	350
20	18 54	064	52 24	105	53 57	149	39 43	193	56 30	252	46 18	313	39 35	349
21	19 14	063	52 45	105	54 09	148	39 39	192	56 09	252	46 01	312	39 30	348
22	19 34	062	53 07	104	54 21	148	39 34	191	55 48	251	45 44	311	39 25	347
23	19 54	061	53 29	103	54 33	147	39 30	191	55 27	250	45 27	310	39 20	345
24	20 13	060	53 51	102	54 45	147	39 26	190	55 06	249	45 10	308	39 14	344
25	20 33	059	54 13	101	54 58	146	39 22	189	54 45	249	44 52	307	39 08	343
26	20 52	058	54 35	101	55 10	146	39 18	189	54 24	248	44 34	306	39 01	342
27	21 11	057	54 57	100	55 23	145	39 15	188	54 03	247	44 16	305	38 53	340
28	21 29	056	55 19	099	55 36	145	39 12	188	53 42	247	43 57	304	38 46	339
29	21 48	055	55 42	098	55 48	145	39 09	187	53 22	246	43 38	303	38 38	338
	◆RIGEL		CANOPUS		Miaplacidus		◆RIGIL KENT		Peacock		◆FOMALHAUT		Diphda	
30	22 06	054	56 04	097	56 02	144	39 06	186	53 01	245	43 19	302	38 29	337
31	22 24	052	56 26	096	56 15	144	39 04	186	52 41	244	43 00	301	38 20	336
32	22 41	051	56 48	095	56 28	143	39 02	185	52 21	244	42 41	299	38 10	334
33	22 59	050	57 11	095	56 42	143	39 00	184	52 01	243	42 21	298	38 00	333
34	23 16	049	57 33	094	56 56	142	38 58	184	51 41	242	42 01	297	37 50	332
35	23 33	048	57 56	093	57 09	142	38 57	183	51 21	242	41 41	296	37 39	331
36	23 50	047	58 18	092	57 23	141	38 56	183	51 01	241	41 21	295	37 28	330
37	24 06	046	58 41	091	57 38	141	38 55	182	50 42	240	41 00	294	37 17	328
38	24 22	045	59 03	090	57 52	140	38 54	181	50 22	239	40 40	293	37 05	327
39	24 38	044	59 26	089	58 06	140	38 54	181	50 03	239	40 19	292	36 52	326
40	24 54	043	59 48	088	58 21	139	38 54	180	49 44	238	39 58	291	36 40	325
41	25 09	042	60 11	087	58 36	139	38 54	179	49 25	237	39 37	290	36 27	324
42	25 24	041	60 33	086	58 51	138	38 54	179	49 06	237	39 16	289	36 13	323
43	25 38	040	60 55	085	59 05	138	38 55	178	48 47	236	38 54	288	35 59	322
44	25 53	039	61 18	084	59 21	137	38 56	178	48 29	235	38 33	287	35 45	320
	RIGEL		◆SIRIUS		Suhail		◆RIGIL KENT		Peacock		◆FOMALHAUT		Diphda	
45	26 07	038	27 44	064	38 54	111	38 57	177	48 10	235	38 11	286	35 31	319
46	26 20	037	28 04	063	39 15	110	38 58	176	47 52	234	37 50	285	35 16	318
47	26 33	036	28 24	062	39 36	110	38 59	176	47 34	233	37 28	284	35 01	317
48	26 46	035	28 44	061	39 58	109	39 01	175	47 16	233	37 06	283	34 45	316
49	26 59	034	29 03	060	40 19	108	39 03	174	46 58	232	36 44	282	34 29	315
50	27 11	032	29 23	059	40 40	107	39 06	174	46 41	231	36 22	281	34 13	314
51	27 23	031	29 42	058	41 02	106	39 08	173	46 23	230	36 00	280	33 57	313
52	27 35	030	30 01	057	41 23	106	39 11	173	46 06	230	35 38	279	33 40	312
53	27 46	029	30 20	056	41 45	105	39 14	172	45 49	229	35 15	278	33 23	310
54	27 56	028	30 38	055	42 07	104	39 17	171	45 32	228	34 53	277	33 06	309
55	28 07	027	30 57	054	42 29	103	39 21	171	45 15	228	34 31	276	32 49	308
56	28 17	026	31 15	053	42 51	102	39 24	170	44 59	227	34 08	275	32 31	307
57	28 26	025	31 32	052	43 13	101	39 28	169	44 42	226	33 46	274	32 13	306
58	28 36	024	31 50	051	43 35	100	39 33	169	44 26	226	33 24	273	31 54	305
59	28 44	022	32 07	050	43 57	100	39 37	168	44 10	225	33 01	272	31 36	304
	RIGEL		◆SIRIUS		Suhail		◆RIGIL KENT		Peacock		◆FOMALHAUT		Diphda	
60	28 53	021	32 24	049	44 19	099	39 42	168	43 54	224	32 39	271	31 17	303
61	29 01	020	32 41	048	44 41	098	39 47	167	43 39	224	32 16	270	30 58	302
62	29 08	019	32 57	046	45 04	097	39 52	166	43 23	223	31 54	269	30 39	301
63	29 16	018	33 14	045	45 26	096	39 57	166	43 08	222	31 31	269	30 20	300
64	29 22	017	33 29	044	45 48	095	40 03	165	42 53	222	31 09	268	30 00	299
65	29 29	016	33 45	043	46 11	094	40 09	164	42 38	221	30 46	267	29 40	298
66	29 35	015	34 00	042	46 33	093	40 15	164	42 23	220	30 24	266	29 20	297
67	29 40	013	34 15	041	46 56	092	40 21	163	42 09	220	30 01	265	29 00	296
68	29 45	012	34 30	040	47 18	092	40 28	163	41 55	219	29 39	264	28 40	295
69	29 50	011	34 44	039	47 41	091	40 35	162	41 40	218	29 17	263	28 19	294
70	29 54	010	34 58	038	48 03	090	40 42	161	41 27	218	28 55	262	27 59	293
71	29 57	009	35 11	036	48 26	089	40 49	161	41 13	217	28 32	261	27 38	292
72	30 01	008	35 24	035	48 48	088	40 57	160	40 59	216	28 10	260	27 17	291
73	30 04	007	35 37	034	49 10	087	41 04	160	40 46	216	27 48	259	26 56	290
74	30 06	006	35 50	033	49 33	086	41 12	159	40 33	215	27 26	259	26 34	289
	RIGEL		◆SIRIUS		Suhail		◆RIGIL KENT		Peacock		◆FOMALHAUT		Diphda	
75	30 08	004	36 02	032	49 55	085	41 21	158	40 20	214	27 04	258	26 13	288
76	30 09	003	36 13	031	50 18	084	41 29	158	40 08	214	26 42	257	25 52	287
77	30 10	002	36 25	030	50 40	083	41 38	157	39 55	213	26 20	256	25 30	286
78	30 11	001	36 36	028	51 02	082	41 47	156	39 43	212	25 58	255	25 08	285
79	30 11	000	36 46	027	51 25	081	41 56	156	39 31	212	25 37	254	24 47	284
80	30 11	359	36 56	026	51 47	080	42 05	155	39 20	211	25 15	253	24 25	283
81	30 10	357	37 06	025	52 09	079	42 15	155	39 08	210	24 54	252	24 03	282
82	30 09	356	37 15	024	52 31	078	42 24	154	38 57	210	24 32	252	23 41	281
83	30 07	355	37 24	022	52 53	077	42 34	153	38 46	209	24 11	251	23 19	280
84	30 05	354	37 32	021	53 15	076	42 45	153	38 35	208	23 50	250	22 56	279
85	30 03	353	37 40	020	53 36	075	42 55	152	38 24	208	23 29	249	22 34	278
86	30 00	352	37 47	019	53 58	074	43 06	151	38 14	207	23 08	248	22 12	277
87	29 56	351	37 55	018	54 20	073	43 16	151	38 04	206	22 47	247	21 50	276
88	29 52	350	38 01	016	54 41	072	43 27	150	37 54	206	22 27	246	21 27	275
89	29 48	348	38 07	015	55 02	071	43 39	150	37 44	205	22 06	245	21 05	274

LHA ♈	Hc	Zn	Hc	Zn	Hc	Zn	Hc	Zn	Hc	Zn	Hc	Zn	Hc	Zn
	◆SIRIUS		Suhail		◆RIGIL KENT		Peacock		◆ACHERNAR		Acamar		RIGEL	
90	38 13	014	55 23	069	43 50	149	37 35	204	59 43	258	53 09	295	29 43	347
91	38 18	013	55 44	068	44 02	148	37 26	204	59 21	257	52 48	294	29 38	346
92	38 23	012	56 05	067	44 14	148	37 17	203	58 59	256	52 28	293	29 32	345
93	38 27	010	56 26	066	44 26	147	37 08	202	58 37	256	52 07	292	29 26	344
94	38 31	009	56 46	065	44 38	147	36 59	202	58 15	255	51 46	291	29 20	343
95	38 34	008	57 06	064	44 51	146	36 51	201	57 54	254	51 25	290	29 13	342
96	38 37	007	57 26	062	45 03	145	36 43	200	57 32	253	51 04	289	29 06	340
97	38 39	005	57 46	061	45 16	145	36 36	200	57 11	253	50 42	288	28 58	339
98	38 41	004	58 06	060	45 29	144	36 28	199	56 49	252	50 21	286	28 50	338
99	38 43	003	58 25	059	45 43	143	36 21	198	56 28	251	49 59	285	28 41	337
100	38 44	002	58 44	058	45 56	143	36 14	198	56 07	250	49 38	284	28 32	336
101	38 44	001	59 03	056	46 10	142	36 07	197	55 46	250	49 16	283	28 23	335
102	38 44	359	59 22	055	46 24	142	36 01	196	55 25	249	48 54	282	28 13	334
103	38 44	358	59 40	054	46 38	141	35 54	196	55 04	248	48 32	281	28 03	333
104	38 43	357	59 58	052	46 52	140	35 48	195	54 43	247	48 10	280	27 53	332
	Alphard		◆Gienah		RIGIL KENT		◆Peacock		ACHERNAR		◆RIGEL		SIRIUS	
105	25 51	041	20 22	087	47 07	140	35 43	194	54 22	247	27 42	330	38 41	356
106	26 06	040	20 44	086	47 21	139	35 37	194	54 02	246	27 30	329	38 39	354
107	26 20	039	21 07	085	47 36	138	35 32	193	53 41	245	27 19	328	38 37	353
108	26 34	038	21 29	084	47 51	138	35 27	192	53 21	244	27 07	327	38 34	352
109	26 48	037	21 51	083	48 06	137	35 22	192	53 01	244	26 54	326	38 31	351
110	27 01	036	22 14	082	48 22	137	35 18	191	52 40	243	26 42	325	38 27	350
111	27 15	035	22 36	081	48 37	136	35 13	190	52 20	242	26 29	324	38 22	348
112	27 27	034	22 58	080	48 53	135	35 09	190	52 01	242	26 15	323	38 18	347
113	27 40	033	23 20	079	49 09	135	35 06	189	51 41	241	26 01	322	38 12	346
114	27 52	032	23 42	078	49 25	134	35 02	188	51 21	240	25 47	321	38 07	345
115	28 03	031	24 04	077	49 41	133	34 59	188	51 02	240	25 33	320	38 00	343
116	28 15	030	24 26	076	49 57	133	34 56	187	50 43	239	25 18	319	37 54	342
117	28 25	028	24 48	075	50 14	132	34 53	186	50 23	238	25 03	318	37 47	341
118	28 36	027	25 10	074	50 31	132	34 51	186	50 04	238	24 48	316	37 39	340
119	28 46	026	25 31	073	50 48	131	34 49	185	49 45	237	24 32	315	37 31	339
	Alphard		◆SPICA		RIGIL KENT		◆Peacock		ACHERNAR		◆RIGEL		SIRIUS	
120	28 56	025	13 36	086	51 05	130	34 47	184	49 27	236	24 16	314	37 23	337
121	29 05	024	13 58	085	51 22	130	34 45	184	49 08	235	24 00	313	37 14	336
122	29 14	023	14 20	085	51 39	129	34 44	183	48 50	235	23 44	312	37 05	335
123	29 23	022	14 43	084	51 57	128	34 43	182	48 31	234	23 27	311	36 55	334
124	29 31	021	15 05	083	52 14	128	34 42	182	48 13	233	23 10	310	36 45	333
125	29 39	020	15 27	082	52 32	127	34 42	181	47 55	233	22 52	309	36 35	332
126	29 46	018	15 50	081	52 50	127	34 41	180	47 38	232	22 35	308	36 24	330
127	29 53	017	16 12	080	53 08	126	34 41	180	47 20	231	22 17	307	36 12	329
128	29 59	016	16 34	079	53 27	125	34 41	179	47 02	231	21 59	306	36 01	328
129	30 05	015	16 56	078	53 45	125	34 42	178	46 45	230	21 41	305	35 49	327
130	30 11	014	17 18	077	54 03	124	34 43	178	46 28	229	21 22	304	35 36	326
131	30 16	013	17 40	076	54 22	123	34 44	177	46 11	229	21 04	303	35 23	325
132	30 21	012	18 01	075	54 41	123	34 45	176	45 54	228	20 45	302	35 10	323
133	30 25	010	18 23	074	55 00	122	34 46	176	45 38	227	20 26	301	34 56	322
134	30 29	009	18 45	073	55 19	121	34 48	175	45 21	227	20 06	300	34 43	321
	Alphard		◆SPICA		RIGIL KENT		◆Peacock		ACHERNAR		◆CANOPUS		SIRIUS	
135	30 32	008	19 06	072	55 38	121	34 50	174	45 05	226	66 05	290	34 28	320
136	30 35	007	19 27	071	55 58	120	34 52	174	44 49	225	65 44	289	34 14	319
137	30 38	006	19 49	070	56 17	120	34 55	173	44 33	225	65 23	288	33 59	318
138	30 40	005	20 10	069	56 37	119	34 58	172	44 17	224	65 01	287	33 44	317
139	30 41	004	20 31	068	56 57	118	35 01	172	44 02	223	64 40	285	33 28	316
140	30 42	002	20 51	067	57 16	118	35 04	171	43 46	223	64 18	284	33 12	315
141	30 43	001	21 12	066	57 36	117	35 08	170	43 31	222	63 56	283	32 56	313
142	30 43	000	21 33	065	57 56	116	35 12	170	43 16	221	63 34	282	32 39	312
143	30 43	359	21 53	064	58 17	116	35 16	169	43 01	221	63 12	281	32 23	311
144	30 43	358	22 13	063	58 37	115	35 20	168	42 47	220	62 50	280	32 06	310
145	30 42	357	22 33	062	58 57	114	35 25	168	42 32	219	62 28	279	31 48	309
146	30 40	355	22 53	061	59 18	114	35 30	167	42 18	219	62 06	278	31 31	308
147	30 38	354	23 13	060	59 39	113	35 35	166	42 04	218	61 43	277	31 13	307
148	30 36	353	23 32	059	59 59	112	35 40	166	41 51	217	61 21	276	30 55	306
149	30 33	352	23 51	058	60 20	112	35 46	165	41 37	217	60 59	275	30 36	305
	◆SPICA		RIGIL KENT		◆Peacock		ACHERNAR		◆CANOPUS		SIRIUS		Alphard	
150	24 10	057	60 41	111	35 52	164	41 24	216	60 36	274	30 18	304	30 29	351
151	24 29	056	61 02	110	35 58	164	41 11	215	60 14	273	29 59	303	30 26	350
152	24 48	055	61 23	109	36 04	163	40 58	215	59 51	272	29 40	302	30 21	349
153	25 06	054	61 45	109	36 11	162	40 45	214	59 29	271	29 21	301	30 17	347
154	25 24	053	62 06	108	36 18	162	40 32	213	59 06	270	29 01	300	30 12	346
155	25 42	052	62 27	107	36 25	161	40 20	213	58 44	269	28 42	299	30 06	345
156	26 00	051	62 49	107	36 32	160	40 08	212	58 21	268	28 22	298	30 00	344
157	26 17	050	63 10	106	36 40	160	39 56	211	57 59	267	28 02	297	29 54	343
158	26 34	049	63 32	105	36 48	159	39 45	211	57 36	266	27 42	296	29 47	342
159	26 51	048	63 54	104	36 56	158	39 33	210	57 14	266	27 21	295	29 40	341
160	27 07	047	64 16	104	37 04	158	39 22	209	56 52	265	27 01	294	29 32	340
161	27 24	046	64 38	103	37 13	157	39 11	209	56 29	264	26 40	293	29 24	338
162	27 40	045	64 59	102	37 22	156	39 00	208	56 07	263	26 19	292	29 16	337
163	27 55	044	65 21	101	37 31	156	38 50	208	55 45	262	25 58	291	29 07	336
164	28 11	043	65 44	101	37 40	155	38 40	207	55 22	261	25 37	290	28 57	335
	◆SPICA		ANTARES		◆Peacock		ACHERNAR		◆CANOPUS		SIRIUS		Alphard	
165	28 26	042	27 10	094	37 50	154	38 30	206	55 00	260	25 16	289	28 48	334
166	28 41	040	27 32	093	38 00	154	38 20	206	54 38	260	24 55	288	28 38	333
167	28 55	039	27 55	092	38 10	153	38 10	205	54 16	259	24 33	287	28 27	332
168	29 09	038	28 17	091	38 20	152	38 01	204	53 54	258	24 12	286	28 16	331
169	29 23	037	28 39	090	38 31	152	37 52	204	53 32	257	23 50	285	28 05	330
170	29 36	036	29 02	089	38 41	151	37 43	203	53 10	256	23 28	284	27 54	328
171	29 49	035	29 24	088	38 52	150	37 34	202	52 48	255	23 06	283	27 42	327
172	30 02	034	29 47	087	39 03	150	37 26	202	52 27	255	22 44	282	27 29	326
173	30 14	033	30 09	086	39 15	149	37 18	201	52 05	254	22 22	281	27 17	325
174	30 26	032	30 32	085	39 26	148	37 10	200	51 44	253	22 00	280	27 04	324
175	30 38	031	30 54	085	39 38	148	37 02	200	51 22	252	21 38	279	26 50	323
176	30 49	029	31 16	084	39 50	147	36 55	199	51 01	251	21 16	278	26 37	322
177	31 00	028	31 39	083	40 03	146	36 48	198	50 40	251	20 53	277	26 22	321
178	31 11	027	32 01	082	40 15	146	36 41	198	50 18	250	20 31	276	26 08	320
179	31 21	026	32 23	081	40 28	145	36 34	197	49 57	249	20 09	275	25 53	319

 LAT 68°S

LHA ♈	Hc Zn	Hc Zn	Hc Zn	Hc Zn	Hc Zn	Hc Zn	Hc Zn
	◆SPICA	ANTARES	◆Peacock	ACHERNAR	◆CANOPUS	SIRIUS	Alphard
180	31 30 025	32 45 080	40 41 145	36 28 196	49 36 248	19 46 274	25 38 318
181	31 40 024	33 07 079	40 54 144	36 21 196	49 15 248	19 24 273	25 23 317
182	31 48 023	33 30 078	41 07 143	36 16 195	48 55 247	19 01 272	25 08 316
183	31 57 022	33 51 077	41 21 143	36 10 194	48 34 246	18 39 271	24 52 314
184	32 05 020	34 13 076	41 35 142	36 04 194	48 14 245	18 16 270	24 36 313
185	32 13 019	34 35 075	41 49 141	35 59 193	47 53 245	17 54 270	24 19 312
186	32 20 018	34 57 074	42 03 141	35 54 192	47 33 244	17 31 269	24 02 311
187	32 26 017	35 18 073	42 17 140	35 50 192	47 13 243	17 09 268	23 45 310
188	32 33 016	35 40 072	42 32 139	35 45 191	46 53 242	16 47 267	23 28 309
189	32 39 015	36 01 071	42 47 139	35 41 190	46 33 242	16 24 266	23 11 308
190	32 44 013	36 22 070	43 02 138	35 37 190	46 13 241	16 02 265	22 53 307
191	32 49 012	36 43 069	43 17 137	35 34 189	45 54 240	15 39 264	22 35 306
192	32 54 011	37 04 068	43 32 137	35 30 188	45 34 239	15 17 263	22 16 305
193	32 58 010	37 25 067	43 48 136	35 27 188	45 15 239	14 55 262	21 58 304
194	33 01 009	37 45 066	44 04 135	35 24 187	44 56 238	14 32 261	21 39 303
	◆SPICA	ANTARES	◆Peacock	ACHERNAR	◆CANOPUS	Suhail	Alphard
195	33 05 008	38 06 065	44 19 134	35 22 186	44 37 237	51 31 279	21 20 302
196	33 07 006	38 26 064	44 36 134	35 19 186	44 18 237	51 08 278	21 01 301
197	33 10 005	38 46 062	44 52 133	35 17 185	44 00 236	50 46 277	20 42 300
198	33 12 004	39 06 061	45 08 132	35 15 184	43 41 235	50 24 276	20 22 299
199	33 13 003	39 25 060	45 25 132	35 14 184	43 23 234	50 01 275	20 03 298
200	33 14 002	39 45 059	45 42 131	35 12 183	43 04 234	49 39 274	19 43 297
201	33 14 001	40 04 058	45 59 130	35 11 182	42 46 233	49 17 273	19 23 296
202	33 14 359	40 23 057	46 16 130	35 11 182	42 29 232	48 54 272	19 02 295
203	33 14 358	40 42 056	46 33 129	35 10 181	42 11 231	48 32 271	18 42 294
204	33 13 357	41 00 055	46 51 128	35 10 180	41 53 231	48 09 271	18 21 293
205	33 12 356	41 18 054	47 09 128	35 10 180	41 36 230	47 47 270	18 01 292
206	33 10 355	41 36 053	47 27 127	35 10 179	41 19 229	47 24 269	17 40 291
207	33 07 354	41 54 051	47 45 126	35 10 178	41 02 229	47 02 268	17 19 290
208	33 05 352	42 12 050	48 03 126	35 11 178	40 45 228	46 39 267	16 58 289
209	33 01 351	42 29 049	48 21 125	35 12 177	40 29 227	46 17 266	16 36 288
	◆ANTARES	Nunki	◆FOMALHAUT	ACHERNAR	CANOPUS	◆Suhail	SPICA
210	42 46 048	30 11 086	13 12 141	35 13 176	40 12 226	45 55 265	32 58 350
211	43 02 047	30 33 085	13 26 140	35 15 176	39 56 226	45 32 264	32 54 349
212	43 18 046	30 56 084	13 41 139	35 17 175	39 40 225	45 10 263	32 49 348
213	43 34 045	31 18 083	13 56 138	35 19 174	39 24 224	44 48 262	32 44 347
214	43 50 043	31 40 082	14 11 137	35 21 174	39 09 224	44 25 262	32 39 345
215	44 05 042	32 03 081	14 26 136	35 24 173	38 53 223	44 03 261	32 33 344
216	44 20 041	32 25 080	14 42 135	35 27 172	38 38 222	43 41 260	32 26 343
217	44 35 040	32 47 079	14 58 134	35 30 172	38 23 222	43 19 259	32 20 342
218	44 49 039	33 09 078	15 14 134	35 33 171	38 08 221	42 57 258	32 12 341
219	45 03 037	33 31 077	15 30 133	35 37 170	37 54 220	42 35 257	32 05 340
220	45 16 036	33 53 076	15 47 132	35 41 170	37 39 219	42 13 256	31 57 338
221	45 29 035	34 15 075	16 04 131	35 45 169	37 25 219	41 51 256	31 48 337
222	45 42 034	34 36 074	16 21 130	35 49 168	37 11 218	41 29 255	31 40 336
223	45 54 032	34 58 073	16 38 129	35 54 168	36 57 217	41 08 254	31 30 335
224	46 06 031	35 19 072	16 56 129	35 59 167	36 44 217	40 46 253	31 21 334
	◆ANTARES	Nunki	◆FOMALHAUT	ACHERNAR	CANOPUS	◆Suhail	SPICA
225	46 17 030	35 41 071	17 13 128	36 04 166	36 31 216	40 25 252	31 10 333
226	46 28 029	36 02 070	17 31 127	36 09 166	36 18 215	40 03 251	31 00 332
227	46 39 027	36 23 069	17 49 126	36 15 165	36 05 215	39 42 251	30 49 331
228	46 49 026	36 44 068	18 08 125	36 21 164	35 52 214	39 21 250	30 38 329
229	46 59 025	37 05 067	18 26 124	36 27 164	35 40 213	39 00 249	30 26 328
230	47 08 023	37 25 066	18 45 123	36 33 163	35 28 212	38 39 248	30 14 327
231	47 16 022	37 46 065	19 04 123	36 40 162	35 16 212	38 18 247	30 02 326
232	47 25 021	38 06 064	19 23 122	36 47 162	35 04 211	37 58 246	29 49 325
233	47 32 020	38 26 063	19 42 121	36 54 161	34 52 210	37 37 246	29 36 324
234	47 40 018	38 46 062	20 01 120	37 01 161	34 41 210	37 17 245	29 23 323
235	47 46 017	39 06 061	20 21 119	37 09 160	34 30 209	36 56 244	29 09 322
236	47 53 016	39 25 060	20 41 118	37 17 159	34 20 208	36 36 243	28 55 321
237	47 58 014	39 45 059	21 01 117	37 25 159	34 09 207	36 16 242	28 40 320
238	48 04 013	40 04 058	21 21 116	37 33 158	33 59 207	35 56 242	28 26 318
239	48 08 012	40 22 056	21 41 116	37 42 157	33 49 206	35 37 241	28 11 317
	ANTARES	◆Nunki	FOMALHAUT	◆ACHERNAR	CANOPUS	◆ACRUX	SPICA
240	48 13 010	40 41 055	22 01 115	37 51 157	33 39 205	68 15 257	27 55 316
241	48 16 009	40 59 054	22 22 114	38 00 156	33 30 205	67 53 256	27 40 315
242	48 20 008	41 18 053	22 42 113	38 09 155	33 20 204	67 32 256	27 24 314
243	48 22 006	41 35 052	23 03 112	38 18 155	33 11 203	67 10 255	27 07 313
244	48 24 005	41 53 051	23 24 111	38 28 154	33 02 203	66 48 254	26 51 312
245	48 26 003	42 10 050	23 45 110	38 38 153	32 54 202	66 27 253	26 34 311
246	48 27 002	42 27 049	24 06 110	38 48 153	32 46 201	66 05 253	26 17 310
247	48 28 001	42 44 047	24 27 109	38 59 152	32 38 200	65 44 252	25 59 309
248	48 28 359	43 00 046	24 49 108	39 10 151	32 30 200	65 22 251	25 42 308
249	48 27 358	43 16 045	25 10 107	39 21 151	32 23 199	65 01 251	25 24 307
250	48 26 357	43 32 044	25 32 106	39 32 150	32 15 198	64 40 250	25 06 306
251	48 25 355	43 47 043	25 53 105	39 43 149	32 08 198	64 19 249	24 47 305
252	48 23 354	44 02 041	26 15 104	39 55 149	32 02 197	63 58 249	24 29 304
253	48 20 353	44 17 040	26 37 103	40 06 148	31 55 196	63 37 248	24 10 303
254	48 17 351	44 32 039	26 59 103	40 19 147	31 49 196	63 16 248	23 51 302
	◆Nunki	FOMALHAUT	◆ACHERNAR	CANOPUS	◆ACRUX	SPICA	ANTARES
255	44 45 038	27 21 102	40 31 147	31 43 195	62 55 247	23 32 301	48 13 350
256	44 59 037	27 43 101	40 43 146	31 38 194	62 35 246	23 12 300	48 09 349
257	45 12 035	28 05 100	40 56 145	31 32 193	62 14 246	22 53 299	48 05 347
258	45 25 034	28 27 099	41 09 145	31 27 193	61 54 245	22 33 298	47 59 346
259	45 37 033	28 49 098	41 22 144	31 22 192	61 33 244	22 13 297	47 54 345
260	45 49 032	29 11 097	41 35 143	31 18 191	61 13 244	21 53 296	47 47 343
261	46 01 030	29 34 096	41 49 143	31 14 191	60 53 243	21 32 295	47 41 342
262	46 12 029	29 56 095	42 02 142	31 10 190	60 33 242	21 12 294	47 34 341
263	46 23 028	30 19 094	42 16 141	31 06 189	60 13 242	20 51 293	47 26 339
264	46 33 027	30 41 094	42 31 141	31 03 189	59 54 241	20 31 292	47 18 338
265	46 43 025	31 03 093	42 45 140	30 59 188	59 34 241	20 10 291	47 09 337
266	46 52 024	31 26 092	42 59 139	30 56 187	59 14 240	19 48 290	47 00 335
267	47 01 023	31 48 091	43 14 139	30 54 186	58 55 239	19 27 289	46 50 334
268	47 10 021	32 11 090	43 29 138	30 51 186	58 36 239	19 06 288	46 40 333
269	47 18 020	32 33 089	43 44 137	30 49 185	58 16 238	18 44 287	46 30 332

LHA ♈	Hc Zn	Hc Zn	Hc Zn	Hc Zn	Hc Zn	Hc Zn	Hc Zn
	◆Nunki	FOMALHAUT	◆ACHERNAR	CANOPUS	◆ACRUX	SPICA	ANTARES
270	47 25 019	32 56 088	44 00 137	30 47 184	57 57 238	18 23 286	46 19 330
271	47 32 017	33 18 087	44 15 136	30 46 184	57 39 237	18 01 285	46 08 329
272	47 39 016	33 41 086	44 31 135	30 45 183	57 20 236	17 39 284	45 56 328
273	47 45 015	34 03 085	44 47 135	30 44 182	57 01 236	17 18 283	45 44 327
274	47 50 013	34 25 084	45 03 134	30 43 181	56 43 235	16 56 282	45 31 325
275	47 55 012	34 48 083	45 19 133	30 42 181	56 24 235	16 34 281	45 18 324
276	48 00 011	35 10 082	45 35 133	30 42 180	56 06 234	16 12 280	45 05 323
277	48 04 009	35 32 081	45 52 132	30 42 179	55 48 233	15 49 279	44 51 322
278	48 07 008	35 55 080	46 09 131	30 43 179	55 30 233	15 27 278	44 37 320
279	48 10 007	36 17 079	46 26 131	30 43 178	55 12 232	15 05 277	44 23 319
280	48 12 005	36 39 078	46 43 130	30 44 177	54 54 232	14 43 276	44 08 318
281	48 14 004	37 01 077	47 00 129	30 46 177	54 37 231	14 20 275	43 53 317
282	48 16 003	37 23 076	47 17 129	30 47 176	54 19 230	13 58 275	43 37 316
283	48 16 001	37 44 075	47 35 128	30 49 175	54 02 230	13 35 274	43 21 314
284	48 17 000	38 06 074	47 53 127	30 51 174	53 45 229	13 13 273	43 05 313
	◆ALTAIR	FOMALHAUT	◆ACHERNAR	CANOPUS	◆RIGIL KENT	ANTARES	Nunki
285	12 33 013	38 28 073	48 11 127	30 53 174	62 34 253	42 48 312	48 16 359
286	12 38 012	38 49 072	48 29 126	30 56 173	62 13 252	42 32 311	48 16 357
287	12 42 011	39 11 071	48 47 125	30 59 172	61 51 251	42 15 310	48 14 356
288	12 46 010	39 32 070	49 06 125	31 02 172	61 30 251	41 57 309	48 12 355
289	12 50 009	39 53 069	49 24 124	31 05 171	61 09 250	41 39 308	48 10 353
290	12 53 008	40 14 068	49 43 123	31 09 170	60 48 249	41 21 306	48 07 352
291	12 56 007	40 35 067	50 02 123	31 13 169	60 27 249	41 03 305	48 04 351
292	12 59 006	40 55 066	50 21 122	31 17 169	60 06 248	40 45 304	48 00 349
293	13 01 005	41 16 065	50 40 121	31 22 168	59 45 247	40 26 303	47 56 348
294	13 02 004	41 36 064	50 59 121	31 27 167	59 25 247	40 07 302	47 51 347
295	13 04 003	41 56 063	51 19 120	31 32 167	59 04 246	39 48 301	47 45 345
296	13 05 002	42 16 062	51 38 119	31 37 166	58 43 245	39 29 300	47 39 344
297	13 05 001	42 36 061	51 58 118	31 42 165	58 23 245	39 09 299	47 33 343
298	13 05 000	42 55 060	52 18 118	31 48 165	58 03 244	38 49 298	47 26 341
299	13 05 359	43 15 059	52 38 117	31 54 164	57 43 243	38 29 297	47 18 340
	◆FOMALHAUT	ACHERNAR	◆CANOPUS	RIGIL KENT	◆ANTARES	Nunki	ALTAIR
300	43 34 057	52 58 116	32 01 163	57 23 243	38 09 296	47 11 339	13 05 358
301	43 53 056	53 18 116	32 07 162	57 03 242	37 49 295	47 02 337	13 04 357
302	44 11 055	53 38 115	32 14 162	56 43 241	37 28 293	46 53 336	13 02 356
303	44 29 054	53 59 114	32 22 161	56 23 241	37 07 292	46 44 335	13 00 355
304	44 48 053	54 19 113	32 29 160	56 04 240	36 47 291	46 34 334	12 58 354
305	45 05 052	54 40 113	32 37 160	55 44 239	36 26 290	46 24 332	12 55 353
306	45 23 051	55 01 112	32 45 159	55 25 239	36 04 289	46 13 331	12 52 352
307	45 40 049	55 22 111	32 53 158	55 06 238	35 43 288	46 02 330	12 49 351
308	45 57 048	55 43 111	33 01 158	54 47 237	35 22 287	45 51 328	12 45 350
309	46 14 047	56 04 110	33 10 157	54 28 237	35 00 286	45 39 327	12 41 349
310	46 30 046	56 25 109	33 19 156	54 09 236	34 39 285	45 26 326	12 36 348
311	46 46 045	56 46 108	33 28 155	53 51 236	34 17 284	45 14 325	12 31 347
312	47 02 043	57 08 108	33 38 155	53 32 235	33 55 283	45 00 324	12 26 346
313	47 17 042	57 29 107	33 47 154	53 14 234	33 33 282	44 47 322	12 20 345
314	47 32 041	57 51 106	33 57 153	52 56 234	33 11 281	44 33 321	12 14 344
	◆FOMALHAUT	ACHERNAR	◆CANOPUS	Miaplacidus	RIGIL KENT	◆ANTARES	Nunki
315	47 46 040	58 12 105	34 08 153	47 48 182	52 38 233	32 49 280	44 19 320
316	48 01 039	58 34 105	34 18 152	47 47 181	52 20 232	32 27 279	44 04 319
317	48 14 037	58 56 104	34 29 151	47 47 181	52 02 232	32 05 278	43 49 317
318	48 28 036	59 18 103	34 40 151	47 47 180	51 45 231	31 42 278	43 34 316
319	48 41 035	59 40 102	34 51 150	47 47 180	51 27 230	31 20 277	43 18 315
320	48 53 033	60 02 101	35 02 149	47 47 179	51 10 230	30 58 276	43 02 314
321	49 06 032	60 24 101	35 14 148	47 47 179	50 53 229	30 35 275	42 45 313
322	49 17 031	60 46 100	35 26 148	47 48 178	50 36 229	30 13 274	42 29 312
323	49 29 030	61 08 099	35 38 147	47 49 178	50 19 228	29 51 273	42 12 310
324	49 39 028	61 30 098	35 50 146	47 50 177	50 03 227	29 28 272	41 55 309
325	49 50 027	61 52 097	36 03 146	47 51 177	49 46 227	29 06 271	41 37 308
326	50 00 026	62 15 096	36 16 145	47 53 176	49 30 226	28 43 270	41 19 307
327	50 09 024	62 37 096	36 29 144	47 54 176	49 14 225	28 21 269	41 01 306
328	50 18 023	62 59 095	36 42 143	47 56 175	48 58 225	27 58 268	40 43 305
329	50 27 022	63 22 094	36 55 143	47 58 175	48 42 224	27 36 267	40 24 304
	◆FOMALHAUT	ACHERNAR	◆CANOPUS	Miaplacidus	RIGIL KENT	◆ANTARES	Nunki
330	50 35 020	63 44 093	37 09 142	48 00 174	48 26 224	27 13 266	40 05 303
331	50 42 019	64 07 092	37 23 141	48 03 173	48 11 223	26 51 265	39 46 302
332	50 49 018	64 29 091	37 37 141	48 06 173	47 56 222	26 29 264	39 27 300
333	50 56 016	64 52 090	37 52 140	48 08 172	47 41 222	26 06 264	39 08 299
334	51 02 015	65 14 089	38 06 139	48 11 172	47 26 221	25 44 263	38 48 298
335	51 07 013	65 37 088	38 21 139	48 15 171	47 11 221	25 22 262	38 28 297
336	51 12 012	65 59 087	38 36 138	48 18 171	46 57 220	24 59 261	38 08 296
337	51 17 011	66 22 086	38 51 137	48 22 170	46 42 219	24 37 260	37 48 295
338	51 21 009	66 44 086	39 06 136	48 26 170	46 28 219	24 15 259	37 27 294
339	51 24 008	67 06 085	39 22 136	48 30 169	46 14 218	23 53 258	37 07 293
340	51 27 006	67 29 083	39 38 135	48 34 169	46 01 217	23 31 257	36 46 292
341	51 29 005	67 51 082	39 54 134	48 38 168	45 47 217	23 09 256	36 25 291
342	51 31 004	68 13 081	40 10 134	48 43 168	45 34 216	22 47 255	36 04 290
343	51 32 002	68 35 080	40 26 133	48 48 167	45 20 216	22 26 255	35 43 289
344	51 32 001	68 58 079	40 43 132	48 53 167	45 07 215	22 04 254	35 21 288
	Diphda	◆CANOPUS	Miaplacidus	RIGIL KENT	◆ANTARES	Nunki	◆FOMALHAUT
345	37 15 032	41 00 131	48 58 166	44 55 214	21 43 253	35 00 287	51 33 359
346	37 26 031	41 17 131	49 03 166	44 42 214	21 21 252	34 38 286	51 32 358
347	37 37 029	41 34 130	49 09 165	44 30 213	21 00 251	34 17 285	51 31 357
348	37 48 028	41 51 129	49 15 165	44 18 212	20 39 250	33 55 284	51 29 355
349	37 59 027	42 08 129	49 21 164	44 06 212	20 18 249	33 33 283	51 27 354
350	38 09 026	42 26 128	49 27 164	43 54 211	19 57 248	33 11 282	51 25 352
351	38 18 025	42 44 127	49 33 163	43 42 211	19 36 248	32 49 281	51 21 351
352	38 27 023	43 02 126	49 40 163	43 31 210	19 15 247	32 27 280	51 18 350
353	38 36 022	43 20 126	49 47 162	43 20 209	18 54 246	32 05 279	51 13 348
354	38 44 021	43 38 125	49 54 162	43 09 209	18 34 245	31 43 278	51 09 347
355	38 52 020	43 57 124	50 01 161	42 58 208	18 14 244	31 20 277	51 03 346
356	39 00 019	44 16 124	50 08 161	42 48 208	17 54 243	30 58 276	50 57 344
357	39 07 017	44 34 123	50 15 160	42 38 207	17 34 242	30 36 275	50 51 343
358	39 13 016	44 53 122	50 23 160	42 27 206	17 14 241	30 13 274	50 44 341
359	39 19 015	45 12 121	50 31 159	42 18 206	16 54 241	29 51 273	50 37 340

LHA ♈	Hc	Zn	Hc	Zn	Hc	Zn	Hc	Zn	Hc	Zn	Hc	Zn	Hc	Zn
	Diphda		◆RIGEL		CANOPUS		Miaplacidus		◆RIGIL KENT		Peacock		◆FOMALHAUT	
0	38 26	014	11 38	082	46 02	120	51 35	158	43 02	205	63 52	271	49 33	339
1	38 31	012	12 00	082	46 21	119	51 43	158	42 53	205	63 31	270	49 25	338
2	38 35	011	12 21	081	46 39	118	51 51	157	42 44	204	63 09	269	49 17	337
3	38 39	010	12 42	080	46 58	118	52 00	157	42 36	204	62 48	268	49 08	335
4	38 43	009	13 03	079	47 18	117	52 08	156	42 27	203	62 26	267	48 59	334
5	38 46	007	13 24	078	47 37	116	52 17	156	42 19	202	62 05	266	48 49	333
6	38 48	006	13 45	077	47 56	115	52 26	155	42 11	202	61 43	265	48 39	331
7	38 50	005	14 06	076	48 16	114	52 35	155	42 03	201	61 22	265	48 28	330
8	38 52	004	14 27	075	48 35	114	52 44	154	41 55	200	61 01	264	48 17	329
9	38 53	003	14 48	074	48 55	113	52 54	154	41 48	200	60 39	263	48 06	327
10	38 54	001	15 08	073	49 15	112	53 03	153	41 41	199	60 18	262	47 54	326
11	38 54	000	15 29	072	49 35	111	53 13	153	41 34	198	59 57	261	47 42	325
12	38 54	359	15 49	071	49 55	111	53 23	152	41 27	198	59 35	260	47 29	324
13	38 53	358	16 09	070	50 15	110	53 33	152	41 21	197	59 14	259	47 17	322
14	38 52	356	16 29	069	50 35	109	53 43	151	41 15	197	58 53	259	47 03	321
	◆RIGEL		CANOPUS		Miaplacidus		◆RIGIL KENT		Peacock		◆FOMALHAUT		Diphda	
15	16 49	068	50 56	108	53 54	151	41 09	196	58 32	258	46 50	320	38 51	355
16	17 09	067	51 16	107	54 04	150	41 03	195	58 11	257	46 36	319	38 49	354
17	17 29	066	51 37	107	54 15	150	40 57	195	57 50	256	46 21	318	38 46	353
18	17 49	065	51 58	106	54 26	149	40 52	194	57 29	255	46 07	316	38 43	352
19	18 08	064	52 18	105	54 37	149	40 47	193	57 09	255	45 52	315	38 40	350
20	18 27	063	52 39	104	54 49	148	40 42	193	56 48	254	45 36	314	38 36	349
21	18 47	062	53 00	103	55 00	148	40 37	192	56 27	253	45 21	313	38 32	348
22	19 05	061	53 21	103	55 12	147	40 33	192	56 07	252	45 05	312	38 27	347
23	19 24	060	53 42	102	55 23	147	40 29	191	55 46	252	44 48	310	38 22	345
24	19 43	059	54 03	101	55 35	146	40 25	190	55 26	251	44 32	309	38 16	344
25	20 01	058	54 24	100	55 47	146	40 21	190	55 06	250	44 15	308	38 10	343
26	20 19	057	54 45	099	56 00	145	40 18	189	54 46	249	43 58	307	38 04	342
27	20 37	056	55 07	098	56 12	145	40 14	188	54 25	249	43 41	306	37 57	341
28	20 55	055	55 28	097	56 24	144	40 11	188	54 06	248	43 23	305	37 50	339
29	21 13	054	55 49	097	56 37	144	40 09	187	53 46	247	43 05	304	37 42	338
	◆RIGEL		CANOPUS		Miaplacidus		◆RIGIL KENT		Peacock		◆FOMALHAUT		Diphda	
30	21 30	053	56 11	096	56 50	143	40 06	186	53 26	246	42 47	302	37 34	337
31	21 47	052	56 32	095	57 03	143	40 04	186	53 06	246	42 29	301	37 25	336
32	22 04	051	56 53	094	57 16	142	40 02	185	52 47	245	42 11	300	37 16	335
33	22 21	050	57 15	093	57 29	142	40 00	185	52 27	244	41 52	299	37 07	334
34	22 37	049	57 36	092	57 43	141	39 58	184	52 08	243	41 33	298	36 57	332
35	22 53	048	57 58	091	57 56	141	39 57	183	51 49	243	41 14	297	36 47	331
36	23 09	047	58 19	090	58 10	140	39 56	183	51 30	242	40 55	296	36 36	330
37	23 25	046	58 41	089	58 24	140	39 55	182	51 11	241	40 35	295	36 25	329
38	23 40	045	59 02	088	58 38	139	39 54	181	50 52	240	40 16	294	36 14	328
39	23 55	044	59 24	087	58 52	139	39 54	181	50 34	240	39 56	293	36 02	327
40	24 10	043	59 45	087	59 06	138	39 54	180	50 15	239	39 36	292	35 50	325
41	24 24	042	60 07	086	59 20	138	39 54	179	49 57	238	39 16	291	35 38	324
42	24 38	041	60 28	085	59 35	137	39 54	179	49 38	238	38 56	290	35 25	323
43	24 52	040	60 50	084	59 50	137	39 55	178	49 20	237	38 36	289	35 12	322
44	25 06	039	61 11	083	60 04	136	39 56	178	49 02	236	38 15	288	34 59	321
	RIGEL		◆SIRIUS		Suhail		◆RIGIL KENT		Peacock		◆FOMALHAUT		Diphda	
45	25 19	038	27 17	064	39 16	111	39 57	177	48 45	236	37 55	287	34 45	320
46	25 32	036	27 37	063	39 36	110	39 58	176	48 27	235	37 34	286	34 31	319
47	25 45	035	27 56	062	39 56	109	39 59	176	48 10	234	37 13	285	34 17	318
48	25 57	034	28 15	061	40 17	108	40 01	175	47 52	233	36 52	284	34 02	316
49	26 09	033	28 33	060	40 37	107	40 03	174	47 35	233	36 31	283	33 47	315
50	26 20	032	28 52	059	40 58	106	40 05	174	47 18	232	36 10	282	33 32	314
51	26 32	031	29 10	058	41 18	106	40 08	173	47 01	231	35 49	281	33 16	313
52	26 43	030	29 28	057	41 39	105	40 10	172	46 44	231	35 28	280	33 00	312
53	26 53	029	29 46	056	42 00	104	40 13	172	46 28	230	35 07	279	32 44	311
54	27 03	028	30 04	055	42 21	103	40 16	171	46 11	229	34 45	278	32 28	310
55	27 13	027	30 21	054	42 42	102	40 20	171	45 55	229	34 24	277	32 11	309
56	27 23	026	30 38	052	43 03	101	40 24	170	45 39	228	34 03	276	31 54	308
57	27 32	025	30 55	051	43 24	100	40 27	169	45 23	227	33 41	275	31 37	307
58	27 41	023	31 12	050	43 45	099	40 31	169	45 08	226	33 20	274	31 20	306
59	27 49	022	31 28	049	44 06	099	40 36	168	44 52	226	32 58	273	31 02	304
	RIGEL		◆SIRIUS		Suhail		◆RIGIL KENT		Peacock		◆FOMALHAUT		Diphda	
60	27 57	021	31 44	048	44 28	098	40 40	167	44 37	225	32 37	272	30 44	303
61	28 05	020	32 00	047	44 49	097	40 45	167	44 22	224	32 15	271	30 26	302
62	28 12	019	32 16	046	45 10	096	40 50	166	44 07	224	31 54	270	30 08	301
63	28 18	018	32 31	045	45 32	095	40 55	166	43 52	223	31 32	269	29 50	300
64	28 25	017	32 46	044	45 53	094	41 01	165	43 37	222	31 11	268	29 31	299
65	28 31	016	33 01	043	46 15	093	41 07	164	43 23	222	30 49	267	29 12	298
66	28 36	014	33 16	042	46 36	092	41 13	164	43 09	221	30 28	266	28 53	297
67	28 42	013	33 30	041	46 58	091	41 19	163	42 55	220	30 07	265	28 34	296
68	28 46	012	33 43	039	47 19	090	41 25	162	42 41	220	29 45	265	28 14	295
69	28 51	011	33 57	038	47 41	090	41 32	162	42 27	219	29 24	264	27 55	294
70	28 55	010	34 10	037	48 02	089	41 39	161	42 14	218	29 02	263	27 35	293
71	28 58	009	34 23	036	48 24	088	41 46	160	42 01	218	28 41	262	27 15	292
72	29 01	008	34 35	035	48 45	087	41 53	160	41 48	217	28 20	261	26 55	291
73	29 04	007	34 48	034	49 07	086	42 01	159	41 35	216	27 59	260	26 35	290
74	29 06	005	34 59	033	49 28	085	42 08	159	41 22	216	27 38	259	26 15	289
	RIGEL		◆SIRIUS		Suhail		◆RIGIL KENT		Peacock		◆FOMALHAUT		Diphda	
75	29 08	004	35 11	031	49 49	084	42 16	158	41 10	215	27 16	258	25 55	288
76	29 09	003	35 22	030	50 11	083	42 24	157	40 58	214	26 55	257	25 34	287
77	29 10	002	35 32	029	50 32	082	42 33	157	40 46	214	26 34	256	25 14	286
78	29 11	001	35 43	028	50 53	081	42 41	156	40 34	213	26 14	256	24 53	285
79	29 11	000	35 53	027	51 15	080	42 50	155	40 22	212	25 53	255	24 32	284
80	29 11	359	36 02	026	51 36	079	42 59	155	40 11	212	25 32	254	24 11	283
81	29 10	358	36 11	024	51 57	078	43 09	154	40 00	211	25 12	253	23 50	282
82	29 09	356	36 20	023	52 18	077	43 18	154	39 49	210	24 51	252	23 29	281
83	29 07	355	36 28	022	52 39	076	43 28	153	39 38	210	24 31	251	23 08	280
84	29 05	354	36 36	021	52 59	075	43 38	152	39 28	209	24 10	250	22 47	279
85	29 03	353	36 44	020	53 20	074	43 48	152	39 17	208	23 50	249	22 26	278
86	29 00	352	36 51	019	53 41	072	43 58	151	39 07	207	23 30	248	22 04	278
87	28 57	351	36 57	017	54 01	071	44 09	150	38 57	207	23 10	248	21 43	277
88	28 53	350	37 04	016	54 21	070	44 19	150	38 48	206	22 50	247	21 22	276
89	28 49	348	37 09	015	54 42	069	44 30	149	38 38	205	22 31	246	21 00	275

LHA ♈	Hc	Zn	Hc	Zn	Hc	Zn	Hc	Zn	Hc	Zn	Hc	Zn	Hc	Zn
	◆SIRIUS		Suhail		◆RIGIL KENT		Peacock		◆ACHERNAR		Acamar		RIGEL	
90	37 15	014	55 02	068	44 41	148	38 29	205	59 54	260	52 43	296	28 45	347
91	37 20	013	55 21	067	44 53	148	38 20	204	59 33	259	52 23	295	28 40	346
92	37 24	011	55 41	066	45 04	147	38 12	203	59 12	258	52 04	294	28 34	345
93	37 28	010	56 01	065	45 16	147	38 03	203	58 51	257	51 44	293	28 29	344
94	37 32	009	56 20	063	45 28	146	37 55	202	58 30	256	51 24	292	28 23	343
95	37 35	008	56 39	062	45 40	145	37 47	201	58 09	256	51 04	291	28 16	342
96	37 38	007	56 58	061	45 53	145	37 39	201	57 49	255	50 44	290	28 09	341
97	37 40	005	57 17	060	46 05	144	37 32	200	57 28	254	50 24	289	28 02	340
98	37 42	004	57 35	059	46 18	143	37 25	199	57 07	253	50 03	288	27 54	338
99	37 43	003	57 53	057	46 31	143	37 18	199	56 47	252	49 43	287	27 46	337
100	37 44	002	58 11	056	46 44	142	37 11	198	56 26	252	49 22	286	27 37	336
101	37 44	001	58 29	055	46 57	142	37 04	197	56 06	251	49 01	284	27 29	335
102	37 44	359	58 47	054	47 11	141	36 58	197	55 46	250	48 40	283	27 19	334
103	37 44	358	59 04	052	47 24	140	36 52	196	55 25	249	48 19	282	27 10	333
104	37 43	357	59 21	051	47 38	140	36 46	195	55 05	249	47 58	281	27 00	332
	Alphard		◆Gienah		RIGIL KENT		◆Peacock		ACHERNAR		◆RIGEL		SIRIUS	
105	25 06	041	20 18	086	47 52	139	36 41	195	54 45	248	26 49	331	37 41	356
106	25 20	040	20 40	085	48 06	138	36 35	194	54 25	247	26 39	330	37 40	354
107	25 34	039	21 01	085	48 21	138	36 30	193	54 06	246	26 28	329	37 37	353
108	25 47	038	21 22	084	48 35	137	36 25	193	53 46	246	26 16	327	37 35	352
109	26 00	037	21 44	083	48 50	136	36 21	192	53 26	245	26 04	326	37 31	351
110	26 13	036	22 05	082	49 05	136	36 16	191	53 07	244	25 52	325	37 28	350
111	26 25	035	22 26	081	49 20	135	36 12	191	52 48	244	25 40	324	37 24	348
112	26 37	034	22 48	080	49 35	135	36 09	190	52 29	243	25 27	323	37 19	347
113	26 49	033	23 09	079	49 51	134	36 05	189	52 09	242	25 14	322	37 14	346
114	27 01	031	23 30	078	50 06	133	36 02	189	51 51	241	25 01	321	37 09	345
115	27 12	030	23 51	077	50 22	133	35 59	188	51 32	241	24 47	320	37 03	344
116	27 22	029	24 12	076	50 38	132	35 56	187	51 13	240	24 33	319	36 57	342
117	27 33	028	24 32	075	50 54	131	35 53	187	50 55	239	24 19	318	36 50	341
118	27 43	027	24 53	074	51 10	131	35 51	186	50 36	239	24 04	317	36 43	340
119	27 52	026	25 14	073	51 26	130	35 49	185	50 18	238	23 49	316	36 35	339
	Alphard		◆SPICA		RIGIL KENT		◆Peacock		ACHERNAR		◆RIGEL		SIRIUS	
120	28 01	025	13 32	086	51 43	129	35 47	185	50 00	237	23 34	315	36 27	338
121	28 10	024	13 53	085	52 00	129	35 45	184	49 42	236	23 19	314	36 19	337
122	28 19	023	14 15	084	52 17	128	35 44	183	49 24	236	23 03	313	36 10	335
123	28 27	022	14 36	083	52 34	127	35 43	183	49 06	235	22 47	312	36 01	334
124	28 35	020	14 57	082	52 51	127	35 42	182	48 49	234	22 31	311	35 52	333
125	28 42	019	15 19	081	53 08	126	35 42	181	48 31	234	22 14	309	35 42	332
126	28 49	018	15 40	080	53 25	126	35 41	180	48 14	233	21 58	308	35 31	331
127	28 55	017	16 01	080	53 43	125	35 41	180	47 57	232	21 41	307	35 21	330
128	29 01	016	16 22	079	54 01	124	35 41	179	47 40	232	21 24	306	35 10	328
129	29 07	015	16 43	078	54 19	124	35 42	178	47 23	231	21 06	305	34 58	327
130	29 12	014	17 04	077	54 37	123	35 43	178	47 07	230	20 49	304	34 46	326
131	29 17	013	17 25	076	54 55	122	35 43	177	46 50	229	20 31	303	34 34	325
132	29 22	011	17 46	075	55 13	122	35 45	176	46 34	229	20 13	302	34 22	324
133	29 26	010	18 06	074	55 31	121	35 46	176	46 18	228	19 54	301	34 09	323
134	29 30	009	18 27	073	55 50	120	35 48	175	46 02	227	19 36	300	33 56	322
	Alphard		◆SPICA		RIGIL KENT		◆Peacock		ACHERNAR		◆CANOPUS		SIRIUS	
135	29 33	008	18 48	072	56 08	120	35 50	174	45 46	227	65 44	292	33 42	320
136	29 36	007	19 08	071	56 27	119	35 52	174	45 31	226	65 24	291	33 28	319
137	29 38	006	19 28	070	56 46	118	35 55	173	45 15	225	65 04	290	33 14	318
138	29 40	005	19 48	069	57 05	118	35 57	172	45 00	225	64 43	289	33 00	317
139	29 41	004	20 08	068	57 24	117	36 00	172	44 45	224	64 23	287	32 45	316
140	29 43	002	20 28	067	57 44	116	36 04	171	44 30	223	64 02	286	32 30	315
141	29 43	001	20 48	066	58 03	115	36 07	170	44 15	223	63 41	285	32 14	314
142	29 43	000	21 07	065	58 22	115	36 11	170	44 01	222	63 21	284	31 59	313
143	29 43	359	21 27	064	58 42	114	36 15	169	43 47	221	63 00	283	31 43	312
144	29 43	358	21 46	063	59 02	113	36 19	168	43 33	221	62 39	282	31 27	311
145	29 42	357	22 05	062	59 21	113	36 23	168	43 19	220	62 18	281	31 10	310
146	29 40	356	22 24	061	59 41	112	36 28	167	43 05	219	61 56	280	30 54	308
147	29 38	354	22 43	060	60 01	111	36 33	166	42 51	219	61 35	279	30 37	307
148	29 36	353	23 01	059	60 21	111	36 38	166	42 38	218	61 14	278	30 19	306
149	29 33	352	23 20	058	60 41	110	36 44	165	42 25	217	60 53	277	30 02	305
	◆SPICA		RIGIL KENT		◆Peacock		ACHERNAR		◆CANOPUS		SIRIUS		Alphard	
150	23 38	057	61 02	109	36 50	164	42 12	217	60 31	276	29 44	304	29 30	351
151	23 56	056	61 22	108	36 55	164	41 59	216	60 10	275	29 26	303	29 27	350
152	24 13	055	61 43	108	37 02	163	41 47	215	59 48	274	29 08	302	29 23	349
153	24 31	054	62 03	107	37 08	162	41 34	215	59 27	273	28 50	301	29 18	348
154	24 48	053	62 24	106	37 15	162	41 22	214	59 05	272	28 32	300	29 13	346
155	25 05	052	62 44	105	37 22	161	41 10	213	58 44	271	28 13	299	29 08	345
156	25 22	051	63 05	105	37 29	160	40 59	213	58 22	270	27 54	298	29 02	344
157	25 38	050	63 26	104	37 36	160	40 47	212	58 01	269	27 35	297	28 56	343
158	25 55	049	63 47	103	37 44	159	40 36	211	57 39	268	27 16	296	28 50	342
159	26 11	048	64 08	102	37 52	158	40 25	211	57 18	267	26 56	295	28 43	341
160	26 26	047	64 29	102	38 00	158	40 14	210	56 56	266	26 37	294	28 36	340
161	26 42	045	64 50	101	38 08	157	40 04	209	56 35	265	26 17	293	28 28	339
162	26 57	044	65 11	100	38 17	156	39 53	209	56 14	264	25 57	292	28 20	338
163	27 12	043	65 32	099	38 26	155	39 43	208	55 52	264	25 37	291	28 12	336
164	27 26	042	65 54	098	38 35	155	39 33	207	55 31	263	25 17	290	28 03	335
	◆SPICA		ANTARES		◆Peacock		ACHERNAR		◆CANOPUS		SIRIUS		Alphard	
165	27 41	041	27 13	093	38 44	154	39 23	207	55 10	262	24 57	289	27 54	334
166	27 55	040	27 35	092	38 53	153	39 14	206	54 48	261	24 36	288	27 44	333
167	28 08	039	27 56	091	39 03	153	39 05	205	54 27	260	24 16	287	27 34	332
168	28 22	038	28 18	091	39 13	152	38 56	205	54 06	259	23 55	286	27 24	331
169	28 35	037	28 39	090	39 23	151	38 47	204	53 45	258	23 34	285	27 13	330
170	28 48	036	29 01	089	39 34	151	38 38	203	53 24	258	23 14	284	27 02	329
171	29 00	035	29 22	088	39 44	150	38 30	203	53 03	257	22 53	283	26 51	328
172	29 12	034	29 44	087	39 55	149	38 22	202	52 42	256	22 32	282	26 39	327
173	29 24	032	30 05	086	40 06	149	38 14	201	52 21	255	22 11	281	26 27	325
174	29 35	031	30 27	085	40 17	148	38 06	201	52 00	254	21 50	280	26 15	324
175	29 46	030	30 48	084	40 29	147	37 59	200	51 40	253	21 28	279	26 02	323
176	29 57	029	31 09	083	40 41	147	37 52	199	51 19	253	21 07	278	25 49	322
177	30 07	028	31 31	082	40 53	146	37 45	199	50 58	252	20 46	277	25 36	321
178	30 17	027	31 52	081	41 05	145	37 38	198	50 38	251	20 24	276	25 22	320
179	30 27	026	32 13	080	41 17	145	37 31	197	50 18	250	20 03	275	25 08	319

LHA ♈	Hc Zn	Hc Zn	Hc Zn	Hc Zn	Hc Zn	Hc Zn	Hc Zn
	◆ SPICA	ANTARES	◆ Peacock	ACHERNAR	◆ CANOPUS	SIRIUS	Alphard
180	30 36 025	32 34 079	41 30 144	37 25 196	49 58 250	19 42 275	24 54 318
181	30 45 024	32 55 078	41 42 143	37 19 196	49 38 249	19 20 274	24 39 317
182	30 53 022	33 16 077	41 55 143	37 13 195	49 18 248	18 59 273	24 25 316
183	31 01 021	33 37 076	42 08 142	37 08 194	48 58 247	18 37 272	24 10 315
184	31 09 020	33 58 075	42 22 141	37 03 194	48 38 246	18 16 271	23 54 314
185	31 16 019	34 19 074	42 35 141	36 58 193	48 19 246	17 54 270	23 38 313
186	31 23 018	34 40 073	42 49 140	36 53 192	47 59 245	17 33 269	23 23 312
187	31 29 017	35 00 072	43 03 139	36 48 192	47 40 244	17 11 268	23 06 311
188	31 35 016	35 21 071	43 17 139	36 44 191	47 20 243	16 50 267	22 50 310
189	31 41 014	35 41 070	43 31 138	36 40 190	47 01 243	16 28 266	22 33 309
190	31 46 013	36 01 069	43 46 137	36 36 190	46 42 242	16 07 265	22 16 308
191	31 50 012	36 21 068	44 01 137	36 33 189	46 23 241	15 45 264	21 59 307
192	31 55 011	36 41 067	44 16 136	36 30 188	46 05 240	15 24 263	21 42 306
193	31 59 010	37 01 066	44 31 135	36 26 188	45 46 240	15 03 262	21 24 305
194	32 02 009	37 20 065	44 46 134	36 24 187	45 27 239	14 41 262	21 06 303
	◆ SPICA	ANTARES	◆ Peacock	ACHERNAR	◆ CANOPUS	Suhail	Alphard
195	32 05 008	37 40 064	45 01 134	36 21 186	45 09 238	51 20 280	20 48 302
196	32 08 006	37 59 063	45 17 133	36 19 186	44 51 237	50 59 279	20 30 301
197	32 10 005	38 18 062	45 33 132	36 17 185	44 33 237	50 38 278	20 12 300
198	32 12 004	38 37 061	45 49 132	36 15 184	44 15 236	50 17 277	19 53 299
199	32 13 003	38 55 060	46 05 131	36 14 184	43 57 235	49 55 276	19 34 298
200	32 14 002	39 14 059	46 21 130	36 12 183	43 40 234	49 34 276	19 15 297
201	32 14 001	39 32 057	46 38 130	36 11 182	43 22 234	49 12 275	18 56 296
202	32 14 359	39 50 056	46 54 129	36 10 182	43 05 233	48 51 274	18 37 296
203	32 14 358	40 08 055	47 11 128	36 10 181	42 48 232	48 30 273	18 17 295
204	32 13 357	40 25 054	47 28 128	36 10 180	42 31 231	48 08 272	17 58 294
205	32 12 356	40 43 053	47 45 127	36 10 180	42 14 231	47 47 271	17 38 293
206	32 10 355	41 00 052	48 02 126	36 10 179	41 58 230	47 25 270	17 18 292
207	32 08 354	41 17 051	48 20 125	36 10 178	41 41 229	47 04 269	16 58 291
208	32 05 352	41 33 050	48 37 125	36 11 178	41 25 229	46 42 268	16 38 290
209	32 02 351	41 49 049	48 55 124	36 12 177	41 09 228	46 21 267	16 17 289
	◆ ANTARES	Nunki	◆ FOMALHAUT	ACHERNAR	CANOPUS	◆ Suhail	SPICA
210	42 05 047	30 06 085	13 58 140	36 13 176	40 53 227	45 59 266	31 59 350
211	42 21 046	30 28 084	14 12 139	36 15 176	40 38 226	45 38 265	31 55 349
212	42 36 045	30 49 083	14 26 139	36 17 175	40 22 226	45 16 264	31 50 348
213	42 51 044	31 11 082	14 40 138	36 19 174	40 07 225	44 55 263	31 46 347
214	43 06 043	31 32 081	14 55 137	36 21 174	39 52 224	44 34 263	31 41 346
215	43 21 042	31 53 080	15 10 136	36 23 173	39 37 224	44 12 262	31 35 344
216	43 35 040	32 14 079	15 25 135	36 26 172	39 22 223	43 51 261	31 29 343
217	43 48 039	32 35 079	15 40 134	36 29 172	39 08 222	43 30 260	31 23 342
218	44 02 038	32 56 078	15 55 133	36 32 171	38 53 221	43 09 259	31 16 341
219	44 15 037	33 17 077	16 11 133	36 36 170	38 39 221	42 48 258	31 09 340
220	44 28 036	33 38 076	16 27 132	36 40 170	38 25 220	42 27 257	31 01 339
221	44 40 034	33 59 075	16 43 131	36 44 169	38 12 219	42 06 256	30 53 338
222	44 52 033	34 20 074	17 00 130	36 48 168	37 58 218	41 45 256	30 45 336
223	45 03 032	34 40 073	17 16 129	36 52 168	37 45 218	41 24 255	30 36 335
224	45 14 031	35 01 072	17 33 128	36 57 167	37 32 217	41 03 254	30 27 334
	◆ ANTARES	Nunki	◆ FOMALHAUT	ACHERNAR	CANOPUS	◆ Suhail	SPICA
225	45 25 029	35 21 071	17 50 127	37 02 166	37 19 216	40 43 253	30 17 333
226	45 35 028	35 41 070	18 07 127	37 07 166	37 06 216	40 22 252	30 07 332
227	45 45 027	36 01 068	18 24 126	37 13 165	36 54 215	40 02 251	29 57 331
228	45 55 026	36 21 067	18 42 125	37 18 164	36 42 214	39 41 251	29 46 330
229	46 04 024	36 41 066	19 00 124	37 24 164	36 30 213	39 21 250	29 35 329
230	46 13 023	37 01 065	19 18 123	37 31 163	36 18 213	39 01 249	29 24 328
231	46 21 022	37 20 064	19 36 122	37 37 162	36 07 212	38 41 248	29 12 326
232	46 28 020	37 39 063	19 54 121	37 44 162	35 55 211	38 21 247	29 00 325
233	46 36 019	37 58 062	20 13 120	37 51 161	35 44 211	38 01 246	28 48 324
234	46 43 018	38 17 061	20 31 120	37 58 160	35 33 210	37 42 246	28 35 323
235	46 49 017	38 36 060	20 50 119	38 05 160	35 23 209	37 22 245	28 22 322
236	46 55 015	38 55 059	21 09 118	38 13 159	35 12 209	37 03 244	28 08 321
237	47 00 014	39 13 058	21 28 117	38 21 158	35 02 208	36 44 243	27 55 320
238	47 05 013	39 31 057	21 47 116	38 29 158	34 52 207	36 25 242	27 41 319
239	47 10 011	39 49 056	22 07 115	38 37 157	34 43 206	36 06 241	27 26 318
	ANTARES	◆ Nunki	FOMALHAUT	◆ ACHERNAR	CANOPUS	◆ ACRUX	SPICA
240	47 14 010	40 07 055	22 26 114	38 46 156	34 33 206	68 28 259	27 12 317
241	47 17 009	40 24 053	22 46 114	38 54 156	34 24 205	68 06 259	26 57 316
242	47 20 007	40 41 052	23 06 113	39 03 155	34 15 204	67 45 258	26 42 315
243	47 23 006	40 58 051	23 25 112	39 13 154	34 06 204	67 24 257	26 26 313
244	47 25 005	41 15 050	23 45 111	39 22 154	33 58 203	67 03 256	26 10 312
245	47 26 003	41 31 049	24 06 110	39 32 153	33 50 202	66 43 256	25 54 311
246	47 27 002	41 47 048	24 26 109	39 42 152	33 42 201	66 22 255	25 38 310
247	47 28 001	42 03 047	24 46 108	39 52 152	33 34 201	66 01 254	25 22 309
248	47 28 359	42 18 046	25 07 107	40 02 151	33 26 200	65 40 254	25 05 308
249	47 27 358	42 34 044	25 27 106	40 13 150	33 19 199	65 20 253	24 48 307
250	47 26 357	42 49 043	25 48 106	40 24 150	33 12 199	64 59 252	24 31 306
251	47 25 355	43 03 042	26 09 105	40 35 149	33 06 198	64 39 251	24 13 305
252	47 23 354	43 17 041	26 30 104	40 46 148	32 59 197	64 19 251	23 55 304
253	47 21 353	43 31 040	26 50 103	40 57 148	32 53 196	63 58 250	23 38 303
254	47 18 352	43 45 038	27 11 102	41 09 147	32 47 196	63 38 249	23 19 302
	◆ Nunki	FOMALHAUT	◆ ACHERNAR	CANOPUS	◆ ACRUX	SPICA	ANTARES
255	43 58 037	27 32 101	41 21 146	32 41 195	63 18 249	23 01 301	47 14 350
256	44 11 036	27 54 100	41 33 145	32 36 194	62 58 248	22 43 300	47 10 349
257	44 23 035	28 15 099	41 45 145	32 31 194	62 38 247	22 24 299	47 06 348
258	44 35 034	28 36 098	41 58 144	32 26 193	62 18 247	22 05 298	47 01 346
259	44 47 032	28 57 098	42 10 143	32 21 192	61 59 246	21 46 297	46 56 345
260	44 58 031	29 19 097	42 23 143	32 17 191	61 39 245	21 27 296	46 50 344
261	45 09 030	29 40 096	42 36 142	32 13 191	61 20 245	21 07 295	46 44 342
262	45 20 029	30 01 095	42 50 141	32 09 190	61 00 244	20 48 294	46 37 341
263	45 30 027	30 23 094	43 03 141	32 05 189	60 41 243	20 28 293	46 30 340
264	45 39 026	30 44 093	43 17 140	32 02 189	60 22 243	20 08 292	46 22 338
265	45 49 025	31 06 092	43 31 139	31 59 188	60 03 242	19 48 291	46 14 337
266	45 57 024	31 27 091	43 45 139	31 56 187	59 44 242	19 28 290	46 05 336
267	46 06 022	31 49 090	43 59 138	31 53 186	59 25 241	19 08 289	45 56 335
268	46 14 021	32 10 089	44 13 137	31 51 186	59 06 240	18 47 288	45 47 333
269	46 21 020	32 32 088	44 28 137	31 49 185	58 47 240	18 27 287	45 37 332

LHA ♈	Hc Zn	Hc Zn	Hc Zn	Hc Zn	Hc Zn	Hc Zn	Hc Zn
	◆ Nunki	FOMALHAUT	◆ ACHERNAR	CANOPUS	◆ ACRUX	SPICA	ANTARES
270	46 28 018	32 53 087	44 43 136	31 47 184	58 29 239	18 06 286	45 27 331
271	46 35 017	33 15 086	44 58 135	31 46 184	58 11 238	17 46 285	45 16 330
272	46 41 016	33 36 085	45 13 135	31 44 183	57 52 238	17 25 284	45 05 328
273	46 47 015	33 58 085	45 29 134	31 44 182	57 34 237	17 04 283	44 54 327
274	46 52 013	34 19 084	45 44 133	31 43 181	57 16 236	16 43 282	44 42 326
275	46 56 012	34 40 083	46 00 133	31 42 181	56 58 236	16 22 281	44 30 325
276	47 01 011	35 02 082	46 16 132	31 42 180	56 41 235	16 01 280	44 17 323
277	47 04 009	35 23 081	46 32 131	31 42 179	56 23 235	15 40 280	44 04 322
278	47 08 008	35 44 080	46 48 131	31 43 179	56 06 234	15 18 279	43 51 321
279	47 10 007	36 05 079	47 04 130	31 43 178	55 48 233	14 57 278	43 37 320
280	47 13 005	36 26 078	47 21 129	31 44 177	55 31 233	14 36 277	43 23 319
281	47 14 004	36 47 077	47 38 129	31 46 176	55 14 232	14 14 276	43 09 317
282	47 16 003	37 08 076	47 55 128	31 47 176	54 57 231	13 53 275	42 54 316
283	47 16 001	37 29 075	48 12 127	31 49 175	54 40 231	13 32 274	42 39 315
284	47 17 000	37 50 074	48 29 126	31 51 174	54 24 230	13 10 273	42 24 314
	◆ ALTAIR	FOMALHAUT	◆ ACHERNAR	CANOPUS	◆ RIGIL KENT	ANTARES	Nunki
285	11 34 013	38 10 073	48 46 126	31 53 174	62 51 255	42 08 313	47 16 359
286	11 39 012	38 31 072	49 04 125	31 55 173	62 30 254	41 52 312	47 16 357
287	11 43 011	38 51 071	49 22 124	31 58 172	62 10 253	41 36 311	47 14 356
288	11 47 010	39 11 070	49 39 124	32 01 172	61 49 253	41 19 309	47 13 355
289	11 51 009	39 31 069	49 57 123	32 05 171	61 29 252	41 03 308	47 11 353
290	11 54 008	39 51 068	50 15 122	32 08 170	61 08 251	40 46 307	47 08 352
291	11 57 007	40 11 066	50 34 122	32 12 169	60 48 250	40 28 306	47 05 351
292	11 59 006	40 31 065	50 52 121	32 16 169	60 28 250	40 11 305	47 01 350
293	12 01 005	40 50 064	51 11 120	32 20 168	60 08 249	39 53 304	46 57 348
294	12 03 004	41 09 063	51 29 119	32 25 167	59 48 248	39 35 303	46 52 347
295	12 04 003	41 29 062	51 48 119	32 30 167	59 28 248	39 17 302	46 47 346
296	12 05 002	41 47 061	52 07 118	32 35 166	59 08 247	38 58 301	46 42 344
297	12 05 001	42 06 060	52 26 117	32 40 165	58 48 246	38 40 299	46 35 343
298	12 05 000	42 25 059	52 45 117	32 46 164	58 29 245	38 21 298	46 29 342
299	12 05 359	42 43 058	53 04 116	32 52 164	58 09 245	38 02 297	46 22 340
	◆ FOMALHAUT	ACHERNAR	◆ CANOPUS	RIGIL KENT	◆ ANTARES	Nunki	ALTAIR
300	43 01 057	53 24 115	32 58 163	57 50 244	37 43 296	46 15 339	12 05 358
301	43 19 056	53 43 114	33 05 162	57 30 243	37 23 295	46 07 338	12 04 357
302	43 37 054	54 03 114	33 11 162	57 11 243	37 04 294	45 58 337	12 02 356
303	43 54 053	54 23 113	33 18 161	56 52 242	36 44 293	45 50 335	12 01 355
304	44 11 052	54 43 112	33 25 160	56 33 241	36 24 292	45 40 334	11 58 354
305	44 28 051	55 03 111	33 33 159	56 14 241	36 04 291	45 31 333	11 56 353
306	44 45 050	55 23 111	33 41 159	55 56 240	35 44 290	45 21 332	11 53 352
307	45 01 049	55 43 110	33 48 158	55 37 239	35 24 289	45 10 330	11 50 351
308	45 17 048	56 03 109	33 57 157	55 19 239	35 04 288	44 59 329	11 46 350
309	45 33 046	56 23 108	34 05 157	55 00 238	34 43 287	44 48 328	11 42 349
310	45 48 045	56 44 108	34 14 156	54 42 237	34 22 286	44 36 327	11 38 348
311	46 03 044	57 04 107	34 23 155	54 24 237	34 02 285	44 24 325	11 33 347
312	46 18 043	57 25 106	34 32 154	54 06 236	33 41 284	44 12 324	11 28 346
313	46 32 042	57 46 105	34 41 154	53 49 235	33 20 283	43 59 323	11 22 345
314	46 46 040	58 06 105	34 51 153	53 31 235	32 59 282	43 46 322	11 17 344
	◆ FOMALHAUT	ACHERNAR	◆ CANOPUS	Miaplacidus	RIGIL KENT	◆ ANTARES	Nunki
315	47 00 039	58 27 104	35 01 152	48 48 182	53 13 234	32 38 281	43 33 320
316	47 13 038	58 48 103	35 11 152	48 47 181	52 56 233	32 17 280	43 19 319
317	47 26 037	59 09 102	35 21 151	48 47 181	52 39 233	31 56 279	43 04 318
318	47 39 035	59 30 101	35 32 150	48 47 180	52 22 232	31 34 278	42 50 317
319	47 51 034	59 51 101	35 43 149	48 47 180	52 05 231	31 13 277	42 35 316
320	48 03 033	60 13 100	35 54 149	48 47 179	51 48 231	30 52 276	42 20 315
321	48 15 032	60 34 099	36 05 148	48 47 179	51 32 230	30 30 275	42 04 313
322	48 26 030	60 55 098	36 16 147	48 48 178	51 15 230	30 09 274	41 49 312
323	48 36 029	61 16 097	36 28 147	48 49 178	50 59 229	29 47 273	41 33 311
324	48 46 028	61 38 096	36 40 146	48 50 177	50 43 228	29 26 272	41 16 310
325	48 56 026	61 59 095	36 52 145	48 51 177	50 27 228	29 04 271	41 00 309
326	49 06 025	62 21 095	37 05 144	48 53 176	50 11 227	28 43 271	40 43 308
327	49 15 024	62 42 094	37 17 144	48 54 175	49 55 226	28 21 270	40 26 307
328	49 23 022	63 03 093	37 30 143	48 56 175	49 40 226	28 00 269	40 08 306
329	49 31 021	63 25 092	37 43 142	48 58 174	49 25 225	27 38 268	39 51 304
	◆ FOMALHAUT	ACHERNAR	◆ CANOPUS	Miaplacidus	RIGIL KENT	◆ ANTARES	Nunki
330	49 38 020	63 46 091	37 56 142	49 00 174	49 10 224	27 17 267	39 33 303
331	49 46 018	64 08 090	38 10 141	49 02 173	48 55 224	26 55 266	39 15 302
332	49 52 017	64 29 089	38 23 140	49 05 173	48 40 223	26 34 265	38 56 301
333	49 58 016	64 51 088	38 37 139	49 08 172	48 25 222	26 13 264	38 38 300
334	50 04 014	65 12 087	38 51 139	49 11 172	48 11 222	25 51 263	38 19 299
335	50 09 013	65 34 086	39 06 138	49 14 171	47 57 221	25 30 262	38 00 298
336	50 14 012	65 55 085	39 20 137	49 17 171	47 42 221	25 09 261	37 41 297
337	50 18 010	66 17 084	39 35 137	49 21 170	47 29 220	24 47 260	37 22 296
338	50 21 009	66 38 083	39 50 136	49 25 170	47 15 219	24 26 260	37 03 295
339	50 24 008	66 59 082	40 05 135	49 29 169	47 01 219	24 05 259	36 43 294
340	50 27 006	67 21 081	40 20 134	49 33 169	46 48 218	23 44 258	36 23 293
341	50 29 005	67 42 080	40 36 134	49 37 168	46 35 217	23 23 257	36 03 292
342	50 31 004	68 03 079	40 51 133	49 42 168	46 22 217	23 02 256	35 43 291
343	50 32 002	68 24 078	41 07 132	49 46 167	46 09 216	22 41 255	35 23 290
344	50 32 001	68 45 077	41 23 132	49 51 167	45 56 216	22 21 254	35 03 289
	Diphda	◆ CANOPUS	Miaplacidus	RIGIL KENT	◆ ANTARES	Nunki	◆ FOMALHAUT
345	36 23 031	41 39 131	49 56 166	45 44 215	22 00 253	34 42 288	50 33 359
346	36 34 030	41 56 130	50 02 166	45 32 214	21 40 252	34 22 287	50 32 358
347	36 45 029	42 12 129	50 07 165	45 20 214	21 19 251	34 01 286	50 31 357
348	36 55 028	42 29 129	50 13 164	45 08 213	20 59 251	33 40 285	50 30 355
349	37 05 027	42 46 128	50 18 164	44 56 212	20 39 250	33 19 284	50 28 354
350	37 15 025	43 03 127	50 25 163	44 45 212	20 18 249	32 58 283	50 25 353
351	37 24 024	43 20 126	50 31 163	44 34 211	19 58 248	32 37 282	50 22 351
352	37 32 023	43 37 126	50 37 162	44 23 210	19 39 247	32 16 281	50 19 350
353	37 40 022	43 55 125	50 44 162	44 12 210	19 19 246	31 55 280	50 15 349
354	37 48 021	44 13 124	50 50 161	44 01 209	18 59 245	31 34 279	50 10 347
355	37 56 020	44 30 124	50 57 161	43 51 209	18 40 244	31 13 278	50 05 346
356	38 03 018	44 48 123	51 05 160	43 41 208	18 20 243	30 51 277	50 00 345
357	38 09 017	45 07 122	51 12 160	43 31 207	18 01 243	30 30 276	49 54 343
358	38 15 016	45 25 121	51 19 159	43 21 207	17 42 242	30 08 275	49 47 342
359	38 21 015	45 43 121	51 27 159	43 12 206	17 23 241	29 47 274	49 40 340

LHA ♈	Hc	Zn	Hc	Zn	Hc	Zn	Hc	Zn	Hc	Zn	Hc	Zn	Hc	Zn
	Diphda		◆ RIGEL		CANOPUS		Miaplacidus		◆ RIGIL KENT		Peacock		◆ FOMALHAUT	
0	37 28	013	11 30	082	46 31	119	52 31	158	43 56	206	63 50	273	48 37	340
2	37 37	011	12 11	080	47 07	117	52 46	157	43 39	205	63 09	271	48 21	337
4	37 43	009	12 51	078	47 44	116	53 03	156	43 22	203	62 28	269	48 05	334
6	37 49	006	13 31	077	48 21	114	53 20	155	43 07	202	61 47	267	47 46	332
8	37 52	004	14 11	075	48 59	113	53 38	154	42 52	201	61 06	265	47 26	329
10	37 54	001	14 50	073	49 37	111	53 57	153	42 38	199	60 25	264	47 04	327
12	37 54	359	15 29	071	50 16	109	54 16	152	42 24	198	59 45	262	46 41	324
14	37 52	356	16 08	069	50 54	108	54 36	150	42 12	197	59 04	260	46 16	322
16	37 49	354	16 46	067	51 34	106	54 56	149	42 01	196	58 24	259	45 50	319
18	37 44	352	17 23	065	52 13	105	55 18	148	41 50	194	57 44	257	45 23	317
20	37 37	349	18 00	063	52 53	103	55 39	147	41 40	193	57 04	255	44 54	315
22	37 29	347	18 36	061	53 33	101	56 02	146	41 32	192	56 24	254	44 25	312
24	37 19	344	19 12	059	54 14	100	56 25	145	41 24	190	55 45	252	43 54	310
26	37 07	342	19 47	057	54 54	098	56 48	144	41 17	189	55 06	251	43 22	308
28	36 53	340	20 21	055	55 35	096	57 13	143	41 11	188	54 28	249	42 49	305
	RIGEL		◆ SIRIUS		Suhail		◆ RIGIL KENT		Peacock		◆ FOMALHAUT		Diphda	
30	20 54	053	22 01	078	35 00	122	41 06	187	53 49	248	42 15	303	36 38	337
32	21 26	051	22 41	076	35 35	121	41 01	185	53 12	246	41 40	301	36 22	335
34	21 58	049	23 21	074	36 11	119	40 58	184	52 34	245	41 05	299	36 04	333
36	22 28	047	24 00	072	36 47	117	40 56	183	51 58	243	40 28	297	35 44	330
38	22 57	045	24 39	070	37 24	116	40 54	181	51 21	242	39 51	295	35 23	328
40	23 26	043	25 17	068	38 01	114	40 54	180	50 45	240	39 14	292	35 01	326
42	23 53	040	25 55	066	38 39	112	40 54	179	50 10	239	38 35	290	34 37	324
44	24 19	038	26 32	064	39 17	111	40 55	178	49 35	237	37 57	288	34 12	321
46	24 44	036	27 09	062	39 56	109	40 58	176	49 01	236	37 17	286	33 46	319
48	25 07	034	27 45	060	40 35	107	41 01	175	48 28	234	36 38	284	33 18	317
50	25 30	032	28 20	058	41 14	106	41 05	174	47 55	233	35 58	282	32 50	315
52	25 51	030	28 55	056	41 54	104	41 10	172	47 22	231	35 18	280	32 20	312
54	26 10	028	29 29	054	42 34	102	41 16	171	46 50	230	34 37	278	31 49	310
56	26 29	025	30 02	052	43 14	100	41 23	170	46 19	229	33 56	276	31 17	308
58	26 46	023	30 33	050	43 55	099	41 30	169	45 49	227	33 16	274	30 45	306
	RIGEL		◆ SIRIUS		Suhail		◆ RIGIL KENT		Peacock		◆ FOMALHAUT		Diphda	
60	27 01	021	31 04	048	44 35	097	41 39	167	45 19	226	32 35	273	30 11	304
62	27 15	019	31 34	046	45 16	095	41 48	166	44 50	224	31 54	271	29 37	302
64	27 27	017	32 03	043	45 57	093	41 59	165	44 21	223	31 13	269	29 01	300
66	27 38	014	32 31	041	46 38	091	42 10	163	43 54	222	30 32	267	28 25	298
68	27 48	012	32 57	039	47 19	089	42 22	162	43 27	220	29 51	265	27 49	296
70	27 56	010	33 22	037	48 00	087	42 35	161	43 01	219	29 10	263	27 11	294
72	28 02	008	33 46	035	48 41	086	42 49	160	42 35	218	28 29	261	26 33	292
74	28 06	005	34 09	032	49 22	084	43 04	158	42 11	216	27 49	260	25 55	290
76	28 10	003	34 30	030	50 03	082	43 20	157	41 47	215	27 08	258	25 16	288
78	28 11	001	34 50	028	50 43	080	43 36	156	41 24	213	26 28	256	24 37	286
80	28 11	359	35 08	025	51 23	078	43 54	154	41 02	212	25 49	254	23 57	284
82	28 09	356	35 25	023	52 03	075	44 12	153	40 40	211	25 09	252	23 17	282
84	28 06	354	35 40	021	52 43	073	44 31	152	40 20	209	24 31	251	22 37	280
86	28 01	352	35 54	018	53 22	071	44 51	151	40 00	208	23 52	249	21 56	278
88	27 54	350	36 06	016	54 00	069	45 11	149	39 42	207	23 14	247	21 16	276
	◆ SIRIUS		Suhail		◆ RIGIL KENT		Peacock		FOMALHAUT		◆ ACHERNAR		RIGEL	
90	36 16	014	54 38	067	45 32	148	39 24	205	22 36	245	60 04	261	27 46	347
92	36 25	011	55 16	064	45 55	147	39 07	204	21 59	244	59 24	260	27 36	345
94	36 32	009	55 53	062	46 18	145	38 51	202	21 23	242	58 44	258	27 25	343
96	36 38	007	56 28	060	46 41	144	38 35	201	20 47	240	58 03	256	27 12	341
98	36 42	004	57 03	057	47 06	143	38 21	200	20 12	238	57 24	255	26 58	339
100	36 44	002	57 38	055	47 31	141	38 08	198	19 37	237	56 44	253	26 42	336
102	36 44	359	58 11	052	47 57	140	37 55	197	19 03	235	56 05	252	26 25	334
104	36 43	357	58 42	050	48 24	139	37 44	196	18 30	233	55 26	250	26 07	332
106	36 40	355	59 13	047	48 51	138	37 33	194	17 58	231	54 48	248	25 47	330
108	36 35	352	59 43	044	49 19	136	37 24	193	17 26	230	54 10	247	25 26	328
110	36 29	350	60 11	042	49 48	135	37 15	191	16 55	228	53 33	245	25 03	326
112	36 21	347	60 37	039	50 17	134	37 08	190	16 25	226	52 55	244	24 39	323
114	36 11	345	61 02	036	50 47	132	37 01	189	15 56	224	52 19	242	24 14	321
116	35 59	343	61 25	033	51 18	131	36 55	187	15 28	223	51 43	241	23 48	319
118	35 46	340	61 47	030	51 49	130	36 50	186	15 00	221	51 07	240	23 20	317
	Suhail		◆ SPICA		RIGIL KENT		Peacock		◆ FOMALHAUT		ACHERNAR		◆ SIRIUS	
120	62 07	027	13 28	086	52 21	128	36 47	185	14 34	219	50 32	238	35 32	338
122	62 25	024	14 08	084	52 53	127	36 44	183	14 09	217	49 57	237	35 16	336
124	62 40	021	14 49	082	53 26	126	36 42	182	13 44	216	49 23	235	34 58	333
126	62 54	018	15 30	080	54 00	124	36 41	180	13 21	214	48 50	234	34 39	331
128	63 06	015	16 10	078	54 34	123	36 41	179	12 58	212	48 17	232	34 18	329
130	63 15	012	16 50	076	55 09	122	36 42	178	12 37	210	47 45	231	33 56	327
132	63 22	008	17 30	074	55 44	120	36 45	176	12 17	209	47 13	230	33 33	324
134	63 27	005	18 09	072	56 19	119	36 48	175	11 58	207	46 42	228	33 09	322
136	63 29	002	18 48	071	56 56	118	36 52	174	11 40	205	46 12	227	32 43	320
138	63 29	359	19 27	069	57 32	116	36 57	172	11 23	203	45 42	225	32 16	318
140	63 27	355	20 04	067	58 09	115	37 03	171	11 07	202	45 13	224	31 47	315
142	63 23	352	20 42	065	58 47	113	37 10	170	10 52	200	44 45	223	31 18	313
144	63 16	349	21 19	063	59 25	112	37 18	168	10 39	198	44 18	221	30 48	311
146	63 07	346	21 55	061	60 03	110	37 27	167	10 27	196	43 51	220	30 16	309
148	62 56	343	22 30	059	60 42	109	37 36	165	10 16	195	43 25	219	29 44	307
	◆ SPICA		ANTARES		◆ Peacock		FOMALHAUT		ACHERNAR		◆ CANOPUS		Suhail	
150	23 05	057	22 14	107	37 47	164	10 06	193	43 00	217	60 24	277	62 42	339
152	23 39	054	22 53	105	37 59	163	09 58	191	42 36	216	59 44	275	62 27	336
154	24 12	052	23 33	103	38 12	161	09 50	189	42 12	214	59 03	273	62 09	333
156	24 44	050	24 13	101	38 25	160	09 44	188	41 49	213	58 22	271	61 50	330
158	25 15	048	24 54	099	38 40	159	09 39	186	41 27	212	57 41	270	61 29	327
160	25 45	046	25 34	097	38 55	157	09 36	184	41 06	210	57 00	268	61 05	324
162	26 14	044	26 15	096	39 12	156	09 34	182	40 46	209	56 19	266	60 41	321
164	26 42	042	26 56	094	39 29	154	09 33	181	40 26	208	55 38	264	60 14	319
166	27 09	040	27 37	092	39 47	153	09 33	179	40 08	206	54 57	262	59 47	316
168	27 34	038	28 18	090	40 06	152	09 34	177	39 50	205	54 17	261	59 17	313
170	27 59	035	28 59	088	40 26	150	09 37	175	39 33	204	53 36	259	58 47	311
172	28 22	033	29 40	086	40 47	149	09 41	173	39 17	202	52 56	257	58 15	308
174	28 44	031	30 21	084	41 08	148	09 46	172	39 02	201	52 16	256	57 42	305
176	29 04	029	31 02	082	41 31	146	09 53	170	38 48	199	51 37	254	57 08	303
178	29 24	027	31 42	080	41 54	145	10 01	168	38 35	198	50 57	252	56 33	301

LAT 70°S

LHA ♈	Hc	Zn	Hc	Zn	Hc	Zn	Hc	Zn	Hc	Zn	Hc	Zn	Hc	Zn
	SPICA		◆ ANTARES		Nunki		FOMALHAUT		◆ ACHERNAR		CANOPUS		◆ Suhail	
180	29 41	024	32 23	078	19 58	112	10 10	166	38 23	197	50 18	251	55 58	298
182	29 58	022	33 03	077	20 37	110	10 20	165	38 11	195	49 40	249	55 21	296
184	30 12	020	33 43	075	21 15	109	10 31	163	38 01	194	49 02	247	54 44	294
186	30 26	018	34 22	073	21 54	107	10 44	161	37 51	193	48 24	246	54 06	291
188	30 37	015	35 01	070	22 34	105	10 58	159	37 43	191	47 47	244	53 27	289
190	30 47	013	35 39	068	23 14	103	11 13	158	37 35	190	47 10	243	52 48	287
192	30 56	011	36 17	066	23 54	101	11 29	156	37 29	189	46 34	241	52 09	285
194	31 03	009	36 54	064	24 34	100	11 46	154	37 23	187	45 58	240	51 29	283
196	31 08	006	37 31	062	25 15	098	12 05	152	37 19	186	45 23	238	50 49	281
198	31 12	004	38 07	060	25 55	096	12 24	151	37 15	184	44 48	237	50 08	279
200	31 14	002	38 42	058	26 36	094	12 45	149	37 12	183	44 14	235	49 28	277
202	31 14	359	39 17	056	27 17	092	13 07	147	37 10	182	43 41	234	48 47	275
204	31 13	357	39 50	053	27 58	090	13 30	145	37 10	180	43 08	232	48 06	273
206	31 10	355	40 22	051	28 39	088	13 53	144	37 10	179	42 36	231	47 25	271
208	31 06	353	40 54	049	29 20	087	14 18	142	37 11	178	42 05	229	46 44	269
	◆ ANTARES		Nunki		◆ FOMALHAUT		ACHERNAR		CANOPUS		◆ Suhail		SPICA	
210	41 24	047	30 01	085	14 44	140	37 13	176	41 34	228	46 03	267	31 00	350
212	41 54	044	30 42	083	15 11	138	37 16	175	41 04	226	45 22	265	30 52	348
214	42 22	042	31 23	081	15 38	137	37 20	174	40 35	225	44 41	264	30 42	346
216	42 49	040	32 03	079	16 07	135	37 26	172	40 06	223	44 00	262	30 32	343
218	43 14	037	32 43	077	16 37	133	37 32	171	39 38	222	43 20	260	30 19	341
220	43 38	035	33 23	075	17 07	131	37 39	169	39 11	220	42 39	258	30 05	339
222	44 01	033	34 02	073	17 38	130	37 47	168	38 45	219	41 59	256	29 50	337
224	44 23	030	34 41	071	18 10	128	37 55	167	38 20	218	41 20	255	29 33	334
226	44 42	028	35 20	069	18 43	126	38 05	165	37 55	216	40 40	253	29 14	332
228	45 01	025	35 58	067	19 16	125	38 16	164	37 31	215	40 01	251	28 54	330
230	45 17	023	36 35	065	19 50	123	38 28	163	37 08	213	39 22	250	28 33	328
232	45 32	020	37 12	063	20 25	121	38 41	161	36 46	212	38 44	248	28 11	326
234	45 45	018	37 48	060	21 01	119	38 54	160	36 25	210	38 06	246	27 47	323
236	45 57	015	38 23	058	21 37	118	39 09	159	36 05	209	37 29	245	27 22	321
238	46 07	012	38 58	056	22 13	116	39 24	157	35 46	207	36 52	243	26 55	319
	ANTARES		◆ Nunki		FOMALHAUT		◆ ACHERNAR		CANOPUS		◆ ACRUX		SPICA	
240	46 15	010	39 32	054	22 51	114	39 40	156	35 27	206	68 37	262	26 28	317
242	46 21	007	40 04	052	23 28	112	39 58	155	35 10	205	67 57	260	25 59	315
244	46 25	005	40 36	049	24 07	110	40 16	153	34 53	203	67 16	259	25 30	313
246	46 27	002	41 07	047	24 45	109	40 35	152	34 37	202	66 36	257	24 59	311
248	46 28	359	41 36	045	25 24	107	40 54	150	34 23	200	65 56	256	24 28	309
250	46 26	357	42 05	043	26 04	105	41 15	149	34 09	199	65 17	254	23 55	307
252	46 23	354	42 32	040	26 44	103	41 37	148	33 56	197	64 37	253	23 22	304
254	46 18	352	42 58	038	27 24	102	41 59	146	33 45	196	63 58	251	22 47	302
256	46 11	349	43 22	035	28 04	100	42 22	145	33 34	194	63 20	250	22 12	300
258	46 03	347	43 45	033	28 45	098	42 46	144	33 24	193	62 41	248	21 37	298
260	45 52	344	44 07	031	29 25	096	43 11	142	33 15	192	62 03	247	21 00	296
262	45 40	341	44 27	028	30 06	094	43 36	141	33 08	190	61 26	246	20 23	294
264	45 26	339	44 45	026	30 47	092	44 03	139	33 01	189	60 48	244	19 45	292
266	45 10	336	45 02	023	31 28	090	44 30	138	32 55	187	60 12	243	19 07	290
268	44 53	334	45 18	021	32 09	089	44 57	137	32 51	186	59 35	242	18 29	288
	◆ Nunki		FOMALHAUT		◆ ACHERNAR		CANOPUS		◆ ACRUX		RIGIL KENT		ANTARES	
270	45 31	018	32 50	087	45 26	135	32 47	184	58 59	240	68 11	269	44 34	331
272	45 43	016	33 31	085	45 55	134	32 44	183	58 24	239	67 30	268	44 14	329
274	45 53	013	34 12	083	46 25	133	32 43	181	57 49	238	66 49	266	43 52	326
276	46 02	010	34 53	081	46 56	131	32 42	180	57 14	236	66 08	264	43 29	324
278	46 08	008	35 33	079	47 27	130	32 43	179	56 40	235	65 27	262	43 04	322
280	46 13	005	36 13	077	47 59	128	32 44	177	56 07	234	64 46	261	42 38	319
282	46 16	003	36 53	075	48 31	127	32 47	176	55 34	233	64 06	259	42 10	317
284	46 17	000	37 32	073	49 04	126	32 50	174	55 02	231	63 26	257	41 42	315
286	46 16	357	38 11	071	49 38	124	32 55	173	54 30	230	62 46	256	41 12	312
288	46 13	355	38 50	069	50 12	123	33 01	171	53 59	229	62 06	254	40 41	310
290	46 08	352	39 28	067	50 47	121	33 07	170	53 28	228	61 27	253	40 09	308
292	46 02	350	40 05	065	51 22	120	33 15	169	52 58	226	60 48	251	39 36	306
294	45 54	347	40 42	063	51 58	118	33 24	167	52 29	225	60 09	250	39 02	303
296	45 44	345	41 18	060	52 35	117	33 33	166	52 00	224	59 31	248	38 28	301
298	45 32	342	41 53	058	53 11	115	33 44	164	51 32	223	58 53	247	37 52	299
	◆ FOMALHAUT		ACHERNAR		◆ CANOPUS		ACRUX		RIGIL KENT		◆ ANTARES		Nunki	
300	42 28	056	53 49	114	33 56	163	51 05	221	58 15	245	37 16	297	45 18	339
302	43 01	054	54 26	112	34 08	161	50 38	220	57 38	244	36 39	295	45 03	337
304	43 34	051	55 05	111	34 22	160	50 12	219	57 01	243	36 01	293	44 46	334
306	44 06	049	55 43	109	34 36	158	49 46	218	56 25	241	35 23	291	44 28	332
308	44 36	047	56 22	108	34 52	157	49 22	216	55 49	240	34 45	289	44 08	330
310	45 05	044	57 01	106	35 08	156	48 58	215	55 14	239	34 06	287	43 46	327
312	45 33	042	57 41	105	35 26	154	48 34	214	54 39	237	33 26	285	43 23	325
314	46 00	040	58 21	103	35 44	153	48 12	213	54 05	236	32 46	283	42 59	322
316	46 26	037	59 01	101	36 04	151	47 50	211	53 31	234	32 06	281	42 33	320
318	46 50	035	59 41	100	36 24	150	47 29	210	52 58	233	31 26	279	42 06	318
320	47 13	032	60 22	098	36 45	148	47 09	209	52 26	232	30 45	277	41 38	315
322	47 34	030	61 03	096	37 07	147	46 49	208	51 54	230	30 04	275	41 08	313
324	47 53	027	61 43	094	37 30	145	46 31	206	51 22	229	29 23	273	40 38	311
326	48 11	025	62 24	093	37 53	144	46 13	205	50 52	228	28 42	271	40 06	308
328	48 27	022	63 05	091	38 18	143	45 56	204	50 22	227	28 01	269	39 33	306
	◆ FOMALHAUT		Diphda		◆ CANOPUS		ACRUX		RIGIL KENT		◆ ANTARES		Nunki	
330	48 42	019	32 17	048	38 43	141	45 39	203	49 52	225	27 20	267	39 00	304
332	48 55	017	32 47	046	39 09	140	45 24	202	49 23	224	26 39	265	38 25	302
334	49 06	014	33 16	043	39 36	138	45 09	200	48 55	223	25 58	264	37 50	300
336	49 15	012	33 44	041	40 04	137	44 55	199	48 28	222	25 17	262	37 14	298
338	49 22	009	34 10	039	40 33	135	44 42	198	48 01	220	24 37	260	36 37	295
340	49 27	006	34 35	037	41 02	134	44 30	197	47 35	219	23 57	258	36 00	293
342	49 31	004	34 59	034	41 32	132	44 19	195	47 10	217	23 17	256	35 22	291
344	49 32	001	35 21	032	42 03	131	44 09	194	46 45	216	22 37	255	34 43	289
346	49 32	358	35 42	030	42 34	129	43 59	193	46 21	215	21 58	253	34 04	287
348	49 30	355	36 02	027	43 06	128	43 50	192	45 58	214	21 19	251	33 25	285
350	49 26	353	36 20	025	43 39	126	43 42	190	45 36	212	20 40	249	32 45	283
352	49 20	350	36 37	023	44 12	125	43 35	189	45 14	211	20 02	247	32 05	281
354	49 12	347	36 52	020	44 46	123	43 29	188	44 54	210	19 24	246	31 25	279
356	49 02	345	37 06	018	45 20	122	43 24	187	44 34	208	18 47	244	30 44	277
358	48 50	342	37 18	016	45 56	120	43 20	185	44 15	207	18 11	242	30 03	275

LHA ♈	Diphda		◆ RIGEL		CANOPUS		Miaplacidus		◆ RIGIL KENT		Peacock		◆ FOMALHAUT	
	Hc	Zn	Hc	Zn	Hc	Zn	Hc	Zn	Hc	Zn	Hc	Zn	Hc	Zn
0	36 29	013	11 22	082	47 00	118	53 26	157	44 50	206	63 46	275	47 40	340
2	36 38	011	12 01	080	47 35	116	53 41	156	44 33	205	63 07	273	47 26	337
4	36 44	008	12 39	078	48 10	115	53 58	155	44 17	204	62 28	271	47 10	335
6	36 49	006	13 17	076	48 45	113	54 14	154	44 02	202	61 49	269	46 53	332
8	36 52	004	13 55	074	49 22	112	54 32	153	43 48	201	61 10	267	46 34	330
10	36 54	001	14 32	072	49 58	110	54 50	152	43 34	200	60 31	265	46 14	327
12	36 54	359	15 10	071	50 35	108	55 08	151	43 21	198	59 52	264	45 52	325
14	36 53	357	15 46	069	51 12	107	55 28	150	43 09	197	59 13	262	45 29	323
16	36 49	354	16 22	067	51 50	105	55 48	149	42 58	196	58 35	260	45 04	320
18	36 45	352	16 58	065	52 28	103	56 08	148	42 48	194	57 56	259	44 39	318
20	36 38	349	17 33	063	53 06	102	56 30	147	42 39	193	57 18	257	44 12	315
22	36 30	347	18 07	061	53 44	100	56 51	145	42 30	192	56 40	255	43 44	313
24	36 21	345	18 41	059	54 23	098	57 14	144	42 23	191	56 03	254	43 15	311
26	36 10	342	19 14	057	55 02	096	57 37	143	42 16	189	55 25	252	42 45	308
28	35 57	340	19 46	055	55 40	095	58 01	142	42 10	188	54 48	250	42 14	306

LHA ♈	RIGEL		◆ SIRIUS		Suhail		◆ RIGIL KENT		Peacock		◆ FOMALHAUT		Diphda	
	Hc	Zn	Hc	Zn	Hc	Zn	Hc	Zn	Hc	Zn	Hc	Zn	Hc	Zn
30	20 18	053	21 48	078	35 32	122	42 05	187	54 12	249	41 42	304	35 43	338
32	20 48	051	22 26	076	36 06	120	42 01	185	53 36	247	41 09	302	35 27	335
34	21 18	048	23 04	074	36 40	118	41 58	184	53 00	246	40 35	300	35 10	333
36	21 47	046	23 42	072	37 14	117	41 56	183	52 24	244	40 01	297	34 52	331
38	22 14	044	24 18	070	37 50	115	41 54	181	51 49	243	39 26	295	34 32	328
40	22 41	042	24 55	068	38 25	113	41 54	180	51 15	241	38 50	293	34 11	326
42	23 07	040	25 31	066	39 01	112	41 54	179	50 41	240	38 14	291	33 49	324
44	23 32	038	26 06	064	39 38	110	41 55	177	50 07	238	37 37	289	33 25	322
46	23 55	036	26 41	062	40 15	108	41 58	176	49 35	237	37 00	287	33 00	320
48	24 17	034	27 15	060	40 52	106	42 01	175	49 02	235	36 23	285	32 34	317
50	24 39	032	27 49	058	41 30	105	42 05	174	48 30	234	35 45	283	32 07	315
52	24 58	030	28 21	056	42 08	103	42 09	172	47 59	232	35 07	281	31 39	313
54	25 17	027	28 53	054	42 46	101	42 15	171	47 29	231	34 28	279	31 10	311
56	25 34	025	29 24	052	43 24	099	42 22	170	46 59	229	33 49	277	30 40	309
58	25 50	023	29 55	049	44 03	098	42 29	168	46 29	228	33 11	275	30 09	307

LHA ♈	RIGEL		◆ SIRIUS		Suhail		◆ RIGIL KENT		Peacock		◆ FOMALHAUT		Diphda	
	Hc	Zn	Hc	Zn	Hc	Zn	Hc	Zn	Hc	Zn	Hc	Zn	Hc	Zn
60	26 05	021	30 24	047	44 42	096	42 37	167	46 00	227	32 32	273	29 37	304
62	26 18	019	30 52	045	45 21	094	42 47	166	45 32	225	31 53	271	29 05	302
64	26 30	016	31 19	043	46 00	092	42 57	164	45 05	224	31 14	269	28 31	300
66	26 40	014	31 45	041	46 39	090	43 08	163	44 38	222	30 34	268	27 57	298
68	26 49	012	32 10	039	47 18	088	43 19	162	44 12	221	29 55	266	27 22	296
70	26 56	010	32 34	036	47 57	086	43 32	160	43 47	219	29 17	264	26 47	294
72	27 02	008	32 56	034	48 36	084	43 45	159	43 23	218	28 38	262	26 11	292
74	27 07	005	33 18	032	49 15	082	44 00	158	42 59	217	27 59	260	25 35	290
76	27 10	003	33 38	030	49 53	080	44 15	157	42 36	215	27 21	258	24 58	288
78	27 11	001	33 56	027	50 32	078	44 31	155	42 14	214	26 43	256	24 20	286
80	27 11	359	34 14	025	51 10	076	44 48	154	41 53	212	26 05	255	23 43	284
82	27 09	356	34 29	023	51 48	074	45 05	153	41 32	211	25 27	253	23 05	282
84	27 06	354	34 44	020	52 25	072	45 23	151	41 12	210	24 50	251	22 26	280
86	27 01	352	34 57	018	53 02	070	45 43	150	40 53	208	24 13	249	21 48	278
88	26 55	350	35 08	016	53 38	068	46 03	149	40 35	207	23 37	247	21 09	276

LHA ♈	◆ SIRIUS		Suhail		◆ RIGIL KENT		Peacock		FOMALHAUT		◆ ACHERNAR		RIGEL	
	Hc	Zn	Hc	Zn	Hc	Zn	Hc	Zn	Hc	Zn	Hc	Zn	Hc	Zn
90	35 18	013	54 14	065	46 23	147	40 18	205	23 01	246	60 12	263	26 48	348
92	35 26	011	54 49	063	46 45	146	40 02	204	22 26	244	59 34	261	26 38	345
94	35 33	009	55 24	061	47 07	145	39 46	203	21 51	242	58 55	260	26 28	343
96	35 38	006	55 58	058	47 30	143	39 31	201	21 17	240	58 17	258	26 16	341
98	35 42	004	56 31	056	47 53	142	39 18	200	20 43	239	57 39	256	26 02	339
100	35 44	002	57 02	054	48 18	141	39 05	199	20 10	237	57 01	255	25 47	337
102	35 44	359	57 33	051	48 43	139	38 53	197	19 38	235	56 23	253	25 31	334
104	35 43	357	58 03	049	49 08	138	38 42	196	19 06	233	55 46	251	25 14	332
106	35 40	355	58 32	046	49 35	137	38 32	194	18 35	232	55 09	250	24 55	330
108	35 36	352	58 59	043	50 02	135	38 22	193	18 05	230	54 33	248	24 35	328
110	35 30	350	59 25	041	50 30	134	38 14	192	17 35	228	53 57	247	24 13	326
112	35 22	348	59 50	038	50 58	133	38 07	190	17 07	226	53 21	245	23 51	324
114	35 13	345	60 13	035	51 27	131	38 00	189	16 39	225	52 46	244	23 27	322
116	35 02	343	60 35	032	51 57	130	37 55	187	16 12	223	52 11	242	23 02	319
118	34 50	341	60 55	029	52 27	129	37 50	186	15 46	221	51 37	241	22 36	317

LHA ♈	Suhail		◆ SPICA		RIGIL KENT		Peacock		◆ FOMALHAUT		ACHERNAR		◆ SIRIUS	
	Hc	Zn	Hc	Zn	Hc	Zn	Hc	Zn	Hc	Zn	Hc	Zn	Hc	Zn
120	61 13	026	13 23	086	52 58	127	37 46	185	15 21	219	51 03	239	34 36	338
122	61 30	023	14 02	084	53 29	126	37 44	183	14 56	218	50 30	238	34 21	336
124	61 44	020	14 41	082	54 01	125	37 42	182	14 33	216	49 57	236	34 04	334
126	61 57	017	15 19	080	54 33	123	37 41	180	14 11	214	49 25	235	33 46	331
128	62 07	014	15 58	078	55 06	122	37 41	179	13 49	212	48 53	233	33 27	329
130	62 16	011	16 36	076	55 40	120	37 42	178	13 29	211	48 22	232	33 06	327
132	62 23	008	17 14	074	56 13	119	37 44	176	13 09	209	47 52	230	32 44	325
134	62 27	005	17 51	072	56 48	118	37 47	175	12 51	207	47 22	229	32 21	322
136	62 29	002	18 28	070	57 23	116	37 51	174	12 34	205	46 53	228	31 57	320
138	62 29	359	19 04	068	57 58	115	37 56	172	12 18	204	46 24	226	31 31	318
140	62 27	356	19 40	066	58 34	113	38 02	171	12 03	202	45 56	225	31 04	316
142	62 23	352	20 16	064	59 10	112	38 09	169	11 49	200	45 29	223	30 37	314
144	62 17	349	20 51	062	59 46	110	38 16	168	11 36	198	45 03	222	30 08	312
146	62 09	346	21 25	060	60 23	109	38 25	167	11 24	196	44 37	221	29 38	309
148	61 58	343	21 59	058	61 00	107	38 34	165	11 14	195	44 12	219	29 08	307

LHA ♈	◆ SPICA		ANTARES		◆ Peacock		FOMALHAUT		ACHERNAR		◆ CANOPUS		Suhail	
	Hc	Zn	Hc	Zn	Hc	Zn	Hc	Zn	Hc	Zn	Hc	Zn	Hc	Zn
150	22 32	056	22 31	106	38 45	164	11 05	193	43 48	218	60 16	279	61 46	340
152	23 04	054	23 09	104	38 56	162	10 56	191	43 24	216	59 37	277	61 32	337
154	23 35	052	23 47	102	39 08	161	10 50	189	43 01	215	58 58	275	61 16	334
156	24 05	050	24 25	101	39 22	160	10 44	188	42 39	214	58 19	273	60 58	331
158	24 35	048	25 03	099	39 36	158	10 39	186	42 18	212	57 40	271	60 38	328
160	25 03	046	25 42	097	39 51	157	10 36	184	41 58	211	57 01	269	60 16	325
162	25 31	044	26 21	095	40 06	155	10 34	182	41 38	209	56 22	267	59 53	323
164	25 57	042	27 00	093	40 23	154	10 33	181	41 19	208	55 43	266	59 29	320
166	26 23	039	27 39	091	40 40	153	10 33	179	41 01	207	55 04	264	59 03	317
168	26 47	037	28 18	089	40 59	151	10 34	177	40 44	205	54 26	262	58 36	314
170	27 10	035	28 57	088	41 18	150	10 37	175	40 28	204	53 47	260	58 07	312
172	27 32	033	29 36	086	41 38	149	10 41	173	40 13	202	53 09	258	57 38	309
174	27 52	031	30 15	084	41 59	147	10 46	172	39 58	201	52 30	257	57 07	307
176	28 12	029	30 54	082	42 20	146	10 52	170	39 45	200	51 53	255	56 35	304
178	28 30	026	31 32	080	42 43	144	10 59	168	39 32	198	51 15	253	56 02	302

LAT 71°S

LHA ♈	SPICA		◆ ANTARES		Nunki		FOMALHAUT		◆ ACHERNAR		CANOPUS		◆ Suhail	
	Hc	Zn	Hc	Zn	Hc	Zn	Hc	Zn	Hc	Zn	Hc	Zn	Hc	Zn
180	28 47	024	32 10	078	20 21	112	11 08	166	39 20	197	50 38	252	55 29	299
182	29 02	022	32 49	076	20 57	110	11 18	165	39 09	196	50 01	250	54 54	297
184	29 16	020	33 26	074	21 34	108	11 29	163	38 59	194	49 24	249	54 19	295
186	29 28	018	34 04	072	22 12	106	11 41	161	38 50	193	48 48	247	53 43	293
188	29 39	015	34 40	070	22 49	105	11 54	159	38 42	191	48 12	245	53 07	290
190	29 49	013	35 17	068	23 27	103	12 08	158	38 35	190	47 37	244	52 30	288
192	29 57	011	35 53	066	24 05	101	12 24	156	38 28	189	47 02	242	51 53	286
194	30 04	009	36 28	064	24 44	099	12 40	154	38 23	187	46 28	241	51 15	284
196	30 09	006	37 03	061	25 22	097	12 58	152	38 18	186	45 54	239	50 37	282
198	30 12	004	37 37	059	26 01	095	13 17	151	38 15	185	45 21	238	49 59	280
200	30 14	002	38 10	057	26 40	094	13 36	149	38 12	183	44 48	236	49 20	278
202	30 14	359	38 42	055	27 19	092	13 57	147	38 10	182	44 16	234	48 41	276
204	30 13	357	39 14	053	27 58	090	14 19	145	38 10	180	43 45	233	48 02	274
206	30 10	355	39 45	051	28 37	088	14 42	144	38 10	179	43 14	231	47 23	272
208	30 06	353	40 14	048	29 16	086	15 05	142	38 11	178	42 44	230	46 44	270

LHA ♈	◆ ANTARES		Nunki		◆ FOMALHAUT		ACHERNAR		CANOPUS		◆ Suhail		SPICA	
	Hc	Zn	Hc	Zn	Hc	Zn	Hc	Zn	Hc	Zn	Hc	Zn	Hc	Zn
210	40 43	046	29 55	084	15 30	140	38 13	176	42 14	228	46 05	268	30 00	350
212	41 11	044	30 34	082	15 56	138	38 16	175	41 45	227	45 26	266	29 53	348
214	41 37	041	31 13	080	16 22	137	38 20	173	41 17	225	44 47	264	29 44	346
216	42 02	039	31 51	078	16 49	135	38 25	172	40 50	224	44 08	263	29 34	344
218	42 26	037	32 29	076	17 18	133	38 31	171	40 23	222	43 30	261	29 22	341
220	42 49	034	33 07	074	17 47	131	38 38	169	39 57	221	42 51	259	29 09	339
222	43 11	032	33 44	072	18 16	129	38 45	168	39 32	220	42 13	257	28 54	337
224	43 31	030	34 21	070	18 47	128	38 54	167	39 07	218	41 35	256	28 38	335
226	43 49	027	34 58	068	19 18	126	39 03	165	38 43	217	40 57	254	28 21	332
228	44 06	025	35 34	066	19 50	124	39 14	164	38 21	215	40 20	252	28 02	330
230	44 22	022	36 09	064	20 23	122	39 25	162	37 59	214	39 43	250	27 42	328
232	44 36	020	36 44	062	20 56	121	39 37	161	37 37	212	39 06	249	27 21	326
234	44 48	017	37 18	060	21 30	119	39 50	160	37 17	211	38 30	247	26 58	324
236	44 59	015	37 52	058	22 04	117	40 04	158	36 57	209	37 54	245	26 35	322
238	45 08	012	38 24	055	22 39	115	40 19	157	36 39	208	37 19	244	26 10	319

LHA ♈	ANTARES		◆ Nunki		FOMALHAUT		◆ ACHERNAR		CANOPUS		◆ ACRUX		SPICA	
	Hc	Zn	Hc	Zn	Hc	Zn	Hc	Zn	Hc	Zn	Hc	Zn	Hc	Zn
240	45 15	010	38 56	053	23 15	114	40 35	156	36 21	206	68 44	265	25 44	317
242	45 21	007	39 27	051	23 51	112	40 52	154	36 04	205	68 05	263	25 17	315
244	45 25	005	39 57	049	24 27	110	41 09	153	35 48	203	67 27	261	24 49	313
246	45 27	002	40 26	047	25 04	108	41 27	151	35 33	202	66 48	260	24 20	311
248	45 28	359	40 53	044	25 42	106	41 47	150	35 19	200	66 10	258	23 50	309
250	45 27	357	41 20	042	26 19	105	42 06	149	35 06	199	65 32	256	23 19	307
252	45 24	354	41 46	040	26 57	103	42 27	147	34 54	198	64 54	255	22 48	305
254	45 19	352	42 10	037	27 35	101	42 49	146	34 42	196	64 17	253	22 15	303
256	45 12	349	42 33	035	28 14	099	43 11	144	34 32	195	63 39	252	21 42	301
258	45 04	347	42 55	033	28 53	097	43 34	143	34 23	193	63 02	250	21 08	299
260	44 55	344	43 15	030	29 31	095	43 58	142	34 14	192	62 26	249	20 33	297
262	44 43	342	43 34	028	30 10	094	44 23	140	34 07	190	61 49	247	19 58	295
264	44 30	339	43 51	025	30 49	092	44 48	139	34 00	189	61 14	246	19 22	293
266	44 15	337	44 07	023	31 28	090	45 14	137	33 55	187	60 38	245	18 46	291
268	43 59	334	44 21	020	32 07	088	45 41	136	33 50	186	60 03	243	18 09	289

LHA ♈	◆ Nunki		FOMALHAUT		◆ ACHERNAR		CANOPUS		◆ ACRUX		RIGIL KENT		ANTARES	
	Hc	Zn	Hc	Zn	Hc	Zn	Hc	Zn	Hc	Zn	Hc	Zn	Hc	Zn
270	44 34	018	32 46	086	46 08	135	33 47	184	59 28	242	68 10	272	43 42	332
272	44 45	015	33 25	084	46 36	133	33 44	183	58 54	240	67 31	270	43 22	329
274	44 55	013	34 04	082	47 05	132	33 43	182	58 20	239	66 52	268	43 02	327
276	45 03	010	34 43	080	47 35	130	33 42	180	57 47	238	66 13	266	42 40	325
278	45 09	008	35 21	078	48 05	129	33 43	179	57 14	236	65 34	264	42 17	322
280	45 13	005	35 59	076	48 36	127	33 44	177	56 42	235	64 55	263	41 52	320
282	45 16	003	36 37	074	49 07	126	33 47	176	56 10	234	64 16	261	41 26	318
284	45 17	000	37 14	072	49 39	125	33 50	174	55 39	232	63 38	259	40 59	315
286	45 16	358	37 51	070	50 11	123	33 54	173	55 08	231	63 00	258	40 31	313
288	45 13	355	38 28	068	50 44	122	34 00	171	54 38	230	62 21	256	40 02	311
290	45 09	352	39 04	066	51 18	120	34 06	170	54 08	229	61 44	255	39 32	308
292	45 03	350	39 39	064	51 52	119	34 14	168	53 39	227	61 06	253	39 01	306
294	44 55	347	40 14	062	52 26	117	34 22	167	53 11	226	60 29	251	38 29	304
296	44 46	345	40 48	060	53 01	116	34 31	165	52 43	225	59 52	250	37 56	302
298	44 35	342	41 21	057	53 37	114	34 42	164	52 16	223	59 16	248	37 23	300

LHA ♈	◆ FOMALHAUT		ACHERNAR		◆ CANOPUS		ACRUX		RIGIL KENT		◆ ANTARES		Nunki	
	Hc	Zn	Hc	Zn	Hc	Zn	Hc	Zn	Hc	Zn	Hc	Zn	Hc	Zn
300	41 54	055	54 12	113	34 53	163	51 49	222	58 39	247	36 48	298	44 22	340
302	42 26	053	54 49	111	35 05	161	51 23	221	58 04	246	36 13	296	44 08	337
304	42 56	051	55 25	110	35 18	160	50 58	220	57 28	244	35 38	293	43 52	335
306	43 26	048	56 02	108	35 32	158	50 34	218	56 53	243	35 02	291	43 35	332
308	43 55	046	56 40	106	35 47	157	50 10	217	56 19	241	34 25	289	43 16	330
310	44 22	044	57 17	105	36 03	155	49 47	216	55 45	240	33 48	287	42 56	328
312	44 49	041	57 55	103	36 20	154	49 24	215	55 11	238	33 11	285	42 34	325
314	45 14	039	58 33	101	36 38	152	49 02	213	54 38	237	32 33	283	42 11	323
316	45 38	037	59 12	100	36 56	151	48 41	212	54 06	236	31 55	281	41 47	320
318	46 00	034	59 50	098	37 16	149	48 21	211	53 34	234	31 16	279	41 21	318
320	46 22	032	60 29	096	37 36	148	48 01	209	53 02	233	30 37	277	40 55	316
322	46 41	029	61 08	094	37 57	146	47 42	208	52 32	231	29 59	275	40 27	314
324	47 00	027	61 47	093	38 19	145	47 24	207	52 01	230	29 20	274	39 58	311
326	47 17	024	62 26	091	38 42	144	47 07	206	51 32	229	28 41	272	39 28	309
328	47 32	022	63 05	089	39 05	142	46 50	204	51 03	227	28 02	270	38 58	307

LHA ♈	◆ FOMALHAUT		Diphda		◆ CANOPUS		ACRUX		RIGIL KENT		◆ ANTARES		Nunki	
	Hc	Zn	Hc	Zn	Hc	Zn	Hc	Zn	Hc	Zn	Hc	Zn	Hc	Zn
330	47 45	019	31 37	047	39 30	141	46 35	203	50 34	226	27 23	268	38 26	305
332	47 57	016	32 05	045	39 55	139	46 20	202	50 06	225	26 44	266	37 53	302
334	48 07	014	32 32	043	40 21	138	46 05	201	49 39	223	26 05	264	37 20	300
336	48 16	011	32 58	041	40 48	136	45 52	199	49 13	222	25 26	262	36 46	298
338	48 23	009	33 23	038	41 15	135	45 40	198	48 47	221	24 47	260	36 11	296
340	48 28	006	33 47	036	41 43	133	45 28	197	48 22	219	24 09	259	35 36	294
342	48 31	003	34 09	034	42 12	132	45 17	196	47 57	218	23 31	257	35 00	292
344	48 32	001	34 30	032	42 41	130	45 07	194	47 33	217	22 53	255	34 23	290
346	48 32	358	34 50	029	43 12	129	44 57	193	47 10	215	22 15	253	33 46	288
348	48 30	356	35 09	027	43 42	127	44 49	192	46 48	214	21 38	251	33 09	286
350	48 26	353	35 26	025	44 14	126	44 41	191	46 27	213	21 01	249	32 31	284
352	48 20	350	35 42	023	44 46	124	44 35	189	46 06	212	20 25	248	31 53	282
354	48 13	348	35 56	020	45 19	123	44 29	188	45 46	210	19 49	246	31 15	280
356	48 04	345	36 09	018	45 52	121	44 24	187	45 26	209	19 13	244	30 36	278
358	47 53	343	36 20	016	46 26	120	44 19	186	45 08	208	18 39	242	29 57	276

LAT 72°S

LHA ♈	Hc	Zn	Hc	Zn	Hc	Zn	Hc	Zn	Hc	Zn	Hc	Zn	Hc	Zn
	Diphda		◆ RIGEL		CANOPUS		Miaplacidus		◆ RIGIL KENT		Peacock		◆ FOMALHAUT	
0	35 31	013	11 14	082	47 27	117	54 21	157	45 44	207	63 40	277	46 44	340
2	35 39	011	11 50	080	48 01	115	54 36	156	45 28	205	63 03	275	46 31	338
4	35 45	008	12 27	078	48 34	114	54 52	155	45 12	204	62 26	273	46 16	335
6	35 49	006	13 03	076	49 09	112	55 08	153	44 58	203	61 49	271	46 00	333
8	35 52	004	13 39	074	49 43	111	55 25	152	44 44	201	61 12	269	45 42	330
10	35 54	001	14 14	072	50 18	109	55 43	151	44 31	200	60 35	267	45 23	328
12	35 54	359	14 49	070	50 53	107	56 01	150	44 18	199	59 58	265	45 03	326
14	35 53	357	15 24	068	51 29	105	56 19	149	44 07	197	59 21	264	44 41	323
16	35 50	354	15 58	066	52 05	104	56 39	148	43 56	196	58 44	262	44 18	321
18	35 45	352	16 32	064	52 41	102	56 59	147	43 46	195	58 08	260	43 54	318
20	35 39	350	17 05	062	53 17	100	57 19	146	43 37	193	57 31	258	43 29	316
22	35 32	347	17 38	060	53 54	099	57 41	145	43 29	192	56 55	257	43 03	314
24	35 23	345	18 10	058	54 31	097	58 02	143	43 22	191	56 19	255	42 35	311
26	35 12	343	18 41	056	55 08	095	58 25	142	43 15	189	55 43	253	42 07	309
28	35 01	340	19 11	054	55 45	093	58 48	141	43 10	188	55 08	252	41 38	307
	RIGEL		◆ SIRIUS		Suhail		◆ RIGIL KENT		Peacock		◆ FOMALHAUT		Diphda	
30	19 41	052	21 36	078	36 03	121	43 05	187	54 33	250	41 08	305	34 47	338
32	20 10	050	22 12	076	36 35	119	43 01	185	53 58	249	40 37	303	34 33	336
34	20 38	048	22 47	074	37 08	118	42 58	184	53 24	247	40 05	300	34 17	333
36	21 05	046	23 23	072	37 41	116	42 56	183	52 50	245	39 33	298	33 59	331
38	21 31	044	23 58	070	38 15	114	42 54	181	52 16	244	39 00	296	33 41	329
40	21 57	042	24 32	068	38 49	113	42 54	180	51 43	242	38 26	294	33 21	327
42	22 21	040	25 06	066	39 23	111	42 54	179	51 11	241	37 52	292	33 00	324
44	22 44	038	25 40	064	39 58	109	42 55	177	50 39	239	37 17	290	32 38	322
46	23 06	036	26 13	062	40 33	107	42 57	176	50 07	238	36 42	288	32 15	320
48	23 28	034	26 45	059	41 09	106	43 00	175	49 36	236	36 07	286	31 50	318
50	23 47	031	27 17	057	41 45	104	43 04	173	49 05	235	35 31	284	31 25	316
52	24 06	029	27 48	055	42 21	102	43 09	172	48 35	233	34 55	282	30 58	313
54	24 24	027	28 18	053	42 57	100	43 14	171	48 06	232	34 18	280	30 31	311
56	24 40	025	28 47	051	43 34	098	43 21	169	47 37	230	33 42	278	30 02	309
58	24 55	023	29 15	049	44 10	097	43 28	168	47 09	229	33 05	276	29 33	307
	RIGEL		◆ SIRIUS		Suhail		◆ RIGIL KENT		Peacock		◆ FOMALHAUT		Diphda	
60	25 09	021	29 43	047	44 47	095	43 36	167	46 41	227	32 28	274	29 03	305
62	25 21	018	30 10	045	45 24	093	43 45	165	46 14	226	31 51	272	28 32	303
64	25 32	016	30 35	043	46 01	091	43 54	164	45 48	224	31 14	270	28 01	301
66	25 42	014	31 00	040	46 38	089	44 05	163	45 23	223	30 37	268	27 29	299
68	25 50	012	31 23	038	47 16	087	44 16	162	44 58	222	30 00	266	26 56	297
70	25 57	010	31 46	036	47 53	085	44 28	160	44 33	220	29 23	264	26 22	295
72	26 03	008	32 07	034	48 29	083	44 41	159	44 10	219	28 46	262	25 48	293
74	26 07	005	32 27	032	49 06	081	44 55	158	43 47	217	28 09	261	25 14	291
76	26 10	003	32 46	029	49 43	079	45 10	156	43 25	216	27 33	259	24 39	289
78	26 11	001	33 03	027	50 19	077	45 25	155	43 04	214	26 56	257	24 04	287
80	26 11	359	33 19	025	50 55	075	45 41	154	42 43	213	26 21	255	23 28	285
82	26 09	356	33 34	023	51 31	073	45 58	152	42 23	212	25 45	253	22 52	283
84	26 06	354	33 48	020	52 06	071	46 16	151	42 04	210	25 09	251	22 15	281
86	26 02	352	34 00	018	52 41	069	46 34	149	41 46	209	24 35	250	21 39	279
88	25 56	350	34 10	016	53 15	066	46 54	148	41 29	207	24 00	248	21 02	277
	◆ SIRIUS		Suhail		◆ RIGIL KENT		Peacock		FOMALHAUT		◆ ACHERNAR		RIGEL	
90	34 20	013	53 49	064	47 14	147	41 12	206	23 26	246	60 19	265	25 49	348
92	34 27	011	54 22	062	47 34	145	40 56	204	22 52	244	59 42	263	25 40	345
94	34 34	009	54 54	060	47 56	144	40 41	203	22 19	243	59 05	261	25 30	343
96	34 39	006	55 26	057	48 18	143	40 27	202	21 46	241	58 29	259	25 19	341
98	34 42	004	55 56	055	48 40	141	40 14	200	21 14	239	57 52	258	25 06	339
100	34 44	002	56 26	052	49 04	140	40 02	199	20 43	237	57 16	256	24 52	337
102	34 44	359	56 55	050	49 28	139	39 50	197	20 12	235	56 40	254	24 37	335
104	34 43	357	57 23	047	49 53	137	39 39	196	19 42	234	56 05	253	24 21	332
106	34 40	355	57 50	045	50 18	136	39 30	195	19 12	232	55 29	251	24 03	330
108	34 36	352	58 15	042	50 44	135	39 21	193	18 43	230	54 55	250	23 44	328
110	34 31	350	58 40	040	51 11	133	39 13	192	18 15	228	54 20	248	23 24	326
112	34 23	348	59 02	037	51 38	132	39 06	190	17 48	227	53 46	246	23 02	324
114	34 15	345	59 24	034	52 06	130	38 59	189	17 22	225	53 12	245	22 40	322
116	34 05	343	59 44	031	52 35	129	38 54	188	16 56	223	52 39	243	22 17	320
118	33 53	341	60 02	028	53 04	128	38 50	186	16 31	221	52 06	242	21 52	318
	Suhail		◆ SPICA		RIGIL KENT		Peacock		◆ FOMALHAUT		ACHERNAR		◆ SIRIUS	
120	60 19	026	13 18	085	53 34	126	38 46	185	16 07	219	51 33	240	33 40	339
122	60 34	023	13 55	084	54 04	125	38 44	183	15 44	218	51 01	239	33 26	336
124	60 48	020	14 32	082	54 34	123	38 42	182	15 22	216	50 30	237	33 11	334
126	60 59	017	15 09	080	55 06	122	38 41	180	15 00	214	49 59	236	32 54	332
128	61 09	014	15 45	078	55 37	121	38 41	179	14 40	212	49 29	234	32 35	329
130	61 17	011	16 21	076	56 09	119	38 42	178	14 20	211	48 59	233	32 16	327
132	61 23	008	16 57	074	56 42	118	38 44	176	14 02	209	48 30	231	31 55	325
134	61 27	005	17 32	072	57 15	116	38 47	175	13 45	207	48 01	230	31 33	323
136	61 29	002	18 07	070	57 48	115	38 51	173	13 28	205	47 33	228	31 10	321
138	61 29	359	18 42	068	58 22	113	38 56	172	13 13	204	47 05	227	30 46	318
140	61 28	356	19 16	066	58 57	112	39 01	171	12 59	202	46 39	226	30 21	316
142	61 24	353	19 50	064	59 31	110	39 08	169	12 45	200	46 13	224	29 55	314
144	61 18	350	20 23	062	60 06	109	39 15	168	12 33	198	45 47	223	29 28	312
146	61 10	347	20 55	060	60 42	107	39 23	166	12 22	197	45 22	221	29 00	310
148	61 01	344	21 27	058	61 17	105	39 32	165	12 12	195	44 58	220	28 31	308
	◆ SPICA		ANTARES		◆ Peacock		FOMALHAUT		ACHERNAR		◆ CANOPUS		Suhail	
150	21 58	056	22 47	106	39 43	164	12 03	193	44 35	218	60 06	281	60 50	341
152	22 28	054	23 23	104	39 53	162	11 55	191	44 12	217	59 29	279	60 36	338
154	22 58	052	23 59	102	40 05	161	11 49	189	43 50	215	58 52	277	60 21	335
156	23 27	050	24 36	100	40 18	159	11 43	188	43 29	214	58 15	275	60 05	332
158	23 54	048	25 12	098	40 31	158	11 39	186	43 09	213	57 38	273	59 47	329
160	24 21	046	25 49	096	40 46	157	11 36	184	42 49	211	57 01	271	59 27	326
162	24 47	043	26 26	095	41 01	155	11 34	182	42 30	210	56 24	269	59 05	324
164	25 12	041	27 03	093	41 17	154	11 33	181	42 12	208	55 47	267	58 43	321
166	25 36	039	27 40	091	41 34	152	11 33	179	41 55	207	55 10	265	58 19	318
168	25 59	037	28 17	089	41 51	151	11 34	177	41 39	206	54 33	263	57 53	316
170	26 21	035	28 54	087	42 10	149	11 37	175	41 23	204	53 57	262	57 27	313
172	26 41	033	29 31	085	42 29	148	11 40	173	41 08	203	53 20	260	56 59	310
174	27 01	031	30 08	083	42 49	147	11 45	172	40 54	201	52 44	258	56 30	308
176	27 19	028	30 45	081	43 10	145	11 51	170	40 41	200	52 07	256	56 01	305
178	27 36	026	31 21	079	43 31	144	11 58	168	40 29	199	51 31	255	55 30	303

LHA ♈	Hc	Zn	Hc	Zn	Hc	Zn	Hc	Zn	Hc	Zn	Hc	Zn	Hc	Zn
	SPICA		◆ ANTARES		Nunki		FOMALHAUT		◆ ACHERNAR		CANOPUS		◆ Suhail	
180	27 52	024	31 58	077	20 43	112	12 06	166	40 17	197	50 56	253	54 59	301
182	28 06	022	32 34	075	21 18	110	12 16	165	40 07	196	50 21	251	54 26	298
184	28 19	020	33 09	073	21 53	108	12 26	163	39 57	194	49 46	250	53 53	296
186	28 31	017	33 45	071	22 28	106	12 38	161	39 49	193	49 11	248	53 20	294
188	28 41	015	34 19	069	23 04	104	12 50	159	39 41	192	48 37	246	52 45	292
190	28 50	013	34 54	067	23 40	102	13 04	157	39 34	190	48 03	245	52 11	289
192	28 58	011	35 28	065	24 17	101	13 19	156	39 27	189	47 30	243	51 36	287
194	29 04	008	36 01	063	24 53	099	13 34	154	39 22	187	46 57	242	51 00	285
196	29 09	006	36 34	061	25 30	097	13 51	152	39 18	186	46 25	240	50 24	283
198	29 12	004	37 06	059	26 07	095	14 09	150	39 15	185	45 53	238	49 48	281
200	29 14	002	37 37	057	26 44	093	14 28	149	39 12	183	45 21	237	49 11	279
202	29 14	359	38 08	054	27 21	091	14 48	147	39 10	182	44 51	235	48 34	277
204	29 13	357	38 37	052	27 58	089	15 08	145	39 10	180	44 21	234	47 58	275
206	29 11	355	39 06	050	28 35	087	15 30	143	39 10	179	43 51	232	47 21	273
208	29 07	353	39 34	048	29 12	085	15 53	142	39 11	178	43 22	231	46 44	271
	◆ ANTARES		Nunki		◆ FOMALHAUT		ACHERNAR		CANOPUS		◆ Suhail		SPICA	
210	40 01	045	29 49	084	16 16	140	39 13	176	42 54	229	46 06	269	29 01	350
212	40 27	043	30 26	082	16 40	138	39 16	175	42 26	228	45 29	267	28 54	348
214	40 52	041	31 02	080	17 06	136	39 20	173	41 59	226	44 52	265	28 46	346
216	41 16	039	31 39	078	17 32	135	39 24	172	41 33	225	44 15	264	28 36	344
218	41 38	036	32 15	076	17 58	133	39 30	171	41 07	223	43 39	262	28 25	342
220	41 59	034	32 50	074	18 26	131	39 37	169	40 42	222	43 02	260	28 13	339
222	42 20	032	33 26	072	18 54	129	39 44	168	40 18	220	42 26	258	27 59	337
224	42 38	029	34 01	070	19 23	127	39 52	166	39 54	219	41 49	256	27 44	335
226	42 56	027	34 35	068	19 53	126	40 01	165	39 31	217	41 14	255	27 28	333
228	43 12	024	35 09	065	20 24	124	40 11	164	39 10	216	40 38	253	27 10	331
230	43 26	022	35 43	063	20 55	122	40 22	162	38 48	214	40 03	251	26 51	328
232	43 39	019	36 16	061	21 26	120	40 34	161	38 28	213	39 28	249	26 31	326
234	43 51	017	36 48	059	21 59	119	40 47	159	38 08	211	38 53	248	26 10	324
236	44 01	014	37 19	057	22 32	117	41 00	158	37 50	210	38 19	246	25 48	322
238	44 09	012	37 50	055	23 05	115	41 14	157	37 32	208	37 46	244	25 24	320
	ANTARES		◆ Nunki		FOMALHAUT		◆ ACHERNAR		CANOPUS		◆ ACRUX		SPICA	
240	44 16	009	38 20	053	23 39	113	41 30	155	37 15	207	68 49	267	25 00	318
242	44 22	007	38 49	050	24 13	111	41 46	154	36 59	205	68 12	265	24 34	316
244	44 25	004	39 17	048	24 48	110	42 02	152	36 43	204	67 35	264	24 08	313
246	44 27	002	39 44	046	25 23	108	42 20	151	36 29	202	66 58	262	23 40	311
248	44 28	359	40 10	044	25 58	106	42 38	150	36 15	201	66 21	260	23 12	309
250	44 27	357	40 35	041	26 34	104	42 58	148	36 03	199	65 45	258	22 43	307
252	44 24	354	40 59	039	27 10	102	43 18	147	35 51	198	65 09	257	22 13	305
254	44 20	352	41 22	037	27 47	101	43 38	145	35 40	196	64 33	255	21 42	303
256	44 14	349	41 44	034	28 23	099	44 00	144	35 30	195	63 57	254	21 11	301
258	44 06	347	42 04	032	29 00	097	44 22	142	35 21	193	63 22	252	20 39	299
260	43 57	344	42 23	030	29 37	095	44 45	141	35 13	192	62 46	251	20 06	297
262	43 46	342	42 41	027	30 14	093	45 09	140	35 06	190	62 12	249	19 33	295
264	43 34	340	42 57	025	30 51	091	45 33	138	35 00	189	61 37	248	18 59	293
266	43 20	337	43 12	022	31 28	089	45 58	137	34 54	187	61 03	246	18 25	291
268	43 05	335	43 25	020	32 05	087	46 24	135	34 50	186	60 29	245	17 50	289
	◆ Nunki		FOMALHAUT		◆ ACHERNAR		CANOPUS		◆ ACRUX		RIGIL KENT		ANTARES	
270	43 37	017	32 42	085	46 50	134	34 47	184	59 56	243	68 07	274	42 49	332
272	43 47	015	33 19	083	47 17	132	34 44	183	59 23	242	67 30	272	42 31	330
274	43 56	013	33 56	082	47 45	131	34 43	182	58 50	241	66 53	270	42 11	327
276	44 04	010	34 32	080	48 13	130	34 42	180	58 18	239	66 15	269	41 51	325
278	44 09	008	35 09	078	48 42	128	34 43	179	57 47	238	65 38	267	41 29	323
280	44 13	005	35 45	076	49 12	127	34 44	177	57 16	236	65 01	265	41 06	320
282	44 16	003	36 20	074	49 42	125	34 46	176	56 45	235	64 25	263	40 42	318
284	44 17	000	36 56	072	50 12	124	34 50	174	56 15	234	63 48	261	40 16	316
286	44 16	358	37 31	069	50 43	122	34 54	173	55 45	232	63 11	260	39 50	314
288	44 13	355	38 05	067	51 15	121	34 59	171	55 16	231	62 35	258	39 23	311
290	44 09	353	38 39	065	51 47	119	35 05	170	54 48	230	61 59	256	38 54	309
292	44 04	350	39 13	063	52 20	118	35 12	168	54 20	228	61 23	255	38 25	307
294	43 57	348	39 45	061	52 53	116	35 20	167	53 52	227	60 47	253	37 55	305
296	43 48	345	40 17	059	53 27	114	35 29	165	53 25	226	60 12	252	37 24	303
298	43 38	343	40 49	057	54 01	113	35 39	164	52 59	224	59 37	250	36 53	300
	◆ FOMALHAUT		ACHERNAR		◆ CANOPUS		ACRUX		RIGIL KENT		◆ ANTARES		Nunki	
300	41 19	054	54 35	111	35 50	162	52 34	223	59 02	249	36 20	298	43 26	340
302	41 49	052	55 10	110	36 02	161	52 09	222	58 28	247	35 47	296	43 12	338
304	42 18	050	55 45	108	36 14	159	51 44	220	57 54	246	35 14	294	42 58	335
306	42 46	048	56 20	106	36 28	158	51 20	219	57 20	244	34 40	292	42 41	333
308	43 13	045	56 56	105	36 42	156	50 57	218	56 47	243	34 05	290	42 24	330
310	43 39	043	57 32	103	36 57	155	50 35	217	56 15	241	33 30	288	42 05	328
312	44 03	041	58 08	101	37 14	153	50 13	215	55 42	240	32 54	286	41 45	326
314	44 27	038	58 44	100	37 31	152	49 52	214	55 11	238	32 19	284	41 23	323
316	44 49	036	59 21	098	37 48	151	49 32	213	54 39	237	31 42	282	41 00	321
318	45 11	034	59 58	096	38 07	149	49 12	211	54 08	235	31 06	280	40 37	319
320	45 30	031	60 35	094	38 27	148	48 53	210	53 38	234	30 29	278	40 11	316
322	45 49	029	61 12	093	38 47	146	48 35	209	53 09	233	29 53	276	39 45	314
324	46 06	026	61 49	091	39 08	145	48 18	207	52 39	231	29 16	274	39 18	312
326	46 22	024	62 26	089	39 30	143	48 01	206	52 11	230	28 39	272	38 50	310
328	46 36	021	63 03	087	39 53	142	47 45	205	51 43	228	28 02	270	38 21	307
	◆ FOMALHAUT		Diphda		◆ CANOPUS		ACRUX		RIGIL KENT		◆ ANTARES		Nunki	
330	46 49	019	30 56	047	40 16	140	47 30	204	51 15	227	27 24	268	37 51	305
332	47 00	016	31 22	045	40 40	139	47 15	202	50 49	226	26 47	266	37 21	303
334	47 09	014	31 48	042	41 05	137	47 01	201	50 22	224	26 10	265	36 49	301
336	47 17	011	32 13	040	41 31	136	46 49	200	49 57	223	25 34	263	36 17	299
338	47 23	009	32 36	038	41 57	134	46 36	198	49 32	222	24 57	261	35 44	297
340	47 28	006	32 58	036	42 24	133	46 25	197	49 08	220	24 20	259	35 11	295
342	47 31	003	33 19	034	42 52	131	46 15	196	48 44	219	23 44	257	34 37	293
344	47 32	001	33 39	031	43 20	129	46 05	195	48 21	217	23 08	255	34 02	291
346	47 32	358	33 58	029	43 49	128	45 56	193	47 59	216	22 32	253	33 28	288
348	47 30	356	34 15	027	44 18	126	45 48	192	47 38	215	21 57	252	32 52	286
350	47 27	353	34 31	025	44 49	125	45 40	191	47 17	213	21 22	250	32 16	284
352	47 21	351	34 46	022	45 19	123	45 34	190	46 57	212	20 47	248	31 40	282
354	47 14	348	35 00	020	45 51	122	45 28	188	46 37	211	20 13	246	31 04	280
356	47 06	345	35 11	018	46 22	120	45 23	187	46 19	209	19 40	244	30 27	278
358	46 56	343	35 22	015	46 55	119	45 19	186	46 01	208	19 06	243	29 51	277

LAT 73°S

LHA ♈	Hc Zn	Hc Zn	Hc Zn	Hc Zn	Hc Zn	Hc Zn	Hc Zn
	Diphda	◆RIGEL	CANOPUS	Miaplacidus	◆RIGIL KENT	Peacock	◆FOMALHAUT
0	34 33 013	11 05 082	47 54 116	55 16 156	46 37 207	63 32 279	45 47 341
2	34 40 011	11 40 080	48 26 114	55 31 155	46 22 206	62 57 277	45 35 338
4	34 45 008	12 14 078	48 58 113	55 46 154	46 07 204	62 22 275	45 21 336
6	34 50 006	12 48 076	49 31 111	56 02 153	45 53 203	61 47 273	45 06 333
8	34 53 004	13 22 074	50 04 109	56 18 152	45 39 202	61 12 271	44 50 331
10	34 54 001	13 56 072	50 37 108	56 35 151	45 27 200	60 37 269	44 32 328
12	34 54 359	14 29 070	51 10 106	56 53 149	45 15 199	60 02 267	44 13 326
14	34 53 357	15 02 068	51 44 104	57 11 148	45 04 198	59 27 265	43 53 324
16	34 50 354	15 34 066	52 18 103	57 29 147	44 54 196	58 52 263	43 32 321
18	34 46 352	16 06 064	52 53 101	57 49 146	44 44 195	58 17 262	43 09 319
20	34 40 350	16 37 062	53 27 099	58 09 145	44 36 194	57 42 260	42 46 317
22	34 33 347	17 08 060	54 02 097	58 29 144	44 28 192	57 08 258	42 21 314
24	34 25 345	17 38 058	54 37 095	58 50 143	44 21 191	56 34 256	41 55 312
26	34 15 343	18 07 056	55 12 094	59 12 141	44 14 190	56 00 255	41 29 310
28	34 04 340	18 36 054	55 47 092	59 34 140	44 09 188	55 26 253	41 02 308
	RIGEL	◆SIRIUS	Suhail	◆RIGIL KENT	Peacock	◆FOMALHAUT	Diphda
30	19 04 052	21 22 077	36 34 120	44 04 187	54 53 251	40 33 305	33 52 338
32	19 31 050	21 57 075	37 04 119	44 01 186	54 19 250	40 04 303	33 38 336
34	19 58 048	22 30 073	37 35 117	43 58 184	53 47 248	39 35 301	33 23 334
36	20 24 046	23 04 071	38 07 115	43 56 183	53 14 247	39 04 299	33 07 331
38	20 48 044	23 37 069	38 39 113	43 54 181	52 42 245	38 33 297	32 50 329
40	21 12 042	24 09 067	39 11 112	43 54 180	52 11 243	38 02 295	32 31 327
42	21 35 040	24 41 065	39 44 110	43 54 179	51 40 242	37 29 293	32 11 325
44	21 57 038	25 13 063	40 17 108	43 55 177	51 09 240	36 57 290	31 50 323
46	22 18 035	25 44 061	40 51 107	43 57 176	50 39 239	36 24 288	31 29 320
48	22 37 033	26 14 059	41 24 105	44 00 175	50 09 237	35 50 286	31 06 318
50	22 56 031	26 44 057	41 58 103	44 04 173	49 40 236	35 16 284	30 42 316
52	23 14 029	27 13 055	42 33 101	44 08 172	49 11 234	34 42 282	30 17 314
54	23 30 027	27 42 053	43 07 099	44 14 171	48 43 233	34 08 280	29 51 312
56	23 46 025	28 09 051	43 42 097	44 20 169	48 15 231	33 33 278	29 24 310
58	24 00 023	28 36 049	44 17 096	44 27 168	47 48 230	32 58 276	28 57 307
	RIGEL	◆SIRIUS	Suhail	◆RIGIL KENT	Peacock	◆FOMALHAUT	Diphda
60	24 13 020	29 02 046	44 52 094	44 34 167	47 22 228	32 24 274	28 29 305
62	24 24 018	29 27 044	45 27 092	44 43 165	46 56 227	31 49 273	28 00 303
64	24 35 016	29 51 042	46 02 090	44 52 164	46 31 225	31 13 271	27 30 301
66	24 44 014	30 14 040	46 37 088	45 02 163	46 06 224	30 38 269	27 00 299
68	24 52 012	30 36 038	47 12 086	45 13 161	45 42 222	30 03 267	26 29 297
70	24 58 010	30 57 036	47 47 084	45 25 160	45 19 221	29 28 265	25 57 295
72	25 03 007	31 17 033	48 22 082	45 37 158	44 56 219	28 53 263	25 25 293
74	25 07 005	31 36 031	48 56 080	45 51 157	44 35 218	28 19 261	24 53 291
76	25 10 003	31 53 029	49 31 078	46 05 156	44 13 216	27 44 259	24 20 289
78	25 11 001	32 10 027	50 05 076	46 19 154	43 53 215	27 10 257	23 46 287
80	25 11 359	32 25 025	50 39 074	46 35 153	43 33 213	26 36 256	23 13 285
82	25 09 357	32 39 022	51 13 072	46 51 152	43 14 212	26 02 254	22 39 283
84	25 07 354	32 51 020	51 46 070	47 08 150	42 56 211	25 28 252	22 04 281
86	25 02 352	33 03 018	52 18 067	47 26 149	42 39 209	24 55 250	21 30 279
88	24 57 350	33 13 015	52 50 065	47 44 148	42 22 208	24 22 248	20 55 277
	◆SIRIUS	Suhail	◆RIGIL KENT	Peacock	FOMALHAUT	◆ACHERNAR	RIGEL
90	33 21 013	53 22 063	48 04 146	42 06 206	23 50 246	60 23 267	24 50 348
92	33 29 011	53 53 061	48 23 145	41 51 205	23 18 245	59 48 265	24 42 346
94	33 34 009	54 23 058	48 44 143	41 37 203	22 47 243	59 14 263	24 33 343
96	33 39 006	54 53 056	49 05 142	41 23 202	22 16 241	58 39 261	24 22 341
98	33 42 004	55 21 054	49 27 141	41 10 201	21 45 239	58 04 259	24 10 339
100	33 44 002	55 49 051	49 50 139	40 58 199	21 15 237	57 30 258	23 57 337
102	33 44 359	56 16 049	50 13 138	40 47 198	20 46 236	56 56 256	23 43 335
104	33 43 357	56 42 046	50 37 137	40 37 196	20 17 234	56 22 254	23 27 333
106	33 41 355	57 07 044	51 01 135	40 28 195	19 49 232	55 48 253	23 11 331
108	33 37 352	57 30 041	51 26 134	40 19 193	19 22 230	55 15 251	22 53 328
110	33 31 350	57 53 038	51 52 132	40 12 192	18 55 229	54 42 249	22 34 326
112	33 25 348	58 14 036	52 18 131	40 05 190	18 29 227	54 09 248	22 14 324
114	33 17 346	58 34 033	52 45 129	39 59 189	18 04 225	53 37 246	21 53 322
116	33 07 343	58 52 030	53 12 128	39 54 188	17 40 223	53 05 244	21 31 320
118	32 57 341	59 09 028	53 40 127	39 49 186	17 16 221	52 34 243	21 08 318
	Suhail	◆SPICA	RIGIL KENT	Peacock	◆FOMALHAUT	ACHERNAR	◆SIRIUS
120	59 25 025	13 14 085	54 09 125	39 46 185	16 53 220	52 03 241	32 44 339
122	59 39 022	13 48 083	54 37 124	39 44 183	16 31 218	51 32 240	32 31 337
124	59 51 019	14 23 081	55 07 122	39 42 182	16 10 216	51 02 238	32 17 334
126	60 02 016	14 58 079	55 37 121	39 41 181	15 50 214	50 32 237	32 01 332
128	60 11 013	15 32 077	56 07 119	39 41 179	15 30 213	50 03 235	31 44 330
130	60 18 010	16 06 075	56 38 118	39 42 178	15 12 211	49 35 234	31 25 328
132	60 24 008	16 40 074	57 09 116	39 44 176	14 55 209	49 07 232	31 06 325
134	60 27 005	17 14 072	57 41 115	39 47 175	14 38 207	48 39 231	30 46 323
136	60 29 002	17 47 070	58 13 113	39 51 173	14 22 205	48 12 229	30 24 321
138	60 29 359	18 19 068	58 45 112	39 55 172	14 08 204	47 46 228	30 01 319
140	60 28 356	18 52 066	59 18 110	40 00 171	13 54 202	47 20 226	29 38 317
142	60 24 353	19 23 064	59 51 109	40 07 169	13 42 200	46 55 225	29 13 314
144	60 19 350	19 54 062	60 25 107	40 14 168	13 30 198	46 31 223	28 48 312
146	60 12 347	20 25 060	60 58 105	40 22 166	13 20 197	46 07 222	28 21 310
148	60 03 344	20 55 058	61 32 104	40 30 165	13 10 195	45 44 220	27 54 308
	◆SPICA	ANTARES	◆Peacock	FOMALHAUT	ACHERNAR	◆CANOPUS	Suhail
150	21 24 056	23 03 105	40 40 163	13 02 193	45 22 219	59 53 283	59 53 341
152	21 53 053	23 37 103	40 50 162	12 54 191	45 00 218	59 19 280	59 41 338
154	22 21 051	24 12 102	41 02 160	12 48 189	44 39 216	58 44 278	59 27 336
156	22 48 049	24 46 100	41 14 159	12 43 188	44 19 215	58 10 276	59 12 333
158	23 14 047	25 21 098	41 27 158	12 39 186	43 59 213	57 35 274	58 55 330
160	23 39 045	25 56 096	41 41 156	12 35 184	43 40 212	57 00 272	58 37 327
162	24 04 043	26 30 094	41 55 155	12 33 182	43 22 210	56 25 270	58 17 325
164	24 27 041	27 06 092	42 11 153	12 33 181	43 05 209	55 50 268	57 56 322
166	24 50 039	27 41 090	42 27 152	12 33 179	42 48 207	55 14 267	57 34 319
168	25 11 037	28 16 088	42 44 150	12 34 177	42 33 206	54 39 265	57 10 317
170	25 32 035	28 51 086	43 01 149	12 36 175	42 18 205	54 05 263	56 45 314
172	25 51 032	29 26 085	43 20 148	12 40 173	42 03 203	53 30 261	56 20 312
174	26 09 030	30 01 083	43 39 146	12 45 172	41 50 202	52 55 259	55 53 309
176	26 26 028	30 35 081	43 59 145	12 50 170	41 37 200	52 21 258	55 25 307
178	26 42 026	31 10 079	44 20 143	12 57 168	41 26 199	51 47 256	54 57 304

LHA ♈	Hc Zn	Hc Zn	Hc Zn	Hc Zn	Hc Zn	Hc Zn	Hc Zn
	SPICA	◆ANTARES	Nunki	FOMALHAUT	◆ACHERNAR	CANOPUS	◆Suhail
180	26 57 024	31 44 077	21 05 111	13 05 166	41 15 197	51 13 254	54 27 302
182	27 11 022	32 18 075	21 38 109	13 14 165	41 05 196	50 39 252	53 57 300
184	27 23 019	32 52 073	22 11 108	13 23 163	40 55 195	50 06 251	53 26 297
186	27 34 017	33 25 071	22 45 106	13 34 161	40 47 193	49 33 249	52 55 295
188	27 44 015	33 58 069	23 19 104	13 46 159	40 39 192	49 00 247	52 23 293
190	27 52 013	34 30 066	23 53 102	13 59 157	40 33 190	48 28 246	51 50 291
192	27 59 011	35 02 064	24 27 100	14 13 156	40 27 189	47 56 244	51 17 288
194	28 05 008	35 34 062	25 02 098	14 28 154	40 22 187	47 25 242	50 44 286
196	28 09 006	36 04 060	25 37 096	14 44 152	40 18 186	46 54 241	50 10 284
198	28 12 004	36 34 058	26 12 094	15 01 150	40 14 185	46 24 239	49 36 282
200	28 14 002	37 04 056	26 47 093	15 19 149	40 12 183	45 54 238	49 01 280
202	28 14 359	37 33 054	27 22 091	15 38 147	40 10 182	45 25 236	48 27 278
204	28 13 357	38 00 052	27 57 089	15 57 145	40 10 180	44 56 235	47 52 276
206	28 11 355	38 27 049	28 32 087	16 18 143	40 10 179	44 27 233	47 17 274
208	28 07 353	38 54 047	29 07 085	16 39 141	40 11 178	44 00 231	46 42 272
	◆ANTARES	Nunki	◆FOMALHAUT	ACHERNAR	CANOPUS	◆Suhail	SPICA
210	39 19 045	29 42 083	17 02 140	40 13 176	43 33 230	46 07 270	28 02 351
212	39 43 043	30 17 081	17 25 138	40 16 175	43 06 228	45 32 268	27 56 348
214	40 06 040	30 51 079	17 49 136	40 19 173	42 40 227	44 57 266	27 48 346
216	40 29 038	31 25 077	18 14 134	40 24 172	42 15 225	44 22 265	27 39 344
218	40 50 036	31 59 075	18 39 133	40 29 170	41 50 224	43 47 263	27 28 342
220	41 10 033	32 33 073	19 05 131	40 35 169	41 27 222	43 12 261	27 17 339
222	41 28 031	33 07 071	19 32 129	40 43 168	41 03 221	42 37 259	27 04 337
224	41 46 029	33 40 069	20 00 127	40 50 166	40 41 219	42 03 257	26 50 335
226	42 02 026	34 12 067	20 28 125	40 59 165	40 19 218	41 29 256	26 34 333
228	42 17 024	34 44 065	20 57 124	41 09 163	39 58 216	40 55 254	26 18 331
230	42 30 022	35 16 063	21 27 122	41 19 162	39 38 215	40 22 252	26 00 329
232	42 43 019	35 46 061	21 57 120	41 31 161	39 18 213	39 48 250	25 41 326
234	42 53 017	36 17 059	22 27 118	41 43 159	39 00 211	39 16 248	25 21 324
236	43 03 014	36 46 056	22 58 116	41 56 158	38 42 210	38 43 247	25 00 322
238	43 11 012	37 15 054	23 30 115	42 09 156	38 25 208	38 11 245	24 38 320
	ANTARES	◆Nunki	FOMALHAUT	◆ACHERNAR	CANOPUS	◆ACRUX	SPICA
240	43 17 009	37 43 052	24 02 113	42 24 155	38 08 207	68 50 270	24 15 318
242	43 22 007	38 10 050	24 35 111	42 39 153	37 53 205	68 15 268	23 51 316
244	43 25 004	38 37 048	25 08 109	42 55 152	37 38 204	67 40 266	23 26 314
246	43 27 002	39 02 045	25 41 107	43 12 151	37 24 202	67 05 264	23 01 312
248	43 28 359	39 27 043	26 15 106	43 30 149	37 11 201	66 31 262	22 34 310
250	43 27 357	39 50 041	26 49 104	43 48 148	36 59 199	65 56 261	22 07 308
252	43 24 355	40 13 039	27 23 102	44 08 146	36 48 198	65 21 259	21 38 305
254	43 20 352	40 34 036	27 57 100	44 27 145	36 38 196	64 47 257	21 09 303
256	43 15 350	40 54 034	28 32 098	44 48 143	36 28 195	64 13 256	20 40 301
258	43 07 347	41 13 032	29 07 096	45 09 142	36 19 193	63 39 254	20 10 299
260	42 59 345	41 31 029	29 42 094	45 31 140	36 12 192	63 05 253	19 39 297
262	42 49 342	41 47 027	30 17 092	45 54 139	36 05 191	62 32 251	19 07 295
264	42 38 340	42 02 024	30 52 091	46 17 137	35 59 189	61 59 249	18 35 293
266	42 25 337	42 16 022	31 27 089	46 41 136	35 54 188	61 26 248	18 03 291
268	42 11 335	42 29 020	32 02 087	47 06 135	35 50 186	60 54 246	17 30 289
	◆Nunki	FOMALHAUT	◆ACHERNAR	CANOPUS	◆ACRUX	RIGIL KENT	ANTARES
270	42 40 017	32 37 085	47 31 133	35 46 185	60 22 245	68 01 277	41 55 333
272	42 49 015	33 12 083	47 57 132	35 44 183	59 50 243	67 26 275	41 39 330
274	42 58 012	33 46 081	48 24 130	35 43 182	59 19 242	66 51 273	41 21 328
276	43 04 010	34 21 079	48 51 129	35 42 180	58 48 241	66 16 271	41 01 326
278	43 10 007	34 55 077	49 19 127	35 43 179	58 18 239	65 41 269	40 41 323
280	43 14 005	35 29 075	49 47 126	35 44 177	57 48 238	65 06 267	40 19 321
282	43 16 003	36 03 073	50 16 124	35 46 176	57 19 236	64 31 265	39 57 319
284	43 17 000	36 36 071	50 45 123	35 49 174	56 50 235	63 56 263	39 33 316
286	43 16 358	37 09 069	51 15 121	35 54 173	56 21 234	63 21 262	39 08 314
288	43 14 355	37 42 067	51 45 120	35 58 171	55 53 232	62 46 260	38 43 312
290	43 10 353	38 14 065	52 16 118	36 04 170	55 26 231	62 12 258	38 16 310
292	43 05 350	38 45 062	52 47 116	36 11 168	54 59 229	61 38 257	37 49 308
294	42 58 348	39 16 060	53 19 115	36 19 167	54 33 228	61 04 255	37 21 305
296	42 50 345	39 46 058	53 51 113	36 27 165	54 07 227	60 30 253	36 52 303
298	42 40 343	40 15 056	54 23 112	36 37 164	53 42 225	59 56 252	36 22 301
	◆FOMALHAUT	ACHERNAR	◆CANOPUS	ACRUX	RIGIL KENT	◆ANTARES	Nunki
300	40 44 054	54 56 110	36 47 162	53 17 224	59 23 250	35 52 299	42 29 340
302	41 12 052	55 29 108	36 58 161	52 53 223	58 50 249	35 21 297	42 17 338
304	41 39 049	56 03 107	37 10 159	52 30 221	58 18 247	34 49 295	42 03 336
306	42 05 047	56 36 105	37 23 158	52 07 220	57 46 245	34 17 293	41 48 333
308	42 30 045	57 10 103	37 37 156	51 45 219	57 14 244	33 44 291	41 32 331
310	42 55 042	57 45 102	37 52 155	51 23 217	56 43 242	33 11 289	41 14 329
312	43 18 040	58 19 100	38 07 153	51 02 216	56 12 241	32 38 287	40 55 326
314	43 40 038	58 54 098	38 23 152	50 42 215	55 42 239	32 04 285	40 35 324
316	44 01 035	59 29 096	38 41 150	50 22 213	55 12 238	31 30 283	40 14 322
318	44 20 033	60 03 095	38 58 149	50 03 212	54 42 237	30 55 281	39 51 319
320	44 39 031	60 39 093	39 17 147	49 45 211	54 13 235	30 21 279	39 28 317
322	44 56 028	61 14 091	39 37 146	49 28 209	53 45 234	29 46 277	39 03 315
324	45 12 026	61 49 089	39 57 144	49 11 208	53 17 232	29 11 275	38 38 313
326	45 27 023	62 24 087	40 18 143	48 55 207	52 49 231	28 36 273	38 12 310
328	45 40 021	62 59 085	40 39 141	48 39 205	52 22 229	28 01 271	37 44 308
	◆FOMALHAUT	Diphda	◆CANOPUS	ACRUX	RIGIL KENT	◆ANTARES	Nunki
330	45 52 018	30 15 046	41 02 140	48 25 204	51 56 228	27 26 269	37 16 306
332	46 02 016	30 40 044	41 25 138	48 11 203	51 30 226	26 51 267	36 48 304
334	46 11 013	31 04 042	41 49 136	47 57 201	51 05 225	26 16 265	36 18 302
336	46 18 011	31 27 040	42 13 135	47 45 200	50 41 224	25 41 263	35 48 299
338	46 24 008	31 49 038	42 38 133	47 33 199	50 17 222	25 06 261	35 17 297
340	46 28 006	32 09 035	43 04 132	47 22 198	49 53 221	24 32 259	34 46 295
342	46 31 003	32 29 033	43 31 130	47 12 196	49 31 220	23 57 258	34 14 293
344	46 32 001	32 48 031	43 58 129	47 03 195	49 09 218	23 23 256	33 41 291
346	46 32 358	33 05 029	44 25 127	46 54 194	48 47 217	22 49 254	33 08 289
348	46 30 356	33 22 027	44 54 126	46 46 192	48 27 215	22 16 252	32 35 287
350	46 27 353	33 37 024	45 22 124	46 39 191	48 07 214	21 43 250	32 01 285
352	46 22 351	33 51 022	45 52 122	46 33 190	47 47 213	21 10 248	31 27 283
354	46 16 348	34 03 020	46 22 121	46 27 188	47 29 211	20 37 247	30 53 281
356	46 08 346	34 14 017	46 52 119	46 23 187	47 11 210	20 05 245	30 18 279
358	45 58 343	34 24 015	47 23 118	46 19 186	46 54 209	19 34 243	29 44 277

LAT 74°S

LHA ♈	Hc Zn	Hc Zn	Hc Zn	Hc Zn	Hc Zn	Hc Zn	Hc Zn
	Diphda	◆ RIGEL	CANOPUS	Miaplacidus	◆ RIGIL KENT	Peacock	◆ FOMALHAUT
0	33 34 013	10 56 081	48 20 115	56 11 156	47 31 208	63 21 281	44 51 341
2	33 41 010	11 29 080	48 50 113	56 25 154	47 16 206	62 49 279	44 39 339
4	33 46 008	12 01 078	49 21 112	56 40 153	47 01 205	62 16 277	44 26 336
6	33 50 006	12 34 076	49 52 110	56 55 152	46 48 204	61 43 275	44 12 334
8	33 53 004	13 06 074	50 23 108	57 11 151	46 35 202	61 10 273	43 57 331
10	33 54 001	13 37 072	50 55 107	57 27 150	46 23 201	60 37 271	43 41 329
12	33 54 359	14 08 070	51 26 105	57 44 149	46 12 199	60 04 269	43 23 327
14	33 53 357	14 39 068	51 58 103	58 01 147	46 01 198	59 31 267	43 04 324
16	33 50 354	15 10 066	52 31 101	58 20 146	45 51 197	58 58 265	42 44 322
18	33 46 352	15 40 064	53 03 099	58 38 145	45 42 195	58 25 263	42 24 320
20	33 41 350	16 09 062	53 36 098	58 57 144	45 34 194	57 52 262	42 02 317
22	33 35 348	16 38 060	54 09 096	59 17 143	45 26 192	57 19 260	41 39 315
24	33 27 345	17 06 058	54 42 094	59 38 141	45 20 191	56 47 258	41 15 313
26	33 18 343	17 34 056	55 15 092	59 58 140	45 14 190	56 15 256	40 50 311
28	33 07 341	18 01 054	55 48 090	60 20 139	45 08 188	55 43 255	40 25 308

LHA ♈	Hc Zn	Hc Zn	Hc Zn	Hc Zn	Hc Zn	Hc Zn	Hc Zn
	RIGEL	◆ SIRIUS	Suhail	◆ RIGIL KENT	Peacock	◆ FOMALHAUT	Diphda
30	18 27 052	21 09 077	37 04 120	45 04 187	55 11 253	39 58 306	32 56 338
32	18 53 050	21 41 075	37 33 118	45 00 186	54 40 251	39 31 304	32 43 336
34	19 18 048	22 13 073	38 02 116	44 58 184	54 08 249	39 03 302	32 29 334
36	19 42 046	22 44 071	38 32 115	44 55 183	53 38 248	38 35 300	32 14 332
38	20 05 044	23 15 069	39 02 113	44 54 181	53 07 246	38 06 297	31 58 329
40	20 27 041	23 46 067	39 33 111	44 54 180	52 37 245	37 36 295	31 41 327
42	20 49 039	24 16 065	40 04 109	44 54 179	52 07 243	37 06 293	31 22 325
44	21 09 037	24 46 063	40 36 107	44 55 177	51 38 241	36 35 291	31 03 323
46	21 29 035	25 15 061	41 07 106	44 57 176	51 09 240	36 04 289	30 42 321
48	21 47 033	25 43 059	41 39 104	45 00 175	50 41 238	35 33 287	30 21 319
50	22 05 031	26 11 057	42 11 102	45 03 173	50 13 237	35 01 285	29 58 316
52	22 21 029	26 39 055	42 44 100	45 08 172	49 46 235	34 29 283	29 35 314
54	22 37 027	27 05 052	43 17 098	45 13 170	49 19 234	33 57 281	29 11 312
56	22 51 025	27 31 050	43 49 097	45 19 169	48 53 232	33 24 279	28 46 310
58	23 04 022	27 56 048	44 22 095	45 25 168	48 27 230	32 51 277	28 20 308

LHA ♈	Hc Zn	Hc Zn	Hc Zn	Hc Zn	Hc Zn	Hc Zn	Hc Zn
	RIGEL	◆ SIRIUS	Suhail	◆ RIGIL KENT	Peacock	◆ FOMALHAUT	Diphda
60	23 16 020	28 20 046	44 55 093	45 33 166	48 01 229	32 19 275	27 54 306
62	23 27 018	28 44 044	45 28 091	45 41 165	47 37 227	31 46 273	27 27 304
64	23 37 016	29 06 042	46 01 089	45 50 164	47 13 226	31 13 271	26 59 302
66	23 46 014	29 28 040	46 34 087	45 59 162	46 49 224	30 39 269	26 30 300
68	23 53 012	29 48 037	47 07 085	46 10 161	46 26 223	30 06 267	26 01 297
70	23 59 010	30 08 035	47 40 083	46 21 159	46 04 221	29 33 265	25 32 295
72	24 04 007	30 27 033	48 13 081	46 33 158	45 43 220	29 00 264	25 02 293
74	24 07 005	30 44 031	48 46 079	46 46 157	45 22 218	28 28 262	24 31 291
76	24 10 003	31 01 029	49 18 077	46 59 155	45 02 217	27 55 260	24 00 289
78	24 11 001	31 16 026	49 50 075	47 13 154	44 42 215	27 23 258	23 29 287
80	24 11 359	31 30 024	50 22 073	47 28 153	44 23 214	26 50 256	22 57 285
82	24 10 357	31 43 022	50 53 071	47 44 151	44 05 213	26 18 254	22 25 283
84	24 07 354	31 55 020	51 24 069	48 00 150	43 48 211	25 47 252	21 52 281
86	24 03 352	32 05 018	51 55 066	48 17 148	43 31 210	25 15 251	21 20 279
88	23 58 350	32 15 015	52 25 064	48 35 147	43 15 208	24 44 249	20 47 278

LHA ♈	Hc Zn	Hc Zn	Hc Zn	Hc Zn	Hc Zn	Hc Zn	Hc Zn
	◆ SIRIUS	Suhail	◆ RIGIL KENT	Peacock	FOMALHAUT	◆ ACHERNAR	RIGEL
90	32 23 013	52 54 062	48 53 146	43 00 207	24 14 247	60 26 268	23 52 348
92	32 30 011	53 23 060	49 12 144	42 45 205	23 43 245	59 53 266	23 44 346
94	32 35 008	53 51 057	49 32 143	42 31 204	23 14 243	59 20 265	23 35 344
96	32 39 006	54 19 055	49 52 141	42 19 202	22 44 241	58 47 263	23 25 341
98	32 42 004	54 45 053	50 13 140	42 06 201	22 16 240	58 14 261	23 14 339
100	32 44 002	55 11 050	50 35 139	41 55 199	21 47 238	57 42 259	23 02 337
102	32 44 359	55 36 048	50 57 137	41 44 198	21 20 236	57 10 257	22 49 335
104	32 43 357	56 00 045	51 20 136	41 35 196	20 52 234	56 37 256	22 34 333
106	32 41 355	56 23 043	51 43 134	41 26 195	20 26 232	56 05 254	22 18 331
108	32 37 353	56 45 040	52 07 133	41 18 194	20 00 231	55 34 252	22 02 329
110	32 32 350	57 06 038	52 32 131	41 10 192	19 35 229	55 02 251	21 44 327
112	32 26 348	57 25 035	52 57 130	41 04 191	19 10 227	54 31 249	21 25 324
114	32 19 346	57 43 032	53 23 128	40 58 189	18 46 225	54 01 247	21 05 322
116	32 10 343	58 00 030	53 49 127	40 53 188	18 23 223	53 30 246	20 45 320
118	32 00 341	58 16 027	54 15 126	40 49 186	18 01 222	53 00 244	20 23 318

LHA ♈	Hc Zn	Hc Zn	Hc Zn	Hc Zn	Hc Zn	Hc Zn	Hc Zn
	Suhail	◆ SPICA	RIGIL KENT	Peacock	◆ FOMALHAUT	ACHERNAR	◆ SIRIUS
120	58 30 024	13 08 085	54 43 124	40 46 185	17 39 220	52 31 243	31 49 339
122	58 43 021	13 41 083	55 10 123	40 43 183	17 18 218	52 02 241	31 36 337
124	58 54 019	14 14 081	55 38 121	40 42 182	16 58 216	51 33 239	31 22 335
126	59 04 016	14 47 079	56 07 120	40 41 181	16 39 215	51 05 238	31 08 332
128	59 13 013	15 19 077	56 36 118	40 41 179	16 21 213	50 37 236	30 52 330
130	59 19 010	15 51 075	57 05 116	40 42 178	16 04 211	50 10 235	30 35 328
132	59 24 007	16 23 073	57 35 115	40 44 176	15 47 209	49 43 233	30 17 326
134	59 28 004	16 54 071	58 05 113	40 47 175	15 31 207	49 17 232	29 57 324
136	59 29 002	17 26 069	58 36 112	40 50 173	15 17 206	48 51 230	29 37 321
138	59 29 359	17 56 067	59 07 110	40 54 172	15 03 204	48 26 229	29 16 319
140	59 28 356	18 27 065	59 38 109	41 00 170	14 50 202	48 02 227	28 54 317
142	59 25 353	18 56 063	60 09 107	41 06 169	14 38 200	47 38 226	28 31 315
144	59 20 350	19 26 061	60 41 105	41 12 167	14 27 198	47 14 224	28 07 313
146	59 14 347	19 54 059	61 13 104	41 20 166	14 17 197	46 52 223	27 42 311
148	59 05 345	20 23 057	61 46 102	41 28 165	14 08 195	46 30 221	27 17 309

LHA ♈	Hc Zn	Hc Zn	Hc Zn	Hc Zn	Hc Zn	Hc Zn	Hc Zn
	◆ SPICA	ANTARES	◆ Peacock	FOMALHAUT	ACHERNAR	◆ CANOPUS	Suhail
150	20 50 055	23 19 105	41 37 163	14 00 193	46 08 220	59 40 284	58 56 342
152	21 17 053	23 51 103	41 47 162	13 53 191	45 47 218	59 07 282	58 45 339
154	21 43 051	24 23 101	41 58 160	13 47 190	45 27 217	58 35 280	58 32 336
156	22 08 049	24 56 099	42 10 159	13 42 188	45 08 215	58 02 278	58 18 333
158	22 33 047	25 29 097	42 22 157	13 38 186	44 49 214	57 29 276	58 03 331
160	22 57 045	26 02 096	42 35 156	13 35 184	44 31 212	56 56 274	57 46 328
162	23 20 043	26 35 094	42 49 154	13 33 182	44 14 211	56 23 272	57 28 325
164	23 42 041	27 08 092	43 04 153	13 33 181	43 57 209	55 50 270	57 08 323
166	24 03 039	27 41 090	43 20 151	13 33 179	43 42 208	55 17 268	56 48 320
168	24 23 036	28 14 088	43 36 150	13 34 177	43 26 206	54 44 266	56 26 318
170	24 42 034	28 47 086	43 53 149	13 36 175	43 12 205	54 11 264	56 03 315
172	25 00 032	29 20 084	44 10 147	13 40 173	42 59 204	53 38 262	55 39 313
174	25 17 030	29 53 082	44 29 146	13 44 172	42 46 202	53 06 261	55 15 310
176	25 33 028	30 25 080	44 48 144	13 49 170	42 34 201	52 33 259	54 49 308
178	25 48 026	30 58 078	45 07 143	13 56 168	42 22 199	52 01 257	54 22 305

LHA ♈	Hc Zn	Hc Zn	Hc Zn	Hc Zn	Hc Zn	Hc Zn	Hc Zn
	SPICA	◆ ANTARES	Nunki	FOMALHAUT	◆ ACHERNAR	CANOPUS	◆ Suhail
180	26 02 024	31 30 076	21 27 111	14 03 166	42 12 198	51 29 255	53 55 303
182	26 15 021	32 02 074	21 58 109	14 11 164	42 02 196	50 57 254	53 27 301
184	26 26 019	32 33 072	22 29 107	14 21 163	41 53 195	50 25 252	52 58 298
186	26 36 017	33 05 070	23 01 105	14 31 161	41 45 193	49 54 250	52 29 296
188	26 46 015	33 36 068	23 33 103	14 42 159	41 38 192	49 23 248	51 59 294
190	26 53 013	34 06 066	24 05 102	14 55 157	41 32 190	48 52 247	51 28 292
192	27 00 010	34 36 064	24 38 100	15 08 156	41 26 189	48 22 245	50 58 290
194	27 05 008	35 05 062	25 10 098	15 22 154	41 21 188	47 52 243	50 26 287
196	27 10 006	35 34 060	25 43 096	15 37 152	41 17 186	47 23 242	49 54 285
198	27 12 004	36 02 057	26 16 094	15 53 150	41 14 185	46 54 240	49 22 283
200	27 14 002	36 30 055	26 49 092	16 10 148	41 12 183	46 26 239	48 50 281
202	27 14 359	36 57 053	27 22 090	16 28 147	41 10 182	45 58 237	48 18 279
204	27 13 357	37 23 051	27 55 088	16 46 145	41 10 180	45 30 235	47 45 277
206	27 11 355	37 48 049	28 28 086	17 06 143	41 10 179	45 03 234	47 12 275
208	27 08 353	38 13 047	29 01 084	17 26 141	41 11 178	44 37 232	46 39 273

LHA ♈	Hc Zn	Hc Zn	Hc Zn	Hc Zn	Hc Zn	Hc Zn	Hc Zn
	◆ ANTARES	Nunki	◆ FOMALHAUT	ACHERNAR	CANOPUS	◆ Suhail	SPICA
210	38 36 044	29 34 082	17 47 139	41 13 176	44 11 231	46 06 271	27 03 351
212	38 59 042	30 07 080	18 09 138	41 15 175	43 46 229	45 33 269	26 57 348
214	39 20 040	30 39 078	18 32 136	41 19 173	43 21 227	45 00 267	26 50 346
216	39 41 038	31 12 076	18 55 134	41 23 172	42 57 226	44 27 266	26 41 344
218	40 01 035	31 44 074	19 20 132	41 28 170	42 34 224	43 54 264	26 31 342
220	40 19 033	32 15 072	19 44 130	41 34 169	42 11 223	43 21 262	26 21 340
222	40 37 031	32 47 070	20 10 129	41 41 167	41 49 221	42 48 260	26 08 337
224	40 53 028	33 18 068	20 36 127	41 49 166	41 27 220	42 16 258	25 55 335
226	41 08 026	33 48 066	21 03 125	41 57 165	41 07 218	41 44 256	25 41 333
228	41 22 024	34 18 064	21 30 123	42 06 163	40 47 217	41 12 255	25 25 331
230	41 35 021	34 48 062	21 58 121	42 16 162	40 27 215	40 40 253	25 09 329
232	41 46 019	35 17 060	22 26 120	42 27 160	40 09 213	40 08 251	24 51 327
234	41 56 016	35 45 058	22 55 118	42 39 159	39 51 212	39 37 249	24 33 325
236	42 05 014	36 13 056	23 25 116	42 51 157	39 34 210	39 07 247	24 13 322
238	42 12 012	36 40 054	23 55 114	43 04 156	39 17 209	38 36 246	23 52 320

LHA ♈	Hc Zn	Hc Zn	Hc Zn	Hc Zn	Hc Zn	Hc Zn	Hc Zn
	ANTARES	◆ Nunki	FOMALHAUT	◆ ACHERNAR	CANOPUS	◆ ACRUX	SPICA
240	42 18 009	37 06 051	24 25 112	43 18 154	39 02 207	68 49 272	23 31 318
242	42 22 007	37 31 049	24 56 111	43 33 153	38 47 206	68 16 270	23 08 316
244	42 26 004	37 56 047	25 27 109	43 48 151	38 33 204	67 43 268	22 45 314
246	42 27 002	38 20 045	25 59 107	44 04 150	38 20 203	67 10 267	22 21 312
248	42 28 359	38 43 043	26 30 105	44 21 149	38 07 201	66 37 265	21 56 310
250	42 27 357	39 05 040	27 03 103	44 39 147	37 56 200	66 04 263	21 30 308
252	42 24 355	39 25 038	27 35 101	44 57 146	37 45 198	65 32 261	21 03 306
254	42 21 352	39 45 036	28 07 099	45 16 144	37 35 197	64 59 259	20 36 304
256	42 15 350	40 04 033	28 40 098	45 36 143	37 26 195	64 27 258	20 08 302
258	42 09 347	40 22 031	29 13 096	45 56 141	37 18 194	63 54 256	19 40 300
260	42 01 345	40 38 029	29 46 094	46 17 140	37 10 192	63 22 254	19 11 298
262	41 52 343	40 54 026	30 19 092	46 39 138	37 04 191	62 51 253	18 41 296
264	41 41 340	41 08 024	30 52 090	47 01 137	36 58 189	62 19 251	18 11 294
266	41 29 338	41 21 022	31 25 088	47 24 135	36 53 188	61 48 250	17 41 292
268	41 16 335	41 32 019	31 58 086	47 48 134	36 49 186	61 17 248	17 10 290

LHA ♈	Hc Zn	Hc Zn	Hc Zn	Hc Zn	Hc Zn	Hc Zn	Hc Zn
	◆ Nunki	FOMALHAUT	◆ ACHERNAR	CANOPUS	◆ ACRUX	RIGIL KENT	ANTARES
270	41 42 017	32 31 084	48 12 132	36 46 185	60 47 247	67 52 279	41 02 333
272	41 51 015	33 04 082	48 37 131	36 44 183	60 16 245	67 20 277	40 46 331
274	41 59 012	33 37 080	49 02 129	36 43 182	59 47 244	66 47 275	40 30 328
276	42 05 010	34 09 078	49 28 128	36 42 180	59 17 242	66 14 273	40 12 326
278	42 10 007	34 41 076	49 55 126	36 43 179	58 48 241	65 41 271	39 53 324
280	42 14 005	35 13 074	50 22 125	36 44 177	58 20 239	65 08 269	39 33 322
282	42 16 002	35 45 072	50 49 123	36 46 176	57 52 238	64 35 267	39 12 319
284	42 17 000	36 16 070	51 17 122	36 49 174	57 24 236	64 02 265	38 49 317
286	42 16 358	36 47 068	51 45 120	36 53 172	56 57 235	63 29 264	38 26 315
288	42 14 355	37 18 066	52 14 118	36 58 171	56 30 233	62 56 262	38 03 313
290	42 10 353	37 48 064	52 44 117	37 03 169	56 04 232	62 23 260	37 38 310
292	42 06 350	38 17 062	53 13 115	37 10 168	55 38 230	61 51 258	37 12 308
294	41 59 348	38 46 060	53 43 114	37 17 166	55 12 229	61 18 257	36 46 306
296	41 52 346	39 14 057	54 14 112	37 25 165	54 48 228	60 46 255	36 19 304
298	41 43 343	39 42 055	54 45 110	37 34 163	54 24 226	60 15 253	35 51 302

LHA ♈	Hc Zn	Hc Zn	Hc Zn	Hc Zn	Hc Zn	Hc Zn	Hc Zn
	◆ FOMALHAUT	ACHERNAR	◆ CANOPUS	ACRUX	RIGIL KENT	◆ ANTARES	Nunki
300	40 08 053	55 16 109	37 44 162	54 00 225	59 43 252	35 22 300	41 33 341
302	40 34 051	55 47 107	37 55 160	53 37 224	59 12 250	34 53 297	41 21 338
304	41 00 049	56 19 105	38 06 159	53 14 222	58 41 248	34 24 295	41 08 336
306	41 24 046	56 51 104	38 19 157	52 53 221	58 10 247	33 53 293	40 54 334
308	41 48 044	57 23 102	38 32 156	52 31 219	57 40 245	33 23 291	40 39 331
310	42 10 042	57 56 100	38 46 154	52 11 218	57 10 244	32 52 289	40 23 329
312	42 32 040	58 29 098	39 01 153	51 50 217	56 41 242	32 20 287	40 05 327
314	42 52 037	59 01 096	39 16 151	51 31 215	56 12 241	31 49 285	39 46 324
316	43 12 035	59 34 095	39 32 150	51 12 214	55 43 239	31 16 283	39 26 322
318	43 30 033	60 07 093	39 50 148	50 54 213	55 15 238	30 44 281	39 06 320
320	43 47 030	60 40 091	40 07 147	50 37 211	54 47 236	30 12 279	38 44 318
322	44 03 028	61 13 089	40 26 145	50 20 210	54 20 235	29 39 277	38 21 315
324	44 18 025	61 47 087	40 45 144	50 04 209	53 53 233	29 06 275	37 57 313
326	44 31 023	62 20 085	41 05 142	49 48 207	53 27 232	28 33 273	37 33 311
328	44 44 021	62 52 083	41 26 140	49 33 206	53 01 230	28 00 271	37 07 309

LHA ♈	Hc Zn	Hc Zn	Hc Zn	Hc Zn	Hc Zn	Hc Zn	Hc Zn
	◆ FOMALHAUT	Diphda	◆ CANOPUS	ACRUX	RIGIL KENT	◆ ANTARES	Nunki
330	44 55 018	29 33 046	41 47 139	49 19 205	52 36 229	27 27 269	36 41 307
332	45 04 016	29 56 044	42 09 137	49 06 203	52 11 227	26 54 267	36 14 304
334	45 12 013	30 19 042	42 32 136	48 53 202	51 47 226	26 21 266	35 46 302
336	45 19 011	30 40 039	42 55 134	48 41 201	51 24 225	25 48 264	35 18 300
338	45 25 008	31 01 037	43 19 133	48 30 199	51 01 223	25 15 262	34 49 298
340	45 29 006	31 21 035	43 44 131	48 20 198	50 38 222	24 42 260	34 20 296
342	45 31 003	31 39 033	44 09 130	48 10 197	50 17 220	24 10 258	33 50 294
344	45 32 001	31 56 031	44 35 128	48 01 195	49 56 219	23 38 256	33 19 292
346	45 32 358	32 13 028	45 01 126	47 52 194	49 35 217	23 06 254	32 48 290
348	45 30 356	32 28 026	45 28 125	47 45 193	49 15 216	22 34 252	32 17 288
350	45 27 353	32 42 024	45 56 123	47 38 191	48 56 215	22 03 251	31 45 286
352	45 23 351	32 55 022	46 24 122	47 32 190	48 38 213	21 32 249	31 13 284
354	45 17 348	33 07 019	46 52 120	47 27 189	48 20 212	21 01 247	30 41 282
356	45 09 346	33 17 017	47 21 118	47 22 187	48 03 210	20 31 245	30 08 280
358	45 01 343	33 26 015	47 50 117	47 18 186	47 46 209	20 01 243	29 36 278

LHA ♈	Hc	Zn	Hc	Zn	Hc	Zn	Hc	Zn	Hc	Zn	Hc	Zn	Hc	Zn
	◆ Diphda		◆ CANOPUS		ACRUX		RIGIL KENT		◆ ANTARES		Peacock		FOMALHAUT	
0	32 35	013	48 45	114	48 15	185	48 24	208	20 00	242	63 09	283	43 54	341
2	32 42	010	49 13	112	48 13	183	48 09	207	19 33	240	62 38	281	43 43	339
4	32 47	008	49 42	111	48 12	182	47 56	205	19 07	238	62 08	279	43 32	337
6	32 50	006	50 12	109	48 11	181	47 43	204	18 40	236	61 37	277	43 19	334
8	32 53	003	50 41	107	48 11	179	47 31	203	18 15	234	61 06	275	43 04	332
10	32 54	001	51 11	105	48 12	178	47 19	201	17 50	233	60 35	273	42 49	329
12	32 54	359	51 41	104	48 13	177	47 08	200	17 26	231	60 04	271	42 33	327
14	32 53	357	52 11	102	48 16	175	46 58	198	17 02	229	59 33	269	42 16	325
16	32 51	354	52 42	100	48 19	174	46 49	197	16 39	227	59 02	267	41 57	322
18	32 47	352	53 13	098	48 22	172	46 40	196	16 16	225	58 31	265	41 38	320
20	32 42	350	53 43	096	48 27	171	46 32	194	15 55	223	58 00	263	41 17	318
22	32 36	348	54 14	094	48 32	170	46 25	193	15 34	222	57 29	261	40 56	316
24	32 29	345	54 45	093	48 38	168	46 18	191	15 14	220	56 59	259	40 34	313
26	32 20	343	55 16	091	48 44	167	46 13	190	14 54	218	56 28	258	40 11	311
28	32 11	341	55 47	089	48 52	166	46 08	189	14 35	216	55 58	256	39 47	309
	RIGEL		◆ SIRIUS		Suhail		◆ RIGIL KENT		Peacock		◆ FOMALHAUT		Diphda	
30	17 50	051	20 55	076	37 33	119	46 04	187	55 28	254	39 23	307	32 00	339
32	18 14	049	21 25	074	38 01	117	46 00	186	54 58	252	38 57	305	31 48	336
34	18 37	047	21 55	072	38 28	116	45 57	184	54 29	251	38 32	302	31 35	334
36	19 00	045	22 24	070	38 57	114	45 55	183	54 00	249	38 05	300	31 21	332
38	19 21	043	22 53	068	39 25	112	45 54	182	53 31	247	37 38	298	31 06	330
40	19 42	041	23 22	066	39 54	110	45 54	180	53 02	246	37 10	296	30 50	328
42	20 02	039	23 50	064	40 24	108	45 54	179	52 34	244	36 42	294	30 33	325
44	20 21	037	24 18	062	40 53	107	45 55	177	52 06	242	36 13	292	30 15	323
46	20 40	035	24 45	060	41 23	105	45 57	176	51 39	241	35 44	290	29 56	321
48	20 57	033	25 12	058	41 53	103	46 00	175	51 12	239	35 15	288	29 36	319
50	21 13	031	25 38	056	42 24	101	46 03	173	50 46	238	34 45	286	29 15	317
52	21 29	029	26 04	054	42 54	099	46 07	172	50 20	236	34 15	284	28 53	315
54	21 43	027	26 28	052	43 25	097	46 12	170	49 54	235	33 45	282	28 31	312
56	21 57	024	26 53	050	43 56	096	46 17	169	49 29	233	33 14	280	28 07	310
58	22 09	022	27 16	048	44 27	094	46 24	168	49 05	231	32 44	278	27 43	308
	RIGEL		◆ SIRIUS		Suhail		◆ RIGIL KENT		Peacock		◆ FOMALHAUT		ACHERNAR	
60	22 20	020	27 39	046	44 58	092	46 31	166	48 41	230	32 13	276	67 49	304
62	22 30	018	28 00	044	45 29	090	46 39	165	48 17	228	31 42	274	67 22	301
64	22 39	016	28 21	041	46 00	088	46 47	163	47 54	227	31 11	272	66 55	299
66	22 47	014	28 41	039	46 31	086	46 57	162	47 32	225	30 40	270	66 28	296
68	22 54	012	29 01	037	47 02	084	47 07	161	47 10	224	30 09	268	66 00	294
70	23 00	009	29 19	035	47 33	082	47 17	159	46 49	222	29 38	266	65 31	291
72	23 04	007	29 36	033	48 03	080	47 29	158	46 28	221	29 07	264	65 02	289
74	23 08	005	29 53	031	48 34	078	47 41	156	46 09	219	28 36	262	64 32	287
76	23 10	003	30 08	028	49 04	076	47 54	155	45 49	218	28 05	260	64 02	284
78	23 11	001	30 22	026	49 34	074	48 07	153	45 31	216	27 35	258	63 32	282
80	23 11	359	30 35	024	50 04	072	48 21	152	45 13	215	27 04	257	63 01	280
82	23 10	357	30 47	022	50 33	070	48 36	151	44 55	213	26 34	255	62 31	278
84	23 07	354	30 58	020	51 02	067	48 52	149	44 39	212	26 05	253	62 00	276
86	23 04	352	31 08	017	51 30	065	49 08	148	44 23	210	25 35	251	61 29	274
88	22 59	350	31 17	015	51 58	063	49 25	146	44 08	209	25 06	249	60 58	272
	◆ SIRIUS		Suhail		◆ RIGIL KENT		Peacock		◆ FOMALHAUT		ACHERNAR		RIGEL	
90	31 24	013	52 25	061	49 43	145	43 53	207	24 37	247	60 27	270	22 53	348
92	31 31	011	52 52	058	50 01	143	43 39	206	24 09	245	59 56	268	22 46	346
94	31 36	008	53 18	056	50 20	142	43 26	204	23 40	244	59 25	266	22 38	344
96	31 40	006	53 44	054	50 39	141	43 14	203	23 13	242	58 54	264	22 28	342
98	31 42	004	54 08	051	50 59	139	43 02	201	22 46	240	58 23	263	22 18	339
100	31 44	002	54 32	049	51 20	138	42 52	200	22 19	238	57 52	261	22 07	337
102	31 44	359	54 55	047	51 41	136	42 42	198	21 53	236	57 22	259	21 54	335
104	31 43	357	55 17	044	52 03	135	42 32	197	21 27	235	56 51	257	21 41	333
106	31 41	355	55 39	042	52 25	133	42 24	195	21 02	233	56 21	255	21 26	331
108	31 38	353	55 59	039	52 48	132	42 16	194	20 38	231	55 51	254	21 10	329
110	31 33	350	56 18	037	53 11	130	42 09	192	20 14	229	55 22	252	20 54	327
112	31 27	348	56 36	034	53 35	129	42 03	191	19 51	227	54 52	250	20 36	325
114	31 20	346	56 52	031	53 59	127	41 57	189	19 29	226	54 23	249	20 18	323
116	31 12	344	57 08	029	54 24	126	41 53	188	19 07	224	53 54	247	19 59	320
118	31 03	341	57 22	026	54 50	124	41 49	186	18 46	222	53 26	245	19 38	318
	Suhail		◆ SPICA		RIGIL KENT		Peacock		◆ FOMALHAUT		ACHERNAR		◆ SIRIUS	
120	57 35	024	13 03	085	55 16	123	41 46	185	18 25	220	52 58	244	30 52	339
122	57 47	021	13 34	083	55 42	121	41 43	183	18 06	218	52 30	242	30 41	337
124	57 58	018	14 05	081	56 09	120	41 42	182	17 47	216	52 03	240	30 28	335
126	58 06	015	14 35	079	56 36	118	41 41	181	17 29	215	51 36	239	30 14	333
128	58 14	013	15 06	077	57 03	117	41 41	179	17 11	213	51 10	237	30 00	330
130	58 20	010	15 36	075	57 31	115	41 42	178	16 55	211	50 44	236	29 44	328
132	58 25	007	16 06	073	58 00	113	41 44	176	16 39	209	50 19	234	29 27	326
134	58 28	004	16 35	071	58 28	112	41 46	175	16 25	208	49 54	233	29 09	324
136	58 29	002	17 04	069	58 57	110	41 50	173	16 11	206	49 29	231	28 50	322
138	58 29	359	17 33	067	59 27	109	41 54	172	15 58	204	49 05	229	28 31	320
140	58 28	356	18 01	065	59 56	107	41 59	170	15 45	202	48 42	228	28 10	317
142	58 25	353	18 29	063	60 26	105	42 04	169	15 34	200	48 19	226	27 48	315
144	58 21	350	18 57	061	60 56	104	42 11	167	15 24	199	47 57	225	27 26	313
146	58 15	348	19 24	059	61 26	102	42 18	166	15 14	197	47 36	223	27 03	311
148	58 08	345	19 50	057	61 57	100	42 26	164	15 06	195	47 15	222	26 39	309
	SPICA		◆ ANTARES		Peacock		FOMALHAUT		◆ ACHERNAR		CANOPUS		◆ Suhail	
150	20 16	055	23 34	104	42 35	163	14 58	193	46 54	220	59 24	286	57 59	342
152	20 41	053	24 04	102	42 44	161	14 52	191	46 34	219	58 54	284	57 49	340
154	21 05	051	24 35	101	42 55	160	14 46	190	46 15	217	58 24	282	57 37	337
156	21 29	049	25 05	099	43 06	158	14 42	188	45 57	216	57 53	279	57 24	334
158	21 52	047	25 36	097	43 18	157	14 38	186	45 39	214	57 22	277	57 10	332
160	22 14	045	26 07	095	43 30	155	14 35	184	45 22	213	56 52	275	56 55	329
162	22 35	043	26 38	093	43 43	154	14 33	182	45 05	211	56 21	273	56 38	326
164	22 56	040	27 09	091	43 57	152	14 33	181	44 50	210	55 50	271	56 20	324
166	23 16	038	27 40	089	44 12	151	14 33	179	44 34	208	55 19	269	56 01	321
168	23 35	036	28 11	087	44 28	149	14 34	177	44 20	207	54 47	268	55 41	319
170	23 52	034	28 42	085	44 44	148	14 36	175	44 06	205	54 16	266	55 20	316
172	24 09	032	29 13	083	45 00	146	14 39	173	43 53	204	53 46	264	54 58	314
174	24 25	030	29 44	081	45 18	145	14 43	172	43 41	202	53 15	262	54 36	311
176	24 40	028	30 15	079	45 36	143	14 48	170	43 30	201	52 44	260	54 12	309
178	24 54	026	30 45	077	45 55	142	14 54	168	43 19	199	52 14	258	53 47	307

LAT 75°S

LHA ♈	Hc	Zn	Hc	Zn	Hc	Zn	Hc	Zn	Hc	Zn	Hc	Zn	Hc	Zn
	SPICA		◆ ANTARES		Nunki		FOMALHAUT		◆ ACHERNAR		CANOPUS		◆ Suhail	
180	25 07	023	31 15	075	21 48	110	15 01	166	43 09	198	51 43	257	53 22	304
182	25 19	021	31 45	073	22 17	109	15 09	164	43 00	197	51 13	255	52 56	302
184	25 29	019	32 15	071	22 47	107	15 18	163	42 51	195	50 43	253	52 29	300
186	25 39	017	32 44	069	23 16	105	15 28	161	42 44	194	50 14	251	52 02	297
188	25 48	015	33 13	067	23 47	103	15 38	159	42 37	192	49 44	250	51 34	295
190	25 55	013	33 41	065	24 17	101	15 50	157	42 31	191	49 16	248	51 06	293
192	26 01	010	34 09	063	24 48	099	16 02	155	42 25	189	48 47	246	50 37	291
194	26 06	008	34 37	061	25 18	097	16 16	154	42 21	188	48 19	244	50 08	289
196	26 10	006	35 04	059	25 49	095	16 30	152	42 17	186	47 51	243	49 38	287
198	26 13	004	35 30	057	26 20	094	16 45	150	42 14	185	47 23	241	49 08	284
200	26 14	002	35 56	055	26 51	092	17 01	148	42 12	183	46 57	239	48 38	282
202	26 14	359	36 21	053	27 22	090	17 18	146	42 10	182	46 30	238	48 07	280
204	26 13	357	36 45	050	27 53	088	17 35	145	42 10	180	46 04	236	47 37	278
206	26 11	355	37 08	048	28 24	086	17 54	143	42 10	179	45 38	235	47 06	276
208	26 08	353	37 31	046	28 55	084	18 13	141	42 11	177	45 13	233	46 35	274
	◆ ANTARES		Nunki		FOMALHAUT		◆ ACHERNAR		CANOPUS		◆ Suhail		SPICA	
210	37 53	044	29 26	082	18 33	139	42 13	176	44 49	231	46 04	272	26 04	351
212	38 14	042	29 57	080	18 54	137	42 15	175	44 25	230	45 33	270	25 58	349
214	38 34	039	30 27	078	19 15	136	42 18	173	44 01	228	45 02	268	25 51	346
216	38 53	037	30 57	076	19 37	134	42 23	172	43 39	227	44 31	267	25 43	344
218	39 12	035	31 27	074	20 00	132	42 28	170	43 16	225	44 00	265	25 34	342
220	39 29	032	31 57	072	20 23	130	42 33	169	42 55	223	43 29	263	25 24	340
222	39 45	030	32 26	070	20 47	128	42 40	167	42 34	222	42 58	261	25 13	338
224	40 00	028	32 55	068	21 12	127	42 47	166	42 13	220	42 28	259	25 01	336
226	40 14	026	33 24	066	21 37	125	42 55	164	41 54	219	41 57	257	24 47	333
228	40 27	023	33 52	064	22 03	123	43 04	163	41 35	217	41 27	255	24 33	331
230	40 39	021	34 19	062	22 29	121	43 13	161	41 16	215	40 57	254	24 17	329
232	40 49	019	34 46	059	22 56	119	43 24	160	40 59	214	40 28	252	24 01	327
234	40 58	016	35 13	057	23 23	117	43 35	158	40 42	212	39 58	250	23 44	325
236	41 06	014	35 39	055	23 51	116	43 46	157	40 25	211	39 29	248	23 25	323
238	41 13	011	36 04	053	24 19	114	43 59	155	40 10	209	39 01	246	23 06	321
	ANTARES		◆ Nunki		FOMALHAUT		◆ ACHERNAR		CANOPUS		◆ ACRUX		SPICA	
240	41 19	009	36 28	051	24 48	112	44 12	154	39 55	208	68 46	275	22 46	319
242	41 23	007	36 52	049	25 17	110	44 26	153	39 41	206	68 15	273	22 25	316
244	41 26	004	37 15	046	25 46	108	44 41	151	39 28	205	67 44	271	22 03	314
246	41 27	002	37 37	044	26 16	106	44 56	150	39 15	203	67 13	269	21 40	312
248	41 28	000	37 58	042	26 46	105	45 12	148	39 03	202	66 42	267	21 17	310
250	41 27	357	38 19	040	27 16	103	45 29	147	38 52	200	66 11	265	20 53	308
252	41 25	355	38 38	038	27 46	101	45 47	145	38 42	198	65 40	263	20 28	306
254	41 21	352	38 56	035	28 17	099	46 05	144	38 32	197	65 09	262	20 03	304
256	41 16	350	39 14	033	28 48	097	46 23	142	38 24	195	64 38	260	19 37	302
258	41 10	348	39 30	031	29 19	095	46 43	141	38 16	194	64 08	258	19 10	300
260	41 03	345	39 46	028	29 50	093	47 03	139	38 09	192	63 38	256	18 43	298
262	40 55	343	40 00	026	30 21	091	47 24	138	38 03	191	63 07	255	18 15	296
264	40 45	340	40 13	024	30 52	089	47 45	136	37 57	189	62 38	253	17 47	294
266	40 34	338	40 25	021	31 23	087	48 07	134	37 53	188	62 08	251	17 19	292
268	40 22	336	40 35	019	31 54	085	48 29	133	37 49	186	61 39	250	16 50	290
	◆ Nunki		FOMALHAUT		◆ ACHERNAR		CANOPUS		◆ ACRUX		RIGIL KENT		ANTARES	
270	40 45	017	32 25	084	48 52	131	37 46	185	61 10	248	67 41	282	40 08	333
272	40 53	014	32 55	082	49 16	130	37 44	183	60 41	247	67 11	280	39 54	331
274	41 00	012	33 26	080	49 40	128	37 43	182	60 13	245	66 40	277	39 38	329
276	41 06	010	33 57	078	50 04	127	37 42	180	59 45	244	66 09	275	39 22	327
278	41 11	007	34 27	076	50 30	125	37 43	179	59 17	242	65 38	273	39 04	324
280	41 14	005	34 57	074	50 55	124	37 44	177	58 50	241	65 07	271	38 46	322
282	41 16	002	35 26	071	51 21	122	37 46	175	58 23	239	64 36	269	38 26	320
284	41 17	000	35 56	069	51 48	120	37 49	174	57 57	238	64 05	268	38 05	318
286	41 16	358	36 24	067	52 15	119	37 52	172	57 31	236	63 34	266	37 44	315
288	41 14	355	36 53	065	52 42	117	37 57	171	57 05	235	63 03	264	37 22	313
290	41 11	353	37 21	063	53 10	116	38 02	169	56 40	233	62 33	262	36 59	311
292	41 06	351	37 48	061	53 38	114	38 09	168	56 15	232	62 02	260	36 35	309
294	41 01	348	38 15	059	54 07	112	38 15	166	55 51	230	61 31	258	36 10	307
296	40 54	346	38 41	057	54 36	111	38 23	165	55 28	229	61 01	257	35 45	304
298	40 45	343	39 07	055	55 05	109	38 32	163	55 05	227	60 31	255	35 19	302
	◆ FOMALHAUT		ACHERNAR		◆ CANOPUS		ACRUX		RIGIL KENT		◆ ANTARES		Nunki	
300	39 32	052	55 34	107	38 41	162	54 42	226	60 01	253	34 52	300	40 36	341
302	39 56	050	56 04	106	38 51	160	54 20	224	59 31	252	34 25	298	40 25	339
304	40 20	048	56 34	104	39 02	159	53 59	223	59 02	250	33 58	296	40 13	336
306	40 42	046	57 05	102	39 14	157	53 38	222	58 33	248	33 29	294	40 00	334
308	41 04	043	57 35	100	39 27	155	53 17	220	58 04	247	33 01	292	39 46	332
310	41 25	041	58 06	098	39 40	154	52 58	219	57 36	245	32 32	290	39 31	329
312	41 45	039	58 36	097	39 54	152	52 38	217	57 08	244	32 02	288	39 15	327
314	42 04	037	59 07	095	40 09	151	52 20	216	56 40	242	31 33	286	38 57	325
316	42 22	034	59 38	093	40 24	149	52 02	215	56 13	240	31 03	284	38 39	323
318	42 39	032	60 09	091	40 40	148	51 44	213	55 46	239	30 32	282	38 20	320
320	42 55	030	60 40	089	40 57	146	51 28	212	55 20	237	30 02	280	37 59	318
322	43 10	027	61 11	087	41 15	145	51 12	211	54 54	236	29 31	278	37 38	316
324	43 24	025	61 42	085	41 33	143	50 56	209	54 28	234	29 00	276	37 16	314
326	43 36	023	62 13	083	41 52	141	50 41	208	54 03	233	28 29	274	36 53	311
328	43 47	020	62 44	081	42 12	140	50 27	206	53 39	231	27 58	272	36 29	309
	◆ FOMALHAUT		ACHERNAR		◆ CANOPUS		ACRUX		RIGIL KENT		◆ ANTARES		Nunki	
330	43 58	018	63 15	079	42 32	138	50 14	205	53 15	230	27 27	270	36 05	307
332	44 06	015	63 45	077	42 53	137	50 01	204	52 51	228	26 56	268	35 40	305
334	44 14	013	64 15	075	43 15	135	49 49	202	52 28	227	26 25	266	35 14	303
336	44 20	011	64 45	072	43 37	134	49 38	201	52 06	225	25 54	264	34 48	301
338	44 25	008	65 14	070	44 00	132	49 27	200	51 44	224	25 23	262	34 21	299
340	44 29	006	65 43	068	44 23	130	49 17	198	51 23	223	24 53	260	33 53	296
342	44 31	003	66 12	065	44 47	129	49 07	197	51 02	221	24 22	258	33 25	294
344	44 32	001	66 40	063	45 12	127	48 59	195	50 42	220	23 52	257	32 57	292
346	44 32	358	67 07	060	45 37	126	48 51	194	50 23	218	23 22	255	32 28	290
348	44 31	356	67 34	058	46 02	124	48 43	193	50 04	217	22 52	253	31 58	288
350	44 28	353	68 00	055	46 28	122	48 37	191	49 45	215	22 22	251	31 29	286
352	44 24	351	68 25	053	46 55	121	48 31	190	49 28	214	21 53	249	30 59	284
354	44 18	349	68 49	050	47 22	119	48 26	189	49 11	212	21 24	247	30 29	282
356	44 11	346	69 12	047	47 49	117	48 22	187	48 54	211	20 56	245	29 58	280
358	44 03	344	69 34	044	48 17	116	48 18	186	48 39	210	20 28	244	29 27	278

LAT 76°S

LHA ♈	Hc	Zn	Hc	Zn	Hc	Zn	Hc	Zn	Hc	Zn	Hc	Zn	Hc	Zn
	◆ Diphda		◆ CANOPUS		ACRUX		RIGIL KENT		◆ ANTARES		Peacock		FOMALHAUT	
0	31 37	012	49 09	113	49 15	185	49 17	209	20 29	242	62 54	285	42 57	342
2	31 43	010	49 36	111	49 13	183	49 03	207	20 03	240	62 26	283	42 47	339
4	31 47	008	50 03	109	49 12	182	48 50	206	19 38	238	61 58	281	42 36	337
6	31 51	006	50 30	108	49 11	181	48 38	204	19 14	236	61 29	278	42 24	335
8	31 53	003	50 58	106	49 11	179	48 26	203	18 50	235	61 00	276	42 11	332
10	31 54	001	51 26	104	49 12	178	48 15	202	18 26	233	60 31	274	41 57	330
12	31 54	359	51 55	102	49 13	176	48 05	200	18 04	231	60 02	272	41 42	328
14	31 53	357	52 23	101	49 15	175	47 55	199	17 41	229	59 33	270	41 26	325
16	31 51	354	52 52	099	49 18	174	47 46	197	17 20	227	59 04	268	41 09	323
18	31 47	352	53 20	097	49 22	172	47 38	196	16 59	225	58 35	267	40 51	321
20	31 43	350	53 49	095	49 26	171	47 30	194	16 38	224	58 06	265	40 33	318
22	31 37	348	54 18	093	49 31	170	47 23	193	16 19	222	57 38	263	40 13	316
24	31 31	346	54 47	091	49 37	168	47 17	192	16 00	220	57 09	261	39 52	314
26	31 23	343	55 16	089	49 43	167	47 12	190	15 41	218	56 40	259	39 31	312
28	31 14	341	55 45	087	49 50	165	47 07	189	15 24	216	56 12	257	39 09	310
	RIGEL		◆ SIRIUS		Suhail		◆ RIGIL KENT		Peacock		◆ FOMALHAUT		Diphda	
30	17 12	051	20 41	076	38 02	118	47 03	187	55 44	256	38 46	307	31 04	339
32	17 35	049	21 09	074	38 28	117	47 00	186	55 16	254	38 23	305	30 53	337
34	17 56	047	21 37	072	38 54	115	46 57	184	54 48	252	37 59	303	30 41	334
36	18 17	045	22 04	070	39 20	113	46 55	183	54 20	250	37 34	301	30 28	332
38	18 38	043	22 31	068	39 47	111	46 54	182	53 53	249	37 09	299	30 14	330
40	18 57	041	22 58	066	40 15	109	46 54	180	53 26	247	36 44	297	29 59	328
42	19 16	039	23 24	064	40 42	108	46 54	179	53 00	245	36 17	295	29 43	326
44	19 33	037	23 50	062	41 10	106	46 55	177	52 34	244	35 51	293	29 27	324
46	19 50	035	24 15	060	41 38	104	46 57	176	52 08	242	35 24	290	29 09	321
48	20 07	033	24 40	058	42 06	102	46 59	174	51 42	240	34 56	288	28 50	319
50	20 22	031	25 05	056	42 35	100	47 02	173	51 17	239	34 29	286	28 31	317
52	20 36	028	25 28	054	43 03	098	47 06	172	50 53	237	34 01	284	28 11	315
54	20 49	026	25 51	052	43 32	097	47 11	170	50 29	235	33 32	282	27 50	313
56	21 02	024	26 14	050	44 01	095	47 16	169	50 05	234	33 04	280	27 28	311
58	21 13	022	26 35	047	44 30	093	47 22	167	49 42	232	32 35	278	27 06	309
	RIGEL		◆ SIRIUS		Suhail		◆ RIGIL KENT		Peacock		◆ FOMALHAUT		ACHERNAR	
60	21 24	020	26 56	045	44 59	091	47 29	166	49 19	231	32 07	276	67 14	306
62	21 33	018	27 17	043	45 28	089	47 37	164	48 57	229	31 38	274	66 50	303
64	21 42	016	27 36	041	45 57	087	47 45	163	48 35	228	31 09	272	66 26	301
66	21 49	014	27 55	039	46 26	085	47 54	162	48 14	226	30 40	270	66 00	298
68	21 55	012	28 13	037	46 55	083	48 03	160	47 53	224	30 11	269	65 35	296
70	22 01	009	28 30	035	47 24	081	48 13	159	47 33	223	29 42	267	65 08	293
72	22 05	007	28 46	032	47 52	079	48 24	157	47 14	221	29 13	265	64 41	291
74	22 08	005	29 01	030	48 21	077	48 36	156	46 55	220	28 44	263	64 14	289
76	22 10	003	29 15	028	48 49	075	48 48	154	46 37	218	28 15	261	63 46	286
78	22 11	001	29 28	026	49 17	073	49 01	153	46 19	217	27 47	259	63 18	284
80	22 11	359	29 40	024	49 44	071	49 14	151	46 02	215	27 18	257	62 50	282
82	22 10	357	29 52	022	50 11	068	49 28	150	45 46	214	26 50	255	62 21	280
84	22 07	354	30 02	019	50 38	066	49 43	149	45 30	212	26 22	253	61 53	278
86	22 04	352	30 11	017	51 04	064	49 59	147	45 15	211	25 54	251	61 24	276
88	22 00	350	30 19	015	51 30	062	50 15	146	45 00	209	25 27	250	60 55	274
	◆ SIRIUS		Suhail		◆ RIGIL KENT		Peacock		◆ FOMALHAUT		ACHERNAR		RIGEL	
90	30 26	013	51 56	060	50 31	144	44 46	208	25 00	248	60 26	272	21 54	348
92	30 32	011	52 20	057	50 49	143	44 33	206	24 33	246	59 57	270	21 48	346
94	30 36	008	52 44	055	51 07	141	44 21	205	24 07	244	59 28	268	21 40	344
96	30 40	006	53 08	053	51 25	140	44 09	203	23 41	242	58 59	266	21 32	342
98	30 43	004	53 31	050	51 44	138	43 58	202	23 16	240	58 30	264	21 22	340
100	30 44	002	53 53	048	52 04	137	43 48	200	22 51	239	58 01	262	21 11	337
102	30 44	359	54 14	046	52 24	135	43 38	198	22 26	237	57 33	260	21 00	335
104	30 43	357	54 34	043	52 44	134	43 30	197	22 02	235	57 04	259	20 47	333
106	30 41	355	54 53	041	53 06	132	43 22	195	21 39	233	56 36	257	20 33	331
108	30 38	353	55 12	038	53 27	131	43 14	194	21 16	231	56 07	255	20 19	329
110	30 34	350	55 29	036	53 50	129	43 07	192	20 53	229	55 39	253	20 04	327
112	30 29	348	55 46	033	54 12	128	43 02	191	20 32	228	55 12	252	19 47	325
114	30 22	346	56 01	031	54 35	126	42 56	189	20 10	226	54 44	250	19 30	323
116	30 15	344	56 15	028	54 59	125	42 52	188	19 50	224	54 17	248	19 12	321
118	30 06	342	56 28	026	55 23	123	42 48	187	19 30	222	53 50	247	18 53	319
	Suhail		◆ SPICA		RIGIL KENT		Peacock		◆ FOMALHAUT		ACHERNAR		◆ SIRIUS	
120	56 40	023	12 57	084	55 48	122	42 45	185	19 11	220	53 24	245	29 56	339
122	56 51	020	13 26	083	56 13	120	42 43	184	18 53	219	52 58	243	29 46	337
124	57 00	018	13 55	081	56 38	118	42 42	182	18 35	217	52 32	242	29 34	335
126	57 09	015	14 23	079	57 04	117	42 41	181	18 18	215	52 07	240	29 21	333
128	57 15	012	14 52	077	57 30	115	42 41	179	18 02	213	51 42	238	29 07	331
130	57 21	010	15 20	075	57 56	114	42 42	178	17 46	211	51 17	237	28 53	328
132	57 25	007	15 48	073	58 23	112	42 44	176	17 32	209	50 53	235	28 37	326
134	57 28	004	16 15	071	58 50	110	42 46	175	17 18	208	50 30	234	28 20	324
136	57 29	002	16 43	069	59 17	109	42 49	173	17 05	206	50 07	232	28 03	322
138	57 29	359	17 09	067	59 45	107	42 53	172	16 52	204	49 44	230	27 45	320
140	57 28	356	17 36	065	60 13	105	42 58	170	16 41	202	49 22	229	27 26	318
142	57 26	353	18 02	063	60 41	104	43 03	169	16 30	200	49 00	227	27 06	316
144	57 22	351	18 28	061	61 09	102	43 09	167	16 21	199	48 39	226	26 45	314
146	57 16	348	18 53	059	61 38	100	43 16	166	16 12	197	48 19	224	26 24	311
148	57 10	345	19 17	057	62 07	098	43 24	164	16 04	195	47 59	223	26 02	309
	SPICA		◆ ANTARES		Peacock		FOMALHAUT		◆ ACHERNAR		CANOPUS		◆ Suhail	
150	19 41	055	23 49	104	43 32	163	15 57	193	47 40	221	59 07	287	57 02	343
152	20 04	053	24 17	102	43 41	161	15 51	191	47 21	219	58 39	285	56 52	340
154	20 27	051	24 46	100	43 51	160	15 45	190	47 03	218	58 11	283	56 42	337
156	20 49	048	25 14	098	44 01	158	15 41	188	46 45	216	57 43	281	56 30	335
158	21 11	046	25 43	096	44 13	157	15 38	186	46 28	215	57 14	279	56 17	332
160	21 31	044	26 12	095	44 25	155	15 35	184	46 12	213	56 45	277	56 03	330
162	21 51	042	26 41	093	44 37	154	15 33	182	45 56	212	56 16	275	55 48	327
164	22 10	040	27 10	091	44 50	152	15 33	181	45 41	210	55 47	273	55 32	325
166	22 29	038	27 39	089	45 04	150	15 33	179	45 27	209	55 18	271	55 14	322
168	22 46	036	28 08	087	45 19	149	15 34	177	45 13	207	54 49	269	54 56	320
170	23 03	034	28 37	085	45 34	147	15 36	175	45 01	206	54 20	267	54 37	317
172	23 18	032	29 06	083	45 50	146	15 39	173	44 48	204	53 51	265	54 17	315
174	23 33	030	29 35	081	46 07	144	15 43	172	44 37	203	53 22	263	53 55	312
176	23 47	027	30 03	079	46 24	143	15 47	170	44 26	201	52 54	261	53 34	310
178	24 00	025	30 32	077	46 42	141	15 53	168	44 16	200	52 25	260	53 11	308

LHA ♈	Hc	Zn	Hc	Zn	Hc	Zn	Hc	Zn	Hc	Zn	Hc	Zn	Hc	Zn
	SPICA		◆ ANTARES		Nunki		FOMALHAUT		◆ ACHERNAR		CANOPUS		◆ Suhail	
180	24 12	023	31 00	075	22 09	110	15 59	166	44 06	198	51 57	258	52 48	305
182	24 23	021	31 28	073	22 36	108	16 07	164	43 57	197	51 28	256	52 24	303
184	24 33	019	31 55	071	23 04	106	16 15	162	43 49	195	51 00	254	51 59	301
186	24 42	017	32 23	069	23 32	104	16 24	161	43 42	194	50 32	252	51 34	298
188	24 49	015	32 49	067	24 00	103	16 34	159	43 35	192	50 05	251	51 08	296
190	24 56	012	33 16	065	24 28	101	16 45	157	43 30	191	49 38	249	50 42	294
192	25 02	010	33 42	063	24 57	099	16 57	155	43 25	189	49 11	247	50 15	292
194	25 07	008	34 07	060	25 26	097	17 10	153	43 20	188	48 44	245	49 48	290
196	25 10	006	34 32	058	25 55	095	17 23	152	43 17	186	48 18	244	49 20	288
198	25 13	004	34 57	056	26 24	093	17 37	150	43 14	185	47 52	242	48 53	286
200	25 14	002	35 21	054	26 53	091	17 52	148	43 12	183	47 27	240	48 24	283
202	25 14	359	35 44	052	27 22	089	18 08	146	43 10	182	47 02	239	47 56	281
204	25 13	357	36 06	050	27 51	087	18 24	144	43 10	180	46 37	237	47 28	279
206	25 12	355	36 28	048	28 20	085	18 42	143	43 10	179	46 13	235	46 59	277
208	25 09	353	36 49	045	28 48	083	19 00	141	43 11	177	45 49	234	46 30	275
	◆ ANTARES		Nunki		FOMALHAUT		◆ ACHERNAR		CANOPUS		◆ Suhail		SPICA	
210	37 10	043	29 17	081	19 18	139	43 12	176	45 26	232	46 01	273	25 04	351
212	37 29	041	29 46	079	19 38	137	43 15	174	45 03	230	45 32	271	24 59	349
214	37 48	039	30 14	077	19 58	135	43 18	173	44 41	229	45 03	269	24 53	346
216	38 05	037	30 42	075	20 18	134	43 22	171	44 20	227	44 34	268	24 46	344
218	38 22	034	31 10	073	20 40	132	43 27	170	43 59	226	44 05	266	24 37	342
220	38 38	032	31 38	071	21 02	130	43 32	169	43 38	224	43 36	264	24 28	340
222	38 53	030	32 05	069	21 24	128	43 38	167	43 18	222	43 07	262	24 17	338
224	39 07	027	32 32	067	21 47	126	43 45	166	42 59	221	42 39	260	24 06	336
226	39 20	025	32 59	065	22 11	124	43 53	164	42 40	219	42 10	258	23 54	334
228	39 32	023	33 25	063	22 35	123	44 01	163	42 22	218	41 42	256	23 40	331
230	39 42	021	33 51	061	23 00	121	44 10	161	42 05	216	41 14	254	23 26	329
232	39 52	018	34 16	059	23 25	119	44 20	160	41 48	214	40 46	253	23 11	327
234	40 01	016	34 40	057	23 51	117	44 30	158	41 32	213	40 18	251	22 54	325
236	40 08	014	35 04	055	24 17	115	44 42	157	41 17	211	39 51	249	22 37	323
238	40 14	011	35 28	052	24 43	113	44 53	155	41 02	210	39 24	247	22 19	321
	ANTARES		◆ Nunki		FOMALHAUT		◆ ACHERNAR		CANOPUS		◆ ACRUX		SPICA	
240	40 19	009	35 50	050	25 10	112	45 06	154	40 48	208	68 39	277	22 01	319
242	40 23	007	36 12	048	25 37	110	45 19	152	40 35	207	68 10	275	21 41	317
244	40 26	004	36 33	046	26 05	108	45 33	151	40 22	205	67 42	273	21 21	315
246	40 27	002	36 54	044	26 33	106	45 48	149	40 10	203	67 13	271	21 00	313
248	40 28	000	37 13	042	27 01	104	46 03	148	39 59	202	66 44	269	20 38	311
250	40 27	357	37 32	039	27 29	102	46 19	146	39 48	200	66 14	267	20 16	308
252	40 25	355	37 50	037	27 57	100	46 36	144	39 39	199	65 46	266	19 53	306
254	40 22	352	38 07	035	28 26	098	46 53	143	39 30	197	65 17	264	19 29	304
256	40 17	350	38 23	033	28 55	096	47 11	141	39 22	196	64 48	262	19 05	302
258	40 12	348	38 38	030	29 24	095	47 29	140	39 14	194	64 19	260	18 40	300
260	40 05	345	38 53	028	29 53	093	47 48	138	39 08	192	63 51	258	18 15	298
262	39 57	343	39 06	026	30 22	091	48 08	137	39 02	191	63 22	257	17 49	296
264	39 48	341	39 18	023	30 51	089	48 28	135	38 57	189	62 54	255	17 23	294
266	39 38	338	39 29	021	31 20	087	48 48	134	38 52	188	62 26	253	16 56	292
268	39 27	336	39 39	019	31 49	085	49 10	132	38 49	186	61 59	252	16 29	290
	◆ Nunki		FOMALHAUT		◆ ACHERNAR		CANOPUS		◆ ACRUX		RIGIL KENT		ANTARES	
270	39 47	016	32 18	083	49 32	131	38 46	185	61 31	250	67 28	284	39 15	334
272	39 55	014	32 46	081	49 54	129	38 44	183	61 04	248	67 00	282	39 01	332
274	40 02	012	33 15	079	50 17	127	38 43	182	60 37	247	66 31	280	38 47	329
276	40 07	009	33 43	077	50 40	126	38 42	180	60 11	245	66 03	278	38 32	327
278	40 11	007	34 11	075	51 04	124	38 43	179	59 45	244	65 34	276	38 15	325
280	40 14	005	34 39	073	51 28	123	38 44	177	59 19	242	65 05	274	37 58	323
282	40 16	002	35 07	071	51 53	121	38 46	175	58 53	240	64 36	272	37 40	320
284	40 17	000	35 34	069	52 18	119	38 48	174	58 28	239	64 07	270	37 21	318
286	40 16	358	36 01	067	52 43	118	38 52	172	58 04	237	63 38	268	37 01	316
288	40 14	355	36 27	065	53 09	116	38 56	171	57 39	236	63 09	266	36 41	314
290	40 11	353	36 53	062	53 35	114	39 01	169	57 16	234	62 40	264	36 19	311
292	40 07	351	37 19	060	54 02	113	39 07	168	56 52	233	62 11	262	35 57	309
294	40 02	348	37 44	058	54 29	111	39 14	166	56 29	231	61 42	260	35 34	307
296	39 55	346	38 08	056	54 56	109	39 21	165	56 07	230	61 14	259	35 11	305
298	39 48	344	38 32	054	55 24	108	39 29	163	55 45	228	60 45	257	34 47	303
	◆ FOMALHAUT		ACHERNAR		◆ CANOPUS		ACRUX		RIGIL KENT		◆ ANTARES		Nunki	
300	38 55	052	55 52	106	39 38	161	55 23	227	60 17	255	34 22	301	39 39	341
302	39 18	050	56 20	104	39 48	160	55 03	225	59 49	253	33 57	299	39 29	339
304	39 39	047	56 48	102	39 58	158	54 42	224	59 22	252	33 31	297	39 18	337
306	40 00	045	57 16	101	40 09	157	54 22	223	58 54	250	33 05	294	39 06	334
308	40 21	043	57 45	099	40 21	155	54 03	221	58 27	248	32 38	292	38 53	332
310	40 40	041	58 14	097	40 34	154	53 44	220	58 00	247	32 11	290	38 39	330
312	40 58	038	58 43	095	40 47	152	53 26	218	57 34	245	31 44	288	38 24	328
314	41 16	036	59 12	093	41 01	150	53 08	217	57 08	243	31 16	286	38 08	325
316	41 33	034	59 41	091	41 16	149	52 51	215	56 42	242	30 48	284	37 51	323
318	41 48	032	60 10	089	41 31	147	52 34	214	56 17	240	30 20	282	37 33	321
320	42 03	029	60 39	087	41 47	146	52 18	213	55 52	239	29 51	280	37 14	319
322	42 17	027	61 08	085	42 04	144	52 03	211	55 27	237	29 23	278	36 55	316
324	42 29	025	61 36	083	42 21	143	51 48	210	55 03	236	28 54	276	36 34	314
326	42 41	022	62 05	081	42 39	141	51 34	208	54 39	234	28 25	274	36 13	312
328	42 51	020	62 34	079	42 58	139	51 21	207	54 16	232	27 56	272	35 51	310
	◆ FOMALHAUT		ACHERNAR		◆ CANOPUS		ACRUX		RIGIL KENT		◆ ANTARES		Nunki	
330	43 00	017	63 02	077	43 17	138	51 08	206	53 53	231	27 27	270	35 29	308
332	43 09	015	63 30	075	43 37	136	50 56	204	53 31	229	26 58	269	35 05	306
334	43 15	013	63 58	073	43 57	135	50 44	203	53 09	228	26 29	267	34 41	303
336	43 21	010	64 26	070	44 18	133	50 33	201	52 48	226	26 00	265	34 17	301
338	43 26	008	64 53	068	44 40	131	50 23	200	52 27	225	25 31	263	33 52	299
340	43 29	006	65 20	066	45 02	130	50 14	199	52 07	223	25 02	261	33 26	297
342	43 32	003	65 46	063	45 24	128	50 05	197	51 47	222	24 34	259	33 00	295
344	43 32	001	66 11	061	45 47	126	49 56	196	51 28	220	24 05	257	32 34	293
346	43 32	358	66 37	058	46 11	125	49 49	194	51 09	219	23 37	255	32 07	291
348	43 31	356	67 01	056	46 35	123	49 42	193	50 52	217	23 09	253	31 39	289
350	43 28	354	67 25	053	47 00	121	49 36	192	50 34	216	22 42	251	31 12	287
352	43 24	351	67 47	051	47 25	120	49 30	190	50 17	215	22 14	250	30 44	285
354	43 19	349	68 09	048	47 50	118	49 25	189	50 01	213	21 47	248	30 16	283
356	43 13	346	68 30	045	48 16	116	49 21	187	49 46	212	21 21	246	29 47	281
358	43 06	344	68 50	042	48 42	115	49 18	186	49 31	210	20 54	244	29 19	279

LHA ♈	Hc	Zn	Hc	Zn	Hc	Zn	Hc	Zn	Hc	Zn	Hc	Zn	Hc	Zn
	◆Diphda		◆CANOPUS		ACRUX		RIGIL KENT		◆ANTARES		Peacock		FOMALHAUT	
0	30 38	012	49 32	112	50 15	185	50 09	209	20 57	242	62 38	287	42 00	342
2	30 44	010	49 57	110	50 13	183	49 56	208	20 33	241	62 12	284	41 51	340
4	30 48	008	50 22	108	50 12	182	49 44	206	20 10	239	61 46	282	41 41	337
6	30 51	006	50 48	107	50 11	181	49 32	205	19 47	237	61 19	280	41 30	335
8	30 53	003	51 14	105	50 11	179	49 21	203	19 24	235	60 53	278	41 18	333
10	30 54	001	51 40	103	50 12	178	49 11	202	19 03	233	60 26	276	41 05	330
12	30 54	359	52 07	101	50 13	176	49 01	200	18 41	231	59 59	274	40 52	328
14	30 53	357	52 33	099	50 15	175	48 52	199	18 20	229	59 32	272	40 37	326
16	30 51	355	53 00	097	50 18	174	48 43	198	18 00	228	59 05	270	40 21	324
18	30 48	352	53 27	095	50 21	172	48 35	196	17 41	226	58 38	268	40 05	321
20	30 44	350	53 54	094	50 25	171	48 28	195	17 22	224	58 11	266	39 47	319
22	30 39	348	54 21	092	50 30	169	48 22	193	17 03	222	57 44	264	39 29	317
24	30 33	346	54 48	090	50 35	168	48 16	192	16 46	220	57 17	263	39 11	315
26	30 25	343	55 15	088	50 41	166	48 11	190	16 28	218	56 51	261	38 51	312
28	30 17	341	55 42	086	50 48	165	48 06	189	16 12	216	56 24	259	38 31	310
	RIGEL		◆SIRIUS		Suhail		◆RIGIL KENT		Peacock		◆FOMALHAUT		Diphda	
30	16 35	051	20 26	076	38 30	118	48 03	187	55 58	257	38 10	308	30 08	339
32	16 55	049	20 52	074	38 54	116	47 59	186	55 32	255	37 48	306	29 58	337
34	17 15	047	21 18	072	39 19	114	47 57	184	55 06	253	37 26	304	29 47	335
36	17 35	045	21 43	070	39 44	112	47 55	183	54 40	252	37 03	302	29 35	333
38	17 54	043	22 08	068	40 09	110	47 54	182	54 14	250	36 40	299	29 22	330
40	18 12	041	22 33	066	40 34	109	47 54	180	53 49	248	36 16	297	29 08	328
42	18 29	039	22 58	064	41 00	107	47 54	179	53 24	247	35 52	295	28 54	326
44	18 45	037	23 22	062	41 26	105	47 55	177	53 00	245	35 27	293	28 38	324
46	19 01	035	23 45	060	41 52	103	47 57	176	52 35	243	35 02	291	28 22	322
48	19 16	032	24 08	057	42 18	101	47 59	174	52 11	241	34 37	289	28 05	320
50	19 30	030	24 31	055	42 45	099	48 02	173	51 48	240	34 11	287	27 47	317
52	19 43	028	24 53	053	43 12	097	48 06	171	51 25	238	33 46	285	27 28	315
54	19 56	026	25 14	051	43 38	096	48 10	170	51 02	237	33 19	283	27 09	313
56	20 07	024	25 35	049	44 05	094	48 15	168	50 40	235	32 53	281	26 49	311
58	20 18	022	25 55	047	44 32	092	48 21	167	50 18	233	32 26	279	26 28	309
	RIGEL		◆SIRIUS		Suhail		◆RIGIL KENT		Peacock		◆FOMALHAUT		ACHERNAR	
60	20 27	020	26 14	045	44 59	090	48 27	166	49 57	232	32 00	277	66 39	308
62	20 36	018	26 33	043	45 26	088	48 34	164	49 36	230	31 33	275	66 17	305
64	20 44	016	26 51	041	45 53	086	48 42	163	49 15	228	31 06	273	65 54	302
66	20 51	014	27 08	039	46 20	084	48 50	161	48 55	227	30 39	271	65 31	300
68	20 57	011	27 25	036	46 47	082	48 59	160	48 36	225	30 12	269	65 08	298
70	21 01	009	27 40	034	47 14	080	49 09	158	48 17	224	29 45	267	64 43	295
72	21 05	007	27 55	032	47 40	078	49 19	157	47 59	222	29 18	265	64 19	293
74	21 08	005	28 09	030	48 06	076	49 30	155	47 41	220	28 51	263	63 54	291
76	21 10	003	28 22	028	48 32	074	49 42	154	47 24	219	28 24	261	63 28	288
78	21 11	001	28 34	026	48 58	072	49 54	152	47 07	217	27 58	260	63 03	286
80	21 11	359	28 45	024	49 24	069	50 07	151	46 51	216	27 31	258	62 36	284
82	21 10	357	28 56	021	49 49	067	50 20	149	46 35	214	27 05	256	62 10	282
84	21 08	354	29 05	019	50 13	065	50 34	148	46 20	213	26 39	254	61 44	280
86	21 05	352	29 14	017	50 38	063	50 49	146	46 06	211	26 13	252	61 17	278
88	21 01	350	29 21	015	51 01	061	51 04	145	45 53	210	25 48	250	60 50	276
	◆SIRIUS		Suhail		◆RIGIL KENT		Peacock		◆FOMALHAUT		ACHERNAR		RIGEL	
90	29 27	013	51 25	058	51 20	143	45 40	208	25 22	248	60 23	274	20 56	348
92	29 33	010	51 47	056	51 36	142	45 27	206	24 58	246	59 56	272	20 50	346
94	29 37	008	52 10	054	51 53	140	45 16	205	24 33	244	59 29	270	20 43	344
96	29 40	006	52 31	052	52 11	139	45 04	203	24 09	243	59 02	268	20 35	342
98	29 43	004	52 52	049	52 29	137	44 54	202	23 45	241	58 35	266	20 26	340
100	29 44	002	53 12	047	52 47	136	44 44	200	23 22	239	58 08	264	20 16	338
102	29 44	359	53 31	045	53 06	134	44 35	199	22 59	237	57 42	262	20 05	335
104	29 43	357	53 50	042	53 26	133	44 27	197	22 36	235	57 15	260	19 53	333
106	29 42	355	54 08	040	53 46	131	44 19	196	22 15	233	56 48	258	19 41	331
108	29 39	353	54 24	037	54 06	130	44 12	194	21 53	232	56 22	257	19 27	329
110	29 35	351	54 40	035	54 27	128	44 06	193	21 32	230	55 56	255	19 13	327
112	29 30	348	54 55	032	54 49	127	44 00	191	21 12	228	55 30	253	18 58	325
114	29 24	346	55 09	030	55 10	125	43 56	190	20 52	226	55 04	251	18 42	323
116	29 17	344	55 22	027	55 33	124	43 51	188	20 33	224	54 39	250	18 26	321
118	29 09	342	55 34	025	55 55	122	43 48	187	20 15	222	54 14	248	18 08	319
	Suhail		◆SPICA		RIGIL KENT		Peacock		◆FOMALHAUT		ACHERNAR		◆SIRIUS	
120	55 45	022	12 51	084	56 19	120	43 45	185	19 57	221	53 49	246	29 00	340
122	55 55	020	13 18	082	56 42	119	43 43	184	19 40	219	53 24	244	28 50	337
124	56 03	017	13 45	080	57 06	117	43 42	182	19 23	217	53 00	243	28 39	335
126	56 11	015	14 12	078	57 30	115	43 41	181	19 07	215	52 36	241	28 28	333
128	56 17	012	14 38	076	57 55	114	43 41	179	18 52	213	52 13	239	28 15	331
130	56 22	009	15 04	074	58 19	112	43 42	177	18 38	211	51 50	238	28 01	329
132	56 26	007	15 30	072	58 45	110	43 44	176	18 24	210	51 27	236	27 47	327
134	56 28	004	15 55	070	59 10	109	43 46	174	18 11	208	51 05	234	27 32	324
136	56 29	001	16 21	068	59 36	107	43 49	173	17 59	206	50 43	233	27 16	322
138	56 30	359	16 46	066	60 02	105	43 53	171	17 47	204	50 22	231	26 59	320
140	56 28	356	17 10	064	60 28	104	43 57	170	17 37	202	50 01	230	26 41	318
142	56 26	354	17 34	062	60 54	102	44 02	168	17 27	201	49 41	228	26 23	316
144	56 22	351	17 58	060	61 21	100	44 08	167	17 18	199	49 21	226	26 04	314
146	56 18	348	18 21	058	61 47	098	44 14	165	17 09	197	49 02	225	25 44	312
148	56 11	346	18 44	056	62 14	096	44 21	164	17 02	195	48 43	223	25 23	310
	SPICA		◆ANTARES		Peacock		FOMALHAUT		◆ACHERNAR		CANOPUS		◆Suhail	
150	19 06	054	24 03	104	44 29	162	16 55	193	48 25	222	58 48	289	56 04	343
152	19 28	052	24 30	102	44 38	161	16 50	191	48 07	220	58 22	287	55 56	341
154	19 49	050	24 56	100	44 47	159	16 45	190	47 50	219	57 56	285	55 46	338
156	20 09	048	25 23	098	44 57	158	16 40	188	47 33	217	57 30	283	55 36	336
158	20 29	046	25 50	096	45 08	156	16 37	186	47 17	215	57 04	280	55 24	333
160	20 48	044	26 17	094	45 19	155	16 35	184	47 02	214	56 37	278	55 11	330
162	21 07	042	26 44	092	45 31	153	16 33	182	46 47	212	56 10	276	54 57	328
164	21 24	040	27 11	090	45 43	152	16 33	181	46 33	211	55 44	274	54 42	325
166	21 41	038	27 38	088	45 57	150	16 33	179	46 20	209	55 17	272	54 27	323
168	21 57	036	28 05	086	46 10	148	16 34	177	46 07	208	54 50	270	54 10	321
170	22 13	034	28 31	084	46 25	147	16 36	175	45 54	206	54 23	268	53 52	318
172	22 27	032	28 58	082	46 40	145	16 38	173	45 43	205	53 56	267	53 34	316
174	22 41	029	29 25	080	46 55	144	16 42	171	45 32	203	53 29	265	53 15	313
176	22 54	027	29 51	078	47 12	142	16 46	170	45 22	202	53 02	263	52 55	311
178	23 06	025	30 18	076	47 29	141	16 52	168	45 12	200	52 35	261	52 34	309

LAT 77°S

LHA ♈	Hc	Zn	Hc	Zn	Hc	Zn	Hc	Zn	Hc	Zn	Hc	Zn	Hc	Zn
	SPICA		◆ANTARES		Nunki		FOMALHAUT		◆ACHERNAR		CANOPUS		◆Suhail	
180	23 17	023	30 44	074	22 29	110	16 58	166	45 03	199	52 09	259	52 13	306
182	23 27	021	31 10	072	22 54	108	17 05	164	44 55	197	51 42	257	51 50	304
184	23 36	019	31 35	070	23 20	106	17 12	162	44 47	196	51 16	255	51 28	302
186	23 44	017	32 01	068	23 46	104	17 21	161	44 40	194	50 50	254	51 05	300
188	23 51	014	32 25	066	24 13	102	17 30	159	44 34	193	50 24	252	50 41	297
190	23 58	012	32 50	064	24 39	100	17 40	157	44 28	191	49 59	250	50 17	295
192	24 03	010	33 14	062	25 06	098	17 51	155	44 24	190	49 33	248	49 52	293
194	24 07	008	33 38	060	25 33	096	18 03	153	44 20	188	49 08	247	49 27	291
196	24 11	006	34 01	058	25 59	094	18 16	152	44 16	186	48 44	245	49 02	289
198	24 13	004	34 23	056	26 26	093	18 29	150	44 13	185	48 20	243	48 36	287
200	24 14	002	34 45	054	26 53	091	18 43	148	44 12	183	47 56	241	48 10	285
202	24 14	359	35 07	051	27 20	089	18 58	146	44 10	182	47 32	240	47 44	282
204	24 14	357	35 27	049	27 47	087	19 13	144	44 10	180	47 09	238	47 17	280
206	24 12	355	35 48	047	28 14	085	19 29	142	44 10	179	46 47	236	46 51	278
208	24 09	353	36 07	045	28 41	083	19 46	141	44 11	177	46 24	235	46 24	276
	◆ANTARES		Nunki		FOMALHAUT		◆ACHERNAR		CANOPUS		◆Suhail		SPICA	
210	36 26	043	29 08	081	20 03	139	44 12	176	46 03	233	45 57	274	24 05	351
212	36 44	041	29 34	079	20 22	137	44 15	174	45 41	231	45 30	272	24 00	349
214	37 01	038	30 01	077	20 40	135	44 18	173	45 20	230	45 03	270	23 55	347
216	37 17	036	30 27	075	21 00	133	44 21	171	45 00	228	44 36	269	23 48	344
218	37 33	034	30 53	073	21 20	131	44 26	170	44 40	226	44 09	267	23 40	342
220	37 47	032	31 18	071	21 40	130	44 31	168	44 21	225	43 42	265	23 31	340
222	38 01	029	31 44	069	22 01	128	44 37	167	44 02	223	43 15	263	23 22	338
224	38 14	027	32 09	067	22 23	126	44 43	165	43 44	221	42 49	261	23 11	336
226	38 25	025	32 33	065	22 45	124	44 50	164	43 27	220	42 22	259	23 00	334
228	38 36	023	32 57	062	23 08	122	44 58	162	43 10	218	41 56	257	22 47	332
230	38 46	020	33 21	060	23 31	120	45 07	161	42 53	217	41 29	255	22 34	330
232	38 55	018	33 44	058	23 54	119	45 16	159	42 38	215	41 03	253	22 20	327
234	39 03	016	34 07	056	24 18	117	45 26	158	42 22	213	40 38	252	22 05	325
236	39 10	013	34 29	054	24 42	115	45 37	156	42 08	212	40 12	250	21 49	323
238	39 15	011	34 51	052	25 07	113	45 48	155	41 54	210	39 47	248	21 33	321
	ANTARES		◆Nunki		FOMALHAUT		◆ACHERNAR		CANOPUS		◆ACRUX		SPICA	
240	39 20	009	35 12	050	25 32	111	46 00	153	41 41	209	68 30	280	21 15	319
242	39 24	006	35 32	048	25 57	109	46 12	152	41 28	207	68 04	278	20 57	317
244	39 26	004	35 51	045	26 23	107	46 25	150	41 16	205	67 37	276	20 39	315
246	39 28	002	36 10	043	26 49	105	46 39	148	41 05	204	67 10	274	20 19	313
248	39 28	000	36 28	041	27 15	104	46 54	147	40 55	202	66 43	272	19 59	311
250	39 27	357	36 46	039	27 41	102	47 09	145	40 45	201	66 16	270	19 38	309
252	39 25	355	37 02	037	28 08	100	47 24	144	40 36	199	65 49	268	19 17	307
254	39 22	353	37 18	034	28 35	098	47 40	142	40 27	197	65 22	266	18 55	305
256	39 18	350	37 33	032	29 01	096	47 57	141	40 19	196	64 55	264	18 33	303
258	39 13	348	37 47	030	29 28	094	48 15	139	40 12	194	64 28	262	18 10	301
260	39 07	346	38 00	028	29 55	092	48 33	138	40 06	193	64 02	260	17 46	299
262	39 00	343	38 12	025	30 22	090	48 51	136	40 01	191	63 35	259	17 22	297
264	38 51	341	38 23	023	30 49	088	49 10	134	39 56	190	63 09	257	16 58	295
266	38 42	339	38 33	021	31 16	086	49 30	133	39 52	188	62 43	255	16 33	293
268	38 32	336	38 42	019	31 43	084	49 50	131	39 48	186	62 17	253	16 08	291
	◆Nunki		FOMALHAUT		◆ACHERNAR		CANOPUS		◆ACRUX		RIGIL KENT		ANTARES	
270	38 50	016	32 10	082	50 10	130	39 46	185	61 51	252	67 12	286	38 21	334
272	38 57	014	32 36	080	50 31	128	39 44	183	61 25	250	66 46	284	38 08	332
274	39 03	012	33 03	078	50 53	126	39 43	182	61 00	248	66 20	282	37 55	330
276	39 08	009	33 29	076	51 15	125	39 42	180	60 35	247	65 54	280	37 41	327
278	39 12	007	33 55	074	51 37	123	39 43	178	60 11	245	65 27	278	37 26	325
280	39 14	005	34 21	072	52 00	122	39 44	177	59 46	243	65 00	276	37 10	323
282	39 16	002	34 47	070	52 23	120	39 46	175	59 22	242	64 33	274	36 54	321
284	39 17	000	35 12	068	52 47	118	39 48	174	58 59	240	64 06	272	36 36	319
286	39 16	358	35 37	066	53 11	117	39 51	172	58 35	239	63 39	270	36 18	316
288	39 14	355	36 01	064	53 35	115	39 55	171	58 12	237	63 12	268	35 59	314
290	39 12	353	36 25	062	54 00	113	40 00	169	57 50	236	62 45	266	35 39	312
292	39 08	351	36 49	060	54 25	111	40 06	167	57 28	234	62 18	264	35 19	310
294	39 03	348	37 12	058	54 50	110	40 12	166	57 06	233	61 52	262	34 58	308
296	38 57	346	37 35	055	55 15	108	40 19	164	56 45	231	61 25	260	34 36	306
298	38 50	344	37 56	053	55 41	106	40 27	163	56 24	230	60 58	259	34 14	303
	◆FOMALHAUT		ACHERNAR		◆CANOPUS		ACRUX		RIGIL KENT		◆ANTARES		Nunki	
300	38 18	051	56 07	104	40 35	161	56 04	228	60 32	257	33 51	301	38 42	342
302	38 38	049	56 33	103	40 44	160	55 44	227	60 06	255	33 28	299	38 33	339
304	38 59	047	57 00	101	40 54	158	55 25	225	59 40	253	33 04	297	38 23	337
306	39 18	045	57 26	099	41 04	156	55 06	224	59 14	252	32 40	295	38 12	335
308	39 36	042	57 53	097	41 15	155	54 48	222	58 49	250	32 15	293	38 00	332
310	39 54	040	58 20	095	41 27	153	54 30	221	58 23	248	31 50	291	37 47	330
312	40 11	038	58 47	093	41 40	152	54 13	219	57 59	246	31 25	289	37 33	328
314	40 27	036	59 14	091	41 53	150	53 56	218	57 34	245	30 59	287	37 19	326
316	40 43	033	59 41	090	42 07	148	53 40	216	57 10	243	30 33	285	37 03	324
318	40 57	031	60 08	088	42 21	147	53 24	215	56 46	242	30 07	283	36 47	321
320	41 10	029	60 35	086	42 36	145	53 09	213	56 22	240	29 40	281	36 29	319
322	41 23	026	61 02	084	42 52	144	52 54	212	55 59	238	29 14	279	36 11	317
324	41 34	024	61 28	081	43 08	142	52 40	210	55 36	237	28 47	277	35 52	315
326	41 45	022	61 55	079	43 25	140	52 27	209	55 14	235	28 20	275	35 33	313
328	41 55	020	62 22	077	43 43	139	52 14	208	54 52	234	27 53	273	35 13	310
	◆FOMALHAUT		ACHERNAR		◆CANOPUS		ACRUX		RIGIL KENT		◆ANTARES		Nunki	
330	42 03	017	62 48	075	44 01	137	52 02	206	54 31	232	27 26	271	34 52	308
332	42 11	015	63 14	073	44 20	135	51 50	205	54 09	230	26 59	269	34 30	306
334	42 17	013	63 39	071	44 39	134	51 39	203	53 49	229	26 32	267	34 08	304
336	42 22	010	64 05	068	44 59	132	51 29	202	53 29	227	26 05	265	33 45	302
338	42 26	008	64 30	066	45 19	131	51 19	200	53 09	226	25 39	263	33 22	300
340	42 30	005	64 54	064	45 40	129	51 10	199	52 50	224	25 12	261	32 59	298
342	42 32	003	65 18	061	46 01	127	51 02	198	52 31	223	24 45	259	32 34	296
344	42 32	001	65 41	059	46 23	126	50 54	196	52 13	221	24 19	257	32 10	294
346	42 32	358	66 04	056	46 45	124	50 47	195	51 56	220	23 52	256	31 45	291
348	42 31	356	66 26	054	47 08	122	50 40	193	51 39	218	23 26	254	31 20	289
350	42 29	354	66 48	051	47 31	120	50 34	192	51 22	217	23 01	252	30 54	287
352	42 25	351	67 08	049	47 54	119	50 29	190	51 07	215	22 35	250	30 28	285
354	42 20	349	67 28	046	48 18	117	50 25	189	50 51	214	22 10	248	30 02	283
356	42 15	347	67 47	043	48 42	115	50 21	188	50 37	212	21 45	246	29 36	281
358	42 08	344	68 05	041	49 07	114	50 17	186	50 22	211	21 21	244	29 09	279

LHA ♈	Hc	Zn	Hc	Zn	Hc	Zn	Hc	Zn	Hc	Zn	Hc	Zn	Hc	Zn
	◆ Diphda		◆ CANOPUS		ACRUX		RIGIL KENT		◆ ANTARES		Peacock		FOMALHAUT	
0	29 40	012	49 53	111	51 15	185	51 01	210	21 24	243	62 20	289	41 03	342
2	29 44	010	50 17	109	51 13	183	50 49	208	21 02	241	61 56	286	40 55	340
4	29 48	008	50 41	107	51 12	182	50 37	207	20 41	239	61 32	284	40 46	338
6	29 51	006	51 05	105	51 11	181	50 26	205	20 19	237	61 08	282	40 36	335
8	29 53	003	51 29	104	51 11	179	50 16	204	19 59	235	60 43	280	40 25	333
10	29 54	001	51 53	102	51 12	178	50 06	202	19 38	233	60 19	278	40 13	331
12	29 54	359	52 18	100	51 13	176	49 57	201	19 19	231	59 54	276	40 01	329
14	29 53	357	52 42	098	51 15	175	49 48	199	18 59	230	59 29	274	39 47	326
16	29 51	355	53 07	096	51 17	173	49 40	198	18 41	228	59 04	272	39 33	324
18	29 49	352	53 32	094	51 21	172	49 33	196	18 22	226	58 39	270	39 18	322
20	29 45	350	53 57	092	51 24	171	49 26	195	18 05	224	58 14	268	39 02	320
22	29 40	348	54 22	090	51 29	169	49 20	193	17 48	222	57 49	266	38 45	317
24	29 34	346	54 47	088	51 34	168	49 15	192	17 31	220	57 24	264	38 28	315
26	29 28	344	55 12	086	51 40	166	49 10	190	17 15	218	57 00	262	38 10	313
28	29 20	341	55 36	084	51 46	165	49 06	189	17 00	217	56 35	260	37 52	311
	RIGEL		◆ SIRIUS		Suhail		◆ RIGIL KENT		Peacock		◆ FOMALHAUT		Diphda	
30	15 57	051	20 11	075	38 58	117	49 02	188	56 11	258	37 33	309	29 12	339
32	16 16	049	20 35	073	39 20	115	48 59	186	55 46	257	37 13	306	29 03	337
34	16 34	047	20 59	071	39 43	113	48 57	185	55 22	255	36 52	304	28 53	335
36	16 52	045	21 22	069	40 06	111	48 55	183	54 58	253	36 32	302	28 42	333
38	17 10	043	21 45	067	40 29	110	48 54	182	54 34	251	36 10	300	28 30	331
40	17 26	041	22 08	065	40 53	108	48 54	180	54 11	250	35 48	298	28 17	329
42	17 42	039	22 31	063	41 17	106	48 54	179	53 47	248	35 26	296	28 04	326
44	17 57	036	22 53	061	41 41	104	48 55	177	53 25	246	35 04	294	27 50	324
46	18 12	034	23 14	059	42 05	102	48 56	176	53 02	244	34 41	292	27 35	322
48	18 25	032	23 36	057	42 30	100	48 59	174	52 40	243	34 17	290	27 19	320
50	18 38	030	23 56	055	42 54	098	49 02	173	52 18	241	33 54	288	27 03	318
52	18 50	028	24 17	053	43 19	097	49 05	171	51 56	239	33 30	286	26 45	316
54	19 02	026	24 36	051	43 44	095	49 09	170	51 35	238	33 06	284	26 28	314
56	19 12	024	24 55	049	44 09	093	49 14	168	51 14	236	32 41	282	26 09	312
58	19 22	022	25 14	047	44 34	091	49 19	167	50 53	234	32 17	280	25 50	309
	RIGEL		◆ SIRIUS		Suhail		◆ RIGIL KENT		Peacock		◆ FOMALHAUT		ACHERNAR	
60	19 31	020	25 32	045	44 59	089	49 25	165	50 33	233	31 52	278	66 01	309
62	19 39	018	25 49	043	45 23	087	49 32	164	50 14	231	31 27	276	65 42	307
64	19 46	016	26 05	040	45 48	085	49 39	162	49 55	229	31 02	274	65 21	304
66	19 52	013	26 21	038	46 13	083	49 47	161	49 36	228	30 37	272	65 00	302
68	19 58	011	26 36	036	46 38	081	49 56	159	49 18	226	30 12	270	64 39	299
70	20 02	009	26 51	034	47 02	079	50 05	158	49 00	224	29 48	268	64 17	297
72	20 06	007	27 04	032	47 27	077	50 14	156	48 43	223	29 23	266	63 55	295
74	20 08	005	27 17	030	47 51	075	50 25	155	48 26	221	28 58	264	63 32	292
76	20 10	003	27 29	028	48 15	073	50 36	153	48 10	220	28 33	262	63 09	290
78	20 11	001	27 40	025	48 39	070	50 47	152	47 54	218	28 08	260	62 45	288
80	20 11	359	27 50	023	49 02	068	50 59	150	47 39	216	27 44	258	62 21	286
82	20 10	357	28 00	021	49 25	066	51 12	149	47 25	215	27 20	256	61 57	284
84	20 08	355	28 08	019	49 48	064	51 25	147	47 11	213	26 55	254	61 33	282
86	20 05	352	28 16	017	50 10	062	51 39	146	46 57	212	26 32	252	61 08	279
88	20 01	350	28 23	015	50 32	060	51 53	144	46 45	210	26 08	251	60 43	277
	◆ SIRIUS		Suhail		◆ RIGIL KENT		Peacock		◆ FOMALHAUT		ACHERNAR		RIGEL	
90	28 29	012	50 53	057	52 08	143	46 32	209	25 45	249	60 19	275	19 57	348
92	28 34	010	51 14	055	52 23	141	46 21	207	25 21	247	59 54	273	19 51	346
94	28 38	008	51 34	053	52 39	140	46 10	205	24 59	245	59 29	271	19 45	344
96	28 41	006	51 53	051	52 56	138	45 59	204	24 36	243	59 04	269	19 38	342
98	28 43	004	52 12	048	53 12	137	45 50	202	24 14	241	58 39	267	19 29	340
100	28 44	002	52 31	046	53 30	135	45 41	201	23 53	239	58 14	266	19 20	338
102	28 44	359	52 48	044	53 48	133	45 32	199	23 31	237	57 49	264	19 10	336
104	28 43	357	53 05	041	54 06	132	45 24	198	23 11	236	57 24	262	19 00	334
106	28 42	355	53 21	039	54 25	130	45 17	196	22 50	234	57 00	260	18 48	331
108	28 39	353	53 36	037	54 44	129	45 10	194	22 30	232	56 35	258	18 36	329
110	28 36	351	53 51	034	55 04	127	45 05	193	22 11	230	56 11	256	18 23	327
112	28 31	348	54 04	032	55 24	126	44 59	191	21 52	228	55 47	254	18 09	325
114	28 26	346	54 17	029	55 44	124	44 55	190	21 34	226	55 23	253	17 54	323
116	28 19	344	54 29	027	56 05	122	44 51	188	21 16	224	54 59	251	17 39	321
118	28 12	342	54 40	024	56 27	121	44 48	187	20 59	223	54 36	249	17 23	319
	Suhail		◆ SPICA		RIGIL KENT		Peacock		◆ FOMALHAUT		ACHERNAR		◆ SIRIUS	
120	54 49	022	12 45	084	56 48	119	44 45	185	20 42	221	54 13	247	28 04	340
122	54 58	019	13 10	082	57 10	117	44 43	184	20 26	219	53 50	246	27 55	338
124	55 06	017	13 35	080	57 33	116	44 42	182	20 11	217	53 27	244	27 45	335
126	55 12	014	13 59	078	57 55	114	44 41	181	19 56	215	53 05	242	27 34	333
128	55 18	012	14 24	076	58 18	112	44 41	179	19 42	213	52 43	241	27 22	331
130	55 23	009	14 48	074	58 41	111	44 42	177	19 29	212	52 21	239	27 10	329
132	55 26	007	15 12	072	59 05	109	44 43	176	19 16	210	52 00	237	26 57	327
134	55 28	004	15 35	070	59 29	107	44 46	174	19 04	208	51 40	236	26 43	325
136	55 29	001	15 59	068	59 53	105	44 48	173	18 53	206	51 19	234	26 28	323
138	55 30	359	16 22	066	60 17	104	44 52	171	18 42	204	50 59	232	26 13	321
140	55 28	356	16 44	064	60 41	102	44 56	170	18 32	202	50 40	231	25 56	318
142	55 26	354	17 06	062	61 06	100	45 01	168	18 23	201	50 21	229	25 39	316
144	55 23	351	17 28	060	61 30	098	45 06	167	18 14	199	50 02	227	25 22	314
146	55 19	349	17 50	058	61 55	096	45 12	165	18 07	197	49 44	226	25 04	312
148	55 13	346	18 11	056	62 20	094	45 19	164	18 00	195	49 26	224	24 45	310
	SPICA		◆ ANTARES		Peacock		FOMALHAUT		◆ ACHERNAR		CANOPUS		◆ Suhail	
150	18 31	054	24 17	103	45 26	162	17 54	193	49 09	222	58 28	291	55 07	344
152	18 51	052	24 42	101	45 34	160	17 48	192	48 53	221	58 04	288	54 59	341
154	19 10	050	25 06	099	45 43	159	17 44	190	48 37	219	57 40	286	54 51	339
156	19 29	048	25 31	097	45 52	157	17 40	188	48 21	218	57 16	284	54 41	336
158	19 47	046	25 56	096	46 02	156	17 37	186	48 06	216	56 52	282	54 30	334
160	20 05	044	26 21	094	46 13	154	17 35	184	47 52	215	56 28	280	54 19	331
162	20 22	042	26 46	092	46 24	153	17 33	182	47 38	213	56 03	278	54 06	329
164	20 38	040	27 10	090	46 36	151	17 33	181	47 24	211	55 38	276	53 53	326
166	20 54	038	27 35	088	46 48	149	17 33	179	47 12	210	55 13	274	53 39	324
168	21 09	035	28 00	086	47 01	148	17 34	177	47 00	208	54 48	272	53 23	321
170	21 23	033	28 25	084	47 15	146	17 35	175	46 48	207	54 23	270	53 07	319
172	21 36	031	28 50	082	47 29	145	17 38	173	46 37	205	53 59	268	52 51	317
174	21 49	029	29 15	080	47 44	143	17 41	171	46 27	204	53 34	266	52 33	314
176	22 00	027	29 39	078	47 59	142	17 45	170	46 17	202	53 09	264	52 15	312
178	22 11	025	30 03	076	48 15	140	17 50	168	46 08	200	52 44	262	51 56	310

LAT 78°S

LHA ♈	Hc	Zn	Hc	Zn	Hc	Zn	Hc	Zn	Hc	Zn	Hc	Zn	Hc	Zn
	SPICA		◆ ANTARES		Nunki		FOMALHAUT		◆ ACHERNAR		CANOPUS		◆ Suhail	
180	22 21	023	30 27	074	22 49	109	17 56	166	46 00	199	52 19	260	51 37	307
182	22 31	021	30 51	072	23 13	107	18 02	164	45 52	197	51 55	258	51 16	305
184	22 39	019	31 15	070	23 37	106	18 10	162	45 45	196	51 30	257	50 56	303
186	22 47	017	31 38	068	24 01	104	18 18	160	45 38	194	51 06	255	50 35	301
188	22 53	014	32 01	066	24 25	102	18 26	159	45 33	193	50 42	253	50 13	298
190	22 59	012	32 23	064	24 50	100	18 36	157	45 27	191	50 19	251	49 51	296
192	23 04	010	32 46	061	25 14	098	18 46	155	45 23	190	49 55	249	49 28	294
194	23 08	008	33 07	059	25 39	096	18 57	153	45 19	188	49 32	248	49 05	292
196	23 11	006	33 28	057	26 04	094	19 08	151	45 16	187	49 09	246	48 42	290
198	23 13	004	33 49	055	26 29	092	19 21	150	45 13	185	48 46	244	48 18	288
200	23 14	002	34 09	053	26 54	090	19 34	148	45 11	184	48 24	242	47 54	286
202	23 14	359	34 29	051	27 19	088	19 47	146	45 10	182	48 02	241	47 30	284
204	23 14	357	34 48	049	27 44	086	20 02	144	45 10	180	47 41	239	47 06	282
206	23 12	355	35 06	047	28 08	084	20 17	142	45 10	179	47 19	237	46 41	279
208	23 09	353	35 24	044	28 33	082	20 32	140	45 11	177	46 59	235	46 17	277
	◆ ANTARES		Nunki		FOMALHAUT		◆ ACHERNAR		CANOPUS		◆ Suhail		SPICA	
210	35 41	042	28 58	080	20 49	139	45 12	176	46 38	234	45 52	275	23 06	351
212	35 58	040	29 22	078	21 05	137	45 14	174	46 18	232	45 27	273	23 02	349
214	36 14	038	29 47	076	21 23	135	45 17	173	45 59	230	45 02	271	22 56	347
216	36 28	036	30 11	074	21 41	133	45 21	171	45 40	229	44 37	270	22 50	345
218	36 43	033	30 35	072	21 59	131	45 25	170	45 21	227	44 12	268	22 43	342
220	36 56	031	30 58	070	22 18	129	45 30	168	45 03	225	43 47	266	22 35	340
222	37 08	029	31 22	068	22 38	127	45 35	167	44 46	224	43 22	264	22 26	338
224	37 20	027	31 45	066	22 58	126	45 41	165	44 29	222	42 58	262	22 16	336
226	37 31	025	32 07	064	23 18	124	45 48	163	44 13	220	42 33	260	22 06	334
228	37 41	022	32 29	062	23 39	122	45 55	162	43 57	219	42 08	258	21 55	332
230	37 50	020	32 51	060	24 01	120	46 03	160	43 41	217	41 44	256	21 42	330
232	37 58	018	33 13	058	24 23	118	46 12	159	43 27	215	41 20	254	21 29	328
234	38 05	015	33 33	056	24 45	116	46 21	157	43 12	214	40 56	252	21 16	326
236	38 11	013	33 54	053	25 07	114	46 31	156	42 59	212	40 32	251	21 01	323
238	38 16	011	34 13	051	25 30	113	46 42	154	42 46	211	40 09	249	20 46	321
	ANTARES		◆ Nunki		FOMALHAUT		◆ ACHERNAR		CANOPUS		◆ ACRUX		SPICA	
240	38 21	009	34 33	049	25 53	111	46 53	153	42 33	209	68 19	282	20 30	319
242	38 24	006	34 51	047	26 17	109	47 05	151	42 22	207	67 54	280	20 13	317
244	38 26	004	35 09	045	26 41	107	47 17	149	42 10	206	67 30	278	19 56	315
246	38 28	002	35 26	043	27 05	105	47 30	148	42 00	204	67 05	276	19 38	313
248	38 28	000	35 43	041	27 29	103	47 44	146	41 50	203	66 40	274	19 20	311
250	38 27	357	35 59	038	27 53	101	47 58	145	41 41	201	66 15	272	19 01	309
252	38 25	355	36 14	036	28 18	099	48 12	143	41 32	199	65 50	270	18 41	307
254	38 23	353	36 28	034	28 42	097	48 28	142	41 24	198	65 25	268	18 21	305
256	38 19	350	36 42	032	29 07	095	48 43	140	41 17	196	65 00	266	18 00	303
258	38 14	348	36 54	030	29 32	093	49 00	138	41 11	194	64 35	264	17 39	301
260	38 09	346	37 06	027	29 57	092	49 17	137	41 05	193	64 11	262	17 17	299
262	38 02	344	37 17	025	30 22	090	49 34	135	40 59	191	63 46	261	16 55	297
264	37 55	341	37 27	023	30 47	088	49 52	134	40 55	190	63 21	259	16 33	295
266	37 46	339	37 37	021	31 12	086	50 10	132	40 51	188	62 57	257	16 10	293
268	37 37	337	37 45	018	31 37	084	50 29	130	40 48	186	62 33	255	15 47	291
	◆ Nunki		FOMALHAUT		◆ ACHERNAR		CANOPUS		◆ ACRUX		RIGIL KENT		ANTARES	
270	37 52	016	32 01	082	50 48	129	40 45	185	62 09	253	66 54	289	37 27	335
272	37 59	014	32 26	080	51 08	127	40 44	183	61 45	252	66 31	286	37 15	332
274	38 04	011	32 50	078	51 28	125	40 43	182	61 21	250	66 06	284	37 03	330
276	38 09	009	33 15	076	51 48	124	40 42	180	60 58	248	65 42	282	36 50	328
278	38 12	007	33 39	074	52 09	122	40 43	178	60 35	247	65 18	280	36 37	326
280	38 15	005	34 03	072	52 31	120	40 44	177	60 12	245	64 53	278	36 22	323
282	38 16	002	34 26	069	52 52	119	40 45	175	59 50	243	64 28	276	36 07	321
284	38 17	000	34 49	067	53 14	117	40 48	174	59 28	242	64 03	274	35 51	319
286	38 16	358	35 12	065	53 37	115	40 51	172	59 06	240	63 38	272	35 34	317
288	38 15	355	35 35	063	54 00	114	40 55	170	58 44	239	63 14	270	35 17	315
290	38 12	353	35 57	061	54 23	112	40 59	169	58 23	237	62 49	268	34 59	313
292	38 09	351	36 18	059	54 46	110	41 04	167	58 03	235	62 24	266	34 40	310
294	38 04	349	36 40	057	55 09	108	41 10	166	57 42	234	61 59	264	34 21	308
296	37 59	346	37 00	055	55 33	107	41 17	164	57 22	232	61 34	262	34 01	306
298	37 53	344	37 20	053	55 57	105	41 24	162	57 03	231	61 09	260	33 41	304
	◆ FOMALHAUT		ACHERNAR		◆ CANOPUS		ACRUX		RIGIL KENT		◆ ANTARES		Nunki	
300	37 40	051	56 21	103	41 32	161	56 44	229	60 45	258	33 20	302	37 45	342
302	37 59	048	56 46	101	41 40	159	56 25	228	60 21	257	32 58	300	37 37	340
304	38 17	046	57 10	099	41 49	158	56 07	226	59 56	255	32 36	298	37 28	337
306	38 35	044	57 35	097	41 59	156	55 49	225	59 32	253	32 14	296	37 18	335
308	38 52	042	58 00	096	42 10	154	55 32	223	59 09	251	31 51	294	37 07	333
310	39 08	040	58 25	094	42 21	153	55 15	222	58 45	250	31 28	292	36 55	331
312	39 24	037	58 50	092	42 32	151	54 59	220	58 22	248	31 05	289	36 42	328
314	39 38	035	59 15	090	42 45	150	54 43	219	57 59	246	30 41	287	36 29	326
316	39 52	033	59 40	088	42 58	148	54 28	217	57 36	245	30 17	285	36 15	324
318	40 05	031	60 04	086	43 11	146	54 13	216	57 14	243	29 53	283	36 00	322
320	40 18	028	60 29	084	43 25	145	53 59	214	56 52	241	29 29	281	35 44	320
322	40 29	026	60 54	082	43 40	143	53 45	213	56 30	240	29 04	279	35 27	317
324	40 40	024	61 19	080	43 56	141	53 32	211	56 09	238	28 40	277	35 10	315
326	40 49	022	61 43	078	44 11	140	53 19	210	55 48	236	28 15	275	34 52	313
328	40 58	019	62 07	075	44 28	138	53 07	208	55 27	235	27 50	273	34 34	311
	◆ FOMALHAUT		ACHERNAR		◆ CANOPUS		ACRUX		RIGIL KENT		◆ ANTARES		Nunki	
330	41 06	017	62 31	073	44 45	136	52 56	207	55 07	233	27 25	271	34 14	309
332	41 13	015	62 55	071	45 02	135	52 45	205	54 47	232	27 00	270	33 55	307
334	41 18	012	63 19	069	45 20	133	52 35	204	54 28	230	26 35	268	33 34	305
336	41 23	010	63 42	067	45 39	131	52 25	202	54 09	228	26 10	266	33 14	302
338	41 27	008	64 04	064	45 58	130	52 16	201	53 51	227	25 45	264	32 52	300
340	41 30	005	64 27	062	46 17	128	52 07	199	53 33	225	25 21	262	32 30	298
342	41 32	003	64 48	060	46 37	126	51 59	198	53 15	224	24 56	260	32 08	296
344	41 32	001	65 10	057	46 57	125	51 52	196	52 58	222	24 32	258	31 46	294
346	41 32	358	65 30	055	47 18	123	51 45	195	52 42	221	24 07	256	31 23	292
348	41 31	356	65 50	052	47 39	121	51 39	194	52 26	219	23 43	254	30 59	290
350	41 29	354	66 10	050	48 01	120	51 33	192	52 10	218	23 19	252	30 36	288
352	41 26	351	66 28	047	48 22	118	51 28	191	51 55	216	22 56	250	30 12	286
354	41 21	349	66 46	044	48 45	116	51 24	189	51 41	214	22 32	248	29 48	284
356	41 16	347	67 03	042	49 07	114	51 20	188	51 27	213	22 09	247	29 24	282
358	41 10	344	67 19	039	49 30	113	51 17	186	51 14	211	21 47	245	28 59	280

LAT 79°S

LHA ♈	Hc	Zn	Hc	Zn	Hc	Zn	Hc	Zn	Hc	Zn	Hc	Zn	Hc	Zn
	◆ Diphda		◆ CANOPUS		ACRUX		RIGIL KENT		◆ ANTARES		Peacock		FOMALHAUT	
0	28 41	012	50 14	110	52 14	185	51 53	211	21 51	243	62 00	290	40 06	342
2	28 45	010	50 36	108	52 13	184	51 42	209	21 31	241	61 38	288	39 58	340
4	28 49	008	50 58	106	52 12	182	51 31	207	21 11	239	61 17	286	39 50	338
6	28 51	006	51 20	104	52 11	181	51 21	206	20 52	237	60 54	284	39 41	336
8	28 53	003	51 42	102	52 11	179	51 11	204	20 33	236	60 32	282	39 31	333
10	28 54	001	52 05	100	52 12	178	51 02	203	20 14	234	60 10	280	39 21	331
12	28 54	359	52 27	099	52 13	176	50 53	201	19 56	232	59 47	278	39 09	329
14	28 53	357	52 50	097	52 15	175	50 45	200	19 38	230	59 24	275	38 57	327
16	28 52	355	53 13	095	52 17	173	50 37	198	19 21	228	59 01	273	38 44	324
18	28 49	352	53 35	093	52 20	172	50 31	197	19 04	226	58 38	271	38 30	322
20	28 46	350	53 58	091	52 24	170	50 24	195	18 48	224	58 16	270	38 16	320
22	28 41	348	54 21	089	52 28	169	50 19	194	18 32	222	57 53	268	38 01	318
24	28 36	346	54 44	087	52 32	167	50 13	192	18 17	221	57 30	266	37 45	316
26	28 30	344	55 07	085	52 38	166	50 09	191	18 02	219	57 07	264	37 29	314
28	28 24	342	55 30	083	52 44	164	50 05	189	17 48	217	56 44	262	37 12	311
	RIGEL		◆ SIRIUS		Suhail		◆ RIGIL KENT		Peacock		◆ FOMALHAUT		Diphda	
30	15 19	051	19 56	075	39 24	116	50 02	188	56 22	260	36 55	309	28 16	339
32	15 36	049	20 18	073	39 45	114	49 59	186	55 59	258	36 37	307	28 07	337
34	15 53	046	20 39	071	40 06	113	49 57	185	55 37	256	36 18	305	27 58	335
36	16 10	044	21 01	069	40 27	111	49 55	183	55 15	254	35 59	303	27 48	333
38	16 25	042	21 22	067	40 49	109	49 54	182	54 53	253	35 40	301	27 38	331
40	16 40	040	21 43	065	41 11	107	49 54	180	54 31	251	35 20	299	27 26	329
42	16 55	038	22 04	063	41 33	105	49 54	179	54 10	249	35 00	297	27 14	327
44	17 09	036	22 24	061	41 55	103	49 55	177	53 48	247	34 39	294	27 01	325
46	17 22	034	22 44	059	42 17	101	49 56	176	53 27	246	34 18	292	26 47	322
48	17 35	032	23 03	057	42 40	099	49 58	174	53 07	244	33 57	290	26 33	320
50	17 46	030	23 22	055	43 03	098	50 01	173	52 46	242	33 35	288	26 18	318
52	17 57	028	23 40	053	43 25	096	50 04	171	52 26	240	33 13	286	26 02	316
54	18 08	026	23 58	051	43 48	094	50 08	170	52 06	239	32 51	284	25 46	314
56	18 17	024	24 16	048	44 11	092	50 13	168	51 47	237	32 29	282	25 29	312
58	18 26	022	24 32	046	44 34	090	50 18	167	51 28	235	32 06	280	25 12	310
	RIGEL		◆ SIRIUS		Suhail		◆ RIGIL KENT		Peacock		◆ FOMALHAUT		ACHERNAR	
60	18 34	020	24 49	044	44 57	088	50 23	165	51 09	234	31 44	278	65 23	311
62	18 42	018	25 04	042	45 20	086	50 30	163	50 51	232	31 21	276	65 05	309
64	18 48	016	25 20	040	45 42	084	50 36	162	50 33	230	30 58	274	64 47	306
66	18 54	013	25 34	038	46 05	082	50 44	160	50 16	229	30 35	272	64 28	304
68	18 59	011	25 48	036	46 28	080	50 52	159	49 59	227	30 12	270	64 09	301
70	19 03	009	26 01	034	46 50	078	51 00	157	49 43	225	29 50	268	63 49	299
72	19 06	007	26 13	032	47 12	076	51 09	156	49 27	224	29 27	266	63 29	297
74	19 09	005	26 25	030	47 35	074	51 19	154	49 11	222	29 04	264	63 08	294
76	19 10	003	26 36	027	47 56	072	51 29	153	48 56	220	28 41	262	62 47	292
78	19 11	001	26 46	025	48 18	069	51 40	151	48 41	219	28 19	261	62 26	290
80	19 11	359	26 55	023	48 39	067	51 51	150	48 27	217	27 56	259	62 04	288
82	19 10	357	27 04	021	49 00	065	52 03	148	48 14	215	27 34	257	61 42	285
84	19 08	355	27 12	019	49 21	063	52 15	147	48 01	214	27 11	255	61 20	283
86	19 06	352	27 19	017	49 41	061	52 28	145	47 48	212	26 49	253	60 57	281
88	19 02	350	27 25	015	50 01	059	52 42	143	47 36	211	26 28	251	60 35	279
	◆ SIRIUS		Suhail		◆ RIGIL KENT		Peacock		◆ FOMALHAUT		ACHERNAR		RIGEL	
90	27 30	012	50 20	056	52 55	142	47 25	209	26 06	249	60 12	277	18 58	348
92	27 35	010	50 39	054	53 10	140	47 14	207	25 45	247	59 49	275	18 53	346
94	27 38	008	50 57	052	53 25	139	47 04	206	25 24	245	59 26	273	18 47	344
96	27 41	006	51 15	050	53 40	137	46 54	204	25 03	243	59 04	271	18 40	342
98	27 43	004	51 32	047	53 56	136	46 45	203	24 43	242	58 41	269	18 33	340
100	27 44	002	51 49	045	54 12	134	46 37	201	24 23	240	58 18	267	18 25	338
102	27 44	359	52 05	043	54 29	132	46 29	199	24 03	238	57 55	265	18 16	336
104	27 44	357	52 20	040	54 46	131	46 21	198	23 44	236	57 32	263	18 06	334
106	27 42	355	52 34	038	55 03	129	46 15	196	23 26	234	57 10	261	17 55	332
108	27 40	353	52 48	036	55 21	128	46 08	195	23 07	232	56 47	260	17 44	330
110	27 36	351	53 01	033	55 40	126	46 03	193	22 49	230	56 24	258	17 32	327
112	27 32	349	53 13	031	55 58	124	45 58	192	22 32	228	56 02	256	17 20	325
114	27 27	346	53 25	029	56 17	123	45 54	190	22 15	227	55 40	254	17 06	323
116	27 22	344	53 35	026	56 37	121	45 50	188	21 59	225	55 18	252	16 52	321
118	27 15	342	53 45	024	56 57	119	45 47	187	21 43	223	54 56	250	16 38	319
	Suhail		◆ SPICA		RIGIL KENT		Peacock		◆ FOMALHAUT		ACHERNAR		◆ SIRIUS	
120	53 54	021	12 39	084	57 17	118	45 45	185	21 28	221	54 35	249	27 08	340
122	54 01	019	13 02	082	57 37	116	45 43	184	21 13	219	54 14	247	26 59	338
124	54 08	016	13 24	080	57 58	114	45 42	182	20 59	217	53 53	245	26 50	336
126	54 14	014	13 47	078	58 19	113	45 41	181	20 45	215	53 32	243	26 40	334
128	54 19	011	14 09	076	58 40	111	45 41	179	20 32	214	53 12	242	26 30	331
130	54 23	009	14 31	074	59 02	109	45 42	177	20 20	212	52 52	240	26 19	329
132	54 26	006	14 53	072	59 23	107	45 43	176	20 08	210	52 32	238	26 06	327
134	54 28	004	15 15	070	59 45	106	45 45	174	19 57	208	52 13	237	25 54	325
136	54 29	001	15 36	068	60 08	104	45 48	173	19 46	206	51 54	235	25 40	323
138	54 30	359	15 57	066	60 30	102	45 51	171	19 37	204	51 36	233	25 26	321
140	54 29	356	16 18	064	60 52	100	45 55	170	19 27	203	51 17	232	25 11	319
142	54 27	354	16 38	062	61 15	098	45 59	168	19 19	201	51 00	230	24 56	317
144	54 24	351	16 58	060	61 38	096	46 05	166	19 11	199	50 42	228	24 40	315
146	54 20	349	17 18	058	62 01	094	46 10	165	19 04	197	50 26	227	24 23	312
148	54 15	346	17 37	056	62 23	093	46 17	163	18 58	195	50 09	225	24 06	310
	SPICA		◆ ANTARES		Peacock		FOMALHAUT		◆ ACHERNAR		CANOPUS		◆ Suhail	
150	17 56	054	24 31	103	46 23	162	18 52	193	49 53	223	58 06	292	54 09	344
152	18 14	052	24 53	101	46 31	160	18 47	192	49 38	222	57 45	290	54 02	342
154	18 32	050	25 16	099	46 39	158	18 43	190	49 23	220	57 23	288	53 55	339
156	18 49	048	25 38	097	46 48	157	18 39	188	49 08	218	57 01	286	53 46	337
158	19 06	046	26 01	095	46 57	155	18 37	186	48 54	217	56 39	283	53 36	334
160	19 22	044	26 24	093	47 07	154	18 35	184	48 41	215	56 17	281	53 26	332
162	19 37	041	26 47	091	47 17	152	18 33	182	48 28	214	55 54	279	53 15	329
164	19 52	039	27 10	089	47 28	151	18 33	181	48 16	212	55 31	277	53 03	327
166	20 06	037	27 33	087	47 40	149	18 33	179	48 04	210	55 09	275	52 50	325
168	20 20	035	27 56	085	47 52	147	18 34	177	47 52	209	54 46	273	52 36	322
170	20 33	033	28 18	083	48 05	146	18 35	175	47 42	207	54 23	271	52 22	320
172	20 45	031	28 41	081	48 18	144	18 38	173	47 31	206	54 00	269	52 07	318
174	20 56	029	29 04	079	48 31	142	18 41	171	47 22	204	53 37	267	51 51	315
176	21 07	027	29 26	077	48 46	141	18 44	170	47 13	202	53 14	265	51 34	313
178	21 17	025	29 48	075	49 00	139	18 49	168	47 04	201	52 51	264	51 17	311

LHA ♈	Hc	Zn	Hc	Zn	Hc	Zn	Hc	Zn	Hc	Zn	Hc	Zn	Hc	Zn
	SPICA		◆ ANTARES		Nunki		FOMALHAUT		◆ ACHERNAR		CANOPUS		◆ Suhail	
180	21 26	023	30 10	073	23 09	109	18 54	166	46 56	199	52 29	262	51 00	308
182	21 35	021	30 32	071	23 30	107	19 00	164	46 49	198	52 06	260	50 41	306
184	21 42	019	30 54	069	23 52	105	19 07	162	46 43	196	51 44	258	50 23	304
186	21 49	016	31 15	067	24 15	103	19 14	160	46 36	195	51 21	256	50 03	302
188	21 55	014	31 36	065	24 37	101	19 22	159	46 31	193	50 59	254	49 44	299
190	22 00	012	31 56	063	25 00	099	19 31	157	46 26	191	50 37	252	49 24	297
192	22 05	010	32 17	061	25 22	097	19 40	155	46 22	190	50 16	251	49 03	295
194	22 08	008	32 36	059	25 45	095	19 50	153	46 18	188	49 54	249	48 42	293
196	22 11	006	32 56	057	26 08	093	20 01	151	46 15	187	49 33	247	48 21	291
198	22 13	004	33 15	055	26 31	092	20 12	149	46 13	185	49 12	245	47 59	289
200	22 14	002	33 33	052	26 54	090	20 24	147	46 11	184	48 51	243	47 38	287
202	22 14	359	33 51	050	27 16	088	20 37	146	46 10	182	48 31	242	47 16	285
204	22 14	357	34 08	048	27 39	086	20 50	144	46 10	180	48 11	240	46 53	283
206	22 12	355	34 25	046	28 02	084	21 04	142	46 10	179	47 52	238	46 31	281
208	22 10	353	34 41	044	28 25	082	21 18	140	46 11	177	47 32	236	46 08	278
	◆ ANTARES		Nunki		FOMALHAUT		◆ ACHERNAR		CANOPUS		◆ Suhail		SPICA	
210	34 57	042	28 47	080	21 33	138	46 12	176	47 13	235	45 46	276	22 07	351
212	35 12	040	29 10	078	21 49	136	46 14	174	46 55	233	45 23	274	22 03	349
214	35 26	037	29 32	076	22 05	135	46 17	173	46 37	231	45 00	272	21 58	347
216	35 40	035	29 54	074	22 22	133	46 20	171	46 19	229	44 37	271	21 52	345
218	35 52	033	30 16	072	22 39	131	46 24	169	46 02	228	44 14	269	21 46	343
220	36 05	031	30 38	070	22 56	129	46 28	168	45 45	226	43 51	267	21 38	340
222	36 16	029	30 59	067	23 14	127	46 33	166	45 29	224	43 28	265	21 30	338
224	36 26	026	31 20	065	23 33	125	46 39	165	45 13	223	43 06	263	21 22	336
226	36 36	024	31 41	063	23 52	123	46 45	163	44 58	221	42 43	261	21 12	334
228	36 45	022	32 01	061	24 11	122	46 52	162	44 43	219	42 20	259	21 02	332
230	36 53	020	32 21	059	24 31	120	47 00	160	44 29	218	41 58	257	20 51	330
232	37 01	018	32 40	057	24 51	118	47 08	158	44 15	216	41 36	255	20 39	328
234	37 07	015	32 59	055	25 11	116	47 17	157	44 02	214	41 14	253	20 26	326
236	37 13	013	33 18	053	25 32	114	47 26	155	43 49	213	40 52	251	20 13	324
238	37 18	011	33 36	051	25 53	112	47 36	154	43 37	211	40 30	250	19 59	322
	ANTARES		◆ Nunki		FOMALHAUT		◆ ACHERNAR		CANOPUS		◆ ACRUX		SPICA	
240	37 21	009	33 53	049	26 14	110	47 46	152	43 26	209	68 05	285	19 45	320
242	37 24	006	34 10	047	26 36	108	47 57	151	43 15	208	67 42	283	19 29	317
244	37 26	004	34 26	044	26 58	106	48 09	149	43 04	206	67 20	280	19 14	315
246	37 28	002	34 42	042	27 20	104	48 21	147	42 55	204	66 57	278	18 57	313
248	37 28	000	34 57	040	27 42	103	48 33	146	42 45	203	66 35	276	18 40	311
250	37 27	357	35 12	038	28 05	101	48 47	144	42 37	201	66 12	274	18 23	309
252	37 26	355	35 25	036	28 27	099	49 00	142	42 29	200	65 49	272	18 05	307
254	37 23	353	35 38	034	28 50	097	49 14	141	42 21	198	65 26	270	17 46	305
256	37 20	351	35 51	031	29 13	095	49 29	139	42 15	196	65 03	268	17 27	303
258	37 16	348	36 02	029	29 35	093	49 44	138	42 09	195	64 40	266	17 08	301
260	37 11	346	36 13	027	29 58	091	50 00	136	42 03	193	64 18	264	16 48	299
262	37 05	344	36 23	025	30 21	089	50 16	134	41 58	191	63 55	263	16 28	297
264	36 58	342	36 32	022	30 44	087	50 33	133	41 54	190	63 32	261	16 07	295
266	36 50	339	36 40	020	31 07	085	50 50	131	41 50	188	63 10	259	15 47	293
268	36 42	337	36 48	018	31 30	083	51 07	129	41 48	187	62 47	257	15 25	291
	◆ Nunki		FOMALHAUT		◆ ACHERNAR		CANOPUS		◆ ACRUX		RIGIL KENT		ANTARES	
270	36 55	016	31 52	081	51 25	128	41 45	185	62 25	255	66 34	291	36 32	335
272	37 00	014	32 15	079	51 44	126	41 44	183	62 03	254	66 13	289	36 22	333
274	37 05	011	32 37	077	52 02	124	41 43	182	61 41	252	65 51	286	36 11	330
276	37 09	009	33 00	075	52 21	123	41 42	180	61 19	250	65 29	284	36 00	328
278	37 12	007	33 22	073	52 41	121	41 43	178	60 58	248	65 06	282	35 47	326
280	37 15	005	33 43	071	53 01	119	41 44	177	60 37	247	64 44	280	35 34	324
282	37 16	002	34 05	069	53 21	118	41 45	175	60 16	245	64 21	278	35 20	322
284	37 17	000	34 26	067	53 41	116	41 47	174	59 55	243	63 58	276	35 06	319
286	37 16	358	34 47	065	54 02	114	41 50	172	59 35	242	63 36	274	34 50	317
288	37 15	356	35 07	063	54 23	112	41 54	170	59 15	240	63 13	272	34 35	315
290	37 13	353	35 28	061	54 44	111	41 58	169	58 55	238	62 50	270	34 18	313
292	37 10	351	35 47	058	55 06	109	42 03	167	58 36	237	62 27	268	34 01	311
294	37 06	349	36 07	056	55 28	107	42 08	165	58 17	235	62 04	266	33 44	309
296	37 01	347	36 25	054	55 50	105	42 14	164	57 59	233	61 41	264	33 25	307
298	36 55	344	36 44	052	56 12	103	42 21	162	57 40	232	61 19	262	33 07	305
	◆ FOMALHAUT		ACHERNAR		◆ CANOPUS		ACRUX		RIGIL KENT		◆ ANTARES		Nunki	
300	37 02	050	56 34	102	42 28	161	57 23	230	60 56	260	32 48	302	36 48	342
302	37 19	048	56 57	100	42 36	159	57 05	229	60 33	258	32 28	300	36 41	340
304	37 35	046	57 19	098	42 45	157	56 48	227	60 11	257	32 08	298	36 32	338
306	37 51	043	57 42	096	42 54	156	56 32	226	59 49	255	31 48	296	36 23	335
308	38 07	041	58 05	094	43 04	154	56 15	224	59 27	253	31 27	294	36 13	333
310	38 22	039	58 28	092	43 14	152	56 00	222	59 05	251	31 06	292	36 03	331
312	38 36	037	58 51	090	43 25	151	55 44	221	58 44	249	30 45	290	35 51	329
314	38 49	035	59 14	088	43 36	149	55 30	219	58 22	248	30 23	288	35 39	327
316	39 02	032	59 36	086	43 48	147	55 15	218	58 01	246	30 01	286	35 26	324
318	39 14	030	59 59	084	44 01	146	55 02	216	57 40	244	29 39	284	35 12	322
320	39 25	028	60 22	082	44 14	144	54 48	215	57 20	243	29 17	282	34 58	320
322	39 35	026	60 45	080	44 28	142	54 35	213	57 00	241	28 54	280	34 43	318
324	39 45	023	61 07	078	44 42	141	54 23	212	56 40	239	28 32	278	34 27	316
326	39 53	021	61 29	076	44 57	139	54 11	210	56 20	238	28 09	276	34 11	314
328	40 01	019	61 51	074	45 12	137	54 00	209	56 01	236	27 46	274	33 54	311
	◆ FOMALHAUT		ACHERNAR		◆ CANOPUS		ACRUX		RIGIL KENT		◆ ANTARES		Nunki	
330	40 08	017	62 13	071	45 28	136	53 49	207	55 43	234	27 23	272	33 37	309
332	40 14	014	62 35	069	45 44	134	53 39	206	55 24	233	27 00	270	33 19	307
334	40 20	012	62 56	067	46 01	132	53 29	204	55 06	231	26 37	268	33 00	305
336	40 24	010	63 17	065	46 18	131	53 20	203	54 49	229	26 15	266	32 41	303
338	40 28	008	63 37	062	46 36	129	53 12	201	54 31	228	25 52	264	32 22	301
340	40 30	005	63 58	060	46 54	127	53 04	200	54 15	226	25 29	262	32 02	299
342	40 32	003	64 17	058	47 12	125	52 56	198	53 58	225	25 06	260	31 42	297
344	40 33	001	64 36	055	47 31	124	52 49	197	53 42	223	24 44	258	31 21	295
346	40 32	358	64 55	053	47 50	122	52 43	195	53 27	221	24 22	256	31 00	293
348	40 31	356	65 13	050	48 10	120	52 37	194	53 12	220	23 59	255	30 39	291
350	40 29	354	65 30	048	48 30	119	52 32	192	52 58	218	23 37	253	30 17	289
352	40 26	352	65 47	045	48 50	117	52 27	191	52 44	217	23 16	251	29 55	286
354	40 23	349	66 03	043	49 11	115	52 23	189	52 30	215	22 54	249	29 33	284
356	40 18	347	66 18	040	49 31	113	52 20	188	52 17	214	22 33	247	29 11	282
358	40 12	345	66 32	038	49 53	111	52 17	187	52 05	212	22 12	245	28 48	280

LAT 80°S

LHA ♈	Hc	Zn	Hc	Zn	Hc	Zn	Hc	Zn	Hc	Zn	Hc	Zn	Hc	Zn
	ACHERNAR		◆SIRIUS		Suhail		ACRUX		◆RIGIL KENT		Peacock		◆FOMALHAUT	
0	65 56	034	14 31	104	35 50	143	53 14	185	52 44	211	61 38	292	39 08	343
2	66 07	031	14 51	102	36 03	141	53 13	184	52 34	210	61 19	290	39 02	340
4	66 17	028	15 11	100	36 17	139	53 11	182	52 24	208	60 59	288	38 55	338
6	66 27	026	15 32	098	36 31	137	53 11	181	52 14	206	60 39	286	38 46	336
8	66 35	023	15 53	096	36 45	135	53 11	179	52 05	205	60 19	283	38 38	334
10	66 43	020	16 13	094	37 00	134	53 12	178	51 57	203	59 59	281	38 28	332
12	66 50	017	16 34	092	37 15	132	53 13	176	51 49	202	59 38	279	38 18	329
14	66 56	015	16 55	090	37 31	130	53 14	175	51 41	200	59 18	277	38 07	327
16	67 00	012	17 16	089	37 47	128	53 17	173	51 34	199	58 57	275	37 55	325
18	67 04	009	17 37	087	38 04	126	53 19	172	51 28	197	58 36	273	37 43	323
20	67 07	006	17 58	085	38 21	125	53 23	170	51 22	196	58 15	271	37 30	321
22	67 09	004	18 18	083	38 38	123	53 27	169	51 17	194	57 54	269	37 16	318
24	67 10	001	18 39	081	38 56	121	53 31	167	51 12	192	57 34	267	37 02	316
26	67 09	358	18 59	079	39 14	119	53 36	166	51 08	191	57 13	265	36 48	314
28	67 08	355	19 20	077	39 32	117	53 41	164	51 04	189	56 52	263	36 32	312
	◆SIRIUS		Suhail		ACRUX		◆RIGIL KENT		Peacock		◆FOMALHAUT		ACHERNAR	
30	19 40	075	39 51	115	53 47	163	51 01	188	56 31	261	36 17	310	67 06	352
32	20 00	073	40 10	114	53 54	161	50 58	186	56 11	260	36 00	308	67 03	350
34	20 20	071	40 29	112	54 01	159	50 56	185	55 50	258	35 44	306	66 58	347
36	20 39	069	40 48	110	54 08	158	50 55	183	55 30	256	35 26	303	66 53	344
38	20 58	067	41 08	108	54 17	156	50 54	182	55 10	254	35 09	301	66 47	341
40	21 17	065	41 28	106	54 25	155	50 54	180	54 50	252	34 51	299	66 40	339
42	21 36	063	41 48	104	54 34	153	50 54	179	54 30	250	34 33	297	66 32	336
44	21 54	060	42 08	102	54 44	152	50 55	177	54 11	249	34 14	295	66 23	333
46	22 12	058	42 29	100	54 54	150	50 56	175	53 52	247	33 55	293	66 13	331
48	22 30	056	42 49	099	55 04	149	50 58	174	53 33	245	33 35	291	66 02	328
50	22 47	054	43 10	097	55 15	147	51 01	172	53 14	243	33 16	289	65 51	325
52	23 04	052	43 31	095	55 27	146	51 04	171	52 55	241	32 56	287	65 39	323
54	23 20	050	43 51	093	55 39	144	51 07	169	52 37	240	32 36	285	65 26	320
56	23 36	048	44 12	091	55 51	143	51 11	168	52 19	238	32 16	283	65 12	318
58	23 51	046	44 33	089	56 04	141	51 16	166	52 02	236	31 55	281	64 58	315
	◆SIRIUS		Suhail		ACRUX		◆RIGIL KENT		Peacock		◆FOMALHAUT		ACHERNAR	
60	24 06	044	44 54	087	56 18	139	51 21	165	51 45	235	31 35	279	64 43	313
62	24 20	042	45 15	085	56 31	138	51 27	163	51 28	233	31 14	277	64 27	310
64	24 34	040	45 35	083	56 46	136	51 33	162	51 11	231	30 54	275	64 11	308
66	24 47	038	45 56	081	57 00	135	51 40	160	50 55	229	30 33	273	63 54	305
68	24 59	036	46 17	079	57 15	133	51 48	158	50 40	228	30 12	271	63 37	303
70	25 11	034	46 37	077	57 31	131	51 55	157	50 25	226	29 51	269	63 19	301
72	25 22	031	46 57	075	57 46	130	52 04	155	50 10	224	29 30	267	63 01	298
74	25 33	029	47 17	073	58 03	128	52 13	154	49 55	223	29 09	265	62 42	296
76	25 42	027	47 37	070	58 19	127	52 22	152	49 42	221	28 49	263	62 24	294
78	25 52	025	47 56	068	58 36	125	52 32	151	49 28	219	28 28	261	62 04	292
80	26 00	023	48 16	066	58 53	123	52 43	149	49 15	218	28 08	259	61 45	289
82	26 08	021	48 35	064	59 11	122	52 54	147	49 03	216	27 47	257	61 25	287
84	26 15	019	48 53	062	59 29	120	53 05	146	48 50	214	27 27	255	61 05	285
86	26 21	017	49 11	060	59 47	118	53 17	144	48 39	213	27 07	253	60 45	283
88	26 27	014	49 29	058	60 05	117	53 30	143	48 28	211	26 47	251	60 24	281
	◆SIRIUS		Suhail		ACRUX		◆RIGIL KENT		Peacock		◆FOMALHAUT		ACHERNAR	
90	26 32	012	49 46	055	60 24	115	53 42	141	48 17	210	26 27	250	60 04	279
92	26 36	010	50 03	053	60 43	113	53 56	139	48 07	208	26 08	248	59 43	277
94	26 39	008	50 20	051	61 03	111	54 09	138	47 58	206	25 49	246	59 22	275
96	26 41	006	50 36	049	61 22	110	54 24	136	47 49	205	25 30	244	59 02	273
98	26 43	004	50 51	046	61 42	108	54 38	135	47 40	203	25 11	242	58 41	271
100	26 44	002	51 06	044	62 02	106	54 53	133	47 33	201	24 53	240	58 20	269
102	26 44	359	51 20	042	62 22	104	55 09	131	47 25	200	24 35	238	57 59	267
104	26 44	357	51 34	040	62 42	103	55 25	130	47 18	198	24 18	236	57 38	265
106	26 42	355	51 47	037	63 02	101	55 41	128	47 12	197	24 01	234	57 18	263
108	26 40	353	51 59	035	63 23	099	55 57	126	47 06	195	23 44	233	56 57	261
110	26 37	351	52 11	033	63 44	097	56 14	125	47 01	193	23 28	231	56 37	259
112	26 33	349	52 22	030	64 04	095	56 32	123	46 57	192	23 12	229	56 16	257
114	26 29	347	52 32	028	64 25	093	56 49	121	46 53	190	22 56	227	55 56	255
116	26 24	344	52 41	026	64 46	091	57 07	120	46 49	189	22 41	225	55 36	254
118	26 18	342	52 50	023	65 07	089	57 25	118	46 47	187	22 27	223	55 16	252
	Suhail		SPICA		◆RIGIL KENT		Peacock		◆FOMALHAUT		ACHERNAR		◆SIRIUS	
120	52 58	021	12 32	084	57 44	116	46 44	185	22 13	221	54 56	250	26 11	340
122	53 04	018	12 53	082	58 03	115	46 43	184	21 59	219	54 37	248	26 04	338
124	53 11	016	13 14	080	58 22	113	46 42	182	21 46	218	54 18	246	25 56	336
126	53 16	014	13 34	078	58 41	111	46 41	181	21 34	216	53 59	245	25 47	334
128	53 20	011	13 54	076	59 01	109	46 41	179	21 22	214	53 40	243	25 37	332
130	53 24	009	14 14	074	59 21	107	46 42	177	21 11	212	53 21	241	25 27	330
132	53 27	006	14 34	072	59 41	106	46 43	176	21 00	210	53 03	239	25 16	327
134	53 29	004	14 54	070	60 01	104	46 45	174	20 50	208	52 46	238	25 04	325
136	53 29	001	15 13	068	60 21	102	46 47	173	20 40	206	52 28	236	24 52	323
138	53 30	359	15 33	066	60 41	100	46 50	171	20 31	205	52 11	234	24 40	321
140	53 29	357	15 51	064	61 02	098	46 54	169	20 23	203	51 54	233	24 26	319
142	53 27	354	16 10	062	61 23	096	46 58	168	20 15	201	51 38	231	24 12	317
144	53 24	352	16 28	060	61 43	094	47 03	166	20 08	199	51 22	229	23 58	315
146	53 21	349	16 46	058	62 04	093	47 08	165	20 01	197	51 06	227	23 43	313
148	53 17	347	17 03	056	62 25	091	47 14	163	19 56	195	50 51	226	23 27	311
	SPICA		◆ANTARES		Peacock		FOMALHAUT		◆ACHERNAR		CANOPUS		◆Suhail	
150	17 20	054	24 44	102	47 20	161	19 50	193	50 37	224	57 43	294	53 11	344
152	17 37	051	25 04	100	47 27	160	19 46	192	50 22	222	57 24	291	53 05	342
154	17 53	049	25 25	098	47 35	158	19 42	190	50 08	221	57 04	289	52 59	340
156	18 08	047	25 45	096	47 43	156	19 39	188	49 55	219	56 44	287	52 51	337
158	18 23	045	26 06	095	47 51	155	19 36	186	49 42	218	56 24	285	52 42	335
160	18 38	043	26 27	093	48 01	153	19 34	184	49 30	216	56 04	283	52 33	332
162	18 52	041	26 48	091	48 10	152	19 33	182	49 18	214	55 44	281	52 23	330
164	19 05	039	27 09	089	48 20	150	19 33	181	49 06	213	55 23	279	52 12	328
166	19 18	037	27 30	087	48 31	148	19 33	179	48 55	211	55 02	277	52 01	325
168	19 31	035	27 50	085	48 42	147	19 34	177	48 45	209	54 42	275	51 49	323
170	19 42	033	28 11	083	48 54	145	19 35	175	48 35	208	54 21	273	51 36	321
172	19 53	031	28 32	081	49 06	143	19 37	173	48 25	206	54 00	271	51 22	318
174	20 04	029	28 52	079	49 19	142	19 40	171	48 17	204	53 39	269	51 08	316
176	20 13	027	29 12	077	49 32	140	19 43	169	48 08	203	53 18	267	50 53	314
178	20 22	025	29 33	075	49 46	138	19 48	168	48 00	201	52 58	265	50 38	312

LHA ♈	Hc	Zn	Hc	Zn	Hc	Zn	Hc	Zn	Hc	Zn	Hc	Zn	Hc	Zn
	SPICA		◆ANTARES		Peacock		FOMALHAUT		◆ACHERNAR		CANOPUS		◆Suhail	
180	20 31	023	29 53	073	50 00	137	19 52	166	47 53	200	52 37	263	50 22	309
182	20 38	020	30 12	071	50 14	135	19 58	164	47 46	198	52 16	261	50 06	307
184	20 45	018	30 32	069	50 29	133	20 04	162	47 40	196	51 56	259	49 49	305
186	20 52	016	30 51	067	50 44	132	20 11	160	47 35	195	51 35	257	49 32	303
188	20 57	014	31 10	064	51 00	130	20 18	158	47 29	193	51 15	255	49 14	300
190	21 02	012	31 29	062	51 16	128	20 26	157	47 25	192	50 55	254	48 56	298
192	21 06	010	31 47	060	51 33	127	20 34	155	47 21	190	50 35	252	48 37	296
194	21 09	008	32 05	058	51 50	125	20 44	153	47 18	188	50 15	250	48 18	294
196	21 11	006	32 23	056	52 07	123	20 54	151	47 15	187	49 56	248	47 59	292
198	21 13	004	32 40	054	52 25	121	21 04	149	47 13	185	49 37	246	47 40	290
200	21 14	002	32 56	052	52 42	120	21 15	147	47 11	184	49 18	244	47 20	288
202	21 14	359	33 12	050	53 01	118	21 26	145	47 10	182	48 59	243	47 00	286
204	21 14	357	33 28	048	53 19	116	21 39	144	47 10	180	48 41	241	46 40	284
206	21 12	355	33 43	046	53 38	114	21 51	142	47 10	179	48 23	239	46 19	282
208	21 10	353	33 58	043	53 57	113	22 04	140	47 11	177	48 05	237	45 59	280
	◆ANTARES		Nunki		◆FOMALHAUT		ACHERNAR		CANOPUS		◆Suhail		SPICA	
210	34 12	041	28 36	079	22 18	138	47 12	176	47 48	236	45 38	277	21 07	351
212	34 25	039	28 57	077	22 32	136	47 14	174	47 31	234	45 18	275	21 04	349
214	34 38	037	29 17	075	22 47	134	47 16	172	47 14	232	44 57	273	20 59	347
216	34 50	035	29 37	073	23 02	132	47 19	171	46 58	230	44 36	271	20 54	345
218	35 02	033	29 57	071	23 18	131	47 23	169	46 42	229	44 15	270	20 49	343
220	35 13	030	30 16	069	23 34	129	47 27	168	46 27	227	43 54	268	20 42	341
222	35 23	028	30 36	067	23 50	127	47 32	166	46 12	225	43 34	266	20 35	338
224	35 33	026	30 55	065	24 07	125	47 37	164	45 57	223	43 13	264	20 27	336
226	35 41	024	31 13	063	24 24	123	47 43	163	45 43	222	42 52	262	20 18	334
228	35 50	022	31 32	061	24 42	121	47 49	161	45 29	220	42 32	260	20 09	332
230	35 57	020	31 50	059	25 00	119	47 56	160	45 16	218	42 11	258	19 59	330
232	36 03	017	32 07	057	25 18	117	48 04	158	45 04	217	41 51	256	19 48	328
234	36 09	015	32 25	055	25 37	115	48 12	156	44 51	215	41 31	254	19 36	326
236	36 14	013	32 41	052	25 56	114	48 20	155	44 40	213	41 11	252	19 25	324
238	36 19	011	32 58	050	26 15	112	48 29	153	44 29	212	40 51	250	19 12	322
	ANTARES		◆Nunki		FOMALHAUT		◆ACHERNAR		CANOPUS		◆ACRUX		SPICA	
240	36 22	008	33 13	048	26 35	110	48 39	152	44 18	210	67 48	287	18 59	320
242	36 25	006	33 29	046	26 55	108	48 49	150	44 08	208	67 28	285	18 45	318
244	36 27	004	33 43	044	27 14	106	49 00	148	43 58	207	67 08	283	18 31	316
246	36 28	002	33 58	042	27 35	104	49 11	147	43 49	205	66 47	281	18 16	314
248	36 28	000	34 11	040	27 55	102	49 23	145	43 41	203	66 27	279	18 01	312
250	36 27	357	34 24	037	28 15	100	49 35	143	43 33	202	66 06	276	17 45	310
252	36 26	355	34 36	035	28 36	098	49 48	142	43 25	200	65 46	274	17 28	307
254	36 24	353	34 48	033	28 57	096	50 01	140	43 19	198	65 25	272	17 12	305
256	36 21	351	34 59	031	29 17	094	50 14	138	43 12	197	65 04	270	16 54	303
258	36 17	348	35 10	029	29 38	092	50 28	137	43 07	195	64 43	268	16 37	301
260	36 12	346	35 19	027	29 59	090	50 43	135	43 02	193	64 22	267	16 19	299
262	36 07	344	35 28	024	30 20	088	50 58	133	42 57	192	64 01	265	16 01	297
264	36 01	342	35 37	022	30 41	086	51 13	132	42 53	190	63 41	263	15 42	295
266	35 54	340	35 44	020	31 01	084	51 29	130	42 50	188	63 20	261	15 23	293
268	35 46	337	35 51	018	31 22	082	51 45	128	42 47	187	63 00	259	15 04	291
	◆Nunki		FOMALHAUT		◆ACHERNAR		CANOPUS		◆ACRUX		RIGIL KENT		ANTARES	
270	35 57	016	31 43	080	52 02	127	42 45	185	62 39	257	66 12	293	35 38	335
272	36 02	013	32 03	078	52 18	125	42 44	183	62 19	255	65 52	291	35 29	333
274	36 06	011	32 24	076	52 36	123	42 43	182	61 59	254	65 33	288	35 19	331
276	36 10	009	32 44	074	52 53	122	42 42	180	61 39	252	65 13	286	35 08	329
278	36 13	007	33 04	072	53 11	120	42 43	178	61 19	250	64 53	284	34 57	326
280	36 15	005	33 23	070	53 29	118	42 43	177	61 00	248	64 32	282	34 45	324
282	36 16	002	33 43	068	53 48	116	42 45	175	60 41	247	64 12	280	34 33	322
284	36 17	000	34 02	066	54 07	115	42 47	173	60 22	245	63 51	278	34 20	320
286	36 16	358	34 21	064	54 26	113	42 50	172	60 03	243	63 31	276	34 06	318
288	36 15	356	34 40	062	54 45	111	42 53	170	59 44	241	63 10	274	33 52	316
290	36 13	353	34 58	060	55 05	109	42 57	169	59 26	240	62 49	272	33 37	314
292	36 10	351	35 16	058	55 24	107	43 01	167	59 08	238	62 28	270	33 22	311
294	36 07	349	35 33	056	55 44	106	43 06	165	58 51	236	62 07	268	33 06	309
296	36 02	347	35 50	054	56 05	104	43 12	164	58 34	235	61 47	266	32 49	307
298	35 57	345	36 07	052	56 25	102	43 18	162	58 17	233	61 26	264	32 33	305
	◆FOMALHAUT		ACHERNAR		◆CANOPUS		ACRUX		RIGIL KENT		◆ANTARES		Nunki	
300	36 23	049	56 45	100	43 25	160	58 00	232	61 05	262	32 15	303	35 51	342
302	36 38	047	57 06	098	43 32	159	57 44	230	60 45	260	31 58	301	35 44	340
304	36 53	045	57 27	096	43 40	157	57 28	228	60 24	258	31 40	299	35 37	338
306	37 08	043	57 47	094	43 48	155	57 13	227	60 04	256	31 21	297	35 29	336
308	37 22	041	58 08	092	43 57	154	56 58	225	59 44	255	31 02	295	35 20	334
310	37 35	039	58 29	090	44 07	152	56 44	224	59 24	253	30 43	293	35 10	331
312	37 48	036	58 50	088	44 17	150	56 29	222	59 04	251	30 24	291	35 00	329
314	38 00	034	59 11	086	44 28	149	56 16	220	58 44	249	30 04	289	34 49	327
316	38 11	032	59 31	084	44 39	147	56 02	219	58 25	247	29 44	287	34 37	325
318	38 22	030	59 52	082	44 51	145	55 50	217	58 06	246	29 24	284	34 25	323
320	38 32	028	60 13	080	45 03	143	55 37	216	57 47	244	29 04	282	34 12	320
322	38 41	025	60 33	078	45 15	142	55 25	214	57 28	242	28 44	280	33 58	318
324	38 50	023	60 54	076	45 28	140	55 14	213	57 10	241	28 23	278	33 44	316
326	38 57	021	61 14	074	45 42	138	55 03	211	56 52	239	28 02	276	33 29	314
328	39 05	019	61 34	072	45 56	137	54 52	209	56 34	237	27 42	274	33 14	312
	◆FOMALHAUT		ACHERNAR		◆CANOPUS		ACRUX		RIGIL KENT		◆ANTARES		Nunki	
330	39 11	016	61 53	070	46 11	135	54 42	208	56 17	236	27 21	273	32 58	310
332	39 16	014	62 13	067	46 26	133	54 33	206	56 00	234	27 00	271	32 42	308
334	39 21	012	62 32	065	46 41	132	54 24	205	55 43	232	26 39	269	32 25	306
336	39 25	010	62 50	063	46 57	130	54 15	203	55 27	231	26 18	267	32 08	304
338	39 28	007	63 09	061	47 13	128	54 07	202	55 11	229	25 58	265	31 51	301
340	39 30	005	63 27	058	47 30	126	54 00	200	54 56	227	25 37	263	31 33	299
342	39 32	003	63 44	056	47 47	125	53 53	199	54 41	226	25 16	261	31 14	297
344	39 33	001	64 01	054	48 04	123	53 46	197	54 26	224	24 56	259	30 56	295
346	39 32	358	64 18	051	48 22	121	53 41	196	54 12	222	24 35	257	30 37	293
348	39 31	356	64 34	049	48 40	119	53 35	194	53 58	221	24 15	255	30 17	291
350	39 30	354	64 49	046	48 58	118	53 30	193	53 44	219	23 55	253	29 58	289
352	39 27	352	65 04	044	49 17	116	53 26	191	53 32	218	23 35	251	29 38	287
354	39 24	349	65 18	041	49 35	114	53 22	190	53 19	216	23 16	249	29 18	285
356	39 19	347	65 31	039	49 55	112	53 19	188	53 07	214	22 56	247	28 58	283
358	39 14	345	65 44	036	50 14	110	53 16	187	52 56	213	22 37	245	28 37	281

 LAT 81°S

LHA ♈	Hc	Zn	Hc	Zn	Hc	Zn	Hc	Zn	Hc	Zn	Hc	Zn	Hc	Zn
	ACHERNAR		◆SIRIUS		Suhail		ACRUX		◆RIGIL KENT		Peacock		◆FOMALHAUT	
0	65 06	032	14 45	104	36 38	142	54 14	185	53 36	212	61 15	294	38 11	343
2	65 15	030	15 04	102	36 49	140	54 12	184	53 26	210	60 58	292	38 05	341
4	65 24	027	15 22	100	37 02	138	54 11	182	53 17	209	60 40	289	37 59	339
6	65 33	025	15 41	098	37 14	137	54 11	181	53 08	207	60 22	287	37 52	336
8	65 40	022	15 59	096	37 27	135	54 11	179	53 00	205	60 04	285	37 44	334
10	65 47	019	16 18	094	37 41	133	54 12	178	52 52	204	59 46	283	37 35	332
12	65 52	017	16 37	092	37 55	131	54 13	176	52 44	202	59 28	281	37 26	330
14	65 57	014	16 55	090	38 09	129	54 14	174	52 38	201	59 09	279	37 16	328
16	66 02	011	17 14	088	38 24	128	54 16	173	52 31	199	58 51	277	37 06	325
18	66 05	009	17 33	086	38 39	126	54 19	171	52 25	198	58 32	275	36 55	323
20	66 07	006	17 52	084	38 54	124	54 22	170	52 20	196	58 13	273	36 43	321
22	66 09	003	18 10	082	39 10	122	54 25	168	52 15	194	57 54	271	36 31	319
24	66 10	001	18 29	080	39 26	120	54 29	167	52 11	193	57 36	269	36 19	317
26	66 09	358	18 47	078	39 42	118	54 34	165	52 07	191	57 17	267	36 06	315
28	66 08	355	19 06	076	39 59	117	54 39	164	52 03	190	56 58	265	35 52	312
	◆SIRIUS		Suhail		ACRUX		◆RIGIL KENT		Peacock		◆FOMALHAUT		ACHERNAR	
30	19 24	074	40 16	115	54 45	162	52 00	188	56 40	263	35 38	310	66 06	353
32	19 42	072	40 33	113	54 51	161	51 58	186	56 21	261	35 23	308	66 04	350
34	20 00	070	40 51	111	54 57	159	51 56	185	56 02	259	35 09	306	66 00	347
36	20 17	068	41 08	109	55 04	157	51 55	183	55 44	257	34 53	304	65 55	345
38	20 34	066	41 26	107	55 11	156	51 54	182	55 26	255	34 37	302	65 50	342
40	20 51	064	41 44	105	55 19	154	51 54	180	55 08	254	34 21	300	65 44	339
42	21 08	062	42 02	103	55 28	153	51 54	179	54 50	252	34 05	298	65 37	337
44	21 25	060	42 21	101	55 37	151	51 55	177	54 32	250	33 48	296	65 29	334
46	21 41	058	42 39	100	55 46	150	51 56	175	54 15	248	33 31	294	65 21	332
48	21 56	056	42 58	098	55 56	148	51 58	174	53 57	246	33 14	292	65 11	329
50	22 12	054	43 16	096	56 06	146	52 00	172	53 40	244	32 56	290	65 01	327
52	22 27	052	43 35	094	56 16	145	52 03	171	53 23	243	32 38	288	64 51	324
54	22 41	050	43 54	092	56 27	143	52 06	169	53 07	241	32 20	285	64 39	322
56	22 56	048	44 13	090	56 39	142	52 10	167	52 51	239	32 02	283	64 27	319
58	23 09	046	44 31	088	56 51	140	52 14	166	52 35	237	31 44	281	64 15	317
	◆SIRIUS		Suhail		ACRUX		◆RIGIL KENT		Peacock		◆FOMALHAUT		ACHERNAR	
60	23 22	044	44 50	086	57 03	138	52 19	164	52 19	236	31 25	279	64 01	314
62	23 35	042	45 09	084	57 15	137	52 24	163	52 04	234	31 07	277	63 48	312
64	23 47	040	45 27	082	57 29	135	52 30	161	51 49	232	30 48	275	63 33	309
66	23 59	037	45 46	080	57 42	134	52 36	160	51 34	230	30 29	273	63 19	307
68	24 10	035	46 04	078	57 56	132	52 43	158	51 20	229	30 11	271	63 03	305
70	24 21	033	46 23	076	58 10	130	52 51	156	51 06	227	29 52	269	62 48	302
72	24 31	031	46 41	074	58 24	129	52 58	155	50 52	225	29 33	268	62 32	300
74	24 40	029	46 59	072	58 39	127	53 07	153	50 39	224	29 14	266	62 15	298
76	24 49	027	47 16	069	58 54	125	53 15	152	50 26	222	28 56	264	61 58	296
78	24 57	025	47 34	067	59 10	124	53 24	150	50 14	220	28 37	262	61 41	293
80	25 05	023	47 51	065	59 26	122	53 34	148	50 02	218	28 19	260	61 24	291
82	25 12	021	48 08	063	59 42	120	53 44	147	49 51	217	28 00	258	61 06	289
84	25 18	019	48 24	061	59 58	118	53 55	145	49 40	215	27 42	256	60 49	287
86	25 24	016	48 41	059	60 15	117	54 06	143	49 29	213	27 24	254	60 30	285
88	25 29	014	48 57	057	60 32	115	54 17	142	49 19	212	27 06	252	60 12	283
	◆SIRIUS		Suhail		ACRUX		◆RIGIL KENT		Peacock		◆FOMALHAUT		ACHERNAR	
90	25 33	012	49 12	054	60 49	113	54 29	140	49 09	210	26 48	250	59 54	280
92	25 37	010	49 27	052	61 06	112	54 41	139	49 00	208	26 31	248	59 35	278
94	25 39	008	49 42	050	61 24	110	54 54	137	48 52	207	26 13	246	59 17	276
96	25 42	006	49 56	048	61 41	108	55 07	135	48 43	205	25 56	244	58 58	274
98	25 43	004	50 10	046	61 59	106	55 20	134	48 36	204	25 39	242	58 39	272
100	25 44	002	50 23	043	62 17	104	55 34	132	48 28	202	25 23	240	58 20	270
102	25 44	359	50 35	041	62 36	103	55 48	130	48 22	200	25 07	239	58 02	268
104	25 44	357	50 47	039	62 54	101	56 02	129	48 15	199	24 51	237	57 43	266
106	25 42	355	50 59	037	63 13	099	56 17	127	48 10	197	24 35	235	57 24	264
108	25 41	353	51 10	034	63 31	097	56 32	125	48 04	195	24 20	233	57 06	263
110	25 38	351	51 20	032	63 50	095	56 48	124	48 00	194	24 05	231	56 47	261
112	25 35	349	51 30	030	64 09	093	57 04	122	47 56	192	23 51	229	56 29	259
114	25 31	347	51 39	027	64 27	091	57 20	120	47 52	190	23 37	227	56 10	257
116	25 26	345	51 47	025	64 46	089	57 36	118	47 49	189	23 24	225	55 52	255
118	25 21	342	51 54	023	65 05	087	57 53	117	47 46	187	23 10	223	55 34	253
	Suhail		SPICA		◆RIGIL KENT		Peacock		◆FOMALHAUT		ACHERNAR		◆SIRIUS	
120	52 01	020	12 26	083	58 10	115	47 44	185	22 58	222	55 16	251	25 15	340
122	52 07	018	12 44	081	58 27	113	47 43	184	22 46	220	54 58	250	25 08	338
124	52 13	016	13 03	079	58 44	111	47 42	182	22 34	218	54 41	248	25 01	336
126	52 18	013	13 21	077	59 02	109	47 41	181	22 22	216	54 24	246	24 53	334
128	52 22	011	13 39	075	59 20	108	47 41	179	22 12	214	54 07	244	24 44	332
130	52 25	008	13 57	073	59 38	106	47 42	177	22 01	212	53 50	242	24 35	330
132	52 27	006	14 15	071	59 56	104	47 43	176	21 52	210	53 33	241	24 25	328
134	52 29	004	14 33	069	60 14	102	47 45	174	21 42	208	53 17	239	24 15	326
136	52 29	001	14 50	067	60 33	100	47 47	172	21 34	207	53 01	237	24 04	324
138	52 30	359	15 08	065	60 51	098	47 50	171	21 26	205	52 46	235	23 53	321
140	52 29	357	15 25	063	61 10	096	47 53	169	21 18	203	52 30	234	23 41	319
142	52 27	354	15 41	061	61 28	095	47 57	168	21 11	201	52 15	232	23 28	317
144	52 25	352	15 58	059	61 47	093	48 01	166	21 05	199	52 01	230	23 15	315
146	52 22	349	16 14	057	62 06	091	48 06	164	20 59	197	51 47	228	23 02	313
148	52 18	347	16 29	055	62 25	089	48 11	163	20 53	195	51 33	227	22 48	311
	SPICA		◆ANTARES		Peacock		FOMALHAUT		◆ACHERNAR		CANOPUS		◆Suhail	
150	16 44	053	24 56	102	48 17	161	20 49	194	51 19	225	57 18	295	52 14	345
152	16 59	051	25 15	100	48 23	159	20 45	192	51 06	223	57 01	293	52 08	342
154	17 14	049	25 33	098	48 30	158	20 41	190	50 54	222	56 44	291	52 02	340
156	17 28	047	25 52	096	48 38	156	20 38	188	50 41	220	56 26	288	51 55	338
158	17 41	045	26 11	094	48 46	154	20 36	186	50 29	218	56 08	286	51 48	335
160	17 54	043	26 29	092	48 54	153	20 34	184	50 18	217	55 50	284	51 40	333
162	18 07	041	26 48	090	49 03	151	20 33	182	50 07	215	55 32	282	51 31	331
164	18 19	039	27 07	088	49 12	149	20 33	181	49 57	213	55 13	280	51 21	328
166	18 30	037	27 26	086	49 22	148	20 33	179	49 47	212	54 55	278	51 11	326
168	18 41	035	27 44	084	49 32	146	20 33	177	49 37	210	54 36	276	51 00	324
170	18 52	033	28 03	082	49 43	144	20 35	175	49 28	208	54 17	274	50 49	321
172	19 02	031	28 22	080	49 54	143	20 37	173	49 19	207	53 59	272	50 37	319
174	19 11	029	28 40	078	50 06	141	20 39	171	49 11	205	53 40	270	50 24	317
176	19 20	027	28 58	076	50 18	139	20 42	169	49 03	203	53 21	268	50 11	315
178	19 28	025	29 17	074	50 30	138	20 46	168	48 56	202	53 02	266	49 58	312

LHA ♈	Hc	Zn	Hc	Zn	Hc	Zn	Hc	Zn	Hc	Zn	Hc	Zn	Hc	Zn
	SPICA		◆ANTARES		Peacock		FOMALHAUT		◆ACHERNAR		CANOPUS		◆Suhail	
180	19 35	022	29 34	072	50 43	136	20 50	166	48 49	200	52 44	264	49 44	310
182	19 42	020	29 52	070	50 56	134	20 55	164	48 43	198	52 25	262	49 29	308
184	19 48	018	30 10	068	51 10	133	21 01	162	48 38	197	52 06	260	49 14	306
186	19 54	016	30 27	066	51 24	131	21 07	160	48 32	195	51 48	258	48 59	304
188	19 59	014	30 44	064	51 38	129	21 14	158	48 28	193	51 30	257	48 43	301
190	20 03	012	31 01	062	51 53	127	21 21	156	48 24	192	51 11	255	48 27	299
192	20 07	010	31 17	060	52 08	126	21 29	155	48 20	190	50 53	253	48 10	297
194	20 10	008	31 33	058	52 24	124	21 37	153	48 17	189	50 36	251	47 53	295
196	20 12	006	31 49	056	52 39	122	21 46	151	48 15	187	50 18	249	47 36	293
198	20 13	004	32 04	054	52 55	120	21 55	149	48 13	185	50 00	247	47 19	291
200	20 14	002	32 19	051	53 12	119	22 05	147	48 11	184	49 43	245	47 01	289
202	20 14	359	32 34	049	53 28	117	22 16	145	48 10	182	49 26	244	46 43	287
204	20 14	357	32 48	047	53 45	115	22 27	143	48 10	180	49 10	242	46 25	285
206	20 13	355	33 01	045	54 02	113	22 38	141	48 10	179	48 53	240	46 07	283
208	20 11	353	33 14	043	54 20	111	22 50	140	48 10	177	48 37	238	45 48	281
	◆ANTARES		Nunki		◆FOMALHAUT		ACHERNAR		CANOPUS		◆Suhail		SPICA	
210	33 27	041	28 25	079	23 03	138	48 12	176	48 21	236	45 30	278	20 08	351
212	33 39	039	28 43	077	23 15	136	48 13	174	48 06	235	45 11	276	20 05	349
214	33 50	037	29 01	075	23 29	134	48 16	172	47 51	233	44 53	274	20 01	347
216	34 01	034	29 19	073	23 42	132	48 18	171	47 36	231	44 34	272	19 56	345
218	34 11	032	29 37	070	23 57	130	48 22	169	47 21	229	44 15	270	19 51	343
220	34 21	030	29 55	068	24 11	128	48 25	167	47 07	228	43 56	269	19 45	341
222	34 30	028	30 12	066	24 26	126	48 30	166	46 54	226	43 38	267	19 39	339
224	34 39	026	30 29	064	24 41	125	48 35	164	46 40	224	43 19	265	19 32	337
226	34 47	024	30 46	062	24 57	123	48 40	163	46 28	222	43 00	263	19 24	334
228	34 54	021	31 02	060	25 13	121	48 46	161	46 15	221	42 42	261	19 15	332
230	35 00	019	31 18	058	25 29	119	48 52	159	46 03	219	42 23	259	19 06	330
232	35 06	017	31 34	056	25 46	117	48 59	158	45 52	217	42 05	257	18 57	328
234	35 11	015	31 50	054	26 03	115	49 07	156	45 40	216	41 47	255	18 47	326
236	35 16	013	32 04	052	26 20	113	49 14	154	45 30	214	41 29	253	18 36	324
238	35 20	011	32 19	050	26 37	111	49 23	153	45 19	212	41 11	251	18 25	322
	ANTARES		◆Nunki		FOMALHAUT		◆ACHERNAR		CANOPUS		◆ACRUX		SPICA	
240	35 23	008	32 33	048	26 55	109	49 32	151	45 10	210	67 29	289	18 13	320
242	35 25	006	32 47	046	27 13	107	49 41	149	45 00	209	67 11	287	18 01	318
244	35 27	004	33 00	043	27 31	105	49 51	148	44 52	207	66 53	285	17 48	316
246	35 28	002	33 13	041	27 49	103	50 01	146	44 43	205	66 35	283	17 34	314
248	35 28	000	33 25	039	28 07	102	50 12	144	44 36	204	66 17	281	17 21	312
250	35 27	357	33 36	037	28 26	100	50 23	143	44 28	202	65 58	279	17 06	310
252	35 26	355	33 47	035	28 44	098	50 35	141	44 22	200	65 40	277	16 52	308
254	35 24	353	33 58	033	29 03	096	50 47	139	44 15	199	65 21	275	16 37	306
256	35 21	351	34 08	031	29 22	094	50 59	138	44 10	197	65 02	273	16 21	304
258	35 18	349	34 17	028	29 40	092	51 12	136	44 05	195	64 44	271	16 06	302
260	35 14	346	34 26	026	29 59	090	51 25	134	44 00	193	64 25	269	15 49	300
262	35 09	344	34 34	024	30 18	088	51 39	133	43 56	192	64 06	267	15 33	298
264	35 04	342	34 41	022	30 37	086	51 53	131	43 52	190	63 47	265	15 16	296
266	34 58	340	34 48	020	30 55	084	52 07	129	43 49	188	63 29	263	14 59	294
268	34 51	338	34 54	018	31 14	082	52 22	127	43 47	187	63 10	261	14 42	292
	◆Nunki		FOMALHAUT		◆ACHERNAR		CANOPUS		◆ACRUX		RIGIL KENT		ANTARES	
270	34 59	015	31 32	080	52 37	126	43 45	185	62 52	259	65 47	295	34 43	335
272	35 04	013	31 51	078	52 52	124	43 43	183	62 33	257	65 30	293	34 35	333
274	35 08	011	32 09	076	53 08	122	43 43	182	62 15	255	65 13	290	34 27	331
276	35 11	009	32 27	074	53 24	120	43 42	180	61 57	254	64 55	288	34 17	329
278	35 13	007	32 45	072	53 40	119	43 43	178	61 39	252	64 37	286	34 07	327
280	35 15	004	33 03	070	53 57	117	43 43	177	61 21	250	64 19	284	33 57	325
282	35 16	002	33 20	068	54 14	115	43 45	175	61 04	248	64 01	282	33 45	323
284	35 17	000	33 38	066	54 31	113	43 47	173	60 46	246	63 42	280	33 34	320
286	35 16	358	33 55	063	54 48	112	43 49	172	60 29	245	63 24	278	33 22	318
288	35 15	356	34 11	061	55 06	110	43 52	170	60 12	243	63 05	276	33 09	316
290	35 13	353	34 27	059	55 24	108	43 56	168	59 56	241	62 46	274	32 55	314
292	35 11	351	34 43	057	55 42	106	44 00	167	59 39	240	62 28	272	32 42	312
294	35 08	349	34 59	055	56 00	104	44 04	165	59 23	238	62 09	270	32 28	310
296	35 04	347	35 14	053	56 18	102	44 09	163	59 08	236	61 50	268	32 13	308
298	34 59	345	35 29	051	56 37	100	44 15	162	58 52	234	61 31	266	31 58	306
	◆FOMALHAUT		ACHERNAR		◆CANOPUS		ACRUX		RIGIL KENT		◆ANTARES		Nunki	
300	35 43	049	56 55	099	44 21	160	58 37	233	61 13	264	31 42	303	34 54	343
302	35 57	047	57 14	097	44 28	158	58 22	231	60 54	262	31 27	301	34 48	340
304	36 11	045	57 32	095	44 35	157	58 08	230	60 36	260	31 10	299	34 41	338
306	36 24	042	57 51	093	44 43	155	57 54	228	60 17	258	30 54	297	34 34	336
308	36 36	040	58 10	091	44 51	153	57 40	226	59 59	256	30 37	295	34 26	334
310	36 48	038	58 29	089	45 00	151	57 27	225	59 41	254	30 20	293	34 17	332
312	36 59	036	58 47	087	45 09	150	57 14	223	59 23	253	30 02	291	34 08	329
314	37 10	034	59 06	085	45 19	148	57 01	221	59 05	251	29 45	289	33 58	327
316	37 20	032	59 25	083	45 29	146	56 49	220	58 47	249	29 27	287	33 48	325
318	37 30	029	59 43	081	45 40	145	56 37	218	58 30	247	29 09	285	33 37	323
320	37 39	027	60 02	079	45 51	143	56 26	217	58 13	245	28 51	283	33 25	321
322	37 47	025	60 20	077	46 02	141	56 15	215	57 56	244	28 32	281	33 13	319
324	37 54	023	60 38	074	46 14	139	56 04	213	57 39	242	28 14	279	33 01	317
326	38 01	021	60 56	072	46 27	138	55 54	212	57 22	240	27 55	277	32 47	315
328	38 08	018	61 14	070	46 40	136	55 44	210	57 06	238	27 37	275	32 34	312
	◆FOMALHAUT		ACHERNAR		◆CANOPUS		ACRUX		RIGIL KENT		◆ANTARES		Nunki	
330	38 13	016	61 32	068	46 53	134	55 35	209	56 50	237	27 18	273	32 20	310
332	38 18	014	61 49	066	47 06	132	55 26	207	56 35	235	26 59	271	32 05	308
334	38 22	012	62 06	064	47 20	131	55 18	205	56 20	233	26 40	269	31 50	306
336	38 26	010	62 22	061	47 35	129	55 10	204	56 05	232	26 22	267	31 35	304
338	38 29	007	62 39	059	47 50	127	55 03	202	55 50	230	26 03	265	31 19	302
340	38 31	005	62 55	057	48 05	125	54 56	201	55 36	228	25 44	263	31 03	300
342	38 32	003	63 10	054	48 20	124	54 50	199	55 22	227	25 26	261	30 47	298
344	38 33	001	63 25	052	48 36	122	54 44	198	55 09	225	25 07	259	30 30	296
346	38 32	358	63 40	050	48 52	120	54 38	196	54 56	223	24 49	257	30 13	294
348	38 32	356	63 54	047	49 08	118	54 33	195	54 43	222	24 31	255	29 55	292
350	38 30	354	64 07	045	49 25	116	54 29	193	54 31	220	24 12	253	29 38	290
352	38 28	352	64 20	042	49 42	115	54 25	191	54 19	218	23 55	252	29 20	288
354	38 25	350	64 32	040	49 59	113	54 21	190	54 07	217	23 37	250	29 02	286
356	38 21	347	64 44	037	50 17	111	54 18	188	53 56	215	23 19	248	28 44	284
358	38 16	345	64 55	035	50 34	109	54 16	187	53 46	214	23 02	246	28 26	282

 LAT 82°S

LHA ♈	Hc Zn	Hc Zn	Hc Zn	Hc Zn	Hc Zn	Hc Zn	Hc Zn
	ACHERNAR	◆SIRIUS	Suhail	ACRUX	◆RIGIL KENT	Peacock	◆FOMALHAUT
0	64 15 031	15 00 104	37 25 142	55 14 185	54 26 213	60 50 295	37 14 343
2	64 23 029	15 16 102	37 35 140	55 12 184	54 18 211	60 35 293	37 09 341
4	64 31 026	15 32 100	37 46 138	55 11 182	54 09 209	60 19 291	37 03 339
6	64 38 024	15 49 098	37 58 136	55 11 181	54 01 208	60 04 289	36 57 337
8	64 44 021	16 05 096	38 10 134	55 11 179	53 54 206	59 48 287	36 50 334
10	64 50 019	16 22 094	38 22 132	55 12 178	53 47 204	59 32 285	36 42 332
12	64 55 016	16 39 092	38 34 131	55 12 176	53 40 203	59 16 283	36 34 330
14	64 59 014	16 55 090	38 47 129	55 14 174	53 34 201	58 59 280	36 26 328
16	65 03 011	17 12 088	39 00 127	55 16 173	53 28 200	58 43 278	36 16 326
18	65 06 008	17 29 086	39 14 125	55 18 171	53 22 198	58 26 276	36 07 324
20	65 08 006	17 45 084	39 28 123	55 21 170	53 17 196	58 10 274	35 57 322
22	65 09 003	18 02 082	39 42 121	55 24 168	53 13 195	57 53 272	35 46 319
24	65 10 001	18 19 080	39 56 120	55 28 166	53 09 193	57 36 270	35 35 317
26	65 09 358	18 35 078	40 11 118	55 32 165	53 05 191	57 19 268	35 23 315
28	65 09 356	18 51 076	40 26 116	55 37 163	53 02 190	57 03 266	35 11 313
	◆SIRIUS	Suhail	ACRUX	◆RIGIL KENT	Peacock	◆FOMALHAUT	ACHERNAR
30	19 07 074	40 41 114	55 42 162	53 00 188	56 46 264	34 59 311	65 07 353
32	19 23 072	40 56 112	55 47 160	52 58 187	56 30 263	34 46 309	65 04 350
34	19 39 070	41 12 110	55 53 158	52 56 185	56 13 261	34 33 307	65 01 348
36	19 55 068	41 27 108	55 59 157	52 55 183	55 57 259	34 19 305	64 57 345
38	20 10 066	41 43 106	56 06 155	52 54 182	55 40 257	34 05 303	64 53 343
40	20 25 064	42 00 104	56 13 154	52 54 180	55 24 255	33 51 300	64 48 340
42	20 40 062	42 16 102	56 21 152	52 54 179	55 08 253	33 37 298	64 42 338
44	20 55 060	42 32 101	56 29 150	52 55 177	54 52 251	33 22 296	64 35 335
46	21 09 058	42 49 099	56 37 149	52 56 175	54 36 249	33 07 294	64 28 333
48	21 23 056	43 05 097	56 46 147	52 57 174	54 21 248	32 51 292	64 20 330
50	21 36 054	43 22 095	56 55 146	52 59 172	54 06 246	32 36 290	64 11 328
52	21 50 052	43 38 093	57 05 144	53 02 170	53 50 244	32 20 288	64 02 325
54	22 03 050	43 55 091	57 15 142	53 05 169	53 36 242	32 04 286	63 52 323
56	22 15 048	44 12 089	57 25 141	53 08 167	53 21 240	31 48 284	63 41 320
58	22 27 045	44 29 087	57 36 139	53 12 166	53 07 238	31 32 282	63 31 318
	◆SIRIUS	Suhail	ACRUX	◆RIGIL KENT	Peacock	◆FOMALHAUT	ACHERNAR
60	22 39 043	44 45 085	57 47 137	53 17 164	52 52 237	31 15 280	63 19 316
62	22 50 041	45 02 083	57 59 136	53 22 162	52 39 235	30 59 278	63 07 313
64	23 01 039	45 18 081	58 11 134	53 27 161	52 25 233	30 42 276	62 55 311
66	23 11 037	45 35 079	58 23 132	53 33 159	52 12 231	30 26 274	62 42 309
68	23 21 035	45 51 077	58 35 131	53 39 157	51 59 230	30 09 272	62 29 306
70	23 31 033	46 07 075	58 48 129	53 45 156	51 46 228	29 52 270	62 15 304
72	23 39 031	46 23 073	59 01 127	53 52 154	51 34 226	29 35 268	62 01 302
74	23 48 029	46 39 071	59 15 126	54 00 153	51 22 224	29 19 266	61 47 299
76	23 55 027	46 55 068	59 28 124	54 08 151	51 11 223	29 02 264	61 32 297
78	24 03 025	47 10 066	59 42 122	54 16 149	51 00 221	28 46 262	61 17 295
80	24 09 023	47 25 064	59 57 120	54 25 148	50 49 219	28 29 260	61 02 293
82	24 16 020	47 40 062	60 11 119	54 34 146	50 39 218	28 13 258	60 46 291
84	24 21 018	47 55 060	60 26 117	54 44 144	50 29 216	27 56 256	60 30 288
86	24 26 016	48 09 058	60 41 115	54 54 143	50 19 214	27 40 254	60 14 286
88	24 30 014	48 23 056	60 56 113	55 04 141	50 10 212	27 24 252	59 58 284
	◆SIRIUS	Suhail	ACRUX	◆RIGIL KENT	Peacock	◆FOMALHAUT	ACHERNAR
90	24 34 012	48 37 054	61 12 112	55 15 139	50 01 211	27 08 250	59 42 282
92	24 37 010	48 50 051	61 27 110	55 26 138	49 53 209	26 53 249	59 26 280
94	24 40 008	49 03 049	61 43 108	55 37 136	49 45 207	26 37 247	59 09 278
96	24 42 006	49 15 047	61 59 106	55 49 134	49 37 206	26 22 245	58 53 276
98	24 43 004	49 27 045	62 15 104	56 01 133	49 30 204	26 07 243	58 36 274
100	24 44 002	49 39 043	62 31 102	56 13 131	49 24 202	25 52 241	58 19 272
102	24 44 359	49 50 040	62 48 101	56 26 129	49 18 201	25 38 239	58 03 270
104	24 44 357	50 00 038	63 04 099	56 39 127	49 12 199	25 24 237	57 46 268
106	24 43 355	50 10 036	63 21 097	56 53 126	49 07 197	25 10 235	57 29 266
108	24 41 353	50 20 034	63 37 095	57 07 124	49 02 196	24 56 233	57 13 264
110	24 39 351	50 29 031	63 54 093	57 21 122	48 58 194	24 43 231	56 56 262
112	24 36 349	50 37 029	64 11 091	57 35 120	48 54 192	24 30 229	56 39 260
114	24 32 347	50 45 027	64 27 089	57 49 119	48 51 191	24 18 228	56 23 258
116	24 28 345	50 52 024	64 44 087	58 04 117	48 48 189	24 06 226	56 07 256
118	24 23 343	50 59 022	65 01 085	58 19 115	48 46 187	23 54 224	55 51 255
	Suhail	SPICA	◆RIGIL KENT	Peacock	◆FOMALHAUT	ACHERNAR	◆SIRIUS
120	51 05 020	12 19 083	58 34 113	48 44 186	23 43 222	55 35 253	24 18 340
122	51 10 018	12 35 081	58 50 112	48 42 184	23 32 220	55 19 251	24 12 338
124	51 15 015	12 52 079	59 05 110	48 42 182	23 21 218	55 03 249	24 06 336
126	51 19 013	13 08 077	59 21 108	48 41 181	23 11 216	54 48 247	23 59 334
128	51 23 011	13 24 075	59 37 106	48 41 179	23 01 214	54 32 245	23 51 332
130	51 25 008	13 40 073	59 53 104	48 42 177	22 52 212	54 17 244	23 43 330
132	51 27 006	13 56 071	60 10 102	48 43 176	22 43 211	54 02 242	23 35 328
134	51 29 004	14 12 069	60 26 100	48 44 174	22 35 209	53 48 240	23 25 326
136	51 30 001	14 27 067	60 42 099	48 46 172	22 27 207	53 33 238	23 16 324
138	51 30 359	14 43 065	60 59 097	48 49 171	22 20 205	53 19 236	23 06 322
140	51 29 357	14 58 063	61 16 095	48 52 169	22 13 203	53 06 235	22 55 320
142	51 28 354	15 12 061	61 32 093	48 55 167	22 07 201	52 52 233	22 44 318
144	51 26 352	15 27 059	61 49 091	48 59 166	22 01 199	52 39 231	22 33 315
146	51 23 350	15 41 057	62 06 089	49 04 164	21 56 197	52 26 229	22 21 313
148	51 20 347	15 55 055	62 22 087	49 08 162	21 51 196	52 14 228	22 08 311
	SPICA	◆ANTARES	Peacock	FOMALHAUT	◆ACHERNAR	CANOPUS	◆Suhail
150	16 08 053	25 09 101	49 14 161	21 47 194	52 01 226	56 52 296	51 16 345
152	16 22 051	25 25 099	49 20 159	21 43 192	51 50 224	56 37 294	51 11 343
154	16 34 049	25 41 097	49 26 157	21 40 190	51 38 222	56 22 292	51 06 340
156	16 47 047	25 58 096	49 32 156	21 38 188	51 27 221	56 06 290	51 00 338
158	16 59 045	26 15 094	49 40 154	21 36 186	51 16 219	55 50 288	50 53 336
160	17 10 043	26 31 092	49 47 152	21 34 184	51 06 217	55 34 286	50 46 334
162	17 21 041	26 48 090	49 55 150	21 33 182	50 56 216	55 18 284	50 38 331
164	17 32 039	27 05 088	50 04 149	21 33 181	50 47 214	55 02 282	50 30 329
166	17 42 037	27 21 086	50 13 147	21 33 179	50 38 212	54 45 279	50 21 327
168	17 52 035	27 38 084	50 22 145	21 33 177	50 29 211	54 29 277	50 12 324
170	18 01 033	27 55 082	50 32 144	21 35 175	50 21 209	54 12 275	50 02 322
172	18 10 031	28 11 080	50 42 142	21 36 173	50 13 207	53 56 273	49 51 320
174	18 18 028	28 27 078	50 52 140	21 39 171	50 05 205	53 39 271	49 40 318
176	18 26 026	28 44 076	51 03 139	21 41 169	49 58 204	53 22 269	49 29 316
178	18 33 024	29 00 074	51 14 137	21 45 167	49 52 202	53 06 267	49 17 313

LHA ♈	Hc Zn	Hc Zn	Hc Zn	Hc Zn	Hc Zn	Hc Zn	Hc Zn
	SPICA	◆ANTARES	Peacock	FOMALHAUT	◆ACHERNAR	CANOPUS	◆Suhail
180	18 40 022	29 16 072	51 26 135	21 49 166	49 46 200	52 49 266	49 05 311
182	18 46 020	29 32 070	51 38 133	21 53 164	49 40 199	52 32 264	48 52 309
184	18 51 018	29 47 067	51 50 132	21 58 162	49 35 197	52 16 262	48 39 307
186	18 56 016	30 02 065	52 03 130	22 03 160	49 30 195	51 59 260	48 25 305
188	19 01 014	30 17 063	52 16 128	22 09 158	49 26 194	51 43 258	48 11 302
190	19 04 012	30 32 061	52 29 126	22 16 156	49 22 192	51 27 256	47 57 300
192	19 08 010	30 47 059	52 43 125	22 23 154	49 19 190	51 11 254	47 42 298
194	19 10 008	31 01 057	52 57 123	22 30 152	49 16 189	50 55 252	47 27 296
196	19 12 006	31 15 055	53 11 121	22 38 151	49 14 187	50 39 250	47 12 294
198	19 13 004	31 28 053	53 25 119	22 47 149	49 12 185	50 23 248	46 57 292
200	19 14 002	31 41 051	53 40 117	22 56 147	49 11 184	50 08 247	46 41 290
202	19 14 359	31 54 049	53 55 116	23 05 145	49 10 182	49 52 245	46 25 288
204	19 14 357	32 07 047	54 10 114	23 15 143	49 10 180	49 37 243	46 09 286
206	19 13 355	32 19 045	54 25 112	23 25 141	49 10 179	49 23 241	45 53 284
208	19 11 353	32 30 043	54 41 110	23 36 139	49 10 177	49 08 239	45 37 282
	◆ANTARES	Nunki	◆FOMALHAUT	ACHERNAR	CANOPUS	◆Suhail	SPICA
210	32 41 040	28 13 078	23 47 137	49 11 175	48 54 237	45 21 279	19 09 351
212	32 52 038	28 29 076	23 58 136	49 13 174	48 40 236	45 04 277	19 06 349
214	33 02 036	28 45 074	24 10 134	49 15 172	48 26 234	44 47 275	19 03 347
216	33 11 034	29 01 072	24 22 132	49 18 171	48 13 232	44 31 273	18 59 345
218	33 21 032	29 17 070	24 35 130	49 21 169	48 00 230	44 14 271	18 54 343
220	33 29 030	29 32 068	24 48 128	49 24 167	47 48 228	43 57 269	18 49 341
222	33 37 028	29 48 066	25 01 126	49 28 166	47 35 227	43 41 268	18 43 339
224	33 45 026	30 03 064	25 15 124	49 32 164	47 23 225	43 24 266	18 37 337
226	33 52 023	30 18 062	25 29 122	49 37 162	47 12 223	43 07 264	18 30 335
228	33 58 021	30 32 060	25 43 120	49 43 161	47 00 221	42 51 262	18 22 333
230	34 04 019	30 46 058	25 58 118	49 48 159	46 50 220	42 34 260	18 14 330
232	34 09 017	31 00 056	26 13 116	49 55 157	46 39 218	42 18 258	18 06 328
234	34 13 015	31 14 054	26 28 115	50 01 155	46 29 216	42 02 256	17 57 326
236	34 17 013	31 27 051	26 44 113	50 08 154	46 19 214	41 46 254	17 47 324
238	34 21 010	31 40 049	26 59 111	50 16 152	46 10 213	41 30 252	17 37 322
	ANTARES	◆Nunki	FOMALHAUT	◆ACHERNAR	CANOPUS	◆ACRUX	SPICA
240	34 23 008	31 53 047	27 14 109	50 24 150	46 01 211	67 08 292	17 27 320
242	34 25 006	32 05 045	27 30 107	50 33 149	45 53 209	66 53 290	17 16 318
244	34 27 004	32 16 043	27 46 105	50 41 147	45 45 207	66 37 287	17 05 316
246	34 28 002	32 27 041	28 03 103	50 51 145	45 38 206	66 21 285	16 53 314
248	34 28 000	32 38 039	28 19 101	51 00 144	45 31 204	66 04 283	16 41 312
250	34 27 357	32 48 037	28 35 099	51 10 142	45 24 202	65 48 281	16 28 310
252	34 26 355	32 58 035	28 52 097	51 21 140	45 18 201	65 32 279	16 15 308
254	34 25 353	33 07 032	29 08 095	51 32 139	45 12 199	65 15 277	16 02 306
256	34 22 351	33 16 030	29 25 093	51 43 137	45 07 197	64 58 275	15 48 304
258	34 19 349	33 24 028	29 42 091	51 55 135	45 02 195	64 42 273	15 34 302
260	34 16 347	33 32 026	29 59 089	52 07 133	44 58 194	64 25 271	15 20 300
262	34 12 344	33 39 024	30 15 087	52 19 132	44 55 192	64 08 269	15 05 298
264	34 07 342	33 45 022	30 32 085	52 32 130	44 51 190	63 52 267	14 50 296
266	34 01 340	33 51 020	30 48 083	52 45 128	44 49 189	63 35 265	14 35 294
268	33 55 338	33 56 017	31 05 081	52 58 126	44 46 187	63 18 263	14 20 292
	◆Nunki	FOMALHAUT	◆ACHERNAR	CANOPUS	◆ACRUX	RIGIL KENT	ANTARES
270	34 01 015	31 21 079	53 11 125	44 45 185	63 02 261	65 21 297	33 49 336
272	34 05 013	31 38 077	53 25 123	44 43 183	62 45 259	65 06 295	33 42 334
274	34 09 011	31 54 075	53 40 121	44 43 182	62 29 257	64 51 292	33 34 331
276	34 11 009	32 10 073	53 54 119	44 42 180	62 13 255	64 35 290	33 26 329
278	34 14 007	32 26 071	54 09 117	44 42 178	61 57 254	64 19 288	33 17 327
280	34 15 004	32 42 069	54 24 116	44 43 177	61 41 252	64 04 286	33 08 325
282	34 16 002	32 57 067	54 39 114	44 44 175	61 25 250	63 47 284	32 58 323
284	34 17 000	33 12 065	54 54 112	44 46 173	61 10 248	63 31 282	32 47 321
286	34 16 358	33 27 063	55 10 110	44 48 172	60 54 246	63 15 280	32 37 319
288	34 15 356	33 42 061	55 26 108	44 51 170	60 39 245	62 58 278	32 25 317
290	34 14 354	33 57 059	55 41 106	44 54 168	60 24 243	62 42 276	32 14 314
292	34 12 351	34 11 057	55 58 105	44 58 166	60 09 241	62 25 274	32 01 312
294	34 09 349	34 25 055	56 14 103	45 02 165	59 55 239	62 08 272	31 49 310
296	34 05 347	34 38 052	56 30 101	45 07 163	59 41 238	61 52 270	31 36 308
298	34 01 345	34 51 050	56 47 099	45 12 161	59 27 236	61 35 268	31 23 306
	◆FOMALHAUT	ACHERNAR	◆CANOPUS	ACRUX	RIGIL KENT	◆ANTARES	Nunki
300	35 04 048	57 03 097	45 17 160	59 13 234	61 18 266	31 09 304	33 57 343
302	35 16 046	57 20 095	45 24 158	58 59 232	61 02 264	30 55 302	33 51 341
304	35 28 044	57 36 093	45 30 156	58 46 231	60 45 262	30 41 300	33 46 338
306	35 39 042	57 53 091	45 37 154	58 34 229	60 29 260	30 26 298	33 39 336
308	35 50 040	58 10 089	45 45 153	58 21 227	60 12 258	30 11 296	33 32 334
310	36 01 038	58 26 087	45 52 151	58 09 226	59 56 256	29 56 294	33 25 332
312	36 10 036	58 43 085	46 01 149	57 57 224	59 40 254	29 41 292	33 16 330
314	36 20 033	59 00 083	46 10 147	57 46 222	59 24 252	29 25 290	33 08 328
316	36 29 031	59 16 081	46 19 146	57 35 221	59 08 251	29 09 288	32 59 326
318	36 37 029	59 33 079	46 28 144	57 24 219	58 52 249	28 53 286	32 49 323
320	36 45 027	59 49 077	46 38 142	57 14 217	58 37 247	28 37 284	32 39 321
322	36 52 025	60 05 075	46 49 140	57 04 216	58 21 245	28 21 282	32 28 319
324	36 59 023	60 21 073	47 00 139	56 54 214	58 06 243	28 04 280	32 17 317
326	37 05 020	60 37 071	47 11 137	56 45 213	57 52 242	27 48 278	32 05 315
328	37 11 018	60 53 068	47 22 135	56 36 211	57 37 240	27 31 276	31 53 313
	◆FOMALHAUT	ACHERNAR	◆CANOPUS	ACRUX	RIGIL KENT	◆ANTARES	Nunki
330	37 16 016	61 08 066	47 34 133	56 28 209	57 23 238	27 14 274	31 41 311
332	37 20 014	61 23 064	47 47 132	56 20 208	57 09 236	26 58 272	31 28 309
334	37 24 012	61 38 062	47 59 130	56 12 206	56 55 235	26 41 270	31 15 307
336	37 27 009	61 53 060	48 12 128	56 05 205	56 41 233	26 24 268	31 01 305
338	37 29 007	62 07 057	48 26 126	55 58 203	56 28 231	26 08 266	30 47 302
340	37 31 005	62 21 055	48 39 125	55 52 201	56 15 229	25 51 264	30 33 300
342	37 32 003	62 34 053	48 53 123	55 46 200	56 03 228	25 35 262	30 18 298
344	37 33 001	62 48 050	49 07 121	55 41 198	55 51 226	25 18 260	30 04 296
346	37 32 358	63 00 048	49 22 119	55 36 197	55 39 224	25 02 258	29 48 294
348	37 32 356	63 12 046	49 36 117	55 31 195	55 27 223	24 45 256	29 33 292
350	37 30 354	63 24 043	49 51 115	55 27 193	55 16 221	24 29 254	29 17 290
352	37 28 352	63 35 041	50 07 114	55 24 192	55 06 219	24 13 252	29 02 288
354	37 26 350	63 46 039	50 22 112	55 20 190	54 55 218	23 58 250	28 46 286
356	37 22 348	63 56 036	50 38 110	55 18 189	54 45 216	23 42 248	28 30 284
358	37 18 345	64 06 034	50 53 108	55 15 187	54 36 214	23 27 246	28 13 282

LAT 83°S

LHA ♈	Hc	Zn	Hc	Zn	Hc	Zn	Hc	Zn	Hc	Zn	Hc	Zn	Hc	Zn
	ACHERNAR		◆ SIRIUS		Suhail		ACRUX		◆ RIGIL KENT		Peacock		◆ FOMALHAUT	
0	63 23	030	15 14	103	38 12	141	56 13	186	55 17	213	60 24	297	36 16	343
2	63 30	028	15 28	101	38 21	139	56 12	184	55 09	212	60 11	295	36 12	341
4	63 37	025	15 42	099	38 31	137	56 11	182	55 01	210	59 57	293	36 07	339
6	63 43	023	15 57	097	38 41	136	56 11	181	54 54	208	59 44	290	36 01	337
8	63 48	021	16 11	096	38 51	134	56 11	179	54 47	207	59 30	288	35 55	335
10	63 53	018	16 26	094	39 02	132	56 11	177	54 41	205	59 16	286	35 49	333
12	63 57	016	16 41	092	39 13	130	56 12	176	54 35	203	59 02	284	35 42	330
14	64 01	013	16 55	090	39 24	128	56 14	174	54 29	202	58 47	282	35 35	328
16	64 04	011	17 10	088	39 36	126	56 15	173	54 24	200	58 33	280	35 27	326
18	64 06	008	17 24	086	39 48	124	56 17	171	54 19	198	58 19	278	35 18	324
20	64 08	006	17 39	084	40 00	123	56 20	169	54 15	197	58 04	276	35 09	322
22	64 09	003	17 53	082	40 13	121	56 23	168	54 11	195	57 50	274	35 00	320
24	64 10	001	18 08	080	40 25	119	56 26	166	54 07	193	57 35	272	34 51	318
26	64 09	358	18 22	078	40 38	117	56 30	164	54 04	192	57 20	270	34 41	316
28	64 09	356	18 36	076	40 51	115	56 34	163	54 02	190	57 06	268	34 30	314
	◆ SIRIUS		Suhail		ACRUX		◆ RIGIL KENT		Peacock		◆ FOMALHAUT		ACHERNAR	
30	18 51	074	41 05	113	56 38	161	53 59	188	56 51	266	34 19	311	64 07	353
32	19 05	072	41 18	111	56 43	160	53 57	187	56 37	264	34 08	309	64 05	351
34	19 18	070	41 32	109	56 49	158	53 56	185	56 22	262	33 57	307	64 03	348
36	19 32	068	41 46	107	56 54	156	53 55	183	56 08	260	33 45	305	63 59	346
38	19 45	066	42 00	105	57 00	155	53 54	182	55 53	258	33 33	303	63 55	343
40	19 59	064	42 14	104	57 07	153	53 54	180	55 39	256	33 20	301	63 51	341
42	20 11	061	42 28	102	57 14	151	53 54	178	55 25	254	33 08	299	63 46	338
44	20 24	059	42 43	100	57 21	150	53 55	177	55 11	253	32 55	297	63 40	336
46	20 37	057	42 57	098	57 28	148	53 56	175	54 57	251	32 42	295	63 34	334
48	20 49	055	43 12	096	57 36	146	53 57	174	54 43	249	32 28	293	63 27	331
50	21 01	053	43 26	094	57 45	145	53 59	172	54 30	247	32 15	291	63 20	329
52	21 12	051	43 41	092	57 53	143	54 01	170	54 16	245	32 01	289	63 12	326
54	21 24	049	43 55	090	58 02	141	54 04	169	54 03	243	31 47	287	63 04	324
56	21 34	047	44 10	088	58 12	140	54 07	167	53 50	241	31 33	285	62 55	322
58	21 45	045	44 25	086	58 21	138	54 10	165	53 37	240	31 19	283	62 46	319
	◆ SIRIUS		Suhail		ACRUX		◆ RIGIL KENT		Peacock		◆ FOMALHAUT		ACHERNAR	
60	21 55	043	44 39	084	58 31	136	54 14	164	53 25	238	31 04	281	62 36	317
62	22 05	041	44 54	082	58 41	135	54 19	162	53 13	236	30 50	279	62 26	315
64	22 14	039	45 08	080	58 52	133	54 23	160	53 01	234	30 36	277	62 15	312
66	22 23	037	45 23	078	59 03	131	54 29	159	52 49	232	30 21	275	62 04	310
68	22 32	035	45 37	076	59 14	129	54 34	157	52 37	231	30 06	273	61 53	308
70	22 40	033	45 51	074	59 25	128	54 40	155	52 26	229	29 52	271	61 41	305
72	22 48	031	46 05	072	59 37	126	54 46	154	52 15	227	29 37	269	61 29	303
74	22 55	029	46 19	070	59 49	124	54 53	152	52 05	225	29 23	267	61 16	301
76	23 02	027	46 32	067	60 01	122	55 00	150	51 55	224	29 08	265	61 04	299
78	23 08	024	46 46	065	60 14	121	55 08	149	51 45	222	28 53	263	60 51	297
80	23 14	022	46 59	063	60 26	119	55 15	147	51 35	220	28 39	261	60 38	294
82	23 19	020	47 12	061	60 39	117	55 24	145	51 26	218	28 25	259	60 24	292
84	23 24	018	47 24	059	60 52	115	55 32	143	51 17	217	28 10	257	60 10	290
86	23 28	016	47 37	057	61 06	114	55 41	142	51 09	215	27 56	255	59 57	288
88	23 32	014	47 49	055	61 19	112	55 50	140	51 00	213	27 42	253	59 43	286
	◆ SIRIUS		Suhail		ACRUX		◆ RIGIL KENT		Peacock		◆ FOMALHAUT		ACHERNAR	
90	23 36	012	48 01	053	61 33	110	56 00	138	50 53	211	27 28	251	59 29	284
92	23 38	010	48 12	050	61 47	108	56 10	137	50 45	210	27 14	249	59 14	282
94	23 41	008	48 23	048	62 01	106	56 20	135	50 38	208	27 01	247	59 00	280
96	23 42	006	48 34	046	62 15	104	56 30	133	50 31	206	26 47	245	58 45	278
98	23 43	004	48 44	044	62 29	102	56 41	131	50 25	204	26 34	243	58 31	276
100	23 44	002	48 54	042	62 43	101	56 52	130	50 19	203	26 21	241	58 16	274
102	23 44	359	49 04	040	62 58	099	57 04	128	50 14	201	26 09	239	58 02	272
104	23 44	357	49 13	037	63 12	097	57 15	126	50 09	199	25 56	237	57 47	270
106	23 43	355	49 22	035	63 27	095	57 27	124	50 04	198	25 44	236	57 32	268
108	23 41	353	49 30	033	63 41	093	57 39	123	50 00	196	25 32	234	57 18	266
110	23 39	351	49 38	031	63 56	091	57 52	121	49 56	194	25 20	232	57 03	264
112	23 37	349	49 45	028	64 11	089	58 05	119	49 53	192	25 09	230	56 49	262
114	23 34	347	49 51	026	64 25	087	58 17	117	49 50	191	24 58	228	56 34	260
116	23 30	345	49 58	024	64 40	085	58 31	115	49 47	189	24 47	226	56 20	258
118	23 26	343	50 03	022	64 54	083	58 44	114	49 45	187	24 37	224	56 06	256
	Suhail		SPICA		◆ RIGIL KENT		Peacock		◆ FOMALHAUT		ACHERNAR		◆ SIRIUS	
120	50 08	019	12 11	083	58 57	112	49 44	186	24 27	222	55 52	254	23 22	341
122	50 13	017	12 26	081	59 11	110	49 42	184	24 17	220	55 38	252	23 16	339
124	50 17	015	12 40	079	59 25	108	49 42	182	24 08	218	55 24	250	23 11	336
126	50 21	013	12 54	077	59 39	106	49 41	181	23 59	216	55 10	249	23 05	334
128	50 24	010	13 09	075	59 53	104	49 41	179	23 51	215	54 57	247	22 58	332
130	50 26	008	13 23	073	60 07	102	49 42	177	23 43	213	54 43	245	22 51	330
132	50 28	006	13 37	071	60 21	101	49 43	176	23 35	211	54 30	243	22 44	328
134	50 29	004	13 50	069	60 36	099	49 44	174	23 28	209	54 17	241	22 36	326
136	50 30	001	14 04	067	60 50	097	49 46	172	23 21	207	54 05	239	22 27	324
138	50 30	359	14 17	065	61 05	095	49 48	170	23 14	205	53 52	238	22 19	322
140	50 29	357	14 30	063	61 20	093	49 51	169	23 08	203	53 40	236	22 09	320
142	50 28	354	14 43	061	61 34	091	49 54	167	23 03	201	53 28	234	22 00	318
144	50 26	352	14 56	059	61 49	089	49 57	165	22 58	199	53 16	232	21 50	316
146	50 24	350	15 08	057	62 03	087	50 01	164	22 53	198	53 05	230	21 39	314
148	50 21	348	15 20	055	62 18	085	50 06	162	22 49	196	52 54	229	21 29	312
	SPICA		◆ ANTARES		Peacock		FOMALHAUT		◆ ACHERNAR		CANOPUS		◆ Suhail	
150	15 32	053	25 20	101	50 10	160	22 45	194	52 43	227	56 25	298	50 18	345
152	15 44	051	25 35	099	50 15	158	22 42	192	52 32	225	56 12	296	50 14	343
154	15 55	049	25 49	097	50 21	157	22 39	190	52 22	223	55 59	293	50 09	341
156	16 06	047	26 04	095	50 27	155	22 37	188	52 12	222	55 45	291	50 04	339
158	16 16	045	26 18	093	50 33	153	22 35	186	52 03	220	55 31	289	49 58	336
160	16 26	043	26 33	091	50 40	152	22 34	184	51 54	218	55 17	287	49 52	334
162	16 36	041	26 47	089	50 47	150	22 33	182	51 45	216	55 03	285	49 46	332
164	16 45	039	27 02	087	50 55	148	22 33	181	51 36	215	54 49	283	49 39	330
166	16 54	037	27 17	085	51 03	146	22 33	179	51 28	213	54 35	281	49 31	327
168	17 03	034	27 31	083	51 11	145	22 33	177	51 20	211	54 20	279	49 23	325
170	17 11	032	27 46	081	51 20	143	22 34	175	51 13	209	54 06	277	49 14	323
172	17 18	030	28 00	079	51 29	141	22 36	173	51 06	208	53 51	275	49 05	321
174	17 26	028	28 14	077	51 38	139	22 38	171	50 59	206	53 37	273	48 56	319
176	17 32	026	28 29	075	51 48	138	22 40	169	50 53	204	53 22	271	48 46	316
178	17 39	024	28 43	073	51 58	136	22 43	167	50 47	203	53 08	269	48 35	314

LHA ♈	Hc	Zn	Hc	Zn	Hc	Zn	Hc	Zn	Hc	Zn	Hc	Zn	Hc	Zn
	SPICA		◆ ANTARES		Peacock		FOMALHAUT		◆ ACHERNAR		CANOPUS		◆ Suhail	
180	17 44	022	28 57	071	52 08	134	22 47	166	50 42	201	52 53	267	48 25	312
182	17 50	020	29 10	069	52 19	132	22 51	164	50 37	199	52 38	265	48 14	310
184	17 54	018	29 24	067	52 30	131	22 55	162	50 32	197	52 24	263	48 02	308
186	17 59	016	29 37	065	52 41	129	23 00	160	50 28	196	52 09	261	47 51	306
188	18 02	014	29 50	063	52 52	127	23 05	158	50 24	194	51 55	259	47 39	303
190	18 06	012	30 03	061	53 04	125	23 11	156	50 21	192	51 41	257	47 26	301
192	18 08	010	30 16	059	53 16	123	23 17	154	50 18	191	51 26	255	47 14	299
194	18 11	008	30 28	057	53 29	122	23 23	152	50 16	189	51 12	253	47 01	297
196	18 12	006	30 40	055	53 41	120	23 30	150	50 14	187	50 58	251	46 47	295
198	18 14	004	30 52	053	53 54	118	23 38	149	50 12	186	50 45	250	46 34	293
200	18 14	002	31 03	050	54 07	116	23 46	147	50 11	184	50 31	248	46 21	291
202	18 14	359	31 15	048	54 20	114	23 54	145	50 10	182	50 18	246	46 07	289
204	18 14	357	31 25	046	54 34	112	24 03	143	50 10	180	50 04	244	45 53	287
206	18 13	355	31 36	044	54 47	111	24 12	141	50 10	179	49 51	242	45 39	285
208	18 12	353	31 46	042	55 01	109	24 21	139	50 10	177	49 39	240	45 24	283
	◆ ANTARES		Nunki		◆ FOMALHAUT		ACHERNAR		CANOPUS		◆ Suhail		SPICA	
210	31 55	040	28 00	078	24 31	137	50 11	175	49 26	238	45 10	280	18 10	351
212	32 05	038	28 14	076	24 41	135	50 13	174	49 14	237	44 56	278	18 07	349
214	32 13	036	28 28	073	24 51	133	50 14	172	49 02	235	44 41	276	18 04	347
216	32 22	034	28 42	071	25 02	131	50 17	170	48 50	233	44 27	274	18 01	345
218	32 30	032	28 56	069	25 13	129	50 19	169	48 38	231	44 12	272	17 57	343
220	32 37	029	29 10	067	25 25	128	50 22	167	48 27	229	43 57	270	17 52	341
222	32 44	027	29 23	065	25 37	126	50 26	165	48 16	227	43 43	268	17 47	339
224	32 50	025	29 36	063	25 49	124	50 30	164	48 05	226	43 28	266	17 41	337
226	32 56	023	29 49	061	26 01	122	50 34	162	47 55	224	43 14	265	17 35	335
228	33 02	021	30 02	059	26 13	120	50 39	160	47 45	222	42 59	263	17 29	333
230	33 07	019	30 14	057	26 26	118	50 44	158	47 36	220	42 45	261	17 22	331
232	33 11	017	30 26	055	26 39	116	50 50	157	47 26	219	42 30	259	17 15	329
234	33 15	015	30 38	053	26 53	114	50 56	155	47 17	217	42 16	257	17 07	327
236	33 19	012	30 50	051	27 06	112	51 02	153	47 09	215	42 02	255	16 59	324
238	33 22	010	31 01	049	27 20	110	51 09	152	47 01	213	41 48	253	16 50	322
	ANTARES		◆ Nunki		FOMALHAUT		◆ ACHERNAR		CANOPUS		◆ ACRUX		SPICA	
240	33 24	008	31 12	047	27 33	108	51 16	150	46 53	211	66 45	294	16 41	320
242	33 26	006	31 22	045	27 47	106	51 24	148	46 45	210	66 31	292	16 31	318
244	33 27	004	31 32	043	28 01	104	51 32	146	46 38	208	66 18	290	16 21	316
246	33 28	002	31 42	041	28 16	102	51 40	145	46 32	206	66 04	287	16 11	314
248	33 28	000	31 51	038	28 30	100	51 48	143	46 25	204	65 50	285	16 00	312
250	33 27	357	32 00	036	28 44	099	51 57	141	46 19	203	65 36	283	15 49	310
252	33 27	355	32 09	034	28 59	097	52 07	139	46 14	201	65 21	281	15 38	308
254	33 25	353	32 17	032	29 14	095	52 16	138	46 09	199	65 07	279	15 26	306
256	33 23	351	32 24	030	29 28	093	52 26	136	46 04	197	64 52	277	15 14	304
258	33 20	349	32 31	028	29 43	091	52 37	134	46 00	196	64 38	275	15 02	302
260	33 17	347	32 38	026	29 57	089	52 47	132	45 56	194	64 23	273	14 50	300
262	33 14	345	32 44	024	30 12	087	52 58	131	45 53	192	64 09	271	14 37	298
264	33 10	342	32 49	021	30 27	085	53 10	129	45 50	190	63 54	269	14 24	296
266	33 05	340	32 55	019	30 41	083	53 21	127	45 48	189	63 39	267	14 11	294
268	33 00	338	32 59	017	30 56	081	53 33	125	45 46	187	63 25	265	13 57	292
	◆ Nunki		FOMALHAUT		◆ ACHERNAR		CANOPUS		◆ ACRUX		RIGIL KENT		ANTARES	
270	33 03	015	31 10	079	53 45	123	45 44	185	63 10	263	64 53	299	32 54	336
272	33 07	013	31 24	077	53 57	122	45 43	184	62 56	261	64 40	297	32 48	334
274	33 10	011	31 38	075	54 10	120	45 42	182	62 41	259	64 27	294	32 41	332
276	33 12	009	31 52	073	54 23	118	45 42	180	62 27	257	64 13	292	32 34	330
278	33 14	006	32 06	071	54 36	116	45 42	178	62 13	255	64 00	290	32 26	328
280	33 15	004	32 20	068	54 49	114	45 43	177	61 59	254	63 46	288	32 18	325
282	33 16	002	32 33	066	55 02	113	45 44	175	61 45	252	63 32	286	32 10	323
284	33 17	000	32 47	064	55 16	111	45 46	173	61 31	250	63 18	284	32 01	321
286	33 16	358	33 00	062	55 30	109	45 48	171	61 17	248	63 04	282	31 51	319
288	33 16	356	33 13	060	55 44	107	45 50	170	61 04	246	62 49	280	31 42	317
290	33 14	354	33 25	058	55 58	105	45 53	168	60 51	244	62 35	277	31 31	315
292	33 12	351	33 38	056	56 12	103	45 56	166	60 38	243	62 20	275	31 21	313
294	33 10	349	33 50	054	56 26	101	46 00	164	60 25	241	62 06	273	31 10	311
296	33 07	347	34 01	052	56 41	099	46 04	163	60 12	239	61 51	271	30 59	309
298	33 03	345	34 13	050	56 55	097	46 09	161	60 00	237	61 36	269	30 47	307
	◆ FOMALHAUT		ACHERNAR		◆ CANOPUS		ACRUX		RIGIL KENT		◆ ANTARES		Nunki	
300	34 24	048	57 10	095	46 14	159	59 47	236	61 22	267	30 35	305	32 59	343
302	34 34	046	57 24	093	46 19	157	59 35	234	61 07	265	30 23	302	32 55	341
304	34 44	044	57 39	092	46 25	156	59 24	232	60 53	264	30 11	300	32 50	339
306	34 54	041	57 53	090	46 31	154	59 12	230	60 38	262	29 58	298	32 44	337
308	35 04	039	58 08	088	46 38	152	59 01	229	60 24	260	29 45	296	32 38	334
310	35 13	037	58 23	086	46 45	150	58 50	227	60 09	258	29 32	294	32 31	332
312	35 22	035	58 37	084	46 52	149	58 40	225	59 55	256	29 18	292	32 24	330
314	35 30	033	58 52	081	47 00	147	58 30	223	59 41	254	29 05	290	32 17	328
316	35 37	031	59 06	079	47 08	145	58 20	222	59 27	252	28 51	288	32 09	326
318	35 45	029	59 20	077	47 17	143	58 10	220	59 13	250	28 37	286	32 01	324
320	35 51	027	59 35	075	47 26	142	58 01	218	59 00	248	28 23	284	31 52	322
322	35 58	024	59 49	073	47 35	140	57 52	217	58 46	247	28 08	282	31 42	320
324	36 04	022	60 03	071	47 44	138	57 43	215	58 33	245	27 54	280	31 33	317
326	36 09	020	60 16	069	47 54	136	57 35	213	58 20	243	27 40	278	31 23	315
328	36 14	018	60 30	067	48 05	134	57 27	212	58 07	241	27 25	276	31 12	313
	◆ FOMALHAUT		ACHERNAR		◆ CANOPUS		ACRUX		RIGIL KENT		◆ ANTARES		Nunki	
330	36 18	016	60 43	065	48 15	133	57 20	210	57 54	239	27 11	274	31 01	311
332	36 22	014	60 56	062	48 26	131	57 13	208	57 41	238	26 56	272	30 50	309
334	36 25	011	61 09	060	48 37	129	57 06	207	57 29	236	26 41	270	30 39	307
336	36 27	009	61 22	058	48 49	127	57 00	205	57 17	234	26 27	268	30 27	305
338	36 30	007	61 34	056	49 01	125	56 54	203	57 05	232	26 12	266	30 15	303
340	36 31	005	61 46	054	49 13	124	56 48	202	56 54	231	25 57	264	30 02	301
342	36 32	003	61 58	051	49 25	122	56 43	200	56 43	229	25 43	262	29 50	299
344	36 33	001	62 09	049	49 38	120	56 38	199	56 32	227	25 29	260	29 37	297
346	36 32	359	62 20	047	49 50	118	56 33	197	56 21	225	25 14	258	29 24	295
348	36 32	356	62 30	044	50 03	116	56 29	195	56 11	224	25 00	256	29 10	293
350	36 31	354	62 40	042	50 17	114	56 26	194	56 01	222	24 46	254	28 57	291
352	36 29	352	62 50	040	50 30	112	56 22	192	55 52	220	24 32	252	28 43	289
354	36 26	350	62 59	037	50 44	111	56 19	190	55 42	219	24 18	250	28 29	287
356	36 24	348	63 07	035	50 57	109	56 17	189	55 33	217	24 04	248	28 15	285
358	36 20	346	63 15	033	51 11	107	56 15	187	55 25	215	23 51	247	28 01	283

LAT 84°S

LHA ♈	Hc Zn	Hc Zn	Hc Zn	Hc Zn	Hc Zn	Hc Zn	Hc Zn
	ACHERNAR	◆ SIRIUS	Suhail	ACRUX	◆ RIGIL KENT	Peacock	◆ FOMALHAUT
0	62 31 029	15 27 103	38 58 141	57 13 186	56 06 214	59 56 299	35 19 344
2	62 37 027	15 40 101	39 06 139	57 12 184	56 00 213	59 45 296	35 15 341
4	62 42 025	15 52 099	39 15 137	57 11 182	55 53 211	59 33 294	35 11 339
6	62 47 022	16 05 097	39 23 135	57 11 181	55 47 209	59 22 292	35 06 337
8	62 52 020	16 17 095	39 33 133	57 11 179	55 41 207	59 10 290	35 01 335
10	62 56 017	16 29 093	39 42 131	57 11 177	55 35 206	58 58 288	34 56 333
12	62 59 015	16 42 091	39 51 129	57 12 176	55 30 204	58 46 286	34 50 331
14	63 02 013	16 55 089	40 01 128	57 13 174	55 25 202	58 34 284	34 43 329
16	63 05 010	17 07 087	40 11 126	57 15 172	55 21 200	58 22 282	34 37 327
18	63 07 008	17 20 085	40 22 124	57 17 171	55 16 199	58 09 280	34 30 324
20	63 08 005	17 32 083	40 32 122	57 19 169	55 12 197	57 57 278	34 22 322
22	63 09 003	17 45 081	40 43 120	57 21 167	55 09 195	57 45 276	34 14 320
24	63 10 001	17 57 079	40 54 118	57 24 166	55 06 194	57 32 274	34 06 318
26	63 10 358	18 09 077	41 05 116	57 28 164	55 03 192	57 20 271	33 58 316
28	63 09 356	18 21 075	41 16 114	57 31 162	55 01 190	57 07 270	33 49 314
	◆ SIRIUS	Suhail	ACRUX	◆ RIGIL KENT	Peacock	◆ FOMALHAUT	ACHERNAR
30	18 33 073	41 28 112	57 35 161	54 59 189	56 54 268	33 40 312	63 08 353
32	18 45 071	41 40 110	57 39 159	54 57 187	56 42 266	33 30 310	63 06 351
34	18 57 069	41 51 108	57 44 157	54 56 185	56 29 264	33 20 308	63 04 349
36	19 09 067	42 03 107	57 49 156	54 55 184	56 17 262	33 10 306	63 01 346
38	19 20 065	42 15 105	57 54 154	54 54 182	56 05 260	33 00 304	62 58 344
40	19 32 063	42 28 103	58 00 152	54 54 180	55 52 258	32 49 302	62 54 342
42	19 43 061	42 40 101	58 06 151	54 54 178	55 40 256	32 39 300	62 50 339
44	19 54 059	42 52 099	58 12 149	54 54 177	55 28 254	32 27 297	62 45 337
46	20 04 057	43 05 097	58 19 147	54 55 175	55 16 252	32 16 295	62 40 334
48	20 15 055	43 17 095	58 26 145	54 57 173	55 04 250	32 05 293	62 34 332
50	20 25 053	43 30 093	58 33 144	54 58 172	54 52 248	31 53 291	62 28 330
52	20 35 051	43 42 091	58 41 142	55 00 170	54 41 246	31 41 289	62 22 327
54	20 44 049	43 55 089	58 49 140	55 03 168	54 29 245	31 30 287	62 15 325
56	20 54 047	44 07 087	58 57 139	55 05 167	54 18 243	31 18 285	62 07 323
58	21 03 045	44 20 085	59 05 137	55 08 165	54 07 241	31 05 283	62 00 320
	◆ SIRIUS	Suhail	ACRUX	◆ RIGIL KENT	Peacock	◆ FOMALHAUT	ACHERNAR
60	21 11 043	44 32 083	59 14 135	55 12 163	53 56 239	30 53 281	61 51 318
62	21 20 041	44 45 081	59 23 133	55 16 161	53 46 237	30 41 279	61 43 316
64	21 28 039	44 57 079	59 32 132	55 20 160	53 35 235	30 28 277	61 34 314
66	21 35 037	45 09 077	59 42 130	55 24 158	53 25 233	30 16 275	61 25 311
68	21 43 035	45 21 075	59 52 128	55 29 156	53 15 232	30 03 273	61 15 309
70	21 50 033	45 34 073	60 02 126	55 34 155	53 05 230	29 51 271	61 05 307
72	21 56 031	45 45 071	60 12 125	55 40 153	52 56 228	29 38 269	60 55 305
74	22 02 028	45 57 069	60 22 123	55 46 151	52 47 226	29 26 267	60 45 303
76	22 08 026	46 09 066	60 33 121	55 52 149	52 38 224	29 13 265	60 34 300
78	22 13 024	46 20 064	60 44 119	55 59 148	52 29 223	29 01 263	60 23 298
80	22 18 022	46 31 062	60 55 117	56 05 146	52 21 221	28 48 261	60 12 296
82	22 23 020	46 42 060	61 06 116	56 13 144	52 13 219	28 36 259	60 01 294
84	22 27 018	46 53 058	61 17 114	56 20 143	52 05 217	28 24 257	59 49 292
86	22 31 016	47 04 056	61 29 112	56 28 141	51 58 216	28 11 255	59 37 290
88	22 34 014	47 14 054	61 41 110	56 36 139	51 50 214	27 59 253	59 25 288
	◆ SIRIUS	Suhail	ACRUX	◆ RIGIL KENT	Peacock	◆ FOMALHAUT	ACHERNAR
90	22 37 012	47 24 052	61 53 108	56 44 137	51 44 212	27 47 251	59 13 285
92	22 39 010	47 34 050	62 04 106	56 53 136	51 37 210	27 36 250	59 01 283
94	22 41 008	47 43 047	62 17 104	57 02 134	51 31 208	27 24 248	58 49 281
96	22 43 006	47 52 045	62 29 103	57 11 132	51 25 207	27 12 246	58 37 279
98	22 44 004	48 01 043	62 41 101	57 20 130	51 20 205	27 01 244	58 24 277
100	22 44 002	48 09 041	62 53 099	57 30 128	51 15 203	26 50 242	58 12 275
102	22 44 359	48 17 039	63 06 097	57 40 127	51 10 201	26 39 240	57 59 273
104	22 44 357	48 25 037	63 18 095	57 50 125	51 05 200	26 28 238	57 47 271
106	22 43 355	48 32 035	63 31 093	58 01 123	51 01 198	26 18 236	57 34 269
108	22 42 353	48 39 032	63 43 091	58 11 121	50 58 196	26 08 234	57 22 267
110	22 40 351	48 46 030	63 56 089	58 22 119	50 54 194	25 57 232	57 09 265
112	22 38 349	48 52 028	64 08 087	58 33 118	50 51 193	25 48 230	56 57 263
114	22 35 347	48 58 026	64 21 085	58 44 116	50 49 191	25 38 228	56 44 261
116	22 32 345	49 03 024	64 33 083	58 56 114	50 47 189	25 29 226	56 32 259
118	22 29 343	49 08 021	64 46 081	59 07 112	50 45 188	25 20 224	56 20 257
	Suhail	SPICA	◆ RIGIL KENT	Peacock	◆ FOMALHAUT	ACHERNAR	◆ SIRIUS
120	49 12 019	12 04 083	59 19 110	50 43 186	25 11 222	56 07 256	22 25 341
122	49 16 017	12 16 081	59 31 108	50 42 184	25 03 221	55 55 254	22 21 339
124	49 19 015	12 29 079	59 43 106	50 41 182	24 55 219	55 43 252	22 16 337
126	49 22 012	12 41 077	59 55 105	50 41 181	24 47 217	55 31 250	22 11 335
128	49 25 010	12 53 075	60 07 103	50 41 179	24 40 215	55 20 248	22 05 332
130	49 27 008	13 05 073	60 19 101	50 42 177	24 33 213	55 08 246	21 59 330
132	49 28 006	13 17 071	60 32 099	50 42 175	24 27 211	54 57 244	21 53 328
134	49 29 004	13 29 069	60 44 097	50 44 174	24 20 209	54 46 242	21 46 326
136	49 30 001	13 40 067	60 56 095	50 45 172	24 14 207	54 35 241	21 39 324
138	49 30 359	13 52 065	61 09 093	50 47 170	24 09 205	54 24 239	21 31 322
140	49 29 357	14 03 063	61 22 091	50 50 168	24 04 203	54 13 237	21 23 320
142	49 28 355	14 14 061	61 34 089	50 52 167	23 59 201	54 03 235	21 15 318
144	49 27 352	14 25 059	61 47 087	50 55 165	23 54 200	53 53 233	21 07 316
146	49 25 350	14 35 057	61 59 085	50 59 163	23 50 198	53 43 231	20 58 314
148	49 22 348	14 46 055	62 12 083	51 02 162	23 47 196	53 33 230	20 49 312
	SPICA	◆ ANTARES	Peacock	FOMALHAUT	◆ ACHERNAR	CANOPUS	◆ Suhail
150	14 56 053	25 31 100	51 07 160	23 44 194	53 24 228	55 56 299	49 20 346
152	15 06 051	25 44 099	51 11 158	23 41 192	53 14 226	55 45 297	49 16 343
154	15 15 049	25 56 097	51 16 156	23 38 190	53 05 224	55 34 295	49 12 341
156	15 25 047	26 09 095	51 21 155	23 36 188	52 57 222	55 23 293	49 08 339
158	15 33 044	26 21 093	51 27 153	23 35 186	52 49 220	55 11 291	49 03 337
160	15 42 042	26 34 091	51 33 151	23 34 184	52 41 219	54 59 288	48 58 335
162	15 50 040	26 46 089	51 39 149	23 33 182	52 33 217	54 47 286	48 53 332
164	15 58 038	26 59 087	51 46 147	23 33 181	52 25 215	54 35 284	48 47 330
166	16 06 036	27 11 085	51 52 146	23 33 179	52 18 214	54 23 282	48 40 328
168	16 13 034	27 24 083	52 00 144	23 33 177	52 12 212	54 10 280	48 33 326
170	16 20 032	27 36 081	52 07 142	23 34 175	52 05 210	53 58 278	48 26 324
172	16 27 030	27 48 079	52 15 140	23 35 173	51 59 208	53 46 276	48 18 321
174	16 33 028	28 01 077	52 23 139	23 37 171	51 53 207	53 33 274	48 10 319
176	16 38 026	28 13 075	52 32 137	23 39 169	51 48 205	53 21 272	48 02 317
178	16 44 024	28 25 073	52 40 135	23 42 167	51 43 203	53 08 270	47 53 315

LHA ♈	Hc Zn	Hc Zn	Hc Zn	Hc Zn	Hc Zn	Hc Zn	Hc Zn
	SPICA	◆ ANTARES	Peacock	FOMALHAUT	◆ ACHERNAR	CANOPUS	◆ Suhail
180	16 49 022	28 37 071	52 49 133	23 45 165	51 38 201	52 56 268	47 44 313
182	16 53 020	28 48 068	52 59 131	23 48 163	51 34 200	52 43 266	47 35 311
184	16 57 018	29 00 066	53 08 130	23 52 162	51 30 198	52 31 264	47 25 309
186	17 01 016	29 11 064	53 18 128	23 56 160	51 26 196	52 18 262	47 15 306
188	17 04 014	29 23 062	53 28 126	24 01 158	51 23 194	52 06 260	47 05 304
190	17 07 012	29 34 060	53 38 124	24 06 156	51 20 193	51 53 258	46 55 302
192	17 09 010	29 44 058	53 49 122	24 11 154	51 17 191	51 41 256	46 44 300
194	17 11 008	29 55 056	54 00 120	24 17 152	51 15 189	51 29 255	46 33 298
196	17 13 006	30 05 054	54 10 119	24 23 150	51 13 187	51 17 253	46 22 296
198	17 14 004	30 15 052	54 22 117	24 29 148	51 12 186	51 05 251	46 10 294
200	17 14 002	30 25 050	54 33 115	24 36 146	51 11 184	50 53 249	45 59 292
202	17 14 359	30 35 048	54 44 113	24 43 144	51 10 182	50 42 247	45 47 290
204	17 14 357	30 44 046	54 56 111	24 50 143	51 10 180	50 30 245	45 35 288
206	17 13 355	30 53 044	55 08 109	24 58 141	51 10 179	50 19 243	45 23 286
208	17 12 353	31 01 042	55 20 107	25 06 139	51 10 177	50 08 241	45 11 284
	◆ ANTARES	Nunki	◆ FOMALHAUT	ACHERNAR	CANOPUS	◆ Suhail	SPICA
210	31 09 040	27 47 077	25 15 137	51 11 175	49 57 239	44 59 281	17 10 351
212	31 17 038	27 59 075	25 23 135	51 12 174	49 46 238	44 46 279	17 08 349
214	31 25 035	28 11 073	25 32 133	51 14 172	49 36 236	44 34 277	17 06 347
216	31 32 033	28 23 071	25 42 131	51 16 170	49 26 234	44 22 275	17 03 345
218	31 38 031	28 35 069	25 51 129	51 18 168	49 16 232	44 09 273	16 59 343
220	31 45 029	28 46 067	26 01 127	51 21 167	49 06 230	43 56 271	16 55 341
222	31 51 027	28 58 065	26 11 125	51 24 165	48 56 228	43 44 269	16 51 339
224	31 56 025	29 09 063	26 22 123	51 27 163	48 47 226	43 31 267	16 46 337
226	32 01 023	29 20 061	26 32 121	51 31 161	48 38 225	43 19 265	16 41 335
228	32 06 021	29 31 059	26 43 119	51 35 160	48 29 223	43 06 263	16 36 333
230	32 10 019	29 41 057	26 54 118	51 40 158	48 21 221	42 54 262	16 30 331
232	32 14 017	29 52 055	27 05 116	51 45 156	48 13 219	42 42 260	16 23 329
234	32 17 014	30 02 053	27 17 114	51 50 154	48 05 217	42 29 258	16 17 327
236	32 20 012	30 12 050	27 28 112	51 56 153	47 58 216	42 17 256	16 10 325
238	32 23 010	30 21 048	27 40 110	52 02 151	47 51 214	42 05 254	16 02 323
	ANTARES	◆ Nunki	FOMALHAUT	◆ ACHERNAR	CANOPUS	◆ ACRUX	SPICA
240	32 25 008	30 30 046	27 52 108	52 08 149	47 44 212	66 20 296	15 54 321
242	32 26 006	30 39 044	28 04 106	52 14 147	47 37 210	66 08 294	15 46 319
244	32 27 004	30 48 042	28 16 104	52 21 146	47 31 208	65 57 292	15 38 317
246	32 28 002	30 56 040	28 28 102	52 29 144	47 25 207	65 45 289	15 29 314
248	32 28 000	31 04 038	28 41 100	52 36 142	47 20 205	65 33 287	15 20 312
250	32 28 357	31 12 036	28 53 098	52 44 140	47 15 203	65 21 285	15 10 310
252	32 27 355	31 19 034	29 06 096	52 52 139	47 10 201	65 09 283	15 01 308
254	32 25 353	31 26 032	29 18 094	53 01 137	47 06 200	64 57 281	14 51 306
256	32 24 351	31 32 030	29 31 092	53 09 135	47 02 198	64 44 279	14 41 304
258	32 22 349	31 38 028	29 43 090	53 18 133	46 58 196	64 32 277	14 30 302
260	32 19 347	31 44 025	29 56 088	53 28 131	46 55 194	64 19 275	14 19 300
262	32 16 345	31 49 023	30 08 086	53 37 130	46 52 192	64 07 273	14 08 298
264	32 12 343	31 54 021	30 21 084	53 47 128	46 49 191	63 54 271	13 57 296
266	32 08 340	31 58 019	30 33 082	53 57 126	46 47 189	63 42 269	13 46 294
268	32 04 338	32 02 017	30 45 080	54 07 124	46 45 187	63 29 267	13 34 292
	◆ Nunki	FOMALHAUT	◆ ACHERNAR	CANOPUS	◆ ACRUX	RIGIL KENT	ANTARES
270	32 05 015	30 58 078	54 18 122	46 44 185	63 17 265	64 23 301	31 59 336
272	32 08 013	31 10 076	54 28 120	46 43 184	63 04 263	64 12 298	31 54 334
274	32 11 011	31 22 074	54 39 119	46 42 182	62 52 261	64 01 296	31 48 332
276	32 13 009	31 34 072	54 50 117	46 42 180	62 39 259	63 50 294	31 42 330
278	32 14 006	31 46 070	55 02 115	46 42 178	62 27 257	63 38 292	31 36 328
280	32 16 004	31 58 068	55 13 113	46 43 177	62 15 255	63 27 290	31 29 326
282	32 16 002	32 09 066	55 25 111	46 44 175	62 03 253	63 15 288	31 22 324
284	32 17 000	32 21 064	55 37 109	46 45 173	61 51 252	63 03 286	31 14 322
286	32 16 358	32 32 062	55 48 107	46 47 171	61 39 250	62 51 284	31 06 319
288	32 16 356	32 43 060	56 00 106	46 49 169	61 27 248	62 38 281	30 58 317
290	32 15 354	32 53 058	56 13 104	46 52 168	61 16 246	62 26 279	30 49 315
292	32 13 352	33 04 056	56 25 102	46 54 166	61 04 244	62 14 277	30 40 313
294	32 11 349	33 14 054	56 37 100	46 58 164	60 53 242	62 01 275	30 31 311
296	32 08 347	33 24 051	56 50 098	47 01 162	60 42 241	61 49 273	30 21 309
298	32 05 345	33 34 049	57 02 096	47 05 161	60 31 239	61 36 271	30 11 307
	◆ FOMALHAUT	ACHERNAR	◆ CANOPUS	ACRUX	RIGIL KENT	◆ ANTARES	Nunki
300	33 43 047	57 15 094	47 10 159	60 21 237	61 24 269	30 01 305	32 02 343
302	33 52 045	57 27 092	47 14 157	60 10 235	61 11 267	29 51 303	31 58 341
304	34 01 043	57 40 090	47 19 155	60 00 233	60 58 265	29 40 301	31 54 339
306	34 09 041	57 52 088	47 25 153	59 50 232	60 46 263	29 29 299	31 49 337
308	34 17 039	58 05 086	47 31 152	59 40 230	60 34 261	29 18 297	31 44 335
310	34 25 037	58 17 084	47 37 150	59 31 228	60 21 260	29 07 295	31 38 333
312	34 32 035	58 30 082	47 43 148	59 22 226	60 09 258	28 55 293	31 32 330
314	34 39 033	58 42 080	47 50 146	59 13 225	59 57 256	28 44 291	31 26 328
316	34 46 030	58 54 078	47 57 145	59 04 223	59 45 254	28 32 289	31 19 326
318	34 52 028	59 06 076	48 05 143	58 56 221	59 33 252	28 20 287	31 12 324
320	34 58 026	59 19 074	48 12 141	58 48 219	59 21 250	28 08 285	31 04 322
322	35 03 024	59 31 072	48 20 139	58 40 218	59 09 248	27 56 283	30 57 320
324	35 08 022	59 42 069	48 29 137	58 32 216	58 57 246	27 43 281	30 48 318
326	35 12 020	59 54 067	48 37 135	58 25 214	58 46 244	27 31 279	30 40 316
328	35 17 018	60 06 065	48 46 134	58 18 213	58 35 243	27 18 277	30 31 314
	◆ FOMALHAUT	ACHERNAR	◆ CANOPUS	ACRUX	RIGIL KENT	◆ ANTARES	Nunki
330	35 20 016	60 17 063	48 56 132	58 12 211	58 24 241	27 06 275	30 22 312
332	35 23 013	60 28 061	49 05 130	58 05 209	58 13 239	26 53 273	30 12 310
334	35 26 011	60 39 059	49 15 128	57 59 208	58 02 237	26 41 271	30 02 308
336	35 28 009	60 49 057	49 25 126	57 54 206	57 52 235	26 28 269	29 52 305
338	35 30 007	61 00 054	49 35 124	57 48 204	57 42 234	26 16 267	29 42 303
340	35 31 005	61 10 052	49 45 123	57 43 202	57 32 232	26 03 265	29 31 301
342	35 32 003	61 19 050	49 56 121	57 39 201	57 22 230	25 51 263	29 21 299
344	35 33 001	61 29 048	50 07 119	57 35 199	57 12 228	25 38 261	29 09 297
346	35 32 359	61 38 045	50 18 117	57 31 197	57 03 226	25 26 259	28 58 295
348	35 32 356	61 47 043	50 29 115	57 27 196	56 54 225	25 14 257	28 47 293
350	35 31 354	61 55 041	50 41 113	57 24 194	56 46 223	25 02 255	28 35 291
352	35 29 352	62 03 039	50 52 111	57 21 192	56 37 221	24 50 253	28 23 289
354	35 27 350	62 11 036	51 04 109	57 18 191	56 29 219	24 38 251	28 11 287
356	35 25 348	62 18 034	51 16 108	57 16 189	56 21 218	24 26 249	27 59 285
358	35 22 346	62 25 032	51 28 106	57 15 187	56 14 216	24 14 247	27 47 283

LAT 85°S

LHA ♈	ACHERNAR Hc	Zn	◆ SIRIUS Hc	Zn	Suhail Hc	Zn	ACRUX Hc	Zn	◆ RIGIL KENT Hc	Zn	Peacock Hc	Zn	◆ FOMALHAUT Hc	Zn
0	61 38	028	15 41	103	39 44	140	58 13	186	56 56	215	59 26	300	34 21	344
2	61 43	026	15 51	101	39 51	138	58 12	184	56 50	213	59 17	298	34 18	342
4	61 48	024	16 02	099	39 58	136	58 11	182	56 44	212	59 08	296	34 15	340
6	61 52	021	16 12	097	40 06	134	58 11	181	56 39	210	58 58	294	34 11	337
8	61 55	019	16 22	095	40 13	133	58 11	179	56 34	208	58 49	292	34 07	335
10	61 59	017	16 33	093	40 21	131	58 11	177	56 29	206	58 39	289	34 02	333
12	62 01	015	16 43	091	40 29	129	58 12	176	56 25	205	58 29	287	33 57	331
14	62 04	012	16 54	089	40 37	127	58 13	174	56 21	203	58 19	285	33 52	329
16	62 06	010	17 04	087	40 46	125	58 14	172	56 17	201	58 09	283	33 46	327
18	62 07	008	17 15	085	40 55	123	58 16	170	56 13	199	57 59	281	33 41	325
20	62 09	005	17 25	083	41 03	121	58 18	169	56 10	198	57 48	279	33 34	323
22	62 09	003	17 35	081	41 12	119	58 20	167	56 07	196	57 38	277	33 28	321
24	62 10	001	17 46	079	41 22	117	58 22	165	56 04	194	57 28	275	33 21	319
26	62 10	358	17 56	077	41 31	115	58 25	164	56 02	192	57 17	273	33 14	317
28	62 09	356	18 06	075	41 41	113	58 28	162	56 00	191	57 07	271	33 07	314

LHA ♈	◆ SIRIUS Hc	Zn	Suhail Hc	Zn	ACRUX Hc	Zn	◆ RIGIL KENT Hc	Zn	Peacock Hc	Zn	◆ FOMALHAUT Hc	Zn	ACHERNAR Hc	Zn
30	18 16	073	41 50	111	58 32	160	55 58	189	56 56	269	32 59	312	62 08	354
32	18 26	071	42 00	110	58 35	158	55 56	187	56 46	267	32 51	310	62 07	351
34	18 36	069	42 10	108	58 39	157	55 55	185	56 35	265	32 43	308	62 05	349
36	18 45	067	42 20	106	58 44	155	55 54	184	56 25	263	32 35	306	62 03	347
38	18 55	065	42 30	104	58 48	153	55 54	182	56 15	261	32 26	304	62 00	344
40	19 04	063	42 40	102	58 53	151	55 54	180	56 04	259	32 18	302	61 57	342
42	19 14	061	42 51	100	58 58	150	55 54	178	55 54	257	32 09	300	61 54	340
44	19 23	059	43 01	098	59 04	148	55 54	177	55 44	255	32 00	298	61 50	338
46	19 32	057	43 11	096	59 09	146	55 55	175	55 34	253	31 50	296	61 46	335
48	19 40	055	43 22	094	59 15	145	55 56	173	55 24	252	31 41	294	61 41	333
50	19 49	053	43 32	092	59 21	143	55 58	171	55 14	250	31 31	292	61 36	331
52	19 57	051	43 43	090	59 28	141	55 59	170	55 04	248	31 21	290	61 31	328
54	20 05	049	43 53	088	59 35	139	56 01	168	54 55	246	31 11	288	61 25	326
56	20 13	047	44 04	086	59 42	137	56 04	166	54 45	244	31 01	286	61 19	324
58	20 20	045	44 14	084	59 49	136	56 06	165	54 36	242	30 51	284	61 13	322

LHA ♈	◆ SIRIUS Hc	Zn	Suhail Hc	Zn	ACRUX Hc	Zn	◆ RIGIL KENT Hc	Zn	Peacock Hc	Zn	◆ FOMALHAUT Hc	Zn	ACHERNAR Hc	Zn
60	20 27	043	44 24	082	59 56	134	56 09	163	54 27	240	30 41	282	61 06	319
62	20 34	041	44 35	080	60 04	132	56 12	161	54 18	238	30 31	280	60 59	317
64	20 41	038	44 45	078	60 12	130	56 16	159	54 09	236	30 21	278	60 52	315
66	20 47	036	44 55	076	60 20	129	56 20	158	54 00	235	30 10	276	60 45	313
68	20 53	034	45 05	074	60 28	127	56 24	156	53 52	233	30 00	274	60 37	311
70	20 59	032	45 15	072	60 36	125	56 28	154	53 44	231	29 49	272	60 29	308
72	21 04	030	45 25	070	60 45	123	56 33	152	53 36	229	29 39	270	60 20	306
74	21 10	028	45 35	068	60 54	121	56 38	150	53 28	227	29 28	268	60 12	304
76	21 14	026	45 44	066	61 03	119	56 44	149	53 20	225	29 18	266	60 03	302
78	21 19	024	45 54	063	61 12	118	56 49	147	53 13	224	29 08	264	59 54	300
80	21 23	022	46 03	061	61 22	116	56 55	145	53 06	222	28 57	262	59 45	298
82	21 27	020	46 12	059	61 31	114	57 01	143	52 59	220	28 47	260	59 36	295
84	21 30	018	46 21	057	61 41	112	57 07	142	52 52	218	28 37	258	59 26	293
86	21 33	016	46 30	055	61 50	110	57 14	140	52 46	216	28 26	256	59 16	291
88	21 36	014	46 38	053	62 00	108	57 21	138	52 40	214	28 16	254	59 06	289

LHA ♈	◆ SIRIUS Hc	Zn	Suhail Hc	Zn	ACRUX Hc	Zn	◆ RIGIL KENT Hc	Zn	Peacock Hc	Zn	◆ FOMALHAUT Hc	Zn	ACHERNAR Hc	Zn
90	21 38	012	46 46	051	62 10	106	57 28	136	52 34	213	28 06	252	58 57	287
92	21 40	010	46 54	049	62 20	104	57 35	134	52 29	211	27 56	250	58 47	285
94	21 42	008	47 02	047	62 31	103	57 43	133	52 24	209	27 47	248	58 36	283
96	21 43	006	47 10	045	62 41	101	57 51	131	52 19	207	27 37	246	58 26	281
98	21 44	004	47 17	042	62 51	099	57 59	129	52 14	206	27 27	244	58 16	279
100	21 44	001	47 24	040	63 01	097	58 07	127	52 10	204	27 18	242	58 05	277
102	21 44	359	47 30	038	63 12	095	58 15	125	52 06	202	27 09	240	57 55	275
104	21 44	357	47 37	036	63 22	093	58 24	124	52 02	200	27 00	238	57 45	273
106	21 43	355	47 43	034	63 33	091	58 33	122	51 58	198	26 51	236	57 34	271
108	21 42	353	47 48	032	63 43	089	58 42	120	51 55	197	26 43	234	57 24	269
110	21 41	351	47 54	030	63 54	087	58 51	118	51 52	195	26 34	232	57 13	267
112	21 39	349	47 59	027	64 04	085	59 00	116	51 50	193	26 26	231	57 03	265
114	21 37	347	48 03	025	64 15	083	59 10	114	51 48	191	26 18	229	56 52	263
116	21 34	345	48 08	023	64 25	081	59 19	112	51 46	189	26 10	227	56 42	261
118	21 31	343	48 12	021	64 35	079	59 29	111	51 44	188	26 03	225	56 32	259

LHA ♈	◆ Suhail Hc	Zn	SPICA Hc	Zn	◆ ANTARES Hc	Zn	Peacock Hc	Zn	FOMALHAUT Hc	Zn	◆ ACHERNAR Hc	Zn	SIRIUS Hc	Zn
120	48 15	019	11 56	083	23 21	129	51 43	186	25 56	223	56 22	257	21 28	341
122	48 18	017	12 06	081	23 29	127	51 42	184	25 49	221	56 11	255	21 25	339
124	48 21	014	12 17	079	23 38	126	51 41	182	25 42	219	56 01	253	21 21	337
126	48 23	012	12 27	077	23 46	124	51 41	181	25 35	217	55 51	251	21 16	335
128	48 25	010	12 37	075	23 55	122	51 41	179	25 29	215	55 42	249	21 12	333
130	48 27	008	12 47	073	24 04	120	51 42	177	25 23	213	55 32	247	21 07	331
132	48 28	006	12 57	071	24 13	118	51 42	175	25 18	211	55 22	246	21 01	329
134	48 29	003	13 07	068	24 23	116	51 43	174	25 13	209	55 13	244	20 56	327
136	48 30	001	13 16	066	24 32	114	51 45	172	25 08	207	55 03	242	20 50	324
138	48 30	359	13 26	064	24 42	112	51 46	170	25 03	205	54 54	240	20 44	322
140	48 29	357	13 35	062	24 51	110	51 48	168	24 59	204	54 45	238	20 37	320
142	48 28	355	13 45	060	25 01	108	51 51	166	24 55	202	54 37	236	20 30	318
144	48 27	352	13 54	058	25 11	106	51 53	165	24 51	200	54 28	234	20 23	316
146	48 26	350	14 02	056	25 21	104	51 56	163	24 48	198	54 20	233	20 16	314
148	48 24	348	14 11	054	25 32	102	51 59	161	24 45	196	54 11	231	20 08	312

LHA ♈	SPICA Hc	Zn	◆ ANTARES Hc	Zn	Peacock Hc	Zn	FOMALHAUT Hc	Zn	◆ ACHERNAR Hc	Zn	CANOPUS Hc	Zn	◆ Suhail Hc	Zn
150	14 19	052	25 42	100	52 03	159	24 42	194	54 03	229	55 27	300	48 21	346
152	14 28	050	25 52	098	52 07	158	24 39	192	53 56	227	55 18	298	48 19	344
154	14 35	048	26 03	096	52 11	156	24 37	190	53 48	225	55 08	296	48 16	342
156	14 43	046	26 13	094	52 15	154	24 36	188	53 41	223	54 59	294	48 12	339
158	14 51	044	26 24	092	52 20	152	24 34	186	53 34	222	54 49	292	48 08	337
160	14 58	042	26 34	090	52 25	150	24 33	184	53 27	220	54 39	290	48 04	335
162	15 05	040	26 44	088	52 30	149	24 33	183	53 20	218	54 30	288	47 59	333
164	15 11	038	26 55	086	52 36	147	24 33	181	53 14	216	54 19	286	47 54	331
166	15 18	036	27 05	084	52 42	145	24 33	179	53 08	214	54 09	284	47 49	329
168	15 24	034	27 16	082	52 48	143	24 33	177	53 02	213	53 59	282	47 44	326
170	15 29	032	27 26	080	52 54	141	24 34	175	52 57	211	53 49	280	47 38	324
172	15 35	030	27 36	078	53 01	140	24 35	173	52 52	209	53 39	278	47 31	322
174	15 40	028	27 46	076	53 08	138	24 36	171	52 47	207	53 28	275	47 25	320
176	15 45	026	27 57	074	53 15	136	24 38	169	52 42	205	53 18	273	47 18	318
178	15 49	024	28 07	072	53 22	134	24 40	167	52 38	204	53 07	271	47 11	316

LHA ♈	SPICA Hc	Zn	◆ ANTARES Hc	Zn	Peacock Hc	Zn	FOMALHAUT Hc	Zn	◆ ACHERNAR Hc	Zn	CANOPUS Hc	Zn	◆ Suhail Hc	Zn
180	15 53	022	28 16	070	53 30	132	24 43	165	52 34	202	52 57	269	47 03	314
182	15 57	020	28 26	068	53 38	130	24 46	163	52 30	200	52 46	267	46 56	311
184	16 00	018	28 36	066	53 46	129	24 49	161	52 27	198	52 36	266	46 48	309
186	16 03	016	28 45	064	53 54	127	24 52	160	52 23	196	52 26	264	46 39	307
188	16 06	014	28 55	062	54 03	125	24 56	158	52 21	195	52 15	262	46 31	305
190	16 08	012	29 04	060	54 11	123	25 00	156	52 18	193	52 05	260	46 22	303
192	16 10	010	29 13	058	54 20	121	25 05	154	52 16	191	51 55	258	46 13	301
194	16 12	008	29 21	056	54 29	119	25 09	152	52 14	189	51 44	256	46 04	299
196	16 13	006	29 30	054	54 39	117	25 15	150	52 13	188	51 34	254	45 55	297
198	16 14	004	29 38	052	54 48	116	25 20	148	52 11	186	51 24	252	45 46	295
200	16 14	002	29 46	050	54 57	114	25 26	146	52 10	184	51 14	250	45 36	293
202	16 14	359	29 54	048	55 07	112	25 32	144	52 10	182	51 05	248	45 26	291
204	16 14	357	30 02	045	55 17	110	25 38	142	52 10	181	50 55	246	45 17	289
206	16 13	355	30 09	043	55 27	108	25 44	140	52 10	179	50 46	244	45 07	287
208	16 12	353	30 16	041	55 37	106	25 51	138	52 10	177	50 36	242	44 56	284

LHA ♈	◆ ANTARES Hc	Zn	Nunki Hc	Zn	FOMALHAUT Hc	Zn	◆ ACHERNAR Hc	Zn	CANOPUS Hc	Zn	◆ Suhail Hc	Zn	SPICA Hc	Zn
210	30 23	039	27 33	077	25 58	136	52 11	175	50 27	240	44 46	282	16 11	351
212	30 29	037	27 43	074	26 06	135	52 12	173	50 18	239	44 36	280	16 09	349
214	30 36	035	27 53	072	26 13	133	52 13	172	50 09	237	44 26	278	16 07	347
216	30 41	033	28 03	070	26 21	131	52 15	170	50 01	235	44 15	276	16 05	345
218	30 47	031	28 13	068	26 29	129	52 17	168	49 52	233	44 05	274	16 02	343
220	30 52	029	28 22	066	26 37	127	52 19	166	49 44	231	43 55	272	15 59	341
222	30 57	027	28 32	064	26 46	125	52 22	165	49 36	229	43 44	270	15 55	339
224	31 02	025	28 41	062	26 55	123	52 25	163	49 28	227	43 34	268	15 51	337
226	31 06	023	28 50	060	27 03	121	52 28	161	49 20	225	43 23	266	15 47	335
228	31 10	021	28 59	058	27 12	119	52 32	159	49 13	224	43 13	264	15 42	333
230	31 13	018	29 08	056	27 22	117	52 35	157	49 06	222	43 02	262	15 37	331
232	31 16	016	29 17	054	27 31	115	52 40	156	48 59	220	42 52	260	15 32	329
234	31 19	014	29 25	052	27 41	113	52 44	154	48 53	218	42 42	259	15 27	327
236	31 21	012	29 33	050	27 50	111	52 49	152	48 46	216	42 32	257	15 21	325
238	31 23	010	29 41	048	28 00	109	52 54	150	48 40	214	42 21	255	15 14	323

LHA ♈	ANTARES Hc	Zn	Nunki Hc	Zn	◆ FOMALHAUT Hc	Zn	ACHERNAR Hc	Zn	◆ CANOPUS Hc	Zn	ACRUX Hc	Zn	◆ RIGIL KENT Hc	Zn
240	31 25	008	29 49	046	28 10	107	52 59	149	48 34	213	65 52	298	65 33	336
242	31 26	006	29 56	044	28 20	105	53 05	147	48 29	211	65 43	296	65 28	334
244	31 27	004	30 03	042	28 30	103	53 11	145	48 24	209	65 34	294	65 24	332
246	31 28	002	30 10	040	28 40	101	53 17	143	48 19	207	65 24	292	65 18	330
248	31 28	000	30 17	038	28 51	099	53 23	141	48 14	205	65 14	289	65 13	327
250	31 28	357	30 23	036	29 01	097	53 30	139	48 10	204	65 04	287	65 07	325
252	31 27	355	30 29	034	29 11	095	53 37	138	48 06	202	64 54	285	65 01	323
254	31 26	353	30 35	031	29 22	093	53 44	136	48 02	200	64 44	283	64 54	320
256	31 24	351	30 40	029	29 32	091	53 51	134	47 59	198	64 34	281	64 48	318
258	31 23	349	30 45	027	29 43	089	53 59	132	47 56	196	64 23	279	64 40	316
260	31 20	347	30 49	025	29 53	087	54 07	130	47 53	194	64 13	277	64 33	314
262	31 18	345	30 54	023	30 04	085	54 15	129	47 50	193	64 03	275	64 25	311
264	31 15	343	30 58	021	30 14	083	54 23	127	47 48	191	63 52	273	64 17	309
266	31 12	341	31 01	019	30 24	081	54 32	125	47 46	189	63 42	271	64 09	307
268	31 08	339	31 04	017	30 35	079	54 40	123	47 45	187	63 31	269	64 01	305

LHA ♈	Nunki Hc	Zn	◆ FOMALHAUT Hc	Zn	ACHERNAR Hc	Zn	◆ CANOPUS Hc	Zn	ACRUX Hc	Zn	◆ RIGIL KENT Hc	Zn	ANTARES Hc	Zn
270	31 07	015	30 45	077	54 49	121	47 44	185	63 21	267	63 52	302	31 04	337
272	31 10	013	30 55	075	54 58	119	47 43	184	63 10	265	63 43	300	31 00	334
274	31 12	011	31 05	073	55 07	117	47 42	182	63 00	263	63 34	298	30 55	332
276	31 14	008	31 15	071	55 17	116	47 42	180	62 50	261	63 24	296	30 50	330
278	31 15	006	31 25	069	55 26	114	47 42	178	62 39	259	63 15	294	30 45	328
280	31 16	004	31 35	067	55 36	112	47 43	176	62 29	257	63 05	292	30 39	326
282	31 16	002	31 44	065	55 46	110	47 44	175	62 19	255	62 56	290	30 33	324
284	31 17	000	31 54	063	55 56	108	47 45	173	62 09	253	62 46	287	30 27	322
286	31 16	358	32 03	061	56 06	106	47 46	171	61 59	251	62 36	285	30 20	320
288	31 16	356	32 12	059	56 16	104	47 48	169	61 49	250	62 25	283	30 13	318
290	31 15	354	32 21	057	56 26	102	47 50	167	61 39	248	62 15	281	30 06	316
292	31 14	352	32 30	055	56 36	100	47 53	166	61 30	246	62 05	279	29 59	314
294	31 12	350	32 38	053	56 47	098	47 55	164	61 20	244	61 55	277	29 51	312
296	31 10	347	32 46	051	56 57	096	47 58	162	61 11	242	61 44	275	29 43	310
298	31 07	345	32 54	049	57 07	094	48 02	160	61 02	240	61 34	273	29 35	307

LHA ♈	◆ FOMALHAUT Hc	Zn	ACHERNAR Hc	Zn	◆ CANOPUS Hc	Zn	ACRUX Hc	Zn	◆ RIGIL KENT Hc	Zn	ANTARES Hc	Zn	Nunki Hc	Zn
300	33 02	047	57 18	092	48 06	158	60 53	238	61 23	271	29 26	305	31 05	343
302	33 10	045	57 28	090	48 10	157	60 44	237	61 13	269	29 18	303	31 01	341
304	33 17	043	57 39	088	48 14	155	60 35	235	61 02	267	29 09	301	30 58	339
306	33 24	041	57 49	086	48 18	153	60 27	233	60 52	265	29 00	299	30 54	337
308	33 30	038	58 00	084	48 23	151	60 19	231	60 42	263	28 51	297	30 50	335
310	33 37	036	58 10	082	48 29	149	60 11	229	60 31	261	28 41	295	30 45	333
312	33 43	034	58 20	080	48 34	148	60 03	228	60 21	259	28 32	293	30 40	331
314	33 49	032	58 31	078	48 40	146	59 55	226	60 11	257	28 22	291	30 35	329
316	33 54	030	58 41	076	48 46	144	59 48	224	60 00	255	28 12	289	30 29	327
318	33 59	028	58 51	074	48 52	142	59 41	222	59 50	254	28 02	287	30 23	325
320	34 04	026	59 01	072	48 59	140	59 34	221	59 40	252	27 52	285	30 17	322
322	34 08	024	59 11	070	49 06	138	59 27	219	59 31	250	27 42	283	30 11	320
324	34 12	022	59 21	068	49 13	136	59 21	217	59 21	248	27 32	281	30 04	318
326	34 16	020	59 30	066	49 20	135	59 14	215	59 11	246	27 22	279	29 57	316
328	34 19	018	59 40	064	49 27	133	59 08	213	59 02	244	27 11	277	29 49	314

LHA ♈	◆ FOMALHAUT Hc	Zn	ACHERNAR Hc	Zn	◆ CANOPUS Hc	Zn	ACRUX Hc	Zn	◆ RIGIL KENT Hc	Zn	ANTARES Hc	Zn	Nunki Hc	Zn
330	34 22	015	59 49	061	49 35	131	59 03	212	58 52	242	27 01	275	29 42	312
332	34 25	013	59 58	059	49 43	129	58 57	210	58 43	240	26 51	273	29 34	310
334	34 27	011	60 07	057	49 51	127	58 52	208	58 34	239	26 40	271	29 26	308
336	34 29	009	60 16	055	50 00	125	58 48	207	58 25	237	26 30	269	29 17	306
338	34 30	007	60 24	053	50 09	123	58 43	205	58 17	235	26 19	267	29 09	304
340	34 32	005	60 32	051	50 17	122	58 39	203	58 08	233	26 09	265	29 00	302
342	34 32	003	60 40	048	50 26	120	58 35	201	58 00	231	25 58	263	28 51	300
344	34 33	001	60 48	046	50 36	118	58 31	200	57 52	229	25 48	261	28 42	298
346	34 32	359	60 55	044	50 45	116	58 28	198	57 44	228	25 38	259	28 32	296
348	34 32	356	61 02	042	50 54	114	58 25	196	57 36	226	25 27	257	28 23	294
350	34 31	354	61 09	040	51 04	112	58 22	194	57 29	224	25 17	255	28 13	292
352	34 30	352	61 16	037	51 14	110	58 20	193	57 22	222	25 07	253	28 03	290
354	34 28	350	61 22	035	51 24	108	58 17	191	57 15	220	24 57	251	27 54	288
356	34 26	348	61 28	033	51 34	106	58 16	189	57 08	219	24 47	249	27 44	286
358	34 24	346	61 33	031	51 44	104	58 14	188	57 02	217	24 38	247	27 33	284

LAT 86°S

LHA ♈	Hc	Zn	Hc	Zn	Hc	Zn	Hc	Zn	Hc	Zn	Hc	Zn	Hc	Zn
	ACHERNAR		◆ SIRIUS		Suhail		ACRUX		◆ RIGIL KENT		Peacock		◆ FOMALHAUT	
0	60 45	027	15 54	103	40 30	140	59 12	186	57 45	216	58 56	301	33 24	344
2	60 49	025	16 02	101	40 36	138	59 12	184	57 40	214	58 49	299	33 21	342
4	60 53	023	16 11	099	40 42	136	59 11	183	57 35	212	58 41	297	33 18	340
6	60 56	021	16 19	097	40 47	134	59 11	181	57 31	211	58 34	295	33 15	338
8	60 58	019	16 27	095	40 54	132	59 11	179	57 27	209	58 26	293	33 12	336
10	61 01	016	16 36	093	41 00	130	59 11	177	57 23	207	58 18	291	33 08	334
12	61 03	014	16 44	091	41 06	128	59 12	175	57 19	205	58 10	289	33 05	331
14	61 05	012	16 52	089	41 13	126	59 13	174	57 16	203	58 02	287	33 00	329
16	61 07	010	17 01	087	41 20	124	59 14	172	57 13	202	57 54	285	32 56	327
18	61 08	007	17 09	085	41 27	122	59 15	170	57 10	200	57 46	283	32 51	325
20	61 09	005	17 17	083	41 34	120	59 16	168	57 07	198	57 38	281	32 47	323
22	61 09	003	17 26	081	41 41	118	59 18	167	57 04	196	57 30	279	32 41	321
24	61 10	001	17 34	079	41 49	116	59 20	165	57 02	194	57 22	277	32 36	319
26	61 10	358	17 42	077	41 56	115	59 23	163	57 00	193	57 13	275	32 30	317
28	61 09	356	17 50	075	42 04	113	59 25	161	56 59	191	57 05	273	32 25	315
	◆ SIRIUS		Suhail		ACRUX		◆ RIGIL KENT		Peacock		◆ FOMALHAUT		ACHERNAR	
30	17 58	073	42 12	111	59 28	160	56 57	189	56 56	271	32 19	313	61 08	354
32	18 06	071	42 20	109	59 31	158	56 56	187	56 48	269	32 12	311	61 07	352
34	18 14	069	42 28	107	59 34	156	56 55	185	56 40	267	32 06	309	61 06	349
36	18 22	067	42 36	105	59 38	154	56 54	184	56 31	265	31 59	307	61 04	347
38	18 29	065	42 44	103	59 42	152	56 54	182	56 23	263	31 52	305	61 02	345
40	18 37	063	42 52	101	59 46	151	56 54	180	56 15	261	31 46	303	61 00	343
42	18 44	061	43 00	099	59 50	149	56 54	178	56 07	259	31 38	301	60 57	340
44	18 51	059	43 09	097	59 54	147	56 54	177	55 58	257	31 31	299	60 54	338
46	18 59	057	43 17	095	59 59	145	56 55	175	55 50	255	31 24	297	60 51	336
48	19 05	054	43 25	093	60 04	144	56 56	173	55 42	253	31 16	295	60 48	334
50	19 12	052	43 34	091	60 09	142	56 57	171	55 34	251	31 08	292	60 44	332
52	19 19	050	43 42	089	60 14	140	56 58	169	55 26	249	31 01	290	60 40	329
54	19 25	048	43 50	087	60 20	138	57 00	168	55 19	247	30 53	288	60 35	327
56	19 31	046	43 59	085	60 25	136	57 02	166	55 11	245	30 45	286	60 30	325
58	19 37	044	44 07	083	60 31	134	57 04	164	55 03	243	30 37	284	60 26	323
	◆ SIRIUS		Suhail		ACRUX		◆ RIGIL KENT		Peacock		◆ FOMALHAUT		ACHERNAR	
60	19 43	042	44 15	081	60 37	133	57 06	162	54 56	241	30 29	282	60 20	321
62	19 48	040	44 24	079	60 44	131	57 09	161	54 49	240	30 20	280	60 15	318
64	19 54	038	44 32	077	60 50	129	57 12	159	54 42	238	30 12	278	60 09	316
66	19 59	036	44 40	075	60 57	127	57 15	157	54 35	236	30 04	276	60 03	314
68	20 04	034	44 48	073	61 03	125	57 19	155	54 28	234	29 55	274	59 57	312
70	20 08	032	44 56	071	61 10	123	57 22	153	54 21	232	29 47	272	59 51	310
72	20 13	030	45 04	069	61 17	122	57 26	152	54 15	230	29 39	270	59 44	308
74	20 17	028	45 11	067	61 24	120	57 30	150	54 08	228	29 30	268	59 38	305
76	20 20	026	45 19	065	61 32	118	57 35	148	54 02	226	29 22	266	59 31	303
78	20 24	024	45 27	063	61 39	116	57 39	146	53 56	225	29 14	264	59 24	301
80	20 27	022	45 34	061	61 47	114	57 44	144	53 50	223	29 05	262	59 16	299
82	20 30	020	45 41	058	61 55	112	57 49	142	53 45	221	28 57	260	59 09	297
84	20 33	018	45 48	056	62 02	110	57 54	141	53 39	219	28 49	258	59 01	295
86	20 35	016	45 55	054	62 10	108	58 00	139	53 34	217	28 41	256	58 54	293
88	20 38	014	46 02	052	62 18	106	58 05	137	53 29	215	28 33	254	58 46	291
	◆ SIRIUS		Suhail		ACRUX		◆ RIGIL KENT		Peacock		◆ FOMALHAUT		ACHERNAR	
90	20 39	012	46 08	050	62 26	105	58 11	135	53 25	213	28 25	252	58 38	289
92	20 41	010	46 15	048	62 34	103	58 17	133	53 20	212	28 17	251	58 30	287
94	20 42	008	46 21	046	62 43	101	58 23	131	53 16	210	28 09	249	58 22	285
96	20 43	006	46 27	044	62 51	099	58 29	130	53 12	208	28 01	247	58 14	282
98	20 44	004	46 32	042	62 59	097	58 36	128	53 08	206	27 53	245	58 06	280
100	20 44	001	46 38	040	63 07	095	58 43	126	53 04	204	27 46	243	57 58	278
102	20 44	359	46 43	038	63 16	093	58 50	124	53 01	202	27 39	241	57 49	276
104	20 44	357	46 48	035	63 24	091	58 57	122	52 58	201	27 31	239	57 41	274
106	20 43	355	46 53	033	63 33	089	59 04	120	52 55	199	27 24	237	57 33	272
108	20 43	353	46 57	031	63 41	087	59 11	118	52 53	197	27 17	235	57 24	270
110	20 42	351	47 01	029	63 49	085	59 18	117	52 50	195	27 11	233	57 16	268
112	20 40	349	47 05	027	63 58	083	59 26	115	52 48	193	27 04	231	57 07	266
114	20 38	347	47 09	025	64 06	081	59 34	113	52 46	192	26 58	229	56 59	264
116	20 36	345	47 12	023	64 14	079	59 41	111	52 45	190	26 51	227	56 51	262
118	20 34	343	47 15	021	64 22	077	59 49	109	52 44	188	26 45	225	56 42	260
	◆ Suhail		SPICA		◆ ANTARES		Peacock		FOMALHAUT		◆ ACHERNAR		SIRIUS	
120	47 18	018	11 48	082	23 59	129	52 43	186	26 40	223	56 34	259	20 32	341
122	47 21	016	11 56	080	24 06	127	52 42	184	26 34	221	56 26	257	20 29	339
124	47 23	014	12 05	078	24 12	125	52 41	182	26 28	219	56 18	255	20 26	337
126	47 25	012	12 13	076	24 19	123	52 41	181	26 23	217	56 10	253	20 22	335
128	47 26	010	12 21	074	24 26	121	52 41	179	26 18	215	56 02	251	20 18	333
130	47 28	008	12 29	072	24 34	119	52 42	177	26 14	213	55 54	249	20 14	331
132	47 29	006	12 37	070	24 41	117	52 42	175	26 09	211	55 46	247	20 10	329
134	47 29	003	12 45	068	24 48	115	52 43	173	26 05	210	55 39	245	20 06	327
136	47 30	001	12 52	066	24 56	113	52 44	172	26 01	208	55 31	243	20 01	325
138	47 30	359	13 00	064	25 04	111	52 45	170	25 57	206	55 24	241	19 56	323
140	47 29	357	13 08	062	25 12	109	52 47	168	25 54	204	55 17	239	19 51	321
142	47 29	355	13 15	060	25 20	107	52 49	166	25 50	202	55 09	237	19 45	319
144	47 28	353	13 22	058	25 28	105	52 51	164	25 47	200	55 02	236	19 40	317
146	47 27	350	13 29	056	25 36	103	52 53	162	25 45	198	54 56	234	19 34	315
148	47 25	348	13 36	054	25 44	102	52 56	161	25 42	196	54 49	232	19 28	312
	SPICA		◆ ANTARES		Peacock		FOMALHAUT		◆ ACHERNAR		CANOPUS		◆ Suhail	
150	13 43	052	25 52	100	52 59	159	25 40	194	54 42	230	54 56	302	47 23	346
152	13 49	050	26 00	098	53 02	157	25 38	192	54 36	228	54 49	299	47 21	344
154	13 56	048	26 09	096	53 05	155	25 37	190	54 30	226	54 41	297	47 19	342
156	14 02	046	26 17	094	53 09	153	25 35	188	54 24	224	54 34	295	47 16	340
158	14 08	044	26 25	092	53 13	152	25 34	186	54 18	222	54 26	293	47 13	338
160	14 13	042	26 34	090	53 17	150	25 33	184	54 13	221	54 18	291	47 09	336
162	14 19	040	26 42	088	53 21	148	25 33	183	54 07	219	54 11	289	47 06	333
164	14 24	038	26 51	086	53 26	146	25 33	181	54 02	217	54 03	287	47 02	331
166	14 29	036	26 59	084	53 31	144	25 33	179	53 57	215	53 55	285	46 58	329
168	14 34	034	27 07	082	53 36	142	25 33	177	53 53	213	53 46	283	46 53	327
170	14 38	032	27 15	080	53 41	141	25 34	175	53 48	211	53 38	281	46 49	325
172	14 43	030	27 24	078	53 46	139	25 34	173	53 44	210	53 30	279	46 44	323
174	14 47	028	27 32	076	53 52	137	25 36	171	53 40	208	53 22	277	46 39	321
176	14 51	026	27 40	074	53 58	135	25 37	169	53 36	206	53 13	275	46 33	319
178	14 54	024	27 48	072	54 04	133	25 39	167	53 33	204	53 05	273	46 27	316

LHA ♈	Hc	Zn	Hc	Zn	Hc	Zn	Hc	Zn	Hc	Zn	Hc	Zn	Hc	Zn
	SPICA		◆ ANTARES		Peacock		FOMALHAUT		◆ ACHERNAR		CANOPUS		◆ Suhail	
180	14 57	022	27 56	069	54 10	131	25 41	165	53 29	202	52 57	271	46 22	314
182	15 00	020	28 03	067	54 16	129	25 43	163	53 26	200	52 48	269	46 16	312
184	15 03	018	28 11	065	54 23	127	25 46	161	53 24	199	52 40	267	46 09	310
186	15 05	016	28 19	063	54 30	126	25 48	159	53 21	197	52 32	265	46 03	308
188	15 08	014	28 26	061	54 37	124	25 52	157	53 19	195	52 23	263	45 56	306
190	15 09	012	28 33	059	54 44	122	25 55	156	53 17	193	52 15	261	45 49	304
192	15 11	010	28 41	057	54 51	120	25 58	154	53 15	191	52 07	259	45 42	302
194	15 12	008	28 47	055	54 58	118	26 02	152	53 13	190	51 59	257	45 35	300
196	15 13	006	28 54	053	55 06	116	26 06	150	53 12	188	51 50	255	45 28	298
198	15 14	004	29 01	051	55 13	114	26 11	148	53 11	186	51 42	253	45 20	296
200	15 14	002	29 07	049	55 21	112	26 15	146	53 10	184	51 34	251	45 13	294
202	15 14	359	29 14	047	55 29	110	26 20	144	53 10	182	51 27	249	45 05	292
204	15 14	357	29 20	045	55 37	108	26 25	142	53 10	181	51 19	247	44 57	290
206	15 14	355	29 25	043	55 45	107	26 31	140	53 10	179	51 11	245	44 49	287
208	15 13	353	29 31	041	55 53	105	26 36	138	53 10	177	51 04	243	44 41	285
	◆ ANTARES		Nunki		FOMALHAUT		◆ ACHERNAR		CANOPUS		◆ Suhail		SPICA	
210	29 36	039	27 19	076	26 42	136	53 11	175	50 56	242	44 33	283	15 12	351
212	29 42	037	27 27	074	26 48	134	53 12	173	50 49	240	44 25	281	15 10	349
214	29 46	035	27 35	072	26 54	132	53 13	171	50 42	238	44 16	279	15 09	347
216	29 51	033	27 43	070	27 00	130	53 14	170	50 35	236	44 08	277	15 07	345
218	29 55	031	27 50	068	27 06	128	53 16	168	50 28	234	44 00	275	15 04	343
220	30 00	029	27 58	066	27 13	126	53 17	166	50 21	232	43 52	273	15 02	341
222	30 03	027	28 06	064	27 20	124	53 20	164	50 15	230	43 43	271	14 59	339
224	30 07	024	28 13	062	27 27	122	53 22	162	50 08	228	43 35	269	14 56	337
226	30 10	022	28 21	060	27 34	121	53 25	161	50 02	226	43 26	267	14 52	335
228	30 13	020	28 28	058	27 41	119	53 28	159	49 56	224	43 18	265	14 49	333
230	30 16	018	28 35	056	27 49	117	53 31	157	49 50	223	43 10	263	14 45	331
232	30 19	016	28 42	054	27 56	115	53 34	155	49 45	221	43 01	261	14 41	329
234	30 21	014	28 48	052	28 04	113	53 38	153	49 40	219	42 53	259	14 36	327
236	30 23	012	28 55	050	28 12	111	53 42	151	49 34	217	42 45	257	14 32	325
238	30 24	010	29 01	048	28 20	109	53 46	150	49 29	215	42 37	255	14 27	323
	ANTARES		Nunki		◆ FOMALHAUT		ACHERNAR		◆ CANOPUS		ACRUX		◆ RIGIL KENT	
240	30 26	008	29 07	046	28 28	107	53 50	148	49 25	213	65 23	300	64 38	337
242	30 27	006	29 13	043	28 36	105	53 55	146	49 20	211	65 16	298	64 34	335
244	30 27	004	29 19	041	28 44	103	54 00	144	49 16	210	65 08	296	64 30	333
246	30 28	002	29 24	039	28 52	101	54 05	142	49 12	208	65 01	294	64 26	331
248	30 28	000	29 29	037	29 00	099	54 10	140	49 08	206	64 53	291	64 22	328
250	30 28	357	29 34	035	29 09	097	54 15	139	49 05	204	64 45	289	64 18	326
252	30 27	355	29 39	033	29 17	095	54 21	137	49 01	202	64 37	287	64 13	324
254	30 26	353	29 43	031	29 25	093	54 27	135	48 58	200	64 29	285	64 08	322
256	30 25	351	29 47	029	29 34	091	54 33	133	48 56	198	64 21	283	64 03	319
258	30 24	349	29 51	027	29 42	089	54 39	131	48 53	197	64 13	281	63 57	317
260	30 22	347	29 55	025	29 50	087	54 45	129	48 51	195	64 05	279	63 51	315
262	30 20	345	29 58	023	29 59	085	54 52	127	48 49	193	63 56	277	63 45	313
264	30 18	343	30 02	021	30 07	083	54 59	126	48 47	191	63 48	275	63 39	311
266	30 15	341	30 04	019	30 15	081	55 05	124	48 46	189	63 40	273	63 32	308
268	30 12	339	30 07	017	30 24	079	55 12	122	48 44	187	63 31	271	63 26	306
	Nunki		◆ FOMALHAUT		ACHERNAR		◆ CANOPUS		ACRUX		◆ RIGIL KENT		ANTARES	
270	30 09	015	30 32	077	55 20	120	48 43	186	63 23	269	63 19	304	30 09	337
272	30 11	013	30 40	075	55 27	118	48 43	184	63 15	267	63 12	302	30 06	335
274	30 13	010	30 48	073	55 34	116	48 42	182	63 06	265	63 05	300	30 02	333
276	30 14	008	30 56	071	55 42	114	48 42	180	62 58	263	62 57	298	29 58	331
278	30 15	006	31 04	069	55 50	112	48 42	178	62 50	261	62 50	296	29 54	328
280	30 16	004	31 11	067	55 58	110	48 43	176	62 41	259	62 42	293	29 49	326
282	30 16	002	31 19	065	56 05	108	48 43	175	62 33	257	62 35	291	29 44	324
284	30 17	000	31 27	063	56 13	106	48 44	173	62 25	255	62 27	289	29 39	322
286	30 16	358	31 34	061	56 21	105	48 46	171	62 17	253	62 19	287	29 34	320
288	30 16	356	31 41	059	56 30	103	48 47	169	62 09	251	62 11	285	29 29	318
290	30 15	354	31 48	057	56 38	101	48 49	167	62 01	249	62 03	283	29 23	316
292	30 14	352	31 55	055	56 46	099	48 51	165	61 53	248	61 54	281	29 17	314
294	30 13	350	32 02	052	56 54	097	48 53	164	61 46	246	61 46	279	29 11	312
296	30 11	348	32 08	050	57 03	095	48 55	162	61 38	244	61 38	277	29 05	310
298	30 09	346	32 15	048	57 11	093	48 58	160	61 31	242	61 30	275	28 58	308
	◆ FOMALHAUT		ACHERNAR		◆ CANOPUS		ACRUX		◆ RIGIL KENT		ANTARES		Nunki	
300	32 21	046	57 19	091	49 01	158	61 23	240	61 21	273	28 51	306	30 07	343
302	32 27	044	57 28	089	49 05	156	61 16	238	61 13	271	28 45	304	30 05	341
304	32 33	042	57 36	087	49 08	154	61 09	236	61 04	269	28 38	302	30 02	339
306	32 38	040	57 44	085	49 12	152	61 02	234	60 56	267	28 30	300	29 59	337
308	32 43	038	57 53	083	49 16	151	60 56	233	60 48	265	28 23	298	29 55	335
310	32 48	036	58 01	081	49 20	149	60 49	231	60 39	263	28 16	296	29 52	333
312	32 53	034	58 09	079	49 24	147	60 43	229	60 31	261	28 08	294	29 48	331
314	32 58	032	58 18	077	49 29	145	60 36	227	60 23	259	28 00	292	29 43	329
316	33 02	030	58 26	075	49 34	143	60 30	225	60 15	257	27 52	290	29 39	327
318	33 06	028	58 34	073	49 39	141	60 25	223	60 07	255	27 44	288	29 34	325
320	33 10	026	58 42	070	49 45	139	60 19	222	59 59	253	27 36	286	29 29	323
322	33 13	024	58 49	068	49 50	138	60 13	220	59 51	251	27 28	284	29 24	321
324	33 17	021	58 57	066	49 56	136	60 08	218	59 43	249	27 20	282	29 19	319
326	33 19	019	59 05	064	50 02	134	60 03	216	59 35	248	27 12	280	29 13	317
328	33 22	017	59 12	062	50 08	132	59 58	214	59 27	246	27 04	278	29 07	315
	◆ FOMALHAUT		ACHERNAR		◆ CANOPUS		ACRUX		◆ RIGIL KENT		ANTARES		Nunki	
330	33 24	015	59 20	060	50 14	130	59 54	213	59 20	244	26 55	276	29 01	313
332	33 27	013	59 27	058	50 21	128	59 49	211	59 12	242	26 47	274	28 55	310
334	33 28	011	59 34	056	50 27	126	59 45	209	59 05	240	26 39	272	28 48	308
336	33 30	009	59 41	054	50 34	124	59 41	207	58 58	238	26 30	270	28 42	306
338	33 31	007	59 47	051	50 41	122	59 37	206	58 51	236	26 22	268	28 35	304
340	33 32	005	59 54	049	50 48	121	59 34	204	58 44	234	26 14	266	28 28	302
342	33 32	003	60 00	047	50 56	119	59 31	202	58 37	233	26 05	264	28 21	300
344	33 33	001	60 06	045	51 03	117	59 28	200	58 30	231	25 57	262	28 14	298
346	33 32	359	60 12	043	51 11	115	59 25	198	58 24	229	25 49	260	28 06	296
348	33 32	356	60 17	041	51 18	113	59 22	197	58 18	227	25 40	258	27 59	294
350	33 31	354	60 23	038	51 26	111	59 20	195	58 12	225	25 32	256	27 51	292
352	33 30	352	60 28	036	51 34	109	59 18	193	58 06	223	25 24	254	27 43	290
354	33 29	350	60 33	034	51 42	107	59 16	191	58 00	221	25 16	252	27 35	288
356	33 28	348	60 37	032	51 50	105	59 15	190	57 55	220	25 08	250	27 27	286
358	33 26	346	60 41	030	51 58	103	59 13	188	57 50	218	25 01	248	27 19	284

 LAT 87°S

LHA ♈	Hc Zn	Hc Zn	Hc Zn	Hc Zn	Hc Zn	Hc Zn	Hc Zn
	ACHERNAR	◆ SIRIUS	Suhail	ACRUX	◆ RIGIL KENT	Peacock	◆ FOMALHAUT
0	59 52 027	16 07 102	41 16 139	60 12 186	58 33 217	58 24 303	32 26 344
2	59 55 025	16 13 100	41 20 137	60 12 184	58 29 215	58 19 301	32 24 342
4	59 57 022	16 20 098	41 24 135	60 11 183	58 26 213	58 13 299	32 22 340
6	59 59 020	16 26 096	41 29 133	60 11 181	58 22 211	58 08 297	32 20 338
8	60 02 018	16 32 094	41 33 131	60 11 179	58 19 210	58 02 295	32 17 336
10	60 03 016	16 38 092	41 38 129	60 11 177	58 16 208	57 56 292	32 15 334
12	60 05 014	16 45 090	41 43 127	60 12 175	58 13 206	57 50 290	32 12 332
14	60 06 012	16 51 088	41 48 125	60 12 174	58 11 204	57 44 288	32 09 330
16	60 07 009	16 57 086	41 53 123	60 13 172	58 08 202	57 38 286	32 05 328
18	60 08 007	17 03 084	41 59 122	60 14 170	58 06 200	57 32 284	32 02 326
20	60 09 005	17 10 082	42 04 120	60 15 168	58 04 198	57 26 282	31 58 324
22	60 09 003	17 16 080	42 10 118	60 17 166	58 02 197	57 20 280	31 55 322
24	60 10 001	17 22 078	42 15 116	60 18 164	58 00 195	57 14 278	31 51 319
26	60 10 358	17 28 076	42 21 114	60 20 163	57 59 193	57 08 276	31 46 317
28	60 09 356	17 34 074	42 27 112	60 22 161	57 57 191	57 01 274	31 42 315
	◆ SIRIUS	Suhail	ACRUX	◆ RIGIL KENT	Peacock	◆ FOMALHAUT	ACHERNAR
30	17 40 072	42 33 110	60 24 159	57 56 189	56 55 272	31 38 313	60 09 354
32	17 46 070	42 39 108	60 26 157	57 55 187	56 49 270	31 33 311	60 08 352
34	17 52 068	42 45 106	60 29 155	57 55 186	56 42 268	31 28 309	60 07 350
36	17 58 066	42 51 104	60 32 153	57 54 184	56 36 266	31 23 307	60 06 348
38	18 04 064	42 57 102	60 35 152	57 54 182	56 30 264	31 18 305	60 04 345
40	18 09 062	43 03 100	60 38 150	57 54 180	56 24 262	31 13 303	60 03 343
42	18 15 060	43 09 098	60 41 148	57 54 178	56 17 260	31 08 301	60 01 341
44	18 20 058	43 15 096	60 44 146	57 54 176	56 11 258	31 02 299	59 59 339
46	18 25 056	43 22 094	60 48 144	57 55 175	56 05 256	30 57 297	59 56 337
48	18 30 054	43 28 092	60 52 142	57 55 173	55 59 254	30 51 295	59 54 335
50	18 36 052	43 34 090	60 56 141	57 56 171	55 53 252	30 45 293	59 51 332
52	18 40 050	43 40 088	61 00 139	57 57 169	55 47 250	30 39 291	59 48 330
54	18 45 048	43 47 086	61 04 137	57 59 167	55 41 248	30 34 289	59 45 328
56	18 50 046	43 53 084	61 08 135	58 00 165	55 35 247	30 28 287	59 41 326
58	18 54 044	43 59 082	61 13 133	58 02 164	55 30 245	30 22 285	59 37 324
	◆ SIRIUS	Suhail	ACRUX	◆ RIGIL KENT	Peacock	◆ FOMALHAUT	ACHERNAR
60	18 59 042	44 05 080	61 17 131	58 04 162	55 24 243	30 15 283	59 34 322
62	19 03 040	44 12 078	61 22 129	58 06 160	55 19 241	30 09 281	59 30 320
64	19 07 038	44 18 076	61 27 128	58 08 158	55 13 239	30 03 279	59 26 317
66	19 10 036	44 24 074	61 32 126	58 10 156	55 08 237	29 57 277	59 21 315
68	19 14 034	44 30 072	61 37 124	58 13 154	55 03 235	29 51 275	59 17 313
70	19 17 032	44 36 070	61 43 122	58 16 153	54 58 233	29 44 273	59 12 311
72	19 21 030	44 42 068	61 48 120	58 19 151	54 53 231	29 38 271	59 07 309
74	19 24 028	44 47 066	61 53 118	58 22 149	54 48 229	29 32 269	59 02 307
76	19 27 026	44 53 064	61 59 116	58 25 147	54 43 227	29 26 267	58 57 305
78	19 29 024	44 59 062	62 05 114	58 29 145	54 39 225	29 19 265	58 52 303
80	19 32 022	45 04 060	62 10 112	58 32 143	54 34 224	29 13 263	58 47 301
82	19 34 020	45 09 058	62 16 110	58 36 141	54 30 222	29 07 261	58 41 298
84	19 36 018	45 15 056	62 22 108	58 40 140	54 26 220	29 01 259	58 36 296
86	19 38 016	45 20 053	62 28 107	58 44 138	54 22 218	28 54 257	58 30 294
88	19 39 014	45 25 051	62 34 105	58 49 136	54 18 216	28 48 255	58 24 292
	◆ SIRIUS	Suhail	ACRUX	◆ RIGIL KENT	Peacock	◆ FOMALHAUT	ACHERNAR
90	19 41 012	45 30 049	62 40 103	58 53 134	54 14 214	28 42 253	58 18 290
92	19 42 010	45 34 047	62 47 101	58 58 132	54 11 212	28 36 251	58 12 288
94	19 43 008	45 39 045	62 53 099	59 02 130	54 08 210	28 30 249	58 06 286
96	19 43 006	45 43 043	62 59 097	59 07 128	54 05 209	28 25 247	58 00 284
98	19 44 004	45 47 041	63 05 095	59 12 126	54 02 207	28 19 245	57 54 282
100	19 44 001	45 51 039	63 11 093	59 17 125	53 59 205	28 13 243	57 48 280
102	19 44 359	45 55 037	63 18 091	59 23 123	53 56 203	28 08 241	57 42 278
104	19 44 357	45 59 035	63 24 089	59 28 121	53 54 201	28 02 239	57 36 276
106	19 44 355	46 02 033	63 30 087	59 33 119	53 52 199	27 57 237	57 29 274
108	19 43 353	46 06 031	63 37 085	59 39 117	53 50 197	27 52 235	57 23 272
110	19 42 351	46 09 029	63 43 083	59 45 115	53 48 196	27 47 233	57 17 270
112	19 41 349	46 12 026	63 49 081	59 50 113	53 47 194	27 42 231	57 10 268
114	19 40 347	46 14 024	63 55 079	59 56 111	53 45 192	27 37 229	57 04 266
116	19 38 345	46 17 022	64 01 077	60 02 109	53 44 190	27 32 227	56 58 264
118	19 37 343	46 19 020	64 07 075	60 08 107	53 43 188	27 28 225	56 52 262
	◆ Suhail	SPICA	◆ ANTARES	Peacock	FOMALHAUT	◆ ACHERNAR	SIRIUS
120	46 21 018	11 40 082	24 37 129	53 42 186	27 23 223	56 45 260	19 35 341
122	46 23 016	11 46 080	24 42 127	53 42 184	27 19 222	56 39 258	19 33 339
124	46 25 014	11 52 078	24 47 125	53 41 183	27 15 220	56 33 256	19 30 337
126	46 26 012	11 59 076	24 52 123	53 41 181	27 11 218	56 27 254	19 28 335
128	46 27 010	12 05 074	24 57 121	53 41 179	27 07 216	56 21 252	19 25 333
130	46 28 008	12 11 072	25 03 119	53 41 177	27 04 214	56 15 250	19 22 331
132	46 29 005	12 17 070	25 08 117	53 42 175	27 00 212	56 09 248	19 19 329
134	46 29 003	12 22 068	25 14 115	53 42 173	26 57 210	56 03 246	19 16 327
136	46 30 001	12 28 066	25 20 113	53 43 171	26 54 208	55 58 244	19 12 325
138	46 30 359	12 34 064	25 25 111	53 44 170	26 51 206	55 52 242	19 08 323
140	46 29 357	12 39 062	25 31 109	53 46 168	26 48 204	55 47 241	19 04 321
142	46 29 355	12 45 060	25 37 107	53 47 166	26 46 202	55 41 239	19 00 319
144	46 28 353	12 50 058	25 43 105	53 49 164	26 44 200	55 36 237	18 56 317
146	46 27 351	12 56 056	25 49 103	53 51 162	26 42 198	55 31 235	18 52 315
148	46 26 349	13 01 054	25 56 101	53 53 160	26 40 196	55 26 233	18 47 313
	SPICA	◆ ANTARES	Peacock	FOMALHAUT	◆ ACHERNAR	CANOPUS	◆ Suhail
150	13 06 052	26 02 099	53 55 158	26 38 194	55 21 231	54 24 303	46 25 346
152	13 11 050	26 08 097	53 57 156	26 37 192	55 16 229	54 19 301	46 23 344
154	13 15 048	26 14 095	54 00 155	26 36 190	55 11 227	54 13 299	46 21 342
156	13 20 046	26 21 093	54 03 153	26 35 188	55 07 225	54 08 297	46 19 340
158	13 24 044	26 27 091	54 06 151	26 34 186	55 02 223	54 02 294	46 17 338
160	13 29 042	26 33 089	54 09 149	26 33 184	54 58 222	53 56 292	46 15 336
162	13 33 040	26 39 087	54 12 147	26 33 183	54 54 220	53 50 290	46 12 334
164	13 37 038	26 46 085	54 15 145	26 33 181	54 50 218	53 44 288	46 09 332
166	13 41 036	26 52 083	54 19 143	26 33 179	54 46 216	53 38 286	46 06 330
168	13 44 034	26 58 081	54 23 142	26 33 177	54 43 214	53 32 284	46 03 328
170	13 48 032	27 04 079	54 27 140	26 33 175	54 39 212	53 26 282	45 59 325
172	13 51 030	27 10 077	54 31 138	26 34 173	54 36 210	53 20 280	45 56 323
174	13 54 028	27 17 075	54 35 136	26 35 171	54 33 208	53 14 278	45 52 321
176	13 57 026	27 23 073	54 40 134	26 36 169	54 30 207	53 08 276	45 48 319
178	13 59 024	27 29 071	54 44 132	26 37 167	54 27 205	53 01 274	45 44 317

LHA ♈	Hc Zn	Hc Zn	Hc Zn	Hc Zn	Hc Zn	Hc Zn	Hc Zn
	SPICA	◆ ANTARES	Peacock	FOMALHAUT	◆ ACHERNAR	CANOPUS	◆ Suhail
180	14 02 022	27 34 069	54 49 130	26 39 165	54 25 203	52 55 272	45 39 315
182	14 04 020	27 40 067	54 54 128	26 41 163	54 22 201	52 49 270	45 35 313
184	14 06 018	27 46 065	54 59 126	26 42 161	54 20 199	52 43 268	45 30 311
186	14 08 016	27 52 063	55 04 124	26 45 159	54 18 197	52 36 266	45 25 309
188	14 09 014	27 57 061	55 09 123	26 47 157	54 17 195	52 30 264	45 20 307
190	14 11 012	28 03 059	55 15 121	26 49 155	54 15 194	52 24 262	45 15 305
192	14 12 010	28 08 057	55 20 119	26 52 153	54 14 192	52 18 260	45 10 303
194	14 13 008	28 13 055	55 26 117	26 55 151	54 12 190	52 11 258	45 05 301
196	14 14 006	28 18 053	55 31 115	26 58 149	54 12 188	52 05 256	44 59 299
198	14 14 004	28 23 051	55 37 113	27 01 147	54 11 186	51 59 254	44 54 297
200	14 14 002	28 28 049	55 43 111	27 05 146	54 10 184	51 53 252	44 48 295
202	14 14 359	28 33 047	55 49 109	27 09 144	54 10 182	51 47 250	44 42 292
204	14 14 357	28 37 045	55 55 107	27 12 142	54 10 181	51 41 248	44 36 290
206	14 14 355	28 41 043	56 01 105	27 16 140	54 10 179	51 36 246	44 31 288
208	14 13 353	28 46 041	56 07 103	27 21 138	54 10 177	51 30 245	44 25 286
	◆ ANTARES	Nunki	FOMALHAUT	◆ ACHERNAR	CANOPUS	◆ Suhail	SPICA
210	28 50 039	27 04 076	27 25 136	54 10 175	51 24 243	44 18 284	14 12 351
212	28 53 037	27 10 073	27 29 134	54 11 173	51 19 241	44 12 282	14 11 349
214	28 57 034	27 16 071	27 34 132	54 12 171	51 13 239	44 06 280	14 10 347
216	29 01 032	27 22 069	27 39 130	54 13 169	51 08 237	44 00 278	14 09 345
218	29 04 030	27 28 067	27 44 128	54 14 168	51 03 235	43 54 276	14 07 343
220	29 07 028	27 33 065	27 49 126	54 16 166	50 58 233	43 48 274	14 05 341
222	29 10 026	27 39 063	27 54 124	54 17 164	50 53 231	43 41 272	14 03 339
224	29 12 024	27 45 061	27 59 122	54 19 162	50 48 229	43 35 270	14 00 337
226	29 15 022	27 50 059	28 04 120	54 21 160	50 43 227	43 29 268	13 58 335
228	29 17 020	27 55 057	28 10 118	54 23 158	50 39 225	43 22 266	13 55 333
230	29 19 018	28 01 055	28 15 116	54 26 156	50 34 223	43 16 264	13 52 331
232	29 21 016	28 06 053	28 21 114	54 28 155	50 30 221	43 10 262	13 49 329
234	29 23 014	28 11 051	28 27 112	54 31 153	50 26 220	43 04 260	13 46 327
236	29 24 012	28 16 049	28 33 110	54 34 151	50 22 218	42 58 258	13 42 325
238	29 25 010	28 20 047	28 39 108	54 37 149	50 18 216	42 51 256	13 39 323
	ANTARES	Nunki	◆ FOMALHAUT	ACHERNAR	◆ CANOPUS	ACRUX	◆ RIGIL KENT
240	29 26 008	28 25 045	28 45 106	54 41 147	50 15 214	64 53 302	63 42 338
242	29 27 006	28 29 043	28 51 104	54 44 145	50 11 212	64 47 300	63 40 336
244	29 27 004	28 33 041	28 57 102	54 48 143	50 08 210	64 42 298	63 37 334
246	29 28 002	28 37 039	29 03 100	54 52 141	50 05 208	64 36 295	63 34 332
248	29 28 000	28 41 037	29 09 098	54 56 140	50 02 206	64 30 293	63 31 329
250	29 28 358	28 45 035	29 15 096	55 00 138	49 59 204	64 24 291	63 28 327
252	29 27 355	28 48 033	29 22 094	55 04 136	49 57 203	64 19 289	63 24 325
254	29 27 353	28 52 031	29 28 092	55 09 134	49 55 201	64 13 287	63 20 323
256	29 26 351	28 55 029	29 34 090	55 13 132	49 53 199	64 07 285	63 16 321
258	29 25 349	28 58 027	29 40 088	55 18 130	49 51 197	64 00 283	63 12 319
260	29 24 347	29 01 025	29 47 086	55 23 128	49 49 195	63 54 281	63 08 316
262	29 22 345	29 03 023	29 53 084	55 28 126	49 47 193	63 48 279	63 04 314
264	29 20 343	29 05 021	29 59 082	55 33 124	49 46 191	63 42 277	62 59 312
266	29 18 341	29 08 019	30 05 080	55 38 122	49 45 189	63 36 275	62 54 310
268	29 16 339	29 09 016	30 12 078	55 44 121	49 44 188	63 29 273	62 50 308
	Nunki	◆ FOMALHAUT	ACHERNAR	◆ CANOPUS	ACRUX	◆ RIGIL KENT	ANTARES
270	29 11 014	30 18 076	55 49 119	49 43 186	63 23 271	62 45 306	29 14 337
272	29 13 012	30 24 074	55 55 117	49 43 184	63 17 269	62 39 304	29 11 335
274	29 14 010	30 30 072	56 00 115	49 42 182	63 11 267	62 34 302	29 09 333
276	29 15 008	30 36 070	56 06 113	49 42 180	63 04 265	62 29 299	29 06 331
278	29 16 006	30 42 068	56 12 111	49 42 178	62 58 263	62 23 297	29 02 329
280	29 16 004	30 47 066	56 18 109	49 43 176	62 52 261	62 18 295	28 59 327
282	29 16 002	30 53 064	56 24 107	49 43 174	62 46 259	62 12 293	28 56 325
284	29 17 000	30 59 062	56 30 105	49 44 173	62 40 257	62 06 291	28 52 323
286	29 17 358	31 04 060	56 36 103	49 45 171	62 33 255	62 00 289	28 48 321
288	29 16 356	31 10 058	56 42 101	49 46 169	62 27 253	61 54 287	28 44 319
290	29 16 354	31 15 056	56 48 099	49 47 167	62 21 251	61 48 285	28 40 317
292	29 15 352	31 20 054	56 54 097	49 49 165	62 16 249	61 42 283	28 35 314
294	29 14 350	31 25 052	57 01 095	49 50 163	62 10 247	61 36 281	28 31 312
296	29 13 348	31 30 050	57 07 093	49 52 161	62 04 245	61 30 279	28 26 310
298	29 11 346	31 35 048	57 13 091	49 54 159	61 58 244	61 23 277	28 21 308
	◆ FOMALHAUT	ACHERNAR	◆ CANOPUS	ACRUX	◆ RIGIL KENT	ANTARES	Nunki
300	31 39 046	57 19 089	49 57 158	61 53 242	61 17 275	28 16 306	29 09 344
302	31 44 044	57 26 087	49 59 156	61 47 240	61 11 273	28 11 304	29 08 342
304	31 48 042	57 32 085	50 02 154	61 42 238	61 05 271	28 06 302	29 06 340
306	31 52 040	57 38 083	50 05 152	61 37 236	60 58 269	28 00 300	29 03 337
308	31 56 038	57 44 081	50 08 150	61 31 234	60 52 267	27 55 298	29 01 335
310	32 00 036	57 51 079	50 11 148	61 26 232	60 46 265	27 49 296	28 58 333
312	32 03 034	57 57 077	50 15 146	61 21 230	60 40 263	27 44 294	28 55 331
314	32 07 032	58 03 075	50 18 144	61 17 228	60 33 261	27 38 292	28 52 329
316	32 10 029	58 09 073	50 22 142	61 12 227	60 27 259	27 32 290	28 49 327
318	32 13 027	58 15 071	50 26 141	61 08 225	60 21 257	27 26 288	28 45 325
320	32 16 025	58 21 069	50 30 139	61 03 223	60 15 255	27 20 286	28 41 323
322	32 18 023	58 27 067	50 34 137	60 59 221	60 09 253	27 14 284	28 38 321
324	32 21 021	58 32 065	50 38 135	60 55 219	60 03 251	27 08 282	28 34 319
326	32 23 019	58 38 063	50 43 133	60 51 217	59 57 249	27 02 280	28 29 317
328	32 25 017	58 43 061	50 48 131	60 47 215	59 51 247	26 56 278	28 25 315
	◆ FOMALHAUT	ACHERNAR	◆ CANOPUS	ACRUX	◆ RIGIL KENT	ANTARES	Nunki
330	32 27 015	58 49 059	50 52 129	60 44 214	59 45 245	26 49 276	28 21 313
332	32 28 013	58 54 056	50 57 127	60 40 212	59 40 243	26 43 274	28 16 311
334	32 29 011	58 59 054	51 02 125	60 37 210	59 34 241	26 37 272	28 11 309
336	32 30 009	59 04 052	51 08 123	60 34 208	59 29 240	26 30 270	28 06 307
338	32 31 007	59 09 050	51 13 121	60 31 206	59 23 238	26 24 268	28 01 305
340	32 32 005	59 14 048	51 18 119	60 29 204	59 18 236	26 18 266	27 56 303
342	32 32 003	59 19 046	51 24 118	60 26 203	59 13 234	26 12 264	27 50 301
344	32 33 001	59 23 044	51 29 116	60 24 201	59 08 232	26 05 262	27 45 299
346	32 32 359	59 27 042	51 35 114	60 22 199	59 03 230	25 59 260	27 39 297
348	32 32 357	59 31 040	51 41 112	60 20 197	58 58 228	25 53 258	27 34 295
350	32 32 354	59 35 037	51 47 110	60 18 195	58 54 226	25 47 256	27 28 293
352	32 31 352	59 39 035	51 53 108	60 16 193	58 49 224	25 41 254	27 22 291
354	32 30 350	59 43 033	51 59 106	60 15 192	58 45 223	25 35 252	27 16 289
356	32 29 348	59 46 031	52 05 104	60 14 190	58 41 221	25 29 250	27 10 287
358	32 28 346	59 49 029	52 11 102	60 13 188	58 37 219	25 23 248	27 04 285

LAT 88°S

LHA ♈	ACHERNAR Hc	Zn	◆ SIRIUS Hc	Zn	Suhail Hc	Zn	ACRUX Hc	Zn	◆ RIGIL KENT Hc	Zn	Peacock Hc	Zn	◆ FOMALHAUT Hc	Zn
0	58 58	026	16 20	102	42 01	138	61 12	186	59 21	218	57 51	304	31 28	344
2	59 00	024	16 24	100	42 04	136	61 11	185	59 18	216	57 47	302	31 27	342
4	59 02	022	16 28	098	42 07	134	61 11	183	59 16	214	57 44	300	31 26	340
6	59 03	020	16 32	096	42 10	133	61 11	181	59 13	212	57 40	298	31 24	338
8	59 04	018	16 36	094	42 13	131	61 11	179	59 11	210	57 36	296	31 22	336
10	59 06	015	16 41	092	42 16	129	61 11	177	59 09	208	57 32	294	31 21	334
12	59 07	013	16 45	090	42 19	127	61 11	175	59 07	207	57 29	292	31 19	332
14	59 08	011	16 49	088	42 23	125	61 12	173	59 05	205	57 25	290	31 17	330
16	59 08	009	16 53	086	42 26	123	61 12	171	59 04	203	57 21	288	31 15	328
18	59 09	007	16 57	084	42 30	121	61 13	170	59 02	201	57 17	286	31 12	326
20	59 09	005	17 01	082	42 33	119	61 14	168	59 01	199	57 13	284	31 10	324
22	59 10	003	17 06	080	42 37	117	61 15	166	58 59	197	57 09	282	31 07	322
24	59 10	001	17 10	078	42 41	115	61 16	164	58 58	195	57 04	280	31 05	320
26	59 10	358	17 14	076	42 45	113	61 17	162	58 57	193	57 00	278	31 02	318
28	59 09	356	17 18	074	42 49	111	61 19	160	58 56	191	56 56	276	30 59	316

LHA ♈	◆ SIRIUS Hc	Zn	Suhail Hc	Zn	ACRUX Hc	Zn	◆ RIGIL KENT Hc	Zn	Peacock Hc	Zn	◆ FOMALHAUT Hc	Zn	ACHERNAR Hc	Zn
30	17 22	072	42 52	109	61 20	158	58 56	190	56 52	274	30 56	314	59 09	354
32	17 26	070	42 56	107	61 22	156	58 55	188	56 48	272	30 53	312	59 09	352
34	17 30	068	43 00	105	61 23	155	58 54	186	56 44	270	30 50	310	59 08	350
36	17 34	066	43 05	103	61 25	153	58 54	184	56 39	268	30 47	308	59 07	348
38	17 37	064	43 09	101	61 27	151	58 54	182	56 35	266	30 43	306	59 06	346
40	17 41	062	43 13	099	61 29	149	58 54	180	56 31	264	30 40	304	59 05	344
42	17 45	060	43 17	097	61 32	147	58 54	178	56 27	262	30 36	302	59 04	342
44	17 48	058	43 21	095	61 34	145	58 54	176	56 23	260	30 33	300	59 02	339
46	17 52	056	43 25	093	61 36	143	58 54	174	56 19	258	30 29	298	59 01	337
48	17 55	054	43 29	091	61 39	141	58 55	173	56 15	256	30 25	296	58 59	335
50	17 59	052	43 34	089	61 42	139	58 55	171	56 11	254	30 22	294	58 57	333
52	18 02	050	43 38	087	61 44	138	58 56	169	56 07	252	30 18	292	58 55	331
54	18 05	048	43 42	085	61 47	136	58 57	167	56 03	250	30 14	290	58 53	329
56	18 08	046	43 46	083	61 50	134	58 58	165	55 59	248	30 10	288	58 51	327
58	18 11	044	43 50	081	61 53	132	58 59	163	55 55	246	30 06	286	58 49	325

LHA ♈	◆ SIRIUS Hc	Zn	Suhail Hc	Zn	ACRUX Hc	Zn	◆ RIGIL KENT Hc	Zn	Peacock Hc	Zn	◆ FOMALHAUT Hc	Zn	ACHERNAR Hc	Zn
60	18 14	042	43 54	079	61 56	130	59 00	161	55 51	244	30 02	284	58 46	323
62	18 17	040	43 59	077	62 00	128	59 02	159	55 47	242	29 58	282	58 44	321
64	18 19	038	44 03	075	62 03	126	59 03	158	55 44	240	29 54	279	58 41	318
66	18 22	036	44 07	073	62 06	124	59 05	156	55 40	238	29 49	277	58 38	316
68	18 24	034	44 11	071	62 10	122	59 07	154	55 37	236	29 45	275	58 35	314
70	18 26	032	44 15	069	62 14	120	59 09	152	55 33	234	29 41	273	58 32	312
72	18 29	030	44 18	067	62 17	118	59 11	150	55 30	232	29 37	271	58 29	310
74	18 31	028	44 22	065	62 21	116	59 13	148	55 26	230	29 33	269	58 26	308
76	18 32	026	44 26	063	62 25	114	59 15	146	55 23	228	29 28	267	58 22	306
78	18 34	024	44 30	061	62 29	113	59 18	144	55 20	227	29 24	265	58 19	304
80	18 36	022	44 33	059	62 32	111	59 20	142	55 17	225	29 20	263	58 15	302
82	18 37	020	44 37	057	62 36	109	59 23	140	55 14	223	29 16	262	58 12	300
84	18 39	018	44 40	055	62 40	107	59 25	139	55 12	221	29 12	260	58 08	298
86	18 40	016	44 44	053	62 44	105	59 28	137	55 09	219	29 08	258	58 04	296
88	18 41	014	44 47	051	62 48	103	59 31	135	55 06	217	29 04	256	58 01	294

LHA ♈	◆ SIRIUS Hc	Zn	Suhail Hc	Zn	ACRUX Hc	Zn	◆ RIGIL KENT Hc	Zn	Peacock Hc	Zn	◆ FOMALHAUT Hc	Zn	ACHERNAR Hc	Zn
90	18 42	012	44 50	049	62 53	101	59 34	133	55 04	215	29 00	254	57 57	292
92	18 43	010	44 53	047	62 57	099	59 37	131	55 02	213	28 56	252	57 53	290
94	18 43	008	44 56	044	63 01	097	59 41	129	54 59	211	28 52	250	57 49	288
96	18 44	006	44 59	042	63 05	095	59 44	127	54 57	209	28 48	248	57 45	286
98	18 44	003	45 02	040	63 09	093	59 47	125	54 55	207	28 44	246	57 41	284
100	18 44	001	45 05	038	63 13	091	59 51	123	54 53	205	28 40	244	57 37	282
102	18 44	359	45 07	036	63 18	089	59 54	121	54 52	204	28 36	242	57 33	280
104	18 44	357	45 09	034	63 22	087	59 58	119	54 50	202	28 33	240	57 28	277
106	18 44	355	45 12	032	63 26	085	60 02	117	54 49	200	28 29	238	57 24	275
108	18 43	353	45 14	030	63 30	083	60 05	115	54 47	198	28 26	236	57 20	273
110	18 43	351	45 16	028	63 34	081	60 09	113	54 46	196	28 22	234	57 16	271
112	18 42	349	45 18	026	63 38	079	60 13	111	54 45	194	28 19	232	57 12	269
114	18 41	347	45 20	024	63 42	077	60 17	110	54 44	192	28 16	230	57 08	267
116	18 40	345	45 21	022	63 46	075	60 21	108	54 43	190	28 13	228	57 03	265
118	18 39	343	45 23	020	63 51	073	60 25	106	54 42	188	28 10	226	56 59	263

LHA ♈	◆ Suhail Hc	Zn	SPICA Hc	Zn	◆ ANTARES Hc	Zn	Peacock Hc	Zn	FOMALHAUT Hc	Zn	◆ ACHERNAR Hc	Zn	SIRIUS Hc	Zn
120	45 24	018	11 32	082	25 14	128	54 42	186	28 07	224	56 55	262	18 38	341
122	45 25	016	11 36	080	25 17	126	54 42	184	28 04	222	56 51	260	18 37	339
124	45 26	014	11 40	078	25 21	124	54 41	183	28 01	220	56 47	258	18 35	337
126	45 27	012	11 44	076	25 24	122	54 41	181	27 58	218	56 43	256	18 33	335
128	45 28	009	11 48	074	25 28	120	54 41	179	27 56	216	56 39	254	18 31	333
130	45 29	007	11 52	072	25 31	118	54 41	177	27 53	214	56 35	252	18 30	331
132	45 29	005	11 56	070	25 35	116	54 42	175	27 51	212	56 31	250	18 27	329
134	45 29	003	12 00	068	25 39	114	54 42	173	27 49	210	56 27	248	18 25	327
136	45 30	001	12 04	066	25 43	112	54 43	171	27 47	208	56 23	246	18 23	325
138	45 30	359	12 08	064	25 47	111	54 43	169	27 45	206	56 19	244	18 20	323
140	45 29	357	12 11	062	25 51	109	54 44	167	27 43	204	56 16	242	18 18	321
142	45 29	355	12 15	060	25 55	107	54 45	165	27 42	202	56 12	240	18 15	319
144	45 29	353	12 19	058	25 59	105	54 46	164	27 40	200	56 08	238	18 12	317
146	45 28	351	12 22	056	26 03	103	54 48	162	27 39	198	56 05	236	18 09	315
148	45 27	349	12 25	054	26 07	101	54 49	160	27 37	196	56 01	234	18 06	313

LHA ♈	SPICA Hc	Zn	◆ ANTARES Hc	Zn	Peacock Hc	Zn	FOMALHAUT Hc	Zn	◆ ACHERNAR Hc	Zn	CANOPUS Hc	Zn	◆ Suhail Hc	Zn
150	12 29	052	26 11	099	54 50	158	27 36	194	55 58	232	53 51	304	45 27	347
152	12 32	050	26 15	097	54 52	156	27 35	192	55 55	230	53 48	302	45 25	345
154	12 35	048	26 19	095	54 54	154	27 35	190	55 52	228	53 44	300	45 24	343
156	12 38	046	26 23	093	54 56	152	27 34	188	55 48	226	53 40	298	45 23	340
158	12 41	044	26 28	091	54 58	150	27 33	186	55 46	224	53 37	296	45 21	338
160	12 44	042	26 32	089	55 00	148	27 33	185	55 43	222	53 33	294	45 20	336
162	12 47	040	26 36	087	55 02	146	27 33	183	55 40	221	53 29	292	45 18	334
164	12 49	038	26 40	085	55 05	144	27 33	181	55 37	219	53 25	290	45 16	332
166	12 52	036	26 44	083	55 07	143	27 33	179	55 35	217	53 21	288	45 14	330
168	12 54	034	26 49	081	55 10	141	27 33	177	55 32	215	53 17	286	45 12	328
170	12 57	032	26 53	079	55 12	139	27 33	175	55 30	213	53 13	284	45 10	326
172	12 59	030	26 57	077	55 15	137	27 34	173	55 28	211	53 09	281	45 07	324
174	13 01	028	27 01	075	55 18	135	27 34	171	55 26	209	53 05	279	45 05	322
176	13 03	026	27 05	073	55 21	133	27 35	169	55 24	207	53 01	277	45 02	320
178	13 04	024	27 09	071	55 24	131	27 36	167	55 22	205	52 56	275	44 59	318

LHA ♈	SPICA Hc	Zn	◆ ANTARES Hc	Zn	Peacock Hc	Zn	FOMALHAUT Hc	Zn	◆ ACHERNAR Hc	Zn	CANOPUS Hc	Zn	◆ Suhail Hc	Zn
180	13 06	022	27 13	069	55 27	129	27 37	165	55 20	203	52 52	273	44 57	316
182	13 07	020	27 17	067	55 31	127	27 38	163	55 18	201	52 48	271	44 54	314
184	13 09	018	27 20	064	55 34	125	27 39	161	55 17	200	52 44	269	44 51	312
186	13 10	016	27 24	062	55 38	123	27 41	159	55 16	198	52 40	267	44 47	310
188	13 11	014	27 28	060	55 41	121	27 42	157	55 14	196	52 35	265	44 44	308
190	13 12	012	27 31	058	55 45	119	27 44	155	55 13	194	52 31	263	44 41	306
192	13 13	010	27 35	056	55 48	117	27 46	153	55 12	192	52 27	261	44 37	304
194	13 13	008	27 38	054	55 52	115	27 48	151	55 12	190	52 23	259	44 34	302
196	13 14	006	27 42	052	55 56	113	27 50	149	55 11	188	52 19	258	44 30	299
198	13 14	004	27 45	050	56 00	112	27 52	147	55 10	186	52 15	256	44 26	297
200	13 14	002	27 48	048	56 04	110	27 54	145	55 10	184	52 11	254	44 23	295
202	13 14	359	27 51	046	56 08	108	27 57	143	55 10	182	52 07	252	44 19	293
204	13 14	357	27 54	044	56 12	106	27 59	141	55 10	181	52 03	250	44 15	291
206	13 14	355	27 57	042	56 16	104	28 02	139	55 10	179	51 59	248	44 11	289
208	13 14	353	28 00	040	56 20	102	28 05	137	55 10	177	51 55	246	44 07	287

LHA ♈	◆ ANTARES Hc	Zn	Nunki Hc	Zn	FOMALHAUT Hc	Zn	◆ ACHERNAR Hc	Zn	CANOPUS Hc	Zn	◆ Suhail Hc	Zn	SPICA Hc	Zn
210	28 03	038	26 49	075	28 08	135	55 10	175	51 51	244	44 03	285	13 13	351
212	28 05	036	26 53	073	28 11	133	55 11	173	51 48	242	43 59	283	13 12	349
214	28 07	034	26 57	071	28 14	131	55 11	171	51 44	240	43 55	281	13 11	347
216	28 10	032	27 01	069	28 17	129	55 12	169	51 40	238	43 51	279	13 10	345
218	28 12	030	27 04	067	28 20	128	55 13	167	51 37	236	43 47	277	13 09	343
220	28 14	028	27 08	065	28 24	126	55 14	165	51 33	234	43 43	275	13 08	341
222	28 16	026	27 12	063	28 27	124	55 15	163	51 30	232	43 38	273	13 07	339
224	28 18	024	27 16	061	28 31	122	55 16	162	51 27	230	43 34	271	13 05	337
226	28 19	022	27 19	059	28 34	120	55 18	160	51 24	228	43 30	269	13 03	335
228	28 21	020	27 23	057	28 38	118	55 19	158	51 21	226	43 26	267	13 02	333
230	28 22	018	27 26	055	28 42	116	55 21	156	51 18	224	43 22	265	13 00	331
232	28 23	016	27 30	053	28 45	114	55 22	154	51 15	222	43 17	263	12 58	329
234	28 24	014	27 33	051	28 49	112	55 24	152	51 12	220	43 13	261	12 55	327
236	28 25	012	27 36	049	28 53	110	55 26	150	51 09	218	43 09	259	12 53	325
238	28 26	010	27 39	047	28 57	108	55 29	148	51 07	217	43 05	257	12 51	323

LHA ♈	ANTARES Hc	Zn	Nunki Hc	Zn	◆ FOMALHAUT Hc	Zn	ACHERNAR Hc	Zn	◆ CANOPUS Hc	Zn	ACRUX Hc	Zn	◆ RIGIL KENT Hc	Zn
240	28 27	008	27 42	045	29 01	106	55 31	146	51 04	215	64 20	304	62 46	339
242	28 27	006	27 45	043	29 05	104	55 33	144	51 02	213	64 17	301	62 45	337
244	28 28	004	27 48	041	29 09	102	55 36	142	51 00	211	64 13	299	62 43	335
246	28 28	002	27 51	039	29 13	100	55 38	141	50 58	209	64 09	297	62 41	332
248	28 28	000	27 53	037	29 18	098	55 41	139	50 56	207	64 06	295	62 39	330
250	28 28	358	27 56	035	29 22	096	55 44	137	50 54	205	64 02	293	62 37	328
252	28 27	356	27 58	033	29 26	094	55 47	135	50 52	203	63 58	291	62 35	326
254	28 27	353	28 00	031	29 30	092	55 50	133	50 51	201	63 54	289	62 32	324
256	28 27	351	28 02	029	29 34	090	55 53	131	50 49	199	63 50	287	62 30	322
258	28 26	349	28 04	027	29 38	088	55 56	129	50 48	197	63 46	285	62 27	320
260	28 25	347	28 06	024	29 43	086	55 59	127	50 47	195	63 42	283	62 24	318
262	28 24	345	28 08	022	29 47	084	56 03	125	50 46	193	63 38	281	62 21	316
264	28 23	343	28 09	020	29 51	082	56 06	123	50 45	192	63 34	279	62 18	314
266	28 22	341	28 11	018	29 55	080	56 10	121	50 44	190	63 29	277	62 15	311
268	28 20	339	28 12	016	29 59	078	56 13	119	50 43	188	63 25	275	62 12	309

LHA ♈	Nunki Hc	Zn	◆ FOMALHAUT Hc	Zn	ACHERNAR Hc	Zn	◆ CANOPUS Hc	Zn	ACRUX Hc	Zn	◆ RIGIL KENT Hc	Zn	ANTARES Hc	Zn
270	28 13	014	30 03	076	56 17	117	50 43	186	63 21	273	62 09	307	28 19	337
272	28 14	012	30 07	074	56 21	115	50 43	184	63 17	271	62 05	305	28 17	335
274	28 15	010	30 11	072	56 25	113	50 42	182	63 13	269	62 02	303	28 15	333
276	28 15	008	30 15	070	56 29	111	50 42	180	63 09	267	61 58	301	28 13	331
278	28 16	006	30 19	068	56 33	109	50 42	178	63 04	265	61 55	299	28 11	329
280	28 16	004	30 23	066	56 36	108	50 43	176	63 00	263	61 51	297	28 09	327
282	28 17	002	30 27	064	56 40	106	50 43	174	62 56	261	61 47	295	28 06	325
284	28 17	000	30 31	062	56 45	104	50 43	172	62 52	259	61 44	293	28 04	323
286	28 17	358	30 34	060	56 49	102	50 44	170	62 48	257	61 40	291	28 01	321
288	28 16	356	30 38	058	56 53	100	50 45	169	62 44	255	61 36	289	27 59	319
290	28 16	354	30 41	056	56 57	098	50 46	167	62 40	253	61 32	287	27 56	317
292	28 15	352	30 45	054	57 01	096	50 47	165	62 36	251	61 28	285	27 53	315
294	28 15	350	30 48	052	57 05	094	50 48	163	62 32	249	61 24	283	27 50	313
296	28 14	348	30 51	049	57 09	092	50 49	161	62 28	247	61 20	281	27 47	311
298	28 13	346	30 54	047	57 14	090	50 51	159	62 24	245	61 15	279	27 44	309

LHA ♈	◆ FOMALHAUT Hc	Zn	ACHERNAR Hc	Zn	◆ CANOPUS Hc	Zn	ACRUX Hc	Zn	◆ RIGIL KENT Hc	Zn	ANTARES Hc	Zn	Nunki Hc	Zn
300	30 57	045	57 18	088	50 52	157	62 20	243	61 11	277	27 40	307	28 12	344
302	31 00	043	57 22	086	50 54	155	62 17	241	61 07	275	27 37	305	28 11	342
304	31 03	041	57 26	084	50 56	153	62 13	239	61 03	273	27 33	303	28 09	340
306	31 06	039	57 30	082	50 58	151	62 09	238	60 59	271	27 30	301	28 08	338
308	31 08	037	57 34	080	51 00	149	62 06	236	60 55	269	27 26	299	28 06	336
310	31 11	035	57 39	078	51 02	147	62 03	234	60 50	267	27 23	297	28 04	334
312	31 13	033	57 43	076	51 04	146	61 59	232	60 46	265	27 19	295	28 02	332
314	31 15	031	57 47	074	51 07	144	61 56	230	60 42	263	27 15	293	28 00	330
316	31 18	029	57 51	072	51 09	142	61 53	228	60 38	261	27 11	291	27 58	328
318	31 20	027	57 55	069	51 12	140	61 50	226	60 34	259	27 07	289	27 56	325
320	31 21	025	57 58	067	51 15	138	61 47	224	60 30	257	27 03	287	27 53	323
322	31 23	023	58 02	065	51 17	136	61 44	222	60 26	255	26 59	285	27 51	321
324	31 25	021	58 06	063	51 20	134	61 41	220	60 22	253	26 55	283	27 48	319
326	31 26	019	58 10	061	51 23	132	61 39	218	60 18	251	26 51	281	27 45	317
328	31 27	017	58 13	059	51 27	130	61 36	217	60 14	249	26 47	279	27 42	315

LHA ♈	◆ FOMALHAUT Hc	Zn	ACHERNAR Hc	Zn	◆ CANOPUS Hc	Zn	ACRUX Hc	Zn	◆ RIGIL KENT Hc	Zn	ANTARES Hc	Zn	Nunki Hc	Zn
330	31 29	015	58 17	057	51 30	128	61 34	215	60 10	247	26 43	277	27 39	313
332	31 30	013	58 20	055	51 33	126	61 31	213	60 06	245	26 38	275	27 36	311
334	31 30	011	58 24	053	51 37	124	61 29	211	60 02	243	26 34	273	27 33	309
336	31 31	009	58 27	051	51 40	122	61 27	209	59 58	241	26 30	271	27 30	307
338	31 32	007	58 30	049	51 44	120	61 25	207	59 55	239	26 26	269	27 27	305
340	31 32	005	58 33	047	51 47	118	61 23	205	59 51	237	26 22	267	27 23	303
342	31 32	003	58 36	045	51 51	116	61 21	203	59 48	235	26 18	265	27 20	301
344	31 33	001	58 39	043	51 55	114	61 20	201	59 44	233	26 13	263	27 16	299
346	31 33	359	58 42	041	51 59	112	61 18	200	59 41	231	26 09	261	27 12	297
348	31 32	357	58 45	039	52 03	111	61 17	198	59 38	229	26 05	259	27 08	295
350	31 32	355	58 47	036	52 07	109	61 16	196	59 35	228	26 01	257	27 05	293
352	31 32	352	58 50	034	52 11	107	61 15	194	59 32	226	25 57	255	27 01	291
354	31 31	350	58 52	032	52 15	105	61 14	192	59 29	224	25 53	253	26 57	289
356	31 30	348	58 54	030	52 19	103	61 13	190	59 26	222	25 49	251	26 53	287
358	31 29	346	58 56	028	52 23	101	61 12	188	59 23	220	25 45	249	26 49	285

LAT 89°S

LHA ♈	ACHERNAR		◆ SIRIUS		Suhail		ACRUX		◆ RIGIL KENT		Peacock		◆ FOMALHAUT	
	Hc	Zn	Hc	Zn	Hc	Zn	Hc	Zn	Hc	Zn	Hc	Zn	Hc	Zn
0	58 04	025	16 32	102	42 45	138	62 11	187	60 08	219	57 16	305	30 30	344
2	58 05	023	16 34	100	42 47	136	62 11	185	60 06	217	57 15	303	30 30	342
4	58 06	021	16 36	098	42 48	134	62 11	183	60 05	215	57 13	301	30 29	340
6	58 06	019	16 38	096	42 50	132	62 11	181	60 04	213	57 11	299	30 28	338
8	58 07	017	16 40	094	42 51	130	62 11	179	60 03	211	57 09	297	30 28	336
10	58 08	015	16 43	092	42 53	128	62 11	177	60 02	209	57 07	295	30 27	334
12	58 08	013	16 45	090	42 55	126	62 11	175	60 01	207	57 06	293	30 26	332
14	58 09	011	16 47	088	42 56	124	62 11	173	60 00	205	57 04	291	30 25	330
16	58 09	009	16 49	086	42 58	122	62 12	171	59 59	203	57 02	289	30 24	328
18	58 09	007	16 51	084	43 00	120	62 12	169	59 58	202	57 00	287	30 23	326
20	58 09	005	16 53	082	43 02	118	62 12	167	59 57	200	56 58	285	30 21	324
22	58 10	003	16 55	080	43 04	116	62 13	165	59 57	198	56 56	283	30 20	322
24	58 10	001	16 57	078	43 06	114	62 14	163	59 56	196	56 54	281	30 19	320
26	58 10	359	16 59	076	43 08	112	62 14	161	59 56	194	56 52	279	30 17	318
28	58 10	356	17 01	074	43 10	110	62 15	160	59 55	192	56 49	277	30 16	316

LHA ♈	◆ SIRIUS		Suhail		ACRUX		◆ RIGIL KENT		Peacock		◆ FOMALHAUT		ACHERNAR	
	Hc	Zn	Hc	Zn	Hc	Zn	Hc	Zn	Hc	Zn	Hc	Zn	Hc	Zn
30	17 03	072	43 11	108	62 16	158	59 55	190	56 47	275	30 15	314	58 09	354
32	17 05	070	43 13	106	62 16	156	59 54	188	56 45	273	30 13	312	58 09	352
34	17 07	068	43 16	104	62 17	154	59 54	186	56 43	271	30 11	310	58 09	350
36	17 09	066	43 18	102	62 18	152	59 54	184	56 41	269	30 10	308	58 08	348
38	17 11	064	43 20	100	62 19	150	59 54	182	56 39	267	30 08	306	58 08	346
40	17 13	062	43 22	098	62 20	148	59 54	180	56 37	265	30 06	304	58 07	344
42	17 15	060	43 24	096	62 22	146	59 54	178	56 35	263	30 05	302	58 07	342
44	17 16	058	43 26	094	62 23	144	59 54	176	56 33	261	30 03	300	58 06	340
46	17 18	056	43 28	092	62 24	142	59 54	174	56 31	259	30 01	298	58 05	338
48	17 20	054	43 30	090	62 25	140	59 54	172	56 29	257	29 59	296	58 05	336
50	17 22	052	43 32	088	62 27	138	59 55	170	56 27	255	29 57	294	58 04	334
52	17 23	050	43 34	086	62 28	136	59 55	169	56 25	253	29 55	292	58 03	332
54	17 25	048	43 36	084	62 30	134	59 55	167	56 23	251	29 53	290	58 02	330
56	17 26	046	43 38	082	62 31	132	59 56	165	56 21	249	29 51	288	58 01	328
58	17 28	044	43 40	080	62 33	130	59 57	163	56 19	247	29 49	286	57 59	326

LHA ♈	◆ SIRIUS		Suhail		ACRUX		◆ RIGIL KENT		Peacock		◆ FOMALHAUT		ACHERNAR	
	Hc	Zn	Hc	Zn	Hc	Zn	Hc	Zn	Hc	Zn	Hc	Zn	Hc	Zn
60	17 29	042	43 43	078	62 34	128	59 57	161	56 17	245	29 47	284	57 58	324
62	17 31	040	43 45	076	62 36	126	59 58	159	56 15	243	29 45	282	57 57	322
64	17 32	038	43 47	074	62 38	124	59 59	157	56 13	241	29 43	280	57 56	320
66	17 33	036	43 49	072	62 39	123	60 00	155	56 11	239	29 41	278	57 54	318
68	17 34	034	43 51	070	62 41	121	60 00	153	56 09	237	29 39	276	57 53	315
70	17 35	032	43 53	068	62 43	119	60 01	151	56 08	235	29 37	274	57 51	313
72	17 36	030	43 54	066	62 45	117	60 03	149	56 06	233	29 35	272	57 50	311
74	17 37	028	43 56	064	62 47	115	60 04	147	56 04	232	29 33	270	57 48	309
76	17 38	026	43 58	062	62 49	113	60 05	145	56 03	230	29 31	268	57 47	307
78	17 39	024	44 00	060	62 51	111	60 06	143	56 01	228	29 29	266	57 45	305
80	17 40	022	44 02	058	62 53	109	60 07	141	56 00	226	29 27	264	57 43	303
82	17 41	020	44 04	056	62 55	107	60 09	139	55 58	224	29 25	262	57 41	301
84	17 41	018	44 05	054	62 57	105	60 10	137	55 57	222	29 22	260	57 40	299
86	17 42	016	44 07	052	62 59	103	60 11	135	55 55	220	29 20	258	57 38	297
88	17 43	014	44 09	050	63 01	101	60 13	133	55 54	218	29 18	256	57 36	295

LHA ♈	◆ SIRIUS		Suhail		ACRUX		◆ RIGIL KENT		Peacock		◆ FOMALHAUT		ACHERNAR	
	Hc	Zn	Hc	Zn	Hc	Zn	Hc	Zn	Hc	Zn	Hc	Zn	Hc	Zn
90	17 43	012	44 10	048	63 03	099	60 15	131	55 53	216	29 16	254	57 34	293
92	17 43	010	44 12	046	63 05	097	60 16	130	55 52	214	29 14	252	57 32	291
94	17 44	007	44 13	044	63 07	095	60 18	128	55 50	212	29 12	250	57 30	289
96	17 44	005	44 15	042	63 09	093	60 19	126	55 49	210	29 10	248	57 28	287
98	17 44	003	44 16	040	63 11	091	60 21	124	55 48	208	29 08	246	57 26	285
100	17 44	001	44 17	038	63 13	089	60 23	122	55 47	206	29 07	244	57 24	283
102	17 44	359	44 19	036	63 15	087	60 25	120	55 46	204	29 05	242	57 22	281
104	17 44	357	44 20	034	63 17	085	60 27	118	55 46	202	29 03	240	57 20	279
106	17 44	355	44 21	032	63 19	083	60 28	116	55 45	200	29 01	238	57 18	277
108	17 44	353	44 22	030	63 22	081	60 30	114	55 44	198	28 59	236	57 16	275
110	17 44	351	44 23	028	63 24	079	60 32	112	55 44	196	28 58	234	57 14	273
112	17 43	349	44 24	026	63 26	077	60 34	110	55 43	194	28 56	232	57 12	271
114	17 43	347	44 25	024	63 28	075	60 36	108	55 43	192	28 54	230	57 09	269
116	17 42	345	44 26	021	63 30	073	60 38	106	55 42	190	28 53	228	57 07	267
118	17 42	343	44 26	019	63 32	071	60 40	104	55 42	188	28 51	226	57 05	265

LHA ♈	◆ Suhail		SPICA		◆ ANTARES		Peacock		FOMALHAUT		◆ ACHERNAR		SIRIUS	
	Hc	Zn	Hc	Zn	Hc	Zn	Hc	Zn	Hc	Zn	Hc	Zn	Hc	Zn
120	44 27	017	11 23	082	25 51	128	55 42	187	28 50	224	57 03	263	17 41	341
122	44 28	015	11 25	080	25 53	126	55 41	185	28 48	222	57 01	261	17 40	339
124	44 28	013	11 27	078	25 54	124	55 41	183	28 47	220	56 59	259	17 40	337
126	44 28	011	11 29	076	25 56	122	55 41	181	28 46	218	56 57	257	17 39	335
128	44 29	009	11 31	074	25 58	120	55 41	179	28 44	216	56 55	255	17 38	333
130	44 29	007	11 33	072	26 00	118	55 41	177	28 43	214	56 53	253	17 37	331
132	44 29	005	11 35	070	26 02	116	55 41	175	28 42	212	56 51	251	17 36	329
134	44 30	003	11 37	068	26 04	114	55 42	173	28 41	210	56 49	249	17 35	327
136	44 30	001	11 39	066	26 06	112	55 42	171	28 40	208	56 47	247	17 34	325
138	44 30	359	11 41	064	26 08	110	55 42	169	28 39	206	56 45	245	17 32	323
140	44 30	357	11 43	062	26 09	108	55 43	167	28 38	204	56 43	243	17 31	321
142	44 29	355	11 45	060	26 11	106	55 43	165	28 37	202	56 42	241	17 30	319
144	44 29	353	11 47	058	26 14	104	55 44	163	28 36	200	56 40	239	17 28	317
146	44 29	351	11 48	056	26 16	102	55 44	161	28 36	198	56 38	237	17 27	315
148	44 29	349	11 50	054	26 18	100	55 45	159	28 35	196	56 36	235	17 25	313

LHA ♈	SPICA		◆ ANTARES		Peacock		FOMALHAUT		◆ ACHERNAR		CANOPUS		◆ Suhail	
	Hc	Zn	Hc	Zn	Hc	Zn	Hc	Zn	Hc	Zn	Hc	Zn	Hc	Zn
150	11 52	052	26 20	098	55 46	157	28 34	194	56 34	233	53 17	305	44 28	347
152	11 53	050	26 22	096	55 47	155	28 34	192	56 33	231	53 15	303	44 28	345
154	11 55	048	26 24	094	55 48	153	28 34	191	56 31	229	53 14	301	44 27	343
156	11 56	046	26 26	092	55 49	151	28 33	189	56 30	227	53 12	299	44 26	341
158	11 58	044	26 28	090	55 50	149	28 33	187	56 28	225	53 10	297	44 26	339
160	11 59	042	26 30	088	55 51	148	28 33	185	56 27	224	53 08	295	44 25	337
162	12 01	040	26 32	086	55 52	146	28 33	183	56 25	222	53 06	293	44 24	335
164	12 02	038	26 34	084	55 53	144	28 33	181	56 24	220	53 04	291	44 23	333
166	12 03	036	26 36	082	55 54	142	28 33	179	56 22	218	53 02	289	44 22	331
168	12 04	034	26 38	080	55 56	140	28 33	177	56 21	216	53 00	287	44 21	329
170	12 05	032	26 40	078	55 57	138	28 33	175	56 20	214	52 58	285	44 20	327
172	12 07	030	26 43	076	55 59	136	28 33	173	56 19	212	52 56	283	44 19	325
174	12 08	028	26 45	074	56 00	134	28 33	171	56 18	210	52 54	281	44 17	323
176	12 08	026	26 47	072	56 02	132	28 34	169	56 17	208	52 52	279	44 16	321
178	12 09	024	26 49	070	56 03	130	28 34	167	56 16	206	52 50	277	44 15	319

LHA ♈	SPICA		◆ ANTARES		Peacock		FOMALHAUT		◆ ACHERNAR		CANOPUS		◆ Suhail	
	Hc	Zn	Hc	Zn	Hc	Zn	Hc	Zn	Hc	Zn	Hc	Zn	Hc	Zn
180	12 10	022	26 51	068	56 05	128	28 35	165	56 15	204	52 48	275	44 13	316
182	12 11	020	26 52	066	56 06	126	28 35	163	56 14	202	52 46	273	44 12	314
184	12 12	018	26 54	064	56 08	124	28 36	161	56 13	200	52 44	271	44 10	312
186	12 12	016	26 56	062	56 10	122	28 37	159	56 13	198	52 42	269	44 09	310
188	12 13	014	26 58	060	56 12	120	28 37	157	56 12	196	52 40	267	44 07	308
190	12 13	012	27 00	058	56 14	118	28 38	155	56 12	194	52 37	265	44 06	306
192	12 14	010	27 02	056	56 15	116	28 39	153	56 11	192	52 35	263	44 04	304
194	12 14	008	27 03	054	56 17	114	28 40	151	56 11	190	52 33	261	44 02	302
196	12 14	006	27 05	052	56 19	112	28 41	149	56 10	188	52 31	259	44 00	300
198	12 14	004	27 07	050	56 21	110	28 42	147	56 10	186	52 29	257	43 58	298
200	12 14	002	27 08	048	56 23	108	28 44	145	56 10	184	52 27	255	43 57	296
202	12 14	359	27 10	046	56 25	106	28 45	143	56 10	183	52 25	253	43 55	294
204	12 14	357	27 11	044	56 27	104	28 46	141	56 10	181	52 23	251	43 53	292
206	12 14	355	27 13	042	56 29	102	28 47	139	56 10	179	52 21	249	43 51	290
208	12 14	353	27 14	040	56 31	100	28 49	137	56 10	177	52 19	247	43 49	288

LHA ♈	◆ ANTARES		Nunki		FOMALHAUT		◆ ACHERNAR		CANOPUS		◆ Suhail		SPICA	
	Hc	Zn	Hc	Zn	Hc	Zn	Hc	Zn	Hc	Zn	Hc	Zn	Hc	Zn
210	27 15	038	26 33	075	28 50	135	56 10	175	52 17	245	43 47	286	12 14	351
212	27 17	036	26 35	073	28 52	133	56 10	173	52 15	243	43 45	284	12 13	349
214	27 18	034	26 37	071	28 53	131	56 10	171	52 14	241	43 43	282	12 13	347
216	27 19	032	26 39	069	28 55	129	56 11	169	52 12	239	43 41	280	12 12	345
218	27 20	030	26 41	067	28 57	127	56 11	167	52 10	237	43 39	278	12 12	343
220	27 21	028	26 43	064	28 58	125	56 12	165	52 08	235	43 37	276	12 11	341
222	27 22	026	26 45	062	29 00	123	56 12	163	52 07	233	43 34	274	12 11	339
224	27 23	024	26 46	060	29 02	121	56 13	161	52 05	231	43 32	272	12 10	337
226	27 24	022	26 48	058	29 04	119	56 14	159	52 03	229	43 30	270	12 09	335
228	27 24	020	26 50	056	29 05	117	56 14	157	52 02	227	43 28	268	12 08	333
230	27 25	018	26 52	054	29 07	115	56 15	155	52 00	225	43 26	266	12 07	331
232	27 26	016	26 53	052	29 09	113	56 16	153	51 59	223	43 24	264	12 06	329
234	27 26	014	26 55	050	29 11	111	56 17	151	51 57	221	43 22	262	12 05	327
236	27 27	012	26 57	048	29 13	109	56 18	149	51 56	219	43 20	260	12 04	325
238	27 27	010	26 58	046	29 15	107	56 19	147	51 55	217	43 18	258	12 03	323

LHA ♈	ANTARES		Nunki		◆ FOMALHAUT		ACHERNAR		◆ CANOPUS		ACRUX		◆ RIGIL KENT	
	Hc	Zn	Hc	Zn	Hc	Zn	Hc	Zn	Hc	Zn	Hc	Zn	Hc	Zn
240	27 27	008	27 00	044	29 17	105	56 21	145	51 54	215	63 46	305	61 50	340
242	27 28	006	27 01	042	29 19	103	56 22	143	51 52	213	63 45	303	61 49	337
244	27 28	004	27 02	040	29 21	101	56 23	142	51 51	211	63 43	301	61 48	335
246	27 28	002	27 04	038	29 23	099	56 24	140	51 50	209	63 41	299	61 48	333
248	27 28	000	27 05	036	29 25	097	56 26	138	51 49	207	63 39	297	61 47	331
250	27 28	358	27 06	034	29 27	095	56 27	136	51 48	206	63 37	295	61 46	329
252	27 28	356	27 07	032	29 30	093	56 29	134	51 47	204	63 35	293	61 44	327
254	27 27	354	27 08	030	29 32	091	56 30	132	51 47	202	63 33	291	61 43	325
256	27 27	352	27 10	028	29 34	089	56 32	130	51 46	200	63 31	289	61 42	323
258	27 27	349	27 10	026	29 36	087	56 33	128	51 45	198	63 29	287	61 41	321
260	27 26	347	27 11	024	29 38	085	56 35	126	51 45	196	63 27	285	61 39	319
262	27 26	345	27 12	022	29 40	083	56 37	124	51 44	194	63 25	283	61 38	317
264	27 25	343	27 13	020	29 42	081	56 39	122	51 44	192	63 23	281	61 37	315
266	27 25	341	27 14	018	29 44	079	56 40	120	51 43	190	63 21	279	61 35	313
268	27 24	339	27 14	016	29 46	077	56 42	118	51 43	188	63 19	277	61 33	311

LHA ♈	Nunki		◆ FOMALHAUT		ACHERNAR		◆ CANOPUS		ACRUX		◆ RIGIL KENT		ANTARES	
	Hc	Zn	Hc	Zn	Hc	Zn	Hc	Zn	Hc	Zn	Hc	Zn	Hc	Zn
270	27 15	014	29 48	075	56 44	116	51 43	186	63 17	275	61 32	309	27 23	337
272	27 15	012	29 50	073	56 46	114	51 42	184	63 15	273	61 30	307	27 22	335
274	27 16	010	29 52	071	56 48	112	51 42	182	63 13	271	61 29	305	27 22	333
276	27 16	008	29 54	069	56 50	110	51 42	180	63 11	269	61 27	303	27 21	331
278	27 16	006	29 56	067	56 52	108	51 42	178	63 09	267	61 25	301	27 20	329
280	27 16	004	29 58	065	56 54	106	51 42	176	63 07	265	61 23	299	27 18	327
282	27 17	002	30 00	063	56 56	104	51 43	174	63 05	263	61 21	297	27 17	325
284	27 17	000	30 02	061	56 58	102	51 43	172	63 02	261	61 19	295	27 16	323
286	27 17	358	30 04	059	57 00	100	51 43	170	63 00	259	61 18	292	27 15	321
288	27 16	356	30 05	057	57 02	098	51 44	168	62 58	257	61 16	290	27 13	319
290	27 16	354	30 07	055	57 04	096	51 44	166	62 56	255	61 14	288	27 12	317
292	27 16	352	30 09	053	57 06	094	51 45	164	62 54	253	61 12	286	27 11	315
294	27 16	350	30 10	051	57 08	092	51 45	162	62 52	251	61 10	284	27 09	313
296	27 15	348	30 12	049	57 10	090	51 46	161	62 50	249	61 08	282	27 08	311
298	27 15	346	30 14	047	57 12	088	51 47	159	62 48	247	61 05	280	27 06	309

LHA ♈	◆ FOMALHAUT		ACHERNAR		◆ CANOPUS		ACRUX		◆ RIGIL KENT		ANTARES		Nunki	
	Hc	Zn	Hc	Zn	Hc	Zn	Hc	Zn	Hc	Zn	Hc	Zn	Hc	Zn
300	30 15	045	57 15	086	51 47	157	62 46	245	61 03	278	27 04	307	27 14	344
302	30 17	043	57 17	084	51 48	155	62 45	243	61 01	276	27 03	305	27 14	342
304	30 18	041	57 19	082	51 49	153	62 43	241	60 59	274	27 01	303	27 13	340
306	30 19	039	57 21	080	51 50	151	62 41	239	60 57	272	26 59	301	27 12	338
308	30 21	037	57 23	078	51 51	149	62 39	237	60 55	270	26 57	299	27 11	336
310	30 22	035	57 25	076	51 52	147	62 37	235	60 53	268	26 55	297	27 11	334
312	30 23	033	57 27	074	51 53	145	62 36	233	60 51	266	26 54	295	27 10	332
314	30 24	031	57 29	072	51 55	143	62 34	231	60 49	264	26 52	293	27 09	330
316	30 25	029	57 31	070	51 56	141	62 32	229	60 47	262	26 50	291	27 07	328
318	30 26	027	57 33	068	51 57	139	62 31	227	60 45	260	26 48	289	27 06	326
320	30 27	025	57 35	066	51 59	137	62 29	225	60 43	258	26 46	287	27 05	324
322	30 28	023	57 37	064	52 00	135	62 28	224	60 41	256	26 44	285	27 04	322
324	30 29	021	57 39	062	52 02	133	62 26	222	60 39	254	26 42	283	27 02	320
326	30 29	019	57 40	060	52 03	131	62 25	220	60 37	252	26 40	281	27 01	318
328	30 30	017	57 42	058	52 05	129	62 24	218	60 35	250	26 38	279	27 00	316

LHA ♈	◆ FOMALHAUT		ACHERNAR		◆ CANOPUS		ACRUX		◆ RIGIL KENT		ANTARES		Nunki	
	Hc	Zn	Hc	Zn	Hc	Zn	Hc	Zn	Hc	Zn	Hc	Zn	Hc	Zn
330	30 31	015	57 44	056	52 06	127	62 23	216	60 33	248	26 36	277	26 58	314
332	30 31	013	57 46	054	52 08	125	62 21	214	60 31	247	26 33	275	26 57	312
334	30 32	011	57 47	052	52 10	123	62 20	212	60 29	245	26 31	273	26 55	310
336	30 32	009	57 49	050	52 12	121	62 19	210	60 27	243	26 29	271	26 53	308
338	30 32	007	57 50	048	52 13	119	62 18	208	60 25	241	26 27	269	26 52	306
340	30 32	005	57 52	046	52 15	117	62 17	206	60 23	239	26 25	267	26 50	304
342	30 32	003	57 53	044	52 17	115	62 16	204	60 21	237	26 23	265	26 48	302
344	30 33	001	57 55	042	52 19	113	62 15	202	60 20	235	26 21	263	26 46	300
346	30 33	359	57 56	040	52 21	111	62 15	200	60 18	233	26 19	261	26 45	298
348	30 32	357	57 58	038	52 23	109	62 14	198	60 16	231	26 17	259	26 43	296
350	30 32	355	57 59	035	52 25	107	62 13	196	60 15	229	26 15	257	26 41	294
352	30 32	353	58 00	033	52 27	105	62 13	194	60 13	227	26 13	255	26 39	292
354	30 32	351	58 01	031	52 29	103	62 12	192	60 12	225	26 11	253	26 37	290
356	30 31	349	58 02	029	52 31	101	62 12	191	60 10	223	26 09	251	26 35	288
358	30 31	346	58 03	027	52 33	099	62 12	189	60 09	221	26 07	249	26 33	286

This page is blank

Typeset by HM Nautical Almanac Office using $\TeX$

MOO TABLE 1 — ALTITUDE CORRECTION FOR CHANGE IN POSITION OF OBSERVER

Rel. Zn	Distance Made Good — nautical miles																				Rel. Zn
	1	2	3	4	5	6	7	8	10	15	20	25	30	35	40	45	50	75	100	150	
°	′	′	′	′	′	′	′	′	′	′	′	′	′	′	′	′	′	′	′	′	°
000	+1·0	+2·0	+3·0	+4·0	+5·0	+6·0	+7·0	+8·0	+10·0	+15·0	+20·0	+25·0	+30·0	+35·0	+40·0	+45·0	+50·0	+75·0	+100·0	+150·0	**000**
002	1·0	2·0	3·0	4·0	5·0	6·0	7·0	8·0	10·0	15·0	20·0	25·0	30·0	35·0	40·0	45·0	50·0	75·0	99·9	149·9	**358**
004	1·0	2·0	3·0	4·0	5·0	6·0	7·0	8·0	10·0	15·0	20·0	24·9	29·9	34·9	39·9	44·9	49·9	74·8	99·8	149·6	**356**
006	1·0	2·0	3·0	4·0	5·0	6·0	7·0	8·0	9·9	14·9	19·9	24·9	29·8	34·8	39·8	44·8	49·7	74·6	99·5	149·2	**354**
008	1·0	2·0	3·0	4·0	5·0	5·9	6·9	7·9	9·9	14·9	19·8	24·8	29·7	34·7	39·6	44·6	49·5	74·3	99·0	148·5	**352**
010	+1·0	+2·0	+3·0	+3·9	+4·9	+5·9	+6·9	+7·9	+ 9·8	+14·8	+19·7	+24·6	+29·5	+34·5	+39·4	+44·3	+49·2	+73·9	+ 98·5	+147·7	**350**
012	1·0	2·0	2·9	3·9	4·9	5·9	6·8	7·8	9·8	14·7	19·6	24·5	29·3	34·2	39·1	44·0	48·9	73·4	97·8	146·7	**348**
014	1·0	1·9	2·9	3·9	4·9	5·8	6·8	7·8	9·7	14·6	19·4	24·3	29·1	34·0	38·8	43·7	48·5	72·8	97·0	145·5	**346**
016	1·0	1·9	2·9	3·8	4·8	5·8	6·7	7·7	9·6	14·4	19·2	24·0	28·8	33·6	38·5	43·3	48·1	72·1	96·1	144·2	**344**
018	1·0	1·9	2·9	3·8	4·8	5·7	6·7	7·6	9·5	14·3	19·0	23·8	28·5	33·3	38·0	42·8	47·6	71·3	95·1	142·7	**342**
020	+0·9	+1·9	+2·8	+3·8	+4·7	+5·6	+6·6	+7·5	+ 9·4	+14·1	+18·8	+23·5	+28·2	+32·9	+37·6	+42·3	+47·0	+70·5	+ 94·0	+141·0	**340**
022	0·9	1·9	2·8	3·7	4·6	5·6	6·5	7·4	9·3	13·9	18·5	23·2	27·8	32·5	37·1	41·7	46·4	69·5	92·7	139·1	**338**
024	0·9	1·8	2·7	3·7	4·6	5·5	6·4	7·3	9·1	13·7	18·3	22·8	27·4	32·0	36·5	41·1	45·7	68·5	91·4	137·0	**336**
026	0·9	1·8	2·7	3·6	4·5	5·4	6·3	7·2	9·0	13·5	18·0	22·5	27·0	31·5	36·0	40·4	44·9	67·4	89·9	134·8	**334**
028	0·9	1·8	2·6	3·5	4·4	5·3	6·2	7·1	8·8	13·2	17·7	22·1	26·5	30·9	35·3	39·7	44·1	66·2	88·3	132·4	**332**
030	+0·9	+1·7	+2·6	+3·5	+4·3	+5·2	+6·1	+6·9	+ 8·7	+13·0	+17·3	+21·7	+26·0	+30·3	+34·6	+39·0	+43·3	+65·0	+ 86·6	+129·9	**330**
032	0·8	1·7	2·5	3·4	4·2	5·1	5·9	6·8	8·5	12·7	17·0	21·2	25·4	29·7	33·9	38·2	42·4	63·6	84·8	127·2	**328**
034	0·8	1·7	2·5	3·3	4·1	5·0	5·8	6·6	8·3	12·4	16·6	20·7	24·9	29·0	33·2	37·3	41·5	62·2	82·9	124·4	**326**
036	0·8	1·6	2·4	3·2	4·0	4·9	5·7	6·5	8·1	12·1	16·2	20·2	24·3	28·3	32·4	36·4	40·5	60·7	80·9	121·4	**324**
038	0·8	1·6	2·4	3·2	3·9	4·7	5·5	6·3	7·9	11·8	15·8	19·7	23·6	27·6	31·5	35·5	39·4	59·1	78·8	118·2	**322**
040	+0·8	+1·5	+2·3	+3·1	+3·8	+4·6	+5·4	+6·1	+ 7·7	+11·5	+15·3	+19·2	+23·0	+26·8	+30·6	+34·5	+38·3	+57·5	+ 76·6	+114·9	**320**
042	0·7	1·5	2·2	3·0	3·7	4·5	5·2	5·9	7·4	11·1	14·9	18·6	22·3	26·0	29·7	33·4	37·2	55·7	74·3	111·5	**318**
044	0·7	1·4	2·2	2·9	3·6	4·3	5·0	5·8	7·2	10·8	14·4	18·0	21·6	25·2	28·8	32·4	36·0	54·0	71·9	107·9	**316**
046	0·7	1·4	2·1	2·8	3·5	4·2	4·9	5·6	6·9	10·4	13·9	17·4	20·8	24·3	27·8	31·3	34·7	52·1	69·5	104·2	**314**
048	0·7	1·3	2·0	2·7	3·3	4·0	4·7	5·4	6·7	10·0	13·4	16·7	20·1	23·4	26·8	30·1	33·5	50·2	66·9	100·4	**312**
050	+0·6	+1·3	+1·9	+2·6	+3·2	+3·9	+4·5	+5·1	+ 6·4	+ 9·6	+12·9	+16·1	+19·3	+22·5	+25·7	+28·9	+32·1	+48·2	+ 64·3	+ 96·4	**310**
052	0·6	1·2	1·8	2·5	3·1	3·7	4·3	4·9	6·2	9·2	12·3	15·4	18·5	21·5	24·6	27·7	30·8	46·2	61·6	92·3	**308**
054	0·6	1·2	1·8	2·4	2·9	3·5	4·1	4·7	5·9	8·8	11·8	14·7	17·6	20·6	23·5	26·5	29·4	44·1	58·8	88·2	**306**
056	0·6	1·1	1·7	2·2	2·8	3·4	3·9	4·5	5·6	8·4	11·2	14·0	16·8	19·6	22·4	25·2	28·0	41·9	55·9	83·9	**304**
058	0·5	1·1	1·6	2·1	2·6	3·2	3·7	4·2	5·3	7·9	10·6	13·2	15·9	18·5	21·2	23·8	26·5	39·7	53·0	79·5	**302**
060	+0·5	+1·0	+1·5	+2·0	+2·5	+3·0	+3·5	+4·0	+ 5·0	+ 7·5	+10·0	+12·5	+15·0	+17·5	+20·0	+22·5	+25·0	+37·5	+ 50·0	+ 75·0	**300**
062	0·5	0·9	1·4	1·9	2·3	2·8	3·3	3·8	4·7	7·0	9·4	11·7	14·1	16·4	18·8	21·1	23·5	35·2	46·9	70·4	**298**
064	0·4	0·9	1·3	1·8	2·2	2·6	3·1	3·5	4·4	6·6	8·8	11·0	13·2	15·3	17·5	19·7	21·9	32·9	43·8	65·8	**296**
066	0·4	0·8	1·2	1·6	2·0	2·4	2·8	3·3	4·1	6·1	8·1	10·2	12·2	14·2	16·3	18·3	20·3	30·5	40·7	61·0	**294**
068	0·4	0·7	1·1	1·5	1·9	2·2	2·6	3·0	3·7	5·6	7·5	9·4	11·2	13·1	15·0	16·9	18·7	28·1	37·5	56·2	**292**
070	+0·3	+0·7	+1·0	+1·4	+1·7	+2·1	+2·4	+2·7	+ 3·4	+ 5·1	+ 6·8	+ 8·6	+10·3	+12·0	+13·7	+15·4	+17·1	+25·7	+ 34·2	+ 51·3	**290**
072	0·3	0·6	0·9	1·2	1·5	1·9	2·2	2·5	3·1	4·6	6·2	7·7	9·3	10·8	12·4	13·9	15·5	23·2	30·9	46·4	**288**
074	0·3	0·6	0·8	1·1	1·4	1·7	1·9	2·2	2·8	4·1	5·5	6·9	8·3	9·6	11·0	12·4	13·8	20·7	27·6	41·3	**286**
076	0·2	0·5	0·7	1·0	1·2	1·5	1·7	1·9	2·4	3·6	4·8	6·0	7·3	8·5	9·7	10·9	12·1	18·1	24·2	36·3	**284**
078	0·2	0·4	0·6	0·8	1·0	1·2	1·5	1·7	2·1	3·1	4·2	5·2	6·2	7·3	8·3	9·4	10·4	15·6	20·8	31·2	**282**
080	+0·2	+0·3	+0·5	+0·7	+0·9	+1·0	+1·2	+1·4	+ 1·7	+ 2·6	+ 3·5	+ 4·3	+ 5·2	+ 6·1	+ 6·9	+ 7·8	+ 8·7	+13·0	+ 17·4	+ 26·0	**280**
082	0·1	0·3	0·4	0·6	0·7	0·8	1·0	1·1	1·4	2·1	2·8	3·5	4·2	4·9	5·6	6·3	7·0	10·4	13·9	20·9	**278**
084	0·1	0·2	0·3	0·4	0·5	0·6	0·7	0·8	1·0	1·6	2·1	2·6	3·1	3·7	4·2	4·7	5·2	7·8	10·5	15·7	**276**
086	0·1	0·1	0·2	0·3	0·3	0·4	0·5	0·6	0·7	1·0	1·4	1·7	2·1	2·4	2·8	3·1	3·5	5·2	7·0	10·5	**274**
088	0·0	0·1	0·1	0·1	0·2	0·2	0·2	0·3	0·3	0·5	0·7	0·9	1·0	1·2	1·4	1·6	1·7	2·6	3·5	5·2	**272**
090	0·0	0·0	0·0	0·0	0·0	0·0	0·0	0·0	0·0	0·0	0·0	0·0	0·0	0·0	0·0	0·0	0·0	0·0	0·0	0·0	**270**
092	0·0	−0·1	−0·1	−0·1	−0·2	−0·2	−0·2	−0·3	− 0·3	− 0·5	− 0·7	− 0·9	− 1·0	− 1·2	− 1·4	− 1·6	− 1·7	− 2·6	− 3·5	− 5·2	**268**
094	0·1	0·1	0·2	0·3	0·3	0·4	0·5	0·6	0·7	1·0	1·4	1·7	2·1	2·4	2·8	3·1	3·5	5·2	7·0	10·5	**266**
096	0·1	0·2	0·3	0·4	0·5	0·6	0·7	0·8	1·0	1·6	2·1	2·6	3·1	3·7	4·2	4·7	5·2	7·8	10·5	15·7	**264**
098	0·1	0·3	0·4	0·6	0·7	0·8	1·0	1·1	1·4	2·1	2·8	3·5	4·2	4·9	5·6	6·3	7·0	10·4	13·9	20·9	**262**
100	0·2	0·3	0·5	0·7	0·9	1·0	1·2	1·4	1·7	2·6	3·5	4·3	5·2	6·1	6·9	7·8	8·7	13·0	17·4	26·0	**260**
102	−0·2	−0·4	−0·6	−0·8	−1·0	−1·2	−1·5	−1·7	− 2·1	− 3·1	− 4·2	− 5·2	− 6·2	− 7·3	− 8·3	− 9·4	−10·4	−15·6	− 20·8	− 31·2	**258**
104	0·2	0·5	0·7	1·0	1·2	1·5	1·7	1·9	2·4	3·6	4·8	6·0	7·3	8·5	9·7	10·9	12·1	18·1	24·2	36·3	**256**
106	0·3	0·6	0·8	1·1	1·4	1·7	1·9	2·2	2·8	4·1	5·5	6·9	8·3	9·6	11·0	12·4	13·8	20·7	27·6	41·3	**254**
108	0·3	0·6	0·9	1·2	1·5	1·9	2·2	2·5	3·1	4·6	6·2	7·7	9·3	10·8	12·4	13·9	15·5	23·2	30·9	46·4	**252**
110	0·3	0·7	1·0	1·4	1·7	2·1	2·4	2·7	3·4	5·1	6·8	8·6	10·3	12·0	13·7	15·4	17·1	25·7	34·2	51·3	**250**
112	−0·4	−0·7	−1·1	−1·5	−1·9	−2·2	−2·6	−3·0	− 3·7	− 5·6	− 7·5	− 9·4	−11·2	−13·1	−15·0	−16·9	−18·7	−28·1	− 37·5	− 56·2	**248**
114	0·4	0·8	1·2	1·6	2·0	2·4	2·8	3·3	4·1	6·1	8·1	10·2	12·2	14·2	16·3	18·3	20·3	30·5	40·7	61·0	**246**
116	0·4	0·9	1·3	1·8	2·2	2·6	3·1	3·5	4·4	6·6	8·8	11·0	13·2	15·3	17·5	19·7	21·9	32·9	43·8	65·8	**244**
118	0·5	0·9	1·4	1·9	2·3	2·8	3·3	3·8	4·7	7·0	9·4	11·7	14·1	16·4	18·8	21·1	23·5	35·2	46·9	70·4	**242**
120	0·5	1·0	1·5	2·0	2·5	3·0	3·5	4·0	5·0	7·5	10·0	12·5	15·0	17·5	20·0	22·5	25·0	37·5	50·0	75·0	**240**
122	−0·5	−1·1	−1·6	−2·1	−2·6	−3·2	−3·7	−4·2	− 5·3	− 7·9	−10·6	−13·2	−15·9	−18·5	−21·2	−23·8	−26·5	−39·7	− 53·0	− 79·5	**238**
124	0·6	1·1	1·7	2·2	2·8	3·4	3·9	4·5	5·6	8·4	11·2	14·0	16·8	19·6	22·4	25·2	28·0	41·9	55·9	83·9	**236**
126	0·6	1·2	1·8	2·4	2·9	3·5	4·1	4·7	5·9	8·8	11·8	14·7	17·6	20·6	23·5	26·5	29·4	44·1	58·8	88·2	**234**
128	0·6	1·2	1·8	2·5	3·1	3·7	4·3	4·9	6·2	9·2	12·3	15·4	18·5	21·5	24·6	27·7	30·8	46·2	61·6	92·3	**232**
130	0·6	1·3	1·9	2·6	3·2	3·9	4·5	5·1	6·4	9·6	12·9	16·1	19·3	22·5	25·7	28·9	32·1	48·2	64·3	96·4	**230**
132	−0·7	−1·3	−2·0	−2·7	−3·3	−4·0	−4·7	−5·4	− 6·7	−10·0	−13·4	−16·7	−20·1	−23·4	−26·8	−30·1	−33·5	−50·2	− 66·9	−100·4	**228**
134	0·7	1·4	2·1	2·8	3·5	4·2	4·9	5·6	6·9	10·4	13·9	17·4	20·8	24·3	27·8	31·3	34·7	52·1	69·5	104·2	**226**
136	0·7	1·4	2·2	2·9	3·6	4·3	5·0	5·8	7·2	10·8	14·4	18·0	21·6	25·2	28·8	32·4	36·0	54·0	71·9	107·9	**224**
138	0·7	1·5	2·2	3·0	3·7	4·5	5·2	5·9	7·4	11·1	14·9	18·6	22·3	26·0	29·7	33·4	37·2	55·7	74·3	111·5	**222**
140	0·8	1·5	2·3	3·1	3·8	4·6	5·4	6·1	7·7	11·5	15·3	19·2	23·0	26·8	30·6	34·5	38·3	57·5	76·6	114·9	**220**
142	−0·8	−1·6	−2·4	−3·2	−3·9	−4·7	−5·5	−6·3	− 7·9	−11·8	−15·8	−19·7	−23·6	−27·6	−31·5	−35·5	−39·4	−59·1	− 78·8	−118·2	**218**
144	0·8	1·6	2·4	3·2	4·0	4·9	5·7	6·5	8·1	12·1	16·2	20·2	24·3	28·3	32·4	36·4	40·5	60·7	80·9	121·4	**216**
146	0·8	1·7	2·5	3·3	4·1	5·0	5·8	6·6	8·3	12·4	16·6	20·7	24·9	29·0	33·2	37·3	41·5	62·2	82·9	124·4	**214**
148	0·8	1·7	2·5	3·4	4·2	5·1	5·9	6·8	8·5	12·7	17·0	21·2	25·4	29·7	33·9	38·2	42·4	63·6	84·8	127·2	**212**
150	0·9	1·7	2·6	3·5	4·3	5·2	6·1	6·9	8·7	13·0	17·3	21·7	26·0	30·3	34·6	39·0	43·3	65·0	86·6	129·9	**210**
152	−0·9	−1·8	−2·6	−3·5	−4·4	−5·3	−6·2	−7·1	− 8·8	−13·2	−17·7	−22·1	−26·5	−30·9	−35·3	−39·7	−44·1	−66·2	− 88·3	−132·4	**208**
154	0·9	1·8	2·7	3·6	4·5	5·4	6·3	7·2	9·0	13·5	18·0	22·5	27·0	31·5	36·0	40·4	44·9	67·4	89·9	134·8	**206**
156	0·9	1·8	2·7	3·7	4·6	5·5	6·4	7·3	9·1	13·7	18·3	22·8	27·4	32·0	36·5	41·1	45·7	68·5	91·4	137·0	**204**
158	0·9	1·9	2·8	3·7	4·6	5·6	6·5	7·4	9·3	13·9	18·5	23·2	27·8	32·5	37·1	41·7	46·4	69·5	92·7	139·1	**202**
160	0·9	1·9	2·8	3·8	4·7	5·6	6·6	7·5	9·4	14·1	18·8	23·5	28·2	32·9	37·6	42·3	47·0	70·5	94·0	141·0	**200**
162	−1·0	−1·9	−2·9	−3·8	−4·8	−5·7	−6·7	−7·6	− 9·5	−14·3	−19·0	−23·8	−28·5	−33·3	−38·0	−42·8	−47·6	−71·3	− 95·1	−142·7	**198**
164	1·0	1·9	2·9	3·8	4·8	5·8	6·7	7·7	9·6	14·4	19·2	24·0	28·8	33·6	38·5	43·3	48·1	72·1	96·1	144·2	**196**
166	1·0	1·9	2·9	3·9	4·9	5·8	6·8	7·8	9·7	14·6	19·4	24·3	29·1	34·0	38·8	43·7	48·5	72·8	97·0	145·5	**194**
168	1·0	2·0	2·9	3·9	4·9	5·9	6·8	7·8	9·8	14·7	19·6	24·5	29·3	34·2	39·1	44·0	48·9	73·4	97·8	146·7	**192**
170	1·0	2·0	3·0	3·9	4·9	5·9	6·9	7·9	9·8	14·8	19·7	24·6	29·5	34·5	39·4	44·3	49·2	73·9	98·5	147·7	**190**
172	−1·0	−2·0	−3·0	−4·0	−5·0	−5·9	−6·9	−7·9	− 9·9	−14·9	−19·8	−24·8	−29·7	−34·7	−39·6	−44·6	−49·5	−74·3	− 99·0	−148·5	**188**
174	1·0	2·0	3·0	4·0	5·0	6·0	7·0	8·0	9·9	14·9	19·9	24·9	29·8	34·8	39·8	44·8	49·7	74·6	99·5	149·2	**186**
176	1·0	2·0	3·0	4·0	5·0	6·0	7·0	8·0	10·0	15·0	20·0	24·9	29·9	34·9	39·9	44·9	49·9	74·8	99·8	149·6	**184**
178	1·0	2·0	3·0	4·0	5·0	6·0	7·0	8·0	10·0	15·0	20·0	25·0	30·0	35·0	40·0	45·0	50·0	75·0	99·9	149·9	**182**
180	1·0	2·0	3·0	4·0	5·0	6·0	7·0	8·0	10·0	15·0	20·0	25·0	30·0	35·0	40·0	45·0	50·0	75·0	100·0	150·0	**180**

Time of fix or computation	Sign from Table	To observed altitude	To tabulated altitude	To intercept	Time of fix or computation	Sign from Table	To observed altitude	To tabulated altitude	To intercept
Later than observation	+ −	Add Subtract	Subtract Add	Add Subtract	**Earlier than observation**	+ −	Subtract Add	Add Subtract	Subtract Add

Rel. Z_n = Relative Azimuth = $Z_n - C$ = True Azimuth − True Track

TABLE 2 — ALTITUDE CORRECTION FOR CHANGE IN POSITION OF BODY

Correction for 1 Minute of Time

MOB

True Zn	Latitude 0°	5°	10°	15°	20°	25°	30°	35°	40°	45°	50°	55°	60°	65°	70°	75°	80°	85°	True Zn
°	′	′	′	′	′	′	′	′	′	′	′	′	′	′	′	′	′	′	°
090	+15·0	+15·0	+14·8	+14·5	+14·1	+13·6	+13·0	+12·3	+11·5	+10·6	+9·7	+8·6	+7·5	+6·4	+5·1	+3·9	+2·6	+1·3	090
093	15·0	15·0	14·8	14·5	14·1	13·6	13·0	12·3	11·5	10·6	9·7	8·6	7·5	6·3	5·1	3·9	2·6	1·3	087
096	15·0	14·9	14·7	14·4	14·1	13·6	13·0	12·3	11·5	10·6	9·6	8·6	7·5	6·3	5·1	3·9	2·6	1·3	084
099	14·9	14·8	14·6	14·3	14·0	13·5	12·9	12·2	11·4	10·5	9·5	8·5	7·4	6·3	5·1	3·8	2·6	1·3	081
102	14·7	14·7	14·5	14·2	13·8	13·3	12·7	12·1	11·3	10·4	9·5	8·4	7·4	6·2	5·0	3·8	2·6	1·3	078
105	+14·5	+14·5	+14·3	+14·0	+13·7	+13·2	+12·6	+11·9	+11·1	+10·3	+9·3	+8·3	+7·3	+6·1	+5·0	+3·8	+2·5	+1·3	075
108	14·3	14·3	14·1	13·8	13·4	13·0	12·4	11·7	11·0	10·1	9·2	8·2	7·2	6·0	4·9	3·7	2·5	1·2	072
111	14·0	14·0	13·8	13·6	13·2	12·7	12·2	11·5	10·8	9·9	9·0	8·1	7·0	5·9	4·8	3·6	2·4	1·2	069
114	13·7	13·7	13·5	13·3	12·9	12·5	11·9	11·3	10·5	9·7	8·8	7·9	6·9	5·8	4·7	3·6	2·4	1·2	066
117	13·4	13·4	13·2	12·9	12·6	12·1	11·6	11·0	10·3	9·5	8·6	7·7	6·7	5·7	4·6	3·5	2·3	1·2	063
120	+13·0	+13·0	+12·8	+12·6	+12·2	+11·8	+11·3	+10·7	+10·0	+9·2	+8·4	+7·5	+6·5	+5·5	+4·5	+3·4	+2·3	+1·1	060
123	12·6	12·6	12·4	12·2	11·9	11·4	10·9	10·3	9·7	8·9	8·1	7·2	6·3	5·3	4·3	3·3	2·2	1·1	057
126	12·2	12·1	12·0	11·8	11·4	11·0	10·5	10·0	9·3	8·6	7·8	7·0	6·1	5·1	4·2	3·1	2·1	1·1	054
129	11·7	11·6	11·5	11·3	11·0	10·6	10·1	9·6	9·0	8·3	7·5	6·7	5·8	4·9	4·0	3·0	2·0	1·0	051
132	11·2	11·1	11·0	10·8	10·5	10·1	9·7	9·2	8·6	7·9	7·2	6·4	5·6	4·7	3·8	2·9	1·9	1·0	048
135	+10·6	+10·6	+10·5	+10·3	+10·0	+9·6	+9·2	+8·7	+8·1	+7·5	+6·8	+6·1	+5·3	+4·5	+3·6	+2·8	+1·8	+0·9	045
138	10·1	10·0	9·9	9·7	9·5	9·1	8·7	8·2	7·7	7·1	6·5	5·8	5·0	4·3	3·4	2·6	1·7	0·9	042
141	9·5	9·4	9·3	9·1	8·9	8·6	8·2	7·8	7·3	6·7	6·1	5·4	4·7	4·0	3·2	2·4	1·6	0·8	039
144	8·8	8·8	8·7	8·5	8·3	8·0	7·7	7·2	6·8	6·3	5·7	5·1	4·4	3·7	3·0	2·3	1·5	0·8	036
147	8·2	8·2	8·1	7·9	7·7	7·4	7·1	6·7	6·3	5·8	5·3	4·7	4·1	3·5	2·8	2·1	1·4	0·7	033
150	+7·5	+7·5	+7·4	+7·3	+7·1	+6·8	+6·5	+6·2	+5·8	+5·3	+4·8	+4·3	+3·8	+3·2	+2·6	+1·9	+1·3	+0·7	030
153	6·8	6·8	6·7	6·6	6·4	6·2	5·9	5·6	5·2	4·8	4·4	3·9	3·4	2·9	2·3	1·8	1·2	0·6	027
156	6·1	6·1	6·0	5·9	5·7	5·5	5·3	5·0	4·7	4·3	3·9	3·5	3·1	2·6	2·1	1·6	1·1	0·5	024
159	5·4	5·4	5·3	5·2	5·1	4·9	4·7	4·4	4·1	3·8	3·5	3·1	2·7	2·3	1·8	1·4	0·9	0·5	021
162	4·6	4·6	4·6	4·5	4·4	4·2	4·0	3·8	3·6	3·3	3·0	2·7	2·3	2·0	1·6	1·2	0·8	0·4	018
165	+3·9	+3·9	+3·8	+3·8	+3·7	+3·5	+3·4	+3·2	+3·0	+2·8	+2·5	+2·2	+1·9	+1·6	+1·3	+1·0	+0·7	+0·3	015
168	3·1	3·1	3·1	3·0	2·9	2·8	2·7	2·6	2·4	2·2	2·0	1·8	1·6	1·3	1·1	0·8	0·5	0·3	012
171	2·4	2·3	2·3	2·3	2·2	2·1	2·0	1·9	1·8	1·7	1·5	1·3	1·2	1·0	0·8	0·6	0·4	0·2	009
174	1·6	1·6	1·5	1·5	1·5	1·4	1·4	1·3	1·2	1·1	1·0	0·9	0·8	0·7	0·5	0·4	0·3	0·1	006
177	0·8	0·8	0·8	0·8	0·7	0·7	0·7	0·6	0·6	0·6	0·5	0·5	0·4	0·3	0·3	0·2	0·1	0·1	003
180	0·0	0·0	0·0	0·0	0·0	0·0	0·0	0·0	0·0	0·0	0·0	0·0	0·0	0·0	0·0	0·0	0·0	0·0	000
183	−0·8	−0·8	−0·8	−0·8	−0·7	−0·7	−0·7	−0·6	−0·6	−0·6	−0·5	−0·5	−0·4	−0·3	−0·3	−0·2	−0·1	−0·1	357
186	1·6	1·6	1·5	1·5	1·5	1·4	1·4	1·3	1·2	1·1	1·0	0·9	0·8	0·7	0·5	0·4	0·3	0·1	354
189	2·4	2·3	2·3	2·3	2·2	2·1	2·0	1·9	1·8	1·7	1·5	1·3	1·2	1·0	0·8	0·6	0·4	0·2	351
192	3·1	3·1	3·1	3·0	2·9	2·8	2·7	2·6	2·4	2·2	2·0	1·8	1·6	1·3	1·1	0·8	0·5	0·3	348
195	3·9	3·9	3·8	3·8	3·7	3·5	3·4	3·2	3·0	2·8	2·5	2·2	1·9	1·6	1·3	1·0	0·7	0·3	345
198	−4·6	−4·6	−4·6	−4·5	−4·4	−4·2	−4·0	−3·8	−3·6	−3·3	−3·0	−2·7	−2·3	−2·0	−1·6	−1·2	−0·8	−0·4	342
201	5·4	5·4	5·3	5·2	5·1	4·9	4·7	4·4	4·1	3·8	3·5	3·1	2·7	2·3	1·8	1·4	0·9	0·5	339
204	6·1	6·1	6·0	5·9	5·7	5·5	5·3	5·0	4·7	4·3	3·9	3·5	3·1	2·6	2·1	1·6	1·1	0·5	336
207	6·8	6·8	6·7	6·6	6·4	6·2	5·9	5·6	5·2	4·8	4·4	3·9	3·4	2·9	2·3	1·8	1·2	0·6	333
210	7·5	7·5	7·4	7·3	7·1	6·8	6·5	6·2	5·8	5·3	4·8	4·3	3·8	3·2	2·6	1·9	1·3	0·7	330
213	−8·2	−8·2	−8·1	−7·9	−7·7	−7·4	−7·1	−6·7	−6·3	−5·8	−5·3	−4·7	−4·1	−3·5	−2·8	−2·1	−1·4	−0·7	327
216	8·8	8·8	8·7	8·5	8·3	8·0	7·7	7·2	6·8	6·3	5·7	5·1	4·4	3·7	3·0	2·3	1·5	0·8	324
219	9·5	9·4	9·3	9·1	8·9	8·6	8·2	7·8	7·3	6·7	6·1	5·4	4·7	4·0	3·2	2·4	1·6	0·8	321
222	10·1	10·0	9·9	9·7	9·5	9·1	8·7	8·2	7·7	7·1	6·5	5·8	5·0	4·3	3·4	2·6	1·7	0·9	318
225	10·6	10·6	10·5	10·3	10·0	9·6	9·2	8·7	8·1	7·5	6·8	6·1	5·3	4·5	3·6	2·8	1·8	0·9	315
228	−11·2	−11·1	−11·0	−10·8	−10·5	−10·1	−9·7	−9·2	−8·6	−7·9	−7·2	−6·4	−5·6	−4·7	−3·8	−2·9	−1·9	−1·0	312
231	11·7	11·6	11·5	11·3	11·0	10·6	10·1	9·6	9·0	8·3	7·5	6·7	5·8	4·9	4·0	3·0	2·0	1·0	309
234	12·2	12·1	12·0	11·8	11·4	11·0	10·5	10·0	9·3	8·6	7·8	7·0	6·1	5·1	4·2	3·1	2·1	1·1	306
237	12·6	12·6	12·4	12·2	11·9	11·4	10·9	10·3	9·7	8·9	8·1	7·2	6·3	5·3	4·3	3·3	2·2	1·1	303
240	13·0	13·0	12·8	12·6	12·2	11·8	11·3	10·7	10·0	9·2	8·4	7·5	6·5	5·5	4·5	3·4	2·3	1·1	300
243	−13·4	−13·4	−13·2	−12·9	−12·6	−12·1	−11·6	−11·0	−10·3	−9·5	−8·6	−7·7	−6·7	−5·7	−4·6	−3·5	−2·3	−1·2	297
246	13·7	13·7	13·5	13·3	12·9	12·5	11·9	11·3	10·5	9·7	8·8	7·9	6·9	5·8	4·7	3·6	2·4	1·2	294
249	14·0	14·0	13·8	13·6	13·2	12·7	12·2	11·5	10·8	9·9	9·0	8·1	7·0	5·9	4·8	3·6	2·4	1·2	291
252	14·3	14·3	14·1	13·8	13·4	13·0	12·4	11·7	11·0	10·1	9·2	8·2	7·2	6·0	4·9	3·7	2·5	1·2	288
255	14·5	14·5	14·3	14·0	13·7	13·2	12·6	11·9	11·1	10·3	9·3	8·3	7·3	6·1	5·0	3·8	2·5	1·3	285
258	−14·7	−14·7	−14·5	−14·2	−13·8	−13·3	−12·7	−12·1	−11·3	−10·4	−9·5	−8·4	−7·4	−6·2	−5·0	−3·8	−2·6	−1·3	282
261	14·9	14·8	14·6	14·3	14·0	13·5	12·9	12·2	11·4	10·5	9·5	8·5	7·4	6·3	5·1	3·8	2·6	1·3	279
264	15·0	14·9	14·7	14·4	14·1	13·6	13·0	12·3	11·5	10·6	9·6	8·6	7·5	6·3	5·1	3·9	2·6	1·3	276
267	15·0	15·0	14·8	14·5	14·1	13·6	13·0	12·3	11·5	10·6	9·7	8·6	7·5	6·3	5·1	3·9	2·6	1·3	273
270	15·0	15·0	14·8	14·5	14·1	13·6	13·0	12·3	11·5	10·6	9·7	8·6	7·5	6·4	5·1	3·9	2·6	1·3	270

Interpolation for Altitude Correction for less than 1m of Time

δt	Value from Table 2: 1′	2′	3′	4′	5′	6′	7′	8′	9′	10′	11′	12′	13′	14′	15′
s	′	′	′	′	′	′	′	′	′	′	′	′	′	′	′
00	0·0	0·0	0·0	0·0	0·0	0·0	0·0	0·0	0·0	0·0	0·0	0·0	0·0	0·0	0·0
10	0·2	0·3	0·5	0·7	0·8	1·0	1·2	1·3	1·5	1·7	1·8	2·0	2·2	2·3	2·5
20	0·3	0·7	1·0	1·3	1·7	2·0	2·3	2·7	3·0	3·3	3·7	4·0	4·3	4·7	5·0
30	0·5	1·0	1·5	2·0	2·5	3·0	3·5	4·0	4·5	5·0	5·5	6·0	6·5	7·0	7·5
40	0·7	1·3	2·0	2·7	3·3	4·0	4·7	5·3	6·0	6·7	7·3	8·0	8·7	9·3	10·0
50	0·8	1·7	2·5	3·3	4·2	5·0	5·8	6·7	7·5	8·3	9·2	10·0	10·8	11·7	12·5
60	1·0	2·0	3·0	4·0	5·0	6·0	7·0	8·0	9·0	10·0	11·0	12·0	13·0	14·0	15·0

Rules of How to Apply the Sign of Tables 1 and 2

Time of fix or computation	Sign from Table	To observed Altitude	To tabulated Altitude	To Intercept
Later than observation	+	Add	Subtract	Add
	−	Subtract	Add	Subtract
Earlier than observation	+	Subtract	Add	Subtract
	−	Add	Subtract	Add

TABLE 3 — CONVERSION OF ARC TO TIME

0°–60°		60°–120°		120°–180°		180°–240°		240°–300°		300°–360°		0′–60′		0″–60″	
°	h m	°	h m	°	h m	°	h m	°	h m	°	h m	′	m s	″	s
0	0 00	60	4 00	120	8 00	180	12 00	240	16 00	300	20 00	0	0 00	0	0·00
1	0 04	61	4 04	121	8 04	181	12 04	241	16 04	301	20 04	1	0 04	1	0·07
2	0 08	62	4 08	122	8 08	182	12 08	242	16 08	302	20 08	2	0 08	2	0·13
3	0 12	63	4 12	123	8 12	183	12 12	243	16 12	303	20 12	3	0 12	3	0·20
4	0 16	64	4 16	124	8 16	184	12 16	244	16 16	304	20 16	4	0 16	4	0·27
5	0 20	65	4 20	125	8 20	185	12 20	245	16 20	305	20 20	5	0 20	5	0·33
6	0 24	66	4 24	126	8 24	186	12 24	246	16 24	306	20 24	6	0 24	6	0·40
7	0 28	67	4 28	127	8 28	187	12 28	247	16 28	307	20 28	7	0 28	7	0·47
8	0 32	68	4 32	128	8 32	188	12 32	248	16 32	308	20 32	8	0 32	8	0·53
9	0 36	69	4 36	129	8 36	189	12 36	249	16 36	309	20 36	9	0 36	9	0·60
10	0 40	70	4 40	130	8 40	190	12 40	250	16 40	310	20 40	10	0 40	10	0·67
11	0 44	71	4 44	131	8 44	191	12 44	251	16 44	311	20 44	11	0 44	11	0·73
12	0 48	72	4 48	132	8 48	192	12 48	252	16 48	312	20 48	12	0 48	12	0·80
13	0 52	73	4 52	133	8 52	193	12 52	253	16 52	313	20 52	13	0 52	13	0·87
14	0 56	74	4 56	134	8 56	194	12 56	254	16 56	314	20 56	14	0 56	14	0·93
15	1 00	75	5 00	135	9 00	195	13 00	255	17 00	315	21 00	15	1 00	15	1·00
16	1 04	76	5 04	136	9 04	196	13 04	256	17 04	316	21 04	16	1 04	16	1·07
17	1 08	77	5 08	137	9 08	197	13 08	257	17 08	317	21 08	17	1 08	17	1·13
18	1 12	78	5 12	138	9 12	198	13 12	258	17 12	318	21 12	18	1 12	18	1·20
19	1 16	79	5 16	139	9 16	199	13 16	259	17 16	319	21 16	19	1 16	19	1·27
20	1 20	80	5 20	140	9 20	200	13 20	260	17 20	320	21 20	20	1 20	20	1·33
21	1 24	81	5 24	141	9 24	201	13 24	261	17 24	321	21 24	21	1 24	21	1·40
22	1 28	82	5 28	142	9 28	202	13 28	262	17 28	322	21 28	22	1 28	22	1·47
23	1 32	83	5 32	143	9 32	203	13 32	263	17 32	323	21 32	23	1 32	23	1·53
24	1 36	84	5 36	144	9 36	204	13 36	264	17 36	324	21 36	24	1 36	24	1·60
25	1 40	85	5 40	145	9 40	205	13 40	265	17 40	325	21 40	25	1 40	25	1·67
26	1 44	86	5 44	146	9 44	206	13 44	266	17 44	326	21 44	26	1 44	26	1·73
27	1 48	87	5 48	147	9 48	207	13 48	267	17 48	327	21 48	27	1 48	27	1·80
28	1 52	88	5 52	148	9 52	208	13 52	268	17 52	328	21 52	28	1 52	28	1·87
29	1 56	89	5 56	149	9 56	209	13 56	269	17 56	329	21 56	29	1 56	29	1·93
30	2 00	90	6 00	150	10 00	210	14 00	270	18 00	330	22 00	30	2 00	30	2·00
31	2 04	91	6 04	151	10 04	211	14 04	271	18 04	331	22 04	31	2 04	31	2·07
32	2 08	92	6 08	152	10 08	212	14 08	272	18 08	332	22 08	32	2 08	32	2·13
33	2 12	93	6 12	153	10 12	213	14 12	273	18 12	333	22 12	33	2 12	33	2·20
34	2 16	94	6 16	154	10 16	214	14 16	274	18 16	334	22 16	34	2 16	34	2·27
35	2 20	95	6 20	155	10 20	215	14 20	275	18 20	335	22 20	35	2 20	35	2·33
36	2 24	96	6 24	156	10 24	216	14 24	276	18 24	336	22 24	36	2 24	36	2·40
37	2 28	97	6 28	157	10 28	217	14 28	277	18 28	337	22 28	37	2 28	37	2·47
38	2 32	98	6 32	158	10 32	218	14 32	278	18 32	338	22 32	38	2 32	38	2·53
39	2 36	99	6 36	159	10 36	219	14 36	279	18 36	339	22 36	39	2 36	39	2·60
40	2 40	100	6 40	160	10 40	220	14 40	280	18 40	340	22 40	40	2 40	40	2·67
41	2 44	101	6 44	161	10 44	221	14 44	281	18 44	341	22 44	41	2 44	41	2·73
42	2 48	102	6 48	162	10 48	222	14 48	282	18 48	342	22 48	42	2 48	42	2·80
43	2 52	103	6 52	163	10 52	223	14 52	283	18 52	343	22 52	43	2 52	43	2·87
44	2 56	104	6 56	164	10 56	224	14 56	284	18 56	344	22 56	44	2 56	44	2·93
45	3 00	105	7 00	165	11 00	225	15 00	285	19 00	345	23 00	45	3 00	45	3·00
46	3 04	106	7 04	166	11 04	226	15 04	286	19 04	346	23 04	46	3 04	46	3·07
47	3 08	107	7 08	167	11 08	227	15 08	287	19 08	347	23 08	47	3 08	47	3·13
48	3 12	108	7 12	168	11 12	228	15 12	288	19 12	348	23 12	48	3 12	48	3·20
49	3 16	109	7 16	169	11 16	229	15 16	289	19 16	349	23 16	49	3 16	49	3·27
50	3 20	110	7 20	170	11 20	230	15 20	290	19 20	350	23 20	50	3 20	50	3·33
51	3 24	111	7 24	171	11 24	231	15 24	291	19 24	351	23 24	51	3 24	51	3·40
52	3 28	112	7 28	172	11 28	232	15 28	292	19 28	352	23 28	52	3 28	52	3·47
53	3 32	113	7 32	173	11 32	233	15 32	293	19 32	353	23 32	53	3 32	53	3·53
54	3 36	114	7 36	174	11 36	234	15 36	294	19 36	354	23 36	54	3 36	54	3·60
55	3 40	115	7 40	175	11 40	235	15 40	295	19 40	355	23 40	55	3 40	55	3·67
56	3 44	116	7 44	176	11 44	236	15 44	296	19 44	356	23 44	56	3 44	56	3·73
57	3 48	117	7 48	177	11 48	237	15 48	297	19 48	357	23 48	57	3 48	57	3·80
58	3 52	118	7 52	178	11 52	238	15 52	298	19 52	358	23 52	58	3 52	58	3·87
59	3 56	119	7 56	179	11 56	239	15 56	299	19 56	359	23 56	59	3 56	59	3·93
60	4 00	120	8 00	180	12 00	240	16 00	300	20 00	360	24 00	60	4 00	60	4·00

a. GHA ♈ AT 00ʰ ON THE FIRST DAY OF EACH MONTH

Year	Jan. 1	Feb. 1	Mar. 1	Apr. 1	May 1	June 1	July 1	Aug. 1	Sept. 1	Oct. 1	Nov. 1	Dec. 1
	° ′	° ′	° ′	° ′	° ′	° ′	° ′	° ′	° ′	° ′	° ′	° ′
2011	100 18	130 52	158 27	189 01	218 35	249 08	278 42	309 16	339 49	9 23	39 56	69 31
2012	100 04	130 37	159 12	189 45	219 20	249 53	279 27	310 00	340 34	10 08	40 41	70 15
2013	100 49	131 22	158 58	189 31	219 05	249 39	279 13	309 46	340 19	9 53	40 27	70 01
2014	100 34	131 08	158 43	189 17	218 51	249 24	278 58	309 32	340 05	9 39	40 12	69 47
2015	100 20	130 53	158 29	189 02	218 36	249 10	278 44	309 17	339 51	9 25	39 58	69 32
2016	100 05	130 39	159 14	189 47	219 21	249 54	279 29	310 02	340 35	10 09	40 43	70 17
2017	100 50	131 23	158 59	189 33	219 07	249 40	279 14	309 48	340 21	9 55	40 28	70 02
2018	100 36	131 09	158 45	189 18	218 52	249 26	279 00	309 33	340 06	9 41	40 14	69 48
2019	100 21	130 55	158 31	189 04	218 38	249 11	278 46	309 19	339 52	9 26	40 00	69 34

b. INCREMENT OF GHA ♈ FOR DAYS AND HOURS

Day	1	2	3	4	5	6	7	8	9	10	11	12	13	14	15	16
h	° ′	° ′	° ′	° ′	° ′	° ′	° ′	° ′	° ′	° ′	° ′	° ′	° ′	° ′	° ′	° ′
00	0 00	0 59	1 58	2 57	3 57	4 56	5 55	6 54	7 53	8 52	9 51	10 51	11 50	12 49	13 48	14 47
01	15 02	16 02	17 01	18 00	18 59	19 58	20 57	21 56	22 56	23 55	24 54	25 53	26 52	27 51	28 50	29 50
02	30 05	31 04	32 03	33 02	34 01	35 01	36 00	36 59	37 58	38 57	39 56	40 55	41 55	42 54	43 53	44 52
03	45 07	46 07	47 06	48 05	49 04	50 03	51 02	52 01	53 01	54 00	54 59	55 58	56 57	57 56	58 55	59 54
04	60 10	61 09	62 08	63 07	64 06	65 06	66 05	67 04	68 03	69 02	70 01	71 00	72 00	72 59	73 58	74 57
05	75 12	76 11	77 11	78 10	79 09	80 08	81 07	82 06	83 05	84 05	85 04	86 03	87 02	88 01	89 00	89 59
06	90 15	91 14	92 13	93 12	94 11	95 10	96 10	97 09	98 08	99 07	100 06	101 05	102 04	103 04	104 03	105 02
07	105 17	106 16	107 16	108 15	109 14	110 13	111 12	112 11	113 10	114 09	115 09	116 08	117 07	118 06	119 05	120 04
08	120 20	121 19	122 18	123 17	124 16	125 15	126 15	127 14	128 13	129 12	130 11	131 10	132 09	133 09	134 08	135 07
09	135 22	136 21	137 20	138 20	139 19	140 18	141 17	142 16	143 15	144 14	145 14	146 13	147 12	148 11	149 10	150 09
10	150 25	151 24	152 23	153 22	154 21	155 20	156 19	157 19	158 18	159 17	160 16	161 15	162 14	163 13	164 13	165 12
11	165 27	166 26	167 25	168 25	169 24	170 23	171 22	172 21	173 20	174 19	175 18	176 18	177 17	178 16	179 15	180 14
12	180 30	181 29	182 28	183 27	184 26	185 25	186 24	187 24	188 23	189 22	190 21	191 20	192 19	193 18	194 18	195 17
13	195 32	196 31	197 30	198 29	199 29	200 28	201 27	202 26	203 25	204 24	205 23	206 23	207 22	208 21	209 20	210 19
14	210 34	211 34	212 33	213 32	214 31	215 30	216 29	217 28	218 28	219 27	220 26	221 25	222 24	223 23	224 22	225 22
15	225 37	226 36	227 35	228 34	229 34	230 33	231 32	232 31	233 30	234 29	235 28	236 27	237 27	238 26	239 25	240 24
16	240 39	241 39	242 38	243 37	244 36	245 35	246 34	247 33	248 33	249 32	250 31	251 30	252 29	253 28	254 27	255 27
17	255 42	256 41	257 40	258 39	259 38	260 38	261 37	262 36	263 35	264 34	265 33	266 32	267 32	268 31	269 30	270 29
18	270 44	271 43	272 43	273 42	274 41	275 40	276 39	277 38	278 37	279 37	280 36	281 35	282 34	283 33	284 32	285 31
19	285 47	286 46	287 45	288 44	289 43	290 43	291 42	292 41	293 40	294 39	295 38	296 37	297 36	298 36	299 35	300 34
20	300 49	301 48	302 48	303 47	304 46	305 45	306 44	307 43	308 42	309 42	310 41	311 40	312 39	313 38	314 37	315 36
21	315 52	316 51	317 50	318 49	319 48	320 47	321 47	322 46	323 45	324 44	325 43	326 42	327 41	328 41	329 40	330 39
22	330 54	331 53	332 52	333 52	334 51	335 50	336 49	337 48	338 47	339 46	340 46	341 45	342 44	343 43	344 42	345 41
23	345 57	346 56	347 55	348 54	349 53	350 52	351 52	352 51	353 50	354 49	355 48	356 47	357 46	358 45	359 45	0 44

Day	17	18	19	20	21	22	23	24	25	26	27	28	29	30	31	32
h	° ′	° ′	° ′	° ′	° ′	° ′	° ′	° ′	° ′	° ′	° ′	° ′	° ′	° ′	° ′	° ′
00	15 46	16 45	17 44	18 44	19 43	20 42	21 41	22 40	23 39	24 38	25 38	26 37	27 36	28 35	29 34	30 33
01	30 49	31 48	32 47	33 46	34 45	35 44	36 44	37 43	38 42	39 41	40 40	41 39	42 38	43 37	44 37	45 36
02	45 51	46 50	47 49	48 49	49 48	50 47	51 46	52 45	53 44	54 43	55 43	56 42	57 41	58 40	59 39	60 38
03	60 54	61 53	62 52	63 51	64 50	65 49	66 48	67 48	68 47	69 46	70 45	71 44	72 43	73 42	74 42	75 41
04	75 56	76 55	77 54	78 53	79 53	80 52	81 51	82 50	83 49	84 48	85 47	86 47	87 46	88 45	89 44	90 43
05	90 59	91 58	92 57	93 56	94 55	95 54	96 53	97 53	98 52	99 51	100 50	101 49	102 48	103 47	104 46	105 46
06	106 01	107 00	107 59	108 58	109 58	110 57	111 56	112 55	113 54	114 53	115 52	116 52	117 51	118 50	119 49	120 48
07	121 03	122 03	123 02	124 01	125 00	125 59	126 58	127 57	128 57	129 56	130 55	131 54	132 53	133 52	134 51	135 51
08	136 06	137 05	138 04	139 03	140 02	141 02	142 01	143 00	143 59	144 58	145 57	146 56	147 56	148 55	149 54	150 53
09	151 08	152 08	153 07	154 06	155 05	156 04	157 03	158 02	159 02	160 01	161 00	161 59	162 58	163 57	164 56	165 55
10	166 11	167 10	168 09	169 08	170 07	171 07	172 06	173 05	174 04	175 03	176 02	177 01	178 01	179 00	179 59	180 58
11	181 13	182 12	183 12	184 11	185 10	186 09	187 08	188 07	189 06	190 06	191 05	192 04	193 03	194 02	195 01	196 00
12	196 16	197 15	198 14	199 13	200 12	201 11	202 11	203 10	204 09	205 08	206 07	207 06	208 05	209 05	210 04	211 03
13	211 18	212 17	213 17	214 16	215 15	216 14	217 13	218 12	219 11	220 11	221 10	222 09	223 08	224 07	225 06	226 05
14	226 21	227 20	228 19	229 18	230 17	231 16	232 16	233 15	234 14	235 13	236 12	237 11	238 10	239 10	240 09	241 08
15	241 23	242 22	243 21	244 21	245 20	246 19	247 18	248 17	249 16	250 15	251 15	252 14	253 13	254 12	255 11	256 10
16	256 26	257 25	258 24	259 23	260 22	261 21	262 20	263 20	264 19	265 18	266 17	267 16	268 15	269 14	270 14	271 13
17	271 28	272 27	273 26	274 26	275 25	276 24	277 23	278 22	279 21	280 20	281 19	282 19	283 18	284 17	285 16	286 15
18	286 31	287 30	288 29	289 28	290 27	291 26	292 25	293 25	294 24	295 23	296 22	297 21	298 20	299 19	300 19	301 18
19	301 33	302 32	303 31	304 30	305 30	306 29	307 28	308 27	309 26	310 25	311 24	312 24	313 23	314 22	315 21	316 20
20	316 36	317 35	318 34	319 33	320 32	321 31	322 30	323 29	324 29	325 28	326 27	327 26	328 25	329 24	330 23	331 23
21	331 38	332 37	333 36	334 35	335 35	336 34	337 33	338 32	339 31	340 30	341 29	342 28	343 28	344 27	345 26	346 25
22	346 40	347 40	348 39	349 38	350 37	351 36	352 35	353 34	354 34	355 33	356 32	357 31	358 30	359 29	0 28	1 28
23	1 43	2 42	3 41	4 40	5 39	6 39	7 38	8 37	9 36	10 35	11 34	12 33	13 33	14 32	15 31	16 30

c. INCREMENT OF GHA ♈ FOR MINUTES AND SECONDS

m	00^s	04^s	08^s	12^s	16^s	20^s	24^s	28^s	m	32^s	36^s	40^s	44^s	48^s	52^s	56^s	60^s	m
m	° ′	° ′	° ′	° ′	° ′	° ′	° ′	° ′	m	° ′	° ′	° ′	° ′	° ′	° ′	° ′	° ′	m
00	0 00	0 01	0 02	0 03	0 04	0 05	0 06	0 07	**00**	0 08	0 09	0 10	0 11	0 12	0 13	0 14	0 15	**00**
01	0 15	0 16	0 17	0 18	0 19	0 20	0 21	0 22	**01**	0 23	0 24	0 25	0 26	0 27	0 28	0 29	0 30	**01**
02	0 30	0 31	0 32	0 33	0 34	0 35	0 36	0 37	**02**	0 38	0 39	0 40	0 41	0 42	0 43	0 44	0 45	**02**
03	0 45	0 46	0 47	0 48	0 49	0 50	0 51	0 52	**03**	0 53	0 54	0 55	0 56	0 57	0 58	0 59	1 00	**03**
04	1 00	1 01	1 02	1 03	1 04	1 05	1 06	1 07	**04**	1 08	1 09	1 10	1 11	1 12	1 13	1 14	1 15	**04**
05	1 15	1 16	1 17	1 18	1 19	1 20	1 21	1 22	**05**	1 23	1 24	1 25	1 26	1 27	1 28	1 29	1 30	**05**
06	1 30	1 31	1 32	1 33	1 34	1 35	1 36	1 37	**06**	1 38	1 39	1 40	1 41	1 42	1 43	1 44	1 45	**06**
07	1 45	1 46	1 47	1 48	1 49	1 50	1 51	1 52	**07**	1 53	1 54	1 55	1 56	1 57	1 58	1 59	2 00	**07**
08	2 00	2 01	2 02	2 03	2 04	2 05	2 06	2 07	**08**	2 08	2 09	2 10	2 11	2 12	2 13	2 14	2 15	**08**
09	2 15	2 16	2 17	2 18	2 19	2 20	2 21	2 22	**09**	2 23	2 24	2 25	2 26	2 27	2 28	2 29	2 30	**09**
10	2 30	2 31	2 32	2 33	2 34	2 35	2 36	2 37	**10**	2 38	2 39	2 40	2 41	2 42	2 43	2 44	2 45	**10**
11	2 45	2 46	2 47	2 48	2 49	2 50	2 51	2 52	**11**	2 53	2 54	2 55	2 56	2 57	2 58	2 59	3 00	**11**
12	3 00	3 01	3 02	3 04	3 05	3 06	3 07	3 08	**12**	3 09	3 10	3 11	3 12	3 13	3 14	3 15	3 16	**12**
13	3 16	3 17	3 18	3 19	3 20	3 21	3 22	3 23	**13**	3 24	3 25	3 26	3 27	3 28	3 29	3 30	3 31	**13**
14	3 31	3 32	3 33	3 34	3 35	3 36	3 37	3 38	**14**	3 39	3 40	3 41	3 42	3 43	3 44	3 45	3 46	**14**
15	3 46	3 47	3 48	3 49	3 50	3 51	3 52	3 53	**15**	3 54	3 55	3 56	3 57	3 58	3 59	4 00	4 01	**15**
16	4 01	4 02	4 03	4 04	4 05	4 06	4 07	4 08	**16**	4 09	4 10	4 11	4 12	4 13	4 14	4 15	4 16	**16**
17	4 16	4 17	4 18	4 19	4 20	4 21	4 22	4 23	**17**	4 24	4 25	4 26	4 27	4 28	4 29	4 30	4 31	**17**
18	4 31	4 32	4 33	4 34	4 35	4 36	4 37	4 38	**18**	4 39	4 40	4 41	4 42	4 43	4 44	4 45	4 46	**18**
19	4 46	4 47	4 48	4 49	4 50	4 51	4 52	4 53	**19**	4 54	4 55	4 56	4 57	4 58	4 59	5 00	5 01	**19**
20	5 01	5 02	5 03	5 04	5 05	5 06	5 07	5 08	**20**	5 09	5 10	5 11	5 12	5 13	5 14	5 15	5 16	**20**
21	5 16	5 17	5 18	5 19	5 20	5 21	5 22	5 23	**21**	5 24	5 25	5 26	5 27	5 28	5 29	5 30	5 31	**21**
22	5 31	5 32	5 33	5 34	5 35	5 36	5 37	5 38	**22**	5 39	5 40	5 41	5 42	5 43	5 44	5 45	5 46	**22**
23	5 46	5 47	5 48	5 49	5 50	5 51	5 52	5 53	**23**	5 54	5 55	5 56	5 57	5 58	5 59	6 00	6 01	**23**
24	6 01	6 02	6 03	6 04	6 05	6 06	6 07	6 08	**24**	6 09	6 10	6 11	6 12	6 13	6 14	6 15	6 16	**24**
25	6 16	6 17	6 18	6 19	6 20	6 21	6 22	6 23	**25**	6 24	6 25	6 26	6 27	6 28	6 29	6 30	6 31	**25**
26	6 31	6 32	6 33	6 34	6 35	6 36	6 37	6 38	**26**	6 39	6 40	6 41	6 42	6 43	6 44	6 45	6 46	**26**
27	6 46	6 47	6 48	6 49	6 50	6 51	6 52	6 53	**27**	6 54	6 55	6 56	6 57	6 58	6 59	7 00	7 01	**27**
28	7 01	7 02	7 03	7 04	7 05	7 06	7 07	7 08	**28**	7 09	7 10	7 11	7 12	7 13	7 14	7 15	7 16	**28**
29	7 16	7 17	7 18	7 19	7 20	7 21	7 22	7 23	**29**	7 24	7 25	7 26	7 27	7 28	7 29	7 30	7 31	**29**
30	7 31	7 32	7 33	7 34	7 35	7 36	7 37	7 38	**30**	7 39	7 40	7 41	7 42	7 43	7 44	7 45	7 46	**30**
31	7 46	7 47	7 48	7 49	7 50	7 51	7 52	7 53	**31**	7 54	7 55	7 56	7 57	7 58	7 59	8 00	8 01	**31**
32	8 01	8 02	8 03	8 04	8 05	8 06	8 07	8 08	**32**	8 09	8 10	8 11	8 12	8 13	8 14	8 15	8 16	**32**
33	8 16	8 17	8 18	8 19	8 20	8 21	8 22	8 23	**33**	8 24	8 25	8 26	8 27	8 28	8 29	8 30	8 31	**33**
34	8 31	8 32	8 33	8 34	8 35	8 36	8 37	8 38	**34**	8 39	8 40	8 41	8 42	8 43	8 44	8 45	8 46	**34**
35	8 46	8 47	8 48	8 49	8 50	8 51	8 52	8 53	**35**	8 54	8 55	8 56	8 57	8 58	8 59	9 00	9 01	**35**
36	9 01	9 02	9 03	9 04	9 05	9 06	9 07	9 08	**36**	9 10	9 11	9 12	9 13	9 14	9 15	9 16	9 17	**36**
37	9 17	9 18	9 19	9 20	9 21	9 22	9 23	9 24	**37**	9 25	9 26	9 27	9 28	9 29	9 30	9 31	9 32	**37**
38	9 32	9 33	9 34	9 35	9 36	9 37	9 38	9 39	**38**	9 40	9 41	9 42	9 43	9 44	9 45	9 46	9 47	**38**
39	9 47	9 48	9 49	9 50	9 51	9 52	9 53	9 54	**39**	9 55	9 56	9 57	9 58	9 59	10 00	10 01	10 02	**39**
40	10 02	10 03	10 04	10 05	10 06	10 07	10 08	10 09	**40**	10 10	10 11	10 12	10 13	10 14	10 15	10 16	10 17	**40**
41	10 17	10 18	10 19	10 20	10 21	10 22	10 23	10 24	**41**	10 25	10 26	10 27	10 28	10 29	10 30	10 31	10 32	**41**
42	10 32	10 33	10 34	10 35	10 36	10 37	10 38	10 39	**42**	10 40	10 41	10 42	10 43	10 44	10 45	10 46	10 47	**42**
43	10 47	10 48	10 49	10 50	10 51	10 52	10 53	10 54	**43**	10 55	10 56	10 57	10 58	10 59	11 00	11 01	11 02	**43**
44	11 02	11 03	11 04	11 05	11 06	11 07	11 08	11 09	**44**	11 10	11 11	11 12	11 13	11 14	11 15	11 16	11 17	**44**
45	11 17	11 18	11 19	11 20	11 21	11 22	11 23	11 24	**45**	11 25	11 26	11 27	11 28	11 29	11 30	11 31	11 32	**45**
46	11 32	11 33	11 34	11 35	11 36	11 37	11 38	11 39	**46**	11 40	11 41	11 42	11 43	11 44	11 45	11 46	11 47	**46**
47	11 47	11 48	11 49	11 50	11 51	11 52	11 53	11 54	**47**	11 55	11 56	11 57	11 58	11 59	12 00	12 01	12 02	**47**
48	12 02	12 03	12 04	12 05	12 06	12 07	12 08	12 09	**48**	12 10	12 11	12 12	12 13	12 14	12 15	12 16	12 17	**48**
49	12 17	12 18	12 19	12 20	12 21	12 22	12 23	12 24	**49**	12 25	12 26	12 27	12 28	12 29	12 30	12 31	12 32	**49**
50	12 32	12 33	12 34	12 35	12 36	12 37	12 38	12 39	**50**	12 40	12 41	12 42	12 43	12 44	12 45	12 46	12 47	**50**
51	12 47	12 48	12 49	12 50	12 51	12 52	12 53	12 54	**51**	12 55	12 56	12 57	12 58	12 59	13 00	13 01	13 02	**51**
52	13 02	13 03	13 04	13 05	13 06	13 07	13 08	13 09	**52**	13 10	13 11	13 12	13 13	13 14	13 15	13 16	13 17	**52**
53	13 17	13 18	13 19	13 20	13 21	13 22	13 23	13 24	**53**	13 25	13 26	13 27	13 28	13 29	13 30	13 31	13 32	**53**
54	13 32	13 33	13 34	13 35	13 36	13 37	13 38	13 39	**54**	13 40	13 41	13 42	13 43	13 44	13 45	13 46	13 47	**54**
55	13 47	13 48	13 49	13 50	13 51	13 52	13 53	13 54	**55**	13 55	13 56	13 57	13 58	13 59	14 00	14 01	14 02	**55**
56	14 02	14 03	14 04	14 05	14 06	14 07	14 08	14 09	**56**	14 10	14 11	14 12	14 13	14 14	14 15	14 16	14 17	**56**
57	14 17	14 18	14 19	14 20	14 21	14 22	14 23	14 24	**57**	14 25	14 26	14 27	14 28	14 29	14 30	14 31	14 32	**57**
58	14 32	14 33	14 34	14 35	14 36	14 37	14 38	14 39	**58**	14 40	14 41	14 42	14 43	14 44	14 45	14 46	14 47	**58**
59	14 47	14 48	14 49	14 50	14 51	14 52	14 53	14 54	**59**	14 55	14 56	14 57	14 58	14 59	15 00	15 01	15 02	**59**

Example. The value of GHA♈ for 2014 June 16 at $21^h\ 33^m\ 07^s$ UT is **(a)** 249° 24′ + **(b)** 330° 39′ + **(c)** 8° 18′ = 228° 21′.

LHA ♈	North latitudes							South latitudes						LHA ♈
	N 80°	N 70°	N 60°	N 50°	N 40°	N 20°	0°	S 20°	S 40°	S 50°	S 60°	S 70°	S 80°	
							2011							
°	′ °	′ °	′ °	′ °	′ °	′ °	′ °	′ °	′ °	′ °	′ °	′ °	′ °	°
0	1·1 200	1·3 217	1·6 228	1·9 236	2·1 240	2·5 245	2·6 247	2·5 245	2·1 241	1·9 236	1·6 230	1·4 219	1·1 203	0
30	1·3 225	1·6 235	1·9 241	2·1 245	2·4 247	2·6 249	2·6 249	2·3 246	1·8 239	1·5 232	1·2 220	1·0 201	0·9 175	30
60	1·4 247	1·8 252	2·1 255	2·3 256	2·5 257	2·6 258	2·5 257	2·0 254	1·4 247	1·0 238	0·7 218	0·5 178	0·7 140	60
90	1·5 269	1·8 269	2·1 269	2·4 269	2·5 269	2·6 269	2·4 269	1·9 269	1·2 269	0·8 268	0·3 265	0·2 100	0·6 093	90
120	1·4 291	1·8 286	2·1 284	2·3 282	2·5 282	2·6 281	2·5 282	2·0 284	1·4 292	1·0 301	0·6 321	0·5 005	0·7 044	120
150	1·3 313	1·6 304	1·9 298	2·2 294	2·4 292	2·6 290	2·6 290	2·3 293	1·7 301	1·4 308	1·2 321	0·9 341	0·9 008	150
180	1·1 337	1·4 321	1·6 310	1·9 304	2·1 299	2·5 295	2·6 293	2·5 295	2·1 300	1·9 304	1·6 312	1·3 323	1·1 340	180
210	0·9 005	1·0 339	1·2 320	1·5 308	1·8 301	2·3 294	2·6 291	2·6 291	2·4 293	2·1 295	1·9 299	1·6 305	1·3 315	210
240	0·7 040	0·5 002	0·7 322	1·0 302	1·4 293	2·0 286	2·5 283	2·6 282	2·5 283	2·3 284	2·1 285	1·8 288	1·4 293	240
270	0·6 087	0·2 080	0·3 275	0·8 272	1·2 271	1·9 271	2·4 271	2·6 271	2·5 271	2·4 271	2·1 271	1·8 271	1·5 271	270
300	0·7 136	0·5 175	0·6 219	1·0 239	1·4 248	2·0 256	2·5 258	2·6 259	2·5 258	2·3 258	2·1 256	1·8 254	1·4 249	300
330	0·9 172	0·9 199	1·2 219	1·4 232	1·7 239	2·3 247	2·6 250	2·6 250	2·4 248	2·2 246	1·9 242	1·6 236	1·3 227	330
360	1·1 200	1·3 217	1·6 228	1·9 236	2·1 240	2·5 245	2·6 247	2·5 245	2·1 241	1·9 236	1·6 230	1·4 219	1·1 203	360
							2012							
0	0·8 196	0·9 214	1·1 227	1·3 234	1·4 239	1·7 245	1·8 247	1·8 246	1·5 241	1·4 237	1·2 231	1·0 222	0·8 207	0
30	0·9 221	1·1 232	1·3 239	1·5 243	1·6 246	1·8 248	1·8 248	1·6 246	1·3 238	1·1 232	0·9 221	0·7 204	0·7 180	30
60	1·0 244	1·2 249	1·4 252	1·6 254	1·7 255	1·8 256	1·7 256	1·4 253	1·0 244	0·8 235	0·5 217	0·4 182	0·5 146	60
90	1·0 266	1·3 266	1·5 267	1·6 267	1·8 267	1·8 268	1·7 267	1·3 267	0·8 264	0·5 261	0·2 249	0·1 125	0·4 100	90
120	1·0 287	1·2 284	1·5 282	1·6 281	1·7 280	1·8 279	1·7 280	1·4 282	0·9 289	0·6 298	0·4 319	0·3 011	0·5 051	120
150	0·9 310	1·1 301	1·4 296	1·5 293	1·7 291	1·8 289	1·8 289	1·5 293	1·2 300	1·0 308	0·8 322	0·6 344	0·6 013	150
180	0·8 333	1·0 318	1·2 309	1·4 303	1·5 299	1·8 294	1·8 293	1·7 295	1·4 301	1·3 306	1·1 313	0·9 326	0·8 344	180
210	0·7 000	0·7 336	0·9 319	1·1 308	1·3 302	1·6 294	1·8 292	1·8 292	1·6 294	1·5 297	1·3 301	1·1 308	0·9 319	210
240	0·5 034	0·4 358	0·5 323	0·8 305	1·0 296	1·4 287	1·7 284	1·8 284	1·7 285	1·6 286	1·4 288	1·2 291	1·0 296	240
270	0·4 080	0·1 055	0·2 291	0·5 279	0·8 276	1·3 273	1·7 273	1·8 272	1·8 273	1·6 273	1·5 273	1·3 274	1·0 274	270
300	0·5 129	0·3 169	0·4 221	0·6 242	0·9 251	1·4 258	1·7 260	1·8 261	1·7 260	1·6 259	1·5 258	1·2 256	1·0 253	300
330	0·6 167	0·6 196	0·8 218	1·0 232	1·2 240	1·5 247	1·8 251	1·8 251	1·7 249	1·5 247	1·4 244	1·1 239	0·9 230	330
360	0·8 196	0·9 214	1·1 227	1·3 234	1·4 239	1·7 245	1·8 247	1·8 246	1·5 241	1·4 237	1·2 231	1·0 222	0·8 207	360
							2013							
0	0·4 187	0·5 207	0·6 222	0·7 232	0·8 238	1·0 244	1·0 247	1·0 246	0·9 243	0·8 239	0·7 234	0·6 227	0·5 214	0
30	0·5 213	0·6 225	0·7 234	0·8 239	0·9 242	1·0 246	1·1 246	1·0 244	0·8 238	0·7 232	0·6 223	0·5 209	0·4 188	30
60	0·6 236	0·7 243	0·8 247	0·9 250	1·0 251	1·1 253	1·0 252	0·9 249	0·6 240	0·5 231	0·4 215	0·3 188	0·3 157	60
90	0·6 258	0·7 261	0·9 262	0·9 263	1·0 263	1·1 263	1·0 263	0·8 261	0·5 256	0·3 248	0·2 225	0·1 152	0·3 116	90
120	0·6 280	0·7 278	0·9 277	0·9 276	1·0 276	1·1 276	1·0 276	0·8 278	0·5 283	0·3 290	0·2 312	0·1 032	0·3 067	120
150	0·6 302	0·7 296	0·8 292	0·9 289	1·0 288	1·1 287	1·0 287	0·9 291	0·6 299	0·5 309	0·4 325	0·3 353	0·3 025	150
180	0·5 326	0·6 313	0·7 306	0·8 301	0·9 297	1·0 294	1·0 293	1·0 296	0·8 302	0·7 308	0·6 318	0·5 333	0·4 353	180
210	0·4 352	0·5 331	0·6 317	0·7 308	0·8 302	1·0 296	1·1 294	1·0 294	0·9 298	0·8 301	0·7 306	0·6 315	0·5 327	210
240	0·3 023	0·3 352	0·4 325	0·5 309	0·6 300	0·9 291	1·0 288	1·1 287	1·0 289	0·9 290	0·8 293	0·7 297	0·6 304	240
270	0·3 064	0·1 028	0·2 315	0·3 292	0·5 284	0·8 279	1·0 277	1·1 277	1·0 277	0·9 277	0·9 278	0·7 279	0·6 282	270
300	0·3 113	0·1 148	0·2 228	0·3 250	0·5 257	0·8 262	1·0 264	1·1 264	1·0 264	0·9 264	0·9 263	0·7 262	0·6 260	300
330	0·3 155	0·3 187	0·4 215	0·5 231	0·6 241	0·9 249	1·0 253	1·1 253	1·0 252	0·9 251	0·8 248	0·7 244	0·6 238	330
360	0·4 187	0·5 207	0·6 222	0·7 232	0·8 238	1·0 244	1·0 247	1·0 246	0·9 243	0·8 239	0·7 234	0·6 227	0·5 214	360

The above table gives the correction to be applied to a position line or a fix for the effects of precession and nutation from the mean equinox of 2015·0. Each entry consists of the distance (in bold type) in nautical miles, and the direction (true bearing) in which the position line or fix is to be moved. The table is entered firstly by the year, then by choosing the column nearest the latitude and finally the entry nearest the LHA♈ of observation; no interpolation is necessary, though in extreme cases near the beginning or end of a year (but not the end of 2014 or the beginning of 2015 when the corrections are zero) values midway towards those of the previous or following years may be taken.

LHA ♈	North latitudes N 80°	N 70°	N 60°	N 50°	N 40°	N 20°	0°	South latitudes S 20°	S 40°	S 50°	S 60°	S 70°	S 80°	LHA ♈
							2014							
°	′ °	′ °	′ °	′ °	′ °	′ °	′ °	′ °	′ °	′ °	′ °	′ °	′ °	°
0	0·2 139	0·1 157	0·1 182	0·1 206	0·2 223	0·2 240	0·3 246	0·3 249	0·3 249	0·3 248	0·3 246	0·3 243	0·2 239	**0**
30	0·2 172	0·2 188	0·2 202	0·2 214	0·2 222	0·3 232	0·3 237	0·3 237	0·3 235	0·3 232	0·3 228	0·2 222	0·2 214	**30**
60	0·2 201	0·2 212	0·2 220	0·3 226	0·3 230	0·3 234	0·3 235	0·3 232	0·3 225	0·2 219	0·2 211	0·2 200	0·2 186	**60**
90	0·2 227	0·2 233	0·3 237	0·3 240	0·3 242	0·3 243	0·3 241	0·3 235	0·2 221	0·2 209	0·2 192	0·1 173	0·2 156	**90**
120	0·2 252	0·3 254	0·3 256	0·3 257	0·3 257	0·3 257	0·3 255	0·2 249	0·1 232	0·1 207	0·1 166	0·1 134	0·1 120	**120**
150	0·2 276	0·3 275	0·3 275	0·3 275	0·3 274	0·3 275	0·3 275	0·2 278	0·1 287	0·0 —	0·0 —	0·1 073	0·1 080	**150**
180	0·2 301	0·3 297	0·3 294	0·3 292	0·3 291	0·3 291	0·3 294	0·2 300	0·2 317	0·1 334	0·1 358	0·1 023	0·2 041	**180**
210	0·2 326	0·2 318	0·3 312	0·3 308	0·3 305	0·3 303	0·3 303	0·3 308	0·2 318	0·2 326	0·2 338	0·2 352	0·2 008	**210**
240	0·2 354	0·2 340	0·2 329	0·2 321	0·3 315	0·3 308	0·3 305	0·3 306	0·3 310	0·3 314	0·2 320	0·2 328	0·2 339	**240**
270	0·2 024	0·1 007	0·2 348	0·2 331	0·2 319	0·3 305	0·3 299	0·3 297	0·3 298	0·3 300	0·3 303	0·2 307	0·2 313	**270**
300	0·1 060	0·1 046	0·1 014	0·1 333	0·1 308	0·2 291	0·3 285	0·3 283	0·3 283	0·3 283	0·3 284	0·3 286	0·2 288	**300**
330	0·1 100	0·1 107	0·0 —	0·0 —	0·1 253	0·2 262	0·3 265	0·3 265	0·3 266	0·3 265	0·3 265	0·3 265	0·2 264	**330**
360	0·2 139	0·1 157	0·1 182	0·1 206	0·2 223	0·2 240	0·3 246	0·3 249	0·3 249	0·3 248	0·3 246	0·3 243	0·2 239	**360**
							2015							
0	0·3 052	0·3 059	0·4 063	0·4 065	0·5 067	0·5 068	0·5 067	0·4 062	0·3 050	0·2 038	0·2 020	0·2 356	0·2 334	**0**
30	0·3 076	0·4 078	0·4 080	0·5 080	0·5 081	0·5 081	0·4 080	0·3 077	0·2 066	0·1 050	0·1 006	0·1 315	0·2 296	**30**
60	0·3 099	0·4 098	0·4 097	0·5 096	0·5 096	0·5 096	0·4 097	0·3 099	0·2 107	0·1 121	0·1 178	0·1 238	0·2 253	**60**
90	0·3 123	0·4 118	0·4 114	0·4 112	0·5 111	0·5 110	0·4 111	0·4 116	0·3 129	0·2 142	0·2 163	0·2 190	0·2 213	**90**
120	0·3 148	0·3 137	0·4 130	0·4 126	0·4 122	0·5 119	0·5 119	0·4 122	0·4 131	0·3 138	0·3 148	0·2 163	0·2 180	**120**
150	0·2 175	0·3 158	0·3 145	0·3 136	0·4 130	0·4 123	0·5 120	0·5 120	0·4 124	0·4 128	0·3 133	0·3 141	0·3 153	**150**
180	0·2 206	0·2 184	0·2 160	0·2 142	0·3 130	0·4 118	0·5 113	0·5 112	0·5 113	0·4 115	0·4 117	0·3 121	0·3 128	**180**
210	0·2 244	0·1 225	0·1 174	0·1 130	0·2 114	0·3 103	0·4 100	0·5 099	0·5 099	0·5 100	0·4 100	0·4 102	0·3 104	**210**
240	0·2 287	0·1 302	0·1 002	0·1 059	0·2 073	0·3 081	0·4 083	0·5 084	0·5 084	0·5 084	0·4 083	0·4 082	0·3 081	**240**
270	0·2 327	0·2 350	0·2 017	0·2 038	0·3 051	0·4 064	0·4 069	0·5 070	0·5 069	0·4 068	0·4 066	0·4 062	0·3 057	**270**
300	0·2 000	0·2 017	0·3 032	0·3 042	0·4 049	0·4 058	0·5 061	0·5 061	0·4 058	0·4 054	0·4 050	0·3 043	0·3 032	**300**
330	0·3 027	0·3 039	0·3 047	0·4 052	0·4 056	0·5 060	0·5 060	0·4 057	0·4 050	0·3 044	0·3 035	0·3 022	0·2 005	**330**
360	0·3 052	0·3 059	0·4 063	0·4 065	0·5 067	0·5 068	0·5 067	0·4 062	0·3 050	0·2 038	0·2 020	0·2 356	0·2 334	**360**
							2016							
0	0·6 036	0·7 048	0·8 055	1·0 060	1·1 063	1·2 066	1·2 067	1·1 064	0·9 057	0·7 051	0·6 041	0·5 025	0·5 004	**0**
30	0·7 059	0·8 066	0·9 069	1·0 072	1·1 073	1·2 074	1·1 073	1·0 070	0·7 061	0·5 051	0·4 034	0·3 004	0·4 331	**30**
60	0·7 082	0·8 083	1·0 084	1·1 085	1·2 085	1·2 085	1·1 085	0·9 083	0·5 079	0·3 073	0·2 051	0·1 318	0·3 289	**60**
90	0·7 104	0·8 101	1·0 099	1·1 099	1·2 098	1·2 098	1·1 098	0·9 100	0·6 107	0·4 115	0·2 140	0·2 204	0·3 240	**90**
120	0·6 126	0·8 119	0·9 114	1·0 111	1·1 110	1·2 108	1·2 109	1·0 112	0·7 121	0·6 130	0·5 145	0·4 171	0·4 200	**120**
150	0·6 150	0·7 136	0·8 128	0·9 122	1·0 119	1·2 115	1·2 114	1·1 116	0·9 122	0·8 128	0·7 137	0·6 150	0·5 169	**150**
180	0·5 176	0·5 155	0·6 139	0·7 129	0·9 123	1·1 116	1·2 113	1·2 114	1·1 117	1·0 120	0·8 125	0·7 132	0·6 144	**180**
210	0·4 209	0·3 176	0·4 146	0·5 129	0·7 119	1·0 110	1·1 107	1·2 106	1·1 107	1·0 108	0·9 111	0·8 114	0·7 121	**210**
240	0·3 251	0·1 222	0·2 129	0·3 107	0·5 101	0·9 097	1·1 095	1·2 095	1·2 095	1·1 095	1·0 096	0·8 097	0·7 098	**240**
270	0·3 300	0·2 336	0·2 040	0·4 065	0·6 073	0·9 080	1·1 082	1·2 082	1·2 082	1·1 081	1·0 081	0·8 079	0·7 076	**270**
300	0·4 340	0·4 009	0·5 035	0·6 050	0·7 059	1·0 068	1·2 071	1·2 072	1·1 070	1·0 069	0·9 066	0·8 061	0·6 054	**300**
330	0·5 011	0·6 030	0·7 043	0·8 052	0·9 058	1·1 064	1·2 066	1·2 065	1·0 061	0·9 058	0·8 052	0·7 044	0·6 030	**330**
360	0·6 036	0·7 048	0·8 055	1·0 060	1·1 063	1·2 066	1·2 067	1·1 064	0·9 057	0·7 051	0·6 041	0·5 025	0·5 004	**360**

Example. In 2012 a fix is obtained in latitude N 23° when LHA♈ is 71°. Entering the table with the year 2012, latitude N 20°, and LHA♈ 60° gives **1′·8** 256° which indicates that the fix is to be transferred 1·8 miles in true bearing 256°.

Example. Early in 2016 a fix is obtained in latitude S 46° when LHA♈ is 247°. Entering the table with the year 2016, latitude S 50°, and LHA♈ 240° gives **1′·1** 095° as compared with **0′·5** 084° for 2015 which indicates that the fix is to be transferred 0·8 miles in true bearing 090°.

LHA ♈	North latitudes							South latitudes						LHA ♈
	N 80°	N 70°	N 60°	N 50°	N 40°	N 20°	0°	S 20°	S 40°	S 50°	S 60°	S 70°	S 80°	
							2017							
°	′ °	′ °	′ °	′ °	′ °	′ °	′ °	′ °	′ °	′ °	′ °	′ °	′ °	°
0	0·9 030	1·1 044	1·3 053	1·5 058	1·6 062	1·9 066	1·9 067	1·8 065	1·5 059	1·3 053	1·1 045	0·9 032	0·8 013	0
30	1·0 053	1·2 061	1·5 066	1·6 069	1·8 070	1·9 072	1·9 071	1·6 068	1·2 060	1·0 052	0·8 037	0·6 013	0·6 343	30
60	1·1 076	1·3 078	1·6 080	1·7 081	1·9 082	1·9 082	1·8 081	1·4 079	0·9 073	0·6 065	0·4 043	0·3 343	0·5 303	60
90	1·1 097	1·3 096	1·6 095	1·7 095	1·9 094	1·9 094	1·8 094	1·4 096	0·9 099	0·6 104	0·3 122	0·2 221	0·5 253	90
120	1·0 119	1·3 113	1·5 110	1·7 107	1·8 106	1·9 105	1·9 106	1·6 109	1·1 117	0·8 126	0·6 144	0·5 175	0·6 209	120
150	0·9 142	1·1 131	1·3 123	1·5 119	1·7 116	1·9 113	1·9 113	1·7 115	1·4 122	1·2 128	1·0 138	0·8 154	0·7 177	150
180	0·8 167	0·9 148	1·1 135	1·3 127	1·5 121	1·8 115	1·9 113	1·9 114	1·6 118	1·5 122	1·3 127	1·1 136	0·9 150	180
210	0·6 197	0·6 167	0·8 143	1·0 128	1·2 120	1·6 112	1·9 109	1·9 108	1·8 110	1·6 111	1·5 114	1·2 119	1·0 127	210
240	0·5 237	0·3 197	0·4 137	0·6 115	0·9 107	1·4 101	1·8 099	1·9 098	1·9 098	1·7 099	1·6 100	1·3 102	1·1 104	240
270	0·5 287	0·2 319	0·3 058	0·6 076	0·9 081	1·4 084	1·8 086	1·9 086	1·9 086	1·7 085	1·6 085	1·3 084	1·1 083	270
300	0·6 331	0·5 005	0·6 036	0·8 054	1·1 063	1·6 071	1·9 074	1·9 075	1·8 074	1·7 073	1·5 070	1·3 067	1·0 061	300
330	0·7 003	0·8 026	1·0 042	1·2 052	1·4 058	1·7 065	1·9 067	1·9 067	1·7 064	1·5 061	1·3 057	1·1 049	0·9 038	330
360	0·9 030	1·1 044	1·3 053	1·5 058	1·6 062	1·9 066	1·9 067	1·8 065	1·5 059	1·3 053	1·1 045	0·9 032	0·8 013	360
							2018							
0	1·2 026	1·4 041	1·7 051	2·0 057	2·2 061	2·6 066	2·7 067	2·5 065	2·1 060	1·9 055	1·6 047	1·3 035	1·1 017	0
30	1·4 050	1·7 058	2·0 064	2·3 067	2·5 069	2·7 071	2·6 070	2·3 067	1·7 059	1·4 052	1·1 038	0·9 016	0·9 348	30
60	1·5 072	1·8 076	2·1 078	2·4 079	2·6 080	2·7 080	2·5 080	2·1 077	1·3 070	1·0 062	0·6 041	0·5 350	0·7 310	60
90	1·5 094	1·9 093	2·2 093	2·4 092	2·6 092	2·7 092	2·5 092	2·0 093	1·2 095	0·8 097	0·3 108	0·2 239	0·6 261	90
120	1·4 116	1·8 110	2·1 107	2·4 105	2·6 104	2·7 103	2·6 104	2·1 107	1·5 115	1·1 124	0·8 143	0·6 178	0·8 215	120
150	1·3 138	1·6 128	1·9 121	2·2 117	2·4 114	2·7 112	2·7 112	2·4 114	1·9 121	1·6 128	1·3 139	1·1 157	1·0 181	150
180	1·1 163	1·3 145	1·6 133	1·9 125	2·1 120	2·5 115	2·7 113	2·6 114	2·2 119	2·0 123	1·7 129	1·4 139	1·2 154	180
210	0·9 192	0·9 164	1·1 142	1·4 128	1·7 121	2·3 113	2·6 110	2·7 109	2·5 111	2·3 113	2·0 116	1·7 122	1·4 130	210
240	0·7 230	0·5 190	0·6 139	1·0 118	1·3 110	2·1 103	2·5 100	2·7 100	2·6 100	2·4 101	2·1 102	1·8 104	1·5 108	240
270	0·6 279	0·2 301	0·3 072	0·8 083	1·2 085	2·0 087	2·5 088	2·7 088	2·6 088	2·4 088	2·2 087	1·9 087	1·5 086	270
300	0·8 325	0·6 002	0·8 037	1·1 056	1·5 065	2·1 073	2·6 076	2·7 077	2·6 076	2·4 075	2·1 073	1·8 070	1·4 064	300
330	1·0 359	1·1 023	1·3 041	1·6 052	1·9 059	2·4 066	2·7 068	2·7 068	2·4 066	2·2 063	1·9 059	1·6 052	1·3 042	330
360	1·2 026	1·4 041	1·7 051	2·0 057	2·2 061	2·6 066	2·7 067	2·5 065	2·1 060	1·9 055	1·6 047	1·3 035	1·1 017	360
							2019							
0	1·5 024	1·8 040	2·2 050	2·5 056	2·9 061	3·3 065	3·5 067	3·3 065	2·8 060	2·5 055	2·1 048	1·7 037	1·5 020	0
30	1·8 048	2·2 057	2·5 062	2·9 066	3·2 068	3·5 070	3·4 070	3·0 067	2·3 059	1·9 052	1·5 039	1·2 019	1·2 351	30
60	1·9 070	2·4 074	2·8 076	3·1 078	3·3 079	3·5 079	3·3 079	2·7 076	1·8 069	1·3 060	0·8 040	0·7 354	0·9 315	60
90	1·9 092	2·4 091	2·8 091	3·1 091	3·4 091	3·5 091	3·2 091	2·5 091	1·6 092	1·0 093	0·4 098	0·2 255	0·8 266	90
120	1·9 114	2·3 109	2·7 106	3·1 104	3·3 103	3·5 102	3·3 103	2·7 106	1·9 114	1·4 123	0·9 142	0·7 181	1·0 219	120
150	1·7 136	2·1 126	2·5 120	2·8 116	3·1 113	3·5 111	3·4 111	3·1 114	2·4 121	2·0 128	1·6 140	1·3 158	1·2 184	150
180	1·5 160	1·7 143	2·1 132	2·5 125	2·8 120	3·3 115	3·5 113	3·3 115	2·9 119	2·5 124	2·2 130	1·8 140	1·5 156	180
210	1·2 189	1·2 161	1·5 141	1·9 128	2·3 121	3·0 113	3·4 110	3·5 110	3·2 112	2·9 114	2·5 118	2·2 123	1·8 132	210
240	0·9 225	0·7 186	0·8 140	1·3 120	1·8 111	2·7 104	3·3 101	3·5 101	3·3 101	3·1 102	2·8 104	2·4 106	1·9 110	240
270	0·8 274	0·2 285	0·4 082	1·0 087	1·6 088	2·5 089	3·2 089	3·5 089	3·4 089	3·1 089	2·8 089	2·4 089	1·9 088	270
300	1·0 321	0·7 359	0·9 038	1·4 057	1·9 066	2·7 074	3·3 077	3·5 078	3·3 077	3·1 076	2·7 074	2·3 071	1·9 066	300
330	1·2 356	1·3 022	1·6 040	2·0 052	2·4 059	3·1 066	3·4 069	3·5 069	3·1 067	2·8 064	2·5 060	2·1 054	1·7 044	330
360	1·5 024	1·8 040	2·2 050	2·5 056	2·9 061	3·3 065	3·5 067	3·3 065	2·8 060	2·5 055	2·1 048	1·7 037	1·5 020	360

The above table gives the correction to be applied to a position line or a fix for the effects of precession and nutation from the mean equinox of 2015·0. Each entry consists of the distance (in bold type) in nautical miles, and the direction (true bearing) in which the position line or fix is to be moved. The table is entered firstly by the year, then by choosing the column nearest the latitude and finally the entry nearest the LHA♈ of observation; no interpolation is necessary, though in extreme cases near the beginning or end of a year (but not the end of 2014 or the beginning of 2015 when the corrections are zero) values midway towards those of the previous or following years may be taken.

Example. In 2019 a fix is obtained in latitude N 57° when LHA♈ is 95°. Entering the table with the year 2019, latitude N 60°, and LHA♈ 90° gives **2′8** 091° which indicates that the fix is to be transferred 2·8 miles in true bearing 091°.

LHA ♈	*Q*	LHA ♈	*Q*	LHA ♈	*Q*	LHA ♈	*Q*	LHA ♈	*Q*	LHA ♈	*Q*	LHA ♈	*Q*	LHA ♈	*Q*
° ′	′	° ′	′	° ′	′	° ′	′	° ′	′	° ′	′	° ′	′	° ′	′
358 13		**86 52**		**124 18**		**158 12**		**231 39**		**288 29**		**322 14**		**0 18**	
	−29		−28		− 5		+18		+39		+16		− 7		−30
0 18		**88 52**		**125 45**		**159 48**		**238 22**		**290 03**		**323 41**		**2 27**	
	−30		−27		− 4		+19		+38		+15		− 8		−31
2 27		**90 48**		**127 11**		**161 26**		**243 01**		**291 35**		**325 09**		**4 42**	
	−31		−26		− 3		+20		+37		+14		− 9		−32
4 42		**92 40**		**128 37**		**163 06**		**246 49**		**293 07**		**326 37**		**7 05**	
	−32		−25		− 2		+21		+36		+13		−10		−33
7 05		**94 30**		**130 03**		**164 47**		**250 08**		**294 38**		**328 05**		**9 36**	
	−33		−24		− 1		+22		+35		+12		−11		−34
9 36		**96 17**		**131 29**		**166 30**		**253 06**		**296 09**		**329 35**		**12 19**	
	−34		−23		0		+23		+34		+11		−12		−35
12 19		**98 02**		**132 56**		**168 16**		**255 50**		**297 38**		**331 05**		**15 16**	
	−35		−22		+ 1		+24		+33		+10		−13		−36
15 16		**99 44**		**134 22**		**170 03**		**258 23**		**299 07**		**332 35**		**18 32**	
	−36		−21		+ 2		+25		+32		+ 9		−14		−37
18 32		**101 25**		**135 48**		**171 54**		**260 47**		**300 35**		**334 07**		**22 18**	
	−37		−20		+ 3		+26		+31		+ 8		−15		−38
22 18		**103 04**		**137 14**		**173 47**		**263 04**		**302 03**		**335 39**		**26 54**	
	−38		−19		+ 4		+27		+30		+ 7		−16		−39
26 54		**104 41**		**138 41**		**175 44**		**265 14**		**303 31**		**337 13**		**33 32**	
	−39		−18		+ 5		+28		+29		+ 6		−17		−40
33 32		**106 17**		**140 07**		**177 45**		**267 20**		**304 58**		**338 48**		**51 33**	
	−40		−17		+ 6		+29		+28		+ 5		−18		−39
51 33		**107 52**		**141 34**		**179 51**		**269 21**		**306 24**		**340 24**		**58 11**	
	−39		−16		+ 7		+30		+27		+ 4		−19		−38
58 11		**109 26**		**143 02**		**182 01**		**271 18**		**307 51**		**342 01**		**62 47**	
	−38		−15		+ 8		+31		+26		+ 3		−20		−37
62 47		**110 58**		**144 30**		**184 18**		**273 11**		**309 17**		**343 40**		**66 33**	
	−37		−14		+ 9		+32		+25		+ 2		−21		−36
66 33		**112 30**		**145 58**		**186 42**		**275 02**		**310 43**		**345 21**		**69 49**	
	−36		−13		+10		+33		+24		+ 1		−22		−35
69 49		**114 00**		**147 27**		**189 15**		**276 49**		**312 09**		**347 03**		**72 46**	
	−35		−12		+11		+34		+23		0		−23		−34
72 46		**115 30**		**148 56**		**191 59**		**278 35**		**313 36**		**348 48**		**75 29**	
	−34		−11		+12		+35		+22		− 1		−24		−33
75 29		**117 00**		**150 27**		**194 57**		**280 18**		**315 02**		**350 35**		**78 00**	
	−33		−10		+13		+36		+21		− 2		−25		−32
78 00		**118 28**		**151 58**		**198 16**		**281 59**		**316 28**		**352 25**		**80 23**	
	−32		− 9		+14		+37		+20		− 3		−26		−31
80 23		**119 56**		**153 30**		**202 04**		**283 39**		**317 54**		**354 17**		**82 38**	
	−31		− 8		+15		+38		+19		− 4		−27		−30
82 38		**121 24**		**155 02**		**206 43**		**285 17**		**319 20**		**356 13**		**84 47**	
	−30		− 7		+16		+39		+18		− 5		−28		−29
84 47		**122 51**		**156 36**		**213 26**		**286 53**		**320 47**		**358 13**		**86 52**	
	−29		− 6		+17		+40		+17		− 6		−29		−28
86 52		**124 18**		**158 12**		**231 39**		**288 29**		**322 14**		**0 18**		**88 52**	

The above table, which does *not* include refraction, gives the quantity *Q* to be applied to the corrected sextant altitude (H_O) of *Polaris* to give the latitude of the observer. In critical cases ascend.

Polaris: Mag. 2·1, SHA 317° 27′, Dec N 89° 20′·0

TABLE 7 — AZIMUTH OF *POLARIS*

LHA ♈	Latitude 0°	30°	50°	55°	60°	65°	70°	LHA ♈	Latitude 0°	30°	50°	55°	60°	65°	70°
°	°	°	°	°	°	°	°	°	°	°	°	°	°	°	°
0	0·5	0·5	0·7	0·8	0·9	1·1	1·3	**180**	359·5	359·5	359·3	359·2	359·1	359·0	358·7
10	0·4	0·4	0·6	0·6	0·7	0·9	1·1	**190**	359·6	359·6	359·4	359·4	359·3	359·2	359·0
20	0·3	0·3	0·4	0·5	0·5	0·6	0·8	**200**	359·7	359·7	359·6	359·6	359·5	359·4	359·3
30	0·1	0·2	0·2	0·3	0·3	0·4	0·4	**210**	359·9	359·8	359·8	359·8	359·7	359·7	359·6
40	0·0	0·0	0·0	0·1	0·1	0·1	0·1	**220**	0·0	0·0	0·0	359·9	359·9	359·9	359·9
50	359·9	359·9	359·9	359·8	359·8	359·8	359·7	**230**	0·1	0·1	0·1	0·1	0·2	0·2	0·2
60	359·8	359·8	359·7	359·6	359·6	359·5	359·4	**240**	0·2	0·2	0·3	0·3	0·4	0·5	0·6
70	359·7	359·6	359·5	359·5	359·4	359·3	359·1	**250**	0·3	0·4	0·5	0·5	0·6	0·7	0·9
80	359·6	359·5	359·4	359·3	359·2	359·0	358·8	**260**	0·4	0·5	0·6	0·7	0·8	0·9	1·2
90	359·5	359·4	359·2	359·1	359·0	358·8	358·5	**270**	0·5	0·6	0·8	0·8	1·0	1·1	1·4
100	359·4	359·3	359·1	359·0	358·9	358·7	358·3	**280**	0·6	0·6	0·9	1·0	1·1	1·3	1·6
110	359·4	359·3	359·0	358·9	358·8	358·5	358·2	**290**	0·6	0·7	1·0	1·1	1·2	1·4	1·8
120	359·3	359·2	359·0	358·9	358·7	358·5	358·1	**300**	0·7	0·8	1·0	1·1	1·3	1·5	1·9
130	359·3	359·2	359·0	358·8	358·7	358·4	358·0	**310**	0·7	0·8	1·0	1·2	1·3	1·6	1·9
140	359·3	359·2	359·0	358·8	358·7	358·4	358·1	**320**	0·7	0·8	1·0	1·2	1·3	1·6	1·9
150	359·4	359·3	359·0	358·9	358·7	358·5	358·2	**330**	0·6	0·7	1·0	1·1	1·3	1·5	1·9
160	359·4	359·3	359·1	359·0	358·8	358·6	358·3	**340**	0·6	0·7	0·9	1·0	1·2	1·4	1·8
170	359·5	359·4	359·2	359·1	359·0	358·8	358·5	**350**	0·5	0·6	0·8	0·9	1·1	1·3	1·6
180	359·5	359·5	359·3	359·2	359·1	359·0	358·7	**360**	0·5	0·5	0·7	0·8	0·9	1·1	1·3

When Cassiopeia is left (right), *Polaris* is west (east).

a. Dip of the Horizon

Ht. of Eye m	Corr^n D ′	Ht. of Eye ft.	Ht. of Eye m	Corr^n D ′	Ht. of Eye ft.
0·00		0·0	13·0		42·8
	−0·3			−6·4	
0·03		0·1	13·4		44·2
	−0·4			−6·5	
0·06		0·2	13·8		45·5
	−0·5			−6·6	
0·09		0·3	14·2		47·0
	−0·6			−6·7	
0·13		0·4	14·7		48·4
	−0·7			−6·8	
0·18		0·5	15·1		49·8
	−0·8			−6·9	
0·23		0·7	15·5		51·3
	−0·9			−7·0	
0·29		0·9	16·0		52·8
	−1·0			−7·1	
0·35		1·1	16·5		54·3
	−1·1			−7·2	
0·42		1·4	16·9		55·8
	−1·2			−7·3	
0·45		1·6	17·4		57·4
	−1·3			−7·4	
0·5		1·9	17·9		58·9
	−1·4			−7·5	
0·6		2·2	18·4		60·5
	−1·5			−7·6	
0·7		2·5	18·8		62·1
	−1·6			−7·7	
0·8		2·8	19·3		63·8
	−1·7			−7·8	
0·9		3·2	19·8		65·4
	−1·8			−7·9	
1·1		3·6	20·4		67·1
	−1·9			−8·0	
1·2		4·0	20·9		68·8
	−2·0			−8·1	
1·3		4·4	21·4		70·5
	−2·1			−8·2	
1·4		4·9	21·9		72·3
	−2·2			−8·3	
1·6		5·3	22·5		74·1
	−2·3			−8·4	
1·7		5·8	23·0		75·8
	−2·4			−8·5	
1·9		6·3	23·5		77·6
	−2·5			−8·6	
2·0		6·9	24·1		79·5
	−2·6			−8·7	
2·2		7·4	24·7		81·3
	−2·7			−8·8	
2·4		8·0	25·2		83·2
	−2·8			−8·9	
2·6		8·6	25·8		85·1
	−2·9			−9·0	
2·8		9·2	26·4		87·0
	−3·0			−9·1	
3·0		9·8	27·0		88·9
	−3·1			−9·2	
3·2		10·5	27·6		90·9
	−3·2			−9·3	
3·4		11·2	28·2		92·9
	−3·3			−9·4	
3·6		11·9	28·8		94·9
	−3·4			−9·5	
3·8		12·6	29·4		96·9
	−3·5			−9·6	
4·0		13·3	30·0		98·9
	−3·6			−9·7	
4·3		14·1	30·6		101·0
	−3·7			−9·8	
4·5		14·9	31·3		103·1
	−3·8			−9·9	
4·7		15·7	31·9		105·2
	−3·9			−10·0	
5·0		16·5	32·6		107·3
	−4·0			−10·1	
5·2		17·4	33·2		109·4
	−4·1			−10·2	
5·5		18·3	33·9		111·6
	−4·2			−10·3	
5·8		19·1	34·5		113·8
	−4·3			−10·4	
6·1		20·1	35·2		116·0
	−4·4			−10·5	
6·3		21·0	35·9		118·2
	−4·5			−10·6	
6·6		22·0	36·6		120·5
	−4·6			−10·7	
6·9		22·9	37·3		122·8
	−4·7			−10·8	
7·2		23·9	38·0		125·1
	−4·8			−10·9	
7·5		25·0	38·7		127·4
	−4·9			−11·0	
7·9		26·0	39·4		129·7
	−5·0			−11·1	
8·2		27·1	40·1		132·1
	−5·1			−11·2	
8·5		28·1	40·8		134·5
	−5·2			−11·3	
8·8		29·2	41·5		136·9
	−5·3			−11·4	
9·2		30·4	42·3		139·3
	−5·4			−11·5	
9·5		31·5	43·0		141·7
	−5·5			−11·6	
9·9		32·7	43·8		144·2
	−5·6			−11·7	
10·3		33·9	44·5		146·7
	−5·7			−11·8	
10·6		35·1	45·3		149·2
	−5·8			−11·9	
11·0		36·3	46·1		151·7
	−5·9			−12·0	
11·4		37·6	46·8		154·3
	−6·0			−12·1	
11·8		38·9	47·6		156·8
	−6·1			−12·2	
12·2		40·1	48·4		159·4
	−6·2			−12·3	
12·6		41·5	49·2		162·1
	−6·3			−12·4	
13·0		42·8	50·0		164·7

b. Refraction for Stars

App. Alt. H_a ° ′	Corr^n R ′	App. Alt. H_a ° ′	Corr^n R ′
0 00	−33·8	3 30	−12·9
0 03	33·2	3 35	12·7
0 06	32·6	3 40	12·5
0 09	32·0	3 45	12·3
0 12	31·5	3 50	12·1
0 15	30·9	3 55	11·9
0 18	−30·4	4 00	−11·7
0 21	29·8	4 05	11·5
0 24	29·3	4 10	11·4
0 27	28·8	4 15	11·2
0 30	28·3	4 20	11·0
0 33	27·9	4 25	10·9
0 36	−27·4	4 30	−10·7
0 39	26·9	4 35	10·6
0 42	26·5	4 40	10·4
0 45	26·1	4 45	10·3
0 48	25·7	4 50	10·1
0 51	25·3	4 55	10·0
0 54	−24·9	5 00	− 9·8
0 57	24·5	5 05	9·7
1 00	24·1	5 10	9·6
1 03	23·7	5 15	9·5
1 06	23·4	5 20	9·3
1 09	23·0	5 25	9·2
1 12	−22·7	5 30	− 9·1
1 15	22·3	5 35	9·0
1 18	22·0	5 40	8·9
1 21	21·7	5 45	8·8
1 24	21·4	5 50	8·7
1 27	21·1	5 55	8·6
1 30	−20·8	6 00	− 8·5
1 35	20·3	6 10	8·3
1 40	19·9	6 20	8·1
1 45	19·4	6 30	7·9
1 50	19·0	6 40	7·7
1 55	18·6	6 50	7·6
2 00	−18·2	7 00	− 7·4
2 05	17·8	7 10	7·2
2 10	17·4	7 20	7·1
2 15	17·1	7 30	6·9
2 20	16·7	7 40	6·8
2 25	16·4	7 50	6·7
2 30	−16·1	8 00	− 6·6
2 35	15·8	8 10	6·4
2 40	15·4	8 20	6·3
2 45	15·2	8 30	6·2
2 50	14·9	8 40	6·1
2 55	14·6	8 50	6·0
3 00	−14·3	9 00	− 5·9
3 05	14·1	9 10	5·8
3 10	13·8	9 20	5·7
3 15	13·6	9 30	5·6
3 20	13·4	9 40	5·5
3 25	13·1	9 50	5·4
3 30	−12·9	10 00	− 5·3

App. Alt. H_a ° ′	Corr^n R ′
9 55	
	−5·3
10 07	
	−5·2
10 20	
	−5·1
10 32	
	−5·0
10 46	
	−4·9
10 59	
	−4·8
11 14	
	−4·7
11 29	
	−4·6
11 44	
	−4·5
12 00	
	−4·4
12 17	
	−4·3
12 35	
	−4·2
12 53	
	−4·1
13 12	
	−4·0
13 32	
	−3·9
13 53	
	−3·8
14 16	
	−3·7
14 39	
	−3·6
15 03	
	−3·5
15 29	
	−3·4
15 56	
	−3·3
16 25	
	−3·2
16 55	
	−3·1
17 27	
	−3·0
18 01	
	−2·9
18 37	
	−2·8
19 16	
	−2·7
19 56	
	−2·6
20 40	
	−2·5
21 27	
	−2·4
22 17	
	−2·3
23 11	
	−2·2
24 09	
	−2·1
25 12	
	−2·0
26 20	
	−1·9
27 34	
	−1·8
28 54	
	−1·7
30 22	
	−1·6
31 58	
	−1·5
33 43	
	−1·4
35 38	
	−1·3
37 45	
	−1·2
40 06	
	−1·1
42 42	
	−1·0
45 34	
	−0·9
48 45	
	−0·8
52 16	
	−0·7
56 09	
	−0·6
60 26	
	−0·5
65 06	
	−0·4
70 09	
	−0·3
75 32	
	−0·2
81 12	
	−0·1
87 03	
	0·0
90 00	

H_a = App. Alt. = Apparent Altitude
= Sextant altitude corrected for index error (IE) & dip (D)
= H_s + IE + D

In critical cases ascend.

c. **Additional Refraction for Non-standard Conditions**

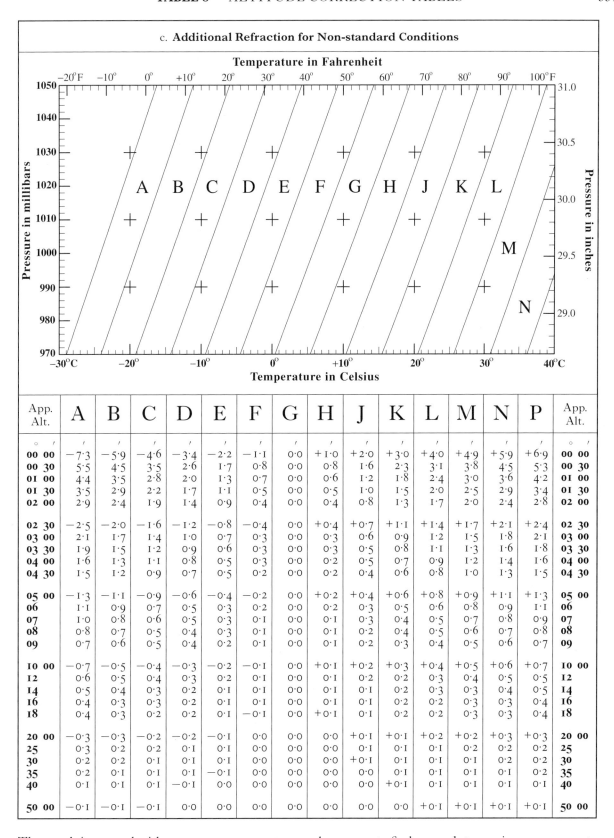

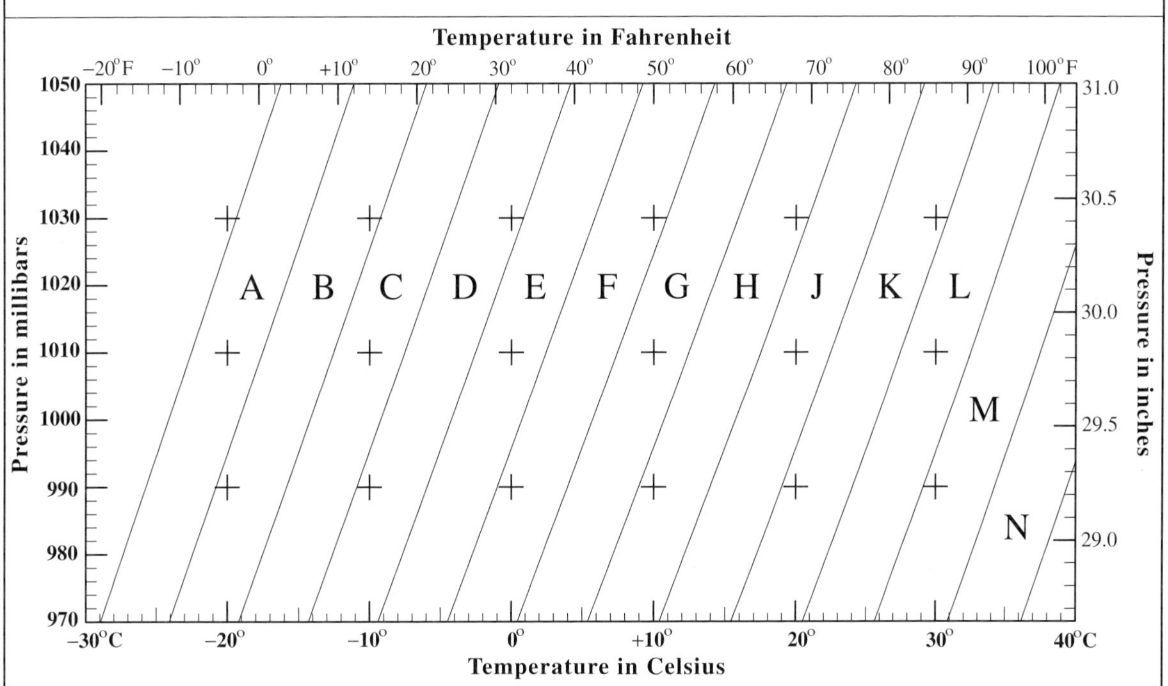

App. Alt.	A	B	C	D	E	F	G	H	J	K	L	M	N	P	App. Alt.
° ′	′	′	′	′	′	′	′	′	′	′	′	′	′	′	° ′
00 00	−7·3	−5·9	−4·6	−3·4	−2·2	−1·1	0·0	+1·0	+2·0	+3·0	+4·0	+4·9	+5·9	+6·9	**00 00**
00 30	5·5	4·5	3·5	2·6	1·7	0·8	0·0	0·8	1·6	2·3	3·1	3·8	4·5	5·3	**00 30**
01 00	4·4	3·5	2·8	2·0	1·3	0·7	0·0	0·6	1·2	1·8	2·4	3·0	3·6	4·2	**01 00**
01 30	3·5	2·9	2·2	1·7	1·1	0·5	0·0	0·5	1·0	1·5	2·0	2·5	2·9	3·4	**01 30**
02 00	2·9	2·4	1·9	1·4	0·9	0·4	0·0	0·4	0·8	1·3	1·7	2·0	2·4	2·8	**02 00**
02 30	−2·5	−2·0	−1·6	−1·2	−0·8	−0·4	0·0	+0·4	+0·7	+1·1	+1·4	+1·7	+2·1	+2·4	**02 30**
03 00	2·1	1·7	1·4	1·0	0·7	0·3	0·0	0·3	0·6	0·9	1·2	1·5	1·8	2·1	**03 00**
03 30	1·9	1·5	1·2	0·9	0·6	0·3	0·0	0·3	0·5	0·8	1·1	1·3	1·6	1·8	**03 30**
04 00	1·6	1·3	1·1	0·8	0·5	0·3	0·0	0·2	0·5	0·7	0·9	1·2	1·4	1·6	**04 00**
04 30	1·5	1·2	0·9	0·7	0·5	0·2	0·0	0·2	0·4	0·6	0·8	1·0	1·3	1·5	**04 30**
05 00	−1·3	−1·1	−0·9	−0·6	−0·4	−0·2	0·0	+0·2	+0·4	+0·6	+0·8	+0·9	+1·1	+1·3	**05 00**
06	1·1	0·9	0·7	0·5	0·3	0·2	0·0	0·2	0·3	0·5	0·6	0·8	0·9	1·1	**06**
07	1·0	0·8	0·6	0·5	0·3	0·1	0·0	0·1	0·3	0·4	0·5	0·7	0·8	0·9	**07**
08	0·8	0·7	0·5	0·4	0·3	0·1	0·0	0·1	0·2	0·4	0·5	0·6	0·7	0·8	**08**
09	0·7	0·6	0·5	0·4	0·2	0·1	0·0	0·1	0·2	0·3	0·4	0·5	0·6	0·7	**09**
10 00	−0·7	−0·5	−0·4	−0·3	−0·2	−0·1	0·0	+0·1	+0·2	+0·3	+0·4	+0·5	+0·6	+0·7	**10 00**
12	0·6	0·5	0·4	0·3	0·2	0·1	0·0	0·1	0·2	0·2	0·3	0·4	0·5	0·5	**12**
14	0·5	0·4	0·3	0·2	0·1	0·1	0·0	0·1	0·1	0·2	0·3	0·3	0·4	0·5	**14**
16	0·4	0·3	0·3	0·2	0·1	0·1	0·0	0·1	0·1	0·2	0·2	0·3	0·3	0·4	**16**
18	0·4	0·3	0·2	0·2	0·1	−0·1	0·0	+0·1	0·1	0·2	0·2	0·3	0·3	0·4	**18**
20 00	−0·3	−0·3	−0·2	−0·2	−0·1	0·0	0·0	0·0	+0·1	+0·1	+0·2	+0·2	+0·3	+0·3	**20 00**
25	0·3	0·2	0·2	0·1	0·1	0·0	0·0	0·0	0·1	0·1	0·1	0·2	0·2	0·2	**25**
30	0·2	0·2	0·1	0·1	0·1	0·0	0·0	0·0	+0·1	0·1	0·1	0·1	0·2	0·2	**30**
35	0·2	0·1	0·1	0·1	−0·1	0·0	0·0	0·0	0·0	0·1	0·1	0·1	0·1	0·2	**35**
40	0·1	0·1	0·1	−0·1	0·0	0·0	0·0	0·0	0·0	+0·1	0·1	0·1	0·1	0·1	**40**
50 00	−0·1	−0·1	−0·1	0·0	0·0	0·0	0·0	0·0	0·0	0·0	+0·1	+0·1	+0·1	+0·1	**50 00**

The graph is entered with arguments temperature and pressure to find a zone letter; using as arguments this zone letter and apparent altitude (sextant altitude corrected for index error and dip), a correction is taken from the table. This correction is to be applied to the sextant altitude in addition to the corrections for standard conditions (Table **8**b).

1 Estimated position at the time of fix:	(See 5.2.4 page xxii)	Navigator	
DR/EP: Lat.	N 24° 15′ Long. W 51° 05′	Height of eye 6 m	
2 Convert Dates/Times:	Year month d h m s	Index Error −2′.1	on arc − off arc +
Fix, local date and time	2014 October 9 18 35 00	Course 356 °T	Temp. 15/10 °C
Zone correction, W + E − ZT	+3	Speed kn	Pressure 1000 mb
Greenwich date & UT UT_f	2014 October 9 21 35 00	Depart	To

Observations of	*Nunki*	*Alphecca*	*Alpheratz*	
Local date	2014 October 9			
	h m s	h m s	h m s	h m s
Local watch time DWT	18 27 01	18 39 52	19 13 16	
Watch error, fast − slow + DWE	−4	−4	−4	
Local time	18 26 57	18 39 48	19 13 12	
Zone correction, W + E − ZT	+3	+3	+3	
UT (Greenwich date) UT	21 26 57 (Oct. 9)	21 39 48	22 13 12	
UT of Fix UT_f			21 35 00	
Fix later + earlier − $UT_f - UT$			− 38 12 earlier	
3 GHA♈: Table 4:	° ′	° ′	° ′	°
Greenwich date (year, mth, 1)	(2014 Oct.) 9 39	9 39	9 39	
Day and hours (b) 9^d	21 323 45	21 323 45	22 338 47	
Minutes and seconds (c)	26 57 6 45	39 48 9 59	13 12 3 19	
Sum = (a) + (b) + (c) GHA♈	21 26 57 340 09	21 39 48 343 23	22 13 12 351 45	
4 AP longitude, E + W −	−51 09	−51 23	−50 45	
Sum	289	292	301	
±360° if required				
GHA♈ + AP *Long* LHA♈	289	292	301	
5 Correct sextant altitudes:	′ ° ′	′ ° ′	′ ° ′	′ °
Sextant altitude H_s	39 54·7	37 53·3	35 18·0	
Index error, on arc − off arc + IE	−2·1	·	·	·
Dip, Table **8**a (ht 6 m) *D*	−4·3	·	·	·
Sum IE + *D*	−6·4 −6·4	· −6·4	· −6·4	·
Apparent altitude H_a	39 48·3	37 46·9	35 11·6	
Refraction, Table **8**b (H_a) *R*	−1·2	−1·2	−1·4	
and Table **8**c (T, P, H_a)	(15°C, 1000 mb) ·	(° ,) ·	(10°C, 1000 mb) ·	(° ,)
Observed altitude H_o	39 47·1	37 45·7	35 10·2	
6 Extract tabulated alt/az:				
(AP latitude, LHA♈) H_c	(24°N, 289°) 39 30·0	(24°N, 292°) 37 49·0	(24°N, 301°) 35 33·0	(° , °)
7 Intercept = $H_o - H_c$ *p*	+17·1	−3·3	−22·8	
Azimuth Z_n	186	286	070	
8 (a) Motion of vessel:			360	
±360° if required			430	
True track of vessel *C*			356	
$Z_n - C$ Rel.Z_n			74	
Table **1**(DMG,Rel.Z_n) MOO	(nm) ·	(nm) ·	(9 nm earlier) −2·5	(nm)
(b) Motion of body: Table**2**	m s	m s	m s	m s
(Lat, Z_n), UT_f−UT MOB	·	·	·	
(c) Precession & nutation:				
Table **5**, (year, Lat, LHA♈)	·	·	·	
9 Intercept, corrected			−25·3	
+ towards − away *p*	*towards* 17·1	*away* 3·3	*away* 25·3	
Azimuth (step 7) Z_n	186	286	070	

Estimated position at the time of fix:		Navigator	
DR/EP: Lat. ° ′	Long. ° ′	Height of eye m/ft	
Convert Dates/Times:	Year month d h m s	Index Error ′	on arc − off arc +
Fix, local date and time	20	Course °T	Temp. °C/F
Zone correction, W + E − ZT		Speed kn	Pressure mb/in
Greenwich date & UT UT_f	20	Depart	To

Observations of				
Local date	20	20	20	20
	h m s	h m s	h m s	h m s
Local watch time DWT				
Watch error, fast − slow + DWE				
Local time				
Zone correction, W + E − ZT				
UT (Greenwich date) UT	( )	( )	( )	( )
UT of Fix UT_f				
Fix later + earlier − $UT_f - UT$				
GHA♈: Table 4:	° ′	° ′	° ′	° ′
Greenwich date (year, mth, 1)	( )			
Day and hours (b) d				
Minutes and seconds (c)				
Sum = (a) + (b) + (c) GHA♈				
AP longitude, E + W −				
Sum				
±360° if required				
GHA♈ + AP *Long* LHA♈	°	°	°	°
Correct sextant altitudes:	′ ° ′	′ ° ′	′ ° ′	′ ° ′
Sextant altitude H_s	.	.	.	.
Index error, on arc − off arc + IE	.	.	.	.
Dip, Table **8**a (ht m/ft) *D*	.	.	.	.
Sum IE + *D*	. .	. .	. .	. .
Apparent altitude H_a	.	.	.	.
Refraction, Table **8**b (H_a) *R*	.	.	.	.
and Table **8**c (T, P, H_a)	(°,) .	(°,) .	(°,) .	(°,) .
Observed altitude H_o	.	.	.	.
Extract tabulated alt/az:				
(AP latitude, LHA♈) H_c	(° , °)	(° , °)	(° , °)	(° , °)
Intercept = $H_o - H_c$ *p*	.	.	.	.
Azimuth Z_n	°	°	°	°
(a) Motion of vessel:				
±360° if required				
True track of vessel *C*				
$Z_n - C$ Rel.Z_n				
Table **1**(DMG, Rel.Z_n) MOO	(nm) .	(nm) .	(nm) .	(nm) .
(b) Motion of body: Table **2**	m s	m s	m s	m s
(Lat, Z_n), $UT_f - UT$ MOB	.	.	.	.
(c) Precession & nutation:				
Table **5**, (year, Lat, LHA♈)	.	.	.	.
Intercept, corrected	.	.	.	.
+ towards − away *p*	.	.	.	.
Azimuth (step 7) Z_n	°	°	°	°

1. *The Astronomical Almanac* contains ephemerides of the Sun, Moon, planets and their natural satellites, as well as data on eclipses and other astronomical phenomena. See also its companion the *The Astronomical Almanac Online* at http://asa.usno.navy.mil/ and mirrored at http://asa.hmnao.com/.

2. *Astronomical Phenomena* contains data on the principal astronomical phenomena of the Sun, Moon and planets (including eclipses), the times of rising and setting of the Sun and Moon at latitudes between S 55° and N 66°, and data on the calendar.

3. *The Nautical Almanac* (NP 314) contains ephemerides at an interval of one hour and auxiliary astronomical data for marine navigation.

4. *Planetary and Lunar Coordinates, 2001–2020* provides low-precision astronomical data for use in advance of the annual ephemerides and for other purposes. It contains heliocentric, geocentric, spherical and rectangular coordinates of the Sun, Moon and planets, eclipse maps, and auxiliary data, such as orbital elements and precessional constants. All the tabular planetary ephemerides are only supplied as ASCII and Adobe's portable document format (pdf) files on an accompanying CD-ROM. The US edition, published by Willmann-Bell Inc., provides all the tabular material in printed form. The CD-ROM only contains the ASCII files.

5. *Rapid Sight Reduction Tables for Navigation* (NP 303/AP 3270), 3 volumes. Volume 1, selected stars for epoch 2015·0, containing the altitude to 1′ and true azimuth to 1° for the seven stars most suitable for navigation, for the complete range of latitudes and hour angles of Aries. Volumes 2 and 3 contain values of the altitude to 1′ and azimuth to 1° for integral degrees of declination from N 29° to S 29°, for latitudes north and south from 0°–40° and 39°–89°, respectively, and for all hour angles at which the zenith distance is less than 95° providing for sights of the Sun, Moon and planets. These volumes were formally entitled *Sight Reduction Tables for Air Navigation*.

6. *The Star Almanac for Land Surveyors* (NP 321) contains the Greenwich hour angle of Aries and the position of the Sun, tabulated for every six hours, and represented by monthly polynomial coefficients. Positions of all stars brighter than magnitude 4·0 are tabulated monthly to a precision of $0^{s}.1$ in right ascension and 1″ in declination. A CD-ROM accompanies the book which contains the data represented compactly in ASCII files and a portable document format (pdf) version of the almanac.

7. *NavPac and Compact Data for 2011–2015* (DP 330) contains ready-to-use software, algorithms and data, which are mainly in the form of polynomial coefficients, for use by astronomers and others to calculate the positions of the Sun, Moon, navigational planets and bright stars. NavPac is supplied on a CD-ROM and enables navigators to compute their position at sea from observations made with a marine sextant using an IBM PC or compatible for the period 1986–2015—please check or web site for updates. In addition times of rising and setting, distance and course between locations, may be calculated. The tabular data are also supplied as ASCII files.

Publications 1–5 are prepared jointly by HM Nautical Almanac Office, and the Nautical Almanac Office of the United States Naval Observatory. Further details about our publications and services may be obtained by writing to H.M. Nautical Almanac Office, or from

http://www.ukho.gov.uk/hmnao

Please refer to the relevant World Wide Web address for further details about the publications and services provided by the following organisations.

- The UK Hydrographic Office (UKHO) at http://www.ukho.gov.uk/
- U.S. Naval Observatory at http://www.usno.navy.mil/USNO

NOTES

NOTES

NOTES

NOTES

NOTES

NOTES

NOTES

NOTES